W0009648

A CHINESE—ENGLISH DICTIONARY

(Revised Edition)

汉英词典

（修 订 版）

北京外国语大学
英语系词典组　编

外语教学与研究出版社
FOREIGN LANGUAGE TEACHING
AND RESEARCH PRESS

(京)新登字 155 号

汉 英 词 典
(修订版)

北京外国语大学 编
英 语 系 词 典 组

* * *

外语教学与研究出版社出版发行

(北京西三环北路 19 号)

新华书店总店北京发行所经销

冶金出版社印刷厂印刷

开本 787×1092　1/16　93.5 印张　5500 千字

1995 年 8 月第 1 版　1995 年 9 月第 2 次印刷

印数：35001—45000 册

* * *

ISBN 7 - 5600 - 0739 - 2
H·456

定价：128.00 元

《汉英词典》修订版编辑人员

主　　编	危东亚
副主编	高厚堃　应曼蓉　陈庆煌
编　　委	危东亚　高厚堃　应曼蓉
	吕　霞　陈庆煌　刘光华
英语顾问	熊德锐 (D. N. Hsiung)
编　　辑	陈兰芳　刘起蓝　孙永勤
	郭士英　沈　毅　戴嘉翔
	李旺盛
责任编辑	吕　霞

《汉英词典》(1978) 编辑人员

主　　编	吴景荣
副主编	王佐良　刘世沐　危东亚　王　般
编　　委	应曼蓉　王晋熙　高厚堃　郑荣成
	吴千之　庄绎传　赵慕昂　林　易
	林学洪　王桂林
英语顾问	大卫·柯鲁克(David Crook)
英语编辑	杜秉洲　陈文伯　王绍坊　张　志
	王　洸　刘国云　杨光慈　吕　霞
	章士法　丁鹏儿
汉语编辑	刘　沫　马耀徽　钟尚钧　林杏光
	陈敦荃
科技编辑	关品枢　王雪华　梁友德　方廷钰
	尚殿元

目　录

前　言

　　《汉英词典》1978年问世后受到国内外广大读者的欢迎。在国外也出了几种版本,学术界多有好评。同时也有一些书评和读者来信提出了一些意见,希望加以修订,使之更加完善。

　　1983年,北京外国语学院(现改名为北京外国语大学)院领导组织英语系几位原来参加编纂《汉英词典》的同志和中文系的几位同志,着手修订《汉英词典》。这项工作受到国家教育委员会的重视,被定为高等学校哲学社会科学博士学科点科研项目。

　　《汉英词典》修订版是一部中型语言工具书,供翻译工作者、英语教师和学习英语的读者使用,对学习汉语的外国朋友也有参考价值。

　　修订工作体现在以下几个方面:

　　1.增添了单字条目800多条,多字条目(包括成语、俗语、谚语等)将近18,000条。全书共收条目约80,000条。增添的条目中有近年来报章书刊中出现的新词以及目前流行而又比较稳定的词语。与此同时,删去了原书中个别条目。

　　2.修改或改编了原来的一些词条:对单字条目中的粘着语素(bound morpheme)作了有别于自由语素(free morpheme)的处理;凡涉及汉英两种语言的多义现象(polysemy),词条释义一般都加注了补充性的说明;增收并阐释了一些词的新义;增添了一些条目的例证,其中有的引自名著,有的采自名家诗词;改正了原来的一些讹误。

　　3.对条目和例证作了全面的审核和调整,使之避免重复,又便于查阅。

　　4.学科门类、词类标注、用法说明等全部改用英语。词类标注仍按照《汉英词典》(1978)限于七类,但标注的范围有所扩大。

　　5.单字条目有的附加了异体字或繁体字,需要分别处理的则分立释义举例。

　　6.词条的注音根据国家语言文字工作委员会、国家教育委员会、广播电视部1985年12月27日联合公布的《普通话异读词审音表》作了调整,使之规范化。

　　修订工作的主要参考书是《现代汉语词典》及其补编。其他参考书有《辞源》、《辞海》、《新华字典》、《现代汉语八百词》、《汉语成语考释词典》等。

　　参加修订工作的除了上述人员外还有几位北京外国语大学英语系的教师。此外,外交学院的陈文伯教授,本校中文系的杨天戈教授和刘宁同志,英语系的王雪华、石成慧同志也参加过一段时间的工作。

　　修订工作得到了原北京外国语学院领导王佐良教授和胡文仲教授、《汉英词典》(1978)主编吴景荣教授的关心和支持,还得到了吕叔湘先生和《汉英词典》(1978)英语顾问大卫·柯鲁克(David Crook)教授的指导和帮助。杨宪益先生和戴乃迭女士的中国古典小说的英译为我们在处理某些词语时提供了有益的借鉴。北京外国语大学图书馆为我们提供了必需的参考书。新华通讯社对外部为我们提供了时事资料。在此,我们一并衷心致谢。

　　修订工作历时十年。由于人力、物力、编辑人员水平的限制,《汉英词典》修订版一定有不少缺点和错误,敬请广大读者批评指正,更希望词书界的同行不吝赐教。

北京外国语大学英语系词典组

一九九五年三月

用 法 说 明

Guide to the Use of the Dictionary

一　条目安排
Arrangement of Entries

1.本词典所收条目分单字条目和多字条目。有的单字条目后附异体字或繁体字。

2.单字条目按汉语拼音字母顺序排列。同音异调的汉字按声调顺序排列。同音同调的汉字按笔划多少排列。

3.多字条目按第一个字分列于单字条目之下。同一单字条目下的多字条目不止一条时,按第二个字的汉语拼音字母顺序和笔划多少排列。第二个字相同时,按第三个字排列,依此类推。儿化词注音中的 r 不计入顺序字母。如:"托儿" tuōr 排在"托³" tuō 之后,"托庇" tuōbì 之前;"肉皮儿" ròupír 排在"肉皮" ròupí 之后,"肉片" ròupiàn 之前;"人缘儿" rényuánr 排在"人员" rényuán 之后,"人猿" rényuán 之前。

4.单字或多字条目字形相同而音或调不同者,分立条目。如:"合" hé 和"合" gě;"温和" wēnhé 和"温和" wēnhuo;"播种" bōzhǒng 和"播种" bōzhòng。分立的条目一般加注 see also 表示"另见"。如:"合" hé 后加注 see also gě;"合" gě 后加注 see also hé。

5.条目形同、音同、调同而在意义上需要分别处理的,予以分立,在条目右上角标注阿拉伯数字。如:"巴¹"、"巴²"、"巴³";"拔火罐儿¹"、"拔火罐儿²"。

6.轻声单字条目,一般紧接在同形的非轻声单字条目之后;带轻声字的多字条目紧接在同形的无轻声字的多字条目之后。如:"出"·chū (参看二3.)排在"出" chū 之后;"大方" dàfang 排在"大方" dàfāng 之后;"地道" dìdao 排在"地道" dìdào 之后,"地道战" dìdàozhàn 之前。但"吧" ba、"了" le、"着" zhe 等轻声单字条目排在该字所属的音节的最后,即去声之后。

7.在同一单字条目下,多字条目意义相同、用字略有差异者,一般只收录其中较常见者。在条目注音后加"(also…)"表示"又作"。如:"百折不挠 bǎi zhé bù náo (also 百折不回 bǎi zhé bù huí)。

8.多字条目能和其他条目组成习语者,最后加 see also…表示"参看"该习语条目。如:

　　天窗 tiānchuāng *archit.* skylight — see also 开天窗 kāi tiānchuāng

二　注　音
Pronunciation

1.条目用汉语拼音字母注音。有些条目的注音根据国家语言文字工作委员会、国家教育委员会、广播电视部1985年12月27日联合公布的《普通话异读词审音表》作了改动。如:"从容"原读 cōngróng,现改读 cóngróng;"事迹"原读 shìjī,现改读 shìjì。

2.声调一般只注原调,不注变调。

3.轻声不加调号。如"喇叭" lǎba。一般轻读,有时重读的字则标以调号,该字的注音前

加圆点。如:"翻腾" fān·téng; 趋向动词"来". ·lái 等。

4. 多字条目的注音中音节界限有可能混淆时,加隔音号"'"。如:"海鸥" hǎi'ōu,"阴暗" yīn'àn,"天安门" Tiān'ānmén。

5. 专名和姓氏的注音中第一个字母大写。如:"中国" Zhōngguó,薛 Xuē。根据国名、地名、人名命名的普通名词的注音第一个字母小写。如:"英尺" yīngchǐ,"京剧" jīngjù,"本生灯" běnshēngdēng。

6. 儿化音只在基本形式后面加 r,不标出语音的实际变化。如:"小孩儿" xiǎoháir,"刨根儿" páogēnr。口语中可儿化可不儿化的,一律不加"儿",不注 r。

7. 多字条目中的并列词和并列结构的四字条目的注音用连字号"-"连接并列成分。如:"山水相连" shān-shuǐ xiānglián,"陈词滥调" chéncí-làndiào,"人仰马翻" rényǎng-mǎfān。

三 释 义
Definitions

1. 专业条目一般用英语注明所属专业或学科名称,用斜体排印。如:*Buddhism* (佛教)。有的标注用略语。如:*bot.* (= botany,植物学)。参看"略语表"。

2. 词类的标注限于六种虚词,即副词、介词、连词、叹词、象声词、助词以及量词,用英语斜体排印,分别为 *adv.*、*prep.*、*conj.*、*interj.*、*onom.*、*part.*、*m.*。参看"略语表"。词类标志仅说明条目的词类,释义所用英语有时与之对应,有时则否。如:

必　bì *adv.*　① certainly; surely; necessarily: … ② must; have to: …

除词类外,有些条目还附有关于风格色彩的标注,用斜体排印。如:*formal* (书面语),*old* (旧时用语)。有的标注用略语,如:*inf.* (= informal,口语)。参看"略语表"。

3. 释义一般用对应的英语词语,无对应的词语时用英语解释。如:

弋阳腔　yìyángqiāng … an opera style of the Ming Dynasty, which originated in Yiyang, Jiangxi Province, and spread to many other places, and which was noteworthy for its use of a chorus as well as of soloists

同一义项下有两个或两个以上释义时,用分号";"隔开;一个条目有两个或两个以上义项时用①②③ 等数码标出顺序。如:

发达　fādá ① developed; flourishing: … ② promote; develop: …

4. 释义中的可替换词语放在圆括号"( )"内,前面加 *or*。如:群起而攻之　qún qǐ ér gōng zhī　all rise (*or* turn) against sb.

5. 由于条目和英语对应词二者的词义范围不同,有的释义用英语加注补充性或限制性说明,放在圆括号内。如:

嫁　jià　① (of a woman) marry: …

鲜　xiān …　③ (of salty dishes or soup) delicious; tasty: …

马克　mǎkè　mark (German monetary unit)

蛐蛐儿　qūqur　*dial.* cricket (an insect)

通条　tōngtiáo　① (stove) poker ② cleaning rod (for a gun)

英语　Yīngyǔ　English (language)

有的则先用英语解释,然后再提供英语对应词。如:

扎猛子　zhā měngzi　*dial.*　swim with the head kept submerged in water; dive

6. 有关用法、语法特征等都用英语说明,放在圆括号内。如:

爱…不… ài... bù... (used before reduplicated verbs, to indicate that the person in question can do as he likes): ...

捉摸 zhuōmō (usu. used in the negative) fathom; ascertain: ～不定 difficult to ascertain;-unpredictable; elusive

都 dōu *adv.* ... (used with 是 to show the cause): ...

呃 e *part.* (used at the end of a sentence, expressing wonder or admiration): ...

7. 某些条目先用英语作字面翻译, 然后释义, 二者之间加破折号 "—"。如:

八仙桌 bāxiānzhuō Eight Immortals table—an old-fashioned square table for eight people

舍车保帅 shějū-bǎoshuài give up a chariot to save the marshal (in Chinese chess) — make minor sacrifices to safeguard major interests

心猿意马 xīnyuán-yìmǎ a heart like a capering monkey and a mind like a galloping horse — restless; perturbed

8. 某些条目在释义后就有关背景、典故等另加补充性说明, 放在圆括号内。如:

五四运动 Wǔ Sì Yùndòng the May 4th Movement of 1919 (an anti-imperialist, anti-feudal, political and cultural movement influenced by the October Revolution and led by intellectuals having the rudiments of Communist ideology)

黄粱美梦 huángliáng měimèng Golden Millet Dream (from the story of a poor scholar who dreamt he had become an official but awoke to find the pot of millet still cooking on the fire) — pipe dream

9. 某些专业条目在释义后加拉丁语学名或其他符号; 某些条目在释义后附英语略语, 均放在圆括号内。如:

半夏 bànxià *Chin. med.* the tuber of pinellia (*pinellia termata*)

钡 bèi *chem.* barium (Ba)

公斤 gōngjīn kilogram (kg.); kilo

石油输出国组织 Shíyóu Shūchūguó Zǔzhī the Organization of Petroleum Exporting Countries (OPEC)

10. 条目如系简称, 一般用 short for 注明全称, 加注音表示 "见" 该全称条目, 不再释义。如:

联大 Liándà short for 联合国大会 Liánhéguó Dàhuì

常用简称, 或无全称条目的简称, 用 short for 注明全称, 不注音, 放在圆括号内。另有释义。如:

人大 Réndà (short for 全国人民代表大会) the National People's Congress

高考 gāokǎo (short for 高等学校招生考试) college entrance examination

文体² wéntǐ (short for 文娱体育) recreation and sports: ～活动…

11. 有的单字条目本身无意义, 只是构词成分, 释义用 see below 表示 "见下", 用 see … 表示 "见…"。如:

蝴 hú see below

佛 fú see 仿佛 fǎngfú

有的多字条目本身无意义, 只能和别的词构成习语, 也用 see… 表示 "见"。如:

小差 xiǎochāi see 开小差 kāi xiǎochāi

12. 不在同一单字条目下的同义多字条目 (参看一 7.), 一般只对较常见者释义, 另一处

用 same as…表示"见"。如:

> 龙盘虎踞 lóngpán-hǔjù a coiling dragon and a crouching tiger — a forbidding strategic point...
>
> 虎踞龙盘 hǔjù-lóngpán same as 龙盘虎踞 lóngpán-hǔjù

13.释义时常用的英语词语有 general name(统称)、common name(通称)、popular name(俗称)、old name(旧称)、another name(别称)等。

四 例 证
Examples

1.条目释义后,根据需要用词、词组或句子作为例证。例证前加冒号":"。例证中的本条目用代字号"～"表示。例证的英语译文不止一个时,如果是词或词组,用分号隔开;如果是句子,用 or 隔开。例证与例证之间用斜线号"/"隔开。如:

> 中途 zhōngtú halfway; midway: ～停留 stop halfway; stop over/.../ 开会不要～退场。Don't leave before the meeting is over. or Don't leave when the meeting is in progress.

例证中的本条目如果中间插入了别的字就不用"～"替代,写出全部汉字。如:

> 说话 shuōhuà ① speak; talk; say: ... 感动得说不出话来 be too moved to say anything ...

2.某些单字条目有具体意义,但常不能单独使用,而多用来构成合成词或固定词组。此种条目释义后用已立条的有关合成词或词组作例证,加注音表示"见"。

> 澈 chè (of water) clear; limpid: 清澈 qīngchè
>
> 涕 tì ① tears: 痛哭流涕 tòngkū liútì ② mucus of the nose; snivel: 鼻涕 bítì

某些单字条目没有具体意义,如后缀,也用同样的方法加例证。如:

> 头 tou (noun suffix) ① (added to a noun, verb, or adjective): 木头 mùtou/看头 kàntou/甜头 tiántou ② (added to a word of locality): 上头 shàngtou/下头 xiàtou /前头 qiántou

某些多字条目常不能单独使用,释义后用同样的方法加例证。如:

> 吹灰之力 chuī huī zhī lì the effort needed to blow away a speck of dust; just a small effort: 不费吹灰之力 bù fèi chuī huī zhī lì

3.例证中可替换部分及其英译放在圆括号内。如:

> 极 jí ... ⑤ adv. extremely; to the greatest extent; exceedingly: ～好(快、慢)extremely good (fast, slow) ...
>
> 联系 liánxì ① contact; touch; connection; relation: ... 事物的内(外)部～ the internal (external) relations of things ...

4.例证英译中可替换词语放在圆括号内,前面加 or。如:

> 拍 pāi ... ④ take (a picture); shoot: ～电影 shoot (or make) a film
>
> 内容 nèiróng content; substance: ... 他的演说毫无～。His speech lacked substance (or content).

5.例证如引自名著或名人,都标明出处。如:

> 败军之将 bàijūn zhī jiàng ...: ～不可以言勇。(《史记》)

枪杆子 qiānggǎnzi ...: 〜里面出政权。（毛泽东）

多情 duōqíng...: ...〜自古伤离别。（柳永）

6.例证如为诗句而不止一句,英译不分行排列,大写字母表示每行开始。如:

渔火 yúhuǒ ... 月落乌啼霜满天,江枫〜对愁眠。（张继）Moonset, rooks caw, frost fills the sky, Maples and fishing lights, and sorrow before my bed.

略 语 表

Abbreviations Used in the Dictionary

acrob. acrobatics 杂技

adj. adjective 形容词

adv. adverb 副词

agric. agriculture 农业

arch. archaic 古义

archaeol. archaeology 考古

archit. architecture 建筑

astron. astronomy 天文学

bacteriol. bacteriology 微生物学

biochem. biochemistry 生物化学

biol. biology 生物学

bot. botany 植物学

chem. chemistry 化学

chem. fibre chemical fibre 化学纤维

Chin. med. Chinese medicine 中医、中药

com. commerce 商业

conj. conjunction 连词

derog. derogatory 贬义

dial. dialect 方言

econ. economics 经济

elec. electricity 电学

electron. electronics 电子学

environ. protec. environmental protection 环
　境保护

euph. euphemistic 婉辞

fig. figurative 比喻

geog. geography 地理

geol. geology 地质

geom. geometry 几何

gram. grammar 语法

hist. history 历史

honor. honorific 尊称

hum. humble 谦辞

humor. humorous 诙谐语

inf. informal 口语

interj. interjection 叹词

leg. legal 法律

linguis. linguistics 语言学

lit. literal(ly) 字面意义

liter. literary 文学语言

log. logic 逻辑学

m. measure word 量词

math. mathematics 数学

mech. mechanics 机械

med. medicine 医学

metall. metallurgy 冶金学

meteorol. meteorology 气象学

mil. military 军事

min. mining 矿业

mus. music 音乐

offens. offensive 骂人话

onom. onomatope 象声词

opp. (as) opposed (to) (与…)相对

pharm. pharmacy 药物

philos. philosophy 哲学

phonet. phonetics 语音学

photog. photography 摄影

phys. physics 物理学

physiol. physiology 生理学

prep. preposition 介词

print. printing 印刷

pol. polite 客套语

psychol. psychology 心理学

text. textile 纺织

theat. theatre 戏剧

vulg. vulgar 粗野话

zool. zoology 动物学

汉语拼音音节索引

Index of Syllables of Hanyupinyin (the Phonetic Transcriptions of Chinese Characters)

A (1—13)

ā 阿啊锕腌　á 啊　ǎ 啊　à 阿啊　a 啊

āi 哎哀埃挨唉娭欸嗳锿　ái 挨骏皑癌　ǎi 欸矮嗳蔼霭　ài 艾砹唉爱隘碍嗳嫒暧嗳

ān 安桉氨谙庵鹌鹌鲅鞍盒　ǎn 俺唵埯铵揞　àn 犴岸按案胺暗黯

āng 肮　áng 昂　àng 盎

āo 凹熬　áo 敖遨嗷廒熬獒鳌聱翱鏊鏖　ǎo 拗袄媪　ào 坳拗傲奡奥骜澳懊鏊

B (14—87)

bā 八巴扒叭芭吧疤耙捌笆　bá 拔菝跋魃蛂　bǎ 把钯靶　bà 把坝爸耙罢鲅霸　ba 吧

bāi 刮掰　bái 白　bǎi 百伯佰柏捭摆　bài 败拜稗

bān 扳班般颁斑搬瘢癍　bǎn 坂板版版　bàn 办半扮伴拌绊瓣

bāng 邦帮浜梆　bǎng 绑榜膀　bàng 蚌谤傍棒蒡磅镑

bāo 包苞孢炮胞剥龅煲褒　báo 雹薄　bǎo 宝饱保鸨葆堡褓　bào 报刨抱豹鲍暴爆曝

bēi 陂杯卑背悲碑鹎　běi 北　bèi 贝狈备背钡悖被倍焙辈惫蓓褙鞴鐾　bei 呗臂

bēn 奔贲锛　běn 本苯畚　bèn 坌奔笨

bēng 崩绷嘣　béng 甭　běng 绷　bèng 迸泵蚌绷镚蹦

bī 屄逼　bí 荸鼻　bǐ 匕比吡妣彼秕笔俾鄙　bì 币必闭毕庇芘荜毖陛狴贲毙铋秘敝婢愊愎弼筚跸痹裨蓖睥辟碧箅蔽薜箅避壁嬖璧襞髀髀壁襞

biān 边砭笾编蝙编鞭　biǎn 贬窆扁匾褊碥　biàn 卞弁抃忭汴苄便遍缏辨辩辫

biāo 标彪骠膘瘭镖飙镳　biǎo 表婊裱　biào 摽鳔

biē 憋瘪鳖　bié 别蹩　biě 瘪　biè 别

bīn 宾彬斌傧滨缤槟镔濒　bìn 摈膑殡髌鬓

bīng 并冰兵槟　bǐng 丙秉炳柄饼屏禀摒　bìng 并病

bō 波拨玻剥钵饽菠播　bó 伯驳泊帛柏勃钹铂舶脖渤博鹁搏魄箔膊镈薄礴　bǒ 跛簸　bò 柏薄檗擘簸　bo 卜啵

bū 逋醭　bǔ 卜卟补捕哺堡鸬　bù 不布步怖钚部埠瓿簿

C (88—174)

cā 拆擦嚓礤　cǎ 礤

cāi 猜　cái 才材财裁　cǎi 采彩睬踩　cài 采菜蔡

cān 参餐　cán 残蚕惭　cǎn 惨穆　càn 灿孱粲璨

cāng 仓伧沧苍鸧舱　cáng 藏

cāo 糙操　cáo 曹漕嘈槽螬艚　cǎo 草

cè 册厕侧测恻策

cèi 瓻

cēn 参　cén 岑涔

cēng 噌　céng 层曾　cèng 蹭

chā 叉杈差插喳馇锸嚓　chá 叉茬茶查搽猹楂槎察碴樨檫　chǎ 叉衩踏镲　chà 汊权岔诧衩刹姹差

chāi 拆钗差　chái 侪柴犲　chǎi 舓　chài 虿瘥

chān 觇掺搀　chán 单婵谗馋孱禅缠廛潺蟾巉　chǎn 产刬诌铲阐蒇幞　chàn 忏划颤羼韂

chāng 伥昌倡菖阊猖娼鲳　cháng 长场肠尝常偿徜裳嫦　chǎng 厂场昶敞氅　chàng 怅畅倡鬯唱

chāo 抄吵钞绰焯超剿　cháo 晁巢朝潮嘲　chǎo 吵炒　chào 耖

chē 车砗　chě 尺扯　chè 彻坼掣澈撤

chēn 抻琛嗔瞋　chén 尘臣沉忱辰陈宸晨谌碜　chèn· 衬称龀趁榇谶　chen 伧碜

chēng 柽称琤蛏铛撑瞠　chéng 丞成呈诚承城成乘盛程惩塍酲醒澄橙　chěng 逞骋　chèng 秤

chī 吃哧蚩鸱眵笞痴嗤媸摛螭魑　chí 池弛驰迟持匙踟墀篪　chǐ 尺呎齿侈移耻豉褫　chì 彳叱斥赤饬炽翅敕啻

chōng 冲充忡茺舂憧瞳　chóng 虫重崇　chǒng 宠　chòng 冲铳

chōu 抽绌搊　chóu 仇俦帱惆绸畴愁稠酬筹踌雠　chǒu 丑瞅　chòu 臭

chū 出初樗　chú 刍除厨锄蜍雏橱躇蹰　chǔ 处杵础楮储褚楚　chù 亍处怵绌畜搐触憷黜矗

chuā 欻

chuāi 揣搋　chuái 膗　chuǎi 揣　chuài 揣踹膪

chuān 川氚穿　chuán 传船遄椽　chuǎn 舛喘　chuàn 串钏

chuāng 创疮窗膆　chuáng 床幢　chuǎng 闯　chuàng 创怆

chuī 吹炊　chuí 垂陲捶棰椎槌锤籲

chūn 春椿蝽　chún 纯唇莼淳鹑醇　chǔn 蠢

chuō 戳　chuò 啜绰辍龊

cī 刺差呲疵趀　cí 词祠茨瓷辞慈磁雌鹚糍　cǐ 此趾　cì 次伺刺赐

cōng 匆囱苁枞铋葱骢聪璁　cóng 从丛淙琮

còu 凑辏腠

cū 粗　cú 殂　cù 卒促猝蔟醋簇蹙蹴

cuān 氽撺镩蹿　cuán 攒　cuàn 窜篡爨

cuī 崔缞催摧榱　cuǐ 璀　cuì 脆淬悴萃啐毳瘁粹翠

cūn 村皴　cún 存蹲　cǔn 忖　cùn 寸时

cuō 搓磋撮蹉　cuó 痤矬嵯　cuò 挫厝措锉错

D (175—250)

dā 叮耷搭嗒答跶褡　dá 打达怛沓答瘩靼鞑　dǎ 打　dà 大　da 垯迖瘩

dāi 呆呔待　dǎi 歹逮傣　dài 大代岱迨贷玳带殆待贷怠袋逮靆戴襶

dān 丹单担眈聃聸酖殚箪　dǎn 胆疸掸　dàn 石旦但担诞萏淡啖蛋萏弹惮氮瘅澹

dāng 当珰裆铛　dǎng 挡党谠　dàng 当凼宕荡挡档砀

dāo 刀叨氘　dáo 捯　dǎo 导岛倒捣祷蹈　dào 到帱悼盗道稻纛

dē 嘚　dé 得锝德　de 地的得赋

děi 得

dèn 扥

dēng 灯登噔簦蹬　děng 等戥　dèng 邓凳澄瞪镫磴蹬

dī 氐低羝堤提滴嘀镝　dí 狄的籴迪荻敌涤笛翟嘀嫡镝　dǐ 诋邸底抵砥骶　dì 地弟的帝递娣谛第棣蒂缔睇碲

diǎ 嗲

diān 掂滇颠巅癫　diǎn 典点碘踮　diàn 电佃甸店玷垫钿淀惦奠殿靛簟癜

diāo 刁叼凋貂碉雕鲷　diǎo 鸟屌　diào 吊钓窎调掉铞铫

diē 爹跌　dié 迭谍堞喋耋牒叠蝶蹀鲽

dīng 丁仃叮玎疔盯钉耵酊靪　dǐng 顶酊鼎　dìng 订钉定啶腚碇锭

diū 丢铥

dōng 东冬咚氡　dǒng 董懂　dòng 动冻侗洞恫峒栋胨胴硐

dōu 兜都兜蔸篼　dǒu 斗抖枓陡蚪　dòu 斗豆逗读痘窦

dū 厾都嘟督　dú 毒独读渎椟犊牍黩髑　dǔ 肚笃堵赌睹　dù 杜肚妒度渡镀蠹

duān 端　duǎn 短　duàn 段断缎煅椴锻簖

duī 堆　duì 队对兑怼敦碓

dūn 吨惇敦墩撴磴蹲　dǔn 盹趸　dùn 沌囤炖砘盾钝顿遁

duō 多咄哆掇裰　duó 夺泽度铎踱　duǒ 朵垛躲　duò 驮剁垛舵堕惰跺

E (251—258)

ē 阿屙婀　é 讹囮俄哦峨娥鹅俄蛾额　ě 恶　è 厄扼呃苊轭垩恶饿鄂愕萼遏腭鹗锷颚鳄鳄　e 呃　ê 欸　é 欸　ě 欸　è 欸

ēn 恩蒽　èn 摁

ér 儿而涟鸸　ěr 尔耳迩饵洱珥铒　èr 二弍贰

F (259—308)

fā 发　fá 乏伐垡罚阀筏　fǎ 法砝　fà 发珐

fān 帆番幡蕃藩翻　fán 凡矾钒烦蕃樊燔繁蹯　fǎn 反返　fàn 犯泛饭范贩畈梵

fāng 方坊芳枋钫　fáng 防坊妨房肪鲂　fǎng 访仿纺舫　fàng 放

fēi 飞妃非啡绯扉菲霏鲱　féi 肥淝腓　fěi 诽匪悱菲斐蜚翡榧　fèi 吠沸狒废痱肺费狒痱镄

fēn 分芬吩纷氛酚雰　fén 汾坟焚棼豮　fěn 粉　fèn 分份奋忿偾粪愤

fēng 丰风沨枫疯砜封峰烽锋蜂酆　féng 冯逢缝　fěng 讽唪　fèng 凤奉俸缝

fó 佛

fǒu 缶否

fū 夫伏呋肤麸趺跗稃孵敷　fú 夫弗伏凫扶芙孚佛拂绋服怫郛绂符茯洑被氟俘浮蚨桴袱菔符匐艴幅福蜉蜉蝠蝮黻　fǔ 父甫抚府斧拊釜俯脯腑腐簠黼　fù 父讣付负妇附阜服咐驸赴复副富赋傅腹缚鲋赙蝮鳆覆馥

G (309—373)

gā 夹旮伽咖嘎　gá 轧钆　gǎ 嘎　gà 尬

gāi 该垓赅　gǎi 改　gài 丐芥钙盖溉概戤

gān 干甘杆玕肝泔矸坩柑竿疳酐尴　gǎn 杆秆赶敢感橄擀　gàn 干旰绀赣

gāng 冈扛刚纲肛缸钢罡　gǎng 岗港　gàng 杠钢戆

gāo 高羔皋膏睾糕篙　gǎo 杲搞缟槁稿镐　gào 告部诰锆膏

gē 戈仡圪纥疙咯哥胳袼鸽割搁歌　gé 革阁阁格胳葛蛤颌搁隔嗝膈槅镉骼　gě 合舸葛　gè 个各虼铬硌

gěi 给

gēn 根跟　gén 哏　gěn 艮　gèn 亘茛

gēng 更庚耕赓鹒羹　gěng 埂耿哽绠梗颈鲠　gèng 更

gōng 工弓公功红攻供肱宫恭蚣躬龚觥　gǒng 巩汞拱栱珙　gòng 共贡供

gōu 勾沟佝钩枸篝鞲　gǒu 苟狗枸　gòu 勾构购诟垢够媾遘彀觏

gū 估沽咕呱孤姑轱骨家菇蛄菰辜箍酤毂篛　gǔ 古汩诂谷股牯骨贾钴蛊鹄鼓毂蛊膨瞽　gù 估固故顾梏雇痼锢

guā 瓜呱刮胍栝鸹　guǎ 剐寡　guà 卦诖挂褂

guāi 乖掴　guǎi 拐　guài 怪

guān 关观纶官冠倌棺鳏　guǎn 馆管　guàn 观贯冠惯掼盥灌鹳罐

guāng 光咣桄胱　guǎng 广犷　guàng 桄逛

guī 归圭龟规瓱闺硅瑰鲑鳜璝　guǐ 宄轨庋诡匦癸鬼晷篡　guì 刽刿柜贵桂桧跪鳜鳜

gǔn 衮绲辊滚磙　gùn 棍

guō 过郭埚聒锅蝈　guó 国掴帼腘　guǒ 果裸椁
裹　guò 过

H (374—441)

hā 哈铪　há 蛤　hǎ 哈　hà 哈

hāi 咳嗨　hái 还孩骸　hǎi 海胲醢　hài 亥骇
害氦嗐

hān 狠顸蚶酣憨鼾　hán 汗含邯函涵焓玲寒韩　hǎn
罕喊锃　hàn 汉汗扞旱悍捍焊菡颔憾撼翰瀚

hāng 夯　háng 行吭杭珩绗航颃　hàng 沆巷

hāo 蒿薅嚆　háo 号蚝毫嗥貉豪壕嚎　hǎo 好郝
hào 号好昊耗浩皓

hē 诃呵喝嗬　hé 禾合纥何河和劾饸曷阂荷核盍涸盒
颌阖貉翮　hè 吓和贺荷喝褐赫鹤壑

hēi 黑嘿

hén 痕　hěn 很狠　hèn 恨

hēng 亨哼脝　héng 姮恒珩桁鸻横衡蘅　hèng 横

hm 噷

hng 哼

hōng 轰哄訇烘薨　hóng 弘红宏闳泓洪虹缸鸿葓黉
hǒng 哄　hòng 讧哄蕻

hōu 齁　hóu 侯喉猴瘊篌糇骺　hǒu 吼　hòu
后厚逅候堠鲎

hū 乎呼忽烀滹惚糊　hú 囫和狐弧胡壶核斛湖葫猢湖
鹕猢煳瑚鹕槲醐蝴醐縠　hǔ 虎浒唬琥　hù 户
互沪护怙戽虎祜笏岵瓠糊

huā 化花晔　huá 划华哗铧滑猾　huà 化划华话画
桦

huái 怀徊淮槐踝　huài 坏　huai 划

huān 欢貛　huán 还环桓锾圜缳鹮鬟　huǎn 缓
huàn 幻奂宦浣涣换唤焕患痪豢漶皖擐

huāng 肓荒慌　huáng 皇黄凰隍惶徨遑煌潢璜蝗篁磺
蟥簧鳇　huǎng 恍晃谎幌　huàng 晃

huī 灰诙恢咴晖辉翚麾徽隳　huí 回洄茴蛔　huǐ
悔毁　huì 汇卉会讳海荟绘恚烩贿彗晦秽惠喙殨慧蕙
蟪

hūn 昏荤惛婚阍　hún 浑珲混馄魂　hùn 诨混溷

huō 耠劐嚄豁撝　huó 和活　huǒ 火伙钬夥
huò 或和货获祸惑霍豁藿镬嚯蠖

J (442—539)

jī 几讥击叽饥圾芨机玑乩肌矶鸡奇唧积屐笄屐姬勣基犄赍稽
期缉跻畸箕稽蓟激墼羁　jí 及汲吉级极即亟佶诘
急笈疾棘集楫戢辑蒺嫉瘠蕺藉籍　jǐ 几己戟虮济挤
给脊戟麂　jì 计记纪伎技芰系忌际妓季剂济荠洎迹既
觊继寄绮寂悸偈绩祭蓟霁跽鲚稷暨髻冀穄鬾鲫骥

jiā 加夹伽佳迦茄枷浃家痂袈笳跏笑傢葭嘉镓　jiá 夹
荚恝铗戛蛱颊　jiǎ 甲岬胛贾钾假斚瘕　jià 价驾
架假嫁稼

jiān 戋尖奸间歼坚肩艰兼监笺渐菅湔缄煎搛缣鹣鲣鰜
鳒　jiǎn 拣茧柬俭检捡剪减谫硷裥睑锏简谫碱戬剪蹇
謇　jiàn 见件间饯建剑荐贱涧舰监健谏渐溅践腱键鉴
键槛箭

jiāng 江将姜豇浆僵缰鳉礓疆　jiǎng 讲奖桨蒋耩膙
jiàng 匠降绛将弶强酱犟糨

jiāo 艽交郊茭浇娇骄姣胶教蛟焦椒鲛蕉礁鹪　jiǎo 矫
嚼　jiǎo 角侥佼狡绞饺皎铰脚矫搅湫剿徼缴　jiào
叫觉校较轿教窖醮噍徼醮醮嚼

jiē 节阶疖皆结接秸揭嗟街嗜　jié 孑节讦劫杰诘洁拮
结桔桀捷婕偈睫竭截碣羯　jiě 姐毑解　jiè 介芥
戒届疥诫界借蚧解褯藉　jie 价家

jīn 巾今斤金津衿矜筋禁襟　jǐn 仅尽卺紧锦谨馑槿
jìn 仅尽进近妗荩浸烬晋赈搢缙禁觐噤

jīng 泾京茎经荆旌惊猄菁晶腈粳睛精兢鲸鶄　jǐng 井
阱刭肼颈景儆憬警　jìng 劲净径经胫痉竟竞敬靓靖境
静镜

jiōng 坰扃　jiǒng 迥炯窘

jiū 纠究鸠赳阄揪啾鬏　jiǔ 九久玖灸韭酒　jiù 旧
臼疚咎枢柏救厩就舅鹫

jū 车拘狙居驹疽掬据琚趄雎裾鞠橘　jú 局侷桔菊焗锔
橘　jǔ 沮咀举枸矩蒟榉踽　jù 巨句讵拒苣具炬
钜俱剧倨惧据距飓窭锯聚踞遽屦

juān 涓捐娟圈鹃镌蠲　juǎn 卷　juàn 卷倦绢隽狷
眷圈

juē 噘撅蹶　jué 孑决诀抉角玦珏觉绝倔掘崛觖厥谲蕨
獗橛噱爵镢蹶矍嚼攫镢镢　juě 蹶　juè 倔

jūn 军均君龟钧菌皲麇　jùn 俊郡浚峻骏菌竣

K (540—575)

kā 咖喀擖　kǎ 卡佧咔咯胩

kāi 开揩锎　kǎi 凯剀铠慨楷　kài 忾欬

kān 刊看勘龛堪戡　kǎn 坎侃砍莰槛　kàn 看阚瞰

kāng 康慷糠䅁鳒　káng 扛　kàng 亢伉抗炕钪

kāo 尻　kǎo 考拷烤栲筹　kào 铐犒靠

kē 坷苛珂柯轲科疴砢钶棵颏窠稞颗榼磕瞌蝌髁　ké
壳咳揢　kě 可坷渴　kè 可克刻客恪课氪骒缂锞
嗑溘

kēi 剋

kěn 肯垦恳啃　kèn 掯

kēng 坑吭阬硁铿

kōng 空倥箜　kǒng 孔恐倥　kòng 空控

kōu 芤抠眍　kǒu 口　kòu 叩扣寇筘蔻

kū 刳矻枯哭窟骷　kǔ 苦　kù 库绔袴裤喾酷

kuā 夸　kuǎ 侉垮　kuà 挎胯跨

kuǎi 蒯擓　kuài 会快块侩郐浍哙狯脍筷鲙

kuān 宽髋　kuǎn 款

kuāng 匡诓哐筐　kuáng 狂诳誆　kuàng 邝圹纩况
旷矿贶框眶

kuī 亏岿盔窥　kuí 奎隗逵馗揆葵喹暌魁睽蝰　kuǐ
傀跬　kuì 匮溃馈愦喟愧聩篑

kūn 坤昆堃裈崑琨醌鲲　kǔn 捆阃悃壸　kùn 困

kuò 扩括蛞阔廓

L (576—650)

lā 拉啦啦邋　lá 旯拉砬喇　lǎ 拉喇　là 拉
剌落腊辣蜡瘌蝲䗖鬎镴　la 啦鞡

lái 来莱徕梾铼　lài 赉睐赖濑癞籁

lán 兰岚拦栏婪阑蓝谰澜褴篮斓镧 　lǎn 览揽缆榄罱漤
懒壈 　làn 烂滥

lāng 啷 　láng 郎狼廊琅榔稂锒螂 　lǎng 朗
làng 郎浪莨埌

lāo 捞 　láo 牢劳唠崂痨铹醪 　lǎo 老佬姥栳铑笔
潦 　lào 涝唠烙落耢酪

lē 肋 　lè 仂乐芳勒鳓 　le 了饹

lēi 勒 　léi 累雷嫘缧擂镭縲赢儡 　lěi 耒诔垒累磊
蕾儡 　lèi 肋泪类累酹擂 　lei 嘞

léng 棱楞 　lěng 冷 　lèng 愣睖

lī 哩 　lí 丽厘离狸骊梨犁喱鹂漓莉缡嫠犛黎鲡篱藜
縭蠡 　lǐ 礼李里俚浬哩娌逦理锂鲤醴醴蠡 　lì 力
历立历吏沥丽励利呖戾例隶枥疠疬栎荔俐郦俪轹莉苈砺
砺栗猁砾粒苙唳蛎疬罾雳痢傈黧 　li 哩蜊璃

liǎ 俩
lián 连夌帘怜涟莲联裢廉鲢臁镰蠊 　liǎn 敛琏脸
liàn 练炼恋殓链楝潋
liáng 良凉莨梁椋量粱粮 　liǎng 两俩啢魉魉 　liàng
亮悢凉谅辆晾量嘹靓踉

liāo 撩 　liáo 辽疗聊寥僚寮撩嘹獠缭嫽潦燎鹩
了钉蓼燎 　liào 尥钌料撂廖瞭镣

liē 咧 　liě 咧裂 　liè 列劣冽洌埒烈捩猎裂趔躐
鬣 　lie 咧

līn 拎 　lín 邻林临淋啉琳粼遴嶙霖辚璘磷鳞麟 　lǐn
凛廪檩 　lìn 吝赁淋蔺膦躏

líng ○伶灵苓吟囹泠玲瓴凌铃鸰陵羚聆菱棂蛉翎绫零龄鲮
lǐng 令岭领 　lìng 另令

liū 溜熘 　liú 刘浏流留琉硫旒遛馏榴飗瘤镏鹠鎏 　liǔ
柳绺 　liù 六陆溜碌遛馏镏鹨蹓

lo 咯
lōng 隆 　lóng 龙泷茏咙珑栊胧眬砻聋笼隆癃窿
lǒng 陇垄拢笼 　lòng 弄

lōu 搂睺 　lóu 娄偻喽楼蝼耧髅 　lǒu 搂篓
陋漏瘘镂露 　lou 喽

lū 噜撸 　lú 卢庐芦炉垆胪栌鸬轳颅舻鲈
庐掳鲁橹镥 　lù 陆录赂鹿绿禄碌路漉辘戮璐簏鹭麓
露 　lu 轳辘

lú 驴闾榈 　lǔ 吕侣旅捋铝稆偻屡缕褛膂履 　lù 律
虑率绿氯葎滤

luán 峦娈孪栾挛鸾脔圞銮 　luǎn 卵 　luàn 乱
lüè 掠略

lūn 抡 　lún 仑伦论沦囵纶苍抡轮 　lùn 论
luō 捋啰 　luó 罗猡啰脶萝猡逻椤锣箩骡螺 　luǒ
裸瘰 　luò 荦洛咯络骆烙珞落摞 　luo 儸哆

M (651—699)

m̄ 姆 　ḿ 呒呣 　m̀ 呣

mā 妈抹麻摩嬷 　má 吗麻蔴 　mǎ 马吗犸玛码蚂
mà 骂蚂 　ma 吗嘛蟆

mái 埋霾 　mǎi 买荬 　mài 迈麦卖脉

mān 颟 　mán 埋蛮谩蔓馒瞒鳗 　mǎn 满螨
màn 曼谩漫蔓慢墁幔缦嫚熳镘

māng 牤 　máng 忙芒杧盲氓茫铓硭
蟒 　mǎng 莽漭

māo 猫 　máo 毛矛茅牦庨猫锚髦蟊蝥 　mǎo 夘
卯昴铆 　mào 茂冒贸袤耄帽瑁瞀貌懋

méi 没玫枚眉莓梅湄嵋猸媒煤楣酶鹛镅霉糜 　měi 每
美浼镁 　mèi 妹袜昧寐媚魅

mēn 闷 　mén 门扪钔 　mèn 闷焖懑 　men 们
mēng 蒙 　méng 氓虻萌蒙盟甍朦檬曚朦矇艨 　měng
勐猛蒙锰蜢獴懵 　mèng 孟梦

mī 咪眯 　mí 弥迷谜眯猕醚糜靡麋 　mǐ 米弭
脒敉靡 　mì 汩泌宓觅秘密幂谧蜜嘧

mián 眠绵棉 　miǎn 免勉眄娩冕沔缅腼黾 　miàn
面腼

miāo 喵 　miáo 苗描瞄鹋 　miǎo 杪秒眇渺淼缈邈
藐 　miào 妙庙缪

miē 乜咩 　miè 灭蔑篾

mín 民旻缗 　mǐn 皿闵泯抿黾悯敏鳘
míng 名明鸣茗冥铭溟暝瞑螟 　mǐng 酩 　mìng 命

miù 谬缪

mō 无摸 　mó 谟馍嫲摹模膜摩磨蘑魔 　mǒ 抹
mò 万末没沫茉抹殁陌脉莫秣漠寞蓦瘼墨默磨貘糢

mōu 哞 　móu 牟侔谋眸蝥缪 　mǒu 某

mú 模 　mǔ 母亩牡拇姆坶姥畝 　mù 术目仫沐苜
牧钼募墓幕睦慕暮穆

N (700—727)

ń 嗯 　ň 嗯 　ǹ 嗯

nā 那南 　ná 拿镎 　nǎ 哪 　nà 那呐纳肭衲钠
娜捺 　na 哪

nǎi 乃艿奶氖哪 　nài 奈柰耐萘褦萘

nān 囡 　nán 男南难喃楠 　nǎn 赧腩蝻 　nàn 难
nāng 囔曩 　náng 囊馕 　nǎng 曩攮馕 　nàng
齉

náo 孬 　náo 呶挠硇铙蛲猱 　nǎo 恼脑瑙 　nào
闹淖

né 哪 　nè 讷那 　ne 呢
něi 哪馁 　nèi 内那
nèn 恁嫩
néng 能

ńg 嗯 　ňg 嗯 　ǹg 嗯

nǐ 妮 　ní 尼泥呢怩倪铌霓鲵 　nǐ 拟你旎 　nì
泥逆昵匿溺睨腻

niān 拈蔫 　nián 年粘鲇黏 　niǎn 捻辇碾撵
niàn 廿念埝

niáng 娘 　niàng 酿
niǎo 鸟茑袅 　niào 尿脲
niē 捏 　nié 苶 　niè 陧聂涅臬啮嗫镊镍颞蹑孽蘖
nín 您
níng 宁拧咛苧狞柠聍凝 　nǐng 拧 　nìng 宁佞泞拧
niū 妞 　niú 牛 　niǔ 忸扭纽狃钮 　niù 拗
nóng 农侬浓哝脓秾 　nòng 弄
nòu 耨
nú 奴孥驽 　nǔ 努弩胬 　nù 怒
nǚ 女钕 　nǜ 衄恧
nuǎn 暖

nüè 疟虐
nuó 挪娜傩　nuò 诺喏搦锘懦糯

O (728—729)

ō 喔噢　ó 哦　ǒ 嚄　ò 哦
ōu 区讴沤欧瓯殴鸥　ǒu 呕偶耦藕　òu 沤怄

P (730—767)

pā 趴派啪葩　pá 扒杷爬耙琶掱筢　pà 怕帕
pāi 拍　pái 排徘牌　pǎi 迫排　pài 派哌蒎湃
pān 潘攀　pán 爿胖盘槃磐蹒蟠　pàn 判泮叛盼
祥畔鋬襻
pāng 乓滂膀　páng 彷庞旁膀磅螃鳑　pǎng 嗙耪
pàng 胖
pāo 抛泡脬　páo 刨庖咆狍炮袍跑　pǎo 跑
pào 泡炮疱
pēi 呸胚　péi 陪培赔锫裴　pèi 沛佩帔配斾辔霈
pēn 喷　pén 盆　pèn 喷
pēng 怦抨砰烹　péng 朋棚彭蓬硼鹏澎篷膨蟛鬅
pěng 捧　pèng 碰
pī 丕批纰坯狉披砒劈噼霹 ・ pí 皮枇毗铍疲蚍啤琵脾裨
鲏蜱罴貔鼙　pǐ 匹圮仳否痞劈擗癖　pì 屁辟媲睥
僻譬鷿
piān 片扁偏犏翩篇　pián 便骈胼蹁　piǎn 谝
piàn 片骗
piāo 剽漂缥飘螵　piáo 朴嫖瓢薸　piǎo 殍漂缥瞟
piào 票漂骠嘌
piē 氕撇瞥　piě 苤撇
pīn 拼姘　pín 贫频嫔蘋颦　pǐn 品　pìn 牝聘
pīng 乒俜娉　píng 平冯评坪苹凭枰屏瓶萍鲆
pō 朴钋泊坡泼颇　pó 婆鄱皤叵钋笸　pò 朴迫珀
破粕魄　po 桲
pōu 剖　póu 抔掊裒　pǒu 掊
pū 仆扑铺潽噗　pú 仆匍菩莆脯葡蒲璞镤　pǔ 朴
浦埔圃普溥谱镨镤曝　pù 铺堡瀑曝

Q (768—827)

qī 七沏妻柒栖桤萋戚期欺缉敧颞漆嘁槭蹊曝　qí 齐
祁芪圻祇祈其奇歧荠俟颀旃耆脐淇萁畦崎骑骐琦祺棋
蛴旗蜞綦蕲鲯麒　qǐ 乞岂企启杞起绮稽　qì 气
讫迄汽弃泣妻咠炁契砌跂葺碛器憩
qiā 掐袷葜　qiá 扴　qiǎ 卡　qià 洽恰髂
qiān 千仟阡芊芉迁金扦钎牵悭铅谦签愆骞搴褰鼹
qián 前钤荨钳虔钱掮乾潜黔　qiǎn 浅遣谴缱
qiàn 欠纤茜倩堑嵌椠歉
qiāng 抢呛羌枪戕斨腔蜣锖锵　qiáng 强墙蔷嫱樯
qiǎng 抢羟强襁镪　qiàng 呛炝戗跄
qiāo 悄硗雀跷跷敲劁锹缲橇　qiáo 乔侨荞桥翘谯憔
樵瞧　qiǎo 巧悄雀愀　qiào 壳俏诮窍峭鞘翘撬
鞘
qiē 切　qié 伽茄　qiě 且　qiè 切妾怯窃挈惬
趄慊箧锲
qīn 亲侵钦衾骎　qín 芹矜秦琴覃禽勤嗪擒噙檎
qǐn 锓寝　qìn 沁吢撳

qīng 青轻氢倾卿清圊蜻鲭　qīng 勍情晴氰綮擎黥
qǐng 苘顷请謦　qìng 庆亲磬罄綮
qióng 穷穹茕劳琼蛩邛
qiū 丘邱秋蚯湫楸鳅鞦　qiú 仇囚犰求虬泅酋俅逑尿赇
球遒巯裘蝤　qiǔ 糗
qū 区曲岖诎驱屈祛胠蛆焌蓲躯趋蛐觑黢嗶　qú 劬鸲
渠蕖磲璩氍朐蘧戵癯衢蠼　qǔ 曲苣取娶龋
去阒趣觑
quān 悛圈　quán 权全诠泉拳辁痊铨筌蜷醛鬈颧
quǎn 犬畎绻　quàn 劝券
quē 炔缺阙　qué 瘸　què 却悫雀阕确阙鹊榷
qūn 逡　qún 裙群麇

R (828—854)

rán 蚺然髯燃　rǎn 冉苒染
rāng 嚷　ráng 瀼禳瓤穰　rǎng 壤攘嚷　ràng
让
ráo 荛饶桡桡　rǎo 扰娆　rào 绕
rě 喏惹　rè 热
rén 人壬仁任　rěn 忍荏稔　rèn 刃认仞任妊纫韧
轫饪衽葚
rēng 扔　réng 仍
rì 日
róng 戎荣茸绒容嵘溶蓉熔榕蝾融　rǒng 冗氄
róu 柔揉糅蹂鞣　ròu 肉
rú 如茹铷儒濡薷嚅孺襦蠕颥　rǔ 汝乳辱擩　rù
入溽缛蓐褥
ruá 挼
ruǎn 阮朊软
ruí 蕤　ruǐ 蕊　ruì 芮枘蚋锐瑞睿
rùn 闰润
ruó 挼　ruò 若偌弱箬爇

S (855—969)

sā 仨撒　sǎ 洒靸撒　sà 卅飒脎萨　sɑ 挲
sāi 塞腮噻鳃　sài 塞赛
sān 三弎叁毵　sǎn 伞散馓糁　sàn 散
sāng 丧桑　sǎng 搡嗓磉颡　sàng 丧
sāo 搔骚缫臊　sǎo 扫嫂　sào 扫梢瘙臊
sè 色涩啬铯塞瑟穑
sēn 森
sēng 僧
shā 杀沙纱杉刹砂莎铩裟煞鲨　shǎ 傻　shà 沙
啥唼厦歃煞嗄霎　shɑ 挲
shāi 筛　shǎi 色　shài 晒
shān 山芟杉删衫苫姗钐珊栅舢扇珊煽潸膻　shǎn 闪
陕睒　shàn 讪汕疝单苫扇掸善禅骟缮擅膳嬗蟮鳝
shāng 伤殇商觞墒熵　shǎng 上垧晌赏　shàng 上
尚绱　shɑng 裳
shāo 烧捎梢稍筲艄鞘　sháo 勺芍苕韶　shāo 少
shào 少邵劭绍捎哨稍潲
shē 奢猞赊畲畬　shé 舌折佘蛇阇　shě 舍　shè
设社舍涉射赦摄慑麝
shéi 谁

shēn 申伸身呻绅参砷莘娠深椮鯵　shén 什神钟
shěn 沈审哂矧谂婶　shèn 肾甚胂渗葚慎蜃瘆
shēng 升生声牲笙甥　shéng 绳　shěng 省眚
shèng 圣胜乘晟盛剩
shī 尸失师虱诗狮鸤施葹著嘘螄鯴　shí 十什石识时实
拾食蚀炻鲥　shǐ 史矢豕使始驶屎　shì 士氏市示
世仕式似试势事侍视拭柿贳是适逝轼舐莳饰弑释
谥筮嗜誓噬螫　shi 匙殖
shōu 收　shóu 熟　shǒu 手守首　shòu 寿受狩
兽授售绶瘦
shū 书殳抒纾枢叔姝殊倏淑菽梳舒疏摅输毹蔬　shú
秫孰赎塾熟　shǔ 黍属暑署数蜀鼠薯曙　shù 术
戍束述树竖恕庶数腧漱墅澍
shuā 刷　shuǎ 耍　shuà 刷
shuāi 衰摔　shuǎi 甩　shuài 帅率蟀
shuān 闩拴栓　shuàn 涮
shuāng 双泷霜媚骦鹴　shuǎng 爽
shuí 谁　shuǐ 水　shuì 说税睡
shǔn 吮　shùn 顺舜瞬
shuō 说　shuò 妁烁铄朔硕数蒴搠槊
sī 司丝私咝思鸶螄锶澌斯缌撕嘶　sǐ 死　sì 巳
四寺似姒祀伺饲泗驷食俟笥耜嗣肆
sōng 松凇淞崧嵩　sóng 㞞　sǒng 怂悚耸竦
sòng 讼宋送诵颂
sōu 溲搜嗖馊飕锼艘螋　sǒu 叟瞍嗾薮擞　sòu 嗽
sū 苏酥窣稣　sú 俗　sù 夙诉肃素速宿骕粟谡溯塑
嗉愫鹔僳蔌觫簌
suān 狻酸　suàn 蒜算
suī 尿虽荽睢濉　suí 绥隋随遂　suǐ 髓　suì 岁
崇遂碎隧燧邃穗
sūn 孙狲荪飧　sǔn 笋损隼榫
suō 娑莎唆梭睃羧嗦嗍蓑缩　suǒ 所索唢琐锁

T (970—1031)

tā 它他她铊趿溻塌遢踏　tǎ 溚塔獭鳎　tà 拓沓挞
闼挞挞遢榻踏蹋
tāi 苔胎　tái 台邰抬苔骀炱鲐薹　tài 太汰态肽钛
泰酞
tān 坍贪滩摊瘫　tán 坛昙谈倓弹覃锬痰谭潭澹燂檀
tǎn 志坦袒钽毯　tàn 叹炭探碳
tāng 汤铴嘡蹚镗蹚　táng 唐堂棠溏搪瑭膛糖螗
镗螳樘　tǎng 帑倘惝淌傥躺镋　tàng 烫趟
tāo 叨涛绦掏滔韬饕　táo 逃咷桃陶淘萄啕梼
tǎo 讨　tào 套
tè 忒忑特铽慝　te 肽
tēi 忒
tēng 熥鼟　téng 疼誊腾滕藤朦
tī 体剔梯踢鹏鶗　tí 黄绨提啼缇鹈题缇醍蹄鳀　tǐ
体屉剃涕洟悌绨偍惕替嚏
tiān 天添黇　tián 田恬畋钿甜阗填　tiǎn 忝殄腆
淟觍舔掭　tiàn 掭
tiāo 佻挑祧　tiáo 条苕迢调笤髫蜩髫　tiǎo 挑朓
tiào 粜眺跳

tiē 帖贴萜　tiě 帖铁　tiè 帖餮
tīng 厅汀听烃桯　tíng 廷亭庭莛停蜓婷霆　tǐng 町
侹挺梃铤艇
tōng 通　tóng 仝同佟彤茼砼桐铜童酮瞳　tǒng
统捅桶筒　tòng 同恸通痛衕
tōu 偷　tóu 头投骰　tǒu 蘣　tòu 透
tū 凸秃突葖　tú 图涂荼途徒屠菟圖酴　tǔ 土吐钍
tù 吐兔堍菟
tuān 湍　tuán 团抟　tuǎn 疃
tuī 忒推　tuí 颓　tuǐ 腿　tuì 退煺蜕褪
tūn 吞暾　tún 屯囤饨豚鲀臀　tǔn 氽　tùn 褪
tuō 托饦拖脱　tuó 驮陀驼沱坨柁砣鸵跎酡橐鼍
tuǒ 妥庹椭　tuò 拓柝唾萚魄箨

W (1032—1074)

wā 洼挖哇娲蛙　wá 娃　wǎ 瓦佤　wà 瓦袜
媪　wa 哇
wāi 歪喎崴　wǎi 崴㩻　wài 外
wān 弯剜湾蜿豌　wán 丸纨完玩顽烷　wǎn 宛莞
挽惋莵晚脘婉绾皖碗　wàn 万萬腕蔓
wāng 汪　wǎng 亡王　wǎng 网柱罔往惘辋蝄魍
wàng 王妄忘旺望
wēi 危委威逶偎隈葳煨微薇巍椝惟帷维帏嵬　wéi
为韦圩违围闱帏桅帷维帷韦鬼　wěi 伪伟苇纬尾炜玮委娓诿萎唯隗猥
卺痿韪鮪　wèi 卫为未位味畏胃谓尉遗喂渭猬蔚慰魏
鳚
wēn 温榅瘟鳁　wén 文纹炆闻蚊雯　wěn 刎抆吻
紊稳　wèn 问汶揾璺
wěng 翁嗡鹟　wěng 蓊　wèng 瓮蕹罋
wō 挝涡倭窝喔蜗踒　wǒ 我　wò 沃肟卧渥握
硪幄龌醒
wū 乌污圬邬巫呜诬屋钨恶唔　wú 无毋吾芜呉梧鼯蜈鼯
鼯　wǔ 五午仵伍妩怃忤武侮捂牾鹉舞　wù 兀乌
勿戊务芴杌坞物误悟恶焐痦靰鹜雾寤骛

X (1075—1160)

xī 夕兮汐西吸希咥昔析矽郗悉茜唏奚牺息浠惜烯硒唏欷
悉晰傒稀腊犀溪锡裼皙徯瘜豨熙僖嘻蹊嬉隰嚱窸熹樨
螅歙蹊蟋羲醯曦鼷巂　xí 习席袭媳隰檄　xǐ 洗
玺徙铣喜葸蓰屣禧蟢　xì 戏系屃细阋鬩舄潟
xiā 呷虾瞎蝦　xiá 匣狎侠峡狭柙遐瑕暇辖霞黠
xià 下吓夏唬厦罅
xiān 仙先纤氙祆籼签掀锨跹酰鲜暹　xián 闲贤弦涎咸
痫娴舷衔鹇痫嫌　xiǎn 洗险显蚬铣筅跣鲜藓燹
xiàn 见苋县现限线宪陷馅羡线腺献霰
xiāng 乡芗相香厢湘箱葙襄骧镶　xiāng 详庠降祥翔
xiǎng 飨享响饷飨想鲞　xiàng 向巷项相象像橡
xiāo 肖枭枵削哓骁消宵逍绡虓魈萧硝销蛸箫潇箫霄魈嚣
xiáo 淆　xiǎo 小晓筱　xiào 孝肖哮效校笑啸
xiē 些揳楔歇蝎　xié 叶协邪胁挟偕斜颉携鞋撷
xiě 写血　xiè 写泻泄绁卸屑械谢亵解榭懈澥廨邂獬
薤燮蟹瀣躞
xīn 心芯辛忻欣锌歆新薪馨鑫　xìn 囟芯信衅
xīng 兴星惺猩腥　xíng 刑邢行形饧型硎　xǐng 省

醒擤 xìng 兴杏性幸姓荇悻
xiōng 凶兄芎匈讻汹胸 xióng 雄熊 xiòng 诇
xiū 休咻修脩羞鸺馐貅髹 xiǔ 朽宿 xiù 秀岫袖绣臭宿锈溴嗅
xū 圩戌吁盱胥须虚需嘘墟歔魆 xú 徐 xǔ 许诩栩醑 xù 旭序洫恤叙畜酗绪续勖絮婿蓄煦 xu 蓿
xuān 轩宣萱喧揎暄煊儇 xuán 玄旋悬漩璇 xuǎn 选烜癣 xuàn 泫券炫绚眩旋渲楦
xuē 削靴薛 xué 穴学茓踅噱 xuě 雪鳕 xuè 血谑
xūn 勋埙熏窨薰曛醺 xún 旬寻巡询洵峋荨浔郇荀循鲟 xùn 讯训驯汛迅逊徇殉巽熏蕈噀

Y (1161—1271)

yā 丫压呀押哑垭鸦桠鸭雅 yá 牙伢芽蚜涯崖睚衙 yǎ 哑雅 yà 轧亚压讶迓砑娅桠氩揠 ya 呀
yān 咽恹烟殷胭淹阉阏焉湮腌鄢嫣燕 yán 延言严芫妍沿炎岩研盐阎筵蜒颜檐 yǎn 奄俨衍掩眼偃罨演魇鼹鼹 yàn 厌砚咽彦宴晏艳唁验谚焰雁堰滟酽餍谳燕赝
yāng 央泱殃秧鸯 yáng 羊阳扬杨炀飏佯疡洋徉烊 yǎng 仰养氧痒 yàng 怏恙样烊漾
yāo 幺夭吆约妖要腰邀 yáo 尧肴姚珧窑谣徭遥摇徭瑶鳐 yǎo 杳咬窈窅舀 yào 疟药要钥勒鹞曜耀
yē 耶倻掖椰噎 yé 爷耶揶 yě 也冶野 yè 业叶页曳夜咽烨晔液掖谒腋靥
yī 一衣伊医依咿铱猗揖壹漪噫繄黟 yí 匜仪圯夷沂诒宜怡迤饴迻贻荑咦姨胰痍移蛇遗颐疑嶷彝 yǐ 乙已以钇矣尾苡迤蚁酏倚椅旖 yì 乂弋义亿忆艺刈艾议亦屹衣异译抑呓邑佚役怿诣易驿绎狭奕弈疫轶益谊挹悒逸翌翊勤溢意裔肄缢蜴瘗薤熠镒毅薏劓臆翼翳瘾镱懿
yīn 因阴音茵洇姻细氤殷铟堙喑 yín 吟垠狺淫寅银龈夤霪 yǐn 尹引饮蚓隐瘾 yìn 印饮茚荫胤䲟窨
yīng 应英莺婴罂嘤缨樱樱璎鹦膺鹰呎吋哩啢噝呏 yíng 迎茔盈荧莹营萤萦滢楹潆蝇羸赢瀛 yǐng 郢颖影瘿 yìng 应映硬媵
yō 哟唷 yo 哟
yōng 佣拥痈邕庸雍慵墉壅臃鳙饔 yóng 喁 yǒng 永甬泳咏俑勇涌恿湧蛹踊鲬 yòng 用佣
yōu 优忧攸呦幽悠 yóu 尤由邮犹油疣柚莜莸铀蚰游鱿鲉猷蝣蝤圝 yǒu 友有卣酉莠铕牖黝 yòu 又右幼有佑侑宥柚囿诱蚴釉鼬
yū 迂吁纡淤瘀 yú 于与予余妤欤盂臾鱼俞竽舁谀娱狳隅萸渔渝腴愉逾揄畲愚瑜榆觎虞舆窬蝓 yǔ 与予宇屿羽伛雨语禹圄圉庾瘐龉窳 yù 与玉驭芋吁聿雨妪育郁语昱狱浴彧钰峪预欲域谕尉阈寓裕遇喻御鹆誉蓣煜愈蜮毓熨豫鹬燠鬻
yuān 鸢冤鸳渊 yuán 元沅芫园员垣爰原袁圆湲媛援鼋源猿缘辕塬螈橼 yuǎn 远 yuàn 苑怨院垸媛掾愿
yuē 曰约矱 yuě 哕 yuè 月乐刖岳钥说栎悦阅钺跃越粤龠瀹
yūn 晕缊氲 yún 云匀芸纭耘筠 yǔn 允陨殒 yùn 孕运郓恽晕酝愠缊韵熨蕴

Z (1272—1387)

zā 扎匝咂拶 zá 杂砸 zǎ 咋 za 臜
zāi 灾甾哉栽 zǎi 仔宰载崽 zài 再在载
zān 糌簪 zán 咱 zǎn 拶攒趱 zàn 暂錾赞
zāng 赃脏臧 zǎng 驵 zàng 脏葬藏奘
zāo 遭糟 záo 凿 zǎo 早枣蚤澡藻 zào 灶皂唣造簉噪燥躁
zé 则责泽择啧帻箦赜 zè 仄昃
zéi 贼鲗
zěn 怎 zèn 谮
zēng 曾憎增缯罾 zèng 综锃缯甑赠
zhā 扎吒咋挓查哳渣喳揸楂劄 zhá 扎札轧闸炸铡喋劄 zhǎ 拃眨砟鲊 zhà 乍诈咋咤炸柞奓栅痄蚱榨
zhāi 斋摘侧 zhái 宅择翟 zhǎi 窄鉙 zhài 债砦寨
zhān 占沾毡旃粘詹谵瞻 zhǎn 斩展盏崭搌辗黵 zhàn 占战栈站绽湛颤蘸璪
zhāng 张章彰嫜獐璋樟蟑 zhǎng 长涨掌礃 zhàng 丈仗杖帐胀涨障幛嶂瘴
zhāo 钊招昭着啁朝 zháo 着 zhǎo 爪找沼 zhào 召兆诏炤赵笊棹照罩肇
zhē 折蜇遮 zhé 折哲辄蛰蜇谪磔辙 zhě 者锗赭褶 zhè 这柘浙蔗䗪鹧 zhe 着
zhèi 这
zhēn 贞针侦珍胗帧祯桢真砧斟甄蓁榛箴臻鱵 zhěn 诊枕轸疹畛缜 zhèn 阵圳鸩振朕赈震镇
zhēng 丁正争怔征挣峥狰症钲睁铮筝蒸 zhěng 拯整 zhèng 正证怔诤郑政挣阐症铮
zhī 之支氏汁只卮芝吱枝知肢织祇胝栀脂蜘 zhí 执直侄值职埴植絷殖跖摭踯蹠 zhǐ 止只旨址芷纸抵祉指枳咫趾黹酯徵 zhì 至忮识志豸治帜炙帙郅质制栉峙陟桎轾致秩挚贽掷窒鸷痔滞痣蛭骘智彘锧置雉稚觯踬疐
zhōng 中忪忠终盅钟衷螽 zhǒng 肿种冢踵 zhòng 中众仲种重
zhōu 州舟诌周洲啁赒粥 zhóu 妯轴 zhǒu 肘帚 zhòu 纣宙㤘绉咒胄荮昼轴皱酎骤籀 zhou 碡
zhū 朱诛侏茱珠株诸猪铢蛛潴 zhú 术竹竺烛逐舳筑瘃蠋躅 zhǔ 主拄渚属煮嘱瞩 zhù 伫苎助住注杼贮驻炷祝柱疰著蛀筑铸翥箸
zhuā 抓挝髽 zhuǎ 爪
zhuāi 拽 zhuǎi 跩 zhuài 拽
zhuān 专砖颛 zhuǎn 转 zhuàn 传转啭赚馔撰篆
zhuāng 妆庄桩装 zhuǎng 奘 zhuàng 壮状僮撞幢戆
zhuī 追骓椎锥 zhuì 坠缀惴缒赘
zhūn 肫窀谆 zhǔn 准
zhuō 拙倬捉桌涿 zhuó 灼卓茁浊斫浞酌诼着啄琢斲濯擢镯
zī 仔吱孜咨姿兹资赀缁滋嗞孳辎越锱龇鲻髭鼒 zǐ

16

子仔姊第籽梓紫滓訾　zì　字自恣渍眦

zōng　宗综棕踪鬃　zǒng　总偬　zòng　纵粽

zōu　邹诹陬　zǒu　走　zòu　奏揍

zū　租　zú　足卒族镞　zǔ　阻诅组祖俎

zuān　钻躜　zuǎn　缵纂　zuàn　钻赚撰

zuǐ　咀嘴　zuì　最罪醉

zūn　尊遵樽鳟　zǔn　撙

zuō　作嘬　zuó　作昨捽琢　zuǒ　左佐撮　zuò　坐作怍柞胙座唑做酢

威妥玛式拼音和汉语拼音音节对照索引

Index of Syllables in the Wade System with Equivalents in the Chinese Phonetic System

威妥玛拼音	汉语拼音	例字	页码	威妥玛拼音	汉语拼音	例字	页码
a	a	啊腌	1	ch'iu	qiu	丘秋	813
ai	ai	哀唉	2	chiung	jiong	窘炯	520
an	an	安庵	6	ch'iung	qiong	穷穹	810
ang	ang	肮昂	11	cho	zhuo	捉桌	1359
ao	ao	凹熬	11	ch'o	chuo	戳绰	162
				chou	zhou	周州	1339
cha	zha	扎渣	1285	ch'ou	chou	抽仇	139
ch'a	cha	叉插	100	chu	zhu	朱诸	1341
chai	zhai	摘宅	1287	ch'u	chu	出初	143
ch'ai	chai	拆柴	105	chü	ju	居具	526
chan	zhan	占展	1288	ch'ü	qu	屈曲	816
ch'an	chan	掺蝉	106	chua	zhua	抓爪	1349
chang	zhang	章丈	1292	ch'ua	chua	欻	152
ch'ang	chang	昌常	109	chuai	zhuai	拽跩	1350
chao	zhao	招兆	1295	ch'uai	chuai	揣踹	152
ch'ao	chao	抄超	115	chuan	zhuan	专撰	1350
chê	zhe	遮折	1300	ch'uan	chuan	川穿	153
ch'ê	che	车扯	118	chüan	juan	娟卷	532
chei	zhei	这	1303	ch'üan	quan	全犬	820
chên	zhen	真侦	1303	chuang	zhuang	庄装	1354
ch'ên	chen	抻晨	119	ch'uang	chuang	窗床	156
chêng	zheng	征争	1308	chüeh	jue	决撅	533
ch'êng	cheng	撑呈	123	ch'üeh	que	缺却	825
chi	ji	基几	442	chui	zhui	追锥	1356
ch'i	qi	七妻	768	ch'ui	chui	吹垂	158
chia	jia	加家	461	chun	zhun	谆准	1358
ch'ia	qia	掐恰	782	ch'un	chun	春唇	160
chiang	jiang	江将	480	chün	jun	君均	536
ch'iang	qiang	腔枪	792	ch'ün	qun	裙群	827
chiao	jiao	交焦	483	chung	zhong	中终	1331
ch'iao	qiao	敲悄	796	ch'ung	chong	充冲	136
chieh	jie	接结	492	chuo(=cho)			
ch'ieh	qie	切且	799	ch'uo(=ch'o)			
chien	jian	尖坚	468	e(=ê)			
ch'ien	qian	千铅	783	ê	e	鹅额	251
chih	zhi	之支	1315	eh	ê	欸	254
ch'ih	chi	吃尺	130	ei(=eh)			
chin	jin	今斤	502	ên	en	恩摁	254
ch'in	qin	侵琴	800	êrh	er	而耳	254
ching	jing	京晶	511				
ch'ing	qing	青轻	803	fa	fa	发伐	259
chiu	jiu	究久	521				

威妥玛拼音	汉语拼音	例字	页码	威妥玛拼音	汉语拼音	例字	页码
fan	fan	帆番	264	jao	rao	饶扰	830
fang	fang	方房	271	jê	re	惹热	831
fei	fei	非飞	277	jên	ren	人忍	833
fên	fen	分焚	283	jêng	reng	扔仍	841
fêng	feng	丰封	289	jih	ri	日	841
fo	fo	佛	295	jo	ruo	弱若	853
fou	fou	否缶	296	jou	rou	柔肉	845
fu	fu	夫父	296	ju	ru	如乳	847
				juan	ruan	软阮	851
ha	ha	哈	374	jui	rui	蕊瑞	852
hai	hai	孩海	374	jun	run	闰润	853
han	han	酣汗	378	jung	rong	容荣	843
hang	hang	杭航	382	juo (＝jo)			
hao	hao	号好	383				
hê	he	喝何	388	ka	ga	嘎尬	309
hei	hei	黑嘿	395	k'a	ka	喀卡	540
hên	hen	很恨	396	kai	gai	该改	309
hêng	heng	亨恒	397	k'ai	kai	揩开	540
hm	hm	噷	398	kan	gan	干甘	312
hng	hng	哼	398	k'an	kan	看刊	545
ho (＝hê)				kang	gang	缸钢	317
hou	hou	后候	403	k'ang	kang	康抗	548
hsi	xi	西希	1075	kao	gao	高羔	319
hsia	xia	瞎下	1085	k'ao	kao	考靠	550
hsiang	xiang	相香	1101	kê	ge	割戈	324
hsiao	xiao	消小	1111	k'ê	ke	刻克	551
hsieh	xie	些协	1121	kei	gei	给	329
hsien	xian	仙先	1092	k'ei	kei	剋	558
hsin	xin	心辛	1126	kên	gen	根亘	330
hsing	xing	星形	1133	k'ên	ken	肯垦	558
hsiu	xiu	休羞	1142	kêng	geng	更耕	331
hsiung	xiong	兄凶	1140	k'êng	keng	坑铿	559
hsü	xu	虚须	1145	ko (＝kê)			
hsüan	xuan	宣轩	1149	k'o (＝k'ê)			
hsüeh	xue	靴雪	1153	kou	gou	勾狗	341
hsün	xun	熏旬	1157	k'ou	kou	口抠	562
hu	hu	呼胡	406	ku	gu	姑骨	343
hua	hua	花划	411	k'u	ku	哭苦	565
huai	huai	淮坏	418	kua	gua	刮瓜	350
huan	huan	寰换	419	k'ua	kua	夸跨	567
huang	huang	荒皇	423	kuai	guai	乖拐	352
hui	hui	灰挥	426	k'uai	kuai	快侩	568
hun	hun	昏混	433	kuan	guan	官惯	353
hung	hong	烘红	399	k'uan	kuan	宽款	570
huo	huo	火活	435	kuang	guang	光逛	359
				k'uang	kuang	匡狂	570
i	yi	一衣	1190	kuei	gui	规龟	362
				k'uei	kui	亏愧	572
jan	ran	然染	828	kun	gun	滚棍	366
jang	rang	嚷让	829	k'un	kun	昆困	574

部首检字表
Radical Index
(一)部首目录

部首左边的号码表示部首的次序

一画	34	宀	71	灬		爿(见丬)	139	西(襾)	171	其
1 丶	35	丬(爿)	72	斗	108	母(毋)	140	页(頁)	172	雨(⻗)
2 一	36	广	73	文	109	水(氺)	141	虍	173	齿(齒)
3 丨	37	门(門)	74	方		**五画**	142	虫	174	黾(黽)
4 丿	38	辶(辶)	75	火	110	穴	143	缶		食(见饣)
5 乙(一乛乚)	39	工	76	心	111	立	144	舌	175	金(釒见钅)
二画	40	土	77	户	112	疒	145	竹(⺮)	176	隹
6 亠	41	士	78	礻(示)	113	衤	146	臼	177	鱼(魚)
7 冫	42	艹	79	王	114	示(礻见礻)	147	自		門(见门)
8 冖	43	大	80	韦(韋)	115	石	148	血		**九画**
9 讠(言)	44	廾(在下)	81	木	116	龙(龍)	149	舟	178	音
10 二	45	尢	82	犬	117	业	150	羽	179	革
11 十	46	寸	83	歹	118	目		聿(见⺺)		頁(见页)
12 厂	47	弋	84	车(車)	119	田	151	(艮)(⻟)	180	骨
13 匚	48	扌	85	戈	120	罒	152	糸(糹见纟)	181	食(飠见饣)
14 卜(⺊)	49	小(⺌)	86	比	121	皿		**七画**	182	鬼
15 刂	50	口	87	瓦	122	钅(金)	153	辛		風(见风)
16 冂	51	囗	88	止	123	矢	154	言(訁见讠)		韋(见韦)
17 八(丷)	52	巾	89	支	124	禾	155	麦(麥)		**十画**
18 人(入)	53	山	90	日	125	白	156	走	183	鬥
19 亻	54	彳	91	曰(日)	126	瓜	157	赤	184	髟
20 勹	55	彡	92	贝(貝)	127	鸟(鳥)	158	豆		馬(见马)
勹(见刀)	56	夕	93	见(見)	128	用		車(见车)		**十一画**
21 儿	57	夂	94	父		氺(见水)	159	酉	185	麻
22 几(幾)	58	犭	95	牛(牜牛)	129	矛	160	辰	186	鹿
23 厶	59	饣(食)	96	手		聿(见⺺)	161	豕		麥(见麦)
24 又(ㄡ)	60	彐(彑彐)	97	毛		(艮)(见⻟)	162	卤(鹵)		鹵(见卤)
25 廴	61	尸	98	气	130	疋(⺪)	163	里		鳥(见鸟)
26 卩(㔾)	62	己(巳)	99	攵	131	皮		貝(见贝)		魚(见鱼)
27 阝(在左)	63	弓	100	片		母(见毋)		見(见见)		**十二画以上**
28 阝(在右)	64	屮	101	斤		**六画**	164	足(⻊)	187	黑
29 凵	65	女	102	爪(爫)	132	衣	165	豸		黽(见黾)
30 刀(⺈)	66	纟	103	月(⺼)	133	羊(⺶⺷)	166	谷	188	鼠
31 力	67	子(孑)	104	欠	134	米	167	釆	189	鼻
巴(见卩)	68	纟(糸)	105	风風	135	耒	168	身		齒(见齿)
三画	69	马(馬)	106	殳	136	老	169	角		龍(见龙)
32 氵	70	巛		小(见⺌)	137	耳		**八画**		
33 忄(心)		**四画**	107	聿(⺺聿)	138	臣	170	青		

（二）检字表

1.字右边的号码指词典正文的页码。
2.带圆括弧的字是繁体字或异体字。

彦 1175　亭 1004　亮 614　衷 2　(亶) 1189

八画
旁 736　衰 939　(歆) 696　衷 1334　高 319　衮 366　离 596

九画
(产) 107　商 872　毫 383　烹 743　孰 934　(衰) 366　裒 665　率 642　939　(率) 939

十至十一画
襃 1125　裔 643　就 525　裒 763　(棄) 781　(廉) 609　(裏) 598　稟 66　稟 66　雍 1231

十二至十四画
(齊) 770　豪 384　(稟) 323　膏 322　324　裹 370　(稟) 323　褒 32　(嬴) 672　(襃) 32　嬴 1227

十五画以上
(齋) 1287　(襃) 1125　襄 1106　嬴 1227　嬴 592　(齏) 1060　(齋) 447　(嬴) 648　(齏) 448

(嬴) 647

(7) 冫部

一至五画
习 1080　斗 235　236　江 480　头 1014　冯 294　759　冲 136　139　次 164　决 533　冰 63　冻 234　况 571　冷 594　泽 250　冶 1187

六至八画
枣 1280　列 618　冼 1097　净 518　(涂) 1020　凉 611　614　凌 623　淞 957　(凍) 234　凄 769　(淨) 518　准 1358　凋 223

九画以上
凑 167　减 473　(飡) 93　寒 379　澌 952　凛 622　(凜) 622　(澤) 250　凝 720　(濱) 239

(8) 冖部

冗 845　写 1124　军 536　罕 380　冠 356　358　冢 1336　冥 688　冤 1257　幂 676　(羃) 676

(9) 讠(言)部

二画
计 456　订 229　讣 303　认 839　讥 442

三画
讦 496　讧 402　讨 983　让 829　讯 1159　汕 870　议 1211　讫 780　(託) 1027　训 1159　记 456

四画
访 275　讲 481　讳 432　讴 728　讵 530　讶 1165　讷 709　论 645　646　讼 958　讽 1140　许 1147　讹 251　(訢) 1130　讽 295　设 883　诀 534

五画
(註) 1347　(詠) 1231　评 759　证 1314　诂 346　诃 388　(訶) 388　诅 1377　识 907　1326　词 1142

诎 817　诊 1306　诈 1286　诉 960　诋 212　诌 1339　译 1212　诒 1204　词 162　诏 1298

六画
诧 104　该 309　详 1106　诨 435　诓 570　诔 592　试 916　诖 351　诗 903　诘 451　496　(誇) 567　诙 427　诚 126　诠 823　诛 1341　话 416　诞 196　诟 343　诡 365　询 1158　诣 1213　(誷) 1140　诤 1314　诩 1147

七画
说 946　948　1266　诚 501　(誖) 41　(誌) 1326　诳 1062　语 1252　1254　诮 798　误 1073　诰 324　诱 1246　海 433　诳 571　诵 959　(誺) 254　(認) 839

八画
谊 1214　谅 614　谆 1358　谈 975　请 811　诸 1342　诺 727　读 237　238　诼 1360　諏 1373　诽 281　课 557　谂 892　(論) 645　646　逯 1051　谁 885　942　谀 1249　调 225　999　谄 108

九画
(諠) 1150　谛 217　谙 8　谚 1176　(諸) 1361　谜 675　谝 751　谎 426　谋 694　谌 122　谍 226　谏 479　谐 1123　谑 1157　谒 1190　谓 1054　谕 1256　谙 921　谗 106　(譚) 432

十画
谤 30　谥 921　谦 786　谧 677　(講) 481　(譁) 415　谟 689　谘 325　谠 199　谡 962　谣 1182　谢 1125　(謥) 1339

十一画
谪 1301　谢 475　谨 507　(譑) 728　漫 657　659　谬 689

十二画
(識) 907　1326　谰 582　谱 766　(譖) 117　谭 976　潘 1283　(譟) 251　谯 797　(譙) 798　(證) 1314　1315　谪 536　(讟) 442

十三至十四画
(議) 1211　(護) 411　譀 1176　谴 791　(譟) 1281　(譯) 1212　(讇) 430　谵 1288　(讔) 1301

十五画以上
(譜) 891　(讞) 475　(讀) 237　238　雠 142　(讎) 140　(協) 1122　(警) 140　(讓) 1176　(讓) 829　谶 123　(讒) 106　(讕) 1213　(讚) 1277　(讜) 199　(讟) 1176

(10) 二部

二 257　干 312　317　于 151　于 1247　亏 572　五 1069　开 540　井 516　元 1258　无 689　1063　云 1267　些 1121　亟 5　亟 192

(11) 十部

十 904

二至六画
支 1316　卉 431　古 345　半 26　(垚) 915　考 550　毕 51　华 414　416　协 1122　甫 301　克 555　(阜) 1280　卒 169　1376　丧 861　861　卓 1359　直 1320　卑 38　阜 305　卖 656　(協) 1122

七至十画
南 700　704　真 1305　(丧) 861　861　啬 863　乾 790　(乾) 312　博 70　(喪) 861　861

十一画以上
(準) 1358　(幹) 317　(嗇) 863　亶 1331　幹 1068　(韓) 317　兢 516　(寇) 1331　翰 381　盎 152

(12) 厂部

厂 113

二至六画
厅 1003　厌 1282　历 601　厄 252　历 603　压 1161　1165　厌 1175　励 604　(匡) 1163　厕 98

七至十画
(庞) 736　厘 596　厚 405　(厔) 1003　厝 173　原 1259　厢 1106　厩 525　厥 536　(厰) 12　厨 149　厦 866　1092　(厤) 601　雁 1176

十一画以上
(厨) 149　厮 952　(属) 603　厰 113　(厭) 1175　厴 1190　厱 1176　魇 1174　(鴈) 1176　(歷) 601　(曆) 601　(厯) 605　赝 1176　(壓) 1161　1165　赝 1175　(鴈) 1176　(曆) 1190　(贋) 1176

(賑) 1174		剌 577	(冏) 428	九至十四画	(夹) 309	仗 1294	佚 721
(賑) 1175	**(15)**	(剌) 577	同 1009	黄 424	463	付 303	估 343
	刂部	(到) 517	1013	兽 929	465	代 189	348
(13)		削 1111	网 1042	普 766	**六至九画**	仙 1092	体 987
匚部	**二至三画**	1153	肉 846	奠 223	舍 882	仪 1203	990
	刘 1211	剐 351	甫 301	曾 100	884	仟 784	何 390
二至五画	刊 545	剑 478	罔 1043	1283	(俞) 645	仡 324	佐 1383
区 728	**四画**	**八画**	(岡) 317	巽 1160	命 688	仫 697	佑 1246
816	刘 628	剁 1037	周 1339	(義) 1210	臾 1248	他 970	(佈) 85
匹 748	刑 1134	剖 763		奥 1248	俞 1249	仞 840	佧 540
巨 529	列 618	(剐) 811	**(17)**	(與) 1248	(俞) 938	仔 1274	(佔) 1289
巨 761	划 414	(剢) 108	**八(丷)部**	1251	俎 1378	1360	攸 1235
匭 1272	416	108		1253	佥 802	1363	但 195
匦 1203	419	捌 283	八 14	(養) 1179	(仓) 94	(仔) 1274	伸 886
匡 570	刚 317	(刚) 317	**一至五画**	舆 1251	拿 700	**四画**	佃 222
匠 482	则 1281	剔 987	丫 1161	冀 461	龛 546	伫 1346	伶 622
臣 120	创 156	(剐) 351	兮 1075	黉 402	盒 394	仿 275	佚 1213
匣 1086	157	剥 32	公 334	黇 996	**十画以上**	伉 549	作 1382
医 1202	刖 1266	69	分 283	(興) 1133	禽 803	伙 439	1384
六画以上	刎 1058	剧 530	288	1138	舒 932	伪 1050	(作) 1386
甌 365	**五画**	**九至十一画**	**九至十一画**	**十五画以上**	畲 882	伕 296	伯 22
匱 714	判 735	副 307	(分) 288	黼 108	畲 882	传 153	69
匪 281	刬 108	割 325	兰 581	黻 532	1250	1353	佟 1011
匾 56	108	(割) 545	半 26	(釁) 402	俞 1078	伟 1050	佣 1230
匮 573	(刦) 496	(创) 156	只 1317		(傘) 859	休 1142	1233
(區) 728	别 61	157	1322	**(18)**	(佥) 785	伎 458	低 210
816	62	剩 900	兴 1133	**人(入部)**	(會) 431	伍 1071	佝 341
(匯) 431	(删) 868	(剮) 108	1138		568	伏 297	你 714
(匵) 607	利 604	剮 568	关 353	人 833	(舖) 767	伛 1252	伺 165
賾 1282	删 868	剽 752	并 63	入 850	(龠) 356	优 1233	956
(匳) 607	刨 36	剿 116	66	**一至三画**	(劍) 478	(伲) 818	佛 295
(匱) 239	737	489	共 340	个 328	龠 1267	伐 262	298
(醫) 1202	到 517	**十二画**	兑 246	(亼) 1042	(龕) 546	伣 748	伽 309
	六画	劁 1285	谷 346	今 502		伝 1033	463
(14)	剂 459	1286	兵 64	从 166	**(19)**	伾 1163	799
卜(卜部)	刻 556	劂 796	弟 216	介 500	**亻部**	仲 1337	**六画**
	刺 162	(劃) 414	**六至八画**	仓 645		价 467	佼 488
卜 72	165	416	卷 532	以 1207	**一至二画**	502	侪 106
72	刳 565	417	533	仑 94	亿 1210	伦 645	依 1202
一至四画	剐 18	419	(並) 66	令 625	仁 838	(㑨) 1334	佯 1178
下 1086	到 203	**十三画以上**	其 771	627	什 889	份 288	(併) 66
上 873	刿 366	劐 435	具 530	全 1009	906	伧 95	侬 723
卞 56	刲 545	劙 366	单 106	从 167	仃 227	123	侠 1086
卡 540	刽 365	(劇) 366	192	**四至五画**	仆 764	伈 1070	佳 463
782	刹 104	剧 530	870	伞 859	765	仵 477	侍 918
占 1288	865	(剑) 478	典 218	全 821	仇 140	任 838	佶 451
1289	制 1328	(創) 365	养 1179	会 431	814	840	佬 590
外 1034	刮 351	(劉) 628	(剙) 157	568	仍 841	伥 109	供 338
卢 637	刭 250	(劑) 459	前 787	合 327	化 411	伤 871	340
(未) 932	(剁) 250	劓 1216	酋 815	389	415	仰 1179	使 912
贞 1303	刷 938		首 927	企 775	仅 505	似 916	佚 971
五画以上	938	**(16)**	兹 1261	众 1336	507	956	侉 567
卣 638	**七画**	**冂部**	(奂) 421	余 169	仂 591	伊 1201	佰 22
卣 1245	前 787	(冄) 828	(粉) 157	余 1027	**三画**	**五画**	侑 1246
卦 351	剃 991	内 710	翁 1060	含 378	们 671	(佇) 1346	例 604
卧 1061	荆 513	冈 317	真 1305	金 785	仁 855	位 1053	侄 1321
卓 1359	剀 558	益 1214	冈 317	佘 882	仕 916	住 1346	侥 488
桌 1359	(剗) 556	(册) 98	兼 471	余 1248		伴 28	侦 1304
				巫 1062			

侣 641	(倀) 109	468	502	兄 1140	炱 973	(廻) 428	六画
侗 234	鄉 1186	(偉) 1050	(儌) 199	充 137	**(24)**	建 477	陕 870
侃 546	借 501	十画	(儂) 721	光 359	**又(又)部**	(疊) 196	陋 636
侧 98	偌 853	傢 465	儇 1150	兕 1182			陌 692
1287	值 1321	傧 63	(儍) 866	(兒) 1140	又 1245	**(26)**	降 482
伶 569	(倈) 581	傍 30	(儉) 472	先 1092	一至六画	**阝(邑)部**	1107
桃 998	(倆) 606	(傲) 1119	(儈) 569	兑 246	叉 100		限 1099
侏 1341	614	储 151	傲 489	克 556	102	卫 1052	七画
倥 1006	倚 1209	傣 189	僻 749	(兒) 254	104	厄 252	院 1264
侨 797	俺 8	傲 12	十四画以上	党 199	支 1316	仓 94	陡 236
侈 134	倒 202	脩 1114	(償) 63	兜 235	友 1240	叩 564	(陝) 870
佩 741	203	(備) 40	(儕) 106	兢 516	反 267	卮 1317	陛 51
俸 694	倾 806	傅 308	儒 849		双 940	印 1223	(隋) 798
七画	倜 980	僳 605	(儔) 140	**(22)**	邓 210	卯 663	陟 1328
信 1132	傲 991	偬 981	(優) 1233	**几(几)部**	(収) 922	危 1045	陧 719
(信) 1132	倬 1359	(條) 981	(儥) 112		劝 824	却 826	陨 1269
俦 140	(倏) 932	(偷) 95	儡 593	几 442	圣 898	即 451	险 1097
俨 1172	倏 932	123	(儘) 505	454	对 244	卷 532	除 149
俪 605	(條) 998	(傴) 1183	(儺) 727	凡 266	发 259	533	(陘) 893
便 57	脩 1143	傒 1078	(儷) 605	(几) 266	264	(卹) 1148	八画
750	俱 530	(傑) 496	(儳) 605	凤 295	戏 1083	卺 505	陪 740
俩 606	倡 109	傕 727	(儳) 1172	朵 250	观 355	(卻) 826	(陸) 633
614	114	十一画	(儸) 650	凤 960	358	卸 1125	638
(侠) 1086	(個) 328	(備) 1230	(儹) 1277	凫 297	欢 419	卿 807	陵 624
俅 815	候 406	僅 505	(儻) 980	壳 553	鸡 444		陬 1373
俏 791	偰 650	507		798	变 56	**(27)**	(陳) 121
修 1142	(保) 91	(傳) 153	**(20)**	秃 1018	取 818	**阝(在左)**	(陰) 1217
俚 599	(偸) 645	1353	**勹部**	凯 545	叔 931	**部**	陲 159
保 33	倭 1065	(偪) 1252		咒 1340	受 928		陶 982
傅 756	倪 713	(僂) 635	一至四画	凭 759	艰 470	二至四画	陷 1100
促 169	俾 49	641	勺 880	凰 425	七画以上	队 243	九画
俘 299	(倫) 40	催 170	匀 1268	(凱) 545	爰 1259	阡 784	(隊) 243
俭 472	個 991	(傷) 871	勿 1072	(凴) 759	叙 1148	防 273	隋 964
俗 960	健 478	(僡) 1373	勾 341	(鳳) 295	叟 959	阮 559	随 964
俐 605	倨 531	傻 866	342	凳 210	难 705	阱 517	(階) 492
俄 251	倔 536	像 1110	句 530		707	阮 851	(隁) 211
侮 1072	536	十二画	(句) 341	**(23)**	桑 861	(陒) 252	(陽) 1177
(係) 1083	九画	僮 1356	342	**厶部**	曼 659	阵 1307	隅 1249
俑 1232	停 1005	(僮) 1012	匆 165		(叢) 940	(阯) 1323	隈 1046
俊 539	偻 635	僧 863	包 30	么 665	(叡) 1285	阳 1177	隍 425
侪 773	641	(催) 350	旬 1157	云 1267	叠 226	阶 492	(隉) 719
956	(偽) 1050	(健) 971	匈 1140	允 1269	(叡) 852	阴 1217	隗 573
侵 801	偏 749	(僥) 488	五画以上	去 819	燮 1125	(阪) 25	1051
侯 403	债 289	僖 1079	甸 222	弁 56	(叢) 167	五画	(隆) 1217
侗 528	做 1386	僦 517	(匊) 527	台 972	(雙) 940	陀 1030	隆 633
八画	偃 1174	僳 962	匐 399	牟 694	矍 536	陆 633	634
倌 356	(偪) 46	(僵) 1092	匍 765	丢 231		638	隐 1222
倥 561	偕 1123	僚 616	(匌) 149	县 1098	**(25)**	际 459	十画以上
561	偿 112	僭 479	匋 300	矣 1209	**廴部**	阿 1	隘 5
倍 42	偶 729	(僕) 765	够 343	叁 859		2	隔 327
俯 302	偈 461	(僞) 1050	(夠) 343	参 92	(巡) 1158	251	隙 1085
(傲) 275	498	僑 797		99	廷 1004	(阿) 2	(隑) 1074
倦 533	偎 1046	(僑) 539	**(21)**	887	延 1167	陇 635	障 1295
倓 976	偷 1014	十三画	**儿部**	畚 45	(廸) 211	陈 121	(隖) 1231
俸 295	傀 573	(億) 1210	十三画	能 712	(廼) 733	阻 1316	(隔) 327
倩 792	(僃) 1277	(儀) 1203	儿 254	(參) 92	761	附 304	(際) 1085
债 1287	惚 1373	僵 481	兀 1072	92	(廻) 703	陂 38	(隣) 459
(倖) 1139	假 466	(價) 467	元 1258	887			(隣) 619

(减) 473
洒 675
渺 681
(湯) 979
湿 904
温 1055
渴 555
渭 1054
溃 573
(溃) 433
湍 1023
溅 479
(溅) 471
滑 415
溇 1261
(沧) 93
渝 1250
湃 734
湫 489
　 814
(渊) 1258
溲 959
湧 1232
溉 312
渥 1061
湄 667

十画

滓 1364
溶 844
滨 63
滂 736
滚 366
漓 597
溏 980
溢 1214
溯 962
滇 688
滟 1176
(沟) 341
溢 558
滢 1227
满 658
溁 662
漠 693
滇 218
溥 766
(减) 682
海 851
(匯) 431
源 1261
(滢) 904
滤 643
滥 583
涸 970
涠 435
滔 981
溪 1079
(沧) 95

滟 52
(滌) 212
漠 1145
溜 627
　 633
(溜) 628
滩 975
溺 715
(溺) 718

十一画

演 1174
滴 211
(滚) 366
漉 640
漩 1151
漾 1181
(滬) 410
漭 1227
(漢) 380
潢 425
滿 658
滞 1329
潇 1114
溇 582
漆 770
漕 96
漱 938
(漚) 728
　 729
漂 752
　 753
　 753
(澗) 638
漫 659
澄 423
激 611
潴 1342
漪 1203
(渗) 892
漏 636
(涨) 1294
　 1295

十二画

澈 119
澜 582
潜 765
(涝) 590
(潔) 496
潜 790
(澄) 971
(浇) 485
澍 938
澎 744
澌 952
潮 117
清 869
(潜) 869
潭 976

潦 616
　 590
(潘) 790
(澁) 863
(澂) 130
潘 734
(浑) 52
涌 881
澳 13
渴 1085
澄 130
　 210

(澄) 760
(浔) 1159
潺 107
(濱) 1160

十三画

濛 672
(浐) 422
濑 581
濒 63
滩 964
(浓) 723
澡 1280
(澤) 1282
(浊) 1359
(澹) 569
激 448
澹 197
　 976
　 1125
(澳) 223

十四画

(溥) 721
(濱) 63
(濠) 384
(濟) 455
　 459
濡 849
(涛) 981
(濫) 583
(潜) 539
(濕) 904
灌 1360
(潤) 575
(灑) 863

十五画

(潴) 891
(瀉) 1124
(澄) 1227
(瀆) 239
(瀦) 1342
(濾) 643
瀑 767
(溅) 479
(瀏) 628

十六画

(瀧) 634

　 941
瀛 1227
(瀿) 1227
瀚 381
(瀟) 1114
(瀝) 603
瀣 1126

十七画

灌 358
渝 1267
(激) 611

十八画以上

(灘) 597
(灘) 975
(灑) 855
(灩) 582
(灣) 1037
(艳) 1176

————

(33)

忄(小)部

一至三画

忆 1211
忙 660
忖 172
忏 108

四画

忏 56
(忧) 548
忧 121
忑 997
忮 1326
怄 728
怀 418
忧 1234
怅 113
忡 137
松 957
　 1334
濡 849
(涛) 981
怆 158
忤 1071
忾 545
忻 1130
快 568
忸 722

五画

怦 743
怔 1309
　 1314
怯 800
怙 411
怵 151
(忧) 151
怖 86
怛 176
怏 1180
怜 607

性 1139
怍 1386
怕 730
怊 1340
怿 1213
怪 353
怡 1204
怩 713
怫 299

六画

恼 708
恽 1270
恸 1013
恃 919
恭 339
恒 397
恓 1077
恢 427
恢 1165
(惟) 353
(恆) 397
恍 426
恫 234
恻 99
恰 782
恬 996
恤 1148
恪 557
(悄) 1323
恨 396

七画

悖 461
惟 1049
悃 141
悃 434
惚 407
惨 94
惯 358

九画

(惬) 800
愤 289
慌 423
福 574
惰 250
愠 1270
惺 1134
愦 573
愕 253
惴 1358
愣 596
愉 1250
愀 798
愎 51
惶 425
愧 573
(惮) 813
慨 545
(恼) 708

十画

慊 800
愫 962
慑 885
慕 698
慎 892
(慄) 605
(怆) 158
(愾) 545
(懊) 1340

十一画

慵 1231
慷 548
(恒) 729
(铿) 786
慢 660
(恸) 1013
(憎) 885
(惨) 94

(怅) 113

十二画

憧 137
(怜) 607
憎 1283
懂 232
憬 517
(惮) 197
憔 797
懊 13

十三画

(忆) 1211
(懔) 673
憷 152
懒 582
憾 381
(悭) 1213
懈 1125
懑 428

十四画以上

懦 727
(懑) 1165
懵 673
(怀) 418
(懶) 419
(懺) 108
(懾) 885
(懼) 531
(懽) 137

————

(34)

宀部

二至四画

宁 719
　 720
(穴) 845
宄 365
它 970
宇 1251
守 926
宅 1287
安 6
字 1364
灾 1273
完 1037
宋 958
宏 401
牢 585

五画

实 909
宓 675
宝 32
宗 1370
定 229
宕 200
宠 139
宜 1204
审 891

宙 1340
官 355
宛 1038

六画

(宲) 959
宣 1149
宦 421
宥 1246
宬 128
室 919
宫 338
宪 1100
客 556

七画

宰 1274
害 377
宽 569
宸 122
家 345
　 463
　 502
宵 1113
宴 1175
窝 1060
宾 63

八画

密 676
寇 564
寅 1220
寄 460
寂 461
宿 962
　 1144
　 1145
(寬) 1257

九至十画

(寗) 719
　 720
寒 379
富 307
寓 1256
寐 670
(寢) 510
寝 803
塞 856
　 856
　 863
骞 787
寞 693

十一画

(寧) 719
　 720
蜜 677
寨 1287
赛 856
寨 787
(寬) 569
(賓) 63

寡 351	店 222	1228	阖 1157	迟 133	370	邀 1182	**四画**
察 104	庙 681	膺 1225	闻 109	**五画**	371	避 1125	坟 287
寥 615	府 301	鹰 1225	阅 1085	述 936	透 1046	52	坊 273
寤 1074	底 212	(龐) 139	阐 434	迪 211	(進) 507	**十四画以上**	274
(寢) 803	庖 738	736	阎 1171	迥 520	(週) 1339	邋 966	坑 559
(寅) 63	庚 332	(廬) 637	**九画**	迭 226	逸 1214	(邇) 256	社 883
(實) 909	废 281	(廳) 1003	阔 575	迤 1204	逮 189	邀 681	坛 975
十二画	**六画**		(闇) 10	1209	192	(邊) 53	坏 418
寮 616	庠 1106	**(37)**	阑 582	迫 733	**九画**	邈 577	(壞) 745
(審) 891	度 240	**门(門)部**	阒 820	761	遊 1239	(邐) 599	址 1323
(寫) 1124	250		阕 826	迦 463	遒 816	(邏) 647	坚 469
十三画以上	庭 1005	门 670	(闌) 1049	迢 999	道 204		坝 17
(憲) 1100	**七画**	(門) 670	**十画以上**	**六画**	遂 965	**(39)**	坐 1383
塞 787	席 1080	**一至三画**	阙 825	迹 459	965	**工部**	(坐) 1386
寶 421	(庑) 365	闩 940	827	送 958	(運) 1269		坌 45
謇 475	座 1386	闪 869	阖 394	进 46	遍 58	工 333	(坋) 45
蹇 475	唐 979	(閂) 1171	阗 997	逆 714	(達) 176	左 1382	坼 771
(寵) 139	**八画**	闭 50	(闐) 572	(酒) 703	逼 46	巧 797	坂 25
(寶) 32	廊 584	问 1059	(闔) 752	(迴) 428	遇 1256	功 337	坍 974
(寶) 32	庶 937	闯 157	阙 548	逃 982	遏 253	式 916	均 538
	庼 1030	**四至五画**	(關) 353	选 1152	遗 1054	巩 339	坎 546
(35)	庵 8	闵 684	(闈) 971	适 920	1205	贡 340	坞 1073
爿(丬部)	庚 1253	闶 670	(闖) 108	追 1356	遄 156	巫 1062	块 569
	庸 1230	671	(闞) 749	近 406	逾 1250	攻 338	坠 1357
爿 734	康 548	闰 853		逢 1204	遑 425	丞 339	(坮) 12
壯 1355	鹿 639	(開) 540	**(38)**	退 1025	遁 247	差 100	**五画**
(壯) 1355	**九画**	闹 1049	**辶(辶)部**	逊 1160	遐 1086	104	坨 1030
妆 1354	(廂) 1106	闲 1095		**七画**	(違) 1048	105	垃 577
(妝) 1354	(廁) 98	闳 402	**二至三画**	(這) 1302	**十画**	162	幸 1139
(牀) 157	(廮) 1256	间 469	边 53	1303	(遜) 962	项 1109	坪 759
状 1356	(廄) 525	477	辽 615	逝 921	遨 12	巯 816	茔 1226
(狀) 1356	(廄) 525	(閏) 469	迁 1247	(逤) 518	遘 343	甄 816	坩 314
戕 793	赓 332	477	达 176	逍 1113	(遠) 1262		坷 551
斨 793	**十画**	1095	迈 656	逞 130	遢 971	**(40)**	555
将 480	廊 575	闸 708	过 367	造 1280	遣 791	**土部**	坯 745
483	廉 609	闸 1285	370	透 1017	遛 971		垄 635
(將) 480	廒 12	**六画**	371	逢 294	遥 1182	土 1021	垆 638
483	(廈) 866	阁 393	迅 1159	逛 362	(遞) 216	**二至三画**	坦 977
(牆) 794	1092	(関) 353	迁 784	通 1006	遛 633	去 819	坤 574
	(廥) 1223	闺 364	迄 780	1013	(遴) 1160	圣 898	坰 12
(36)	**十一画**	闻 1058	(池) 1204	逡 827	**十一至十二画**	圹 571	坿 520
广部	(廣) 361	阅 971	1209	**八画**	(適) 920	圩 1048	(坵) 813
	腐 302	闽 684	巡 1158	逵 573	遮 1300	1145	(埘) 304
广 361	廖 617	闾 641	**四画**	(逵) 45	遭 1278	圬 1062	坼 119
二至四画	**十二画**	阁 326	这 1302	逻 647	遰 247	圭 363	坡 760
邝 571	(廚) 149	(阁) 394	1303	367	遴 621	在 1275	坳 12
庄 1354	(廝) 952	阀 263	进 507	**十三画**	遵 1381	寺 956	坶 696
庆 812	(廟) 681	阁 326	远 1262	邃 532	(邁) 656	至 1325	(坤) 974
应 1224	(廠) 113	阐 1315	运 1269	(還) 374	(遼) 615	尘 120	**六画**
1228	廛 107	**七画**	违 1048	420	遏 1094	圪 324	垓 310
庐 637	(廢) 281	阅 1266	还 374		遷 133	圳 1307	型 1138
床 157	(慶) 812	阐 574	420		(選) 1152	坂 443	垭 1162
庋 365	**十三画以上**	阄 521	连 606		**十三画**	圮 748	垩 252
库 566	(廊) 571	**八画**	迓 1165		邃 532	圯 1203	垣 1259
庇 51	廪 622	阂 1167	迕 1071		(還) 374	地 207	垯 189
序 1148	(廩) 622	阉 108	近 509		420	213	垮 567
五画	廨 1125	阊 882	返 269			场 111	城 128
庞 736	(應) 1224	阈 1256	迎 1225			113	垫 222

堡 262
坰 873
垢 343
垛 250
　 250
（塆）250
　 250
垒 593
垠 1219
垦 558
（坯）8

七画

垸 1264
埔 766
埂 332
埋 655
　 657
埌 584
埙 1157
埚 367
袁 1260
埒 618
埃 3

八画

培 740
堲 574
（执）1319
堵 239
（埻）1162
（堅）252
基 446
埴 1322
（塾）1187
域 1256
（堅）469
埯 8
堙 792
堂 979
（塭）367
埰 91
埝 717
堆 243
埠 87
块 1022
（埮）546
堕 250
（隓）250
　 428

九画

（报）35
（堘）130
（堯）1182
堪 546
堞 226
塔 971
堰 1176
埂 1219
（城）475

（墙）492
堤 211
（场）111
　 113
堡 35
　 73
　 767
（块）569
塅 406
（壻）1149

十画

（塗）1020
塞 856
　 856
　 863
（塙）826
塘 980
塑 962
（垄）1226
（塚）1336
墓 698
填 997
塌 970
（塢）1073
塍 130

十一画

境 520
墒 873
塾 934
墉 1231
（塵）120
墙 794
（塾）222
（塼）1351
墟 1147
（墟）1145
墅 938
墁 660
（增）971
（场）111
　 113
（坠）1357
（隓）250
赫 394

十二画

墩 246
增 1284
（墝）796
（填）287
（壗）189
（壈）975
墨 693
墀 134

十三至十四画

壎 583
（壇）975
（壜）583

雍 1231
（墙）794
（墼）558
壁 53
壕 384
（壙）571
壑 394
（壖）1157

十五画以上

（壜）1032
（壘）593
（壟）635
（壢）635
（壩）418
壚 638
（壪）975
疆 481
壤 829
壩 17
（壥）798

(41)
士部

士 914

三至四画

壮 1355
吉 449
志 1326
壳 798
　 553
劳 585
声 896
（壮）1355

七至九画

壶 408
壸 574
壹 1203
（壺）408
（喆）1301
喜 1082
　 818
芽 1163
芷 1323
（芇）828
芮 852
莧 1098
苏 165
芥 311
　 500
芬 286
苍 95
花 411
芹 802
芪 771
芡 792
芴 1073
芟 868
苡 1209

(42)
艹部

一至二画

艺 1211
艾 4
　 1211
芄 483
芍 703
节 492
　 495
芳 591

三画

芒 661
芝 1317
芋 1254
芊 784
芍 880
芨 443
芎 1140
芑 1102
苎 1346
苄 56
芳 273
芯 1129
　 1132
芦 637
　 638
劳 585
芙 298
芫 1170
　 1258
芜 1069
芸 1268
苇 1050
芰 458
范 252
苣 530
　 818

五画

范 271
苧 720
（苧）1346
茋 1155
茎 1226
茕 813
苹 759
茉 692
苷 314
苦 565
苯 45
苛 551
茏 754
若 853
茂 664
茏 634
苫 869
　 870
苜 698
苗 680
苒 828
英 1224
茚 811
苗 1359
苓 623
茶 719
苻 299
茑 718
苑 1263
茚 1223
苟 341
苞 31
茎 511
苔 971
　 972
茅 663
苕 880
　 999
茄 463
　 799
（莓）667

六画

茫 661
荡 200
茭 485
荠 459
莱 580
（华）414
　 416
茬 47
茨 547
（荟）1140
（荳）236
荤 434
荸 648

荚 465
荆 513
茸 843
茜 792
　 1077
荏 102
荐 478
荑 987
　 1204
莛 830
草 97
茧 472
茼 1011
茵 1219
茴 430
荟 433
（荅）176
　 176
茶 102
茱 1341
莛 1005
荞 797
茯 299
荏 839
荇 1140
茗 688
荀 1159
荚 656
荨 789
　 1159
茛 331
荩 510
荫 1223
茹 848
荔 605
（兹）1361
莳 1340
药 1184
荪 966

七画

莎 865
莞 1039
莠 813
莘 887
莹 1226
莨 584
　 612
莺 1225
莱 580
（华）414
　 416
莩 47
莰 547
（荟）1140
（荳）236
莆 765
莽 661

（荚）465
莲 608
（茎）511
莫 693
蒔 921
荫 1060
萎 964
莶 1094
茶 1020
莉 605
莠 1245
莓 667
莅 605
荷 393
　 394
莜 1239
获 211
获 440
莸 1239
（莊）1354
莼 161

八画

萍 760
菠 69
菪 200
菅 472
菀 1039
菩 765
萃 171
（萊）1165
萤 1227
营 1226
萦 1227
菁 514
菾 997
菱 624
著 1348
（著）1303
　 1360
其 773
菘 957
菫 506
黄 424
菾 704
（菴）8
（菜）580
姜 769
菝 16
（菢）36
萍 1031
菲 280
　 281
苕 196
菽 932
菖 109
萌 672
菇 1002
萝 647

菌 539
（蒿）1060
菜 91
菱 1051
黄 1249
菊 528
菔 300
菟 1021
　 1022
萄 983
萏 817
萧 1113
萨 855
菇 345
菌 381
菰 345

九画

（滽）760
蒗 734
落 590
　 577
　 648
萱 1150
葵 1019
蒂 217
蒋 482
葜 782
葚 841
　 892
（葉）1188
　 1188
葫 409
葙 1106
葳 1046
葴 108
葬 1278
（韭）522
募 698
葺 781
萬 1041
（万）1040
葛 327
　 328
葸 1083
黄 573
葶 253
葿 345
董 232
葆 35
（蓧）887
（蒐）959
葩 730
葎 643
葡 765
葱 166
葵 573
葭 465
（韩）1050

	12	捐	532	(捨)	882	搜	959	(撾)	1285	擂	592	号	383
	722	损	966	(掄)	645	(搥)	159	(搜)	635		594		387
拇	696	挹	1214		645	(搯)	399		636	**(49) 小(⺌)部**		卟	72
六画		捌	16	捶	159	搀	106	摆	617			占	1288
挖	1032	捋	641	推	1023	搔	861	摆	650	小	1114		1289
挓	1285		646	掉	22	揆	573	(摑)	352	**一至四画**		只	1317
按	9	授	851	掀	1094	揉	846		369	少	880		1322
挤	455		853	掬	527	搦	67	搋	170		880	叭	15
拼	754	挫	173	捆	1340	搂	1225	攥	1225	尔	255	史	912
挥	427	捡	472	掏	981	握	1061	(樋)	1060	尘	120	句	530
挟	1123	捣	202	(掏)	983	搂	1264		1350	尖	468	兄	1140
(挟)	463	换	422	掐	782	**十画**		(摺)	1300	光	359	叱	135
拭	919	挽	1039	掺	106	(搾)	1286	(摻)	106	(未)	932	叽	442
挂	351	捅	1013	掇	249	摈	63	**十二画**		劣	618	叹	977
持	133	挨	3	(掃)	862	搞	323	撵	170	当	197	台	972
拮	496		3		862	摘	133	撞	1356		199	司	950
拷	550	**八画**		据	527	搪	980	撤	246	肖	1111	叼	223
挗	1165	控	562		531	搐	151	撤	119		1119	叫	489
拱	339	掊	763	掘	536	搛	472	撑	1382	**五至八画**		叩	564
挞	971		764	掼	358	搠	950	(撈)	584	尚	878	叨	201
挎	567	接	492	**九画**		(搲)	869	撵	717	尝	111		201
挝	1060	掠	644	搅	489	(摧)	827	(撻)	971	省	898		981
	1350	捽	1382	揎	1150	(搨)	553	(撓)	707		1138	召	1298
挠	707	掂	218	搿	553	摄	885	撷	1124	党	199	另	627
挡	199	披	1186	揩	9	摸	689	撕	952	堂	979	加	461
	200		1190	搁	325	搏	90	撒	855	常	111	**三画**	
拽	1350	掷	1329		327	摅	933		855	雀	796	问	1059
	1350	(捲)	532	搓	173	(搅)	426	撬	540		798	吁	1145
(拽)	1189	(捵)	744	楼	635	(搅)	971	(撣)	195		826		1247
拴	940	掸	195		636	摁	254	撩	615	**九至十画**			1254
拾	911		870	揰	1033	摆	22		616	棠	980	吓	394
挑	998	掖	618	搜	1121	摇	1182	(撩)	617	赏	873		1091
	1000	掮	790	揾	409	(搨)	981	撅	533	掌	1294	吐	1022
挺	1006	探	977	揍	1375	(搇)	803	(撐)	124	辉	427		1022
括	575	捧	744	搽	103	(搶)	792	撑	124	(當)	197	吉	449
指	1324	掭	998	搭	175		794	(撲)	764		199	(叻)	700
挣	1310	(掛)	351	揸	1285	携	1123	撮	173	赵	1098		713
	1315	(控)	1165	(揀)	472	(搗)	202		1383	(尠)	1098	时	173
挬	1096	(掺)	1340	握	1165	(搞)	1072	(撏)	195	**十一画以上**			1225
挪	727	捫	1186	揩	545	搋	152		870	裳	879	吕	641
拯	1310	措	173	(揹)	38	搬	25	**十四画**			113	吊	224
挼	1272	描	680	(揰)	498	(操)	1286	摛	803	(甞)	111	合	327
	1277	捺	702	援	1261	(捅)	1013	播	69	(黨)	199		389
七画		掩	1172	揄	1250	摊	975	(撏)	207	耀	1186	吒	1285
(抄)	856	(揑)	3	(揲)	1172	操	861	撬	798	**(50) 口部**		(吃)	1286
	866	捯	201	揪	803	振	1289	攒	170	口	562	吃	130
	967	捷	498	揪	521	揭	727		1277	**二画**		向	1109
捞	584	排	731	插	101	**十一画**		**十五至十七画**		叶	1122	后	403
捕	73		733	(揑)	718	摘	1287	攮	829		1188	(吆)	1181
捂	1072	掯	558			摭	1322	(攙)	106	古	345	名	684
(挟)	1123	掉	225			(摭)	651	(攔)	581	右	1246	各	328
振	1307	掳	638			摔	939	**十八画以上**		叮	227	吸	1076
捎	879	捆	352			撒	753	(攛)	170	可	553	吆	1181
	881		369				754	(攝)	885		555	吗	651
捍	381	(換)	119			**十三画**		(攜)	1123				654
捏	718	授	929			擅	871	(攤)	975				654
捉	1359	(採)	90			拥	1230	(攪)	199			**四画**	
捆	574	捻	717			撒	959		199			(叫)	489

第一列

字	页
（孃）	582
（孃）	717
嬺	941
（孌）	643

(66) 幺部

字	页
幺	1181
乡	1101
幻	421
幼	1246
兹	1361
幽	1235
（幾）	442
	454
畿	448

(67) 子（孑）部

字	页
子	1362
孑	533
孓	495

一至四画

字	页
孔	561
孕	1269
存	172
孙	966
（孝）	1153
孝	1119
孚	298
孜	1361

五至八画

字	页
学	1153
享	1107
孟	673
孤	344
孢	32
孥	725
孪	643
孩	375
（娩）	678
（孫）	966
孰	934

九画以上

字	页
孳	1362
孵	297
（學）	1153
孺	849
（孿）	719
（孌）	643

(68) 纟（糹）部

一至三画

字	页
纠	521

第二列

字	页
纩	571
纤	1247
红	338
	399
纣	1340
纤	792
	1093
纥	324
	390
约	1181
	1264
纨	1037
级	450
纪	455
	457
纫	841

四画

字	页
纹	1058
（纹）	1060
纺	275
纭	1269
纬	1050
纯	161
纰	745
纱	865
纲	318
纳	702
纵	1373
纶	355
纷	286
纸	1323
纾	931
纽	722

五画

字	页
（絃）	1096
绊	29
线	1100
绀	317
绁	1124
绂	299
练	610
组	1377
绅	887
细	1084
绌	140
（绌）	141
织	1319
绌	151
终	1334
绉	1340
绎	1213
经	511
	519
绋	298
绍	881
给	190

第三列

六画

字	页
绞	488
统	1012
绑	29
绒	843
结	492
	496
绖	189
绮	567
绕	830
（綖）	1124
绢	1219
绘	433
给	329
	455
绗	382
绛	483
络	648
绚	1153
绝	535
（絲）	950

七画

字	页
继	460
绨	988
	991
绠	332
（經）	511
	519
绡	1113
绤	574
绢	533
绥	964
绣	1144
绦	981

八画

字	页
综	1284
	1370
绽	1292
绾	1040
绻	824
绩	461
绫	624
绪	1148
续	1148
绮	778
（綫）	1100
绡	879
绯	280
绰	115
	162
绲	366
绳	898
绶	930
（綠）	91
（綢）	355

第四列

字	页
	645
维	1049
绵	677
绺	632
绷	45
	46
	46
绸	141
（緔）	684
缀	1357
绿	639
	642
缁	1362

九画

字	页
缔	217
缕	642
（總）	1371
缂	558
缭	1124
（練）	610
缄	472
缅	678
缆	582
缇	989
缈	681
缉	770
	447
缊	1267
	1270
缓	421
缎	243
缠	58
（縛）	35
线	1101
缃	1358
缜	684
（緯）	1050
缘	1262

十画

字	页
缤	63
缥	170
缟	323
缡	597
缠	107
缢	1215
缣	472
缙	510
缜	1306
缚	308
缛	851
（緻）	1329
（縚）	981
（縑）	981
缝	294
	295
（縐）	1340

第五列

十一画

字	页
缩	967
（縡）	792
缥	752
	753
（縷）	642
缦	660
缧	592
（繃）	45
	46
	46
（繙）	684
缫	1225
（總）	1371
（縱）	1373
缪	682
	689
	695
缲	862

十二画

字	页
（纖）	1319
缮	871
缯	1284
（縫）	189
（繞）	830
缴	859
（繢）	966
缭	616
（繩）	898
（繰）	796

十三至十四画

字	页
缱	481
缲	791
缳	796
（繯）	862
（繹）	1213
缵	421
（繪）	433
缴	489
（繡）	1144
（纘）	63
（續）	571

十五画以上

字	页
（纏）	107
（纘）	1148
纛	592
（纛）	592
	593
缵	1378
（纜）	829
（變）	56
（纖）	1093
（纜）	88
（纘）	643
（纘）	582

(69) 马（馬）部

字	页
马	652
（馬）	652

二至四画

字	页
驭	1254
闯	157
驮	250
	1029
驯	1159
驰	133
驴	641
驱	817
驳	70

五画

字	页
驼	1030
驻	1348
驵	1278
驶	913
（駡）	654
驷	956
驸	305
驹	527
驿	1213
驺	972
驽	725
驾	467

六画

字	页
（駮）	70
骀	377
骈	750
骁	1111
骂	654
骄	486
骆	648

七画

字	页
骊	597
骋	130
验	1175
骏	539
骓	4
骒	802

八画

字	页
骐	773
骑	773
骒	558
（駸）	1175
骓	1357
骗	962

九画

字	页
骗	751
（騔）	751
	1052
骘	97
骚	861

第六列

字	页
鸳	1074

十至十一画

字	页
骞	787
蓦	693
骟	871
腾	987
（骟）	817
骠	59
	753
骤	647
骢	166
骛	13

十二至十三画

字	页
（骁）	1111
（骜）	513
（骄）	486
（驿）	1213
（骏）	1175
（骟）	962

十四画以上

字	页
骤	1341
骥	461
（驴）	641
骧	1106
骊	941
（骊）	597

(70) 巛部

字	页
（災）	1273
甾	1273
邕	1230
巢	116

(71) 灬部

四至七画

字	页
杰	496
炁	781
（為）	1047
	1052
点	218
羔	322
烈	618
热	831
（烏）	1061
烹	743
焉	1167

八至九画

字	页
煮	1346
（焉）	1047
	1052
（無）	689
	1063

第七列

字	页
焦	487
然	828
煎	472
蒸	1310
煦	1149
照	1298
煞	865
	866

十画以上

字	页
熬	11
	12
熙	1079
黑	748
熏	1157
	1160
熊	1142
熟	924
	934
（熱）	831
熹	1080
燕	1167
	1176
（羆）	748

(72) 斗部

字	页
斗	235
	236
戽	411
料	617
（斞）	467
斜	1123
斛	408
斝	467
斟	1306
斡	1061
斠	1000

(73) 文部

字	页
文	1055
刘	628
齐	770
斉	622
（孛）	1153
斋	1287
虔	789
紊	1058
斑	25
斌	63
斐	281
斒	448
斓	582

(74) 方部

方 271
二至五画
房 274
(於) 1247
放 275
(旆) 742
施 904
六画
旁 736
㔾 742
旄 663
旌 1288
旎 773
(旇) 774
旅 641
七画以上
旌 513
族 1376
旒 714
旋 1150
1153
旗 631
旗 774
旖 1210
(旛) 264

(75) 火部

火 437
(火) 439
一至三画
灭 682
灰 426
灯 207
灾 1273
灶 1280
灿 94
灸 522
灼 1359
灵 622
炀 1178
(灾) 1273
四画
炆 1058
炕 550
炎 1170
炉 637
炜 1051
炬 530
炖 247
炒 117
炝 796
炙 1327

炊 159
炔 825
五画
炷 1348
炫 1153
烂 583
荧 1226
炳 65
炤 912
炼 610
炽 135
炭 977
(炭) 977
炯 520
烀 407
炸 1286
1286
(烁) 813
炮 32
738
739
烁 949
烃 1004
炱 973
炤 1298
六画
烫 981
烊 1179
1180
烤 551
耿 332
烘 399
烜 1152
烦 266
烧 879
烛 1343
烟 1165
烩 433
烨 1189
烙 590
烬 510
七画
烷 1038
焖 671
(焗) 854
焐 1074
焊 1004
焊 381
焙 379
烯 1078
烽 294
焕 422
焌 817
焗 528
八画
焙 42
(焯) 171

歘 152
焚 287
焯 115
焰 1176
九画
煊 1150
(桊) 813
(辉) 427
煸 55
煤 667
(煤) 1286
煳 409
(煉) 610
(煙) 1165
(煥) 726
煜 1257
(煬) 1178
煨 1046
(煖) 726
煅 243
煲 32
煌 425
(煺) 1026
煴 1026
(煒) 1051
十画
熔 845
(熒) 1226
(榮) 843
(燁) 1189
煽 869
(熗) 796
熄 1079
熘 628
熥 986
十一画
熵 873
(摰) 1026
熳 660
熠 1215
1271
十二画
(燙) 981
(熾) 135
(燉) 247
(燐) 621
燧 966
(營) 1226
(燒) 879
燀 976
燎 616
617
燔 266
燠 1257
燃 828
(镢) 1176
(燈) 207

十三至十四画
(燦) 94
爆 1281
(爛) 1343
(燴) 433
(熜) 430
(榛) 811
燹 1098
爆 1189
(燻) 1157
(爐) 510
十五画以上
(爕) 1125
爆 38
(爍) 949
(爐) 637
(鶯) 1225
(爛) 583
爨 170

(76) 心部

心 1126
一至三画
必 50
忘 1044
闷 670
671
忑 985
志 1326
忒 985
986
1023
志 977
(旨) 803
忌 458
忍 838
四至五画
态 974
忠 1334
怂 958
念 717
忿 289
忽 407
总 1371
惩 51
思 951
怎 1283
怨 1263
(忽) 165
急 451
怼 246
怠 191
怒 725
六画
恋 610

恣 1370
恙 1180
恝 465
恚 433
恐 561
恶 252
1063
1074
(耻) 332
恧 726
虑 642
恩 254
恁 711
息 1077
恳 558
恕 937
七画
悫 826
悬 1151
患 422
悉 1078
悠 1235
您 719
(恩) 165
惠 1232
八画
(恶) 252
1063
1074
惹 831
惠 433
惑 441
悲 39
崽 1274
惩 129
急 42
九画
意 1214
慈 163
(恭) 161
(愿) 800
想 1107
感 316
愚 1250
(爱) 4
愈 1257
愁 141
愆 786
十画
(愿) 1232
愿 986
(慇) 826
愿 1264
(態) 974
十一画
(慶) 812
憋 61

慧 433
(慭) 826
(懃) 94
(感) 769
(憂) 1234
(慮) 642
(慈) 1256
(慸) 782
(慫) 958
憨 378
慰 1054
十二至十三画
(憲) 1100
(憑) 759
(懇) 782
(懱) 42
懑 671
(應) 1224
1228
懋 665
(懇) 558
十四画以上
(懣) 671
(懞) 1165
(懟) 246
(懲) 129
(懸) 1151
懿 1216
(戀) 610
戆 319
1356

(77) 户部

户 410
一至五画
(乞) 252
启 775
戽 411
房 274
戾 604
肩 470
所 967
扁 55
749
扃 520
六画以上
扇 869
870
扈 411
扉 280
雇 350

(78) 礻(示)部

一至三画
礼 598
祁 771
社 883
祀 956
四画
袄 1094
祉 1324
视 918
祈 771
祇 771
(祇) 1322
五画
(祕) 51
676
祛 817
祜 411
(祐) 1246
袚 299
祖 1377
神 889
祝 1348
祚 1386
祇 1319
祠 163
六至七画
祥 1107
祷 998
祯 1304
祸 440
八至十一画
禅 107
871
祺 773
(禍) 440
禄 639
十二画以上
禧 1083
(禪) 107
871
(禮) 598
(禱) 202
襀 829

(79) 王部

王 1042
1043
一至三画
主 1344
玉 1253
玎 227
全 821

玑 444
弄 635
724
玖 522
玛 654
玕 314
四画
玩 1038
玮 1051
环 420
现 1098
玫 667
玦 534
玢 287
五画
珏 534
珐 264
珂 552
珑 634
玷 222
(珊) 869
玲 623
珍 1304
玳 190
珀 761
皇 424
珊 869
六画
班 24
珲 434
莹 1226
珥 257
珙 339
珰 198
珧 1182
珠 1341
珩 382
397
珞 648
(珮) 741
珺 123
玺 1082
七画
琉 631
望 1044
琅 584
球 815
琏 609
琐 969
理 599
琇 379
八画
(琺) 264
琮 167
琼 813
斑 25

(鼀)	116	扃	1084	赌	239	觌	212	**七至八画**		**(97)**		(氫)	1165	(徽)	668
曙	936	贮	1347	赍	447	觎	997	(牽)	785	**毛部**		氯	643		
(暖)	5	责	1282	(資)	581	(親)	800	牾	1072			氲	1267	**(100)**	
十四画以上		贤	1095	赎	934		812	犁	597	**(99)**				**片部**	
(曠)	571	贪	974	(賢)	1095	觊	1251	(牺)	168	**攵部**		片	749		
(曨)	1052	贬	55	(賤)	478	觏	343	犊	239				751	版	26
曛	770	贫	754	赏	873	(覰)	460	犄	447	(攵)	550	牍	239
曘	1157	败	23	赐	165	觐	511	(犐)	597	收	922	(牋)	471
曜	1186	货	439	赑	51	觑	818	犍	472	攻	337	牌	733
曝	38	质	1327	(質)	1327	**九画以上**		犀	1079	攸	1235	牒	226
	767	贩	271	(賙)	1339	(覵)	818	**九画以上**		改	310	牕	157
(叠)	226	购	343	**九画以上**			820	犏	750	孜	1361	(牘)	1285
(曤)	634	贯	358	赖	581	(覷)	818	犒	551	放	275	(牎)	157
曦	1080	**五画**		(賚)	510		820	(犖)	648	败	23	牖	1245
馨	1131	(貯)	1347	赛	856	(覺)	490	(犗)	660	政	1314	(牘)	239
曩	707	贰	258	赚	1353		534	(犛)	1086	故	349		
(曬)	867	贱	478		1379	矗	364	犛	597	畋	997	**(101)**	
(91)		贲	43	赘	1358	(覽)	582	靠	551	(敏)	564	**斤部**	
日(曰)部			51	(購)	343	(覿)	647	犟	483	**六至七画**		斤	503
日	1264	贯	919	赙	308	(觀)	212	(犢)	239	效	1119	斥	135
二至七画		贴	1001	(贅)	1329	(觀)	355	(犧)	1077	敖	11	(劤)	510
曲	816	(貼)	1001	赜	1282		358			致	1329	斩	1288
	818	贵	366	赠	1284			**(96)**		敌	211	斧	302
旨	1323	贶	572	赞	1277	**(94)**		**手部**		敉	51	所	967
曳	1189	(買)	655	赡	871	**父部**		手	924	(敔)	773	欣	1130
者	1302	贷	191	(贐)	510			**四至八画**		(教)	70	斯	793
杳	176	贸	665	(贓)	1278	父	301	承	127	赦	885	顾	773
	971	贻	1204	(臟)	1278		303	拜	23	教	486	断	242
(者)	1302	费	282	(贖)	934	爷	1186	(拏)	700		491	斯	952
冒	664	贺	394	(屭)	1084	斧	302	挈	643	救	136	新	1130
曷	393	**六至七画**		(蠶)	1378	爸	18	拳	824	救	524	斲	1360
耆	773	赃	1278			釜	302	挚	800	敛	609	(斷)	242
(書)	930	资	1361	**(93)**		爹	226	挛	1329	(敘)	1148		
曹	96	赅	310	**见(見)部**		(爺)	1186	拿	700	敏	684	**(102)**	
(勗)	1148	贼	1282	见	475			挲	856	敢	315	**爪(爫)部**	
曼	659	贾	347		1098	**(95)**			866	**八至九画**		爪	1297
冕	678		466	(見)	475	**牛(牜牛)**			967	敦	246		1350
八画		贿	433		1098	**部**		掌	1294		246	妥	1030
曾	100	赀	1329	**二至七画**		牛	721	掰	18	散	860	孚	298
	1283	赁	1362	观	355	**二至四画**		掣	119		860	受	928
替	991	赁	622		358	牝	755	弄	730	敬	519	采	90
最	1379	(賵)	1148	视	918	牟	694	**九画以上**		敞	113		91
(嘗)	111	赂	639	现	1098	牢	585	搴	787	数	935	觅	676
		赈	510	规	363	牦	660	摹	689		937	(爭)	1308
(92)		(賔)	63	(覓)	676	牡	696	摩	651		950	爬	730
贝(貝)部		(實)	909	觅	676	告	323		690	(敫)	1177	乳	849
贝	40	赉	581	觉	490	(牠)	970	(摯)	1329	**十一画以上**		爱	1259
(貝)	40	赈	1307		534	牥	663	擎	811	(敵)	211	爰	4
二至四画		赇	815	觇	106	牧	698	(擊)	442	敷	297	舀	1184
贞	1303	赊	881	览	582	物	1073	(舉)	528	(數)	935	奚	1077
则	1281	**八画**		觊	647	**五至六画**		擘	72		937	舜	947
负	303	赔	740	觋	460	荦	648	(擘)	18		950	(爲)	1047
贡	339	赓	332	舰	478	牯	347	攀	734	整	1310		1052
财	89	赋	307	**八画以上**		牵	785	(攣)	643	(斂)	609	(愛)	4
员	1259	赌	811	觌	520	牲	898			(變)	56		
		(贊)	1277		615	特	985			(戲)	1249		
		(賬)	1295	(觀)	239	牺	1077						
		(賣)	656										

(亂) 643
叆 5
孵 297
爵 536
(靉) 5

(103)
月(⺼)部

月 1265
一至三画
(肊) 1216
有 1240
1246
刖 1266
肌 444
肋 590
593
肓 423
肝 314
肟 1061
肛 318
肚 239
240
肘 1340
肖 1111
1119
(肐) 325
肠 111
四画
肪 275
肮 11
育 1254
肩 470
(肨) 737
肤 296
肼 517
朊 851
肢 1319
肺 282
肽 974
(肧) 740
肱 328
(肬) 1239
肫 1358
肯 558
肾 892
肿 1336
肭 702
肴 1182
胀 1295
朋 743
股 346
肥 280
服 298
305
胁 1122
五画
胖 734
737
脉 657
692
胠 817
胡 408
胚 740
胧 634
胨 234
胩 540
背 38
41
胪 638
胆 195
胛 466
胂 892
胃 1054
胄 1340
胗 1304
胜 899
胙 1386
胍 351
胝 1319
胞 32
胫 519
胎 971
胥 1145
六画
胺 10
脐 773
胶 486
脊 455
脑 708
脏 1278
1278
胲 377
朕 1307
胼 751
脒 675
朔 949
朗 584
脓 724
胯 567
胰 1204
胱 361
胴 234
胭 1166
脍 569
脎 855
脁 1000
(脈) 657
692
(胮) 736
胳 325
327
脆 171
胸 1141
(胷) 1141
(脃) 171
脂 1319
能 712
(脇) 1122
(脅) 1122
七画
脘 1039
脝 397
望 1044
脱 1028
脦 207
986
脖 70
脚 488
脯 302
765
(脣) 161
豚 1027
(脛) 519
脶 647
脬 737
脸 609
(膃) 1058
脲 718
八画
腚 230
腔 793
腕 1041
腋 1190
腑 302
(勝) 899
腈 514
(脹) 1295
期 447
769
(朞) 447
腊 578
1079
朝 116
1296
(腖) 234
(腎) 892
腌 2
1167
腓 281
腘 370
腆 997
(腡) 647
腴 1250
脾 748
腱 479
九画
腟 130
媵 1230
腾 987
腻 715
腠 168
腩 707
腰 1181
腼 678
(腸) 111
腽 1033
腥 1134
腮 856
腭 253
腧 938
(腳) 488
(腫) 1336
腹 308
腺 1101
鹏 744
腿 1025
(腦) 708
十至十二画
膑 63
膀 30
736
737
膏 322
324
膂 642
(膆) 962
膜 690
膊 71
膈 327
滕 987
膝 1079
膘 59
膛 980
(膚) 296
(膕) 370
膗 152
(膠) 486
膪 153
膳 871
膦 622
膨 744
(膢) 578
臄 482
十三画以上
臆 1216
膻 869
臁 609
膺 1225
臃 1231
(膯) 986
(賸) 900
臌 348
朦 673
(膿) 724
臊 862
862
(膾) 569
(臉) 609
(膽) 195
臀 1027
臂 42
53
十四画以上
(臏) 63
(臍) 773
臞 987
(臕) 59
(臘) 578
(朧) 634
(臙) 1166
(臚) 638
臢 1273
(臟) 1278

(104)
欠部

欠 791
二至八画
次 164
欢 419
欤 1248
欧 728
软 851
欣 1130
欬 545
(欨) 388
欷 1078
欲 1256
(欵) 570
欸 3
4
254
欻 152
款 570
欺 770
九画以上
歆 1130
歇 1121
歃 866
歉 792
歌 325
(歎) 977
(歐) 728
歔 1147
(歘) 152
歙 1080
(歟) 1248
(歗) 1121
(歡) 419

(105)
风(風)部

风 289
(風) 289
飏 1178
飒 855
(颱) 972
(颳) 351
飓 531
(颺) 1178
飕 959
飗 632
飘 752
(飄) 752
(飆) 60
飙 60
(飇) 60

(106)
殳部

殳 931
四至八画
殴 728
殁 692
段 242
(殺) 864
般 25
殷 1166
1219
(殼) 553
798
(殺) 237
(發) 259
九画以上
毂 345
348
彀 343
骰 1017
毁 430
殿 223
(毀) 534
毅 1215
(穀) 346
(毆) 728
觳 409

(107)
聿(肀⺻)部

聿 1254
隶 605
(書) 930
肃 961
(晝) 1340
(畫) 417
肆 957
肄 1215
(肇) 1300
肇 1300
(肅) 961
(盡) 507

(108)
毋(母)部

毋 1069
母 695
每 668
毑 498
毒 237
贯 358
毓 1257
(緐) 266

(109)
水(氺)部

水 942
一至五画
(氷) 63
永 1231
(氹) 200
求 814
汆 1027
氽 169
凼 200
汞 339
录 638
隶 605
尿 718
964
沓 176
971
泰 974
泵 46
泉 823
六画以上
浆 481
(漿) 483
淼 681
黎 597
滕 987
(漿) 481

(110)
穴部

穴 1153
一至五画
穷 812
究 521
空 559
561
帘 607
穸 1077
穹 813
(穽) 517
突 1019
窀 1358
窃 800
穿 153
窆 55
窍 798
窅 1184
容 844
窄 1287
窎 225
窈 1184
六至七画
窒 1329
窕 1000
窑 1182
(窓) 157
窜 170
窝 1060
窖 492
窗 157
窘 521
八至九画
窣 960
窥 572
窦 237
窠 552
(窩) 1060
窟 565
(窪) 1032
窨 1157
1224
窭 531
窬 1251
十画以上
(窯) 1182
(窮) 812
窳 1253
(窰) 1182
(窶) 531
窸 1080
(窻) 157
窿 635
(竅) 798
(竄) 170
(竈) 1280
(竇) 237
(竊) 800

(111)
立部

立 602
一至六画
产 107
妾 800
亲 800
812
竖 937
彦 1175
飒 855

二至四画
盯 227 | 盲 661 | 盰 1145 | 眈 194 | 相 1102 / 1110 | 眄 678 / 680 | 眍 562 | 眮 246 | 眇 681 | 省 898 / 1138 | 眨 1286 | 盼 736 | 看 546 / 547 | 盾 247 | (䀠) 142 | 眉 667

五画
眩 1153 | 眬 634 | 眚 898 | 眠 677

六画
眷 533 | 眯 674 / 675 | 眶 572 | 眦 1370 | (眥) 1370 | 眺 1000 | 眵 132 | 睁 1310 | 眸 695 | 眼 1172

七画
睇 217 | 睐 581 | 睑 870 | (䁀) 574 | 睑 474 | 睃 967 | 鼎 228

八画
(睄) 533 | (睒) 870 | 睛 514 | 睦 698 | 睃 596 | 睹 239 | 瞄 681 | (睞) 581 | 睨 1164 | 睫 498 | 督 237

睬 91 | 睡 946 | 睢 964 | 睨 715 | 睥 52 / 749

九画
(睰) 674 / 675 | 睽 635 | 睿 852 | 瞅 142 | 瞍 959 | 瞑 573 | 督 665

十画
瞌 1085 | 瞇 688 | 瞰 553 | 瞒 658 | 瞋 119

十一画
瞥 753 | (瞞) 658 | (縣) 1098 | (瞘) 562 | 瞟 753 | 瞳 124 | (瞜) 635 | 瞰 548

十二画
瞳 1012 | 瞭 617 | (瞭) 616 | 瞬 947 | 瞧 797 | 瞪 210 | 瞩 1346

十三画以上
瞽 348 | 矇 673 | (矓) 672 | 矍 818 | (瞼) 474 | 瞻 1288 | (矚) 634 | (矙) 548 | (矚) 1346

(119) 田部
田 996 | 甲 466 | 申 885 | 由 1236 | 电 220

二至三画
亩 696 | 町 1006 | 甸 222 | 男 704 | (叱) 672 | 界 51 | (叫) 1307 | 备 40 | 甾 1273

四画
思 951 | 畎 824 | 畏 1054 | 毗 747 | (毘) 747 | 胃 1054 | 界 501 | 畋 997 | 畈 271

五至六画
(畞) 696 | 畜 151 / 1148 | 畔 736 | (畢) 51 | 畛 1023 | 畛 1306 | 留 630 | 畚 45 | 畦 773 | (異) 1211 | 略 644 | (畧) 644 | 累 592 / 593 / 593

七至十画
富 307 | 畴 141 | (畱) 630 | 畲 882 | 畬 882 / 1250 | 番 264 | (畫) 417 | 替 976 | 畸 447 | (當) 197 / 199 | 畿 448

十一画以上
(奮) 288 | (畴) 873 | 疃 1023 | (疊) 593 | (疇) 141 | 疊 592

纍 592 | (纝) 592 / 593 | (疊) 226

(120) 罒部
四 954

三至五画
罗 646 | 罚 263 | 罡 319 | 罢 18 | (罢) 18

六至八画
罥 605 | (買) 655 | 署 935 | 罨 1174 | 置 1330 | 罪 1380 | 罩 1300 | 蜀 935

九至十一画
黑 748 | 罱 582 | (罰) 263 | (罵) 654 | (罷) 18 / 18 | 罹 597

十二画以上
罾 1284 | 羁 449 | (羆) 748 | (羅) 646 | 蠲 532

(121) 皿部
皿 684

三至四画
孟 1248 | 孟 673 | (盉) 394 | (盃) 38 | 盅 1335 | 盆 743 | 盈 1226

五画
益 1214 | 盏 1289 | 盐 1171 | 盍 394 | 监 471 / 478

盎 11 | (盌) 1040

六画
盗 204 | 盖 311 | 盔 572 | 盛 129 / 900 | 蛊 347 | 盒 394 | 盘 734

八至十一画
(盞) 1289 | 盟 672 | (監) 471 / 478 | (盡) 507 | (盤) 734 | 盐 348 | (盧) 637 | 盦 8 | 盥 358

十二画以上
(盪) 200 | (蠱) 347 | (鹽) 1171 | (豔) 1175

(122) 钅(金)部

一至二画
钇 1209 | 钌 309 | 针 1303 | 钉 227 / 229 | 钋 760 | 钊 1295 | 钉 617 / 617

三画
钍 671 | (釺) 381 | 钛 1022 | (釦) 564 | 钎 785 | 钏 156 | 钐 869 | 钓 224 | 钒 266 | 钗 105 | 钕 726

四画
钘 273 | 钪 550 | 钬 439

钙 311 | 钛 974 | 钚 86 | 钜 530 | (鉅) 529 | 钝 247 | 钞 115 | (鈔) 115 | 钟 1335 | 钡 41 | 钠 702 | 钢 318 / 319 | 铃 789 | 纵 166 | 钩 538 | 钥 1186 / 1266 | 钦 802 | 钧 341 | 钨 1063 | 钮 722 | 钯 17 | (鈀) 730

五画
铊 970 | (鉈) 1030 | 钸 921 | 铋 51 | 钰 1255 | 钱 789 | 钲 1310 | 钳 789 | 钴 347 | 钵 69 | 钶 552 | 钷 761 | 钹 70 | 钺 1266 | 钻 1378 / 1378 | 铈 638 | 钼 698 | 钽 977 | 钾 466 | 钿 223 / 997 | 铀 1239 | 钟 891 | 铃 624 | 铁 1002 | 铂 70 | (鈎) 341 | 铅 786 | 铆 664 / 767

铌 713 | 铍 747

六画
铵 9 | 铷 979 | 铲 108 | 铰 488 | 铱 1203 | 铳 139 | 铗 465 | 铙 590 | 铐 551 | 铛 661 | 铒 257 | 铺 1245 | (銤) 1002 | 铩 708 | 铟 124 / 199 | 铝 641 | 铜 1011 | 锦 226 | 铠 545 | 铡 1286 | 铨 824 | 铢 865 | 铪 374 | 铫 226 | 铢 1342 | 铣 1082 / 1098 | 铥 231 | 铤 1006 | 铧 415 | 铭 688 | 铬 329 | 铮 1310 / 1315 | 铯 863 | 银 1220 | 铷 848

七画
锌 1130 | 锎 545 | 铜 474 | 锐 852 | 锑 987 | 银 584 | 铼 581 | 铽 986 | 铸 1348 | 锗 586 | 铺 764 / 767 | (鋏) 465 | 链 610 | 销 1113

锁 969 | 铎 380 | 铿 559 | (銲) 381 | 铤 1284 | 锂 600 | 锄 149 | (鋤) 1360 | 锅 367 | 锉 174 | 锆 323 | 锈 1145 | 锇 252 | 锋 294 | 锓 803 | 铜 527 / 528 | 铜 2

八画
锭 230 | 锫 741 | 锯 584 | (錶) 60 | 锗 1302 | 错 174 | 锘 727 | 锚 663 | (鍊) 581 | 锛 43 | (錢) 789 | (鋼) 318 / 319 | 锝 207 | 锞 558 | 锡 1079 | 锢 350 | 锣 647 | (鍋) 367 | 锤 159 | 锥 1357 | 锦 506 | 锧 1330 | 锨 1094 | 键 479 | (錄) 638 | 锯 531 | (鋸) 527 | 锰 673 | 镏 1362

九画
锲 793 | 镍 3 | 镀 240 | 镁 669 | 镂 636 | 锶 800 | (鍊) 610 / 610

(三)难检字笔画索引

(字右边的号码指词典正文的页码)

						二十一至二十三画	二十四画以上
寰 1331	(夥) 439	肄 192	噩 253	(隶) 605	(夔) 232	赣 317	蠹 205
截 498	(暢) 114	(寰) 1331	整 1310	(斃) 51	(豎) 1202	(赢) 648	(巍) 798
赫 394	舞 1072	赜 1206	臻 1306	(虜) 572	(歸) 362	蠱 748	蠱 152
(壽) 928	毓 1257	(憂) 1234	(舘) 356	爵 536	**十九画**	鼙 755	(艶) 1175
斡 1061	辜 322	(舖) 767	(舉) 528	黏 716	赢 592	懿 1216	(赣) 402
(幹) 317	孵 297	輦 551	餤 1176	(嚮) 1109	(賬) 108	囊 707	(鬓) 5
聚 531	蕭 704	豫 1257	(龜) 363	**十八画**	疆 481	(孋) 108	鼍 986
兢 516	暨 461	**十六画**	538	幪 108	**二十画**	齋 448	(霽) 1133
(爾) 255	疑 1206	赢 1227	**十七画**	(蘆) 596	馨 1131	(赢) 647	(豔) 1175
臧 1278	**十五画**	(隶) 605	赢 1227	1083	耀 1186	灝 532	(鬱) 1254
(甎) 816	犖 597	黏 996	戴 192	鬻 364	(譽) 567		
夥 439	(熬) 663	翰 381	(韓) 380	(鼀) 1032			

A

ā

阿　ā　*dial.*　① (a prefix used before pet names, monosyllabic surnames, or numbers denoting order of seniority in a family, to form terms of endearment): 〜宝 A Bao／〜唐 A Tang; Tang／〜大 A Da; the eldest　② (a prefix used before kinship terms): 〜爸 dad; pop; pa／〜妹 younger sister; sister ——see also à; ē

阿鼻地狱　Abí Dìyù　*Buddhism*　the Avici Hell, the last and deepest of the eight hot hells (as opposed to the eight cold hells), where the condemned go through endless cycles of suffering, death, and rebirth without intermission

阿波罗　Ābōluó　Apollo (the Greek and Roman god of the sun); a handsome young man

阿昌族　Āchāngzú　the Achang nationality; or the Achangs, inhabiting Yunnan Province

阿的平　ādīpíng　*pharm.*　atabrine

阿爹　ādiē　*dial.*　① dad　② granddad (on father's side)

阿斗　Ā Dǒu　① the infant name of Liu Shan (刘禅, 207-271), last emperor of Shu Han (蜀汉, 221-263), known for his lack of ability and weakness of character　② a weak-minded and ne'er-do-well person; a failure or fool: 扶不起的〜 a disappointing person; a hopeless case／不要把群众看作〜。Don't treat the masses as if they were fools.

阿尔巴尼亚　Ā'ěrbāníyà　Albania

阿尔巴尼亚人　Ā'ěrbāníyàrén　Albanian

阿尔巴尼亚语　Ā'ěrbāníyàyǔ　Albanian (language)

阿尔卑斯山脉　Ā'ěrbēisī Shānmài　the Alps

阿尔法粒子　ā'ěrfǎ lìzǐ　*phys.*　alpha particle

阿尔法射线　ā'ěrfǎ shèxiàn　*phys.*　alpha ray

阿尔及利亚　Ā'ěrjílìyà　Algeria

阿尔及利亚人　Ā'ěrjílìyàrén　Algerian

阿飞　āfēi　a young street rowdy; a (teenager) hoodlum or hooligan

阿伏伽德罗定律　Āfújiādéluó dìnglǜ　*chem.*　Avogadro's law

阿芙蓉　āfúróng　another name for 鸦片 yāpiàn

阿富汗　Āfùhàn　Afghanistan

阿富汗人　Āfùhànrén　Afghan

阿哥　āgē　*dial.*　① elder brother　② an affectionate form of address between men of about the same age ——see also àgē

阿根廷　Āgēntíng　Argentina

阿根廷人　Āgēntíngrén　Argentine

阿公　āgōng　*dial.*　① grandpa; granddad　② husband's father; father-in-law　③ a term of respect for any elderly man

阿家阿翁　āgū-āwēng　(also 阿家翁 āgūwēng)　① husband's father and mother; parents-in-law　② the head of a house: 不痴不聋，不作阿家翁。Unless you're deaf or obtuse, you'll never do as head of the house.

阿訇　āhōng　*Islam*　ahung; imam (the officiating priest of a mosque)

阿基米德原理　Ājīmǐdé yuánlǐ　*phys.*　Archimedes' principle

阿Q　Ā Kiū　① Ah Q, the main character in Lu Xun's *The True Story of Ah Q* (《阿Q正传》), a victim of social injustice who seeks consolation in interpreting his defeats as moral victories　② a person who interprets his defeats as moral victories

阿拉　ālā　*dial.*　① I or me　② we or us

阿拉伯半岛　Ālābó Bàndǎo　the Arabian Peninsula; Arabia

阿拉伯国家　Ālābó guójiā　Arab countries (*or* states)

阿拉伯国家联盟　Ālābó Guójiā Liánméng　the League of Arab States; the Arab League

阿拉伯胶　ālābójiāo　gum arabic; gum acacia

阿拉伯联合酋长国　Ālābó Liánhéqiúzhǎngguó　the United Arab Emirates

阿拉伯人　Ālābórén　Arab

阿拉伯数码　Ālābó shùmǎ　(also 阿拉伯数字 Ālābó shùzì)　Arabic numerals

阿拉伯语　Ālābóyǔ　Arabic (language)

阿鲁巴　Ālǔbā　Aruba

阿罗汉　āluóhàn　same as 罗汉 luóhàn

阿妈　āmā　*dial.*　① woman servant; amah　② mom; mum; mummy ——see also àma

阿曼　Āmàn　Oman

阿曼人　Āmànrén　Omani

阿芒拿　āmángná　*chem.*　ammonal

阿猫阿狗　āmāo-āgǒu　(also 阿狗阿猫 āgǒu-āmāo)　*dial. derog.*　people of small importance; Tom, Dick, and Harry

阿门　āmén　(used at the end of a Christian's prayer) amen

阿米巴　āmǐbā　amoeba

阿米巴痢疾　āmǐbā lìji　amoebic dysentery

阿米妥　āmǐtuǒ　*pharm.*　amytal

阿摩尼亚　āmóníyà　ammonia

阿姆哈拉语　Āmǔhālāyǔ　Amharic

阿木林　āmùlín　*dial.*　a stupid fellow; dullard; country bumpkin

阿尼林　ānílín　*chem.*　aniline (oil)

阿片　āpiàn　*pharm.*　opium

阿片制剂　āpiàn zhìjì　*pharm.*　opiate

阿婆　āpó　*dial.*　① grandma　② husband's mother; mother-in-law　③ a term of respect for any elderly woman

阿朴吗啡　āpǔmǎfēi　*pharm.*　apomorphine

阿塞拜疆　Āsàibàijiāng　Azerbaijan

阿是穴　āshìxué　*Chin. med.*　Ashi Point, any nerve point on the affected part of the body other than those specified for acupuncture-moxibustion

阿司匹林　āsīpǐlín　*pharm.*　aspirin

阿嚏　ātì　*onom.*　the sound of sneezing; atishoo; ahchoo

阿托品　ātuōpǐn　*pharm.*　atropine

阿伊马拉语　Āyīmǎlāyǔ　Aymara (language)

阿姨　āyí　① *dial.*　mother's sister; aunt　② a form of address for a woman of one's parents' generation; auntie　③ a nursemaid in a family or a childcare work-

er in a nursery school or kindergarten
阿扎尼亚 Āzāníyà Azania
阿扎尼亚人 Āzāníyàrén Azanian

啊（呵） ā *interj.* (expressing surprise or admiration): ～, 出虹了! Oh, there's a rainbow! / ～, 这菊花真美! Ah, these chrysanthemums are simply gorgeous! / ～! 黄河! 你是中华民族的摇篮。O! Huanghe, cradle of the Chinese nation!

啊哈 āhā *interj.* ① (expressing surprise): ～, 你在这儿呀! Oh, so you're here! ② (expressing admiration or praise): ～, 这活儿做得真不错呀! Wow! That's a really good bit of work. ③ (expressing realization): ～, 你又来捉弄我了。Ha-ha, so you're teasing me again! ④ (expressing triumph): ～, 我又赢了! Aha, I've won again!

啊呀 āyā *interj.* ① (expressing surprise): ～, 这消息传得真快呀! How fast the news got round! ② (expressing resentment, dissatisfaction or embarrassment): ～, 这事可不好办! Oh, that would really be a hard job.

啊哟 āyō (also 啊唷 āyō) *interj.* (expressing surprise, sudden pain, etc.): ～, 我的钱包丢了! Oh, no, I've lost my purse! / ～, 今天的天气太糟糕了! What terrible weather this is! / ～, 疼死我了! Ow, that (*or* it) hurts!

锕 ā *chem.* actinium (Ac)
锕系元素 ā xì yuánsù *chem.* actinides

腌 ā see below —— see also yān
腌臜 ā·zā *dial.* ① filthy; dirty ② unhappy; ruffled

á

啊（呵） á *interj.* (pressing for an answer or asking for a repetition of sth. just said): ～? 你说什么? Eh? *or* Pardon? / ～, 你明儿倒是去不去呀? Well, are you going tomorrow or not?

ǎ

啊（呵） ǎ *interj.* (expressing puzzled surprise): ～? 他还没来啊! What! Isn't he here yet?

à

阿 à see below —— see also ā; ē
阿哥 àgē ① (a Manchu term of address) son ② the title of a Manchu Emperor's son not yet of age —— see also āgē
阿妈 àmā (a Manchu term of address) father; dad —— see also āmā

啊（呵） à *interj.* ① (expressing agreement or compliance): ～, 我就来。All right, I'm coming. ② (expressing sudden realization): ～, 原来是你呀! Ah, so it's you.

a

啊（阿、呵） a *part.* ① (used at the end of a sentence to express enthusiasm): 多好的天儿～!

What a fine day! / 这次参观收获不小～! What a lot of things we've learned during this visit! ② (used at the end of a sentence to express obviousness or impatience): 你这话说得是～。What you say is quite true. / 我没有去是因为我病了～。I didn't go because I was ill. / 我也没说你全错了～。I didn't say you were entirely wrong. ③ (used at the end of an order, warning, etc.): 快走～! Hurry up! / 你可要小心～! Do be careful! ④ (used at the end of a sentence to express doubtful questioning): 是谁～? Who is it? / 这消息是真的～? Is this really true? / 这本书你倒是要不要～? Do you really want this book? / 你想吃苹果呢还是吃梨～? Would you like to have an apple or a pear? ⑤ (used to indicate a deliberate pause): 你～, 老这样下去可不行! Look, you can't go on like this. / 去年～, 去年这会儿～, 我还在上海呢。Last year—about this time last year, I was still in Shanghai. ⑥ (used in enumerating items): 茄子～, 黄瓜～, 洋白菜～, 西红柿～, 各种蔬菜摆满了货架。The shelves were filled with all sorts of vegetables—eggplants, cucumbers, cabbages, tomatoes. / 这～, 那～, 她说了一大堆。She talked about this, that and the other—oh, she said such a lot of things.

āi

哎（嗳） āi *interj.* ① (showing surprise or disapproval): ～! 是老刘啊! Why, it's Lao Liu! / ～, 你怎么不早跟我说呢? But why didn't you tell me sooner? ② (used to remind sb. of sth.): ～, 咱们这回可不能再迟到啦! Now, we mustn't be late again this time. / ～, 小心油漆! Mind the wet paint! / ～, 别把凳子碰倒了! Watch out! Don't knock the stool over.

哎呀 āiyā *interj.* ① (expressing surprise or amazement): ～, 这水真甜哪! Ah, this water is really sweet! / ～! 好不容易见面哪! So we meet again. / ～, 好大的雨呀! My God! It's raining buckets! *or* It's pouring! ② (expressing complaint or showing impatience): ～, 你怎么来得这么晚呢! Goodness, why have you come so late? / ～, 你又忘啦! Oh dear, you've forgotten again!

哎哟 āiyō *interj.* (expressing astonishment or pain): ～, 壶漏啦! Hey, the kettle leaks! / ～, 真烫。Ouch! (*or* Ow!) It's hot. / ～! 我把钥匙弄断了! Damn, I've broken the key! / ～! 我肚子好疼! Oh, I've got an awful stomachache! *or* My stomach hurts!

哀 āi ① grieved; sorrowful: 悲哀 bēi'āi ② mourning: 志哀 zhì'āi ③ pity: 哀怜 āilián

哀兵必胜 āibīng bì shèng an army burning with indignation is bound to win
哀愁 āichóu be distressed: 无限～ be extremely distressed
哀辞 āicí a formal expression of sorrow or mourning, esp. in verse; elegy
哀悼 āidào mourn for the deceased; grieve over sb.'s death; lament sb.'s death: 向死者家属表示深切的～ express one's heartfelt condolences to the family of the deceased
哀的美敦书 āidīměidūnshū same as 最后通牒 zuìhòu tōngdié
哀而不伤 āi ér bù shāng sorrow without self-injury
哀告 āigào beg piteously; supplicate
哀歌 āigē ① dirge; elegy ② croon plaintively
哀号 āiháo cry piteously; wail
哀嚎 āiháo ① same as 哀号 āiháo ② wail mournfully: 饿狼在野外～。Famished (*or* Hungry) wolves were howling in the wilds.

哀鸿遍野 āihóng biànyě　famished refugees swarming over the land; disaster victims moaning everywhere

哀毁骨立 āi huǐ gǔ lì　be emaciated with grief at the loss of one's father or mother

哀矜 āijīn　*formal*　feel compassion for; pity

哀怜 āilián　feel compassion for; pity

哀鸣 āimíng　whine plaintively: 那是天鹅临死前的～。It's the plaintive call of the dying swan. / 没落阶级的～lamentations of the declining classes

哀莫大于心死 āi mòdàyú xīnsǐ　there is no grief greater than the death of the mind

哀戚 āiqī　*formal*　look woeful: 面容～ have a woebegone look

哀启 āiqǐ　a brief biographical sketch of the deceased, usu. attached to an obituary written by his kinsmen

哀泣 āiqì　weep plaintively

哀求 āiqiú　entreat; implore: 苦苦哀求　kǔkǔ āiqiú

哀荣 āiróng　*formal*　posthumous honour: 他生前鞠躬尽瘁, 死后备极～。He gave his best till his dying day and was accorded the highest of honours posthumously.

哀伤 āishāng　be grieved and heartbroken

哀思 āisī　sad memories (of the deceased); grief: 寄托～ give expression to one's grief over sb.'s death

哀叹 āitàn　sigh sorrowfully for; lament; bewail; bemoan: 他～自己命运不济。He bemoaned his fate. / 她的死讯引起一片～。The news of her death caused widespread lamentation.

哀痛 āitòng　mourn sorrowfully; grieve deeply for; lament: 我们～失去了一位亲密的战友。We lament the death of a very close friend of ours.

哀艳 āiyàn　*formal*　(of poetry, etc.) poignantly sensual

哀怨 āiyuàn　aggrieved; resentful

哀乐 āiyuè　funeral music; dirge

哀子 āizǐ　a son bereaved of his mother

埃¹

āi　see 尘埃 chén'āi

埃²

āi　*phys.*　angstrom (Å)

埃及 Āijí　Egypt

埃及人 Āijírén　Egyptian

埃米尔 āimǐ'ěr　emir (a Muslim ruler)

埃塞俄比亚 Āisài'ébǐyà　Ethiopia

埃塞俄比亚人 Āisài'ébǐyàrén　Ethiopian

挨

āi　① be or get close to; be next to: ～着窗口坐 sit by the window / 那两家铺子紧～着。The two shops are next to each other. / 路旁的白杨树一棵～一棵的, 非常整齐。The white poplars stand in a neat row along the road. / 别挤了! 一个～一个进去。Don't push. Go in one by one. ② follow a regular order or sequence; do sth. in sequence or by turns: ～家送牛奶 go from house to house delivering milk / 他就住在这一带, 你～着门找找。He lives somewhere around here. Try to find him by going from door to door. / 还没～到我吧? It isn't my turn yet, is it? ——see also ái

挨边儿 āibiānr　*inf.*　① keep close to the edge: 上了大路要挨着边儿走。Keep close to one side when walking on the road. ② be near; be close to: 我都六十一～了。I'm getting on for sixty. ③ be connected with the subject; be relevant: 你说的跟现在讨论的问题一点儿也不～。Your remark is completely irrelevant to the present problem.

挨次 āicì　take turns (doing sth.); do sth. one after another or in turn: ～上车 get on the bus one after another / ～入场 file in / ～检查机器上的零件 examine the machine parts in due order

挨个儿 āigèr　*inf.*　do sth. by turns or one by one: 检查身体 have medical check-ups in turn / 把他们～找来问问。Bring them here one at a time for questioning.

挨肩 āijiān　sit or stand shoulder to shoulder: ～坐着 be sitting very close to each other

挨肩儿 āijiānr　*inf.*　(of brothers or sisters one succeeding the other in birth) be close in age: 她们姐儿俩～, 就差一岁。The two sisters are close in age, with only one year's difference.

挨肩擦膀 āijiān-cābǎng　rub shoulders—be jostling; be crowded together

挨近 āijìn　get close to; be near to: 我们村～火车站。Our village is close to the railway station. / 别～我! 离我远点儿! Don't come near me! Keep your distance! / 我近视, 要挨得很近才看得清。I'm near-sighted and have to get very close in order to see things clearly. / 侦察员悄悄地～敌人哨所。The scouts sneaked up to the enemy sentry post.

挨门挨户 āimén-āihù　(also 挨家挨户 āijiā-āihù)　go from house to house (or from door to door): ～搜查 make a house-to-house search

挨门逐户 āimén-zhúhù　go from house to house (or from door to door)

唉

āi　*interj.*　(expressing sadness, weariness, regret or disappointment) alas ——see also ài

唉声叹气 āishēngtànqì　heave deep sighs (of grief, worry or anguish); moan and groan: 不要受了一点挫折就～。Don't moan and groan because of a little setback. / 她怎么整天～, 愁眉苦脸的? Why is she looking so depressed and sighing all the time?

唉呀 āiyā　*interj.*　same as 哎呀 āiyā

娭

āi　see below

娭毑 āijiě　*dial.*　① grandma ② a term of respect for any elderly woman

欸

āi　same as 唉 āi ——see also ǎi; ê̌; ê̌; ê̌; ề

嗳(嗳)

āi　same as 哎 āi ——see also ǎi; ài

镰

āi　*chem.*　einsteinium (Es)

ái

挨(捱)

ái　① suffer; endure: ～饿 suffer from hunger; go hungry / ～骂 get a scolding; get a dressing-down / ～批评 be criticized / ～了一记耳光 got a box on the ear ② struggle to pull through (hard times); drag out: ～日子 suffer day after day; drag out a miserable existence / 咱们总算～过来了。We've pulled through at long last. ③ delay; stall; put off: 快走吧! 别～时间了。Get going and stop dawdling. or Quit stalling. / 为什么非要～到下个月不可? Why must we put it off till next month? ——see also āi

挨呲儿 áicīr　*inf.*　get a talking-to; get a tongue-lashing: 这孩子淘气, 老～。The boy is a regular little mischief. He gets a good talking-to every now and then.

挨打 áidǎ　① take a beating; get a thrashing: 他挨了骂不算, 还挨了一顿打。On top of a tongue-lashing, he got a beating as well. ② come under attack: 处于被动～的地位 be passive and vulnerable to attack / 侵略军一进入山地, 就处处～。Once they got into the mountainous area, the invaders took a beating wherever they went.

挨浇 áijiāo　*inf.*　get caught in a pouring rain

挨尅 áikēi　*inf.*　① get a talking-to; be told off; get a dressing-down ② take a beating; get licked

挨整 áizhěng　be the target of criticism or attack

挨揍　áizòu　*inf.*　① take a beating; get a thrashing ② come under attack

骏　ái　*formal.*　stupid; idiotic: 痴骏 chī'ái

皑(皑)　ái　*liter.*　pure white; snow white
皑皑　ái'ái　(of snow, frost, etc.) pure white: 白雪～ an expanse of white snow / ～的雪山 a snowcapped mountain

癌　ái　cancer; carcinoma: 肝癌 gān'ái / 肺癌 fèi'ái
癌变　áibiàn　canceration
癌扩散　áikuòsàn　metastasis (or proliferation) of cancer
癌细胞　áixìbāo　cancer cell
癌症　áizhèng　cancer

ǎi

欸　ǎi　see below ——see also āi; ê; ê; ê; ê
欸乃　ǎinǎi　*onom. liter.* the creak of an oar while rowing

矮　ǎi　① short (of stature): 我个子～。I'm short. / 他比他哥哥～一头。He's a head shorter than his brother. ② low: ～墙 a low wall ③ low in rank or grade: 她在中学里比我～一级。She was a grade lower than me in middle school.
矮凳　ǎidèng　a low stool
矮墩墩　ǎidūndūn　pudgy; dumpy; stumpy
矮杆品种　ǎigǎn pǐnzhǒng　*agric.*　short–stalked variety; short–straw variety
矮个儿　ǎigèr　(also 矮个子 ǎigèzi) a low-built person; a short person
矮林　ǎilín　coppice; brushwood
矮胖　ǎipàng　short and stout; squat; dumpy; roly-poly
矮人　ǎirén　① a short person; dwarf ② Pigmy (or Pygmy)
矮人看戏，随人说　ǎirén kànxì, suí rén shuō　a dwarf watching a show applauds or boos along with the others—have no definite views of one's own; have no independent mind
矮小　ǎixiǎo　short and small; low and small; under-sized: 身材～ short and slight in figure / ～的房屋 a small, low house
矮星　ǎixīng　*astron.*　dwarf star; dwarf
矮壮素　ǎizhuàngsù　*agric.*　cycocel
矮子　ǎizi　a short person; dwarf
矮子里拔将军　ǎizili bá jiāngjūn　choose a general from among the dwarfs—pick the best out of a mediocre bunch

嗳(嗳)　ǎi　*interj.*　(expressing disagreement or negation): ～，没有这回事，你别信他。No, it isn't true. Don't believe what he says. / ～，你搞混啦。No, no, you're all mixed up. ——see also ài; ài
嗳气　ǎiqì　belch; eructation
嗳酸　ǎisuān　rising up of acid from the stomach (a symptom of hyperacidity of the gastric juice)

蔼¹
蔼²　ǎi　friendly; amiable: 和蔼 hé'ǎi
蔼蔼　ǎi'ǎi　*liter.*　① lush; luxuriant ② dim; dark
蔼然可亲　ǎirán kěqīn　kindly; amiable; affable

霭　ǎi　*formal*　mist; haze: 暮霭 mù'ǎi

ài

艾¹　ài　① *bot.* Chinese mugwort (*Artemisia argyi*) ②(Ài) a surname
艾²　ài　*formal*　end; stop: 方兴未艾 fāngxīng-wèi'ài
艾³　ài　*formal*　beautiful; fair: 少艾 shào'ài ——see also yì
艾绒　àiróng　moxa
艾窝窝　àiwōwo　steamed cake made of glutinous rice with sweet filling
艾炷　àizhù　moxa cone
艾炷灸　àizhùjiǔ　(also 艾灸 àijiǔ) *Chin. med.* mox-ibustion
艾滋病　àizībìng　AIDS (acquired immunodeficiency syn-drome)

砹　ài　*chem.* astatine (At)

唉　ài　① *interj.* (a sigh of sadness or regret): ～，要是老张在这儿该多好啊! Oh, if only Lao Zhang were here. / ～，谁能想到啊! Well, who'd have thought of that? / ～，真可惜! What a pity! ② (a response to a call, order, etc.): 快开门去。一～。Open the door, quick!—Right. / 小王! 一～，来啦。Xiao Wang!—Yes. Coming. ——see also āi

爱(愛)　ài　① love: ～祖国 love one's country / ～孩子～得要命 dote on one's children / 他们俩相～已经多年。They have been in love for a number of years. / 他～上她了。He has fallen in love with her. ② like; be fond of; be keen on: ～游泳 be fond of swim-ming / ～干净 like cleanliness / 只～听恭维话, 不～听批评话 be fond of flattery but deaf to criticism / 我不～跟他来往。I don't like to have anything to do with him. ③ cherish; treasure; hold dear; take good care of: ～公物 take good care of public property / ～集体荣誉 cherish the good name of the collective / ～厂如家 hold the factory as dear as one's family ④ be apt to; be in the habit of: 他～头疼。He gets headaches easily. / 我～晕车。I'm apt to get carsick. / 她老～发脾气。She's always losing her temper. / 铁～生锈。Iron rusts easily.
爱…不…　ài…bù…　(used before reduplicated verbs, to indicate that the person in question can do as he likes): 你爱信不信。Believe it or not. / 反正我通知到了, 你爱去不去。Anyway I've notified you. You can go or not, for all I care. / 就剩这一辆车了, 你爱买不买。That's the only bike left. Take it or leave it.
爱不释手　ài bù shìshǒu　be so fond of sth. that one will not let it out of one's hand: 她拿着那副耳环～。The moment she got hold of those earrings, she took a fan-cy to them and wouldn't let go of them.
爱财如命　ài cái rú mìng　love money as one loves one's life; love money as much as life itself; be greedy for money; be a money-grubber
爱称　àichēng　term of endearment; pet name
爱戴　àidài　love and esteem: ～自己的领袖 venerate one's leader / 老师博得了同学们的～。The teacher has won the love and esteem of his students.
爱尔兰　Ài'ěrlán　Ireland
爱尔兰人　Ài'ěrlánrén　the Irish; Irishman
爱尔兰语　Ài'ěrlányǔ　Irish (language)
爱抚　àifǔ　show tender care for: 她用～的眼光看着那个婴儿。She looked at the baby tenderly.
爱国　àiguó　love one's country; be patriotic: 他很～。

He is very patriotic. / ～同胞们! Patriotic fellow-countrymen! / ～一家,～不分先后. All patriots belong to one big family, whether they rally to the common cause early or late.

爱国人士 àiguó rénshì patriotic personage

爱国统一战线 àiguó tǒngyī zhànxiàn the patriotic united front

爱国卫生运动 àiguó wèishēng yùndòng the patriotic health campaign

爱国心 àiguóxīn patriotic feeling; patriotism

爱国者 àiguózhě patriot

爱国主义 àiguózhǔyì patriotism

爱好 àihào ① take great pleasure in; have sth. as a hobby; be keen on: ～音乐 like music / ～京剧 be keen on Beijing opera / ～体育 go in for sports ② interest; hobby: 她的～是多方面的. She has a wide range of interests. / 你在文娱方面有什么～? What kind of recreation do you go in for?

爱好者 àihàozhě lover (of art, sports, etc.); enthusiast; fan: 音乐～ music-lover / 体育～ sports enthusiast; sports fan

爱护 àihù cherish; treasure; take good care of: 互相～ care for each other / ～群众的积极性 cherish the initiative of the masses / ～公物 take good care of public property / ～儿童 take good care of children; bring up children with loving care / ～祖国的一草一木 cherish every tree and every blade of grass in our country

爱克斯光 àikèsīguāng X ray; Roentgen ray: 照～ take an X-ray; have an X-ray taken

爱克斯光机 àikèsīguāngjī X-ray apparatus

爱克斯光透视 àikèsīguāng tòushì fluoroscopy; X-ray examination

爱克斯光照片 àikèsīguāng zhàopiàn roentgenogram; X-ray; radiograph

爱克斯光诊断 àikèsīguāng zhěnduàn X-ray diagnosis; roentgen diagnosis

爱理不理 àilǐbùlǐ (also 爱答不理 àidābùlǐ) look cold and indifferent; be standoffish: 我去向他请教,他～的,不太愿意帮助我. I went to consult him, but he was cold and indifferent and not very willing to help me out.

爱丽舍宫 Àilìshě Gōng the Élysée Palace

爱怜 àilián show tender affection for: 她用～的目光看着那些孤儿. She looked at the orphans with love and sympathy.

爱恋 àiliàn be in love with; feel deeply attached to: 他深深地～着那位姑娘. He is head over heels in love with the girl. / 对乡土的～ attachment to one's native soil

爱侣 àilǚ lovers; sweethearts

爱美 àiměi set great store by one's appearance; love to make up and wear beautiful clothes

爱面子 ài miànzi be concerned about face-saving; be sensitive about one's reputation

爱莫能助 ài mò néng zhù be willing to help but unable to do so: 对不起,实在～! I'm sorry. I'd love to help you but my hands are tied.

爱慕 àimù adore; admire: 相互～ adore each other / ～虚荣 be vain; be given to vanity

爱情 àiqíng love (between man and woman): 他们之间已经有了很深的～. They have a deep love for each other already. / ～专一 be constant in love

爱人儿 àirénr dial. lovable; lovely: 这孩子长得多～! What a lovely child!

爱人 àiren ① husband or wife: 您～好吗? How is your husband (or wife)? / 你不知道他们是～关系吗? Don't you know they are husband and wife? ② sweetheart; lover

爱沙尼亚 Àishāníyà Estonia

爱沙尼亚人 Àishāníyàrén Estonian

爱沙尼亚语 Àishāníyàyǔ Estonian (language)

爱神 àishén god of love; Cupid

爱斯基摩人 Àisījīmórén Eskimo

爱窝窝 àiwōwo same as 艾窝窝 àiwōwo

爱屋及乌 ài wū jí wū love for a person extends even to the crows on his roof; love me, love my dog

爱惜 àixī value highly and use prudently; treasure: 他不知道～东西. He doesn't know what it is to treasure things. / ～人力物力 use manpower and materials with prudence / ～人才 treasure men of talent / ～时间 make the best use of one's time; use time efficiently

爱小 àixiǎo be keen on gaining petty advantages; go after petty advantages

爱因斯坦方程 Àiyīnsītǎn fāngchéng phys. Einstein equation

爱憎分明 ài-zēng fēnmíng understand what to love and what to hate; know whom to love and whom to hate

隘

隘 ài ① narrow: ～巷 a narrow lane; alley ② a narrow pass: 要隘 yào'ài

隘口 àikǒu mountain pass

隘路 àilù defile; narrow passage

碍(礙)

碍 ài hinder; obstruct; be in the way of: 在这儿呆着吧,你～不着我. Stay where you are. You're not in my way. / 有～团结 be harmful (or detrimental) to unity

碍口 àikǒu be too embarrassing to mention: 这事有点～,不好说. It's rather embarrassing; I don't know how to bring it up.

碍面子 ài miànzi just to spare sb.'s feelings: 碍着他爸爸的面子,我不好说什么. I didn't say anything for fear of hurting his father's feelings.

碍难 àinán formal find it difficult (to do sth.): ～照办 find it difficult to comply / ～照准 cannot approve

碍事 àishì inf. ① be in the way; be a hindrance: 这桌子放在门口太～了. This table is too close to the door, it gets in the way. / 要是我在这儿碍你们的事,我可以挪别处去. If I'm in your way, I can move to some other place. ② (usu. used in the negative) be of consequence; matter: 这不～. It doesn't matter. or It's of no consequence. / 她来不了不～. It doesn't matter if she can't come. / 受了点凉,不～. It's just a slight cold, nothing serious.

碍手碍脚 àishǒu-àijiǎo be in the way; be a hindrance: 你走开! 别在这儿～的! Get out of the way! / 过道里放满了自行车,～的. The corridor is crowded with bikes which get in everybody's way.

碍眼 àiyǎn be unpleasant to look at; offend the eye; be an eyesore: 那些广告牌真～. Those billboards are a real eyesore.

碍于情面 àiyú qíngmiàn for fear of hurting sb.'s feelings; out of consideration for sb.'s feelings

嗳(嗳)

嗳 ài interj. (expressing regret or annoyance): ～,早知道就好了. Oh! If only I'd known sooner. ——see also ǎi; ài

嫒(嬡)

嫒 ài beloved daughter: 令嫒 lìng'ài

暧(曖)

暧 ài formal (of daylight) dim

暧昧 àimèi ① ambiguous; equivocal: 态度～ assume an ambiguous attitude ② shady; dubious: 关系～ dubious relationship

瑷(璦)

瑷 ài see below

瑷珲 àidài formal cloudy

ān

安[1]　ān　① peaceful; at ease; undisturbed; tranquil; calm: ～睡 sleep peacefully ② set (sb.'s mind) at ease; calm: 安神 ānshén　③ rest content; be satisfied: 安于现状 ānyú xiànzhuàng ④ safe; secure; in good health: ～抵拉萨 arrive in Lhasa safely (or safe and sound) ⑤ place in a suitable position; find a place for: 把我～在哪儿都行 I'll be happy with any job I'm assigned to. or I'll fit in contentedly anywhere. ⑥ install; fix; fit: ～电灯 install electric lights / 窗玻璃～上了。 The windowpanes have been put in. / 门上～把锁。 Fit a lock on the door. / 暖气片～得不是地方。 The radiator wasn't put in the right place. ⑦ set up: 咱们这儿～上电视转播站了。 A TV relay station has been set up here. ⑧ bring (a charge against sb.); give (sb. a nickname): ～罪名 bring charges against; put the blame on: 我连去都没去，这个罪名可～不到我头上。 I wasn't even there. There's no way they can put the blame on me. ⑨ harbour (an intention): 安心[2] ānxīn ⑩ (Ān) a surname

安[2]　ān　formal ① where: 其故～在? Wherein lies the cause? ② (used in rhetorical questions) how: ～能袖手旁观? How can one stand by and do nothing?

安[3]　ān　short for 安培 ānpéi

安邦定国　ānbāng-dìngguó　(of a ruler) bring peace and stability to the country

安不忘危　ān bù wàng wēi　mindful of possible danger in times of peace

安步当车　ān bù dàng chē　stroll over instead of riding in a carriage; walk rather than ride

安瓿　ānbù　med. ampoule

安插　ānchā　① place (sb.) in a certain position; assign to a job: 新徒工就～在我们车间好吗? Could the new apprentice be assigned to our shop? / 请你把他～在你们单位。 Please find him a position in your unit. / 这么多人叫我往哪儿～? Where can I find positions for so many people? / ～亲信 put one's trusted followers in key positions ② insert (an episode, etc.)into a story, play, article, etc.: 作者在这里～了一段倒叙。 At this point the writer puts in a flashback.

安常处顺　āncháng-chǔshùn　stick to the status quo; go along with things as they are

安厝　āncuò　keep a coffin in a temporary shelter pending burial, or lay it in a temporary burial place to be reburied permanently later

安道尔　Āndào'ěr　Andorra

安道尔人　Āndào'ěrrén　Andorran

安的列斯群岛　Āndìlièsī Qúndǎo　the Antilles Islands

安第斯山脉　Āndìsī Shānmài　the Andes (Mountains)

安定　āndìng　① stable; quiet; settled:～的生活 a stable (or settled) life / ～的社会环境 a stable social environment / 时局～。 The current political situation is stable and quiet. / ～团结的政治局面 political stability and unity ② stabilize; maintain: ～社会秩序 maintain social order / ～人心 reassure the public; set people's minds at rest / 考试前我的心情怎么也～不下来。 No matter how hard I try, I can't possibly keep calm before an exam. ③ pharm. diazepam

安堵　āndǔ　formal live in peace and security

安顿　āndùn　① help settle down (or in); get sth. or everything arranged; find a place for: 家里都～好了吗? Have you got everything settled at home? / 妈妈把女儿～在托儿所里。 The woman found a place for her

daughter in a nursery. ② undisturbed; peaceful: 病人吃了药，睡觉～多了。 The patient slept much better after taking the medicine.

安放　ānfàng　put in a proper place; lay: 烈士墓前～着花圈。 Wreaths were laid at the martyr's tomb. / 把仪器～好。 Put the instruments in their proper places. / 这张两用沙发没有合适的地方～。 There's nowhere to put the sofa bed.

安分　ānfèn　not go beyond one's bounds; be law-abiding; know one's place: 这孩子在课堂上一点也不～，老要搞小动作。 The boy doesn't behave himself in class; he's always playing some prank or other.

安分守己　ānfèn-shǒujǐ　abide by the law and behave oneself; be content with one's lot and act one's part; know one's place: 我知道你是个老实人，你是～的。 I know you are an honest man, content with your lot and not causing any trouble.

安抚　ānfǔ　aid and comfort (or console); reassure and pacify; appease: ～伤员 aid and comfort the wounded / ～人心 reassure and pacify the public / ～政策 a policy aimed at appeasing the people

安富尊荣　ānfù-zūnróng　be content with one's wealth and rank

安哥拉　Āngēlā　Angola

安哥拉人　Āngēlārén　Angolan

安哥拉兔　āngēlātù　Angora rabbit

安圭拉　Ānguīlā　Anguilla

安好　ānhǎo　safe and sound; well: 全家～，请勿挂念。 You will be pleased to know that everyone in the family is well.

安徽　Ānhuī　Anhui (Province)

安家　ānjiā　① settle down: 他们在新疆安了家。 They settled in Xinjiang. ② set up a home; get married: 他收入不高，还没有条件～。 He isn't earning enough to get married and start a family.

安家费　ānjiāfèi　allowance for setting up a home in a new place; settling-in allowance; family allowance

安家落户　ānjiā-luòhù　make one's home (or take up residence) in a new place; settle: 他们已经在海南岛～。 They have settled in Hainan.

安靖　ānjìng　① quiet; peaceful; tranquil: 地方～。 The district is at peace. ② formal make tranquil; pacify

安静　ānjìng　① quiet; peaceful: 这个地方很～。 It is very quiet here. / ～的环境 tranquil surroundings / 病人需要～。 The patient needs peace and quiet. / 保持～! Keep quiet! ② calm; undisturbed: 周围安安静静的，没有任何异常情况。 Everything around was still and quiet. Nothing unusual happened. / 孩子们都已～地入睡了。 The children are all sound asleep. ③ quiet down: 大幕一拉开，观众顿时～下来。 As soon as the curtain rose, the audience quieted down.

安居乐业　ānjū-lèyè　live and work in peace and contentment

安康　ānkāng　in good health: 祝您～! Wishing you the best of health!

安拉　ānlā　Islam Allah

安澜　ānlán　forml ① (of a stream, etc.) calm; unruffled ② peaceful

安乐　ānlè　peaceful and happy; free from worry

安乐死　ānlèsǐ　mercy killing; euthanasia

安乐窝　ānlèwō　a cosy nest

安乐椅　ānlèyǐ　easy chair

安理会　Ānlǐhuì　short for 安全理事会 Ānquán Lǐshìhuì

安谧　ānmì　formal (of a place) tranquil; quiet; peaceful

安眠　ānmián　sleep peacefully

安眠药　ānmiányào　sleeping pill (or tablet); soporific

安眠酮　ānmiántóng　pharm. methaqualone; hyminal

安民　ānmín　pacify the people; reassure the public: ～

政策 policies to reassure the public

安民告示 ānmín gàoshì ① a notice to reassure the public ② advance notice (of an agenda, etc.)

安那其主义 ānnàqízhǔyì same as 无政府主义 wúzhèngfǔzhǔyì

安乃近 ānnǎijìn *pharm.* analgin

安宁 ānníng ① peaceful; tranquil: ～的生活 a peaceful life / 确保两国边境～ ensure tranquillity on the border of the two countries / 两口子成天吵架，闹得左邻右舍不得～。The couple are always bickering. They gave their neighbours no peace. ② calm; composed; free from worry: 心里很不～ feel rather worried

安宁片 ānníngpiàn *pharm.* meprobamate

安排 ānpái arrange (matters); plan in detail; dispose (manpower): 为外宾～参观游览 arrange visits and sightseeing trips for foreign guests / ～好下个年度的生产 have everything well planned for next year's production / 长计划，短～ long-term plans with short-term arrangements / 每周～一个下午的政治学习 set aside one afternoon a week for political study / 妥善～时间 budget one's time well / 合理～人力 dispose available manpower rationally / ～好休养人员的生活 make adequate arrangements for the recuperators' daily life / 给新来的人员～工作 assign the newcomers adequate jobs / 给每个组～一项任务 allot a task to each group / ～版面 plan the layout (of printed matter) / 日程～得太紧了。Our schedule is much too packed. / 一切由你们～，我们没有意见。You can make all the arrangements for us. We won't have any objection whatever. / 对失业工人作了适当的～。Adequate arrangements have been made for the unemployed.

安培 ānpéi *elec.* ampere

安培计 ānpéijì ammeter; amperemeter

安培小时 ānpéi xiǎoshí ampere-hour

安贫乐道 ānpín-lèdào be content with poverty, caring only for one's principles or the Way

安琪儿 ānqí'ér angel (a transliteration)

安寝 ānqǐn sleep (peacefully)

安全 ānquán safe; secure: 转移到一个比较～的地方 move to a safer place / ～到达 arrive safely / 保证～生产 ensure safety in production / ～行车 safe driving / ～正点 safe and punctual running (of trains, buses, etc.) / ～操作 safe operation / ～停车距离 safe stopping distance / ～高度 safe altitude / ～措施 safety measures / ～设施 safety devices / ～规程 safety regulations / 交通～ traffic safety / ～第一! Safety first!

安全玻璃 ānquán bōli safety glass

安全带 ānquándài safety belt; seat belt

安全岛 ānquándǎo safety island; pedestrian island

安全灯 ānquándēng ① *min.* safety lamp ② *photog.* safelight

安全阀 ānquánfá safety valve

安全感 ānquángǎn sense of security

安全角 ānquánjiǎo *mil.* safety angle

安全界 ānquánjiè *mil.* safety limit

安全理事会 Ānquán Lǐshìhuì the (U. N.) Security Council

安全帽 ānquánmào safety helmet

安全梯 ānquántī emergency staircase; fire escape

安全剃刀 ānquán tìdāo same as 保险刀 bǎoxiǎndāo

安全通行证 ānquán tōngxíngzhèng safe-conduct

安全网 ānquánwǎng safety netting

安全系数 ānquán xìshù safety coefficient (*or* factor)

安然 ānrán ① safe: ～脱险 be out of danger ② be free from worry; feel at ease: ～入睡 go to sleep peacefully / 只有把这件事告诉他，他心里才会～。He will never feel at ease unless we tell him about this.

安然无恙 ānrán wúyàng safe and sound; (escape) unscathed

安如磐石 ān rú pánshí as firm (*or* solid) as a rock

安如泰山 ān rú Tàishān as solid as Mount Tai; as firm (*or* solid) as a rock

安山岩 ānshānyán *geol.* andesite

安设 ānshè install; set up: 在山顶上～一个气象观测站 set up a weather station on the mountaintop

安身 ānshēn have a roof over one's head; take shelter: 无处～ have no roof over one's head; have nowhere to live; be homeless and shelterless / 在破庙里～ take shelter in a dilapidated temple

安身立命 ānshēn-lìmìng settle down and get on with one's work

安神 ānshén ① calm (*or* soothe) the nerves ② *Chin. med.* relieve uneasiness of body and mind

安神药 ānshényào *Chin. med.* sedative; tranquillizer

安生 ān·shēng ① peaceful; restful: 过～日子 live a peaceful and restful life / 那帮小青年吵得邻居们不得～。Those youngsters raised such a ruckus. They gave their neighbours no peace. / 为了抢修机器，他几天没有吃过一顿～饭。To get the machine repaired quickly, he didn't enjoy a leisurely meal for several days. ② (usu. of children) quiet; still; untroublesome: 这孩子一会儿也不～。The child simply will not keep quiet for a moment. *or* The child is always making some trouble or other. / 这孩子即便睡觉也不～。The kid won't keep still, not even in sleep.

安适 ānshì quiet and comfortable: ～的环境 a quiet and comfortable environment / 他们在养老院里过着～的生活。They are enjoying a quiet and comfortable life in an old people's home.

安提瓜和巴布达 Āntíguādǎo hé Bābùdá Antigua and Barbuda

安替比林 āntìbǐlín *pharm.* antipyrine

安土重迁 ān tǔ zhòng qiān love one's homeland and not wish to leave it; hate to leave one's native land

安妥 āntuǒ antu (a rat poison)

安危 ān-wēi safety and danger; safety: 不顾个人～ be heedless of one's personal safety / 护士把伤员们的～冷暖时刻挂在心上。The nurses have the safety and well-being of the wounded constantly at heart.

安慰 ānwèi ① be comforted; feel encouraged: 我听了这些话心里很～。I felt much comforted at hearing these words. ② comfort; console: 我～了他几句。I said a few words to comfort him (*or* gave him a few words of comfort). / 他没考上大学，你多～～他。He failed his college entrance exams. Try to comfort him as best as you can. / 自我～ console oneself ③ consolation; comfort: 同志们的关怀是对我的极大～。The comrades' solicitude was a great comfort (*or* consolation) to me. / 孩子成了她唯一的～。The child became her only consolation.

安慰剂 ānwèijì *med.* placebo

安慰奖 ānwèijiǎng consolation prize

安慰赛 ānwèisài *sports* consolation event (*or* match)

安稳 ānwěn ① smooth and steady: 船走得很～。The boat sailed smoothly. / 睡得很～ sleep peacefully / 飞机安安稳稳地降落在跑道上。The plane landed smoothly on the runway. ② *dial.* calm and poised

安息 ānxī ① rest; go to sleep ② rest in peace: 烈士们，～吧! May the revolutionary martyrs rest in peace!

安息 Ānxī Parthia (an ancient country)

安息日 ānxīrì Sabbath (day)

安息香 ānxīxiāng benzoin (the plant, the resin, or the perfume)

安息香酸 ānxīxiāngsuān same as 苯甲酸 běnjiǎsuān

安闲 ānxián peaceful and carefree; relaxed; leisurely: ～自在 leisurely and carefree / ～的心情 a relaxed mood

安详 ānxiáng serene; composed; unruffled: 举止～ behave with composure / 在那危急的时刻，他还保持着～

的神态。At the critical juncture, he still kept his composure.

安歇 ānxiē　go to bed; retire for the night

安心[1] ānxīn　① feel at ease; be relieved; set one's mind at rest: 他怎么也安不下心来做事。He simply can't set his mind to work. / 考试还没完，大家都安不下心来。None of us will feel at ease until all the exams are over. / 听到这个消息，她就～了。She was relieved at the news. / 希望你～休养。You just get better and don't worry. ② keep one's mind on sth.: ～工作 keep one's mind on one's work; work contentedly / 回乡～生产 go home and settle down to productive work

安心[2] ānxīn　harbour an (evil) intention: 你安的什么心？What are you up to? / 不安好心 have evil intentions; not have good intentions

安逸 ānyì　easy and comfortable; easy: ～的生活 an easy life

安营 ānyíng　pitch a camp; camp: 大军在那片树林里～造饭。The army camped in the forest and started to prepare food.

安营扎寨 ānyíng-zhāzhài　pitch a camp; camp: 民工们在水库工地上～。The farmer-labourers working on the conservancy project camped at the worksite.

安于 ānyú　be content or satisfied with a state of affairs: ～落后，不求上进 be quite satisfied with one's backward state (or be satisfied with oneself) and not wish to do any better

安于现状 ānyú xiànzhuàng　be content with things as they are; be satisfied with the existing state of affairs

安葬 ānzàng　bury (the dead): 把他的遗骸送回去～ escort his remains back to his home town for burial / 举行了隆重的～仪式。A solemn burial service was held.

安枕 ānzhěn　arrange the pillow—go to bed: 祸根不除，大家不得～。We can't rest in peace if this evil is not eradicated.

安之若素 ān zhī ruò sù　① bear (hardship, etc.) with equanimity ② regard (wrongdoing, etc.) with indifference

安置 ānzhì　find a suitable place, position, job, etc. for; arrange for the placement of: 把行李～好 put the luggage in the right place / 复员军人得到了适当的～。Proper arrangements have been made for the placement of demobilized soldiers. / 我们把家～好了再说。We'll see about it after we have set up our home. / 今年我们～了一百名待业青年。This year we've found jobs for a hundred young people hitherto unemployed. / 她把小女儿暂时～在邻居家。She arranged for her youngest daughter to stay with a neighbour.

安置费 ānzhìfèi　placement or settlement allowance

安装 ānzhuāng　install; fix; set up: ～电话 install a telephone / ～机器 install machinery / ～扩音器 set up a megaphone / 推进器的叶片已经～好了。The propeller blades have been mounted. / 在工厂里没呆多久，他就把机器的拆卸和～都学会了。He hadn't been at the factory for long before he had learned how to disassemble and assemble the machines.

桉 ān　bot. eucalyptus

桉树 ānshù　eucalyptus

桉油 ānyóu　volatile oil extracted from eucalyptus' leaves or twigs

氨 ān　chem. ammonia: 合成～ synthetic ammonia

氨苯磺胺 ānběnhuáng'àn　pharm. sulfanilamide

氨茶碱 ānchájiǎn　pharm. aminophylline

氨化 ānhuà　ammoniation

氨基 ānjī　amino; amino-group

氨基比林 ānjībǐlín　pharm. aminopyrine

氨基酸 ānjīsuān　amino acid

氨碱法 ānjiǎnfǎ　chem. ammonia soda process

氨硫脲 ānliúniào　pharm. thiacetazone

氨水 ānshuǐ　ammonia solution; ammonia (water); aqua ammoniae

谙 ān　formal　know well: 不～水性 not know how to swim / 素～针灸之术 be highly skilled in administering acupuncture and moxibustion

谙练 ānliàn　formal　conversant; skilled; proficient

谙熟 ānshú　be proficient in; be conservant with: ～汉语 be well versed in the Chinese language

庵（菴） ān　① formal hut: 草～ a thatched hut ② nunnery; Buddhist convent

庵堂 āntáng　dial.　nunnery; Buddhist convent

唵 ān　interj.　① (expressing affirmation) yes: 处长，您开完会啦？——～。Is your meeting over, chief?——Yes. ② (used to impress sth. on sb.'s mind): 你的责任更重了，更要加油干哪，～！Now you're shouldering even heavier responsibility. You should put in extra effort. / 你们出的点子，～，我看很不错嘛! Your suggestions are not at all bad. ——see also ǎn

鹌 ān　see below

鹌鹑 ānchun　quail (a bird)

鮟 ān　see below

鮟鱇 ānkāng　goosefish; angler

鞍 ān　saddle

鞍部 ānbù　a ridge connecting two higher elevations; saddle (of a hill or mountain)

鞍鞯 ānchàn　saddle and saddle blanket

鞍架 ānjià　saddletree

鞍鞯 ānjiān　formal　saddle and saddle blanket

鞍马 ānmǎ　① sports pommelled horse; side horse ② formal saddle and horse—horseback riding: ～生活 life on horseback—soldiering

鞍马劳顿 ānmǎ láodùn　be fatigued by a long journey; be travel-worn

鞍桥 ānqiáo　pommel and cantle; cantle

鞍屉 āntì　① saddle cloth; saddle blanket ② saddle

鞍子 ānzi　saddle

盦[1] ān　ancient food container

盦[2] ān　same as 庵 ān

ǎn

俺 ǎn　dial.　① we or our (the person spoken to not included): ～村 our village ② I or my: ～爹 my father

俺们 ǎnmen　dial.　we or us

唵 ǎn　interj.　(expressing interrogation) eh: ～，你把钥匙弄到哪儿去了? Eh, where have you left the key? / 怎么这两天你都没过来呀，～? Why haven't you been around these past few days, eh? ——see also ān

埯（垵） ǎn　① a hole to dibble seeds ② dibble: ～豆 dibble in the beans ③ m. (for crops planted by dibbling): 一～花生 a cluster of peanut seedlings

铵 ǎn *chem.* ammonium

揞 ǎn apply medicinal powder to (a wound): 你手上的伤口比较深，最好～上一点儿消炎粉。The cut in your hand is rather deep. You'd better apply some powder to it.

àn

犴 àn see 狴犴 bì'àn

岸[1] àn ① bank; shore; coast: 江～ the bank of a river; river bank／上～ go ashore／小河两～柳树成行。On either bank of the stream stand rows of willow trees.

岸[2] àn *formal* ① lofty; tall and big: 伟岸 wěi'àn ② proud: 傲岸 ào'àn

岸标 ànbiāo shore beacon

岸然 ànrán *formal* in a solemn manner: 道貌岸然 dàomào ànrán

按[1] àn ① press; push down: ～电钮 press (*or* push) a button／～门铃 ring a doorbell／～手印 put one's fingerprint on (a document, etc.)／把他一倒在地 push him down on the ground／这是水泥墙，图钉～不进去。This is a cement wall. Thumbtacks won't go into it. ② leave aside; shelve: ～下此事不提 leave this aside for the moment ③ restrain; control: ～不住心头怒火 be unable to restrain (*or* control) one's anger ④ keep one's hand on; keep a tight grip on: ～住操纵杆 keep a tight grip on the control lever ⑤ *prep.* according to; in accordance with; in the light of; on the basis of: ～制度办事 act in accordance with rules and regulations／～计划执行任务 carry out the task according to plan／～质定价 fix the price according to the quality／～比例发展 develop in proportion; proportional development／～年代顺序排列 arrange in chronological order

按[2] (案) àn ① *formal* check; refer to: 有原文可～。There's the original to refer to. ② (of an editor or author) make a comment: 编者～ editor's note

按兵不动 àn bīng bù dòng ① hold one's troops where they are; not throw one's troops into battle ② take no action; bide one's time: 大家都干起来了，你怎么还～呢? Everybody else has started work. Why do you sit there doing nothing?

按部就班 ànbù-jiùbān follow the prescribed order; keep to conventional ways of doing things: 学习应该～，循序渐进。In studying it is imperative to follow the proper order and advance step by step.／时间来不及了，没法～地搞下去了。There isn't enough time. We can't keep to the conventional way of doing things any more.

按成 ànchéng according to percentage; proportionately: ～计算 reckon in terms of percentages／～分配红利 distribute the bonuses proportionately

按次 àncì in due order; in sequence: ～发言 speak in due order

按件计工 àn jiàn jì gōng reckon by the piece: 实行～ adopt the piecework system

按酒 ànjiǔ *old* meat dishes to go with liquor

按扣儿 ànkòur snap fastener

按劳分配 ànláo fēnpèi distribution according to work ——see also 各尽所能，按劳分配 gè jìn suǒ néng, àn láo fēnpèi

按理 ànlǐ (also 按理说 ànlǐshuō) according to principle or reason; in the ordinary course of events; normally: 他们村遭了灾，～可以免交农业税,可他们就是不干。As a village hit by natural calamity, they were entitled to exemption from agrarian tax, but they rejected it.／这种病～不该有并发症。Normally there are no complications with this illness.／～不应当这么办。Logically, it shouldn't be done this way.

按脉 ànmài feel (*or* take) the pulse

按摩 ànmó massage

按摩疗法 ànmó liáofǎ *med.* massotherapy

按捺 ànnà (also 按纳 ànnà) restrain; control

按捺不住 ànnà bù zhù cannot control (*or* contain) oneself: ～激动的心情 be unable to suppress one's excitement／～心中的仇恨 be unable to suppress any longer the bitterness in one's heart

按钮 ànniǔ push button

按钮控制 ànniǔ kòngzhì push-button control; dash control

按期 ànqī on schedule; on time: 这项工作我们必须～完成。We must complete this job on schedule.／～交货 deliver goods on schedule／～出版 publish on schedule; come out on time

按时 ànshí on time; on schedule: ～到达 arrive on time／我们一定～开会,不要迟到。We will begin the meeting at the appointed hour. Don't be late.

按说 ànshuō in the ordinary course of events; ordinarily; normally: ～这时候该下雪了。Ordinarily it should be snowing at this time of the year.／～现在是蔬菜的淡季,可是你们这里的供应还不错。This is supposed to be an off season for vegetables but you seem to have a good supply here.

按图索骥 àn tú suǒ jì look for a steed with the aid of its picture—① try to find sth. by following up a clue ② deal with (*or* handle) a matter in a mechanical way

按蚊 ànwén anopheles; malarial mosquito

按下葫芦浮起瓢 àn xià húlu fúqǐ piáo hardly has one gourd been pushed under water when another bobs up—solve one problem only to find another cropping up

按需分配 àn xū fēnpèi distribution according to need ——see also 各尽所能,按需分配 gè jìn suǒ néng, àn xū fēnpèi

按压 ànyā ① press down with one's hand: 他做了个往下～的手势。He made a gesture with his hand pressing downward. ② suppress; restrain: ～不住心头怒火 can't suppress one's anger

按验 ànyàn same as 案验 ànyàn

按语 ànyǔ a note or comment (by an author or editor on a piece of writing or certain parts of it)

按照 ànzhào *prep.* according to; in accordance with; in the light of; on the basis of: ～宪法规定的基本原则 according to the fundamental principles laid down in the constitution／～等价交换的原则 in accordance with the principle of exchange of equal values／～自愿原则组合 form groups on a voluntary basis／～实际情况决定工作方针 determine working policies in the light of actual conditions／～贡献大小,分别给以奖励。Awards are to be given each according to his contribution.／计划已～群众的意见修改了。The plan has been revised in accordance with the opinions of the masses.／～计划,这座楼房应于年底交工。The building is scheduled to be completed and handed over by the end of the year.

案[1] àn ① an old-fashioned long, narrow table or desk: 条案 tiáo'àn／书案 shū'àn ② a long board propped up to serve as a table or counter: ～上摆着各色日用小百货。A variety of small articles of daily use are

displayed on the propped-up counter.

案²

àn ① law case; case: 破案 pò'àn ② record; file: 在案 zài'àn ③ a plan submitted for consideration; proposal: 提案 tí'àn / 草案 cǎo'àn ④ same as 按² àn

案板 ànbǎn　kneading or chopping board (usu. rectangular)

案秤 ànchèng　counter scale

案牍 àndú　*formal* official documents or correspondence

案犯 ànfàn　*leg.* criminals involved in a case

案件 ànjiàn　*law* case; case: 刑事～ a criminal case / 反革命～ a counterrevolutionary case

案酒 ànjiǔ　same as 按酒 ànjiǔ

案卷 ànjuàn　records; files; archives

案例 ànlì　*leg.* case: ～分析 case analysis

案情 ànqíng　details of a case; case: 了解～ investigate the details of a case / ～相当复杂。The case is quite complicated.

案头 àntóu　on the table or desk: ～放着几本参考书。There are some reference books on the desk. / 这项计划还剩下一些～工作要做。There is still some desk work to be done before we can finish the project.

案头剧 àntóujù　closet play; closet drama

案头日历 àntóu rìlì　desk calendar

案验 ànyàn　*formal* investigate the evidence of a case

案由 ànyóu　the main points (or a brief summary) of a case; brief

案语 ànyǔ　same as 按语 ànyǔ

案子¹ ànzi　a long, narrow table or a long board propped up to serve as a table or counter: 乒乓球～ ping-pong table / 肉～ meat counter

案子² ànzi　*inf.* law case; case

胺

àn　*chem.* amine

胺化 ànhuà　amination

胺盐 ànyán　amine salt

暗¹(闇)

àn　① dark; dim; dull: 天色渐渐～下来了。It's getting dark. / 灯光很～。The light is rather dim. / 这间屋子光线太～。This room is too dark. / ～紫色 dull purple / ～绿 dark green ② unclear; hazy: 若明若暗 ruòmíng-ruò'àn

暗²

àn　hidden; secret: ～下决心 make up one's mind secretly

暗暗 àn'àn　secretly; inwardly; to oneself: ～跟踪 secretly follow sb. / 我～吃了一惊。I was startled but didn't show it. / 他～发誓要为牺牲的同志报仇。He vowed to himself to avenge his martyred comrades.

暗坝 ànbà　underwater dam

暗堡 ànbǎo　*mil.* bunker

暗病 ànbìng　same as 暗疾 ànjí

暗藏 àncáng　hide; conceal: ～枪枝 conceal firearms; illegally possess firearms / ～的反革命分子 a hidden counterrevolutionary

暗娼 ànchāng　a disguised prostitute; unlicensed (or unregistered) prostitute

暗场 ànchǎng　details in a play not acted out on stage, but told through dialogues or monologues

暗潮 àncháo　undercurrent (fig.)

暗处 ànchù　① a dark place: 猫头鹰白天躲在～。Owls stay in dark places in the daytime. ② a secret place; a covert place; cover: 我们在明处, 敌特在～, 可得提防着他们点儿。The enemy agents are acting under cover while we are in the open. So we must be on our guard.

暗袋 àndài　*photog.* camera bag (for changing film)

暗淡 àndàn　dim; faint; dismal; gloomy: ～的颜色 a dull colour / ～的景象 a dismal picture / 屋里灯光～。The

room is dimly lit. / 当时经济发展的前景颇为～。The prospects for economic development then were rather dismal.

暗地里 àndìli　(also 暗地 àndì)　secretly; inwardly; on the sly: ～做了些不可告人的事 do something secretly which cannot be told to anybody / ～搞鬼 secretly make trouble / 我们～替他高兴。We inwardly rejoiced for him.

暗渡陈仓 àn dù Chéncāng　(of a man and a woman) enter into a secret liaison ——see also 明修栈道, 暗渡陈仓 míng xiū zhàndào, àn dù Chéncāng

暗沟 àngōu　underground drainage ditch; underground drain

暗害 ànhài　① kill secretly ② stab in the back

暗含 ànhán　imply: 他的回答～着对我们工作的批评。His reply implied a criticism of our work.

暗号 ànhào　a secret signal (or sign); countersign; watchword

暗合 ànhé　be in complete agreement without prior consultation; (happen to) coincide

暗河 ànhé　underground river

暗盒 ànhé　*photog.* magazine; cassette

暗花儿 ànhuār　a veiled design incised in porcelain or woven in fabric

暗疾 ànjí　a disease one is ashamed of; unmentionable disease

暗记儿 ànjìr　secret mark

暗间儿 ànjiānr　inner room (usu. used as a bedroom or storeroom)

暗箭 ànjiàn　an arrow shot from hiding—an attack by a hidden enemy; a stab in the back

暗箭伤人 ànjiàn shāng rén　stab sb. in the back; injure sb. by underhand means

暗礁 ànjiāo　① submerged reef (or rock) ② latent obstacle

暗井 ànjǐng　*min.* blind shaft; winze

暗扣 ànkòu　a veiled or covered button (on clothing)

暗流 ànliú　undercurrent (lit. or fig.)

暗楼子 ànlóuzi　attic storeroom accessible through an opening in the ceiling by using a ladder

暗昧 ànmèi　① dim; obscure ② ignorant

暗门子 ànménzi　*old* unlicensed (or unregistered) prostitute

暗盘 ànpán　*old* secretly negotiated price

暗器 ànqì　hidden weapon (as darts hidden inside sleeves)

暗色 ànsè　dark colours

暗杀 ànshā　assassinate

暗伤 ànshāng　① internal (or invisible) injury ② indiscernible damage

暗射 ànshè　insinuate

暗射地图 ànshè dìtú　a map with locations marked but not labelled (a teaching aid to train learners in identifying places on a map)

暗示 ànshì　① drop a hint; hint; suggest: 他～我快走开。He hinted that he wanted me to leave at once. / 她没有懂我的～。She didn't take my hint. ② *psychol.* suggestion

暗事 ànshì　clandestine or illicit action: 明人不做暗事 míngrén bù zuò ànshì

暗室 ànshì　*photog.* darkroom

暗适应 ànshìyìng　*psychol.* dark adaptation

暗送秋波 àn sòng qiūbō　make eyes at sb.; give sb. the glad eye; ogle; make secret overtures to sb.

暗算 ànsuàn　plot against: 遭人～ fall a prey to a plot / ～别人 plot against sb.

暗锁 ànsuǒ　built-in lock

暗滩 àntān　hidden shoal

暗探 àntàn　secret agent; spy

暗无天日 àn wú tiānrì complete darkness—total absence of justice: 旧社会～。The old society was an abyss of darkness.

暗喜 ànxǐ feel pleased but not show it: 不由得心中～ cannot help feeling secretly pleased

暗线光谱 ànxiàn guāngpǔ *phys.* dark-line spectrum

暗香疏影 ànxiāng-shūyǐng secret fragrance and dappled shadows—a poetic epithet for the plum blossom, the two metonymic images referring to its smell and shape respectively (from a famous couplet on the plum blossom by the poet-recluse Lin Bu 林逋 of the early Northern Song: 疏影横斜水清浅，暗香浮动月黄昏。Dappled shadows hang aslant over clear shallow water; Secret fragrance wafts in the moonlit dusk.)

暗箱 ànxiāng *photog.* camera bellows; camera obscura

暗笑 ànxiào ① laugh in (*or* up) one's sleeve ② sneer secretly at

暗影 ànyǐng ① shadow ② *astron.* umbra

暗语 ànyǔ code word

暗喻 ànyù metaphor

暗中 ànzhōng ① in the dark: 我在～什么也看不见。I couldn't see anything in the dark. ② in secret; on the sly; surreptitiously: ～操纵 pull strings from behind the scenes / ～支持 give secret support to / ～串通 collude with; conspire

暗中摸索 ànzhōng mōsuo grope in the dark

暗转 ànzhuǎn *theat.* blackout in the middle of a scene or act (to indicate either a change in time, or, with a quick change of setting, a change in place)

暗自 ànzì inwardly; to oneself; secretly: ～落泪 cry to oneself; shed a tear in secret

暗自庆幸 ànzì qìngxìng congratulate oneself; consider oneself lucky

黯 àn dim; gloomy

黯淡 àndàn same as 暗淡 àndàn

黯然 ànrán *formal* ① dark and dim-looking: 工地上千万盏电灯光芒四射，连天上的星月也～无光。The worksite was ablaze with thousands of lights so that even the moon and the stars appeared lustreless in comparison. ② dejected; low-spirited; downcast: 神色～ appear dejected / 听到那消息，她不禁～泪下。The news dampened her spirits and set tears rolling down her cheeks.

黯然神伤 ànrán shénshāng feel dejected (*or* depressed)

黯然失色 ànrán shīsè be cast into the shade; be overshadowed; be eclipsed; pale into insignificance

黯然销魂 ànrán xiāohún be deeply grieved (as at parting): ～者，惟别而已矣。(江淹) There is no sorrow like sorrow at parting. *or* O what pain it is to part!

āng

肮(骯) āng see below

肮脏 āngzāng ① dirty; filthy: ～的衣服 dirty clothes / ～的阴沟 a filthy sewer / 这孩子浑身上下肮里肮脏的。The boy was covered all over with dirt. ② vile; mean; foul; dirty: ～的勾当 dirty work; a foul deed / ～的政治交易 a dirty political deal / 他的外表漂亮，可是灵魂～。His handsome appearance belies a dark soul.

áng

昂 áng ① hold (one's head) high: ～起头，挺起胸 hold up one's head and throw out one's chest; chin up and chest out ② high; soaring: 战天斗地志气～ battle against nature with high resolve

昂昂 áng'áng high-spirited; brave-looking: 雄赳赳，气昂昂 xióngjiūjiū, qì'áng'áng

昂藏 ángcáng *formal* tall and imposing: ～七尺之躯 a tall strapping man; a manly man

昂奋 ángfèn (of spirits or enthusiasm) run high

昂贵 ángguì expensive; costly: 价格～ be high-priced / ～的首饰 costly jewels

昂然 ángrán chin up and chest out; upright and unafraid: 他～直入。He strode in, chin up and chest out.

昂首阔步 ángshǒu-kuòbù stride along with one's chin up; stride proudly ahead

昂首望天 ángshǒu wàng tiān hold one's head high and gaze at the sky—disdain to investigate conditions at the lower levels

昂扬 ángyáng high-spirited: ～的歌声 spirited singing

àng

盎¹ àng an ancient vessel with a big belly and a small mouth

盎² àng *formal* brimming; abundant

盎格鲁撒克逊人 Ànggélǔ-Sākèxùnrén Anglo-Saxon

盎然 àngrán abundant; full; exuberant: 趣味～ be full of interest

盎司 àngsī (also 盎斯 àngsī) ounce

āo

凹 āo concave; sunken; dented: ～鼻梁儿 a flat nose / 这张床中间～下去了。This bed sags in the middle. ——see also wā

凹岸 āo'àn concave bank

凹版 āobǎn *print.* intaglio; gravure: 照相～ photogravure

凹版印刷 āobǎn yìnshuā intaglio (*or* gravure) printing

凹版印刷机 āobǎn yìnshuājī intaglio (*or* gravure) press

凹版制版 āobǎn zhìbǎn gravure plate-making

凹度 āodù concavity

凹面镜 āomiànjìng concave mirror

凹透镜 āotòujìng concave lens

凹凸不平 āo-tū bù píng full of bumps and holes; uneven

凹凸压花 āo-tū yāhuā *text.* embossing

凹凸印刷 āo-tū yìnshuā embossing; die stamping

凹凸印刷机 āo-tū yìnshuājī embossing (*or* die stamping) press

凹陷 āoxiàn cave in; sink: 地面～。The ground caved in. / 双颊～ have sunken (*or* hollow) cheeks

熬 āo stew (vegetables, etc.) in water: ～白菜 stewed cabbage / 豆腐～好了没有? Has the tofu been stewed long enough? ——see also áo

áo

敖 áo ① same as 遨 áo ② (Áo) a surname

敖包 áobāo a pile of stones, earth or grass used by Mongolians as a road sign or a boundary sign

遨 áo stroll; saunter

遨游 áoyóu go on a pleasure tour; travel: ～海上 go on a cruise / ～太空 travel through space

嗷 áo see below

嗷嗷 áo'áo *onom.* the sound of crying (of certain birds or animals, or of human beings in pain or suffering): 疼得～叫 howl with pain / 雁群～地飞过。Flocks of honking geese flew past.

嗷嗷待哺 áo'áo dài bǔ (of starving people or young animals) cry piteously for food

廒（厫） áo *formal* storehouse for grain, etc.; granary; barn

熬 áo ① cook (cereals, etc.) into porridge or thick soup: ～粥 make gruel / ～一锅汤 prepare a pot of soup / 汤快～干了。The soup is overstewed, it's nearly dried up. / 用微火～ simmer ② extract sth.'s essence by long boiling: ～盐 make salt by boiling seawater / ～油 extract grease by melting animal fat / ～药 decoct Chinese medicine by boiling and simmering medicinal herbs, etc. in water ③ endure (distress, hard times, etc.); hold out: ～过苦难的岁月 endure years of suffering and deprivation / 他眼睛都～红了。His eyes are bloodshot through staying up late all night. / 这种苦日子我再也～不下去了。She can't put up with such hardship any longer. / 孩子大了，她总算～出头了。Now that her kids have grown up, her hard years are over at last. / 他的病怕～不过冬天了。I doubt if he will live through the winter. ——see also āo

熬煎 áojiān suffering; torment; torture: 受尽～ be subjected to all kinds of sufferings (*or* afflictions) / 她经不住这样的～，过早地离开了人世。Unable to endure such torments, she came to an untimely end.

熬夜 áoyè stay up late or all night: 天天～，谁受得了？Who can keep on staying up late night after night? / 她熬一回夜就病一回。Every time she stays up all night, she's taken ill the next day.

獒 áo a large fierce dog; mastiff

螯 áo chela; pincers (of crustaceans, etc.)

聱 áo see 佶屈聱牙 jíqū áoyá

翱（翱） áo *formal* take wing

翱翔 áoxiáng hover; soar: 海鸥在惊涛骇浪上～。Seagulls hover over the surging waves. / ～长空的女飞行员 women pilots soaring in the skies

翱翔机 áoxiángjī sailplane

鳌（鼇） áo a huge legendary turtle

鏖 áo *formal* engage in fierce battle

鏖兵 áobīng *formal* fight hard; engage in fierce battle

鏖战 áozhàn *formal* fight hard; engage in fierce battle: 两军～三日。The two armies were fiercely engaged for three days. / 两队～九十分钟，不分胜负。After a fierce 90-minute contest, the score was even.

ǎo

拗（抝） ǎo *dial.* bend or twist so as to break: 把甘蔗～断 bend and break a piece of sugarcane in two —— see also ào; niù

拗陷 ǎoxiàn *geol.* depression

袄（襖） ǎo a lined Chinese-style coat or jacket: 小～ a short close-fitting jacket

媪 ǎo *formal* an old woman

ào

坳（坳、圳） ào low-lying land between or amidst higher points in a mountain range; col: 珠峰北～ the North Col of Mount Qomolangma (Mount Everest)

拗（抝） ào defy; disobey: 违拗 wéi'ào ——see also ǎo; niù

拗口 àokǒu be hard to pronounce (esp. rapidly); be awkward reading: 这两句念起来～。These two lines do not read smoothly.

拗口令 àokǒulìng tongue twister

傲 ào ① proud; haughty: 这个人～得很，可不好接近了。That fellow is extremely haughty and standoffish. ② refuse to yield to; brave; defy: 红梅～雪凌霜开。Braving snow and frost, the plum trees blossomed defiantly.

傲岸 ào'àn *formal* proud; haughty: ～的青松 a proud and towering pine tree

傲岸不群 ào'àn bù qún haughty and standoffish; proud and aloof

傲骨 àogǔ unbending backbone——lofty and unyielding character: 他生就一身～，宁折不弯。A man of unyielding character, he would rather break than bend.

傲慢 àomàn arrogant; haughty; overbearing: 态度～ be arrogant; put on airs; give oneself airs; hold one's nose in the air / 他的～无礼激起了大家的愤怒。His overbearing insolence angered everyone.

傲气 àoqì ① air of arrogance; haughtiness: ～十足 full of arrogance; extremely haughty ② arrogant; haughty: 她可～了。She's very haughty.

傲然 àorán lofty and proud-looking; unyielding: ～挺立的山峰 a mountain peak towering proudly into the skies

傲视 àoshì regard with disdain; turn up one's nose at; show disdain for

奡 ào *formal* ① vigorous: 排奡 pái'ào ② same as 傲 ào

奥[1] ào ① profound and difficult to understand; abstruse: 深奥 shēn'ào ② *formal* the southwestern corner or the innermost part of a house: 堂奥 táng'ào ③ (Ào) short for 奥地利 Àodìlì

奥[2] ào *phys.* short for 奥斯特 àosītè

奥博 àobó *formal* ① extensive and profound in meaning ② (of a person) widely read

奥得河 Àodéhé the Oder River

奥地利 Àodìlì Austria

奥地利人 Àodìlìrén Austrian

奥林匹克运动会 Àolínpǐkè Yùndònghuì the Olympic Games

奥纶 àolún *text.* orlon

奥秘 àomì profound mystery: 探索宇宙的～ probe the mysteries of the universe

奥妙 àomiào profound and subtle: 神奇～ mysterious and profound / ～无穷 extremely subtle / 不难看出其中

的 ～。It's not difficult to see what's behind it.／其中定有 ～。There must be more to it than meets the eye.

奥氏体 àoshìtǐ *metall.* austenite: ～钢 austenitic steel

奥斯曼帝国 Àosīmàn Dìguó the Ottoman Empire (1290–1922)

奥斯特 àosītè *phys.* oersted (Oe)

奥陶纪 Àotáojì *geol.* the Ordovician Period

奥陶系 Àotáoxì *geol.* the Ordovician system

奥匈帝国 Ào-Xiōng Dìguó Austro-Hungary (1867–1918)

奥援 àoyuán *formal derog.* power behind the scenes; powerful backing

奥运会 Àoyùnhuì short for 奥林匹克运动会 Àolínpǐkè Yùndònghuì

骜 ào *formal* ① a good horse; steed ② same as 傲 ào

澳[1] ào ① (usu. used as part of a place name) an inlet of the sea; bay: 三都 ～ Sandu Bay ② (Ào) short for Aomen (Macao): 港 ～同胞 compatriots in Hong Kong and Macao

澳[2] Ào short for 澳大利亚 Àodàlìyà

澳大利亚 Àodàlìyà Australia

澳大利亚抗原 Àodàlìyà kàngyuán *med.* Australia antigen; hepatitis-associated antigen (HAA)

澳大利亚人 Àodàlìyàrén Australian

澳抗 Àokàng short for 澳大利亚抗原 Àodàlìyà kàngyuán

澳门 Àomén Aomen (Macao)

澳洲 Àozhōu Australia (the continent)

懊 ào ① regretful; remorseful: 懊悔 àohuǐ ② annoyed; vexed: 懊恼 àonǎo

懊悔 àohuǐ feel remorse; repent; regret: 我 ～不该错怪了她。I regretted having blamed her unjustly.／现在你不好好学习，将来你自会 ～的。If you don't study hard now, you will regret it in the future.

懊恼 àonǎo be annoyed, vexed or upset; fret: 他工作没做好，心里很 ～。He was quite upset at not having done his work well.／她正为自己丢失了钱包而 ～呢。She's fretting over the loss of her purse.

懊丧 àosàng feel dejected or depressed.

鏖 ào see below

鏖子 àozi griddle

B

bā

八 bā eight: ～公斤 eight kilos / ～个班 eight classes / ～班 the eighth class; class 8 / 电视～厂 No. 8 Television Factory

八拜之交 bā bài zhī jiāo sworn brotherhood: 我和他有～。 He and I are sworn brothers.

八宝 bābǎo eight treasures (choice ingredients of certain special dishes)

八宝儿 bābǎor common name for 景天 jǐngtiān

八宝菜 bābǎocài eight-treasure pickles; assorted soy-sauce pickles

八宝饭 bābǎofàn eight-treasure rice pudding (steamed glutinous rice with bean paste, lotus seeds, preserved fruits, etc.)

八倍体 bābèitǐ *biol.* octoploid

八辈子 bābèizi eight lifetimes—a long time: 这简直是倒了～霉了。 What interminable rotten luck!

八成 bāchéng ① eighty per cent: ～新 eighty per cent new; practically new / 事情有了～啦。 It's almost as good as settled. *or* There's a fair chance of success. ② most probably; most likely: ～儿他不来了。 Most probably he isn't coming.

八带鱼 bādàiyú octopus

八斗才 bādǒucái unusual literary talent; superb talent

八度 bādù *mus.* octave

八方 bāfāng the eight points of the compass; all directions: 一方有难，～支援。 When trouble occurs at one spot, help comes from all quarters. ——see also 四面八方 sìmiàn-bāfāng

八方呼应 bāfāng hūyìng responses from every direction; cooperation from all

八分音符 bāfēn yīnfú *mus.* quaver; eighth note

八分之一决赛 bāfēnzhīyī juésài *sports* eighth-finals

八纲 bāgāng *Chin. med.* the eight principal syndromes: *yin* and *yang* (阴阳), exterior and interior (表里), cold and heat (寒热), hypofunction and hyperfunction (虚实)

八纲辨证 bāgāng biànzhèng *Chin. med.* analysis and differentiation of pathological conditions in accordance with the eight principal syndromes

八哥儿 bāgēr *zool.* myna

八股 bāgǔ ① eight-part essay (a literary composition prescribed for the imperial civil service examinations, known for its rigidity of form and poverty of ideas) ② stereotyped writing

八卦 bāguà the Eight Trigrams (eight combinations of three lines—all solid, all broken, or a combination of solid and broken lines—joined in pairs to form 64 hexagrams, formerly used in divination)

八国联军 Bāguó Liánjūn the Eight-Power Allied Forces (aggressive troops sent by Britain, the United States, Germany, France, tsarist Russia, Japan, Italy and Austria in 1900, to suppress the anti-imperialist Yihetuan Movement 义和团运动 of the Chinese people, known to the West as the Boxer Rebellion)

八行书 bāhángshū (also 八行 bāháng) ① (also 八行纸 bāhángzhǐ) letter paper with eight vertical lines to the page ② letter

八会穴 bāhuìxué *Chin. med.* the Eight Strategic Nerve Points

八级风 bājífēng *meteorol.* force 8 wind; fresh gale

八级工 bājígōng eight-grade worker (highest on the eight-grade wage scale); top-grade worker

八级工资制 bājí gōngzīzhì eight-grade wage scale (*or* system)

八极 bājí *formal* the ends of the earth; remotest places

八角 bājiǎo *bot.* ① anise; star anise ② aniseed

八角枫 bājiǎofēng *bot.* alangium

八角帽 bājiǎomào octagonal cap

八角形 bājiǎoxíng octagon

八进位制 bājìnwèizhì octal (number) system

八九不离十 bā jiǔ bù lí shí *inf.* about right; pretty close; very near: 猜个～ make a very close guess / 这些估计虽然不是绝对保险，但也～。 These calculations, though not always one hundred percent accurate, were never far out.

八开 bākāi *print.* octavo; 8vo

八开本 bākāiběn octavo

八路军 Bālùjūn the Eighth Route Army (led by the Chinese Communist Party during the War of Resistance Against Japan)

八面光 bāmiànguāng (also 八面见光 bāmiàn jiànguāng) same as 八面玲珑 bāmiàn línglóng

八面玲珑 bāmiàn línglóng be smooth and slick (in establishing social relations)

八面威风 bāmiàn wēifēng an aura of awesome might; a commanding presence

八旗 bāqí the "Eight Banners" (military-administrative organizations of the Man nationality in the Qing Dynasty)

八仙 Bāxiān ① the Eight Immortals (in Taoist mythology, usu. identified as Han Zhongli 汉钟离, Zhang Guolao 张果老, Lü Dongbin 吕洞宾, Li Tieguai 李铁拐, Han Xiangzi 韩湘子, Cao Guojiu 曹国舅, Lan Caihe 蓝采和, and He Xiangu 何仙姑; much represented in art) ② *dial.* same as 八仙桌 bāxiānzhuō

八仙过海，各显神通 Bāxiān guò hǎi, gè xiǎn shéntōng like the Eight Immortals crossing the sea, each one showing his or her special prowess: 没有统一计划，你们就～吧。 There's no unified plan, so you'll all be on your own resources and prove your worth.

八仙桌 bāxiānzhuō Eight Immortals table—an old-fashioned square table for eight people

八小时工作制 bāxiǎoshí gōngzuòzhì eight-hour day

八一建军节 Bā-Yī jiànjūnjié Army Day (August 1, anniversary of the founding of the Chinese People's Liberation Army)

八一南昌起义 Bā-Yī Nánchāng Qǐyì the August 1 Nanchang Uprising (1927), which fired the first shot against the KMT reactionaries and marked the beginning of the Chinese Communist Party's independent

leadership of the revolutionary war

八音盒 bāyīnhé (also 八音琴 bāyīnqín) musical (*or* music) box

八月 bāyuè ① August ② the eighth month of the lunar year; the eighth moon

八月节 Bāyuèjié the Mid-Autumn Festival (15th day of the 8th lunar month)

八字 bāzì Eight Characters (in four pairs, indicating the year, month, day and hour of a person's birth, each pair consisting of one Heavenly Stem 天干 and one Earthly Branch 地支, formerly used in fortune-telling)

八字步 bāzìbù a measured gait with the toes pointing outwards: 迈着～ walk in a deliberate way, with the feet turned outwards

八字还没一撇儿 bā zì hái méi yī piěr there's not even the first stroke of the character 八—things aren't even starting to take shape yet; there's not the slightest sign of success yet: 你的喜事准备得怎么样了？——～呢。How are the wedding preparations going?—Oh, we haven't even got off the ground yet.

八字胡 bāzìhú mustache shaped like character 八

八字脚 bāzìjiǎo splayfoot

八字眉 bāzìméi slanted eyebrows

八字帖儿 bāzìtiěr a card with the horoscope of a boy or girl sent as a proposal for betrothal

八字宪法 bā zì xiànfǎ short for 农业八字宪法 nóngyè bā zì xiànfǎ

巴¹ bā ① hope earnestly; wait anxiously: 巴望 bāwàng ② cling to; stick to: 爬山虎～在墙上。The ivy clings to the wall. / 粥～了锅了。The porridge has stuck to the pot. ③ crust: 锅巴 guōbā ④ *dial.* be close to; be next to: 前不巴村，后不巴店 qián bu bā cūn, hòu bu bā diàn ⑤ *dial.* open; spread: ～着眼瞧瞧 stare wide-eyed / 天气干燥，桌子都～缝啦。The table-top is cracked because of the dry weather.

巴² Bā ① an ancient state in the eastern part of what is now Sichuan Province ② the eastern part of Sichuan Province ③ a surname

巴³ bā *phys.* bar: 微～ microbar

巴巴多斯 Bābāduōsī Barbados

巴巴多斯人 Bābāduōsīrén Barbadian

巴比伦 Bābǐlún Babylon

巴比特合金 bābǐtè héjīn babbitt (metal)

巴比妥 bābǐtuǒ *pharm.* barbitone; barbital

巴布亚新几内亚 Bābùyà Xīnjǐnèiyà Papua New Guinea

巴布亚新几内亚人 Bābùyà Xīnjǐnèiyàrén Papua New Guinean

巴不得 bābude *inf.* be only too anxious (to do sth.); eagerly look forward to; earnestly wish: 他～立刻回到工作岗位。He is only too anxious to get back to work right away. / 我～天快晴。I wish it would clear up soon. / 这是～的好事。This is the best thing we can wish for.

巴斗 bādǒu same as 笆斗 bādǒu

巴豆 bādòu *bot.* (purging) croton

巴豆霜 bādòushuāng *Chin. med.* defatted croton seed powder

巴尔干半岛 Bā'ěrgàn Bàndǎo the Balkan Peninsula

巴尔干国家 Bā'ěrgàn guójiā Balkan states; the Balkans

巴儿狗 bārgǒu ① pekingese (a breed of dog) ② sycophant; toady

巴哈马 Bāhāmǎ the Bahamas

巴哈马人 Bāhāmǎrén Bahamian

巴基斯坦 Bājīsītǎn Pakistan

巴基斯坦人 Bājīsītǎnrén Pakistani

巴结 bājie ① fawn on; curry favour with; make up to: ～阔人 fawn on rich people ② *dial.* try hard; make great efforts: 他工作很～。He works very hard.

巴克夏猪 bākèxiàzhū Berkshire (swine)

巴枯宁主义 Bākūníngzhǔyì Bakuninism

巴拉圭 Bālāguī Paraguay

巴拉圭人 Bālāguīrén Paraguayan

巴勒斯坦 Bālèsītǎn Palestine

巴勒斯坦解放组织 Bālèsītǎn Jiěfàng Zǔzhī the Palestine Liberation Organization (PLO)

巴勒斯坦人 Bālèsītǎnrén Palestinian

巴黎公社 Bālí Gōngshè the Paris Commune (the world's first dictatorship of the proletariat, established by the French working class after smashing the old state machine, 1871)

巴黎绿 bālílǜ *chem.* Paris green

巴里纱 bālǐshā *text.* organdy

巴林 Bālín Bahrain

巴林人 Bālínrén Bahraini

巴龙霉素 bālóngméisù *pharm.* paromomycin

巴拿马 Bānámǎ Panama

巴拿马人 Bānámǎrén Panamanian

巴拿马运河 Bānámǎ Yùnhé the Panama Canal

巴士 bāshì bus (a transliteration)

巴士底狱 Bāshìdǐyù the Bastille

巴松管 bāsōngguǎn popular name for 大管 dàguǎn

巴头探脑儿 bātóutànnǎor pop one's head in and look about

巴望 bāwàng *dial.* ① look forward to; hope: 我真～我们再也不分开了。I hope we'll never separate again. ② good prospects: 这事总算有了～了。Things are looking up now.

巴西 Bāxī Brazil

巴西人 Bāxīrén Brazilian

巴眨 bāzha *dial.* blink; wink

巴掌 bāzhang palm; hand: 拍～ clap one's hands / 打他一～ give him a slap / 现在连～大的地方都利用上了。Now, every square inch of land is utilized.

扒 bā ① hold on to; cling to: 孩子们～着窗台看游行队伍。Holding on to the window sill, the children watched the parade. ② dig up; rake; pull down: ～土 rake earth / ～了旧房盖新房 pull down the old house to build a new one in its place / 城墙～了个豁口。A breach was made in the city wall. ③ push aside: ～开芦苇 push aside the reeds ④ strip off; take off: ～兔皮 skin a rabbit / 他把棉袄一～就干起活来。Stripping off his padded coat, he set to work at once. ——see also pá

扒车 bāchē climb onto a slow-going train, etc.

扒钉 bādīng cramp

扒拉 bāla push lightly: 把压在苗上的土一～开 flick the earth off the seedlings / ～算盘子儿 move the beads of an abacus up and down; click away at an abacus ——see also pála

扒头儿 bātour *inf.* handhold

叭 bā same as 吧 bā

叭儿狗 bārgǒu same as 巴儿狗 bārgǒu

芭 bā a fragrant plant (mentioned in ancient texts)

芭蕉 bājiāo *bajiao* banana

芭蕉扇 bājiāoshàn palm-leaf fan

芭蕾舞 bālěiwǔ ballet: 跳～ dance ballet

芭蕾舞剧 bālěiwǔjù ballet: 《天鹅湖》是一个古典～。*Swan Lake* is a classical ballet.

芭蕾舞女演员 bālěiwǔ nǚyǎnyuán ballerina

芭蕾舞设计 bālěiwǔ shèjì choreography

芭蕾舞演员 bālěiwǔ yǎnyuán ballet dancer

吧

吧 bā ① *onom.*: ～的一声，弦断了。 The string broke with a snap. ／～～两声枪响。 Crack! Crack! Two shots rang out. ② *dial.* draw on (*or* pull at) one's pipe, etc.: 他～了一口烟，才开始说话。 He didn't start to speak until he had taken a puff at his pipe. ——see also ba

吧嗒 bādā *onom.*: ～一声，门关上了。 The door clicked shut.

吧嗒 bāda ① smack one's lips (in surprise, alarm, etc.): 他～了一下嘴，一声也不言语。 He smacked his lips but did not utter a word. ②*dial.* pull at (a pipe, etc): 他～着叶子烟打主意。 He puffed at his pipe as he wondered what to do.

吧唧 bājī *onom.*: 她光着脚～～地在泥里走。 She squelched barefoot through the mud.

吧唧 bāji ① smack one's lips ② *dial.* pull at (a pipe, etc.)

疤

疤 bā scar: 刀伤在他的膝盖上留下了一个～。 The cut left a scar on his knee. ／香烟在桌面上烧了一个～。 The burning cigarette left a mark on the top of the table.

疤痕 bāhén scar

疤瘌 bāla (also 疤拉 bāla) scar

疤瘌眼儿 bālayǎnr ① an eye with a scar on the eyelid ② a person who has such an eye

粑

粑 bā *dial.* cake: 糖～ sweet cake

粑粑 bābā *dial.* cake: 玉米～ corn cake

捌

捌 bā eight (used for the numeral 八 on cheques, etc. to avoid mistakes or alterations)

笆

笆 bā basketry: 竹篾～ bamboo basketry

笆斗 bādǒu round-bottomed basket

笆篱 bālí *dial.* bamboo or twig fence

笆篱子 bālízi *dial.* prison; jail

bá

拔

拔 bá ① pull out; pull up: ～草 pull up weeds; weed ／～麦子 harvest wheat (by pulling it up) ／～牙 pull out (*or* extract) a tooth ／～剑 draw one's sword ② suck out; draw: 把火～一～。 Put a chimney on the stove to make the fire draw. ③ choose; select; pick: 选拔 xuǎnbá ④ lift; raise: ～起嗓子直嚷 shout at the top of one's voice ⑤ stand out among; surpass: 海拔 hǎibá ⑥ capture; seize: 连～敌人五个据点 capture five enemy strongholds in succession ⑦ *dial.* cool in water: 把西瓜放在冰水里～一～ cool a watermelon in ice water ⑧ *mech.* drawing: 冷拔 lěngbá

拔白 bábái *dial.* dawn

拔步 bábù same as 拔腿 bátuǐ

拔不出腿 bábuchūtuǐ be tied up

拔除 báchú pull out; remove: ～敌军哨所 wipe out an enemy sentry post

拔萃 bácuì *formal* stand out from one's fellows; be out of the common run: ～出群 stand head and shoulders above others; be outstanding

拔地 bádì rise sheer (*or* steeply) from level ground; tower: ～而起的高楼 a towering building

拔钉锤 bádīngchuí claw hammer

拔顶 bádǐng ① *petroleum* topping ② *dial.* become bald

拔毒 bádú *Chin. med.* draw out pus by applying a plaster to the affected part

拔份儿 báfènr push oneself forward; be pushy

拔罐子 bá guànzi *Chin. med.* cupping

拔海 báhǎi same as 海拔 hǎibá

拔河 báhé tug-of-war

拔火罐儿[1] báhuǒguànr *dial. Chin. med.* cupping

拔火罐儿[2] báhuǒguànr (also 拔火筒 báhuǒtǒng) detachable stove chimney

拔尖儿 bájiānr *inf.* ① tiptop; top-notch: 他的学习成绩是～的。 He is a top-notch student. ② push oneself forward; be pushy

拔脚 bájiǎo same as 拔腿 bátuǐ

拔节 bájié *agric.* jointing: ～期 jointing (*or* elongation) stage

拔举 bájǔ select and propose sb. for an office; recommend

拔锚 bámáo weigh anchor

拔苗助长 bá miáo zhù zhǎng try to help the shoots grow by pulling them upward—spoil things by excessive enthusiasm

拔群 báqún stand head and shoulders above others

拔染 bárǎn *text.* discharge: ～剂 discharging agent; discharge

拔丝 básī ① *mech.* wire drawing: ～机 wire drawing bench (*or* machine) ② candied floss: ～山药 hot candied yam

拔腿 bátuǐ ① lift the foot (and begin to run, chase, etc.): ～就跑 start running away at once; immediately take to one's heels ／～就追 give instant chase ② leave (one's work); get away; free oneself: 他事情太多，拔不开腿。 He is too busy with his work to get away.

拔秧 báyāng *agric.* pull up seedlings (for transplanting)

拔营 báyíng *mil.* strike camp

拔招 bázhāo *inf.* retract a false move in a chess game

拔擢 bázhuó *formal* promote (a person)

菝

菝 bá see below

菝葜 báqiā *bot.* chinaroot greenbrier

跋[1]

跋 bá cross mountains

跋[2]

跋 bá postscript (to a book)

跋扈 báhù domineering; bossy

跋前疐后 báqián-zhìhòu (also 跋前踬后 báqián-zhìhòu) encounter obstacles ahead and behind; be beset with difficulties

跋山涉水 báshān-shèshuǐ scale mountains and ford streams—travel afar under difficult conditions

跋涉 báshè trudge; trek: 长途跋涉 chángtú báshè

跋文 báwén postscript (to a book)

魃

魃 bá see 旱魃 hànbá

跋

跋 bá see 蹉跋 tuóbá

bǎ

把[1]

把 bǎ ① hold; grasp: ～住栏杆 hold on to a railing ／～着手教 take sb. by the hand and teach him how to do sth. ／～犁 handle a plough ② hold (a baby while it relieves itself): 给孩子～尿 hold a baby out to let it urinate ③ control; monopolize; dominate: 要充分发挥群众的积极性，不要什么都～着不放手。 You must give full play to the initiative of the masses and not keep such a tight control on things. ④ guard; watch: 把门 bǎmén ⑤ *inf.* be close; be located at: ～墙角儿站着

stand in the corner of the wall / ～着胡同口儿有个小饭馆。 There is a small restaurant at the entrance of the alley. ⑥ *dial.* give (of a pushcart, etc.): 自行车～ the handlebars of a bicycle ⑧ bundle; bunch: 草～ a bundle of straw ⑨ *m.* ⓐ (for sth. with a handle): 一～刀 a knife / 一～茶壶 a teapot / 一～扇子 a fan ⓑ handful of: 一～米 a handful of rice / 一～花 a bunch of flowers ⓒ (for certain abstract ideas): 有一～年纪 be getting on in years / 有～力气 be quite strong / 加～劲 make an extra effort; put on a spurt / 一～好手 an efficient or skillful worker ⓓ (for sth. done with the hand): 拉他一～ give him a tug; give (*or* lend) him a hand / 帮他一～ give him a helping hand; pull him out of difficulties

把² 　bǎ　*prep.* (used to shift the object to before the verb, which must be reduplicated or accompanied by some other word or expression): ～衣服洗洗 have the clothes washed / ～头一扭 toss one's head / ～衣服撕了个口子 tear a hole in one's jacket / ～方便让给别人，～困难留给自己 take difficulties on oneself and leave what is easy to others / ～人急死 worry one to death / 这一趟可～他累坏了。 That trip really tired him out. / 正在这节骨眼上偏偏～老张病了。 It was right at the moment we needed Lao Zhang most that he fell ill. / 别害怕，他能～你怎么样? Don't be afraid. What can he do to you? / 他不～我当人。 He doesn't treat me like a human being. / 她简直不～这点困难放在眼里。 She simply thinks nothing at all of this difficulty.

把³ 　bǎ　*part.* (used after 百,千,万,里,丈,顷,斤,个, etc., the combination admitting of no numeral) about; or so: 个～月 about a month; a month or so / 百～人 some hundred people

把⁴ 　bǎ　sworn: ～兄 a sworn brother / ～嫂 a sworn sister-in-law
——see also bà

把柄 bǎbǐng handle: 给人抓住～ give sb. a handle (against oneself) / 他抓住了你什么～? What hold does he have on you? / 不要给别人留下～。 Don't do anything that others can hold against you.

把持 bǎchí ① *derog.* dominate; monopolize: ～一切 monopolize everything / ～一部分权力 seize a certain amount of power ② control (one's feelings, etc.)

把舵 bǎduò hold the rudder; hold (*or* take, be at) the helm; steer

把风 bǎfēng keep watch (for one's partners in a clandestine activity); be on the lookout

把关 bǎguān ① guard a pass ② check on: 层层～ make checks at all levels / 把好质量关 guarantee the quality (of products) / 把好政治关 ensure political soundness

把角儿 bǎjiǎor street corner

把酒 bǎjiǔ ① raise one's wine cup: 明月几时有,～问青天。(苏轼) When did the moon begin to shine? Lifting my cup I ask of Heaven. ② fill a wine cup for sb.

把揽 bǎlǎn monopolize; take on everything; arrogate: ～大权 arrogate all powers to oneself

把牢 bǎláo *dial.* (usu. used in the negative) steady; reliable: 桩子不打深不～。 Piles won't be steady unless driven in deep. / 他做事一向马马虎虎,不～。 He's careless and unreliable in everything he does.

把理 bǎlǐ *dial.* reasonable; sensible; right: 说话～ give a reasonable statement

把门 bǎmén ① guard a gate: ～很严。 The gate was closely guarded. / 我说话嘴上缺个～的。 I can't keep my mouth shut. ② be a goalkeeper (in football, etc.)

把势 bǎshi (also 把式 bǎshi) ① *inf.* *wushu* (武术): martial arts: 练～ practise *wushu* ② *inf.* a person skilled in *wushu*; a person skilled in a trade: 论庄稼活,他可真是个好～。 He's a highly skilled farmer. ③ *dial.* skill: 学会木工的全套～ learn all the skills of carpentry

把守 bǎshǒu guard: ～城门 guard a city gate / 分兵～ divide up one's forces for defence

把手 bǎshou *dial.* ① shake hands ② handle; grip; knob

把水搅浑 bǎ shuǐ jiǎo hún muddy the water—create confusion

把头 bǎ·tóu labour contractor; gangmaster

把稳 bǎwěn *dial.* trustworthy; dependable: 他办事很～。 He is dependable in what he does.

把握 bǎwò ① hold; grasp: 司机～着方向盘。 The driver was holding the steering wheel. / 透过现象,～本质 see through the phenomenon to grasp the essence / ～时机 seize the opportunity; seize the right time ② assurance; certainty: 没有成功的～ have no certainty of success / 他有～通过考试。 He feels confident of passing the examination. / 他很有～地回答了所有的问题。 He answered all the questions with assurance. / 做这项工作,他很有～。 He's quite sure he can do this job. / 不打无准备之仗,不打无～之仗。Fight no battle unprepared, fight no battle you are not sure of winning.

把晤 bǎwù *formal* (of friends) meet and shake hands; see each other

把戏 bǎxì ① acrobatics; jugglery: 耍～ play tricks; juggle ② cheap trick; game: 不知道他玩的是什么～。 I wonder what trick he is up to. / 他玩的～我都看穿了。 I saw through his game.

把兄弟 bǎxiōngdì sworn brothers

把盏 bǎzhǎn *formal* raise a wine cup (in a toast to a guest)

把捉 bǎzhuō grasp (abstract things): ～事物的本质 grasp the essence of the matter

把子¹ bǎzi *m.* ① *derog.* group; band ② bundle: 一～韭菜 a bundle of chives ③ (for certain abstract ideas): 加～劲儿 make an extra effort; put on a spurt

把子² bǎzi ① general name for the weapons used in traditional operas ② fighting and fencing in such operas

把子³ bǎzi see 拜把子 bài bǎzi

钯 　bǎ　*chem.* palladium (Pd)

靶 　bǎ　target: 打中了～ hit the target

靶标 bǎbiāo target

靶场 bǎchǎng shooting range; range

靶船 bǎchuán target ship

靶壕 bǎháo marking pit; pit

靶机 bǎjī target drone

靶心 bǎxīn centre of a target; bull's-eye

靶纸 bǎzhǐ target sheet

靶子 bǎzi target

bà

把（欛） 　bà　① grip; handle: 茶壶～儿 the handle of a teapot / 枪～儿 rifle butt ② stem (of a leaf, flower or fruit): 花～儿 a flower stem ——see also bǎ

把子 bàzi handle: 刀把子 dāobàzi

坝（壩） 　bà　① dam ② dyke; embankment ③ *dial.* sandbar ④ (usu. used as part of a place name) flatland; plain

爸 bà *inf.* pa; dad; father
爸爸 bàba papa; dad; father

耙(耮) bà ① harrow ② draw a harrow over (a field); harrow: 那块地已经～过两遍了。 That piece of land has already been harrowed twice. ——see also pá

罢(罷) bà ① stop; cease: 欲罢不能 yù bà bùnéng ② dismiss: 罢官 bàguān ③ *dial.* finish: 说～，他就走了。 With these words he left.
罢笔 bàbǐ put down the pen—stop writing
罢斥 bàchì remove an official from his position
罢黜 bàchù *formal* ① dismiss from office ② ban; reject: 汉武帝～百家，独尊儒术。Emperor Wu (156-87 B.C.) of the Han Dynasty proscribed all non-Confucian schools of thought and espoused Confucianism as the orthodox state ideology.
罢工 bàgōng strike; go on strike: 号召～ call for a strike / 工人已经罢了三天工了。 The workers have been on strike for three days now.
罢官 bàguān dismiss from office: 《海瑞～》 *Hai Rui Dismissed from Office* (a play)
罢教 bàjiào teachers' strike
罢课 bàkè students' strike
罢了 bàle *part.* (used at the end of a declarative sentence) that's all; nothing else: 这没有什么，我不过做了我应该做的事～。 It's nothing. I've only done what I ought to do. / 你就是不想去～。 You just don't want to go, that's all.
罢了 bàliǎo let it pass; be done with it: 他不愿意来也就～。 Let him stay away if he wishes. / 他不肯来也～，连个回信也不给。 I wouldn't have minded his refusing, but he didn't even answer my letter.
罢论 bàlùn abandoned idea: 此事已作～。 The idea has already been dropped.
罢免 bàmiǎn recall: 常委由代表大会选举或者～。Members of the standing committee are elected and subject to recall by the congress.
罢免权 bàmiǎnquán right of recall; recall
罢市 bàshì shopkeepers' strike
罢手 bàshǒu give up: 不试验成功，我们决不～。 We will never stop until the experiment succeeds.
罢休 bàxiū (usu. used in the negative) give up; let the matter drop: 不达目的，决不～。 We'll not stop until we reach our goal.
罢职 bàzhí remove from office; dismiss

釟 bà *dial.* bucktooth: ～牙 bucktooth

鲅(鮊) bà Spanish mackerel
鲅鱼 bàyú Spanish mackerel

霸(覇) bà ① leader of feudal lords: 春秋五～ the Five Overlords of the Spring and Autumn Period (770-476 B.C.) ② tyrant; despot; bully: 他是地方一～。 He is a local despot. ③ hegemonist power; hegemonism; hegemony: 争霸 zhēngbà ④ dominate; lord it over; tyrannize over: 军阀割据，各～一方。 The country was torn by warlordism, with each warlord dominating a region.
霸道 bàdào ① (in ancient political thought) rule by force; overbearing; high-handed; unreasonable: 他这个人很～，你没法儿跟他说。 That guy is very unreasonable; there's no use arguing with him.
霸道 bàdao (of liquor, medicine, etc.) strong, potent: 这酒真～，少喝点吧。 This liquor is pretty strong; you'd better go easy.

霸权 bàquán hegemony; supremacy
霸权主义 bàquánzhǔyì hegemonism
霸头 bàtou ① labour contractor; gangmaster ② overlord; hegemon
霸王 bàwáng ① (Bàwáng) Hegemon King (a title assumed by Xiang Yu 项羽, 232-202 B.C.) ② overlord; despot
霸王鞭 bàwángbiān ① a rattle stick used in folk dancing ② rattle stick dance
霸业 bàyè achievements of a leader of feudal lords
霸占 bàzhàn forcibly occupy; seize: ～别国领土 forcibly occupy the territory of another country
霸主 bàzhǔ ① a powerful leader of feudal lords (of the Spring and Autumn Period, 770-476 B.C.) ② overlord; hegemon: 海上～ maritime overlord

ba

吧(罷、罷) ba *part.* ① (indicating a suggestion, a request or a mild command): 咱们走～。 Let's go. / 你好好儿想想～! Just think it over. ② (indicating consent or approval): 好～，就这么办～! O.K. Let's do it this way. / 明天就明天～。 All right, let's make it tomorrow. ③ (forming a leading question which asks for confirmation of a supposition): 他会来～? He'll come, won't he? / 你是中国人～? You are Chinese, I suppose (*or* I take it)? ④ (indicating some doubt in the speaker's mind): 他们走了～。 I suppose they've left. / 他好像是这么说的～。 That's what he said, it seems. ⑤ (marking a pause after suppositions as alternatives): 去～，不好; 不去～，也不好。 If I go, it's no good; if I don't, it's no good either. ——see also bā

bāi

刮 bāi see below
刮划 bāihuai *dial.* ① deal with; arrange ② repair; renovate

掰(擘) bāi break off with the fingers and thumb: 把饼～成两半 break the cake in two / ～玉米 break off corncobs / 一分钱～成两半花 watch every penny / ～着手指算 count on one's fingers
掰开揉碎 bāikāi-róusuì *inf.* break apart and crumble to bits—(explain) in great detail; (ask) repeatedly: 我～地劝你，你只当耳旁风。 I tried again and again to persuade you, but you wouldn't listen.
掰腕子 bāi wànzi hand wrestling

bái

白[1] bái ① white: 几根～发 a few white (*or* grey) hairs / 皮肤～ have a fair complexion ② clear: 真相大白 zhēnxiàng dàbái ③ pure; plain; blank: ～纸 a blank sheet of paper ④ *adv.* in vain; to no purpose; for nothing: ～忙了半天 go to a lot of trouble for nothing / ～跑一趟 make a fruitless trip / 烈士们的鲜血没有～流。 The martyrs did not shed their blood in vain. / 我的活儿全～干了。 All my work was wasted. ⑤ *adv.* free of charge; gratis: ～看戏 go to a theatre free of charge / ～送 give away free (of charge) / ～给我也不要。 I wouldn't take it even as a gift. ⑥ White (as a

symbol of reaction): 白军 báijūn ⑦ look at sb. with the white of the eye—give sb. a supercilious look; coldly stare at sb.: 我～了他一眼。 I gave him a supercilious look. ⑧ (Bái) a surname

白² bái (of a Chinese character) wrongly written or mispronounced: 我把这字念～了。 I've mispronounced the character.

白³ bái ① state; explain: 自白 zìbái / 表白 biǎobái ② spoken part in opera, etc.: 独白 dúbái / 对白 duìbái ③ dialect: 苏～ Suzhou (in Jiangsu Province) dialect

白皑皑 bái'ái'ái (of snow, frost, etc.) pure white: ～的雪铺满田野。 The fields were all covered with pure white snow.

白矮星 bái'ǎixīng astron. white dwarf

白案 bái'àn white (kneading) board—cooking that deals with staple food, both rice and flour ——see also 红案 hóng'àn

白白 báibái adv. in vain; to no purpose; for nothing: 这个问题我们～地讨论了几次。 We have discussed the problem several times but to no purpose. / 不要让时光～过去。 Don't let time slip by. / 我有一小笔资金，～地搁在银行里。 I have a bit of capital in the bank doing nothing. / 眼看这些水～流掉，觉着挺可惜的。 It's a pity to see all that water running to waste.

白班儿 báibānr inf. day shift: 上～ be on day shift

白报纸 báibàozhǐ newsprint

白璧微瑕 báibì wēi xiá a slight flaw in white jade—a minor blemish in a thing of beauty; a slight defect in a person of integrity

白璧无瑕 báibì wú xiá flawless white jade—impeccable moral integrity

白醭 báibú mould (on the surface of vinegar, soy sauce, etc.)

白卜鲔 báibǔwěi zool. wavyback skipjack

白布 báibù plain white cloth; calico

白不呲咧 báibucīliē dial. colourless or tasteless: 这件衣服晒得～的了。 The colour of this coat has faded through too much exposure to the sun. / 菜里酱油放少了，～的。 This dish is tasteless because there is not enough sauce in it.

白菜 báicài Chinese cabbage

白痴 báichī ① idiocy ② idiot

白炽 báichì same as 白热 báirè

白炽电灯 báichì diàndēng incandescent lamp

白搭 báidā inf. no use; no good: 和他辩也是～。 It's no use arguing with him.

白大褂 báidàguà inf. doctor's coat; doctor's overall

白带 báidài med. leucorrhoea; whites

白蛋白 báidànbái biochem. albumin

白道 báidào astron. moon's path

白瞪 bái·dèng look at sb. with the white of the eye: ～某人一眼 give sb. a supercilious look

白癜风 báidiànfēng med. vitiligo

白丁 báidīng a person without academic titles or official ranks (in feudal times); commoner

白俄罗斯 Bái'éluósī Belarus

白垩 bái'è chalk (a type of limestone)

白垩纪 Bái'èjì geol. the Cretaceous Period

白发苍苍 báifà cāngcāng hoary; hoary-headed: ～的老人 a hoary-headed old man

白矾 báifán alum

白匪 báifěi White bandits

白费 báifèi waste: ～力气 waste one's energy / ～心思 bother one's head for nothing / 再等下去是～时间。 It's waste of time to wait any longer.

白费唇舌 báifèi chúnshé same as 徒费唇舌 túfèi chúnshé

白粉病 báifěnbìng agric. powdery mildew

白干儿 báigānr same as 白酒 báijiǔ

白宫 Bái Gōng the White House

白姑鱼 báigūyú white Chinese croaker

白骨 báigǔ white bones (of the dead); bleached bones: 君不见青海头, 古来～无人收。(杜甫) Have you not seen, beside Lake Koko Nor, Bleached bones unburied from ancient times?

白骨顶 báigǔdǐng zool. coot

白骨精 báigǔjīng the White Bone Demon (in the novel Pilgrimage to the West《西游记》)

白圭之玷 báiguī zhī diàn a flaw in a piece of jade—damages suffered through careless speech

白果 báiguǒ bot. ginkgo; gingko

白鹤 báihè zool. white crane

白喉 báihóu med. diphtheria

白狐 báihú arctic fox

白虎 báihǔ the White Tiger—① a collective name for the western group (Nos. 15-21) of the twenty-eight constellations (二十八宿) ② the guardian spirit of the west in Taoism

白花花 báihuāhuā shining white: ～的胡子 silky white beard / ～的银子 gleaming silver (coins) / ～的流水 foaming water

白花蛇 báihuāshé long-noded pit viper (Agkistrodon acutus)

白化病 báihuàbìng albinism: ～人 albino

白话¹ báihuà exaggerated statement or groundless talk: 空口说白话 kōngkǒu shuō báihuà

白话² báihuà vernacular

白话诗 báihuàshī free verse written in the vernacular

白话文 báihuàwén writings in the vernacular

白话文运动 báihuàwén yùndòng the Vernacular Movement (1917–1919)

白桦 báihuà bot. white birch

白晃晃 báihuǎnghuǎng shining and bright; gleaming; glaring

白灰 báihuī common name for 石灰 shíhuī

白芨 báijī Chin. med. the tuber of hyacinth bletilla (Bletilla striata)

白鳖豚 báijìtún same as 白鳍豚 báiqítún

白僵蚕 báijiāngcán Chin. med. the larva of a silkworm with batrytis

白金 báijīn ① platinum ② ancient name for silver

白金汉宫 Báijīnhàn Gōng Buckingham Palace

白净 báijìng (of skin) fair and clear: 这孩子长得白白净净的。 The child has a fair complexion.

白酒 báijiǔ spirit usu. distilled from sorghum or maize; white spirit

白驹过隙 báijū guò xì a glimpse of a white colt flashing past a chink in a wall (said of the fleeting of time): 人生一世间, 如～。(《史记》) Man's life in this world is as brief as a glimpse of a white colt flashing past a chink in a wall.

白卷 báijuàn a blank examination paper; an examination paper unanswered ——see also 交白卷 jiāo báijuàn

白军 báijūn the White army (the reactionary bourgeois troops, in China referring to the Kuomintang army during the Second Revolutionary Civil War, 1927-1937)

白开水 báikāishuǐ plain boiled water

白口 báikǒu spoken parts in traditional operas

白口铁 báikǒutiě white iron

白蜡 báilà white wax; insect wax

白蜡虫 báilàchóng wax insect

白镴 báilà solder

白兰地 báilándì brandy (a transliteration)

白痢 báilì ① Chin. med. dysentery characterized by white mucous stool ② husbandry white diarrhoea

白鲢 báilián silver carp

白脸 báiliǎn white face, face painting in Beijing opera,

etc., traditionally for the villain ——see also 唱白脸 chàng báiliǎn

白磷　báilín　*chem.*　white phosphorus

白蛉　báilíng　(also 白蛉子 báilíngzi)　sand fly

白蛉热　báilíngrè　*med.*　sand-fly fever

白令海　Báilìnghǎi　the Bering Sea

白榴石　báiliúshí　leucite (a mineral)

白鹭　báilù　egret

白露　Báilù　① White Dew—the 15th of the 24 solar terms ② the day marking the beginning of the 15th solar term (Sept. 7, 8, or 9) ——see also 节气 jiéqì; 二十四节气 èrshí sì jiéqì

白茫茫　báimángmáng　(of mist, snow, floodwater, etc.) a vast expanse of whiteness: 下了一场大雪, 田野上一一片。After the heavy snow, the fields were a vast expanse of whiteness.

白茅　báimáo　*bot.*　cogongrass (*Imperata cylindrica*)

白茅根　báimáogēn　*Chin. med.*　cogongrass rhizome

白煤　báiméi　① *dial.*　anthracite; hard coal ② white coal; waterpower

白蒙蒙　báiměngměng　(of smoke, fog, steam, etc.) hazy; misty: 山村笼罩在一片一的晨雾中。A haze of morning mist veiled the mountain village.

白米　báimǐ　(polished) rice: 一饭 (cooked) rice

白棉纸　báimiánzhǐ　stencil tissue paper

白面　báimiàn　wheat flour; flour

白面儿　báimiànr　heroin

白面书生　báimiàn shūshēng　pale-faced scholar; pasty-faced bookworm

白描　báimiáo　① line drawing in traditional ink and brush style ② simple, straightforward style of writing

白沫　báimò　frothy saliva; foam: 口吐一 foam at the mouth

白木耳　báimù'ěr　tremella

白内障　báinèizhàng　*med.*　cataract: 一摘除术 cataract extraction

白嫩　báinèn　(of skin) fair and clear; delicate

白砒　báipī　*chem.*　white arsenic; arsenic trioxide

白皮书　báipíshū　white paper; white book

白皮松　báipísōng　(also 白果松 báiguǒsōng)　lacebark pine

白旗　báiqí　white flag (a signal of surrender or truce): 挂一 fly the white flag

白鳍豚　báiqítún　white-flag dolphin

白铅　báiqiān　popular name for 锌 xīn

白镪　báiqiǎng　ancient silver currency

白切　báiqiē　white cut (a dish of slices of boiled meat or chicken served cold with a dip of soy sauce, sesame oil, and mashed garlic): 一鸡 white cut chicken / 一肉 white cut pork

白区　báiqū　White area (the Kuomintang-controlled area during the Second Revolutionary Civil War, 1927-1937)

白屈菜　báiqūcài　*bot.*　greater celandine

白饶　báiráo　① give sth. extra free of charge ② *dial.* no use; no good: 咱们干的全算一, 得打头儿重来。We did the work for nothing. We have to start all over again.

白热　báirè　white heat; incandescence

白热化　báirèhuà　turn white-hot: 争论达到了一的程度。The debate became white-hot.

白人　báirén　white man or woman

白刃　báirèn　naked sword

白刃战　báirènzhàn　bayonet charge; hand-to-hand combat

白日做梦　báirì zuòmèng　spin daydreams; indulge in wishful thinking; build castles in the air

白肉　báiròu　plain boiled pork

白润　báirùn　(of skin) fair; delicate

白色　báisè　① white (colour) ② White (as a symbol of reaction): 一据点 White stronghold; stronghold of reaction / 一政权 White regime

白色恐怖　báisè kǒngbù　White terror

白色人种　báisè rénzhǒng　the white race

白色体　báisètǐ　*bot.*　leucoplast

白芍　báisháo　*Chin. med.*　(peeled) root of herbaceous peony (*Paeonia lactiflora*)

白手起家　báishǒu qǐjiā　(also 白手成家 báishǒu chéngjiā)　build up from nothing; start from scratch: 他一开了这家饭馆。He started his restaurant from scratch.

白首　báishǒu　*formal*　hoary head; old age

白薯　báishǔ　sweet potato

白水泥　báishuǐní　*archit.*　white cement

白苏　báisū　*bot.*　common perilla (*Perilla frutescens*)

白汤　báitāng　clear soup (meat or vegetable soup without soy sauce)

白糖　báitáng　(refined) white sugar

白陶　báitáo　*archaeol.*　white pottery (of the Shang Dynasty, c. 16th-11th century B.C.)

白体　báitǐ　*print.*　lean type

白天　báitiān　daytime; day: 一我睡不着。I cannot sleep in the daytime. / 冬季一时间短。The day is shorter in winter. / 一比较暖和, 晚上可是很冷。The days are warmer, but the nights are very cold.

白条　báitiáo　(also 白条子 báitiáozi)　a promissory note with little binding force

白铁　báitiě　common name for 镀锌铁 dùxīntiě

白铁皮　báitiěpí　tinplate; galvanized iron sheet

白厅　Bái Tīng　Whitehall

白铜　báitóng　copper-nickel alloy; paktong

白头　báitóu　① hoary head; old age ② unsigned; anonymous

白头翁[1]　báitóuwēng　*zool.*　Chinese bulbul

白头翁[2]　báitóuwēng　*Chin. med.*　the root of Chinese pulsatilla

白头偕老　báitóu xiélǎo　live in conjugal bliss to a ripe old age; remain a devoted couple to the end of their lives; remain happily married to a ripe old age

白脱　báituō　butter (a transliteration)

白文　báiwén　① the text of an annotated book ② an unannotated edition of a book ③ intaglied characters (on a seal)

白钨矿　báiwūkuàng　scheelite

白皙　báixī　*formal*　(of skin) fair and clear: 皮肤一 have a fair complexion; be fair-complexioned

白细胞　báixìbāo　*physiol.*　white blood cell; leucocyte

白鲜　báixiān　*bot.*　shaggy-fruited dittany (*Dictamnus dasycarpus*)

白鲜皮　báixiānpí　*Chin. med.*　the root bark of shaggy-fruited dittany

白鹇　báixián　*zool.*　silver pheasant

白相　báixiàng　*dial.*　play; enjoy oneself

白相人　báixiàngrén　*dial.*　hoodlum; hooligan; gangster

白熊　báixióng　polar bear; white bear

白絮　báixù　① white cotton (fibre) ② *liter.*　cotton fluff—snowflake: 雪压冬云一飞, 万花纷谢一时稀。(毛泽东) Winter clouds snow-laden, cotton fluff flying, None or few the unfallen flowers.

白血病　báixuèbìng　leukaemia

白血球　báixuèqiú　*physiol.*　white blood cell; leucocyte

白鲟　báixún　Chinese paddlefish

白眼　báiyǎn　supercilious look: 一看人 treat people superciliously; look upon people with disdain / 遭人一 be treated with disdain

白眼珠　báiyǎnzhū　*inf.*　the white of the eye

白杨　báiyáng　*bot.*　white poplar

白药　báiyào　*Chin. med.*　baiyao, a white medicinal powder for treating haemorrhage, wounds, bruises, etc.

白夜　báiyè　*astron.*　white night

白衣战士　báiyī zhànshì　**warrior in white; medical worker**

白蚁　báiyǐ　termite; white ant

白翳　báiyì　*Chin. med.*　slight corneal opacity; nebula

白银　báiyín　silver

白鱼　báiyú　whitefish

白云苍狗　báiyún cānggǒu　white clouds change into grey dogs—the changes in human affairs often take freakish forms

白云母　báiyúnmǔ　muscovite; white mica (a mineral)

白云石　báiyúnshí　dolomite (a mineral)

白芷　báizhǐ　*Chin. med.*　the root of Dahurian angelica

白纸黑字　báizhǐ-hēizì　(written) in black and white: 这些条件～，一清二楚，想抵赖是抵赖不掉的。 These terms are clearly written in black and white. You can never deny them.

白种　báizhǒng　the white race

白昼　báizhòu　daytime; day

白术　báizhú　*Chin. med.*　the rhizome of large-headed atractylodes (*Atractylodes macrocephala*)

白浊　báizhuó　*Chin. med.*　gonorrhoea

白字　báizì　a character misused or mispronounced through confusion with one that sounds or looks like it: 写(读)～ write a wrong character (pronounce a character wrongly) in mistake for one that resembles it (e.g. write 定 for 淀, pronounce 淀 diàn the same as 定 dìng)

白字连篇　báizì liánpiān　reams of wrong characters; (of speech or writing) full of mispronounced or wrong words: 这篇文章～。 There're so many wrong characters in this piece.

白族　Báizú　the Bai (Pai) nationality, or the Bais, inhabiting Yunnan

bǎi

百　bǎi　① hundred ② numerous; all kinds of: ～花盛开 a hundred flowers in bloom / ～忙之中 in the midst of pressing affairs; despite many claims on one's time

百儿八十　bǎirbāshí　*inf.*　about a hundred; a hundred or so

百般　bǎibān　in a hundred and one ways; in every possible way; by every means: ～咒骂 abuse in every possible way; heap abuse on / ～抵赖 try by every means to deny / ～奉承 flatter sedulously / ～照顾 show sb. every consideration

百般刁难　bǎibān diāonàn　create obstructions of every description; put up innumerable obstacles; raise all manner of difficulties

百倍　bǎibèi　a hundredfold; a hundred times: 展望未来，信心～ look to the future with full confidence

百弊　bǎibì　① all kinds of maladies or evils ② many drawbacks or disadvantages

百病　bǎibìng　all kinds of diseases and ailments

百步穿杨　bǎi bù chuān yáng　shoot an arrow through a willow leaf at a hundred paces; split a willow wand at a hundred paces; shoot with great precision

百部　bǎibù　*Chin. med.*　the tuber of stemona (*Stemona japonica* or *Stemona sessilifolia*)

百尺竿头, 更进一步　bǎichǐ gāntóu, gèng jìn yī bù　make still further progress; further improve one's work

百出　bǎichū　*derog.*　numerous; full of; plenty of: 矛盾～ full of contradictions

百川归海　bǎi chuān guī hǎi　all rivers flow to the sea —all things tend in one direction; everyone turns to sb. for guidance

百读不厌　bǎi dú bù yàn　be worth reading a hundred times; can be read a hundred times with delight: 这本书～。 You never get tired of reading this book.

百端待举　bǎi duān dài jǔ　a hundred things remain to be done; numerous tasks have yet to be undertaken

百发百中　bǎifā bǎizhòng　a hundred shots, a hundred bull's-eyes; every shot hits the target; shoot with unfailing accuracy; be a crack shot: 他是我们班里的神枪手, 打靶时总是～。 He's the crack shot of our squad and never misses the bull's-eye in target practice.

百废俱兴　bǎi fèi jù xīng　(also 百废具兴 bǎi fèi jù xīng) all neglected tasks are being undertaken; all that was left undone is now being undertaken

百分比　bǎifēnbǐ　percentage: 失业～ unemployment percentage / 按～计算 in terms of percentage / 癌症病人的～在不断上升。 The percentage of cancer patients keeps rising. / 这一班女生所占的～比较高。 There's a higher percentage of girl students in this class.

百分点　bǎifēndiǎn　one percentage point: 增加一个～ an increase of one percentage point

百分号　bǎifēnhào　percentage symbol (％)

百分率　bǎifēnlǜ　percentage; per cent

百分数　bǎifēnshù　percentage (expressed with ％, e.g. 5％)

百分之百　bǎifēnzhībǎi　hundred-percent; out and out; absolutely: 有～的把握 be a hundred per cent sure; be absolutely certain / 这是～的谎话! That's an out-and-out lie!

百分制　bǎifēnzhì　hundred-mark system

百感交集　bǎi gǎn jiāojí　all sorts of feelings well up in one's heart

百合　bǎihé　*bot.*　lily

百花齐放　bǎihuā qífàng　let a hundred flowers bloom —free development of different forms and styles in the arts

百花齐放, 百家争鸣　bǎihuā qífàng, bǎijiā zhēngmíng　let a hundred flowers blossom and a hundred schools of thought contend (a policy set forth by Mao Zedong for promoting the progress of the arts and the sciences and the development of a flourishing socialist culture)

百花齐放, 推陈出新　bǎihuā qífàng, tuī chén chū xīn　let a hundred flowers blossom, weed through the old to bring forth the new (a policy set forth by Mao Zedong for transforming and developing theatrical art)

百花争艳　bǎihuā zhēngyàn　(also 百花争妍 bǎihuā zhēngyán) a hundred flowers contend in beauty; the flowers are a riot of colour

百喙莫辩　bǎi huì mò biàn　(also 百口莫辩 bǎi kǒu mò biàn) a hundred mouths can't explain it away; no one can argue it away

百货　bǎihuò　general merchandise: 日用～ articles of daily use

百货公司　bǎihuò gōngsī　department store

百货商店　bǎihuò shāngdiàn　general store; department store

百家争鸣　bǎijiā zhēngmíng　① contention of a hundred schools of thought (during the Spring and Autumn and the Warring States Periods, 770-221 B.C.) ② let a hundred schools of thought contend

百脚　bǎijiǎo　*dial.*　centipede

百洁布　bǎijiébù　scouring pad

百科全书　bǎikē quánshū　encyclopaedia

百孔千疮　bǎikǒng-qiānchuāng　riddled with gaping wounds; afflicted with all ills

百里挑一　bǎi lǐ tiāo yī　one in a hundred; cream of the crop: ～的美人 an exceptional beauty

百炼成钢　bǎi liàn chéng gāng　be tempered into steel: 在革命斗争中～ be tempered in revolutionary struggle

百灵　bǎilíng　lark

百米赛跑　bǎimǐ sàipǎo　100-metre dash

百慕大　Bǎimùdà　Bermuda

百慕大人　Bǎimùdàrén　Bermudan

百衲本　bǎinàběn　an edition or text (usu. of an ancient book) containing selections from various editions or texts: ～《二十四史》a *bainaben* edition of *The Twenty-Four Histories*

百衲衣　bǎinàyī　① another name for 袈裟 jiāshā ② a heavily patched garment

百乃定　*pharm*. panadin

百年　bǎinián　① a hundred years; a century: ～大业 a cause of vital and lasting importance ② lifetime: 祝你们～好合。Wishing you life-long happiness and perfect harmony.

百年不遇　bǎinián bù yù　not seen once in a hundred years: ～的大水灾 the biggest flood in a century

百年大计　bǎinián dàjì　a matter of fundamental importance for generations to come; a project of vital and lasting importance; a major project: 基本建设是～，要求质量第一。Capital construction projects, which are to last for generations, call above all for good quality.

百年纪念　bǎinián jìniàn　centenary; centennial

百年树人　bǎinián shù rén　see 十年树木，百年树人 shí-nián shù mù, bǎinián shù rén

百年之后　bǎinián zhīhòu　*euph.* when sb. has passed away; after sb.'s death

百鸟朝凤　bǎi niǎo cháo fèng　all birds paying homage to the phoenix—peace under a wise ruler

百日咳　bǎirìké　whooping cough; pertussis: ～疫苗 pertussis vaccine

百日维新　Bǎirì Wéixīn　old name for 戊戌变法 Wùxū Biànfǎ

百十　bǎishí　a hundred or so: ～户人家 about a hundred households

百事通　bǎishìtōng　① knowledgeable person ② know-all

百思不解　bǎi sī bù jiě　still puzzled after pondering a hundred times; remain perplexed despite much thought

百岁老人　bǎisuì lǎorén　centenarian

百听不厌　bǎi tīng bù yàn　worth hearing a hundred times: 这个故事～。You never get tired of hearing this story.

百万　bǎiwàn　million

百万吨级　bǎiwàndūnjí　megaton

百万富翁　bǎiwàn fūwēng　millionaire

百万雄师　bǎiwàn xióngshī　a million bold warriors; a mighty army: 钟山风雨起苍黄，～过大江。(毛泽东) Over Zhongshan swept a storm, headlong, Our mighty army, a million strong, has crossed the Great River.

百闻不如一见　bǎi wén bùrú yī jiàn　it is better to see once than to hear a hundred times; seeing for oneself is better than hearing from others

百问不厌，百拿不烦　bǎi wèn bù yàn, bǎi ná bù fán　(of a shop assistant) patiently answer the customers' questions and show them the goods they want; serve the customers patiently and tirelessly

百无禁忌　bǎi wú jìnjì　all taboos in abeyance (a magic formula credited with the power of neutralizing offences against taboos)

百无聊赖　bǎi wú liáolài　bored to death; bored stiff; overcome with boredom: ～时我就随手抓过一本书来，强迫自己看下去。In times of sheer boredom I would pick up a book and force myself to read.

百无一失　bǎi wú yī shī　no danger of anything going wrong; no risk at all; perfectly safe; surefire

百姓　bǎixìng　common people

百业凋敝　bǎiyè diāobì　all business declining

百叶窗　bǎiyèchuāng　shutter; blind; jalousie

百叶窗帘　bǎiyèchuānglián　Venetian blinds

百叶箱　bǎiyèxiāng　*meteorol.* thermometer screen

百依百顺　bǎiyī-bǎishùn　docile and obedient; all obedience: 这位当妈妈的宠爱儿子，对他可真是～。The mother doted on her son so much that she complied with all his whims.

百战百胜　bǎizhàn-bǎishèng　fight a hundred battles, win a hundred victories—emerge victorious in every battle; be ever-victorious

百折不挠　bǎi zhé bù náo　(also 百折不回 bǎi zhé bù huí) keep on fighting in spite of all setbacks; be undaunted by repeated setbacks; be dauntless; be indomitable; be unrelenting: ～的努力 unrelenting effort / 用～的毅力去克服所有的困难 overcome all difficulties with an indomitable will / 只要～地奋斗下去，最后的胜利必属于我们。As long as we keep on fighting in spite of all setbacks, the final victory will be ours.

百褶裙　bǎizhěqún　pleated skirt; accordion-pleated skirt

百足之虫，死而不僵　bǎi zú zhī chóng, sǐ ér bù jiāng　a centipede does not topple over even when dead; a centipede dies but never falls down; old institutions die hard

伯　bǎi　see 大伯子 dàbǎizi ——see also bó

佰　bǎi　hundred (used for the numeral 百 on cheques, etc. to avoid mistakes or alterations)

柏（栢）　bǎi　cypress ——see also bó; bò

柏树　bǎishù　cypress

柏油　bǎiyóu　common name for 沥青 lìqīng

柏子仁　bǎizǐrén　*Chin. med.* the seed of Oriental arborvitae

捭　bǎi　see 纵横捭阖 zònghéng-bǎihé

摆¹（擺）　bǎi　① put; place; arrange: 把药瓶～在架子上 put the medicine bottles on the shelf / 把碗筷～好 set (*or* lay) the table / 各种标本～了一桌子。The table was loaded with all kinds of specimens. / 西边一字儿～开十几条渔船。In the west lay a dozen fishing boats in a row. / ～在我们面前的任务 the task confronting us / 把问题～到桌面上来 place the problem on the table; bring the issue out into the open / ～正个人和集体的关系 put oneself in a correct relationship to the collective / 水库工地～战场。The reservoir construction site was like a battlefield, seething with activity. ② lay bare; state clearly: ～矛盾 lay bare the contradictions / 把有利和不利的条件～一～ set forth the advantages and disadvantages ③ put on; assume: ～威风 give oneself airs; put on airs / ～出一副吓人的架势 assume an intimidating posture / ～老资格 flaunt one's seniority; put on the airs of a veteran ④ sway; wave: 钟摆～来～去。The pendulum swung backwards and forwards. ⑤ *phys.* pendulum: 单摆 dānbǎi / 复摆 fùbǎi ⑥ *dial.* talk; say: 我们来～～，好吗? Let's talk it over, OK?

摆²（擺、襬）　bǎi　see 下摆 xiàbǎi

摆布　bǎibu　① decorate; arrange: 这间屋子～得十分雅致。The room is tastefully furnished. ② order about; manipulate: 任人～ allow oneself to be ordered about; be at the mercy of others

摆荡　bǎidàng　swing; sway

摆荡吊环　bǎidàng diàohuán　*sports* swinging rings

摆动　bǎidòng　swing; sway: 柳条迎风～。The willows swayed in the breeze. / 指示针来回～。The pointer flickered.

摆渡　bǎidù　① cross a river by boat; ferry ② ferryboat; ferry

摆饭　bǎifàn　lay out a meal; lay the table

摆放　bǎifàng　put; place; lay

摆供　bǎigòng　present offerings

摆晃　bǎihuàng　swing; sway: 这个醉汉一边走，一边～。The drunk man swayed as he walked along the road.

摆架子　bǎi jiàzi　put on airs; give oneself airs: 摆出一副大官的架子 affect the pose of a high official

摆酒　bǎijiǔ　spread a feast; give a feast: ～款待 entertain sb. to a dinner

摆款儿　bǎikuǎnr　put on airs; give oneself airs

摆阔　bǎikuò　parade one's wealth; be ostentatious and extravagant

摆列　bǎiliè　put; place; lay

摆龙门阵　bǎi lóngménzhèn　*dial.* chat; gossip; spin a yarn

摆轮　bǎilún　(also 摆盘 bǎipán) balance (of a watch or clock); balance wheel

摆门面　bǎi ménmiàn　put up a front; maintain an outward show; keep up appearances

摆弄　bǎinòng　① move back and forth; fiddle with: 你别来回～那几盆花了。Don't move those flower pots back and forth. ② order about; manipulate

摆平　bǎipíng　be fair to; be impartial to: ～关系 be impartial in dealings with people / 两边要～ must be fair to both parties

摆谱儿　bǎipǔr　*dial.* keep up appearances; be ostentatious

摆设　bǎishè　furnish and decorate (a room): 屋子里～得很整齐。The room is decorated neatly.

摆设儿　bǎisher　① ornaments; decorations: 客厅里的～朴素大方。The decorations in the drawing-room are simple but in good taste. ② objects or articles merely for show

摆事实，讲道理　bǎi shìshí, jiǎng dàoli　present the facts and reason things out

摆手　bǎishǒu　① shake one's hand in admonition or disapproval ② beckon; wave: 她向我摆了摆手，要我跟着她。She beckoned me to follow her. / 他～叫我走开。He waved me away.

摆摊子　bǎi tānzi　(also 摆摊儿 bǎitānr) ① set up a stall ② maintain a large staff or organization

摆脱　bǎituō　shake off; cast off; break away from; free (*or* extricate) oneself from: 飞行员驾着飞机扎进云层，打算～敌人的歼击机。The pilot dived into a bank of cloud in an attempt to shake off the enemy fighter. / ～殖民主义的桎梏 cast off the yoke of colonialism / ～贫穷落后的状态 be lifted out of poverty and backwardness / 有助于妇女～繁重的家务劳动 help to free women from household chores / ～困境 extricate oneself from a predicament

摆尾　bǎiwěi　wag the tail

摆样子　bǎi yàngzi　do sth. for show: 他的自我批评是认真的，不是～的。His self-criticism was serious and not made for show.

摆针　bǎizhēn　pointer (on a meter, scales, etc.)

摆钟　bǎizhōng　pendulum clock

摆轴　bǎizhóu　balance staff (of a balance wheel)

摆子　bǎizi　*dial.* malaria

bài

败　bài　① be defeated; lose: 垓下一战，项羽～于刘邦。Xiang Yu was defeated by Liu Bang in the battle of Gaixia. / 这次比赛他～了。He was beaten in the contest. / 主队以二比三～于客队。The home team lost to the visitors 2 to 3. ② defeat; beat: 击败 jíbài ③ fail: 成败 chéng-bài ④ spoil: 事情可能就～在他手里。He may spoil the whole show. ⑤ counteract: 败毒 bàidú ⑥ decay; wither: 枯枝～叶 dead twigs and withered leaves / 开不～的花朵 a flower that will not fade

败北　bàiběi　*formal* suffer defeat; lose a battle

败笔　bàibǐ　① a faulty stroke in calligraphy or painting ② a faulty expression or flaw in writing: 电影里这段三角恋爱故事是个～。The love triangle in this film is a flaw in an otherwise very good plot.

败兵　bàibīng　a defeated army; an army in flight; defeated troops

败草　bàicǎo　withered grass

败毒　bàidú　*Chin. med.* relieve internal heat or fever

败坏　bàihuài　ruin; corrupt; undermine: ～名誉 discredit; defame / 道德～ morally degenerate / ～风俗 corrupt morals; exert a bad moral influence / ～社会风气 corrupt social values

败火　bàihuǒ　*Chin. med.* relieve inflammation or internal heat

败绩　bàijī　*formal* be utterly defeated; be routed: 屡遭～ be badly defeated again and again; has sustained severe defeats time and again

败家　bàijiā　dissipate a family fortune

败家子　bàijiāzǐ　spendthrift; wastrel; prodigal

败局　bàijú　lost game; losing battle: ～已定。The game is as good as lost.

败军之将　bàijūn zhī jiàng　the general of a defeated army; a defeated general: ～不可以言勇。(《史记》) The general of a defeated army has no right to talk of bravery.

败类　bàilèi　scum of a community; degenerate: 民族～ scum of a nation

败柳残花　bàiliǔ-cánhuā　same as 残花败柳 cánhuā-bàiliǔ

败露　bàilù　(of a plot, etc.) fall through and stand exposed: 阴谋终于～。In the end the conspiracy was brought to light.

败落　bàiluò　decline (in wealth and position): 这部小说反映了一个封建家庭的～。This novel reflects the decline of a feudal family.

败衄　bàinù　*formal* be defeated; suffer a defeat

败色　bàishǎi　lose colour; fade

败诉　bàisù　lose a lawsuit

败退　bàituì　retreat in defeat

败亡　bàiwáng　be defeated and destroyed

败胃　bàiwèi　spoil one's appetite (by eating certain food or taking certain medicines)

败谢　bàixiè　wither and fall

败兴　bàixìng　have one's spirits dampened; feel disappointed

败兴而归　bàixìng ér guī　come back disappointed ——see also 乘兴而来 chéngxìng ér lái

败血症　bàixuèzhèng　*med.* septicaemia

败意　bàiyì　*formal* have one's spirits dampened; feel disappointed

败仗　bàizhàng　lost battle; defeat: 打～ be defeated in battle; suffer a defeat / 吃了个大～ have suffered a crushing defeat

败阵　bàizhèn　be defeated on the battlefield or be beaten in a contest: ～而逃 lose the field and take to flight / 败下阵来 lose a battle or be beaten in a contest

败子回头　bàizǐ huítóu　return of the prodigal son

败走　bàizǒu　flee after defeat

拜　bài　① do obeisance: 拜佛 bàifó ② pay a courtesy call: 回拜 huíbài ③ congratulate (on a certain occasion): 拜年 bàinián ④ visit; pay a visit: 新搬来的张同志刚才～街坊来了。The new neighbour, Comrade Zhang, came to visit us. ⑤ confer a title on

sb. ; appoint: ～相 confer the title of Prime Minister on sb. ; appoint sb. as Prime Minister ⑥ acknowledge sb. as one's master, godfather, etc.: 我～他为师学钢琴。 I became a piano student of his. ⑦ *pol.* (used before a verb): ～谢 express one's thanks

拜把子 bài bǎzi　become sworn brothers

拜别 bàibié　(also 拜辞 bàicí) *pol.*　take leave of

拜赐 bàicì　same as 拜领 bàilǐng

拜倒 bàidǎo　prostrate oneself; fall on one's knees; grovel: ～在某人脚下 grovel (*or* lie prostrate) at the feet of sb.

拜读 bàidú　*pol.*　read with respect; have the pleasure of reading an essay, etc. : ～ 大作 have the pleasure of perusing your work

拜访 bàifǎng　pay a visit; call on: 正式～ formal visit / 专程～ make a special trip to call on sb. / ～亲友 pay a visit to one's relatives and friends

拜佛 bàifó　prostrate oneself before the image of Buddha; worship Buddha

拜服 bàifú　*pol.*　admire greatly; worship

拜候 bàihòu　call to pay one's respects; call on

拜会 bàihuì　(usu. used on diplomatic occasions) pay an official call; call on: 告别～ farewell call / 礼节性～ courtesy call / 私人～ personal visit (*or* call)

拜火教 Bàihuǒjiào　Zoroastrianism; Mazdaism

拜见 bàijiàn　① pay a formal visit; call to pay respects ② meet one's senior or superior

拜金主义 bàijīnzhǔyì　money worship

拜客 bàikè　pay visits; make calls

拜聆 bàilíng　*pol.*　have the privilege of hearing (sb. speak): ～ 高论. I had the privilege of hearing your brilliant views.

拜领 bàilǐng　*pol.*　have the pleasure of receiving (a gift, etc.); accept with thanks

拜门 bàimén　① call on sb. and express one's thanks ② formally become a pupil to a master

拜年 bàinián　pay a New Year call; wish sb. a Happy New Year: 给军属～ pay New Year calls to servicemen's families / 大妈，我们给您～来啦! Auntie, we've come to wish you a Happy New Year. / 给您拜个早(晚)年. Let me wish you an early (belated, late) Happy New Year.

拜上 bàishàng　*pol.*　(used in ending a letter, after the name of the writer) with my respectful bows

拜师 bàishī　formally become a pupil to a master

拜识 bàishí　*pol.*　have the pleasure of making sb.'s acquaintance: ～ 尊颜. I had the pleasure of making your acquaintance.

拜寿 bàishòu　congratulate an elderly person on his birthday; offer birthday felicitations

拜堂 bàitáng　*old*　(of bride and groom) make ceremonial obeisances—perform the marriage ceremony

拜天地 bài tiāndì　same as 拜堂 bàitáng

拜托 bàituō　*pol.*　request sb. to do sth.: ～您捎个信给他。 Would you be kind enough to take a message to him?

拜望 bàiwàng　*pol.*　call to pay one's respects; call on

拜物教 bàiwùjiào　fetishism: 商品～ commodity fetishism

拜谒 bàiyè　*formal*　① pay a formal visit; call to pay respects ② pay homage (at a monument, mausoleum, etc.)

拜占庭帝国 Bàizhàntíng Dìguó　the Byzantine Empire (395–1453)

稗 bài　① barnyard grass ②*formal* insignificant; unofficial: 稗史 bàishǐ

稗贩 bàifàn　*formal*　①small retailer; pedlar ②*derog.* copy or apply indiscriminately

稗官野史 bàiguān-yěshǐ　books of anecdotes

稗记 bàijì　books of anecdotes

稗史 bàishǐ　① unofficial history ② books of anecdotes

稗子 bàizi　*bot.*　barnyard grass; barnyard millet

bān

扳 bān　pull; turn: ～倒 pull down / ～枪栓 pull back the bolt of a rifle / ～道岔 pull railway switches / ～着指头算 count on one's fingers / ～成平局 equalize the score

扳不倒儿 bānbudǎor　*inf.*　tumbler; roly-poly

扳道员 bāndàoyuán　pointsman; switchman

扳机 bānjī　trigger

扳手 bānshou　① spanner; wrench ② lever (on a machine)

扳指儿 bānzhir　thumb-ring (made of jade; originally an archery ring worn on the thumb of the right hand to prevent it from being cut by the taut bowstring)

扳子 bānzi　spanner; wrench

班 bān　① class; team: 甲～ class A / 作业～ work team / ～上有十五个学生. There're fifteen students in the class. ② shift; duty: 三～倒 work in three shifts / 今天晚上是我的～儿。 I'll be on duty tonight. ③*mil.* squad ④ *m.* ⓐ a group of people: 这～年轻人真了不起。 They're a fine bunch of young people. ⓑ a trip by bus, boat, etc.: 搭下一～火车 take the next train / 一路公共汽车每隔三分钟就有一～。 There's a Number One bus every three minutes. ⑤ regularly-run; regular; scheduled: 班机 bānjī ⑥ *old* used as part of the name of a theatrical troupe ⑦ move troops; withdraw troops: 班师 bānshī ⑧ (Bān) a surname

班巴拉语 Bānbālāyǔ　Bambara (language)

班禅喇嘛 Bānchán Lǎma　the Panchen Lama

班车 bānchē　regular bus (service)

班次 bāncì　① order of classes or grades at school: 在学校时，她～比我高。 At school she was in a higher class than me. ② number of runs or flights: 增加货车～ increase the number of runs of freight trains

班底 bāndǐ　① ordinary members of a theatrical troupe ② core members of an organization

班房 bānfáng　*inf.*　jail: 坐～ be (put) in jail

班机 bānjī　airliner; regular air service: 京沪～ scheduled flights between Beijing and Shanghai / 两国首都之间有～来往。 There's a regular air service between the two capitals.

班级 bānjí　classes and grades in school: 我们在中学是同一个～。 We used to be in the same class when at high school.

班轮 bānlún　regular passenger or cargo ship; regular steamship service

班门弄斧 Bān mén nòng fǔ　show off one's skill with the axe before Lu Ban (鲁班) the master carpenter—display one's slight skill before an expert: 在你面前～，太不好意思了. I'm making a fool of myself trying to show off before an expert like you.

班配 bānpèi　same as 般配 bānpèi

班期 bānqī　schedule (for flights, voyages, etc.): ～表 a table of scheduled flights, voyages, etc.; timetable

班师 bānshī　*formal*　withdraw troops from the front; return after victory

班头儿 bāntóur　group leader

班图人 Bāntúrén　Bantu

班图语 Bāntúyǔ　Bantu (language)

班务会 bānwùhuì　a routine meeting of a squad, team or class

班长　bānzhǎng　① class monitor ② *mil.* squad leader ③ (work) team leader

班指　bānzhi　same as 扳指儿 bānzhir

班主　bānzhǔ　*old* head of a theatrical troupe

班主任　bānzhǔrèn　a teacher in charge of a class (in a primary or middle school); form master

班子　bānzi　① *old* theatrical troupe ② organized group: 生产～ a team in charge of production /专业～ a special, full-time group

班组　bān-zǔ　teams and groups (in factories, etc.): ～竞赛 emulation between teams or groups; emulation at the team or group level

般　bān　*part.* same as; just like: 闪电～地 like lightning /暴风雨～的掌声 stormy (*or* thunderous) applause /兄弟～的情谊 fraternal feelings

般配　bānpèi　*dial.* well matched (in marriage, etc.); well suited: 这小两口儿倒挺～的。 This young couple is a very good match indeed. /这身儿打扮跟他的身份不大～。 The way he dresses is not quite suitable for his position.

颁　bān　promulgate; issue

颁布　bānbù　promulgate; issue; publish: ～法令 promulgate (*or* issue) a decree

颁发　bānfā　① issue; promulgate: ～嘉奖令 issue an order of commendation ② award: ～奖章 award a medal

颁示　bānshì　*formal* make known to the world; reveal to the public

颁行　bānxíng　issue for enforcement

斑　bān　① spot; speck; speckle; stripe: 油～ oil stains; grease spots ② spotted; striped: 斑马 bānmǎ

斑白　bānbái　grey; grizzled: 头发～ with grizzled hair; grey-haired

斑斑　bānbān　full of stains or spots: 血迹～ blood-stained

斑鬓　bānbìn　greying hair on the temples

斑驳　bānbó　*formal* mottled; motley

斑驳陆离　bānbó-lùlí　of many colours; many-hued

斑翅山鹑　bānchì shānchún　partridge

斑点　bāndiǎn　spot; stain; speckle

斑痕　bānhén　mark; trace

斑鸠　bānjiū　turtledove

斑斓　bānlán　*formal* gorgeous; bright-coloured; multi-coloured: 五彩～ a riot of colour /～的玛瑙 gorgeous agates

斑羚　bānlíng　goral

斑马　bānmǎ　zebra

斑马线　bānmǎxiàn　zebra crossing

斑蝥　bānmáo　*zool.* Chinese blister beetle; cantharides

斑铜矿　bāntóngkuàng　bornite

斑秃　bāntū　*med.* alopecia areata

斑纹　bānwén　stripe; streak: 斑马有黑白相间的～。 A zebra has black and white stripes.

斑岩　bānyán　*geol.* porphyry

斑疹　bānzhěn　*med.* macula

斑疹伤寒　bānzhěn shānghán　typhus

斑竹　bānzhú　mottled bamboo

搬(般)　bān　① take away; move; remove: 把桌子～走 take the table away /～山填沟 raze hills to fill gullies /～掉绊脚石 remove a stumbling block /把小说里的故事～到舞台上 adapt a story for performance on the stage; dramatize a novel ② move (house): 他早就～走了。 He moved out long ago. ③ apply indiscriminately; copy mechanically: 生搬硬套 shēngbān-

yìngtào

搬兵　bānbīng　(also 搬救兵 bān jiùbīng) call in reinforcement; ask for help

搬不倒儿　bānbùdǎor　same as 扳不倒儿 bānbudǎor

搬动　bāndòng　① move; remove; shift ② employ; draw on; dispatch

搬家　bānjiā　① move (house): 我们下星期～。 We're moving next week. ② remove; move: 把这个箱子搬搬家，别挡路。 Please move the box out of the way.

搬弄　bānnòng　① move sth. about; fiddle with: 别～枪栓。 Don't fiddle with the rifle bolt. ② show off; display: ～学问 parade one's erudition /他总好～自己的那点儿知识。 He is apt to show off what he knows. ③ instigate; sow discord

搬弄是非　bānnòng shìfēi　sow discord; tell tales; make mischief : ～的人 a talebearer

搬起石头打自己的脚　bānqǐ shítou dǎ zìjǐde jiǎo　pick up a stone only to drop it on one's own feet; lift a rock only to drop it on one's own toes

搬迁　bānqiān　move; transfer; remove: 这一家是新～来的。 The family has moved here recently. /我们的办事处从西区～到东区了。 Our office has moved from the west to the east district.

搬唆　bānsuō　incite; instigate

搬移　bānyí　move; remove; shift

搬用　bānyòng　apply mechanically; use indiscriminately

搬运　bānyùn　carry; transport: ～货物 transport goods

搬运工人　bānyùn gōngrén　porter (at a railway station); docker (at a seaport)

搬指　bānzhi　same as 扳指儿 bānzhir

瘢　bān　scar

瘢痕　bānhén　scar

癍　bān　abnormal pigmentary deposits on the skin; flecks

bǎn

坂(阪)　bǎn　*formal* slope

坂上走丸　bǎn shàng zǒu wán　balls rolling rapidly down a slope—a rapidly developing situation

板　bǎn　① board; plank; plate: 切菜～ chopping block /混凝土～ concrete slab ② shutter: 铺子都上了～儿了。 The shops have all put up the shutters. ③ *table tennis* bat ④ *mus.* clappers ⑤ an accented beat in traditional Chinese music; time; measure: 板眼 bǎnyǎn[①] ⑥ hard: 地～了，锄不动。The ground is too hard to hoe. ⑦ stiff; unnatural: 我这张照片照得太～了。 I look too stiff in this picture. ⑧ stop smiling; look serious: ～起面孔 put on a stern expression /～着脸 keep a straight face

板板六十四　bǎnbǎn liùshí sì　unaccommodating; inflexible

板报　bǎnbào　*inf.* short for 黑板报 hēibǎnbào

板壁　bǎnbì　wooden partition

板擦儿　bǎncār　blackboard eraser

板车　bǎnchē　a flatbed cart

板床　bǎnchuáng　plank bed

板锉　bǎncuò　flat file

板凳　bǎndèng　wooden bench or stool

板斧　bǎnfǔ　broad axe

板鼓　bǎngǔ　a small drum for marking time

板规　bǎnguī　*mech.* plate gauge

板胡　bǎnhú　a bowed stringed instrument with a thin wooden soundboard

板结 bǎnjié　harden: 〜的土壤 hardened and impervious soil

板块 bǎnkuài　*geol.*　plate

板块构造学 bǎnkuài gòuzàoxué　*geol.*　plate tectonics

板栗 bǎnlì　Chinese chestnut

板梁桥 bǎnliángqiáo　plate girder bridge

板皮 bǎnpí　*forestry*　slab

板球 bǎnqiú　① cricket ② cricket ball

板上钉钉 bǎn shàng dìng dīng　that clinches it; that's final; no two ways about it

板式 bǎnshì　modes in Chinese operatic music

板实 bǎnshi　① (of soil) firm and hard ② (of dress material, etc.) smooth and stiff

板书 bǎnshū　① write on the blackboard ② words written on the blackboard; blackboard writing: 这位老师的〜漂亮。 The teacher writes a beautiful hand on the blackboard.

板刷 bǎnshuā　scrubbing brush

板条 bǎntiáo　*archit.*　lath

板条箱 bǎntiáoxiāng　crate

板鸭 bǎnyā　pressed (*or* dried) salted duck

板牙 bǎnyá　① *dial.*　front tooth; incisor ② *dial.*　molar ③ *mech.*　screw die; threading die

板牙扳手 bǎnyá bānshou　stock and die

板烟 bǎnyān　plug (of tobacco)

板岩 bǎnyán　*geol.*　slate

板眼 bǎnyǎn　① *mus.*　accented and unaccented beats in traditional Chinese music; measure; time: 一板三眼 one accented beat and three unaccented beats in a bar, similar to 4/4 time ② orderliness; system; method: 她做事很有〜。 There is method in what she does. *or* She is very methodical in her work. / 他做事没〜。 He lacks method in his work. ③ *dial.*　idea; trick: 他〜多。 He's full of ideas (*or* tricks). ——see also 有板有眼 yǒubǎn-yǒuyǎn

板油 bǎnyóu　leaf fat; leaf lard

板羽球 bǎnyǔqiú　① battledore and shuttlecock ② shuttlecock

板纸 bǎnzhǐ　paperboard; board: 草〜 strawboard / 牛皮〜 kraft board

板滞 bǎnzhì　(of writing, drawing, manner, etc.) stiff; dull

板桩 bǎnzhuāng　*archit.*　sheet pile

板子 bǎnzi　① board; plank ② bamboo or birch for corporal punishment

版 bǎn　① printing plate (*or* block): 铜版 tóngbǎn ② edition: 新〜 new edition / 《现代汉语词典》(第二〜) *A Dictionary of Modern Chinese* (Second Edition) / 香港〜 Hong Kong edition ③ page (of a newspaper): 第四〜 Page 4 / 国内新闻〜 home news section

版本 bǎnběn　edition (as in different forms, bindings, etc. or by different publishers): 这本书有三个〜。 This book has three editions.

版次 bǎncì　the order in which editions are printed

版画 bǎnhuà　a picture printed from an engraved or etched plate; print

版刻 bǎnkè　carving; engraving

版面 bǎnmiàn　① space of a whole page ② layout (*or* makeup) of a printed sheet: 〜设计 layout

版权 bǎnquán　copyright: 此书〜归出版社所有。 The publisher has the copyright of the book. / 〜所有, 不准翻印。 All rights reserved.

版权页 bǎnquányè　copyright page; colophon

版式 bǎnshì　format

版税 bǎnshuì　royalty (on books)

版图 bǎntú　domain; territory: 〜辽阔 vast in territory

舨 bǎn　see 舢舨 shānbǎn

---

bàn

办(辦) bàn　① do; handle; manage; tackle; attend to: 我该怎么〜? What shall I do? / 你看着〜吧。 Do whatever you think is best. / 缺少经费, 这事没法〜。 It is impossible to do the job without the necessary funds. / 这点事她一个人〜得了。 She can handle (*or* tackle) this by herself. / 我有点事得〜一〜。 I have something to attend to. / 在中央的统一计划下, 让地方〜更多的事。 Let the localities undertake more work under unified central planning. ② set up; run: 〜工厂 run a factory / 〜教育 carry out education / 村里新〜了一所学校。 A new school has been set up in the village. ③ buy a fair amount of; get sth. ready: 〜年货 do New Year shopping; do shopping for the Spring Festival / 〜酒席 prepare a feast / 他们刚〜完喜事。 They've recently got married. ④ punish (by law); bring to justice: 〜了几个为首的 have punished the ringleaders

办案 bàn'àn　① handle a legal case ② apprehend (a criminal)

办报 bànbào　run a newspaper

办到 bàndào　get sth. done; accomplish: 原来认为办不到的事, 现在〜了。 What was thought impossible has now been done. / 时代不同了, 男女都一样。 男同志能〜的事情, 女同志也能办得到。 Times have changed, and today men and women are equal. Whatever men comrades can accomplish, women comrades can too.

办法 bànfǎ　way; means; measure: 找出克服困难的〜 find a way to overcome a difficulty / 用切实的〜来改进我们的工作 adopt effective measures to improve our work / 他这个人〜多。 He is resourceful. / 借钱不是个〜。 Borrowing money is no way out. / 我们总得想个〜把它完成。 We must get it finished by some means or other. / 你说的〜可以考虑。 What you propose is worth considering.

办公 bàngōng　handle official business; work (usu. in an office): 〜时间 office hours / 你在什么地方〜? Where do you work? *or* Where is your office?

办公费 bàngōngfèi　administrative expenses

办公室 bàngōngshì　office

办公厅 bàngōngtīng　general office

办公桌 bàngōngzhuō　desk; bureau

办货 bànhuò　make purchases for an organization or enterprise; purchase

办结 bànjié　handle and wind up a legal case

办理 bànlǐ　handle; conduct; transact: 〜进出口业务 handle imports and exports / 〜手续 go through the formalities (*or* procedure) / 这些事情你可以斟酌〜。 You may handle these matters as you see fit.

办事 bànshì　handle affairs; work: 〜公正 be fair and just in handling affairs / 〜认真 be conscientious in one's work / 按原则〜 act according to principles

办事处 bànshìchù　office; agency

办事机构 bànshì jīgòu　administrative body; working body

办事员 bànshìyuán　office worker

办事组 bànshìzǔ　administrative group

办学 bànxué　run a school: 〜方针 guiding principle for running a school

办置 bànzhì　buy (durables); purchase

办罪 bànzuì　punish sb. (for a crime)

半 bàn　① half; semi-: 〜小时 half an hour / 一个〜月 a month and a half; one and a half months / 〜年 six months; half a year / 〜机械化 semi-mechanized / 增

加一倍～ increase by 150% ② in the middle; halfway: ～山腰 halfway up a hill ③ very little; the least bit: 他连一句话都不说。He wouldn't breathe a word. ④ *adv.* partly; about half: ～开玩笑地说 say sth. half jokingly / 房门一～开着。The door was left half open.

半百 bànbǎi fifty (years of age): 年近～ getting on for fifty; approaching fifty

半…半… bàn…bàn… (used before two antonyms indicating the simultaneous existence of two states): 半文半白 half literary, half vernacular / 半饥半饱 underfed / 半心半意 half-hearted / 半嗔半喜 half-annoyed, half-pleased / 半吞半吐 hesitate in speech; hem and haw; mutter and mumble

半半拉拉 bànbanlālā *inf.* incomplete; unfinished: 这点活儿干完了，别剩下～的。Let's finish the job off. Don't leave a lot of loose ends hanging over. / 这篇稿子写得～的就丢下了。The manuscript was put aside unfinished.

半辈子 bànbèizi half a lifetime: 我活了～了，还不知道这个吗? How can a person of my age be ignorant of such a thing?

半壁江山 bànbì jiāngshān (also 半壁河山 bànbì héshān) half of the country (usu. referring to the unoccupied part of an invaded country)

半边 bànbiān half of sth.; one side of sth.: ～身子 left or right side of the body / 这个苹果～儿红，～儿绿。One half of the apple is red, the other half is green.

半边莲 bànbiānlián *Chin. med.* Chinese lobelia (*Lobelia chinensis*)

半边人 bànbiānrén *dial.* widow

半边天 bànbiāntiān ① half of the sky: 夕阳映红了～。The setting sun tinted half of the sky with a reddish hue. *or* Half the sky shone red in the glow of the sunset. ② women of the new society; womenfolk (from Mao Zedong's saying 妇女能顶～。Women can hold up half of the sky.)

半彪子 bànbiāozi *dial.* a brash (esp. middle-aged) man

半病子 bànbìngzi a person in poor health; semi-ablebodied or part-time worker

半…不… bàn…bù… (used in the same way as 半…半… bàn…bàn…): 半明不暗 not very bright; dimly lit

半场 bànchǎng *sports* ① half of a game or contest: 上～ the first half (of a game) ② half-court: (in basketball) ～紧逼 half-court press

半成品 bànchéngpǐn semi-manufactured goods; semi-finished articles; semi-finished products

半大 bàndà medium-sized; biggish: ～桌子 a table of medium size

半大小子 bàndà xiǎozi an adolescent boy; boy teenager; lad

半导体 bàndǎotǐ semiconductor: ～存储器 semiconductor store (*or* memory) / ～集成电路 semiconductor integrated circuit

半导体收音机 bàndǎotǐ shōuyīnjī transistor radio (*or* receiver)

半岛 bàndǎo peninsula

半道儿 bàndàor same as 半路 bànlù

半点 bàndiǎn the least bit: 没有～慌张 not the least bit flurried / 原则问题～也不能动摇。One should never waver on matters of principle. / 这是一个科学问题，来不得～虚伪。This is a matter of science, which permits no dishonesty.

半吊子 bàndiàozi ① dabbler; smatterer ② tactless and impulsive person

半封建 bànfēngjiàn semi-feudal

半复赛 bànfùsài *sports* eighth-finals

半工半读 bàngōng-bàndú part work, part study; work-study programme

半公开 bàngōngkāi semi-overt; more or less open

半官方 bànguānfāng semi-official: 据～人士称 according to semi-official sources

半规管 bànguīguǎn *physiol.* semicircular canal

半酣 bànhān half drunk

半价 bànjià half price: ～出售 sell at half price

半截 bànjié half (a section): ～香肠 half of a sausage / 话只说了～儿 finish only half of what one has to say / 把这两～儿粘上 stick the two halves together / ～子革命 one who gives up the cause of revolution halfway / 他走到～儿就回来了。He walked halfway there and then came back.

半截入土 bànjié rùtǔ with one foot in the grave

半斤八两 bànjīn-bāliǎng six of one and half a dozen of the other; not much to choose between the two; two of a kind: 他们俩的技术～, 差不多。So far as their skills are concerned, it's six of one and half a dozen of the other. / 这两人半斤对八两，都不是好东西。The two of them are equally bad.

半径 bànjìng radius: 爆炸声在～十公里范围内都能听到。The explosion could be heard within a radius of ten kilometres.

半决赛 bànjuésài *sports* semifinals

半开门儿 bànkāiménr half-open door—unlicensed (*or* unregistered) prostitute

半空中 bànkōngzhōng *inf.* in midair; in the air: 悬在～ hang in midair

半拉 bànlǎ *inf.* half: ～苹果 half an apple

半拉子 bànlǎzi *dial.* ① half ② *old* child farm labourer

半劳动力 bànláodònglì (also 半劳力 bànláolì) one able to do light manual labour only; semi-ablebodied or part-time (farm) worker

半老徐娘 bàn lǎo Xúniáng an attractive middle-aged woman—see also 徐娘半老, 风韵犹存 Xúniáng bàn lǎo, fēngyùn yóu cún

半流体 bànliútǐ semifluid

半路 bànlù halfway; midway; on the way: 走到～, 天就黑了。We had got only halfway when it began to get dark. / ～上遇到熟人 run into a friend on the way

半路出家 bànlù chūjiā become a monk or nun late in life—switch to a job one was not trained for

半面之交 bànmiàn zhī jiāo sb. only seen or met once before

半票 bànpiào half-price ticket; half fare

半瓶醋 bànpíngcù *inf.* half a bottle of vinegar—dabbler; smatterer: 他的法文是半瓶子醋。He has a smattering of French.

半旗 bànqí half-mast: 下半旗 xià bànqí

半球 bànqiú hemisphere: 东～ the Eastern Hemisphere / 北～ the Northern Hemisphere

半人半鬼 bànrén-bànguǐ half man, half ghost—an inhuman person or one living in conditions that are inhuman

半人马座 Bànrénmǎzuò *astron.* Centaurus

半日制学校 bànrìzhì xuéxiào half-day (*or* double-shift) school

半晌 bànshǎng *dial.* ① half of the day: 前半晌 qiánbànshǎng ② a long time; quite a while: 他想了～才想起来。It took him a long time to recall it. / 他去了～, 不见回。He's been away quite a while, and hasn't returned yet.

半晌午 bànshǎngwu *inf.* a little before noon; about noon

半身不遂 bànshēn bùsuí *med.* hemiplegia

半身像 bànshēnxiàng ① half-length photo or portrait ② bust

半生 bànshēng half a lifetime: ～戎马 led a soldier's life for many years

半生不熟　bànshēng-bùshú　half cooked; underdone

半失业　bànshīyè　semi-employed; partly employed; underemployed

半世　bànshì　half a lifetime

半熟练　bànshúliàn　semi-skilled

半数　bànshù　half the number; half: ～以上 more than half; majority

半衰期　bànshuāiqī　phys.　half-life

半死　bànsǐ　half-dead: 被打个～ be beaten within an inch of one's life / 气得～ be half-dead from anger; nearly faint with rage / 庄稼旱得～。 The drought nearly ruined the crops.

半死不活　bànsǐ-bùhuó　half-dead; more dead than alive

半天　bàntiān　① half of the day: 前～ morning / 后～ afternoon ② a long time; quite a while: 他～说不出话来。 He remained tongue-tied for a long time.

半头　bàntóu　① half a head: 高(矮)～ half a head taller (shorter) ② half a piece

半透明　bàntòumíng　translucent; semitransparent

半透明体　bàntòumíngtǐ　phys.　translucent body

半透明纸　bàntòumíngzhǐ　onionskin

半途　bàntú　formal　halfway; midway: ～拆伙 part company halfway

半途而废　bàntú ér fèi　give up halfway; leave sth. unfinished: 改革必须坚持到底, 不能～。 Reforms must be carried through to the end and not abandoned halfway.

半推半就　bàntuī-bànjiù　yield with a show of reluctance; give way after making a show of declining: 说了几句客气话, 他也就～地把礼物收下了。 He accepted the gift after making a polite show of declining.

半脱产　bàntuōchǎn　partly released from productive labour; partly released from one's regular work

半文盲　bànwénmáng　semiliterate

半无产阶级　bànwúchǎnjiējí　semi-proletariat

半夏　bànxià　Chin. med.　the tuber of pinellia (Pinellia ternata)

半硝革　bànxiāogé　crust leather

半新不旧　bànxīn-bùjiù　no longer new; showing signs of wear: 他穿着一身～的衣服。 His suit, though not shabby, was far from new.

半信半疑　bànxìn-bànyí　half-believing, half-doubting; not quite convinced: 他抱着～的态度去试一试。 Not quite convinced, he went to try it himself. / 她～地摇摇头。 Still a little sceptical, she shook her head.

半歇　bànxiē　dial.　a long time; quite a while

半星儿　bànxīngr　a tiny bit; a very small amount: 他这话并没有～埋怨的意思。 There wasn't the slightest suggestion of complaint in his words.

半休　bànxiū　half-day rest: 大夫建议～两周。 The doctor prescribed a fortnight's half-day rest.

半掩门儿　bànyǎnménr　half-closed door—unlicensed (or unregistered) prostitute

半腰　bànyāo　middle; halfway: 山～ halfway up a hill

半夜　bànyè　midnight; in the middle of the night: 会议一直开到～。 The meeting went on far into the night.

半夜三更　bànyè-sāngēng　in the depth of night; late at night: ～的, 你起来干什么? Why are you getting up at this time of night?

半音　bànyīn　mus.　semitone

半音音阶　bànyīn yīnjiē　mus.　chromatic scale

半影　bànyǐng　phys.　penumbra: ～锥 penumbra cone

半语子　bànyǔzi　a person with faulty pronunciation and articulation due to defective vocal chord

半元音　bànyuányīn　phonet.　semivowel

半圆　bànyuán　semicircle

半月瓣　bànyuèbàn　physiol.　semilunar valve

半月刊　bànyuèkān　semimonthly (a periodical); fortnightly

半载　bànzài　transportation　half load

半真半假　bànzhēn-bànjiǎ　① half-genuine, half-sham; partly true, partly false ② half in jest, half in earnest

半支莲　bànzhīlián　bot.　sun plant

半殖民地　bànzhímíndì　semi-colony: ～半封建社会 semi-colonial, semi-feudal society

半制浆　bànzhìjiāng　paper making　half stuff; semi-pulp

半制品　bànzhìpǐn　same as 半成品 bànchéngpǐn

半中间　bànzhōngjiān　middle; halfway: 他一气儿游到河的～。 He swam halfway across the river at a stretch. / 这事～出了岔儿。 Something went wrong when the work was in progress.

半中腰　bànzhōngyāo　inf.　middle; halfway: 山的～有一座亭子。 A pavilion is halfway up the hill. / 他的话说到～就停住了。 He broke off in the middle of a sentence.

半子　bànzǐ　half son—son-in-law

半自动　bànzìdòng　semi-automatic

半自动步枪　bànzìdòng bùqiāng　semi-automatic rifle

半自耕农　bànzìgēngnóng　semi-tenant peasant; semi-owner peasant

扮

扮　bàn　① be dressed up as; play the part of; disguise oneself as: 他在戏里～一位老贫农。 In the opera he plays the part of an old poor peasant. / 侦察员～作一个商人。 The scout disguised himself as a merchant. ② put on (an expression): ～鬼脸 make grimaces; make faces

扮戏　bànxì　① (of a traditional opera singer) put on makeup; make up ② old　put on a play; act in a play

扮相　bànxiàng　the appearance of an actor or actress in costume and makeup: ～好 cut a good figure when in costume and makeup

扮演　bànyǎn　play the part of; act: 她在《白毛女》里～喜儿。 She played the part of (or acted) Xi'er in The White-Haired Girl.

扮装　bànzhuāng　(of an actor, etc.) put on makeup; make up

伴

伴　bàn　① companion; partner: 我得找个～儿一块儿去。 I have to find someone to go with me. / 跟我一起旅游的都是挺不错的～儿。 My fellow tourists were all good companions. ② accompany: 行政命令必须～之以说服教育。 Administrative regulations must be accompanied by persuasion and education.

伴唱　bànchàng　① vocal accompaniment ② accompany (a singer)

伴君如伴虎　bàn jūn rú bàn hǔ　being close to the emperor is like being close to a tiger

伴郎　bànláng　groomsman; best man

伴侣　bànlǚ　companion; mate; partner

伴娘　bànniáng　bridesmaid

伴陪　bànpéi　accompany; keep sb. company

伴生气　bànshēngqì　petroleum　associated gas

伴送　bànsòng　see sb. off; accompany: 他～我到火车站。 He saw me off at the railway station.

伴随　bànsuí　accompany; follow: 肖邦的夜曲～我度过了这个晚上。 Chopin's nocturnes accompanied me throughout the night. / ～着生产的大发展, 必将出现一个文化高潮。 An upsurge in culture is bound to follow the rapid advance in production.

伴舞　bànwǔ　① accompanying dancer ② (hired) dancing girl; escort

伴星　bànxīng　astron.　companion (star)

伴奏　bànzòu　accompany (with musical instruments): 钢琴～ piano accompaniment / 手风琴～: 张小芳 Accompanied on the accordion by Zhang Xiaofang / ～者 accompanist

拌 bàn mix: 〜匀 mix thoroughly / 〜饲料 mix fodder / 〜鸡丝 shredded chicken salad / 〜黄瓜 cucumber salad / 香椿〜豆腐 bean curd and toon buds salad / 〜海蜇皮 jellyfish salad

拌和 bàn·huò mix and stir; blend

拌面 bànmiàn noodles served with soy sauce, sesame butter, etc.

拌种 bànzhǒng *agric.* seed dressing

拌种机 bànzhǒngjī seed dresser

拌嘴 bànzuǐ bicker; squabble; quarrel: 我一时忍不住，和她拌了几句嘴。 I couldn't control myself and exchanged a few hot words with her.

绊 bàn (cause to) stumble; trip: 他被树根〜了一下。 He stumbled over the root of a tree. / 差点儿〜了我一交。 I tripped and almost fell. / 别让日常事务把你〜住了。 Don't get yourself bogged down in routine work. / 〜手〜脚 be in the way

绊绊磕磕 bànbankēkē same as 磕磕绊绊 kēkebànbàn

绊脚石 bànjiǎoshí stumbling block; obstacle: 害怕批评是进步的〜。 Your fear of criticism is an obstacle to your ideological progress.

瓣 bàn ① petal: 这朵花儿掉了一个〜儿。 This flower has lost one petal. ② segment or section (of a tangerine, etc.); clove (of garlic) ③ valve; lamella: 三尖瓣 sānjiānbàn / 鳃瓣 sāibàn ④ fragment; piece: 摔成几〜 be broken into several pieces ⑤ *m.*: 一〜儿蒜 a clove of garlic

瓣膜 bànmó *physiol.* valve

bāng

邦(邦) bāng nation; state; country: 邻邦 línbāng

邦国 bāngguó *formal* nation; state; country

邦家 bāngjiā *formal* nation; state; country

邦交 bāngjiāo relations between two countries; diplomatic relations: 建立(断绝, 恢复)〜 establish (sever, resume) diplomatic relations

邦联 bānglián confederation

邦人 bāngrén *formal* fellow countryman; compatriot

帮¹(幫) bāng ① help; assist; aid: 你〜我翻译一下这首诗好吗？ Will you please help me to translate this poem? / 我〜他搬了行李。 I helped him with his luggage. / 她今天要〜大夫做手术。 She's going to assist the doctor in an operation today. / 你能〜我们弄两张票吗？ Could you get two tickets for us? / 〜人要〜到底。 When you help someone, you should make a thorough job of it. ② be hired: 〜短工 serve as a seasonal labourer

帮²(幫) bāng ① side (of a boat, truck, etc.) or upper (of a shoe): 船帮 chuánbāng① / 鞋帮 xiébāng ② outer leaf (of cabbage, etc.): 菜帮儿 càibāngr

帮³(幫) bāng ① gang; band; clique: 匪帮 fěibāng ② *m.* group: 来了一〜孩子。 Here comes a group of children. ③ secret society; underworld gang: 青帮 Qīngbāng

帮办 bāngbàn ① *old* assist in managing: 〜军务 assist in handling military affairs ② deputy: 副国务卿〜 Deputy Under Secretary (of the U. S. Department of State) / 助理国务卿〜 Deputy Assistant Secretary (of the U. S. Department of State)

帮厨 bāngchú help in the mess kitchen

帮凑 bāngcòu pool or contribute money, etc. to help sb. out: 我需要钱花，父亲〜了我。 My father helped me out with money when I needed it.

帮倒忙 bāng dàománg be more of a hindrance than a help; do sb. a disservice: 她替儿子做作业，反而帮了倒忙。 She did her son a disservice by doing his homework for him.

帮扶 bāngfú help; assist; aid

帮工 bānggōng ① help with farm work ② casual labourer (in pre-liberation countryside); seasonal labourer; helper

帮会 bānghuì secret society; underworld gang

帮伙 bānghuǒ *derog.* gang; band; clique

帮忙 bāngmáng help; give (*or* lend) a hand; do a favour; do a good turn: 我要请她〜。 I'll ask her to help. / 他来找人〜。 He came for help. / 他帮了大忙。 He's been a great help. *or* He's given a lot of help. / 请你帮个忙。 Will you give me a hand? / 他帮不上我什么忙。 There's hardly anything he can help me with. / 他帮过我们的忙。 He once did us a good turn. / 〜把这封信寄一下好吗？ Will you do me a favour and mail this letter? / 我能帮什么忙吗？ Can I be of any assistance?

帮派 bāngpài faction: 〜体系 factionalist setup

帮腔 bāngqiāng ① *mus.* vocal accompaniment in some traditional Chinese operas ② speak in support of sb.; echo sb.; chime in with sb.: 他看见没有人〜，也就不再坚持了。 When he saw nobody supporting him, he no longer insisted.

帮手 bāngshou helper; assistant

帮闲 bāngxián ① hang on to and serve the rich and powerful by literary hack work, etc. ② literary hack

帮闲文人 bāngxián wénrén literary hack

帮凶 bāngxiōng accomplice; accessary

帮佣 bāngyōng ① work or be hired as a labourer, servant, etc. ② hired labourer; servant

帮助 bāngzhù help; assist; aid: 〜消化 aid digestion / 他〜我学外文。 He helped me learn a foreign language. / 希望你从思想上多给我〜。 I hope you will give me as much help as you can to improve myself. / 我们需要〜。 We need help. / 这本手册没有多大〜。 This handbook isn't of much help. / 我每个月〜他十块钱。 I help him out with 10 *yuan* each month. / 谢谢你的〜。 Thank you for your help (*or* assistance).

帮助犯 bāngzhùfàn *leg.* abettor

帮子¹ bāngzi ① outer leaf (of cabbage, etc.) ② upper (of a shoe)

帮子² bāngzi same as 帮³ bāng②

浜 bāng *dial.* (usu. used as part of a place name) creek; streamlet: 张华〜 Zhanghuabang (in Shanghai)

梆 bāng ① watchman's clapper ② *onom.* rat-tat; rat-a-tat: 〜〜〜的敲门声 a rat-a-tat at the door

梆子 bāngzi ① watchman's clapper ② *mus.* wooden clappers with bars of unequal length ③ same as 梆子腔 bāngziqiāng

梆子腔 bāngziqiāng ① clapper opera (a general term for local operas in Shanxi, Shaanxi, Henan, Hebei, etc.) performed to the accompaniment of *bangzi* or clappers ② the music of such operas

bǎng

绑 bǎng ① bind; tie: 〜个三脚架 tie three sticks

together to make a tripod ②bind sb.'s hands behind him; truss up

绑带 bǎngdài ① bandage ② puttee

绑匪 bǎngfěi　kidnapper

绑架 bǎngjià ① kidnap ② *agric.* staking: 下午咱们给黄瓜～。We're going to stake the cucumbers this afternoon.

绑票 bǎngpiào　kidnap (for ransom)

绑腿 bǎngtuǐ　leg wrappings; puttee

绑扎 bǎngzā ① wrap up; bind up: ～伤口 bind up (or dress) a wound ② tie up; bundle up; pack: ～行李 tie up baggage

榜

榜 bǎng ① a list of names posted up: 发榜 fābǎng ② same as 榜文 bǎngwén

榜首 bǎngshǒu　the first place on a list of successful candidates; the first place in a contest, etc.: 位居～ rank first; come first

榜文 bǎngwén　*arch.* proclamation; notice

榜眼 bǎngyǎn　title conferred on the one who won second place in the highest imperial examination in the Ming and Qing Dynasties

榜样 bǎngyàng　example; model: 以大庆为～ take Daqing as the model / ～的力量是无穷的。A fine example has boundless power.

膀

膀 bǎng ① upper arm; arm ② shoulder: 肩膀 jiānbǎng ③ wing (of a bird): 翅膀 chìbǎng ——see also pāng; páng

膀臂 bǎngbì ① *dial.* upper arm; arm ② capable assistant; reliable helper; right-hand man

膀阔腰圆 bǎngkuò-yāoyuán (also 膀大腰圆 bǎngdà-yāoyuán) broad-shouldered and solidly-built; hefty; husky

膀子 bǎngzi ① upper arm; arm: 光着～ be stripped to the waist ② wing (of a bird): 鸭～ duck wings

bàng

蚌

蚌 bàng　freshwater mussel; clam ——see also bèng

谤

谤 bàng　*formal* slander; defame; vilify: 诽谤 fěibàng

谤议 bàngyì　*formal* slander; calumny; libel

傍

傍 bàng ① be close to (in distance); draw near: 船～了岸。The boat drew alongside the bank. ② close to (in time): 傍晚 bàngwǎn

傍近 bàngjìn　be close to; near: ～身边 by one's side / ～晌午 about noon

傍明 bàngmíng　*dial.* dawn; daybreak

傍人门户 bàng rén ménhù　live under another's roof; depend on sb. for a living

傍晚 bàngwǎn　toward evening; at nightfall; at dusk

傍午 bàngwǔ　about noon

棒

棒 bàng ① stick; club; cudgel: 木～ wooden stick / 垒球～ softball bat ②*inf.* good; fine; excellent; strong: 字写得～ write a good hand / 庄稼长得真～。The crops are excellent. / ～小伙子 a strong young fellow / 你干得～极了。You've done a first-rate job.

棒冰 bàngbīng　*dial.* ice-lolly; popsicle; ice-sucker; frozen sucker

棒槌 bàngchuí　wooden club (used to beat clothes in washing)

棒硫 bàngliú　*chem.* roll sulphur

棒磨机 bàngmójī　*min.* rod mill

棒球 bàngqiú　baseball: ～场 baseball field

棒糖 bàngtáng　lollipop; sucker

棒子 bàngzi ① stick; club; cudgel ② *dial.* maize; corn ③ *dial.* ear of maize (or corn); corncob

棒子面 bàngzimiàn　cornmeal; corn flour: ～粥 cornmeal porridge (or mush)

蒡

蒡 bàng　see 牛蒡 niúbàng

磅¹

磅 bàng ① pound (a measure of weight) ② scales: 把行李搁在～上看有多重。Put the luggage on the scales and see how much it weighs. ③ weigh: ～体重 weigh oneself or sb. on the scales

磅²

磅 bàng　*print.* point (type): 六～字太小了。6-point type is too small. ——see also páng

磅秤 bàngchèng　platform scale; platform balance

镑

镑 bàng　pound (a currency): 英镑 yīngbàng

bāo

包

包 bāo ① wrap: 把东西～起来 wrap things up / 头上～着一条白毛巾 with a white towel wrapped round one's head / ～书 wrap up a book in a piece of paper; put a jacket (or cover) on a book / ～饺子 make *jiaozi* (dumplings) ② bundle; package; pack; packet; parcel: 邮包 yóubāo ③ bag; sack: 书包 shūbāo ④ *m.* package; bundle: 一大～衣服 a big bundle of clothes / 一～香烟 a packet (or pack) of cigarettes / 两～大米 two sacks of rice / 一～棉纱 a bale of cotton yarn ⑤ protuberance; swelling; lump: 脑门上碰了个～ have (or get) a bump on one's forehead / 腿上起了个～ have a swelling in the leg ⑥ yurt: 蒙古包 měnggǔbāo ⑦ surround; encircle; envelop: 浓雾～住了群山。The hills were enveloped in dense fog. ⑧ include; contain: 包含 bāohán ⑨ undertake the whole thing: 这事～在我身上。Just leave it all to me. ⑩ assure; guarantee: ～你满意。You'll like it, I assure you. *or* Satisfaction guaranteed. ⑪ hire; charter: ～一只船 hire (or charter) a boat / ～三桌酒席 reserve three banquet tables ⑫ (Bāo) a surname

包办 bāobàn ① take care of everything concerning a job: 这件事你一个人～了吧。You'd better do the whole job yourself. ② run the whole show; monopolize everything

包办代替 bāobàn-dàitì　take away sb. else's work; run things all by oneself without consulting others: 要指导和帮助子女而不要～。Guide and help your children rather than do their work for them.

包办婚姻 bāobàn hūnyīn　an arranged marriage

包背装 bāobèizhuāng　*print.* wrapped-ridge binding

包庇 bāobì　shield; harbour; cover up: 互相～ shield each other / ～坏人坏事 harbour evildoers and cover up their evil deeds

包藏 bāocáng　contain; harbour; conceal: 大海～着许多秘密。The sea contains many mysteries.

包藏祸心 bāocáng huòxīn　harbour evil intentions

包产 bāochǎn　make a production contract; take full responsibility for output quotas: ～合同 contract for fixed output / ～指标 targets stated in a contract for fixed output

包产到户 bāochǎn dào hù　fixing of farm output quotas for each household ——see also 三自一包 sānzì yībāo

包场 bāochǎng　book a whole theatre or cinema; make

a block booking

包抄 bāochāo outflank; envelop: 从两翼～逃敌 outflank the fleeing enemy on both wings / 骑兵分三路～过去。The cavalry closed in on the enemy in a three-pronged attack.

包车 bāochē ① charter a bus, etc. ② *old* a private vehicle (esp. a rickshaw) ③ *old* a vehicle (esp. a rickshaw) hired for one's exclusive use

包乘 bāochéng ① charter (a plane, etc.) ② *transportation* adopt responsible crew system

包乘制 bāochéngzhì *transportation* responsible crew system

包乘组 bāochéngzǔ *transportation* (responsible) crew

包虫病 bāochóngbìng echinococcosis; hydatid disease

包打天下 bāo dǎ tiānxià undertake to conquer the country all by oneself—take away sb. else's work; run things all by oneself without consulting others

包打听 bāodǎtīng *dial.* ① detective ② nosy parker; snooper

包饭 bāofàn ① get or supply meals at a fixed rate; board: 在附近的饭馆里～ board at a nearby restaurant ② meals thus arranged

包袱 bāofu ① cloth-wrapper ② a bundle wrapped in cloth ③ millstone round one's neck; load; weight; burden: 思想～ a load (*or* weight) on one's mind / 不要把成绩当～ not allow one's merits to become a hindrance to one's progress

包袱底儿 bāofudǐr *dial.* ① family property, esp. valuables, accumulated over a long time; resources ② one's secrets; private matters one wants to hide ③ unique skill; consummate skill: 抖搂～ make an exhibition of one's skills; show off

包袱皮儿 bāofupír cloth-wrapper

包干儿 bāogānr be responsible for a task until it is completed: 分片～ divide up the work and assign a part to each individual or group / 剩下的活儿由我们小组～。You can trust our team to finish up the rest of the job.

包干制 bāogānzhì a system of payment partly in kind and partly in cash ——see also 供给制 gōngjǐzhì

包工 bāogōng ①(also 包活 bāohuó) undertake to perform work within a time limit and according to specifications; contract for a job ② contractor

包工头 bāogōngtóu labour contractor

包谷 bāogǔ *dial.* maize; corn

包管 bāoguǎn assure; guarantee: 这件活三天完成,～没问题。We'll finish this job in three days without fail. / ～退换。Merchandise will be exchanged if found unsatisfactory. / 吃这个方子,～你三天痊愈。If you take this prescription, you are sure to fully recover within three days.

包裹 bāoguǒ ① wrap up; bind up: 用布把伤口～起来。Bandage up the wound. ② bundle; package; parcel: 今天上午我收到一个邮寄来的～。I got a parcel in the post this morning.

包裹单 bāoguǒdān parcel form

包含 bāohán contain; embody; include: 没有什么事物是不～矛盾的。There is nothing that does not contain contradiction. / 他的建议～不少合理的因素。His proposal contains much that is reasonable. / 群众的意见常常～着许多深刻的道理。The opinions of the masses often embody profound truths. / 这句话～好几层意思。This statement has quite a few implications.

包涵 bāohán *pol.* excuse; forgive; bear with: 我唱得不好,请多多～。Excuse (me for) my poor singing.

包伙 bāohuǒ same as 包饭 bāofàn

包机 bāojī ① charter a plane ② a chartered plane

包剿 bāojiǎo encircle and suppress

包金 bāojīn ① cover with gold leaf; gild ② same as 包

银 bāoyín

包举 bāojǔ *formal* include; embrace: ～无遗 all-embracing

包括 bāokuò include; consist of; comprise; incorporate: 房租每月四元,水电费～在内。The rent is 4 *yuan* a month, including water and electricity. / 联合王国～英格兰、威尔士、苏格兰和北爱尔兰。The United Kingdom comprises (*or* embraces) England, Wales, Scotland, and Northern Ireland. / 委员会中～老、中、青三部分人。The committee consists of old, middle-aged and young people. / 我们的设计已经～了你们的意见。Our design has incorporated your suggestions. / 他的报告～三个方面。His report contained three aspects.

包揽 bāolǎn undertake the whole thing; take on everything: 这样多的事,一个人～不了。No one person can take on so much work.

包揽词讼 bāolǎn císòng engage in pettifoggery

包罗 bāoluó include; cover; embrace: 民间艺术～甚广。Folk art covers a wide range.

包罗万象 bāoluó wànxiàng all-embracing; all-inclusive

包赔 bāopéi guarantee to pay compensations

包皮 bāopí ① wrapping; wrapper ② *physiol.* prepuce; foreskin

包皮环切术 bāopí huánqiēshù *med.* circumcision

包票 bāopiào old name for 保单 bǎodān ——see also 打包票 dǎ bāopiào

包容 bāoróng ① pardon; forgive: 大度包容 dàdù bāoróng ② contain; hold

包身工 bāoshēngōng indentured labourer

包探 bāotàn *old* detective

包围 bāowéi surround; encircle: 以农村～城市,最后夺取城市 encircle the cities from the rural areas and then capture them / 亭子被茂密的松林～着。The pavilion is surrounded by a thick pine forest.

包围圈 bāowéiquān ring of encirclement

包厢 bāoxiāng box (in a theatre or concert hall)

包销 bāoxiāo ① have exclusive selling rights ② be the sole agent for a production unit or a firm

包心菜 bāoxīncài *dial.* cabbage

包衣 bāoyī coating (on pills)

包银 bāoyín wages paid to traditional opera singers by a theatre

包圆儿 bāoyuánr *inf.* ① buy the whole lot: 你少算一点的话,这些我～了。If you give me a reduction, I'll buy the whole lot. ② finish up (*or* off): 剩下的活儿我一个人～了。I'll finish off what's left of the work.

包月 bāoyuè ① make monthly payment ② *old* hire (as a rickshaw) by the month: 拉～ have a monthly job as a rickshaw boy

包蕴 bāoyùn contain; embody; include

包扎 bāozā wrap up; bind up; pack: ～伤口 bind up (*or* dress) a wound / 待运的自行车已经～好了。The bicycles to be transported are packed.

包治百病 bāozhì bǎibìng guarantee a cure for all ills; be guaranteed to cure all ills: ～的药方 a remedy for all ills; panacea; cure-all

包装 bāozhuāng pack (commodities); package

包装车间 bāozhuāng chējiān packing department

包装设计 bāozhuāng shèjì packing design

包装箱 bāozhuāngxiāng packing box (*or* case)

包装纸 bāozhuāngzhǐ wrapping (*or* packing) paper

包准 bāozhǔn assure; guarantee; vouch for

包子 bāozi steamed stuffed bun

包租 bāozū ① *old* rent land or a house for subletting ② *old* fixed rent for farmland (to be paid no matter how bad the harvest might be) ③ hire (a car, boat, etc.) for a period of time; charter

 苞[1] bāo bud: 花苞 huābāo

苞² 　bāo　*formal*　luxuriant; profuse; thick: 竹～松茂 bamboos and pines growing in profusion

孢 　bāo　see below
孢粉 bāofěn　general name for 孢子 bāozǐ and 花粉 huāfěn
孢子 bāozǐ　*bot.*　spore: ～体 sporophyte
孢子生殖 bāozǐ shēngzhí　*bot.*　sporogony
孢子植物 bāozǐ zhíwù　cryptogam

炮 　bāo　① quick-fry; *sauté*: ～羊肉 quick-fried mutton ② dry by heat: 湿衣服搁在热炕上, 一会儿就～干了。Put the damp clothes on a hot *kang* and they'll soon dry. ——see also páo; pào

胞 　bāo　① (human) afterbirth ② born of the same parents: ～兄弟 full (*or* blood) brothers
胞衣 bāoyī　*Chin. med.*　(human) afterbirth

剥 　bāo　shell; peel; skin: ～花生 shell peanuts / ～香蕉 peel a banana / ～兔皮 skin a rabbit ——see also bō

鲍 　bāo　see below
鲍牙 bāoyá　bucktooth

煲 　bāo　*dial.*　① a kind of deep pot: 电饭煲 diànfànbāo ② use this kind of pot for cooking

褒(襃) 　bāo　①praise; honour; commend:褒扬 bāoyáng ②*formal*　(of clothes) loose; large: ～衣博带 a loose gown with wide girdle
褒贬 bāo-biǎn　pass judgment on; appraise: ～人物 pass judgment on people / 不加～ make no comment, complimentary or otherwise; neither praise nor censure
褒贬 bāobian　speak ill of; cry down: 别在背地里～人。Don't speak ill of anybody behind his back.
褒奖 bāojiǎng　praise and honour; commend and award
褒扬 bāoyáng　praise; commend
褒义 bāoyì　commendatory (*or* complimentary) sense: "崇高"总带有～。The word 崇高 is always commendatory.
褒义词 bāoyìcí　commendatory term

báo

雹 　báo　hail
雹暴 báobào　hailstorm
雹灾 báozāi　disaster caused by hail
雹子 báozi　hail; hailstone

薄 　báo　①thin; flimsy: ～纸 thin paper / ～布 flimsy cloth ② weak; light: 酒味很～。This is a light wine. ③ lacking in warmth; cold: 待他不～ treat him quite well ④ infertile; poor: ～地 poor land ——see also bó; bò
薄板 báobǎn　*metall.*　sheet metal; sheet: 不锈钢～ stainless sheet steel / ～轧机 sheet rolling mill
薄饼 báobǐng　thin pancake
薄脆 báocuì　crisp fritter
薄壳结构 báoqiào jiégòu　*archit.*　shell structure
薄纱织物 báoshā zhīwù　muslin
薄页纸 báoyèzhǐ　① tissue paper ② flimsy

bǎo

宝(寶、寶) 　bǎo　① treasure: 粮食是～中之～。Grain is the treasure of treasures. ② precious; treasured: 宝刀 bǎodāo ③ *honor.*　your: ～眷 your wife and children; your family / ～号 your firm; your shop
宝爱 bǎo'ài　love dearly; treasure; be very fond of
宝宝 bǎo·bǎo　(a pet name for a child) darling; baby
宝贝 bǎobèi　① treasured object; treasure ② darling; baby ③ (used ironically) good-for-nothing or queer character: 这人真是个～! What a fellow!
宝贝疙瘩 bǎobèigēda　*inf.*　parents' darling
宝刹 bǎochà　① pagoda in a temple ② *honor.*　your temple (*or* monastery)
宝刀 bǎodāo　a precious (*or* treasured) sword; a fine sword
宝刀不老 bǎodāo bù lǎo　the man is old, but not his sword—he is still at the height of his powers
宝典 bǎodiǎn　a treasured book; a revered book
宝贵 bǎoguì　① valuable; precious: ～意见 valuable suggestion / ～经验 valuable experience / ～文物 precious cultural relics ② value; treasure; set store by: 你不希罕, 他可是～得很。You don't care for it, but he treasures it dearly.
宝剑 bǎojiàn　a double-edged sword
宝库 bǎokù　treasure-house: 中国医药学是一个伟大的～。Chinese medicine and pharmacology are a great treasure-house.
宝蓝 bǎolán　sapphire blue
宝山空回 bǎoshān kōng huí　return empty-handed from a mountain of treasure—fail to benefit from a visit to a great master, a seat of learning, etc.
宝石 bǎoshí　precious stone; gem
宝书 bǎoshū　a treasured book
宝塔 bǎotǎ　pagoda
宝塔菜 bǎotǎcài　*bot.*　Chinese artichoke
宝塔筒子 bǎotǎtǒngzi　*text.*　cone
宝物 bǎowù　treasure
宝藏 bǎozàng　precious (mineral) deposits: 发掘地下～ unearth buried treasure; tap mineral resources / 民间艺术的～真是无穷无尽。Folk art is a truly inexhaustible treasure trove.
宝重 bǎozhòng　value greatly; treasure
宝座 bǎozuò　throne

饱 　bǎo　① have eaten one's fill; be full: 吃～喝足 eat and drink one's fill / 我～了, 一点也吃不下了。I've had enough. I can't eat any more. ② full; plump: 谷粒很～。The grains are quite plump. ③ fully; to the full: ～尝旧社会的辛酸 taste to the full the bitterness of life in the old society / ～览海岛的美丽风光 drink in the beauty of the island scenery / 她的眼眶里～含着幸福的热泪。Her eyes filled with tears of joy. / 旧中国～经忧患。Old China suffered untold tribulations. ④ satisfy: 饱眼福 bǎo yǎnfú
饱餐 bǎocān　eat to one's heart's content: ～一顿 eat and drink one's fill / ～秀色 feast one's eyes on a beauty
饱读 bǎodú　be well-read: ～诗书 be well-read in classics
饱嗝儿 bǎogér　belch; burp: 打～ hiccup; give a burp
饱汉不知饿汉饥 bǎohàn bù zhī èhàn jī　the well-fed don't know how the starving suffer
饱和 bǎohé　saturation: ～点 saturation point / 相对湿度为百分之百时空气即呈～。When the relative humid-

ity reaches 100 per cent the air is saturated. / 城市里对黑白电视机的需求已趋～. In the cities, the black and white TV market has reached saturation point.

饱和差 bǎohéchā *meteorol.* saturation deficit (or deficiency)

饱和轰炸 bǎohé hōngzhà saturation bombing

饱和剂 bǎohéjì *chem.* saturant

饱和器 bǎohéqì saturator

饱和溶液 bǎohé róngyè *chem.* saturated solution

饱和压力 bǎohé yālì saturation pressure

饱和脂肪 bǎohé zhīfáng saturated fat

饱经沧桑 bǎo jīng cāngsāng have experienced many vicissitudes of life: 她一生～. She has experienced the vicissitudes of life.

饱经风霜 bǎo jīng fēngshuāng weather-beaten; having had one's fill of hardships: ～的面容 a weather-worn face / 一位～的老渔民 an old fisherman who has survived the hardships of life

饱看 bǎokàn watch to one's heart's content; take a good look at

饱满 bǎomǎn full; plump: 颗粒～的小麦 plump-eared wheat / 精神～ full of vigour (or vitality); energetic

饱满度 bǎomǎndù *agric.* plumpness (of seeds)

饱暖 bǎonuǎn being well-fed and well-clad—easy circumstances: ～思淫欲. Easy circumstances breed lewd thoughts.

饱食终日,无所用心 bǎoshí zhōngrì, wú suǒ yòngxīn eat all day without exerting one's mind; eat three square meals a day and do no work; be sated with food and lead an idle life

饱受 bǎoshòu suffer enough from; have one's fill of: ～虐待 be subjected to every kind of maltreatment

饱私囊 bǎo sīnáng commit embezzlement; line one's pockets; feather one's nest

饱学 bǎoxué learned; erudite; scholarly

饱学之士 bǎoxué zhī shì an erudite person; a learned scholar; a man of learning

饱眼福 bǎo yǎnfú feast one's eyes on sth.; enjoy to the full (watching a scene, show, etc.)

饱以老拳 bǎo yǐ lǎoquán give sb. a proper pummelling

饱雨 bǎoyǔ *dial.* saturating (or soaking) rain; soaker

保[1] bǎo ① protect; defend: ～家卫国 protect our homes and defend our country ② keep; maintain; preserve: 这种热水瓶能～暖二十四小时. This kind of thermos flask keeps water hot for 24 hours. / ～水～肥 preserve moisture and fertility (in the soil) ③ guarantee; ensure: 旱涝～收 ensure stable yields despite drought or waterlogging / 西瓜～甜. Watermelon sweetness guaranteed. ④ stand guarantor (or surety) for sb.; bail: 他把儿子从派出所～了出来. He bailed his son out from the police substation. ⑤ guarantor: 作保 zuòbǎo

保[2] Bǎo an old administrative system organized on the basis of households, each *Bao* being made up of 10 *Jia* (甲) ——see also 保甲制度 bǎojiǎ zhìdù

保安 bǎo'ān ① ensure public security ② ensure safety (for workers engaged in production): ～措施 security measures / ～规程 safety regulations / ～装置 protective device

保安队 bǎo'ānduì peace preservation corps (under KMT and warlord rule)

保安人员 bǎo'ān rényuán security personnel

保安族 Bǎo'ānzú the Bonan (Paoan) nationality, the Bonans, inhabiting Gansu

保本保值 bǎoběn-bǎozhí (deposits) with principal and interest safeguarded against price increases

保膘 bǎobiāo keep domestic animals fat

保镖 bǎobiāo bodyguard

保不定 bǎobudìng same as 保不住 bǎobuzhù

保不住 bǎobuzhù most likely; more likely than not; may well: 这个天儿很难说,～会下雨. The weather is rather uncertain; most likely it's going to rain. / 他～把这事儿全给忘了. He may well have forgotten all about it.

保藏 bǎocáng keep in store; preserve: 食品～ food preservation / 把这幅画好好～起来. Preserve the painting carefully.

保持 bǎochí keep; maintain; preserve: ～安静 keep quiet / ～冷静的头脑 keep a cool head; keep cool / 跟群众～密切联系 keep close to the masses / ～中立 remain neutral; maintain neutrality / ～警惕 maintain vigilance; be on the alert / ～艰苦奋斗的作风 preserve (or keep up) the style of plain living and hard struggle / ～跳高记录 retain the high jump record

保存 bǎocún preserve; conserve; keep: ～实力 preserve one's strength; conserve one's forces / ～自己,消灭敌人 preserve oneself and destroy the enemy / 这批文物～得很好. These cultural relics are well preserved. / 他还～着长征时戴的那顶帽子. He still keeps the cap he wore on the Long March.

保单 bǎodān guarantee slip; warranty

保管 bǎoguǎn ① take care of: 负责～农具 be responsible for the care of farm tools / 图书～工作 the care of library books / 这个仓库的粮食～得很好. The grains in this barn are well preserved. ② warehouseman; storeman; storekeeper ③ certainly; surely: 他～不知道. He certainly doesn't know. / 你只要努力,～能学好汉语. I assure you that you can learn Chinese if you make the effort.

保管费 bǎoguǎnfèi storage charges; storage fee

保管室 bǎoguǎnshì storeroom

保管员 bǎoguǎnyuán warehouseman; storeman; storekeeper

保户 bǎohù the insured; policy holder

保护 bǎohù protect; safeguard: ～眼睛 protect one's eyes / ～环境,防止污染 protect the environment against pollution / ～人民的利益 safeguard the people's interests / ～现场 keep intact the scene of a crime or accident / 体操运动员都学会了互相～和自我～. The gymnasts have all learnt to protect each other and themselves against injuries.

保护地 bǎohùdì protectorate; dependent territory

保护关税 bǎohù guānshuì protective tariff

保护国 bǎohùguó protectorate

保护贸易政策 bǎohù màoyì zhèngcè policy of protection; protectionism

保护鸟 bǎohùniǎo protected birds

保护人 bǎohùrén guardian

保护伞 bǎohùsǎn umbrella (a protecting power)

保护色 bǎohùsè *zool.* protective coloration

保护涂剂 bǎohù tújì protective coating

保护性拘留 bǎohùxìng jūliú protective custody; protective detention

保护主义 bǎohùzhǔyì protectionism

保皇党 bǎohuángdǎng royalists

保加利亚 Bǎojiālìyà Bulgaria

保加利亚人 Bǎojiālìyàrén Bulgarian

保加利亚语 Bǎojiālìyàyǔ Bulgarian (language)

保甲制度 bǎojiǎ zhìdù the *Bao-Jia* system (an old administrative system organized on the basis of households, each *Jia* being made up of 10 households, and each *Bao* of 10 *Jia*)

保价信 bǎojiàxìn a kind of registered mail for sending cashable coupons; an insured letter

保驾 bǎojià *humor.* escort the Emperor: 放心吧,我给你～. Don't worry. I'll escort you.

保荐 bǎojiàn recommend sb. (for a job, etc.) with

guarantee

保健 bǎojiàn health protection; health care: 妇 幼～ maternal and child hygiene; mother and child care

保健按摩 bǎojiàn ànmó keep-fit massage

保健操 bǎojiàncāo setting-up exercises

保健费 bǎojiànfèi health subsidies

保健网 bǎojiànwǎng health care network

保健箱 bǎojiànxiāng medical kit

保健员 bǎojiànyuán health worker

保健站 bǎojiànzhàn health station (or centre)

保洁 bǎojié keep a public place clean; do sanitation work

保洁箱 bǎojiéxiāng litter-bin

保举 bǎojǔ (of a high-ranking court official) recommend sb. (for office) with personal guarantee

保龄球 bǎolíngqiú ① tenpin bowling; tenpins; bowling ② bowling ball

保留 bǎoliú ① continue to have; retain: 他还～着战争年代的革命朝气。He still retains the revolutionary fervour of the war years. / 这个地方还～着原来的面貌。The place still looks the same as before. ② hold (or keep) back; reserve: 无～地同意 agree unreservedly (or without reservation) / 以后再答复的权利 reserve the right to reply at a later date / 持～意见 have reservations / 票给你～到明天中午。We'll reserve (or hold) the ticket for you till tomorrow noon. / 有意见～谈出来，不要～。Don't hold back anything you want to say.

保留地 bǎoliúdì reservation (as Indian reservations in the U.S.)

保留剧目 bǎoliú jùmù repertory; repertoire

保留条款 bǎoliú tiáokuǎn reservation clause

保媒 bǎoméi old be a matchmaker (or go-between); arrange a match

保密 bǎomì maintain secrecy; keep sth. secret: 这事绝对～。This must be kept absolutely secret. or This is strictly confidential. / 我说的事儿你可要～。Keep mum about what I said.

保密级别 bǎomì jíbié security classification

保密条例 bǎomì tiáolì security regulations

保密文件 bǎomì wénjiàn classified document

保苗 bǎomiáo agric. keep a full stand of seedlings

保命 bǎomìng save one's life; survive

保姆 bǎomǔ ① housemaid; housekeeper ② (children's) nurse

保票 bǎopiào same as 包票 bāopiào

保全 bǎoquán ① save from damage; preserve: ～名誉 preserve one's reputation / 由于战士们的抢救, 这一批物资终于～了。Thanks to the soldiers' rescue operations, the supplies were finally saved. / ～面子 save face ② maintain; keep in good repair: ～工 maintenance worker

保人 bǎorén same as 保证人 bǎozhèngrén

保墒 bǎoshāng agric. preservation of soil moisture

保释 bǎoshì leg. release on bail; bail: 准予 (不准)～ accept (refuse) bail

保守 bǎoshǒu ① guard; keep: ～国家机密 guard state secrets ② conservative: ～观点 conservative point of view / ～思想 conservative ideas (or thinking) / ～的估计 a conservative estimate / ～派 conservatives / 这计划定得有些～。This is rather a conservative plan.

保守党 Bǎoshǒudǎng Conservative Party (as in Britain)

保守疗法 bǎoshǒu liáofǎ med. conservative treatment

保守主义 bǎoshǒuzhǔyì conservatism

保送 bǎosòng recommend sb. for admission to school (without taking the entrance examination), etc.: ～北京大学 recommend sb. for immediate admission to Beijing University / ～留学生 a student recommended to study abroad

保胎 bǎotāi prevent miscarriages

保泰松 bǎotàisōng pharm. phenylbutazone

保外就医 bǎo wài jiùyī leg. be released on bail for medical treatment; remain out of custody and obtain medical treatment

保外执行 bǎowài zhíxíng leg. serve a sentence on bail

保卫 bǎowèi defend; safeguard: ～祖国 defend one's country / ～国家主权和领土完整 safeguard state sovereignty and territorial integrity / ～大桥 guard a bridge

保卫部门 bǎowèi bùmén public security bodies

保卫工作 bǎowèi gōngzuò security work

保卫科 bǎowèikē security section (of an organization)

保温 bǎowēn heat preservation: 积雪可以～保墒。A layer of snow can preserve soil moisture and prevent it from freezing. / 这个暖瓶不～。This thermos flask doesn't keep the heat well.

保温杯 bǎowēnbēi thermos mug

保温材料 bǎowēn cáiliào thermal insulation material

保温层 bǎowēncéng achit. (thermal) insulating layer

保温车 bǎowēnchē railway refrigerator wagon (or car)

保温瓶 bǎowēnpíng vacuum flask (or bottle); thermos

保鲜 bǎoxiān keep vegetables, fruit, etc. fresh; preserve freshness

保鲜纸 bǎoxiānzhǐ handi-wrap

保险 bǎoxiǎn ① insurance: 人寿 (海损)～ life (maritime) insurance / 你的汽车保了险没有? Is your car insured? / 保了火险 have insured against fire ② safe: 骑车太快可不～。It's not safe to cycle too fast. / 你还是带上雨衣吧, ～点儿。You'd better take your raincoat just to be on the safe side. ③ be sure; be bound to: 他明天～会来。He is sure to come tomorrow. / ～能行! It's bound to work. / 你依我的话, ～不会出错。If you follow my advice, then I can assure you that nothing will go wrong.

保险带 bǎoxiǎndài safety belt

保险单 bǎoxiǎndān insurance policy

保险刀 bǎoxiǎndāo safety razor

保险费 bǎoxiǎnfèi insurance premium

保险粉 bǎoxiǎnfěn text. sodium hydrosulphite

保险杆 bǎoxiǎngān mech. bumper bar

保险杠 bǎoxiǎngàng bumper (on a car)

保险公司 bǎoxiǎn gōngsī insurance company

保险柜 bǎoxiǎnguì strongbox; safe

保险盒 bǎoxiǎnhé fuse box

保险机 bǎoxiǎnjī safety (of a firearm)

保险客户 bǎoxiǎn kèhù the insured; policy holder

保险人 bǎoxiǎnrén the insurer; assurer

保险丝 bǎoxiǎnsī elec. fuse; fuse-wire: ～烧断了。The fuse has blown.

保险弹簧 bǎoxiǎn tánhuáng relief spring

保险箱 bǎoxiǎnxiāng strongbox; safe

保险装置 bǎoxiǎn zhuāngzhì safety device

保修 bǎoxiū guarantee to keep sth. in good repair: 这只表～一年。There is a year's guarantee with this watch. or This watch is guaranteed for a year.

保养 bǎoyǎng ① take good care of (or conserve) one's health: 他很会～, 六十岁了, 还显得很年轻。He certainly knows how to take care of himself, looking so young at the age of 60. ② maintain; keep in good repair: 机器～ maintenance (or upkeep) of machinery / 这条路～得很好。This road is in good repair.

保养费 bǎoyǎngfèi maintenance cost; upkeep

保养工 bǎoyǎnggōng maintenance worker

保有 bǎoyǒu possess; have: ～土地 possess land

保佑 bǎoyòu bless and protect: 我们相信人定胜天, 不靠老天～。We believe in man's conquest of nature and don't rely on blessings from heaven.

保育　bǎoyù　child care; child welfare
保育员　bǎoyùyuán　child-care worker; nurse
保育院　bǎoyùyuàn　nursery school
保障　bǎozhàng　ensure; guarantee; safeguard: ～人民言论自由 guarantee freedom of speech for the people / 在这里职业有～。Jobs are secure here.
保真度　bǎozhēndù　electron. fidelity: 高～ high fidelity
保证　bǎozhèng　pledge; guarantee; assure; ensure: ～完成任务 pledge (or guarantee) to fulfil a task / 不再发生类似事件 guarantee against the occurrence of similar incidents / 我～说到做到。I assure you I'll do what I say. / ～供应。There's a guaranteed supply. / 谁能～他不再犯错误。Nobody can say for sure he won't make any more mistakes. / 妇女在产前产后有充分的休息。Adequate rest is ensured for women during pregnancy and after childbirth.
保证单位　bǎozhèng dānwèi　guarantor unit
保证金　bǎozhèngjīn　① earnest money; cash deposit ② leg. bail
保证人　bǎozhèngrén　leg. ① guarantor ② bail
保证书　bǎozhèngshū　written pledge; guarantee; guaranty; letter of guarantee
保质保量　bǎozhì-bǎoliàng　guarantee both quality and quantity
保重　bǎozhòng　(used in expressing one's concern about sb.'s health) take care of oneself: 多多～。Take good care of yourself. or Look after yourself.
保住　bǎozhù　keep; retain; hold on to: 那座城一定要～。That city must be held at all costs. / 他该的钱太多了，恐怕他的房子保不住了。He owes so much money that he probably won't be able to keep his house. / 这场比赛我们一定要赢，这样才保得住不败的记录。We must win the game so as to keep a perfect record.
保准　bǎozhǔn　① reliable; dependable; trustworthy: 他说话不～。His words cannot be relied on. ② guarantee; assure; ensure: 我～办到。I guarantee to get it done. / 我～不会出问题。I assure you everything will be all right.

鸨　bǎo　① zool. bustard ② procuress: 老鸨 lǎobǎo
鸨母　bǎomǔ　(also 鸨儿 bǎo'ér) a woman running a brothel; procuress; madam

葆¹　bǎo　formal preserve; nurture: 永～青春 keep alive the fervour of youth

葆²　bǎo　formal luxuriant growth (of grass)

堡　bǎo　fort; fortress: 地堡 dìbǎo ——see also bǔ
堡礁　bǎojiāo　barrier reef
堡垒　bǎolěi　fort; fortress; stronghold; blockhouse: ～是最容易从内部攻破的。The easiest way to capture a fortress is from within. / 把党支部建设成坚强的战斗～ build the Party branch into a powerful fighting force
堡垒战　bǎolěizhàn　blockhouse warfare

褓（緥）　bǎo　see 襁褓 qiǎngbǎo

bào

报（報）　bào　① report; announce; declare: ～公安局 report to the public security bureau / ～上级批准 report (or submit) sth. to the higher authorities for approval ② reply; respond; reciprocate: ～友人书 a (letter in) reply to a friend / ～以热烈的掌声 respond with warm applause ③ recompense; requite: 无以为～

be unable to repay a kindness ④ revenge: 报仇 bàochóu ⑤ retribution; judgment: 果报 guǒbào ⑥ newspaper: 日报 rìbào ⑦ periodical; journal: 画报 huàbào ⑧ bulletin; report: 战报 zhànbào ⑨ telegram; cable: 发报 fābào
报案　bào'àn　report a case to the security authorities
报表　bàobiǎo　forms for reporting statistics, etc.; report forms
报偿　bàocháng　repay; recompense
报仇　bàochóu　revenge; avenge: 为父～ avenge one's father / 报私仇 settle personal scores
报仇雪耻　bàochóu-xuěchǐ　avenge a wrong and wipe out a humiliation
报仇雪恨　bàochóu-xuěhèn　avenge oneself; take revenge
报酬　bàochou　reward; remuneration; pay: 不计～ not concerned about pay; irrespective of remuneration / 在发展生产的基础上逐步提高劳动～ gradually increase payment for labour on the basis of increased production / 工作很累，～不多 get very little in reward for one's hard work / 她找到了一个～比较好的工作。She has found a more remunerative job.
报答　bàodá　repay; requite: 以实际行动～党的关怀 repay the Party's kindness with one's deeds / 我怎么也～不了您的恩情。How can I ever repay you for your kindness?
报单　bàodān　① taxation form; declaration form ② same as 报条 bàotiáo
报到　bàodào　report for duty; check in; register: 向部里～ report for duty at the ministry / 向大会秘书处～ check in at the secretariat of the congress / 新生已开始～。The new students have started registering.
报道　bàodào　(also 报导 bàodǎo) ① report (news); cover: ～考古新发现 report new archaeological finds / ～会议情况 cover the conference / 据～ it is reported that / 据新华社三月二日自北京～ according to a Xinhua News Agency dispatch datelined Beijing, March 2 / 各报都在第一版～了这个消息。This was front-paged in all the papers. ② news report; story: 一篇关于奥运会的～ a news report about the Olympic Games
报德　bàodé　repay a kindness
报端　bàoduān　space in a newspaper: 这条广告已见～。The advertisement has appeared in the paper.
报恩　bào'ēn　pay a debt of gratitude
报废　bàofèi　① report sth. as worthless ② discard as useless; reject; scrap: 使～矿井复生 reopen an abandoned mine / 这架机器太旧，快～了。This machine is so old it will soon have to be scrapped.
报分　bàofēn　sports call the score
报复　bàofu　make reprisals; retaliate: 图谋～ nurse thoughts of revenge / ～性打击 vindictive blow; retaliatory strike / 杀害人质作为～ retaliate by killing hostages
报告　bàogào　① report; make known: 向上级～ report to the higher authorities / ～大家一个好消息。Here's a piece of good news for us all. / 现在～新闻。Here is the news. / 国务院对全国人民代表大会负责并～工作。The State Council is responsible and accountable to the National People's Congress. / ～! Reporting! ② report; speech; talk; lecture: 作～ give a talk or lecture / 总结～ summing-up report / 动员～ mobilization speech / ～会 public lecture / ～人 speaker; lecturer
报告文学　bàogào wénxué　reportage
报关　bàoguān　declare sth. at customs; apply to customs: 你有什么东西要～吗? Have you got anything to declare?
报关表　bàoguānbiǎo　declaration form; customs declaration: 进出口货物～ customs declaration for imports and exports
报馆　bàoguǎn　popular name for 报社 bàoshè

报国　bàoguó　dedicate oneself to the service of one's country: 以身～ lay down one's life for one's country

报户口　bào hùkǒu　apply for a residence permit: 报临时户口 apply for a temporary residence permit / 给新生婴儿～ register the birth of a child

报话机　bàohuàjī　handie-talkie

报价　bàojià　*econ.*　quoted price

报捷　bàojié　report a success; announce a victory

报界　bàojiè　the press; journalistic circles; the journalists: 向～发表谈话 make a statement to the press

报警　bàojǐng　① report (an incident) to the police: 报火警 report a fire ② give an alarm: 鸣钟～ sound the alarm bell

报刊　bàokān　newspapers and periodicals; the press

报考　bàokǎo　enter oneself for an examination: ～清华大学 register for the entrance examinations to Qinghua University; apply for entrance to Qinghua University

报密　bàomì　inform against sb.

报名　bàomíng　enter one's name; sign up: ～参加百米赛跑 enter one's name for the 100-metre dash / ～参军 enlist in the army / ～参加比赛的共有五十人。There are fifty entries (*or* entrants) altogether. / 他已在夜大学～了。He has signed up for the evening university.

报命　bàomìng　*formal*　report on one's mission

报幕　bàomù　announce the items on a (theatrical) programme: ～员 announcer

报批　bàopī　report (*or* submit) sth. to the higher authorities for approval

报屁股　bàopìgu　insignificant space on the inside pages of a newspaper

报聘　bàopìn　*old*　return a state visit (on behalf of one's government)

报请　bàoqǐng　(used in official communications) submit a report asking for: ～上级批准 report (*or* submit) sth. to the higher authorities for approval

报社　bàoshè　general office of a newspaper; newspaper office: 他在一家～工作。He works for a newspaper.

报审　bàoshěn　report (*or* submit) sth. to the higher authorities for examination

报失　bàoshī　report the loss of sth. to the authorities concerned: 已向保卫部门～。The loss has been reported to the security department.

报时　bàoshí　give the correct time

报时器　bàoshíqì　chronopher

报时台　bàoshítái　(telephone) time inquiry service

报数　bàoshù　number off: ～! (word of command) Count off!

报税　bàoshuì　declare dutiable goods; make a statement of dutiable goods

报摊　bàotān　news-stand; news stall

报条　bàotiáo　an official announcement of a candidate's success in the imperial examinations or of an official's promotion

报童　bàotóng　*old*　newsboy

报头　bàotóu　masthead (of a newspaper, etc.); nameplate

报务员　bàowùyuán　telegraph operator; radio operator

报喜　bàoxǐ　announce good news; report success: 我给大家～来了。I've come with good news for all of you.

报喜不报忧　bào xǐ bù bào yōu　report the good news but not the bad; hold back unpleasant information

报系　bàoxì　newspaper chain; syndicate

报销　bàoxiāo　① submit an expense account; apply for reimbursement: 向财务科～ submit an expense account to the treasurer's office / 旅费凭票～。Travelling expenses can be reimbursed on handing in the tickets. ② hand in a list of expended articles ③ *inf.* write off; wipe out: 敌人马上～了。This enemy force was wiped out right away.

报晓　bàoxiǎo　(of a cock, bell, etc.) herald the break of day; be a harbinger of dawn: 晨鸡～。The crowing of roosters at dawn heralded the break of day. / 远处传来～的钟声。From afar came the chimes of a bell announcing the break of day.

报效　bàoxiào　render service to repay sb's kindness: 我参军是为了～祖国。I enlisted in order to serve my country.

报谢　bàoxiè　express appreciation (for sb.'s kindness or hospitality); acknowledge

报信　bàoxìn　notify; inform: 赶快给他报个信儿。Let him know as soon as possible.

报应　bàoyìng　① *Buddhism* retribution; judgment ② due punishment: 这是他应得的～。He's getting what he deserves. / 他净干坏事，现在可遭～了。He's getting paid back for all the bad things he's done.

报章　bàozhāng　newspapers: ～杂志 newspapers and magazines

报帐　bàozhàng　render an account; submit an expense account; apply for reimbursement: 修理费用可以～。Costs of repairs may be reimbursed.

报纸　bàozhǐ　① newspaper: ～夹 newspaper holder ② newsprint

报子　bàozi　*old*　① a man who brings news of appointment, promotion, or success in imperial examinations, in expectation of a reward ② same as 报条 bàotiáo

刨(鉋、鑢)

　bào　① plane sth. down; plane: ～木板 plane a board ② plane; planer; planing machine ——see also páo

刨冰　bàobīng　water ice (powdered or in shavings)

刨程　bàochéng　*mech.*　planing length

刨齿　bàochǐ　*mech.*　gear-shaping: ～机 gear shaper

刨床　bàochuáng　planer; planing machine

刨刀　bàodāo　*mech.*　① planer tool ② plane iron

刨工　bàogōng　① planing ② planing machine operator; planer

刨花　bàohuā　wood shavings

刨花板　bàohuābǎn　*archit.*　shaving board

刨刃儿　bàorènr　(also 刨铁 bàotiě) plane iron

刨子　bàozi　plane (a carpenter's tool)

抱¹

　bào　① hold or carry in the arms; embrace; hug: 把小孩子～起来 take a child in one's arms / 不要～住错误观点不放。Don't stick to your wrong views. ② have one's first child or grandchild: 她快～孙子了。She'll soon be a grandmother. ③ adopt (a child): 他的女儿是～的。His daughter is adopted. ④ *dial.* hang together: ～成一团 gang up; hang together ⑤ *dial.* (of shoes and clothes) fit: 这件上衣～身。This jacket fits well. ⑥ cherish; harbour: ～很大希望 entertain high hopes / ～正确的态度 adopt (*or* take) a correct attitude / 不～幻想 cherish no illusions ⑦ *m.* armful of: 一～草 an armful of hay / 这颗树有一～粗。You can just get your arms around this tree trunk.

抱²(菢)

　bào　hatch (eggs); brood

抱病　bàobìng　be ill; be in bad health: ～工作 go on working in spite of ill health

抱不平　bàobùpíng　be outraged by an injustice (done to sb. else): 有人替他～。Some felt indignant on his behalf. ——see also 打抱不平 dǎ bàobùpíng

抱残守缺　bàocán-shǒuquē　cherish the outmoded and preserve the outworn—be conservative; be an anachronism

抱粗腿　bàocūtuǐ　(also 抱大腿 bàodàtuǐ) latch on to the rich and powerful; throw oneself under the protection of someone of influence or power

抱蛋　bàodàn　*dial.*　sit (on eggs); brood; hatch

抱佛脚　bàofójiǎo　clasp Buddha's feet—profess devotion only when in trouble; make a hasty last-minute effort ——see also 急来抱佛脚 jí lái bàofójiǎo

抱负　bàofù　aspiration; ambition: 很有～ have high aspirations; cherish high ambitions

抱恨　bàohèn　have a gnawing regret

抱恨终天　bàohèn zhōngtiān　feel bitter regret to the end of one's days; have an aching void in one's heart: 今老母已丧,～。(《三国演义》) Now my dear old mother has died, leaving an aching void in my heart. / 辱命而返,～ bitterly lament the non-fulfilment of one's mission upon returning home

抱疚　bàojiù　*formal*　feel compunction; have qualms of conscience

抱愧　bàokuì　feel ashamed

抱歉　bàoqiàn　be sorry; feel apologetic; regret: 叫你久等了,很～。Very sorry to have kept you waiting. / 这书晚还了两天,很～。I apologize for keeping the book two days overdue.

抱屈　bàoqū　feel wronged

抱厦　bàoshà　① a veranda in front of a house ② a lean-to at the back of a house

抱头鼠窜　bàotóu shǔcuàn　cover the head and sneak away like a rat; scurry (*or* scamper) off like a frightened rat

抱头痛哭　bàotóu tòngkū　weep in each other's arms; cry on each other's shoulders

抱团儿　bàotuánr　*inf.*　gang up; hang together

抱窝　bàowō　sit (on eggs); brood; hatch: 母鸡～了。The hen is sitting.

抱娃娃　bàowáwa　give birth to a child: 她快～了。She is expecting a baby.

抱薪救火　bào xīn jiùhuǒ　carry faggots to put out a fire—adopt a wrong method to save a situation and end up by making it worse; do something counterproductive

抱养　bàoyǎng　adopt (a child)

抱恙　bàoyàng　*formal*　be ill; be in bad health

抱腰　bàoyāo　*dial.*　give support to sb.; back sb. up

抱冤　bàoyuān　feel wronged; nurse a grievance

抱怨　bào·yuàn　complain; grumble: 不要总是～别人对你帮助不够。Don't always complain that you haven't been given enough help. / 他～自己的工资低。He grumbled about his low pay.

抱柱　bàozhù　a thick pillar; a massive pillar

抱罪　bàozuì　be conscious of one's guilt; be conscience-stricken

豹　bào　leopard; panther

豹猫　bàomāo　leopard cat

豹死留皮,人死留名　bào sǐ liú pí, rén sǐ liú míng　when a leopard dies, it leaves its skin; when a man dies, he leaves his name

豹子　bàozi　leopard; panther

鲍　bào　① see 鲍鱼¹ bàoyú ② see 鲍鱼² bàoyú ③ (Bào) a surname

鲍鱼¹　bàoyú　*formal*　salted fish

鲍鱼²　bàoyú　abalone

鲍鱼之肆　bàoyú zhī sì　a shop which sells salted fish ——see also 如入鲍鱼之肆 rú rù bàoyú zhī sì

暴¹　bào　① sudden and violent: 暴雷 bàoléi ② cruel; savage; fierce: 残暴 cánbào ③ short-tempered; hot-tempered: 脾气～ have a hot temper

暴²　bào　stick out; stand out; bulge: 急得头上的青筋都～出来了 be so agitated that the veins on one's forehead stand out

暴³　bào　*formal*　waste; ruin; spoil: 自暴自弃 zìbào-zìqì

暴病　bàobìng　sudden attack of a serious illness: 得～ be suddenly seized with a severe illness / ～而死 die of a sudden illness

暴跌　bàodiē　steep fall (in price); slump: 股票价格～。There was a slump in share prices.

暴动　bàodòng　insurrection; rebellion; riot: 举行～ raise an insurrection; stage a riot

暴发　bàofā　① break out: 山洪～。Torrents of water rushed down the mountain. ② *derog.* suddenly become rich or important; get rich quick: ～户 upstart

暴风　bàofēng　① storm wind ② storm (force 11 wind)

暴风雪　bàofēngxuě　snowstorm; blizzard

暴风雨　bàofēngyǔ　rainstorm; storm; tempest: 遇上～ be caught in a storm / 革命的～ a storm of revolution; a revolutionary tempest / ～般的掌声 thunderous applause

暴风骤雨　bàofēng-zhòuyǔ　violent storm; hurricane; tempest: 其势如～ with the force of a hurricane

暴富　bàofù　suddenly become rich; get rich quick

暴光　bàoguāng　same as 曝光 bàoguāng

暴洪　bàohóng　a sudden, violent flood; flash flood

暴虎冯河　bàohǔ-pínghé　fight a tiger with bare hands and cross a river without a boat—foolishly brave; foolhardy

暴君　bàojūn　tyrant; despot

暴客　bàokè　*formal*　brigand; bandit

暴雷　bàoléi　violent thunderclaps

暴力　bàolì　violence; force: ～行为 an act of violence / 电影里的～镜头 violence (*or* violent scenes) shown in films / ～革命 violent revolution

暴利　bàolì　sudden huge profits

暴戾　bàolì　*formal*　ruthless and tyrannical; cruel and fierce

暴戾恣睢　bàolì-zìsuī　cruel and despotic; tyrannical

暴烈　bàoliè　violent; fierce: 性情～ have a fiery temper

暴露　bàolù　expose; reveal; lay bare: ～思想 lay bare one's thoughts / ～目标 give away one's position / ～在光天化日之下 be exposed to the light of day / 矛盾还没有充分～。The contradictions have not yet been fully revealed.

暴露文学　bàolù wénxué　literature of exposure (exposing the dark side of a society)

暴露无遗　bàolù wú yí　be thoroughly exposed: 这伙侵略者的狰狞面貌～。The ferocious features of these aggressors were completely unmasked.

暴乱　bàoluàn　riot; rebellion; revolt: 平定反革命～ suppress (*or* put down, quell) a counterrevolutionary rebellion

暴民　bàomín　mob

暴怒　bàonù　violent rage; fury

暴虐　bàonüè　brutal; tyrannical

暴弃　bàoqì　*formal*　give oneself up as hopeless; have no urge to make progress; be resigned to one's backwardness

暴晒　bàoshài　be exposed to the sun (for a long time)

暴死　bàosǐ　die of a sudden illness

暴殄天物　bàotiǎn tiānwù　a reckless waste of the products of nature

暴跳如雷　bàotiào rú léi　stamp with fury; fly into a rage: 气得～ stamp frantically in anger / 他～地发了一顿脾气。He stormed and raged in a fit of temper.

暴徒　bàotú　ruffian; thug

暴行　bàoxíng　savage act; outrage; atrocity

暴性子　bàoxìngzi　a violent temper

暴饮暴食　bàoyǐn-bàoshí　eat and drink too much at one

meal

暴雨 bàoyǔ torrential rain; rainstorm: 下了一阵～。 There was a heavy downpour.

暴躁 bàozào irascible; irritable: 脾气～ be irritable by nature; be hot-tempered

暴涨 bàozhǎng (of floods, prices, etc.) rise suddenly and sharply: 河水～。 The river suddenly rose. / 物价～。 Prices soared (or skyrocketed).

暴政 bàozhèng tyranny; despotic rule

暴卒 bàozú die of a sudden illness; die suddenly

爆 bào ① explode; burst: 车胎～了。 The tyre's burst. / 子弹打在石头上，～起许多火星。 The bullet hit the rock and sent sparks flying from it. ② quick-fry; quick-boil: 葱～牛肉 quick-fried beef with scallions

爆豆 bàodòu ① pop beans: 说话像～似的 chatter away like popping beans / 一片～似的枪声 a continuous rattle of gunfire ② popped beans

爆肚儿 bàodǔr quick-boiled tripe

爆发 bàofā erupt; burst out; break out: 火山～ volcanic eruption / 战争～。 War broke out. / 人群中～出一片欢呼声。 The crowd burst into cheers.

爆发力 bàofālì sports explosive force

爆发音 bàofāyīn phonet. plosive

爆管 bàoguǎn cartridge igniter; squib

爆花 bàohuā ① snuff (of a wick) ② same as 爆米花儿 bàomǐhuār

爆冷门 bào lěngmén (of a contest, etc.) produce an unexpected winner; a dark horse bobbing up

爆裂 bàoliè burst; crack: 豌豆过熟就会～。 Pea pods burst open when overripe.

爆满 bàomǎn ① (of a theatre, cinema, etc.) have a full house; house full ② (of a stadium, etc.) be filled to capacity

爆米花儿 bàomǐhuār ① puffed rice ② popcorn

爆破 bàopò blow up; demolish; dynamite; blast: 连续～ successive demolitions / ～敌人的碉堡 blow up an enemy's pillbox / ～手 dynamiter / ～英雄 demolition hero; ace dynamiter / ～组 demolition team

爆破弹 bàopòdàn blasting cartridge

爆破筒 bàopòtǒng bangalore (torpedo)

爆破音 bàopòyīn phonet. plosive

爆破炸弹 bàopò zhàdàn demolition bomb

爆腾 bàoteng inf. raise (or kick up) a dust; whirling up a dust

爆音 bàoyīn aviation sonic boom; shock-wave noise

爆炸 bàozhà explode; blow up; detonate: ～力 explosive force / 炸弹～了。 A bomb exploded. / 敌人的军火库～了。 The enemy ammunition dump blew up. / ～一个核装置 detonate a nuclear device / ～性的局势 an explosive situation

爆炸极限 bàozhà jíxiàn explosive limit

爆炸物 bàozhàwù explosive

爆竹 bàozhú (also 爆仗 bàozhang) firecracker: 放～ let off firecrackers / ～没响。 The firecracker didn't go off.

曝 bào see below

曝光 bàoguāng ① photog. exposure: 多次～ multiple exposure / ～表 exposure meter / ～宽容度 exposure latitude ② make (sth. bad) public; expose

bēi

陂 bēi ① pond ② formal waterside; bank ③ formal mountain slope

杯(盃) bēi ① cup: 一～茶 a cup of tea ② (alcoholic) drink: 咱们喝一～。 Let's have a drink. / 多喝了几～ have a drop (or glass) too much ③ (prize) cup; trophy: 世界～ World Cup

杯弓蛇影 bēigōng-shéyǐng mistaking the reflection of a bow in the cup for a snake—beset with imaginary fears; extremely suspicious

杯酒 bēijiǔ (usu. used in invitations to a feast) a cup of wine: ～言欢 hobnob

杯盘狼藉 bēi-pán láng jí wine cups and dishes strewn in disorder (after a feast): 看核既尽，～。相与枕藉于舟中，不知东方之既白。(苏轼) When we had finished the dishes, and cups and plates lay about us in disorder, we stretched out in the boat and did not notice the coming of dawn in the east.

杯赛 bēisài cup (a competition): 去年我们参加了那次～。 We played in the cup last year.

杯水车薪 bēishuǐ chēxīn trying to put out a blazing cartload of faggots with a cup of water—an utterly inadequate measure

杯中物 bēizhōngwù formal the contents of the cup—wine

杯子 bēizi cup; glass

卑 bēi ① low: 地势～湿 low-lying and damp ② inferior: 自卑 zìbēi ③ formal modest; humble: 卑辞厚礼 bēicí-hòulǐ

卑鄙 bēibǐ base; mean; contemptible; despicable: ～行为 a base (or mean) action; sordid conduct; abject behaviour / ～手段 contemptible means; dirty tricks / ～勾当 a dirty deal / 他这个人很～，欺负人家孤儿寡母。 He is unprincipled, swindling the widow and her orphan.

卑鄙龌龊 bēibǐ wòchuò sordid; foul; base; mean

卑鄙无耻 bēibǐ wúchǐ base and shameless

卑不足道 bēi bùzú dào too insignificant or trivial to be worth mentioning; inconsiderable

卑辞厚礼 bēicí-hòulǐ humble words and handsome gifts

卑恭 bēigōng servile; obsequious; cringing

卑躬屈节 bēigōng-qūjié (also 卑躬屈膝 bēigōng-qūxī) bow and scrape; cringe; act servilely (or obsequiously)

卑贱 bēijiàn ① lowly; humble: ～者最聪明，高贵者最愚蠢。 The lowly are most intelligent; the élite are most ignorant. ② mean and low

卑劣 bēiliè base; mean; despicable: ～手法 a mean (or despicable) trick

卑劣行径 bēiliè xíngjìng base conduct; dishonourable behaviour

卑陋 bēilòu ① humble; mean: ～的茅屋 a mean thatched cottage ② lowly; degrading

卑怯 bēiqiè mean and cowardly; abject: ～行为 abject behaviour

卑屈 bēiqū obsequiously submissive; cringing

卑弱 bēiruò formal ① decline; wane ② weak; delicate

卑视 bēishì look down upon; despise; scorn

卑微 bēiwēi petty and low

卑污 bēiwū despicable and filthy; foul

卑下 bēixià base; low

卑之无甚高论 bēi zhī wú shèn gāolùn the discourse is far from lofty; there is nothing brilliant about the idea

卑职 bēizhí old hum. (used by subordinate officials in addressing superiors) your humble subordinate; I

背(揹) bēi ① carry on the back: ～着孩子 carry a baby on one's back ② bear; shoulder: 我怕～不起这样的责任。 I'm afraid I can't shoulder such a responsibility. ——see also bèi

背包 bēibāo ① knapsack; rucksack; infantry (or field)

pack; backpack ② *mil.* blanket roll

背包袱 bēibāofu carry baggage—have a weight (*or* load) on one's mind: 你不要因此～。Don't let it weigh on your mind.

背带 bēidài ① braces; suspenders ② sling (for a rifle); straps (for a knapsack)

背负 bēifù bear; carry on the back; have on one's shoulder: ～着衣包 carry a bundle of clothes on one's back / ～着人民的希望 with people's expectations always on one's mind

背黑锅 bēihēiguō *inf.* be made a scapegoat; be unjustly blamed: 他倒称心如意了，却叫我一人～。He got what he wanted and left me in the lurch as a scapegoat.

背饥荒 bēijīhuang run into debt; owe a debt

背篓 bēilǒu a basket carried on the back

背篓商店 bēilǒu shāngdiàn a mobile shop with shop assistants carrying goods in baskets on their backs to sell in mountain areas; mobile shop with goods carried in baskets; pack-basket shop

背头 bēitóu swept-back hair

背债 bēizhài be in debt; be saddled with debts: 背了一屁股债 be heavily in debt; be up to one's eyes in debt

悲 bēi ① sad; sorrowful; melancholy: ～不自胜 be overcome with grief ② compassion: 慈悲 cíbēi

悲哀 bēi'āi grieved; sorrowful

悲惨 bēicǎn miserable; tragic: ～的遭遇 a tragic experience / ～的过去 the bitter past / 小姑娘又冷又饿，样子很～。Suffering from cold and hunger, the little girl looked very miserable.

悲恻 bēicè *formal* sad; grieved; sorrowful

悲楚 bēichǔ *formal* grief; sorrow

悲从中来 bēi cóng zhōng lái feel sadness welling up

悲悼 bēidào mourn; grieve over sb.'s death

悲愤 bēifèn grief and indignation

悲愤填膺 bēifèn tián yīng be filled with grief and indignation

悲感 bēigǎn ① recall wih grief ② sadness; grief

悲歌 bēigē ① sad melody; stirring strains: 国际～歌一曲, 狂飙为我从天落。(毛泽东) To the *Internationale's* stirring strains A wild whirlwind swoops from the sky. ② *mus.* elegy; dirge; threnody ③ sing with solemn fervour

悲哽 bēigěng choke with grief: 说到这里, 她满眼泪花, 声音～, 不能说下去了。At this point her eyes filled with tears and, her voice choked with sobs, she was unable to go on.

悲观 bēiguān pessimistic: ～情绪 pessimism / ～厌世 be pessimistic and world-weary / 持～看法 take a pessimistic (*or* gloomy) view / 尽管不断遭受挫折, 可他们从不～。They have never been disheartened in spite of repeated setbacks.

悲观失望 bēiguān shīwàng pessimistic and despondent; disheartened

悲观主义 bēiguānzhǔyì pessimism

悲号 bēiháo cry piteously; wail

悲欢离合 bēi-huān-lí-hé joys and sorrows, partings and reunions—vicissitudes of life

悲剧 bēijù tragedy

悲苦 bēikǔ grief; sorrow

悲凉 bēiliáng sad and dreary; forlorn; desolate

悲悯 bēimǐn feel compassion for; pity

悲鸣 bēimíng utter sad calls; lament: 深秋时节, 寒蝉～。In late autumn, the cicadas sadly bemoaned their fate.

悲凄 bēiqī plaintive; mournful

悲泣 bēiqì weep with grief

悲切 bēiqiè *formal* mournful; grieved

悲秋 bēiqiū melancholy thoughts associated with autumn; autumnal melancholy

悲伤 bēishāng sad; grieved; sorrowful: 人生的欢乐和～ the joys and sorrows of life

悲酸 bēisuān grieved; sad; bitter

悲叹 bēitàn sigh mournfully; lament

悲啼 bēití ① sob with grief; cry mournfully ② (of certain birds and animals) utter sad cries

悲天悯人 bēitiān-mǐnrén bemoan the state of the universe and pity the fate of mankind: 装出一副～的样子 pretend to bewail the times and pity the people; be sanctimonious; assume a compassionate tone

悲恸 bēitòng be deeply grieved; be filled with deep sorrow

悲痛 bēitòng grieved; sorrowful: 感到深切的～ be deeply grieved; be filled with deep sorrow / 化～为力量 turn grief into strength

悲喜交集 bēi-xǐ jiāojí mixed feelings of grief and joy; grief and joy intermingled; joy tempered with sorrow: 两人久别重逢, ～。The reunion after a long separation brought mixed feelings of joy and sorrow to both of them.

悲喜剧 bēixǐjù tragicomedy

悲壮 bēizhuàng solemn and stirring; moving and tragic: ～的歌曲 a solemn and stirring song

碑 bēi an upright stone tablet; stele: 立一块～纪念死者 put up a tablet or erect a monument in memory of the dead

碑额 bēi'é the top part of a tablet

碑记 bēijì a record of events inscribed on a tablet

碑碣 bēijié *formal* an upright stone tablet; stele

碑林 Bēilín Forest of Steles (in Xi'an)

碑铭 bēimíng same as 碑文 bēiwén

碑帖 bēitiè a rubbing from a stone inscription (usu. as a model for calligraphy)

碑亭 bēitíng a pavilion housing a stone tablet

碑文 bēiwén an inscription on a tablet

碑阴 bēiyīn the reverse side of a stone tablet

碑志 bēizhì same as 碑记 bēijì

鹎 bēi *zool.* bulbul

běi

北[1] běi north: 城～ north of the city / ～屋 a room with a southern exposure / 往～走 go north

北[2] běi *formal* be defeated: 连战皆～ be defeated in one battle after another; suffer repeated defeats

北半球 běibànqiú the Northern Hemisphere

北边 běibiān ① north; the northern side: 加拿大在美国的～。Canada lies north of the United States of America. ② same as 北方 běifāng[2]

北冰洋 Běibīngyáng the Arctic (Ocean)

北朝 Běi Cháo the Northern Dynasties (386–581), namely, the Northern Wei Dynasty (北魏, 386–534), the Eastern Wei Dynasty (东魏, 534–550), the Western Wei Dynasty (西魏, 535–556), the Northern Qi Dynasty (北齐, 550–577) and the Northern Zhou Dynasty (北周, 557–581)

北辰 Běichén *arch.* the North Star

北大荒 Běidàhuāng the Great Northern Wilderness (in northeast China)

北大西洋公约组织 Běi Dàxīyáng Gōngyuē Zǔzhī the North Atlantic Treaty Organization (NATO)

北斗星 Běidǒuxīng the Big Dipper; the Plough

北伐军 Běifájūn the Northern Expeditionary Army

北伐战争 Běifá Zhànzhēng the Northern Expedition (1926–1927) ——see also 第一次国内革命战争 Dìyīcì Guónèi Gémìng Zhànzhēng

北方 běifāng ① north: ～刮来的风沙 sand blown from the north ② the northern part of the country, esp. the area north of the Huanghe River; the North: ～话 northern dialect / ～人 Northerner

北风 běifēng north wind

北国 běiguó liter. the northern part of the country; the North: 好一派～风光! What magnificent northern scenery!

北海 Běihǎi the North Sea

北海道 Běihǎidào Hokkaido

北寒带 běihándài the north frigid zone

北回归线 běihuíguīxiàn the Tropic of Cancer

北货 běihuò delicacies from north China (such as dried persimmons, etc.)

北极 běijí ① the North Pole; the Arctic Pole ② the north magnetic pole

北极光 běijíguāng astron. northern lights; aurora borealis

北极狐 běijíhú another name for 白狐 báihú

北极圈 běijíquān the Arctic Circle

北极星 Běijíxīng Polaris; the North Star; the polestar

北极熊 běijíxióng polar bear

北京 Běijīng Beijing (Peking)

北京时间 Běijīng shíjiān Beijing Time (the standard time in China)

北京鸭 Běijīngyā Beijing Duck

北京猿人 Běijīng yuánrén (also 北京人 Běijīngrén) archaeol. Peking Man (Sinanthropus pekinensis)

北马里亚纳 Běimǎlǐyànà the Northern Mariana Islands

北美洲 Běi Měizhōu North America

北面[1] běimiàn face north——be a subject or vassal: ～称臣 acknowledge one's allegiance as a subject or vassal ——see also 南面 nánmiàn

北面[2] běimiàn north; the northern side

北欧 Běi Ōu Northern Europe (including Denmark, Norway, Sweden, Finland and Iceland)

北齐 Běi Qí the Northern Qi Dynasty (550–577), one of the Northern Dynasties

北上 běishàng go up north

北宋 Běi Sòng the Northern Song Dynasty (960–1127)

北天极 běitiānjí astron. north pole; north celestial pole

北纬 běiwěi north (or northern) latitude

北魏 Běi Wèi the Northern Wei Dynasty (386–534), one of the Northern Dynasties

北温带 běiwēndài the north temperate zone

北洋 Běiyáng the Qing Dynasty name for the coastal provinces of Liaoning, Hebei and Shandong

北洋军阀 Běiyáng Jūnfá the Northern Warlords (1912–1927)

北岳 Běi Yuè the Northern Mountain (another name for 恒山 Mount Heng in Shanxi Province) ——see also 五岳 Wǔyuè

北周 Běi Zhōu the Northern Zhou Dynasty (557–581), one of the Northern Dynasties

bèi

贝(貝)

bèi ① shellfish ② cowrie: 虎斑～ tiger cowrie ③ (Bèi) a surname

贝雕 bèidiāo arts & crafts shell carving: ～画 shell picture; shell mosaic

贝加尔湖 Bèijiā'ěrhú Lake Baikal

贝壳 bèiké shell (of shellfish)

贝壳学 bèikéxué conchology

贝劳 Bèiláo Belau

贝类 bèilèi shellfish; molluscs

贝母 bèimǔ Chin. med. the bulb of fritillary (Fritillaria thunbergii)

贝宁 Bèiníng Benin

贝宁人 Bèiníngrén Beninian

贝丘 bèiqiū archaeol. shell mound

狈

bèi see 狼狈 lángbèi

备(備、俻)

bèi ① be equipped with; have: 各种农业机械无一不～ be equipped with all sorts of farm machinery / ～有样品。Samples are available. ② prepare; get ready: 把料～齐 get all the materials ready ③ provide (or prepare) against; take precautions against: 以～万一 prepare against all eventualities ④ equipment: 设备 shèbèi ⑤ fully; in every possible way: ～受虐待 be subjected to every kind of maltreatment / 艰苦～尝 suffer untold hardships / ～受欢迎 enjoy great popularity; be very popular

备案 bèi'àn put on record (or on file); enter (a case) in the records: 报上级党委～ report to the next higher Party committee for the record

备办 bèibàn prepare (things needed): ～酒席 (嫁妆) prepare a feast (a trousseau)

备不住 bèibuzhù dial. perhaps; possibly: ～他一会儿来。Perhaps he'll come in a little while. / 今年～又是个丰收年。This year may possibly be another good year.

备查 bèichá for future reference: 所有重要文件都要存档～。All important documents should be kept on file for reference.

备而不用 bèi ér bù yòng have sth. ready just in case; keep sth. for possible future use

备耕 bèigēng make preparations for ploughing and sowing

备荒 bèihuāng prepare against natural disasters

备件 bèijiàn spare parts

备考 bèikǎo (an appendix, note, etc.) for reference

备课 bèikè (of a teacher) prepare lessons

备料 bèiliào ① get the materials ready ② prepare feed (for livestock)

备品 bèipǐn machine parts or tools kept in reserve; spare parts

备取 bèiqǔ be on the waiting list (for admission to a school)

备忘录 bèiwànglù diplomacy memorandum; aide-mémoire ② memorandum book

备细 bèixì ① formal detailed; minute: ～地解释一番 give a detailed explanation ② old detailed information; details; particulars

备用 bèiyòng reserve; spare; alternate: ～物资 reserve goods and materials / ～轮胎 spare tyre / ～款项 reserve funds

备用航空站 bèiyòng hángkōngzhàn alternate airport

备用机器 bèiyòng jīqì standby machine

备用燃油箱 bèiyòng rányóuxiāng reserve fuel tank

备战 bèizhàn ① prepare for war: 扩军～ arms expansion and war preparations ② be prepared against war

备至 bèizhì to the utmost; in every possible way: 颂扬～ praise profusely

备置 bèizhì get (things) ready

备注 bèizhù remarks

备注栏 bèizhùlán remarks column: 可在～内附加说明。Further information can be given in the remarks column.

背[1]

bèi ① the back of the body: ～痛 backache

② the back of an object: 椅～ the back of a chair / 墨透纸～. The ink blotted on the paper.

背² bèi ① with the back towards: ～着太阳坐 sit with one's back to the sun / ～着手 with one's hands clasped behind one's back / ～山面海 with hillls behind and the sea in front ② turn away: 把脸～过去 turn one's face away ③ leave; go away: 背井离乡 bèijǐng-líxiāng ④ hide sth. from; do sth. behind sb.'s back: ～着人说话 talk behind sb.'s back / 没有什么～人的事 have nothing to hide from anyone / 这孩子～着父母抽烟。The child smoked behind his parents' backs. ⑤ recite from memory; learn by heart; learn by rote): 一台词speak one's lines / 书～熟了。I've learnt the lesson by heart. or I have the lesson off pat. ⑥ act contrary to; violate; break: ～着良心说话 talk against good conscience ⑦ out-of-the-way: ～街 back street; side street / 那地方很～. It is an out-of-the-way place. or That place is off the beaten track. ⑧ inf. unlucky: 手气～ have bad luck (at mahjong playing, etc.) ⑨ hard of hearing: 耳朵有点～ be a bit hard of hearing
——see also bēi

背榜 bèibǎng old be the last on the list of successful candidates (published after an examination)

背不住 bèibuzhù same as 备不住 bèibuzhù

背场儿 bèichǎngr inf. a quiet place

背城借一 bèi chéng jiè yī make a last-ditch stand before the city wall; fight to the last ditch; put up a desperate struggle

背褡 bèidā dial. a sleeveless garment

背道儿 bèidàor a quiet path

背道而驰 bèi dào ér chí run in the opposite direction; run counter to: 和党的方针～ in diametrical opposition to the Party's policy / 同改革的要求～ contradict the whole purpose of reforms / 和他们的愿望～ run counter to their intentions

背地里 bèidìli behind sb.'s back; privately; on the sly : 他当着面恭维你，～净使坏. He flatters you to your face while playing dirty tricks behind your back.

背风 bèifēng out of the wind; on the lee side; leeward: ～处 lee side; sheltered side

背躬 bèigōng (in traditional opera) aside: 打～ utter an aside (the actor lifting his sleeve or stepping to one side of the stage when doing so)

背光 bèiguāng be in a poor light; do sth. with one's back to the light; stand in one's own light

背后 bèihòu ① behind; at the back; in the rear: 门～ behind the door / 房子～ at the back of the house / 从～袭击敌人 attack the enemy from the rear ② behind sb.'s back: 当面不说，～乱说 say nothing to people to their faces but gossip about them behind their backs / ～搞鬼 plot (or scheme) behind the scenes; play underhand tricks / ～下毒手 stab in the back

背悔 bèihui same as 悖晦 bèihui

背货 bèihuò unfashionable and unsalable (or slow-selling) goods; a drug on the market

背脊 bèijǐ the back of the human body

背剪 bèijiǎn with one's hands clasped or tied behind one's back

背井离乡 bèijǐng-líxiāng leave one's native place (esp. against one's will); be away from home

背景 bèijǐng background; backdrop: 这幅画的～是一片森林。The painting shows the woods in the background. / 历史～ historical background (or setting) / 这个案子～复杂。This case has a complicated background. 这事肯定有～。Someone must be behind this. / 这人有～。He has powerful connections.

背静 bèijing quiet and secluded

背靠背 bèikàobèi ① back to back: ～坐着 sit back to

back ② criticize or expose sb. without his knowledge

背离 bèilí deviate from; depart from: ～奥林匹克精神 deviate from the Olympic spirit / ～社会主义的言论 views departing from socialism

背理 bèilǐ contrary to reason; unreasonable

背面 bèimiàn the back; the reverse side; the wrong side: 信封的～ the back of an envelope / 请阅～ please turn over (P.T.O.); see overleaf

背谬 bèimiù same as 悖谬 bèimiù

背叛 bèipàn betray; forsake: ～马克思主义 betray Marxism / 忘记过去就意味着～. Forgetting the past means betrayal. / ～原来的阶级 forsake one's original class; rebel against one's own class

背鳍 bèiqí zool. dorsal fin

背弃 bèiqì abandon; desert; renounce: ～原来的立场 abandon one's original stand / ～自己的诺言 go back on one's word

背时 bèishí dial. ① behind the times ② unlucky

背书¹ bèishū recite a lesson from memory; repeat a lesson

背书² bèishū econ. endorsement (on a cheque)

背水一战 bèi shuǐ yī zhàn fight with one's back to the river—fight to win or die

背诵 bèisòng recite; repeat from memory

背销 bèixiāo (of goods) slow-selling

背斜 bèixié geol. anticline: ～层 anticlinal strata

背心 bèixīn a sleeveless garment: 西服～ waistcoat / 毛～ sleeveless woollen sweater / 棉～ cotton-padded waistcoat

背信弃义 bèixìn-qìyì break faith with sb.; be perfidious: ～的行为 a breach of faith; perfidy / ～地撕毁协定和合同 perfidiously tear up agreements and contracts

背眼 bèiyǎn (of places) not easily seen: 海报不要贴在～的地方。Don't put up posters where they cannot easily be seen. / 双双对对的青年男女在公园里～的地方谈情说爱。There were pairs of young lovers billing and cooing at hidden spots in the park.

背阴 bèiyīn in the shade; shady: ～处 shady spot

背影 bèiyǐng a view of sb.'s back; a figure viewed from behind: 凝望着他逐渐消失的～ gazing at his receding figure

背约 bèiyuē break an agreement; go back on one's word; fail to keep one's promise

背运 bèiyùn ① bad luck; ill luck: 走～ go through an unlucky period ② have bad luck; be out of luck

钡 bèi chem. barium (Ba)

钡餐 bèicān med. barium meal

悖（誖） bèi formal ① be contrary to; go against: 悖理 bèilǐ ② perverse; erroneous: 悖谬 bèimiù

悖晦 bèihui dial. (usu. of old people) muddle-headed; confused: 爷爷上了年纪，行事不免有点儿～。Well on in years, Grandpa often got mixed up in doing things.

悖理 bèilǐ formal contrary to reason

悖谬 bèimiù formal absurd; preposterous

悖逆 bèinì formal disloyal; treasonable; rebellious

悖入悖出 bèirù-bèichū ill-gotten, ill-spent

被¹ bèi quilt: 做一床～ make a new quilt

被² bèi formal ① cover (with): 被覆 bèifù ② suffer: ～灾 suffer from a disaster

被³ bèi ① prep. (used in a passive sentence to introduce either the doer of the action or the action if the doer is not mentioned): 他～对手击倒。He was knocked down by his opponent. / 那棵树～大风刮倒了。The tree was uprooted by the gale. / 她～选为主席。She

was elected chairwoman. ② *part.* (used to form a set phrase with a passive meaning): ～捕 be arrested; be under arrest

被剥削阶级　bèibōxuējiējí　exploited class

被乘数　bèichéngshù　*math.*　multiplicand

被除数　bèichúshù　*math.*　dividend

被袋　bèidài　bedding bag

被单　bèidān　(also 被单子 bèidānzi) (bed) sheet

被单布　bèidānbù　sheeting

被动　bèidòng　passive: 陷入～地位 land oneself in a passive position; be thrown into passivity / 变～为主动 regain the initiative

被动式　bèidòngshì　*gram.*　passive form

被动免疫　bèidòng miǎnyì　*med.*　passive immunity

被动吸烟　bèidòng xīyān　passive smoking; secondhand smoking

被动语态　bèidòng yǔtài　*gram.*　passive voice

被服　bèifú　bedding and clothing (esp. for army use): ～厂 clothing factory

被俘　bèifú　be captured; be taken prisoner

被覆　bèifù　① cover ② plant cover; natural vegetation cover: 滥伐森林，破坏了地面～。Severe deforestation has destroyed the natural vegetation cover.

被告　bèigào　*leg.* (also 被告人 bèigàorén) defendant; the accused

被告席　bèigàoxí　defendant's seat; dock

被管制分子　bèiguǎnzhìfènzǐ　a person under the surveillance of the masses

被害人　bèihàirén　*leg.*　the injured party; the victim

被加数　bèijiāshù　*math.*　summand

被减数　bèijiǎnshù　*math.*　minuend

被里　bèilǐ　the underneath side of a quilt

被面　bèimiàn　the facing of a quilt: 绣花～ an embroidered quilt cover

被难　bèinàn　be killed in a disaster, political incident, etc.

被迫　bèipò　be compelled; be forced; be constrained: 敌人～放下武器。The enemy were compelled to lay down their arms. / ～承认错误 be forced to admit one's mistakes

被侵略者　bèiqīnlüèzhě　victim of aggression

被褥　bèirù　bedding; bedclothes

被上诉人　bèishàngsùrén　*leg.*　appellee

被套　bèitào　① bedding bag ② (bag-shaped) quilt cover; slipcover for a quilt ③ cotton wadding for a quilt

被统治者　bèitǒngzhìzhě　the ruled

被窝儿　bèiwōr　a quilt folded to form a sleeping bag

被卧　bèiwo　quilt

被选举权　bèixuǎnjǔquán　the right to be elected

被压迫民族　bèiyāpòmínzú　oppressed nation

被罩　bèizhào　(bag-shaped) quilt cover; slipcover for a quilt

被子植物　bèizǐ zhíwù　angiosperm

被子　bèizi　quilt

倍

倍　bèi　① times; -fold: 四～ four times; fourfold / 二的五～是十。Five times two is ten. / 十是五的两～。Ten is twice as much as five. / 大一～ twice as big; twice the size / 增长了五～ increase by 500%; register a 500% increase; be six times as much / 战胜了两～于我的敌人。We defeated an enemy outnumbering us two to one. / 产量成～增长。Output has doubled and redoubled. ② double; twice as much: 勇气～增 with redoubled courage

倍儿　bèir　*dial.*　awfully; terribly: ～棒。It's awfully good. *or* Great! / ～聪明 terribly clever / ～新 brand-new; up-to-the-minute

倍频器　bèipínqì　*electron.*　frequency multiplier

倍数　bèishù　*math.*　multiple

倍塔　bèitǎ　beta

倍塔粒子　bèitǎ lìzǐ　*phys.*　beta particle

倍塔射线　bèitǎ shèxiàn　*phys.*　beta ray

倍增器　bèizēngqì　*electron.*　multiplier: 光电～ photo-electric multiplier

焙

焙　bèi　bake over a slow fire: ～干 dry over a fire / ～制 cure sth. by drying it over a fire

焙烧　bèishāo　roast; bake: ～炉 roaster

辈

辈　bèi　① people of a certain kind; the like: 无能之～ people without ability ② generation: 他比我长（小）一～。He's one generation my senior (junior). / 他俩同～。They belong to the same generation. ③ lifetime: 后半～儿 the latter part of one's life

辈出　bèichū　come forth in large numbers: 英雄～的时代 an age of heroes

辈分　bèifen　(also 辈行 bèiháng) order of seniority in the family or clan; position in the family hierarchy: 她的～比我小。She ranks as my junior in the clan.

辈数儿　bèishùr　order of seniority in the family or clan; position in the family hierarchy: 他岁数小，～大。He is young in years but ranks high in family seniority (has e.g. nephews or grandnephews).

辈子　bèizi　all one's life; lifetime: 她家三～都当工人。Hers has been a working-class family for three generations.

惫(憊)

惫(憊)　bèi　exhausted; fatigued: 疲惫 píbèi

惫乏　bèifá　*formal*　tired; weary

惫倦　bèijuàn　*formal*　tired out and sleepy

惫懒　bèilǎn　tired out; exhausted

惫累　bèilèi　tired; weary

惫色　bèisè　*formal*　a tired look: 面带～ look tired

蓓

蓓　bèi　see below

蓓蕾　bèilěi　bud

褙

褙　bèi　stick one piece of cloth or paper on top of another: 裱褙 biǎobèi

鞴¹

鞴　bèi　put a saddle, etc. on a horse

鞴²

鞴　bèi　see 鞲鞴 gōubèi

鐾

鐾　bèi　grind or sharpen (a knife): ～刀 sharpen a knife

bei

唄

唄　bei　*part.* ① (indicating that sth. is obvious): 你不会骑车就学～。You can't ride a bike? Well, learn to. ② (expressing resignation): 你一定要去，就去～。Well, go if you insist.

臂

臂　bei　see 胳臂 gēbei ——see also bì

bēn

奔

奔　bēn　① run quickly: ～马 a galloping horse ② hurry; hasten; rush: ～向共产主义明天 march on towards the Communist future ③ flee: 东奔西窜 dōngbēn-xīcuàn ——see also bèn

奔波　bēnbō　rush about; be busy running about: 两地～ shuttle back and forth between two places / 为了生计，他不得不经常在外～。In order to make a living, he had

to go from place to place hunting for jobs.

奔驰 bēnchí　run quickly; speed: 骏马在草原上～。Sturdy steeds gallop on the grasslands. / 火车向前～。The train sped on.

奔窜 bēncuàn　run helter-skelter: 敌军被打得四处～。The enemy forces were routed and fled in disorder.

奔放 bēnfàng　bold and unrestrained; untrammelled: 豪爽～的性格 a forthright and uninhibited nature / ～不羁的风格 a bold and flowing style / 李白的诗潇洒～。Li Bai's poems are known for their freedom and naturalness of expression.

奔赴 bēnfù　hurry to (a place); rush to: ～前线 hurry to the front

奔雷 bēnléi　a sudden peal of thunder; thunderbolt

奔流 bēnliú　① flow at great speed; pour: ～入海 flow into the sea / 铁水～ molten iron pouring out in a stream ② racing current

奔忙 bēnmáng　be busy rushing about; bustle about: 秋收季节, 农民们一天到晚～着。During the autumn harvest, the farmers were busy working day and night. / 他似乎一天到晚～不休。He seems to be on the move all day long.

奔命 bēnmìng　rush about on errands; be kept on the run: 疲于奔命 píyú bēnmìng ——see also bēnmìng

奔跑 bēnpǎo　run: 一路～去请医生 run all the way to fetch a doctor / 母亲一喊, 孩子们都～过来。The children came running when their mother called them.

奔泉 bēnquán　gushing spring: 泪如～ tears gushing from one's eyes

奔丧 bēnsāng　hasten home for the funeral of a parent or grandparent

奔逝 bēnshì　(of time) fly past; (of waters) rush by: 岁月～。The days flew past. / ～的河水 a rushing river

奔淌 bēntǎng　(of waters) flow swiftly

奔逃 bēntáo　flee; run away: 四散～ flee in all directions; flee helter-skelter; stampede

奔腾 bēnténg　① gallop: 那马～疾驰而去。The horse galloped off at full speed. ② surge forward; roll on in waves: 浩浩长江, ～不息。The mighty waters of the Changjiang roll on incessantly. / 革命的洪流～向前。The tide of revolution is surging ahead.

奔突 bēntū　run wild; run amok

奔湍 bēntuān　① swift current ② (of waters) flow swiftly; rush by: 一股溪水～流过。A stream rushed by.

奔袭 bēnxí　*mil.* long-range raid

奔泻 bēnxiè　(of torrents) rush down; pour down: 怒涛滚滚, ～千里。An angry torrent rolls thunderously on for a thousand *li.*

奔涌 bēnyǒng　flow swiftly; pour; surge: 大江～。The great river flows swiftly. / 热泪～ tears welling up in one's eyes / 激情～ overflowing with passion

奔逐 bēnzhú　run after; chase: 孩子们在田野里～着。The children were chasing each other in the fields.

奔注 bēnzhù　(of waters) rush into

奔走 bēnzǒu　① run ② go around (in order to accomplish certain goals); rush about; be busy running about: 我父亲一生辛苦, ～于外。My father had a hard life going from place to place all the year round.

奔走呼号 bēnzǒu hūháo　go around crying for help or campaigning for a cause: ～, 为灾民募款 go around trying to raise a relief fund for the victims of the disaster

奔走相告 bēnzǒu xiānggào　run around spreading the news; lose no time in telling each other the news: 喜讯传来, 人们～。On hearing the good news, they lost no time telling everybody.

贲 bēn　see below ——see also bì

贲门 bēnmén　*physiol.* cardia

锛 bēn　① adze ② cut with an adze

锛子 bēnzi　adze

běn

本¹ běn　① the root or stem of a plant: 水有源, 木有～。A stream has its source; a tree has its roots. ② foundation; basis; origin: 兵民是胜利之～。The army and the people are the foundation of victory. ③ capital; principal: 还本 huánběn ④ principal; major; central: 本部 běnbù ⑤ *adv.* originally; at first: 我～想不去。Originally I didn't want to go. ⑥ one's own; native: ～厂 this factory ⑦ current; this; present: ～周 this week; the current week / ～决议 this resolution ⑧ be based on: 每句话都有所～。Every statement is well-founded.

本² běn　① book: 笔记本 bǐjìběn ② manuscript; copy: 抄本 chāoběn ③ script: 剧本 jùběn ④ edition; version: 普及本 pǔjíběn ⑤ *m.* (for books, parts of a serial, etc.): 两～书 two books / 这部电影有十二～。This is a twelve-reel film.

本本 běnběn　written or printed documents; books; papers

本本主义 běnběnzhǔyì　book worship; bookishness

本币 běnbì　short for 本位货币 běnwèi huòbì

本部 běnbù　headquarter: 校～ main campus

本埠 běnbù　this town or city (where one is)

本草 běncǎo　a class of traditional Chinese medical literature consisting of herbals which focus on descriptions of individual drugs

本草纲目 Běncǎo Gāngmù　*Compendium of Materia Medica* (by Li Shizhen 李时珍 1518-1593)

本朝 běncháo　the present dynasty

本初子午线 běnchū zǐwǔxiàn　the first meridian; the prime meridian

本大利宽 běndà-lìkuān　large capital and big profit——a big business

本岛 běndǎo　the island proper

本底 běndǐ　*phys.* background: 放射性～ radioactive background

本底噪声 běndǐ zàoshēng　background noise

本地 běndì　this locality: ～风光 local colour / ～口音 local accent / ～货 local (*or* native) goods / 我是～人。I'm a native of this place. *or* I was born here.

本笃会 Běndǔhuì　*Catholicism* the Benedictine Order

本分 běnfèn　① one's duty: 尽～ do one's duty (*or* bit) / 为人民服务是我们的～。To serve the people is our duty. ② honest; decent: ～人 an honest person / 他这个人很～。He never goes beyond what is proper. *or* He's a decent person.

本干 běngàn　trunk (of a tree)

本根 běngēn　origin; source

本固枝荣 běngù-zhīróng　when the root is firm, the branches flourish

本国 běnguó　one's own country: ～资源 national resources

本国语 běnguóyǔ　native language; mother tongue

本行 běnháng　one's line; one's own profession: 搞建筑是他的～。Architecture is his line.

本号 běnhào　this shop; our shop

本怀 běnhuái　original idea; real intention

本籍 běnjí　ancestral home

本纪 běnjì　basic annals (a leading section of a dynastic history, giving a dated chronological outline of events centred round an emperor): 《秦始皇～》 the

"Basic Annals of the First Emperor of Qin"(in the *Shi Ji* 《史记》)

本家 běnjiā　a member of the same clan; a distant relative with the same family name

本家儿 běnjiār　*dial.*　the person or party concerned

本届 běnjiè　current; this year's: ～联合国大会 the current session of the U. N. General Assembly / ～毕业生 this year's graduates

本金 běnjīn　capital; principal

本科 běnkē　(as distinguished from a preparatory course, a correspondence course, etc.) regular college course; undergraduate course

本科学生 běnkē xuéshēng　undergraduate

本来 běnlái　① original: ～的意思 original meaning (or intention) / 事物～的辩证法 the dialectics inherent in things ② *adv.*　originally; at first: 大会～定星期五举行。The meeting was originally fixed for Friday. / 他～身体很瘦弱。He used to be thin and weak. ③ *adv.*　it goes without saying; of course: ～ 就该这样办。Of course it should be handled that way. / 你～用不着着急。You needn't have worried about it. / 这样的事～不应该发生。Such a thing should never have been allowed to happen in the first place.

本来面目 běnlái miànmù　true colours; true features: 认清他们的～ see them in their true colours / 还其～ reveal sth. in its true colours / 恢复历史的～ restore historical truth / 按照历史的～ according to what actually occurred in history

本垒 běnlěi　*baseball softball*　home base; home plate; home; the plate

本利 běnlì　principal and interest

本领 běnlǐng　skill; ability; capability: 组织生产的～ ability to organize production / 苦练杀敌的～ train hard to increase one's combat efficiency / 掌握为人民服务的～ master the skills needed for serving the people / 他的～很大。He's very capable. / 凡是他要的东西他都有～弄到手。He is resourceful enough to get whatever he is after.

本命年 běnmìngnián　every 12th year after the year of one's birth ——see also 生肖 shēngxiào

本末 běn-mò　① the whole course of an event from beginning to end; ins ad outs: 详述～ tell the whole story from beginning to end ② the fundamental and the incidental

本末倒置 běn-mò dàozhì　take the branch for the root; put the incidental before the fundamental: 强调方法而忽视内容是～。To put emphasis on method at the expense of content is to put the cart before the horse.

本能 běnnéng　instinct: 出于～ by instinct / 大多数动物都有保护幼仔的～。Most animals have an instinct to protect their young.

本年度 běnniándù　this year; the current year: ～计划 this year's plan / ～国家预算 the national budget for this fiscal year

本票 běnpiào　cashier's cheque

本钱 běnqián　① capital: 没～做生意 have no capital to start a business ② what is capitalized on; sth. used to one's own advantage

本人 běnrén　① I (me, myself): ～认为 in my opinion ② oneself; in person: 我想见政委～。I'd like to see the commissar himself. / 必须你～来。You must come in person.

本色 běnsè　true (or inherent) qualities; distinctive character: 劳动人民的～ the true qualities of the labouring people

本色 běnshǎi　natural colour

本色布 běnshǎibù　unbleached and undyed cloth; grey cloth

本身 běnshēn　itself; in itself: 院子里杂草丛生, 但房子～完好无损。The yard is full of weeds, but the house itself is in good condition. / 广交会～标志着我国对外贸易的发展。The Guangzhou Trade Fair is in itself a symbol of the growth of China's foreign trade. / 条约～ the treaty *per se*

本生 běnshēng　an adopted child's own parents

本生灯 běnshēngdēng　Bunsen burner

本事 běnshì　source material; original story: 这些诗词的～, 年久失考。The original story these poems were based on has long been lost. / 电影～ synopsis of a film

本事 běnshi　same as 本领 běnlǐng

本题 běntí　the subject under discussion; the point at issue: 请不要离开～。Please keep (or stick) to the point. / 这跟～无关。This has nothing to do with the point at issue. or This is quite irrelevant.

本体 běntǐ　① *philos.*　noumenon; thing-in-itself ② main part of a machine or a project

本体论 běntǐlùn　*philos.*　ontology

本土 běntǔ　① one's native country (or land) ② metropolitan territory

本位 běnwèi　① *econ.*　standard: 金本位 jīnběnwèi ② one's own department or unit: ～工作 the work of one's own department; one's own job (or work)

本位号 běnwèihào　*mus.*　natural (♮)

本位货币 běnwèi huòbì　the basic monetary unit of a country's currency (e.g. *yuan* of China, dollar of the U. S.)

本位主义 běnwèizhǔyì　selfish departmentalism; departmental selfishness

本文 běnwén　① this text, article, etc.: ～谈的是我国经济方面的一些问题。This article deals with certain problems in our national economy. ② the original text; the original

本息 běnxī　principal (or capital) and interest

本乡本土 běnxiāng-běntǔ　native soil; native land; home village: 大家都是～的, 有话好说嘛。As we're all natives of this village, no problems are too difficult to settle among us.

本相 běnxiàng　true colours; true features: ～毕露 show one's true colours; be revealed for what one is

本小利微 běnxiǎo-lìwēi　small capital and little gain—a small business: 我们～, 实在周转不过来。Ours is a very small business, and we just don't have enough cash to carry on.

本心 běnxīn　original intention; true intention

本性 běnxìng　natural instincts (or character, disposition); nature; inherent quality: ～好战 be belligerent by nature

本性难移 běnxìng nán yí　it is hard to change one's nature; the leopard can't change his spots ——see also 江山易改, 本性难移 jiāngshān yì gǎi, běnxìng nán yí

本义 běnyì　original meaning; literal sense: "兵"字的～是武器。The original meaning of "兵" is weapon. / 这个词不能按～去理解。This word should not be taken in its literal sense.

本意 běnyì　original idea; real intention: 我看这不是她的～。I don't think that is her real intention. / 他～是好的, 只是说话方式不好。He meant well, though he said it in an inappropriate way.

本影 běnyǐng　*phys.*　umbra

本源 běnyuán　origin; source

本着 běnzhe　*prep.*　in line with; in conformity with; in the light of: ～我们一贯的立场 in line with our consistent stand / ～为人民服务的精神 motivated by a desire to serve the people / ～增进两国之间友好关系的愿望 actuated by a desire to promote friendly relations between our two countries / ～平等互利、互通有无的原则 adhering to the principles of equality, mutual benefit

and helping to meet each other's needs／办一切事业都要～节约的原则。In running all enterprises we should observe the principle of frugality.

本职 běnzhí one's job (*or* duty): 做好～工作 do one's own job well

本旨 běnzhǐ ① original intention ② main purpose

本质 běnzhì essence; nature; innate character; intrinsic quality: ～方面 an essential aspect／非～方面 a nonessential aspect／～差别 an essential distinction／透过现象看～ see through the appearance to the essence

本州 Běnzhōu Honshu

本主儿 běnzhǔr ① the person concerned: ～一会儿就来, 你问他得了。The man concerned will be here soon, so you'd better ask him.／你应该向～了解情况。You should ask for information from the party concerned. ② the owner of a lost article: 这辆招领的自行车, ～还没来取。The owner of this bicycle has not yet come to claim it.

本子 běnzi ① book; notebook: 改～ go over students' written exercises; correct papers ② edition: 这两个～都是宋本。Both of these are Song Dynasty block-printed editions.

本族语 běnzúyǔ native language; mother tongue

苯 běn *chem.* benzene; benzol: ～中毒 benzene poisoning; benzolism

苯胺 běn'àn *chem.* aniline

苯胺革 běn'àngé aniline leather

苯胺染料 běn'àn rǎnliào aniline dyes

苯胺印刷 běn'àn yìnshuā aniline printing; flexography

苯胺紫 běn'ànzǐ mauve

苯巴比妥 běnbābǐtuǒ *pharm.* phenobarbital; phenobarbitone; luminal

苯酚 běnfēn *chem.* phenol

苯海拉明 běnhǎilāmíng *pharm.* diphenhydramine; benadryl

苯甲酸 běnjiǎsuān *chem.* benzoic acid

苯妥英纳 běntuǒyīngnà *pharm.* phenytoin sodium; dilantin

苯乙烯 běnyǐxī *chem.* styrene

畚 běn ① a bamboo or wicker scoop ② *dial.* scoop up with a dustpan

畚箕 běnjī *dial.* ① a bamboo or wicker scoop ② dustpan

bèn

坌[1] bèn *dial.* dig: ～地 dig the ground

坌[2] (坋) bèn *formal* dust

坌[3] bèn *formal* ① gather; bring together: ～集 gather together ② of poor quality

奔 (逩) bèn ① go straight towards; head for: 直～实验室 head straight for the laboratory／这条路～天津。This road goes (*or* leads) to Tianjin.／咱们是一心～现代化。Our minds are set on the goal of modernization. ② approach; be getting on for: 他是～六十的人了。He's getting on for sixty. ③ *prep.* towards: 汽车～广场驶去。The car sped by towards the square. ④ busy oneself about: 给厂里～材料 busy oneself procuring raw materials for the factory ——see also bēn

奔命 bènmìng *inf.* be in a desperate hurry ——see also bēnmìng

奔头儿 bèntour sth. to strive for; prospect: 大有～ have a bright prospect

笨 bèn ① stupid; dull; foolish: ～人 a stupid person; fool／脑子～ stupid; slow-witted ② clumsy; awkward: 我的手太～, 干不了这活。I'm all thumbs and no good for this. ③ cumbersome; awkward; unwieldy: 这把锄头太～。This is an awkward hoe.／这大柜子太～了。This cabinet is too large and clumsy.

笨笨磕磕 bènbenkēkē speak slowly and indistinctly; be inarticulate: 他一着急, 说话就～的。He becomes inarticulate when he is anxious.

笨伯 bènbó *formal* a stupid person

笨蛋 bèndàn *offens.* fool; idiot: 真是个大～! What a fool!

笨活儿 bènhuór *inf.* heavy manual labour

笨货 bènhuò *offens.* fool; idiot

笨口拙舌 bènkǒu-zhuōshé awkward in speech; slow of speech; inarticulate

笨鸟先飞 bèn niǎo xiān fēi clumsy birds have to start flying early—the slow need to start early (usu. said self-depreciatingly)

笨手笨脚 bènshǒu-bènjiǎo clumsy; awkward: 他这人～。He is clumsy. *or* His fingers are all thumbs.

笨重 bènzhòng heavy; cumbersome; unwieldy: ～的家具 heavy (*or* cumbersome) furniture／通过技术革新, 我们车间摆脱了～的体力劳动。Through technical innovations, our workshop has got rid of heavy manual labour.

笨拙 bènzhuō clumsy; awkward; stupid: 动作～ clumsy (*or* awkward) in movement／～的伎俩 stupid tricks

bēng

崩 bēng ① collapse: 山崩 shānbēng ② burst: 把气球吹～了 burst a balloon／他们谈～了。Their negotiations broke down. ③ (of sth. bursting) hit sb. or sth.: 爆竹～了他的手。The firecracker went off in his hand. ④ *inf.* execute by shooting; shoot ⑤ (of an emperor) die: 驾崩 jiàbēng

崩解 bēngjiě disintegrate; collapse; crumble

崩决 bēngjué (of a dyke, etc.) burst

崩溃 bēngkuì collapse; crumble; fall apart: 敌军全线～。The enemy collapsed all along the line.／殖民主义的～ the collapse of colonialism

崩裂 bēngliè burst (*or* break) apart; crack: 炸药轰隆一声, 山石～。Boom! The dynamite sent the rocks flying.

崩龙族 Bēnglóngzú old name for 德昂族 Dé'ángzú

崩漏 bēnglòu *Chin. med.* uterine bleeding

崩塌 bēngtā collapse; crumble

崩陷 bēngxiàn fall in; cave in

崩症 bēngzhèng *Chin. med.* metrorrhagia

绷[1] (繃) bēng ① stretch (*or* draw) tight: 在绷子上～一块绸子 stretch a piece of silk on an embroidery frame／弓弦一定要～紧。The bowstring must be drawn tight. ② spring; bounce: 盒子一打开, 弹簧就～出来了。When the box was opened, the spring jumped out. ③ baste; tack; pin: ～着金字的横幅红布 a red cloth streamer with golden papercut characters pinned on it ④ *dial.* manage to do sth. with difficulty: ～场面 keep up appearances

绷[2] (繃) bēng *dial.* swindle; cheat sb. out of money: 坑～拐骗 resort to all sorts of deception ——see also běng; bèng

绷带 bēngdài bandage

绷簧 bēnghuáng *dial.* spring

绷子　bēngzi　embroidery frame; hoop; tambour

嘣

嘣　bēng　*onom.*　the sound of palpitations or explosions: 我心里～～直跳。My heart is thumping. / 爆竹～地一响。The firecracker went bang.

嘣豆儿　bēngdòur　*dial.*　roasted broad bean

béng

甭

甭　béng　*dial.*　don't; needn't: ～再说了。Don't say any more. / 有这样好的徒工，老师傅～提有多高兴了。Needless to say, the old master worker was happy to have such good apprentices. / 你～管! None of your business! / 您～管了。Don't bother. Leave it to me.

běng

绷（繃）

绷　běng　*inf.*　① look serious: ～着脸 look displeased; pull a long face ② strain oneself: 咬住牙～住劲 clench one's teeth and strain one's muscles ——see also bēng; bèng

bèng

迸

迸　bèng　spout; spurt; burst forth: 火星乱～ sparks flying in all directions / 他怎么突然～出这句话来? What made him blurt out such a remark?

迸脆　bèngcuì　① (of biscuits, etc.) crisp ② (of voice) clear and sharp; crisp

迸发　bèngfā　burst forth; burst out: 锤子打在岩石上,～了好些火星儿。Sparks flew out as the sledge hammer hit the rock. / 大厅里～出一阵笑声。There was an outburst of laughter in the hall. / 热烈的掌声,有如春雷~。Applause broke out like spring thunder.

迸飞　bèngfēi　fly in all directions

迸裂　bèngliè　split; burst (open): 脑浆～ have one's brains dashed out

迸流　bèngliú　gush; pour; spurt: 伤口鲜血～。Blood poured (*or* spurt) from the wound.

迸射　bèngshè　strafe

泵

泵　bèng　pump: 高扬程～ high lift pump

泵房　bèngfáng　pump house

泵排量　bèngpáiliàng　pumpage; pump delivery

蚌

蚌　Bèng　short for 蚌埠 (city in Anhui Province) ——see also bàng

绷（繃）

绷　bèng　① split open; crack: 玻璃～了一条缝儿。The glass has a crack in it. ② *inf.* (used before certain adjectives) very: ～脆 very crisp / ～硬 hard as a rock; stiff as a board / ～直 exceptionally straight / ～亮 shining bright ——see also bēng; běng

绷瓷　bèngcí　crackled glaze

镚

镚　bèng　see below

镚儿　bèngr　(also 镚子 bèngzi) *inf.*　small coin: 镚子儿不值 not worth a penny; worthless

甏

甏　bèng　*dial.*　an earthen jar

蹦

蹦　bèng　leap; jump; spring: 他使劲一～就过了沟。With one powerful leap he crossed the ditch. / 这件事

还没处理完,那件事又～出来了。One problem had scarcely been solved when another cropped up.

蹦蹦儿戏　bèngbèngrxì　old name for 评剧 píngjù

蹦蹦跳跳　bèngbèngtiàotiào　bouncing and vivacious: 孩子们～地进了教室。The children bounced into the classroom.

蹦达　bèngda　jump about (in a desperate struggle)

bī

屄（屄）

屄　bī　vaginal orifice

逼（偪）

逼　bī　① force; compel; press: ～对方取守势 force one's opponent onto the defensive / ～某人招供 try to force sb. to talk / 他拿枪～着她交出钱来。He forced her at gun point to give him her money. ② press for; extort: 逼债 bīzhài ③ press on towards; press up to; close in on: 直～城下 press up to the city wall ④ *formal*　narrow: 逼仄 bīzè

逼宫　bīgōng　(of ministers, etc.) force the king or emperor to abdicate

逼供　bīgòng　extort a confession: 严刑～ extort a confession by cruel torture

逼供信　bī-gòng-xìn　obtain confessions by compulsion and give them credence: 要重证据,重调查研究,严禁～。Stress should be laid on the weight of evidence and on investigation and study, and it is strictly forbidden to obtain confessions by compulsion and to give them credence.

逼和　bīhé　(in chess, etc.) force a draw

逼近　bījìn　press on towards; close in on; approach; draw near: 我军已～运河。Our troops were pressing on towards the canal. / ～敌主力 close in on the main force of the enemy / 天色已经～黄昏。Dusk is closing in.

逼勒　bīlè　force; coerce

逼命　bīmìng　press (*or* push) hard

逼迫　bīpò　force; compel; coerce: 他们～他辞职。They forced him to resign.

逼人　bīrén　pressing; threatening: 形势～。The situation spurs us on. / 寒气～。There is a cold nip in the air.

逼人太甚　bī rén tài shèn　press (*or* push) people too hard

逼上梁山　bī shàng Liángshān　be driven to join the Liangshan rebels (a band of peasant rebels of the Song Dynasty, who had their stronghold on Liangshan Mountain)—be driven to revolt

逼视　bīshì　look at from close-up; watch intently: 光采夺目,不可～。At close range the glare dazzles one's eyes.

逼死　bīsǐ　hound sb. to death

逼问　bīwèn　① force sb. to answer ② question closely

逼肖　bīxiào　*formal*　bear a close resemblance to; be the very image of

逼仄　bīzè　*formal*　narrow; cramped

逼窄　bīzhǎi　narrow; cramped

逼债　bīzhài　press for payment of debts; dun

逼真　bīzhēn　① lifelike; true to life: 这幅湘竹画得十分～。This painting of mottled bamboos is really true to life. ② distinctly; clearly: 听得～ hear distinctly / 看得～ have a clear view of sth.

逼真度　bīzhēndù　*electron.*　fidelity

逼租　bīzū　press for payment of (land) rent

bí

荸　bí　see below

荸荠　bí·qí　water chestnut (*Eleocharis tuberosa*), the plant or its tuber

鼻

鼻　bí　① nose ② *formal*　start; initiate: 鼻祖 bízǔ

鼻儿　bír　① a hole in an implement, utensil, etc., for sth. to be inserted into; eye: 门鼻儿 ménbír ② *dial.* whistle: 火车拉～了。The engine is whistling.

鼻翅儿　bíchìr　common name for 鼻翼 bíyì

鼻窦　bídòu　common name for 鼻旁窦 bípángdòu

鼻窦炎　bídòuyán　nasosinusitis

鼻观　bíguàn　*formal*　nostril

鼻化元音　bíhuàyuányīn　*phonet.*　nasalized vowel

鼻甲　bíjiǎ　concha

鼻尖　bíjiān　(also 鼻子尖儿 bízijiānr) tip of the nose

鼻镜　bíjìng　*med.*　rhinoscope: 电光～ nasoscope

鼻疽　bíjū　same as 马鼻疽 mǎbíjū

鼻孔　bíkǒng　nostril

鼻梁儿　bíliángr　bridge of the nose

鼻牛儿　bíniúr　*dial.*　hardened mucus in nostrils

鼻衄　bínǜ　*med.*　nosebleed; epistaxis

鼻旁窦　bípángdòu　*physiol.*　paranasal sinus

鼻腔　bíqiāng　*physiol.*　nasal cavity

鼻青脸肿　bíqīng-liǎnzhǒng　a bloody nose and a swollen face; badly battered: 被打得～ have one's face bashed in; be beaten black and blue

鼻塞　bísè　have a stuffy nose

鼻饲　bísì　*med.*　nasal feeding

鼻涕　bítì　nasal mucus; snivel: 流～ have a running nose

鼻涕虫　bítìchóng　popular name for 蛞蝓 kuòyú

鼻头　bítou　*dial.*　nose

鼻息　bíxī　breath: 听见均匀的～声 hear sb.'s regular and even breathing

鼻烟　bíyān　snuff

鼻烟盒　bíyānhé　snuffbox

鼻烟壶　bíyānhú　snuff bottle

鼻炎　bíyán　*med.*　rhinitis

鼻翼　bíyì　the alae of the nose

鼻音　bíyīn　*phonet.*　nasal sound: 说话带～ speak with a twang／～化 nasalize

鼻渊　bíyuān　*Chin. med.*　nasosinusitis

鼻韵母　bíyùnmǔ　*phonet.*　(in Chinese pronunciation) a vowel followed by a nasal consonant (e.g. an, ian, en, in, un, ang, ing, ong, etc.)

鼻针疗法　bízhēn liáofǎ　*Chin. med.*　nose-acupuncture therapy

鼻中隔　bízhōnggé　*physiol.*　nasal septum

鼻子　bízi　nose: 高～ high-bridged nose; high nose／塌～ snub nose; pug nose／不要只顾～底下的小事。Don't get bogged down in trivial matters.——see also 哭鼻子 kūbízi; 牵鼻子 qiān bízi; 有鼻子有眼儿 yǒubízi-yǒuyǎnr

鼻子眼儿　bíziyǎnr　*inf.*　nostril

鼻祖　bízǔ　*formal*　the earliest ancestor; originator (of a tradition, school of thought, etc.)

bǐ

匕　bǐ　an ancient type of spoon

匕鬯不惊　bǐ-chàng bù jīng　strict military discipline

匕首　bǐshǒu　dagger

比¹

比¹　bǐ　① compare; contrast: ～得上 can compare with; compare favourably with／想想过去，～～现在 recall the past and contrast it with the present ② emulate; compete; match: 学先进，～先进 emulate the advanced／这家旅馆的服务质量谁也～不上。This hotel can't be matched for its good service.／咱俩～一～，看谁高。Let's stand back to back and see who is taller. ③ gesture; gesticulate: 连说带～ gesticulate as one talks ④ *dial.*　aim at; direct towards: 警察用枪～着罪犯。The policeman pointed his gun at the criminal. ⑤ copy; model after: ～着旧衣裁新衣 pattern a new garment on an old one／用尺～着画。Use a ruler when drawing this. ⑥ draw an analogy; liken to; compare to: 我们这小小的公司可以～作一个大家庭。Our little company can be likened to a big family. ⑦ ratio; proportion: 这里小麦同水稻的年产量约为一与三之～。Here the annual yield of wheat and rice is in a ratio of about one to three. ⑧ to (in a score): 甲队以二～一胜乙队。Team A beat team B (by a score of) two to one.／现在几～几? What's the score? ⑨ *prep.*　than: 许多同志都～我干得好。Many comrades have done better than I.／他吃的～平常少。He's eating less than usual.／我～你早来一个钟头。I came an hour earlier than you did.／人民的生活一年～一年好。The life of the people is getting better and better each year.

比²

比²　bǐ　*formal*　① close together; next to: 比肩 bǐjiān ② cling to; collude with: 朋比为奸 péngbǐ wéi jiān ③ lately: 比来 bǐlái

比比皆是　bǐbǐ jiē shì　can be found everywhere; such is the case everywhere: 好人好事，～。Good people and good deeds can be found everywhere.

比方　bǐfang　① analogy; instance: 打～ draw an analogy／拿盖房子作～ take for instance the building of a house／这不过是个～。This is only by way of analogy. ② suppose: 听说他待人热情，～我求他帮个忙，他不会拒绝吧?I hear he's very warm-hearted, so I don't suppose he would refuse me help if I ask him. ③ same as 比如 bǐrú

比分　bǐfēn　*sports*　score: 场上～是三比二。The score is 3 to 2.／离比赛结束只剩十秒钟时，两队～是82比81。The score stood at 82 to 81 with 10 seconds left in the game.／双方～十分接近。It's a close game.

比附　bǐfù　*formal*　make a farfetched comparison

比号　bǐhào　colon (used between numbers in a proportion) (∶)

比葫芦画瓢　bǐ húlu huà piáo　same as 照葫芦画瓢 zhào húlu huà piáo

比画　bǐhua　(also 比划 bǐhua) gesture; gesticulate: 他～着讲。He made himself understood with the help of gestures.

比及　bǐjí　*formal*　when; by the time

比价　bǐjià　① price relations; parity; rate of exchange: 工农业产品～ the price parities between industrial and agricultural products／英镑和美元的～ the rate of exchange between the pound sterling and the U.S. dollar／粮棉～ the price ratios between grain and cotton ② compare bids or prices

比肩　bǐjiān　*formal*　shoulder to shoulder: ～作战 fight shoulder to shoulder

比肩继踵　bǐjiān-jìzhǒng　same as 摩肩接踵 mójiān-jiēzhǒng

比较　bǐjiào　① compare; contrast: 有～才能鉴别。Only by comparing can one distinguish the difference.／把译文和原文～一下 check the translation against the original／真理是跟谬误相～，并且同它作斗争发展起来的。Truth stands in contrast to falsehood and develops in struggle with it. ② *prep.*　(used to compare a difference

in degree): ～去年有显著的增长 show a marked increase over last year ③ *adv.* fairly; comparatively; relatively; quite; rather: ～快 relatively fast / 两个都可以, 不过这个～好一点儿。Either will do, but this one is a bit better. / 这里条件～艰苦。Conditions are rather tough here.

比较级 bǐjiàojí *gram.* comparative degree

比较价格 bǐjiào jiàgé another name for 不变价格 bùbiàn jiàgé

比较文学 bǐjiào wénxué comparative literature

比来 bǐlái *formal* recently; of late

比利时 Bǐlìshí Belgium

比利时人 Bǐlìshírén Belgian

比例 bǐlì ① proportion: 不合～ out of proportion / 按～发展 develop in proportion; proportionate development / 安排积累和消费的适当～ establish a proper ratio between accumulation and consumption ② scale: 按～绘制 be drawn to scale / 这个模型是按准确的～做的。This model is made exactly to scale.

比例尺 bǐlìchǐ ① *surveying & drawing* scale: 这张地图的～是四十万分之一。The scale of the map is 1:400,000. ② architect's scale; engineer's scale

比例税 bǐlìshuì *econ.* proportional tax

比量 bǐliang ① take rough measurements (with the hand, a stick, string, etc.) ② make gestures

比邻 bǐlín ① neighbour; next-door neighbour ② near; next to: 跟车站～的那个工厂 the factory next to the railway station

比邻星 bǐlínxīng *astron.* the self-luminous star nearest to the sun

比率 bǐlǜ ratio; rate

比美 bǐměi compare favourably with; rival

比目鱼 bǐmùyú flatfish; flounder

比拟 bǐnǐ ① compare; draw a parallel; match: 难以～ beyond compare ② analogy; metaphor

比年 bǐnián (also 比岁 bǐsuì) *formal* ① recent years; the past few years ② every year

比配 bǐpèi be equally matched; match well

比丘 bǐqiū *Buddhism* monk

比丘尼 bǐqiūní *Buddhism* nun

比热 bǐrè *phys.* specific heat

比容 bǐróng *phys.* specific volume

比如 bǐrú for example; for instance; such as

比赛 bǐsài match; competition: 足球～ football match / 自行车～ bicycle race / 射击～ shooting contest / 象棋～ chess tournament / ～规则 rules of a game; rules of a contest

比赛项目 bǐsài xiàngmù event

比色分析 bǐsè fēnxi *chem.* colorimetric analysis

比色计 bǐsèjì *chem.* colorimeter

比上不足, 比下有余 bǐ shàng bùzú, bǐ xià yǒuyú not up to those above, but above those below—middling; passable; tolerable

比湿 bǐshī *meterol.* specific humidity

比试 bǐshi ① have a competition: 不信咱俩～～。If you don't believe me, let's have a competition and see. ② make gestures: 两个小演员拿长枪一～, 就开始对打起来。With a flourish of their spears, the two little performers started sparring with each other.

比手画脚 bǐshǒu-huàjiǎo (make oneself understood) with the help of gestures

比索 bǐsuǒ peso

比特 bǐtè *computer* bit (a transliteration)

比武 bǐwǔ take part in a *wushu* contest

比学赶帮超 bǐ-xué-gǎn-bāng-chāo emulate, learn from, catch up with, help and in turn surpass each other

比翼 bǐyì fly wing to wing: ～齐飞 pair off wing to wing; fly side by side

比翼鸟 bǐyìniǎo fabulous birds that had only one wing each and thus had to fly in pairs (used in poetry as an epithet for a loving couple): 在天愿作～, 在地愿为连理枝。(白居易) We wish to fly in heaven, two birds with the wings of one, And to grow together on earth, two branches of one tree.

比喻 bǐyù metaphor; analogy; figure of speech: 这只是一个～的说法。This is just a figure of speech. / 人们常用青松来～坚贞不屈的革命者。Steadfast revolutionaries are often likened to pine trees.

比喻义 bǐyùyì metaphorical meaning

比照 bǐzhào ① according to; in the light of: 我们可以～其它厂的做法拟定计划。We can draw up our plan in the light of the experience of other factories. / ～着实物绘图 draw with an object as a model ② contrast: 两相～ contrasting the two

比值 bǐzhí ratio; rate

比重 bǐzhòng ① *phys.* specific gravity ② proportion: 工业在整个国民经济中的～ the proportion of industry in the national economy as a whole / 农业～大的省 predominantly agricultural provinces

比重计 bǐzhòngjì hydrometer

比重选种 bǐzhòng xuǎnzhòng *agric.* specific gravity selection (of seeds)

吡 bǐ see below

吡啶 bǐdìng *chem.* pyridine

吡咯 bǐluò *chem.* pyrrole

姒 bǐ *formal* one's deceased mother: 先姒 xiānbǐ

彼 bǐ ① that; those; the other; another: ～时 at that time ② the other party: 要知己知～。You must know both your opponent and yourself.

彼岸 bǐ'àn ① *Buddhism* Faramita ② the other side or bank of a river; the opposite shore: 太平洋的～ the opposite shore of the Pacific

彼此 bǐcǐ ① each other; one another: ～呼应 support each other; act in coordination with each other / ～之间无话不谈 be so intimate as to keep no secrets from each other ② *pol.* (used in reduplication as a reply) me too or you too: 您辛苦啦!—～～! You must have taken a lot of trouble. —So must you!

彼一时, 此一时 bǐ yīshí, cǐ yīshí that was one situation, and this is another; times have changed: ～, 不要拿老眼光看新事物。Times have changed, you know, so don't judge new things by old standards.

秕(粃) bǐ (of grain) not plump; blighted: ～粒 blighted seeds

秕糠 bǐkāng ① chaff ② worthless stuff

秕子 bǐzi blighted grain

笔(筆) bǐ ① pen, pencil or writing brush: 一枝～ a pen or pencil / 一管～ a writing or painting brush ② technique of writing, calligraphy or drawing: 文笔 wénbǐ ③ write: ～之于书 put down in black and white ④ stroke; touch: "天"字有四～。The character 天 has four strokes. / 这里再添几～, 情节就更生动了。Add a few touches here and the episode will be more lively. / 你给他写信时, 替我带一～。Please remember me to him when you write. ⑤ *m.* ⓐ (for sums of money, financial accounts, debts, etc.): 一～钱 a sum of money; a fund / 我们有三～帐要算。We have three scores to settle. ⓑ (for skill in calligraphy or painting): 写得一～好字 write a good hand / 能画几～山水画 be a landscape painter of sorts

笔触 bǐchù brush stroke in Chinese painting or calligraphy; brushwork; style of drawing or writing: 简洁

的～ simple, light touches; a succinct style / 他以锋利的～揭露社会的阴暗面。He wrote with a caustic pen exposing the dark side of society.

笔床 bǐchuáng same as 笔架 bǐjià

笔答 bǐdá answer questions in writing

笔胆 bǐdǎn (also 笔囊 bǐnáng) barrel (in a fountain pen)

笔刀 bǐdāo graver (for engraving characters on a seal, etc.); burin

笔道儿 bǐdàor strokes of a Chinese character

笔底生花 bǐ dǐ shēng huā flowers blooming under the brush—brilliant writing

笔底下 bǐdǐxia ability to write: ～不错 write well / ～来得快 write with ease (or facility)

笔调 bǐdiào (of writing) tone; style: 讽刺的～ a satirical tone / 他用通俗的～写了许多科学读物。He wrote many books on science in a popular style.

笔陡 bǐdǒu precipitous

笔端 bǐduān *formal* tip of the brush—style of writing or painting: ～妙趣横生 write in a witty and pleasing style

笔伐 bǐfá condemn or denounce in writing ——see also 口诛笔伐 kǒuzhū-bǐfá

笔法 bǐfǎ technique of writing, calligraphy or drawing

笔锋 bǐfēng ① the tip of a writing brush ② vigour of style in writing; stroke; touch: ～犀利 write in an incisive style; wield a pointed pen

笔杆子 bǐgānzi (also 笔杆儿 bǐgǎnr) ① the shaft of a pen or writing brush; penholder ② pen: 耍～ wield the pen ③ a facile writer; a literary spokesman: 他是编辑部的～。He is the most effective writer of the editorial department.

笔耕 bǐgēng live by one's pen

笔供 bǐgòng a written confession

笔管 bǐguǎn the shaft of a writing brush

笔管条直 bǐguǎntiáozhí *inf.* stand erect (or upright)

笔画 bǐhuà strokes of a Chinese character

笔会 Bǐhuì PEN (the International Association of Poets, Playwrights, Editors, Essayists, and Novelists)

笔记 bǐjì ① take down (in writing) ② notes: 记～ take notes ③ pen jottings (a type of literature consisting mainly of short sketches): 《阅微草堂～》 *Jottings from the Thatched Abode of Close Observations*

笔记本 bǐjìběn notebook

笔记小说 bǐjì xiǎoshuō literary sketches; sketchbook

笔迹 bǐjì a person's handwriting; hand: 对～ identify sb.'s handwriting / ～潦草难以辨认 an illegible scribble

笔架 bǐjià pen rack; penholder

笔尖 bǐjiān ① nib; pen point ② the tip of a writing brush or pencil

笔据 bǐjù a written pledge

笔力 bǐlì vigour of strokes in calligraphy or drawing; vigour of style in literary composition: ～雄健 powerful strokes / 这篇文章没有表现出作者平素的～。This essay lacks the vigour and vitality which characterize the author's usual style.

笔立 bǐlì stand erect (or upright)

笔录 bǐlù ① put down (in writing); take down ② notes; record

笔路 bǐlù ① same as 笔法 bǐfǎ ② one's train of thought in the process of writing

笔帽 bǐmào the cap of a pen, pencil or writing brush

笔名 bǐmíng pen name; pseudonym

笔墨 bǐmò pen and ink; words; writing: 我们激动的心情难以用～来形容。Words can hardly describe how excited we were. / 把无关紧要的话删去, 不要浪费～。To save space leave out superfluous words and sentences.

笔墨官司 bǐmò guānsi written polemics (or controversy); a battle of words

笔铅 bǐqiān pencil lead

笔峭 bǐqiào precipitous

笔石 bǐshí graptolite

笔试 bǐshì written examination

笔势 bǐshì ① style of brushwork ② vigour of literary style

笔受 bǐshòu *formal* take down what is dictated

笔顺 bǐshùn order of strokes observed in calligraphy

笔算 bǐsuàn ① do a sum in writing ② written calculation

笔谈 bǐtán ① conversation by writing ② comment in writing; give a written statement ③ pen conversations (often used in book titles): 《梦溪～》 *Dream Pool Essays*

笔套 bǐtào ① the cap of a pen, pencil or writing brush ② the sheath of a pen (made of cloth, silk or thread)

笔挺 bǐtǐng ① (standing) very straight; straight as a ramrod; bolt upright: 战士们～地站着, 听候发令。The soldiers stood at attention, waiting for orders. ② well-ironed; trim: 穿着一身～的制服 be dressed in a trim uniform

笔筒 bǐtǒng pen container; brush pot

笔头儿 bǐtóur ① same as 笔尖 bǐjiān ② ability to write; writing skill: 你～快, 你写吧。You're good at writing. You do it. ③ written; in written form: ～练习 written exercises

笔误 bǐwù ① make a slip in writing ② a slip of the pen

笔洗 bǐxǐ a writing-brush washer

笔下 bǐxià ① same as 笔底下 bǐdǐxia ② the wording and purport of what one writes: 刘鹗～的济南城, 是家家泉水, 户户垂杨, 比那江南风景, 更为有趣。The city of Jinan, as described by Liu E, had flowing streams by every house and willow trees by every door, which delighted one even more than the scenery of the South.

笔下超生 bǐxià chāoshēng (of a judge) spare a life by a stroke of the brush; refrain from passing a death sentence

笔下留情 bǐxià liúqíng be charitable in writing critical comments: 对于反动派, 鲁迅是从来不讲什么～的。In his writings, Lu Xun was never sparing in his criticism of the reactionaries.

笔心 bǐxīn (also 笔芯 bǐxīn) ① pencil lead ② refill (for a ball-point pen)

笔形 bǐxíng the form of a stroke or a combination of strokes (in Chinese characters)

笔削 bǐxuē *pol.* please correct or improve my writing

笔译 bǐyì written translation

笔意 bǐyì artistic conception revealed in the work of a calligrapher, painter, or writer

笔友 bǐyǒu pen friend; pen pal

笔札 bǐzhá ① stationery; writing materials ② writings

笔债 bǐzhài a commissioned contribution (to a magazine, newspaper, etc.)

笔战 bǐzhàn written polemics

笔者 bǐzhě the present writer; the author

笔直 bǐzhí perfectly straight; straight as a ramrod; bolt upright: ～的马路 straight avenues / ～走 go straight on (or ahead) / 身子挺得～ stand straight as a ramrod; draw oneself up to one's full height

笔资 bǐzī *old* fees for writing

笔走龙蛇 bǐ zǒu lóng-shé dragons and snakes following the writing brush—a vigorous calligraphic style

俾 bǐ *formal* in order to; so that: 对该项工程应予大力支持, ～能按期完成。We should give this project every support so that it may be completed on schedule.

俾众周知 bǐ zhòng zhōuzhī for the information of all; so

as to make it known to everyone

鄙

bǐ ① low; mean; vulgar: 粗鄙 cūbǐ ② *hum.* my: ～意 my humble opinion; my idea ③ *formal* despise; disdain; scorn: 可～ despicable ④ *formal* an out-of-the-way place: 边鄙 biānbǐ

鄙薄 bǐbó *formal* despise; scorn: 不应～技术工作。One should not despise technical work.

鄙夫 bǐfū *formal* ① a mean person; an ignorant person ② *hum.* your humble servant; I

鄙见 bǐjiàn *hum.* my humble opinion; my idea

鄙贱 bǐjiàn *formal* ① lowly; humble ② despise; disdain

鄙俚 bǐlǐ *formal* vulgar; philistine

鄙吝 bǐlìn *formal* ① vulgar ② stingy; miserly; mean

鄙陋 bǐlòu superficial; shallow: ～无知 shallow and ignorant

鄙弃 bǐqì disdain; loathe: ～这种庸俗作风 disdain such vulgar practices

鄙人 bǐrén *hum.* your humble servant; I

鄙视 bǐshì despise; disdain; look down upon: 有些人～体力劳动者。Some people look down on manual workers.

鄙俗 bǐsú vulgar; philistine

鄙夷 bǐyí *formal* look down upon; despise

鄙意 bǐyì *hum.* my humble opinion

bì

币 (幣)

bì money; currency: 外币 wàibì / 银币 yínbì

币值 bìzhí currency value: ～稳定 a stable currency

币制 bìzhì currency (or monetary) system

币制改革 bìzhì gǎigé currency (or monetary) reform

必

bì *adv.* ① certainly; surely; necessarily: 我明天下午三点～到。I'll definitely be there at 3 p.m. tomorrow. / 你们这次访问～将增强两国人民之间的友谊。Your visit will certainly strengthen the friendship between our two peoples. ② must; have to: ～读书目 a list of required reading / 事物的发展～有一定的条件。Things can only develop under certain conditions.

必不可少 bì bùkě shǎo absolutely necessary; indispensable; essential

必得 bǐděi *adv.* must; have to: 你～去一趟。You simply must go.

必定 bìdìng *adv.* ① must; have to: 他～知道。He must have known it. ② be bound to; be sure to: 明天我们～把图纸送到。We'll be sure to send you the blueprints tomorrow.

必恭必敬 bìgōng-bìjìng reverent and respectful; extremely deferential: ～听着 listening with the utmost deference

必然 bìrán ① inevitable; certain: ～结果 an inevitable outcome / ～趋势 an inexorable trend / ～的结论 a logical conclusion ② *adv.* be bound to; be sure to: 他～失败。He's bound to fail. ③ *philos.* necessity

必然规律 bìrán guīlǜ inexorable law

必然王国 bìrán wángguó *philos.* realm of necessity

必然性 bìránxìng necessity; inevitability; certainty

必修课 bìxiūkè a required (or obligatory) course

必须 bìxū *adv.* must; have to: ～指出 it must be pointed out that / 共产党员～勇于批评和自我批评。A Communist must be bold in criticism and self-criticism. / ～厉行节约。It is imperative to practise economy. / 学习～刻苦。Study demands diligence.

必需 bìxū essential; indispensable: 发展工业所～的原料 raw materials essential for industrial development / 应该把国家建设资金用在最～的地方。Our national construction funds should be spent where they are most needed.

必需品 bìxūpǐn necessities; necessaries

必要 bìyào necessary; essential; indispensable: ～条件 essential condition; prerequisite / 国家为这个国营农场提供了～的资金。The state provided the requisite capital for this state farm. / 没有～再讨论了。There's no need to discuss it any more.

必要产品 bìyào chǎnpǐn *econ.* necessary product

必要劳动 bìyào láodòng *econ.* necessary labour

必要前提 bìyào qiántí prerequisite; precondition

必要性 bìyàoxìng necessity

必由之路 bì yóu zhī lù the road one must follow or take; the only way: 人民群众得到解放的～ the only road to liberation for the people

闭

bì ① shut; close: ～门 shut the door / ～上眼 close one's eyes / ～嘴! Hold your tongue! or Shut up! / 他笑得～不上嘴。He just couldn't stop laughing. ② stop up; obstruct: 闭气 bìqì

闭关锁国 bìguān-suǒguó cut off one's country from the outside world

闭关政策 bìguān zhèngcè closed-door policy

闭关自守 bìguān zì shǒu close the country to international intercourse; follow a policy of national isolation; adopt a closed-door policy: 独立自主并不意味着～。Independence does not mean isolation from other countries. / ～只能越来越落后。Closing the country to external contact will result only in increasing backwardness.

闭合 bìhé close

闭合电路 bìhé diànlù closed circuit

闭合度 bìhédù *geol.* closure

闭合生态 bìhé shēngtài *space* closed ecology

闭会 bìhuì close (or end, adjourn) a meeting: 委员会～期间 when the committee is not in session

闭架式 bìjiàshì closed shelves (a system of library management which denies readers open access to bookshelves)

闭经 bìjīng *med.* amenorrhoea

闭口不谈 bìkǒu bù tán refuse to say anything about; avoid mentioning

闭口无言 bìkǒu wú yán remain silent; be tongue-tied; be left speechless

闭路电视 bìlù diànshì closed-circuit television; closed circuit

闭门羹 bìméngēng (usu. used in) 飨以～ shut the door in sb.'s face—refuse to receive sb. / 吃～ find the door closed on one—be denied a reception

闭门思过 bìmén sīguò shut oneself up and ponder over one's mistakes; ponder over one's mistakes in seclusion

闭门谢客 bìmén xièkè close the door to visitors; stop receiving visitors

闭门造车 bìmén zào chē make a cart behind closed doors——work behind closed doors; divorce oneself from the masses and from reality; act blindly

闭目塞听 bìmù-sètīng shut one's eyes and stop one's ears—cut oneself off from reality: 一个～、同客观外界根本绝缘的人, 是无所谓认识的。For a person who shuts his eyes, stops his ears and totally cuts himself off from the objective world there can be no such thing as knowledge.

闭幕 bìmù ① the curtain falls; lower the curtain: 在观众热烈掌声中～。The curtain fell to the loud applause of the audience. ② close; conclude: 会议已胜利～。The conference has come to a successful close.

闭幕词 bìmùcí　closing address (*or* speech)

闭幕式 bìmùshì　closing ceremony

闭气 bìqì　① stop breathing: 他跌了一交, 闭住气了。He fell over and almost stopped breathing· ② hold one's breath: 护士放轻脚步闭住气走近病人床前。The nurse held her breath and walked quietly towards the patient's bed.

闭塞 bìsè　① stop up; close up: 鼻孔～ with one's nose stuffed up ② hard to get to; out-of-the-way; inaccessible: 以前这一带交通～。In the past this district was very hard to get to. ③ unenlightened: 消息～ ill-informed ④ *elec.* blocking

闭塞信号 bìsè xìnhào　*railway* block signal

闭塞眼睛捉麻雀 bìsè yǎnjing zhuō máquè　try to catch sparrows with one's eyes blindfolded—act blindly

闭市 bìshì　suspend business; close

闭锁 bìsuǒ　deadlock; occlusion

闭音节 bìyīnjié　*phonet.* closed syllable

闭元音 bìyuányīn　*phonet.* close vowel

闭月羞花 bìyuè-xiūhuā　(of feminine beauty) outshine the moon and put the flowers to shame ——see also 沉鱼落雁 chényú-luòyàn

毕 (畢)
bì　① finish; accomplish; conclude: 阅～请放回原处。Please replace after reading. ② *formal* fully; altogether; completely: 毕力 bìlì ③ the nineteenth of the twenty-eight constellations (二十八宿) into which the celestial sphere was divided in ancient Chinese astronomy (consisting of eight stars, six in Hyades and two in Taurus) ④ (Bì) a surname

毕恭毕敬 bìgōng-bìjìng　same as 必恭必敬 bìgōng-bìjìng

毕竟 bìjìng　*adv.* after all; all in all; when all is said and done; in the final analysis: 她的缺点同她的成绩相比, ～是第二位的。Compared with her achievements, her shortcomings are, after all, only secondary. / 这部书虽然有缺页, 但～是珍本。This book is a rare edition, though there are several pages missing.

毕力 bìlì　make every effort; do all one can; try one's best

毕命 bìmìng　*formal* end one's life; die a violent death; meet with a sudden death

毕其功于一役 bì qí gōng yú yī yì　accomplish the whole task at one stroke

毕生 bìshēng　all one's life; lifetime: ～事业 lifework; work of a lifetime / 他～为革命事业奋斗。He fought all his life for the revolutionary cause.

毕肖 bìxiào　*formal* resemble closely; be the very image of: 画得神情～ paint a lifelike portrait of sb.

毕业 bìyè　graduate; finish school: 还有一年, 他就大学～了。He'll graduate from college next year. / 他中学还没～就参了军。He enlisted before he had finished middle school.

毕业班 bìyèbān　graduating class

毕业典礼 bìyè diǎnlǐ　graduation (ceremony); commencement

毕业分配 bìyè fēnpèi　job assignment on graduation

毕业论文 bìyè lùnwén　graduation thesis (*or* dissertation)

毕业设计 bìyè shèjì　graduation project

毕业生 bìyèshēng　graduate

毕业实习 bìyè shíxí　graduation field work

毕业证书 bìyè zhèngshū　diploma; graduation certificate

庇
bì　shelter; protect; shield: 包庇 bāobì

庇护 bìhù　shelter; shield; put under one's protection; take under one's wing

庇护权 bìhùquán　right of asylum

庇护所 bìhùsuǒ　sanctuary; asylum

庇荫 bìyìn　① (of a tree, etc.) give shade ② shield

庇佑 bìyòu　*formal* bless; prosper

畀
bì　*formal* confer; give: ～以重任 entrust sb. with an important task

毖
bì　*formal* caution

哔 (嗶)
bì　see below

哔叽 bìjī　*text.* serge

陛
bì　*formal* a flight of steps leading to a palace hall

陛辞 bìcí　*formal* leave the capital after bidding farewell to the emperor in audience

陛见 bìjiàn　*formal* have an audience with the emperor

陛下 bìxià　① Your Majesty ② His or Her Majesty

狴
bì　see below

狴犴 bì'àn　*formal* prison (originally a legendary beast the image of which was painted on prison doors)

赉
bì　*formal* beautifully adorned ——see also bēn

赉临 bìlín　*formal pol.* (of distinguished guests) honour my house, firm, etc. with your presence

毙 (斃)
bì　① die; get killed: 倒毙 dǎobì ② *inf.* kill or execute by shooting; shoot: 愤怒的群众要求～了这个杀人犯。The angry masses demanded that the murderer be shot. ③ *formal* fall down

毙命 bìmìng　*derog.* meet a violent death; get killed: 两名匪徒当场～。Two of the bandits were killed on the spot.

毙伤 bìshāng　kill and wound; inflict casualties

铋
bì　*chem.* bismuth (Bi)

秘 (祕)
bì ——see also mì

秘鲁 Bìlǔ　Peru

秘鲁人 Bìlǔrén　Peruvian

敝
bì　① *formal* shabby; worn-out; ragged: ～衣 ragged clothing; shabby (*or* worn-out) clothes ② *hum.* my; our; this: ～处 my place / ～校 my school / ～姓陈。My name is Chen.

敝旧 bìjiù　ragged; worn-out; shabby

敝俗 bìsú　corrupt customs; bad habits

敝屣 bìxǐ　*formal* worn-out shoes; a worthless thing: 弃之如敝屣 qì zhī rú bìxǐ

敝帚千金 bìzhǒu qiānjīn　cherish an old broom as if it were a thousand pieces of gold—cherish a possession of little value

敝帚自珍 bìzhǒu zì zhēn　value one's own old broom—cherish sth. of little value simply because it is one's own (usu. used as a self-depreciatory expression)

婢
bì　slave girl; servant-girl: 奴婢 núbì

婢女 bìnǚ　slave girl; servant-girl

赑
bì　see below

赑屃 bìxì　① *formal* straining hard ② a fabulous tortoise (formerly a motif for the base of heavy stone tablets)

愊
bì　see 悃愊 kǔnbì

愎
bì　wilful; self-willed: 刚愎 gāngbì

弼(弻) bì *formal* assist

筚(篳) bì a bamboo or wicker fence: 蓬门筚户 péngmén-bìhù

筚路蓝缕 bìlù-lánlǚ drive a cart in ragged clothes to break fresh ground—endure hardships in pioneer work

筚门圭窦 bìmén-guīdòu a poor family

跸(蹕) bì *formal* clear the road for the emperor

痹(痺) bì *Chin. med.* pain or numbness caused by cold, damp, etc. ; rheumatism

裨 bì *formal* benefit; advantage: 无～于事。It won't help matters. *or* It won't do any good. ——see also pí

裨补 bìbǔ *formal* ① make up; remedy ② benefit; advantage; profit

裨益 bìyì *formal* benefit; advantage; profit: 大有～ be of great benefit

蓖 bì see below

蓖麻 bìmá *bot.* castor-oil plant

蓖麻蚕 bìmácán castor silkworm

蓖麻油 bìmáyóu castor oil

蓖麻子 bìmázǐ castor bean

睥 bì see below

睥睨 bìnì *formal* look at sb. disdainfully out of the corner of one's eye: ～一切 consider everyone and everything beneath one's notice; be overweening

辟¹ bì *formal* monarch; sovereign: 复辟 fùbì

辟² bì ① *formal* ward off; keep away ② same as 避 bì ——see also pì

辟邪 bìxié exorcise evil spirits

滗(潷) bì decant; strain; drain: 别把壶里的茶～干了。Don't drain the teapot dry. / ～一下，把渣子去掉 decant it to keep the sediment away / ～汤药 strain the decoction

碧 bì ① *formal* green jade ② bluish green; blue: ～海 the blue sea / ～空 a clear blue sky; an azure sky

碧波万顷 bìbō wànqǐng a boundless (*or* vast) expanse of blue water

碧草如茵 bìcǎo rú yīn a carpet of green grass

碧空如洗 bìkōng rú xǐ a cloudless blue sky

碧蓝 bìlán dark blue: ～的海洋 the blue sea

碧绿 bìlù dark green: ～的田野 green fields

碧螺春 bìluóchūn (also 碧萝春 bìluóchūn) a green tea

碧落 bìluò *liter.* the green void; the blue empyrean; the blue sky: 上穷～下黄泉，两处茫茫皆不见。(白居易) Above, he searched the Green Void, below, the Yellow Springs; But he failed, in either place, to find the one he looked for.

碧瓦 bìwǎ green, glazed tile

碧血 bìxuè blood shed in a just cause

碧血丹心 bìxuè-dānxīn loyalty unto death

碧油油 bìyōuyōu bright green: ～的麦苗 green wheat seedlings

碧玉 bìyù jasper

箅 bì see below

箅子 bìzi grate; grating; grid

蔽 bì cover; shelter; hide: ～风雨 shelter from the wind and rain / 浮云～日。The clouds shut out the sun.

蔽匿 bìnì *formal* hide; conceal

弊 bì ① fraud; abuse; malpractice: 舞弊 wǔbì ② disadvantage; harm: ～多利少。The disadvantages outweigh the advantages.

弊病 bìbìng ① malady; evil; malpractice: 资本主义所固有的社会～ social evils inherent in capitalism ② drawback; disadvantage: 这种做法～不少。This method has quite a few drawbacks (*or* disadvantages).

弊端 bìduān malpractice; abuse; corrupt practice

弊绝风清 bìjué-fēngqīng abuses swept away and the air cleared; with all corrupt practices done away with, a healthful atmosphere prevails

弊政 bìzhèng *formal* misgovernment; maladministration

薜 bì see below

薜荔 bìlì *bot.* climbing fig

箆(箆) bì comb (hair) with a double-edged fine-toothed comb: ～头 comb one's hair with such a comb

箆子 bìzi a double-edged fine-toothed comb

避 bì ① avoid; evade; shun: ～而不谈 evade the question; avoid the subject; keep silent about the matter / ～而不答 avoid making a reply / ～雨 seek shelter from the rain / ～开敌人岗哨 keep clear of enemy sentries ② prevent; keep away; repel: 避孕 bìyùn

避弹坑 bìdànkēng *mil.* foxhole

避风 bìfēng ① take shelter from the wind ② (also 避风头 bìfēngtou) lie low; stay away from trouble: 避一避风头 lie low until it blows over

避风港 bìfēnggǎng (sometimes fig.) haven; harbour

避讳 bìhuì avoid a taboo (on the personal names of emperors, one's elders, etc.): 公元 313 年，因避晋愍帝司马邺讳，改建邺(今南京市)为建康。In 313, to avoid the taboo on the personal name of Emperor Min of the Jin, Jianye (modern Nanjing) was changed to Jiankang.

避讳 bìhui (also 避忌 bìjì) ① a word or phrase to be avoided as taboo; taboo ② evade; dodge: ～这个问题 evade the issue

避坑落井 bì kēng luò jǐng dodge a pit only to fall into a well; out of the frying pan into the fire

避雷器 bìléiqì lightning arrester

避雷针 bìléizhēn lightning rod

避乱 bìluàn flee from social upheaval; seek refuge from war

避免 bìmiǎn avoid; refrain from; avert: ～错误 avoid mistakes / ～轻率行动 refrain from any rash action / 设法～了一场事故 succeed in averting an accident / ～挫伤群众的积极性 see that the enthusiasm of the masses is not dampened

避难就易 bì nán jiù yì shirk the difficult and take the easy; take the easier way out; choose the easier of the two alternatives

避难 bìnàn take refuge; seek asylum

避难港 bìnàngǎng port of refuge

避难所 bìnànsuǒ refuge; sanctuary; haven

避其锐气，击其惰归 bì qí ruìqì, jī qí duò guī avoid the enemy when he is fresh, strike him when he is tired and withdraws: 孙子说的"～"，就是指的使敌疲劳沮丧，以求减杀其优势。(毛泽东) When Sun Wu Zi said, "Avoid the enemy when he is full of vigour, strike when he is fatigued and withdraws", he was referring to tiring and demoralizing the enemy so as to reduce

his superiority.

避让　bìràng　① avoid; clude; dodge ② get out of the way; step aside; make way

避实就虚　bì shí jiù xū　stay clear of the enemy's main force and strike at his weak points

避世　bìshì　retire from the world; withdraw from society

避暑　bìshǔ　① be away for the summer holidays; spend a holiday at a summer resort: 暑假我们将去海边～. We're going to spend our summer holidays at a seaside resort. ② prevent sunstroke

避暑山庄　Bìshǔ Shānzhuāng　Mountain Estate for Escaping the Heat (the former summer residence of the Qing emperors at Chengde)

避暑胜地　bìshǔ shèngdì　summer resort

避暑药　bìshǔyào　medicine for preventing sunstroke; preventive against sunstroke

避蚊剂　bìwénjì　mosquito repellent

避嫌　bìxián　avoid doing anything that may arouse suspicion; avoid arousing suspicion

避孕　bìyùn　contraception

避孕栓　bìyùnshuān　contraceptive suppository

避孕套　bìyùntào　condom

避孕丸药　bìyùn wányào　the pill

避孕药膏　bìyùn yàogāo　contraceptive jelly

避孕用品　bìyùn yòngpǐn　contraceptives

避重就轻　bì zhòng jiù qīng　evade major responsibility and take minor; avoid the important and dwell on the trivial

壁

　bì　① wall ② sth. resembling a wall: 细胞壁 xìbāobì　③ cliff: 峭壁 qiàobì　④ rampart; breastwork ⑤ the fourteenth of the twenty-eight constellations (二十八宿) into which the celestial sphere was divided in ancient Chinese astronomy (consisting of two stars in a straight line, one in Pegasus and the other in Andromeda)

壁报　bìbào　wall newspaper: 办～ put up a regular wall newspaper

壁橱　bìchú　a built-in wardrobe or cupboard; closet

壁灯　bìdēng　wall lamp; bracket light

壁挂　bìguà　(wall) hanging

壁柜　bìguì　same as 壁橱 bìchú

壁虎　bìhǔ　zool. gecko; house lizard

壁画　bìhuà　mural (painting); fresco: 敦煌～ the Dunhuang murals

壁脚　bìjiǎo　dial. the foot of a wall

壁龛　bìkān　niche

壁垒　bìlěi　rampart; barrier: 贸易～ trade barrier / ～分明 be diametrically opposed; be sharply divided / 唯物主义和唯心主义是哲学中的两大～。Materialism and idealism are two rival camps in philosophy (or two diametrically opposed philosophical theories).

壁垒森严　bìlěi sēnyán　① closely guarded; strongly fortified: 早已森严壁垒, 更加众志成城。(毛泽东) Already our defence is iron-clad, Now our wills unite like a fortress. ② sharply divided; rival camps confronting each other

壁立　bìlì　(of cliffs, etc.) stand like a wall; rise steeply: ～千尺 a sheer rise of a thousand feet / ～的山峰 a sheer cliff

壁炉　bìlú　fireplace

壁炉台　bìlútái　mantelpiece

壁球　bìqiú　squash rackets; squash

壁上观　bìshàngguān　see 作壁上观 zuò bìshàngguān

壁虱　bìshī　① tick ② dial. bedbug

壁毯　bìtǎn　tapestry (used as a wall hanging)

壁厢　bìxiāng　old side: 这～ here / 那～ there

壁纸　bìzhǐ　wallpaper

壁钟　bìzhōng　① wall clock ② bracket clock

嬖

　bì　arch.　① show favour to ② enjoy favour ③ a favourite

嬖人　bìrén　arch.　a favourite

屄

　bì　see below

屄篥　bìlì　the Tartar pipe (an ancient musical instrument)

臂

　bì　① arm: 左～ the left arm ② upper arm ——see also bei

臂板信号　bìbǎn xìnhào　railway　semaphore

臂膀　bìbǎng　arm

臂膊　bìbó　dial.　arm

臂纱　bìshā　(black) armband: 戴～ wear a black armband

臂弯　bìwān　crook of the arm: 她把包夹在～里。She carried the parcel in the crook of her arm.

臂腕　bìwàn　wrist

臂章　bìzhāng　① armband; armlet ② mil.　shoulder emblem (or patch)

臂肘　bìzhǒu　elbow

臂助　bìzhù　formal　① help ② assistant

髀

　bì　formal　① thigh ② thighbone

髀肉复生　bìròu fùshēng　one's hips are becoming heavy (said when sighing over a life of inactivity)

璧

　bì　a round flat piece of jade with a hole in its centre (used for ceremonial purposes in ancient China)

璧还　bìhuán　pol.　① return (a borrowed object) with thanks ② decline (a gift) with thanks

璧谢　bìxiè　pol.　decline (a gift) with thanks

襞

　bì　① formal　folds in a garment ② physiol.　folds (of the stomach, intestines, etc.)

biān

边¹ (邊)

　biān　① side (of a geometrical figure): 三角形的一～ one side of a triangle ② side; margin; edge; brim; rim: 街道两～ both sides of the street / 每页～上的批注 notes in the margin on every page / 湖～那座扬水站 the pumping station on the edge of the lake / 田～地头 edges of fields / 碗～儿 the rim of a bowl / 宽～草帽 broad-brimmed hat / 衬衣的～ the hem of a shirt ③ border; frontier; boundary: 边城 biānchéng　④ limit; bound: 外层空间没个～儿。Outer space is boundless. / 这话可太没～儿了。That's just absurd. ⑤ the place next to a person or thing: 身边 shēnbiān　⑥ (Biān) a surname

边² (邊)

　bian　(suffix of nouns of locality) side: 东～ east side

边隘　biān'ài　frontier pass

边鄙　biānbǐ　formal　frontier region; remote district

边币　biānbì　Border Region currency (consisting of the currency notes issued by the Border Region governments during the War of Resistance Against Japan and the War of Liberation)

边…边…　biān…biān…　(used with two verbs to indicate the simultaneous progression or development of two actions): 他边唱歌边工作。He sang as he worked. / 边干边学 learn while working; learn on the job / 边读边议 read sth. and discuss it as one goes along / 边发展边巩固 expand while consolidating

边城　biānchéng　border (or frontier) town
边陲　biānchuí　formal　border area; frontier
边地　biāndì　border district; borderland
边防　biānfáng　frontier (or border) defence
边防部队　biānfáng bùduì　frontier guards
边防检查　biānfáng jiǎnchá　frontier inspection: ～站 frontier inspection station
边防军　biānfángjūn　frontier force
边防哨　biānfángshào　border sentry
边防战士　biānfáng zhànshì　frontier guard
边防站　biānfángzhàn　frontier station
边锋　biānfēng　(in football, etc.) wing; wing forward: 左边锋 zuǒbiānfēng
边幅　biānfú　see 不修边幅 bù xiū biānfú
边关　biānguān　frontier pass: 镇守～ guard a frontier pass; hold a frontier command
边患　biānhuàn　trouble on the frontier (as caused by foreign invasion)
边际　biānjì　limit; bound; boundary: 绿色的田野, 望不到～。Before me is a boundless stretch of green fields.
边际效用论　biānjìxiàoyònglùn　econ. the theory of marginal utility
边疆　biānjiāng　border area; borderland; frontier; frontier region: 支援～建设 support the construction of the border areas / 保卫～ guard the frontier
边角料　biānjiǎoliào　leftover bits and pieces (of industrial material)
边界　biānjiè　boundary; border: 越过～ cross a boundary; cross the border
边界实际控制线　biānjiè shíjì kòngzhìxiàn　line of actual control on the border
边界事件　biānjiè shìjiàn　border incident
边界谈判　biānjiè tánpàn　border talks
边界线　biānjièxiàn　boundary line
边界现状　biānjiè xiànzhuàng　status quo on the border; status quo of the boundary
边界协定　biānjiè xiédìng　boundary agreement
边界争端　biānjiè zhēngduān　boundary dispute
边界走向　biānjiè zǒuxiàng　alignment of the boundary line
边境　biānjìng　border; frontier
边境冲突　biānjìng chōngtū　border clash (or conflict)
边境贸易　biānjìng màoyì　frontier trade
边境市镇　biānjìng shìzhèn　border town
边框　biānkuàng　frame; rim: 镜子的～ the rim of a mirror
边门　biānmén　side door; wicket door (or gate): 请走～。Side door, please.
边民　biānmín　people living on the frontiers; inhabitants of a border area
边卡　biānqiǎ　border checkpoint
边区　biānqū　border area (or region): 陕甘宁～ the Shaanxi-Gansu-Ningxia Border Region
边塞　biānsài　frontier fortress
边线　biānxiàn　① sports sideline ② baseball softball foul line
边沿　biānyán　edge; fringe: 森林～ the edge (or fringe) of a forest / 市镇～地带 the periphery of a town
边音　biānyīn　phonet. lateral (sound)
边缘　biānyuán　① edge; fringe; verge; brink; periphery: 在特区的～ on the border of the special administrative zone / 悬崖的～ the edge of a precipice / 临近经济破产的～ on the verge of economic bankruptcy ② marginal; borderline
边缘地区　biānyuán dìqū　border district; borders
边缘海　biānyuánhǎi　marginal sea
边缘科学　biānyuán kēxué　frontier science
边远　biānyuǎn　far from the centre; remote; outlying: ～省份 remote border provinces / ～地区 an outlying district

边寨　biānzhài　borderland village

砭　biān　① a stone acupuncture needle (used in ancient times) ② perform acupunctures with stone needles (as in ancient times) ③ pierce (fig.): 冷风～骨。The cold wind cuts one to the marrow. / 痛～时弊 castigate the abuses of the time

笾(籩)　biān　a bamboo container for fruit, dried meat, etc. (used at banquets or sacrifices in ancient times)

编　biān　① weave; plait: ～柳条筐 weave wicker baskets / ～辫子 plait one's hair ② organize; group; arrange: ～班 group into classes / 把他～在我们组吧。Put him in our group. ③ edit; compile: ～教材 compile teaching material / ～杂志 edit a magazine; work in the editorial department of a magazine ④ write; compose: ～剧本 write a play / ～儿童歌曲 compose songs for children ⑤ fabricate; invent; make up; cook up: 这事儿是他～出来的。He made the whole thing up. ⑥ (often used in book titles) book; copy: 人手一～。Everyone has a copy. /《故事新～》A New Book of Stories ⑦ part of a book; book; volume: 上～ Book I; Volume I; Part I
编贝　biānbèi　well-arranged shells—(of teeth) white and lovely
编次　biāncì　order of arrangement
编凑　biāncòu　fabricate; invent; make up; cook up: 你可真会瞎～! You're quite good at making up stories! / 歌词是几个人～起来的。The words of the song were thrown together by several hands. / 剧本作者精心～了这段情节。The playwright showed great ingenuity in inventing this episode.
编导　biāndǎo　① write and direct (a play, film, etc.): 这个话剧是由两位青年作家～的。The play was written and directed by two young writers. ② playwright-director (of a play); choreographer-director (of a ballet); scenarist-director (of a film)
编订　biāndìng　(also 编定 biāndìng) compile and edit: 鲁迅～了《唐宋传奇集》。Lu Xun compiled and edited the Literary Tales of the Tang-Song Period.
编队　biānduì　① form into columns; organize into teams ② formation (of ships or aircraft)
编队飞行　biānduì fēixíng　formation flight (or flying)
编队轰炸　biānduì hōngzhà　formation bombing
编发　biānfā　edit and release (news reports, etc.)
编法儿　biānfǎr　try every means; do everything possible
编号　biānhào　① number: 给树苗～ number the saplings ② serial number
编后　biānhòu　editorial afterword
编辑　biānjí　① edit; compile: ～图书索引 compile an index (of books) ② editor; compiler: 总～ editor-in-chief; chief editor
编辑部　biānjíbù　editorial department
编辑人员　biānjí rényuán　editorial staff
编辑委员会　biānjí wěiyuánhuì　editorial board
编剧　biānjù　① write a play, scenario, etc. ② playwright ③ screenwriter; scenarist
编码　biānmǎ　coding
编目　biānmù　① make a catalogue; catalogue: 新到的图书正在～。The new books are being catalogued. ② catalogue; list
编目部　biānmùbù　cataloguing department
编目员　biānmùyuán　cataloguer
编年史　biānniánshǐ　annalistic history; annals; chronicle
编年体　biānniántǐ　annalistic style (in historiography)

编排 biānpái arrange; lay out: 文字和图片的～ the lay-out of pictures and articles／课文要按难易程度～。The texts should be graded in order of difficulty.

编派 biānpai *dial.* invent stories about others

编遣 biānqiǎn reorganize (troops, etc.) and discharge surplus personnel

编磬 biānqìng a set of musical stones; stone chimes

编审 biānshěn ① read and edit ② senior editor

编外 biānwài (of personnel) not on the permanent staff; not on the regular payroll: ～人员 personnel not on the permanent staff; personnel not on the regular payroll

编舞 biānwǔ ① choreography ② choreographer

编写 biānxiě ① compile: ～教科书 compile a textbook ② write; compose: ～歌剧 compose an opera／～剧本 write a play

编选 biānxuǎn select and edit; compile

编演 biānyǎn write and produce (a play, etc.)

编译 biānyì ① translate and edit ② translator-editor

编印 biānyìn compile and print; publish

编余 biānyú (of personnel) redundant after reorganization: ～人员 surplus personnel

编造 biānzào ① compile; draw up; work out: ～预算 draw up a budget／～表册 compile statistical tables ② fabricate; invent; concoct; make up; cook up: ～谎言 fabricate lies／～情节 falsify the details of an event; invent (*or* make up) a story ③ create out of the imagination: 古代人民～的神话 myths invented by the ancients

编者 biānzhě editor; compiler

编者按 biānzhě'àn (also 编者案 biānzhě'àn) editor's note; editorial note

编织 biānzhī weave; knit; plait; braid: ～地毯 weave a rug／～草席 weave a straw mat／～毛衣 knit a sweater

编制 biānzhì ① weave; plait; braid: ～竹器 weave bamboo articles ② work out; draw up: ～生产计划 work out a production plan／～教学大纲 draw up a teaching programme ③ authorized strength; establishment: 部队～ establishment (for army units)／政府机关的～ authorized size of a government body／缩小～ reduce the staff／控制人员～ control the manning quotas; limit the size of the personnel force

编钟 biānzhōng a set of bells; chimes

编著 biānzhù compile; write

编撰 biānzhuàn compile; write

编组 biānzǔ ① organize into groups ② *railway* marshalling: ～场 marshalling (*or* classification) yard

编纂 biānzuǎn compile: ～词典 compile a dictionary

煸 biān *dial.* stir-fry before stewing

蝙 biān see below

蝙蝠 biānfú bat (an animal)

蝙蝠衫 biānfúshān an upper outer garment with bat-wing sleeves

鳊（鯿） biān bream

鳊鱼 biānyú bream

鞭 biān ① whip; lash ② an iron staff used as a weapon in ancient China ③ sth. resembling a whip: 教鞭 jiàobiān ④ a string of small firecrackers: 放～ let off firecrackers／一挂～ a string of firecrackers ⑤ *formal* flog; whip; lash: ～马 whip a horse

鞭策 biāncè spur on; urge on: 要经常～自己, 为祖国努力学习。We should constantly urge ourselves on to study hard for our country.／领导的表扬是对我们的～。The leadership's praise will spur us on.

鞭长莫及 biān cháng mò jí beyond the reach of one's power (*or* authority); too far away to be helped

鞭笞 biānchī *formal* flog; lash

鞭虫 biānchóng whipworm

鞭打 biāndǎ whip; lash; flog; thrash

鞭痕 biānhén welt; whip scar; lash mark

鞭毛 biānmáo *zool.* flagellum

鞭毛虫 biānmáochóng flagellate

鞭炮 biānpào ① firecrackers ② a string of small fire-crackers

鞭辟入里 biān pì rù lǐ (also 鞭辟近里 biān pì jìn lǐ) penetrating; trenchant; incisive

鞭挞 biāntà *formal* lash; castigate: 影片对吃人的旧社会进行了无情的～。The film mercilessly castigates the cannibalistic old society.

鞭子 biānzi whip

biǎn

贬 biǎn ① (in imperial times) demote; relegate: ～为庶民 be degraded to commoner status ② reduce; devalue: ～价出售 sell at a reduced price ③ censure; depreciate: ～得一钱不值 condemn as worthless

贬斥 biǎnchì ① *formal* demote ② denounce

贬黜 biǎnchù *formal* demote

贬词 biǎncí same as 贬义词 biǎnyìcí

贬低 biǎndī belittle; depreciate; play down: ～其重要性 belittle the importance of sth./她想～他在这件事里起的作用, 夸大自己的作用。She tried to play down his part in the affair and play up her own.

贬毁 biǎnhuǐ disparage and defame

贬价 biǎnjià reduce the price; mark down: ～出售 sell at a reduced price

贬损 biǎnsǔn belittle; disparage

贬义 biǎnyì derogatory sense: 这个词常用于～。This word is often used in a derogatory sense.

贬义词 biǎnyìcí derogatory term; expression of censure

贬抑 biǎnyì belittle; depreciate

贬谪 biǎnzhé (in imperial times) banish from the court; relegate: 苏轼为官一生, 屡遭～。Su Shi was frequently banished during his official career.

贬值 biǎnzhí *econ.* ① devalue; devaluate: 一九六七年英国政府宣布英镑～。The British government devalued the pound in 1967. ② depreciate: 由于恶性通货膨胀, 该国货币大大～了。Owing to runaway inflation, that country's currency has greatly depreciated.

贬职 biǎnzhí demote

窆 biǎn *arch.* bury

扁 biǎn flat: 一只～盒子 a flat case; a shallow box／纸箱子压～了。The cardboard box was crushed.
——see also piān

扁虫 biǎnchóng flatworm

扁蝽 biǎnchūn flat bug

扁担 biǎndan carrying pole; shoulder pole

扁担没扎, 两头打塌 biǎndan méi zā, liǎngtóu dǎtā when the loads are not secured at both ends of the pole, they slip off—try to grab both but end up with neither

扁豆 biǎndòu hyacinth bean: 小～ lentil

扁骨 biǎngǔ *physiol.* flat bone

扁坯 biǎnpī *metall.* slab

扁平足 biǎnpíngzú same as 平足 píngzú

扁桃 biǎntáo ① almond tree ② almond ③ *dial.* flat peach

扁桃体 biǎntáotǐ (also 扁桃腺 biǎntáoxiàn) *physiol.* tonsil

扁桃体肥大 biǎntáotǐ féidà hypertrophy of tonsils

扁桃体切除术　biǎntáotǐ qiēchúshù　tonsillectomy

扁桃腺炎　biǎntáoxiànyán　tonsillitis

扁体字　biǎntǐzì　squat-shaped handwriting

扁形动物　biǎnxíng dòngwù　flatworm; platyhelminth

扁圆　biǎnyuán　oblate

匾　biǎn　① a horizontal inscribed board ② a silk banner embroidered with words of praise: 绣金～ embroidering a silk banner with words of gold ③ a big round shallow basket

匾额　biǎn'é　a horizontal inscribed board

褊　biǎn　formal　narrow; cramped

褊急　biǎnjí　formal　narrow-minded and short-tempered

褊狭　biǎnxiá　formal　narrow; cramped: 居处～ live in cramped quarters / 气量～ small-minded

褊小　biǎnxiǎo　narrow and small; narrow

褊窄　biǎnzhǎi　① narrow; cramped: 房子～ a cramped house ② small-minded

藊　biǎn　see below

藊豆　biǎndòu　same as 扁豆 biǎndòu

biàn

卞　biàn　① formal irritable; irascible: ～急 irascible; testy ② (Biàn) a surname

弁　biàn　① a man's cap used in ancient times ② old a low-ranking military officer: 马弁 mǎbiàn

弁言　biànyán　formal　foreword; preface

抃　biàn　arch.　clap one's hands; applaud

忭　biàn　formal　glad; happy: 欢忭 huānbiàn

汴　Biàn　another name for 开封 (city in Henan Province)

苄　biàn　chem.　benzyl

苄基　biànjī　chem.　benzyl

变(變)　biàn　① become different; change: 情况～了。The situation has changed. / 这地方～了样了。The place looks quite different now. ② change into; become: 天气～暖和了。The weather became warmer. / 旱地～水田。Dry land has been turned into paddy fields. / 牛奶～酸了。The milk has gone sour. ③ transform; change; alter: ～废为宝 change waste material into things of value; recycle waste material / ～害为利 turn bane into boon ④ changeable; changed: 变态biàntài ⑤ sell off (one's property): 变产biànchǎn ⑥ an unexpected turn of events: 事变 shìbiàn ⑦ short for 变文 biànwén

变把戏　biàn bǎxì　perform conjuring tricks; conjure; juggle: ～的 conjurer; magician

变本加厉　biàn běn jiā lì　become aggravated; be further intensified: 资本家～地剥削工人。The capitalists are intensifying their efforts to exploit the workers.

变产　biànchǎn　sell off one's property

变成　biànchéng　change into; turn into; become; transform into: 贫穷落后的旧中国已经～了初步繁荣昌盛的社会主义国家。Poor and backward old China has changed into a socialist country with the beginnings of prosperity. / 在一定的条件下，坏事能够～好事。Under given conditions, bad things can be turned into good things. / 蝌蚪会～青蛙。A tadpole transforms into a frog.

变蛋　biàndàn　another name for 松花 sōnghuā

变电站　biàndiànzhàn　(transformer) substation

变调　biàndiào　① phonet. tone sandhi (i.e. the occurrence of allophonic and phonemic changes when tones come together; e.g., when a 3rd tone is followed by another 3rd, the first one changes to a 2nd tone, thus 很好 hěn hǎo is said hén hǎo) ② same as 转调 zhuǎndiào

变动　biàndòng　① alteration; change: 国际局势发生了很大的～。Great changes have taken place in the international situation. / 文字上作一些～ make some changes (or alterations) in the wording / 人事没有什么～。There is not much change of personnel. ② change: 你安排得不错，不用～了。Your arrangement is not bad. There is no need to change it.

变法　biànfǎ　hist.　introduce institutional reforms: 王安石～，推行新政。Wang Anshi introduced reforms and initiated new policies.

变法儿　biànfǎr　try different ways: 食堂里总是～把伙食搞得好一些。The mess hall is always trying to provide better food.

变法维新　biànfǎ wéixīn　Constitutional Reform and Modernization (1898)

变分法　biànfēnfǎ　math.　calculus of variations

变革　biàngé　transform; change: ～自然 transform nature / 社会～ social change / 你要有知识，你就得参加～现实的实践。If you want knowledge, you must take part in the practice of changing reality.

变更　biàngēng　change; alter; modify: 所有制方面的～ changes in the system of ownership / ～作息时间 alter the daily timetable / 我们的计划稍有～。We have modified our plan.

变工　biàngōng　exchange work (or labour)

变工队　biàngōngduì　work-exchange team (an agricultural producers' mutual-aid organization)

变宫　biàngōng　mus.　a note of the ancient Chinese seven-tone scale, corresponding to 7 in numbered musical notation

变故　biàngù　an unforeseen event; accident; misfortune: 发生了～。Something quite unforeseen has happened.

变卦　biànguà　go back on one's word; break an agreement: 昨天说得好好的，怎么～了? Yesterday you agreed. What made you change your mind?

变化　biànhuà　change; vary: 气温的～ variations (or fluctuations) of temperature / 我家乡有了很大的～。Great changes have taken place in my home village. / 他发球～多端。He's always changing his way of serving.

变化无常　biànhuà wúcháng　constantly changing; changeable; capricious: 高山天气～。In high mountains the weather is changeable.

变幻　biànhuàn　change irregularly; fluctuate

变幻莫测　biànhuàn mò cè　changeable; unpredictable

变换　biànhuàn　vary; alternate: ～手法 vary one's tactics / ～位置 shift one's position

变价　biànjià　appraise at the current rate: ～出售 sell at the current price

变焦距镜头　biànjiāojù jìngtóu　photog.　zoom lens

变节　biànjié　make a political recantation; turn one's coat

变节分子　biànjiéfènzǐ　recanter; turncoat

变脸　biànliǎn　suddenly turn hostile: 他跟我～了。我哪儿得罪他了? He turned on me. What did I do to offend him?

变量　biànliàng　math.　variable

变流器　biànliúqì　elec.　converter

变乱　biànluàn　turmoil; social upheaval

变卖　biànmài　sell off (one's property): ～产业 sell off

one's estate

变频 biànpín *electron.* frequency conversion: 〜管 converter tube

变迁 biànqiān changes; vicissitudes: 李家庄的〜 changes in Li Village / 社会〜 social changes / 人事〜 the vicissitudes of life / 时代〜 the changes of the times

变色 biànsè ① change colour; discolour: 这种墨水不会〜。This ink will not change colour. / 脸不〜心不跳 one's face does not change colour, nor does one's heart beat faster—without a trace of fear / 保证我国社会主义江山永不〜 ensure that socialist China will never change her political colour ② change countenance; become angry

变色镜 biànsèjìng light-sensitive glasses

变色龙 biànsèlóng ① chameleon ② a changeable or fickle person (esp. in politics)

变生肘腋 biàn shēng zhǒuyè trouble is brewing close at hand

变声 biànshēng change of voice (at puberty)

变数 biànshù *math.* variable

变速 biànsù *mech.* speed change; gearshift

变速比 biànsùbǐ gear ratio

变速器 biànsùqì gearbox; transmission

变速运动 biànsù yùndòng *phys.* variable motion

变态 biàntài ① *biol.* metamorphosis ② abnormal; anomalous

变态反应 biàntài fǎnyìng *med.* allergy

变态心理 biàntài xīnlǐ abnormal psychology

变态心理学 biàntài xīnlǐxué abnormal psychology (a science)

变天 biàntiān ① change of weather: 太闷热了, 看来要〜。The weather is bound to change soon, it's so close. ② change of heavens—restoration of reactionary rule

变天帐 biàntiānzhàng restoration records (of usurious loans, former land holdings, etc., kept secretly by members of the overthrown classes dreaming of a comeback)

变通 biàntōng be flexible; accommodate (*or* adapt) sth. to circumstances: 〜办法 accommodation; adaptation / 根据不同情况作适当的〜 make appropriate adaptations in the light of specific conditions

变为 biànwéi change into; turn into: 把荒漠〜绿色的原野 turn the wilderness into green fields

变温层 biànwēncéng another name for 对流层 duìliúcéng

变温动物 biànwēn dòngwù poikilothermal (*or* cold-blooded) animal

变文 biànwén a popular form of narrative literature flourishing in the Tang Dynasty (618-907), with alternate prose and rhymed parts for recitation and singing (often on Buddhistic themes): 《大目乾连冥间救母〜》 *The Great Maudgalyayana Rescues His Mother from Hell*

变戏法 biàn xìfǎ perform conjuring tricks; conjure; juggle

变相 biànxiàng in disguised form; covert: 〜体罚 corporal punishment in disguised form / 〜的剥削行为 a covert act of exploitation / 〜涨价 a disguised price hike

变心 biànxīn cease to be faithful; change loyalties; break faith

变星 biànxīng *astron.* variable (star)

变形 biànxíng be out of shape; become deformed: 这箱子压得〜了。The box has been crushed out of shape. / 病人的脊椎骨已经〜。The patient has a deformed spine.

变形虫 biànxíngchóng amoeba

变形虫痢疾 biànxíngchóng lìji amoebic dysentery

变形体 biànxíngtǐ *biol.* plasmodium

变性 biànxìng *chem.* denaturation

变性蛋白质 biànxìng dànbáizhì denatured protein

变性酒精 biànxìng jiǔjīng denatured alcohol

变压器 biànyāqì *elec.* transformer

变样 biànyàng change in shape or appearance: 几年没见, 你还没〜。You haven't changed any since I saw you last. / 这个地方已经大〜了。This place has changed a lot.

变异 biànyì *biol.* variation: 〜性 variability

变易 biànyì change

变造 biànzào *leg.* alter in order to deceive; doctor: 伪造或〜公文 forge or alter official documents

变徵 biànzhǐ *mus.* a note of the ancient Chinese seven-tone scale, corresponding to 4 in numbered musical notation

变质 biànzhì ① go bad; deteriorate: 这肉〜了。The meat has gone bad. ② *geol.* metamorphism

变质岩 biànzhìyán *geol.* metamorphic rock

变种 biànzhǒng ① *biol.* mutation; variety ② variety; variant: 机会主义的〜 a variety of opportunism

变奏 biànzòu *mus.* variation: 〜曲 variations (on a theme)

变阻器 biànzǔqì *elec.* rheostat

便[1] biàn ① convenient; handy: 近便 jìnbiàn ② a convenient situation or time: 得便 débiàn ③ informal; plain; ordinary: 便饭 biànfàn ④ piss or shit; urine or excrement: 粪便 fènbiàn ⑤ relieve oneself: 大便 dàbiàn / 小便 xiǎobiàn

便[2] biàn (used in the same way as, and more formal than, 就) ① *adv.* soon afterwards: 车开不久, 天〜亮了。It was light soon after the train had started. ② *adv.* in that case; then: 这几天不是刮风, 〜是下雨。During the last few days, if it was not blowing, then it was raining. ③ *conj.* even if: 〜是累了, 我也要来。I'll come even if I'm tired. ——see also pián

便步走 biànbùzǒu *mil.* march at ease; route step: 〜! (word of command) At ease, march! *or* Route step, march!

便车 biànchē sb.'s car in which one may have a ride: 我要找个〜带我进城。I'm looking for a ride to town. *or* I'm looking for someone who can give me a lift to town.

便池 biànchí urinal

便当 biàndang convenient; handy; easy: 房子里家具不多, 收拾起来很〜。There isn't too much furniture in the room. We can easily tidy it up.

便道 biàndào ① shortcut: 抄〜走 take a shortcut ② pavement; sidewalk: 行人走〜。Pedestrians walk on the pavement. ③ makeshift road

便毒 biàndú *Chin. med.* bubo (in the groin)

便饭 biànfàn an ordinary meal; a simple meal; potluck: 跟我们一块儿吃顿〜吧。Come along and take potluck with us.

便服 biànfú ① everyday clothes; informal dress ② civilian clothes

便函 biànhán an informal letter sent by an organization

便壶 biànhú (bed) urinal; chamber pot

便笺 biànjiān ① (informal) note ② notepaper; memo; memo pad

便捷 biànjié ① convenient ② quick; nimble

便览 biànlǎn brief guide: 交通〜 roadbook / 旅游〜 guidebook

便利 biànlì ① convenient; easy: 交通〜 have convenient communications; have good transport facilities;

be conveniently located / 附近就有百货公司, 买东西很～。It's easy to shop here since there's a department store nearby. ② facilitate: 为～居民, 新盖了一个副食商场。A new food market has been built for the convenience of the residents. / 为对方建立使馆提供～ provide the other side with facilities for the establishment of its embassy

便了 biànliǎo *part. old* (used at the end of a sentence, meaning the same as 就是了)

便路 biànlù　shortcut: 走～ take a shortcut

便帽 biànmào　cap

便门 biànmén　side door; wicket door

便秘 biànmì　comstipation

便民 biànmín　for the convenience of the people: ～措施 facilities for the convenience of the people (e.g. day nurseries, neighbourhood service centres, etc.) / ～商店 convenience shop (a retail shop that goes out of its way to cater to the needs of its customers, as by doing business during odd hours, delivering goods to the customer's home, etc.)

便溺 biànniào　urinate or defecate; relieve oneself

便盆 biànpén　bed pan

便桥 biànqiáo　temporary (*or* makeshift) bridge

便人 biànrén　somebody who happens to be on hand for an errand: 如有～, 请把那本书捎来。Please send the book by anyone who happens to come this way.

便士 biànshì　penny

便所 biànsuǒ　lavatory; toilet; W.C.

便条 biàntiáo　(also 便签 biànqiān) (informal) note

便桶 biàntǒng　chamber pot

便席 biànxí　informal dinner

便鞋 biànxié　cloth shoes; slippers

便血 biànxiě　*med.* having (*or* passing) blood in one's stool

便宴 biànyàn　informal dinner: 设～招待 give a dinner for sb.

便衣 biànyī　① civilian clothes; plain clothes: ～警察 plainclothes policeman / ～公安人员 plainclothes public security personnel; public security personnel in plain clothes ② plainclothesman

便宜 biànyí　convenient; advantageous ——see also piányi

便宜行事 biànyí xíng shì　(authorized to) act at one's discretion; act as one sees fit

便于 biànyú　easy to; convenient for: ～携带 easy to carry

便中 biànzhōng　at one's convenience; when it's convenient: 我替你捎来一双鞋, 望～来取。I've brought you a pair of shoes. Please come for them whenever it's convenient. / ～请告知。Please let me know at your convenience.

便装 biànzhuāng　same as 便服 biànfú

便酌 biànzhuó　informal dinner

遍 (徧)

biàn　① all over; everywhere: 我找～了也没找着。I have looked everywhere, but I can't find it. / 走～全省 travel all over the province / 我们的朋友～天下。We have friends all over the world. ② *m.* (for actions) once through; a time: 这本书我从头到尾看过两～。I've read the book twice from cover to cover. / 请再说一～。Please say it again.

遍布 biànbù　be found everywhere; spread all over: 乡镇企业～全国。Enterprises run by townships and villages can be found all over the country. / 公路～全省。Highways extend over the whole province.

遍地 biàndì　all over the place; everywhere

遍地开花 biàndì kāihuā　blossom everywhere; spring up all over the place

遍及 biànjí　extend (*or* spread) all over

遍体鳞伤 biàntǐ línshāng　be covered all over with cuts and bruises; be beaten black and blue; be a mass of bruises

缠

biàn　see 草帽缏 cǎomàobiàn

辨

biàn　differentiate; distinguish; discriminate: 不～真伪 fail to distinguish between truth and falsehood; be unable to tell the true from the false

辨白 biànbái　same as 辩白 biànbái

辨别 biànbié　differentiate; distinguish; discriminate: ～真假 distinguish the true from the false / ～方向 take one's bearings

辨尝 biànchǎng　taste; sample; savour

辨惑 biànhuò　straighten out confusing points

辨明 biànmíng　make a clear distinction; distinguish

辨认 biànrèn　identify; recognize: 他的笔迹容易～。His handwriting is easy to identify. / 相片已经模糊, 不能～。The photo has faded beyond recognition.

辨析 biànxī　differentiate and analyse; discriminate: 同义词～ synonym discrimination

辨正 biànzhèng　determine and rectify: 《性命古训～》A Critical Study of the Traditional Theories of Human Nature and Destiny

辨证 biànzhèng　same as 辩证 biànzhèng①

辨证论治 biànzhèng lùnzhì　(also 辨证施治 biànzhèng shīzhì) *Chin. med.* diagnosis and treatment based on an overall analysis of the illness and the patient's condition

辩 (辯)

biàn　argue; dispute; debate: 真理愈～愈明。The more truth is debated, the clearer it becomes.

辩白 biànbái　offer an explanation; plead innocence; try to defend oneself

辩驳 biànbó　dispute; refute: 无可～ beyond all dispute; indisputable; irrefutable

辩才 biàncái　*formal* eloquence: 颇有～ be quite eloquent; have a silver tongue

辩辞 biàncí　(also 辩词 biàncí) explanation; argument

辩护 biànhù　① speak in defence of; argue in favour of; defend: 不要替他～了。Don't try to defend him. ② *leg.* plead; defend: 为被告人～ plead for the accused / 出庭～ (of a lawyer) defend a case in court / 被告人有权获得～。The accused has the right to defence.

辩护权 biànhùquán　right to defence

辩护人 biànhùrén　defender; counsel

辩护士 biànhùshì　apologist

辩解 biànjiě　provide an explanation; try to defend oneself: 错了就错了, 不要～。A mistake is a mistake. Don't try to explain it away.

辩论 biànlùn　argue; debate: ～个水落石出 argue the matter out

辩论会 biànlùnhuì　a debate: 举行～ hold a debate

辩难 biànnàn　*formal* retort with challenging questions; debate

辩士 biànshì　orator; sophist

辩说 biànshuō　argue; debate

辩诬 biànwū　defend oneself against false accusations

辩正 biànzhèng　same as 辨正 biànzhèng

辩证 biànzhèng　① investigate; authenticate: 《长门赋》"Authentication of the 'Tall Gate Rhapsody'" ② dialectical: ～的统一 dialectical unity / ～地看问题 look at things dialectically / 事物发展的～规律 the dialectical law of the development of things

辩证法 biànzhèngfǎ　dialectics

辩证逻辑 biànzhèng luóji　dialectical logic

辩证唯物主义 biànzhèngwéiwùzhǔyì　dialectical materialism: ～的认识论 the dialectical materialist theory of

knowledge／～观点 a dialectical materialist point of view／～者 dialectical materialist

辫(辮)
biàn　plait; braid; pigtail: 蒜～ a braid of garlic

辫子 biànzi ① plait; braid; pigtail: 梳～ braid one's hair／留～ wear one's hair in braids ② a mistake or shortcoming that may be exploited by an opponent; handle ——see also 梳辫子 shū biànzi; 抓辫子 zhuā biànzi

biāo

标(標)
biāo ① mark; sign: 路标·lùbiāo ② put a mark, tag or label on; label: ～上号码 put a number on／～界 demarcate a boundary／商品都～了价格。 Every article has a price tag on it. ③ prize; award: 夺标 duóbiāo ④ outward sign; symptom: 治标 zhìbiāo ⑤ tender; bid: 招标 zhāobiāo

标榜 biāobǎng ① flaunt; advertise; parade: ～自由平等 flaunt the banner of liberty and equality ② boost; excessively praise: 互相～ boost each other; exchange excessive praise

标本 biāoběn ① specimen; sample: 昆虫～ insect specimen ② Chin. med. the root cause and symptoms of a disease: ～同治 treat a disease by looking into both its root cause and symptoms

标本虫 biāoběnchóng zool. spider beetle

标兵 biāobīng ① parade guards (usu. spaced out along parade routes) ② example; model; pacesetter: 树立～ set sb. up as a pacemaker／石油战线上的～ a pacesetter on the oil production front

标尺 biāochǐ ① surveyor's rod; staff ② water conservancy staff gauge ③ common name for 表尺 biǎochǐ

标灯 biāodēng ① beacon light; beacon ② sign lamp (as outside a post office, chemist, etc. at night)

标点 biāodiǎn ① punctuation ② punctuate

标点符号 biāodiǎn fúhào punctuation mark

标定 biāodìng ① demarcate: ～边界线 demarcate a boundary by setting up boundary markers (done jointly by the two parties concerned) ② standardize ③ check according to set standards ④ standard; standardized

标杆 biāogān ① surveyor's pole ② model; example

标高 biāogāo surveying & drawing elevation; level

标号 biāohào grade: 水泥～ grade of cement／高～水泥 high-grade cement

标记 biāojì sign; mark; symbol: 探清地雷，作出～ locate the landmines and mark their location

标记原子 biāojì yuánzǐ same as 示踪原子 shìzōng yuánzǐ

标价 biāojià ① mark a price ② marked price

标量 biāoliàng phys. scalar quantity

标明 biāomíng mark; indicate: 货箱上～"小心轻放"。 The crate is marked "Handle with care".／在这幅地图上北京是用一颗红星～的。 Beijing is indicated on the map by a red star.

标签 biāoqiān label; tag: 贴上～ stick on a label／价目～ price tag

标枪 biāoqiāng javelin

标示 biāoshì mark; indicate

标题 biāotí title; heading; headline; caption

标题音乐 biāotí yīnyuè programme music

标新立异 biāoxīn-lìyì start sth. new just in order to be different; do sth. unconventional or unorthodox; create sth. new and original

标样 biāoyàng a trade sample

标音 biāoyīn transcription: 宽式～ broad transcription／严式～ narrow transcription

标语 biāoyǔ slogan; poster: 张贴～ put up slogans (or posters)

标语牌 biāoyǔpái placard

标语塔 biāoyǔtǎ slogan pylon

标志 biāozhì (also 标识 biāozhì) ① sign; mark; symbol: 兴旺发达的～ a sign of vigour and prosperity ② indicate; mark; symbolize: 中华人民共和国的成立，～着我国新的历史阶段的开始。 The founding of the People's Republic of China marked the beginning of a news historical period in our country.

标志层 biāozhìcéng geol. marker bed

标致 biāozhì (usu. of women) beautiful; handsome

标桩 biāozhuāng (marking) stake

标准 biāozhǔn ① standard; criterion: 合乎～ up to standard／按我们的～来看 by our standards／用高～要求自己 set high demands on oneself／真理的～只能是社会的实践。 Only social practice can be the criterion of truth. ② serving as or conforming to a standard

标准层 biāozhǔncéng geol. key bed

标准大气压 biāozhǔn dàqìyā phys. standard atmosphere

标准化 biāozhǔnhuà standardize

标准局 biāozhǔnjú bureau of standards

标准时 biāozhǔnshí standard time

标准时区 biāozhǔn shíqū same as 时区 shíqū

标准台 biāozhǔntái agric. standard unit (a unit for measuring the power of a tractor, equal to 15 horse-power): 一台东方红拖拉机等于2.4个～。 An "East Is Red" tractor equals 2.4 standard units.／这个拖拉机站有拖拉机四十个～，负责十万亩地的农活。 This tractor station possesses 40 standard units and is responsible for 100,000 mu of land.

标准像 biāozhǔnxiàng official portrait

标准音 biāozhǔnyīn standard pronunciation

标准语 biāozhǔnyǔ standard speech

彪
biāo formal a young tiger

彪炳 biāobǐng formal shining; splendid: ～显赫的历史功绩 splendid achievements in history／篇之～，章无疵也；章之明靡，句无玷也；句之清英，字不妄也。(刘勰《文心雕龙》) The brilliance of a literary piece depends on the faultlessness of each paragraph; the clarity of the paragraph depends on the flawlessness of each sentence; and the purity of the sentence depends on a happy choice of words.

彪炳千古 biāobǐng qiāngǔ shine through the ages: 其功业将～。 The glory of his achievements will shine through the ages.

彪悍 biāohàn intrepid; doughty; valiant

彪形大汉 biāoxíng dàhàn burly chap; husky fellow; hefty fellow

彪壮 biāozhuàng tall and husky; hefty: 身材～ of great stature／～的小伙子 a hefty young man

骠
biāo see 黄骠马 huángbiāomǎ ——see also piào

骠实 biāoshi same as 膘实 biāoshi

膘(臕)
biāo fat (of a domestic animal): 牲口～肥体壮。 The animals are plump and sturdy.／这块肉～厚。 This piece of meat has got a lot of fat on it.

膘实 biāoshi (of a domestic animal) plump

瘭
biāo see below

瘭疽 biāojū Chin. med. pyogenic infection of the pad of a finger

镖　biāo　a dartlike weapon (used in former times)

镖局　biāojú　(in former times) a professional establishment which provided armed escorts

镖客　biāokè　(also 镖师 biāoshī) (in former times) armed escort (of travellers or merchants' caravans)

飙（飇、飚）　biāo　*formal*　violent wind; whirlwind: 狂飙 kuángbiāo

镳¹　biāo　*formal*　bit (of a bridle): 分道扬镳 fēndào yángbiāo

镳²　biāo　same as 镖 biāo

biǎo

表¹　biǎo　① surface; outside; external: 表面 biǎomiàn ② the relationship between the children or grandchildren of a brother and a sister or of sisters: 表哥 biǎogē ③ show; express: 深～同情 show deep sympathy /～决心 express (*or* declare) one's determination ④ *Chin. med.*　administer medicine to bring out the cold ⑤ model; example: 表率 biǎoshuài ⑥ memorial to an emperor: 诸葛亮《出师～》Zhuge Liang's "Memorial on Going to War" ⑦ table; form; list: 价目～ price list / 登记～ registration form ⑧ meter; gauge: 水表 shuǐbiǎo

表²（錶）　biǎo　watch (a timepiece)

表白　biǎobái　express or state clearly; explain; clarify; explain oneself: ～诚意 assert one's sincerity / 我们看一个人，不是根据他的～，而是根据他的行动。We judge a person not by what he says but by what he does.

表报　biǎobào　statistical tables and reports

表册　biǎocè　statistical forms; book of tables or forms: 公文报告～ documents, written reports and statistical forms

表层　biǎocéng　surface layer

表尺　biǎochǐ　*mil.*　rear sight

表尺座　biǎochǐzuò　rear sight base

表达　biǎodá　express; convey; voice: 我激动的心情难以用语言来～。Words can hardly express my excitement. / ～群众的感情 voice the feelings of the masses / ～人民的坚强意志 demonstrate the firm will of the people

表带　biǎodài　watchband; watch strap

表弟　biǎodì　the son of one's father's sister or of one's mother's brother or sister, who is younger than oneself; younger male cousin; cousin

表哥　biǎogē　the son of one's father's sister or of one's mother's brother or sister, who is older than oneself; older male cousin; cousin

表格　biǎogé　form; table: 填写～ fill in a form

表功　biǎogōng　① brag about one's deeds ② *formal*　praise; commend

表观　biǎoguān　*phys.*　apparent

表观运动　biǎoguān yùndòng　apparent motion

表观质量　biǎoguān zhìliàng　apparent mass

表汗　biǎohàn　induce perspiration (as by drugs); diaphoresis

表记　biǎojì　*formal*　sth. given as a token; souvenir

表姐　biǎojiě　the daughter of one's father's sister or of one's mother's brother or sister, who is older than oneself; older female cousin; cousin

表决　biǎojué　decide by vote; vote: 我们现在～。Let's take a vote. / 付～ put to the vote; take a vote / 投票～ decide (*or* vote) by ballot / 举手～ vote by a show of hands / 唱名～ vote by roll call; roll-call vote / 口头～ voice vote; vote by "yes" and "no" / 起立～ vote by sitting and standing /～通过 be voted through

表决程序　biǎojué chéngxù　voting procedure

表决机器　biǎojué jīqì　voting machine

表决权　biǎojuéquán　the right to vote; the vote: 行使～ exercise the right to vote / 有(无)～ have the right (no right) to vote

表决指示牌　biǎojué zhǐshìpái　vote indicator

表里　biǎo-lǐ　① outside and inside; one's outward show and inner thoughts: ～为奸 collusion between those within and those without ② *Chin. med.*　exterior and interior

表里不一　biǎo-lǐ bù yī　think one way and act another

表里如一　biǎo-lǐ rú yī　think and act in one and the same way

表链　biǎoliàn　watch chain

表露　biǎolù　show; reveal: 他很着急，但并没有～出来。He was very worried, but didn't show it.

表妹　biǎomèi　the daughter of one's father's sister or of one's mother's brother or sister, who is younger than oneself; younger female cousin; cousin

表蒙子　biǎoméngzi　watch glass; crystal

表面¹　biǎomiàn　surface; face; outside; appearance: 地球的～ the surface of the earth / 你不能只看事情的～。You must not look only at the surface of things. / 他～上好象很和气。He seems very friendly on the surface.

表面²　biǎomiàn　*dial.*　dial plate; dial

表面处理　biǎomiàn chǔlǐ　surface treatment

表面光　biǎomiànguāng　attractive on the surface; cheaply showy: 这产品～，质量却很差。This product looks nice, but proves to be poor in quality.

表面化　biǎomiànhuà　come to the surface; become apparent: 矛盾～了。The contradiction has become apparent.

表面价值　biǎomiàn jiàzhí　face value

表面文章　biǎomiàn wénzhāng　show; ostentation: 我们讲求实际效果，不要形式主义和～。We want solid results, not show and formalism. / 他那番话不过是～。He was merely paying lip service.

表面现象　biǎomiàn xiànxiàng　superficial phenomenon

表面硬化　biǎomiàn yìnghuà　*metall.*　case-hardening

表面张力　biǎomiàn zhānglì　*phys.*　surface tension

表明　biǎomíng　make known; make clear; state clearly; indicate: ～立场 make known one's position; declare one's stand / 有迹象～会谈即将恢复。There are indications that the talks will be resumed soon.

表盘　biǎopán　dial plate; dial

表皮　biǎopí　*biol.*　epidermis; cuticle

表亲　biǎoqīn　① cousin ② cousinship

表情　biǎoqíng　① express one's feelings: 她演戏善于～。Her acting is very expressive. ② expression: 她唱歌很有～。She sings with great expression. / 面部～ facial expression / ～不自然 look awkward; wear an unnatural expression

表示　biǎoshì　① show; express; indicate: ～关切 show concern / ～愤慨 voice (*or* express) one's indignation / ～热烈欢迎 extend a warm welcome / 我们谨向你们～衷心的祝贺。We wish to convey to you our hearty congratulations. / 发高烧～有病。A high fever indicates that a person is sick. ② expression; indication: 友好的～ an expression of friendship; a friendly gesture

表述　biǎoshù　explain; state: ～己见 state (*or* air) one's views

表率　biǎoshuài　example; model: 老师要做学生的～。A teacher must set an example (*or* a good example) to his students.

表态　biǎotài　make known one's position; declare where one stands; commit oneself: 明确～ take a clear-

cut stand / 她没有～。 She didn't say which side she was on. *or* She didn't commit herself. / 作～性发言 make a statement of one's position

表土　biǎotǔ　surface soil; topsoil

表现　biǎoxiàn　① show; display; manifest: 他心里很不高兴，可是没有～出来。 He was unhappy, but he didn't show it. / ～出极大的勇敢和智慧 display immense courage and wisdom / 一贯～积极 be always active; always show great initiative / ～战争的文学作品 literary works depicting war ② expression; manifestation; display: 这是他无知的又一种～。 This is yet another manifestation of his ignorance. / 政治是经济的集中～。 Politics is the concentrated expression of economics. ③ behaviour; performance: 他在工作中的～很好。 He is doing very well in his work. ④ show off: 好～ like to show off

表现手法　biǎoxiàn shǒufǎ　technique of expression

表现形式　biǎoxiàn xíngshì　form of expression; manifestation

表现型　biǎoxiànxíng　*biol.*　phenotype

表象　biǎoxiàng　*psychol.*　idea

表兄　biǎoxiōng　same as 表哥 biǎogē

表演　biǎoyǎn　① perform; act; play: ～节目 give a performance; put on a show / 她～得很好。 She performed very well. ② performance; exhibition: 杂技～ acrobatic performance / 体育～ sports exhibition / 航空模型～ model planes exhibition ③ demonstrate: ～新操作方法 demonstrate new techniques of operation

表演唱　biǎoyǎnchàng　singing with actions

表演赛　biǎoyǎnsài　exhibition match

表扬　biǎoyáng　praise; commend: ～好人好事 praise good people and good deeds / 大会～了十个先进集体。 The conference commended ten advanced units.

表扬信　biǎoyángxìn　commendatory letter

表意文字　biǎoyì wénzì　ideograph; ideogram; ideography

表音文字　biǎoyīn wénzì　phonography

表语　biǎoyǔ　*gram.*　predicative

表彰　biǎozhāng　cite (in dispatches); commend: 六连的出色战功得到～。 The 6th Company was cited for its distinguished service in the battle. / 为了～他生前的事迹 in recognition of his deeds in his lifetime

表针　biǎozhēn　indicator; pointer

表证　biǎozhèng　*Chin. med.*　illness that has not attacked the vital organs of the human body

表字　biǎozì　(also 表号 biǎohào)　*old*　courtesy name; style: 朱买臣，～翁子，会稽郡人氏。 Zhu Maichen, styled Wengzi, came from the prefecture of Guiji.

婊　biǎo　see below

婊子　biǎozi　prostitute; whore

裱　biǎo　① mount (a picture, etc.): 把画拿去～一下。 Go and have the painting mounted. ② paper (a wall, ceiling, etc.)

裱褙　biǎobèi　(also 裱贴 biǎotiē) mount (a picture, etc.)

裱糊　biǎohú　paper (a wall, ceiling, etc.)

裱装　biǎozhuāng　mount (a picture, etc.)

biào

摽¹　biào　① tie; bind; fasten: 桌子腿活动了，用铁丝～住吧。 The table is shaky. Let's fasten its legs with iron wire. ② lock together: 母女俩～着胳膊走。 Mother and daughter walked arm in arm. ③ be glued to: 他小妹妹老～在他身边。 His little sister always stays glued to his side.

摽²　biào　*formal*　① fall down ② strike

摽劲儿　biào·jìnr　① be in a huff with sb.; be at odds with sb.: 他正跟我～呢，能听我的吗？ How can you expect him to listen to me, when he's in a huff with me? ② compete with sb. and try to get the upper hand of him

鳔　biào　① swim bladder; air bladder ② same as 鳔胶 biàojiāo

鳔胶　biàojiāo　isinglass; fish glue

biē

憋　biē　① suppress; hold back: ～不住 be unable to hold oneself back; can't contain oneself / ～住气 hold one's breath / ～了一肚子火 be filled with pent-up anger / ～足了劲儿 be bursting with energy / 我们都～着不笑。 We all held ourselves from laughing. / 别老在家里～着。 Don't stay cooped up at home all the time. ② suffocate; feel oppressed: 心里～得慌 feel very much oppressed / 屋里太闷，～得人透不过气来。 The room was so stuffy, one could hardly breathe. ③ *dial.* force: ～他说出来。 Force him to say it. ④ *dial.* ponder; contemplate: 他心里～什么呢？ What is he thinking about? / 他～出这样一个主意来。 He thought about it and then came up with this idea. ⑤ *dial.* keep watch on: 猫～耗子。 The cat watched for the mouse. / 我这儿～着你呢。 I'm watching you. ⑥ *dial.* be destroyed (by inner pressure): 保险丝～了。 The fuse has blown out.

憋闷　biēmen　feel oppressed; be depressed; be dejected

憋气　biēqì　① feel suffocated (*or* oppressed) ② choke with resentment; feel injured and resentful: 憋着一肚子气 have pent-up grievances

癟（癟）　biē　see below ——see also bié

癟三　biēsān　*dial.*　a wretched-looking tramp who lives by begging or stealing

鳖（鱉）　biē　soft-shelled turtle

鳖甲　biējiǎ　*Chin. med.*　turtle shell

鳖裙　biēqún　(also 鳖边 biēbiān) calipash

bié

别¹　bié　① leave; part: ～故乡 leave one's native place ② other; another: ～处 another place; elsewhere ③ *dial.* turn; change: 她把头～了过去。 She turned her head away. / 这个人的脾气一时～不过来。 There is no changing his temper.

别²　bié　① differentiate; distinguish: ～其真伪 determine whether it's true or false ② difference; distinction: 男女有～ make a distinction between the sexes ③ classification; category: 性别 xìngbié

别³　bié　① fasten with a pin or clip: 把表格～在一起 pin (*or* clip) the forms together / 胸前～着大红花 with a big red flower pinned on one's breast ② stick in: 腰里～着旱烟袋 with a pipe stuck in one's belt / 把门～上。 Bolt the door.

别⁴　bié　*adv.*　① (used in giving commands or advice) don't; had better not: ～忘了。 Don't forget. / ～

忙! No hurry. *or* Take your time. ② (used in expressing anxiety that sth. bad may happen): 明天可～下雨。I hope it doesn't rain tomorrow. / 他～睡过头了, 误了火车。 Maybe he's overslept and missed the train. ——see also bié

别本 biéběn ① a separate copy (of a manuscript) ② a different version (of a book)

别才 biécái (also 别材 biécái) unusual ability or talent

别称 biéchēng another name; alternative name: 湘是湖南的～。 Xiang is another name for Hunan.

别出机杼 bié chū jīzhù (of literary compositions) be original in conception

别出心裁 bié chū xīncái adopt an original approach; try to be different

别动队 biédòngduì ① special detachment; commando ② an armed secret agent squad

别风淮雨 biéfēng-huáiyǔ strange wind and torrential rain (wrongly written for 列风淫雨 "strong wind and continuous rain", as in the *Shangshu Dazhuan* 《尚书大传》)—corruptions in ancient texts

别管 biéguǎn *conj.* no matter (who, what, etc.): ～是谁, 一律按原则办事。No matter who it is, we'll act according to principle.

别号 biéhào *old* another name; alias: 李白, 字太白, ～青莲居士。 Li Bai, whose courtesy name was Taibai, was also known as the Hermit of Green Lotus.

别集 biéjí a separate (*or* individual) collection (i.e. an author's collected works, opp. 总集 zǒngjí)

别价 biéjie *dial.* please don't

别具肺肠 bié jù fèi-cháng harbour sinister designs; have evil intentions

别具匠心 bié jù jiàngxīn show ingenuity; have originality: 园中布置～。 The layout of the garden shows the designer's ingenuity.

别具一格 bié jù yī gé have a style of one's own; have a unique (*or* distinctive) style: 这个舞蹈刚健清新, ～。 There is something unique about the liveliness and vigour of the dance.

别具只眼 bié jù zhī yǎn be able to see what others cannot; have an original view

别开生面 bié kāi shēngmiàn start sth. new (*or* original); break a new path; break fresh ground: 一次～的现场会 an entirely new sort of on-the-spot meeting / 这首诗可谓命意新奇, ～。 This poem can be considered fresh and original, quite a new approach to the subject.

别来无恙 bié lái wúyàng you have been well, I trust, since we parted?

别离 biélí take leave of; leave: ～家乡, 踏上征途 leave home and start on a long journey

别论 biélùn another or a different matter: 又当～ should be regarded as a different matter

别名 biémíng another name; alternative name: 铁牛是拖拉机的～。 Iron-ox is another name for tractor.

别情 biéqíng sorrow of separation

别趣 biéqù peculiar charm

别人 biérén someone else: 家里只有母亲和我, 没有～。 There are only my mother and I in our family—nobody else.

别人 biéren other people; others; people: 认真考虑～的意见 consider other people's suggestions seriously / ～恐怕不这样看。 People won't view it this way, I'm afraid.

别史 biéshǐ a separate history (i.e. a privately compiled history, opp. 正史 zhèngshǐ)

别是 biéshì *adv.* (used in expressing anxiety that sth. bad may happen): 他这时还没来, ～不肯来吧? He hasn't come yet. I hope he is not unwilling to come. / ～他不来了吧? Maybe he isn't coming.

别树一帜 bié shù yī zhì set up a new banner; found a new school of thought; have a style of one's own

别墅 biéshù villa

别说 biéshuō *conj.* to say nothing of; not to mention; let alone: ～在下雨, 你现在出去也太晚了。 It's far too late for you to go out, not to mention the fact that it's raining. / 这种动物我连听也没听说过, ～见过了。 I haven't even heard of such an animal, let alone seen it.

别提 biétí *inf.* no need to mention; you can well imagine: 他那个高兴劲儿啊, 就～了。 You can well imagine how happy he was.

别体 biétǐ a varied form of a Chinese character

别无长物 bié wú chángwù have nothing other than: 他是一介寒士, 除书以外, ～。 A poor scholar, he possessed nothing but his books.

别无二致 bié wú èr zhì without the slightest difference; just the same; identical

别绪 biéxù sorrow of separation

别筵 biéyán farewell dinner party

别样 biéyàng ① other; different ② a different style

别业 biéyè *formal* villa

别有风味 bié yǒu fēngwèi have a distinctive flavour

别有天地 bié yǒu tiān-dì a place of unique beauty; scenery of exceptional charm; an altogether different world

别有用心 bié yǒu yòngxīn have ulterior motives; have an axe to grind

别择 biézé appraise and select

别针 biézhēn ① safety pin; pin ② brooch

别致 biézhì unique; unconventional: 天坛的建筑结构非常～。 The architecture of the Temple of Heaven is unique.

别传 biézhuàn separate biography (i.e. an anecdotal biography, as distinct from an official one): 张荫麟《张衡～》 Zhang Yinlin's *Separate Biography of Zhang Heng*

别庄 biézhuāng villa

别字 biézì ① same as 白字 báizì ② same as 别号 biéhào

蹩

biè *dial.* sprain (one's ankle or wrist)

蹩脚 biéjiǎo *dial.* inferior; shoddy: ～的宣传家 an incompetent propagandist / 他的英语很～。 His English is very poor.

蹩脚货 biéjiǎohuò inferior goods; poor stuff; shoddy work

biě

瘪（癟）

biě shrivelled; shrunken: ～花生 blighted peanuts / 车胎～了。 The tyre is flat. / 没牙～嘴儿 have a toothless, sunken mouth ——see also biē

瘪螺痧 biěluóshā *Chin. med.* cholera (with dehydration)

biè

别（彆）

biè *dial.* persuade sb. to change his opinion or give up his idea (usu. used in 别不过): 我想不依他, 可是又～不过他。 I'd hate to let him have his own way, but I can't talk him round. ——see also bié

别扭 bièniu ① awkward; difficult; uncomfortable: 这两天我心里很～。 I've been feeling depressed the past few days. / 这个人真～。 That chap is really difficult to deal with (*or* is really contrary). / 她刚来牧区的时候, 生活上

感到有点～。When she first came to this pastoral area, she found life here a bit difficult to get used to. / 事情老是这样～。Things never seem to go smoothly. / 这天气真～，一会儿冷，一会儿热。The weather is unpredictable—now cold, now hot. ② not see eye to eye; disagree: 两个人素来有些别别扭扭的。The two of them often have difficulty with each other. ③ (of speech or writing) unnatural; awkward: 这句话听起来有点～。This sentence sounds a bit awkward. ——see also 闹别扭 nào bièniu

bīn

宾（賓、賓）　bīn　guest: 贵宾 guìbīn
宾白 bīnbái　spoken parts in an opera
宾词 bīncí　*log.*　predicate
宾东 bīndōng　*old*　host and guest; superior and subordinate; employer and employee; master and servant
宾服 bīnfú　*formal*　submit
宾服 bīnfu　*dial.*　admire
宾格 bīngé　*gram.*　the objective case
宾馆 bīnguǎn　guesthouse
宾客 bīnkè　guests; visitors
宾客盈门 bīnkè yíng mén　a house always full of visitors
宾礼 bīnlǐ　courtesy due to a guest: 以～相待 treat sb. with courtesy due to a guest
宾朋 bīnpéng　friends and guests; guests: ～满座。There was a houseful of guests. *or* Visitors filled all the seats.
宾铁 bīntiě　same as 镔铁 bīntiě
宾语 bīnyǔ　*gram.*　object
宾至如归 bīn zhì rú guī　where guests feel at home (said of a hotel, etc.); a home from home: 在这家饭店住宿的旅客都有～的感觉。All travellers find this hotel a home from home.
宾主 bīnzhǔ　host and guest: ～频频举杯。Host and guests proposed repeated toasts.

彬　bīn　see below
彬彬 bīnbīn　*formal*　refined
彬彬有礼 bīnbīn yǒu lǐ　refined and courteous; urbane: 他扣上上衣的扣子，～地走上一步。He buttoned up his jacket and moved forward with ceremonious deference.

斌　bīn　same as 彬 bīn

傧（儐）　bīn　see below
傧相 bīnxiàng　attendant of the bride or bridegroom at a wedding

滨（濱）　bīn　① bank; brink; shore: 湘江之～ on the banks of the Xiangjiang River ② be close to (the sea, a river, etc.); border on: ～海城市 a city bordering on the sea / ～海地区 a coastal region / 江～公园 a riverside park

缤（繽）　bīn　see below
缤纷 bīnfēn　*formal*　in riotous profusion: 五彩缤纷 wǔcǎi bīnfēn

槟（檳、梹）　bīn　see below ——see also bīng
槟子 bīnzi　*binzi*, a species of apple which is slightly sour and astringent

镔（鑌）　bīn　see below

镔铁 bīntiě　wrought iron

濒　bīn　① be close to (the sea, a river, etc.); border on: ～湖 border on the shores of a lake / 东～大海 face the sea on the east ② be on the brink of; be on the point of: 濒死 bīnsǐ / 濒行 bīnxíng
濒近 bīnjìn　close to; close on
濒临 bīnlín　be close to; border on; be on the verge of: 河北省～渤海。Hebei Province is on the Bohai. / 春秋末期奴隶社会～瓦解。By the end of the Spring and Autumn Period (770-476 B.C.) slave society was on the verge of disintegration.
濒死 bīnsǐ　be dying
濒危 bīnwēi　*formal*　① be in imminent danger: 我国有354种珍稀植物～。In our country 354 species of rare plants are on the brink of extinction (*or* are dying out). ② be critically ill
濒行 bīnxíng　be about to start on a journey
濒于 bīnyú　be on the brink of: ～破产 be on the brink of bankruptcy / ～崩溃 verge on collapse / ～灭亡 near extinction / ～绝境 face an impasse

bìn

摈（擯）　bìn　*formal*　discard; get rid of: ～而不用 reject / ～诸门外 shut (*or* lock) sb. out
摈斥 bìnchì　*formal*　reject; dismiss: ～异己 dismiss those who hold different opinions
摈除 bìnchú　discard; get rid of; dispense with: ～繁文缛节 dispense with all unnecessary formalities
摈弃 bìnqì　abandon; discard; cast away: ～陈旧的道德观念 cast away antiquated moral values

膑（臏）　bìn　same as 髌 bìn
殡（殯）　bìn　① lay a coffin in a memorial hall ② carry a coffin to the burial place: 出殡 chūbìn
殡车 bìnchē　hearse
殡殓 bìnliàn　encoffin a corpse and carry it to the grave
殡仪馆 bìnyíguǎn　the undertaker's; funeral parlour (*or* home)
殡葬 bìnzàng　funeral and interment

髌（髕）　bìn　① kneecap; patella ② chopping off the kneecaps (a punishment in ancient China)
髌骨 bìngǔ　kneecap; patella

鬓（鬢、鬂）　bìn　temples; hair on the temples: 双～斑白 greying at the temples
鬓发 bìnfà　hair on the temples: ～苍白 greying at the temples
鬓角 bìnjiǎo　(also 鬓脚 bìnjiǎo) temples; hair on the temples

bīng

并　Bīng　another name for 太原 Tàiyuán ——see also bìng

冰（氷）　bīng　① ice ② put on the ice; ice: 把那瓶啤酒～上。Ice the bottle of beer. ③ feel cold: 这水～手。This water is freezing cold.
冰棒 bīngbàng　*dial.*　same as 冰棍儿 bīnggùnr
冰雹 bīngbáo　hail; hailstone: 下～了。It's hailing.
冰场 bīngchǎng　skating (*or* ice) rink; ice stadium; ice

arena

冰川　bīngchuān　glacier

冰川湖　bīngchuānhú　glacial lake

冰川期　bīngchuānqī　glacial epoch; ice age

冰川舌　bīngchuānshé　glacier tongue

冰川学　bīngchuānxué　glaciology

冰川作用　bīngchuān zuòyòng　glaciation

冰床　bīngchuáng　sled; sledge; sleigh

冰醋酸　bīngcùsuān　*chem.* glacial acetic acid

冰镩　bīngcuān　ice chisel

冰袋　bīngdài　*med.* ice bag

冰蛋　bīngdàn　frozen eggs

冰刀　bīngdāo　*sports* (ice) skates

冰岛　Bīngdǎo　Iceland

冰岛人　Bīngdǎorén　Icelander

冰岛语　Bīngdǎoyǔ　Icelandic (language)

冰灯　bīngdēng　ice lantern

冰点　bīngdiǎn　*phys.* freezing point

冰点测定器　bīngdiǎn cèdìngqì　cryoscope

冰雕　bīngdiāo　① ice carving ② carved ice; ice sculpture

冰冻　bīngdòng　① freeze ② *dial.* ice

冰冻季节　bīngdòng jìjié　freezing season

冰冻区　bīngdòngqū　frost zone

冰冻三尺，非一日之寒　bīng dòng sān chǐ, fēi yī rì zhī hán　it takes more than one cold day for the river to freeze three *chi* deep—the trouble has been brewing for quite some time

冰冻食物　bīngdòng shíwù　frozen foods

冰斗　bīngdǒu　cirque

冰帆　bīngfān　① iceboat ② *sports* iceboating

冰封　bīngfēng　① (of a river, lake, etc.) freeze over; be blocked up with ice: 这湖～了，可以在上面走。The lake has frozen over; you can walk on it. / 北国风光，千里～，万里雪飘。(毛泽东) North country scene: A hundred leagues locked in ice, A thousand leagues of whirling snow. ② icebound: ～的港口 an icebound harbour

冰峰　bīngfēng　an icy mountain peak

冰盖　bīnggài　*geol.* ice sheet

冰糕　bīnggāo　*dial.* ① same as 冰激凌 bīngjīlíng ② same as 冰棍儿 bīnggùnr

冰镐　bīnggǎo　ice axe

冰棍儿　bīnggùnr　ice-lolly; popsicle; ice-sucker; frozen sucker

冰河　bīnghé　same as 冰川 bīngchuān

冰河时代　bīnghé shídài　same as 冰川期 bīngchuānqī

冰花　bīnghuā　① frost (on windows); frostwork ② (soft) rime

冰激凌　bīngjīlíng　ice cream

冰肌玉骨　bīngjī-yùgǔ　flesh of ice and bones of jade—① a beautiful woman ② noble and unsullied

冰窖　bīngjiào　icehouse

冰晶　bīngjīng　*meteorol.* ice crystal

冰晶石　bīngjīngshí　cryolite

冰冷　bīnglěng　ice-cold

冰凉　bīngliáng　ice-cold: ～的酸梅汤 ice-cold sweet-sour plum juice / 他两手冻得～。His hands were freezing.

冰凌　bīnglíng　ice

冰轮　bīnglún　*liter.* the moon

冰凝器　bīngníngqì　*phys.* cryophorus

冰排　bīngpái　ice raft; ice floe

冰片　bīngpiàn　*Chin. med.* borneol

冰期　bīngqī　same as 冰川期 bīngchuānqī

冰淇淋　bīngqílín　same as 冰激凌 bīngjīlíng

冰碛　bīngqì　*geol.* moraine: ～物 till / ～岩 tillite

冰橇　bīngqiāo　sled; sledge; sleigh

冰清玉洁　bīngqīng-yùjié　same as 玉洁冰清 yùjié-bīngqīng

冰球　bīngqiú　*sports* ① ice hockey ② puck

冰染染料　bīngrǎn rǎnliào　azoic dyes

冰人　bīngrén　*formal* matchmaker; go-between

冰山　bīngshān　① an icy mountain ② iceberg ③ an individual or a group not to be relied upon for long

冰上运动　bīngshàng yùndòng　ice-sports: ～会 ice-sports meet

冰舌　bīngshé　same as 冰川舌 bīngchuānshé

冰释　bīngshì　*formal* (of misgivings, misunderstandings, etc.) disappear; vanish; be dispelled: 涣然冰释 huànrán bīngshì

冰霜　bīngshuāng　*formal* ice and frost—① moral integrity ② austerity: 冷若冰霜 lěng ruò bīngshuāng

冰塔　bīngtǎ　*geol.* serac

冰坛　bīngtán　the ice-sports world

冰炭不相容　bīng-tàn bù xiāng róng　as incompatible (or irreconcilable) as ice and hot coals

冰糖　bīngtáng　crystal sugar; rock candy

冰糖葫芦　bīngtánghúlu　candied haws on a stick

冰天雪地　bīngtiān-xuědì　a world of ice and snow

冰隙　bīngxì　*geol.* crevasse

冰箱　bīngxiāng　icebox; refrigerator; freezer

冰消瓦解　bīngxiāo-wǎjiě　melt like ice and break like tiles—disintegrate; dissolve; be dispelled: 通过谈心，他们两人之间的误会已经～。The misunderstandings between the two of them were cleared up (or removed) after a heart-to-heart talk.

冰鞋　bīngxié　skating boots; skates

冰心　bīngxīn　moral purity

冰雪聪明　bīngxuě cōngmíng　extremely intelligent; remarkably bright; brilliant

冰镇　bīngzhèn　iced: ～西瓜 iced watermelon / ～汽水 iced soda water

冰洲石　bīngzhōushí　Iceland spar

冰柱　bīngzhù　icicle

冰砖　bīngzhuān　ice-cream brick

冰锥　bīngzhuī　(also 冰锥子 bīngzhuīzi) same as 冰柱 bīngzhù

兵

兵　bīng　① weapons; arms: 坚甲利兵 jiānjiǎ-lìbīng ② soldier: 当兵 dāngbīng ③ rank-and-file soldier; private: 官兵 guānbīng ④ army; troops: 骑兵 qíbīng ⑤ military: 纸上谈兵 zhǐ shàng tán bīng ⑥ pawn, one of the pieces in Chinese chess

兵败如山倒　bīng bài rú shān dǎo　an army in flight is like a landslide

兵变　bīngbiàn　mutiny

兵不血刃　bīng bù xuè rèn　with blades innocent of blood—win victory without shedding a drop of blood or firing a shot: 第二次世界大战爆发前数年，希特勒～，吞并了欧洲的部分地区。In the years immediately preceding the outbreak of World War II, Hitler succeeded in annexing various parts of Europe without firing a shot.

兵不厌诈　bīng bù yàn zhà　there can never be too much deception in war; all's fair in war

兵部　Bīngbù　the Board of War ——see also 六部 Liùbù

兵操　bīngcāo　*old* military drill

兵差　bīngchāi　*old* conscript labour

兵车　bīngchē　① *old* (war) chariot ② military vehicle

兵船　bīngchuán　man-of-war; naval vessel; warship

兵丁　bīngdīng　*old* rank-and-file soldiers; privates

兵端　bīngduān　*formal* hostilities; war: 猝启～。War broke out.

兵多将广　bīngduō-jiàngguǎng　a very large army with many able generals—very powerful military forces

兵法　bīngfǎ　art of war; military strategy and tactics

兵符　bīngfú　① (in former times) military tally (used as evidence of authority) ② same as 兵书 bīngshū

兵戈　bīnggē　*formal* ① weapons; arms: 不动～ without resorting to force ② fighting; war: ～扰攘 war-torn

兵工　bīnggōng　war industry

兵工厂　bīnggōngchǎng　munitions (*or* ordnance) factory; arsenal

兵贵神速　bīng guì shénsù　speed is what counts in war; in war it's speed that counts

兵荒马乱　bīnghuāng-mǎluàn　the turmoil and chaos of war

兵火　bīnghuǒ　flames of war: ～连天 flames of war raging fiercely

兵祸　bīnghuò　disaster of war

兵家　bīngjiā　① military strategist in ancient China ② military commander; soldier: ～必争之地 a place contested by all strategists; strategic point

兵舰　bīngjiàn　warship

兵精粮足　bīngjīng-liángzú　have well-trained troops and abundant supplies

兵来将挡，水来土掩　bīng lái jiàng dǎng, shuǐ lái tǔ yǎn　confront soldiers with generals and stem water with earth—take such measures as the situation calls for

兵力　bīnglì　military strength; armed forces; troops: ～对比 relative military strength / 分散～ disperse one's troops; spread one's forces too thin / ～不足 be short of men (*or* armed forces) / ～转移 transfer of troops / ～部署 troop disposition; battle array

兵连祸结　bīnglián-huòjié　ravaged by successive wars; war-torn; war-ridden

兵临城下　bīng lín chéng xià　the enemy host has reached the city gates; the city is under siege

兵乱　bīngluàn　turmoil caused by war

兵马　bīngmǎ　troops and horses; military forces

兵马未动，粮草先行　bīngmǎ wèi dòng, liángcǎo xiān xíng　food and fodder should go ahead of troops and horses—proper preparations should be made ahead of time

兵马俑　bīngmǎyǒng　wood or clay figures of warriors and horses buried with the dead

兵痞　bīngpǐ　army riffraff; army ruffian; soldier of fortune

兵器　bīngqì　weaponry; weapons; arms

兵强马壮　bīngqiáng-mǎzhuàng　strong soldiers and sturdy horses—a well-trained and powerful army

兵权　bīngquán　military leadership; military power: 掌握～ hold military power

兵戎　bīngróng　arms; weapons

兵戎相见　bīngróng xiāngjiàn　resort (*or* appeal) to arms; open hostilities; cross swords with; meet on the battleground

兵士　bīngshì　rank-and-file soldiers; privates

兵势　bīngshì　military strength; armed forces; troops

兵书　bīngshū　a book on the art of war

兵团　bīngtuán　large (military) unit; formation; corps

兵燹　bīngxiǎn　*formal* ravages of war

兵饷　bīngxiǎng　*old* soldier's pay and provisions

兵械　bīngxiè　ordnance; armament

兵蚁　bīngyǐ　soldier ant; dinergate

兵役　bīngyì　military service: 服～ serve in the army; perform military service

兵役法　bīngyìfǎ　military service law

兵役制　bīngyìzhì　system of military service

兵营　bīngyíng　military camp; barracks

兵油子　bīngyóuzi　*old* army riffraff; army ruffian

兵员　bīngyuán　soldiers; troops: 五十万～ 500,000 troops; an army 500,000 strong

兵源　bīngyuán　manpower resources (for military service); sources of troops

兵灾　bīngzāi　disaster of war

兵站　bīngzhàn　army service station; military depot

兵种　bīngzhǒng　a combat branch of one of the armed forces; arm: 步兵是陆军～之一。The infantry is one of the arms of the army.

兵卒　bīngzú　*old* soldiers

槟（檳、梹）

bīng　see below——see also bīn

槟榔　bīnglang　areca; betel palm

槟榔子　bīnglangzǐ　*Chin. med.* betel (*or* areca) nut

bǐng

丙

bǐng　① the third of the ten Heavenly Stems (天干) (see also 干支 gān-zhī) ② third: ～等 the third grade; grade C / ～种维生素 vitamin C

丙纶　bǐnglún　*text.* polypropylene fibre

丙酮　bǐngtóng　*chem.* acetone

丙酮树脂　bǐngtóng shùzhī　acetone resin

丙烯酸　bǐngxīsuān　*chem.* acrylic acid

丙烯酸绘画　bǐngxīsuān huìhuà　acrylic painting

丙种射线　bǐngzhǒng shèxiàn　*phys.* gamma ray

秉

bǐng　① *liter.* grasp; hold: ～笔 hold a pen / ～烛 hold a candle ② *formal* control; preside over: ～政 hold political power; be in power

秉承　bǐngchéng　*formal* take (orders); receive (commands): ～其主子的旨意 act on the orders of one's master

秉持　bǐngchí　adhere to (principles, etc.); hold onto: ～公心，指摘时弊 castigate the error of the times out of unselfish motives

秉赋　bǐngfù　① possess; be endowed with ② natural endowment; gift

秉公　bǐnggōng　justly; impartially

秉公办理　bǐnggōng bànlǐ　handle a matter impartially; act with justice

秉国　bǐngguó　*formal* hold state power; rule a nation

秉钧　bǐngjūn　*formal* hold political power; be in power

秉性　bǐngxìng　same as 禀性 bǐngxìng

秉钺　bǐngyuè　*formal* wield military power; have command of the armed forces

秉正　bǐngzhèng　*formal* fair-minded; honest; upright

秉政　bǐngzhèng　*formal* be at the helm of the state; be in power; be in office

秉直　bǐngzhí　*formal* honest; upright

秉烛夜游　bǐng zhú yè yóu　wander about at night carrying a lamp—make merry while one may

炳

bǐng　*formal* bright; splendid; remarkable: 彪炳 biāobǐng

柄

bǐng　① handle: 刀～ the handle of a knife / 斧～ the shaft of an axe; helve ② stem (of a flower, leaf or fruit): 花～ the stem of a flower ③ anything affording an advantage or pretext to an opponent: 话柄 huàbǐng ④ *formal* control: ～国 rule a country / ～政 hold political power ⑤ *formal* power; authority: 国柄 guóbǐng ⑥ *m. dial.* (for things with handles): 两～斧头 two axes

柄臣　bǐngchén　*formal* a powerful minister (of a monarchy)

柄权　bǐngquán　*formal* be in power; exercise control

饼

bǐng　① a round flat cake: 月饼 yuèbǐng ② sth. shaped like a cake: 柿饼 shìbǐng

饼铛　bǐngchēng　baking pan

饼饵　bǐng'ěr　*formal* cakes; pastry

饼肥　bǐngféi　cake (fertilizer)

饼干 bǐnggān biscuit; cracker
饼子 bǐngzi (maize or millet) pancake

屏[1] bǐng hold (one's breath): ～着呼吸 hold one's breath

屏[2] (摒) bǐng reject; get rid of; abandon: 屏除 bǐngchú
——see also píng

屏除 bǐngchú get rid of; dismiss; brush aside: ～杂念 dismiss distracting thoughts

屏居 bǐngjū *formal* retire from public life; live in seclusion

屏绝 bǐngjué dismiss; brush aside; abandon

屏气 bǐngqì hold one's breath: 他放轻脚步屏住气向病房走去。Holding his breath, he stepped lightly towards the ward.

屏气凝神 bǐngqì-níngshén hold one's breath in concentration: ～地听讲 listen with rapt attention

屏弃 bǐngqì discard; reject; throw away; abandon

屏去 bǐngqù ① get rid of; eliminate; remove ② order retainers, servants, etc. to retire

屏声 bǐngshēng hold one's breath and keep quiet: ～倾听 listen in rapt silence

屏退 bǐngtuì ① order retainers, servants, etc. to retire: ～左右 order one's attendants to clear out ② *formal* (of an official) retire from public life; go into retirement

屏息 bǐngxī hold one's breath: ～静听 listen with bated breath

禀 (稟) bǐng ① *formal* report (to one's superior or senior); petition: 禀报 bǐngbào ② *old* an official report; petition: 禀帖 bǐngtiě ③ receive; be endowed with: 禀赋 bǐngfù

禀报 bǐngbào *formal* report (to one's superior or senior)

禀呈 bǐngchéng *formal* present or submit (to one's superior or senior)

禀承 bǐngchéng same as 秉承 bǐngchéng

禀复 bǐngfù *formal* report back (to one's superior or senior)

禀赋 bǐngfù natural endowment; gift: ～聪明 be gifted with keen intelligence

禀告 bǐnggào *formal* report (to one's superior or senior)

禀见 bǐngjiàn *formal* call on (one's superior)

禀明 bǐngmíng explain (to one's superior or senior)

禀受 bǐngshòu possess; be endowed with

禀帖 bǐngtiě *old* a report or petition to government authorities

禀性 bǐngxìng natural disposition: ～纯厚 be simple and honest by nature

bìng

并[1] (併) bìng combine; merge; incorporate: 几个小厂～成一个大厂。Several small factories merged into a big one.

并[2] (並、竝) bìng ① stand or place side by side: 并肩 bìngjiān ② *adv.* side by side; equally; simultaneously: 并存 bìngcún ③ *adv.* (used to reinforce a negative) actually; definitely: 你以为他糊涂，他～不糊涂。You thought he was foolish, but actually he isn't. / 所谓团结，～非一团和气。When we speak of unity, we do not mean unprincipled peace. ④ *conj.*

and; besides: 我完全同意～拥护这个报告。I fully agree with and endorse this report.
——see also Bīng

并存 bìngcún exist side by side: 多种经济成分～。Multiple sectors of the economy exist side by side. / 两说～。The two statements are compatible.

并蒂莲 bìngdìlián twin lotus flowers on one stalk—a devoted married couple

并发 bìngfā be complicated by; erupt simultaneously

并发症 bìngfāzhèng *med.* complication

并激 bìngjī *elec.* shunt excitation

并激电动机 bìngjī diàndòngjī shunt motor

并激绕组 bìngjī ràozǔ shunt winding

并驾齐驱 bìngjià-qíqū run neck and neck; keep abreast of sb.; keep pace with sb.; be on a par with sb.

并肩 bìngjiān shoulder to shoulder; side by side; abreast: 四人～而行。The four of them walked abreast. / 互帮互学，～前进 help and learn from each other and advance together

并肩作战 bìngjiān zuòzhàn fight side by side; fight shoulder to shoulder

并进 bìngjìn advance side by side: 齐头并进 qítóu bìngjìn

并举 bìngjǔ carry on (two things) at the same time; develop concurrently

并卷机 bìngjuǎnjī *text.* ribbon lap machine

并力 bìnglì *formal* join forces; pool efforts

并立 bìnglì exist side by side; exist simultaneously

并联 bìnglián *elec.* parallel connection: ～电路 parallel circuit

并列 bìngliè stand side by side; be juxtaposed: ～第二名 be both runners-up; tie for second place

并列分句 bìngliè fēnjù *gram.* coordinate clause

并列句 bìnglièjù *gram.* compound sentence

并拢 bìnglǒng close up; join together

并排 bìngpái side by side; abreast: 不要～骑车。Don't all cycle abreast.

并辔 bìngpèi ride bridle to bridle; ride abreast

并且 bìngqiě *conj.* and; besides; moreover; furthermore: 任务艰巨，～时间紧迫。The task is difficult and, moreover, time is pressing. / 这本书内容好，～写得很生动。This book is sound in content and lively in style.

并日 bìngrì *formal* ① on the same day ② for days on end; day after day

并日而食 bìng rì ér shí eat once every two or three days—live in poverty

并入 bìngrù merge into; incorporate into: 1955年西康省撤销，金沙江以东地区～四川省。In 1955 Xikang Province was abolished, and the region east of the Jinshajiang was incorporated into Sichuan Province.

并纱 bìngshā *text.* doubling: ～机 doubling winder

并世 bìngshì of the time; of the day: ～无第二人 the best of the time (*or* day); peerless; unrivalled

并条 bìngtiáo *text.* drawing: ～机 drawing frame

并吞 bìngtūn swallow up; annex; absorb: 大垄断资本集团～中小企业。Big monopoly capitalist groups swallow up medium and small enterprises.

并行 bìngxíng ① walk abreast; run side by side ② carry on (two things) at the same time

并行不悖 bìngxíng bù bèi both can be accomplished without coming into conflict; not be mutually exclusive

并用 bìngyòng use two things simultaneously: 手脚～ use both hands and feet

并重 bìngzhòng lay equal stress on; pay equal attention to: 预防和治疗～ lay equal stress on prevention and cure

病 bìng ① disease; illness; sickness: 他有～。He is ill. / 他的～已经好了。He is well again. ② ill; sick:

他～了。He is ill. / 他～得很利害。He is seriously ill. ③ malady; evil: 弊病 bìbìng ④ fault; defect: 不足为～ can't count as a fault ⑤ *formal* do harm to; injure: 祸国～民 wreck the country and ruin the people ⑥ *formal* be distressed about; disapprove of: 为世所～ draw public censure

病案　bìng'àn　same as 病历 bìnglì

病包儿　bìngbāor　*inf.* a person who is always falling ill; chronic invalid

病变　bìngbiàn　pathological changes

病病歪歪　bìngbìngwāiwāi　(usu. followed by 的) sickly-looking

病残　bìngcán　illness and disability

病程　bìngchéng　course of disease

病虫害　bìng-chónghài　plant diseases and insect pests

病床　bìngchuáng　① hospital bed: 这所医院有三百张～。The hospital has three hundred beds. ② sickbed: 我在他～旁边守了好几夜。I watched beside his sickbed for several nights.

病从口入，祸从口出　bìng cóng kǒu rù, huò cóng kǒu chū　disease goes in by the mouth and trouble comes out of the mouth; illness comes from food and trouble from speech

病倒　bìngdǎo　be down with an illness; be laid up

病毒　bìngdú　*med.* virus: ～病 virosis

病毒性肝炎　bìngdúxìng gānyán　viral hepatitis

病毒学　bìngdúxué　virology

病笃　bìngdú　*formal* be critically ill; be terminally ill

病房　bìngfáng　ward (of a hospital); sickroom: 隔离～ isolation ward / 内科～ medical ward

病夫　bìngfū　sick man

病根　bìnggēn　① an incompletely cured illness; an old complaint ② the root cause of trouble: 他犯错误的～在于私心太重。His error stems from selfishness.

病故　bìnggù　die of illness

病骸　bìnghái　ailing body

病害　bìnghài　(plant) disease

病号　bìnghào　sick personnel; person on the sick list; patient: 老～ one who is always ill; chronic invalid

病号饭　bìnghàofàn　patient's diet; special food for patients

病患　bìnghuàn　disease; illness; sickness

病机　bìngjī　*Chin. med.* interpretation of the cause, onset and process of an illness; pathogenesis

病急乱投医　bìng jí luàn tóu yī　men at death's door will turn in desperation to any doctor—men in a desperate plight will try anything

病家　bìngjiā　① a patient and his family ② patient

病假　bìngjià　sick leave: 请～ ask for sick leave / 休～ be on sick leave / 给三天～ grant three days' sick leave

病假条　bìngjiàtiáo　certificate for sick leave

病句　bìngjù　a faulty sentence (grammatically or logically)

病剧　bìngjù　*formal* be critically ill; be terminally ill

病菌　bìngjūn　pathogenic bacteria; germs

病苦　bìngkǔ　suffering caused by illness

病况　bìngkuàng　state of an illness; patient's condition

病来如山倒，病去如抽丝　bìng lái rú shān dǎo, bìng qù rú chōu sī　sickness comes like an avalanche but goes like reeling silk; illness strikes like a landslide, recovery is as slow as reeling silk; agues come on horseback, but go away on foot

病理　bìnglǐ　pathology

病理学　bìnglǐxué　pathology

病历　bìnglì　medical record; case history: ～室 records room

病例　bìnglì　case (of illness): 流感～ a case of influenza

病脉　bìngmài　*Chin. med.* abnormal pulse

病魔　bìngmó　the demon of disease—serious illness: ～缠身 be possessed by the demon of disease—be afflicted with a lingering disease

病情　bìngqíng　state of an illness; patient's condition: 孩子的～有好转。The child's condition took a favourable turn. *or* The child's condition was improving.

病情公报　bìngqíng gōngbào　medical bulletin

病躯　bìngqū　a sick body

病人　bìngrén　① a sick person; invalid: 他是～。He's a sick man. / 我家有～。Someone in my family is ill. / 重～ a serious case ② patient: 这家医院医生不够，～太多。This hospital has not enough doctors and too many patients. / 这医生有好几个～等着他看。The doctor had several patients waiting to see him.

病容　bìngróng　sickly look: 面带～ look ill; look unwell

病入膏肓　bìng rù gāohuāng　the disease has attacked the vitals—beyond cure

病弱　bìngruò　sick and weak

病史　bìngshǐ　medical history; case history

病势　bìngshì　degree of seriousness of an illness; patient's condition: 针灸以后，～略为减轻。The patient became a bit better after the acupuncture treatment.

病逝　bìngshì　*formal* die of illness

病死　bìngsǐ　die of illness

病榻　bìngtà　*formal* sickbed

病态　bìngtài　morbid (*or* abnormal) state

病态心理　bìngtài xīnlǐ　morbid psychology (*or* mentality)

病体　bìngtǐ　a sick body

病痛　bìngtòng　slight illness; indisposition; ailment

病退　bìngtuì　resign from office on account of one's illness

病危　bìngwēi　be critically ill; be terminally ill

病象　bìngxiàng　symptom (of a disease)

病休　bìngxiū　be on sick leave

病恹恹　bìngyānyān　(usu. followed by 的) sickly-looking

病秧子　bìngyāngzi　same as 病包儿 bìngbāor

病因　bìngyīn　cause of disease; pathogeny

病友　bìngyǒu　a friend made in hospital or people who become friends in hospital; wardmate

病愈　bìngyù　recover (from an illness)

病员　bìngyuán　sick personnel; person on the sick list; patient

病原　bìngyuán　cause of disease; pathogeny

病原虫　bìngyuánchóng　same as 原虫 yuánchóng

病原菌　bìngyuánjūn　same as 病菌 bìngjūn

病原体　bìngyuántǐ　pathogen

病原学　bìngyuánxué　aetiology

病院　bìngyuàn　a specialized hospital: 传染病院 chuán-rǎn bìngyuàn

病灶　bìngzào　*med.* focus (of a disease): 肺结核～ a tuberculous focus in the lungs

病征　bìngzhēng　symptom (of a disease)

病症　bìngzhèng　disease; illness

病重　bìngzhòng　be seriously ill

病株　bìngzhū　diseased or infected plant

病状　bìngzhuàng　symptom (of a disease)

摒

摒　bìng　get rid of; brush aside; dismiss ——see also 屏 bǐng

摒挡　bìngdàng　*formal* arrange; put in order; get ready: ～行李 get one's luggage ready

摒绝　bìngjué　get rid of; dismiss; brush aside: ～杂念 dismiss distracting thoughts

摒弃　bìngqì　discard; reject; throw away; abandon

bō

波　bō　① wave: 水波 shuǐbō ② *phys.* wave: 声波

shēngbō ③ an unexpected turn of events: 风波 fēngbō

波长 bōcháng　wavelength

波长计 bōchángjì　wavemeter; cymometer

波茨坦公告 Bōcítǎn Gōnggào　Potsdam Proclamation (1945)

波荡 bōdàng　heave; surge: 海水～。 The sea surges.

波导 bōdǎo　*phys.* wave guide

波导管 bōdǎoguǎn　wave guide

波导通信 bōdǎo tōngxìn　wave guide communication

波动 bōdòng ① undulate; fluctuate: 物价～ price fluctuation / 情绪～ in an anxious state of mind ② *phys.* wave motion

波动说 bōdòngshuō　*phys.* wave theory

波段 bōduàn　*radio* wave band: ～开关 band switch; waver

波多黎各 Bōduōlígè　Puerto Rico

波多黎各人 Bōduōlígèrén　Puerto Rican

波尔多液 bō'ěrduōyè　*agric.* Bordeaux mixture

波尔卡 bō'ěrkǎ　polka (a dance)

波峰 bōfēng　*phys.* wave crest

波幅 bōfú　*phys.* amplitude: ～失真 amplitude distortion

波谷 bōgǔ　*phys.* trough

波-黑共和国 Bō-Hēi Gònghéguó　Republic of Bosnia-Herzegovena

波及 bōjí　spread to; involve; affect: 经济危机～整个资本主义世界。 The economic crisis affected the entire capitalist world.

波谲云诡 bōjué-yúnguǐ　same as 云谲波诡 yúnjué-bōguǐ

波兰 Bōlán　Poland

波兰人 Bōlánrén　Pole

波兰语 Bōlányǔ　Polish (language)

波澜 bōlán　great waves; billows

波澜起伏 bōlán qǐfú　(of a piece of writing) with one climax following another

波澜壮阔 bōlán zhuàngkuò　surging forward with great momentum; unfolding on a magnificent scale: ～的民族解放运动 the surging national liberation movement / 一首～、气势磅礴的史诗 a mighty and magnificent epic; an epic of magnificent sweep

波浪 bōlàng　wave: ～起伏 waves rising and falling / ～式前进 advance wave upon wave

波浪热 bōlàngrè　same as 波状热 bōzhuàngrè

波浪鼓 bōlànggǔ　same as 拨浪鼓 bōlanggǔ

波棱盖 bōlenggài　*dial.* knee

波利尼西亚 Bōlìníxīyà　Polynesia

波利尼西亚人 Bōlìníxīyàrén　Polynesian

波利尼西亚语 Bōlìníxīyàyǔ　Polynesian (language)

波罗的海 Bōluódìhǎi　the Baltic (Sea)

波罗蜜 bōluómì　another name for 木菠萝 mùbōluó

波罗蜜多 bōluómìduō　*Buddhism* paramita

波罗乃兹 bōluónǎizī　*mus.* polonaise

波美比重计 bōměibǐzhòngjì　(also 波美表 bōměibiǎo) Baumé hydrometer

波美度 bōměidù　*chem.* Baumé degrees

波谱 bōpǔ　*phys.* spectrum

波俏 bōqiào　handsome; pretty

波束 bōshù　*phys.* beam

波斯 Bōsī　Persia

波斯猫 bōsīmāo　Persian cat; Persian

波斯语 Bōsīyǔ　Persian (language)

波速 bōsù　*phys.* wave velocity

波涛 bōtāo　great waves; billows: ～滚滚 waves rolling

波涛汹涌 bōtāo xiōngyǒng　waves surging turbulently; waves running high

波特 bōtè　*telecommunications* baud

波纹 bōwén ① ripple ② corrugation

波纹管 bōwénguǎn　*mech.* bellows; corrugated pipe

波纹铁 bōwéntiě　corrugated iron

波纹纸板 bōwén zhǐbǎn　corrugated cardboard

波音 bōyīn　*mus.* mordent: 逆～ inverted mordent

波音 Bōyīn　Boeing: ～747 Boeing 747

波折 bōzhé　twists and turns: 事情发生了～。 Events took an unexpected turn.

波状热 bōzhuàngrè　*med.* undulant fever; brucellosis

波状云 bōzhuàngyún　*meteorol.* undulatus

拨（撥） bō ① move or adjust with the hand, the foot, a stick, etc.: ～算盘 move the beads on an abacus / ～火 poke a fire / ～钟 set a clock / ～电话号码 dial a telephone number / ～到北京电台 tune in to Radio Beijing ② set aside; assign; allocate: ～两间房子给词典组 set aside two rooms for the dictionary group / ～了五名青年工人到我们车间。 Five young workers have been assigned to our workshop。/ 国家～出大批资金, 发展支农工业。 The state allocates huge funds for the development of aid-agriculture industries. ③ turn round: ～转马头 turn the horse round ④ *m.* (for people) group; batch: 民工分成两～儿挖渠道。 The labourers divided themselves into two groups for digging the channel.

拨付 bōfù　appropriate (a sum of money): ～经费 appropriate funds

拨工 bōgōng　*dial.* exchange work (or labour)

拨号盘 bōhàopán　(telephone) dial

拨火棍 bōhuǒgùn　poker

拨款 bōkuǎn ① appropriate money: 市政府～筹建一所新中学。 The municipal government appropriated money for a new middle school. ② money appropriated: 军事～ military appropriations / 财政～ financial allocations

拨剌 bōlà　*onom. liter.* the sound of splashing made by a fish

拨拉 bōla　move or adjust with the hand, the foot, a stick, etc.: ～算盘子儿 move the beads on an abacus

拨浪鼓 bōlanggǔ　a drum-shaped rattle (used by pedlars or as a toy); rattle-drum

拨乱反正 bō luàn fǎn zhèng　bring order out of chaos; set to rights what has been thrown into disorder; restore things to order

拨弄 bōnong ① move to and fro with the hand, the foot, a stick, etc.; fiddle with: ～火盆里的木炭 poke the charcoal in the brazier / ～琴弦 pluck the strings of a fiddle ② stir up: ～是非 stir things up

拨冗 bōrǒng　*pol.* find time in the midst of pressing affairs: 务希～出席。 Your presence is cordially requested.

拨弦乐器 bōxián yuèqì　plucked string (or stringed) instrument; plucked instrument

拨云见日 bō yún jiàn rì　(also 拨云见天 bō yún jiàn tiān) dispel the clouds and see the sun (fig.): 得蒙先生指教, 如～, 感激不尽。 You have dispelled the clouds to let me see the sun, sir. I can't say how grateful I am for your advice. / 咱家乡自从来了共产党, ～得解放。 The Communist Party came to our home village, swept away the dark clouds and brought us the light of liberation.

拨正 bōzhèng　set right; correct: ～航向 correct the course

拨子 bōzi ① *mus.* plectrum; pick ② *m.* (for people) group; batch: 刚才有一～队伍从这里过去了。 A group of soldiers passed by just now.

拨奏 bōzòu　*mus.* pizzicato

玻 bō　see below

玻利维亚　Bōlìwéiyà　Bolivia

玻利维亚人　Bōlìwéiyàrén　Bolivian

玻璃　bōli　① glass ② *inf.* nylon; plastic

玻璃板　bōlibǎn　glass plate; plate glass; glass top (of a desk)

玻璃版　bōlibǎn　*print.* collotype

玻璃杯　bōlibēi　glass; tumbler

玻璃布　bōlibù　glass cloth

玻璃厂　bōlichǎng　glassworks

玻璃刀　bōlidāo　glass cutter; glazier's diamond

玻璃粉　bōlifěn　glass dust

玻璃钢　bōligāng　glass fibre reinforced plastic

玻璃棉　bōlimián　(also 玻璃绒 bōliróng) glass wool

玻璃片　bōlipiàn　sheet glass

玻璃纱　bōlishā　*text.* organdy

玻璃丝　bōlisī　glass silk

玻璃体　bōlitǐ　*physiol.* vitreous body

玻璃纤维　bōli xiānwéi　glass fibre

玻璃纸　bōlizhǐ　cellophane; glassine

玻璃砖　bōlizhuān　glass block

玻意耳定律　Bōyì'ěr dìnglǜ　*phys.* Boyle's law

剥　bō (meaning the same as 剥 bāo, limited to use in compound words and idiomatic phrases) ——see also bāo

剥采比　bōcǎibǐ　*min.* stripping-to-ore ratio; stripping ratio

剥夺　bōduó　deprive; expropriate; strip: ～政治权利 deprive sb. of political rights / 被～的阶级 the expropriated classes / ～权力 divest sb. of his power

剥离　bōlí　(of tissue, skin, covering, etc.) come off; peel off; be stripped: 表土～ topsoil stripping

剥落　bōluò　come off; peel off: 门上的漆已～了。The paint on the door has peeled off.

剥蚀　bōshí　denude; corrode; erode: 由于风雨～，碑文已无法辨认。Owing to the ravages of wind and rain, the inscription on the stone tablet is already undecipherable.

剥蚀作用　bōshí zuòyòng　*geol.* denudation

剥脱　bōtuō　① strip off ② come off; peel off

剥削　bōxuē　exploit: 消灭人～人的制度 abolish the system of exploitation of man by man / ～收入 income from exploitation

剥削阶级　bōxuējiējí　exploiting class

剥削者　bōxuēzhě　exploiter: ～与被剥削者 exploiter and exploited

剥啄　bōzhuó　*onom. liter.* a tap on a door or window

钵（缽）　bō　① earthen bowl ② alms bowl (of a Buddhist monk)

钵盂　bōyú　alms bowl (of a Buddhist monk)

钵子　bōzi　*dial.* earthen bowl

饽　bō　see below

饽饽　bōbo　*dial.* ① pastry ② (steamed) bun; cake: 玉米～ maize cake

菠　bō　see below

菠菜　bōcài　spinach

菠萝　bōluó　pineapple

菠萝蜜　bōluómì　① pineapple ② jackfruit

播　bō　① sow; seed: 夏～ summer sowing / ～下革命的种子 sow the seeds of revolution ② broadcast: ～出《东方红》乐曲 broadcast the music of *The East Is Red* ③ *formal* remove; go into exile: ～迁 remove to another place

播荡　bōdàng　① jolt; bump; toss: 船在惊涛骇浪里～得厉害。The ship tossed wildly in the rough sea. ②

formal become destitute and homeless; wander about homeless

播发　bōfā　broadcast: ～新闻 broadcast news

播放　bōfàng　① broadcast ② broadcast a T.V. programme

播幅　bōfú　the width of a row of planted seeds

播讲　bōjiǎng　talk over the radio: ～故事 tell a story over the radio / ～卫生常识 give a radio talk on health and hygiene

播弄　bōnong　① order sb. about ② stir up

播弄是非　bōnong shìfēi　stir things up; stir up trouble; sow dissension; tell tales

播散　bōsàn　① send out; diffuse; emit ② distribute; issue; give out

播送　bōsòng　broadcast; transmit; beam: ～新闻 broadcast news / ～电视节目 broadcast a T.V. programme / 向东南亚～的节目 programme beamed to Southeast Asia

播音　bōyīn　transmit; broadcast: 这次～到此结束。That concludes our programme for this transmission.

播音室　bōyīnshì　broadcasting studio

播音员　bōyīnyuán　announcer

播映　bōyìng　broadcast a T.V. programme (usu. a film)

播种　bōzhǒng　sow seeds; sow; seed

播种机　bōzhòngjī　seeder; planter; grain drill

播种　bōzhòng　sowing; seeding

播种面积　bōzhòng miànjī　sown area; seeded area

播种期　bōzhòngqī　sowing (*or* seeding) time

bó

伯¹　bó　① father's elder brother; uncle ② the eldest among brothers: ～兄 the eldest brother

伯²　bó　earl; count: 伯爵 bójué ——see also bǎi

伯伯　bóbo　*inf.* ① father's elder brother; uncle: 二～ second uncle ② a term of address for a man of one's father's generation who is older than one's father; uncle: 张～ Uncle Zhang

伯父　bófù　① father's elder brother; uncle ② a term of address for a man of one's father's generation who is older than one's father; uncle

伯公　bógōng　*dial.* ① one's paternal grandfather's elder brother; great-uncle ② the elder brother of one's husband's father

伯爵　bójué　earl; count

伯爵夫人　bójué fūrén　countess

伯劳　bóláo　*zool.* shrike

伯乐　Bólè　① a legendary connoisseur of horses ② a good judge of talent: 世有～，然后有千里马。千里马常有，而～不常有。(韩愈) Only when there is a Bole can there be a thousand-*li* horse. While thousand-*li* horses are not uncommon, men like Bole are rare to find.

伯力　Bólì　see 哈巴罗夫斯克 Hābāluófūsīkè

伯利兹　Bólìzī　Belize

伯母　bómǔ　wife of father's elder brother; aunt

伯婆　bópó　*dial.* ① wife of (paternal) grandfather's elder brother; great-aunt ② wife of the elder brother of one's husband's father

伯仲　bó-zhòng　*formal* the first and the second brother—not much difference: 相～ about the same

伯仲叔季　bó-zhòng-shū-jì　eldest, second, third and youngest of brothers; order of seniority among brothers

伯仲之间　bó-zhòng zhī jiān　almost on a par; about the same; equally matched

伯祖 bózǔ (paternal) grandfather's elder brother; grand-uncle (or great-uncle)

伯祖母 bózǔmǔ wife of (paternal) grandfather's elder brother; grandaunt (or great-aunt)

驳[1] **(駁)** bó refute; contradict; gainsay: 他老～我。 He's always contradicting me. ／他的建议被～回来了。 His proposal was rejected. ／真理不怕人～。 Truth fears no refutation.

驳[2] **(駁)** bó formal parti-coloured; variegated: 斑驳 bānbó

驳[3] bó ① transport by lighter: 起驳 qǐbó ② barge; lighter: 油驳 yóubó ③ dial. extend or widen (a bank or a dike): 这条堤还不够宽, 最好再～出去一米。 This dike is not wide enough and should be widened by one metre.

驳岸 bó'àn a low stone wall built along the water's edge to protect an embankment; revetment

驳斥 bóchì refute; rebut; contradict: ～谬论 refute a fallacy

驳船 bóchuán barge; lighter

驳倒 bódǎo demolish sb.'s argument; refute; argue sb. down; outargue: 我一句话把他～了。 I refuted him in one sentence. ／真理是驳不倒的。 Truth is irrefutable.

驳回 bóhuí reject (an appeal, request, proposal, etc.); turn down; overrule: ～上诉 reject an appeal ／法院～了他的无理要求。 The court overruled his unreasonable claim.

驳价 bójià (of a buyer) haggle over prices

驳壳枪 bókéqiāng Mauser pistol

驳面子 bó miànzi not spare sb.'s sensibilities; not show due respect for sb.'s feelings

驳难 bónàn formal condemn as false or erroneous

驳卸 bóxiè unload by lighter

驳议 bóyì ① criticize and correct; refute ② (written) criticism or refutation

驳运 bóyùn transport by lighter; lighter

驳运费 bóyùnfèi lighterage

驳杂 bózá multifarious; heterogeneous: 这本书三分历史, 七分科学, 内容非常～。 This book is a heterogeneous mass of information, being three parts history and seven parts science.

驳正 bózhèng criticize and correct

泊 bó ① be at anchor; moor; berth: ～岸 anchor alongside the shore ／船～港外。 The ship was lying at anchor outside the harbour. ② stay for a time; stop: 漂泊 piāobó ——see also pō

泊位 bówèi berth (for a ship): 深水～ deepwater berth

泊位费 bówèifèi berthage

帛 bó formal silks

帛画 bóhuà painting on silk

帛书 bóshū a book copied on silk

柏 bó (used only in 柏林 Bólín, the transliteration of "Berlin") ——see also bǎi; bò

勃 (教) bó formal vigorous; thriving: 蓬勃 péngbó

勃勃 bóbó thriving; vigorous; exuberant: 生气勃勃 shēngqì bóbó

勃发 bófā formal ① thrive; prosper: 生机～ full of life ／英姿～ dashing and spirited ／游兴～ be seized with a desire to travel ② break out: 战争～。 War broke out.

勃郎宁 bólángníng Browning (a type of automatic pistol)

勃然 bórán ① agitatedly; excitedly: ～变色 agitatedly change colour; be visibly stung ② vigorously: 第三世界～兴起。 The Third World is rising as a vigorous new force.

勃然大怒 bórán dànù fly into a rage; flare up

勃谿 bóxī (also 勃豀 bóxī) formal family quarrel; tiff; squabble

勃兴 bóxīng formal rise suddenly; grow vigorously: 一个工业城市的～ the vigorous growth of an industrial town ／十三世纪蒙古之～ the phenomenal rise of the Mongols in the thirteenth century

钹 bó mus. cymbals

铂 bó chem. platinum (Pt)

舶 bó oceangoing ship: 巨～ a huge ship

舶来品 bóláipǐn old imports

脖 bó ① neck: 脖子 bózi ② sth. shaped like a neck: 这个瓶子～儿长。 The bottle has a long neck.

脖颈儿 bógěngr (also 脖梗儿 bógěngr) back of the neck; nape

脖颈子 bógěngzi (also 脖梗子 bógěngzi) back of the neck; nape

脖子 bózi neck ——see also 抹脖子 mǒ bózi

渤 Bó short for 渤海 Bóhǎi

渤海 Bóhǎi the Bohai Sea

博[1] bó ① rich; abundant; plentiful: 渊博 yuānbó ② erudite; well-informed: 博古通今 bógǔ-tōngjīn ③ formal loose; big: 宽衣～带 in loose garments

博[2] bó win; gain: 聊～一笑 just for your entertainment

博[3] **(簙)** bó gamble: ～徒 gambler ／～局 a gambling party

博爱 bó'ài universal fraternity (or brotherhood); universal love: 自由、平等、～ liberty, equality, and fraternity

博采众议 bó cǎi zhòngyì adopt good advice from all quarters

博茨瓦纳 Bócíwǎnà Botswana

博茨瓦纳人 Bócíwǎnàrén (sing.) Motswana; (pl.) Batswana

博大 bódà broad; extensive

博大精深 bódà-jīngshēn have extensive knowledge and profound scholarship

博得 bódé win; gain: ～同情 win sympathy ／～全场喝采 draw loud applause from the audience; bring the house down ／～好评 have a favourable reception

博而不精 bó ér bù jīng have wide but not expert knowledge; know something about everything

博古 bógǔ ① conversant with things of the past ② paintings of ancient objects

博古通今 bógǔ-tōngjīn possess a wide knowledge of things ancient and modern——erudite and informed

博览 bólǎn read extensively (or widely): ～群书 be well-read

博览会 bólǎnhuì (international) fair

博取 bóqǔ try to gain; court: ～同情 seek (or enlist) sb.'s sympathy ／～欢心 curry favour ／～信任 try to win sb.'s confidence

博识 bóshí learned; erudite: 多闻～ well-informed

and learned

博识洽闻 bóshí-qiàwén experienced and knowledgeable; erudite

博士 bóshì ① doctor: 哲学～ Doctor of Philosophy (Ph. D.)／张～ Doctor Zhang／念～ study (or read) for a doctorate ② hist. court academician

博士后 bóshìhòu ① postdoctoral student or researcher ② postdoctoral study or research ③ postdoctoral; postdoctorate: ～科研 postdoctoral research／～科研人员 postdoctoral researchers

博士学位 bóshì xuéwèi doctor's degree; doctorate: 念～ study (or read) for a doctorate

博闻强记 bówén-qiángjì (also 博闻强识, 博闻强志 bówén-qiángzhì) possessed of wide learning and a powerful memory; have encyclopaedic knowledge

博物 bówù old general name for zoology, botany, mineralogy, physiology, etc.

博物馆 bówùguǎn museum: 中国革命～ the Museum of the Chinese Revolution

博物馆学 bówùguǎnxué museology

博物院 bówùyuàn museum

博学 bóxué learned; erudite: ～之士 learned scholar; erudite person

博学多才 bóxué-duōcái learned and versatile

博雅 bóyǎ learned: ～之士 a scholar of profound knowledge

博弈 bóyì formal play chess; have a game of chess

鹁 bó see below

鹁鸽 bógē pigeon

鹁鸪 bógū wood-pigeon

搏 bó ① wrestle; fight; combat; struggle: 肉搏 ròubó ② pounce on: 恶狼～羊。The wolf pounced on the sheep. ③ beat; throb: 脉搏 màibó

搏动 bódòng (of the heart, the blood, or the pulse) beat rhythmically; throb; pulsate

搏斗 bódòu wrestle; fight; struggle: 他同歹徒进行了～。He struggled with the ruffian.／与风浪～ battle with the winds and waves／生死～ a life-and-death struggle／保守派和激进派之间的一场大～ a tug-of-war between the conservatives and the radicals

搏击 bójī struggle with; fight with: ～风浪 battle with the winds and waves

搏杀 bóshā ① fight with a weapon ② (in chess games) be locked in a fierce contest

搏噬 bóshì (of an animal) pounce on and bite

魄 bó see 落泊 (魄) luòbó ——see also pò; tuò

箔[1] bó ① screen (of reeds, sorghum stalks, etc.): 苇箔 wěibó ② a bamboo tray for rearing silkworms: 蚕箔 cánbó

箔[2] bó ① foil; tinsel: 金箔 jīnbó ② paper tinsel burnt as offerings to the dead: 锡箔 xībó

膊 bó arm: 赤膊 chìbó

镈 bó ① a large bell used as a musical instrument in ancient times ② a hoe-like tool used in ancient times

踣 bó arch. fall; tumble

薄[1] bó ① slight; meagre; small: ～酬 small reward; meagre remuneration ② ungenerous; unkind; mean: 薄待 bódài ③ frivolous: 轻薄 qīngbó ④ de-

spise; belittle: 鄙薄 bǐbó ⑤ (Bó) a surname

薄[2] bó formal approach; near: 日薄西山 rì bó xīshān ——see also báo; bò

薄产 bóchǎn a small property

薄待 bódài treat sb. ungenerously

薄地 bódì unfertile land

薄海同欢 bóhǎi tóng huān the whole world or nation joins in the jubilation

薄厚 bóhòu same as 厚薄 hòubó

薄技 bójì hum. my slight skill

薄近 bójìn same as 薄礼 bólǐ

薄酒 bójiǔ light wine (said by a host of his own wine)

薄礼 bólǐ hum. my small (or unworthy) gift

薄利 bólì small profits: ～多销 small profits but quick turnover

薄面 bómiàn hum. for my sake

薄明 bómíng dawn; daybreak

薄命 bómìng (usu. of women) born under an unlucky star; born unlucky

薄膜 bómó ① membrane ② film: 塑料～ plastic film

薄膜电阻 bómó diànzǔ film resistor

薄暮 bómù liter. dusk; twilight

薄片 bópiàn thin slice; thin section

薄片分析 bópiàn fēnxi geol. thin section analysis

薄情 bóqíng inconstant in love; fickle: ～郎 a heartless (man) lover

薄弱 bóruò weak; frail: 意志～ weak-willed／能力～ lacking in ability／技术力量～ lack qualified technical personnel／～环节 weak link; vulnerable spot

薄胎瓷器 bótāi cíqì eggshell china

薄物细故 bówù-xìgù trifles; trivialities; trivia

薄雾 bówù mist; haze

薄晓 bóxiǎo shortly before daybreak; before dawn

薄行 bóxíng ① frivolous conduct ② frivolous; dissipated

薄幸 bóxìng formal inconstant in love; fickle; heartless: ～贼! You heartless brute!／十年一觉扬州梦, 赢得青楼～名。(杜牧) Once waking up from my ten-year dream in Yangzhou, I've won the name of a fickle man among blue mansions.

薄油层 bóyóucéng petroleum oil sheet

礴 bó see 磅礴 pángbó

bǒ

跛 bǒ lame: ～了一只脚 lame in one leg／一颠一～ walk with a limp; limp along

跛鳖千里 bǒ biē qiān lǐ a lame tortoise can walk a thousand li—success can be gained by steady continuous effort

跛脚 bǒjiǎo lame

跛腿 bǒtuǐ lame

跛子 bǒzi a lame person; cripple

簸 bǒ winnow with a fan; fan: ～谷 winnow away the chaff; fan the chaff ——see also bò

簸荡 bǒdàng roll; rock: 船～得很厉害。The ship was rolling heavily.

簸动 bǒdòng ① jolt; bump; toss ② old strike (a gong)

簸箩 bǒluo shallow basket

簸扬 bǒyáng winnow

bò

柏 bò see 黄柏 same as 黄檗 huángbò ——see also bǎi; bó

薄 bò see below ——see also báo; bó
薄荷 bòhe field mint; peppermint
薄荷醇 bòhechún (alse 薄荷脑 bòhenǎo) *chem.* menthol; peppermint camphor
薄荷糖 bòhetáng peppermint drops
薄荷酮 bòhetóng menthone
薄荷油 bòheyóu peppermint oil

檗(蘗) bò see 黄檗(柏) huángbò

擘 bò *formal* thumb
擘画 bòhuà (also 擘划 bòhuà) *formal* plan; arrange: 此事尚待～。 This has yet to be arranged.
擘肌分理 bòjī-fēnlǐ make a detailed analysis

簸 bò see below ——see also bǒ
簸箕 bòji ① dustpan ② winnowing fan ③ loop (of a fingerprint)

bo

卜(葡) bo see 萝卜 luóbo ——see also bǔ

啵 bo *part. old* same as 吧 ba

bū

逋 bū *formal* ① flee: 逋逃 būtáo ② owe: 逋债 būzhài
逋欠 būqiàn be behind in payment; be in arrears; default
逋逃 būtáo ① flee; abscond ② fugitive
逋逃薮 būtáosǒu *formal* refuge for fugitives
逋亡 būwáng *formal* flee; abscond
逋债 būzhài owe a debt

bú

醭 bú mould (on the surface of soy sauce, vinegar, etc.)

bǔ

卜 bǔ ① divine; tell fortunes: ～卦 divine by the Eight Trigrams ② *formal* foretell; predict: 生死未～。 It is hard to tell whether the person is alive or not. / 行期未～。 The date of departure remains undecided. / 胜败可～。 Victory or defeat can be predicted. *or* We can forecast the outcome. ③ *formal* choose (a place): ～宅 choose a house / ～邻 choose a neighbourhood ④ (Bǔ) a surname ——see also bo

卜辞 bǔcí oracle inscriptions of the Shang Dynasty (c. 16th-11th century B.C.) on tortoiseshells or animal bones
卜居 bǔjū *formal* choose a dwelling-place
卜课 bǔkè divination; fortune-telling
卜筮 bǔshì divination; fortune-telling
卜昼卜夜 bǔzhòu-bǔyè day and night; round the clock

卟 bǔ see below
卟吩 bǔfēn *chem.* porphin (e)

补(補) bǔ ① mend; patch; repair: ～衣服 mend (or patch) clothes / ～鞋 repair (or mend) shoes / ～袜子 darn socks / ～车胎 mend a puncture / 修桥～路 build bridges and repair roads ② fill; supply; make up for: 把漏了的字～上 supply the missing words / 我们还得～两个人。 We have two vacancies to be filled. *or* We need two more people. ③ nourish: ～身体 build up one's health (with nourishing food or tonics) ④ *formal* benefit; use; help: 空言无补 kōngyán wú bǔ
补白 bǔbái filler (in a newspaper or magazine)
补报 bǔbào ① make a report after the event; make a supplementary report: 调查结果以后～。 Findings will be reported later. ② repay a kindness
补偿 bǔcháng compensate; make up: ～所受的损失 compensate sb. for a loss / ～差额 make up a deficiency
补偿电容器 bǔcháng diànróngqì compensation condenser
补偿费 bǔchángfèi compensatory payment; compensation
补偿贸易 bǔcháng màoyì compensation trade
补充 bǔchōng ① replenish; supplement; complement; add: ～人力 replenish manpower / ～兵员 fill up (an army unit) to full strength; replace losses / ～库存 replenish the stock / ～两点意见 have two points to add / 互相～ complement each other; be mutually complementary ② additional; complementary; supplementary: ～规定 additional regulations / ～说明 additional remarks
补充读物 bǔchōng dúwù supplementary reading material
补丁 bǔding (also 补钉, 补靪 bǔding) patch: 打～ put (or sew) a patch on; patch up
补发 bǔfā supply again (sth. lost, etc.); reissue; pay retroactively: 材料丢失, 不予～。 The material will not be reissued if lost. / ～增加的工资 pay increased wages retroactively / 上次没领到工作服的, 现由总务处～。 Those who were not issued workclothes last time can get them at the general affairs office now.
补法 bǔfǎ *Chin. med.* ① treatment involving the use of tonics to restore the patient's health ② reinforcing method (in acupuncture)
补过 bǔguò make amends for one's faults ——see also 将功补过 jiāng gōng bǔguò
补花 bǔhuā *arts & crafts* appliqué
补给 bǔjǐ *mil.* supply
补给点 bǔjǐdiǎn supply point
补给品 bǔjǐpǐn supplies
补给线 bǔjǐxiàn supply line
补给站 bǔjǐzhàn depot
补假 bǔjià days off for having worked overtime
补角 bǔjiǎo *math.* supplementary angle
补救 bǔjiù remedy: ～办法 remedial measure; remedy / 无可～ be past (or beyond) remedy; irremediable; irreparable
补苴 bǔjū *formal* make up (deficiencies): ～罅漏 make up deficiencies

补考　bǔkǎo　make-up examination

补课　bǔkè　① make up a missed lesson: 教师给学生～。 The teacher helped his pupils make up the lesson they had missed. ② do over again sth. not well done

补炉　bǔlú　*metall.* fettling

补苗　bǔmiáo　*agric.* fill the gaps with seedlings

补偏救弊　bǔpiān-jiùbì　remedy defects and rectify errors; rectify a deviation and correct an error

补票　bǔpiào　buy one's ticket after the normal time

补品　bǔpǐn　tonic

补葺　bǔqì　repair; renovate: ～一新 take on a new look after renovation; be completely renovated

补情　bǔqíng　repay a kindness

补缺　bǔquē　fill a vacancy; supply a deficiency

补缺选举　bǔquē xuǎnjǔ　by-election

补色　bǔsè　complementary colour

补税　bǔshuì　① pay a tax one has evaded ② pay an overdue tax

补台　bǔtái　lend sb. a hand; help sb. out

补体　bǔtǐ　*med.* complement (in blood serum): ～结合试验 complement fixation test

补贴　bǔtiē　① subsidize: 由国家给予～ be subsidized by the state ② subsidy; allowance: 粮食～ grain subsidy／价格～ price subsidy／出口～ export subsidy／生活～ living allowances; subsistence allowances

补习　bǔxí　take lessons after school or work; take a make-up course

补习学校　bǔxí xuéxiào　continuation school

补泻　bǔxiè　*Chin. med.* reinforcing and reducing methods (in acupuncture)

补休　bǔxiū　days off for having worked overtime

补选　bǔxuǎn　by-election: ～人民代表 hold a by-election for a people's deputy

补血　bǔxuè　build (or enrich) the blood: 猪肝据说能～。 Pork liver is said to be a blood-builder.

补血剂　bǔxuèjì　blood (or haematic) tonic

补牙　bǔyá　fill a tooth; have a tooth stopped

补养　bǔyǎng　take a tonic or nourishing food to build up one's health

补药　bǔyào　tonic

补液　bǔyè　*med.* fluid infusion

补遗　bǔyí　addendum; supplement: 《文选》～ Supplement to the *Wenxuan* (a book title)

补益　bǔyì　*formal*　① benefit; help: 有所～ be of some help (or benefit) ② be of help (or benefit)

补语　bǔyǔ　*gram.* complement

补正　bǔzhèng　supplement and correction: 《庄子》～ Emended Text of the *Zhuang Zi* (a book title)

补种　bǔzhòng　reseed; resow; replant

补助　bǔzhù　① help financially; subsidize ② subsidy; allowance: 实物～ subsidy in kind／煤火～ heating allowance

补助金　bǔzhùjīn　grant-in-aid; subsidy

补缀　bǔzhuì　mend (clothes); patch: 缝连～ mend and darn／～成文 put together some sort of an article; produce a patchwork of an article

补足　bǔzú　bring up to full strength; make up a deficiency; fill (a vacancy, gap, etc.): ～缺额 fill all the vacancies

捕　bǔ　catch; seize; arrest: ～鸟 catch birds／被～ be arrested; be under arrest

捕虫叶　bǔchóngyè　*bot.* insect-catching leaf

捕打　bǔdǎ　catch and kill (injurious insects, etc.)

捕房　bǔfáng　same as 巡捕房　xúnbǔfáng

捕风捉影　bǔfēng-zhuōyǐng　chase the wind and clutch at shadows—speak or act on hearsay evidence

捕俘　bǔfú　*mil.* capture enemy personnel (for intelligence purposes)

捕获　bǔhuò　catch; capture; seize; 当场～ catch sb. redhanded

捕获法　bǔhuòfǎ　*leg.* law of prize

捕获量　bǔhuòliàng　catch (of fish, etc.)

捕鲸船　bǔjīngchuán　whaler; whale catcher

捕快　bǔkuài　(in former times) a *yamen* officer charged with hunting down criminals; constable; sheriff

捕捞　bǔlāo　fish for (aquatic animals and plants); catch: ～对虾 catch prawns

捕捞能力　bǔlāo nénglì　fishing capacity

捕猎　bǔliè　catch (wild animals); hunt

捕拿　bǔná　arrest; apprehend; capture; catch

捕杀　bǔshā　catch and kill

捕食　bǔshí　① (of an animal) hunt for food; prey: 猫头鹰在夜间～。 Owls prey at night. ② (of an animal) hunt and eat (another animal); prey on: 猫头鹰～鼠、麻雀等小动物。 Owls prey (or feed) on mice, sparrows, and other small animals.

捕鼠器　bǔshǔqì　mousetrap

捕头　bǔtóu　police officer (in former foreign concessions)

捕鱼　bǔyú　catch fish; fish: 出海～ go fishing on the sea

捕捉　bǔzhuō　hunt; chase; catch; seize: ～逃犯 hunt escaped prisoners／～蝴蝶 chase butterflies／～战机 seize the opportunity for battle; seize the right moment to strike／～镜头 catch a good shot; take a candid shot／～信息 hunt for information

哺　bǔ　*formal*　① feed (a baby); nurse ② the food in one's mouth

哺乳　bǔrǔ　breast-feed; suckle; nurse

哺乳动物　bǔrǔ dòngwù　mammal: ～学 mammalogy

哺乳室　bǔrǔshì　nursing room (where mothers leave their babies when at work and breast-feed them during breaks)

哺喂　bǔwèi　feed

哺养　bǔyǎng　*formal*　feed; rear

哺育　bǔyù　① *formal* feed: ～雏鸟 (of mother birds) feed little birds ② nurture; foster: 青年一代在党的～下茁壮成长 Nurtured by the Communist Party, the younger generation is growing up strong and healthy.

堡　bǔ　same as 堡子, usu. used as part of a place name: 吴～ Wubu (in Shaanxi Province) ——see also bǎo

堡子　bǔzi　*dial.*　① a town or village surrounded with earthen walls ② village

鹐　bǔ　see　地鹐 dìbǔ

bù

不　bù　*adv.*　① (used before verbs, adjectives, and other adverbs; never before 有) not; won't; not want to: 他的病～(很) 严重。 His illness is not (very) serious.／他～是学生。 He isn't a student.／我～会。 I don't know how.／我～去。 I'm not going. or I won't go.／他昨天～来, 可是今天来了。 He didn't want to come yesterday, but he came today. ② (used before certain nouns to form an adjective) un-; in-: 不法 bùfǎ／不轨 bùguǐ　③ (used by itself or with a particle in responses) not so; no: 他知道吗?—～, 他不知道。 Does he know? —No, he doesn't.／他不知道吗?—～, 他知道。 He doesn't know, does he? —Yes, he does.／他是上海人。—～~吧。 He comes from Shanghai. —No, I doubt it./

您再吃一点儿吧。——～了，谢谢。 How about having some more? —No more, thanks. ④ *dial.* (used at the end of a sentence to indicate that it is a question): 他现在身体好～? Is he in good health now? ⑤ (used between a verb and its complement) cannot: 进～去 cannot go in / 拿～动 find sth. too heavy to carry ⑥ (inserted within a reduplication, usu. preceded by 什么) no matter (how, where, etc.): 什么难学～难学，我保证学会。No matter how hard it is, I'll learn how to do it. / 什么学历～学历，要有真才实学才行。 It doesn't matter how much formal schooling you've had; what matters is whether you have real ability and learning. ⑦ (used correlatively with 就) if not... (then...): 晚上他～是看书，就是看报。In the evening if he is not reading a book, then he is reading a newspaper. / 他这会儿～是在教室，就是在图书馆。He's now either in the classroom or in the library. ⑧ (used in polite formulas only) don't; needn't: 不谢　**bùxiè**

不安　bù'ān　① intranquil; unpeaceful; unstable: 动荡不安 dòngdàng bù'ān　② uneasy; disturbed; restless: 听了这消息我心里很～。 I was rather disturbed by the news. ③ *pol.* sorry: 老来麻烦您，真是～。 I'm sorry to trouble you so often.

不白之冤　bù bái zhī yuān　unrighted wrong; unredressed injustice: 蒙受～ be grievously wronged

不败之地　bù bài zhī dì　invincible position: 立于不败之地 lì yú bù bài zhī dì

不饱和脂肪　bùbǎohé zhīfáng　unsaturated fat

不卑不亢　bùbēi-bùkàng　same as 不亢不卑 bùkàng-bùbēi

不备　bùbèi　① unprepared; off guard: 乘其～ catch sb. off guard / 伺其～ watch for a chance to take sb. by surprise ② *formal* (used at the end of a letter) there is more than I can tell you in this letter

不比　bùbǐ　unlike: 北方～南方，春天老刮风。 The north of China, unlike the south, is windy in spring.

不比不知道，一比吓一跳　bù bǐ bù zhīdao, yī bǐ xià yī tiào　if you don't compare, you're in the dark; the moment you do, you get a shock

不必　bùbì　*adv.* need not; not have to: ～担心(惊慌)。 There is no need to worry (panic). / 你～去了。 You don't have to go now.

不避艰险　bù bì jiānxiǎn　shrink (*or* flinch) from no difficulty or danger; make light of difficulties and dangers

不变价格　bùbiàn jiàgé　*econ.* fixed price; constant price: 国民收入按～计算增加了 1.31 倍。National income increased by 131% at constant prices.

不变资本　bùbiàn zīběn　*econ.* constant capital

不便　bùbiàn　① inconvenient; inappropriate; unsuitable: 交通～ have poor transport facilities; not be conveniently located / 给治疗带来～ hamper medical treatment / 在场的人很多，～同他长谈。 With so many people around, it wasn't convenient to have a long talk with him. / 如果对你没有什么～的话，我想把时间提早一点。 I'd like to make it earlier, if that's not inconvenient to you. ② *inf.* short of cash: 手头～ be short of cash; be hard up

不辨菽麦　bù biàn shū-mài　be unable to tell beans from wheat—have no knowledge of practical matters

不…不…　bù...bù...　① (used with two words or expressions which are similar in meaning; an emphatic negative form): 不理不睬 take no notice of; ignore ② (used with two words or expressions which are opposite in meaning) neither... nor.: 不大不小 neither too big nor too small; just right / 不多不少 neither too much nor too little; just right / 不中不西 neither Chinese nor Western / 不盈不亏 neither gain nor lose; break even ③ if not... then not...: 他不吃饭不喝酒。 He won't drink unless he's eating. *or* He

only drinks at meals.

不才　bùcái　*formal hum.* I (lit. "without ability")

不测　bùcè　accident; mishap; contingency: 以防～ be prepared for any contingency / 如有～ if anything untoward should happen / 险遭～ have a narrow escape / 应付各种可能发生的～事件 cope with a variety of unpredictable possibilities

不曾　bùcéng　never (have done sth.): 我～到过那里。 I have never been there.

不差累黍　bù chā lěishǔ　not a whit (*or* an iota) of difference

不成　bùchéng　① won't do: 只说不做，那是～的。Mere talk and no action won't do. ② *part.* (used at the end of a rhetorical question beginning with 难道 or 莫非): 难道就这样算了～? How can we let it go at that? / 莫非说起重机不到，大家就坐等～? Are we going to sit back and do nothing until the cranes arrive?

不成材　bùchéngcái　(also 不成器 bùchéngqì) good-for-nothing; worthless; ne'er-do-well

不成话　bùchénghuà　same as 不像话 bù xiànghuà

不成体统　bù chéng tǐtǒng　most improper; downright outrageous

不成文法　bùchéngwénfǎ　*leg.* unwritten law

不承认主义　bùchéngrènzhǔyì　policy of nonrecognition

不逞之徒　bùchěng zhī tú　desperado; the unruly

不齿　bùchǐ　*formal* despise; hold in contempt: 为世人所～ held in contempt by the people / ～于人类的狗屎堆 filthy and contemptible as dog's dung

不耻下问　bù chǐ xià wèn　not feel ashamed to ask one's subordinates or people below

不啻　bùchì　*formal* ① not less than: 工程所需，～万金。 The project requires a tremendous amount of money. ② as; like; as good as: ～沧海一粟 like a drop in the ocean / ～是当头一棒 like a blow on the head / 人民盼望解放军，～大旱之望云霓。 The people longed for the coming of the People's Liberation Army as one longs for rain during a drought.

不出所料　bù chū suǒ liào　as expected: ～，她轻而易举地通过了考试。 As expected, she passed the exam easily.

不揣冒昧　bù chuǎi màomèi　I venture to; may I take the liberty of

不辞而别　bù cí ér bié　go away without taking leave; leave without saying goodbye

不辞辛苦　bù cí xīnkǔ　spare no effort; take pains; take the trouble to; go to the trouble of doing sth.: 感谢同志们～来支援我们。 Thank you comrades for all the trouble you have taken to help us.

不错[1]　bùcuò　① correct; right: 这个答案一点儿～。This answer is perfectly correct. ② (used by itself to express agreement) yes: ～，他是这么说的。Yes, that's what he said.

不错[2]　bùcuò　*inf.* not bad; pretty good: 这个主意～。 This idea is not bad. / 这个录音～。 The recording is pretty good. / 庄稼长得挺～。 The crops are doing quite well.

不打不成相识　bù dǎ bù chéng xiāngshí　out of blows friendship grows; no discord, no concord

不打紧　bùdǎjǐn　*dial.* it's not serious; it doesn't matter

不打自招　bù dǎ zì zhāo　confess without being pressed; make a confession without duress; give oneself away

不大　bùdà　*adv.* ① not very; not too: ～好 not very good / ～清楚 not too clear ② not often: 他最近～来。 He hasn't been coming around much recently. / 我～吃鱼。 I don't eat fish often. *or* I'm not too keen on fish.

不大离儿　bùdàlír　*inf.* ① pretty close; just about right: 你这个子打篮球还～。 You're about the right height for a basketball player. ② not bad: 这块地的麦子长得～。

The wheat on this field is not bad.

不待见 bùdàijian dislike; loathe; be disgusted with

不待说 bùdàishuō needless to say; it goes without saying

不丹 Bùdān Bhutan

不丹人 Bùdānrén Bhutanese

不丹语 Bùdānyǔ Bhutanese (language)

不单 bùdān ① not the only: 获奖的～是这几部影片。These are not the only films that have won the prizes. ② conj. not merely; not simply: 人民解放军～是战斗队，也是工作队和生产队。The PLA is not merely a fighting force, but a working force and a production corps as well.

不但 bùdàn conj. (used correlatively with 而且, 并且, 也 or 还) not only: 我们的产品～要求数量多, 而且要求质量好。In production, we demand not only quantity but also quality. / 他～会讲英语, 还会讲法语。He can speak not only English but also French.

不惮 bùdàn not fear; not be afraid of: ～其烦 not mind taking the trouble; take great pains; be very patient

不当 bùdàng unsuitable; improper; inappropriate: 处理～ not be handled properly / 措辞～ inappropriate wording

不倒翁 bùdǎowēng self-righting doll; tumbler; roly-poly

不到长城非好汉 bù dào Chángchéng fēi hǎohàn if you fail to reach the Great Wall you are not a man

不到黄河心不死 bù dào Huánghé xīn bù sǐ not stop until one reaches the Huanghe River—not stop until one reaches one's goal; refuse to give up until all hope is gone

不道德 bùdàodé immoral; unethical: 淫人妻女是～的。It is immoral to defile the womenfolk of others. / 拆阅别人信件是～的。Opening other people's letters and reading them is unethical.

不得 bùdé must not; may not; not be allowed: ～将参考书携出阅览室。Reference books may not be taken out of the reading room. / ～有误。Let there be no mistake.

不得 bude (used after a verb) must not: 去～ must not go / 马虎～ mustn't (or can't afford to) be careless / 这件事你做～。You must never do this.

不得不 bùdébù have no choice (or option) but to; cannot but; have to: 我～去。There's nothing I can do but go. / 铁证如山, 那个坏家伙～低头认罪。Confronted with ironclad evidence the scoundrel had to plead guilty.

不得而知 bùdé ér zhī unknown; unable to find out: 作者是谁, ～。The name of the author is unknown. / 情况如何, ～。We are unable to find out how things stand.

不得劲 bùdéjìn ① inf. awkward; unhandy: 这把铁锹使起来～。This is an awkward spade. ② inf. be indisposed; not feel well: 我今天有点～儿。I'm not feeling too well today. ③ dial. feel embarrassed: 大家都看着他, 弄得他怪～儿的。He was embarrassed by so many people staring at him.

不得了 bùdéliǎo ① no way out; no end of trouble: 要是这样做, 那可～。If you do it this way, there'll be no end of trouble. / 让人口这样增长下去, 那可～。If population is allowed to grow like this, disaster will overtake us. / 成绩不夸跑不了, 缺点不找～。If we don't speak of our achievements, they won't run away. If we don't find out our faults, we'll be in a bad way. / 没有什么～的事。There's nothing really serious. / 哎呀, ～, 着火了! Oh, how awful! Fire! Fire! ② (used after 得 as a complement) extremely; exceedingly: 高兴得～ be extremely happy; be wild with joy / 坏得～ be very bad; couldn't be worse / 后悔得～ regret it very much;

be overcome with remorse

不得其门而入 bù dé qí mén ér rù can't find the door and get in; can't find one's way in; can't gain admission

不得人心 bù dé rénxīn not enjoy popular support; be unpopular: 这个政策很～。This policy is very unpopular.

不得要领 bù dé yàolǐng fail to grasp the main point; not see what sb. is driving at: 他讲了半天, 我还是～。He talked at great length, but I just couldn't see what he was driving at.

不得已 bùdéyǐ act against one's will; have no alternative but to; have to: 实在～, 她只好请几天假。She had no alternative but to ask for a few days' leave. / 他们这样做是出于～。They did it that way because they had no choice.

不得已而求其次 bùdéyǐ ér qiú qí cì have to be content with the second best

不得已而为之 bùdéyǐ ér wéi zhī do sth. against one's will; have no alternative but to do sth.

不登大雅之堂 bù dēng dàyǎ zhī táng too low to enter polite company; not appeal to refined taste; be unrefined; be unpresentable

不等 bùděng vary; differ: 数量～ vary in amount / 大小～ differ (or vary) in size / 每包的重量从三斤到十斤～。The packages vary in weight from 3 to 10 jin.

不等边三角形 bùděngbiān sānjiǎoxíng math. scalene triangle

不等号 bùděnghào math. sign of inequality

不等价交换 bùděngjià jiāohuàn econ. exchange of unequal values

不等式 bùděngshì math. inequality

不抵抗主义 bùdǐkàngzhǔyì policy of nonresistance

不第[1] bùdì fail in an imperial examination

不第[2] bùdì conj. formal not only

不点儿 bùdiǎnr very few or very small; tiny

不迭 bùdié (used after a verb) ① cannot cope; find it too much: 忙～ hasten (to do sth.) / 后悔～ too late for regrets ② incessantly: 称赞～ praise profusely

不丁点儿 bùdīngdiǎnr very few or very small

不定 bùdìng ① adv. hard to say; hard to predict: 他一天～来多少次。He comes I don't know how many times a day. / 我明天还～去不去呢。It's not at all certain whether I'll go tomorrow. / 事情还～怎么样呢。It's hard to predict how things will turn out. ② indefinite; indeterminate

不定变异 bùdìng biànyì biol. indeterminate variation

不定方程 bùdìng fāngchéng math. indeterminate equation

不定根 bùdìnggēn bot. adventitious root

不定冠词 bùdìng guàncí gram. indefinite article

不定积分 bùdìng jīfēn math. indefinite integral

不定式 bùdìngshì gram. infinitive

不定芽 bùdìngyá bot. adventitious bud

不动产 bùdòngchǎn real estate; immovable property; immovables

不动声色 bù dòng shēngsè (also 不露声色 bù lù shēngsè) maintain one's composure; stay calm and collected; not turn a hair; not bat an eyelid: 他～, 镇静如常。He remained unperturbed and was as calm as usual.

不冻港 bùdònggǎng ice-free port; open port

不独 bùdú conj. not only: 养猪～可以改善人民生活, 还能多积肥料。Pig-breeding not only improves the people's diet; it makes more manure available.

不端 bùduān improper; dishonourable: 品行～ having bad conduct; ill-behaved

不断 bùduàn unceasing; uninterrupted; continuous; constant: 促进生产力的～发展 promote the uninterrupted (or continuous) growth of the productive

forces / 人类社会总是～进步的。Human society makes unceasing progress. / 先进单位～涌现。Advanced units are constantly emerging. / 使针刺麻醉～完善 bring about steady improvement in acupuncture anaesthesia

不断革命论 bùduàn gémìnglùn the theory of uninterrupted revolution

不对[1] bùduì ① incorrect; wrong: 这样做～。It's wrong to act like that. / 他没有什么～的地方。He's not in the wrong. ② (used by itself to express disagreement) no: ～，我没有那么说。No, I didn't say that.

不对[2] bùduì ① amiss; abnormal; queer: 这机器声音～。The machine makes a queer noise. / 她今天神色有点儿～。She doesn't quite look her usual self today. ② be in disagreement; be at odds: 他们俩素来～。The two of them have always been in disagreement.

不对茬儿 bùduìchár inf. not proper; not fit for the occasion: 他觉得自己说的话～，就停住了。He found what he was saying was not proper for the occasion and he stopped short.

不对头 bùduìtóu same as 不对[1] bùduì①; 不对[2] bùduì①

不…而… bù…ér… do... without doing...: 不战而胜 win without fighting a battle; win hands down

不二法门 bù èr fǎmén the one and only way; the only proper course to take

不二价 bùèrjià fixed prices; uniform prices

不发达国家 bùfādá guójiā an underdeveloped country

不乏 bùfá formal there is no lack of

不乏其人 bùfá qí rén such people are not rare; there is no lack of such people

不乏先例 bùfá xiānlì there is no lack of precedents

不法 bùfǎ lawless; illegal; unlawful: ～行为 unlawful practice; an illegal act / ～商人 lawbreaking merchants

不法之徒 bùfǎ zhī tú a lawless person

不凡 bùfán out of the ordinary; out of the common run: 自命不凡 zì mìng bùfán

不妨 bùfáng adv. there is no harm in; might as well: 你～现在就告诉他。You might as well tell him right now. / ～一试。There is no harm in trying. / 你～同他联系一下。You might get in touch with him.

不费吹灰之力 bù fèi chuī huī zhī lì as easy as blowing off dust; as easy as falling off a log

不分彼此 bù fēn bǐcǐ make no distinction between one's own and sb. else's; share everything; be on very intimate terms: 如果你要用钱，我可以给你，我们姐妹俩还分什么彼此。If you need money, I'll give you some. You and I are sisters—what's the difference between yours and mine?

不分青红皂白 bù fēn qīng-hóng-zào-bái (also 不分皂白 bù fēn zào-bái) make no distinction between right and wrong; indiscriminately: 如果～，一概拒绝向外国学习，就只能使中国永远处于落后地位。If we indiscriminately refused to learn anything from foreign countries, China would remain backward forever.

不分胜负 bù fēn shèng-fù tie; draw; come out even: 一场～的比赛 a drawn game / 两队～。The two teams tied. or The two teams came out even.

不分轩轾 bù fēn xuān-zhì equally matched; on a par

不分畛域 bù fēn zhěnyù make no distinctions

不忿 bùfèn take offence; be resentful

不孚众望 bù fú zhòngwàng not inspire popular confidence

不服 bùfú refuse to obey (or comply); refuse to accept as final; remain unconvinced by; not give in to: ～指导 refuse to obey instructions / ～裁判 refuse to accept the referee's ruling / 对批评表示～ express disagreement with the criticism

不服水土 bù fú shuǐtǔ (of a stranger) not accustomed to the climate of a new place; not acclimatized

不符 bùfú not agree (or tally, square) with; not conform to; be inconsistent with: 言行～ deeds not matching words / 名实～ have an undeserved reputation / 与事实～ be inconsistent (or at variance) with the facts / 他说话前后～。What he said was self-contradictory. or What he said didn't hang together.

不复 bùfù no longer: ～存在 no longer exist

不干 bùgān have nothing to do with

不干不净 bùgān-bùjìng unclean; filthy: 嘴里～ be foul-mouthed

不干涉 bùgānshè noninterference; nonintervention

不干涉政策 bùgānshè zhèngcè policy of noninterference (or nonintervention)

不甘 bùgān unreconciled to; not resigned to; unwilling

不甘后人 bùgān hòu rén not content to lag behind; hate to be outdone

不甘寂寞 bùgān jìmò hate to be neglected or overlooked

不甘落后 bùgān luòhòu not content to lag behind

不甘示弱 bùgān shìruò unwilling to be outshone; not to be outdone

不甘心 bùgānxīn not reconciled to; not resigned to: ～于自己的失败 will not take one's defeat lying down / 我们输给那么个队，我真～。We lost to such a team—I simply can't take it.

不敢 bùgǎn ① not dare to do sth. ② same as 不敢当 bùgǎndāng

不敢当 bùgǎndāng pol. (used in reply to a compliment or a complimentary gesture) I really don't deserve this; it's too much of an honour; I'm overwhelmed; I'm much obliged; you flatter me: 您中国话说得真好。— ～。You speak Chinese very well. — I'm flattered. / 请上坐。— ～。Please take the seat of honour. — I really don't deserve it.

不敢问津 bùgǎn wènjīn not dare to inquire (as about the price of expensive goods)

不敢越雷池一步 bùgǎn yuè Léichí yī bù not dare to go one step beyond the limit

不更事 bùgēngshì have not seen the world; have not experienced life; be inexperienced ——see also 少不更事 shào bù gēng shì

不公 bùgōng unjust; unfair: 办事～ be unfair in handling matters

不攻自破 bù gōng zì pò collapse of itself: 这种谣言在事实面前将～。These rumours will declare their own bankruptcy when confronted with the facts. or Facts will eventually scotch these rumours.

不恭 bùgōng disrespectful: 言词～ use disrespectful language

不共戴天 bù gòng dài tiān will not live under the same sky (with one's enemy)—absolutely irreconcilable: ～的敌人 a sworn enemy; a mortal foe / ～之仇 inveterate hatred

不苟 bùgǒu not lax; not casual; careful; conscientious: 一丝不苟 yī sī bùgǒu

不苟言笑 bùgǒu yán-xiào reserved; reticent; taciturn; sober; sedate

不够 bùgòu not enough; insufficient; inadequate: 我做得很～。I haven't done nearly enough. / 他们人力～。They haven't enough manpower. / 分析～深入。The analysis lacks depth. / 准备～ be inadequately prepared

不顾 bùgù in spite of; regardless of: ～后果 regardless of the consequences / ～事实 fly in the face of the facts; have no regard for the truth / ～大局 show no consideration for the general interest; ignore the larger issues / ～信义 be guilty of bad faith

不关 bùguān have nothing to do with

不关痛痒 bù guān tòng-yǎng of no consequence; immaterial

不管　bùguǎn　*conj.* regardless of; no matter (what, who, etc.): ～他来不来，我们得走了。No matter whether he comes or not, we've got to leave. / 在党的领导下，～多大的困难，我们都能克服。Under the leadership of the Party, we can overcome any difficulty, however great. / ～怎样我不想去。In any case I don't want to go.

不管部部长　bùguǎnbù bùzhǎng　minister without portfolio

不管三七二十一　bù guǎn sān qī èrshí yī　casting all caution to the winds; regardless of the consequences; recklessly: ～，我要照计划行事。I'll carry out the plan, regardless of the consequences.

不光　bùguāng　*inf.* ① not the only one: 报名参加的～是他一个人。He was not the only one to sign up. ② *conj.* not only: 我们县～出煤，而且出铁。Our county produces not only coal, but iron.

不规则　bùguīzé　irregular: 这种结晶体呈～菱形。This kind of crystal takes the shape of an irregular rhombus.

不规则动词　bùguīzé dòngcí　*gram.* irregular verb

不轨　bùguǐ　against the law or discipline

不过　bùguò　① (used as an intensifier after an adjective): 那再好～了！It couldn't be better! *or* That would be superb! ② *adv.* only; merely; no more than: 她参军的时候～十七岁。She was only seventeen when she joined the army. ③ *conj.* but; however; only: 病人精神还不错，～胃口不大好。The patient feels pretty well, but he hasn't much of an appetite.

不过尔尔　bùguò ěr'ěr　not better than that—only just so-so; merely mediocre; just middling

不过如此　bùguò rú cǐ　only just so-so

不过意　bùguòyì　be sorry; feel apologetic: 叫您受累了，真～。I'm terribly sorry to have given you such a lot of trouble.

不含糊　bùhánhu　*inf.* ① unambiguous; unequivocal; explicit: 以毫～的语言作出回答 answer in clear and unequivocal terms; answer in explicit language / 在原则问题上绝～ stand firm on matters of principle ② not ordinary; really good: 他那乒乓球可～。He is a very good table-tennis player. / 他这活儿做得真～。He's really made a good job of it. ③ not be afraid of: ～你们。I am not afraid of you.

不寒而栗　bù hán ér lì　shiver all over though not cold ——tremble with fear; shudder

不好惹　bùhǎorě　not to be trifled with; not to be pushed around; stand no nonsense: 他这个人可是～的。He's not a man to be trifled with.

不好意思　bùhǎoyìsi　① feel embarrassed; be ill at ease: 她被夸得～了。She felt embarrassed by so much praise. / 让你久等了，真～。I'm sorry to have kept you waiting. ② find it embarrassing (to do sth.): ～推辞 find it difficult to refuse / ～再问 hesitate to ask again

不合　bùhé　① not conform to; be unsuited to; be out of keeping with: ～规定 not conform to the rules / ～当前的需要 be unsuited to present needs / ～客观情况 be out of keeping with the objective conditions / ～标准 not up to the (required) standard; below the mark / 脾气～ be temperamentally incompatible / ～她的口味 not be to her taste; not appeal to her / ～当地习俗 not comform to the customs of the locality ② *formal* should not; ought not: 早知如此，当初～叫他去。Had we foreseen that, we would not have let him go. ③ not get along well; be on bad terms

不合时宜　bùhé shíyí　be out of keeping with the times; be incompatible with present needs; be inopportune or inappropriate

不和　bùhé　① not get along well; be on bad terms; be at odds: 兄弟～ brothers on bad terms with each other

② discord: 制造～ sow discord

不怀好意　bù huái hǎoyì　harbour evil designs; not with the best of intentions

不欢而散　bùhuān ér sàn　part on bad terms: 会议～。The conference broke up in discord.

不慌不忙　bùhuāng-bùmáng　unhurried; calm; leisurely: 他慢慢地，～地从椅子上站起来，然后开始讲话。Slowly and deliberately he rose from his chair and began to speak.

不遑　bùhuáng　*formal* have no time; be too busy: ～顾及 have no time to attend to

不讳　bùhuì　*formal* ① without concealing anything: 直言不讳 zhíyán bùhuì ② *euph.* die

不会　bùhuì　① be unlikely; will not (act, happen, etc.): 她～不知道。It's not likely that she doesn't know. / 人～多的。There won't be too many people. ② have not learned to; be unable to: 我～游泳。I don't know how to swim. / 谢谢你，我～抽烟。No, thanks. I don't smoke. ③ (used to express reproach for the non-performance of an action): 你就～打个电话问一问？Couldn't you have phoned up and asked? / 你不能来，～早点儿告诉我吗？You might have told me earlier you couldn't come.

不惑　bùhuò　*formal* be free from doubts (used esp. in) ～之年 the age of forty (from Confucius' saying 四十而不惑 "At forty I came to be free from doubts") / 年逾～ be over forty

不羁　bùjī　*formal* unruly; uninhibited: 放荡不羁 fàngdàng bùjī

不羁之才　bùjī zhī cái　outstanding abilities

不及　bùjí　① not as good as; inferior to: 这台录音机～那台好。This recorder is not as good as that one. / 我学习～他刻苦。I don't study as hard as he does. ② find it too late: 躲避～ too late to dodge / 后悔～ too late for regrets

不及物动词　bùjíwù dòngcí　*gram.* intransitive verb

不即不离　bùjí-bùlí　be neither familiar nor distant; keep sb. at arm's length

不急之务　bù jí zhī wù　a matter of no great urgency; business requiring no immediate attention

不计其数　bù jì qí shù　countless; innumerable: 每日过往客人～。There are countless travellers coming and going every day.

不记名投票　bùjìmíng tóupiào　secret ballot

不济　bùjì　*inf.* not good; of no use: 我眼力～了。My eyesight is failing.

不济事　bùjìshì　no good; of no use; not of any help: 这是项突击任务，人少了～。This is a shock task. It'll be no good to be short of hands.

不假辞色　bù jiǎ císè　look at sb. with a solemn mien and speak harshly; be severe in speech and countenance

不假思索　bù jiǎ sīsuǒ　(also 不加思索 bù jiā sīsuǒ) (act, respond, etc.) without thinking; without hesitation; readily; offhand: 这些句子是摇笔即来，～的。Such phrases flow unsought at the flourish of a pen.

不检　bùjiǎn　be indiscreet (in one's speech and conduct); be careless (about one's words and acts): 行为～ depart from correct conduct

不减当年　bù jiǎn dāngnián　just like one's old self (in appearance, bearing, etc.): 他的精力～。He is as energetic as ever.

不简单　bùjiǎndān　① not simple; rather complicated: 这事～，需要进一步调查。The matter is not so simple; it requires further investigation. ② remarkable; marvellous: 他有这么大的进步真～。It's remarkable he's made such good progress.

不见　bùjiàn　not see; not meet: 好久～。Haven't seen you for a long time. / 这孩子一年～，长这么高了。It's

only a year since I last saw the child and he's grown so tall.

不见不散 bù jiàn bù sàn (let's) not leave without seeing each other (said when making an appointment): 咱们两点钟左右在大门口碰头，～。Let's meet at the gate around two o'clock and not leave without seeing each other.

不见得 bùjiànde not necessarily; not likely: ～对 not necessarily correct / 他今晚～会来。He's not likely to come tonight.

不见棺材不落泪 bù jiàn guāncai bù luò lèi not shed a tear until one sees the coffin—refuse to be convinced until faced with grim reality

不见经传 bù jiàn jīngzhuàn not to be found in the classics—not authoritative; unknown: 此人名～。He is not a well-known figure. *or* He is a nobody.

不见了 bùjiànle disappear; be missing: 我的钢笔～。My pen's disappeared.

不骄不躁 bùjiāo-bùzào not conceited or rash; free from arrogance and rashness

不教而诛 bù jiào ér zhū punish without prior warning

不结盟 bùjiéméng nonalignment

不结盟国家 bùjiéméng guójiā nonaligned countries

不结盟政策 bùjiéméng zhèngcè nonalignment policy: 奉行～ pursue a policy of nonalignment

不解 bùjiě ① not understand: ～其意 not understand what he means ② indissoluble

不解之谜 bùjiě zhī mí an unsolved riddle (*or* puzzle); enigma; mystery

不解之缘 bùjiě zhī yuán an indissoluble bond; an irrevocable commitment: 他早年就和文学结下了～。Early in his life he was irrevocably committed to literature.

不价 bùjie *dial.* ① no: 是在下雨吗?—～，在下雪。Is it raining? — No, it's snowing. ② not: 你来不来?—我才～呢。Will you come? —No, I won't.

不禁 bùjīn *adv.* can't help (doing sth.); can't refrain from: 看他那滑稽的样子，我～笑了起来。He looked so funny that I couldn't help laughing.

不仅 bùjǐn ① not the only one: 这～是我一个人的看法。I'm not the only one who holds this view. ② same as 不但 bùdàn

不进则退 bù jìn zé tuì move forward, or you'll fall behind——see also 逆水行舟 nì shuǐ xíng zhōu

不近人情 bù jìn rénqíng not amenable to reason; unreasonable

不经一事，不长一智 bù jīng yī shì, bù zhǎng yī zhì you can't gain knowledge without practice; wisdom comes from experience

不经意 bùjīngyì carelessly; by accident: 他～把茶杯碰倒了。He accidentally knocked over a cup.

不经之谈 bù jīng zhī tán absurd statement; cock-and-bull story

不景气 bùjǐngqì ① *econ.* depression; recession; slump ② in a depressed state: 最近生意～。Business is bad these days.

不胫而走 bù jìng ér zǒu get round fast; spread like wildfire: 此书一经问世，～。As soon as it was published, the book had a big circulation.

不久 bùjiǔ ① soon; before long: 水库～就能完工。The reservoir will soon be completed. ② not long after; soon after: 插完秧～就下了一场雨。It rained soon after we had transplanted the rice seedlings.

不咎既往 bù jiù jìwǎng (*also* 不究既往 bù jiū jìwǎng) forgive sb.'s past misdeeds; not censure sb. for his past misdeeds

不拘 bùjū ① not stick to; not confine oneself to: 字数～。No limit is set on the length (for an article). ② no matter (what, who, etc.); whatever: ～什么任务，只要对人民有益的，我都愿意接受。I'm ready to accept

any job whatever, so long as it is in the interest of the people.

不拘小节 bùjū xiǎojié not bother about trifles; not niggling

不拘形迹 bùjū xíngjì without formality; not standing on ceremony

不拘形式 bùjū xíngshì not particular about form; informal: 请你给墙报写些东西。～，文章、诗，都可以。Please write something for the wall newspaper. Any form will do—poetry or prose. /～的讨论 an informal discussion

不拘一格 bùjū yī gé not stick to one pattern; not limited to one type (*or* style): 文学作品只要内容健康，形式方面可以～。So long as the content of a literary work is healthy, it need not be limited to any one form. /～选拔人才 recruit all kinds of talented people (*or* talent of all sorts) / 我劝天公重抖擞，～降人才。(龚自珍) O Heaven! Bestir yourself, I beseech you, And send down men of all the talents.

不倦 bùjuàn tireless; untiring; indefatigable: 诲人不倦 huì rén bù juàn

不具 bùjù *formal* ① incomplete; insufficient ② same as 不备 bùbèi②

不绝如缕 bù jué rú lǚ ① hanging by a thread; very precarious; almost extinct ② (of sound) linger on faintly: 余音袅袅，～。(苏轼) The notes trailed on and on like a thread of gossamer.

不刊之论 bù kān zhī lùn same as 不易之论 bù yì zhī lùn

不堪 bùkān ① cannot bear; cannot stand: ～其苦 cannot bear the hardships ② (used after words of bad meaning) utterly; extremely: 疲惫～ be in a state of utter exhaustion; be dog-tired / 穿得破烂～ be dressed in rags (*or* tatters) ③ extremely undesirable: 他这个人太～了。He is impossible.

不堪回首 bùkān huíshǒu cannot bear to look back on; find it unbearable to recall

不堪入耳 bùkān rù'ěr intolerable to the ear; revolting; disgusting

不堪入目 bùkān rùmù most unsightly; not fit to be seen; revolting; disgusting

不堪设想 bùkān shèxiǎng too ghastly (*or* dreadful) to contemplate: 后果将～。The consequences would be too ghastly to contemplate. *or* The consequences would be disastrous. / 困难到了～的地步。The difficulties defy the imagination.

不堪一击 bùkān yī jī cannot withstand a single blow; collapse at the first blow

不看僧面看佛面 bù kàn sēng miàn kàn fó miàn not for the monk's sake, but for the Buddha's—(do sth. for a person) out of deference to sb. else

不亢不卑 bùkàng-bùbēi neither haughty nor humble; neither supercilious nor obsequious; neither overbearing nor servile

不可 bùkě ① cannot; should not; must not: 你～随便说话。You cannot say whatever you wish. /～一概而论 must not make sweeping generalizations /～剥夺的权利 an inalienable right /～抗拒的历史潮流 an irresistible historical trend ② (used in 非…～): 今天这个会很重要，我非去～。Today's meeting is very important. I simply must go. / 非你去～。It won't do unless you go (with stress on "you").

不可多得 bùkě duō dé hard to come by; rare: ～的佳作 a rare specimen of good writing /～的人才 a man of rare ability

不可分割 bùkě fēngē inseparable: 社会主义民主和社会主义法制～。Socialist democracy is inseparable from a socialist legal system. /～的一部分 an integral part

不可告人 bùkě gào rén not to be divulged; hidden: ～的动机 motives that cannot bear the light of day; ulterior motives /～的勾当 a sinister trick

不可估量 bùkě gūliàng inestimable; incalculable; immeasurable; beyond measure: ～的损失 an immeasurable loss

不可或缺 bùkě huò quē indispensable

不可救药 bùkě jiùyào incurable; incorrigible; hopeless: 人总是要犯错误的, 但可救的却很少。Everyone makes mistakes, but few are incorrigible.

不可开交 bùkě kāijiāo (used as a complement after 得 to indicate a hopeless state of affairs): 忙得～ be up to one's eyes in work; be awfully (or terribly) busy / 打得～ be locked in a fierce struggle / 争得～ be engaged in a heated argument

不可抗力 bùkěkànglì leg. force majeure

不可理喻 bùkě lǐyù be impervious to reason; won't listen to reason

不可名状 bùkě míngzhuàng (also 不可言状 bùkě yánzhuàng) beggar description; be indescribable; beyond description

不可磨灭 bùkě mómiè indelible: ～的印象 an indelible impression / ～的贡献 an everlasting contribution / ～的功绩 ineffaceable merit; unforgettable meritorious deeds

不可逆转 bùkě nìzhuǎn irreversible: ～的历史潮流 an irreversible trend of history

不可偏废 bùkě piānfèi cannot do one thing and neglect the other: 我们必须注意, 集体领导和个人负责, 二者～。We must take care that neither collective leadership nor personal responsibility is overemphasized to the neglect of the other.

不可企及 bùkě qǐjí matchless; inimitable

不可侵犯权 bùkěqīnfànquán diplomacy inviolability

不可胜数 bùkě shèngshǔ countless; innumerable: 缴获的武器装备～。The military equipment captured was beyond counting.

不可收拾 bùkě shōushi irremediable; unmanageable; out of hand; hopeless: 事情到了～的地步。The situation got out of hand.

不可思议 bùkě sīyì inconceivable; unimaginable; unthinkable: 不久以前, 登月旅行还是～的事情。Travel to the moon was inconceivable until recently.

不可同日而语 bùkě tóngrì ér yǔ cannot be mentioned in the same breath; there's no comparison between them

不可望其项背 bùkě wàng qí xiàngbèi can't (or not be fit to) hold a candle to sb.

不可言宣 bùkě yánxuān cannot be explained in words; be beyond expression

不可一世 bùkě yīshì consider oneself unexcelled in the world; be overweeningly (or insufferably) arrogant: 声势汹汹, ～ bluster and swagger like a conquering hero / 他晋级以后, 盛气凌人, ～。As soon as he was promoted, he began to act high-and-mighty.

不可移易 bùkě yíyì cannot be changed; immutable: ～的自然规律 immutable laws of nature

不可逾越 bùkě yúyuè impassable; insurmountable; insuperable: ～的鸿沟 an impassable chasm; an unbridgeable gulf / ～的障碍 an insurmountable (or insuperable) barrier / ～的发展阶段 an unavoidable stage in development

不可知论 bùkězhīlùn philos. agnosticism: ～者 agnostic

不可终日 bùkě zhōng rì be unable to carry on even for a single day; be in a desperate situation ——see also 惶惶不可终日 huánghuáng bùkě zhōng rì

不可捉摸 bùkě zhuōmō difficult to ascertain; unpredictable; elusive: ～的概念 an elusive concept / ～的哲理文章 intangible philosophical essays / 情况～。The situation is hard to size up.

不克 bùkè be unable to; cannot: ～胜任 be unequal to the job

不客气 bùkèqì ① impolite; rude; blunt: 说句～的话 to put it bluntly / 你再这样, 我可就要～了。If you go on like this, I won't be so easy on you. ② pol. you're welcome; don't mention it; not at all ③ pol. please don't bother; I'll help myself

不快 bùkuài ① be unhappy; be displeased; be in low spirits: 心中～ feel unhappy / 精神～ feel depressed ② be indisposed; feel under the weather; be out of sorts

不愧 bùkuì be worthy of; deserve to be called; prove oneself to be: ～为建设社会主义的积极分子 be worthy of the title of activist in socialist construction / 他们～为中国人民的好儿女。They have proved themselves to be fine sons and daughters of the Chinese people. / 她～是律师的女儿。She was not the daughter of an attorney for nothing.

不愧不怍 bùkuì-bùzuò open and aboveboard

不赖 bùlài dial. not bad; good; fine: 今年的庄稼可真～。This year's crops are really fine.

不稂不莠 bùláng-bùyǒu (also 不郎不秀 bùláng-bùxiù) useless; worthless; good-for-nothing

不劳动者不得食 bù láodòngzhě bùdé shí he who does not work, neither shall he eat

不劳而获 bù láo ér huò reap without sowing; profit by or reap the fruits of other people's toil

不老少 bùlǎoshǎo dial. a good few; quite a few: 这次音乐会来的人～。A good few (or quite a few) people came to the concert.

不离儿 bùlír dial. ① not bad; pretty good: 你看他画得还真～呢。Look, he is really drawing well. ② pretty close

不理 bùlǐ refuse to acknowledge; pay no attention to; take no notice of; ignore: 见了人～ cut sb. dead / 别～他, 要帮助他。Don't ignore him; help him. / 我才不～那些闲话呢。I don't pay attention to such gossip.

不力 bùlì not do one's best; not exert oneself: 办事～ not do one's best in one's work; be slack in one's work / 领导～ not exercise effective leadership

不利 bùlì ① unfavourable; disadvantageous; harmful; detrimental: 化～因素为有利因素 turn unfavourable factors into favourable ones ② unsuccessful: 首战～ lose the first battle

不良 bùliáng bad; harmful; unhealthy: ～倾向 harmful trends / ～现象 unhealthy tendencies / ～影响 harmful (or adverse) effects / 存心～ harbour evil intentions; have ulterior motives

不了 bùliǎo (used after a verb plus 个) without end: 一天到晚忙个～ busy from morning till night / 大雨下个～。The rain kept pouring down.

不了了之 bùliǎo liǎo zhī settle a matter by leaving it unsettled; end up with nothing definite: 这件案子因证据不足, 也就～了。Prosecution of the case fizzled out for lack of conclusive evidence.

不料 bùliào conj. unexpectedly; to one's surprise: 早上天气还好好的, ～下午竟下起雹子来了。It was so fine this morning. Who would have thought it would hail in the afternoon!

不吝 bùlìn pol. (used in asking advice) not stint; not grudge; be generous with

不吝指教 bùlìn zhǐjiào not be stinting with comments or criticism: 尚希～。We hope that you will not spare your comments. or We hope that you will not be stinting with your criticism.

不灵 bùlíng not work; be ineffective: 这机器～了。The machine doesn't work. / 老太太手脚有点～了。The old lady has trouble moving about.

不露声色 bù lù shēngsè not show (or betray) one's feelings, intentions, etc.: 他～地说… He said without any change of expression (or without betraying what

was going through his mind)...

不伦不类 bùlún-bùlèi　neither fish nor fowl; nondescript: 〜的比喻 an inappropriate metaphor; a far-fetched analogy

不论 bùlùn　*conj.* (often used correlatively with 都 or 总) no matter (what, who, how, etc.); whether...or...; regardless of: 〜性别年龄 regardless (*or* irrespective) of sex and age / 〜他来不来, 我们都得做。Whether he comes or not, we'll have to do it. / 全村〜男女老幼, 都参加了抗旱斗争。All the villagers, men and women, old and young, took part in the battle against the drought.

不落窠臼 bù luò kējiù　not follow the beaten track; have an original style; show originality; be unconventional: 不落前人窠臼 depart from the beaten track of one's predecessors

不落俗套 bù luò sútào　conform to no conventional pattern; depart from convention

不满 bùmǎn　resentful; discontented; dissatisfied: 心怀〜 nurse a grievance / 他对这件事, 非常〜。He is very unhappy about this matter.

不蔓不枝 bùmàn-bùzhī　neither spreading about nor branching out—concise; succinct

不忙 bùmáng　there's no hurry; take one's time: 这件事你先去调查一下, 〜表态。Don't be in a hurry to say what you think about this. First find out the facts.

不毛之地 bù máo zhī dì　barren land; desert

不免 bùmiǎn　*adv.* cannot avoid; cannot help but: 谁碰到这种事也〜要发牢骚。Anyone in such a situation cannot help but complain. / 这段路太窄, 交通有时〜堵塞。This section of the road is so narrow that there are bound to be traffic jams now and then.

不妙 bùmiào　(of a turn of events) not too encouraging; far from good; anything but reassuring: 情况〜。Things are none too encouraging.

不敏 bùmǐn　*formal* not intelligent (used in self-deprecation)

不名数 bùmíngshù　*math.* abstract number

不名一文 bù míng yī wén　(also 不名一钱 bù míng yī qián) without a penny to one's name; penniless

不名誉 bùmíngyù　disreputable; disgraceful

不明 bùmíng　① not clear; unknown: 失踪的渔船至今下落〜。The whereabouts of the missing fishing boat is still unknown. / 〜国籍的飞机 a plane of unidentified nationality; an unidentified aircraft ② fail to understand: 〜事理 lack common sense / 〜是非 confuse right and wrong / 〜真相 be unaware of the truth; be ignorant of the facts

不明不白 bùmíng-bùbái　obscure; doubtful; dubious: 死得〜 meet a mysterious death

不明飞行物 bùmíng fēixíngwù　unidentified flying object (UFO); the flying saucer

不摸头 bùmōtóu　*inf.* not acquainted with the situation; not up on things: 我刚来, 对地方情况〜。I'm a newcomer and so not well up on local affairs.

不谋而合 bù móu ér hé　agree without prior (*or* previous) consultation; happen to hold the same view: 我们的意见〜。Our views happened to coincide.

不睦 bùmù　*formal* not get along well; be on bad terms; be at odds

不能 bùnéng　cannot; must not; should not: 我〜收这份儿礼。I cannot accept this gift. / 我们决〜一见成绩就自满起来。We must not become complacent the moment we have some success.

不能不 bùnéngbù　have to; cannot but: 〜表示惋惜 cannot but express regret / 〜指出 it must be pointed out that / 我们〜提起某些历史事实。We cannot very well avoid mentioning certain historical facts.

不能赞一辞 bùnéng zàn yī cí　unable to say a word (in criticism of an impeccable piece of writing)

不能自拔 bùnéng zìbá　unable to extricate oneself (from one's plight): 他染上了吸毒的恶习, 〜。He cannot extricate himself from the drug habit.

不能自已 bùnéng zì yǐ　cannot control oneself; lose self-control; can't help; be beside oneself: 度假日即将到来, 她兴奋得〜。She was beside herself with excitement as the day of her holiday approached.

不念旧恶 bù niàn jiù'è　not bear a grudge; forgive and forget

不宁唯是 bù nìng wéi shì　moreover; and what is more

不佞 bùnìng　*formal hum.* I

不怕不识货, 就怕货比货 bù pà bù shíhuò, jiù pà huò bǐ huò　don't worry about not knowing much about the goods; just compare them and you will see which is better

不怕官, 只怕管 bù pà guān, zhǐ pà guǎn　it is the clerk, not the official, that is to be feared—it is the man in direct control, however low his position, that is to be reckoned with

不怕慢, 只怕站 bù pà màn, zhǐ pà zhàn　it's better to move slowly than just to mark time

不偏不倚 bùpiān-bùyǐ　even-handed; impartial; unbiased

不平 bùpíng　① injustice; unfairness; wrong; grievance ② indignant; resentful: 消除心中的〜 allay one's resentment

不平等条约 bùpíngděng tiáoyuē　unequal treaty

不平衡 bùpínghéng　disequilibrium: 工农业发展〜 the disequilibrium between the development of industry and agriculture

不平则鸣 bùpíng zé míng　injustice provokes outcry; where there is injustice, there will be protest

不破不立 bù pò bù lì　there is no construction without destruction; there's no making without breaking; to make you must break

不欺暗室 bù qī ànshì　be scrupulously honest even when there is no one around

不期而遇 bù qī ér yù　meet unexpectedly (*or* by chance); have a chance encounter

不期然而然 bù qī rán ér rán　(also 不期而然 bù qī ér rán) happen unexpectedly; contrary to one's expectations

不起眼 bùqǐyǎn　*dial.* not attract attention; not be noticeable; not be attractive: 这座厂房并不〜, 但产品却是第一流的。The factory building doesn't attract much attention, but the products are first-class. / 别看这人〜儿, 人家可是一肚子学问。He is not taken much notice of, but he is a very learned man.

不巧 bùqiǎo　unfortunately; as luck would have it: 我到那儿, 〜他刚走。As luck would have it, he had just left when I arrived.

不切实际 bù qiè shíjì　unrealistic; unpractical; impracticable: 〜的计划 an impracticable plan / 〜的幻想 unrealistic notions; fanciful ideas

不情之请 bù qíng zhī qǐng　*pol.* my presumptuous request

不求甚解 bù qiú shèn jiě　not seek deep understanding; be content with a superficial understanding; not seek to understand things thoroughly

不屈 bùqū　unyielding; unbending: 坚强〜 iron-willed and unyielding

不屈不挠 bùqū-bùnáo　unyielding; indomitable; dauntless: 〜再接再厉的斗争 an unrelenting and persistent struggle / 〜, 前仆后继 dauntlessly step into the breach as others fall

不然 bùrán　① not so: 其实〜。Actually this is not so. ② (used at the beginning of a sentence to express disagreement) no: 〜, 事情没有那样简单。No, it's not as simple as that. ③ *conj.* or else; otherwise; if not: 我得早点去, 〜就赶不上火车了。I've got to leave a bit

early, otherwise I'll miss the train. / 要去就别迟到，～，就甭去了。Either be there on time, or don't go at all.

不人道 bùréndào inhuman: 那些战俘受到了～的待遇，世界舆论为之震惊。Inhuman treatment of the prisoners of war shocked world opinion.

不仁 bùrén ① not benevolent; heartless ② numb: 麻木不仁 mámù bùrén

不忍 bùrěn cannot bear to: 我～看到老年人生活穷困，无人照料。I cannot bear to see old people living in poverty and neglect.

不忍坐视 bùrěn zuòshì cannot bear to stand idly by

不日 bùrì *formal* within the next few days; in a few days' time: 我～到京，请准备住处。I'll be in Beijing in a few days. Please find me accommodation.

不容 bùróng not tolerate; not allow; not brook: ～外国干涉 tolerate no foreign interference / ～耽搁 allow of no delay / ～歪曲 brook no distortion / ～怀疑 admit of no doubt

不容置辩 bùróng zhìbiàn indisputable; incontestable

不容置喙 bùróng zhìhuì not allow others to interfere; brook no intervention

不容置疑 bùróng zhìyí allow (or admit) of no doubt; not be open to doubt; be beyond doubt

不如 bùrú ① not equal to; not as good as; inferior to: 论手巧，一般人都～她。Few can equal (or compare with) her in manual dexterity. / 今天～昨天暖和。Today is not as warm as yesterday. ② *adv.* it would be better to: 我看～派老王去。I think it would be better to send Lao Wang instead. / 要是这样我还～呆在家里。In that case I might as well stay at home.

不入虎穴，焉得虎子 bù rù hǔxué, yān dé hǔzǐ how can you catch tiger cubs without entering the tiger's lair; nothing venture, nothing gain (or have)

不三不四 bùsānbùsì ① dubious; shady: ～的人 a person of dubious (or shady) character / 交些个～的朋友 make friends with a lot of dubious characters ② neither one thing nor the other; neither fish nor fowl; nondescript: 自己生造的～的词句 nondescript expressions of one's own coinage / 说些～的话 make frivolous remarks; talk twaddle

不塞不流，不止不行 bù sè bù liú, bù zhǐ bù xíng there is no flowing without damming and no motion without rest

不衫不履 bùshān-bùlǚ be dressed with studied negligence; not properly dressed

不善 bùshàn ① bad; ill: 来意～ come with ill intent / 处理～ not handle properly; mishandle ② (also 不善于 bùshànyú) not good at: ～管理 not good at managing things ③ (also 不善乎 bùshànhu) *dial.* not to be pooh-poohed; quite impressive: 别看他身体不强，干起农活来可～。He does not look strong, but he does all right in farm work.

不上不下 bùshàng-bùxià be suspended in mid air; be in a fix

不设防城市 bùshèfáng chéngshì open city

不甚了了 bù shèn liǎo liǎo not know much (about sth.); not be too clear (about sth.)

不声不响 bùshēng-bùxiǎng quiet; silent: 这小伙子平时～，只是埋头工作。The young man was usually very quiet and devoted to his work. / 他～地走进屋来。He slipped into the room without a word.

不胜 bùshèng ① cannot bear (or stand); be unequal to: 体力～ be physically unequal to (a task); be physically incapable of coping with (a job) ② (used between two identical verbs to indicate difficulty or impossibility of fulfilment): 看～看 find it difficult to read so many books, etc. ③ (used in expressing feelings) very; extremely: ～遗憾 be very sorry; much to one's regret / ～感激 be very much obliged; be deeply grateful

不胜枚举 bùshèng méi jǔ too numerous to mention individually (or one by one): 诸如此类的事情，～。Things like these defy enumeration.

不胜其烦 bùshèng qí fán be pestered beyond endurance

不失时机 bù shī shíjī not let the opportunity slip; seize the opportune moment; lose no time: 用兵贵在～。The great thing in war is to seize your opportunities before they're gone.

不失为 bùshīwéi can yet be regarded as; may after all be accepted as: 这～一个办法。This, after all, is one way of doing it.

不识大体 bù shí dàtǐ fail to see the larger issues; ignore the general interest

不识时务 bù shí shíwù ① show no understanding of the times ② lack judgment

不识抬举 bù shí táiju fail to appreciate sb.'s kindness; not know how to appreciate favours

不时 bùshí ① *adv.* frequently; often: 他～来看我。He comes to see me from time to time. ② at any time: 不时之需 bùshí zhī xū

不时之需 bùshí zhī xū a possible period of want or need: 以备～ for emergency needs; to provide against a rainy day

不食人间烟火 bù shí rénjiān yānhuǒ not interested in, or out of touch with, mundane affairs; above the material attractions of the world

不是玩儿的 bùshì wánrde *inf.* it's no joke: 你正在养伤，受了寒可～! It's no joke catching a chill when you are recovering from an injury.

不是味儿 bùshìwèir (also 不是滋味儿 bùshì zīwèir) *inf.* ① not the right flavour; not quite right; a bit off: 这个菜炒得～。This dish doesn't taste quite right. / 他的京剧唱得～。The way he sings Beijing opera is a bit off. ② fishy; queer; amiss: 他的作风，我越看越～。I feel more and more that there's something wrong with his way of doing things. ③ feel bad; be upset: 听了他的话，我心里感到～。I was upset by what he said.

不是冤家不聚头 bùshì yuānjiā bù jùtóu only the ones with mutual bonds will be thrown together; enemies and lovers are destined to meet

不是 bùshi fault; blame: 落个～ get blamed in the end / 这就是你的～了。It's your fault. or You're to blame.

不适 bùshì unwell; indisposed; out of sorts: 胃部～ have a stomach upset / 略感～ feel a bit unwell

不受欢迎的人 bù shòu huānyíng de rén *diplomacy* persona non grata

不受理 bùshòulǐ ① *leg.* reject a complaint ② *diplomacy* refuse to entertain (a proposal)

不爽[1] bùshuǎng not well; out of sorts; in a bad mood

不爽[2] bùshuǎng without discrepancy; accurate: 丝毫～ not deviate a hair's breadth; be perfectly accurate; be right in every detail

不死不活 bùsǐ-bùhuó neither dead nor alive; half dead; lifeless; lethargic

不死心 bùsǐxīn unwilling to give up; unresigned: 失败了还～ not be reconciled to one's failure

不送 bùsòng *pol.* don't bother to see me out

不送气 bùsòngqì *phonet.* unaspirated: ～音 unaspirated sound (e.g. Chinese b, d, g, z, zh, j)

不速之客 bù sù zhī kè uninvited (or unexpected) guest; gate-crasher

不随意肌 bùsuíyìjī *physiol.* involuntary muscle

不遂 bùsuì *formal* fail; fail to materialize: 谋事～ fail to carry out one's plan

不碎玻璃 bùsuì bōli shatterproof (or safety) glass

不特 bùtè *conj. formal* not only

不祧之祖 bù tiāo zhī zǔ revered earliest ancestor

不通 bùtōng ① be obstructed; be blocked up; be impassable: 管子～。The pipe is blocked. / 电话～。The line's dead. ② not make sense; be illogical; be ungrammatical: 文章写得～。The article is badly written.

不同 bùtóng not alike; different; distinct: 两个～的革命阶段 two distinct revolutionary stages / 在～的程度上 to varying degrees

不同凡响 bùtóng fánxiǎng (usu. of literary and artistic works) outstanding; out of the ordinary; out of the common run

不痛不痒 bùtòng-bùyǎng scratching the surface; superficial; perfunctory: ～的批评 superficial criticism / 讲些～的话 make some perfunctory remarks

不透明 bùtòumíng opaque

不透明色 bùtòumíngsè body colour

不透明体 bùtòumíngtǐ opaque body

不透明性 bùtòumíngxìng opacity

不透气 bùtòuqì airtight: 尼龙布～。Nylon cloth is airtight. / 屋里～。The room is stuffy.

不透水 bùtòushuǐ waterproof; watertight; impermeable

不透水层 bùtòushuǐcéng *geol.* impermeable stratum; impervious bed

不图 bùtú ① not seek; not strive for: ～名利 not seek fame or gain ② *conj. formal* unexpectedly; contrary to expectation

不吐气 bùtǔqì same as 不送气 bùsòngqì

不妥 bùtuǒ not proper; inappropriate: 这样处理, 恐怕～。I'm afraid this isn't the proper way to handle the case. / 没有调查研究就作决定是～的。It's not right to make a decision without investigation and study. / 觉得有些～ feel that something is amiss

不外 bùwài (also 不外乎 bùwàihu) not beyond the scope of; nothing more than: ～两种可能。There are only two possibilities.

不完全统计 bùwánquán tǒngjì incomplete statistics: 据～ according to incomplete statistics

不完全叶 bùwánquányè *bot.* incomplete leaf

不完全中立 bùwánquán zhōnglì *leg.* imperfect neutrality

不为已甚 bù wéi yǐ shèn not go too far; refrain from going to extremes; never go beyond reasonable limits

不违农时 bùwéi nóngshí not miss the farming season; do farm work in the right season

不惟 bùwéi *conj. formal* not only

不谓 bùwèi *conj. formal* unexpectedly; to one's surprise

不闻不问 bùwén-bùwèn not bother to ask or to listen; show no interest in sth.; be indifferent to sth.: 同志们有困难我们不能～。We can't be indifferent when a comrade is in difficulty. / 采取～的态度 adopt a "none of my business" attitude

不稳平衡 bùwěn pínghéng *phys.* unstable equilibrium

不问 bù wèn ① pay no attention to; disregard; ignore: ～年龄大小 irrespective of age / ～事实真相 ignore the facts / ～是非曲直 make no distinction between right and wrong; not look into the rights and wrongs of the case ② let go unpunished; let off: 胁从～。Those who acted under duress shall go unpunished.

不无小补 bùwú xiǎobǔ not be without some advantage; be of some help

不务正业 bù wù zhèngyè ① not do honest work; not live by honest labour ② ignore one's proper occupation; not attend to one's duties

不惜 bùxī ① not stint; not spare: ～一切代价 at all costs; at any cost ② not hesitate (to do sth.); not scruple (to do sth.): 为革命～牺牲自己的一切 not hesitate to sacrifice one's all for the revolution

不惜工本 bùxī gōngběn spare no expense

不暇 bùxiá have no time (for sth.); be too busy (to do sth.): ～顾及 be too busy to attend to sth.

不下于 bùxiàyú ① (also 不下 bùxià) as many as; no less than: 展出的新产品～二百种。There are as many as 200 new products on show. / 参加五一节游园活动的～五十万人。No less than half a million people took part in the May Day festivities. ② not inferior to; as good as; on a par with: 这个街道小厂的产品, 质量～一些国营大厂。The products of this small neighbourhood factory are as good as those turned out by some large state-run plants.

不相干 bùxiānggān be irrelevant; have nothing to do with: ～的话 irrelevant remarks / 那件事跟你～。That has nothing to do with you.

不相容 bùxiāngróng incompatible

不相上下 bù xiāng shàngxià equally matched; about the same; almost on a par: 能力～ of about equal ability; equally able / 这两种水稻都是良种, 产量～。Both strains of rice are good and will give about the same yield.

不详 bùxiáng *formal* ① not well known; not quite clear: 吴昌龄(元戏曲作家)生平事迹～。Very little is known about the life of Wu Changling (a Yuan playwright). / 吴承恩生卒年月～。Wu Cheng'en's dates are unknown. / 言之～ be stated too briefly; not be given in detail ② (used in letters) no need to go into details; let me spare you the details

不祥 bùxiáng ominous; inauspicious

不祥之兆 bùxiáng zhī zhào an ill (*or* evil) omen

不想 bùxiǎng unexpectedly: 我本想去看电影, ～来了客人。I wanted to go to the movies, but guests came unexpectedly.

不像话 bùxiànghuà ① unreasonable: 要你们自己掏钱就～了。It would be unreasonable for you to pay out of your own pockets. ② shocking; outrageous: 这种行为真～。Such behaviour is really shocking.

不像样 bùxiàngyàng ① in no shape to be seen; unpresentable: 这活儿～, 拿不出手。This is a shoddy piece of work, it's hardly presentable. ② (used as a complement after 得) beyond recognition: 瘦得～ extremely thin; worn to a mere shadow / 破得～ worn to shreds

不消 bùxiāo *dial.* not need: ～说 needless to say; it goes without saying / ～一会儿工夫, 这个消息就传开了。The news got about in no time.

不肖 bùxiào *formal* (of children) unworthy: ～子 an unworthy son

不肖子孙 bùxiào zǐsūn unworthy descendants

不孝 bùxiào be an unfilial son or daughter; act contrary to filial piety: ～有三, 无后为大。(《孟子》) There are three ways of being a bad son. The most serious is to have no heir.

不屑 bùxiè (also 不屑于 bùxièyú) disdain to do sth.; think sth. not worth doing; feel it beneath one's dignity to do sth.: ～答复 disdain to reply

不屑一顾 bùxiè yī gù will not spare a glance for; regard as beneath one's notice

不谢 bùxiè *pol.* don't mention it; not at all

不懈 bùxiè untiring; unremitting; indefatigable: 作～的努力 make unremitting efforts; make a sustained effort

不信任案 bùxìnrèn'àn no-confidence motion

不信任投票 bùxìnrèn tóupiào vote of no-confidence

不信邪 bùxìnxié not believe in heresy; refuse to be taken in by fallacies; not be scared by evil forces

不兴 bùxīng ① out of fashion; outmoded: 现在～中山装了。The Chinese tunic suit is out of fashion now. ② impermissible; not allowed: ～这样做。That's not allowed. ③ (only used in a rhetorical question) can't: 你干吗嚷嚷, 就～小点儿声吗？Why shout? Can't you lower your voice a little?

不行 bùxíng ① not be allowed; won't do; be impossi-

ble: 开玩笑可以, 欺负人可～。 To have a joke is all right, but to bully people just won't do. / 我们没你～。 We can't do without you. / 这本书今天不还～。 This book must be returned today. ② be no good; won't work: 这个方法～。 This method just won't work. / 我的脑子～, 还不大懂。 My mind is no good; I still don't quite understand. / 他教书不大行。 He's not much good as a teacher. / 他干这种工作身体～。 He is physically unfit for this kind of work. ③ not be good; be poor: 料子不错, 手工～。 The material is fine, but the workmanship is poor. ④ (used as a complement after 得) awfully; extremely: 大街上热闹得～。 The streets are awfully busy. / 我可困得～了。 I'm terribly sleepy.

不行了 bùxíngle on the point of death; dying: 病人快要～。 The patient is failing fast.

不省人事 bù xǐng rénshì lose consciousness; be unconscious; be in a coma

不幸 bùxìng ① misfortune; adversity: 遭～ meet with a misfortune ② unfortunate; sad: ～的消息 sad news ③ unfortunately: 他～以身殉职。 To our great sorrow he died at his post.

不幸而言中 bùxìng ér yán zhòng the prophecy unfortunately comes true: 现在怎么样? ～了吧。 Now, you see what has happened. Unfortunately my prediction has come true.

不幸之幸 bùxìng zhī xìng good fortune in the midst of bad; a stroke of good luck in a stretch of bad; a redeeming feature of a piece of misfortune

不休 bùxiū (used as a complement) endlessly; ceaselessly: 争论～ argue endlessly; keep on arguing

不修边幅 bù xiū biānfú not care about one's appearance; be slovenly

不朽 bùxiǔ immortal: ～的著作 an immortal masterpiece / ～的功勋 immortal deeds

不锈钢 bùxiùgāng stainless steel

不虚此行 bù xū cǐ xíng the journey has not been made in vain; the journey has been well worthwhile; it's been a worthwhile journey

不许 bùxǔ ① not allow; must not: ～说谎。 You mustn't tell lies. / 熄灯后～说话。 No talking after lights out. ② inf. (used in a rhetorical question) can't: 何必非等我, 你就～自己去吗? Why wait for me? Can't you go yourself?

不宣而战 bù xuān ér zhàn open hostilities without declaring war; start an undeclared war

不学无术 bùxué-wúshù have neither learning nor skill; be ignorant and incompetent

不逊 bùxùn formal rude; impertinent: 出言不逊 chūyán bùxùn

不雅观 bùyǎguān offensive to the eye; unbecoming: 随地吐痰既～也不卫生。 Spitting in public places is not only unbecoming but also unsanitary.

不言不语 bùyán-bùyǔ not say a word; keep silent

不言而喻 bù yán ér yù it goes without saying; it is self-evident

不厌 bùyàn not mind doing sth.; not tire of; not object to

不厌其烦 bù yàn qí fán not mind taking the trouble; take great pains; be very patient

不厌其详 bù yàn qí xiáng go into details; dwell at length upon: 她～地向她朋友诉说她的遭遇。 She told her friend in detail all the things she'd gone through.

不扬 bùyáng not good-looking: 其貌不扬 qí mào bùyáng

不要 bùyào don't: ～麻痹大意。 Don't slacken your vigilance. / ～总是以为自己对。 Don't think you are always right.

不要紧 bùyàojǐn ① it's not serious; it doesn't matter; never mind: 有点伤风, ～。 Just a slight cold, nothing

serious. / 路远也～, 我们可以骑车去。 It doesn't matter how far it is; we can go by bike. ② it looks all right, but: 你这一嚷～, 把大家都吵醒了。 You may think it's all right for you to shout, but you've woken everybody up.

不要脸 bùyàoliǎn offens. have no sense of shame; shameless: 只有～的人才能做出这样～的事。 Only those who have no sense of shame can do such shameful things. / 真～! What a nerve!

不一 bùyī vary; differ: 质量～ vary in quality / 长短～ differ in length

不一而足 bù yī ér zú no isolated case; numerous: 凡此种种, ～。 There are countless similar cases. or Such instances are legion.

不依 bùyī ① not comply; not go along with: 我们劝他休息, 他怎么也～。 We advised him to have a rest, but he simply wouldn't hear of it. / 孩子要什么, 她没有～。 She always lets her child have his own way. ② not let off easily; not let sb. get away with it: 你要是再这样, 我可～你。 If you do this again, I won't let you off so easily.

不宜 bùyí not suitable; inadvisable: ～操之过急。 It's no good being overhasty. / 这一点～过分强调。 It's inadvisable to overemphasize this point. / 这种土壤～种花生。 This kind of soil is not suitable for growing peanuts.

不遗余力 bù yí yúlì spare no pains (or effort); do one's utmost

不已 bùyǐ endlessly; incessantly: 赞叹～ praise again and again / 风雨如晦, 鸡鸣～。《诗经》 Through the wind and rain all looks dark, And the cock crows without ceasing.

不以人废言 bù yǐ rén fèi yán not reject an opinion because of the person expressing it: 君子不以言举人, ～。《论语》 The gentleman does not recommend a man on account of what he says, neither does he dismiss what is said on account of the speaker.

不以为然 bù yǐ wéi rán object to; take exception to; not approve of: 他父母对他抽烟颇～。 His parents strongly disapprove of his smoking. / 也许你～, 但我是出自肺腑。 You may not agree with me, but I'm speaking from my heart.

不以为意 bù yǐ wéi yì pay no attention to; take no notice of; not mind

不义之财 bùyì zhī cái ill-gotten wealth (or gains)

不亦乐乎 bù yì lè hū (used as a complement after 得) extremely; awfully: 忙得～ be awfully (or terribly) busy

不易之论 bù yì zhī lùn perfectly sound proposition; undeniable truth; irrefutable argument

不意 bùyì formal ① unexpectedly: ～大雨如注, 无法启程。 Unexpectedly it poured with rain and it was impossible to start off. ② unawareness; unpreparedness: 利用敌人的错觉和～来争取自己的主动 exploit the enemy's misconceptions and unpreparedness to gain the initiative

不翼而飞 bù yì ér fēi ① (of an object) disappear without trace; vanish into thin air: 他一掏口袋, 皮夹子已～。 He reached into his pocket for the wallet only to find it was missing. ② spread fast as if on wings; spread like wildfire: 这消息传得这样快, 简直是～。 The news has spread fast, as if on wings.

不阴不阳 bùyīn-bùyáng neither yin nor yang — assume an ambiguous (or equivocal) attitude

不用 bùyòng adv. need not: ～着急。 You needn't worry. or There is no need to worry. / ～说 it goes without saying; needless to say

不由得 bùyóude can't help; cannot but: 他说得这么透彻, ～你不信服。 He spoke so cogently that you couldn't help being convinced.

不由分说 bùyóu fēnshuō (also 不容分说 bùróng fēn-

shuō) allowing no explanation; without so much as a "by your leave"; without listening to sb.'s protests: 他们把他抓住，～，痛打一顿。They seized him, and without waiting for an explanation gave him a severe beating.

不由自主 bùyóu zìzhǔ can't help; involuntarily: ～地流下了眼泪 cannot help shedding tears; be unable to hold back one's tears; shed tears in spite of oneself

不虞 bùyú *formal* ① unexpected: 不虞之誉 bùyú zhī yù ② eventuality; contingency: 以备不虞 yǐ bèi bùyú ③ not worry about: ～匮乏 fear no shortage of material resources; not worry about running out of supplies

不虞之誉 bùyú zhī yù unexpected praise: 有～，有求全之毁。(《孟子》) There is unexpected praise; equally, there is perfectionist criticism.

不予 bùyǔ not grant: ～批准 not grant approval / ～考虑 refuse to take into consideration; will not consider

不育性 bùyùxìng (also 不孕性 bùyùnxìng) *agric.* sterility

不育症 bùyùzhèng *med.* sterility; barrenness

不豫 bùyù *formal* ① displeased; discontented: 面有～之色 look displeased ② *euph.* unwell; indisposed; under the weather

不远千里 bù yuǎn qiān lǐ make light of travelling a thousand *li*; make light of travelling from afar; go to the trouble of travelling a long distance: 孟子见梁惠王。王曰：“叟！～而来，亦将有以利吾国乎？”(《孟子》) Mencius went to see King Hui of Liang. "Sir," said the King. "You have come all this distance, thinking nothing of a thousand *li*. You must surely have some way of profiting my state?"

不约而同 bù yuē ér tóng do or think the same without prior consultation; happen to coincide: 她一讲完，大家～都鼓起掌来。Spontaneous applause broke out as soon as she finished speaking. / 他们都～地提出了这个问题。They all raised the question as if by prior agreement. / 三个人～地大笑起来。Simultaneously, the three of them burst out laughing.

不悦 bùyuè displeased; annoyed

不在 bùzài not be in; be out: 你找老王吗? 他～。Are you looking for Lao Wang? He's out.

不在乎 bùzàihu see 在乎 zàihu③

不在话下 bù zài huà xià be nothing difficult; be a cinch: 两个月拿下这项任务，～。It will be a cinch to get the job done in two months. / 她摩托车都会骑，自行车更～了。She can ride a motorcycle, to say nothing of a bicycle. / 有这样的决心，再大的困难也～。For people with such determination, no difficulty amounts to much.

不在了 bùzàile *euph.* be dead: 他爷爷早就～。His grandfather has been dead a long time.

不在其位，不谋其政 bù zài qí wèi, bù móu qí zhèng he who holds no rank in a state does not discuss its policies

不在意 bùzàiyì ① pay no attention to; take no notice of; not mind: 别人背后议论，他毫～。He doesn't care at all what people say behind his back. ② negligent; careless: 人家托你的事，你别～。When people ask you to do something, you should take it seriously.

不赞一词 bù zàn yī cí not say a word; keep silent; make no comment: 我对这个问题不清楚，只能～。I'm not clear about this matter, so I had better keep quiet.

不择手段 bù zé shǒuduàn by fair means or foul; by hook or by crook; unscrupulously: 他为了达到个人目的，可以～。He'd stop at nothing (*or* stoop to anything) to get what he wants.

不怎么 bùzěnme not very; not particularly: 这块地～大。This plot isn't very big. / 我～想去。I'm not particularly keen on going. / 他～爱说话。He doesn't talk

much.

不怎么样 bùzěnmeyàng not up to much; very indifferent: 这幅画画得～。This isn't much of a painting. / 他的英语怎么样? ——～。Is his English any good? —It doesn't amount to much.

不战不和 bùzhàn-bùhé no war, no peace: ～的局面 a stalemate of "no war, no peace"

不折不扣 bùzhé-bùkòu ① hundred-percent; to the letter: ～地贯彻党的政策 implement the Party's policies to the letter ② out-and-out: ～的伪君子 an out-and-out hypocrite / ～的老实人 an honest man through and through / ～的欺骗 a fraud pure and simple

不争气 bùzhēngqì be disappointing; fail to live up to expectations: 他这个人真～。This chap has let us down. / 我这腿～，最后一圈跑不动了。My legs failed me and I wasn't able to run the last lap.

不正之风 bù zhèng zhī fēng unhealthy tendency; malpractice: 纠正行业～ correct malpractices in all trades and professions

不知不觉 bùzhī-bùjué unconsciously; unwittingly: ～已过了三个月。Before we knew it three months had passed.

不知凡几 bù zhī fán jǐ can't tell how many there are—there are countless similar cases

不知分寸 bù zhī fēncùn lack tact; have no sense of propriety: 说话～ talk tactlessly

不知好歹 bù zhī hǎo-dǎi (also 不识好歹 bù shí hǎo-dǎi) can't tell good from bad; not know what's good for one

不知进退 bù zhī jìn-tuì have no sense of propriety; not know where to stop

不知人间有羞耻事 bù zhī rénjiān yǒu xiūchǐshì be lost to all sense of shame

不知死活 bù zhī sǐhuó act recklessly; do sth. regardless of danger

不知所措 bù zhī suǒ cuò be at a loss; be at one's wits' end: 茫然～ be at a complete loss what to do

不知所以 bù zhī suǒyǐ not know why it is so

不知所云 bù zhī suǒ yún ① scarcely know what one has said: 今当远离，临表涕泣，～。(诸葛亮) Knowing that I face distant separation from Your Majesty, I write amid my tears, unwitting of my words. ② not understand what sb. is driving at: 他说了半天，听的人还是～。He talked on and on, but the audience couldn't make out what he was driving at. / 这篇文章写得太乱，使人看了～。This is such a chaotic piece of writing that it is practically unintelligible.

不知天高地厚 bù zhī tiāngāo-dìhòu not know the height of the heavens or the depth of the earth—have an exaggerated opinion of one's abilities; not understand things

不值 bùzhí not worth: 我看～那么多。I don't think it's worth that much. / ～一提 not worth mentioning / 跑这一趟～。The trip is not worthwhile.

不值识者一笑 bùzhí shízhě yī xiào beneath the contempt of the discerning

不值一驳 bùzhí yī bó not worth refuting

不值一文 bùzhí yī wén utterly worthless

不止 bùzhǐ ① incessant; without end: 愚公毫不动摇，每天挖山～。Unshaken in his conviction, the Foolish Old Man kept on digging at the mountain every day. / 大笑～ roar with laughter ② more than; not limited to: ～一次 more than once; not just once / 他恐怕～六十岁了。He is probably over sixty. / 这水库带来的好处～是在农业方面。The benefit which the reservoir brings is not limited to agriculture.

不只 bùzhǐ *conj.* not only; not merely: 河水～可供灌溉，且可用来发电。River waters can be used not only for irrigation but also for the generation of electricity.

不至于 bùzhìyú cannot go so far; be unlikely: 他～连这一点道理也不明白。He must have more sense than that. / 如果你事先作好准备，也～那么被动。If you had prepared in advance, you wouldn't be in such an awkward position.

不忮不求 bùzhì-bùqiú free from jealousy and greed

不治之症 bùzhì zhī zhèng incurable disease

不致 bùzhì not in such a way as to; not likely to: 事先做好准备，就～临时手忙脚乱了。If you arrange everything in advance, you won't be in a rush at the last moment.

不置可否 bù zhì kě-fǒu decline to comment; not express an opinion; be noncommittal; hedge: 你是负责人，你怎么能对这个问题～？You are in charge of the job. How could you evade the issue? / 她～地"唔"了一声。She gave a noncommittal grunt in reply.

不中用 bùzhōngyòng unfit for anything; no good; useless: 这铁锹～，我去换一把吧。This spade is no good. I'll go and get another one. / 老了，～啦! I'm getting old and useless!

不周 bùzhōu not attentive and satisfactory; thoughtless; inconsiderate: 计划～ not well planned; not planned carefully enough / 招待～ not be attentive enough to guests

不周延 bùzhōuyán log. undistributed

不准 bùzhǔn not allow; forbid; prohibit: 此处～吸烟。Smoking is not allowed here. or No Smoking! / ～停车! No parking! / ～入内。No admittance.

不着边际 bù zhuó biānjì not to the point; wide of the mark; neither here nor there; irrelevant: ～的长篇大论 a long rambling talk / 他越讲越～。The more he talked, the further he strayed from the point.

不着痕迹 bù zhuó hénjì leave no trace

不着陆飞行 bùzhuólù fēixíng nonstop flight

不赀 bùzī formal immeasurable; incalculable: 工程浩大，所费～。The project is on such a gigantic scale that the cost is hard to calculate.

不自量 bùzìliàng not take a proper measure of oneself; overrate one's own abilities

不自量力 bù zì liàng lì not have a proper measure of oneself; overrate one's own abilities; overreach oneself

不自由，毋宁死 bùzìyóu, wúnìng sǐ give me liberty, or give me death

不足 bùzú ① not enough; insufficient; inadequate: 资源～ inadequate resources / 给养～ be short of supplies / 人手～ be shorthanded; be understaffed / 估计～ underestimate / 信心～ lack confidence / ～之处 deficiency; inadequacy / ～一千 less than a thousand / ～以引起人们的注意 not enough to attract attention ② not worth: 不足道 bùzúdào ③ cannot; should not: 非团结～图存。We cannot survive unless we unite.

不足道 bùzúdào not worth mentioning; inconsiderable; of no consequence: 我这方面的这点知识是～的。What little I know on the subject is not worth mentioning.

不足挂齿 bù zú guàchǐ not worth mentioning; nothing to speak of: 区区微劳，～。My paltry efforts are not worth mentioning.

不足轻重 bù zú qīng-zhòng worthless; negligible

不足为凭 bù zú wéi píng cannot be taken as evidence; afford little or no evidence

不足为奇 bù zú wéi qí not at all surprising; nothing to be surprised at

不足为训 bù zú wéi xùn not fit to serve as a model; not to be taken as an example; not an example to be followed; not to be taken as authoritative: 书本上讲的也有～的。What is stated in books is not always true.

不足为外人道 bù zú wéi wàirén dào this is not to be mentioned to outsiders; this is strictly between ourselves

不做声 bùzuòshēng keep silent; not say a word

布¹ bù ① cotton cloth; cloth: 把车用块干净的～擦一擦。Wipe the car with a clean cloth. ② an ancient coin

布²（佈） bù ① declare; announce; publish; proclaim: 公布 gōngbù ② spread; disseminate: 传布 chuánbù ③ dispose; arrange; deploy: ～好阵势 deploy the troops in battle formation

布帛 bùbó cloth and silk; cotton and silk textiles

布帛菽粟 bù-bó-shū-sù cloth, silk, beans and grain —food and clothing; daily necessities

布菜 bùcài serve out food (to guests at a meal)

布达拉宫 Bùdálā Gōng the Potala (the former palace of the Dalai Lamas, in Lhasa, Xizang)

布道 bùdào preach the Gospel; evangelize

布店 bùdiàn cloth store; draper's; piece-goods store

布丁 bùdīng pudding

布尔乔亚 bù'ěrqiáoyà bourgeoisie (a transliteration)

布尔什维克 Bù'ěrshíwéikè Bolshevik

布尔什维主义 Bù'ěrshíwéizhǔyì Bolshevism

布防 bùfáng place troops on garrison duty; organize a defence

布告 bùgào notice; bulletin; proclamation: 张贴～ paste up a notice

布告栏 bùgàolán notice board; bulletin board

布谷鸟 bùgǔniǎo cuckoo

布鼓雷门 bùgǔ léimén display one's slight skill before an expert

布褐 bùhè coarse cloth clothing

布基纳法索 Bùjīnàfǎsuǒ Burkina Faso

布景 bùjǐng ① composition (of a painting) ② theat. setting: ～设计师 set designer

布局 bùjú ① overall arrangement; layout; distribution: 新市区的～ the layout of a new urban district / 工业的合理～ a rational distribution of industry / ～整齐的农村 neatly arranged villages / 合理调整城乡经济～ make rational adjustments in the distribution of urban and rural economies / 我们一定要建成～合理，相互配套的科研体系。We are determined to set up a complete, rationally distributed scientific and technological research system. ② composition (of a picture, piece of writing, etc.) ③ position (of pieces on a chessboard)

布拉吉 bùlāji another name for 连衣裙 liányīqún (a transliteration of Russian platye)

布莱尔盲字 bùlái'ěr mángzì Braille

布朗基主义 Bùlǎngjīzhǔyì Blanquism

布朗运动 Bùlǎng yùndòng phys. Brownian movement

布朗族 Bùlǎngzú the Blang (Pulang) nationality, or the Blangs, inhabiting Yunnan

布雷 bùléi lay mines; mine: 在港口～ mine a harbour

布雷舰艇 bùléi jiàntǐng minelayers

布雷区 bùléiqū minefield

布列斯特和约 Bùlièsītè Héyuē the Treaty of Brest-Litovsk (1918)

布隆迪 Bùlóngdí Burundi

布隆迪人 Bùlóngdírén Burundian

布鲁氏菌 bùlǔshìjūn brucella

布鲁氏菌病 bùlǔshìjūnbìng brucellosis; undulant fever

布面 bùmiàn cloth cover (of a book)

布面精装本 bùmiàn jīngzhuāngběn clothbound de luxe edition

布匹 bùpǐ cloth; piece goods

布匹染色 bùpǐ rǎnsè piece dyeing

布票 bùpiào cloth coupon; clothing coupon cloth

布施 bùshī formal alms giving; charitable

布头 bùtóu ① leftover of a bolt of cloth ② odd bits of cloth

布网船　bùwǎngchuán　*mil.*　netlayer

布纹纸　bùwénzhǐ　wove paper

布线　bùxiàn　*elec.*　wiring

布线图　bùxiàntú　wiring diagram

布鞋　bùxié　cloth shoes

布衣　bùyī　① cotton clothes ② *arch.* commoner

布衣蔬食　bùyī-shūshí　coarse clothes and simple fare—a thrifty and simple life

布依族　Bùyīzú　the Bouyei (Puyi) nationality, or the Bouyeis, inhabiting Guizhou

布置　bùzhì　① fix up; arrange; decorate: ～会场 fix up a place for a meeting / ～展品 arrange exhibits / 礼堂～得很漂亮。The auditorium was beautifully decorated. ② assign; make arrangements for; give instructions about: ～工作 assign work; give instructions about an assignment / ～政治学习 make arrangements for political study / 今天～的算术作业是十道题。Today's assignment in arithmetic consists of ten problems.

步¹　bù　① step; pace: 只有几～路了。It's only a few steps away. / 大～前进 advance with big strides / 走一～棋 make a move (in chess, etc.) ② stage; step: 下一～怎么办? What's the next step (*or* move)? / 这只好一～一～地去做。This will have to be done step by step. ③ condition; situation; state: 事情怎么发展到这一～? How did things get into such a state? ④ an old measure of length, equivalent to 5 *chi* ⑤ walk; go on foot: ～入会场 walk into the assembly hall ⑥ *formal* tread: 步人后尘 bù rén hòuchén ⑦ *dial.* measure by paces; pace out: ～一～这块地够不够三亩。Pace out this piece of land and see if it's three *mu* in area.

步²　bù　(same as 埠, usu. used as part of a place name): 盐～ Yanbu (in Guangdong Province)

步兵　bùbīng　① infantry; foot ② infantryman; foot soldier

步步　bùbù　step by step; at every step: ～进逼 press forward steadily

步步登高　bùbù dēnggāo　ascend step by step; rise steadily in one's career

步步为营　bùbù wéi yíng　advance gradually and dig in at every step; consolidate at every step; act cautiously

步测　bùcè　measure by paces; pace out

步调　bùdiào　pace; step: 统一～ concert action

步调一致　bùdiào yīzhì　march in step; keep in step; act in unison: ～才能得胜利。Only if we coordinate our efforts can we win victory.

步伐　bùfá　step; pace: 加快～ quicken one's steps (*or* pace) / ～整齐 (march) in step / 跟上时代的～ keep pace with the times

步法　bùfǎ　footwork (in dancing, sports, etc.)

步弓　bùgōng　another name for 弓 gōng③

步话机　bùhuàjī　walkie-talkie

步进制　bùjìnzhì　*postal service* step-by-step system

步犁　bùlí　walking plough

步履　bùlǚ　*formal* walk

步履蹒跚　bùlǚ pánshān　walk haltingly; hobble along

步履维艰　bùlǚ wéi jiān　have difficulty walking; walk with difficulty

步枪　bùqiāng　rifle

步人后尘　bù rén hòuchén　follow in sb.'s footsteps

步哨　bùshào　sentry; sentinel

步谈机　bùtánjī　same as 步话机 bùhuàjī

步武　bùwǔ　*formal* ① a pace and a half—a very short distance ② follow in sb.'s footsteps: ～前贤 emulate the examples of the former worthies

步行　bùxíng　go on foot; walk

步行虫　bùxíngchóng　ground beetle

步行机　bùxíngjī　popular name for 步话机 bùhuàjī

步韵　bùyùn　use the rhyme sequence of a poem (when replying to it)

步骤　bùzhòu　step; move; measure: 有计划有～地进行工作 carry on the work step by step in a planned way / 采取适当的～ take proper steps / 这是增产的一个具体～。This is a practical move to increase production.

步子　bùzi　step; pace: ～轻快 walk with springy steps / 队伍的～走得很整齐。The soldiers marched in step. / 技术革新的～越迈越大。Technical innovations are being made at a faster and faster pace.

怖　bù　fear; be afraid of: 恐怖 kǒngbù

钚　bù　*chem.* plutonium (Pu)

部　bù　① part; section: 分为三～ divide into three parts (*or* sections) / 南～ the southern part ② unit; ministry; department; board: 解放军某～ a certain PLA unit ③ headquarters: 指挥部 zhǐhuībù ④ troops; forces ⑤ *formal* control; command: 所部 suǒbù ⑥ *m.* (for books and films): 两～字典 two dictionaries / 一～电影 a film ⑦ *m. dial.* (for machines and vehicles): 一～机器 a machine / 两～汽车 two cars

部队　bùduì　① army; armed forces ② troops; force; unit: 通讯兵～ signal troops / 人民解放军北京～ PLA units under the Beijing Command / ～就要出发了。The troops are about to set out. / 这是一支野战～。This is a field army unit.

部队代号　bùduì dàihào　code designation (of a military unit)

部分　bùfen　part; section; share: 我们看问题, 不但要看到～, 而且要看到全体。In approaching a problem we should see the whole as well as the parts. / 他完成了自己的那～工作以后, 又去帮助别人。After finishing his share of the work he went to help the others. / 我们～地改变了原计划。We've altered the original plan to some extent.

部件　bùjiàn　parts; components; assembly

部件分解图　bùjiàn fēnjiětú　exploded view

部将　bùjiàng　*old* officers under one's control

部类　bùlèi　category; division

部落　bùluò　tribe

部落社会　bùluò shèhuì　tribal society

部门　bùmén　department; branch: 政府各～ various government departments / 工业和农业是国民经济的两个重要～。Industry and agriculture are the two important sectors of the national economy.

部首　bùshǒu　radicals by which characters are arranged in traditional Chinese dictionaries

部属　bùshǔ　① same as 部下 bùxià ② affiliated to a ministry: ～机构 organizations affiliated to the ministry

部署　bùshǔ　dispose; deploy: ～兵力 dispose (*or* deploy) troops for battle / 改革的～和实施 the planning and implementation of the reform / 大会为我国社会主义现代化作出了重大～。The Congress drew up an important plan for the socialist modernization of our country.

部头　bùtóu　size (of a voluminous work)

部委　bùwěi　ministries and commissions: 国务院各～ ministries and commissions under the State Council

部位　bùwèi　(usu. used of parts of the human body) position; place: 发音时舌的～ the position of the tongue in pronunciation; tongue position / 受伤～ the location of an injury

部下　bùxià　① troops under one's command ② subordinate

部长　bùzhǎng　minister; head of a department (under the Party Central Committee): 外贸部～ Minister of

Foreign Trade／对外联络部～ Head of the International Liaison Department／省委宣传部～ Director of the Propaganda Department of a provincial Party committee

部长会议 bùzhǎng huìyì Council of Ministers

部长级会议 bùzhǎngjí huìyì conference at ministerial level

部长助理 bùzhǎng zhùlǐ assistant minister

埠

bù ① wharf; pier ② port

埠头 bùtóu *dial.* wharf; pier

瓿

bù *arch.* a small jar

簿

bù notebook; book: 帐簿 zhàngbù

簿册 bùcè books for taking notes or keeping accounts

簿籍 bùjí account books, registers, records, etc.

簿记 bùjì bookkeeping: 复(单)式～ double-entry (single-entry) bookkeeping

簿录 bùlù *formal* ① make an inventory of a criminal's possessions and confiscate them ② a record of things or events ③ a catalogue of books

簿子 bùzi notebook; book

C

cā

拆 cā *dial.* discharge (faeces or urine); shit or piss ——see also chāi

拆烂污 cā lànwū *dial.* do sloppy work; scamp a job; leave things in a mess; be irresponsible: 他工作～，受到了批评。He was criticized for his sloppy work.

擦 cā ① rub: ～根火柴点烟 strike a match and light a cigarette / 他～伤了膝盖。He skinned his knee. / 没关系，就～破了一点皮。Nothing serious. Just a scratch. ② wipe: ～桌子(地板, 玻璃, 自行车) wipe a table (mop the floor, clean a pane of glass, clean a bike) / 你～～汗吧, 这儿有毛巾。Wipe the sweat away, here's a towel. / 他的皮鞋～得很亮。His shoes are well shined. ③ apply or spread sth. on: ～药水或药膏 apply medicinal lotion or ointment (to an affected spot) / ～粉 powder one's face / 我的皮鞋该～点儿油了。My shoes need a shine. ④ touch lightly or come close to in passing; shave; brush: 他～着我的肩膀走过去了。He brushed past me. / 飞机～着山顶飞过。The plane swept the hilltops. ⑤ scrape into shreds: 把萝卜～成丝儿。Shred the turnips.

擦棒球 cābàngqiú foul tip (in baseball, soft ball, etc.)

擦背 cābèi rub one's back with a towel while bathing

擦边球 cābiānqiú *table tennis* edge ball; touch ball

擦菜板 cācàibǎn (also 擦子 cāzi) grater

擦黑儿 cāhēir *dial.* dusk: 他～才回到家。He didn't come back home until dusk.

擦亮眼睛 cāliàng yǎnjīng remove the scales from one's eyes; sharpen one's vigilance: 我们要～识破他们的阴谋。We should sharpen our vigilance and guard against their schemes.

擦屁股 cā pìgu clear up the mess left by sb. else

擦拭 cāshì wipe clean; cleanse: ～枪支 clean firearms

擦网球 cāwǎngqiú net ball (in table tennis, volleyball, etc.)

擦洗 cāxǐ clean (with water or alcohol): 这个手表该～了。This watch needs cleaning.

擦音 cāyīn *phonet.* fricative

擦澡 cāzǎo rub oneself down with a wet towel

嚓 cā *onom.*: 汽车～的一声停住了。The car screeched to a halt. ——see also chā

礤 cā see 礓礤 jiāngcā

cǎ

礤 cǎ *formal* coarse stone

礤床儿 cǎchuángr shredder (for vegetables)

cāi

猜 cāi ① guess; conjecture; speculate: 你～谁来了? Guess who's here. / 他准～不着。He's sure to guess wrong. / 这个谜语真难～。This riddle is really difficult to solve. ② suspect: 我～他和这件事有点牵连。I suspect that he is somewhat involved in the affair.

猜测 cāicè guess; conjecture; surmise: 那都是～。That's pure conjecture. / 妄加～ make wild guesses / 考古新发现否定了过去对这个问题的～。The new archaeological finds have disproved previous conjectures on this subject.

猜度 cāiduó surmise; conjecture: 他心里在～, 这位老人家是谁? He was wondering who that old man could be.

猜忌 cāijì be suspicious and jealous: 自己没有私心, 就不会～别人。If you didn't have selfish motives, you wouldn't be suspicious and jealous of others.

猜谜儿 cāimèir ① guess a riddle ② guess: 快说吧, 别让我们～了。Now out with it. Don't keep us guessing.

猜破 cāipò guess right: 他的意思我早就～了。I guessed what he meant long ago.

猜拳 cāiquán same as 划拳 huáquán

猜透 cāitòu guess right: 他的意图我早就～了。I guessed his intentions long ago. / 我猜不透她的心事。I can't figure out what's on her mind.

猜想 cāixiǎng suppose; guess; suspect: 我～她又到商店去了。I suppose she's gone shopping again. / 我～他病了。I suspect he is ill. / 你这种～不一定正确。This supposition of yours might be wrong.

猜哑谜 cāi yǎmí try to guess a riddle—guess at sth.

猜疑 cāiyí harbour suspicions; be suspicious; have misgivings: 不要随便～。Don't let your suspicions get out of hand.

猜中 cāizhòng guess right: 谁～这个谜语可得奖。Whoever guesses the riddle will get a prize.

cái

才[1] cái ① ability; talent: 才能 cáinéng / 德才兼备 dé-cái jiānbèi ② a capable person: 人才 réncái ③ people of a certain type: 奴才 núcai

才[2] (纔) cái *adv.* ① a moment ago; just: 你怎么～来就要走? You've only just come. Why do you want to leave so soon? / 他～回到家里, 老徐就来找他了。He had just got home when Lao Xu came looking for him. ② (preceded by an expression of time) not until: 他九点钟～来, 太晚了。He didn't come until 9 o'clock. That was too late. / 大风到晚上～住了。The gale didn't stop until evening. / 他走了两个钟头～走到。It took him two hours to get there. / 你为什么这会儿～说呢? How come you didn't say anything till now? ③

(preceded by an expression of reason or condition) not unless; not until; then and only then; for no other reason: 他吃了三碗～饱。 He wasn't full until he had eaten three bowls. / 经他解释之后，我～明白是怎么回事。 I didn't understand what was going on until he explained it to me. / 他说行～行。 It's O. K. only if he says so. / 只有依靠群众，～能把工作做好。 Only by relying on the people can we do our work well. / 正因为有困难，～派我们去。 We were sent precisely because there were problems there. ④ (followed by a numerical expression) only: 现在～八点钟，还早着呢。 It's only 8 o'clock, so there's still plenty of time. / 一～五块钱吗？真便宜。 Only five dollars? That's really cheap. / 这孩子～五岁，已经认得不少字了。 The child is only five, and he already knows quite a few characters. ⑤ (used in an assertion or contradiction, emphasizing what comes before 才, usu. with 呢 at the end of the sentence) actually; really: 这～好呢! Now this is really good! / 你以为他傻吗？他～不傻呢! You think he's stupid? Not him! / 我～懒得管呢! I can't be bothered! or I couldn't care less. / 你～是撒谎! You are the one who's lying. / 他要是不知道～怪呢! I'd be really surprised if he didn't know.

才干 cáigàn ability; competence: 长～ enhance one's abilities / 他很有～。 He is very capable. / 这件事充分显示了他的～。 This fully shows his ability.

才高八斗 cái gāo bā dǒu be endowed with unusual literary talents

才华 cáihuá literary or artistic talent: 她是一位很有～的青年作家。 She is a gifted young writer.

才华横溢 cáihuá héngyì brim with talent; have superb talent: 李白是唐代一位～的诗人。 Li Bai was a Tang poet of superb talent.

才具 cáijù formal capability; ability: ～有限 be of limited capability

才力 cáilì capability; ability

才略 cáilüè ability and sagacity (in political and military affairs): 雄才大略 xióngcái-dàlüè

才貌 cáimào talent and appearance

才貌出众 cáimào chūzhòng of exceptional talent and distinguished appearance

才貌双全 cáimào shuāngquán be endowed with both beauty and talent

才能 cáinéng ability; capability; talent: 有～ have ability; be capable / 在工厂的经营管理方面，她显示出非凡的～。 She shows rare capability in factory management.

才女 cáinǚ a gifted female scholar

才气 cáiqì same as 才华 cáihuá

才气横溢 cáiqì héngyì same as 才华横溢 cái huá héngyì

才情 cáiqíng literary or artistic talent; imaginative power

才识 cáishí ability and insight: ～过人 be gifted with talent and insight far beyond the average person

才疏学浅 cáishū-xuéqiǎn pol. have little talent and less learning

才思 cáisī imaginative power and creativeness (in writing): ～敏捷 have a facile imagination

才学 cáixué talent and learning; scholarship: 他读书万卷，～出众。 He's read volumes and is an outstanding scholar.

才智 cáizhì ability and wisdom: 充分发挥人民群众的聪明～ give full play to the wisdom and creativity of the people / ～过人 far surpass others in ability and wisdom

才子 cáizǐ a talented scholar

才子佳人 cáizǐ-jiārén genius and beauty (the hero and heroine in a type of romance in which a talented young man and a beautiful girl meet and fall in love and, after overcoming many obstacles, marry and live happily ever after): 这些书就是一套子，左不过是些佳人才子，最没趣儿。（《红楼梦》） There is a sameness about all these tales. They're so stereotyped—all about talented scholars and lovely ladies.

材 cái ① timber: 木材 mùcái ② coffin: 寿材 shòucái ③ material: 教材 jiàocái / 钢材 gāngcái ④ ability; talent; aptitude: 因材施教 yīn cái shī jiào ⑤ a capable person: 成材 chéngcái

材积 cáijī forestry volume of timber

材料 cáiliào ① material: 做个书架需要些什么～？ What materials do you need to make a bookcase? ② data; material: 学习～ material for study / 档案～ archival material / 调查～ data; findings / 搜集～ gather material; collect data / 根据现有～还不能得出肯定的结论。 We cannot draw any definite conclusion from the available data. ③ makings; stuff: 她不是演戏的～。 She hasn't the makings of an actress.

材料力学 cáiliào lìxué mechanics of materials

财 cái wealth; money: 发财 fācái / 财政 cáizhèng

财宝 cáibǎo money and valuables

财帛 cáibó wealth; money

财产 cáichǎn property: 公共～ public property / 国家～ state property / 私人～ private property / ～保险 property insurance

财产权 cáichǎnquán property right

财产税 cáichǎnshuì property tax

财大气粗 cáidà-qìcū he who has wealth speaks louder than others

财东 cáidōng old ① shopowner; store owner ② moneybags

财阀 cáifá financial magnate; plutocrat; tycoon

财富 cáifù wealth; riches: 自然～ natural wealth / 精神～ spiritual wealth / 物质～ material wealth

财货 cáihuò money and property

财经 cáijīng finance and economics: ～工作 work in the field of finance and economics / ～学校 schools of finance and economics / ～纪律 financial discipline

财会 cáikuài finance and accounting: ～人员 accountants

财礼 cáilǐ same as 彩礼 cǎilǐ

财力 cáilì financial resources (or capacity): ～雄厚 have abundant financial resources / ～不足 have insufficient financial resources / ～有限 have limited financial resources

财贸 cáimào finance and trade (or commerce)

财贸系统 cáimào xìtǒng departments of finance and trade and affiliated organizations

财迷 cáimí moneygrubber; miser: 他是个老～。 He's an old miser.

财迷心窍 cái mí xīnqiào be mad about money; be money-grubbing

财权 cáiquán ① ownership of property; property right ② financial power; control over money matters: 她在单位里是掌～的。 She has control over financial matters in her unit (or organization).

财神 cáishén (also 财神爷 cáishényé) the God of Wealth: 请～ invoke the God of Wealth

财势 cáishì wealth and influence: 依仗～ count on one's or sb. else's wealth and influence

财团 cáituán financial group: 国际～ consortium

财务 cáiwù financial affairs: ～报告 financial statement (or report) / ～行政 financial administration

财务科 cáiwùkē finance section

财物 cáiwù money and goods; property (estate not included): 个人～ personal property; personal effects / 公共～ public property

财雄势大 cáixióng-shìdà　be of great wealth and influence

财源 cáiyuán　financial resources; source of revenue: ～茂盛 rich in financial resources / 广开～ explore all possible ways of bringing in money or revenue

财运 cáiyùn　luck in making money: 他～不错,一下子赚了十几万。 He's very lucky. He's made over a hundred thousand *yuan* in one deal.

财政 cáizhèng　(public) finance: ～危机 financial crisis / ～收入 revenue / ～支出 expenditure / ～收支平衡 balance of revenue and expenditure / ～政策 financial (*or* fiscal) policy / ～机关 financial organ or administration; fiscal organ or administration

财政部 cáizhèngbù　the Ministry of Finance

财政赤字 cáizhèng chìzì　financial deficits

财政年度 cáizhèng niándù　financial (*or* fiscal) year

财主 cáizhu　rich man; moneybags: 他是本地有名的～。 He's one of the well-known rich men in these parts.

裁 cái　① cut (paper, cloth, etc.) into parts: 把一张纸～成条儿 cut a sheet of paper into strips / 一件新衣服 cut out a new garment / 这块料子可以～两套衣服。 Two suits can be cut out of this piece of material. ② reduce; cut down; dismiss: 这家公司去年～了十个人。 This company dismissed ten people last year. ③ judge; decide: 裁决 cáijué / 独裁 dúcái ④ check; sanction: 制裁 zhìcái ⑤ mental planning: 别出心裁 bié chū xīncái

裁并 cáibìng　cut down and merge (organizations): 这个科已～到总务处。 This section has been merged into the general affairs department.

裁撤 cáichè　dissolve (an organization): 这个机构应该～。 This organization should be dissolved. / 我们已经～了两个科室。 We have dissolved two offices already.

裁处 cáichǔ　consider and solve; decide and take action: 这件事由你～。 This matter will be left in your hands. / 这事太复杂,一时很难～。 This is too complicated a matter to be settled right away.

裁定 cáidìng　*leg.*　decide or declare judicially; rule: 法官～他的证词有效。 The judge ruled that his testimony was valid.

裁断 cáiduàn　consider and decide: 此事如何处理,请您～。 Please consider the problem and decide how to handle it.

裁夺 cáiduó　same as 裁断 cáiduàn

裁缝 cáifeng　tailor; dressmaker

裁剪 cáijiǎn　cut out (a garment): 我这件大衣请你照这个式样～。 Please cut out my overcoat according to (*or* after) this pattern.

裁减 cáijiǎn　reduce; cut down: ～机关工作人员 reduce (*or* cut down) the staff of an organization / ～军备 reduce armaments

裁决 cáijué　adjudicate; rule: 依法～ adjudicate according to law / 会议主席作出了～。 A ruling was given by the chairman.

裁军 cáijūn　reduce armaments: ～谈判 disarmament talks

裁判 cáipàn　① *leg.*　judge ② *sports*　act as referee ③ *sports*　referee; judge; umpire: 他应邀为这场排球赛担任～。 He is asked to referee this volleyball match.

裁判权 cáipànquán　jurisdiction: 有～ have jurisdiction / 取消～ deprive sb. of his jurisdiction

裁判员 cáipànyuán　same as 裁判③

裁判长 cáipànzhǎng　*sports*　head referee; head judge

裁汰 cáitài　*formal*　weed out the superfluous and unqualified: ～冗员 weed out superfluous personnel

裁员 cáiyuán　cut down the number of persons employed; reduce the staff: 这家饭店已～二十人。 The hotel has dismissed twenty people from its staff.

裁纸机 cáizhǐjī　paper cutter; (paper) trimmer

cǎi

采[1]（採）　cǎi　① pick, pluck or gather: ～茶 pick tea / ～药 gather medicinal herbs / 潜水～珠 dive for pearls ② mine; extract: 采煤 cǎiméi / 采油 cǎiyóu ③ choose; select: 采取 cǎiqǔ / 采用 cǎiyòng

采[2]　cǎi　manner, air or spirit (of a person): 神采 shéncǎi / 风采 fēngcǎi

采[3]　cǎi　same as 彩 cǎi
——see also cài

采办 cǎibàn　select and purchase on a considerable scale (esp. for a special occasion): ～年货 make special purchases for the Spring Festival

采茶戏 cǎicháxì　tea-pickers' opera (a local opera popular in Jiangxi, Hubei, Guangxi, Anhui, etc., developed from folk songs and dances)

采场 cǎichǎng　*min.*　stope

采出 cǎichū　*petroleum*　extraction

采伐 cǎifá　cut timber; lumber: ～原始森林 open up a primeval forest for logging / 他从事～多年。 He has been engaged in the lumbering business for years.

采伐迹地 cǎifájìdì　cutover

采伐量 cǎifáliàng　(timber) cut

采访 cǎifǎng　① hunt for and collect: 图书～工作 the work of finding and collecting books for libraries ② gather news; cover: ～新闻 cover a news item / ～一位名演员 interview a famous actor / 她负责～证券交易所。 She covers the stock exchange. / 他～了竞选活动的全过程。 He covered the election campaign from start to finish.

采风 cǎifēng　collect folk songs

采购 cǎigòu　make purchases for an organization or enterprise; purchase: ～建筑材料 purchase building materials

采购员 cǎigòuyuán　purchasing agent

采购站 cǎigòuzhàn　purchasing station

采光 cǎiguāng　*archit.*　(natural) lighting; daylighting

采集 cǎijí　gather; collect: ～标本 collect specimens / 原始部落靠渔猎～为生。 Primitive tribes lived by fishing, hunting and gathering.

采掘 cǎijué　*min.*　excavate: ～设备 equipment for excavation

采矿 cǎikuàng　mining: 露天～ opencut (*or* opencast) mining / ～工程 mining engineering / ～工业 mining (industry)

采莲船 cǎiliánchuán　same as 跑旱船 pǎohànchuán

采录 cǎilù　collect and record: ～民歌 collect and record folk songs

采买 cǎimǎi　① select and purchase ② purchasing agent: 我可以当～。 I can handle the purchasing job. *or* I can do all the purchasing for the occasion.

采煤 cǎiméi　coal mining; coal extraction; coal cutting: ～工作面 coal face / ～回收率 coal recovery

采棉机 cǎimiánjī　cotton picker (farming machine)

采纳 cǎinà　accept (opinions, suggestions, requests, etc.): ～群众建议 accept suggestions made by the masses

采暖 cǎinuǎn　heating: 蒸气～ steam heating / ～设备 heating equipment (*or* facilities)

采取 cǎiqǔ　adopt; assume or take: ～紧急措施 take emergency measures / ～主动 take the initiative / ～攻势 take the offensive / ～说服教育的办法 use the

method of persuasion and education / ～拖延战术 employ stalling tactics / ～强制手段 resort to compulsion / 咱们不能～消极的态度。We mustn't assume a passive attitude.

采石场 cǎishíchǎng　stone pit; quarry

采撷 cǎixié　*formal* ① pick; pluck ② gather

采写 cǎixiě　(of a journalist) interview and write about

采薪之忧 cǎixīn zhī yōu　a slight indisposition (referring to one's own illness)

采样 cǎiyàng　*min.* sampling

采用 cǎiyòng　select and use; adopt: ～新技术 adopt new techniques / ～有效的工作方法 use effective work methods / 中国～拉丁字母作为汉语拼音字母。The Chinese have adopted the Latin alphabet as the Chinese phonetic alphabet.

采油 cǎiyóu　*petroleum* oil extraction; oil recovery: 二次～ secondary recovery

采油队 cǎiyóuduì　oil production crew

采择 cǎizé　choose; select: 提出以下几种办法, 以供～。Now, I propose the following measures for you to choose from.

采摘 cǎizhāi　pick (fruit, flowers, leaves, etc.); pluck: ～苹果(棉花) pick apples (cotton)

采脂 cǎizhī　*forestry* resin tapping

采制 cǎizhì　gather and process: ～中草药 gather medicinal herbs and prepare them for use

采种 cǎizhǒng　*agric.* seed collecting

彩[1]　cǎi ① colour: 五彩 wǔcǎi / 彩色 cǎisè ② applause; cheer: 彩声 cǎishēng ③ variety; brilliance; splendour: 丰富多彩 fēngfù duōcǎi ④ prize: 中彩 zhòngcǎi ⑤ blood from a wound: 挂彩 guàcǎi

彩[2]（綵）　cǎi coloured silk; variegated silk: 剪彩 jiǎncǎi / 张灯结彩 zhāngdēng-jiécǎi

彩蚌 cǎibàng　*arts & crafts* painted clam shell (a clam shell with a colour painting done on its inside)

彩笔 cǎibǐ　colour pencil; crayon

彩车 cǎichē　① float (in a parade) ② bridal car

彩绸 cǎichóu　coloured silk

彩带 cǎidài　coloured ribbon (*or* streamer)

彩旦 cǎidàn　the feminine counterpart to the *chou* (丑) role, or female comedians (portraying a shrew, a dangerous woman, or the ever-present matchmaker 媒婆, all comic, lowly, and mean)

彩蛋 cǎidàn　① *arts & crafts* painted eggshell (an emptied eggshell with a colour painting done on its outside, with or without decorative silk tassels) ② *dial.* preserved egg

彩灯 cǎidēng　coloured lights

彩电 cǎidiàn　① (short for 彩色电视) colour television (broadcasting): 北京～中心 the Beijing Colour Television Centre ② (short for 彩色电视机) colour television set; colour TV: 一台20英寸～ a 20″ colour TV

彩调 cǎidiào　a local opera of the Guangxi Zhuang Autonomous Region, popular in its southern part

彩坊 cǎifāng　same as 彩牌楼 cǎipáilou

彩凤随鸦 cǎi fèng suí yā　a phoenix mating with a crow —a beautiful woman married to a worthless man

彩号 cǎihào　a soldier wounded in action

彩虹 cǎihóng　rainbow

彩绘 cǎihuì　coloured drawing or pattern: ～瓷器 porcelain decorated with coloured drawings / ～陶俑 painted pottery figurine

彩轿 cǎijiào　same as 花轿 huājiào

彩扩 cǎikuò　(short for 彩色扩印) *photog.* make enlargements of 135 colour films

彩礼 cǎilǐ　betrothal gifts (from the bridegroom to the bride's family); bride-price: 要（收, 送）～ ask for (accept, present) betrothal gifts

彩练 cǎiliàn　coloured ribbon

彩门 cǎimén　same as 彩牌楼 cǎipáilou

彩排 cǎipái　dress rehearsal: 明天晚上进行～。We are having a dress rehearsal tomorrow evening.

彩牌楼 cǎipáilou　a decorated archway (erected on a festive occasion)

彩棚 cǎipéng　a decorated tent (set up on a festive occasion); marquee

彩票 cǎipiào　lottery ticket

彩旗 cǎiqí　coloured banner; bunting

彩球 cǎiqiú　coloured silk ball (for decorative purposes)

彩券 cǎiquàn　lottery ticket

彩色 cǎisè　multicolour; colour: ～铅笔 colour pencil; crayon

彩色玻璃 cǎisè bōli　stained glass

彩色电视 cǎisè diànshì　colour television (broadcasting)

彩色电视机 cǎisè diànshìjī　colour television set; colour TV

彩色胶卷 cǎisè jiāojuǎn　*photog.* colour film

彩色片儿 cǎisèpiānr　*inf.* colour film

彩色片 cǎisèpiàn　colour film

彩色印刷 cǎisè yìnshuā　colour printing

彩声 cǎishēng　cheering: 掌声～一浪高一浪。There was wave after wave of cheering and applause.

彩塑 cǎisù　painted sculpture: ～泥人 a painted clay figurine

彩陶 cǎitáo　painted pottery (of a Neolithic culture)

彩陶文化 cǎitáo wénhuà　the painted pottery culture (another name for 仰韶文化 Yǎngsháo wénhuà)

彩头 cǎitóu　good luck in business, contests or lotteries

彩霞 cǎixiá　rosy (*or* pink) clouds

彩印 cǎiyìn　short for 彩色印刷 cǎisè yìnshuā

彩釉陶 cǎiyòutáo　glazed coloured pottery

睬（倸）　cǎi pay attention to; take notice of: 别～他。Take no notice of him. or Ignore him. / 嘿! 人家对你说话呢, 你怎么能～也不～? Hey, he's talking to you. How can you pay no attention to what he says?

踩（踹）　cǎi step on; trample: 当心～坏了庄稼。Mind you don't tread on the crops. / 对不起, ～了您的脚。Sorry for stepping on your toe! / 他～在凳子上挂窗帘。He stepped onto the stool to put up the curtains. / 不小心一脚～到烂泥里了。I stepped into the mud before I knew it.

踩水 cǎishuǐ　*sports* tread water

踩线 cǎixiàn　*sports* ① foot fault ② commit a foot fault; footfault

踩闸 cǎizhá　step on the brake

cài

采（埰）　cài see below ——see also cǎi

采地 càidì　(also 采邑 càiyì) fief; vassalage

菜　cài ① vegetable; greens: 种～ grow vegetables ② (non-staple) food: 上街买～ go to the market to buy food ③ dish; course: 一道～ a course / 川～ Sichuan dishes; Sichuan cuisine / 做～ prepare the dishes; do the cooking / 做四道～ prepare a four-course meal ④ (edible) wild herbs: 吃糠咽～ barely keep alive on chaff and wild herbs

菜案 cài'àn　same as 红案 hóng'àn

菜板 càibǎn　chopping board

菜帮 càibāng　outer leaves (of a cabbage, etc.)

菜场　càichǎng　food market

菜单　càidān　menu; bill of fare

菜刀　càidāo　kitchen knife

菜地　càidì　vegetable plot

菜豆　càidòu　kidney bean

菜墩子　càidūnzi　chopping block

菜粉蝶　càifěndié　cabbage butterfly

菜瓜　càiguā　snake melon

菜馆　càiguǎn　*dial.*　restaurant

菜花　càihuā　① cauliflower ② rape flower

菜窖　càijiào　vegetable cellar

菜篮子　càilánzi　① shopping basket (for food); food basket ② food supply: 关心人民群众的～ see that the people have plenty to eat

菜篮子工程　càilánzi gōngchéng　shopping basket programme—a programme for increasing food production

菜码儿　càimǎr　*dial.*　shredded or sliced vegetables to go with noodles

菜牛　càiniú　beef cattle

菜农　càinóng　vegetable grower

菜圃　càipǔ　vegetable garden; vegetable farm

菜谱　càipǔ　① menu; bill of fare ② cookery book

菜畦　càiqí　small sections of a vegetable plot; vegetable bed

菜青　càiqīng　dark greyish green

菜青虫　càiqīngchóng　cabbage caterpillar

菜色　càisè　a sickly pallor of one living on wild herbs; a famished (*or* emaciated) look: 面有～ look famished

菜市　càishì　food market

菜蔬　càishū　① vegetables or greens ② (vegetable and meat) dishes prepared for a meal or a feast

菜薹　càitái　tender flower stalk (of garlic, rape, mustard, etc.)

菜摊　càitān　vegetable stall

菜心　càixīn　heart (of a cabbage, etc.)

菜肴　càiyáo　cooked dishes (usu. meat dishes)

菜油　càiyóu　rapeseed oil; rape oil

菜园　càiyuán　vegetable garden; vegetable farm

菜子　càizǐ (also 菜籽 càizǐ)　① vegetable seeds ② rapeseed

菜子饼　càizǐbǐng　rapeseed cake (usu. used as a fertilizer)

菜子油　càizǐyóu　same as 菜油 càiyóu

蔡[1]　Cài　a surname

蔡[2]　cài　*arch.*　turtle; tortoise

cān

参[1](參)　cān　① join; enter; take part in: 参战 cānzhàn　② refer; consult: 参阅 cānyuè

参[2](參)　cān　① call to pay one's respects to: 参谒 cānyè／参拜 cānbài　② impeach an official before the emperor: ～一本 present a memorial to the emperor impeaching an official
——see also cēn; shēn

参拜　cānbài　① pay one's respects to (a superior); present oneself to: 大礼～ present oneself to sb. ceremoniously ② pay homage to sb. (before his tomb or image)

参半　cānbàn　half; half-and-half: 疑信～ half believing, half doubting

参禅　cānchán　(of Buddhists) sit in deep meditation

参股　cāngǔ　purchase of shares in enterprises

参观　cānguān　visit; have a look around: ～工厂 visit a factory／～名胜古迹 go on sightseeing trips to scenic spots and historical monuments／～游览 visit places of interest; go sightseeing／欢迎～。Visitors are welcome.

参观团　cānguāntuán　visiting group

参加　cānjiā　① join (a group, organization, etc.); take part in (an activity): ～革命 join the revolutionary ranks／～政党 join a political party／～晚会 go to an evening party／积极～社会主义建设 take an active part in socialist construction／～生产劳动 participate in productive labour／～管理国家大事 participate in the management of state affairs／～会议 attend a meeting／～会谈 take part in talks／～比赛的人都是经过严格挑选的。Every participant in the contest has been rigidly selected.／要是她～进来，这场辩论就更热闹了。The debate would have been even more heated if she had joined in. ② give (advice, suggestion, etc.): 这件事你也来～点儿意见吧？Come and give us your view on the matter, won't you?

参见[1]　cānjiàn　see (used in references): ～第九章。See Chapter 9.

参见[2]　cānjiàn　pay one's respects to (a superior, etc.)

参军　cānjūn　join the army; join up; enlist: 这个青年要报名～。That boy wants to enlist.／他参了一年军，身体更结实了。After being in the army for a year, he's become fitter than ever before.

参看　cānkàn　① see (used in references): ～下面注释。See note below.／～第二十二页。See page 22. ② read sth. for reference; consult: 他～了不少有关书刊。He consulted a number of relevant books and periodicals.／学习语法可以～这篇文章。If you are studying grammar, you might read this article for reference.

参考　cānkǎo　① consult; refer to: ～历史文献 consult historical documents ② reference: 仅供～。For reference only.

参考书　cānkǎoshū　reference book

参考书目　cānkǎo shūmù　a list of reference books; bibliography

参考资料　cānkǎo zīliào　reference material

参谋　cān·móu　① *mil.*　staff officer ② give advice: 这事可以让老张给你～一下。You might ask Lao Zhang for advice on this matter.／请你给我们～～看怎么办才好。Please give us some advice as to what is the best way to do it.

参谋长　cānmóuzhǎng　*mil.*　chief of staff

参赛　cānsài　participate in a match or contest: ～选手 contestant

参事　cānshì　counsellor; adviser

参数　cānshù　*math.*　parameter

参天　cāntiān　(of trees, etc.) reach to the sky; tower: ～古树 towering old trees／松柏～，浓荫蔽日。Pines and cypresses reach high up to the sky, blotting out the sunlight.

参透　cāntòu　thoroughly understand: ～他的机关 see through his tricks

参谒　cānyè　*formal*　① pay one's respects to (a superior) ② pay homage to sb. (before his tomb or image)

参议　cānyì　*formal*　counsel; advise

参议员　cānyìyuán　senator

参议院　cānyìyuàn　senate

参与　cānyù (also 参预 cānyù)　participate in; have a hand in; involve oneself in: ～其事 have a hand in the matter／～制订计划 participate in the drawing up of a plan／这种事我不～。I don't want to have a hand (*or* be involved) in such things.

参阅　cānyuè　same as 参看 cānkàn

参杂　cānzá　mix; mingle

参赞　cānzàn　① counsellor: 商务～ commercial counsellor／文化～ cultural attaché ② *formal*　participate in planning; serve as an adviser: ～军务 participate in

military planning

参战 cānzhàn　enter a war; take part in a battle

参战国 cānzhànguó　belligerent state

参照 cānzhào　consult and follow: ～原文作必要的修改 consult the original and make some necessary changes / 翻译这个句子非～上下文不可。We can't translate this sentence without reference to the context. / ～具体情况作出适当安排。Make appropriate arrangements in the light of the situation. / 他们这个办法最好, 值得～实行。Their way of doing it is best. It's well worth trying.

参政 cānzhèng　participate in government and political affairs

参酌 cānzhuó　consider (a matter) in the light of actual conditions; deliberate: 以上意见仅供～, 切勿机械执行。The afore-mentioned suggestions are for your consideration only. They are not to be followed blindly.

餐（飧、湌）

cān　① eat: 聚餐 jùcān　② food; meal: 西餐 xīcān / 中餐 zhōngcān　③ m. (for meals): 一日三～ three meals a day

餐车 cānchē　restaurant car; dining car; diner: 列车上有一节～。There is a dining car on the train.

餐风宿露 cānfēng-sùlù　same as 风餐露宿 fēngcān-lùsù

餐馆 cānguǎn　restaurant

餐巾 cānjīn　table napkin

餐巾纸 cānjīnzhǐ　napkin paper; paper napkin; serviette

餐具 cānjù　tableware; dinner service; dinner set

餐室 cānshì　dining room

餐厅 cāntīng　① dining room; dining hall ② restaurant

餐桌 cānzhuō　dining table

cán

残（殘）

cán　① incomplete; deficient: ～稿 an incomplete manuscript / 这部书很好, 可惜～了。It is a very good book, but unfortunately it's incomplete. ② remnant; remaining: ～敌 remnants of the enemy forces / ～冬 the last days of winter ③ injure; damage: 身～志不～ broken in health but not in spirit ④ cruel; savage; barbarous; ferocious: 凶残 xiōngcán / 残暴 cánbào

残暴 cánbào　cruel and ferocious; brutal; savage

残杯冷炙 cánbēi-lěngzhì　the crumbs which fall from one's master's table; leftovers from a rich man's table

残本 cánběn　a book with a part or some pages missing

残兵败将 cánbīng-bàijiàng　remnants of a routed army: 收拾～, 企图东山再起 muster the remnants of the army, intending to stage a comeback

残部 cánbù　remnants of sb.'s defeated troops: 胡匪～已遁入深山老林。The remnants of Hu's routed bandit groups have fled into the thickly forested mountains.

残存 cáncún　be left alive; survive: 大熊猫是一种～的古动物。The giant panda is one of the surviving ancient animal species.

残废 cánfèi　① become disabled; be crippled: 他的双腿去年就～了。He lost the use of both legs last year. ② a disabled person; cripple

残废军人 cánfèi jūnrén　disabled armyman

残废证 cánfèizhèng　*mil.* certificate of disability

残羹剩饭 cángēng-shèngfàn　(also 残茶剩饭 cánchá-shèngfàn) remains of a meal; leftovers; crumbs from the table: 她把～倒进垃圾桶里。She dumped the leftovers into the rubbish bin.

残骸 cánhái　remains (of a person or animal); wreckage (of a building, machine, vehicle, etc.): 敌机～ the wreckage of an enemy plane

残害 cánhài　cruelly injure or kill: ～肢体 cause bodily injury / 侵略者到处～无辜老百姓。Wherever they went the invaders slaughtered innocent civilians.

残花败柳 cánhuā-bàiliǔ　faded flowers and withered willows—fallen women

残货 cánhuò　damaged or substandard goods; shopworn goods

残迹 cánjì　a remaining trace, sign, etc.; vestiges

残疾 cánji　deformity: 他的腿有～, 行动不便。He's got a deformed leg, so he has difficulty getting about.

残疾人 cánjírén　a disabled (or handicapped) person

残局 cánjú　① the final phase of a game of chess ② the situation after the failure of an undertaking or after social unrest: 收拾～ clear up the mess; pick up the pieces

残酷 cánkù　cruel; brutal; ruthless: ～的剥削 ruthless exploitation / ～的殖民统治 brutal colonial rule / ～的现实 the harsh reality / ～地杀害 kill sb. in cold blood

残留 cánliú　remain; be left over: 这里还～着战争的痕迹。Traces of war still remain here.

残年 cánnián　① the evening of life; declining years ② the last days of the year

残虐 cánnüè　① cruel and tyrannical ② maltreat

残篇断简 cánpiān-duànjiǎn　same as 断编残简 duànbiān-cánjiǎn

残品 cánpǐn　damaged article; defective goods

残破 cánpò　broken; dilapidated: 有些器皿在出土时已经～。Some utensils were already broken when they were unearthed.

残缺 cánquē　incomplete; with parts missing: 迄今仍未发现竹简的～部分。The missing parts of the inscribed bamboo slips have not yet been discovered.

残缺不全 cánquē bù quán　incomplete; fragmentary: 一套～的茶具 an incomplete tea set / 那套书已～。That set of books is no longer complete.

残忍 cánrěn　cruel; ruthless: 他这样对待老年人, 太～了。It's really cruel of him to treat old people like that.

残杀 cánshā　murder in cold blood; slaughter: ～无辜 kill the innocent

残山剩水 cánshān-shèngshuǐ　the ravaged territory of an invaded country

残生 cánshēng　① one's remaining years ② one's wretched life

残阳 cányáng　the setting sun

残余 cányú　remnants; remains; survivals; vestiges: 封建～ remnants of feudalism; feudal remnants / ～势力 remaining (or surviving) forces / 剥削阶级思想～ vestiges of the ideology of the exploiting classes

残垣断壁 cányuán-duànbì　same as 断垣残壁 duànyuán-cánbì

残月 cányuè　① the waning moon ② the setting moon: 晓风～ breezes at dawn and the fading moon

残渣余孽 cánzhā-yúniè　dregs of the old society

残照 cánzhào　sunset glow; evening glow: 天边只留下一抹～。There was only a trace of sunset glow left on the horizon.

蚕（蠶）

cán　silkworm: 养～ raise silkworms

蚕宝宝 cánbǎobao　*dial.* silkworm

蚕箔 cánbó　a bamboo tray for breeding silkworms

蚕蔟 cáncù　a small bundle of straw, etc., for silkworms to spin cocoons on

蚕豆 cándòu　broad bean (the plant, the pod or the seed)

蚕蛾 cán'é　silk moth

蚕茧 cánjiǎn　silkworm cocoon

蚕眠 cánmián　the inactive state of the silkworm before it sheds its skin

蚕农 cánnóng　silkworm breeder; sericulturist

蚕桑 cánsāng silkworm breeding and mulberry growing (as an industry)

蚕沙 cánshā silkworm excrement

蚕山 cánshān *dial.* a cone-shaped bundle of straw, etc., for silkworms to spin cocoons on

蚕食 cánshí nibble: ～别国领土 nibble at another country's territory

蚕食政策 cánshí zhèngcè the policy of nibbling at another country's territory

蚕食鲸吞 cánshí-jīngtūn nibble away like a silkworm or swallow like a whale—seize another country's territory by piecemeal encroachment or wholesale annexation

蚕丝 cánsī natural silk; silk

蚕蚁 cányǐ newly-hatched silkworm

蚕蛹 cányǒng silkworm chrysalis

蚕蛹油 cányǒngyóu silkworm chrysalis oil

蚕纸 cánzhǐ silkworm egg sheet (a sheet of paper on which silk moths have laid eggs)

蚕子 cánzǐ silkworm egg

惭(慚) cán feel ashamed: 惭愧 cánkuì ／羞惭 xiūcán

惭愧 cánkuì be ashamed: 我没有完成任务，感到很～。I feel quite ashamed that I have not fulfilled the task.

惭怍 cánzuò *formal* feel ashamed

cǎn

惨(慘) cǎn ① miserable; tragic: 他死得很～。He died a tragic death. ② cruel; brutal; merciless: ～遭杀害 be murdered in cold blood; be brutally killed ③ to a serious degree; disastrously: 他们愈是捣乱，就失败得愈～。The more trouble they make, the worse will be their downfall.

惨案 cǎn'àn massacre: 五卅～ the May 30th Massacre (1925, in Shanghai)

惨白 cǎnbái deathly pale: 脸色～ look deathly pale

惨败 cǎnbài be crushingly (or disastrously) defeated: 入侵之敌～而退。The invaders retreated after suffering a crushing defeat.

惨变 cǎnbiàn a tragic turn of fortune

惨不忍睹 cǎn bùrěn dǔ too horrible (or tragic) to look at

惨淡 cǎndàn ① gloomy; dismal; dim: 在～的星光下 in the dim starlight／天色～。It was gloomy weather.／市面～。Business was dull. ② taking great pains: 惨淡经营 cǎndàn jīngyíng

惨淡经营 cǎndàn jīngyíng keep (an enterprise, etc.) going by painstaking effort; take great pains to carry on one's work under difficult circumstances

惨祸 cǎnhuò a horrible disaster; a frightful calamity: 球迷们疯狂地争斗起来，看台倒坍，酿成～。When the football fans got into a frenzied fight, the spectators' stand collapsed and a horrible disaster occurred.

惨叫 cǎnjiào give a horrible shriek; give a blood-curdling scream

惨景 cǎnjǐng a tragic sight; a miserable scene

惨境 cǎnjìng an extremely miserable condition; dire straits

惨剧 cǎnjù a dreadful, fatal event; a tragic event; calamity; disaster: 渡船翻了，一场～发生了。The ferry capsized and a disaster occurred.

惨绝人寰 cǎn jué rénhuán tragic beyond compare in this human world; extremely tragic: ～的暴行 an atrocity of unparalleled savagery／一场～的浩劫 a holocaust tragic beyond compare

惨绿愁红 cǎnlǜ-chóuhóng weather-beaten leaves and flowers

惨然 cǎnrán saddened; grieved: 他听到这个不幸的消息，不禁～。He couldn't but feel deeply grieved at this sad news.

惨杀 cǎnshā massacre; murder

惨死 cǎnsǐ die a tragic death: 他～于车祸。He died a tragic death in a traffic accident.

惨痛 cǎntòng distressingly grievous; excruciatingly painful; bitter; agonizing: ～的教训 a bitter lesson／一起～的事件 a most distressing incident

惨无人道 cǎn wú réndào inhuman; brutal: 遭受～的迫害 be subjected to inhuman persecution

惨笑 cǎnxiào a sad smile

惨遭不幸 cǎn zāo bùxìng die a tragic death; meet a sad end

惨重 cǎnzhòng heavy; grievous; disastrous: 损失～ suffer heavy (or grievous) losses／～失败 a disastrous defeat／伤亡～ suffer heavy casualties

惨状 cǎnzhuàng a miserable condition; a pitiful or horrible sight: 一声爆炸，霎时间血肉横飞，其～不忍卒睹。A loud explosion sent flesh and blood flying in every direction—a sight too horrible to look at.／你可以想见灾民的那种～。You can well imagine the miserable condition of the disaster victims.

穇(穇) cǎn see below

穇子 cǎnzi billion-dollar grass (the plant or its edible seed)

càn

灿(燦) càn see below

灿烂 cànlàn magnificent; brilliant; resplendent; splendid: ～的阳光 the bright sun; brilliant sunshine／～的民族文化 splendid national culture／前途光辉～。Our prospects are bright.

灿然 cànrán bright; brilliant; resplendent

屪 càn same as 屪 chán, limited to use in 屪头 càntou——see also chán

屪头 càntou *dial. offens.* weakling; coward

粲 càn *formal* ① bright; beaming ② smile beamingly: 以博一～ just for your amusement

粲然 cànrán ① bright; beaming ② smiling broadly: ～一笑 give a beaming smile; grin with delight

璨 càn ① fine jade ② same as 粲 càn

cāng

仓(倉) cāng storehouse; warehouse: 粮食满～。The granary is bursting with grain.

仓廒 cāng'áo *formal* granary

仓储 cāngchǔ keep grain, goods, etc. in a storehouse: 尽量避免商品在～过程中的损耗。Avoid as much as possible the spoilage of goods during storage.

仓促 cāngcù (also 仓猝, 仓卒 cāngcù) hurried; hasty: 我走得太～。I left in too great a hurry.／应战不要～ accept battle in haste／不要～下结论。Don't jump to conclusions.／时间～，咱们还是马上出发边走边谈的好。Time is pressing. We'd better leave right now and talk it over on our way.／时间太～，我没有能完成你交待的全部任务。The time was too short for me to fulfil all your assignments.／在～之间，她也没有留下地址就走

了。She left in such a hurry that she didn't even leave her address.

仓房 cāngfáng　warehouse; storehouse

仓庚 cānggēng　same as 鸧鹒 cānggēng

仓皇 cānghuáng　(also 仓黄 cānghuáng) in a flurry; in panic: ～逃窜 flee in confusion; flee in panic; flee helter-skelter / ～退却 retreat in haste

仓皇失措 cānghuáng shīcuò　be scared out of one's wits; be panic-stricken

仓库 cāngkù　warehouse; storehouse; depository: 清理～ take stock; check warehouse stocks

仓库保管员 cāngkù bǎoguǎnyuán　warehouseman

仓廪 cānglǐn　*formal* granary

仓廪实而知礼节 cānglǐn shí ér zhī lǐjié　when the granaries are full, men appreciate rites and obligations

仓鼠 cāngshǔ　hamster

仓租 cāngzū　warehouse storage charges

伧（傖）
cāng　rude; rough ——see also chen

伧俗 cāngsú　vulgar

沧（滄）
cāng　(of the sea) deep blue

沧海 cānghǎi　the deep blue sea; the sea

沧海横流 cānghǎi héng liú　the seas in turbulence—the country or the world in chaos

沧海桑田 cānghǎi-sāngtián　from seas into mulberry fields and from mulberry fields into seas—time brings great changes to the world

沧海一粟 cānghǎi yī sù　a drop in the ocean: 个人的力量和群众的力量相比, 不过是～。The strength of an individual, as compared with that of the masses, is but a drop in the ocean.

沧海遗珠 cānghǎi yízhū　a pearl left in the depths of the sea—a talent left unrecognized

沧桑 cāngsāng　short for 沧海桑田 cānghǎi-sāngtián

苍（蒼）
cāng　① dark green or blue: ～松 green pines ② grey; ashen: ～髯 a grey beard

苍白 cāngbái　① pale; pallid; wan: 她脸色～。She looks pale. ② lifeless; flat: 这篇文章～无力。This article is flat writing.

苍苍 cāngcāng　*liter.* ① grey: 他年近七十, 两鬓～。He is nearly seventy and greying at the temples. ② dark blue: 天～, 野茫茫。The sky is blue, blue: And the steppe wide, wide. ③ luxuriant

苍翠 cāngcuì　(of trees, grass, etc.) green; verdant: 山峦～。The hills are verdant.

苍耳 cāng'ěr　Siberian cocklebur (*Xanthium sibiricum*)

苍耳子 cāng'ěrzǐ　*Chin. med.* the achene of Siberian cocklebur (*Xanthium sibiricum*)

苍黄[1] cānghuáng　① greenish yellow: 病人面色～。The patient has a sallow complexion. / 时近深秋, 竹林变得～了。It was almost late autumn. The bamboos were turning a greenish yellow. ② *formal* black or yellow—changeable (from the Mohist saying 染于苍则苍, 染于黄则黄 "White silk can be dyed either black or yellow")

苍黄[2] cānghuáng　same as 仓皇 cānghuáng

苍劲 cāngjìng　① (of trees) old and hardy: 古松～挺拔。The sturdy old pines stand tall and straight. ② (of calligraphy or painting) vigorous; bold: 笔力～ write or paint in bold, vigorous strokes / 他的书法～有力。His calligraphy is bold and vigorous.

苍老 cānglǎo　① old (in appearance); hoary: (of an old man's voice) hoarse: 他显得～多了。He looks much older than before. / "谁呀?"一个～的声音从室内传出来。"Who is it?" An old man's voice was heard from the room. ② (of calligraphy or painting) vigorous; forceful: 这幅画笔势～遒劲, 显出画家功力深厚。This

painting exhibits a force and vigour characteristic of a master's hand.

苍凉 cāngliáng　desolate; bleak: 过去满目～的乡村, 现在已经完全变了样。The once desolate countryside has changed entirely.

苍龙 cānglóng　the Green Dragon— ① a collective name for the eastern group (Nos.1—7) of the twenty-eight constellations (二十八宿) ② an evil spirit: 今日长缨在手, 何时缚住～? (毛泽东) Today we hold the long cord in our hands, When shall we bind fast the Green Dragon?

苍鹭 cānglù　heron

苍茫 cāngmáng　① vast; boundless: ～大地 boundless land / ～的大海 vast seas / 一片～的海天景色 a vast expanse of sea and sky ② indistinct: 夜色～。The shades of dusk are deepening.

苍莽 cāngmǎng　same as 苍茫 cāngmáng

苍穹 cāngqióng　*liter.* the vault of heaven; the firmament

苍生 cāngshēng　*formal* the common people

苍天 cāngtiān　Heaven

苍头 cāngtóu　*old* ① servant ② soldier

苍哑 cāngyǎ　(of voice) hoarse

苍鹰 cāngyīng　goshawk

苍蝇 cāngying　fly; housefly

苍蝇拍 cāngyingpāi　(also 苍蝇拍子 cāngying pāizi) flyswatter

苍郁 cāngyù　*formal* (of grass, trees, etc.) verdant and luxuriant

苍术 cāngzhú　① *bot.* Chinese atractylodes (*Atractylodes chinensis*) ② *Chin. med.* the rhizome of Chinese atractylodes

鸧（鶬）
cāng　see below

鸧鹒 cānggēng　oriole

舱（艙）
cāng　① cabin (of an airplane or ship): 客舱 kècāng / 货舱 huòcāng ② module (of a spacecraft): 指挥舱 zhǐhuīcāng

舱壁 cāngbì　bulkhead

舱单 cāngdān　*transportation* manifest

舱口 cāngkǒu　hatchway; hatch

舱口盖 cāngkǒugài　hatch door; hatch cover

舱面 cāngmiàn　deck

舱面货 cāngmiànhuò　deck cargo

舱内货 cāngnèihuò　underdeck cargo

舱室 cāngshì　cabin

舱位 cāngwèi　① cabin seat or berth ② shipping space

cáng

藏
cáng　① hide; conceal: 钱～在箱子里。The money was hidden in a trunk. / 老大娘把八路军伤员～在自己家里。Grandma hid the wounded Eighth Route Army man in her house. / 这人肚子里～不住话。This chap can't keep anything to himself. ② store; lay by: 阁楼上可以～好多东西。We can store a lot of things in the attic. / ～粮于民 store grain among the people ——see also zàng

藏躲 cángduǒ　same as 躲藏 duǒcáng

藏垢纳污 cánggòu-nàwū　(also 藏污纳垢 cángwū-nàgòu) shelter evil people and countenance evil practices: ～之所 a sink of iniquity

藏奸 cángjiān　① harbour evil intentions: 笑里～ hide one's evil intentions behind one's smiles ② *dial.* be unwilling to help others

藏龙卧虎 cánglóng-wòhǔ　(used esp. in) ～之地 a place

where dragons and tigers are hiding—a place where people of unusual ability are to be found

藏猫儿 cángmāor *inf.* play hide-and-seek

藏闷儿 cángmēnr *dial.* play hide-and-seek

藏匿 cángnì conceal; hide; go into hiding: 那个罪犯在一个远房亲戚家里～了三个星期。The criminal remained in hiding at a distant relative's place for three weeks.

藏身 cángshēn hide oneself; go into hiding: 无处～ have no place to hide /～之处 hiding-place; hideout

藏书 cángshū ① collect books: 他有～的爱好。His hobby is book-collecting. ② a collection of books; library: 他有很多珍贵的～。He has a large collection of valuable books.

藏头露尾 cángtóu-lùwěi hide the head but show the tail—hide one part of sth. only to reveal another

藏头诗 cángtóushī a verse with a hidden head—a verse in which the initial characters of the lines form a word or phrase which conveys the intended meaning; acrostic (e. g., Wu Yong's verse in the *Shui Hu Zhuan*, which conceals the name of 卢俊义反 "Lu Junyi the rebel": 芦花丛里一扁舟, 俊杰皆从此地游。义士手提三尺剑, 反身定斩逆臣头。)

藏掖 cángyē ① try to cover up: 他做错了事, 从不～躲闪。He never tries to cover up or explain away his mistakes. ② cover-up: 我全说了, 没有一点儿～。I've told you everything. I haven't held anything back.

藏拙 cángzhuō hide one's inadequacy by keeping quiet

藏踪 cángzōng conceal one's tracks

cāo

糙 cāo rough; coarse: ～纸不好写字。Rough paper is no good for writing. / 这活儿做得太～。This is very slipshod work.

糙粮 cāoliáng *dial.* coarse food grain (e.g. maize, sorghum, millet, etc. as distinct from wheat flour and polished rice)

糙米 cāomǐ brown rice; unpolished rice

糙皮病 cāopíbìng pellagra

操 cāo ① grasp; hold: 他～刀就砍了过去。He grabbed a knife and struck with it. ② do; operate: 操劳 cāoláo / 操作 cāozuò ③ speak (a language or dialect): ～本地口音 speak with a local accent / 他～一口流利的英语。He speaks fluent English. ④ drill; exercise: 体操 tǐcāo / 早操 zǎocāo ⑤ conduct; behaviour: 操行 cāoxíng / 贞操 zhēncāo

操办 cāobàn manage affairs; make preparations or arrangements for: ～婚事 make preparations for a wedding / 这次宴会, 经理已交给秘书去～了。The manager has left the arrangement for the banquet in his secretary's hands.

操必胜之券 cāo bì shèng zhī quàn be certain of success; be sure to win

操场 cāochǎng playground; sports ground; drill ground

操持 cāo·chí manage; handle: ～家务 manage household affairs / 这件事由你～。I'll leave the matter in your hands.

操典 cāodiǎn *mil.* drill regulations; drill manual; drill book

操舵室 cāoduòshì wheelhouse; pilothouse; steering room

操法 cāofǎ methods and rules for military drill or physical exercise

操课 cāokè *mil.* military drill; lecture as part of military training: ～时间 time for military drill or lecture

操劳 cāoláo ① work hard: 她～过度, 病倒了。She overworked herself and fell ill. / 终年为集体～ work hard for the collective all the year round / 父亲～了多半辈子, 勉强顾上一家人的温饱。For the greater part of his life, Father worked extremely hard to keep the wolf from the door. ② take care; look after: 这事请您多～。Would you mind looking after this?

操练 cāoliàn drill; train

操切 cāoqiè rash; hasty: 不要～从事。Don't act with undue haste.

操琴 cāoqín play the *huqin* as an accompanist (esp. in Beijng opera)

操神 cāoshén take trouble: 让您～受累了。Sorry to have put you to so much trouble.

操守 cāoshǒu personal integrity

操心 cāoxīn worry; take trouble; take pains: 这件事, 你不必～了。You needn't worry about it. / 为了抗旱, 支书可没少～。The Party secretary has put his heart and soul into the task of combatting the drought. / 多少父母为子女操碎了心。Many parents go to a lot of trouble for their children.

操行 cāoxíng behaviour or conduct (usu. of a student at school)

操演 cāoyǎn drill: 学生在为运动会开幕式加紧～。The students are drilling hard for the opening ceremony of the coming sports meet.

操之过急 cāo zhī guò jí act with undue haste: 这事可～。This shouldn't be done in haste. / 不宜～。It's no good being overhasty (*or* overzealous). / 要慢慢儿说服她, ～会引起反感。When we try to talk her around, we must be patient. Rushing things will put her back up.

操舟 cāozhōu *formal* steer a boat

操纵 cāozòng ① operate; control: 培养～新机器的工人 train workers to operate the new machines / 无线电～ radio control / 这套设备将用电子计算机～。These installations will be operated by computer. ② manipulate; rig: ～市场 rig the market / ～表决机器 tamper with the voting machine; manipulate the voting / 幕后～ manipulate from behind the scenes; pull strings

操纵杆 cāozònggǎn operating lever; control rod; control stick

操纵台 cāozòngtái control panel

操作 cāozuò operate; manipulate: 避免～上的疏忽。Avoid carelessness in manipulation. / 他能独立～了。He can operate the machines by himself. / 这台新机器须按新规程～。This new machine should be operated in accordance with the new rules.

操作程序 cāozuò chéngxù operation sequence

操作程序图 cāozuò chéngxùtú flow diagram; flow chart

操作规程 cāozuò guīchéng operating rules and regulations

操作性能 cāozuò xìngnéng *mech.* serviceability

cáo

曹[1] cáo *formal* people of the same kind: 尔～ all of you; you

曹[2] Cáo a surname

曹白鱼 cáobáiyú Chinese herring

漕 cáo water transport (esp. of grain)

漕船 cáochuán a boat for carrying grain to the capital in former times

漕河 cáohé a river (i.e. the Grand Canal) for transporting grain to the capital in former times

漕粮 cáoliáng grain transported to the capital by water

in former times

漕运 cáoyùn the transport of grain by water to the capital in former times

嘈 cáo noisy

嘈杂 cáozá noisy: 人声～ a hubbub of voices / 机器声～刺耳。The machine makes a deafening noise.

槽 cáo ① trough: 水～ water trough ② groove; notch: 开个～ cut a notch / 这个～挖得太深了。The groove is made too deep.

槽床 cáochuáng troughstand

槽坊 cáofang old brewery; distillery

槽钢 cáogāng (also 槽铁 cáotiě) metall. channel iron

槽糕 cáogāo dial. cakes with moulded designs

槽谷 cáogǔ geol. trough valley

槽距 cáojù mech. slot pitch

槽口 cáokǒu mech. notch

槽探 cáotàn min. trenching

槽头 cáotóu trough (in a livestock shed): ～兴旺 a manger full of sturdy livestock

槽牙 cáoyá molar

槽子 cáozi same as 槽 cáo

槽子糕 cáozigāo same as 槽糕 cáogāo

螬 cáo see 蛴螬 qícáo

艚 cáo see below

艚子 cáozi a wooden cargo boat with a cabin before the helm

cǎo

草[1] (艸) cǎo ① grass: 羊在山上吃～。The sheep are grazing on the hillside. ② straw: ～可以做饲料，也可以造纸。Straw can be used both for fodder and for papermaking.

草[2] (艸) cǎo ① careless; rough: 这几个字写得太～。These characters are written in a sloppy hand. ② same as 草书 cǎoshū ③ the running or cursive hand of a phonetic alphabet ④ draft: 起草 qǐcǎo / 草拟 cǎonǐ

草[3] (艸、騲) cǎo inf. female livestock or poultry: 草鸡 cǎojī / 草驴 cǎolú

草案 cǎo'àn draft (of a plan, law, etc.): 拟订一个计划～ make out a draft plan

草包 cǎobāo ① straw bag; straw sack ② a bungling oaf

草本 cǎoběn herbaceous

草本植物 cǎoběn zhíwù herbs

草编 cǎobiān straw-woven ware: ～提篮 a straw-woven basket

草标儿 cǎobiāor a wisp of straw stuck on a second-hand article offered for sale (usu. at a country fair)

草草 cǎocǎo carelessly; hastily: 今天的报纸我只～地看过一遍。I've only skimmed through today's newspapers.

草草了事 cǎocǎo liǎoshì get a job done any old way

草草收场 cǎocǎo shōuchǎng hastily wind up a matter

草测 cǎocè make a preliminary survey

草叉 cǎochā pitch-fork

草场 cǎochǎng meadow; pasture; grassland

草虫 cǎochóng grass-and-insect painting

草创 cǎochuàng start (an enterprise, etc.): ～时期 initial (or pioneering) stage

草刺儿 cǎocìr a very tiny thing

草苁蓉 cǎocōngróng another name for 列当 lièdāng

草丛 cǎocóng a thick growth of grass

草底儿 cǎodǐr inf. rough draft; preliminary draft

草地 cǎodì ① grassland; meadow; pasture ② lawn

草甸子 cǎodiànzi dial. grassy marshland

草垫子 cǎodiànzi straw mattress; pallet

草豆蔻 cǎodòukòu same as 豆蔻 dòukòu

草垛 cǎoduò haystack; hayrick

草房 cǎofáng thatched cottage

草稿 cǎogǎo rough draft; preliminary draft: 打个～ make a rough draft

草菇 cǎogū straw mushroom

草果 cǎoguǒ ① caoguo (Amomum tsao-ko) (the plant or its seed) ② dial. strawberry ③ same as 豆蔻 dòukòu

草狐 cǎohú a fox with greyish-yellow fur

草花 cǎohuā ① showy flowers of herbaceous plants ② club (a playing card)

草荒 cǎohuāng neglected farmland with more weeds than crops

草灰 cǎohuī ① plant ash ② ash grey

草鸡 cǎojī dial. ① hen ② a chicken-hearted person

草菅人命 cǎojiān rénmìng treat human life as if it were not worth a straw; act with utter disregard for human life

草荐 cǎojiàn pallet; straw mattress

草浆 cǎojiāng straw pulp (for making paper)

草芥 cǎojiè trifle; mere nothing; trash: 视如～ regard as worthless; treat like dirt

草棵 cǎokē (also 草棵子 cǎokēzi) same as 草丛 cǎocóng

草寇 cǎokòu old robbers in the greenwood; brigands

草兰 cǎolán cymbidium; orchid

草帘 cǎolián (also 草帘子 cǎoliánzi) straw screen or mat

草料 cǎoliào forage; fodder: 我去给马喂点～。I'll go and feed the horse.

草蛉 cǎolíng (also 草蜻蛉 cǎoqīnglíng) Chrysopa perla (an insect which is a natural enemy of the plant louse 蚜虫)

草驴 cǎolú jenny ass; jenny

草履虫 cǎolǚchóng paramecium

草绿 cǎolǜ grass green

草莽 cǎomǎng ① a rank growth of grass ② uncultivated land; wilderness

草莽英雄 cǎomǎng yīngxióng a hero of the greenwood

草帽 cǎomào straw hat

草帽缏 cǎomàobiàn (also 草帽辫 cǎomàobiàn) plaited straw (for making hats, baskets, etc.)

草莓 cǎoméi strawberry (the plant or the fruit)

草煤 cǎoméi same as 草炭 cǎotàn

草昧 cǎomèi formal uncivilized; primitive

草棉 cǎomián the cotton plant

草茉莉 cǎomòli same as 紫茉莉 zǐmòli

草木 cǎomù grass and trees; plants and trees

草木灰 cǎomùhuī plant ash

草木皆兵 cǎo mù jiē bīng every bush and tree looking like an enemy soldier—a state of extreme suspicion and fear: 你们不要神经过敏，弄得～了。Don't be over-sensitive and suspect everybody. ——see also 风声鹤唳，草木皆兵 fēngshēng-hèlì, cǎo mù jiē bīng

草木犀 cǎomùxī bot. sweet clover

草拟 cǎonǐ draw up; draft: 请你～一个开会通知。Please draft a notice for the meeting.

草棚 cǎopéng a thatched shack; a thatched shed

草皮 cǎopí sod; turf (used for making lawns or protecting dams, banks, etc., or as fertilizer)

草坪 cǎopíng lawn

草器 cǎoqì *arts & crafts* articles woven of straw; straw articles

草签 cǎoqiān initial: 〜协定 initial an agreement / 协议书已由双方代表 〜。Representatives from both sides have initialled the agreement.

草裙舞 cǎoqúnwǔ hula; hula-hula

草苫子 cǎoshānzi straw mat

草石蚕 cǎoshícán *bot.* ① Chinese artichoke (*Stachys sieboldii*) ② the plant's pagoda-shaped stem tuber (popularly known as 宝塔菜 bǎotǎcài)

草食 cǎoshí herbivorous: 〜动物 herbivorous animal; herbivore

草书 cǎoshū (in Chinese calligraphy) cursive script

草率 cǎoshuài sloppy; careless; slapdash; perfunctory: 这件事你做得太 〜 了。You did a sloppy job.

草率从事 cǎoshuài cóngshì act rashly; take hasty action

草酸 cǎosuān *chem.* oxalic acid

草台班子 cǎotáibānzi a small, scantily-equipped travelling theatrical troupe giving shows in villages and small towns

草炭 cǎotàn peat composed of rotten mosses

草堂 cǎotáng *liter.* grass hut; thatched hut; cottage (esp. as a poet's or recluse's retreat): 杜甫 〜 Du Fu Cottage (at Chengdu, a shrine built in the poet's memory on the site where his modest house used to stand)

草体 cǎotǐ ① same as 草书 cǎoshū ② cursive hand of a phonetic alphabet

草头王 cǎotóuwáng king of the bushes—a bandit chief

草图 cǎotú sketch

草屋 cǎowū thatched hut

草席 cǎoxí straw mat

草鞋 cǎoxié straw sandals: 打一双 〜 weave a pair of straw sandals

草鞋没样, 边打边像 cǎoxié méi yàng, biān dǎ biān xiàng straw sandals need no last, the shape comes with the weaving—work things out as you go along

草写 cǎoxiě cursive hand

草药 cǎoyào herbal medicine

草野 cǎoyě the common people

草鱼 cǎoyú grass carp

草原 cǎoyuán grasslands; prairie

草约 cǎoyuē draft treaty; draft agreement; protocol

草泽 cǎozé ① grassy marsh; swamp ② *formal* the common people

草纸 cǎozhǐ ① rough straw paper ② toilet paper

草子 cǎozǐ grass seed

草字 cǎozì a Chinese character written in the cursive hand

cè

册[1] **(冊)** cè ① volume; book: 装订成 〜 be bound into book form ② *m.* copy; volume: 这本书已销售十万 〜。100,000 copies of the book have been sold. / 这部书一共六 〜。This book is in six volumes.

册[2] **(冊)** cè ① an imperial order to confer a title ② confer a title

册封 cèfēng (of a king, emperor, etc.) confer a title upon sb.: 皇帝 〜 她为贵妃。The emperor bestowed on her the title of imperial concubine of the highest rank.

册页 cèyè an album of paintings or calligraphy

册子 cèzi book; volume

厕[1] **(廁)** cè lavatory; toilet; washroom; W.C.: 男 〜 men's (room *or* toilet) / 女 〜 women's (room *or* toilet)

厕[2] **(廁)** cè *formal* mingle with; participate in

厕身 cèshēn *formal pol.* occupy an unimportant place in; be an unqualified member of: 〜教育界 happen to move in educational circles

厕所 cèsuǒ lavatory; toilet; W.C.

厕足 cèzú *formal* set foot in; participate in: 〜 其间 set foot there; get involved

侧 cè ① side: 左 (右) 〜 the left (right) side / 公路两 〜 种着杨树。Poplars are planted on both sides of the highway. ② incline to one side: 〜着身子睡 sleep on one's side ——see also zhāi

侧柏 cèbǎi *bot.* oriental arborvitae

侧吹转炉 cèchuīzhuànlú *metall.* side-blown converter

侧耳 cè'ěr incline the ear; strain one's ears: 〜 而听 listen attentively; be all ears

侧根 cègēn *bot.* lateral root

侧光 cèguāng *photog.* sidelight

侧航 cèháng *aeron.* crabbing

侧击 cèjī make a flank attack

侧记 cèjì (usu. used in news report headings) sidelights: 《出口商品展览会〜》 *Sidelights on the Export Commodities Exhibition*

侧力 cèlì side force; lateral force

侧门 cèmén side door; side entrance: 入场请走正门, 退场请走〜。Please enter through the main entrance and exit through the side doors.

侧面 cèmiàn side; flank; aspect: 他们从 〜 向敌人进攻。They made a flank attack on the enemy. / 我们要从 〜 了解一下情况。We should find out about the situation from indirect sources. / 这篇短篇小说反映了当前农村改革的一个 〜。This short story presents one aspect of the present agricultural reform.

侧面图 cèmiàntú same as 侧视图 cèshìtú

侧面像 cèmiànxiàng profile

侧目 cèmù cast sidelong glances (with fear or indignation): 权尊势重, 朝野〜。Exalted and powerful, he was feared by officials and common citizens alike.

侧目而视 cèmù ér shì look askance at sb. (with fear or indignation) ——see also 重足而立, 侧目而视 chóng zú ér lì, cèmù ér shì

侧身 cèshēn ① turn or move sideways: 你侧着身就能挤过去。You can squeeze through sideways. / 战士们 〜 匍匐前进。The soldiers advanced crawling on their sides. ② same as 厕身 cèshēn

侧石 cèshí kerbstone; kerb

侧视 cèshì look sideways

侧视图 cèshìtú side view; profile

侧室 cèshì side room—a concubine

侧手翻 cèshǒufān *sports* cartwheel; turn a cartwheel

侧卫 cèwèi *mil.* flank guard

侧卧 cèwò lie on one's side

侧线 cèxiàn lateral line (of fishes, amphibians, round worms, etc.)

侧旋 cèxuán *sports* sidespin; cut a sidespin

侧压力 cèyālì *phys.* lateral pressure

侧芽 cèyá *bot.* axillary bud

侧翼 cèyì *mil.* flank

侧影 cèyǐng profile; silhouette

侧泳 cèyǒng *sports* sidestroke; do the sidestroke

侧重 cèzhòng lay special emphasis on: 这篇文章 〜讨论交通运输问题。In this article, special emphasis is laid on problems of communications and transportation.

测 cè ① survey; fathom; measure: 〜 雨量 gauge rainfall / 〜 温度 gauge temperature / 〜 风向 determine the wind direction / 〜 深浅 measure the depth

of; fathom／我国测绘工作者 ～ 得珠穆朗玛峰海拔高程为八千八百四十八点一三米。Chinese cartographers determined the height of Mount Qolmolangma (Mount Everest) to be 8,848.13 metres above sea level. ② infer; conjecture: 变幻莫测 biànhuàn mò cè

测程仪 cèchéngyí mileage meter; (navigation) log

测电笔 cèdiànbǐ test pencil (for detecting and measuring electricity)

测定 cèdìng ascertain by measuring or surveying; determine: ～ 船只方位 take a ship's bearings／航线已经 ～。The route (of a ship or plane) has been surveyed and determined.

测度 cèdù *math.* measure

测度 cèduó estimate; infer: 根据风向 ～, 今天不会下雨。Judging by the direction of the wind, it won't rain today.

测风经纬仪 cèfēng jīngwěiyí pilot balloon theodolite

测风气球 cèfēng qìqiú pilot balloon

测杆 cègān surveying rod; measuring staff

测候 cèhòu *meteorol.* astronomical and meteorological observation

测候网 cèhòuwǎng *meteorol.* reseau

测谎器 cèhuǎngqì polygraph; lie detector

测绘 cèhuì survey and drawing; mapping; cartography: 地形 ～ topographical survey

测绘飞机 cèhuì fēijī air-mapping plane

测绘员 cèhuìyuán surveyor-draftsman; surveyor-cartographer

测井 cèjǐng *petroleum* well logging

测距仪 cèjùyí range finder

测力计 cèlìjì *phys.* dynamometer

测量 cèliáng survey; measure; gauge: ～ 地形 survey the topography／～ 河道 survey the river course／大地 ～ geodetic survey／航空 ～ air survey／～ 仪器 surveying instrument

测量学 cèliángxué surveying

测量员 cèliángyuán surveyor

测漏 cèlòu track down a leak

测深仪 cèshēnyí fathometer; depth-sounder

测试 cèshì ① test (a machine, meter or apparatus): 产品须经 ～ 方能出厂。All products must be tested before leaving the factory.／把新机器 ～ 一下。Put the new machine to the test.／要 ～ 新仪表的精确度。We must test the precision of the newly-acquired meters. ② test (a student's proficiency): ～ 英语水平 give (students) an English proficiency test

测算 cèsuàn measure and calculate

测图摄影机 cètú shèyǐngjī mapping camera

测向仪 cèxiàngyí goniometer

测斜仪 cèxiéyí inclinometer

测验 cèyàn ① put to the test; test: ～ 机器的性能 test the performance of a machine／老师 ～ 学生的拼写。The teacher tested the students in spelling. ② test; quiz: 算术～ an arithmetic test (*or* quiz)

测云气球 cèyún qìqiú *meteorol.* ceiling balloon

测云器 cèyúnqì *meteorol.* nephoscope

测震学 cèzhènxué seismometry

测字 cèzì fortune-telling by analysing the component parts of a Chinese character; glyphomancy

测字先生 cèzì xiānsheng glyphomancer

恻 cè sorrowful; sad: 凄恻 qīcè

恻恻 cècè *formal* ① grieved; sorrowful ② earnest; sincere

恻隐 cèyǐn *formal* feel compassion for sb.

恻隐之心 cèyǐn zhī xīn compassion: ～, 人皆有之。Compassion is common to all men.／他对那个孤儿起了 ～。His heart went out to the orphan.

策[1]（筞） cè ① bamboo or wooden slips used for writing on in ancient China ② questions on current affairs set for the imperial examinations ③ plan; scheme: 献计献 ～ suggest ways and means

策[2]（筞） cè ① a riding crop ② whip (a horse) with a riding crop: ～ 马前进 whip a horse on

策动 cèdòng instigate; engineer; stir up: ～ 政变 plot to stage a *coup d'état*／～ 农民造反 engineer a peasant rebellion

策反 cèfǎn instigate rebellion within the enemy camp; incite defection

策划 cèhuà plan; plot; scheme: ～ 作战方案 make a battle plan／～ 阴谋 hatch a plot／幕后 ～ plot behind the scenes

策励 cèlì encourage; spur on: 时刻 ～ 自己 constantly spur oneself ahead／～ 青年们努力工作 encourage the young people to work hard

策略 cèlüè ① tactics: 制订对敌斗争的 ～ work out the tactics of our struggle against the enemy ② tactful: 这样做很不 ～。That's not a very tactful way to do it.

策论 cèlùn an essay on current affairs presented to the emperor as advice on government policy

策士 cèshì counsellor

策应 cèyìng *mil.* support by coordinated action

策源地 cèyuándì place of origin; source (of a war or a social movement): 战争 ～ a source of war; a hotbed of war／北京是五四运动的 ～。Beijing was where the May 4th Movement started.

cèi

瓻 cèi *inf.* (of glass, china, etc.) break: 小心别把玻璃 ～ 了! Be careful! Don't break the glass. *or* Take care not to break the glass.

cēn

参（參） cēn see below ——see also cān; shēn

参差 cēncī uneven; not uniform

参差不齐 cēncī bù qí uneven; not uniform: 同学们的汉语水平 ～。The students have different levels of proficiency in Chinese.

cén

岑 cén ① *formal* a high hill ② (Cén) a surname

岑寂 cénjì *liter.* quiet and still; lonely: 四周都 ～ 了, 只有几处蝉声, 断断续续地送来。The deep silence reigning all around was broken now and then by the trills of the cicadas.

涔 cén *formal* rainwater in puddles

涔涔 céncén *formal* dripping; streaming: 汗 ～ 下 sweat streaming down; dripping with sweat

cēng

噌 cēng *dial.* scold; give a talking-to: 他挨了 ～

了。He got a scolding.

céng

层(層) céng ① *m.* ⓐ storey; floor: 十五 ～ 大楼 a fifteen-storey building / 我住一 ～。I live on the ground floor. / 她住二 ～。She lives on the first floor. ⓑ a component part in a sequence: 这段文章有两 ～ 意思。This article has two levels of discourse. / 我听了那话，又多了一 ～ 顾虑。When I heard this, my misgivings increased. / 他这话还有一 ～ 意思。What he said has further implications. ⓒ layer; stratum: 一 ～ 薄膜 a thin layer of plastic film / 涂上一 ～油漆 give sth. a coat of paint / 桌上积了厚厚的一 ～ 灰尘。The desk is covered with a thick layer of dust. / 湖上结了一 ～ 薄冰。A thin layer of ice formed on the lake. ② level: 层次 céngcì ③ one on top of another; overlapping: 层峦叠嶂 céngluán-diézhàng

层报 céngbào report a matter to the higher authorities level by level: 此事已经 ～ 备案。The matter has been reported to our superiors at each level for the record.

层层 céngcéng layer upon layer; ring upon ring: ～ 包围 surround ring upon ring / ～ 设防 set up successive lines of defence; erect defensive works in depth / ～ 把关 check at each level / ～ 下达 make known to each of the levels below / ～ 建立责任制 devise a responsibility system at each level

层出不穷 céng chū bù qióng emerge in an endless stream: 新生事物 ～。New things are emerging one after another.

层次 céngcì ① arrangement of ideas (in writing or speech): 这篇文章 ～ 不清。This article lacks unity and coherence. ② administrative levels: 为了提高工作效率，必须减少办事机构的 ～，精简人员。To raise efficiency, we should simplify the administrative structure and reduce the staff. ③ *photog.* gradation

层叠 céngdié one on top of another: 层层叠叠的雪峰 range upon range of snow-capped mountains

层积云 céngjīyún *meteorol.* stratocumulus

层见叠出 céngjiàn-diéchū occur frequently; appear repeatedly

层理 cénglǐ *geol.* bedding; stratification

层林 cénglín row upon row of trees: 看万山红遍，～ 尽染。(毛泽东) I see a thousand hills crimsoned through By their serried woods deep-dyed.

层流 céngliú *phys.* laminar flow

层峦 céngluán range upon range of hills: ～ 叠翠 range upon range of green hills / ～ 起伏 range upon range of undulating hills

层峦叠嶂 céngluán-diézhàng peaks rising one upon another; range upon range of hills

层压 céngyā *chem.* lamination

层压玻璃 céngyā bōli laminated glass

层云 céngyún *meteorol.* stratus

层子 céngzǐ *phys.* straton

层子模型 céngzǐ móxíng *phys.* straton model

曾 céng *adv.* (indicating that an action once happened or a state once existed): 几年前我 ～ 见过她一面。I met her once several years ago. / 我未 ～ 听说过这样的事。I've never heard of such a thing. ——see also zēng

曾几何时 céng jǐ hé shí before long; not long after: 猖獗一时的侵略者，～，遭到了彻底失败。The invaders were on the rampage for a time, but before long they were completely defeated.

曾经 céngjīng *adv.* (indicating that an action once happened or a state once existed): 她 ～ 参加过校队。She once played for the school team. / 这顶军帽是他参加长征时 ～ 戴过的。This army cap was worn by him on the Long March. / 我 ～ 在美国住过两年。I lived in the United States for two years.

曾经沧海 céng jīng cānghǎi have sailed the seven seas—have much experience of life; have seen much of the world

曾经沧海难为水 céng jīng cānghǎi nán wéi shuǐ one who has seen the ocean thinks nothing of mere rivers—to a sophisticated person there is nothing new under the sun (from Yuan Zhen's 元稹 lines: ～，除却巫山不是云。Speak not of lakes and streams to him who has once seen the sea; The clouds that circle Wushan are the only clouds for me.)

cèng

蹭 cèng ① rub; scrape; scratch: 小猫在桌子腿上 ～ 痒痒。The kitten is scratching its back against the table leg. / 我的手 ～ 破了皮。I grazed my hand. ② rub against sth. and get stained: 油漆没干，留神别～了。The paint is not dry. Be careful that you don't stain your clothes. / 你上哪儿去了? ～ 了一身泥。Where have you been? Your clothes are all muddy. ③ move slowly: 他的腿疼得厉害，只能一步一步地往前 ～。His legs hurt terribly. He could only drag himself along inch by inch. / 快干吧! 别～时间了。Get on with your work. Don't dawdle. ④ *dial.* cadge; scrounge: 他常吃～喝。He's always cadging meals and drinks. / 坐～车 go on a bus or train without buying a ticket

蹭蹬 cèngdèng *formal* meet with setbacks; be down on one's luck

chā

叉¹ chā ① fork: 钢 ～ steel fork / 干草 ～ hayfork; pitchfork / 餐 ～ (table) fork ② X-sign; cross: 在每个错别字上打个 ～ put a cross above each wrongly written word

叉²(扠) chā work with a fork; fork: ～ 草上垛 pitch hay onto a stack / ～ 鱼 spear fish ——see also chá; chǎ

叉车 chāchē forklift

叉烧 chāshāo grill (marinated pork): ～肉 grilled pork / ～包 steamed buns stuffed with diced grilled pork

叉手 chāshǒu raise one's folded hands to one's chin to salute sb.

叉丝 chāsī *phys.* cross hair; spider line

叉腰 chāyāo akimbo: 她双手 ～ 站着。She stood with arms akimbo.

叉子 chāzi fork

杈 chā wooden fork; hayfork; pitchfork ——see also chà

差 chā ① difference; dissimilarity: 差别 chābié / 时差 shíchā ② *math.* difference ③ *formal* only just; barely: ～可 barely passable ——see also chà; chāi; cī

差别 chābié difference; disparity: 年龄 ～ disparity in age / 数量与质量上的 ～ quantitative and qualitative differences / 二者之间 ～ 很大。There is a world of difference between the two. / 两者之间没有什么～。There

isn't much to choose between the two.

差别关税 chābié guānshuì differential rates of duty; differential duties

差别阈限 chābié yùxiàn *psychol.* difference limen (*or* threshold)

差池 chāchí *dial.* ① error; mistake: 如有半点 ～, 我决不轻饶你。I'll never forgive you if you make the slightest error. ② accident; mishap; untoward event: 你好好看住他, 万一有个 ～, 你我都不好办。Keep an eye on him, or we'll get into trouble if anything happens to him.

差错 chācuò ① mistake; error; slip: 她抄的这个文件没有一点儿 ～。There is not a single mistake in the paper she copied. / 工作认真负责, 就会少出 ～。If we work conscientiously, we won't make many mistakes. / 这笔账目里有 ～。There's an accounting error in this entry. / 几个月来这部机器一直运转正常, 没有出过 ～。This machine has been running without a hitch for months. ② mishap; accident: 万一这孩子出了 ～ 怎么办? What if anything should happen to the child?

差动 chādòng *mech.* differential: ～ 齿轮 differential gear / ～ 滑轮 differential pulley

差额 chā'é difference; differential; balance; margin: 补足 ～ make up the balance (*or* difference)

差额选举 chā'é xuǎnjǔ multi-candidate election

差价 chājià price difference: 地区 ～ regional price differences / 季节 ～ seasonal price differences; seasonal variations in price

差价关税 chājià guānshuì variable import levy

差距 chājù ① gap; disparity: 在成绩面前找 ～。Try to find out where you fall short when you have achieved success. / 我们和先进单位比还有很大的 ～。Compared with advanced units, we still have a long way to go. ② *mech.* difference: 检测工件与设计标准之间的 ～ see if there's any difference between the part and the set standard

差强人意 chā qiáng rényì just passable

差数 chāshù *math.* difference

差忒 chātè *formal* error; mistake

差误 chāwù mistake; error; slip

差异 chāyì difference; divergence; discrepancy; diversity: 这两个地区气候 ～ 很大。These two regions differ greatly in climate. / 操作方法不同, 生产效率就会有相当大的 ～。Different methods of operation will bring about considerable discrepancy in work efficiency.

差之毫厘, 谬以千里 chā zhī háolí, miù yǐ qiānlǐ (also 差之毫厘, 失之千里 chā zhī háolí, shī zhī qiānlǐ) an error the breadth of a single hair can lead you a thousand *li* astray

插 chā ① stick in; insert: 把插头 ～ 上 insert the plug in a socket; plug in / 把双手 ～ 在口袋里 put one's hands in one's pockets / 把门 ～ 上 bolt the door / 山峰高 ～ 人云。The peaks penetrate into the clouds. / 一定要把红旗 ～ 上顶峰。We are determined to plant the red flag on the peak. ② interpose; insert: 他说个没完, 别人半句话也 ～ 不进。He talked on and on and nobody else could get a word in.

插班 chābān (of a new or transferred student) join a class in the middle of the course; be placed in an appropriate class

插翅难飞 chā chì nán fēi (also 插翅难逃 chā chì nán táo) unable to escape even if given wings: 密密层层的天罗地网, 我看他 ～。He's closely hemmed in on all sides. I don't think he could possibly get away even if he grew wings.

插床 chāchuáng *mech.* slotting machine; slotter: 齿轮 ～ gear slotter

插戴 chādài women's head ornaments

插刀 chādāo *mech.* slotting tool

插断 chāduàn interrupt (sb. speaking): 她讲话时, 好多次被别人 ～。While she was speaking, she was interrupted many times.

插队 chāduì (of school graduates in cities) be sent to live and work in the countryside as a member of a production team for a number of years (a practice during the 1960's and 1970's)

插队落户 chāduì-luòhù (of school graduates in cities) be sent to settle in the countryside as a regular and permanent member of a production team

插队知青 chāduì zhīqīng a school graduate sent to live and work in the countryside as a member of a production team

插管 chāguǎn *med.* intubate

插管法 chāguǎnfǎ *med.* intubation

插花 chāhuā ① arrange flowers in a vase, basket, etc. ② insert sth. amidst things of another kind; mix; mingle: 玉米地里还 ～ 着种大豆。Soya beans have been sown between the rows of maize. or Soya beans are intercropped with maize.

插话 chāhuà ① interpose a remark, etc.; chip in: 这时老张插了话, 补充了一些新例子。At this point Lao Zhang chipped in with some fresh examples. ② a remark interposed: 支书的发言和几位老同志的 ～ 都很有意思。The Party branch secretary's speech and the occasional remarks added by some of the old comrades were all very interesting. ③ digression; episode: 这一段 ～ 使她的报告生动多了。This digression added to the liveliness of her talk.

插画 chāhuà illustration (in a book); plate

插肩袖 chājiānxiù raglan sleeve

插脚 chājiǎo ① (usu. used in the negative) put one's foot in: 屋里坐得满满的, 几乎没有 ～ 的地方。The room was so crowded that there was standing room only, and even then, people could hardly find a place to put their feet. ② participate in (some activity): 今天这个聚会纯粹是我们姑娘家的事, 你们小伙子休想 ～。Today's gathering is for girls only, boys are not allowed.

插科打诨 chākē-dǎhùn (of actors) make impromptu comic gestures and remarks; make gags

插口[1] chākǒu same as 插嘴 chāzuǐ

插口[2] chākǒu *elec.* socket; jack

插屏 chāpíng *arts & crafts* table plaque

插曲 chāqǔ ① *mus.* interlude ② a song in a film or play ③ episode; interlude: 双方谈判中的一个 ～ an episode in the negotiations between the two parties

插入 chārù ① insert: 这本书再版时 ～ 了新的一章。A new chapter is included in the second edition. ② *elec.* plug in: ～ 部件 plug-in unit

插入语 chārùyǔ *gram.* parenthesis

插身 chāshēn ① squeeze in; edge in: 很难 ～ difficult to squeeze in ② take part in; get involved in: 他不想 ～ 在这场纠纷中间。He doesn't want to get involved in this dispute.

插手 chāshǒu ① take part; lend a hand: 人够多了, 您就不用 ～ 了。You don't have to join in, there are more than enough people on the job already. / 我真想帮忙, 可又插不上手。I really wanted to help but didn't know how. ② have a hand in; poke one's nose into; meddle in: 想不到她会插上一手。We never thought she would poke her nose into this.

插条 chātiáo ① transplant a cutting ② cutting

插头 chātóu *elec.* plug: 三脚 ～ a three-pin plug

插图 chātú illustration (artistic or scientific in nature); plate: 书中有几幅彩色 ～。The book has several colour plates.

插图本 chātúběn illustrated edition

插销 chāxiāo ① bolt (for a door, window, etc.) ②

elec. plug

插叙 chāxù narration interspersed with flashbacks

插言 chāyán same as 插话 chāhuà①

插秧 chāyāng transplant rice seedlings (*or* rice shoots)

插秧机 chāyāngjī rice transplanter

插页 chāyè insert; inset

插枝 chāzhī same as 插条 chātiáo

插足 chāzú same as 插脚 chājiǎo②

插嘴 chāzuǐ interrupt; chip in: 别人说话，你别 ～。You shouldn't interrupt when others are talking. / 她真爱 ～。She always loves to chip in her own two cents' worth. / 他说起话来，谁也插不上嘴。When he talks, nobody else can get a word in.

插座 chāzuò *elec.* socket; outlet: 弹簧 ～ cushion socket

喳
chā see below ——see also zhā

喳喳 chāchā a whispering sound: 喊喊喳喳 qīqi chāchā

喳喳舞 chāchāwǔ cha-cha

喳喳 chāchā whisper: 她在她妈妈耳边～了两句。She whispered a few words in her mother's ear. ——see also 打喳喳 dǎchāchā

馇
chā ① cook and stir (feed for pigs or dogs): ～ 猪食 cook and stir feed for pigs ② *dial.* stew: ～ 粥 cook gruel

锸(臿)
chā spade

嚓
chā *onom.* see 喀嚓 kāchā; 啪嚓 pāchā ——see also cā

chá

叉
chá *dial.* block up; jam: 游行队伍把路口全都 ～ 住了。Traffic was completely held up by the procession (*or* paraders). ——see also chā; chǎ

茬
chá ① stubble: 麦 ～ wheat stubble ② crop: 这块菜地一年种几 ～? How many crops can this vegetable plot produce a year? / 二 ～ 韭菜 the second crop of Chinese chives / 一 ～ 新干部成长起来了。A whole new crop of cadres has matured. ③ same as 碴儿 chár

茬口 chákǒu ① crops for rotation: 选好～, 实行合理轮作 select the right crops and rotate them rationally ② soil on which a crop has been planted and harvested: 西红柿 ～ 壮, 种白菜挺合适。A crop of tomatoes enriches the soil and makes it suitable for growing cabbage. ③ *dial.* chance; opportunity

茬子 cházi stubble: 刨 ～ dig up the stubble

茶
chá ① tea (the plant or its leaves): 种 ～ grow tea / 采 ～ pick tea (leaves) / 这儿产 ～。Tea is produced here. ② tea (the drink): 沏 ～ make tea / 浓(淡) ～ strong (weak) tea / 咱们喝点儿 ～ 吧。Let's have some tea. / 请你给我倒杯 ～。Please give me a cup of tea. ③ certain kinds of drink or liquid food: 杏仁 ～ almond paste

茶杯 chábēi teacup

茶博士 chábóshì *old* teahouse keeper

茶场 cháchǎng tea plantation

茶匙 cháchí teaspoon

茶炊 cháchuī tea-urn

茶底儿 chádǐr tea dregs: 把茶壶里的 ～ 倒掉。Pour the dregs out of the teapot.

茶点 chádiǎn tea and pastries; refreshments

茶碟儿 chádiér saucer (for holding a teacup)

茶饭 cháfàn tea and rice—food and drink; food: 不思～ have no appetite

茶房 cháfang *old* waiter (who serves tea and does odd jobs in a hotel, teahouse, or theatre, or on a ship or train)

茶缸子 chágāngzi mug

茶倌 cháguān *old* teahouse waiter

茶馆 cháguǎn teahouse: 开 ～ run a teahouse

茶褐色 cháhèsè dark brown

茶壶 cháhú teapot

茶花 cháhuā camellia

茶话会 cháhuàhuì a tea party at which the participants chat or give talks

茶会 cháhuì tea party

茶几 chájī tea table; teapoy; side table

茶鸡蛋 chájīdàn same as 茶叶蛋 cháyèdàn

茶巾 chájīn tea cloth

茶晶 chájīng citrine; yellow quartz

茶镜 chájìng glasses with citrine or brown-coloured lenses; sunglasses

茶具 chájù tea set; tea-things; tea service

茶客 chákè ① customer of a teahouse ② *old* tea dealer; tea merchant

茶楼 chálóu a teahouse with two or more storeys

茶卤儿 chálǔr strong tea (to be diluted before drinking)

茶末 chámò tea dust

茶农 chánóng tea grower

茶盘 chápán (also 茶盘子 chápánzi) tea tray; teaboard

茶钱 cháqian ① payment for tea (in a teahouse) ② *old* tip

茶青 cháqīng dark brownish green

茶色 chásè dark brown: ～ 玻璃 brown-coloured glass

茶食 cháshi cakes and sweetmeats

茶树 cháshù tea shrub; tea tree

茶水 cháshuǐ tea or plain boiled water (supplied to walkers, trippers, etc.)

茶水站 cháshuǐzhàn tea-stall set up for an occasion: 沿途群众为游行队伍设了 ～。Along the way there were tea-stalls set up for the paraders.

茶肆 chásì *formal* teahouse

茶摊 chátān roadside tea-stall: 那姑娘摆过 ～, 卖过大碗茶。That girl once set up a roadside stall and sold big bowls of tea to passersby.

茶亭 chátíng tea-booth; tea-kiosk

茶托 chátuō saucer (for holding a teacup)

茶碗 cháwǎn (handleless) teacup; tea-bowl

茶味儿 cháwèir tea flavour: 这种茶冲两次 ～ 才出来。The full flavour of this kind of tea doesn't come out until it has been steeped twice. *or* With this kind of tea the second cup is always better. / 祁门红茶 ～ 香甜。Keemun black tea has a sweet taste and smell (*or* both smells and tastes sweet).

茶锈 cháxiù tea stain

茶叶 cháyè tea leaves; tea: 买一百克 ～ buy 100 grams of tea

茶叶蛋 cháyèdàn tea eggs (i.e. eggs stewed in tea)

茶叶罐 cháyèguàn tea caddy; tea canister

茶叶花 cháyèhuā another name for 罗布麻 luóbùmá

茶役 cháyì same as 茶房 cháfang

茶油 cháyóu tea-seed oil; tea oil

茶余饭后 cháyú-fànhòu (also 茶余酒后 cháyú-jiǔhòu) over a cup of tea or after a meal: 这些轶事可作 ～ 的谈助。These anecdotes are good topics for after-dinner conversation.

茶园 cháyuán ① tea plantation ② a place where tea and soft drinks are served; tea garden

茶盅 cházhōng　handleless teacup

茶砖 cházhuān　tea brick

茶资 cházī　payment for tea

茶座 cházuò　① tea-stall with seats: 树阴下面有 〜 儿。 There's a tea-stall with seats under the shady trees. ② seats in a teahouse or tea garden: 这家茶馆有五十多个 〜 儿。 There are over fifty seats in this teahouse.

查 chá　① check; examine: 〜 卫生 make a public health and sanitation check (or inspection) / 〜 血 have a blood test ② look into; investigate: 〜 一 事故的原因 find out the cause of an accident / 〜 过他的履历吗?Have you looked into his antecedents? or Have you checked his *curriculum vitae*? ③ look up; consult: 〜 字典 look up a word in the dictionary; consult a dictionary / 〜 资料 consult reference materials (on a subject) ——see also zhā

查办 chábàn　investigate and deal with accordingly: 撤职 〜 dismiss (or discharge) sb. from his post and prosecute him

查抄 cháchāo　make an inventory of a criminal's possessions and confiscate them

查处 cháchǔ　investigate and prosecute

查档 chádàng　consult the files

查点 chádiǎn　check the number or amount of; make an inventory of: 〜 出席人数 check the number of people present; check the attendance / 〜 存货 make an inventory of the goods in stock; take stock

查对 cháduì　check and verify: 〜 材料 check the data / 〜 原文 check against the original (text, manuscript, etc.) / 〜 数字 verify the figures / 〜 无误 examined and found correct; verified

查房 cháfáng　(of doctors, nurses, etc.) make (or go) the rounds of the wards: 值班护士每夜查两次房。 Nurses on duty make two rounds of the wards during the night.

查访 cháfǎng　go around and make inquiries; investigate: 〜 案情 investigate the details of a crime / 经过公安人员到处 〜,他终于和失散多年的亲人重新团聚了。 Thanks to long investigations by security personnel, he was finally reunited with his family.

查封 cháfēng　seal up; close down: 〜 伪政府大楼 seal up the office building of the puppet government / 〜 敌产 seal up and confiscate enemy property

查岗 chágǎng　same as 查哨 cháshào

查号台 cháhàotái　(at a telephone exchange) directory inquiries; information

查核 cháhé　check (accounts, etc.)

查户口 chá hùkǒu　check residence cards; check on household occupants

查获 cháhuò　hunt down and seize; ferret out; track down: 〜 一部秘密电台 discover and seize a secret transmitter / 〜 逃犯 track down a fugitive criminal / 〜 大批走私毒品 track down and seize a large shipment of smuggled drugs

查禁 chájìn　ban; prohibit; suppress: 依法 〜 淫秽书刊 have pornographic literature banned according to law / 严格 〜 走私活动 rigorously suppress smuggling

查究 chájiū　investigate; try to ascertain (cause, responsibility, etc.); look into and find out: 〜 责任 find out who should be held responsible / 如有渎职现象, 必须依法 〜。 Malfeasance must be looked into and dealt with according to law.

查勘 chákān　survey; prospect: 〜地形 survey the terrain / 〜地界 survey the boundaries of a piece of land / 〜 矿产资源 prospect for mineral deposits

查看 chákàn　look over; examine: 〜 证件 check the certificates / 〜 帐目 examine the accounts / 〜 水情 look into the water or flood situation / 〜 机器运转的

情况 see how the machine is working

查考 chákǎo　investigate; try to ascertain; do research on: 〜 中国古时有关地震的全部文献 study all available literature about earthquakes in ancient China / 〜 一批新出土文物的年代 try to ascertain the date of a new lot of unearthed relics

查明 chámíng　prove through investigation; find out; ascertain: 〜 事实真相 find out the truth; ascertain the facts / 〜 起因 find out the cause / 现已 〜 it has been established that; investigation reveals that

查票 chápiào　examine (or check) tickets

查铺 chápù　*mil.* go the rounds of the beds (in barracks) at night; bed check: 干部坚持 〜 制度。 The officers make it a regular practice to go the rounds of the men's beds at night.

查讫 cháqì　checked

查清 cháqīng　make a thorough investigation of; check up on: 某人的来历 find out sb.'s background; check up on sb. / 一件事情的来龙去脉 find out how sth. started and developed / 事情已经彻底 〜。 A thorough investigation has been made into the matter and everything has come to light.

查哨 cháshào　*mil.* go the rounds of guard posts; inspect the sentries

查实 cháshí　check and verify: 案情已经 〜。 The case has been verified after a thorough investigation.

查收 cháshōu　(usu. used in a letter, note, etc.) check and accept (what is sent herewith): 寄上样品十种, 请 〜。 Please find ten samples enclosed herewith.

查税 cháshuì　make a tax inspection

查问 cháwèn　① inquire about ② question; interrogate: 〜 证人 interrogate a witness / 〜 口令 challenge for a password

查无实据, chá wú shíjù　investigation reveals no evidence (against the suspect): 事出有因,〜。 An investigation was called for, but no evidence was found. / 〜, 恐怕是诬告。 No evidence has been found in the case so far and therefore it is probably a libellous suit.

查询 cháxún　inquire about: 〜 地址 inquire about sb.'s address / 〜 行李下落 inquire about the whereabouts of the luggage

查验 cháyàn　check; examine: 〜 护照 examine a passport / 海关凭原入境申报单 〜 放行。 Customs clearance shall be based on inspection of the original declaration made at the time of entry. / 出入境人员应接受口岸检查机关的 〜。 All personnel who enter and leave the country shall submit to inspection by the inspection office at the port.

查夜 cháyè　① go the rounds at night ② night patrol

查阅 cháyuè　consult (books, magazines, papers, etc.); look up: 〜 技术资料 consult technical data; look up technical literature

查帐 cházhàng　check (or audit) accounts: 下星期要查你们单位的帐。 We'll start to audit your accounts next week.

查找 cházhǎo　look for: 〜 失主 try to find the owner of the lost property / 〜 资料 gather data

查照 cházhào　*formal* please note (and act accordingly): 希 〜 办理。 Please note and take appropriate action.

查证 cházhèng　investigate and verify; check: 证据必须 〜 核实。 Evidence must be examined and verified. / 〜 属实 be checked and found to be true; be verified

搽 chá　put (powder, ointment, etc.) on the skin; apply: 〜 雪花膏 put on vanishing cream / 〜 药 apply ointment, lotion, etc. / 〜 粉 powder one's face, etc.

猹 chá　badger-like wild animal

楂 chá ① short, bristly hair or beard; stubble: 胡子 ～ a stubbly beard ② same as 茬 chá ——see also zhā

槎[1] chá *formal* raft

槎[2] chá same as 茬 chá

察 chá examine; look into; scrutinize: 观察 guānchá

察察为明 cháchá wéi míng be astute in trivial matters

察访 cháfǎng make firsthand observations and inquiries; make an investigation trip: 暗中 ～ make a secret investigation trip

察觉 chájué be conscious of; become aware of; perceive: ～ 到一个盗窃国家机密的阴谋 discover a plot to steal government secrets / 开始我没有 ～ 到他有病。At first I wasn't aware that he was ill.

察勘 chákān survey

察看 chákàn watch; look carefully at; observe; inspect: ～ 风向 watch which way the wind is blowing / ～ 现场 inspect the scene / ～ 杀虫药的治虫效果 check the effectiveness of the insecticide / ～.四周的动静 peer in all directions to see if anything is afoot / 他仔细 ～ 了庄稼的生长情况。He looked carefully to see how the crops were coming along.

察其言, 观其行 chá qí yán, guān qí xíng check a person's words and watch his deeds; check what a person says against what he does

察言观色 cháyán-guānsè carefully weigh up a person's words and closely watch his expression; watch a person's every mood: 她善于 ～, 理会经理的心思。She is good at watching the manager's every mood and guessing his thoughts.

碴 chá *dial.* be cut (by broken glass, china, etc.): 小心别让碎玻璃 ～ 了手! Mind you don't cut yourself on the broken glass!

碴儿 chár ① broken pieces; fragments: 冰 ～ small pieces of ice / 玻璃 ～ fragments of glass ② sharp edge of broken glass, china, etc.: 碰到碗 ～ 上, 手指头拉了个口子。I happened to touch the sharp edge of the broken bowl and cut my finger. ③ feeling of animosity; grudge; the cause of a quarrel: 他们俩过去有 ～, 现在又和好了。They had grudges against each other in the past, but now they are on good terms again. ④ sth. said or mentioned: 接不上 ～ cannot take the cue; cannot take the hint

楂 chá see below

楂子 cházi *dial.* coarsely ground maize (*or* corn)

檫 chá sassafras (a tree)

---

chǎ

叉 chǎ part so as to form a fork; fork: ～ 着腿站着 stand with one's legs apart ——see also chā; chá

衩 chǎ see 裤衩 kùchǎ ——see also chà

踏 chǎ trudge (in mud, snow, etc.): 我的鞋都 ～ 湿了。My shoes got soaked as I trudged along.

镲 chǎ small cymbals

---

chà

汉 chà a branch of a river

汉港 chàgǎng a branching stream

汉流 chàliú same as 岔流 chàliú

汉子 chàzi same as 汉 chà

杈 chà (tree) branch: 树杈 shùchà ——see also chā

杈子 chàzi (tree) branch

岔 chà ① branching off; forked: 岔路 chàlù / 三岔路口 sānchà lùkǒu ② turn off the main road: 自行车下了公路 ～ 上了小道。The cyclist turned off the highway onto a side road. ③ same as 岔子 chàzi[2] ④ *dial.* (of voice) sound unnatural; become hoarse: 她越说越伤心, 嗓音都 ～ 了。As she talked, she became sadder and sadder until her voice broke.

岔开 chàkāi ① branch off; diverge: 线路在这儿 ～ 了。The line branches here. ② diverge to (another topic); change the subject (of conversation): 两个人正要争吵, 我给 ～ 了。A quarrel was starting between the two of them, but I headed it off. / 她伤心得要流泪了, 我赶紧把话题 ～。When she came near to tears, I quickly changed the subject. ③ stagger: 把休假日 ～ stagger the days off

岔口 chàkǒu fork (in a road): 他们一直把他送到 ～。They saw him straight to the fork in the road.

岔流 chàliú a branch of a river

岔路 chàlù (also 岔道儿 chàdàor) branch road; byroad; side road

岔气 chàqì feel a pain in the chest when breathing

岔子 chàzi ① same as 岔路 chàlù ② accident; trouble: 拖拉机出了什么～? What's wrong with the tractor? / 他开了好几年卡车, 从没有出过 ～。He has been a truck driver for years and never had an accident. / 你放心吧, 出不了 ～。Don't worry, nothing will go wrong.

诧 chà be surprised: 诧异 chàyì

诧异 chàyì be surprised; be astonished: ～ 的神色 a surprised look / 听到这个突如其来的消息, 我们都十分 ～。We were all astonished at the unexpected news.

衩 chà vent or slit in the sides of a garment ——see also chǎ

刹 chà Buddhist temple or monastery: 古 ～ an ancient Buddhist temple ——see also shā

刹地利 Chàdìlì Kshatriya

刹那 chànà (also 刹时 chàshí) instant; a split second: 一～ in an instant; in a flash; in the twinkling of an eye / ～ 间, 他倒在地上, 不省人事。Suddenly he collapsed and lost consciousness.

姹(奼) chà *liter.* beautiful

姹紫嫣红 chàzǐ-yānhóng deep purples and bright reds —beautiful flowers: 公园里百花盛开, ～, 十分绚丽。With lovely flowers everywhere, the park is a blaze of colour.

差 chà ① differ from; fall short of: 我们离父母的要求还 ～ 得远。We still fall far short of what our parents expect of us. ② wrong: 这你可说 ～ 了。You're wrong there. ③ be less than; be short of: 一个月 ～ 两天 two days less than a month / ～ 七天不到一年 seven days short of a year / ～ 十分四点 ten (minutes)

to four / ～ 两个人 two people short / 我还 ～ 你两块钱。I still owe you two *yuan*. / 还 ～ 一道工序。There's still one more step in the process. / 木料还～多少?—～ 不了多少了。How much more timber is needed? —Not much. ④ not up to standard; poor: 成绩不算太 ～。The results are by no means poor. / 这个街道工厂设备 ～, 可是产品并不 ～。The neighbourhood factory's equipment is not up to much, but its products are not at all bad. ——see also chā; chāi; cī

差不点儿 chàbudiǎnr *adv.* almost; very nearly; practically: 她委屈得 ～ 要哭出来。She felt so hurt that she could hardly keep back her tears.

差不多 chàbuduō ① about the same; similar: 姐妹俩长相 ～。The two sisters look very much alike. / 他们俩高矮 ～。The two of them are about the same height. / 这两种看法 ～。These two views are similar. ② just about right; just about enough; not far off; not bad: 麦子熟得 ～ 了, 该割了。The wheat is just about ripe enough to be cut. / 那只麻袋你扛不动, 我扛还 ～。That sack is too heavy for you, but I may be able to manage it. ③ *adv.* almost; nearly: 我 ～ 等了两个小时。I waited for nearly two hours. / 你比我 ～ 高一头。You're almost a head taller than me. / ～ 一半同学都学过英语。Nearly half the students have learned some English before. / 这座大楼 ～ 快完工了。The building is nearing completion. / 她离开学校 ～ 三十年了。It's almost thirty years since she left school.

差不多的 chàbuduōde the average person: 这包大米一百公斤重, ～ 还扛不起来。This sack of rice weighs 100 kg.; no ordinary person can carry it. / 都知道这件事了, 你还不知道? Practically everyone knows all about it, and you don't?

差不离 chàbulí same as 差不多 chàbuduō

差点儿 chàdiǎnr ① not quite up to the mark; not good enough: 她的技术还 ～。Her technique is not quite up to the mark. / 这块布料质量挺好, 就是颜色 ～。The quality of this cloth is fine, but the colour is not quite right. *or* The cloth is quite good except for the colour. / 这支笔比那支笔 ～。This pen is not as good as that one. ② *adv.* almost; nearly; on the verge of: 我 ～ 没赶上车。I almost missed the bus. / 那个问题可难了, 我～没答上来。The question was so difficult I almost failed to answer it. / 她 ～ (没)哭出来。She was on the verge of tears. / 你 ～ (没)触电。You narrowly escaped getting a shock. / 老太太 ～ (没)摔倒。The old lady stumbled and nearly fell over.

差劲 chàjìn (of quality, ability, etc.) no good; disappointing: 这条路坑坑洼洼的, 太 ～ 了。The road is no good, it's rough and full of holes. / 真 ～, 麦子刚上场就下起雨来了! Too bad! We'd just got the wheat to the threshing ground when it started to rain. / 你这人真 ～, 说话不算数。You didn't keep your word; you disappointed me.

chāi

拆 chāi ① tear open; take apart: ～ 信 open a letter / ～ 机器 disassemble a machine; take a machine apart; strip a machine / 把这个组 ～ 了。Break up the group. ② pull down; dismantle: ～ 房子 pull down a house / ～桥 dismantle a bridge / ～帐篷 strike a tent / 把旧毛衣 ～ 了重新织一下 unravel an old sweater and reknit it ——see also cā

拆白 chāibái *dial.* swindle

拆白党 chāibáidǎng *dial.* a gang of swindlers

拆除 chāichú dismantle; tear down; demolish: ～ 城墙 tear down (*or* demolish) a city wall / ～ 破房子 pull down a dilapidated old house / ～ 军事基地 dismantle a military base / ～ 障碍物 dismantle (*or* remove) obstacles

拆穿 chāichuān expose; unmask: ～ 骗局 expose a fraud

拆穿西洋镜 chāichuān xīyángjìng strip off the camouflage; expose sb.'s tricks

拆东墙, 补西墙 chāi dōngqiáng, bǔ xīqiáng tear down the east wall to repair the west wall—reinforce one place at the expense of another; rob Peter to pay Paul

拆毁 chāihuǐ demolish; pull down; tear down: 侵略军强行 ～ 民房。The invading troops tore down the people's houses.

拆伙 chāihuǒ dissolve a partnership; part company

拆借 chāijiè *dial.* a short-term loan made at a daily interest

拆开 chāikāi take apart; open; separate: 把机器 ～ disassemble a machine / 这两个字构成一个词, 不能 ～。The two characters form a single word, they cannot be separated. / 他能摸着黑儿把机枪 ～ 再装上。He can strip and reassemble a machine gun in the dark.

拆卖 chāimài sell by the piece (things usu. sold by the set): 这套家具不～。This set of furniture cannot be sold by the piece.

拆迁 chāiqiān have an old building pulled down and its occupants move elsewhere

拆墙脚 chāi qiángjiǎo undermine; pull away a prop: 投机倒把是拆社会主义的墙脚。Speculation undermines socialism.

拆散 chāisǎn break (a set): 这是整套的, 别 ～ 了。These pieces belong together. Don't break the set.

拆散 chāisàn break up (a marriage, family, group, etc.)

拆台 chāitái cut the ground from under sb.'s feet; pull away a prop: 工作要互相支持, 不要互相 ～。We should help and not hinder each other in our work. / 你一定来, 可别拆我的台。Be sure to come. Don't let me down.

拆息 chāixī a daily interest rate on private loans or deposits

拆洗 chāixǐ wash after removing the padding or lining; take apart and clean: ～ 棉被 wash a quilt after removing the padding / ～ 打字机 take apart and clean a typewriter

拆线 chāixiàn take out stitches (in surgery)

拆线刀 chāixiàndāo seam ripper

拆卸 chāixiè dismantle; disassemble; dismount

拆帐 chāizhàng payment by a share of the takings

拆字 chāizì same as 测字 cèzì

钗 chāi hairpin (formerly worn by women for adornment): 金 ～ a gold hairpin

差 chāi ① send on an errand; dispatch: ～ 人去送封信 send a letter by messenger / ～ 他去办件事 send (*or* dispatch) him on an errand ② errand; job: 兼差 jiānchāi ——see also chā; chà; cī

差拨 chāibō ① send; assign; dispatch ② *yamen* runner

差旅费 chāilǚfèi allowances for a business trip

差遣 chāiqiǎn send sb. on an errand or mission; dispatch; assign: 听候 ～ await assignment / 我听候您的 ～。I'm at your disposal.

差使 chāishǐ send; dispatch; assign

差使 chāishi official post; billet; commission; job: 我一点也不喜欢我这新 ～。I don't like this new job of mine at all.

差事 chāishi ① errand; assignment: 给你们一件 ～。Here's a job for you. ② same as 差使 chāishi

差役 chāiyì ① corvée ② runner or bailiff in a *yamen*

chái

侪（儕） chái *formal* people of the same generation; fellows; associates: 吾 ～ we; people like us

侪辈 cháibèi (also 侪类 cháilèi) *formal* people of the same generation

柴[1] chái ① firewood ② (Chái) a surname

柴[2]（瘥） chái *dial.* ① (of food) tough; dry: 火鸡肉 ～。Turkey (meat) is dry. / 煎饼搁凉了就 ～。Pancakes get hard and dry when they are cold. ② no good; poor; inferior; low-grade; second-rate: 这种皮鞋太 ～ 了。These shoes are too shoddy. / 他的棋下得 ～。He's a poor chess-player. *or* He's no good at chess.

柴草 cháicǎo faggot; firewood

柴扉 cháifēi *formal* wicker gate

柴胡 cháihú ① *bot.* Chinese thorowax (*Bupleurum chinense*) ② *Chin. med.* the root of Chinese thorowax

柴火 cháihuo faggot; firewood

柴门 cháimén wicker gate—a poor family

柴米夫妻 cháimǐ fūqī a couple who live from hand to mouth

柴米油盐 chái-mǐ-yóu-yán fuel, rice, oil and salt—chief daily necessities

柴爿 cháipán *dial.* kindling; firewood

柴炭 cháitàn ① faggot and charcoal; firewood ② charcoal

柴油 cháiyóu diesel oil

柴油机 cháiyóujī diesel engine: 船用 ～ marine diesel engine / 陆用 ～ stationary diesel engine

柴油机车 cháiyóu jīchē diesel locomotive

豺 chái jackal

豺狼 cháiláng jackals and wolves—cruel and evil people

豺狼成性 cháiláng chéng xìng wolfish by nature; rapacious and ruthless

豺狼当道 cháiláng dāngdào jackals and wolves hold sway—the cruel and the wicked are in power: ～, 安问狐狸。When the wolf is rampant, why pick on the fox?

chǎi

碴 chǎi ground beans or maize: 玉米 ～ 儿 ground maize (*or* corn)

chài

虿（蠆） chài a kind of scorpion

瘥 chài *formal* be recovered: 久病初 ～ have just recovered from a long illness

chān

觇 chān *formal* observe; survey

觇标 chānbiāo surveyor's beacon

掺（摻） chān same as 搀[2] chān

搀[1]（攙） chān support sb. by the arm; support sb. with one's hand: 把老大娘 ～ 进屋 help the old lady into the room / ～着他点儿。Help him along. / 把盲人 ～ 过马路 help a blind person across the street / 这位老先生太胖,我一个人 ～ 不起他来。The old gentleman was too heavy, I wasn't able to help him up alone.

搀[2]（攙） chān mix: 往沙子里 ～ 石灰 mix lime into sand / 油和水 ～ 不到一块儿。Oil and water do not mix. / 往饲料里再 ～ 点儿水。Add a little more water to the feed. / 初期白话文, ～ 用文言成分的比较多。Most of early *baihua* writings had an admixture of classical Chinese.

搀兑 chānduì mix different substances (esp. liquids): 把酒精跟水 ～ 起来。Mix the alcohol with water.

搀扶 chānfú support sb. by the arm

搀混 chānhùn mix up: 两种药给 ～ 在一起了。The two drugs have been mixed up.

搀和 chānhuo ① mix: 粗粮细粮 ～ 着吃 have a mixed diet of fine and coarse grain ② meddle; disturb; cause trouble: 别人正忙着呢,你别在这儿瞎 ～。We are busy. Don't hang around interfering.

搀假 chānjiǎ adulterate: 这批中草药 ～ 了。This batch of herbal medicine has been adulterated.

搀杂 chānzá mix up; jumble up: 别把这两种菜籽 ～ 在一起。Don't mix up these two kinds of vegetable seeds.

chán

单（單） chán see below ——see also dān; Shàn

单于 chányú the title of the chief of the Xiongnu (匈奴)

婵（嬋） chán see below

婵娟 chánjuān *liter.* ① (of a woman) lovely; beautiful ② the moon: 但愿人长久,千里共 ～。(苏轼) Would that we could live a long life And together share the moonlight a thousand miles away!

婵媛[1] chányuán same as 婵娟 chánjuān

婵媛[2] chányuán *formal* be joined; be related

谗（讒） chán slander; backbite

谗害 chánhài calumniate or slander sb. in order to have him persecuted; frame sb. up

谗佞 chánnìng *formal* slanderer

谗言 chányán slanderous talk; calumny

馋（饞） chán greedy; gluttonous: 别这么～, 留点儿给大家吃吧。Don't be so greedy—leave some of the food for the rest of us. / 这么多好吃的,真 ～ 人哪! Oh, it makes my mouth water to see so much delicious food. / 看见下棋他就 ～ 得慌。His fingers itch at the sight of a game of chess.

馋痨 chánláo greedy; gluttonous; piggish: ～ 鬼! You greedy pig!

馋涎欲滴 chánxián yù dī mouth drooling with greed: 使他 ～ make his mouth water / 他那贪婪的眼光露出 ～ 的神情。There was a look of unrestrained greed in his covetous eyes.

馋嘴 chánzuǐ ① gluttonous ② glutton; a greedy eater: 你这 ～,把个苹果排全吃了! You've eaten the whole apple pie, you glutton!

孱
chán　frail; weak——see also càn

孱羸　chánléi　*formal*　thin and frail; emaciated

孱弱　chánruò　*formal*　① frail (of physique); delicate in health: 体质～ have a frail constitution ② weak and incompetent ③ insubstantial; thin

禅（禪）
chán　*Buddhism*　① prolonged and intense contemplation; deep meditation; dhyana: 坐禅 zuòchán　② relating to Buddhism; Buddhist: 禅堂 chántáng／禅杖 chánzhàng——see also shàn

禅房　chánfáng　① Buddhist monks' living quarters ② Buddhist temple

禅机　chánjī　Buddhist allegorical word or gesture

禅林　chánlín　Buddhist temple

禅师　chánshī　honorific title for a Buddhist monk

禅堂　chántáng　a room or hall in a Buddhist monastery set apart for meditation; meditation room or hall

禅杖　chánzhàng　a Buddhist monk's staff

禅宗　chánzōng　the Chan sect; Dhyana; Zen

缠（纏）
chán　① twine; wind: 把线～在线轴上。Wind the thread onto the reel.／把毛线～成球。Wind the knitting wool into balls.／他手上～着绷带。His hand was bandaged. ② tangle; tie up; pester: 这两股线～在一起了。The two threads got tangled up.／他被事情～住了，没能来。He couldn't come because he was tied up.／小孩子总～着妈妈要这要那。Children are always pestering their mothers for this and that.／干吗老～着我? Why do you keep pestering me?／这孩子真～人。That kid is a real pesterer (*or* pest, nuisance). ③ *dial.*　deal with: 这人真难～。This fellow is really hard to deal with.

缠绵　chánmián　① (of an illness or emotion) be lingering: ～病榻 be bedridden with a lingering disease／乡思～ be tormented by homesickness ② melodious and moving: 歌声是那样柔和～。The singing was so soft and sweet.

缠绵悱恻　chánmián-fěicè　(of a story, poem, etc.) exceedingly sentimental; full of pathos

缠磨　chánmo　*inf.*　pester; bother: 这孩子老～人。The child is really a pest.／许多事情～着他,搞得他老是晕头转向的。He's got so much on his plate he's always in a muddle.／这件事一直～着她。This problem has long been bothering her.

缠绕　chánrào　① twine; bind; wind: 大树上～着藤萝。There is a wisteria twining round the big tree. ② pester; bother; harass: 孩子们～着我不让我走。The children kept pestering me and would not let me go.

缠绕植物　chánrào zhíwù　twining plant; twiner

缠手　chánshǒu　(of a matter) be troublesome; be hard to deal with; (of an illness) be hard to cure: 这件事有些～。That's a rather troublesome matter.／这病真～。This is a very difficult case.

缠足　chánzú　same as 裹脚 guǒjiǎo

蝉（蟬）
chán　cicada

蝉联　chánlián　continue to hold (a post or title): 多次～全国冠军 win the national championship several times running

蝉蜕　chántuì　① cicada slough (used as a Chinese medicine) ② *formal*　free (*or* extricate) oneself

蝉翼　chányì　cicada's wings: 薄如～的轻纱 gauze as thin as a cicada's wings

蝉翼纱　chányìshā　*text.*　organdie

廛
chán　① housing ground allotted to a commoner in a city in ancient times ② commoners' houses: ～里 the common people's houses and the officials' residences; the residential area of a city in ancient times

潺
chán　see below

潺潺　chánchán　*onom.*　murmur; babble; purl: ～流水 a murmuring stream

潺湲　chányuán　*liter.*　slowly flowing: 秋水～。Gently flow the autumn streams.

蟾
chán　short for 蟾蜍 chánchú

蟾蜍　chánchú　① toad ② the fabled three-legged toad in the moon ③ *liter.*　the moon

蟾宫　chángōng　*liter.*　Toad Palace—the moon

蟾宫折桂　chángōng zhé guì　pluck the laurel branch from Toad Palace—obtain a *jinshi* (进士) degree

蟾酥　chánsū　the dried venom of toads; toad-cake (used as a Chinese medicine)

巉
chán　*formal*　dangerously steep; precipitous

巉峻　chánjùn　*formal*　steep and precipitous: ～的悬崖 a sheer overhanging cliff

巉岩　chányán　*formal*　an overhanging rock: ～林立 a forest of precipitous rocks

chǎn

产（産）
chǎn　① give birth to; be delivered of: 蚕娥～卵了。The silk moths are laying eggs. ② produce; yield: ～油 produce oil／～煤 produce coal／水稻主要～在南方。Rice is grown chiefly in the south. ③ product; produce: 土产 tǔchǎn／特产 tèchǎn ④ property; estate: 房地产 fángdìchǎn／家产 jiāchǎn

产床　chǎnchuáng　obstetric table

产蛋鸡　chǎndànjī　laying hen; layer

产地　chǎndì　place of production (*or* origin); producing area: 甘蔗～ a sugarcane growing area／原料～ sources of raw materials／金丝猴～ the native haunt of the golden monkey

产地证明书　chǎndì zhèngmíngshū　certificate of origin

产犊　chǎndú　*animal husbandry*　calving

产儿　chǎn'ér　① newborn baby ② result; product: 这种新工具正是技术革新运动的～。This new kind of implement is a product of the technical innovation drive.

产房　chǎnfáng　delivery room

产妇　chǎnfù　a lying-in woman; a woman in childbirth; puerpera

产羔　chǎngāo　*animal husbandry*　lambing; kidding

产供销　chǎn-gōng-xiāo　*econ.*　production, supply and marketing: 企业有权安排自己的～活动。Enterprises have the right to plan their production, supply and marketing.

产后　chǎnhòu　postnatal; postpartum: ～护理 postnatal care; puerperal care

产后出血　chǎnhòu chūxuè　postpartum haemorrhage

产假　chǎnjià　maternity leave

产驹　chǎnjū　*animal husbandry*　foaling

产科　chǎnkē　① obstetrical department; maternity department ② obstetrics

产科病房　chǎnkē bìngfáng　obstetrical ward; maternity ward

产科学　chǎnkēxué　obstetrics

产科医生　chǎnkē yīshēng　obstetrician

产科医院　chǎnkē yīyuàn　maternity hospital

产量　chǎnliàng　output; yield: 今年煤的～ this year's output of coal／杂交水稻的亩～超过普通水稻的百分之十五至二十。The per *mu* yield of hybrid rice exceeds that of ordinary rice by 15 to 20 percent.

产卵 chǎnluǎn (of birds) lay eggs; (of fishes, frogs, etc.) spawn; (of insects) oviposit

产品 chǎnpǐn product; produce: 农 ～ farm produce / 畜 ～ livestock products / 工业 ～ industrial products / ～成本 cost of goods / ～ 销售 sale of goods / ～ 销售利润 profit on sales (of products) / ～ 质量 the quality of products

产婆 chǎnpó *old* midwife

产前 chǎnqián antenatal; prenatal; antepartum

产前检查 chǎnqián jiǎnchá antenatal (*or* prenatal) examination

产钳 chǎnqián obstetric forceps

产权 chǎnquán (short for 财产权) property right: ～ 要求 property claim

产褥期 chǎnrùqī *med.* puerperium

产褥热 chǎnrùrè puerperal fever; childbed fever

产生 chǎnshēng (used with immaterial things) give rise to; bring about; evolve; emerge; come into being: ～ 好的结果 produce good results / ～ 很大的影响 exert a great influence / 最近我对围棋～了很大的兴趣。I've become very interested in *go* recently. / 实践使我们的认识 ～ 了新的飞跃。Practice (*or* Practical experience) brings about a new leap in our knowledge. / 在中国几千年的历史中, ～ 了极其丰富灿烂的文化。China has evolved a very rich, splendid culture in her long history of several thousand years. / 正确的路线是在实践中 ～ 和发展起来的。A correct line emerges and develops only in the course of practice. / 旧的问题解决了, 新的问题又 ～ 了。New problems will crop up when old ones get solved. / 当初我们根本没有料到会 ～ 这样多的矛盾。We never expected that so many problems would arise.

产物 chǎnwù outcome; result; product: 这个方案是领导意见和群众意见相结合的 ～。This plan is the result of combining the ideas of the leadership with those of the masses.

产销 chǎn-xiāo production and marketing: ～ 平衡 coordination of production and marketing / ～ 两旺。Both production and marketing are thriving. / 要使 ～ 直接挂钩。Direct contact is to be established between the producing and marketing departments.

产业 chǎnyè ① estate; property: 他们祖上传下来的 ～ 早就变卖掉了。They sold their ancestral estate long ago. ② industry: 第三产业 dìsān chǎnyè

产业革命 chǎnyè gémìng the Industrial Revolution

产业工人 chǎnyè gōngrén industrial worker

产业后备军 chǎnyè hòubèijūn industrial reserve army; reserve army of labour

产业结构 chǎnyè jiégòu industrial structure; structure of production: 实现 ～ 合理化 rationalize the structure of production

产业军 chǎnyèjūn the army (*or* body) of industrial workers

产业资本 chǎnyè zīběn industrial capital

产值 chǎnzhí value of output; output value

产仔 chǎnzǐ (of a mammal) give birth to its young: 熊猫每胎 ～ 一到二只。A female panda bears only one or two young per litter. / 大白猪 ～了。The big white sow is farrowing.

刬（剗）

chǎn same as 铲^2 chǎn ——see also chàn

刬除 chǎnchú same as 铲除 chǎnchú

谄

chǎn fawn on; curry favour with; toady to

谄媚 chǎnmèi fawn on; toady to; curry favour with

谄上欺下 chǎnshàng-qīxià be servile to one's superiors and tyrannical to one's subordinates; fawn on those above and bully those below

谄笑 chǎnxiào give an ingratiating smile; smile obsequiously: 胁肩谄笑 xiéjiān chǎnxiào

谄谀 chǎnyú flatter servilely

铲^1（鏟）

chǎn shovel; spade: 煤铲 méichǎn / 锅铲 guōchǎn

铲^2（鏟、剷）

chǎn work with a shovel or spade: ～ 煤 shovel coal / 把 地 ～ 平 scrape the ground even; level the ground with a spade

铲车 chǎnchē forklift truck

铲齿车床 chǎnchǐ chēchuáng relieving lathe; backing-off lathe

铲除 chǎnchú root out; uproot; eradicate: ～ 杂草 root out weeds; weed / ～ 封建旧习俗 eradicate old feudal customs

铲球 chǎnqiú *football* sliding tackle

铲土机 chǎntǔjī spading machine; earth-scraper

铲运机 chǎnyùnjī carry-scraper; scraper

铲子 chǎnzi shovel; spade

阐（闡）

chǎn explain

阐发 chǎnfā elucidate: 这篇文章 ～了在我国发展商品经济的意义。This article elucidates the significance of developing a commodity economy in our country.

阐明 chǎnmíng expound; clarify: ～ 社会发展规律 expound the laws of social development / ～ 观点 clarify one's views / 我们支持声明中所～的正义立场。We support the just stand expounded in the statement.

阐释 chǎnshì explain; expound; interpret: 她对各项规定作了明确的 ～。She gave a clear explanation of each of the rules and regulations.

阐述 chǎnshù expound; elaborate; set forth: 进行系统的 ～ make a systematic exposition / ～ 人民群众在历史上的伟大作用 expound the great role played in history by the masses of the people / 各方 ～ 了自己对这一问题的立场。Each side set forth its position on this question.

阐扬 chǎnyáng expound and propagate: ～ 教义 expound and propagate religious doctrines

蒇

chǎn *formal* finish; complete: ～ 事 have finished the work; have accomplished the job

冁（囅，辴）

chǎn *formal* smiling; laughing: ～ 然而笑 break into a smile; burst out laughing

chàn

忏（懺）

chàn repent

忏悔 chànhuǐ ① repent; be penitent ② confess (one's sins) to God or to a priest

刬（剗）

chàn see 一 刬 yīchàn ——see also chǎn

颤

chàn quiver; tremble: 她的手 ～ 得利害。Her hands shook violently. / 我两腿直 ～。My legs kept shaking. ——see also zhàn

颤动 chàndòng vibrate; quiver: 声带 ～ vibration of the vocal chords / 树叶在微风中 ～。The leaves quivered in the breeze.

颤抖 chàndǒu shake; tremble; quiver; shiver: 冻得全身 ～ shiver all over with cold / 吓得两腿 ～ shake in one's shoes

颤巍巍 chànwēiwēi (usu. of aged people) tottering; faltering: 老太太 ～ 地走出屋来。The old lady came

tottering out of her room.

颤音 chànyīn ① *phonet.* trill ② *mus.* trill; shake

颤悠 chànyou shake; quiver; flicker: 〜 的灯光 a flickering light / 这块桥板直 〜。 This board on the bridge is shaky. / 他挑起担子 〜 〜 地走了。 He shouldered the loaded carrying pole and walked off with a swing.

屪 chàn　mix up; jumble up

屪杂 chànzá　same as 搀杂 chānzá

鹯 chàn　see 鞍鹯　ānchàn

chāng

伥(倀) chāng the ghost of one devoured by a tiger, who helps the tiger to devour others: 为虎作伥 wèi hǔ zuò chāng

伥鬼 chāngguǐ　same as 伥 chāng

昌 chāng ① prosperous; flourishing ② (Chāng) a surname

昌明 chāngmíng (of government, culture, etc.) flourishing; thriving; well-developed; advanced: 科学 〜。 Science is flourishing.

昌盛 chāngshèng prosperous: 建设一个繁荣 〜 的社会主义国家 build a prosperous socialist country

昌言 chāngyán *formal* ① proper words or comments ② speak openly: 〜 无忌 speak openly without reservation

倡 chāng ① *formal* singer, dancer or musician ② same as 娼 chāng ——see also chàng

倡伴 chāngyàng　same as 徜徉 chángyáng

倡优 chāngyōu *formal* ① singers, dancers or entertainers ② prostitutes and actors or actresses

菖 chāng　see below

菖兰 chānglán gladiolus (*Gladiolus gandavensis*)

菖蒲 chāngpú calamus

阊 chāng　see below

阊阖 chānghé *formal* ① the gate of heaven ② the gate of a palace

猖 chāng *formal* ferocious

猖獗 chāngjué rampant; raging; running wild: 〜 多年的天花，终于灭迹了。 Smallpox, rampant for ages, has at last been eliminated. / 这个地区过去风沙 〜。 The area used to be struck by raging sandstorms.

猖獗一时 chāngjué yīshí be rampant for a while; run wild for a time

猖狂 chāngkuáng savage; furious: 〜 的挑衅 reckless provocation / 〜 的攻击 a furious attack / 打退敌人的〜进攻 beat back the enemy's savage onslaught

娼 chāng prostitute

娼妇 chāngfù *offens.* bitch; whore

娼妓 chāngjì prostitute; streetwalker

娼寮 chāngliáo brothel; whorehouse

鲳 chāng silvery pomfret; butterfish

鲳鱼 chāngyú silvery pomfret; butterfish

cháng

长(長) cháng ① (of space or time) long: 这条河很 〜。 This is a long river. / 夏季昼 〜 夜短。 In summer the days are long and the nights short. / 〜 〜 的柳条垂到湖面。 The long willow twigs hang low, brushing against the surface of the lake. ② length: 南京长江大桥全 〜 六千七百七十二米。 The overall length of the Changjiang River Bridge at Nanjing is 6,772 metres. ③ strong point; forte: 取人之 〜，补己之短 overcome one's shortcomings by learning from others' strong points ④ be good at; be proficient in: 她 〜 于刺绣。 She is good at embroidery. *or* Embroidery is her forte. ——see also zhǎng

长安 Cháng'ān Chang'an, capital of China in the Han and Tang Dynasties

长臂猿 chángbìyuán *zool.* gibbon

长波 chángbō long wave

长波通讯 chángbō tōngxùn long-wave communication

长策 chángcè an effectual scheme; a sound plan; a long-term plan

长长短短 chángchángduǎnduǎn of uneven length

长城 chángchéng ① (Chángchéng) the Great Wall ② impregnable bulwark: 人民解放军是我们祖国的钢铁 〜。 The People's Liberation Army is China's great wall of steel.

长虫 chángchong *inf.* snake

长抽短吊 chángchōu-duǎndiào (in table tennis, badminton, etc.) combine long drives with drop shots

长处 chángchu good qualities; strong points: 他有许多 〜。 He has many good qualities. / 有联系群众的 〜 have the strong point of maintaining close contact with the masses / 国无大小，都各有 〜 和短处。 Every nation, big or small, has its strong and weak points.

长川 chángchuān same as 常川 chángchuān

长传 chángchuán (in ball games) throw a long pass

长春 Chángchūn Changchun (capital of Jilin Province)

长蝽 chángchūn chinch bug (an insect): 高粱 〜 sorghum chinch bug

长辞 chángcí leave forever—die; pass away: 与世长辞 yǔ shì chángcí

长此以往 cháng cǐ yǐ wǎng (also 长此下去 cháng cǐ xiàqu) if things go on like this; if things continue this way: 这些青少年不好好念书，却成天玩牌，〜，怎么得了？ These teenagers don't work hard at their studies; instead, they play cards all the time. If they go on like this, what will become of them?

长存 chángcún live forever

长凳 chángdèng backless bench

长笛 chángdí flute

长度 chángdù length: 测量黄河的 〜 survey the length of the Yellow River / 两者 〜 相同。 The two are of equal length. / 这条跑道的 〜 是多少？ What is the length of the track?

长短 chángduǎn ① length: 这两条扁担 〜 差不多。 The two carrying poles are about the same length. / 这件上衣 〜 正合适。 This coat is just the right length. ② accident; mishap: 万一这孩子的母亲有个 〜，怎么办？ What if anything should happen to the child's mother? / 渔民出海捕鱼，家里人总是提心吊胆，唯恐有个 〜。 When fishermen went out to sea, their folks would be left in constant fear of possible accidents. ③ right and wrong; strong and weak points: 背地里议论别人 〜 是不应该的。 It is not right to gossip about a person behind his back. ④ *dial.* in any case; anyhow: 明天的联欢会你 〜 要来。 You must come to tomorrow's party,

no matter what.

长短句 chángduǎnjù ① long and short verse (a pre-Tang verse form consisting chiefly of seven-character lines interspersed with shorter or longer ones) ② another name for 词 cí③

长吨 chángdūn　long ton

长法儿 chángfǎr　(usu. used in the negative) a long-term plan or solution: 头痛医头, 脚痛医脚, 这不是个 ～. Treating the symptoms and not the disease is no long-term solution.

长方体 chángfāngtǐ　rectangular parallelepiped; cuboid

长方形 chángfāngxíng　rectangle: ～ 的脸 a long, squarish face

长风破浪 chángfēng pòlàng　same as 乘风破浪 chéngfēng pòlàng

长歌当哭 chánggē dàng kū　compose and recite poems to vent one's grief and indignation

长庚 chánggēng astron. ancient Chinese name for Venus

长工 chánggōng　farm labourer hired by the year; long-term hired hand

长骨 chánggǔ physiol. long bone

长鼓 chánggǔ　a long drum, narrowing towards the middle, used by the Korean and Yao nationalities

长跪 chángguì formal kneel with the back straight

长号 chánghào mus. trombone

长河 chánghé　long river—endless flow: 历史的 ～ the long process (or span) of history

长话短说 cháng huà duǎn shuō　to make a long story short

长活 chánghuó ① long-term job (of a farm labourer): 他早先给地主扛过 ～. He used to be a long-term labourer for a landlord. ② dial. long-term labourer

长假 chángjià　long leave of absence; resignation: 请 ～ ask for a long leave of absence; hand in one's resignation

长江 Chángjiāng　the Changjiang (Yangtze) River: ～后浪推前浪, 一代更比一代强. As in the Yangtze River the waves behind drive on those before, so each new generation excels the last one.

长颈鹿 chángjǐnglù　giraffe

长久 chángjiǔ　for a long time; permanently: 他打算在这儿～住下去. He's thinking of living here permanently. / 这种发夹外形美观, 但用不～. These hairpins look nice but won't last.

长久之计 chángjiǔ zhī jì　a long-term plan; a permanent solution: 不是 ～ not a permanent solution; just a makeshift arrangement

长距离 chángjùlí　long distance: ～ 赛跑 a long-distance race

长空 chángkōng　the vast sky: 万里～ the vast expanse of the sky

长裤 chángkù　trousers; slacks; pants

长廊 chángláng ① a covered corridor or walk; gallery ② the Long Corridor (of the Summer Palace in Beijing)

长龙 chánglóng　long dragon—a long queue or line

长毛 chángmáo derog. long-haired rebels (referring to the Taiping rebels)

长毛绒 chángmáoróng　plush

长矛 chángmáo　long spear; lance

长眠 chángmián euph. have an eternal sleep; be dead: ～ 地下 be dead and buried

长明灯 chángmíngdēng　an altar lamp that is kept burning day and night

长命百岁 chángmìng bǎisuì　(usu. used in expressing good wishes for a child) a life of a hundred years; live to be a hundred; live to a ripe old age: 姑奶奶定依我这名字, 必然～.(《红楼梦》) If you agree to this name,

madam, she's sure to live to a ripe old age.

长年 chángnián　all the year round: 筑路工人～奋战在风雪高原. The road builders brave the wind and snow on the plateaus all the year round. ——see also zhǎngnián

长年累月 chángnián-lěiyuè　year in year out; over the years: 他～在大西北从事野外工作. Year in year out he has been doing fieldwork in the Northwest. / ～ 没修理, 墙上的灰泥都剥落了. The plaster on the wall had peeled off through years of neglect.

长袍儿 chángpáor　long gown (worn by men)

长跑 chángpǎo　long-distance running; long-distance race: 他每天 ～. He goes long-distance running every day. / 这次运动会, 我参加了五千米～. I ran the 5,000-metre race at the sports meet.

长篇大论 chángpiān-dàlùn　a lengthy speech or article: 只要有机会, 他就要～地讲起来. He seized every chance to make long, high-sounding speeches. / 注意简明扼要, 不要～. Be sure to make it clear and concise and avoid long-windedness. / 有不少人说话了, 有～的, 也有三言两语的. Quite a few people spoke, some at considerable length, some just saying a word or two.

长篇小说 chángpiān xiǎoshuō　novel

长期 chángqī　over a long period of time; long-term; long-lasting: ～规划 a long-term plan / 天气预报 a long-range weather forecast / ～存在的问题 a long-standing problem / ～无息贷款 a long-term interest-free loan / ～战争 a protracted war / 作～打算 take a long view; make long-term plans / 经受～斗争锻炼 be tempered in long years of struggle / ～的战乱给人民带来极大的苦难. The long-drawn-out war caused the people extreme suffering.

长期共存, 互相监督 chángqī gòngcún, hùxiāng jiāndū long-term coexistence and mutual supervision (a principle upheld by the Chinese Communist Party in its relations with China's other democratic parties)

长期性 chángqīxìng　of a protracted nature

长崎 Chángqí　Nagasaki

长枪 chángqiāng ① spear ② long-barrelled gun; rifle

长驱 chángqū　(of an army) make a long drive; push deep: ～千里 make a long drive of 1,000 li

长驱直入 chángqū zhí rù　drive straight in: 我军 ～, 所向披靡. Our army drove straight in, carrying everything before it.

长拳 chángquán　the long punch (a style of Chinese boxing)

长日照植物 chángrìzhào zhíwù　long-day plant

长沙 Chángshā　Changsha (capital of Hunan Province)

长衫 chángshān　unlined long gown (worn by men)

长舌 chángshé　long tongue—a gossipy person; gossip-monger: ～ 妇 a gossipy woman

长蛇阵 chángshézhèn　single-line battle array: 排成一字 ～ deploy the troops in a long line; string out in a long line

长蛇座 Chángshézuò astron. Hydra

长生不老 chángshēng bùlǎo　live forever and never grow old: ～ 药 elixir of life

长生果 chángshēngguǒ dial. peanut

长绳系日 chángshéng jì rì　use a long rope to tie the sun—try to stop the passage of time

长石 chángshí　feldspar (a mineral)

长时记忆 chángshí jìyì psychol. long-term memory

长逝 chángshì　pass away; be gone forever

长寿 chángshòu　a long life; longevity: 祝 您健康～. I wish you good health and a long life.

长丝 chángsī text. filament

长随 chángsuí　personal attendant (of an official)

长叹 chángtàn　deep sigh: ～ 一声 heave a deep sigh

长条校样 chángtiáo jiàoyàng print. galley proof

长挑　chángtiāo　tall and slender

长亭　chángtíng　travellers' pavilion (a small roadside pavilion built every ten *li* in ancient China for travellers to rest in): ～ 话别 bid farewell at a travellers' pavilion

长统皮靴　chángtǒng píxuē　high boots

长统袜　chángtǒngwà　stockings

长途　chángtú　① a long distance: 经过 ～ 飞行 after a long-distance flight ② short for 长途电话 chángtú diànhuà

长途跋涉　chángtú báshè　make a long, arduous journey; trudge a long distance; trek a long way

长途奔袭　chángtú bēnxí　*mil.* make a long-distance raid

长途电话　chángtú diànhuà　long-distance telephone call

长途电话局　chángtú diànhuàjú　long-distance telephone exchange

长途电信局　chángtú diànxìnjú　long-distance telecommunications bureau

长途汽车　chángtú qìchē　long-distance bus; coach

长途运输　chángtú yùnshū　long-distance transport

长网　chángwǎng　*paper making* fourdrinier wire

长网造纸机　chángwǎng zàozhǐjī　fourdrinier (machine)

长尾鹟　chángwěiwēng　paradise flycatcher (a bird)

长物　chángwù　① surplus ② a presentable thing: 身无长物 shēn wú chángwù

长线　chángxiàn　(of products) be in oversupply: ～产品 products in oversupply

长效　chángxiào　enduring effect

长效磺胺　chángxiào huáng'àn　*med.* sulphamethoxy-pyridazine (SMP)

长啸　chángxiào　utter a long and loud cry: 仰天 ～ look up to heaven and utter a long, mournful cry

长性　chángxìng　perseverance; constancy

长袖善舞，多财善贾　cháng xiù shàn wǔ, duō cái shàn gǔ　if you have long sleeves, you'll be good at dancing; if you have much money, you'll be good at business—given the facilities, success is assured

长吁短叹　chángxū-duǎntàn　utter sighs and groans; moan and groan: 他在床上翻来覆去，不时地 ～。 He tossed about in bed, moaning and groaning from time to time.

长须鲸　chángxūjīng　finback (a whale)

长阳人　Chángyángrén　Changyang Man (a type of primitive man whose fossil remains were found in Changyang, Hubei Province, in 1956 and 1957)

长夜　chángyè　*liter.* ① eternal night ② all night: 作 ～ 饮 carouse all night long

长揖　chángyī　make a deep bow with hands clasped in front of one's chest

长缨　chángyīng　*formal* long tassel; long ribbon

长于　chángyú　be good at; be adept in: 她 ～ 绘画。 She is good at painting. / 他 ～ 舞蹈。 He is adept in dancing.

长元音　chángyuányīn　*phonet.* long vowel

长圆　chángyuán　oval; egg-shaped

长远　chángyuǎn　long-term; long-range: ～ 的利益 long-term interests / ～ 规划 a long-term (*or* long-range) plan / ～ 目标 long-range objectives / 从 ～ 的观点看问题 consider a problem from a long-term point of view

长斋　chángzhāi　a Buddhist's permanent abstention from meat, fish, etc.

长征　chángzhēng　① expedition; long march ② the Long March (a major strategic movement of the Chinese Workers' and Peasants' Red Army which succeeded in reaching the revolutionary base in northern Shaanxi after traversing eleven provinces and covering 25,000 *li*, or 12,500 kilometres, 1934–1935)

长至　chángzhì　same as 夏至 xiàzhì

长治久安　chángzhì-jiǔ'ān　a long period of peace and order; lasting political stability

长住　chángzhù　live in a place for long; settle

长足　chángzú　*formal* leaps and bounds: 有了 ～ 的进展 have made considerable progress

长足进步　chángzú jìnbù　make great strides; make rapid progress

场（場、塲）

cháng　① a level open space (often used as a threshing ground, etc.): 麦子已经上 ～。 The wheat has been taken to the threshing ground. ② *dial.* country fair; market: 赶场 gǎnchǎng ③ *m.* spell; period: 那是一～ 硬仗。 That was a hard battle. / 昨夜下了一～ 大雪(雨)。 There was a heavy fall of snow (rain) last night. / 她害了一 ～ 大病。 She was seriously ill. / 为了参加下届奥运会，我们要大干一 ～。 We must go all out for the coming Olympic Games. ——see also chǎng

场院　chángyuàn　threshing ground

肠（腸）

cháng　intestines: 大 ～ large intestine / 小 ～ small intestine

肠儿　chángr　sausage

肠穿孔　chángchuānkǒng　intestinal perforation; enterobrosis

肠断　chángduàn　*liter.* heartbroken

肠肥脑满　chángféi-nǎomǎn　same as 脑满肠肥 nǎomǎn-chángféi

肠梗阻　chánggěngzǔ　intestinal obstruction

肠激酶　chángjīméi　*biochem.* enterokinase

肠结核　chángjiéhé　tuberculosis of the intestines

肠扭转　chángniǔzhuǎn　volvulus

肠套叠　chángtàodié　intussusception

肠胃　chángwèi　intestines and stomach; stomach; belly: ～ 不好 suffer from stomach trouble

肠胃炎　chángwèiyán　enterogastritis

肠炎　chángyán　enteritis

肠衣　chángyī　casing for sausages

肠痈　chángyōng　*Chin. med.* appendicitis

肠子　chángzi　intestines

尝¹（嘗、嚐）

cháng　taste; try the flavour of: ～ ～味道。 Try it and see if it tastes all right. / ～ 到甜头 become aware of the benefits of; come to know the good of

尝²（嘗）

cháng　ever; once: 未尝 wèicháng / 何尝 hécháng

尝鼎一脔　cháng dǐng yī luán　try one morsel and you'll know the whole potful—get to know the whole from sampling a part

尝试　chángshì　attempt; try: 为了增产，他们曾 ～ 过各种方法。 They have tried various ways to increase production. / 最后一次 ～ 成功了。 The last try was a success.

尝受　chángshòu　have a personal experience of (hardship, misery, etc.); taste (the bitterness of life, etc.)

尝味　chángwèi　try the flavour; taste; savour: 这是一道名菜，你一定要～一下。 Do have a taste of this well-known dish.

尝鲜　chángxiān　have a taste of a delicacy; have a taste of what is just in season

尝新　chángxīn　have a taste of what is just in season

常

cháng　① ordinary; common; normal: 人情之 ～ natural and normal ② constant; invariable: 冬夏 ～ 青 remain green throughout the year; evergreen ③ *adv.* frequently; often; usually: ～ 来～ 往 exchange

frequent visits; pay frequent calls / 她 ～ 去听音乐会。 She goes to concerts quite often. / 我们 ～ 见面。 We see quite a lot of each other. ④ (Cháng) a surname

常备不懈 cháng bèi bù xiè always be on the alert; be ever prepared (against war): 人民解放军 ～ 地守卫着祖国边疆。 The People's Liberation Army, ever on the alert, guards the borders of our country.

常备军 chángbèijūn standing army

常常 chángcháng *adv.* frequently; often; many a time; more often than not: 她 ～ 工作到深夜。 She often works far into the night. / 他俩 ～ 通信, 交换学术上的看法。 The two of them frequently write to each other, exchanging views on academic questions.

常川 chángchuān frequently; constantly: ～ 往来 keep in constant touch / ～ 供给 keep sb. constantly supplied

常春藤 chángchūnténg *bot.* Chinese ivy

常规 chángguī ① convention; common practice; routine: 按照 ～ 办事 follow the old routine / 打破 ～ break with convention ② *med.* routine: 血 ～ routine blood test / 尿 ～ routine urine test

常规疗法 chángguī liáofǎ *med.* routine treatment
常规武器 chángguī wǔqì conventional weapons
常规战争 chángguī zhànzhēng conventional war
常轨 chángguī normal practice (*or* course): 这类事情, 可以遵循 ～ 解决。 We can follow the usual procedures when dealing with this sort of thing.

常衡 chánghéng (also 常衡制 chánghéngzhì) avoirdupois (weight)

常会 chánghuì regular meeting; regular session: 委员会每半年举行一次 ～。 The committee holds regular meetings once every six months.

常见 chángjiàn be common: 这儿的春天, 风沙是 ～ 的。 Duststorms are common here in spring.

常见病 chángjiànbìng common disease; common ailment

常客 chángkè a frequent guest or customer; frequenter (of a theatre, restaurant, ballroom, etc.)

常礼 chánglǐ common courtesy; etiquette (in everyday life): 这是违反社交 ～ 的。 This is against social etiquette.

常理 chánglǐ general rule; what is normal: 按 ～ normally

常例 chánglì common practice

常量 chángliàng *phys.* constant

常绿植物 chánglù zhíwù evergreen plants; evergreens

常年 chángnián ① throughout the year; year in year out: ～ 坚持体育锻炼 persist in physical training all the year round / ～ 从事农业生产 be engaged in agricultural production year in year out ② an average year: 这儿小麦 ～ 亩产三百公斤。 In this area the per *mu* yield of wheat for an average year is 300 kilograms.

常青 chángqīng evergreen: 四季 ～ have green leaves throughout the year / 冷杉和松树是 ～ 树。 Firs and pines are evergreens.

常情 chángqíng reason; sense: 按照 ～, 他会提出这个问题同你讨论的。 It stands to reason that he will take up the matter with you. / 既然这事合乎 ～, 我不反对。 Since this is a sensible thing to do, I have no objections.

常人 chángrén ordinary person; the man in the street

常任 chángrèn permanent; standing: 安理会 ～ 理事国 permanent member of the Security Council / ～ 代表 permanent representative / ～ 制的国家公务员 public servants whose tenure in office is permanent

常山 chángshān ① *bot.* antipyretic dichroa (*Dichroa febrifuga*) ② *Chin. med.* the root or leaves of antipyretic dichroa

常设 chángshè (of an organization) standing; permanent: ～ 机构 standing body; permanent organization / ～ 秘书处 permanent secretariat / ～ 委员会 permanent committee

常胜将军 chángshèng jiāngjūn an ever-victorious general

常胜军 chángshèngjūn an invincible army

常识 chángshí ① general knowledge; elementary knowledge: 卫生 ～ elementary knowledge of hygiene and sanitation / 科学 ～ general knowledge of science / ～ 课 general knowledge course ② common sense: 天冷了要穿得暖一点儿, 这是 ～。 It's common sense to dress more warmly when it gets cold.

常时 chángshí ① often; frequently; regularly ② *dial.* sometimes

常事 chángshì a common happening; routine: 工作到深夜对他来说是 ～。 It's his routine to work late into the night.

常数 chángshù *math.* constant

常态 chángtài normal behaviour or conditions; normality; normalcy: 恢复 ～ return to normal (*or* normalcy)

常态曲线 chángtài qūxiàn *statistics* normal curve

常套 chángtào convention; a usual pattern: 摆脱才子佳人小说的 ～ break away from the pattern of the "genius and beauty" romance

常委 chángwěi short for 常务委员 chángwù wěiyuán

常委会 chángwěihuì short for 常务委员会 chángwù wěiyuánhuì

常温 chángwēn ① normal atmospheric temperature (between 15° and 25°C) ② *zool.* homoiothermy

常温动物 chángwēn dòngwù homoiothermal animal; homoiotherm

常务 chángwù day-to-day business; routine: 主持 ～ in charge of day-to-day business

常务理事 chángwù lǐshì managing director

常务委员 chángwù wěiyuán member of the standing committee

常务委员会 chángwù wěiyuánhuì standing committee

常性 chángxìng perseverance; tenacity: 没有 ～ lack perseverance / 有 ～ show tenacity of purpose

常压塔 chángyātǎ atmospheric tower

常言 chángyán saying: ～ 道 as the saying goes / ～ 说得好 as the saying aptly puts it; it is well said that...

常业犯 chángyèfàn same as 惯犯 guànfàn

常用 chángyòng in common use: ～ 药材 medicinal herbs most in use

常用词语 chángyòng cíyǔ everyday expressions

常住 chángzhù ① permanently reside at a place: 有 ～ 户口 be a permanent resident ② *Buddhism* changeless; permanent ③ *Buddhism* (short for 常住物) a temple and its assets

常驻 chángzhù resident; permanent: ～ 联合国代表团 a permanent mission to the United Nations

常驻大使 chángzhù dàshǐ resident ambassador

常驻代表 chángzhù dàibiǎo permanent representative

常驻记者 chángzhù jìzhě resident correspondent

偿 (償)

cháng ① repay; compensate for: ～ 债 pay (*or* discharge) a debt ② meet; fulfil: 得 ～ 夙愿 have fulfilled one's long-cherished wish

偿付 chángfù pay back; pay: 延期 ～ delay the payment of a debt

偿还 chánghuán repay; pay back: ～ 债务 pay a debt / 如数 ～ pay back the exact amount

偿命 chángmìng pay with one's life (for a murder); a life for a life

偿清 chángqīng pay back in full; clear (a debt): ～ 债务 clear one's debts

徜　chǎng　see below
徜徉　chángyáng　*formal*　wander about unhurriedly; roam leisurely

裳　cháng　skirt (worn in ancient China) ——see also shang

嫦　cháng　see below
嫦娥　Cháng'é　the Lady in the Moon (the Chinese moon goddess figuring prominently in legend and literature, who in mortal life stole the herb of immortality and fled to the moon, where she became immortal but was cloistered forever)

chǎng

厂（厰、廠）　chǎng　① factory; mill; plant; works: 鞋 ～ shoe factory / 面粉 ～ flour mill / 机床 ～ machine tool plant / 钢铁 ～ iron and steel works / 制糖 ～ sugar refinery / 造船 ～ shipyard / ～ 办食堂 factory-run canteen ② yard; depot: 煤 ～ coal yard
厂房　chǎngfáng　① factory building ② factory workshop
厂家　chǎngjiā　factory; mill: 有些 ～ 濒临破产。 Some of the factories are verging on bankruptcy.
厂矿　chǎng-kuàng　factories and mines
厂矿企业　chǎng-kuàng qǐyè　factories, mines and other enterprises; industrial enterprises
厂礼拜　chǎnglǐbài　a factory's weekly holiday (usu. on a weekday): 星期二是我们厂的 ～。 Tuesday is our factory's weekly holiday.
厂商　chǎngshāng　① factory owner: 承包 ～ contractor ② factories and stores
厂丝　chǎngsī　*text.*　filature silk
厂校挂钩　chǎng-xiào guàgōu　establish a hookup between a school and a factory
厂休　chǎngxiū　a factory's day of rest (usu. on a weekday): 今天我们 ～。 Today is our factory's day of rest.
厂长　chǎngzhǎng　factory director
厂址　chǎngzhǐ　the site (*or* location) of a factory: 选择 ～ choose a site for building a factory
厂主　chǎngzhǔ　factory owner; millowner
厂子　chǎngzi　① *inf.*　factory; mill ② yard; depot

场（場、塲）　chǎng　① a large place used for a particular purpose: 会场 huìchǎng / 操场 cāochǎng / 市场 shìchǎng / 剧场 jùchǎng / 农场 nóngchǎng / 养鸡场 yǎngjīchǎng ② stage: 上场 shàngchǎng / 开场 kāichǎng ③ *theat.*　scene: 第二幕第三 ～ Act II, Scene iii ④ *m.* (for recreational or sports activities): 一 ～ 电影 a film show / 一 ～ 球赛 a match; a ball game / 加演一 ～ give an extra performance or show / 第二 ～ 两点开始。 The second show starts at two. ⑤ *phys.*　field: 电场 diànchǎng / 磁场 cíchǎng ——see also chǎng
场磁铁　chǎngcítiě　*elec.*　field magnet
场次　chǎngcì　the number of showings of a film, play, etc.
场地　chǎngdì　space; place; site: 体育比赛 ～ sports arena; sports ground; court / 施工 ～ construction site / 由于 ～ 有限，他们只展出了部分产品。 They displayed only a part of their products because space was limited.
场合　chǎnghé　occasion; situation: 外交 ～ a diplomatic occasion / 这种 ～ 你不能穿得太随便。 You should be properly dressed for such an occasion.
场记　chǎngjì　① log (for film shooting, theatrical performance, etc.) ② log keeper
场界灯　chǎngjièdēng　boundary lights (in an airfield)
场论　chǎnglùn　*phys.*　field theory
场面　chǎngmiàn　① scene (in drama, fiction, etc.); spectacle: 电影里的动人 ～ a moving scene in a film / 油画再现了红军过雪山的雄伟 ～。 The painting conjures up the grand spectacle of the Red Army crossing the snowcapped mountains. / 作者很善于描写大的 ～。 The author is adept in depicting grand scenes. ② occasion; scene: 盛大的 ～ a grand occasion / 热烈友好的 ～ a scene of warm friendship ③ appearance; front; facade: 撑场面 chēng chǎngmiàn
场所　chǎngsuǒ　place; arena: 公共 ～ a public place / 娱乐 ～ place of recreation / 帝国主义角逐的 ～ an arena of imperialist rivalry / 蚊蝇孳生的 ～ a breeding ground of flies and mosquitoes / 这里通常是举行纪念活动的 ～。 This is the usual place for commemorative activities.
场子　chǎngzi　a place where people gather for various purposes (e. g. theatre, hall, sports ground, etc.): 这个 ～ 够大，可是音响效果不好，不适合用来开音乐会。 The place is big enough, but the acoustics are not good enough for a concert.

昶　chǎng　*formal*　① a long day ② same as 畅
chàng

敞　chǎng　① (of a house, courtyard, etc.) spacious; roomy: 这屋子太 ～。 This room is too big. ② open; be uncovered: ～ 着门 leave the door open; with the door open
敞车　chǎngchē　① open wagon; open freight car ② a railway flatcar
敞怀　chǎnghuái　have one's shirt unbuttoned; bare one's chest
敞开　chǎngkāi　open wide: 把门 ～open the door wide / 大门 ～ 着。 The gate was left wide open. / ～ 思想 say what's in (*or* on) one's mind; get things off one's chest
敞开儿　chǎngkāir　*inf.*　unlimitedly; unrestrictedly: 啤酒有的是，大家 ～ 喝吧。 There's plenty of beer. Drink to your hearts' content. / ～ 供应 have an unlimited (*or* open-ended) supply of sth. / 你有什么意见就 ～ 说吧。 Don't hesitate to tell me if you have any complaints.
敞亮　chǎngliàng　① light and spacious: 这间屋子很 ～。 This room is light and spacious. ② (of one's thinking) clear: 学习了这篇社论，心里更 ～ 了。 After I studied the editorial, things seemed much clearer.
敞喷　chǎngpēn　*petroleum*　open flow
敞篷车　chǎngpéngchē　open car
敞着口儿　chǎngzhekǒur　① be uncovered; be unsealed; be unsettled: 他的伤还 ～ 呢。 His wound hasn't healed up yet. / 这个问题还 ～ 呢。 This is still an open question. ② *dial.*　be unrestrained: 生活好了，也不能 ～ 过日子。 Things are much better than they were, but still we mustn't spend too freely.

氅　chǎng　cloak: 大氅 dàchǎng

chàng

怅（悵）　chàng　disappointed; sorry: 惆怅 chóuchàng
怅怅　chàngchàng　*formal*　frustrated and disconsolate; disappointed and unhappy
怅恨　chànghèn　feel bitter at one's frustration; feel

disappointed and resentful

怅然 chàngrán disappointed; upset: ～而返 come away disappointed

怅惘 chàngwǎng distracted; listless: 轮船在远处消失了，而她仍然～地站在江边。Even after the steamship had sailed out of sight, she still stood in a daze on the pier.

畅（暢）

chàng ① smooth; unimpeded: 流畅 liúchàng ② free; uninhibited: ～饮 drink one's fill

畅达 chàngdá fluent; smooth: 译文～。The translation reads smoothly. / 交通～ have a good transport and communications network

畅怀 chànghuái to one's heart's content: ～痛饮 drink to one's heart's content

畅快 chàngkuài free from inhibitions and happy; carefree: 心情～ have ease of mind; be carefree and happy / 大家都玩得非常～。We all had a wonderful time.

畅抒 chàngshū freely express: ～己见 air one's own views freely

畅顺 chàngshùn same as 顺畅 shùnchàng

畅所欲言 chàng suǒ yù yán pour out all that one wishes to say; speak without any inhibitions; speak one's mind freely; speak out freely

畅谈 chàngtán talk freely and to one's heart's content: ～国内外大好形势 speak glowingly of the excellent situation at home and abroad

畅通 chàngtōng unimpeded; unblocked: 前面道路～无阻。The road ahead is clear of obstructions. or Open road ahead. / 这里过去很偏僻，现在铁路公路都～了。This formerly inaccessible place can now be easily reached by road and rail.

畅想 chàngxiǎng give full play to one's imagination

畅销 chàngxiāo sell well; have a ready market; be in great demand: 中国丝绸～国外。Chinese silk fabrics sell well on foreign markets. / 秋天是毛织品～的季节。Autumn is a lively season for the wool market.

畅销书 chàngxiāoshū best seller

畅行无阻 chàng xíng wú zǔ pass unimpeded; proceed without hindrance

畅叙 chàngxù chat cheerfully (usu. about old times): ～友情 relive an old friendship

畅游 chàngyóu ① have a good swim: ～长江 have a good swim in the Changjiang River ② enjoy a sightseeing tour: ～名胜古迹 enjoy a trip to places of historic interest

倡

chàng initiate; advocate: 提倡 tíchàng / 倡议 chàngyì——see also chāng

倡导 chàngdǎo initiate; propose: ～和平共处五项原则 initiate the Five Principles of Peaceful Coexistence

倡始 chàngshǐ initiate; start; found

倡始人 chàngshǐrén initiator; founder

倡言 chàngyán formal propose; initiate

倡议 chàngyì propose; initiate: ～召开国际会议 propose the calling of an international conference / 在他的～下 at his suggestion / 提出利用废料的～ put forward a proposal to make use of waste material / 他的～得到了大家一致的赞同。His proposal met with unanimous approval.

倡议权 chàngyìquán diplomacy initiative

倡议书 chàngyìshū written proposal; proposal

倡议者 chàngyìzhě initiator

鬯¹

chàng a wine used at ancient sacrificial ceremonies

鬯²

chàng same as 畅 chàng

唱

chàng ① sing: ～国歌 sing the national anthem / ～女高音 sing the soprano / 颂歌一曲～北京 sing a song in praise of Beijing / ～～农村新面貌 sing of the new look of the countryside ② call; cry: 鸡～三遍。The cock has crowed for the third time. ③ a song or a singing part of a Chinese opera

唱白脸 chàng báiliǎn wear the white mask of the villain—play the villain; pretend to be harsh and severe (often used in contrast to 唱红脸)

唱本 chàngběn the libretto or script of a ballad-singer

唱酬 chàngchóu formal same as 唱和 chànghè②

唱词 chàngcí libretto; words of a ballad

唱独角戏 chàng dújiǎoxì (also 唱独脚戏 chàng dújiǎoxì) put on a one-man show; go it alone

唱段 chàngduàn aria: 京剧～ an aria from a Beijing opera

唱对台戏 chàng duìtáixì put on a rival show; enter into rivalry with sb.

唱反调 chàng fǎndiào sing a different tune; speak or act contrary to

唱高调 chàng gāodiào mouth high-sounding words; say fine-sounding things; affect a high moral tone: 少～，你要是能干，就来试试。None of your high-sounding words. If you can do it, come and have a try.

唱歌 chànggē sing (a song): 她很会～。She is a good singer.

唱工 chànggōng (also 唱功 chànggōng) theat. art of singing; singing

唱工戏 chànggōngxì Chinese opera featuring singing (rather than acrobatics, etc.)

唱和 chànghè ① one singing a song and the others joining in the chorus: 此唱彼和。When one starts singing, another joins in. ② an exchange of poems (i. e. one person writing a poem and another writing one in reply, both using the same rhyme scheme)

唱红脸 chàng hóngliǎn wear the red mask of the hero—play the hero; pretend to be generous and kind (often used in contrast to 唱白脸): 一个～，一个唱白脸。One coaxes, the other coerces.

唱机 chàngjī phonograph; record player; gramophone

唱空城计 chàng kōngchéngjì perform The Stratagem of the Empty City—present a bold front to conceal a weak defence; have an absentee staff

唱名 chàngmíng ① read out a list of names ② mus. sol-fa syllables (do, re, mi, fa, sol, la and ti)

唱名表决 chàngmíng biǎojué vote by roll call; roll-call vote

唱名法 chàngmíngfǎ mus. sol-fa; solmization: 固定～ fixed-do system / 首调～ movable-do system

唱盘 chàngpán turntable (of a record player)

唱片 chàngpiàn phonograph (or gramophone) record; disc: 放～ play a phonograph record / 灌～ cut a disc

唱票 chàngpiào call out the names of those voted for while counting ballot-slips

唱票人 chàngpiàorén teller

唱腔 chàngqiāng vocal music in a Chinese opera

唱喏 chàngrě dial. make a bow with hands clasped in front

唱诗班 chàngshībān choir

唱双簧 chàng shuānghuáng ① give a two-man comic show (with one speaking or singing while hiding behind the other who gesticulates) ② collaborate with each other

唱头 chàngtóu pickup (of a phonograph)

唱戏 chàngxì inf. sing and act in a traditional opera: 她从小就跟她爸爸学～。She began to learn opera singing and acting from her father when she was a mere child.

唱针　chàngzhēn　gramophone needle; stylus

唱做念打　chàng-zuò-niàn-dǎ　singing, gesticulating, elocution and acrobatics—elements of the art of acting in traditional opera

chāo

抄[1]（钞）　chāo　① copy; transcribe: ～书 copy from a book／请把稿件～一下。Please make a fair copy of the manuscript.／照～原文 make a verbatim transcription of the original ② plagiarize; lift: ～别人的文章 plagiarize (from) somebody else's writing／逐字逐句地～人家的作业 copy another student's written work word by word

抄[2]　chāo　① search and confiscate; make a raid upon: ～土匪的老窝 destroy the bandits' den ② take a shortcut: ～到他们前面 outstrip them by taking a shortcut ③ fold (one's arms): ～着手站在一边 stand by with folded arms ④ grab; take up: ～起一把铁锹就干 take up a spade and plunge into the job／谁拿我的字典～走了？Who's gone off with my dictionary?

抄靶子　chāo bǎzi　*dial.* search a person; frisk

抄本　chāoběn　hand-copied book; transcript:《红楼梦》～ a handwritten copy of *A Dream of Red Mansions*

抄道　chāodào　① take a shortcut ② *inf.* shortcut: 走～去要近两公里路。If you take the shortcut, it will be two kilometres closer.

抄后路　chāo hòulù　outflank and attack (the enemy) in the rear; turn the enemy's rear

抄获　chāohuò　search out; ferret out

抄家　chāojiā　search sb.'s house and confiscate his property

抄件　chāojiàn　duplicate; copy: 现将报告的～转发给你们。A copy of the report is forwarded herewith.

抄近儿　chāojìnr　take a shortcut

抄录　chāolù　make a handwritten copy of; copy: 这段引文是从报上～来的。This quotation is copied (*or* taken) from a newspaper article.／他读了这首诗爱不释手，一定要～一份。He loved the poem so much that he insisted on making a copy of it.

抄掠　chāolüè　*formal* loot; plunder: 所有的商店都被～一空。All the shops were looted and stripped clean.

抄身　chāoshēn　search a person; frisk

抄手　chāoshǒu　*dial. won ton*; dumpling soup

抄送　chāosòng　make a copy for; send a duplicate to

抄网　chāowǎng　dip net

抄袭[1]　chāoxí　① plagiarize; lift: ～行为 (an act of) plagiarism ② borrow indiscriminately from other people's experience

抄袭[2]　chāoxí　launch a surprise attack on the enemy by making a detour

抄写　chāoxiě　copy (by hand); transcribe

抄写员　chāoxiěyuán　copyist

抄用　chāoyòng　copy indiscriminately (experience, a method, etc.)

吵　chāo　see below ——see also chǎo

吵吵　chāochao　*dial.* make a row; kick up a racket: 一个一个地说，别～。Speak one at a time. Don't make such a row.

钞[1]　chāo　bank note; paper money: 现～ cash

钞[2]　chāo　same as 抄[1] chāo

钞票　chāopiào　bank note; paper money; bill: 五元一张的～ a five-*yuan* bill

钞票纸　chāopiàozhǐ　bank-note paper

绰[1]　chāo　grab; take up: ～起一根棍子 grab a stick／～起活儿就干 plunge right into the job

绰[2]　chāo　same as 焯 chāo ——see also chuò

焯　chāo　dip vegetables in boiling water for a few seconds; scald: 先把菠菜～一下。First, scald the spinach.

超　chāo　① exceed; surpass; overtake: 赶先进，～先进 catch up with and surpass the advanced／亩产～千斤 produce over 1,000 *jin* per *mu*; exceed 1,000 *jin* in per *mu* yield ② ultra; super; extra: 超高温 chāogāowēn ③ transcend; go beyond: ～现实 transcend realism

超编　chāobiān　overstaff: ～人员 excess personnel

超产　chāochǎn　overfulfil a production target (*or* quota): ～百分之二十 exceed the production quota by 20%

超产粮　chāochǎnliáng　grain output in excess of a production target

超常　chāocháng　be above average; be above the common run: 智力～ be a person of extraordinary intelligence

超车　chāochē　overtake (a car, a person in a dream, etc.): 别～, 对面来车了! Don't try to overtake—there's a car coming the other way.／不准～! No overtaking! *or* No passing!

超尘拔俗　chāochén-báosú　avoid earthly concerns and hold oneself aloof from the vulgar

超出　chāochū　overstep; go beyond; exceed: ～范围 go beyond the scope (*or* bounds)／～定额 exceed the quota／～预料 exceed one's expectations／我们今天仍然远没有～社会主义初级阶段。We still have a long way to go before we can advance beyond the primary stage of socialism.

超导　chāodǎo　*phys.* superconduction

超导材料　chāodǎocáiliào　*phys.* superconductor

超导电性　chāodǎodiànxìng　*phys.* superconductivity

超导体　chāodǎotǐ　*phys.* superconductor

超等　chāoděng　of superior grade; extra fine: ～质量 extra good quality; superfine

超低空飞行　chāodīkōng fēixíng　minimum altitude flying; hedgehopping

超低量喷雾器　chāodīliàng pēnwùqì　ultra-low-volume sprayer

超低温　chāodīwēn　ultralow temperature

超度　chāodù　redeem lost souls by making offerings and saying prayers

超短波　chāoduǎnbō　ultrashort wave

超短裙　chāoduǎnqún　miniskirt

超额　chāo'é　above quota: ～完成生产指标 overfulfil the production quota; surpass the production target

超额利润　chāo'é lìrùn　superprofit

超额剩余价值　chāo'é shèngyú jiàzhí　excess surplus value

超凡　chāofán　① transcend the worldly ② out of the ordinary; extraordinary; uncommon

超凡入圣　chāofán-rùshèng　transcend worldliness and attain holiness

超负荷　chāofùhè　excess load; overload

超高频　chāogāopín　ultrahigh frequency (uhf): ～变压器 ultrahigh-frequency transformer

超高温　chāogāowēn　superhigh temperature

超高压　chāogāoyā　① *phys.* superhigh pressure ② *elec.* extrahigh voltage (*or* tension): ～线路带电作业

working on live extrahigh tension power lines

超高真空 chāogāozhēnkōng ultrahigh vacuum

超过 chāoguò outstrip; surpass; exceed: ～规定的速度 exceed the speed limit / ～限度 go beyond the limit / ～历史最高水平 top all previous records / ～世界先进水平 surpass advanced world levels / 有利条件～困难条件。 The favourable conditions outweigh the difficulties. / 到会的代表已～百分之九十。 More than 90 per cent of the delegates to the conference have arrived.

超级 chāojí super: ～间谍 superspy

超级大国 chāojí dàguó superpower

超级公路 chāojí gōnglù superhighway

超级市场 chāojí shìchǎng supermarket

超级油轮 chāojí yóulún supertanker

超假 chāojià overstay one's leave

超阶级 chāojiējí transcend classes

超经济剥削 chāojīngjì bōxuē extraeconomic exploitation

超巨星 chāojùxīng astron. supergiant star

超绝 chāojué unique; superb; extraordinary: 技艺～ exhibit superb skill

超龄 chāolíng overage: 因为她已～，那家公司没有要她。 The company wouldn't have her because she was overage.

超伦 chāolún be above the rank and file

超期服役 chāoqī fúyì mil. extended active duty; extended service in the army

超迁 chāoqiān formal (of an official) be promoted more than one grade at a time

超前 chāoqián elec. lead

超前角 chāoqiánjiǎo elec. angle of lead

超群 chāoqún head and shoulders above all others; preeminent: 武艺～ be extremely skilful in martial arts

超群绝伦 chāoqún-juélún incomparably superior; preeminent

超然 chāorán aloof; detached: 他对那件事持～的态度。 He took a detached attitude to the matter.

超然物外 chāorán wù wài hold oneself aloof from the world; be above worldly considerations; stay away from the scene of contention

超人 chāorén ① be out of the common run: ～的记忆力 exceptionally good memory ② superman (as defined by Nietzsche)

超深井 chāoshēnjǐng petroleum extradeep well

超升 chāoshēng Buddhism (of a dead person's soul) rise to the Western Paradise

超生 chāoshēng ① Buddhism be reincarnated ② spare sb.'s life; be merciful: 笔下超生 bǐ xià chāoshēng

超声波 chāoshēngbō ultrasonic (wave); supersonic (wave): ～探伤仪 ultrasonic flaw detector

超声波疗法 chāoshēngbō liáofǎ ultrasonic therapy

超声物理学 chāoshēng wùlǐxué ultrasonic physics

超声学 chāoshēngxué ultrasonics

超速 chāosù ① exceed the speed limit ② hypervelocity

超速粒子 chāosù lìzǐ phys. hypervelocity particle

超脱 chāotuō ① unconventional; original: 他的字，信笔写来，十分～。 His effortless calligraphy has an unconventional grace of its own. ② be detached; stand (or hold, keep) aloof: ～现实是不可能的。 It's impossible to detach oneself from reality.

超外差 chāowàichā electron. superheterodyne; superhet

超外差式收音机 chāowàichāshì shōuyīnjī superheterodyne (radio set)

超细纤维 chāoxì xiānwéi superfine fibre

超显微镜 chāoxiǎnwēijìng ultramicroscope

超现实主义 chāoxiànshízhǔyì surrealism

超小型管 chāoxiǎoxíngguǎn electron. subminiature tube

超新星 chāoxīnxīng astron. supernova

超逸 chāoyì unconventionally graceful; free and natural

超音速 chāoyīnsù supersonic speed

超音速喷气机 chāoyīnsù pēnqìjī superjet

超音速战斗机 chāoyīnsù zhàndòujī supersonic fighter-plane; supersonic fighter

超铀元素 chāoyóu yuánsù transuranic (or transuranium) element

超员 chāoyuán (of a conveyance, etc.) exceed seating capacity; be overloaded: ～六人 exceed seating capacity by six passengers

超越 chāoyuè surmount; overstep; transcend; surpass: ～障碍 surmount an obstacle / ～职权范围 go beyond one's terms of reference; overstep one's authority / 该代理人～了代理权限。 The agent exceeded his power.

超越射击 chāoyuè shèjī mil. overhead fire

超载 chāozài transportation overload: ～能力 overload capacity

超支 chāozhī overspend: 从不～ never live beyond one's income

超重 chāozhòng ① overload ② overweight: ～信件 overweight letter / ～行李 excess luggage

超重量级 chāozhòngliàngjí sports super-heavyweight

超重氢 chāozhòngqīng chem. tritium (T or H³)

超轴 chāozhóu railway over haulage: ～牵引 trains hauling above-normal tonnage

超擢 chāozhuó promote sb. more than one grade at a time

超子 chāozǐ phys. hyperon

超自然 chāozìrán supernatural

剿(勦)

chāo formal plagiarize ——see also jiǎo

剿袭 chāoxí plagiarize

cháo

晁(鼂)

Cháo a surname

巢

cháo nest (of birds, ants, etc.): 小鸟回～了。 The bird has returned to the nest.

巢菜 cháocài common vetch

巢蛾 cháo'é ermine moth

巢居 cháojū dwell in trees

巢鼠 cháoshǔ harvest mouse

巢穴 cháoxué lair; den; nest; hideout: 匪徒的～ a bandits' lair

朝

cháo ① royal court; government: 上朝 shàngcháo ② dynasty: 唐～ the Tang Dynasty ③ (a sovereign's) reign: 康熙～ the reign of Emperor Kangxi ④ an assembly held by a sovereign; court: 早～ a morning court held by a sovereign ⑤ make a pilgrimage to: 朝圣 cháoshèng ⑥ prep. facing; towards: ～南走 go southward / 他背～我站着。 He stood there with his back towards me. / 这门～里开还是～外开? Does the door open inwards or outwards? ——see also zhāo

朝拜 cháobài ① make obeisances to (a sovereign) ② pay religious homage to; worship: 这座寺庙常有善男信女来～。 Devotees often come to this temple to worship.

朝臣 cháochén courtier

朝代 cháodài dynasty

朝顶 cháodǐng (of Buddhists) make a pilgrimage to a

temple on a mountain

朝奉 cháofèng *old* a term of address for a rich man or a pawnshop assistant

朝服 cháofú court dress

朝贡 cháogòng (of envoys from a vassal state or a foreign country) present tribute to an emperor

朝见 cháojiàn have an audience with a sovereign: 进宫～皇上 be presented at court

朝觐 cháojìn ① *formal* have an audience with a sovereign ② go on a pilgrimage to a shrine or a sacred place

朝山 cháoshān (of Buddhists) make a pilgrimage to a temple on a famous mountain

朝圣 cháoshèng (of religious people) make a pilgrimage to a sacred place

朝廷 cháotíng ① royal or imperial court ② royal or imperial government

朝鲜 Cháoxiǎn Korea

朝鲜人 Cháoxiǎnrén Korean

朝鲜语 Cháoxiǎnyǔ Korean (language)

朝鲜族 Cháoxiǎnzú ① the Korean nationality, or the Koreans, distributed over Jilin, Heilongjiang and Liaoning Provinces ② the Koreans (of Korea)

朝香 cháoxiāng go to a temple to burn incense

朝向 cháoxiàng turn towards; face: 向日葵总是～太阳。 Sunflowers always turn towards the sun.

朝阳 cháoyáng have a sunny, usu. southern, exposure: 这间屋～。 The room has a southern exposure. ——see also zhāoyáng

朝阳花 cháoyánghuā sunflower

朝野 cháo-yě ① the court and the commonalty ② the government and the public

朝政 cháozhèng (in imperial times) court administration; affairs of state: ～日非，人心思乱。 Court administration continued to worsen, and men's thoughts turned to rebellion.

朝中有人好做官 cháozhōng yǒu rén hǎo zuòguān having a friend at court helps an official

朝珠 cháozhū a string of coral or agate beads worn by court officials of the Qing Dynasty

潮[1] cháo ① tide: 早～ morning tide / 花如海，歌如～。 A sea of flowers; a tidal wave of songs. ② social upsurge; current; tide: 工潮 gōngcháo / 思潮 sīcháo ③ damp; moist: 火柴～了。 The matches have got damp. / 这屋子太～。 The room is too damp.

潮[2] Cháo short for 潮州 Chaozhou (a prefecture with its seat in modern 潮安 Chao'an, Guangdong Province)

潮红 cháohóng flush (of the face)

潮呼呼 cháohūhū damp; dank; clammy: 下了七八天雨，屋子里什么都是～的。 After a week's rain, everything in the house became damp and clammy.

潮解 cháojiě *chem.* deliquescence

潮剧 cháojù Chao opera (a local opera popular in Chao'an 潮安 and Shantou 汕头 in Guangdong Province)

潮流 cháoliú ① tide; tidal current ② trend: 历史～ historical trend / 顺应世界之～ adapt oneself to (or go along with) world trends

潮气 cháoqì moisture in the air; humidity: 仓库里～太大，粮食就容易发霉。 The grain is liable to mildew when the humidity in the barn is too high.

潮热 cháorè *Chin. med.* hectic fever

潮湿 cháoshī moist; damp: 这间屋子太～，不适宜住人。 This room is too damp to live in.

潮水 cháoshuǐ tidewater; tide: ～上涨了。 The tide is coming in. / 欢乐的人群～般地涌向天安门广场。 Crowds of joyous people streamed into Tian'anmen Square from all directions.

潮位 cháowèi the level of the tidal current at its flow or ebb; tidemark

潮汐 cháoxī morning and evening tides

潮汐表 cháoxībiǎo tide table

潮汐测站 cháoxīcèzhàn tide station

潮汐能 cháoxīnéng tidal energy

潮信 cháoxìn tidewater; tide

潮汛 cháoxùn spring tide

潮涌 cháoyǒng roll like the tide: 心事如～ one's mind seething with all kinds of thoughts

嘲（謿）

cháo ridicule; deride: 解嘲 jiěcháo /

嘲弄 cháonòng

嘲讽 cháofěng sneer at; taunt: 她带着～的神情斜了他一眼。 She gave him a sideway glance with a sneering look on her face.

嘲弄 cháonòng mock; poke fun at: ～历史的人必将被历史所～。 Those who mock history will be mocked by history.

嘲笑 cháoxiào ridicule; deride; jeer at; laugh at: 反正我觉得该做的就做，不别人～。 I will do what I think I should do and fear no ridicule.

chǎo

吵 chǎo ① make a noise: 别～！ Don't make so much noise! / ～得慌 terribly noisy / 瞧，孩子被你们～醒了。 Look! You've woken the child. / 别～他。 Don't disturb him. ② quarrel; wrangle; squabble: 不要为一点小事就～起来。 Don't squabble over trifles. / 我不跟他～。 I will not quarrel with him. / ～翻了天 kick up a terrific row ——see also chāo

吵架 chǎojià quarrel; have a row; wrangle: 我跟他～了。 I had a quarrel with him.

吵闹 chǎonào ① wrangle; kick up a row: 他们俩各不相让，～不休。 As neither of them was willing to give ground, they quarrelled on and on. ② harass; disturb: 这孩子～得我整整一上午不得安宁。 The child has been harassing me all morning. ③ din; hubbub: 院子里一片～声。 A hubbub was heard in the courtyard.

吵嚷 chǎorǎng make a racket; shout in confusion; clamour

吵嘴 chǎozuǐ quarrel; bicker: 她从来不跟别人～。 She has never quarrelled with anybody.

炒 chǎo ① stir-fry; *sauté*: ～肉丝 stir-fried shredded pork / ～黄瓜 *sautéed* cucumber / ～鸡蛋 scrambled eggs ② roast while stirring: 糖～栗子 chestnuts roasted (in sand) with brown sugar / ～花生 roasted peanuts ③ *inf.* speculate (on the stock exchange, etc.): ～股票(汇) speculate in shares (foreign exchange)

炒菜 chǎocài ① make dishes: 我～，你做饭。 I'll make the dishes while you cook the rice. ② a stir-fried dish: 我要了两个～一个汤。 I ordered two dishes and a soup.

炒货 chǎohuò roasted seeds and nuts

炒冷饭 chǎo lěngfàn stir-fry leftover rice—say or do the same old thing; dish up the same old stuff; rehash

炒买炒卖 chǎomǎi-chǎomài buy quick and sell quick; speculate

炒米 chǎomǐ ① parched rice ② millet stir-fried in butter (staple food of the Mongolians)

炒米花 chǎomǐhuā puffed rice

炒面 chǎomiàn ① fried noodles with shredded meat and vegetables; *chow mein* ② parched flour

炒勺 chǎosháo round-bottomed frying pan; *wok*

炒鱿鱼 chǎoyóuyú *inf.* give sb. the sack; sack; fire: 被～ get the sack

chào

耖 chào ① a harrow-like implement for pulverizing soil ② level land with such an implement

chē

车(車) chē ① vehicle: ～已经开了。The car (bus, etc.) has already left. / 骑～ ride a bike ② a wheeled instrument: 纺车 fǎngchē / 水车 shuǐchē ③ machine: 这台～停了。This machine has stopped. ④ lathe; turn: ～机器零件 lathe a machine part / ～光 smooth sth. on a lathe ⑤ lift water by waterwheel: 把河里的水～到稻田里。Lift some water from the river into the paddy fields. ⑥ (Chē) a surname ——see also jū

车把 chēbǎ handlebars (of a bicycle, motor cycle, etc.); shaft (of a wheelbarrow, handcart, etc.)

车把式 chēbǎshi (also 车把势 chēbǎshi) cart-driver; carter

车床 chēchuáng lathe: 多刀～ multicut lathe

车次 chēcì ① train number ② coach number (indicating order of departure)

车带 chēdài *inf.* tyre

车刀 chēdāo lathe tool; turning tool: 木工～ wood turning tool

车到山前必有路 chē dào shānqián bì yǒu lù the cart will find its way round the hill when it gets there—things will eventually sort themselves out

车道 chēdào (traffic) lane; roadway

车道沟 chēdàogōu ① rut; furrow; groove ② a rutted path

车灯 chēdēng general name for lights on a vehicle (e.g. headlights, bicycle lamp, etc.)

车队 chēduì motorcade

车费 chēfèi (passenger's) fare: 到动物园～多少? What's the fare to the Zoo?

车夫 chēfū *old* carter; driver; rickshaw puller; chauffeur

车工 chēgōng ① lathe work ② turner; lathe operator: ～车间 turning shop

车沟 chēgōu rut; furrow; groove

车钩 chēgōu *railway* coupling

车轱辘 chēgūlu *inf.* wheel (of a vehicle)

车轱辘话 chēgūluhuà *dial.* repetitive talk: 他的～说起来没完。You'd never hear the last of his long-winded, repetitious talk.

车号 chēhào license number (of a vehicle)

车祸 chēhuò traffic accident; road accident: 昨天出了两起～, 死伤四人。There were two traffic accidents yesterday, with four casualties.

车技 chējì *acrob.* trick-cycling

车驾 chējià imperial carriage

车架 chējià frame (of a car, bicycle, etc.)

车间 chējiān workshop; shop

车库 chēkù garage

车辆 chēliàng vehicles: 来往～ traffic / 铁路机车及～ rolling stock

车辆周转率 chēliàng zhōuzhuǎnlǜ *railway* average turnround rate of rolling stock

车裂 chēliè tearing apart by five chariots (a punish-ment in ancient China)

车流 chēliú ① traffic: ～不息 an incessant stream of vehicles—heavy traffic ② the rate of traffic flow

车轮 chēlún wheel (of a vehicle)

车轮战 chēlúnzhàn the tactic of several persons taking turns in fighting one opponent to tire him out

车马费 chēmǎfèi travel allowance

车马坑 chēmǎkēng *archaeol.* chariot pit

车马盈门 chē mǎ yíngmén the gateway is thronged with horses and carriages; the house is honoured with a host of rich and distinguished guests

车幔 chēmàn same as 车帷 chēwéi

车牌 chēpái license plate

车篷 chēpéng awning for a vehicle

车皮 chēpí railway wagon or carriage; flatcar or freight car: 两～货物 two freight cars of goods

车票 chēpiào train or bus ticket; ticket

车前草 chēqiáncǎo *bot.* Asiatic plantain (*Plantago asiatica*)

车钱 chēqian *inf.* (passenger's) fare

车身 chēshēn the body of a vehicle

车水马龙 chēshuǐ-mǎlóng an incessant stream of horses and carriages—heavy traffic: 那天真是～, 游览的人络绎不绝。The tourist traffic was very busy that day. There was an endless stream of visitors. / 门前～。The courtyard was thronged with visitors.

车速 chēsù speed of a motor vehicle: ～太快! The car is going too fast! / 现在～为每小时五十公里。The car is travelling at 50 km. per hour.

车胎 chētāi tyre

车条 chētiáo *inf.* spokes (of a wheel)

车头 chētóu ① the front of a vehicle ② engine (of a train); locomotive

车帷 chēwéi curtain in a carriage

车尾 chēwěi the rear of a vehicle

车厢 chēxiāng railway carriage; railroad car

车削 chēxiāo *mech.* turning

车辕 chēyuán shaft (of a cart, etc.)

车载斗量 chēzài-dǒuliáng enough to fill carts and be measured by the bushel—common and numerous: 在我们那里像我这样的人～, 不可胜数。Where I come from, people like me come by the bushel.

车闸 chēzhá brake (of a car, bicycle, etc.): 我的～不灵, 要修理一下。My brakes don't work very well and need to be fixed.

车站 chēzhàn station; depot; stop

车照 chēzhào driving license

车辙 chēzhé rut

车轴 chēzhóu axletree; axle

车资 chēzī same as 车钱 chēqian

车子 chēzi ① a small vehicle (such as a car, pushcart, etc.) ② *dial.* bicycle

砗 chē see below

砗磲 chēqú *zool.* giant clam; tridacna

chě

尺 chě *mus.* a note of the scale in *gongchepu* (工尺谱), corresponding to 2 in numbered musical notation ——see also chǐ

扯(撦) chě ① pull: ～着他的袖子 pull him by the sleeve / ～住绳子不放 hold onto the rope / ～着嗓子喊 shout at the top of one's voice / 这是两个问题, 不能往一块儿～。These two questions should not be lumped together. ② tear: 把信～得粉碎 tear the letter

to pieces / ～下假面具 tear off the mask ③ *inf.* buy (cloth, thread, etc.): ～三尺布 buy three *chi* of cloth ④ chat; gossip: 咱俩好好～一～。Let's have a good chat. / 别～远了。Don't wander from the subject. *or* Stick to the point.

扯白 chěbái　*dial.* tell a lie; lie

扯淡 chědàn　*dial.* talk nonsense: 别瞎～! Don't talk nonsense!

扯后腿 chě hòutuǐ　hold sb. back (from action); be a drag on sb.; be a hindrance to sb.: 他要去参军，你不要扯他的后腿。He wants to enlist. Don't try to hold him back. / 不发展教育，就会扯现代化的后腿。Arrested development in education will hinder modernization.

扯谎 chěhuǎng　tell a lie or fib; lie: 我对他扯了个谎，他真信了。I told him a fib, and he swallowed it whole.

扯家常 chě jiācháng　talk about everyday matters; engage in small talk; chitchat

扯皮 chěpí　dispute over trifles; argue back and forth; bicker: 政府机构互相～ government organizations pass the buck to each other

扯臊 chěsào　*dial.* talk sheer nonsense; tell shameless lies: 尽是瞎～。This is utter nonsense! *or* Bare-faced lies!

扯谈 chětán　engage in small talk; chitchat

扯腿 chětuǐ　① same as 扯后腿 chě hòutuǐ ② (usu. used in) ～就跑 immediately take to one's heels

chè

彻(徹)
chè　thorough; penetrating: 透彻 tòuchè / 彻骨 chègǔ

彻查 chèchá　make a thorough investigation (of a case)

彻底 chèdǐ　thorough; thoroughgoing: 屋子打扫得很～。The room has been given a thorough cleaning. / ～失败 end in utter failure / ～地为人民的利益工作 work entirely in the people's interests / ～性 (degree of) thoroughness

彻骨 chègǔ　penetrate to the bone: 寒风～。The bitter wind chills one to the bone.

彻头彻尾 chètóu-chèwěi　out and out; through and through; downright: ～的坏蛋 an out-and-out villian / ～的骗局 a downright (*or* sheer) fraud; deception from beginning to end / ～的谎言 an absolute lie

彻悟 chèwù　fully recognize the truth; come to understand thoroughly

彻夜 chèyè　all night; all through the night; from dusk to dawn: ～不眠 lie awake all night / 工地上灯火～明。The lights were ablaze at the worksite all through the night.

坼
chè　*formal* split open; crack: 天旱地～。The ground cracked after a long drought.

坼裂 chèliè　*formal* split open; crack

掣
chè　① pull; tug: 掣肘 chèzhǒu ② draw: 他赶紧～回手去。He quickly drew back his hand. ③ flash past: 电～雷鸣。Lightning flashed and thunder rolled.

掣肘 chèzhǒu　hold sb. back by the elbow—impede sb. from doing sth.: 这件事办得很顺利，没有人～。As there was no one making things difficult for us, we settled the matter smoothly.

澈
chè　(of water) clear; limpid: 清澈 qīngchè

澈底 chèdǐ　same as 彻底 chèdǐ

撤
chè　① remove; take away: 把障碍物～了 remove the obstacle / 把盘子、碗～了 clear away the

dishes ② dismiss: 他的职务给～了。He was dismissed from his post. ③ withdraw; evacuate: 向后～ withdraw; retreat / 把伤员～走 evacuate the wounded

撤兵 chèbīng　withdraw troops

撤差 chèchāi　*old* dismiss (*or* discharge) sb. from his official post; remove sb. from office

撤除 chèchú　remove; dismantle: ～军事设施 dismantle military installations / 外国空军基地应立即～。Foreign air bases should be removed immediately.

撤佃 chèdiàn　(of a landlord) take back the land rented to a tenant

撤防 chèfáng　withdraw a garrison; withdraw from a defended position

撤换 chèhuàn　dismiss and replace; recall; replace

撤回 chèhuí　① recall; withdraw: ～军队 recall troops / ～步哨 withdraw the guard ② revoke; retract; withdraw: ～起诉 withdraw charges; revoke a court action / ～提案 withdraw a proposal

撤军 chèjūn　withdraw troops

撤离 chèlí　withdraw from; leave; evacuate: ～阵地 abandon a position / ～现场 quit the scene / ～一座城市 evacuate a city

撤诉 chèsù　(of the plaintiff) withdraw an accusation; drop a lawsuit

撤退 chètuì　withdraw; pull out: 向安全地区～ withdraw to a safe place / ～方向 the line of withdrawal / 安全～ make good one's retreat

撤席 chèxí　clear the table (after a feast): ～以后，端上水果。Fruits were served after the table was cleared.

撤消 chèxiāo　(also 撤销 chèxiāo) cancel; rescind; revoke: ～职务 dismiss sb. from his post / ～一项决议 annul a decision / ～处分 rescind (*or* annul) a penalty / ～原计划 rescind the original plan / ～命令 countermand an order / ～法令 repeal a decree

撤职 chèzhí　dismiss (*or* discharge) sb. from his post; remove sb. from office: ～查办 discharge sb. from his post and prosecute him

撤走 chèzǒu　withdraw; leave: ～军用物资 withdraw and transfer military supplies / ～使馆人员家属 withdraw the families of the embassy staff

chēn

抻(捵)
chēn　*inf.* pull out; draw out; stretch: 把你的衣服～一～。Stretch and smooth out your clothes.

抻面 chēnmiàn　① hand-pulled noodles ② make noodles by drawing out the dough by hand: 他～抻得好极了。He's really good at making hand-pulled noodles.

琛
chēn　*formal* treasure

嗔
chēn　① be angry; be displeased: 生～ get angry ② be annoyed (with sb.): 嗔斥 chēnchì

嗔斥 chēnchì　rebuke; reproach; scold

嗔怪 chēnguài　blame; rebuke

嗔怒 chēnnù　get angry

嗔色 chēnsè　an angry or sullen look: 微露～ look somewhat displeased / 她面带～。She looks sullen. *or* She's wearing a sullen expression.

嗔着 chēnzhe　*inf.* blame sb. for sth.: 他～我说错了话。He blamed me for saying the wrong thing.

瞋
chēn　*formal* stare angrily; glare

瞋目 chēnmù　stare angrily; glare; glower

瞋目而视 chēnmù ér shì　stare at sb. angrily; glare defiance or hatred at sb.

chén

尘(塵) chén ① dust; dirt: 灰尘 huīchén ② this world: 红尘 hóngchén

尘埃 chén'āi dust

尘埃传染 chén'āi chuánrǎn *med.* dust infection

尘暴 chénbào dust storm

尘凡 chénfán the present world; the mortal world

尘肺 chénfèi *med.* pneumoconiosis

尘封 chénfēng be covered with dust; be dust-laden

尘垢 chéngòu dust and dirt; dirt

尘海 chénhǎi same as 尘世 chénshì

尘寰 chénhuán same as 尘世 chénshì

尘芥 chénjiè dust and weed—trifles; rubbish; garbage

尘世 chénshì this world; this mortal life

尘俗 chénsú ① this world; this mortal life ② mundane affairs

尘土 chéntǔ dust: 卡车开过，～飞扬。The truck stirred up a cloud of dust as it drove by. / 满身～ be covered all over with dust

尘嚣 chénxiāo (also 尘喧 chénxuān) hubbub; uproar

尘烟 chényān (also 尘雾 chénwù) ① a cloud of dust: ～滚滚 clouds of dust churning ② smoke and dust: ～弥漫 be heavy with smoke and dust

尘缘 chényuán the bonds of this world; carnal thoughts: ～未断 have not broken free the bonds of this world

臣 chén ① an official under a feudal ruler; subject; minister: 君～ the monarch and his subjects ② your servant (a form of self-address used by a subject when speaking to a ruler)

臣服 chénfú *formal* ① submit oneself to the rule of; acknowledge allegiance to ② serve a ruler as his subject

臣僚 chénliáo civil and military officials in feudal times

臣民 chénmín subjects of a feudal ruler

臣属 chénshǔ ① an official in feudal times ② same as 臣服 chénfú①

臣子 chénzǐ an official in feudal times

沉(沈) chén ① sink: 船～了。The boat sank. / ～底儿 sink to the bottom / 月落星～。The moon is down and the stars have set. ② (fig.) keep down; lower; sink: ～下脸来 pull a long face; put on a serious expression / 我的心直往下～。My heart sank. ③ deep; profound: 睡得很～ be in a deep sleep; be fast asleep; sleep like a log; sleep soundly ④ heavy: 这只箱子很～。This trunk is very heavy. ⑤ feel heavy: 我觉得头有点～。My head feels a bit heavy. / 胳膊～ have a stiff arm / 两条腿～得迈不动步。My legs were heavy and I could hardly move a step.

沉沉 chénchén ① heavy: 穗子～地垂下来。The ears hang heavy on the stalks. ② deep: ～入睡 sink into a deep sleep / 暮霭～。Dusk is falling.

沉甸甸 chéndiàndiàn heavy: ～的一口袋稻种 a heavy sack of rice seed / ～的谷穗 heavy ears of millet / 任务还没有完成，我心里老是～的。The thought of the unfinished task weighed heavily on my mind.

沉淀 chéndiàn form a sediment; precipitate: 墨水～了。There is some sediment in the ink. / 水太浑啦，～一下再用。The water is muddy; let it settle for a while.

沉淀池 chéndiànchí *environ. protec.* precipitating tank

沉淀剂 chéndiànjì *chem.* precipitating agent

沉淀物 chéndiànwù sediment; precipitate

沉浮 chénfú ① sink and rise; bob on water ② ups and downs of fortune; vicissitudes: 宦海～ vicissitudes of an official career

沉痼 chéngù *formal* ① a chronic disease; a serious illness ② an incurable bad habit

沉积 chénjī ① deposit: 泥沙～河底。The silt is deposited in the riverbed. ② *geol.* (also 沉积作用 chénjī zuòyòng) sedimentation: ～旋回 cycle of sedimentation

沉积物 chénjīwù deposit; sediment

沉积岩 chénjīyán sedimentary rock

沉寂 chénjì ① quiet; still: ～的深夜 in the still of (the) night / 入夜后，四野一片～。Night fell, and it was all quiet in the open country. ② no news: 消息～。There has been no news whatsoever.

沉降 chénjiàng subside

沉降缝 chénjiàngfèng *archit.* settlement joint

沉浸 chénjìn be immersed in; be steeped in; be permeated with: ～在幸福的回忆中 be immersed in happy memories / 整个首都～在节日的欢乐气氛中。The entire capital was permeated with a festive atmosphere.

沉井 chénjǐng *archit.* open caisson

沉静 chénjìng ① quiet; calm: 夜深了，村子里～下来。It was late at night, and all was quiet in the village. ② calm; serene; placid: ～的神色 a serene look / 这姑娘性格～。She is a placid girl.

沉疴 chénkē *formal* a severe and lingering illness; a serious chronic disease

沉沦 chénlún sink into vice, degradation, depravity, etc.

沉落 chénluò sink; fall: 心绪～ be in very low spirits; be downhearted

沉脉 chénmài *Chin. med.* deep pulse (which can be felt only by pressing hard)

沉闷 chénmèn ① (of weather, atmosphere, etc.) dreary; gloomy; oppressive; depressing: 那里的气氛太～了，令人无法忍受。The atmosphere there is unbearably oppressive. ② depressed; in low spirits: 心情～ feel depressed ③ not outgoing; withdrawn: 他这个人很～。He's rather withdrawn.

沉迷 chénmí be confused; be bewildered

沉眠 chénmián sleep soundly; be fast asleep

沉湎 chénmiǎn *formal* indulge in; wallow in; be given to: ～于酒 be given to heavy drinking

沉没 chénmò sink; founder: 军舰被鱼雷击中，立即～。The warship was torpedoed and sank at once. / 渔船于暴风雨中～。The fishing boat foundered in a hurricane.

沉默 chénmò ① reticent; taciturn; uncommunicative: 从此，他变得更～了。He has become even more reticent since then. ② silent: 保持～ remain silent / 他～了一会儿又继续说下去。After a moment's silence he went on.

沉默寡言 chénmò-guǎyán reticent; taciturn; uncommunicative: 他一向～。He has always been a man of few words.

沉溺 chénnì wallow or indulge in (vices, etc.): ～于声色 wallow in sensual pleasures

沉潜 chénqián ① stay or hide under water: 这种鱼常～于海底。This kind of fish usually stays at the bottom of the sea. ② *formal* reserved; self-possessed ③ concentrate one's energies (on work, study, etc.): ～在研究工作中 devote oneself to research work

沉砂池 chénshāchí *environ. protec.* grit chamber

沉睡 chénshuì be sunk in sleep; be fast asleep; be sound asleep

沉思 chénsī ponder; meditate; be lost in thought: 他为这个问题～了好久。He pondered over this problem for a long time. / 陷入～之中 be lost in thought; be deep in meditation

沉潭 chéntán drown a person in a pond (a clan punishment in former times)

沉痛 chéntòng ① with a deep feeling of grief or remorse; heavy at heart: 怀着～的心情 be deeply grieved／表示～的哀悼 express profound condolences／他对自己的错误感到十分～。He felt deep remorse for his error. ② deeply felt; bitter: 应该接受这个～的教训。It is necessary to learn a lesson from this bitter experience.

沉稳 chénwěn ① steady; staid; sedate: 这个人很～，处理问题细密周到。A sober and steady type, he is meticulous and thoughtful in handling matters. ② untroubled; sound: 睡得很～ sleep soundly (or peacefully)

沉陷 chénxiàn ① sink; cave in: 地震后路基～了。The earthquake made the roadbed cave in. ② archit. settlement: 不均匀～ unequal settlement

沉香 chénxiāng bot. agalloch eaglewood (Aquilaria agallocha; Aquilaria sinensis)

沉箱 chénxiāng archit. caisson

沉毅 chényì steady and strong: 这位将军～果断。The general was steady and resolute.

沉吟 chényín mutter to oneself, unable to make up one's mind: 他～了一会儿才去打电话。He hesitated for a while before he made the phone call.

沉吟不决 chényín bù jué hesitate; be irresolute; be undecided

沉鱼落雁 chényú-luòyàn (of feminine beauty) make fish sink and birds alight: 有～之容, 闭月羞花之貌 have features that can make fish sink and birds alight, and looks that can outshine the moon and put the flowers to shame

沉郁 chényù depressed; gloomy

沉冤 chényuān gross injustice; unrighted wrong: 他的十年～终于得到昭雪。After being a victim of gross injustice for ten long years, he was finally rehabilitated.

沉冤莫白 chényuān mò bái grievous wrongs that can never be redressed

沉渣 chénzhā ① sediment; dregs ② dregs of society

沉滞 chénzhì formal stagnant; stalemated

沉重 chénzhòng ① heavy: ～的脚步 heavy steps／～的打击 a heavy blow／心情～ with a heavy heart ② serious; critical: 病情～ critically ill

沉重儿 chénzhòngr inf. burden; heavy responsibility: 他作事不肯担一点～。He wouldn't shoulder any heavy responsibility.

沉舟侧畔千帆过, 病树前头万木春 chénzhōu cèpàn qiān fān guò, bìngshù qiántóu wàn mù chūn a thousand sails pass by the sunken ship, ten thousand saplings shoot up beyond the withered tree

沉舟破釜 chénzhōu-pòfǔ same as 破釜沉舟 pòfǔ-chénzhōu

沉住气 chénzhùqì keep calm; keep cool; be steady: ～, 等敌人靠近了再打。Steady, don't fire till the enemy come closer.／不要一听到不同意见就沉不住气。Don't get excited the moment you hear a differing opinion.／你真沉得住气。都八点了, 还不走。You're really a cool customer. It's already eight o'clock and you still don't go.

沉着 chénzhuó cool-headed; composed; steady; calm: 勇敢～ brave and steady／～应战 meet the attack calmly／引擎出了点故障, 飞行员很～, 飞机安全降落。Although he was having some trouble with the engine, the pilot kept a stiff upper lip and landed the plane safely.

沉子 chénzǐ sinker

沉滓 chénzǐ same as 沉渣 chénzhā

沉醉 chénzuì (fig.) get drunk; become intoxicated: ～在节日的欢乐里 be intoxicated with the spirit of the festival

忱 chén formal sincere feeling; true sentiment:

谢忱 xièchén／热忱 rèchén

辰[1] chén ① celestial bodies: 星辰 xīngchén ② any of the traditional twelve two-hour periods of the day: 时辰 shíchen ③ time; day; occasion: 寿辰 shòuchén

辰[2] chén the fifth of the twelve Earthly Branches (地支) (see also 干支 gān-zhī)

辰光 chénguāng dial. time; time of the day

辰砂 chénshā cinnabar; vermillion

辰时 chénshí the period of the day from 7 a.m. to 9 a.m.

辰星 Chénxīng the Chronographic Star (old name for 水星 Shuǐxīng)

陈[1] **(陳)** chén ① lay out; put on display: 陈列 chénliè ② state; explain: 此事当另函详～。The matter will be explained in detail in a separate letter.

陈[2] **(陳)** chén old; stale: ～米 old rice

陈[3] **(陳)** Chén the Chen Dynasty (557–589), one of the Southern Dynasties ② a surname

陈兵 chénbīng mass (or deploy) troops: ～边境 mass troops along the border／～百万 deploy a million troops

陈陈相因 chén chén xiāng yīn follow a set routine; stay in the same old groove

陈词[1] chéncí (also 陈辞 chéncí) present one's views: ～恳切 set forth one's opinions in an earnest tone

陈词[2] chéncí stale words; hackneyed words

陈词滥调 chéncí-làndiào hackneyed and stereotyped expressions; clichés

陈醋 chéncù mature vinegar

陈放 chénfàng lay out; set out; display: 条案上～着香炉、烛台和各色供品。On the long narrow table were set out an incense burner, candlesticks, and offerings of all kinds.

陈腐 chénfǔ old and decayed; stale; outworn: ～的词句 stale phrases／重男轻女的～观念 the outworn concept of regarding men as superior to women

陈谷子烂芝麻 chéngǔzi-lànzhīma old millet and stale sesame—stale topics of conversation

陈规 chénguī outmoded conventions: 打破～ break with outmoded conventions

陈规陋习 chénguī-lòuxí outmoded regulations and irrational practices; bad customs and habits

陈货 chénhuò old stock; shopworn goods

陈迹 chénjì a thing of the past

陈酒 chénjiǔ old wine; mellow wine

陈旧 chénjiù outmoded; obsolete; old-fashioned; out-of-date: ～的观点 an outmoded notion／～的设备 outdated equipment／～的词语 obsolete words and expressions

陈列 chénliè display; set out; exhibit: 玻璃柜里～着各种矿物标本。Ore specimens are on display in showcases.

陈列馆 chénlièguǎn exhibition hall

陈列柜 chénlièguì showcase

陈列品 chénlièpǐn exhibits; articles on display

陈列室 chénlièshì exhibition room; showroom

陈年 chénnián of long standing; preserved for a long time: ～老酒 old vintage wine／～老帐 an old (or longstanding) debt

陈皮 chénpí Chin. med. dried tangerine or orange peel

陈皮梅 chénpíméi preserved prune

陈情 chénqíng formal give a full account

陈请 chénqǐng plead; petition

陈设 chénshè ① display; set out: 屋子里～着几件工艺品。There is some artware set out in the room. ② furnishings: 房间里的～朴素大方。The room was furnished simply and in good taste.

陈胜吴广起义 Chén Shèng-Wú Guǎng Qǐyì the Chen Sheng-Wu Guang Uprising (209 B.C.), the first large-scale peasant uprising in China's history

陈述 chénshù state: ～自己的意见 state one's views

陈述句 chénshùjù gram. declarative sentence

陈说 chénshuō state; explain: ～利害 explain the advantages and disadvantages (of a situation, course of action, etc.)

陈诉 chénsù state; recount: ～委屈 state one's grievances

陈言[1] chényán speak out; air one's views

陈言[2] chényán hackneyed phrases: 写文章务去～。Hackneyed words and expressions should be avoided in writing.

陈帐 chénzhàng old debts; longstanding debts: ～未清, 免开尊口。While old debts are still unpaid, you might as well save your breath.

宸 chén formal ① a great mansion ② imperial palace ③ the throne; the emperor

宸衷 chénzhōng the emperor's wishes

晨 chén morning: 清晨 qīngchén

晨操 chéncāo morning exercises

晨光 chénguāng the light of the early morning sun; dawn

晨光熹微 chénguāng xīwēi the first faint rays of dawn

晨昏 chén-hūn formal morning and evening: ～定省 pay respects to one's parents in the morning and in the evening

晨夕 chén-xī morning and evening: ～相处 be together from morning till evening; be very close

晨曦 chénxī the first rays of the morning sun

晨星 chénxīng ① stars at dawn ② astron. morning star

晨钟暮鼓 chénzhōng-mùgǔ same as 暮鼓晨钟 mùgǔ-chénzhōng

谌 Chén, also Shèn a surname

chěn

碜 (硶、磣) chěn (of food) be gritty ——see also chen

chèn

衬 (襯) chèn ① line; place sth. underneath: ～着驼绒的大衣 a fleece-lined overcoat / ～上一层纸 put a piece of paper underneath / 里面～一件背心 wear a vest underneath ② lining; liner: 领～ collar lining / 袖～ cuff lining / 钢～ steel liner / 管～ liner tube ③ provide a background for; set off; serve as a foil to: 白雪～着红梅, 景色十分美丽。The red plum blossoms set off by the white snow were a beautiful sight.

衬布 chènbù lining cloth

衬层 chèncéng mech. lining

衬垫 chèndiàn mech. liner: 接合～ joint liner

衬裤 chènkù underpants; pants

衬里 chènlǐ lining

衬领 chènlǐng detachable collar (affixed to the inside of the collar of a Chinese tunic)

衬裙 chènqún underskirt; slip; petticoat

衬衫 chènshān ① shirt ② blouse

衬套 chèntào mech. bush; bushing: 隔离～ dividing bushing / 减震～ shock absorbing bushing

衬托 chèntuō set off; serve as a foil to: 红花要有绿叶～。Red flowers must have green leaves as a foil.

衬衣 chènyī ① underclothes; undergarments ② shirt

衬映 chènyìng same as 映衬 yìngchèn

衬纸 chènzhǐ slip sheet; interleaving paper

衬字 chènzì word inserted in a line of verse for balance or euphony (e.g. 那个 in 北风那个吹, 雪花那个飘。)

称 (稱) chèn fit; match; suit: 相称 xiāngchèn / 对称 duìchèn ——see also chēng

称钱 chènqián same as 趁钱 chènqián

称身 chènshēn (of a garment) fit: 这件外套你穿了挺～的。This coat fits you perfectly.

称体裁衣 chèn tǐ cái yī same as 量体裁衣 liàng tǐ cái yī

称心 chènxīn find sth. satisfactory; be gratified: 我这辆自行车买得很～。This bicycle is quite satisfactory—just the thing I want. / 这孩子一不～就发脾气。The child will kick up a row if he doesn't get his own way. / 这老人晚年过得很～。The man spent his old age in contentment.

称心如意 chènxīn-rúyì after one's own heart; very gratifying and satisfactory: ～的工作 a most satisfying job / 天底下的事未必都那么～。In this world, things don't always turn out the way you want. / 你想要什么尽管说, 我包你～。Just tell me what you want, and I'll see that your wishes are met.

称意 chènyì same as 称心 chènxīn

称愿 chènyuàn be gratified (esp. at the misfortune of a rival)

称职 chènzhí prove oneself competent at one's job; fill a post with credit; be well qualified for a post: 他在公司里担任过好几种职务, 都很～。He has held several different posts in the firm and proved himself competent at all of them.

龀 chèn formal ① grow permanent teeth ② childhood

趁 (趂) chèn ① prep. take advantage of (time, opportunity, etc.); avail oneself of: 我想～这个机会讲几句话。I'd like to take this opportunity to say a few words. / 这面～热吃吧。Eat the noodles while they are hot. / ～风起帆 set sail when the wind is fair ② dial. be possessed of; be rich in: ～好多衣服 have a large wardrobe / ～几头牲口 own a few head of cattle / 我连辆自行车都不～。I don't even own a bicycle. / 他可～啦! He's rolling in money. or He's awfully rich.

趁便 chènbiàn when it is convenient; at one's convenience: 你回去的时候, ～给我带个口信。When you go back would you take a message for me? / 我回来的路上～去书店看了看。I stopped at the bookstore on my way home.

趁火打劫 chèn huǒ dǎjié loot a burning house—take advantage of sb.'s misfortune to do him harm; fish in troubled waters

趁机 chènjī take advantage of the occasion; seize the chance: ～捣乱 seize the opportunity to make trouble

趁空 chènkòng use one's spare time; avail oneself of leisure time: 我～去看了看老王。I went to see Lao Wang when I happened to have a few minutes to spare.

趁亮儿 chènliàngr do sth. while it is light: 咱们～走吧。Let's start while it is still light.

趁钱　chènqián　*dial.*　have pots of money: 他可～啦! He's rolling in money.

趁热打铁　chèn rè dǎtiě　strike while the iron is hot

趁墒　chènshāng　sow while there is sufficient moisture in the soil

趁势　chènshì　take advantage of a favourable situation: 他越过对方后卫,～把球踢入球门。He dribbled past the full back and scored a goal.

趁手　chènshǒu　*dial.*　conveniently; without extra trouble: 请你～把门带上。Please shut the door after you.

趁水和泥　chèn shuǐ huóní　prepare the plaster when there is water—seize the opportunity

趁心　chènxīn　same as 称心 chènxīn

趁圩　chènxū　*dial.*　go to market; go to a village fair

趁愿　chènyuàn　same as 称愿 chènyuàn

趁早　chènzǎo　as early as possible; before it is too late; at the first opportunity: 咱们～动身,争取十点以前赶到。Let's start off early and try to get there by ten. / 我们还是～把场打完,免得雨淋。We'd better finish threshing as soon as possible, in case it rains. / 你脸色不好,～去看看吧。You don't look well. You'd better go and see a doctor right away.

槻(櫬)　chèn　*formal*　coffin

谶　chèn　*formal*　augury

谶纬　chènwěi　divination combined with mystical Confucianist belief (prevalent during the Eastern Han Dynasty, 25–220)

谶语　chènyǔ　a prophecy believed to have been fulfilled

chen

伧(傖)　chen　see 寒碜 (寒伧) hánchen
——see also cāng

碜(碜、硶)　chen　see 牙碜 yáchen; 寒碜 hánchen ——see also chěn

chēng

柽(檉)　chēng　see below
柽柳　chēngliǔ　*bot.*　Chinese tamarisk

称[1](稱)　chēng　① call: 我们都～他老李。We all call him Lao Li. ② name: 俗～ popular name / 青藏高原素有世界屋脊之～。The Qinghai-Xizang Plateau has long been known as the roof of the world. ③ say; state: 连声～好 say "good, good" again and again / 据外交部发言人～ according to the Foreign Ministry spokesman ④ *formal*　commend; praise: 称许 chēngxǔ

称[2](稱)　chēng　weigh: 用秤～一～。Weigh it in the balance. / 给我～一公斤苹果。I'd like one kilo of apples, please.
——see also chèn

称霸　chēngbà　seek hegemony; dominate: ～世界 dominate the world

称便　chēngbiàn　find sth. a great convenience: 商店日夜服务,群众无不～。Shops that stay open twenty-four hours a day are a great convenience to the public.

称兵　chēngbīng　*formal*　start military operations

称病　chēngbìng　claim to be ill; offer illness as an excuse; plead illness: ～辞职 resign on grounds of ill health

称臣　chēngchén　declare oneself a vassal or subject; acknowledge one's allegiance to a ruler

称贷　chēngdài　ask for a loan; borrow money

称道　chēngdào　speak approvingly of; praise; acclaim: 值得～ be praiseworthy / 无足～ not worth mentioning; of no consequence

称得起　chēngdeqǐ　deserve to be called; be worthy of the name of: 他～一位伟大的改革家。He deserves to be called a great reformer.

称帝　chēngdì　proclaim oneself emperor

称孤道寡　chēnggū-dàoguǎ　style oneself king—act like an absolute monarch

称号　chēnghào　title; name; designation: 她获得了先进工作者的～。She has won the title of advanced worker.

称呼　chēnghu　① call; address: 我该怎么～她? What should I call her? *or* How should I address her? ② a form of address: 工人中最流行的～是"师傅"。*Shifu* ("master") is the most popular form of address among workers.

称斤掂两　chēngjīn-diānliǎng　same as 掂斤播两 diānjīn-bōliǎng

称快　chēngkuài　express one's gratification; express joy and jubilation

称量　chēngliáng　weigh

称量体重　chēngliáng tǐzhòng　*sports*　weigh in

称美　chēngměi　praise

称赏　chēngshǎng　extol; speak highly of

称述　chēngshù　relate; narrate; state

称说　chēngshuō　say the name of sth.; name

称颂　chēngsòng　praise; extol; eulogize: 人人～他的崇高品德。Everyone extols his noble qualities.

称叹　chēngtàn　sigh in admiration; highly praise: 连声～ be full of praise

称王　chēngwáng　proclaim oneself king

称王称霸　chēngwáng-chēngbà　act like an overlord; lord it over; domineer

称为　chēngwéi　call or be called; be known as: 食盐在化学上～氯化钠。Sodium chloride is the chemical term for table salt.

称谓　chēngwèi　appellation; title

称羡　chēngxiàn　express one's admiration or envy: ～不已 express profuse admiration

称谢　chēngxiè　express one's thanks; thank: ～不止 thank sb. again and again

称兄道弟　chēngxiōng-dàodì　call each other brothers; be on intimate terms

称雄　chēngxióng　hold sway over a region; rule the roost: 割据～ break away from central authority and exercise local power; set up separatist rule

称许　chēngxǔ　praise; commendation: 他的工作博得普遍的～。His work received high praise from everyone.

称扬　chēngyáng　praise: 极口～ praise in highest terms

称誉　chēngyù　sing the praises of; praise; acclaim: 《国际歌》被列宁～为全世界无产阶级之歌。The *Internationale* was acclaimed by Lenin as the song of the world proletariat.

称赞　chēngzàn　praise; acclaim; commend: 我们都～她办事公道。We all praise her for her impartiality. / 他们获得全国人民的～。They have won the acclaim of the people all over the country.

琤(琤)　chēng　see below
琤琤　chēngchēng　*onom.*　a jangling, twanging, or gurgling sound

蛏(蟶)　chēng　razor clam
蛏干　chēnggān　dried razor clam
蛏田　chēngtián　razor clam farm

蛏子 chēngzi   razor clam

铛(鐺)   chēng   a shallow, flat pan; griddle ——see also dāng

撑(撐)   chēng ① prop up; support: 他一手～起身子，一手投弹。He propped himself up on one hand and threw a grenade with the other. / 两手～着下巴 rest one's chin in both hands ② push or move with a pole; pole: ～船 pole a boat; punt ③ maintain; keep up: 他～不住，笑了。He could not help laughing. / 他连着打了两场球，再打恐怕～不住劲儿了。I'm afraid he won't be able to go on with another game; he's played two in a row already. ④ open; unfurl: ～伞 open an umbrella / 把麻袋～开 hold open the sack ⑤ fill to the point of bursting: 我已经有点～，不能再吃了。I'm rather full and can't eat any more. / 别装得太多，把口袋～破了。Don't stuff the sack too full or it'll burst. ⑥ mech. brace; stay: 角～ corner brace

撑臂 chēngbì   mech. brace

撑场面 chēng chǎngmiàn (also 撑门面 chēng ménmiàn) keep up appearances: 他们为了～，借了很多钱大摆喜筵。In order to keep up appearances, they borrowed a lot of money to give a big wedding party.

撑持 chēngchí   prop up; shore up; sustain: ～局面 shore up a shaky situation

撑得慌 chēngdehuang   have eaten too much and feel uncomfortable

撑杆 chēnggān   vaulting pole

撑杆跳高 chēnggān tiàogāo   pole vault; pole jump

撑篙 chēnggāo   punt-pole

撑条 chēngtiáo   mech. stay: 斜～ diagonal stay / 横～ cross stay

撑腰 chēngyāo   support; back up; bolster up: 有他给你～，你还怕什么?He's backing you up, so what's there to fear?

撑腰打气 chēngyāo-dǎqì   bolster and pep up

瞠   chēng   formal stare

瞠乎其后 chēng hū qí hòu   stare helplessly at the vanishing back of the runner ahead—despair of catching up

瞠目 chēngmù   stare (in alarm, embarrassment, confusion, etc.): ～不知所答 stare blankly, at a loss for a suitable reply / ～相视 stare fixedly in each other's face

瞠目结舌 chēngmù-jiéshé   stare tongue-tied; stare dumbfounded

瞠然 chēngrán   staring blankly: ～木立 staring blankly transfixed to the spot / ～若失 staring blankly in a daze

瞠视 chēngshì   stare at

chéng

丞   chéng   an assistant to an official (in ancient China): 县～ county magistrate's assistant

丞相 chéngxiàng   prime minister (in ancient China); chief minister

成¹   chéng ① accomplish; succeed: 事～之后 after this is achieved / 他～不了大事。He can't accomplish anything significant. / 筐编～了。I've finished weaving the basket. ② become; turn into: 两个人～了好朋友。The two of them became good friends. / 雪化～水了。The snow melted into water. / 绿树～荫。The trees give welcome shade. ③ achievement; result: 坐享其成 zuò xiǎng qí chéng ④ fully developed or fully grown: 成人 chéngrén / 成虫 chéngchóng ⑤ established; ready-made:

成规 chéngguī / **成药** chéngyào ⑥ in considerable numbers or amounts: ～排的新房 row upon row of new houses / 产量～倍增长。Output has doubled and redoubled. ⑦ all right; O.K.: ～! 就这么办吧。O.K. Go ahead. / 你不去可不～。No, you must go. / 什么时候都～。Any time will do. ⑧ capable; able: 说起口译，他可真～! When it comes to oral interpretation, he really knows his job. ⑨ (Chéng) a surname

成²   chéng   m. one tenth: 增产两～ a 20% increase in output; output increased by 20 per cent

成案 chéng'àn ① precedent ② legal precedent; judicial precedent

成败 chéng-bài   success or failure: ～在此一举。Success or failure hinges on this one action.

成败利钝 chéng-bài lì-dùn   success or failure, smooth going or rough: ～尚难逆料。Whether this will succeed or not is still hard to tell.

成本 chéngběn   cost: 生产～ production cost / 固定～ fixed cost / 可变～ variable cost / 直接(间接)～ direct (indirect) cost / ～核算 cost accounting / ～价格 cost price / ～帐 cost accounts

成本会计 chéngběn kuàijì   cost accounting

成材 chéngcái ① grow into useful timber: 这棵树已经～了。This tree has grown to full size. ② become a useful person: 不让孩子经风雨见世面，怎么能～呢? How can a child grow up to be useful if he is not allowed to face the world and brave the storm? / 他长大了一定能～。He'll grow up to be somebody.

成材林 chéngcáilín   standing timber; mature timber

成虫 chéngchóng   zool. adult insect; imago

成仇 chéngchóu   become enemies

成丁 chéngdīng   (of a boy) come of age

成都 Chéngdū   Chengdu (capital of Sichuan Province)

成堆 chéngduī   form a pile; be in heaps: 菜市场门外摆着～的蔬菜。Vegetables are piled (or heaped) up outside the food market. / 我们不要等问题成了堆才去解决。We shouldn't wait until problems pile up before we try to solve them.

成法 chéngfǎ ① established laws ② tried methods

成方 chéngfāng   Chin. med. set prescription

成分 chéngfen (also 成份 chéngfen) ① composition; component part; ingredient: 化学～ chemical composition / 肥料的～ the composition of a fertilizer ② one's class status; one's profession or economic status: 定～ determine sb.'s class status / ～好，出身好 of good class status and family background

成风 chéngfēng   become a common practice; become the order of the day: 国内旅游～。Tourism has become very popular in this country. / 勤俭～。Diligence and frugality are now the order of the day.

成佛 chéngfó   become a Buddha; attain Buddhahood

成服 chéngfú ① formal (of relatives of the deceased) put on mourning clothes for the funeral service ② ready-made clothes; ready-to-wear

成个儿 chénggèr ① grow to a good size: 苹果已经～了。The apples have grown to a good size. ② be well formed; be in the proper form: 他的字写得不～。His handwriting lacks form. / 怎么我捏的饺子成不了个儿? How come the dumplings I make aren't the right shape?

成功 chénggōng   succeed; be a success: 大会开得很～。The congress was a great success. / 试验～了吗? Did the experiment come off all right? / 这项革新一定能够～。The innovation is bound to be a success.

成规 chéngguī   established practice; set rules; groove; rut

成果 chéngguǒ   achievement; fruit; gain; positive result: 科研～ achievements in scientific research / 劳动～ the

fruits of labour / 改革的～ successes scored in reform / 会谈取得了一些～。 The talks have yielded some positive results.

成婚 chénghūn get married

成活 chénghuó survive: 新栽的树苗都已～。 The new seedlings have all survived.

成活率 chénghuólǜ survival rate

成绩 chéngjì result (of work or study); achievement; success: 取得很大～ achieve great successes / 在比赛中取得良好的～ get good results in a tournament / 学习～不太好 not do very well in one's studies / 在我们的工作中～是主要的。 Our achievements are the main aspect of our work. / 他们的工作是有～的。 Their work has been fruitful.

成绩单 chéngjìdān school report; report card; transcript

成家[1] chéngjiā (of a man) get married: 他还没有～。 He's not married yet.

成家[2] chéngjiā become a specialist or expert ——see also 成名成家 chéngmíng-chéngjiā

成家立业 chéngjiā-lìyè marry and embark on a career

成见 chéngjiàn preconceived idea; prejudice: 有～ be prejudiced / ～很深 be deeply prejudiced / 消除～ dispel prejudices / 我对他毫无～。 I have no prejudice against him at all.

成交 chéngjiāo strike a bargain; conclude a transaction; clinch a deal

成交额 chéngjiāo'é volume of business

成就 chéngjiù ① achievement; success; attainment; accomplishment: 他是个很有～的科学家。 He is an accomplished scientist. / 没什么～ haven't achieved anything / 剧本的艺术～ artistic merits of a play ② achieve; accomplish: ～革命大业 accomplish a great revolutionary task

成句 chéngjù form a complete sentence: 他的英语说不～。 He speaks broken English.

成矿作用 chéngkuàng zuòyòng mineralization

成了 chéngle inf. ① that's enough; that'll do: ～, 够我用两个月的了。 That's enough. It'll last me a couple of months. ② be done; be ready: 裁缝说你的套装～。 The tailor says your suit is ready.

成立 chénglì ① found; establish; set up: 中华人民共和国于1949年10月1日～。 The People's Republic of China was founded on October 1st, 1949. / 一所学校 set up (or establish) a school / 举行～大会 hold an inaugural meeting ② be tenable; hold water: 这个论点不能～。 That argument is untenable (or does not hold water).

成例 chénglì precedent; existing model: 这件事没有～可援。 There is no precedent for this. / 有～可循。 There is a precedent to follow. / 援引～ cite a precedent

成粒器 chénglìqì mech. granulator

成殓 chéngliàn be encoffined

成林 chénglín (of young trees) grow up into a wood

成龙配套 chénglóng-pèitào fill in the gaps to complete a chain (of equipment, construction projects, etc.); link up the parts to form a whole: 使排灌设备～ complete a drainage and irrigation network / 大小沟渠, ～。 The canals and ditches formed a complete irrigation system.

成眠 chéngmián formal fall asleep; go to sleep: 夜不～ lie awake all night

成名 chéngmíng become famous; make a name for oneself: 他早就成了名。 He made a name for himself long ago.

成名成家 chéngmíng-chéngjiā establish one's reputation as an authority in one's field

成命 chéngmìng an order already issued: 收回成命 shōuhuí chéngmìng

成年[1] chéngnián grow up; come of age: ～人 grown-ups; adults / ～树 full-grown trees / 尚未～ be under age; have not grown up yet / 在我国, 年满十八岁为～。 In China, a person comes of age at eighteen.

成年[2] chéngnián inf. all year: ～在外 be away from home all year

成年累月 chéngnián-lěiyuè year in year out; for years on end

成批 chéngpī group by group; in batches: ～的新钢材 batches of new-type steel products / ～生产 serial production; mass production

成品 chéngpǐn end product; finished product

成气候 chéng qìhou (usu. used in the negative) make good: 成不了什么气候 will not get anywhere

成器 chéngqì grow up to be a useful person: 他那儿子将来成不了器。 His boy will never come to anything.

成千上万 chéngqiān-shàngwàn (also 成千成万 chéngqiān chéngwàn, 成千累万 chéngqiān-lěiwàn) thousands and tens of thousands; thousands upon thousands: ～的人 tens of thousands of people

成亲 chéngqīn inf. get married: 他们是去年成的亲。 They got married last year.

成全 chéngquán help sb. achieve his aim

成群 chéngqún in groups; in great numbers: ～的牛羊 herds (or droves) of cattle and sheep / ～的狼(猎狗) packs of wolves (hounds) / ～的鸟 flocks of birds / ～的鱼 schools of fish / ～的蜜蜂 swarms of bees / ～的对虾 shoals of prawns

成群结队 chéngqún-jiéduì in crowds: 孩子们～地到海滩上玩儿去了。 Groups of children went to the beach to play.

成人 chéngrén ① be grown up; become full-grown: 长大～ be grown to manhood ② adult; grown-up

成人教育 chéngrén jiàoyù adult education

成人之美 chéng rén zhī měi help sb. to fulfil his wish; aid sb. in doing a good deed: 君子～。 A gentleman is always ready to help others attain their aims.

成仁 chéngrén formal die for a righteous cause: 不成功, 便～。 Fulfil your mission or, failing that, lay down your life.

成日 chéngrì dial. the whole day; all day long

成日成夜 chéngrì-chéngyè day and night

成色 chéngsè ① the percentage of gold or silver in a coin, etc.; the relative purity of gold or silver: 这条金项链～好。 This is a fine gold necklace. ② quality: 看～定价钱 fix the prices according to the quality

成式 chéngshì an accepted way of doing sth.; a set rule

成事 chéngshì ① accomplish sth.; succeed: 你这样做成不了事, 只会误事。 If you go at it this way you'll never succeed. Instead you'll make a mess of things. ② formal a thing that is past or finished

成事不足, 败事有余 chéng shì bùzú, bài shì yǒuyú unable to accomplish anything but liable to spoil everything; never able to achieve, always able to ruin; never make, but always mar

成书 chéngshū ① be published in book form ② a book already in circulation

成熟 chéngshú ripe; mature: 桃子快～了。 The peaches will soon be ripe. / 她到十六岁发育～。 She had reached maturity by the time she was sixteen. / 改革的条件已经～。 Conditions were ripe for reform. / 时机～。 The time is ripe. / 计划已经～。 Now we have a well-thought-out plan. / 政治上～ politically mature / ～的经验 ripe experience / ～的意见 well-considered opinions / 我的意见还不～。 I haven't thought this idea through.

成熟林 chéngshúlín mature forest

成熟期 chéngshúqī agric. mature period; maturity

成数[1] chéngshù round number

成数[2] chéngshù percentage; ratio; rate

成双 chéngshuāng　form a pair

成说 chéngshuō　an accepted theory or formulation: 进行科学研究, 不能囿于～, 要敢于创新。In scientific research, one should break new paths and not be fettered by accepted theories.

成诵 chéngsòng　*formal* be able to recite; be able to repeat from memory: 熟读～ read again and again until one knows by heart; learn by rote

成俗 chéngsú　become social custom

成算 chéngsuàn　a preconceived idea or plan: 我是走一步看一步, 心里没什么～。I am just groping along without any preconceived plans.

成套 chéngtào　form a complete set: 这些仪器是～的, 不要拆散。These instruments form a complete set. Don't separate them. / ～家具 complete sets of furniture / ～设备 complete sets of equipment; complete plants and equipment / ～唱腔 a complete score for voices (in an opera) / 提供～项目和技术援助 supply whole plants as well as technical aid

成体 chéngtǐ　*zool.* adult

成天 chéngtiān　*inf.* all day long; all the time: ～忙忙碌碌 be kept busy all day long / ～不在家 be out all the time

成为 chéngwéi　become; turn into: ～工程师 become an engineer / 把我国建设～社会主义的现代化强国 build China into a powerful modern socialist country

成文 chéngwén　① existing writings: 抄袭～ copy existing writings; follow a set pattern ② written: 规则已经归纳～。The rules are all put together in written form.

成文法 chéngwénfǎ　written laws; statute law; statutory law

成问题 chéng wèntí　be a problem; be open to question (*or* doubt, objection): 雨再不停, 明天的比赛就要～了。If the rain doesn't stop, I doubt if we can have the game tomorrow. / 这活干得这么粗, 真～。The job has been done very carelessly; this is really serious. / 那不～。That's no problem. / 完成生产指标不～。We will fulfil the quota without fail.

成仙 chéngxiān　become an immortal

成象 chéngxiàng　*phys.* formation of image; imagery

成效 chéngxiào　effect; result: ～显著 produce a marked effect; achieve remarkable success / ～甚少 achieve little / 初见～ win initial success / 这种药连着吃下去一定会有～。This medicine will be effective if you keep on taking it for a time. / 几年来计划生育收到了巨大的～。Family planning has had marked success the last few years.

成心 chéngxīn　intentionally; on purpose; with deliberate intent: 别生气, 他不是～的。Don't be angry. He didn't mean it. / 他～让我难堪。He purposely embarrassed me.

成行 chéngxíng　*formal* embark on a (planned) journey: 代表团已于 5 日～。The delegation left as planned on the 5th. / 未能～ didn't leave as planned

成形 chéngxíng　① take shape: 我们的计划开始～了。Our plan is beginning to take shape. ② shaping; forming: 爆炸～ explosive forming / 冷滚～ cold roll forming

成型 chéngxíng　(of workpieces or products) be in finished form

成性 chéngxìng　by nature; become sb.'s second nature: 好斗～ be belligerent by nature / 这家伙偷盗窃～。Stealing has become that rascal's second nature.

成宿 chéngxiǔ　*inf.* the whole night; all night long: 他～翻来覆去睡不着觉。He tossed and turned all night, unable to sleep.

成样儿 chéngyàngr　(usu. used in the negative) seemly; presentable: 这么做太不～了。Such conduct is most unseemly.

成药 chéngyào　pharmacist-prepared medicine; patent medicine

成夜 chéngyè　the whole night; all night long: 她～～地打麻将。She spends whole nights playing mahjong.

成衣 chéngyī　① *old* tailoring ② ready-made clothes; ready-to-wear

成衣匠 chéngyījiàng　*old* tailor; dressmaker

成衣铺 chéngyīpù　*old* tailor's shop; tailor's; dressmaker's

成议 chéngyì　an agreement already reached: 此事已有～。An agreement has already been reached on this issue.

成因 chéngyīn　cause of formation; contributing factor: 海洋的～ the origin of seas and oceans

成鱼 chéngyú　adult fish

成语 chéngyǔ　set phrase (usu. composed of four characters); idiom

成员 chéngyuán　member (of a group or family): 正式～ a full member / 家庭主要～ the chief members of a family / 全社会～ every member of society

成员国 chéngyuánguó　member state

成约 chéngyuē　a signed treaty or agreement; an existing agreement

成灾 chéngzāi　cause disaster; result in disaster: 暴雨～。The heavy rainstorm caused a disastrous flood.

成长 chéngzhǎng　grow up; grow to maturity: 果树正苗壮～。The fruit trees are growing well. / 关心年轻一代的健康～ take an active interest in the healthy growth of the younger generation / 大批少数民族干部已经～起来。Many members of minority nationalities have become mature cadres.

成竹在胸 chéngzhú zài xiōng　same as 胸有成竹 xiōng yǒu chéngzhú

成总儿 chéngzǒngr　*inf.* ① in round numbers; in full: 这笔钱我～付吧。I'll pay in a lump sum. ② in whole batches; in large amounts: 这东西～买便宜, 零买贵。It's cheaper to buy these things in batches than in pieces.

呈

　chéng　① assume (form, colour, etc.): 叶～椭圆形。The leaf is oval in shape. ② submit or present (a report, etc.) to a superior ③ petition; memorial

呈报 chéngbào　submit a report; report a matter (to a superior): ～上级机关备案 report the matter to a higher level for the record

呈递 chéngdì　present; submit: ～国书 present credentials (*or* letters of credence)

呈览 chénglǎn　submit sth. to a higher authority for perusal

呈请 chéngqǐng　apply (to the higher authorities for consideration or approval): ～上级审批 apply to the higher level for approval

呈文 chéngwén　a document submitted to a superior; memorial; petition

呈现 chéngxiàn　present (a certain appearance); appear; emerge: 农村～出一派繁荣景象。The countryside is one vast scene of prosperity.

呈献 chéngxiàn　respectfully present: ～花圈 lay a wreath with due formality

呈正 chéngzhèng　(also 呈政 chéngzhèng) *formal* present for criticism or correction

呈子 chéngzi　a petition (usu. from the common people) to the authorities

诚

　chéng　① sincere; honest: 忠诚 zhōngchéng / 诚心 chéngxīn ② *formal* really; actually; indeed: ～非易事。It is by no means easy. / ～有此事。There actually was such a thing.

诚笃 chéngdǔ　sincere and earnest: 他为人～, 可以信

赖。He's sincere and earnest, and so can be trusted.

诚服 chéngfú submit oneself willingly (to sb.): 心悦诚服 xīn yuè chéngfú

诚惶诚恐 chénghuáng-chéngkǒng with reverence and awe; in fear and trepidation

诚恳 chéngkěn sincere: 态度～ be sincere in what one does and says / 作～的自我批评 make a sincere self-criticism / ～地接受别人的意见 listen to other people's criticisms with an open mind

诚朴 chéngpǔ honest; sincere and simple: 一个～的青年 an honest youth / ～的工作作风 a simple and honest work style

诚然 chéngrán ① *adv.* truly; really: 她喜爱她的小狗，那小狗也～可爱。She loves her puppy, and the puppy is really lovable. ② *conj.* (used correlatively with 但是) no doubt; to be sure; it is true: 旱情～是严重的，但是它吓不倒我们。True, the drought is serious, but it can't scare us.

诚实 chéngshí honest: ～可靠 honest and dependable / ～劳动 honest work

诚心 chéngxīn ① sincere desire; sincerity; whole-heartedness: 一片～ in all sincerity ② sincere and earnest; devout: 她长年吃斋念佛，可～了。Over the years she's been abstaining from meat and praying to Buddha. She's such a devout Buddhist.

诚心诚意 chéngxīn-chéngyì earnestly and sincerely: 我们要～地积极帮助少数民族发展经济建设和文化建设。We must sincerely and actively help the minority nationalities to develop their economy and culture.

诚意 chéngyì good faith; sincerity: 表明～ show one's good faith / 缺乏～ lack sincerity / 谁也不怀疑你的～。No one doubts your sincerity.

诚挚 chéngzhì sincere; cordial: ～友好的气氛 a sincere and friendly atmosphere / 致以～的谢意 extend one's heartfelt thanks to sb. / 给予～的接待 accord sb. a cordial reception

承 chéng ① bear; hold; carry: 那座木桥～得住这样重的卡车吗? Can that wooden bridge carry such heavy trucks? ② undertake; contract (to do a job): ～印名片 undertake the printing of visiting cards ③ *formal* be indebted (to sb. for a kindness); be granted a favour: ～您过奖。You flatter me. / 咋～盛情款待, 不胜感激。I am much indebted to you for the kind hospitality shown me yesterday. ④ continue; carry on: 继承 jìchéng

承办 chéngbàn undertake: ～土木工程 undertake civil engineering projects / 这件事由他一手～。He has taken the whole task upon himself.

承包 chéngbāo contract: ～桥梁工程 contract to build a bridge / ～一万吨水泥的供应 contract for the supply of ten thousand tons of cement

承包商 chéngbāoshāng contractor

承包责任制 chéngbāo zérènzhì contract and responsibility system; system of contracted responsibility

承保 chéngbǎo undertake to provide insurance; accept insurance: 这家公司为工矿企业～火险。The company undertakes to provide fire insurance for factories, mines and other enterprises. / ～范围 insurance coverage

承保人 chéngbǎorén insurer

承保通知书 chéngbǎo tōngzhīshū cover note

承尘 chéngchén ① *formal* canopy ② *dial.* ceiling

承担 chéngdān bear; undertake; assume: ～一切费用 bear all the costs / ～责任 shoulder (*or* bear) the responsibility / ～由此而产生的一切严重后果 bear responsibility (*or* be held responsible) for all the serious consequences arising therefrom / ～新设备的全部安装任务 undertake to install all the new equipment /

～义务 undertake the obligation / ～不首先使用核武器的义务 commit oneself not to be the first to use nuclear weapons / ～额外工作 take on extra work / 对一切损失～全部责任 commit oneself to answer for all the losses incurred / 各自～相应的责任。Each party shall be commensurately liable.

承当 chéngdāng ① bear; take on: 一切责任由我～。I'll bear all the responsibility. ② *dial.* agree (to do sth.); promise

承佃 chéngdiàn hold tenancy of land (from a landlord)

承兑 chéngduì honour; accept: ～支票 honour a cheque / ～汇票 accept a bill

承兑人 chéngduìrén acceptor

承乏 chéngfá *formal pol.* (said in self-depreciation) be unworthy of a post; fill a post until a better man is found

承管 chéngguǎn take full charge of and bear responsibility for; be held fully responsible (for): 此事当由外事组～。The foreign affairs section should take full charge of this.

承欢 chénghuān *formal* please one's parents or sovereign: ～膝下 take good care of one's parents and make them happy / ～侍宴无闲暇,春从春游夜专夜。(白居易《长恨歌》) Constantly she amused and feasted with him, Accompanying him on his spring outings, Spending all the nights with him.

承继 chéngjì ① be adopted as heir to one's uncle ② adopt one's brother's son (as one's heir)

承建 chéngjiàn contract for the building of; undertake the construction of: 宾馆由第二建筑公司～。The No. 2 Building Company has undertaken the construction of the hotel.

承教 chéngjiào *pol.* thanks for your advice, instructions, etc.

承接 chéngjiē ① hold out a vessel to have a liquid poured into it ② continue; carry on: ～上文 continued from the preceding paragraph ③ undertake the task of; contract to accept: ～来料加工 accept customers' materials for processing; undertake the processing of supplied materials

承揽 chénglǎn contract to do a whole job; undertake an entire project: ～物资运输业务 undertake the transportation of materials

承梁 chéngliáng *mech.* bolster: 防松～ check bolster

承溜 chéngliù *formal* eaves gutter; gutter

承蒙 chéngméng *pol.* be accorded (a kindness); be granted (a favour): ～热情接待,不胜荣幸。I feel greatly honoured to be given such a warm reception. / ～照顾,十分感谢。I am very grateful to you for the kind treatment you accorded me.

承诺 chéngnuò promise to undertake; undertake to do sth.: 双方～为进一步开展文化交流创造便利条件。Both sides undertake to facilitate further cultural exchanges. / 我无法作出肯定的～。I can't make a definite promise.

承平 chéngpíng *formal* peaceful: ～岁月 piping times of peace; time of peace

承情 chéngqíng *pol.* be much obliged; owe a debt of gratitude

承认 chéngrèn ① admit; acknowledge; recognize: ～错误 admit one's mistake; acknowledge one's fault / 大家都～这个规划还很不完善。Everybody agreed that the plan was far from perfect. / ～党的章程 accept the constitution of a party / 得到群众的～和信任 win the recognition and trust of the people / ～生产力的决定作用 recognize the decisive role of the productive forces ② give diplomatic recognition; recognize: ～中华人民共和国政府为中国的唯一合法政府 recognize the Government of the People's Republic of China as the sole legal government of China

承上启下 chéngshàng-qǐxià (also 承上起下 chéngshàng-qǐxià) form a connecting link between what comes before and what goes after (as in a piece of writing, etc.)

承受 chéngshòu ① bear; support; endure: 这桥～得住很大的重量。The bridge can bear a tremendous weight. / ～住种种考验 be able to stand every kind of trial ② inherit (a legacy, etc.)

承桃 chéngtiāo become heir to one's uncle who has no son

承望 chéngwàng (usu. used in the negative) expect: 不～您帮了这个忙，太感谢了。Thank you very much for your unexpected help.

承袭 chéngxí ① adopt; follow (a tradition, etc.): ～旧制 follow the old system ② inherit (a peerage, etc.)

承先启后 chéngxiān-qǐhòu (also 承前启后 chéngqián-qǐhòu) inherit the past and usher in the future; serve as a link between past and future

承销 chéngxiāo act as sales agent

承销人 chéngxiāorén sales agent; salesman

承应 chéngyìng same as 应承 yìngchéng

承允 chéngyǔn agree; promise: 满口～ agree or promise readily

承运[1] chéngyùn *formal* (of a ruler) be ordained by Heaven

承运[2] chéngyùn (of transportation companies, etc.) undertake the transportation of (goods)

承运人 chéngyùnrén carrier

承载 chéngzài bear the weight of: ～能力 bearing (or carrying) capacity; load-bearing capacity

承造 chéngzào undertake to manufacture, build or construct for others

承制 chéngzhì undertake to manufacture for others: ～配套器材 accept orders for manufacturing necessary accessories

承重 chéngzhòng load-bearing; bearing

承重墙 chéngzhòngqiáng *archit.* bearing (or load-bearing) wall

承重孙 chéngzhòngsūn eldest grandson acting as chief mourner during his grandfather's funeral instead of his dead father

承转 chéngzhuǎn assume the responsibility of forwarding (a document) to the level above or below

承做 chéngzuò undertake to make for others: 我店～中式服装。We accept orders for Chinese-style clothes.

城

chéng ① city wall; wall: ～外 outside the city wall; outside the city ② city: 外～ outer city / 内～ inner city / 东～ the eastern part of the city ③ town: 城乡 chéngxiāng

城邦 chéngbāng city-state

城堡 chéngbǎo castle

城池 chéngchí *formal* city wall and moat; city

城堞 chéngdié battlements

城垛 chéngduǒ battlements

城垛口 chéngduǒkǒu crenel (of battlements)

城垛子 chéngduǒzi merlon (of battlements)

城防 chéngfáng city defence: ～巩固。The city is closely guarded.

城防部队 chéngfáng bùduì city garrison

城防工事 chéngfáng gōngshì defence works of a city

城府 chéngfǔ *formal* a mind hard to fathom; subtle thinking: ～很深 shrewd and deep; subtle

城根 chénggēn sections of a city close to the city wall

城关 chéngguān the area just outside a city gate

城郭 chéngguō inner and outer city walls; city walls

城壕 chénghào moat

城狐社鼠 chénghú-shèshǔ a fox in the city wall and a rat in the village temple—evil-doers with strong backing

城隍 chénghuáng town god (in Taoist legend)

城隍庙 chénghuángmiào town god's temple

城建 chéngjiàn (short for 城市建设) urban construction; city building: ～规划 city planning; construction programme for a city

城郊 chéngjiāo outskirts of a town

城里 chénglǐ inside the city; in town: ～人 city dwellers; townspeople / ～很热闹。The city is bustling with activity.

城楼 chénglóu a tower over a city gate; gate tower: 在天安门～上 on the rostrum of Tian An Men

城门 chéngmén city gate

城门失火，殃及池鱼 chéngmén shīhuǒ, yāng jí chíyú when the city gate catches fire, the fish in the moat come to grief—innocent people suffering from what happens to others

城墙 chéngqiáng city wall

城区 chéngqū the city proper: ～和郊区 the city proper and the suburbs

城阙 chéngquè *formal* ① the watch tower on either side of a city gate ② imperial palace

城市 chéngshì town or city: ～规划 city planning / ～环境 urban environment / ～居民 city dwellers; urban population

城市建设 chéngshì jiànshè urban construction; city building

城市贫民 chéngshì pínmín urban poor; city poor

城头 chéngtóu ① the top of a city wall: ～飘扬着红旗。Red flags are flying on top of the city wall. ② gate tower

城下之盟 chéng xià zhī méng a treaty concluded with the enemy who have reached the city wall; terms accepted under duress; a treaty signed under coercion

城乡 chéngxiāng town and country; urban and rural areas; the city and the countryside: ～居民 urban and rural residents / ～差别 the difference between town and country / ～物资交流 flow of goods and materials between town and country (or urban and rural areas); exchange of goods and materials between the city and the countryside

城厢 chéngxiāng the city proper and areas just outside its gates

城邑 chéngyì *formal* cities and towns

城垣 chéngyuán *formal* city wall

城镇 chéngzhèn cities and towns

宬

chéng *arch.* a room for keeping books: 皇史～ the Imperial Library (in Ming and Qing times)

乘[1]

chéng ① ride: ～公共汽车 ride in a bus; go by bus / ～出租汽车到火车站去 take a taxi to the railway station / ～火车 (飞机、轮船) 旅行 travel by train (plane, boat) / 他们～车前往宾馆。They drove to the guesthouse. ② take advantage of; avail oneself of: ～夜出击 attack under cover of night / ～敌不备 take the enemy unawares ③ Buddhist teaching considered as a vehicle for bringing the truth to men: 大乘 dàchéng / 小乘 xiǎochéng

乘[2]

chéng *math.* multiply: 五～三等于十五。Five times three is fifteen. *or* 5 multiplied by 3 is 15. ——see also shèng

乘便 chéngbiàn when it is convenient; at one's convenience: 请你～把那本书带给我。Please bring me the book whenever it's convenient.

乘法 chéngfǎ *math.* multiplication

乘法表 chéngfǎbiǎo multiplication table

乘方 chéngfāng *math.* ① involution ② power: n 的五次～ the fifth power of n; n (raised) to the

power of 5; n^5

乘风凉 chéng fēngliáng *dial.* relax in a cool place

乘风破浪 chéngfēng pòlàng ride the wind and cleave the waves; brave the wind and the waves: 舰艇～巡逻在祖国的海疆。Braving the wind and the waves, the warships patrol our territorial waters.

乘号 chénghào *math.* multiplication sign (×)

乘火打劫 chéng huǒ dǎjié same as 趁火打劫 chèn huǒ dǎjié

乘机 chéngjī seize the opportunity: ～反攻 seize the opportunity to counterattack

乘积 chéngjī *math.* product

乘坚策肥 chéngjiān-cèféi ride in a fine carriage drawn by well-fed horses—live a luxurious life

乘客 chéngkè passenger

乘凉 chéngliáng enjoy the cool; relax in a cool place

乘龙快婿 chéng lóng kuài xù an excellent or ideal son-in-law (usu. of high social or official position)

乘幂 chéngmì *math.* power

乘骑 chéngqí ① ride (a horse, donkey, etc.) ② saddle horse; mount ③ rider

乘人之危 chéng rén zhī wēi take advantage of sb.'s precarious position

乘胜 chéngshèng exploit (*or* follow up) a victory: ～追击 follow up a victory with hot pursuit / ～前进 advance on the crest of a victory; push on in the flush of victory

乘时 chéngshí take the opportunity

乘势 chéngshì same as 趁势 chènshì

乘数 chéngshù *math.* multiplier

乘务员 chéngwùyuán attendant on a train

乘隙 chéngxì take advantage of a loophole; turn sb.'s mistake to one's own account: ～突围 seize an opportunity to break through the encirclement (*or* siege) / 乘敌之隙 exploit the enemy's blunder

乘兴 chéngxìng while one is in high spirits: ～作了一首诗 improvise a poem while in a joyful mood

乘兴而来 chéngxìng ér lái arrive in high spirits; set out cheerfully: ～，兴尽而返 arrive in high spirits and depart well content / ～，败兴而归 set out cheerfully and come back disappointed

乘虚 chéngxū take advantage of a weak point (*or* an opening) in an opponent's defence; act when sb. is off guard

乘虚而入 chéngxū ér rù (*also* 乘隙而入 chéngxì ér rù) break through at a weak point; act when one's opponent is off guard; exploit one's opponent's weakness: 我军～，势如破竹。Our troops took advantage of the enemy's weakened position and cut in like a knife slicing down a length of bamboo.

盛 chéng ① fill; ladle: ～饭 fill a bowl with rice / 把菜～出来 ladle food from the pot; dish out food / ～汤 ladle out soup / 缸里～满了酒。The crock is filled with wine. ② hold; contain: 这麻袋可以～一百多公斤粮食。This sack can hold more than 100 kilos of grain. / 这间屋子太小，～不了这么多东西。The room is too small to hold all these things. / 这个礼堂能～一千人。This hall is big enough for a thousand people. ——see also **shèng**

盛殓 chéngliàn encoffin

盛器 chéngqì vessel; receptacle

程 chéng ① rule; regulation: 章程 zhāngchéng ② order; procedure: 议程 yìchéng ③ journey; stage of a journey: 送他一～ accompany him part of the way / 送了一～又一～ accompany (a guest, traveller, etc.) league after league before parting ④ distance: 行程 xíngchéng ⑤ (Chéng) a surname

程度 chéngdù ① level; degree: 文化～ level of education; degree of literacy / 生产社会化～还很低。Socialization of production is still at a very low level. ② extent; degree: 在很大(一定)～上 to a great (certain) extent / 在不同～上 in varying degrees / 在不少环节上还不同～存在着官僚主义和腐败现象。Bureaucratism and corruption still exist to varying degrees in many sectors.

程控 chéngkòng short for 程序控制 chéngxù kòngzhì

程控电话 chéngkòng diànhuà program-controlled telephone

程门立雪 Chéng mén lì xuě stand in snow at the gate of Cheng's house—a pupil showing reverence for his master (a reference to the Song scholar Cheng Yi 程颐)

程式 chéngshì form; pattern; formula: 公文～ forms and formulas of official documents / ～动作 stylized movements (as in Beijing opera)

程式化 chéngshìhuà stylize

程限 chéngxiàn *formal* ① patterns and restrictions: 创作是没有一定的～的。Creative writing knows no rules or formulas. ② a fixed rate of progress: 读书日有～ be making progress in one's studies

程序 chéngxù ① order; procedure; course; sequence: 工作～ working procedure / 法律～ legal procedure / ～事项 procedural matters / ～问题 a question of procedure; a point of order / 符合～ be in order / ～性动议 procedural motion ② *automation* program: 编～ write programs for computers; program

程序法 chéngxùfǎ *leg.* procedural law

程序教学 chéngxù jiàoxué programmed instruction or learning

程序控制 chéngxù kòngzhì *automation* pre-programmed automatic control

程序设计 chéngxù shèjì *automation* programming

程序设计语言 chéngxù shèjì yǔyán programming language; program language

程序设计员 chéngxù shèjìyuán (*also* 程序员 chéngxùyuán) programmer

程仪 chéngyí *formal* a gift of money for a friend going on a journey

程子 chéngzi *dial.* a period of time; a number of days: 那～我很忙。I was busy at that time.

惩(懲) chéng punish; penalize: 惩罚 chéngfá / 严惩 yánchéng

惩办 chéngbàn punish: 依法～ punish according to law / 严加～ punish severely / ～和宽大相结合 combine punishment with leniency

惩处 chéngchǔ penalize; punish: 依法～ punish in accordance with the law

惩恶劝善 chéng'è-quànshàn punish evil-doers and encourage people to do good

惩罚 chéngfá punish; penalize: 受到一次严厉的～ pay a severe penalty / 侵略者受到了应得的～。The aggressors got what they deserved.

惩戒 chéngjiè punish sb. to teach him a lesson; discipline sb. as a warning; take disciplinary action against: 吊销执照，以示～ revoke sb.'s licence as a punishment

惩前毖后 chéngqián-bìhòu learn from past errors to avoid future mistakes: ～，治病救人 learn from past mistakes to avoid future ones, and cure the sickness to save the patient

惩一儆百 chéng yī jǐng bǎi (*also* 惩一警百 chéng yī jǐng bǎi) punish one to warn a hundred; make an example of sb.: 重办这个为首的，～。Severely punish the ringleader as a warning to the rest.

惩艾 chéngyì *formal* punish; mete out punishment to

惩治 chéngzhì punish; mete out punishment to

塍(堘) chéng *dial.* a path between fields: 田塍 tiánchéng

醒 chéng *formal* be drunk; be fuddled; have a hangover

澄(澂) chéng ① (of water, air, etc.) clear; transparent; limpid: 澄空 chéngkōng ② clear up; clarify ——see also dèng

澄碧 chéngbì clear blue: 湖水～。The lake water is a clear blue.

澄彻 chéngchè (also 澄澈 chéngchè) *formal* transparently clear; crystal clear: 江水～见底。The river is so clear that you can see to the bottom.

澄空 chéngkōng a clear, cloudless sky

澄清 chéngqīng ① clear; transparent: 湖水碧绿～。The water of the lake is green and clear. ② clear up; clarify: ～误会 clear up a misunderstanding / ～事实 clarify some facts / 要求～ demand clarification ——see also dèngqīng

橙 chéng ① orange (the tree and the fruit): 甜～ sweet orange ② orange colour

橙黄 chénghuáng orange colour

橙子 chéngzi orange (the fruit)

chěng

逞 chěng ① show off; flaunt: ～英雄 pose as a hero / ～威风 show off one's strength or power; swagger about ② carry out (an evil design); succeed (in a scheme): 得逞 déchěng ③ indulge; give free rein to: 逞性子 chěng xìngzi

逞能 chěngnéng show off one's skill or ability; parade one's ability: 他的缺点是好～。The trouble with him is that he likes to show off.

逞强 chěngqiáng flaunt one's superiority: ～好胜 parade one's superiority and strive to outshine others

逞性子 chěng xìngzi self-willed; wilful; wayward; headstrong

逞凶 chěngxiōng act violently; act with murderous intent

骋 chěng *formal* ① gallop: 驰骋 chíchěng ② give free rein to

骋怀 chěnghuái *formal* give free rein to one's thoughts and feelings

骋目 chěngmù *formal* look as far as the eye can see; look into the distance: ～远眺 scan distant horizons

chèng

秤(称) chèng balance; steelyard: 拿～称称 weigh it in a balance (*or* on the scales) / 一杆～ a steelyard

秤锤 chèngchuí the sliding weight of a steelyard

秤杆 chènggǎn the arm (*or* beam) of a steelyard

秤钩 chènggōu steelyard hook

秤纽 chèngniǔ (also 秤毫 chènghǎo) the lifting cord of a steelyard

秤盘 chèngpán ① the pan or dish of a steelyard ② either of the pans or dishes of a balance; scale

秤砣 chèngtuó *inf.* the sliding weight of a steelyard

秤星 chèngxīng gradations marked on the beam of a steelyard

chī

吃¹(喫) chī ① eat; take: ～苹果 eat an apple / ～药 take medicine / ～糖 have some sweets / ～得很饱 have eaten one's fill ② have one's meals; eat somewhere: ～食堂 have one's meals in the mess ③ live on (*or* off): ～利钱 live on interest / ～劳保 live on labour insurance ④ annihilate; wipe out: ～掉敌军一个师 annihilate an enemy division / ～一个子儿 take a piece (in chess) ⑤ exhaust; be a strain on: 吃力 chīlì ⑥ absorb; soak up: 这种纸不～墨水。This kind of paper does not absorb ink. / 茄子很～油。Eggplant calls for a lot of oil in cooking. ⑦ suffer; bear; incur: 腿上～了一枪 get wounded by a shot in the leg / 连～败仗 suffer one defeat after another / 我可不～这一套。I won't take all this lying down.

吃² chī see 口吃 kǒuchī

吃白饭 chībáifàn ① eat nothing but plain cooked rice ② live off others: 他不干活, 专～。He doesn't work and just lives off others.

吃白食 chībáishí eat food that isn't earned; not earn an honest living; live off others: 他不务正业, 惯～。He does not do any honest work and lives off others.

吃饱了撑的 chībǎole chēngde restless from overeating (said of sb. doing sth. silly or senseless)

吃瘪 chībiē *dial.* be beaten; acknowledge defeat

吃不饱 chībùbǎo ① not have enough to eat ② (of factories, etc.) cannot operate at full capacity; operate under capacity: 由于原料缺乏, 我们厂长期处于～状态。Owing to a constant shortage of raw materials, our factory has not been running at full capacity.

吃不得 chībùdé ① cannot eat; cannot be eaten: 他胃不好, ～油腻的东西。He has stomach trouble and cannot eat oily food. / 这苹果太酸了, ～。This apple is too sour to eat. ② cannot bear; cannot suffer: ～苦 cannot stand any hardships

吃不服 chībùfú not be accustomed to eating sth.; not be used to certain food: 生冷的东西我总～。Cold and raw things never agree with me.

吃不开 chībùkāi be unpopular; won't work: 这种工作作风到哪儿都～。Such a work style isn't popular anywhere. / 你这老一套现在可～了。Your old ways of doing things won't work now.

吃不来 chībùlái not be fond of certain food: 芥末我～。I'm not especially fond of mustard. / 很多南方人～生蒜。Many southerners do not eat raw garlic.

吃不了 chībùliǎo cannot finish (all the food): 这么一大碗面条我实在～。I really can't finish such a bowlful of noodles.

吃不了兜着走 chībùliǎo dōuzhe zǒu get more than one bargained for; land oneself in serious trouble: 这件事你如果说出去, 我叫你～! If you let this leak out, I'll make you sorry for it! / 你可别得罪了上头, 回头～。You must take care not to offend your superiors, or you'll land yourself in real trouble.

吃不上 chībùshàng ① be unable to get something to eat: ～一顿饱饭 be unable to get a square meal ② miss a meal: 快走吧, 再晚就什么也～了。Hurry up, or we'll be too late to get anything to eat.

吃不下 chībùxià not feel like eating; be unable to eat any more: 他不太舒服, ～饭。He's not very well and doesn't feel like eating. / 谢谢, 我实在～了。Thanks, but I really can't eat any more. *or* Thanks, I've really had enough.

吃不消 chībuxiāo be unable to stand (exertion, fatigue, etc.): 走这么多的路恐怕你～。It may be too much for you to walk such a long way. / 这文章写得又长又难懂，真让看的人～。No reader can put up with such a long-winded article. / 她连续做了五天夜班，身体渐渐～了。She had been on night shift five days running, and it was gradually becoming more than she could bear.

吃不住 chībuzhù be unable to bear or support: 机器太沉，这个架子～。The stand is not strong enough for this heavy machine. / 在我军的强大攻势下，敌人～了。In the face of our strong attacks, the enemy couldn't stand their ground.

吃吃 chīchī onom. titter; chuckle: 她～地笑出声来。She tittered.

吃吃喝喝 chīchīhēhē derog. indulge oneself in eating and drinking; wine and dine

吃穿 chī-chuān food and clothing: ～不愁 not have to worry about food and clothing / 她很讲究～。She's fastidious about her food and clothing.

吃醋 chīcù be jealous (usu. of a rival in love): 他不过请你女朋友跳了两次舞，你干吗～啊! He's only had a couple of dances with your girlfriend. Why should you eye him with such jealousy?

吃大锅饭 chīdàguōfàn ① eat in the cafeteria the same as everyone else; mess together ② eat from the same big pot—get the same reward or pay as everyone else regardless of one's performance in work

吃大户 chīdàhù mass seizure and eating of food in the homes of landlords during famines (as in pre-liberation China)

吃刀 chīdāo mech. (of the cutting tool on a lathe, etc.) penetrate a certain depth into a workpiece

吃得苦中苦，方为人上人 chī dé kǔzhōngkǔ, fāng wéi rénshàngrén only if you can stand the hardest of hardships can you hope to rise in society

吃得开 chīdekāi be popular; be much sought after: 吹牛的人在那儿～。Braggarts can get along all right there. / 只要技术好，到哪儿都～。A person who has expertise is welcome anywhere.

吃得来 chīdelái be able to eat; not mind eating: 辣椒我～，但不特别喜欢。I can eat red pepper, though I'm not overfond of it.

吃得上 chīdeshàng ① be able to get sth. to eat; can afford to eat: 解放前吃糠咽菜的人家现在也～大米白面了。Families who lived on chaff and wild herbs before liberation can now afford rice and wheat flour. / 鱼塘和鸡场多了，大家都～鲜鱼、鲜蛋了。There are plenty of fish ponds and chicken farms, supplying everybody with fresh fish and eggs. ② be in time for a meal; be able to get a meal: 十二点半以前赶回去还～饭。If we get back before twelve thirty, we won't be too late for lunch. / 工人们不管什么时候到食堂去，都～热饭。The workers can get a hot meal any time they go to the canteen.

吃得下 chīdexià be able to eat: 还有一点，你～吗? There's still a bit left. Can you eat some more? / 她已经好多了，饭也～了。She's much better; she's got an appetite now.

吃得消 chīdexiāo be able to stand (exertion, fatigue, etc.): 再干一个夜班，我也完全～。I can easily stand working another night shift. or I'm certainly good for another night shift. / 高空飞行，要身体结实才～。One needs a strong physique for high altitude flying.

吃得住 chīdezhù be able to bear or support: 再重的卡车，这座桥也～。This bridge can bear the weight of the heaviest lorry.

吃地面儿 chīdìmiànr live off the locality—live by extorting money from the people in the locality

吃豆腐 chī dòufu dial. ① flirt with a woman: 你别想

吃她豆腐! Don't try to flirt with her. ② crack a joke ③ visit the bereaved to offer one's condolences

吃独食 chī dúshí have food all to oneself; refuse to share one's food with others

吃耳光 chī ěrguāng dial. get a slap in the face

吃饭 chīfàn ① eat; have a meal: 吃了饭再走吧! Don't go. Stay for dinner. / 吃过饭了吗? (lit. "Have you eaten?") Hello! ② keep alive; make a living: 靠打猎～ make a living by hunting / 只有增加生产，才能解决～问题。Only by increasing production can we solve the problem of feeding the whole population.

吃饭防噎 chīfàn fáng yē be careful not to get choked while eating—be very cautious

吃挂落 chī guà·lào dial. be involved in trouble: 这孩子再这么胡闹，父母都得跟着他～。If the boy is allowed to fool around like this, he'll soon get his parents into trouble.

吃官司 chī guānsi inf. get into trouble with the law; serve a jail term

吃馆子 chī guǎnzi inf. eat in a restaurant; dine out: 他要请我们～。He's going to invite us out to dinner. / 我难得～。I seldom dine out.

吃惯 chīguàn be used to (eating) certain food: ～了大米，一下子习惯不了吃面食。Being used to rice, I can't take readily to wheaten food.

吃喝不分 chī-hē bù fēn share food and drink — be close friends

吃喝拉撒睡 chī-hē-lā-sā-shuì eat, drink, shit, piss and sleep—the routine of daily life

吃喝嫖赌 chī-hē-piáo-dǔ go dining, wining, whoring and gambling—lead a dissipated life

吃喝玩乐 chī-hē-wán-lè eat, drink and be merry—idle away one's time in pleasure-seeking

吃喝儿 chīher inf. food and drink: 他把钱都花在～上。He spends all his money on food and drink.

吃黑枣儿 chīhēizǎor inf. eat a black date—get shot

吃后悔药 chīhòuhuǐyào feel remorse; regret: 你要先考虑好再去，免得～。Think it over before you go so that you won't regret it later.

吃花酒 chīhuājiǔ go to a dinner party with singsong girls in attendance

吃回扣 chī huíkòu get commission

吃荤 chīhūn eat meat: 胃口不好，不想～ have no appetite for meat

吃紧 chījǐn be critical; be hard pressed: 形势～。The situation was critical. / 前后方都～ be hard pressed both at the front and in the rear

吃劲 chījìn entail much effort; be a strain: 他挑一百五十斤也不～。He can carry 150 jin on a pole without straining himself.

吃惊 chījīng be startled; be shocked; be amazed; be taken aback: 大吃一惊 be flabbergasted / 他那坚强的毅力使人～。His will power is amazing.

吃空额 chī kòng'é (also 吃空缺 chī kòngquē) (of army officers) line one's pockets with the salaries allotted to soldiers existing only in name on the payroll; embezzle by misrepresenting the payroll

吃苦 chīkǔ bear hardships: 怕～，就干不成大事。Those who fear hardships will not accomplish anything great. / 他小时候吃了不少苦。He suffered a great deal in his childhood.

吃苦耐劳 chīkǔ-nàiláo bear hardships and stand hard work; work hard and endure hardships: 他工作很努力，能～。He was hard-working and unafraid of hardships.

吃苦在前，享乐在后 chīkǔ zài qián, xiǎnglè zài hòu be the first to bear hardships and the last to enjoy comforts

吃亏 chīkuī ① suffer losses; come to grief; get the worst of it: 有备才能无患，无备必定～。If one is pre-

pared, one will be safe; if not, one will suffer. *or* Preparedness ensures security; unpreparedness invites disaster. / 有的人～，就在于不老实。 Some people come to grief on account of their dishonesty. / 机械地搬用外国的东西是要吃大亏的。 Mechanical copying of things foreign would be disastrous. ② be at a disadvantage; be in an unfavourable situation: 他跑得不快，踢足球～。 He can't run fast and that puts him at a disadvantage as a footballer.

吃老本 chīlǎoběn　live off one's past gains; rest on one's laurels

吃里爬外 chīlǐ-páwài　live off one person while secretly helping another

吃力 chīlì　① entail strenuous effort; be a strain: 他身体好，干这点儿活不算～。 He's strong; this bit of work won't be too much for him. / 热情帮助学习上感到～的同学 warm-heartedly help classmates who have difficulty in their studies ② *dial.*　tired; fatigued: 我跑了一天路，感到很～。 After a long day's journey, I felt exhausted.

吃力不讨好 chīlì bù tǎohǎo　same as 费力不讨好 fèilì bù tǎohǎo

吃粮 chīliáng　*old*　serve as a soldier

吃奶 chīnǎi　suck the breast: ～的孩子 a sucking child; suckling / 使尽～的力气 strain every muscle

吃排头 chīpáitou　*dial.*　be scolded; be criticized; get a talking-to

吃枪子儿 chīqiāngzǐr　*offens.*　get shot; be shot dead

吃请 chīqǐng　accept an invitation to dinner (extended as a bribe)

吃人不吐骨头 chī rén bù tǔ gǔtou　devour a man without spitting out the bones—treat people ruthlessly and cruelly

吃软不吃硬 chīruǎn bù chīyìng　be open to persuasion, but not to coercion

吃烧饼 chīshāobing　eat a sesame seed cake—miss the target in shooting practice

吃生活 chīshēnghuo　*dial.*　get a beating

吃食 chīshí　(of animals or birds) feed: 小鸡正在～。 The chickens were feeding.

吃食 chīshi　*inf.*　food; eatables: 到处找～ look here and there for something to eat

吃水[1] chīshuǐ　*dial.*　drinking water: 过去这里～很困难。 It used to be difficult to get drinking water here.

吃水[2] chīshuǐ　absorb water: 这块地不～。 This plot of land absorbs little water. / 这种大米～。 You need a lot of water in cooking this kind of rice.

吃水[3] chīshuǐ　*navigation*　have a draught (*or* draft) of: 这船～三米。 The ship has a draught of 3 metres. / 满载～ load draught / 空载～ light draught

吃水线 chīshuǐxiàn　*navigation*　waterline

吃素 chīsù　abstain from eating meat; be a vegetarian

吃太平饭 chītàipíngfàn　enjoy a peaceful life

吃透 chītòu　have a thorough grasp: ～文件精神 understand a document thoroughly; grasp the spirit of a document

吃瓦片儿 chīwǎpiànr　*dial.*　live on tiles—live on the rent from one's houses

吃闲饭 chīxiánfàn　lead an idle life; be a loafer or sponger

吃闲话 chīxiánhuà　be gossiped about; cause a lot of talk

吃现成饭 chī xiànchéngfàn　(also 吃现成 chī xiànchéng) eat what is already prepared—enjoy the fruits of others' work

吃香 chīxiāng　*inf.*　be very popular; be much sought after; be well-liked: 这种花布在群众中很～。 This kind of cotton print is very popular.

吃香的喝辣的 chī xiāngde hē làde　*inf.*　have tasty food

and strong drinks—eat well

吃心 chīxīn　*dial.*　① be oversensitive; be suspicious: 你别～，我们没说你。 Don't be so oversensitive. We were not talking about you. ② be absorbed in sth.: 他捧着一本书，～地阅读，忘掉了一切。 He was holding a book in both hands, reading so absorbedly as to forget about everything else.

吃鸭蛋 chīyādàn　eat the duck's egg—score nothing in a game or get a zero in an exam

吃夜草 chīyècǎo　*inf.*　eat midnight fodder—moonlight

吃一堑，长一智 chī yī qiàn, zhǎng yī zhì　a fall into the pit, a gain in your wit

吃硬不吃软 chīyìng bù chīruǎn　be open to coercion, but not to persuasion

吃斋 chīzhāi　practise abstinence from meat (as a religious exercise); be a vegetarian for religious reasons

吃着碗里看着锅里 chīzhe wǎnli kànzhe guōli　*inf.*　keep one's eyes on the pot while eating from a bowl—be greedy

吃重 chīzhòng　① arduous; strenuous: 这个任务很～。 This is a hard job. *or* The task is arduous. ② carrying (*or* loading) capacity: 这辆卡车～多少？ What's the carrying capacity of this truck?

吃准 chīzhǔn　*dial.*　be sure; be certain; be positive: 他～小王过三两天就会回来。 He is quite sure Xiao Wang will be back in a couple of days.

吃租 chīzū　live on rent

吃罪 chīzuì　bear (*or* take) the blame: ～不轻 bear much of the blame / ～不起 cannot take the blame

哧

chī　*onom.*: ～的一声撕下一块布来 rip off a piece of cloth with a sharp tearing sound / ～～地笑 titter

哧溜 chīliū　*onom.*　the sound of slipping or sliding: ～一下，她滑了一交。 Swish! She slipped and fell.

蚩

chī　*formal*　ignorant; stupid

鸱

chī　sparrow hawk (used in ancient texts)

鸱尾 chīwěi　a pottery figure of a grotesque animal placed at either end of a roof ridge as an ornament

鸱吻 chīwěn　same as 鸱尾 chīwěi

鸱鸮 chīxiāo　(also 鸱枭 chīxiāo) *zool.*　strigidae (the family of birds to which owls belong)

鸱鸺 chīxiū　another name for 猫头鹰 māotóuyīng

眵

chī　gum (in the eyes)

眵目糊 chīmuhū　*dial.*　gum (in the eyes)

笞

chī　*formal*　beat with a stick, cane, etc.: 鞭笞 biānchī

笞刑 chīxíng　flogging as a punishment

痴（癡）

chī　① silly; idiotic ② crazy about sb. or sth. ③ *dial.*　insane; mad: 发痴 fāchī

痴骏 chī'ái　slow-witted; stupid; clumsy

痴呆 chīdāi　① dull-witted; stupid ② *med.*　dementia

痴肥 chīféi　abnormally fat; obese

痴楞 chīléng　dumbstruck; in a daze; in a trance: 她～地望着她妈，半晌说不出话来。 She stared blankly at her mother, speechless.

痴迷 chīmí　infatuated; obsessed; crazy

痴男怨女 chīnán-yuànnǚ　pining lovers (usually those who for some reason cannot marry each other)

痴念 chīniàn　crazy ideas; stupid notions; foolish thoughts

痴情 chīqíng　① unreasoning passion; infatuation ② be infatuated

痴人说梦 chīrén shuō mèng　idiotic nonsense; lunatic

ravings

痴想 chīxiǎng　wishful thinking; illusion

痴笑 chīxiào　laugh foolishly; giggle

痴心 chīxīn　infatuation: 一片～ sheer infatuation／他对那姑娘真是一片～, 可是姑娘却看不上他。He is infatuated with the girl, but she doesn't think much of him.

痴心女子负心汉 chīxīn nǚzǐ fùxīnhàn　an innocent girl infatuated with a heartless man (the common theme of many old love stories)

痴心妄想 chīxīn-wàngxiǎng　wishful thinking; fond dream

痴长 chīzhǎng　pol. be older but not wiser (than the person spoken to): 我～你几岁, 可也没多学到什么东西。I'm several years your senior, but I'm no more knowledgeable than you are.

痴子 chīzi　dial. ① idiot ② a mad person

嗤 chī　formal sneer

嗤嗤 chīchī　onom. the sound of ripping, tittering, frying, burning, etc.: 两个小姑娘交头接耳一～笑着。The two little girls tittered and whispered in each other's ears.

嗤溜 chīliū　same as 哧溜 chīliū

嗤笑 chīxiào　laugh at; sneer at: 为人～ be sneered at

嗤之以鼻 chī zhī yǐ bí　give a snort of contempt; turn up one's nose at; despise

媸 chī　formal ugly; unsightly; hideous

摛 chī　formal spread

摛藻 chīzǎo　formal write in a flowery style

螭 chī　① hornless dragon (a decorative motif) ② same as 魑 chī

魑 chī　see below

魑魅 chīmèi　formal way man-eating mountain spirit

魑魅魍魉 chīmèi-wǎngliǎng　formal evil spirits; demons and monsters

chí

池 chí　① pool; pond: 养鱼～ fishpond ② an enclosed space with raised sides: 花池子 huāchízi／乐池 yuèchí ③ stalls (in a theatre); orchestra ④ formal moat: 城池 chéngchí ⑤ (Chí) a surname

池汤 chítāng　common bathing pool (in a bathhouse)

池塘 chítáng　pond; pool

池盐 chíyán　lake salt

池鱼之殃 chíyú zhī yāng　a disaster for the fish in the moat—trouble not of one's own making ——see also 城门失火, 殃及池鱼 chéngmén shīhuǒ, yāng jí chíyú

池浴 chíyù　bathing in a common bathing pool

池沼 chízhǎo　a large pond

池中物 chízhōngwù　formal a mediocre person

池子 chízi　inf. ① pond ② common bathing pool (in a bathhouse) ③ dance floor (in a ballroom) ④ stalls (in a theatre); orchestra

池座 chízuò　stalls (in a theatre); orchestra

弛 chí　formal relax; slacken: 松弛 sōngchí

弛废 chífèi　formal same as 废弛 fèichí

弛缓 chíhuǎn　relax; calm down: 他听了这一番话, 紧张的心情渐渐～下来。On hearing this he calmed down.／局势渐趋～。Things are easing up.

弛禁 chíjìn　formal annul a prohibition; lift a ban

弛懈 chíxiè　formal slack; lax

弛张热 chízhāngrè　med. remittent fever

驰 chí　① (of vehicles, horses, etc.) speed; gallop: 飞驰 fēichí ② spread: 驰名 chímíng ③ formal (of thoughts) turn eagerly towards: 心驰神往 xīnchí-shénwǎng

驰骋 chíchěng　gallop: ～在辽阔的原野上 gallop across the vast plain／～文坛 play an outstanding role in the literary world; bestride the literary stage

驰马 chímǎ　gallop (on a horse)

驰名 chímíng　be known far and wide; be famous; be renowned: 世界～的万里长城 the world-famous Great Wall／～中外 be renowned at home and abroad

驰念 chíniàn　formal think longingly of sb. far away

驰驱 chíqū　① gallop ② do one's utmost in sb.'s service

驰思 chísī　same as 驰念 chíniàn

驰突 chítū　formal charge: 往来～, 如入无人之境 charge back and forth, smashing all resistance

驰骛 chíwù　formal (of horses) speed; gallop

驰行 chíxíng　(of vehicles) go at full speed; speed: 火车向北～。The train was speeding north.

驰誉 chíyù　same as 驰名 chímíng

驰援 chíyuán　rush to the rescue

驰骤 chízhòu　formal gallop: 纵横～ gallop freely about

驰逐 chízhú　① ride in full chase ② race a horse

迟（遲） chí　① slow; tardy: ～于作复, 歉甚。I'm sorry I have not been able to reply sooner. ② late: 对不起, 来～了。I'm sorry I'm late. ③ (Chí) a surname

迟迟 chíchí　slow; tardy: ～不表态 not state one's position even after stalling for a long time／他为什么～不来? Why is he taking so long to come?

迟到 chídào　be (or come, arrive) late: ～五分钟 be five minutes late／上班从不～ never be late for work

迟钝 chídùn　slow (in thought or action); obtuse: 反应～ be slow in reacting; react slowly

迟缓 chíhuǎn　slow; tardy; sluggish: 进展～ make slow progress／行动～ act slowly／这件事要赶快办, 不能～。This must be done at once. There must be no delay.

迟留 chíliú　stay; linger on

迟脉 chímài　Chin. med. retarded pulse (less than 60 beats per minute)

迟慢 chímàn　slow; tardy

迟暮 chímù　① dusk; twilight ② formal past one's prime; late in one's life

迟误 chíwù　delay; procrastinate: 不得～ admit of no delay

迟效肥料 chíxiào féiliào　slow-acting fertilizer

迟延 chíyán　delay; retard: 毫不～地执行命令 carry out orders without delay

迟疑 chíyí　hesitate: 毫不～地接受了任务 accept an assignment without hesitation

迟疑不决 chíyí bù jué　hesitate to make a decision; be irresolute; be undecided: 你要是再～, 就失去机会了。If you remain undecided, you'll let the chance slip.／你的一生, 误事就误在"～"四个字上! The trouble with you all your life has been that you hesitate too much.

迟早 chízǎo　sooner or later: 他～会来的。He will come sooner or later.

迟滞 chízhì　① slow-moving; sluggish: 河道淤塞, 水流～。The river is silted up and the water flows sluggishly. ② mil. delaying (action)

迟重 chízhòng　slow and heavy: 老人脚步～, 行走艰难。The old man trudged (or plodded) along.

持 chí　① hold; grasp: ～枪 hold a gun／～相反意见 hold a contrary opinion／～保留态度 have reserva-

tions ② support; maintain: 支持 zhīchí / 维持 wéichí ③ manage; run: 主持 zhǔchí / 操持 cāochí ④ oppose: 相持 xiāngchí

持法 chífǎ enforce the law; execute the law

持己 chíjǐ same as 持身 chíshēn

持家 chíjiā run one's home; keep house: ～有方 be good at running one's home

持节 chíjié hold the imperial insignia (as credentials)—serve as a diplomatic envoy

持久 chíjiǔ lasting; enduring; protracted: 作～打算 plan on a long-term basis / ～和平 lasting peace / 他们之间的感情是不会～的。Their love won't last. / 没有正确的领导, 群众的积极性就不可能～。Without correct leadership, the enthusiasm of the masses cannot be sustained.

持久力 chíjiǔlì staying power; stamina; endurance

持久战 chíjiǔzhàn protracted war; protracted warfare

持论 chílùn present an argument; put a case; express a view: ～公平 state a case fairly / ～有据 put forward a well-grounded argument

持平 chípíng unbiased; fair

持平之论 chípíng zhī lùn a fair argument; an unbiased view

持球 chíqiú *sports* holding

持身 chíshēn make demands on oneself: ～严正 make strict demands on oneself

持续 chíxù continue; sustain: 两国的文化交流已经～了一千多年。Cultural interchange between the two countries has gone on for more than a thousand years. / 保证交通运输业以较高的速度～发展 ensure a sustained and reasonably rapid development of communications and transportation / 使国民经济～稳定增长 bring about a sustained, stable growth in the national economy / ～射击 sustained fire

持有 chíyǒu hold: ～护照 hold a passport / ～不同意见 hold differing views

持之以恒 chí zhī yǐ héng persevere: 刻苦学习, ～ study assiduously and perseveringly

持之有故 chí zhī yǒu gù have grounds for one's views

持重 chízhòng prudent; cautious; discreet: 老成持重 iǎochéng chízhòng

匙
chí spoon: 汤匙 tāngchí ——see also shi

匙子 chízi spoon

踟
chí see below

踟蹰 chíchú (also 踟躇 chíchú) hesitate; waver

踟蹰不前 chíchú bù qián hesitate to move forward

墀
chí *formal* steps (leading up to a palace hall): 丹墀 dānchí

篪 (箎、篪)
chí bamboo flute (an ancient musical instrument)

chǐ

尺
chǐ ① *chi*, a traditional unit of length ② short for 市尺 shìchǐ ③ rule; ruler: 折尺 zhéchǐ / 尺子 chǐzi ④ an instrument in the shape of a ruler: 计算尺 jìsuànchǐ ——see also chě

尺寸 chǐcun ① measurement; dimensions; size: 衣服的～ measurements of a garment / 量～ take sb.'s measurements / 这块木板～正好。This board is just the right size. / 轮廓～ overall size / 名义～ nominal size / 加工～ finish size / ～比例尺 dimension scale ② *inf.* proper limits for speech or action; sense of

propriety: 他办事很有～。He knows what to do and what not to do.

尺动脉 chǐdòngmài *physiol.* ulnar artery

尺牍 chǐdú ① a model of epistolary art ② correspondence (of an eminent writer)

尺度 chǐdù yardstick; measure; scale: 检验真理的～ yardstick of truth

尺短寸长 chǐduǎn-cùncháng short for 尺有所短,寸有所长 chǐ yǒu suǒ duǎn, cùn yǒu suǒ cháng

尺幅千里 chǐfú qiānlǐ a thousand-mile view on a one-foot scroll—rich content within a small compass

尺骨 chǐgǔ *physiol.* ulna

尺蠖 chǐhuò *zool.* looper; inchworm; measuringworm; geometer; 桑～ mulberry looper

尺蠖蛾 chǐhuò'é *zool.* geometrid moth

尺码 chǐmǎ size; measures: 你穿多大～的鞋? What size shoes do you wear?

尺素 chǐsù a foot-long white silk scroll (used for painting, letter writing, etc.)——① a painting of small size ② letter; correspondence

尺有所短,寸有所长 chǐ yǒu suǒ duǎn, cùn yǒu suǒ cháng sometimes a foot may prove short while an inch may prove long—everyone has his strong and weak points

尺子 chǐzi rule; ruler

呎
chǐ, also yīngchǐ old form for 英尺 yīngchǐ

齿 (齒)
chǐ ① tooth ② a tooth-like part of anything: 锯齿儿 jùchǐr ③ *formal* age: 稚～ very young / ～德俱尊 advanced in age and moral integrity ④ *formal* mention: 不足～数 not worth mentioning

齿唇音 chǐchúnyīn *phonet.* labio-dental sound

齿及 chǐjí *formal* mention; touch upon

齿冷 chǐlěng *formal* laugh sb. to scorn: 令人齿冷 lìng rén chǐlěng

齿轮 chǐlún gear wheel; gear: 正～ spur gear / 斜～ helical gear / 伞～ bevel gear / ～传动 gear drive / ～间隙 gear clearance / ～箱 gear box / ～组 gear cluster

齿条 chǐtiáo *mech.* rack

齿舞 Chǐwǔ Habomai

齿音 chǐyīn *phonet.* dental sound

齿龈 chǐyín *physiol.* gums

侈
chǐ *formal* ① wasteful; extravagant: 奢侈 shēchǐ ② exaggerate: 侈谈 chǐtán

侈论 chǐlùn *formal* gross exaggerations; high-sounding talk

侈靡 chǐmí *formal* extravagant and wasteful; excessively extravagant

侈谈 chǐtán talk glibly about; prate about; prattle about: ～永久和平 prate about eternal peace / 不能脱离生产实际去～技术革新。One should not prattle about technical innovations and disregard actual production.

耻 (恥)
chǐ shame; disgrace; humiliation: 引以为～ regard as a disgrace

耻骨 chǐgǔ *physiol.* pubic bones; pubis

耻骂 chǐmà abuse; insult

耻辱 chǐrǔ shame; disgrace; humiliation

耻笑 chǐxiào hold sb. to ridicule; sneer at; mock

豉
chǐ see 豆豉 dòuchǐ

褫
chǐ *formal* strip; deprive: ～职 deprive sb. of his post; remove sb. from office

褫夺 chǐduó strip; deprive: ～公权 deprive sb. of civil rights

褫革 chǐgé *formal* remove sb. from office; discharge

sb. from his post

chì

彳　chì　see below

彳亍　chìchù　*formal*　walk slowly: 独自在河边～ take a solitary walk along a river

叱　chì　*formal*　loudly rebuke; shout at

叱呵　chìhē　(also 叱喝 chìhē) shout at; bawl at

叱骂　chìmà　scold roundly; curse; abuse

叱责　chìzé　scold; upbraid; rebuke

叱咤　chìzhà　*formal*　shout or bawl angrily

叱咤风云　chìzhà fēngyún　commanding the wind and the clouds; shaking heaven and earth; all-powerful: ～的英雄气概 earthshaking heroism

斥¹　chì　① upbraid; scold; denounce; reprimand: 痛斥 tòngchì　② repel; exclude; oust: 同电相～。 Two like electric charges repel each other. ③ *formal* open up; expand: ～地 expand territory

斥²　chì　*formal*　reconnoitre; scout: 斥候 chìhòu

斥革　chìgé　*formal*　dismiss from office

斥候　chìhòu　*old*　① reconnoitre ② scout

斥力　chìlì　*phys.*　repulsion

斥骂　chìmà　reproach; upbraid; scold

斥退　chìtuì　① *old* dismiss sb. from his post ② *old* expel from a school ③ shout at sb. to go away

斥责　chìzé　reprimand; rebuke; denounce: 厉声～ severely reprimand; excoriate

斥逐　chìzhú　expel; oust; drive away

斥资　chìzī　*formal*　furnish funds for; fund: ～创办医院 furnish funds for setting up hospitals

赤　chì　① red: ～色 red colour ② *old* revolutionary; Communist: 赤卫队 chìwèiduì　③ loyal; sincere; single-hearted: 赤心 chìxīn　④ bare: 赤膊 chìbó / 赤脚 chìjiǎo

赤背　chìbèi　barebacked

赤膊　chìbó　barebacked: 打～ be stripped to the waist

赤膊上阵　chìbó shàngzhèn　go into battle stripped to the waist—throw away all disguise; come out into the open

赤忱　chìchén　*formal*　① same as 赤诚 chìchéng　② absolute sincerity

赤诚　chìchéng　absolutely sincere: ～待人 treat people with absolute sincerity

赤胆忠心　chìdǎn-zhōngxīn　utter devotion; whole-hearted dedication; ardent loyalty: ～为人民 serve the people with utter devotion

赤道　chìdào　① the equator ② *astron.* the celestial equator

赤道几内亚　Chìdào Jǐnèiyà　Equatorial Guinea

赤道几内亚人　Chìdào Jǐnèiyàrén　Equatorial Guinean

赤道面　chìdàomiàn　the equatorial plane

赤道无风带　chìdào wúfēngdài　the equatorial calm belt

赤道仪　chìdàoyí　equatorial telescope

赤地千里　chìdì qiānlǐ　a thousand *li* of barren land—a scene of utter desolation (after a drought or an insect plague): 那年，华北平原大旱，～。That year the North China Plain was visited by a great drought that seared vast expanses of farmland.

赤豆　chìdòu　*dial.*　red bean

赤褐色　chìhèsè　russet

赤红　chìhóng　crimson

赤狐　chìhú　red fox

赤脚　chìjiǎo　barefooted; barefoot: 赤着脚在稻田里干活 work barefooted in the paddy fields / 打～ go barefoot

赤脚医生　chìjiǎo yīshēng　barefoot doctor (a nickname for part-time paramedical workers in rural areas trained in simple techniques of diagnosis and treatment)

赤金　chìjīn　pure gold; solid gold

赤经　chìjīng　*astron.*　right ascension

赤口毒舌　chìkǒu-dúshé　venomous tongue; vile language

赤佬　chìlǎo　*dial.*　① ghost; ② scoundrel; rascal

赤痢　chìlì　*Chin. med.*　dysentery characterized by blood in the stool

赤练蛇　chìliànshé　Dinodon rufozonatum (a poisonless snake)

赤磷　chìlín　red phosphorus

赤露　chìlù　bare: ～着胸口 with bared chest

赤裸　chìluǒ　① bare: ～着上身 barebacked; stripped to the waist / 全身～ stark naked ② undisguised

赤裸裸　chìluǒluǒ　① without a stitch of clothing; stark naked ② undisguised; naked; out-and-out: ～的勾结 undisguised collusion / ～的强盗行径 plain robbery / ～的侵略 naked aggression / ～的威胁 a naked threat

赤霉素　chìméisù　*biochem.*　gibberellin

赤贫　chìpín　in abject poverty; utterly destitute

赤日　chìrì　scorching sun

赤芍　chìsháo　*Chin. med.*　the (unpeeled) root of herbaceous peony (Paeonia lactiflora)

赤身　chìshēn　naked

赤身露体　chìshēn-lùtǐ　stark naked; not wearing a stitch

赤手空拳　chìshǒu-kōngquán　bare-handed; unarmed: 巡捕用警棍对付～的示威学生。The police in the foreign concessions used truncheons against the unarmed demonstrating students.

赤松　chìsōng　Japanese red pine (Pinus densiflora)

赤陶　chìtáo　terra-cotta

赤条条　chìtiáotiáo　have not a stitch on; be stark naked

赤铁矿　chìtiěkuàng　red iron ore; hematite

赤铜矿　chìtóngkuàng　red copper ore; cuprite

赤纬　chìwěi　*astron.*　declination

赤卫队　chìwèiduì　Red Guards (armed units of the masses in the revolutionary base areas during the Second Revolutionary Civil War, 1927–1937)

赤县神州　Chìxiàn-Shénzhōu　Red Territory and Divine Land (a poetic name for China)

赤小豆　chìxiǎodòu　red bean

赤心　chìxīn　sincere heart; genuine sincerity; whole-hearted devotion: ～相待 treat sb. with all sincerity

赤血盐　chìxuèyán　*chem.*　potassium ferricyanide; red prussiate of potash

赤眼蜂　chìyǎnfēng　trichogramma

赤子　chìzǐ　① a newborn baby ② *formal* the people: 海外～ overseas compatriots

赤子之心　chìzǐ zhī xīn　the heart of a newborn babe—utter innocence: 大人者，不失其～者也。《孟子》A great man is one who retains the heart of a newborn babe.

赤字　chìzì　deficit: ～开支 deficit spending / 财政(贸易)～ financial (trade) deficit / 弥补～ make up (or meet) a deficit

赤足　chìzú　barefooted; barefoot

饬　chì　*formal*　① put in order; readjust: 整饬 zhěngchì　② orderly; well-behaved: 谨饬 jǐnchì　③ (usu. used in official documents) order: 严～ issue strict orders

饬令　chìlìng　(usu. used in official documents) order

炽(熾)　chì　flaming; ablaze

炽烈　chìliè　burning fiercely; flaming; blazing: 炉火～。The stove is burning fiercely. / ～的气氛 a fervent

atmosphere.

炽热 chìrè ① red-hot; blazing: ～的钢水 red-hot molten steel / ～的阳光 a blazing sun ② passionate: ～的情感 passionate feelings

炽盛 chìshèng　flaming; ablaze; flourishing: 火势～。The fire is blazing.

炽燥 chìzào　hot and dry; parching hot

炽灼 chìzhuó ① (of a fire) blazing; raging ② powerful; influential ③ burn; scorch; singe

翅 (翄)
chì ① wing ② shark's fin

翅膀 chìbǎng　wing

翅果 chìguǒ　bot. samara

翅脉 chìmài　vein (of the wings of an insect)

翅鞘 chìqiào　same as 鞘翅 qiàochì

翅席 chìxí　a banquet with shark's fin as the crowning feature

敕 (勅、勑)
chì　imperial order; edict

敕封 chìfēng　appoint sb. to a post or confer a title on sb. by imperial order

敕令 chìlìng　(also 敕命 chìmìng) imperial order; edict

畜
chì　formal only 畜 bùchì

chōng

冲¹ (沖、衝)
chōng ① thoroughfare; important place: 要冲 yàochōng ② charge; rush; dash: 向敌人～去 charge the enemy / 哪里有困难就～向哪里。Rush to wherever there are difficulties to tackle. / 他～进着火的房子，救出了两个小孩。He dashed into the burning house and rescued two children. ③ clash; collide: 冲突 chōngtū ④ astron. opposition; 大冲 dàchōng

冲² (沖)
chōng ① pour boiling water on: ～茶 make tea ② rinse; flush: 把盘子一一～ rinse the plates / 便后～水。Flush the toilet after use. / 秧苗给大水～走了。The seedlings were washed away by the flood. ③ photog. develop: ～胶卷 develop a roll of film

冲³ (沖)
chōng　dial. a stretch of flatland in a hilly area
——see also chòng

冲程 chōngchéng　mech. stroke: 四～发动机 four-stroke engine

冲冲 chōngchōng　in a state of excitement: 怒气～ in a great rage

冲刺 chōngcì　sports spurt; sprint: 向终点线～ make a spurt (or dash) towards the tape / 最后～ a final sprint; a sprint at the finish / ～速度 dash speed

冲淡 chōngdàn ① dilute: 把溶液～ dilute the solution ② water down; weaken; play down: 官方报纸故意～这次罢工的意义。The government newspapers played down the significance of the strike. / ～戏剧效果 weaken the dramatic effect / 不要因次要问题而～了中心任务。Don't stress minor issues at the expense of the central task.

冲荡 chōngdàng　rinse out; wash away

冲动 chōngdòng ① impulse: 出于一时～ act on impulse ② get excited; be impetuous: 他很容易～。He easily gets excited.

冲断层 chōngduàncéng　geol. thrust fault

冲犯 chōngfàn　offend; affront: 他控制不住自己，说了几句话，～了他叔父。He forgot himself and said something that offended his uncle.

冲锋 chōngfēng　charge; assault: 打退敌人的～ beat back the enemy assault / 在改革中，他们～在前。They are in the vanguard of the movement for reform.

冲锋号 chōngfēnghào　a bugle call to charge

冲锋枪 chōngfēngqiāng　submachine gun; tommy gun

冲锋陷阵 chōngfēng-xiànzhèn　charge and shatter enemy positions; charge the enemy lines; charge forward: 冒着枪林弹雨～ charge under a hail of bullets; charge under heavy fire

冲服 chōngfú　take (medicine) after mixing it with water, wine, etc.

冲沟 chōnggōu　mil. stormed crack

冲昏头脑 chōnghūn tóunǎo　turn sb.'s head: 胜利～ be dizzy with success; be carried away by success

冲击 chōngjī ① lash; pound: 海浪～着礁石，飞起像珠子般的水花。The waves lashed at the rocks, sending up pearly spray. ② charge; assault: 向敌人阵地发起～ charge an enemy position / 各国人民的革命斗争～着旧世界。The revolutionary struggles of the people of various countries are pounding at the old world. / 在文化大革命中受到～ came under attack during the Cultural Revolution / 向世界纪录展开猛烈～ make vigorous attempts to break the world records

冲击波 chōngjībō　phys. shock wave; blast wave

冲击机 chōngjījī　old name for 强击机 qiángjījī

冲积 chōngjī　geol. alluviation

冲积层 chōngjīcéng　geol. alluvium

冲积平原 chōngjī píngyuán　alluvial plain

冲积扇 chōngjīshàn　geol. alluvial fan

冲积土 chōngjītǔ　alluvial soil

冲剂 chōngjì　medicine to be taken after being mixed with boiling water, wine, etc.

冲决 chōngjué　burst; smash: ～堤防 burst the dykes / ～束缚他们的罗网 smash the trammels that bind them

冲口而出 chōng kǒu ér chū　say sth. unthinkingly; blurt out

冲垮 chōngkuǎ　burst; shatter: 洪水～了堤坝。The flood waters burst the dykes. / ～敌军防线 shatter the enemy lines

冲浪 chōnglàng　sports surfing; surfboarding: ～板 surfboard

冲力 chōnglì　impulsive force; momentum

冲凉 chōngliáng　dial. have a shower

冲量 chōngliàng　phys. impulse

冲破 chōngpò　break through; breach: ～重重障碍 break through one barrier after another; surmount all obstacles / ～敌军包围 break through the enemy encirclement / ～传统观念的束缚 smash the bonds of tradition / ～僵化的经济体制 break down the rigid economic structure

冲散 chōngsàn　break up; scatter; disperse: ～人群 disperse a crowd / 游行队伍让马队给～了。The demonstrators were scattered by the mounted police.

冲杀 chōngshā　charge; rush ahead: 在枪林弹雨中～ charge head-on against a hail of bullets

冲沙闸 chōngshāzhá　scouring sluice

冲晒 chōngshài　photog. develop and print

冲绳 Chōngshéng　Okinawa

冲刷 chōngshuā ① wash and brush; wash down: 把汽车～得干干净净 give the car a thorough wash-down / ～旧社会遗留下来的污泥浊水 wash away the dirt and filth left over from the old society ② erode; wash away: 垒起石坝，防止雨水～梯田。Stone banks were built to prevent erosion of the terraced fields. / 岩石上有被洪水～过的痕迹。The rocks carry marks left by a flood.

冲塌 chōngtā　(of floodwater, etc.) cause to collapse; burst: ～堤坝 burst dykes and dams / ～房屋 dash

against the houses and wash them away

冲天　chōngtiān　towering; soaring: ～干劲 boundless enthusiasm / 怒气～ be in a towering rage

冲突　chōngtū　conflict; clash: 武装～ an armed conflict / 边境～ a border clash / 利害～ conflict of interests / 避免～ avoid clashes / 这两个会的时间～了。The two meetings clash.

冲洗　chōngxǐ　① rinse; wash: 用消毒药水～伤口 wash a wound with a disinfectant ② *photog.* develop: ～照片 develop prints

冲喜　chōngxǐ　"warding-off" wedding (formerly, a wedding arranged for a young man who was dangerously ill, in the hope that the joyous occasion would ward off the danger of imminent death)

冲霄　chōngxiāo　shoot up into the sky: ～的高楼 sky-high buildings; skyscrapers

冲泻　chōngxiè　rush down in torrents

冲要　chōngyào　(of a place) strategically important

冲澡　chōngzǎo　*inf.* take a shower: 我冲个澡再说。I'll take a shower before I leave.

冲帐　chōngzhàng　*accounting* ① strike a balance ② reverse an entry

冲撞　chōngzhuàng　① collide; bump; ram: 渔船遭到敌舰的～。The fishing boat was rammed by an enemy warship. ② give offence; offend: 我没想到这句话竟～了他。I didn't expect him to take offence at that remark.

充　chōng　① sufficient; full: 充分 chōngfēn ② fill; stuff: 充电 chōngdiàn / 充塞 chōngsè ③ serve as; act as: ～向导 serve as a guide ④ pretend to be; pose as; pass sth. off as: ～内行 pretend to be an expert / ～好汉 pose as a hero

充畅　chōngchàng　① (of the flow of commodities) free and smooth ② (of writing) smooth and fluent

充斥　chōngchì　*derog.* flood; congest; be full of: 市场上～着外国商品。The markets were flooded with foreign goods.

充当　chōngdāng　serve as; act as; play the part of: ～翻译 act as interpreter / ～辩护士 play the part of an apologist

充电　chōngdiàn　charge (a battery)

充电器　chōngdiànqì　charger

充耳不闻　chōng ěr bù wén　stuff one's ears and refuse to listen; turn a deaf ear to: 对于别人的批评，他们是～的。They turned a deaf ear to other people's criticisms. / 日日夜夜跟她讲，她～，我又有什么法子呢？I talked to her day and night, but she wouldn't listen; what else could I do?

充分　chōngfēn　① full; ample; abundant: ～协商 full consultation / ～证据 ample evidence / 我们有～理由相信这消息是可靠的。We have every reason to believe that the news is true. / 准备工作做得很～。Ample preparations were made. ② to the full; as fully as possible: ～利用 fully utilize; make full use of / ～发动群众 fully arouse the masses

充公　chōnggōng　confiscate: 他受贿的财物全部充了公。The bribes and gifts that he took were all confiscated.

充饥　chōngjī　allay (*or* appease) one's hunger: 靠野菜～ allay one's hunger with wild herbs

充军　chōngjūn　be transported to a distant place for penal servitude; banish

充满　chōngmǎn　① fill: 欢呼声～了会场。Loud cheers filled the assembly hall. ② be filled with; be full of; brim with; be permeated (*or* imbued) with: 屋子里～着阳光。The room is full of sunshine. / 大厅里～了孩子们的欢笑声。The hall resounded with the laughter of children. / ～热情的讲话 a speech brimming with warmth / 这首诗～革命乐观主义。This poem is imbued with revolutionary optimism.

充沛　chōngpèi　plentiful; abundant; copious: 雨水～ abundant rainfall / ～的革命热情 unflagging revolutionary enthusiasm

充其量　chōngqíliàng　(also 充其极 chōngqíjí) at most; at best: 这点给养～只够维持三天。The provisions can last three days at most. / ～十天就可以完成这项任务。The job will be finished in ten days at most.

充任　chōngrèn　fill the post of; hold the position of: 聘请老工程师～顾问 ask senior engineers to be our advisers / 他～经理很合适。He's well suited for the position of manager.

充塞　chōngsè　fill (up); cram: 我心里～着喜悦的情绪。My heart is filled with joy.

充实　chōngshí　① substantial; rich: 内容～ substantial in content ② substantiate; enrich; replenish: ～论据 substantiate one's argument / ～库存 replenish the stocks / 下放干部，～基层 transfer cadres to strengthen organizations at the grass roots

充数　chōngshù　make up the number; serve as a stopgap: 参加你们队，我只能充个数。I'll only be an also-ran in your team.

充填　chōngtián　fill up; stuff: 有的气球是用氢气～的，有的用氦气。Some balloons are filled with hydrogen, some with helium.

充血　chōngxuè　*med.* hyperaemia; congestion

充溢　chōngyì　be full to the brim; be exuberant; be overflowing: 孩子们的脸上～着幸福的笑容。The children's faces beamed with happy smiles. / 祖国大地～春意。There is spring in the air all over our country.

充盈　chōngyíng　① plentiful; full: 仓廪～。The granaries are full. ② *formal* (of muscles) well-developed

充裕　chōngyù　abundant; ample; plentiful: 时间～ have ample (*or* plenty of) time / 经济～ well-off

充足　chōngzú　adequate; sufficient; abundant; ample: 经费～ have sufficient (*or* ample) funds / 阳光～ full of sunshine; sunny

充足理由律　chōngzúlǐyóulǜ　*log.* the law of sufficient reason

忡（懤）　chōng　see below

忡忡　chōngchōng　laden with anxiety; careworn: 忧心忡忡 yōuxīn chōngchōng

茺　chōng　see below

茺蔚　chōngwèi　same as 益母草 yìmǔcǎo

舂　chōng　pound (in a mortar); pestle: ～米 husk rice with mortar and pestle / ～药 pound medicinal substances into powder

憧　chōng　see below

憧憧　chōngchōng　flickering; moving to and fro: 树影～ flickering shadows of trees / 人影～ shadows of people moving about

憧憬　chōngjǐng　yearn for; long for; look forward to: ～着更为美好的未来 yearning for a better and brighter future / 青年的～ yearnings of young people / 我们～着四个现代化的实现。We look forward to the realization of the "four modernizations".

艟　chōng　see 艨艟 méngchōng

chóng

虫（蟲）　chóng　insect or worm

虫草　chóngcǎo　short for 冬虫夏草 dōngchóng-xiàcǎo

虫害　chónghài　insect pest

虫积　chóngjī　*Chin. med.*　parasitic diseases (mainly in the stomach or intestines)

虫胶　chóngjiāo　shellac

虫胶清漆　chóngjiāo qīngqī　shellac (varnish)

虫媒花　chóngméihuā　*bot.*　entomophilous flower

虫情　chóngqíng　pest situation: ～测报 pest forecasting

虫蚀　chóngshí　worm-eaten; moth-eaten

虫牙　chóngyá　popular name for 龋齿　qǔchǐ

虫瘿　chóngyǐng　gall (on plants)

虫灾　chóngzāi　a plague of insects

虫豸　chóngzhì　*formal*　insects

虫子　chóngzi　insect or worm

重　chóng　① repeat; duplicate: 这两个例子～了。 These two examples duplicate each other. / 书买～了。 Two copies of the same book have been bought by mistake. ② *adv.*　again; once more: ～启战端 renew hostilities / 把生词～抄一遍。 Copy the new words over again. ③ layer: 越过万～山 climb over countless mountains / 突破一～又一～的障碍 break through barrier after barrier ——see also zhòng

重版　chóngbǎn　① (of books, periodicals, etc.) be republished ② republication

重播　chóngbō　① rebroadcast a programme (from the same station) ② resow (the same field)

重操旧业　chóng cāo jiùyè　resume one's old profession; take up one's old trade again

重唱　chóngchàng　*mus.*　an ensemble of two or more singers, each singing one part: 四～ (vocal) quartet

重重　chóngchóng　layer upon layer; ring upon ring: 陷入～包围之中 be encircled ring upon ring / 克服～困难 overcome one difficulty after another; surmount numerous difficulties

重床叠屋　chóngchuáng-diéwū　same as 叠床架屋 diéchuáng-jiàwū

重打锣鼓另开张　chóng dǎ luógǔ lìng kāizhāng　reopen a business to the beating of gongs and drums; start all over again: 他得～，打头来! He would have to start from scratch all over again.

重蹈覆辙　chóng dǎo fùzhé　follow the track of the overturned cart—follow the same old road to ruin

重叠　chóngdié　one on top of another; overlapping: 山峦～ range upon range of mountains / 精简～的行政机构 streamline (*or* simplify) overlapping administrative organizations

重发球　chóngfāqiú　*sports*　let service; let

重返　chóngfǎn　return: ～前线 go back to the front / ～家园 return to one's homeland

重返大气层　chóngfǎn dàqìcéng　reentry (of a spaceship, rocket, etc.): ～运载工具 reentry vehicle

重犯　chóngfàn　repeat (an error or offence): 吸取教训，避免～错误 draw a lesson from past errors so as to prevent their recurrence

重逢　chóngféng　meet again; have a reunion: 旧友～ reunion of old friends

重复　chóngfù　repeat; duplicate: 避免不必要的～ avoid unnecessary repetition / 他一再～他的观点。 He reiterated his views over and over again. / 任何历史现象都不会是简单的～。 No historical phenomenon is a mere repetition of the past.

重合　chónghé　*math.*　coincide

重婚　chónghūn　*leg.*　(commit) bigamy

重见天日　chóng jiàn tiānrì　once more see the light of day—be delivered from oppression or persecution

重建　chóngjiàn　rebuild; reconstruct; reestablish; rehabilitate: 战后的～工作 postwar reconstruction / ～家园 rehabilitate one's homeland; rebuild one's home village or town

重九　Chóngjiǔ　the Double Ninth Festival (the 9th day of the 9th lunar month)

重峦叠嶂　chóngluán-diézhàng　same as 层峦叠嶂 céngluán-diézhàng

重名儿　chóngmíngr　bear the same name: 他和我～。 He is my namesake.

重起炉灶　chóng qǐ lúzào　begin all over again; make a fresh start

重庆谈判　Chóngqìng Tánpàn　the Chongqing Negotiations (August-October 1945, peace talks between the representatives of the Chinese Communist Party and those of the Kuomintang)

重申　chóngshēn　reaffirm; reiterate; restate: ～前令 reaffirm an existing decree / ～党的纪律 affirm anew the discipline of the Party / ～我国政府的一贯立场 reiterate the consistent stand of our government

重审　chóngshěn　*leg.*　retrial

重生父母　chóngshēng fùmǔ　same as 再生父母 zàishēng fùmǔ

重施故技　chóng shī gùjì　play the same old trick; repeat a stock trick

重适　chóngshì　*formal*　(of a woman) remarry

重孙　chóngsūn　*inf.*　son's grandson; great-grandson

重孙女　chóngsūnnǚ　son's granddaughter; great-granddaughter

重弹老调　chóng tán lǎodiào　same as 老调重弹 lǎodiào chóng tán

重提　chóngtí　bring up again: 旧事～ bring up an old case; recall past events

重围　chóngwéi　tight encirclement: 杀出～ break through a tight encirclement

重温　chóngwēn　review: ～第二次世界大战的历史 review the history of World War II

重温旧梦　chóngwēn jiùmèng　revive an old dream; relive an old experience

重现　chóngxiàn　reappear: 当年的战斗场面又～在他眼前。 The battle scenes of those years reappeared in his mind's eye.

重霄　chóngxiāo　*liter.*　the empyrean; heaven (from the ancient belief that the heavens have nine layers or spheres)

重新　chóngxīn　*adv.*　again; anew; afresh: ～考虑 reconsider / ～部署 rearrange; redeploy / ～发起进攻 launch a fresh offensive

重新做人　chóngxīn zuòrén　start one's life afresh; turn over a new leaf

重行　chóngxíng　begin doing sth. again; take up sth. again: ～公布 republish / ～审查 reexamine

重修　chóngxiū　① renovate; rebuild: ～教堂 renovate a church building ② revise: ～《汉英词典》 revise the *Chinese-English Dictionary*

重修旧好　chóng xiū jiùhǎo　renew cordial relations; become reconciled; bury the hatchet

重言　chóngyán　another name for 叠字 diézì

重檐　chóngyán　*archit.*　double-eaved roof

重演　chóngyǎn　① put on an old play, etc. ② recur; reenact; repeat: 历史的错误不许～。 Past mistakes should not be repeated.

重阳　Chóngyáng　the Double Ninth Festival (the 9th day of the 9th lunar month)

重洋　chóngyáng　the seas and oceans: 远隔重洋 yuǎn gé chóngyáng

重样　chóngyàng　of the same pattern

重译　chóngyì　retranslate

重印　chóngyìn　reprint

重印本　chóngyìnběn　reprint

重圆　chóngyuán　be reunited: 破镜重圆 pòjìng chóngyuán

重张　chóngzhāng　*old*　restart a business; reopen a shop

重振军威 chóng zhèn jūnwēi restore the prestige of an army; make an army's might felt once again

重整旗鼓 chóng zhěng qígǔ rally one's forces (after a defeat)

重奏 chóngzòu *mus.* an ensemble of two or more instrumentalists, each playing one part: 四～ (instrumental) quartet

重足而立，侧目而视 chóng zú ér lì, cèmù ér shì stand transfixed with fear and eye sb. askance: 使通国之人～者，无过于此辈穷凶极恶之特务人员。Ordinary people everywhere recoil and turn away in fear from these fiendish brutes of agents.

崇
chóng ① high; lofty; sublime: 崇山峻岭 chóngshān-jùnlǐng ② esteem; worship: 尊崇 zūnchóng ③ (Chóng) a surname

崇拜 chóngbài worship; adore: 她很～她父亲。She worships her father. / ～偶像 worship of idols; idolatry

崇奉 chóngfèng believe in (a religion); worship

崇高 chónggāo lofty; sublime; high: ～的理想 a lofty ideal / ～的威望 high prestige / 顺致最～的敬意。I avail myself of this opportunity to renew to you the assurances of my highest consideration.

崇敬 chóngjìng esteem; respect; revere: 我很～这位老教授。I have great respect for the old professor. / 怀着十分～的心情 cherish a feeling of great reverence for / 革命英雄永远受到人民的～。Revolutionary heroes will always be held in esteem by the people.

崇论闳议 chónglùn-hóngyì lofty and brilliant discourse

崇山峻岭 chóngshān-jùnlǐng lofty ridges and towering mountains

崇尚 chóngshàng uphold; advocate: ～勤俭 advocate industry and thrift

崇信 chóngxìn believe in; trust: ～伊斯兰教 believe in Islamism / ～奸邪 put one's trust in crafty and evil persons

崇洋媚外 chóngyáng-mèiwài worship foreign things and toady to foreign powers

崇洋迷外 chóngyáng-míwài worship and have blind faith in things foreign

chǒng

宠（寵）
chǒng dote on; bestow favour on: 他太～小女儿了。He dotes on his youngest daughter too much. / 别把孩子～坏了。Don't spoil the child.

宠爱 chǒng'ài make a pet of sb.; dote on: 奶奶特别～小孙儿。Grandma dotes on her little grandson.

宠儿 chǒng'ér pet; favourite; darling: 小红是她全家的～。Xiao Hong is the family darling. / 命运的～ the darling of fortune / 时代的～ the idol of the day

宠惯 chǒngguàn pamper (a child); indulge

宠姬 chǒngjī *formal* favourite concubine

宠辱不惊 chǒng-rǔ bù jīng remain indifferent whether favoured or humiliated

宠物 chǒngwù pet (e.g. a cat or a dog)

宠信 chǒngxìn be specially fond of and trust unduly (a subordinate)

宠幸 chǒngxìng patronize; bestow favour on

chòng

冲¹（衝）
chòng *inf.* ① with vim and vigour; with plenty of dash; vigorously: 这小伙子干活儿真～。This young fellow does his work with vim and vigour. /

水流得很～。The water flows with great force. / 他说话很～。He speaks bluntly. ② (of smell) strong; pungent: 这药味很～。This medicine has a strong smell.

冲²（衝）
chòng *prep. inf.* ① facing; towards: 窗户～南开。The window faces south. / 这话是～他说的。That remark was aimed at him. ② on the strength of; on the basis of; because: ～他们这股子干劲儿，没有克服不了的困难。With such drive, there's no difficulty that they can't overcome.

冲³（衝）
chòng *mech.* punching: 冲压 chòngyā
——see also chōng

冲床 chòngchuáng *mech.* punch (press); punching machine

冲盹儿 chòngdǔnr *dial.* doze off; nod off

冲劲儿 chòngjìnr ① vim and vigour; dash ② strength (of liquor); kick: 这二锅头～大。This *erguotou* has a lot of kick in it.

冲孔 chòngkǒng *mech.* ① punching ② punched hole

冲模 chòngmú *mech.* die

冲模插床 chòngmú chāchuáng *mech.* die slotting machine

冲头 chòngtóu *mech.* drift; punch pin

冲压 chòngyā *mech.* stamping; punching

冲压机 chòngyājī another name for 冲床 chòngchuáng

冲子 chòngzi punching pin (a tool)

铳
chòng blunderbuss: 鸟～ an old kind of fowling piece

铳子 chòngzi same as 冲子 chòngzi

chōu

抽¹
chōu ① take out (from in between): 从文件夹里～出一份申请书 take an application out of the file ② take (a part from a whole): ～出一部分劳力去抗旱 release part of the labour force from other work to combat the drought / 把他～出来管仓库 release him from his job and put him in charge of the warehouse / 开会前请～时间把文件看一下。Try and find time to read the document before the meeting. ③ (of certain plants) put forth: ～枝 branch out; sprout / 小树～出了嫩芽。The saplings are budding. ④ obtain by drawing, etc.: ～血 draw blood (for a test or transfusion)

抽²
chōu ① shrink: 这种布一洗就～。This cloth shrinks in the wash. ② lash; whip; thrash: ～陀螺 whip a top / ～牲口 lash a draught animal ③ *sports* drive

抽巴 chōuba *inf.* contract; shrink

抽查 chōuchá carry out selective examinations; make spot checks; spot-check

抽成 chōuchéng same as 提成 tíchéng

抽抽儿 chōuchour *inf.* ① shrink: 这块布一洗就～。This cloth shrinks in the wash. ② shrivel: 这些枣儿都～了。These dates have shrivelled up.

抽搐 chōuchù ① twitch ② *med.* tic

抽打 chōudǎ lash; whip; thrash: 农奴主用皮鞭～农奴。The serf owner lashed the serf with a whip.

抽打 chōuda beat (a carpet, blanket, etc.): 毯子得好好～一下。The blanket needs a good beating.

抽搭 chōuda *inf.* sob: 抽抽搭搭地哭了起来 break into sobs

抽地 chōudì (of a landlord) take land back from a tenant

抽调 chōudiào transfer (personnel or material): ～部分

兵力向北增援 move part of the troops to the north as reinforcements / ～干部支援农业 transfer cadres to strengthen the agricultural front

抽丁 chōudīng　press-gang

抽动 chōudòng　twitch; have a spasm; jerk spasmodically

抽斗 chōudǒu　dial. drawer

抽肥补瘦 chōuféi-bǔshòu　take from the fat to pad the lean; take from those with much and give to those with little

抽风[1] chōufēng　① med. convulsions ② inf. go crazy; lose one's senses: 别～了! Don't be crazy!

抽风[2] chōufēng　pump air: 这车间设有～装置。This workshop has air-pumping equipment.

抽风机 chōufēngjī　air pump

抽功夫 chōu gōngfu　same as 抽空 chōukòng

抽换 chōuhuàn　change (or replace) part of a whole: 这个课本～了三篇课文。Three of the lessons in the textbook have been superseded.

抽筋 chōujīn　① pull out a tendon ② inf. cramp: 腿～ have a cramp in the leg

抽空 chōukòng　manage to find time: 他工作很忙, 可是还～学习英语。Despite the pressure of work, he manages to find time to study English. / 抽不出空来 be unable to find time

抽冷子 chōulěngzi　do sth. when people are off guard: 医生让他在医院里再呆几天, 他却～跑回了工地。The doctor had told him to stay in hospital a few more days, but he slipped back to the worksite.

抽搦 chōunuò　same as 抽搐 chōuchù

抽气机 chōuqìjī　air exhauster; air extractor; air pump

抽泣 chōuqì　sob: 低声～ weep in choking sobs

抽签 chōuqiān　draw (or cast) lots

抽球 chōuqiú　sports drive

抽取 chōuqǔ　① draw; collect: ～版税 receive a royalty / ～百分之三佣金 charge a commission of 3%

抽纱 chōushā　arts & crafts drawnwork

抽身 chōushēn　leave one's work; extricate oneself; get away: 我七点钟以前恐怕抽不出身来。I'm afraid I'll be tied up until 7 o'clock. or I'm afraid I won't be free until 7 o'clock. / 及早～ hasten to extricate oneself from a difficult situation

抽水[1] chōushuǐ　draw (or pump) water: 从河里～ pump water from a river

抽水[2] chōushuǐ　(of cloth through wetting) shrink

抽水机 chōushuǐjī　water pump

抽水马桶 chōushuǐ mǎtǒng　flush toilet; water closet

抽水站 chōushuǐzhàn　pumping station

抽税 chōushuì　levy a tax

抽丝 chōusī　reel off raw silk from cocoons

抽穗 chōusuì　(of cereal plants) put forth ears; ear: 小麦正在～。The wheat is in the ear.

抽穗期 chōusuìqī　earing stage (or period); heading stage (or period)

抽缩 chōusuō　shrink; contract

抽薹 chōutái　(of garlic, chives, rape, etc.) bolt: 油菜～了。The rape is bolting.

抽提 chōutí　chem. extraction: ～蒸馏 extractive distillation

抽屉 chōuti　drawer

抽头[1] chōutóu　take a percentage (or cut) of the winnings in gambling

抽头[2] chōutóu　elec. tap: ～电路 tap circuit

抽闲 chōuxián　manage to find time: 我们～去十三陵玩玩。Let's find time for a trip to the Ming Tombs.

抽象 chōuxiàng　① abstract: ～的概念 an abstract concept / 科学的～ scientific abstraction / 不要这样～地谈问题。Don't speak in such abstract terms. ② form a general idea from particular instances: 从客观事物中～

出正确的结论 draw a correct conclusion from objective facts

抽象劳动 chōuxiàng láodòng　econ. abstract labour

抽象名词 chōuxiàng míngcí　abstract noun

抽象派 chōuxiàngpài　abstractionist school

抽象数 chōuxiàngshù　math. abstract number

抽象思维 chōuxiàng sīwéi　abstraction

抽象艺术 chōuxiàng yìshù　abstract art

抽薪止沸 chōuxīn zhǐfèi　take out the fuel to stop the pot boiling—take drastic measures to stop sth.

抽绣 chōuxiù　arts & crafts punchwork

抽选 chōuxuǎn　select; choose

抽芽 chōuyá　put forth buds; bud; sprout: 柳树开始～了。The willow trees have begun to bud.

抽烟 chōuyān　smoke (a cigarette or a pipe): 你～吗? Do you smoke? / 请～。Have a smoke. / 抽一袋烟 smoke a pipe

抽演 chōuyǎn　formal deduction

抽样 chōuyàng　sampling (in statistics and research)

抽样调查 chōuyàng diàochá　statistics sample survey; sampling

抽样分布 chōuyàng fēnbù　statistics sampling distribution

抽样误差 chōuyàng wùchā　statistics sampling error

抽噎 chōuyē　sob: 一个小姑娘坐在角落里～着。A little girl sat sobbing in the corner.

抽印 chōuyìn　offprint: ～学报的头一篇文章 offprint the first article of the journal / ～三百份 offprint 300 copies (of an article, etc.); make 300 offprints

抽印本 chōuyìnběn　offprint

抽油烟机 chōuyóuyānjī　range hood

抽壮丁 chōu zhuàngdīng　same as 抽丁 chōudīng

绌

绌 chōu　formal draw out

绌绎 chōuyì　formal expound; set forth

瘳

瘳 chōu　formal ① recover from an illness ② harm

chóu

仇 (讎、讐)

仇 chóu ① enemy; foe: 仇敌 chóudí ② hatred; enmity: 有～ have a score to settle / 这～一定要报。This wrong must be avenged. ——see also Qiú

仇雠 chóuchóu　formal enemy; foe: ～敌战之国 hostile or warring countries

仇敌 chóudí　foe; enemy

仇恨 chóuhèn　① hatred; enmity; hostility: 满腔～ seething with hatred ② feel great enmity towards; hate

仇家 chóujiā　personal enemy

仇人 chóurén　personal enemy

仇人相见, 分外眼红 chóurén xiāngjiàn, fènwài yǎnhóng　when enemies come face to face, their eyes blaze with hate

仇杀 chóushā　kill in revenge

仇视 chóushì　regard as an enemy; look upon with hatred; be hostile to

仇冤 chóuyuān　same as 冤仇 yuānchóu

仇怨 chóuyuàn　grudge; hatred; spite

仇隙 chóuxì　formal bitter quarrel; feud

俦 (儔)

俦 chóu　formal companion

俦类 chóulèi　formal people (esp. friends or companions) of the same generation or class

俦侣 chóulǚ　formal companion

帱（幬）
chóu *formal* ① bed curtain ② carriage curtain ——see also dào

惆
chóu see below

惆怅 chóuchàng sad; disconsolate; melancholy: 他这一走，她似乎有些～。She seems rather melancholy now that he has gone away.

绸（䌷）
chóu silk fabric; silk: 那连衣裙是～的。The dress is made of silk.

绸缎 chóuduàn silks and satins

绸缪 chóumóu *formal* ① be sentimentally attached: 情意～ be head over heels in love ② see 未雨绸缪 wèi yǔ chóumóu

绸子 chóuzi silk fabric

畴（疇）
chóu *formal* ① farmland: 平～千里 a vast expanse of cultivated land ② kind; division: 范畴 fànchóu

畴辈 chóubèi *formal* people of the same generation

畴类 chóulèi same as 俦类 chóulèi

畴日 chóurì *formal* in former times

畴昔 chóuxī *formal* in former times

愁
chóu worry; be anxious: 不～吃，不～穿 not have to worry about food and clothing / 你别～，病人很快会好的。Don't worry. The patient will soon recover. / 我们不～完不成任务。We know for certain we'll fulfil our task. / 这件事可把我～死了。This is really worrying me to death.

愁肠 chóucháng pent-up feelings of anxiety or sadness

愁肠百结 chóucháng bǎi jié with anxiety gnawing at one's heart; weighed down with anxiety

愁苦 chóukǔ anxiety; distress

愁眉 chóuméi knitted brows; worried look

愁眉不展 chóuméi bù zhǎn with a worried frown; with knitted brows: 她成天～，唉声叹气的。She looked terribly distressed and was sighing all the time.

愁眉苦脸 chóuméi-kǔliǎn wear a worried look; pull a long face: 我看你这两天～的，有什么心事吧？I've noticed these last few days you've been looking rather unhappy. There must be something worrying you. / 他～地抬起头来看了看我。He looked up at me miserably.

愁眉锁眼 chóuméi-suǒyǎn with knitted brows and lowered eyes; wearing a deep frown on one's face: 大家以为有了出路，～的姿态为之一扫。There is a general feeling that a way out of the impasse has been found, and people no longer knit their brows in despair.

愁闷 chóumèn feel gloomy; be in low spirits; be depressed: 他工作不顺利，心里十分～。He was very cast down by setbacks in his work.

愁容 chóuróng worried look; anxious expression: ～满面 look extremely worried / 面带～ look rather worried

愁思 chóusī sad thoughts; feelings of anxiety

愁绪 chóuxù *formal* gloomy mood: 小女儿的欢笑使他～全消。His little daughter's bright smiles dispelled all his gloom.

愁云 chóuyún gloomy clouds ——gloom; melancholy: 喜讯传来，人们脸上的～消散了。The gloomy expressions on their faces disappeared at the good news.

愁云惨雾 chóuyún-cǎnwù gloomy clouds and sad mists—gloom; melancholy

稠
chóu ① thick: 粥很～。The porridge is very thick. ② dense: 地窄人～ small in area but densely populated

稠密 chóumì dense: 人口～ densely populated; popu-

lous / 交通网～ a dense communications network

稠人广众 chóurén-guǎngzhòng a large crowd; a big gathering: 在～面前说话，她还是第一回呢。It was the first time she had ever spoken before such a big audience.

酬（酧、醻）
chóu ① *formal* propose a toast; toast ② reward; payment: 稿酬 gǎochóu ③ friendly exchange: 应酬 yìngchou ④ fulfil; realize: 壮志未酬 zhuàngzhì wèi chóu

酬报 chóubào requite; reward; repay; recompense

酬宾 chóubīn bargain sales

酬唱 chóuchàng present each other with poems

酬答 chóudá ① thank sb. with a gift ② respond with a poem or speech

酬对 chóuduì reply; answer

酬和 chóuhè respond (to a poem) with a poem

酬金 chóujīn monetary reward; remuneration: 优厚的～ a generous remuneration

酬劳 chóuláo ① repay; reward; recompense: 他们辛苦了一天，得好好～他们一下。We should reward them generously for a hard day's work. ② repayment; reward; recompense: 我自愿帮忙，不要任何～。I volunteered to help and expected no reward.

酬谢 chóuxiè thank sb. with a gift: 他帮了我们大忙，我不知道该怎么～他才好。He has given us a lot of help. I don't know what to give him to express my thankfulness.

酬应 chóuyìng same as 应酬 yìngchou①

酬庸 chóuyōng *formal* recompense; reward

酬酢 chóuzuò *formal* ① exchange of toasts ② friendly intercourse

筹（籌）
chóu ① chip; counter: 竹筹 zhúchóu ② prepare; plan: ～款 raise money (or funds)

筹办 chóubàn make preparations; make arrangements: ～国家行政学院 make preparations to found a state administrative college / 这次越野赛跑由我们厂负责～。Our factory is to make arrangements for the cross-country race.

筹备 chóubèi prepare; arrange: ～建校事宜 make preparations for the setting up of a school / ～工作 preparatory work; preparations / ～会议 preparatory (or preliminary) meeting / ～委员会 preparatory committee

筹措 chóucuò raise (money): ～旅费 raise money for travelling expenses

筹划 chóuhuà plan and prepare: 合作医疗站正～种植中草药。The cooperative medical service centre is planning to grow medicinal herbs. / 这里正在～建设一座水力发电站。Plans are being drawn up to build a hydroelectric station here.

筹集 chóují accumulate; raise (money): ～基金 raise funds

筹建 chóujiàn prepare to construct or establish sth.: 这个车间从去年开始～。Preparations were started last year for the construction of the workshop. / ～研究所 make preparations for the setting up of a research institute

筹借 chóujiè try to get a loan: ～款项 try to borrow money

筹略 chóulüè astuteness and resourcefulness; strategy

筹码 chóumǎ chip; counter: 麻将～ mahjong counters / 政治交易的～ bargaining counters in political deals

筹谋 chóumóu lay plans; devise strategies

筹募 chóumù collect (funds): ～福利基金 collect welfare funds

筹商 chóushāng (also 筹议 chóuyì) discuss; consult: ～对策 discuss what countermeasures to take

筹算 chóusuàn ① calculate with chips (in ancient times) ② calculate; reckon

踌（躊） chóu see below

踌躇 chóuchú hesitate; shilly-shally

踌躇不决 chóuchú bù jué hesitating; irresolute

踌躇不前 chóuchú bù qián hesitate to move forward; hesitate to make a move

踌躇满志 chóuchú mǎn zhì enormously proud of one's success; smug; complacent

雠¹ **（讎、讐）** chóu collate; proofread: 校雠 jiàochóu

雠² **（讎、讐）** chóu same as 仇 chóu

chǒu

丑¹ chǒu the second of the twelve Earthly Branches （地支）——see also 干支 gān-zhī

丑² **（醜）** chǒu ① ugly; unsightly; hideous: 长得不～ not bad-looking ② disgraceful; shameful; scandalous: 这种事太～了，不要说出去。This is really disgraceful. Don't breathe a word of it to anyone.

丑³ chǒu comic role (one of the four main roles in traditional opera, the other three being 生 shēng, 旦 dàn, and 净 jìng; recognized by the patch of white paint around the eyes and nose, sometimes outlined in black, and representing foolish, awkward, or stingy people, though not necessarily evil ones); comedian; clown

丑八怪 chǒubāguài inf. a very ugly person

丑表功 chǒubiǎogōng brag shamelessly about one's deeds; claim undeserved credit: 他做了一点儿小事，就到处～。He always swaggers around boasting about any little thing he has done.

丑诋 chǒudǐ formal hurl insults at; use bad language against; revile

丑恶 chǒu'è ugly; repulsive; hideous: ～灵魂 an ugly soul / ～面目 ugly features / ～表演 a disgusting performance / 露出～的嘴脸 show one's ugly face; reveal one's hideous features

丑化 chǒuhuà smear; uglify; defame; vilify: 这出戏～了劳动人民的形象。This play vilifies the working people.

丑话 chǒuhuà ① vulgar language; abusive words ② blunt words: 我把～说在前头，事情办糟了你可得负责。I must tell you bluntly that should anything go wrong you will be held responsible.

丑剧 chǒujù farce

丑角 chǒujué ① same as 丑³ chǒu ② (in real life) clown; comedian; buffoon

丑类 chǒulèi the bad sort; rascals; crooks

丑陋 chǒulòu ugly

丑婆子 chǒupózi old comedienne (in traditional opera)

丑时 chǒushí the period of the day from 1 a.m. to 3 a.m.

丑事 chǒushì a disgraceful affair; scandal

丑态 chǒutài ugly (or ludicrous) performance; buffoonery

丑态百出 chǒutài bǎi chū act like a buffoon; cut a contemptible figure

丑态毕露 chǒutài bì lù be utterly shameless; be extremely nauseating

丑闻 chǒuwén scandal: 水门事件是1972年发生在美国的一件政治～。The Watergate affair was a U.S. political scandal that broke in 1972.

丑媳妇总得见公婆 chǒuxífu zǒngděi jiàn gōngpó an ugly daughter-in-law will have to face her parents-in-law sooner or later—one's work whatever its faults or shortcomings, must be shown to others

丑行 chǒuxíng disgraceful conduct; shameful (or scandalous) behaviour

瞅（瞅） chǒu dial. look at: 让我～～。Let me have a look. / 她～了我一眼。She took a look (or glance) at me.

瞅见 chǒujiàn dial. see: 你～他没有? Did you see him? / 啥也瞅不见 can't see anything

瞅空儿 chǒukòngr (also 瞅空子 chǒukòngzi) inf. find time: 这件事你～和他谈谈。Try to find time to talk to him about this.

chòu

臭 chòu ① smelly; foul; stinking: ～味儿 stink; offensive odour; foul smell / ～鸡蛋 a rotten egg / ～不可闻 give off an unbearable stink ② disgusting; disgraceful: 他的名声早就～了。He has long been discredited. ③ severely: 被～骂了一顿 get a tongue-lashing; get a dressing down / 挨了一顿～打 get a good beating ④ dial. dud: 这颗子弹～了。This bullet is a dud. ——see also xiù

臭吃臭喝 chòuchī-chòuhē inf. eat and drink greedily

臭虫 chòuchóng bedbug

臭椿 chòuchūn bot. tree of heaven (Ailanthus altissima)

臭大姐 chòudàjiě popular name for a kind of stinkbug

臭弹 chòudàn a bullet, grenade, shell or bomb that fails to go off; dud

臭豆腐 chòudòufu strong-smelling preserved bean curd

臭烘烘 chòuhōnghōng stinking; foul-smelling; smelly

臭乎乎 chòuhūhū somewhat smelly; a bit off: 这块猪肉～的，最好不吃。This piece of pork is a bit off. Better not eat it.

臭美 chòuměi inf. show off shamelessly; be disgustingly smug: 你看她打扮得花里胡哨的，真～! Look how gaudily she is dressed, what a shameless display! / 你摇头晃脑的，～什么劲儿? What makes you so smug, swaggering like that?

臭名远扬 chòumíng yuǎn yáng notorious

臭名昭著 chòumíng zhāozhù of ill repute; notorious

臭皮囊 chòupínáng Buddhism the vile skin-bag; the human body; this mortal flesh

臭棋 chòuqí inf. a lousy chess move or game: 他走了一步～，结果输了。He made a lousy move and lost the game. / 他们俩下的这～没啥看头儿。They are playing a lousy chess game; it's not worth watching. / ～婆子 a lousy chess-player

臭气 chòuqì bad (or offensive) smell; stink: ～熏天 stink to high heaven

臭钱 chòuqián stinking money; filthy money: 你别以为手里有几个～就可以为所欲为! Don't think you can do whatever you like with your stinking money.

臭球 chòuqiú inf. a lousy pass, stroke, or shot in a ball game; a lousy game or match

臭水沟 chòushuǐgōu sewage ditch

臭死 chòusǐ inf. to death: 累得～ be dog-tired / 把他打了个～ beat him within an inch of his life

臭味相投 chòuwèi xiāngtóu be birds of a feather; be two of a kind

臭熏熏 chòuxūnxūn same as 臭烘烘 chòuhōnghōng

臭氧 chòuyǎng chem. ozone

臭氧层 chòuyǎngcéng ozonosphere; ozone layer

臭鼬 chòuyòu *zool.* skunk

chū

出[1] chū ① go or come out: ~城 go out of town / ~站 come out of the station ② exceed; go beyond: ~月 after this month; next month / 不 ~ 三 年 within three years / 球 ~了边线。The ball went beyond the sideline. ③ issue; put out: ~证明 issue a certificate / ~杂志 publish a magazine / ~主意 offer advice; supply ideas; make suggestions / ~ 布 告 post an announcement; put up a notice / 我们村 ~一百个民工参加水库建设。Our village is to send a hundred workers to help build the reservoir. / 今晚比赛, 你们 ~谁? Who's going to play for your side in tonight's match? ④ produce; turn out: 多 ~煤, ~好煤。Produce more coal, and good coal, too. / 要多 ~人才。We must turn out a greater number of qualified personnel. / 我们部队 ~过不少战斗英雄。Our unit has produced quite a few combat heroes. ⑤ arise; happen: 这事 ~在三十年前。It happened thirty years ago. / ~问题 go wrong; go amiss / 防止 ~事故 prevent accidents ⑥ put forth; vent: 树上 ~了不少花蕾。The tree has put forth many buds. / ~疹子 have measles ⑦ rise well (with cooking); grow in volume: 出饭 chūfàn / 出数儿 chūshùr ⑧ pay out; expend: 量入为出 liàng rù wéi chū ⑨ *dial.* (used with 往, indicating an outward direction): 散会了, 大家往 ~走。The meeting ended and people came out.

出[2]（齣） chū *m.* (for operas or plays): 一~戏 an opera; a play

出 ·chū ① (used after a verb to indicate an outward direction): 从大厅里走 ~两个人。Two people came out of the hall. / 电报已经发 ~。The telegram has been dispatched. / 拿 ~证件 produce one's papers / 派 ~代表团参加会议 send a delegation to attend a conference ② (used after a verb to indicate completion or succeeding): 做 ~显著成绩 achieve remarkable results / 选~新的中央委员会 elect a new central committee / 看 ~问题 see where the problem lies; realize that there's something wrong / 想 ~办法 work out a solution ③ (used between an adjective and a numeral-measure word to indicate a higher degree): 他高 ~我一头了。He's a head taller than me now. / 这条裙子再长 ~一寸就好了。If only the skirt were an inch longer!

出版 chūbǎn come off the press; publish; put out or come out: 这本书什么时候 ~? When will the book be published? / ~自由 freedom of the press

出版社 chūbǎnshè publishing house

出版物 chūbǎnwù publication

出榜 chūbǎng ① publish a list of successful candidates or examinees: 考试后三日 ~。The list of successful examinees will be published three days after the exams. ② *old* put up a notice: ~安民 put up a notice to reassure the public

出奔 chūbēn leave one's home or country under compulsion; run away; flee

出殡 chūbìn carry a coffin to the cemetery; hold a funeral procession

出兵 chūbīng dispatch (*or* send) troops

出操 chūcāo go out for drill or a workout: 民兵今天下午 ~。The militia will have drill this afternoon. / 每周出两次操 have two workouts every week

出差 chūchāi go or be away on official business; go or be on a business trip: 去上海 ~ go on a business trip to Shanghai / 出了几天差 have been away a few days on business / ~费 allowances for a business trip

出产 chūchǎn ① yield or manufacture; produce: 江西景德镇 ~精美的瓷器。Jingdezhen in Jiangxi Province produces fine porcelain. ② product; produce

出厂 chūchǎng (of products) be dispatched from the factory: ~价格 producer price; ex-factory price / ~日期 date of production (*or* manufacture) / ~检验 delivery inspection

出场 chūchǎng ① come on the stage; appear on the scene: 她一 ~, 台下就响起了热烈的掌声。There was enthusiastic applause as soon as she came on the stage. / 他们是今晚 ~的演员。They are the actors and actresses appearing tonight. ② enter the arena: ~的运动员名单 list of players for the match / 他 ~准赢。If he enters the contest, he's sure to win.

出超 chūchāo favourable balance of trade; export surplus

出车 chūchē ① dispatch a vehicle: 公共汽车早五点~。Bus service starts at 5 a.m. ② be out driving a vehicle: 老王~去了。Lao Wang is out with the car.

出乘 chūchéng be on duty as a crewperson; serve on board

出丑 chūchǒu make a fool of sb. or oneself: 上次我已经出过一回丑, 今天我可不唱了。I sang and made a fool of myself last time. I'm not going to sing again today.

出处 chūchǔ *formal* take and leave office

出处 chūchù source (of a quotation or allusion): 注明 ~ indicate the source; give references / 查明引文 ~ find out the source of a quotation / 你知道这个典故的 ~ 吗? Do you know the original source of this allusion?

出错 chūcuò make a mistake: 他管帐很少~。He seldom makes a mistake in the accounts. / 用典~ make mistakes in using allusions

出倒 chūdǎo sell up (a shop, factory, etc.)

出点子 chū diǎnzi offer advice; make suggestions: 怎么办? 大家来出出点子。What's to be done? Let's put our heads together. / 有人在背后出坏点子。Someone is directing the show from behind the scenes.

出典 chūdiǎn ① the source of an allusion: 这个成语的~ 见《论语》。This idiom is an allusion to *The Analects.* ② *old* mortgage: 把房屋 ~给人 mortgage one's house

出顶 chūdǐng *dial.* sublet a house or room

出动 chūdòng ① set out; start off: 小分队提前 ~了。The detachment set off ahead of schedule. / 待命 ~ await orders to set out (*or* go into action) / 全连 ~救火。The whole company turned out to fight the fire. ② send out; dispatch: ~军舰 dispatch warships / ~飞机二十架次 fly 20 sorties / ~医护人员 send out medical personnel / 反动当局 ~军队镇压罢工。The reactionary authorities called out troops to put down the strike.

出动机场 chūdòng jīchǎng departure airfield

出尔反尔 chū ěr fǎn ěr go back on one's word; contradict oneself: 你怎么说话不算数, ~? Why do you go back on your word? Doesn't what you promised still count?

出发 chūfā ① set out; start off: 部队于拂晓前~。The troops set out before dawn. / 医疗队今晚就要~了。The medical team is leaving tonight. ② take... as a starting point in consideration; proceed from: 从国家利益 ~ proceed from the considerations of national interests / 从长远的观点 ~ from a long-term point of view

出发点 chūfādiǎn ① the starting point of a journey ② starting point (in a discussion, argument, etc.); point of departure: 研究问题的 ~ the starting point for a study of the problem / 全心全意地为人民服务, 一切为了人民

的利益, 这就是我们的 ~。Our point of departure is to serve the people wholeheartedly and to proceed in all cases from the interests of the people.

出发港 chūfāgǎng　port of departure

出饭 chūfàn　*inf.*　(of rice, millet, etc.) rise well with cooking: 这种米真 ~。This kind of rice rises well when it's cooked.

出访 chūfǎng　go abroad on an official visit: ~西欧四国 go on an official visit to four Western European countries

出份子 chū fènzi　club together (to present a gift to sb.)

出风头 chū fēngtou　(also 出锋头 chū fēngtou) seek or be in the limelight: 喜欢 ~ like to be in the limelight; seek the limelight; enjoy being the centre of attention / 出够了风头 have been in the limelight enough

出伏 chūfú　the *fu* days end; the hottest days of the year are over: 今天 ~。The *fu* days end today. / 出了伏, 天气就明显地凉快起来。The weather gets noticeably cooler when the *fu* days are over. ——see also 三伏 sānfú

出钢 chūgāng　tap molten steel; produce steel: 这座平炉年底可以 ~。This open-hearth furnace will be ready to produce steel by the end of the year.

出港 chūgǎng　clear a port; leave port

出港呈报表 chūgǎng chéngbàobiǎo　bill of clearance

出港证 chūgǎngzhèng　clearance papers; clearance

出阁 chūgé　*formal*　(of a girl) get married; marry

出格 chūgé　① be out of the ordinary; be outstanding ② overstep the bounds; exceed what is proper: 他这样做太 ~了。What he's doing is most improper. / 你这话有点 ~了。That's going a bit too far.

出工 chūgōng　show up for work; go to work: 准时 ~ show up on time for work / 大忙季节, 农民天不亮就 ~了。During the busy seasons the farmers go to work before dawn.

出恭 chūgōng　go to the lavatory (for a bowel movement)

出乖露丑 chūguāi-lùchǒu　make an exhibition of oneself

出轨 chūguǐ　① go off the rails; be derailed ② overstep the bounds; exceed what is proper: ~行为 improper behaviour

出国 chūguó　go abroad: ~旅行 go travelling abroad / ~留学 go abroad to study / 他出过两次国。He has been abroad twice.

出海 chūhǎi　go to sea; put out to sea: ~捕鱼 go fishing on the sea / 货轮已经 ~。The freighter has put out to sea.

出汗 chūhàn　perspire; sweat: 我热得直 ~。I'm so hot that I'm dripping with sweat. / 出一身汗 break into a sweat; sweat all over

出航 chūháng　(of a ship or plane) set out on a voyage or flight: 飞机 ~侦察。The plane set out on a reconnaissance flight. / 班轮按时 ~。The liner set sail on schedule.

出号[1] chūhào　*old*　(of a salesclerk) leave a store for good; give up one's job in a store

出号[2] chūhào　be extra-large: 他得穿~的鞋。He's got to wear extra-large shoes.

出乎意料 chūhū yìliào　exceeding one's expectations; contrary to one's expectations; unexpectedly: 这件事出乎我的意料。This is something quite contrary to my expectations. / ~之外, 却在情理之中 unexpected but not surprising / 试验结果 ~地好。The experiment turned out to be even more successful than was expected.

出花儿 chūhuār　get smallpox

出活 chūhuó　yield results in work; get a lot done: 这样干~快。We'll get quicker results if we do it this way. / 我们下午虽然只干了两个钟头, 可是很 ~。We worked

only two hours in the afternoon, but we accomplished a lot. / 新式农具既轻巧, 又 ~。The improved farm tools are efficient as well as easy to handle. / 她笔头快, ~。She is good at writing and is a quick, efficient worker.

出击 chūjī　① launch an attack; hit out; make a sally: 四面 ~ hit out in all directions ② fight against (evil, crime, etc.)

出继 chūjì　be adopted as a son: 他一岁时就 ~给大伯父了。He was adopted by his eldest uncle when he was just one year old.

出家 chūjiā　renounce the family (to become a monk or nun)

出家人 chūjiārén　a monk or a nun

出价 chūjià　offer a price; bid: 你出个价吧! Would you name a price for it? / 你 ~多少? How much would you pay for it?

出嫁 chūjià　(of a woman) get married; marry

出尖 chūjiān　① push oneself to the front ② *dial.*　be full to the brim

出将入相 chūjiàng-rùxiàng　be a general in the field or a minister at court—hold high office

出结 chūjié　*old*　sign an undertaking

出界 chūjiè　*sports*　out-of-bounds; outside; out

出借 chūjiè　lend (things other than money)

出境 chūjìng　① leave the country: 限期 ~ leave the country within the specified time / 办理 ~手续 go through exit formalities / ~登记 departure registration / ~签证 exit visa / ~许可证 exit permit ② leave a certain region

出九 chūjiǔ　the coldest days of the year end: 虽说还没有 ~, 可天气已暖和起来了。Although the coldest days of the year are not quite over, the weather is already getting warmer.

出局 chūjú　out (in baseball, soft ball, etc.)

出圈 chūjuàn　same as 出栏 chūlán

出科 chūkē　*old*　finish one's professional training and become a full member of a traditional opera troupe

出客 chūkè　*dial.*　go to a party; be a guest: 我这套衣服只 ~时才穿。I don't wear this suit except to parties.

出口[1] chūkǒu　① speak; utter: 这话我很难 ~。I'd be too embarrassed to bring that up. ② (of a ship) leave port: 证件不齐, 这条船不能~。Since the necessary papers are not in order, the ship cannot yet leave port. ③ export: ~大米 export rice / ~信贷担保 export credit guarantee / ~产业和产品 export-oriented industries and products

出口[2] chūkǒu　exit: 地铁 ~ subway exit / 剧场的 ~ (theatre) exit

出口补贴 chūkǒu bǔtiē　export subsidy

出口成章 chū kǒu chéng zhāng　words flow from the mouth as from the pen of a master; talk in literature

出口货 chūkǒuhuò　exported goods; exports; outbound freight; exportation

出口检疫 chūkǒu jiǎnyì　export quarantine

出口贸易 chūkǒu màoyì　export trade

出口伤人 chūkǒu shāng rén　say things that will hurt others' feelings; speak bitingly

出口商 chūkǒushāng　exporter

出口商品 chūkǒu shāngpǐn　export commodities

出口税 chūkǒushuì　export duties

出口许可证 chūkǒu xǔkězhèng　export license

出来 chū‧lái　① come out: 太阳 ~了。The sun has come out. / 你 ~, 我跟你说句话。Come out, will you? I have something to tell you. / 对不起, 我今天有事出不来。Sorry, I can't come out today because I'm tied up. / 全村的人都~观看表演。The whole village turned out to watch the performance. ② emerge; arise; appear: 要是 ~新问题怎么办? What should we do if a new prob-

lem crops up? /经过讨论,～两种相反的意见。After a discussion, two opposite views emerged.

出来 ·chū·lái ① (used after a verb, indicating motion out towards the speaker): 他刚从监狱里放～。He's just been released from prison. /从屋里走出一个人来。Someone came out of the room. ② (used after a verb, indicating the completion of an action): 她那篇论文写～了。She's finished writing her thesis. /他们终于把这种优质钢炼～了。They finally succeeded in making the high-grade steel. ③ (used after a verb, indicating revealing, detecting, etc.): 我一眼就认出他来了。I recognized him the moment I saw him. /她的话是什么意思,我听不～。I couldn't make out what she meant. /这几首诗把他的爱国热情充分表达～了。These poems give full expression to his patriotic feelings. /有什么困难说～。If you have any difficulty, just let me know.

出栏 chūlán ① (of livestock) become full-grown and ready for slaughter ② dial. remove manure from a pigsty, sheepfold, etc.

出类拔萃 chūlèi-bácuì stand out from one's fellows; be out of the common run; be pre-eminent: ～的人物 an outstanding figure

出力 chūlì put forth one's strength; exert oneself: 他为我们县的医疗卫生工作出过不少力。He has done quite a lot for the medical and health work of our county. /每人多出把力,任务就可以提前完成。If everyone puts in a bit more effort, the job will be finished ahead of time.

出列 chūliè mil. leave one's place in the ranks: ～! (word of command) Fall out!

出猎 chūliè go on a hunting trip

出溜 chūliu dial. slip; slide: 他脚底下一～,摔了一交。He slipped and fell.

出笼 chūlóng ① come out of the steamer: 刚～的包子 hot stuffed buns just out of the steamer ② derog. come forth; appear: 那本坏书是什么时候～的? When did that filthy book come out?

出娄子 chū lóuzi dial. get into trouble; go wrong: 你这样下去非～不可。You are bound to get (or run) into trouble if you go on like this.

出路 chūlù ① a way out; outlet: 他们在森林里迷失了方向,找不到～。They lost their bearings in the forest and couldn't find their way out. /河道淤塞,水无～。The riverbed is silted up, so there's no outlet for the floodwater. /给以生活～ provide sb. with the opportunity to earn a living /坚持错误思想是没有～的。You won't get anywhere if you cling to your wrong ideas. /农业的根本～在于机械化。The fundamental way out for agriculture lies in mechanization. ② an outlet for goods: 给滞销商品找个～ find an outlet for unsalable goods

出乱子 chū luànzi go wrong; get into trouble: 你放心,出不了什么乱子。Don't worry. There won't be any trouble.

出落 chūluo (of a young person, esp. a young girl) grow (prettier, etc.): 三年不见,这姑娘～得更漂亮了。The girl has grown prettier than ever since I last saw her three years ago.

出马 chūmǎ go into action; take the field: 亲自～ take up the matter oneself; attend to the matter personally; take personal charge of the matter

出卖 chūmài ① offer for sale; sell ② sell out; betray: ～原则 barter away principles /～民族利益 betray the interests of the nation

出满月 chū mǎnyuè ① same as 出月子 chū yuèzi ② (of a baby) be one month old

出毛病 chū máobing be or go out of order; malfunction: 机器～了。The machine is out of order. or There's some trouble with the machine. /汽车～了。Something has gone wrong with the car. /一路上没出什么毛病。Nothing went wrong on the journey.

出梅 chūméi the rainy season ends ——see also 黄梅季 huángméijì

出门 chūmén ① go out: 他刚～,一会儿就回来。He's just gone out, he'll be back soon. ② leave home; go on a journey: ～在外,要多加小心。Look after yourself when you're away from home. /我年纪大了,不能出远门了。I'm too old to go on long trips any more. ③ dial. (of a woman) get married; marry

出门子 chūménzi dial. (of a woman) get married; marry

出面 chūmiàn appear personally; act in one's own capacity or on behalf of sb.: ～调停 act as a mediator /部长亲自～向大使们说明情况。The minister personally explained the matter to the ambassadors. /双方由民间团体～商谈贸易。Trade talks are to be held by non-governmental organizations of both sides. /为什么你自己不～? Why didn't you take up the matter yourself? /我愿出力,不愿～。I'm willing to help out but not to act on anyone's behalf.

出苗 chūmiáo (of seedlings) emerge; come out; sprout

出苗率 chūmiáolù agric. the rate of emergence

出名 chūmíng ① be famous; be well known: 四川菜在国内外都很～。Sichuan cuisine is famous both at home and abroad. /这儿是战争时期～的游击区。This was a famous guerrilla zone during the war. /哈密瓜～地甜。Hami melons are known for their sweetness. ② lend one's name (to an occasion or enterprise); use the name of: 今晚由学生会～,召开迎新晚会。This evening the Students' Union will give a party to welcome the new students.

出没 chūmò appear and disappear; haunt: 大熊猫～于川西山区。The mountainous areas of western Sichuan are the haunt of the giant panda.

出没无常 chūmò wúcháng appear and disappear unexpectedly; come and go unpredictably

出谋划策 chūmóu-huàcè give counsel; mastermind: 躲在背后～ mastermind a scheme from behind the scenes

出纳 chūnà ① receipt and payment of money or bills ② cashier; teller ③ lending and receiving books

出纳台 chūnàtái ① cashier's (or teller's) desk ② circulation desk (in a library)

出纳员 chūnàyuán cashier; teller

出盘 chūpán dial. sell up (a shop, factory, etc.)

出品 chūpǐn ① make; produce; manufacture: 光明化工厂～ manufactured (or made) by Guangming Chemical Plant ② product: 这是本厂的新～。This is a new product of our factory.

出聘 chūpìn ① (of a woman) get married; marry ② formal serve as an envoy abroad

出妻 chūqī old ① divorce a wife ② a divorced wife

出其不意 chū qí bù yì take sb. by surprise; catch sb. unawares: ～地袭击敌人,很快地解决战斗 take the enemy by surprise and bring battles to a quick decision /攻其无备,～。(《孙子》) Attack the unprepared; do the unexpected.

出奇 chūqí unusual; extraordinary: 今年夏天热得～。It's unusually hot this summer. /那天清晨,大海～地宁静。The sea was extraordinarily calm that morning. /这个人忽而右得要命,忽而"左"得～。He can be extremely Right at one time and extraordinarily "Left" at another.

出奇制胜 chū qí zhì shèng defeat one's opponent by a surprise move: 我们不是冒险,是～! We wouldn't be running any risk, we'd be winning by means of a surprise attack!

出气 chūqì give vent to one's anger; vent one's spleen: 是她得罪了你,可别在我身上～。She's the one who

offended you. Don't take it out on me.

出气口 chūqìkǒu　gas outlet; air vent

出气筒 chūqìtǒng　*dial.* punching bag (fig.)

出勤 chūqín　① turn out for work: 她已经三天没 ～了。She's been absent from work for three days. / 全体～ full attendance ② be or go out on business

出勤率 chūqínlǜ　attendance rate; attendance

出去 chū·qù　go out; get out: ～走走 go out for a walk (*or* stroll) / 他刚 ～。 He's just gone out. / 门口太拥挤, 一时出不去。The exit is too crowded for us to get out yet.

出去 ·chū·qù　(used after a verb, indicating motion out away from the speaker): 把桌子搬～。Move the table out. / 把客人送出大门去。See the guests out of the gate. / 走 ～向群众征求意见 go out among the masses to ask for their opinions

出圈儿 chūquānr　*dial.* overstep the bounds; go too far: 说话出了圈儿 go too far in what one says

出缺 chūquē　(of a high post) fall vacant

出让 chūràng　sell (one's own things): 自行车减价～ sell one's bicycle at a reduced price

出人命 chū rénmìng　cause the loss of lives; cause deaths: 这件事弄不好, 会 ～的。If this case is not handled with great care, a death or two may occur.

出人头地 chū rén tóu dì　rise head and shoulders above others; stand out among one's fellows

出人意料 chū rén yìliào　(also 出人意表 chū rén yìbiǎo) exceeding all expectations; beyond all expectations: 疗效之佳 ～。The curative effect exceeded all expectations.

出任 chūrèn　*formal* take up the post of: ～县长 take up the post of county magistrate / 你们准备推荐谁 ～此职? Who are you going to recommend for the post?

出入 chūrù　① come in and go out: 机房不能随便～。You can't come in and go out of the motor room as you please. / ～大门请下车! Cyclists please dismount at the gate. ② discrepancy; divergence: 他说的和你说的 有 ～。There's some discrepancy between your account and his. / 现款跟帐上的数目没有 ～。Cash on hand tallies with the figure in the accounts.

出入证 chūrùzhèng　pass (identifying a staff member, etc.)

出塞 chūsài　go out of the frontier pass (i.e. beyond the Great Wall)

出赛 chūsài　take part in a match or contest

出丧 chūsāng　same as 出殡 chūbìn

出色 chūsè　outstanding; remarkable; splendid: 干得很 ～ do a remarkable job; acquit oneself splendidly / 他们 ～地完成了任务。They accomplished their task with flying colours.

出山 chūshān　① leave the mountain area ② come out of retirement and take up an official post

出身 chūshēn　① be descended from; come of (*or* from): ～书香门第 come from a family of scholars / ～工人家庭 come from a worker's family ② family background; (class) origin: 他 ～很好。He's of good class origin. *or* He has a good class background. / 咱俩都是穷苦 ～。We are both from poor families. ③ one's previous experience or occupation: 工人 ～的技术员 a technician promoted from among the workers / 那位将军是铁匠 ～。The general began life as a blacksmith.

出神 chūshén　be spellbound; be in a trance; be lost in thought: 青年钢琴家的演奏使她听得出了神。She was held spellbound by the performance of the young pianist. / 他坐在那里 ～。He sat there, lost in thought. / 你看什么书看得这么 ～? What's that book you are so absorbed in?

出神入化 chūshén-rùhuà　reach the acme of perfection; be superb: 他的表演艺术～。His performance was superb.

出生 chūshēng　be born: 我是1930年 ～的。I was born in 1930. / 他 ～在美国。He was born in the United States. / ～登记 registration of birth / ～日期 date of birth

出生地 chūshēngdì　birthplace

出生率 chūshēnglǜ　birthrate

出生入死 chūshēng-rùsǐ　go through fire and water; brave untold dangers; at the risk of life and limb: 革命战争中 ～的战士 a fighter who risked death in the revolutionary wars

出生证 chūshēngzhèng　birth certificate

出声 chūshēng　make a sound; speak: 大家别～, 先仔细听听。Don't make a sound, any of you. Just listen carefully. / 不管我怎么问她, 她就是不 ～。No matter what questions I asked her, she just remained silent.

出师[1] chūshī　complete one's apprenticeship

出师[2] chūshī　*formal* dispatch troops to fight; send an army to battle: ～不利 lost the first battle or game; meet with initial setbacks / ～未捷身先死, 长使英雄泪满襟。(杜甫) How sad that he had to die before he gained victory, Leaving great men of succeeding generations to grieve for him.

出使 chūshǐ　serve as an envoy abroad; be sent on a diplomatic mission: ～西班牙 be sent as an envoy to Spain; be accredited to Spain

出示 chūshì　① show; produce: 请 ～车票。Please show your ticket. / ～证件 produce one's papers ② *formal* put up a notice: ～安民 put up a notice to reassure the public

出世 chūshì　① come into the world; be born; come into being: 他 ～才三天, 他妈妈就去世了。His mother died three days after he was born. / 旧制度要灭亡, 新制度要～了。The old system is dying out; a new system is coming into being. ② renounce the world; keep aloof from worldly affairs ③ rise high above the world: 横空～, 莽昆仑, 阅尽人间春色。(毛泽东) Far above the earth, into the blue, You, wild Kunlun, have seen All that was fairest in the world of men.

出世作 chūshìzuò　*old* maiden work; first effort

出仕 chūshì　*old* take up an official post; become an official

出事 chūshì　meet with a mishap; have an accident: 飞机 ～了。The plane crashed. / 我开车没出过事。I've never had an accident driving a car. / 出了什么事? What's wrong? *or* What's happening? / 放心吧, 出不了事。Don't worry. Nothing will go wrong. / ～地点 the site of an accident

出手[1] chūshǒu　① get (hoarded goods, etc.) off one's hands; dispose of; sell: 货物已经 ～了。The goods have been disposed of. ② give out: 他相当大方, 一一就给了一百块。He was quite generous and gave 100 *yuan* offhand.

出手[2] chūshǒu　① the length of a sleeve: 你 ～大约有70厘米 吧? Your sleeves must be about 70cm. long. Right? ② skill displayed in making opening moves (in *wushu,* chess, etc.): 出手不凡 chūshǒu bù fán ③ see 打出手 dǎ chūshǒu

出手不凡 chūshǒu bù fán　make skilful (*or* masterly) opening moves (in *wushu,* chess, etc.)

出首 chūshǒu　① denounce sb. as a criminal (to the authorities) ② *old* confess one's crime; give oneself up

出售 chūshòu　offer for sale; sell

出书 chūshū　publish books: 出版社明年计划 ～三百种。The publishing house plans to put out 300 new titles next year. / 他才三十岁, 就已经出了十本书。He's only 30, but already has 10 books to his credit.

出数儿 chūshùr　*inf.* (of rice) rise well with cooking: 这种米做饭很 ～。This kind of rice rises well when it's

cooked.

出水 chūshuǐ ① appear above water: ～新莲 lotus flowers just appearing above the water ② send out water: 他们的井 ～了。Their well is sending up water. ③ *old* (of a prostitute) get out of the brothel and start a new life

出水芙蓉 chūshuǐ fúróng **same as** 芙蓉出水 fúróng chūshuǐ

出死入生 chūsǐ-rùshēng **same as** 出生入死 chūshēng-rùsǐ

出台 chūtái ① appear on the stage ② make a public appearance

出逃 chūtáo flee: ～国外 flee the country

出题 chūtí ① set a question; set a test paper ② set a topic

出挑 chū·tiāo ① see 出落 chūluo ② develop (in skill, etc.): 不满一年，他就～成一个好司机。In less than a year he developed into a good driver.

出粜 chūtiào sell (grain)

出铁 chūtiě tap molten iron; tap a blast furnace: 新炉 ～了。They have started tapping the new blast furnace. / 出一炉铁 tap a heat of molten iron

出铁口 chūtiěkǒu *metall.* taphole; iron notch

出庭 chūtíng appear in court: ～作证 appear in court as a witness

出头 chūtóu ① hold up one's head; free oneself (from misery, persecution, etc.): 穷苦人有了 ～的日子。Poor people can now hold up their heads. ② appear in public; come forward: 他要肯 ～，咱们这件事准能成功。If he's willing to come forward on our behalf, we're sure to succeed. ③ (used after a round number) a little over; odd: 他三十 ～了。He's a little over thirty. / 三百 ～ three hundred odd

出头的椽子先烂 chūtóude chuánzi xiān làn the rafters that jut out rot first—one who wants to be to the fore will get into trouble

出头露面 chūtóu-lùmiàn appear in public; be in the limelight: ～的人物 a public figure / 喜欢 ～ be fond of being in the limelight; enjoy being the centre of attention / 只要有～的机会，他总是走在头里。Wherever there's a chance of being in the limelight, he always pushes to the front.

出徒 chūtú complete one's apprenticeship

出土 chūtǔ ① be unearthed; be excavated: ～文物 unearthed artifacts; archaeological finds ② come up out of the ground: 小苗刚 ～。The sprouts have just come up.

出脱 chūtuō ① manage to sell; dispose of: 那批货一时 ～不了。We can't sell off those goods just now. ② same as 出落 chūluo ③ acquit; absolve: 你的罪名无法 ～。You can never clear yourself of that charge.

出外 chūwài go away from home; leave home: ～谋生 leave home and seek a living elsewhere

出亡 chūwáng *formal* flee from one's home or country; go into exile

出污泥而不染 chū wūní ér bù rǎn emerge unstained from the filth

出息 chū·xī ① prospects; a bright future: 有 ～ have prospects of success in life; show promise / 这人真没 ～。This chap is a good-for-nothing. ② *dial.* make good progress: 这孩子比去年 ～多了。The boy is doing much better than he did last year. ③ *dial.* profits; gains: 咱这儿种稻子比种高粱 ～大。It's more profitable to grow rice than sorghum here.

出席 chūxí be present (at a meeting, social gathering, etc.); attend: ～会议 attend a meeting / ～宴会 be present at a banquet / ～人数 number of persons present; attendance

出险 chūxiǎn ① be or get out of danger: 救人 ～ res-

cue sb. from danger ② (of dykes, dams, etc.) be in danger; be threatened: 河堤 ～，全村的人都赶去抢修。When the dyke was in danger, the whole village rushed out to repair it.

出现 chūxiàn appear; arise; emerge: 天上 ～一片乌云。Black clouds appeared in the sky. / 她的 ～使人感到意外。Her appearance was quite unexpected. / ～了新情况。A new situation arose. / 工地上 ～了你追我赶的社会主义竞赛场面。The construction site presented an exciting scene of each one vying with the other in the socialist emulation campaign. / 我们将以一个具有高度文化的民族 ～于世界。We shall take our place in the world as a nation with an advanced culture.

出线 chūxiàn *sports* qualify for the next round of competitions

出项 chūxiàng item of expenditure; expenses; outlay

出行 chūxíng go on a journey

出血 chūxuè ① lose blood; bleed: 她出了大量的血。She's lost a lot of blood. ② *med.* haemorrhage; bleeding: 大（内、胃）～ massive (internal, gastric) haemorrhage

出巡 chūxún go on an inspection tour

出芽 chūyá put forth buds; bud; sprout

出言不逊 chūyán bù xùn make impertinent remarks; speak insolently

出演 chūyǎn ① same as 演出 yǎnchū ② play the part of; act

出洋 chūyáng *old* go abroad: ～留学 go abroad to study

出洋相 chū yángxiàng make an exhibition of oneself; make a spectacle of oneself

出以公心 chū yǐ gōngxīn keep the public interest in mind; act without selfish considerations

出迎 chūyíng go or come out to meet

出油井 chūyóujǐng *petroleum* producing well

出游 chūyóu go on a sightseeing tour

出于 chūyú start from; proceed from; stem from: ～对工作的责任感 proceed from a sense of duty / ～对同志的关怀 out of concern for one's comrades / ～不可告人的目的 actuated by ulterior motives / ～自愿 on a voluntary basis; of one's own accord

出于无奈 chūyú wúnài as it cannot be helped; there being no alternative

出渔 chūyú set out on a fishing voyage

出狱 chūyù be released from prison

出院 chūyuàn (of an inpatient) leave hospital: 病愈 ～ be discharged from hospital after recovery / ～证明 hospital discharge certificate

出月 chūyuè after the end of this month: 恐怕要～才能完工。I'm afraid it won't be finished until after the end of this month.

出月子 chū yuèzi (of a woman after childbirth) complete her month of confinement

出渣口 chūzhākǒu *metall.* slag notch; cinder notch

出战 chūzhàn go to war; go into battle

出帐 chūzhàng ① enter an item of expenditure in the accounts ② *dial.* items of expenditure

出蛰 chūzhé (of hibernating animals) come out of hibernation

出诊 chūzhěn (of a doctor) visit a patient at home; pay a home visit; make a house call

出阵 chūzhèn ① go into battle; go into action ② pitch in

出征 chūzhēng go on an expedition; go out to battle: ～的战士 soldiers sent on an expedition

出众 chūzhòng be out of the ordinary; be outstanding: 人才～ a person of exceptional ability / 成绩 ～ get outstanding results in study or work

出资 chūzī provide funds or capital: 此项工程由市政府

〜兴建。The municipal government is going to provide funds for this construction project. / 我厂 〜百万。Our factory has put in a capital of a million *yuan*.

出自 chūzì　come from; originate from; stem from: 〜肺腑 straight from the heart; from the depths of one's heart / 这个典故 〜何处? Where does this quotation come from?

出走 chūzǒu　leave one's home or country under compulsion; run away; flee: 仓卒〜 leave in a hurry / 五四时代有许多青年为了参加革命而离家 〜。During the May Fourth Movement period many young people had to leave their kith and kin in order to join the revolution.

出租 chūzū　hire out; rent; let: 游船按小时 〜。Rowboats for hire by the hour. / 房屋 〜。Houses to let. / 这家公司 〜汽车、大轿车。This company has cars and buses for hire.

出租汽车 chūzū qìchē　taxicab; taxi; cab

初 chū　① the beginning of; the early part of: 八月 〜 early in August; in early August / 本世纪 〜 the beginning of this century ② first (in order): 〜雪 first snow / 〜战 first battle / 〜一 (五、十) the first (fifth, tenth) day of the lunar month ③ for the first time; just beginning: 感冒〜起 with the first symptoms of a cold / 〜具规模 be just beginning to take shape / 〜上阵的战士 soldiers going into action for the first time ④ elementary; rudimentary: 初级 chūjí / 初等 chūděng ⑤ original: 和好如 〜 become good friends again; become reconciled ⑥ (Chū) a surname

初版 chūbǎn　① first edition ② be first published: 这部词典于1978年 〜。This dictionary was first published in 1978.

初步 chūbù　initial; preliminary; tentative: 〜方案 a tentative programme / 〜设想 a tentative idea / 〜估计 preliminary estimates / 〜繁荣昌盛的社会主义国家 a socialist country with the beginnings of prosperity / 获得 〜成果 reap first fruits; get initial results / 〜交换意见 have a preliminary exchange of views

初产妇 chūchǎnfù　primipara

初潮 chūcháo　first menses

初出茅庐 chū chū máolú　just come out of one's thatched cottage—at the beginning of one's career; young and inexperienced: 〜的电视节目主持人 a fledgling TV host

初创 chūchuàng　newly established: 〜阶段 initial stage

初春 chūchūn　early spring; first spring month (i.e. the first month of the lunar year)

初次 chūcì　the first time: 〜见面 see sb. for the first time / 〜登台 appear for the first time on the stage; make one's *début*

初等 chūděng　elementary; primary: 〜数学 elementary mathematics

初等教育 chūděng jiàoyù　elementary education

初等小学 chūděng xiǎoxué　*old* lower primary school

初冬 chūdōng　early winter; first winter month (i.e. the tenth month of the lunar year)

初度 chūdù　*formal* birthday: 三十 〜 one's 30th birthday

初犯 chūfàn　① first offender ② first offence

初伏 chūfú　① the first *fu*—the first of the three ten-day periods of the hot season ② the first day of the first *fu* (falling in mid-July)——see also 三伏 sānfú

初稿 chūgǎo　first draft; draft

初会 chūhuì　first encounter; first meeting

初婚 chūhūn　① first marriage ② newly married

初级 chūjí　elementary; primary: 〜产品 primary products / 〜读本 primer

初级阶段 chūjí jiēduàn　primary stage: 社会主义 〜 the primary stage of socialism

初级农业生产合作社 chūjí nóngyè shēngchǎn hézuòshè　elementary agricultural producers' cooperative (in which distribution was according to the amount of work each member did and the amount of land he contributed)

初级社 chūjíshè　short for 初级农业生产合作社 chūjí nóngyè shēngchǎn hézuòshè

初级线圈 chūjí xiànquān　*elec.* primary coil

初级小学 chūjí xiǎoxué　lower primary school

初级中学 chūjí zhōngxué　junior middle school

初交 chūjiāo　new acquaintance: 我和他是 〜, 对他还不太了解。We've just got acquainted, so I don't know much about him.

初亏 chūkuī　*astron.* first contact (the beginning of an eclipse)——see also 食相 shíxiàng

初恋 chūliàn　① first love: 一个人的 〜是最难以忘怀的。One can never forget one's first love. ② the first stage of falling in love: 他们老两口儿还像〜那会儿那样亲昵。The old couple still dote on each other just as when they first fell in love.

初露锋芒 chū lù fēngmáng　display one's talent for the first time

初露头角 chū lù tóujiǎo　begin to show ability or talent: 〜的新作家 budding writers

初年 chūnián　① the first years of a historical period: 民国 〜 in the first years of the Republic ② *formal* first spring month (i.e. the first month of the lunar year)

初期 chūqī　initial stage; early days: 战争 〜 in the early days of the war / 解放 〜 during the initial post-liberation period; just (*or* right) after liberation

初秋 chūqiū　early autumn; first autumn month (i.e. the seventh month of the lunar year)

初赛 chūsài　preliminary contest; preliminary

初审 chūshěn　*leg.* trial of first instance; first trial: 〜案件 case of first instance / 〜法庭 court of first instance

初生之犊不畏虎 chū shēng zhī dú bù wèi hǔ　newborn calves are not afraid of tigers—young people are fearless

初始 chūshǐ　initial; first; primary

初试 chūshì　① first try: 贾宝玉〜云雨情 Jia Baoyu having his first taste of love ② preliminary examination

初霜 chūshuāng　first frost

初速度 chūsùdù　*phys.* initial velocity

初岁 chūsuì　*formal* the beginning (*or* the first days) of a year

初头 chūtóu　*dial.* the first days of a year or a month: 一九四七年 〜 the beginning of 1947 / 八月 〜 the first few days of August or the eighth lunar month

初夏 chūxià　early summer; first summer month (i.e. the fourth month of the lunar year)

初小 chūxiǎo　short for 初级小学 chūjí xiǎoxué

初心 chūxīn　*formal* one's original desire, aspiration, or intention: 事虽如此, 不改 〜 will not change one's original intention in spite of what has happened

初选 chūxuǎn　primary election

初学 chūxué　begin to learn; be a beginner: 我是 〜, 还不会拉曲子。I'm just a beginner; I can't play a tune yet.

初旬 chūxún　the first ten days of a month

初叶 chūyè　early years (of a century): 二十世纪 〜 early in the twentieth century

初夜 chūyè　① early evening ② wedding night

初夜权 chūyèquán　right of first night; *jus primae noctis*

初愿 chūyuàn　one's original intention

初月 chūyuè　waxing moon; crescent

初诊 chūzhěn　one's first visit to a doctor or hospital

初值　chūzhí　*math.*　initial value
初志　chūzhì　one's original ambition or aspiration
初中　chūzhōng　short for 初级中学　chūjí zhōngxué
初衷　chūzhōng　one's original intention: 虽经挫折，不改～ will not change one's original intention despite the setbacks one has suffered

樗
chū　tree of heaven (*Ailanthus altissima*)

chú

刍（芻）
chú　*formal*　① hay; fodder: 反刍 fǎnchú　② cut grass: 刍荛　chúráo

刍狗　chúgǒu　*formal*　straw dogs (used as offerings in ancient sacrifices, brought in with pomp but thrown away afterwards): 天地不仁，以万物为～；圣人不仁，以百姓为～。《道德经》Heaven and earth are ruthless, and treat the myriad creatures as straw dogs; the sage is ruthless, and treats the people as straw dogs.
刍粮　chúliáng　*formal*　fodder and food
刍秣　chúmò　*formal*　fodder; forage
刍荛　chúráo　*formal*　① cut grass and firewood ② one who gathers grass and firewood ③ (used in self-deprecation) boor; rustic: ～之言 my superficial remarks
刍言　chúyán　*formal*　(my) superficial remarks; (my) humble opinion
刍议　chúyì　*formal*　(my) modest proposal; (my) tentative suggestion: 考试制度改革～ a modest proposal (*or* tentative suggestions) for the reform of the examination system

除¹
chú　① get rid of; eliminate; remove: 除草 chúcǎo／铲除 chǎnchú　② *prep.*　except: ～此而外 with the exception of this; excepting this ③ *prep.* besides: ～水稻外，我们还种棉花和小麦。Besides rice, we grow cotton and wheat. ④ *math.*　divide: 八～以四得二。8 divided by 4 is 2.／二～六得三。2 goes into 6 three times.／十能被五～尽。10 divides by 5. *or* 5 goes into 10. ⑤ *formal*　appoint to office

除²
chú　*formal*　steps to a house; doorsteps: 庭除　tíngchú

除暴安良　chúbào-ānliáng　get rid of bullies and bring peace to good people
除草　chúcǎo　remove weeds; weed
除草机　chúcǎojī　weeder
除草剂　chúcǎojì　weed killer; herbicide
除尘器　chúchénqì　dust remover: 真空～ vacuum cleaner
除虫菊　chúchóngjú　Dalmatian chrysanthemum
除恶务尽　chú è wù jìn　one must be thorough in exterminating an evil
除法　chúfǎ　*math.*　division
除非　chúfēi　*conj.*　① (used correlatively with 才) only if; only when: ～你跟我去，我才去。I'll go only if you go with me.／～他做不了，他才会找我帮忙。Only when he can't do it does he ask me for help. ② (usu. used correlatively with 否则，不然，*or* 要不然) (not) ... unless: ～你跟我去，否则我不去。I won't go unless you go with me.／～便宜，要不然我不买。I won't buy it unless it's cheap.／他不会答应的，～你劝得动他。He won't agree unless you could persuade him. ③ (preceded by a clause with 要) must needs; necessarily: 要想取得第一手资料，～你亲自去作调查。If you want firsthand information, you'll have to find out for yourself.／要相逢，～是梦里团圆。Meeting again is impossible—except in a dream.
除服　chúfú　take off mourning clothes (at the end of the mourning period)
除根　chúgēn　dig up the roots; cure once and for all; root out: 斩草必须～。When you're weeding, you must dig up the roots.／这病很难～。It's difficult to find a permanent cure for this disease.
除号　chúhào　division sign (÷)
除籍　chújí　*formal*　strike sb.'s name off the rolls
除旧布新　chújiù-bùxīn　get rid of the old to make way for the new; do away with the old and set up the new
除旧更新　chújiù-gēngxīn　replace the old with the new
除开　chúkāi　same as 除了 chúle
除了　chúle　*prep.*　① except: ～老王，我都通知到了。I've notified everyone except Lao Wang.／那条山路，～这位老猎人，谁也不熟悉。Nobody knows the mountain path well except the old hunter.／～下雨，我每天都坚持长跑。I practise long-distance running every day except on rainy days. ② (used correlatively with 还，也，etc.) besides; in addition to: 懂日语的，～我还有两个人。There are two others besides me who know some Japanese.／～教课，他还负责学校里青年团的工作。Besides teaching, he's in charge of the school's Youth League work. ③ (used correlatively with 就是) if not... (then...); either ... (or...): 刚生下来的孩子，～吃就是睡。If a newborn baby isn't eating, then it's sleeping.／这几天～刮风，就是下雨。Recently we've been having either windy or rainy days.
除名　chúmíng　remove sb.'s name from the rolls; strike sb.'s name off the rolls; expunge sb.'s name from a list
除却　chúquè　except
除丧　chúsāng　*formal*　take off mourning clothes (at the end of the mourning period)
除授　chúshòu　*formal*　appoint sb. to an official position
除数　chúshù　*math.*　divisor
除霜　chúshuāng　defrost: 自动～ auto-defrosting／手动～ manual defrosting／快速～ fast defrosting
除四害　chú sì hài　eliminate the four pests (usu. referring to rats, bedbugs, flies and mosquitoes)
除外　chúwài　except; not counting; not including: 展览会每天开放，星期一～。The exhibition is open every day except Monday.／一共五件行李，药箱～。There are five pieces of luggage, not counting the medical kit.
除夕　chúxī　New Year's Eve
除夜　chúyè　New Year's Eve
除莠剂　chúyǒujì　herbicide

厨（廚、厨）
chú　kitchen: 下～ go to the kitchen (to do cooking)

厨房　chúfáng　kitchen: ～用具 kitchen (*or* cooking) utensils
厨娘　chúniáng　*old*　woman cook
厨师　chúshī　cook; chef
厨子　chúzi　*old*　cook

锄（鋤）
chú　① hoe ② do hoeing: ～草 hoe up weeds; weed with a hoe ③ uproot; eliminate; wipe out: 锄奸 chújiān

锄地　chúdì　hoe the fields; do hoeing: 锄玉米地 hoe the cornfields
锄奸　chújiān　eliminate traitors; ferret out spies: ～工作 elimination of traitors; anti-espionage work
锄强扶弱　chúqiáng-fúruò　suppress the strong and aid the weak
锄头　chútou　① pickaxe (used in southern China) ② *dial.* hoe

蜍 chú see 蟾蜍 chánchú

雏（雛） chú young (bird): ～燕 young swallow

雏儿 chúr inf. ① a young bird; nestling: 燕～ young swallow / 鸭～ duckling ② a young, inexperienced person; fledgling

雏凤 chúfèng young phoenix—a talented young man or a promising young student: ～清于老凤声。A young phoenix sings better than an old one (said of a son surpassing his father or of a student surpassing his master).

雏鸡 chújī chick; chicken

雏鸟 chúniǎo nestling; fledgling

雏形 chúxíng ① a rudimentary, undeveloped form of an organism; an embryonic form: 蛹显示出成虫的触角、腿、翅膀的～。The undeveloped forms of the adult insect's antennae, legs and wings are embodied in the pupa. / 龙山文化时期已产生了阶级的～。Classes appeared in an embryonic form as early as the age of the Longshan Culture. ② miniature

橱（櫥） chú cabinet; closet; wardrobe: ～顶上放着两只皮箱。There are two suitcases on the top of the wardrobe. / 玻璃～里放着许多小摆设。A lot of bric-a-brac is displayed in the glass-fronted cabinet.

橱窗 chúchuāng ① show (or display) window; showcase; shopwindow ② glass-fronted billboard

橱柜 chúguì ① cupboard ② a cupboard that also serves as a table; sideboard

蹰 chú see 踌蹰 chóuchú

蹰（躕） chú see 踟蹰 chíchú

chǔ

处（處、処、处） chǔ ① formal dwell: 穴居野处 xuéjū-yěchǔ ② get along (with sb.): 容易相～ easy to get along with / 他们俩～得很好。They get along quite well. / 这个人不好～。This fellow is hard to get along with. ③ be situated in; be in a certain condition: 昔阳县地～太行山区。Xiyang County is located in the Taihang Mountains. / 我们正～在一个伟大的历史时代。We are living in a great historic era. ④ manage; handle; deal with: 处事 chǔshì ⑤ punish; sentence: ～以两年徒刑 sentence sb. to two years' imprisonment ——see also chù

处罚 chǔfá punish; penalize

处方 chǔfāng ① write out a prescription; prescribe ② prescription; recipe

处分 chǔfèn ① take disciplinary action against; punish: 免予～ exempt sb. from punishment / 按情节轻重予以～ punish a person according to the seriousness of his case / 予以警告～ give sb. disciplinary warning / 党内～ disciplinary action within the Party / 行政～ administrative disciplinary measure ② formal handle; manage; deal with

处境 chǔjìng unfavourable situation; plight: ～困难 be in a sorry plight; be in a predicament; be in a difficult situation / ～危险 be in a dangerous (or precarious) situation; be in peril

处决 chǔjué ① put to death; execute: 依法～ put to death in accordance with the law / 被秘密～ be executed in secret ② manage and make decisions: 大会休会期间，一切事项由常委会～。When the Congress is

not in session, all affairs are handled by the standing committee.

处理 chǔlǐ ① handle; deal with; dispose of: 正确～人民内部矛盾 correctly handle contradictions among the people / 必须严加～ should be dealt with sternly / ～国家大事 conduct state affairs / ～日常事务 handle day-to-day work; deal with routine matters / 我～完家务就来。I'll come along as soon as I'm through with my household chores. / 这事请保卫科～。Please refer the matter to the security section. / 垃圾～ garbage disposal ② treat (a workpiece or product) by a special process: 用硫酸～ treat with sulphuric acid ③ sell at reduced prices: ～积压商品 sell old stock at reduced prices / ～价格 reduced price; bargain price

处理机 chǔlǐjī processor: 数据～ data processor / 文字～ word processor / 中央～ central processor

处理品 chǔlǐpǐn goods (usu. shopworn or substandard) sold at reduced prices

处女 chǔnǚ virgin; maiden

处女地 chǔnǚdì virgin land (or soil)

处女航 chǔnǚháng maiden voyage or flight

处女膜 chǔnǚmó physiol. hymen

处女作 chǔnǚzuò maiden work; first effort

处身 chǔshēn place oneself; settle: ～在异常艰险的环境中 place oneself amid great hardships and dangers / ～涉世 the way one conducts oneself in society

处士 chǔshì recluse

处世 chǔshì conduct oneself in society: ～哲学 philosophy of life

处事 chǔshì handle affairs; deal with matters: 他～严肃，态度却十分和蔼。He handles affairs in a businesslike yet friendly way.

处暑 Chǔshǔ ① the End of Heat—the 14th of the 24 solar terms ② the day marking the beginning of the 14th solar term (Aug. 22, 23, or 24, when summer is really over) ——see also 节气 jiéqì, 二十四节气 èrshísìjiéqì

处死 chǔsǐ put to death; execute

处心积虑 chǔxīn-jīlǜ derog. deliberately plan (to achieve evil ends); incessantly scheme: ～地破坏革命队伍的团结 be bent on undermining the unity of the revolutionary ranks

处刑 chǔxíng leg. condemn; sentence

处于 chǔyú be (in a certain condition): ～有利的地位 find oneself in an advantageous position / ～平等地位 be on an equal footing / ～优势 have the advantage / ～高潮 be at high tide / ～水深火热之中 live in the abyss of suffering / ～昏迷状态 be in a coma

处之泰然 chǔ zhī tàirán take things calmly; remain unruffled

处治 chǔzhì punish

处置 chǔzhì ① handle; deal with; manage; dispose of: 妥善地～各种复杂情况 handle complex situations aptly / ～失当 mismanage; mishandle ② punish

处子 chǔzǐ formal virgin

杵 chǔ ① pestle: ～臼 mortar and pestle ② a wooden club used to beat clothes in washing ③ poke: 用手指头～他一下 give him a poke / 把纸～个窟窿 poke a hole in the paper

杵臼时代 chǔjiù shídài the mortar-and-pestle age; the age of the hand-pestle

杵乐 chǔyuè (also 杵舞 chǔwǔ) pestle dance (a song-and-dance form popular among the Gaoshan people in Taiwan Province)

杵状指 chǔzhuàngzhǐ clubbed finger

础（礎） chǔ plinth: ～石 the stone base of a column; plinth

楮 chǔ ① paper mulberry ② *formal* paper
楮实 chǔshí *Chin. med.* paper mulberry fruit

储 chǔ ① store. up: 〜粮备荒 store up grain against natural disasters / 冬〜白菜 cabbages stored for the winter ② (Chǔ) a surname
储备 chǔbèi ① store for future use; lay in; lay up: 〜过冬饲料 lay up fodder for the winter / 〜粮食 store up grain; build up supplies of grain ② reserve: 黄金〜 gold reserve / 外汇〜 foreign exchange reserve
储备基金 chǔbèi jījīn reserve fund
储备粮 chǔbèiliáng grain reserves
储藏 chǔcáng ① save and preserve; store; keep: 鲜果〜 preservation (*or* storage) of fresh fruit ② deposit: 我国有丰富的石油〜。Our country abounds in oil deposits.
储藏量 chǔcángliàng *min.* reserves
储藏室 chǔcángshì storeroom
储存 chǔcún lay in; lay up; store; stockpile; deposit: 〜余粮 store up surplus grain / 〜战略物资 stockpile strategic materials / 把钱〜在银行里 deposit the money in a bank
储放 chǔfàng store; leave in sb.'s care: 把行李〜在寄存处 check one's luggage at the checkroom
储宫 chǔgōng *formal* crown prince
储户 chǔhù depositor
储积 chǔjī ① store up; save: 〜余粮，以备急需 store up surplus grain for use in time of need ② stock; savings
储集 chǔjí store up; save
储集层 chǔjícéng *petroleum* reservoir bed
储君 chǔjūn crown prince
储量 chǔliàng *min.* reserves: 远景〜 prospective reserves / 探明〜 proved reserves / 可采〜 recoverable (*or* workable) reserves / 〜等级 ore reserve classification
储气 chǔqì gas storage
储气构造 chǔqì gòuzào gas-bearing structure
储气罐 chǔqìguàn gas tank
储蓄 chǔxù save; deposit: 提倡〜 encourage saving / 城乡〜迅速增加。Savings deposits in both urban and rural areas have shown a rapid increase.
储蓄存款 chǔxù cúnkuǎn savings deposit
储蓄代办所 chǔxù dàibànsuǒ savings agency
储蓄额 chǔxù'é total savings deposits
储蓄所 chǔxùsuǒ savings bank
储油 chǔyóu *petroleum* oil storage
储油构造 chǔyóu gòuzào *petroleum* oil-bearing structure
储油罐 chǔyóuguàn *petroleum* oil storage tank; oil tank

褚 Chǔ a surname

楚¹ chǔ ① clear; neat: 清楚 qīngchǔ ② *formal* pang; suffering: 苦楚 kǔchǔ

楚² Chǔ ① one of the Warring States into which China was divided during the Eastern Zhou period (770–256 B.C.), occupying what is now Hubei and northern Hunan ② a name for what is now Hubei and Hunan (esp. the former) ③ a surname
楚材晋用 Chǔ cái Jìn yòng the talents of Chu used by Jin—the intellectual resources of one country used by another
楚楚 chǔchǔ ① tidy; neat; spotlessly clean: 衣冠楚楚 yīguān chǔchǔ ② delicate; dainty
楚楚可怜 chǔchǔ kělián (of a young woman) delicate and charming

楚辞 Chǔcí *The Songs of the South*
楚馆秦楼 Chǔguǎn-Qínlóu same as 秦楼楚馆 Qínlóu-Chǔguǎn
楚剧 chǔjù Chu opera (a local opera popular in Hubei and part of Jiangxi)
楚囚对泣 Chǔ qiú duì qì the captives from Chu weeping with each other (said of people lamenting a common fate)
楚腰 chǔyāo a slender waist (of a woman); a slim figure

chù

亍 chù see 彳亍 chìchù

处（處、處、处） chù ① place: 别〜 another place; elsewhere / 停车〜 parking place; car park ② point; part: 有相同之〜 bear a resemblance; have something in common ③ *m.* (for places or for occurrences or activities in different places): 几〜人家 several homesteads / 发现两〜印刷错误 find two misprints ④ department; office: 总务〜 general affairs department ——see also chǔ
处处 chùchù *adv.* everywhere; in all respects: 〜严格要求自己 set strict demands on oneself in all respects / 〜以革命利益为重 always put the interests of the revolution first / 〜关心同学 show the students every consideration / 祖国〜有亲人。All over our country one can find friends and dear ones.
处所 chùsuǒ place; location
处长 chùzhǎng the head of a department or office; section chief

怵（怵） chù fear: 〜惕 feel apprehensive
怵然 chùrán apprehensive; frightened
怵头 chùtóu *dial.* same as 憷头 chùtóu

绌 chù *formal* inadequate; insufficient: 相形见绌 xiāng xíng jiàn chù

畜 chù domestic animal; livestock: 牲畜 shēngchù ——see also xù
畜肥 chùféi animal manure
畜圈 chùjuàn (also 畜舍 chùshè) pen; fold; sty; shed
畜类 chùlèi domestic animals
畜力 chùlì animal power: 〜车 animal-drawn cart / 〜农具 animal-drawn farm implements
畜生 chùsheng ① domestic animals ② *offens.* beast; dirty swine
畜疫 chùyì epidemic disease of domestic animals

搐 chù jerk; twitch
搐动 chùdòng (of muscles, etc.) jerk; twitch

触（觸） chù ① touch; contact: 〜到痛处 touch a sore spot; touch sb. to the quick ② strike; hit: 〜雷 strike (*or* touch off) a mine ③ move sb.; stir up sb.'s feelings: 〜起前情 awaken one's old love
触电 chùdiàn get an electric shock: 小心〜! Danger! Electricity! *or* Danger! Live wire!
触动 chùdòng ① touch sth., moving it slightly: 他在暗中摸索着，忽然〜了什么东西。Groping in the dark, he suddenly touched something. / 敌人的诽谤〜不了我们一根毫毛。The enemy's slanders can't do us the slightest harm. ② move sb.; stir up sb.'s feelings: 有所〜 be somewhat moved / 这句话〜了他的心事。That remark reminded him of something he'd had on his mind for a

long time. / 群众的批评对我们 ～很大。The masses' criticisms shook us up a lot.

触发 chùfā　detonate by contact; touch off; spark; trigger: ～热核聚变 trigger thermonuclear fusion / ～乡思 touch off a train of home thoughts; provoke nostalgic longing

触发地雷 chùfā dìléi　contact mine

触发电路 chùfā diànlù　trigger circuit

触发器 chùfāqì　trigger

触犯 chùfàn　offend; violate; go against: ～法律 violate (or break) the law / ～人民利益 encroach on the interests of the people / 我什么地方 ～了你? What have I done to offend you?

触感 chùgǎn　tactile impression

触击 chùjī　① strike: 钢镚儿 ～的声音 the sound of coins striking against each other; the jingling of coins ② sports　bunt

触及 chùjí　touch: ～人们的灵魂 touch people to their very souls / ～事物的本质 get to the essence of a matter / 这本书仅仅 ～而没有深刻揭示封建社会的主要矛盾。The book merely touches on the main contradiction of feudal society; it does not go into it deeply.

触礁 chùjiāo　run (up) on rocks; strike a reef (or rock)

触角 chùjiǎo　zool.　antenna; feeler

触景生情 chù jǐng shēng qíng　the sight strikes a chord in one's heart: 他～, 想起家乡, 不觉泪下。He was moved by the occasion to thoughts of home, and despite himself he began to weep.

触觉 chùjué　physiol.　tactile (or tactual) sensation; sense of touch

触觉器官 chùjué qìguān　tactile organ

触类旁通 chù lèi páng tōng　grasp a typical example and you will grasp the whole category; comprehend by analogy

触媒 chùméi　chem.　catalyst; catalytic agent

触霉头 chù méitóu　dial.　have a stroke of bad luck; be unfortunate; come to grief

触摸 chùmō　touch; feel: 请勿～展品。Please don't touch the exhibits.

触目 chùmù　① meet the eye: 触目皆是　chùmù jiē shì ② eye-catching; striking; conspicuous: ～的广告 eye-catching posters

触目皆是 chùmù jiē shì　can be seen everywhere; be everywhere in evidence

触目惊心 chùmù-jīngxīn　startling; shocking

触怒 chùnù　make angry; infuriate; enrage

触杀剂 chùshājì　contact insecticide

触手 chùshǒu　zool.　tentacle

触痛 chùtòng　① touch a tender (or sore) spot; touch sb. to the quick ② med.　tenderness

触网 chùwǎng　sports　touch net

触须 chùxū　zool.　cirrus: 鱼类～ barbel / 无脊椎动物～ palp

触眼 chùyǎn　dial.　eye-catching; striking; conspicuous

触诊 chùzhěn　med.　palpation

憷 chù　fear; shrink from: 这孩子 ～见生人。The child is afraid of strangers.

憷场 chùchǎng　dial.　feel nervous before a large audience

憷头 chùtóu　dial.　shrink from difficulties; be timid

黜 chù　formal　remove sb. from office; dismiss

黜免 chùmiǎn　formal　dismiss (a government official)

黜陟 chùzhì　formal　demote and promote (officials)

矗 chù　formal　stand tall and upright

矗立 chùlì　stand tall and upright; tower over sth.: 人民英雄纪念碑 ～在天安门广场上。The Monument to the People's Heroes towers aloft in Tian'anmen Square.

chuā

欻（歘）chuā　onom.　the sound of heavy steps: 一队队民兵 ～ ～地走过去, 非常整齐。Tramp, tramp, tramp, columns of militiamen marched by in perfect step.

欻拉 chuālā　onom.　a hissing sound: ～一声, 把菜倒进了滚油锅里。The vegetables dropped into the boiling oil with a sizzle.

chuāi

揣 chuāi　① hide or carry in one's clothes: ～在怀里 hide in the bosom; tuck into the bosom / 这封信一直 ～在我口袋里。The letter has been in my pocket all this time. ② dial.　cram oneself with food; overeat: 我 ～得太饱了。I'm overfull. ③ dial.　cram sb. with food; overfeed: 别净 ～孩子。Don't keep cramming the child with food. ——see also chuǎi; chuài

揣手儿 chuāishǒur　tuck each hand in the opposite sleeve

搋 chuāi　① rub; knead: ～面 knead dough / 这衣服没洗干净, 再～两下。These clothes haven't been washed clean. Let me give them another rub or two. ② clear a drain with a suction pump

搋子 chuāizi　suction pump

chuái

膗 chuái　dial.　fat and flabby: 瞧他那 ～样。See how fat and flabby he is.

chuǎi

揣 chuǎi　formal　estimate; surmise; conjecture: 揣测　chuǎicè ——see also chuāi; chuài

揣测 chuǎicè　guess; conjecture: 据我 ～, 他已经离开太原了。My guess is that he's already left Taiyuan.

揣度 chuǎiduó　formal　estimate; appraise; conjecture: ～敌情 make an appraisal of the enemy's situation

揣摩 chuǎimó　try to fathom; try to figure out: 我始终 ～不透他的用意。I simply couldn't figure out his intention.

揣想 chuǎixiǎng　guess; think: 她心里～着接下去会发生什么情况。She was trying to figure out what would happen next.

chuài

揣 chuài　see 挣揣　zhèngchuài ——see also chuāi; chuǎi

踹 chuài　① kick: 一脚把门 ～开 kick the door open ② tread; stamp: 一脚 ～在水坑里 step in a puddle ③ undermine; sap; sabotage: 这桩买卖让人给 ～

了。This business deal has been sabotaged by some-one. ④ *dial.* kick the bucket; kick off

踹腿儿 chuàituǐr *dial.* kick the bucket; turn up one's toes; die

膪

膪 chuài see 囊膪 nāngchuài

chuān

川

川 chuān ① river: 高山大 ～ high mountains and big rivers ② plain: 米粮川 mǐliángchuān ③ (Chuān) short for 四川 Sìchuān

川贝 chuānbèi *Chin. med.* tendril-leaved fritillary bulb of Sichuan origin

川菜 chuāncài Sichuan food; Sichuan cuisine

川剧 chuānjù Sichuan opera (a local opera popular in Sichuan and in parts of Guizhou and Yunnan)

川流不息 chuān liú bù xī flowing past in an endless stream; never-ending: 顾客 ～。Customers came in an endless stream. *or* Customers kept pouring in. / 公路上车辆 ～。There was an endless stream of traffic on the highway.

川芎 chuānxiōng *Chin. med.* the rhizome of *chuanxiong* (*Ligusticum wallichii*)

川资 chuānzī travelling expenses

氕

氕 chuān *chem.* tritium (T *or* H³)

氕核 chuānhé *phys.* triton

穿

穿 chuān ① pierce through; penetrate: ～个窟窿 pierce (*or* bore) a hole / 鞋底磨 ～了。The sole of the shoe was worn through. ② pass through; cross: 飞机 ～云下降。The plane descended through the clouds. ③ wear; put on; be dressed in: ～上工作服 put on work clothes / ～灰大衣的那个女的 the woman in a grey overcoat / 衣服 ～旧了。The clothes show signs of wear. / 这种鞋小点不要紧，～ ～就大了。It doesn't matter if the shoes feel a bit tight. They'll stretch with wearing. / ～得这么少，不冷吗? Aren't you cold with so little on? ④ string together: 用珠子 ～成一串项链 string the beads into a necklace

穿不出去 chuānbuchūqù cannot be seen in such clothes; be unpresentable (because of colour, style, or shabbiness): 这件衣服式样太老，我实在 ～。I don't want to be seen in such an old-fashioned dress.

穿不得 chuānbude cannot wear (because it does not fit): 这件衣裳肥得 ～。This coat is too loose for me.

穿不起 chuānbuqǐ cannot afford to wear: 这么贵的绸缎我可 ～。I cannot afford such expensive silk dresses.

穿不住 chuānbuzhù cannot go on wearing (because the weather is too warm): 天热了，毛衣～了。It's too warm to wear woollen sweaters now.

穿插 chuānchā ① alternate; do in turn: 施肥和除草 ～进行 do manuring and weeding in turn ② weave in; insert: 他在报告中 ～了一些生动的例子。His talk was spiced with vivid examples. ③ subplot; interlude; episode ④ *mil.* thrust deep into the enemy forces: 打 ～fight a deep-thrust battle / ～分割敌人 penetrate and cut up the enemy forces

穿插营 chuānchāyíng *mil.* deep-thrust battalion

穿刺 chuāncì *med.* puncture: 肝 (腰椎) ～ liver (lumbar) puncture

穿戴 chuāndài apparel; dress: ～整齐 be neatly dressed and adorned / 不讲究～ not be particular about one's dress

穿耳 chuān'ěr have the earlobes pierced (for earrings)

穿过 chuānguò go across or through; cross; penetrate: ～马路 cross a street / ～地道 pass through a tunnel / ～树林 go through a forest / 从人群中 ～ thread one's way through the crowd / 咱们从操场～去吧。Let's take the shortcut across the sports field. / 子弹 ～头盔射入他的头部。The bullet penetrated his helmet and hit his head.

穿甲弹 chuānjiǎdàn armour-piercing projectile; armour-piercing shell or bullet; armour piercer

穿孔 chuānkǒng ① bore (*or* punch) a hole; perforate: ～卡片 punched card / ～纸带 punched tape ② *med.* perforation: 胃 (阑尾) ～ gastric (appendicular) perforation

穿孔机 chuānkǒngjī punch; perforator

穿箔机 chuānkòujī *text.* reeding machine

穿廊 chuānláng a covered corridor on either side of the second gate in an old-style Chinese compound

穿连裆裤 chuān liándāngkù *dial.* band together; collude; gang up

穿颅术 chuānlúshù *med.* craniotomy

穿山甲 chuānshānjiǎ ① *zool.* pangolin ② *Chin. med.* pangolin scales

穿梭 chuānsuō shuttle back and forth: ～轰炸 shuttle bombing / ～外交 shuttle diplomacy

穿堂儿 chuāntángr a hallway connecting two courtyards in an old-style Chinese compound

穿堂风 chuāntángfēng draught

穿堂门 chuāntángmén passageway; alley gate

穿透 chuāntòu pierce through; run through: 钉子 ～了木板。The nail ran through the board.

穿小鞋 chuān xiǎoxié (usu. used in) 给某人～ give sb. tight shoes to wear—make things hard for sb. by abusing one's power; make it hot for sb.

穿孝 chuānxiào be in mourning; wear mourning: 为母亲～ wear mourning for one's mother

穿心莲 chuānxīnlián *Chin. med.* creat

穿新鞋，走老路 chuān xīnxié, zǒu lǎolù tread the old path in new shoes—make no real change

穿一条裤子 chuān yītiáo kùzi share the same pair of trousers—band together; collude; gang up

穿衣镜 chuānyījìng full-length mirror

穿窬 chuānyú *formal* cut through or climb over a wall (in order to rob the house): 口谈道德，而志在 ～ contemplate burglary while mouthing morality; talk of virtue but think of vice / ～之盗 burglar

穿越 chuānyuè pass through; cut across: 铁路 ～原始森林。The railway cuts through a primeval forest. / ～国境 cross the border

穿云裂石 chuānyún-lièshí cloud-piercing and rock-splitting— (of singing, the piping of a flute, etc.) penetrating

穿凿 chuānzáo give a farfetched (*or* strained) interpretation; read too much into sth.

穿凿附会 chuānzáo-fùhuì give strained interpretations and draw farfetched analogies

穿针 chuānzhēn thread a needle

穿针器 chuānzhēnqì needle threader

穿针引线 chuānzhēn-yǐnxiàn act as a go-between

穿着 chuānzhuó dress; apparel: ～朴素整洁 be plainly but neatly dressed

chuán

传(傳)

传(傳) chuán ① pass; pass on: 此件请按名单顺序向下 ～。Please pass on this document in the order of the name list. ② hand down: 这种药方没能 ～下来。That herbal prescription has been lost to posterity. / 这是古代 ～下来的文化遗产。This is a cultural

heritage handed down from ancient times. ③ pass on (knowledge, skill, etc.); impart; teach: 老师傅把他的技术全 ～给徒弟了。The old master passed all his skills on to his apprentices. ④ spread: 消息很快 ～开了。The news spread quickly. *or* The news soon got around. / 喜讯～来，欢声雷动。The glad tidings gave rise to thunderous cheers. / 这个秘密是他 ～出去的。He's the one who let out the secret. ⑤ transmit; conduct: ～热 transmit heat / 铜 ～电。Copper conducts electricity. ⑥ convey; express: 传神 chuánshén / 传情 chuánqíng ⑦ summon: ～证人 summon a witness ⑧ infect; be contagious: 小心别让你孩子 ～上流感。Mind that your children don't catch the flu. ——see also zhuàn

传帮带 chuán-bāng-dài　pass on experience, give help and set an example (in training new hands)

传播 chuánbō　① disseminate; propagate; spread: ～花粉 carry pollen (from flower to flower); pollinate / ～马克思主义 propagate (*or* disseminate) Marxism / ～知识（消息）spread knowledge (news) / 制止疾病的 ～ check the spread of the disease ② *phys.* propagation: 直线 ～ rectilinear propagation / 散射 ～ scatter propagation

传播媒介 chuánbō méijiè　mass media; the media

传布 chuánbù　disseminate; propagate; spread: ～基督教 spread Christianity

传抄 chuánchāo　make private copies of (a manuscript, document, etc. which is being circulated)

传出神经 chuánchū shénjīng　*physiol.* efferent nerve

传达 chuándá　① pass on (information, etc.); transmit; relay; communicate: ～命令 transmit an order / 听 ～报告 hear a relayed report / 把上级的指示 ～到基层 communicate the instructions of a higher leading body to grass-roots units ② reception and registration of callers at a public establishment ③ janitor

传达室 chuándáshì　reception office; janitor's room

传代 chuándài　pass on from generation to generation

传单 chuándān　leaflet; handbill

传导 chuándǎo　① *phys.* conduct (heat, electricity, etc.): 金属都有 ～作用。All metals are conductive. / 热的～ the conduction of heat ② *physiol.* transmit: 神经纤维把外界的刺激 ～给大脑。Nerve fibres transmit external stimuli to the brain.

传道 chuándào　① deliver a sermon; preach ② propagate Confucianist doctrines: 古之学者必有师。师者，所以 ～授业解惑也。(韩愈) In ancient times scholars always had teachers. It takes a teacher to transmit wisdom, impart knowledge, and resolve doubts.

传递 chuándì　transmit; deliver; transfer: ～信件 deliver mail / ～信息 transmit messages

传动 chuándòng　*mech.* transmission; drive: 变速 ～ change drive / 齿轮 ～ gear drive (*or* transmission)

传动比 chuándòngbǐ　drive ratio; ratio of transmission; transmission ratio

传动齿轮 chuándòng chǐlún　transmission (*or* drive) gear

传动带 chuándòngdài　transmission belt

传动箱 chuándòngxiāng　transmission case

传动轴 chuándòngzhóu　transmission shaft

传动装置 chuándòng zhuāngzhì　gearing

传粉 chuánfěn　*bot.* pollination: ～媒介 pollination medium

传感器 chuángǎnqì　*elec.* sensor; transducer: 激光 ～ laser sensor

传告 chuángào　pass on (news or word); spread: ～喜讯 pass on (*or* tell each other) the good news / 奔走～ go around spreading the news

传观 chuánguān　pass sth. round for a look

传呼 chuánhū　(of a trunk-line operator or public telephone custodian) pass on a telephone message or call sb. to answer the phone

传呼电话 chuánhū diànhuà　neighbourhood telephone service

传话 chuánhuà　pass on a message

传唤 chuánhuàn　*leg.* summon to court; subpoena

传家 chuánjiā　pass on (*or* hand down) from generation to generation in a family

传家宝 chuánjiābǎo　① family heirloom: 这块玉珮是咱们家的 ～。This jade pendant is our family heirloom. ② a cherished tradition or heritage: 艰苦朴素的作风是中国人民的 ～。Hard work and plain living is a cherished heritage of the Chinese people.

传见 chuánjiàn　call in (a subordinate)

传教 chuánjiào　do missionary work

传教士 chuánjiàoshì　missionary

传戒 chuánjiè　*Buddhism* initiation ceremony for monks or nuns

传经送宝 chuánjīng-sòngbǎo　pass on one's valuable experience

传看 chuánkàn　pass sth. round for a look: 他拿出几本相册让大家～。He took out some photo albums and passed them round.

传令 chuánlìng　transmit (*or* dispatch) orders: ～嘉奖 cite sb. in a dispatch

传流 chuánliú　same as 流传 liúchuán

传票 chuánpiào　① *leg.* (court) summons; subpoena: 发出 ～ issue a summons ② *accounting* voucher

传奇 chuánqí　① tales of the marvellous (short stories of the Tang-Song period, written in the literary style; e.g. 元稹《莺莺传》Yuan Zhen's "The Story of Yingying," 杜光庭《虬髯客传》Du Guangting's "The Curly-bearded Hero"): 《唐宋 ～集》*Literary Tales of the Tang and Song*　(selected and edited by Lu Xun 鲁迅) ② a form of drama of the Ming-Qing period, immensely long with an average of forty or more scenes (the songs are chanted by several characters in the play, the bamboo flute being the chief musical instrument; e.g. 汤显祖《牡丹亭》Tang Xianzu's *The Peony Pavilion*, 孔尚任《桃花扇》Kong Shangren's *The Peach Blossom Fan*) ③ legend; romance:《少帅～》*The Legend of the Young Marshal*　(a TV drama) / ～式的人物 a legendary figure

传情 chuánqíng　express amorous feelings: 借诗 ～ convey one's feelings through a poem

传球 chuánqiú　pass the ball to a teammate

传染 chuánrǎn　infect; be contagious: 接触～ contagion / 空气～ infection through air / 水～ waterborne infection / 这 病 不 ～。This disease is not contagious (*or* infectious). / 感冒很容易 ～。Colds are highly infectious.

传染病 chuánrǎnbìng　infectious (*or* contagious) disease

传染病院 chuánrǎnbìngyuàn　hospital for infectious diseases; isolation hospital

传染性 chuánrǎnxìng　infectiousness; contagion: ～很强 be highly infectious / ～肝炎 infectious hepatitis

传人 chuánrén　① pass on a skill or craft to others: 过去梨园行对技艺是保密的。除非是家里人，名角都不会轻易将绝技 ～。The traditional stage world was not remarkable for its altruism in professional matters, and famous actors would think twice about passing on their technical secrets to those outside the family circle. ② *formal* successor; exponent: 梅派 ～ the foremost exponent of the Mei school (of Beijing opera) ③ summon sb.: ～问话 summon sb. for questioning ④ be contagious; be infectious: 这种病～。This disease is contagious.

传入神经 chuánrù shénjīng　*physiol.* afferent nerve

传神 chuánshén　vivid; lifelike: 他的画很能 ～。His

paintings are lifelike.

传神之笔 chuánshén zhī bǐ a vivid touch (in writing or painting)

传审 chuánshěn *leg.* summon for interrogation

传声器 chuánshēngqì microphone

传声清晰度 chuánshēng qīngxīdù *radio* articulation

传声筒 chuánshēngtǒng ① megaphone; loud hailer ② one who parrots another; sb.'s mouthpiece

传世 chuánshì be handed down from ancient times: ～珍宝 a treasure handed down from ancient times / 他有两部作品～。Two of his works have been handed down to posterity.

传授 chuánshòu pass on (knowledge, skill, etc.); impart; teach: ～知识 impart knowledge to; teach / 向年轻人～技术 teach young people skills; give technical instruction to young people

传输 chuánshū *elec.* transmission: ～损耗 transmission loss

传输线 chuánshūxiàn *elec.* transmission line

传述 chuánshù same as 传说 chuánshuō①

传说 chuánshuō ① pass from mouth to mouth; it is said; they say: 村里～他叔要从国外回来了。The villagers are all saying that his uncle is soon coming home from abroad. / ～如此。So the story goes. ② legend; tradition: 鲁班的～ the legend of Lu Ban / 民间～ folklore; popular legend

传诵 chuánsòng be widely read; be on everybody's lips: 为世人所～ be read with admiration by people all over the world / ～一时 be on everybody's lips at the time

传送 chuánsòng convey; deliver: ～信息 convey information / 村里的邮件都由他～。He's the postal delivery man in his village.

传送带 chuánsòngdài *mech.* conveyer belt

传颂 chuánsòng be told from mouth to mouth with approbation; be on everybody's lips: 当地群众中～着工农红军的英雄事迹。The heroic deeds of the Workers' and Peasants' Red Army are continually on the lips of the local inhabitants.

传统 chuántǒng tradition: 发扬优良～ carry on a fine tradition / 革命～ revolutionary tradition / ～友谊 traditional (ties of) friendship / ～观念 traditional ideas / ～剧目 traditional theatrical pieces

传为佳话 chuán wéi jiāhuà become a favourite topic or a much-told tale: 他二人的破镜重圆在这儿～。The couple's reunion has become a favourite topic among the people here.

传为美谈 chuán wéi měitán pass from mouth to mouth with approbation: 老作家捐献十万元作奖学金, 在知识界～。The old writer's donation of 100,000 *yuan* for the scholarship has won widespread approbation among intellectuals.

传闻 chuánwén ① it is said; they say ② hearsay; rumour; talk: 这只是～, 我不相信。That's only hearsay. I don't believe it. / ～失实。The rumour was unfounded.

传闻异辞 chuánwén-yìcí different versions of hearsay

传习 chuánxí learn and pass on (knowledge or skills): ～民间传统技艺 learn and pass on traditional skills

传檄 chuánxí *formal* (in former times) send out a war proclamation, setting forth the purpose of the expedition and exposing the evil done by the enemy

传写 chuánxiě *formal* make private copies of (a manuscript, document, etc. which is being circulated)

传讯 chuánxùn *leg.* summon for interrogation or trial; subpoena; cite: ～有关人员 summon the persons concerned for interrogation

传言 chuányán ① hearsay; rumour: 不可轻信～! Give no credence to rumours! / ～非虚。It's not just hear-

say. ② pass on a message: 我不愿给人家～送语, 你自己找他说去。I don't like to act as a messenger. Go and speak to him yourself. ③ *formal* deliver a speech

传扬 chuányáng spread (from mouth to mouth): ～四方 spread far and wide / 这件事不要～出去。Don't let a word of this get around.

传阅 chuányuè pass round (*or* circulate) for perusal: 这篇稿子请大家～。Please pass the draft round. / 文件正在委员中～。The document is being circulated among the members of the committee.

传真 chuánzhēn ① portraiture ② facsimile; fax: 无线电～ radio facsimile; radiophotography

传真电报 chuánzhēn diànbào phototelegraph

传真照片 chuánzhēn zhàopiàn radiophoto

传旨 chuánzhǐ deliver an imperial order: ～嘉奖 deliver an imperial commendation

传种 chuánzhǒng propagate; reproduce

传宗接代 chuánzōng-jiēdài produce a male heir to continue the family line

船(舩)

船(舩) chuán boat; ship: 上～ board a ship; go on board; embark / 乘～去大连 go to Dalian by boat; embark (on a ship) for Dalian

船板 chuánbǎn deck of a small wooden boat

船帮 chuánbāng ① the side of a boat; shipboard ② merchant fleet

船舶 chuánbó shipping; boats and ships

船舶登记证书 chuánbó dēngjì zhèngshū ship's certificate of registry

船舶证书 chuánbó zhèngshū ship's papers

船埠 chuánbù wharf; quay

船舱 chuáncāng ① ship's hold ② cabin

船次 chuáncì ① number indicating a ship's order of departure ② number of voyages taken by a ship

船到江心补漏迟 chuán dào jiāngxīn bǔ lòu chí it's too late to plug the leak when the boat is in midstream

船东 chuándōng shipowner

船队 chuánduì fleet; flotilla

船方 chuánfāng *com.* the ship: ～不负担装货费用 free in (F.I.) / ～不负担卸货费用 free out (F.O.) / ～不负担装、卸、理仓费用 free in and out and stowed (F.I.O.S.)

船夫 chuánfū *old* boatman

船夫曲 chuánfūqǔ boatmen's song

船工 chuángōng ① boatman; junkman ② boatwright

船棺葬 chuánguānzàng *archaeol.* boat-coffin burial

船户 chuánhù ① same as 船家 chuánjia ② *dial.* boat dweller

船级 chuánjí ship's classification (*or* class)

船级社 chuánjíshè (ships') classification society: 劳氏～ Lloyd's Register of Shipping

船级证书 chuánjí zhèngshū ship's classification certificate

船籍 chuánjí the nationality of a ship

船籍港 chuánjígǎng port of registry; home port

船家 chuánjia *old* one who owns a boat and makes a living as a boatman; boatman

船脚 chuánjiǎo ① boatman; junkman ② shipping freight

船壳 chuánké hull

船老大 chuánlǎodà *dial.* ① the chief crewman of a wooden boat ② boatman

船龄 chuánlíng the age of a ship

船篷 chuánpéng ① the mat or wooden roofing of a boat ② sail

船票 chuánpiào steamer ticket: 预订去青岛的～ book one's passage to Qingdao

船期 chuánqī sailing date

船期表 chuánqībiǎo sailing schedule

船钱 chuánqian boat fare; money to hire a boat

船桥 chuánqiáo (ship's) bridge
船蛆 chuánqū shipworm
船艄 chuánshāo stern
船身 chuánshēn hull (of a ship): ～倾斜。The boat is tilted to one side.
船首 chuánshǒu stem; bow; prow
船首楼 chuánshǒulóu forecastle
船台 chuántái (building) berth; shipway; slipway; slip: 干式～ dry shipway
船台周期 chuántái zhōuqī berth period
船体 chuántǐ the body of a ship; hull
船尾 chuánwěi stern
船尾部 chuánwěibù quarter
船尾楼 chuánwěilóu poop
船尾轴 chuánwěizhóu stern shaft
船位 chuánwèi ① accommodation on a ship: 订～ book one's passage (on a ship) ② ship's position: 测定～ fix a ship's position (at sea); position finding / ～推算法 dead reckoning
船坞 chuánwù dock; shipyard: 浮～ floating dock / 干～ dry (or graving) dock
船坞费 chuánwùfèi dockage
船舷 chuánxián side (of a ship or boat)
船用油 chuányòngyóu bunker oil
船员 chuányuán (ship's) crew
船闸 chuánzhá (ship) lock
船长 chuánzhǎng captain; skipper
船只 chuánzhī shipping; vessels: 往来～ shipping traffic / 载货～ carrying vessels / ～失事 shipwreck
船主 chuánzhǔ ① the captain of a vessel; skipper ② the owner of a boat or ship

遄 chuán formal quickly: ～返 return quickly

椽 chuán rafter
椽笔 chuánbǐ a writing brush as big as a rafter— your masterpiece; your masterly writing
椽条 chuántiáo rafter
椽子 chuánzi rafter

chuǎn

舛 chuǎn formal ① error: 舛错 chuǎncuò ② mishap: 命途多舛 mìngtú duō chuǎn ③ run counter
舛错 chuǎncuò ① error; mistake: 音韵～ errors in rhyming ② accident: 万一有个～,后悔也就晚了。If anything should happen, it would be too late for regrets. ③ irregular; uneven: 互相～ crisscrossed
舛误 chuǎnwù formal error; mishap

喘 chuǎn ① breathe heavily; gasp for breath; pant ② asthma
喘咳 chuǎnké pant and cough
喘气 chuǎnqì ① breathe (deeply); pant; gasp: 喘不过气来 gasp for breath; be out of breath / 大口大口地～ puff and blow ② take a breather: 喘口气儿再干。Let's take a breather before we go on.
喘息 chuǎnxī ① pant; gasp for breath ② breather; breathing spell; respite: 不让敌人有～的机会。Do not allow the enemy a breathing spell.
喘息未定 chuǎnxī wèi dìng before catching one's breath; before one has a chance to catch one's breath: 敌人～,即予以迎头痛击。Deal a head-on blow before the enemy has a chance to catch his breath.
喘哮 chuǎnxiāo same as 哮喘 xiàochuǎn
喘吁吁 chuǎnxūxū puff and blow

chuàn

串 chuàn ① string together: 把鱼～起来 string the fish together ② conspire; gang up: 串通 chuàntōng ③ get things mixed up: 电话～线 get the (telephone) lines crossed / (收音机)～台 get two or more (radio) stations at once / 字印得太小, 很容易看～行。The print is too small, you can easily miss (or skip) a line. ④ go from place to place; run about; rove: 到处乱～ run about aimlessly / ～亲戚 go visiting one's relatives ⑤ play a part (in a play); act: 客串 kèchuàn ⑥ m. (for a string of things) string; bunch; cluster: 一～珠子 a string of beads / 一～钥匙 a bunch of keys / 一～葡萄 a cluster of grapes
串并联 chuànbìnglián elec. series-parallel connection
串供 chuàngòng act in collusion to make each other's confessions tally
串儿红 chuànrhóng scarlet sage (Salvia splendens)
串激 chuànjī elec. series excitation: ～电动机 series motor / ～发电机 series generator; series dynamo
串讲 chuànjiǎng (of a teacher) ① explain a text sentence by sentence ② give a summing-up of a text after going over it paragraph by paragraph
串联 chuànlián ① establish ties; contact: 一九五一年秋, 他～了几户贫农, 组织起一个互助组。In the autumn of 1951 he contacted several poor peasant families and organized a mutual-aid team. ② elec. series connection: ～电池组 series battery / ～电阻 series resistance
串铃 chuànlíng ① a hollow metal ring with small metal balls in it, used in old times by pedlars, fortune-tellers, and itinerant doctors ② a string of bells hung round the neck of a horse, mule, etc.
串门子 chuànménzi (also 串门儿 chuànménr) inf. call at sb.'s home; drop in: 有空来～。Drop in when you're free.
串骗 chuànpiàn conspire in a fraud; gang up and swindle sb.; collude
串通 chuàntōng gang up; collaborate; collude
串通一气 chuàntōng yīqì gang up; collaborate; work hand in glove; collude: 两人～, 互相包庇。Acting in collaboration, the two of them shielded each other. / 你们～来算计我! You're all in league against me.
串味 chuànwèi absorb the smell of sth.; become tainted inflavour: 茶叶与化妆品放在一起就会～。Tea stored close to cosmetics will become tainted in flavour.
串戏 chuànxì (of an amateur actor) play a part in a professional performance
串乡 chuànxiāng travel from village to village (as a travelling salesman, performer, etc.)
串演 chuànyǎn play (or act) the role of
串秧儿 chuànyāngr inf. crossbreed; interbreed
串珠 chuànzhū a string of beads

钏 chuàn bracelet: 金～ gold bracelet

chuāng

创 (創) chuāng wound: 创伤 chuāngshāng ——see also chuàng
创痕 chuānghén scar
创巨痛深 chuāngjù-tòngshēn badly injured and in great pain—in deep distress
创口 chuāngkǒu wound; cut: ～很大 a gaping wound

创伤 chuāngshāng wound; trauma: 精神上的 ～ a mental scar; a traumatic experience / 医治战争的 ～ heal the wounds of war

创痍 chuāngyí same as 疮痍 chuāngyí

疮(瘡)

chuāng ① sore; skin ulcer: 我手上长的～挺疼的。The sore on my hand hurts. ② wound: 刀～ a sword wound

疮疤 chuāngbā scar: 脸上的 ～ a scar on the face ——see also 揭疮疤 jiē chuāngbā

疮痕 chuānghén scar

疮痂 chuāngjiā med. scab

疮口 chuāngkǒu the open part of a sore

疮痍 chuāngyí formal wounds; traumata—devastation caused by a war or a natural calamity

疮痍满目 chuāngyí mǎnmù everywhere a scene of devastation meets the eye

窗(窓、牎)

chuāng window: 开 ～ open the window / 看～外 look out of the window

窗玻璃 chuāngbōli windowpane

窗洞 chuāngdòng an opening in a wall (to let in light and air)

窗扉 chuāngfēi casement

窗格子 chuānggézi window lattice

窗户 chuānghu window; casement

窗花 chuānghuā paper-cut for window decoration

窗口 chuāngkǒu window: 坐在 ～ sit at (or by) the window / 去上海的火车票在那个 ～ 卖。Train tickets to Shanghai are sold at that window. / 在对外开放中发挥 ～作用 serve as a window open to the outside world

窗框 chuāngkuàng window frame

窗帘 chuānglián window curtain

窗棂 chuānglíng (also 窗棂子 chuānglíngzi) dial. window lattice

窗幔 chuāngmàn window curtain

窗明几净 chuāngmíng-jījìng with bright windows and clean tables; bright and clean

窗纱 chuāngshā gauze for screening windows; window screening

窗扇 chuāngshàn casement

窗台 chuāngtái windowsill

窗帷 chuāngwéi (also 窗纬 chuāngwéi) window curtain

窗沿 chuāngyán windowsill

窗友 chuāngyǒu old fellow student; schoolmate

窗子 chuāngzi window

牕(牎)

chuāng same as 窗 chuāng

chuáng

床(牀)

chuáng ① bed: 小孩 ～ child's cot; baby's crib / 躺在 ～上 lie in bed / 卧病在 ～ take to one's bed; be laid up ② sth. shaped like a bed: 车床 chēchuáng / 河床 héchuáng ③ m. (for bedding): 一 ～被子 one quilt / 两 ～毯子 two blankets / 三 ～铺盖 three sets of bedding

床单 chuángdān sheet

床单布 chuángdānbù sheeting

床垫 chuángdiàn mattress

床架 chuángjià bedstead

床铺 chuángpù bed

床蓐 chuángrù bedding: 卧病～ take to one's bed; be laid up

床身 chuángshēn mech. lathe bed

床虱 chuángshī bedbug

床榻 chuángtà bed; couch

床头 chuángtóu the head of a bed; bedside

床头灯 chuángtóudēng bedside lamp; bedlamp

床头柜 chuángtóuguì bedside cupboard

床头箱 chuángtóuxiāng mech. headstock

床位 chuángwèi berth; bunk; bed

床沿 chuángyán the edge of a bed

床罩 chuángzhào bedspread; counterpane

床笫 chuángzǐ formal bed mat—the bed as a place of conjugal intimacies

床笫之间 chuángzǐ zhī jiān conjugal intimacies

床笫之言 chuángzǐ zhī yán private talk between husband and wife; pillow talk

床子 chuángzi ① lathe ② dial. a bed-shaped shelf for goods

幢

chuáng ① a pennant or streamer used in ancient China ② a stone pillar inscribed with Buddha's name or Buddhist scripture ——see also zhuàng

幢幢 chuángchuáng (of shadows) flickering; dancing: 人影 ～ shadows of people moving about / 树影 ～ the dancing shadows of the trees

chuǎng

闯

chuǎng ① rush; dash; charge: ～进来 rush in; break in; force one's way in ② temper oneself (by battling through difficulties and dangers); venture out into the world: 他是自己 ～出来的。He has hewed out his path on his own. / 我们必须 ～出一条新路子。We must break a new path.

闯荡 chuǎngdàng make a living away from home

闯关东 chuǎng Guāndōng brave the journey to the Northeast (to eke out an existence in the old society)

闯祸 chuǎnghuò get into trouble; bring disaster: 你 ～了! Look what you've done! / 你开车要小心, 千万别 ～。Drive carefully and be sure not to have an accident.

闯江湖 chuǎng jiānghú (also 闯荡江湖 chuǎngdàng jiānghú) make a living wandering from place to place (as a fortune-teller, acrobat, quack doctor, etc.)

闯将 chuǎngjiàng a daring general; pathbreaker: 他是技术革新的 ～。He's a pathbreaker in technical innovation.

闯劲 chuǎngjìn the spirit of a pathbreaker; pioneering spirit: 搞改革就要有一股不怕困难的 ～。To go in for reforms, one must have the fearless spirit of a pathbreaker.

闯练 chuǎngliàn leave home to temper oneself; be tempered in the world: 让青年人到社会上去～ ～。Let young people temper themselves in society.

闯路 chuǎnglù blaze a trail; open a way; break a path

闯南走北 chuǎngnán-zǒuběi same as 走南闯北 zǒunán-chuǎngběi

chuàng

创(創、刱、剙)

chuàng start (doing sth.); achieve (sth. for the first time): 排万难, ～高产 surmount all difficulties and achieve higher output / ～记录 set a record; chalk up a record / 该厂钢产量 ～历史最高水平。The plant's steel output was an all-time high. ——see also chuāng

创办 chuàngbàn establish; set up: ～农具修理厂 set up a farm implement repair shop

创编 chuàngbiān compose or write (a play); design and arrange (a dance)

创汇 chuànghuì earn foreign exchange: 出口～能力 capacity to earn foreign exchange through export

创获 chuànghuò new discovery; original findings: 他专攻化学, 有不少～。He specializes in chemistry and has made a number of new discoveries.

创见 chuàngjiàn original idea: 有～的思想家 an original thinker

创建 chuàngjiàn found; establish: ～一个政党 found a (political) party / 这所学校是一九七八年冬～的。This school was set up in the winter of 1978.

创举 chuàngjǔ pioneering work (or undertaking): 伟大的～ a great beginning

创刊 chuàngkān start publication: 《人民日报》于一九四八年六月十五日～。 Renmin Ribao started publication on June 15, 1948.

创刊号 chuàngkānhào first issue (or number)

创立 chuànglì found; originate: 马克思和恩格斯～了科学社会主义理论。Marx and Engels founded the theory of scientific socialism. / ～新学派 found a new academic school

创设 chuàngshè ① found; create; set up: ～一个新的研究所 set up a new research institute ② create (conditions, etc.): 为我们的学习～有利的条件 create favourable conditions for our studies

创始 chuàngshǐ originate; initiate; found: 处在～阶段 be in the initial stage / 中国是联合国的～会员国之一。China is a founding member of the United Nations.

创始人 chuàngshǐrén founder; originator; initiator

创世纪 Chuàngshìjì Genesis

创树 chuàngshù originate; be the first to cultivate or foster: ～新的艺术风格 foster a new artistic style

创新 chuàngxīn bring forth new ideas; blaze new trails: 在艺术上不断～ constantly bring forth new ideas in the arts / 勇于实践, 大胆～。Be bold in putting things into practice and blazing new trails.

创业 chuàngyè start an undertaking; do pioneering work: 为社会主义～ be builders of socialism / ～的艰辛 hardships endured in pioneering work

创议 chuàngyì ① propose ② proposal

创造 chuàngzào create; produce; bring about: ～有利条件 create favourable conditions / ～优异成绩 produce excellent results / ～新记录 set (or create) a new record / ～奇迹 create miracles; work wonders; achieve prodigious feats / 人民是～世界历史的动力。The people are the motive force in the making of world history. / 中华民族政治智慧的伟大～ a great innovation showing the political wisdom of the Chinese nation

创造力 chuàngzàolì creative power (or ability)

创造性 chuàngzàoxìng creativeness; creativity

创制 chuàngzhì formulate; institute; create: ～拼音文字 formulate an alphabetic system of writing

创作 chuàngzuò ① create; produce; write: ～反映现实生活的美术作品 produce works of art that reflect real life / ～技巧 artistic technique; craftsmanship / ～经验 creative experience / ～思想 ideas guiding artistic or literary creation ② creative work; creation: 文艺～ literary and artistic creation / 划时代的～ epoch-making creative work

怆 (愴)

chuàng formal sorrowful: 凄怆 qīchuàng

怆恻 chuàngcè formal grieved; sad; sorrowful

怆恍 chuànghuǎng (also 怆悦 chuànghuǎng) formal disheartened; discouraged

怆然 chuàngrán formal sad; sorrowful: ～泪下 burst into sorrowful tears

chuī

吹

chuī ① blow; puff: ～火 blow a fire / 把灯～灭 blow out the lamp / ～一口气 give a puff / 门～开了。The door blew open. / 什么风把你给～来了? What brings you here? ② play (wind instruments): ～笛子 play the flute / ～起床号 sound the reveille ③ inf. boast; brag: 先别～, 做出具体成绩来再说。Don't brag about what you're going to do. Get something done. / ～得天花乱坠 boast in the most fantastic terms ④ inf. break off; break up; fall through: 他们俩～了。That couple have broken up. / 原来的计划～了。The original plan has fallen through.

吹吹打打 chuīchuīdǎdǎ beating drums and blowing trumpets; piping and drumming

吹吹拍拍 chuīchuīpāipāi boasting and toadying: 这个人～, 到处钻营。That man is given to boasting and flattering, trying to secure personal gain wherever he goes.

吹打 chuīdǎ ① beat drums and blow trumpets; play wind and percussion instruments ② a sudden attack (of wind and rain): 经受暴风雨的～ withstand the tribulations of tempests

吹打 chuīda ① blow away (dust, etc.) ② dial. sting; hurt: 说话～人 say things which hurt people's feelings ③ dial. boast; brag; talk big

吹打乐 chuīdǎyuè mus. an ensemble of Chinese wind and percussion instruments

吹灯拔蜡 chuīdēng-bálà dial. blow out the lamp and snuff the candle— ① die; kick the bucket ② be finished; be done with

吹风 chuīfēng ① be in a draught; catch a chill: 你病还没有好, 不要～。Don't get in a draught, you aren't well yet. ② dry (hair, etc.) with a blower; blow-dry ③ blow-dryer; blower (for drying hair) ④ inf. let sb. in on sth. in advance: 下次会要讨论什么, 你给我们吹吹风吧。Will you give us some idea of what will be taken up at the next meeting? / ～会 briefing

吹风机 chuīfēngjī ① blower (for drying hair); blow-dryer ② air-blower; blower

吹拂 chuīfú ① (of a breeze) sway; stir: 晨风～着垂柳。The morning breeze is swaying the weeping willows. ② formal praise and recommend sb.

吹歌 chuīgē traditional instrumental music popular in certain rural areas (usu. with the suona horn leading)

吹鼓手 chuīgǔshǒu ① music makers at old-time weddings or funerals ② derog. eulogist

吹管 chuīguǎn mech. blowpipe: 氢氧～ oxyhydrogen blowpipe / 氧乙炔～ oxyacetylene blowpipe

吹胡子瞪眼 chuīhúzi-dèngyǎn froth at the mouth and glare with rage; foam with anger: 老王气得～的。Lao Wang is fuming, his eyes glaring.

吹灰之力 chuī huī zhī lì the effort needed to blow away a speck of dust; just a small effort ——see also 不费吹灰之力 bùfèi chuī huī zhī lì

吹拉弹唱 chuī-lā-tán-chàng blow, bow, pluck, and sing —be very musical: ～他样样都会。He plays every instrument of the band and sings as well.

吹喇叭, 抬轿子 chuī lǎba, tái jiàozi blow the trumpet and carry sb. in a sedan chair—flatter (rich and influential people); sing the praises of; boost

吹冷风 chuī lěngfēng blow a cold wind over; throw cold water on; make discouraging remarks

吹炼 chuīliàn metall. blowing

吹毛求疵 chuī máo qiú cī find fault; pick holes; nitpick: 总的说来, 这是一本好书, 若对不足之处过多指摘, 未

免～。On the whole it's a good book; and it would be nitpicking to dwell on those small defects.

吹牛 chuīniú boast; brag; talk big: 他就爱～。He's a boastful person.

吹牛拍马 chuīniú-pāimǎ boast and flatter

吹拍 chuīpāi boast and flatter: 惯于～ be given to boasting and flattering

吹捧 chuīpěng flatter; laud to the skies; lavish praise on: 互相～ flatter each other

吹求 chuīqiú same as 吹毛求疵 chuī máo qiú cī

吹蚀 chuīshí *geol.* deflation; wind erosion

吹手 chuīshǒu *old* wind instrument player

吹台 chuītái *inf.* ① end in failure; fall through; break off: 我早就料到他俩的事要～。I knew long ago that they two wouldn't make it together. ② kick the bucket

吹弹 chuī-tán play music; strike up a tune

吹嘘 chuīxū lavish praise on oneself or others; boast

吹皱一池春水 chuī zhòu yīchí chūnshuǐ a spring breeze rippling the surface of the pond—a slight disturbance

吹奏 chuīzòu play (wind instruments)

吹奏乐 chuīzòuyuè band music; wind music

炊 chuī cook a meal: 无米之炊 wú mǐ zhī chuī

炊饼 chuībǐng *old* steamed cake

炊爨 chuīcuàn make a fire and do cooking

炊具 chuījù cooking utensils

炊事 chuīshì cooking; kitchen work: ～用具 kitchen (or cooking) utensils

炊事班 chuīshìbān cookhouse (or mess, kitchen) squad

炊事员 chuīshìyuán a cook or the kitchen staff

炊烟 chuīyān smoke from kitchen chimneys

炊帚 chuīzhou a brush for cleaning pots and pans; pot-scouring brush

chuí

垂 chuí ① hang down; droop; let fall: ～泪 shed tears; weep ② *formal* bequeath to posterity; hand down: 功～竹帛 be recorded in history in letters of gold / ～法后世 set an example for posterity ③ *formal* nearing; approaching ④ ～亡 be dying out ④ *formal pol.* (of one's elders or superiors) condescend: ～问 condescend to inquire / ～念 show kind concern for (me)

垂爱 chuí'ài *pol.* (usu. used in correspondence) have gracious concern for (me)

垂成 chuíchéng be approaching success or completion

垂钓 chuídiào fish with a hook and line; go angling

垂挂 chuíguà hang from above

垂老 chuílǎo approaching old age; getting on in years

垂帘听政 chuí lián tīng zhèng (of an empress regent) sit behind a screen to receive ministerial reports; hold court from behind a screen (an empress regent was supposed to be concealed from the sight of ministers at audience)

垂柳 chuíliǔ weeping willow

垂落 chuíluò hang down; drop down; fall: 她两行眼泪簌簌地～下来。Tears streamed down her cheeks. / 夜幕～。Night has fallen.

垂暮 chuímù *formal* dusk; towards sunset; just before sundown: ～之年 in old age

垂盆草 chuípéncǎo *bot.* stringy stonecrop (*Sedum sarmentosum*)

垂青 chuíqīng *formal* show appreciation for sb.; look upon sb. with favour

垂手 chuíshǒu with one's hands at one's side: ～侍立

stand respectfully in attendance

垂手可得 chuíshǒu kě dé extremely easy to obtain

垂首 chuíshǒu hang (or bow) one's head: ～默哀 bow one's head in silent mourning

垂首帖耳 chuíshǒu-tiē'ěr same as 俯首帖耳 fǔshǒu-tiē'ěr

垂死 chuísǐ moribund; dying: ～的命运 approaching doom

垂死挣扎 chuísǐ zhēngzhá be in one's death throes; put up a last-ditch (or deathbed) struggle

垂体 chuítǐ *physiol.* hypophysis; pituitary body (or gland)

垂体后叶素 chuítǐhòuyèsù *pharm.* pituitrin

垂髫 chuítiáo *formal* early childhood

垂头 chuítóu hang (or bow) one's head: ～叹息 hang one's head and sigh

垂头丧气 chuítóu-sàngqì be crestfallen; be dejected

垂危 chuíwēi ① be critically ill; be at one's last gasp ② (of a nation) be in great peril

垂涎 chuíxián drool; slaver; covet

垂涎三尺 chuíxián sān chǐ spittle three feet long—drool with envy

垂涎欲滴 chuíxián yù dī same as 馋涎欲滴 chánxián yù dī

垂询 chuíxún *formal pol.* deign (or condescend) to inquire into sth.

垂直 chuízhí perpendicular; vertical: ～平面 vertical plane / ～发射 vertical firing (or launching) / ～俯冲 steep dive; nose dive / ～降落 vertical landing / ～起飞 vertical takeoff / 两线～相交。The two lines meet at right angles. / 由某人～领导 be under the direct leadership of sb. / ～贸易 vertical trade / ～起落飞机 vertical takeoff and landing aircraft; VTOL aircraft / ～天线 vertical antenna / ～线 perpendicular line; vertical line

垂注 chuízhù *formal* ① gaze down ② be kept for permanent record; be permanently recorded: ～史册 be written into the annals of history; go down in history

陲 chuí *formal* frontiers; borders: 边陲 biānchuí

捶（搥） chuí beat (with a stick or fist); thump; pound: ～背 pound sb.'s back (as in massage) / ～鼓 beat a drum / ～门 bang on the door

捶打 chuídǎ ① beat; pound; thump: ～衣服 beat clothes (when washing them) / 用榔头～铁板 hammer away at the iron plate / ～凸纹 hammer repoussé

捶打 chuída ① beat with quick, light blows: 她用拳头～酸痛的腿。She beat on her aching leg with her fist. ② temper; steel; toughen: 让青年人到艰苦的斗争中去～～。Let our young people steel themselves in arduous struggle.

捶胸顿足 chuíxiōng-dùnzú beat one's breast and stamp one's feet (in sorrow, etc.)

棰 chuí *formal* ① rod; cane ② beat with a cane ③ same as 箠 chuí ④ same as 槌 chuí

椎 chuí ① same as 槌 chuí ② same as 捶 chuí ——see also zhuī

椎心泣血 chuíxīn-qìxuè beat one's breast and shed tears of blood—be heartbroken

槌 chuí mallet; beetle: 棒槌 bàngchui / 鼓槌 gǔchuí

锤（鎚） chuí ① hammer: 铁～ iron hammer / 手～ hand hammer ② mace ③ hammer into shape: ～金箔 hammer gold into foil ④ weight: 调节～ *mech.* governor weight / 平衡～ *mech.* balance weight

锤骨　chuígǔ　*physiol.*　malleus; hammer

锤光　chuíguāng　*mech.*　planish

锤炼　chuíliàn　① hammer into shape ② temper oneself; steel oneself ③ (of an artist, writer, etc.) try to perfect one's skill or technique by strenuous effort; hammer out; polish: ～钢琴演奏技巧 work hard to perfect one's piano technique／～词句 polish a piece of writing

锤子　chuízi　hammer

箠　chuí　*formal*　① a whip ② flog with a whip; whip

chūn

春　chūn　① spring: 温暖如～ as warm as spring ② love; lust: 春心 chūnxīn／怀春 huáichūn ③ life; vitality: 枯木逢春 kūmù féng chūn ④ (Chūn) a surname

春饼　chūnbǐng　spring pancake (usu. eaten on Beginning of Spring day 立春)

春播　chūnbō　spring sowing: ～作物 spring-sown crops

春不老　chūnbùlǎo　*dial.*　potherb mustard

春茶　chūnchá　spring tea (tea leaves picked in spring or tea made with them)

春潮　chūncháo　spring tide

春凳　chūndèng　spring bench (an old-fashioned bench)

春分　Chūnfēn　① the Spring Equinox—the 4th of the 24 solar terms ② the day marking the beginning of the 4th solar term (March 20 or 21)——see also 节气 jiéqì; 二十四节气　èrshí sì jiéqì

春风　chūnfēng　① spring breeze ② a kindly and pleasant countenance

春风得意　chūnfēng déyì　be flushed with success

春风化雨　chūnfēng huà yǔ　life-giving spring breeze and rain—salutary influence of education

春风满面　chūnfēng mǎnmiàn　beaming with satisfaction; radiant with happiness

春耕　chūngēng　spring ploughing: ～大忙季节 busy spring ploughing season

春宫　chūngōng　① living quarters of the crown prince ② pornographic pictures

春灌　chūnguàn　*agric.*　spring irrigation

春光　chūnguāng　sights and sounds of spring; spring scenery

春光明媚　chūnguāng míngmèi　a sunlit and enchanting scene of spring

春寒料峭　chūn hán liàoqiào　there is a chill in the air in early spring

春旱　chūnhàn　a long dry spell in spring; spring drought

春华秋实　chūnhuá-qiūshí　spring flowers and fall fruit—literary talent and moral integrity

春化　chūnhuà　*agric.*　vernalization

春画　chūnhuà　pornographic pictures

春荒　chūnhuāng　grain shortage in spring

春晖　chūnhuī　*formal*　spring sunshine—parental love

春季　chūnjì　spring; springtime

春假　chūnjià　spring holidays

春节　Chūnjié　the Spring Festival

春卷　chūnjuǎn　spring roll (a thin sheet of dough, rolled, stuffed and fried)

春兰　chūnlán　another name for 兰花 lánhuā

春兰秋菊　chūnlán-qiūjú　orchids in spring and chrysanthemums in autumn—each has a charm all its own

春雷　chūnléi　spring thunder

春雷霉素　chūnléiméisù　*pharm.*　kasugarnycin

春联　chūnlián　Spring Festival couplets (pasted on gateposts or door panels conveying one's best wishes for the year); New Year couplets

春令　chūnlìng　① spring ② spring weather: 冬行～ a springlike winter; a very mild winter

春梦　chūnmèng　spring dream—transient joy

春暖花开　chūn nuǎn huā kāi　spring has come and the flowers are in bloom

春情　chūnqíng　stirrings of love

春秋[1]　chūnqiū　① spring and autumn; year: ～多佳日。There are many fine days in spring and autumn.／几度～ several years ② age: ～已高 be advanced in years

春秋[2]　Chūnqiū　① the Spring and Autumn Period (770-476 B.C.) ② *The Spring and Autumn Annals* (see also 五经 wǔjīng) ③ (chūnqiū) annals; chronicle:《海岛～》*The Chronicle of an Island* (a short story)

春秋笔法　Chūnqiū bǐfǎ　the style of the *Spring and Autumn Annals*—the use of subtle and guarded language in criticism

春秋鼎盛　chūnqiū dǐngshèng　in the prime of manhood

春秋衫　chūnqiūshān　a jacket for spring and autumn wear

春秋正富　chūnqiū zhèng fù　in the prime of life

春日　chūnrì　① spring ② *formal*　the spring sun

春色　chūnsè　① spring's colours; spring scenery: 水乡～ spring in a waterside village／～恼人。Spring's hues are teasing. ② joyful look; wine-flushed face

春色满园　chūnsè mǎnyuán　spring's colours fill the garden: ～关不住，一枝红杏出墙来。(叶绍翁) Spring's colours fill the garden but cannot all be contained, For one spray of red apricot blossom peeps out from the wall.

春上　chūnshang　*inf.*　in spring: 今年～雨水多。We have had plenty of rain this spring.

春事　chūnshì　*formal*　spring farming; esp. spring ploughing

春笋　chūnsǔn　bamboo shoots in spring

春天　chūntiān　spring; springtime

春条　chūntiáo　*dial.*　Spring Festival scroll

春帖　chūntiě　① Spring Festival scroll ② same as 春联 chūnlián

春宵　chūnxiāo　spring night: ～苦短。A spring night is rather too short.

春小麦　chūnxiǎomài　spring wheat

春心　chūnxīn　thoughts of love; stirrings of love; budding love: 动了～ feel the first stirrings of love

春汛　chūnxùn　① spring flood ② *fishery*　spring (fishing) season

春药　chūnyào　aphrodisiac

春意　chūnyì　① spring in the air; the beginning (*or* awakening) of spring: 树梢发青，现出了几分～。The tops of the trees are turning green; spring is in the air.／红杏枝头～闹。(宋祁) Red apricot blossoms along the branch—the breath of spring stirs. ② thoughts of love

春意盎然　chūnyì àngrán　spring is in the air

春意阑珊　chūnyì lánshān　spring is on the wane: 帘外雨潺潺，～。(李煜) Outside the curtains the rain goes splash, splash; Spring's mood languishes.

春游　chūnyóu　spring outing

春雨贵如油　chūnyǔ guì rú yóu　rain in spring is as precious as oil

春种　chūnzhòng　spring sowing

春装　chūnzhuāng　spring clothing; spring costume

椿　chūn　*bot.*　① Chinese toon ② tree of heaven

椿白皮　chūnbáipí　*Chin. med.*　the bark of the root or stem of the tree of heaven

椿庭　chūntíng　*formal honor.*　your father

椿象　chūnxiàng　stinkbug; shieldbug

椿萱 chūnxuān *formal* father and mother; parents: ～并茂。Both parents are living and in good health.

蝽 chūn same as 椿象 chūnxiàng

chún

纯 chún ① pure; unmixed: ～毛 pure wool / ～金 pure (*or* solid) gold / ～白 pure white / ～黑 all black ② skilful; practised; well versed: 功夫不～ not skilful enough ③ *adv.* purely; sheerly; wholly: 这件事的发生～属偶然。It all happened by sheer chance.

纯粹 chúncuì ① pure; unadulterated: 陶器是用比较～的黏土制成的。Pottery is made from unadulterated clay. / 一个～的人 a pure person ② *adv.* purely; sheerly; wholly: 我帮助她～是为了友谊。I helped her purely out of friendship. / 那～是浪费时间。It was a sheer waste of time.

纯度 chúndù degree of purity
纯厚 chúnhòu same as 淳厚 chúnhòu
纯化 chúnhuà purification
纯碱 chúnjiǎn *chem.* soda ash; sodium carbonate
纯洁 chúnjié ① pure; clean and honest: 心地～ be pure of heart ② purify: ～组织 purify an organization
纯净 chúnjìng pure; clean: ～的水是透明的。Pure water is transparent.
纯利 chúnlì (also 纯利润 chún lìrùn) net profit
纯良 chúnliáng kind and honest
纯朴 chúnpǔ honest; simple; unsophisticated: ～敦厚 simple and honest / ～爽朗 honest and frank / 文风～ simplicity of style
纯然 chúnrán *adv.* simply; purely: 这～是捏造。This is sheer fabrication.
纯收入 chúnshōurù net income
纯熟 chúnshú skilful; practised; well versed: 技术～ highly skilled
纯损 chúnsǔn net loss
纯文学 chúnwénxué pure literature; belles-lettres
纯一 chúnyī single; simple: 目标～ singleness of purpose
纯音 chúnyīn *phys.* pure (*or* simple) tone
纯贞 chúnzhēn pure and faithful: ～的爱情 pure and faithful love
纯真 chúnzhēn pure; sincere: ～无邪 pure and innocent
纯正 chúnzhèng pure; unadulterated: 动机～ have pure motives / 他说的是～的普通话。He speaks pure *putonghua*.
纯挚 chúnzhì pure and sincere: ～的友情 pure and sincere friendship
纯种 chúnzhǒng thoroughbred; purebred: ～马 thoroughbred horse / ～牛 purebred cattle; pedigree cattle

唇(脣) chún lip: 上～ upper lip / 下～ lower lip
唇齿相依 chún-chǐ xiāngyī be as close as lips and teeth; be closely related and mutually dependent: ～的兄弟邻邦 fraternal neighbouring countries as closely related as lips and teeth
唇齿音 chúnchǐyīn *phonet.* labiodental (sound)
唇膏 chúngāo lipstick
唇焦舌敝 chúnjiāo-shébì same as 舌敝唇焦 shébì-chúnjiāo
唇裂 chúnliè harelip; cleft lip
唇枪舌剑 chúnqiāng-shéjiàn cross verbal swords; engage in a battle of words
唇舌 chúnshé words; argument: 费唇舌 fèi chúnshé
唇亡齿寒 chúnwáng-chǐhán if the lips are gone, the teeth will be cold; if one (of two interdependent things) falls, the other is in danger; share a common lot
唇音 chúnyīn *phonet.* labial (sound)

莼(蓴) chún see below
莼菜 chúncài *bot.* water shield
莼鲈之思 chún lú zhī sī longing for home (esp. of sb. holding office far from home)

淳 chún *formal* pure; honest
淳厚 chúnhòu pure and honest; simple and kind
淳美 chúnměi pure and sweet: 她的音色～。Her voice has a pure and sweet timbre.
淳朴 chúnpǔ honest; simple; unsophisticated: ～的庄稼人 an honest peasant; unsophisticated countryfolk
淳于 Chúnyú a two-character surname

鹑 chún quail
鹑衣 chúnyī *formal* ragged clothes
鹑衣百结 chúnyī bǎijié in rags

醇 chún ① *formal* mellow wine; good wine ② *formal* pure; unmixed ③ *chem.* alcohol
醇和 chúnhé (of quality, taste, etc.) mellow; pure
醇厚 chúnhòu ① mellow; rich: 酒味～。The wine is (*or* tastes) mellow. ② same as 淳厚 chúnhòu
醇化 chúnhuà ① refine; purify; perfect ② *chem.* alcoholization
醇化物 chúnhuàwù alcoholate
醇解 chúnjiě *chem.* alcoholysis
醇酒 chúnjiǔ good wine
醇酒妇人 chúnjiǔ fùrén wine and women—debauchery
醇醪 chúnláo strong wine
醇美 chúnměi pure and sweet; mellow: 酒味～。The wine is mellow and full-bodied. / ～的嗓音 a pure and sweet voice
醇朴 chúnpǔ same as 淳朴 chúnpǔ
醇醛 chúnquán *chem.* alcohol aldehyde
醇酸 chúnsuān *chem.* alcohol (*or* alcoholic) acid
醇酸树脂 chúnsuān shùzhī alkyd resin
醇香 chúnxiāng sweet-smelling; aromatic

chǔn

蠢¹ chǔn *formal* wriggle

蠢²(惷) chǔn stupid; foolish; dull; clumsy
蠢笨 chǔnbèn clumsy; awkward; stupid
蠢材 chǔncái *offens.* idiot; fool
蠢蠢 chǔnchǔn *formal* ① wriggling ② restive; restless
蠢蠢欲动 chǔnchǔn yù dòng ready to start wriggling—ready to make trouble: 敌人又在～。The enemy is going to start something again.
蠢动 chǔndòng ① wriggle ② create disturbances; carry on disruptive activities
蠢货 chǔnhuò *offens.* blockhead; dunce; idiot
蠢驴 chǔnlǘ *offens.* idiot; donkey; ass
蠢然 chǔnrán ① wriggling: ～思动 ready to start wriggling—ready to make trouble ② stupid-looking
蠢人 chǔnrén fool; blockhead
蠢事 chǔnshì a stupid thing: 我再也不干那种～了。I will never do such a stupid thing again.
蠢头蠢脑 chǔntóu-chǔnnǎo stupid-looking
蠢猪 chǔnzhū *offens.* idiot; stupid swine; ass

chuō

戳 chuō ① jab; poke; stab: 小心！你的竹竿儿别～了他的眼睛。Be careful! Don't jab his eye out with your bamboo pole. / 在纸上～了一个洞 poke a hole in the paper / 一～就破 break at the slightest touch ② *dial.* sprain; blunt: 打排球～了手 sprain one's wrist while playing volleyball / 钢笔尖儿～了。The nib is blunted. ③ *dial.* stand sth. on end: 把秫秸～起来 stand the bundle of sorghum stalks on end / 有话进来说，别在门口儿～着。Don't stand in the doorway. Come in if you have something to say.

戳壁脚 chuō bìjiǎo *dial.* speak ill of others

戳不住 chuōbuzhù cannot bear up

戳穿 chuōchuān ① puncture: 笔尖把纸～了。The sharp nib scratched through the paper. ② lay bare; expose; explode: ～谣言和诡辩 lay bare sb.'s lies and sophistry / ～纸老虎 punch holes in the paper tiger; expose sb. or sth. as a paper tiger

戳得住 chuōdezhù can bear up

戳脊梁骨 chuō jǐlianggǔ backbite: 办事要公正，别让人家～。Try to play fair so that people won't talk behind your back.

戳记 chuōjì stamp; seal

戳破 chuōpò same as 戳穿 chuōchuān

戳子 chuōzi (also 戳儿 chuōr) *inf.* stamp; seal: 在文件上盖个～ put a seal (*or* stamp) on a document / 橡皮～ rubber stamp

chuò

啜 chuò *formal* ① sip; suck: ～茗 sip tea ② sob

啜泣 chuòqì sob

绰 chuò *formal* ample; spacious ——see also chāo

绰绰有余 chuòchuò yǒu yú (also 绰有余裕 chuò yǒu yú yù) more than sufficient; enough and to spare

绰号 chuòhào nickname: 他的～叫小老虎。He has got the nickname of "Young Tiger". *or* He is nicknamed "Young Tiger".

绰约 chuòyuē *formal* (of a girl) graceful

绰约多姿 chuòyuē duō zī (of a girl) graceful

辍 chuò *formal* stop; cease: ～工 stop work / 时作时～ on and off; by fits and starts

辍笔 chuòbǐ stop in the middle of writing or painting

辍学 chuòxué discontinue one's studies; drop out of school

辍演 chuòyǎn stop staging (a play, show, etc.)

辍止 chuòzhǐ stop; cease

龊 chuò see 龌龊 wòchuò

cī

刺 cī *onom.*: ～的一声，他滑了一个跟头。Swish! He slipped and fell. / 花炮点着后，～～地直冒火星。The firecracker spattered sparks the moment it was lit. ——see also cì

刺啦 cīlā *onom.* the sound of ripping, tearing, or scratching: ～一声，她划着了火柴。Scratch! She struck a match.

刺棱 cīlēng *onom.* the sound of a quick movement: 猫～一下跑了。The cat scampered away.

刺溜 cīliū *onom.* the sound of slipping, sliding, etc.: ～一下滑倒了 slip and fall / 子弹～～地从他耳边擦过去。The bullets whistled past his ears.

差 cī see 参差 cēncī ——see also chā; chà; chāi

呲 cī *inf.* give a talking-to; give a tongue-lashing: 挨了一顿～儿 get a good talking-to

疵 cī flaw; defect; blemish: 小～ a trifling defect / 无～ flawless; impeccable

疵点 cīdiǎn flaw; fault; defect

疵毛 cīmáo defective wool

疵品 cīpǐn defective goods

疵瑕 cīxiá same as 瑕疵 xiácī

跐 cī slip: 他脚一～，差点儿摔倒了。His foot slipped and he nearly fell. ——see also cǐ

跐溜 cīliū ① slip: 他～一滑，摔了个脸朝天。He slipped and fell flat on his back. ② move quickly

cí

词 cí ① word; term: 这个～略带贬义。This word is slightly derogative. / 调子我记得，可是～儿我忘了。I remember the tune all right, but I've forgotten the words. ② speech; statement: 开幕词 kāimùcí ③ ci, poetry written to certain tunes with strict tonal patterns and rhyme schemes, in fixed numbers of lines and words, originating in the Tang Dynasty (618-907) and fully developed in the Song Dynasty (960-1279)

词不达意 cí bù dá yì the words fail to convey the idea

词典 cídiǎn dictionary

词典学 cídiǎnxué lexicography

词调 cídiào tonal patterns and rhyme schemes of ci poetry ——see also 词 cí③

词法 cífǎ *linguis.* morphology

词锋 cífēng vigour or pungency of style

词赋 cífù same as 辞赋 cífù

词干 cígàn *linguis.* stem

词根 cígēn *linguis.* root

词华 cíhuá ornate diction

词话 cíhuà ① notes and comments on ci poetry (see also 词 cí③) ② storytelling interspersed with songs and ballads, popular in the Song Dynasty (960-1279) ③ novel with parts in verse, common in the Ming Dynasty (1368-1644)

词汇 cíhuì vocabulary; words and phrases: 常用～ common words

词汇表 cíhuìbiǎo word list; vocabulary; glossary

词汇学 cíhuìxué lexicology

词句 cíjù words and phrases; expressions: 空洞的～ empty phrases

词类 cílèi *gram.* parts of speech

词令 cílìng same as 辞令 cílìng

词律 cílù the prosody of ci poems ——see also 词 cí③

词牌 cípái names of the tunes to which ci poems are composed ——see also 词 cí③

词谱 cípǔ a collection of tunes of ci poems ——see also 词 cí③

词曲 cíqǔ a general term for ci（词）and qu（曲）——see also 词 cí③; 曲 qǔ①

词人 círén ① ci writer; ci master ② a man of literary ability

词讼 císòng legal cases

词素 císù *linguis.* morpheme

词头 cítóu *linguis.* prefix

词尾 cíwěi *linguis.* ① suffix ② inflectional ending

词形 cíxíng *linguis.* morphology: ～变化 morphological changes; inflections

词性 cíxìng *linguis.* syntactical functions and morphological features that help to determine a part of speech

词序 cíxù *linguis.* word order

词严义正 cíyán-yìzhèng same as 义正词严 yìzhèng-cíyán

词义 cíyì *linguis.* the meaning (*or* sense) of a word

词语 cíyǔ words and expressions; terms

词源 cíyuán *linguis.* the origin of a word; etymology

词韵 cíyùn ① rhyme of *ci* poems ② rhyming dictionary (of *ci* poems) ——see also 词 cí ③

词藻 cízǎo same as 辞藻 cízǎo

词章 cízhāng same as 辞章 cízhāng

词缀 cízhuì *linguis.* affix

词宗 cízōng same as 辞宗 cízōng

词组 cízǔ *gram.* word group; phrase

祠 cí ancestral hall (*or* temple); memorial temple: 宗祠 zōngcí

祠堂 cítáng ancestral hall (*or* temple); memorial temple

茨 cí *formal* ① thatch (a roof) ② *bot.* puncture vine

茨冈人 Cígāngrén another name for 吉卜赛人 Jíbǔsàirén

茨菰 cígu same as 慈姑 cígu

茨茛 cíliáng another name for 薯莨 shǔliáng

瓷 (甆) cí porcelain; china: ～碗 china bowl / 细～ fine china

瓷雕 cídiāo porcelain carving

瓷公鸡，一毛不拔 cígōngjī, yī máo bù bá a porcelain cock, from which not a single feather can be plucked——a stingy person; miser

瓷刻 cíkè porcelain carving

瓷瓶 cípíng ① china vase ② popular name for 绝缘子 juéyuánzǐ

瓷漆 cíqī enamel paint; enamel

瓷器 cíqì porcelain; chinaware

瓷实 císhi *dial.* solid; firm; substantial: 他身体很～。He is solidly built. / 打夯以后，地基就～了。The foundation becomes solid after tamping.

瓷土 cítǔ porcelain clay; china clay

瓷窑 cíyáo porcelain kiln; china kiln

瓷砖 cízhuān ceramic tile; glazed tile

辞¹ (辭、辤) cí ① diction; phraseology: 修辞 xiūcí ② a type of classical Chinese literature: 《楚～》The Songs of Chu ③ a form of classical poetry: 《木兰～》The Ballad of Mulan

辞² (辭、辤) cí ① take leave: 告辞 gàocí ② decline; resign: 他～了科长的职务。He resigned his post of section chief. / 固～ firmly decline ③ dismiss; discharge: 老板把他给～了。His boss dismissed him. ④ shirk: 推辞 tuīcí / 不辞辛苦 bù cí xīnkǔ

辞别 cíbié bid farewell (to); say goodbye (to); take one's leave (of): ～父母 say goodbye to one's parents

辞呈 cíchéng (written) resignation: 提出～ submit (*or* hand in) one's resignation

辞典 cídiǎn dictionary

辞赋 cífù a style of metrical composition like that of the *fu* (赋)

辞工 cígōng ① dismiss (a labourer or employee); discharge: 东家辞了他的工。The boss dismissed him. ② quit one's job; resign: 他～不干了。He's quit his job.

辞活 cíhuó quit one's job

辞灵 cílíng bow to a coffin before it is carried to the grave

辞令 cílìng language appropriate to the occasion: 外交～ diplomatic language / 善于～ be gifted with a silver tongue

辞却 cíquè resign (a post); decline (an offer)

辞让 círàng politely decline: 他～了一番，才在前排就座。After first politely declining, he eventually took a seat in the front row.

辞色 císè *formal* one's speech and facial expression: ～严厉 severe in speech and countenance / 假以～ look at sb. encouragingly

辞世 císhì depart this life; pass away

辞书 císhū dictionary; lexicographical work (e.g. wordbook, etc.)

辞岁 císuì bid farewell to the outgoing year; see the old year out; celebrate the lunar New Year's Eve

辞退 cítuì dismiss; discharge

辞谢 cíxiè politely decline; decline with thanks

辞行 cíxíng say goodbye (to one's relatives, friends, etc.) before setting out on a journey

辞严义正 cíyán-yìzhèng same as 词严义正 cíyán-yìzhèng

辞藻 cízǎo flowery language; rhetoric; ornate diction: 堆砌～ string together ornate phrases

辞灶 cízào same as 送灶 sòngzào

辞章 cízhāng ① poetry and prose; prose and verse ② art of writing; rhetoric

辞职 cízhí resign; hand in one's resignation

辞宗 cízōng *formal* the dean of writers

慈 cí ① kind; loving: 心～ tenderhearted; kindhearted ② *formal* mother: 家慈 jiācí

慈爱 cí'ài love (of an older person for a younger one); affection; kindness

慈悲 cíbēi mercy; benevolence; pity: 发～ have pity; be merciful / 对敌人的～就是对人民的残忍。Kindness to the enemy means cruelty to the people.

慈姑 cígu *bot.* arrowhead (the plant or its edible corm)

慈和 cíhé kindly and amiable

慈眉善目 címéi-shànmù a benign countenance

慈命 címìng mother's commands

慈母 címǔ loving mother; mother

慈善 císhàn charitable; benevolent; philanthropic: ～机关 charitable institution (*or* organization) / ～事业 charities; good works; philanthropy

慈善家 císhànjiā philanthropist

慈祥 cíxiáng kindly: ～的面容 a kindly face

慈颜 cíyán kindly face (of one's parents or elders)

磁¹ cí *phys.* magnetism: 磁场 cíchǎng / 地磁 dìcí

磁² cí same as 瓷 cí

磁暴 cíbào *phys.* magnetic storm: ～记录器 magnetic storm monitor

磁北 cíběi the magnetic north

磁场 cíchǎng *phys.* magnetic field

磁场强度 cíchǎng qiángdù *phys.* magnetic field intensity

磁畴 cíchóu *phys.* magnetic domain

磁带 cídài (magnetic) tape

磁带录音机 cídài lùyīnjī tape recorder

磁感应 cígǎnyìng *phys.* magnetic induction

磁钢　cígāng　magnet steel

磁化　cíhuà　*phys.* magnetization

磁化率　cíhuàlǜ　*phys.* magnetic susceptibility

磁化器　cíhuàqì　magnetizer

磁极　cíjí　*phys.* magnetic pole

磁极强度　cíjí qiángdù　magnetic pole strength

磁力　cílì　*phys.* magnetic force: ～测定 magnetometry / ～勘探 magnetic prospecting / ～选矿 magnetic dressing

磁力探矿仪　cílì tànkuàngyí　magnetic detector (for ore deposits)

磁力探伤器　cílì tànshāngqì　magnetic flaw detector; magnetic fault finder

磁力线　cílìxiàn　*phys.* magnetic line of force

磁力仪　cílìyí　magnetometer

磁疗　cíliáo　magnetotherapy

磁盘　cípán　*computer* magnetic disk

磁盘存储器　cípán cúnchǔqì　*computer* magnetic disk memory

磁偏角　cípiānjiǎo　*phys.* magnetic declination

磁石　císhí　① magnetite ② *elec.* magnet

磁石发电机　císhí fādiànjī　magneto

磁石检波器　císhí jiǎnbōqì　magneto detector

磁体　cítǐ　*phys.* magnetic body; magnet

磁铁　cítiě　*phys.* magnet: 马蹄形～ horseshoe magnet / 永久～ permanent magnet

磁铁矿　cítiěkuàng　magnetite

磁通量　cítōngliàng　*phys.* magnetic flux

磁头　cítóu　magnetic head (of a recorder)

磁心　cíxīn　*computer* (magnetic) core

磁心存储器　cíxīn cúnchǔqì　*computer* core memory

磁性　cíxìng　*phys.* magnetism; magnetic

磁性水雷　cíxìng shuǐléi　magnetic mine

磁性炸弹　cíxìng zhàdàn　magnetic bomb

磁选　cíxuǎn　*min.* magnetic separation: 湿法～ wet magnetic separation / ～厂 magnetic ore dressing plant

磁针　cízhēn　magnetic needle

磁子　cízǐ　*phys.* magneton

雌　cí　female

雌伏　cífú　① submit to another's control ② lie low; be retiring

雌花　cíhuā　*bot.* female (or pistillate) flower

雌黄　cíhuáng　① orpiment ② see 信口雌黄 xìnkǒu cíhuáng

雌老虎　cílǎohǔ　tigress—virago; shrew

雌蕊　círuǐ　*bot.* pistil

雌性　cíxìng　female

雌雄　cí-xióng　① male and female ② victory and defeat: 决一雌雄 jué yī cí-xióng

雌雄同体　cí-xióng tóng tǐ　*zool.* hermaphroditism; monoecism

雌雄同株　cí-xióng tóng zhū　*bot.* monoecism

雌雄异体　cí-xióng yì tǐ　*zool.* gonochorism; dioecism

雌雄异株　cí-xióng yì zhū　*bot.* dioecism

雌蚁　cíyǐ　female ant; gyne

鹚　cí　see 鸬鹚 lúcí

糍　cí　see below

糍粑　cíbā　cooked glutinous rice pounded into paste; glutinous rice cake

cǐ

此　cǐ　① this: ～处 this place; here / ～等 this kind; such as these / 由～往南 go south from here ② here and now: 就此 jiùcǐ / 从此 cóngcǐ

此岸　cǐ'àn　*Buddhism* this shore; temporality

此辈　cǐbèi　people of this type (or ilk); such people: 勿与～来往。Don't associate with such people.

此道　cǐdào　this kind of thing (usu. sth. bad): 精于～ be good at this kind of (crooked or dishonest) practice

此地　cǐdì　this place; here: ～人 local people

此地无银三百两　cǐdì wú yín sānbǎiliǎng　no 300 taels of silver buried here (the sign put up by the man in the folk tale over the place where he had hidden some money)—a clumsy denial resulting in self-exposure

此伏彼起　cǐfú-bǐqǐ　same as 此起彼伏 cǐqǐ-bǐfú

此后　cǐhòu　after this; hereafter; henceforth: 她一九五八年到农村去，～一直在那儿工作。She went to the countryside in 1958 and has worked there ever since.

此呼彼应　cǐhū-bǐyìng　as one calls out, another responds; echo and reecho: 口号声～。Shouts of slogans resounded back and forth.

此际　cǐjì　*formal* this moment; now; at present

此间　cǐjiān　around here; here: ～已有传闻。It has been so rumoured here.

此举　cǐjǔ　this measure, action or step

此刻　cǐkè　this moment; now; at present

此路不通　cǐ lù bù tōng　dead end; blind alley: ～! (street sign) Not a Through Road.

此起彼伏　cǐqǐ-bǐfú　as one falls, another rises; rise one after another: ～的农民起义 repeated peasant uprisings / 欢呼声～。Loud cheers rang out continuously.

此生　cǐshēng　this life

此时　cǐshí　this moment; right now: ～此刻 at this very moment / ～此地 here and now

此外　cǐwài　*adv.* besides; in addition; moreover: ～，还要讨论一下分工问题。In addition, we'll discuss the question of division of labour. / 我们家新买了一台拖拉机，～还买了一台水泵。We have just bought a tractor, and a pump as well. / 他一生就写过这两部书，～没有别的著作了。Besides these two books, he didn't produce any other work during his lifetime.

此一时，彼一时　cǐ yīshí, bǐ yīshí　same as 彼一时，此一时 bǐ yīshí, cǐ yīshí

此致　cǐzhì　I hereby communicate (used at the close of an official report or a business letter): ～敬礼! Salutations! or With best regards. / ～徐总经理。I hereby submit the above to General Manager Xu.

此中　cǐzhōng　in this; herein: ～定有文章。There must be something behind this.

跐　cǐ　① step on: ～着门槛儿 with one foot on the doorsill (or threshold) ② stand on tiptoe: ～着脚往前头看 stand on tiptoe to look into the distance ——see also cì

cì

次　cì　① order; position in a series; place in a sequence: 依次 yīcì / 车次 chēcì ② second; next: ～子 second son / ～年 the next year ③ second-rate; inferior: ～棉 poor quality cotton / 这本书真～。This book is really no good. / 我的字写得可～了。My handwriting is terrible. ④ *chem.* hypo-: ～氯酸 hypochlorous acid ⑤ *m.* occurrence; time: 三～ three times / 首～ first time; first / 进行几～会谈 hold several talks ⑥ *formal* stopping place on a journey; stopover: 旅次 lǚcì

次大陆　cìdàlù　subcontinent

次等　cìděng　second-class; second-rate; inferior

次第　cìdì　① order; sequence ② one after another: ～入座 take seats one after another

次货 cìhuò inferior goods; substandard goods

次级线圈 cìjí xiànquān *elec.* secondary coil

次品 cìpǐn substandard products; defective goods

次轻量级 cìqīngliàngjí *weight lifting* featherweight

次日 cìrì the next day

次生 cìshēng *geol.* secondary: ～矿床 secondary deposit／～矿物 secondary mineral

次生林 cìshēnglín second growth

次声 cìshēng (also 次声波 cìshēngbō) *phys.* infrasonic sound; infrasonic wave

次数 cìshù number of times; frequency: ～不多 not very often／练习的～越多,熟练的程度越高。The more you practise, the more skilful you'll become.

次序 cìxù order; sequence: 按～入场 enter in proper order／文件的～不对。The papers are not in the right order.

次要 cìyào less important; secondary; subordinate; minor: ～问题 secondary questions／～矛盾 secondary contradiction／把这个问题推到～地位 relegate the problem to a position of secondary importance

次长 cìzhǎng vice-minister

次之 cìzhī take second place: 该省矿藏,以锡最多,铜～。Among the mineral deposits of the province, tin occupies first place; copper comes second.

次中音号 cìzhōngyīnhào *mus.* tenor horn

次重量级 cìzhòngliàngjí *weight lifting* middle heavyweight

次最轻量级 cìzuìqīngliàngjí *weight lifting* flyweight

伺 cì see below ——see also sì

伺候 cìhou wait upon; serve: 难～ hard to please; fastidious

刺 cì ① thorn; splinter: 手上扎了个～ get a thorn (or splinter) in one's hand／他说话总带～儿。There's always a sting in his words. ② stab; prick: ～伤 stab and wound ③ assassinate: 被～ be assassinated ④ irritate; stimulate: ～鼻 irritate the nose; assail one's nostrils ⑤ pry; spy: 刺探 cìtàn ⑥ criticize: 讽刺 fěngcì ⑦ *formal* visiting card: 投～ send in one's card ——see also cī

刺柏 cìbǎi another name for 桧 guì

刺儿菜 cìrcài common name for 小蓟 xiǎojì

刺刺不休 cìcì bù xiū talk incessantly; chatter on and on

刺丛 cìcóng prickly bushes

刺刀 cìdāo bayonet: 上～! (order of command) Fix bayonets!／下～! (order of command) Unfix bayonets!／拼～ bayonet-fighting

刺耳 cì'ěr grating on the ear; jarring; ear-piercing; harsh: 这声音太～。The sound is too piercing.／～的话 harsh words; sarcastic remarks

刺骨 cìgǔ piercing to the bones; piercing; biting: 寒风～。The cold wind chills one to the bone.

刺儿话 cìrhuà scathing remarks; biting words

刺槐 cìhuái locust (tree)

刺激 cìjī ① stimulation; stimulus; incentive: 强～ a strong stimulus／竞争给产业以有力的～。Competition is a strong incentive to industry. ② stimulate; urge on; encourage: 咖啡能～神经。Coffee can stimulate one's nerves.／～生产 stimulate production／成绩能～人们作出更大的努力。Success will stimulate people to further efforts. ③ provoke; irritate; upset: 别～他。Don't provoke him.／这一不幸的消息给了她很大的～。She was badly upset by the sad news.

刺激物 cìjīwù stimulus; stimulant

刺激性毒剂 cìjīxìng dújì irritant agent

刺客 cìkè assassin

刺目 cìmù same as 刺眼 cìyǎn

刺挠 cìnao *inf.* itchy: 浑身～ itching all over

刺配 cìpèi tattoo the face of a criminal and send him into exile (a punishment in feudal China)

刺取 cìqǔ *formal* ① adopt; take ② spy out

刺杀 cìshā ① assassinate ② *mil.* bayonet charge: 练～ practise bayonet fighting

刺参 cìshēn a kind of sea cucumber (*stichopus japonicus*)

刺史 cìshǐ (in imperial times) provincial or prefectural governor

刺探 cìtàn make roundabout or secret inquiries; pry; spy: ～军情 spy out military secrets; gather military intelligence

刺铁丝 cìtiěsī (also 刺丝 cìsī) barbed wire

刺儿头 cìrtóu *dial.* a person hard to deal with; a hard nut to crack

刺网 cìwǎng *fishery* gill net: 三层～ trammel net

刺猬 cìwei hedgehog

刺绣 cìxiù ① embroider ② embroidery

刺绣品 cìxiùpǐn embroidery

刺眼 cìyǎn dazzling; offending to the eye: 亮得～ dazzlingly bright／打扮得～ be loudly dressed

刺痒 cìyang *inf.* itchy: 我被蚊子咬了一下,好～。I have an itch from a mosquito bite.

刺鱼 cìyú stickleback (a fish)

刺字 cìzì ① tattoo ② (in former times) brand a criminal by tattooing

赐 cì ① bestow; confer: ～恩 bestow favours／～爵 confer a title of nobility／～福 bless ② *pol.* favour; grant: 请即～复。Please favour me with an early reply.／盼～示。I await your instructions. ③ *pol.* gift: 厚～受之有愧。I feel unworthy of the precious gift you have bestowed on me.

赐光 cìguāng same as 赏光 shǎngguāng

赐婚 cìhūn (of the emperor) give a bride to sb. for his meritorious service; sanction a marriage

赐教 cìjiào *pol.* condescend to teach; grant instruction: 不吝～ please favour (or enlighten) me with your instructions; be so kind as to give me a reply

赐死 cìsǐ commit suicide by imperial order (as a mark of imperial favour, so as to be spared the indignity of execution)

赐予 cìyǔ grant; bestow

cōng

匆 (悤、怱) cōng hastily; hurriedly

匆匆 cōngcōng hurriedly: ～吃了一顿饭 take a hurried meal; hurry through a meal／来去～ come and go in a hurry

匆促 cōngcù hastily; in a hurry: ～起程 set out hastily／时间～ be pressed for time

匆忙 cōngmáng hastily; in a hurry: ～作出决定 make a hasty decision／临行～,未能向你告别。I left in such a hurry that I didn't have time to say good-bye to you.／他匆匆忙忙吃了几口东西,又回车间去了。He bolted down a few mouthfuls of food and hurried back to the workshop.

囱 cōng see 烟囱 yāncōng

苁 (蓯) cōng see below

苁蓉 cōngróng *bot.* desert cistanche (*Cistanche deserticola*)

枞 (樅) cōng *bot.* fir

钡（鏦） cōng　short spear (a weapon used in ancient times)

葱（蔥） cōng　① onion; scallion ② green: 葱绿 cōnglǜ

葱白 cōngbái　very light blue

葱白儿 cōngbáir　scallion stalk

葱翠 cōngcuì　fresh green; luxuriantly green: ～的竹林 a green bamboo grove

葱花 cōnghuā　chopped green onion

葱花饼 cōnghuābǐng　green onion pancake

葱黄 cōnghuáng　light yellow; greenish yellow

葱茏 cōnglóng　verdant; luxuriantly green: 草木～ luxuriant vegetation

葱绿 cōnglǜ　pale yellowish green; light green; verdant: ～的田野 verdant fields / 麦苗一片～。The wheat shoots are a lush green.

葱茂 cōngmào　(of vegetation) verdant and luxuriant

葱头 cōngtóu　onion

葱郁 cōngyù　verdant; luxuriantly green: ～的松树林 a verdant pine wood

骢 cōng　formal a piebald horse

聪（聰） cōng　① formal faculty of hearing: 左耳失～ become deaf in the left ear ② acute hearing: 耳聪目明 ěrcōng-mùmíng

聪慧 cōnghuì　bright; intelligent

聪明 cōngming　intelligent; bright; clever: ～能干 bright and capable / 这孩子很～。This child is very clever.

聪明才智 cōngming cáizhì　intelligence and wisdom: 充分发挥人民群众的～ give full play to the wisdom and creativeness of the people

聪明反被聪明误 cōngming fǎn bèi cōngming wù　clever people may be victims of their own cleverness; cleverness may overreach itself

聪明一世，糊涂一时 cōngming yīshì, hútu yīshí　clever all one's life but stupid this once; smart as a rule, but this time a fool

聪颖 cōngyǐng　formal intelligent; bright; clever: ～过人 far surpass others in intelligence; be exceptionally bright

璁 cōng　formal a jadelike stone; jadeite

璁珑 cōnglóng　formal bright and clear

cóng

从¹（從） cóng　① follow; comply with; obey: ～俗 follow the general custom; conform to custom ② join; be engaged in: 从军 cóngjūn ③ in a certain manner; according to a certain principle: ～宽处理 handle leniently; treat with leniency / ～轻发落 deal with an offender leniently / ～严治党 be strict with Party members / 训练要～严。Training should be hard and strict. ④ follower; attendant: 随从 suícóng ⑤ secondary; accessary: 主从 zhǔcóng / 从犯 cóngfàn ⑥relationship between cousins, etc. of the same paternal grandfather or great-grandfather: ～兄弟 cousins on the paternal side; cousins

从²（從） cóng　① prep. from (a time, a place, or a point of view): ～上海到北京 from Shanghai to Beijing / ～现在起 from now on / ～这儿往西 go west from here; west of here / ～全局出发 proceed from the situation as a whole / ～根本上说 essentially;

in essence ② prep. via, through, or past (a place): ～门缝里往外看 peep outside through a crevice in the door / 你～桥上过，我～桥下走。You go over the bridge, I'll go under it. / ～学校门前经过 pass the school gate ③ adv. (followed by a negative) ever: ～没听说过。Never heard of it. / 她在成绩面前～不骄傲。Her head was never turned by success. / ～不计较个人的名誉地位 never give any consideration to personal fame or position

从长计议 cóng cháng jìyì　give the matter further thought and discussion; take one's time in reaching a decision

从此 cóngcǐ　adv. from this time on; from now on; from then on; henceforth; thereupon

从…到… cóng…dào…　from… to…: 从上到下 from top to bottom; from the higher levels to the grass roots / 从无到有 grow out of nothing / 从早到晚 from dawn to dusk; from morning till night / 从古到今 from ancient times to the present; from time immemorial / 革命力量的发展总是从弱到强，从小到大。The development of revolutionary forces is always from weak to strong and from small to large.

从动 cóngdòng　mech. driven: ～齿轮 driven gear / ～构件 driven member

从而 cóng'ér　conj. thus; thereby: 农业迅速发展，～为轻工业提供了充足的原料。Agriculture has developed rapidly, thus providing light industry with ample raw materials.

从犯 cóngfàn　accessary criminal; accessary

从父 cóngfù　formal (paternal) uncle

从价税 cóngjiàshuì　econ. ad valorem duties

从简 cóngjiǎn　conform to the principle of simplicity: 一切～ dispense with all unnecessary formalities

从谏如流 cóng jiàn rú liú　(of a ruler) follow good advice as a stream follows its course

从井救人 cóng jǐng jiù rén　jump into a well to save sb. who's fallen in—(originally) try to do a good deed in the wrong way; try to save sb.'s life at the risk of one's own

从句 cóngjù　gram. subordinate clause

从军 cóngjūn　join the army; enlist

从来 cónglái　adv. from the past till the present; always; at all times; all along: 世界各国人民的革命斗争～都是互相支持的。The people of all countries have always supported each other in their revolutionary struggle. / 我～没有见过他。I've never seen him before.

从良 cóngliáng　(of a prostitute) get married and start a new life

从量税 cóngliàngshuì　econ. specific duties

从略 cónglüè　be omitted: 此处引文～。The quotation is omitted here.

从命 cóngmìng　do sb.'s bidding; comply with sb.'s wish; obey an order: 欣然～ gladly comply with sb.'s wish

从母 cóngmǔ　formal (maternal) aunt

从女 cóngnǚ　formal brother's daughter; niece

从前 cóngqián　before; formerly; in the past: 咱们村跟～大不一样了。Our village is very different from what it was before. / ～，有一个老人，名叫"愚公"。Once upon a time, there lived an old man called Yu Gong.

从权 cóngquán　as a matter of expediency: ～处理 do what is expedient

从戎 cóngróng　formal join the army; enlist: 投笔从戎 tóu bǐ cóngróng

从容 cóngróng　① calm; unhurried; leisurely: 举止～ deport oneself in a calm, unhurried manner ② plentiful: 时间很～。There's still plenty of time. / 手头～ be quite well off at the moment

从容不迫 cóngróng bù pò　calm and unhurried: ～地对

and smashing rotten wood

摧眉折腰 cuīméi-zhéyāo bowing and scraping

摧折 cuīzhé *formal* ① break; snap ② setback

猫

cuī see 猥猫 wěicuī

cuǐ

璀

cuǐ see below

璀璨 cuǐcàn *formal* bright; resplendent: ～夺目 dazzling

cuì

脆（脃）

cuì ① fragile; brittle: 这纸太～。This kind of paper is too fragile. / ～金属 brittle metal ② crisp: 这种梨又甜又～。These pears are sweet and crisp. ③ (of voice) clear; crisp: 听她的嗓音多～! What a crisp voice she has! ④ *dial.* neat: 这件事办得很～。That was a neat job.

脆骨 cuìgǔ gristle (as food)

脆快 cuìkuài *dial.* straightforward; direct

脆亮 cuìliàng (of sound or voice) clear and sharp

脆美 cuìměi ① (of food) crisp and tasteful; crisp and delicious ② (of sound or voice) clear and sweet

脆嫩 cuìnèn tender and crisp

脆弱 cuìruò fragile; frail; weak: 感情～ be easily upset

脆生 cuìsheng (also 脆生生 cuìshēngshēng) *inf.* ① crisp: 这黄瓜～爽口。The cucumbers are crisp and refreshing. ② (of sound or voice) clear and sharp

脆爽 cuìshuǎng ① (of food) crisp and refreshing ② (of sound or voice) clear and sharp

脆响 cuìxiǎng loud and clear

脆性 cuìxìng *metall.* brittleness

脆枣 cuìzǎo crisp dates (a dialectal name for 焦枣 jiāozǎo)

淬（焠）

cuì temper (a metal workpiece) by dipping in water, oil, etc.; quench

淬火 cuìhuǒ quench: ～硬化 quench hardening

淬火剂 cuìhuǒjì hardening agent; quenching liquid

淬砺 cuìlì *formal* temper oneself through severe trials

悴

cuì see 憔悴 qiáocuì

萃

cuì *formal* ① come together; assemble: 荟萃 huìcuì ② a gathering of people or a collection of things: 出类拔萃 chūlèi-bácuì

萃萃蝇 cuìcuìyíng tsetse fly

萃集 cuìjí gather; assemble: 港口船舶～ ships gathering in harbour

萃聚 cuìjù gather; assemble: 群英～ heroes of our time getting together

萃取 cuìqǔ *chem.* extraction

啐

cuì ① spit; expectorate: ～他一口 spit at him / ～一口唾沫 throw out some spittle ② *interj. old* (expressing scorn, reproach or disgust) bah; pah; phooey

毳

cuì *formal* fine hair on birds or animals; down

瘁

cuì *formal* overworked; tired: 心力交瘁 xīn-lì jiāo cuì / 鞠躬尽瘁 jūgōng jìn cuì

粹

cuì ① pure: ～白 pure white / ～而不杂 pure and unadulterated ② essence; the best: 精粹 jīngcuì

粹美 cuìměi *formal* perfect; flawless: 品学～ a man of flawless character and eminent scholarship

翠

cuì ① emerald green; green: ～竹 green bamboos ② kingfisher ③ jadeite: 珠翠 zhūcuì

翠菊 cuìjú *bot.* China aster (*Callistephus chinensis*)

翠蓝 cuìlán bright blue; azure: ～的天空 the azure sky

翠绿 cuìlǜ emerald green; jade green

翠鸟 cuìniǎo kingfisher

翠生生 cuìshēngshēng fresh and green: ～的秧苗 fresh and green rice seedlings

翠微 cuìwēi *liter.* ① blue mountain mists: 高高～里, 遥见石梁横。(孟浩然) High, high amid the azure mists Afar I see the Bridge of Stone stretch before me. ② green mountains: 九嶷山上白云飞, 帝子乘风下～。(毛泽东) White clouds are sailing above Mount Jiuyi; Riding the wind, the Princesses descend the green hills.

翠玉 cuìyù another name for 翡翠 fěicuì

cūn

村（邨）

cūn ① village; hamlet: 渔～ a fishing village / 一个小～儿 a hamlet ② rustic; boorish: 村野 cūnyě

村夫 cūnfū villager; countryman

村姑 cūngū village girl; country wench

村口 cūnkǒu entrance to a village

村落 cūnluò village; hamlet

村民 cūnmín villager; village people

村舍 cūnshè cottage

村史 cūnshǐ village history

村市 cūnshì village fair; village market

村俗 cūnsú coarse; rustic; unrefined; vulgar

村头 cūntóu the edge of a village; entrance to a village

村坞 cūnwù *formal* village; hamlet

村圩 cūnxū *dial.* ① village fair; village market ② village; hamlet

村学 cūnxué (also 村塾 cūnshú) (in former times) village school

村野 cūnyě ① villages; countryside ② rustic; countrified

村姬 cūnyù an old village woman

村寨 cūnzhài stockaded village; village: ～相望 neighbouring villages within sight of each other

村长 cūnzhǎng village head

村镇 cūnzhèn villages and small townships

村庄 cūnzhuāng village; hamlet

村子 cūnzi village; hamlet

皴

cūn ① (of skin) be chapped from the cold: 孩子的手～了。The child's hands were chapped from the cold. ② interior brush texturing (the use of brush-strokes or dabs that give texture to the pictorial elements of a traditional Chinese painting)

皴法 cūnfǎ texturing methods, or types of texture strokes (e.g. for trees, rocks, mountains, etc.) ——see also 皴 cūn②

皴裂 cūnliè (of skin) be chapped from the cold: 手足～。Both one's hands and feet were chapped from the cold.

cún

存 cún ① exist; live; survive: 父母俱～. Both parents are still living. ② store; keep: ～粮 store up grain／新水库～了大量的水. A large quantity of water is stored in the new reservoir.／天气热, 西红柿～不住. Tomatoes won't keep in hot weather. ③ accumulate; collect: 一下雨, 洼地里就～了好些水. Whenever it rains, a lot of water accumulates in the low-lying land. ④ deposit: 把钱～在银行里 deposit money in a bank ⑤ leave with; check: 行李先～在这里, 回头再来取. Let's check our luggage here and come back for it later.／～自行车 leave one's bicycle in a bicycle park ⑥ reserve; retain: 他有什么说什么, 肚子里～不住话. He always says what he thinks; he can't hold anything back. ⑦ remain on balance; be in stock: 收支相抵, 净～两千元. The accounts show a surplus of 2,000 *yuan*. ⑧ cherish; harbour: ～着很大的希望 cherish high hopes／不～幻想 harbour no illusions

存案 cún'àn register with the proper authorities

存查 cúnchá file for reference

存车处 cúnchēchù parking lot (for bicycles); bicycle park (*or* shed)

存储 cúnchǔ *electron.* memory; storage: ～二极管 storage diode／～容量 memory capacity／～元件 memory element

存储器 cúnchǔqì memory (of a computer)

存单 cúndān deposit receipt: 定期～ time certificate (bearing specific maturity date)

存档 cúndàng keep in the archives; place on file; file

存底儿 cúndǐr keep the original draft; keep a file copy

存而不论 cún ér bù lùn leave the question open

存放 cúnfàng ① leave with; leave in sb.'s care: 我把箱子～在朋友那里了. I've left my suitcase with a friend of mine. ② deposit (money): 把节余的钱～在银行里. Put your savings in the bank.

存根 cúngēn counterfoil; stub: 支票～ cheque stub

存户 cúnhù depositor

存活 cúnhuó survive

存活率 cúnhuólǜ survival rate

存货 cúnhuò ① stock up ② goods in stock; existing stock

存据 cúnjù a written statement (e.g. a certificate, receipt, etc.) kept as evidence or as a record

存款 cúnkuǎn ① deposit money (in a bank) ② deposit; bank savings: 个人～ personal savings account

存栏 cúnlán *animal husbandry* livestock on hand: 牲畜～总头数比去年增加了一倍. The total livestock number is twice as large as it was last year.

存身 cúnshēn take shelter; make one's home: 无处～ find no shelter; have no place to call one's home

存食 cúnshí suffer from indigestion

存亡 cún-wáng live or die; survive or perish: 抗日战争是一场关系民族～的战争. The War of Resistance Against Japan was a life-and-death struggle for the Chinese nation.／与阵地共～ defend one's position to the death

存亡绝续 cún-wáng jué-xù survive or perish; stand or fall: ～的关头 at a critical moment; when one's very existence is at stake

存问 cúnwèn *formal* send one's regards to

存息 cúnxī interest on a deposit

存项 cúnxiàng credit balance; balance

存心 cúnxīn ① cherish certain intentions: ～不良 cherish evil designs (*or* intentions)／他说这番话, 不知存着什么心. It's hard to say what his intentions were in saying that. ② intentionally; deliberately; on purpose: 我不是～这么做的. I didn't do it on purpose.

存休 cúnxiū (also 存假 cúnjià) accumulated holidays

存疑 cúnyí leave a question open; leave a matter for future consideration: 这件事情暂时～吧. Let's put this matter aside for the time being.

存余 cúnyú sth. left over; surplus; remainder: 原料略有～. There is a little surplus of raw materials.

存在 cúnzài exist; be: 那个问题已经不～了. That problem no longer exists.／人们的社会～决定人们的思想. It is man's social being that determines his thinking.／矛盾～于一切事物发展的过程中. Contradiction is present in the process of development of all things.

存照 cúnzhào ① file a document ② a document on file

存折 cúnzhé deposit book; bankbook

存执 cúnzhí counterfoil; stub

存贮 cúnzhù same as 贮存 zhùcún

存贮器 cúnzhùqì same as 存储器 cúnchǔqì

蹲

cún *dial.* injure one's foot by bringing it down too heavily ——see also dūn

cǔn

忖 cǔn turn over in one's mind; ponder; speculate

忖度 cǔnduó speculate; conjecture; surmise

忖量 cǔnliàng ① think over; turn over in one's mind: 她～了半天, 还拿不定主意. She turned the matter over in her mind for a long while but still could not come to a decision. ② conjecture; guess: 我一边走, 一边～着他说的那番话的意思. As I walked along I kept wondering what he really meant.

忖摸 cǔnmo reckon; estimate; conjecture

cùn

寸 cùn ① *cun*, a traditional unit of length ② short for 市寸 shìcùn ③ very little; very short; small: 寸功 cùngōng

寸步 cùnbù a tiny step; a single step

寸步不离 cùnbù bù lí follow sb. closely; keep close to sb.; be always at sb.'s elbow

寸步不让 cùnbù bù ràng refuse to yield an inch; not budge an inch

寸步难行 cùnbù nán xíng be unable to move even a single step—be unable to do anything: 市场困难, 头寸短少, 真是～. Markets were difficult, ready cash was in short supply—in fact it was virtually impossible to do anything.

寸草不留 cùncǎo bù liú leave not even a blade of grass; be devastated

寸草春晖 cùncǎo chūnhuī young grass and spring sunshine—children owe to parents what young grass owes to spring sunshine: 谁言寸草心, 报得三春晖. (孟郊) Who says that the heart of an inch-long plant Can requite the radiance of full Spring?

寸长 cùncháng *formal* modest ability; small ability

寸断 cùnduàn break into pieces: 肝肠～ a heart broken into pieces—a broken heart

寸功 cùngōng a small achievement (*or* contribution): 身无～ have achieved nothing at all; have not the slightest merit

寸关尺 cùn-guān-chǐ *Chin. med.* cun, guan and chi, three places at the wrist where the pulse is usually

taken

寸金难买寸光阴 cùn jīn nán mǎi cùn guāngyīn money can't buy time; time is more precious than gold

寸进 cùnjìn a little progress; a small advance: 略有～ have made just a little progress / ～尺退 advance by inches, retreat by feet; more regressing than progressing

寸劲儿 cùnjìnr *dial.* ① coincidence: 瞧这～, 你前脚才走, 他后脚就来了。 As luck would have it, he turned up just after you left. ② appropriate strength (in doing things): 砸钉子又快又不弯, 全靠～。 To drive in a nail straight and quickly, you have to apply just the right force.

寸铁 cùntiě a small weapon: 手无寸铁 shǒu wú cùntiě

寸头 cùntóu crew cut: 留～ wear a crew cut / 我要理个～。 I want my hair cropped short.

寸土 cùntǔ an inch of land—a very small piece of land: 一寸金。 An inch of land is an inch of gold.

寸土必争 cùntǔ bì zhēng fight for (*or* contest) every inch of land

寸心 cùnxīn ① feelings: 聊表～ as a small token of my feelings; just to show my appreciation ② heart; mind: ～不忘 bear it in mind

寸阴 cùnyīn *formal* time indicated by a shadow moving a *cun*—a very short time

寸衷 cùnzhōng same as 寸心 cùnxīn

吋

cùn, also yīngcùn old form for 英寸 yīngcùn

cuō

搓

cuō ① rub with the hands: ～手取暖 rub one's hands together to warm them / ～麻绳 make cord by twisting hemp fibres between the palms / ～纸捻 roll paper spills / 这件上衣太脏了, 洗时要多～～。 This jacket is very dirty; give it a good scrubbing. / 急得她直～手。 She wrung her hands in anxiety. ② *sports* (in tennis, table tennis, cricket, etc.) chop: 一板一板地把球～过去 return every shot with a chop

搓板 cuōbǎn washboard

搓弄 cuō·nòng rub, knead, or twist idly: 她手里～着手绢, 一言不发。 She sat twiddling her handkerchief, saying not a word.

搓球 cuōqiú *sports* chopping

搓揉 cuōróu rub; knead; twist: 她把那封信～成一团, 扔进了字纸篓。 She crumpled the letter into a ball and threw it into the wastepaper basket.

搓手顿脚 cuōshǒu-dùnjiǎo wring one's hands and stamp one's feet—get anxious and impatient

搓洗 cuōxǐ hand-wash (clothes)

搓澡 cuōzǎo give or get a rubdown with a damp towel

磋

cuō consult

磋磨 cuōmó *formal* exchange views; compare notes

磋切 cuōqiè *formal* learn from each other by exchanging views

磋商 cuōshāng consult; exchange views: 与各有关部门进行～ hold consultations with all departments concerned

撮

cuō ① *formal* gather; bring together ② scoop up (with a dustpan or shovel): ～起一簸箕土 scoop up a dustpan of dirt ③ *dial.* pick up or hold (dust, powder, etc.) between the thumb and the first finger: ～一点儿盐 take a pinch of salt ④ extract; summarize: 撮要 cuōyào ⑤ *cuo*, a traditional unit of capacity ⑥ short for 市撮 shìcuō ⑦ *m.* ⓐ *dial.* pinch:

一～盐 a pinch of salt / 一～儿米 a small pinch of rice ⓑ handful (of bad people): 一小～法西斯匪徒 a handful of fascist gangsters ——see also zuǒ

撮合 cuōhé make a match; act as go-between

撮合山 cuōhéshān *old* matchmaker

撮口呼 cuōkǒuhū *phonet.* a class of syllables with ü as the final 韵母 or a final beginning with ü (e.g. 女 nǚ, 略 lüè) ——see also 四呼 sìhū

撮弄 cuōnòng ① make fun of; play a trick on; tease ② abet; instigate; incite

撮要 cuōyào ① make an abstract; outline essential points: 把工作情况～上报 submit an outline report on one's work ② abstract; synopsis; extracts: 论文～ an abstract of a thesis

蹉

cuō see below

蹉跌 cuōdiē *formal* trip and fall—make a slip

蹉跎 cuōtuó waste time: 一再～ let one opportunity after another slip away

蹉跎岁月 cuōtuó suìyuè let time slip by accomplishing nothing; idle away one's time

cuó

痤

cuó see below

痤疮 cuóchuāng acne (a skin disease)

矬

cuó *dial.* short: ～个儿 a short person

矬子 cuózi *dial.* a short person; dwarf

嵯

cuó see below

嵯峨 cuó'é *formal* (of mountains) lofty and rugged

cuò

挫

cuò ① defeat; frustrate: 受挫 shòucuò ② subdue; lower: ～敌人的锐气, 长自己的威风 deflate the enemy's arrogance and boost one's own morale / ～其锋芒 blunt the edge of sb.'s advance

挫败 cuòbài frustrate; foil; defeat: 遭到严重的～ suffer a serious defeat / ～侵略计划 frustrate plans for aggression / ～扩张主义者的阴谋 foil the schemes of the expansionists

挫伤 cuòshāng ① *med.* contusion; bruise ② dampen; blunt; discourage: 不要～群众的积极性。 Don't dampen the enthusiasm of the masses.

挫折 cuòzhé setback; reverse: 屡遭～ suffer repeated setbacks (*or* reverses)

厝

cuò *formal* ① lay; place ② place a coffin in a temporary shelter pending burial

厝火积薪 cuòhuǒ-jīxīn a fire beneath a pile of faggots—a hidden danger

措

cuò ① arrange; manage; handle: 惊慌失措 jīnghuāng shīcuò ② make plans: 筹措 chóucuò

措辞 cuòcí wording; diction: ～不当 inappropriate wording / ～严厉 couched in harsh terms / ～强硬 strongly worded

措大 cuòdà *old* a miserable poor scholar

措施 cuòshī measure; step: 采取重大～ adopt an important measure / 十分指标, 十二分～。 If the target is ten, take measures to achieve twelve—make ample preparations to guarantee success.

措手不及 cuò shǒu bù jí be caught unprepared; be

caught unawares: 打他个～ make a surprise attack on them

措置 cuòzhì　handle; manage; arrange

措置得当 cuòzhì dédàng　handle properly

措置裕如 cuòzhì yùrú　handle with ease; manage very well

锉

cuò　① file: 方～ square file / 圆～ round file / 木～ (wood) rasp ② make smooth with a file; file: ～光 file sth. smooth

锉刀 cuòdāo　file

锉屑 cuòxiè　filing

错¹

cuò　① interlocked and jagged; intricate; complex: 交错 jiāocuò / 错落 cuòluò ② grind; rub: ～牙 grind one's teeth (in one's sleep) ③ make way; move out of the way: 劳驾往那边一～一～。 Would you mind making room for me? ④ alternate; stagger: 这两个会不能同时开, 得～一下。 We can't hold the two meetings at the same time. We must stagger them. ⑤ be out of alignment: 这行没排齐, 中间～进去了一点儿。 This line is not straight. It's a little crooked in the middle. ⑥ wrong; mistaken; erroneous: 你弄～了。 You've got it wrong. / 拿～东西 take sth. by mistake / 从头～到底 completely wrong ⑦ fault; demerit: 这是他的～, 不怨你。 You are not to blame. It's his fault. ⑧ (used in the negative) bad; poor: 今年的收成～不了。 This year's harvest is sure to be good.

错²

cuò　*formal*　inlay with gold, silver, etc.: 错金 cuòjīn

错³

cuò　*formal*　① grindstone for polishing jade: 他山之石, 可以为～。 Stones from other hills may serve to polish the jade of this one—advice from others may help one overcome one's shortcomings. ② polish jade

错爱 cuò'ài　*pol.*　undeserved kindness or favour

错案 cuò'àn　*leg.*　misjudged case

错别字 cuòbiézì　wrongly written or mispronounced characters

错彩镂金 cuòcǎi-lòujīn　elaborately carved and colourfully embellished—literary brilliance

错车 cuòchē　one vehicle gives another the right of way: 地方太小, 错不开车。 The space is too narrow for vehicles to make way for each other.

错处 cuòchu　fault; demerit

错待 cuòdài　treat unfairly; treat badly: 他们不会～你的, 你放心好了。 You can rest assured that you'll be

treated well.

错讹 cuò'é　error (in writing or recording)

错愕 cuò'è　*formal*　stunned; dumbfounded

错非 cuòfēi　*dial.*　except: ～这种药, 没法儿治他的病。 His illness can't be cured except by taking this medicine.

错怪 cuòguài　blame sb. wrongly

错过 cuòguò　① miss; let slip: ～机会 miss an opportunity / ～这趟汽车, 今天就走不成了。 If we miss this bus, we won't be able to go today. ② same as 过错 guòcuò

错话 cuòhuà　improper remarks

错踝 cuòhuái　dislocation of the ankle

错角 cuòjiǎo　*math.*　alternate angle

错金 cuòjīn　inlay with gold: ～器皿 gold-inlaid ware; metal-inlaid ware

错觉 cuòjué　illusion; misconception; wrong impression: 这样会给人造成～。 This will give people a false impression.

错开 cuòkāi　stagger: 把日子～ stagger the days off / 三场球赛应～进行。 We should stagger the three ball games.

错漏 cuòlòu　mistakes and omissions

错乱 cuòluàn　in disorder; in confusion; deranged: 颠倒～ topsy-turvy

错落 cuòluò　in disorderly profusion: 苍松翠柏～其间 dotted with green pines and cypresses; with pines and cypresses interspersed

错落不齐 cuòluò bù qí　disorderly and uneven

错落有致 cuòluò yǒu zhì　in picturesque disorder

错位 cuòwèi　*med.*　dislocation: 肘关节～ dislocation of the elbow

错误 cuòwù　① wrong; mistaken; erroneous: ～思想 wrong thinking; a mistaken idea / ～的结论 wrong conclusion / ～路线 an erroneous line ② mistake; error; blunder: 犯～ make a mistake; commit an error

错误百出 cuòwù bǎi chū　riddled with errors; full of mistakes

错银 cuòyín　inlay with silver: ～首饰盒 a silver-inlaid jewel box

错杂 cuòzá　mixed; heterogeneous; jumbled; of mixed content

错字 cuòzì　① wrongly written character ② misprint

错综 cuòzōng　crisscross; intricate

错综复杂 cuòzōng-fùzá　intricate; complex: 这部小说的情节～, 引人入胜。 The plot of the novel is intricate and fascinating.

D

dā

叮 dā *onom.* (uttered by a person driving a draft animal, directing it to go faster) gee; gee-up; giddyap

奆 dā *formal* big-eared

奆拉 dāla droop; hang down: ～着脑袋 hang one's head / 他眼皮～下来，一会儿就睡着了。His eyelids drooped and he was soon asleep.

搭 dā ① put up; build: ～一个临时舞台 put up a makeshift stage / ～窝 build a nest / ～帐篷 pitch a tent ② hang over; put over: 把洗好的衣服～在绳上 hang the washing on a line / 他肩膀上～着一块毛巾。He had a towel over his shoulder. ③ come into contact; join: 那两根电线～上了。The two wires are touching. / ～上关系 strike up a relationship with; establish contact with ④ throw in more (people, money, etc.); add: 你忙不过来，给你一个人吧。You're terribly busy. We'll send someone to help you. / 为了救他，我差点儿把命都～进去了。In trying to save him I nearly lost my own life, too. ⑤ lift sth. together: 帮我把这包大米～上卡车。Help me lift the bag of rice onto the truck. / 咱们俩把这筐土～走。Let's carry this basket of earth away. ⑥ take (a ship, plane, etc.); travel (*or* go) by: ～轮船去上海 go to Shanghai by boat / ～飞机 go by plane / ～长途汽车 travel by coach / ～他们的车走 get a lift in their car

搭班 dābān ① *old* temporarily join a theatrical troupe ② temporarily join in a group's work

搭班子 dā bānzi ① set up a theatrical troupe ② organize personnel for a job

搭伴 dābàn join sb. on a trip; travel together: 他也到新疆去，你们搭个伴儿吧。He's going to Xinjiang too, so you may as well travel together.

搭补 dābǔ *dial.* subsidize

搭茬儿 dāchár same as 答茬儿 dāchár

搭乘 dāchéng travel by (plane, car, ship, etc.)

搭档 dādàng ① cooperate; work together: 咱俩～吧。Let us two team up. ② partner: 老～ old partner; old workmate

搭调 dādiào ① be in tune: 他唱起歌来老不～。He always gets out of tune when he sings. ② be reasonable; stand to reason: 你这话说得可太不～。What you say is utterly unreasonable. ③ match; go together (with): 这首插曲与影片不～。The song doesn't go well with the film.

搭盖 dāgài put up (sth. simple and crude, as a shed)

搭钩 dāgōu establish contact or connection with: 他们厂跟一家港商搭上钩了。Their factory has established a relationship with a Hong Kong business firm.

搭话 dāhuà ① make conversation; get a word in: 十几个年轻人围着他，抢着跟他～。About a dozen boys and girls crowded round him, all trying to enter into a con-

versation with him. ② send word

搭伙[1] dāhuǒ join as partner: 他们明天去参观故宫，我也想～去。They're going to visit the Palace Museum tomorrow and I'd like to join them.

搭伙[2] dāhuǒ eat regularly in (a mess, etc.): 我们都在厂里食堂～。We all eat in the factory cafeteria.

搭架子 dā jiàzi ① build a framework; get (an undertaking, etc.) roughly into shape: 先搭好架子，再充实内容。First make an outline, then fill in the content. ② *dial.* put on airs; assume great airs

搭肩 dājiān ① help to shoulder sth. heavy ② stand on another's shoulders (in order to climb up): 他们～爬上墙头。They climbed up the wall by standing on one another's shoulders.

搭建 dājiàn ① put up (a shed, etc.) ② set up (an organization): ～领导班子 organize a leading group

搭脚儿 dājiǎor *dial.* get a lift or a free ride; hitchhike

搭界 dājiè ① have a common boundary: 两省～的地方 the place where the two provinces meet ② *dial.* (usu. used in the negative) have some contact with; have sth. to do with: 我跟这件事不～。This has nothing to do with me. / 你少跟这种人～。Better not have anything to do with these people.

搭救 dājiù rescue; go to the rescue of: ～落水儿童 rescue a drowning child

搭客 dākè ① passenger ② *dial.* take on passengers

搭拉 dāla same as 奆拉 dāla

搭理 dāli same as 答理 dāli

搭凉棚 dā liángpéng ① set up a mat-awning ② shade one's eyes with one's hand: 他手～，四处观望。Shading his eyes with his hand, he looked around.

搭配 dāpèi ① arrange in pairs or groups: 她和小王～参加混合双打。She paired up with Xiao Wang in the mixed doubles. ② *linguis.* collocation: 这两个词～不当。These two words don't collocate.

搭腔 dāqiāng ① answer; respond: 我问了两遍，没人～。I repeated my question, but nobody answered. ② talk to each other: 以前他俩合不来，彼此不～。In the past the two of them did not get on at all well; they weren't even on speaking terms.

搭桥 dāqiáo ① put up (*or* build) a bridge ② (also 搭鹊桥 dā quèqiáo) act as a matchmaker

搭讪 dāshàn (also 搭赸 dā·shàn) strike up a conversation with sb.; say sth. to smooth over an embarrassing situation: 他很尴尬，～着走开了。Feeling embarrassed, he muttered a few words and walked off. / 他总是一边卖东西一边和顾客～。While doing business he would strike up a conversation with his customers.

搭手 dāshǒu give a hand; help: 我也很想帮忙，但人太多，搭不上手。I wanted to help but there were already too many helping hands. / 她忙不过来，你去给她搭把手。She's too busy to manage everything. Please go and give her some help. / 他赶紧跑来～。He hurried over to give me a hand.

搭售 dāshòu pair unsalable goods up with goods that sell well, making the purchase of the former compulsory for anyone who wants to buy the latter

搭载 dāzài (of trucks, freighters, etc.) pick up extra

passengers or freight

搭坐 dāzuò　same as 搭乘 dāchéng

嗒(噠) dā *onom.*: ～～的马蹄声 clatter of horses' hoofs／机枪～～地响着。The machine guns rattled away. ——see also tà

答(荅) dā see below ——see also dá

答茬儿 dāchár *dial.* pick up the thread of a conversation and take part in it: 这问题我还没有仔细考虑，没法～。I haven't thought it over, so I can't say anything.／又没问你，你答什么茬儿! Nobody asked you, so why butt in?

答理 dāli (usu. used in the negative) acknowledge (sb.'s greeting, etc.); respond; answer: 我跟他打招呼，他没～我。I greeted him but he didn't respond.／不爱～人 be standoffish／他生气地坐在那里，谁也不～。She sat there sulking and wouldn't speak to anyone.

答腔 dāqiāng　same as 搭腔 dāqiāng

答应 dāying ① answer; reply; respond: 敲了半天门没人～。I knocked again and again but there was no answer.／我在楼下喊你半天，你怎么不～? I kept calling to you from downstairs—how come you didn't answer?／我～了好几声他才听见。I answered several times before he heard me. ② agree; promise; comply with: 我们请他来参加座谈会，他已经～了。We asked him to attend our discussion, and he agreed to come.／他～八点半到。He promised to be here at 8:30.／无论如何你必须～我们的要求。You've got to agree to our request, no matter what.

跶 dā see 踢跶 tīdā

褡 dā see below

褡包 dābao (also 褡膊 dābo; 褡布 dābù) a long, broad girdle

褡裢 dā·lián ① a long, rectangular bag sewn up at both ends with an opening in the middle (usu. worn round the waist or across the shoulder) ② a jacket, made of several layers of cloth, worn by wrestlers

褡子 dāzi　same as 褡裢 dā·lián①

dá

打 dá *m.* dozen: 一～铅笔 a dozen pencils／论～出售 sell by the dozen ——see also dǎ

达(達) dá ① extend: 直达 zhídá／四通八达 sìtōng-bādá ② reach; attain; amount to: 全县粮食平均亩产～千斤。The per *mu* grain yield for the whole county has reached 1,000 *jin*.／我们不～目的决不罢休。We will never cease our efforts until we achieve our aim.／听众鼓掌～两分钟之久。The audience applauded for two whole minutes.／灌溉面积共～五十万亩。The irrigated area amounts to 500,000 *mu*. ③ understand thoroughly: 通达 tōngdá ④ express; communicate: 传达 chuándá ⑤ eminent; distinguished: 达官贵人 dáguān-guìrén

达标 dábiāo　reach a set standard

达卜 dábǔ　a small drum similar to the tambourine, used by the Uygur nationality

达成 dáchéng　reach (agreement): 双方就会议议程～协议。The two parties reached agreement on the agenda of the meeting.／～交易 strike a bargain

达旦 dádàn　until dawn: 通宵～ tōngxiāo-dádàn

达到 dádào　achieve; attain; reach: ～目的 achieve (*or* attain) the goal／～高潮 reach a high tide; come to a

climax／～世界先进水平 come up to advanced world standards／你要求太高，我恐怕达不到。Your expectations are too high. I'm afraid I can't live up to them.／货物运量将～四千万吨。The volume of freight handled will amount to 40 million tons.

达尔文主义 Dá'ěrwénzhǔyì　Darwinism

达观 dáguān　take things philosophically

达官贵人 dáguān-guìrén　high officials and noble lords; VIPs: 周旋于～之间 move in high society

达赖喇嘛 Dálài Lǎma　the Dalai Lama

达姆弹 dámǔdàn　*mil.* dumdum (bullet)

达人 dárén　*formal* ① an intelligent, well-informed person ② a person who takes everything philosophically

达斡尔族 Dáwò'ěrzú　the Daur (Tahur) nationality, or the Daurs (Tahurs), distributed over Heilongjiang Province, the Inner Mongolia Autonomous Region, and the Xinjiang Uygur Autonomous Region

达意 dáyì　express (*or* convey) one's ideas: 抒情～ express one's thoughts and feelings

达因 dáyīn　*phys.* dyne

怛 dá　*formal* grieved; distressed

沓 dá　*m.* pile (of paper, etc.); pad: 一～报纸 a pile of newspapers／一～信纸 a pad of letter paper／一～钞票 a wad of bank notes ——see also tà

沓子 dázi　pile (of paper, etc.); pad: 一大～十元钞票 a thick wad of 10-*yuan* notes

答(荅) dá ① answer; reply; respond: 一问一～ one asking and the other answering／这个问题他～不上来。He couldn't answer the question. ② return (a visit, etc.); reciprocate: ～礼 return a salute ——see also dā

答案 dá'àn　answer; solution; key: 找不到问题的～ find no solution to the problem／练习的～ key to an exercise

答拜 dábài　pay a return visit (*or* call)

答辩 dábiàn　reply (to a charge, query or an argument): 保留公开～的权利 reserve the right of public reply／进行论文～ defend one's thesis

答词 dácí　thank-you speech; answering speech; reply

答对 dáduì　(usu. used in the negative) answer sb.'s question; reply: 被问得没法～ be baffled by the question

答访 dáfǎng　pay a return visit (*or* call)

答非所问 dá fēi suǒ wèn　give an irrelevant answer

答复 dáfù　answer; reply: ～他的询问 reply to his inquiry

答话 dáhuà　(usu. used in the negative) answer; reply: 人家问你，你怎么不～? I've asked you a question. Why don't you answer?

答卷 dájuàn ① answer the questions or solve the problems in a test paper ② an answered test paper: 标准～ standard answers to a test paper

答数 dáshù　answer (to an arithmetic problem)

答问 dáwèn ① answer a question ② a question-and-answer form of writing

答谢 dáxiè　express appreciation (for sb.'s kindness or hospitality); acknowledge: 我们简直不知道怎样～你们的热情招待。We simply don't know how to repay your kind hospitality.

答谢宴会 dáxiè yànhuì　a return banquet

答疑 dáyí　(of a teacher, speaker, etc.) answer questions: 留下半小时～ set aside half an hour for questions and answers (*or* for answering questions)

瘩 dá see below ——see also da

瘩背　dábèi　*Chin. med.*　carbuncle on the back

鞑　dá　see 鞑靼 Dádá

鞑（韃）　dá　see below

鞑靼　Dádá　Tartar

dǎ

打¹　dǎ　① strike; hit; knock: ～门 knock at the door / ～稻子 thresh rice / 钟～了十下。The clock struck ten. ② break; smash: 我～了一个碗。I broke a bowl. / 窗玻璃～破了。The windowpane is broken. ③ beat; fight; attack: 不许～他! You mustn't beat him! / 两个人～了起来。The two men came to blows. / 他们又～下了一座县城。They've captured another town. / ～硬仗 fight a hard battle / 你们～得好。You're putting up a good fight. ④ deal with sb. or sth.: 打交道 dǎ jiāodao / 打官司 dǎ guānsi ⑤ construct; build: ～坝 construct a dam / ～田埂 build low ridges between paddy fields ⑥ make (articles of daily use or food): ～一把刀 forge a knife / ～家具 make furniture / ～烧饼 make sesame seed cakes ⑦ mix; stir; beat: ～鸡蛋 beat eggs / ～糨子 mix paste ⑧ tie up; pack: ～行李 pack one's luggage; pack up / ～成一捆 tie (things) up in a bundle / ～裹脚 wind a puttee ⑨ knit; weave: ～草鞋 weave straw sandals / ～毛衣 knit a sweater ⑩ draw; paint; make a mark on: ～方格儿 draw squares / ～手印 put one's fingerprint on a document / ～一个问号 put a question mark; put a query ⑪ spray; spread: ～农药 spray insecticide / 在地板上～蜡 wax the floor ⑫ open; dig: ～井 dig (*or* sink) a well / ～炮眼 drill a blasting hole ⑬ hold up; hoist; raise: ～灯笼 carry a lantern / ～伞 hold up an umbrella / ～起精神来 cheer up one's spirits; cheer up ⑭ send; dispatch; project: ～电报 send a telegram / ～电话 make a phone call / ～信号 give a signal; signal / ～炮 fire a cannon / ～手电 flash a torch ⑮ issue or receive (a certificate, etc.): ～介绍信 write a letter of introduction (for sb.); get a letter of introduction (from one's organization) ⑯ remove; get rid of: ～蛔虫 take medicine to get rid of roundworms; take worm medicine ⑰ ladle; draw: ～粥 ladle gruel / ～一盆水 fetch a basin of water / 从井里～水 draw water from a well ⑱ buy: ～酱油 buy soy sauce (in a small quantity with one's own container) / ～票 buy a (train, bus, etc.) ticket / ～五分钱的醋 buy vinegar for five *fen* ⑲ catch; hunt: ～鱼 catch fish / ～鸟 shoot birds / ～野鸭 go duck-hunting ⑳ gather in; collect; reap: ～柴 gather firewood / ～了八百斤麦子 get in 800 *jin* of wheat ㉑ estimate; calculate; reckon: 成本～二百块钱 estimate (*or* reckon) the cost at 200 *yuan* / 损耗已经～进去了。Allowances have been made for damages. ㉒ work out: ～草稿 work out a draft ㉓ do; engage in: ～短工 work as a day or seasonal labourer; be a temporary worker / ～夜班 go on night shift ㉔ play: ～篮球 play basketball / ～扑克 play cards / ～秋千 have a swing ㉕ go through (some physical action): ～手势 make a gesture; gesticulate / ～喷嚏 sneeze / ～一个跟斗 turn (*or* do) a somersault ㉖ adopt; use: ～一个比方 draw an analogy ㉗ (used to give a clue to the answer when setting a riddle): 画时圆，写时方；寒时短，热时长。——～一字。(谜底: 日) When drawn it is round, but when written it is square; in cold weather it is short, and in hot weather long. — A character. (Answer: the character 日 "sun, day")

打²　dǎ　*prep.*　from; since: ～那以后 since then

你～哪儿来? Where have you come from? / 他～门缝里往外看。He looked out through the crack in the door. / 他～心眼里感到高兴。It warmed the cockles of his heart.
——see also dá

打熬　dǎ'áo　① endure; bear; suffer: 他在旧社会～了三十年。He suffered for thirty years in the old society. ② suffering; hardship: 经得住任何～ can endure hardships of any kind ③ temper; steel; toughen: ～筋骨 build up one's physique

打靶　dǎbǎ　target (*or* shooting) practice

打靶场　dǎbǎchǎng　target range

打摆子　dǎ bǎizi　*dial.*　suffer from malaria

打败　dǎbài　① defeat; beat; worst ② suffer a defeat; be defeated

打板子　dǎ bǎnzi　flog; cane

打扮　dǎban　① dress up; make up; deck out: 孩子们～得像春天的花朵一样。The gaily-dressed children looked like spring flowers. / 节日的天坛～得格外壮丽。The Temple of Heaven was magnificently decked out for the festive occasion. / 把自己～成英雄 pose as a hero ② way or style of dressing: 她虽然在城里工作多年，还是那副农村妇女的朴素～。Although she has worked in the city a long time, she still dresses in the simple style of a countrywoman. / 学生～ be dressed like a student

打包　dǎbāo　① bale; pack: ～费 packing charges ② unpack

打包机　dǎbāojī　baling press

打包票　dǎ bāopiào　(also 打保票 dǎ bǎopiào) vouch for; guarantee: 我敢～，机器一定准时送到。I guarantee that the machines will be delivered on time. / 这件事你可不能给人～。This is not a matter in which you can vouch for other people. / 他最适合做这件事，我敢～。He's the right man for this job, I can give you my word.

打苞　dǎbāo　(of wheat, sorghum, etc.) form ears; ear up

打抱不平　dǎ bàobùpíng　take up the cudgels for the injured party; defend sb. against an injustice; be the champion of the oppressed: 他是个爱～的人。He was always ready to defend the weak and helpless. ——see also 抱不平 bàobùpíng

打奔儿　dǎbēnr　*dial.*　① stumble (in speech) ② stumble (in walking)

打比　dǎbǐ　① draw an analogy; use a metaphor or simile: 讲抽象的事情，拿具体的东西来～，就容易使人明白。When you talk about abstract things, people can understand you better if you draw concrete analogies. ② *dial.* compare: 他六十多岁了，怎么能跟小伙子～呢? He's over sixty, so how can you compare him with a young man?

打边鼓　dǎ biāngǔ　same as 敲边鼓 qiāo biāngǔ

打并　dǎbìng　① pack; get ready: ～行装 pack one's luggage; pack up one's things ② *old* piece together; gather together: ～得五十块大洋 scrape together fifty silver dollars

打不住　dǎbuzhù　*inf.*　① be more than: 这块地麦子亩产三百公斤也～。This field of wheat will yield more than 300 kilos per *mu*. ② not be enough: 这么多准备工作，三天时间是～的。Three days isn't enough for so much preparatory work.

打草¹　dǎcǎo　cut grass

打草²　dǎcǎo　*dial.*　work out a draft

打草惊蛇　dǎ cǎo jīng shé　beat the grass and startle the snake—act rashly and alert the enemy

打喳喳　dǎchāchā　*dial.*　whisper

打杈　dǎchà　prune: 给棉花～ prune cotton plants / 打旁杈 prune the side branches

打岔　dǎchà　interrupt; cut in: 他们在谈正经事儿, 别～。Don't interrupt them; they're talking business. / 我说话的时候你别～。Don't butt in while I'm talking.

打禅　dǎchán　(of a Buddhist) sit in meditation

打场　dǎcháng　thresh grain (on the threshing ground)

打成一片　dǎchéng yīpiàn　become one with; identify oneself with; merge with: 和群众～ be (or become) one with the masses / 同工人农民～ identify oneself with the workers and peasants / 要官兵～, 军民～。The officers must be integrated with the men and the army with the people.

打冲锋　dǎchōngfēng　① charge (in a battle) ② be in the vanguard

打抽丰　dǎchōufēng　same as 打秋风 dǎqiūfēng

打出手　dǎ chūshǒu　① (in traditional opera) throw weapons back and forth ② start a fight; come to blows

打从　dǎcóng　prep. inf. ① since: ～那时候起 since then ② (used with 经过) past; by: ～邮局门口经过 go past the post office

打打闹闹　dǎdǎnàonào　have boisterous fun; horseplay

打蛋器　dǎdànqì　egg-whisk; whisk

打倒　dǎdǎo　overthrow: ～帝国主义! Down with imperialism!

打道　dǎdào　clear the way (for officials in imperial times)

打得火热　dǎ de huǒrè　be very thick with each other; be as thick as thieves: 两人正在谈情说爱, ～。The two of them were billing and cooing together; they were obviously very engrossed.

打灯谜　dǎ dēngmí　guess lantern riddles (as a game or pastime)

打的　dǎdī　inf.　go by taxi; take a taxi

打底　dǎdǐ　① eat sth. before having a drink ② feel secure 心里不～ feel insecure ③ same as 打底子 dǎ dǐzi ④ text. bottoming

打底机　dǎdǐjī　padding machine

打底子　dǎ dǐzi　① sketch a plan, picture, etc.: 这篇文章我先打个底子, 再请你修改。I'll make a draft of the essay and then ask you to revise it. ② lay a foundation: 学英语应该在中学就打好底子。Learners of English should be given a good grounding in middle school.

打点　dǎdian　① get (luggage, etc.) ready: ～行李, 准备出发。Pack the luggage and make ready to depart. ② bribe officials

打掉　dǎdiào　destroy; knock out; wipe out: 把敌人的探照灯～ knock out the enemy's searchlight / ～敌人一个师 wipe out an enemy division

打叠　dǎdié　pack; arrange; prepare: ～行李 pack one's luggage

打动　dǎdòng　move; touch: 这番话～了他的心。He was moved (or touched) by these words.

打洞机　dǎdòngjī　(also 打眼机 dǎyǎnjī) perforator

打赌　dǎdǔ　bet; wager: 我敢～他明天准来。I bet he'll come tomorrow.

打短儿　dǎduǎnr　inf.　① work as a casual labourer ② be dressed in a Chinese-style jacket and trousers

打断　dǎduàn　① break: 他的腿给弹片～了。A shrapnel broke his leg. ② interrupt; cut short: ～思路 interrupt sb.'s train of thought / 别～他, 让他说完。Don't cut him short; let him finish. / 他的讲话不时被热烈的掌声～。His speech was punctuated with warm applause.

打盹儿　dǎdǔnr　doze off; take (or have) a nap: 午饭后他总要打个盹儿。He always takes (or has) a nap after lunch.

打趸儿　dǎdǔnr　inf.　buy in batches

打顿　dǎdùn　make a pause (in a speech, recitation, etc.)

打呃　dǎ'è　same as 打嗝儿 dǎgér

打耳光　dǎ ěrguāng　box sb.'s ears; slap sb. in the face

打发　dǎfa　① send; dispatch: 赶快～人去请大夫。Send for a doctor at once. ② dismiss; send away: 他把孩子们～走了, 坐下来工作。He sent the children away and sat down to work. ③ while away (one's time)

打幡儿　dǎfānr　(of the son of the deceased) hold a streamer in a funeral procession

打翻　dǎfān　overturn; strike down: 一个大浪把小船～了。A huge wave overturned the boat. / 把人～在地 strike sb. down

打翻身仗　dǎ fānshēnzhàng　work hard to bring about a decisive turn for the better

打榧子　dǎ fěizi　snap the fingers

打分　dǎfēn　give a mark; mark students' papers, etc.

打稿　dǎgǎo　(also 打稿子 dǎ gǎozi) work out a draft

打嗝儿　dǎgér　inf.　① hiccup ② belch; burp

打更　dǎgēng　sound the night watches

打埂　dǎgěng　agric.　ridging

打工　dǎgōng　dial.　do manual work

打躬　dǎgōng　make a bow; bow

打躬作揖　dǎgōng-zuōyī　bow and raise one's clasped hands in salute; fold the hands and make deep bows; bow and scrape

打谷场　dǎgǔcháng　threshing ground (or floor)

打鼓　dǎgǔ　① beat a drum ② feel uncertain (or nervous): 心里直～ feel extremely diffident

打卦　dǎguà　divine by casting lots

打官腔　dǎguānqiāng　speak in a bureaucratic tone; talk like a bureaucrat; stall with official jargon

打官司　dǎ guānsi　① go to court (or law); engage in a lawsuit ② inf.　squabble: 打不完的官司 endless squabbles

打光棍　dǎguānggùn　remain a bachelor: 你快结婚吧, 哪能打一辈子光棍。You'd better get married soon. How could you be a bachelor all your life? / 他决心打一辈子光棍。He's a confirmed bachelor.

打滚　dǎgǔn　roll about: 小毛驴在地上～。The little donkey rolled on the ground. / 疼得直～ writhe with pain

打棍子　dǎgùnzi　beat with a big stick—criticize unsparingly or unfoundedly

打哈哈　dǎhāha　make fun; crack a joke: 别拿我～。Don't make fun of me. / 这是正经事, 可别～。This is a serious matter; let's not joke about it.

打哈欠　dǎ hāqian　(also 打呵欠 dǎhēqian) yawn

打鼾　dǎhān　snore

打夯　dǎhāng　ramming; tamping

打夯机　dǎhāngjī　ramming machine; rammer; tamper

打横　dǎhéng　take the least important seat at a square table

打横炮　dǎhéngpào　raise unexpected difficulties; deliberately complicate matters

打呼　dǎhū　snore

打滑　dǎhuá　① skid around: 我们的车陷在泥坑里, 车轮直～。Our car got stuck in the mud and the wheels just skidded around. ② slip (on slippery ground)

打晃儿　dǎhuàngr　wobble on one's feet

打回票　dǎhuípiào　dial.　send back; give back: 送出去的货不少～的。Quite a number of delivered goods were returned to the store.

打诨　dǎhùn　see 插科打诨 chākē-dǎhùn

打火　dǎhuǒ　strike sparks from a flint; strike a light

打火机　dǎhuǒjī　lighter

打伙儿　dǎhuǒr　inf.　join together; form a group: 几个人～上山采药。They went together to gather herbs in the mountains.

打击　dǎjī　hit; strike; attack: ～投机倒把活动 crack down on speculation and profiteering / ～歪风 take strong measures against unhealthy tendencies / ～反动

派的气焰 puncture the arrogance of the reactionaries / ～报复 make vindictive attacks on sb.; retaliate / 狠狠～敌人 strike relentless blows at the enemy

打击乐器 dǎjī yuèqì percussion instrument

打饥荒 dǎjīhuang *dial.* be in straitened circumstances or be in debt

打家劫舍 dǎjiā-jiéshè loot; plunder

打架 dǎjià come to blows; fight; scuffle

打尖[1] dǎjiān stop for refreshment when travelling; have a snack (at a rest stop)

打尖[2] dǎjiān *agric.* topping; pinching

打江山 dǎ jiāngshān fight to win state power

打浆 dǎjiāng *paper making* beating: ～机 beating engine; beater

打桨 dǎjiǎng pull an oar: 打得一手好桨 pull a good oar

打交道 dǎ jiāodao come into (or make) contact with; have dealings with: 两个厂经常～。 The two factories maintain frequent contacts. / 我没跟他打过交道。 I've never had any dealings with him.

打脚 dǎjiǎo *dial.* (of tight shoes) pinch

打搅 dǎjiǎo disturb; trouble: 人家正在工作, 别去～他了。 He's working. Don't disturb him. / 对不起, ～您了! Sorry to have bothered you. / ～您一下。 May I trouble you a minute?

打醮 dǎjiào perform a Taoist ritual

打劫 dǎjié rob; plunder; loot ——see also 趁火打劫 chèn huǒ dǎjié

打结 dǎjié tie a knot: 打个结 tie a knot / 眉头～ knit one's brows / 舌头～ be tongue-tied

打结器 dǎjiéqì *chem. fibre* knotter

打紧 dǎjǐn *dial.* (usu. used in the negative) urgent; serious: 这事不～。 It's not serious. *or* It doesn't matter.

打救 dǎjiù rescue

打开 dǎkāi ① open; unfold: 把门～ open the door / ～盖子 take off the lid / ～包袱 untie a bundle / ～缺口 make a breach / ～眼界 widen one's horizon / ～局面 open up a new prospect; make a breakthrough ② turn on; switch on: ～收音机(电灯) turn on the radio (light)

打开天窗说亮话 dǎkāi tiānchuāng shuō liànghuà frankly speaking; let's not mince matters; let's be frank and put our cards on the table

打瞌睡 dǎ kēshuì doze off; nod

打垮 dǎkuǎ defeat completely; rout: 把敌军的精锐部队～ put the enemy's crack troops to rout

打来回 dǎ láihuí make a round trip

打捞 dǎlāo ① get out of the water; salvage: ～沉船 salvage a sunken ship / ～尸体 retrieve a corpse from the water ② *petroleum* fishing: ～工具 fishing tool

打雷 dǎléi thunder: 远处在～。 It's thundering in the distance.

打擂 dǎlèi join in an open competition or contest

打冷枪 dǎ lěngqiāng ① shoot from a hiding-place; snipe ② attack in a sly way

打量 dǎliang ① measure with the eye; look sb. up and down; size up: 门卫上下～着那个陌生人。 The sentry looked the stranger up and down. ② think; suppose; reckon: 你～她这点事都干不了? Do you think she can't do a little job like that?

打猎 dǎliè go hunting

打铃 dǎlíng ring a bell: ～了! There goes the bell!

打卤面 dǎlǔmiàn noodles served with thick gravy

打乱 dǎluàn throw into confusion; upset: ～敌人的阵脚 throw the enemy into confusion / ～计划 disrupt a plan; upset a scheme / 他的突然到来把一切都给～了。 His unexpected arrival threw everything into confusion.

打骡子惊马 dǎ luózi jīng mǎ beat the mule and scare the horse—punish one and frighten another

打落水狗 dǎ luòshuǐgǒu beat a drowning dog—completely crush a defeated enemy

打马虎眼 dǎmǎhuyǎn *dial.* pretend to be ignorant of sth. (in order to gloss it over); act dumb

打埋伏 dǎ máifu ① lie in ambush; set an ambush; ambush ② hold sth. back for one's own use; keep sth. in reserve

打闷棍 dǎ mēngùn ① (of a robber) give sb. a staggering blow with a cudgel ② give sb. a stunning blow (fig.)

打鸣儿 dǎmíngr *inf.* (of a rooster) crow

打磨 dǎmó polish; burnish; shine

打牌 dǎpái play mahjong or cards

打泡 dǎpào get blisters

打棚 dǎpéng *dial.* kid; jest; joke

打屁股 dǎ pìgu ① beat on the buttocks; spank ② *inf.* take sb. to task

打破 dǎpò break; smash: ～僵局 break a deadlock; find a way out of a stalemate / ～记录 break a record / ～界线 break down barriers / ～平衡 upset a balance / ～超级大国的核垄断 break the nuclear monopoly of the superpowers / ～常规, 尽量采用先进技术。 Break free from conventions and use advanced techniques as much as possible.

打破砂锅问到底 dǎpò shāguō wèn dàodǐ insist on getting to the bottom of the matter: 小明老爱问为什么, 老爱～。 Xiaoming always asks why and he'll never be satisfied until he knows everything.

打破碗花花 dǎpòwǎnhuāhuā *bot.* Hubei anemone (Anemone hupehensis)

打气 dǎqì ① inflate; pump up: 给车胎～ inflate (or pump up) a tyre ② bolster up (or boost) the morale; encourage; cheer up: 给他打打气 try to encourage him

打气筒 dǎqìtǒng inflater; tyre pump

打千 dǎqiān salute by going down on one knee

打钎 dǎqiān drill a blasting hole in rock with a hammer and a drill rod

打前失 dǎqiánshī (of horses or mules) stumble

打前站 dǎ qiánzhàn act as an advance party; set out in advance to make arrangements

打钱 dǎqián (formerly, of a street-performer) collect money from the audience

打情骂俏 dǎqíng-màqiào fool around and banter in flirtation

打秋风 dǎqiūfēng try to sponge on people

打趣 dǎqù banter; tease; make fun of

打圈子 dǎquānzi circle: 飞机在机场上空～。 The plane circled over the airfield. / 不要在枝节问题上～。 Don't get bogged down in minor issues.

打拳 dǎquán shadowbox

打群架 dǎ qúnjià engage in a gang fight

打扰 dǎrǎo same as 打搅 dǎjiǎo

打入冷宫 dǎrù lěnggōng banish (a queen or concubine) to the cold palace—consign to limbo; put on the back shelf

打入十八层地狱 dǎrù shíbācéng dìyù banish to the lowest depths of hell—condemn to eternal damnation

打散 dǎsǎn break up; scatter: 把原来的组～重编 break up the existing groups to form new ones

打扫 dǎsǎo sweep; clean: ～房间 clean a room / ～垃圾 sweep away rubbish / ～战场 clean up the battlefield / 把院子～干净 sweep the courtyard clean

打闪 dǎshǎn (of lightning) flash: 打了两个闪。 Lightning flashed twice.

打扇 dǎshàn fan sb.

打食[1] dǎshí (of birds and beasts) seek food

打食[2] dǎshí use medicine to aid digestion or ease constipation

打手 dǎshou hired roughneck (or thug); hatchet man:

充当反动派的～ serve as a hatchet man for the reactionaries

打死老虎 dǎ sǐlǎohǔ　beat a dead tiger—attack sb. who has already lost his power

打算盘 dǎ suànpan　① calculate on an abacus ② calculate; scheme: 打小算盘 be calculating; be petty and scheming / 打错算盘 miscalculate

打算 dǎsuan　plan; intend: 代表团～去延安访问。The delegation plans to visit Yan'an. / 他～当教师。He intends to become a teacher. / 作最坏的～ be prepared for the worst / 各有各的～。Each has a plan of his own. or Each has his own calculations.

打碎 dǎsuì　break into pieces; smash; destroy: 玻璃杯～了。The glass is smashed to pieces. / ～旧的国家机器 smash (or destroy) the old state machinery

打胎 dǎtāi　have an (induced) abortion

打太极拳 dǎ tàijíquán　① practise (or do) taijiquan; do taijiquan exercises (or calisthenics) ② dodge and shirk

打天下 dǎ tiānxià　①(of rebels) seize state power ② win success in a big enterprise

打铁 dǎtiě　forge iron; work as a blacksmith

打铁先得本身硬 dǎtiě xiān děi běnshēn yìng　if you want to work with iron, you must be tough yourself—one must be ideologically sound and professionally competent to do arduous work

打挺儿 dǎtǐngr　dial. bend backwards: 这孩子怕吃药，在妈妈的怀里直～。The child refused to take the medicine and bent backwards in his mother's arms.

打听 dǎting　ask about; inquire about: 跟您～一件事。I'd like to ask you about something. / ～战友的消息 inquire about one's comrades-in-arms

打通 dǎtōng　get through; open up: 电话打不通 be unable to get through (on the telephone) / 两家的院墙～了。An opening has been made in the wall between the two courtyards. / ～思想 straighten out sb.'s thinking; talk sb. round

打通宵 dǎ tōngxiāo　work all night: 打了两个通宵 worked two whole nights

打头[1] dǎtóu　take the lead: 老师傅～，青年人跟着上。The old worker took the lead and the youngsters followed suit.

打头[2] dǎtóu　dial. from the beginning: 咱们再～儿来。Let's do the job all over again.

打头[3] dǎtóu　same as 抽头 chōutóu①

打头炮 dǎ tóupào　fire the first shot; be the first to speak or act

打头阵 dǎ tóuzhèn　fight in the van; spearhead the attack; take the lead

打退 dǎtuì　beat back (or off); repulse: ～敌人的进攻 repulse an enemy attack

打退堂鼓 dǎ tuìtánggǔ　retreat; withdraw: 不能遇到点困难就～呀。You can't give up the moment you run up against difficulty. / 你既然答应了，就别～。You've given your word; don't try to back out.

打弯 dǎwān　① (of limbs) bend ② change one's mind or behaviour ③ talk in a roundabout way

打碗花 dǎwǎnhuā　Chin. med. ivy glorybind (calystegia hederacea)

打围 dǎwéi　encircle and hunt down (animals)

打破 dǎwō　operate a rammer

打先锋 dǎ xiānfēng　fight in the van; be a pioneer

打响 dǎxiǎng　① start shooting; begin to exchange fire: 先头部队～了。The advance detachment has engaged the enemy. / 武昌起义～了推翻封建廷的第一枪。The Wuchang Uprising fired the first shot against the feudal imperial regime. ② win initial success: 这一炮～了，下一步就好办了。Success at this stage will make the next step easier. / ～了春耕第一炮。The spring

ploughing got off to a good start.

打响鼻 dǎ xiǎngbí　(of animals) snort

打消 dǎxiāo　give up (an idea, etc.); dispel (a doubt, etc.): 她～了春节回家的念头。She gave up the idea of going home for the Spring Festival. / ～顾虑 dispel misgivings

打小报告 dǎ xiǎobàogào　be an informer

打旋 dǎxuán　turn round and round; spin

打雪仗 dǎ xuězhàng　have a snowball fight; throw snowballs

打鸭子上架 dǎ yāzi shàng jià　same as 赶鸭子上架 gǎn yāzi shàng jià

打牙 dǎyá　① one's teeth chatter with cold ② crack a joke; jest; make fun of sb.

打牙祭 dǎ yájì　dial. have sth. special to eat

打眼[1] dǎyǎn　punch (or bore) a hole; drill

打眼[2] dǎyǎn　dial. catch the eye; attract attention

打眼[3] dǎyǎn　dial. be cheated when buying goods

打掩护 dǎ yǎnhù　provide cover for; shield: 为主力部队～ provide cover for the main force

打样 dǎyàng　① draw a design ② print. make a proof

打样机 dǎyàngjī　print. proof press

打烊 dǎyàng　dial. (of shops) put up the shutters; close for the night

打药[1] dǎyào　dial. go and buy Chinese medicine

打药[2] dǎyào　① laxative; cathartic; purgative ② ointment for wounds and injuries sold by quacks

打嗝 dǎyē　① hiccup or belch ② be choked by a piece of food

打夜作 dǎ yèzuō　work late into the night; put in extra time at night: 他已经一连打了两个夜作了。He has already worked overtime for two nights running.

打印[1] dǎyìn　put a seal on; stamp

打印[2] dǎyìn　cut a stencil and mimeograph; mimeograph

打油 dǎyóu　① scoop up oil—buy oil (in a small quantity with one's own container) ② dial. extract oil

打油诗 dǎyóushī　doggerel; ragged verse

打游击 dǎyóují　① fight as a guerrilla: 上山～ join the guerrillas in the mountains; wage guerrilla warfare in the mountains ② humor. operate like a guerrilla—work, eat, sleep, etc. at no fixed place

打鱼 dǎyú　try to catch fish; fish: ～为生 fish for a living

打冤家 dǎ yuānjia　blood feud

打圆场 dǎ yuánchǎng　mediate a dispute; smooth things over

打援 dǎyuán　attack (or ambush) enemy reinforcements: 围点～ besiege an enemy stronghold in order to strike at the reinforcements

打杂儿 dǎzár　do odds and ends: 我不会做菜，只能在厨房打打杂儿。I can't cook, so I can only do odds and ends in the kitchen.

打砸抢 dǎ-zá-qiǎng　beating, smashing and looting: 严禁～。Acts of smashing and grabbing are strictly forbidden. / ～者 smash-and-grabber

打早 dǎzǎo　inf. ① long ago: 我～就想来看你的。I wanted to come and see you a long time ago. ② as early as possible; at the first opportunity: 还是～动身的好。Better start as early as possible.

打斋 dǎzhāi　(of a Buddhist monk) beg for food from door to door

打颤 dǎzhàn　(also 打战 dǎzhàn) shiver; tremble; shudder: 浑身～ shiver all over / 冷得我直～。I was so cold that I kept shivering.

打仗 dǎzhàng　fight; go to war; make war

打招呼 dǎ zhāohu　① greet sb.; say hello: 他俩见面不～，仿佛谁也不认得谁。The two of them never greet

each other and behave as if they were strangers. ②
notify; let sb. know: 你什么时候去开封，给我打个招呼。
When you go to Kaifeng, please let me know. ③ warn;
remind: 事先已跟他们打过招呼了。I've already warned
them.

打照面儿 dǎ zhàomiànr ① meet unexpectedly (*or* by
chance); have a chance encounter: 那天我在街上跟他
打了个照面儿。I bumped into him the other day in the
street. ② show one's face; make a brief appearance: 她
打了个照面儿就走了。She just showed her face and
left.

打折扣 dǎ zhékòu ① sell at a discount; give a discount
② fall short of a requirement or promise: 说到做到，
不～ carry out one's pledge to the letter

打着灯笼没处找 dǎzhe dēnglong méi chù zhǎo　not to be
found even with a lantern—hard to come by; rare

打针 dǎzhēn　give or have an injection

打制 dǎzhì　make (by hammering, chipping, etc.): ～镰
刀 make sickles

打制石器 dǎzhì shíqì　*archaeol.*　chipped stone implement

打肿脸充胖子 dǎzhǒngliǎn chōng pàngzi　slap one's face
until it's swollen in an effort to look imposing—puff
oneself up to one's own cost

打中 dǎzhòng　hit the mark (*or* target); hit: ～一艘敌舰
hit an enemy vessel / ～要害 hit on the vital spot; hit
where it really hurts

打皱 dǎzhòu　*dial.*　crumple; crease

打主意 dǎ zhǔyì ① think of a plan; evolve an idea: 打
定主意 make up one's mind / 打错主意 miscalculate;
make a wrong decision ② try to obtain; seek: 他们正在
打你的主意，要你帮忙呢。They are thinking of asking
you to help.

打住 dǎzhù　come to a halt; (in speech or writing)
stop: 他说到这儿突然～了。He suddenly stopped when
he came to that point.

打转 dǎzhuàn　spin; rotate; revolve: 卡车轮子在烂泥里
直～。The truck's wheels kept spinning in the mud. /
不要老在个人利益的小圈子里～。Don't keep going
round and round pursuing your own selfish interests.

打桩 dǎzhuāng　pile driving; piling

打桩机 dǎzhuāngjī　pile driver

打字 dǎzì　typewrite; type

打字带 dǎzìdài　typewriter ribbon

打字稿 dǎzìgǎo　typescript

打字机 dǎzìjī　typewriter

打字员 dǎzìyuán　typist

打字纸 dǎzìzhǐ　typing-paper

打总儿 dǎzǒngr　*inf.*　at one go; in a batch: ～算帐 settle an account once and for all

打嘴 dǎzuǐ ① slap sb.'s face ② *dial.*　slap one's own
face—fail to make good one's boast

打嘴巴 dǎ zuǐba　slap sb.'s face: 我打了他一嘴巴。I
gave him a slap on the cheek. / 打自己的嘴巴 slap
one's own face—be self-contradictory

打坐 dǎzuò　(of a Buddhist or Taoist monk) sit in
meditation

dà

大¹　dà ① big; large; great: ～城市 big city / ～眼
睛 big eyes / ～救星 great liberator / 这张照片不够～。
The picture isn't large enough. ② heavy (rain, etc.);
strong (wind, etc.): 雪下得很～。The snow is falling
heavily. / 风太～，你没法放风筝。The wind is too
strong to fly your kite. / 外面风～。It's blowing hard. /
团结起来力量～。Unity is strength. ③ loud: 声音太～

too loud / 收音机开～点。Turn the radio up a bit louder. ④ general; main; major: ～马路 main street / ～问
题 major issue; big problem / ～手术 major operation /
～反攻 general counteroffensive ⑤ size: 那间屋子有这
间两个～。That room is twice the size of this one. / 你
穿多～的鞋? What size shoes do you wear? ⑥ age: 你
的孩子多～了? How old is your child? / 他～我两岁。
He's two years my senior. ⑦ *adv.*　greatly; fully: ～长
中国人民的志气 greatly heighten the morale of the
Chinese people / ～笑 laugh heartily / 天已～亮。It's
already broad daylight. ⑧ *adv.*　in a big way; on a big
(*or* large) scale; with all-out efforts; vigorously: ～删～
改 do a thorough job in revising / ～搞农田水利 go all
out with irrigation and water conservancy ⑨ eldest: ～
哥 eldest brother / ～房 senior branch of a family ⑩
honor.　your: ～札 your letter / ～作 your writing ⑪
(used before a time word, etc. to show emphasis): ～
清早 early in the morning ⑫ see 不大 bùdà

大²　dà　*dial.* ① father ② father's brother; uncle
——see also dài

大白¹ dàbái　*dial.*　whiting: ～浆 whitewash

大白² dàbái　come out; become known: 真相已～于天
下。The truth has become known to all.

大白菜 dàbáicài　Chinese cabbage

大白话 dàbáihuà　colloquial speech

大白天 dàbáitiān　broad daylight; daytime

大白天说梦话 dàbáitiān shuō mènghuà　daydream talk;
sheer nonsense

大伯子 dàbǎizi　*inf.*　husband's elder brother; brother-
in-law

大败 dàbài ① defeat utterly; put to rout: ～敌军 inflict
a crushing defeat on the enemy ② suffer a crushing
defeat

大班¹ dàbān　*dial.*　big boss (a term for the manager
of a foreign firm in old China); comprador; *taipan*

大班² dàbān　the top class in a kindergarten

大阪 Dàbǎn　Osaka

大板车 dàbǎnchē　large flatbed tricycle

大办 dàbàn　go in for sth. in a big way (*or* on a big
scale): ～农业 go in for agriculture in a big way; make
great efforts to develop agriculture

大半 dàbàn　*adv.* ① more than half; the greater part;
most; more often than not: ～天 the greater part of a
day; most of the day / 这个突击队的队员～是青年人。
Most of the members of this shock team are young. ②
most probably; most likely: 他～不来了。Most probably
he isn't coming. / 这火车～要晚点了。The train will
most likely be late.

大棒 dàbàng　big stick—means of intimidation: "～加
胡萝卜"政策 the stick-and-carrot policy; the policy of
the stick and the carrot

大包干 dàbāogān　all-round contract system

大本营 dàběnyíng ① supreme headquarters ② base
camp: 登山队～ the base camp of a mountaineering
expedition

大笔 dàbǐ ① pen: ～一挥 with one stroke of the pen
② *honor.*　your writing; your handwriting: 这是您的～
吧? Isn't this your handwriting?

大笔如椽 dàbǐ rú chuán　a writing brush as big as a rafter—powerful strokes or forceful writing

大便 dàbiàn ① defecate; have a bowel movement; shit:
～不通 (suffer from) constipation / 通～ ease constipation ② stool; human excrement; shit; faeces: 去化验～
have one's stool examined

大辩论 dàbiànlùn　great (*or* mass) debate

大兵 dàbīng　common soldier

大兵团 dàbīngtuán　large troop formation: ～作战 large
formation warfare; grand (*or* major) tactics

大饼　dàbǐng　a kind of large flatbread

大伯　dàbó　① father's elder brother; uncle ② uncle (a polite form of address for an elderly man)

大脖子病　dàbózibìng　*dial.*　goitre

大不　dàbù　*adv.*　very much not: ～相同 differ widely; be very different / 有没有准备～一样。It makes a world of difference whether preparations are made or not. / 家里的光景已经～如前。The family is in a greatly reduced state compared with what it used to be.

大不列颠　Dàbùlièdiān　Great Britain

大不了　dàbuliǎo　① at the worst; if the worst comes to the worst: ～我们走着回去。If the worst comes to the worst, we'll walk back. ② (usu. used in the negative) alarming; serious: 划破点皮, 没有什么～的。It's nothing serious, just a scratch.

大步流星　dàbù liú xīng　with vigorous strides: 他在这条小路上～地走着。He strode along the path.

大部　dàbù　the greater part: 歼敌～ annihilate the greater part of the enemy

大部头　dàbùtóu　a voluminous work

大材小用　dàcái xiǎoyòng　large material put to small use—one's talent wasted on a petty job; not do justice to sb.'s talents

大菜　dàcài　① the last course of a feast (usu. a whole chicken or duck, or a leg of pork) ② *old*　Western-style food

大餐　dàcān　① a sumptuous meal ② Western-style food

大肠　dàcháng　*physiol.*　large intestine

大肠杆菌　dàcháng gǎnjūn　colon bacillus

大氅　dàchǎng　overcoat; cloak; cape

大潮　dàcháo　spring tide

大车¹　dàchē　cart

大车²　dàchē　a respectful term for an engine driver or the chief engineer of a ship

大车店　dàchēdiàn　an inn for carters

大臣　dàchén　minister (of a monarchy)

大成殿　dàchéngdiàn　the main hall of a Confucian temple

大乘　dàchéng　Great Vehicle (a school of Buddhism); Mahayana

大吃大喝　dàchī-dàhē　(also 大吃八喝 dàchī-bāhē) eat and drink to one's heart's content; eat and drink extravagantly: 反对～, 注意节约。Oppose extravagant eating and drinking and pay attention to thrift and economy.

大吃一惊　dà chī yī jīng　be greatly surprised; be quite taken aback

大冲　dàchōng　*astron.*　favourable opposition

大虫　dàchóng　*dial.*　tiger

大出血　dàchūxuè　*med.*　massive haemorrhage

大处落墨　dàchù luòmò　(also 大处着墨 dàchù zhuómò) concentrate on the key points

大处着眼, 小处着手　dàchù zhuóyǎn, xiǎochù zhuóshǒu　keep the general goal in sight while taking hold of the daily tasks

大吹大擂　dàchuī-dàlèi　make a great fanfare; make a big noise; beat the drum

大吹法螺　dà chuī fǎluó　blow one's own trumpet; talk big; brag

大锤　dàchuí　sledgehammer

大春　dàchūn　① spring ② same as 大春作物 dàchūn zuòwù

大春作物　dàchūn zuòwù　crops sown in spring (rice, corn, etc.)

大醇小疵　dàchún-xiǎocī　sound on the whole though defective in details

大词　dàcí　*log.*　major term

大慈大悲　dàcí-dàbēi　infinitely compassionate and merciful

大葱　dàcōng　green Chinese onion

大错特错　dàcuò tècuò　completely mistaken; absolutely wrong

大打出手　dà dǎ chūshǒu　come to blows; get into a fight

大大　dàdà　*adv.*　greatly; enormously: 生产效率～提高。Productivity has risen greatly. / 革命～推动了社会生产力的发展。The revolution has given an enormous impetus to the social productive forces. / 今年的棉花产量～超过了去年。This year's cotton production exceeded last year's by a big margin.

大…大…　dà…dà…　(used before nouns, verbs, or adjectives to show a high degree): 大鱼大肉 plenty of meat and fish; rich food / 大红大绿 loud colours / 大吵大闹 kick up a row ; make a scene

大大咧咧　dàdàliēliē　*dial.*　careless; casual: 别看他～的, 什么事他都很在心。He seems unconcerned, but nothing escapes his attention.

大大落落　dàdaluōluō　*dial.*　natural and poised

大袋鼠　dàdàishǔ　kangaroo

大胆　dàdǎn　bold; daring; audacious: ～的革新 a bold innovation / ～! How dare you!

大刀　dàdāo　broadsword

大刀阔斧　dàdāo-kuòfǔ　bold and resolute; drastic: ～地进行改革 carry out drastic reforms

大道　dàdào　① main road ② the way of justice ③ the Great Tao; the Great Way: ～之行也, 天下为公。《礼记》When the Great Tao prevailed, the whole world was one community.

大道理　dàdàolǐ　major principle; general principle; great truth: 这些～人人都懂, 真正做到可不容易啊! These general principles are widely known, but it isn't easy to live up to them. / 小道理要服从～。Minor principles should be subordinated to major ones.

大灯　dàdēng　headlight (of a car)

大敌　dàdí　formidable enemy; archenemy

大敌当前　dàdí dāng qián　a formidable enemy stands before one; be faced with a formidable foe

大抵　dàdǐ　*adv.*　generally speaking; in the main; on the whole: ～相同 basically the same; more or less alike

大地　dàdì　earth; mother earth: 阳光普照～。The sun illuminates every corner of the land. / ～回春。Spring returns to the earth. *or* Spring is here again. / 走遍祖国～ travel all over the land

大地测量学　dàdì cèliángxué　geodesy

大地构造学　dàdì gòuzàoxué　geotectology; tectonics

大地水准面　dàdì shuǐzhǔnmiàn　geoid

大典　dàdiǎn　① grand ceremony: 开国～ founding ceremony (of a state) ② a body of classical writings; canon: 《永乐～》 Yongle Canon

大殿　dàdiàn　① audience hall ② main hall of a Buddhist temple

大调　dàdiào　*mus.*　major: C～ 奏鸣曲 sonata in C major

大动干戈　dà dòng gāngē　go to war; get into a fight

大动肝火　dà dòng gānhuǒ　fly into a rage; be furious; be very angry

大动脉　dàdòngmài　① *physiol.*　main artery; aorta ② main line of communication; main communications artery: 南北交通的～ the main artery of communications between north and south

大豆　dàdòu　soybean; soya bean

大都　dàdū　*adv.*　for the most part; mostly: 这些诗歌～是工人写的。Most of these poems were written by workers. / 我发现这个作曲家的音乐～还悦耳动听。In the main, I find this composer's music pleasant listening.

大肚子　dàdùzi　*inf.*　① pregnant ② big eater ③

potbelly

大度 dàdù *formal* magnanimous: 豁达大度 huòdá dàdù

大度包容 dàdù bāoróng regard with kindly tolerance; be magnanimous and tolerant; be magnanimous

大端 dàduān *formal* main aspects (*or* features); salient points: 仅举其～ merely point out the main features

大队 dàduì ① a military unit corresponding to the battalion or regiment; group ② production brigade (of a rural people's commune); brigade ③ a large body of: ～人马 a large contingent of troops; a large body of marchers, paraders, etc.

大多 dàduō *adv.* for the most part; mostly: 出席大会的代表～是先进工作者。 The representatives present at the meeting are mostly advanced workers. / 树上的苹果～已经成熟。 Most of the apples on the tree have ripened. / 现代音乐～难以欣赏。 Most modern music is difficult to appreciate. / 这次测验, 学生的成绩～很好。 In the main, the pupils did well on the test.

大多数 dàduōshù great majority; vast majority; the bulk: 团结～ unite with the great majority / 人口的～ the bulk of the population / 为中国和世界的～人谋利益 work for the interests of the vast majority of the people of China and of the whole world

大而化之 dà ér huà zhī carelessly; casually; sloppily

大而无当 dà ér wú dàng large but impractical; unwieldy: ～的计划 a grandiose but impractical plan

大发雷霆 dà fā léitíng be furious; fly into a rage; bawl at sb. angrily: 他一, 跳起脚来骂我。 He flew into a rage and jumped up and shouted at me.

大法 dàfǎ fundamental laws and principles (of a state); constitution

大凡 dàfán *adv.* generally; in most cases: ～坚持锻炼的, 身体抵抗力都比较强。 Generally those who exercise regularly have high resistance to disease.

大方¹ dàfāng *formal* expert; scholar: 贻笑大方 yíxiào dàfāng

大方² dàfāng a kind of green tea

大方 dàfang ① generous; liberal ② natural and poised; easy; unaffected: 举止～ have an easy manner; have poise; carry oneself with ease and confidence ③ in good taste; tasteful: 这种料子的颜色和花样很～。 The pattern and colour of this fabric are in good taste.

大方向 dàfāngxiàng general orientation

大方之家 dàfāng zhī jiā scholar; a learned man; expert

大放厥词 dà fàng jué cí talk a lot of nonsense; spout a stream of empty rhetoric

大分子 dàfēnzǐ *chem.* macromolecule

大粪 dàfèn human excrement; night soil

大风 dàfēng ① *meteorol.* fresh gale ② gale; strong wind: 外面刮着～。 There's a gale blowing. *or* It's blowing hard.

大风大浪 dàfēng-dàlàng wind and waves; great storms: 人类社会是从～中发展起来的。 It is amid great storms that human society progresses.

大风子 dàfēngzǐ *bot.* chaulmoogra (*Hydnocarpus anthelmintica*): ～油 chaulmoogra oil

大夫 dàfū a senior official in feudal China ——see also 大夫 dàifu

大伏天 dàfútiān *inf.* the *fu* days—the hottest days of the year ——see also 三伏 sānfú

大副 dàfù first (*or* chief) mate; mate; chief officer

大腹贾 dàfùgǔ potbellied merchant; rich merchant

大腹皮 dàfùpí *Chin. med.* the shell of areca nut

大腹便便 dàfù piánpián potbellied; big-bellied

大概 dàgài ① general idea; broad outline: 我只知道个～。 I have only a general idea. / 我～跟他说了说。 I told him briefly. ② general; rough; approximate: 作一

个～的分析 make a general analysis / ～的数字 an approximate figure / ～的估计 a rough estimate ③ *adv.* probably; most likely; presumably: 会议～要延期。 The meeting will probably be postponed. / 你～知道他吧。 Presumably you know him. / ～将有五百人出席。 There will be approximately 500 people present.

大概其 dàgàiqí *dial.* general; rough: 这本书我没细看, 只～翻了翻。 I didn't read the book carefully; I only skimmed through it. / 他说了半天, 我只听了个～。 He talked at length, but I only caught the general idea.

大干 dàgàn work energetically; go all out; make an all-out effort

大干快上 dàgàn-kuàishàng get going and go all out

大纲 dàgāng outline: 世界史～ an outline history of the world / 《土地法～》 Outline Land Law

大哥 dàgē ① eldest brother ② elder brother (a polite form of address for a man about one's own age)

大哥大 dàgēdà ① popular name for 移动电话 yídòng diànhuà ② *inf.* man with power; boss

大革命 dàgémìng ① great revolution: 法国～ the French Revolution ② the Great Revolution in China (1924–1927)

大公 dàgōng grand duke

大公国 dàgōngguó grand duchy

大公无私 dàgōng-wúsī ① selfless; unselfish ② perfectly impartial

大功 dàgōng great merit; extraordinary service: 立了～ have performed exceptionally meritorious services

大功告成 dàgōng gàochéng be brought to successful completion; be accomplished; be crowned with success

大功率 dàgōnglǜ *elec.* high-power: ～可控硅 high-power silicon controlled rectifier

大恭 dàgōng *formal* faeces: 出～ empty the bowels

大姑子 dàgūzi *inf.* husband's elder sister; sister-in-law

大骨节病 dàgǔjiébìng Kaschin-Beck disease

大鼓 dàgǔ ① *mus.* bass drum ② dagu, versified story sung to the accompaniment of a small drum and other instruments

大褂 dàguà unlined long gown

大关 dàguān ① an important pass; a pass of vital importance ② high point; the highest level: 工业总产值已突破了百万元～。 The gross value of industrial output has reached a new high of 1,000,000 *yuan*.

大观 dàguān grand sight; magnificent spectacle: 蔚为大观 wèi wéi dàguān

大管 dàguǎn *mus.* bassoon

大规模 dàguīmó large-scale; extensive; massive; mass: ～生产 large-scale production / ～兴修水利 launch a large-scale (*or* extensive) water conservancy project / ～进攻 launch a massive attack / 举行～罢工 stage a massive strike / ～毁灭性武器 weapon of mass destruction

大锅饭 dàguōfàn food prepared in a large canteen cauldron; mess ——see also 吃大锅饭 chī dàguōfàn

大国沙文主义 dàguóshāwénzhǔyì (also 大国主义 dàguózhǔyì) great-nation chauvinism

大过 dàguò serious offence: 记～一次 record a serious mistake

大海捞针 dàhǎi lāo zhēn fish for a needle in the ocean; look for a needle in a haystack

大寒 Dàhán ① Greater Cold—the last of the 24 solar terms ② the day marking the beginning of the last solar term (Jan. 20 or 21), after which the weather grows slowly warmer) ——see also 节气 jiéqì, 二十四节气 èrshí sì jiéqì

大喊大叫 dàhǎn-dàjiào ① shout at the top of one's

voice ② conduct vigorous propaganda

大汉 dàhàn big (*or* hefty, burly) fellow

大汉族主义 dà-Hànzúzhǔyì Han chauvinism

大旱望云霓 dàhàn wàng yúnní long for a rain cloud during a drought—look forward to relief from distress

大好 dàhǎo very good; excellent: 形势～。The situation is very good. / ～时机 opportune moment; golden opportunity; finest hour

大好河山 dàhǎo héshān beautiful rivers and mountains (of a country); one's beloved country

大号 dàhào ① large size: ～的鞋 large-size shoes ② *mus.* tuba; bass horn ③ *honor.* your (given) name

大合唱 dàhéchàng cantata; chorus:《黄河～》The Yellow River Cantata

大河 dàhé ① great river ② the Mighty River (a literary name for 黄河)

大河有水小河满，大河无水小河干 dàhé yǒu shuǐ xiǎohé mǎn, dàhé wú shuǐ xiǎohé gān the small streams rise when the main stream is high; when the main stream is low, the small streams run dry—individual well-being depends on collective prosperity

大亨 dàhēng *old* big shot; bigwig; magnate

大轰大嗡 dàhōng-dàwēng make a terrific din; raise a hue and cry

大红 dàhóng bright red; scarlet

大后方 dàhòufāng ① rear area ② the area under KMT rule during the War of Resistance Against Japan

大后年 dàhòunián three years from now

大后天 dàhòutiān (also 大后儿 dàhòur) three days from now

大户 dàhù ① rich and influential family ② large family——see also 卖大户 mài dàhù

大花脸 dàhuāliǎn big flowery face (a division of the flowery-face role 花脸, which requires more skill in singing than in acting including roles like the black face 黑头)

大话 dàhuà big (*or* tall) talk; boast; bragging: 说～ talk big; brag

大荒 dàhuāng ① a great famine: ～之年 a year of famine ② vast tracts of wasteland: 北大荒 Běidàhuāng

大黄蜂 dàhuángfēng hornet

大黄鱼 dàhuángyú large yellow croaker

大茴香 dàhuíxiāng *bot.* anise; star anise

大会 dàhuì ① plenary session; general membership meeting: 党支部～ a general membership meeting of a Party branch ② mass meeting; mass rally: 庆祝～ a celebration meeting

大伙儿 dàhuǒr (also 大家伙儿 dàjiāhuǒr) *inf.* we all; you all; everybody

大祸临头 dàhuò líntóu disaster is imminent; disaster is hanging over one

大惑不解 dà huò bù jiě be extremely puzzled; be unable to make head or tail of sth.

大吉 dàjí ① very lucky; highly auspicious: 万事大吉 wànshì dàjí ② (used ironically in)关门大吉 guānmén dàjí; 溜之大吉 liū zhī dàjí

大吉大利 dàjí-dàlì good luck and great prosperity (an expression of good wishes)

大戟 dàjí *Chin. med.* the root of Beijing euphorbia (*Euphorbia pekinensis*)

大计 dàjì a major programme of lasting importance; a matter of fundamental importance: 共商～ discuss matters of vital importance

大蓟 dàjì *bot.* setose thistle (*Cephalanoplos setosum*)

大家[1] dàjiā ① a great master; authority: 书法～ a great master of calligraphy; a noted calligrapher ② an old and well-known family; a distinguished (*or* prominent) family

大家[2] dàjiā all; everybody: ～知道，中国是一个发展中国家。As everybody knows, China is a developing country. / ～的事～管。Everybody's business should be everybody's responsibility. / 我报告～一个好消息。I have some good news for you all. / ～请坐好，现在开会了。Take your seats, please. Let's start the meeting. / 你给～弹肖邦的曲子。Please play Chopin for us. / 明天咱们～开个会谈谈。We'll have a meeting to discuss it tomorrow.

大家闺秀 dàjiā guīxiù a girl from a good family; a well-bred girl; lady

大家庭 dàjiātíng big family; community: 李家是个～，有三代人。The Lis are a big family with three generations.

大驾 dàjià *honor.* your good self—you

大建 dàjiàn a lunar month of 30 days

大江 dàjiāng ① a great river ② the Great River (a literary name for 长江): ～东去。The Great River flows to the east.

大将 dàjiàng ① senior general ② high-ranking officer

大脚 dàjiǎo unbound or natural feet (opp. 小脚 "bound feet")

大教堂 dàjiàotáng cathedral

大街 dàjiē main street; street: 逛～ go window-shopping; stroll around the streets

大街小巷 dàjiē-xiǎoxiàng streets and lanes: ～彩旗飘扬。The streets and lanes are decked with bunting.

大节 dàjié political integrity

大捷 dàjié great victory

大姐 dàjiě ① eldest sister ② elder sister (a polite form of address for a woman about one's own age)

大姐大 dàjiědà *inf.* woman with powr; boss

大解 dàjiě go to the lavatory (to defecate); have a bowel movement

大襟 dàjīn the front of a Chinese garment which buttons on the right

大尽 dàjìn same as 大建 dàjiàn

大惊失色 dàjīng shīsè turn pale with fright

大惊小怪 dàjīng-xiǎoguài be surprised or alarmed at sth. quite normal; make a fuss about nothing: 有什么值得～的? What's there to be surprised at? / 是什么要紧的事，这么～! Why get so excited over a little thing like this?

大净 dàjìng *Islam* Ghusl

大静脉 dàjìngmài *physiol.* vena cava

大舅子 dàjiùzi *inf.* wife's elder brother; brother-in-law

大局 dàjú overall (*or* general, whole) situation: 事关～。It's an issue that concerns the overall situation. / ～已定。The outcome is a foregone conclusion.

大举 dàjǔ carry out (a military operation) on a large scale: ～进攻 mount a large-scale offensive; attack in force

大军 dàjūn ① main forces; army: 我们是先头部队，～随后就到。We are the advance detachment. The main forces will be here soon. / ～过处，秋毫无犯。Wherever the troops went, they never infringed on the people's interests. ② large contingent: 筑路～ a large contingent of road builders / 百万～ an army a million strong

大卡 dàkǎ *phys.* kilocalorie; large (*or* great) calorie

大楷 dàkǎi ① regular script in big characters, as used in Chinese calligraphy exercises ② block letters; blockwriting

大考 dàkǎo end-of-term examination; final exam

大可不必 dà kě bùbì not at all necessary: 其实这种担心～。As a matter of fact there's no need to worry about it at all.

大客车 dàkèchē (also 大轿车 dàjiàochē) bus; coach

大课 dàkè a lecture given to a large number of students; enlarged class

大口径 dàkǒujìng heavy-calibre: ～机枪 heavy-calibre

machine gun

大跨径桥 dàkuàjìngqiáo long-span bridge

大快人心 dà kuài rénxīn (usu. of the punishment of an evil-doer) affording general satisfaction; most gratifying to the people; to the immense satisfaction of the people

大块头 dàkuàitóu *dial.* a fat person; a person of big build; fatty

大块文章 dàkuài wénzhāng a long article

大款 dàkuǎn *inf.* tycoon; moneybags

大牢 dàláo *inf.* prison; jail

大老粗 dàlǎocū uncouth fellow; uneducated person; rough and ready fellow

大老远 dàlǎoyuǎn *inf.* very far away

大礼拜 dàlǐbài an extended Sunday—an alternate Sunday on which one has a day off; a fortnightly holiday: 休～have every other Sunday off

大理石 dàlǐshí marble

大力 dàlì energetic; vigorous: ～支援农业 give energetic support to agriculture / ～发展教育事业 devote major efforts to developing education

大力士 dàlìshì a man of unusual strength, esp. a weight-lifter

大丽花 dàlìhuā dahlia

大殓 dàliàn encoffining ceremony

大梁 dàliáng ridgepole; ridgepiece

大量 dàliàng ① a large number; a great quantity: 为国家积累～资金 accumulate large funds for the state / ～生产拖拉机 mass-produce tractors / ～杀伤敌人 inflict heavy casualties on the enemy / 收集～科学资料 collect a vast amount of scientific data / ～财富 enormous wealth; large fortune / ～事实 a host of facts / ～库存 huge stocks ② generous; magnanimous: 宽宏大量 kuānhóng-dàliàng

大料 dàliào *dial.* aniseed

大龄未婚青年 dàlíng wèihūn qīngnián a single man or woman of around thirty who is in want of a spouse

大楼 dàlóu multi-storied building: 居民～ apartment house; block of flats

大陆 dàlù continent; mainland: 中国～ the mainland of China

大陆架 dàlùjià continental shelf

大陆隆 dàlùlóng *geol.* continental rise

大陆漂移 dàlù piāoyí continental drift: ～说 the theory of continental drift

大陆坡 dàlùpō continental slope

大陆性气候 dàlùxìng qìhòu continental climate

大路 dàlù main road; highway

大路货 dàlùhuò popular goods of dependable quality

大略 dàlüè ① general idea; broad outline: 我只知道个～。I have only a general idea. / 时间不多了，你～说说吧。There isn't much time left. Could you speak just briefly? ② bold vision: 雄才大略 xióngcái-dàlüè ③ same as 大致 dàzhì

大妈 dàmā ① father's elder brother's wife; aunt ② aunt (an affectionate or respectful form of address for an elderly woman)

大麻 dàmá ① hemp ② marijuana

大麻哈鱼 dàmáhāyú (also 大马哈鱼 dàmǎhāyú) chum salmon; dog salmon

大麦 dàmài barley

大忙 dàmáng very busy: ～季节 rush (*or* busy) season

大忙人 dàmángrén busy bee

大猫熊 dàmāoxióng giant panda

大毛 dàmáo long-haired pelt

大帽子 dàmàozi a big hat—an exaggerated epithet used to categorize a person; unwarranted charge; political label: 别拿～压人。Don't you try to intimidate

people by pinning political labels on them

大媒 dàméi *inf.* matchmaker; go-between

大门 dàmén entrance (*or* front) door; gate

大米 dàmǐ (husked) rice

大面儿 dàmiànr *dial.* general appearance; surface: ～上还过得去。It's basically all right.

大民主 dàmínzhǔ great (*or* extensive) democracy

大民族主义 dàmínzúzhǔyì big-nationality chauvinism

大名 dàmíng ① one's formal personal name ② *honor.* your (given) name

大名鼎鼎 dàmíng dǐngdǐng famous; celebrated; well-known: 他已经是～的人物了。He has become a celebrity.

大鸣大放 dàmíng-dàfàng free airing of views

大螟 dàmíng pink rice borer (Sesamia inferens)

大谬不然 dà miù bùrán entirely wrong; grossly mistaken

大模大样 dàmú-dàyàng in an ostentatious manner; with a swagger: 我看见他穿着一身新衣服，～地在街上走。I saw him swaggering along the street in his new suit.

大姆哥 dàmugē *dial.* thumb

大姆指 dàmuzhǐ *inf.* thumb: 竖起～叫好 hold up one's thumb in approval

大拿 dànά *inf.* ① person with power; boss ② authority; expert: 技术～ a technical expert

大难 dànàn catastrophe; disaster

大难不死，必有后福 dànàn bù sǐ, bì yǒu hòufú after surviving a great disaster, one is bound to have good fortune in later years

大难临头 dànàn líntóu with great disaster hanging over one; be faced with imminent disaster

大脑 dànǎo *physiol.* cerebrum

大脑半球 dànǎo bànqiú cerebral hemisphere

大脑脚 dànǎojiǎo cerebral peduncle

大脑皮层 dànǎo pícéng cerebral cortex

大鲵 dàní *zool.* giant salamander

大逆不道 dà nì bù dào treason and heresy; worst offence; greatest outrage

大年 dànián ① good year; bumper year; (for fruit trees) on-year ② a lunar year in which the last month has 30 days ③ the Spring Festival

大年初一 dàniánchūyī *inf.* first day of the lunar year; lunar New Year's Day

大年夜 dàniányè *dial.* lunar New Year's Eve

大娘 dàniáng *inf.* ① wife of father's elder brother; aunt ② aunt (a respectful form of address used for an elderly woman)

大排行 dà páiháng order of seniority among cousins in an extended family or descendants of the same paternal grandfather

大炮 dàpào ① artillery; big gun; cannon ② *inf.* one who speaks boastfully or forcefully; one who noisily overstates things

大批 dàpī ① large quantities (*or* numbers, amounts) of: ～轻工业品运往农村。Large quantities of light industrial products are transported to the countryside. / ～干部深入基层。Large numbers of cadres go to the grass-roots level. ② mass criticism

大批判 dàpīpàn mass criticism; mass criticism and repudiation

大辟 dàpì capital punishment (in feudal times); decapitation ——see also 五刑 wǔxíng

大藻 dàpiāo *bot.* water lettuce; water cabbage

大谱儿 dàpǔr general idea: 究竟怎么做，心里应该先有个～。Before you start anything, you ought to have a general idea of what you're going to do.

大谱表 dàpǔbiǎo *mus.* great stave

大气 dàqì ① *meterol.* atmosphere; air ② heavy

breathing: 跑得直喘～ breathe heavily from running / 吓得连～也不敢出 catch (or hold) one's breath in fear

大气层 dàqìcéng atmospheric layer; atmosphere

大气电 dàqìdiàn atmospheric electricity

大气干扰 dàqì gānrǎo atmospheric interference

大气候 dàqìhòu ① *meterol.* macroclimate ② general tendency; general political climate

大气环流 dàqì huánliú atmospheric circulation; general circulation of atmosphere

大气科学 dàqì kēxué atmospheric sciences

大气磅礴 dàqì pángbó of great momentum; powerful; grand and magnificent

大气污染 dàqì wūrǎn air (or atmospheric) pollution

大气压 dàqìyā atmospheric pressure; atmosphere

大气折射 dàqì zhéshè atmospheric (or astronomical) refraction

大器 dàqì *formal* ① treasure ② a man of great talent

大器晚成 dàqì wǎn chéng great vessels take years to produce—great minds mature slowly

大千世界 dàqiān shìjiè the boundless universe

大前年 dàqiánnián three years ago

大前提 dàqiántí *log.* major premise

大前天 dàqiántiān (also 大前儿 dàqiánr) three days ago

大钳 dàqián tongs

大巧若拙 dàqiǎo ruò zhuō great skill seems awkward

大庆 dàqìng ① grand celebration of an important event; great occasion: 十年～ the festive occasion of the 10th anniversary ② the birthday of an old person who commands respect: 七十～ seventieth birthday ③ (Dàqìng) Daqing Oilfield

大秋 dàqiū ① harvest season in autumn ② crops harvested in autumn; autumn harvest

大秋作物 dàqiū zuòwù crops sown in spring and reaped in autumn; autumn-harvested crops

大曲 dàqū ① yeast for making hard liquor ② a hard liquor made with such yeast

大权 dàquán power over major issues; authority: ～在握 hold power in one's hands

大权独揽 dàquán dú lǎn centralize power in one person's hands; have sole power; arrogate all authority to oneself

大权旁落 dàquán pángluò lose one's power to others (usu. one's subordinates)

大犬座 Dàquǎnzuò *astron.* Canis Major

大人 dàrén *old honor.* (used in a letter to address one's parents or people of an older generation): 父亲～ Dear Father

大人 dàren ① adult; grown-up ② *old* Your Excellency or His Excellency

大人物 dàrénwù important person; great personage; big shot; VIP

大肉 dàròu pork

大扫除 dàsǎochú general cleaning; thorough cleanup: 节日～ thorough cleanup before a holiday

大嫂 dàsǎo ① eldest brother's wife; sister-in-law ② elder sister (a polite form of address for a woman about one's age)

大杀风景 dà shā fēngjǐng (also 大煞风景 dàshā fēngjǐng) utterly spoil the fun

大厦 dàshà ① large building ② mansions (used in names of large buildings): 上海～ Shanghai Mansions

大厦将倾 dàshà jiāngqīng a great mansion on the point of collapse—the situation is hopeless

大少爷 dàshàoye ① eldest son (of a rich family) ② a spoilt son of a rich family; spendthrift: ～作风 behaviour typical of the spoilt son of a rich family; extravagant ways

大舌头 dàshétou *inf.* a thick-tongued person; one who lisps; lisper

大赦 dàshè amnesty; general pardon

大婶儿 dàshěnr aunt (an affectionate or respectful form of address for a woman about one's mother's age)

大声疾呼 dàshēng jíhū raise a cry of warning; loudly appeal to the public: 我们要～，唤醒这些同志: 速速改变保守思想! To awaken these comrades we must raise our voices and cry out to them: get rid of your consevative ideas without delay!

大牲口 dàshēngkou (also 大牲畜 dàshēngchù) draught animal

大失所望 dàshī suǒ wàng greatly disappointed; to one's great disappointment

大师 dàshī ① great master; master: 国画～ a great master of traditional Chinese painting ② Great Master, a courtesy title used to address a Buddhist monk

大师傅 dàshīfu cook; chef

大使 dàshǐ ambassador: 特命全权～ ambassador extraordinary and plenipotentiary

大使馆 dàshǐguǎn embassy

大使级会谈 dàshǐjí huìtán talks at ambassadorial level; ambassadorial talks

大使衔 dàshǐxián ambassadorial rank

大事 dàshì ① great (or major) event; important matter; major issue: 头等～ a matter of prime (or paramount) importance / 关心国家～ concern oneself with affairs of state / 当前国际政治中的一件～ a major event in current international politics / 完成了一桩～ have accomplished an important task / 抓～ grasp major issues / 你们要把它作为一件～去做。 You should make this a top priority. ② overall (or general) situation: ～不好。 A disaster is imminent. ③ in a big way: ～渲染 enormously exaggerate; play up

大事记 dàshìjì chronicle of events

大事化小, 小事化了 dàshì huà xiǎo, xiǎoshì huà liǎo reduce major issues to minor ones and minor ones to nothing; turn big problems into small ones and small ones into no problems at all

大势 dàshì general trend of events

大势所趋 dàshì suǒ qū the trend of the times; the general trend: ～, 人心所向 the trend of the times and the desire of the people; the general trend and popular feeling

大势已去 dàshì yǐ qù the situation is hopeless; the game is as good as lost; it's all up with sb.

大是大非 dàshì-dàfēi major matters of principle; cardinal questions of right and wrong: 分清～ draw clear distinctions concerning cardinal issues of right and wrong; distinguish between right and wrong on cardinal issues

大手笔 dàshǒubǐ ① the work of a well-known writer ② a well-known writer

大手大脚 dàshǒu-dàjiǎo wasteful; extravagant: 他 是～过惯了的。He has been used to extravagance. / 现在人们好像都变得～了。It seems people have become very free with their money these days.

大书 dàshū professional storytelling in a local dialect

大书特书 dàshū-tèshū record in letters of gold; write volumes about

大叔 dàshū ① younger brother of one's father; uncle ② uncle (a polite form of address for a man about one's father's age)

大暑 Dàshǔ ① Greater Heat—the 12th of the 24 solar terms ② the day marking the beginning of the 12th solar term (July 22, 23, or 24, in the midst of the three *fu* 伏 or ten-day periods when the heat is greatest) see also 节气 jiéqì, 二十四节气 èrshí sì jiéqì

大水 dàshuǐ flood; floodwater

大肆 dàsì without restraint; wantonly: ～攻击 wantonly vilify; launch an unbridled (or all-out) attack against / ～鼓吹 noisily advocate / ～宣扬 indulge in unbridled propaganda for; give enormous publicity to

大苏打 dàsūdá chem. sodium thiosulfate; sodium hyposulfite; hypo

大蒜 dàsuàn garlic: 一头～ a head of garlic

大踏步 dàtàbù in big strides: ～前进 stride along

大堂 dàtáng the court room in a yamen

大…特… dà…tè… (with a word repeated for emphasis): 大改特改 make drastic changes (in writing, etc.)

大提琴 dàtíqín violoncello; cello

大体 dàtǐ ① cardinal principle; general interest: 识～, 顾大局 have the cardinal principles in mind and take the overall situation into account ② adv. roughly; more or less; on the whole; by and large; approximately: ～相同 more or less alike; about the same / 收支～平衡 Income and expenditure roughly balance. / 我～上同意你的看法。On the whole I agree with you. / 事情的进展～上还不错。By and large, things are going quite well. / 他这个意见～上还行。On the whole, this idea of his is good. / 生产总值～上翻了一番。The total output value has approximately doubled.

大天白日 dàtiān-báirì inf. broad daylight: ～的, 你怎么走迷了路! How could you have got lost in broad daylight.

大田 dàtián land for growing field crops

大田作物 dàtián zuòwù field crop

大厅 dàtīng hall

大庭广众 dàtíng guǎngzhòng (before) a big crowd; (on) a public occasion: ～之中 in public; before a large audience

大同 dàtóng Great Harmony (an ideal or perfect society)

大同小异 dàtóng-xiǎoyì much the same but with minor differences; alike except for slight differences; very much the same

大头 dàtóu ① head mask ② a silver dollar coined in the early years of the Republic (1912–1916) with the head of Yuan Shikai (袁世凯) on the obverse side ③ the bigger end; the main part: 抓～儿 grasp the main part ④ derog. spendthrift; wastrel: 拿～ sponge on a spendthrift

大头菜 dàtóucài bot. rutabaga

大头针 dàtóuzhēn pin

大团圆 dàtuányuán ① happy reunion ② happy ending

大腿 dàtuǐ thigh

大腕 dàwàn inf. ① star (usu. referring to actors, singers, etc.) ② past master; master-hand

大王 dàwáng ① king; magnate: 煤油～ oil king; oil magnate ② a person of the highest class or skill in sth.; ace: 足球～ an ace footballer; a football hero ——see also dàiwang

大为 dàwéi adv. to a large extent; greatly; considerably: ～感动 be greatly moved / ～改观 have changed considerably

大尉 dàwèi senior captain

大我 dàwǒ (opp. 小我) the big self—the collective

大无畏 dàwúwèi dauntless; utterly fearless; indomitable: ～的英雄气概 dauntless heroism

大西洋 Dàxīyáng the Atlantic (Ocean)

大喜 dàxǐ inf. ① great rejoicing: 在这～的日子里 in these days of great rejoicing / 您～啦! Congratulations! ② wedding: 哪天是你们～的日子? When will your wedding take place?

大喜过望 dàxǐ guò wàng be delighted that things are better than one expected

大戏 dàxì ① a full-scale traditional opera ② dial. Beijing opera

大虾 dàxiā prawn

大显身手 dà xiǎn shēnshǒu display one's skill to the full; give full play to one's abilities; distinguish oneself; give a good account of oneself: 你～的时机到啦! Now's your chance to distinguish yourself.

大显神通 dàxiǎn shéntōng give full play to one's remarkable skill (or abilities); display one's prowess

大相径庭 dà xiāng jìng tíng widely divergent; entirely different; poles apart

大小 dàxiǎo ① big or small: ～水库十座 ten reservoirs of varying sizes / 国家不论～, 应该一律平等。All countries, big or small, should be equal. ② size: 这双鞋我穿上～正合适。These shoes are just my size. ③ degree of seniority: 说话没个～ speak impolitely to elderly people ④ adults and children: 全家～五口。There are five people in the family altogether. / ～平安。All's well in the family.

大校 dàxiào senior colonel

大协作 dàxiézuò large-scale cooperation; a major pooling of efforts

大写 dàxiě ① the capital form of a Chinese numeral: ～金额 amount in words ② capitalization: ～字母 capital letter

大兴 dàxīng go in for sth. in a big way: ～调查研究之风 energetically encourage the practice of conducting investigations and studies

大兴土木 dàxīng tǔmù go in for large-scale construction; be busy putting up buildings: 始皇初定天下, ～; 造宫殿, 建陵墓。Once the First Emperor had unified the empire, he launched an immense construction project which included a palace and his own mausoleum.

大兴问罪之师 dàxīng wèn zuì zhī shī angrily point an accusing finger at; scathingly condemn

大猩猩 dàxīngxing gorilla

大行星 dàxíngxīng astron. major planet

大行政区 dàxíngzhèngqū the six administrative areas of the People's Republic of China (1951–1954)

大型 dàxíng large-scale; large: ～企业 large enterprise / ～彩色记录片 full-length colour documentary film / ～运输机 giant transport aircraft; air freighter / ～轧钢厂 heavy steel rolling plant

大雄宝殿 Dàxióng Bǎodiàn the Precious Hall of the Great Hero (the main hall of a Buddhist temple, in which Sakyamuni 释迦牟尼 is the central figure of a triad enthroned upon lotus pedestals, the two others being usu. Ananda and Kasyapa, his two favourite disciples)

大熊猫 dàxióngmāo giant panda

大熊座 Dàxióngzuò astron. Ursa Major; the Great Bear

大修 dàxiū mech. overhaul; heavy repair

大选 dàxuǎn general election

大学 dàxué ① university; college ② The Great Learning (see also 四书 sìshū)

大学生 dàxuéshēng university (or college) student

大雪 Dàxuě ① Greater Snow—the 21st of the 24 solar terms ② the day marking the beginning of the 21st solar term (Dec. 6, 7, or 8) ——see also 节气 jiéqì, 二十四节气 èrshí sì jiéqì

大循环 dàxúnhuán physiol. systemic circulation

大牙 dàyá ① molar ② front tooth (see also 笑掉大牙 xiào diào dàyá)

大雅 dàyǎ elegance; refinement; good taste: 不登大雅之堂 bù dēng dàyǎ zhī táng

大烟 dàyān common name for 鸦片 yāpiàn

大烟鬼 dàyānguǐ opium addict

大言不惭 dàyán bù cán brag unblushingly; talk big

大盐 dàyán crude salt

大雁 dàyàn wild goose

大洋　dàyáng　① ocean ② silver dollar

大洋洲　Dàyángzhōu　Oceania; Oceanica

大样　dàyàng　① *print.* full-page proof ② *archit.* detail drawing

大摇大摆　dàyáo-dàbǎi　strutting; swaggering: 优胜者～地走上前去领奖。 The winner proudly stepped forward to receive his prize. / 显然小偷是从这里～出去的。 Obviously the thief had simply walked out this way as bold as brass.

大要　dàyào　main points; gist: 文章的～ the gist of an article

大爷　dàyé　son of the idle rich: ～作风 the ways of the idle rich

大爷　dàye　*inf.* ① father's elder brother; uncle ② uncle (a respectful form of address for an elderly man)

大业　dàyè　great cause; great undertaking: 革命～ the great cause of revolution / 创～ become pioneers in a great undertaking

大衣　dàyī　overcoat; topcoat

大姨　dàyí　*inf.* mother's eldest sister; aunt

大姨子　dàyízi　*inf.* wife's elder sister; sister-in-law

大义　dàyì　cardinal principles of righteousness; righteous cause: 深明～ be deeply conscious of the righteousness of a cause

大义凛然　dàyì lǐnrán　inspiring awe by upholding justice; with stern righteousness: 刘胡兰临刑时，～，视死如归。 Liu Hulan faced the executioner's ax with a fortitude that commanded admiration and respect.

大义灭亲　dàyì miè qīn　place righteousness above loyalty to one's family; sacrifice ties of blood to righteousness

大异其趣　dà yì qí qù　have very different tastes and interests

大意　dàyì　general idea; main points; gist; tenor: 段落～ the gist of a paragraph / 把他讲话的～记下来就行了。 Just jot down the main ideas (*or* points) of what he says.

大意　dàyi　careless; negligent; inattentive: 千万不可粗心～ must never on any account be negligent / 他真～，竟把她的地址给丢了。 He was so careless that he lost her address.

大音阶　dàyīnjiē　*mus.* major scale

大印　dàyìn　great seal—the seal of power

大油　dàyóu　*inf.* lard

大有　dàyǒu　① there is much: ～区别。 There is a great difference / ～希望。 There is great promise for the future. ② *formal* abundance: ～之年 a year of abundance

大有可为　dàyǒu kě wéi　be well worth doing; have bright prospects; 淡水养鱼～。 There are bright prospects for freshwater fish farming.

大有人在　dàyǒu rén zài　there are plenty of such people; such people are by no means rare

大有文章　dàyǒu wénzhāng　there's something behind all this; there's more to this than meets the eye

大有作为　dàyǒu zuòwéi　have full scope for one's talents; be able to develop one's ability to the full; have great possibilities: 农村是一个广阔的天地，在那里是可以～的。 The countryside is a vast world where much can be accomplished. / 青年人在这里是可以～的。 There are plenty of opportunities for young people here.

大雨　dàyǔ　heavy rain

大雨如注　dàyǔ rú zhù　the rain is pouring down; it's raining cats and dogs; it's raining in torrents: 不意～，无法启程。 Unexpectedly it began to pour with rain and it was impossible to start off.

大元帅　dàyuánshuài　generalissimo

大员　dàyuán　*old* high-ranking official: 委派～ appoint high-ranking officials

大远　dàyuǎn　far away: ～的路 a long way off / 你～地走来，累了吧! You must be tired after walking such a long distance.

大院　dàyuàn　courtyard; compound: 居民～ residential compound

大约　dàyuē　*adv.* ① approximately; about: ～有十二个人。 There were around a dozen people. / ～一小时的路程。 It's about an hour's journey. / ～将有五百人出席。 There will be approximately 500 people present. ② probably: 他～是到车间去了。 He has probably gone to the workshop.

大月　dàyuè　greater month—a solar month of 31 days; a lunar month of 30 days

大跃进　Dàyuèjìn　the Great Leap Forward (1958)

大运河　Dàyùnhé　the Grand Canal

大杂烩　dàzáhuì　hodgepodge; hotchpotch

大杂院儿　dàzáyuànr　a compound occupied by many households

大早　dàzǎo　very early in the morning: 起个大早 get up unusually early / 她一～就出去了。 She went out very early this morning.

大灶　dàzào　ordinary mess

大张旗鼓　dà zhāng qí-gǔ　on a grand scale; in a big way: ～地宣传新时期的总任务 give wide publicity to the general task in the new period

大张挞伐　dà zhāng tàfá　make a massive assault

大丈夫　dàzhàngfu　true man; real man; man

大政方针　dàzhèng fāngzhēn　fundamental policy (of a state); major policy: 中央的责任是提出～和进行监督。 The central authorities determine major policies and exercise supervision.

大指　dàzhǐ　thumb

大志　dàzhì　high aim; lofty aim; exalted ambition; high aspirations: 胸怀～ cherish high ideals; have lofty aspirations

大治　dàzhì　great order: ～之年 a year of great order

大致　dàzhì　*adv.* roughly; approximately; more or less: ～相同 roughly (*or* about) the same / 这项工程～两年可以完工。 This project will take about two years to complete. / 这活儿他们已经～干完了。 They've more or less finished the job. / 小孩儿～在一岁左右就开始学走路了。 Babies usually learn to walk when they are about one year old.

大智若愚　dà zhì ruò yú　a man of great wisdom often seems slow-witted

大众　dàzhòng　the masses; the people; the public; the broad masses of the people: ～歌曲 popular songs / ～文艺 art and literature for the masses; popular literature

大众化　dàzhònghuà　popularize: ～的饭菜 popular low-priced dishes / 语言～ use the language of the ordinary people

大洲　dàzhōu　continent

大轴子　dàzhòuzi　the last (usu. the major) item on a theatrical programme

大主教　dàzhǔjiào　archbishop

大专　dà-zhuān　short for 大专院校 dà-zhuān yuànxiào

大专　dàzhuān　college for professional training

大专学校　dà-zhuān xuéxiào　universities and colleges for professional training

大专院校　dà-zhuān yuànxiào　universities and colleges; institutions of higher education

大篆　dàzhuàn　an ancient style of calligraphy, current in the Zhou Dynasty (c. 11th century-256 B.C.)

大资产阶级　dàzīchǎnjiējí　the big bourgeoisie

大子儿　dàzǐr　a former large copper coin worth 20 cash: 一个～也没有 be penniless

大字报　dàzìbào　dazibao; big-character poster

大字本 dàzìběn *print.* large-character edition; large-type edition

大自然 dàzìrán nature: 征服～ conquer nature

大宗 dàzōng ① a large amount (*or* quantity): ～款项 a large amount of money; large sums ② staple: ～产品 staple product／本地出产以棉花为～。Cotton is the staple crop here.

大作 dàzuò ① *honor.* your writing: 拜读～ have the pleasure of perusing your work ② spring up; break out: 霎时狂风～。A violent wind suddenly sprang up.／枪声～。Shots rang out.

da

垯（墶） da see 圪垯 gēda

縼（縺） da see 纥縼 gēda

瘩 da see 疙瘩 gēda ——see also dá

dāi

呆（獃） dāi ① slow-witted; dull: 这孩子大病之后变～了。After recovering from a serious illness, the child became slow-witted.／这人怎么那么～! What a silly man! ② blank; wooden: ～～地望着 stare at sth. blankly／吓～了 be stupefied; be scared stiff; be dumbstruck ③ *inf.* stay: ～在家里 stay at home／我在那家饭店～了三个晚上。I stayed three nights at that hotel.

呆板 dāibǎn stiff and awkward; rigid; not natural; inflexible: 动作～ stiff and awkward movements／表情～ a stony expression／样子～ look stiff／～的公式 a rigid formula／这篇文章写得太～。This article is rather hackneyed.／这个人真～。This person is inflexible.

呆痴 dāichī stupid; slow-witted

呆气 dāiqì stupidity; foolishness

呆若木鸡 dāi ruò mùjī dumb as a wooden chicken; dumbstruck; transfixed (with fear or amazement): 他站在那里, 吓得～。He stood there transfixed with horror.

呆头呆脑 dāitóu-dāinǎo stupid-looking

呆小症 dāixiǎozhèng *med.* cretinism

呆性物质 dāixìng wùzhì *chem.* inert material

呆帐 dāizhàng bad debt

呆滞 dāizhì ① dull: 两眼～无神 with a dull look in one's eyes／她注视着远方, 目光是～的。She gazed into the distance with her eyes blank. ② idle: 避免资金～ prevent capital from lying idle

呆子 dāizi idiot; simpleton; blockhead

呔（�） dāi *interj. old* (used to call attention)

待 dāi *inf.* stay: 他在广州～了三天。He stayed in Guangzhou for three days. ——see also dài

待会儿 dāihuìr in a moment: 你先走, 我～就来。You go first. I'll be along presently (*or* in a moment).

dǎi

歹 dǎi bad; evil; vicious: 为非作歹 wéifēi-zuòdǎi

歹毒 dǎidú *dial.* sinister and vicious

歹人 dǎirén *dial.* villain; gangster or robber

歹徒 dǎitú scoundrel; ruffian; evildoer

歹心 dǎixīn (*also* 歹意 dǎiyì) malice; malicious intent: 把别人的好心当作歹意 take sb.'s goodwill for evil intent

逮 dǎi capture; catch: 猫～老鼠。Cats catch mice. ——see also dài

傣 Dǎi see below

傣族 Dǎizú the Dai (Tai) nationality, or the Dais (Tais), inhabiting Yunnan Province

dài

大 dài see below ——see also dà

大夫 dàifu *inf.* doctor; physician ——see also dàfū

大黄 dàihuáng *bot.* Chinese rhubarb

大王 dàiwang great king (a term of address for a king or a bandit chief, used in traditional operas and novels) ——see also dàwáng

代[1] dài ① take the place of; be in place of: 主任不在时由老王～。Lao Wang acts for the director during his absence.／请～我向他致意。Please give him my regards. ② acting: ～部长 acting minister

代[2] dài ① historical period: 汉～ the Han Dynasty ② *geol.* era: 古生代 Gǔshēngdài ③ generation: ～～相传 pass on (*or* hand down) from generation to generation／一～新人在成长。A new generation is growing up.

代办 dàibàn ① do sth. for sb.; act on sb.'s behalf: 这件事请你～吧。Could you do this for me? *or* Could you act on my behalf? ② *diplomacy* chargé d'affaires: 临时～ chargé d'affaires ad interim

代办处 dàibànchù *diplomacy* Office of the Chargé d'Affaires

代办所 dàibànsuǒ agency: 储蓄～ savings agency／邮政～ postal agency

代笔 dàibǐ write (a letter, etc.) for sb.; be a ghost writer: 老太太求我～给她儿子写封信。The old woman asked me to write a letter for her to her son.

代表 dàibiǎo ① deputy; delegate; representative: 全国人大～ deputy to the National People's Congress／党代会～ delegate to the Party Congress／双方～ representatives from both sides／常驻～ permanent representative (*or* delegate) ② represent; stand for: ～无产阶级利益 represent the interests of the proletariat／这三个人～三种不同性格。These three persons represent three different types of character.／～时代精神 embody the spirit of the era ③ on behalf of; in the name of: ～我国政府表示衷心的感谢 express heartfelt thanks on behalf of our government／～全厂工人讲话 speak in the name of the workers of the factory

代表大会 dàibiǎo dàhuì congress; representative assembly (*or* conference): 中国共产党全国～ the National Congress of the Communist Party of China

代表权 dàibiǎoquán representation

代表人物 dàibiǎo rénwù representative figure (*or* personage); typical representative; leading exponent

代表团 dàibiǎotuán delegation; mission; deputation

代表性 dàibiǎoxìng representativeness: 这些候选人具有较广泛的～。These candidates represent broader sections of the people.

代表资格 dàibiǎo zīgé qualifications of a representative

代表资格审查委员会 dàibiǎo zīgé shěnchá wěiyuánhuì

(delegates') credentials committee

代表作 dàibiǎozuò　representative work

代步 dàibù　*formal*　ride instead of walk

代词 dàicí　*gram*.　pronoun

代父 dàifù　same as 教父 jiàofù

代耕 dàigēng　① *formal*　make a living by doing sth. other than farming: 以笔 ～ make a living by writing ② village-organized tilling for armymen's or revolutionary martyrs' families (before the agricultural cooperative movement) ③ (of a tractor station, etc.) help collective or individual farmers with tilling

代沟 dàigōu　generation gap

代购 dàigòu　buy on sb.'s behalf; act as a purchasing agent: 本店为顾客办理 ～ 业务。This store will act as a purchasing agent for customers.

代购代销点 dàigòudàixiāodiǎn　purchasing and marketing agency

代号 dàihào　code name

代价 dàijià　price; cost: 不惜任何 ～ prepared to pay any price; at any cost; at all costs / 战士们为了攻下这座山付出了巨大的～。The soldiers took the hill at great cost.

代金 dàijīn　cash equivalent

代课 dàikè　take over a class for an absent teacher

代劳 dàiláo　do sth. for sb.; take trouble on sb.'s behalf: 这事请你老李～吧。Will you do this for us, Lao Li?

代理 dàilǐ　① act on behalf of sb. in a responsible position: 总经理病了, 工作由他～。He acted for the general manager who was ill. / ～ 厂长 acting manager of a factory ② act as agent (*or* proxy, procurator)

代理人 dàilǐrén　① agent; deputy; proxy ② *leg*. procurator; attorney

代脉 dàimài　*Chin. med*.　slow, intermittent pulse

代名词 dàimíngcí　① same as 代词 dàicí ② synonym: 诸葛亮在民间传说中成了智慧的 ～。Zhuge Liang is a synonym for wisdom in folklore.

代母 dàimǔ　same as 教母 jiāomǔ

代庖 dàipáo　*formal*　do what is sb. else's job; act in sb.'s place ——see also 越俎代庖 yuèzǔ-dàipáo

代人受过 dài rén shòu guò　suffer for the faults of another; bear the blame for sb. else; be made a scapegoat

代乳粉 dàirǔfěn　milk powder substitute

代售 dàishòu　be commissioned to sell sth. (usu. as a sideline): 此处 ～ 邮票。Stamps sold here.

代数 dàishù　algebra

代数方程 dàishù fāngchéng　algebraic equation

代数式 dàishùshì　algebraic expression

代数数论 dàishù shùlùn　algebraic theory of numbers

代替 dàitì　replace; substitute for; take the place of: 用国产品 ～ 进口货 substitute homemade products for imported goods / 有些外科手术可用针麻 ～ 药麻。In some surgical operations, acupuncture anaesthesia may be used instead of medicinal anaesthetics. / 社会主义制度终究要 ～ 资本主义制度。The socialist system will eventually replace the capitalist system. /你要是自己不能去, 可以找个人来。If you cannot go yourself, try to find someone to substitute for you.

代为 dàiwéi　(used before verbs) on behalf of; for (sb.): ～说项 put in a good word for sb. / 请～致意。Please give him my regards.

代销 dàixiāo　sell goods (for the state) on a commission basis; be commissioned to sell sth. (usu. as a sideline); act as a commission agent: ～ 店 shop commissioned to sell certain goods; commission agent

代谢 dàixiè　① supersession: 新旧事物的 ～ the supersession of the old by the new ② *biol*. metabolize: 分解 ～ catabolism /组成 ～ anabolism ——see also 新陈代谢 xīn-chén dàixiè

代谢病 dàixièbìng　metabolic disease

代谢期 dàixièqī　*biol*.　metabolic stage

代谢物 dàixièwù　*biol*.　metabolite

代谢作用 dàixiè zuòyòng　*biol*.　metabolism

代行 dàixíng　act on sb.'s behalf: ～ 职权 function in an acting capacity

代序 dàixù　an article used in lieu of a preface (*or* by way of introduction)

代言人 dàiyánrén　spokesman; mouthpiece

代议制 dàiyìzhì　the representative system (of government): ～ 机构 representative institution

代营食堂 dàiyíng shítáng　neighbourhood cafeteria

代用 dàiyòng　substitute: ～ 材料 substitute (*or* ersatz) materials

代用品 dàiyòngpǐn　substitute; ersatz

代远年湮 dài yuǎn nián yān　be of remote antiquity and buried in oblivion

代职 dàizhí　hold a position in an acting capacity

代字号 dàizìhào　swung dash (～)

岱 Dài　another name for 泰山 Tàishān

岱岳 Dàiyuè　another name for 泰山 Tàishān

岱宗 Dàizōng　another name for 泰山 "Tai Mountain": ～ 夫如何, 齐鲁青未了。(杜甫) And what is Tai Mountain like? Over Qi and Lu a green unceasing.

迨 dài　*formal*　① wait till ② before sth. happens: ～ 天之未阴雨 before it rains

绐 dài　*formal*　cheat; fool

甙 dài　*chem*.　glucoside

玳(瑇) dài　see below

玳瑁 dàimào　*zool*.　hawksbill turtle

带¹(帶) dài　① belt; girdle; ribbon; band; tape: 皮带 pídài /丝带 sīdài /磁带 cídài ② tyre: 自行车 ～ bicycle tyre ③ zone; area; belt: 他在这一 ～ 打过游击。He used to be a guerrilla fighter in these parts. ④ same as 白带 báidài

带²(帶) dài　① take; bring; carry: 我可以 ～ 多少行李? How much luggage can I take? /别忘了 ～ 雨衣。Don't forget to take your raincoat along. /连队走到哪里, 就把老红军的传统 ～ 到哪里。Wherever it goes, the company passes on to the people the glorious tradition of the Red Army. /请人 ～ 个话儿给她。Ask somebody to take her a message. /我没有 ～ 钱。I haven't any money on me. ② do sth. incidentally: 上街时给 ～ 点茶叶来。When you go out, get me some tea. /你在信上给我 ～ 一笔, 问你父亲好。Remember me to your father in your letter. /你出去请把门 ～ 上。Please pull the door to when you go out. ③ bear; have: ～ 有时代的特点 bear the imprint of the times /面 ～ 笑容 wear a smile / ～ 刺的灌木 a thorny bush /一项 ～ 根本性的措施 a measure of fundamental importance ④ having sth. attached; simultaneous: ～ 叶的橘子 tangerines with their leaves on / ～ 电脑的收录机 a programmable cassette recorder /这几个茶杯是 ～ 碟儿的。There are saucers to go with these cups. /放牛 ～ 割草 cut grass while tending cattle /玉米地里 ～ 着种点黄豆 grow some soybeans in the maize field ⑤ lead; head: ～ 队 lead (*or* be the leader of) a group of people / ～ 兵 lead (*or* be in command of) troops / ～ 研究生 direct (*or* be a tutor of) postgraduates ⑥ look after; bring up; raise: ～ 孩子 look after children /他是由一位贫农大娘 ～ 大的。He was brought up by a poor peasant woman. ⑦ drive; spur on; bring along: 他

这样一来～得大家都勤快了。His example has spurred everybody on to work harder.

带病 dàibìng in spite of illness: 他～坚持工作。He went on working in spite of his illness.

带材 dàicái *metall.* strip

带刺儿 dàicìr with veiled sarcasm: 说话别～。Don't be sarcastic.

带电 dàidiàn electrified; live; charged: ～导线 live wire

带电粒子 dàidiàn lìzǐ *phys.* charged particle

带电体 dàidiàntǐ charged (or electrified) body

带电作业 dàidiàn zuòyè live-wire work

带动 dàidòng drive; spur on; bring along: 用拖拉机上的发动机～打谷机 use the tractor motor to power the thresher / 先进～后进。The more advanced bring along the less advanced. / 抓好典型，～全局 take firm hold of typical examples to promote the work as a whole / 改革～了生产。The reforms have given an impetus to production.

带钢 dàigāng strip steel

带好儿 dàihǎor give regards to: 你见了他，替我带个好儿。When you see him, give him my best regards.

带花 dàihuā (also 带彩 dàicǎi) be wounded in action: 打过仗，带过花 have fought and been wounded

带劲 dàijìn ① energetic; forceful: 他干起活来可～了。He works like a horse. / 这篇文章写得真～。This is a very forceful piece of writing. ② interesting; exciting; wonderful: 这场比赛真～。This is really a terrific match. / 下棋不～，咱们游泳去吧。Chess is no fun; let's go swimming. / 什么时候我学会开拖拉机，那才～呢。It'll be wonderful if I can drive a tractor some day.

带锯 dàijù *mech.* band saw

带菌 dàijūn carry disease germs

带菌者 dàijūnzhě *med.* carrier

带累 dàilěi implicate; involve; get sb. into trouble: 我病成这样，可不能再～你了。I'm so ill. I shouldn't trouble you any more.

带领 dàilǐng lead; guide: 他～全家出海捕鱼。He led the whole family out to sea to catch fish. / 老师～同学们去参观中国历史博物馆。The teacher took the pupils to the Museum of Chinese History.

带路 dàilù (also 带道 dàidào) show (or lead) the way; act as a guide: 老猎户给我们～。The old hunter acted as our guide.

带路人 dàilùrén guide

带身子 dàishēnzi *inf.* be in the family way; be pregnant

带头 dàitóu take the lead; be the first; take the initiative; set an example: ～冲锋 lead the charge / 起～作用 play a leading (or vanguard) role / ～发言 be the first to speak; break the ice / 带个好头 set a good example

带头羊 dàitóuyáng bellwether

带徒弟 dài túdi train (or take on) an apprentice

带下 dàixià *Chin. med.* morbid leucorrhoea

带孝 dàixiào wear mourning for a parent, relative, etc.; be in mourning: 给母亲～ wear mourning for one's mother / 带了一个月的孝 have been in mourning for one month

带信儿 dàixìnr take or bring a message: 请你带个信儿给我妈，说我今晚要晚点儿回去。Please tell my mother that I'll be home late tonight.

带音 dàiyīn *phonet.* voiced

带引 dàiyǐn guide; lead the way

带鱼 dàiyú hairtail

带职 dàizhí in service; on the job: ～学习 on-the-job training

带状疱疹 dàizhuàng pàozhěn *med.* herpes zoster; zoster

带子 dàizi belt; girdle; ribbon; band; tape

殆 dài *formal* ① dangerous; perilous: 危殆 wēidài ② *adv.* nearly; almost: 敌人伤亡～尽。The enemy were practically wiped out.

待[1] dài ① treat; deal with: ～人诚恳 treat people sincerely; be sincere with people / 他们～我如家人。They treated me as one of the family. ② entertain: ～客 entertain a guest

待[2] dài ① wait for; await: ～机 await an opportunity; bide one's time / 尚～解决的问题 a problem awaiting solution; an outstanding issue ② need: 自不待言 zì bù dài yán ③ going to; about to: 我正～出门，有人来了。I was about to go out when someone came. ——see also dāi

待到 dàidào by the time; when: ～来年冰雪消融时，我们再相会。Let's meet again when the thaw comes in.

待价而沽 dàijià ér gū wait to sell at a good price; wait for the highest bid

待考 dàikǎo need checking; remain to be verified: 此说是否正确～。Whether or not this is true remains to be verified.

待命 dàimìng (also 待令 dàilìng) await orders: ～出发 await orders to set off / 原地～ stay where one is, pending orders; stand by

待人处世 dàirén-chǔshì the way one treats people and conducts oneself in society

待人接物 dàirén-jiēwù the way one gets along with people

待时 dàishí *formal* bide one's time

待续 dàixù to be continued

待业 dàiyè job-waiting; unemployed: ～青年 job-waiting youth / ～人员 job-waiting people; the unemployed

待遇 dàiyù ① treatment; reception: 冷淡的～ cold reception; cold shoulder / 受到良好～ have received good treatment / 政治～ political treatment ② remuneration; pay; wages; salary: 优厚～ excellent pay and conditions / 这家公司～很高。This company pays very high salaries.

待字闺中 dàizì guīzhōng (of a girl) staying in the boudoir waiting to be betrothed—not yet betrothed

贷 dài ① loan: 农贷 nóngdài ② borrow or lend: 银行～给工厂大量款项。The bank granted a large loan to the factory. ③ shift (responsibility); shirk: 责无旁贷 zé wú páng dài ④ pardon; forgive: 严惩不贷 yánchéng bù dài

贷方 dàifāng *bookkeeping* credit side; credit

贷款 dàikuǎn ① provide (or grant) a loan; extend credit to; make an advance to: 银行给他们贷了款。The bank granted a loan to them. / 向银行～ ask for a bank loan ② loan; credit: 无息～ interestfree loans / 未偿～ outstanding loans / ～对象 prospective borrower / ～计划 borrowing plan / ～利率 interest rate on a loan / ～期限 terms of a loan / ～条件 conditions for a loan / ～帐户 a loan account / ～种类 types of loans

怠 dài idle; remiss; slack: 懈怠 xièdài

怠惰 dàiduò idle; lazy; indolent

怠工 dàigōng slow down; go slow: 工人以～作为斗争的一种方式。Workers went slow as a form of struggle.

怠忽 dàihū be indolent and neglectful: ～职守 be neglectful of one's duties

怠倦 dàijuàn be indolent and listless; be languid and idle

怠慢 dàimàn ① cold-shoulder; slight: 不要 ～ 了客人。 See that none of the guests are neglected. ② *pol.* (used by the host at the end of a reception, etc.): ～了! I'm afraid I have been a poor host.

袋 dài ① bag; sack; pocket; pouch: 旅行袋 lǚxíngdài／工具袋 gōngjùdài／口袋 kǒudài ② *m.* 一 ～面粉 a sack of flour／一 ～ 烟的功夫 time needed to smoke a pipe

袋泡茶 dàipàochá teabag

袋兽 dàishòu marsupial

袋鼠 dàishǔ kangaroo

袋装 dàizhuāng in bags: ～ 奶粉 milk powder in bags

袋子 dàizi sack; bag

逮[1] dài *formal.* reach: 力有未 ～ beyond one's reach (*or* power)

逮[2] dài see below
——see also dǎi

逮捕 dàibǔ arrest; take into custody: ～ 法办 arrest and deal with according to law; bring to justice／你被 ～ 了。 You are under arrest.

逮捕证 dàibǔzhèng arrest warrant

逮(靆) dài see 叆叇 àidài

戴 dài ① put on; wear: ～ 上手套 put on one's gloves／～ 眼镜 wear glasses ② respect; honour: 爱戴 àidài ③ (Dài) a surname

戴高帽子 dài gāomàozi ① flatter; lay it on thick: 爱 ～ be fond of flattery／他爱给有钱有势的人 ～。 He is always ready to flatter rich and influential people. ② wear a tall paper hat (as a mark of shame); wear a dunce's cap: ～ 游街 have a tall paper hat clapped on one's head and be paraded through the streets

戴绿帽 dài lǜmào (also 戴绿头巾 dài lǜtóujīn) be a cuckold

戴帽子 dài màozi be branded as; be labelled: 戴上反革命帽子 be branded as a counterrevolutionary; be officially declared a counterrevolutionary

戴胜 dàishèng *zool.* hoopoe

戴孝 dàixiào same as 带孝 dàixiào

戴月披星 dàiyuè-pīxīng same as 披星戴月 pīxīng-dàiyuè

戴罪立功 dàizuì lìgōng atone for one's crimes by doing good deeds; redeem oneself by good service

黛 dài a black pigment used by women in ancient times to paint their eyebrows

黛绿 dàilǜ *formal* dark green

褦 dài see 褦襶 nàidài

dān

丹 dān ① red: ～ 枫 a flaming maple ② *Chin. med.* pellet or powder

丹忱 dānchén a sincere heart; absolute sincerity

丹墀 dānchí (also 丹陛 dānbì) vermilion steps leading up to a palace hall

丹顶鹤 dāndǐnghè red-crested crane; red-crowned crane

丹毒 dāndú *med.* erysipelas

丹方 dānfāng same as 单方 dānfāng

丹桂 dānguì *bot.* orange osmanthus

丹麦 Dānmài Denmark

丹麦人 Dānmàirén Dane

丹麦语 Dānmàiyǔ Danish (language)

丹皮 dānpí *Chin. med.* the root bark of the tree peony

丹青 dānqīng *liter.* red and green colours—painting

丹青妙笔 dānqīng miàobǐ superb artistry (in painting); the superb touch of a great painter; the touch of a master

丹砂 dānshā same as 朱砂 zhūshā

丹参 dānshēn *Chin. med.* the root of red-rooted salvia (*Salvia miltiorrhiza*)

丹田 dāntián the pubic region: ～ 之气 deep breath controlled by the diaphragm

丹心 dānxīn a loyal heart; loyalty

单(單) dān ① one; single: ～ 扇门 a single-leaf door ② odd: ～ 只袜子 an odd sock ③ single; solitary: 形单影只 xíngdān-yǐngzhī ④ *adv.* only; alone: 我 ～ 看见小李。 I only saw Xiao Li.／她一个人就拿了三块金牌。 She alone won 3 gold medals.／不要 ～ 凭热情去工作。 Don't work by enthusiasm alone.／他为什么 ～ 在这时候来? Why does he show up at a time like this? ／～ 凭主观愿望 rely simply (*or* solely) on one's own subjective will／把这几件东西 ～ 放在一个地方。 Keep these things in a separate place. ⑤ simple: 简单 jiǎndān ⑥ thin; weak: 单薄 dānbó ⑦ unlined (clothing): 单衣 dānyī ⑧ sheet: 床单 chuángdān ⑨ bill; list: 名单 míngdān／菜单 càidān ——see also chán; Shàn

单摆 dānbǎi *phys.* simple pendulum

单板 dānbǎn veneer

单板微型机 dānbǎn wēixíngjī single board microcomputer

单帮 dānbāng a travelling trader working on his own: 跑 ～ travel around trading on one's own

单倍体 dānbèitǐ *biol.* monoploid; haploid

单本位制 dānběnwèizhì *econ.* monometallic standard; monometallism

单比 dānbǐ *math.* digital ratio

单比例 dānbǐlì *math.* digital ratio equation

单边 dānbiān *econ.* unilateral: ～ 进(出)口 unilateral import (export)

单兵 dānbīng ① individual soldier ② *formal* an isolated force

单兵教练 dānbīng jiàoliàn *mil.* individual drilling

单兵装备 dānbīng zhuāngbèi *mil.* individual equipment

单薄 dānbó ① (of clothing) thin: 穿得 ～ be thinly clad ② thin and weak; frail: 身体 ～ have a poor physique ③ insubstantial; flimsy; thin: 论据 ～ a feeble argument

单产 dānchǎn per unit area yield

单车 dānchē *dial.* bicycle

单程 dānchéng one way: ～ 车票 one-way (*or* single) ticket

单程清棉机 dānchéng qīngmiánjī *text.* single process scutcher

单传 dānchuán ① pass on a skill from a master to a single disciple ② a patrilineal line of descent with only one son in each generation

单纯 dānchún ① simple; pure: 思想 ～ pure in mind; unsophisticated／问题决不象我们当初想象的那么 ～。 The problem is by no means as simple as we first thought. ② alone; purely; merely: 不 ～ 追求数量 not concentrate on quantity alone

单纯词 dānchúncí *linguis.* single-morpheme word

单词 dāncí ① individual word; word ② same as 单纯词 dānchúncí

单打 dāndǎ *sports* singles: 男子(女子) ～ men's (women's) singles／少年男子(女子) ～ boys' (girls') singles／她只参加 ～。 She's only playing in the singles.

单打一 dāndǎyī ① concentrate on one thing only ② have a one-track mind

单单 dāndān *adv.* only; alone: 别人都来了，～ 他没来。He's the only one absent. Everybody else is here. *or* Everybody has come except him. / 你 ～ 吃米饭是不行的。You can't live on rice alone. / 为什么 ～ 要我去呢? Why ask me to go, of all people?

单刀 dāndāo ① short-hilted broadsword ② *martial arts* single-broadsword event

单刀直入 dāndāo zhí rù come straight to the point; speak out without beating about the bush: 我 ～ 地问他到底要干什么。I asked him point-blank what he wanted to do. / 他说话喜欢 ～, 不绕弯子。He likes to come straight to the point without beating about the bush.

单调 dāndiào monotonous; dull; drab: 声音 ～ in a monotonous tone / 色彩 ～ dull colouring / 昨天的节目比较 ～。Yesterday's programme was rather dull.

单丁 dāndīng *old* an only son; a young man without brothers

单独 dāndú alone; by oneself; on one's own; single-handed; independent: ～一个人干不了这个活儿。Nobody can do this job alone (*or* by himself). / 采取 ～ 行动 take independent action / 她 ～ 住一间屋子。She has a room to herself. / 我要和他 ～ 谈一谈。I want to have a talk with him alone. / 这东西我 ～ 一个人拿不了, 太重。I can't carry it on my own; it's too heavy.

单发 dānfā *mil.* single shot: ～ 射击 single shot

单方 dānfāng folk prescription; home remedy

单方面 dānfāngmiàn one-sided; unilateral: ～ 撕毁协定 unilaterally tear up an agreement

单飞 dānfēi *aviation* solo flight

单峰驼 dānfēngtuó one-humped camel; dromedary; Arabian camel

单幅 dānfú *text.* single width

单干 dāngàn ① work on one's own; go it alone; work by oneself; do sth. single-handed ② individual farming: ～ 户 a peasant family still farming on its own after agricultural cooperation

单杠 dāngàng *sports* ① horizontal bar ② horizontal bar gymnastics

单个儿 dāngèr ① individually; alone: 最好集体去, 不要 ～ 去。We'd better go in a group, not individually. ② an odd one: 这副手套只剩下 ～ 了。There's only an odd glove left. / ～ 棋子不卖。Chessmen aren't sold by the piece.

单根独苗 dāngēn-dúmiáo an only son or daughter; an only child

单挂号 dānguàhào ordinary registered mail (which does not require a receipt for the sender)

单轨 dānguǐ single track

单号 dānhào odd numbers (of tickets, seats, etc.)

单簧管 dānhuángguǎn *mus.* clarinet

单级火箭 dānjí huǒjiàn single-stage rocket

单季稻 dānjìdào single cropping of rice

单价 dānjià ① *econ.* unit price ② *chem. biol.* univalent

单间儿 dānjiānr separate room (in a hotel, restaurant, etc.)

单键 dānjiàn *chem.* single bond

单交 dānjiāo *agric.* single cross

单脚跳 dānjiǎotiào *sports* hop

单晶硅 dānjīngguī *electron.* monocrystalline silicon

单晶体 dānjīngtǐ *phys.* monocrystal

单句 dānjù *gram.* simple sentence

单据 dānjù documents attesting to the giving or receiving of money, goods, etc., such as receipts, bills, vouchers and invoices: 货运 ～ shipping documents

单孔目 dānkǒngmù *zool.* Monotremata: ～ 动物 mono-treme

单口 dānkǒu *quyi* (曲艺) solos: ～ 相声 solo *xiangsheng*; comic monologue

单跨 dānkuà *archit.* single span

单利 dānlì *econ.* simple interest

单恋 dānliàn one-sided love; unrequited love

单另 dānlìng *inf.* separately and exclusively: 稍等一下, 我 ～ 给你做吃的。Just wait a while. I'll fix something specially for you.

单轮射箭 dānlún shèjiàn *sports* single round archery: 女子三十米 ～ women's 30-metre single round archery event

单名 dānmíng single-character given name

单宁酸 dānníngsuān *chem.* tannic acid

单偶婚 dān'ǒuhūn monogamy

单皮 dānpí single-skin drum (made of heavy circles of wood over which is stretched thick pigskin; the leading instrument in the orchestra in traditional opera, beating the time and thus having the other instruments play in unison)

单片眼镜 dānpiàn yǎnjìng monocle

单枪匹马 dānqiāng-pǐmǎ (also 单人独马 dānrén-dúmǎ) single-handed; all by oneself; alone

单亲家庭 dānqīn jiātíng one-parent family

单人床 dānrénchuáng single bed

单人房 dānrénfáng single-bed room

单人舞 dānrénwǔ solo dance: 跳～ dance a solo

单日 dānrì odd-numbered days (of the month)

单弱 dānruò thin and weak; frail

单色 dānsè monochromatic: ～电视 monochrome television

单色光 dānsèguāng *phys.* monochromatic light

单色画 dānsèhuà monochrome (painting)

单色胶印机 dānsè jiāoyìnjī single-colour offset press

单身 dānshēn ① unmarried; single ② not be with one's family; live alone: ～ 在外 live alone away from home

单身汉 dānshēnhàn unmarried man; bachelor

单身宿舍 dānshēn sùshè quarters for unmarried men or women; bachelor quarters

单生花 dānshēnghuā *bot.* solitary flower

单式 dānshì *bookkeeping* single entry

单数 dānshù ① odd number ② *gram.* singular number

单丝 dānsī *text.* monofilament

单丝不成线, 孤树不成林 dān sī bù chéng xiàn, gū shù bù chéng lín one strand of silk doesn't make a thread; one tree doesn't make a forest

单瘫 dāntān *med.* monoplegia

单糖 dāntáng *chem.* monose; monosaccharide

单体 dāntǐ *chem.* monomer

单条 dāntiáo a vertically-hung scroll of painting or calligraphy (not in a set); wall scroll

单位 dānwèi ① unit (as a standard of measurement): 长度～ a unit of length / 货币～ monetary unit / ～面积产量 yield per unit area / 以秒为～计算时间 measure time by the second ② unit (as an organization, department, division, section, etc.): 行政 ～ administrative unit / 生产 ～ production unit / 基层 ～ basic (*or* grass-roots) unit

单位圆 dānwèiyuán *math.* unit circle

单位制 dānwèizhì system of unit

单细胞 dānxìbāo unicellular

单细胞动物 dānxìbāo dòngwù unicellular animal

单弦儿 dānxiánr *danxianr*, story-telling to musical accompaniment

单线 dānxiàn ① single line ② one-way (contact); singleline (link): 做地下工作时, 他和我 ～ 联系。When we were doing underground work, he was my only

contact. ③ *transportation* single track

单线铁路 dānxiàn tiělù single-track railway; single-track line

单相思 dānxiāngsī unrequited love

单向 dānxiàng one-way; unidirectional: ～ 电路 one-way circuit / ～ 交通 one-way traffic

单项 dānxiàng *sports* individual event: ～ 比赛 individual competition

单相 dānxiàng single-phase; monophase: ～ 电动机 single-phase motor / ～ 合金 single-phase alloy

单斜 dānxié *geol.* monocline: ～层 monoclinal stratum

单行本 dānxíngběn ① separate edition ② offprint

单行法规 dānxíng fǎguī special (*or* separate) regulations

单行条例 dānxíng tiáolì specific regulations

单行线 dānxíngxiàn one-way road

单姓 dānxìng single-character surname

单性花 dānxìnghuā *bot.* unisexual flower

单性生殖 dānxìng shēngzhí *biol.* parthenogenesis; parthenogenetic propagation (*or* reproduction)

单眼 dānyǎn *zool.* simple eye

单眼皮 dānyǎnpí single-edged eyelid

单叶 dānyè *bot.* simple leaf

单一 dānyī single; unitary: ～ 的生产资料全民所有制 a unitary system of the ownership of the means of production by the whole people / 管理方式陈旧 ～。The methods of management are outdated and simplistic.

单一经济 dānyī jīngjì single-product economy

单一种植 dānyī zhòngzhí monoculture; one-crop farming

单衣 dānyī unlined garment

单翼机 dānyìjī monoplane

单音词 dānyīncí *linguis.* monosyllabic word; monosyllable

单元 dānyuán unit: 运算 ～ arithmetic unit / 三号楼丙 ～ 四号 No.4, Entrance C, Building 3

单渣操作 dānzhā cāozuò *metall.* single-slag practice

单质 dānzhì *chem.* simple substance

单子 dānzǐ *philos.* monad

单子 dānzi ① list; bill; form: 开个 ～ make out a list / 填写 ～ fill in a form ② bed sheet: 床 ～ bed sheet

单子叶植物 dānzǐyè zhíwù monocotyledon

单字 dānzì ① individual character (of the Chinese language) ② separate word (of a foreign language)

单座飞机 dānzuò fēijī single-seater (aeroplane)

担 (擔)

dān ① carry on a shoulder pole: ～ 水 carry water (with a shoulder pole and buckets) ② take on; undertake: 咱们把任务 ～ 起来。Let's take on the job. / 不怕 ～ 风险 be ready to face any danger; not be afraid of running risks ——see also dàn

担保 dānbǎo assure; guarantee; vouch for: 这事交给她办, ～ 错不了。I assure you that she can be trusted to do the work well. *or* I'll vouch for her as the best person for the job. / 出口信贷 ～ export credit guarantees

担保企业 dānbǎo qǐyè guarantor enterprise

担保人 dānbǎorén guarantor; guarantee

担不起 dānbuqǐ ① be unable to shoulder (the responsibility); be unequal to (a task): 我 ～ 如此重任。I am unequal to such a responsible task. ② *hum.* I really don't deserve this; you flatter me: 对我这样夸奖, 我可 ～。I really don't deserve such praise.

担不是 dān bùshì take the blame: 出了问题, 由我一个人 ～。If anything goes wrong, I'll take the blame.

担承 dānchéng bear; undertake; assume the responsibility for: ～ 任务 undertake a task / ～ 全部责任 bear full responsibility; be held fully responsible

担待 dāndài *inf.* ① be magnanimous; be tolerant ② bear the responsibility: 你放心吧, 一切由我 ～。Have

no fear. I'll bear all the responsibility.

担当 dāndāng take on; undertake; assume: ～ 重任 take on heavy responsibilities / 无论什么工作, 他都敢于 ～。He's willing to take on any kind of job.

担负 dānfù bear; shoulder; take on; be charged with: ～ 责任 shoulder responsibility / ～ 费用 bear an expense / ～ 领导工作 hold a leading post

担搁 dānge same as 耽搁 dānge

担架 dānjià stretcher; litter: ～ 队 stretcher-team / ～ 员 stretcher-bearer

担惊受怕 dānjīng-shòupà feel alarmed; be in a state of anxiety

担名 dānmíng bear a certain name: 担罪 名 bear the guilt / 担了个虚名 bear an empty title

担任 dānrèn assume the office of; hold the post of: ～ 工会主席 be the chairman of a trade union / ～ 会议主席 take the chair / 请他们 ～ 校外辅导员 invite them to be advisers on after-school activities / 他 ～ 外交部长。He assumed office as Foreign Minister. / 她 ～ 什么职务? What office does she hold?

担险 dānxiǎn run a risk

担心 dānxīn worry; feel anxious: 我真 ～ 她的健康。I do worry about her health. / 快给老大娘写信, 免得她 ～。Write to the old lady at once so as to set her mind at rest.

担忧 dānyōu worry; be anxious: 不要为我的身体 ～。Don't worry about my health.

眈

dān see 虎视眈眈 hǔ shì dāndān

耽¹ (躭)

dān delay: 耽误 dānwu

耽²

dān *formal* abandon oneself to; indulge in: ～ 乐 indulge in pleasure

耽待 dāndài same as 担待 dāndài

耽搁 dānge ① stop over; stay: 我去天津途中可能在济南 ～ 一下。I may have a stopover at Jinan on my way to Tianjin. / 我不打算在这里 ～ 多久。I won't be here for long. ② delay: 毫不 ～ without delay / 不得 ～ admit of no delay / 一分钟也不能～。Not a single minute is to be lost. / 事情忙, 把回信给 ～ 了。I've been very busy and failed to write back in time.

耽溺 dānnì indulge in; abandon oneself to : ～ 酒色 abandon oneself to wine and women; indulge in sensual pursuits / ～ 于幻想之中 indulge in fantasy

耽误 dānwu delay; hold up: ～ 了整个工程 hold up (*or* delay) the whole project / ～ 功夫 waste time / 把 ～ 的时间夺回来 make up for lost time / 她从不为个人事情 ～ 工作。She never allows her private affairs to interfere with her work. / 都是你, 一个人 ～ 了大伙儿。It was all because of you that we failed to finish the job in time. / 过去 ～ 的时间太多了。We lost too much time.

耽延 dānyán delay; hold up: ～ 时日 lose time

耽忧 dānyōu same as 担忧 dānyōu

聃 (耼)

dān used in 老聃, another name for 老子 (the philosopher)

酖

dān be addicted to alcoholic drinks

殚 (殫)

dān *formal* use up; exhaust: ～ 心 devote one's entire mind

殚见洽闻 dānjiàn-qiàwén have seen all and heard all—erudite; learned

殚竭 dānjié *formal* use up; exhaust: 国用 ～。The national treasury was exhausted.

殚精竭力 dānjīng-jiélì do one's utmost; go all out; use every ounce of one's energy: 他 ～, 终于夺得了金牌。

He went all out and won the gold medal.

殚精竭虑 dānjīng-jiélǜ (also **殚思极虑** dānsī-jílǜ) tax one's ingenuity; rack (or cudgel) one's brains

殚力 dānlì strive; endeavour

箪 (簞)
dān *arch.* a bamboo utensil for holding cooked rice

箪食壶浆 dānsì-hújiāng (welcome an army with) food and drink

箪食瓢饮 dānsì-piáoyǐn live on a bowlful of rice and a ladleful of water—live in poverty

dǎn

胆 (膽)
dǎn ① gallbladder ② courage; guts; bravery: 壮胆 zhuàngdǎn ③ a bladder-like inner container: 热水瓶 ～ the glass liner of a vacuum flask

胆大 dǎndà bold; audacious

胆大包天 dǎndà bāo tiān audacious in the extreme

胆大妄为 dǎndà wàngwéi bold and reckless; daredevil

胆大心细 dǎndà-xīnxì bold but cautious

胆矾 dǎnfán *chem.* chalcanthite; blue vitriol

胆敢 dǎngǎn dare; have the audacity to: 敌人 ～ 来侵犯，就坚决消灭它。 If the enemy dare to invade us, we'll resolutely wipe them out.

胆固醇 dǎngùchún *biochem.* cholesterol

胆管 dǎnguǎn *physiol.* bile duct

胆管炎 dǎnguǎnyán cholangitis

胆管造影 dǎnguǎn zàoyǐng cholangiography

胆寒 dǎnhán be terrified; be struck with terror

胆红素 dǎnhóngsù *biochem.* bilirubin

胆碱 dǎnjiǎn *biochem.* choline

胆力 dǎnlì courage and boldness

胆量 dǎnliàng courage; guts; pluck; spunk: 很有 ～ have plenty of guts (or spunk)

胆略 dǎnlüè courage and resourcefulness: ～ 过人 have unusual courage and resourcefulness

胆囊 dǎnnáng *physiol.* gallbladder

胆囊炎 dǎnnángyán cholecystitis

胆瓶 dǎnpíng a vase with a slender neck and a bulging belly

胆破心惊 dǎnpò-xīnjīng be scared to death

胆气 dǎnqì courage

胆怯 dǎnqiè timid; cowardly: 他不喜欢自己的工作，可又 ～，不敢另找一个。 He does not like his job, but is too timid to try to find another.

胆石 dǎnshí *med.* cholelith; gallstone

胆石病 dǎnshíbìng cholelithiasis

胆识 dǎnshí courage and insight

胆酸 dǎnsuān *biochem.* cholic acid

胆小 dǎnxiǎo timid; cowardly: 这孩子 ～，怕黑。 The timid child was afraid of the dark.

胆小鬼 dǎnxiǎoguǐ coward

胆小如鼠 dǎnxiǎo rú shǔ as timid as a mouse; chicken-hearted: 表面上气壮如牛，实际上 ～ outwardly fierce as a bull, but inwardly timid as a mouse

胆虚 dǎnxū afraid; scared; timid

胆战心惊 dǎnzhàn-xīnjīng tremble with fear; be terror-stricken: 使人 ～ strike terror into sb.; be terrifying

胆汁 dǎnzhī *physiol.* bile

胆壮 dǎnzhuàng bold; fearless; courageous

胆子 dǎnzi courage; guts; nerve: 放开 ～ pluck up courage; stop being afraid / 好大的 ～! What a nerve! / 你大着 ～ 去，不要怕。 Go right ahead and don't be afraid.

疸
dǎn see 黄疸 huángdǎn

掸 (撢、撢、担)
dǎn brush lightly; whisk: ～掉身上的雪花 brush (or whisk) the snow off one's coat / ～～衣服 brush the dust off one's clothes / 墙壁和天花板都～得很干净。 The walls and the ceiling were all dusted clean.

掸子 dǎnzi duster (usu. made of chicken feathers or strips of cloth): 鸡毛 ～ feather duster

dàn

石
dàn *dan*, a unit of dry measure for grain (=1 hectolitre) ——see also shí

旦[1]
dàn ① *formal* dawn; daybreak: 通宵达旦 tōngxiāo-dádàn ② day: 元旦 yuándàn

旦[2]
dàn female role (one of the four main roles in traditional opera, the other three being 生 shēng, 净 jìng, and 丑 chǒu; subdivided into 青衣 qīngyī, 花旦 huādàn, 武旦 wǔdàn, 老旦 lǎodàn, etc.)

旦[3]
dàn *text.* denier

旦角儿 dànjuér same as 旦[2] dàn or, specifically, 青衣 qīngyī or 花旦 huādàn

旦暮 dànmù ① morning and evening ② in a brief span of time

旦夕 dànxī *formal* this morning or evening—in a short while: 危在旦夕 wēi zài dànxī

旦夕之间 dànxī zhī jiān between morning and evening—in a day's time; overnight

但
dàn ① *conj.* but; yet; still; nevertheless: 这孩子用功～不怎么聪明。 He's a hardworking but not very intelligent boy. / 他早已年过六十，～毫不见老。 He's well over sixty, but he doesn't look at all old. / 他很努力，～还是失败了。 He worked hard, yet he failed. / 这消息可能出乎意料，～却是真实的。 The news may be unexpected; nevertheless, it is true. ② only; merely: 明哲保身，～求无过 be worldly-wise and play safe and seek only to avoid blame / 在辽阔的原野上，～见麦浪随风起伏。 On the vast fields, one sees nothing but the wheat billowing in the wind.

但凡 dànfán *adv.* in every case; without exception; as long as: ～ 过路的人，没有一个不停下来欣赏这儿的风景的。 Whoever passes here stops to admire the scenery. / ～ 同志们有困难，他没有不热情帮助的。 Whenever a comrade needs help, he is ready to give it.

但是 dànshì *conj.* but; yet; still; nevertheless: 一个宏大～不切实际的计划 a grandiose but impracticable plan / 他虽然很能干，～ 这个问题太难，他也不好解决。 He's an able man, but the problem is too hard for him. / 我原以为我能去，～ 去不了啦。 I thought I could go, but I can't. / 尽管他相当和霭可亲，～ 我不喜欢他。 He's pleasant enough, yet I don't like him. / 我不能听从你，～ 我感谢你说了这番话。 I can't follow your advice. Nevertheless, thank you for giving it.

但书 dànshū *leg.* proviso

但愿 dànyuàn if only; I wish: ～ 天气赶快放晴。 If only it would clear up soon!

但愿如此 dànyuàn rúcǐ I wish it were true; let's hope so

担 (擔)
dàn ① *dan*, a unit of weight (=50 kilograms) ② a carrying (or shoulder) pole and the loads on it; load; burden: 货郎担 huòlángdàn ③ *m.* shoulder-pole load: 一 ～ 水 two buckets of water

(carried on a shoulder pole) ——see also dàn

担担面　dàndanmiàn　*dial.*　street vendor's noodles (served with sauce only)

担子　dànzi　① a carrying (*or* shoulder) pole and the loads on it; load; burden ② task: 我们不怕～重,一定要把事情办好。We're not afraid of the heavy task and are determined to do a good job.

诞[1]

dàn　① birth: 诞辰 dànchén　② birthday: 华～ your birthday

诞[2]

dàn　absurd; fantastic: 荒诞 huāngdàn

诞辰　dànchén　*formal*　birthday

诞日　dànrì　birthday

诞生　dànshēng　be born; come into being; emerge: 新中国的～ the birth of New China / 在斗争的烈火中～ emerge from the flames of struggle

诞生地　dànshēngdì　birthplace

疍 (蜑)

dàn　see below

疍民　dànmín　boat dwellers

淡

dàn　① thin; light: ～酒 light wine / 云～风轻。The clouds are pale and a light breeze is blowing. ② bland; tasteless; weak; without enough salt: ～茶 weak tea / ～酒 weak wine / 这个汤太～。There's not enough salt in this soup. *or* This soup is too bland for me. ③ (of colour) light; pale: ～黄 light yellow / ～紫 pale purple; lilac ④ indifferent; cool: 淡然 dànrán　⑤ slack; dull: 淡季 dànjì　⑥ *dial.* meaningless; trivial: 扯淡 chědàn

淡泊　dànbó　*formal*　not seek fame and wealth: 他一生～,生活简朴。All through the years he led a simple life without worldly desires.

淡泊明志　dànbó míng zhì　show high ideals by simple living

淡薄　dànbó　① thin; light: 朝雾渐渐地～了。The morning mist gradually thinned. ② tasteless; weak: 酒味～。The wine tastes weak. ③ become indifferent; flag: 他对象棋的兴趣逐渐～了。His interest in chess has begun to flag. ④ faint; dim; hazy: 时间隔得太久,印象也就～了。With the passage of time, these impressions became dim.

淡菜　dàncài　same as 贻贝 yíbèi

淡出　dànchū　*film*　fade out

淡淡　dàndàn　① thin; light; pale: ～的浮云 thin clouds floating in the sky / ～的香水味 a faint smell of perfume ② indifferent; cool: ～地答应了一声 answer drily ③ *liter.*　(of ripples) undulating gently

淡而无味　dàn ér wú wèi　tasteless; insipid

淡饭　dànfàn　simple food: 粗衣～ simple food and clothing—a frugal life

淡化　dànhuà　desalinate: 海水～ desalination of sea water

淡积云　dànjīyún　*meteorol.*　cumulus humilis

淡季　dànjì　slack (*or* dull, off) season: 争取做到蔬菜～不淡,旺季不烂 strive for an ample supply of vegetables in the off seasons and avoid waste in the peak periods

淡漠　dànmò　① indifferent; apathetic; nonchalant ② faint; dim; hazy: 这件事在我脑子里已很～了。The event has left only faint memories in my mind.

淡墨　dànmò　light ink

淡青　dànqīng　light greenish blue

淡然　dànrán　indifferent; cool: ～一笑 smile drily / ～地回答 answer drily (*or* coolly)

淡然处之　dànrán chǔ zhī　treat with indifference; regard coolly

淡入　dànrù　*film*　fade in

淡食　dànshí　① a salt-free diet: 吃～ go on a salt-free diet / 医生让患肾病的病人吃～。Doctors prescribe a salt-free diet for patients with kidney disease. ② eat saltless food; live without salt

淡水　dànshuǐ　fresh water: ～养鱼 freshwater fish-farming

淡水湖　dànshuǐhú　freshwater lake

淡水鱼　dànshuǐyú　freshwater fish

淡忘　dànwàng　fade from one's memory: 这件事我早已～。It has long since faded from my memory.

淡雅　dànyǎ　simple but elegant; quietly elegant; unadorned and in good taste: 衣着～ be tastefully dressed in a simple style; be dressed with sober refinement / 刺绣品有的鲜艳,有的～。Some of the embroideries are in bold, bright colours; others are quietly elegant.

淡竹　dànzhú　*bot.*　henon bamboo (*phyllostachys nigra* var. *henonis*)

淡妆　dànzhuāng　be lightly made up

淡妆浓抹　dànzhuāng-nóngmǒ　(of a woman) whether lightly or heavily made up: 欲把西湖比西子,～总相宜。(苏轼) For symbol of the Western Lake the Western Maid you well may take, Whether adorned with white and rose Or in unpainted grace she goes.

啖 (啗、噉)

dàn　*formal*　① eat ② feed ③ entice; lure

蛋

dàn　① egg ② an egg-shaped thing: 泥～儿 mud ball

蛋白　dànbái　① egg white; albumen ② protein

蛋白酶　dànbáiméi　*biochem.*　protease; proteinase

蛋白尿　dànbáiniào　*med.*　albuminuria

蛋白石　dànbáishí　opal

蛋白质　dànbáizhì　protein: ～塑料 protein plastics

蛋粉　dànfěn　powdered eggs; egg powder

蛋糕　dàngāo　cake

蛋羹　dàngēng　egg custard

蛋黄　dànhuáng　yolk

蛋鸡　dànjī　laying hen; layer

蛋壳　dànké　eggshell

蛋品　dànpǐn　egg products

蛋青　dànqīng　pale blue

蛋清　dànqīng　*inf.*　egg white

蛋用鸡　dànyòngjī　layer (a hen)

蛋子　dànzi　an egg-shaped thing

萏

dàn　see 菡萏 hàndàn

弹 (彈)

dàn　① ball; pellet: 泥～儿 mud ball ② bullet; bomb: 燃烧弹 ránshāodàn ——see also tán

弹道　dàndào　trajectory

弹道弧线　dàndào húxiàn　ballistic curve

弹道火箭　dàndào huǒjiàn　ballistic rocket

弹道式导弹　dàndàoshì dǎodàn　ballistic missile

弹道学　dàndàoxué　ballistics: 内(外)～ interior (exterior) ballistics

弹弓　dàngōng　catapult; slingshot

弹痕　dànhén　bullet or shell hole; shot mark: ～累累 be riddled with bullets

弹夹　dànjiā　(cartridge) clip; charger

弹尽粮绝　dànjìn-liángjué　run out of ammunition and provisions

弹尽援绝　dànjìn-yuánjué　ammunition has run out and no aid is forthcoming

弹壳　dànké　shell case; cartridge case

弹坑　dànkēng　(shell) crater

弹幕　dànmù　barrage

弹盘　dànpán　cartridge drum; magazine

弹片　dànpiàn　shell fragment (*or* splinter); shrapnel

弹膛　dàntáng　chamber (of a gun)
弹头　dàntóu　bullet; projectile nose; warhead
弹丸　dànwán　① pellet; shot; bullet ② *liter.* (of a place) very small; tiny: ～小邑 a very small town
弹丸之地　dànwán zhī dì　a tiny little place
弹匣　dànxiá　*mil.*　magazine
弹药　dànyào　ammunition
弹药库　dànyàokù　ammunition depot (or storehouse)
弹药手　dànyàoshǒu　ammunition man (or bearer)
弹药所　dànyàosuǒ　ammunition supply (or refilling) point
弹药箱　dànyàoxiāng　ammunition chest; cartridge box
弹着　dànzhuó　*mil.*　impact: ～点 point of impact; hitting point / ～角 angle of impact / ～区 impact (or objective) area
弹着观察　dànzhuó guānchá　*mil.*　spotting: ～兵 spotter
弹子　dànzi　① a pellet shot from a slingshot ② marble: 打～ play marbles ③ *dial.* billiards: ～房 billiard room
弹子锁　dànzisuǒ　spring lock

惮(憚)
dàn　*formal*　fear; dread: 不～烦 not be afraid of trouble

氮
dàn　*chem.*　nitrogen (N)
氮肥　dànféi　nitrogenous fertilizer

瘅(癉)
dàn　*formal*　① illness caused by overwork ② detest; denounce; condemn: 彰善瘅恶 zhāngshàn-dàn'è

澹
dàn　*formal*　quiet; peaceful ——see also tán
澹泊　dànbó　same as 淡泊 dànbó
澹澹　dàndàn　(of ripples) dancing gently
澹然　dànrán　same as 淡然 dànrán

dāng

当¹(當)
dāng　① equal: 门当户对 méndāng-hùduì ② ought to; should; must: 能省的就省，～用的还是得用。Save what you can, but use what you must. ③ *prep.* in sb.'s presence; to sb.'s face: ～着大家谈一谈。Speak out in the presence of everyone. ④ *prep.* just at (a time or place): ～莫扎特只有四岁的时候，就在写一些小步舞曲了。When only four, Mozart was composing minuets.

当²(當)
dāng　① work as; serve as; be: 选他～组长 elect him group leader / 他解放前～长工。He worked as a farmhand before liberation. / 我长大要～飞行员。I want to be a pilot when I grow up. / ～官做老爷 hold an official post and act like an overlord ② bear; accept; deserve: 敢做敢～ dare to act and to take the consequences / 我可～不起这样的夸奖。I just don't deserve such praise. ③ direct; manage; be in charge of: 当家 dāngjiā

当³(當、噹)
dāng　*onom.* the sound of a gong or a bell: ～～的钟声 the tolling of a bell ——see also dàng
当儿　dāngr　*inf.* ① this or that very moment ② space in between: 两张床中间留两米宽的～。There's a two-metre-wide space between the two beds.
当班　dāngbān　be on a shift: 他病了，我得替他去～。He's ill, so I've got to work his shift.
当兵　dāngbīng　be a soldier; serve in the army
当差　dāngchāi　*old* ① be a petty official or an orderly

② manservant
当场　dāngchǎng　on the spot; then and there: ～拒绝他们的要求 turn down their request on the spot / 他～表演了这种新的操作方法。He gave a demonstration of the new technique then and there. / ～抓住 catch red-handed (or in the act)
当场出彩　dāngchǎng chūcǎi　① make a spectacle of oneself ② give the show away on the spot
当朝　dāngcháo　① *formal* the present dynasty ② the reigning sovereign or the present prime minister ③ be in control of court administration
当初　dāngchū　*adv.* originally; at the outset; in the first place; at that time: ～打算在这儿盖一座大楼。It was originally planned to put up a big building here. / ～这儿是一片荒野，如今工厂林立。Factories now stand where there used to be a wilderness. / 我～怎么对你讲的? What did I tell you, eh? / ～你就不该这么做。You should never have acted the way you did in the first place. / 早知今日，何必～? If I had known it would come to this, I would have acted differently.
当代　dāngdài　the present age; the contemporary era: 毛泽东是～最伟大的人物之一。Mao Zedong was one of the greatest men of our time. / ～著名作家 a famous contemporary writer
当道　dāngdào　① blocking the way: 别在～站着。Don't stand in the way. ② *derog.* be in power; hold sway: 坏人～，好人受害。When evildoers are in power, good people suffer.
当地　dāngdì　at the place in question; in the locality; local: ～土特产 special local products / ～人民 local people; local inhabitants / ～时间 local time
当东　dāngdōng　(short for 当东道主) play the host; act as host
当断不断　dāng duàn bù duàn　fail to make a decision when one should; hesitate when decision is needed
当关　dāngguān　① guard a pass or checkpoint ② *formal* gatekeeper; guard
当归　dāngguī　*Chin. med.* Chinese angelica
当行出色　dānghàng-chūsè　excel in one's own field
当回事　dānghuíshì　take sth. seriously
当机立断　dāng jī lì duàn　decide quickly; make a prompt decison: 情况紧急，需要我们～! In this crisis we've got to make a quick decision.
当即　dāngjí　*adv.* at once; right away: ～表示同意 give one's consent right away
当家　dāngjiā　manage (household) affairs: 我妻子很会～。My wife is a very good housekeeper. / 他是厂里的好～。He does a good job as director of the factory.
当家的　dāngjiāde　① *inf.* the head of a family ② *dial.* husband ③ *inf.* the head monk of a Buddhist temple; Buddhist abbot
当家作主　dāngjiā zuòzhǔ　be master in one's own house; be the master of one's own affairs (or destiny): 人民～。The people are the masters of their own country.
当间儿　dāngjiànr　*dial.* in the middle: 堂屋～放着一张大方桌。There is a big square table in the middle of the hall.
当街　dāngjiē　① facing the street ② *dial.* in the street
当今　dāngjīn　① now; at present; nowadays: ～之世 in the world of today; at the present time ② *old* the emperor on the throne; the reigning emperor
当紧　dāngjǐn　*dial.* critical; important: 他遇到～的事，就用笔记下。He always made a note of anything important.
当局　dāngjú　the authorities: 政府(学校)～ the government (school) authorities
当局者迷，旁观者清　dāngjúzhě mí, pángguānzhě qīng　the spectators see the chess game better than the players;

the onlooker sees most of the game

当空 dāngkōng high above in the sky: 明月 ～。A bright moon is shining in the sky.

当口儿 dāngkǒur *inf.* this or that very moment: 就在这 ～ at the very moment; just at that time

当啷 dānglāng *onom.* clank; clang

当量 dāngliàng *chem.* equivalent (weight): 电化 ～ electrochemical equivalent / 克 ～ gram equivalent / ～ 比例定律 the law of equivalent proportions / ～ 浓度 equivalent concentration

当令 dānglìng in season: 现在是伏天, 西瓜正 ～。These are the dog days; watermelons are just in season.

当炉 dānglú (also 当炉 dānglú) sell alcoholic drinks

当路 dānglù same as 当道 dāngdào

当面 dāngmiàn *adv.* to sb.'s face; in sb.'s presence: ～ 撒谎 tell a barefaced lie / ～ 弄清楚 straighten things out face to face / 信是我 ～ 交给主任的。I handed the letter to the director personally.

当面锣对面鼓 dāngmiànluó-duìmiàngǔ direct confrontation and face-to-face argument

当面说好话, 背后下毒手 dāngmiàn shuō hǎohuà, bèihòu xià dúshǒu say nice things to sb.'s face, then stab him in the back

当年 dāngnián ① in those years (*or* days): ～ 家里穷, 无力抚养孩子。In those years we were too poor to bring up our children properly. / 想 ～, 这里还没有火车呢! Well, in those days there was no railway here. / 他的精力不减 ～。He is as energetic as ever. ② the prime of life: 他正在 ～。He is in his prime. ——see also dàngnián

当前 dāngqián ① before one; facing one: 一事 ～, 应该先想到国家的利益。Whenever something crops up, one should first think of the interests of the state. ② present; current: ～的中心任务 the central task at present / ～世界的主要倾向 the main trend in the world today / ～利益 immediate interests / ～的国际形势 the current (*or* present) international situation

当枪使 dāngqiāngshǐ serve as hatchet man

当权 dāngquán be in power; hold power: ～ 派 person in power; people in authority

当然 dāngrán ① *adv.* without doubt; certainly; of course; to be sure: 这样做～最好。Of course this is the best way to do it. / 借你的笔用一下可以吗?—～ 可以。May I borrow your pen?—Certainly! (*or* Sure!) / 他这个人～挺好, 可就是不那么聪明。He's a nice person, to be sure, but not very clever. / 同志有困难～要帮助。It goes without saying that we should help a comrade in difficulty. ② natural: ～ 同盟军 natural ally / 你取得成功是～的。It is quite natural that you should succeed. ③ ex officio: ～成员 an ex officio member (of a committee, etc.) / ～继承人 heir apparent

当仁不让 dāng rén bù ràng not decline to shoulder a responsibility; not leave to others what one ought to do oneself; not pass on to others what one is called upon to do: 那件事你可 ～ 啊! That's what you should do by rights.

当时 dāngshí *adv.* then; at that time: ～ 我并不知道。I didn't know then. ——see also dàngshí

当事 dāngshì ① be in charge; be in control: 坏人 ～, 好人倒霉。When bad people are in control, good people suffer. ② concerned; involved ③ the authorities or the parties concerned ——see also dàngshì

当事国 dāngshìguó the state directly involved; the country concerned

当事人 dāngshìrén ① *leg.* party (to a lawsuit); litigant ② person (*or* party) concerned; interested parties: 经济合同 ～ parties to an economic contract

当堂 dāngtáng *old* in court: ～作证 bear witness in court

当天 dāngtiān same as 当空 dāngkōng ——see also dàngtiān

当庭 dāngtíng in court

当头 dāngtóu ① right overhead; right on sb.'s head; head on: 烈日 ～ 照。The hot sun is shining right overhead. / 给他 ～ 一瓢冷水 pour cold water on him ② facing (*or* confronting) one; imminent: 那时候正是国难 ～, 爱国青年都纷纷到抗敌前线去。The country was in imminent danger, and large numbers of patriotic young people left for the front to fight the enemy. ——see also dàngtou

当头棒喝 dāngtóu bànghè a blow and a shout—a sharp (*or* severe) warning

当头炮 dāngtóupào direct criticism

当头一棒 dāngtóu yī bàng (also 当头棒 dāngtóubàng) a head-on blow

当午 dāngwǔ midday; noon: 锄禾日～, 汗滴禾下土。(李绅) As at noontide they hoe their crops, Sweat on the grain to earth drops.

当务之急 dāng wù zhī jí the most pressing matter of the moment; a top priority task; urgent matter

当下 dāngxià *adv.* instantly; immediately; at once: 我一听这话, ～ 就警惕起来了。Hearing this, I was instantly on the alert.

当先 dāngxiān in the van; in the front ranks; at the head: 奋勇 ～ fight bravely in the van

当心[1] dāngxīn take care; be careful; look out: ～ 别把试管打碎了。Take care not to break the test tube. / ～ 别踩了庄稼。Be careful not to step on the crops. / ～ ! 汽车来了。Look out! There's a car coming. *or* Mind that car. / ～ 路滑。Watch your step. The road is slippery.

当心[2] dāngxīn *dial.* the centre of the chest; centre

当选 dāngxuǎn be elected: 他 ～ 为全国人大代表。He was elected a deputy to the National People's Congress.

当选总统 dāngxuǎn zǒngtǒng president-elect

当腰 dāngyāo the middle part (of a long object): 两头细, ～ 粗 thin at both ends and thick in the middle

当一天和尚撞一天钟 dāng yītiān héshang zhuàng yītiān zhōng same as 做一天和尚撞一天钟 zuò yītiān héshang zhuàng yītiān zhōng

当政 dāngzhèng be in power; be in office

当之无愧 dāng zhī wúkuì fully deserve (a title, an honour, etc.); be worthy of: 劳动英雄的称号, 他 ～。He is worthy of the title of labour hero.

当之有愧 dāng zhī yǒukuì not deserve (a title, an honour, etc.); not be worthy of

当值 dāngzhí (also 当直 dāngzhí) *old* be on duty

当中 dāngzhōng ① in the middle; in the centre: 河 ～ 水流最急。The current is swiftest in the middle of the river. / 坐在主席台 ～ be seated in the centre of the rostrum ② among: 工人 ～ 出现了许多技术革新能手。Many technical innovators have emerged from among the workers.

当中间儿 dāngzhōngjiànr *inf.* right in the middle; right in the centre

当众 dāngzhòng in the presence of all; in public: ～ 认错 acknowledge one's mistakes in public

当众出丑 dāngzhòng chūchǒu make an exhibition of oneself

当子 dāngzi *dial.* space in between ——see also dàngzi

珰(璫) dāng *formal* ① earring ② eunuch

珰珰 dāngdāng *onom.* same as 铛铛 dāngdāng

裆(襠) dāng ① crotch (of trousers) ② *physiol.* crotch

铛(鐺)

dāng *onom.* clank; clang ——see also chēng

铛铛 dāngdāng *onom.* clank; clang: 铜锣敲得～响。The bronze gong clanked.

dǎng

挡(擋、攩)

dǎng ① keep off; ward off; block: ～雨 keep off the rain; shelter one from the rain / ～风 shelter sth. from (or keep out) the wind / 防护林带～住了风沙。The shelterbelt kept the sand in check. / 喝一口～～夜里的寒气。Have a drop. It'll ward off the cold of the night. ② block; get in the way of: ～路 be (or get) in the way / ～光 be (or get) in the light / 山高～不住太阳。The highest mountains can't shut out the sun. / 绝不能让私利～住了眼睛。Never be blinded by private interests. ③ fender; blind: 炉～儿 (fire) fender; fire screen / 窗～子 window blind (or shade) ④ gear (of a car): 前进(倒)～ forward (reverse) gear / 高速(低速)～ top (bottom) gear ——see also dàng

挡车 dǎngchē be in charge of looms and check the quality and quantity of the products

挡驾 dǎngjià *euph.* turn away a visitor with some excuse; decline to receive a guest

挡箭牌 dǎngjiànpái ① shield ② excuse; pretext

挡泥板 dǎngníbǎn mudguard (of a car); fender

挡土墙 dǎngtǔqiáng *archit.* retaining wall

党(黨)

dǎng ① political party; party ② the Party (the Communist Party of China): ～的生活 Party life ③ clique; faction; gang: 死党 sǐdǎng ④ *formal* be partial to; take sides with: 党同伐异 dǎngtóng-fáyì ⑤ *formal* kinsfolk; relatives: 父党 fùdǎng ⑥ (Dǎng) a surname

党八股 dǎngbāgǔ stereotyped Party writing; Party jargon

党报 dǎngbào ① party newspaper (or organ) ② the organ of the Chinese Communist Party; the Party organ

党部 dǎngbù party headquaters (of the Kuomintang)

党代表 dǎngdàibiǎo Party representative (a political worker of the Chinese Communist Party in the Red Army before 1929): ～制 the system of Party representatives

党阀 dǎngfá a despotic political party leader; party tyrant

党费 dǎngfèi party membership dues

党风 dǎngfēng a party's work style; party members' conduct

党纲 dǎnggāng party programme

党棍 dǎnggùn party boss; party man

党籍 dǎngjí party membership: 开除～ expel from the party

党纪 dǎngjì party discipline

党纪国法 dǎngjì-guófǎ Party discipline and the law of the land

党课 dǎngkè Party class; Party lecture: 听(讲)～ attend (give) a Party lecture

党魁 dǎngkuí *derog.* party chieftain (or chief, boss)

党龄 dǎnglíng party standing: 多年～的老党员 a Communist Party member of many years' standing

党内 dǎngnèi within (or inside) the party; inner-party: ～斗争 inner-party struggle / ～民主 democracy within the Party; inner-Party democracy

党派 dǎngpài political parties and groups; party groupings: ～关系 party affiliation

党旗 dǎngqí party flag

党人 dǎngrén ① members of a political party ② *formal* partisans

党参 dǎngshēn *Chin. med.* dangshen (*Codonopsis pilosula*)

党同伐异 dǎngtóng-fáyì defend those who belong to one's own faction and attack those who don't; be narrowly partisan

党徒 dǎngtú *derog.* ① member of a clique or a reactionary political party ② henchman

党团 dǎng-tuán ① political parties and other organizations ② the Chinese Communist Party and the Chinese Communist Youth League; the Party and the League: ～员 Party and League members ③ parliamentary group of a political party

党外 dǎngwài outside the party: ～人士 non-Party personages

党委 dǎngwěi Party committee: ～制 the Party committee system (a system for ensuring collective leadership in the Party)

党务 dǎngwù party work; party affairs

党小组 dǎngxiǎozǔ Party group (a small group under a branch committee in the Party)

党校 dǎngxiào Party school

党性 dǎngxìng Party spirit; Party character: ～不纯的表现 a sign of impurity in Party spirit

党羽 dǎngyǔ *derog.* members of a clique; adherents; henchmen

党员 dǎngyuán party member: ～大会 general membership meeting of a party organization; meeting of all party members

党章 dǎngzhāng party constitution

党证 dǎngzhèng party card

党支部 dǎngzhībù Party branch: ～书记 Party branch secretary

党中央 dǎngzhōngyāng the Party Central Committee; the central leading body of the Party

党总支 dǎngzǒngzhī general Party branch

党组 dǎngzǔ leading Party members' group (in a state organ, of ministerial level)

谠(讜)

dǎng *formal* outspoken

谠论 dǎnglùn *formal* outspoken criticisms

谠言 dǎngyán *formal* outspoken remarks

dàng

当¹(當)

dàng ① proper; right; appropriate: 以上意见～否，请批示。We are awaiting your comment on the proposals set forth above. ② match; equal to: 他一个人能～两个人用。He can do the work of two persons put together. ③ treat as; regard as; take for: 不要把支流～主流。Don't take minor aspects for major ones. ④ think: 我～你不知道。I thought you didn't know. ⑤ that very (day, etc.): 当月 dàngyuè

当²(當、儅)

dàng ① pawn: ～衣服 pawn one's clothes; put one's clothes in pawn ② sth. pawned; pawn; pledge: 赎当 shúdàng ——see also dāng

当成 dàngchéng regard as; treat as; take for

当当 dàngdàng pawn things

当家子 dàngjiāzi *dial.* a member of the same clan; a distant relative with the same family name

当年 dàngnián the same year; that very year: 这个水库一修成，～就受益。The reservoir provided benefits the same year it was completed. ——see also dāngnián

当票　dàngpiào　pawn ticket

当铺　dàngpù　pawnshop: ～ 老板 pawnbroker

当日　dàngrì　the same day; that very day: ～ 有效 good for the date of issue only

当时　dàngshí　*adv.*　right away; at once; immediately: 他一接到电报，～ 就赶回去了。He hurried back the moment he received the telegram. / 她一听到这消息，～ 就晕倒了。She fainted on hearing the news. ——see also dāngshí

当事　dàngshì　① treat sth. as a serious matter; take sth. seriously: 他根本不拿工作当回事儿。He doesn't take the job seriously at all. ② be important; count: 她说话不 ～。What she says doesn't count. ——see also dāngshì

当天　dàngtiān　the same day; that very day: 你可以 ～ 来回。You can go and come back on the same day. / ～ 的事 ～ 做完。Today's work must be done today.

当头　dàngtou　*inf.*　sth. pawned; pawn; pledge ——see also dāngtóu

当晚　dàngwǎn　the same evening; that very evening

当押　dàngyā　pawn or mortgage

当夜　dàngyè　the same night; that very night

当月　dàngyuè　the same month; that very month

当真　dàngzhēn　① take seriously: 我只是开个玩笑，何必 ～ 呢? I was only joking. Why take it seriously? ② (really) true: 这话 ～? Is it really true? ③ *adv.*　really; sure enough: 他说要来，～ 来了。He said he would come and, sure enough, he did.

当子　dàngzi　same as 档子 dàngzi ——see also dāngzi

当做　dàngzuò　treat as; regard as; look upon as: 农奴主把农奴 ～ 会说话的牲口。Serf owners regarded their serfs as animals that could talk. / 我们把雷锋 ～ 学习的榜样。We take Lei Feng as our model. / 退休老工人把教育下一代 ～ 自己应尽的责任。The retired workers regard it as their duty to educate the younger generation. / 白求恩把中国人民的解放事业 ～ 他自己的事业。Norman Bethune adopted the cause of the Chinese people's liberation as his own.

凼(氹)　dàng　*dial.*　water hole; a manure pit in the fields

凼肥　dàngféi　wet compost; watter-logged compost

宕　dàng　*formal*　delay: 延宕 yándàng

宕帐　dàngzhàng　a debt long overdue

荡¹(蕩、盪)　dàng　① swing; sway; wave: ～ 秋千 play on a swing / ～ 桨 pull on the oars ② loaf about: 游荡 yóudàng ③ rinse: 冲荡 chōngdàng ④ clear away; sweep off: 扫荡 sǎodàng

荡²(蕩)　dàng　loose in morals: 淫荡 yíndàng

荡³(蕩)　dàng　a shallow lake; marsh: 芦苇 ～ a reed marsh

荡船　dàngchuán　swingboat

荡涤　dàngdí　cleanse; clean up; wash away: ～ 旧社会遗留下来的污泥浊水 clean up the filth and mire left over from the old society

荡妇　dàngfù　*formal*　① a loose woman ② prostitute

荡平　dàngpíng　wipe out; quell; stamp out

荡气回肠　dàngqì-huícháng　same as 回肠荡气 huícháng-dàngqì

荡然无存　dàngrán wú cún　all gone; nothing left: 大火之后，庙里过去那些雄伟建筑 ～。After the fire, nothing remained of the once magnificent temple buildings.

荡漾　dàngyàng　ripple; undulate: 湖水 ～。There were ripples on the lake. / 歌声 ～。The song rose and fell like waves. / 金黄的小麦在微风中 ～。The golden wheat rippled in the breeze.

荡子　dàngzǐ　vagrant; wanderer

挡(擋)　dàng　see 摒挡 bìngdàng ——see also dǎng

档(檔)　dàng　① shelves (for files); pigeonholes: 归档 guīdàng ② files; archives: 查档 chádàng ③ crosspiece (of a table, etc.) ④ grade: 这一～ 的羊毛可低价出售。This grade of wool can be sold at a lower price.

档案　dàng'àn　files; archives; record; dossier: ～ 管理员 archivist

档案馆　dàng'ànguǎn　archives

档案柜　dàng'ànguì　filing cabinet

档次　dàngcì　grade: 拉开职工收入的 ～ widen the difference between the income brackets of workers and staff members / ～ 较高的消费品 high-grade (*or* better quality) consumer goods

档子　dàngzi　*dial. m.*　① (for affairs or matters): 这～ 事我来管吧。I'll take care of this matter. ② (for groups of players): 两 ～ 龙灯 two groups of dragon lantern players

砀　dàng　see 莨砀 làngdàng

dāo

刀　dāo　① knife; sword ② *mech.*　cutting tool; tool: 铣刀 xǐdāo ③ sth. shaped like a knife: 冰～ ice skates ④ *m.*　one hundred sheets (of paper)

刀把子　dābàzi　(also 刀把儿 dāobàr) ① the handle of a knife ② (sword) hilt ③ military power; power: 旧社会劳动人民受压迫就是因为没有掌握～、印把子。It was because they had neither arms nor power that the working people were oppressed in the old society. ④ *dial.*　sth. that may be used against one; a handle

刀背　dāobèi　the back of a knife blade

刀笔　dāobǐ　writing of indictments, appeals, etc.; pettifoggery: ～ 吏 petty official who draws up indictments, etc.; pettifogger

刀币　dāobì　a knife-shaped ancient coin

刀兵　dāobīng　① weapons; arms ② fighting; war: 动 ～ resort to arms; resort to force

刀兵之灾　dāobīng zhī zāi　the calamities of war; war

刀叉　dāo-chā　knife and fork

刀豆　dāodòu　sword bean (the plant or the pods it bears)

刀法　dāofǎ　skill in using a kitchen knife in cookery or a chisel in engraving, or in wielding a sword in martial arts

刀锋　dāofēng　the point or edge of a knife

刀斧手　dāofǔshǒu　*old*　executioner; headsman

刀耕火种　dāogēng-huǒzhòng　slash-and-burn cultivation: 那个偏僻山区，过去是 ～。In those remote mountains people used to farm by the slash-and-burn method.

刀功　dāogōng　(in preparing food) cutting and slicing skill

刀光剑影　dāoguāng-jiànyǐng　the glint and flash of daggers and swords

刀痕　dāohén　a mark or scar left by a knife-cut

刀架　dāojià　*mech.*　tool carrier; tool carriage

刀架导轨　dāojià dǎoguǐ　*mech.*　tool guide

刀具　dāojù　*mech.*　cutting tool; tool

刀口　dāokǒu　① the edge of a knife ② where a thing

can be put to best use; the crucial point; the right spot: 把劲儿使在 ～上 bring efforts to bear on the right spot / 钱要花在～上。 Use your money where it's needed most. ③ cut; incision

刀马旦 dāomǎdàn sword-and-horse *dan*—a subdivision of the *wudan* (武旦) role (portraying horse-women and female warriors, who wear tight-fitting clothes, twirl weapons, and perform acrobatic feats)

刀片 dāopiàn ① razor blade ② *mech.* (tool) bit; blade

刀枪 dāo-qiāng sword and spear; weapons

刀枪不入 dāo-qiāng bù rù (of a human body) arms-proof

刀枪入库，马放南山 dāo-qiāng rù kù, mǎ fàng nánshān put the weapons back in the arsenal and graze the war horses on the hillside—relax vigilance against war

刀鞘 dāoqiào sheath; scabbard

刀刃 dāorèn ① the edge of a knife ② where a thing can be put to best use; the crucial point: 好钢用在刀刃上 hǎogāng yòng zài dāorèn shang

刀山火海 dāoshān-huǒhǎi a mountain of swords and a sea of flames—most dangerous places; most severe trials: 刀山敢上，火海敢闯 dare to climb a mountain of swords or plunge into a sea of flames; be ready to undergo the most severe trials

刀伤 dāoshāng a wound inflicted with a knife or sword; gash or stab

刀鱼 dāoyú *dial.* hairtail

刀子 dāozi *inf.* small knife; pocketknife

刀子嘴 dāozizuǐ ① a sharp tongue ② a sharp-tongued person

刀俎 dāozǔ *formal* butcher's knife and chopping block—oppressor; persecutor: 人为刀俎，我为鱼肉 rén wéi dāozǔ, wǒ wéi yúròu

叨 dāo see below ——see also dáo; tāo

叨叨 dāodao talk on and on; chatter away: 别一个人～了，听听大家的意见吧。 Don't say the same thing over and over again. Listen to what other people have to say.

叨登 dāodeng *inf.* ① turn things over; move things around: 把衣服～出来晒晒。 Turn your clothes out to air them. ② harp on things past: 事情已经过去了，还～什么? Why harp on things already over and done with?

叨唠 dāolao *inf.* talk on and on; chatter away: 他～了半天，人都不爱听。 He chattered for a long time and bored everybody.

氘 dāo *chem.* deuterium (H^2 or D)

氘核 dāohé *chem.* deuteron

dáo

叨 dáo see below ——see also dāo; tāo

叨咕 dáogu mutter; grumble

捯 dáo *dial.* ① wind (string, yarn, or thread): 把风筝～回来。 Pull in the kite. ② find the clue to sth.: 这件事已经 ～出头儿来了。 We've finally found the clue to the matter.

捯根儿 dáogēnr *dial.* get to the root of a matter

dǎo

导(導) dǎo ① lead; guide: ～淮入海 channel the Huaihe River into the sea ② transmit; conduct:

导电 dǎodiàn ③ instruct; teach; give guidance to: 教导 jiàodǎo

导弹 dǎodàn guided missile: 反辐射～ anti-radiation missile / 反坦克～ anti-tank missile / 空中截击～ air intercept missile

导弹发射场 dǎodàn fāshèchǎng missile (launching) site; launching site

导弹发射井 dǎodàn fāshèjǐng launching silo

导弹发射器 dǎodàn fāshèqì missile launcher

导弹发射台 dǎodàn fāshètái (missile) launching pad

导弹核潜艇 dǎodàn héqiántǐng nuclear submarine armed with guided missiles

导弹基地 dǎodàn jīdì missile base

导弹驱逐舰 dǎodàn qūzhújiàn guided missile destroyer

导弹巡洋舰 dǎodàn xúnyángjiàn guided missile cruiser

导电 dǎodiàn transmit electric current; conduct electricity: ～性 electric conductivity

导风板 dǎofēngbǎn *aviation* baffle

导管 dǎoguǎn ① *mech.* conduit; pipe; duct: 冷却～ cooling duct / 金属～ metal conduit ② *biol.* vessel; duct

导轨 dǎoguǐ *mech.* slideway; guide: 刀架～ tool guide

导轨磨床 dǎoguǐ móchuáng *mech.* slideway grinder

导航 dǎoháng navigation: 无线电(雷达，天文)～ radio (radar, celestial) navigation

导航台 dǎohángtái guidance station; nondirection radio beacon (NDB)

导火索 dǎohuǒsuǒ *mil.* (blasting) fuse

导火线 dǎohuǒxiàn ① (blasting) fuse ② a small incident that touches off a big one: 战争的 ～ an incident that touches off a war

导流 dǎoliú *water conservancy* diversion: ～隧洞 diversion tunnel

导轮 dǎolún *mech.* guide pulley; pilot wheel

导论 dǎolùn introduction (to a thesis, etc.); introductory remarks

导尿 dǎoniào *med.* catheterization

导盘 dǎopán *chem. fibre* godet

导热 dǎorè *phys.* conduct heat ～系数 thermal conductivity

导师 dǎoshī ① tutor; teacher ② guide of a great cause; teacher: 无产阶级的伟大 ～ great teacher of the proletariat

导数 dǎoshù *math.* derivative

导体 dǎotǐ *phys.* conductor

导线 dǎoxiàn *elec.* lead; (conducting) wire: 玻璃纤维～ fibreglass wire / ～管 conduit

导向 dǎoxiàng ① direct sth. towards: 这次会谈～两国关系的正常化。 These talks were directed towards the normalization of the relations between the two countries. ② direct the course of sth.; guide: 舆论～ the guidance of public opinion (as by news media)

导言 dǎoyán introduction (to a piece of writing); introductory remarks

导演 dǎoyǎn ① direct (a film, play, etc.) ② director

导引 dǎoyǐn ① guide; lead ② Taoist breathing exercises

导游 dǎoyóu ① conduct a sightseeing tour ② tourist guide ③ guidebook: ～图 tourist map

导源 dǎoyuán ① (of a river) have its source: 黄河 ～ 于青海。 The Huanghe River rises in Qinghai Province. ② originate; derive: 认识～于实践。 Knowledge derives from practice.

导致 dǎozhì lead to; bring about; result in; cause: ～第二次世界大战的一些事件 the events that led up to World War Ⅱ / 理论上的错误必然 ～实践上的失败。 Errors in theory inevitably result in failures in practice.

岛(島) dǎo island

岛国 dǎoguó country consisting of one or more islands; island country

岛屿 dǎoyǔ islands and islets; islands

倒[1]

dǎo ① fall; topple: 摔～ fall over / 风把树刮～了。The gale uprooted the tree. / 我～在床上就睡着了。I threw myself down on the bed and fell asleep immediately. / 他把对手击～了。He felled his opponent. / 他把我问～了。He stumped me. ② collapse; fail: 内阁～了。The cabinet collapsed. ③ close down; go bankrupt; go out of business: 这家公司～了。The company went bankrupt. ④ (of voice) become hoarse: 他的嗓子～了。He has lost his voice.

倒[2]

dǎo ① change; exchange: ～肩 shift a burden from one shoulder to the other / 请你们两位把座位～一下。Will you two please swop (or change) seats? ② move around: 地方太小，～不开身。There is no room to move around.

——see also dào

倒把 dǎobǎ engage in profiteering; speculate: 投机倒把 tóujī-dǎobǎ

倒班 dǎobān change shifts; work in shifts; work by turns: 昼夜～ work in shifts round the clock

倒闭 dǎobì close down; go bankrupt; go into liquidation: 企业～ bankruptcy of an enterprise

倒毙 dǎobì drop dead: ～街头 drop dead in the street

倒仓 dǎocāng ① take grain out of a granary to sun it ② transfer grain from one granary to another

倒茬 dǎochá agric. rotation of crops

倒车 dǎochē change trains or buses: 这趟车直达徐州，不用～。This is a through train to Xuzhou. You don't have to change. ——see also dàochē

倒动 dǎodòng ① move; shift ② dial. buy and sell; deal in: ～香烟 deal in cigarettes

倒伏 dǎofú (of crops) lodging: 抗～力强的稻种 a strain of rice with strong resistance to lodging

倒戈 dǎogē change sides in a war; turn one's coat; transfer one's allegiance

倒阁 dǎogé force the government to resign; bring down a cabinet: 反对派发动了～运动。The opposition launched a campaign to bring down the government.

倒海翻江 dǎohǎi-fānjiāng same as 翻江倒海 fānjiāng-dǎohǎi

倒换 dǎohuàn ① rotate; take turns: 几种作物～着种 rotate several crops / ～着护伤员 take turns looking after the wounded ② rearrange (sequence, order, etc.); replace

倒嚼 dǎojiào (also 倒噍 dǎojiào) ruminate; chew the cud

倒卖 dǎomài resell at a profit; scalp: ～火车票 scalp train tickets

倒霉 dǎoméi (also 倒楣 dǎoméi) have bad luck; be out of luck; be down on one's luck: 真～，赶到车站车刚开走。What lousy luck! When I reached the station, the train had just left.

倒弄 dǎonong ① move; shift ② buy and sell; deal in: ～粮食 deal in grain ③ make a fool of; deceive

倒嗓 dǎosǎng (of a singer) lose one's voice

倒手 dǎoshǒu (of merchandise, etc.) change hands: 这批货他一～就赚了了一千元。As soon as this batch of goods passed through his hands, he made a 1,000-*yuan* profit.

倒塌 dǎotā (also 倒坍 dǎotān) collapse; topple down

倒台 dǎotái fall from power; downfall

倒腾 dǎoteng inf. ① turn; move: 把粪～到地里去 spread the manure over the field ② buy and sell; deal in

倒头 dǎotóu touch the pillow; lie down: ～就睡 tumble into bed

倒胃口 dǎo wèikou spoil one's appetite: 这东西吃多了容易～。Too much of this food will spoil your appetite. / 这样的电视剧真叫人～。I've no stomach for such TV dramas.

倒卧 dǎowò lie down: ～在地 lie down on the ground

倒卧 dǎowo dial. the body of one who has dropped dead by the roadside

倒休 dǎoxiū change one's shift to get leave later

倒牙 dǎoyá dial. set (or put) one's teeth on edge

倒爷 dǎoyé inf. usu. derog. profiteer

倒运[1] dǎoyùn dial. have bad luck; be out of luck; be down on one's luck

倒运[2] dǎoyùn profiteer by buying cheap and selling dear

倒灶 dǎozào dial. ① decline (in wealth and position) ② have bad luck; be out of luck; be down on one's luck

倒帐 dǎozhàng a bad debt

捣（搗、擣）

dǎo ① pound with a pestle, etc.; beat; smash: ～药 pound medicine in a mortar / ～米 husk rice with a pestle and mortar / ～衣 beat clothes (in washing) / 他用胳膊肘～了我一下。He poked me with his elbow. ② harass; disturb

捣蛋 dǎodàn make or cause trouble: 这孩子老在班上～。The boy is always making trouble in class. / 他的牙又在～了，他得看牙科医生去。His teeth are giving him trouble again; he needs to see a dentist.

捣动[1] dǎodòng ① turn over ② dial. stir up; incite

捣动[2] dǎodòng same as 倒动 dǎodòng

捣固 dǎogù make firm by ramming or tamping

捣鼓 dǎogu dial. move back and forth; fiddle with

捣鬼 dǎoguǐ play tricks; do mischief: 不老实的买卖人有时候会～。Dishonest businessmen sometimes use tricks. / 你别跟我～，我要知道事情的真相。Don't play tricks on me—I want to know the truth. / 你在捣什么鬼？What mischief are you up to?

捣毁 dǎohuǐ smash up; demolish; destroy: ～敌军据点 destroy enemy strongpoints

捣乱 dǎoluàn make or cause trouble; create a disturbance: 有人想在会上～。Some people tried to make trouble at the meeting. / 他专门～。He's a real troublemaker. / 叔叔忙着呢，你别～。Uncle's busy. Don't disturb him.

捣麻烦 dǎo máfan inf. seek a quarrel; stir up or make trouble

捣弄 dǎonong ① move back and forth; fiddle with ② same as 倒弄 dǎonong①②

捣碎 dǎosuì pound to pieces

祷（禱）

dǎo ① pray: 祈祷 qídǎo ② (used in an old-style letter) ask earnestly; beg: 望即赐复为～。I beg for an early reply.

祷告 dǎogào pray; say one's prayers

祷念 dǎoniàn say a prayer

祷文 dǎowén prayer

祷祝 dǎozhù pray for sb.

蹈

dǎo ① formal tread; step: 赴汤蹈火 fùtāng-dǎohuǒ ② skip; trip: 舞蹈 wǔdǎo

蹈常袭故 dǎocháng-xígù go on in the same old way; get into a rut; follow a set routine

蹈海 dǎohǎi formal commit suicide by throwing oneself into the sea

蹈袭 dǎoxí follow slavishly: ～前人 slavishly follow one's predecessors

dào

到 dào ① arrive; reach: 火车～站了。The train has arrived at the station. / ～了多少人? How many people were present? / 时间～了。Time's up. / ～! (answer to roll call) Here! ② go to; leave for: ～兰州去 go to Lanzhou / ～群众中去 go among the masses; go into the midst of the masses ③ *prep.* up until; up to: 从星期三～星期五 from Wednesday to Friday / ～目前为止 up to the present; until now; so far / 工作～深夜 work late into the night / 温度降～零下二十度。The temperature dropped to minus twenty degrees centigrade. ④ (used as a verb complement to show the result of an action): 办得～ can be done / 说～做～ be as good as one's word / 想不～你来了。I didn't expect you would come. / 我到处找那本书, 终于在床底下找～了。I looked everywhere for the book, and finally found it under the bed. ⑤ thoughtful; considerate: 不～之处请原谅。Please excuse me if I have been inconsiderate in any way.

到岸价格 dào'àn jiàgé cost, insurance and freight (C. I. F.)

到场 dàochǎng be present; show up; turn up: 市长～为展览会剪了彩。The mayor was present and cut the ribbon for the exhibition.

到处 dàochù *adv.* at all places; everywhere: 侵略者～挨打。The invaders were attacked wherever they went. / 烟头不要～乱扔。Don't drop cigarette ends about.

到处碰壁 dàochù pèngbì run into snags everywhere

到达 dàodá arrive; get to; reach: 代表团于今晨～广州。The delegation arrived in Guangzhou this morning. / 按现在的速度, 我们三点以前可以～。We can get there before three o'clock at this speed.

到达港 dàodágǎng port of arrival

到达站 dàodázhàn destination

到底[1] dàodǐ to the end; to the finish: 打～ fight to the finish / 将革命进行～。Carry the revolution through to the end.

到底[2] dàodǐ *adv.* ① at last; in the end; finally: 新方法～试验成功了。The new method has finally proved to be a success. ② (used in a question for emphasis): 你～是什么意思? What on earth do you mean? / 你那样干～是为什么? What in the world did you do that for? ③ after all; in the final analysis: 他～是新手, 干活还不熟练。After all, he's new to the work and isn't very skilful at it yet.

到点 dàodiǎn it's time to do sth.; time is up: ～了, 该下班了。It's time to knock off. / ～了, 一律交卷! Time is up! Hand in your papers, everybody.

到顶 dàodǐng reach the summit (*or* peak, limit); cannot be improved

到会 dàohuì be present at a meeting; attend a meeting: ～人数很多。There was a large attendance.

到家 dàojiā reach a very high level; be perfect; be excellent: 把思想工作做～ do ideological work really well / 这活儿做得很～。This is excellent workmanship. / 他这笔字写得还不～。His calligraphy is far from perfect.

到来 dàolái arrival; advent: 迎接技术革新高潮的～ hail the arrival of a high tide of technical innovation / 一个社会主义的文化建设高潮正在～。A new high tide in the development of socialist culture is in the offing.

到了儿 dàoliǎor *dial.* at last; in the end; finally

到期 dàoqī become due; mature; expire: 这本书已经～了。This book is due for return. / 这张票据什么时候～? When does this bill mature (*or* become due)? / 签证下月～。The visa expires next month.

到期日 dàoqīrì date due

到任 dàorèn take office; arrive at one's post

到手 dàoshǒu in one's hands; in one's possession: 眼看就要～的粮食, 决不能让洪水冲走。The grain is nearly in our hands. We mustn't allow the flood to carry it away.

到头 dàotóu to the end; at an end: 这条街走～就有一个邮局。There's a post office at the end of the street.

到头来 dàotóulái *adv.* in the end; finally: 不老实的人～总是要栽跟头的。Dishonest people are bound to come a cropper in the end.

到职 dàozhí take office; arrive at one's post

倒[1] dào ① upside down; inverted; inverse; reverse: 次序～了。The order is reversed. / 小孩把画挂～了。The child hung the picture upside down. ② move backwards; turn upside down: 火车～回去了。The train backed up. ③ pour; tip: ～一杯茶 pour a cup of tea / ～垃圾 tip (*or* dump) rubbish / 他把一肚子冤屈都～出来。He poured out all his grievances.

倒[2] dào *adv.* ① (indicating sth. unexpected): 本想省事, 没想～费事了。We wanted to save ourselves some trouble but actually we gave ourselves more. / 你还有什么要说的, 我～要听听。I'd like to hear what else you've got to say. ② (indicating contrast): 你说得～容易, 做起来可不容易。It's easy for you to say that, but it's not so easy to do it. *or* That's easier said than done. ③ (indicating concession): 我跟他认识～认识, 就是不太熟。Yes, I know him, but not very well. / 那本书好～是好, 可是太贵。That book is good all right, but it's too expensive. ④ (used to press sb. for an answer): 你～去不去呀! Do you want to go or don't you? / 你～是说话呀! Can't you say something?

——see also 到

倒背如流 dào bèi rú liú can recite sth. backwards — know sth. by heart

倒背手 dàobèishǒu with one's hands behind one (when pacing to and fro or strolling)

倒不如 dàobùrú it would be better to

倒彩 dàocǎi booing; hooting; catcall: 喝～ make catcalls; boo and hoot

倒插门 dàochāmén (of a man) marry into the wife's family: ～女婿 a live-in son-in-law

倒车 dàochē back a car: 他倒着车开进车库。He backed his car into the garage. ——see also dǎochē; 开倒车 kāi dǎochē

倒持太阿 dào chí Tài'ē same as 太阿倒持 Tài'ē dào chí

倒刺 dàocì hangnail; agnail

倒打一耙 dào dǎ yī pá make unfounded countercharges; put the blame on one's victim; recriminate: 他自己错了不承认, 反而～。So far from admitting his own mistake, he falsely accused his critic.

倒挡 dàodǎng reverse gear

倒飞 dàofēi *aviation* inverted (*or* upside down) flight

倒粪 dàofèn turn over a heap of manure or a compost heap and pile it up afresh

倒挂 dàoguà ① hang upside down: 他左肩～着一支冲锋枪。He had a tommy gun slung muzzle down over his left shoulder. ② reversal of the natural order of things: 购销价格～ purchasing prices higher than selling prices / 脑体～ manual workers earning more than mental workers

倒挂金钟 dàoguàjīnzhōng *bot.* fuchsia

倒灌 dàoguàn (of floodwaters, tidal currents, etc.) flow from a lower to a higher place; (of smoke) pour in down a chimney

倒果为因 dào guǒ wéi yīn take effect for cause

倒过儿 dàoguòr *dial.* transpose; switch the order: 这两个字写倒了 过儿了。These two characters should switch places. / 把号码倒个过儿就对了。Transpose the two digits and then the number is correct.

倒好儿 dàohǎor booing; hooting; catcall: 叫～ make catcalls; boo and hoot

倒睫 dàojié *med.* trichiasis

倒经 dàojīng *med.* vicarious menstruation

倒立 dàolì ① stand upside down: 宝塔的影子～在水里。The pagoda is reflected upside down in the water. ② *sports* handstand

倒流 dàoliú flow backwards: 河水不能～。Rivers don't flow backwards. / 防止商品运输上的～ avoid transporting goods back to their place of origin

倒轮闸 dàolúnzhá backpedalling brake (of a bicycle); coaster brake

倒赔 dàopéi lose money instead of making money

倒片 dàopiàn *film* rewind: ～机 rewinder

倒摄遗忘 dàoshè yíwàng *psychol.* retroactive (*or* retrograde) amnesia

倒收付息 dàoshōu fùxī *econ.* negative interest

倒数 dàoshǔ count from bottom to top or from rear to front; count backwards: ～第三行 the third line from the bottom / 我住在这条胡同里～第二家。I live in the last house but one in this lane.

倒数计时 dàoshǔ jìshí countdown

倒数 dàoshù *math.* reciprocal

倒算 dàosuàn seize back confiscated property ——see also 反攻倒算 fǎngōng-dàosuàn

倒锁 dàosuǒ lock sb. in: 她把小孩儿～在屋里，出门去买东西。She locked her baby in the room and went shopping.

倒贴 dàotiē ① pay instead of getting paid ② (of a woman) pay for the upkeep of her paramour; keep a gigolo

倒退 dàotuì go backwards; fall back: 迎面一阵狂风把我刮得～了好几步。A gust of strong wind pushed me a few steps backwards. / ～三十年，我也是个壮小伙子。Thirty years ago, I was a strapping young fellow too. / 坚持进步，反对～ persist in progress and oppose retrogression

倒像 dàoxiàng *phys.* inverted image

倒行逆施 dàoxíng-nìshī ① go against the trend of the times; try to put the clock back; push a reactionary policy ② perverse acts: 反动派的～从反面教育了人民。The perverse acts of the reactionaries taught the people by negative example.

倒许 dàoxǔ but perhaps; or maybe: 她对学外语不感兴趣，让她学学绘画看，～合适。She is not interested in foreign languages. Let her try painting; maybe she has an aptitude for that.

倒叙 dàoxù flashback

倒悬 dàoxuán *formal* hang by the feet—be in sore straits

倒因为果 dào yīn wéi guǒ take cause for effect

倒影 dàoyǐng inverted image; inverted reflection in water

倒栽葱 dàozāicōng fall head over heels; fall headlong: 飞机引擎失灵，一个～掉到海里了。The engine failed and the plane fell headlong into the sea.

倒置 dàozhì place upside down; invert: 轻重倒置 qīng-zhòng dàozhì

倒转 dàozhuǎn ① turn the other way round; reverse: ～来说，也是这样。The same is true the other way round. ② *dial.* contrary to reason or one's expectation: 你把事情搞糟了，～来怪我。You messed up the whole thing yourself and now you put the blame on me.

倒装词序 dàozhuāng cíxù *gram.* inverted word order

帱（幬） dào *formal* cover ——see also chóu

悼 dào mourn; grieve: 哀悼 āidào

悼词 dàocí memorial speech: 致～ deliver a memorial speech

悼念 dàoniàn mourn; grieve over: 沉痛～ mourn with deep grief

悼亡 dàowáng *formal* ① mourn a deceased wife ② be bereaved of one's wife

盗 dào ① steal; rob: 被～ be stolen ② thief; robber: 强盗 qiángdào

盗案 dào'àn a theft case; a case of larceny

盗伐 dàofá fell trees unlawfully: ～森林 surreptitious felling of a forest; illegal lumbering

盗匪 dàofěi bandits; robbers: 肃清～ exterminate banditry

盗汗 dàohàn *med.* night sweat

盗魁 dàokuí a robber or bandit chief

盗卖 dàomài steal and sell (public property)

盗名欺世 dàomíng-qīshì same as 欺世盗名 qīshì-dàomíng

盗墓 dàomù rob a tomb (*or* grave): ～人 grave robber

盗窃 dàoqiè steal: ～国家机密 steal state secrets

盗窃犯 dàoqièfàn thief

盗窃罪 dàoqièzuì *leg.* larceny

盗取 dàoqǔ steal; embezzle

盗薮 dàosǒu *formal* bandits' (*or* robbers') den

盗用 dàoyòng embezzle; usurp: ～公款 embezzle public funds / ～名义 usurp a name

盗贼 dàozéi robbers; bandits

道[1] dào ① road; way; path: 这是往古北口去的～儿。This road goes (*or* leads) to Gubeikou. / 山间小～ a mountain path ② channel; course: 河道 hédào ③ way; method: 养生之道 yǎngshēng zhī dào ④ doctrine; principle; the Tao; the Way: 孔孟之道 Kǒng-Mèng zhī dào ⑤ Taoism; Taoist: 道士 dàoshì ⑥ superstitious sect: 会道门 huìdàomén ⑦ line: 画一条斜～儿 draw a slanting line ⑧ *m.* ⓐ (for long and narrow objects): 一～河 a river / 万～金光 myriads of golden rays / 一～缝儿 a crack ⓑ (for doors, walls, etc.): 两～门 two successive doors / 三～防线 three lines of defence ⓒ (for orders, questions, etc.): 一～命令 an order / 出五～题 set five questions (for an examination, etc.) ⓓ (for courses in a meal, stages in a procedure, etc.): 上四～菜 serve four courses / 省一～手续 save one step in the process / 上三～漆 apply three coats of paint

道[2] dào circuit (an administrative division of a province in former times): ～台 intendant of a circuit

道[3] dào ① say; talk; speak: 能说会道 néngshuōhuìdào ② say (polite words): 道谢 dàoxiè ③ say (the words quoted): 她笑～: "你说对了!" She said with a smile, "You're right!" ④ think; suppose: 我～是老周呢，原来是你。So it's you! I thought it was Lao Zhou.

道白 dàobái spoken parts in an opera

道班 dàobān railway or highway maintenance squad

道别 dàobié bid farewell; say goodbye

道不拾遗 dào bù shí yí no one picks up what's left by the wayside—honesty prevails throughout society: ～，夜不闭户。People do not take any articles left by the wayside and doors are not bolted at night.

道不同，不相为谋 dào bù tóng, bù xiāng wèi móu there is no point in people taking counsel together who follow different ways

道岔 dàochà *railway* switch; points

道场　dàochǎng　① Taoist or Buddhist rites (performed to save the souls of the dead) ② place where such rites are performed

道床　dàochuáng　*railway*　roadbed: 整体～ monolithic roadbed

道道儿　dàodaor　*dial.*　way; method: 找到增产的新～ find new ways of increasing production / 说出个～来 give a convincing explanation

道德　dàodé　morals; morality; ethics: ～品质 moral character / ～教育 education in ethics / 旧～观念 old moral concepts / 共产主义～ communist morality (*or* ethics) / 体育～ sportsmanship / ～败坏 morally degenerate / 商业～ business ethics

道德经　dàodéjīng　The Classic of the Virtue of the Tao

道地　dàodì　same as 地道 dìdao①

道钉　dàodīng　*railway*　(dog) spike

道乏　dàofá　thank sb. for taking the trouble: 他还要亲自来给你～呢。He is coming himself to thank you for taking all that trouble.

道高一尺，魔高一丈　dào gāo yī chǐ, mó gāo yī zhàng　as virtue rises one foot, vice rises ten; the more illumination, the more temptation

道姑　dàogū　Taoist nun

道观　dàoguàn　Taoist temple

道号　dàohào　Taoist name

道贺　dàohè　congratulate

道家　Dàojiā　Taoist school (a school of thought in the Spring and Autumn and Warring States Periods, 770-221 B.C.); Taoists

道教　Dàojiào　the Taoist religion; Taoism

道具　dàojù　stage property; prop

道口儿　dàokǒur　① road junction ② level crossing

道劳　dàoláo　same as 道乏 dàofá

道理　dàolǐ　① principle; truth; hows and whys: 讲解深耕细作的～ explain the principles of deep ploughing and intensive cultivation / 言语不多～深。The words were few, but they contained profound truth. / 我自有～。I shall find a way. ② reason; argument; sense: 你的话很有～。What you said is quite reasonable (*or* right). / 讲不出一点～ unable to come up with any convincing argument; unable to justify oneself in any way

道林纸　dàolínzhǐ　glazed printing paper

道路　dàolù　road; way; path: ～泥泞。The road is muddy. / 走前人没有走过的～ break paths none have explored before / 为两国首脑会谈铺平～ pave the way for summit talks between the two countries

道路以目　dàolù yǐ mù　(of people living under tyranny) exchange glances when meeting on the road (not daring to speak out openly)

道貌岸然　dàomào ànrán　pose as a person of high morals; be sanctimonious: 好一个～的伪君子! What a sanctimonious hypocrite!

道木　dàomù　same as 枕木 zhěnmù

道袍　dàopáo　Taoist robe

道破　dàopò　point out frankly; lay bare; reveal: 一语道破 yī yǔ dàopò

道歉　dàoqiàn　apologize; make an apology: 你把她的生日给忘了，应该向她～。You should apologize to her for forgetting her birthday. / 我得向你～。I owe you an apology.

道情　dàoqíng　chanting folk tales to the accompaniment of simple percussion instruments

道人　dàoren　a respectful form of address for a Taoist priest

道士　dàoshi　Taoist priest

道听途说　dàotīng-túshuō　hearsay; rumour; gossip: 这是～，不足为信。This is only hearsay, and is not to be taken seriously.

道统　dàotǒng　Confucian orthodoxy

道徒　dàotú　a follower of Taoism

道喜　dàoxǐ　congratulate sb. on a happy occasion

道谢　dàoxiè　express one's thanks; thank

道行　dàoxíng　*inf.*　the attainments of a Taoist priest

道学　dàoxué　① same as 理学 lǐxué ② rigidly and stubbornly adhering to outworn rules and ideas; pedantic: ～先生 a scholar rigidly adhering to principles, esp. Confucian principles; pedant

道义　dàoyì　morality and justice: ～上的支持 moral support

道藏　dàozàng　the Taoist Canon (collected Taoist scriptures)

道砟　dàozhǎ　*railway*　ballast

稻

稻　dào　rice; paddy

稻白叶枯病　dàobáiyèkūbìng　bacterial blight of rice

稻苞虫　dàobāochóng　rice plant skipper

稻草　dàocǎo　rice straw

稻草人　dàocǎorén　scarecrow

稻恶苗病　dào'èmiáobìng　Bakanae disease of rice

稻谷　dàogǔ　paddy

稻糠　dàokāng　rice chaff

稻壳　dàoké　rice husk (*or* hull)

稻烂秧　dàolànyāng　seedling blight of rice

稻螟虫　dàomíngchóng　rice borer

稻田　dàotián　(rice) paddy; rice field; paddy field

稻田皮炎　dàotián píyán　*med.*　paddy-field dermatitis

稻瘟病　dàowēnbìng　(also 稻热病 dàorèbìng) rice blast

稻纹枯病　dàowénkūbìng　sheath and culm blight of rice

稻秧　dàoyāng　rice seedlings; rice shoots

稻子　dàozi　*inf.*　rice; paddy

稻纵卷叶螟　dàozòngjuǎnyèmíng　rice leaf roller

纛

纛　dào　a big army banner used in ancient times

dē

嘚

嘚　dē　*onom.*　the clatter of a horse's hoofs

嘚啵　dēbo　*dial.*　chatter; jabber

dé

得¹

得　dé　① get; obtain; gain: ～第一名 get a first; win first place / ～了一大笔钱 have obtained a large sum of money / 这次选举他只～了五票。He only received (*or* got) 5 votes at the election. / 他～了个坏名声。He gained a bad reputation. / ～了结核病 have (*or* contract) tuberculosis / 今天的幸福生活～来不易。The happy life we have today was not easily won. ② (of a calculation) result in: 二三～六。Twice three is six. ③ fit; proper: 得用 déyòng ④ *formal*　satisfied; complacent: 自得 zìdé ⑤ *inf.*　be finished; be ready: 饭～了。Dinner is ready. ⑥ *inf.* (expressing approval or prohibition): ～，就这么办。All right! Just go ahead. / ～了，别再说了。That's enough. Let it go at that. ⑦ *inf.* (expressing helplessness or frustration): ～，又搞错了! Look! I've got it wrong again!

得²

得　dé　(usu. used in laws and decrees before verbs to express permission): 国家在必要时～设立特别行政区。The state may establish special administrative regions when necessary.

——see also de; děi

得便 débiàn　when it's convenient: 这几样东西,请你～捎给他。Please take these things to him whenever it's convenient.

得标 débiāo　have one's tender accepted

得病 débìng　fall ill; contract a disease: 突然～be suddenly taken ill / 得了重病 be seriously ill / 得了传染病 contract a contagious disease

得不偿失 dé bù cháng shī　the loss outweighs the gain; the game is not worth the candle: 不打～的消耗战。Avoid battles of attrition in which we lose more than we gain.

得步进步 dé bù jìn bù　same as 得寸进尺 dé cùn jìn chǐ

得逞 déchěng　derog. have one's way; prevail; succeed: 阴谋未能～。The plot fell through.

得宠 déchǒng　derog. find favour with sb.; be in sb.'s good graces

得出 déchū　reach (a conclusion); obtain (a result)

得寸进尺 dé cùn jìn chǐ　reach for a yard after getting an inch; give him an inch and he'll take a yard (or a mile, an ell); be insatiable

得当 dédàng　apt; appropriate; proper; suitable: 安排～be properly arranged / 措词～aptly worded; appropriate wording

得到 dédào　get; obtain; gain; receive: ～及时治疗 get timely medical treatment / ～群众的支持 enjoy the support of the masses / 退休工人～很好的照顾。Retired workers are all well provided for.

得道 dédào　① attain the Way ② support a just cause

得道多助,失道寡助 dédào duō zhù, shīdào guǎ zhù　a just cause enjoys abundant support while an unjust cause finds little; a just cause gains great support, an unjust one gains little

得法 défǎ　do sth. in the proper way; get the knack: 管理～be properly managed / 讲授不甚～not teach in the right (or proper) way

得分 défēn　score: 客队的六号～最多。Player No. 6 of the visiting team scored the most points. / 连得四分 win four points in a row

得过且过 dé guò qiě guò　get by however one can; muddle along; drift along: 敷衍了事,～ work perfunctorily and muddle along / 像他这样～,有什么出息? What future will a man ever have if he keeps dragging along like this?

得计 déjì　succeed in one's scheme

得奖 déjiǎng　win (or be awarded) a prize: ～人 prizewinner / ～单位 prizewinning unit

得劲 déjìn　① feel well: 他这几天身体不大～。He hasn't been feeling well for the last few days. ② fit for use; handy: 这把锹我用起来很～。This spade is just right for me.

得救 déjiù　be saved (or rescued): 病人～了。The patient was saved.

得空 dékōng　have leisure; be free: 老想来看你,总不～。I've been meaning to come and see you but haven't had the time.

得了 déle　① (expressing a suggestion): 你走～,剩下的事我干。You just go, and I'll finish the rest. ② that's enough; that's that: ～,我才不信呢! That's enough! I don't believe a word of it.

得力 délì　① benefit from; get help from: ～于平时勤学苦练 profit from diligent study and practice / 我得他的力很不小。I benefited a lot from his help. ② capable; competent: ～助手 capable assistant; right-hand man / ～干部 competent cadre / 办事～ do things efficiently

得了 déliǎo　(used in rhetorical questions) really serious; awful: 这还～吗? Isn't it awful?

得陇望蜀 dé Lǒng wàng Shǔ　covet Shu after getting Long—have insatiable desires

得气 déqì　Chin. med.　bring about the desired sensation (in acupuncture treatment)

得人心 dé rénxīn　have the support of the people; be popular: 他做那件事很～。That was a very popular move on his part.

得胜 déshèng　win a victory; triumph: ～归来 return in triumph; return with flying colours

得胜回朝 déshèng huícháo　return to court a victor—return in triumph

得失 dé-shī　① gain and loss; success and failure: ～相当 gains and losses balance each other; break even / 从不计较个人～ never give a thought to personal gain or loss ② advantages and disadvantages; merits and demerits: 两种办法各有～。Each of the two methods has its advantages and disadvantages.

得势 déshì　① be in power ② get the upper hand; be in the ascendant

得手 déshǒu　go smoothly; come off; do fine; succeed: 歼敌左翼,～后,迅速扩大战果 wipe out the enemy's left flank and, this accomplished, swiftly exploit the victory

得数 déshù　same as 答数 dáshù

得体 détǐ　befitting one's position or suited to the occasion; appropriate: 讲话～ speak in appropriate terms / 她打扮得很～。She was suitably dressed.

得天独厚 dé tiān dú hòu　be richly endowed by nature; abound in gifts of nature; enjoy exceptional advantages: 长江三角洲是～的鱼米之乡。The Changjiang Delta, richly endowed by nature, is a land of plenty.

得悉 déxī　hear of; learn about: ～病体康复,不胜欣慰。I rejoice to hear of your recovery.

得闲 déxián　have leisure; be free: 病中～ have a little leisure when convalescing

得心应手 déxīn-yìngshǒu　① with facility; with high proficiency: 他画起马来真可谓～。He is in his element when painting horses. ② serviceable; handy: 这支笔写起来～。This pen writes very well.

得样儿 déyàngr　dial.　look smart

得宜 déyí　proper; appropriate; suitable: 措置～ handle properly

得以 déyǐ　so that...can (or may)...: 放手发动群众,让群众的意见～充分发表出来 boldly mobilize the masses so that they can fully express their opinions / 为求本联合声明～有效执行 with a view to the effective implementation of this joint declaration

得益 déyì　benefit; profit: 读者的意见使他～不少。He benefits considerably from the readers' comments.

得意 déyì　proud of oneself; pleased with oneself; complacent: 对自己取得的成功感到～ be proud of one's success

得意门生 déyì ménshēng　a favourite pupil

得意忘形 déyì wàngxíng　grow dizzy with success; have one's head turned by success: 工作有了成绩,可不能～。We mustn't let our achievements turn our heads. / ～地吹嘘 boast elatedly

得意扬扬 déyì yángyáng　(also 得意洋洋 déyì yángyáng)　be immensely proud; look triumphant

得用 déyòng　fit for use; handy: 这把剪子很～。This is a very handy pair of scissors.

得鱼忘筌 dé yú wàng quán　forget the trap as soon as the fish is caught; forget the means by which the end is attained; forget the things or conditions which bring one success

得知 dézhī　have learned of sth.; have heard of sth.: ～平安到达,甚感欣慰。I'm relieved to hear that you have arrived safely.

得志 dézhì　achieve one's ambition; have a successful career: 少年～ enjoy success when young

得中 dézhōng　moderate; appropriate

得中 dézhòng　① pass the imperial examinations ② get the winning number (in a lottery): ～头奖 win the

first prize in a lottery

得罪 dé·zuì offend; displease: 不怕～人 not be afraid of giving offence / 我的话把他给～了。My words offended him.

锝 dé chem. technetium (Tc)

德(悳)

dé ① virtue; morals; moral character: 品德 pǐndé ② heart; mind: 同心同德 tóngxīn-tóngdé ③ kindness; favour: 以怨报德 yǐ yuàn bào dé ④ (Dé) short for 德国 Déguó

德昂族 Dé'ángzú the De'ang nationality, or the De'angs, inhabiting Yunnan Province

德才兼备 dé-cái jiānbèi have both ability and integrity: ～的干部 cadres who combine ability with political integrity

德高望重 dégāo-wàngzhòng (of an old person) be of noble character and high prestige; enjoy high prestige and command universal respect

德国 Déguó Germany

德国人 Déguórén German

德黑兰 Déhēilán Teheran

德谟克拉西 démókèlāxī democracy (a transliteration, now replaced by 民主 mínzhǔ)

德望 déwàng moral prestige

德行 déxíng moral integrity; moral conduct

德行 déxíng dial. disgusting; shameful: 那个家伙真～。That fellow is really disgusting. ·

德性 déxìng moral character; moral integrity

德性 déxìng same as 德行 déxíng

德语 Déyǔ German (language)

德育 déyù moral education; education in ethics

德政 dézhèng benevolent rule

德治 dézhì rule of virtue

de

地

de part. (used after an adverbial): 实事求是～处理问题 handle problems in a practical and realistic way / 天渐渐～冷了。The weather is getting cold. ——see also dì

的

de part. ① (used after an attribute): 铁～纪律 iron discipline / 已经站起来～中国人民 the Chinese people who have stood up / 我～母亲 my mother / 无产阶级～政党 a party of the proletariat / 今天开会是你～主席。You will chair today's meeting. / 别开他～玩笑了。Don't make fun of him. ② (used to form a noun phrase or nominal expression): 赶大车～ a carter / 我爱吃辣～。I like hot (or peppery) food. / 菊花开了，有红～，有黄～。The chrysanthemums are in bloom; some are red and some yellow. / 他说他～，我干我～。Let him say what he likes; I'll just get on with my work. / 火车上看书～看书，聊天～聊天。On the train some people were reading and some were chatting. / 我要两个三毛～。I want two of the three-*mao* ones. / 无缘无故～，你着什么急? why do you get excited for no reason at all? / 这里用不着你，你只管睡你～去。We don't need you here. You just go to bed. ③ (used after a verb or between a verb and its object to stress an element of the sentence): 谁买～? Who bought it? / 你嗓子怎么哑了?一唱～。Why are you so hoarse?—From singing. / 是我打～稿子, 他上～色。I made the sketch; he filled in the colours. / 他是昨天进～城。He went to town yesterday. / 我是在车站打～票。I bought the ticket at the station. ④ (used at the end of a declarative sentence for emphasis): 你们这两天真够辛苦～。

You've really been working hard the past few days. ⑤ (used to express the idea of "of that kind"): 针头线脑～ things like needles and threads ⑥ inf. (used to express multiplication or addition): 这间屋子是五米～三米, 合十五平方米。This room is five metres by three, or fifteen square metres. / 两个～三个, 一共五个。Two pieces and three pieces—there're five in all. ——see also dí; dì

的话 dehuà part. (used to express a condition): 如果你有事～, 就不要来了。Don't come if you're busy. / 如果我是你～, 我绝对不干。If I were you, I definitely wouldn't do it.

得

de part. ① (used after a verb or an adjective to express possibility or capability): 吃～ eatable / 做不～ must not be done / 这双鞋穿～。These shoes fit well. / 这个人批评不～。He's not a man to criticize. / 咱们可粗心不～。We can't afford to be careless. / 她去～, 我为什么去不～? If she can go, why can't I? / 这个料子洗～洗不～? Is this material washable? ② (inserted between a verb and its complement to express possibility or capability): 我拿～动。I can carry it. / 那办～到。That can be done. / 他做～好做不好? Can he do it well? ③ (used to link a verb or an adjective to a complement which describes the manner or degree): 写～非常好 very well written / 唱～不好 not sing well / 冷～打哆嗦 shiver with cold / 笑～肚子痛 laugh till one's sides split / 好～很 very good / 他吵～我工作不下去。He made so much noise that I couldn't go on working. ——see also dé; děi

赋

de see 肋赋 lēde

děi

得

děi inf. ① need: 这个工程～三个月才能完。This project will take three months to complete. ② must; have to: 有错误就～批评。Wherever mistakes occur, they must be criticized. ③ certainly will: 要不快走, 我们就～迟到了。We'll be late if we don't hurry. ——see also dé; de

dèn

扽(撙)

dèn pull with sharp tugs; yank: 把袖子一～一～ pull out one's sleeve / 你～住绳子, 不要松手。Pull the rope tight. Don't relax your grip.

dēng

灯(燈)

dēng ① lamp; lantern; light: 突然所有的～都灭了。Suddenly all the lights went out. ② valve; tube: 五～收音机 a five-valve radio set ③ burner: 酒精灯 jiǔjīngdēng

灯标 dēngbiāo beacon light; beacon; light buoy

灯彩 dēngcǎi ① coloured-lantern making ② coloured lanterns (formerly used on the stage)

灯草 dēngcǎo rush (used as lampwick)

灯船 dēngchuán lightship; light vessel

灯光 dēngguāng ① the light of a lamp; lamplight: ～很暗。The light is rather dim. ② (stage) lighting: ～渐暗 lights slowly dim; lights fade to dark / 舞台～ stage lights; lighting

灯光球场　dēngguāng qiúchǎng　floodlit (*or* illuminated) court, field, etc.

灯红酒绿　dēnghóng-jiǔlǜ　red lanterns and green wine—feasting and revelry: 豪门～，街头啼饥号寒。While the houses of the rich and powerful presented a scene of feasting and revelry, cries of hunger and cold were heard out in the streets.

灯花　dēnghuā　snuff (of a candlewick)

灯会　dēnghuì　lantern festival

灯火　dēnghuǒ　lights: ～熄了。The lights went out.

灯火管制　dēnghuǒ guǎnzhì　blackout (enforced during wartime)

灯火辉煌　dēnghuǒ huīhuáng　brilliantly illuminated; ablaze with lights: 宴会在～的人民大会堂举行。The banquet was held in the brightly-lit Great Hall of the People.

灯节　Dēngjié　the Lantern Festival (the 15th of the first lunar month)

灯具　dēngjù　lamps and lanterns

灯笼　dēnglong　lantern: 点～ light a lantern／打～ carry a lantern／挂～ hang a lantern

灯笼椒　dēnglongjiāo　*dial.* bell pepper

灯笼裤　dēnglongkù　knee-length or ankle-length sports trousers; knickerbockers

灯谜　dēngmí　riddles written on lanterns; lantern riddles: 猜～ guess a lantern riddle

灯捻　dēngniǎn　(also 灯捻子 dēngniǎnzi) lampwick

灯泡　dēngpào　*inf.* (electric) bulb; light bulb: 螺口(卡口)～ screw- (bayonet-) socket bulb／乳白～ opal bulb

灯市　dēngshì　lantern fair (on the 15th of the first lunar month)

灯丝　dēngsī　filament (in a light bulb or valve)

灯塔　dēngtǎ　lighthouse; beacon

灯台　dēngtái　lampstand

灯头　dēngtóu　① lamp holder; electric light socket: 螺口～ screw socket／开关～ switch socket ② a holder for the wick and chimney of a kerosene lamp

灯心　dēngxīn　lampwick; wick

灯心草　dēngxīncǎo　*bot.* rush

灯心绒　dēngxīnróng　*text.* corduroy

灯油　dēngyóu　lamp-oil; kerosene; paraffin oil

灯语　dēngyǔ　lamp signal

灯盏　dēngzhǎn　oil lamps (without a chimney)

灯罩　dēngzhào　① lampshade ② lamp-chimney (for an oil lamp)

灯烛　dēngzhú　lamps and candles — lights: ～辉煌 ablaze with lights; brilliantly illuminated

灯炷　dēngzhù　lampwick; wick

灯柱　dēngzhù　lamppost

灯座　dēngzuò　lampstand

登¹

dēng　① ascend; mount; scale (a height):～上讲台 mount the platform／～上峰顶 reach the summit／在旧社会，穷孩子上大学比～天还难。In the old society, for poor children to go to college was harder than climbing to heaven. ② publish; record; enter: ～帐 enter an item in an account book／～广告 advertise (in a newspaper)／最近一期《中国建设》～了几篇有关四个现代化的文章。The latest issue of *China Reconstructs* carries (*or* has) several articles about the four modernizations. ／他的名字～上了光荣榜。His name appeared on the honour roll. ③ be gathered and taken to the threshing ground: 五谷丰登 wǔgǔ fēngdēng

登²

dēng　① press down with the foot; pedal; treadle: ～三轮车 pedal a pedicab ② step on; tread: ～在窗台儿上擦玻璃 step onto the sill to clean the window ③ *dial.* put on (shoes or trousers): ～上鞋 put one's shoes on／脚～高跟鞋 wearing high-heeled shoes

登岸　dēng'àn　go ashore; land

登报　dēngbào　publish in the newspaper: ～声明 make a statement in the newspaper

登场　dēngcháng　be gathered and taken to the threshing ground: 小麦已经～。The wheat has been carried to the threshing ground.

登场　dēngchǎng　come on stage

登场人物　dēngchǎng rénwù　characters in a play; *dramatis personae*

登程　dēngchéng　start (off) on a journey; set out

登第　dēngdì　pass the imperial examinations (esp. the palace examination 殿试)

登峰造极　dēngfēng-zàojí　reach the peak of perfection; have a very high level (of scholastic attainment or technical skill); reach great heights: 他的人物画在当时可谓～。His painting of people attained a level never known before.

登高　dēnggāo　① ascend a height: ～远眺 ascend a height to enjoy a distant view ②climb hills or mountains on the Double Ninth Festival (重阳节)

登革热　dēnggérè　*med.* dengue fever

登机　dēngjī　board a plane

登基　dēngjī　ascend the throne; be enthroned

登极　dēngjí　same as 登基 dēngjī

登记　dēngjì　register; check in; enter one's name: 结婚～ marriage registration／向有关部门～ register with the proper authorities ／在旅馆～住宿 check in at a hotel

登记簿　dēngjìbù　register; registry

登记处　dēngjìchù　registration (*or* registry) office

登科　dēngkē　(in imperial times) pass the civil service examinations: ～及第，光耀门楣 pass the imperial examinations, placing high on the list of successful candidates, and bring honour to one's family

登临　dēnglín　① climb a hill, a tall building, etc. which commands a broad view ② visit famous mountains, places of interest, etc.

登龙门　dēnglóngmén　mount the dragon gate—find a powerful patron or pass the imperial examinations

登陆　dēnglù　land; disembark: 盟军在诺曼底海滩～。The Allied troops landed on the beaches of Normandy. ／台风将于明晨～。The typhoon will land tomorrow morning.

登陆部队　dēnglù bùduì　landing force

登陆场　dēnglùchǎng　beachhead

登陆地点　dēnglù dìdiǎn　debarkation (*or* landing) point

登陆舰　dēnglùjiàn　landing ship

登陆母舰　dēnglù mǔjiàn　landing-craft carrier

登陆艇　dēnglùtǐng　landing craft

登陆作战　dēnglù zuòzhàn　landing operations

登门　dēngmén　call at sb.'s house: ～拜访 pay sb. a visit

登攀　dēngpān　climb; clamber; scale

登山　dēngshān　mountain-climbing; mountaineering: ～队 mountaineering party (*or* expedition)

登山鞋　dēngshānxié　climbing (*or* mountaineering) boot

登山运动　dēngshān yùndòng　mountaineering: ～员 mountaineer

登时　dēngshí　*adv.* immediately; at once; then and there: 说干就干，大家～动起手来了。Once agreed, everyone set to work straight away.

登台　dēngtái　mount a platform; go up on the stage: 想～表演一番 strive to take the stage and perform

登堂入室　dēngtáng-rùshì　pass through the hall into the inner chamber—reach a higher level in one's studies or become more proficient in one's profession

登徒子　dēngtúzǐ　*liter.* lecher

登载　dēngzǎi　publish (in newspapers or magazines); carry: 各报在显著位置～了这条消息。The newspapers

gave prominent coverage to the news.

噔 dēng *onom.* thump; thud: 听见楼梯上 ～ ～的脚步声 hear heavy footsteps on the stairs

蹬 dēng press down with the foot; pedal; treadle ——see also dèng

蹬技 dēngjì *acrob.* juggling with the feet

蹬腿 dēngtuǐ ① kick one's legs ② *inf. humor.* kick the bucket; turn up one's toes

děng

等[1] děng ① class; grade; rank: 分为三～ classify into three grades ② kind; sort: 这～事 this sort of thing / 此～人 this kind of person ③ equal: 相等 xiāngděng ④ same as 戥 děng

等[2] děng ① wait; await: ～车 wait for a train, bus, etc. / ～上级批准 await approval by the higher authorities / 请～一下。Would you mind waiting a minute, please. / 别～我吃饭。Don't wait for me for dinner. / 我回家要晚, 你先睡, 别～我。I'll be late, so don't wait up for me. ② when; till: ～我做完再走。Stay till I'm through.

等[3] děng *part.* ① *formal* (used after a personal pronoun or a personal name to show plurality): 我～ we / 彼～ they / 该犯～ the aforesaid criminals ② and so on; and so forth; etc.; 购置书籍、纸张、文具～ buy books, stationery and so on / 赴沈阳、鞍山～地视察 go to Shenyang, Anshan and other places on a tour of inspection ③ (indicating the end of an enumeration): 长江、黄河、黑龙江、珠江～四大河流 the four large rivers —the Changjiang, the Huanghe, the Heilongjiang and the Zhujiang

等边三角形 děngbiān sānjiǎoxíng equilateral triangle

等差 děngchā *formal* place in a series; grade

等次 děngcì place in a series; grade: 产品按质量划分～。The products are graded according to quality.

等待 děngdài wait; await: ～时机 await a favourable opportunity; wait for a chance; bide one's time / 抓紧时间, 不要～。Don't waste time. Go ahead.

等到 děngdào by the time; when: ～敌军赶到, 游击队已经转移了。By the time the enemy troops arrived, the guerrilla force had already disappeared.

等等 děngděng *part.* and so on; and so on and so forth; etc.: 标点符号有逗号、句号、冒号～。Punctuation marks are commas, full stops, colons, etc.

等等 děngdeng wait a minute

等第 děngdì *formal* ① grade in an imperial examination ② place in a competition

等而下之 děng ér xià zhī from that grade down; lower down: 好的尚且如此, ～的就不必谈了。Even those higher up are not worth much, to say nothing of those lower down.

等份 děngfèn equal divisions; equal portions

等风速线 děngfēngsùxiàn *meteorol.* isotach

等高线 děnggāoxiàn *geol.* contour (line): ～地图 contour map

等号 děnghào *math.* equal-sign; equality sign

等候 děnghòu wait; await; expect: ～命令 wait for instructions; await orders

等级 děngjí ① grade; rank: 棉花按～收购 pay for cotton according to its grade ② order and degree; social estate; social stratum: 封建社会～森严。Feudal society was rigidly stratified.

等级制度 děngjí zhìdù hierarchy; social estate system

等价 děngjià of equal value; equal in value: ～交换 exchange of equal values; exchange at equal value / ～有偿的原则 principle of making compensation for equal value

等价物 děngjiàwù *econ.* equivalent

等距离 děngjùlí equidistance: A 和 B 同 C 是～。Points A and B are equidistant from C.

等距离外交 děngjùlí wàijiāo equidistant diplomacy

等离子体 děnglízǐtǐ *phys.* plasma: ～激光器 plasma laser / ～加速器 plasmatron

等离子体物理学 děnglízǐtǐ wùlǐxué plasma physics

等量齐观 děngliàng-qíguān equate; put on a par: 这两部小说差得太远了, 怎么能～呢? There is a world of difference between these two novels. How can you equate one with the other?

等内 děngnèi (of goods) be up to standard

等日照线 děngrìzhàoxiàn *meteorol.* isohel

等熵面 děngshāngmiàn *meteorol.* isentropic surface

等深线 děngshēnxiàn *geog.* isobath

等式 děngshì *math.* equality

等速运动 děngsù yùndòng same as 匀速运动 yúnsù yùndòng

等同 děngtóng equate; be equal: 你不能把现象和本质～起来。You must not equate the appearance with the essence.

等同语 děngtóngyǔ equivalent word; equivalent

等外 děngwài substandard: ～品 substandard product

等温线 děngwēnxiàn *meteorol.* isotherm

等闲 děngxián *formal* ① ordinary; unimportant: 红军不怕远征难, 万水千山只～。(毛泽东) The Red Army fears not the trials of the Long March, Holding light ten thousand crags and torrents. ② aimlessly; thoughtlessly: 大好时光, 不可～度过。Don't fritter away your precious time.

等闲视之 děngxián shì zhī regard as unimportant; treat lightly (*or* casually): 这样的违法行为不可～。Such an illegal act should not be treated lightly.

等效 děngxiào *elec.* equivalent: ～电抗 equivalent reactance / ～天线 equivalent antenna

等压面 děngyāmiàn *meteorol.* isobaric surface; constant pressure surface

等压线 děngyāxiàn *meteorol.* isobar; isobaric line

等腰三角形 děngyāo sānjiǎoxíng isosceles triangle

等因奉此 děngyīn-fèngcǐ ① *old* (used in official documents) in view of the above, we therefore... ② officialese

等音 děngyīn *mus.* enharmonic

等于 děngyú ① equal to; equivalent to: 一公里～二华里。One kilometre is equal to two li. / 三加二～五。Three plus two is five. / 我们厂去年的产量～一九六五年的五倍。Last year our factory produced five times as much as in 1965. ② amount to; be tantamount to: 这～拒绝执行命令。This is tantamount to refusal to carry out orders. / 抓而不紧, ～不抓。Not to grasp firmly is not to grasp at all. / 吸烟～慢性自杀。Smoking is suicidal; every cigarette you smoke is a nail in your coffin. / 发展商品经济并不～搞资本主义。Developing the commodity economy does not necessarily mean practising capitalism.

等雨量线 děngyǔliàngxiàn *meteorol.* isohyet

等着瞧 děngzheqiáo wait and see: ～的政策 wait-and-see policy

等震线 děngzhènxiàn *geol.* isoseismal line; isoseismic line

等值线 děngzhíxiàn *meteorol.* isopleth; isoline; isogram: ～图 isogram

等子 děngzi same as 戥子 děngzi

戥（等） děng weigh with a small steelyard

戥子 děngzi a small steelyard for weighing precious metal, medicine, etc.

dèng

邓（鄧） Dèng a surname

凳（櫈） dèng stool or bench: 方～ square stool / 长～ bench

凳子 dèngzi stool

澄 dèng (of a liquid) settle ——see also chéng

澄清 dèngqīng (of a liquid) settle; become clear: 这水太浑, 等～了再用。 This water is too muddy. Wait till it has settled before you use it. ——see also chéngqīng

澄沙 dèngshā sweetened bean paste

瞪 dèng open (one's eyes) wide; stare; glare: 他注视着这个景象, 眼睛都～圆了。 He gazed at the scene with round eyes. / 她不高兴地～着他。 She glared at him with displeasure.

瞪眼 dèngyǎn ① open one's eyes wide; stare; glare: 别瞪着眼叫那流氓溜了。 Don't let the hooligan get away from right under your nose. ② glower and glare at sb.; get angry with sb.: 我生气地瞪了他一眼。 I gave him an angry look. / 你怎么老爱跟人～? Why are you always glowering at people? ——see also 干瞪眼 gāndèngyǎn

镫 dèng stirrup

镫骨 dènggǔ physiol. stapes; stirrup bone

镫子 dèngzi inf. stirrup

磴 dèng ① stone steps ② m. (for steps or stairs): 这楼梯有三十来～。 This flight of stairs has about thirty steps.

蹬 dèng see 蹭蹬 cèngdèng ——see also dēng

dī

氐 dī ① the third of the twenty-eight constellations (二十八宿) into which the celestial sphere was divided in ancient Chinese astronomy (consisting of four stars in the shape of a measure in Libra) ② (Dī) Di (Ti), an ancient nationality in China

低 dī ① low: ～水位 low water level / 情绪～ be low-spirited / 压～嗓门 lower one's voice / 飞机飞得很～。 The plane flew very low. / 这个音女声唱太～。 The note is too low for a female voice. / ～年级学生 students of the junior years (or lower grades) / 我比他～一年级。 I am one grade below him. ② let droop; hang down: 他把头～了下来。 He hung his head.

低标号 dībiāohào low grade: 400号以下的水泥是～水泥。 Cement under No. 400 is low-grade cement.

低产 dīchǎn low yield: ～田 low-yield (or low-yielding) land / ～作物 low-yielding crop

低产井 dīchǎnjǐng petroleum stripper well; stripped well

低潮 dīcháo low tide; low ebb: 处于～ be at a low tide; be at a low ebb / ～线 low water mark

低沉 dīchén ① overcast; lowering: ～的天空 an overcast sky ② (of voice) low and deep ③ low-spirited; downcast

低垂 dīchuí hang low: 乌云～。 Black clouds hang low.

低档 dīdàng ① low gear ② low grade: ～商品 low-grade goods; cheap goods

低等动物 dīděng dòngwù lower animal; invertebrate

低地 dīdì lowland

低调 dīdiào ① low-key ② photog. low tone

低估 dīgū underestimate; underrate: 这篇她翻译得不错, 过去我们～了她的英语水平。 She translated this piece quite well. We had underestimated her English level.

低谷 dīgǔ all-time low

低合金钢 dīhéjīngāng metall. low-alloy steel

低回 dīhuí (also 低徊 dīhuí) formal ① pace up and down ② linger; be loath to part

低级 dījí ① elementary; rudimentary; lower ② vulgar; low

低级趣味 dījí qùwèi vulgar interests; bad taste

低贱 dījiàn low and degrading; humble

低空 dīkōng low altitude; low level: ～飞行 low-altitude (or low-level) flying / ～轰炸 low-level bombing / ～扫射 low-level strafing; ground strafing

低栏 dīlán sports low hurdles

低廉 dīlián cheap; low: 价格～。 Prices are low.

低劣 dīliè inferior; low-grade: 质量～ of inferior quality

低落 dīluò low; downcast: 情绪～ be low-spirited

低眉顺眼 dīméi-shùnyǎn submissive; meek

低能 dīnéng mental deficiency; feeble-mindedness

低能儿 dīnéng'ér imbecile; retarded child

低频 dīpín low frequency: ～变压器 low-frequency transformer / ～放大器 low-frequency amplifier

低频扬声器 dīpín yángshēngqì woofer

低气压 dīqìyā meteorol. low pressure; depression

低人一等 dī rén yī děng inferior to others: ～的工作 inferior jobs

低三下四 dīsān-xiàsì ① lowly; humble; degrading: 他们不是什么～的人家。 Theirs is a respectable family. ② servile; obsequious; cringing: 从来没有向人～ have never gone crawling to anyone / ～地求情 go bowing and scraping to sb. for a favour

低烧 dīshāo med. low fever; slight fever

低声 dīshēng in a low voice; under one's breath; with bated breath

低声波 dīshēngbō phys. infrasonic wave

低声下气 dīshēng-xiàqì speak humbly and under one's breath; be meek and subservient; be obsequious: ～地乞求施舍 humbly beg for alms

低首下心 dīshǒu-xiàxīn bow and scrape; be obsequiously submissive

低俗 dīsú vulgar; low

低速挡 dīsùdǎng bottom gear

低碳钢 dītàngāng metall. low-carbon steel

低头 dītóu ① lower (or bow, hang) one's head: ～默哀 bow one's head in silent mourning ② yield; submit: 决不向困难～ never bow to difficulties

低头认罪 dītóu rènzuì hang one's head and admit one's guilt; plead guilty

低洼 dīwā low-lying: ～地 low-lying land

低微 dīwēi ① (of a voice or sound) low: ～的呻吟 low groans ② lowly; humble: 出身～ of humble origin

低纬度 dīwěidù low latitudes

低温 dīwēn ① low temperature ② meteorol. microtherm: ～气候 microthermal climate ③ med. hypothermia: ～麻醉 hypothermic anaesthesia

低温恒温器 dīwēn héngwēnqì phys. cryostat

低温生物学 dīwēn shēngwùxué cryobiology

低温学 dīwēnxué cryogenics

低息 dīxī low interest: ～贷款 a low-interest loan

低下 dīxià (of status or living standards) low; lowly: 经

济地位～ be of low economic status

低陷 dīxiàn　sunken; hollow; depressed: 两颊～ have sunken (or hollow) cheeks

低消耗 dīxiāohào　low consumption (of raw materials, fuel, etc.): 保持高产、优质、～ maintain a record of high production, good quality and low consumption

低血糖 dīxuètáng　med. hypoglycemia

低压 dīyā　① phys. low pressure ② elec. low tension; low voltage: ～水银蒸气灯 low-tension mercury-vapour lamp ③ meteorol. low pressure; depression: ～气流 low-pressure air current ④ med. minimum pressure

低压槽 dīyācáo　meteorol. trough

低哑 dīyǎ　low and hoarse: 声音～ speak in a hoarse, low voice

低音提琴 dīyīn tíqín　double bass; contrabass

低语 dīyǔ　speak in a low voice; whisper

低云 dīyún　meteorol. low clouds

羝 dī　formal ram; billy goat

堤(隄) dī　dyke; embankment

堤岸 dī'àn　embankment

堤坝 dībà　dykes and dams

堤防 dīfáng　dyke; embankment: 加固～ strengthen the dykes / ～工程 dyke building; embankment project

堤埂 dīgěng　an earth dyke (or embankment)

堤围 dīwéi　dyke; embankment

提 dī　see below ——see also tí

提防 dīfang　take precautions against; be on guard against; beware of: ～恐怖主义分子的破坏 guard against sabotage by terrorists

提溜 dīliu　dial. carry: 他手里～着一个小提包。He was carrying a small bag.

提溜着心 dīliuzhexīn　have one's heart in one's mouth

滴 dī　① drip: 他脸上的汗水直往下～。Sweat kept dripping from his face. / 往轴承里～油 put a few drops of lubricating oil in the bearings; oil the bearings / ～眼药 put drops in one's eyes ② m. drop: 一～水 a drop of water

滴虫 dīchóng　trichomonad

滴虫病 dīchóngbìng　trichomoniasis

滴答 dīdā　onom. tick; ticktack; ticktock: 夜很静, 只有钟摆～ ～地响。The night was very quiet except for the ticktack of the clock. / 发报机滴滴答答不停地发出电报。The transmitter ticked (or tapped) out message after message. / 雨～ ～地下个不停。The rain kept pitter-pattering.

滴答 dīda　(also 滴嗒 dīda) drip: 屋顶上的雪化了,～着水。The snow on the roof melted and dripped down.

滴滴涕 dīdītì　DDT (dichloro-diphenyl-trichloroethane)

滴定 dīdìng　chem. titration: 比浊～ heterometric titration / 碘量～ iodometry / ～度 titre / ～管 burette / ～剂 titrant

滴管 dīguǎn　dropper

滴灌 dīguàn　agric. drip irrigation; trickle irrigation

滴剂 dījì　med. drops: 滴鼻剂 nose drops

滴沥 dīlì　onom. the sound of rain pattering: 雨～ ～下个不停。The rain pattered on and on.

滴里搭拉 dīlidālā　(also 滴里耷拉 dīlidālā) hanging loose

滴溜儿 dīliūr　① perfectly round: 他两眼睁得～圆。He opened his eyes wide. ② turning round quickly 忙得～转 be terribly busy

滴漏 dīlòu　water clock; clepsydra; hourglass

滴滤池 dīlùchí　environ. protec. trickling filter

滴水不进 dī shuǐ bù jìn　not take even a drop of water —unable to eat or drink

滴水不漏 dī shuǐ bù lòu　① watertight (fig.) ② tightly packed or completely enclosed

滴水成冰 dī shuǐ chéng bīng　(so cold that) the water freezes as it drips; freezing cold: ～的天气 freezing weather

滴水穿石 dī shuǐ chuān shí　same as 水滴石穿 shuǐ dī shí chuān

滴水石 dīshuǐshí　dripstone

滴水瓦 dīshuǐwǎ　drip-tile (placed at either end of an eaves)

嘀 dī　see below ——see also dí

嘀嗒 dīda　same as 滴答 dīda

嘀里嘟噜 dīlidūlū　mumbling; muttering

镝 dī　chem. dysprosium (Dy) ——see also dí

dí

狄 Dí　① an ancient name for the tribes in the north ② a surname

的 dí　true; really: 的确 díquè ——see also de; dì

的当 dídàng　formal apt; appropriate; proper; suitable: 这个评语十分～。This appraisal is quite appropriate.

的款 díkuǎn　a sum of money definitely available

的确 díquè　adv. indeed; really: 听到这消息我～很高兴。I was indeed very glad to hear the news. / 我～不知道。I really don't know.

的确良 díquèliáng　dacron; terylene

籴(糴) dí　buy in (grain)

迪(廸) dí　formal enlighten; guide: 启迪 qǐdí

迪斯科 dísīkē　disco (a transliteration): ～舞厅 discotheque

获 dí　a kind of reed

敌(敵) dí　① enemy; foe: 引～向东 induce the enemy to move east / 先打分散和孤立之～ attack dispersed, isolated enemy forces first / ～机 an enemy plane ② oppose; fight; resist: 与人民为～的人绝不会有好下场。Those who oppose the people will come to no good end. ③ match; equal: 军民团结如一人, 试看天下谁能～? If the army and the people are united as one, who in the world can match them?

敌百虫 díbǎichóng　agric. dipterex

敌稗 díbài　agric. Stam F-34 (dichloropropionanilide)

敌敌畏 dídíwèi　DDVP; dichlorvos

敌对 díduì　hostile; antagonistic: ～阶级 antagonistic(or hostile) classes / ～行为 a hostile act / ～行动 hostilities / ～分子 a hostile element / ～情绪 hostility; enmity / ～双方 opposing sides; parties to hostilities

敌国 díguó　enemy state

敌后 díhòu　enemy's rear area: 深入～ penetrate into the enemy's rear area / 建立～根据地 establish base areas behind the enemy lines

敌军 díjūn　enemy troops; the enemy; hostile forces

敌忾 díkài　formal hatred towards the enemy ——see also 同仇敌忾 tóngchóu-díkài

敌情 díqíng　the enemy's situation: 侦察～ make a reconnaissance of the enemy's situation / ～的变化 changes on the enemy's side / ～严重。Enemy activities present a serious threat.

敌情观念 díqíng guānniàn　alertness to the presence of the enemy: ～强 be keenly aware of the enemy's pres-

ence / 要有～ must not relax our vigilance against the enemy

敌酋 díqiú　the leader of the enemy; enemy chieftain

敌人 dírén　enemy; foe

敌视 díshì　be hostile (*or* antagonistic) to; adopt a hostile attitude towards

敌手 díshǒu　① match; opponent; adversary ② enemy hands: 落人～ fall into enemy hands

敌台 dítái　enemy broadcasting station

敌探 dítàn　enemy spy

敌特 dítè　enemy spy; enemy agent

敌伪 díwěi　the enemy and the puppet regime (during the War of Resistance Against Japan): ～人员 enemy and puppet personnel / ～时期 the period of Japanese occupation; during the Japanese occupation

敌我矛盾 dí-wǒ máodùn　contradictions between ourselves and the enemy

敌意 díyì　hostility; enmity; animosity

敌阵 dízhèn　the enemy's position

涤（滌） dí *formal* wash; cleanse: 洗涤 xǐdí

涤除 díchú　wash away; do away with; eliminate: ～旧习 do away with old customs

涤荡 dídàng　wash away; clean up; cleanse

涤纶 dílún *text.* polyester fibre: ～长丝 polyester filament / ～短纤维 polyester staple fibre / ～絮棉 polyester cotton

涤瑕荡垢 díxiá-dànggòu　(also 涤瑕荡秽 díxiá-dànghuì) remove the stains and cleanse the filth—eradicate bad habits and customs

笛 dí　① bamboo flute ② whistle: 汽笛 qìdí

笛子 dízi *dizi*, bamboo flute

觌（覿） dí *formal* meet: 觌面 dímiàn

觌面 dímiàn *formal* meet each other

嘀（啾） dí　see below——see also dī

嘀咕 dígu　① whisper; talk in whispers: 两个女孩子嘀嘀咕咕地不知谈些什么。The two girls were talking in whispers. I couldn't hear a word. ② have misgivings about sth.; have sth. on one's mind: 我心里直～这件事。It's been on my mind all the while.

嫡 dí　① of or by the wife (as distinguished from a concubine under the feudal-patriarchal system): ～长子 the wife's eldest son ② of lineal descent; closely related

嫡传 díchuán　be handed down in a direct line from the master

嫡母 dímǔ　a term of address used to the wife by the children of a concubine

嫡派 dípài　① same as 嫡系 díxì ② disciples taught by the master himself

嫡亲 díqīn　blood relations; close paternal relations: ～弟兄 blood brothers; whole brothers

嫡堂 dítáng　relationship between cousins of the same paternal grandfather: ～兄弟 (male) cousins of the same paternal grandfather

嫡系 díxì　① direct line of descent ② one's own clique: ～部队 troops under one's direct control; one's own (*or* personal) troops

镝 dí *formal* arrowhead: 鸣～ whistling arrow ——see also dī

诋 dǐ *formal* slander; defame: 丑诋 chǒudǐ

诋毁 dǐhuǐ　slander; vilify; calumniate; defame

邸 dǐ　the residence of a high official: 官邸 guāndǐ

底[1] dǐ　① bottom; base: 井～ the bottom of a well ② the heart of a matter; ins and outs: 交底 jiāodǐ ③ rough draft ④ a copy kept as a record: 留个～儿 keep a copy on file; duplicate and file (a letter, etc.) ⑤ end of a year or month: 年底 niándǐ ⑥ ground; background; foundation: 白～红花 red flowers on a white background ⑦ *formal* end up with; come to: 终底于成 zhōng dǐ yú chéng

底[2] dǐ *formal* what: ～处 what place; where / 干卿～事? What has that to do with you?

底版 dǐbǎn　photographic plate; negative

底本 dǐběn　① a copy for the record or for reproduction; master copy ② a text against which other texts are checked; original text

底财 dǐcái　real estate; real property

底册 dǐcè　a bound copy of a document kept on file

底层 dǐcéng　① (British) ground floor; (American) first floor ② bottom; the lowest rung: 旧中国劳动妇女被压在社会的最～。In old China working women were kept at the bottom of society.

底肥 dǐféi　base fertilizer

底稿 dǐgǎo　draft; manuscript

底工 dǐgōng　basic skill or training (of actors and performers)

底火 dǐhuǒ　① the fire in a stove before fuel is added ② *mil.* primer; ignition cartridge

底价 dǐjià　base price

底架 dǐjià *mech.* chassis

底角 dǐjiǎo　base angle

底孔 dǐkǒng *water conservancy* bottom outlet

底里 dǐlǐ　the inside story; the ins and outs; exact details: 不知～ not know the ins and outs of the matter

底牌 dǐpái　cards in one's hand; hand: 亮～ show one's hand

底盘 dǐpán　chassis (of a car)

底片 dǐpiàn　photographic plate; negative

底栖生物 dǐqī shēngwù　benthon

底漆 dǐqī　priming paint; primer

底气 dǐqì　lung power: ～足 have good lungs

底色 dǐsè *text.* bottom

底墒 dǐshāng *agric.* soil moisture (before sowing or planting)

底视图 dǐshìtú *mech.* bottom view

底数 dǐshù　① the truth or root of a matter; how a matter actually stands: 心中有～ know how the matter stands ② *math.* base number

底图 dǐtú *geog.* base map

底细 dǐxì　ins and outs; exact details: 我们不了解这件事的～。We don't know the ins and outs of the matter.

底下 dǐxia　① under; below; beneath: 树～ under the tree / 手～工作多 have one's hands full / 笔～不错 write well ② next; later; afterwards: 他们～说的话我就听不清了。I didn't catch what they said next. / ～再交换意见吧。We can exchange views after the meeting.

底下人 dǐxiarén *old* servant

底限 dǐxiàn　the lowest limit; minimum

底线 dǐxiàn　① same as 端线 duānxiàn ② under thread ③ a planted agent

底蕴　dǐyùn　*formal*　inside information; details

底止　dǐzhǐ　*formal*　end; limit: 永无～。There is no end (*or* limit) to it.

底子　dǐzi　① bottom; base: 鞋～ the sole of a shoe ② foundation: ～薄 have a poor foundation to start with / 他的英文～好。He has a good grounding in English. ③ rough draft or sketch: 画画儿要先打个～。When drawing a picture, first make a rough sketch. ④ a copy kept as a record: 发出的文件要留～。Keep a copy of each document sent out. ⑤ remnant: 货～ remnants of stock ⑥ ground; background; foundation: 一件浅灰色～淡蓝色条子的上衣 a light grey jacket with light blue stripes

底座　dǐzuò　base; pedestal; foundation

抵¹　dǐ　① support; sustain; prop: 用手～着下巴颏儿 prop one's chin in one's hands / 用东西把门～住, 别让风刮开。Prop something against the door so that it won't blow open. ② resist; withstand: ～住来自外面的压力 withstand the pressure from outside ③ compensate for; make good: 抵命 dǐmìng ④ mortgage: 用房屋做～ mortgage a house ⑤ balance; set off: 以定金～作价款 balance the deposit against the price ⑥ be equal to: 干活他一个能～我们两个。He can do the work of two of us.

抵²　dǐ　*formal*　reach; arrive at: 日内～京 will arrive in Beijing in a day or two

抵补　dǐbǔ　make up for; compensate

抵偿　dǐcháng　compensate for; make good; give sth. by way of payment for: 用货物～欠款 give merchandise in payment for a debt / ～损失 compensate for (*or* make good) a loss

抵触　dǐchù　conflict; contradict: 在个人利益和集体利益有～的时候, 应服从集体利益。When individual and collective interests conflict, those of the collective should prevail. / 与法律相～ contravene (*or* go against) the law / ～情绪 resentment; resistance

抵达　dǐdá　arrive; reach: 总理及其一行于昨晚～巴黎。The Premier and his party arrived in Paris last night.

抵挡　dǐdǎng　keep out; ward off; check; withstand: ～风寒 keep out the wind and the cold / ～洪水 keep the flood in check / ～突然袭击 withstand a sudden attack

抵换　dǐhuàn　substitute for; take the place of

抵近射击　dǐjìn shèjī　*mil.*　point-blank firing

抵拒　dǐjù　resist: 无法～ irresistible

抵抗　dǐkàng　resist; stand up to: 奋起～ rise in resistance / 增强对疾病的～力 build up one's resistance to disease

抵赖　dǐlài　deny; disavow: 不容～ brook no denial / 事实是～不了的。Denying the facts is futile. *or* Facts cannot be denied.

抵命　dǐmìng　pay with one's life (for a murder, etc.); a life for a life

抵塞　dǐsè　① stall sb. off; do sth. perfunctorily ② contradict; reply defiantly

抵事　dǐshì　*dial.*　(usu. used in the negative) be useful; be of great help: 人少了不～! Just a few people won't help much.

抵数　dǐshù　make up the number; serve as a stopgap

抵死　dǐsǐ　even at the cost of one's life; unto death; till death: ～一战 a fight to the death / ～不从 refuse to submit even unto death

抵牾　dǐwǔ　contradiction

抵瑕蹈隙　dǐxiá-dǎoxì　pick holes in; find fault with

抵消　dǐxiāo　offset; cancel out; counteract: ～影响 offset an influence / ～药物的作用 counteract the effect of a medicine

抵押　dǐyā　mortgage: 以某物作～ raise a mortgage on sth.; leave sth. as a pledge

抵押放款　dǐyā fàngkuǎn　mortgage loan; secured loan; loan on security

抵押品　dǐyāpǐn　security; pledge

抵用　dǐyòng　be of use; be of help; serve the purpose: 她吓得浑身打颤, 腿也不～了。She was trembling all over with fear and could hardly stand on her legs.

抵御　dǐyù　resist; withstand: ～侵略 resist aggression / ～自然灾害 withstand natural calamities / 建立防风林带～风沙的侵袭 build a shelter belt against sandstorms

抵债　dǐzhài　pay a debt in kind or by labour

抵帐　dǐzhàng　pay a debt in kind or by labour

抵制　dǐzhì　resist; boycott: ～会议 boycott a meeting

抵罪　dǐzuì　be punished for a crime

柢　dǐ　root (of a tree): 根深柢固 same as 根深蒂固 gēnshēn-dìgù

砥　dǐ　*formal*　whetstone

砥砺　dǐlì　① temper: ～革命意志 temper one's revolutionary will ② encourage: 互相～ encourage each other

砥柱　dǐzhù　mainstay: 中流砥柱 zhōngliú dǐzhù

骶　dǐ　see below

骶骨　dǐgǔ　*physiol.*　sacrum

dì

地　dì　① the earth: 大地 dàdì ② land; soil: 山地 shāndì ③ fields: 在～里干活儿 work in the fields / 麦～ wheat field ④ ground; floor: 水泥～ cement floor ⑤ place; locality: 每到一～ wherever one goes / 各～党组织 Party organizations of all localities / ～处山区 be located in a mountain area ⑥ position; situation: 不败之地 bù bài zhī dì ⑦ background; ground: 一块白～黑字的木牌 a board with black characters on a white background / 白～红花的大碗 a big white bowl with a pattern of red flowers on it ⑧ distance travelled (measured in *li* 里 or stops 站): 学校离村子有一里～。The school is one *li* away from the village. / 我家离工厂只有两站～。My home is only a couple of bus stops from the factory. ——see also *de*

地巴唑　dìbāzuò　*pharm.*　dibazol

地板　dìbǎn　① floor board ② floor: 水泥～ cement floor

地堡　dìbǎo　*mil.*　bunker; blockhouse; pillbox

地表　dìbiǎo　the earth's surface

地表水　dìbiǎoshuǐ　*geol.*　surface water

地鳖虫　dìbiēchóng　*Chin. med.*　ground beetle (*Eupolyphage sinensis*)

地鵏　dìbǔ　*zool.*　bustard

地步　dìbù　① condition; plight: 你怎么闹到这样的～? How did you get into such a mess? / 事情到了不可收拾的～。The situation got out of hand. ② extent: 发展到公开对抗的～ develop to the point of an open clash / 兴奋到不能入睡的～ be so excited that one can't get to sleep ③ room for action: 留～ leave room for manoeuvre; have some leeway; give oneself elbowroom

地财　dìcái　valuables buried by landlords or rich peasants

地蚕　dìcán　*dial.*　① cutworm ② grub

地槽　dìcáo　*geol.*　geosyncline

地槽学说　dìcáo xuéshuō　theory of geosyncline

地层　dìcéng　*geol.*　stratum; layer: ～层序 stratigraphic succession (*or* sequence) / ～对比 stratigraphic cor-

relation /～图 stratigraphic map

地层学 dìcéngxué　stratigraphy

地产 dìchǎn　landed estate; landed property; real estate

地秤 dìchèng　weighbridge

地磁 dìcí　*phys.*　terrestrial magnetism; geomagnetism: ～场 terrestrial magnetic field; geomagnetic field

地磁极 dìcíjí　geomagnetic pole

地磁记录仪 dìcí jìlùyí　magnetograph

地磁仪 dìcíyí　magnetometer

地磁异常 dìcí yìcháng　magnetic anomaly

地大物博 dìdà-wùbó　vast territory and abundant resources; a vast land with rich resources; a big country abounding in natural wealth: 中国～, 人口众多。China is a vast country with a large population and abundant resources.

地带 dìdài　district; region; zone; belt: 沙漠(森林)～ a desert (forest) region /危险～ a danger zone

地道 dìdào　tunnel

地道 dìdao　① from the place noted for the product; genuine: ～的吉林人参 genuine Jilin ginseng ② pure; typical: 她的上海话说得真～。She speaks pure Shanghai dialect. /讲一口～的英语 speak idiomatic English ③ well-done; thorough: 他干的活儿真～。He does excellent work.

地道战 dìdàozhàn　tunnel warfare

地地道道 dìdidàodào　out-and-out; outright; hundred-percent: ～的伪君子 a thoroughgoing hypocrite /～的反动分子 a dyed-in-the-wool reactionary

地点 dìdiǎn　place; site; locale: 开会～ place for a meeting; venue /故事发生的～ the locale (*or* scene) of a story /在这里建个百货商店,～倒适中。This would be a suitable site for a new department store.

地电 dìdiàn　terrestrial electricity

地动 dìdòng　*inf.*　earthquake; quake

地动山摇 dìdòng-shānyáo　earthshaking

地动仪 dìdòngyí　seismograph as invented by the Chinese scientist Zhang Heng (张衡) in A. D. 132

地洞 dìdòng　a hole in the ground; burrow

地段 dìduàn　a sector (*or* section) of a town, etc.; area: 这个～商店多。There're quite a few shops in this area.

地对地导弹 dì duì dì dǎodàn　ground-to-ground (guided) missile; surface-to-surface missile

地对空导弹 dì duì kōng dǎodàn　ground-to-air (guided) missile; surface-to-air missile

地盾 dìdùn　*geol.*　shield

地方 dìfāng　① locality (as distinct from the central administration): 党的～组织 Party organizations in the localities /充分发挥中央和～两个积极性 give full play to the initiative of both central and local authorities ② local: ～政权机关 local state organs /～武装 local armed forces /～观念 localistic way of thinking; localism /～军 local forces; regional troops

地方 dìfang　① place; space; room: 你是什么～人? Where are you from? /这张桌子太占～。That desk takes up too much space (*or* room). /给钢琴腾出～ make room for the piano /我这个～有点疼。I've got a pain here. ② part; respect: 你说的话有对的～, 也有不对的～。What you say is partly right and partly wrong.

地方病 dìfāngbìng　endemic disease

地方国营 dìfāng guóyíng　state-owned but locally-administered: ～企业 locally-administered state enterprise /～农场 state farm under local administration

地方民族主义 dìfāngmínzúzhǔyì　local nationalism; local-nationality chauvinism

地方气候 dìfāng qìhòu　microclimate

地方时间 dìfāng shíjiān　local time

地方税 dìfāngshuì　local taxes

地方戏 dìfāngxì　local opera; local drama

地方志 dìfāngzhì　local chronicles; annals of local history

地方主义 dìfāngzhǔyì　regionalism; localism

地肤 dìfū　*bot.*　summer cypress (*Kochia scoparia*)

地肤子 dìfūzǐ　*Chin. med.*　the fruit of summer cypress

地府 dìfǔ　the underworld; Hades

地覆天翻 dìfù-tiānfān　same as 天翻地覆 tiānfān-dìfù

地高辛 dìgāoxīn　*pharm.*　digoxin

地宫 dìgōng　① underground palace—the coffin chamber of an emperor's tomb ② terrestrial palace—a shrine housing Buddhist relics

地沟 dìgōu　underground drainage

地骨皮 dìgǔpí　*Chin. med.*　the root bark of Chinese wolf-berry (*Lycium chinense*)

地瓜 dìguā　*dial.*　① yam bean ② sweet potato

地光 dìguāng　flashes of light preceding an earthquake

地广人稀 dìguǎng-rénxī　a vast but thinly populated area; a vast territory with a sparse population: 那个边区～, 只有五十万人口。The border region has only 500,000 inhabitants, a small population for so large an area.

地滚球 dìgǔnqiú　① *baseball* ground ball; grounder ② same as 保龄球 bǎolíngqiú

地核 dìhé　*geol.*　the earth's core

地黄 dìhuáng　*bot.*　glutinous rehmannia (*Rehmannia glutinosa*)

地积 dìjī　measure of land; area

地基 dìjī　① ground ② foundation

地极 dìjí　*geog.*　terrestrial pole

地甲病 dìjiǎbìng　(short for 地方性甲状腺肿) endemic goitre

地价 dìjià　land price

地角 dìjiǎo　① the ends of the earth; a remote place ② cape; promontory ③ the lower jaw

地脚 dìjiǎo　lower margin (of a page)

地脚螺栓 dìjiǎo luóshuān　*mech.*　foundation bolt

地窖 dìjiào　cellar

地界 dìjiè　the boundary of a piece of land

地锦 dìjǐn　*bot.*　humid euphorbia (*Euphorbia humifusa*)

地久天长 dìjiǔ-tiāncháng　same as 天长地久 tiāncháng-dìjiǔ

地窨 dìkū　① cellar ② cave

地块 dìkuài　*geol.*　massif

地蜡 dìlà　earth wax; ozocerite: 纯～ ceresin wax

地牢 dìláo　dungeon

地老虎 dìlǎohǔ　cutworm

地老天荒 dìlǎo-tiānhuāng　till the end of the world; for all eternity

地雷 dìléi　(land) mine: 埋～ plant (*or* lay) mines /防坦克～ antitank mine

地雷场 dìléichǎng　minefield

地雷战 dìléizhàn　(land) mine warfare

地垒 dìlěi　*geol.*　horst

地理 dìlǐ　① geographical features of a place: 熟悉～民情 be familiar with the place and its people ② geography: 自然(经济)～ physical (economic) geography /～发现 geographical discovery /～分布 geographical distribution /～环境 geographical conditions /～特点 geographical features /～位置 geographical position

地理先生 dìlǐxiānsheng　geomancer

地理学 dìlǐxué　geography: ～家 geographer

地理政治学 dìlǐ zhèngzhìxué　same as 地缘政治学 dìyuán zhèngzhìxué

地理坐标 dìlǐ zuòbiāo　geographical coordinates

地力 dìlì　soil fertility

地利 dìlì　① favourable geographical position; topographical advantages ② land productivity

地利人和 dìlì-rénhé　favourable terrain and friendly people

地沥青　dìlìqīng　asphalt; bitumen

地裂　dìliè　the ground cleaves: 山崩地裂 shānbēng-dìliè

地灵人杰　dìlíng-rénjié　a remarkable place produces outstanding people

地龙　dìlóng　*Chin. med.* earthworm

地龙墙　dìlóngqiáng　*archit.* sleeper wall

地漏　dìlòu　*archit.* floor drain

地脉　dìmài　the veins of the earth (believed to exist by geomancers)

地幔　dìmàn　*geol.* (the earth's) mantle

地貌　dìmào　the general configuration of the earth's surface; landforms

地貌图　dìmàotú　geomorphologic map

地貌学　dìmàoxué　geomorphology: ～家 geomorphologist

地面　dìmiàn　① the earth's surface; ground: 高出～两米 two metres above ground level ② *archit.* ground; floor: 水磨石～ terrazzo floor ③ *inf.* region; area; territory: 这里已经进入山东～。We're now in the Province of Shandong.

地面部队　dìmiàn bùduì　ground forces

地面沉降　dìmiàn chénjiàng　*geol.* surface subsidence

地面辐射　dìmiàn fúshè　*meteorol.* terrestrial surface radiation

地面灌溉　dìmiàn guàngài　surface irrigation

地面卫星站　dìmiàn wèixīngzhàn　(also 地面站 dìmiànzhàn) ground satellite station

地面遥测装置　dìmiàn yáocè zhuāngzhì　ground telemetering equipment

地面砖　dìmiànzhuān　*archit.* floor tile

地名　dìmíng　place name: ～辞典 dictionary of place names; gazetteer

地名学　dìmíngxué　toponomy; toponymy

地膜　dìmó　plastic film for covering young plants

地亩　dìmǔ　land; fields

地盘　dìpán　territory under one's control; domain: 军阀互相争夺～。The warlords competed for spheres of influence.

地皮　dìpí　① land for building ② ground: 雨停了,～还没有干。The ground is still wet after the rain.

地痞　dìpǐ　local ruffian; local riffraff

地平俯角　dìpíng fǔjiǎo　*surveying & drawing* dip of the horizon

地平经度　dìpíng jīngdù　*astron.* azimuth

地平经纬仪　dìpíng jīngwěiyí　*astron.* altazimuth

地平纬度　dìpíng wěidù　*astron.* altitude

地平线　dìpíngxiàn　horizon

地平坐标　dìpíng zuòbiāo　*astron.* horizontal coordinates

地铺　dìpù　shakedown: 用稻草和毯子在地板上打个～ make a shakedown of straw and blankets on the floor

地气　dìqì　① ground vapour (water vapour over the surface of the ground) ② (ground) temperature; climate

地契　dìqì　(also 地券 dìquàn) title deed for land

地堑　dìqiàn　*geol.* graben

地壳　dìqiào　*geol.* the earth's crust

地壳均衡　dìqiào jūnhéng　isostasy

地壳运动　dìqiào yùndòng　crustal movement

地勤　dìqín　*aviation* ground service: ～人员 ground crew; ground personnel

地球　dìqiú　the earth; the globe

地球化学　dìqiú huàxué　geochemistry

地球科学　dìqiú kēxué　geoscience

地球同步卫星　dìqiú tóngbù wèixīng　geostationary satellite; synchronous satellite

地球卫星　dìqiú wèixīng　earth satellite

地球物理学　dìqiú wùlǐxué　geophysics

地球仪　dìqiúyí　(terrestrial) globe

地区　dìqū　① area; district; region: 北京～ the Beijing area / 多山～ a mountainous district / 这个～最适宜种小麦。This area is most suitable for growing wheat. ② prefecture: 河北省保定～ the Baoding Prefecture of Hebei Province

地区冲突　dìqū chōngtū　regional conflict

地权　dìquán　land ownership: 平均～ equalization of land ownership

地热　dìrè　(also 地下热 dìxiàrè) *geol.* the heat of the earth's interior; terrestrial heat

地热电力　dìrè diànlì　geothermal power

地热能源　dìrè néngyuán　geothermal energy resources

地热学　dìrèxué　geothermics

地热资源　dìrè zīyuán　geothermal resources

地声　dìshēng　earthquake sounds

地史学　dìshǐxué　historical geology

地势　dìshì　physical features of a place; relief; terrain; topography: ～险要。The terrain is strategically situated and difficult of access.

地刷　dìshuā　scrubbing brush; scrubber

地税　dìshuì　land tax

地台　dìtái　*geol.* platform

地摊　dìtān　street vendor's stand or stall (with goods spread out on the ground for sale)

地毯　dìtǎn　carpet; rug

地毯式轰炸　dìtǎnshì hōngzhà　carpet bombing

地铁　dìtiě　short for 地下铁道 dìxià tiědào

地头¹　dìtóu　① edge of a field: 在～休息一会儿 rest for a moment at the edge of a field (while doing farm work) ② *dial.* destination ③ *dial.* the place: 你～熟悉,联系起来方便。You know the place well, so you can easily make contacts there.

地头²　dìtóu　lower margin (of a page) ——see also 天地头 tiāndìtóu

地头蛇　dìtóushé　a snake in its old haunts—local villain (or bully)

地图　dìtú　map

地图集　dìtújí　atlas

地图投影　dìtú tóuyǐng　map projection

地图学　dìtúxué　cartography

地推子　dìtuīzi　wheeled push broom; mechanized or semi-mechanized sweeper

地委　dìwěi　prefectural Party committee

地位　dìwèi　① position; standing; place; status: 政治～ political position (or standing) / 国际～ international standing / 经济～ economic status / 社会～ social position (or status) / ～平等 equal in status; on an equal footing / 一定的历史～ a proper or definite place in history / 他～变了,但普通劳动者的本色没有变。His status has changed but he's kept the fine qualities of an ordinary labourer. ② place (as occupied by a person or thing)

地温　dìwēn　*meteorol.* ground (or earth) temperature

地温表　dìwēnbiǎo　ground (or earth) thermometer

地温梯度　dìwēn tīdù　geothermal gradient

地文学　dìwénxué　physical geography; physiography

地物　dìwù　surface features (usu. man-made features of a region)

地峡　dìxiá　isthmus: 巴拿马～ the Isthmus of Panama

地下　dìxià　① underground; subterranean: ～仓库 underground storehouse / ～宫殿 underground palace ② secret (activity); underground: 转入～ go underground / 被打入～ be driven underground / 搞～工作 do underground work / ～党 underground Party; underground Party organization

地下　dìxia　on the ground: 掉在～ fall on the ground / 从～拣起 pick up from the ground

地下管道　dìxià guǎndào　underground piping

地下河流　dìxià héliú　subterranean river (or stream)

地下核试验　dìxià héshìyàn　underground nuclear test

地下茎　dìxiàjīng　*bot.* subterranean stem

地下渗流　dìxià shènliú　underground percolation

地下室　dìxiàshì　basement

地下水　dìxiàshuǐ　groundwater

地下水位　dìxià shuǐwèi　groundwater level; water table

地下铁道　dìxià tiědào　underground (railway); tube; subway

地线　dìxiàn　*elec.* ground (*or* earth) wire

地心　dìxīn　the earth's core

地心引力　dìxīn yǐnlì　terrestrial gravity; gravity

地形　dìxíng　topography; terrain: 〜优越 enjoy topographical advantages / 中国〜复杂。China has a varied topography. / 〜测量 topographic survey / 〜侦察 terrain reconnaissance

地形图　dìxíngtú　topographic map; relief map

地形学　dìxíngxué　topography

地形雨　dìxíngyǔ　*meteorol.* orographic rain

地形云　dìxíngyún　*meteorol.* orographic cloud

地衣　dìyī　*bot.* lichen

地窨子　dìyìnzi　*inf.* ① basement ② cellar

地应力　dìyìnglì　*geol.* crustal stress: 〜场 (crustal) stress field

地榆　dìyú　*bot.* garden burnet

地舆图　dìyútú　*old* atlas

地狱　dìyù　hell; inferno

地域　dìyù　region; district: 〜辽阔 vast in territory / 〜观念 regionalism

地缘政治学　dìyuán zhèngzhìxué　geopolitics

地震　dìzhèn　earthquake; seism: 这次〜为里氏七点一级。The shock was of 7.1 magnitude on the Richter scale. / 〜观测 seismological observation / 〜活动 seismic activity / 〜勘探 seismic prospecting

地震波　dìzhènbō　seismic (*or* earthquake) wave: 〜曲线 seismogram

地震带　dìzhèndài　seismic belt

地震海啸　dìzhèn hǎixiào　seismic sea wave; tsunami

地震检波器　dìzhèn jiǎnbōqì　geophone

地震烈度　dìzhèn lièdù　earthquake intensity

地震区　dìzhènqū　seismic area (*or* region)

地震台站　dìzhèn táizhàn　seismograph (*or* seismic) station

地震学　dìzhènxué　seismology

地震仪　dìzhènyí　seismograph

地震预报　dìzhèn yùbào　earthquake prediction; earthquake forecasting

地震震级　dìzhèn zhènjí　(earthquake) magnitude

地支　dìzhī　the twelve Earthly Branches, used in combination with the ten Heavenly Stems (天干) to designate years, months, days and hours

地址　dìzhǐ　address: 回信〜 return address

地志学　dìzhìxué　topology

地质　dìzhì　geology: 〜调查 geological survey

地质构造　dìzhì gòuzào　geological structure

地质勘探　dìzhì kāntàn　geological prospecting: 〜队 geological prospecting party (*or* team)

地质力学　dìzhìlìxué　geomechanics

地质年代学　dìzhìniándàixué　geochronology

地质时代　dìzhì shídài　geologic age (*or* period)

地质图　dìzhìtú　geologic map

地质学　dìzhìxué　geology: 〜家 geologist

地中海　Dìzhōnghǎi　the Mediterranean (Sea)

地轴　dìzhóu　the earth's axis

地主　dìzhǔ　①landlord ②host: 尽〜之谊 perform the duties of the host

地主阶级　dìzhǔjiējí　the landlord class

地啄木　dìzhuómù　*zool.* wryneck

地子　dìzi　background; ground: 红〜上绣金龙 a golden dragon embroidered on a red background

地租　dìzū　land rent; ground rent; rent: 〜剥削 exploitation through land rent

弟

弟　dì　①younger brother ② *hum.* (used between male friends, usu. in old-style letters) I

弟弟　dìdi　younger brother; brother

弟妇　dìfù　younger brother's wife; sister-in-law

弟妹　dìmèi　① younger brother and sister ② *inf.* younger brother's wife; sister-in-law

弟兄　dìxiong　brothers: 亲〜 blood brothers / 阶级〜 class brothers / 他就〜一个。He is the only son of the family.

弟子　dìzǐ　disciple; pupil; follower

的

的　dì　target; bull's-eye: 目的 mùdì ——see also de;
dí

帝

帝　dì　① the Supreme Being; god: 上帝 shàngdì ② emperor: 称帝 chēngdì ③ short for 帝国主义 dìguózhǔyì

帝俄　Dì'É　tsarist Russia

帝国　dìguó　empire: 英〜 the British Empire

帝国主义　dìguózhǔyì　imperialism: 〜分子 imperialist element; imperialist / 〜者 imperialist

帝号　dìhào　imperial title

帝君　dìjūn　a title of reverence added to the names of gods: 关圣〜 the god of war / 文昌〜 the god of literature

帝王　dìwáng　emperor; monarch

帝王将相，才子佳人　dì-wáng-jiàng-xiàng, cáizǐ-jiārén　kings and princes, generals and ministers, scholars and beauties—leading characters in traditional novels, dramas, etc.

帝汶岛　Dìwèndǎo　Timor

帝制　dìzhì　autocratic monarchy; monarchy

帝雉　dìzhì　*zool.* mikado pheasant

递（遞）

递（遞）　dì　① hand over; pass; give: 把报〜给我。Hand me the newspaper, please. / 给他〜个口信 take a message to him ② successively; in the proper order: 递升 dìshēng

递补　dìbǔ　fill vacancies in the proper order

递和气　dìhéqì　*inf.* be friendly towards sb.; make a friendly gesture

递加　dìjiā　progressively (*or* successively) increase; increase by degrees

递减　dìjiǎn　decrease progressively (*or* successively); decrease by degrees: 产品的成本随着生产率提高而〜。Increase in productivity is accompanied by a progressive decrease in production costs.

递降　dìjiàng　fall progressively; fall by degrees

递交　dìjiāo　hand over; present; submit: 〜国书 (of an ambassador) present one's credentials / 〜抗议书 lodge a protest / 〜一份声明 send in a statement / 〜入党申请书 submit an application for Party membership

递解　dìjiè　escort (a criminal) from one place to another: 〜回籍 send (a convict, etc.) to his native place under escort

递进　dìjìn　① go forward one by one ② increase progressively; increase by degrees

递升　dìshēng　promote to the next rank

递送　dìsòng　send; deliver: 〜情报 send out (*or* pass on) information / 〜信件 deliver letters

递推公式　dìtuī gōngshì　*math.* recurrence formula

递眼色　dì yǎnsè　tip sb. the wink; wink at sb.: 他给我递了个眼色，要我保持沉默。He winked at me to keep silent.

递增　dìzēng　increase progressively; increase by degrees: 产量平均每年〜百分之十五。The output in-

creased at an average rate of 15 per cent a year. *or* The output showed a yearly average increase of 15 per cent.

娣 dì *arch*. ① the wife of one's husband's younger brother; sister-in-law ② a woman's younger sister

谛 dì *formal* ① carefully; attentively: ～听 listen attentively / ～视 examine closely; scrutinize ② meaning; significance: 真谛 zhēndì

第[1] dì ① (used before numerals to form ordinal numbers):《～五交响曲》The Fifth Symphony; Symphony No.5 / 宪法～三条 Article 3 of the Constitution ② *formal* grades into which successful candidates in the imperial examinations were placed: 及第 jídì

第[2] dì the residence of a high official: 府第 fǔdì

第[3] dì *formal* but; only: ～恐 I only fear that...

第二产业 dì'èr chǎnyè secondary industry

第二次国内革命战争 Dì'èrcì Guónèi Gémìng Zhànzhēng the Second Revolutionary Civil War or the Agrarian Revolutionary War (1927-1937), waged by the Chinese people under the leadership of the Chinese Communist Party against KMT rule

第二次世界大战 Dì'èrcì Shìjiè Dàzhàn the Second World War (1939-1945); World War II

第二次鸦片战争 Dì'èrcì Yāpiàn Zhànzhēng the Second Opium War (1856-1860)

第二国际 Dì'èr Guójì the Second International (1889-1914)

第二审 dì'èrshěn *leg*. second instance: ～法院 court of second instance

第二声 dì'èrshēng *phonet*. rising tone, the second of the four tones in modern standard Chinese pronunciation

第二世界 dì'èr shìjiè the second world

第二信号系统 dì'èr xìnhào xìtǒng *physiol*. the second signal system

第二性 dì'èrxìng *philos*. secondary

第三产业 dìsān chǎnyè tertiary industry; the service sector

第三次国内革命战争 Dìsāncì Guónèi Gémìng Zhànzhēng the Third Revolutionary Civil War or the War of Liberation (1945-1949), in which the Chinese people, under the wise leadership of the Chinese Communist Party and Chairman Mao Zedong, finally overthrew KMT rule and founded the People's Republic of China

第三国际 Dìsān Guójì the Third International (1919-1943)

第三纪 Dìsānjì *geol*. the Tertiary Period

第三声 dìsānshēng *phonet*. falling-rising tone, the third of the four tones in modern standard Chinese pronunciation

第三世界 dìsān shìjiè the third world

第三者 dìsānzhě a third party (to a dispute, a divorce proceeding, etc.)

第四纪 Dìsìjì *geol*. the Quaternary Period

第四声 dìsìshēng *phonet*. falling tone, the fourth of the four tones in modern standard Chinese pronunciation

第五纵队 dìwǔ zòngduì fifth column

第一 dìyī first; primary; foremost: 党委～书记 the first secretary of the Party committee / 做出～等的工作 do first-rate work / ～号种子选手 No.1 seeded player / 获得～名 win first place; get a first; win a championship / 他跑百米得了～。He came in first in the 100-metre

dash. / 把劳动看作生活的～需要 regard labour as life's prime want / 以革命利益为～生命 look upon the interests of the revolution as one's very life

第一把手 dìyībǎshǒu first in command; number one man; a person holding primary responsibility

第一产业 dìyī chǎnyè primary industry

第一次国内革命战争 Dìyīcì Guónèi Gémìng Zhànzhēng the First Revolutionary Civil War (1924-1927), waged by the Chinese people under the leadership of the Chinese Communist Party against the imperialists and the Northern warlords

第一次世界大战 Dìyīcì Shìjiè Dàzhàn the First World War (1914-1918); World War I

第一国际 Dìyī Guójì the First International (1864-1876)

第一审 dìyīshěn *leg*. first instance: ～法院 court of first instance

第一声 dìyīshēng *phonet*. high and level tone, the first of the four tones in modern standard Chinese pronunciation

第一世界 dìyī shìjiè the first world

第一手 dìyīshǒu firsthand: ～材料 firsthand material

第一线 dìyīxiàn forefront; front line; first line: 生产～ the forefront of production / 教学～ the first-line work of a school—teaching

第一线飞机 dìyīxiàn fēijī first-line aircraft

第一信号系统 dìyī xìnhào xìtǒng *physiol*. the first signal system

第一性 dìyīxìng *philos*. primary: 物质是～的, 意识是第二性的。Matter is primary and consciousness is secondary.

棣[1] dì ① see 棣棠 dìtáng ② see 棠棣 tángdì

棣[2] dì *formal* younger brother

棣棠 dìtáng *bot*. kerria

蒂(蔕) dì the base of a fruit: 并蒂莲 bìngdìlián

缔 dì form (a friendship); conclude (a treaty)

缔交 dìjiāo ① establish diplomatic relations ② form (*or* contract) a friendship

缔结 dìjié conclude; establish: ～条约 conclude a treaty / ～邦交 establish diplomatic relations

缔盟 dìméng form an alliance

缔姻 dìyīn form a marriage alliance

缔约 dìyuē conclude (*or* sign) a treaty: ～双方 both contracting parties

缔约国 dìyuēguó signatory (state) to a treaty; party to a treaty; (high) contracting party

缔造 dìzào found; create: ～者 founder / 毛泽东等同志～了中国工农红军。Mao Zedong and his comrades founded the Chinese Workers' and Peasants' Red Army.

睇 dì *formal* look askance; cast a sidelong glance

碲 dì *chem*. tellurium (Te)

diǎ

嗲 diǎ *dial*. ① flirtatious: 说话～声～气 speak in a coquettish voice ② acting spoiled ③ good; nice

diān

掂（战） diān weigh in the hand: ～～这有多重。Weigh this in your hand.

掂对 diāndui *dial.* ① weigh up; consider ② exchange; swop

掂斤播两 diānjīn-bōliǎng (also 掂斤簸两 diānjīn-bǒliǎng) engage in petty calculations; be calculating in small matters

掂量 diānliàng *dial.* ① weigh in the hand: 你～一下有多重。Try to feel its weight. ② think over; weigh up: 你～着办得了。Just do as you think fit. / 听到什么话要～～，看它代表谁的利益。We must weigh up what we hear and see whose interests it represents.

掂算 diānsuàn estimate; calculate; weigh

滇

滇 Diān .another name for 云南 Yúnnán

滇红 diānhóng Yunnan black tea

颠[1] diān ① crown (of the head) ② top; summit: 山～ mountain top / 塔～ the top of a pagoda

颠[2] diān ① jolt; bump: 路不平，卡车～得厉害。As the road was rough, the truck jolted badly. ② fall; turn over; topple down: 颠覆 diānfù ③ *dial.* run; go away: 整天跑跑～～ be on the go all day long / 对不起，我得～儿了。Sorry, I've got to be on my way.

颠[3] diān same as 癫 diān

颠簸 diānbǒ jolt; bump; toss: 卡车在土路上～着前进。The truck bumped along the dirt road. / 风更大了，船身～起来。As the wind grew stronger, the boat was tossed about by the waves.

颠达 diāndá (also 颠搭 diāndá) ① jolt; joggle ② *dial.* rush about; bustle about

颠倒 diāndǎo ① put (*or* turn) upside down; transpose; reverse; invert: 这一头朝上，别放～了。This is the top; don't put it upside down. / 把这两个字～过来句子就顺了。Transpose these two words and the sentence will read right. / 主次～ reverse the order of importance / 把被～的历史再～过来 reverse the reversal of history; set the record of history straight / ～敌我关系 take enemies for comrades and comrades for enemies ② confused; disordered: 神魂颠倒 shénhún diāndǎo

颠倒黑白 diāndǎo hēi-bái confound black and white; confuse right and wrong; stand facts on their heads

颠倒是非 diāndǎo shì-fēi confound (*or* reverse) right and wrong; confuse truth and falsehood; turn things upside down

颠覆 diānfù overturn; subvert: 火车出轨～了。The train derailed and overturned. / ～活动 subversive activities; subversion

颠来倒去 diānlái-dǎoqù over and over: 就那么点事，他却～说个没完。It was only a small matter but he kept harping on it. / 如果一篇文章～总是那么几个词，人家就不愿看。No one cares to read an article that merely rings the changes on a few terms.

颠连[1] diānlián *formal* hardship; trouble; difficulty

颠连[2] diānlián *formal* peak upon peak

颠末 diānmò *formal* beginning and end——the whole story

颠沛流离 diānpèi-liúlí drift from place to place, homeless and miserable; wander about in a desperate plight; lead a vagabond life: 他们～，含辛茹苦地过了大半生。They spent the greater part of their lives wandering from place to place and enduring all kinds of hardships.

颠扑不破 diānpū bù pò be able to withstand heavy battering; irrefutable; indisputable: ～的真理 irrefutable truth

颠茄 diānqié *pharm.* belladonna

颠三倒四 diānsān-dǎosì incoherent; disorderly; confused

颠踬 diānzhì ① dodder along; stagger along ② be in dire straits

巅

巅 diān mountain peak; summit: 泰山之～ the summit of Mount Tai

巅峰 diānfēng summit; peak; pinnacle: 我们的运动员正处于～状态。Our athletes are in top form.

癫

癫 diān mentally deranged; insane: 疯癫 fēngdiān

癫狂 diānkuáng ① demented; mad; insane ② frivolous

癫痫 diānxián *med.* epilepsy

diǎn

典[1] diǎn ① standard; law; canon: 典范 diǎnfàn ② standard work of scholarship: 词典 cídiǎn ③ allusion; literary quotation: 用～ use allusions ④ ceremony: 盛典 shèngdiǎn ⑤ *formal* be in charge of: 典狱 diǎnyù

典[2] diǎn mortgage; pawn

典当 diǎndàng mortgage; pawn

典范 diǎnfàn model; example; paragon

典故 diǎngù allusion; literary quotation

典籍 diǎnjí ancient codes and records; ancient books and records: 先秦～ pre-Qin books and records

典礼 diǎnlǐ ceremony; celebration

典卖 diǎnmài mortgage

典型 diǎnxíng ① typical case (*or* example); model; type: 抓～ grasp typical cases / 理论与实践相结合的～ a model of the integration of theory and practice ② typical; representative: ～人物 a typical character / ～事例 a typical instance (*or* case) / ～的中国村庄 a representative Chinese village / 文艺作品所反映的生活应该比实际生活更～。Life as reflected in works of art and literature ought to be more typical than actual everyday life. / ～性 typicalness; representativeness

典押 diǎnyā mortgage; pawn

典雅 diǎnyǎ (of diction, etc.) refined; elegant

典狱 diǎnyù prison warden

典狱长 diǎnyùzhǎng prison warden

典章 diǎnzhāng institutions; decrees and regulations

典质 diǎnzhì mortgage; pawn

典制 diǎnzhì laws and institutions

点[1]（點） diǎn ① drop (of liquid): 雨点 yǔdiǎn ② spot; dot; speck: 墨～ ink spots ③ dot stroke (in Chinese characters) ④ *math.* point: 两～成一直线。A line is formed by connecting two points. ⑤ decimal point; point: 三～儿五 three point five (3.5) ⑥ *m.* a little; a bit; some: 给我～纸。Give me some paper, will you? / 读～鲁迅 read some of Lu Xun's works / 他今天好～了。He's feeling a bit better today. / 人的认识一～也不能离开实践。Human knowledge can in no way be separated from practice. ⑦ *m.* (for items): 我有几～不成熟的想法。I have some tentative suggestions. ⑧ place; point: 突破一～ make a breakthrough at one point ⑨ aspect; feature: 从这～上看 viewed from this aspect / 对这一～没人怀疑。Nobody has any doubt about that. ⑩ put a dot: ～三个点表示省略 put

three dots to show that something has been omitted ⑪ touch on very briefly; skim: 他用篙一～就把船撑开了。He pushed the boat off with a shove of the pole. / 她发言时～了这件事。She touched on the matter in her speech. ⑫ drip: ～眼药 put drops in the eyes ⑬ sow in holes; dibble: ～豆子 dibble beans ⑭ check one by one: 请你把钱～一～。Please check and see if the money is right. / ～货 check over goods; take stock ⑮ select; choose: 他～了牛排。He ordered a steak. ⑯ hint; point out: 一～他就明白了。He quickly took the hint. ⑰ light; burn; kindle: ～灯 light a lamp / 他是火爆性子，一～就着。He's got a fiery temper and flares up at the slightest provocation. ⑱ embellish; decorate: 装点 zhuāngdiǎn

点²(點) diǎn ① o'clock: 上午九～钟 nine o'clock in the morning / 现在几～了？What time is it now? ② appointed time: 到点 dàodiǎn

点³(點) diǎn refreshments: 茶点 chádiǎn

点⁴(點) diǎn *print.* point, a unit of measurement for type

点兵 diǎnbīng *old* muster troops (for inspection)

点播¹ diǎnbō *agric.* dibble seeding; dibbling: ～器 dibbler

点播² diǎnbō request a programme from a radio station: 听众～的节目 a programme by request; (listeners') request / 听众～的爵士乐 jazz for the asking

点拨 diǎnbo *inf.* give directions; show how (to do sth.); coach

点补 diǎnbu have a snack to stave off hunger; have a bite: 这里有点吃的，谁饿了可以先～～。Here's a bite to eat if anyone's hungry.

点菜 diǎncài choose dishes from a menu; order dishes (in a restaurant)

点唱 diǎnchàng (of an audience) request a number (a song, an aria from a traditional opera, etc.)

点穿 diǎnchuān bring sth. out into the open; lay bare

点窜 diǎncuàn make some alterations in wording

点滴 diǎndī ① a bit: 这批资料是点点滴滴积累起来的。This fund of information has been accumulated bit by bit. ② *med.* intravenous drip: 打葡萄糖～ have an intravenous glucose drip

点定 diǎndìng *formal* make corrections in a piece of writing

点乩 diǎndū add a few touches to a painting

点焊 diǎnhàn spot (*or* point) welding

点画¹ diǎnhuà strokes and dots (in Chinese calligraphy)

点画² diǎnhuà ① point with the finger or gesticulate ② embellish; adorn: 晚霞把西半边天空～得绚丽多彩。Sunset clouds tinted the western sky with gorgeous colours.

点火 diǎnhuǒ ① light a fire ② ignition ③ stir up trouble

点饥 diǎnjī have a snack to stave off hunger

点将 diǎnjiàng ① (in traditional operas) call the muster roll of officers and assign them tasks ② name a person for a particular job

点交 diǎnjiāo hand over item by item

点金成铁 diǎn jīn chéng tiě touch gold and turn it into iron—miscorrect a piece of writing

点睛 diǎnjīng (short for 画龙点睛, used in) ～之笔 a finishing touch added to a painting; an apt word added to clinch the point

点卯 diǎnmǎo *old* (in *yamen*) call the roll in the morning (from 5 a.m. to 7 a.m.)

点名 diǎnmíng ① call the roll: 晚～ evening roll call /

老师点了名。The teacher called the roll. / 我到的时候刚要～。I arrived just before roll call. ② mention sb. by name: 他～要你去。He named you as the one he wanted. / ～攻击 attack sb. by name / ～批判 criticize sb. by name

点名册 diǎnmíngcè roll book; roll

点明 diǎnmíng point out; put one's finger on: ～问题所在 put one's finger on the cause of the trouble

点派 diǎnpài same as 指派 zhǐpài

点破 diǎnpò bring sth. out into the open; lay bare; point out bluntly: 我没有～他的真实意图。I didn't point out what he was really after.

点球 diǎnqiú *football* penalty kick

点燃 diǎnrán light; kindle; ignite: ～火把 light a torch / ～革命之火 kindle the flames of revolution

点染 diǎnrǎn ① add details to a painting ② touch up (*or* polish) a piece of writing

点射 diǎnshè *mil.* ① fixed fire ② firing in bursts

点石成金 diǎn shí chéng jīn touch a stone and turn it into gold—turn a crude essay into a literary gem

点收 diǎnshōu check and accept: 按清单～货物 acknowledge receipt of goods after checking them against a list

点数 diǎnshù check the number (of pieces, etc.); count: 找你的钱别忘了点点数。Don't forget to count your change.

点题 diǎntí bring out the theme

点铁成金 diǎn tiě chéng jīn touch iron and turn it into gold—turn a crude essay into a literary gem

点头 diǎntóu nod one's head; nod: ～同意 nod assent / ～打招呼 nod to sb. (as a greeting) / ～示意 signal by nodding / 他已经～了。He's already given the go-ahead. *or* He's already OK'd it.

点头哈腰 diǎntóu-hāyāo *inf.* bow unctuously; bow and scrape

点头之交 diǎntóu zhī jiāo nodding (*or* bowing) acquaintance: 我和他只是～。I have only a nodding acquaintance with him. *or* He and I are only nodding acquaintances.

点心 diǎnxin light refreshments; pastry

点穴 diǎnxué (in Chinese boxing) touch vital points on the adversary's body to cause internal injury

点验 diǎnyàn examine item by item

点阵 diǎnzhèn *phys.* lattice

点种 diǎnzhòng dibble in the seeds

点种 diǎnzhòng same as 点播¹ diǎnbō

点缀 diǎnzhuì ① embellish; ornament; adorn: 几株红梅把雪后的园林～得格外美丽。Embellished with the red blossoms of the plum trees, the garden looked more beautiful than ever after the snow. ② use sth. merely for show: 贴几张标语～～ put up some slogans for more atmosphere

点字 diǎnzì braille

点子¹ diǎnzi ① drop (of liquid): 雨～ raindrops ② spot; dot; speck: 油～ grease spot ③ beat (of percussion instruments): 鼓～ drumbeat

点子² diǎnzi ① key point: 工作抓到～上 get to grips with the essentials in one's work; put one's finger on the right spot / 这话说到～上了。This remark gets to the heart of the matter. ② idea; pointer: 他～多。He's full of ideas. ——see also 出点子 chū diǎnzi

碘 diǎn *chem.* iodine (I)

碘酊 diǎndīng *pharm.* tincture of iodine

碘仿 diǎnfǎng *chem.* iodoform

碘化银 diǎnhuàyín silver iodide

碘酒 diǎnjiǔ same as 碘酊 diǎndīng

跕(跕) diǎn stand on tiptoe: 他得～着脚才够

得着架子。He had to stand on tiptoe to reach the shelf. / 护士～着脚走到病人床边。The nurse tiptoed to the bedside of the patient.

diàn

电（電） diàn ① electricity ② give or get an electric shock: 电门有毛病,～了我一下。There was something wrong with the switch and I got a shock. ③ telegram; cable: ～上级请示 telegraph the higher authorities for instructions

电棒 diànbàng *dial.* (electric) torch; flashlight

电报 diànbào telegram; cable: 无线～ radiotelegram / 有线～ wire telegram / 打～ send a telegram; cable / 打～让他回来 wire him to come back

电报等级 diànbào děngjí telegram message precedence

电报挂号 diànbào guàhào cable address; telegraphic address

电报机 diànbàojī telegraph

电报局 diànbàojú telegraph office

电报音响器 diànbào yīnxiǎngqì telegraph sounder

电笔 diànbǐ popular name for 测电笔 cèdiànbǐ

电表 diànbiǎo ① any meter for measuring electricity, such as ammeter or voltmeter ② kilowatt-hour meter; watt-hour meter; electric meter

电冰箱 diànbīngxiāng (electric) refrigerator; fridge; freezer: 单门～ single-door refrigerator / 双门～ double-door refrigerator

电波 diànbō same as 电磁波 diàncíbō

电铲 diànchǎn power shovel

电场 diànchǎng electric field: ～强度 electric field intensity

电唱机 diànchàngjī electric gramophone (*or* phonograph); record player

电唱头 diànchàngtóu pickup (of a record player)

电唱针 diànchàngzhēn (gramophone) stylus; needle

电车 diànchē ① tram; tramcar; streetcar ② trolleybus; trolley

电池 diànchí (electric) cell; battery: 干～ dry cell / 太阳能～ solar cell / ～组 battery

电传 diànchuán telex

电传打字电报机 diànchuán dǎzì diànbàojī teletypewriter; teleprinter

电传机 diànchuánjī short for 电传打字电报机 diànchuán dǎzì diànbàojī

电磁 diàncí electromagnetism

电磁波 diàncíbō electromagnetic wave

电磁感应 diàncí gǎnyìng electromagnetic induction

电磁铁 diàncítiě electromagnet

电磁学 diàncíxué electromagnetics

电大 diàndà short for 电视大学 diànshì dàxué

电导 diàndǎo conductance: ～仪 conductivity gauge

电灯 diàndēng electric lamp; electric light: 偏僻的山村现在有了～。Electric light has now reached remote mountain villages.

电灯泡 diàndēngpào electric (light) bulb

电动 diàndòng motor-driven; power-driven; power-operated; electric: ～泵 motor-driven pump; electric pump / ～车 electrically operated motor car / ～发电机 motor generator / ～割草机 power-operated mower / ～葫芦 electric hoist (*or* block) / ～回转罗盘 electric gyro-compass / ～记分牌 electric scoreboard

电动机 diàndòngjī (electric) motor

电动力学 diàndònglìxué electrodynamics

电动势 diàndòngshì electro-motive force (EMF)

电度表 diàndùbiǎo kilowatt-hour meter; watt-hour meter; electric meter

电镀 diàndù electroplate: 无氰～ electroplating without using cyanide

电法勘探 diànfǎ kāntàn *min.* electrical prospecting

电饭煲 diànfànbāo *dial.* (electric) rice cooker

电饭锅 diànfànguō (electric) rice cooker

电风扇 diànfēngshàn same as 电扇 diànshàn

电复 diànfù reply by telegraph

电杆 diàngān (wire) pole; telephone pole

电感 diàngǎn inductance: ～电桥 inductance bridge

电告 diàngào notify or report by telegraph

电工 diàngōng ① electrical engineering: ～技术 electrotechnics / ～器材 electrical appliances ② electrician

电工学 diàngōngxué electrical engineering; electrotechnics

电功率 diàngōnglù electric power: ～计 electrodynamometer

电灌站 diànguànzhàn electric pumping station (*or* house)

电光 diànguāng light produced by electricity; lightning

电光工艺 diànguāng gōngyì *text.* schreinering

电滚子 diàngǔnzi *dial.* ① generator; dynamo ② (electric) motor

电棍 diàngùn electric prod

电焊 diànhàn electric welding: ～机 electric welding machine; electric welder

电焊工 diànhàngōng electric welder

电焊条 diànhàntiáo welding electrode; welding rod

电贺 diànhè telegraph one's congratulations to sb.; cable a message of congratulations

电荷 diànhè electric charge; charge: 正(负)～ positive (negative) charge

电弧 diànhú electric arc: ～割切机 arc cutting machine / ～炉 arc furnace

电弧焊接 diànhú hànjiē (electric) arc welding

电化当量 diànhuà dāngliàng electrochemical equivalent

电化教育 diànhuà jiàoyù education with electrical audio-visual aids; audio-visual education programme

电化学 diànhuàxué electrochemistry

电话 diànhuà ① telephone; phone: 请别把～挂上。Hold the line, please. / 他把～挂了。He's hung up. ② phone call: 打～ make a phone call; phone sb.; call (*or* ring) sb. up; give sb. a ring / 他正在打～。He's on the phone. / 有你的～。There's a phone call for you. *or* You're wanted on the phone.

电话簿 diànhuàbù telephone directory (*or* book)

电话分机 diànhuà fēnjī extention (telephone)

电话号码 diànhuà hàomǎ telephone number

电话会议 diànhuà huìyì telephone conference; teleconference

电话机 diànhuàjī telephone (set)

电话间 diànhuàjiān telephone box (*or* booth, kiosk); call box

电话交换台 diànhuà jiāohuàntái telephone exchange (*or* switchboard)

电话局 diànhuàjú telephone office (*or* exchange)

电话亭 diànhuàtíng telephone booth; telephone kiosk; call box

电话用户 diànhuà yònghù telephone subscriber

电话增音机 diànhuà zēngyīnjī telephone repeater

电汇 diànhuì telegraphic money order; remittance by telegram; telegraphic transfer: ～汇率 rate for telegraphic transfer

电火花 diànhuǒhuā electric spark: ～加工 electric spark machining

电击 diànjī electric shock

电机 diànjī electrical machinery: ～厂 electrical machinery plant / ～工程 electrical engineering

电机车 diànjīchē electric locomotive

电积 diànjī *metall.* electrodeposition

电吉他 diànjítā *mus.* electric guitar

电极 diànjí electrode: 阳～ anode; positive electrode / 阴～ cathode; negative electrode

电价键 diànjiàjiàn *chem.* electrovalent bond

电键 diànjiàn telegraph key; key; button

电教 diànjiào short for 电化教育 diànhuà jiàoyù

电解 diànjiě electrolysis

电解质 diànjiězhì electrolyte

电介质 diànjièzhì dielectric

电锯 diànjù electric saw

电抗 diànkàng reactance: ～器 reactor

电烤箱 diànkǎoxiāng electric oven; electric grill; electric roaster

电缆 diànlǎn electric cable; cable

电烙铁 diànlàotie ① electric iron ② electric soldering iron

电离 diànlí ionization

电离层 diànlícéng *meteorol.* ionosphere

电力 diànlì electric power; power: ～工程 electric power project / ～工业 power industry / ～供应 supply of electricity / ～机械 electrical power equipment / ～系统 power system / ～消耗 power consumption

电力机车 diànlì jīchē electric locomotive

电力网 diànlìwǎng power network

电力线 diànlìxiàn power line; electric line of force

电疗 diànliáo *med.* electrotherapy: 短波～ shortwave therapy / 超短波～ ultrashort-wave therapy

电料 diànliào electrical materials and appliances

电铃 diànlíng ① electric bell ② doorbell

电令 diànlíng ① cable orders; send orders by telegraph ② orders sent by telegraph; cabled orders

电流 diànliú electric current: 载波～ carrier current / 反向～ reverse current / ～强度 current intensity

电流表 diànliúbiǎo same as 安培计 ānpéijì

电流计 diànliújì galvanometer

电溜子 diànliūzi *min.* chain conveyor; face conveyor

电炉 diànlú ① electric stove; hot plate ② electric furnace: ～钢 electric steel / ～炼钢法 electric furnace process

电路 diànlù (electric) circuit

电路图 diànlùtú circuit diagram

电码 diànmǎ (telegraphic) code: 莫尔斯～ Morse code / ～本 code book

电鳗 diànmán *zool.* electric eel

电门 diànmén (electric) switch

电母 diànmǔ the goddess of lightning

电木 diànmù *chem.* bakelite

电木粉 diànmùfěn phenolic moulding powder

电纳 diànnà *phys.* susceptance

电脑 diànnǎo popular name for 电子计算机 diànzǐ jìsuànjī

电钮 diànniǔ push button; button: 按～ press (*or* push) a button

电耙 diànpá *min.* scraper

电瓶 diànpíng common name for 蓄电池 xùdiànchí

电瓶车 diànpíngchē storage battery car; electromobile

电气 diànqì electric: ～机车 electric locomotive / ～设备 electrical equipment

电气化 diànqìhuà electrify: 全国铁路系统几乎全部～了。The national railway system has nearly all been electrified. / 农业～ electrification of agriculture / ～铁路 electric railway

电气石 diànqìshí tourmaline

电器 diànqì electrical equipment (*or* appliance): 家用～ household (electrical) appliances

电热 diànrè electric heat; electrothermal

电热杯 diànrèbēi electric heating jug

电热丝 diànrèsī heating wire

电热毯 diànrètǎn ① *med.* electrothermal pad ② electric blanket

电热针灸 diànrè zhēnjiǔ electrothermal acupuncture

电容 diànróng electric capacity; capacitance: ～率 permittivity

电容器 diànróngqì condenser; capacitor

电熔炼 diànróngliàn *metall.* electric smelting

电扇 diànshàn electric fan

电渗析 diànshènxī *chem.* electrodialysis

电石 diànshí *chem.* calcium carbide

电石气 diànshíqì same as 乙炔 yǐquē

电示 diànshì notify *or* give instructions by telegraph; cable a notice *or* directive

电势 diànshì same as 电位 diànwèi

电视 diànshì television; TV: 看～ watch television / 彩色 (黑白, 立体)～ colour (black-and-white, stereoscopic) television

电视大学 diànshì dàxué TV university

电视电话 diànshì diànhuà video telephone; video-phone

电视电影 diànshì diànyǐng telecine

电视发射机 diànshì fāshèjī television transmitter

电视广播 diànshì guǎngbō television broadcasting; telecasting; videocast

电视机 diànshìjī common name for 电视接收机 diànshì jiēshōujī

电视讲座 diànshì jiǎngzuò telecourse

电视接收机 diànshì jiēshōujī television receiver; television set

电视剧 diànshìjù TV drama; TV play

电视雷达导航仪 diànshì léidá dǎohángyí teleran

电视片 diànshìpiàn telefilm

电视屏幕 diànshì píngmù television screen

电视摄影机 diànshì shèyǐngjī television camera; telecamera

电视塔 diànshìtǎ television tower

电视台 diànshìtái television station

电视网 diànshìwǎng television network

电视转播 diànshì zhuǎnbō television relay

电视转播卫星 diànshì zhuǎnbō wèixīng television transmission satellite

电枢 diànshū armature: ～绕组 armature winding

电刷 diànshuā *mech.* brush: ～触点 brush contact

电台 diàntái ① transmitter-receiver; transceiver ② broadcasting (*or* radio) station

电烫 diàntàng permanent hair styling (*or* waving); permanent wave; perm

电梯 diàntī lift; elevator: ～司机 lift operator; elevator runner

电筒 diàntǒng (electric) torch; flashlight

电网 diànwǎng electrified wire netting; live wire entanglement

电位 diànwèi (electric) potential: ～差 potential difference

电文 diànwén the text of a telegram

电线 diànxiàn (electric) wire: ～杆子 (wire) pole; telephone pole

电信 diànxìn telecommunications: ～业务 telecommunication service

电信局 diànxìnjú telecommunication bureau

电刑 diànxíng ① torture by electricity ② electrocution; the electric chair; the chair

电学 diànxué electricity (as a science)

电讯 diànxùn ① (telegraphic) dispatch: 世界各地发来的～ dispatches from all parts of the world ② telecommunications: ～设备 telecommunication equipment

电压 diànyā voltage

电压表 diànyābiǎo (also 电压计 diànyājì) voltmeter

电眼 diànyǎn electric eye; magic eye

电唁 diànyàn send a telegram (*or* message) of condo-

lence

电邀 diànyāo　send an invitation by telegraph; cable an invitation

电冶金 diànyějīn　electrometallurgy

电椅 diànyǐ　the electric chair

电影 diànyǐng　film; movie; motion picture: 有声（无声）～ sound (silent) film／彩色（黑白）～ colour (black-and-white) film／～发行公司 film distribution corporation／～放映队 film projection unit (or team)／～放映网 film projection network／～译制厂 film dubbing studio／～制片厂 (film) studio

电影放映机 diànyǐng fàngyìngjī　(film) projector; cine-projector

电影剪辑机 diànyǐng jiǎnjíjī　film editing machine

电影胶片 diànyǐng jiāopiàn　cinefilm; motion-picture film

电影节 diànyǐngjié　film festival

电影界 diànyǐngjiè　film (or movie) circles

电影剧本 diànyǐng jùběn　scenario

电影明星 diànyǐng míngxīng　film star; movie star

电影摄影机 diànyǐng shèyǐngjī　cinecamera; film camera

电影摄影师 diànyǐng shèyǐngshī　cinematographer; cameraman

电影说明书 diànyǐng shuōmíngshū　film synopsis

电影演员 diànyǐng yǎnyuán　film actor or actress

电影院 diànyǐngyuàn　cinema; movie (house)

电影招待会 diànyǐng zhāodàihuì　film reception

电影周 diànyǐngzhōu　film week

电影字幕 diànyǐng zìmù　(film) caption

电泳 diànyǒng　*phys.* electrophoresis

电玉粉 diànyùfěn　*chem.* urea-formaldehyde moulding powder

电谕 diànyù　send instructions, directives, etc. by telegraph

电源 diànyuán　power supply; power source; mains: 接上～ connect with the mains

电源变压器 diànyuán biànyāqì　power transformer; mains transformer

电灶 diànzào　electric cooking stove (or range)

电渣焊 diànzhāhàn　electroslag welding

电渣炉 diànzhālú　*metall.* electroslag furnace

电闸 diànzhá　main switch; master switch

电针疗法 diànzhēn liáofǎ　*Chin. med.* acupuncture with electric stimulation; galvano-acupuncture

电针麻醉 diànzhēn mázuì　*Chin. med.* galvano-acupuncture anaesthesia

电钟 diànzhōng　electric clock

电珠 diànzhū　small bulb (as in a flashlight)

电铸版 diànzhùbǎn　*print.* electrotype

电子 diànzǐ　electron: 热～ thermal electron／正～ positron／负～ negatron／～工业 electronics industry／～器件 electronic device

电子表 diànzǐbiǎo　common name for 石英手表 shíyīng shǒubiǎo

电子秤 diànzǐchèng　electronic-weighing system

电子伏特 diànzǐ fútè　electron-volt

电子管 diànzǐguǎn　electron tube; valve

电子管收音机 diànzǐguǎn shōuyīnjī　valve radio set

电子光学 diànzǐ guāngxué　electron optics

电子回旋加速器 diànzǐ huíxuán jiāsùqì　betatron

电子计算机 diànzǐ jìsuànjī　electronic computer

电子刻版机 diànzǐ kèbǎnjī　*print.* electronic engraving machine

电子枪 diànzǐqiāng　electron gun

电子壳层 diànzǐqiàocéng　electron shell

电子琴 diànzǐqín　electronic organ; electronic keyboard

电子束 diànzǐshù　electron beam

电子玩具 diànzǐ wánjù　electronic toys

电子望远镜 diànzǐ wàngyuǎnjìng　electron telescope

电子物理学 diànzǐ wùlǐxué　electron physics

电子显微镜 diànzǐ xiǎnwēijìng　electron microscope: 八十万倍～ an electron microscope with a magnification of 800,000 times

电子学 diànzǐxué　electronics

电子游戏 diànzǐ yóuxì　video game; TV game

电子游戏机 diànzǐ yóuxìjī　video game player; TV game player

电子云 diànzǐyún　electron cloud

电子照相术 diànzǐ zhàoxiàngshù　electrophotography

电子钟 diànzǐzhōng　common name for 石英钟 shíyīngzhōng

电阻 diànzǔ　*elec.* resistance: ～率 resistivity; specific resistance

电阻对焊 diànzǔ duìhàn　*mech.* upset butt welding

电阻炉 diànzǔlú　*metall.* resistance furnace

电钻 diànzuàn　electric drill

佃　diàn　rent land (from a landlord)

佃户 diànhù　tenant (farmer)

佃农 diànnóng　tenant-peasant; tenant farmer

佃契 diànqì　tenancy contract

佃权 diànquán　tenant right

佃租 diànzū　land rent

甸　diàn　(usu. used as part of a place name) pasture: 桦～ Huadian (in Jilin Province)

甸子 diànzi　*dial.* pasture

店　diàn　① shop; store: 服装～ clothing store／文具～ stationer's ② inn: 住～ stop at an inn

店东 diàndōng　*old* ① shopkeeper ② innkeeper

店家 diànjiā　① *old* shopkeeper ② *old* innkeeper; restaurateur ③ *dial.* shop; store

店铺 diànpù　shop; store

店堂 diàntáng　the business quarter of a shop (or store); commodity section

店小二 diànxiǎo'èr　*old* waiter; attendant

店员 diànyuán　shop assistant; salesclerk; clerk; salesman or saleswoman

玷　diàn　① a flaw in a piece of jade: 白圭之玷 báiguī zhī diàn ② blemish; disgrace: 玷污 diànwū

玷辱 diànrǔ　bring disgrace on; be a disgrace to

玷污 diànwū　stain; sully; tarnish: 他这种行为～了共产党员的光荣称号。By such behaviour he has sullied the honour of a Communist.

垫（墊）　diàn　① put sth. under sth. else to raise it or make it level; fill up; pad: ～路 repair a road by filling the holes／桌子腿底下～点儿纸就平了。Put a wad of paper under the leg of the table to make it level.／正戏还没开演，咱们先～一出小戏。Let's put in a short skit before the major item. ② pad; cushion; mat: 椅～ chair cushion ③ pay for sb. and expect to be repaid later: 你先给我～上，以后再还你。Would you mind paying for me? I'll pay you back later.

垫背 diànbèi　*dial.* act as a cushion—bear the blame for others; be made a scapegoat

垫补 diànbu　*dial.* ① make up the deficiency by borrowing money or using money intended for other purposes ② have a snack

垫底儿 diàndǐr　① put sth. at the bottom: 鱼缸里是用细沙～的。The bottom of the fish bowl is covered with a layer of fine sand. ② have a bite to stave off hunger pains (before taking a regular meal) ③ do spadework; lay a foundation

垫付 diànfù　(also 垫支 diànzhī) pay for sb. and expect to be repaid later

垫肩 diànjiān　shoulder pad (or padding)

垫脚石 diànjiǎoshí　stepping-stone

垫圈 diànjuàn　bed down the livestock; spread earth in a pigsty, cowshed, etc. ——see also diànquān

垫款 diànkuǎn　money advanced for sb. to be paid back later

垫密片 diànmìpiàn　*mech.* gasket: 气缸～ cylinder gasket

垫片 diànpiàn　*mech.* ① spacer: 绝缘～ insulation spacer ② shim: 轴承～ bearing shim

垫平 diànpíng　level up: 把篮球场～ level a basketball court

垫圈 diànquān　*mech.* washer: 毡～ felt washer / 锁紧～ locking washer / 开口～ snap washer ——see also diànjuàn

垫上运动 diànshàng　yùndòng　*sports* mat tumbling; mat work

垫子 diànzi　mat; pad; cushion: 蹭鞋～ doormat / 体操～ gym mat / 沙发～ sofa cushion / 弹簧～ spring mattress / 茶杯～ teacup mat; coaster

钿 diàn　see 螺钿 luódiàn ——see also tián

淀¹（澱） diàn　form sediment; settle; precipitate

淀² diàn　(usu. used as part of a place name) shallow lake: 白洋～ Baiyangdian Lake (in Hebei Province)

淀粉 diànfěn　starch; amylum

淀粉酶 diànfěnméi　*biochem.* amylase

淀积作用 diànjī zuòyòng　*geol.* illuviation

惦 diàn　remember with concern; be concerned about; keep thinking about: 我一直～着这件事。I've been thinking about that all the time.

惦记 diànjì　remember with concern; be concerned about; keep thinking about: 她老～着给孩子打件毛衣。She's always thinking of knitting a sweater for her child. / 她一下班就～着照顾街面儿上的老人。When she gets home from work, she concerns herself with looking after the old people in the neighbourhood.

惦念 diànniàn　(also 惦挂 diànguà) keep thinking about; be anxious about; worry about: 我一切都好，请您不要～。Everything's fine with me. Don't worry.

奠¹ diàn　establish; settle: 奠都 diàndū

奠² diàn　make offerings to the spirits of the dead: 祭奠 jìdiàn

奠定 diàndìng　establish; settle: ～基础 lay a foundation

奠都 diàndū　establish (*or* found) a capital: 太平天国～南京。The Taiping Heavenly Kingdom made Nanjing its capital.

奠基 diànjī　lay a foundation: ～礼 foundation stone laying ceremony / ～人 founder / ～石 foundation stone; cornerstone

奠酒 diànjiǔ　pour out a libation of wine

奠仪 diànyí　a gift of money made on the occasion of a funeral

殿¹ diàn　hall; palace; temple: 太和～ the Hall of Supreme Harmony (in the former Imperial Palace)

殿² diàn　at the rear: 殿后 diànhòu

殿后 diànhòu　bring up the rear

殿军 diànjūn　① rearguard ② a person who comes last in a contest or last among the winners; the last of the successful candidates

殿试 diànshì　the palace examination (the final imperial

examination, presided over by the emperor)

殿堂 diàntáng　① palace or temple buildings ② palace or temple halls

殿下 diànxià　*honor.* Your Highness or His or Her Highness

靛 diàn　① indigo ② indigo-blue

靛蓝 diànlán　indigo: ～色 indigo-blue

靛青 diànqīng　① indigo-blue ② *dial.* indigo

簟 diàn　*dial.* bamboo mat

癜 diàn　purplish or white patches on the skin: 紫癜 zǐdiàn

diāo

刁 diāo　① tricky; artful; sly: 放刁 fàngdiāo ② (used in) ～卡 make things difficult for sb. ③ (Diāo) a surname

刁悍 diāohàn　cunning and fierce

刁横 diāohèng　crafty and rude

刁滑 diāohuá　cunning; crafty; artful

刁民 diāomín　*old* unruly people

刁难 diāonàn　create difficulties; make things difficult: 故意～ deliberately make things difficult for others

刁顽 diāowán　cunning and stubborn

刁钻 diāozuān　cunning; artful; wily: 发球～ tricky service

刁钻古怪 diāozuān gǔguài　sly and capricious: ～的人 a strange crafty person / ～的脾气 a strange cranky temper

叼 diāo　hold in the mouth: 嘴里～着烟卷 with a cigarette dangling from one's lips / 黄鼠狼～走一只小鸡。A weasel ran off with a chick in its mouth.

凋（彫） diāo　wither: 苍松翠柏, 常绿不～。The pine and the cypress remain green all the year round.

凋敝 diāobì　① (of life) hard; destitute: 民生凋敝 mínshēng diāobì ② (of business) depressed: 百业凋敝 bǎiyè diāobì

凋残 diāocán　① broken; dilapidated: 一座～的古庙 a dilapidated ancient temple ② (of flowers) withered and fallen ③ *formal* (of life) hard; destitute

凋零 diāolíng　① (of flowers and plants) wither ② decline; be on the wane: 百业～。All business languished. ③ die: 老辈～。The older generation is dying off.

凋落 diāoluò　wither and fall

凋萎 diāowěi　wither; fade

凋谢 diāoxiè　① wither and fall ② die of old age: 老成凋谢 lǎochéng diāoxiè

貂（貂） diāo　marten

貂皮 diāopí　fur or pelt of marten; marten

貂裘 diāoqiú　marten coat

貂熊 diāoxióng　same as 狼獾 lánghuān

碉 diāo　see below

碉堡 diāobǎo　pillbox; blockhouse

碉楼 diāolóu　watchtower

雕¹（彫、琱） diāo　carve; engrave: 这个像是用大理石～成的。This statue is carved out of marble.

雕[2]**（鵰）** diāo *zool.* vulture

雕虫小技 diāo chóng xiǎo jì insignificant skill (esp. in writing); the trifling skill of a scribe; literary skill of no high order

雕花 diāohuā ① carve patterns or designs on woodwork ② carving: 〜家具 carved furniture

雕花玻璃 diāohuā bōli cut glass

雕画 diāohuà (also 雕绘 diāohuì) carve and paint

雕刻 diāokè carve; engrave: 玉石〜 jade carving / 整个成昆铁路的模型是用四根象牙〜成的。The entire model of the Chengdu-Kunming Railway is carved out of four pieces of ivory. / 〜刀 carving tool; burin / 〜品 carving / 〜工艺 artistic carving

雕栏玉砌 diāolán-yùqì carved balustrades and marble steps—richly ornamented palace buildings: 〜应犹在, 只是朱颜改。(李煜) Carved railings and marble stairs should still be there, Only these ruddy cheeks have changed.

雕梁画栋 diāoliáng-huàdòng carved beams and painted rafters—a richly ornamented building

雕漆 diāoqī carved lacquerware

雕砌 diāoqì write in a laboured and ornate style

雕饰 diāoshì ① carve; engrave ② carvings; engravings ③ too elaborate; overwrought

雕塑 diāosù sculpture

雕像 diāoxiàng statue: 大理石〜 marble statue / 半身〜 bust / 小〜 statuette

雕琢 diāozhuó ① cut and polish (jade, etc.); carve ② write in an ornate style

鲷 diāo porgy

鸟（鳥） diǎo same as 屌 diǎo, used in old novels as a term of abuse ——see also niǎo

屌 diǎo *inf.* penis

吊[1]**（弔）** diào ① hang; suspend: 门前〜着两盏红灯。There were two red lanterns hanging over the door. ② lift up or let down with a rope, etc.: 把和好的水泥〜上去。Hoist up the mixed cement. ③ put in a fur lining: 〜皮袄 line a coat with fur ④ revoke; withdraw: 吊销 diàoxiāo ⑤ crane: 塔吊 tǎdiào

吊[2]**（弔）** diào a former coinage unit, equal to a string of 1,000 cash

吊[3]**（弔）** diào condole; mourn: 吊丧 diàosāng

吊膀 diàobàng (also 吊膀子 diàobàngzi) *dial.* (of a man) try to get fresh with a woman; flirt

吊钹 diàobó *mus.* suspension cymbal

吊车 diàochē crane; hoist: 〜梁 crane beam

吊床 diàochuáng hammock

吊打 diàodǎ hang up and beat sb.

吊灯 diàodēng pendent lamp

吊斗 diàodǒu cableway bucket

吊儿郎当 diào'erlángdāng *inf.* careless and casual; slovenly: 他从来不干什么工作, 整天〜的。He never does any work; he just fools around all day long.

吊杆 diàogān ① *inf.* well-sweep; sweep ② *mech.*

boom; jib: 起重机〜 crane boom / （船用）起重〜 derrick

吊杠 diàogàng *sports* trapeze

吊钩 diàogōu *mech.* (lift) hook; hanger

吊古 diàogǔ visit a historical site and muse over the past

吊罐 diàoguàn *min.* cage

吊环 diàohuán *sports* rings: 摆荡（静止）〜 swinging (still) rings

吊货盘 diàohuòpán platform (or tray) sling

吊货网 diàohuòwǎng cargo net

吊架 diàojià *mech.* hanger: 平衡〜 balance hanger

吊景 diàojǐng *theat.* drop scene

吊具 diàojù hoist (for lifting heavy things)

吊卡 diàokǎ *petroleum* elevator: 油管〜 tubing elevator

吊坎儿 diàokǎnr same as 调侃儿 diàokǎnr

吊客 diàokè one who visits the bereaved to offer condolences

吊兰 diàolán *Chlorophytum comosum*

吊雷 diàoléi *mil.* hanging mine

吊链 diàoliàn chain sling; sling chain

吊楼 diàolóu (also 吊脚楼 diàojiǎolóu) *dial.* house projecting over the water

吊民伐罪 diàomín-fázuì console the people and punish their oppressive ruler (a slogan often used by rebels in ancient China)

吊铺 diàopù hanging bed; hammock

吊桥 diàoqiáo ① suspension bridge ② drawbridge

吊丧 diàosāng visit the bereaved to offer one's condolences; pay a condolence call

吊嗓子 diào sǎngzi train (or exercise) one's voice

吊扇 diàoshàn ceiling fan

吊死 diàosǐ hang by the neck; hang oneself

吊索 diàosuǒ sling: 钢丝〜 wire sling / 绳〜 rope sling

吊塔 diàotǎ same as 塔吊 tǎdiào

吊梯 diàotī hanging ladder; rope ladder

吊桶 diàotǒng well-bucket; bucket

吊袜带 diàowàdài garters; suspenders

吊胃口 diào wèikǒu tantalize

吊慰 diàowèi (also 吊问 diàowèn) offer condolences

吊线 diàoxiàn plumb-line

吊销 diàoxiāo revoke; withdraw: 〜驾驶执照 revoke a driving licence / 〜护照 withdraw a passport

吊孝 diàoxiào *inf.* visit the bereaved to offer one's condolences; pay a condolence call

吊唁 diàoyàn condole; offer one's condolences: 〜函电 messages of condolence

吊影 diàoyǐng *formal* have only one's own shadow for company—be extremely lonely ——see also 形影相吊 xíng-yǐng xiāng diào

吊钟花 diàozhōnghuā another name for 倒挂金钟 dàoguàjīnzhōng

吊装 diàozhuāng *archit.* hoisting

吊子 diàozi same as 铫子 diàozi

钓 diào ① fish with a hook and line; angle: 你今天〜了几条? How many fish did you catch today? ② pursue (personal fame and gain): 沽名钓誉 gūmíng-diàoyù

钓饵 diào'ěr bait

钓竿 diàogān fishing rod

钓钩 diàogōu fishhook

钓具 diàojù fishing tackle

钓丝 diàosī fishline; fishing-line

钓鱼 diàoyú go fishing; angle

钓鱼岛 Diàoyúdǎo Diaoyu Island

钓鱼郎 diàoyúláng another name for 翠鸟 cuìniǎo

窎 diào deep; distant

窎远 diàoyuǎn far off; distant

调[1] diào transfer; shift; move: ～干部 transfer cadres / ～挡 shift gears / ～军队 move troops / 改变南粮北～的局面 put an end to the state of affairs in which grain has to be sent from the south to the north / 她～到这个小组来了。 She has been transferred to this group.

调[2] diào ① accent: 这人说话带山东～儿。 This person speaks with a Shandong accent. ② *mus.* key: C～ the key of C ③ air; tune; melody: ～寄《沁园春》 to the tune of *Qinyuanchun* ④ *phonet.* tone; tune: 升调 shēngdiào / 降调 jiàngdiào ——see also tiáo

调包 diàobāo same as 掉包 diàobāo

调兵遣将 diàobīng-qiǎnjiàng ① dispatch officers and men; move troops; deploy forces ② muster and organize manpower (according to needs)

调拨 diàobō allocate and transfer (goods or funds); allot: ～款项购置图书 allocate funds for books / 国家给他们～了大量化肥。 The state allotted them large quantities of chemical fertilizer.

调查 diàochá investigate; inquire into; look into; survey: 作社会～ make a social investigation / ～原因 investigate the cause / 农村～ rural survey / ～报告 findings report / ～会 fact-finding meeting / ～提纲 outline for investigation; questionnaire / ～团 fact-finding mission

调查问卷 diàochá wènjuàn questionnaire: 发出～ distribute questionnaires / 回答～ respond to a questionnaire / 设计～ formulate a questionnaire

调车场 diàochēchǎng *railway* switchyard

调调 diàodiào ① *mus.* key ② tune; melody ③ point of view; argument

调动 diàodòng ① transfer; shift: ～工作 transfer sb. to another post ② move (troops); manoeuvre; muster: ～十万军队, 一千辆坦克 muster a hundred thousand troops and a thousand tanks / 部队～频繁。 There have been numerous troop movements. ③ bring into play; arouse; mobilize: ～一切积极因素 bring every positive factor into play / ～群众的积极性 arouse (*or* mobilize) the enthusiasm of the masses

调度 diàodù ① dispatch (trains, buses, etc.) ② dispatcher: 他是电车公司的～。 He is a dispatcher at the trolleybus company. ③ manage; control: 生产～ production management

调度室 diàodùshì dispatcher's office; control room

调度员 diàodùyuán dispatcher; controller

调防 diàofáng *mil.* relieve a garrison

调干学员 diàogàn xuéyuán (also 调干生 diàogànshēng) a college student enrolled from among cadres; cadre student

调号 diàohào ① *phonet.* tone mark ② *mus.* key signature

调虎离山 diào hǔ lí shān lure the tiger out of the mountains—lure the enemy away from his base

调换 diàohuàn same as 掉换 diàohuàn

调回 diàohuí recall (troops, etc.): 把某人～北京 recall sb. to Beijing / ～驻外使节 recall a diplomatic envoy (stationed overseas)

调集 diàojí assemble; muster: ～兵力 assemble forces / ～二十个师 concentrate twenty divisions

调卷 diàojuàn ask for files for examination

调侃儿 diàokǎnr *dial.* (also 调坎儿 diàokǎnr) talk in professional jargon

调类 diàolèi *phonet.* tone category

调离 diàolí be transferred from: 她已～该部门。 She has been transferred from that department.

调令 diàolìng transfer order: 她的～已到。 The order for her transfer has arrived.

调门儿 diàoménr *inf.* ① pitch: 请把～定低点儿。 Please pitch the tune in a lower key. / 他说话～高。 He has a high-pitched voice. ② point of view; argument

调派 diàopài send; assign: ～大批干部下乡 assign large numbers of cadres to the countryside

调配 diàopèi allocate; deploy: ～原材料 allocation of raw materials / 合理～劳动力 rational deployment of manpower ——see also tiáopèi

调遣 diàoqiǎn dispatch; assign: ～军队 dispatch troops / 听从～ (be ready to) accept an assignment

调任 diàorèn be transferred to another post: 他已～车间主任。 He has been transferred to be head of a workshop.

调式 diàoshì *mus.* mode

调头 diàotóu point of view; argument

调头 diàotou *dial.* ① tune; melody ② manner of speaking

调研 diàoyán (short for 调查研究) investigation and research; survey and study

调演 diàoyǎn gather performers from different localities or various troupes for a joint performance or a theatrical festival

调用 diàoyòng transfer (under a unified plan): ～干部 transfer cadres (to a specific job) / ～物资 allocate materials

调阅 diàoyuè call for (documents, data, etc.) for consultation

调运 diàoyùn allocate and transport: ～大批工业品到农村 allocate and ship large quantities of industrial products to the rural areas

调值 diàozhí *phonet.* tone pitch

调职 diàozhí be transferred to another post

调子 diàozi ① tune; melody: 这个～倒挺熟的。 The tune is quite familiar. / 两个人唱的是一个～。 Both men sang the same tune. ② tone (of speech); note: 定～ set the tone (*or* keynote)

掉[1] diào ① fall; drop; shed; come off: ～下几滴眼泪 shed a few tears / 被击伤的敌机～在海里了。 The damaged enemy plane dropped into the sea. / 镐头～了。 The pick-head has come off. ② fall behind: 他脚上打了泡, ～在后面了。 He got blisters on his feet, so he lagged behind. ③ lose; be missing: 我把钥匙～了。 I've lost my key. / 这本书～了两页。 Two pages are missing from the book. ④ reduce; drop: 他害了一场大病, 体重～了十多斤。 During his serious illness he lost over ten *jin*.

掉[2] diào ① wag; swing: ～尾巴 wag the tail / ～臂而去 leave in a flurry ② turn: 把车头～过来 turn the car round ③ change; exchange: ～座位 change (*or* exchange) seats; swop places with sb.

掉[3] diào (used after certain verbs to indicate removal): 洗～ wash out / 扔～ throw away / 擦～ wipe off / 改～坏习气 correct bad habits

掉包 diàobāo stealthily substitute one thing for another

掉膘 diàobiāo (of a domestic animal) lose flesh

掉点儿 diàodiǎnr *inf.* start to rain: ～了。 It's starting to rain.

掉队 diàoduì drop out (*or* off); fall behind: 在三天的急行军中, 没有一个～的。 No one dropped out in the three days' forced march. / 继续革命, 永不～ continue to make revolution and never fall behind

掉过儿 diàoguòr　change (*or* exchange) places; swop places with sb.: 你跟他掉个过儿, 就看得见台上的人了。You can see the·people on the stage if you change seats with him.

掉换 diàohuàn　exchange; change; swop: 咱们俩的上班时间～一下好吗? Would you mind swopping shifts with me? / ～工作 be assigned a new job; be transferred to another post

掉魂 diàohún　be frightened out of one's wits

掉价 diàojià　fall (*or* drop) in price; go down in price: 西红柿～了。The price of tomatoes has come down.

掉枪花 diàoqiānghuā　*dial.* get up to tricks; play tricks

掉色 diàoshǎi　lose colour; fade: 这种料子不～。This material won't fade. *or* This material is colourfast.

掉书袋 diàoshūdài　a walking satchel—a person who lards his speech with quotations and allusions

掉头 diàotóu　turn round; turn about: 这地方太窄, 汽车不好～。The place is too narrow for the truck to turn around. / 敌人见势不妙, ～就跑。Seeing that the situation was getting hot for them, the enemy turned tail and fled.

掉以轻心 diào yǐ qīng xīn　lower one's guard; relax one's vigilance; treat sth. lightly: 大敌当前, 我们决不可～。Faced with a formidable enemy, we must not lower our guard.

掉转 diàozhuǎn　turn round; make a U-turn: ～身子 turn round / ～枪口 turn one's gun (against one's superiors or old associates)

锦 diào　see 钉锦儿 liàodiàor

铫 diào　same as 铫子 diàozi

铫子 diàozi　a small pot with a handle and a spout for boiling water or herbal medicine

---

diē

爹 diē　*inf.* father; dad; daddy; pa: ～娘 father and mother; mum and dad; ma and pa; parents

爹爹 diēdie　*dial.* ① father; dad; daddy; pa ② grandfather

跌 diē　① fall; tumble: 他～伤了。He fell down and injured himself. / ～进泥坑 fall into a quagmire ② drop; fall: 跌价 diējià

跌膘 diēbiāo　(of a domestic animal) lose flesh

跌打损伤 diē-dǎ sǔnshāng　injuries from falls, fractures, contusions and strains

跌宕 diēdàng　(also 跌荡 diēdàng) *liter.* ① free and easy; bold and unconstrained ② flowing rhythm

跌倒 diēdǎo　fall; tumble: 他滑了一下, ～在地。He slipped and fell over. / 在哪儿～就从哪儿爬起来。Pick yourself up from where you fell—correct your mistake where you made it.

跌跌撞撞 diēdiēzhuàngzhuàng　dodder along; stagger along: 他～地出了门。He staggered out of the house.

跌跟头 diē gēntou　same as 栽跟头 zāi gēntou

跌价 diējià　fall (*or* drop) in price; go down in price: 收音机～了。The prices of radio sets have gone down.

跌交 diējiāo　① trip (*or* stumble) and fall; fall: 跌了一交 have a fall ② make a mistake; meet with a setback

跌落 diēluò　fall; drop

跌水 diēshuǐ　*water conservancy* drop

跌足 diēzú　stamp one's foot (in bitter remorse, sorrow or despair)

---

dié

迭 dié　① alternate; change: 更迭 gēngdié ② *adv.* repeatedly; again and again: ～挫强敌 inflict repeated reverses on a formidable enemy / 近二十年来, 地下文物～有发现。Over the last 20 years, archaeological finds have been made one after another. ③ in time for: 不迭 bùdié

迭次 diécì　*adv.* repeatedly; again and again: ～磋商 repeatedly consult each other

迭忙 diémáng　hurry; hasten; make haste

迭起 diéqǐ　occur repeatedly; happen frequently: 入冬以来, 车祸～。Since winter began, there have been frequent traffic accidents.

谍 dié　① espionage: 谍报 diébào ② intelligence agent; spy: 间谍 jiàndié

谍报 diébào　information obtained through espionage; intelligence report; intelligence: ～员 intelligence agent; spy

堞 dié　battlements: 城堞 chéngdié

喋 dié　see below

喋喋不休 diédié bùxiū　chatter away; rattle on; talk endlessly

喋血 diéxuè　*liter.* bloodshed; bloodbath

耋 dié　*formal* ① septuagenarian ② advanced in years

牒 dié　an official document or note; certificate: 通牒 tōngdié

叠 (疊、壘) dié　① pile up; repeat: 重叠 chóngdié ② fold: 把信～好 fold the letter / ～被子 fold up a quilt; make the bed (after getting up)

叠床架屋 diéchuáng-jiàwū　pile one bed upon another or build one house on top of another—needless duplication: 这样～, 文章就太啰嗦了。So much needless repetition makes the article long-winded.

叠句 diéjù　reiterative sentence

叠罗汉 dié luóhàn　*sports* pyramid

叠印 diéyìn　*photog.* double exposure

叠韵 diéyùn　*linguis.* rhyming compound (a compound consisting of two syllables that rhyme with one another; e.g. 徘徊 páihuái, 宛转 wǎnzhuǎn)

叠字 diézì　*linguis.* reduplicated word; reduplication (e.g. 皎皎 jiǎojiǎo, 年年 niánnián, 妹妹 mèimei, 坛坛罐罐 tántán-guànguàn)

碟 dié　small plate; small dish: 一～炒黄豆 a dish of fried soya beans

碟子 diézi　small dish; small plate

蝶 (蜨) dié　butterfly: 蝴蝶 húdié

蝶骨 diégǔ　*physiol.* sphenoid bone

蝶形花 diéxínghuā　papilionaceous flower

蝶泳 diéyǒng　butterfly stroke

蹀 dié　*formal* stamp one's foot

蹀躞 diéxiè　*formal* ① walk in small steps ② pace about

鲽 dié　right-eyed flounder; flatfish

dīng

丁[1] dīng ① man: 成丁 chéngdīng ② members of a family; population: 添丁 tiāndīng ③ a person engaged in a certain occupation: 园丁 yuándīng ④ (Dīng) a surname

丁[2] dīng ① the fourth of the ten Heavenly Stems (天干) (see also 干支 gān-zhī) ② fourth: ～等 the fourth grade; grade D / ～种维生素 vitamin D

丁[3] dīng small cubes of meat or vegetable; cubes: 黄瓜～儿 diced cucumber

丁[4] dīng formal encounter; incur: 丁忧 dīngyōu
——see also zhēng

丁坝　dīngbà　spur dike; spur

丁苯橡胶　dīngběn xiàngjiāo　butadiene styrene rubber

丁村人　Dīngcūnrén　Dingcun Man, a type of primitive man of about 100,000 years ago whose fossil remains were found in Dingcun, Shanxi Province, in 1954

丁当　dīngdāng　onom.　ding-dong; jingle; clatter: 碟子碗碰得丁丁当当的。The dishes and bowls slid together with a clatter. / 铃儿～响。The bell jingled. / 穷得～响 be penniless; be broke

丁点儿　dīngdiǎnr　dial.　a tiny bit: 这套茶具连一～毛病都没有。There isn't the slightest flaw in this tea set. / 这一～事不必放在心上。Don't bother about such trifles.

丁东　dīngdōng　(also 丁冬 dīngdōng) onom.　tinkle

丁赋　dīngfù　(also 丁税 dīngshuì) formal　poll tax

丁零　dīnglíng　onom.　tinkle; jingle: ～～的自行车铃声 the jingling of bicycle bells

丁零当郎　dīnglíngdānglāng　onom.　jinglejangle; cling-clang

丁宁　dīngníng　urge again and again; warn; exhort: 她一再～儿子向牧民们学习。She repeatedly urged her son to learn from the herdsmen.

丁宁周至　dīngníng zhōuzhì　give thoughtful advice (or instructions)

丁是丁，卯是卯　dīng shì dīng, mǎo shì mǎo　keep ding (a Heavenly Stem) distinct from mao (an Earthly Branch) —be strict; be precise; be unaccommodating

丁酸　dīngsuān　chem.　butyric acid

丁烷　dīngwán　chem.　butane: ～气 butagas

丁烯　dīngxī　chem.　butene

丁香　dīngxiāng　bot.　① lilac ② clove: ～油 clove oil

丁忧　dīngyōu　formal　be in mourning for a parent

丁字尺　dīngzìchǐ　T-square

丁字钢　dīngzìgāng　(also 丁字铁 dīngzìtiě) T-steel

丁字街　dīngzìjiē　T-shaped road junction

丁字形　dīngzìxíng　T-shaped

仃 dīng　see 伶仃 língdīng

叮 dīng ① sting; bite: 腿上叫蚊子～了一下 get a mosquito bite on the leg ② say or ask again to make sure: 我～了他一句，他才说了真话。I asked him again, and at last he came out with the truth.

叮当　dīngdāng　same as 丁当 dīngdāng

叮咛　dīngníng　same as 丁宁 dīngníng

叮问　dīngwèn　dial.　question closely; make a detailed inquiry

叮嘱　dīngzhǔ　urge again and again; warn; exhort: 父亲再三～我们要谦虚谨慎。Father urged us again and again to be modest and prudent.

玎 dīng　see below

玎珰　dīngdāng　same as 丁当 dīngdāng

玎玲　dīnglíng　onom.　clink; jingle; tinkle

疔 dīng　malignant boil (or furuncle)

疔疽　dīngjū　miliary vesicle under the nose or on either side of the mandible

盯 dīng　fix one's eyes on; gaze at; stare at: 他两眼～着雷达荧光屏。His eyes were fixed on the radar screen. / ～住这个坏蛋。Keep a close watch on the scoundrel.

盯梢　dīngshāo　same as 钉梢 dīngshāo

钉[1] dīng　nail; tack: 螺丝钉 luósīdīng

钉[2] dīng ① follow closely; tail: 紧紧～住敌长机 keep on the tail of the enemy's lead plane ② urge; press: 你要～着他吃药，别让他忘了。You must remind him to take his medicine, in case he forgets. ③ same as 盯 dīng
——see also dìng

钉齿耙　dīngchǐbà　spike-tooth harow

钉锤　dīngchuí　nail hammer; claw hammer

钉螺　dīngluó　zool.　oncomelania (a kind of freshwater snail, which is the intermediate host of the blood fluke); snail

钉帽　dīngmào　the head of a nail

钉耙　dīngpá　(iron-toothed) rake

钉人　dīngrén　sports　watch (or mark) an opponent in a game: ～防守 man-for-man (or man-to-man) defence

钉梢　dīngshāo　shadow sb.; tail sb.: 他觉得有人钉他的梢。He felt he was being shadowed.

钉是钉，铆是铆　dīng shì dīng, mǎo shì mǎo　same as 丁是丁，卯是卯 dīng shì dīng, mǎo shì mǎo

钉鞋　dīngxié　spiked shoes; spikes

钉子　dīngzi ① nail ② saboteur: 安插～ plant a saboteur ——see also 碰钉子 pèng dīngzi

耵 dīng　see below

耵聍　dīngníng　earwax; cerumen

酊 dīng　tincture: 碘酊 diǎndīng ——see also dǐng

酊剂　dīngjì　pharm.　tincture

靪 dīng　mend the sole of a shoe

dǐng

顶 dǐng ① the crown of the head: 秃顶 tūdǐng ② top: 此山之～有一古庙。There is an old temple at the top of the mountain. ③ carry on the head: 头上～着一罐水 carry a pitcher of water on one's head / 农民们～着月亮抢收稻子。The peasants did a rush job reaping the rice in the moonlight. ④ gore; butt: 这牛爱～人。This bull gores people. ⑤ go against: ～风雪，战严寒 face blizzards and brave severe cold ⑥ push from below or behind; push up; prop up: 嫩芽把土～起来了。The sprouts have pushed up the earth. / 用千斤顶把汽车～起来 jack up a car ⑦ retort; turn down: 我～了他几句。I said a few words to him in retort. / 把抗议～回去 reject a protest ⑧ cope with; stand up to: 负担虽重，他们两个也～下来了。The load was heavy, but the two of them coped with it all right. ⑨ take the place of; substitute; replace: ～别人的名字 assume sb. else's name / 不能拿次货～好货卖。You shouldn't pass in-

ferior goods off as high-quality goods and sell them. ⑩ equal; be equivalent to: 一台收割机能～几十个人。 One harvester can do the work of scores of people. ⑪ old take over or turn over: 顶盘 dǐngpán ⑫ m. (for things which have a top): 一～帽子 a cap; a hat / 一～帐子 a mosquito net ⑬ adv. very; most; extremely: ～有用 very useful / ～小的那个孩子 the youngest (or smallest) child / 我～喜欢贝多芬的音乐。 I'm very fond of Beethoven's music.

顶班 dǐngbān ① work on regular shifts; work full time: 领导干部经常下车间～劳动。 Leading cadres often go to the workshops to work regular shifts. ② work as a substitute for sb. absent

顶板 dǐngbǎn min. roof: 直接～ immediate (or nether) roof / ～下沉 roof-to-floor convergence; roof convergence

顶吹 dǐngchuī metall. top-blown: ～转炉 top-blown converter

顶戴 dǐngdài ① formal salute; pay one's respects to ② buttons worn on Qing Dynasty officials' hats as a sign of rank

顶灯 dǐngdēng dome light (of a car)

顶点 dǐngdiǎn ① apex; zenith; acme; pinnacle ② math. vertex; apex

顶端 dǐngduān ① top; peak; apex ② end: 我们走到大桥的～。 We walked to the end of the bridge.

顶多 dǐngduō at (the) most; at best: 屋里～不过十个人。 There were at most ten people in the room. / 我们～只能干上星期的活儿的一半。 At best we can do only half as much as last week.

顶风 dǐngfēng ① against the wind: ～骑车 cycle against the wind / 开～船 sail against the wind ② head wind

顶风冒雨 dǐngfēng-màoyǔ brave wind and rain; be undeterred by wind and rain; in spite of wind and rain

顶峰 dǐngfēng peak; summit; pinnacle

顶骨 dǐnggǔ physiol. parietal bone

顶呱呱 dǐngguāguā (also 顶刮刮 dǐngguāguā) tip-top; first-rate; excellent

顶光 dǐngguāng photog. top light

顶好 dǐnghǎo ① very good ② had better; it would be best: 我们～现在就动身回去。 We'd better be starting back now.

顶花坛 dǐng huātán acrob. balancing a jar on the head

顶价 dǐngjià ① top price; ceiling price ② dial. rent deposit

顶尖 dǐngjiān ① tip ② mech. centre: 死～ dead centre

顶交 dǐngjiāo agric. topcross

顶角 dǐngjiǎo math. vertex angle

顶礼 dǐnglǐ prostrate oneself before sb. and press one's head against his feet (a Buddhist salute of the highest respect)

顶礼膜拜 dǐnglǐ-móbài usu. derog. prostrate oneself in worship; make a fetish of; pay homage to

顶梁柱 dǐngliángzhù pillar (fig.); backbone

顶门儿 dǐngménr the front top of the head

顶名 dǐngmíng ① assume sb. else's name (to cheat) ② nominal; only in name

顶命 dǐngmìng a life for a life; pay with one's life (for a first-degree murder)

顶牛儿 dǐngniúr lock horns like bulls; clash; be at loggerheads: 他们两人一谈就～。 The two of them began to wrangle the moment they got talking.

顶盘 dǐngpán old take over a business

顶棚 dǐngpéng ceiling

顶球 dǐngqiú football head (a ball)

顶少 dǐngshǎo at (the) least: 这～得五块钱。 It costs at least 5 yuan.

顶事 dǐngshì be useful; serve the purpose: 这孩子可～啦! The boy is a great help!

顶数 dǐngshù ① serve as a fill-in; make up the number ② (usu. used in the negative) useful; effective: 你说的不～。 What you say carries little weight.

顶替 dǐngtì ① take sb.'s place; replace: 他走了谁来～他? Who's going to take his place after he leaves? ② get a job at one's parent's place of work when the parent retires or dies

顶天立地 dǐngtiān-lìdì of gigantic stature; of indomitable spirit; dauntless: 做一个～的英雄汉 be a dauntless hero

顶头 dǐngtóu ① coming directly towards one: ～风 head wind ② top; end: 这条胡同的～有个公用电话。 There is a public telephone (booth) at the end of this lane.

顶头上司 dǐngtóu shàngsi inf. one's immediate (or direct) superior

顶碗 dǐngwǎn acrob. balancing a stack of bowls on the head; pagoda of bowls

顶芽 dǐngyá bot. terminal bud

顶叶 dǐngyè bot. terminal leaf

顶用 dǐngyòng be of use (or help); serve the purpose: 等她毕了业就～了。 She'll be a help when she finishes school. / 我去也不～。 I can't be of any help even if I go. / 你干着急顶什么用? What's the use of just worrying and doing nothing about it?

顶真 dǐngzhēn dial. conscientious; serious: 什么事他都很～。 He takes everything seriously.

顶针 dǐngzhen thimble

顶住 dǐngzhù withstand; stand up to; hold out against: ～压力 withstand pressure / ～逆流 stand up against an adverse current / ～风浪 weather a storm

顶撞 dǐngzhuàng contradict (one's elder or superior): ～父母 contradict one's parents

顶租 dǐngzū ① pay rent in kind or by labour ② dial. rent deposit

顶嘴 dǐngzuǐ inf. reply defiantly (usu. to one's elder or superior); answer back; talk back: 你不该跟你奶奶～。 You shouldn't talk back to your grandmother.

顶罪 dǐngzuì bear the blame for sb. else

酊   dǐng   see 酩酊大醉 mǐngdǐng dàzuì ——see also dīng

鼎¹   dǐng   ① an ancient cooking vessel with two loop handles and three or four legs: 三足～ tripod / 四足～ quadripod ② dial. pot

鼎²   dǐng   formal enter upon a period of: 鼎盛 dǐngshèng

鼎鼎大名 dǐngdǐng dàmíng same as 大名鼎鼎 dàmíng dǐngdǐng

鼎沸 dǐngfèi formal like a seething cauldron; noisy and confused: 人声鼎沸 rénshēng dǐngfèi

鼎革 dǐnggé formal change of dynasty or regime; dynastic change ——see also 革故鼎新 gégù-dǐngxīn

鼎力 dǐnglì pol. your kind effort: 多蒙～协助,无任感谢。 We are extremely grateful to you for the trouble you have taken on our behalf.

鼎立 dǐnglì (of three antagonists confronting one another) stand like the three legs of a tripod; tripartite confrontation; tripartite balance of forces

鼎盛 dǐngshèng in a period of great prosperity; at the height of power and splendour: ～时期 a period of full bloom; prime; heyday

鼎新 dǐngxīn formal make innovations: 革故鼎新 gégù-dǐngxīn

鼎彝 dǐngyí ancient sacrificial vessels engraved with inscriptions commemorating worthy men's deeds

鼎峙 dǐngzhì *formal* tripartite confrontation

鼎助 dǐngzhù *formal pol.* your kind and generous help

鼎足 dǐngzú the three legs of a tripod—three rival powers: 势成～ a situation of tripartite confrontation

鼎足而立 dǐngzú ér lì (also 鼎足而三 dǐngzú ér sān) (of three rival powers) stand like the legs of a tripod

鼎足之势 dǐngzú zhī shì tripartite balance of forces; triangular balance of power: 赤壁之战决定了魏、蜀、吴三国～。The battle of the Red Cliffs determined the triangular balance of power of the three kingdoms, Wei, Shu, and Wu.

dǐng

订 dǐng ① conclude; draw up; agree on: ～条约 conclude a treaty / ～合同 enter into (*or* make) a contract / ～计划 draw up (*or* work out) a plan / ～日期 fix (*or* agree on) a date / ～生产指标 set a production target ② subscribe to (a newspaper, etc.); book (seats, tickets, etc.); order (merchandise, etc.): ～《中国日报》 subscribe to *China Daily* / ～房间 make room (*or* hotel) reservations / ～座 make reservations for seats in a restaurant, theatre, etc. ③ make corrections; revise: 修订 xiūdìng ④ staple together: 他把两封信～在一起。He stapled the two letters together.

订单 dìngdān order for goods; order form

订费 dìngfèi subscription (rate)

订购 dìnggòu order (goods); place an order for sth.: ～一套家具 order a set of furniture / 欢迎～。Customers are welcome to place orders.

订户 dìnghù ① subscriber (to a newspaper or periodical) ② a person or household with a standing order for milk, etc.

订婚 dìnghūn be engaged (to be married); be betrothed

订货 dìnghuò order goods; place an order for goods: ～确认书 confirmation of order

订交 dìngjiāo pledge friendship; establish friendly relations with each other

订立 dìnglì conclude (a treaty, agreement, etc.); make (a contract, etc.): ～收购合同 conclude a purchasing contract

订书机 dìngshūjī ① stapler; stapling-machine ② book-binding machine

订约 dìngyuē conclude a contract or treaty

订阅 dìngyuè subscribe to (a newspaper, periodical, etc.)

订正 dìngzhèng make corrections; emend: ～了第一版中的错误。Corrections have been made to the first edition.

钉 dīng ① nail: ～马掌 nail on horseshoes / ～钉子 drive in a nail / 把窗子～死 nail up a window ② sew on: ～扣子 sew a button on —see also dìng

定 dìng ① calm; stable: 天下大～。General stability has been achieved in the country. ② decide; fix; set: 开会时间～在明天上午。The meeting is fixed for tomorrow morning. / 代表团～于今日离京。The delegation is due to leave Beijing today. / ～方针 decide on a policy / ～计划 make a plan ③ fixed; settled; established: 定见 dìngjiàn ④ subscribe to (a newspaper, etc.); book (seats, tickets, etc.); order (merchandise, etc.) ⑤ *adv. formal* surely; certainly; definitely: ～可

取胜 be sure to win

定案 dìng'àn ① decide on (*or* pass) a verdict; reach a conclusion on a case ② verdict; final decision

定本 dìngběn definitive edition

定比定律 dìngbǐ dìnglǜ *chem.* the law of definite (*or* constant) proportions

定编 dìngbiān delimit the organizational structure

定产 dìngchǎn a system of fixed quotas for grain production ——see also 三定 sāndìng

定场白 dìngchǎngbái (in traditional opera) lines that actually open the play (lines delivered by an actor giving a detailed account of himself, his family, or the drama, after he has spoken both his prologue 引子 and poetic lines 定场诗 and has announced his name 通名)

定场诗 dìngchǎngshī (in traditional opera) poetry that opens the play (four introductory lines of poetry recited by an actor after he has delivered the prologue 引子 and has seated himself)

定单 dìngdān order for goods; order form

定调子 dìng diàozi set the tone (*or* keynote)

定都 dìngdū choose a site for the capital; establish a capital: ～北京 make Beijing the capital; decide on Beijing as the capital

定夺 dìngduó make a final decision; decide: 讨论后再行～。We won't make any decision until after the discussion.

定额 dìng'é quota; norm: 生产～ production quota

定额工资制 dìng'é gōngzīzhì wages based on work quotas

定高气球 dìnggāo qìqiú constant-level balloon

定稿 dìnggǎo ① finalize a manuscript, text, etc. ② final version or text

定购 dìnggòu ① order (goods); place an order for sth. ② a system of fixed quotas for purchasing ——see also 三定 sāndìng

定冠词 dìngguàncí *gram.* definite article

定规 dìngguī ① established rule or practice; set pattern: 并无～。There's no hard and fast rule. ② *dial.* be bent on; be determined

定户 dìnghù same as 订户 dìnghù

定婚 dìnghūn be engaged (to be married); be betrothed

定货 dìnghuò same as 订货 dìnghuò

定级 dìngjí decide grade and level

定计 dìngjì devise a stratagem; work out a scheme

定价 dìngjià ① fix a price: 你给这批货定个价吧。Could you set a price for this batch of goods, please? ② fixed price: 这种衬衫每件～十元。The marked price of these shirts is 10 *yuan* each. ③ list price

定见 dìngjiàn definite opinion; set view: 这事儿请你们讨论，我没有～。Please discuss the matter among yourselves. I have no definite opinion about it.

定金 dìngjīn deposit (put down on sth. for future purchase)

定睛 dìngjīng fix one's eyes upon: ～细看 look fixedly and scrutinize

定居 dìngjū settle down: 回乡～ return to settle in one's native place / 我决定在北京～。I've decided to settle down in Beijing.

定居点 dìngjūdiǎn settlement (of herdsmen, fishermen, etc.)

定局 dìngjú ① foregone conclusion; inevitable outcome: 今年丰收已成～。It's a foregone conclusion that we'll have a bumper harvest this year. ② settle finally: 事情还没有～，明天可以再议。The matter isn't settled yet. We can take it up again tomorrow.

定礼 dìnglǐ same as 彩礼 cǎilǐ

定理 dìnglǐ theorem: 基本～ fundamental theorem

定例 dìnglì usual practice; set pattern; routine: 每星期

六我们学校总是放场电影，这已成～了。It's a usual practice in our school to have a film shown every Saturday.

定量 dìngliàng ① fixed quantity; ration: ～供应 rationing ② determine the amounts of the components of a substance

定量分析 dìngliàng fēnxi *chem.* quantitative analysis

定律 dìnglǜ (scientific) law: 万有引力～ the law of universal gravitation

定论 dìnglùn final conclusion: 这个问题尚无～。No final conclusion has yet been reached on this matter. *or* This is still an open question. ／此事已有～，不必再议。The question is decided already. There is no need for further discussion.

定苗 dìngmiáo *agric.* final singling (of seedlings)

定名 dìngmíng name; denominate: 这个厂～为东风造船厂。It was named Dongfeng Shipyard.

定盘星 dìngpánxīng ① zero point on a steelyard ② (usu. used in the negative) decided ideas: 他做事没～。He works in a haphazard way.

定评 dìngpíng accepted opinion; final conclusion

定期 dìngqī ① fix (*or* set) a date ② regular; at regular intervals; periodical: ～体格检查 regular physical checkups ／～轮换 rotate at regular intervals ／～汇报工作 regularly report back on one's work ／ ～刊物 periodical publication; periodical ／ 不～刊物 nonperiodic publication

定期存款 dìngqī cúnkuǎn fixed deposit; time deposit

定期租船 dìngqī zūchuán time charter

定钱 dìngqian deposit; earnest (money)

定亲 dìngqīn engagement (usu. arranged by parents); betrothal: 她已跟李家的儿子定了亲。She is betrothed to a son of the Li family.

定情 dìngqíng pledge love

定然 dìngrán *adv.* certainly; definitely: 这件事他～不会同意。He definitely won't agree to it.

定神 dìngshén ① collect oneself; compose oneself; pull oneself together: 一开头她吓坏了，后来才定下神来。At first she was terrified, then she pulled herself together. ② concentrate one's attention: 听见有人叫我，～一看，原来是小李。I heard someone calling me and, looking hard, saw that it was Xiao Li.

定时器 dìngshíqì timer

定时炸弹 dìngshí zhàdàn time bomb

定数 dìngshù ① fix a number or amount ② a fixed number or amount

定数[2] dìngshù fate; destiny: 在迷信的人看来，什么事都有一个～。Superstitious people see everything as decided by fate.

定说 dìngshuō ① affirm; assert: 她～她讲的是实话。She affirmed that she was telling the truth. ② an accepted argument: 这种病的起因尚无～。The cause of the disease is still a matter of dispute.

定位 dìngwèi ① fixed position; location; orientation ② orientate; position

定位器 dìngwèiqì *min.* positioner

定息 dìngxī fixed interest (an annual rate of interest paid by the state to the national bourgeoisie on the money value of their assets for a given period of time, after the 1956 conversion of capitalist industry and commerce into joint state-private enterprises)

定弦 dìngxián ① tune a stringed instrument ② *dial.* make up one's mind

定限 dìngxiàn ① a fixed limit (to quantity, or degree) ② a fixed time limit

定向爆破 dìngxiàng bàopò directional blasting

定向地雷 dìngxiàng dìléi oriented mine

定向培育 dìngxiàng péiyù *agric.* directive breeding

定向天线 dìngxiàng tiānxiàn directional antenna

定向仪 dìngxiàngyí *meteorol.* direction finder

定心[1] dìngxīn *mech.* centering: ～装置 centering device

定心[2] dìngxīn feel relieved; feel at ease: 那笔钱找到了，这一下她可～了。Now that the money was found, she could feel relieved.

定心丸 dìngxīnwán sth. capable of setting sb.'s mind at ease: 吃了～ be reassured

定形 dìngxíng ① *chem. fibre* setting: 热～ heat setting ② *knitting* boarding: ～机 boarding machine

定型 dìngxíng finalize the design; fall into a pattern: 这种插秧机正在试制，尚未～。This type of rice transplanter is being trial-produced; the design hasn't been finalized.

定省 dìngxǐng *formal* inquire after the health of one's parents

定性 dìngxìng ① determine the nature (of an offence or a case): 他的错误还没调查清楚，暂不能～。His offences are still being investigated, so we can't yet determine their nature. ② determine the chemical composition of a substance

定性分析 dìngxìng fēnxi *chem.* qualitative analysis

定义 dìngyì definition: 下～ give a definition; define

定音鼓 dìngyīngǔ *mus.* kettledrums; timpani

定影 dìngyǐng *photog.* fixing; fixation: ～罐 fixing tank ／～剂 fixer ／～液 fixing bath

定于一尊 dìng yú yī zūn look up to one man as the highest authority

定语 dìngyǔ *gram.* attribute: ～从句 attributive clause

定员 dìngyuán fixed number of staff members or passengers: 这节车厢～一百二十人。This carriage has a seating capacity of 120 people.

定约 dìngyuē ① same as 订约 dìngyuē ② contract (in contract bridge)

定则 dìngzé *phys.* rule: 左手（右手）～ left-hand (right-hand) rule

定植 dìngzhí *bot.* field planting (*or* setting)

定制 dìngzhì ① have sth. made to order; have sth. custom-made: ～家具 have furniture made to order ／ 欢迎选购和～。Orders for ready-made or custom-made articles are welcome. ② an established rule or practice

定置网 dìngzhìwǎng *fishery* set (*or* fixed) net

定准 dìngzhǔn ① a set standard ② *adv.* certainly; surely: 你看见了～满意。You are sure to like it when you see it.

定子 dìngzǐ *elec.* stator: ～绕组 stator winding

定罪 dìngzuì declare sb. guilty; convict sb. (of a crime)

定做 dìngzuò have sth. made to order (*or* measure): ～的衣服 tailor-made clothes; clothes made to measure ／ 这双鞋是～的。This pair of shoes was made to order. ／ 这件上衣不合身，我要～一件。This jacket doesn't fit. I want to have one made to order.

啶 dìng see 吡啶 bǐdìng

腚 dìng *dial.* buttocks

碇（矴、椗） dìng a heavy stone used as an anchor; killick

碇泊 dìngbó anchor; berth

锭 dìng ① ingot-shaped tablet (of medicine, metal, Chinese ink, etc.) ② *text.* spindle ③ *m.* (for ingot-shaped objects): 一～墨 an ink stick

锭剂 dìngjì *pharm.* lozenge; pastille; troche

锭模 dìngmú *metall.* ingot mould

锭子 dìngzi *text.* spindle

diū

丢（丟） diū ① lose; mislay: 这套书～了一本。There's a book missing from the set. / 我把钳子～哪儿了？Where have I left my pliers? ② throw; cast; toss: 把菜帮子～给小兔吃 throw the outer leaves to the rabbit / 不要随地～果皮。Please don't litter. / 劳动人民的本色不能～。We mustn't lose the good qualities of the working people. ③ put (or lay) aside: ～在脑后 let sth. pass out of one's mind; clean forget; completely ignore / 我的法语～了好几年了，都忘得差不多了。I haven't used my French for years and have forgotten almost all of it. / 只有这件事～不开。That's the one thing that keeps worrying me. or That's my only worry.

丢丑 diūchǒu lose face; be disgraced: 简直是～! It's really a disgrace!

丢掉 diūdiào ① lose: 我～了一支笔。I've lost my pen. ② throw away; cast away; discard: ～幻想 cast away illusions / ～错误观点 discard mistaken views / ～官气 shed one's bureaucratic airs

丢魂落魄 diūhún-luòpò same as 失魂落魄 shīhún-luòpò

丢盔卸甲 diūkuī-xièjiǎ (also 丢盔弃甲 diūkuī-qìjiǎ) throw away one's helmet and coat of mail; throw away everything in headlong flight: 打得敌人～，狼狈逃窜。The enemy were so badly battered that they threw away everything and fled helter-skelter.

丢脸 diūliǎn lose face; be disgraced: 这不是～的事。There's nothing to be ashamed of.

丢面子 diū miànzi lose face: 有了错误要作自我批评，不要怕～。Criticize yourself when you've made a mistake. Don't be afraid of losing face.

丢弃 diūqì abandon; discard; give up

丢人 diūrén lose face; be disgraced: 真～! What a disgrace!

丢人现眼 diūrén-xiànyǎn make a fool of oneself; make a spectacle of oneself

丢三落四 diūsān-làsì forget this and that; be always forgetting things: 他老是这么～的。你看，又把房门钥匙锁在屋子里了。He's so scatterbrained. Look, he's locked his key inside his room again.

丢失 diūshī lose

丢手 diūshǒu wash one's hands of; give up: 他～不管了。He washed his hands of the matter.

丢眼色 diū yǎnsè wink at sb.; tip sb. the wink: 他朝我丢了个眼色, 转身走了。He winked at me, turned, and left.

丢卒保车 diū zú bǎo jū give up a pawn to save a chariot—sacrifice minor things to save major ones

铥 diū chem. thulium (Tm)

dōng

东（東） dōng ① east: 城～ east of the city / ～城 the eastern part of the city / ～郊 eastern suburbs ② master; owner: 房东 fángdōng ③ host: 今天是我的～。I'll be the host today. or It's my treat today.

东半球 dōngbànqiú the Eastern Hemisphere

东北 dōngběi ① northeast ② (Dōngběi) northeast China; the Northeast

东北抗日联军 Dōngběi Kàng Rì Liánjūn the Anti-Japanese Amalgamated Army of the Northeast (organized and led by the Communist Party of China after the September 18th Incident of 1931)

东奔西窜 dōngbēn-xīcuàn flee in all directions

东奔西跑 dōngbēn-xīpǎo run around here and there; bustle about; rush about (or around): 采购员天天为备料～。The purchasing agent rushes around everyday to secure materials. / 为找职业而～ be driven from pillar to post seeking employment

东不拉 dōngbùlā same as 冬不拉 dōngbùlā

东窗事发 dōngchuāng shì fā the plot has come to light; the secret is out

东床 dōngchuáng eastern bed—a son-in-law 〔from an anecdote about the celebrated calligrapher Wang Xizhi 王羲之 (321-379), who as a young man once remained lying on the eastern bed with his belly naked when a man came to his family to choose a son-in-law for the tutor of the crown prince, and who was chosen for his independence of mind in preference to his well-behaved brothers〕: ～快婿 a good son-in-law

东倒西歪 dōngdǎo-xīwāi leaning; unsteady; tottering: 三间～的屋子 three tumbledown rooms / 这个醉鬼～地在马路上走。The drunk man staggered along the road.

东道 dōngdào (also 东道主 dōngdàozhǔ) one who treats sb. to a meal; host: 做～ play the host; stand treat

东道国 dōngdàoguó host country

东帝汶 Dōngdìwèn East Timor

东方 dōngfāng ① the east: ～欲晓。Dawn is breaking. ② (Dōngfāng) the East; the Orient ③ (Dōngfāng) a two-character surname

东风 dōngfēng ① east wind; spring wind ② driving force of revolution

东风带 dōngfēngdài meteorol. easterlies

东风吹马耳 dōngfēng chuī mǎ'ěr like the east wind blowing at the ear of a horse—go in one ear and out the other

东宫 dōnggōng ① the Eastern Palace (the residence of the crown prince) ② the crown prince

东郭先生 Dōngguō Xiānsheng Master Dongguo (the soft-hearted scholar who narrowly escaped being eaten by a wolf which he had helped to hide from a hunter)—a naive person who gets into trouble through being soft-hearted to evil people

东海 Dōnghǎi the Donghai Sea; the East China Sea

东汉 Dōng Hàn the Eastern Han Dynasty (25-220)

东家长, 西家短 dōng jiā cháng, xī jiā duǎn gossip about various people

东家 dōngjia a form of address formerly used by an employee to his employer or a tenant-peasant to his landlord; master; boss

东晋 Dōng Jìn the Eastern Jin Dynasty (317-420)

东经 dōngjīng geog. east longitude: 北京位于～116度, 北纬40度。Beijing is located at 40°N and 116°E.

东拉西扯 dōnglā-xīchě drag in irrelevant matters; talk at random; ramble: 他做起报告来～, 不着边际。When he lectures he often strays from the subject.

东鳞西爪 dōnglín-xīzhǎo odds and ends; bits and pieces; fragments: ～地收集材料 glean scraps of information

东面[1] dōngmiàn face east: ～而坐 take a seat facing east

东面[2] dōngmiàn the east: 在火车站～ east of the railway station

东南 dōngnán ① southeast ② (Dōngnán) southeast China; the Southeast

东南亚 Dōngnán Yà Southeast Asia

东南亚国家联盟 Dōngnán Yà Guójiā Liánméng the Association of Southeast Asian Nations (ASEAN)

东欧 Dōng Ōu Eastern Europe

东跑西颠 dōngpǎo-xīdiān rush here and hurry there;

rush about

东拼西凑 dōngpīn-xīcòu　scrape together; knock together: 他～地借到了一笔钱。He scraped together a sum of money by borrowing left and right. / 那篇文章是～来的。That article is just scissors-and-paste work.

东萨摩亚 Dōngsàmóyà　Eastern Samoa

东三省 Dōngsānshěng　the Three Eastern Provinces (i.e. Liaoning, Jilin, and Heilongjiang; old name for 东北 Dōngběi)

东沙群岛 Dōngshā Qúndǎo　the Dongsha Islands

东山再起 Dōngshān zài qǐ　stage a comeback; resume one's former position

东施效颦 Dōngshī xiào pín　Dongshi, an ugly woman, knitting her brows in imitation of the famous beauty Xishi（西施）, only to make herself uglier—crude imitation with ludicrous effect

东涂西抹 dōngtú-xīmǒ　scribble; daub

东魏 Dōng Wèi　the Eastern Wei Dynasty (534-550), one of the Northern Dynasties

东西 dōng-xī　① east and west ② from east to west: 这地方～三里, 南北五里。This district is three *li* across from east to west and five *li* from north to south.

东…西… dōng… xī…　here … there: 东一个, 西一个 (of things) be scattered here and there / 东一句, 西一句 talk incoherently

东西 dōngxi　① thing: 他收拾好～就走了。He packed his things and left. / 一成不变的～是没有的。Nothing is immutable. / 她买～去了。She's out shopping. / 分析形势要注意全局性的～。In analysing a situation, pay attention to things that concern the situation as a whole. ② (referring to a person or animal) thing; creature: 这小～真可爱。What a sweet little thing! / 真不是～! What a despicable creature!

东乡族 Dōngxiāngzú　the Dongxiang (Tunghsiang) nationality, or the Dongxiangs (Tunghsiangs), inhabiting Gansu Province

东亚 Dōng Yà　East Asia

东洋 Dōngyáng　old name for 日本 Rìběn

东洋车 dōngyángchē　*old* rickshaw

东一锤头, 西一棒子 dōng yī lángtou, xī yī bàng zi　hammer here and batter there; act or speak haphazardly; act in a hit-or-miss fashion

东瀛 dōngyíng　*formal* ① the Donghai Sea; the East China Sea ② Japan

东岳 Dōng Yuè　the Eastern Mountain (another name for 泰山 Mount Tai in Shandong Province) ——see also 五岳 Wǔyuè

东张西望 dōngzhāng-xīwàng　gaze (or peer) around; glance this way and that; look in every direction: 她在车站外～了一会, 看不见有接她的人。She stood outside the station, looking round in all directions, but apparently no one had come to meet her.

东正教 Dōngzhèngjiào　the Orthodox Eastern Church

东周 Dōng Zhōu　the Eastern Zhou Dynasty (770-256 B.C.)

冬¹ dōng　winter: ～寒 winter cold

冬²（鼕） dōng　*onom.* the sound of beating a drum, knocking at a door, etc.; rub-a-dub; rat-tat; rat-a-tat

冬不拉 dōngbùlā　*mus.* a plucked stringed instrument, used by the Kazak nationality

冬菜 dōngcài　preserved, dried cabbage or mustard greens

冬虫夏草 dōngchóngxiàcǎo　*Chin. med.* Chinese caterpillar fungus (*Cordyceps sinensis*)

冬储 dōngchǔ　store away in winter

冬耕 dōnggēng　winter ploughing

冬菇 dōnggū　dried mushrooms (picked in winter)

冬瓜 dōngguā　wax gourd; white gourd

冬灌 dōngguàn　*agric.* winter irrigation

冬烘 dōnghōng　shallow but pedantic

冬烘先生 dōnghōng xiānsheng　pedant

冬候鸟 dōnghòuniǎo　winter bird

冬花 dōnghuā　another name for 款冬 kuǎndōng

冬季 dōngjì　winter

冬季施工 dōngjì shīgōng　winter construction

冬季体育运动 dōngjì tǐyù yùndòng　winter sports

冬季作物 dōngjì zuòwù　winter crops

冬节 dōngjié　same as 冬至 dōngzhì

冬令 dōnglìng　① winter ② winter weather: 春行～ wintry weather in spring

冬麦 dōngmài　same as 冬小麦 dōngxiǎomài

冬眠 dōngmián　*biol.* winter sleep; hibernation

冬青 dōngqīng　*bot.* Chinese ilex

冬日 dōngrì　*formal* the winter sun: ～融融 the winter sun radiating warmth

冬笋 dōngsǔn　winter bamboo shoots

冬天 dōngtiān　winter

冬瘟 dōngwēn　*Chin. med.* epidemic febrile diseases in winter

冬闲 dōngxián　slack winter season (in farming)

冬小麦 dōngxiǎomài　winter wheat

冬汛 dōngxùn　*fishery* winter fishing season

冬衣 dōngyī　winter clothes

冬泳 dōngyǒng　winter outdoor swimming

冬月 dōngyuè　the eleventh month of the lunar calendar; the eleventh moon

冬蛰 dōngzhé　*formal* hibernation

冬至 Dōngzhì　① the Winter Solstice—the 22nd of the 24 solar terms ② the day marking the beginning of the 22nd solar term (Dec. 21, 22, or 23) ——see also 节气 jiéqi, 二十四节气 èrshí sì jiéqì

冬装 dōngzhuāng　winter dress (or clothes)

咚 dōng　same as 冬² dōng

氡 dōng　*chem.* radon (Rn)

dǒng

董 dǒng　① *formal* direct; superintend; supervise: ～其成 supervise the project until its completion ② director; trustee: 校董 xiàodǒng ③ (Dǒng) a surname

董事 dǒngshì　director; trustee

董事会 dǒngshìhuì　board of directors (in an enterprise); board of trustees (in an educational institution)

董事长 dǒngshìzhǎng　chairman (or president) of the board of directors

懂 dǒng　understand; know: ～英语 know English / ～礼貌 have good manners / 不要不～装～。Don't pretend to know (or understand) when you don't. / 干部必须～政策。Cadres must have a good grasp of policy. / 他的话我听～了。I understand what he said.

懂得 dǒngde　understand; know; grasp: ～革命道理 understand revolutionary principles / 你～这句话的意思吗? Do you understand the meaning of this sentence? / 这一事件使我们更清楚地～了问题的复杂性。This incident brought home to us the complex nature of the problem. / 用群众所熟悉和～的词句 use words which are familiar and intelligible to the masses

懂行 dǒngháng　*dial.* know the business; know the ropes

懂事 dǒngshì sensible; intelligent: ～的孩子 a sensible child / 你怎么这样不～? How can you be so thoughtless?

dòng

动(動)

dòng ① move; stir: 他扭了腰,～不了。He's strained his back and can't move. / 微风吹～树叶。A breeze stirred the leaves. / 这东西一个人拿不～。No one can carry that single-handed. / 你一～,我就开枪。Move one step, and I fire. ② act; get moving: 经过动员,群众普遍地～起来了。After the mobilization meetings, the masses all got moving. ③ change; alter: 这句话只要～一两个字就顺了。Just change one or two words and the sentence will read smoothly. ④ use: ～脑筋 use one's head ⑤ touch (one's heart); arouse: ～了公愤 have aroused public indignation / ～感情 be carried away by emotion; get worked up / 不为甜言蜜语所～ not be swayed by fine words ⑥ dial. (usu. used in the negative) eat or drink: 不～荤腥 never touch meat or fish; be a vegetarian ⑦ easily; frequently: 影片一经上演,观众～以万计。Immediately on release, the film drew an audience tens of thousands.

动笔 dòngbǐ take up the pen; start writing: 他最近很少～。He hasn't done much writing recently. / 想清楚了再～。Think it all out before you start writing.

动宾词组 dòng-bīn cízǔ gram. verb-object word group

动兵 dòngbīng send out troops to fight

动不动 dòngbudòng easily; frequently; at every turn: ～就感冒 catch cold easily / ～就发脾气 be apt to lose one's temper; often get into a temper / 他～就训人。He is always lecturing people.

动产 dòngchǎn movable property; movables; personal property

动词 dòngcí gram. verb: ～不定式 infinitive

动荡 dòngdàng turbulence; upheaval; unrest: ～的局势 a turbulent situation

动荡不安 dòngdàng bù'ān turbulent; in turmoil: 世界局势～。The world situation is characterized by turbulence and intranquility.

动电学 dòngdiànxué electrokinetics

动肝火 dòng gānhuǒ get angry; flare up

动工 dònggōng ① begin construction; start building: 新的电视塔～了。Construction of the new television tower has started. ② construct: 这里正在～,车辆不能通过。Construction site ahead. No thoroughfare.

动画片 dònghuàpiàn animated cartoon (or drawing); cartoon

动换 dònghuan inf. move; stir: 风车不～了。The windmill has stopped.

动火 dònghuǒ inf. get angry; flare up

动机 dòngjī motive; intention: 出于自私的～ be actuated by selfish motives / ～不纯 have impure motives / 他的～是好的。His intentions are good. or He means well.

动静 dòngjìng ① the sound of sth. astir: 屋子里静悄悄的,一点～也没有。It was quiet in the room; nothing was stirring. ② movement; activity: 发现可疑～ spot something suspicious / 一有～就来报告。Report as soon as anything happens.

动觉 dòngjué psychol. kinaesthesia

动力 dònglì ① motive power; power ② motive (or driving) force; impetus: 社会发展的～ the motive force of the development of society / 改革是推进一切工作的～。Reform motivates us in all our work.

动力机 dònglìjī same as 发动机 fādòngjī

动力学 dònglìxué dynamics; kinetics

动量 dòngliàng phys. momentum: 广义～ generalized momentum / ～矩 moment of momentum

动量守恒定律 dòngliàng shǒuhéng dìnglǜ phys. the law of conservation of momentum

动令 dònglìng mil. command of execution

动乱 dòngluàn turmoil; disturbance; upheaval; turbulence: ～时期 a time of turmoil; a time of storm and stress / 社会～ social upheaval / ～年代 years of upheaval

动脉 dòngmài physiol. artery: ～脉搏 arterial pulse

动脉弓 dòngmàigōng arch of aorta

动脉血压 dòngmài xuèyā arterial pressure

动脉炎 dòngmàiyán arteritis

动脉硬化 dòngmài yìnghuà arteriosclerosis

动脉粥样硬化 dòngmài zhōuyàng yìnghuà atherosclerosis

动名词 dòngmíngcí gram. gerund

动能 dòngnéng phys. kinetic energy

动怒 dòngnù lose one's temper; flare up

动气 dòngqì inf. take offence; get angry

动情 dòngqíng ① get worked up; become excited ② become enamoured; have one's (sexual) passions aroused

动人 dòngrén moving; touching: ～的情景 a moving scene / ～的事迹 stirring deeds / ～的故事 a touching story

动人心弦 dòng rén xīnxián tug at one's heartstrings; be deeply moving

动容 dòngróng formal change countenance; be visibly moved

动身 dòngshēn go (or set out) on a journey; leave (for a distant place): 行李都打好了,我们明天早上就～。We've already packed and will leave tomorrow morning.

动手 dòngshǒu ① start work; get to work: 早点儿～,早点儿完成。The sooner we start, the sooner we finish. / ～修建一座高炉 start building a blast furnace / 大家～干了起来。Everyone set to work. ② touch; handle: 爱护展品,请勿～。Please don't touch the exhibits. ③ raise a hand to strike; hit out: 谁先动的手? Who struck the first blow?

动手动脚 dòngshǒu-dòngjiǎo get fresh with sb.: 别～的。Keep your hands to yourself.

动手术 dòng shǒushù ① perform an operation; operate on sb. ② have an operation; be operated on

动态 dòngtài ① trends; developments: 科技新～ recent developments in science and technology / 了解敌军的～ find out about enemy troop movements / 油井～ behaviour (or performance) of an oil well ② dynamic state: ～电阻 dynamic resistance

动态平衡 dòngtài pínghéng phys. dynamic equilibrium

动态特性 dòngtài tèxìng elec. dynamic characteristic

动弹 dòngtan move; stir: 机器不～了。The machine has stopped.

动弹不得 dòngtanbude cannot move: 车里太挤,～。The bus was so crowded that nobody could move.

动听 dòngtīng interesting or pleasant to listen to: 他能把极平常的事儿说得很～。He can make ordinary things sound interesting. / 她唱得很～。She sings beautifully.

动土 dòngtǔ break ground; start building

动问 dòngwèn dial. pol. may I ask: 不敢～,您是从北京来的吗? Excuse me, but are you from Beijing?

动窝 dòngwō dial. start moving; make a move: 不管你说什么,他就是不～。No matter what you say, he just won't stir.

动武 dòngwǔ use force; start a fight; come to blows

动物 dòngwù animal: ～界 the animal kingdom

动物胶 dòngwùjiāo chem. animal size (or glue)

动物区系　dòngwù qūxì　fauna

动物生态学　dòngwù shēngtàixué　animal ecology

动物学　dòngwùxué　zoology

动物油　dòngwùyóu　animal oil

动物园　dòngwùyuán　zoo; zoological garden

动物志　dòngwùzhì　fauna

动响　dòngxiǎng　same as 响动 xiǎngdong

动向　dòngxiàng　trend; tendency: 新～ new trends / 密切注意敌人～。Keep a close watch on the enemy's movements.

动心　dòngxīn　one's mind is perturbed; one's desire, enthusiasm or interest is aroused

动刑　dòngxíng　subject sb. to torture; torture

动眼神经　dòngyǎnshénjīng　oculomotor nerve

动摇　dòngyáo　shake; vacillate; waver: ～分子 wavering (*or* vacillating) element / 坚决走社会主义道路, 绝不～ never waver in one's determination to take the socialist road / 环境再艰苦也～不了他们征服自然的决心。No difficulties can shake their resolve to conquer nature.

动摇军心　dòngyáo jūnxīn　shake the morale

动议　dòngyì　motion: 紧急～ an urgent motion / 提出一项～ put forward a motion

动用　dòngyòng　put to use; employ; draw on: ～大量人力 employ a tremendous amount of manpower / ～库存 draw on stock

动员　dòngyuán　mobilize; arouse: 全国～, 大干四化 mobilize the whole nation and work energetically for the four modernizations / 作一番～ give a mobilization (*or* pep) talk / 整个医院都～起来, 抢救伤员。The whole hospital was galvanized into action to save the wounded.

动员报告　dòngyuán bàogào　mobilization speech

动员大会　dòngyuán dàhuì　mobilization meeting

动员令　dòngyuánlìng　mobilization order

动辄　dòngzhé　*formal* easily; frequently; at every turn: ～发怒 fly into a rage on the slightest provocation

动辄得咎　dòngzhé dé jiù　be constantly taken to task; be blamed for whatever one does

动作　dòngzuò　① movement; motion; action: ～敏捷 (缓慢) quick (slow) in one's movements / 优美的舞蹈 graceful dance movements ② act; start moving: 且看他下一步如何～。Let's see how he acts next.

冻（凍）
dòng　① freeze: 水管里的水～了。The water in the pipes froze. / 不能让这些白菜～坏。We mustn't let the cabbages be damaged by frost. ② jelly: 肉冻 ròudòng　③ feel very cold; freeze; be frostbitten: 多穿些, 别～着了。Put on more clothes so you don't catch cold. / 她手都～了。Her hands were frostbitten. / 真～得够呛! Brr, I'm freezing!

冻冰　dòngbīng　freeze: 河上～了。The river is frozen.

冻疮　dòngchuāng　chilblain: 生～ have chilblains

冻豆腐　dòngdòufu　frozen bean curd

冻害　dònghài　*agric.* freeze injury

冻僵　dòngjiāng　frozen stiff; numb with cold

冻结　dòngjié　① freeze; congeal ② (of wages, prices, etc.) freeze: 工资～ wage freeze / ～的资产 frozen assets

冻馁　dòngněi　cold and hunger

冻凝　dòngníng　congeal: ～点 congealing point

冻肉　dòngròu　frozen meat

冻伤　dòngshāng　frostbite

冻死　dòngsǐ　freeze to death; freeze and perish; die of frost: 昨天来寒流时, ～了两只小羊。When the cold snap set in yesterday, two lambs froze to death.

冻土　dòngtǔ　frozen earth (*or* ground, soil)

冻土学　dòngtǔxué　cryopedology

冻雨　dòngyǔ　*meteorol.* sleet

冻原　dòngyuán　another name for 苔原 táiyuán

侗
Dòng　see below

侗族　Dòngzú　the Dong (Tung) nationality, or the Dongs (Tungs), distributed over Guizhou Province, Hunan Province, and the Guangxi Zhuang Autonomous Region

洞
dòng　① hole; cavity: 城门～儿 archway of a city gate / 衬衣破了一个～ have a hole in one's shirt ② used in place of 零 when speaking figures ③ *formal* penetratingly; thoroughly: 洞晓 dòngxiǎo

洞察　dòngchá　see clearly; have an insight into: ～力 insight; discernment; acumen / ～是非 see clearly the rights and wrongs of the case / ～一切 have a keen insight into matters

洞彻　dòngchè　understand thoroughly; see clearly: ～事理 be sensible and perfectly aware

洞穿　dòngchuān　① pierce: 一颗子弹～他的右肺。A bullet pierced his right lung. ② have an insight into; understand fully

洞达　dòngdá　understand thoroughly: ～事理 be sensible

洞房　dòngfáng　bridal (*or* nuptial) chamber

洞房花烛　dòngfáng huāzhú　wedding festivities; wedding

洞府　dòngfǔ　cave-dwelling (of immortals)

洞黑　dònghēi　dark; gloomy: ～的峡谷 a dark valley

洞见症结　dòngjiàn zhēngjié　see clearly the crux of the matter; get to the heart of the problem

洞鉴　dòngjiàn　*formal* see clearly; have an insight into: ～积弊 see clearly the age-old malpractices

洞开　dòngkāi　(of doors, windows, etc.) be wide open: 门户～。The door was wide open.

洞若观火　dòng ruò guān huǒ　see sth. as clearly as a blazing fire

洞天　dòngtiān　cave heaven—fairyland; a heavenly abode: 别有～ a place of unique, enchanting beauty

洞天福地　dòngtiān fúdì　cave heaven and blessed region—fairyland; a heavenly abode

洞悉　dòngxī　know clearly; understand thoroughly

洞箫　dòngxiāo　*dongxiao*, a vertical bamboo flute

洞晓　dòngxiǎo　have a clear knowledge of: ～其中利弊 have a clear understanding of the advantages and disadvantages

洞穴　dòngxué　cave; cavern

洞穴墓　dòngxuémù　catacomb

洞烛　dòngzhú　see through; discern clearly: ～其阴谋 see through his scheme

洞烛其奸　dòngzhú qí jiān　see through sb.'s tricks

恫
dòng　*formal* fear

恫吓　dònghè　threaten; intimidate

峒
dòng　(usu. used as part of a place name) cave; cavern: ～中 Dongzhong (in Guangdong Province)

栋（棟）
dòng　① *formal* ridgepole ② *m.* (for buildings): 一～楼房 a building

栋梁　dòngliáng　ridgepole and beam—pillar of the state

栋梁之材　dòngliáng zhī cái　one with the makings of a statesman

胨（腖）
dòng　*biochem.* peptone

胴
dòng　① trunk; torso ② *formal* large intestine

胴体　dòngtǐ　trunk; (esp. of a slaughtered animal)

硐
dòng　cave; cave dwelling; pit

dōu

哝 dōu *interj. old* expressing anger

都 dōu *adv.* ① all: 大家～到了吗? Is everybody here? / 我们的干部～是人民的勤务员。Our cadres are all servants of the people. / 我父母～不在了。My parents are both dead. / 不管做什么, ～应该考虑到人民的利益。Whatever we do, we should take the interests of the people into consideration. / 什么～行。Anything will do. ② (used with 是 to show the cause): ～是你老磨蹭, 害得我们迟到了。It was all because of your dawdling that we were late. / ～是党的领导, 我们才有今天幸福的生活。Thanks to the leadership of the Party, we are leading a happy life today. / ～是你, 把他灌成这样。It's all your fault; you made him drunk. ③ even: 今天天气真怪, 中午比早晨～冷。Strange weather we're having today. It's even colder at noon than it was early in the morning. / 连他～不知道。Even he doesn't know it. ④ already: 他～八十岁了, 身子骨还那么硬朗。He's already eighty but still going strong. ——see also dū

兜[1] dōu ① pocket; bag: 他站着, 两手插在～里。He stood with his hands in his pockets. / 钥匙在我上衣～里。The key is in my coat pocket. ② wrap up in a piece of cloth, etc.: 用毛巾～着几个鸡蛋 carry a few eggs wrapped up in a towel ③ move round: 我们乘车在城里～了一圈。We went for a drive around in town. ④ canvass; solicit: ～了一号买卖 have canvassed a business order ⑤ take upon oneself; take responsibility for sth.: 没关系, 出了问题我～着。Don't worry. If anything goes wrong, I'll take responsibility for it. ⑥ see 兜底 dōudǐ ⑦ same as 篼 dōu

兜[2] dōu same as 蔸 dōu

兜捕 dōubǔ surround and seize; round up: ～一伙走私犯 close in on the gang of smugglers

兜抄 dōuchāo close in from the rear and both flanks; round up

兜底 dōudǐ *inf.* reveal all the details (of a person's disreputable background, etc.); disclose the whole inside story: 千万别兜他的底儿! Don't you bring up anything about his past!

兜兜 dōudou *inf.* same as 兜肚 dōudu

兜兜裤儿 dōudoukùr sunsuit (for a child)

兜肚 dōudu an undergarment covering the chest and abdomen

兜翻 dōufān *dial.* ① rummage through (old things) ② dig up (old stories) ③ expose (a secret)

兜风 dōufēng ① catch the wind: 帆破了, 兜不住风。The sails are torn; they won't catch the wind. ② *dial.* go for a drive, ride or sail; go for a spin: 在河边骑车兜兜风, 很有意思。It's fun to take a spin on your bicycle along the riverbank.

兜揽 dōulǎn ① canvass; solicit: ～生意 solicit custom; drum up trade ② take upon oneself (sb. else's work, etc.): 这是你～来的事, 我不管。You've taken this on yourself. I'm not going to get involved in it.

兜圈子 dōu quānzi ① go around in circles; circle: 飞机在森林上空～。The aeroplane circled over the forest. ② beat about the bush

兜售 dōushòu peddle; hawk: ～劣货 hawk low-quality goods / ～军火 peddle munitions

兜销 dōuxiāo same as 兜售 dōushòu

兜子 dōuzi ① pocket; bag ② same as 篼子 dōuzi

蔸 (槐) dōu *dial.* ① root and stem of certain plants ② *m.*: 一～树 a tree / 一～白菜 a (head of) Chinese cabbage

篼 dōu container made of bamboo, wicker, ratten, etc.

篼子 dōuzi a bamboo chair for one person carried on two poles by two men

dǒu

斗 dǒu ① *dou*, a unit of dry measure for grain (= 1 decalitre) ② a *dou* measure ③ an object shaped like a cup or dipper: 漏斗 lòudǒu ④ whorl (of a fingerprint) ⑤ the eighth of the twenty-eight constellations (二十八宿) into which the celestial sphere was divided in ancient Chinese astronomy (consisting of six stars in the shape of a ladle in Sagittarius) ⑥ (short for 北斗星) the Big Dipper; the Dipper: 少焉, 月出于东山之上, 徘徊于～牛之间。(苏轼) Shortly after, the moon rose above the eastern mountain and hovered between the Dipper and the Cowherd. ⑦ same as 陡 dǒu ——see also dòu

斗柄 dǒubǐng the handle of the Dipper: 楼上栏杆横～, 露寒人远鸡相应。(周邦彦) Now, on the upper balcony lies aslant the Dipper's handle; The dew is cold, the man far away, only the cocks answer each other.

斗车 dǒuchē trolley (in a mine or at a construction site); tram

斗胆 dǒudǎn *hum.* make bold; venture: 我～说一句, 这件事您做错了。May I make bold to suggest that you were wrong to do so.

斗方 dǒufāng ① a square sheet of paper used for painting or calligraphy ② painting or calligraphy done on a (one- or two-*chi*) square sheet of paper

斗方名士 dǒufāng míngshì a pretender to culture and refinement

斗拱 dǒugǒng (in monumental buildings) sets of brackets on top of the columns supporting the beams within and roof eaves without (each set consisting of tiers of outstretching arms called *gong*, cushioned with trapezoidal blocks called *dou*)

斗箕 dǒuji (also 斗记 dǒujì) fingerprint

斗笠 dǒulì bamboo hat

斗篷 dǒupeng ① cape; cloak ② *dial.* bamboo hat

斗渠 dǒuqú *water conservancy* lateral canal

斗筲 dǒushāo *formal* a bamboo *dou* measure used in ancient times: ～之材 a person of limited capacity

斗式提升机 dǒushì tíshēngjī *mech.* bucket elevator

斗室 dǒushì *liter.* a small room

斗烟丝 dǒuyānsī pipe tobacco

斗转参横 dǒuzhuǎn-shēnhéng the Dipper turns and Orion slants—day dawns

斗转星移 dǒuzhuǎn-xīngyí same as 星移斗转 xīngyí-dǒuzhuǎn

抖 dǒu ① tremble; shiver; quiver: 浑身直～ tremble all over ② shake; jerk: 把衣服上的雪～掉 shake the snow off one's clothes / ～一～缰绳 give the reins a jerk / ～空竹 play with a diabolo / ～开棉被 spread the quilt with a flick ③ rouse; stir up: ～起精神 pluck up one's spirits ④ (used sarcastically) get on in the world

抖颤 dǒuchàn same as 颤抖 chàndǒu

抖动 dǒudòng shake; tremble; vibrate

抖搂 dǒulou *dial.* ① shake off; shake out of sth.: 把包里的东西～出来 shake a bag to empty it ② expose;

bring to light: 把她干的那些坏事给大伙～～。Let everyone know all the wicked things she has done. ③ waste; squander: 别把钱～光了。Don't waste all the money.

抖落 dǒuluo　same as 抖搂 dǒulou

抖擞 dǒusǒu　enliven; rouse: 精神抖擞 jīngshén dǒusǒu

抖擞精神 dǒusǒu jīngshén　brace up; pull oneself together

抖威风 dǒu wēifēng　throw one's weight about

枓
dǒu　see below

枓栱 dǒugǒng　same as 斗拱 dǒugǒng

陡
dǒu　① steep; precipitous: 山～路险。The hill is steep, and the climb is dangerous. ② adv. suddenly; unexpectedly; abruptly: 天气～变。The weather changed suddenly. / 狂风～起。A sudden gale struck.

陡壁 dǒubì　cliff; precipice; steep

陡槽 dǒucáo　water conservancy chute

陡度 dǒudù　phys. gradient: 压力～ pressure gradient

陡峻 dǒujùn　high and precipitous

陡立 dǒulì　rise steeply

陡坡 dǒupō　a steep slope

陡峭 dǒuqiào　precipitous: ～的山崖 a sheer precipice

陡然 dǒurán　adv. suddenly; unexpectedly; abruptly: ～下降 fall suddenly

陡削 dǒuxuē　precipitous: ～的山崖 a sheer precipice

蚪
dǒu　see 蝌蚪 kēdǒu

dòu

斗 (鬥、鬭、鬬)
dòu　① fight; tussle: 拳～ fist fight; fisticuffs ② struggle against; denounce ③ contest with; contend with: 很少人～得过他。Few people can get the better of him. / 狐狸再狡猾也～不过好猎手。The craftiest fox can't escape the skilled hunter. ④ make animals fight (as a game): ～蛐蛐 hold a cricketfight ⑤ fit together: ～榫 fit the tenon into the mortise; dovetail / 大家～一～情况。Let's pool our information and size up the situation. ——see also dǒu

斗法 dòufǎ　① exercise magic powers against each other ② use stratagems

斗富 dòufù　vie with each other in wealth

斗鸡 dòujī　① gamecock ② cockfighting

斗鸡眼 dòujīyǎn　cross-eye

斗劲 dòujìn　compete in strength

斗口 dòukǒu　quarrel; bicker; squabble

斗口齿 dòu kǒuchǐ　dial. ① squabble; bicker ② banter

斗牛 dòuniú　bullfight

斗牛士 dòuniúshì　bullfighter; matador

斗殴 dòu'ōu　fight; scuffle

斗牌 dòupái　play cards or dominoes

斗气 dòuqì　quarrel or contend with sb. on account of a personal grudge

斗巧 dòuqiǎo　① luckily; fortunately: 真不～! 他刚出门。What bad luck! He's just gone out. ② compete in ingenuity

斗趣儿 dòuqùr　same as 逗趣儿 dòuqùr

斗士 dòushì　fighter (for a cause)

斗心眼儿 dòu xīnyǎnr　fight a battle of wits

斗眼 dòuyǎn　cross-eye

斗争 dòuzhēng　① struggle; fight; combat: 作坚决的～ fight resolutely against / 同一切不正确的思想和行为作不疲倦的～ wage a tireless struggle against all incorrect ideas and actions / 新与旧的～ conflict between the new and the old ② accuse and denounce at a meeting: ～恶霸地主 publicly denounce (or struggle against) a despotic landlord ③ strive for; fight for: 为完成五年计划而～ strive for the fulfilment of the five-year plan

斗争会 dòuzhēnghuì　public accusation meeting

斗争性 dòuzhēngxìng　fighting spirit; militancy

斗志 dòuzhì　will to fight; fighting will: 鼓舞群众的～ arouse the fighting will of the masses

斗志昂扬 dòuzhì ángyáng　have high morale; be full of fight; be militant

斗智 dòuzhì　fight a battle of wits

斗嘴 dòuzuǐ　① quarrel; bicker; squabble ② banter

豆¹
dòu　an ancient stemmed cup or bowl

豆² (荳)
dòu　pod-bearing plant or its seeds: 扁豆 biǎndòu

豆³
dòu　a bean-shaped thing: 花生豆儿 huāshēngdòur

豆瓣酱 dòubànjiàng　thick broad-bean sauce

豆包 dòubāo　steamed bun stuffed with sweetened bean paste

豆饼 dòubǐng　agric. soya-bean cake; bean cake

豆豉 dòuchǐ　fermented soya beans, salted or otherwise

豆腐 dòufu　bean curd

豆腐房 dòufufáng　bean-curd plant

豆腐干 dòufugān　dried bean curd

豆腐脑儿 dòufunǎor　jellied bean curd

豆腐皮 dòufupí　① skin of soya-bean milk ② dial. thin sheets of bean curd

豆腐乳 dòufurǔ　fermented bean curd

豆花儿 dòuhuār　dial. bean jelly (a dessert)

豆荚 dòujiá　pod

豆浆 dòujiāng　soya-bean milk

豆角儿 dòujiǎor　inf. fresh kidney beans

豆秸 dòujiē　beanstalk (left after threshing)

豆科 dòukē　bot. the pulse family; bean or pea family

豆科植物 dòukē zhíwù　legume; leguminous plant

豆蔻 dòukòu　bot. round cardamom (Amomum cardamomum)

豆蔻年华 dòukòu niánhuá　(of a girl) in one's early teens

豆绿 dòulǜ　(also 豆青 dòuqīng) pea green

豆面 dòumiàn　bean flour

豆娘 dòuniáng　zool. damselfly

豆萁 dòuqí　dial. beanstalk

豆蓉 dòuróng　fine bean mash, used as stuffing in cakes

豆乳 dòurǔ　soya-bean milk

豆沙 dòushā　sweetened bean paste

豆薯 dòushǔ　yam bean

豆象 dòuxiàng　zool. bean weevil

豆芽儿 dòuyár　bean sprouts

豆雁 dòuyàn　zool. bean goose

豆油 dòuyóu　soya-bean oil

豆渣 dòuzhā　residue from beans after making soya-bean milk; bean dregs

豆汁 dòuzhī　① a fermented drink made from ground beans ② dial. soya-bean milk

豆纸 dòuzhǐ　coarse toilet paper

豆制品 dòuzhìpǐn　bean products

豆子 dòuzi　① pod-bearing plant or its seeds ② bean-shaped thing

逗¹ (鬥、鬭、鬬)
dòu　① tease; play with: ～孩子玩 play with a child / 别～了。You're kidding! ② provoke (laughter, etc.); amuse: 这小女孩～人

喜欢。She's a lovable little girl. ③ *dial.* funny: 这话真～! What a funny remark!

逗² dòu ① stay; stop: 逗留 dòuliú ② same as 读 dòu

逗点 dòudiǎn same as 逗号 dòuhào

逗哏 dòugén (esp. in *xiangsheng* performances) crack jokes; play the fool

逗号 dòuhào comma (,)

逗乐儿 dòulèr *dial.* try to make people laugh; clown around

逗留 dòuliú (also 逗遛 dòuliú) stay; stop: 他们中途在西安～了几天。They stopped over in Xi'an for several days. / 禁止～! No loitering!

逗闷子 dòu mènzi *dial.* crack a joke; joke; make fun of

逗弄 dòunong tease; kid; make fun of: 他～你呢。He's kidding you.

逗趣儿 dòuqùr *dial.* set people laughing (by funny remarks, etc.); amuse: 他真会～! He's really very amusing!

逗笑儿 dòuxiàor *dial.* amusing

逗引 dòuyǐn tease: ～孩子玩儿 amuse oneself by teasing with the kids / 这孩子被～哭了。The child has been teased to tears.

读(讀) dòu a slight pause in reading: 句读 jùdòu ——see also dú

痘 dòu ① smallpox ② smallpox pustule ③ (bovine) vaccine: 种痘 zhòngdòu

痘苗 dòumiáo (bovine) vaccine

窦(竇) dòu ① hole ② *physiol.* sinus: 鼻窦 bídòu ③ (Dòu) a surname

dū

氜(毀) dū lightly touch with a finger, writing brush, stick, etc.

都 dū ① capital (of a country): 建都 jiàndū ② big city; metropolis: 鞍山是我国的钢～。Anshan is our country's steel metropolis. ——see also dōu

都城 dūchéng capital (of a country)

都督 dūdu ① commander-in-chief in ancient China ② provincial military governor in the early Republican period who was also in charge of civil administration

都会 dūhuì a big city; metropolis

都市 dūshì a big city; metropolis

嘟¹ dū *onom.* toot; honk: 汽车喇叭～～响。The car tooted.

嘟² dū *dial.* pout: 生气地～起了嘴 pout sulkily

嘟噜 dūlu *inf.* ① *m.* bunch; cluster: 一～葡萄 a bunch of grapes / 一～钥匙 a bunch of keys ② hang down in a bunch ③ trill: 打～儿 pronounce with a trill; trill

嘟囔 dūnang (also 嘟哝 dūnong) mutter to oneself; mumble: 他嘴里嘟嘟囔囔的，也不知道在说什么。He was mumbling to himself and was barely intelligible.

督 dū superintend and direct: ～战 supervise (military) operations

督办 dūbàn supervise and manage

督察 dūchá superintend; supervise

督促 dūcù supervise and urge: ～大家及时归还工具 urge everybody to return the tools on time / 已经布置了的工作, 应当认真～检查。We must supervise and speed up fulfilment of assigned tasks.

督军 dūjūn provincial military governor in the early Republican period

督励 dūlì urge and encourage

督率 dūshuài (also 督帅 dūshuài) lead; command: ～百万大军 command an army a million strong

督学 dūxué *old* educational inspector

督造 dūzào supervise the manufacture: ～兵器 supervise arms manufacture

dú

毒 dú ① poison; toxin: 服毒 fúdú ② narcotics; (narcotic) drugs: 吸毒 xīdú ③ poisonous; noxious; poisoned: ～蜘蛛 poisonous spider / 有～气体 noxious gas / ～箭 a poisoned arrow ④ kill with poison; poison: ～老鼠 poison rats ⑤ malicious; cruel; fierce: 他的心肠真～! How cruel he is! / 那时太阳正～, 晒得他汗珠直往下滚。The sun was at its fiercest and beads of sweat kept rolling down his face. / ～打 beat up ⑥ poison (sb.'s mind): 放毒 fàngdú②

毒扁豆 dúbiǎndòu *bot.* calabar bean

毒扁豆碱 dúbiǎndòujiǎn *pharm.* physostigmine; eserine

毒草 dúcǎo ① poisonous weeds ② harmful speech, writing, etc.

毒蛾 dú'é tussock moth

毒饵 dú'ěr poison bait

毒谷 dúgǔ poison grains (planted with seeds to kill harmful insects)

毒害 dúhài ① murder by poisoning; poison ② poison (sb.'s mind): 用资产阶级思想～青年 poison young people with bourgeois ideology

毒化 dúhuà poison; spoil: ～会谈的气氛 poison the atmosphere of the talks / ～社会风气 debase social morality

毒计 dújì venomous scheme; deadly trap

毒剂 dújì toxic; toxicant

毒辣 dúlà sinister; diabolic: 阴险～ sinister and ruthless / 手段～ vicious means

毒瘤 dúliú malignant tumour; cancer

毒品 dúpǐn narcotics; (narcotic) drugs

毒气 dúqì poisonous (or poison) gas

毒气弹 dúqìdàn gas shell; gas bomb

毒气室 dúqìshì gas chamber

毒区 dúqū contaminated area (in chemical warfare); gassed area

毒杀 dúshā kill with poison; poison

毒杀芬 dúshāfēn *agric.* toxaphene; octachlorocamphene

毒砂 dúshā *min.* arsenopyrite; mispickel

毒蛇 dúshé poisonous (or venomous) snake; viper

毒手 dúshǒu violent treachery; murderous scheme ——see also 下毒手 xià dúshǒu

毒死 dúsǐ kill with poison; poison: 这药～了三个人。Three people were poisoned by this chemical.

毒素 dúsù ① *biol.* toxin ② poison: 清除封建～ eliminate feudal poison

毒瓦斯 dúwǎsī poisonous (or poison) gas

毒物 dúwù poisonous substance; poison

毒腺 dúxiàn *zool.* poison gland

毒刑 dúxíng cruel corporal punishment; horrible torture

毒性 dúxìng toxicity; poisonousness

毒蕈　dúxùn　poisonous fungus; toadstool

毒牙　dúyá　poison (*or* venom) fang

毒药　dúyào　poison; toxicant

毒液　dúyè　venom

毒汁　dúzhī　venom

独 (獨)

dú　① only; single: ～子 only son ② *adv.* solely; only: 大家都到了，～有他还没来。He's the only one who isn't here yet. ③ *adv.* alone; by oneself; in solitude: ～居 live a solitary existence／～坐 sit alone ④ old people without offspring; the childless: 鳏寡孤独 guān-guǎ-gū-dú　⑤ *inf.* standoffish: 他这个人真～。He's rather standoffish.

独霸　dúbà　dominate exclusively; monopolize

独霸一方　dúbà yīfāng　lord it over a district; be a local despot

独白　dúbái　soliloquy; monologue

独步　dúbù　be unrivalled: ～文坛 be the unrivalled literary colossus of the age

独步一时　dúbù yīshí　have no equal in one's time: 她歌喉极佳，演歌剧～。Gifted with a rare voice, she was an outstanding star among the opera singers.

独裁　dúcái　dictatorship; autocratic rule: ～者 autocrat; dictator／～政治 autocracy

独唱　dúchàng　(vocal) solo

独唱会　dúchànghuì　recital (of a vocalist)

独出心裁　dú chū xīncái　show originality; be original

独创　dúchuàng　original creation: ～精神 creative spirit／～性 originality

独创一格　dúchuàng yīgé　create a style all one's own; have a unique (*or* distinctive) style

独词句　dúcíjù　*gram.* one-member sentence

独当一面　dú dāng yīmiàn　take charge of a department or locality; assume responsibility for a certain sector: 他成长很快，已经可以～了。He's matured quickly. He can now take charge of the whole locality.

独到　dúdào　original: ～的见解 original view

独到之处　dúdào zhī chù　distinctive qualities; specific characteristics

独断　dúduàn　arbitrary; dictatorial

独断独行　dúduàn-dúxíng　(also 独断专行 dúduàn-zhuānxíng) make arbitrary decisions and take peremptory action; act arbitrarily

独夫　dúfū　a bad ruler forsaken by all; autocrat

独夫民贼　dúfū-mínzéi　autocrat and traitor to the people

独个　dúgè　alone; by oneself: 她～住一套房子。She lives in a flat all by herself.

独根　dúgēn　same as 独苗 dúmiáo

独孤　Dúgū　a two-character surname

独家　dújiā　sole; the only one; exclusive: ～经销 sole agent

独家新闻　dújiā xīnwén　*Journalism* exclusive

独角戏　dújiǎoxì　(also 独脚戏 dújiǎoxì) ① monodrama; one-man show ② same as 滑稽 huájī

独居石　dújūshí　*min.* monazite

独具匠心　dú jù jiàngxīn　show ingenuity; have originality

独具只眼　dú jù zhǐ yǎn　be able to see what others cannot; have exceptional insight

独来独往　dúlái-dúwǎng　coming and going all alone—unsociable; aloof: 她老是～的。She kept pretty much to herself.

独揽　dúlǎn　arrogate; monopolize: ～大权 arrogate all powers to oneself

独力　dúlì　by one's own efforts; on one's own: ～经营 manage affairs on one's own

独立　dúlì　① stand alone: ～山巅的苍松 a pine tree standing alone on a mountain peak ② independence: 宣布～ proclaim independence ③ independent; on one's own: ～营 (团、师) independent battalion (regiment, division)／～分析问题和解决问题的能力 ability to analyse and solve problems on one's own

独立成分　dúlì chéngfen　*gram.* independent element

独立国　dúlìguó　independent state

独立核算单位　dúlì hésuàn dānwèi　independent accounting unit

独立王国　dúlì wángguó　independent kingdom (fig.)

独立性　dúlìxìng　independent character; independence: 闹～ assert one's "independence"—refuse to obey the leadership

独立自主　dúlì-zìzhǔ　maintain independence and keep the initiative; act independently and with the initiative in one's own hands

独联体　Dúliántǐ　the Commonwealth of Independent States

独龙族　Dúlóngzú　the Drung (Tulung) nationality, or the Drungs (Tulungs), inhabiting Yunnan Province

独轮车　dúlúnchē　wheelbarrow

独门儿　dúménr　special skill (of an individual or a family)

独门独院　dúmén-dúyuàn　a *siheyuan* (四合院) occupied by a single family: 他们家是～。They have a *siheyuan* to themselves.

独苗　dúmiáo　(also 独苗苗 dúmiáomiáo) only son and heir

独木不成林　dú mù bù chéng lín　one tree doesn't make a forest—one person alone can't accomplish much

独木难支　dú mù nán zhī　one log can't prop up a tottering building—one person alone can't save the situation

独木桥　dúmùqiáo　① single-plank (*or* single-log) bridge ② difficult path

独木舟　dúmùzhōu　dugout canoe

独幕剧　dúmùjù　one-act play

独辟蹊径　dú pì xījìng　open a new road for oneself; develop a new style or a method of one's own

独善其身　dú shàn qí shēn　maintain one's own integrity

独身　dúshēn　① separated from one's family: ～在外 be away from home and family ② unmarried; single: 她现在还是～。She's still single.

独身主义　dúshēnzhǔyì　celibacy

独生女　dúshēngnǚ　only daughter

独生子　dúshēngzǐ　only son

独生子女　dúshēng zǐnǚ　only child

独树一帜　dú shù yīzhì　fly one's own colours—develop a school of one's own

独特　dútè　unique; distinctive: ～的风格 a unique style

独体字　dútǐzì　(also 独体 dútǐ) single character (e.g. 日, 月, 上, 下, etc.)

独吞　dútūn　take exclusive possession of sth.

独舞　dúwǔ　solo dance

独行其是　dú xíng qí shì　do what one thinks is right regardless of others' opinions

独眼龙　dúyǎnlóng　*derog.* a person blind in one eye; one-eyed person

独一无二　dúyī-wú'èr　unique; unparalleled; unmatched

独占　dúzhàn　have sth. all to oneself; monopolize

独占鳌头　dúzhàn áotóu　come out first; head the list of successful candidates; be the champion

独占资本　dúzhàn zīběn　*econ.* monopoly capital

独资　dúzī　exclusive investment

独资企业　dúzī qǐyè　exclusive investment in enterprises; enterprises solely owned by sb.

独自　dúzì　alone; by oneself: 他～一人走向公园。He walked on alone towards the park.

独奏　dúzòu　(instrumental) solo: 钢琴～ piano solo

独奏会　dúzòuhuì　recital (of an instrumentalist)

读 (讀)

dú　① read; read aloud: 这部小说值

得一～。This novel is worth reading. / ～报 read the newspaper aloud / 老师～一句，同学们跟着～一句。The students read after the teacher sentence by sentence. ② attend school: ～完大学 finish college ——see also dòu

读本 dúběn reader; textbook: 汉语～ a Chinese reader

读后感 dúhòugǎn thoughts on reading sth.:《宋诗选注》～ thoughts on reading *Annotated Selection of Song Poetry*

读书 dúshū ① read; study: ～是学习，使用也是学习，而且是更重要的学习。Reading is learning, but applying is also learning and the more important kind of learning at that. / 她～很用功。She studies hard. ② attend school

读书班 dúshūbān study class

读书笔记 dúshū bǐjì reading notes

读书破万卷 dúshū pò wànjuàn have read ten thousand volumes—be well read: ～，下笔如有神。(杜甫) I have read ten thousand volumes, And it is as if I were guided by the spirits when I write.

读书人 dúshūrén *old* a scholar; an intellectual

读数 dúshù reading: 温度计～ thermometer reading / 标度～ scale reading

读图 dútú interpret blueprints; interpret drawings

读物 dúwù reading matter (*or* material): 儿童～ children's books / 通俗～ popular literature

读音 dúyīn pronunciation: 他把这个字的～忘了。He forgot the pronunciation of this word.

读者 dúzhě reader (of a book, newspaper, etc.)

读者来信 dúzhě láixìn readers' letters; letters to the editor

渎[1]（瀆、凟） dú *formal* show disrespect or contempt: 亵渎 xièdú

渎[2]（瀆） dú *formal* ditch; drain

渎职 dúzhí malfeasance; dereliction of duty

椟（櫝、匵） dú *formal* casket; case; box: 买椟还珠 mǎi dú huán zhū

犊（犢） dú calf: 初生之犊不畏虎 chū shēng zhī dú bù wèi hǔ

牍（牘） dú ① wooden tablets or slips for writing (in ancient times) ② documents; archives; correspondence: 文牍 wéndú

黩（黷） dú *formal* ① blacken; defile ② act wantonly

黩武 dúwǔ *formal* militaristic; warlike; bellicose: 穷兵黩武 qióngbīng-dúwǔ

黩武主义 dúwǔzhǔyì militarism: ～者 militarist

髑 dú see below

髑髅 dúlóu *liter.* skull (of a dead person)

dǔ

肚 dǔ tripe: 拌～丝儿 slices of pork tripe and cucumber in soy sauce ——see also dù

肚子 dǔzi tripe ——see also dùzi

笃 dǔ ① sincere; earnest: 感情弥～ have an ever deeper affection for each other; be more passionately attached to each other ② (of an illness) serious; critical: 病笃 bìngdǔ

笃定 dǔdìng *dial.* ① sure; certain ② calm and unhurried; leisurely

笃厚 dǔhòu sincere and magnanimous

笃实 dǔshí ① honest and sincere ② solid; sound: 学问～ sound scholarship

笃信 dǔxìn sincerely believe in; be a devout believer in

笃学 dǔxué diligent in study; devoted to study; studious

笃志 dǔzhì be steadfast in one's purpose; devote oneself to: ～学习 devote oneself to study / 博学而～ study widely and with set purpose

笃挚 dǔzhì *formal* sincere; true: 友谊～ sincere friendship

堵 dǔ ① stop up; block up: 把老鼠洞～死 stop up mouseholes / 我鼻子～了。My nose is all blocked up. / 别～着门！Don't stand in the doorway! / 黄继光舍身～枪眼。Defying death, Huang Jiguang threw himself against the embrasure of the enemy's blockhouse. ② stifled; suffocated; oppressed: 胸口～得慌 feel suffocated; feel a tightness in the chest / 心里～得难受 have a load on one's mind ③ *formal* wall: 观者如～。There was a crowd of spectators. ④ *m.* 一～墙 a wall

堵挡 dǔdǎng stop up; block up

堵击 dǔjī intercept and attack: ～逃敌 intercept the fleeing enemy

堵截 dǔjié intercept: ～不明国籍的飞机 intercept an unidentified airplane

堵塞 dǔsè stop up; block up: 交通～ traffic jam / ～漏洞 stop up a loophole; plug a hole

堵嘴 dǔzuǐ gag sb.; silence sb.: 你别想堵住我的嘴。You can't stop me from speaking out.

赌 dǔ ① gamble: ～了个通宵 gamble all night ② bet: 打赌 dǎdǔ

赌本 dǔběn ① money to gamble with ② resources for risky ventures

赌博 dǔbó gambling

赌场 dǔchǎng gambling house

赌东道 dǔ dōngdào (also 赌东儿 dǔdōngr) bet on sth. for which the loser has to stand treat

赌棍 dǔgùn hardened (*or* professional) gambler

赌局 dǔjú gambling party; gambling joint

赌具 dǔjù gambling paraphernalia; gambling device

赌窟 dǔkū gambling-den

赌气 dǔqì feel wronged and act rashly: 他觉得受了委屈，一～就走了。Feeling he had been wronged, he went off in a fit of pique.

赌钱 dǔqián gamble

赌誓 dǔshì vow; pledge; swear

赌徒 dǔtú gambler

赌咒 dǔzhòu take an oath; swear

赌注 dǔzhù stake

睹（覩） dǔ see: 目睹 mùdǔ

睹物思人 dǔ wù sī rén seeing the thing one thinks of the person—the thing reminds one of its owner

dù

杜[1] dù ① birch-leaf pear ② (Dù) a surname

杜[2]（斁） dù shut out; stop; prevent: 以～流弊 so as to put an end to abuses

杜蘅 dùhéng (also 杜衡 dùhéng) *bot.* wild ginger

杜渐防微 dùjiàn-fángwēi same as 防微杜渐 fángwēi-dùjiàn

杜鹃[1] dùjuān *zool.* cuckoo

杜鹃[2] dùjuān *bot.* azalea

杜绝 dùjué stop; put an end to: ～弊端 stop all corrupt practices／～浪费 put an end to waste

杜康 dùkāng *liter.* wine: 何以解忧，惟有～。(曹操) Sorrows naught allays, Save the cup, since ancient days.

杜口裹足 dùkǒu-guǒzú speechless and motionless with fear

杜梨 dùlí birch-leaf pear

杜门谢客 dù mén xiè kè close one's door to visitors; live in seclusion

杜灭芬 dùmièfēn *pharm.* domiphen

杜塞 dùsè stop up; block up: ～言路 stifle criticisms and suggestions

杜松子酒 dùsōngzijiǔ gin

杜宇 dùyǔ *zool.* cuckoo

杜仲 dùzhòng *Chin. med.* the bark of eucommia (*Eucommia ulmoides*)

杜仲胶 dùzhòngjiāo gutta-percha

杜撰 dùzhuàn fabricate; make up: 他讲的是真有其事，不是～的。 The story he told is true, not made up.

肚 dù belly; abdomen; stomach ——see also dǔ

肚肠 dùcháng ① intestines and stomach; stomach: 饿～ go hungry ② heart: 热心热～ warm-hearted

肚带 dùdài bellyband; girth

肚量 dùliàng same as 度量 dùliàng

肚皮 dùpí *dial.* belly

肚脐 dùqí (also 肚脐眼儿 dùqíyǎnr) navel; belly button

肚子 dùzi ① belly; abdomen: ～疼 have a stomachache; suffer from abdominal pain／笑得～疼 laugh till one's sides split／一～气 absolutely exasperated; full of pent-up anger ② a belly-shaped thing: 腿肚子 tuǐdùzi ——see also dǔzi

妒(妬) dù be jealous (*or* envious) of; envy: 同行相～ professional jealousy

妒火中烧 dùhuǒ zhōng shāo be burning with jealousy

妒忌 dùjì be jealous (*or* envious) of; envy

妒贤嫉能 dùxián-jínéng be jealous of the worthy and the able

度 dù ① linear measure: 度量衡 dùliànghéng ② degree of intensity: 硬度 yìngdù／湿度 shīdù ③ a unit of measurement for angles, temperature, etc.; degree: 直角为九十～。 A right angle is an angle of 90 degrees.／北纬三十八～ latitude 38° N.／水的沸点是摄氏一百～。 The boiling point of water is 100 degrees centigrade.／这种酒五十～。 This spirit contains 50 per cent alcohol.／您的眼镜多少～? What's the strength of the lenses of your glasses? ④ *elec.* kilowatt-hour (kwh) ⑤ limit; extent; degree: 将玻璃管加热，以能弯曲为～。 Heat the glass tube to the point that it can bend. ⑥ tolerance; magnanimity: 度量 dùliàng ⑦ consideration: 置之度外 zhì zhī dù wài ⑧ *m.* occasion; time: 一年一～ once a year ⑨ spend; pass: 在农村～过童年 spend one's childhood in the countryside ⑩ (of Buddhist monks or nuns, or Taoist priests) preach; try to convert ——see also duó

度牒 dùdié (formerly for Buddhist monks) clerical certificate; ordination diploma

度荒 dùhuāng tide over a lean year

度假 dùjià spend one's holidays (*or* vacation); go vacationing

度冷丁 dùlěngdīng *pharm.* dolantin

度量 dùliàng tolerance; magnanimity: ～大 broadminded; magnanimous／～小 narrow-minded

度量衡 dùliànghéng length, capacity and weight; weights and measures

度量衡学 dùliànghéngxué metrology

度命 dùmìng drag out a miserable existence: 靠糠菜～ manage to keep oneself alive with bran and wild herbs

度曲 dùqǔ *formal* ① write music; compose ② sing according to the music score

度日 dùrì subsist (in hardship); eke out an existence: 过去他靠什么～的? What did he do for a living in the old days?

度日如年 dùrì rú nián one day seems like a year; the days drag on like years

度数 dùshu number of degrees; reading: 那个表上的～是多少? What does that meter read?

渡 dù ① cross (a river, the sea, etc.): ～河 cross a river／飞～太平洋 fly (across) the Pacific ② tide over; pull through: ～过难关 tide over a difficulty; pull through ③ ferry (people, goods, etc.) across ④ (usu. used as part of a place name) ferry crossing: 深～ Shendu (in Anhui Province) ——

渡槽 dùcáo aqueduct

渡场 dùchǎng *mil.* crossing site

渡船 dùchuán ferryboat; ferry

渡河点 dùhédiǎn point of crossing

渡口 dùkǒu ferry crossing

渡轮 dùlún ferry steamer; ferryboat

渡头 dùtóu same as 渡口 dùkǒu

渡鸦 dùyā *zool.* raven

渡越 dùyuè get over; surmount: ～险阻 get over dangers and difficulties

镀 dù plating: ～镍 nickel-plating／～铝钢 aluminium-plated steel

镀金 dùjīn ① gold-plating; gilding ② get gilded (formerly said of students who went abroad to study in order to enhance their social status)

镀锡 dùxī tin-plating; tinning

镀锡铁 dùxītiě tinplate

镀锌 dùxīn zinc-plating; galvanizing

镀锌铁 dùxīntiě galvanized iron

镀银 dùyín silver-plating; silvering

蠹(蠧、螙、蠧) dù ① a kind of insect that eats into books, clothing, etc.; moth: 书～ bookworm ② moth-eaten; worm-eaten: 流水不腐，户枢不蠹 liúshuǐ bù fǔ, hùshū bù dù

蠹弊 dùbì *formal* malpractice; abuse; corrupt practice

蠹虫 dùchóng ① a kind of insect that eats into books, clothing, etc.; moth ② a harmful person; vermin

蠹害 dùhài harm; endanger: ～人民 do great harm to the people

蠹鱼 dùyú silverfish; fish moth

蠹蚀 dùzhù be moth-eaten; be worm-eaten

duān

端[1] duān ① end; extremity: 两～ both ends／岛的南～ the southern tip (*or* end) of the island ② beginning: 开端 kāiduān ③ point; item: 举其一～ for instance; just to mention one example ④ reason; cause: 无端 wúduān／借端 jièduān

端[2] duān ① upright; proper: ～坐 sit up straight ② hold sth. level with both hands; carry: ～盘子 carry a tray／～饭上菜 serve a meal／～进两杯茶来 bring in two cups of tea／给病人～大小便 carry bedpans for

the patients / 有什么想法都～出来。 Whatever you think, come out with it.

端底 duǎndǐ ① actually; exactly: 你～要啥呢? What exactly do you want? ② the bottom of a matter; the ins and outs: 查明事情～ get to the bottom of the matter

端的 duǎndì *old* ① actually; exactly: 这人～是谁? Who actually is this man? ② as expected; sure enough; really; truly: ～是好! Truly remarkable! ③ the bottom of a matter; the ins and outs: 我一问起, 方知～。 I asked and then got to know what it was all about.

端方 duǎnfāng *formal* proper; correct: 她品格～, 容貌美丽。 She is a proper, charming young lady.

端架子 duǎn jiàzi *dial.* put on airs

端节 Duǎnjié same as 端午节 Duǎnwǔjié

端丽 duǎnlì comely; graceful: 姿容～ have comely features / 字体～ write a graceful hand

端量 duǎnliang look sb. up and down

端木 Duānmù a two-character surname

端倪 duānní ① clue; inkling: 略有～ have an inkling of the matter ② predict: 千变万化, 不可～。 Things are constantly changing and unpredictable.

端平 duǎnpíng ① fair; just; impartial ② hold sth. level with both hands

端日 duǎnrì *formal* the first day of the lunar year; the Lunar New Year's Day

端视 duǎnshì look closely: ～良久 look closely for quite a while

端午节 Duānwǔjié the Dragon Boat Festival (the 5th day of the 5th lunar month)

端线 duǎnxiàn *sports* end line

端详 duǎnxiáng ① details: 细说～ give a full and detailed account; give full particulars ② dignified and serene: 举止～ behave with serene dignity

端详 duǎnxiang look sb. up and down: 我～了半天, 才认出来她是小张。 I looked her over for a long time before I recognized her as Xiao Zhang.

端绪 duǎnxù inkling; clue: 我们谈了半天, 仍然毫无～。 We talked the matter over for quite some time but didn't get anywhere.

端砚 duǎnyàn a kind of high-quality ink-slab made in Duanxi (端溪), Guangdong Province

端阳 Duānyáng same as 端午节 Duānwǔjié

端月 duǎnyuè *formal* the first lunar month; the first moon

端正 duǎnzhèng ① upright; regular: 五官～ have regular features / 把画像端端正正地挂起来 hang the portrait straight ② proper; correct: 品行～ having good conduct; well-behaved ③ rectify; correct: ～思想 correct one's thinking; straighten out one's ideas / ～学习态度 take a correct attitude towards study

端庄 duǎnzhuāng dignified; sedate

duǎn

短 duǎn ① short; brief: 她头发剪得～～的。 She had her hair cut short. / 这条路最～。 This is the shortest way. / 冬季日～夜长。 In winter the days are short and the nights long. / 我给他写了封～信。 I dropped him a few lines. / 开个～会 have a brief meeting ② lack; owe: 一个月～两天 two days short of a month; a month less two days / 别人都来了, 就～他一个。 All the others are here; he's the only one missing. / ～你三块钱。 I owe you three *yuan*. ③ weak point; fault: 揭短 jiēduǎn

短兵相接 duǎnbīng xiāng jiē fight at close quarters; en-

gage in hand-to-hand fighting (*or* close combat)

短波 duǎnbō shortwave

短不了 duǎnbuliǎo ① cannot do without: 人～水。 Man cannot do without water. ② cannot avoid; have to: 以后～还要请你帮忙。 Most likely I'll have to ask you for help again.

短长 duǎn-cháng ① strong and weak points; good points and shortcomings: 识其～而量才使用 know his strong and weak points and give him work suited to his abilities ② good and bad; right and wrong: 议论别人的～ gossip about people / 不争一日之～ not strive for temporary superiority ③ accident; mishap: 如妈有个～, 速来电。 If anything should happen to Mother, cable me at once.

短程 duǎnchéng short distance; short range

短秤 duǎnchèng give short weight: 那家铺子卖货经常～。 They give short weights in that store.

短绌 duǎnchù fall short; be short of: 现金～。 There is a shortage of cash. / 他们劳力～。 They are short of hands.

短处 duǎnchu shortcoming; failing; fault; weakness

短传 duǎnchuán *sports* short pass

短促 duǎncù of very short duration; very brief: 呼吸～ be short of breath; gasp; pant / 舒伯特～的一生里, 六百多首歌曲从他的笔端流泻出来。 During Schubert's brief life, more than 600 songs poured from his pen.

短打 duǎndǎ ① *theat.* hand-to-hand fight in tights ② same as 短装 duǎnzhuāng

短大衣 duǎndàyī short overcoat; car coat

短笛 duǎndí *mus.* piccolo

短吨 duǎndūn short ton

短工 duǎngōng casual labourer; seasonal labourer

短骨 duǎngǔ *physiol.* short bone

短号 duǎnhào *mus.* cornet

短见 duǎnjiàn ① shortsighted view ② suicide: 自寻～ attempt suicide; commit suicide

短角牛 duǎnjiǎoniú shorthorn

短斤缺两 duǎnjīn-quēliǎng same as 缺斤短两 quējīn-duǎnliǎng

短距离 duǎnjùlí short distance

短距离赛跑 duǎnjùlí sàipǎo short-distance run; dash; sprint

短裤 duǎnkù shorts

短路 duǎnlù ① *elec.* short circuit ② *dial.* waylay; hold up

短命 duǎnmìng die young; be short-lived: ～的军阀政权 a short-lived warlord regime

短跑 duǎnpǎo short-distance run; dash; sprint: ～运动员 dash man; sprinter

短篇小说 duǎnpiān xiǎoshuō short story

短片 duǎnpiàn short film; short

短评 duǎnpíng short commentary; brief comment

短期 duǎnqī short-term: 在～内 in a short time; in a brief space of time / ～贷款 short-term loan / ～轮训 short-term training in rotation / ～周转资金 short-term revolving fund

短气 duǎnqì lose heart; get discouraged; be disheartened

短浅 duǎnqiǎn narrow and shallow: 见识～ lacking knowledge and experience; shallow

短欠 duǎnqiàn ① owe; be in arrears ② be short of

短枪 duǎnqiāng short arm; handgun

短球 duǎnqiú (in tennis, etc.) short ball; drop shot

短拳 duǎnquán the short jab (a style of Chinese boxing)

短缺 duǎnquē shortage: ～产品 products in short supply / 资金～ short of funds

短日照植物 duǎnrìzhào zhíwù short-day plant

短衫 duǎnshān a short Chinese-style unlined garment;

a short gown

短少 duǎnshǎo deficient; short; missing: ～一页。There is one page missing. / 你们需要的钢材我们保证供应，一吨也不～。We guarantee to supply the steel you need, and not fall short by a single ton.

短时记忆 duǎnshí jìyì *psychol.* short-term memory

短视 duǎnshì ① nearsightedness; myopia ② lack foresight; be shortsighted

短寿 duǎnshòu be short-lived; die young

短统靴 duǎntǒngxuē ankle boots

短途 duǎntú short distance: ～运输 short-distance transport; short haul

短袜 duǎnwà socks

短尾猴 duǎnwěihóu stump-tailed macaque (or monkey)

短纤维 duǎnxiānwéi ① short-staple: ～棉花 short-staple cotton ② *text.* staple (fibre): ～切断器 staple cutter

短线 duǎnxiàn (of products) be in short supply; be in pressing demand: ～产品 products in short supply

短小 duǎnxiǎo short and small; short; small: 身材～ of small stature / ～的序幕 a brief prologue

短小精悍 duǎnxiǎo jīnghàn ① not of imposing stature but strong and capable ② (of a piece of writing) short and pithy; terse and forceful

短讯 duǎnxùn news in brief; brief dispatch

短训班 duǎnxùnbān short-term training course

短语 duǎnyǔ *gram.* phrase

短元音 duǎnyuányīn *phonet.* short vowel

短暂 duǎnzàn of short duration; transient; brief: 她的一生是～而光荣的一生。Her life was short but glorious.

短装 duǎnzhuāng be dressed in a Chinese-style jacket and trousers

duàn

段 duàn ① *m.* section; segment; part: 一～铁路 a section of railway / 一～衣料 a length of dress material / 这一～历史 this phase of history / 一～时间 a period of time / 边界东～ the eastern sector of the boundary ② paragraph; passage: 另起一～ start a new paragraph / 这是钢琴五重奏《鳟鱼》里我最喜欢的一～。That is my favourite passage from the piano quintet, *The Trout*. ③ (Duàn) a surname

段落 duànluò ① paragraph: 这篇文章～清楚。This article is well paragraphed. ② phase; stage: 第一期工程已经告一～。The first phase of the project has been completed.

断¹（斷） duàn ① break; snap: 喀嚓一声，～成两截 break in two with a snap / 他给小提琴调弦的时候，E 弦～了。When he was tuning his violin, the E string snapped. ② break off; cut off; stop: ～水 cut off the water supply / ～敌退路 cut off the enemy's retreat / 与指挥部的联系～了 lose contact with headquarters ③ give up; abstain from: ～烟 give up (or quit) smoking

断²（斷） duàn ① judge; decide: 诊断 zhěnduàn ② *adv. formal* (usu. used in the negative) absolutely; decidedly: ～不可信 absolutely incredible / ～无此理 absolutely untenable (or unreasonable); the height of absurdity

断案 duàn'àn ① settle a lawsuit ② *log.* conclusion (of a syllogism)

断壁 duànbì ① dilapidated walls: 残垣断壁 cányuán-duànbì ② cliff; precipice; steep

断编残简 duànbiān-cánjiǎn (also 断简残编 duànjiǎn-cánbiān) stray fragments of text

断层 duàncéng *geol.* fault: 倾向（走向）～ dip (strike) fault / ～带 fault zone /～面 fault plane / ～作用 faulting

断层地震 duàncéng dìzhèn *geol.* fault earthquake

断层湖 duàncénghú *geol.* fault lake

断层山 duàncéngshān *geol.* fault mountain

断肠 duàncháng heartbroken

断炊 duànchuī run out of rice and fuel; can't keep the pot boiling; go hungry

断代 duàndài division of history into periods: 文学史的～研究 the study of the history of literature by period

断代史 duàndàishǐ dynastic history

断档 duàndàng be out of stock; be sold out

断定 duàndìng conclude; form a judgment; decide; determine: 我们有理由可以～，会议推迟了。We may reasonably conclude that the meeting has been postponed. / 他一～机器出了毛病了。He came to the conclusion that the machine was out of order.

断断 duànduàn *adv.* (usu. used in the negative) absolutely: ～使不得。That will never do. or That simply won't do.

断断续续 duànduàn-xùxù off and on; intermittently: ～读过四年书 had four years of schooling off and on / ～地说 speak haltingly

断顿 duàndùn can't afford the next meal; go hungry

断根 duàngēn ① be completely cured; effect a permanent cure ② have no heir; have no progeny

断后 duànhòu ① *old* bring up the rear; cover a retreat ② have no progeny

断乎 duànhū *adv.* (usu. used in the negative) absolutely: ～不可 absolutely impermissible

断魂 duànhún be overwhelmed with sorrow: 清明时节雨纷纷，路上行人欲～。(杜牧) The rain falls thick and fast on All Souls' festive day, The men and women sadly move along the way.

断交 duànjiāo ① break off a friendship ② sever (or break off) diplomatic relations

断井颓垣 duànjǐng-tuíyuán dilapidated wells and crumbling walls—a scene of devastation

断句 duànjù ① make pauses in reading unpunctuated ancient writings ② punctuate

断绝 duànjué break off; cut off; sever: ～外交关系 sever (or break off) diplomatic relations / ～交通 stop traffic

断绝地 duànjuédì *mil.* broken terrain (or ground)

断口 duànkǒu *geol.* fracture

断粮 duànliáng run out of grain (or food)

断裂 duànliè ① split; crack ② *geol.* rift

断流器 duànliúqì *elec.* cutout: 安全～ safety cutout

断路 duànlù *elec.* ① open circuit; broken circuit：～器 circuit breaker ② waylay; hold up: 一伙武装匪徒拦劫旅客的钱财。A band of armed bandits held up the passengers and took all their money.

断面 duànmiàn *surveying & drawing* section: ～图 sectional drawing; section

断奶 duànnǎi (also 断乳 duànrǔ) wean: 给孩子～ wean a child / 宝宝已经断了奶，改吃固体食物了。The baby has been weaned on to solid foods.

断念 duànniàn give up all hope; abandon oneself to despair: 他在一切都已～的情况下走上自杀的绝路。In utter despair he committed suicide.

断片 duànpiàn part; passage; extract; fragment

断七 duànqī hold a service on the 49th day after sb.'s death

断气 duànqì ① breathe one's last; die ② cut off the gas

断然 duànrán ① resolute; drastic: 采取～措施 take drastic measures ② *adv.* absolutely; flatly; categorically: ～不能接受 absolutely inacceptable / ～拒绝 flatly refuse / ～否认 categorically deny

断送 duànsòng forfeit (one's life, future, etc.); ruin: 这件丑闻～了他的前程。The scandal ruined his career.

断头 duàntóu *text.* ① broken end ② end breaking: ～率 end breaking rate

断头台 duàntóutái guillotine

断尾 duànwěi *animal husbandry* docking

断弦 duànxián snap the lute string—lose one's wife

断线 duànxiàn ① a string being broken: 啊唷, 风筝～啦! Oh, the (kite's) string is broken! ② disconnect; sever; break off: 有的学科后继乏人, 面临～的危险。Certain disciplines lack successors and face the danger of being discontinued.

断线风筝 duànxiàn fēngzheng a kite with a broken string—gone beyond recall

断言 duànyán say (*or* state) with certainty; assert categorically; affirm

断语 duànyǔ conclusion; judgment: 遽下～ jump to conclusions

断狱 duànyù *old* try a case in court; hear and pass judgment on a case

断垣残壁 duànyuán-cánbì (also 断壁颓垣 duànbì-tuíyuán) dilapidated walls—a desolate scene

断章取义 duàn zhāng qǔ yì quote out of context; garble a statement, etc.

断肢再植 duànzhī zàizhí *med.* replantation of a severed limb

断子绝孙 duànzǐ-juésūn *offens.* may you die sonless (*or* without sons); may you be the last of your line

断奏 duànzòu *mus.* staccato

缎
duàn satin: 绸缎 chóuduàn

缎纹 duànwén satin weave

缎子 duànzi satin

煅
duàn ① forge: ～铁 forge iron ② calcine

煅烧 duànshāo calcine

煅石膏 duànshígāo another name for 熟石膏 shúshígāo

椴
duàn *bot.* (Chinese) linden

锻
duàn forge

锻锤 duànchuí forging hammer

锻工 duàngōng ① forging: ～车间 forging shop; forge ② forger; blacksmith

锻工钳 duàngōngqián band jaw tongs

锻件 duànjiàn forging

锻接 duànjiē forge welding

锻炼 duànliàn ① take exercise; have physical training: 每天～半小时 take half an hour's exercise every day/ ～身体, 保卫祖国 build up a good physique to defend the country / 在大江大海中游泳, 既可以～身体, 又可以～意志。Swimming in big rivers and seas helps to build up both physical strength and willpower. ② temper; steel; toughen: 劳动～ temper oneself through manual labour

锻炉 duànlú forge

锻模 duànmú forging die

锻铁 duàntiě ① wrought iron ② forge iron

锻压 duànyā forging and pressing

锻压机 duànyājī forging press

锻冶 duànyě forging and smelting

锻造 duànzào forging; smithing: 压力～ press forging

籪 (籪)
duàn bamboo weir (for catching fish, etc.)

duī

堆
duī ① pile up; heap up; stack: 把麦秸～在场上 stack the wheat-stalks on the threshing ground / 桌上～满了书。The desk was piled with books. / 粮食～满仓, 果子～成山。Storehouses are bursting with grain, and fruit is piled high on the ground. / 他把盒子～在桌子上。He piled the boxes on the table. ② heap; pile; stack: 柴火～ a pile (*or* stack) of firewood / 土～ mound / 草～ haystack ③ *m.* heap; pile; crowd: 一～垃圾 a garbage (*or* rubbish) heap / 一～人 a crowd of people ④ (used as part of a place name) hillock; mound: 双～集 Shuangduiji (in Anhui Province)

堆存 duīcún store up

堆垛机 duīduòjī (hay) stacker

堆放 duīfàng pile up; stack: 库房里～着许多农具。A lot of farm tools are piled in the storehouse.

堆房 duīfáng storeroom

堆肥 duīféi *agric.* compost

堆积 duījī ① pile up; heap up: 工地上建筑材料～如山。Building materials are piled up mountain-high on the construction site. ② *geol.* accumulation

堆金积玉 duījīn-jīyù piles of gold and jade—a vast fortune

堆聚 duījù pile up; heap up: ～成山 be piled up mountain-high

堆垒数论 duīlěishùlùn *math.* additive theory of numbers

堆漆 duīqī *arts & crafts* embossed lacquer

堆砌 duīqì ① pile up (hewn rocks, etc. to build sth.) ② load one's writing with fancy phrases: ～辞藻 string together ornate phrases

堆石坝 duīshíbà *water conservancy* rock-fill dam

堆笑 duīxiào put on a smile: 满脸～ face wreathed in smiles; smiling from ear to ear

堆栈 duīzhàn storehouse; warehouse

duì

队 (隊)
duì ① a row of people; line: 排成两～ fall into two lines ② team; group: 篮球～ basketball team ③ (short for 少年先锋队) Young Pioneers: 队日 duìrì ④ *m.*: 一～战士 a file of soldiers

队部 duìbù the office or headquarters of a team, etc.: 勘探队～ the prospecting team headquarters

队礼 duìlǐ Young Pioneer's salute

队列 duìliè formation: ～教练 (military) drill; formation drill

队旗 duìqí *sports* team pennant: 互赠～ exchange team pennants

队日 duìrì Young Pioneer's Day (a day of collective activity for Young Pioneers)

队伍 duìwu ① troops: ～就要出发了。The troops are about to set out. ② ranks; contingent: 游行～ contingents of marchers; procession; parade /革命～ the revolutionary ranks; battalions of the revolution / 马克思主义理论～ a contingent of Marxist theoretical workers

队形 duìxíng formation: 成战斗～ in battle formation / 以密集(散开)～前进 advance in close (open) order

队形变换 duìxíng biànhuàn evolutions (of troops, dancers, etc.)

队员 duìyuán team member

队长 duìzhǎng ① *sports* captain: 排球队～ the captain of a volleyball team ② team leader: 生产队～ pro-

duction team leader

对 (對)

duì ① answer; reply: 无言以～ have nothing to say in reply ② treat; cope with; counter: 刀～刀，枪～枪 sword against sword and spear against spear / 上海队～北京队 the Shanghai team versus the Beijing team ③ be trained on; be directed at: 枪口～着敌人 train the gun on the enemy / 她的话不是～着你的。What she said was not directed at you. ④ mutual; face to face: ～骂 call each other names / ～坐 sit facing each other / ～饮 (two people) have a drink together ⑤ opposite; opposing: ～岸 the opposite bank; the other side of the river ⑥ bring (two things) into contact; fit one into the other: ～暗号 exchange code words / 这个榫头～不上。This tenon won't fit. ⑦ suit; agree; get along: ～心眼儿 suit one down to the ground / ～胃口 suit one's taste ⑧ compare; check; identify: ～笔迹 identify the handwriting / ～号码 check numbers ⑨ set; adjust: ～表 set one's watch; synchronize watches / ～好望远镜的距离 adjust the focus of a telescope ⑩ right; correct: 猜～了 guess right / 这事你做得～。You did the right thing. / 你说得很～。What you say is quite true. / ～，就这么办。All right, just go ahead. / 他今天神色不～。He doesn't look himself today. ⑪ mix; add: 茶太浓了，给我～点儿水。Add some water to the tea, it's too strong for me. ⑫ divide into halves: ～股劈 go halves; split fifty-fifty ⑬ antithetical couplet; couplet: 喜～ wedding couplet ⑭ m. pair; couple: 一～花瓶 a pair of vases / 一～夫妇 a married couple ⑮ prep. with regard to; concerning; to: ～敌狠，～己和 ruthless to the enemy, kind to one's comrades / ～这个问题的不同意见 different views on this question / ～青少年的教育工作 educational work among young people / ～无产阶级革命事业的必胜信念 a firm belief in the ultimate triumph of the proletarian revolution / ～犯罪分子实行法律制裁 carry out legal sanctions against criminals / ～健康不利 be bad for one's health /他～他父亲很尊敬。He has a great respect for his father. / 这录音机～我来说是够好的了。This recorder is good enough for me.

对氨水杨酸钠 duì'ān shuǐyángsuānnà pharm. sodium para-aminosalicylate (PASNa)

对案 duì'àn diplomacy counterproposal

对白 duìbái dialogue

对半 duìbàn ① half-and-half; fifty-fifty: ～儿分 divide half-and-half; go halves ② double: ～儿利 a double profit

对比 duìbǐ ① contrast; balance: 今昔～ contrast the present with the past / 构成鲜明的～ form a sharp contrast / 阶级力量的～ the balance of class forces / 敌我力量的～ the relative strength of the enemy forces and our own / 如果你把马克思和黑格尔的著作～一下，你就会发现有很大的差别。If you compare Marx's work with Hegel's you'll find many differences. ② ratio: 双方人数～是一对四。The ratio between the two sides (or parties) is one to four.

对比剂 duìbǐjì med. contrast medium

对簿 duìbù formal face a charge: ～公堂 be interrogated in court

对不起 duìbuqǐ (also 对不住 duìbuzhù) ① pol. I'm sorry; sorry; excuse me; pardon me; I beg your pardon: ～，给你添麻烦了。Sorry to have given you so much trouble. / ～，是我的错。Pardon me. It was my fault. / ～，我得走了。Excuse me, but I'll have to go now. / ～，请你再讲一遍好吗? I beg your pardon, but would you repeat what you said? or I beg your pardon? ② let sb. down; be unworthy of; do a disservice to; be unfair to: 球队输了球，大伙儿觉得～教练。The team lost and felt they had let the coach down. / 他～她，本来答应跟她结婚，后来又把她甩了。He wronged her by first promising to marry her and then leaving her.

对策 duìcè the way to deal with a situation; countermeasure; countermove

对策论 duìcèlùn math. game theory

对茬儿 duìchár dial. tally; agree: 他们两人说的话对不上茬儿。The two stories they told didn't tally.

对唱 duìchàng musical dialogue in antiphonal style; antiphonal singing

对称 duìchèn symmetry

对答 duìdá answer; reply: ～不上来 can't answer the question

对答如流 duìdá rú liú answer fluently; answer questions without hesitation

对待 duìdài treat; approach; handle: ～同志象春天般的温暖 treat one's comrades with the warmth of spring / 用无产阶级观点～一切问题 approach all problems from the proletarian point of view /正确地～群众 adopt a correct attitude towards the masses

对得起 duìdeqǐ (also 对得住 duìdezhù) not let sb. down; treat sb. fairly; be worthy of : 你要我做的事情我都做了。我总算～你了。I've done everything you asked me to do. I didn't let you down in the least.

对等 duìděng reciprocity; equity: 在～的基础上 on the basis of reciprocity; on a reciprocal basis

对调 duìdiào exchange; swop: ～工作 exchange jobs / ～座位 exchange (or swop) seats

对顶角 duìdǐngjiǎo math. vertical angles

对方 duìfāng the other (or opposite) side; the other party

对付 duìfu ① deal with; cope with; counter; tackle: 那人好～。That man is easy to deal with. / 用人民战争～侵略战争 counter a war of aggression with people's war / 他只学了几个月的文化，写信也能～了。He has had only a few months' schooling, but he can manage to write a letter. ② make do: 这把锹你先～着用吧。Try to make do with this spade for now.

对歌 duìgē singing in antiphonal style

对光 duìguāng photog. set (or focus) a camera: 自动～ automatic focusing / 对好光再拍照。Focus the camera before you take the picture.

对过 duìguò opposite; across the way: 他就住在～。He lives just across the way. / 我家～就是邮局。The post office is just opposite my house.

对号[1] duìhào ① check the number: ～入座 take one's seat according to the number on the ticket; sit in the right seat ② fit; tally: 这张图纸有几个数据对不上号。There are a few figures on this blueprint that don't tally. / 他说的和做的不～。His deeds don't match his words.

对号[2] duìhào check mark (✓); tick

对话 duìhuà dialogue: 两国政府已开始～。The two governments have opened a dialogue. / 南北～ North-South dialogue

对换 duìhuàn change or exchange

对火 duìhuǒ use sb.'s lighted cigarette to light one's own: 对个火儿。Give me a light, please.

对角线 duìjiǎoxiàn math. diagonal (line)

对接 duìjiē space dock

对接焊 duìjiēhàn mech. butt welding

对襟 duìjīn a kind of Chinese-style jacket with buttons down the front

对劲儿 duìjìnr ① be to one's liking; suit one: 这把锄我使着很～。This hoe suits me very well. ② normal; right: 这件事我越想越觉得不～。The more I think of it, the more I'm convinced there's something fishy about it. ③ get along (well): 他们俩一向很～。The two of them have always got along very well.

对进突击 duìjìn tūjī mil. two-pronged assault from

opposite directions

对酒当歌 duì jiǔ dāng gē cup to cup calls for song: 〜，人生几何?譬如朝露, 去日苦多。(曹操) Cup to cup calls for song. Man's life—how long? A morning's dew? Alas! Many a day is done.

对局 duìjú play a game of chess, etc.: 我跟他对了一局, 输了。I played a game of chess with him and lost.

对开 duìkāi ① (of trains, buses or ships) run from opposite directions ② divide into two halves; go fifty-fifty ③ *print.* folio

对抗 duìkàng ① antagonism; confrontation: 阶级〜 class antagonism / 两国之间的〜 confrontation between two states ② resist; oppose

对抗赛 duìkàngsài *sports* dual meet

对抗性 duìkàngxìng antagonism

对抗性矛盾 duìkàngxìng máodùn antagonistic contradiction

对空监视哨 duìkōng jiānshìshào antiaircraft lookout (or scout); ground observer; aircraft spotter

对空射击 duìkōng shèjī antiaircraft firing

对口 duìkǒu ① (of two performers) speak or sing alternately ② be geared to the needs of the job; fit in with one's vocational training or speciality: 〜训练 training geared to the needs of the job / 专业〜 a job suited to one's special training ③ counterpart

对口唱 duìkǒuchàng musical dialogue in antiphonal style; antiphonal singing

对口疮 duìkǒuchuāng *Chin. med.* a boil on the nape

对口词 duìkǒucí rhymed dialogue

对口会谈 duìkǒu huìtán *diplomacy* talks between representatives of similar organizations of two countries; counterpart conversations

对口赛 duìkǒusài emulation between counterpart organizations

对口相声 duìkǒu xiàngsheng cross talk; comic dialogue

对垒 duìlěi stand facing each other, ready for battle; be pitted against each other: 两军〜 two armies pitted against each other

对立 duìlì oppose; set sth. against; be antagonistic to: 消灭城乡〜 abolish the antithesis between town and country / 〜情绪 antagonism / 不要把学习和工作〜起来。Don't think of study as conflicting with work. / 把依靠群众和加强领导〜起来是错误的。It is wrong to set reliance on the masses against strengthening the leadership.

对立面 duìlìmiàn *philos.* opposite; antithesis: 矛盾着的〜 the opposites in a contradiction / 为自己树立〜 create one's own antithesis

对立统一 duìlì tǒngyī *philos.* unity of opposites: 〜规律是宇宙的根本规律。The law of the unity of opposites is the fundamental law of the universe.

对立物 duìlìwù opposite; antithesis

对联 duìlián antithetical couplet (written on scrolls, etc.)

对流 duìliú *phys.* convection

对流层 duìliúcéng *meteorol.* troposphere

对流雨 duìliúyǔ *meteorol.* convective rain

对硫磷 duìliúlín *agric.* parathion

对路 duìlù ① satisfy the need: 这种货到农村正〜。These goods are the very thing the countryside needs. ② be to one's liking; suit one: 一句话不〜, 两个人就要拌嘴。One word out of turn, the two of them would quarrel.

对门 duìmén ① (of two houses) face each other ② the building or room opposite: 照相馆〜是家餐厅。Opposite the photo studio is a restaurant.

对面 duìmiàn ① opposite: 他家就在我家〜。His house is opposite mine. ② right in front: 〜来了一位解放军。A PLA man came towards us. ③ face to face: 这事儿得

他们本人〜儿谈。They should talk about this face to face. / 他俩〜坐着。The two of them sat facing each other.

对内 duìnèi internal; domestic; at home: 〜政策 domestic (or internal) policy / 〜搞活经济 enliven the domestic economy

对牛弹琴 duì niú tánqín play the lute to a cow—address the wrong audience; talk over sb.'s head

对偶 duì'ǒu ① antithesis ——see also 对仗 duìzhàng ② *math.* dual: 〜运算 dual operations

对偶原理 duì'ǒu yuánlǐ *math.* principle of duality

对脾味 duì píwèi get along well

对瓶 duìpíng *arts & crafts* a twin vase

对日照 duìrìzhào *astron.* counterglow

对生 duìshēng *bot.* opposite: 〜叶 opposite leaf

对事不对人 duì shì bù duì rén concern oneself with facts and not with individuals (when trying to settle a question)

对手 duìshǒu ① opponent; adversary ② match; equal: 他不是你的〜。He's no match for you.

对数 duìshù *math.* logarithm: 〜函数 logarithmic function

对数表 duìshùbiǎo logarithmic table

对台戏 duìtáixì rival show: 演〜 put on a rival show ——see also 唱对台戏 chàng duìtáixì

对头 duìtóu ① correct; on the right track: 方法〜, 效率就高。When the method is correct, efficiency is high. or Good methods make for high efficiency. / 你的思想不〜。Your thinking is not on the right track. or You're not thinking along the right lines. ② (usu. used in the negative) normal; right: 你的脸色不〜。You're not looking well. ③ (usu. used in the negative) get on well; hit it off: 过去他俩不大〜, 现在却合得来了。The two didn't get along in the past but now they hit it off well.

对头 duìtou ① enemy: 死〜 sworn enemy ② opponent; adversary

对外 duìwài external; foreign: 〜工作 external work; work in the field of external relations / 〜关系 external (or foreign) relations / 〜援助 aid to foreign countries / 〜政策 external (or foreign) policy

对外开放 duìwài kāifàng (the policy of) opening to the outside world; the open policy

对外贸易 duìwài màoyì foreign trade: 〜逆差 foreign trade deficit; unfavourable balance of trade / 〜顺差 foreign trade surplus; favourable balance of trade

对位 duìwèi *mus.* counterpoint

对味儿 duìwèir ① to one's taste; tasty ② (usu. used in the negative) seem all right: 他的发言不大〜。What he said didn't sound quite right.

对虾 duìxiā prawn

对象 duìxiàng ① target; object: 革命〜 targets of the revolution / 研究〜 an object of study / 党的发展〜 a prospective Party member / 这本书的〜是中学生。This book is intended for middle school students. / 讲话或写文章要看〜。One should not speak or write without considering one's audience. ② boy or girl friend: 找〜 look for a partner in marriage ——see also 搞对象 gǎo duìxiàng

对消 duìxiāo offset; cancel each other out

对眼 duìyǎn cross-eye

对弈 duìyì (of two people) play chess

对应 duìyìng corresponding; homologous: 〜物 homologue

对应原理 duìyìng yuánlǐ *phys.* correspondence principle

对于 duìyú *prep.* with regard to; concerning; to: 〜每个具体问题要进行具体分析。We should make a concrete analysis of each specific question. / 〜他的工作我没有什么意见。I have no complaints with regard to

his work. / 她～你的建议有什么反应? How did she react to your suggestion? / ～一个革命者来说, 为人民服务就是最大的幸福。Nothing makes a revolutionary happier than serving the people. / 我～音乐没有鉴赏力。I have no ear for music.

对仗 duìzhàng (in poetry, etc.) a matching of both sound and sense in two lines, sentences, etc. usu. with the matching words in the same part of speech; antithesis

对照 duìzhào contrast; compare: 形成鲜明的～ form a sharp contrast / 用共产党员标准～检查自己 measure oneself by the standards of a Communist / ～原文修改译文 check the translation against the original and make corrections / 英汉～读本 an English-Chinese bilingual textbook

对折 duìzhé 50% discount

对着干 duìzhegàn ① do the very opposite of what sb. is doing ② try to beat sb. at what he is doing

对阵 duìzhèn ① (of two opposing armies) be poised for battle ② (of two teams) play each other

对证 duìzhèng verify; check: ～事实 verify the facts

对症下药 duì zhèng xià yào suit the medicine to the illness; suit the remedy to the case; prescribe the right remedy for an illness

对质 duìzhì confrontation (in court): 让被告与原告～ confront the accused with his accuser

对峙 duìzhì stand facing each other; confront each other: 两山～。The two mountains stand facing each other. / 武装～ military confrontation

对准 duìzhǔn ① aim at: 把枪口～敌人 aim a gun at the enemy ② mech. alignment: 轴～ shaft alignment

对酌 duìzhuó (of two people) drink together

对子 duìzi ① a pair of antithetical phrases, etc.: 对～ supply the antithesis to a given phrase, etc. ——see also 对仗 duìzhàng ② same as 对联 duìlián

兑 duì ① exchange; convert: 用纸币～黄金 convert notes into gold ② add (water, etc.): 这酒是～了水的。The wine has been watered.

兑付 duìfù cash (a cheque, etc.): ～人民币 cash a cheque, etc. in Renminbi

兑换 duìhuàn exchange; convert: 把外币～成人民币 exchange foreign money for Renminbi

兑换率 duìhuànlǜ rate of exchange (between two currencies)

兑换券 duìhuànquàn bank draft; money order ——see also 外汇兑换券 wàihuì duìhuànquàn

兑现 duìxiàn ① cash (a cheque, etc.) ② honour (a commitment, etc.); fulfil; make good: 他们的声明是不准备～的。They had no intention of carrying out what they had publicly undertaken to do. / 说话不～ not live up to one's promise; fail to make good one's promise

怼 (懟) duì formal rancour; resentment

敦 dūn
duì archaeol. grain receptacle ——see also

碓 duì a treadle-operated tilt hammer for hulling rice

dūn

吨 (噸) dūn ton (t.)

吨公里 dūngōnglǐ ton kilometre

吨海里 dūnhǎilǐ ton sea (or nautical) mile

吨时 dūnshí ton hour

吨位 dūnwèi tonnage

惇
敦 dūn sincere and honest

dūn honest; sincere: 敦请 dūnqǐng ——see also duì

敦促 dūncù urge; press: ～他早日启程 urge him to start on his journey early

敦厚 dūnhòu honest and sincere: 质朴～ simple and honest; unsophisticated

敦煌石窟 Dūnhuáng Shíkū the Dunhuang Caves, Gansu Province, dating from 366 A.D., containing Buddhist statues, frescoes, and valuable manuscripts

敦睦 dūnmù formal promote friendly relations:～邦交 promote friendly diplomatic relations between two countries

敦聘 dūnpìn formal cordially invite sb. (to serve in some capacity)

敦请 dūnqǐng cordially invite; earnestly request

敦劝 dūnquàn earnestly urge

敦实 dūnshi stocky: 他长得很～。He's stockily built. / 这个坛子真～。This jar is rather squat.

墩 dūn ① mound: 土～ mound ② a block of stone or wood: 树墩 shùdūn / 桥墩 qiáodūn ③ m. cluster: 栽稻秧三万～ transplant 30,000 clusters of rice seedlings

墩布 dūnbù mop; swab

墩子 dūnzi a block of wood or stone: 菜～ chopping block

撴 dūn dial. hold tight; seize

礅 dūn a big and heavy stone

蹲 dūn ① squat on the heels: 两人～下就聊起来了。Squatting down, the two of them started to have a chat. ② stay: 他在实验室里一～就是好几个小时。He would stay for hours at a stretch in the laboratory.

蹲班 dūnbān same as 留级 liújí

蹲班房 dūn bānfáng inf. be put in jail; be imprisoned

蹲膘 dūnbiāo (of cattle, etc.) fatten in the shed

蹲点 dūndiǎn (of cadres) stay at a selected grass-roots unit to help improve its work and gain firsthand experience for guiding overall work: 县委书记到一个村～去了。The county Party secretary has gone to stay in a village to gain firsthand experience.

蹲伏 dūnfú squat; crouch

蹲坑 dūnkēng ① squat over a pit to relieve oneself ② latrine pit

蹲苗 dūnmiáo agric. restrain the growth of seedlings (for root development)

dǔn

不 dǔn see below

不子 dǔnzi dial. ① a block of wood or stone ② a brick of porcelain clay

盹 dǔn short light sleep; doze: 打盹儿 dǎdǔnr

趸 (躉) dǔn ① wholesale: 趸批 dǔnpī ② buy wholesale: ～货 buy goods wholesale

趸船 dǔnchuán landing stage; pontoon

趸买 dǔnmǎi buy wholesale

趸卖 dǔnmài (also 趸售 dǔnshòu) sell wholesale

趸批 dǔnpī wholesale: ～买进(卖出) buy (sell)

wholesale

dùn

沌 dùn see 混沌 hùndùn

囤 dùn a grain bin——see also tún

炖 (燉) dùn ① stew: ～一只鸡 stew a chicken ② warm sth. by putting the container in hot water: ～酒 warm (up) wine

砘 dùn ram the loose soil with a stone-roller after sowing

盾 dùn shield
盾牌 dùnpái ① shield ② pretext; excuse

钝 dùn ① blunt; dull: 刀～了。The knife is blunt. ② stupid; dull-witted: 迟钝 chídùn
钝化 dùnhuà *chem.* passivation; inactivation: ～剂 passivator
钝角 dùnjiǎo *math.* obtuse angle: ～三角形 obtuse triangle
钝性物质 dùnxìng wùzhì *chem.* inactive substance
钝滞 dùnzhì blunt; dull: ～的眼光 dull eyes; lacklustre eyes

顿[1] dùn ① pause: 他～了一下，又接着往下说。After a short pause, he went on. ② (in Chinese calligraphy) pause in writing in order to reinforce the beginning or ending of a stroke ③ arrange; settle: 安顿 āndùn ④ touch the ground (with one's head) ⑤ stamp (one's foot) ⑥ *adv.* suddenly; immediately; at once: ～悟 suddenly realize the truth, etc.; attain enlightenment ⑦ *m.*: 一天三～饭 three meals a day / 说了他一～ give him a dressing down

顿[2] dùn fatigued; tired: 劳顿 láodùn
顿挫 dùncuò pause and transition in rhythm or melody: 抑扬顿挫 yìyáng-dùncuò
顿号 dùnhào a slight-pause mark used to set off items in a series (、)
顿河 Dùnhé the Don
顿开茅塞 dùn kāi máo sè suddenly see the light; be suddenly enlightened: 闻兄大教，～。Your excellent advice has opened my eyes.
顿时 dùnshí *adv.* suddenly; immediately; at once: 喜讯传来，人们～欢呼起来。People broke into cheers as soon as they heard the good news.
顿首 dùnshǒu kowtow (usu. used after the signature in old-fashioned letters)
顿足捶胸 dùnzú-chuíxiōng same as 捶胸顿足 chuíxiōng-dùnzú
顿钻钻井 dùnzuàn zuànjǐng churn drilling; percussion drilling; cable tool drilling

遁 (遯) dùn escape; flee; fly: 远～ flee to a far-away place
遁北 dùnběi *formal* lose the field and take to flight
遁词 dùncí subterfuge; quibble
遁迹 dùnjì *formal* live in seclusion
遁甲 dùnjiǎ same as 奇门 qímén
遁入空门 dùn rù kōngmén become a monk or nun

duō

多[1] duō ① many; much; more: 很～人 many people / 要办的事情很～。There are many things to attend to. / 时间紧迫，我不能～考虑。Time is running out; I can't give it much thought. / 请～～帮助。Please give me all the help you can. / 人～议论～。More people mean a greater ferment of ideas. / 他～喝了一点儿。He's had a drop too much. / 我们比原计划～打了十口井。We have sunk 10 wells more than the plan called for. / ～思。Think more. / 我在那儿～住了几天。I stayed there a few days longer. / 这样简单～了。This is much simpler. / 昨天很热，今天凉快～了。It was quite hot yesterday; today it's a lot cooler. / 病人今天好～了。The patient is much better today. ② have (a specified amount) more or too much: 这个句子～了一个字。There is one word too many in this sentence. / 班上～了三个新同学。There are three more new students in the class. / ～上两天就不成问题了。Two days more and there would be no problem. / 昨晚上结帐～出三角五分。When we made up the accounts last night, we found there was an extra 35 fen. ③ have sth. in abundance: 南方～水，利于灌溉。Irrigation is easy in the South because of the abundance of water. /这里春天～风，夏天～雨。Here we have a lot of wind in spring and a lot of rain in summer. /夏天～痢疾。There is a high incidence of dysentery in summer. ④ excessive: ～疑 oversensitive; oversuspicious; given to suspicion ⑤ over a specified amount; and more: 三个～月 more than three months; three months and more / 六十～岁 over sixty years old / 十斤～ ten *jin* and more / 十～斤 dozen or more *jin* / 一百～个人 more than 100 people / 全书一千～页。It's a book of 1,000-odd pages.

多[2] duō *adv.* ① (used in questions) to what extent: 他～大年纪了？How old is he? / 天安门有～高？How high is Tian'anmen? / ～厚的木板才能做桌面呢？How thick must a piece of wood be if it is to be made into a table top? ② (used in exclamations) to what an extent: 这天儿～闷哪！How sultry it is! / 看她～漂亮！Look how pretty she is! ③ to an unspecified extent: 有～大劲儿使～大劲儿。Put out all the strength you have. / ～复杂的算术题他都能做出来。He can do any arithmetic problem, no matter how complicated it is. / 走出不～远，他又回来了。He turned back before he had gone very far.
多儿 duōr *dial.* ① whatever amount; no matter how much: 他有～钱一下子都会花掉。No matter how much money he has, he'll spend it all in no time. ② what time; when: 你～回来的？When did you get back?
多半 duōbàn *adv.* ① the greater part; most; more often than not: 这支足球队的成员～是工人。Most of the members of this football team are workers. / 星期天他～上这儿来。He comes over on Sunday more often than not. ② most probably; very likely: 他这会儿还不来，～不来了。Since he hasn't come yet, he probably isn't coming.
多宝槅 duōbǎogé a lattice framework for curios or bric-a-brac; curio shelves
多倍体 duōbèitǐ *physiol.* polyploid: ～植物 polyploid plant
多臂机 duōbìjī *text.* dobby
多边 duōbiān multilateral: ～会谈 multilateral talks / ～贸易 multilateral trade / ～条约 multilateral treaty
多边形 duōbiānxíng *math.* polygon
多变 duōbiàn changeable; changeful; varied: ～的战术

varied tactics /山区气候～, 小心感冒。The weather in the mountains is very changeable. Be careful not to catch cold.

多才多艺 duōcái-duōyì versatile; gifted in many ways: 一位～的表演艺术家 a versatile performer

多财善贾 duō cái shàn gǔ (also 多钱善贾 duō qián shàn gǔ) see 长袖善舞 cháng xiù shàn wǔ

多产 duōchǎn ① prolific: ～作家 a prolific writer ② *med.* multiparity: ～妇 a multiparous woman

多吃多占 duōchī-duōzhàn eat or take more than one is entitled to; grab more than one's share

多愁善感 duōchóu-shàngǎn sentimental and susceptible

多此一举 duō cǐ yī jǔ make an unnecessary move: 何必～? Why take the trouble to do that?

多次 duōcì many times; time and again; repeatedly; on many occasions: 她曾～访问中国。She's visited China many times. / 他在部队里～立功。He repeatedly distinguished himself in the PLA.

多弹头 duōdàntóu multiple warhead: ～导弹 multiple warhead missile / ～分导重返大气层运载工具 multiple independently targeted reentry vehicle (MIRV)

多党 duōdǎng multi-party: 共产党领导下的～合作和协商制度 the system of multi-party cooperation and consultation under the leadership of the Communist Party

多刀切削 duōdāo qiēxiāo *mech.* multiple cut; multicut

多多益善 duōduō yì shàn the more the better

多发病 duōfābìng frequently-occurring disease

多方 duōfāng in many ways; in every way: ～设法 try all possible means; make every effort / ～协助 render all manner of help

多方面 duōfāngmiàn many-sided; in many ways: 这条水渠给农民带来的好处是～的。The canal has proved useful to the peasants in many ways.

多哥 Duōgē Togo

多哥人 Duōgērén Togolese

多功能 duōgōngnéng multi-functional; multi- (or all-) purpose: ～收录机 multi-functional tape recorder / ～、现代化的经济中心 a modern, multi-functional economic centre / ～厅 multi-purpose hall

多寡 duō-guǎ number; amount: ～不等 vary in amount or number

多管 duōguǎn *mil.* multibarrel: ～高射机关炮 pom-pom / ～火箭炮 multibarrel (rocket) launcher / ～炮 multibarreled gun

多国公司 duōguó gōngsī multinational corporation

多核苷酸 duōhégānsuān *biochem.* polynucleotide

多铧犁 duōhuálí multishare (or multifurrow) plough

多会儿 duōhuir *inf.* ① when: 你是～来的? When did you come? ② ever; at any time: 我～有空～去。I'll go there when I'm free.

多级火箭 duōjí huǒjiàn multistage rocket

多极 duōjí *elec.* multipolar: ～发电机 multipolar generator

多极化 duōjíhuà multipolarization: 世界出现了～的趋势。The world is moving towards multipolarization.

多晶硅 duōjīngguī *electron.* polycrystalline silicon

多晶体 duōjīngtǐ *phys.* polycrystal

多孔 duōkǒng porous

多孔动物 duōkǒng dòngwù porifera

多孔砖 duōkǒngzhuān porous brick; perforated brick

多口词 duōkǒucí rhymed dialogue performed by more than two persons

多口相声 duōkǒu xiàngsheng cross talk (or comic dialogue) performed by more than two persons

多跨 duōkuà *archit.* multispan: ～结构 multispan structure / ～桥 multiple span bridge

多快好省 duō-kuài-hǎo-shěng more, faster, better, cheaper—achieve greater, faster, better and more economical results

多亏 duōkuī *adv.* thanks to; luckily: ～你的帮助 thanks to your help / ～你给我们带路。We were lucky to have you as our guide.

多劳多得 duōláo-duōdé more pay for more work

多虑 duōlù be full of anxiety; worry too much

多么 duōme *adv.* ① (used in questions, often replaced by 多 in spoken language) to what extent: 洛阳离这里有～远? How far is Luoyang from here? ② (used in exclamations) to what an extent: ～新鲜的水果啊! How fresh the fruit is! *or* What fresh fruit! / 这是～高尚的精神! What a noble spirit this is! ③ to an unspecified extent: 不管天～冷, 他都坚持户外锻炼。However cold it was, he never stopped taking outdoor exercise.

多米尼加岛 Duōmǐníjiādǎo Dominica

多米尼加共和国 Duōmǐníjiā Gònghéguó the Dominican Republic

多米尼加人 Duōmǐníjiārén Dominican

多米诺骨牌 duōmǐnuògǔpái dominoes

多米诺骨牌理论 duōmǐnuògǔpái lǐlùn the domino theory

多面角 duōmiànjiǎo *math.* polyhedral angle

多面手 duōmiànshǒu a many-sided person; a versatile person; an all-rounder

多面体 duōmiàntǐ *math.* polyhedron

多民族国家 duōmínzú guójiā a multi-nationality country

多明我会 Duōmíngwǒhuì *Catholicism* the Dominican Order

多谋善断 duōmóu-shànduàn resourceful and decisive; sagacious and resolute

多幕剧 duōmùjù a play of many acts; a full-length drama

多难兴邦 duō nàn xīng bāng much distress regenerates a nation; deep distress resurrects a nation

多瑙河 Duōnǎohé the Danube

多年 duōnián many years: ～不见啦! Haven't seen you for ages!

多年生 duōniánshēng *bot.* perennial: ～植物 perennial plant

多尿症 duōniàozhèng polyuria

多普勒效应 Duōpǔlè xiàoyìng *phys.* Doppler effect

多情 duōqíng full of tenderness or affection (for a person of the opposite sex): 他对她很是～。He feels great affection for her. / 转盼～ a loving (or soulful) glance / ～自古伤离别。(柳永) Lovers have suffered since ancient times the sorrows of parting.

多刃刀具 duōrèn dāojù *mech.* multiple-cutting-edge tool; multipoint tool

多如牛毛 duō rú niúmáo as many as the hairs on an ox; countless; innumerable

多色 duōsè polychrome: ～染料 polygenetic dyes / ～印刷 polychrome printing

多少 duōshǎo ① number; amount: ～不等 vary in amount or number ② *adv.* more or less; to some extent: ～有点失望 feel somewhat disappointed / 他讲的～有点道理。There's something in what he says. / 她对这消息～是相信的。She believes more or less in the news. / 我～有点喜欢他, 不过他很骄傲。I like him in a way, but he is very proud. / 他～会说几句英语。He speaks a little English.

多少 duōshao ① how many; how much: 这一班有～学生? How many pupils are there in this class? / 这药我每次吃～? How much of the medicine do I take each time? / 这里的粮食亩产量是～? What is the per *mu* yield of grain here? ② (expressing an unspecified amount or number): 我跟你说过不知～次了。I've told you I don't know how many times. / 我知道～说～。I'll

tell all I know. / 不论有～困难，都不能阻止我们前进。No matter what the difficulties, nothing can stop our advance.

多神教 duōshénjiào polytheism

多时 duōshí a long time: 等候～ have waited a long time

多事 duōshì ① meddlesome: 怪我～。I shouldn't have poked my nose into this. *or* I shouldn't have interfered. ② eventful: 多事之秋 duōshì zhī qiū

多事之秋 duōshì zhī qiū an eventful period or year; troubled times

多数 duōshù majority; most: 绝对～ an overwhelming majority / 微弱的～ a small majority / 必要的～ the requisite majority / 简单～ a simple majority / 相对～ a relative majority / 特定～ a qualified majority / 三分之二的～ a two-thirds majority / 我们是～。We are in the majority. / 团结～, 孤立少数 unite with the many and isolate the few

多数表决 duōshù biǎojué decision by majority

多数党 duōshùdǎng the majority party; the majority: ～领袖 the majority leader

多数票 duōshùpiào majority vote: 以～当选 be elected by a majority

多肽 duōtài *biochem.* polypeptide: ～酶 polypeptidase

多糖 duōtáng *chem.* polysaccharide; polysaccharose: ～酶 polysaccharase; polyase

多头 duōtóu ① (on the stock exchange) bull; long ② many chiefs or bosses: 领导～ with too many bosses

多头政治 duōtóu zhèngzhì polyarchy

多退少补 duōtuì-shǎobǔ (in subscribing to sth. or doing business) refund for any overpayment or demand a supplemental payment for any difference in price

多细胞生物 duōxìbāo shēngwù multicellular organism

多相 duōxiàng *chem.* heterogeneous: ～催化 heterogeneous catalysis / ～聚合 heterogeneous polymerization

多项式 duōxiàngshì *math.* multinomial; polynomial

多谢 duōxiè *pol.* many thanks; thanks a lot

多心 duōxīn oversensitive; paranoid: 你别～, 我只是就一般而论。Don't get me wrong; I'm speaking in general. / 他听了这话～了。He became paranoid when he heard this.

多芯电缆 duōxīn diànlǎn multicore cable

多行不义必自毙 duō xíng bùyì bì zì bì he who is unjust is doomed to destruction

多样 duōyàng diversified: 形式～ diversified in form

多样化 duōyànghuà diversify; make varied: 使农作物～ diversify the crops / ～的艺术风格 a variety of artistic styles

多一半 duōyībàn same as 多半 duōbàn

多一事不如少一事 duō yī shì bùrú shǎo yī shì the less trouble the better; avoid trouble whenever possible: 有些人得过且过, 采取 "～" 的态度。Some people do just enough work to get by, believing "the less trouble the better."

多义词 duōyìcí *linguis.* polysemant

多余 duōyú unnecessary; surplus; superfluous; uncalled-for: 删掉～的词语 cut out superfluous words and phrases / 把～的农产品卖给国家 sell surplus farm products to the state / 事实证明我们的担心是～的。Facts proved that our worries were uncalled-for.

多元论 duōyuánlùn *philos.* pluralism: ～历史观 the pluralistic concept of history

多元酸 duōyuánsuān *chem.* polybasic acid

多元体 duōyuántǐ another name for 多倍体 duōbèitǐ

多云 duōyún *meteorol.* cloudy

多咱 duōzan *dial.* what time; when: 咱们～走? When

are we leaving?/ 这是～的事? When did that happen? *or* When was that?

多早晚 duōzǎowǎn same as 多咱 duōzan

多种多样 duōzhǒng-duōyàng varied; manifold: 满足人民群众～的需要 meet the manifold needs of the people / 音乐创作的形式是～的。The forms of musical composition are many and varied.

多种经营 duōzhǒng jīngyíng diversified economy; diversification: 以粮为纲, ～, 全面发展。Take grain as the key link, develop a diversified economy and ensure an all-round development. / ～方式 various methods of business operation

多足动物 duōzú dòngwù myriopod

多嘴 duōzuǐ speak out of turn; shoot off one's mouth: ～多舌 gossipy and meddlesome; long-tongued / 要不是他～, 事情也不至于搞僵。If he hadn't shot his mouth off, things wouldn't have been so awkward. / 你不了解情况, 别～! You don't know the facts, so keep your mouth shut!

咄 duō tut-tut

咄咄 duōduō *interj.* tut! tut!

咄咄逼人 duōduō bī rén overbearing; aggressive: 他说话时的神气～。He spoke with an overbearing air.

咄咄怪事 duōduō guàishì monstrous absurdity: 岂非～? Isn't it absurd? *or* Isn't it a strange business?

咄嗟立办 duōjiē lì bàn can be done at once

哆 duō see below

哆嗦 duōsuo tremble; shiver: 气得直～ tremble with rage /冷得打～ shiver with cold

掇（掇） duō pick up: 拾掇 shíduo

掇弄 duōnòng *dial.* ① fix up: 经他一～机器就好了。The machine worked again after he fixed it up. ② stir up (trouble, etc.); incite

掇拾 duōshí *formal* ① tidy up; put in order ② collect; gather

裰 duō ① mend (clothing) ② see 直裰 zhíduō

duó

夺[1]**（奪）** duó ① take by force; seize; wrest: 从暴徒手上～下刀子 wrest a knife from a hooligan / 从甲队手里～走冠军 take the championship from team A ② force one's way: ～门而出 force open the door and rush out; force one's way out / 眼泪～眶而出。Tears started from one's eyes. ③ contend for; compete for; strive for: ～红旗 contend for the red banner / ～高产 strive for high yields / ～得冠军 carry off the first prize ④ deprive: 剥夺 bōduó ⑤ *formal* miss; let slip: 勿～农时 not miss the farming season

夺[2]**（奪）** duó *formal* decide: 定夺 dìngduó

夺[3]**（奪）** duó *formal* (of words in a text) be left out; be omitted; be missing: 此处～一 "之" 字。The character 之 is missing here.

夺标 duóbiāo ① win the championship: ～呼声很高 be a likely champion ② have one's tender accepted

夺佃 duódiàn eviction of peasants from land leased to them by landlords or rich peasants

夺冠 duóguàn (also 夺魁 duókuí) carry off the first prize; win first place; win the championship

夺回 duóhuí recapture; retake; seize back: ～阵地 recapture a position / ～一局 win a game (after losing

one or more); pull up by a game / ～发球权 win back service / ～失去的时间 make up for lost time

夺目 duómù dazzle the eyes: 光彩夺目 guāngcǎi duómù

夺取 duóqǔ ① capture; seize; wrest: ～敌人的据点 capture an enemy stronghold / ～主动权 seize the initiative / 武装～政权 seize state power by armed force ② strive for: ～社会主义建设的新胜利 strive for new victories in socialist construction

夺权 duóquán seize power; take over power

夺印 duóyìn seize the seal—seize power

泽(澤) duó see 凌泽 língduó

度 duó formal surmise; estimate: 揣度 chuǎiduó ——see also dù

度德量力 duódé-liànglì estimate one's own moral and material strength; make an appraisal of one's own position

铎(鐸) duó a kind of bell used in ancient China when issuing proclamations or in times of war

踱 duó pace; stroll: ～来～去 pace to and fro; pace up and down / ～方步 walk with measured tread

duǒ

朵(朶) duǒ m.: 一～花 a flower / 一～云 a cloud

朵儿 duǒr ① flower ② same as 朵 duǒ

朵颐 duǒyí formal munch; chew: 大快～ eat with great relish

垛(垜) duǒ ① buttress ② battlements ——see also duò

垛口 duǒkǒu (also 垛堞 duǒdié) crenel

垛子 duǒzi ① buttress ② battlements: 城垛子 chéngduǒzi

躲(躱) duǒ ① hide (oneself): ～进深山老林 hide in a mountain forest / 我去～在门背后。I'll hide behind the door. / 你快～起来! Quick, hide yourself! ② avoid; dodge: 你怎么老～着他? Why do you keep avoiding him?/车来了, 快～开! Look out! A truck's coming! Get out of the way. / ～雨 take shelter from the rain

躲避 duǒbì ① hide (oneself): 这几天他好像有意～我。He seems to have been hiding from me these days. / 你还是～起来为好。You had better hide. ② avoid; elude; dodge: ～困难 avoid difficulties

躲藏 duǒcáng ① hide (or conceal) oneself; go into hiding: 他～在哪儿? Where is he hiding? / 他被迫一起来。He was forced to go into hiding. / 被赶得没处～be so hounded that one can find no place to hide ② avoid; dodge: 暴风雨快要来了, 鸟儿都～起来。As the

storm approached, the birds were seeking shelter.

躲躲闪闪 duǒduǒshǎnshǎn be evasive; hedge; equivocate

躲风 duǒfēng ① take shelter from the wind ② lie low until sth. blows over

躲懒 duǒlǎn shy away from work; shirk

躲让 duǒràng dodge; get out of the way: 卡车飞驰而过, 他及时一开了。He dodged just in time to avoid the speeding truck.

躲闪 duǒshǎn dodge; evade: 小王～不及, 和我撞了个满怀。It was too late for Xiao Wang to dodge and I bumped into him.

躲债 duǒzhài avoid a creditor

duò

驮 duò see below ——see also tuó

驮子 duòzi ① a load carried by a pack-animal; pack ② m.: 三～货 three packs of goods

剁(刴) duò chop; cut: 把柳条～成三段 chop a willow branch into three pieces / ～肉馅 chop up (or mince) meat

垛(垜、稞) duò ① pile up neatly; stack: 把木头～起来 pile up the logs ② pile; stack: 柴火～ a pile of faggots / 麦～ a stack of wheat ——see also duǒ

舵(柁) duò rudder; helm: 方向舵 fāngxiàngduò

舵工 duògōng (also 舵公 duògōng) steersman; helmsman

舵轮 duòlún (also 舵盘 duòpán) steering wheel

舵手 duòshǒu steersman; helmsman

堕(墮) duò fall; sink: ～地 fall on the ground

堕落 duòluò degenerate; sink low: 走上～、犯罪的道路 embark on the road of degeneration and crime / 政治上～be politically degenerate / ～成罪犯 degenerate into a common criminal

堕落风尘 duòluò fēngchén be driven to prostitution

堕入 duòrù sink (or lapse) into; land oneself in: ～陷阱 fall into a trap

堕胎 duòtāi ① induced abortion ② have an (induced) abortion

惰 duò lazy; indolent: 懒惰 lǎnduò

惰性 duòxìng inertia

惰性气体 duòxìng qìtǐ chem. inert gas

惰性元素 duòxìng yuánsù chem. inert element

跺(跥、跢) duò stamp (one's foot): 气得直～脚 stamp one's foot with fury

E

ē

阿[1]　ē　play up to; pander to: 法不～贵。The law cannot fawn on the noble.

阿[2]　Ē　short for 东阿县 (Dong E County of Shandong Province): 阿胶 ējiāo ——see also ā

阿附　ēfù　*formal*　fawn on and echo; toady to and chime in with: ～权贵 fawn on the noble

阿胶　ējiāo　*Chin. med.*　E-gelatin, a traditional Chinese tonic for nourishing the blood (named after its place of origin, Dong E County of Shandong Province)

阿弥陀佛　Ēmítuófó　① *Buddhism Amitābha* Buddha (who presides over the Western Paradise and whose name is used as an incantation repeated by the faithful) ② (used as an exclamation) may Buddha preserve us; Buddha be praised

阿其所好　ē qí suǒ hào　play up to sb.'s whims; pander to sb.'s weaknesses

阿魏　ēwèi　*Chin. med.*　asafoetida (a gum resin obtained from the roots of the plant *Ferula asafoetida*)

阿谀　ēyú　fawn on; flatter

阿谀逢迎　ēyú-féngyíng　flatter and toady to; fawn upon

阿谀奉承　ēyú-fèngcheng　flatter; toady to

屙　ē　*dial.*　discharge (excrement or urine)

婀　ē　see below

婀娜　ēnuó　(of a woman's carriage) lithe and graceful; supple and graceful: 体态～ have a supple, graceful carriage / 柳枝迎风摇曳，～多姿。Willow branches are fluttering (*or* swaying) gracefully in the breeze.

é

讹[1]（譌）　é　erroneous; mistaken: ～字 wrong words (in a text)

讹[2]　é　extort under false pretences; blackmail: 这不是～人吗？Isn't this blackmail!

讹传　échuán　false (*or* unfounded) rumour

讹舛　échuǎn　*formal*　(of words in a text) erroneous; mistaken

讹夺　éduó　*formal*　error or omission (in a text)

讹赖　élài　*dial.*　extort; blackmail

讹谬　émiù　mistake; error

讹脱　étuō　error or omission (in a text)

讹误　éwù　error (in a text)

讹言　éyán　① *formal* rumour ② wild talk; raving: 口出～ talk nonsense; rave

讹诈　ézhà　extort under false pretences; blackmail: ～钱财 extort money under false pretences

囮　é　see below

囮子　ézi　decoy bird

俄[1]　é　very soon; presently; suddenly: 俄顷 éqǐng

俄[2]　É　① short for 俄罗斯帝国 Éluósī Dìguó ② short for 俄罗斯联邦 Éluósī Liánbāng

俄而　é'ér　(also 俄尔 é'ěr) very soon; in a moment; in a little while; presently: ～日出。Presently the sun emerged.

俄罗斯帝国　Éluósī Dìguó　the Russian Empire (1721–1917)

俄罗斯联邦　Éluósī Liánbāng　the Russian Federation

俄罗斯人　Éluósīrén　Russian

俄罗斯族　Éluósīzú　① the Russian nationality, or the Russians, distributed over the Xinjiang Uygur Autonomous Region and Heilongjiang Province ② the Russians (of Russia)

俄顷　éqǐng　*formal*　in a moment; presently

俄然　érán　suddenly; all of a sudden: ～消失 vanish suddenly

俄延　éyán　delay; retard; put off

俄语　Éyǔ　Russian (language)

哦　é　*formal*　softly chant (a poem): 吟哦 yín'é ——see also ó; ò

峨（峩）　é　*formal*　high: 巍峨 wēi'é

峨冠博带　éguān-bódài　a high-topped hat and a broad waist band (the attire of an official or an intellectual in ancient times)

峨嵋山　Éméishān　Mount Emei

娥　é　a pretty young woman: 宫娥 gōng'é

娥眉　éméi　*liter.*　① the beautiful eyebrows of a woman ② a beautiful woman ——see also 蛾眉 éméi

娥眉月　éméiyuè　crescent moon; crescent; waxing moon

鹅（鵝、䳘）　é　goose

鹅蛋脸　édànliǎn　an oval face

鹅黄　éhuáng　light yellow

鹅颈管　éjǐngguǎn　*mech.*　gooseneck

鹅口疮　ékǒuchuāng　thrush (a children's disease characterized by whitish spots and ulcers on the membranes of the mouth, fauces, etc.)

鹅卵石　éluǎnshí　cobblestone; cobble

鹅毛　émáo　① goose feather ② sth. as light as a goose feather: 下了一场～大雪。Snow fell in big feathery flakes.

鹅绒　éróng　goose down

鹅行鸭步　éxíng-yābù　waddle along like a duck or a goose

鹅掌风　ézhǎngfēng　*Chin. med.*　fungal infection of the hand; tinea manuum

鹅掌楸　ézhǎngqiū　Chinese tulip tree

锇　é　*chem.* osmium (Os)

蛾　é　moth

蛾眉　éméi　*liter.* ① moth eyebrows—the fine and delicate eyebrows of a woman (suggesting the dainty sweep of a moth's antennae): 云鬓轻笼蝉翼，～淡拂春山。(《京本通俗小说·碾玉观音》) The cloudlike hair above her temples is like a cicada's wings; Her moth eyebrows, lightly painted, are like the mountains in spring. ② a beautiful woman: 六军不发无奈何，宛转～马前死。(白居易) The army would no longer march—there was no choice: The dainty-browed beloved one died before the horses.

蛾子　ézi　moth

额[1]　é　① forehead ② a horizontal tablet; a horizontal inscribed board

额[2]　é　a specified number or amount: 贸易～ volume of trade

额定功率　édìng gōnglǜ　rated power
额定马力　édìng mǎlì　rated horsepower
额骨　égǔ　*physiol.* frontal bone
额角　éjiǎo　frontal eminence
额门　émén　forehead: ～宽阔 a broad forehead / ～突出 a prominent forehead / 他～上冒出了豆大的汗珠。Sweat stood in beads on his forehead.
额手称庆　éshǒu chēng qìng　raise one's hand to one's forehead in joy—be overjoyed
额数　éshù　a specified number, figure or amount
额头　étóu　forehead
额外　éwài　extra; additional; added: ～开支 extra expenses / ～收入 additional income / ～负担 added burden

ě

恶 (惡、噁)　ě see below ——see also è; wū; wù

恶心　ěxin　① feel like vomiting; feel nauseated; feel sick: 我一坐海船就感到～。I always feel sick (or nauseated) at sea. ② be nauseating; disgust: 看了这事真～。It was a disgusting sight to see. ③ *dial.* rotten; lousy: 他的棋下得可～。He is a lousy chess-player.

è

厄[1] (阨、戹)　è　*formal* a strategic point: 险～ a strategic pass

厄[2] (戹)　è　① adversity; disaster; hardship: 遭～ meet with disaster ② be in distress; be stranded: 渔船～于风暴。The fishing boat was caught in a storm.

厄尔尼诺　È'érnínuò　El Niño
厄瓜多尔　Èguāduō'ěr　Ecuador
厄瓜多尔人　Èguāduō'ěrrén　Ecuadorian
厄境　èjìng　a difficult situation; adversity: 处于～ be in a difficult situation / 在～中保持乐观 remain cheerful in adversity
厄立特里亚　Èlìtèlǐyà　Eritrea
厄难　ènàn　disaster; distress
厄运　èyùn　adversity; misfortune

扼　è　*formal* ① clutch; grip: ～住他的咽喉 clutch at his throat ② guard; control: 扼制 èzhì

扼吭拊背　èháng-fǔbèi　(also 扼喉抚背　èhóu-fǔbèi) seize by the throat and hit at the spine—hold the best strategic position and render the enemy helpless
扼流圈　èliúquān　*elec.* choke
扼杀　èshā　strangle; smother; throttle: ～在摇篮里 strangle in the cradle / ～在萌芽状态中 nip in the bud / ～新生事物 stifle new things
扼守　èshǒu　hold (a strategic point); guard: 战士们～住山口，打退了敌人的进犯。The soldiers held the mountain pass and beat back the intruders.
扼死　èsǐ　strangle; throttle
扼腕　èwàn　*formal* hold one's own wrist (in excitement, disappointment, etc.): ～叹息 sighing and wringing one's hands
扼要　èyào　to the point: 简明～ brief and to the point / 请～说明。Please explain the main points briefly.
扼制　èzhì　control; restrain; check; bring under control

呃　è　hiccups ——see also e

呃逆　ènì　hiccups

苊　è　*chem.* acenaphthene

轭　è　yoke

垩 (堊)　è　① chalk (a soft, white, powdery limestone) ② whiten with chalk

恶 (惡)　è　① evil; vice; wickedness: 罪大恶极 zuìdà-èjí ② fierce; ferocious: 一场～战 a fiece battle / ～骂 vicious abuse / ～狗 a ferocious (or vicious) dog; cur ③ bad; evil; wicked: ～行 evil (or wicked) conduct / ～势力 evil forces ——see also ě; wū; wù

恶霸　èbà　local tyrant (or despot)
恶霸地主　èbà dìzhǔ　despotic landlord
恶报　èbào　retribution for evildoing; judgment: 善有善报，恶有恶报 shàn yǒu shànbào, è yǒu èbào
恶变　èbiàn　*med.* cancerate; grow into a cancer
恶病质　èbìngzhì　cachexia (general ill health with emaciation, due to a serious chronic disease, as cancer)
恶臭　èchòu　a foul smell; stench: 伤口溃烂，散发出一股～。The wound is festering and stinking.
恶斗　èdòu　a fierce (or furious) fight: 一场～之后 after a fierce fight
恶毒　èdú　vicious; malicious; venomous: ～的诬蔑 venomous slander / ～攻击 viciously attack / ～的语言 vile language / 用心极其～ entertain most evil designs
恶恶实实　è'eshíshí　*dial.* fierce; ferocious
恶感　ègǎn　ill feeling; malice: 我对他并无～。I bear him no malice.
恶贯满盈　è guàn mǎnyíng　be guilty of countless crimes and deserve to come to judgment; be steeped in evil and deserve damnation
恶鬼　èguǐ　① evil spirit ② *offens.* devil
恶棍　ègùn　ruffian; scoundrel; bully
恶果　èguǒ　evil consequence; disastrous effect: 不注意环境保护造成的～ the evil consequences of the neglect of environmental protection
恶耗　èhào　same as 噩耗 èhào
恶狠狠　èhěnhěn　fierce; ferocious: 她～地瞪了他一眼。She gave him a ferocious stare.
恶化　èhuà　worsen; deteriorate; take a turn for the worse: 他的病情～了。His condition has worsened. / 局势愈来愈～。The situation is getting worse and worse. / 这场边境争端～了两国关系。The border dispute worsened the relationship between the two countries.

恶疾　èjí　a foul (or nasty) disease

恶口　èkǒu　an abusive tongue; a foul tongue; a wicked tongue: ～伤人 hurt people with one's abusive tongue

恶浪　èlàng　① fierce waves; monstrous waves: ～滔天 monstrous billows rising to the skies ② evil forces

恶劣　èliè　odious; abominable; disgusting: ～作风 abominable behaviour / ～行径 disgusting conduct / 手段～ mean (or dirty) tricks / ～环境 adverse circumstances / 品质～ unprincipled; base / 影响～ make a very bad impression / 作案的情节十分～。 The way in which the crime was committed was absolutely vile. / 他对这种～的服务态度感到十分气愤。 He is very angry at the bad service. / 由于气候～,登山队不得不延期出发。 The mountaineering party delayed its departure because of the foul weather.

恶露　èlù　Chin. med. lochia

恶眉恶眼　èméi-èyǎn　a very fierce expression

恶梦　èmèng　nightmare

恶名　èmíng　a bad name; a bad reputation; infamy

恶魔　èmó　demon; devil; evil spirit (lit. and fig.)

恶癖　èpǐ　a pernicious habit; addiction: 沾染了赌博～ be addicted to gambling

恶气　èqì　① a bad odor; a foul smell ② insult; outrage ③ grievance; resentment: 出口～ vent one's grievance ④ anger; fury: 恶声恶气 èshēng-èqì

恶人　èrén　an evil person; a vile creature; villain

恶人先告状　èrén xiān gàozhuàng　the villain sues his victim before he himself is prosecuted; the guilty party files the suit

恶煞　èshà　① devil; fiend ② a fiendish person

恶少　èshào　a young ruffian: 洋场～ a young rake in a gay cosmopolitan city (as in preliberation Shanghai)

恶声　èshēng　① angry voice; abusive language: ～对骂 shout abuse at each other ② formal vulgar music ③ formal a bad reputation

恶声恶气　èshēng-èqì　angry voices and hard words

恶事传千里　èshì chuán qiānlǐ　bad news spreads far and wide

恶岁　èsuì　formal a bad year; a lean year; a terrible famine year

恶习　èxí　a bad (or pernicious) habit: 染上～ contract a bad habit; fall into evil ways / ～不改 persist in one's evil ways

恶行　èxíng　evil-doing; vicious behaviour; bad conduct

恶性　èxìng　malignant; pernicious; vicious: ～事故 a fatal accident / ～通货膨胀 galloping (or runaway) inflation

恶性贫血　èxìng pínxuè　pernicious anaemia

恶性循环　èxìng xúnhuán　vicious circle

恶性肿瘤　èxìng zhǒngliú　malignant tumour

恶言　èyán　rude language; abusive language: ～相向 exchange hot words / 口出～ use abusive language; wag one's vicious tongue

恶衣恶食　èyī-èshí　poor clothes and coarse fare

恶意　èyì　evil (or ill) intentions; ill will; malice: ～攻击 malicious attacks / 她对你并无～。 She bore you no malice (or ill will).

恶语中伤　èyǔ zhòngshāng　viciously slander; calumniate

恶运　èyùn　bad luck: 我交了～。 Luck is against me.

恶兆　èzhào　ill (or bad) omen

恶浊　èzhuó　foul; filthy: 空气～ foul air / ～的社会环境 a very bad social environment

恶阻　èzǔ　Chin. med. vomiting during early pregnancy; morning sickness

恶作剧　èzuòjù　a practical joke; a mischievous prank; mischief: 这孩子十分淘气,喜欢～。 The child is very naughty and likes to play practical jokes. / 别～了! No more of your practical jokes !

饿　è　① hungry: 挨～ go hungry / 孩子～了。 The child is hungry. / 可把我～坏了。 I feel famished. or I'm starving. ② cause to starve; starve: 别～着小猪。 Don't starve the piglets. / 好好～他一顿就好了。 He'll feel better if you let him miss a meal.

饿饭　èfàn　dial. go hungry; go without food

饿鬼　èguǐ　① a hungry ghost (a sinner condemned to perpetual starvation after death) ② a piggish eater

饿虎扑食　èhǔ pū shí　like a hungry tiger pouncing on its prey: 守门员来了个～,把球扑住了。 The goalkeeper pounced like a tiger and caught the ball.

饿狼　èláng　ravenous wolf—a greedy person

饿殍　èpiǎo　formal bodies of the starved

饿殍遍野　èpiǎo biànyě　the fields strewn with the bodies of the starved

鄂　È　① another name for Hubei Province ② a surname

鄂博　èbó　same as 敖包 áobāo

鄂伦春族　Èlúnchūnzú　the Oroqen (Olunchun) nationality, or the Oroqens (Olunchuns), inhabiting Heilongjiang Province

鄂温克族　Èwēnkèzú　the Ewenki (Owenk) nationality, or the Ewenkis (Owenks), inhabiting Heilongjiang Province

愕　è　stunned; astounded

愕然　èrán　stunned; astounded: ～四顾 look around in astonishment / 消息传来,大家为之～。 Everyone was stunned by the news.

愕视　èshì　stare in astonishment

萼　è　bot. calyx

萼片　èpiàn　bot. sepal

遏　è　check; hold back: 怒不可遏 nù bùkě è

遏抑　èyì　suppress; restrain: 不可～的怒火 uncontrollable fury

遏止　èzhǐ　check; hold back: 一股无法～的激情 an uncheckable wave of emotion / 不可～的改革洪流 the irresistible tide of reform

遏制　èzhì　keep within limits; contain: ～不住的笑声 uncontrollable laughter / ～愤怒的情绪 check one's anger / 不可～的欲望 an irrepressible desire

遏制政策　èzhì zhèngcè　policy of containment

腭（齶）　è　physiol. palate: 硬腭 yìng'è / 软腭 ruǎn'è

腭裂　èliè　cleft palate

鹗　è　osprey; fish hawk; sea eagle

锷　è　formal the blade of a sword

颚　è　① mandibles (of arthropods) ② same as 腭

噩　è　shocking; upsetting

噩耗　èhào　sad news of the death of a beloved person: ～传来,犹如晴天霹雳。 The grievous news came like a bolt from the blue.

噩梦　èmèng　a frightening (or horrible) dream; nightmare: 这一切犹如一场～。 The whole thing was a nightmare.

噩运　èyùn　same as 恶运 èyùn

噩兆　èzhào　same as 恶兆 èzhào

鳄（鱷）　è　crocodile; alligator

鳄鱼　èyú　crocodile; alligator
鳄鱼眼泪　èyú yǎnlèi　crocodile tears

e

呃　e *part.* (used at the end of a sentence, expressing wonder or admiration): 红霞映山崖～! Oh, look at the red glow over the cliff-face! ——see also è

ē

欸（誒）　ē *interj.* (used to call attention): ～, 你快来! Hey! Come over here. ——see also āi; ǎi; é; ě; è

é

欸（誒）　é or éi *interj.* (used to express surprise): ～, 他怎么走了! Why, he's gone! ——see also āi; ǎi; ē; ě; è

ě

欸（誒）　ě or ěi *interj.* (used to express disapproval): ～, 话可不能这么说呀! Now, you can't say that. ——see also āi; ǎi; ē; é; è

è

欸（誒）　è or èi *interj.* (used to express assent or polite attentiveness): ～, 我这就来! Yes, I'm coming in a minute. or Coming. / ～, 就这么办! All right. That's settled. ——see also āi; ǎi; ē; é; ě

ēn

恩　ēn　kindness; favour; grace: 施～ bestow favours
恩爱　ēn'ài　(of a married couple) be deeply in love with each other: ～夫妻 an affectionate couple / 小两口儿十分～。 The young couple love each other tenderly.
恩宠　ēnchǒng　① imperial favour ② show special favour to a minister
恩赐　ēncì　① bestow (favours, charity, etc.): 独立是被压迫民族斗争得来的, 不是什么人～的。 Independence is won by the oppressed nations through struggle; it is not bestowed as a favour. ② favour; charity: 大自然的～ the bounty of Nature
恩德　ēndé　benevolence; favour; kindness; grace
恩典　ēndiǎn　· ① favour; grace: 这是皇上的～。 This is an imperial favour. ② bestow (favours): 求老爷～～! I beg your excellency's grace.
恩公　ēngōng　benefactor
恩惠　ēnhuì　a favour bestowed or received; bounty: 小恩小惠 xiǎo'ēn-xiǎohuì
恩将仇报　ēn jiāng chóu bào　requite kindness with enmity; return hate for love; bite the hand that feeds one

恩情　ēnqíng　loving-kindness: 我一辈子也忘不了义母对我的～。 I shall never forget my foster mother's loving-kindness to me as long as I live. / 共产党的～说也说不完。 We can never say enough about our gratitude to the Party.
恩人　ēnrén　benefactor
恩深义重　ēnshēn-yìzhòng　a great debt of gratitude
恩同再造　ēn tóng zàizào　a favour tantamount to giving sb. a new lease of life
恩威并用　ēn-wēi bìng yòng　make a combined use of favour and disfavour (as in controlling one's subordinates); use both the mailed fist and the velvet glove
恩遇　ēnyù　*formal* ① treat with kindness ② kind treatment
恩怨　ēn-yuàn　① feeling of gratitude or resentment: ～分明 know clearly to whom to show gratitude and against whom to feel resentment ② resentment; grievance; old scores: 不计较个人～ not allow oneself to be swayed by personal feelings
恩泽　ēnzé　bounties bestowed by a monarch or an official
恩重如山　ēn zhòng rú shān　sb.'s great kindness is as weighty as a mountain
恩准　ēnzhǔn　graciously grant

蒽　ēn　*chem.* anthracene
蒽酸　ēnsuān　anthroic acid

èn

摁　èn　press (with the hand or finger): ～电钮 press (*or* push) a button / ～住不放 press sth. down and hold it there / ～电铃 ring an electric bell
摁钉儿　èndīngr　*inf.* drawing pin; thumbtack
摁扣儿　ènkòur　*inf.* snap fastener

ér

儿¹（兒）　ér　① child: 婴儿 yīng'ér ② youngster; youth (esp. a young man): 健儿 jiàn'ér / 男儿 nán'ér ③ son: 他有一～一女。 He has a son and a daughter. ④ male: 儿马 érmǎ

儿²（兒）　ér　(transcribed as r) *suffix* ① (added to nouns to express smallness): 小猫～ kitten / 穗～ an ear of grain ② (added to verbs to form nouns): 吃～ something to eat / 唱～ a song or a singing part in a Chinese opera ③ (added to adjectives to form nouns): 亮～ a light / 热闹～ a thrilling sight; fun ④ (added to concrete nouns to change them into abstract nouns): 门 ～ a way to do sth. / 根～ cause; origin ⑤ (added to nouns to form nouns with different meaning): 白面 wheat flour—白面～ heroin ⑥ (a verb suffix very much restricted in use): 玩～牌 play cards / 火～了 flare up
——see also 儿化 érhuà
儿茶　érchá　① *bot.* Acacia catechu ② *Chin. med.* catechu
儿歌　érgē　children's song; nursery rhymes
儿化　érhuà　*linguis.* suffixation of a nonsyllabic 儿 (r) to nouns and sometimes verbs or adjectives, causing a retroflexion of the preceding vowel, typical of the pronunciation of standard Chinese and of some dialects
——see also 儿² ér
儿皇帝　érhuángdì　puppet emperor

儿科　érkē　(department of) paediatrics

儿科医生　érkē yīshēng　paediatrician

儿郎　érláng　*formal* ① man ② son; boy ③ rank-and-file soldiers; men

儿马　érmǎ　*inf.* male horse

儿男　érnán　① man ② boy; son: 中华民族的好～ good sons of the Chinese nation

儿女　ér-nǚ　① sons and daughters; children: 大儿大女 grown-up sons and daughters / 中国人民的优秀～ fine sons and daughters of the Chinese people / ～都已长大成人。The children have all grown up. ② young man and woman (in love)

儿女情长　ér-nǚ qíng cháng　love between man and woman is long: 英雄气短，～。Brief is the spirit of a hero, but love between man and woman is long (said of a man who turns from duty for the sake of love).

儿时　érshí　childhood

儿孙　érsūn　children and grandchildren; descendants; posterity: ～满堂 with generations of offspring filling the house (formerly regarded as a sign of prosperity)

儿孙自有儿孙福　érsūn zì yǒu érsūn fú　each one of your sons and your grandsons must find his own way as he ought; you cannot determine your children's fortune

儿童　értóng　children

儿童节　Értóngjié　(International) Children's Day (June 1)

儿童团　Értóngtuán　the Children's Corps

儿童文学　értóng wénxué　children's (*or* juvenile) literature

儿童医院　értóng yīyuàn　children's hospital

儿媳妇儿　érxífur　daughter-in-law

儿戏　érxì　trifling matter: 这样重要的工作可不能当～。You shouldn't regard such important work as a trifling matter. / 视同～ regard as a mere trifle

儿韵　éryùn　*linguis.* r-ending retroflexion

儿子　érzi　son

而　ér　*conj.* ① and; as well as: 伟大～艰巨的任务 a great and arduous task / 这篇文章长～空。This article is long-winded and lacks substance. ② and yet; but; while on the other hand: 有其名～无其实 in name but not in reality / 这里的气候有利于种小麦，～不利于种水稻。The climate here is favourable to the growth of wheat but unfavourable to the growth of rice. / 中看～不中吃。It looks good but doesn't taste good. / 你喜欢爱体育运动，～我呢，情愿看书。You like sports, while I'd rather read. ③ so that; in order to: 不要因失败～灰心，也不要因成功～骄傲。Don't be discouraged by failure or get dizzy with success. / 全国人民正在为早日实现四个现代化～奋斗。The whole nation is striving for an early realization of the four modernizations. ④ (used with 由, 从, 自, etc.) to: 由南～北 from south to north / 自远～近 approach from a distance / 由童年～少年，～壮年 from childhood to teenage, then to middle age ⑤ (connecting an adverbial element to a verb): 匆匆～去 leave in haste / 顺流～下 go down the stream / 盘旋～上 spiral up ⑥ (used between a subject and a predicate expressing a condition, to be followed by a clause indicating result) if: 作家～不深入群众，那就写不出好的作品来。If a writer does not go deep among the masses, he cannot expect to turn out good writings.

而后　érhòu　*conj.* after that; then: 先小组酝酿～由大会讨论。First exchange ideas in small groups and then hold a general discussion.

而今　érjīn　now; at the present time

而况　érkuàng　same as 何况 hékuàng

而立　érlì　*formal* (used esp. in): ～之年 the age of thirty (from Confucius' saying 三十而立 "At thirty I took my stand") / 年近～ be nearly thirty

而且　érqiě　*conj.* ① and also: 这屋子很宽敞，～光线充足。The room is spacious and bright. ② but also: 我们不但战胜了灾害，～获得了丰收。We not only came through the natural calamity, but also won a bumper harvest.

而外　érwài　① besides; aside from; apart from: 她除了打乒乓～，还喜欢游泳、滑冰。Besides table tennis, she goes in for swimming and skating. ② except; with the exception of; but: 他除了做饭～，什么家务活都干。He does all the housework except cooking.

而已　éryǐ　*part.* that is all; nothing more: 我不过是个学生～。I'm just a student, that's all. / 如此～，岂有他哉! That's all there is to it! / 以上只是几个例子～，类似的情况还很多。I've given only a few examples; similar cases are too many to mention.

洏　ér　see 涟洏 lián'ér

鸸　ér　see below

鸸鹋　érmiáo　*zool.* emu

ěr

尔 (爾)　ěr　*formal* ① thou; you: 非～之过。It's not your fault. *or* You are not to blame. ② like that; so: 果～ if so ③ that: ～日 that day / ～时 at that time ④ *suffix*: 率尔 shuài'ěr / 莞尔 wǎn'ěr

尔曹　ěrcáo　*formal* you people; you and your kind

尔曹身与名俱灭，不废江河万古流　ěrcáo shēn yǔ míng jù miè, bù fèi jiānghé wàngǔ liú　your bodies and names will perish, but the river will flow on for ever—the names of you ordinary men will be forgotten, but those of great men will live

尔代节　Ěrdàijié　another name for 开斋节 Kāizhāijié

尔尔　ěr'ěr　so-so: 不过～ just so-so

尔格　ěrgé　*phys.* erg

尔后　ěrhòu　*formal* thereafter; subsequently; henceforth: ～的战斗 the subsequent battles

尔来　ěrlái　*formal* since then; recently; lately: ～二十有一年矣。Twenty-one years have passed since then.

尔许　ěrxǔ　*formal* so; such; like that: ～高 just that tall (*or* high) / ～多 just that much; just so many

尔雅　ěryǎ　*formal* elegant; refined; cultured: 温文尔雅 wēnwén-ěryǎ

尔虞我诈　ěryú-wǒzhà　(also 尔诈我虞 ěrzhà-wǒyú) each trying to cheat the other: 各派勾心斗角，～。All the factions intrigued against each other, resorting to deception and fraud.

耳¹　ěr　① ear: 内耳 nèi'ěr / 外耳 wài'ěr ② any ear-like thing: 鼎～ the ears of a tripod ③ on both sides; flanking; side: 耳房 ěrfáng

耳²　*part. formal.* only; just: 距此不过五里～。It is only five *li* from here. / 想当然～。It is mere conjecture.

耳报神　ěrbàoshén　informer

耳背　ěrbèi　be hard of hearing: 老太太有点儿～，你说话大声点儿。The old lady is a bit hard of hearing. Louder, please.

耳鼻喉科　ěr-bí-hóukē　① E.N.T. (ear-nose-throat) department; otolaryngological department ② otolaryngology

耳鼻喉科医生　ěr-bí-hóukē yīshēng　E.N.T. specialist; otolaryngologist

耳边风　ěrbiānfēng　a puff of wind passing the

ear—unheeded advice: 当作～ let sth. go in one ear and out the other; turn a deaf ear to sth.

耳鬓厮磨 ěrbìn sīmó ear to ear and temple to temple—(of a boy and a girl) have close childhood friendship: 宝玉从幼时和黛玉～, 心情相对。(《红楼梦》) Since childhood, Baoyu had been intimate with Daiyu, finding her a kindred spirit.

耳沉 ěrchén (also 耳朵沉 ěrduochén) dial. be hard of hearing

耳垂 ěrchuí physiol. earlobe

耳聪目明 ěrcōng-mùmíng have good ears and eyes —— have a clear understanding (of the situation)

耳珰 ěrdāng ear pendants

耳底 ěrdǐ eardrum

耳朵 ěrduo ear: ～尖 have sharp ears / 穿～ have one's earlobes pierced (for wearing earrings)

耳朵底子 ěrduodǐzi dial. inflammation of the middle ear; otitis media

耳朵软 ěrduoruǎn credulous; easily influenced; susceptible to flattery: 他～, 架不住人家三句好话, 就相信了。He was credulous, and fell for words of flattery.

耳朵眼儿 ěrduoyǎnr ① the external opening of the ear ② holes pierced in the earlobes for wearing earrings

耳房 ěrfáng side rooms (flanking the principal room)

耳福 ěrfú the good fortune of hearing sth. rare or beautiful: 大饱～ enjoy to the full listening to music, singing, etc.

耳根 ěrgēn ① the basal part (or root) of the ear ② dial. ear ③ Buddhism the ear taken as a source of sin

耳根清净 ěrgēn qīngjìng peace of heart or mind attained by staying away from, or shutting one's ears to, worldly discord

耳垢 ěrgòu earwax

耳鼓 ěrgǔ same as 鼓膜 gǔmó

耳刮子 ěrguāzi same as 耳光 ěrguāng

耳掴子 ěrguāizi dial. a slap in the face; a box on the ear

耳光 ěrguāng (also 耳光子 ěrguāngzi) a slap in the face; a box on the ear: 打～ slap sb.'s face; box sb.'s ears / 我搧了他一个～。I gave him a box on the ear. / 事实给了他们一记响亮的～。The facts have given them a slap in the face.

耳郭 ěrguō physiol. auricle; pinna

耳锅 ěrguō eared pot

耳环 ěrhuán earrings

耳机 ěrjī earphone; earpiece: 戴上～ put on the earphones

耳际 ěrjì in the ears: 几天来他的话一直在我～萦绕。For days his words have been ringing in my ears.

耳镜 ěrjìng med. otoscope

耳孔 ěrkǒng same as 外耳门 wài'ěrmén

耳廓 ěrkuò same as 耳郭 ěrguō

耳力 ěrlì power of hearing; hearing: 我的～不大好。My hearing is not very good. / 他的～不济了。His hearing is getting worse

耳聋 ěrlóng be deaf

耳轮 ěrlún physiol. helix

耳帽 ěrmào (also 耳朵帽儿 ěrduomàor) earmuffs

耳门 ěrmén side doors (flanking the main gate)

耳鸣 ěrmíng have a ringing sensation in the ears; tinnitus: 我～。My ears are ringing.

耳膜 ěrmó tympanic membrane; eardrum

耳目 ěrmù ① what one sees and hears; knowledge; information: ～不广 not well-informed ② one who spies for sb. else: 他～众多, 你说话要小心。His men are everywhere. Be careful what you say.

耳目闭塞 ěrmù bìsè ill-informed; uninformed; ignorant

耳目所及 ěrmù suǒ jí from what one sees and hears;

from what one knows: 就～, 只觉得这几年的变化可真不小。From what I hear and see, things have changed a lot in these last few years.

耳目一新 ěrmù yī xīn find everything fresh and new: 他们一到那里就感到～。They found themselves in an entirely new world the moment they arrived.

耳旁风 ěrpángfēng same as 耳边风 ěrbiānfēng

耳屏 ěrpíng physiol. tragus

耳热 ěrrè have burning ears: 她激动得脸红～。In her excitement her cheeks reddened and her ears burned.

耳濡目染 ěrrú-mùrǎn be imperceptibly influenced by what one sees and hears

耳软心活 ěrruǎn-xīnhuó credulous and pliable

耳塞 ěrsāi earplug

耳塞 ěrsai inf. earwax

耳扇 ěrshàn ① earflaps; earlaps ② auricle; pinna: 一支纸烟夹在～上 with a cigarette held behind one's ear

耳生 ěrshēng unfamiliar to the ear; strange-sounding: 外面说话的声音听着～。The voice outside sounds unfamiliar to me.

耳食 ěrshí formal believe what one is told

耳食之谈 ěrshí zhī tán hearsay; rumour

耳屎 ěrshǐ inf. earwax: 挖～ pick one's ears

耳饰 ěrshì ear ornaments

耳熟 ěrshú familiar to the ear: 这个名字好～, 好像在广播里听到过。The name sounds so familiar. I seem to have heard it mentioned over the radio.

耳熟能详 ěrshú néng xiáng what's frequently heard can be repeated in detail

耳顺 ěrshùn ① formal ear attuned (used esp. in): ～之年 the age of sixty (from Confucius' saying 六十而耳顺 "At sixty my ear was attuned") / 年近～ be nearly sixty ② pleasing to the ear

耳提面命 ěrtí-miànmìng pour earnest advice into sb.'s ears; give earnest exhortations

耳听为虚, 眼见为实 ěr tīng wéi xū, yǎn jiàn wéi shí what you hear may be false, what you see is true

耳挖勺儿 ěrwāsháor dial. earpick

耳挖子 ěrwāzi earpick

耳闻 ěrwén hear of (or about): 这事略有～, 详细情况不很清楚。I've heard a little about it, but I don't know the details.

耳闻不如目见 ěrwén bùrú mùjiàn seeing for oneself is better than hearing from others

耳闻目睹 ěrwén-mùdǔ (also 耳闻目击 ěrwén-mùjī) what one sees and hears: 其间～的事, 算起来也很不少。During that time I witnessed or heard about a lot of things.

耳蜗 ěrwō physiol. cochlea; acoustic labyrinth

耳下腺 ěrxiàxiàn same as 腮腺 sāixiàn

耳穴 ěrxué the acupuncture points on the ears

耳熏目染 ěrxūn-mùrǎn same as 耳濡目染 ěrrú-mùrǎn

耳咽管 ěryānguǎn physiol. Eustachian tube; auditory tube

耳音 ěryīn power of hearing; hearing: 我的～越来越不行了。My hearing is getting worse. / 瞧你这～, 连我的声音也听不出来了。What's the matter with your hearing? You can't even recognize my voice.

耳语 ěryǔ whisper in sb.'s ear; whisper: 大夫看了看我的伤口, 跟护士～了几句便出去了。After examining my wound, the doctor whispered something in the nurse's ear and left.

耳针疗法 ěrzhēn liáofǎ Chin. med. auriculotherapy; ear-acupuncture therapy

耳坠子 ěrzhuìzi (also 耳坠儿 ěrzhuìr) inf. eardrops

耳子 ěrzi ears or side handles of a utensil

迩 (邇) ěr formal near; close: 遐迩闻名 xiá'ěr wénmíng

迩来　ěrlái　*formal*　recently; lately; hitherto

饵　ěr　① cakes; pastry: 果～ candies and cakes; confectionery ② (fish) bait ③ *formal* entice: ～以重利 use great wealth as a bait; entice sb. with prospects of great wealth

饵敌　ěrdí　set a trap for the enemy

饵子　ěrzi　(fish) bait

洱　ěr　see 普洱茶 pǔ'ěrchá

珥　ěr　*formal* jade or pearl earrings

铒　ěr　*chem.* erbium (Er)

èr

二　èr　① two: ～公斤 two kilograms / ～～得四。 Twice two is four. / 第～遍 the second time / ～路公共汽车 No. 2 bus / ～哥 one's second elder brother / ～层楼 (British) first floor; (American) second floor / 一百～ a hundred and twenty / 三千～ three thousand two hundred / 六万～ sixty-two thousand / 把这个班一分为～。 Divide the class in two. ② different: 二心 èrxīn / 不二价 bù'èrjià

二八　èrbā　sixteen: 年方～ be only sixteen years of age

二把刀　èrbǎdāo　*dial.* ① have a smattering of a subject ② smatterer

二百二　èrbǎi'èr (also 二百二十 èrbǎi'èrshí) common name for 汞溴红 gǒngxiùhóng

二百五　èrbǎiwǔ　① *inf.* a stupid person: 他是个～。 He's a rather stupid person. *or* He's not all there. ② *dial.* dabbler; smatterer

二倍体　èrbèitǐ　*biol.* diploid

二遍苦，二茬罪　èr biàn kǔ, èr chá zuì (usu. used in): 吃二遍苦，受二茬罪 suffer oppression and exploitation all over again

二部制　èrbùzhì　two-shift system (in schools); two part-time shifts (with half of the pupils coming to classes in the mornings and half in the afternoons): ～学校 a school with two part-time shifts; two-shift school

二重唱　èrchóngchàng　*mus.* (vocal) duet

二重性　èrchóngxìng　dual character (*or* nature); duality

二重奏　èrchóngzòu　*mus.* (instrumental) duet

二传手　èrchuánshǒu　setter (in volleyball)

二次方程　èrcì fāngchéng　*math.* quadratic equation

二次曲面　èrcì qūmiàn　*math.* quadratic surface

二次曲线　èrcì qūxiàn　*math.* conic section

二道贩子　èrdàofànzi　a person who resells at inflated prices

二等　èrděng　second-class; second-rate

二等兵　èrděngbīng　(U. S. and Brit. Army, U. S. Marine Corps) private; (U. S. Navy) seaman second class; (Brit. Navy) able seaman; (U. S. Air Force) airman second class; (Brit. Air Force) leading aircraftsman; (Brit. Marine Corps) marine second class

二等残废军人　èrděng cánfèi jūnrén　disabled soldier, second class

二等舱　èrděngcāng　second-class cabin

二等功　èrděnggōng　Merit Citation Class II

二等奖　èrděngjiǎng　second prize

二等秘书　èrděng mìshū　*diplomacy* Second Secretary

二等品　èrděngpǐn　second-class or inferior goods; seconds

二地主　èrdìzhǔ　sub-landlord

二叠纪　Èrdiéjì　*geol.* the Permian Period

二叠系　Èrdiéxì　*geol.* the Permian System

二房　èrfáng　① the second branch of an extended family (*or* a big family) ② concubine

二房东　èrfángdōng　sublessor (of a room or house); sub-landlord

二分点　èrfēndiǎn　*astron.* the equinoxes

二分裂　èrfēnliè　*biol.* binary fission

二分音符　èrfēn yīnfú　*mus.* minim; half note

二伏　èrfú　the second *fu* (another name for 中伏 zhōngfú)

二副　èrfù　second mate; second officer

二鬼子　èrguǐzi　traitor (a term applied to sb. who aided the Japanese invaders during the War of Resistance against Japan)

二锅头　èrguōtóu　a strong, colourless liquor distilled from sorghum (so called because it is distilled twice)

二胡　èrhú　erhu, a two-stringed bowed instrument with a lower register than *jinghu* (京胡)

二乎　èrhu　*dial.* ① shrink from fear: 他在困难面前向来不～。 He never shrank from difficulty. ② hesitant; undecided: 你越说越把我弄～了。 The more you say, the less able I am to make up my mind. ③ not promising; not hopeful: 我看这件事～了，你说呢? I think the prospects are rather dim. Don't you think so?

二花脸　èrhuāliǎn　a type of the painted face in Beijing opera, a male role characterized by his postures and acting rather than singing

二化螟　èrhuàmíng　striped rice borer (*Chilo suppressalis*)

二话　èrhuà　(often used in the negative) demur; objection: ～不说 without demur / 需要他干什么，他就干什么，从来没有～。 Whatever he is required to do, he does it readily.

二荒地　èrhuāngdì　cultivated land running to waste

二黄　èrhuáng (also 二簧 èrhuáng) *theat.* erhuang, one of the two chief types of music in traditional Chinese operas

二婚头　èrhūntóu (also 二婚儿 èrhūnr) *derog.* a remarried woman

二混子　èrhùnzi　*dial.* loafer; ne'er-do-well

二级风　èrjífēng　*meteorol.* force 2 wind; light breeze

二级准尉　èrjí zhǔnwèi　(Brit. Army, Navy, Air Force and Marine Corps) warrant officer (Class II); (U. S. Army and Air Force) warrant officer, junior grade; (U. S. Navy and Marine Corps) warrant officer

二极管　èrjíguǎn　*electron.* diode

二尖瓣　èrjiānbàn　*physiol.* mitral valve

二尖瓣狭窄　èrjiānbàn xiázhǎi　mitral stenosis

二进制　èrjìnzhì　binary system

二进制标度　èrjìnzhì biāodù　binary scale

二进制数　èrjìnzhìshù　binary number

二进制数字　èrjìnzhì shùzi　binary digit

二赖子　èrlàizi　*dial.* a shameless loafer

二郎腿　èrlángtuǐ　*dial.* a sitting posture with the legs crossed and one foot poised in the air: 跷起～ sit cross-legged, poising one foot in the air

二老　èrlǎo　father and mother; parents: ～健在? Your parents are in good health, aren't they?

二愣子　èrlèngzi　a rash fellow

二流子　èrliúzi　loafer; idler; bun

二硫化物　èrliúhuàwù　*chem.* bisulphide

二路儿　èrlùr　second-rate: ～货 inferior goods; inferior stuff

二门　èrmén　inner gate

二米饭　èrmǐfàn　(cooked) rice and millet mixed

二面角　èrmiànjiǎo　*math.* dihedral angle

二名法　èrmíngfǎ　*biol.* binomial nomenclature

二拇指　èrmuzhǐ　*inf.* forefinger; index finger

二年生　èrniánshēng　*bot.* biennial

二年生植物　èrniánshēng zhíwù　biennial plant

二七大罢工 **Èr Qī Dà Bàgōng** the Great Strike of February 7, 1923 (an anti-imperialist, anti-warlord strike of the Beijing-Hankou Railway workers led by the Chinese Communist Party)

二全音符 **èrquán yīnfú** *mus.* breve

二人台 **èrréntái** ① a song-and-dance duet popular in Inner Mongolia ② a new type of folk drama evolved from the song-and-dance duet

二人转 **èrrénzhuàn** ① a song-and-dance duet popular in Heilongjiang, Jilin and Liaoning Provinces ② the provincial drama newly evolved from the song-and-dance duet, also known as Jilin drama 吉剧

二十八星瓢虫 **èrshí bā xīng piáochóng** potato ladybug; potato ladybird

二十八宿 **èrshí bā xiù** the twenty-eight constellations into which the celestial sphere was divided in ancient Chinese astronomy (seven of these constellations were allotted to each of the four quadrants of the vault of heaven: the eastern quadrant, called the "Green Dragon" 苍龙, comprising *jiao* 角, *kang* 亢, *di* 氐, *fang* 房, *xin* 心, *wei* 尾, and *ji* 箕; the northern quadrant, called the "Black Warrior" or "Black Tortoise" 玄武, comprising *dou* 斗, *niu* 牛, *nü* 女, *xu* 虚, *wei* 危, *shi* 室, and *bi* 壁; the western quadrant, called the "White Tiger" 白虎, comprising *kui* 奎, *lou* 娄, *wei* 胃, *mao* 昴, *bi* 毕, *zi* 觜, and *shen* 参; and the southern quadrant, called the "Scarlet Bird" 朱雀, comprising *jing* 井, *gui* 鬼, *liu* 柳, *xing* 星, *zhang* 张, *yi* 翼, and *zhen* 轸)

二十四节气 **èrshí sì jiéqì** the twenty-four solar terms (i.e. 立春 Lìchūn, 雨水 Yǔshuǐ, 惊蛰 Jīngzhé, 春分 Chūnfēn, 清明 Qīngmíng, 谷雨 Gǔyǔ, 立夏 Lìxià, 小满 Xiǎomǎn, 芒种 Mángzhòng, 夏至 Xiàzhì, 小暑 Xiǎoshǔ, 大暑 Dàshǔ, 立秋 Lìqiū, 处暑 Chǔshǔ, 白露 Báilù, 秋分 Qiūfēn, 寒露 Hánlù, 霜降 Shuāngjiàng, 立冬 Lìdōng, 小雪 Xiǎoxuě, 大雪 Dàxuě, 冬至 Dōngzhì, 小寒 Xiǎohán, 大寒 Dàhán) ——see also 节气 jiéqì

二十四开 **èrshí sì kāi** ① 24-carat gold; pure gold ② (of book or paper size) 24 mo

二十四史 **èrshí sì shǐ** ① the Twenty-Four Histories (dynastic histories from remote antiquity till the Ming Dynasty) ② a long intricate story: 一部～, 不知从何说起。It's such a long and complicated story, I hardly know where to start.

二十一条 **èrshí yī tiáo** the Twenty-one Demands (forced by Japan on Yuan Shikai 袁世凯 in 1915 for domination of China)

二手 **èrshǒu** ① assistant: 让我给你当～怎么样? Will you take me as your assistant? ② secondhand: ～资料 secondhand materials／～货 secondhand goods

二四滴 **èrsìdī** *agric.* 2,4-D; 2,4-dichlorophenoxyacetic acid

二踢脚 **èrtījiǎo** *inf.* double-kick (popular name for 双响 shuāngxiǎng)

二天 **èrtiān** *dial.* another day; some other day; in a day or two

二五眼 **èrwuyǎn** *dial.* ① of inferior ability or quality ② an incompetent person

二项式 **èrxiàngshì** *math.* binomial

二象性 **èrxiàngxìng** *phys.* dual property; duality: 物质的～ the dualistic nature of matter／波粒～ wave-particle duality

二心 **èrxīn** ① disloyalty ② halfheartedness

二性子 **èrxìngzi** common name for 两性人 liǎngxìngrén

二氧化物 **èryǎnghuàwù** *chem.* dioxide (e.g. 二氧化碳 carbon dioxide; 二氧化硅 silicon dioxide; silica

二一添作五 **èr yī tiān zuò wǔ** go halves; go fifty-fifty

二意 **èryì** same as 二心 èrxīn

二意 **èryi** *inf.* hesitate

二元 **èryuán** ① *math.* duality ② *chem.* binary

二元论 **èryuánlùn** *philos.* dualism

二元酸 **èryuánsuān** *chem.* binary acid

二元体 **èryuántǐ** another name for 二倍体 èrbèitǐ

二月 **èryuè** ① February ② the second month of the lunar year; the second moon

二者必居其一 **èr zhě bì jū qí yī** either one or the other: 或者把老虎打死, 或者被老虎吃掉,～。Either kill the tiger or be killed by him——one way or the other.

二指 **èrzhǐ** forefinger; index finger

二至点 **èrzhìdiǎn** *astron.* the solstices

二致 **èrzhì** different: 并无～ there is no difference whatever

弍　**èr** same as 二 èr

貳　**èr** ① two (used for the numeral 二 on cheques, banknotes, etc. to avoid mistakes or alterations) ② defect; turn one's coat: 贰臣 èrchén

贰臣 **èrchén** an official who retains his position after capitulating to the new dynasty; turncoat official

贰心 **èrxīn** same as 二心 èrxīn

F

fā

发 (發) fā ① send out; issue; emit; give forth; shoot: ～电报 send a telegram / ～传单 distribute leaflets / ～命令 issue an order / ～信号 give a signal / ～炮 fire shells / ～工资 pay out wages / ～了三条新闻。Three items of news have been released. / 万箭齐～。Ten thousand arrows shot at once. ② utter; express: ～一通议论 speak at length ③ come or bring into existence: 发电 fādiàn / 发芽 fāyá ④ become; come to be: 脸色～白 become pale; lose colour / 树叶～黄了。The leaves are turning yellow. / 肉～臭了。The meat smells a bit off. *or* The meat smells bad. ⑤ (of foodstuffs) rise or expand when leavened or soaked: 面～起来了。The dough has risen. / ～海参 puff up dried sea cucumbers (by soaking them in water) ⑥ develop; expand: 发育 fāyù ⑦ open up; expose: 发掘 fājué / 揭发 jiēfā ⑧ feel; have a feeling: 嘴里～苦 have a bitter taste in the mouth / ～麻 tingle / ～痒 itch ⑨ start; set out: 车船齐～ All the boats and carts set out at the same time. ⑩ *m.* (for bullets and shells): 一～炮弹 one shell / 两百～子弹 two hundred rounds of ammunition; two hundred cartridges ——see also fà

发榜 fābǎng publish a list of successful candidates or applicants: 高考过后，同学们都焦急地等待着～。After the college entrance examinations, the students were all waiting anxiously for the results to be published.

发包 fābāo give out a contract for a project

发报 fābào transmit messages by radio, telegraphy, etc.

发报机 fābàojī radio transmitter

发背 fābèi *Chin. med.* carbuncle on the back

发表 fābiǎo publish; issue: ～文章 publish an article / ～声明 issue (*or* make) a statement / ～意见 express an opinion; state one's views / ～演说 make (*or* deliver) a speech / ～社论 carry an editorial / 这项任命尚未正式～。The appointment has not yet been officially announced.

发兵 fābīng send out troops; dispatch troops

发病 fābìng (of a disease) come on: 他是昨天半夜发的病，现在还在抢救。He came down with the illness about midnight and is still under emergency treatment.

发病率 fābìnglǜ incidence of a disease: 近几年这种病的～大大降低了。The incidence of this disease has dropped considerably in the past few years.

发布 fābù issue; release: ～命令 issue orders / ～新闻 release news

发财 fācái get rich; make a fortune; make a pile: 他做股票生意发了大财。He made a fortune buying and selling stocks.

发颤 fāchàn quiver; tremble: 他激动得说话声音都～了。He was so overcome with emotion that his voice quivered. —— see also fāzhàn

发潮 fācháo become damp: 衣服有点儿～。The clothes feel a bit damp.

发车场 fāchēchǎng *railway* departure track; departure yard

发痴 fāchī *dial.* ① stare blankly; be in a daze; be in a trance ② go mad; go crazy; become insane

发愁 fāchóu worry; be anxious: 不要为这事～。Don't worry about it. / 你发什么愁啊? What are you so anxious about?

发出 fāchū issue; send out; give out: ～指示 issue a directive / ～警告 send out a warning / ～阵阵清香 send forth wafts of delicate fragrance / ～警报 sound the alarm / 原子反应堆～大量的热能。The atomic reactor generates enormous amounts of thermal energy. / 通知已经～了。The notice has already been sent out.

发怵 fāchù (also 发憷 fāchù) feel timid; grow apprehensive: 新演员初次上台总有点～。New actors are invariably keyed up for their first stage appearance.

发喘 fāchuǎn breathe heavily; gasp for breath; pant

发达 fādá ① developed; flourishing: 肌肉～ have well-developed muscles / 交通～ have a well-developed transportation system / 工商业很～。Industry and commerce are flourishing. ② promote; develop: ～贸易 develop (*or* promote) trade

发达国家 fādá guójiā developed country

发呆 fādāi stare blankly; be in a daze; be in a trance: 他话也不说，坐在那里～。He said nothing but sat there staring blankly. *or* He said nothing but sat there as if in a trance.

发嗲 fādiǎ *dial.* ① speak or act coquettishly ② act like a spoilt child

发电 fādiàn generate electricity (*or* electric power)

发电厂 fādiànchǎng power plant; power station: 水力 (火力) ～ hydraulic (thermal) power plant / 地热～ geothermal power plant / 原子能～ atomic power plant / ～容量 station capacity

发电机 fādiànjī generator; dynamo: 双水内冷汽轮～ turbogenerator with inner water-cooled stator and rotor / 永磁～ magneto generator / ～容量 generator capacity / ～组 generating set

发电量 fādiànliàng generated energy; electric energy production

发电站 fādiànzhàn power station

发动 fādòng ① start; launch: ～机器 start a machine; set a machine going / ～战争 launch (*or* unleash) a war ② call into action; mobilize; arouse: ～群众 arouse the masses to action; mobilize the masses

发动机 fādòngjī engine; motor

发抖 fādǒu shiver; shake; tremble: 冷得～ shiver (*or* shake) with cold / 吓得～ tremble with fear; shake in one's shoes / 气得～ tremble with anger

发堵 fādǔ feel oppressed; be depressed

发端 fāduān make a start

发凡 fāfán formal introduction (to a subject or a book): 《修辞学～》*An Introduction to Rhetoric*

发烦 fāfán be vexed; be annoyed

发放 fāfàng provide; grant; extend: ～贷款 grant a

loan / 救灾物资很快～到灾区人民手里。 Relief goods were quickly handed out to the people in the stricken area.

发粉 fāfěn baking powder

发奋 fāfèn ① work energetically ② same as 发愤 fāfèn

发愤 fāfèn make a firm resolution; make a determined effort: ～工作 put all one's energies into one's work

发愤图强 fāfèn túqiáng work with a will to make the country strong

发愤忘食 fāfèn wàngshí be so buried in one's work as to forget one's meals; work so hard as to forget to eat

发疯 fāfēng go mad; go crazy; become insane; be out of one's mind

发福 fāfú pol. (usu. said to older people) grow stout; put on weight: 您～了。 You have put on weight.

发绀 fāgàn med. cyanosis

发糕 fāgāo steamed sponge cake

发稿 fāgǎo ① distribute news dispatches ② send manuscripts to the press

发给 fāgěi issue; distribute; grant: ～护照 issue a passport / ～复员费 issue (or give) demobilization pay / ～学员学习材料 distribute study material among the students

发光 fāguāng ① give off light; shine; be luminous: ～发热 emit light and heat / 群星闪闪～。 The stars twinkled. / 有一分热， 发一分光 give as much light as the heat can produce—do one's best, however little it may be ② phys. luminescence: 场致～ electroluminescence / ～度 luminosity

发光漆 fāguāngqī luminous paint

发光体 fāguāngtǐ luminous body; luminary; luminophor

发汗 fāhàn induce perspiration (as by drugs); diaphoresis

发汗药 fāhànyào sudorific; diaphoretic

发号施令 fāhào-shīlìng issue orders; order people about: 干部要深入群众， 不要只是坐在办公室里～。 Cadres should get out among the people, not just sit in their offices issuing orders. / 你有什么资格向别人～？ What right have you to order people about?

发狠 fāhěn ① make a determined effort: 他们一～， 三天的任务一天就完成了。 With a determined effort, they finished the three-day task in a single day. ② be angry

发横 fāhèng act in an unreasonable (or brutal) way

发花 fāhuā (of the eyes) grow dim; see things in a blur

发话 fāhuà ① give (verbal) orders or instructions ② speak angrily

发话器 fāhuàqì telephone transmitter

发还 fāhuán return sth. (usu. to one's subordinate); give (or send) back: 把作业～给学生 return the homework to the pupils / 把计划～原单位去讨论修改 send the plan back where it came from for discussion and revision

发慌 fāhuāng feel nervous; get flustered; get flurried: 她虽是第一次当众讲话， 却一点都不～。 She didn't feel a bit nervous though it was the first time she'd spoken in public.

发挥 fāhuī ① bring into play; give play to; give free rein to: 充分～群众的积极性 bring the initiative of the masses into full play / ～专长 give full play to one's professional knowledge or skill / ～水利设施的最大效益 make the most of the water conservancy works / ～想像力 give free rein to one's imagination / 我们没有充分～他的才干。 We're not doing justice to his talents. ② develop (an idea, a theme, etc.); elaborate: 这一论点有待进一步～。 This point needs further elaboration.

发昏 fāhūn ① feel giddy (or dizzy): 我的头有点儿～。 I feel a bit giddy. ② lose one's head; become confused:

你～啦! Are you out of your mind?

发火 fāhuǒ ① catch fire; ignite ② detonate; go off: 他打了一枪， 没有～。 He pulled the trigger but the gun didn't go off. ③ dial. (of a stove) draw well ④ dial. a fire breaking out ⑤ get angry; flare up; lose one's temper: 你别～， 咱们慢慢儿谈。 Don't get excited. Let's talk it over calmly.

发火点 fāhuǒdiǎn phys. ignition point

发货 fāhuò send out goods; deliver goods

发货单 fāhuòdān dispatch list

发货人 fāhuòrén consignor; shipper

发急 fājí become impatient or excited: 等得～ waiting impatiently / 他一输棋， 就会～。 Every time he lost a game of chess, he got excited.

发迹 fājì (of a poor man) gain fame and fortune; rise to power and position

发家 fājiā build up a family fortune

发家致富 fājiā-zhìfù build up a family fortune

发奖 fājiǎng award prizes: ～仪式 prize-giving ceremony

发酵 fājiào ferment

发酵饲料 fājiào sìliào fermented feed

发紧 fājǐn ① (of the chest muscles) become taut ② feel nervous; be keyed up

发酒疯 fā jiǔfēng get drunk and behave sillily; have a drunken fit

发觉 fājué find; detect; discover: 错误一经～， 就应改正。 Mistakes should be corrected as soon as they are detected. / 火扑灭了以后， 他才～自己受了伤。 He didn't realize that he was injured until the fire had been put out.

发掘 fājué excavate; unearth; explore: ～古墓 excavate an ancient tomb / ～文物 unearth cultural relics / ～人才 seek gifted (or talented) people / ～祖国的医药学遗产 explore the legacy of traditional Chinese medicine and pharmacology

发刊词 fākāncí foreword (or introduction) to a periodical: 《共产党人》～ Introducing The Communist

发狂 fākuáng go mad; go crazy

发聩振聋 fākuì-zhènlóng same as 振聋发聩 zhènlóng-fākuì

发困 fākùn inf. feel sleepy (or drowsy)

发蓝 fālán same as 烤蓝 kǎolán

发懒 fālǎn feel lazy (or sluggish)

发冷 fālěng feel cold (or chilly): 我有点～， 没准儿发烧了。 I feel chilly, maybe I am running a fever.

发楞 fālèng inf. stare blankly; be in a daze; be in a trance

发亮 fāliàng shine: 把机器擦得～ polish the machine till it shines / 东方～了。 The gleam of dawn shimmered in the east.

发令 fālìng ① issue an order; give orders ② give a password

发令枪 fālìngqiāng sports starting gun (or pistol)

发聋振聩 fālóng-zhènkuì same as 振聋发聩 zhènlóng-fākuì

发落 fāluò deal with (an offender): 从轻～ deal with sb. leniently

发毛 fāmáo ① inf. be scared; get gooseflesh ② dial. lose one's temper

发霉 fāméi go mouldy; become mildewed

发闷 fāmēn ① be stuffy; be close: 天气～。 The weather is close. ② (of a sound) be muffled ——see also fāmèn

发闷 fāmèn feel depressed; be in low spirits ——see also fāmēn

发蒙 fāmēng inf. get confused; get into a muddle

发蒙 fāméng old teach a child to read and write; teach a child his ABC

发面 fāmiàn ① leaven dough ② leavened dough: ～饼 leavened pancake

发明 fāmíng ① invent: 印刷术是中国首先～的。Printing was first invented by the Chinese. ② invention: 最新～ the latest invention ③ *formal* expound: 本书对《老子》的哲理颇多～。This book does much to expound the philosophy of the *Lao Zi*.

发木 fāmù be numb: 我手～。My hands are numb.

发奶 fānǎi stimulate the secretion of milk; promote lactation

发难 fānàn ① rise in revolt; launch an attack ② same as 问难 wènnàn

发腻 fānì sickening; nasty; offensive; disgusting

发蔫 fāniān ① be fading; be withering; be shrivelled up ② be listless; be spiritless; be droopy

发茶 fāniě same as 发蔫 fāniān②

发怒 fānù get angry; flare up; lose one's temper

发排 fāpái send a manuscript to the compositor

发胖 fāpàng put on (*or* gain) weight; get fat: 我近来好像～。I seem to have put on some weight lately.

发泡剂 fāpàojì *chem.* foaming (*or* blowing) agent

发配 fāpèi *old* be transported to a distant place for penal servitude

发脾气 fā píqi lose one's temper; get angry: 有理慢慢儿说, 何必～。Speak calmly if you think you're in the right; there's no need to get angry. / 他从来没发过脾气。He has never lost his temper.

发票 fāpiào (also 发货票 fāhuòpiào) invoice: 开～ make an invoice

发起 fāqǐ ① initiate; sponsor: 这次会议是由十四个国家～的。The meeting was sponsored by 14 countries. / 这个歌咏队是我们～成立的。This singing group was formed on our initiative. ② start; launch: ～反攻 launch a counterattack

发起国 fāqǐguó sponsor nation

发起人 fāqǐrén initiator; sponsor

发气 fāqì *dial.* ① get angry; lose one's temper: 她从来没有像今天那样～过。She has never been so angry before. ② give vent to one's anger: 他哪天工作不顺心, 回家就拿老婆孩子来～。After a bad day at work, he would come home and take it out on his wife and children.

发情 fāqíng *zool.* ① oestrus: 同步～ synchronization of oestrus ② be in heat

发情期 fāqíngqī heat period; oestrus

发情周期 fāqíng zhōuqī oestrous cycle

发球 fāqiú serve a ball: 该谁～? Whose service is it? / ～得分 ace / ～不过网 serve a ball into the net / 他～发得好。He has a very good serve. / 他发了一个怪球。He made a tricky serve.

发球区 fāqiúqū service area

发热 fārè ① have (*or* run) a fever; have (*or* run) a temperature: 我好像有点儿～。I feel as if I'm running a fever. ② give out heat; generate heat: 恒星本身发光。A fixed star can emit light and heat by itself. ③ be hotheaded; be impetuous: 别头脑～! Don't be so impetuous!

发热量 fārèliàng *chem.* calorific capacity

发人深省 fā rén shēnxǐng (also 发人深醒 fā rén shěnxǐng; 发人深思 fā rén shěnsī) set people thinking; call for deep thought; provide food for thought

发轫 fārèn *formal* set sth. afoot; commence an undertaking

发散 fāsàn ① (of rays, etc.) diverge ② *Chin. med.* disperse the internal heat with sudorifics: 吃点药～一下 take a sudorific to sweat out a cold

发散度 fāsàndù *phys.* divergency

发丧 fāsāng ① announce a death; send out an obituary ② arrange a funeral

发色团 fāsètuán *text.* chromophore

发痧 fāshā *dial.* have a heatstroke

发烧 fāshāo have (*or* run) a fever; have (*or* run) a temperature

发射 fāshè ① launch; project; discharge; shoot; fire: ～导弹 launch a guided missile / ～人造卫星 launch a man-made satellite / ～炮弹 fire shells ② *phys.* transmit; emit

发射场 fāshèchǎng launching site

发射光谱 fāshè guāngpǔ emission spectrum

发射架 fāshèjià launcher

发射井 fāshèjǐng launching silo

发射台 fāshètái launching stand; launching (*or* firing) pad

发身 fāshēn puberty

发神经 fā shénjīng go mad; go crazy; be out of one's mind

发生 fāshēng happen; occur; take place: ～了意外。Something unexpected happened. / 那里～了强烈地震。A violent earthquake occurred there. / ～了巨大的变化。Tremendous changes have taken place. / ～新的困难。New difficulties cropped up (*or* arose). / 机器～故障。The machine broke down. / 故事～在一九六二年秋天。The story is set in the autumn of 1962. / 她对养蜂～了兴趣。She's become interested in apiculture.

发生器 fāshēngqì *chem.* generator: 氨～ ammonia generator

发声 fāshēng sound production

发誓 fāshì vow; pledge; swear: 他们～要为死难烈士报仇。They vowed to avenge the martyrs.

发售 fāshòu sell; put on sale: 这些杂志在全国各地书店均有～。These magazines are sold at bookstores throughout the country. / 新的纪念邮票将于下星期～。The new commemorative stamps will be put on sale next week.

发抒 fāshū (also 发舒 fāshū) express; voice: ～己见 express one's personal views / ～革命豪情 voice lofty revolutionary sentiments

发水 fāshuǐ flood: 过去一下暴雨, 这条河就发大水。This river used to get flooded whenever there was a rainstorm.

发思古之幽情 fā sī gǔ zhī yōuqíng muse over things of the remote past

发送 fāsòng ① transmit by radio: ～密码电报 transmit a coded message ② dispatch (letters, etc.)

发酸 fāsuān ① turn sour; taste sour: 牛奶～了。The milk has turned sour. / 碱放少了, 馒头就～。Steamed bread will taste sour if there isn't enough soda in the dough. ② feel a tingle in one's eyes or nose (when about to break down and weep): 她觉得两眼～, 泪水止不住流了下来。She felt a tingle in her eyes and could hardly keep from shedding tears. ③ ache slightly: 腰有点～ have a slight backache

发条 fātiáo *mech.* spiral power spring; clockwork spring

发文 fāwén outgoing message; dispatch: ～簿 register of outgoing documents, letters, etc.

发问 fāwèn ask (*or* pose, raise) a question

发现 fāxiàn ① discover; find: 一四九二年哥仑布～美洲。Columbus discovered America in 1492. / ～一个新方法 discover a new method / ～一些线索 find some clues / 敌机被我们的雷达～了。Enemy planes were picked up by our radar. ② discovery; find: 物理学方面一个划时代的～ an epoch-making discovery in physics / 考古方面的重大～ important archaeological finds ③ find; realize; perceive; notice: 我们～他有神经病。We found him to be a mental case. / 我～他好像有什么心事。I noticed that he seemed to have something on his mind.

发祥地 fāxiángdì　place of origin; birthplace: 黄河流域是我国古代文化的～。The Yellow River Basin was the birthplace of China's ancient culture.

发饷 fāxiǎng　*old*　issue pay (esp. to soldiers)

发笑 fāxiào　burst into laughter; laugh: 令人～ make one laugh; provoke laughter; be ridiculous

发泄 fāxiè　give vent to; let off: ～不满情绪 express one's discontent; air one's grievances / 有气就～出来比闷在心里要好得多。It's much healthier to give vent to your anger than to try to control it.

发心 fāxīn　make up one's mind (to do sth.)

发薪 fāxīn　pay wages or salary

发信 fāxìn　post a letter: 我接连发了两封信，催他快来。I sent off two letters in succession, urging him to come at once. / ～人 addresser

发行 fāxíng　issue; publish; distribute; put on sale: ～货币（债券，股票）issue currency (bonds, stocks) / ～书刊 publish books and magazines / ～影片 release a film / 由新华书店～ distributed by Xinhua Bookstore / 将在全国各地～ will be put on sale throughout the country / ～者 publisher

发行银行 fāxíng yínháng　bank of issue

发虚 fāxū　① feel apprehensive; feel diffident ② feel feeble and weak

发芽 fāyá　germinate; sprout: 种子还没有～。The seeds haven't sprouted yet. / ～率 germination percentage / ～试验 germination test

发言 fāyán　speak; make a statement or speech; take the floor: 他在会上～了吗? Did he speak at the meeting? / 要求～ ask to be heard; ask for the floor / 他的～很精彩。He made a brilliant speech. / ～稿 the text of a statement or speech

发言权 fāyánquán　right to speak: 我们对这事当然有～。Of course we have a say in this matter. / 他们对这个问题最有～。They are best qualified to speak on this question. / 没有调查就没有～。No investigation, no right to speak.

发言人 fāyánrén　spokesman; spokeswoman: 政府～ government spokesman or spokeswoman

发炎 fāyán　*med.*　inflammation: 伤口～了。The wound has become inflamed.

发扬 fāyáng　① develop; carry on (or forward): ～民主作风 develop a democratic style of work / ～艰苦奋斗的作风 keep up the practice of plain living and hard struggle / ～优良传统 carry forward the fine traditions / ～成绩，纠正错误。Add to your achievements and correct your mistakes. / ～正气，打击歪风。Encourage healthy trends and combat unhealthy ones. ② make the most of; make full use of: ～火力，消灭敌人 make full use of firepower to destroy the enemy

发扬踔厉 fāyáng chuōlì　(also 发扬蹈厉 fāyáng dǎolì) full of spirit; mettlesome

发扬光大 fāyáng guāngdà　carry forward; develop; enhance: 延安精神～。Carry forward the Yan'an spirit.

发洋财 fā yángcái　make a big fortune

发疟子 fā yàozi　have an attack of malaria; suffer from malarial fever

发音 fāyīn　pronounce; enunciate: 这个字怎么～? How do you pronounce this word? / 在 doubt 这个词中，b 这个字母不～。The letter b in the word "doubt" is silent (*or* not pronounced). / 她～清晰。She enunciates her words clearly. / 他～不清楚。His articulation is poor.

发音部位 fāyīn bùwèi　points of articulation

发音困难 fāyīn kùnnan　*med.*　dysphonia

发音器官 fāyīn qìguān　vocal organs; speech organs

发育 fāyù　grow; develop: ～健全 physically well developed / 婴儿～情况良好。The baby is coming along well.

发育不全 fāyù bùquán　*med.*　hypoplasia

发育异常 fāyù yìcháng　*med.*　dysplasia

发源 fāyuán　rise; originate: 长江～于青海。The Changjiang River rises in Qinghai Province. / 一切真知都是从直接经验～的。All genuine knowledge originates in direct experience.

发源地 fāyuándì　place of origin; source; birthplace

发晕 fāyūn　feel dizzy (*or* giddy)

发展 fāzhǎn　① develop; expand; grow: ～轻工业 expand the light industry / ～组织 expand an organization; increase the membership / 跟不上形势的～ cannot keep up with the changing situation / 用～的眼光看人 look at a person with an eye on the course of his development / ～经济，保障供给。Develop the economy and ensure supplies. / 我国社会主义建设事业蓬勃～。China's socialist construction is forging rapidly ahead. ② recruit; admit: ～新党员 recruit new party members

发展经济学 fāzhǎn jīngjìxué　development economics

发展中国家 fāzhǎnzhōng guójiā　developing country

发颤 fāzhàn　(also 发战 fāzhàn) tremble; shiver; shake: 气得浑身～ shake all over with rage ——see also fāchàn

发胀 fāzhàng　① swell: 肚子～ feel bloated / 头脑～ have a swelled head ② feel distended (under acupuncture treatment)

发怔 fāzhèng　be stupefied

发咒 fāzhòu　swear; take an oath; vow

发作 fāzuò　① break out; show effect: 昨天她的心脏病又～了。She had another heart attack yesterday. / 酒性开始～。The liquor began to show its effect. ② have a fit of anger; flare up: 他有些生气，但当着大家的面又不好～。He was angry, but with everybody present, he could not very well show it. / 歇斯底里大～ have a bad fit of hysterics

fá

乏 fá　① lack: 不乏其人 bùfá qí rén ② tired; weary: 走～了 be tired from a long walk ③ *dial.* exhausted; worn-out: ～地 exhausted soil; poor land / 火～了，该续煤了。The fire's going out. Put on some more coal.

乏货 fáhuò　*dial.*　good-for-nothing; ne'er-do-well

乏困 fákùn　tired; fatigued: 旅途～ tired from travelling; travel-worn

乏味 fáwèi　dull; insipid; drab; tasteless: 语言～ dull (*or* drab) language / 这项工作枯燥～。This is dull and tedious work.

伐[1] fá　① fell; cut down: ～了几棵树 cut down a few trees ② send an expedition against; strike; attack: 讨伐 tǎofá

伐[2] fá　*formal*　boast about: ～善 boast about one's own goodness / 不矜不～ not be conceited or boastful

伐柯 fákē　*formal*　act as matchmaker: ～人 matchmaker

伐木 fámù　lumbering; felling; cutting: ～工人 lumberman

伐木业 fámùyè　lumbering

伐区 fáqū　*forestry*　cutting area; felling area

伐罪 fázuì　*formal*　send a punitive expedition against a despotic ruler: 吊民伐罪 diàomín-fázuì

垡 fá　*dial.*　① turn up soil ② upturned soil

垡子 fázi　(also 垡头 fátóu) *dial.*　upturned soil

罚（罰）

fá　punish; penalize: 挨～ be punished／～他唱个歌。Let him sing a song as a forfeit.

罚不当罪 fá bù dāng zuì　the punishment exceeds the crime; be punished too severely

罚出场 fá chūchǎng　*sports*　be ordered off the field for foul play; foul out

罚金 fájīn　fine; forfeit: 处以～ impose a fine on sb.; fine sb.

罚酒 fájiǔ　be made to drink as a forfeit: 我打赌输了，被罚了两大杯酒。I lost the bet and had to drink two glassfuls of wine as a forfeit.

罚款 fákuǎn　① impose a fine or forfeit: 违反交通规则要～。Fines are imposed for breaches of traffic rules. ② fine; forfeit; penalty

罚球 fáqiú　(in basketball) foul shot; free throw; (in football) penalty kick

阀¹

fá　a powerful person or family: 军阀 jūnfá／财阀 cáifá

阀²

fá　*mech.*　valve: 安全阀 ānquánfá

阀门 fámén　*mech.*　valve

阀阅 fáyuè　*formal*　① meritorious service ② a powerful and distinguished family

筏

fá　raft: 橡皮～ rubber raft／竹～ bamboo raft

筏道 fádào　log chute; logway

筏子 fázi　raft

fǎ

法

fǎ　① law: 守法 shǒufǎ ② method; way; mode: 教～ teaching method／表达～ mode of expression ③ standard; model: 法书 fǎshū ④ follow; model after: 效法 xiàofǎ ⑤ *Buddhism* the Law; dharma ⑥ magic arts: 作法 zuòfǎ ⑦ (Fǎ) short for 法国 Fǎguó

法案 fǎ'àn　proposed law; bill

法办 fǎbàn　deal with according to làw; punish by law; bring to justice: 将贪污分子逮捕～ have the grafters arrested and brought to justice

法宝 fǎbǎo　① *Buddhism* the Sutras ② a magic weapon or formula

法币 fǎbì　paper currency issued by the KMT government from 1935 onwards

法场 fǎchǎng　*old* execution ground: 押赴～ be taken under escort to the execution ground／劫～ raid an execution ground to rescue the condemned

法典 fǎdiǎn　code; statute book

法定 fǎdìng　legal; statutory: 按照～手续办理 do sth. according to legal procedure

法定代理人 fǎdìng dàilǐrén　legal representative

法定汇率 fǎdìng huìlǜ　official rate (of exchange); pegged rate of exchange; pegged exchange parity

法定货币 fǎdìng huòbì　legal tender

法定假期 fǎdìng jiàqī　official holiday

法定年龄 fǎdìng niánlíng　lawful (*or* legal) age

法定期限 fǎdìng qīxiàn　*leg.*　prescription

法定人数 fǎdìng rénshù　quorum: 已足～。We have a quorum now.／～不足。We haven't a quorum.

法度 fǎdù　① law ② moral standard

法官 fǎguān　judge; justice

法规 fǎguī　laws and regulations; statutes: 经济～ economic statutes

法国 Fǎguó　France

法国大革命 Fǎguó Dàgémìng　the French Revolution (1789–1799)

法国人 Fǎguórén　the French; Frenchman

法国梧桐 fǎguówútóng　plane tree

法号 fǎhào　same as 法名 fǎmíng

法纪 fǎjì　law and discipline: 目无～ act in utter disregard of law and discipline; flout law and discipline／遵守～ observe law and discipline

法家 Fǎjiā　Legalists (a school of thought in the Spring and Autumn and Warring States Periods, 770–221 B.C.)

法警 fǎjǐng　bailiff

法拉 fǎlā　*phys.*　farad

法拉第定律 Fǎlādì dìnglǜ　*phys.*　Faraday's law

法兰 fǎlán　*mech.*　flange

法兰盘 fǎlánpán　flange plate

法兰绒 fǎlánróng　flannel

法郎 fǎláng　franc

法老 fǎlǎo　Pharaoh (the title of the ruler of ancient Egypt)

法理 fǎlǐ　legal principle; theory of law

法理学 fǎlǐxué　jurisprudence

法力 fǎlì　① power of the Buddhist doctrine; dharma power ② magic power: 使～ exercise one's magic power

法令 fǎlìng　laws and decrees; decree: 政府～ government decree

法律 fǎlǜ　law; statute: ～保护 legal protection／～地位 legal status／～根据 legal basis／～规定 legal provisions／～手续 legal procedure／～制裁 legal sanction／～面前人人平等。All are equal before the law.

法律承认 fǎlǜ chéngrèn　*de jure* recognition

法律顾问 fǎlǜ gùwèn　legal adviser

法轮 fǎlún　*Buddhism* the Wheel of the Law (an emblem of the power of the Buddhist doctrine, which crushes all delusions and superstitions just as a wheel crushes anything it passes over)

法罗群岛 Fǎluó Qúndǎo　the Faeroe Islands

法螺 fǎluó　① *zool.* triton (shell) ② conch: 自吹～ blow one's own trumpet

法盲 fǎmáng　a person ignorant of the law; one who lacks legal knowledge

法门 fǎmén　① *Buddhism* gateway to the Law: ～寺 the Temple of the Law Gate ② way; method: 不二法门 bù èr fǎmén

法名 fǎmíng　religious name (the name one adopts on becoming a Buddhist monk or nun)

法器 fǎqì　musical instruments used in a Buddhist or Taoist mass

法权 fǎquán　right; privilege

法人 fǎrén　*leg.*　person; artificial person; corporation

法人团体 fǎrén tuántǐ　body corporate; corporation

法师 fǎshī　Master of the Law (a title of respect for a Buddhist or Taoist priest)

法式 fǎshì　rule; method; model:《营造～》A Treatise on Architectural Methods (c. 1100)

法事 fǎshì　religious services or rituals (either Buddhist or Taoist)

法书 fǎshū　① model calligraphy ② *pol.* your calligraphy

法术 fǎshù　① (in Legalist thought) the law and the methods of governing —— the former for guiding and keeping in line the officials and the people at large, and the latter for guiding the ruler in wielding authority and controlling the men under him ② magic arts

法堂 fǎtáng　① *old* law court ② a hall for preaching the Buddhist doctrine

法帖 fǎtiè　model calligraphy

法庭 fǎtíng　court; tribunal

法统 fǎtǒng　legally constituted authority

法网 fǎwǎng　the net of justice; the arm of the law: 逃不出人民的～ be unable to escape the net of justice

spread by the people

法西斯 fǎxīsī fascist: ～化 fascistization
法西斯蒂 fǎxīsīdì the Fascisti (1922–1943)
法西斯主义 fǎxīsīzhǔyì fascism
法线 fǎxiàn *math.* normal (line)
法相 fǎxiàng ① *Buddhism* the aspects of things ② an image of Buddha
法像 fǎxiàng an image of Buddha
法学 fǎxué the science of law; law
法学家 fǎxuéjiā jurist
法眼 fǎyǎn same as 慧眼 huìyǎn
法衣 fǎyī garments worn by a Buddhist or Taoist priest at a religious ceremony
法医 fǎyī legal medical expert
法医学 fǎyīxué medical jurisprudence; forensic medicine
法语 Fǎyǔ French (language)
法院 fǎyuàn court of justice; law court; court
法则 fǎzé ① rule; law: 自然～ law of nature ② *formal* laws and regulations ③ *formal* model
法治 fǎzhì rule by law
法制 fǎzhì legal system; legal institutions; legality: 加强社会主义～ strengthen the socialist legal system／～教育 education in legality
法子 fǎzi way; method: 我们得想个～解决这个问题。We'll have to think of a way to solve the problem. *or* We must find a way out.

砝 fǎ see below

砝码 fǎmǎ weight (used on a balance)

fà

发(髮) fà hair: 白～ white hair ——see also fā

发辫 fàbiàn plait; braid; pigtail
发菜 fàcài flagelliform nostoc (*Nostoc commune*)
发短心长 fàduǎn-xīncháng with hair sparse from age and a mind mature from experience—be old and wise
发际 fàjì hairline
发髻 fàjì hair worn in a bun or coil
发夹 fàjiā hairpin; bobby pin
发蜡 fàlà pomade
发妻 fàqī *old* first wife ——see also 结发夫妻 jiéfà fūqī
发卡 fàqiǎ hairpin
发乳 fàrǔ hair cream; pomade
发式 fàshì hairstyle; hairdo; coiffure
发刷 fàshuā hairbrush
发网 fàwǎng hairnet
发型 fàxíng hairstyle; hairdo; coiffure: ～美观大方 a tasteful hairstyle／流行～ a stylish coiffure
发绣 fàxiù *arts and crafts* hair embroidery (done with human hair instead of silk thread)
发癣 fàxuǎn ringworm of the scalp; tinea capitis
发油 fàyóu hair oil
发指 fàzhǐ one's hair bristling up with anger: 令人发指 lìngrén fàzhǐ

珐(琺) fà see below

珐琅 fàláng enamel
珐琅质 fàlángzhì enamel (of the teeth)

fān

帆 fān sail: 把～扯起来。Raise the sails.

帆板 fānbǎn windsurfer; sailboard
帆板运动 fānbǎn yùndòng windsurfing; sailboarding
帆布 fānbù canvas: ～包 canvas bag; kit bag／～床 cot; campbed／～篷 canvas roof; awning／～鞋 plimsolls; sneakers
帆船 fānchuán sailing boat or ship; sailboat; junk
帆船运动 fānchuán yùndòng sailboating; sailing
帆篷 fānpéng sail
帆樯 fānqiáng mast: ～林立 a forest of masts

番¹ fān ① aborigines: 生番 shēngfān ② foreign; barbarian: 番邦 fānbāng ③ (used in names for certain plants originally introduced from abroad): 番茄 fānqié／番薯 fānshǔ

番² fān *m.* ① (for actions, deeds, etc.): 下过一～功夫 have put in a lot of time and effort／费了一～口舌才使他回心转意 It took a lot of talking to bring him round.／她上上下下打量了我一～。She looked me up and down.／她考虑了一～，终于同意了我们的要求。After some deliberation, she finally agreed to our request.／经过几～周折，这笔交易总算做成了。After several setbacks, the deal was finally clinched. ② (used with the numeral 一 only) kind: 洞里别有一～天地。The cave is an altogether different world. ③ (used after the verb 翻) times; -fold: 翻番 fānfān

番邦 fānbāng *old* a foreign (*or* barbarian) land
番瓜 fānguā *dial.* pumpkin
番号 fānhào the designation of a military unit
番木鳖 fānmùbiē same as 马钱子 mǎqiánzǐ
番木鳖碱 fānmùbiējiǎn *pharm.* strychnine
番木瓜 fānmùguā papaya (the tree or its fruit)
番茄 fānqié tomato: ～酱 tomato ketchup (*or* catsup); tomato sauce／～汁 tomato juice
番薯 fānshǔ *dial.* sweet potato

幡(旛) fān a long narrow flag; streamer

幡儿 fānr funeral streamer
幡然 fānrán same as 翻然 fānrán

蕃 fān same as 番¹ fān ——see also fán

藩 fān ① hedge; fence: 藩篱 fānlí ② *formal* screen; barrier: 屏藩 píngfān ③ vassal; feudatory: 三～之乱 the Revolt of the Three Feudatories (1673–1681)

藩国 fānguó vassal state
藩篱 fānlí hedge; fence; barrier
藩属 fānshǔ vassal state
藩镇 fānzhèn Tang Dynasty military governor (usu. in control of outlying prefectures)

翻 fān ① turn upside down or inside out; turn over: ～谷子 turn over the grain (to dry)／船～了。The ship capsized.／车～了。The cart overturned.／我把茶杯碰～了。I knocked the teacup over. ② look through; search: ～参考书 look through reference works／抽屉我都～一遍了，还是找不到。I rummaged all the drawers, but still couldn't find it. ③ reverse: 翻案 fān'àn ④ cross; get over: ～过山头 cross a mountaintop／～墙 climb over a wall ⑤ multiply; double: 翻番 fānfān ⑥ translate: 把英文～成中文 translate the English into Chinese／～电报 decode a telegram ⑦ *inf.* fall out; break up: 他们闹～了。They fell out.／谁把他惹～了? Who made him so angry?

翻案 fān'àn reverse a verdict
翻案文章 fān'àn wénzhāng an article presenting differing views on a historical incident or personage
翻白眼 fān báiyǎn show the whites of one's eyes (as from emotion or illness): 她以为我们在议论她，直朝我

们～。She kept glaring at us, thinking that we had been talking about her.

翻版 fānbǎn reprint; reproduction; refurbished version

翻本 fānběn win back all the money lost (in gambling)

翻茬 fānchá plough under the stubble after the harvest

翻场 fāncháng turn over the grain on the threshing ground

翻车 fānchē ① (of a car) overturn: 在公路拐弯处发生了一起～事故。A car turned over at the road bend. ② run into difficulties ③ *dial.* have a row ④ *dial.* go back on one's word

翻车机 fānchējī *min.* tipper; dumper; tipple

翻车鱼 fānchēyú ocean sunfish; headfish

翻地 fāndì turn up the soil; plough up the fields

翻斗 fāndǒu tipping bucket; skip bucket

翻斗车 fāndǒuchē skip car; tipcart

翻斗卡车 fāndǒu kǎchē tipping lorry; tip lorry; tip truck

翻番 fānfān increase by a specified number of times: 十年内学生人数翻了一番。The school's enrolment doubled in ten years.

翻飞 fānfēi ① (of birds, butterflies, etc.) fly up and down; flit to and fro ② (of flags, etc.) flutter in the wind

翻覆 fānfù ① turn over; turn upside down: 车辆～。Cars turned over. / 天地～ heaven and earth turning upside down — cataclysmic changes ② toss and turn: ～不能眠 toss and turn in bed, being unable to sleep ③ *formal* vacillate

翻改 fāngǎi remake (old clothes)

翻盖 fāngài rebuild or renovate (a house)

翻杠子 fān gàngzi *sports* do gymnastics on a horizontal bar or on parallel bars

翻个儿 fāngèr *inf.* turn over; turn upside down or inside out: 把饼翻个个儿再烙一会儿。Turn the cake over and bake it some more. / 这件上衣～也能穿。This jacket can be worn inside out. *or* This is a reversible jacket.

翻跟头 fān gēntou turn a somersault; loop the loop: 飞机连翻了三个跟头。The plane looped the loop three times.

翻供 fāngòng withdraw a confession; retract one's testimony

翻滚 fāngǔn ① seethe; churn: 白浪～。The waves rolled and foamed. ② roll about; toss about: 痛得忍不住地～ writhing in pain

翻过儿 fānguòr turn over a specified number of times: 我把抽屉翻了个过儿也没有找到。I turned over everything in the drawers, but still couldn't find it.

翻悔 fānhuǐ back out (of a commitment, promise, etc.): 一经答应，就别～。Once you've given your word, don't try to back out.

翻检 fānjiǎn look through (books, papers, etc.)

翻江倒海 fānjiāng-dǎohǎi holding back rivers and overturning seas—overwhelming; tremendous; earth-shaking: 以～之势 with the momentum of an avalanche

翻浆 fānjiāng (of road surfaces) burst and become muddy when a thaw sets in

翻来覆去 fānlái-fùqù ① toss and turn; toss from side to side: 他在床上～睡不着。He tossed and turned in bed, unable to sleep. ② again and again; repeatedly: 这种话，她～不知说过多少遍了。This is what she has been saying over and over again—I don't know how many times.

翻老帐 fān lǎozhàng (also 翻旧帐 fān jiùzhàng) rake up old scores (*or* grievances)

翻脸 fānliǎn fall out; suddenly turn hostile: 他俩从来没

有翻过脸。The two of them have never quarrelled.

翻脸不认人 fānliǎn bù rèn rén turn against a friend

翻脸无情 fānliǎn wúqíng turn against a friend and show him no mercy; be treacherous and ruthless

翻领 fānlǐng turndown collar

翻录 fānlù pirate recordings

翻拍 fānpāi *photog.* reproduction (from a photograph)

翻然 fānrán (change) quickly and completely

翻然改图 fānrán gǎi tú quickly change one's plans

翻然悔悟 fānrán huǐwù wake up to one's error; make an effort to atone for one's misdeeds

翻砂 fānshā *mech.* ① founding ② moulding; casting

翻砂车间 fānshā chējiān foundry shop

翻砂工 fānshāgōng ① foundry worker ② caster

翻山越岭 fānshān-yuèlǐng cross over mountain after mountain; tramp over hill and dale

翻身 fānshēn ① turn (the body) over: 他翻了个身又睡着了。He turned over in bed and fell asleep again. / 一～从床上爬起来 roll off the bed ② free oneself; stand up: ～农奴 emancipated serfs / ～做主人 stand up and be master of one's fate

翻身仗 fānshēnzhàng see 打翻身仗 dǎ fānshēnzhàng

翻绳儿 fānshéngr cat's cradle

翻腾 fānténg *sports* tuck dive: 向内(前)～两周半 backward (forward) tuck dive with two-and-a-half somersaults

翻腾 fān·teng ① seethe; rise; churn: 波浪～ seething (*or* turbulent) waves / 许多问题在他脑子里～着。His mind was seething with problems. ② turn sth. over and over: 几个箱子都～遍了也没有找到。I rummaged through all the boxes but still could not find it. / 过去的事，别再去～了。Don't rake up the past.

翻天 fāntiān ① overturn the heavens —— overthrow the government ② (used after 吵 or 闹) behave wildly: 吵～ kick up a terrific row / 孩子们闹～了。The children are really cutting up.

翻天覆地 fāntiān-fùdì earth-shaking; world-shaking: ～的变化 an earth-shaking change

翻蔓儿 fānwànr turn the vines (of sweet potato, etc.)

翻胃 fānwèi same as 反胃 fǎnwèi

翻箱倒柜 fānxiāng-dǎoguì (also 翻箱倒箧 fānxiāng-dǎoqiè) rummage through chests and cupboards; ransack boxes and chests

翻新 fānxīn renovate; recondition; make over: 旧大衣可以～。Old overcoats can be reconditioned. / ～车胎 retread a tyre —— see also 花样翻新 huāyàng fānxīn

翻修 fānxiū rebuild or renovate: ～房屋 have the house rebuilt or renovated / ～地板 relay a wooden floor / ～马路 repair the roads

翻译 fānyì ① translate; interpret: 请你帮我～一下好吗? Would you mind translating (*or* interpreting) this for me? / 这部书早就～成中文了。This book was translated into Chinese a long time ago. / ～电码 decode; decipher ② translator; interpreter: 担任～ act as interpreter

翻译本 fānyìběn translation

翻译片 fānyìpiàn dubbed film

翻印 fānyìn reprint; reproduce

翻阅 fānyuè leaf through; thumb through; look over; glance over: ～报章杂志 look over newspapers and magazines / ～目录 glance through a catalogue

翻越 fānyuè get over; surmount: ～障碍物 surmount obstacles

翻云覆雨 fānyún-fùyǔ produce clouds with one turn of the hand and rain with another—be given to playing tricks; keep shifting one's ground

翻造 fānzào rebuild or renovate (a building, bridge, etc.)

fán

凡¹ **（凣）** fán ① commonplace; ordinary: 非凡 fēifán ② this mortal world; the earth: 下凡 xiàfán

凡² **（凣）** fán *adv. formal* ① all; every; any: 在我国，～年满十八岁的公民，都有选举权与被选举权。In our country every citizen who has reached the age of 18 has the right to vote and stand for election. / ～属我国文化遗产中有用的东西，都应当继承。All of our cultural heritage which is useful should be inherited. ② altogether; in all: 全书～二十卷。The set consists of 20 volumes altogether. ③ general idea; outline: 发凡 fāfán

凡³ **（凣）** fán *mus.* a note of the scale in *gongchepu* (工尺谱), corresponding to 4 in numbered musical notation

凡尘 fánchén this world; this mortal life

凡尔 fán'ěr valve

凡夫俗子 fánfū-súzǐ ordinary people; the common herd

凡立丁呢 fánlìdīngní *text.* valitin

凡例 fánlì notes on the use of a book etc.; guide to the use of a book, etc.

凡人 fánrén ① *formal* ordinary person ② mortal

凡士林 fánshìlín vaseline; petrolatum

凡事 fánshì everything: ～应该用脑筋好好想一想。We should always use our brains and think everything over carefully.

凡事预则立，不预则废 fán shì yù zé lì, bù yù zé fèi preparedness ensures success, unpreparedness spells failure

凡是 fánshì *adv.* every; any; all: ～正义的事业都是不可战胜的。A just cause is invincible. / ～认识他的人，没有不称赞他的。All who know him speak highly of him.

凡响 fánxiǎng common music; ordinary music: 非同～out of the ordinary

凡庸 fányōng (usu. of humans) commonplace; ordinary: ～之辈 the common herd

矾（礬） fán *chem.* vitriol

矾土 fántǔ alumina (a mineral): ～水泥 alumina cement

钒 fán *chem.* vanadium (V): ～钢 vanadium steel

烦 fán ① be vexed; be irritated; be annoyed: 孩子老哭，真～人！How annoying it is to have a kid crying all the time! / 你～什么? What are you getting so annoyed about? ② be tired of: 这话我都听～了。I'm fed up with this kind of talk. ③ superfluous and confusing: 要言不烦 yàoyán bù fán ④ *pol.* trouble (sb. to do sth.); bother: ～交某人 please forward this to so-and-so / ～您给她捎个信儿。May I trouble you to pass on a message to her? / ～请贵公司尽速将货样寄来。Please mail us a sample of the merchandise as soon as possible.

烦劳 fánláo ① trouble (sb. to do sth.): ～您带几本书给他。Would you mind taking a few books to him? ② depressed; feeling low

烦忙 fánmáng same as 繁忙 fánmáng

烦闷 fánmèn be unhappy; be depressed; be moody: 雨下个不停，真叫人～。When will the rain ever stop? How depressing! / 你干吗这样～? Why are you so un-happy? / 他一上午都没说话，心里一定很～。There must be something weighing on his mind, he's been so quiet all morning.

烦难 fánnán same as 繁难 fánnán

烦恼 fánnǎo vexed; worried: 何必为这些小事～? Why should you fret over such trifles?

烦腻 fánnì same as 腻烦 nìfan

烦扰 fánrǎo ① bother; disturb ② feel disturbed

烦冗 fánrǒng ① (of one's affairs) diverse and complicated ② (of speech or writing) lengthy and tedious; prolix

烦神 fánshén spend time and energy; take great trouble: 这些事就不用您～了。You needn't trouble yourself about these things.

烦琐 fánsuǒ loaded down with trivial details: ～的手续 overelaborate procedure; tedious formalities / ～的考证 pedantic textual criticism; overelaborate research / 这篇文章写得太～。This article is too long and wordy.

烦琐哲学 fánsuǒ zhéxué ① scholasticism ② *inf.* overelaboration; hairsplitting

烦嚣 fánxiāo *formal* noisy and annoying: 住在乡间，城里～的声音一点也听不到。As I live out of the city, I'm not harassed by the racket of urban life.

烦心 fánxīn annoying; vexatious; troublesome: 她从不把～的事对人讲。She never confides her troubles to anybody.

烦言 fányán *formal* ① complaint: 口无～ make no complaints whatsoever ② tedious talk

烦言碎辞 fányán-suìcí loquacities; verbosities

烦躁 fánzào fidgety; agitated: 某些动物～不安可能是地震临震前的预兆。Agitated activity by certain animals may be a sign of an impending earthquake.

蕃 fán ① (of trees, grass, etc.) be luxuriant; grow in abundance: ～茂 luxuriant; lush ② multiply; proliferate: 蕃息 fánxī ——see also fān

蕃息 fánxī multiply; propagate

蕃衍 fányǎn same as 繁衍 fányǎn

樊 fán ① *formal* fence ② (Fán) a surname

樊篱 fánlí ① fence ② barriers; restriction: 冲破～ break down barriers; cast off trammels

樊笼 fánlóng bird cage (fig.): 久在～里，复得返自然。(陶潜) Too long a captive in a cage, I have now come back to Nature.

燔 fán *formal* ① burn ② roast

繁（緐） fán ① in great numbers; numerous; manifold: ～星满天 a starry sky ② propagate; multiply: 农场自～自养的牲畜 livestock bred and reared by the farm itself

繁本 fánběn unabridged version

繁多 fánduō various: 花色～ a great variety

繁分数 fánfēnshù *math.* complex fraction

繁复 fánfù heavy and complicated: 有了计算机，～的计算工作在几秒钟之内就可以完成。A computer does complicated calculations in a few seconds.

繁花 fánhuā full-blown flowers; flowers of different colours: ～似锦 flowers in full bloom, brilliant as brocade

繁华 fánhuá flourishing; bustling; busy: 城里最～的地区 the busiest section of town; the downtown district

繁忙 fánmáng busy: ～的收获季节 the busy harvest season / 工作～ be very busy with one's work; be busi-engaged

繁茂 fánmào lush; luxuriant: 草木～ a lush growth of trees and grass / 枝叶～ with luxuriant foliage

繁密 fánmì dense: 林木～ densely wooded / ～的鞭炮声 the sound of firecrackers going off uninterruptedly

繁难 fánnán hard to tackle; troublesome: 校对是一件～的工作。Proofreading is a troublesome task.

繁荣 fánróng ① flourishing; prosperous; booming: ～的文化事业 flourishing cultural undertakings / ～富强 rich, strong and prosperous / 经济～。The economy is booming. / 市场～。The market is brisk. ② make sth. prosper: ～经济 bring about a prosperous economy; promote economic prosperity / ～文学创作 promote literary creation

繁荣昌盛 fánróng chāngshèng thriving and prosperous: 祝贵国～，人民幸福。We wish your country prosperity and her people happiness.

繁冗 fánrǒng same as 烦冗 fánrǒng

繁缛 fánrù overelaborate: ～的礼节 overelaborate formalities / 这张地毯花纹～，色彩也过于艳丽。This carpet has an overelaborate and garish pattern.

繁盛 fánshèng thriving; flourishing; prosperous: 这个城市越来越～了。The city is becoming more and more prosperous.

繁琐 fánsuǒ same as 烦琐 fánsuǒ

繁体字 fántǐzì the original complex form of a simplified Chinese character

繁文缛节 fánwén-rùjié unnecessary and overelaborate formalities; red tape

繁芜 fánwú loaded with unnecessary words; wordy; verbose: 此书引证过多，文字～。Heavily documented, the book is long-winded and verbose.

繁细 fánxì overloaded with details; excessively detailed

繁嚣 fánxiāo same as 烦嚣 fánxiāo

繁衍 fányǎn formal multiply; increase gradually in number or quantity

繁育 fányù breed: ～优良品种 breed good strains

繁杂 fánzá many and diverse; miscellaneous: ～的日常事务 daily chores of all sorts

繁殖 fánzhí breed; reproduce; propagate: 自我～ self-reproduction; autosynthesis / ～牲畜 breed livestock / 靠种子～的植物 plants which propagate themselves by seeds

繁殖力 fánzhílì reproductive capacity; fecundity; fertility

繁殖率 fánzhílǜ rate of reproduction; breeding rate

繁重 fánzhòng heavy; strenuous; onerous: ～的劳动 strenuous labour / 任务～。The tasks are arduous.

繁滋 fánzī formal multiply profusely

蹯 fán formal animal's paw: 熊蹯 xióngfán

fǎn

反 fǎn ① in an opposite direction; reverse; inside out: 你的袜子穿～了。You have put your socks on inside out. / ～绑着手 with one's hands tied behind one's back / 这件上衣正～两面都可以穿。This coat is reversible, you can wear it inside out. ② turn over; reverse: 反败为胜 fǎn bài wéi shèng ③ return; counter: 反击 fǎnjī / 反问 fǎnwèn ④ revolt; rebel; turn against: ～朝廷 rebel against the imperial government ⑤ oppose; combat: ～贪污 combat corruption / ～侵略 oppose aggression ⑥ short for 反革命 fǎngémìng or 反动派 fǎndòngpài ⑦ adv. on the contrary; instead: 他不但不支持我，～把我批评了一顿。Instead of supporting me, he criticized me. / 这样做不但于事无补，～会把事情弄糟。This won't do any good; on the contrary, it will make things even worse. ⑧ short for 反切 fǎnqiè

⑨ prefix anti-; counter-: ～法西斯 anti-fascist / ～间谍 counterespionage / ～科学 contrary to science / 颠覆与～颠覆 subversion and anti-subversion

反霸 fǎnbà ① struggle against local despots (in land reform) ② oppose hegemonism: 第三世界的～斗争 the struggle of the third world countries against hegemonism

反败为胜 fǎn bài wéi shèng turn defeat into victory; turn the tide

反比 fǎnbǐ ① inverse relation; inverse proportion: 与…成～ be inversely proportional to...; be in inverse proportion to... ② same as 反比例 fǎnbǐlì

反比例 fǎnbǐlì math. inverse ratio; inverse proportion: 分数值与分母值成～。The value of a fraction is inversely proportional to that of the denominator.

反驳 fǎnbó refute; rebut: 作出强有力的～ refute (or rebut) with convincing arguments / ～对方的指责 refute the other party's accusations

反哺 fǎnbǔ feed mother birds in return when fully grown—repay one's parents for their upbringing when they get old: ～之情 filial piety

反侧 fǎncè formal ① toss about (in bed); toss and turn ② behave capriciously; chop and change

反差 fǎnchā photog. contrast

反常 fǎncháng unusual; abnormal; strange: 最近天气有点儿～。The weather is a bit unusual these days. / 他昨天的表现有点儿～。His behaviour yesterday was a bit strange.

反衬 fǎnchèn set off by contrast; serve as a foil to

反冲 fǎnchōng recoil; kick

反冲核 fǎnchōnghé phys. recoil nucleus

反冲力 fǎnchōnglì phys. recoil

反刍 fǎnchú ruminate; chew the cud

反刍动物 fǎnchú dòngwù ruminant

反刍胃 fǎnchúwèi ruminant stomach

反串 fǎnchuàn (in traditional opera) play a reversed role, i.e. a role that one is not trained for (as when a female impersonator plays a male role)

反唇相讥 fǎn chún xiāng jī answer back sarcastically: 他对同志们的批评置若罔闻，甚至～。He not only ignored the criticism of his comrades but went so far as to answer back (or retort) sarcastically.

反导弹导弹 fǎndǎodàn dǎodàn antimissile missile

反倒 fǎndào adv. inf. on the contrary; instead

反帝 fǎndì oppose imperialism; be anti-imperialist: ～斗争 anti-imperialist struggle

反动 fǎndòng ① reactionary: ～势力 reactionary forces ② reaction: 他弃家出走，是对旧社会婚姻压迫的～。He finally left home in an effort to counter the tyranny of arranged marriage in the old society.

反动分子 fǎndòng fènzǐ reactionary element; reactionary

反动会道门 fǎndòng huìdàomén reactionary secret society

反动派 fǎndòngpài reactionaries

反对 fǎnduì oppose; be against; fight; combat: ～种族歧视 oppose racial discrimination / ～官僚主义 combat bureaucracy / ～贪污浪费 fight against corruption and waste / 有～意见吗？Any objections? / 我～这个提议。I am against this proposal. / 这门亲事遭到全家的～。The marriage was opposed by the whole family.

反对党 fǎnduìdǎng opposition party; the Opposition

反对派 fǎnduìpài opposition faction

反对票 fǎnduìpiào dissenting vote; negative vote

反而 fǎn'ér adv. on the contrary; instead: 风不但没停，～更大了。Instead of going down, the wind blew even harder. / 困难吓不倒我们，～激起我们更大的干劲。We were not cowed by difficulties. On the contrary, they inspired us to even greater efforts.

反封建　fǎn fēngjiàn　anti-feudal; against feudalism

反复　fǎnfù　① repeatedly; again and again: ～解释 explain over and over again / ～思考 think a lot about sth; turn sth. over in one's mind again and again / ～辩论 argue back and forth / 这个计划是经过～讨论产生的. The plan was born out of repeated discussions. ② back out; chop and change: 说一是一, 说二是二, 决不～. I mean what I say and I'll never go back on my word. / 他的态度反反复复, 叫人难以捉摸. He's always chopping and changing, and you just can't tell where he stands. ③ reversal; relapse: 你的病虽然好了, 可要防止～. You're well now, but mind you don't have a relapse. / 思想上有～ have ideological relapses

反复记号　fǎnfù jìhào　mus. repeat

反复无常　fǎnfù wúcháng　behave capriciously; blow hot and cold; chop and change: 这个人～, 很不可靠. This fellow is always chopping and changing; he's very unreliable.

反感　fǎngǎn　be disgusted with; be averse to; dislike; take unkindly to: 我对他的话很～. I'm disgusted with what he said. / 对这种人极其～ have a strong aversion to such people; feel a repugnance to such people

反戈一击　fǎn gē yī jī　turn one's weapon around and strike—turn against one's own side

反革命　fǎngémìng　① counterrevolutionary: ～罪行 a counterrevolutionary crime ② a counterrevolutionary: 镇压～ suppress counterrevolutionaries

反攻　fǎngōng　launch a counteroffensive; counterattack: 敌人已无力～. The enemy hasn't the strength to counterattack. / 发动猛烈的～ launch a fierce counterattack (on sb.)

反攻倒算　fǎngōng-dàosuàn　(of members of an overthrown reactionary class) counterattack to settle old scores; launch a vindictive counterattack; retaliate

反躬自问　fǎngōng zìwèn　examine oneself; examine one's conscience

反顾　fǎngù　formal　look back; turn back: 义无反顾 yì wú fǎngù

反光　fǎnguāng　① reflect light: 白墙～, 屋里显得很敞亮. With the white walls reflecting the light, the room looks bright and spacious. ② reflection of light: 湖面上的～把我的眼睛都照花了. The reflections of sunlight in the lake dazzled my eyes.

反光灯　fǎnguāngdēng　reflector lamp

反光镜　fǎnguāngjìng　reflector

反过来　fǎn·guò·lái　① in reverse order; in an opposite direction: 我把帐目～又算了一遍. I added up the account items all over again in reverse order. ② conversely; the other way round: ～也是一样. It's the same the other way round. / 这话～说就不一定对. The converse of this statement may not be true.

反函数　fǎnhánshù　math.　inverse function

反话　fǎnhuà　an ironic remark; irony

反悔　fǎnhuǐ　go back on one's word (or promise): 一言为定, 决不～. I give you my word and I'll never go back on it.

反击　fǎnjī　strike back; beat back; counterattack: 自卫～ counterattack in self-defence / 对挑衅给予有力的～ answer provocation with a vigorous counterblow

反剪　fǎnjiǎn　① have one's hands tied behind one's back ② hold one's hands behind one's back

反间　fǎnjiàn　sow distrust or dissension among one's enemies; set one's enemies at odds (by spreading rumours, etc.)

反间计　fǎnjiànjì　a stratagem of sowing distrust or discord among one's enemies: 不要中了敌人的～. Don't fall into the enemy's plot of sowing discord among us.

反建议　fǎnjiànyì　counterproposal

反骄破满　fǎnjiāo-pòmǎn　oppose arrogance and shatter complacency; combat arrogance and complacency

反诘　fǎnjié　ask in retort; counter with a question

反抗　fǎnkàng　revolt; resist: ～侵略 resist aggression / ～精神 spirit of revolt; rebellious spirit / 哪里有压迫, 哪里就有～. Where there is oppression, there is resistance.

反客为主　fǎn kè wéi zhǔ　turn from guest into host—gain the initiative

反空降　fǎnkōngjiàng　mil.　anti-airborne defence

反馈　fǎnkuì　① electron. feedback: 正 (负) ～ positive (negative) feedback ② feedback (a response): 公司欢迎消费者对他们产品的～. The company welcomes feedback from consumers who use their products.

反馈抑制　fǎnkuì yìzhì　physiol.　feedback inhibition

反雷达涂层　fǎnléidá túcéng　antiradar coating

反粒子　fǎnlìzǐ　phys.　antiparticle

反面　fǎnmiàn　① reverse side; wrong side; back: 唱片的～ the reverse side of a disc / 料子的～ the wrong side of the cloth ② the reverse side of a state of affairs, a problem, etc.: 我们必须学会全面地看问题, 不但要看到事物的正面, 也要看到它的～. We must learn to look at problems from all sides, seeing the reverse as well as the obverse side of things. ③ opposite; negative side: 走向～ change (or turn) into one's opposite / ～的教训 a lesson learnt from negative (or bitter) experience; wisdom won from hard knocks

反面教材　fǎnmiàn jiàocái　negative example which may serve as a lesson; bad experience which teaches us what not to do

反面教员　fǎnmiàn jiàoyuán　teacher by negative example

反面人物　fǎnmiàn rénwù　villain; negative character; negative role

反目　fǎnmù　(usu. of husband and wife) fall out; have a falling-out

反派　fǎnpài　villain (in drama, etc.); negative character: 演～人物 act the part of the villain; play a negative role

反叛　fǎnpàn　revolt; rebel: ～朝廷 rebel against the imperial government

反叛　fǎnpan　inf.　traitor; turncoat

反批评　fǎnpīpíng　counter-criticism

反扑　fǎnpū　(of a beast of prey or an enemy) pounce on sb. again after being beaten off; (of enemy forces) launch a counteroffensive to retrieve lost ground: 打退敌人一次又一次的～ repulse the repeated counterattacks of the enemy

反璞归真　fǎnpú-guīzhēn　same as 归真反璞 guīzhēn-fǎnpú

反其道而行之　fǎn qí dào ér xíng zhī　act in a diametrically opposite way; do exactly the opposite

反气旋　fǎnqìxuán　meteorol.　anticyclone

反潜　fǎnqián　defend (maritime space) against enemy submarines

反潜机　fǎnqiánjī　antisubmarine plane

反潜舰艇　fǎnqián jiàntǐng　antisubmarine vessels

反切　fǎnqiè　a traditional method of indicating the pronunciation of a character by taking two other characters, one with the same initial and the other with the same final as the character in question (e.g., the pronunciation of 同 tóng is indicated as 徒红切 or 徒红反, that is, 徒 t(ú) ＋ 红 (h)óng, taking the initial of the first character and the final of the second)

反求诸己　fǎn qiú zhū jǐ　seek the cause in oneself (instead of in sb. else)

反射　fǎnshè　① reflect (light, heat, sound, etc.): 镜子能～光线. Mirrors reflect light. ② physiol. reflex: 条件反射 tiáojiàn fǎnshè

反射比　fǎnshèbǐ　phys.　reflectance

反射测云器 fǎnshè cèyúnqì reflecting nephoscope

反射弧 fǎnshèhú *physiol.* reflex arc

反射计 fǎnshèjì reflectometer

反射镜 fǎnshèjìng reflector

反射炉 fǎnshèlú reverberatory furnace

反射望远镜 fǎnshè wàngyuǎnjìng reflecting telescope

反噬 fǎnshì *formal* trump up a false countercharge against one's accuser; make a false countercharge

反手 fǎnshǒu ① backhand: ～抽球 backhand drive / ～接住飞盘 catch the Frisbee backhand (*or* backhanded) ② same as 反掌 fǎnzhǎng

反水 fǎnshuǐ *dial.* turn one's coat; defect

反诉 fǎnsù *leg.* countercharge; counterclaim

反锁 fǎnsuǒ ① be locked in ② be locked out

反坦克炮 fǎntǎnkèpào antitank gun

反特 fǎntè prevent or thwart enemy espionage; engage in counterespionage: ～影片 spy film; counterespionage film

反题 fǎntí *philos.* antithesis

反铁电现象 fǎntiědiànxiànxiàng antiferroelectricity

反围盘 fǎnwéipán *mech.* reverse repeater (used in steel rolling)

反胃 fǎnwèi have a gastric disorder; feel nauseated; feel queasy

反问 fǎnwèn ① ask a question in reply ② *gram.* rhetorical question

反响 fǎnxiǎng repercussion; echo; reverberation: 在世界上引起广泛的～ evoke worldwide repercussions / 在很多人心中引起～ find an echo in the hearts of many people

反向 fǎnxiàng opposite direction; reverse

反向铲 fǎnxiàngchǎn backhoe

反向电流 fǎnxiàng diànliú reverse current

反向卫星 fǎnxiàng wèixīng retrograde satellite

反斜面 fǎnxiémiàn *mil.* reverse slope; rear slope

反信风 fǎnxìnfēng *meteorol.* antitrades

反省 fǎnxǐng engage in introspection, self-examination or soul-searching: 停职～ be temporarily relieved of one's post for self-examination

反宣传 fǎnxuānchuán ① counterpropaganda ② slander campaign

反咬一口 fǎn yǎo yī kǒu trump up a countercharge against one's accuser; make a false countercharge

反义词 fǎnyìcí *gram.* antonym

反应 fǎnyìng ① response; repercussion; reaction: ～不一。Reactions vary. / 作出～ make a response / ～冷淡。The response was far from warm. / 这位青年科学家的研究报告在科学界引起了强烈的～。The young scientist's research paper evoked strong repercussions in scientific circles. ② react; respond: 他对你的建议～怎么样? How did he react to your suggestion? / 对老师的提问，他～很快。He responds very quickly to the teacher's questions. ③ *physiol. med.* reaction: 过敏～ allergic reaction / 阳性(阴性)～ positive (negative) reaction / 病人打针(化验)以后的～ a patient's reaction to an injection (a medical test) ④ *chem. phys.* reaction: 链式反应 liànshì fǎnyìng

反应本领 fǎnyìng běnlǐng *phys.* reaction capacity

反应堆 fǎnyìngduī *phys.* reactor: 高温～ high-temperature reactor / 浓缩铀～ enriched uranium reactor / 增殖～ breeder reactor / 石墨减速～ graphite-moderated reactor / 热中子～ thermal reactor / 轻水慢化～ light-water-moderated reactor

反应塔 fǎnyìngtǎ reaction tower

反应物 fǎnyìngwù *chem.* reactant

反映 fǎnyìng ① reflect; mirror: 这张报纸～知识分子的看法和意见。The newspaper reflects the intellectuals' views and opinions. / 这部小说真实地～了拓荒者的生活。This novel gives a faithful representation of (*or* is

a mirror of) the life of the pioneers. / ～新时代的特点 mirror the features of our new age / 这个决定～了广大人民的根本利益。This decision represents the fundamental interests of the people. ② report; make known: 向上级～ report to the higher level / 把群众的呼声及时地～上去 transmit the voices of the people to the leading bodies without delay / 我将经常向您～进度。I'll keep you informed of the progress made.

反映论 fǎnyìnglùn *philos.* theory of reflection: 唯物论的～ the materialist theory of reflection / 能动的革命的～ the dynamic revolutionary theory of knowledge as the reflection of reality

反右派斗争 fǎnyòupài dòuzhēng the Anti-Rightist Campaign (1957)

反语 fǎnyǔ irony

反掌 fǎnzhǎng turn one's hand over——a most easy thing to do: 易如反掌 yì rú fǎnzhǎng

反照 fǎnzhào reflection of light: 夕阳～ evening (*or* sunset) glow

反照镜 fǎnzhàojìng rearview mirror

反正 fǎnzhèng come over from the enemy's side

反正 fǎnzheng *adv.* ① (often used correlatively with 不管, 无论, etc.) in any case; at any rate; anyway: 不管怎么样，～工作不能停。Come what may, the work must go on. / 无论你怎么说，～我不答应。No matter what you say, I won't agree. / 老王来不来还没决定，～小张一定来。Lao Wang hasn't made up his mind whether to come or not; anyway Xiao Zhang is coming. ② since; as: ～得去一个人，就让我去吧! Since someone has to go anyway, let me go. / ～你不是外人，我也就不客气了。Since you're my friend, I won't stand on ceremony. / ～路不远，咱们就走着去吧! As it's not far, we might as well go on foot.

反证 fǎnzhèng disproof; counterevidence

反证法 fǎnzhèngfǎ reduction to absurdity; *reductio ad absurdum*

反之 fǎnzhī *conj. formal* whereas; on the other hand; conversely: 谁愿意为人民服务，人民就欢迎他；～，谁只为自己打算，人民就不欢迎他。Those who have the welfare of the people at heart are popular, whereas those who think only of themselves are unpopular.

反殖 fǎnzhí anti-colonialist

反治 fǎnzhì *Chin. med.* treatment by reverse process, e.g. administering medicine of a hot nature to treat a pseudofebrile disease

反质子 fǎnzhìzǐ *phys.* antiproton

反中子 fǎnzhōngzǐ *phys.* antineutron

反转 fǎnzhuǎn reverse

反转来 fǎnzhuǎnlái same as 反过来 fǎn·guò·lái

反转片 fǎnzhuǎnpiàn reversal film

反坐 fǎnzuò *leg.* sentence the accuser to the punishment facing the person he falsely accused

反作用 fǎnzuòyòng counteraction; reaction: 上层建筑对经济基础的～ the reaction of the superstructure on the economic base / 你要起好作用，不要起～。You should set a good example, not a bad one.

反作用力 fǎnzuòyònglì *phys.* reacting force

返

返 fǎn return; come or go back: ～沪 return to Shanghai

返场 fǎnchǎng (of a performer) give an encore: 那位青年歌手～三次。The young singer gave three encores.

返潮 fǎncháo get damp: 雨季里东西容易～。Things get damp easily in the rainy season.

返程 fǎnchéng return journey

返防 fǎnfáng *mil.* return to stations

返工 fǎngōng do poorly done work over again: 这项工作必须～。This job will have to be done over again. / 当初要是听了我的意见，今天哪至于～呢! If you had

listened to me, you wouldn't have to do it all over again.

返航 fǎnháng (of ships, planes, etc.) return to base or port: 在～途中 on the homebound voyage or flight / 这支舰队在完成任务后, 已安然～。 After completing its voyage, the fleet safely returned to base.

返还 fǎnhuán return; give or send back: 请求～定金 claim the return of a deposit

返回 fǎnhuí return; come or go back: ～原地 return to the starting point / ～港口 put back to port / 使人造地球卫星～地面 recover a man-made earth satellite / ～工作岗位 return to one's post

返魂 fǎnhún revive after death; return from the grave

返碱 fǎnjiǎn accumulation of salt in the surface soil

返老还童 fǎnlǎo-huántóng recover one's youthful vigour; feel rejuvenated

返里 fǎnlǐ *formal* return to one's native place; return home

返青 fǎnqīng *agric.* (of winter crops or transplanted seedlings) turn green

返任 fǎnrèn return to one's post

返销 fǎnxiāo (of state-purchased grain) be sold back to a grain-producing area (in cases of natural disaster, etc.): 吃～粮 eat "resold grain"

返校 fǎnxiào (of students) return to school: ～日 a day set for schoolchildren to return to school during the vacation to have homework checked

返修 fǎnxiū repair again sth. poorly repaired

返盐 fǎnyán same as 返碱 fǎnjiǎn

返照 fǎnzhào same as 反照 fǎnzhào

返祖现象 fǎnzǔ xiànxiàng (also 返祖遗传 fǎnzǔ yíchuán) *biol.* atavism; reversion

fàn

犯

fàn ① violate; offend (against the law, etc.): ～纪律 violate discipline / ～校规 offend (or break) a school rule ② attack; invade; work against: 犯境 fànjìng ③ criminal: 战犯 zhànfàn ④ have a recurrence of (an old illness); revert to (a bad habit): 他的气喘病又～了。 He's got another attack of asthma. / ～脾气 get angry; fly into a temper; be in a bad temper ⑤ commit (a mistake, crime, etc.): ～错误 make a mistake / ～官僚主义 commit the error of bureaucracy

犯案 fàn'àn (of a criminal) be found out and brought to justice

犯病 fànbìng have an attack of one's old illness: 她妈又～了。 Her mother is ill again. / 这孩子三天两头～。 This child gets ill too often. / 别理他, 他又～了。 Leave him alone! He's in one of his moods again.

犯不着 fànbuzháo (also 犯不上 fànbushàng) *inf.* not worthwhile: 在枝节问题上～花这么多时间。 It isn't worthwhile spending so much time on minor problems. / 这种不讲理的人, ～和他计较。 It's not worthwhile to argue with such an unreasonable man.

犯愁 fànchóu worry; be anxious: 你犯什么愁? What are you worrying about?

犯怵 fànchù *dial.* feel timid; grow apprehensive

犯得着 fàndezháo (also 犯得上 fàndeshàng) *inf.* (usu. used in rhetorical questions) is it worthwhile: 为这么点小事～和他吵吗? Is it worthwhile quarrelling with him over such a trifling matter? / ～冒这种风险吗? Is it worthwhile taking such risks?

犯嘀咕 fàn dígu have misgivings; have doubts: 心里直～ feel uneasy

犯法 fànfǎ violate (or break) the law: ～行为 an offence against the law / 重婚是～的。 Bigamy is against

the law.

犯规 fànguī ① break the rules ② *sports* foul: 侵人～ personal foul / 三号队员已经犯了四次规。 Player No. 3 has already fouled four times in the game.

犯急 fànjí become impatient; get excited

犯忌 fànjì violate a taboo: 几年前～的话题, 我们现在可以谈论了。 Now we can discuss topics that would have been taboo a few years ago.

犯节气 fàn jiéqi suffer from a seasonal illness

犯禁 fànjìn violate a ban (or prohibition)

犯境 fànjìng invade the frontiers of another country; encroach upon another country's territory; make inroads into another country

犯科 fànkē *formal* violate the law

犯困 fànkùn feel sleepy; feel drowsy; be half asleep

犯赖 fànlài ① be perverse; act shamelessly ② feel languid (or listless)

犯难 fànnán feel embarrassed; feel awkward

犯人 fànrén prisoner; convict

犯傻 fànshǎ *dial.* ① pretend to be naive, ignorant, or stupid: 你心里很清楚, 别～啦。 You know perfectly well. Don't pretend not to know. ② do a foolish thing: 我真～, 竟信了她的话! What a fool I was to believe what she said. ③ be in a daze; stare blankly

犯上 fànshàng go against the king or emperor (in former times); defy one's elders, superiors, etc.

犯上作乱 fànshàng zuòluàn defy one's superiors and start a rebellion; rebel: 你一放松, 他们就～无所不为了。 Once the lid is loose, there'll be a deluge of rebellion and they'll take the law into their own hands.

犯事 fànshì commit a crime (or an offence)

犯嫌疑 fàn xiányí arouse suspicion; come under suspicion

犯性 fànxìng lose one's temper; get angry

犯颜 fànyán *formal* have no regard for sb.'s face (esp. a ruler's): ～直谏 voice outspoken criticisms that bring scowls to the emperor's face

犯疑 fànyí (also 犯疑心 fànyíxīn) become suspicious

犯罪 fànzuì commit a crime (or an offence): ～行为 a criminal offence / ～团伙 a criminal gang / ～分子 offender; criminal / 浪费这么好的粮食简直是～。 It's a crime to waste such good food.

泛¹（汎）

fàn ① *formal* float: ～舟西湖 go boating on the West Lake ② drift out; spread out: 从厨房里～出阵阵香味。 Delicious aromas wafted out of the kitchen. / 她的脸色黑里～红。 She has a tanned and glowing face. / 脸上～出红晕 with one's cheeks suffused with blushes ③ extensive; general; nonspecific: 泛读 fàndú

泛²（汎、氾）

fàn flood; inundate: 黄泛区 huángfànqū

泛称 fànchēng general term

泛读 fàndú extensive reading

泛泛 fànfàn general; not deep-going; not going into detail: 他只是～地一说。 He merely touched on the subject.

泛泛而谈 fànfàn ér tán speak in general terms; talk in generalities

泛泛之交 fànfàn zhī jiāo a casual acquaintance

泛光灯 fànguāngdēng floodlight

泛函分析 fànhán fēnxi *math.* functional analysis

泛碱 fànjiǎn same as 返碱 fǎnjiǎn

泛览 fànlǎn read extensively

泛滥 fànlàn be in flood; overflow; inundate: 河水～。 The river was flooding. *or* The river overflowed its banks. / 不能让错误思想自由～。 Under no circumstances should erroneous ideas be allowed to spread

unchecked.

泛滥成灾 fànlàn chéng zāi　flood; run rampant; run wild: 江水决堤，～。The river overflowed its banks and caused serious flooding. / 表格之多，闹得～。There is such a flood of statistical forms that they become a scourge.

泛论 fànlùn　a general survey or discussion

泛美主义 Fànměizhǔyì　Pan-Americanism

泛神论 fànshénlùn *philos.*　pantheism

泛酸 fànsuān *chem.*　pantothenic acid

泛溢 fànyì　overflow; flood: 江水～。The river overflowed. / 大地～着青草的气味。The earth was redolent of grass.

泛音 fànyīn *mus.*　overtone; harmonic

泛音列 fànyīnliè *mus.*　harmonic series

泛指 fànzhǐ　make a general reference; be used in a general sense: 他的发言是～一般情况，不是针对某一个人的。His statement refers to people in general, not to anyone in particular.

饭 fàn　① cooked rice or other cereals: 小米～ (cooked) millet ② meal: 一天三顿饱～ three square meals a day / ～前洗手。Wash your hands before meals.

饭菜 fàncài　① meal; repast: ～可口，服务周到 tasty food and good service ② dishes to go with rice, steamed buns, etc.

饭单 fàndān　① table napkin ② *dial.* menu; bill of fare ③ *dial.* apron ④ *dial.* bib

饭店 fàndiàn　① hotel: 北京～ Beijing Hotel ② *dial.* restaurant

饭馆 fànguǎn　(small) restaurant; eating house: 下～ eat (or dine) in a restaurant

饭锅 fànguō　① pot for cooking rice; rice cooker ② means of living; livelihood: 砸～ lose one's livelihood; lose one's job

饭盒 fànhé　lunch-box; mess tin; dinner pail

饭局 fànjú *old*　dinner party; feast

饭来张口，衣来伸手 fàn lái zhāngkǒu, yī lái shēnshǒu　have only to open one's mouth to be fed and hold out one's arms to be dressed—lead an easy life, with everything provided; be waited on hand and foot

饭粒 fànlì　grains of cooked rice: 饭桌上剩下不少～。The table was littered with grains of rice.

饭量 fànliàng　appetite: ～很大 have an enormous appetite; be a big eater / 她的～比你小多了。She eats much less than you do.

饭囊 fànnáng　rice bag—good-for-nothing

饭票 fànpiào　meal ticket; mess card

饭铺 fànpù　(small) restaurant; eating house

饭食 fànshí　food provided by a canteen, restaurant, boarding house, etc. (esp. with regard to its quality); fare: 那儿的～挺不错。You get pretty good food there.

饭摊 fàntān　quick-meal stall

饭堂 fàntáng *dial.*　dining room; mess hall; canteen

饭厅 fàntīng　dining hall; dining room; mess hall: 这个～可容三百人就餐。The dining hall can seat 300 people.

饭桶 fàntǒng　① rice bucket ② a big eater; a piggish eater ③ fathead; good-for-nothing

饭碗 fànwǎn　① rice bowl ② *inf.* job; means of livelihood: 丢～ lose one's job / 找～ hunt for a job / 你要加倍小心，这事弄不好会把你的～砸了。Be extra cautious. It may cost you your job if anything goes wrong.

饭庄 fànzhuāng　(also 饭庄子 fànzhuāngzi) (big) restaurant

饭桌 fànzhuō　dining table

范[1] **（範）** fàn　① *formal* mould; matrix; pat-

tern ② model; example: 典范 diǎnfàn ③ limits: 就范 jiùfàn ④ *formal* restriction: 防范 fángfàn

范[2] Fàn　a surname

范本 fànběn　a model for calligraphy or painting: 习字～ a model for calligraphy

范畴 fànchóu　① category: 这些概念属于美学的～。These concepts belong in the field of aesthetics. ② type; scope

范例 fànlì　example; model: 这是厉行节约的一个出色～。This is an outstanding example of strict economy.

范围 fànwéi　① limits; scope; range: 在法律许可～内 within the limits permitted by law / 国家管辖～ the limits of national jurisdiction / 势力～ sphere of influence / 我们谈话的～很广。Our talk covered a wide range of subjects. / ～狭小 be limited in scope / 实际控制～ the extent of actual control / 在协定规定的～内 within the framework of the agreement / 这不属于我们研究的～。This is outside the scope of our study. ② *formal* set limits to; limit the scope of

范文 fànwén　model essay; anthology piece

范性 fànxìng　same as 塑性 sùxìng

贩 fàn　① (of traders) buy to resell: ～牲口 buy and sell draught animals ② trader; monger; pedlar (or peddler): 小贩 xiǎofàn

贩毒 fàndú　traffic in narcotics

贩夫 fànfū *old*　pedlar (or peddler); hawker

贩卖 fànmài　traffic; peddle; sell: ～皮货 be in the fur trade / ～军火 traffic in arms / ～腐朽思想 peddle decadent ideas

贩卖人口 fànmài rénkǒu　traffic in human beings; human traffic; (specifically) traffic in women; the white-slave trade; white slavery

贩私 fànsī　traffic in smuggled goods

贩运 fànyùn　transport goods for sale; traffic: 解放前他靠～食盐过日子。Before liberation, he made a living by transporting and selling salt. / 在广州和东北之间搞长途～ transport goods for sale between Guangzhou and the Notheast

贩子 fànzi　trader; monger: 马～ horse trader / 鱼～ fishmonger

畈 fàn *dial.*　① (usu. used in place names) field; land ② *m.* (for large tracts of land): 一～田 a big tract of farmland

梵 fàn　① of ancient India: 梵文 Fànwén ② Buddhist: ～刹 Buddhist temple

梵蒂冈 Fàndìgāng　the Vatican

梵宫 fàngōng　Buddhist temple

梵文 Fànwén　Sanskrit

梵哑铃 fànyǎlíng　violin (a transliteration)

梵宇 fànyǔ　Buddhist temple

梵语 Fànyǔ　Sanskrit

fāng

方[1] fāng　① square: 这块板子是～的。This is a square board. ② *math.* involution; power: 二的四次～是十六。The fourth power of 2 is 16. / 三的三次～是二十七。The third power (or cube) of 3 is 27. ③ *m.* (for square things): 三～图章 three seals / 一～手帕 a handkerchief ④ short for square metre or cubic metre: 一～木材 a cubic metre of lumber / 铺地板十五～ lay 15 square metres of floorboards ⑤ upright; honest: 方

正 fāngzhèng ⑥ (Fāng) a surname

方² fāng ① direction: 东方 dōngfāng / 前方 qiánfāng ② side; party: 我～ our side ③ place; region; locality: 远方 yuǎnfāng

方³ fāng ① method; way: 有方 yǒufāng ② prescription: 这～儿专治腰痛。This prescription is especially good for backaches.

方⁴ fāng adv. formal ① just when; at the time when: 方今 fāngjīn ② only; just: 年～二十 be just twenty years old

方案 fāng'àn scheme; plan; programme: 提出初步～ put forward a preliminary plan

方便 fāngbiàn ① convenient: 这儿交通～。Transportation is convenient here. / 什么时候～，什么时候来。Drop in whenever it's convenient. / 这件事让我去办很～。It's quite convenient for me to do that. / 这儿说话不～。It's not convenient to talk here. or This isn't the right place to talk. / 把困难留给自己，把～让给别人 take the difficulties on oneself and make things easy for others ② make things convenient for sb.: ～群众 make things convenient for the people ③ euph. have money to spare or lend: 手头不～ have little money to spare ④ euph. inf. go to the lavatory: 你要不要～一下? Do you want to use the lavatory (or wash your hands)? / 稍候，我去～～。Wait a few minutes. I'm just going to wash my hands.

方便面 fāngbiànmiàn instant noodles

方便食品 fāngbiàn shípǐn convenience food

方便之门 fāngbiàn zhī mén convenience: 大开～ do everything to suit sb.'s convenience

方步 fāngbù measured steps: 迈～ walk with measured steps

方才 fāngcái ① just now: ～的情形，你都知道了。You know what has just happened. / ～我到他家去了。I went to his place just now. / 她～还在这儿。She was here just a moment ago. ② (only) just; not until: 等到天黑，他～回来。He didn't come back until after dark.

方材 fāngcái a long thick piece of timber shaped like a square pillar

方策 fāngcè formal ① strategy; general plan ② (also 方册 fāngcè) ancient books and records

方程 fāngchéng math. equation: 三次～ cubic equation / 高次～ equation of higher degree / 线性～ linear equation

方程式 fāngchéngshì ① same as 方程 fāngchéng ② (chemical) equation

方尺 fāngchǐ square chi (= 1/9 square metre)

方寸 fāngcùn ① square cun (= 1/9 square decimetre) ② liter. heart

方寸已乱 fāngcùn yǐ luàn with one's heart troubled and in turmoil; with one's mind in a turmoil; greatly agitated

方法 fāngfǎ method; way; means: 学习～ study method / 看问题的～ the way one approaches a problem (or looks at things) / 用各种～ in all sorts of ways; by every means / 用某种～ by some means or other; one way or another

方法论 fāngfǎlùn philos. methodology

方钢 fānggāng metall. square steel

方格 fānggé a pattern of squares; check: ～桌布 a checked (or check) tablecloth / ～纹 trellis design / ～纸 squared paper; graph paper

方根 fānggēn math. root

方剂 fāngjì Chin. med. prescription; recipe

方济各会 Fāngjìgèhuì the Franciscan Order

方尖碑 fāngjiānbēi obelisk

方解石 fāngjiěshí calcite (a mineral)

方巾 fāngjīn kerchief worn by male scholars of the Ming Dynasty

方巾气 fāngjīnqì (of thoughts, ideas or behaviour) conservative; pedantic

方今 fāngjīn now; nowadays: ～盛世 in this age of prosperity

方块 fāngkuài diamond (in cards)

方块字 fāngkuàizì square-shaped characters—Chinese characters

方框 fāngkuàng square frame

方括号 fāngkuòhào square brackets ([ ])

方略 fānglüè general plan: 建国～ a general plan for national reconstruction

方面 fāngmiàn respect; aspect; side; field: 在这～ in this respect / 在工业、商业、财政～ in the fields of industry, commerce and finance / 站在我们这～ stand on our side; take our side / 考虑各～的意见 consider opinions from different quarters / 这个问题可以从两～来看。This subject may be viewed from two aspects. / 我们两国的关系在各个～都有了显著的进展。The relations between our two countries have improved markedly in every aspect.

方面军 fāngmiànjūn front army: 中国工农红军第一～ the First Front Army of the Chinese Workers' and Peasants' Red Army

方铅矿 fāngqiānkuàng galena

方枘圆凿 fāngruì-yuánzáo same as 圆凿方枘 yuánzáo fāngruì

方士 fāngshì ① necromancer ② alchemist

方式 fāngshì way; fashion; pattern: 生活～ way (or mode) of life; life-style / 斗争～ form of struggle / 领导～ style of leadership / 一反过去因袭的～ depart from the formula followed in the past / 做工作应注意～方法。In doing our work, we must pay attention to method and style.

方术 fāngshù medicine, divination, and similar arts

方糖 fāngtáng sugar cube; lump sugar

方外 fāngwài ① beyond this world: ～之友 Buddhist monks or Taoist priests ② formal foreign lands

方位 fāngwèi ① points of the compass: 东、南、西、北为基本～。East, west, north and south are the cardinal points of the compass. ② direction and position; bearings: 确定～ find one's bearings

方位词 fāngwèicí gram. noun of locality; localizer

方位角 fāngwèijiǎo astron. azimuth

方位罗盘 fāngwèi luópán surveying azimuth compass

方位天文学 fāngwèi tiānwénxué positional astronomy

方位物 fāngwèiwù mil. topographic marker; landmarker

方向 fāngxiàng direction; orientation: 他朝学校的～走了。He went in the direction of the school. / 她深信已在生活中找到了新的～。She is confident that she has found a new orientation in life. / 坚定正确的政治～ a firm and correct political orientation / 党为全国人民指明了前进的～。The Party has pointed out the way forward for the whole nation.

方向 fāngxiàng dial. situation; circumstances; trend of events: 看～做事 act according to the circumstances

方向舵 fāngxiàngduò rudder (of an airplane)

方向盘 fāngxiàngpán steering wheel

方兴未艾 fāngxīng-wèi'ài be fast unfolding; be in the ascendant: 这场运动～。The movement is now in the ascendant.

方形 fāngxíng square-shaped; square

方言 fāngyán dialect

方言学 fāngyánxué dialectology

方音 fāngyīn ① the phonetic aspect of a dialect ② a dialectal accent: 他说话～很重。He speaks with a

strong accent.

方圆 fāngyuán ① neighbourhood; vicinity: ～左近的人,他都认识。 He knows everyone in the neighbourhood. ② circumference: 那个湖～八百公里。 The lake has a circumference of 800 kilometres.

方丈 fāngzhàng square *zhang* (= 11 1/9 square metres)

方丈 fāngzhang ① Buddhist abbot ② abbot's room

方针 fāngzhēn policy; guiding principle: 基本～ fundamental policy (*or* principle) / ～政策 general and specific policies / 文艺～ guiding principles for literature and art / ～任务 guiding principles and specific tasks

方正 fāngzhèng ① upright and foursquare: 字要写得～。 In writing, make the characters square and upright. ② straightforward; upright; righteous: 他为人～。 He is an upright man.

方志 fāngzhì local records

方舟[1] fāngzhōu *formal* two boats sailing abreast

方舟[2] fāngzhōu Noah's Ark

方桌 fāngzhuō a square table

方子 fāngzi ① prescription: 开～ write out a prescription ② directions for mixing chemicals; formula ③ same as 方材 fāngcái

方钻杆 fāngzuàngǎn *petroleum* kelly (bar)

坊 fāng ① lane (usu. as part of a street or lane name): 白纸～ White Paper Lane (a street in Beijing) ② see 牌坊 páifāng——see also fáng

坊本 fāngběn *old* block-printed edition prepared by a bookshop

坊间 fāngjiān in the streets (esp. with reference to the bookshops): 此书～少见。 This book is rarely seen in the bookshops.

芳 fāng ① sweet-smelling; fragrant: ～草 fragrant grass ② good (name or reputation); virtuous: 流芳百世 liúfāng bǎishì

芳菲 fāngfēi *formal* ① the fragrance of flowers and plants ② flowers and plants

芳邻 fānglín *pol.* neighbours

芳龄 fānglíng *old* the age of a young woman

芳名 fāngmíng *old* ① the name of a young woman ② a good reputation

芳烃 fāngtīng *chem.* aromatic hydrocarbon

芳香 fāngxiāng (esp. of flowers or plants) fragrant

芳香剂 fāngxiāngjì an aromatic drug; aromatic

芳心 fāngxīn the heart of a young woman

芳泽 fāngzé ① scented hair oil used by women in former times ② fragrance

芳族 fāngzú *chem.* aromatics: ～化合物 aromatic compound; aromatic / ～酸 aromatic acid

枋[1] fāng a tree mentioned in ancient texts as timber for vehicles

枋[2] fāng same as 枋子 fāngzi ①

枋子 fāngzi ① a long thick piece of timber shaped like a square pillar ② *dial.* coffin

钫[1] fāng *chem.* francium (Fr)

钫[2] fāng ① *archaeol.* a bronze square-mouthed, roundbellied wine vessel ② *formal* pot; pan

fáng

防 fāng ① guard against; provide against: ～病 prevent disease / ～霜冻 protect plants against severe frosts ② defend: 国防 guófáng / 防御 fángyù ③ dyke; embankment: 堤防 dīfáng

防暴警察 fángbào jǐngchá riot squad; riot police

防备 fángbèi guard against; take precautions against: ～敌人突然袭击 be prepared for surprise attacks by the enemy / 采取措施～发生事故 take precautions against accidents / 他们事先没有一点～。 They didn't take any precautions whatever. *or* They threw precautions to the winds.

防波堤 fángbōdī breakwater; mole

防不胜防 fáng bùshèng fáng hard to guard against; cannot reckon with all eventualities: 他的球路多变, 打得对手～。 His opponent couldn't stand up to his varied and fast-changing tactics.

防潮 fángcháo ① dampproof; moistureproof: ～纸 moistureproof paper; tarred paper / ～砖 moistureproof brick ② give protection against the tide: ～堰堤 tidal barrage

防潮层 fángcháocéng *archit.* dampproof course; damp course

防潮火药 fángcháo huǒyào moistureproof powder; nonhygroscopic powder

防尘 fángchén dustproof

防尘圈 fángchénquān *mech.* dust ring

防尘罩 fángchénzhào dust cover

防除 fángchú prevent and kill off: ～害虫 prevent and kill off insect pests

防磁 fángcí *phys.* protect against magnetization; be antimagnetic: ～表 antimagnetic watch

防弹 fángdàn bulletproof; shellproof: ～背心 bulletproof vest / ～玻璃 bulletproof glass

防盗 fángdào guard against theft; take precautions against burglars

防地 fángdì *mil.* defence sector; station (of a unit)

防冻 fángdòng prevent frostbite: ～药品 frostbite preventive

防毒 fángdú protect (men or animals) against poisonous substances; protect against poison gas: ～器材 gas protection equipment / ～衣 protective clothing

防毒面具 fángdú miànjù gas mask

防范 fángfàn be on guard; keep a lookout: 严加～ take strict precautions

防风[1] fángfēng ① *bot.* fangfeng (*Saposhnikovia divaricata*) ② *Chin. med.* the root of fangfeng

防风[2] fángfēng protect against the wind; provide shelter from the wind

防风林 fángfēnglín windbreak (forest)

防风障 fángfēngzhàng windbreak

防辐射 fángfúshè protect against radiation

防腐 fángfǔ ① antiseptic: ～纱布 antiseptic gauze ② antirot: ～材料 antirot material

防腐剂 fángfǔjì antiseptic; preservative

防腐蚀 fángfǔshí ① anticorrosive ② guard against corruption

防旱 fánghàn take precautions against drought

防洪 fánghóng prevent or control flood: ～措施 flood control measures / ～工程 flood control works

防护 fánghù protect; shelter: 人体～ physical protection / ～涂层 protective coating

防护堤 fánghùdī (protection) embankment

防护林 fánghùlín shelter-forest: ～带 shelterbelt

防滑链 fánghuálián tyre chain; skid chain

防化学兵 fánghuàxuébīng (also 防化兵 fánghuàbīng) antichemical warfare corps

防患未然 fáng huàn wèi rán (also 防患于未然 fáng huàn yú wèi rán) take preventive measures; provide against possible trouble: 与其补救于已然, 不如防患于未然。 To forestall is better than to amend. *or* Prevention is better than cure.

防火 fánghuǒ ① prevent fires ② fireproof

防火隔离线 fánghuǒ gélíxiàn *forestry* fire lane

防火墙 fánghuǒqiáng fire wall

防己 fángjǐ ① *bot.* fangji (*Stephania tetrandra*) ② *Chin. med.* the root of *fangji*

防空 fángkōng air defence: ～导弹 air defence missile; interceptor missile / ～演习 air defence exercise; air-raid drill

防空部队 fángkōng bùduì air defence forces

防空洞 fángkōngdòng ① air-raid shelter ② a hideout for evildoers; a cover for wrong thoughts

防空壕 fángkōnghào air-raid dugout

防空警报 fángkōng jǐngbào air-raid warning; air-raid siren

防老剂 fánglǎojì *chem.* antideteriorant

防涝 fánglào prevent waterlogging

防凌 fánglíng reduce the menace of ice run

防区 fángqū defence area; garrison area

防染剂 fángrǎnjì *text.* resist

防身 fángshēn defend oneself against violence: ～武器 weapons for self-defence

防守 fángshǒu defend; guard: ～阵地 defend one's position (in battle)

防暑 fángshǔ prevent heatstroke (*or* sunstroke): ～措施 measures taken to prevent heatstroke / ～药 heatstroke preventive

防水 fángshuǐ waterproof: ～表 waterproof watch / ～布 waterproof cloth / ～水泥 waterproof cement

防水层 fángshuǐcéng *archit.* waterproof layer

防缩 fángsuō *text.* shrinkproof: ～整理 shrinkproof finish; shrinkage control finish

防坦克 fángtǎnkè antitank defence: ～地雷 antitank mine / ～壕 tank (*or* antitank) ditch / ～炮 antitank gun / ～阵地 antitank position

防特 fángtè guard against enemy agents

防微杜渐 fángwēi-dùjiàn nip in the bud; check at the outset

防卫 fángwèi defend: ～作战能力 defence capability

防务 fángwù matters pertaining to defence; defence

防线 fángxiàn line of defence: 突破敌人～ break through the enemy's line of defence

防修 fángxiū prevent revisionism

防锈 fángxiù rust-resist; rustproof: 不要让自行车在雨里淋，注意～。 Don't leave the bike in the rain and let it rust. / ～漆 antirust paint / ～脂 antirust grease

防锈剂 fángxiùjì rust inhibitor; antirust agent

防汛 fángxùn flood prevention or control: 组成一支～大军 organize an army of flood-fighters / ～指挥部 flood-control headquarters

防疫 fángyì epidemic prevention

防疫站 fángyìzhàn epidemic prevention station

防疫针 fángyìzhēn (prophylactic) inoculation

防雨布 fángyǔbù waterproof cloth; tarpaulin

防御 fángyù defend; guard: ～国家外部敌人的颠覆和侵略 guard against subversion and aggression by external enemies / 积极 (消极) ～ active (passive) defence / 纵深～ defence in depth / 加强～力量 strengthen defence capabilities / 由～转入进攻 go over from the defensive to the offensive

防御部队 fángyù bùduì defending force (*or* troops, unit)

防御部署 fángyù bùshǔ defensive disposition

防御工事 fángyù gōngshì defences; fortifications; defence works

防御战 fángyùzhàn defensive warfare

防御阵地 fángyù zhèndì defensive position; defended post

防御正面 fángyù zhèngmiàn frontage in defence; front of defence

防灾 fángzāi take precautions against natural calamities

防震 fángzhèn ① shockproof: ～表 shockproof watch ② take precautions against earthquakes: ～措施 precautions against earthquakes

防止 fángzhǐ prevent; guard against; forestall; avoid: ～煤气中毒 guard against gas poisoning / ～浪费人力 avoid waste of manpower / ～骄傲自满 guard against conceit and complacency / ～交通事故 try to forestall traffic accidents

防治 fángzhì provide prevention and cure; administer prophylaxis and treatment: ～血吸虫病 the prevention and cure of schistosomiasis / ～病虫害 the prevention and control of plant diseases and elimination of pests

坊 fāng handicraftsmen's workplace; workshop; mill: 染坊 rǎnfáng / 油坊 yóufáng —— see also fǎng

妨 fáng ① hinder; hamper; impede; obstruct: 妨碍 fáng'ài ② (used in the negative or interrogative) harm: 何妨 héfáng / 不妨 bùfáng

妨碍 fáng'ài hinder; hamper; impede; obstruct: ～团结 hinder unity / ～交通 block traffic / ～生产的发展 hamper the growth of production / 这不～我们按期动工。 This won't stop us from starting the project on schedule. / 这不应该～我们两国之间良好关系的发展。 This should not present an obstacle to the development of good relations between our two countries. / 请你说话轻些，不要～别人学习。 Please speak softly so as not to disturb those who are studying.

妨害 fánghài impair; jeopardize; be harmful to: 吃得不好会～健康。 A poor diet is harmful to one's health.

房[1] fáng ① house: 一所砖～ a brick house ② room; bedroom: 三间～ three rooms / 两～一厅 two bedrooms and a living room ③ a house-like structure: 莲～ lotus pod ④ a branch of an extended family: 三～ the third branch, i.e. the third son and his family ⑤ *m.* (for daughters-in-law or concubines): 有两～儿媳妇 have two daughters-in-law / 娶一～小老婆 take a concubine ⑥ the fourth of the twenty-eight constellations (二十八宿) into which the celestial sphere was divided in ancient Chinese astronomy (consisting of four stars nearly in a straight line in Scorpio) ⑦ (Fáng) a surname

房[2] fáng same as 坊 fāng

房舱 fángcāng passenger's cabin in a ship

房产 fángchǎn house property

房产主 fángchǎnzhǔ an owner of houses for rent; landlord

房地产 fángdìchǎn real estate: ～经纪人 estate agent; house agent; realtor

房顶 fángdǐng roof

房东 fángdōng the owner and lessor of a house or room; landlord or landlady

房荒 fánghuāng housing shortage

房基 fángjī foundations (of a building)

房间 fángjiān room: 一套～ a suite; an apartment; a flat

房客 fángkè tenant (of a room or house); lodger

房契 fángqì title deed (for a house)

房钱 fángqian house rent; room rent

房事 fángshì sexual intercourse (usu. between a married couple)

房屋 fángwū　houses or buildings; housing
房檐 fángyán　eaves
房主 fángzhǔ　house-owner
房柱 fángzhù　pillars of a house
房子 fángzi　① house; building ② room, apartment, etc.: 我弄到了一套两室一厅的～。 I've got a flat with two bedrooms and a living room.
房租 fángzū　rent (for a house, flat, etc.); rental

肪

fáng　see 脂肪 zhīfáng

鲂

fáng　triangular bream (*Megalobrama terminalis*)

鲂鮄 fángfú　gurnard

fǎng

访

fǎng　① visit; call on: ～友 call on a friend ② seek by inquiry or search; try to get: 采访 cǎifǎng / 访求 fǎngqiú

访查 fǎngchá　go about making inquiries; investigate
访古 fǎnggǔ　search for ancient relics: 河套～ in quest of antiquities at the Great Bend
访求 fǎngqiú　search for: ～民间丹方 search for folk remedies
访视 fǎngshì　make a house call (to see a patient, lying-in woman, etc.)
访问 fǎngwèn　visit; call on; interview: ～亲友 call on friends and relatives / ～延安 visit Yan'an / 记者～了那位知名人士。 A reporter interviewed the well-known personage. / 正式（非正式）～ an official (unofficial) visit / 国事～ a state visit / 进行一次亲善～ pay a goodwill visit
访问学者 fǎngwèn xuézhě　visiting scholar

仿（倣）

fǎng　① imitate; copy: 仿造 fǎngzào ② resemble; be like: 相仿 xiāngfǎng ③ characters written after a calligraphy model: 写一张～ write a page of characters after a calligraphy model
仿单 fǎngdān　instructions for use (of a commodity, esp. a medicine)
仿佛 fǎngfú　① *adv.* seemingly; as if: 这事她～已经知道了。 She seems to know about it already. / 他的身体, 看外表～很好, 其实有高血压病。 He appears to be healthy, but has high blood pressure. / 读着这些故事, 我～进入了一个童话世界。 As I read these stories, I felt as if I was entering a fairyland. ② be more or less the same; be alike: 这两个人的年纪相～。 These two persons are about the same age. / 他的模样还和十年前相～。 He looks about the same as he did ten years ago.
仿古 fǎnggǔ　modelled after an antique; in the style of the ancients: ～青铜器 an imitation of an ancient bronze
仿生学 fǎngshēngxué　bionics
仿宋 fǎngsòng　(also 仿宋体 fǎngsòngtǐ) *print.* imitation Song-Dynasty-style typeface
仿效 fǎngxiào　imitate; follow the example of: 她是个好榜样, 我们应当～她。 We ought to follow her good example. / 他～那位名歌唱家的唱法, 已经达到无懈可击的地步。 His imitation of that famous singer is perfect.
仿行 fǎngxíng　follow an example; follow suit
仿形 fǎngxíng　*mech.* profile modelling: ～车床 copying lathe; repetition lathe / ～机械 profiling mechanism
仿造 fǎngzào　copy; be modelled on
仿照 fǎngzhào　imitate; follow: 这个办法很好, 各地可以～办理。 This is a good method. It might well be adopted by other localities. / 这个公园是～《红楼梦》里大观园设计的。 This park is laid out in imitation of the Garden of Grand View in *A Dream of Red Mansions*.
仿制 fǎngzhì　copy; imitate; be modelled on
仿制品 fǎngzhìpǐn　an imitation; replica; copy

纺

fǎng　① spin: 把棉花～成纱 spin cotton into yarn ② a thin silk cloth
纺车 fǎngchē　spinning wheel
纺绸 fǎngchóu　a soft plain-weave silk fabric
纺锤 fǎngchuí　spindle
纺锭 fǎngdìng　*text.* spindle
纺纱 fǎngshā　spinning: ～工人 spinner / ～机 spinning machine
纺丝 fǎngsī　*chem. fibre* spinning: ～泵 spinning pump / ～罐 spinning box / ～机 spinning machine / ～浴 spinning bath
纺液染色 fǎngyè rǎnsè　*chem. fibre* dope dyeing: ～纤维 dope-dyed fibre
纺织 fǎngzhī　spinning and weaving: ～厂 textile mill / ～工人 textile worker / ～工业 textile industry
纺织娘 fǎngzhīniáng　*zool.* katydid; long-horned grasshopper
纺织品 fǎngzhīpǐn　textile; fabric

舫

fǎng　boat: 画舫 huàfǎng

fàng

放

fàng　① let go; set free; release: ～他走 let him go / 抓住绳子不～ won't let go of the rope / 把俘房～了 release the captives / 把游泳池里的水～掉 let the water out of the swimming pool ② give way to; let oneself go: 放声 fàngshēng / 放胆 fàngdǎn ③ put out to feed: ～牛 put cattle out to pasture; graze cattle / ～鸭子 put ducks out to feed in a pond, stream, etc. ④ let off; give off or out: ～枪 fire a gun / ～箭 shoot an arrow / ～爆竹 set off firecrackers / ～风筝 fly a kite / 蒸汽机～汽了。 The engine is letting off steam. / 月亮本身不～光。 The moon does not give off light by itself. ⑤ show (a film, etc.); play (a record, etc.): ～录音 play back a recording / ～录像 play a video tape / ～幻灯片 show some lantern slides / ～点儿音乐听听 play some music records or tapes / ～电视 switch on the TV ⑥ light; kindle: 放火 fànghuǒ ⑦ lend (money) at interest; loan: 他的钱全～出去了, 一时收不回来。 All his money has been loaned out. He can't get it back for the moment. ⑧ make larger or longer; let out; let down: ～几张相片 have a few photos enlarged / 把这条裙子～长一点儿。 Let out the hem on this skirt a little. / 裤腰要～一厘米。 Please let these trousers out 1 cm. at the waist. ⑨ moderate (one's action, attitude or behaviour): ～老实点儿! You behave yourself! / ～明白些。 Be sensible. / 请你脚步～轻些! Tread softly, please. / 把速度～慢点儿。 Slow down a little. / ～低声音慢慢地说。 Lower your voice and speak slowly. ⑩ (of flowers) blossom; open: 百花齐放 bǎihuā qífàng / 心花怒放 xīnhuā nùfàng ⑪ put; place; lay: 把书～在桌上。 Put the book on the desk. / 你来～碗筷。 Will you set the table for dinner? / 她～下笔, 拿起书。 She laid down her pen and took up a book. / 汤里～点胡椒粉。 Put some pepper in the soup. / 把人民利益～在个人利益之上。 Place the interests of the people above personal interests. ⑫ *inf.* cause sth. or sb. to fall to the ground: 上山～树 go to the mountains to fell trees / 他三下两下就把那个坏蛋～倒了。 With just a few blows, he knocked the

hooligan down to the ground. ⑬ lay aside; store away (for future use); keep: 这事不急, 先～一～再说。It's not an urgent matter. Let's lay it aside for the moment. / 鲜牛奶不能～得太久。Fresh milk won't keep long. / 这鱼怕～不住。This fish won't keep, I'm afraid. ⑭ (followed by 着…不…) allow sth. to remain (undone, untaken, unused, etc.): 怎么了, ～着觉不睡, 却到处乱跑? Why are you running around instead of going to bed? / ～着这么多好书不看, 多可惜! What a pity all these fine books are left untouched !

放长线, 钓大鱼 fàng chángxiàn, diào dàyú　throw a long line to catch a big fish——adopt a long-term plan to secure sth. big

放大 fàngdà　enlarge; magnify; amplify: 把照片～ make enlargements of a photograph; have a photo enlarged / 这台显微镜可以把细菌～三千倍。This microscope can magnify bacteria three thousand times their actual size. / 本位主义是～了的个人主义。Departmentalism is magnified individualism.

放大尺 fàngdàchǐ　pantograph

放大机 fàngdàjī　*photog.* enlarger

放大镜 fàngdàjìng　magnifying glass; magnifier

放大率 fàngdàlǜ　magnifying power

放大炮 fàng dàpào　① brag; boast; talk big ② shoot off one's mouth (usu. at a meeting)

放大器 fàngdàqì　*electron.* amplifier

放大照片 fàngdà zhàopiàn　enlarged photograph; enlargement; blowup

放大纸 fàngdàzhǐ　*photog.* enlarging paper; bromide paper

放胆 fàngdǎn　act boldly and with confidence: 你尽管～去干! Don't hesitate to forge ahead!

放诞 fàngdàn　wild in speech and behaviour

放荡 fàngdàng　① dissolute; dissipated: 她决不是一个～的女人。She's definitely not a woman of easy virtue. ② unconventional

放荡不羁 fàngdàng bùjī　unconventional and unrestrained

放电 fàngdiàn　*phys.* (electric) discharge: 火花～ spark discharge / 尖端～ point discharge / 闪电是自然界的～现象。Lightning is a natural discharge of electricity.

放刁 fàngdiāo　make difficulties for sb.; act in a rascally manner

放毒 fàngdú　① put poison in food, water, etc.; poison ② make vicious remarks; spread poisonous ideas

放对 fàngduì　① *dial.* be rivals in a *wushu* contest ② *dial.* set oneself against sb. ③ mate (animals)

放风 fàngfēng　① let in fresh air ② let prisoners out for exercise or to relieve themselves ③ leak certain information; spread news or rumours ④ *dial.* be on the lookout; act as a lookout

放高利贷 fàng gāolìdài　lend money at an excessively high rate of interest; practise usury

放工 fànggōng　get out of work; knock off: 我们是下午六点钟放的工。We got out of work at six o'clock in the afternoon. / 大多数工厂五点～。Most factories knock off work at five.

放过 fàngguò　let sb. off; let sth. slip by: 我们决不冤枉一个好人, 也决不～一个坏人。We will never wrong a single good person nor let off a single bad one. / 这是个好机会, 不要～。Don't let this good opportunity slip by.

放虎归山 fàng hǔ guī shān　same as 纵虎归山 zòng hǔ guī shān

放怀 fànghuái　to one's heart's content; as much as one likes: ～畅饮 drink to one's heart's content

放还 fànghuán　① release; let go: 交保～ release (a detained person) on bail / ～原主 let (an animal) go back

to its owner ② return (*or* restore) sth. to its former place: 架上期刊, 阅后～原处。Please return the periodicals to their places on the shelves.

放火 fànghuǒ　① set fire to; set on fire; commit arson: 游击队～烧了敌人的仓库。The guerrillas burned down the enemy's depot. ② create disturbances

放火犯 fànghuǒfàn　arsonist

放假 fàngjià　have a holiday or vacation; have a day off: 你们什么时候放暑假? When is your summer vacation? / 三八节妇女～半天。Women have a half-day holiday on March 8.

放开 fàngkāi　have a free hand in doing sth.: 让外贸企业～经营 give foreign trade enterprises full authority over management

放空 fàngkōng　(of a car, truck, etc.) travel empty (unloaded or without passengers)

放空炮 fàng kōngpào　talk big; spout hot air; indulge in idle boasting: 不要～, 拿出行动来。Now, none of your empty talk. Let's see how you act.

放空气 fàng kōngqì　drop a hint; spread word; create an impression: 放出紧张空气 try to create the impression that the situation is tense

放宽 fàngkuān　relax restrictions; relax: ～尺度 relax the requirements / ～期限 extend a time limit / ～条件 soften the terms

放款 fàngkuǎn　make loans; loan: 短 (中, 长) 期～ short-term (medium-term, long-term) loan

放浪 fànglàng　*formal* ① unrestrained ② dissolute

放浪形骸 fànglàng xínghái　refuse to be bound by convention; be defiant of convention

放冷风 fàng lěngfēng　spread slanderous rumours

放冷箭 fàng lěngjiàn　shoot from a hidden position——injure sb. by underhand means; snipe

放量 fàngliàng　(eat or drink) to the limit of one's capacity; to one's heart's content

放疗 fàngliáo　short for 放射疗法 fàngshè liáofǎ

放牧 fàngmù　put out to pasture; graze; herd: ～牛羊 herd (*or* graze) sheep and cattle

放牧期 fàngmùqī　grazing season

放牛娃 fàngniúwá　child cowherd

放排 fàngpái　① set a raft going (downstream): ～喽! Here goes the raft! ② rafting (a way of transporting logs)

放盘 fàngpán　*old* (of a shop) sell at reduced prices or buy in at raised prices

放炮 fàngpào　① fire a gun: 放三炮 fire three gunshots ② set off firecrackers ③ blast: ～, 危险! Danger! Blasting in progress! ④ (of a tyre, etc.) blow out: 车胎～了! The tyre's had a blowout. ⑤ shoot off one's mouth: 不了解情况不要乱～! Don't shoot off your mouth if you don't know the facts.

放屁 fàngpì　① break wind; fart ② *offens.* talk nonsense: ～! Shit! *or* What crap!

放弃 fàngqì　abandon; give up; renounce: ～原来计划 abandon the original plan / ～表决权 abstain from voting / ～原则 forsake one's principles

放青 fàngqīng　put (cattle, etc.) out to graze

放青苗 fàng qīngmiáo　*old* (of landlords *or* merchants) purchase standing crops at extremely low prices from poor peasants who run short before the harvest; buy standing crops dirt cheap

放情 fàngqíng　to one's heart's content; as much as one likes

放晴 fàngqíng　clear up (after rain): 天一～咱们就开镰收麦子。We'll begin harvesting the wheat as soon as it clears up.

放热 fàngrè　*chem.* exothermic

放热反应 fàngrè fǎnyìng　*chem.* exothermic reaction

放任 fàngrèn　① not interfere; let alone ② noninterfer-

ence; *laissez-faire*: 采取～态度 take a *laissez-faire* attitude

放任自流 fàngrèn zìliú let things drift (*or* slide)

放散 fàngsàn (of smoke, scent, etc.) diffuse; disperse; dissipate

放哨 fàngshào be on sentry or on patrol: 站岗～ stand sentry; stand sentinel; go on sentry duty / 巡逻～ go on patrol; patrol

放射 fàngshè radiate: 初升的太阳～出万道金光。The rising sun radiated myriads of golden rays.

放射病 fàngshèbìng radiation sickness

放射疗法 fàngshè liáofǎ radiotherapy

放射线 fàngshèxiàn radioactive rays

放射现象 fàngshè xiànxiàng *phys.* radioactivity

放射性 fàngshèxìng *phys.* radioactivity; activity

放射性示踪物 fàngshèxìng shìzōngwù radioactive tracer

放射性碳素断代法 fàngshèxìngtànsù duàndàifǎ *archaeol.* radiocarbon dating

放射性同位素 fàngshèxìng tóngwèisù radio isotope: 人造～ induced radio isotope

放射性微尘 fàngshèxìng wēichén radioactive dust; fallout

放射性污染 fàngshèxìng wūrǎn radioactive pollution

放射性元素 fàngshèxìng yuánsù radioactive element; radioelement

放射性沾染 fàngshèxìng zhānrǎn radioactive contamination

放射性战剂 fàngshèxìng zhànjì radioactive agent

放生 fàngshēng free captive animals; (of Buddhists) buy captive fish or birds and set them free

放声 fàngshēng raise one's voice to its utmost: ～歌唱 sing heartily / ～大哭 cry loudly

放手 fàngshǒu ① let go; let go one's hold: 他一～, 笔记本就掉了。He let go his hold and the notebook dropped to the ground. / 你抓紧, 我要～了。Hold tight. I'm going to let go. ② have a free hand; go all out: 让他们～工作 give them a free hand in their work / ～发动群众 go all out to mobilize the masses; fully arouse the masses / 我们信得过你, 你～干吧。We trust you. Just go ahead with your work. ③ release one's control; hand over to sb. else: 我要他交给小张去办, 可他就是不～。I told him to let Xiao Zhang take over the job, but he refused to hand it over.

放水 fàngshuǐ ① turn on the water: 给浴缸里放上水。Turn on the water in the bathtub. ② draw off some water (from a reservoir, etc.)

放肆 fàngsì unbridled; wanton: ～的行为 unbridled behaviour / ～诬蔑 wantonly vilify / 极为～ throw all restraint to the winds / 胆敢如此～! How dare you take such liberties!

放松 fàngsōng relax; slacken; loosen: ～鞋带 loosen up the shoelaces / ～肌肉 relax one's muscles / ～警惕 relax one's vigilance / 计划生育工作～不得。We should never loosen up on the rules for family planning.

放送 fàngsòng broadcast; send out (over a loudspeaker, etc.): ～大会实况录音 broadcast the live recording of the conference

放下 fàngxià lay down; put down: ～手头的工作 put aside the work on hand / 命令敌军～武器 order the enemy to lay down their arms / ～架子, 拜群众为师 drop pretentious airs and learn from the masses

放下屠刀, 立地成佛 fàngxià túdāo, lìdì chéngfó drop one's cleaver and become a Buddha—achieve salvation as soon as one gives up evil

放线菌 fàngxiànjūn *bacteriol.* actinomyces

放像机 fàngxiàngjī videocassette player; videotape player

放血 fàngxiě *slang* purposely make sb. bleed profusely, even to death; intentionally inflict fatal wounds on

sb.: 那伙流氓威胁说要放他的血。The hooligans threatened to make him bleed to death. ——see also fàngxuè

放心 fàngxīn ① set one's mind at rest; be at ease; rest assured; feel relieved: 你～, 一切都会安排好的。You can rest assured that everything will be all right. / 她来了电报, 我们才～。We were worried about her until her telegram came. / 我～不下。I can't set my mind at ease. *or* I'm still worried. ② have confidence in sb.; trust sb.: 我对他不大～。I don't quite trust him. / 你怎么老不～别人? Why do you have no confidence in others?

放行 fàngxíng let sb. or sth. pass: 申请～ request clearance / 免税～ tax-free clearance

放学 fàngxué ① classes are over; school lets out: 他们学校下午五点～。Their school lets out (*or* closes) at five p. m. / 孩子们都～回家了。The children have all left school and gone home for the day. ② have a holiday or vacation

放血 fàngxuè phlebotomy; bloodletting: 大夫给他放了血, 他感觉好多了。He felt much better after the doctor did a phlebotomy on him. ——see also fàngxiě

放眼 fàngyǎn take a broad view; scan widely: 他～远望, 只见万里长江, 奔腾东去。He looked ahead and saw the mighty Changjiang rolling and surging towards the east.

放眼世界 fàngyǎn shìjiè have the whole world in view; open one's eyes to the whole world: 胸怀祖国, ～ have the whole country in mind and the whole world in view

放养 fàngyǎng put (fish, insects, etc.) in a suitable place to breed: 水库里～了许多种鱼。Various kinds of fish are being bred in the reservoir.

放样 fàngyàng *shipbuilding* lofting

放音机 fàngyīnjī cassette player; tape recording player

放映 fàngyìng show (a film); project: 剧院有时也用来～电影。Occasionally theatres are used for film shows. / 今晚新华电影院～《红高粱》。*Red Sorghum* is being shown at the Xinhua Cinema this evening.

放映队 fàngyìngduì film projection team

放映机 fàngyìngjī (film) projector

放映室 fàngyìngshì projection room

放映员 fàngyìngyuán projectionist

放淤 fàngyū *agric.* warp: ～肥田 fertilize the soil by warping

放债 fàngzhài (also 放帐 fàngzhàng) lend money at interest

放赈 fàngzhèn *formal* distribute relief to the people in stricken areas

放之四海而皆准 fàng zhī sìhǎi ér jiē zhǔn universally applicable; valid everywhere: ～的普遍真理 universally applicable truth

放置 fàngzhì lay up; lay aside: ～不用 lay up (machinery, equipment, etc.); lie idle

放逐 fàngzhú send into exile; exile; banish

放纵 fàngzòng ① let sb. have his own way; indulge: 你太～孩子了。You are too indulgent with your child. ② self-indulgent; undisciplined

fēi

飞 (飛) fēi ① (of birds or insects) fly; flit: 小鸟～了。The bird flew away. / 老鹰～得高。Eagles fly high. / 蜜蜂在花丛中～来～去。Bees are flitting from flower to flower. ② (of an aircraft or its occupants) fly: 我明天～广州。I'm flying to Guangzhou tomorrow. / 那架飞机从北京直～广州。That plane flies nonstop from

Beijing to Guangzhou. ③ hover or flutter in the air: 〜鸢 a hovering kite / 〜絮 willow catkins fluttering in the air / 〜雪花了。It's snowing. ④ (move) swiftly: 飞奔 fēibēn / 飞驶 fēishǐ ⑤ *inf.* disappear through volatilization: 樟脑丸放久了会〜净的。Camphor balls will disappear as time goes on. ⑥ unexpected; accidental; unfounded; groundless: 〜祸 unexpected disaster ⑦ *dial.* free wheel (of a bicycle)

飞白　fēibái　a style of calligraphy characterized by hollow strokes, as if done with a half-dry brush

飞奔　fēibēn　dash; tear along

飞镖　fēibiāo　① a dartlike weapon ② darts (a game)

飞播　fēibō　aerial sowing

飞车走壁　fēi chē zǒu bì　*acrobatics* stunt cycling, driving or motorcycling on the inner surface of a cylindrical wall

飞驰　fēichí　(of trains, cars, horses, etc.) speed along: 火车〜而过。A train sped by.

飞虫　fēichóng　winged insect

飞船　fēichuán　① airship; dirigible ② spaceship; spacecraft

飞弹　fēidàn　① missile ② stray bullet

飞地　fēidì　① land of one province or county enclosed by that of another ② enclave; exclave

飞碟　fēidié　① *sports* skeet shooting; skeet; trapshooting ② flying saucer; UFO

飞短流长　fēiduǎn-liúcháng　spread embroidered stories and malicious gossip

飞蛾投火　fēi'é tóu huǒ　(also 飞蛾扑火 fēi'é pū huǒ) a moth darting into a flame—bring destruction upon oneself; seek one's own doom

飞红　fēihóng　bright red; scarlet; crimson: 她羞得满脸〜。She was crimson with embarrassment.

飞花　fēihuā　① cotton wad (of worn-out or torn cotton-padded clothes, shoes, etc.) is showing ② *text.* flyings; fly

飞黄腾达　fēihuáng téngdá　make rapid advances in one's career; have a meteoric rise

飞蝗　fēihuáng　migratory locusts

飞机　fēijī　aircraft; aeroplane; plane: 我坐〜去上海。I'll go to Shanghai by plane.

飞机场　fēijīchǎng　airfield; airport; aerodrome

飞机库　fēijīkù　hangar

飞机制造业　fēijīzhìzàoyè　aircraft industry; aviation industry

飞架　fēijià　(of a great bridge, viaduct, etc.) arch high over; span: 一桥〜南北，天堑变通途。(毛泽东) A bridge will fly to span the north and south, Turning a deep chasm into a thoroughfare.

飞溅　fēijiàn　splash: 浪花〜到甲板上。The waves splashed on the deck. / 钢花〜 sparks flying off molten steel

飞快　fēikuài　① very fast; at lightning speed: 以〜的速度前进 forge ahead at full speed / 他〜地向出事地点奔去。He tore along to the site of the accident. ② extremely sharp; razorsharp: 把镰刀磨得〜。Sharpen the sickles till they are like razors.

飞来横祸　fēilái hènghuò　unexpected disaster

飞掠　fēilüè　fly past or over: 子弹嗖嗖地从身边〜而过。Bullets whistled by him.

飞轮　fēilún　① *mech.* flywheel ② free wheel (of a bicycle)

飞毛腿　fēimáotuǐ　① fleet-footed; swift of foot ② a fleet-footed runner

飞沫　fēimò　flying particles of liquid; splattered drops

飞沫传染　fēimò chuánrǎn　*med.* infection through breathing in flying particles of the saliva or phlegm of a sick person

飞盘　fēipán　Frisbee disk; frisbee: 孩子们玩〜，大人聊天。Kids flip frisbees while their elders chat.

飞跑　fēipǎo　run very fast; fly

飞蓬　fēipéng　*bot.* bitter fleabane

飞禽　fēiqín　birds

飞禽走兽　fēiqín-zǒushòu　birds and beasts

飞泉　fēiquán　cliffside spring

飞绕　fēirào　wind high above: 红旗渠〜太行山, 宛如长龙。The Red Flag Canal winds like a long dragon through the Taihang Mountains.

飞散　fēisàn　① (of smoke, mist, etc.) disperse; dissipate ② (of birds) fly away in different directions; scatter; disperse: 麻雀听到枪声而〜。The sparrows scattered at the sound of the gun.

飞沙走石　fēishā-zǒushí　sand flying about and stones hurtling through the air (as in a windstorm)

飞升　fēishēng　① ascend to heaven—become an immortal ② rise; ascend; fly up

飞虱　fēishī　plant hopper

飞驶　fēishǐ　(of vehicles) travel at a tremendous speed; speed: 一辆摩托车〜而过。A motorcycle sped past.

飞逝　fēishì　(of time, etc.) slip by (*or* past); fly; elapse: 时光〜。Time just flies.

飞鼠　fēishǔ　flying squirrel

飞速　fēisù　at full speed: 列车在〜前进。The train is running at express speed. / 这个县的轻重工业都在〜发展。This county is making rapid strides in both light and heavy industries.

飞腾　fēiténg　fly swiftly upward; soar: 烟雾〜。A smoke-laden fog rose quickly and soon filled the air.

飞天　fēitiān　*arts* flying *Apsaras* (as in the frescoes of the Dunhuang Caves)

飞艇　fēitǐng　airship; dirigible

飞吻　fēiwěn　blow a kiss

飞舞　fēiwǔ　dance in the air; flutter: 雪花〜。Snow-flakes are dancing in the air. / 蝴蝶在花丛中〜。Butterflies fluttered about among the flowers.

飞翔　fēixiáng　circle in the air; hover: 展翅〜 spread wings and fly / 雄鹰在山谷中〜着。An eagle was hovering over the valley.

飞行　fēixíng　(of an aircraft, missile, etc. or of a pilot) fly; make a flight: 〜速度 flying speed / 〜表演 demonstration (*or* exhibition) flight / 上〜课 take flying lessons / 她受过〜训练。She had some flight training. / 他是一位有二十多年〜经验的驾驶员。He is a pilot with over twenty years' flying experience. / 新飞机胜利地完成了她的首次〜。The plane's maiden flight was a success. / 火箭正以惊人的速度向高空〜。The rocket is shooting into the sky at a breathtaking speed.

飞行半径　fēixíng bànjìng　flying radius

飞行服　fēixíngfú　flying suit

飞行管制　fēixíng guǎnzhì　air traffic control

飞行记录簿　fēixíng jìlùbù　flight log

飞行帽　fēixíngmào　aviator's helmet

飞行器　fēixíngqì　aircraft

飞行人员　fēixíng rényuán　aircrew; aircrewman

飞行员　fēixíngyuán　pilot; aviator; flyer

飞旋　fēixuán　fly in circles: 鸟儿在空中〜。Birds were wheeling in the air. / 一对对舞伴在舞池中〜。Couples were revolving quickly on the dance floor.

飞檐　fēiyán　*archit.* upturned eaves

飞檐走壁　fēiyán-zǒubì　(of swordsmen, etc. in old Chinese novels) leap onto roofs and vault over walls

飞眼　fēiyǎn　make eyes; ogle: 她直向他〜。She kept making eyes at him.

飞扬　fēiyáng　fly upward; rise: 尘土〜 clouds of dust flying up / 到处〜着欢乐的歌声。Songs of joy were floating in the air. / 大风起兮云〜，威加海内兮归故乡。(刘邦) A great wind came forth, the clouds rose on high. Now that my might rules all within the seas, I

have returned to my old village.

飞扬跋扈 fēiyáng-báhù arrogant and domineering

飞鱼 fēiyú flying fish

飞语 fēiyǔ rumours; gossip: 流言飞语 liúyán-fēiyǔ

飞跃 fēiyuè ① leap: 我国的石油工业正～地发展。China's oil industry is developing by leaps and bounds. ② *philos.* leap: 认识过程的一次～ a leap in the process of cognition

飞越 fēiyuè ① fly over or across: ～太平洋 make a flight across the Pacific ② fly upward; become elevated or uplifted: 心神～ in high spirits; in an elevated mood

飞灾 fēizāi unexpected disaster

飞贼 fēizéi ① a burglar who makes his way into a house over walls and roofs ② an intruding enemy airman; air marauder (or pirate)

飞涨 fēizhǎng (of prices, water level, etc.) soar; shoot up; skyrocket: 物价～。Prices were skyrocketing. / 水位～，大堤出现险情。The water level kept rising and the dykes were in peril.

飞针走线 fēizhēn-zǒuxiàn ply one's needle nimbly; do skilful needlework: 她那～的手艺，见到的人无不惊叹。The skill with which she plied her needle astounded all who saw her.

妃 fēi ① imperial concubine ② the wife of a prince

妃红 fēihóng light pink

妃色 fēisè light pink

妃子 fēizi imperial concubine

非[1] fēi ① wrong; wrongdoing: 是非 shìfēi ② not conform to; run counter to: 非法 fēifǎ ③ censure; blame: 无可厚非 wúkě hòufēi ④ *formal* be not: 当时的情景～言语所能形容。The occasion defies description. / 这件事～你我所能解决。This cannot be decided by either you or me. ⑤ *prefix* non-: ～党员 non-Party member / ～无产阶级思想 non-proletarian ideology (or ideas) ⑥ *inf.* have got to; simply must: 不行，我今天～去! No, I simply must go there today. / 他不来就算了，为什么～叫他来? If he doesn't want to come, that's fine. Why should we insist on him coming? / 干这种活儿～要有耐心才成。You've got to have patience in doing this kind of work.

非[2] Fēi short for 非洲 Fēizhōu

非比寻常 fēi bǐ xúncháng unusual; out of the ordinary

非病原菌 fēibìngyuánjūn nonpathogenic bacteria

非…不… fēi…bù… ① must; have to: 非说不可 have to speak out / 我非参加这次登山活动不可。I simply must join this mountaineering expedition. / 要学好中文，非下苦功不行。You can't get a good grasp of the Chinese language without making a painstaking effort. / 难道非你去处理这件事不成? Are you really the only one who can handle the matter? ② will inevitably; be bound to: 一味蛮干的人非碰壁不可。One who acts rashly and arbitrarily is bound to come to grief.

非常 fēicháng ① extraordinary; unusual; special: ～会议 extraordinary session / ～支出 a special expenditure / ～措施 emergency measures ② *adv.* very; extremely; highly: ～必要 highly necessary / ～重要 extremely important / ～精彩 simply marvellous / ～清楚 perfectly clear / ～重视 attach great importance to / ～抱歉 awfully (or terribly) sorry / 问题～之复杂。The case is extremely complicated. / 街上热闹～。The street is a hive of activity.

非常任 fēichángrèn nonpermanent: ～代表 nonpermanent representative / 安理会～理事国 nonpermanent member of the UN Security Council

非常时期 fēicháng shíqī time of emergency

非此即彼 fēi cǐ jí bǐ either this or that; one or the other

非但 fēidàn *conj.* not only: 他～自己干得好，还肯帮助别人。He not only does his own work well, but is also ready to help others. / ～学生答不出，连老师也答不出。Not only the students couldn't answer, the teacher didn't know the answer either.

非导体 fēidǎotǐ *phys.* nonconductor

非得 fēiděi (followed by 不 or 才) have got to; must: 做校对工作～仔细才行。You've got to be very careful when you do proofreading. / 这病～马上开刀不可。This disease calls for an immediate operation. / 这笔基金～全体委员通过才能动用。To use this fund, it is necessary to get the approval of all the members of the committee.

非独 fēidú *formal* not merely: ～无益，而且有害 not merely useless, but harmful

非对抗性 fēiduìkàngxìng nonantagonistic: ～矛盾 nonantagonistic contradiction

非法 fēifǎ illegal; unlawful; illicit: ～活动 unlawful (or illegal) activities / ～收入 illicit income / ～入境 illegal entry (into a country) / 被宣布为～ be outlawed; be declared illegal; be illegalized

非凡 fēifán outstanding; extraordinary; uncommon: ～的成就 outstanding achievements; extraordinary successes / ～的英雄气概 outstanding courage / ～的经营才能 exceptional administrative ability / 热闹～ bustling with activity

非…非… fēi…fēi… neither…nor…: 非亲非故 fēiqīn-fēigù / 非驴非马 fēilǘ-fēimǎ

非分 fēifèn overstepping one's bounds; assuming; presumptuous: ～的要求 presumptuous demands

非分之想 fēifèn zhī xiǎng inordinate ambitions

非公莫入 fēi gōng mò rù no admittance except on business

非官方 fēiguānfāng unofficial: ～消息 information from unofficial sources

非婚生子女 fēihūnshēng zǐnǚ children born out of wedlock; illegitimate children

非…即… fēi…jí… either…or…: 非亲即友 either relative or friend

非交战国 fēijiāozhànguó nonbelligerent

非金属 fēijīnshǔ nonmetal: ～材料 nonmetallic materials / ～元素 nonmetallic elements

非晶体 fēijīngtǐ amorphous body; noncrystal

非晶质 fēijīngzhì *chem.* noncrystalline; amorphous

非军事化 fēijūnshìhuà demilitarize: ～计划 demilitarization programme

非军事区 fēijūnshìqū demilitarized zone

非军事人员 fēijūnshì rényuán civilian personnel

非劳动收入 fēiláodòng shōurù unearned income

非礼 fēilǐ ① improper; indecorous; rude: ～之举 improper conduct; indecorous behaviour ② assault (a woman) sexually; violate: 欲行～ attempt to violate a woman

非驴非马 fēilǘ-fēimǎ neither ass nor horse—neither fish, flesh, nor fowl

非轮回亲本 fēilúnhuí qīnběn *agric.* nonrecurrent parent

非卖品 fēimàipǐn (articles) not for sale

非贸易外汇收入 fēimàoyì wàihuì shōurù foreign exchange earned from sources other than trade

非命 fēimìng an unnatural death; a violent death: 死于非命 sǐ yú fēimìng

非难 fēinàn (usu. used in the negative) blame; censure; reproach: 他的品德是无可～的。His character is irreproachable.

非农产业 fēinóngchǎnyè non-agricultural industries

非亲非故 fēiqīn-fēigù neither relative nor friend; neither

kith nor kin: 我跟他~, 跟你也无冤无仇, 我不偏向哪个, 只说几句良心话。He's not my relative, and you are not my enemy. I don't favour either one of you. I only want to say a few honest words.

非人 fēirén ① *formal* not the right person: 所用~ choose the wrong person for a job ② inhuman: ~待遇 inhuman treatment

非生产部门 fēishēngchǎnbùmén nonproductive departments

非生产劳动 fēishēngchǎnláodòng nonproductive labour

非生产性 fēishēngchǎnxìng unproductive; nonproductive: ~开支 nonproductive (*or* unproductive) expenditure

非条件刺激 fēitiáojiàncìjī *physiol.* unconditioned stimulus

非条件反射 fēitiáojiànfǎnshè *physiol.* unconditioned reflex

非同小可 fēi tóng xiǎokě no small (*or* trivial) matter: 这件事~, 我们一定要抗议! This is no trivial matter; we must raise our voices against it.

非徒 fēitú (also 非特 fēitè) *formal* not only: ~无益, 而且有害。It's not only useless but harmful too.

非刑 fēixíng brutal torture (not permitted by the law)

非刑拷打 fēixíng kǎodǎ put sb. to the torture

非议 fēiyì (usu. used in the negative) reproach; censure: 无可非议 wú kě fēiyì

非约束性条款 fēiyuēshùxìngtiáokuǎn permissive provision

非战斗人员 fēizhàndòurényuán *mil.* noncombatant

非正规军 fēizhèngguījūn irregular troops; irregulars

非正式 fēizhèngshì unofficial; informal: ~译文 unofficial translation / ~访问 unofficial (*or* informal) visit / ~会议 informal meeting

非正统 fēizhèngtǒng unorthodox

非正义战争 fēizhèngyìzhànzhēng an unjust war

非洲 Fēizhōu Africa

非洲统一组织 Fēizhōu Tǒngyī Zǔzhī the Organization of African Unity (OAU)

非主要矛盾 fēizhǔyào máodùn nonprincipal contradiction

菲[1] fēi ① (of flowers and grass) luxuriant and rich with fragrance: 芳菲 fāngfēi ② (Fēi) short for 菲律宾 Fēilǜbīn

菲[2] fēi *chem.* phenanthrene ——see also fěi

菲菲 fēifēi *liter.* ① luxuriant and beautiful ② richly fragrant

菲林 fēilín *dial.* a roll of film; film

菲律宾 Fēilǜbīn the Philippines

菲律宾人 Fēilǜbīnrén Filipino

啡 fēi see 咖啡 kāfēi; 吗啡 mǎfēi

绯 fēi red

绯红 fēihóng bright red; crimson; scarlet: ~的晚霞 rosy evening clouds / 脸羞得~ blush with shame

扉 fēi *formal* door leaf: 柴~ faggot door

扉页 fēiyè *print.* title page

蜚 fēi *formal* same as 飞 fēi ——see also fěi

蜚短流长 fēiduǎn-liúcháng same as 飞短流长 fēiduǎn-liúcháng

蜚声 fēishēng *formal* make a name; become famous: ~文坛 be famous in literary circles / 我国的工艺美术品~海外。China's arts and crafts enjoy a high reputation abroad.

蜚语 fēiyǔ same as 飞语 fēiyǔ

霏 fēi *liter.* ① (of rain or snow) fall thick and fast: 雨 (yù) 雪其~。It's snowing thick and fast. ② thin, floating clouds; mist: 夕~ evening mist

霏霏 fēifēi *liter.* (of rain, snow, mist, cloud, etc.) thick and fast; heavy: 淫雨~。It has been raining heavily for days. / 云~。Clouds are gathering thick and fast.

鲱 fēi Pacific herring

féi

肥 féi ① fat: ~猪 a big porker / 这肉太~了。The meat is too fat. ② fertile; rich: 这里的地~极了。The soil here is extremely fertile. ③ fertilize: 肥田粉 féitiánfěn ④ fertilizer; manure: 上点儿~ spread some manure on the soil / 这些庄稼需要~。The flowers are in need of fertilizer. ⑤ become rich by illegal means or income ⑥ loose-fitting; loose; large: 这条裤子太~了。These trousers are too baggy.

肥肠 féicháng pig's large intestines (used as food)

肥大 féidà ① loose; large: ~的衣服 a loose garment ② fat; plump; corpulent: ~的鲤鱼 a fat carp / 果实~ lush and plump fruit ③ *med.* hypertrophy: 心脏(扁桃体)~ hypertrophy of the heart (tonsils)

肥分 féifèn *agric.* (the percentage of) nutriment in a fertilizer

肥甘 féigān *formal* delicious food; delicacy

肥厚 féihòu ① plump; fleshy: 果肉~。The pulp is full and fleshy. / 嘴唇~ have thick lips ② thick and fertile: 土层~ thick and fertile topsoil ③ *formal* (of food) rich and tasty

肥力 féilì *agric.* fertility (of soil)

肥料 féiliào fertilizer; manure: 有机~ organic fertilizer / 细菌~ bacterial fertilizer

肥溜溜 féiliūliū ① (of animals) stout and sleek; (of fruit, nuts, etc.) fleshy and shiny ② *dial.* well-off; well-to-do; prosperous: 过着~的日子 live a comfortable life

肥马轻裘 féimǎ-qīngqiú sleek horses and soft furs—an extravagant way of living; a luxurious life

肥煤 féiméi a kind of bituminous coal used in coking

肥美 féiměi ① fertile; rich: ~的土地 rich soil; fertile land ② luxuriant; plump; fleshy; fat: 水草~牛羊壮 rich pastures and thriving herds / ~的北京鸭 plump, tender-fleshed Beijing ducks

肥胖 féipàng fat; corpulent

肥胖病 féipàngbìng obesity

肥缺 féiquē a lucrative post

肥实 féishi ① fat; stout: 这匹马很~。This is a stout horse. ② rich in fat: 这块肉很~。The meat is fatty.

肥瘦 féishòu ① the girth of a garment: 你看这件外衣的~怎么样? Look and see if this coat is a good fit. ② the proportion of fat and lean: 这块肉~正好。This chunk of meat is not too fat and not too lean.

肥瘦儿 féishòur *dial.* partly fat and partly lean meat

肥硕 féishuò ① (of fruit) big and fleshy ② (of limbs and body) large and firm-fleshed

肥田[1] féitián fertile land: 五亩~ five *mu* of fertile land

肥田[2] féitián fertilize (*or* enrich) the soil: 草木灰可以用来~。Plant ash can be used to fertilize the soil.

肥田草 féitiáncǎo fabaceous herbs (as clover, Chinese milk vetch, etc.); herbal fertilizer

肥田粉 féitiánfěn *inf.* ammonium sulphate

肥头大耳 féitóu-dà'ěr (of a child) round and plump; chubby; (of a man) fat and bulky; (of a pig) fat; plump

肥土 féitǔ　fertile (*or* good) soil

肥沃 féiwò　fertile; rich: 这里土地～。The land here is rich and fertile.

肥效 féixiào　*agric.* fertilizer efficiency (*or* effect)

肥腴 féiyú　*formal* ① fertile (soil or land) ② fat; plump; corpulent

肥育 féiyù　*animal husbandry* fatten

肥育期 féiyùqī　*animal husbandry* stage of fattening

肥育猪 féiyùzhū　fattening pig

肥源 féiyuán　*agric.* source of manure

肥皂 féizào　soap: ～泡 soap bubble

肥皂粉 féizàofěn　soap powder

肥皂剧 féizàojù　soap opera

肥皂片 féizàopiàn　soap flakes

肥皂水 féizàoshuǐ　soapsuds

肥壮 féizhuàng　stout and strong: 牛羊～ thriving herds of sheep and cattle

泚
Féi　short for 泚河 Féihé

泚河 Féihé　(also 泚水 Féishuǐ) the name of a river in Anhui Province

腓¹
féi　calf (of the leg)

腓²
féi　*formal* diseased; withered: 百卉俱～。The plants are all withering.

腓骨 féigǔ　*physiol.* fibula

---

fěi

诽
fěi　slander

诽谤 fěibàng　slander; calumniate; libel: 我要以～罪控告你。I'll sue you for libel.

匪¹
fěi　bandit; brigand; robber: 盗匪 dàofěi / 土匪 tǔfěi

匪²
fěi　*adv. formal* not: 获益～浅 reap no little benefit

匪帮 fěibāng　bandit gang; a felonious political gang: 法西斯～ the Fascist gangsters

匪巢 fěicháo　bandits' lair

匪患 fěihuàn　the evil of banditry; banditry

匪军 fěijūn　bandit troops

匪窟 fěikū　bandits' lair

匪酋 fěiqiú　*formal* bandit chieftain (*or* chief)

匪首 fěishǒu　bandit chieftain (*or* chief)

匪徒 fěitú　gangster; bandit

匪穴 fěixué　bandits' lair; enemy's entrenchment

匪夷所思 fěi yí suǒ sī　*formal* (of ideas) unimaginably queer; fantastic

悱
fěi　*formal* be at a loss for words

悱恻 fěicè　*formal* laden with sorrow; sad at heart: 缠绵悱恻 chánmián-fěicè

菲
fěi　① *arch.* radish or its like ② *hum.* poor; humble; unworthy: ～材 my humble talent ——see also fēi

菲薄 fěibó　① humble; poor: ～的礼物 a small gift ② belittle; despise: 妄自菲薄 wàng zì fěibó

菲仪 fěiyí　(also 菲敬 fěijìng) *hum.* my small (*or* unworthy) gift

菲酌 fěizhuó　*hum.* (used in invitation cards) a simple meal with wine: 敬备～，恭候光临。You are cordially invited to a simple dinner with us.

斐
fěi　*formal* (of literary talent) striking; brilliant

斐济 Fěijì　Fiji

斐济人 Fěijìrén　Fijian

斐济语 Fěijìyǔ　Fijian (language)

斐然 fěirán　*formal* striking; brilliant; splendid: 文采～ with striking (*or* brilliant) literary talent / 成绩～ (achieve) splendid results

斐然成章 fěirán chéng zhāng　show striking literary merit

蜚
fěi　*arch.* an insect ——see also fēi

蜚蠊 fěilián　another name for 蟑螂 zhāngláng

翡
fěi　*arch.* a kind of bird with red feathers

翡翠 fěicuì　① halcyon (a bird) ② jadeite (a mineral)

榧
fěi　Chinese torreya (tree)

榧子 fěizi　*bot.* ① Chinese torreya (tree) ② Chinese torreya nut

---

fèi

吠
fèi　(of a dog) bark; yap; yelp: 狂～ bark furiously

吠叫 fèijiào　(of a dog) bark; yap; yelp

吠舍 Fèishè　Vaisya

吠影吠声 fèiyǐng-fèishēng　(also 吠形吠声 fèixíng-fèishēng) when one dog barks at a shadow all the others join in—blindly follow others

沸
fèi　boil: ～油 boiling oil / ～水 boiling water

沸点 fèidiǎn　boiling point

沸反盈天 fèi fǎn yíng tiān　all is uproar; pandemonium breaks loose

沸沸扬扬 fèifèiyángyáng　bubbling and gurgling; in a hubbub: 大家～地嚷起来。A general hubbub arose. / 消息～地传开了。The news spread like wildfire.

沸滚 fèigǔn　boiling

沸泉 fèiquán　*geol.* near-boiling spring (a spring with waters hotter than 80℃)

沸热 fèirè　boiling hot; steaming hot

沸石 fèishí　another name for 泡沸石 pàofèishí

沸腾 fèiténg　① *phys.* boiling; ebullition ② seethe with excitement; boil over: 工地上一片～。The construction site was seething with excitement. / 大会主席宣布选举结果后，全场顿时～起来。When the chairman announced the election results, the whole assembly clapped and cheered.

沸扬 fèiyáng　(of feelings, sentiments, or voices and sounds) seethe with excitement; boil over

怫
fèi　a variant pronunciation for 佛 fú

废（廢）
fèi　① give up; abandon; abolish; abrogate: 秦始皇～封建，设郡县。The First Emperor of Qin (221–206 B.C.) abolished principalities and established prefectures and counties. / 不以人～言 not reject an opinion because of the speaker / 把条约～了 abrogate (*or* nullify) the treaty ② waste; useless; disused: ～热 waste heat / ～棉 cotton waste / ～井 a disused well / ～矿 an abandoned mine ③ disabled; maimed: ～疾 disability

废弛 fèichí　(of a law, custom, discipline, etc.) cease to be binding; become lax

废除 fèichú　abolish; abrogate; annul; repeal: ～一切不

平等条约 abrogate all unequal treaties／～烦琐的礼节 do away with tedious formalities

废黜 fèichù　dethrone; depose: ～王位 dethrone／～国王 dethrone the king／太子被～了。The crown prince was deposed (by the emperor).

废帝 fèidì　a dethroned emperor

废耕 fèigēng　(of farmland) be allowed to lie waste; be left uncultivated

废话 fèihuà　superfluous words; nonsense; rubbish: 我说的也可能是～, 不过还是请你再考虑考虑。What I said may seem superfluous, but I do hope you'll give it a little more thought.／～! 我还不知道? You're wasting your breath! Do you think I don't know that? ／少～! No more nonsense!

废话连篇 fèihuà liánpiān　pages of nonsense; reams of rubbish: 这篇文章简直是～。This article is just so much nonsense.

废旧 fèijiù　(of things) old and useless: ～物资 waste materials; scrap

废料 fèiliào　waste material; waste; scrap: ～堆 scrap heap; waste heap

废票 fèipiào　① invalidated ticket ② invalidated ballot

废品 fèipǐn　① waste product; reject: ～率 reject rate ② scrap; waste: 你可以把这东西当～卖。You could sell it for scrap.

废品回收 fèipǐn huíshōu　waste recovery; salvage of waste material

废品收购站 fèipǐn shōugòuzhàn　salvage station (where waste materials may be turned in for payment)

废气 fèiqì　waste gas or steam

废弃 fèiqì　discard; abandon; cast aside: ～陈规旧习 discard outdated regulations and customs／～多年的旧机器零件 old machine parts discarded for years

废寝忘食 fèiqǐn-wàngshí　forget to eat and sleep: ～地工作 forget to eat and sleep while working

废人 fèirén　① disabled person ② good-for-nothing

废水 fèishuǐ　waste water; liquid waste: ～渗透 waste water infiltration

废水处理场 fèishuǐ chǔlǐchǎng　waste water processing station

废水处理池 fèishuǐ chǔlǐchí　purification tank for liquid waste

废丝 fèisī　*text.*　waste silk

废铁 fèitiě　scrap iron

废物 fèiwù　waste material; trash: ～利用 make use of waste material; convert waste into useful material

废物 fèiwu　*offens.*　good-for-nothing: 他什么事也不会干, 简直是个～! He's really a good-for-nothing!

废墟 fèixū　ruins: 地震把那座城市变为一片～。The earthquake reduced that city to ruins.

废学 fèixué　discontinue one's schooling

废液 fèiyè　same as 废水 fèishuǐ

废渣 fèizhā　waste residue

废止 fèizhǐ　nullify; annul; abolish (a law, decree, regulation, etc.): 科举制是在1905年～的。The imperialist examinations system was abolished in 1905.／这个法令早就～了。This decree has long been annulled.

废纸 fèizhǐ　waste paper: 不要乱扔～。Don't litter the place with waste paper.／他们的那个条约不过是一张～而已。That treaty of theirs is a mere scrap of paper.

废置 fèizhì　put aside as useless: 这样珍贵的资料竟被～在一边, 真是太可惜了。It's a great pity such precious documents should be cast aside as useless.

狒

狒　fèi　see below

狒狒 fèifèi　baboon (a mammal)

肺

肺　fèi　lung

肺癌 fèi'ái　carcinoma of the lungs; lung cancer

肺病 fèibìng　*inf.*　pulmonary tuberculosis (TB)

肺动脉 fèidòngmài　*physiol.*　pulmonary artery

肺腑 fèifǔ　the bottom of one's heart: 出自～ straight from the heart; from the depths of one's heart

肺腑之言 fèifǔ zhī yán　words from the bottom of one's heart

肺活量 fèihuóliàng　vital capacity

肺结核 fèijiéhé　pulmonary tuberculosis (TB)

肺静脉 fèijìngmài　*physiol.*　pulmonary vein

肺痨 fèiláo　*inf.*　consumption; tuberculosis

肺脓肿 fèinóngzhǒng　pulmonary abscess

肺泡 fèipào　*physiol.*　pulmonary alveolus

肺气肿 fèiqìzhǒng　pulmonary emphysema

肺切除术 fèiqiēchúshù　pneumonectomy

肺吸虫 fèixīchóng　(also 肺蛭 fèizhì) lung fluke

肺吸虫病 fèixīchóngbìng　paragonimiasis

肺循环 fèixúnhuán　*physiol.*　pulmonary circulation

肺炎 fèiyán　pneumonia

肺叶 fèiyè　*physiol.*　a lobe of the lung

肺鱼 fèiyú　lungfish

肺脏 fèizàng　lungs

费

费　fèi　① fee; dues; expenses; charge: 生活～ living expenses／订报～ subscription for a newspaper／医药～ medical expenses ② cost; spend; expend: 买这部电影机～了我们不少钱。This projector cost us a lot of money.／买东西～时间。Shopping takes time. ③ consume too much; expend sth. too quickly; be wasteful: 这部汽车～油。This car consumes too much gasoline.／这孩子穿鞋太～。This child wears out his shoes much too quickly. ④ (Fèi) a surname

费边主义 Fèibiānzhǔyì　(also 费边社会主义 Fèibiānshèhuìzhǔyì) Fabianism

费唇舌 fèi chúnshé　take a lot of talking or explaining: 那得费一番唇舌。That'll take a lot of arguing.／事已如此, 我就不必多～了。Now it's done, I might as well save my breath.

费工 fèigōng　take a lot of work; require much labour: 这种活儿～。This is a difficult job.／做这样的衣裳不太～。This kind of dress isn't too hard to make.／你绣这块台布费了多少工? How long did it take you to embroider this tablecloth?

费工夫 fèi gōngfu　(also 费功夫 fèi gōngfu) take time and energy; be time-consuming; be exacting; be demanding: 他费了好多工夫才把电视机修好。It took him a lot of time to get the TV set repaired.／编词典很～。Dictionary making is exacting (or demanding) work.／做思想工作要不怕～。You shouldn't stint your time and energy when doing ideological work.

费话 fèihuà　take a lot of talking or explaining: 一说她就明白, 用不着人～。Just mention it and she'll catch on. It won't take much talking.／我费了不少话才把他说服。It took me a lot of explaining to convince him.

费解 fèijiě　hard to understand; obscure; unintelligible: 这段文章实在～。This passage is really hard to understand.

费尽心机 fèijìn xīnjī　rack one's brains (in scheming); tax one's ingenuity

费劲 fèijìn　*inf.*　need or exert great effort; be strenuous: 安装这台机器真～。It really took a lot of effort to install this machine.／他看英文参考书一点不～。He can read reference books in English without difficulty.／我在这件事上已经费了好大的劲。I have already spent a great deal of effort on this matter.／这山越往上爬越～。The higher we went up the mountain, the more strenuous the climb became.

费力 fèilì　need or exert great effort; be strenuous: 有了这种机器, 插秧就不那么～了。With this kind of machine it is no longer a strain to transplant rice

seedlings. / 他有气喘病, 呼吸很～。Asthma causes him great difficulty in breathing. / 我们费了大力才把这件事办好。It took us a lot of effort to get this done.

费力不讨好 fèilì bùtǎohǎo ① work hard but get little result; do a hard but thankless job ② arduous but fruitless: ～的差使 a tough but thankless job; an exacting but unrewarding task

费钱 fèiqián cost a lot; be costly: 做广告挺～。Advertising costs a good deal of money. / 修这样的水电站不很～。It doesn't cost much to build hydroelectric stations of this kind. / 这不是白～吗? Isn't this a sheer waste of money?

费神 fèishén ① need or exert great mental effort: 孩子进了幼儿园以后, 你就不用那么操心～了。It will be a load off your mind when your child enters kindergarten. ② pol. (used in making a request or giving thanks) may I trouble you (to do sth.); would you mind (doing sth.): 我这篇稿子您～给看看好吗? Would you mind going over this article for me? / 让您～了, 多谢, 多谢! Thanks a lot for the trouble you've taken to help us!

费时 fèishí take time; be time-consuming: 手工操作既～又费力。It takes both time and effort to do it by hand.

费事 fèishì give or take a lot of trouble: 别给我们烧水了, 太～了。——一点儿也不～。Don't bother to boil any water for us. —Oh, it's no trouble at all. / 他费了不少事才把材料找齐。He went to a lot of trouble to find all the necessary materials. / 做中餐比做西餐～。To prepare a Chinese meal is more work than to prepare a Western meal.

费手脚 fèi shǒujiǎo need or exert great effort

费心 fèixīn ① give a lot of care; take a lot of trouble: 她为这些孩子可费了不少心。She devoted a lot of care to these children. ② pol. (used in making a request or giving thanks) may I trouble you (to do sth.); would you mind (doing sth.): 您见到他时, ～把这封信交给他。Will you be so kind as to give him this letter when you see him? / 您帮了我们大忙, ～～! You've helped us a lot. Thank you very much for taking all that trouble.

费用 fèiyong cost; expenses: 生产～ production cost / 这笔～由我们负担。We'll bear the expenses.

费嘴皮子 fèi zuǐpízi talk nonsense; waste one's breath

捌 (跰) fèi cutting off the feet (a punishment in ancient China) ——see also 五刑 wǔxíng

痱 (疿) fèi see below

痱子 fèizi med. prickly heat

痱子粉 fèizifěn prickly-heat powder

篚 (籆) fèi arch. bamboo mat

镄 fèi chem. fermium (Fm)

fēn

分 fēn ① divide; separate; part: 一年～四季。The year is divided into four seasons. / 一条河把那个县城～成两部分。A river divides the county town into two parts. / ～阶段实行 carry out stage by stage / ～组讨论 hold discussions in groups / 这药～三次吃。This medicine is to be taken in three separate doses. / 这里的树木大致～为三类。The trees grown here fall roughly into three categories. /他们几个人把钱～了。They divided the money among them. / 他的头发是往右边～的。He parts his hair on the right side. ② distribute;

assign; allot: 音乐会的票都已经～完了。The tickets for the concert have all been distributed. / 把这个任务～给我们吧。Assign (or Give) this task to us, please. / 她～到了一套新房子。She has been allotted a new flat. / 他大学毕业后就～到外交部去工作了。After his graduation from college, he was assigned to work at the Foreign Ministry. ③ distinguish; differentiate: 是非不～ make no distinction between right and wrong / 现在还～不出个胜负来。It's still quite impossible to tell who'll win. / 这对双胞胎长得一模一样, 简直～不出谁是谁。The twins look so much alike that you can hardly tell them apart. ④ branch (of an organization): 新华社上海～社 the Shanghai Branch of the Xinhua News Agency ⑤ fraction: 约分 yuēfēn / 分母 fēnmǔ ⑥ (used in spoken forms of fractions and percentages): 三～之一 one-third / 十～之七 seven-tenths / 百～之四 four per cent ⑦ one tenth (of certain units of the metric system): 分克 fēnkè / 分米 fēnmǐ / 分升 fēnshēng ⑧ fen (also called 市分 shìfēn, of the traditional system of weights and measures) ⓐ a unit of length equal to 0.1 cun 寸 or 0.01 chi 尺 ⓑ a unit of area equal to 0.1 mu 亩 ⓒ a unit of weight equal to 0.1 qian 钱 or 0.01 liang 两 ⑨ fen, equal to one hundredth of a yuan 元: 六元三角五～ 6.35 yuan ⑩ minute, equal to one sixtieth of an hour ⑪ minute, equal to one sixtieth of a degree of angle or arc: 成36度30～角 form an angle of 36 degrees 30 minutes (36°30′) / 东经129度15～ 129 degrees 15 minutes (129°15′) east longitude ⑫ a unit of interest rate ⓐ 1% monthly interest: 月利一～二厘 1.2% monthly interest ⓑ 10% annual interest: 年利一～二厘 12% annual interest ⑬ point; mark: 60～为及格。Sixty is the passing mark. / 甲队罚球连得二～。Team A scored two successive points by free throws. / 他今天考试得了100～。He got full marks in today's exam. ⑭ m. (for nonphysical things) one-tenth: 七～成绩, 三～错误 70 per cent achievements, 30 per cent mistakes / 这消息使我多了一～希望。The news raised my hopes a little. / 我的牙痛好了几～。My toothache has been partly relieved. / 他已经有三～醉了。He's a bit tipsy already. ——see also fèn

分贝 fēnbèi phys. decibel (db)

分崩离析 fēnbēng-líxī disintegrate; fall to pieces; come apart: 抗日战争使全国～的局面变成比较团结的局面。The Anti-Japanese War changed a disunited China into a relatively united country.

分辨[1] fēnbiàn distinguish; differentiate; tell: ～真假 distinguish truth from falsehood / 他～不出人家奏的是什么曲子。He couldn't tell what tune they were playing. / 很难～谁是谁非。It's hard to tell who is right and who is wrong.

分辨[2] fēnbiàn phys. resolution: ～率 resolving power

分辩 fēnbiàn defend oneself (against a charge); offer an explanation: 不容～ allowing no explanation to be offered

分别[1] fēnbié part; leave each other: 我们～快两年了。It's almost two years since we parted. / 他们～不久又见面了。They met again after a short separation.

分别[2] fēnbié ① distinguish; differentiate: ～善恶 distinguish good from evil ② difference: 两者之间没有任何～。There is no difference between the two. ③ adv. in different ways; differently: 对他们两人应该～对待。You should treat the two of them differently. / 根据具体情况, ～处理。Deal with the cases in different ways, according to specific conditions. ④ adv. separately; individually; respectively: 你还是～跟他们谈谈的好。You'd better have a talk with each of them separately. / 会长和秘书长～接见了他。The chairman and the secretary-general each granted an interview to him. / 他们～代表本国政府在协定上签了字。They signed the

agreement on behalf of their respective governments. / 老周和老陈～提升为主任和副主任。 Lao Zhou and Lao Chen have been promoted to director and deputy director respectively.

分兵 fēnbīng　divide forces: ～把守 divide the forces for defence / ～两路前进。 The troops separated and advanced by two different routes.

分拨 fēnbō　① allocate (goods, materials, etc.) ② assign (persons) to different tasks ③ group (persons) into batches

分布 fēnbù　be distributed (over an area); be dispersed; be scattered: 彝族主要～在云南、四川、贵州三省。 The Yis are distributed mainly over Yunnan, Sichuan and Guizhou Provinces. / 气象站～在广阔的平原和山区。 Weather stations are scattered all over the vast plains and the mountain regions. / 我国石油资源～范围很广。 Oil deposits are widely dispersed over our country.

分册 fēncè　a separately published part of a book; fascicle: 第二～ Book Two

分杈 fēnchà　agric. ① branching ② branch

分成 fēnchéng　divide into tenths: 四六～ divide into two shares of four and six tenths (or 40% and 60%)

分词 fēncí　gram. participle: 现在 (过去) ～ present (past) participle / ～短语 participial phrase

分爨 fēncuàn　formal (of brothers) cook separately —— live apart

分寸 fēncun　proper limits for speech or action; sense of propriety; sense of proportion: 他说话很有～。 He knows what to say and what not to say. / 她说话做事都没有～。 She has no sense of propriety in what she does or says. / 批评要注意掌握～。 Don't go too far in criticism.

分担 fēndān　share responsibility for: ～费用 shoulder part of the expenses; share the expenses / 提倡男女～家务劳动 Men and women are encouraged to share household duties. / 抚养子女的责任应由夫妇双方～。 Both partners should share in rearing the family.

分道 fēndào　sports lane: 第一～ the first lane

分道扬镳 fēndào yángbiāo　go different ways; part company

分等 fēnděng　grade; classify: 产品按质～ grade products according to quality / 商品～论价 grade commodities and fix prices accordingly; fix prices according to the different grades of commodities

分店 fēndiàn　branch (of a shop)

分度 fēndù　graduation (of a measuring instrument)

分队 fēnduì　a troop unit corresponding to the platoon or squad; element

分而治之 fēn ér zhì zhī　divide and rule

分发 fēnfā　① distribute; hand out; issue (to individuals): 把课本～给同学们 hand out textbooks to the students / 给优胜者～奖品 distribute prizes to the winners / ～证件 issue certificates individually ② assign to a post; appoint to a job

分肥 fēnféi　share out ill-gotten gains; divide booty

分封制 fēnfēngzhì　the system of enfeoffment (of the Western Zhou Dynasty, c. 11th. century–771 B.C., investing the nobility with hereditary titles, territories and slaves)

分赴 fēnfù　leave for different destinations: ～不同的工作岗位 go to take up different posts

分付 fēn·fù　same as 吩咐 fēn·fù

分割 fēngē　cut apart; break up; carve up: ～围歼入侵之敌 break up the invading enemy forces into many pockets and wipe them out one by one; carve up and wipe out the invaders / 民主和集中这两方面，任何时候都不能～开。 Democracy and centralism can at no time be separated.

分隔 fēngé　separate; divide: 把一间房～成两小间 parti-

tion a room into two small ones

分工 fēngōng　division of labour: ～负责 division of labour with individual responsibility / 咱们怎么～? How shall we divide up the work? / 社会～ social division of labour

分工合作 fēngōng-hézuò　share out the work and help one another

分管 fēnguǎn　be assigned personal responsibility for; be put in charge of: 工会委员中有专人～妇女工作。 One of the members of the trade union committee is in charge of women's affairs.

分光计 fēnguāngjì　phys. spectrometer

分光镜 fēnguāngjìng　phys. spectroscope

分规 fēnguī　same as 分线规 fēnxiànguī

分行 fēnháng　branch (of a bank, business firm, etc.): 国内～ home (or domestic) branch / 国外～ overseas branch

分毫 fēnháo　fraction; iota: 不差～ without the slightest error; just right

分号[1] fēnhào　semicolon (;)

分号[2] fēnhào　branch (of a shop, firm, etc.): 本店只此一家, 别无～。 Our shop is the only one bearing the name; there are no branches.

分红 fēnhóng　draw (or receive) dividends; share profits: 股份～ dividends on shares; dividends to the shareholders

分洪 fēnhóng　flood diversion: ～工程 flood-diversion project

分洪区 fēnhóngqū　flood-diversion area

分洪闸 fēnhóngzhá　flood-diversion sluice

分户帐 fēnhùzhàng　ledger

分化 fēnhuà　① become divided; break up: 随着私有制的产生, 人类便～为阶级。 With the emergence of private ownership, humanity was divided into classes. ② split up: 把一部分人从敌人营垒中间～出来 split off a number of people from the enemy camp ③ biol. (of cells or tissues) differentiate

分化瓦解 fēnhuà wǎjiě　disintegrate; divide and demoralize

分会 fēnhuì　branch (of a society, committee, association, etc.); chapter

分机 fēnjī　(telephone) extension

分级 fēnjí　grade; classify: 这几筐苹果还没～。 These baskets of apples have not been graded yet.

分级机 fēnjíjī　agric. grader; sorter: 水果～ fruit grader / 马铃薯～ potato sorter

分家 fēnjiā　① divide up family property and live apart; break up the family and live apart ② separate; break up: 咱俩分工不～。 Let's divide the work but still work together.

分解 fēnjiě　① phys. math. resolve: 力的～ the resolution of forces / ～成因式 resolve into factors ② chem. decompose; resolve: 水可以～为氢和氧。 Water can be decomposed (or resolved) into hydrogen and oxygen. ③ mediate: 让我替你们～～。 Let me try to mediate your dispute. ④ disintegrate; split up: 促使敌人内部～ try to bring about a split-up of the enemy ⑤ explain (used in traditional novels): 毕竟不知此去吉凶如何, 且听下回～。 (《西游记》) We do not know whether good or ill will befall him after he leaves, and you must listen to the explanation in the next chapter.

分解代谢 fēnjiě dàixiè　biol. catabolism

分解反应 fēnjiě fǎnyìng　chem. decomposition reaction

分解热 fēnjiěrè　chem. decomposition heat

分界 fēnjiè　① have as the boundary; be demarcated by: 这两个县以运河～。 The two counties have the canal as their common boundary. / 河北省和辽宁省在山海关～。 Hebei and Liaoning Provinces have a common border at Shanhaiguan. ② dividing line; line of de-

marcation: 这两块地之间有一排大树作为～。There is a row of trees on the line of demarcation between the two pieces of land.

分界线 fēnjièxiàn line of demarcation; boundary: 军事～ a military demarcation line

分斤掰两 fēnjīn-bāiliǎng ① pinch pennies; pinch and scrape ② niggle over personal gain

分进合击 fēnjìn-héjī *mil.* concerted attack by converging columns

分居 fēnjū ① (of family members) live apart: 她的兄弟都成了家,～各地。All her brothers are married and live in different parts of the country. ② (of husband and wife) live separately; separate: 他们夫妻结婚十年就～了。They separated after ten years of marriage.

分句 fēnjù *gram.* clause

分开 fēnkāi ① come apart; separate; part: 弟兄俩～已经三年了。It is three years since the two brothers parted. / 他们结婚才一年就～了。They separated after only one year's marriage. ② cause to separate; sort: 把好的和坏的～ sort out the good ones from the bad / 老赵～人群,挤到台前。Lao Zhao elbowed his way through the crowd till he got to the front of the stage. / 这两个问题咱们～来谈。Let's discuss the two problems separately. / 动机和效果是分不开的。Motive is inseparable from effect.

分克 fēnkè decigram (dg.)

分类 fēnlèi classify: 把这些资料加以～ classify the data / 按题材～ classify according to subjects

分类法 fēnlèifǎ classification

分类数字 fēnlèi shùzì breakdown figures

分类索引 fēnlèi suǒyǐn classified index

分类学 fēnlèixué taxology; taxonomy; systematics: 植物(动物)～ systematic botany (zoology)

分类帐 fēnlèizhàng ledger

分厘 fēnlí a very small amount; a tiny bit: ～之差也不容许。Not even the slightest error is permissible.

分离 fēnlí ① (of things) separate; sever: 从空气中把氮～出来 separate nitrogen from air / 理论和实践是不可～的。Theory and practice cannot be separated. / 医院决定对这对连体婴儿作～手术。The hospital decided to perform a separation operation on the Siamese twins. ② (of people) leave; part; separate: ～多年的好友又重逢了,他们非常高兴。The friends were glad to meet after so long a separation.

分离器 fēnlíqì *chem.* separator

分理处 fēnlǐchù a small local branch (of a bank)

分力 fēnlì *phys.* component (of force)

分列式 fēnlièshì *mil.* march-past

分裂 fēnliè ① *biol. phys.* fission: 核～ nuclear fission / 细胞～ cell division ② split; divide; break up: ～革命队伍 split the revolutionary ranks / 这些人是从保守党～出来加入民主党的。These people broke away from the Conservative Party to join the Democratic Party.

分裂生殖 fēnliè shēngzhí *biol.* fission

分裂主义 fēnlièzhǔyì splittism: ～分子 splittist

分馏 fēnliú *chem.* fractional distillation; fractionation

分馏塔 fēnliútǎ fractionating tower; fractional column

分路 fēnlù ① go along separate routes or from several directions: ～前进 advance along separate routes / ～出击 attack from several directions ② *elec.* shunt: ～电流 branch current / ～电阻 shunt resistance

分袂 fēnmèi *formal* leave each other; part company; part

分门别类 fēnmén-biélèi put into different categories; classify

分米 fēnmǐ decimetre (dm.)

分泌 fēnmì *biol.* secrete: ～胃液 secrete gastric juice

分泌物 fēnmìwù secretion

分娩 fēnmiǎn childbirth; parturition

分秒 fēnmiǎo every minute and second; instant: 时间不饶人,～赛黄金。Time waits for no man; every minute is as precious as gold.

分秒必争 fēnmiǎo bì zhēng seize every minute and second; every second counts; not a second is to be lost

分明 fēnmíng ① be clear; be distinct; be unmistakable: 这件事情是非～,无可争辩。The rights and wrongs of the case are perfectly clear and admit of no dispute. ② *adv.* clearly; evidently; obviously: ～是你不对。Obviously you are in the wrong.

分母 fēnmǔ *math.* denominator

分蘖 fēnniè *agric.* tiller: 有效～ effective tillering / 麦子正在～。The wheat is tillering.

分蘖节 fēnnièjié tillering node

分蘖期 fēnnièqī tillering stage

分派 fēnpài assign (to different persons or groups); apportion: 队长给各个组都～了任务。The team leader has assigned a task to each group.

分配 fēnpèi ① distribute; allot: ～土地 distribute land / ～住房 allot dwelling houses ② assign; dispose: 合理～劳力 rational disposition of manpower / 服从组织～ accept the job that the organization assigns to one / 她毕业后被～到县医院工作。She was assigned to work at a county hospital after graduation. ③ *econ.* distribution: ～制度 distribution system

分配律 fēnpèilǜ *math.* distributive law

分批 fēnpī in batches; group by group; in turn: ～轮流参加训练班 go to a training course in turn / 实习医生～到市医院实习。Interns go group by group to work at the city hospital. / 代表团～出发。The delegation set out in different batches.

分片包干 fēn piàn bāogān divide up the work and assign a part to each

分期 fēnqī by stages: ～实行 implement by stages / ～分批 by stages and in groups; group after group at different times

分期付款 fēnqī fùkuǎn payment by instalments; hire purchase; instalment plan

分歧 fēnqí difference; divergence: 意见～ divergence of views; differences of opinion / 原则～ a difference in principle / 制造～ sow discord; create dissension / 消除～ iron out differences / 在这个问题上我们的看法有～。Our views are divergent on this question. *or* We are divided in opinion on this question.

分清 fēnqīng distinguish; draw a clear distinction between; draw a clear line of demarcation between: ～是非 distinguish right from wrong / ～敌我友 draw a distinction between ourselves, our friends and the enemy / 分不清真假 cannot distinguish between genuine and sham

分权 fēnquán a division of power or authority

分群 fēnqún (of bees) hive off

分润 fēnrùn share in the benefit (*or* profit)

分散 fēnsàn ① scattered; dispersed; diverted; decentralized: ～的落后的个体经济 a scattered and backward individual economy / 注意力～ with one's attention diverted (*or* distracted) to something else / 兵力太～。The soldiers were dispersed along too wide a front. / ～指挥 decentralized command / 集中领导,～经营 unified leadership and decentralized management ② disperse; distribute: ～传单 disperse handbills

分散剂 fēnsànjì *chem.* dispersing agent

分散染料 fēnsàn rǎnliào disperse dyes

分散主义 fēnsànzhǔyì decentralism

分色机 fēnsèjī *print.* colour scanner

分身 fēnshēn (usu. used in the negative) spare time from one's main work to attend to sth. else: 他实在太忙,无法～。He is really too busy to attend to anything

else. / 一直想去看您，可总是分不开身。Though I've been wanting to go and see you, I just haven't been able to find the time.

分神 fēnshén *pol.* give some attention to: 请～照顾一下这孩子。Would you mind keeping an eye on the child?

分升 fēnshēng decilitre (dl.)

分手 fēnshǒu part company; say good-bye: 我们是在车站～的。We said good-bye to each other at the station. / 他们因意见分歧而～了。They parted company due to a difference of opinion.

分数 fēnshù ① *math.* fraction ② mark; grade

分水岭 fēnshuǐlǐng ① *geol.* watershed; divide ② line of demarcation; dividing line

分水线 fēnshuǐxiàn same as 分水岭 fēnshuǐlǐng①

分水闸门 fēnshuǐzhámén *water conservancy* bifurcation gate

分税制 fēnshuìzhì a system of tax distribution: 实行中央和地方～ institute a system of tax distribution between the central and local authorities

分说 fēnshuō *formal* defend oneself (against a charge); explain matters: 不由分说 bùyóu fēnshuō

分送 fēnsòng send; distribute: 把学习材料～给各组。Distribute the study materials to all the groups.

分摊 fēntān apportion; share: ～费用 share the expenses

分庭抗礼 fēntíngkànglǐ stand up to sb. as an equal; act independently and defiantly

分头[1] fēntóu *adv.* separately; severally: 这事咱们～去做吧。Let's go about the work separately.

分头[2] fēntóu parted hair: 他理了个小～。He has a new hair parting.

分文 fēnwén a single cent (or penny): 身无～ have not a penny to one's name

分文不取 fēnwén bù qǔ not take (or charge) a cent; free of charge

分析 fēnxi analyse: ～句子成分 parse a sentence / 培养～问题和解决问题的能力 cultivate the ability to analyse and solve problems / 善于～形势 be proficient in sizing up a situation / 老师把这篇课文～得很精辟。The teacher made a penetrating analysis of the text.

分析化学 fēnxi huàxué analytical chemistry

分析天平 fēnxi tiānpíng *chem.* analytical balance

分析语 fēnxiyǔ *gram.* analytical language

分线规 fēnxiànguī dividers

分享 fēnxiǎng share (joy, rights, etc.); partake of: ～胜利的喜悦 share the joys of victory

分相 fēnxiàng *elec.* split phase

分相电动机 fēnxiàng diàndòngjī split-phase motor

分相器 fēnxiàngqì phase splitter

分销店 fēnxiāodiàn retail shop

分晓 fēnxiǎo ① (usu. used after 见) outcome; solution: 此事明天就见～。We'll know the outcome of the whole affair tomorrow. ② sth. seen or understood clearly: 问个～ inquire about and get to the bottom of a matter ③ (usu. used with 没) reason: 没～的话 unreasonable remarks

分校 fēnxiào a branch school

分心 fēnxīn ① divert (or distract) one's attention: 她工作起来，什么事也不能使她～。Nothing can divert her attention once she starts working. / 孩子多了～。Parents cannot concentrate on their work if they have too many children. ② *pol.* may I trouble you (to do sth.); would you mind (doing sth): 这件事您多～吧。Would you be kind enough to take care of the matter?

分压器 fēnyāqì *elec.* voltage divider

分野 fēnyě dividing line: 无产阶级世界观和资产阶级世界观的～ the dividing line between a proletarian and a bourgeois world outlook

分一杯羹 fēn yī bēi gēng take a share of the spoils or profits

分阴 fēnyīn a second; an instant: 惜～ use every second efficiently; make the best use of every single second

分忧 fēnyōu share sb.'s cares and burdens; help sb. to get over a difficulty: 孩子懂事了，学会为妈妈～了。The boy has really grown up and is beginning to share his mother's worries.

分赃 fēnzāng divide the spoils; share the booty (or loot): 他们由于～不均而争吵。They quarrelled over the spoils。

分针 fēnzhēn minute hand (of a clock or watch)

分支 fēnzhī subdivision; branch: 银行的～机构 branches of a bank

分子 fēnzǐ ① *math.* numerator (in a fraction) ② *chem.* molecule ——see also fēnzǐ

分子病 fēnzǐbìng molecular disease

分子仿生学 fēnzǐ fǎngshēngxué molecular bionics

分子结构 fēnzǐ jiégòu molecular structure

分子量 fēnzǐliàng molecular weight

分子溶液 fēnzǐ róngyè *chem.* molecular solution

分子筛 fēnzǐshāi molecular sieve

分子生物学 fēnzǐ shēngwùxué molecular biology

分子式 fēnzǐshì molecular formula

分子遗传学 fēnzǐ yíchuánxué molecular genetics

分组 fēnzǔ divide into groups: ～讨论 discuss in groups; group discussion

芬

fēn sweet smell; fragrance

芬芳 fēnfāng ① sweet-smelling; fragrant: ～的花朵 sweet-smelling flowers ② sweet smell; fragrance: 空气里弥漫着玫瑰的～。The sweet smell of roses fills the air.

芬兰 Fēnlán Finland

芬兰人 Fēnlánrén Finn; Finlander

芬兰语 Fēnlányǔ Finnish (language)

吩

fēn see below

吩咐 fēn·fù *inf.* ① tell; instruct: 父亲～孩子好生照看小马驹。The father told his son to take good care of the foal. / 我们该做什么，请您～。Please tell us what we should do. ② instructions: 听候～ await instructions / 您有什么～? Have you any instructions to give?

纷

fēn ① confused; tangled; disorderly: 纷扰 fēnrǎo ② many and various; profuse; numerous: 纷飞 fēnfēi

纷繁 fēnfán numerous and complicated: 头绪～ have too many things to take care of; have too many irons in the fire; be highly complicated / 从～的现象中抓住本质的东西 grasp the essentials from a variety of phenomena; sort out the essentials from a mass of detail

纷飞 fēnfēi (of thick-falling snowflakes, flowers, etc.) swirl in the air; fly all over: 大雪～。Snowflakes were falling thick and fast. *or* It was snowing hard.

纷纷 fēnfēn ① numerous and confused: 落叶～。Leaves fell in profusion. / 敌军～逃窜。The enemy troops fled pell-mell. / 锦城丝管日～，半入江风半入云。(杜甫) In the city of Brocade the lutes and the pipes all day make riot; Half of the music is lost in the river breezes, and half in the clouds. ② one after another; in succession: 年青人～要求参军。Young people volunteered to join the army one after another. / 世界各地～来电祝贺。Congratulatory telegrams poured in from all parts of the world.

纷纷扬扬 fēnfēnyángyáng (of snowflakes, flowers, leaves, etc.) flying or fluttering in profusion: 鹅毛大雪～。Snowflakes were fluttering like feathers in the

air. *or* It was snowing heavily.

纷乱 fēnluàn numerous and disorderly; helter-skelter; chaotic: ～的脚步声 hurried footsteps / ～的局面 a state of chaos

纷忙 fēnmáng be very busy; be in a rush and a muddle: 终日～ be in a mad rush all day

纷披 fēnpī *formal* spreading out in all directions: 枝叶～ branches and leaves spreading out in all directions

纷扰 fēnrǎo confusion; turmoil: 内心的～使他无法入睡。His mind was in such a turmoil that he couldn't get to sleep.

纷纭 fēnyún diverse and confused: 头绪～ have too many things to attend to

纷杂 fēnzá numerous and disorderly: 思绪～ a confused train of thought; a confused state of mind

纷争 fēnzhēng dispute; wrangle: ～不已 endless dispute

纷至沓来 fēnzhì-tàlái come in a continuous stream; come thick and fast; keep pouring in

坋
fēn see 赛璐坋 sàilùfēn

氛
fēn atmosphere: 气氛 qìfēn

氛围 fēnwéi atmosphere: 人们在欢乐的～中迎来了新的一年。People saw in the New Year in a happy and gay atmosphere.

酚
fēn *chem.* phenol

酚醛 fēnquán *chem.* phenolic aldehyde

酚醛树脂 fēnquán shùzhī phenolic resin

酚醛塑料 fēnquán sùliào phenolic plastics; phenolics; phenoplast

酚酞 fēntài *chem.* phenolphthalein

酚酞试纸 fēntài shìzhǐ phenolphthalein test paper

雰
fēn *formal* mist; air

雰雰 fēnfēn *liter.* (of snow, frost, etc.) heavy: 雨（yù）雪～。It is snowing heavily.

雰围 fēnwéi same as 氛围 fēnwéi

fén

汾
Fén the name of a river in Shanxi Province

汾酒 fénjiǔ a colourless liquor distilled in Fenyang (汾阳) of Shanxi Province

坟(墳)
fén grave; tomb

坟包 fénbāo (also 坟堆 fénduī) grave mound

坟地 féndì (also 坟场 fénchǎng) graveyard; cemetery

坟墓 fénmù grave; tomb

坟丘 fénqiū grave mound; tomb; grave

坟头 féntóu grave mound

坟茔 fényíng ① grave; tomb ② graveyard; cemetery

焚
fén burn: ～香 burn incense

焚风 fénfēng *meteorol.* foehn

焚膏继晷 fén gāo jì guǐ burn the midnight oil

焚化 fénhuà incinerate; cremate

焚化炉 fénhuàlú incinerator; cremator

焚毁 fénhuǐ destroy by fire; burn down

焚琴煮鹤 fénqín-zhǔhè burn a lute for fuel and cook a crane for food—offend against good taste; act like a philistine; philistine behaviour

焚烧 fénshāo burn; set on fire: 起义农民～了地主庄园。The peasant rebels burned down the manor houses.

焚尸扬灰 fén shī yáng huī burning the corpse and scattering the ashes (considered a most merciless treatment of the dead in feudal times)

焚书坑儒 fén shū kēng rú burning books and burying Confucian scholars alive (by 秦始皇 Qin Shi Huang or the First Emperor of Qin)

焚香 fénxiāng burn incense or joss sticks: ～拜佛 burn incense before Buddha / ～操琴 light some joss sticks and begin to pluck the *guqin* (古琴)

棼
fén *formal* confused; tangled: 治丝益棼 zhì sī yì fén

鼢
fén see below

鼢鼠 fénshǔ *zool.* zokor

fěn

粉
fěn ① powder: 磨成～ grind into powder or flour ② cosmetics in powder form: 脸上擦～ put on face powder; powder one's nose ③ noodles or vermicelli made from bean or sweet potato starch: 菠菜炒～ bean noodles stir-fried with spinach ④ *dial.* become powder ⑤ *dial.* whitewash: 墙刚～过。The wall has just been whitewashed. ⑥ white: ～底布鞋 cloth shoes with white soles ⑦ pink: ～色 pink colour / 系上～绸带 tie with a pink ribbon

粉白黛绿 fěnbái-dàilǜ (also 粉白黛黑 fěnbái-dàihēi) (of a woman) with face powdered and eyebrows darkened

粉笔 fěnbǐ chalk: 两支～ two chalks

粉笔画 fěnbǐhuà chalk drawing; crayon

粉彩 fěncǎi *arts and crafts* mixed glaze

粉肠 fěncháng sausage stuffed mainly with bean starch paste

粉尘 fěnchén dust

粉刺 fěncì common name for 痤疮 cuóchuāng

粉翠 fěncuì Beijing jade

粉黛 fěndài ① face powder and eyebrow pigment (cosmetics for women in ancient China) ② beautiful women: 回眸一笑百媚生，六宫～无颜色。(白居易) Glancing, one single smile she gave, which shed Such radiance that through the palace halls Each painted, pencill'd dame seemed pale and wan.

粉底霜 fěndǐshuāng foundation cream

粉蝶 fěndié *zool.* white (butterfly): 菜～ cabbage butterfly

粉红 fěnhóng pink; rosy: 一张～的圆脸 a round face with rosy cheeks / 一条～色的裙子 a pink skirt

粉剂 fěnjì ① *med.* powder ② *agric.* dust

粉瘤 fěnliú sebaceous cyst

粉末 fěnmò powder

粉末冶金 fěnmò yějīn powder metallurgy

粉墨登场 fěnmò dēngchǎng make oneself up and go on stage—embark upon a political venture

粉嫩 fěnnèn (of young women or children's skin) fair and tender; soft and fair

粉皮 fěnpí sheet jelly made from bean or sweet potato starch

粉扑 fěnpū powder puff

粉芡 fěnqiàn pasty mixture of starch and water (for cooking)

粉墙 fěnqiáng plaster wall

粉砂 fěnshā silt

粉身碎骨 fěnshēn-suìgǔ have one's body smashed to pieces and one's bones ground to powder; die the most cruel death

粉饰 fěnshì gloss over; whitewash

粉饰太平 fěnshì tàipíng present a false picture of peace

and prosperity

粉刷 fěnshuā ① whitewash: ～一新 take on a new look after whitewashing ② *dial.* plaster

粉丝 fěnsī vermicelli made from bean starch, etc.

粉碎 fěnsuì ① broken to (or into) pieces: 茶杯摔得～。 The cup was smashed to pieces. ② smash; shatter; crush: ～经济封锁 smash an economic blockade / ～军事进攻 shatter a military attack / ～反动派的阴谋 crush the conspiracy of the reactionaries

粉碎机 fěnsuìjī pulverizer; grinder; kibbler: 饲料～ fodder grinder / 球磨～ ball mill pulverizer

粉碎性骨折 fěnsuìxìng gǔzhé comminuted fracture

粉条 fěntiáo noodles made from bean or sweet potato starch

粉头 fěntóu *old* prostitute

粉线 fěnxiàn tailor's chalk line

粉蒸肉 fěnzhēngròu pork steamed with ground glutinous rice

粉装玉琢 fěnzhuāng-yùzhuó silvery white (said of a snow scene): 大雪整整下了一夜，晨起一看窗外变成了一个～的世界。 It snowed all night, and looking out of the window in the morning, I found a world of silvery white.

fèn

分[1] fèn ① component: 盐～ salt content ② what is within one's rights or duty: 本分 běnfèn / 过分 guòfèn ③ same as 份 fèn

分[2] fèn *formal* think; expect: 自～不能肩此重任 be aware of one's inability to shoulder such a heavy responsibility ——see also fēn

分际 fènjì *formal* proper limits for speech or action

分量 fèn·liàng weight: 给足～ give full measure / ～给得不足 give short measure / 称称～ weigh it / 这个铺盖卷没多少～，我拿得动。 This bedding roll isn't heavy at all, I can manage it. / 这个南瓜重～不下二十斤。 This pumpkin weighs no less than twenty *jin*. / 掂掂这个问题的～ consider the significance of the question; weigh the matter carefully / 他这话说得很有～。 What he said should not be taken lightly. *or* What he has said carries a lot of weight.

分内 fènnèi one's job or duty: 从思想上关心学生是教师～的事。 It's a teacher's duty to be concerned about the students' ideology. / 这是我～的工作。 This is my share of the work.

分外 fènwài ① *adv.* particularly; especially: ～高兴 particularly happy / ～香 especially fragrant / 战友重逢～亲。 Meeting again after a long separation, comrades-in-arms are drawn to each other more closely than ever. ② not one's job or duty: 革命工作不分分内和～。 In revolutionary work there's no such thing as "that's not my job". / 不要把帮助别人看作～的工作。 Don't think that helping others is not one's job. *or* Never say "Helping others is not my job."

分子 fènzǐ member; element: 工人阶级一～ a member of the working class / 反动～ reactionary element; reactionary ——see also fēnzǐ

份（分） fèn ① share; part; portion: 把钱平分成三～。 Divide the money into three equal shares. / 这一～是你的。 This share is yours. ② (combined with 年, 月, 省 or 县 to form units for differentiation): 年份 niánfèn / 月份 yuèfèn / 省份 shěngfèn / 县份 xiànfèn ③ *m.* ⓐ part; portion: 送一～礼去 send a gift / 为祖国出一～

力量 do one's bit for one's country / 两～客饭、三～冰淇淋 two set meals and three ice creams / 跟大伙儿一样，我也为她担着一～儿心呢! I'm worried about her just as you are. ⓑ (for certain nonphysical things, used after 这 or 那): 瞧他那～儿神气! Look what airs he puts on! / 我心里那～儿痛快就甭提了。 Needless to say, I was overjoyed. ⓒ (for documents, newspapers, periodicals, etc.) copy: 一～《人民日报》 a copy of *Renmin Ribao* / 这篇报告请复印三～。 Xerox three copies of this paper, please. / 协议一式两～，每～都用汉语和英语写成，两种文本具有同等效力。 The agreement is in duplicate, in the Chinese and English languages, both texts being equally authentic.

份儿 fènr *inf.* degree; extent: 到这～上你该死心了。 You should give up when things have come to this.

份额 fèn'é share; portion

份儿饭 fènrfàn *table d'hôte;* set meal

份子 fènzi ① one's share of expenses for a joint undertaking, as in buying a gift for a mutual friend: 凑份子 còu fènzi / 出份子 chū fènzi ②.a gift of money

奋（奮） fèn ① exert oneself; act vigorously: 振奋 zhènfèn ② raise; lift: ～臂高呼 raise one's arm and call out aloud / ～笔疾书 wield one's brush furiously

奋不顾身 fèn bù gù shēn dash ahead regardless of one's safety: ～的斗志 a fighting will that defies personal danger / 他～地抢救遇险同志。 Completely disregarding his own safety, he rushed to rescue the comrades in danger.

奋斗 fèndòu struggle; fight; strive: ～到底 struggle to the end / ～目标 the objective of a struggle / 为共产主义事业～终身 fight all one's life for the cause of communism; dedicate one's life to the struggle for communism

奋发 fènfā rouse oneself; exert oneself: 一个～有为的青年 a promising enterprising youth

奋发图强 fènfā túqiáng go all out to make the country strong; work hard for the prosperity of the country: 自力更生～的革命精神 the revolutionary spirit of relying on our own efforts and working hard for the prosperity of the country

奋击 fènjī strike out with great force; make a spirited attack

奋激 fènjī be roused to enthusiasm: 群情～。 Popular feeling runs high.

奋力 fènlì do all one can; spare no effort: 骑兵战士冲入敌群，～砍杀。 The cavalrymen charged into the enemy ranks, slashing furiously. / ～实现生产指标 do all one can to fulfil the production quota

奋袂而起 fènmèi ér qǐ *formal* throw up the sleeves and rise—get ready for action

奋勉 fènmiǎn make a determined effort

奋乃静 fènnǎijìng *pharm.* perphenazine

奋起 fènqǐ ① brace up; exert oneself; rise with force and spirit: ～抗敌 rise against the enemy / ～自卫 rise in self-defence ② raise or lift sth. with all one's strength

奋起直追 fènqǐ zhí zhuī do all one can to catch up

奋然 fènrán energetic; animated

奋勇 fènyǒng summon up all one's courage and energy: ～前进 advance bravely; forge ahead courageously

奋战 fènzhàn fight bravely; work strenuously: ～到底 fight to the bitter end / ～七天 fight for seven days on end; work without a letup for seven days / 经过四个月的～，他们终于成功地完成了试验。 After four months of strenuous labour, they succeeded in the experiment.

奋志 fènzhì resolve to dedicate oneself to (a cause): 他～从事民众教育。 He is determined to dedicate his

life to popular education.

忿[1]　fèn　same as 愤 fèn

忿[2]　fèn　see 不忿 bùfèn; 气不忿儿 qìbùfènr

债　fèn　*formal*　spoil; ruin

债事　fènshì　*formal*　spoil an affair: 胆大而心不细, 只能~。Impetuosity will only make things worse.

粪（糞）　fèn　① excrement; faeces; dung; droppings ② *formal*　apply manure: ～田 manure the fields ③ *formal*　clear away; wipe out: ～除 wipe out

粪便　fènbiàn　excrement and urine; night soil: ～检查 stool examination

粪车　fènchē　dung-cart; night-soil cart

粪池　fènchí　manure pit

粪堆　fènduī　dunghill; manure pile (*or* heap)

粪肥　fènféi　muck; manure; dung

粪夫　fènfū　*old*　night-soil collector

粪箕子　fènjīzi　manure basket

粪坑　fènkēng　manure pit

粪筐　fènkuāng　manure basket

粪桶　fèntǒng　night-soil bucket; manure bucket

粪土　fèntǔ　dung and dirt; muck: ～当年万户侯。(毛泽东) We counted the mighty as no more than muck.

愤　fèn　indignation; anger; resentment: 公愤 gōngfèn / 气愤 qìfèn

愤愤不平　fènfèn bùpíng　be indignant; feel aggrieved; be resentful: 人们为他受到的不公正待遇~。People are indignant at the unfair treatment he received. / 他还是有些~的情绪。He was still smouldering with indignation.

愤恨　fènhèn　indignantly resent; detest

愤激　fènjī　excited and indignant; roused to indignation

愤慨　fènkǎi　*formal*　(righteous) indignation: 表示~ express one's indignation / 这起儿子虐待老人的事件, 引起了群众的极大~。The maltreatment of the old man by his son aroused great public indignation.

愤懑　fènmèn　*formal*　depressed and discontented; resentful

愤怒　fènnù　indignation; anger; wrath: 激起群众的极大~ rouse the masses to great indignation / ～的烈火在胸中燃烧 burn with anger; boil with rage

愤然　fènrán　angry; indignant: ～离去 leave in anger; walk off in a huff

愤世嫉俗　fènshì-jísú　detest the world and its ways; be cynical

fēng

丰[1]**（豐）**　fēng　① abundant; plentiful: 丰收 fēngshōu ② great: 丰功伟绩 fēnggōng-wěijī ③ (Fēng) a surname

丰[2]　fēng　fine-looking; handsome: 丰姿 fēngzī

丰碑　fēngbēi　① monument: 周总理的光辉业绩在中国人民心中立下了不朽的~。Premier Zhou's illustrious deeds are an everlasting monument in the hearts of the Chinese people. ② monumental work: 这部著作不愧为中国新文化运动的~。This book is a monumental work worthy of China's new cultural movement.

丰采　fēngcǎi　same as 风采 fēngcǎi①

丰产　fēngchǎn　high yield; bumper crop: ～田 a high-yield plot / ～经验 experience in getting bumper crops

丰登　fēngdēng　bumper harvest: 五谷丰登 wǔgǔ fēng-

丰度[1]　fēngdù　same as 风度 fēngdù

丰度[2]　fēngdù　*phys.*　abundance: 同位素~ isotopic abundance

丰富　fēngfù　① rich; abundant; plentiful: 资源~ rich in natural resources / 积累~ 的资料 accumulate a wealth of data / 他的教学经验很~。He has a great deal of teaching experience. ② enrich: ～自己的生活经验 enrich one's experience of life / 向各方面学习, ～自己的知识 learn from every possible source to widen one's knowledge

丰富多彩　fēngfù duōcǎi　rich and varied; rich and colourful: ～的节日活动 varied and colourful festival activities / 演出~的节目 present a varied and interesting programme / ～的传统出口商品 a rich array of traditional products for export

丰功伟绩　fēnggōng-wěijī　great achievements; signal contributions: 他为祖国的解放事业建立了~。He made great contributions to the liberation of the country.

丰厚　fēnghòu　① thick: 绒毛~ rich and thick fur ② rich and generous: ～的礼品 generous gifts

丰满　fēngmǎn　① plentiful: 粮仓~。The granaries are full. ② full and round; well-developed; full-grown: ～的脸盘 a chubby (*or* plump) face / 体态~ have a well filled-out figure / 她比去年生病的时候~多了。She's rounded out quite a bit since she fell ill last year.

丰茂　fēngmào　luxuriant; lush

丰美　fēngměi　lush: 水草~ lush pasture

丰年　fēngnián　a bumper harvest year; a good year

丰沛　fēngpèi　plentiful: 雨水~ have plenty of rain

丰饶　fēngráo　rich and fertile: ～的草原 fertile grassland

丰稔　fēngrěn　*formal*　bumper crop; good harvest

丰润　fēngrùn　plump and smooth-skinned: 肤色~ have smooth and velvety skin

丰盛　fēngshèng　rich; sumptuous: ～的酒席 a sumptuous feast

丰收　fēngshōu　bumper harvest: 连年~ bumper harvests for years running / ～在望。A good harvest is in sight.

丰硕　fēngshuò　plentiful and substantial; rich: 取得~的成果 reap rich fruits; score great successes

丰衣足食　fēngyī-zúshí　have ample food and clothing; be well-fed and well-clothed: 过着~的生活 live a life of plenty

丰盈　fēngyíng　① full and round; well-developed: 体态~ have a full figure ② plentiful: 衣食~ have plenty to eat and wear

丰腴　fēngyú　① full and round; plump; buxom and fair ② rich and fertile: ～的草场 a rich pasture ③ sumptuous: ～的酒席 a sumptuous feast

丰裕　fēngyù　well provided for; in plenty: 生活~ live in plenty; be comfortably off

丰韵　fēngyùn　same as 风韵 fēngyùn

丰姿　fēngzī　same as 风姿 fēngzī

丰足　fēngzú　abundant; plentiful: 衣食~ have plenty of food and clothing

风（風）　fēng　① wind: 一阵~ a gust of wind / 起~了。The wind is rising. / ～停了。The wind has stopped. ② air-dry; winnow: 晒干~净 sun-dried and well winnowed / ～鸡 air-dried chicken / ～肉 air-dried meat ③ swift as the wind: 风发 fēngfā / 风行 fēngxíng ④ practice; custom; tendency: 此~不可长。This tendency is not to be encouraged. ⑤ scene; view: 风光 fēngguāng ⑥ style; attitude: 作风 zuòfēng / 文风 wénfēng ⑦ news; information: 他刚听见一点~儿就来打听。He came to ask the moment he got wind of it. ⑧ rumoured; unfounded: 风闻 fēngwén ⑨ one of the

three sections of *The Book of Songs* (《诗经》), consisting of ballads: 采风 cǎifēng ⑩ *Chin. med.* (used in the names of certain diseases): 羊痫风 yángxiánfēng

风暴 fēngbào ① windstorm; storm: 海上～ a storm at sea ② a violent commotion; storm; tempest: 革命～ the storm of revolution

风泵 fēngbèng ① air pump ② air compressor

风痹 fēngbì *Chin. med.* wandering arthritis

风标 fēngbiāo weathercock; weather vane

风波 fēngbō wind and waves—disturbance; storm (fig.): ～迭起。Disturbances arose repeatedly. / 平地起～ a storm out of nowhere

风伯 Fēngbó God of Wind

风采 fēngcǎi ① *formal* elegant demeanour; graceful bearing: ～动人 have a strikingly elegant and graceful bearing ② *formal* literary grace ③ *arch.* integrity (of government officials): 举朝惮其～。All the other court officials were awestruck by his strict rectitude.

风餐露宿 fēngcān-lùsù eat in the wind and sleep in the dew—endure the hardships of an arduous journey

风操 fēngcāo character and conduct; personal integrity

风潮 fēngcháo agitation; unrest: 闹～ agitate (for a strike, etc.)

风车 fēngchē ① windmill ② winnower; winnow ③ pinwheel (a child's toy)

风尘 fēngchén ① wind and dust—travel fatigue: 满面～ travel-stained ② hardships or uncertainties in an unstable society, esp. in the officials' circle ③ the life of a prostitute: 沦落～ be driven to prostitution ④ *formal* chaos caused by war: ～之警 the menace of war

风尘仆仆 fēngchén púpú have endured the hardships of a long journey; be travel-stained; be travel-worn and weary

风驰电掣 fēngchí-diànchè swift as the wind and quick as lightning: 列车～般闪过。The train flashed past.

风传 fēngchuán (of news or rumours) get about (*or* round); be rumoured (*or* said); they say: ～内阁即将改组。The rumour is getting about that there's going to be a reshuffle of the cabinet.

风吹草动 fēngchuī-cǎodòng the rustle of leaves in the wind—a sign of disturbance or trouble: 不要一有～就惊慌失措。Don't fly into a panic at the mere rustle of leaves in the wind. / 工商界有点～，我们总经理早就知道了。There only has to be the slightest movement in the business world and our general manager knows all about it.

风吹浪打 fēngchuī-làngdǎ be beaten by wind and waves; be battered by a storm: ～不动摇 never waver in the storm and stress of struggle

风吹雨打 fēngchuī-yǔdǎ be buffeted by wind and rain; be exposed to the weather: 经不起～ cannot withstand natural calamities

风锤 fēngchuí pneumatic hammer

风挡 fēngdǎng *automobile* windscreen; windshield

风刀霜剑 fēngdāo-shuāngjiàn piercing wind and biting frost—① severe cold ② adverse circumstances

风灯 fēngdēng lantern

风笛 fēngdí bagpipes; pipes

风动工具 fēngdòng gōngjù pneumatic tools

风洞 fēngdòng *aviation* wind-tunnel

风斗 fēngdǒu wind scoop

风度 fēngdù demeanour; bearing: 有～ have poise / ～大方 have an easy manner / 他的举止动作完全是军人～。He carries himself every inch like a soldier.

风度翩翩 fēngdù piānpiān (of a young man) have an elegant and smart carriage

风铎 fēngduó *formal* wind-bells

风发 fēngfā ① swift as the wind ② energetic: 意气风发 yìqì fēngfā

风帆 fēngfān ① sail: 扬起～ unfurl the sails ② sailing boat or ship

风范 fēngfàn *formal* ① demeanour; bearing; poise ② style; manner; air

风风火火 fēngfēnghuǒhuǒ ① hustling and bustling: 他～地闯了进来。He came bustling into the room. ② stirring: ～的战斗年代 the stirring war years

风风雨雨 fēngfēngyǔyǔ ① difficulties and hardships ② groundless gossip

风干 fēnggān air-dry: 木材经过～可以防止腐烂。Air-drying can prevent wood rotting away. / ～栗子 air-dried chestnuts / ～腊肉 air-dried bacon

风镐 fēnggǎo pneumatic pick; air pick

风格 fēnggé style; manner; mode: ～高 behave in a generous manner / 发扬～ go out of one's way to help others / 运动员们赛出了水平，赛出了～。The athletes gave a good account of themselves and displayed fine sportsmanship. / 京剧有其独特的艺术～。Beijing opera has a distinctive artistic style. / 作者的～是喜爱作细腻的描述。The author's style is characterized by a fondness for detailed descriptions.

风格学 fēnggéxué *linguis.* stylistics

风骨 fēnggǔ ① strength of character ② vigour of style (in writing, painting or of calligraphy)

风光 fēngguāng scenery; scene; view; sight: 北国～ typical northern scenery / 青山绿水好～ a splendid view of green mountains and blue waters

风光 fēngguang *dial.* grand; impressive; in style

风害 fēnghài damage caused by a windstorm

风寒 fēnghán chill; cold: 只是受了点儿～。It's nothing but a chill. / 经常洗冷水澡可以抵御～。Taking cold baths regularly can heighten one's resistance to colds.

风和日丽 fēnghé-rìlì (also 风和日暖 fēnghé-rìnuǎn) a bright sun and a gentle breeze; warm and sunny weather: 又是～、万木争荣的时节了。It was a time of sunshine and gentle breezes, of trees and shrubs bursting into glorious blossom.

风戽 fēnghù wind-powered waterwheel (for irrigation)

风花雪月 fēng-huā-xuě-yuè wind, flowers, snow and the moon—referring originally to certain types of literary works and later to effete and sentimental writings in general

风华 fēnghuá *formal* elegance and intellectual brilliance

风华正茂 fēnghuá zhèng mào at life's full flowering; in one's prime

风化[1] fēnghuà morals and manners; decency: 有伤～ an offence against decency

风化[2] fēnghuà ① *geol.* weathering ② *chem.* efflorescence

风级 fēngjí *meteorol.* wind scale: ～表 wind scale; Beaufort scale

风纪 fēngjì conduct and discipline; discipline

风纪扣 fēngjìkòu hook and eye on the collar of a uniform

风井 fēngjǐng *min.* ventilating shaft; air shaft

风景 fēngjǐng scenery; landscape: 欣赏～ admire the scenery / 桂林以～优美著称。Guilin is famous for its scenic beauty. / 西湖～如画。The West Lake is as beautiful as a painting. / 昆明是一座～美丽的城市。Kunming is a picturesque city.

风景画 fēngjǐnghuà landscape painting

风景林 fēngjǐnglín scenic forest

风景区 fēngjǐngqū scenic spot

风镜 fēngjìng goggles

风卷残云 fēng juǎn cányún a strong wind scattering the last clouds—make a clean sweep of sth.

风口 fēngkǒu ① a place where there is a draught: 别站在～上, 小心着凉。Don't stand in the draught. You may catch cold. ② geol. wind gap ③ metall. (blast) tuyere: 渣～ slag tuyere

风口浪尖 fēngkǒu-làngjiān where the wind and the waves are highest—where the struggle is fiercest

风快 fēngkuài swift as the wind; at lightning speed; very fast: 消息～地传遍全城。The news quickly spread through the town.

风浪 fēnglàng ① stormy waves; storm: ～大, 船颠簸得很利害。There was a heavy sea and the ship tossed terribly. ② a stormy experience: 久经～ have weathered many a storm

风雷 fēngléi wind and thunder; tempest: 革命的～ the storm of revolution

风雷激荡 fēngléi jīdàng a storm raging in all its fury

风力 fēnglì ① wind-force: 测试～大小 gauge the wind's intensity ② wind power: 以～为动力 wind-powered; wind-driven

风力发电机 fēnglì fādiànjī wind-driven generator; windmill generator

风力发电站 fēnglì fādiànzhàn wind power station

风力输送机 fēnglì shūsòngjī pneumatic conveyor

风力提水机 fēnglì tíshuǐjī wind-driven water pump; wind pump

风里来, 雨里去 fēngli lái, yǔli qù come in the wind and go in the rain—carry out one's task in the teeth of wind and rain

风凉 fēngliáng cool: 大家坐在～的地方休息。All of us were sitting in a cool place for a rest.

风凉话 fēngliánghuà irresponsible and sarcastic remarks: 说～ make sarcastic comments

风铃 fēnglíng wind-bells (hung on the eaves of pagodas or temple buildings)

风流 fēngliú ① refined and tasteful: 唐诗如贵介公子, 举止～。《四溟诗话》Tang poetry is like a noble prince whose behaviour is refined and tasteful. ② unrestrained in spirit and behaviour: 吾爱孟夫子, ～天下闻。(李白) I love the Master, Meng Haoran (孟浩然), A free spirit known the whole world through. ③ romantic; amorous; licentious: ～年少 a romantic young man / ～才子 a gallant young scholar / ～寡妇 a merry widow / ～韵事 romantic deeds; amorous encounters

风流人物 fēngliú rénwù ① a man of untrammelled spirit: 大江东去, 浪淘尽, 千古～。(苏轼) The Great River flows to the east: Its waves have washed away All the men of untrammelled spirit of a thousand ages. / 俱往矣, 数～, 还看今朝。(毛泽东) All are past and gone! For truly great men Look to this age alone. ② a romantic person

风流云散 fēngliú-yúnsàn dispersed by the wind and scattered like the clouds—(usu. of old companions) separated and scattered

风流蕴藉 fēngliú yùnjiè graceful but not showy; urbanely charming

风马牛不相及 fēng mǎ niú bù xiāng jí have nothing to do with each other; be totally unrelated: 这和我们的谈话内容, 有点～啊! I don't see it has anything to do with what we're talking about.

风帽 fēngmào ① a cowl-like hat worn in winter ② hood

风貌 fēngmào ① style and features: 民间艺术的～ the style and features of folk art ② view; scene: 农村新～ the new look of the countryside ③ elegant appearance and bearing

风玫瑰图 fēngméiguìtú wind rose (another name for 风向图)

风媒传粉 fēngméi chuánfěn wind pollination

风媒花 fēngméihuā bot. anemophilous flower

风门 fēngmén ① min. air door; ventilation door ② same as 风门子 fēngménzi

风门子 fēngménzi storm door (put up in winter in northern China)

风靡 fēngmǐ be fashionable: 今夏超短裙又～京沪了。Miniskirts have become fashionable again in Beijing and Shanghai this summer.

风靡一时 fēngmǐ yìshí become fashionable for a while; be all the rage at the time

风磨 fēngmò windmill (for grinding grain)

风鸟 fēngniǎo zool. bird of paradise

风派 fēngpài (also 风派人物 fēngpài rénwù) timeserver; trimmer

风平浪静 fēngpíng-làngjìng the wind has dropped and the waves have subsided; calm and tranquil: ～的海面 an unruffled sea / 他的生活总是～的。His life had been uneventful.

风起云涌 fēngqǐ-yúnyǒng ① winds rising and clouds scudding; rolling on with full force; surging forward

风气 fēngqì general mood; atmosphere; common (or established) practice: 促进整个社会～的改变 help to change the general mood of society / 全厂出现了大搞技术革新的～。It has become the regular practice in the factory to go in for technical innovations.

风切变 fēngqiēbiàn meteorol. wind shear

风琴 fēngqín organ: 弹～ play the organ

风情 fēngqíng ① information about wind direction, wind-force, etc. ② formal bearing; demeanour ③ formal feelings ④ amorous feelings; flirtatious expressions: 卖弄～ play the coquette; coquet; flirt ⑤ local conditions and customs

风趣 fēngqù humour; wit: 他是一个很有～的人。He is a man of charm and wit. / 她说话很有～。She is a witty talker.

风圈 fēngquān solar or lunar halo

风骚¹ fēngsāo formal literary excellence: 江山代有才人出, 各领～数百年。(赵翼) Each age brings forth new genius on this noble land, And each will rule its own domain for years to come.

风骚² fēngsāo coquettish; flirtatious: 卖弄～ play the coquette; coquet; flirt

风色 fēngsè ① how the wind blows: ～突然变了, 由南往北刮。The wind suddenly veered round to the north. ② how things stand: ～不对。Things are going against one. ——see also 看风色 kàn fēngsè

风沙 fēngshā sand blown by the wind: 这里春天～很大。It's very windy and dusty here in spring.

风扇 fēngshàn electric fan; fan: 散热～ radiator fan / 通风～ draught fan

风尚 fēngshàng prevailing custom (or practice, habit): 勤俭节约的新～ a new habit of diligence and frugality / 时代～ the vogue of the day

风神 fēngshén bearing; demeanour

风声 fēngshēng ① the sough of the wind: ～萧萧。The wind is soughing. ② rumour: 听到～ get wind of sth. / ～很紧。The situation is getting tense.

风声鹤唳, 草木皆兵 fēngshēng-hèlì, cǎo mù jiē bīng scared by the moan of the wind and the cry of the cranes, and seeing the enemy in every bush and tree (said of the extreme nervousness of a fleeing army)

风湿 fēngshī med. rheumatism

风湿性关节炎 fēngshīxìng guānjiéyán rheumarthritis

风蚀 fēngshí geol. wind erosion; deflation

风势 fēngshì ① the force or speed of the wind: 到了傍晚, ～越来越大了。Towards evening the wind was blowing harder and harder. ② situation; circumstances: 他一看～不对, 拔腿就跑。Seeing that things were going against him, he took to his heels.

风霜 fēngshuāng wind and frost—hardships of a jour-

ney or of one's life: 饱经风霜 bǎo jīng fēngshuāng

风水　fēngshuǐ　the location of a house or tomb, supposed to have an influence on the fortune of a family; geomantic omen: 这栋房子～好。or This house is of high geomantic quality. / 那家人说在那儿施工挖掘，破了他家祖坟的～。The family charged that some construction excavations had disturbed the geomantic configuration of its ancestral tombs.

风水先生　fēngshuǐ xiānsheng　geomancer

风丝　fēngsī　a slight wind; a breath of wind: 今天闷热，一点～儿也没有。It's heavy today. There's not a breath of wind.

风俗　fēngsú　custom: ～习惯 customs and habits

风俗画　fēngsúhuà　genre painting; genre

风速　fēngsù　wind speed; wind velocity

风速表　fēngsùbiǎo　anemometer

风速计　fēngsùjì　anemograph; registering anemometer

风速器　fēngsùqì　wind gauge

风瘫　fēngtān　common name for 瘫痪 tānhuàn

风调雨顺　fēngtiáo-yǔshùn　good weather for the crops; favourable weather: ～，五谷丰登。Good weather brings good harvests. / ～，国泰民安。The elements were propitious, the country prospered and the people were at peace.

风头　fēngtóu　the way the wind blows: 船老大仔细观察～和水势。The boatman kept a sharp eye on the wind and water.

风头　fēngtou　① the trend of events (as affecting a person): 避避～ lie low until sth. blows over / 看～办事 act according to circumstances ② (usu. derog.) the publicity one receives: ～十足 be very much in the limelight

风土　fēngtǔ　natural conditions and social customs of a place

风土人情　fēngtǔ-rénqíng　local conditions and customs

风土驯化　fēngtǔ xúnhuà　agric. acclimatization

风味　fēngwèi　special flavour; local colour (or flavour): 家乡～ the pleasing taste of the cooking of one's native place; local flavour / 这首诗有民歌～。This poem has a distinctive balladic air.

风味菜　fēngwèicài　typical local dishes; local delicacies

风味小吃　fēngwèi xiǎochī　local delicacies: 中国每个地区都有自己的～。Each region of China boasts its local delicacies.

风闻　fēngwén　learn through hearsay; get wind of

风物　fēngwù　scenery (typical of a place)

风险　fēngxiǎn　risk; hazard: 冒～ take risks / 要改革就不怕担～。A true reformist fears no dangers. / ～补偿 income to compensate for risk-taking

风箱　fēngxiāng　bellows

风向　fēngxiàng　wind direction

风向标　fēngxiàngbiāo　wind vane

风向袋　fēngxiàngdài　wind sleeve; wind sock; wind cone

风向计　fēngxiàngjì　registering weather vane

风向图　fēngxiàngtú　wind rose

风向仪　fēngxiàngyí　anemoscope

风心病　fēngxīnbìng　med. rheumatic heart disease

风信　fēngxìn　① scent or sound brought by a wind —news; wind: 他一听到～就赶去了。As soon as he got wind of it, he went at once. ② formal seasonal wind

风信子　fēngxìnzǐ　bot. hyacinth

风信子石　fēngxìnzǐshí　another name for 锆石 gàoshí

风行　fēngxíng　be in fashion (or vogue); be popular: ～全国 be popular all over the country

风行一时　fēngxíng yīshí　be popular for a while; be all the rage for a time

风选　fēngxuǎn　agric. selection by winnowing (or wind)

风选机　fēngxuǎnjī　winnowing machine; winnower

风雪　fēngxuě　wind and snow; snowstorm: ～交加 a raging snowstorm / 柴门闻犬吠，～夜归人。(刘长卿) A dog barks at the brushwood gate, As someone heads home this windy, snowy night.

风压　fēngyā　meteorol. wind pressure

风雅　fēngyǎ　① literary pursuits ② elegant; refined: 举止～ have refined manners

风雅颂　fēng-yǎ-sòng　the three sections in which The Book of Songs (《诗经》) is divided ——see also 风 fēng⑨; 雅¹ yǎ④; 颂 sòng

风言风语　fēngyán-fēngyǔ　groundless talk; slanderous gossip

风衣　fēngyī　windcheater; windbreaker; wind-jacket

风雨　fēngyǔ　wind and rain; the elements; trials and hardships: 迎着～去战斗 go into battle braving wind and rain

风雨灯　fēngyǔdēng　same as 风灯 fēngdēng

风雨交加　fēng-yǔ jiāojiā　it's raining and blowing hard; it's wet and windy

风雨飘摇　fēng-yǔ piāoyáo　swaying in the midst of a raging storm; precarious; tottering: ～的年代 precarious times; troubled times

风雨如晦　fēng-yǔ rú huì　wind and rain sweeping across a gloomy sky—a grim situation

风雨同舟　fēng-yǔ tóng zhōu　in the same storm-tossed boat—stand together through thick and thin: 两国人民在共同对敌的长期斗争中～，患难与共。The two peoples went through storm and stress together, sharing weal and woe in their protracted struggle against common enemies.

风雨无阻　fēng-yǔ wú zǔ　stopped by neither wind nor rain—regardless of the weather; rain or shine: 我们郊游的日期已定，～。We've fixed the date for the outing and we'll go regardless of wind or rain.

风雨衣　fēngyǔyī　a rainproof windcheater; mackintosh

风月　fēngyuè　① wind and moon—scene; view: ～清幽 a tranquil and exquisite scene ② romantic affairs: ～场中 in the arena (or tournaments) of love

风云　fēngyún　wind and cloud—a stormy or unstable situation

风云变幻　fēngyún biànhuàn　constant change of events; a changeable situation: ～的时代 an age of rapid change / 国际政治～。World politics are constantly changing.

风云人物　fēngyún rénwù　man of the hour

风云突变　fēngyún tūbiàn　a sudden change in the situation

风韵　fēngyùn　(usu. a woman's) graceful bearing; charm

风灾　fēngzāi　disaster caused by a windstorm: 遭受～ be hit by a windstorm

风凿　fēngzáo　pneumatic chipping chisel

风闸　fēngzhá　mech. pneumatic brake

风障　fēngzhàng　agric. windbreak

风疹　fēngzhěn　med. nettle rash; urticaria

风筝　fēngzheng　kite: 放～ fly a kite

风中之烛　fēng zhōng zhī zhú　a candle guttering in the wind—① a person who may die at any moment ② a thing that may perish at any moment

风烛残年　fēngzhú cánnián　old and ailing like a candle guttering in the wind

风姿　fēngzī　graceful bearing; charm: ～秀逸 have elegant bearing

风钻　fēngzuàn　pneumatic drill

汲　fēng　liter.　the sound of flowing water

枫　fēng　① same as 枫树 fēngshù ② maple

枫树　fēngshù　(also 枫香树 fēngxiāngshù) Chinese sweet gum (*Liquidambar formosana*)

枫叶　fēngyè　leaves of Chinese sweet gum, maple, etc. which turn red in autumn

疯

fēng ① mad; insane; crazy: 他～了。He's gone mad. ② (of a plant, grain crop, etc.) spindly and not likely to bear much fruit or seed: 这些棉花长～了。These cotton-plants are growing too tall and spindly (*or* are overgrowing).

疯癫　fēngdiān　same as 疯 fēng①

疯疯癫癫　fēngfengdiāndiān　mentally deranged; acting like a lunatic; flighty

疯狗　fēnggǒu　mad dog; rabid dog

疯话　fēnghuà　mad talk; ravings; nonsense

疯狂　fēngkuáng　① insane ② frenzied; unbridled: ～咒骂 frenzied vilification / ～反扑 a desperate counterattack / ～掠夺 unbridled plunder / ～叫嚣 frenzied clamouring

疯人院　fēngrényuàn　madhouse; lunatic asylum

疯瘫　fēngtān　same as 风瘫 fēngtān

疯长　fēngzhǎng　*agric.* overgrowing; spindling: 防止～ prevent spindling

疯枝　fēngzhī　(also 疯权 fēngchà) spindling branch

疯子　fēngzi　lunatic; madman

砜

fēng　*chem.* sulphone (*or* sulfone)

封¹

fēng　① confer (a title, territory, etc.) upon: ～王 be made a prince / 分～诸侯 grant titles and territories to the nobles ② short for 封建主义 fēngjiànzhǔyì ③ (Fēng) a surname

封²

fēng　① seal: 把信～上 seal a letter / 大雪纷飞，江河冰～。It is snowing hard, and rivers and streams have frozen over. ② bank (a fire): 炉子～了吗? Have you banked up the fire? ③ wrapper; envelope: 赏～ an envelope with money reward sealed in; an enveloped money reward ④ *m.* (for sth. enveloped): 一～信 a letter

封闭　fēngbì　① seal: 用蜡～瓶口 seal a bottle with wax ② seal off; close: ～机场 close an airport / ～的社会 a closed society

封闭层　fēngbìcéng　*petroleum* confining bed

封闭疗法　fēngbì liáofǎ　block therapy

封存　fēngcún　seal up for safekeeping

封底　fēngdǐ　*bookbinding* back cover

封地　fēngdì　fief; feud; manor

封顶　fēngdǐng　① (of a plant) cease growing any taller ② impose a ceiling (on prices, wages, bonuses, etc.): 奖金不～。There is no ceiling on bonuses.

封冻　fēngdòng　(of a river, the ground, etc.) freeze

封冻期　fēngdòngqī　a period of freezing weather; freeze

封二　fēng'èr　*bookbinding* inside front cover (also called 封里)

封港　fēnggǎng　close a port or harbour

封官许愿　fēngguān xǔyuàn　*derog.* offer official posts and make lavish promises; promise high posts and other favours

封罐机　fēngguànjī　tin seamer; can seamer

封火　fēnghuǒ　bank a fire

封建　fēngjiàn　① the system of enfeoffment (see also 分封制 fēnfēngzhì) ② feudalism ③ feudal; feudalistic: 头脑～ feudal-minded

封建把头　fēngjiàn bǎtóu　feudal gangmaster

封建割据　fēngjiàn gējù　feudal separationist rule

封建社会　fēngjiàn shèhuì　feudal society

封建主　fēngjiànzhǔ　feudal lord

封建主义　fēngjiànzhǔyì　feudalism

封建专制主义　fēngjiànzhuānzhìzhǔyì　feudal autocracy

封疆　fēngjiāng　borders; frontiers

封疆大吏　fēngjiāng dàlì　general name for high provincial officials in Ming and Qing times

封禁　fēngjìn　① close (a place) ② prohibit; ban: ～黄色书刊 ban pornographic books and periodicals

封口　fēngkǒu　① seal: 这封信还没～。The letter hasn't been sealed yet. ② heal: 腿上的伤已经～了。The leg wound has healed. ③ say sth. definitive so as to prevent further discussion

封蜡　fēnglà　sealing wax

封里　fēnglǐ　*bookbinding* ① inside front cover ② inside back cover

封门　fēngmén　① seal up a door ② same as 封口 fēngkǒu③

封面　fēngmiàn　*bookbinding* ① the title page of a thread-bound book ② the front and back cover of a book ③ front cover

封泥　fēngní　① sealing clay ② *metall.* lute

封皮　fēngpí　*dial.* ① same as 封条 fēngtiáo ② same as 封面 fēngmiàn ③ paper wrapping ④ envelope

封妻荫子　fēngqī-yìnzǐ　(of the emperor) confer titles of honour on the wife of a deserving official and hereditary ranks on his descendants

封三　fēngsān　*bookbinding* inside back cover (also called 封里)

封山　fēngshān　seal (*or* close) a mountain pass: 大雪～。Heavy snow has sealed the mountain passes.

封山育林　fēngshān-yùlín　close hillsides (to livestock grazing and fuel gathering) to facilitate afforestation

封豕长蛇　fēngshǐ-chángshé　like a big boar and a long serpent—rapacious and ruthless

封四　fēngsì　*bookbinding* back cover (also called 封底)

封锁　fēngsuǒ　block or seal off (through military or other compulsory means); blockade: ～港口 blockade a port / ～边境 close the border / ～消息 block the passage of information / 经济～ economic blockade

封锁线　fēngsuǒxiàn　blockade line; blockade

封套　fēngtào　big envelope (for holding documents, books, etc.)

封条　fēngtiáo　a strip of paper used for sealing (doors, drawers, etc.); paper strip seal

封土　fēngtǔ　① grave mound ② *formal* fief; feud; manor

封网　fēngwǎng　*volleyball* block: 她那一下～可精彩了! She made a brilliant block.

封檐板　fēngyánbǎn　*archit.* eaves board

封一　fēngyī　*bookbinding* front cover (also called 封面)

封印　fēngyìn　seal (on mail)

封斋　fēngzhāi　the Islamic day of fasting

封装　fēngzhuāng　seal and package

峰 (峯)

fēng　① peak; summit; crest: 孤～ a solitary peak / 浪～ the crest of a wave ② hump: 驼峰 tuófēng ③ *m.* (only for camels): 四～骆驼 four camels

峰巅　fēngdiān　mountain peak; summit

峰回路转　fēnghuí-lùzhuǎn　amidst surrounding elevations and winding roads: 山行六七里，渐闻水声潺潺而泻出于两峰之间者，酿泉也。～，有亭翼然临于泉上者，醉翁亭也。(欧阳修) After journeying on the mountainside for six or seven *li*, one begins to hear the sound of flowing water. It is the Niang Spring rushing out from between two peaks. Placed amidst surrounding elevations and winding roads is a pavilion which juts out over the spring like the wing of a bird. This is the Old Drunkard's Pavilion.

峰立 fēnglì tower aloft like a mountain peak
峰峦 fēngluán ridges and peaks
峰态 fēngtài *math.* kurtosis
峰值 fēngzhí *elec.* peak value; crest value

烽
fēng beacon

烽火 fēnghuǒ ① beacon-fire (used to give border alarm in ancient times); beacon ② flames of war
烽火连天 fēnghuǒ liántiān flames of battle raging everywhere
烽火台 fēnghuǒtái beacon tower
烽烟 fēngyān beacon-fire; beacon

锋
fēng ① a sharp point or cutting edge (of a knife, sword, etc.): 刀锋 dāofēng / 笔锋 bǐfēng ② vanguard: 先锋 xiānfēng ③ *meteorol.* front

锋镝 fēngdí *formal* swords and arrows—weapons; war: ～余生 survivors of a war
锋钢 fēnggāng high-speed steel; rapid steel
锋快 fēngkuài ① (of a knife, sword, etc.) sharp; keen ② penetrating; incisive; sharp: ～的反诘 a sharp retort
锋利 fēnglì ① sharp; keen: ～的钢刀 a sharp knife ② incisive; sharp; poignant: ～泼辣的笔调 a sharp and pungent style
锋芒 fēngmáng (also 锋铓 fēngmáng) ① cutting edge; spearhead: 斗争的～ the spearhead of struggle ② talent displayed; abilities: 不露～ refrain from showing one's ability; be able but modest
锋芒逼人 fēngmáng bīrén trenchant; poignant
锋芒毕露 fēngmáng bìlù make a display of one's abilities
锋芒所向 fēngmáng suǒ xiàng target of attack
锋面 fēngmiàn *meteorol.* frontal surface
锋面低压 fēngmiàn dīyā *meteorol.* frontal low
锋刃 fēngrèn cutting edge (of a knife, sword, etc.)
锋锐 fēngruì ① (of a knife, sword, etc.) sharp; keen: ～的匕首 a sharp dagger ② penetrating; incisive; sharp: ～的评论 incisive comments / 目光～ have sharp eyes ③ a person's impulsive force; drive; push
锋头 fēngtou ① same as 风头 fēngtou② ② sharpness; incisiveness; vigour (of writing, speech, etc.)

蜂 (蠭)
fēng ① bee; honeybee ② wasp ③ in swarms: 蜂集 fēngjí

蜂虿有毒 fēng-chài yǒudú the sting of a bee has poison —beware of the harm done by small things
蜂巢 fēngcháo honeycomb
蜂巢胃 fēngcháowèi *zool.* honeycomb stomach; reticulum
蜂刺 fēngcì the sting of a bee or wasp
蜂毒 fēngdú bee venom
蜂房 fēngfáng any of the six-sided wax cells in a honeycomb
蜂糕 fēnggāo steamed sponge cake (made of wheat or rice flour)
蜂虎 fēnghǔ *zool.* bee eater
蜂皇精 fēnghuángjīng same as 蜂王精 fēngwángjīng
蜂集 fēngjí (also 蜂聚 fēngjù) gather in smarms; swarm together: 上千人～在广场上。About a thousand people thronged the square.
蜂蜡 fēnglà beeswax
蜂蜜 fēngmì honey
蜂鸣器 fēngmíngqì buzzer
蜂鸟 fēngniǎo hummingbird
蜂农 fēngnóng beekeeper; apiarist
蜂起 fēngqǐ rise in swarms
蜂群 fēngqún (bee) colony
蜂乳 fēngrǔ royal jelly
蜂王 fēngwáng ① queen bee ② queen wasp

蜂王精 fēngwángjīng royal jelly
蜂窝 fēngwō ① common name for 蜂巢 fēngcháo ② a honeycomb-like thing; honeycomb
蜂窝炉 fēngwōlú honeycomb briquet stove
蜂窝煤 fēngwōméi honeycomb briquet (or briquette)
蜂窝织炎 fēngwōzhīyán *med.* cellulitis; phlegmon; phlegmona
蜂窝组织 fēngwō zǔzhī *physiol.* cellular tissue; areolar tissue
蜂箱 fēngxiāng beehive; hive
蜂响器 fēngxiǎngqì another name for 蜂鸣器 fēngmíngqì
蜂拥 fēngyōng swarm; flock: 车门一开，乘客～而上。As soon as the door opened, passengers swarmed onto the bus.
蜂拥而来 fēngyōng ér lái come swarming; swarm forward: 四面八方的人向广场～。People came swarming into the square from all directions.

鄷
Fēng a surname

鄷都 Fēngdū a county in Sichuan Province (now written 丰都)
鄷都城 Fēngdūchéng the Capital of Hell

fēng

冯
Féng a surname

逢
féng meet; come upon: ～人便问 ask whoever happens to come one's way / ～双(单)日开放 open on even (odd) days of the month

逢场作戏 féng chǎng zuò xì join in the fun on occasion: 咱们搞这行的只不过是"～"嘛。We of this trade know too well that we are only playing a game.
逢集 féngjí market day: 我们进村的那天正好～。The day we arrived at the village happened to be market day.
逢年过节 féng nián guò jié on New Year's Day or other festivals: ～我总回家。On New Year's Day and other festivals, I always go back home.
逢人说项 féng rén shuōxiàng praise a person before everybody
逢山开路，遇水搭桥 féng shān kāilù, yù shuǐ dāqiáo cut paths through mountains and build bridges across rivers
逢凶化吉 féng xiōng huà jí ill luck turns into good: 因为他在外边的朋友多，遇啥事都能～。He has many connections, and he can always find some way of tiding over a crisis.
逢迎 féngyíng make up to; fawn on; curry favour with: 百般～上司 curry favour with one's superior sedulously

缝
féng stitch; sew: ～被子 stitch a quilt cover on / ～扣子 sew a button on / 刀口刚～好。The incision has just been stitched up. ——see also fèng

缝补 féngbǔ sew; mend (by sewing): ～衣服 mend clothes
缝缝连连 féngféngliánlián sewing and mending: 拆拆洗洗、～的活儿，她都很在行。She is quite good at washing and sewing.
缝合 fénghé *med.* suture; sew up: ～伤口 sew up (or suture) a wound
缝合线 fénghéxiàn ① another name for 缝线 féngxiàn ② *geol.* stylolite
缝纫 féngrèn sewing; tailoring: ～车间 tailoring shop
缝纫机 féngrènjī sewing machine
缝线 féngxiàn *med.* suture: 吸收性～ absorbable su-

ture／羊肠〜 catgut suture

缝叶莺　féngyèyīng　tailorbird

缝制　féngzhì　make (clothes, bedding, etc.)

缝缀　féngzhuì　sew on; patch: 把领章〜在军装领子上 sew the badge onto the collar of the uniform／〜破衣服 patch torn or worn-out clothes

fěng

讽　fěng　① satirize; mock: 嘲讽 cháofěng ② *formal* chant; intone: 讽诵 fěngsòng

讽嘲　fěngcháo　sneer at; taunt

讽刺　fěngcì　① satirize: 这是一部〜封建文人的作品。This is a satire on feudal scholars. ② ridicule; taunt; mock: 别〜他了。Don't ridicule him.／我受不了这种〜。I can't stand such taunts (*or* sarcasm).

讽刺画　fěngcìhuà　caricature

讽刺诗　fěngcìshī　satirical poem

讽刺文学　fěngcì wénxué　satire

讽刺小品　fěngcì xiǎopǐn　satirical essay

讽诵　fěngsòng　*formal* read with intonation and expression

讽喻诗　fěngyùshī　allegorical poem

唪　fěng　chant in a loud voice

唪经　fěngjīng　(of Buddhists or Taoists) recite or chant the scriptures in a loud voice

fèng

凤（鳳）　fèng　phoenix: 凤凰 fènghuáng

凤蝶　fèngdié　swallowtail butterfly; swallowtail

凤冠　fèngguān　phoenix coronet (worn by an empress or imperial concubine and also used formerly as a bride's headdress)

凤凰　fènghuáng　phoenix (凤 being the male and 凰 being the female)

凤凰木　fènghuángmù　royal poinciana (*Delonix regia*); flamboyant (tree)

凤凰于飞　fènghuáng yúfēi　a couple of phoenixes flying together—marital felicity

凤凰竹　fènghuángzhú　hedge bamboo (*Bambusa multiplex*)

凤凰座　Fènghuángzuò　*astron.* Phoenix

凤梨　fènglí　pineapple (the plant and its fruit)

凤毛麟角　fèngmáo-línjiǎo　(precious and rare as) phoenix feathers and unicorn horns; rarity of rarities

凤尾鱼　fèngwěiyú　common name for 鲚 jì

凤尾竹　fèngwěizhú　fernleaf hedge bamboo (*Bambusa multiplex* var. *nana*)

凤仙花　fèngxiānhuā　garden balsam; balsam

奉　fèng　① give or present with respect: 双手〜上 present respectfully with both hands／〜上新书一册。I am forwarding you a new book. ② receive (orders, etc.): 〜上级指示, 暂停开放。Temporarily closed on orders from above. ③ esteem; revere: 〜为典范 look upon as a model ④ believe in: 素〜佛教 have always believed in Buddhism ⑤ wait on; attend to: 侍奉 shìfèng ⑥ *pol.* have the honour to: 〜访未晤, 甚怅。Much to my regret you weren't at home when I called.

奉承　fèngcheng　flatter; fawn on; toady to: 你别信他的, 他只不过是在〜你罢了。Don't believe him. He was simply flattering you.／许多人〜他就因为他有钱。Many people fawn on him only because of his wealth.

奉承话　fèngchenghuà　flattery: 他爱听别人的〜。He's apt to fall for flattery.

奉告　fènggào　*pol.* let sb. know; inform: 详情容后〜。I'll give you the details later.

奉公守法　fènggōng-shǒufǎ　be law-abiding

奉还　fènghuán　*pol.* return sth. with thanks

奉命　fèngmìng　(also 奉令 fènglìng) receive orders; act under orders: 〜出发 receive orders to set off／〜于危难之间 be entrusted with a mission at a critical and difficult moment／奉市长命 by order of the mayor／我〜来此报到。I'm here to report for duty as ordered.／中国代表团〜就这一问题阐明中国政府的立场。The Chinese Delegation has been instructed to state the position of the Chinese Government on this question.

奉命唯谨　fèngmìng wéi jǐn　obey orders scrupulously

奉陪　fèngpéi　*pol.* keep sb. company: 恕不〜。Sorry I won't be able to keep you company.

奉陪到底　fèngpéi dàodǐ　have the honour of keeping sb. company until the end: 今天晚上来和我们玩桥牌, 好吗?—好极啦, 我一定〜。Will you come and join us at a bridge party this evening? —Yes, I'll be glad to, and I'll stay at the party until the very end.／他们要打, 我们就〜。If they want to attack us, we'll take them on and fight to the finish.

奉劝　fèngquàn　*pol.* may I offer a piece of advice: 〜你少喝点儿酒。I'd like to advise you not to drink too much.／〜你还是听听大家的意见为好。You would be well advised to listen to the opinions of others.

奉若神明　fèng ruò shénmíng　worship sb. or sth.; make a fetish of sth.

奉送　fèngsòng　*pol.* offer as a gift; give away free

奉为圭臬　fèng wéi guīniè　look up to as a standard; hold up as a model

奉为楷模　fèng wéi kǎimó　hold up as a model

奉献　fèngxiàn　offer as a tribute; present with all respect

奉行　fèngxíng　pursue (a policy, etc.): 〜不结盟政策 pursue a policy of nonalignment

奉行故事　fèngxíng gùshì　follow established practice

奉养　fèngyǎng　support and wait upon (one's parents, etc.)

奉迎　fèngyíng　①same as 逢迎 féngyíng ② *pol.* be honoured to welcome (*or* meet).you

奉赠　fèngzèng　*pol.* present with respect

奉召　fèngzhào　be summoned: 大使已〜回国。The ambassador has been summoned home.

奉赵　fèngzhào　*formal* return sth. intact to its owner; return sth. with thanks ——see also 完璧归赵 wánbì guī Zhào

奉旨　fèngzhǐ　by order of the emperor; by imperial decree

俸　fèng　pay; salary: 薪俸 xīnfèng

俸给　fèngjǐ　same as 俸禄 fènglù

俸禄　fènglù　*old* an official's salary; government salary

缝　fèng　① seam: 缭〜儿 sew a seam ② crack; crevice; fissure: 院墙上裂了一道〜儿。There is a crack in the courtyard wall. ——see also féng

缝隙　fèngxì　chink; crack; crevice

缝子　fèngzi　*inf.* chink; crack; crevice: 门板裂了一条〜。There is a crack in the door planks.

fó

佛　fó　① Buddha (short for 佛陀 Fótuó) ② Buddhism: 信〜 believe in Buddhism ③ an image of Bud-

dha; Buddha: 一尊铜～ a bronze statue of Buddha / 大殿上塑着三尊～。 There are three Buddhas in the main hall of the temple. ——see also fú

佛得角 Fódéjiǎo Cape Verde

佛得角人 Fódéjiǎorén Cape Verdean

佛法 fófǎ ① Buddha dharma; Buddhist doctrine: 传布～ spread Buddhism ② power of Buddha

佛法僧 fófǎsēng Buddha-dharma-sangha ——see also 三宝 sānbǎo

佛家 Fójiā Buddhists

佛教 Fójiào Buddhism

佛教徒 Fójiàotú Buddhist

佛经 Fójīng Buddhist Scripture; Buddhist sutra; Buddhist sacred literature

佛龛 fókān a niche for a statue of Buddha

佛口蛇心 fókǒu-shéxīn a Buddha's mouth but a viper's heart—honeyed words but evil intent

佛兰芒人 Fólánmángrén the Flemish; Fleming

佛兰芒语 Fólánmángyǔ Flemish (language)

佛门 fómén Buddhism: ～弟子 followers of Buddhism; Buddhists / 皈依～ be converted to Buddhism

佛事 fóshì Buddhist ceremony (or service)

佛手 fóshǒu (also 佛手柑 fóshǒugān) bot. Buddha's-hand; fingered citron

佛寺 fósì Buddhist temple

佛堂 fótáng family hall for worshipping Buddha

佛头着粪 fótóu zhuó fèn smear Buddha's head with dung—desecrate

佛陀 Fótuó Buddha—a title for Sakyamuni or a person who has attained enlightenment

佛像 fóxiàng an image of Buddha; Buddha

佛学 fóxué Buddhist philosophy

佛牙 fóyá sacred tooth relic of Buddha

佛爷 fóye Buddha

佛珠 fózhū beads; rosary

佛祖 fózǔ Buddhist patriarch

fǒu

缶 fǒu ① formal a narrow-necked earthen jar ② an ancient percussion instrument made of clay

否 fǒu ① negate; deny: 否认 fǒurèn ② inf. turn down: 我的建议被他～了。 He turned down my offer. ③ formal nay; no: 这是妥当的办法吗? ～! Is that the right way to do it? No! / 你这样说合适吗? ～! Is it right for you to say so? No! ④ formal (used at the end of a sentence to indicate that the sentence is a question): 知其事～? Do you know anything about it? ⑤ (used with 是, 能, 可, etc.) whether or not: 明日能～出发须视天气而定。 Whether or not we can start off tomorrow will depend on the weather. ——see also pǐ

否定 fǒudìng ① negate; deny: 你不能～他的话是合乎事实的。 You cannot deny the truth of his statement. / 事实～了他的看法。 Facts have refuted his views. / 采取一切～的态度 adopt an attitude of negating everything ② negative: ～的答复 a negative answer; an answer in the negative ③ philos. negation: ～之～ the negation of negation

否决 fǒujué vote down; veto; overrule: ～提案 veto a proposal / 动议被大会～了。 The motion was voted down at the assembly. or The assembly rejected the motion.

否决权 fǒujuéquán veto power; veto: 行使～ exercise the veto

否认 fǒurèn deny; repudiate: 她～跟我讲过这事。 She denied that she had told me about it. / 他～做过任何违

法的事。 He denied doing anything illegal. / 不能～, 雹灾给我们带来了一些困难。 There is no denying the fact that the hailstorm has brought us some difficulties. / 我们断然～这种无理指责。 We categorically reject this groundless charge.

否则 fǒuzé conj. otherwise; if not; or else: 快点走,～要迟到了。 Hurry up, or we'll be late. / 他一定有要紧事找你,～不会接连打三次电话来。 He must have something urgent to discuss with you, otherwise he wouldn't have phoned you three times. / 我们必须加强基础工业的建设,～经济发展就没有后劲。 Basic industries must be strengthened; otherwise economic development cannot be sustained.

fū

夫 fū ① husband: 夫妻 fūqī ② man: 匹夫 pǐfū ③ a manual worker: 船夫 chuánfū / 渔夫 yúfū ④ (in former times) a conscripted labourer: 拉夫 lāfū ——see also fú

夫唱妇随 fūchàng-fùsuí the husband sings and the wife follows—domestic harmony; conjugal felicity

夫妇 fūfù husband and wife: 新婚～ a newly married couple; newlyweds

夫君 fūjūn formal my husband

夫妻 fūqī man and wife

夫妻店 fūqīdiàn a small shop run by husband and wife

夫妻无隔夜之仇 fūqī wú géyè zhī chóu enmity between husband and wife doesn't last the night

夫权 fūquán authority of the husband: ～是封建宗法制度束缚妇女的一条绳索。 The authority of the husband was one of the thick ropes with which the feudal-patriarchal system bound women.

夫人 fūren ① a lady of high rank; the wife of a feudal lord; the wife of a high official ② the wife of a diplomat: 各国使节和～ foreign diplomatic envoys and their wives ③ Mrs.; Madame (Mme); Lady: 孙～ Madame Sun / 第一～ First Lady ④ pol. wife: 您的～好吗? How is your wife?

夫婿 fūxù formal husband

夫役 fūyì (in former times) servants; coolies; conscripted labourers

夫子 fūzǐ ① old (a respectful term of address for a scholar or a teacher) master: 孔～ Master Kong; Confucius ② old my husband ③ pedant: ～气 pedantry

夫子自道 fūzǐ zì dào what the Master says is a description of himself (said of a person criticizing others when he himself is open to the same charge)

伕 fū same as 夫 fū④

伕子 fūzi dial. (in former times) a conscripted labourer

呋 fū see below

呋喃 fūnán chem. furan

呋喃妥英 fūnántuǒyīng pharm. nitrofurantoin

呋喃西林 fūnánxīlín pharm. nitrofurazone; furacin

肤(膚) fū skin: 皮肤 pífū

肤泛 fūfàn superficial; shallow: ～之论 shallow views

肤觉 fūjué physiol. dermal sensation

肤皮潦草 fūpí liáocǎo cursory; casual; perfunctory

肤浅 fūqiǎn superficial; shallow: 我对这个问题的认识很～。 I have only a superficial understanding of the problem.

肤色 fūsè colour of skin: 不同国度、不同～的运动员欢聚一堂。 Players from different lands and of different colours were gathered happily in the same hall. / 不论种族、信仰或～ without regard to race, creed, or colour

麸（麱）

fū　(wheat) bran

麸皮　fūpí　(wheat) bran

麸皮面包　fūpí miànbāo　whole wheat bread; brown bread

麸子　fūzi　(wheat) bran

跌

fū　instep

跌坐　fūzuò　(of Buddhists) sit cross-legged in meditation (with the legs locked firmly and the soles directed fully upwards)

跗

fū　instep (i.e. the arching area of the middle of the human foot)

跗骨　fūgǔ　*physiol.*　tarsus; tarsal bones

跗面　fūmiàn　instep (i.e. the upper surface of the arching area of the human foot)

跗蹠　fūzhí　the shank of a bird; tarsometatarsus

稃

fū　same as 麸 fū

孵

fū　hatch; brood; incubate: ～小鸡 hatch chicks / ～出来了十只小鸭子。Ten ducklings have hatched.

孵化　fūhuà　hatch; incubate: 这台孵卵器一次能～的蛋要比一百只母鸡还多。This incubator can hatch more eggs at a time than a hundred hens.

孵化场　fūhuàchǎng　hatchery (for poultry, etc.)

孵化池　fūhuàchí　hatchery (for fish, etc.)

孵卵　fūluǎn　brood; hatch; incubate: ～鸡 brooding hen

孵卵期　fūluǎnqī　incubation period

孵卵器　fūluǎnqì　incubator

孵育　fūyù　hatch; incubate: 刚～出来的小鸡就会走会啄食。Newly hatched chicks can walk and peck.

敷

fū　① apply (powder, ointment. etc.): ～粉 apply powder / 在创口上～药膏 dress the wound with ointment ② spread; lay out: 敷设 fūshè ③ be sufficient for: 入不敷出 rù bù fū chū

敷料　fūliào　*med.*　dressing

敷设　fūshè　① lay (pipes, etc.): ～管道 lay pipelines / ～铁轨 lay a railway track / ～电缆 lay electricity cables ② lay (mines): ～水雷 lay mines in water

敷贴　fūtiē　apply ointment or plaster (to an affected part of the body)

敷衍　fūyǎn　(also 敷演 fūyǎn)　*formal*　elaborate; expound: ～经文要旨 elaborate the main ideas of the scriptures

敷衍　fūyan　① act in a perfunctory manner; go through the motions; do just enough to satisfy sb.: 干这种活儿可～不得。You mustn't be perfunctory in doing this kind of work. / 他做事老是采取～的态度，很不认真。He's in the habit of working perfunctorily and half-heartedly. / 他那些话分明是～你的。Obviously, he said that just to satisfy you. / 他～了几句就走了。He made a few casual remarks and left. ② barely get by; just manage: 这几个钱只够我～几天的。This money is barely enough for me to get by (*or* manage) a few days.

敷衍了事　fūyan liǎoshì　muddle through one's work: 她办事认真，从不～。She is very conscientious and never skimps her work.

敷衍塞责　fūyan-sèzé　perform one's duty in a perfunctory manner

夫

fú

fú　*formal*　① this; that: 此～鲁国之巧伪人孔丘非邪?《庄子》This must be none other than that crafty hypocrite Kong Qiu from the state of Lu! ② this person; that person: ～也不良。That man is not good. ③ *part.* ⓐ (used at the beginning of a sentence to introduce a new subject): ～人必自侮而后人侮之。A man must despise himself before others will. ⓑ (used at the end of a sentence with exclamatory force): 逝者如斯～! Thus do things flow away! ——see also fū

弗

fú　*adv. formal*　not: 自愧～如 feel ashamed of one's inferiority

弗拉芒语　Fúlāmángyǔ　Flemish (language)

伏[1]

fú　① lean over; bend over: ～几而卧 fall asleep against a table ② lie prostrate: ～地不动 lie still on the ground, face downwards ③ subside; go down: 起伏 qǐfú ④ hide: 昼～夜出 hide by day and come out at night ⑤ yield; admit (defeat, guilt, etc.): 伏输 fúshū ⑥ subdue; vanquish: 降伏 xiángfú / 降龙伏虎 xiánglóngfúhǔ ⑦ the hottest days of the year: 入伏 rùfú / 初伏 chūfú ⑧ (Fú) a surname

伏[2]

fú　short for 伏特 fútè

伏安　fú'ān　*elec.*　volt-ampere

伏案　fú'àn　bend over or lean over a table: ～读书 (作画) bend over one's desk reading (painting) / ～入睡 fall asleep against a table

伏笔　fúbǐ　a hint foreshadowing later developments in a story, essay, etc.; foreshadowing: 这件事为以后故事情节的发展埋下了～。This episode carries a foreshadowing of what is to follow later on in the story.

伏兵　fúbīng　troops in ambush; ambush

伏尔加河　Fú'ěrjiāhé　the Volga

伏法　fúfǎ　be executed; be put to death

伏击　fújī　ambush: 遭到～ fall into (*or* get caught in) an ambush / 进行～ attack from (an) ambush / ～敌人 ambush the enemy

伏击圈　fújīquān　ambush ring

伏流　fúliú　*geol.*　subterranean drainage; underground stream

伏侍　fúshi　same as 服侍 fúshi

伏输　fúshū　same as 服输 fúshū

伏暑　fúshǔ　the torrid weather of the year's hottest days

伏特　fútè　*elec.*　volt

伏特计　fútèjì　voltmeter

伏特加　fútèjiā　vodka

伏天　fútiān　the *fu* days—the hottest days of the year ——see also 三伏 sānfú

伏帖　fútiē　① at ease; content; comfortable: 心里很～ feel perfectly content ② same as 服帖 fútiē①

伏贴　fútiē　fit perfectly: 这身衣服穿着很～。This suit fits perfectly.

伏卧　fúwò　lie prostrate; take a prone position; lie on one's stomach

伏羲　Fúxī　a legendary ruler of great antiquity, the first of the Three August Ones (三皇), credited with the invention of hunting and fishing and the domestication of animals

伏线　fúxiàn　same as 伏笔 fúbǐ

伏汛　fúxùn　summer flood (*or* freshet)

伏诛　fúzhū　*formal*　be executed

伏罪　fúzuì　same as 服罪 fúzuì

凫（鳧）

fú　① wild duck ② swim: ～水 swim

凫翁　fúwēng　*zool.*　water cock

扶

fú　① support with the hand; place a hand on sb. or sth. for support: ～着栏杆上楼 walk upstairs

with one's hand on the banisters / 你～着点梯子,我上去。Hold the ladder while I climb up. ② help sb. up; straighten sth. up: ～苗 straighten up the seedlings / 护士～起伤员,给他换药。The nurse propped up the wounded soldier and changed the dressing on his wound. ③ help; assist; support: 扶持 fúchí

扶病　fúbìng　(do sth.) in spite of illness: ～出席会议 go to a meeting in spite of one's illness

扶持　fúchí　① support sb. with one's hand; help sb. to stand or walk: 伤员们互相～着练习走路。Leaning on each other for support, the wounded men practised walking. ② help sustain; give aid to; support: 疾病相～。When one is ill, the others take good care of him. / 荷花虽好,也要绿叶～。For all its beauty the lotus needs its green leaves to set it off.

扶乩　fújī　(also 扶箕 fújī) a form of planchette writing

扶老携幼　fúlǎo-xiéyòu　holding the old by the arm and the young by the hand; bringing along the old and the young

扶犁　fúlí　put one's hand to the plough; follow the plough

扶鸾　fúluán　same as 扶乩 fújī

扶贫　fúpín　aid-the-poor programme (a government programme for providing assistance for poor areas of the country)

扶弱抑强　fúruò-yìqiáng　same as 抑强扶弱 yìqiáng-fúruò

扶桑[1]　fúsāng　① a legendary mulberry tree located at the extreme eastern limits of the world, from which the sun is supposed to rise ② (Fúsāng) an archaic poetic name for 日本 (Japan)

扶桑[2]　fúsāng　another name for 朱槿 zhūjǐn

扶手　fúshou　① handrail; rail; banisters ② armrest

扶手椅　fúshouyǐ　armchair

扶疏　fúshū　formal　luxuriant and well-spaced: 枝叶～。The branches and leaves are luxuriant but well-spaced.

扶梯　fútī　① staircase ② dial.　ladder

扶危济困　fúwēi-jìkùn　help those in distress and aid those in peril

扶养　fúyǎng　① provide for; support and assist: 夫妻间有互相～的义务。Husband and wife have the duty to support and assist each other. ② same as 抚养 fǔyǎng

扶养费　fúyǎngfèi　payment for support and assistance (for one's former spouse); alimony

扶摇直上　fúyáo zhí shàng　soar on the wings of a cyclone; rise steeply; skyrocket

扶掖　fúyè　formal　support; help

扶正　fúzhèng　① set sth. upright or straight: 把杆子～ set the pole upright ② (of a concubine) be raised to the status of wife ③ Chin. med.　build up one's resistance to disease

扶植　fúzhí　foster; prop up: ～新生力量 foster new rising forces / ～傀儡政权 prop up a puppet regime

扶助　fúzhù　help; assist; support: ～老弱 help the old and the weak

芙
fú　see below

芙蕖　fúqú　liter.　lotus

芙蓉　fúróng　bot.　① cottonrose hibiscus ② another name for 荷花 héhuā

芙蓉出水　fúróng chūshuǐ　a lotus flower just appearing above the water (said of a beautiful poem or painting or of a beautiful woman)

芙蓉国　Fúróngguó　the land of hibiscus (poetic name for 湖南 Húnán): ～里尽朝晖(毛泽东) the land of hibiscus glowing in the morning sun

孚
fú　inspire confidence in sb.: 深～众望 enjoy great popularity; enjoy high prestige

佛[1]
fú　see 仿佛 fǎngfú

佛[2]
fú　formal　same as 拂 fú③ ——see also fó

佛戾　fúlì　formal　go against; run counter to

拂
fú　① stroke: 春风～面 a spring breeze stroking the face ② whisk; flick: ～去桌上的尘土 whisk the dust off the desk ③ go against (sb.'s wishes): 拂意 fúyì

拂尘　fúchén　horsetail whisk

拂荡　fúdàng　sway gently; swing slightly; wave gracefully: 低垂的柳枝在微风中～。The drooping willows swayed gently in the breeze.

拂动　fúdòng　brush against; stroke; caress: 和风～着姑娘的披肩秀发。A gentle breeze brushed against (or caressed) the girl's beautiful long hair.

拂拂　fúfú　(of the wind) blow gently: 凉风～。A cool breeze was blowing gently.

拂逆　fúnì　go against; run counter to: 他不敢～父母的意旨。He dare not go against his parents' wishes.

拂拭　fúshì　whisk or wipe off

拂晓　fúxiǎo　daybreak; dawn: ～出发 set off at dawn / ～前发起总攻 start the general offensive before dawn

拂袖而去　fú xiù ér qù　leave with a flick of one's sleeve ——go off in a huff

拂煦　fúxù　formal　(of the wind) be blowing warm: 微风～。A light breeze is blowing warm.

拂意　fúyì　go against sb.'s wishes: 不忍拂其意 not have the heart to go against sb.'s wishes; not wish to refuse sb. / 稍有～,他就大发雷霆。He would flare up at the slightest provocation.

绋
fú　formal　① a long, thick rope ② a long cord guiding the hearse: 执绋 zhífú

服
fú　① clothes; dress: 工作服 gōngzuòfú ② mourning apparel: 有～在身 be wearing mourning clothes; be in mourning ③ wear or put on (clothes): 服丧 fúsāng ④ take (medicine): 日～三次,每次两片。To be taken three times a day, two (tablets) each time. ⑤ serve: ～兵役 serve in the army; perform military service ⑥ be convinced; obey: 你说得有道理,我～了。What you've said is reasonable. I'm convinced. ⑦ be accustomed to: 不服水土 bù fú shuǐtǔ ——see also fù

服从　fúcóng　obey; submit (oneself) to; be subordinated to: ～命令 obey orders / 少数～多数。The minority should submit to the majority. / 个人利益应当～集体利益。One's personal interests should be subordinated to the interests of the collective.

服毒　fúdú　take poison: ～自杀 commit suicide by taking poison

服法[1]　fúfǎ　submit to the law: 认罪～ admit one's guilt and submit oneself to the law

服法[2]　fúfǎ　directions about how to take a medicine

服老　fúlǎo　accept old age and declining health: 不～ refuse to give in to old age

服满　fúmǎn　the period of mourning is over

服气　fúqì　be convinced: 他批评得对,你别不～。His criticism is justified. You shouldn't take it amiss.

服劝　fúquàn　be amenable to advice

服软　fúruǎn　① admit defeat; acknowledge a mistake: 他明知自己错了,可嘴上还不～。He knew perfectly well he was in the wrong, but stubbornly refused to admit it. ② yield to persuasion: ～不服硬 yield to persuasion but not to coercion

服丧　fúsāng　be in mourning (for the death of a kinsman, etc.)

服色　fúsè　the style and colour of clothes: 民族～ the styles and colours of ethnic garments

服饰 fúshì　dress and personal adornment; dress

服侍 fúshi　(also 服事 fúshì) wait upon; attend: ～父母 attend one's parents / 他生病的时候，同志们轮流来～他。His comrades took turns looking after him when he was ill.

服输 fúshū　admit (or acknowledge) defeat

服帖 fútiē　① docile; obedient; submissive: 他对老板很～。He is obedient to his boss. / 反动统治阶级总是要人民服服帖帖地忍受剥削和压迫。The reactionary ruling classes always wanted the people to endure exploitation and oppression submissively. ② appropriate; fitting; well arranged: 把事情都弄得服服帖帖的 arrange everything smoothly

服务 fúwù　give service to; be in the service of; serve: 为人民～。Serve the people. / ～周到 provide good service / 提高～质量 improve one's service / 他在邮局～了三十年。He served in the post-office for thirty years. / 这个饭店的～非常好。The hotel provides very good service.

服务行业 fúwù hángyè　service trades

服务台 fúwùtái　service desk (or counter); information and reception desk

服务态度 fúwù tàidu　attitude in attending to or waiting on guests, customers, etc.

服务员 fúwùyuán　attendant

服务站 fúwùzhàn　service centre

服刑 fúxíng　serve a sentence: ～期满 complete a term of imprisonment / 他已～三年。He has served three years in prison.

服药 fúyào　take medicine

服役 fúyì　① be on active service; enlist in the army: 他在海军～。He's serving in the Navy. / ～期间 during one's term of military service; during the period of enlistment / ～期满 complete one's term of service ② (in former times) do corvée labour

服膺 fúyīng　formal　① bear in mind ② feel deeply convinced ——see also 拳拳服膺 quánquán fúyīng

服用 fúyòng　① formal　clothing and articles for daily use: ～甚俭 be frugal in one's habits ② take (medicine)

服装 fúzhuāng　dress; clothing; costume: ～整齐 be neatly dressed / 民族～ national or ethnic costume / 她负责保管这出戏的～。She's the wardrobe mistress of this play.

服罪 fúzuì　plead guilty; admit one's guilt: 不～ plead not guilty

怫　fú　formal　looking angry; glowering

郛　fú　the outer wall of a city

绂　fú　① a silk ribbon for holding a jade seal through its nose ② same as 黻 fú

苻　fú　① the membrane inside the rush stalk ② (Fú) a surname

茯　fú　see below

茯苓 fúlíng　fuling (Poria coccus), an edible fungus, often used as a herbal medicine

茯苓饼 fúlíngbǐng　fuling cake

洑　fú　① (of flowing water) whirl in eddies ② whirlpool; eddy ——see also fù

袚　fú　① an ancient exorcistic ceremony ② cleanse; purify

氟　fú　chem.　fluorine (F)

氟化氢 fúhuàqīng　chem.　hydrogen fluoride

氟化物 fúhuàwù　chem.　fluoride

氟利昂 fúlì'áng　chem.　freon

氟石 fúshí　fluorite; fluorspar (a mineral)

俘　fú　① capture; take prisoner: 被～ be taken prisoner ② prisoner of war; captive: 遣～ repatriate prisoners of war

俘获 fúhuò　① capture; seize: 我军～甚众。Our army captured a lot of enemy soldiers and weapons. ② phys.　capture: 中子～ neutron capture / 裂变～ fission capture

俘虏 fúlǔ　① capture; take prisoner: 那一仗他们～敌军一千二百名。They captured twelve hundred enemy soldiers in that battle. ② captive; captured personnel; prisoner of war (P.O.W.): 执行宽待～的政策 carry out the policy of lenient treatment of prisoners of war

浮　fú　① float: 木头能～在水面上。Wood floats on water. / 潜水员～上来了。The diver has emerged. / 干部要深入群众，不能～在上面。Cadres should go deep among the masses, not remain on the surface. / 她脸上～起了笑容。A faint smile played on her face. ② dial.　swim: 他一口气～到了对岸。He swam across at one go. ③ on the surface; superficial: 浮土 fútǔ ④ movable: 浮财 fúcái ⑤ temporary; provisional: ～支 expenditure not in the regular account ⑥ shallow and frivolous; superficial: 他这个人太～，办事不踏实。He is too frivolous to do solid work. ⑦ hollow; inflated: 浮夸 fúkuā ⑧ excessive; surplus: ～额 surplus number

浮报 fúbào　give inflated figures in a report

浮标 fúbiāo　buoy

浮冰 fúbīng　floating ice; (ice) floe

浮财 fúcái　old　movable property

浮尘 fúchén　floating dust; surface dust

浮尘子 fúchénzǐ　zool.　leafhopper

浮沉 fúchén　now sink, now emerge; drift along: 宦海～ the ups and downs in officialdom; the vicissitudes of an official career

浮船坞 fúchuánwù　floating dock; floating dry dock

浮词 fúcí　unfounded remarks

浮厝 fúcuò　place a coffin in a temporary shelter pending burial

浮袋 fúdài　water wings

浮荡 fúdàng　float in the air: 歌声在空中～。The air resounded with singing.

浮雕 fúdiāo　relief (sculpture): ～群像 a relief sculpture of a group of people

浮雕压印 fúdiāo yāyìn　embossing

浮吊 fúdiào　mech.　floating crane

浮动 fúdòng　① float; drift: 树叶在水面上～。Leaves were floating on the water. ② be unsteady; fluctuate: 物价飞涨，人心～。With the soaring of prices, there was a growing feeling of insecurity. ③ econ.　float: 货币共同～ a joint currency float

浮动工资 fúdòng gōngzī　floating wages

浮动价格 fúdòng jiàgé　floating prices

浮动汇率 fúdòng huìlǜ　floating exchange rate

浮动利率 fúdòng lìlǜ　floating interest rate

浮动轴 fúdòngzhóu　mech.　floating axle

浮泛 fúfàn　① formal　float about: 轻舟～ a light boat gliding past ② reveal; display: 她的脸上～着愉快的神情。Her face beamed with joy. ③ superficial; too abstract: 他的发言内容～。His speech was superficial and full of generalities.

浮光掠影 fúguāng-lüèyǐng　skimming over the surface; hasty and casual; cursory

浮华 fúhuá　showy; ostentatious; flashy: 文辞～ florid language; an ornate style / ～的生活 a showy and luxu-

rious life style

浮滑 fúhuá slick and frivolous

浮记 fújì keep a tally of a transaction before entering it in the regular accounts; keep a temporary account

浮夸 fúkuā boastful; exaggerating: ～作风 proneness to boasting and exaggeration

浮雷 fúléi mil. floating mine

浮力 fúlì phys. buoyancy

浮码头 fúmǎtou floating pier

浮脉 fúmài Chin. med. surface pulse which can be felt when touched only lightly

浮面 fúmiàn surface: 把～的一层泥铲掉 scrape the mud off the surface / 汤一开锅就把～的油撇掉。Skim the grease from the soup when it starts to boil.

浮名 fúmíng an empty name: ～身后有谁知? After death who remembers an empty name?

浮沤 fú'ōu ① bubbles on water; froth ② the transience of human life; the inconstancy of human relationships

浮皮儿 fúpír ① outer skin ② surface

浮皮蹭痒 fúpí cèngyǎng scratching the surface; superficial

浮皮潦草 fúpí liǎocǎo same as 肤皮潦草 fūpí liǎocǎo

浮漂 fúpiāo (of work or study) cursory; superficial

浮萍 fúpíng bot. duckweed

浮签 fúqiān a detachable note stuck on the margin of a page

浮浅 fúqiǎn superficial; shallow: 一种～的看法 a superficial view

浮桥 fúqiáo pontoon bridge; floating bridge

浮生 fúshēng ① floating (or fleeting) life: 《～六记》Six Chapters of a Floating Life ② grow floating on water: 浮萍～在池塘中。Duckweeds float on ponds.

浮生若梦 fúshēng ruò mèng this fleeting life of ours is like an empty dream

浮石 fúshí pumice (stone)

浮水 fúshuǐ swim

浮筒 fútǒng float; pontoon; buoy

浮头 fútóu (of fish for want of oxygen) raise the nose above water to breathe

浮头儿 fútóur dial. surface

浮屠 fútú (also 浮图 fútú) Buddhism ① same as 佛陀 Fótuó ② a title applied by Buddhists to a monk ③ Buddhist pagoda or stupa: 救人一命胜造七级～。There is greater merit in saving one life than in building a seven-tier pagoda.

浮土 fútǔ dust collected on furniture, clothing, etc.; surface dust

浮文 fúwén verbiage; padding

浮现 fúxiàn appear before one's eyes: 往事～在我眼前。Scenes of the past rose before my eyes. or The past came back to my mind.

浮想 fúxiǎng ① thoughts flashing across one's mind ② recollections

浮想联翩 fúxiǎng liánpiān thoughts thronging one's mind: ～，夜不能寐。Thoughts thronged my mind and I could not sleep.

浮选 fúxuǎn min. flotation

浮选剂 fúxuǎnjì flotation agent

浮言 fúyán unfounded remarks

浮漾 fúyàng float about; drift along: 一叶扁舟在随波～ a leaf of a boat drifting along with the waves / 她脸上～着欣慰的微笑 her face beaming with satisfaction

浮游 fúyóu ① swim; float ② formal go on a pleasure trip

浮游生物 fúyóu shēngwù plankton

浮游资金 fúyóu zījīn floating fund

浮云 fúyún floating clouds

浮躁 fúzào impetuous; impulsive

浮渣 fúzhā metall. dross

浮肿 fúzhǒng dropsy; edema

浮子 fúzi ① fishing float ② automobile carburettor float

蚨 fú see 青蚨 qīngfú

桴[1] fú ① formal small wooden raft ② dial. smaller beams supporting the main beam; joists

桴[2]（枹） fú formal drumstick

桴鼓相应 fú-gǔ xiāngyìng the drum responding perfectly to the drumsticks—work in perfect coordination

袱（幞、襆） fú cloth-wrapper; cloth covering

袱子 fúzi dial. ① cloth-wrapper; a bundle wrapped in cloth ② kerchief ③ handkerchief

蕧 fú see 莱蕧 láifú

符 fú ① a tally issued by a ruler to generals, envoys, etc., as credentials in ancient China: 兵符 bīngfú ② symbol: 音符 yīnfú ③ tally with; accord with: 与事实不～ not tally with the facts ④ magic figures drawn by Taoist priests to invoke or expel spirits and bring good or ill fortune: 画了一张～ draw a magic figure ⑤ (Fú) a surname

符号 fúhào ① symbol; mark: 注音～ phonetic symbol / 标点～ punctuation mark / 代数～ algebraic symbol / 文字是记录语言的～。The written word is a symbol for recording human speech. ② insignia

符合 fúhé ① accord with; tally with; conform to; be in keeping with: ～要求 accord with the demands / ～实际情况 tally with the actual situation; conform to reality / ～当前政策 be in line with the current policy / 不～或不完全～条件 not qualified or not fully qualified / ～各国人民的愿望 be in keeping with the aspirations of the people of all countries ② phys. coincidence

符合摆 fúhébǎi phys. coincidence pendulum

符节 fújié a tally used in ancient times as credentials or a warrant

符拉迪沃斯托克 Fúlādíwòsītuōkè Vladivostok

符咒 fúzhòu Taoist magic figures or incantations

匐 fú see 匍匐 púfú

舮 fú formal an angry look: ～然不悦 look annoyed and ill-humoured

幅 fú ① width of cloth: 宽～白布 extra wide white cloth ② size: 大～照片 a large-sized photo ③ m. (for cloth, picture, etc.): 一～画 a picture; a painting / 一～布 a breadth of cloth

幅度 fúdù range; scope; extent: 病人血压变化的～不大。The patient's blood pressure fluctuates within a narrow range. / 粮食产量大～增长。There was a big increase in grain production. or Grain output increased by a big margin.

幅面 fúmiàn width of cloth

幅员 fúyuán the area of a country's territory; the size of a country: ～广大 vast in territory

幅员辽阔 fúyuán liáokuò have a vast territory: ～的国家 a country with a vast territory

福 fú ① good fortune; blessing; happiness: ～寿双全 enjoy both happiness and longevity ② (of a woman in former times) make a curtsy: ～了一～ make a curtsy ③ (Fú) short for 福建 Fújiàn

福地　fúdì　a place of perfect (or ideal) happiness

福尔马林　fú'ěrmǎlín　chem. formalin

福分　fúfen　inf. good luck; good fortune; a happy lot: 我们可没有你这样的～。 We don't have such good luck as you do.

福建　Fújiàn　Fujian (Province)

福克兰群岛　Fúkèlán Qúndǎo　the Falkland Islands

福利　fúlì　① material benefits; well-being; welfare: 为人民谋～ work for the well-being of the people ② formal better one's living conditions: 发展轻工业，～人民 better people's living conditions by developing light industry

福利费　fúlìfèi　welfare funds

福利国家　fúlì guójiā　welfare state

福利设施　fúlì shèshī　welfare facilities

福利事业　fúlì shìyè　welfare project (or services)

福气　fúqi　good luck; good fortune; a happy lot: 这位老太太有～，儿女都很孝顺。 The old lady is fortunate in having such dutiful children.

福如东海　fú rú dōnghǎi　happiness as boundless as the eastern seas (a stock term of congratulations): 爷爷! 祝您老人家～，寿比南山! I wish you long life and happiness, Grandpa!

福无双至，祸不单行　fú wú shuāng zhì, huò bù dān xíng blessings never come in pairs; misfortunes never come singly

福相　fúxiàng　a face showing good fortune

福星　fúxīng　lucky star; mascot: ～高照。 The lucky star is in the ascendant.

福音　fúyīn　① Christianity Gospel: ～书 the Gospels (in the Bible) ② glad tidings

福祉　fúzhǐ　formal happiness; blessedness

福至心灵　fú zhì xīn líng　when good fortune comes the mind works well

福州　Fúzhōu　Fuzhou (the capital of Fujian Province)

辐　fú　spoke (of a wheel)

辐辏　fúcòu　(also 辐凑 fúcòu) formal converge like the spokes of a wheel at the hub: 人烟～，车马骈阗。 People are clustered together like the spokes of a wheel; carts and horses are everywhere, side by side.

辐合　fúhé　meteorol. convergence

辐散　fúsàn　meteorol. divergence: ～场 divergence field

辐射　fúshè　① radiate (from a central point): 八条大道从广场呈～形伸展出去。 Eight roads radiate from the square. ② phys. radiation: 热～ thermal radiation / 电磁～ electromagnetic radiation / 受激～ stimulated radiation / 自发～ spontaneous radiation

辐射带　fúshèdài　meteorol. radiation zone

辐射计　fúshèjì　radiometer

辐射剂量　fúshè jìliàng　radiation dosage

辐射能　fúshènéng　radiant energy

辐射频率　fúshè pínlǜ　radiation frequency

辐射容限　fúshè róngxiàn　radiotolerance

辐射损伤　fúshè sǔnshāng　① radiation injury ② radiation damage

辐射体　fúshètǐ　radiant body

辐射学　fúshèxué　radiology

辐射育种　fúshè yùzhǒng　agric. radioactive breeding

辐射源　fúshèyuán　radiant

辐条　fútiáo　inf. spoke (of a wheel)

辐照　fúzhào　phys. irradiation

辐照度　fúzhàodù　phys. irradiance

蜉　fú　see below

蜉蝣　fúyóu　zool. mayfly

鲱　fú　see 鲂鲱 fāngfú

蝠　fú　zool. bat: 蝙蝠 biānfú

幞　fú　① a kind of headdress in ancient China ② same as 袱 fú

黻　fú　an embroidered pattern of black and blue on ancient official robes

fǔ

父　fǔ　① formal a term of respect for an elderly man: 渔～ an old fisherman ② same as 甫[1] fǔ ——see also fù

甫[1]　fǔ　old one's courtesy name: 台甫 táifǔ

甫[2]　fǔ　adv. formal just; only: 年～二十 have just reached the age of twenty / 惊魂～定 have just recovered from a fright

抚(撫)　fǔ　① comfort; console: 安抚 ānfǔ ② nurture; foster: 抚养 fǔyǎng ③ stroke: ～琴 play the zither ④ same as 拊 fǔ

抚爱　fǔ'ài　caress; fondle

抚躬自问　fǔgōng zìwèn　same as 反躬自问 fǎngōng zìwèn

抚今追昔　fǔjīn-zhuīxī　recall the past and compare it with the present; reflect on the past in the light of the present

抚摩　fǔmó　stroke: 他轻轻地～着我的头发。 He was gently stroking my hair.

抚弄　fǔnòng　stroke; fondle: 她双手不停地～着她的辫子。 She kept on stroking her braids.

抚慰　fǔwèi　comfort; console; soothe: ～灾区人民 console the people in afflicted areas

抚恤　fǔxù　comfort and compensate a bereaved family

抚恤金　fǔxùjīn　pension for the disabled or for the family of the deceased

抚养　fǔyǎng　foster; raise; rear; bring up: 父母对子女有～教育的义务。 Parents have the duty to rear and educate their children. / 她一人把那三个孤儿～成人。 She brought up the three orphans all by herself.

抚养费　fǔyǎngfèi　payment for the upbringing of one's children (as after divorce)

抚育　fǔyù　foster; nurture; tend: ～烈士子女 bring up the children of revolutionary martyrs / 森林～ the tending of woods

抚掌　fǔzhǎng　clap one's hands

府　fǔ　① seat of government; government office: 政府 zhèngfǔ ② old government repository: 府库 fǔkù ③ official residence; mansion: 总统府 zǒngtǒngfǔ ④ honor. your home: 贵～ your home ⑤ prefecture (from the Tang to the Qing Dynasty): 济南～ the Prefecture of Jinan

府绸　fǔchóu　poplin: 山东～ Shandong pongee; shantung

府第　fǔdì　(also 府邸 fǔdǐ) mansion (of nobles, high officials, big landlords, etc.); mansion house

府库　fǔkù　government repository (in former times)

府上　fǔshang　honor. ① your home; your family: 改日再来～拜访。 I'll pay a visit to your home some other day. / ～都好吗? How is everybody in your family? ② your native place: 您～哪里? Where are you from?

府尹　fǔyǐn　the governor of a prefecture

府治　fǔzhì　the seat of a prefecture

斧 fǔ　axe; hatchet

斧柯 fǔkē *formal* ① the handle of a hatchet ② authority; political power; state power

斧头 fǔtóu　axe; hatchet

斧钺 fǔyuè　executioner's axe and battle-axe (used in ancient China)—capital punishment

斧凿 fǔzáo ① hatchet and chisel ② conscious artistry (in literary works)

斧凿痕 fǔzáohén *formal* marks of hatchet and chisel —traces of conscious artistry: 不露～ (of literary works) be free from traces of conscious artistry; be natural and spontaneous

斧正 fǔzhèng (also 斧政 fǔzhèng) *pol.* (please) make corrections

斧锧 fǔzhì　executioner's block and cleaver (used in ancient China)

斧子 fǔzi　axe; hatchet

斧足类 fǔzúlèi *zool.* pelecypoda (comprising oysters, clams, scallops, etc.)

拊 fǔ *formal* clap: ～手 clap hands

拊膺 fǔyīng *formal* beat one's chest (in distress): ～长叹 beat one's chest and heave a deep sigh of grief

拊掌 fǔzhǎng *formal* clap hands: ～大笑 clap hands and laugh heartily

釜 fǔ　a kind of cauldron used in ancient China

釜底抽薪 fǔ dǐ chōu xīn　take away the firewood from under the cauldron—take drastic measures to deal with an emergency

釜底游鱼 fǔ dǐ yóuyú　a fish swimming in the bottom of a cauldron—a person whose fate is sealed

俯 fǔ ① bow (one's head): 俯视 fǔshì ② *pol. old* (used in official documents or letters) condescend to: ～允 condescend to give permission / ～察 deign to examine

俯冲 fǔchōng *aviation* dive: ～轰炸 dive-bomb

俯冲角 fǔchōngjiǎo　dive angle

俯伏 fǔfú　lie prostrate; lie prone

俯角 fǔjiǎo *surveying and drawing* angle of depression

俯就 fǔjiù ① *pol.* condescend to accept (a job) ② adapt oneself to; make the best of; make do with

俯瞰 fǔkàn　look down at; overlook: 从飞机上～海面 look down at the sea from a plane

俯瞰摄影 fǔkànshèyǐng *photog.* crane shot; boom shot

俯临 fǔlín　look out on: 岩洞～着波光闪烁的河流。The cavern looks out on a shimmering river.

俯念 fǔniàn *pol.* condescend to consider (said to one's superior)

俯拍 fǔpāi　take a crane (or boom) shot

俯摄 fǔshè　short for 俯瞰摄影 fǔkànshèyǐng

俯身 fǔshēn　bend over; bend down: 她～亲亲睡在摇篮里的孩子。She bent down to kiss the baby in the crib.

俯拾即是 fǔ shí jí shì　be found everywhere; be extremely common: 这类事例～。Such instances are extremely common.

俯视 fǔshì　look down at; overlook: 站在山上～蜿蜒的公路 stand on the top of the hill looking down at the winding highway below

俯视图 fǔshìtú　vertical view

俯首 fǔshǒu　bow one's head (in submission): ～就范 meekly submit; surrender without a struggle

俯首甘为孺子牛 fǔshǒu gān wéi rúzǐ niú　head bowed, like a willing ox I serve the children ——see also 横眉冷对千夫指, 俯首甘为孺子牛 héngméi lěng duì qiānfū zhǐ, fǔshǒu gān wéi rúzǐ niú

俯首帖耳 fǔshǒu-tiē'ěr　be docile and obedient; be all obedience; be servile: 我知道这是他拉拢我，好让我～地为他效劳。I knew he was trying to wheedle me into being at his beck and call.

俯首听命 fǔshǒu tīngmìng　bow down to obey submissively; be at sb.'s beck and call

俯卧 fǔwò　lie prostrate; lie face down (on the ground)

俯卧撑 fǔwòchēng *sports* push-up

俯仰 fǔ-yǎng *formal* a bending or lifting of the head—a simple move or action: 随人～ be at sb.'s beck and call

俯仰角 fǔyǎngjiǎo *aviation* angle of pitch

俯仰无愧 fǔ-yǎng wúkuì　have done nothing to be ashamed of

俯仰由人 fǔ-yǎng yóu rén　be at others' beck and call

俯仰运动 fǔ-yǎng yùndòng *mech.* pitching movement

俯仰之间 fǔ-yǎng zhījiān　in the twinkling of an eye; in an instant; in a flash

脯 fǔ ① dried meat: 鹿～ dried venison ② sun-dried candied fruit; preserved fruit: 桃脯 táofǔ——see also pú

辅 fǔ　assist; complement; supplement: 自力更生为主，争取外援为～ rely mainly on one's own efforts while making external assistance subsidiary

辅币 fǔbì　fractional currency (or money): 硬～ subsidiary coin; minor coin

辅弼 fǔbì *formal* assist a ruler in governing a country

辅车相依 fǔ-chē xiāngyī　as dependent on each other as the jowls and the jawbone; as close as the jowls and the jaws

辅导 fǔdǎo　give guidance in study or training; coach: 学习这篇文章，你给我们～～好不好? Could you give us some guidance in studying this article? / ～孩子们练武术 coach the children in *wushu* exercises / 个别～ individual coaching (or tutorial) / ～报告 guidance lecture (supplementary lecture on background, study method, etc.) / ～材料 guidance material

辅导员 fǔdǎoyuán　(political and ideological) assistant; instructor: 政治～ political assistant / 理论～ instructor in political theory

辅课 fǔkè　subsidiary course

辅料 fǔliào　subsidiary material; supplementary material

辅音 fǔyīn *phonet.* consonant

辅助 fǔzhù ① assist: 多加～ assist (sb.) as much as possible ② supplementary; auxiliary; subsidiary: ～劳动 auxiliary labour (or jobs) / ～仪器 supplementary instruments

辅助机构 fǔzhù jīgòu　auxiliary body

辅助舰船 fǔzhù jiànchuán　auxiliary vessels

辅助人员 fǔzhù rényuán　auxiliary staff members

辅助授粉 fǔzhù shòufěn *agric.* supplementary pollination

辅佐 fǔzuǒ (also 辅翼 fǔyì) *formal* assist a ruler in governing a country

腑 fǔ　see 脏腑 zàngfǔ

腐 fǔ ① rotten; putrid; stale; corroded: ～肉 rotten meat ② tofu; beancurd

腐败 fǔbài ① rotten; putrid; decayed: ～的食物 putrid food / 油漆涂在木材上，可以防止～。Paint is put on wood as a protection against rotting. ② corrupt; rotten: ～无能 corrupt and incompetent / 消除～现象 put an end to corrupt dealings / 政治～ political corruption

腐臭 fǔchòu　emitting a smell of decay; decaying and stinking; smelly

腐恶　fǔ'è　corrupt and evil: ～势力 evil influences / 惩～ chastise the corrupt and evil

腐化　fǔhuà　① degenerate; become corrupt, dissolute or depraved: ～生活 lead a dissolute (or dissipated) life ② rot; decay; decompose

腐化堕落　fǔhuà duòluò　degenerate and decadent; leading a dissolute (or dissipated) life

腐化分子　fǔhuà fènzǐ　degenerate; a depraved person

腐烂　fǔlàn　① decompose; become putrid (or rotten): 一大批水果～了。A large supply of fruit rotted. / ～的树叶是好肥料。Decomposed leaves make good fertilizer. ② corrupt; rotten

腐泥煤　fǔnímái　sapropelic coal

腐儒　fǔrú　pedantic scholar; pedant

腐乳　fǔrǔ　fermented tofu (or beancurd)

腐生　fǔshēng　biol. living on nonliving organic matter; saprophytic: ～细菌 saprophytic bacteria / ～植物 saprophyte

腐蚀　fǔshí　① chem. corrode; etch ② corrupt; corrode: 警惕资产阶级思想的～ be on guard against the corrosive influence of bourgeois ideas / ～性 corrosiveness

腐蚀版　fǔshíbǎn　print. etched plate

腐蚀机　fǔshíjī　print. etching machine

腐蚀剂　fǔshíjì　chem. corrosive; corrodent

腐熟　fǔshú　agric. (of compost, etc.) become thoroughly decomposed

腐刑　fǔxíng　another name for 宫刑 gōngxíng

腐朽　fǔxiǔ　① rotten; decayed: 这些木材已经～了。The timber has rotted. ② decadent; degenerate: ～庸俗的作风 decadent and philistine ways / 封建主义～思想 decadent feudal ideology

腐殖煤　fǔzhímái　humic coal

腐殖酸　fǔzhísuān　agric. humic acid: ～类肥料 humic acid fertilizers

腐殖土　fǔzhítǔ　agric. humus soil

腐殖质　fǔzhízhì　humus

腐竹　fǔzhú　dried rolls of bean milk cream

簠　fǔ　archaeol. a square grain receptacle used at sacrificial ceremonies in ancient China

黼　fǔ　an embroidered pattern of black and white on ancient official robes

fù

父　fù　① father: ～与子 father and son ② male relative of a senior generation: 伯父 bófù / 祖父 zǔfù ——see also fǔ

父辈　fùbèi　people of father's generation

父本　fùběn　bot. male parent: ～植株 paternal plant

父党　fùdǎng　father's kinsfolk

父老　fùlǎo　elders (of a country or district): ～兄弟 elders and brethren

父母　fùmǔ　father and mother; parents

父母官　fùmǔguān　father-mother official (formerly, a popular term for a county magistrate 知县)

父母之命，媒妁之言　fùmǔ zhī mìng, méishuò zhī yán　the command of parents and the good offices of a go-between—(in former times) the proper way of contracting a marriage

父亲　fùqin　father

父权制　fùquánzhì　patriarchy

父系　fùxì　① paternal: ～亲属 paternal relatives ② patrilineal: ～家族制度 patrilineal family system / ～氏族公社 patrilineal clan commune

父兄　fùxiōng　① father and elder brothers ② head of a family

父执　fùzhí　formal father's friends

父子　fùzǐ　father and son: 他们家～四人都是教师。The father and his three sons are all schoolteachers.

讣　fù　① announce sb.'s death ② obituary

讣告　fùgào　① announce sb.'s death ② obituary

讣闻　fùwén　(also 讣文 fùwén) obituary

付[1]　fù　① hand (or turn) over to; commit to: ～表决 put to the vote; take a vote on / ～诸实施 put into effect ② pay: ～房租 pay rent (for a house, flat or room) / ～税 pay taxes / 票钱已经～了。I've paid for the tickets.

付[2]　fù　same as 副[2] fù

付丙　fùbǐng　(also 付丙丁 fùbǐngdīng) formal burn (a letter, etc.)

付出　fùchū　pay; expend: ～现款 pay in cash / ～代价 pay a price / 为人类解放事业不惜～自己的生命 be ready to give one's life for the emancipation of mankind / ～辛勤的劳动 put in a lot of hard work

付方　fùfāng　bookkeeping credit side; credit

付刊　fùkān　send to the press; put into print

付款　fùkuǎn　pay a sum of money: 货到～ cash on delivery (C.O.D.) / 凭单～ cash against documents / ～办法 methods of payment

付款凭证　fùkuǎn píngzhèng　payment voucher

付款人　fùkuǎnrén　payer; drawee

付排　fùpái　print. send to the compositor

付讫　fùqì　(of a bill) paid

付清　fùqīng　pay in full; pay off; clear (a bill): 一次～ pay off in one lump sum

付托　fùtuō　put sth. in sb.'s charge; entrust: ～得人 have entrusted the matter to the right person / ～重任 charge sb. with a heavy responsibility / 他把家产～给他的好友照管。He entrusted his best friend with the care of his property.

付息　fùxī　pay interest

付现　fùxiàn　pay in cash

付型　fùxíng　print. make paper moulds (or paper matrices)

付印　fùyìn　① send to the press ② turn over to the printing shop (after proofreading)

付邮　fùyóu　send by post; take to the post; post; mail: 贺年片本周内必须全部～。All the New Year cards must be posted off this week.

付帐　fùzhàng　pay a bill: 我付过帐了。I've already paid the bill.

付之一炬　fù zhī yī jù　commit to the flames

付之一笑　fù zhī yī xiào　dismiss with a laugh

付诸东流　fù zhū dōngliú　(also 付之东流 fù zhī dōngliú, 付之流水 fù zhī liúshuǐ) thrown into the eastward flowing stream—all one's efforts wasted; irrevocably lost

付梓　fùzǐ　formal send to the press; put into print

负　fù　① formal carry on the back or shoulder: ～薪 carry firewood on one's back ② shoulder; bear: 身～重任 shoulder an important task / ～责任 assume the responsibility ③ have at one's back; rely on: ～险固守 put up a stubborn defence by relying on one's strategic position ④ suffer: 负伤 fùshāng ⑤ enjoy: 久～盛名 have long enjoyed a good reputation ⑥ owe: 负债 fùzhài ⑦ fail in one's duty, obligation, etc.; betray: 负约 fùyuē ⑧ lose (a battle, game, etc.); be defeated: 一比二—于对方 lose the match 1:2 / 该队以两胜一一的成绩取得小组第二名。The team finished second in its group with two wins and one loss. ⑨ math. less

than zero; minus; negative: 〜乘〜得正。A negative number multiplied by another negative number makes the product positive. / 〜一点五 minus one point five (—1.5) ⑩ *elec.*　negative: 负极 fùjí

负戴 fùdài *formal*　carry (a load) on the back or on the head—do heavy manual labour

负担 fùdān ① bear (a burden); shoulder: 旅费由东道国〜。All the travelling expenses will be borne by the host country. ② burden; load; encumbrance: 财政〜 financial burden / 家庭〜 family burden (esp. financial) / 工作〜 workload / 思想〜 a load on one's mind; mental burden / 减轻学生〜 lighten the students' load / 解除精神〜 free one's mind of encumbrances

负电 fùdiàn　negative electricity

负电荷 fùdiànhè　negative (electric) charge

负电极 fùdiànjí　negative electrode; cathode

负电子 fùdiànzǐ　electron; negatron

负号 fùhào *math.*　negative sign

负荷 fùhè ① *formal*　carry on one's back and shoulder; bear; shoulder: 〜重任 shoulder important responsibilities ② load (that a person or machine is expected to perform); work load: 满〜 full-load / 超〜 overload

负极 fùjí *elec.*　negative pole

负笈 fùjí *formal*　carry a case of books—leave home to study: 〜从师 leave home to study under a master / 〜游学 pursue one's studies away from home

负加速度 fùjiāsùdù *phys.*　negative acceleration

负荆请罪 fùjīng qǐngzuì　proffer a birch and ask for a flogging—offer a humble apology

负疚 fùjiù *formal*　feel apologetic; have a guilty conscience

负累 fùlěi ① burden; load; encumbrance: 他家人口多，〜大。He had a large family, which proved to be a heavy burden. ② *old*　implicate; involve

负离子 fùlízǐ *phys.*　anion

负片 fùpiàn *photog.*　negative

负气 fùqì　do sth. in a fit of pique: 〜而去 leave in a fit of pique

负情 fùqíng　forsake one's love; be unfaithful in love

负伤 fùshāng　be wounded; be injured: 负重伤 be badly wounded / 光荣〜 be wounded in action

负手 fùshǒu　with one's hands clasped behind one's back: 〜散步 stroll along with one's hands clasped behind one's back

负数 fùshù *math.*　negative number

负像 fùxiàng *phys.*　negative image

负心 fùxīn　ungrateful (esp. in love); untrue; heartless

负隅顽抗 fùyú wánkàng　(of an enemy or a robber) fight stubbornly with one's back to the wall; put up a desperate struggle

负约 fùyuē ① break a promise; go back on one's word ② fail to keep an appointment

负载 fùzài *elec. mech.*　load: 高峰〜 peak load / 工作〜 operating load / 调整〜 load regulation

负责 fùzé ① be responsible for; be in charge of: 他〜保卫工作。He is in charge of security affairs. / 本着对工作〜的精神 motivated by a desire to do one's job well / 向人民〜 hold oneself responsible to the people / 由此产生的一切后果由你方〜。Your side will be held responsible for all the consequences arising therefrom. ② conscientious: 她对工作很〜。She is very conscientious in her work.

负责干部 fùzé gànbù　cadre in a responsible position; responsible cadre; cadre in charge

负责人 fùzérén　person in charge; leading cadre

负债 fùzhài ① be in debt; incur debts: 她〜从来不还。She never repays her debts. / 他负了上千元的债。His debts amount to nearly a thousand *yuan*. ② liabilities: 资产与〜 assets and liabilities

负债累累 fùzhài lěilěi　be heavily in debt; be up to one's ears in debt

负重 fùzhòng ① carry a heavy load on one's back ② shoulder a heavy task

负重致远 fùzhòng zhìyuǎn　bear a heavy burden and go a long way—shoulder heavy responsibilities

负罪 fùzuì *formal*　bear the blame

妇 (婦)

fù ① woman: 妇孺 fùrú ② married woman: 少妇 shàofù ③ wife: 夫妇 fūfù

妇产科 fùchǎnkē　(department of) gynaecology and obstetrics

妇产医院 fùchǎn yīyuàn　a hospital for gynaecology and obstetrics

妇道 fùdào　female virtues

妇道 fùdao　women; womenfolk

妇道人家 fùdao rénjiā *derog.*　women; womenfolk

妇姑勃谿 fù-gū bóxī　squabbles between mother-in-law and daughter-in-law; family squabbles; petty squabbles

妇科 fùkē　(department of) gynaecology

妇科医生 fùkē yīshēng　gynaecologist

妇联 fùlián　short for 妇女联合会 fùnǚ liánhéhuì

妇女 fùnǚ　woman: 〜队长 woman leader (in charge of women's affairs in a production team)

妇女病 fùnǚbìng　gynaecological (*or* women's) disease

妇女节 Fùnǚjié　short for 国际劳动妇女节 Guójì Láodòng Fùnǚjié

妇女联合会 fùnǚ liánhéhuì　the Women's Federation: 全国〜 the All-China Women's Federation

妇人 fùrén　married woman

妇孺 fùrú *formal*　women and children: 〜皆知 known even to women and children

妇婴 fù-yīng　women and infants; mothers and babies: 〜卫生 maternity and infant hygiene

妇幼 fù-yòu　women and children: 〜保健站 health centre for women and children; maternity and child-care centre / 〜卫生 maternity and child hygiene

附 (坿)

fù ① add; attach; enclose: 〜上一笔 add a word or two (in a letter, etc.) / 〜表三张 with three lists or charts attached / 〜寄照片四张，希查收。Please find enclosed four snapshots. ② get close to; be near: 〜在耳边低声说话 whisper in sb.'s ear ③ depend on; rely on; comply with: 附议 fùyì / 附骥 fùjì

附笔 fùbǐ　additional remarks (in a letter, document, etc.): 内人〜问好。I'd like to add that my wife asked to be remembered to you.

附带 fùdài ① *adv.*　in passing: 〜说一下 mention in passing; by the way; incidentally ② attach: 我们提供的援助不〜任何条件。The aid we provide has no strings attached. ③ subsidiary; supplementary: 从事〜劳动 do supplementary labour

附点 fùdiǎn *mus.*　dot: 〜音符 dotted note

附耳 fù'ěr　move close to sb.'s ear: 〜低语 whisper in sb.'s ear / 他们俩〜谈了几句。They whispered a few words to each other.

附凤攀龙 fùfèng-pānlóng　same as 攀龙附凤 pānlóng-fùfèng

附睾 fùgāo *physiol.*　epididymis

附睾炎 fùgāoyán *med.*　epididymitis

附和 fùhè　echo; chime in with: 〜别人的意见 echo other people's views

附会 fùhuì　draw wrong conclusions by false analogy; strain one's interpretation

附骥 fùjì　(also 附骥尾 fùjìwěi) *pol.*　(I am) merely following the lead of a great man

附加 fùjiā ① add; attach: 文件后面〜两项说明。The document has two explanatory notes attached to it. ② additional; attached; appended

附加费　fùjiāfèi　extra charge; surcharge

附加税　fùjiāshuì　surtax; additional tax; supertax

附加条款　fùjiā tiáokuǎn　additional article; memorandum clause

附加文件　fùjiā wénjiàn　*diplomacy* appended document

附加议定书　fùjiā yìdìngshū　*diplomacy* additional protocol

附件　fùjiàn　① appendix; annex: 作为调查报告的～ as an appendix to the investigation report ② enclosure ③ *mech.* accessories; attachment: 车床～ lathe accessories / 铲工～ backing-off attachment

附近　fùjìn　① nearby; neighbouring: ～地区 nearby regions / ～的城市 neighbouring (*or* adjacent) towns ② in the vicinity of; close to: 住在工厂～ live close to the factory / ～有没有邮局? Is there a post office near here? / 就在～，几分钟就可走到。It's only a few minutes' walk from here.

附丽　fùlì　*formal*　depend on; attach oneself to

附录　fùlù　appendix (to a book): 词典的十二个～ the twelve appendices to the dictionary

附上　fùshàng　be enclosed herewith: 随信～商品目录一份。A catalogue of commodities is enclosed herewith. / ～样稿一份，请查收。Enclosed please find a set of sample sheets.

附设　fùshè　have as an attached institution: 这个学院～一所中学。There is a middle school attached to the institute. / 这个商店～了一个早晚服务部。This store has set up an after-hours department.

附身　fùshēn　(of an evil spirit, demon, etc.) possess a person: 巫婆装作妖魔～。The sorceress acted as if possessed by an evil spirit.

附生　fùshēng　(of a plant) grow nonparasitically upon another plant

附生兰　fùshēnglán　epiphytic orchid; epidendrum

附生植物　fùshēng zhíwù　*bot.*　epiphyte; air plant

附属　fùshǔ　subsidiary; auxiliary; attached; affiliated: 医学院～医院 a hospital attached to a medical college / ～机构 subsidiary body

附属国　fùshǔguó　dependency

附属品　fùshǔpǐn　accessory; appendage

附属小学　fùshǔ xiǎoxué　a primary school attached to a middle school; attached primary school

附属中学　fùshǔ zhōngxué　a middle school attached to a college or university; attached middle school

附图　fùtú　attached map or drawing; figure: 见～一。See Figure 1.

附小　fùxiǎo　short for 附属小学 fùshǔ xiǎoxué

附言　fùyán　postscript (P. S.)

附议　fùyì　second a motion; support a proposal: 我～! I second the motion!

附庸　fùyōng　① dependency; vassal ② appendage: 语言文字学在清代还只是经学的～。During the Qing Dynasty, philology was a mere handmaid of classical studies.

附庸风雅　fùyōng fēngyǎ　(of landlords, merchants, etc.) mingle with men of letters and pose as a lover of culture

附则　fùzé　supplementary articles (appended to a treaty, decree, etc.)

附肢　fùzhī　*zool.*　appendage

附中　fùzhōng　short for 附属中学 fùshǔ zhōngxué

附注　fùzhù　notes appended to a book, etc.; annotations

附赘悬疣　fùzhuì-xuányóu　swelling tumours and protruding wens—superfluities

附着　fùzhuó　adhere to; stick to: 地衣～在岩石、树干上。Lichens adhere to rocks and tree trunks. / 这种病菌～在病人使用过的东西上。This germ is found on the

things used by the patients.

附着力　fùzhuólì　*phys.*　adhesive force; adhesion

附子　fùzǐ　*Chin. med.*　monkshood

阜　fù　*formal*　① mound ② abundant: 物阜民丰 wùfù-mínfēng

服　fù　*m.*　(for Chinese medicine) dose: 一～中药 a dose of Chinese medicine ——see also fú

咐　fù　see 吩咐 fēn·fù; 嘱咐 zhǔ·fù

驸　fù　a horse hitched up by the side of the shaft-horse (to assist the pulling of a vehicle)

驸马　fùmǎ　husband of an emperor's daughter or sister; emperor's son-in-law or brother-in-law

洑　fù　swim: ～过河去 swim across the river ——see also fú

洑水　fùshuǐ　swim

赴　fù　① go to; attend: 离京～美 leave Beijing for U. S. A. ② same as 讣 fù

赴敌　fùdí　*formal*　go to meet the enemy

赴会　fùhuì　attend a meeting; keep an appointment (to meet sb.)

赴难　fùnàn　go to the aid of one's country; go to help save the country from danger

赴任　fùrèn　go to one's post; be on the way to one's post

赴汤蹈火　fùtāng-dǎohuǒ　go through fire and water; defy all difficulties and dangers

赴宴　fùyàn　go to a feast; attend a banquet

赴约　fùyuē　keep an appointment

复¹(複)　fù　①. duplicate: 复写 fùxiě ② compound; complex: ～光谱 complex spectrum

复²(復)　fù　① turn round; turn over: 反复无常 fǎnfù wúcháng ② reply; answer: 请即电～。Cable reply immediately.

复³(復)　fù　① recover; resume: 复职 fùzhí / 康复 kāngfù ② revenge: 报复 bàofù

复⁴(復)　fù　*adv.*　again: 复查 fùchá / 复活 fùhuó

复摆　fùbǎi　*phys.*　compound pendulum

复背斜　fùbèixié　*geol.*　anticlinorium

复本　fùběn　duplicate

复本位制　fùběnwèizhì　*econ.*　bimetallism

复辟　fùbì　restore a dethroned monarch or the old order: 1814年法国波旁王朝在法国。The Bourbons were restored to power in France in 1814. / ～活动 restorationist activities (*or* manoeuvres)

复波　fùbō　*phys.*　complex wave

复查　fùchá　check; reexamine: 一个月后到医院～。Come back to the hospital for a check in a month's time.

复仇　fùchóu　revenge; avenge: ～心理 vindictiveness; a desire for revenge / 他发誓要～。He vowed to avenge himself.

复仇主义　fùchóuzhǔyì　revanchism

复聪　fùcōng　recover lost hearing

复电　fùdiàn　① send a telegram in reply: 我已给家里复了电。I've already telegraphed my family in reply. ② a telegram in reply: ～已发。A telegram has been sent in reply to the one received.

复调音乐　fùdiào yīnyuè　*mus.*　polyphony

复发 fùfā　have a relapse; recur: 旧病～ have an attack of an old illness; have a relapse / 他的关节炎～了。He's suffering from arthritis again.

复返 fùfǎn　return: 一天之内去而～ make a one-day trip to the place and back; make a round trip on the same day

复方 fùfāng　① Chin. med. a prescription composed of two or more recipes of herbal medicines ② med. medicine made of two or more ingredients; compound: ～阿斯匹林 aspirin compound (APC) / ～甘草合剂 brown mixture

复分解反应 fùfēnjiěfǎnyìng　chem. double decomposition reaction

复辅音 fùfǔyīn　phonet. consonant cluster

复根 fùgēn　chem. compound radical

复工 fùgōng　return to work (after a strike or layoff)

复古 fùgǔ　restore ancient ways; return to the ancients

复古主义 fùgǔzhǔyì　the doctrine of "back to the ancients"

复果 fùguǒ　bot. multiple fruit; compound fruit; collective fruit

复合 fùhé　compound; complex; composite

复合词 fùhécí　gram. compound word; compound

复合电路 fùhé diànlù　compound circuit

复合肥料 fùhé féiliào　compound fertilizer

复合句 fùhéjù　gram. compound or complex sentence

复合量词 fùhé liàngcí　Chin. gram. compound classifier

复合元音 fùhé yuányīn　phonet. diphthong (as ei, uo) or triphthong (as uai, iao)

复核 fùhé　① check: 把数字～一下 check the figures ② leg. (of the Supreme People's Court) review a case in which a death sentence has been passed by a lower court

复会 fùhuì　resume a session (or sitting)

复婚 fùhūn　(of a divorced couple) remarry each other

复活 fùhuó　① come back to life; revive: 防止法西斯主义～ guard against the revival of fascism ② Christianity Resurrection

复活节 Fùhuójié　Christianity Easter

复激 fùjī　elec. compound excitation: ～发电机 compound generator

复交 fùjiāo　① resume (once broken) relations ② diplomacy reestablish (or resume) diplomatic relations

复旧 fùjiù　restore (or revive) old ways; return to the past

复句 fùjù　Chin. gram. a sentence of two or more clauses

复卷机 fùjuǎnjī　papermaking rewinding machine; rewinder

复刊 fùkān　(of magazines or newspapers) resume publication

复课 fùkè　resume classes

复理层 fùlǐcéng　geol. flysch

复利 fùlì　econ. compound interest

复明 fùmíng　recover lost eyesight

复命 fùmìng　report back after carrying out an order

复赛 fùsài　sports intermediary heat; semi-finals

复审 fùshěn　① reexamine ② leg. review a case

复生 fùshēng　come back to life

复式 fùshì　bookkeeping double entry

复式车床 fùshì chēchuáng　mech. double lathe

复试 fùshì　reexamination; final examination

复述 fùshù　① repeat: ～命令 repeat an order ② retell (in language learning): 把故事～一遍 retell a story

复数 fùshù　① gram. plural (number) ② math. complex number

复丝 fùsī　chem. fibre multifilament

复苏 fùsū　① come back to life or consciousness; resuscitate ② recovery; resurgence: 经济～ economic resurgence

复位 fùwèi　① med. reduce ② be restored to the throne

复位术 fùwèishù　med. reduction

复胃 fùwèi　complex stomach (of a ruminant); ruminant stomach

复习 fùxí　review; revise: ～功课 review (or revise) lessons

复线 fùxiàn　transportation multiple track

复现 fùxiàn　reappear: 往事一幕幕在脑海中～。Scene after scene of past events reappeared in my mind.

复向斜 fùxiàngxié　geol. synclinorium

复写 fùxiě　make carbon copies; duplicate

复写纸 fùxiězhǐ　carbon paper

复信 fùxìn　① write a letter in reply; reply: 我给他复了三封信，他说都没收到。He says he has received none of the three letters I wrote back to him. ② a letter in reply

复兴 fùxīng　revive; rejuvenate: 民族～ national rejuvenation / ～国家 rejuvenate one's country

复姓 fùxìng　compound surname; two-character surname: 司马在汉族姓氏里是～。司马 (Sīmǎ) is a compound surname among Chinese surnames.

复学 fùxué　go back to school (after prolonged absence for health reasons, etc.); resume one's interrupted studies

复盐 fùyán　chem. double salt

复眼 fùyǎn　zool. compound eye (of insects)

复业 fùyè　① take up one's old trade again ② reopen or restart business

复叶 fùyè　bot. compound leaf

复议 fùyì　reconsider (a decision)

复音 fùyīn　phys. complex tone

复音词 fùyīncí　disyllabic or polysyllabic word

复印 fùyìn　xerox; duplicate: ～文件 xerox (or duplicate) documents

复印机 fùyìnjī　xerox (machine); duplicator

复印纸 fùyìnzhǐ　duplicating paper

复员 fùyuán　① return to peacetime conditions ② (of servicemen) be demobilized: 小王是一九八二年从部队～的。Xiao Wang was demobilized from the army in 1982.

复员费 fùyuánfèi　demobilization pay

复员军人 fùyuán jūnrén　a demobilized serviceman; an ex-serviceman

复员令 fùyuánlìng　demobilization order

复原 fùyuán　① (also 复元 fùyuán) recover from an illness; be restored to health: 他身体已经～了。He's already recovered. ② be restored; be rehabilitated: ～后的金缕玉衣充分显示出中国古代劳动人民的精湛工艺。The restored jade burial suit fully reveals the consummate skill of the labouring people of ancient China. / 这座在战争中惨遭破坏的城市已经～。The city, which was destroyed in the war, has been restored.

复圆 fùyuán　astron. fourth contact of a total eclipse; last contact of a partial eclipse; end of an eclipse

复杂 fùzá　complicated; complex: 情况～。The situation is complicated. / 故事情节～。The story is very complicated. / ～的心情 mixed feelings / 使问题～化 make things complicated; complicate matters / 低估问题的～性 underestimate the complexity of the problem

复照 fùzhào　diplomacy a note in reply

复诊 fùzhěn　further consultation (with a doctor); subsequent visit

复职 fùzhí　resume one's post; be reinstated

复制 fùzhì　duplicate; reproduce; make a copy of: ～模型 reconstructed model

复制片 fùzhìpiàn duplicated film; copy of a film

复制品 fùzhìpǐn replica; reproduction

复种 fùzhòng *agric.* multiple cropping

复种面积 fùzhòng miànjī multiple cropping area

复种指数 fùzhòng zhǐshù multiple crop index

复壮 fùzhuàng *agric.* rejuvenation

副¹

fù ① deputy; assistant; vice-: ～主席 vice-chairman / ～总理 vice-premier / ～部长 vice-minister / ～领事 vice-consul / ～书记 deputy secretary / ～秘书长 deputy secretary-general / ～主任 deputy director / ～经理 deputy manager / ～主编 associate editor in chief / ～司令员 assistant commanding officer (*or* commandant) / (飞机) ～驾驶员 copilot ② assistant post; a person who takes an assistant post: 大副 dàfù / 二副 èrfù ③ auxiliary; subsidiary; secondary: ～泵 auxiliary pump ④ correspond to; fit: 名不副实 míng bù fù shí

副²

fù *m.* ① for a set of sth.: 一～手套 a pair of gloves ② for facial expression: 一～笑脸 a smiling face / 装出一～庄严的面孔 put on solemn looks; assume a solemn face

副本 fùběn duplicate; transcript; copy

副标题 fùbiāotí subheading; subtitle

副产品 fùchǎnpǐn (also 副产物 fùchǎnwù) by-product

副赤道带 fùchìdàodài *meteorol.* subequatorial belt

副词 fùcí ① *Chin. gram.* adverbial word, any of a class of words that are used mainly to modify a verb or an adjective ② *Eng. gram.* adverb

副歌 fùgē *mus.* refrain

副官 fùguān adjutant; aide-de-camp

副虹 fùhóng *meteorol.* secondary bow

副交感神经 fùjiāogǎnshénjīng *physiol.* parasympathetic nerve

副教授 fùjiàoshòu associate professor

副井 fùjǐng *min.* auxiliary shaft

副刊 fùkān supplement: 文学～ literary supplement

副品 fùpǐn substandard goods

副热带 fùrèdài another name for 亚热带 yàrèdài

副伤寒 fùshānghán *med.* paratyphoid (fever)

副神经 fùshénjīng *physiol.* accessory nerve

副食 fùshí non-staple food

副食品 fùshípǐn non-staple food (*or* foodstuffs): ～加工厂 non-staple food processing factory

副食商店 fùshí shāngdiàn grocer's; grocery

副室 fùshì *old* concubine

副手 fùshǒu assistant

副署 fùshǔ countersign

副题 fùtí subtitle; subheading

副研究员 fùyánjiūyuán associate research fellow

副业 fùyè sideline; side occupation: ～生产 sideline (*or* supplementary, subsidiary) production / 家庭～ household sideline production

副翼 fùyì *aviation* aileron

副油箱 fùyóuxiāng *aviation* ① auxiliary tank ② drop tank

副职 fùzhí the position of a deputy to the chief of an office, department, etc.

副轴 fùzhóu *mech.* countershaft; layshaft

副作用 fùzuòyòng ① side effect; by-effect: 麻醉药物的～ side effects from the use of anaesthetics / 这种新药已经发现有～。 The new drug was found to have harmful side effects. ② *mech.* secondary action

富

fù ① rich; wealthy; abundant: 他不是很～的。 He is not very rich. / ～日子当穷日子过。 Be thrifty even in days of abundance. / 村里多数人逐渐～起来了。 Most of the villagers are getting rich. ② resource; property: 财富 cáifù ③ be rich in: ～于养分 be rich in nutrition / ～于自我批评精神 be imbued with the spirit of self-criticism / ～于创造性 be highly creative ④ (Fù) a surname

富富有余 fùfù yǒuyú have enough and to spare

富贵 fùguì riches and honour; wealth and rank: ～人家 a rich and powerful family

富贵病 fùguìbìng a rich man's disease (i.e. one which calls for a long period of rest and an expensive diet)

富国强兵 fùguó-qiángbīng make one's country rich and build up its military might

富豪 fùháo rich and powerful people

富矿 fùkuàng *min.* rich ore; high-grade ore

富矿体 fùkuàngtǐ ore shoot

富丽堂皇 fùlì tánghuáng beautiful and imposing; in majestic splendour; sumptuous: ～的建筑 magnificent buildings

富农 fùnóng rich peasant

富强 fùqiáng (of a country) prosperous and strong: 使祖国更加繁荣～ make our country more prosperous and powerful

富饶 fùráo richly endowed; fertile; abundant: 美丽～的国家 a beautiful and richly endowed country / ～的土地 fertile land

富人 fùrén the rich; rich people

富实 fù·shí well-off; substantial

富士山 Fùshìshān Fujiyama

富庶 fùshù rich and populous

富岁 fùsuì *formal* a good year; a bumper harvest year

富态 fùtai *euph. dial.* portly; stout

富翁 fùwēng man of wealth; moneybags

富有 fùyǒu ① rich; wealthy: 他家非常～。 His family is very rich. ② be rich in; be full of: ～经验 be rich in experience; be very experienced / ～战斗性 be very militant / ～代表性 be typical / ～生命力 be full of vitality

富裕 fùyù prosperous; well-to-do; well-off: 日子过得挺～ lead a well-to-do life / 中国农民一天天～起来了。 Peasants in China are getting more prosperous day by day.

富裕中农 fùyù zhōngnóng well-to-do middle peasant

富余 fùyu have more than needed; have enough and to spare: 我们还～两张票。 We have two tickets to spare. / 你有～的钱吗? Have you any money to spare? / 粮食有～。 There is a surplus of grain.

富源 fùyuán natural resources

富足 fùzú plentiful; abundant; rich

赋¹

fù *formal* bestow; grant

赋²

fù *old* land tax

赋³

fù ① an intricate literary form combining elements of poetry and prose (much cultivated from Han times to the Six Dynasties period; variously translated as "rhyme prose," "poetic prose," "prose poem," "rhapsody," etc.; often transliterated as *fu*): 班固《两都～》 Ban Gu's "Rhapsody on Two Capitals" *or* "Two Capitals Rhapsody" / 陆机《文～》 Lu Ji's "*Fu* on Literature" / 苏轼《赤壁～》 Su Shi's "*Fu* on the Red Cliff" ② compose (verses): ～诗 compose verses / ～诗一首 compose a poem

赋格曲 fùgéqǔ *mus.* fugue

赋课 fùkè *formal* land tax, etc.; taxes

赋敛 fùliǎn *formal* levy taxes

赋税 fùshuì taxes

赋闲 fùxián be out of office; be out of employment

赋形剂 fùxíngjì *pharm.* excipient

赋性 fùxìng inborn nature: ～刚强 be strong by nature; be of an unyielding nature

赋役 fùyì taxes and corvée

赋有 fùyǒu be endowed with (qualities or characteristics): 劳动人民～忠厚质朴的性格. Working people are endowed with an honest, kindly nature.

赋予 fùyǔ entrust (an important task) to sb.: 实现四个现代化是历史～我们的使命. History has entrusted to us the task of realizing the four modernizations.

傅¹

fù ① teach; instruct ② teacher; instructor: 师傅 shīfu ③ (Fù) a surname

傅²

fù *arch.* lay on; apply: ～彩 lay on colours / ～粉 put powder on; powder (the face, etc.)

傅会 fùhuì same as 附会 fùhuì

傅科摆 fùkēbǎi Foucault pendulum

腹

fù ① belly (of the body); abdomen; stomach ② belly (of a bottle, etc.): 一个～大颈细的瓶子 a narrow-necked, big-bellied bottle

腹背受敌 fù-bèi shòu dí be attacked front and rear

腹地 fùdì hinterland

腹诽 fùfěi (also 腹非 fùfēi) *formal* unspoken criticism

腹稿 fùgǎo a draft worked out in one's mind: 打～ work out a draft in one's mind

腹股沟 fùgǔgōu *physiol.* groin

腹膜 fùmó *physiol.* peritoneum

腹膜炎 fùmóyán *med.* peritonitis

腹鳍 fùqí *zool.* ventral fin

腹腔 fùqiāng *physiol.* abdominal cavity

腹腔镜 fùqiāngjìng *med.* peritoneoscope

腹水 fùshuǐ *med.* ascites: 抽～ tap the abdomen

腹痛 fùtòng abdominal pain

腹泻 fùxiè diarrhoea

腹心 fùxīn ① vital organs; key parts: 腹心之患 fùxīn zhī huàn ② trusted subordinate; reliable agent ③ true thoughts and feelings: 敢布～ venture to air some of my views

腹心之患 fùxīn zhī huàn disease in one's vital organs —danger from within; serious hidden trouble

腹胀 fùzhàng abdominal distension

腹足 fùzú *zool.* abdominal leg; proleg

腹足类 fùzúlèi *zool.* gastropod

缚

fù tie up; bind fast: 手脚都被～住 have one's hands and feet tied up

鲋

fù crucian carp ——see also 涸辙之鲋 hé zhé zhī fù

赙

fù *formal* present a gift (of money, etc.) to a bereaved family

赙金 fùjīn *formal* money presented to a bereaved family

赙仪 fùyí *formal* a gift to a bereaved family

赙赠 fùzèng *formal* present a gift to a bereaved family

蝮

fù see below

蝮蛇 fùshé Pallas pit viper

鳆

fù see below

鳆鱼 fùyú abalone

覆

fù ① *formal* cover: 种子播下后～土大约要十厘米厚. The sown seeds shall be covered with about 10cm. of soil. ② *formal* overturn; upset: ～舟 capsized boat ③ same as 复² fù

覆败 fùbài be utterly defeated

覆被 fùbèi cover: 森林～率 forest cover

覆巢无完卵 fù cháo wú wánluǎn when the nest is overturned no egg stays unbroken—when disaster befalls a family, etc., no member can escape unscathed

覆车之戒 fù chē zhī jiè a warning taken from the overturned cart ahead—a lesson drawn from another's mistake

覆盖 fùgài ① cover: 积雪～着地面. The ground is covered with snow. ② plant cover; vegetation

覆盖层 fùgàicéng *geol.* overburden

覆灭 fùmiè destruction; complete collapse

覆没 fùmò ① *formal* (of a ship) capsize and sink ② (of an army) be overwhelmed; be annihilated: 全军覆没 quánjūn fùmò ③ *formal* be occupied by the enemy: 中原～. The Central Plains were occupied by the enemy.

覆盆之冤 fù pén zhī yuān a wrong that can never be righted; irremediable wrong

覆盆子 fùpénzǐ *Chin. med.* Korean raspberry

覆水难收 fù shuǐ nán shōu spilt water can't be gathered up—what is done can't be undone

覆亡 fùwáng fall (of an empire, nation, etc.)

覆辙 fùzhé the track of an overturned cart: 重蹈覆辙 chóng dǎo fùzhé

馥

fù *formal* fragrance

馥馥 fùfù *formal* strongly fragrant; sweet-smelling

馥郁 fùyù *formal* strongly fragrant; sweet-scented; sweet-smelling: ～的花香 the sweet scent of flowers

G

gā

夹（夾） gā see below ——see also jiā; jiá

夹肢窝 gāzhiwō armpit

旮 gā see below

旮旯旯儿 gālalálár *dial.* every nook and cranny: ～都打扫干净了。Every nook and cranny has been swept clean.

旮旯儿 gālár *dial.* ① nook; corner: 墙～ a corner formed by two walls; corner ② out-of-the-way place: 山～ a mountain recess

伽 gā see below ——see also jiā; qié

伽马射线 gāmǎ shèxiàn *phys.* gamma ray

咖 gā see below ——see also kā

咖喱 gālí curry: ～牛肉 beef curry / ～粉 curry powder

嘎 gā *onom.* a loud, high-pitched sound: 汽车～的一声刹住了。The car screeched to a halt. ——see also gǎ

嘎巴 gābā *onom.* a cracking or snapping sound: 手杖～一声断成两截了。Crack! The stick broke in two.

嘎巴 gāba *dial.* ① form into a crust; crust: 瞧，浆糊都～在你袖子上了。Look, the paste has crusted on your sleeve. ② crust: 粥～儿 porridge crust

嘎嘣脆 gābēngcuì *inf.* ① (of food) crisp: 德州大枣享有盛名，咬一口～。Dezhou dates are famous for their crispness. ② (of voice) clear and brisk: 人们评价这位演员的唱腔特点是～。Everyone says the singer has a clear and brisk voice.

嘎嘎 gāgā *onom.* the quacking sound made by a duck; quack

嘎吱 gāzhī *onom.* (usu. reduplicated) the creaking sound of objects that are under great stress: 行李压得扁担～～直响。The shoulder pole creaked under the weight of the luggage.

gá

轧 gá *dial.* ① press hard against each other ② make friends: 轧朋友 gápéngyou ③ check: ～帐 check the accounts ——see also yà; zhá

轧朋友 gápéngyou *dial.* ① make friends with sb. ② go steady

轧姘头 gápīntou *dial.* live illicitly as husband and wife; cohabit; take a lover

钆 gá *chem.* gadolinium (Gd)

gǎ

嘎 gǎ *dial.* ① eccentric; bad-tempered ② naughty; mischievous ——see also gā

gà

尬 gà see 尴尬 gāngà

gāi

该[1] gāi ① ought to be; should be: 十五斤分三份，每份～五斤。When 15 *jin* is divided into three equal portions, each ought to be 5 *jin*. / 按岁数排，～老潘排第一。By seniority, first place goes to Lao Pan. ② be sb.'s turn, duty, or lot: 这回～我了吧? It's my turn now, isn't it? / 下一个～谁发言? Who's the next speaker? / 这个工作～老张来担任。This is a job for Lao Zhang to take on. / 你要是听了他的话，就～你倒霉。You're in for trouble if you've followed his advice. ③ (used alone) deserve the punishment; serve sb. right: ～! 谁叫他不守纪律。It serves him right; he shouldn't have broken the rules. / ～! 还得严加管教。He deserves it, and needs even stricter discipline. ④ must; should; ought to: 我～走了。I must be off now. / 我不～来。I shouldn't have come. / 昨天的会你不～不来。You should have come to yesterday's meeting. / ～做的一定要做。What needs to be done must be done. / ～有个长远打算。There ought to be a long-term plan. / 别人已经赶到前头去了，咱们～不～加把劲儿干? ——～! They've got ahead of us. Shouldn't we work harder? ——Yes, we should! / ～上班了。Time to go to work. ⑤ (no negative form; not to be used alone in answering a question) will probably; can be reasonably or naturally expected to: 他是昨天动的身，今天～到了。He started out yesterday, so he ought to get here today. / 不久又～冷了。It will soon be cold again. / 再不浇水，花儿都～蔫儿了。If we don't water the flowers soon, they'll wither. / 你女儿今年～高中毕业了吧? ——高中毕业了。Your daughter is finishing senior middle school this year? ——Yes, she is. / 这么粗枝大叶，～会给工作造成多大的损失! The work will suffer a lot from such carelessness! / 接到这封信，你～可以放心了吧? Surely this letter can set your mind at rest? ⑥ (used in exclamatory sentences): 等这些树木都长大成林，风景～(有)多美! When these trees grow into a forest, how beautiful the scenery will be! / 再过十年，这里～有多大的变化啊! Another ten years, and what great changes will have taken place here! / 要是水泵今天就运到，～多好哇! If only the pump could arrive today!

该[2]　gāi　owe (money or debt): 这钱是～你的。I owe you this money. / 我～他五元钱。I owe him five *yuan*. / 没带钱不要紧, 先～着吧。It doesn't matter if you haven't brought any money with you. You can have it on credit. / 这笔帐～了快一年了。The debt has been owed for almost a year.

该[3]　gāi　*formal* this; that; the said; the above-mentioned: ～厂 this (*or* the said) factory / ～校 that (*or* the above-mentioned) school / ～项工作 the job (*or* work) in question / ～同志工作一贯认真。The said comrade has always been conscientious in the performance of his duties. / ～地区交通非常便利。That area has excellent communications.

该[4]　gāi　same as 赅 gāi

该博　gāibó　same as 赅博 gāibó

该当　gāidāng　① deserve: ～何罪? What punishment do you think you deserve? ② should: 集体的事, 我们～尽力。It's for the collective and we should do our best.

该死　gāisǐ　*inf.* (used to show one's abomination or anger): ～的天气! What wretched weather! / 这牛又在吃麦子啦! Damn it! That cow's eating the wheat again! / ～的猫又叼去一条鱼! That damned cat stole a fish again! / ～! 我又忘了带钥匙了。Oh, no! I've forgotten my key again.

该应　gāiyīng　*dial.* should; ought to

该帐　gāizhàng　be in debt: 他在银行还该一笔帐呢。He still owes the bank a sum. / ～该多了, 就不好还了。If you run up your bills, you'll have difficulty paying them.

该着　gāizháo　decreed by fate; predestined: 排了半天队, 什么也没买着, ～我倒霉。I queued up all this time for nothing. Just my luck!

垓　gāi　*arch.* one hundred million

赅　gāi　*formal* ① complete; full: 言简意赅 yán-jiǎn-yìgāi ② include in; embrace: 举一赅百 jǔ yī gāi bǎi

赅博　gāibó　broad and profound; erudite: 学问～ erudite; learned

赅括　gāikuò　summarize; generalize; epitomize

gǎi

改　gǎi　① change; transform: 几年没来, 这儿完全～样了。I've been away for only a few years, but the place has completely changed. / ～洼地为稻田 transform lowlands into paddy fields ② alter; revise: ～灶节煤 make alterations in an oven so that it will burn less coal / 请把这条裤子～短一些。Please have this pair of trousers shortened. / 这个戏已经～了好多次了。The play has been revised many times. / 他写完这篇文章以后, 又～了～。After he finished writing the essay he made a few more changes in it. ③ correct; rectify; put right: ～作业 correct students' homework or papers / 有错误一定要～。Any mistakes you've made must be corrected. ④ (followed by a verb) switch over to (doing sth. else): ～种水稻 switch over to growing rice / ～乘五路公共汽车 change to a No. 5 bus / ～用良种 begin to use improved varieties / 他现在～踢左后卫。He's playing left-back now.

改版　gǎibǎn　*print.* correcting

改编　gǎibiān　① adapt; rearrange; revise: 这支歌已～成小提琴曲。The music of the song has been rearranged (*or* adapted) for the violin. / 经过～, 戏的主题更突出了。The theme of the play stands out even more clearly now that it's been revised. / 根据这本小说～的剧本 a stage version of the novel ② reorganize; redesignate: 把七个师～为六个师 reorganize seven divisions into six / 抗日战争时期红军～为八路军、新四军。During the War of Resistance Against Japan the Red Army was redesignated as the Eighth Route Army and the New Fourth Army.

改变　gǎibiàn　change; alter; transform: ～主意 change one's mind / 人们的精神面貌～了。People's spiritual complexion has changed. / 五年不见, 他的样子看来没有多大的～。It's been 5 years since I last saw him, but he hasn't changed much. / 历史发展的总趋势是不可～的。The general trend of history is unalterable. / 情况变了, 你那计划也该～～。The situation has changed, so you should make some changes in your plans.

改朝换代　gǎicháo-huàndài　change of dynasty or regime; dynastic changes

改窜　gǎicuàn　same as 窜改 cuàngǎi

改道　gǎidào　① change one's route: 他们决定～先去延安。They decided to change their route and go to Yan'an first. ② (of a river) change its course: 历史上, 黄河曾多次～。The Huanghe River has changed its course many times over the centuries.

改掉　gǎidiào　give up; drop: 睡懒觉的坏习惯我已经～了。I've given up the bad habit of getting up late.

改订　gǎidìng　reformulate; rewrite: ～规章制度 draw up new rules and regulations

改动　gǎidòng　change; alter; modify: 这篇文章我只～了一些词句。I just polished a few sentences in this essay. / 文字上作许少～ make a few changes in wording / 这学期的课程没有大的～。There are no big changes in this term's curriculum.

改恶从善　gǎi'è-cóngshàn　abandon evil and do good; turn over a new leaf; mend one's ways

改革　gǎigé　reform: ～经济管理体制 reform the economic management system / 工具～ improvement of tools

改观　gǎiguān　change the appearance (*or* face) of: 第二次世界大战后, 世界的面貌大大～了。The face of the world has changed greatly since the Second World War. / 这一胜利使战争形势为之～。This victory changed the complexion of the war. / 昔日荒山已经大为～。The barren hills of yesterday have changed considerably.

改过　gǎiguò　mend one's ways; correct one's mistakes: 勇于～ have the courage to correct one's mistakes

改过自新　gǎiguò zìxīn　correct one's errors and make a fresh start; mend one's ways; turn over a new leaf

改行　gǎiháng　change one's profession (*or* occupation, trade): 他原先在学校教书, 后来～当记者。He started off as a schoolteacher, but later left the professions and became a journalist.

改换　gǎihuàn　change over to; change: ～一套新的做法 change over to new ways; adopt a new approach / ～日期 change the date / ～名称 rename / 这句话不好懂, 最好～一个说法。This sentence is difficult to understand. You'd better try to put it another way.

改悔　gǎihuǐ　repent: 毫无～之意 show not the least sign of repentance; be absolutely unrepentant

改嫁　gǎijià　(of a woman) remarry: 丈夫死了以后, 她～了。She got remarried after her husband's death.

改建　gǎijiàn　reconstruct; rebuild: 把仓库～为厂房 remodel a storehouse for use as a workshop

改醮　gǎijiào　*old* (of a woman) remarry

改进　gǎijìn　improve; make better: ～工作作风 improve one's work style / 服务态度有很大的～。The service has improved a lot.

改口　gǎikǒu　withdraw or modify one's previous re-

mark; correct oneself: 他发现自己说错了，连忙～。He corrected himself as soon as he realized he'd made a mistake. / 他原来是那么说的，现在～了。That's what he said at first, but he's changed it now.

改良 gǎiliáng ① improve; ameliorate: ～土壤 improve (or ameliorate) the soil / ～家畜品种 improve the breed of domestic animals ② reform

改良主义 gǎiliángzhǔyì reformism: ～对旧制度主张修修补补，反对革命。Reformism aims at patching up the old system; it is opposed to revolution.

改判 gǎipàn *leg.* change the original sentence; commute; amend a judgment: 由死刑～无期徒刑 commute the death sentence to life imprisonment

改期 gǎiqī change the date (usu. to a later date); postpone: 会议～举行。The meeting has been put off. / 由于下大雨，足球赛不得不～。The soccer match had to be postponed because of heavy rain.

改任 gǎirèn change to another post: 他从上月起～车间主任。He has been at his new post as workshop superintendent since last month.

改日 gǎirì same as 改天 gǎitiān

改善 gǎishàn improve; ameliorate: ～劳动条件 improve working conditions / ～人民的生活 improve the people's livelihood / 今天我们～生活。We have something especially good to eat today. / 两国关系有所～。The relations between the two countries have shown some improvement.

改天 gǎitiān some other day; another day: 咱们～再商量吧。Let's talk it over another day. / ～见! See you later.

改天换地 gǎitiān-huàndì transform heaven and earth; change the world: 以～的气概 in a spirit of changing heaven and earth

改头换面 gǎitóu-huànmiàn change the appearance but not the essence; dish up the same old stuff in a new form: 他把别人著作中的话～算作自己的意见。He took pieces of another author's works, changed them around a little, and then tried to pass them off as his own ideas.

改土 gǎitǔ *agric.* improve the soil

改弦更张 gǎixián-gēngzhāng adopt new ways; make a fresh start

改弦易辙 gǎixián-yìzhé change one's course; strike out on a new path

改邪归正 gǎixié-guīzhèng give up vice and return to virtue; turn over a new leaf

改写 gǎixiě rewrite; adapt: 经过～，文章生动多了。Rewriting has livened up the article. / 这篇课文是根据《中国文学》上的一个故事～的。This text is adapted from a story in *Chinese Literature*.

改性 gǎixìng *chem.* be modified

改选 gǎixuǎn reelect: 班委会每年～一次。A new class committee is elected every year.

改削 gǎixuē shorten and improve a piece of writing: 这篇文章很不成熟，请你大力～。This is only a rough draft, so please shorten and improve it in any way you like.

改易 gǎiyì *formal* change; alter

改元 gǎiyuán change the designation of an imperial reign; change the title of a reign

改造 gǎizào transform; reform; remould; remake: ～思想 remould one's ideology / ～盐碱地 transform saline-alkali land / ～自然 remake nature / 把罪犯～成新人 reform a criminal, making a new man out of him

改正 gǎizhèng correct; amend; put right: ～错误 correct one's mistakes

改正液 gǎizhèngyè correction fluid

改制 gǎizhì *formal* change a social system; reform

改装 gǎizhuāng ① change one's costume or dress ②

repackage; repack ③ reequip; refit: ～一辆卡车 refit a truck

改锥 gǎizhuī screwdriver

改组 gǎizǔ reorganize; reshuffle: ～管理机构 reorganize the management / ～内阁 reshuffle the cabinet

改嘴 gǎizuǐ *inf.* withdraw or modify one's previous remark: 你话已出口，～已来不及了。You can't unsay what you've just said.

gài

丐 gài *formal* ① beg ② beggar ③ give; grant; bestow

芥 gài see below ——see also jiè

芥菜 gàicài *bot.* leaf mustard ——see also jiècài

芥蓝 gàilán *bot.* cabbage mustard

钙 gài *chem.* calcium (Ca)

钙化 gàihuà *med.* calcify

钙镁磷肥 gàiměilínféi calcium magnesium phosphate

盖¹(蓋) gài ① lid; cover: 茶壶～ teapot lid / 轴承～ bearing cap (or cover) ② shell (of a tortoise, crab, etc.) ③ canopy: 华盖 huágài ④ put a cover on; cover: 盖儿～得不紧。The lid isn't on tight. / 用塑料薄膜～住秧苗 cover the seedlings with plastic sheeting / 箱子没～严。The lid of the box hasn't been put on right. or The box isn't closed properly. / 他昨天晚上被子没～好，着凉了。He didn't cover himself up well last night and now he's got a cold. / 丑事想～也～不住。Scandals cannot be covered up. ⑤ affix (a seal): 盖戳 gàichuō ⑥ surpass: 大桥通车了，欢庆的锣鼓声～过了江上的浪涛声。When the bridge was opened to traffic, the joyful sounds of gongs and drums drowned the roar of the river. / 他的跳高成绩～过了所有的选手。He excelled all the other contestants in the high jump. / 他的嗓门很大，把别人的声音都～下去了。His voice was so loud that it drowned out everyone else's voice. ⑦ build: ～新房 build new houses / 这栋楼～得真漂亮。This building is really nice-looking. ⑧ (Gài) a surname

盖²(蓋) gài *formal* ① *adv.* approximately; about; around: 与会者～一千人。About a thousand people attended the meeting. ② *conj.* for; because: 有所不知，～未学也。If there are things we do not know, it is because we haven't learnt them.

盖菜 gàicài leaf mustard (a vegetable)

盖层 gàicéng *petroleum* cap rock

盖戳 gàichuō *inf.* affix one's seal; put a stamp on

盖饭 gàifàn (also 盖浇饭 gàijiāofàn) rice served with meat and vegetables on top

盖棺论定 gài guān lùn dìng final judgment can be passed on a person only when the lid is on his coffin; no final verdict can be pronounced on a man until after his death

盖然性 gàiránxìng *log.* probability

盖世 gàishì *formal* unparalleled; matchless; peerless: 力拔山兮气～。《史记》My strength plucked up the hills, My might shadowed the world.

盖世太保 Gàishìtàibǎo Gestapo

盖世无双 gàishì wúshuāng unparalleled anywhere on earth; matchless throughout the world; peerless; unrivalled

盖世英雄 gàishì yīngxióng a peerless (or matchless) hero

盖头 gàitou headkerchief (used to cover the head of

the bride)

盖碗儿 gàiwǎnr　teacup with lid and saucer

盖章 gàizhāng　affix one's seal; seal; stamp: 由本人签字～ to be signed and sealed by the recipient or applicant / 这份合同他已盖过章了。He has affixed his seal to the contract.

盖盅儿 gàizhōngr　(also 盖杯 gàibēi) teacup with a lid

盖子 gàizi　① lid; cover; cap; top: 水壶～ the lid of a kettle / 瓶～ bottle top ② shell (of a tortoise, etc.) ——see also 捂盖子 wǔ gàizi

溉 gài　see 灌溉 guàngài

概¹（槩） gài　① general idea; broad outline: 梗概 gěnggài ② adv. generally; approximately: ～而论之 generally speaking ③ adv. without exception; categorically: ～不追究 no action will be taken (against sb. for his past offences) / 货物售出，～不退换。Goods sold are not returnable.

概² gài　the manner of carrying oneself; deportment: 气概 qìgài

概而不论 gài ér bù lùn　not worry at all; not care in the least; give (or take) no heed

概观 gàiguān　(usu. used in book titles) general survey

概况 gàikuàng　general situation; survey: 我把这里的～介绍一下。I'll give a brief account of how things are in this place. /《非洲～》A Survey of Africa

概括 gàikuò　① summarize; generalize; epitomize: 这部小说的优点～起来有以下几方面。The good points of the novel may be summarized as follows. / ～起来说 to sum up / 高度的艺术～ a highly artistic condensation ② brief and to the point: ～地说 to put it briefly / 请把你的看法～地讲一讲。Please give your views in broad outline.

概括性 gàikuòxìng　generality: 最后这段话～很强。The last paragraph is a succinct summary.

概率 gàilǜ　math. probability

概略 gàilüè　outline; summary: 这只是故事的～。This is only an outline of the story.

概论 gàilùn　(usu. used in book titles) outline; introduction:《地质学～》An Introduction to Geology

概貌 gàimào　general picture: 反映人民生活的～ give a general picture of the life of the people

概莫能外 gài mò néng wài　admit of no exception whatsoever: 古今中外，～。There is no exception to this in modern times or ancient, in China or abroad.

概念 gàiniàn　concept; conception; notion; idea: 基本～ fundamental concept / 基本～ basic concept / 玩弄～ juggle with concepts / 经过反复实践，人们的脑子里就产生了～。As a result of repeated practical experience, concepts are formed in men's minds. / 我对汉语语法只有一点模糊的～。I have only a hazy idea about Chinese grammar.

概念化 gàiniànhuà　deal in generalities; write or speak in abstract terms: 公式化、～的作品 literary works which tend to formularize and generalize

概述 gàishù　give a brief account of (an event, etc.)

概数 gàishù　approximate number; round number

概算 gàisuàn　econ. budgetary estimate

概要 gàiyào　(usu. used in book titles) essentials; outline:《汉语语法～》Essentials of Chinese Grammar /《汉语方言～》Outline of Chinese Dialects

戤 gài　dial. ① counterfeit ② lean against ③ rely on

gān

干¹ gān　arch. shield

干² gān　① formal offend: 干犯 gānfàn ② have to do with; be concerned with; be implicated in: 与你何～? What has this to do with you? / 这事与我无～。It has nothing to do with me. or It's none of my business. ③ formal seek (official positions, emoluments, etc.): ～禄 seek official emoluments

干³ gān　formal waterside; bank: 江～ riverbank

干⁴ gān　short for 天干 tiāngān ——see also 干支 gān-zhī

干⁵（乾） gān　① dry: 这天气洗衣服～得慢。The washing dries slowly in this weather. / 池塘快～了。The pond is drying up. / 口～ feel thirsty / 油漆未～。Wet paint. ② dried food: 萝卜～儿 dried radish / 牛肉～儿 dried beef; jerked beef ③ empty; hollow; dry: 钱都花～了。All the money has been spent. / ～号 cry aloud but shed no tears; affected wailing ④ taken into nominal kinship: 干亲 gānqīn ⑤ adv. in vain; to no purpose; for nothing: 他们上午不来，咱们别～等了。They're not coming this morning. Let's not waste time waiting for them. ⑥ dial. (of speech) too rude and blunt: 你说话别那么～，要不，他会生气的。Don't say it too bluntly, or he'll get angry. ⑦ dial. embarrass sb. by making sarcastic remarks or complaining just in front of him: 我又～了他一顿。I embarrassed him again. ⑧ dial. leave sb. out in the cold; give sb. the cold shoulder: 她不高兴地走进卧室，把客人～在客厅里。She went into the bedroom sullenly, leaving her guests in the living room to fend for themselves. ——see also gàn

干巴巴 gānbābā　dull and dry; insipid; dryasdust; dull as ditchwater: ～的土地 parched land / 文章写得～的。The article is dull. / 这个人～的，毫无意思。The man is so insipid—not the slightest bit interesting.

干巴 gānba　inf. dried up; shrivelled; wizened: 枣儿都晒～了。The dates have all dried up in the sun. / 人老了，皮肤就变得～了。When a person grows old, his skin becomes wizened. / 这本书内容很～。This book is dryasdust.

干板 gānbǎn　photog. dry plate

干杯 gānbēi　drink a toast: 为我们的合作成功干一杯! Let's drink a toast to the success of our cooperative effort! / 我提议为两国人民的友谊～! I now propose a toast to the friendship between our two peoples—to our friendship! / 为朋友们的健康～! Here's to the health of our friends—to your health! / 老王，～! Lao Wang, cheers!

干贝 gānbèi　dried scallop (adductor)

干瘪 gānbiě　① dry: 墙上挂着的丝瓜都已经给风吹～了。The towel gourds hanging on the wall have been dried out by the wind. ② shrivelled; wizened: ～老太婆 a wizened old woman ③ (of writing) dull; drab; dryasdust

干冰 gānbīng　chem. dry ice

干菜 gāncài　dried vegetable

干草 gāncǎo　hay: ～垛 haystack

干柴烈火 gānchái-lièhuǒ　dry wood near a fierce fire—① a man and a woman burning with passion ② an explosive situation

干城 gānchéng　formal shield and city wall—defend-

ing army; defender

干脆 gāncuì ① clear-cut; straightforward: 他回答得很～。His answer was simple and straightforward. *or* He gave a clear-cut reply. / 我～跟你说吧。I'll be frank with you. / ～一点嘛! Make it snappy! *or* Be quick about it! ② simply; just; altogether: 你～说"行"还是"不行"。Just say yes or no. / 她～不承认有这回事。She simply denied that such a thing had ever happened.

干打雷,不下雨 gān dǎléi bù xiàyǔ all thunder but no rain—much noise but no action

干打垒 gāndǎlěi a house with walls of rammed earth; rammed-earth construction

干瞪眼 gāndèngyǎn *inf.* stand by anxiously, unable to help; look on in despair: 他气得说不出话来,只会～。He was speechless with anger, and could only stand by helplessly.

干电池 gāndiànchí dry cell: ～组 dry battery

干爹 gāndiē (nominally) adoptive father; godfather

干儿子 gān'érzi (nominally) adopted son

干犯 gānfàn *formal* offend; encroach upon: ～法纪 break the law and violate discipline

干饭 gānfàn cooked rice

干纺 gānfǎng dry spinning: ～纱 dry-spun yarn

干粉 gānfěn ① dried vermicelli made from bean starch, etc. ② dried noodles made from bean or sweet potato starch

干戈 gāngē weapons of war—war: 动～ take up arms; go to war

干戈扰攘 gāngē rǎorǎng in the tumult of war

干果 gānguǒ ① dry fruit (e. g. nuts) ② dried fruit

干旱 gānhàn (of weather or soil) arid; dry

干嚎 gānháo cry aloud without tears

干涸 gānhé dry up; run dry: 河道～。The river dried up.

干货 gānhuò dried food and nuts (as merchandise)

干急 gānjí same as 干着急 gānzhāojí

干季 gānjì dry season

干结 gānjié dry and hard: 大便～ constipated

干净 gānjìng ① clean; neat and tidy: 把院子扫～ sweep the yard clean / 他穿得干干净净的。His clothes are neat and tidy. / 屋子收拾得挺～。The room is neat and tidy. / 干干净净过春节 give every place a thorough cleaning for the Spring Festival / 不干不净, 吃了生病。Unclean food can make you ill. ② complete; total: 把谷子扬～ winnow the grain thoroughly / 忘得干干净净 have completely forgotten; clean forgot

干净利落 gānjìng-lìluo neat and tidy; neat; efficient: 他办事～。He's very efficient. / 这一仗打得～。The battle was neatly won.

干咳 gānké have a dry cough

干渴 gānkě very thirsty; (feeling) parched

干枯 gānkū dried-up; withered; shrivelled; wizened: ～的树木 withered trees / ～的皮肤 wizened skin / 小河～了。The stream has dried up.

干酪 gānlào cheese

干酪素 gānlàosù same as 酪素 làosù

干冷 gānlěng dry and cold (weather)

干粮 gānliang solid food (prepared for a journey); field rations; rations for a journey: 明天郊游, 请自带～。Bring your own food on tomorrow's outing. / ～袋 haversack; ration bag

干裂 gānliè crack because of dryness; be dry and cracked: 嘴唇～ parched lips

干馏 gānliú *chem.* dry distillation

干妈 gānmā (nominally) adoptive mother; godmother

干女儿 gānnǚ'ér (nominally) adopted daughter

干呕 gàn'ǒu *med.* retch

干亲 gānqīn nominal kinship: 认～ enter into an adoptive relationship

干扰 gānrǎo ① disturb; interfere; obstruct: 把收音机开小点儿, 别～人家。Turn down the radio, or you'll disturb people. ② *radio* interference; jam: ～台 jamming station

干扰素 gānrǎosù *biochem.* interferon

干鞣法 gānróufǎ *leather* dry tannage

干涉 gānshè ① interfere; intervene; meddle: 外来～ external interference / 武装～ armed intervention / 互不～内政 noninterference in each other's internal affairs ② relation: 二者了无～。There is no relation whatsoever between the two. ③ *phys.* interference: 相长(相消)～ constructive (destructive) interference

干涉仪 gānshèyí interferometer

干湿表 gānshībiǎo *meteorol.* psychrometer

干瘦 gānshòu skinny and wizened; bony

干丝 gānsī *dial.* dried bean curd cut into shreds; shredded dried bean curd

干洗 gānxǐ dry-clean

干系 gānxi responsibility; implication: 逃脱不了～ cannot shirk the responsibility / 他同这桩案子有～。He is implicated in the case.

干舷 gānxián freeboard

干笑 gānxiào laugh hollowly; force a smile

干薪 gānxīn salary drawn for a sinecure: 领～ hold a sinecure

干选 gānxuǎn *min.* dry separation

干血痨 gānxuèláo *Chin. med.* type of tubercular disease found in women, usu. characterized by menostasis, recurrent low fever and general debility

干眼症 gānyǎnzhèng *med.* xerophthalmia

干谒 gānyè *formal* seek favour; seek an interview: ～权贵 seek favours from influential officials

干预 gānyù (also 干与 gānyù) intervene; interpose; meddle: 这是你们内部的事情, 我们不便～。This is your internal affair; it is not for us to interfere.

干哕 gānyue feel sick; be nauseated; retch: 他一闻到汽油味就～。The smell of gasoline always makes him retch.

干燥 gānzào ① dry; arid: 气候～ arid climate / 大便～ constipated; costive ② dull; uninteresting: ～无味 dryasdust; dull

干燥剂 gānzàojì drier; drying agent; desiccating agent

干燥器 gānzàoqì *chem.* desiccator

干着急 gānzhāojí be anxious but unable to do anything: 他什么事也不会干, 只会～! He could do nothing but worry. / 这件事她～没办法。She had to stand by helplessly and couldn't do anything about it.

干支 gān-zhī the Heavenly Stems (天干) and Earthly Branches (地支) (two sets of signs, with one being taken from each set to form 60 pairs, designating years, formerly also months and days)

甘 gān ① sweet; pleasant: ～泉 sweet spring water ② willingly; of one's own accord: ～当群众的小学生 be a willing pupil of the masses ③ short for 甘肃 Gānsù ④ (Gān) a surname

甘拜下风 gān bài xiàfēng candidly acknowledge one's inferiority (in knowledge, ability, etc.); bow to sb.'s superiority

甘草 gāncǎo *Chin. med.* licorice root

甘汞 gānggǒng *chem.* calomel; mercurous chloride: ～电池 calomel cell

甘结 gānjié (in former times) a written pledge given to the government authorities

甘居中游 gān jū zhōngyóu be resigned to mediocrity; be content to stay mediocre

甘苦 gānkǔ ① sweetness and bitterness; joys and sorrows; weal and woe: 同～ share the joys and sorrows ② hardships and difficulties experienced in work: 没有

搞过这种工作，就不知道其中的～。You don't know how difficult the job is, unless you have done it yourself.

甘蓝 gānlán *bot.* wild cabbage

甘霖 gānlín a good rain after a long drought; timely rainfall

甘露 gānlù ① sweet dew ② *pharm.* manna ③ another name for 草石蚕 cǎoshícán

甘美 gānměi sweet and refreshing: 泉水～。The spring water is sweet and refreshing.

甘薯 gānshǔ sweet potato

甘薯黑斑病 gānshǔ hēibānbìng sweet potato black rot

甘薯软腐病 gānshǔ ruǎnfǔbìng sweet potato soft rot

甘肃 Gānsù Gansu (Province)

甘遂 gānsuì *Chin. med.* the root of gansui (*Euphorbia kansui*)

甘甜 gāntián sweet: ～可口 sweet and delicious

甘心 gānxīn ① do sth. willingly; be ready and willing ② be reconciled to; resign oneself to; be content with: 敌人对于他们的失败是不会～的。The enemy will not resign themselves to defeat.

甘心情愿 gānxīn-qíngyuàn willingly and gladly

甘休 gānxiū be willing to give up: 不试验成功，决不～。We won't give up until the experiment succeeds.

甘油 gānyóu *chem.* glycerine

甘油炸药 gānyóu zhàyào dynamite

甘于 gānyú be willing to; be ready to; be happy to: ～牺牲个人利益 be ready to sacrifice one's personal interests

甘愿 gānyuàn do sth. willingly; be ready and willing: 谁也没有强迫他，是他～这么做的。Nobody forced him to do it; he did it of his own free will.

甘蔗 gānzhe sugarcane: ～渣 bagasse ／ ～渣浆厂 bagasse-pulp mill

甘蔗板 gānzhebǎn *archit.* cane fibre board

甘蔗没有两头甜 gānzhe méiyǒu liǎngtóu tián sugarcane is never sweet at both ends—you can't have it both ways

甘之如饴 gān zhī rú yí enjoy sth. bitter as if it were malt sugar—gladly endure hardship

甘旨 gānzhǐ *formal* delicious food; delicacy

甘紫菜 gānzǐcài *bot.* laver (*Porphyra tenera*)

杆 gān pole; staff: 旗杆 qígān ——see also gǎn

杆子 gānzi pole: 电线～ wire pole; telephone pole

玕 gān see 琅玕 lánggān

肝 gān liver

肝癌 gān'ái cancer of the liver

肝肠寸断 gāncháng cùnduàn be heartbroken; be deeply grieved

肝胆 gāndǎn ① open-heartedness; sincerity ② heroic spirit; courage

肝胆过人 gāndǎn guòrén far surpass others in daring

肝胆相照 gāndǎn xiāngzhào (of friends) treat each other with all sincerity; be devoted to each other heart and soul

肝功能 gāngōngnéng liver function: ～试验 liver function test ／ ～正常。The liver is functioning normally.

肝火 gānhuǒ irascibility: ～旺 hot-tempered; irascible

肝脑涂地 gānnǎo tú dì spill one's liver and brains on the ground—lay down one's life (in fighting for one's sovereign)

肝气 gānqì ① *Chin. med.* diseases with such symptoms as costal pain, vomiting, diarrhoea, etc. ② irritability

肝素 gānsù *pharm.* heparin

肝泰乐 gāntàilè *pharm.* glucurolactone; glucurone

肝吸虫 gānxīchóng liver fluke

肝炎 gānyán hepatitis

肝硬变 gānyìngbiàn (also 肝硬化 gānyìnghuà) cirrhosis (of the liver)

肝脏 gānzàng liver

肝蛭 gānzhì another name for 肝吸虫 gānxīchóng

肝肿大 gānzhǒngdà hepatomegaly

泔 gān swill; slops; hogwash

泔水 gānshuǐ swill; slops; hogwash

矸 gān see below

矸石 gānshí waste (rock)

矸子 gānzi common name for 矸石 gānshí

坩 gān see below

坩埚 gānguō *chem.* crucible: 石墨～ graphite (or carbon) crucible

坩埚炉 gānguōlú *metall.* crucible furnace

苷 gān see 糖苷 tánggān

柑 gān mandarin orange

柑橘 gānjú ① oranges and tangerines ② citrus

柑橘酱 gānjújiàng marmalade

柑子 gānzi mandarin orange

竿 gān pole; rod: 钓～ fishing rod

竿子 gānzi bamboo pole

疳 gān same as 疳积 gānjī

疳积 gānjī *Chin. med.* infantile malnutrition due to digestive disturbances or intestinal parasites

酐 gān short for 酸酐 suāngān

尴（尷、尲） gān see below

尴尬 gāngà ① (of the situation one is in) awkward; hard to deal with: 处境～ in an awkward position; in a dilemma ／ 他觉得去也不好，不去也不好，实在～。He felt it would be bad to go and bad not to go. He was in a real quandary. ② *dial.* embarrassed: 样子十分～ look very much embarrassed

gǎn

杆（桿） gǎn ① the shaft or arm of sth.: 钢笔～儿 penholder ／ 枪～ the barrel of a rifle ② *m.* (for a long and thin cylindrical object): 一～秤 a steelyard ／ 一～枪 a rifle ／ 一～红旗 a red flag ——see also gān

杆秤 gǎnchèng steelyard

杆菌 gǎnjūn bacillus: ～载体 bacillus carrier

秆（稈） gǎn stalk: 高粱～ sorghum stalk ／ 麻～ hemp stalk

赶（趕） gǎn ① catch up with; overtake: ～先进 catch up with the advanced ／ 落在后面的人～上来了。Those who lagged behind have caught up. ／ 要说摘棉花，可谁也～不上她。Nobody can keep up with her in picking cotton. ／ 她已经～到大伙儿前头去了。She's shot ahead of all the rest of us. ② try to catch; make a dash for; rush for: ～头班车 catch the first bus ／ 火车七点三十分开，我们～得及吗？The train leaves at 7:30. Can we make it? ③ hurry (*or* rush) through: ～任务 rush through one's job ／ 他连夜～写了一份报告。He dashed off a report that very night. ／ ～调了一个团到灾

区去帮助救灾。A regiment was rushed to the stricken area to help with relief work. ④ drive: ～大车 drive a cart / 把羊～到山上去吃草。Herd the sheep up the hill to graze. ⑤ drive away; expel: 把敌人～走 drive the enemy away; throw out the enemy / 辛亥革命～跑了一个皇帝，但是没有摧毁封建统治的基础。The 1911 Revolution sent an emperor packing, but failed to demolish the foundation of feudal rule. / ～苍蝇 whisk the flies off; brush away a fly ⑥ happen to; find oneself in (a situation); avail oneself of (an opportunity): ～上一场雨 run into a rain / 我去了两趟，正～上他下厂去了。I went there twice, but he happened to be away at the factory each time. / 得～这好天把被子晒一晒。We should air the bedding while the good weather lasts. ⑦ prep. till: 咱俩的婚事～年下再办吧。Let's put off our wedding till the Spring Festival. / ～响午我就走。I'll be leaving at noon. / 这事～以后再谈吧。Let's discuss the matter later.

赶不及 gǎnbují there's not enough time (to do sth.); it's too late (to do sth.): 火车七点开，动身晚了就～了。The train leaves at seven, and we won't catch it if we start off too late.

赶不上 gǎnbushàng ① be unable to catch up with: 他已经走远了，～了。He's pretty far away by now and we won't be able to catch up with him. / 我们的认识常常～形势的发展。Our knowledge often fails to keep pace with the march of events. ② there's not enough time (to do sth.); it's too late (to do sth.): 离开车只有十分钟，恐怕～了。The train is going to leave in ten minutes. I'm afraid we'll be too late. ③ be unable to meet with or chance upon: 几个星期天都～好天气。We never met with good weather these past few Sundays.

赶场 gǎnchǎng dial. go to the village fair or market

赶场 gǎnchǎng (of a performer) hurry from one performance to a second one in another place

赶超 gǎnchāo catch up with and surpass

赶车 gǎnchē drive a cart

赶道 gǎndào hurry on with one's journey

赶得及 gǎndejí there is still time; be able to do sth. in time; be able to make it: 马上就动身还～。There's still time if we start at once.

赶得上 gǎndeshàng ① be able to catch up: 你先走吧，我～你的。You go first. I'll be able to catch up with you. ② there is still time; be able to do sth. in time; be able to make it: 他们还没有走，你现在去还～和他们告别。They haven't left yet. If you go there right away, you'll be just in time to say good-bye to them.

赶海 gǎnhǎi dial. gather seafood on the beach when the tide is ebbing

赶活 gǎnhuó speed up (or rush through) one's work in order to meet a deadline: 赶合同的活 rush a contract through

赶集 gǎnjí go to market; go to a fair

赶脚 gǎnjiǎo lead a donkey or mule for hire

赶紧 gǎnjǐn adv. hastily; without losing time: ～刹车 quickly put on the brakes / ～解释 hasten to explain / 发现情况，～报告。If you find anything unusual, report at once. / 他～吃了饭就上工地去了。He had a hurried meal and made for the construction site.

赶尽杀绝 gǎnjìn-shājué kill all; wipe out the whole lot; spare none; be ruthless

赶考 gǎnkǎo take the imperial examinations: 进京～ go to the capital to sit for the imperial examinations

赶快 gǎnkuài adv. at once; quickly: ～跟我走。Come along with me at once. / ～把这块地收完。Let's finish harvesting this plot quickly. / ～! Be quick! or Hurry up!

赶浪头 gǎn làngtou follow the trend

赶路 gǎnlù hurry on with one's journey: 快休息吧，明天一早还要～呢。Let's go to bed right away. We must push on with our journey early tomorrow morning. / 赶了一天路，累了吧? Aren't you tired after such a hard day's journey?

赶忙 gǎnmáng adv. hurriedly; hastily: 他从自行车上摔下来，我～过去把他扶了起来。He fell off his bicycle and I hurried over to help him up. / 他～道歉。He hastened to apologize.

赶庙会 gǎnmiàohuì go to a temple fair

赶明儿 gǎnmíngr dial. one of these days; another day

赶前不赶后 gǎn qián bù gǎn hòu it's better to hurry at the beginning than to rush at the last moment

赶巧 gǎnqiǎo happen to; it so happened that: 这次进城，～跟张大爷同车。On my way to the city, I happened to ride in the same bus as Grandpa Zhang. / 上午我去找他，～他不在家。I went to see him this morning, but he happened to be away.

赶上 gǎnshàng ① overtake; catch up with; keep pace with: ～先进单位 catch up with the advanced units / ～时代的发展 keep abreast of the times ② run into (a situation); be in time for: 我到北京那天正～过国庆。It happened to be National Day when I arrived in Beijing. / 你要～渔汛来，就能跟我们一块儿出海了。If you come during the fishing season, you'll be able to go out to sea with us. / 我没～车。I missed the bus.

赶时髦 gǎn shímáo follow the fashion; try to be in style

赶趟儿 gǎntàngr inf. be in time for: 我们要不快点儿走，就赶不上趟儿了。We'll be late if we don't hurry. / 他正好赶上趟儿。He was just in time.

赶鸭子上架 gǎn yāzi shàng jià drive a duck onto a perch—try to make sb. do sth. entirely beyond him: 我不会唱，你偏叫我唱，这不是～吗? I can't sing. But if you insist on my singing, it'll be like driving a duck onto a perch.

赶早 gǎnzǎo do sth. as early as possible: 看样子要下雨，我们～走吧! It looks like rain. We'd better leave at once.

赶锥 gǎnzhuī same as 改锥 gǎizhuī

敢¹

gǎn ① bold; courageous; daring: 勇敢 yǒnggǎn ② be brave enough; dare: ～想、～说、～干 dare to think, to speak and to act / 过去连想都不～想的事，现在变成了现实。What one couldn't even imagine in the past has now become reality. ③ have the confidence to; be certain; be sure: 我～说他一定乐于接受这个任务。I'm confident he will be willing to undertake the task. / 我不～说他究竟哪一天来。I'm not sure just what day he will come. ④ formal pol. make bold; venture: ～问 I venture to ask; may I ask

敢²

gǎn dial. perhaps; I'm afraid

敢保 gǎnbǎo ① guarantee; assure: 我～你会喜欢它。I guarantee that you'll like it. ② certainly; surely: 他～会按时到。I'm sure he'll be here on time.

敢怒而不敢言 gǎn nù ér bùgǎn yán be forced to keep one's resentment to oneself; choke with silent fury

敢情 gǎnqing adv. dial. ① (used when sth. is discovered or seen for the first time) why; so; I say: ～这屋子都笼上火啦! Oh, so there's a fire in the room already! ② of course; indeed; really: 去西安参观? 那～好! We're going to visit Xi'an? That'll be really wonderful.

敢是 gǎnshì adv. dial. perhaps; I'm afraid: 这不像是去颐和园的道儿，～走错了吧? This doesn't seem to be the way to the Summer Palace. I'm afraid we may have taken the wrong road.

敢死队 gǎnsǐduì dare-to-die corps; suicide squad

敢于 gǎnyú dare to; be bold in; have the courage to: ～斗争，～胜利 dare to struggle and dare to win

敢作敢当 gǎnzuò-gǎndāng have the courage to take the blame for what one does

敢作敢为 gǎnzuò-gǎnwéi bold and decisive in action

感

gǎn ① feel; sense: 身体略～不适 not feel very well; be under the weather; be out of sorts ② move; touch; affect: 深有所～ be deeply moved; be greatly touched ③ be grateful; be obliged: 请早日寄下为～。 I should be grateful if you would send it to me at an early date. ④ *Chin. med.* be affected: 外感 wàigǎn ⑤ sense; feeling: 民族自豪～ a sense of national pride / 读后～ reaction to (*or* impressions of) a book or an article / 给人以一种新鲜～ engender a feeling of freshness ⑥ *photog.* sensitize: 感光 gǎnguāng

感触 gǎnchù thoughts and feelings; feeling: 深有～地说 say with deep feeling / 故乡的巨大变化引起了我很多～。 Great changes in my home village give me much food for thought.

感戴 gǎndài feel gratitude and respect for (one's superior)

感到 gǎndào feel; sense: ～疲倦 feel tired / ～幸福 feel happy / 这件事结局没想到是这样，我真～遗憾。 I never thought it would turn out this way. I do regret it. / 我胸部～疼痛。 I have a pain in my chest. / 他～自己错了。 He sensed that he himself was wrong. / 她对草原上的一切都～新鲜。 She found everything on the grasslands new and attractive. / 我为你取得的成就～骄傲。 I take pride in your achievements.

感动 gǎndòng move; touch: ～得流下眼泪 be moved to tears / 深为他的精神所～ be deeply touched by his spirit / 他的话深深地～了在座的人。 What he said deeply moved everyone present.

感恩 gǎn'ēn feel grateful; be thankful: ～不尽 be extremely grateful

感恩戴德 gǎn'ēn-dàidé be deeply grateful; be overwhelmed with gratitude

感恩节 Gǎn'ēnjié Thanksgiving Day

感恩图报 gǎn'ēn tú bào be grateful to sb. and seek ways to return his kindness

感奋 gǎnfèn be moved and inspired; be fired with enthusiasm: 老红军的报告令人～。 Everybody was moved and inspired by the veteran Red Army man's talk.

感官 gǎnguān short for 感觉器官 gǎnjué qìguān

感光 gǎnguāng *photog.* sensitize: ～度 (light) sensitivity / ～计 sensitometer / ～纸 sensitive paper

感荷 gǎnhè be thankful for; feel gratitude for

感化 gǎnhuà help (a misguided or erring person) to change by persuasion, setting an example, etc.

感怀 gǎnhuái ① recall with emotion: ～往事 recall past events with deep feeling ② reflections; thoughts; recollections: 新春～ thoughts on the Spring Festival

感激 gǎnjī feel grateful; be thankful; feel indebted: 不胜～ be deeply grateful; feel very much indebted / 很～你给我的帮助。 I'm very grateful for your help.

感激涕零 gǎnjī-tìlíng shed grateful tears; be moved to tears of gratitude

感觉 gǎnjué ① sense perception; sensation; feeling: 概念同～的区别 the difference between concepts and sense perceptions / ～和思想只是外部世界的反映。 Sensations and ideas are only reflections of the external world. / 这只是我个人的～。 That's only my personal feeling. / 他给人以亲切的～。 He gives you the impression that he's a very kind man. ② feel; perceive; become aware of: 一场秋雨过后就～有点冷了。 I felt a little bit cold after the autumn rain. / 他～到了问题的严重性。 He became aware of the seriousness of the matter. / 你～怎么样？ How do you feel now?

感觉论 gǎnjuélùn *philos.* sensualism

感觉器官 gǎnjué qìguān sense (*or* sensory) organ

感觉神经 gǎnjué shénjīng sensory nerve

感觉阈限 gǎnjué yùxiàn *psychol.* sense limen; sense threshold

感慨 gǎnkǎi sigh with emotion: 提起过去那段经历，他无限～。 When he spoke of those hard times, he sighed a great sorrow.

感慨万端 gǎnkǎi wànduān all sorts of feelings well up in one's mind

感慨系之 gǎnkǎi xì zhī sigh with deep feeling

感喟 gǎnkuì *formal* sigh with emotion

感冒 gǎnmào common cold: 患～ catch cold; have a cold

感念 gǎnniàn remember with gratitude; recall with deep emotion: ～不忘 always recall sb. with deep emotion

感情 gǎnqíng ① emotion; feeling; sentiment: 动～ be carried away by one's emotions; get worked up / 伤～ hurt sb.'s feelings / 思想～开始发生变化 experience a change in one's thoughts and feelings ② affection; attachment; love: 我们对延安的一草一木都怀有深厚的～。 We cherish a deep affection for every tree and bush in Yan'an. / 这些年来，她对他产生了～。 She formed an attachment for him over the years. / 他对母亲的～很深。 He has a deep love for his mother.

感情用事 gǎnqíng yòngshì be swayed by one's emotions; act impetuously

感染 gǎnrǎn ① infect: 细菌～ bacterial infection / 手术后～ postoperative infection / 身体不好，容易～流行性感冒。 If one is feeling physically low, it's easy to catch the flu. ② influence; infect; affect: 她的乐观态度～了周围的人。 Her optimism was infectious. / 诗人的激情～了每一个读者。 The poet's passion affected all his readers.

感染力 gǎnrǎnlì power to move the feelings; appeal: 艺术～ artistic appeal

感人 gǎnrén touching; moving: ～的故事 a moving story / 他的先进事迹十分～。 His meritorious deeds are very moving.

感人肺腑 gǎn rén fèifǔ touch one to the depths of one's soul; move one deeply

感纫 gǎnrèn *formal* my gratitude (used in letters)

感伤 gǎnshāng sad; sorrowful; sentimental

感生电流 gǎnshēng diànliú same as 感应电流 gǎnyìng diànliú

感受 gǎnshòu ① be affected by: ～风寒 be affected by the cold; catch cold ② experience; feel: 我才来几天，就～到这个革命集体的温暖。 I've been here only a few days and I've already experienced the warmth of this revolutionary collective. / 这次去东北参观～很深。 My visit to the Northeast made a deep impression on me.

感受器 gǎnshòuqì *physiol.* receptor

感叹 gǎntàn sigh with feeling

感叹词 gǎntàncí interjection; exclamation

感叹号 gǎntànhào exclamation mark; exclamation point (!)

感叹句 gǎntànjù exclamatory sentence

感同身受 gǎn tóng shēn shòu *pol.* I shall appreciate it as a personal favour (said when making a request on behalf of a friend)

感悟 gǎnwù come to realize

感想 gǎnxiǎng impressions; reflections; thoughts: 请你谈谈看了这部影片后的～。 Please tell us your impressions of the film. *or* Tell us what you think of the film. / 把～当政策 substitute one's personal feelings for policy

感谢 gǎnxiè thank; be grateful: 表示衷心的～ express heartfelt thanks / 非常～你的帮助。 Thank you very much for your help.

感谢信 gǎnxièxìn letter of thanks

感性　gǎnxìng　(sense) perception: 认识的～阶段 the perceptual stage of cognition

感性认识　gǎnxìng rènshi　*philos.*　perceptual knowledge

感性运动　gǎnxìng yùndòng　*biol.*　nastic movement

感性知觉　gǎnxìng zhījué　*psychol.*　sense impressions

感应　gǎnyìng　① response; reaction; interaction: 凡是动物都有对外界的刺激发生比较灵敏的～的特性。Reaction to strong stimuli from the outside world is a characteristic of all animals. ② *biol.* irritability ③ *elec.* induction: 电磁～ electromagnetic induction / 静电～ electrostatic induction / ～干扰 inductive interference / ～式话筒 inductor microphone

感应电流　gǎnyìng diànliú　induced current

感应率　gǎnyìnglǜ　inductivity

感应圈　gǎnyìngquān　induction coil; inductor

感召　gǎnzhào　move and inspire; impel: 在党的政策～下 under the influence of the Party's policy

感知　gǎnzhī　mental perception through sensory organs

橄　gǎn　see below

橄榄　gǎnlǎn　*bot.*　① Chinese olive (*Canarium album*); the fruit of the canary tree ② olive

橄榄绿　gǎnlǎnlǜ　olive green

橄榄球　gǎnlǎnqiú　*sports*　rugby; American football

橄榄石　gǎnlǎnshí　olivine (a mineral)

橄榄岩　gǎnlǎnyán　*geol.*　peridotite

橄榄油　gǎnlǎnyóu　olive oil

橄榄枝　gǎnlǎnzhī　olive branch—a symbol of peace

擀（扞）　gǎn　① roll (dough, etc.): ～饺子皮 roll out dumpling wrappers / ～面条 make noodles ② *dial.* polish; shine: 用湿布把玻璃窗擦完后，再用干布～一～。When you've finished cleaning the windows with a wet towel, polish them with a dry one.

擀面杖　gǎnmiànzhàng　rolling pin

擀面杖吹火——一窍不通　gǎnmiànzhàng chuī huǒ, yī qiào bù tōng　try to blow the fire with a rolling pin—know nothing about sth.

gàn

干¹（幹、榦）　gàn　① trunk; main part: 树干 shùgàn / 骨干 gǔgàn ② short for 干部 gànbù

干²（幹）　gàn　① do; work: 咱们～吧! Let's get cracking! *or* Let's get started! / 叫我～什么都行。I'll do whatever job I'm given. / ～革命 make (*or* wage) revolution / ～社会主义 build socialism; work for socialism ② work as; go in for: 他～过队长。He used to be a team leader. ③ *dial.* (of things) going wrong; involving trouble: 要～! It's going wrong! ④ capable; able: ～员 a capable official
——see also gān

干部　gànbù　cadre: 各级领导～ leading cadres at all levels / ～政策 policy towards cadres; cadre policy

干部学校　gànbù xuéxiào　a school for cadres; cadre school

干才　gàncái　① ability; capability: 这个人还有点～。The man is quite capable. ② a capable (*or* able) person: 他是个～。He's a capable person.

干得过儿　gàndeguòr　be worth doing

干掉　gàndiào　*inf.*　kill; get rid of; put sb. out of the way: 先～敌人的哨兵。Get rid of the enemy sentry first.

干活　gànhuó　work; work on a job: ～去吧。Let's get to work. / 他们都在～呢。They are all at work. *or* They are all on the job. / 今儿你干什么活啊?What's your job for today?

干架　gànjià　① quarrel ② come to blows

干将　gànjiàng　capable person; go-getter

干劲　gànjìn　drive; vigour; enthusiasm: 鼓～ rouse one's enthusiasm / ～十足 be full of vigour (*or* drive)

干了　gànle　*dial.*　too bad; what a mess: ～, 车闸坏了。That does it; the brakes are out of order.

干练　gànliàn　capable and experienced: 他的确是一个精明～的人才。He's a really bright and capable man.

干流　gànliú　trunk stream; mainstream

干吗　gànmá　*inf.*　① why on earth; whatever for: ～这么大规矩? Why all this formality? ② what to do: 今儿下午～? What are we going to do this afternoon? / 你想～? What are you up to?

干渠　gànqú　trunk canal; main canal

干群关系　gàn-qún guānxi　relations between cadres and the masses; cadre-mass relations

干上了　gànshàngle　have a quarrel: 他们俩～了! The two of them started quarrelling.

干什么　gànshénme　same as 干吗 gànmá

干事　gànshi　a secretary (*or* clerical worker) in charge of sth.: 文娱～ person in charge of recreational activities

干头儿　gàntour　(usu. preceded by 有 or 没有 to mean worth doing or not worth doing): 这事没什么～。This isn't worth doing.

干线　gànxiàn　main line; trunk line; artery: 公路～ arterial or main highway / 交通～ main lines of communication (*or* transportation)

干校　gànxiào　short for 干部学校 gànbù xuéxiào

干仗　gànzhàng　*dial.*　come to blows or have a row

旰　gàn　*formal*　late at night

旰食　gànshí　*formal*　eat late

绀　gàn　dark purple; dark red

绀青　gànqīng　dark purple; prune purple

赣　Gàn　another name for 江西 Jiāngxī

gāng

冈（岡、岗）　gāng　ridge (of a hill): 景阳～ the Jingyang Ridge

冈比亚　Gāngbǐyà　the Gambia

冈比亚人　Gāngbǐyàrén　Gambian

扛　gāng　① lift with both hands ② *dial.* (of two or more people) carry together ——see also káng

刚¹（剛）　gāng　firm; strong; indomitable: 他的性情太～。He has a very strong character. / 她的舞蹈柔中有～。There is strength as well as grace in her dancing.

刚²（剛）　gāng　*adv.*　① just; exactly: 这双鞋大小～合适。This pair of shoes is just the right size. *or* This pair of shoes fits perfectly. ② barely; only; just: 我参加八路军时, ～跟枪一般高。When I joined the Eighth Route Army, I was barely the height of a rifle. / 天还很黑, ～能看出人的轮廓。It was still dark and I could just make out the outlines of people. / 他～十八岁, 有了选举权。He just turned 18 and has the right to vote. / 他回家时～碰上大雨。On his way home, he got caught in the rainstorm. ③ only a short while ago; just: 她～走。She just left. / 她～来过。She was here just now. / 他～到农村时, 连麦子韭菜都分不清。When

he first came to the countryside, he couldn't tell wheat from Chinese chives.

刚愎 gāngbì　headstrong; opinionated

刚愎自用 gāngbì zìyòng　self-willed; headstrong; opinionated

刚才 gāngcái　a moment ago; just now: 别把～跟你说的事忘了。Don't forget what I told you just now. / 他～还说要去呢。He was saying only a moment ago that he wanted to go. / ～还不到一点，怎么现在已经两点了? Just a moment ago it was one o'clock. How did it get to be two o'clock already. / 吃了片阿司匹林，现在比～舒服些了。I took an aspirin and now I feel a little better. / ～的消息可靠吗? Is that information we just got reliable? / 这就是～那个人。That's the man (who came here a moment ago).

刚刚 gānggāng　adv. ① just; only; exactly: 上次讨论会到现在～一个月。It's only a month since the last discussion. / 那时候天～亮。It was just beginning to get light. ② a moment ago; just now: 报纸～到。The newspaper came just now. / 他～走，你快去追吧! He left just a minute ago. Run and try to catch him.

刚果 Gāngguǒ　the Congo

刚果河 Gāngguǒhé　the Congo (River)

刚果红 gāngguǒhóng　Congo red

刚果人 Gāngguǒrén　Congolese

刚果语 Gāngguǒyǔ　Congolese (language)

刚好 gānghǎo　adv. ① just; exactly: 我们～赶上末班车。We just managed to catch the last bus. / 这件上衣你穿着不大不小，～。This jacket fits you beautifully. / 我体重～五十公斤。I weigh just 50 kilograms, no more, no less. / 你们来得～。You've come in the nick of time. ② by chance; by coincidence: 他们两人～编在一个组里。The two of them happened to be in the same group. / ～校长在这儿，你就跟他谈谈吧。The Chancellor happens to be here. You'd better talk it over with him.

刚架 gāngjià　archit. rigid frame: ～结构 rigid-framed structure

刚健 gāngjiàn　vigorous; energetic; robust: ～的舞姿 vigorous movements of a dancer

刚劲 gāngjìng　bold; vigorous; sturdy: 笔力～ write in a bold hand / ～的松枝 sturdy boughs of a pine

刚…就 gāng…jiù　as soon as; no sooner than; immediately: 他刚开完会回来，就下地干活去了。As soon as he got back from the conference, he went to work in the fields. / 刚过立春，天气就异乎寻常地热。It got unusually hot just after the Beginning of Spring.

刚烈 gāngliè　fiery and forthright; upright and unyielding

刚毛 gāngmáo　zool. bristle; seta; chaeta

刚强 gāngqiáng　firm; staunch; unyielding: 性格～ be of firm character

刚巧 gāngqiǎo　adv. by chance; by coincidence: 明天～有车进城。It just so happens that there's a bus going to the city tomorrow.

刚柔相济 gāng-róu xiāng jì　couple hardness with softness (in dealing with people); temper toughness with gentleness

刚体 gāngtǐ　phys. rigid body

刚性 gāngxìng　phys. rigidity: ～结构 rigid structure

刚毅 gāngyì　resolute and steadfast: 在斗争中表现得非常～和机智 display both fortitude and resourcefulness in the struggle

刚玉 gāngyù　corundum (a mineral)

刚正 gāngzhèng　upright; honourable; principled

刚正不阿 gāngzhèng bù ē　upright and above flattery

刚直 gāngzhí　upright and outspoken

纲 (綱)

gāng　① the headrope of a fishing net ② key link; guiding principle: 纲举目张 gāngjǔmùzhāng ③ outline; programme: 总纲 zǒnggāng ④ biol. class: 哺乳动物～ the class of mammals / 亚～ subclass ⑤ transportation of goods under convoy (in feudal China): 盐～ salt transported under convoy; salt convoy

纲常 gāngcháng　see 三纲五常 sāngāng wǔcháng

纲纪 gāngjì　formal law and order; discipline

纲举目张 gāngjǔ-mùzhāng　once the headrope of a fishing net is pulled up, all its meshes open—once the key link is grasped, everything falls into place

纲领 gānglǐng　programme; guiding principle: ～性文件 programmatic document

纲目 gāngmù　(usu. used in book titles) detailed outline (of a subject); outline; compendium: 《本草～》 Compendium of Materia Medica

纲要 gāngyào　① outline; sketch: 他把意见写成～，准备在会上发言。He made an outline of his views and got ready to present them at the meeting. ② (usu. used in book titles) essentials; compendium: 《英语语法～》 Essentials of English Grammar / 《全国农业发展～》 The National Programme for Agricultural Development

肛

gāng　anus: 脱肛 tuōgāng

肛裂 gāngliè　med. anal fissure

肛瘘 gānglòu　med. anal fistula

肛门 gāngmén　anus

缸 (甌)

gāng　① vat; jar; crock: 水～ water vat / 一～咸菜 a jar of salted vegetables / 金鱼～ goldfish bowl / 一口大～ a big vat ② a compound of sand, clay, etc. for making earthenware: 缸盆 gāngpén ③ a jar-shaped vessel: 汽缸 qìgāng

缸管 gāngguǎn　earthen pipe

缸盆 gāngpén　glazed earthen basin

缸瓦 gāngwǎ　a compound of sand, clay, etc. for making earthenware

缸砖 gāngzhuān　clinker (tile); quarry tile

缸子 gāngzi　mug; bowl: 茶～ (tea) mug / 糖～ sugar bowl

钢 (鋼)

gāng　steel: ～是用铁炼成的。Steel is made from iron. ——see also gàng

钢板 gāngbǎn　① steel plate; plate: 锅炉～ boiler plate / 造船～ ship plate ② spring (of a motorcar, etc.) ③ stencil steel board

钢镚儿 gāngbèngr　inf. small coin

钢笔 gāngbǐ　pen; fountain pen

钢笔画 gāngbǐhuà　pen-and-ink drawing

钢笔水 gāngbǐshuǐ　inf. ink

钢材 gāngcái　steel products; steels; rolled steel

钢尺 gāngchǐ　steel rule

钢锭 gāngdìng　steel ingot

钢骨水泥 gānggǔ shuǐní　reinforced concrete

钢管 gāngguǎn　steel tube (or pipe): 无缝～ seamless steel tube / 焊接～ welded steel pipe

钢轨 gāngguǐ　rails (for trains, etc.); tracks

钢轨探伤仪 gāngguǐ tànshāngyí　rail flaw detector

钢号 gānghào　metall. steel grade

钢花 gānghuā　spray (or sparks) of molten steel

钢化玻璃 gānghuà bōli　toughened glass

钢结构 gāngjiégòu　archit. steel structure

钢筋 gāngjīn　reinforcing bar

钢筋混凝土 gāngjīn hùnníngtǔ　reinforced concrete

钢精 gāngjīng　(also 钢种 gāngzhǒng) aluminium (as used for utensils): ～锅 aluminium pan

钢锯 gāngjù　hacksaw: ～架 hacksaw frame / ～条 hacksaw blade

钢口儿 gāngkǒur　the edge of a knife

钢筘 gāngkòu *text.* reed

钢盔 gāngkuī (steel) helmet

钢坯 gāngpī *metall.* billet: 大～ bloom

钢片琴 gāngpiànqín *mus.* celesta

钢钎 gāngqiān drill rod; drill steel

钢琴 gāngqín piano: 大～ grand piano / 竖式～ upright piano / ～家 pianist

钢水 gāngshuǐ *metall.* molten steel: ～包 steel ladle

钢丝 gāngsī (steel) wire: ～垫子 spring mattress

钢丝床 gāngsīchuáng spring bed

钢丝锯 gāngsījù fret saw; scroll saw

钢丝录音机 gāngsī lùyīnjī wire recorder

钢丝钳 gāngsīqián combination pliers; cutting pliers

钢丝绳 gāngsīshéng steel cable; wire rope

钢铁 gāngtiě ① iron and steel; steel: ～厂 steelworks / ～工业 iron and steel industry / ～公司 iron and steel company / ～联合企业 integrated iron and steel works; iron and steel complex ② strong; firm; staunch: ～意志 iron will / ～运输线 an unbreakable transportation line / ～战士 a dauntless fighter / 解放军是保卫祖国的～长城。The PLA is a great wall of steel guarding our country.

钢印 gāngyìn ① steel seal; embossing seal ② embossed stamp

钢珠 gāngzhū steel ball (in a ball bearing); ball bearing; ball

罡 gāng see below

罡风 gāngfēng ① *Taoism* winds in the empyrean ② strong winds

gǎng

岗（崗） gǎng ① hillock; mound: ～峦起伏 undulating hills ② ridge; welt; wale: 他眉毛脱了,只剩下两道肉～儿。Only the two superciliary ridges are left there since his eyebrow hair fell out. ③ sentry; post: 布～ post sentries

岗警 gǎngjǐng policeman on point duty

岗楼 gǎnglóu watchtower

岗卡 gǎngqiǎ checkpost

岗哨 gǎngshào ① lookout post ② sentry; sentinel: 设置～ post sentries

岗亭 gǎngtíng sentry box; police box

岗位 gǎngwèi post; station: 战斗～ fighting post; battle station / 坚守～ stand fast at one's post; stick to one's guns / 走上新的～ take up a new post; take on a new job

岗位责任制 gǎngwèi zérènzhì system of personal responsibility (for each section of a production line, etc.)

岗子 gǎngzi ① hillock; mound: 土～ earth hillock ② ridge; wale; welt: 他胸口上肿起一道～。There's a welt on his chest.

港 gǎng ① port; harbour: 天然～ natural harbour / 停靠～ port of call ② (Gǎng) short for 香港 Xiānggǎng

港币 gǎngbì Hong Kong dollar

港汊 gǎngchà branching stream

港口 gǎngkǒu port; harbour: 沿海～ coastal port / ～规章 harbour regulations / ～吞吐量 traffic (of a port) / ～税 port dues

港湾 gǎngwān harbour

港务费 gǎngwùfèi harbour dues

港务监督 gǎngwù jiāndū harbour superintendency administration

港务局 gǎngwùjú port office

gàng

杠（槓） gàng ① a thick stick ② *sports* bar: 单杠 dāngàng / 双杠 shuānggàng ③ rod-like spare parts used for machine tools: 丝杠 sīgàng ④ stout poles used to carry a coffin ⑤ cross out; delete: 她把草稿中不必要的词句都～掉了。She crossed out all the superfluous words and phrases in the draft.

杠棒 gàngbàng a stout carrying pole

杠房 gàngfáng *old* an undertaker's shop

杠夫 gàngfū *old* professional coffin bearer

杠杆 gànggǎn lever: ～臂 lever arm / ～原理 lever principle / ～率 leverage / 经济～ economic levers

杠铃 gànglíng *sports* barbell: ～片 disc (of a barbell)

杠子 gàngzi ① a thick stick; a stout carrying pole ② same as 杠 gàng② ③ thick line (drawn beside or under words in reading, correcting papers, etc.)

钢（鋼） gàng ① sharpen; whet; strop: ～菜刀 sharpen a kitchen knife / ～镰刀 whet a sickle / ～剃刀 strop a razor ② reinforce the edge (of a knife, etc.) by adding steel and retempering: 这口铡刀该～了。The fodder chopper needs to be reinforced. ——see also gāng

钢刀布 gàngdāobù (razor) strop

戆 gàng *dial.* rash; reckless ——see also zhuàng

gāo

高 gāo ① tall; high: 这里地势很～。The terrain here is very high. / 她比小红一头。She is a head taller than Xiao Hong. / 坝～四十米。The dam is 40 metres high (*or* in height). / 这片地中间～起一块。There is a mound in the middle of the field. ② of a high level or degree; above the average: ～速度 high speed / ～年级 higher (*or* senior) grades / ～质量 high (*or* good) quality / 体温～ have a fever / 他的思想境界比我～。He has nobler thoughts than I. / 他的见解比谁都～。He has more original ideas than others do. / ～风格 fine style / ～难度动作 exceedingly difficult movements; operations of extraordinary difficulty / 这主意真～! What a brilliant idea! ③ loud: 嗓门～ have a loud voice / ～喊 shout loudly; raise a cry ④ high-priced; dear; expensive: 要价太～ ask too high a price ⑤ *honor.* your: 高见 gāojiàn ⑥ *chem.* containing one more oxygen atom in an acid or a chemical compound: 高锰酸钾 gāoměngsuānjiǎ ⑦ (Gāo) a surname

高矮 gāo'ǎi height: 这两棵树～差不多。The two trees are about the same height.

高昂 gāo'áng ① hold high (one's head, etc.): 骑兵队伍～着头通过了广场。The mounted troops passed the square with their heads held high. ② high; elated; exalted: 情绪～ be in high spirits / 大会在～的《国际歌》声中结束。The meeting ended with the inspiring strains of *The Internationale.* ③ dear; expensive; exorbitant

高傲 gāo'ào ① supercilious; arrogant; haughty ② proud; self-respecting; high-minded

高保真 gāobǎozhēn high fidelity; hi-fi

高标号 gāobiāohào high grade: ～水泥 high-grade cement

高不成,低不就 gāo bù chéng, dī bù jiù ① be unfit for a higher post but unwilling to take a lower one ② be unable to achieve one's heart's desire but unwilling to

accept less

高不可攀 gāo bùkě pān too high to reach; unattainable

高才生 gāocáishēng (also 高材生 gāocáishēng) a brilliant (or outstanding) student

高参 gāocān (short for 高级参谋) ① senior staff officer ② counsellor; mentor

高层云 gāocéngyún meteorol. altostratus

高产 gāochǎn high yield; high production: ～品种 high-yield variety / ～田 high-yield field / ～作物 high-yield crop; highly productive crop

高唱 gāochàng ① sing loudly; sing with spirit: ～战歌 sing battle songs ② talk glibly about; call out loudly for

高唱入云 gāochàng rù yún piercing the clouds with song—singing loud and clear

高超 gāochāo superb; excellent: 技艺～ superb skill / 见解～ excellent ideas

高超音速 gāochāoyīnsù phys. hypersonic speed: ～火箭 hypersonic rocket

高潮 gāocháo ① high tide; high water: ～线 high-water mark (or line) ② upsurge; high tide: 迎接社会主义建设的新～ greet the new high tide of socialist construction ③ (of fiction, drama and films) climax: 全剧的～ the climax of the play

高次方程 gāocì fāngchéng math. equation of higher degree

高醋 gāocù top-quality vinegar

高大 gāodà ① tall and big; tall: 身材～ be of tall and sturdy stature / ～的建筑物 tall buildings / ～明亮的车间 a big, bright, high-ceilinged workshop ② lofty: 革命英雄的～形象 the lofty image of a revolutionary hero

高蛋白 gāodànbái high protein

高档 gāodàng high (or top) grade; superior quality: ～商品 high-grade goods; expensive goods / ～服装 superior quality clothing

高等 gāoděng higher: ～哺乳动物 higher mammal

高等教育 gāoděng jiàoyù higher education

高等数学 gāoděng shùxué higher mathematics

高等学校 gāoděng xuéxiào institutions of higher learning; colleges and universities

高低 gāodī ① height: 山崖的～ the height of a cliff / 声调的～ the pitch of a voice ② relative superiority or inferiority: 争个～ vie with each other to see who is better / 难分～ hard to tell which is better ③ sense of propriety; discretion: 不知～ not know what's proper; have no sense of propriety ④ adv. dial. on any account; just; simply: 不管大家怎么劝说，他～不听。No matter how hard everyone tried to persuade him, he just wouldn't listen. ⑤ adv. dial. at long last: 经过几天的苦战，～把涵洞修好了。After days of hard work, the culvert was at last completed. / 这本书找了好几天，～找到了。We'd been looking for the book for quite a few days before we finally found it.

高低杠 gāodīgàng sports uneven (parallel) bars

高低角 gāodījiǎo mil. angle of site

高地 gāodì ① highland; upland; elevation: ～田 an upland field ② mil. height: 拿下三三二～ capture Height 332

高调 gāodiào ① lofty tone; high-sounding words ② photog. high tone —— see also 唱高调 chàng gāodiào

高度 gāodù ① altitude; height: 飞行～ flying altitude / 山的～ the height of a mountain ② a high degree: ～赞扬 pay high tribute to; speak highly of / 给予～重视 attach great importance to / ～现代化的工厂 a highly modernized plant / 没有充分的民主，就不可能有～的集中。Without ample democracy, it is impossible to have a high degree of centralism.

高度表 gāodùbiǎo (also 高度计 gāodùjì) altimeter

高尔夫球 gāo'ěrfūqiú ① golf: ～场 golf course; golf

links ② golf ball

高尔基体 gāo'ěrjītǐ biol. golgiosome

高飞远走 gāofēi-yuǎnzǒu same as 远走高飞 yuǎnzǒu-gāofēi

高分子 gāofēnzǐ chem. high polymer; macromolecule: ～化学 (high) polymer chemistry

高分子化合物 gāofēnzǐ huàhéwù macromolecular compound; high-molecular compound

高分子聚合物 gāofēnzǐ jùhéwù high polymer

高风亮节 gāofēng-liàngjié noble character and sterling integrity

高峰 gāofēng peak; summit; height: 珠穆朗玛峰是世界第一～。Mount Qomolangma (Everest) is the world's highest peak. / 攀登科学的～ scale the heights of science / 人口出生～期 a baby boom

高峰时间 gāofēng shíjiān peak-hour; rush hour

高干 gāogàn short for 高级干部 gāojí gànbù

高高在上 gāogāo zài shàng set oneself high above the masses; be far removed from the masses and reality

高高手儿 gāogāoshǒur same as 高抬贵手 gāo tái guì shǒu

高歌 gāogē sing heartily

高歌猛进 gāogē měngjìn stride forward singing songs of triumph; advance triumphantly

高个儿 gāogèr (also 高个子 gāogèzi) a tall person

高根 gāogēn bot. coca

高跟鞋 gāogēnxié high-heeled shoes

高官厚禄 gāoguān-hòulù high position and handsome salary; high position with high pay

高贵 gāoguì ① morally elevated; magnanimous; noble: ～品质 noble quality ② highly privileged; elitist

高寒 gāohán high and cold: ～地带 a high and cold area

高合金钢 gāohéjīngāng metall. high-alloy steel

高呼 gāohū shout loudly; cheer: ～口号 shout slogans loudly

高积云 gāojīyún meteorol. altocumulus

高级 gāojí ① senior; high-ranking; high-level; high: ～将领 high-ranking general officers / ～官员 high-ranking official ② high-grade; high-quality; advanced: ～染料 high-grade dyestuff / ～墨水 high-quality ink / ～读本 advanced reader / 这个旅馆真～! This hotel is really first-class.

高级干部 gāojí gànbù senior cadre

高级农业生产合作社 gāojí nóngyè shēngchǎn hézuòshè advanced agricultural producers' cooperative (in which the land and other chief means of production were collectively owned by the co-op and the distribution system was based on the principle of "from each according to his ability, to each according to his work")

高级人民法院 gāojí rénmín fǎyuàn higher people's court

高级社 gāojíshè short for 高级农业生产合作社 gāojí nóngyè shēngchǎn hézuòshè

高级神经活动 gāojí shénjīng huódòng physiol. higher nervous activity

高级小学 gāojí xiǎoxué higher primary school

高级研究员 gāojí yánjiūyuán senior research fellow

高级知识分子 gāojí zhīshifènzǐ higher intellectual

高级中学 gāojí zhōngxué senior middle school

高技术 gāojìshù high-technology; high-tech

高加索山脉 Gāojiāsuǒ Shānmài the Caucasus Mountains

高价 gāojià high price: ～收买 buy over at a high price / ～货物 expensive goods

高架桥 gāojiàqiáo viaduct

高架铁道 gāojià tiědào overhead railway; elevated railway

高见 gāojiàn *honor.* your brilliant idea; your opinion: 有何～? What do you think about it? / 不知～以为如何? I wonder if you would be kind enough to enlighten us on this matter. / 老兄～. What a brilliant idea, man.

高洁 gāojié noble and unsullied

高精尖 gāo-jīng-jiān high-grade, precision and advanced (industrial products)

高就 gāojiù *pol.* move up to a higher position (usu. in another place): 哎哟! 怎么你要～了! Oh! So you're moving up! / 另有～ have landed a better job

高举 gāojǔ hold high; hold aloft: 他～着奖杯向观众致意. He held the cup high for all the audience to see.

高聚物 gāojùwù *chem.* high polymer

高踞 gāojù stand above; set oneself above; lord it over: 共产党员绝不可～于群众之上. A Communist must never set himself above the masses.

高峻 gāojùn high and steep

高亢 gāokàng ① loud and sonorous; resounding: ～的歌声 sonorous singing ② (of terrain) high ③ *formal* supercilious; arrogant; haughty

高考 gāokǎo (short for 高等学校招生考试) college entrance examination

高空 gāokōng high altitude; upper air: ～飞行 high-altitude flight / ～核试验 high-altitude nuclear test / ～适应 high-altitude adaptation

高空病 gāokōngbìng altitude sickness

高空气象学 gāokōng qìxiàngxué aerology

高空作业 gāokōng zuòyè work high above the ground

高栏 gāolán *sports* high hurdles

高丽 Gāolí old name for 朝鲜 Cháoxiān

高丽参 gāolíshēn Korean ginseng

高利 gāolì very high interest (on a loan)

高利贷 gāolìdài usury; usurious loan: 放～ practise usury / ～者 usurer; loan shark / ～资本 usurer's capital

高良姜 gāoliángjiāng *bot.* (lesser) galangal (Alpinia officinarum)

高粱 gāoliang *kaoliang*; Chinese sorghum

高粱酒 gāoliangjiǔ spirit distilled from sorghum

高粱米 gāoliangmǐ husked *kaoliang*

高粱饴 gāoliangyí sweets (or candy) made of sorghum syrup; sorghum candy

高龄 gāolíng *pol.* advanced age (usu. over 60); venerable age: 八十～ the venerable age of 80

高岭石 gāolǐngshí kaolinite

高岭土 gāolǐngtǔ kaolin

高楼大厦 gāolóu-dàshà high buildings and large mansions

高炉 gāolú *metall.* blast furnace: ～利用系数 capacity factor of a blast furnace / ～煤气 blast furnace gas / ～寿命 life of a blast furnace

高氯酸 gāolǜsuān *chem.* perchloric acid

高论 gāolùn *pol.* enlightening remarks; brilliant views

高迈 gāomài *formal* advanced in years

高帽子 gāomàozi ① tall paper hat (worn as a sign of humiliation); dunce's cap ② flattery ——see also 戴高帽子 dài gāomàozi

高门 gāomén *old* wealthy family

高锰酸钾 gāoměngsuānjiǎ *chem.* potassium permanganate

高妙 gāomiào ingenious; masterly: 手艺～ masterly craftsmanship / 笔法～ masterly writing skills

高明 gāomíng ① brilliant; wise: 群众比我们～. The masses are wiser than we are. / 他这一手一点也不～. This move of his is not at all clever. / 见解～ brilliant ideas ② a wise person: 另请高明 lìng qǐng gāomíng

高能 gāonéng high energy: ～粒子 high-energy particle; energetic particle

高能燃料 gāonéng ránliào high-energy fuel

高能物理学 gāonéng wùlǐxué high-energy physics

高攀 gāopān make friends or claim ties of kinship with someone of a higher social position: 不敢～. I dare not be so presumptuous as to make friends with someone so high up.

高朋满座 gāopéng mǎn zuò a great gathering of distinguished guests

高频 gāopín *radio* high frequency: 甚～ very high frequency (vhf) / 超～ ultrahigh frequency (uhf) / ～扬声器 tweeter

高频电波 gāopín diànbō high-frequency electric wave

高气压 gāoqìyā high atmospheric (or barometric) pressure: ～区 high-pressure area; region of high barometric pressure

高腔 gāoqiāng a style of opera characterized by high-pitched singing to the accompaniment of percussion instruments only

高强 gāoqiáng excelling in: 武艺～ excel in martial arts

高强度 gāoqiángdù high strength: ～钢 high-strength steel; high-tensile steel

高跷 gāoqiāo stilts: 踩～ walk on stilts

高球 gāoqiú *sports* high ball; lob: 放～ send a ball in a lob; lob

高热 gāorè same as 高烧 gāoshāo

高人 gāorén ① a man of noble character; a man of great sanctity ② a man of superior attainments; past master; master-hand

高人一等 gāo rén yī děng a cut above other people: 他老以为自己～. He always thinks he's a cut above others. / 他看问题确是～. He stood head and shoulders above others in the way he looked at problems.

高僧 gāosēng eminent monk

高山病 gāoshānbìng mountain sickness

高山反应 gāoshānfǎnyìng altitude reaction

高山景行 gāoshān-jǐngxíng a high mountain and a great road—great nobility of character

高山流水 gāoshān-liúshuǐ high mountains and flowing waters—① sublime music ② understanding friends (a reference to an anecdote of the two great friends 伯牙 and 钟子期)

高山植物 gāoshān zhíwù alpine plant

高山族 Gāoshānzú the Gaoshan (Kaoshan) nationality, or the Gaoshans (Kaoshans), inhabiting Taiwan Province

高尚 gāoshàng ① noble; lofty: ～的人 a noble-minded person / ～的理想 lofty ideals ② meaningful; not in poor taste: ～的娱乐 tasteful entertainment

高烧 gāoshāo high fever: 发～ have (or run) a high fever

高射机关枪 gāoshè jīguānqiāng antiaircraft machine gun

高射炮 gāoshèpào antiaircraft gun (or artillery)

高深 gāoshēn advanced; profound; recondite: ～的学问 great learning (or scholarship)

高深莫测 gāoshēn mò cè same as 莫测高深 mò cè gāoshēn

高升 gāoshēng be promoted

高士 gāoshì same as 高人 gāorén①

高视阔步 gāoshì-kuòbù carry oneself proudly; strut; swagger; prance

高手 gāoshǒu past master; master-hand; ace: 象棋～ master (Chinese) chess player / 他在外科手术上是有名的～. He's a well-known master-hand in surgery.

高寿 gāoshòu ① longevity; long life ② *pol.* your venerable age: 老大爷, 您今年～? May I ask how old you are, Grandpa?

高耸 gāosǒng (stand) tall and erect; towering: ～入云 reach to the sky; tower into the clouds / ～的纪念碑 a towering monument

高速 gāosù high speed: ～前进 advance at high speed／～发展 develop by leaps and bounds; develop at top speed／～转弯很危险。It's dangerous to turn a corner at high speed.

高速挡 gāosùdǎng top gear; high gear

高速钢 gāosùgāng high-speed steel; rapid steel

高速公路 gāosù gōnglù expressway; freeway

高台定车 gāotái dìngchē *acrob.* a bicycle balancing act on an elevated stand

高抬贵手 gāo tái guì shǒu be magnanimous; be generous; not be too hard on sb.

高谈阔论 gāotán-kuòlùn indulge in loud and empty talk; talk volubly or bombastically

高碳钢 gāotàngāng *metall.* high-carbon steel

高汤 gāotāng ① soup-stock ② thin soup

高堂 gāotáng ① big hall; main hall ② *formal* one's parents

高挑儿 gāotiǎor *dial.* tall and lanky

高徒 gāotú ① *honor.* your (brilliant) student ② a brilliant student ——see also 名师出高徒 míngshī chū gāotú

高纬度 gāowěidù high latitudes

高位 gāowèi a high position: 身居～ hold a high position

高温 gāowēn high temperature: ～计 pyrometer／～气候 megathermal climate

高温切削 gāowēn qiēxiāo *mech.* high-temperature machining

高温作业 gāowēn zuòyè high-temperature operation

高卧 gāowò ① sleep with one's head on a high pillow ② live in seclusion; be a hermit

高屋建瓴 gāowū jiàn líng pour water off a steep roof—sweep down irresistibly from a commanding height; operate from a strategically advantageous position

高下 gāoxià relative superiority or inferiority: 两个人的技术不分～。The two of them are equally matched in their skills.

高香 gāoxiāng high-quality slender joss stick (burned when offering sacrifices to gods or ancestors) ——see also 烧高香 shāo gāoxiāng

高小 gāoxiǎo short for 高级小学 gāojí xiǎoxué

高校 gāoxiào short for 高等学校 gāoděng xuéxiào

高薪 gāoxīn high salary; high pay

高兴 gāoxìng ① glad; happy; cheerful: 看到孩子们有进步,心里很～。He was very pleased to see that the kids had made progress. / 小强高高兴兴地上学去了。Xiao Qiang cheerfully went off to school. / 他平时话不多,～的时候才说上几句。He's usually reticent and only talks a little when in high spirits. / 把这消息告诉你爷爷,叫他老人家也～～。Tell Grandpa the good news, so that he can share our joy. / 两个人谈得可～了。The two of them chatted merrily. / 我们昨天玩得真～。We had a wonderful time yesterday. / 他们～得太早了。They rejoiced too soon. ② be willing to; be happy to: 他就是～看电影,看戏不感兴趣。He's fond of seeing films, and not at all interested in watching plays. / 你不～去就甭去了。You needn't go if you don't feel like it.

高血压 gāoxuèyā *med.* hypertension; high blood pressure

高压 gāoyā ① *phys. meteorol.* high pressure ② *elec.* high tension; high voltage: ～电力网 high-tension network ③ *med.* maximum pressure ④ high-handed (persecution): 反动政权的～政策 the high-handed policy of a reactionary regime

高压泵 gāoyābèng *mech.* high-pressure pump

高压电缆 gāoyā diànlǎn high-tension cable

高压锅 gāoyāguō pressure cooker

高压脊 gāoyājǐ *meteorol.* ridge of high pressure; pressure ridge

高压灭菌器 gāoyā mièjūnqì autoclave

高压水龙 gāoyā shuǐlóng water cannon

高压线 gāoyāxiàn high-tension line (*or* wire)

高雅 gāoyǎ refined; elegant

高研 gāoyán short for 高级研究员 gāojí yánjiūyuán

高眼鲽 gāoyǎndié *zool.* plaice

高音喇叭 gāoyīn lǎba tweeter

高原 gāoyuán plateau; highland; tableland: 青藏～ the Qinghai-Xizang Plateau

高燥 gāozào (of land) high and dry

高瞻远瞩 gāozhān-yuǎnzhǔ stand high and see far; take a broad and long view; show great foresight

高涨 gāozhǎng rise; upsurge; run high: 群众热情～。The enthusiasm of the masses ran high. / 物价～。Prices were skyrocketing.

高招 gāozhāo (also 高着儿 gāozhāor) *inf.* clever move; brilliant idea: 我看他也没有什么～。I don't think he can come up with any clever move. / 你有什么～,快说说。What have you got up your sleeve? Out with it!

高枕无忧 gāo zhěn wú yōu shake up the pillow and have a good sleep; sit back and relax

高知 gāozhī short for 高级知识分子 gāojí zhīshifènzǐ

高枝儿 gāozhīr higher branches—one's superiors or betters: 攀～ play up to one's superiors or betters

高中 gāozhōng short for 高级中学 gāojí zhōngxué

高姿态 gāozītài lofty stance; magnanimous attitude

高足 gāozú *honor.* your brilliant disciple; your pupil

高祖 gāozú (paternal) great-great-grandfather

高祖母 gāozǔmǔ (paternal) great-great-grandmother

羔 gāo lamb; kid; fawn: 羊羔 yánggāo

羔皮 gāopí lambskin; kidskin; kid

羔羊 gāoyáng lamb—an innocent and helpless person or a scapegoat

羔子 gāozi lamb; kid; fawn: 小猪～ piglet

皋（皐） gāo *formal* highland on the banks of a river

膏 gāo ① fat; grease; oil: 春雨如～。Rain in spring is as precious as oil. ② paste; cream; ointment: 雪花膏 xuěhuāgāo ——see also gào

膏肓 gāohuāng see 病入膏肓 bìng rù gāohuāng

膏剂 gāojì *pharm.* medicinal extract; electuary

膏粱 gāoliáng *liter.* fat meat and fine grain; rich food: 居处于～锦绣之中 living in the lap of luxury

膏粱子弟 gāoliáng zǐdì good-for-nothing sons of the idle rich

膏血 gāoxuè human fat and blood—the fruits of hard toil

膏药 gāoyao *Chin. med.* medicated plaster; plaster: 贴～ apply a plaster to

膏腴 gāoyú *formal* fertile: ～之地 fertile land

膏子 gāozi *inf.* ointment-like medicine for oral or plastering use

睾 gāo see below

睾丸 gāowán testis; testicle

睾丸炎 gāowányán orchitis

糕（餻） gāo cake; pudding

糕点 gāodiǎn cake; pastry

糕干 gāogan sweetened rice flour (sometimes fed to infants as a substitute for powdered milk)

糕干粉 gāoganfěn powdered rice-cereal

篙 gāo punt-pole

gǎo

杲 gǎo *liter.* bright: ～日升空。The bright sun rises into the void.

杲杲 gǎogǎo *liter.* (of the sun) shining brightly

搞 gǎo ① do; carry on; be engaged in: ～调查研究 do some investigation and study; do surveys / ～改革 carry on reforms / ～生产 engage in production / ～社会主义 practise socialism / ～阴谋诡计的人注定要失败。Those who go in for intrigues and conspiracy are doomed to failure. / 他是～建筑的。He's in the building industry. *or* He's in building. ② make; produce; work out: ～个计划 draw up a plan / 我们～一点核武器完全是为了自卫。It is purely for self-defence that we have produced some nuclear weapons. / 我们要～一期短篇小说专刊。We're going to put out a special issue of short stories. / 别～那么多菜了。Don't make so many dishes. ③ set up; start; organize: 这家工厂是由一个个体户～起来的。This factory was started by a self-employed worker. / 我们打算在这里～个发电站。We're thinking of putting up a power station here. ④ get; get hold of; secure: 你去给我们～点吃的来。Go and get us something to eat. / ～钱 raise money; make money ⑤ (followed by a complement): 把事情～糟了 have made a mess of things / 把某人～臭 make sb.'s name stink; discredit sb. / 把问题～清楚 get a clear understanding of the question (*or* problem) / 别把机器～坏了。Don't break the machine. / 我把你们的名字～混了。I've mixed up your names. / 他思想一～通了，精神也就愉快了。Once he straightened out his ideas, he became cheerful again.

搞对象 gǎo duìxiàng go steady

搞法 gǎofǎ way of doing or making a thing; method: 不是这么个～。This is not the right way of doing it. / 他训练游泳运动员的那种～我不赞成。I don't much like his methods of training swimmers.

搞鬼 gǎoguǐ play tricks; be up to some mischief: 提防有人暗中～。Beware of foul play! / 你究竟在搞什么鬼？这么神秘。What on earth are you up to? You're being so mysterious.

搞好 gǎohǎo make a good job of; do well: ～团结 strengthen unity / ～军民关系 build good relations between the army and the people / 这块地～了，每亩地可以收一千斤。If this plot of land is handled well, it can yield 1,000 *jin* per *mu*. / 搞不好还得重来。If things go wrong we'll have to start all over again. / 要么不搞，要搞就要～。We either do a good job of it, or we don't do it at all.

搞活 gǎohuó vitalize; enliven: ～经济 enliven the economy / ～企业 invigorate the enterprises

缟 gǎo a thin white silk used in ancient China

缟素 gǎosù white mourning apparel

槁（槀） gǎo withered: 枯槁 kūgǎo

槁木 gǎomù a withered tree

槁木死灰 gǎomù-sǐhuī dead trees and cold ashes—complete apathy

稿¹（稾） gǎo *formal* stalk of grain; straw: 稿荐 gǎojiàn

稿²（稾） gǎo ① draft; sketch: 先打个～儿再画 make a sketch before painting ② a rough draft (of a document); draft: 拟～ make a draft

稿本 gǎoběn manuscript (of a book, etc.)

稿酬 gǎochóu same as 稿费 gǎofèi

稿费 gǎofèi payment for an article or book published; contribution fee; author's remuneration: 这家出版社的～标准较高。This publisher offers a better rate of remuneration.

稿件 gǎojiàn manuscript; contribution

稿荐 gǎojiàn straw mattress; pallet

稿约 gǎoyuē notice to contributors (to a magazine, etc.)

稿纸 gǎozhǐ standardized writing paper with squares or lines

稿子 gǎozi ① draft; sketch: 起个～ make a draft ② manuscript; contribution: 给黑板报写～ write sth. for the blackboard newspaper / 这篇～是谁写的？Who wrote this article? ③ idea; plan: 我心里还没个准～。I haven't got any definite plan yet.

镐 gǎo pick; pickaxe

镐头 gǎotou pick; pickaxe

gào

告 gào ① tell; inform; notify: 何时启程, 盼～。Please inform me of your date of departure. ② go to law against sb.; sue; take sb. to court: 到法院去～他。Go to court and sue him. ③ ask for; request; solicit: 告假 gàojià ④ declare; announce: 不～而别 go away without taking leave; leave without saying good-bye ⑤ reach (a particular state): ～一段落 come to the end of a stage; be brought to a temporary close

告白 gàobái a public notice or announcement

告便 gàobiàn *euph.* ask permission to absent oneself briefly (to relieve oneself): 对不起, 我先～一下。Will you please excuse me for a moment?

告别 gàobié ① leave; part from: 我们～了这个地方, 继续向前进。We left the place and went on with our journey. / 他把信交给了队长, 就匆匆～了。He hurried off after giving the letter to the team leader. ② bid farewell to; say good-bye to: 挥手～ wave farewell / 我向你～来了。I've come to say good-bye to you. / 向遗体～ pay one's last respects to the deceased

告别词 gàobiécí farewell speech; valediction

告别宴会 gàobié yànhuì farewell banquet

告别仪式 gàobié yíshì farewell ceremony

告禀 gàobǐng report (to one's superior)

告病 gàobìng ask for sick leave; resign on account of illness

告成 gàochéng (of a major task or project) be completed or accomplished: 这部巨著历时十年方始～。This magnum opus took ten years to complete.

告吹 gàochuī *inf.* fizzle out; fail: 由于资金不足, 计划～。The plan fizzled out due to lack of funds.

告辞 gàocí take leave (of one's host): 我怕耽误他的时间, 谈了一会儿就～了。I took leave after a brief talk so as not to take up too much of his time.

告贷 gàodài ask for a loan: 四处～ borrow money from everyone / 奔走～ run around trying to raise money / ～无门 be unable to get a loan from any source

告发 gàofā report (an offender); inform against; lodge an accusation against: 向政府～了他的卖国罪行 report his treasonous act to the government / 他逃税漏税的事早就被人～了。He has already been reported concerning his tax-evasion.

告乏 gàofá be inadequate; be in short supply: 资金～。Funds are inadequate.

告急 gàojí ① be in a state of emergency: 洪水猛涨,大坝～。The dam was in danger because of the rising flood. ② report an emergency; ask for emergency help: 前线频频～。The front-line units repeatedly signalled for help.

告假 gàojià ask for leave: 告三天假 ask for a three-day leave

告捷 gàojié ① win victory (in war or games): 首战～ win in the very first battle or game ② report a victory

告诫 gàojiè warn; admonish; exhort: 师长经常～我们要提高警惕。The division commander constantly exhorted us to heighten our vigilance. / 他再三～自己,不要轻举妄动。Again and again, he cautioned himself against rashness.

告警 gàojǐng report an emergency; give (or sound) an alarm

告竣 gàojùn be completed: 治河工程全部～。The whole project for harnessing the river has been completed.

告老 gàolǎo retire on account of age

告老还乡 gàolǎo huánxiāng old (of a government official) retire and return to one's native place

告密 gàomì inform against sb.: 他做地下工作时,曾因叛徒～而被捕。When he was doing underground work he was arrested because a renegade informed against him. / ～者 informer

告罄 gàoqìng run out; be exhausted: 弹药～。Ammunition has run out. / 库存～ be out of stock

告饶 gàoráo beg for mercy; ask pardon: 求情～ plead for mercy

告示 gàoshi ① notify; announce: 我们按照海报上～的钟点,准时进入会场。We went to the meeting hall at the time as announced in the poster. ② official notice; bulletin; placard ③ old slogan; poster

告诉 gàosù leg. file a legal complaint; bring a complaint

告诉 gàosu tell; let know: ～他们别等了。Tell them not to wait. / 有什么消息,～我一声。Let me know if there's any news. / 我～你,下回可不许这样。Let me tell you, don't do it again.

告退 gàotuì ask for leave to withdraw from a meeting, etc.: 兄弟在此不便久留,就此～。I should not stay here too long. I wish you good day. / 随着仪式结束,客人全部～。As the ceremony came to a close, all the guests departed. ② old resign from an office

告慰 gàowèi ① comfort; console ② feel relieved

告语 gàoyǔ formal tell; let know: 互相～ tell one another the news / 无可～。There is nothing to tell.

告御状 gào yùzhuàng bring an accusation against sb. before the emperor

告枕头状 gào zhěntouzhuàng make complaints in private to one's husband about sb. or sth.

告知 gàozhī inform; notify: 他问起许多老同学的近况,我一一～。He inquired about many of our old classmates, and I told him about each of them. / 我将这事～了有关人员。I informed those concerned of this matter.

告终 gàozhōng come to an end; end up: 以失败～ end in failure / 以损人开始,以害己～ start with the aim of harming others and end up by harming oneself

告状 gàozhuàng inf. ① go to law against sb.; bring a lawsuit against sb. ② lodge a complaint against sb. with his superior: 他在老师面前告了我一状。He lodged a complaint against me with the teacher.

告罪 gàozuì ask for forgiveness; apologize

郜 Gào a surname

诰 gào ① arch. (of superiors) admonish; enjoin ② arch. a written admonition ③ imperial mandate: 诰封 gàofēng

诰封 gàofēng the conferment of honorary titles by imperial mandate

诰命 gàomìng ① imperial mandate ② old a titled lady

锆 gào chem. zirconium (Zr)

锆鞣 gàoróu zirconium tanning: ～革 zirconium tanned leather

锆石 gàoshí zircon (a mineral)

膏 gào ① lubricate: ～车 lubricate the axle of a cart / 在轴上～点儿油 put some lubricant on the axle ② dip a writing brush in ink and smooth it on an inkstone before writing: ～笔 smooth a (ink-dipped) writing brush on the edge of an inkstone ——see also gāo

gē

戈 gē ① dagger-axe (an ancient weapon) ② (Gē) a surname

戈壁 gēbì ① geol. gobi ② (Gēbì) the Gobi Desert

仡 gē see below

仡佬族 Gēlǎozú the Gelo (Kelao) nationality, or the Gelos (Kelaos), inhabiting Guizhou Province

圪 gē see below

圪垯 gēda (also 圪塔 gēda) ① same as 疙瘩 gēda ② mound; knoll

纥 gē see below ——see also hé

纥繨 gēda lump; knot

疙 gē see below

疙瘩 gēda ① a swelling on the skin; pimple; lump ② lump; knot: 线结成了～。The thread has got tangled (or got into a knot). ③ a knot in one's heart; hang-up: 解开心上的～ get rid of one's hang-up / 我们帮助他们解开了～。We helped to dispel the misunderstanding between them.

疙瘩汤 gēdatāng dough drop soup

疙疙瘩瘩 gēgedādā (also 疙里疙瘩 gēligēdā) inf. rough; knotty; bumpy: 路上净是石头子儿,～的,差点绊倒。The road was full of gravel and very bumpy. I almost stumbled. / 这事情～的,很不好办。It was a tricky problem to deal with.

咯 gē see below ——see also kǎ; lo; luò

咯噔 gēdēng onom.: ～～的皮靴声 the click of boots (on a floor)

咯咯 gēgē onom. ① the sound made by a hen; cluck; chuckle; cackle: 母鸡下完蛋后,～地叫个不停。The hen started clucking after she laid an egg. ② the sound of laughing; chuckle; titter: 她～地笑个不停,眼泪都笑出来了。She chuckled herself to tears.

咯吱 gēzhī onom.: 扁担压得～～地直响。The carrying pole creaked under the load.

格 gē see below ——see also gé

格格 gēgē onom. the sound of laughing; chuckle; titter

格格 gēge a Manchu term for a princess, a young lady, or a daughter

哥 gē ① (elder) brother: 大～ the eldest of one's

brothers ② a friendly term of address for male older acquaintances: 李二～ Brother Li'er

哥儿 gēr ① brothers: 你们～几个? How many of you boys are there altogether in your family? / 他们～仨都是运动员。All three brothers are athletes. ② boys (of rich families, etc.): 公子哥儿 gōngzǐgēr

哥瓷 gēcí porcelain with crackled glaze; crackle-china

哥德巴赫猜想 Gēdébāhè cāixiǎng math. Goldbach's conjecture

哥哥 gēge (elder) brother

哥伦比亚 Gēlúnbǐyà Colombia

哥伦比亚人 Gēlúnbǐyàrén Colombian

哥罗仿 gēluófǎng chem. chloroform

哥儿们 gērmen inf. ① brothers ② buddies; pals: 穷～ we, the poor / ～义气 brotherhood loyalty; gang spirit

哥斯达黎加 Gēsīdálíjiā Costa Rica

哥斯达黎加人 Gēsīdálíjiārén Costa Rican

哥特式 gētèshì archit. Gothic: ～教堂 Gothic cathedral (or church)

哥特体 gētètǐ print. gothic (type)

胳（肐） gē see below ——see also gé

胳臂 gēbei arm

胳膊 gēbo arm

胳膊扭不过大腿 gēbo niǔbuguò dàtuǐ the arm is no match for the thigh—the weaker can't contend with the stronger

胳膊腕子 gēbowànzi wrist

胳膊肘儿 gēbozhǒur elbow

袼 gē see below

袼褙 gēbei pieces of old cloth or rags pasted together to make cloth shoes

谞 gē formal ① song ② sing

鸽 gē pigeon; dove: 家鸽 jiāgē / 野鸽 yěgē

鸽哨 gēshào a whistle tied to a pigeon

鸽子 gēzi pigeon; dove: ～笼 dovecote; pigeon house; loft

割 gē cut: ～麦子 cut (or reap) wheat / ～草 cut grass; mow / ～破手指 cut one's finger

割爱 gē'ài give up what one treasures; part with some cherished possession: 这盘磁带请你～让给我吧。Would you be willing to part with this cassette and give it to me please?

割草机 gēcǎojī mower

割除 gēchú cut off; remove; excise: ～肿瘤 remove a tumour

割地 gēdì cede territory: 帝国主义列强多次强迫清廷～赔款。The imperialist powers repeatedly forced the Qing government to cede territory and pay indemnities.

割断 gēduàn sever; cut off: ～电话线 cut telephone wires / 我们不能～历史看问题。We mustn't consider a question apart from its historical context.

割鸡焉用牛刀 gē jī yān yòng niúdāo why use an ox-cleaver to kill a chicken; why break a butterfly on the wheel

割胶 gējiāo tap rubber

割炬 gējù mech. cutting torch

割据 gējù set up a separatist regime by force of arms: 封建～ feudal separatist rule / 军阀～ separatist warlord regimes / 诸侯～称雄的封建国家 a feudal state torn apart by rival principalities / 工农武装～ an armed independent regime of workers and peasants (during the Second Revolutionary Civil War)

割捆机 gēkǔnjī agric. self-binder; binder

割礼 gēlǐ religion circumcision

割裂 gēliè cut apart; separate; isolate: 这两点是互相联系的, 不能～。The two points are related and cannot be taken separately. / 不应把这种政策同当时的环境～开来。One must not isolate this policy from its historical context.

割漆 gēqī tap a lacquer tree

割让 gēràng cede: ～领土 cession of territory

割晒机 gēshàijī agric. swather; windrower

割舍 gēshě give up; part with: 难以～ find it hard to part with

割线 gēxiàn math. secant

搁 gē ① put: 把箱子～在行李架上。Put the suitcase on the luggage-rack. / 你把东西～下。Put down your things. / 汤里～点盐。Put some salt in the soup. / 把东西～在这儿吧。Just leave your things here. / 箱子这么大, 所有东西都～得下。This suitcase is big enough to hold all the things. / 这屋子太热, 种子～不住。This room is too hot; the seeds won't keep. ② put aside; leave over; shelve: 这件事得～一～再办。We'll have to put the matter aside for the time being. / 你把手里活儿～下, 歇一会儿。Stop what you're doing and take a rest. ——see also gé

搁笔 gēbǐ lay down the pen or brush; stop writing or painting

搁浅 gēqiǎn ① run aground; be stranded: 船～了。The ship got stranded (or ran aground). ② reach a deadlock: 谈判～了。The negotiations have come to a deadlock.

搁置 gēzhì shelve; lay aside; pigeonhole: ～一项动议 shelve a motion / 他要出国留学, 婚事只好～不提。Since he was going abroad to study, he had to shelve his marriage plans.

歌 gē ① song: 唱支～儿 sing a song ② sing: 高歌 gāogē

歌本 gēběn songbook

歌唱 gēchàng ① sing: 尽情～ sing to one's heart's content / ～家 singer; vocalist ② praise (through songs, poems, etc.): ～祖国的繁荣昌盛 sing (in praise) of the prosperity of our country

歌词 gēcí words of a song

歌功颂德 gēgōng-sòngdé eulogize sb.'s virtues and achievements; sing the praises of sb.

歌喉 gēhóu (singer's) voice; singing voice: ～婉转 have a sweet (or beautiful) voice

歌剧 gējù opera: 小～ operetta / ～剧本 libretto / ～团 opera troupe (or company) / ～院 opera house

歌诀 gējué formulas or directions put into rhyme: 汤头歌诀 tāngtóu gējué

歌女 gēnǚ old singing-girl

歌片儿 gēpiānr song sheet

歌谱 gēpǔ music score of a song; music of a song

歌曲 gēqǔ song

歌声 gēshēng sound of singing; singing: ～四起。Sounds of singing were heard from all around. / 嘹亮的～ loud and clear singing / 那山鸟欢乐的～ the joyous song of the blackbird

歌手 gēshǒu singer; vocalist

歌颂 gēsòng sing the praises of; extol; eulogize: ～劳动英雄 sing the praises of labour heroes / ～共产主义风格 extol the communist style of behaviour

歌台舞榭 gētái-wǔxiè halls for the performance of songs and dances

歌坛 gētán the circle of singers: ～新秀 a new singing star

歌舞 gēwǔ song and dance

歌舞伎　gēwǔjì　kabuki (a popular Japanese dramatic form)

歌舞剧　gēwǔjù　song and dance drama

歌舞升平　gēwǔ shēngpíng　sing and dance to extol the good times—put on a show of peace and prosperity

歌舞团　gēwǔtuán　song and dance ensemble (or troupe)

歌星　gēxīng　a singing star

歌行　gēxíng　an old song form: 长～ long-song lay / 短～ short-song lay

歌谣　gēyáo　ballad; folk song; nursery rhyme: 民间～ folk songs; popular ballads

歌吟　gēyín　① sing ② recite a poem

歌咏　gēyǒng　singing: ～比赛 singing contest / ～队 singing group; chorus

歌子　gēzi　song

gé

革¹　gé　① leather; hide: 皮革 pígé　② (Gé) a surname

革²　gé　① change; transform: 变革 biàngé　② remove sb. from office; expel: 革职 gézhí

革出　géchū　expel

革除　géchú　① abolish; get rid of; eliminate: ～陈规陋习 abolish outmoded regulations and eliminate irrational practices ② expel; dismiss; remove sb. from office

革故鼎新　gégù-dǐngxīn　discard the old and introduce the new

革履　gélǚ　leather shoes

革面洗心　gémiàn-xǐxīn　same as 洗心革面 xǐxīn-gémiàn

革命　gémìng　① cause great social change; rise in revolt; take part in revolution: ～到底 carry the revolution through to the end; remain a revolutionary to the end of one's life / 农民起来革地主的命。The peasants rose in revolt against the landlords. ② revolution: 技术～ technological revolution / ～理论 revolutionary theory / 工人阶级是最～的阶级。The working class is the most dedicated class to the cause of the revolution.

革命发展阶段论　gémìng fāzhǎn jiēduànlùn　the theory of the development of revolution by stages

革命化　gémìnghuà　revolutionize; do things in a revolutionary way

革命回忆录　gémìng huíyìlù　reminiscences of earlier revolutionary times

革命家　gémìngjiā　revolutionary; revolutionist

革命军人委员会　gémìng jūnrén wěiyuánhuì　revolutionary armymen's committee (a mass organization of a company, elected by all its members)

革命浪漫主义　gémìnglàngmànzhǔyì　revolutionary romanticism

革命人道主义　gémìngréndàozhǔyì　revolutionary humanitarianism

革命现实主义　gémìngxiànshízhǔyì　revolutionary realism

革命性　gémìngxìng　revolutionary character (or quality, spirit): 无产阶级的～ the revolutionary character of the proletariat / 这本教科书～和科学性结合得很好。This textbook successfully combines revolutionary spirit with scientific methodology.

革命英雄主义　gémìngyīngxióngzhǔyì　revolutionary heroism

革囊　génáng　a leather bag

革新　géxīn　innovate; improve: 技术～ technological innovation / 传统的手工艺技术不断～。Traditional handicraft techniques are being steadily improved.

革职　gézhí　remove sb. from office; dismiss sb. from his post; cashier: 他因贻误军机被朝廷～查办。The imperial court removed him from office and prosecuted him for delaying the fulfilment of a military plan.

革制品　gézhìpǐn　leather goods

阁　gé　① pavilion (usu. two-storeyed) ② cabinet (of a government): 内阁 nèigé　/ 组阁 zǔgé　③ old boudoir: 出阁 chūgé　④ formal shelf: 束之高阁 shù zhī gāogé

阁楼　gélóu　attic; loft; garret

阁下　géxià　honor. Your Excellency or His or Her Excellency: 大使～ Your Excellency Mr. Ambassador or His Excellency the Ambassador

阁员　géyuán　member of a cabinet

阖　gé　formal ① a small side door ② same as 阁 gé

格¹　gé　① squares formed by crossed lines; check: 把字写在～儿里。Write the characters in the squares. / 在纸上打～儿 square off the paper ② division (horizontal or otherwise): 横～纸 ruled paper / 四～儿的书架 a bookcase with four shelves / 每服一小～。Dose one measure each time. ③ standard; pattern; style: 合格 hégé　④ formal impede; obstruct; bar: ～于成例 be hindered by conventions

格²　gé　gram. case: 主～ the nominative case / 宾～ the objective case

格³　gé　examine; study: 格物 géwù

格⁴　gé　fight: 格斗 gédòu
——see also gē

格调　gédiào　① (literary or artistic) style: ～豪放 a vigorous and flowing style / 这首诗～很老成。This poem is written in a grand style. ② formal one's style of work as well as one's moral quality: 他这个人～不高。He's rather vulgar.

格斗　gédòu　grapple; wrestle; fistfight: 徒手～ fight with bare fists

格格不入　gégé bù rù　incompatible with; out of tune with; out of one's element; like a square peg in a round hole: 他的计划和我的意图是～的。His plan is incompatible with my intentions.

格局　géjú　pattern; setup; structure: 外交～ the pattern of a country's foreign affairs / 在这场足球比赛中我队始终保持"四三三"的～。Throughout the football match our team kept to the 4–3–3 pattern (or formation). / 这几个菜市场的～差不多。These food markets have more or less the same setup. / 这篇文章写得很乱，简直不成个～。This article is badly written without any structure. / 我很欣赏这个花园的～。I admire the layout of this garden.

格林纳达　Gélínnàdá　Grenada

格林纳达人　Gélínnàdárén　Grenadian

格林威治时间　Gélínwēizhì shíjiān　Greenwich mean time (GMT)

格陵兰　Gélínglán　Greenland

格鲁吉亚　Gélǔjíyà　Georgia

格律　gélǜ　rules and forms of classical poetic composition (with respect to tonal pattern, rhyme scheme, etc.)

格杀勿论　géshā wùlùn　(also 格杀不论 géshā bùlùn) kill on the spot with the authority of the law

格式　géshì　form; pattern: 公文～ the form (or standardized style) of an official document

格外 géwài *adv.* ① especially; particularly; all the more: 雪地上骑车要～小心。You've got to be especially careful when you cycle on snow. /国庆节，天安门显得～壮丽。Tian An Men looks especially magnificent on National Day. /他对计算机～感兴趣。He's particularly interested in computers. /雨后天空～蓝。The sky is extremely blue after the rain. /这个问题解决得～令人满意。The problem was solved most satisfactorily. /打败一名种子选手～不容易。It's extremely difficult to beat a seeded player. ② additionally: 卡车装不下，～找了一辆大车。As the truck couldn't hold all the goods, an additional cart was ordered.

格物 géwù investigate things

格物致知 géwù-zhìzhī to investigate things is to attain knowledge

格言 géyán maxim; motto; aphorism

格致 gézhì short for 格物致知, used during the closing years of the Qing Dynasty (1644–1911) to refer to natural science in general

格子 gézi squares formed by crossed lines; check; chequer: 用尺打～ square (the page) off with a ruler

格子布 gézibù checked fabric; check

格子窗 gézichuāng lattice window

格子花呢 gézi huāní tartan

胳

胳 gé see below ——see also gē

胳肢 gézhi *dial.* tickle sb.

葛
Gě

葛 gé ① *bot.* kudzu vine ② poplin ——see also

葛布 gébù ko-hemp cloth

葛根 gégēn *Chin. med.* the root of kudzu vine

蛤

蛤 gé clam ——see also há

蛤蚧 géjiè red-spotted lizard

蛤蜊 géli clam

颌

颌 gé *formal* mouth ——see also hé

搁

搁 gé bear; stand; endure: ～不住压 cannot stand crushing ——see also gē

隔（隔）

隔 gé ①separate; cut off; partition: 把一间屋～成两间 partition a room into two /龟蛇二山～江相望。Tortoise and Snake Hills (in Hubei Province) face each other across the (Changjiang) River. /一座山就是水库。The reservoir is just on the other side of the hill. ② be apart from; be at a distance from: 相～千里 a thousand *li* away from each other /每棵树苗要～开五米。The saplings should be five metres apart. /你～两天再来吧。Come back in two days' time. /～两周去一次 go there every third week /请～行写。Please write on every other line. /～四小时服一次。To be taken once every four hours.

隔岸观火 gé àn guān huǒ watch a fire from the other side of the river—look on at sb.'s trouble with indifference

隔壁 gébì next door: ～邻居 next-door neighbour /住在～ live next door /～第二间 next door but one

隔断 géduàn cut off; separate; obstruct: 洪水把村子同县城的交通～了。The flood cut the village off from the county town. /高山大海隔不断我们两国人民的友好往来。Mountains and seas cannot obstruct the friendly exchanges between our two peoples.

隔断 géduan *archit.* partition (wall, board, etc.)

隔行 géháng of different trades or professions

隔行如隔山 géháng rú gé shān different trades are separated as by mountains (i.e. the outsider knows no more of the secrets of the craft than he knows of another country)

隔阂 géhé estrangement; misunderstanding: 制造～ foment feelings of estrangement /经过批评和自我批评，他们消除了～。Through criticism and self-criticism they cleared up their misunderstanding (or ended their estrangement). ② barrier: 语言的～ language barrier

隔火墙 géhuǒqiáng fire division wall; fire wall

隔绝 géjué cut off; separate; obstruct: 和外界～ be cut off from the outside world /他走了以后就与我们音信～了。He has never been heard of since he left us. or There's been no news of him since he left.

隔离 gélí keep apart; isolate; segregate: 种族～ racial segregation; apartheid /病人已经～了一周。The patient has been in isolation for a week.

隔离病房 gélí bìngfáng isolation ward

隔膜 gémó ① lack of mutual understanding: 他们之间有些～。They are somewhat estranged from each other. ② be unfamiliar with: 我对那里的情况很～。I know very little about the situation there.

隔年黄历 génián huánglì last year's calendar—something obsolete; yesterday's paper

隔片 gépiàn *mech.* spacer

隔墙 géqiáng *archit.* partition (wall)

隔墙有耳 gé qiáng yǒu ěr walls have ears; beware of eavesdroppers

隔热 gérè *archit.* insulate against heat

隔日 gérì ① the next day ② every other day: ～吃一片 take a tablet every other day

隔山 géshān separation by a mountain—relationship between half-brothers or half-sisters by the same father: ～兄弟 half-brothers by the same father

隔扇 géshan partition board

隔声 géshēng *archit.* insulate against sound: ～板 sound insulating board /～材料 sound insulator

隔世之感 géshì zhī gǎn (it seems as if) a whole generation has passed

隔靴搔痒 gé xuē sāoyǎng scratch an itch from outside one's boot—fail to get to the root of the matter; fail to strike home; take totally ineffective measures

隔夜 géyè of the previous night: 把～的菜热一热 warm up last night's leftovers /～的茶最好别喝。You'd better not drink last night's tea. /过去那日子，真是家无～粮啊。In the old days, we never had any food at home to tide us over the next day.

隔音 géyīn give sound insulation

隔音符号 géyīn fúhào syllable-dividing mark (')

隔音室 géyīnshì soundproof room

嗝

嗝 gé ① hiccup ② belch; burp

膈

膈 gé diaphragm

膈膜 gémó diaphragm

槅

槅 gé ① a latticed door or partition board; lattice ② a set of latticed shelves: 多宝槅 duōbǎogé

槅门 gémén a latticed door; lattice

槅扇 géshan same as 隔扇 géshan

镉

镉 gé *chem.* cadmium (Cd)

骼

骼 gé see 骨骼 gǔgé

gě

合

合 gě *ge*, a unit of dry measure for grain (=1 decilitre) ——see also hé

舸 gě *liter.* barge: 漫江碧透，百～争流。(毛泽东) A hundred barges were vying over crystal blue waters.

葛 Gě a surname ——see also gé

葛仙米 gěxiānmǐ *bot.* nostoc

gè

个[1]**(個、箇)** gè ① *m.* (before nouns without special measure words of their own): 三～苹果 three apples / 一～故事 a story / 两～星期 two weeks; a fortnight / 一～心眼儿 be of one mind / 第五～年头 the fifth year ② *m.* (used to replace certain measure words): 一～ (*or* 所) 学校 a school / 一～ (*or* 家) 工厂 a factory / 两～ (*or* 只) 耳朵 two ears ③ *m.* (before an approximate number): 他每星期来一～或两次 every week. / 这点活儿有～两三天就干完了。 This bit of work can easily be finished in a couple of days. / 哥儿俩也不过差～两三岁。 There's only a two or three years difference between the two brothers. ④ *m.* (between a verb and its object): 洗～澡 have a bath / 睡～好觉 have a good sleep / 他在农村待了两年, 扶～犁, 赶～车, 都拿得起来。 After a couple of years in the countryside, he was quite good at handling a plough and driving a cart. / 你有～正经没有? Can't you ever be a little bit serious? / 没～错儿, 就是这样。 That's it, and no mistake! ⑤ *m.* (between a verb and its complement): 砸～稀巴烂 smash sth. to smithereens / 忙～不停 be as busy as a bee / 扫得～干干净净 have given a thorough sweeping / 雨下～不停。 It kept raining. ⑥ *m.* (after in certain phrases to indicate suddenness): 他一～箭步窜了上去。 With a sudden big stride, he leapt forward. / 一～失手我把茶杯瓶了。 I accidentally dropped the cup and broke it. ⑦ individual: 个别 gèbié / 个人 gèrén

个[2]**(個、箇)** gè ① (used as a suffix after 些): 那些～花儿 all those flowers / 这些～书哪能看完? How can I finish reading so many books? ② *dial.* (used after 昨儿, 今儿, 明儿, etc.): 明儿～ tomorrow ——see also gě

个儿 gèr ① size; height; stature: 别看她～不大, 劲儿可不小。 She's not big, but she's strong. / 瞧这棉桃的～! Look, what huge bolls these are! ② persons or things taken singly: 挨～握手 shake hands with each one / 论～卖 be sold by the piece

个把 gèbǎ one or two; a couple of: 多～人也住得下。 There is enough room to put up one or two more people. / 再过～月, 我就要回国了。 In a couple of months, I'll be going back to my country. / 会只开了～小时就散了。 The meeting ended after only a couple of hours.

个别 gèbié ① individual; specific: ～辅导 individual coaching / ～照顾 special consideration for individual cases / 一般号召和～指导相结合 combine the general call with particular guidance / 领导找她一～谈话 The leading comrade had a private talk with her. ② very few; one or two: 只有～人请假。 Only one or two people asked for leave. / 这是极其～的事例。 Such instances are very rare. / 这是～情况。 These are isolated cases.

个别差异 gèbié chāyì *psychol.* individual differences

个个 gègè each and every one; all: 这些战士～都是好样的。 Each and every one of these soldiers has proved his mettle. / 这次劳动竞赛, 人人奋发, ～争先。 During the emulation campaign, everyone went all out, and each tried to outdo the other.

个人 gèrén ① individual (person): ～利益 personal interests / 关心集体比关心～为重 be more concerned about the collective than about oneself / 集体领导和～负责相结合 combine collective leadership with individual responsibility / 用他～的名义 in his own name ② I: ～认为 in my opinion / 我～并不反对你这样干。 Personally I see no objection to your doing so.

个人迷信 gèrén míxìn cult of the individual; personality cult

个人项目 gèrén xiàngmù *sports* individual events

个人野心 gèrén yěxīn personal ambition: ～家 careerist

个人英雄主义 gèrényīngxióngzhǔyì individualistic heroism

个人主义 gèrénzhǔyì individualism

个体 gètǐ individual: ～农业经营 individual farming

个体户 gètǐhù ① privately owned small enterprise ② self-employed labourer (*or* worker)

个体经济 gètǐ jīngjì individual economy

个体劳动者 gètǐ láodòngzhě a person who works on his own; self-employed labourer (*or* worker)

个体生产者 gètǐ shēngchǎnzhě individual producer

个体所有制 gètǐ suǒyǒuzhì individual (*or* private) ownership

个头儿 gètóur size; height: 这种西瓜～大。 This kind of watermelon is remarkable for its size. / 这小伙子～不小。 This young chap is very tall.

个性 gèxìng individual character; individuality; personality: 共性和～ the general and specific character of sth. / 这孩子～很强。 The boy has a strong character.

个中 gèzhōng *formal* therein: ～奥妙 the inside story; the secret of it

个中人 gèzhōngrén a person in the know

个中事 gèzhōngshì inside information; inside story: ～局外人无从知晓。 Outsiders have no way to know the inside story.

个子 gèzi height; stature; build: 高～ a tall person / 小～ a small fellow; a short person

各 gè ① each; every; various; different: ～人有～人的优点。 Each has his merits. / ～式糕点 various kinds of cakes and pastries / 自由主义有～种表现。 Liberalism manifests itself in various ways. / 世界～国 every country in the world; all the nations in the world / 全国～地 all over the country / 她～科成绩都很好。 She does very well in all the subjects. / ～派政治力量 different political forces ② *adv.* variously; respectively: 这三人～按其能力分配了工作。 The three men were given work according to their respective abilities. / 两侧～有一门。 There's a door on either side. / 三种办法～有优点, 也～有缺点。 Each of the three methods has its strong and weak points. / 上半时双方～进一球。 In the first half, each side scored a goal. / ～不相同 have nothing in common with each other

各半 gèbàn half and half; fifty-fifty: 成败的可能性～。 The chances of success are fifty-fifty. / 我们排党员和非党员～。 Half of the men in our platoon are Party members.

各奔前程 gè bèn qiánchéng each pursues his own course; each goes his own way

各别 gèbié ① distinct; different: ～对待 treat differently; treat each on its (his, etc.) own merits ② *dial.* out of the ordinary; peculiar: 这只闹钟式样很～。 This alarm clock is quite unusual-looking. ③ odd; eccentric; funny: 这人的脾气真～。 He's a really eccentric character.

各不相让 gè bù xiāng ràng neither is willing to give ground; each is trying to outdo the other

各持己见 gè chí jǐjiàn (also 各执己见 gè zhí jǐjiàn) each sticks to his own view

各吹各的号,各唱各的调 gè chuī gède hào, gè chàng gède diào each blows his own bugle and sings his own song—each does things in his own way

各打五十大板 gè dǎ wǔshí dàbǎn punish the wronged and the wrong-doer alike; punish the guilty and the innocent alike; blame both sides without discrimination

各得其所 gè dé qí suǒ each is in his proper place; each is properly provided for; each has a role to play

各个儿 gègěr *dial.* oneself: 你甭管了,我～做吧。 Don't bother, I'll do it myself.

各个击破 gègè jīpò destroy (*or* crush) one by one

各个 gègè ① each; every; various: ～厂矿 each factory and mine / ～方面 all the various aspects / 社会上的～阶级 the various classes in society ② one by one: ～解决 resolve problems one at a time / 集中优势兵力,～歼灭敌人。 Concentrate a superior force to destroy the enemy forces one by one.

各行各业 gèháng-gèyè all trades and professions; all walks of life

各级 gèjí all or different levels: ～领导机关 leading organizations at all levels / ～人民代表大会 the people's congresses at different levels

各界 gèjiè all walks of life; all circles: ～人士 personages of various circles

各尽所能 gè jìn suǒ néng each doing his best; from each according to his ability

各尽所能,按劳分配 gè jìn suǒ néng, àn láo fēnpèi from each according to his ability, to each according to his work—the socialist principle of distribution

各尽所能,按需分配 gè jìn suǒ néng, àn xū fēnpèi from each according to his ability, to each according to his needs—the communist principle of distribution

各就位 gè jiùwèi *sports* (word of command) on your marks

各取所需 gè qǔ suǒ xū each takes what he needs

各人自扫门前雪 gèrén zì sǎo mén qián xuě each one sweeps the snow from his own doorstep—each one minds his own business: ～,莫管他家瓦上霜。 Each one sweeps the snow from his own doorstep and heeds not the frost on his neighbour's roof.

各色 gèsè of all kinds; of every description; assorted: 商店里～货物,一应俱全。 The shop is well stocked with goods of all kinds.

各抒己见 gè shū jǐjiàn each airs his own views

各位 gèwèi ① everybody (a term of address): ～请注意! Attention please, everybody. ② every: ～代表 fellow delegates

各向同性 gèxiàngtóngxìng *phys.* isotropy

各向异性 gèxiàngyìxìng *phys.* anisotropy

各行其是 gè xíng qí shì each does what he thinks is right; each goes his own way

各有千秋 gè yǒu qiānqiū each has something to recommend him; each has his strong points

各有所长 gè yǒu suǒ cháng each has his own strong points

各有所好 gè yǒu suǒ hào each has his likes and dislikes; each follows his own bent

各有一本难念的经 gè yǒu yīběn nánniànde jīng each has a difficult scripture to recite—each has his own hard nut to crack; each has his own troubles

各执一词 gè zhí yī cí each sticks to his own version or argument

各自 gèzì each; respective: 我们根据～的情况,订出了具体的学习计划。 We worked out study plans that would suit each individual. / 散会的时候已经很晚了,大家就～回家了。 When the meeting ended, it was already very late, so everyone just went home. / 研究社会各阶级的相互关系和～状况 study the mutual relations and respective conditions of the various classes

in society / 既要～努力,也要彼此帮助。 There must be both individual effort and mutual help.

各自为政 gèzì wéi zhèng each does things in his own way

各族人民 gèzú rénmín people of all nationalities: 全国～ the Chinese people of all nationalities

屹

屹 gè see below

屹螂 gèláng dung beetle

屹蚤 gèzao *inf.* flea

铬

铬 gè *chem.* chromium (Cr)

铬钢 gègāng *metall.* chromium steel; chrome steel

铬镍钢 gèniègāng chrome-nickel steel

铬鞣 gèróu chrome tanning: ～革 chrome leather

铬铁 gètiě ferrochrome

铬铁矿 gètiěkuàng chromite

硌

硌 gè *inf.* (of sth. hard or bulging) press or rub against: 褥子没有铺平,躺在上面～得难受。 That rumpled mattress was terribly uncomfortable. / 鞋里有砂子,～脚。 There's some grit in the shoe, and it hurts my foot.

硌窝儿 gèwōr cracked (egg): ～蛋 a cracked egg

gěi

给

给 gěi ① give; grant: 我哥～了我一块表。 My brother gave me a watch. / 公司～他一个月的假。 The company granted him a month's leave. / 杭州～我的印象很好。 Hangzhou left a very good impression on me. / 这本书是～你的。 This book is for you. / ～我一杯水喝。 Give me a cup of water (to drink). / ～我一点儿开水沏茶。 Give me some boiling water to make tea. / 他～了我一脚。 He gave me a kick. / ～敌人一个沉重的打击 strike a heavy blow at the enemy / 我～他一个不理睬。 I just ignored him. ② let; allow; make: ～我看看。 Let me have a look. / 开完运动会,～我累得够呛。 After the sports meet, I was tired out. ③ *prep.* (used after a verb indicating the handing over of sth.): 信已经交～他了。 I've handed the letter to him. / 把锤子递～我。 Pass me the hammer. / 我把钥匙留～你。 I'll leave the key with you. ④ *prep.* for the benefit of; for the sake of; for: 她～旅客送水倒茶。 She brought drinking water and tea for the passengers. / 我～你当翻译。 I'll act as interpreter for you. / 大夫～孩子们种牛痘。 The doctor vaccinated the children (against smallpox). ⑤ *prep.* (used to introduce the recipient of an action): 他～我道歉了。 He's apologized to me. / 小朋友～老师行了礼。 The children saluted their teacher. ⑥ *prep.* (used in a passive sentence to introduce either the doer of the action or the action if the doer is not mentioned): 这股敌人全～游击队消灭了。 The whole horde of enemy soldiers was wiped out by the guerrillas. / 我们的衣服～汗水湿透了。 Our clothes were soaked with sweat. / 反动统治～推翻了。 The reactionary regime was overthrown. ⑦ *part. inf.* (used before a verb for emphasis): 质量不合格～换。 Substandard products will be exchanged. / 把纸收起来,别叫风～刮散了。 Put away all the paper. Don't let it get blown about. / 我差点儿把这事～忘了。 I almost forgot that. ——see also jǐ

给脸 gěiliǎn do sb. a favour; save sb.'s face: 董事长来打了个照面儿,也算是～了。 As a favour, the president put in a brief appearance.

给脸不要脸 gěiliǎn bùyàoliǎn be fool enough to reject a face-saving offer

给以 gěiyǐ (usu. with abstract nouns as direct object)

give; grant: ～充分的重视 pay ample attention to／～适当照顾 show due consideration for／对触犯刑律的人一定要～法律制裁。 People who violate criminal law must be punished according to that law.／精湛的演出给观众以深刻的印象。 The superb performance made a profound impression on the audience.／他学习有困难，我们一定要给他以热情的帮助。 He's having difficulties with his studies. We must give him all the help we can.

gēn

根 gēn ① root (of a plant): 树～ roots of a tree ② descendants; offspring: 单～独苗 the sole male descendant (or heir) ③ short for 方根 fānggēn ④ math. solution of an algebraic equation ⑤ chem. radical: 酸～ acid radical ⑥ root; foot; base: 舌～ the root of the tongue／城墙～ the foot (or base) of a city wall ⑦ cause; origin; source; root: 只有坚持走社会主义道路才能挖掉穷～。 Only by sticking to the socialist road can we do away with the root cause of poverty.／我们是老街坊，彼此都知～知底的。 We are old neighbours, so we know each other's background very well. ⑧ thoroughly; completely: 根除 gēnchú ⑨ m. (for long, thin objects): 一～火柴 a match／一～小绳子 a piece of string

根本 gēnběn ① foundation; base: 从～上改变农村缺医少药的现象 put an end once and for all to the lack of doctors and medicine in the rural areas／千头万绪抓～。 Faced with a great variety of problems, one must concentrate on what is of basic importance. ② basic; fundamental; essential; cardinal: ～原因 basic reason; root cause／～原则 cardinal principle／一件带～性的大事 a major measure of fundamental importance ③ adv. (usu. used in the negative) at all; simply: 我～就不赞成你的主张。 I don't agree with you at all.／奴隶主～不把奴隶当人看待。 The slave owners simply did not treat the slaves as human beings.／我～没说过这话。 I've never said this. ④ adv. radically; thoroughly: 两种～对立的世界观 two diametrically opposed world outlooks／必须～改变我们这里的落后面貌。 We must thoroughly overcome our backwardness.／问题已经得到～解决。 The problem has been settled once and for all.

根本法 gēnběnfǎ fundamental law (i.e. a constitution): 宪法是国家的～。 The Constitution is the fundamental law of the state.

根除 gēnchú thoroughly do away with; eradicate; root out; eliminate: ～一切形式的殖民主义 eradicate all forms of colonialism／～水患 eliminate the scourge of floods

根底 gēndǐ ① foundation: ～浅 have a shaky foundation／他的英文～很好。 He has a solid foundation in English. ② cause; root: 追问～ inquire into the cause of the matter／你了解这个人的～吗? Do you know that fellow's background?

根雕 gēndiāo   tree-root carving (a handicraft)
根腐病 gēnfǔbìng   agric.   root rot
根冠 gēnguān   bot.   root cap
根号 gēnhào   math.   radical sign
根基 gēnjī ① foundation; basis: 打好～ lay a solid foundation／～牢固 a firm foundation／～动摇 be shaken to the very foundations ② property accumulated over a long time; resources: 公司刚成立，～还很差。 The company has just been established and is still on unsound footing.
根茎 gēnjīng   (also 根状茎 gēnzhuàngjīng) bot.   rhizome
根究 gēnjiū   make a thorough investigation of; get to

the bottom of; probe into: ～缘由 probe into the cause

根据 gēnjù ① prep. on the basis of; according to; in the light of; in line with: ～天气预报，明天要下雨。 According to the weather forecast, it's going to rain tomorrow.／我们～具体情况制订了这个计划。 We made the plan in the light of the specific conditions.／～这样的考虑 in line with these considerations／～公报的精神 in the spirit of the communiqué／～同名小说拍摄的影片 a film based on the novel of the same title ② basis; grounds; foundation: 说话要有～。 One should avoid making assertions without good grounds.／毫无～ utterly groundless

根据地 gēnjùdì   base area; base
根绝 gēnjué   stamp out; eradicate; exterminate: ～血吸虫病 stamp out snail fever／～事故 eliminate accidents
根瘤 gēnliú   bot.   root nodule
根瘤菌 gēnliújūn   nodule bacteria
根毛 gēnmáo   bot.   root hair
根苗 gēnmiáo ① root and shoot ② source; root ③ old (usu. male) offspring
根深蒂固 gēnshēn-dìgù   (also 根深柢固 gēnshēn-dǐgù) deep-rooted; ingrained; inveterate: ～的偏见 deep-rooted (or inveterate) prejudice
根深叶茂 gēnshēn-yèmào   have deep roots and luxuriant leaves—be well eatablished and vigorously developing
根式 gēnshì   math.   radical (expression)
根外追肥 gēnwài zhuīféi   agric.   foliage dressing; foliage spray
根由 gēnyóu   cause; origin: 追问～ make detailed inquiries about the cause of sth.
根源 gēnyuán ① source; origin; root: 实践是一切科学知识的～。 Practical experience is the source of all scientific knowledge.／认识～ cognitive roots／分析犯错误的思想～ analyse the ideological roots of the mistakes ② originate; stem from: 经济危机～于资本主义制度。 Economic crisis originates in the capitalist system.
根治 gēnzhì   effect a radical cure; cure once and for all; bring under permanent control: ～支气管炎 effect a radical cure of bronchitis／～海河 bring the Haihe River under permanent control; permanently harness the Haihe River
根治手术 gēnzhì shǒushù   med.   radical operation
根轴系 gēnzhóuxì   bot.   root system
根子 gēnzi   inf. ① root (of a plant) ② cause; origin; source; root

跟 gēn ① heel: 脚跟 jiǎogēn ② follow: ～我来。 Come along with me. or Follow me.／～紧～形势 keep abreast of the current situation／请～我念。 Please read after me.／你们走得太快，我～不上。 You all walk too fast. I can't keep up with you. ③ (of a woman) marry sb.: 他要是老这样游手好闲，我就不～他。 I won't marry him if he doesn't stop fooling around. ④ prep. (used to indicate accompaniment, relationship, involvement, etc.) with: ～父母住在一块儿 live with one's parents／这件事～他没有关系。 It has nothing to do with him.／我不～这个人见面。 I'm not going to meet this person.／我～这个人不相识。 I'm not acquainted with this person.／我没～这个人见面。 I didn't meet this person.／有事要～群众商量。 Consult the masses when a problem crops up. ⑤ prep. (used to introduce the recipient of an action): 我有几句话～你讲。 There's something I want to talk to you about.／他刚来～我告别了。 He came to say good-bye to me just now.／快～大伙儿说说。 Tell us all about it.／～错误思想作斗争 combat wrong ideas ⑥ prep. (used to show comparison): 今天的活儿～往常一样。 Our job today is the same as before.／～去年相比，产量增加了百分之十。

Output has increased by 10% over last year. ⑦ *conj.* and: 种子～农药都准备好了。The seeds and the pesticide are both ready. / 他～我都是四川人。He and I are both from Sichuan.

跟班[1]　gēnbān　join a regular shift or class: ～劳动 (of a leading comrade) go to work in a workshop for a specified period of time / ～听课 audit a class

跟班[2]　gēnbān　(also 跟班儿的 gēnbānrde) *old* footman

跟包　gēnbāo　*old* attendant of a stage actor

跟差　gēnchāi　*old* manservant of an official; attendant; footman

跟斗　gēndou　*dial.* ① fall: 跌～ have a fall ② somersault

跟脚　gēnjiǎo　*dial.* ① (of shoes) fit well ② close upon sb.'s heels: 你刚走，他～儿就来找你。He came to see you just after you left. ③ wait upon one's master when going out: ～的 footman ④ (of children) not be willing to leave one's parents

跟进　gēnjìn　*mil.* follow-up

跟前　gēnqián　① the area in front of sb. or sth.: 他把我叫到～又讲了几句。He told me to come closer and said a few more words. / 桌子～靠着一支猎枪。A shotgun leans against the table. ② the time just before: 春节～ shortly before the Spring Festival

跟前　gēnqian　(of one's children) living with one: 他～有一儿一女。He has a son and a daughter living with him.

跟人　gēnrén　*inf.* (of a woman) get married

跟上　gēn·shàng　keep pace with; catch up with; keep abreast of: 快～! Hurry and catch up! / ～亿万人民前进的步伐 keep pace with the onward march of the millions / 跟不上形势的需要 fall short of the demands of the times / 跟不上形势的发展 cannot keep up with the changing situation

跟随　gēnsuí　① follow: 他从小就～着爸爸在山里打猎。He used to go hunting with his father in the mountains when he was a boy. / 这条狗紧紧～在主人身后。The dog followed closely behind his master. ② retinue: 他每次出门，后面总有一大批～。Whenever he goes out, he always has a whole entourage following him.

跟头　gēntou　① tumble; fall: 摔～ have a fall ② somersault: 翻个～ turn a somersault

跟头虫　gēntouchóng　wiggler; wriggler

跟着　gēnzhe　follow in the wake of: 我们听完报告～就讨论。We held a discussion right after the speech.

跟踪　gēnzōng　follow the tracks of: 雪地～ follow sb.'s tracks in the snow / ～追击 go in hot pursuit of / ～敌舰 shadow the enemy warships / 他发现后面有人～，赶忙躲进一条小巷。When he realized that he was being shadowed, he quickly hid himself in a narrow alley.

gén

哏　gén　*dial.* ① amusing; comical; funny: 这段相声真～。This comic dialogue is really funny. / 这孩子笑的样子真有点儿～。The way the child laughs is quite funny. ② clownish speech or behaviour; clowning; antics: 他说话带～。There's humour in his words.

gěn

艮[1]　gěn　*dial.* blunt; straightforward; forthright: 这人真～! That fellow is really blunt! / 他说的话太～。He put it too sharply.

艮[2]　gěn　*dial.* (of food) tough; leathery: 发～ turn tough / ～萝卜不好吃。Tough radish is not good to eat.

gèn

亘（亙）　gèn　extend; stretch: 绵亘 miángèn

亘古及今　gèngǔ jí jīn　from time immemorial down to the present day

亘古未有　gèngǔ wèiyǒu　no such thing from days of old—unheard-of; unprecedented

茛　gèn　see 毛茛 máogèn

gēng

更[1]　gēng　① change; replace: 变更 biàngēng ② *formal* experience: 少不更事 shào bù gēng shì

更[2]　gēng　one of the five two-hour periods into which the night was formerly divided; watch: 打更 dǎgēng
——see also gèng

更迭　gēngdié　alternate; change: 内阁～ a change of cabinet

更动　gēngdòng　change; alter: 人事～ personnel changes / 图案已有所～。The design has been altered.

更番　gēngfān　by turns; alternately: ～出差 go on business trips by turns

更夫　gēngfū　*old* night watchman

更改　gēnggǎi　change; alter: 不可～的决定 an unalterable decision / 由于天气恶劣，飞机不得不～航线。Owing to bad weather the plane had to change its course.

更换　gēnghuàn　change; replace: ～位置 change places / ～衣裳 change one's clothes / 农展馆的展品常有～。The exhibits in the agricultural exhibition centre keep changing.

更楼　gēnglóu　*old* a night watch tower

更名　gēngmíng　change one's name

更年期　gēngniánqī　climacteric or menopause; change of life

更仆难数　gēng pú nán shǔ　too many to count; innumerable; countless

更深人静　gēngshēn-rénjìng　deep is the night and all is quiet: 在～的时候 at dead of night; in the quiet of the night

更生　gēngshēng　① regenerate; revive: 自力更生 zìlì gēngshēng ② renew: 可～和不可～的海洋资源 renewable and nonrenewable marine resources

更生霉素　gēngshēngméisù　*pharm.* actinomycin D

更始　gēngshǐ　*formal* make a new beginning

更事　gēngshì　*formal* experienced: ～不多 have little experience; be inexperienced

更替　gēngtì　replace: 生产方式的～ the replacement of one mode of production by another

更新　gēngxīn　① replace: 设备～ renewal of equipment / 渔船在不断～。Old fishing vessels are continually being replaced by new ones. / 消费品的～换代 the updating and upgrading of consumer goods ② (of forest, plants, etc.) renew; rejuvenate: 他们采用科学方法～草场。They have adopted scientific methods to rejuvenate the pastures.

更新伐　gēngxīnfá　*forestry* regeneration felling (or cutting)

更新世　Gēngxīnshì　*geol.*　the Pleistocene Epoch

更新造林　gēngxīn zàolín　reforestation

更衣　gēngyī　① change one's clothes ② *euph.* go to the toilet

更衣室　gēngyīshì　changeroom; locker room

更易　gēngyì　change; alter

更张　gēngzhāng　tune a stringed instrument—reform ——see also 改弦更张 gǎixián-gēngzhāng

更正　gēngzhèng　make corrections (of errors in published statements or articles): 文章有了错误, 应当在报纸上～。 If there is a mistake in any of the articles, the newspaper should correct it.

庚

　gēng　① the seventh of the ten Heavenly Stems (天干) (see also 干支 gān-zhī) ② age: 年庚 niángēng

庚帖　gēngtiě　same as 八字帖儿 bāzìtiěr

耕

　gēng　plough; till: 春耕 chūngēng

耕畜　gēngchù　farm animal

耕地　gēngdì　① plough; till: 耕了两亩地 plough two *mu* of land ② cultivated land: ～面积 area under cultivation; cultivated area

耕具　gēngjù　tillage implements

耕牛　gēngniú　farm cattle

耕田　gēngtián　plough; till

耕耘　gēngyún　plough and weed; cultivate: 一分～, 一分收获。 The more ploughing and weeding, the better the crop. —no gains without pains

耕者有其田　gēngzhě yǒu qí tián　land to the tiller

耕种　gēngzhòng　till; cultivate

耕作　gēngzuò　tillage; cultivation; farming

耕作方法　gēngzuò fāngfǎ　methods of cultivation; farming methods

耕作机械　gēngzuò jīxiè　tillage machinery

耕作技术　gēngzuò jìshù　farming technique

耕作园田化　gēngzuò yuántiánhuà　garden-style cultivation of farmland; gardenization

耕作制度　gēngzuò zhìdù　cropping system

赓

　gēng　*formal*　continue

赓续　gēngxù　*formal*　continue

鹒

　gēng　see 鸧鹒 cānggēng

羹

　gēng　a thick soup: 鸡蛋～ egg custard (usu. salty)

羹匙　gēngchí　soup spoon; tablespoon

gěng

埂

　gěng　① a low bank of earth between fields: 田埂 tiángěng ② a long, narrow mound: 山～ a hill mound ③ an earth dyke (*or* embankment): 堤埂 dīgěng

耿

　gěng　① *liter.*　bright ② honest and just; upright ③ (Gěng) a surname

耿耿　gěnggěng　① *liter.*　bright: ～星河 the bright Milky Way ② devoted; dedicated: 忠心～为革命 be dedicated heart and soul to the revolution ③ having sth. on one's mind; worried: ～不寐 lose sleep over sth.

耿耿于怀　gěnggěng yú huái　brood on (an injury, one's neglected duty, etc.); take sth. to heart

耿介　gěngjiè　*formal*　upright; honest and frank

耿直　gěngzhí　honest and frank; upright: 秉性～ be upright by nature / 他是个～人, 一向知无不言, 言无不尽。 He is honest and frank, and always says everything he knows without reserve.

哽

　gěng　choke (with emotion); feel a lump in one's throat: 他心里一酸, 喉咙～得说不出话来。 He felt a pang of sadness, and got so choked up he couldn't speak.

哽咽　gěngyè　choke with sobs: 她怎么也忍不住, ～了一声泪水便夺眶而出。 Unable to control herself any longer, she began to sob and her tears fell in torrents. / 她用～了的嗓音苦苦哀求。 She implored piteously, in a voice choked with sobs.

绠

　gěng　*formal*　a well rope

绠短汲深　gěngduǎn-jíshēn　a short rope for a deep well —ability inadequate for the task

梗

　gěng　① stalk; stem: 荷～ lotus stem / 菠菜～儿 spinach stalk ② a slender piece of wood or metal: 火柴～ matchstick ③ straighten: ～着脖子 straightening up one's neck ④ frank; forthright: 梗直 gěngzhí ⑤ *formal* obstinate; stubborn: 顽梗 wángěng ⑥ obstruct; block: 梗塞 gěngsè

梗概　gěnggài　broad outline; main idea; gist: 故事的～ the gist of a story; synopsis

梗塞　gěngsè　① block; obstruct; clog: 交通～ traffic jam ② *med.*　infarction

梗死　gěngsǐ　*med.*　infarction: 心肌～ myocardial infarction

梗直　gěngzhí　same as 耿直 gěngzhí

梗阻　gěngzǔ　① block; obstruct; hamper: 山川～ be separated by mountains and rivers; be far away from each other / 横加～ unreasonably obstruct or raise obstacles ② *med.*　obstruction: 肠～ intestinal obstruction

颈 (頸)

　gěng　see 脖颈儿 bógěngr ——see also jǐng

鲠 (骾)

　gěng　① fishbone ② (of a fishbone) get stuck in one's throat: 如～在喉 like having a fishbone caught in one's throat (said of a person who has a criticism that he must express)

鲠直　gěngzhí　same as 耿直 gěngzhí

gèng

更

　gèng　*adv.*　① more; still more; even more: 他没有放慢速度, 反而把车开得～快了。 He didn't slow down. On the contrary, he drove faster. / 刮了一夜北风, 天～冷了。 The weather has got even colder since the north wind blew all night. / 他讲话的最后部分～重要。 The last section of his speech is particularly important. / 不能压制批评, ～不能打击报复。 One must not suppress criticism, still less retaliate on one's critics. ② *formal*　further; furthermore; what is more: ～进一步地阐明观点 go still one step further to explain one's position / ～有甚者 what is more ——see also gēng

更加　gèngjiā　(also 更其 gèngqí) *adv.*　more; still more; even more: 问题～复杂了。 The problem became even more complicated. / 图书馆的书, 应该～爱护。 You should take even better care of books from the library. / 天色渐亮, 星星～稀少。 The stars faded as day dawned.

更上一层楼　gèng shàng yī céng lóu　climb one storey higher—attain a yet higher goal; scale new heights: 欲穷千里目, ～。 (王之涣) Would you command a prospect of a thousand *li*? Climb yet one storey higher.

更为 gèngwéi *adv.* more; still more; even more: ～重要的是要坚持下去。 Persistence is even more important.

gōng

工[1] gōng ① worker; workman; the working class: 女工 nǚgōng / 工农联盟 gōng-nóng liánméng ② work; labour: 上～ go to work / 既省料又省～ save both material and labour ③ (construction) project: 动工 dònggōng ④ industry: ～交战线 the industry and communications front; industry and communications ⑤ man-day: 这项工程需要五千个～。 This project will take 5,000 man-days to complete. ⑥ skill; craftsmanship: 唱工 chànggōng ⑦ be versed in; be good at: ～诗善画 be well versed in painting and poetry ⑧ exquisite; fine: 工巧 gōngqiǎo

工[2] gōng *mus.* a note of the scale in *gongchepu* (工尺谱), corresponding to 3 in numbered musical notation

工本 gōngběn cost (of production)

工笔 gōngbǐ traditional Chinese realistic painting characterized by fine brushwork and close attention to detail

工兵 gōngbīng engineer (in an army): 坑道～ sapper / 轻～ pioneer

工部 Gōngbù the Board of Works ——see also 六部 Liùbù

工厂 gōngchǎng factory; mill; plant; works: 铁～ iron works / ～区 factory district

工场 gōngchǎng workshop

工潮 gōngcháo workers' demonstration or protest movement; strike movement: 闹～ go on strike

工尺 gōngchě *gongche,* a traditional Chinese musical scale

工尺谱 gōngchěpǔ *mus.* **gongchepu** a traditional Chinese muscial notation

工程 gōngchéng ① engineering: 土木 (机械,电机,采矿)～ civil (mechanical, electrical, mining) engineering ② project: 水利～ water conservancy project / ～浩大 a gigantic project; a tremendous amount of work

工程兵 gōngchéngbīng engineer (in an army): ～部队 engineer troops (*or* units)

工程地质学 gōngchéng dìzhìxué engineering geology

工程队 gōngchéngduì construction brigade

工程技术人员 gōngchéng jìshù rényuán engineers and technicians

工程师 gōngchéngshī engineer

工程塑料 gōngchéng sùliào engineering plastics

工程验收 gōngchéng yànshōu *archit.* acceptance of work

工党 gōngdǎng the Labour Party

工地 gōngdì building site; construction site: ～上一片繁忙景象。 The construction site was a scene of bustling activity.

工读学校 gōngdú xuéxiào reform school; approved school

工段 gōngduàn ① a section of a construction project ② workshop section

工段长 gōngduànzhǎng section chief

工分 gōngfēn workpoint (a unit indicating the quantity and quality of labour performed, and the amount of payment earned, in rural people's communes): ～值 cash value of a workpoint

工蜂 gōngfēng worker (bee)

工夫 gōngfū *old* casual labourer; temporary worker

工夫 gōngfu ① time: 他三天～就学会了滑冰。 It took him only three days to learn to skate. / 她去了没多大～就回来了。 She didn't take long to get there and come back. / 明天有～再来吧。 Come again tomorrow if you have time. ② *dial.* at that time: 我当闺女那～,连大门都不敢出。 When I was a girl, I didn't even dare to go outdoors. ③ workmanship; skill; art: 练～ (of actors, athletes, etc.) practise / 这位杂技演员可真有～! The acrobat's skill is really superb! ④ effort; work: 花了好大～ put in a lot of work

工会 gōnghuì trade union; labour union

工架 gōngjià movements and postures of actors (in traditional operas)

工间操 gōngjiāncāo work-break exercises

工件 gōngjiàn workpiece; work: ～夹具 workpiece holder; (work) fixture

工匠 gōngjiàng craftsman; artisan

工具 gōngjù tool; instrument; implement; means: 木工～ carpenter's tools / 生产～ implements of production / 运输～ means of transport / 爱护～ take good care of the tools / ～改革 improvement of tools / 语言是人们交流思想的～。 Language is the means for exchanging thoughts between people.

工具车床 gōngjù chēchuáng toolmaker lathe

工具袋 gōngjùdài kit bag; workbag

工具房 gōngjùfáng toolhouse; tool storeroom

工具钢 gōngjùgāng tool steel

工具书 gōngjùshū reference book

工具箱 gōngjùxiāng toolbox; tool kit; workbox

工楷 gōngkǎi (in Chinese calligraphy) neat regular script

工科 gōngkē engineering course: ～大学 college of engineering

工力 gōnglì ① skill; craftsmanship: ～深厚 remarkable craftsmanship / 颇见～ show the hand of a master ② manpower (needed for a project)

工力悉敌 gōnglì xī dí rival each other in artistry or workmanship

工联主义 gōngliánzhǔyì (also 工会主义 gōnghuìzhǔyì) (trade) unionism

工料 gōngliào labour and materials (for a building project)

工龄 gōnglíng length of service; standing; seniority: 一个有三十年～的老工人 an old worker of thirty years' standing

工农 gōng-nóng workers and peasants: ～大众 the broad masses of workers and peasants / ～干部 cadres of worker-peasant origin; worker and peasant cadres

工农兵 gōng-nóng-bīng workers, peasants and soldiers

工农差别 gōng-nóng chābié the difference between industry and agriculture

工农联盟 gōng-nóng liánméng alliance of workers and peasants; worker-peasant alliance

工农业总产值 gōngnóngyè zǒngchǎnzhí gross output value of industry and agriculture

工棚 gōngpéng ① builders' temporary shed ② work shed

工期 gōngqī time limit for a project: 提高效率,缩短～。 Increase efficiency and shorten the time limit for the project.

工钱 gōngqian ① money paid for odd jobs; charge for a service: 做这套衣服要多少～? How much should I pay for having the suit made? ② *inf.* wages; pay

工巧 gōngqiǎo exquisite; fine

工区 gōngqū work area (a grass-roots unit of an industrial enterprise)

工人 gōngrén worker; workman: 产业～ industrial worker

工人干部 gōngrén gànbù worker-cadre

工人贵族 gōngrén guìzú labour aristocracy; aristocrats of labour

工人阶级 gōngrén jiējí the working class

工人纠察队 gōngrén jiūcháduì workers' pickets

工人运动 gōngrén yùndòng labour (or workers') movement

工伤 gōngshāng injury suffered on the job; industrial injury: ～事故 industrial accident

工商界 gōngshāngjiè industrial and commercial circles; business circles

工商联 gōngshānglián short for 工商业联合会 gōng-shāngyè liánhéhuì

工商业 gōngshāngyè industry and commerce: 私营～ privately owned industrial and commercial enterprises／～者 industrialists and businessmen (or merchants)

工商业联合会 gōng-shāngyè liánhéhuì association of industry and commerce

工时 gōngshí man-hour

工事 gōngshì fortifications; defence works: 修筑～ build fortifications (or defence works)

工头 gōngtóu foreman; overseer

工团主义 gōngtuánzhǔyì syndicalism

工稳 gōngwěn apt; well chosen: 造句～ well-turned phrases

工效 gōngxiào work efficiency: 提高～ raise (or improve) work efficiency

工休日 gōngxiūrì day off; holiday

工序 gōngxù working procedure; process

工业 gōngyè industry

工业病 gōngyèbìng professional diseases of industrial workers

工业粉尘 gōngyè fěnchén industrial dust: ～污染 industrial dust pollution

工业革命 gōngyè gémìng the Industrial Revolution

工业国 gōngyèguó industrialized (or industrial) country

工业化 gōngyèhuà industrialize

工业基地 gōngyè jīdì industrial base

工业酒精 gōngyè jiǔjīng industrial alcohol

工业品 gōngyèpǐn industrial products; manufactured goods

工业企业 gōngyè qǐyè industrial enterprise

工业气压 gōngyè qìyā technic atmosphere

工业体系 gōngyè tǐxì industrial system

工业无产阶级 gōngyè wúchǎnjiējí the industrial proletariat

工业总产值 gōngyè zǒngchǎnzhí gross value of industrial output

工蚁 gōngyǐ worker (ant); ergate

工艺 gōngyì technology; craft: 手工艺 shǒugōngyì

工艺流程 gōngyì liúchéng technological process

工艺美术 gōngyì měishù industrial art; arts and crafts

工艺品 gōngyìpǐn handicraft article; handiwork; handicraft

工艺设计 gōngyì shèjì technological design

工艺水平 gōngyì shuǐpíng technological level

工艺要求 gōngyì yāoqiú technological requirements

工友 gōngyǒu a manual worker such as janitor, cleaner, etc. in a school or government office

工于心计 gōngyú xīnjì adept at scheming; very calculating

工欲善其事, 必先利其器 gōng yù shàn qí shì, bì xiān lì qí qì a workman must first sharpen his tools if he is to do his work well

工贼 gōngzéi scab; blackleg

工长 gōngzhǎng section chief (in a workshop, or on a building site); foreman

工整 gōngzhěng careful and neat: 字迹～ neatly lettered／他把自己的名字工工整整地写在书的衬页上。He carefully printed his name on the flyleaf.

工致 gōngzhì exquisite; delicate: 那幅花鸟画画得很～。The flower-and-bird painting was executed with great delicacy.

工种 gōngzhǒng type of work in production

工装裤 gōngzhuāngkù overalls

工资 gōngzī wages; pay

工资表 gōngzībiǎo payroll; pay sheet

工资袋 gōngzīdài pay packet

工资改革 gōngzī gǎigé reform of the wage system

工资级别 gōngzī jíbié wage scale

工资率 gōngzīlǜ wage rate

工资制 gōngzīzhì wage system

工字钢 gōngzìgāng I-steel

工字形 gōngzìxíng I-shaped

工作 gōngzuò ① work; operate: 努力～ work hard／机器正在～。The machine is in operation. ② work; job: 分配～ assign jobs (or work)／做研究～ do research work／懂外语的人比较容易找到～。People who know a foreign language can find jobs more easily.／他是做消防～的。He works in the fire brigade.

工作本 gōngzuòběn working copy

工作单位 gōngzuò dānwèi an organization in which one works; place of work

工作队 gōngzuòduì work team; working force

工作服 gōngzuòfú work clothes; boiler suit

工作会议 gōngzuò huìyì working conference

工作量 gōngzuòliàng amount of work; work load

工作面 gōngzuòmiàn ① min. face: 采煤～ coal face／回采～ stope／～运输机 face conveyor ② mech. working surface

工作母机 gōngzuò mǔjī machine tool

工作人员 gōngzuò rényuán working personnel; staff member; functionary

工作日 gōngzuòrì workday; working day

工作台 gōngzuòtái mech. working table; bench

工作样片 gōngzuò yàngpiàn film rushes

工作语言 gōngzuò yǔyán working language

工作者 gōngzuòzhě worker: 教育～ educational worker／文艺～ literary and art workers; writers and artists／美术～ art worker; artist／音乐～ musician／新闻～ journalist

工作证 gōngzuòzhèng employee's card; I. D. card

工作周期 gōngzuò zhōuqī mech. action cycle

弓

gōng ① bow: 用～和箭射鹿 shoot a deer with a bow and arrow ② anything bow-shaped: 弹棉花用的绷～儿 bow used to tease cotton ③ wooden land-measuring dividers ④ an old unit of length for measuring land, equal to five chi (尺) ⑤ bend; arch; bow: ～着背 arch one's back; bend low／～着腿坐着 sitting with arched legs

弓箭 gōngjiàn bow and arrow

弓箭步 gōngjiànbù forward lunge (in wushu 武术 or gymnastics)

弓弩 gōngnǔ bow and crossbow; bow and arrow

弓弦 gōngxián bowstring

弓弦乐器 gōngxián yuèqì bowed stringed (or string) instrument; bowed instrument

弓形 gōngxíng ① math. segment of a circle ② bow-shaped; arched; curved

弓腰 gōngyāo bend over; bend down

弓子 gōngzi ① bow (of a stringed instrument) ② anything bow-shaped

弓钻 gōngzuàn bow drill

公¹

gōng ① public; state-owned; collective: ～私要分清 make a clear distinction between public and private interests ② common; general: ～分母 common

denominator ③ of the world; international; universal: 公海 gōnghǎi ④ make public: 公布 gōngbù ⑤ equitable; impartial; fair; just: 公买公卖 gōngmǎi-gōngmài ⑥ public affairs; official business: 因～外出 be away on official business ⑦ (Gōng) a surname

公² gōng ① duke: 公爵 gōngjué ② (a respectful term of address for an elderly man): 张～ the revered Mr. Zhang ③ husband's father; father-in-law ④ male (animal): ～象 male (or bull) elephant / 这只小鸡是～ 的。It's a cockerel. / 你的狗是～的还是母的? Is your dog a he or a she? / ～狼 he-wolf

公安 gōng'ān public security: ～人员 public security officer (or man) / ～部队 public security troops / ～机关 public security organs

公安部 gōng'ānbù the Ministry of Public Security

公安局 gōng'ānjú public security bureau

公案 gōng'àn old ① court table (used by a judge) ② a complicated legal case ③ a much discussed issue; a sensational affair

公案小说 gōng'àn xiǎoshuō a short piece of fictional writing which involves the committing of a crime and its subsequent legal handling, the actions of a clever judge often being the centre of attention (e.g.《龙图公案》The Cases of Longtu, a collection of gong'an stories with Lord Bao 包公, the fictionalized version of the Northern Song official Bao Zheng 包拯, as the titular hero)

公报 gōngbào communiqué; bulletin: 新闻～ press communiqué / 政府～ (government) bulletin

公报私仇 gōng bào sīchóu avenge personal wrongs in the name of public interests; abuse public power to retaliate against a personal enemy

公倍数 gōngbèishù math. common multiple: 最小～ least (or lowest) common multiple

公布 gōngbù promulgate; announce; publish; make public: ～法令 promulgate a decree / ～罪状 announce sb.'s crimes / ～名单 publish a name list / ～帐目 publish the accounts

公厕 gōngcè short for 公共厕所 gōnggòng cèsuǒ

公差 gōngchā ① math. common difference ② mech. tolerance: 制造（安装）～ manufacturing (location) tolerance

公差 gōngchāi ① public errand; official business; noncombatant duty: 出～ go on a public errand; go on official business; perform noncombatant duty ② a person on a public errand (or noncombatant duty): 连里叫咱们班出两个～。The company has assigned two men from our squad to noncombatant duty. ③ old corvée ④ old runner or bailiff in a feudal yamen

公产 gōngchǎn public property

公称 gōngchēng mech. nominal: ～尺寸 nominal dimension

公尺 gōngchǐ metre (m.)

公出 gōngchū be away on official business

公畜 gōngchù male animal (kept for breeding); stud

公担 gōngdàn quintal (q.)

公道 gōngdào justice: 主持～ uphold justice

公道 gōngdao fair; just; reasonable; impartial: 说句～ 话 to be fair; in fairness to sb. / 价钱～。The price is reasonable. / 办事～ be evenhanded; be impartial

公德 gōngdé public morality (concerned with a regulated behaviour pattern in a community); social ethics

公德心 gōngdéxīn public spirit: 有～ be public-spirited

公敌 gōngdí public enemy: 人民～ an enemy of the people; a public enemy

公牍 gōngdú formal official document

公断 gōngduàn ① arbitrate: 听候众人～ await the verdict of the public ② consider and decide impartially

公吨 gōngdūn metric ton (MT)

公而忘私 gōng ér wàng sī so devoted to public service as to forget private interests; selfless: ～的共产主义风格 a selfless communist spirit; the communist style of working selflessly for the public interest / 自古道：“～, 国而亡家。” As the proverb says, "Public business comes before private affairs. The state comes before the family."

公法 gōngfǎ leg. public law

公房 gōngfáng public housing

公费 gōngfèi (at) public (or state) expense: ～留学 study abroad on state scholarship

公费医疗 gōngfèi yīliáo free medical service (or care); public health services

公分 gōngfēn ① centimetre (cm.) ② gram (g.)

公愤 gōngfèn public indignation; popular anger: 激起～ arouse public indignation

公干 gōnggàn official business: 有何～? What important business brings you here?

公告 gōnggào announcement; proclamation

公共 gōnggòng public; common; communal: ～财产 public property / ～场所 public places / ～建筑 public buildings / ～食堂 canteen; mess; cafeteria / ～秩序 public order

公共厕所 gōnggòng cèsuǒ public conveniences; public latrine

公共关系 gōnggòng guānxi public relations

公共积累 gōnggòng jīlěi common accumulation; accumulation fund

公共汽车 gōnggòng qìchē bus: ～线路 bus line / ～站 bus stop

公共卫生 gōnggòng wèishēng public health (or hygiene)

公公 gōnggong ① husband's father; father-in-law ② dial. (paternal) grandfather ③ dial. (maternal) grandfather ④ (a respectful term of address for an elderly man) grandpa; grandad: 刘～ Grandpa Liu ⑤ old a form of address for a court eunuch

公股 gōnggǔ government share (in a joint state-private enterprise)

公关 gōngguān short for 公共关系 gōnggòng guānxi

公馆 gōngguǎn old residence (of a rich or important person); mansion

公国 gōngguó duchy; dukedom

公海 gōnghǎi high seas

公害 gōnghài social effects of pollution; environmental pollution

公函 gōnghán official letter

公会 gōnghuì trade council; trade association; guild

公鸡 gōngjī cock; rooster

公积金 gōngjījīn accumulation fund (of a socialist economic collective)

公祭 gōngjì public memorial ceremony

公家 gōngjia inf. the state; the public; the organization: 咱们宁可个人受损失，也决不让～吃亏。We would rather sustain personal losses than let the state suffer. / ～的财产就是人民的财产。Public property is the people's property.

公检法 gōng-jiǎn-fǎ public security organs, procuratorial organs and people's courts

公教人员 gōng-jiào rényuán old government employees and teachers

公斤 gōngjīn kilogram (kg.); kilo

公举 gōngjǔ elect by public nomination: 我们～他当代表。We elected him as our representative.

公爵 gōngjué duke

公爵夫人 gōngjué fūren duchess

公开 gōngkāi ① open; overt; public: ～论战 open pole-

mics / 〜审判 public (or open) trial / 〜的秘密 an open secret / 〜的和暗藏的敌人 overt and covert enemies / 〜的场合 a public occasion / 〜指名攻击 attack publicly by name ② make public; make known to the public: 把事情〜出去 make the matter known to the public

公开化 gōngkāihuà come out into the open; be brought into the open

公开信 gōngkāixìn open letter

公款 gōngkuǎn public money (or fund)

公厘 gōnglí millimetre (mm.)

公里 gōnglǐ kilometre (km.)

公理 gōnglǐ ① generally acknowledged truth; self-evident truth ② math. axiom

公理宗 Gōnglǐzōng Christianity the Congregational Church

公历 gōnglì the Gregorian calendar

公立 gōnglì established and maintained by the government; public

公例 gōnglì general rule

公粮 gōngliáng agricultural tax paid in grain; grain delivered to the state; public grain: 交〜 deliver tax grain to the state

公量 gōngliàng text. conditioned weight

公路 gōnglù highway; road: 〜交通 highway communication / 〜运输 highway (or road) transportation

公路桥 gōnglùqiáo highway bridge

公路容量 gōnglù róngliàng highway capacity

公论 gōnglùn public opinion; verdict of the masses

公买公卖 gōngmǎi-gōngmài be fair in buying and selling; buy and sell at reasonable prices

公民 gōngmín citizen: 中华人民共和国〜 a citizen of the People's Republic of China

公民权 gōngmínquán civil rights; citizen's rights

公民投票 gōngmín tóupiào referendum; plebiscite

公亩 gōngmǔ are (a.)

公墓 gōngmù cemetery

公牛 gōngniú bull

公判 gōngpàn ① pronounce judgment in public ② verdict of the public

公平 gōngpíng fair; just; impartial; equitable: 〜合理 fair and reasonable / 买卖〜 be fair in buying and selling; buy and sell at reasonable prices / 〜交易 fair deal / 〜的协议 an equitable agreement / 社会〜 social equity / 〜税负的原则 the principle of keeping taxation fair and reasonable / 太不〜了。 It's grossly unfair.

公婆 gōng-pó husband's father and mother; parents-in-law ② dial. husband and wife: 两〜 the husband and his wife; the couple

公仆 gōngpú public servant: 人民的〜 a servant of the people

公切线 gōngqiēxiàn math. common tangent

公勤人员 gōng-qín rényuán service personnel in an office; office attendants

公顷 gōngqǐng hectare (ha.)

公然 gōngrán derog. openly; undisguisedly; brazenly: 〜背叛 openly betray / 〜撕毁协议 brazenly tear up an agreement

公认 gōngrèn generally acknowledge (or recognize); (universally) accept; establish: 〜的国际关系原则 generally recognized principles governing international relations / 〜的国际法准则 established principles of international law / 大家〜他为领袖。 He was acknowledged as their leader.

公山羊 gōngshānyáng he-goat; billy goat

公设 gōngshè math. postulate

公社 gōngshè ① primitive commune ② commune: 巴黎〜 the Paris Commune ③ people's commune

公社化 gōngshèhuà be organized into people's communes: 我们县在一九五八年实现了〜。 People's com-

munes were organized throughout our county in 1958.

公审 gōngshěn leg. public (or open) trial

公升 gōngshēng litre

公使 gōngshǐ envoy; minister: 〜衔参赞 counsellor with the rank of minister; minister-counsellor

公使馆 gōngshǐguǎn legation

公式 gōngshì formula

公式化 gōngshìhuà ① formulism (in art and literature) ② formulistic; stereotyped

公事 gōngshì ① public affairs; official business (or duties): 还是〜要紧。 Public affairs should come first. / 我还有很多〜要办。 I still have a lot of official duties to attend to. ② inf. official document: 我每天上午看〜。 I read official documents every morning.

公事包 gōngshìbāo briefcase; portfolio

公事房 gōngshìfáng office (room or building)

公事公办 gōngshì gōng bàn do official business according to official principles; not let private affairs interfere with public duty; business is business

公署 gōngshǔ government office

公说公有理，婆说婆有理 gōng shuō gōng yǒulǐ, pó shuō pó yǒulǐ each says he is right; both parties claim to be in the right

公司 gōngsī company; corporation: 钢铁〜 iron and steel company / 进出口〜 import and export corporation

公私 gōng-sī public and private: 〜兼顾 give concurrent consideration to public and private interests / 〜两利 benefit both public and individual interests / 〜分明 make (or draw) a clear distinction between public and private interests

公私合营 gōng-sī héyíng joint state-private ownership (the principal form of state capitalism adopted during the socialist transformation of capitalist enterprises in China)

公诉 gōngsù leg. public prosecution: 对罪犯提起〜 institute legal proceedings against an offender

公诉人 gōngsùrén public prosecutor; the prosecution

公孙 Gōngsūn a two-character surname

公堂 gōngtáng ① old law court; tribunal ② ancestral hall (or temple); memorial temple

公推 gōngtuī recommend by general acclaim

公文 gōngwén official document: 〜程式 forms and formulas of official documents

公文袋 gōngwéndài document envelope

公文纸 gōngwénzhǐ paper for copying official documents

公务 gōngwù public affairs; official business: 办理〜 handle official business / 执行国家〜 perform official duties

公务护照 gōngwù hùzhào service passport

公务人员 gōngwù rényuán government functionary

公务员 gōngwùyuán ① orderly ② government office worker; civil servant

公物 gōngwù public property

公心 gōngxīn ① public spirit ② fairness

公休 gōngxiū general holiday; official holiday

公演 gōngyǎn perform in public; give a performance: 青年剧院下月〜曹禺名剧《日出》。 The Youth Theatre is presenting Cao Yu's famous play Sunrise next month.

公羊 gōngyáng ram

公羊 Gōngyáng a two-character surname

公议 gōngyì have a public or mass discussion: 自报〜 self-assessment and public discussion / 交由群众〜 pass on to the masses for discussion

公益 gōngyì public good; public welfare: 热心〜 be public-spirited

公益金 gōngyìjīn public welfare fund (of a socialist economic collective)

公意　gōngyì　public will; will of the public

公因子　gōngyīnzǐ　*math.* common factor: 最大～ greatest common factor (*or* divisor)

公营　gōngyíng　publicly-owned; publicly-operated; public: ～经济 the public sector of the economy; public economy / ～企业 public enterprise

公用　gōngyòng　for public use; public; communal: ～电话 public telephone / 这个操场是两校～的。 This sports ground is shared by the two schools.

公用事业　gōngyòng shìyè　public utilities

公有　gōngyǒu　publicly-owned; public: ～财产 public property

公有化　gōngyǒuhuà　transfer to public ownership; socialize

公有制　gōngyǒuzhì　public ownership (of means of production)

公余　gōngyú　leisure hours (after work)

公寓　gōngyù　① block of flats; apartment house ② *old* lodging house

公元　gōngyuán　the Christian era: ～一二○○年 A.D. 1200 / ～前二二一年 221 B.C.

公园　gōngyuán　park

公约　gōngyuē　① convention; pact: 日内瓦～ Geneva Convention ② joint pledge: 爱国卫生～ patriotic public health pledge / 服务～ service pledge (given by workers in the service trades)

公约数　gōngyuēshù　*math.* common divisor: 最大～ greatest common divisor

公允　gōngyǔn　just and sound; fair and equitable; evenhanded: 持论～ be just and fair in argument

公债　gōngzhài　(government) bonds: 经济建设～ economic construction bonds

公章　gōngzhāng　official seal: 盖～ affix an official seal

公正　gōngzhèng　just; fair; impartial; fair-minded: ～的舆论 fair-minded public opinion / 有个裁判不～。 One of the judges was partial. / 历史将对这些人作出最～的判决。 History will pass the fairest judgment on such people.

公证　gōngzhèng　notarization

公证处　gōngzhèngchù　notary office

公证人　gōngzhèngrén　notary public; notary

公之于世　gōng zhī yú shì　make known to the world; reveal to the public

公职　gōngzhí　public office; public employment: 担任～ hold public office / 开除～ discharge sb. from public employment; take sb.'s name off the books

公职人员　gōngzhí rényuán　civil servant

公制　gōngzhì　the metric system: ～尺寸 metric size

公制螺纹　gōngzhì luówén　*mech.* metric thread

公众　gōngzhòng　the public: ～领袖 leader of the public / 制造谎言欺骗～ fabricate lies to deceive the public

公诸同好　gōng zhū tónghào　share enjoyment with those having similar tastes

公猪　gōngzhū　boar

公主　gōngzhǔ　princess

公转　gōngzhuàn　*astron.* revolution

公子　gōngzǐ　son of a feudal prince or high official

公子哥儿　gōngzǐgēr　a pampered son of a wealthy or influential family

公子王孙　gōngzǐ-wángsūn　sons of princes and nobles; sons of the aristocracy and the rich

功

功　gōng　① meritorious service (*or* deed); merit; achievement: 他的～大于过。 His achievements outweighed his errors. ② result; effect; success: 教育之～ the fruits of education ③ skill: 基本功 jīběngōng ④ *phys.* work: 机械～ mechanical work

功败垂成　gōng bài chuí chéng　fail on the verge of success; suffer defeat when victory is within reach

功臣　gōngchén　a person who has rendered outstanding service: 治淮～ meritorious workers in harnessing the Huaihe River / 开国～ founders of a state / 不要以～自居。 Don't give yourself the airs of a hero.

功成不居　gōng chéng bù jū　claim no credit for one's service

功成名遂　gōngchéng-míngsuì　(also 功成名立 gōngchéng-mínglì) be successful and famous

功成身退　gōngchéng-shēntuì　retire after winning merit

功成业就　gōngchéng-yèjiù　(of a person's career) be crowned with success

功到自然成　gōng dào zìrán chéng　constant effort yields sure success

功德　gōngdé　① merits and virtues: 歌颂人民英雄的～ extol the merits and virtues of the people's heroes ② *Buddhism* charitable and pious deeds; benefaction; beneficence; works

功德无量　gōngdé wúliàng　boundless beneficence; great service: 谁要是能够找到治疗癌症的方法，那真是～。 Whoever finds a cure for cancer will render a great service to mankind.

功底　gōngdǐ　grounding in basic skills: ～扎实 have a good grounding (*or* be well grounded) in basic skills

功夫　gōngfu　same as 工夫 gōngfu, esp. 工夫③

功过　gōngguò　merits and demerits; contributions and blunders

功过是非　gōngguò-shìfēi　merits and demerits, right and wrong

功绩　gōngjì　merits and achievements; contribution: 为革命事业建立不朽的～ make immortal contributions to the revolutionary cause

功架　gōngjià　same as 工架 gōngjià

功课　gōngkè　① schoolwork; homework: 做～ do homework ② a school subject: 他在学校里门门～都很好。 He does well in every subject at school.

功亏一篑　gōng kuī yī kuì　fail to build a mound for want of one final basket of earth—fall short of success for lack of a final effort

功劳　gōngláo　contribution; meritorious service; credit: 她的～可不小啊! She has certainly made no small contribution! *or* 我在研究工作中取得了一点成绩，这里面也有我妻子的一份～。 Some of the credit for my success in my research work goes to my wife. / 绝不能把一切～归于自己。 One must never claim all the credit for oneself.

功劳簿　gōngláobù　record of merits: 不要躺在自己的～上。 Don't rest on your laurels.

功力　gōnglì　① efficacy; effect ② same as 工力 gōnglì①

功利　gōnglì　utility; material gain

功利主义　gōnglìzhǔyì　utilitarianism: ～者 utilitarian

功烈　gōngliè　*formal* achievements: ～著而不灭。 The glory of his achievements never fades.

功率　gōnglǜ　*phys.* power: ～计 dynamometer

功名　gōngmíng　scholarly honour or official rank (in feudal times): 上京赶考，求取～ go to the capital to take the imperial examination in the hopes of winning an official rank

功名利禄　gōngmíng-lìlù　position and wealth

功能　gōngnéng　function: ～锻炼 functional training / ～性障碍 functional disorder / 这种机器具有多种～。 This gadget can perform many different functions. / 肝～正常。 The liver is functioning normally.

功效　gōngxiào　efficacy; effect: 此药～非常显著。 This medicine is most efficacious.

功勋　gōngxūn　exploit; meritorious service: 为祖国为人民立下了不朽的～ have performed immortal feats for the nation and the people / ～卓著 notable exploits

功业　gōngyè　exploits; achievements

功用 gōngyòng　function; use

功状 gōngzhuàng　an account of sb.'s meritorious service

红
攻 gōng　see 女红 nǚgōng ——see also hóng

攻 gōng ① attack; take the offensive: ～城 attack a city / ～入敌阵 storm into the enemy position / 进攻受阻,～不进去。The attack hit a snag and made no headway. / 全～型选手 an all-out attack player ② accuse; charge: 群起而攻之 qún qǐ ér gōng zhī ③ study; specialize in: 专攻 zhuāngōng

攻城略地 gōngchéng-lüèdì　attack cities and seize territories

攻错 gōngcuò　other people's advice is of help

攻打 gōngdǎ　attack; assault: ～一座城市 attack a city

攻读 gōngdú ① assiduously study; diligently study: 刻苦～ study assiduously ② specialize in: ～法律 study law / ～博士学位 study for a doctorate

攻伐 gōngfá　send an expedition against; attack; invade

攻关 gōngguān ① storm a strategic pass ② tackle key problems: 攻下这一关,其他问题就好办了。Once this difficulty is overcome, other problems will be easy to solve.

攻击 gōngjī ① attack; assault; launch an offensive: 发起总～ launch a general offensive ② accuse; charge; vilify: 恶毒～ viciously attack / 无端的～ groundless charges / 人身～ personal attack

攻击机 gōngjījī　another name for 强击机 qiángjījī

攻坚 gōngjiān　storm fortifications; assault fortified positions: ～部队 assault troops

攻坚战 gōngjiānzhàn　storming of heavily fortified positions

攻讦 gōngjié　formal　rake up sb.'s past and attack him; expose sb.'s past misdeeds

攻克 gōngkè　capture; take: ～敌军据点 capture an enemy stronghold / ～技术难关 surmount (or overcome) a technical difficulty; solve a difficult technical problem

攻破 gōngpò　make a breakthrough; breach: ～敌军防线 break through (or penetrate) the enemy defence lines / 这个堡垒是攻不破的。This is an impregnable fortress.

攻其不备 gōng qí bù bèi　strike where or when the enemy is unprepared; take sb. by surprise; catch sb. unawares

攻其一点,不及其余 gōng qí yī diǎn, bù jí qí yú　pounce on one point and ignore all others—attack sb. for a single fault without considering his other aspects

攻取 gōngqǔ　storm and capture; attack and seize: ～据点 capture a stronghold

攻势 gōngshì　offensive: 采取～ take the offensive / 政治～ political offensive / 客队～凌厉。The visiting team maintained a powerful offensive.

攻守同盟 gōng-shǒu tóngméng　an offensive and defensive alliance—an agreement between partners in crime not to give each other away; a pact to shield each other

攻丝 gōngsī　mech.　tapping: ～机 tapping machine

攻无不克 gōng wú bù kè　all-conquering; ever-victorious: 战无不胜,～ take every objective one attacks and win every battle one fights

攻陷 gōngxiàn　capture; storm: 1644年,李自成军～北京。In 1644, Li Zicheng's army captured Beijing.

攻心 gōngxīn ① attack the mind; make a psychological attack: 政策～ try to win over or obtain a confession from a person by explaining the Party's policy ② Chin. med. be in a coma or remain in a stupor (because of sorrow or hatred), or be in danger of dying (from severe burns or gangrene)

攻心为上 gōngxīn wéi shàng　psychological offensive is the best of tactics: 用兵之道,～,攻城为下。In war, to attack the mind is first, to attack a city second.

攻占 gōngzhàn　attack and occupy; storm and capture

供 gōng ① supply; feed: ～不上 run out; be in short supply / ～不起 unable to meet the demand; unable to afford the cost / 你～砖,我来砌。You pass the bricks to me, and I'll lay them. ② provide sb. with sth. (for the use or convenience of): 仅～参考 for your reference only / 这个饭厅可～五百人同时用饭。This dining hall can accommodate five hundred people at a time. ——see also gòng

供不应求 gōng bù yìng qiú　supply falls short of demand; demand exceeds supply

供电 gōngdiàn　supply electricity; supply power: ～调度员 load dispatcher / ～干线 supply main

供电局 gōngdiànjú　power supply bureau

供电系统 gōngdiàn xìtǒng　same as 电力网 diànlìwǎng

供过于求 gōng guò yú qiú　supply exceeds demand

供给 gōngjǐ　supply; provide; furnish: 原料由国家～。Raw materials are provided by the state.

供给制 gōngjǐzhì　the supply system—a system of payment in kind (practised during the revolutionary wars and in the early days of the People's Republic, providing working personnel and their dependents with the primary necessities of life)

供暖 gōngnuǎn　heating: 热水～ hot water heating / 蒸汽～ steam heating / 这幢楼正在安装～设备。A heating system is being installed in this building.

供暖系统 gōngnuǎn xìtǒng　heating system

供气 gōngqì　mech.　air feed

供求 gōngqiú　supply and demand: ～关系 the relation between supply and demand / 调剂市场物资,使商品～平衡 redistribute goods and materials in the market in order to strike a balance between supply and demand

供销 gōng-xiāo　supply and marketing

供销合作社 gōng-xiāo hézuòshè　(also 供销社 gōng-xiāoshè) supply and marketing cooperative

供养 gōngyǎng　provide for (one's parents or elders); support: ～老人 support the elders (esp. one's aged parents or grandparents) ——see also gòngyǎng

供应 gōngyìng　supply: 大量～ supply in large quantity / 计划～ planned supply / 市场～ supply of commodities; market supplies / 合同规定农民养一头猪,～一百斤饲料。The contract states that a farmer will be supplied with 100 jin of fodder for each pig he raises.

供应点 gōngyìngdiǎn　supply centre

供应线 gōngyìngxiàn　supply line

肱 gōng　formal　the upper arm; arm: 曲～而枕 sleep with one's head resting on one's bent arm

肱骨 gōnggǔ　physiol.　humerus

宫¹ gōng ① imperial palace ② a house in which supernatural beings live; heavenly palace: 天宫 tiāngōng ③ temple (used in a name): 雍和～ the Lama Temple of Peace and Harmony (in Beijing) ④ a place for cultural activities and recreation: 工人文化～ the Workers' Cultural Palace ⑤ physiol. womb; uterus: 宫颈 gōngjǐng ⑥ (Gōng) a surname

宫² gōng　mus.　a note of the ancient Chinese five-tone scale, corresponding to 1 in numbered musical notation

宫灯 gōngdēng　palace lantern

宫殿 gōngdiàn　palace: ～式建筑 palatial architecture

宫调 gōngdiào　mus.　modes of ancient Chinese music

宫娥 gōng'é same as 宫女 gōngnǚ

宫禁 gōngjìn ① palace prohibitions ② palace precincts

宫颈 gōngjǐng same as 子宫颈 zǐgōngjǐng

宫内节育器 gōngnèi jiéyùqì intrauterine device (IUD)

宫女 gōngnǚ a maid in an imperial palace; maid of honour

宫阙 gōngquè imperial palace

宫扇 gōngshàn round fan

宫室 gōngshì palace

宫廷 gōngtíng ① palace ② royal or imperial court; court

宫廷政变 gōngtíng zhèngbiàn palace coup

宫外孕 gōngwàiyùn med. ectopic pregnancy; extrauterine pregnancy

宫闱 gōngwéi formal palace chambers: ～秘事 palace secrets

宫刑 gōngxíng castration (a punishment in ancient China)——see also 五刑 wǔxíng

恭 gōng respectful; reverent: ～而有礼 be polite and respectful / 执礼甚～ treat sb. with great respect

恭贺 gōnghè pol. congratulate: ～新禧 Happy New Year

恭候 gōnghòu pol. await respectfully: ～光临。We request the pleasure of your company.

恭谨 gōngjǐn respectful and cautious

恭敬 gōngjìng respectful: 学生们恭恭敬敬地向老师行了个礼。The students bowed respectfully to their teacher.

恭敬不如从命 gōngjìng bùrú cóng mìng it is better to accept deferentially than to decline courteously (on accepting gifts, etc. from one's elders)

恭请 gōngqǐng pol. invite respectfully: ～光临。We request the honour of your presence.

恭顺 gōngshùn respectful and submissive

恭桶 gōngtǒng closestool; nightstool; commode

恭维 gōngwei (also 恭惟 gōngwéi) flatter; compliment: ～话 flattery; compliments / 我～了他几句。I said a few words complimenting him. / 他那几句英语，我实在不敢。I can't compliment him on his English.

恭喜 gōngxǐ pol. congratulate: ～！～！～你们试验成功! Congratulations! Congratulations! I congratulate you on the success of your experiment. / ～你得了个千金。Let me congratulate you on the birth of your daughter. / ～发财! Congratulations and may you be prosperous! or Wishing you happiness and prosperity! (a Spring Festival greeting)

恭正 gōngzhèng ① reverently ② carefully and neatly: 写得很～ neatly written

蚣 gōng see 蜈蚣 wú·gōng

躬（躳） gōng ① formal personally: ～行实践 practise what one preaches ② bend forward; bow: ～身 bend at the waist

躬逢其盛 gōng féng qí shèng be present in person on the grand occasion

躬亲 gōngqīn attend to personally: 事必躬亲 shì bì gōngqīn

龚（龔） Gōng a surname

觥 gōng archaeol. an ancient bronze wine vessel in the shape of a composite animal

觥筹交错 gōngchóu jiāocuò wine cups and mora chips lying about in disorder—a hilarious party

gōng

巩（鞏） gǒng ① consolidate: 巩固 gǒnggù ② (Gǒng) a surname

巩固 gǒnggù ① consolidate; strengthen; solidify: ～阵地 consolidate a position / ～政权 consolidate political power / ～工农联盟 strengthen the worker-peasant alliance ② consolidated; strong; solid; stable: 建立～的革命根据地 build stable revolutionary base areas / ～的国防 strong national defence / 两国人民的友谊是～的。The people of the two nations have strong ties of friendship.

巩膜 gǒngmó physiol. sclera

巩膜炎 gǒngmóyán scleritis

巩皮病 gǒngpíbìng another name for 硬皮病 yìngpíbìng

汞 gǒng chem. mercury; hydrargyrum (Hg)

汞弧灯 gǒnghúdēng mercury-arc lamp

汞化 gǒnghuà chem. mercurate; mercurize: ～物 mercuride

汞溴红 gǒngxiùhóng pharm. mercurochrome

拱[1] gǒng ① cup one hand in the other before the chest (in salutation): 拱手 gǒngshǒu ② surround: 四山环～的大湖 a large lake surrounded by mountains ③ hump up; arch: 猫～了～腰。The cat arched its back. ④ archit. arch: ～道 archway / ～式涵洞 arch culvert

拱[2] gǒng ① push with the shoulders or head: 用肩膀把门～开 push the door open with one's shoulder / 一个小孩儿从人群里～出去了。A child wormed his way out of the crowd. / 猪用嘴～地。Pigs dig earth with their snouts. / 蚯蚓从地下～出许多土来。The earthworms wriggled their way out, pushing up a lot of earth. ② sprout up through the earth: 苗儿～出土了。The sprouts are coming out of the earth.

拱坝 gǒngbà water conservancy arch dam

拱抱 gǒngbào surround: 群峰～的山坞 a cove surrounded by cliffs

拱点 gǒngdiǎn astron. apsis; apse

拱顶 gǒngdǐng archit. vault

拱门 gǒngmén archit. arched door

拱桥 gǒngqiáo archit. arch bridge: 双曲～ double-curvature arch bridge

拱手 gǒngshǒu make an obeisance by cupping one hand in the other before the chest: 两人～作别，互道珍重。The two men bid farewell to each other with a cupped-hand salute, each asking the other to take good care of himself.

拱手让人 gǒngshǒu ràng rén surrender sth. submissively; hand sth. over on a silver platter

拱卫 gǒngwèi surround and protect: 大半精兵都驻扎在山下，～着设在山上的指挥部。More than half of the crack troops were stationed at the foot of the mountain, surrounding and protecting the mountaintop command post.

拱券 gǒngxuàn archit. arch

栱 gǒng see 枓栱 dǒugǒng

珙 gǒng formal a kind of jade

珙桐 gǒngtóng bot. dove tree

gòng

共　gòng ① common; general: 共性 gòngxìng ② share: ～命运 share a common fate; throw in one's lot with sb. ③ *adv.* together; in company: ～进午餐 have lunch together / 与国土～存亡 defend the homeland to the death / 两国人民～饮一江水。The people of our two countries drink from the same river. ④ *adv.* altogether; in all; all told: 这个集子～收小说十二篇。There are altogether twelve short stories in this collection. / 我们小组～有十人。There are ten of us in the group. ⑤ short for 共产党 gòngchǎndǎng

共产党　gòngchǎndǎng the Communist Party: ～人 Communist / ～员 member of the Communist Party; Communist; Party member

共产党宣言　Gòngchǎndǎng Xuānyán *Manifesto of the Communist Party; Communist Manifesto*

共产国际　Gòngchǎn Guójì the Communist International (1919–1943); Comintern

共产主义　gòngchǎnzhǔyì communism: ～道德 communist morality / ～风格 communist style (*or* spirit) / ～觉悟 communist consciousness / ～人生观 communist outlook on life / ～者 communist

共产主义青年团　gòngchǎnzhǔyì qīngniántuán the Communist Youth League

共处　gòngchǔ coexist: 每一个矛盾的两个方面～于一个统一体中。The two aspects of every contradiction coexist in a single entity.

共存　gòngcún coexist

共电制　gòngdiànzhì common-battery system: ～电话机 common-battery telephone / ～电话局 common-battery telephone exchange

共度　gòngdù spend (an occasion) together: ～佳节 celebrate a festival together

共轭　gòng'è *math. phys.* conjugate

共轭点　gòng'èdiǎn *math.* conjugate point

共轭角　gòng'èjiǎo *math.* conjugate angles

共轭象　gòng'èxiàng *phys.* conjugate image

共发射极　gòngfāshèjí *electron.* common emitter

共犯　gòngfàn *leg.* accomplice

共管　gòngguǎn short for 国际共管 guójì gòngguǎn

共和　gònghé republicanism; republic

共和党　Gònghédǎng the Republican Party (in U. S.)

共和国　gònghéguó republic

共基极　gòngjījí *electron.* common base

共计　gòngjì amount to; add up to; total: 两项开支～三十元。These two items of expenditure come to thirty *yuan.* / 参观展览会的～二十万人。Altogether 200,000 people visited the exhibition.

共价　gòngjià *chem.* covalence: ～键 covalent bond

共聚　gòngjù *chem.* copolymerization: ～物 copolymer

共聚一堂　gòng jù yī táng gather in the same hall; gather together: 各族人民的代表～,商讨国家大事。Representatives of different nationalities gather in the same hall to discuss affairs of state.

共勉　gòngmiǎn encourage each other: 愿～之。Let us encourage each other in our endeavours. / 毕业时同学们互相题词～。At graduation the students presented each other with valedictory inscriptions.

共鸣　gòngmíng ① *phys.* resonance: ～器 resonator ② sympathetic response: 引起～ arouse sympathy; strike a sympathetic chord

共栖　gòngqī *biol.* commensalism

共青团　gòngqīngtuán short for 共产主义青年团 gòngchǎnzhǔyì qīngniántuán

共青团员　gòngqīngtuányuán member of the Communist Youth League; League member

共生　gòngshēng ① *geol.* intergrowth; paragenesis ② *biol.* symbiosis: ～细菌 symbiotic bacteria

共生次序　gòngshēng cìxù *geol.* paragenesis

共生矿　gòngshēngkuàng mineral intergrowth

共识　gòngshí common understanding

共事　gòngshì work together (at the same organization); be fellow workers: ～多年 have been colleagues for many years

共通　gòngtōng applicable to both or all: 这两者之间有～的道理。The same argument applies to both cases.

共同　gòngtóng ① shared; common: ～语言 common language / ～敌人 common enemy / ～关心的问题 matters of common concern; issues of common interest / 有～之处 have something in common ② *adv.* together; jointly: ～战斗 fight side by side / ～努力 make joint efforts / ～对敌 join forces to oppose the enemy / ～行动 act in concert

共同点　gòngtóngdiǎn common ground

共同市场　Gòngtóng Shìchǎng the Common Market

共同体　gòngtóngtǐ community: 欧洲经济～ the European Economic Community (EEC) / 加勒比～ the Caribbean Community (CARICOM)

共析　gòngxī *metall.* eutectoid: ～钢 eutectoid steel

共享　gòngxiǎng enjoy together; share: ～胜利的喜悦 share the joys of victory

共性　gòngxìng general character; generality

共振　gòngzhèn *phys.* resonance: ～器 resonator / ～腔 resonant cavity / ～示波器 resonoscope

共总　gòngzǒng *adv.* altogether; in all; in the aggregate: 这几笔帐～多少? How much do all these accounts add up to? / 今年全厂～有二百名工人超额完成定量。There are altogether 200 workers in the factory who overfulfilled their production quotas this year.

共轴　gòngzhóu coaxial

贡　gòng ① tribute: 进贡 jìngòng ② (Gòng) a surname

贡品　gòngpǐn articles of tribute; tribute

贡税　gòngshuì tribute and taxes

贡献　gòngxiàn ① contribute; dedicate; devote: 他把自己全部的藏书都～给了图书馆。He contributed all his collections of books to the library. / 为祖国的建设～一份力量 do one's bit for the construction of the motherland / 她为和平事业～了自己的一生。She devoted her life to the cause of peace. ② contribution; dedication; devotion: 中国应当对人类有较大的～。China ought to make a greater contribution to humanity. / 爱因斯坦最大的～是创立了相对论。The theory of relativity was Einstein's greatest contribution.

供[1]　gòng ① present (offerings): 遗像前～着鲜花。Fresh flowers were laid out before the portrait of the deceased. ② offerings: 上供 shànggòng

供[2]　gòng ① confess; own up: 据该犯～称 as was confessed by the culprit / 他～出了主犯的名字。He gave the name of the chief culprit. ② confession; deposition: 问了半天也问不出～来。No confession was forthcoming during the lengthy interrogation.
——see also gōng

供案　gòng'àn altar table

供词　gòngcí a statement made under examination; confession

供奉　gòngfèng ① enshrine and worship; consecrate ② actors who gave command performances (in the Qing

Dynasty)

供具 gòngjù sacrificial vessel
供品 gòngpǐn offerings
供认 gòngrèn confess
供认不讳 gòngrèn bù huì candidly confess; confess everything
供养 gòngyǎng make offerings to; offer sacrifices to; enshrine and worship; consecrate ——see also gòngyǎng
供职 gòngzhí hold office
供状 gòngzhuàng written confession; deposition
供桌 gòngzhuō altar table

gōu

勾[1]（句） gōu ① cancel; cross out; strike out; tick off: 把他的名字～掉 cross out his name; strike his name off the register／～了这笔帐·cancel the debt／把重要的项目～出来 tick off the important items ② delineate; draw:～出一个轮廓 draw an outline ③ fill up the joints of brickwork with mortar or cement; point: ～墙缝 point a brick wall ④ thicken: ～芡 thicken soup ⑤ induce; evoke; call to mind: 这件事～起了我对童年的回忆。This evoked memories of my childhood. ⑥ collude with; gang up with: 他们这帮人怎么～上的? How did these people come to form a gang?

勾[2]（句） gōu old name for the shorter leg of a right triangle
——see also gòu
勾除 gōuchú delete; strike out; cancel
勾搭 gōuda ① gang up with: 这四个坏家伙～上了。The four scoundrels ganged up.／那家伙跟投机倒把分子勾勾搭搭。That fellow works hand in glove with speculators. ② carry on (or have a carry-on) with sb.: 她丈夫和隔壁那个女人勾勾搭搭的。Her husband is carrying on with the woman next door.
勾股定理 gōugǔ dìnglǐ math. the Pythagorean theorem (or proposition)
勾股形 gōugǔxíng old name for 直角三角形 zhíjiǎo sānjiǎoxíng
勾画 gōuhuà draw the outline of; delineate; sketch: 寥寥数笔，就把这高利贷者贪婪的嘴脸～出来了。A few words successfully bring out the greediness of the usurer.
勾魂 gōuhún captivate sb.'s soul—enchant; bewitch
勾结 gōujié collude with; collaborate with; gang up with: 与敌人相～ collude with the enemy
勾栏 gōulán (also 勾阑 gōulán) arch. ① theatre ② brothel
勾勒 gōulè ① draw the outline of; sketch the contours of: 他只用简单的几笔就～出了马的轮廓。He sketched the outline of a horse with just a few rapid strokes. ② give a brief account of; outline
勾脸 gōuliǎn paint the face (in traditional opera)
勾留 gōuliú stop over; break one's journey at: 我们回京途中，在保定稍作～。We stopped over at Baoding on our way back to Beijing.
勾通 gōutōng collude with; work hand in glove with
勾销 gōuxiāo liquidate; write off; strike out: ～债务 liquidate a debt
勾心斗角 gōuxīn-dòujiǎo same as 钩心斗角 gōuxīn-dòujiǎo
勾引 gōuyǐn tempt; entice; seduce: ～少女 seduce young girls

沟（溝） gōu ① ditch; channel; trench: 排

水～ drainage ditch; drain／交通～ communication trench ② groove; rut; furrow: 开～播种 make furrows for sowing seeds／拖拉机在泥路上轧出两道～。The tractor made ruts in the dirt road. ③ gully; ravine: 七～八梁 seven gullies and eight ridges; full of gullies and ridges／乱石～ boulder-strewn gully
沟灌 gōuguàn agric. furrow irrigation
沟壑 gōuhè gully; ravine: ～纵横 a crisscross network of gullies
沟坎 gōukǎn ditch; trench
沟堑 gōuqiàn ditch; trench
沟渠 gōuqú irrigation canals and ditches: 田野上～纵横。The fields are crisscrossed by irrigation canals and ditches.
沟通 gōutōng link up: ～南方各省的新铁路 the new railways that link up the southern provinces／～两大洋的运河 an interoceanic canal／～思想 promote mutual understanding／早在两千年前，著名的"丝绸之路"就～了中国和西亚各国的文化。As far back as 2,000 years ago, the famous Silk Road facilitated the flow of culture between China and the countries of West Asia.
沟沿儿 gōuyánr banks of a ditch or canal

佝 gōu see below
佝偻病 gōulóubìng rickets

钩（鉤） gōu ① hook: 钓鱼～ fishhook／挂衣～ clothes-hook ② hook stroke (in Chinese characters) ③ check mark; tick ④ secure with a hook; hook: 杂技演员用脚～住绳圈儿。The acrobat hooked his foot into the loop.／他的袖子给钉子～住了。His sleeve caught on a nail.／他把掉到井里的水桶～上来了。He fished up the bucket which had dropped into the well. ⑤ crochet: ～花边 crochet lace ⑥ sew with large stitches: ～贴边 sew on an edging ⑦ a spoken form for the numeral 九
钩虫 gōuchóng hookworm
钩虫病 gōuchóngbìng hookworm disease; ancylostomiasis
钩端螺旋体病 gōuduānluóxuántǐbìng leptospirosis
钩吻 gōuwěn bot. elegant jessamine
钩心斗角 gōuxīn-dòujiǎo intrigue against each other; jockey for position
钩针 gōuzhēn crochet hook
钩子 gōuzi ① hook: 有挂衣服的～吗? Is there a hook to hang my coat on? ② a hook-like thing: 蝎子的～有毒。The sting of a scorpion is poisonous.
钩嘴鹛 gōuzuǐméi scimitar babbler

枸 gōu see below ——see also gǒu; jǔ
枸橘 gōujú another name for 枳 zhǐ

篝 gōu formal cage
篝火 gōuhuǒ bonfire; campfire: 举行～晚会 give a campfire party／宿营地上燃起熊熊的～。A bright bonfire was built at camp.

鞲 gōu see below
鞲鞴 gōubèi piston

gǒu

苟[1] gǒu careless; negligent; indifferent (to right or wrong): 不苟 bùgǒu
苟[2] gǒu conj. formal if: ～能坚持, 必将胜利。If you can persist, you are sure to win. or Given persis-

tence, victory is certain.

苟安 gǒu'ān　seek a moment's peace however one can; be content with temporary ease and comfort

苟合 gǒuhé　illicit sexual relations

苟活 gǒuhuó　drag out an ignoble existence; live on in degradation

苟简 gǒujiǎn　*formal*　too brief to be intelligible; slipshod: 终身大事, 不当～. Marriage is a major affair in one's life and should be celebrated in style.

苟且 gǒuqiě　① drift along; be resigned to circumstances ② perfunctory; careless: ～了事 dispose of sth. perfunctorily / 他做翻译, 一字一句都不敢～. In doing translation work, he chose every word with great care. ③ illicit (sexual relations); improper

苟且偷安 gǒuqiě-tōu'ān　seek a moment's peace however one can; be content with temporary ease and comfort

苟且偷生 gǒuqiě-tōushēng　drag out an ignoble existence

苟全 gǒuquán　aimlessly preserve (one's own life)

苟全性命 gǒuquán xìngmìng　barely manage to survive: ～于乱世 barely secure personal safety in a troubled age

苟同 gǒutóng　*formal*　(usu. used in the negative) agree without giving serious thought; readily subscribe to (sb.'s view): 不敢～ beg to differ; cannot agree

苟延残喘 gǒuyáncánchuǎn　be on one's last legs; linger on in a steadily worsening condition

狗

gǒu　① dog ② *offens.*　damned; cursed: ～东西 that son of a bitch

狗宝 gǒubǎo　*Chin. med.*　the stone of a dog's gallbladder, kidney or bladder

狗吃屎 gǒuchīshǐ　*derog.*　a dog eating dung—a heavy fall or a fall flat on the face

狗胆包天 gǒudǎn bāo tiān　monstrously audacious

狗颠屁股 gǒu diān pìgu　a dog wagging its behind —cringing; sycophantic

狗窦 gǒudòu　hole in the wall for a dog to come in and out

狗苟蝇营 gǒugǒu-yíngyíng　same as 蝇营狗苟 yíngyíng-gǒugǒu

狗獾 gǒuhuān　badger

狗急跳墙 gǒu jí tiào qiáng　a cornered beast will do something desperate

狗脊蕨 gǒujǐjué　*bot.*　chain fern

狗拿耗子, 多管闲事 gǒu ná hàozi, duō guǎn xiánshì　a dog trying to catch mice—poke one's nose into other people's business

狗皮膏药 gǒupí gāoyao　*Chin. med.*　① dogskin plaster (a plaster for rheumatism, strains, contusions, etc., formerly spread on dogskin, but now usu. on cloth) ② quack medicine ——see also 卖狗皮膏药 mài gǒupí gāoyao

狗屁 gǒupì　*offens.*　horseshit; rubbish; nonsense

狗屁不通 gǒupì bù tōng　unreadable rubbish; mere trash: 这篇文章写得～. This article is mere trash.

狗屎堆 gǒushǐduī　a heap of dog's droppings; a pile of dog's dung: 不齿于人类的～ filthy and contemptible as dog's dung

狗头军师 gǒutóu jūnshī　① a person who offers bad advice; inept adviser ② villainous adviser

狗腿子 gǒutuǐzi　*inf.*　hired thug; lackey; henchman

狗尾草 gǒuwěicǎo　*bot.*　green bristlegrass

狗尾续貂 gǒuwěi xù diāo　a dog's tail joined to sable—(of a literary work) a wretched sequel to a fine work

狗窝 gǒuwō　kennel; doghouse: 房间里乱得像～。The room is such a mess that it resembles a doghouse.

狗血喷头 gǒuxiě pēn tóu　(usu. used in) 骂得～ let loose a stream of abuse against sb.; pour out a flood of invective against sb.

狗熊 gǒuxióng　① black bear ② coward

狗眼看人低 gǒuyǎn kàn rén dī　be a bloody snob

狗咬狗 gǒu yǎo gǒu　dog-eat-dog: 傀儡集团内部～的斗争 a dog-eat-dog struggle within a puppet clique

狗咬吕洞宾 gǒu yǎo Lǚ Dòngbīn　snarl and snap at Lü Dongbin (one of the eight immortals in Chinese mythology)—wrong a kind-hearted person: 你别～, 不识好人心。我是好心好意劝你, 倒粘到我身上来了。Don't snap and snarl at me when I'm trying to do my best for you. I give you my advice with the best will in the world and you turn round and lay the blame on me.

狗蝇 gǒuyíng　dog louse fly

狗鱼 gǒuyú　pike (a fish)

狗崽子 gǒuzǎizi　*offens.*　son of a bitch

狗蚤 gǒuzǎo　dog flea

狗仗人势 gǒu zhàng rén shì　like a dog threatening people on the strength of its master's power—be a bully with the backing of a powerful person

狗彘不如 gǒu-zhì bùrú　worse than a cur or a swine

狗嘴里吐不出象牙 gǒuzuǐli tǔbuchū xiàngyá　no ivory issues from the mouth of a dog; a filthy mouth can't utter decent language; what can you expect from a dog but a bark

枸

gǒu　see below ——see also gōu; jǔ

枸骨 gǒugǔ　*bot.*　Chinese holly

枸杞子 gǒuqǐzi　*Chin. med.*　the fruit of Chinese wolfberry (*Lycium chinense*)

gòu

勾(句)

gòu　see below ——see also gōu

勾当 gòudàng　*derog.*　business; deal: 罪恶～ criminal activities / 肮脏～ a dirty deal

构(構)

gòu　① construct; form; compose: ～词 form a word ② fabricate; make up: 虚构 xūgòu ③ literary composition: 佳～ a good piece of writing

构成 gòuchéng　constitute; form; compose; make up: ～威胁 constitute (*or* pose) a threat / 西沙群岛是由珊瑚礁～的。The Xisha Archipelago is formed of coral reefs. / ～部分 component part

构词法 gòucífǎ　*linguis.*　word-building; word-formation

构件 gòujiàn　① *archit.*　(structural) member; component ② *mech.*　component (part)

构思 gòusī　(of a writer or artist) work out the plot of a story or the composition of a painting: 他正在～一部小说。He is working out the plot of a novel. / 故事的～相当巧妙。The plot of the story is ingeniously conceived. / 大胆的～ boldness of conception

构图 gòutú　composition (of a picture)

构陷 gòuxiàn　make a false charge against sb.; frame sb. up

构想 gòuxiǎng　idea; conception; concept: 我有个经济体制改革的～。I have an idea for restructuring the economy. / 按照"一国两制"～, 促进祖国和平统一! Promote the peaceful unification of the motherland according to the concept of "one country, two systems"! (a slogan) / 这部小说, ～和行文都不高明。This novel is none too satisfactory, either in conception or in execution.

构造 gòuzào　① structure; construction: 人体～ the structure of the human body / 句子的～ the structure

of a sentence / 这种机器~简单, 使用方便。This machine is simple in construction and easy to handle. ② *geol.* tectonic; structural: ~体系 structural system / ~序次 structural generation

构造地震 gòuzào dìzhèn　tectonic earthquake

构造地质学 gòuzào dìzhìxué　structural geology

构造运动 gòuzào yùndòng　*geol.*　tectonic movement

构筑 gòuzhù　construct (military works); build: ~工事 construct field works (*or* fortifications); build defences; dig in

构筑物 gòuzhùwù　*archit.*　structures

购（購）

gòu　purchase; buy: ~粮 purchase grain / 此书~于北京新华书店。The book was bought in the Beijing Xinhua Bookstore.

购办 gòubàn　buy (goods, supplies, etc.)

购货单 gòuhuòdān　order form; order

购买 gòumǎi　purchase; buy: 实验室计划~大量设备。The laboratory plans to buy a lot of equipment.

购买力 gòumǎilì　purchasing power

购销 gòu-xiāo　purchase and sale; buying and selling: ~两旺 brisk buying and selling

购置 gòuzhì　purchase (durables): ~农具 purchase farm implements / 学校~了大量的实验设备。Our school bought a large amount of lab equipment.

诟

gòu　*formal*　① shame; humiliation: ~感之情 sentiments of shame and thankfulness ② revile; talk abusively: 诟病 gòubìng

诟病 gòubìng　*formal*　denounce; castigate: 为世~ become an object of public denunciation

诟骂 gòumà　*formal*　revile; abuse; vilify: 当众~ vilify sb. in public

垢

gòu　① *formal*　dirty; filthy: 蓬头垢面 péngtóu-gòumiàn　② dirt; filth: 油~ grease stain ③ *formal* disgrace; humiliation: 含垢忍辱 hángòu-rěnrǔ

垢泥 gòuní　deposit of oil, sweat and dirt on the skin

够（夠）

gòu　① enough; sufficient; adequate: 你钱~不~? Do you have enough money? / 我吃~了。I've had enough. / 这里只举一个例子就~了。Here a single example will suffice. / 钱不~买一本字典。The money is not enough to buy a dictionary. / 这活儿~我们忙几天的。This job will keep us busy for several days. ② *adv.*　enough (to reach a certain extent); sufficiently: ~好了。It's good enough. / 今儿~冷的。It's quite cold today. / 今天你们可~辛苦了。You've really done a hard day's work. ③ reach (sth. by stretching): 你~得着那些桑葚儿吗? Can you reach those mulberries? / 我~不着书架的最上一层。I can't reach the top shelf of the bookcase. ④ reach (a standard or level): ~标准 be up to standard / ~资格 be qualified

够本 gòuběn　① make enough money to cover the cost; break even ② the gains balancing the losses

够格 gòugé　be qualified; be up to standard: 当代表, 他满~。He's well qualified to be a representative.

够交情 gòu jiāoqing　same as 够朋友 gòu péngyou

够劲儿 gòujìnr　*inf.*　① (of an onerous task, etc.) almost too much to cope with: 他一个人担任那么多工作, 真~。He really has a tough job having to attend to so many things. ② strong (in taste, strength, etc.): 这辣椒真~。This pepper is really hot. / 这茅台酒真~。This *maotai* is certainly powerful stuff.

够朋友 gòu péngyou　*inf.*　deserve to be called a true friend; be a friend indeed

够呛 gòuqiàng　(also 够戗 gòuqiàng) *dial.*　unbearable; terrible: 疼得~ unbearably painful / 她的脚冻得~。

Her feet were terribly frostbitten. / 他的伤势怎么样? ——~! How's his wound?—Pretty bad! / 这家伙真~! He's simply impossible.

够瞧的 gòuqiáode　really awful; too much: 天热得真~。The weather is terribly hot. *or* The weather is really scorching. / 这个人脾气说犯就犯, 真~。It's really awful the way that man loses his temper so easily.

够受的 gòushòude　quite an ordeal; hard to bear: 累得~ be dog-tired / 他这一跤摔得真~。He had a really bad fall.

够数 gòushù　sufficient in quantity; enough: 你领的镰刀不~。You didn't get enough sickles to go round.

够味儿 gòuwèir　*inf.*　just the right flavour; just the thing; quite satisfactory: 最后这两句你唱得真~! The way you sang the last two lines was just superb!

够意思 gòu yìsi　① really something; terrific: 这场球赛可真~。That was a really terrific game. ② generous; really kind: 不~ unfriendly; ungrateful

媾

gòu　*formal*　① wed: 婚~ marriage ② reach an agreement: 媾和 gòuhé ③ coition: 交媾 jiāogòu

媾和 gòuhé　make peace: 单独~ make peace without consulting one's allies; make a separate peace

遘

gòu　*formal*　encounter

彀¹

gòu　draw a bow to the full

彀²

gòu　same as 够 gòu

彀中 gòuzhōng　*formal*　① shooting range: 尽入~ have all come within shooting range (*or* come under control) ② trap; snare: 入我~ fall into my trap

觏

gòu　*formal*　meet: 罕觏 hǎngòu

gū

估

gū　estimate; appraise: 你~一~这堆西红柿有几斤。Can you tell how many *jin* of tomatoes there are in this heap。——see also gù

估产 gūchǎn　① estimate the yield: 这块地~八百斤。The estimated yield of this plot of land is 800 *jin*。② appraise the assets; assess

估堆儿 gūduīr　estimate the number or value of a lot

估计 gūjì　estimate; appraise; reckon: 我~这项工作要三个月才能完成。I estimate that it will take three months to finish the work. / 我~他会来。I reckon he will come. / 清醒地~当前的形势 make a clearheaded appraisal of the present situation / 这种可能性我们必须~到。We must take this possibility into account. / ~今年又是一个丰收年。It looks as if there'll be another good harvest this year. / 这只是一种~, 实际情况也许不是这样。This is just an estimate. The actual situation might be different. / ~错误 miscalculate / 过高~ overestimate / 过低~ underestimate

估价 gūjià　① appraise; evaluate: 这件家具请你估一估价。Evaluate this piece of furniture, please. / 对自己要有正确的~。One must have a correct estimate of oneself. / 对历史人物的~不能脱离具体的历史条件。In evaluating historical personages, we should not lose sight of specific historical conditions. ② *econ.* appraised price

估量 gūliang　appraise; estimate; assess; reckon: ~双方力量的对比 assess the balance of strength between the two sides / 你~他挣多少? How much do you reckon he earns?

估摸 gūmo　*inf.*　reckon; guess: 我~着她月底就能回

来。I reckon she'll be back by the end of this month.

估算 gūsuàn estimate; appraise; reckon: ～产量 estimate the yield / ～到几种可能性 reckon with several possibilities

沽[1] gū *formal* ① buy: ～酒 buy wine ② sell: 待价而沽 dài jià ér gū

沽[2] Gū another name for 天津 Tiānjīn

沽名钓誉 gūmíng-diàoyù fish for fame and compliments

咕 gū *onom.* the clucking of a hen; the cooing of a pigeon: 鸽子一边儿吃，一边儿～～地叫。The pigeon was eating and cooing at the same time.

咕咚 gūdōng *onom.* the sound of a heavy thing falling down; thud; splash; plump: 大石头～一声掉到水里去了。The rock fell into the water with a splash. / 他～一声倒在地上了。He fell to the ground with a thud.

咕嘟 gūdū *onom.* bubble; gurgle: 泉水～～地往外冒。The spring kept bubbling up. / 他端起一碗水，～～地喝了下去。He took up a bowl of water and gulped it down.

咕嘟 gūdu ① boil for a long time: 白菜早就～烂了。The cabbage is overcooked. ② *dial.* purse (one's lips): 不高兴地～着嘴 purse one's lips in displeasure

咕唧 gūjī (also 咕叽 gūjī) *onom.* a squelching sound: 水牛拉着犁，在稻田里～～地走着。The water buffalo squelched up and down the paddy fields, pulling the plough. / 他在雨地里走着，脚底下～～地直响。He walked along in the rain, the water squelching in his boots.

咕唧 gūji (also 咕叽 gūji) whisper; murmur: 他俩～了半天。They whispered to each other for a long time. / 他一边儿想心事，一边儿～。He was murmuring to himself as he thought about something.

咕隆 gūlōng *onom.* rumble; rattle; roll: 远处雷声～～地响。Thunder rumbled in the distance. / 行李车在月台上～～地跑着。The luggage trolley rattled along the platform.

咕噜 gūlū *onom.* rumble; roll: 他的肚子～～直响。His stomach kept rumbling. / 粗大的圆木～～地从山坡上滚下来。Large logs came rolling down the slope.

咕噜 gūlu same as 咕哝 gūnong

咕哝 gūnong murmur; mutter; grumble: 他在～些什么? What is he muttering about?

咕容 gūrong *dial.* (of a snake, etc.) wriggle

呱 gū see below ——see also guā

呱呱 gūgū *formal* the cry of a baby: ～而泣 mewl ——see also guāguā

呱呱坠地 gūgū zhuì dì (of a baby) come into the world with a cry; raise the first cry of life; be born

孤 gū ① (of a child) fatherless or orphaned: 孤儿 gū'ér ② solitary; isolated; alone: ～雁 a solitary wild goose / 众鸟高飞尽，～云独去闲。(李白) Flocks of birds fly high and vanish; A single cloud, alone, calmly drifts on. ③ I (used by feudal princes)

孤哀子 gū'āizǐ a son bereaved of both parents (used in obituaries)

孤傲 gū'ào proud and aloof: 去掉～习气 rid oneself of aloofness and arrogance

孤本 gūběn the only copy extant; the only existing copy

孤臣孽子 gūchén-nièzǐ a minister in disgrace and the son of a concubine out of favour——a supporter of a doomed dynasty or a lost cause

孤单 gūdān ① alone; lonely: 孤孤单单一个人 all alone;

all by oneself; a lone soul / 感到～ feel lonely ② weak: 力量～ weak and helpless

孤胆 gūdǎn fighting single-handed: ～英雄 a lone fighter

孤岛 gūdǎo an isolated island

孤独 gūdú lonely; solitary: 过着～的生活 live in solitude / 同学们都回家去了，剩下自己一个人不免感到～、烦闷。The other students have all gone home, leaving me here all alone, and I can't help feeling lonely and depressed.

孤儿 gū'ér ① a fatherless child ② orphan

孤儿寡妇 gū'ér-guǎfù (also 孤儿寡母 gū'ér-guǎmǔ) a widow and her child

孤儿院 gū'éryuàn orphanage

孤芳自赏 gūfāng zì shǎng a solitary flower in love with its own fragrance; a lone soul admiring his own purity; indulge in self-admiration

孤高 gūgāo *formal* haughty and aloof

孤寡 gūguǎ ① same as 孤儿寡妇 gū'ér-guǎfù ② lonely; solitary: 家里只剩下她一个～老婆儿。The old woman is the only one left in the family.

孤拐 gūguai *dial.* ① cheekbone ② the ball of the foot

孤寂 gūjì lonely

孤家寡人 gūjiā-guǎrén a person who is utterly isolated: 关门主义的策略则是～的策略。(毛泽东) The tactics of closed-doorism are, on the contrary, the tactics of the regal isolationist.

孤军 gūjūn an isolated force

孤军深入 gūjūn shēnrù an isolated force penetrating deep into enemy territory

孤军作战 gūjūn zuòzhàn fight in isolation; fight a lone battle

孤苦伶仃 gūkǔ-língdīng orphaned and helpless; alone and uncared for; friendless and wretched

孤老 gūlǎo lonely old people

孤老院 gūlǎoyuàn old folks' home; home for the aged

孤立 gūlì ① isolated: 处境～ find oneself in an isolated position / ～无援 isolated and cut off from help / 任何事物都不是～地存在着的。Nothing exists in isolation. ② isolate: ～敌人 isolate the enemy

孤立主义 gūlìzhǔyì isolationism

孤零零 gūlínglíng solitary; lone; all alone

孤陋寡闻 gūlòu-guǎwén ignorant and ill-informed

孤僻 gūpì unsociable and eccentric: 性情～ of an uncommunicative and eccentric disposition

孤身 gūshēn alone: ～前往 go there alone / 他哥哥去世后，家里只剩下他～一人了。After the death of his brother, he was the only one left in the family.

孤孀 gūshuāng widow

孤行己见 gū xíng jǐ jiàn follow one's bigoted course

孤掌难鸣 gūzhǎng nán míng it's impossible to clap with one hand——it's hard to succeed without support

孤注一掷 gū zhù yī zhì stake all on a single throw; risk everything on a single venture; put all one's eggs in one basket

孤子 gūzǐ ① orphan ② a son bereaved of his father

姑[1] gū ① father's sister; aunt ② husband's sister; sister-in-law ③ *arch.* husband's mother; mother-in-law ④ nun: 尼姑 nígū

姑[2] gū *adv. formal* tentatively; for the moment: ～置勿论 leave sth. aside for the moment

姑表 gūbiǎo the relationship between the children of a brother and a sister; cousinship: ～兄弟 male cousins (the father of one and the mother of the other being brother and sister)

姑夫 gūfu (also 姑父 gūfu) the husband of one's fa-

ther's sister; uncle

姑姑 gūgu *inf.* father's sister; aunt

姑舅 gūjiù same as 姑表 gūbiǎo

姑宽 gūkuān be sympathetic and forgiving

姑老爷 gūlǎoye a form of address for a man used by members of his wife's family

姑妈 gūmā *inf.* father's (married) sister; aunt

姑母 gūmǔ father's (married) sister; aunt

姑奶奶 gūnǎinai *inf.* ① married daughter ② the sister of one's paternal grandfather; grandaunt ③ your grandaunt (used by a woman in mentioning herself when quarrelling)

姑娘 gūniáng *dial.* ① father's (married) sister; aunt ② husband's sister; sister-in-law

姑娘 gūniang ① girl ② *inf.* daughter

姑婆 gūpó ① husband's aunt ② paternal grandaunt

姑且 gūqiě *adv.* tentatively; for the moment: 你～试一试。Have a try, anyhow. *or* Suppose you give it a try. / 我这里有支钢笔，你～用着。I have a pen here. You can use it for the moment. / 费用问题～不谈，要在一年内完成这项工程是不可能的。Even leaving aside the question of cost, it will be impossible to complete the project in a year.

姑嫂 gūsǎo a woman and her brother's wife; sisters-in-law

姑妄听之 gū wàng tīng zhī see no harm in hearing what sb. has to say

姑妄言之 gū wàng yán zhī tell sb. sth. for what it's worth

姑息 gūxī appease; indulge; tolerate: 不应该～他的错误。We shouldn't be indulgent towards his mistakes. / 对个人主义不能过分地～迁就。When it comes to individualism, we can't afford to be excessively tolerant or accommodating.

姑息疗法 gūxī liáofǎ *med.* palliative treatment

姑息养奸 gūxī yǎng jiān to tolerate evil is to abet it

姑爷爷 gūyéye *inf.* paternal grandaunt's husband

姑嫜 gūzhāng *formal* a woman's parents-in-law

姑丈 gūzhàng the husband of one's father's sister; uncle

姑子 gūzi *inf.* Buddhist nun

轱 gū see below

轱辘 gūlu (also 轱轳 gūlu) ① *inf.* wheel ② roll: 把桶推一下就～过来了。Give the barrel a push and it'll roll over here.

轱辘鞋 gūluxié roller skates

骨 gū see below —— see also gǔ

骨朵儿 gūduor *inf.* flower bud

骨碌 gūlu roll: 皮球在地上～。The ball is rolling on the ground. / 他一～从床上爬起来。He rolled out of bed.

鸪 gū see 鹁鸪 bógū; 鹧鸪 zhègū

家 gū see 阿家阿翁 āgū-āwēng —— see also jiā

菇 gū mushroom: 香菇 xiānggū

蛄 gū see 蝼蛄 huìgū; 蝼蛄 lóugū —— see also gǔ

菰 gū ① wild rice ② same as 菇 gū

辜 gū ① guilt; crime: 无辜 wúgū ② (Gū) a surname

辜负 gūfù let down; fail to live up to; be unworthy of; disappoint: 我们决不～党的期望。We will never let the

Party down. *or* We'll certainly live up to the expectations of the Party. / ～群众的信任 be unworthy of the trust the masses place in one; let the masses down / 你～了他的一片好心。You're unworthy of his kindness.

觚 gū ① *archaeol.* wine vessel; beaker; goblet ② *arch.* a wooden writing tablet: 操～ engage in literary composition ③ *arch.* edges and corners

菩 gū see below

菩葖 gūtū *bot.* follicle

酤 gū *formal* ① light wine ② buy (wine) ③ sell (wine)

觳 gū see below —— see also gǔ

觳辘 gūlu same as 轱辘 gūlu

箍 gū ① bind round; hoop: 用铁丝把桶～上 bind a bucket with wire / 他头上～着条毛巾。He had a towel wound round his head. ② hoop; band: 铁～ iron hoop

箍桶匠 gūtǒngjiàng cooper; hooper

箍子 gūzi *dial.* (finger) ring

gǔ

古 gǔ ① ancient; age-old; palaeo-: ～时候 in ancient times; in olden days / ～画 ancient paintings / ～瓷 old china / 这座庙～得很。This temple is very old. ② short for 古体诗 gǔtǐshī ③ (Gǔ) a surname

古奥 gǔ'ào (usu. of writing) archaic and abstruse

古巴 Gǔbā Cuba

古巴人 Gǔbārén Cuban

古板 gǔbǎn old-fashioned and inflexible

古刹 gǔchà an ancient temple

古代 gǔdài ① the period in Chinese history from remote antiquity down until the mid-19th century ② the age of slave society; ancient times; antiquity: ～文化 ancient civilization / ～史 ancient history

古道热肠 gǔdàorèicháng warm-hearted and compassionate

古典 gǔdiǎn ① classical allusion ② classical: ～作品 classic

古典文学 gǔdiǎn wénxué classical literature

古典音乐 gǔdiǎn yīnyuè classical music

古典主义 gǔdiǎnzhǔyì classicism

古董 gǔdǒng ① antique; curio: ～鉴赏家 connoisseur of curios ② old fogey

古动物学 gǔdòngwùxué palaeozoology

古都 gǔdū ancient capital

古尔邦节 Gǔ'ěrbāngjié *Islam* Corban

古方 gǔfāng an ancient prescription

古风 gǔfēng ① ancient customs; antiquities ② same as 古体诗 gǔtǐshī

古怪 gǔguài eccentric; odd; strange: ～脾气 eccentric character / 样子～ odd-looking

古汉语 gǔ Hànyǔ archaic Chinese

古话 gǔhuà old saying: ～说，有志者事竟成。As the old saying goes, where there's a will there's a way.

古籍 gǔjí ancient books

古迹 gǔjì historic site; place of historic interest

古今中外 gǔ-jīn-zhōng-wài ancient and modern, Chinese and foreign; at all times and in all lands: 在战役和战斗上面争取速决，～都是相同的。(毛泽东) Quick decision is sought in campaigns and battles, and this is true at all times and in all countries.

古旧 gǔjiù antiquated; archaic: ～词语 archaic words and expressions; archaisms

古柯 gǔkē *bot.* coca

古柯碱 gǔkējiǎn another name for 可卡因 kěkǎyīn

古来 gǔlái since time immemorial

古兰经 Gǔlánjīng *Islam* the Koran

古老 gǔlǎo ancient; age-old: ～的传说 legend／～的文明 an old civilization／～的风俗 ancient (*or* old) customs／～的中国变年轻了。 Old China has been rejuvenated.

古朴 gǔpǔ (of art, architecture, etc.) simple and unsophisticated; of primitive simplicity

古琴 gǔqín *guqin,* a seven-stringed plucked instrument in some ways similar to the zither

古人 gǔrén the ancients; our forefathers

古人类学 gǔrénlèixué palaeoanthropology: ～家 palaeoanthropologist

古色古香 gǔsè-gǔxiāng (also 古香古色 gǔxiāng-gǔsè) antique; quaint: 这个鼎土花斑驳，～。 This tripod has a beautiful patina and an air of great antiquity.

古生代 Gǔshēngdài *geol.* the Palaeozoic Era

古生界 Gǔshēngjiè *geol.* Palaeozoic Erathem

古生物学 gǔshēngwùxué palaeontology

古诗 gǔshī ① ancient poetry ② same as 古体诗 gǔtǐshī

古书 gǔshū ancient books

古塔胶 gǔtǎjiāo *chem.* gutta-percha

古体诗 gǔtǐshī a form of pre-Tang poetry, usu. having five or seven characters to each line, without strict tonal patterns or rhyme schemes

古田会议 Gǔtián Huìyì the Gutian Congress (the 9th Party Congress of the 4th Army of the Chinese Workers' and Peasants' Red Army, presided over by Comrade Mao Zedong in December 1929 at Gutian, Shanghang County, Fujian Province)

古田会议决议 Gǔtián Huìyì ·Juéyì the Gutian Congress Resolution (entitled *On Correcting Mistaken Ideas in the Party,* drawn up by Comrade Mao Zedong, a programme for building the people's armed forces on a Marxist-Leninist basis)

古铜色 gǔtóngsè bronze-coloured; bronze

古玩 gǔwán antique; curio: ～店 antique shop

古往今来 gǔwǎng-jīnlái throughout the ages; from time immemorial

古为今用 gǔ wéi jīn yòng make the past serve the present: ～，洋为中用。 Make the past serve the present and foreign things serve China.

古文 gǔwén ① prose written in the classical literary style; ancient Chinese prose ② Chinese script before the Qin Dynasty (221–206 B.C.)

古文字 gǔwénzì ancient writing

古文字学 gǔwénzìxué palaeography

古物 gǔwù ancient objects; antiquities: ～陈列馆 museum of antiquities

古稀 gǔxī seventy years of age: 年近～ getting on for seventy

古新世 Gǔxīnshì *geol.* the Palaeocene Epoch

古训 gǔxùn an old maxim (*or* adage)

古雅 gǔyǎ (of material things, literary works, etc.) of classic beauty and in elegant taste; of classic elegance

古谚 gǔyàn old proverb; old saw

古语 gǔyǔ ① archaism ② an old saying

古筝 gǔzhēng same as 筝 zhēng①

古植物学 gǔzhíwùxué palaeobotany

古装 gǔzhuāng ancient costume

古拙 gǔzhuō primitive and crude: 这个石刻虽然形式～,但是很有艺术价值。 Though primitive and crude in form, this stone carving has very high artistic value.

汩　gǔ *formal* (of running water) gurgle

汩汩 gǔgǔ gurgle: 渠水～地流入稻田。 Gurgling water flowed from the irrigation ditch into the paddy fields.

诂　gǔ explain archaic or dialectal words in current language: 训诂 xùngǔ

谷[1]　gǔ ① valley; gorge: 深～ a deep valley; gorge ② (Gǔ) a surname

谷[2] **(穀)**　gǔ ① cereal; grain: 谷类作物 gǔlèi zuòwù ② millet ③ *dial.* unhusked rice

谷氨酸 gǔ'ānsuān *pharm.* glutamic acid

谷仓 gǔcāng granary; barn

谷草 gǔcǎo ① millet straw ② *dial.* rice straw

谷蛾 gǔ'é grain moth

谷坊 gǔfāng *water conservancy* check dam

谷贱伤农 gǔ jiàn shāng nóng low prices for grain hurt the peasants; cheap grain harms the peasants

谷壳 gǔké husk (of rice)

谷类作物 gǔlèi zuòwù general name for rice, wheat, millet, sorghum, maize, etc.; cereal crops

谷维素 gǔwéisù oryzanol

谷物 gǔwù ① cereal; grain ② common name for 谷类作物 gǔlèi zuòwù

谷雨 Gǔyǔ ① Grain Rain—the 6th of the 24 solar terms ② the day marking the beginning of the 6th solar term (April 19, 20, or 21, which is the right time to sow wheat) ——see also 节气 jiéqì; 二十四节气 èrshí sì jiéqì

谷子 gǔzi ① millet ② *dial.* unhusked rice

谷子白发病 gǔzi báifàbìng *agric.* downy mildew of millet

股[1]　gǔ ① thigh ② section (of an office, enterprise, etc.): 人事～ personnel section ③ strand; ply: 三～的绳子 a three-strand rope／双～的毛线 two-ply wool／把线捻成～儿。 Twist the threads into yarn. ④ share in a company or one of several equal parts of property: 分～ divide into equal parts／每～五百元。 Five hundred *yuan* for each share. ⑤ *m.* ⓐ (for a long, narrow thing): 一～线 a skein of thread／一～泉水 a stream of spring water／上山有两～道。 There are two roads (*or* paths) going up the hill. ⓑ (for strength, smell, etc.): 一～香味 a whiff of fragrance／一～热气 a stream (*or* puff) of hot air／一～劲 a burst of energy ⓒ *derog.* (for a group of people): 两～土匪 two gangs of bandits／一～敌军 a horde of enemy soldiers; an enemy detachment

股[2]　gǔ old name for the longer leg of a right triangle

股本 gǔběn capital stock

股东 gǔdōng shareholder; stockholder

股匪 gǔfěi gang of bandits

股份 gǔfèn (also 股分 gǔfèn) share; stock

股份公司 gǔfèn gōngsī joint-stock company; stock company

股份有限公司 gǔfèn yǒuxiàn gōngsī limited-liability company; limited company (Ltd.)

股份资本 gǔfèn zīběn share capital

股肱 gǔgōng *formal* right-hand man

股骨 gǔgǔ *physiol.* thighbone; femur

股金 gǔjīn money paid for shares (in a partnership or cooperative)

股利 gǔlì same as 股息 gǔxī

股票 gǔpiào share certificate; share; stock

股票行市 gǔpiào hángshì current prices of stocks; quotations on the stock exchange

股票交易 gǔpiào jiāoyì buying and selling of stocks

股票交易所　gǔpiào jiāoyìsuǒ　stock exchange

股票经纪人　gǔpiào jīngjìrén　stockbroker; stockjobber

股票市场　gǔpiào shìchǎng　stock market

股息　gǔxī　dividend

股线　gǔxiàn　*text.*　plied yarn

股长　gǔzhǎng　section chief

股子　gǔzi　① share in a company ② *m.* (for strength, smell, etc.): 这小伙子有一～使不完的劲。The youngster just doesn't know what it is to be tired.

牯　gǔ　bull

牯牛　gǔniú　bull

骨　gǔ　① bone ② skeleton; framework: 伞～ umbrella frame; the ribs of an umbrella ③ character; spirit: 媚骨 mèigǔ ——see also gū

骨刺　gǔcì　*med.*　spur

骨雕　gǔdiāo　bone carving

骨顶鸡　gǔdǐngjī　*zool.*　coot

骨董　gǔdǒng　same as 古董 gǔdǒng

骨粉　gǔfěn　(also 骨肥 gǔféi) bone meal; bone dust

骨干　gǔgàn　① *physiol.*　diaphysis ② backbone; mainstay: 起～作用 be a mainstay / 科技队伍的～力量 the backbone of the scientific and technological contingents / 治淮～工程 key projects for harnessing the Huaihe River / 在每个工业部门中，都应该有一些大型的企业作为～。Each sector of industry should have a few large enterprises which can act as a mainstay.

骨干分子　gǔgàn fènzǐ　core member; key member

骨骼　gǔgé　*physiol.*　skeleton

骨骼肌　gǔgéjī　skeletal muscle

骨鲠在喉　gǔgěng zài hóu　(like) having a fishbone caught in one's throat: 如～，不吐不快 feel as if one has a fishbone in one's throat and be unable to rest until one has spat it out; have a criticism that one must express

骨骺　gǔhóu　*physiol.*　epiphysis

骨化　gǔhuà　*physiol.*　ossify

骨灰　gǔhuī　① bone ash ② ashes of the dead

骨灰盒　gǔhuīhé　cinerary casket

骨架　gǔjià　skeleton; framework: 房屋的～ the framework of a house / 小说的～已经有了。The framework of the novel has been worked out.

骨胶　gǔjiāo　*chem.*　bone glue

骨节　gǔjié　*physiol.*　joint

骨结核　gǔjiéhé　bone tuberculosis; TB bone

骨科　gǔkē　(department of) orthopaedics

骨科医生　gǔkē yīshēng　orthopaedist

骨刻　gǔkè　bone sculpture (*or* carving)

骨痨　gǔláo　*Chin. med.*　tuberculosis of bones and joints

骨力　gǔlì　strength of calligraphic strokes

骨料　gǔliào　*archit.*　aggregate: 轻～ light aggregate

骨瘤　gǔliú　*med.*　osteoma

骨膜　gǔmó　*physiol.*　periosteum

骨膜炎　gǔmóyán　periostitis

骨牌　gǔpái　dominoes

骨盆　gǔpén　*physiol.*　pelvis

骨气　gǔqì　① strength of character; moral integrity; backbone: 有～的人 a man of integrity / 我们中国人是有～的。We Chinese have backbone. ② strength of calligraphic strokes: 他的字写得很有～。His writing shows strength in the strokes.

骨器　gǔqì　bone object; bone implement

骨肉　gǔròu　flesh and blood; kindred: 亲生～ one's own flesh and blood / ～情谊 kindred feelings; feelings of kinship

骨肉团聚　gǔròu tuánjù　a family reunion

骨肉相连　gǔròu xiānglián　as closely linked as flesh and blood

骨肉兄弟　gǔròu xiōngdì　blood brothers; one's own brothers

骨肉之亲　gǔròu zhī qīn　blood relations

骨软化　gǔruǎnhuà　*med.*　osteomalacia

骨殖　gǔshi　skeleton (of a human body after decomposition)

骨瘦如柴　gǔ shòu rú chái　lean as a rake; worn to a shadow; a mere skeleton; a bag of bones: 他渐渐饮食不进，～。Gradually he lost his appetite and wasted away till he was nothing but skin and bones.

骨髓　gǔsuǐ　*physiol.*　marrow

骨髓炎　gǔsuǐyán　osteomyelitis

骨碎补　gǔsuìbǔ　*Chin. med.*　the rhizome of davallia (*Davallia mariesii*)

骨炭　gǔtàn　bone black; animal charcoal

骨头　gǔtou　① bone ② moral character: 他～很硬。He is a person of great moral integrity. ③ *dial.* sharpness; bitterness: 他话里有～。His words had a bite to them.

骨头架子　gǔtoujiàzi　*inf.*　① skeleton: 瘦得只剩个～ be reduced to a skeleton; be all skin and bones ② a very thin person

骨学　gǔxué　osteology

骨血　gǔxuè　flesh and blood—one's offspring

骨折　gǔzhé　*med.*　fracture: 粉碎性～ comminuted fracture / 开放性～ open (*or* compound) fracture / 他摔了一交，右臂～了。He fell and fractured his right arm.

骨子　gǔzi　frame; ribs: 伞～ umbrella frame; the ribs of an umbrella

骨子里　gǔzilǐ　① *derog.*　in the bones—beneath the surface; in one's innermost nature; in substance: 他表面上和和气气，～却阴险狠毒。He had a frank friendly look, but at heart he was crafty and ruthless. ② (also 骨子里头 gǔzilǐtou) *dial.*　private; secret: 这是他们～的事，你不用管。This is their private affair; don't bother about it.

贾　gǔ　① *formal*　merchant: 书贾 shūgǔ ② engage in trade: 多财善贾 duō cái shàn gǔ ③ buy ④ *formal*　incur; court: 贾祸 gǔhuò ⑤ *formal*　sell; afford: 余勇可贾 yúyǒng kě gǔ ——see also jiǎ

贾祸　gǔhuò　court disaster

贾怨　gǔyuàn　court grudge against oneself; invite resentment

钴　gǔ　*chem.*　cobalt (Co)

蛄　gǔ　see 蝲蝲蛄 làlagǔ; 蝲蛄 làgǔ ——see also gū

蛊（蠱）　gǔ　a legendary venomous insect

蛊惑　gǔhuò　poison and bewitch

蛊惑人心　gǔhuò rénxīn　confuse and poison people's minds; resort to demagogy: ～的口号 demagogic slogans

鹄　gǔ　*formal*　target (in archery): 中～ hit the target ——see also hú

鹄的　gǔdì　*formal*　① bull's eye; target: 三发连中～。All the three shots hit the target. ② purpose; aim

鼓　gǔ　① drum: 打～ beat a drum / ～声 drumbeats ② a thing like a drum: 耳鼓 ěrgǔ ③ beat; strike; sound: ～琴 play the zither ④ blow with bellows, etc.: ～风 work a bellows ⑤ rouse; agitate; pluck up: ～起勇 pluck up (*or* muster) one's courage ⑥ bulge; swell: 钱包很～。The purse is bulging. / 把口袋塞得～～的 fill one's pockets till they bulge / ～着嘴 pout

鼓板　gǔbǎn　*mus.* clappers

鼓包　gǔbāo　① bulge; swell ② swelling; lump; bump

鼓吹　gǔchuī　① advocate: ～革命 advocate revolution ② *derog.* preach; advertise; play up

鼓槌　gǔchuí　drumstick

鼓儿词　gǔrcí　lyrics to *dagu* ——see also 大鼓 dàgǔ

鼓捣　gǔdao　*dial.* ① tinker with; fiddle with: 他最爱～收音机。 He likes to tinker with radios. ② egg on; incite: 在背后～ egg on from behind the scenes / ～别人去干坏事 incite people to do evil

鼓点子　gǔdiǎnzi　① drumbeats ② clapper beats which set the tempo and lead the orchestra in traditional Chinese operas

鼓动　gǔdòng　① agitate; arouse: 做宣传～工作 conduct propaganda and agitation / ～群众 arouse the masses ② instigate; incite: 这些坏事是谁～你干的？ Who put you up to all these dirty tricks?

鼓风　gǔfēng　*metall.* (air) blast: 富氧～ oxygen-enriched (air) blast

鼓风机　gǔfēngjī　air-blower; blower

鼓风炉　gǔfēnglú　blast furnace

鼓鼓囊囊　gǔgunāngnāng　bulging: 背包里装满了工具，～的。 The backpack is bulging with tools.

鼓角　gǔjiǎo　ancient battle drums and horns

鼓劲　gǔjìn　rouse one's enthusiasm

鼓揪　gǔjiu　same as 鼓秋 gǔqiu

鼓励　gǔlì　encourage; urge: 首长对我们讲了许多～的话。 The leading cadres said a lot to encourage us. / 老师～大家学习英语。 Our teacher encouraged us to learn English.

鼓楼　gǔlóu　drum-tower

鼓膜　gǔmó　*physiol.* tympanic membrane; eardrum

鼓膜穿孔　gǔmó chuānkǒng　*med.* perforation of the tympanic membrane

鼓弄　gǔnong　*inf.* fiddle with; play with

鼓秋　gǔqiu　① tinker with; fiddle with: 他最爱～手表。 He likes to tinker with watches. ② egg on; incite

鼓舌　gǔshé　wag the tongue (esp. in honeyed talk): 鼓其如簧之舌 talk glibly

鼓师　gǔshī　the conductor of a Chinese opera band who keeps time on a small drum with two thin drumsticks

鼓室　gǔshì　*physiol.* tympanum

鼓手　gǔshǒu　drummer

鼓书　gǔshū　same as 大鼓 dàgǔ

鼓舞　gǔwǔ　inspire; encourage; hearten: ～群众的积极性 arouse the enthusiasm of the masses / ～士气 boost the morale of the soldiers / 形势令人～。 The present state of affairs is quite heartening. / 在大好形势～下 inspired by the very good situation / 工作进展很快, 这给我很大的～。 The rapid progress I have made in my work is a great encouragement to me.

鼓舞人心　gǔwǔ rénxīn　inspiring; heartening: ～的消息 most heartening news

鼓乐　gǔyuè　strains of music accompanied by drumbeats: ～齐鸣, 万众欢腾。 The cheers of the jubilant crowds mingled with *crescendos* of music.

鼓噪　gǔzào　make an uproar; raise a hubbub; clamour: ～一时 make a great to-do about sth. for a time

鼓掌　gǔzhǎng　clap one's hands; applaud: 热烈～ warmly applaud / ～通过 approve by acclamation

鼓子词　gǔzicí　a form of *dagu* in the Song Dynasty (960–1279) ——see also 大鼓 dàgǔ

鼓足干劲　gǔ zú gànjìn　go all out: ～, 力争上游, 多快好省地建设社会主义。 Go all out, aim high and gain greater, faster, better and more economical results in building socialism.

轂　gǔ　hub ——see also gū

蠱　gǔ　see below

蠱子　gǔzi　a kind of deep pot, usu. made of earth

臌　gǔ　see below

臌胀　gǔzhàng　*Chin. med.* distension of abdomen caused by accumulation of gas or fluid due to dysfunction of liver and spleen; tympanites

瞽　gǔ　*arch.* blind: ～者 a blind person / ～说 stupidities

gù

估　gù　see below ——see also gū

估衣　gùyi　secondhand clothes or clothes badly tailored and of poor material

固¹　gù　① solid; firm: 基础已～。 The foundation is solid. ② solidify; consolidate; strengthen: ～堤 strengthen the dyke ③ firmly; resolutely: ～辞 resolutely refuse; firmly decline / ～请 insistently request

固²　gù　*formal* ① *adv.* originally; in the first place; as a matter of course: ～当如此。 It is just as it should be. ② *conj.* (used in the same way as 固然 gùrán): 乘车～可, 乘船亦无不可。 Admittedly we can make the journey by train, but there is no harm in our travelling by boat.

固步自封　gù bù zì fēng　same as 故步自封 gù bù zì fēng

固氮菌　gùdànjūn　*bacteriol.* nitrogen-fixing bacteria; azotobacter

固氮作用　gùdàn zuòyòng　*agric.* nitrogen fixation; azofication

固定　gùdìng　① fixed; regular: ～职业 permanent occupation / ～价格 fixed price / 电台的～节目 a regular (*or* scheduled) radio programme / 不要用～眼光看问题。 Don't take a static view of things. ② fix; regularize: 把灯座～在车床上 fix the lampstand on the lathe / 把业务学习时间～下来 set a regular time for vocational study

固定工资制　gùdìng gōngzīzhì　fixed-wage system

固定汇率　gùdìng huìlǜ　fixed (exchange) rate

固定机库　gùdìng jīkù　permanent hangar

固定基金　gùdìng jījīn　fixed fund

固定平价　gùdìng píngjià　fixed parity

固定式平炉　gùdìngshì pínglú　*metall.* stationary open-hearth furnace

固定资本　gùdìng zīběn　fixed capital

固定资产　gùdìng zīchǎn　fixed assets

固化　gùhuà　*chem.* solidify: ～酒精 solidified alcohol

固件　gùjiàn　*computer* firmware

固井　gùjǐng　*petroleum* well cementation

固陋　gùlòu　*formal* ignorant; provincial

固然　gùrán　*conj.* (admitting a point that goes or does not go against the main argument of the sentence) though of course; admittedly; no doubt; it is true: 这样办～稳当些, 可就是要慢一些。 No doubt it would be safer to do it that way, but it would be slower. / 这里条件～艰苦些, 但正是我们锻炼的好地方。 True, conditions are tougher here, but that gives us a chance to temper ourselves. / 他～不对, 可是你也不对。 He's not right, it's true; but you aren't either. / 他能来～很好, 不来也没关系。 If he can come, well and good; but if he can't, it doesn't matter.

固若金汤　gù ruò jīn tāng　strongly fortified; impregnable

固涩　gùsè　*Chin. med.* astringent or styptic treatment

for spontaneous sweating, seminal emission, chronic diarrhoea, anal prolapse, uterine bleeding, etc.

固沙林 gùshālín　sand-fixation forest; dune-fixing forest

固守 gùshǒu ① defend tenaciously; be firmly entrenched in: ～阵地 tenaciously defend one's position ② stick to: ～老一套的办法 stick to the old ways

固态 gùtài *phys.* solid state

固态物理学 gùtài wùlǐxué　solid-state physics

固体 gùtǐ　solid body; solid

固体废物 gùtǐ fèiwù　solid waste

固体酱油 gùtǐ jiàngyóu　solidified soy sauce

固体燃料 gùtǐ ránliào　solid fuel

固体燃料发动机 gùtǐ ránliào fādòngjī　solid propellant engine; solid engine

固有 gùyǒu　intrinsic; inherent; innate: ～的属性 intrinsic attributes / 资本主义制度～的矛盾 the contradictions inherent in the capitalist system / 人的正确思想不是自己头脑里～的。Correct ideas are not innate in the mind.

固执己见 gùzhí jǐjiàn　stubbornly persist in one's opinions: ～，拒不接受别人的经验 adhere stubbornly to one's own opinions and reject other people's experience

固执 gùzhi ① obstinate; stubborn: 她很～，不会改变主意的。She's very obstinate and won't change her mind. ② persist in; cling to

故¹

gù ① incident; happening: 事故 shìgù ② reason; cause: 该生不知何～缺席。The reason for the student's absence remains unknown. ③ *adv.* on purpose; intentionally: ～作镇静 pretend to be calm / ～作惊讶 put on a show of surprise; feign surprise ④ *conj.* hence; therefore; so; for this reason: 无私～能无畏。Fearlessness stems from selflessness. / 今日大雨倾盆，～未如期起程。It was pouring today, and therefore I didn't start out as scheduled.

故²

gù ① former; old: 黄河～道 the old course of the Yellow River ② friend; acquaintance: 亲故 qīngù ③ (of people) die; dead: 他父母早～。His parents died when he was very young. *or* He was left an orphan when very young.

故步自封 gù bù zìfēng　stand still and refuse to make progress; be complacent and conservative

故此 gùcǐ　*conj.* and so; therefore; hence

故地 gùdì　an old haunt: ～重游 revisit an old haunt

故都 gùdū　onetime capital

故而 gù'ér　*conj.* and so; therefore; hence

故宫 gùgōng　imperial palace

故宫 Gùgōng　the Imperial Palace (in Beijing)

故宫博物院 Gùgōng Bówùyuàn　the Palace Museum (in Beijing)

故国 gùguó　*liter.* native land; native soil; native place: 小楼昨夜又东风，～不堪回首月明中。(李煜) The east wind visited again my small chamber last night; I could not bear to look back to my native land in the clear moonlight.

故伎 gùjì　(also 故技 gùjì) stock trick; old tactics

故伎重演 gùjì chóngyǎn　be up to one's old tricks; play the same old trick

故家 gùjiā ① an old family ② *old* the family of a high official

故交 gùjiāo　*formal* an old friend

故旧 gùjiù　old friends and acquaintances

故居 gùjū　former residence (*or* home): 鲁迅～ the former residence of Lu Xun

故里 gùlǐ　native place; hometown: 荣归～ return home with honours

故弄玄虚 gù nòng xuánxū　purposely make a mystery of simple things; be deliberately mystifying

故去 gùqù　(of one's elders) die; pass away: 他父亲早就～了。His father passed away a long time ago.

故人 gùrén　an old friend: ～西辞黄鹤楼，烟花三月下扬州。(李白) You have left me behind, old friend, at the Yellow Crane Terrace, On your way to visit Yangzhou in the misty month of flowers.

故杀 gùshā　*leg.* premeditated (*or* wilful) murder

故实 gùshí　historical facts or anecdotes (esp. as holding moral lessons)

故世 gùshì　die; pass away

故事 gùshì　old practice; routine: 奉行～ follow established practice mechanically

故事 gùshi ① story; tale: 讲～ tell a story / 红军长征的～ stories about the Long March of the Red Army / ～员 storyteller ② plot: 这部小说～性很强。The novel has an interesting plot.

故事会 gùshihuì　a gathering at which stories are told; story-telling session

故事片 gùshipiàn　feature film

故态复萌 gùtài fù méng　slip back into one's old ways

故土 gùtǔ　native land; native place; birthplace; hometown: 怀念～ long for home

故乡 gùxiāng　old home; native place; birthplace: 北京已经成了我的第二～。Beijing has become a second home to me. / 举头望明月，低头思～。(李白) Raising my head, I look at the bright moon; Bending my head, I think of my old home.

故意 gùyì　*adv.* intentionally; wilfully; deliberately; on purpose: 他～让我生气。He made me angry on purpose. / 他是～侮辱人。His insults were deliberate. / 对不起，我不是～的。I'm sorry, I didn't do it on purpose. *or* I'm sorry, I didn't mean it. / ～刁难 place obstacles in sb.'s way

故友 gùyǒu　a departed friend

故园 gùyuán　*liter.* old home; native place; native soil: ～东望路漫漫，双袖龙钟泪不干。(岑参) On the great highway looking back to the east, far far from his native place, With his sleeves an old man wiped the tears as they trickled down his face.

故障 gùzhàng　hitch; breakdown; stoppage; trouble: 排除～ fix a breakdown; clear a stoppage / 发动机出了～。The engine has broken down. *or* The engine is out of order. / 出了什么～? What's gone wrong?

故知 gùzhī　*formal* an old friend: 他乡遇故知 tāxiāng yù gùzhī

故址 gùzhǐ　site (of an ancient monument, etc.)

故纸堆 gùzhǐduī　*derog.* a heap of musty old books or papers: 他埋头于～中，不问世事。He buried himself in his musty old books and took no notice of the outside world.

故作高深 gù zuò gāoshēn　pretend to be learned and profound

故作姿态 gù zuò zītài　strike a pose; put on airs

顾¹ (顧)

gù ① turn round and look at; look at: 相顾 xiānggù ② attend to; take into consideration: 你别只～自己。Don't just think of yourself. / 这么多事你一个人～得过来吗? You've got so many things to attend to. Can you manage all by yourself? / 医生～不得吃饭就去抢救病人。The doctor immediately attended to the emergency case without stopping for a meal. ③ visit; call on: 三顾茅庐 sān gù máolú ④ customer: 主顾 zhǔgù ⑤ (Gù) a surname

顾² (顧)

gù　*formal* ① *conj.* but; however ② *adv.* on the contrary; instead

顾此失彼 gùcǐ-shībǐ　cannot attend to one thing without neglecting the other; have too many things to take

care of at the same time

顾及 gùjí take into account; attend to; give consideration to: 无暇～ have no time to attend to the matter / 事前应该～事后的效果。Before taking an action, one should consider what effect it may have. / ～可能产生的后果 take the possible consequences into account / 我顾不及这些零碎事儿。I can't spare the time for those miscellaneous items.

顾忌 gùjì scruple; misgiving: 毫无～ without scruple; have no scruples / 不能不有所～ have to think twice (before doing sth.); be unable to overcome certain misgivings

顾家 gùjiā look after one's family: 他工作太忙, 很少～。 He's so busy at work that he hardly looks after his family.

顾客 gùkè customer; shopper; client: ～至上。Customers First.

顾虑 gùlǜ misgiving; apprehension; worry: 打消～ dispel one's misgivings (or worries) / 你不必有任何～。 You needn't have any misgivings whatsoever. / 他毫无～地谈出了自己的想法。He spoke his mind without the slightest hesitancy.

顾虑重重 gùlǜ chóngchóng have no end of worries; be full of misgivings

顾面子 gù miànzi ① save face; keep up appearances ② spare sb.'s feelings: 为了顾她的面子, 我没有说她这事做得有多糟。I tried to spare her feelings by not telling her what a poor job she had done.

顾名思义 gù míng sī yì seeing the name of a thing one thinks of its function; just as its name implies; as the term suggests: 变频器,～, 它的功能是改变交流电路的频率。The frequency converter, as the term suggests, serves to change the frequency of an alternating-current circuit. / 心理学,～, 是研究人们心理的科学。 Psychology is by definition the scientific study of the mind.

顾念 gùniàn think about; be concerned about: ～人民 be concerned about the well-being of the people

顾盼 gùpàn formal look around: 左右～ glance right and left

顾盼自雄 gùpàn zì xióng look about complacently

顾前不顾后 gù qián bù gù hòu drive ahead without considering the consequences; act rashly

顾全 gùquán show consideration for and take care to preserve: ～面子 save sb.'s face; spare sb.'s feelings

顾全大局 gùquán dàjú take the interests of the whole into account; consider the situation as a whole: 我们历来的原则, 就是提倡～, 互助互让。(毛泽东) It is our consistent principle to advocate consideration for the general interest and mutual help and accommodation.

顾问 gùwèn adviser; consultant: 法律～ legal adviser

顾问委员会 gùwèn wěiyuánhuì consultative (or advisory) committee

顾惜 gùxī value; care for: ～自己的身体 look after one's health

顾影自怜 gù yǐng zì lián ① look at one's reflection and admire oneself ② look at one's shadow and lament one's lot

顾主 gùzhǔ customer; client; patron

桍 gù formal wooden handcuffs: 桎桍 zhìgù

雇 (僱) gù hire; employ: 我们大家～了一只船。We hired a boat between us. / 我想～个保姆。I want to hire a maid. / 他家里～了好些用人。Many servants were employed in his house.

雇工 gùgōng ① hire labour; hire hands ② hired labourer (or hand, worker) ③ same as 雇农 gùnóng

雇农 gùnóng farmhand; farm labourer

雇请 gùqǐng hire or employ (a person)

雇佣 gùyōng employ; hire

雇佣兵役制 gùyōng bīngyìzhì mercenary system

雇佣观点 gùyōng guāndiǎn hired hand mentality—the attitude of one who will do no more than he is paid for

雇佣军 gùyōngjūn mercenary army (or troops); mercenaries

雇佣劳动 gùyōng láodòng wage labour: 资本的生存条件是～。The condition for capital is wage labour.

雇佣劳动者 gùyōng láodòngzhě wage labourer

雇佣奴隶 gùyōng núlì wage slave

雇员 gùyuán employee

雇主 gùzhǔ employer

痼 gù chronic; inveterate: 痼疾 gùjí

痼弊 gùbì age-old malpractice; long-standing abuse

痼疾 gùjí chronic (or obstinate) illness: 医学的发达, 使很多所谓～都能治好。Advances in medical science have made it possible to cure many so-called chronic diseases. / 经济危机是资本主义制度的～。Economic crises are a chronic malady of capitalism.

痼癖 gùpǐ addiction

痼习 gùxí inveterate (or confirmed) habit: ～难改。Confirmed habits are difficult to break.

锢 gù ① plug with molten metal; run metal into cracks ② formal hold in custody; imprison

锢弊 gùbì formal age-old malpractice; long-standing abuse

锢疾 gùjí formal chronic (or obstinate) illness

锢囚 gùqiú meteorol. occlusion: ～气旋 occluded cyclone

guā

瓜 guā melon, gourd, etc.

瓜德罗普 Guādéluópǔ Guadeloupe

瓜分 guāfēn cut up a melon—carve up; dismember; partition; divide up: 几个战胜国无情地～了这个战败国, 各自攫取了同样大小的一片土地。The victors mercilessly carved up the defeated country, each taking an equal share.

瓜葛 guāgé connection; implication; association: 他跟投机倒把分子有～。He's got mixed up with speculators.

瓜葛亲 guāgéqīn distant relatives

瓜农 guānóng melon grower

瓜皮帽 guāpímào a kind of skullcap resembling the rind of half a watermelon; skullcap

瓜片 guāpiàn a green tea produced in Anhui Province

瓜仁 guārén edible kernel of melon seeds

瓜熟蒂落 guāshú-dìluò when a melon is ripe it falls off its stem—things are easily settled once conditions are ripe

瓜田李下 guātián-lǐxià in a melon patch or under a plum tree—in suspicious circumstances or surroundings: 瓜田不纳履, 李下不正冠。Don't put on your shoes in a melon patch; don't adjust your cap under a plum tree—don't do anything to arouse suspicion.

瓜条 guātiáo sweetened melon strips

瓜子 guāzǐ melon seeds: 嗑～儿 crack melon seeds

瓜子脸 guāzǐliǎn an oval face

呱 guā see below——see also gū

呱嗒 guādā (also 呱哒 guādā) ① onom. clip-clop; clack: 她在人行道上走着, 脚底下～～地响。Her heels

clacked as she walked on the pavement. ② *dial.* speak sarcastically or ironically: ～人 make sarcastic remarks

呱嗒 guāda (also 呱哒 guāda) *dial.* ① (used in)～着脸 pull a long face ② talk foolishly: 乱～一阵 talk a lot of nonsense

呱嗒板儿 guādabǎnr ① *inf.* bamboo clappers ② *dial.* clogs

呱呱 guāguā *onom.* the quacking of a duck; the croaking of a frog; the cawing of a crow: 鸭子～地叫。 A duck quacks. ——see also gūgū

呱呱叫 guāguājiào *inf.* tiptop; top-notch

呱唧 guāji *onom.* the sound of hands being clapped

刮¹ guā ① scrape; shave: 把墙上的漆～下去 scrape the paint off the wall / ～锅子 scrape a pot clean / ～鱼鳞 scale a fish / ～胡子 shave the beard / 就～破一点皮。 It's only a scratch. ② smear with (paste, etc.): ～糨子 stiffen (cloth) by spreading paste over it ③ plunder; fleece; extort: 他当知县时～了不少的钱。 While holding office as county magistrate, he made a lot of money by extortion.

刮² (颳) guā (of the wind) blow: ～大风了。 It's blowing hard. *or* There's a gale blowing. / 土～得满天飞。 Dust was blown into the air. / 把～倒的树苗扶起来 straighten up the saplings that have been blown down / 什么风把你～来了? What brings you here?

刮刀 guādāo scraping cutter; scraper: 三角～ triangular scraper

刮地皮 guādìpí scrape off the earth—(of reactionary rulers) extort money from the people

刮宫 guāgōng *med.* dilatation and curettage (D. and C.)

刮垢磨光 guāgòu-móguāng scrape and polish—① take pains to teach and train a person or to improve oneself ② be meticulous and painstaking

刮刮叫 guāguājiào same as 呱呱叫 guāguājiào

刮脸 guāliǎn shave (the face): 我天天早上～。 I shave every morning.

刮脸刀 guāliǎndāo razor

刮脸皮 guā liǎnpí *dial.* rub the forefinger against one's own cheek (to indicate scorn for sb.); point the finger of scorn at sb.

刮目相看 guā mù xiāng kàn (also 刮目相待 guā mù xiāngdài) look at sb. with new eyes; treat sb. with increased respect: 古人云，"士别三日便当～。" The ancients say, "A scholar who has been away three days must be looked at with new eyes."

刮痧 guāshā *Chin. med.* a popular treatment for sunstroke by scraping the patient's neck, chest or back

刮削 guāxiāo scrape: ～器 scraper

胍 guā *chem.* guanidine

栝 guā *arch.* ① Chinese juniper ② the protuberance on the end of an arrow which catches the bowstring

栝楼 guālóu *bot.* Chinese trichosanthes (*Trichosanthes kirilowii*)

栝楼皮 guālóupí *Chin. med.* the fruit-rind of Chinese trichosanthes

鸹 guā see 老鸹 lǎogua

guǎ

剐 (剮) guǎ ① cut to pieces (a form of capital punishment in ancient times); dismember: 千刀万剐 qiāndāo-wànguǎ ② cut; slit: 手上～了个口子 cut one's hand

寡 guǎ ① few; scant: 以寡敌众 yǐ guǎ dí zhòng ② bland; tasteless: 清汤寡水 qīngtāng-guǎshuǐ ③ widowed: 鳏～ widowers and widows

寡不敌众 guǎ bù dí zhòng be hopelessly outnumbered; fight against hopeless odds

寡断 guǎduàn indecisive; irresolute

寡妇 guǎfu widow

寡妇门前是非多 guǎfu ménqián shìfēi duō slanders cluster round a widow's door

寡欢 guǎhuān joyless; unhappy: 郁郁寡欢 yùyù-guǎhuān

寡居 guǎjū live alone as a widow

寡廉鲜耻 guǎlián-xiǎnchǐ lost to shame; shameless

寡情 guǎqíng unfeeling; cold-hearted; heartless

寡人 guǎrén I, your unworthy king (corresponding to the English "royal we"): 梁惠王曰："～之于国也，尽心焉耳矣。"(《孟子》) King Hui of Liang said, "I have done my best for my state."

寡头 guǎtóu oligarch: 金融～ financial oligarch; financial magnate / ～垄断 oligopoly

寡头政治 guǎtóu zhèngzhì oligarchy

寡言 guǎyán taciturn: 沉默寡言 chénmò-guǎyán

寡欲 guǎyù have few desires; be ascetic: 清心寡欲 qīngxīn-guǎyù

guà

卦 guà divinatory symbols: 占卦 zhānguà

诖 guà *formal* ① cheat; deceive ② error; mistake

诖误 guàwù be punished for a mistake made by sb. else

挂 (掛) guà ① hang; put up: 把地图～在墙上。 Put (*or* Hang) the map up on the wall. / 天上～着一轮明月。 A bright moon hung in the sky. / 把这件事先～一～再说。 Let's leave the matter aside for the moment. ② hang up; ring off: 我还没有来得及问他名字，他就把电话～了。 He hung up (*or* rang off) before I could ask his name. / 你先别～，等我查一下。 Hold the line while I find out. ③ *dial.* call (*or* phone, ring) up; put sb. through to: 我呆会儿再给他～电话。 I'll ring him up again. / 请给我～北京饭店。 Give me the Beijing Hotel, please. *or* Please put me through to the Beijing Hotel. ④ hitch; get caught: 把拖车～上。 Hitch up the trailer. / 她的衣服给钉子～住了。 Her dress got caught on a nail. / ⑤ *dial.* be concerned about: 时刻把群众的利益～在心上 always have the welfare of the masses at heart / 队长总是～着小李的病。 Our team leader is very worried about Xiao Li's illness. ⑥ *dial.* be covered with; be coated with: 他脸上～了一层尘土。 His face was covered with dust. / 瓦盆里面～一层釉子。 The earthen pot is glazed inside. ⑦ register (at a hospital, etc.): 我要～外科。 I want to register for surgery. *or* Surgery, please. ⑧ *m.* a set or string (of things): 一～大车 a horse and cart / 十多～鞭炮 a dozen strings of firecrackers / 一～珠子 a string of pearls

挂碍　guà'ài　worries: 心中没有～ have no worries

挂表　guàbiǎo　*dial.* pocket watch

挂不住　guàbuzhù　*dial.* lose control of one's feelings (in embarrassment)

挂彩　guàcǎi　① decorate with coloured silk festoons; decorate for festive occasions ② be wounded in action: 他在战争中挂了两回彩。He was wounded twice in the war.

挂车　guàchē　trailer

挂齿　guàchǐ　mention: 何足挂齿 hé zú guàchǐ

挂锄　guàchú　put away the hoe (for the winter); finish hoeing

挂挡　guàdǎng　put into gear: 挂高速挡 change to (or put into) high gear / 挂头挡 engage the first gear

挂斗　guàdǒu　trailer

挂钩　guàgōu　① *transportation* couple (two railway coaches); articulate ② link up with; establish contact with; get in touch with: 产销直接～，减少中间环节。With direct contact between producing and marketing departments, the number of intermediate steps are reduced. / 大学应该与科研单位～。Universities should establish close contact with research institutes.

挂冠　guàguān　*old* resign from office

挂果　guàguǒ　bear fruit

挂号　guàhào　① register (at a hospital, etc.): 请排队～。Please queue (or line) up to register. / 你挂的是几号? What's your registration number? ② send by registered mail: 你这封信要不要～? Do you want to have this letter registered?

挂号处　guàhàochù　registration office

挂号费　guàhàofèi　registration fee

挂号信　guàhàoxìn　registered letter (or mail)

挂红　guàhóng　hang up red festoons

挂花　guàhuā　be wounded in action: 他腿上挂过两次花。He was twice wounded in the leg.

挂怀　guàhuái　have sth. weighing on one's mind; be concerned (or worried) about

挂火　guàhuǒ　*dial.* be furious; flare up

挂记　guàjì　worry about; be anxious about; keep thinking about

挂历　guàlì　monthly calender hung up on the wall; wall calender

挂镰　guàlián　*agric.* put away the sickle; complete the year's harvest

挂零　guàlíng　odd: 这个人看样子顶多不过四十～。This man is about forty odd at most. / 到会人数五百～。Five hundred odd were present at the meeting.

挂漏　guàlòu　same as 挂一漏万 guà yī lòu wàn

挂虑　guàlù　be anxious about; worry about: 孩子由她姥姥照看，用不着～。The child is being looked after by his grandmother, so there's no need to worry.

挂免战牌　guà miǎnzhànpái　hang up a truce sign—① refuse battle ② *humor.* refuse debate

挂面　guàmiàn　fine dried noodles; vermicelli

挂名　guàmíng　titular; nominal; only in name: 我只是～委员，没有什么事儿干。I'm only a titular committee member, having little or nothing to do. / 他挂着主任的名，可实际工作并没干多少。Although he held the title of director, he didn't actually do much of the work.

挂念　guàniàn　worry about sb. who is absent; miss: ～亲人 miss one's folks at home / 我身体很好，请勿～。I'm in good health. Please don't worry.

挂牌　guàpái　hang out one's shingle; put up one's brass plate: 他行医多年，在天津和北京都挂过牌。He practised medicine for many years and opened clinics of his own in both Tianjin and Beijing.

挂屏　guàpíng　a set of hanging scrolls of painting or calligraphy

挂牵　guàqiān　worry; care

挂失　guàshī　report the loss of (identity papers, cheques, etc.): 他存折丢了，赶紧去银行～。He lost his bankbook, and hurried to the bank to report it.

挂帅　guàshuài　be in command; assume (or take) command; assume leadership: 所长亲自～进行这项工作。The director himself took charge of the project.

挂锁　guàsuǒ　padlock

挂毯　guàtǎn　tapestry

挂图　guàtú　① wall map ② hanging chart

挂线疗法　guàxiàn liáofǎ　*Chin. med.* ligating method for treating anal fistula

挂孝　guàxiào　wear mourning

挂心　guàxīn　be on one's mind

挂靴　guàxuē　(also 挂鞋 guàxié) (of a footballer) retire

挂羊头，卖狗肉　guà yángtóu, mài gǒuròu　hang up a sheep's head and sell dogmeat—try to palm off sth. inferior to what it purports to be

挂一漏万　guà yī lòu wàn　for one thing cited, ten thousand may have been left out—the list is far from complete

挂衣钩　guàyīgōu　clothes-hook

挂钟　guàzhōng　wall clock

挂轴　guàzhóu　hanging scroll (of Chinese painting or calligraphy)

褂　guà　a Chinese-style unlined garment; gown: 短～儿 short gown

褂子　guàzi　a Chinese-style unlined upper garment; short gown

guāi

乖¹　guāi　① (of a child) well-behaved; good: 真是个～孩子。There's a dear. ② clever; shrewd; alert: 学～了 become a little wiser

乖²　guāi　*formal* ① perverse; contrary to reason: 有～常理 run counter to reason ② (of character, behaviour, etc.) irregular; abnormal: 乖谬 guāimiù

乖舛　guāichuǎn　*formal* mistake; error

乖乖　guāiguāi　① well-behaved; obedient: 孩子们都～儿地坐着听老师讲故事。The children all sat quietly listening to the teacher telling stories. / 被围困的敌人见无路可走，只好～地缴械投降。The enemy, totally surrounded, saw that they had no choice but to drop their weapons and meekly surrender. ② (to a child) little dear; darling ③ *interj.* good gracious

乖觉　guāijué　alert; quick: 松鼠～得很，听到一点儿响声就溜跑了。The squirrel is very alert, and will run away as soon as it hears the slightest sound.

乖剌　guāilà　*formal* perverse; contrary to reason

乖戾　guāilì　perverse; unreasonable; disagreeable

乖谬　guāimiù　absurd; abnormal

乖僻　guāipǐ　eccentric; odd

乖巧　guāiqiǎo　① clever; ingenious ② cute; lovely

乖张　guāizhāng　eccentric and unreasonable; perverse; recalcitrant

掴（摑）　guāi　slap; smack: ～耳光 box sb.'s ears; slap sb. on the face ——see also guó

guǎi

拐¹　guǎi　① turn: ～过墙角 turn the corner of a house / ～进一条胡同 turn into an alley / 往左～ turn

to the left / 前面走不通了, 咱们～回去吧。We can't get through here, let's turn back. ② *dial.* corner; turning: 墙～ a corner formed by two walls ③ limp: 他一一～地走。He limped along. *or* He walked with a limp. ④ a spoken form for the numeral 七

拐² (枴)
guǎi　crutch: 走路架着双～ walk on crutches

拐³
guǎi　① swindle; make off with: ～款潜逃 abscond with funds ② abduct; kidnap

拐脖儿 guǎibór elbow (of a stove pipe)

拐带 guǎidài kidnap (women or children); abduct

拐棍 guǎigùn walking stick: 拄着～ leaning on a stick

拐角 guǎijiǎo corner; turning: 胡同～有个邮筒。There is a postbox at the street corner.

拐卖 guǎimài kidnap and sell; engage in slavery: ～妇女儿童 abduct and sell women and children

拐骗 guǎipiàn abduct; swindle: ～钱财 swindle money (out of sb.)

拐弯 guǎiwān ① turn a corner; make a turn: ～要慢行。Slow down when turning a corner. / 往前走向左一～就到了。Go straight ahead, turn left and you'll be there. ② change one's opinion to another point of view; pursue a new course: 他思想一时还拐不过弯来。He hasn't straightened out his thoughts yet. / 他话说得离题太远, 不容易拐过弯儿来。He strayed too far away to come back to the point. ③ corner; turning

拐弯抹角 guǎiwān-mòjiǎo talk in a roundabout way; beat about the bush: 说话不要～。Get to the point. Don't beat about the bush. / 他～地提到这件事 He referred to it obliquely.

拐杖 guǎizhàng walking stick

拐子¹ guǎizi *inf.* cripple

拐子² guǎizi ① I-shaped spool or reel ② crutch

拐子³ guǎizi abductor; swindler

guài

怪¹ (恠)
guài　① strange; odd; queer; bewildering: ～现象 something quite unusual / 你说不～? Isn't this strange? / 他这个人真～! He's rather odd. / 他不来才～呢。I would be surprised if he doesn't come. / 小李也～。他干吗不跟我们一块儿来呢? Funny about Xiao Li. Why didn't he come with us? ② find sth. strange; wonder at: 那有什么可～的? Is that anything to be surprised at? ③ *adv. inf.* quite; rather: ～不好意思的 feel rather embarrassed / 箱子～沉的。The suitcase is rather heavy. / 瞧, 这些葡萄～水灵的。Look, how fresh and juicy those grapes are. ④ monster; demon; evil being: 鬼怪 guǐguài

怪² (恠)
guài　blame: 不能～他们。They're not to blame. *or* It's not their fault. / ～我没讲清楚。I'm to blame for not having made it clearer.

怪不得¹ guàibude no wonder; so that's why; that explains why: ～多一张票, 她把自己的让出来了。So that's why (*or* No wonder) there's an extra ticket. She has given hers up. / ～我最近没有看到他, 原来他到西安去了。So that's why I haven't seen him lately—he's gone to Xi'an.

怪不得² guàibude not to blame: 他来晚了, ～他, 因为开会时间通知错了。He's not to blame for arriving late. He was told the wrong time for the meeting.

怪诞 guàidàn weird; strange: ～的传说 a strange legend

怪诞不经 guàidàn bù jīng weird and uncanny; fantastic

怪道 guàidào *dial.* no wonder; so that's why; that explains why: 她是我过去的学生, ～觉得很眼熟。She is my former student; no wonder she looked so familiar.

怪话 guàihuà cynical remark; grumble; complaint: 说～ make cynical remarks

怪里怪气 guàiliguàiqì eccentric; peculiar; queer: ～的人 an eccentric fellow / 她的声音～的。Her voice sounds queer.

怪模怪样 guàimú-guàiyàng queer-looking; grotesque: 这条小狗长得～的。The little dog is queer-looking. / 你穿着这衣服显得～的。You look grotesque in those clothes.

怪癖 guàipǐ strange hobby

怪僻 guàipì eccentric: 性情～ eccentric

怪声怪气 guàishēng-guàiqì (speak in) a strange voice or an affected manner

怪事 guàishì strange thing: 我的表刚才还在桌上的呢, 怎么转眼就不见了, 真是～! Strange! My watch was on the desk a minute ago, and now it has disappeared.

怪胎 guàitāi monster; teratism

怪题 guàití queer (*or* odd) questions (in an examination)

怪物 guàiwu ① monster; monstrosity; freak ② an eccentric person; a queer bird; oddball

怪异 guàiyì ① monstrous; strange; unusual: 听到一些～的声音我吃了一惊。Queer noises startled me. ② strange phenomenon; portent; prodigy

怪罪 guàizuì blame sb.

guān

关 (關、関)
guān　① shut; close: 把门～上。Shut the door. / 这扇窗户～不上。This window won't shut. ② turn off: ～收音机 turn (*or* switch) off the radio / ～电灯 turn off the light ③ shut in; lock up: 别把孩子们整天～在屋里。Don't keep the children inside all day. / 他昨天一天都～在书房里。He was cooped up in his study all day yesterday. / ～进监狱 lock up (in prison); put behind bars ④ (of a business) close down: 镇上～了好几家店铺。Quite a few shops in the town closed down. ⑤ mountain pass; a guarded passage: 玉门～ the Yumen Pass ⑥ customs house: 海关 hǎiguān ⑦ barrier; a critical juncture: 大考是一～。The final exam is a barrier to be passed. / 只要突破这一～, 就好办了。Once we have got over this difficulty, it will be plain sailing. ⑧ a key factor: 关键 guānjiàn ⑨ concern; involve: 这不～他的事。That doesn't concern him. / 这些见解至～重要。These views are of extreme importance. ⑩ *old* give out or draw (pay): ～饷 (of soldiers, policemen, etc.) get paid ⑪ (Guān) a surname

关隘 guān'ài *formal* (mountain) pass

关碍 guān'ài hinder; obstruct

关闭 guānbì ① close; shut: 门窗都紧紧～着。The doors and windows were all tightly closed. ② (of a shop or factory) close down; shut down: 那家工厂无人订货, 被迫～。The factory had to close down through lack of orders.

关岛 Guāndǎo Guam

关东 Guāndōng east of the Pass (i.e. 山海关 Shanhaiguan "Pass Between Mountain and Sea")—the Northeast; northeast China

关东糖 guāndōngtáng a kind of malt candy (originating in the Northeast)

关防 guānfáng ① security measures: ～严密 tight security measures ② *old* government or army seal (usu. rectangular in shape)

关怀 guānhuái show loving care for; show solicitude for: 在老师的～下，这次考试我取得了良好的成绩。Thanks to my teacher's concern I got good results in the exam. / 党和国家非常～少年儿童的健康成长。The Party and the state pay great attention to the healthy growth of children. / 祖国人民对海外侨胞深为～。The Chinese residents overseas are much in the thoughts of the people at home.

关怀备至 guānhuái bèizhì show the utmost solicitude

关键 guānjiàn ① door bolt; door bar ② key; hinge; crux: 问题的～ the key to the question; the crux (or heart) of the matter / ～时刻 a critical (or crucial) moment / ～的一年 a year of crucial importance / ～在于要有决心和行动。What counts is determination and action. / 这着棋很～，关系全局的胜负。This is a decisive move which will determine the outcome of the game.

关节 guānjié ① physiol. joint: 指～ finger joints ② a key (or crucial) link; a key (or crucial) point: 应该注意那些涉及全局的重要～。Attention should be centred on the links that have a bearing on the situation as a whole. / 黛玉因识得宝钗后方吐真情，宝钗亦识得黛玉后方肯戏也。此是大～大章法，非细心看不出。Daiyu begins to reveal her real feelings only because she has now come to know Baochai, and Baochai too begins to show willingness to tease Daiyu only after having come to know her. This is a crucial point, and very good writing. Unless we are careful, we won't notice this. ③ see 通关节 tōng guānjié ——see also 买关节 mǎi guānjié

关节炎 guānjiéyán arthritis

关口 guānkǒu ① strategic pass ② juncture

关里 Guānlǐ same as 关内 Guānnèi

关联 guānlián be related; be connected: 国民经济各部门是互相～互相依存的。The various branches of the national economy are interrelated and interdependent. / 数学和天文学是互相～的科学。Mathematics and astronomy are cognate sciences.

关贸总协定 guān-mào zǒngxiédìng (short for 关税及贸易总协定) General Agreement on Tariffs and Trade (GATT)

关门 guānmén ① (of a shop, etc.) close: 展览馆下午六点半～。The exhibition centre closes at 6:30 p. m. ② inf. (of a business) close down: 公司因为管理不善，最后只好～。The company had no choice but to close down in the end due to mismanagement. ③ refuse discussion or consideration; slam the door on sth.: 对方在谈判中还没有～。The other side hasn't yet slammed the door on further negotiations. / 采取～态度 adopt a closed-door attitude ④ be behind closed doors: 我们不能～办报。We must not run a newspaper behind closed doors.

关门打狗 guānmén dǎ gǒu bolt the door and beat the dog—block the enemy's retreat and then destroy him

关门大吉 guānmén dàjí humor. (of a factory, business, etc.) close down for good

关门主义 guānménzhǔyì closed-doorism; closed-door policy; exclusivism

关内 Guānnèi inside the Pass—the area to the west of Shanhaiguan (山海关) or to the east of Jiayuguan (嘉峪关)

关卡 guānqiǎ an outpost of a tax office; checkpoint

关切 guānqiè ① considerate; thoughtful: 他待人非常和蔼、～。He's very kind and thoughtful. ② be deeply concerned; show one's concern over: 感谢同志们对我的～。I'm grateful to you comrades for your deep concern. / 表示严重～ show grave concern over / 获悉贵国遭受地震，我们极为～。We are deeply concerned at the news that your country has been struck by an earthquake.

关山 guānshān frontier passes and mountains

关涉 guānshè involve; concern; be related to

关税 guānshuì customs duty; customs; tariff: 这种东西～很重。The duty on this sort of goods is awfully high.

关税壁垒 guānshuì bìlěi tariff barrier

关税豁免 guānshuì huòmiǎn exemption from customs duties

关税同盟 guānshuì tóngméng customs (or tariff) union

关税优惠 guānshuì yōuhuì tariff preference

关税自主 guānshuì zìzhǔ tariff autonomy

关说 guānshuō formal speak on sb.'s behalf; speak in sb.'s favour

关头 guāntóu juncture; key moment: 在革命的重要～ at important junctures of the revolution / 生死存亡的紧要～ a critical moment of life-and-death importance

关外 Guānwài outside the Pass (another name for 关东 Guāndōng)

关系 guānxi ① connections; relations; relationship: 夫妻～ relations between husband and wife / 家庭～ family connections / 社会～ social connections / 军民～ relationship between the army and the people / 外交～ diplomatic relations / 两国间的友好合作～ friendly relations and cooperation between the two countries / 搞好～ build (or establish) good personal relations / 他们两个人是什么～? What is the relationship between the two of them? / 他们的～不好。They are not on good terms. / 她和上司的～很好。She's well in with her superior. / 发生～ have sexual relations with sb. (not as husband and wife) ② relevance; bearing; influence; significance: 这件事跟我没有～。This matter has nothing to do with me. / 你回答的话跟他所问的我看不出有什么～。I don't see any connection between your answer and his question. / 这一点对今后工作～重大。This has an important bearing on our future work. / 你上午去还是下午去，～不大。It won't make much difference whether you go in the morning or in the afternoon. ③ (usu. used with 由于 or 因为 to indicate cause or reason): 由于时间～，就谈到这里吧。Since time is limited, I'll have to stop here. ④ credentials showing membership in or connection with an organization: 党员调动工作时要转党的～。When a Party member is transferred to another place of work, his Party credentials are sent there. / 组织～带来了吗? Have you brought your membership credentials with you? ⑤ concern; affect; have a bearing on; have to do with: 农业～国计民生极大。Agriculture is of vital importance to the nation's economy and the people's livelihood. / 交通运输是～到工农业生产的重要部门。Transport and communications play a very important part in industrial and agricultural production. ——see also 没关系 méi guānxi

关系户 guānxihù persons or groups having dealings with each other that promote their common interests

关系学 guānxixué humor. the art of cultivating good personal relations

关厢 guānxiāng a neighbourhood outside of a city gate

关心 guānxīn be concerned about; show solicitude for; care for; be interested in: 我很～你。I'm very concerned about you. / 我们要～国家大事。We should concern ourselves with affairs of state. / 这是咱们组里的事，希望大家多关点儿心。This matter is our group's concern. I hope everyone will take an active interest in it. / 一切革命队伍的人都要互相～，互相爱护，互相帮助。All people in the revolutionary ranks must care for each other, must love and help each other. / 双方共同～的问题 matters of interest to both sides

关押 guānyā lock up; put under detention; put in pris-

on: ～犯人 put a criminal in prison / 这就是过去农奴主–农奴的地牢。 This is the dungeon where the serf owner used to lock up his serfs.

关于 guānyú *prep.* about; on; with regard to; concerning: 这是一个～龙的故事。 This is a story about dragons. / 他读了几本～政治经济学的书。 He read a few books on political economy. / ～这件事我没有意见。 I have no suggestions concerning this. / ～教学质量问题,我们准备开会研究。 We are preparing to hold a meeting in which we will look into problems regarding the quality of education. / 《～保护森林的若干规定》 *Regulations Concerning the Protection of Forests*

关张 guānzhāng *dial.* (of a shop) close down; go out of business

关照 guānzhào ① (often used in asking or thanking sb. for help) look after; take care of; keep an eye on: 我走后,这里的工作就靠你多～了。 When I'm gone, you'll have to look after the work here. / 我儿子在那儿做事,请你多～。 My son is working there; please look after him a bit. / 感谢你的～。 Thank you for the trouble you've taken on my behalf. ② notify by word of mouth; tell: 你走的时候请～一声。 Please let me know when you're ready to go. / 医生再三～不许你再抽烟。 The doctor ordered you again and again to stop smoking.

关中 Guānzhōng within the Pass (i.e. 函谷关 the Hangu Pass)—the central Shaanxi plain

关注 guānzhù follow with interest; pay close attention to; show solicitude for: 我们对那个地区的局势十分～。 We're paying a good deal of attention to what's going on in that area. / 海外赤子都异常～祖国的现代化建设。 Overseas Chinese follow the modernization of their motherland with great interest. / 物价问题引起了大家的～。 The question of prices has aroused general concern.

关子 guānzi climax (in a story or drama) ——see also 卖关子 mài guānzi

观（觀）

guān ① look at; watch; observe: 登泰山,～日出 ascend Taishan Mountain to see the sunrise ② sight; view: 奇观 qíguān ③ outlook; view; concept: 世界观 shìjièguān ——see also guàn

观测 guāncè ① observe and survey: ～气象 make weather observations / 气球～ balloon observation ② observe; watch: ～敌情 watch enemy movements

观测站 guāncèzhàn observation station

观察 guānchá observe; watch; survey: ～地形 survey the terrain / ～动静 watch what is going on / 这个病人需要住院～。 This patient should be hospitalized for observation.

观察机 guānchájī observation aircraft

观察家 guānchájiā observer (a pseudonym used by a political commentator)

观察所 guānchásuǒ *mil.* observation post

观察员 guāncháyuán *diplomacy* observer (who has the right to make a speech, but not to vote)

观潮派 guāncháopài a person who takes a wait-and-see attitude; onlooker; bystander

观点 guāndiǎn point of view; viewpoint; standpoint: 阶级～ class viewpoint / 马克思列宁主义的～ Marxist-Leninist standpoint / 阐明～ explain one's position

观风 guānfēng be on the lookout; serve as a lookout

观感 guāngǎn impressions; observations: 对新中国的～ impressions of New China / 我就自己～所及,写了一篇通讯。 I wrote a news report based on my own observations.

观光 guānguāng go sightseeing; visit; tour: ～市容 tour the city / 南京长江大桥建成后有不少外宾前来～。 Many foreign visitors have come to see the Nanjing Chang-

jiang Bridge since its construction. / ～者 sightseer

观光团 guānguāngtuán sightseeing party; tour group

观看 guānkàn watch; view: ～排球比赛 watch a volleyball match / ～话剧《茶馆》(舞剧《天鹅湖》) see the play *Teahouse* (the ballet *Swan Lake*)

观礼 guānlǐ attend a celebration or ceremony: 国庆～代表 a representative attending National Day celebrations

观礼台 guānlǐtái reviewing stand; visitors' stand

观摩 guānmó inspect and learn from each other's work; view and emulate: ～演出 give a performance before fellow artists for the purpose of discussion and emulation / ～教学 learn how to teach by observing other teachers' classes and emulating their teaching methods

观念 guānniàn sense; idea; concept: 组织～ sense of organization / 私有～ private ownership mentality / 破除旧的传统～ break away from outdated traditional modes of thought

观念形态 guānniàn xíngtài same as 意识形态 yìshi xíngtài

观赏 guānshǎng view and admire; enjoy the sight of: 我们～了几位名演员的表演。 We watched with enjoyment the performances of several famous actors.

观赏艺术 guānshǎng yìshù the visual arts

观赏鱼 guānshǎngyú fishes for display (e.g. goldfish)

观赏植物 guānshǎng zhíwù ornamental (or decorative) plant

观通站 guāntōngzhàn *mil.* observation and communication post (of the naval service)

观望 guānwàng ① wait and see; look on (from the sidelines): 采取～态度 take a wait-and-see attitude ② look around: 四下～ look around

观象台 guānxiàngtái observatory

观音 Guānyīn (also 观世音 Guānshìyīn) *Buddhism* Guanyin; the Goddess of Mercy; (Sanskrit) *Avalokitesvara* (lit. "looking on or hearing the voices of the suffering")

观音土 guānyīntǔ (also 观音粉 guānyīnfěn) a kind of white clay (eaten by famine victims to appease their hunger in the old society)

观音竹 guānyīnzhú fernleaf hedge bamboo (*Bambusa multiplex* var. *nana*)

观瞻 guānzhān the appearance of a place and the impressions it leaves; sight; view: 有碍观瞻 yǒu'ài guānzhān

观战 guānzhàn ① watch a battle; watch other people fight ② watch a match or contest

观众 guānzhòng spectator; viewer; audience

纶（綸）

guān see below ——see also lún

纶巾 guānjīn a kind of silk kerchief formerly worn by men ——see also 羽扇 yǔshàn

官¹

guān ① government official; officer; officeholder: 大～ a high official / 他做过什么～? What official positions has he held? ② governmental; official: 官办 guānbàn / 官费 guānfèi ③ public: ～厕所 a public W.C. (or toilet) ④ (Guān) a surname

官²

guān organ (a part of the body): 感官 gǎnguān

官办 guānbàn run by the government; operated by official bodies: ～企业 state enterprise

官报私仇 guān bào sīchóu same as 公报私仇 gōng bào sīchóu

官逼民反 guān bī mín fǎn oppressive government drives the people to rebellion

官兵 guānbīng ① officers and men: ～一致 unity be-

tween officers and men ② *old* government troops

官舱 guāncāng *old* cabin class on a steamer

官差 guānchāi public errand: 出～ go on a public errand; go on official business

官场 guānchǎng *derog.* officialdom; official circles

官倒 guāndǎo official-speculator

官邸 guāndǐ official residence; official mansion: 首相～ prime minister's residence

官方 guānfāng of the government; official: ～人士 government officials / ～消息 news from government sources; official sources / 以～身分 in an official capacity / ～宣传 official propaganda; government publicity

官费 guānfèi *old* (at) public (*or* state) expense

官俸 guānfèng *old* salaries of government officials

官府 guānfǔ *old* ① local authorities ② feudal official

官复原职 guān fù yuán zhí restore an official to his original post; be reinstated

官官相护 guān guān xiāng hù officials protect each other; bureaucrats shield one another

官话 guānhuà ① *old* (now replaced by 普通话 pǔtōnghuà) official dialect; Mandarin ② bureaucratic jargon

官宦 guānhuàn *old* government official

官家 guānjiā *old* ① the government authorities ② the emperor

官价 guānjià official price (*or* rate)

官架子 guānjiàzi the airs of an official; bureaucratic airs: 摆～ put on bureaucratic airs

官阶 guānjiē an official's rank

官爵 guānjué offices and titles; ranks and titles

官军 guānjūn *old* government troops

官吏 guānlì *old* government officials

官僚 guānliáo bureaucrat: 封建～ feudal bureaucrat / 清除～习气 get rid of bureaucratic practices / 这人真～! What a bureaucrat that fellow is!

官僚机构 guānliáo jīgòu bureaucratic apparatus

官僚主义 guānliáozhǔyì bureaucracy; bureaucratism: ～作风 bureaucratic style of work; bureaucratic way of doing things; bureaucratic practices

官僚资本 guānliáozīběn capital owned by the bureaucrat-capitalist class; bureaucratic capital

官僚资产阶级 guānliáozīchǎnjiējí the bureaucrat-capitalist class

官迷 guānmí a person who hankers after public office; office seeker

官名 guānmíng *old* one's formal name (as opposed to infant or pet name)

官能 guānnéng (organic) function; sense: 视、听、嗅、味、触这五种～ the five senses of sight, hearing, smell, taste and touch

官能团 guānnéngtuán *chem.* functional group

官能症 guānnéngzhèng functional disease

官气 guānqì bureaucratic airs; bureaucratism: ～十足 full of bureaucratic airs

官腔 guānqiāng bureaucratic tone; official jargon ——see also 打官腔 dǎ guānqiāng

官人 guānrén *old* wife's term of address for husband

官商 guānshāng ① government commerce; state-operated commerce ② government merchant; a bureaucratic operator of a commercial enterprise: ～作风 the style of government merchants; a bureaucratic way of handling commerce

官书 guānshū *old* a book compiled or published by a government agency

官署 guānshǔ *old* government office

官司 guānsi *inf.* lawsuit

官太太 guāntàitai *derog.* the wife of an official

官厅 guāntīng *old* government office

官衔 guānxián official title

官样文章 guānyàng wénzhāng officialese; bureaucratic

red tape; mere formalities

官窑 guānyáo (in former times) a government porcelain kiln

官瘾 guānyǐn *derog.* love for public office; anxiety to be an official

官员 guānyuán official: 外交～ diplomatic official

官运 guānyùn official career; fortunes of officialdom

官运亨通 guānyùn hēngtōng have a successful official career

官长 guānzhǎng *old* ① government official ② army officer

官职 guānzhí government post; official position

官制 guānzhì civil service system

官秩 guānzhì official grades or ranks; the ranking of officials

官佐 guānzuǒ *old* army officer

冠 guān ① hat: 衣冠 yīguān ② corona; crown: 树冠 shùguān ③ crest; comb: 鸡冠 jīguān ——see also guàn

冠盖 guāngài *formal* official hats and canopies——officials

冠盖如云 guāngài rú yún (also 冠盖云集 guāngài yúnjí) a large gathering of high officials

冠盖相望 guāngài xiāng wàng constant exchange of high officials' visits between two nations

冠冕 guānmiǎn ① royal crown; official hat ② stately; ceremonious

冠冕堂皇 guānmiǎn tánghuáng highfalutin; high-sounding: ～的理由 high-sounding excuses / 他说得～，干的却是种种见不得人的事。 He talks in a dignified, high-sounding way, but engages in all sorts of underhand activities.

冠心病 guānxīnbìng coronary heart disease

冠周炎 guānzhōuyán pericoronitis

冠状动脉 guānzhuàng dòngmài coronary artery

冠状动脉硬化 guānzhuàng dòngmài yìnghuà coronary arteriosclerosis

冠子 guānzi crest; comb: 鸡～ cockscomb

倌 guān ① a keeper of domestic animals; herdsman: 马～儿 groom ② *old* a hired hand in certain trades: 堂倌 tángguān

棺 guān coffin: 棺材 guāncai

棺材 guāncai coffin

棺床 guānchuáng *archaeol.* coffin platform

棺椁 guānguǒ *archaeol.* inner and outer coffins

棺架 guānjià bier

棺木 guānmù coffin

鳏 guān wifeless; widowered: ～居 live as a widower

鳏夫 guānfū *formal* an old wifeless man; bachelor or widower

鳏寡孤独 guān-guǎ-gū-dú widowers, widows, orphans and the childless—those who have no kith and kin and cannot support themselves

guǎn

馆（舘） guǎn ① accommodation for guests: 旅馆 lǚguǎn ② embassy; legation or consulate: 使馆 shǐguǎn ③ (of service trades) shop: 茶馆 cháguǎn ④ a place for cultural activities: 博物馆 bówùguǎn ⑤ *old* an old-style private school: 他教过三年～。He taught in a private school for three years.

馆藏 guǎncáng (of a library or a museum) ① have a collection of: ～图书二十万册 have a collection of 200,000 volumes ② collection: ～丰富 have a fine library; have a fine collection of books, paintings, etc.

馆子 guǎnzi restaurant; eating house: 下～ eat at a restaurant

管¹

guǎn ① tube; pipe: 钢管 gāngguǎn ② wind instrument: 单簧管 dānhuángguǎn ③ *electron.* valve; tube: 电子管 diànzǐguǎn ④ *m.* (for long, thin cylinder-shaped things): 一～毛笔 a writing brush / 一～牙膏 a tube of toothpaste ⑤ (Guǎn) a surname

管²

guǎn ① manage; run; control; take care of; be in charge of: ～家务 manage a household; run a house / ～孩子 take care of children / ～伙食 be in charge of the mess / 这些文件归他～。These documents are in his charge. / 他又～人事又～钱。He has control over both money and personnel. / 每个工人～好几台机器。Each worker minds (*or* tends) several machines. / 学生难～。Students are hard to handle. ② have jurisdiction over; administer: 这个市～着十个县。This city has jurisdiction over ten counties. / 警察归市政府～。The police force is under the control of the city government. ③ discipline (children or students): 孩子要～，但更要引导。Children need discipline, but they need guidance even more. ④ be concerned about; care about; bother about; intervene: 他只～自己，不～别人。He's only concerned about himself, not about others. / 去不去随你，我不～。Go or not as you like, I don't care. / 那个你别～，我来做。Don't bother about that, I'll do it. / 有些地区滥伐林木非常严重，政府得～一～了。Excessive tree-felling is very serious in some areas, and it's high time the government stepped in. ⑤ provide; guarantee: ～吃～住 provide meals and accommodation / ～接不～送 provide transportation to come, but not to go / 不好～换。We guarantee to change it if it isn't any good. ⑥ *prep. inf.* (used in the pattern 管……叫 "call sb. sth. address sb., as sth."): 我们～他叫张先生。We address him as Mr. Zhang. / 大家～他叫小淘气。People call him "little rogue." *or* He's known as "little rogue." ⑦ *conj. dial.* no matter (who, what, how, etc.): ～你怎么说，我也要再试一下。No matter what you say, I'll try again. / ～它下不下雨，我们都得马上出发。We've got to be off immediately, whether it rains or not.

管饱 guǎnbǎo guarantee adequate food: 每天三顿～。Three square meals a day guaranteed.

管保 guǎnbǎo guarantee; assure: 我～你吃了这药就好。I guarantee that if you take this medicine, you'll soon get well. / 他～不知道。I'm sure he doesn't know.

管不了 guǎnbuliǎo (also 管不住 guǎnbuzhù) be unable to control or manage: 这孩子非常淘气，连他父亲都～他。The child is very naughty and even his father cannot manage him.

管不着 guǎnbuzháo have no right to interfere; (it's) none of your concern (*or* business): 这是我们家里事，你～! This is something within the family, and you have no right to interfere.

管道 guǎndào pipeline; piping; conduit; tubing: 煤气～ gas piping / ～安装 piping erection

管得宽 guǎndekuān make everything one's own business: 我去哪儿你都要问，你也管得太宽了。Whenever I go out, you always ask where I'm going. You bother about too many things.

管儿灯 guǎnrdēng *inf.* fluorescent lamp

管饭 guǎnfàn include board; have free meals provided: 这木匠给我们家干活，我们～。We provide the carpenter who is working for us with free meals.

管风琴 guǎnfēngqín *mus.* pipe organ; organ

管家 guǎnjiā ① manage a household; run a house ② *old* steward; butler ③ manager (of a work unit); housekeeper

管见 guǎnjiàn *hum.* my humble opinion; my limited understanding: 容陈～。Let me state my humble opinion.

管见所及 guǎnjiàn suǒ jí in my humble opinion; in the light of my limited experience

管教 guǎnjiào *dial.* certainly; assuredly; surely: 听他的话，～没错。Surely you won't go wrong if you follow his advice.

管教 guǎnjiao discipline (children or students); correct: 他母亲经常～他。His mother corrects him from time to time. / 她从不～孩子，现在管不住了。She never disciplines her children and they are uncontrollable.

管井 guǎnjǐng *water conservancy* tube well

管窥 guǎnkuī look at sth. through a bamboo tube—have a restricted view: ～所及 in my humble opinion

管窥蠡测 guǎnkuī-lícè look at the sky through a bamboo tube and measure the sea with a calabash—be restricted in vision and shallow in understanding

管理 guǎnlǐ ① manage; run; administer; govern; take care of: 他们请了一个人来～那个买卖。They hired a man to manage the business. / 妇女同样能～国家大事。Women, too, can administer state affairs. / 大城市不容易～。Big cities are not easy to govern. / ～财务 be in charge of financial affairs / ～图书 take care of the library books / ～群众生活 look after the everyday life of the masses / 工商～ industrial and commercial management / 城市～ city government / 加强企业～ strengthen the management (*or* administration) of enterprises / 因为～不善，销路日减。Sales have been falling off due to mismanagement. ② control (people or animals): ～罪犯 keep criminals under control / ～牲口 tend and control draught animals

管理处 guǎnlǐchù administrative (*or* management) office

管理费 guǎnlǐfèi management expenses; costs of administration

管理委员会 guǎnlǐ wěiyuánhuì management committee; board of management

管理员 guǎnlǐyuán a person managing some aspect of daily work within an organization

管路 guǎnlù *mech.* pipeline: ～铺设 pipe laying / ～输送能力 carrying capacity of a pipeline; delivery capacity

管纱 guǎnshā *text.* cop

管事 guǎnshì ① run affairs; be in charge: 这里谁～? Who's in charge here? ② *inf.* of use; effective: 这药很～儿。This medicine helps a lot (*or* is very effective). / 找他不～。It's no use asking him. / 他说的话不～。What he says doesn't count for much. ③ *old* manager; steward

管束 guǎnshù restrain; check; control: 严加～ keep sb. under strict control

管辖 guǎnxiá have jurisdiction over; exercise control over; administer: 在～范围之内 come within the jurisdiction of / 这个市由中央直接～。This municipality is directly under the Central Government.

管辖权 guǎnxiáquán jurisdiction

管闲事 guǎnxiánshì be meddlesome; be a busybody: 他爱～。He's a real busybody. / 这是他们内部问题，你别～。This is their own problem, keep your nose out of it.

管弦乐 guǎnxiányuè orchestral music

管弦乐队 guǎnxián yuèduì orchestra

管弦乐法 guǎnxiányuèfǎ orchestration

管线 guǎnxiàn pipes and power lines

管押 guǎnyā　take sb. into custody; keep in custody; detain

管用 guǎnyòng　same as 管事 guǎnshì[2]

管乐队 guǎnyuèduì　wind band; band

管乐器 guǎnyuèqì　wind instrument

管帐 guǎnzhàng　keep accounts: 他在一家书店～。He keeps accounts for a bookshop.

管制 guǎnzhì　① control: ～物价 control prices / ～灯火 enforce a blackout / 军事～ military control / 外汇～ foreign exchange control ② put (a criminal, etc.) under surveillance: 交群众～ put sb. under public surveillance / ～劳动 labour under surveillance

管中窥豹 guǎn zhōng kuī bào　look at a leopard through a bamboo tube—have a limited view of sth.

管中窥豹，可见一斑 guǎn zhōng kuī bào, kě jiàn yī bān　look at one spot on a leopard and you can visualize the whole animal; conjure up the whole thing through seeing a part of it

管状花 guǎnzhuànghuā　bot. tubular flower

管子 guǎnzi　tube; pipe: 自来水～ tap water pipe

管子工 guǎnzigōng　plumber; pipe fitter

guàn

观（觀） guàn　Taoist temple: 白云～ Baiyun (White Cloud) Temple (in Beijing) ——see also guān

贯 guàn　① pass through; pierce: 纵贯 zòngguàn ② be linked together; follow in a continuous line: 贯珠 guànzhū ③ (in former times) a string of 1,000 cash: 《十五～》 Fifteen Strings of Cash (a play) ④ (Guàn) a surname

贯彻 guànchè　carry out; carry through; go through with; put into effect; implement: ～党的路线 implement the Party line / ～十三大精神 act in the spirit of the thirteenth Party Congress / ～群众路线 follow the mass line / ～执行党委的决议 carry out the Party Committee's decisions consistently and thoroughly / 艰苦奋斗的精神要～始终。We must always adhere to the principle of plain living and hard struggle.

贯穿 guànchuān　① run through; penetrate: 这条公路～十几个县。This highway runs through a dozen counties. ② permeate: 友爱的精神～在我们的班里。Our class is permeated with the spirit of camaraderie.

贯穿辐射 guànchuān fúshè　penetrating radiation

贯串 guànchuàn　spread through; run through; permeate: 李清照的词～着一种缠绵悱恻之情。A languid melancholy runs through the ci poetry of Li Qingzhao. / 事物发展的每一过程都～着矛盾。Each phase of the development of any phenomenon is permeated with contradictions.

贯通 guàntōng　① have a thorough knowledge of; be well versed in: ～中西医学 have a thorough knowledge of both Western and traditional Chinese medicine ② link up; thread together: 大运河～五大河流。The Grand Canal links up five big rivers. / 这条铁路已全线～。The whole railway line has been linked up.

贯众 guànzhòng　Chin. med. the rhizome of cyrtomium (Cyrtomium fortunei)

贯珠 guànzhū　a string of pearls: 声如～。The notes rang out like a string of pearls.

贯注 guànzhù　① concentrate on; be absorbed in: 把精力～在工作上 concentrate one's energy on one's work ② be connected in meaning or feeling: 这两句是一气～下来的。These two sentences are closely connected. or These two sentences hang together.

冠 guàn　① formal put on a hat ② precede; crown with: 英语的名词可以～以一个叫做"冠词"的单音词。In English a noun may be preceded by a monosyllable called an article. ③ first place; the best: 这里的棉花产量为全国之～。This area ranks first in the whole country for cotton output. ——see also guān

冠词 guàncí　gram. article

冠军 guànjūn　champion

冠军赛 guànjūnsài　another name for 锦标赛 jǐnbiāosài

惯 guàn　① be used to; be in the habit of: 这里空气比较稀薄，～了就好了。The air is rather thin here, but you'll get used to it in time. / 老大爷劳动～了，闲着就不舒服。Grandpa is used to physical labour. He'll feel uncomfortable if he's idle. / 这孩子～说假话。This child has got into the habit of lying. / 用圆珠笔写字我还不～。I'm still not used to writing with a ball-point pen. ② indulge; spoil: 他爷爷奶奶～着他，他要什么就给什么。His grandparents indulge him by giving him anything he asks for. / 别把孩子～坏了。Don't spoil the child. / 那个孩子真～得不成样子。That child is terribly spoilt.

惯犯 guànfàn　habitual offender; hardened criminal; recidivist; repeater

惯匪 guànfěi　hardened bandit; professional brigand

惯技 guànjì　derog. customary tactic; old trick

惯家 guànjia　derog. an old hand

惯例 guànlì　convention; usual practice: 按照国际～ according to international practice / 打破～ do away with convention; break with usual practice / 因循～ follow convention or usual practice

惯量 guànliàng　phys. inertia

惯骗 guànpiàn　hardened swindler

惯窃 guànqiè　hardened thief

惯偷 guàntōu　hardened thief

惯性 guànxìng　phys. inertia: ～矩 moment of inertia

惯性定律 guànxìng dìnglǜ　the law of inertia

惯性飞行导弹 guànxìng fēixíng dǎodàn　coasting missile; coaster

惯性领航 guànxìng lǐnghǎng　inertial navigation

惯用 guànyòng　derog. ① habitually practise; consistently use: ～两面派的手法 consistently use double-faced tactics ② habitual; customary: ～伎俩 customary tactics; old tricks / ～手法 habitual practice

惯贼 guànzéi　hardened thief

惯纵 guànzòng　pamper; spoil; indulge

掼 guàn　dial. ① throw; toss; cast: ～手榴弹 throw a hand grenade / ～稻 thresh rice ② fall; throw down: 他～了一个跟头。He had a fall. / 他把对手一～倒在地。He flung his opponent down on the ground.

掼交 guànjiāo　dial. tumble; trip and fall

掼纱帽 guàn shāmào　dial. throw away one's official's hat in a huff; resign in resentment; quit office

盥 guàn　formal wash (the hands or face)

盥漱 guànshù　wash one's face and rinse one's mouth

盥洗 guànxǐ　wash one's hands and face: ～用具 toilet articles

盥洗室 guànxǐshì　washroom

盥洗台 guànxǐtái　washstand

灌 guàn　① irrigate: ～田 irrigate the fields ② pour; fill: 把剩下的牛奶～到那个瓶里。Pour the rest of the milk into that bottle. / ～药 pour medicine down the throat / 暖瓶都～满了。The thermos flasks have all been filled. / 他～了我三杯。He made me drink three drinks. / ～醉 get sb. drunk / 冷风往屋里直～。The

cold air poured into the room. ③ record (sound, music, etc. on a tape or disc): ～唱片 make a gramophone record; cut a disc

灌肠　guàncháng　*med.* give an enema (*or* clyster)

灌肠　guàncháng　sausage

灌溉　guàngài　irrigate: ～农田 irrigate the fields / 提水～ irrigation by pumping

灌溉面积　guàngài miànjī　area under irrigation; irrigated area

灌溉渠　guàngàiqú　irrigation canal

灌溉网　guàngàiwǎng　irrigation network

灌溉系统　guàngài xìtǒng　irrigation system

灌浆　guànjiāng　① *archit.* grout ② *agric.* (of grain) be in the milk ③ *med.* form a vesicle (during smallpox or after vaccination)

灌迷魂汤　guàn míhúntāng　try to ensnare sb. with honeyed words

灌米汤　guàn mǐtāng　lay it on thick; butter sb. up

灌木　guànmù　bush; shrub: ～丛 shrubbery

灌区　guànqū　irrigated area

灌输　guànshū　① divert running water for use elsewhere ② instil into; inculcate; imbue with: 向农民～科学知识 imbue the peasants with scientific knowledge / 给学生～爱国思想 instil patriotism into the students

灌音　guànyīn　have one's voice recorded

灌注　guànzhù　pour into: 把铁水～到砂型里 pour molten iron into a sand mould

鹳
鹳　guàn　stork

罐(鑵)
罐　guàn　① jar; pot; tin: 一～苹果酱 a jar of apple jam / 茶叶～ tea caddy / 水～ water pitcher ② *min.* coal tub

罐车　guànchē　tank car; tank truck; tanker

罐笼　guànlóng　*min.* cage

罐头　guàntou　① *dial.* pot; jar; pitcher; jug ② tinned (*or* canned) food: 吃～ eat tinned (*or* canned) food / ～牛肉 tinned (*or* canned) beef

罐头食品　guàntou shípǐn　tinned (*or* canned) food (*or* goods)

罐子　guànzi　pot; jar; pitcher; jug: 这个～是空的。The caddy is empty. / 两～水 two jugs of water

guāng

光
光　guāng　① light: 太阳～ the light of the sun; sunlight / 就着蜡烛～看书 read by the light of a candle / ～很暗。The light is dim. ② scenery: 风光 fēngguāng ③ honour; glory: 儿子没出息，父母脸上也无～。A worthless son is a disgrace to his parents. ④ (used in polite formulas): 光临 guānglín ⑤ *formal* glorify; bring honour to: 光前裕后 guāngqián-yùhòu ⑥ brightness; lustre: 两眼无～ dull-eyed ⑦ smooth; glossy; polished: 这个桌子面儿很～。The surface of this table is smooth. / 正面儿是～的，反面儿不是。The face is polished, the other side isn't. ⑧ all gone; used up; nothing left: 他的钱都～了。All his money is gone. / 墨水用～了。The ink's used up. / 把敌人消灭～ wipe out the enemy ⑨ bare; naked: 别～着脚走。Don't walk around barefoot. / ～着膀子 be stripped to the waist ⑩ *adv.* only; alone: 她～笑不说话。She just smiled and said nothing. / 一～你一个人没法儿抬这架钢琴。You can't lift the piano alone. / 不～是我才这样想。I'm not the only one who thinks this way. / 干革命～凭一股子热情是不够的。It's not enough to rely on enthusiasm alone in waging revolution.

光斑　guāngbān　*astron.* facula

光板儿　guāngbǎnr　① worn-out fur ② (in former times) a copper coin without a distinctive stamp

光泵　guāngbèng　optical pump

光波　guāngbō　light wave

光彩　guāngcǎi　① lustre; splendour; radiance: ～绚丽的贝雕吸引了许多观众。The brilliant lustre of the shell carving attracted many visitors. ② honourable; honoured; glorious: 扮演一个极不～的角色 play a most inglorious part / 小李评上了劳动模范，全组都感到～。The whole group felt honoured to have Xiao Li named as model worker. / 谁说当模特儿不～? Who says it's not respectable to work as an artist's model?

光彩夺目　guāngcǎi duómù　with dazzling brightness; brilliant; resplendent: ～的钻石 dazzling diamonds

光灿灿　guāngcàncàn　shining

光赤　guāngchì　stark naked: 他～着身子在地里干活。He is working bare-backed in the field.

光宠　guāngchǒng　*formal* honours or favours (granted)

光大　guāngdà　*formal* ① glorify; carry forward; develop: 发扬光大 fāyáng guāngdà ② wide; extensive

光导管　guāngdǎoguǎn　another name for 光敏电阻 guāngmǐn diànzǔ

光导纤维　guāngdǎo xiānwéi　another name for 光学纤维 guāngxué xiānwéi

光电　guāngdiàn　*phys.* photoelectricity: ～发射 photoelectric emission; photoemission

光电导体　guāngdiàn dǎotǐ　photoconductor

光电管　guāngdiànguǎn　photocell; phototube

光电子　guāngdiànzǐ　*phys.* photoelectron

光度　guāngdù　*phys.* luminosity

光度计　guāngdùjì　photometer

光风霁月　guāngfēng-jìyuè　like a light breeze and a clear moon—open and aboveboard

光辐射　guāngfúshè　ray radiation: ～伤害 ray radiation injury

光复　guāngfù　recover (lost territory); restore (old glory, etc.)

光复旧物　guāngfù jiùwù　recover what has been lost (to an invader)

光杆儿　guānggǎnr　① a bare trunk or stalk: ～牡丹 peony on a bare stalk ② a man who has lost his family ③ a person without a following

光杆司令　guānggǎn sīlìng　a general without an army; a leader without a following

光顾　guānggù　*pol.* (used by a shop owner or a shop assistant) patronize: 如蒙～，无任欢迎。Your patronage is cordially invited.

光怪陆离　guāngguài-lùlí　grotesque in shape and gaudy in colour; bizarre and motley: ～的广告 grotesque and gaudy advertisements

光棍　guānggùn　① ruffian; hoodlum ② *dial.* a clever (*or* wise) person: ～不吃眼前亏。A wise man doesn't fight against impossible odds.

光棍儿　guānggùnr　unmarried man; bachelor: 打光棍儿 dǎ guānggùnr

光合作用　guānghé zuòyòng　*bot.* photosynthesis

光华　guānghuá　brilliance; splendour: 日月～ the brilliance of the sun and the moon

光滑　guānghuá　smooth; glossy; sleek: 这个桌子面儿很～。The surface of this table is very smooth. / 她的皮肤～细腻。Her skin is smooth and delicate. / 她在地板上打蜡，让它～美观。She waxed the floor to give it a nice gloss.

光化　guānghuà　*chem.* ① actinic: ～射线 actinic ray ② photochemical

光化作用　guānghuà zuòyòng　photochemical action

光环　guānghuán　① a ring of light (round a planet): 土星周围沿赤道面有三个～。Saturn is encircled by a

system of three rings lying in the plane of its equator. ② halo (round the head of a holy person)

光辉 guānghuī ① radiance; brilliance; glory: 太阳的～ the brilliance of the sun / 一轮红日冉冉升起, 放射出耀眼的～。 A red sun is slowly rising, shedding rays of dazzling brilliance. / 敌人的诽谤无损于我党的～。 The slanderous attacks of enemies cannot diminish the glory of our Party. ② brilliant; magnificent; glorious: 马列主义的～著作 magnificent works of Marxism-Leninism / ～形象 a glorious image / ～典范 a glorious model / ～榜样 a shining example / ～的一生 a glorious life

光辉灿烂 guānghuī-cànlàn glorious and magnificent; brilliant and dazzling

光火 guānghuǒ dial. flare up; fly into a rage

光洁 guāngjié bright and clean: 在灯光照耀下, 平滑的大理石显得格外～。 In the lamp light the smooth marble looks especially bright and clean.

光洁度 guāngjiédù mech. smooth finish

光介子 guāngjièzǐ phys. photomeson

光景 guāngjǐng ① scene: 看到这排窑洞, 当年延安的～又重现在眼前。 The sight of the caves brought back scenes of our life at Yan'an. ② situation; circumstances; conditions: 他的～挺不错。 He's quite comfortably off. / 过去我们工人做梦也想不到会有今天这样的好～啊! We workers never dreamed of such a happy life as we enjoy today. / 家境萧索, 不比先时的～。 The family is in a greatly reduced state compared with what it used to be. ③ prospects: 今天太闷热, ～是要下雨。 The weather is stifling. It looks like rain. / 看～得这样办。 I think it has to be done this way after all. ④ (used after time and numerical expressions) about; around: 离这儿有十里～。 It's about 10 li away from here. / 半夜～起了风。 A wind sprang up around midnight.

光刻 guāngkè phys. photoetching

光亮 guāngliàng bright; luminous; shiny: ～的窗子 bright windows / 这套家具油漆得挺～。 This set of furniture has a very shiny coat of paint.

光疗 guāngliáo med. phototherapy

光临 guānglín pol. (of a guest or visitor) honour sb. with one's presence: 各国朋友～我国首都, 一起欢度佳节。 We are honoured with having foreign friends in our capital to join us in celebrating the festival. / 欢迎你们～指导。 We welcome you and would appreciate your advice. / 敬请～。 Your presence is cordially requested.

光溜溜 guāngliūliū ① smooth; slippery: ～的大理石地面 a smooth marble floor / 她走在～的冰上有点害怕。 She was a bit nervous walking on the slippery ice. / 她把头梳得～的。 She combed her hair smooth. ② bare; naked: 孩子们脱得～的在河里游泳。 The children stripped off their clothes and swam naked in the river.

光溜 guāngliu inf. smooth; glossy; slippery: ～的纸 glossy paper

光芒 guāngmáng rays of light; brilliant rays; radiance: 旭日东升, ～四射。 The morning sun rises in the east, shedding its rays in all directions. / 延安精神永放～。 The Yan'an spirit will shine for ever.

光芒万丈 guāngmáng wàn zhàng shining with boundless radiance; gloriously radiant; resplendent

光面 guāngmiàn plain noodles (without meat or vegetables)

光敏 guāngmǐn phys. photosensitive

光敏电阻 guāngmǐn diànzǔ photoresistance

光敏二极管 guāngmǐn èrjíguǎn photodiode

光明 guāngmíng ① light: 黑暗中的一线～ a streak of light in the darkness / 是共产党把中国引向～。 It was the Communist Party that led China to the light. ② bright; promising: 世界的前途是～的。 The future of the world is bright. / 社会主义的～大道 the bright road of socialism ③ openhearted; guileless: 心地～ upright and pure in mind

光明磊落 guāngmíng-lěiluò open and aboveboard: 我们应该～, 应该随时公开说出自己的政治见解。 We must be open and aboveboard, always ready to express our political views openly.

光明正大 guāngmíng-zhèngdà just and honourable; open and aboveboard: 这件事我认为～, 可以跟任何人谈。 This business is quite open and aboveboard so far as I'm concerned. I don't care who knows.

光年 guāngnián astron. light-year

光谱 guāngpǔ phys. spectrum: 明(暗)线～ bright-line (dark-line) spectrum / 太阳～ solar spectrum

光谱比较仪 guāngpǔ bǐjiàoyí spectrocomparator

光谱分析 guāngpǔ fēnxi spectrum (or spectral) analysis

光谱学 guāngpǔxué spectroscopy: ～家 spectroscopist

光气 guāngqì chem. phosgene

光前裕后 guāngqián-yùhòu bring honour to one's ancestors and prosperity to one's descendants (said of one attaining high position)

光球 guāngqiú astron. photosphere

光圈 guāngquān (also 光孔 guāngkǒng, 光阑 guānglán) photog. diaphragm; aperture; stop: 你用多大～? What aperture are you using? / 比 f／3.5 大一档的～是 f／2。 The next stop smaller than f／3.5 is f／2.

光荣 guāngróng ① honourable; honoured; glorious: ～传统 a glorious tradition / ～的行为 a glorious deed / ～军属 the honoured family of a PLA man; soldier's family / ～使者 an honoured envoy / ～称号 a title of honour / 我们的国家有很～的历史。 Our country has a glorious history. / ～地加入了中国共产党 have the honour of being admitted into the Communist Party of China / 他有这么好的儿子, 觉得很～。 He feels very proud having such a wonderful son. ② honour; glory; credit: ～归于祖国。 The honour (or credit) goes to the country. / 我们国家的～ the glory of our country

光荣榜 guāngróngbǎng honour roll; a roster of honour

光荣花 guāngrónghuā rosette (presented as a mark of honour to combat heroes, model workers, recruits to the army, etc.)

光荣之家 guāngróng zhī jiā an honourable family (the family of a PLA man on active service, usu. inscribed on the door of the house)

光润 guāngrùn (of skin) smooth

光栅 guāngshān phys. grating

光渗 guāngshèn phys. irradiation

光束 guāngshù phys. light beam: 参考～ reference beam

光速 guāngsù phys. velocity of light

光趟 guāngtang (also 光烫 guāngtang) dial. fine and smooth: 他的脸刮得光光趟趟的。 His face was clean shaven.

光天化日 guāngtiān-huàrì broad daylight; the light of day: 一起抢劫案竟在～之下发生在一条热闹大街上。 A holdup took place in broad daylight in a crowded street. / 我要把他们的伪善面貌暴露在～之下。 I'll expose their hypocrisy to the light of the day.

光通量 guāngtōngliàng phys. luminous flux

光头 guāngtóu ① bare one's head: 他不习惯戴帽子, 一年四季总光着头。 He is not used to wearing a hat and goes bareheaded all year round. ② shaven head: 剃个～ have one's head shaved

光秃秃 guāngtūtū bare; bald: ～的山坡 bare hillsides / ～的树枝 naked branches

光纤 guāngxiān short for 光学纤维 guāngxué xiānwéi

光鲜 guāngxiān bright and new: 穿着一身～的衣服 be

dressed in a bright new suit

光线 guāngxiàn light; ray: 这间屋子～不够。There's not enough light in this room. / 别在～不好的地方看书。Don't read in poor light.

光行差 guāngxíngchā *astron.* aberration

光学 guāngxué optics: 几何～ geometrical optics / 非线性～ nonlinear optics / ～影象 optical image

光学玻璃 guāngxué bōli optical glass

光学录音 guāngxué lùyīn optical recording: ～机 photographic sound recorder

光学容限 guāngxué róngxiàn *phys.* optical tolerance

光学纤维 guāngxué xiānwéi light guide; optical fibre

光学仪器 guāngxué yíqì optical instrument

光焰 guāngyàn radiance; flare

光洋 guāngyáng *dial.* silver dollar

光耀 guāngyào ① brilliant light; brilliance: ～夺目 dazzling ② honour; glory; credit ③ glorify; carry forward; develop: ～祖国 bring honour to one's country

光阴 guāngyīn time available; time: ～很宝贵。Time is precious. / ～荏苒, 不觉又过了两年。Little by little time slipped away, and two more years passed by unnoticed.

光阴似箭 guāngyīn sì jiàn time flies like an arrow; how time flies: ～, 不觉残年将尽。Time went by like an arrow, and before I knew it the year was drawing to a close.

光源 guāngyuán *phys.* light source; illuminant

光泽 guāngzé lustre; gloss; sheen: 这些珍珠的～都很好。These pearls have a fine lustre. / 经过半年疗养, 他脸上有了～。After a six months' recuperation, his cheeks were glowing with health.

光照 guāngzhào *bot.* illumination: ～阶段 photostage

光制 guāngzhì *mech.* finishing: 最后～ final finishing / ～品 finished product

光质子 guāngzhìzǐ *phys.* photoproton

光柱 guāngzhù light beam; beam: 手电的～刺破了这片黑暗。The beam from the flashlight penetrated the darkness.

光子 guāngzǐ (also 光量子 guāngliàngzǐ) *phys.* photon: ～火箭 photon rocket

光宗耀祖 guāngzōng-yàozǔ bring honour to one's ancestors

呪 guāng *onom.* bang: ～的一声, 关上了大门。The door closed with a bang.

桄 guāng see below —— see also guàng

桄榔 guānglāng *bot.* gomuti palm

胱 guāng see 膀胱 pángguāng

guǎng

广¹(廣) guǎng ① wide; broad; vast; extensive: 知识面～ have a wide range of knowledge / 他见识很～。He's a man of wide experience. / 她兴趣相当～。Her interests are fairly broad. / 交游甚～ have a large circle of friends / 这次造林植树面积之～是前所未有的。Such extensive afforestation is unprecedented. / 这支小调流行很～。This ditty is very popular. / 丰收不忘～积粮。When we reap a good harvest, we must make a point of storing grain everywhere. ② numerous: 大庭广众 dàtíng-guǎngzhòng ③ expand; spread: 以～流传 so that it may spread far and wide

广²(廣) Guǎng short for 广东 Guǎngdōng or 广州 Guǎngzhōu (广西 Guǎngxī is not abbreviated to 广

except in the old term 两广 "the two Guangs, i. e. Guangdong and Guangxi")

广板 guǎngbǎn *mus.* largo

广播 guǎngbō ① broadcast: 那个电台每天～二十四小时。That radio station broadcasts (*or* is on the air) 24 hours a day. / 电台反复～这条重要消息。The radio station repeatedly broadcast this important piece of news. / 现在全文～《人民日报》社论。We now bring you the full text of the *Renmin Ribao* editorial. / 开始(停止)～ go on (off) the air ② radio broadcast: 我每天晚上听新闻～。I listen to the news broadcast every evening. / 实况～ live broadcast; live transmissions over the radio or television / 听北京台～ tune in to Radio Beijing

广播电视大学 guǎngbō diànshì dàxué radio and television university; college on the air

广播电台 guǎngbō diàntái broadcasting (*or* radio) station

广播稿 guǎngbōgǎo broadcast script

广播讲话 guǎngbō jiǎnghuà broadcast speech; radio talk

广播节目 guǎngbō jiémù broadcast (*or* radio) programme

广播剧 guǎngbōjù radio play

广播喇叭 guǎngbō lǎba loudspeaker

广播体操 guǎngbō tǐcāo setting-up (*or* callisthenic) exercises to radio music

广播网 guǎngbōwǎng rediffusion (*or* broadcasting) network

广播卫星 guǎngbō wèixīng broadcasting satellite

广播员 guǎngbōyuán (radio) announcer; broadcaster

广播站 guǎngbōzhàn broadcasting station (of a factory, school, etc.); rediffusion station

广博 guǎngbó (of a person's knowledge) extensive; broad; wide: 知识～ have extensive knowledge; be erudite

广场 guǎngchǎng public square; square: 天安门～ Tian'anmen Square

广大 guǎngdà ① (of an area or space) vast; wide; extensive: 幅员～ vast in territory / ～地区 vast areas; extensive regions / ～农村 the vast countryside; extensive rural areas ② large-scale; widespread: 掀起～的增产节约运动 set off a large-scale emulation drive to increase production and practise economy ③ (of people) numerous: ～人民群众 the broad masses of the people / ～干部 vast numbers of cadres / ～青年学生 the mass of student youth / ～官兵 the broad ranks of officers and men / ～读者 the reading public

广岛 Guǎngdǎo Hiroshima

广东 Guǎngdōng Guangdong (Province)

广东戏 Guǎngdōngxì same as 粤剧 yuèjù

广东音乐 Guǎngdōng yīnyuè Guangdong folk music

广度 guǎngdù scope; range: 人类利用自然资源的～将日益扩大。The scope of man's use of natural resources will steadily grow. / 这篇文章讲国民经济, 具有一定的～和深度。This article is a fairly comprehensive and in-depth study of the national economy. / 向生产的～和深度进军 develop the range and quality of production

广而言之 guǎng ér yán zhī speaking generally; in a general sense

广泛 guǎngfàn broad; extensive; wide-ranging; widespread: ～的兴趣 wide interests / ～而深入的影响 a widespread and profound influence / ～的统一战线 a broad united front / ～征求意见 solicit opinions from all sides / ～宣传计划生育的好处 give wide publicity to the advantages of family planning / 双方会谈的内容十分～。The two sides discussed a wide range of subjects.

广柑 guǎnggān a kind of orange (produced in Guangdong, Sichuan and Taiwan Provinces)

广告 guǎnggào advertisement: 登～ put an advertisement in a newspaper, magazine, etc. / 做～ advertise / 贴～ post a bill

广告画 guǎnggàohuà poster

广告栏 guǎnggàolán advertisement column (in a newspaper, etc.)

广告牌 guǎnggàopái billboard

广告色 guǎnggàosè poster colour

广告学 guǎnggàoxué (the study of) advertising

广寒宫 Guǎnghán Gōng the Moon Palace (the mythical palace in the moon)

广交会 Guǎngjiāohuì the Guangzhou Export Commodities Fair

广角镜头 guǎngjiǎo jìngtóu wide-angle lens

广开才路 guǎng kāi cáilù open all avenues for people of talent

广开言路 guǎng kāi yánlù provide wide opportunities for airing views; encourage the free airing of views

广阔 guǎngkuò vast; wide; broad: ～的前景 broad prospects / 交游～ have a wide circle of acquaintances; have a large circle of friends / 中国国土～，资源丰富。 China is a vast country abundant in natural resources.

广阔天地，大有作为 guǎngkuò tiāndì, dà yǒu zuòwéi a vast world where much can be accomplished; a vast field for using one's talents

广袤 guǎngmào formal length and breadth of land: ～千里的黄土高原 a vast expanse of loess plateau a thousand li across

广漠 guǎngmò vast and bare: 在～的沙滩上 on the bare expanse of the beach

广木香 guǎngmùxiāng Chin. med. costusroot (Saussurea lappa)

广厦 guǎngshà liter. a spacious mansion: 安得～千万间，大庇天下寒士俱欢颜，风雨不动安如山！(杜甫) Oh, for a great mansion with thousands of rooms Where all the poor on earth could find welcome shelter, Steady through every storm, secure as a mountain!

广土众民 guǎngtǔ-zhòngmín a vast territory and a large population

广西 Guǎngxī short for 广西壮族自治区 Guǎngxī Zhuàngzú Zìzhìqū

广西壮族自治区 Guǎngxī Zhuàngzú Zìzhìqū the Guangxi Zhuang Autonomous Region

广延 guǎngyán phys. extension: ～量 extensive quantity

广义 guǎngyì ① broad sense: ～地说 in a broad sense; broadly speaking / "古典音乐" 这个名称有～和狭义之分。 The term "classical music" can be used in a broad and a narrow sense. ② phys. generalized: ～空间 generalized space / ～坐标 generalized coordinates

广种薄收 guǎng zhòng bó shōu extensive cultivation

广州 Guǎngzhōu Guangzhou (formerly Canton; capital of Guangdong Province)

广州起义 Guǎngzhōu Qǐyì the Guangzhou Uprising of Dec. 11, 1927 (organized by the revolutionary soldiers and workers of the city, under the leadership of the Chinese Communist Party—one of the three major uprisings of this period, the other two being the Nanchang and Autumn Harvest Uprisings)

犷(獷) guǎng formal rustic; uncouth; boorish: 粗犷 cūguǎng

犷悍 guǎnghàn tough and intrepid

guàng

桄 guàng ① reel (thread or wire on a revolving frame): 把线～上 reel the thread ② a reel of thread: 线～儿 reels of thread ③ m. (for thread) reel: 一～线 a reel of thread ——see also guāng

桄子 guàngzi reel

逛 guàng stroll; ramble; roam: ～公园 go for a walk in the park / ～大街 stroll around the streets; go window-shopping / 咱们今天下午到城里～～去，看商店有什么东西卖。 Let's just roam around the town this afternoon, looking in the shop windows. / 咱们哪天到上海～～去吧。 Let's go sightseeing in Shanghai sometime.

逛荡 guàngdang derog. loiter; loaf about

逛窑子 guàng yáozi old dial. visit a brothel

guī

归(歸) guī ① go back to; return: 归期 guīqī ② give back to; return sth. to: 物归原主 wù guī yuánzhǔ ③ converge; come together: 千条江河～大海，各族人民一条心。 A thousand rivers find their way to the sea; the hearts of all nationalities unite as one. / 把性质相同的问题～为一类 group together problems of a similar nature ④ turn over to; put in sb.'s charge: ～集体所有 be turned over to the collective; be owned by the collective / 颗粒～仓 every grain to the granary / 消防工作～我们管。 We are in charge of fire fighting. ⑤ (used between two identical verbs) regardless of; despite: 玩笑～玩笑，事情可得认真去办。 It's all right to crack jokes but you must do your job seriously. / 批评～批评，他就是不改。 Despite our repeated criticisms, he simply won't mend his ways. ⑥ math. division on the abacus with a one-digit divisor ⑦ (Guī) a surname

归案 guī'àn bring to justice: 缉拿～ arrest and bring to justice

归并 guībìng ① incorporate into; merge into: 这个厂后来～到另一个工厂里去了。 This factory was later incorporated into another one. / 把两组～成一组 merge the two groups into one ② lump together; add up: 这三笔帐～起来是四百五十元。 The three accounts add up to 450 yuan.

归程 guīchéng return journey

归除 guīchú math. division on the abacus with a divisor of two or more digits

归档 guīdàng place on file; file away: 把文件～ place a document on file; file a document / 那封信你～了吗? Did you file that letter?

归队 guīduì ① rejoin one's unit: 他的伤已经好了，可以～了。 Now that his wound has healed, he can go back to his unit. ② return to the profession one was trained for: 前几年改行做其他工作的教师，现在逐渐～了。 Those teachers who went in for other jobs during the past few years are now gradually returning to their teaching posts.

归附 guīfù submit to the authority of another: ～国法 obey the law of the state

归根结底 guīgēn-jiédǐ (also 归根结柢 guīgēn-jiédǐ) in the final analysis; fundamentally: 人类社会的发展，～，是由生产力的发展决定的。 The development of human society is, in the final analysis, conditioned by the de-

velopment of the productive forces.

归功 guīgōng give the credit to; attribute the success to: 教练把球队的胜利～于平时的训练。 The coach attributed the team's victory to training and practice. / 他们把一切成就都～于党和人民。 They owe all their achievements to the Party and the people.

归国 guīguó return to one's country: ～观光 return to one's homeland on a sightseeing tour

归国华侨 guīguó huáqiáo returned overseas Chinese

归航 guīháng *aviation* homing: ～飞行 homing flight / ～台 homer

归还 guīhuán return; revert: 向图书馆借书要按时～。 Books borrowed from the library should be returned on time.

归结 guījié ① come to a conclusion; sum up; put in a nutshell: 原因很多，～起来不外三个方面。 There is a variety of reasons, which can be summed up in three points. ② end (of a story, etc.): 剧本是以主人公之死作为～的。 The play ends with the hero's death.

归咎 guījiù impute to; attribute a fault to; put the blame on: 不要把你的错误都～于客观原因。 Don't attribute all your mistakes to objective causes.

归来 guīlái return; come back; be back: 海外～ return from abroad / 放学～ return after school

归类 guīlèi sort out; classify: 请你把这些文件整理～，分别存档。 Please sort out, classify and file these documents.

归里包堆 guīlǐbāozuī *dial.* in all; altogether: 这个月的开支～是一百二十元。 This month's expenditure totalled 120 *yuan*. / 家里头～就是他爱人跟一个老太太。 There're altogether two people in the family—his wife and his old mother.

归拢 guīlǒng put together: 你把工具～一下。 Please put the tools together.

归谬法 guīmiùfǎ same as 反证法 fǎnzhèngfǎ

归纳 guīnà induce; conclude; sum up: 请你把这篇文章的大意～一下。 Will you please sum up the main ideas of this article? / 学生的意见～起来，不外乎是要求改进教学方法。 To sum up, the students' complaints call for an improvement of teaching methods. / 这是他从大量事实中～出来的结论。 This is a conclusion which he has drawn from numerous facts.

归纳法 guīnàfǎ the inductive method; induction

归宁 guīníng *formal* (of a married woman) visit her parents

归期 guīqī date of return

归齐 guīqí *dial.* result; outcome: 他张罗了好几天，～还是没去成。 He had been busy preparing for quite a few days, but still he failed to go in the end.

归侨 guīqiáo short for 归国华侨 guīguó huáqiáo

归去 guīqù *formal* go back; return

归入 guīrù classify; include: 这些问题可～一类。 These questions may be included in the same category.

归属 guīshǔ belong to; come under the jurisdiction of: 无所～ belong nowhere / 该岛的～早已确定无疑。 The ownership of the island has long been established beyond dispute.

归顺 guīshùn come over and pledge allegiance

归宿 guīsù a home to return to; a permanent home; a final settling place: 这位流浪多年的老人，到解放后才在我们村找到了～。 After long years of wandering, the old man at last found a home in our village after liberation.

归天 guītiān *euph.* pass away; die

归途 guītú homeward journey; one's way home

归西 guīxī *euph.* pass away; die

归降 guīxiáng surrender

归向 guīxiàng turn towards (the righteous side); incline to: 人心～ the inclination of the hearts of the

people

归心 guīxīn ① thoughts of returning home; homesickness ② *formal* submit willingly; pledge one's allegiance to

归心似箭 guīxīn sì jiàn with one's heart set on speeding home; impatient to get back; anxious to return

归依 guīyī same as 皈依 guīyī

归于 guīyú ① belong to; be attributed to: 光荣～伟大的祖国。 Glory to the great motherland. ② result in; end in: 经过长时间的辩论，大家的意见～一致。 The long debate finally ended in agreement. *or* Agreement was reached after a long debate.

归着 guīzhe *inf.* put in order; tidy up: ～屋子 tidy up the room / 行李～好了吗? Have you finished packing?

归真反璞 guīzhēn-fǎnpú (drop all affectation and) return to original purity and simplicity

归置 guīzhi *inf.* put in order; tidy up: 把东西～～，马上就要动身了。 Put everything in order. We'll be starting out soon.

归终 guīzhōng *dial.* finally; in the end: 我为他忙了半天，～还说我是多管闲事。 For all I have done for him, I've been blamed for being a busybody.

归总 guīzǒng put (items, etc.) together; sum up: ～一句话 to put it in a nutshell / 大家提的问题我还没来得及～。 I haven't had time yet to make a list of all your questions.

归罪 guīzuì put the blame on; impute to: ～于人 lay the blame on others / 实验失败不能～于他一个人。 You can't blame the failure of the experiment on him alone.

圭[1] guī an elongated pointed tablet of jade held in the hands by ancient rulers on ceremonial occasions

圭[2] guī a unit of dry measure for grain used in ancient China

圭表 guībiǎo an ancient Chinese sundial consisting of an elongated dial (*gui*) and one or two gnomons (*biao*), used for measuring the length of the year and of the 24 solar terms

圭臬 guīniè *formal* criterion; standard: 奉为圭臬 fèng wéi guīniè

圭亚那 Guīyànà Guyana

圭亚那(法) Guīyànà (Fǎ) French Guiana

圭亚那人 Guīyànàrén Guyanese

龟 (龜) guī tortoise; turtle: 乌龟 wūguī ——see also jūn

龟板 guībǎn *Chin. med.* tortoise plastron

龟背 guībèi *Chin. med.* curvature of the spinal column

龟卜 guībǔ divination by the shell of the tortoise; scapulimancy

龟趺 guīfū the base of a stone tablet carved in the form of a tortoise

龟甲 guījiǎ tortoise-shell

龟鉴 guījiàn (also 龟镜 guījìng) lessons of the past held up as a mirror for the present and future

龟龄 guīlíng longevity

龟纽 guīniǔ the turtle-shaped knob of a seal

龟缩 guīsuō huddle up like a turtle drawing in its head and legs; withdraw into passive defence; hole up: 敌人～在几个孤立的据点里。 The enemy was holed up in a few isolated strongholds.

龟头 guītóu *physiol.* glans penis

规 (槼) guī ① compasses; dividers: 圆规 yuánguī ② regulation; rule: 校规 xiàoguī ③ admonish; advise: 规劝 guīquàn ④ plan; map out: 规划 guīhuà ⑤

mech. gauge: 线规 xiànguī

规避 guībì evade; dodge; avoid: ～问题的实质 evade the substance of the issue

规避战术 guībì zhànshù evasion tactics

规程 guīchéng rules; regulations: 操作～ rules of operation

规定 guīdìng ① stipulate; provide; prescribe: 宪法～妇女享有与男子完全相同的权利。 The Constitution stipulates (*or* provides) that women enjoy exactly the same rights as men. / 学校～不许抽烟。 The school made a regulation forbidding smoking. / 我们～每人出五块钱。 We have decided that each person will contribute five *yuan*. / 中国革命的特点～了我党的战略和战术。 The characteristics of the Chinese revolution determined the strategy and tactics of our Party. / 在～的地点集合 assemble at an assigned spot / 在～的时间内 within the fixed time / ～的表格 prescribed forms / ～的指标 a set quota ② rule; regulation; stipulation: 遵守党章的～ abide by the stipulations of the Party Constitution / 关于出国留学问题，最近有了某些新～。 Certain new regulations concerning study abroad have been laid down recently.

规定动作 guīdìng dòngzuò *sports* compulsory exercise

规定数额 guīdìng shù'é *econ.* quota

规范 guīfàn standard; norm: 合乎～ conform to the standard / 这个词的用法不～。 This is not the normal way of using the word.

规范化 guīfànhuà standardize

规格 guīgé specifications; standards; norms: 统一的～ unified standards / 不合～ not be up to standard; fall short of specifications

规格化 guīgéhuà standardize

规划 guīhuà ① programme; plan: 城市～ city planning / 长远～ a long-term programme; long-term planning ② make a programme; draw up a plan: 兴修水利,应当全面～。 An overall plan should be made for the construction of water conservancy projects.

规诫 guījiè *formal* admonish; advise; warn

规矩准绳 guījǔ-zhǔnshéng compasses, set square, spirit level and plumb line—standards; norms; criteria

规矩 guīju ① rules of a community or organization; established practice; custom: 损坏东西要赔,是我们解放军的老～。 To pay compensation for damage done is an old rule in our PLA. / 按照中国～,写信时日期写在最后。 In Chinese usage, the date of a letter is placed at the end. ② customary rules of good behaviour; social etiquette; manners: 守～ abide by the rules; behave oneself / 这个孩子没～。 This child has no manners. ③ proper in behaviour; well-behaved; well-disciplined: 你(放)～点儿。 Behave properly. / 他这个老头儿不～。 He's an old man of loose morals. / 他的字写得很～。 His handwriting shows care and training. / 规规矩矩 well-behaved; law-abiding

规律 guīlǜ law; regular pattern: 客观～ objective law / 历史发展的～ law of the development of history / 自然界的～ the laws of nature / 生活有～ live a regular life

规律性 guīlǜxìng regularity; law

规模 guīmó ① scale; scope; extent; dimensions: 那个公司的～很大。 The scope of that company is very extensive. / 这个工程～宏大。 The project is of a grand scale. / ～空前的盛会 a grand gathering of unprecedented size / 这所大学开办只有三年,现已初具～。 This university, founded only three years ago, is now beginning to take shape. ② large-scale: ～经济 large-scale production

规劝 guīquàn admonish; advise: 好意～ give well-meaning advice

规行矩步 guīxíng-jǔbù ① behave correctly and cautiously ② stick to established practice; follow the

beaten track

规约 guīyuē stipulations of an agreement

规整 guīzhěng ① regular; standardized ② put in order; sort out; straighten out

规则 guīzé ① rule; regulation: 交通～ traffic regulations / 篮球比赛～ basketball competition rules ② regular: 这条河流的水道原来很不～。 The course of this river used to be quite irregular.

规章 guīzhāng rules; regulations: ～制度 rules and regulations

皈 guī see below

皈依 guīyī ① the ceremony of proclaiming sb. a Buddhist ② be converted to Buddhism or some other religion: 他晚年退隐山林,～佛教。 In his later years he retired from public life, went into the mountains and was converted to Buddhism.

闺 guī ① *arch.* a small door ② lady's chamber; boudoir: 深闺 shēnguī

闺房 guīfáng *old* lady's chamber; boudoir

闺阁 guīgé *old* lady's chamber; boudoir

闺门旦 guīméndàn (in traditional opera) a *dan* or female role of the maidenly type, elegant, attractive, and graceful

闺女 guīnü ① girl; maiden ② *inf.* daughter

闺秀 guīxiù *old* a young lady

闺怨 guīyuàn *liter.* boudoir repinings (a favourite subject in, *ci* poetry 词)

硅 guī *chem.* silicon (Si)

硅肺 guīfèi *med.* silicosis

硅钢 guīgāng *metall.* silicon steel

硅华 guīhuá *geol.* siliceous sinter; silica sinter

硅胶 guījiāo *chem.* silica gel

硅可控整流器 guīkěkòng zhěngliúqì *electron.* silicon-controlled rectifier; thyristor

硅铝带 guīlǚdài *geol.* sial

硅镁带 guīměidài *geol.* sima

硅锰钢 guīměnggāng silico-manganese steel

硅石 guīshí silica

硅酸 guīsuān *chem.* silicic acid

硅酸钠 guīsuānnà *chem.* sodium silicate

硅酸盐 guīsuānyán *chem.* silicate: ～砖 silicate brick

硅铁 guītiě ferrosilicon

硅藻 guīzǎo *bot.* diatom

硅藻土 guīzǎotǔ diatomaceous earth; diatomite

硅砖 guīzhuān silica brick

瑰 guī *formal* rare; marvellous

瑰宝 guībǎo rarity; treasure; gem: 敦煌壁画是我国古代艺术中的～。 The Dunhuang frescoes are gems of ancient Chinese art.

瑰丽 guīlì surpassingly beautiful; magnificent: 南京长江大桥的夜景雄伟～。 The view of the Nanjing Changjiang bridge at night is magnificent. / 这些作品为我国的文学艺术增添了新的～的花朵。 These works are new additions to the glories of our country's literature and art.

瑰玮 guīwěi (also 瑰伟 guīwěi) *formal* ① (of one's character) remarkable ② (of language or style) ornate

鲑 guī salmon

鬹 guī *archaeol.* a pitcher with three legs

瓌 guī ① *arch.* a jade-like stone ② same as 瑰 guī

guǐ

宄 guǐ see 奸宄 jiāngguǐ

轨 guǐ ① rail; track: 铁轨 tiěguǐ ② course; path: 正轨 zhèngguǐ

轨道 guǐdào ① track: 地铁～ underground railway track ② orbit; trajectory: 人造卫星已进入～。The man-made satellite is now in orbit. ③ the proper way of doing things; a proper course: 工作已走上～。The work has got onto the right track.

轨道变换 guǐdào biànhuàn *space* orbital transfer

轨道衡 guǐdàohéng *railway* track scale

轨道火箭 guǐdào huǒjiàn orbital rocket

轨道交角 guǐdào jiāojiǎo *space* orbit inclination

轨道空间站 guǐdào kōngjiānzhàn *space* orbital space station

轨道平面 guǐdào píngmiàn *space* orbit plane

轨道运动 guǐdào yùndòng *astron.* orbital motion

轨范 guǐfàn standard; criterion

轨迹 guǐjī ① *math.* locus ② *astron.* orbit

轨距 guǐjù *railway* gauge: 标准～ standard gauge

轨枕 guǐzhěn *railway* sleeper; tie: 纵向～ longitudinal sleeper / ～板 concrete slab sleeper

庋（庪） guǐ *formal* ① shelf ② keep; preserve: ～藏 store up; preserve

诡 guǐ ① deceitful; tricky; cunning: 诡诈 guǐzhà ② *formal* weird; eerie: 诡异 guǐyì

诡辩 guǐbiàn ① quibble; indulge in sophistry ② sophistry; sophism; quibbling: ～改变不了事实。Sophistry won't alter facts.

诡辩术 guǐbiànshù sophistry

诡称 guǐchēng falsely allege; pretend: 敌特～自己是公安人员。The enemy agent pretended that he was one of our own security men.

诡辞 guǐcí artful words; sophistry

诡计 guǐjì a crafty plot; a cunning scheme; trick; ruse

诡计多端 guǐjì duōduān have a whole bag of tricks; be very crafty

诡谲 guǐjué *formal* ① strange and changeful ② weird; eccentric; odd: 言语～ speak cryptically ③ crafty; cunning; treacherous

诡雷 guǐléi *mil.* booby mine; booby trap

诡秘 guǐmì furtive; surreptitious; secretive: 行踪～ surreptitious in one's movements

诡异 guǐyì (also 诡奇 guǐqí) strange; abnormal

诡诈 guǐzhà crafty; cunning; treacherous

匦 guǐ box: 票匦 piàoguǐ

癸 guǐ the last of the ten Heavenly Stems (天干)——see also 干支 gān-zhī

鬼 guǐ ① ghost; spirit; apparition: 不信～, 不信神 believe in neither ghosts nor gods ② *offens.*: 懒～ lazy bones / 讨厌～ a bore ③ stealthy; surreptitious: 鬼鬼祟祟 guǐguǐsuìsuì ④ sinister plot; dirty trick: 有鬼 yǒuguǐ ⑤ terrible; damnable: ～天气 terrible weather / ～地方 a damnable place ⑥ *inf.* clever; smart; quick: 这家伙真～。He's an artful devil. ⑦ the twenty-third of the twenty-eight constellations (二十八宿) into which the celestial sphere was divided in ancient Chinese astronomy (consisting of four stars in Cancer)

鬼把戏 guǐbǎxì sinister plot; dirty (*or* underhand) trick: 耍～ play dirty tricks

鬼聪明 guǐcōngmíng clever in a shallow way

鬼点子 guǐdiǎnzi *dial.* wicked idea; devilish trick: 出～ give devilish advice; make a wicked suggestion / 他～多。He's full of wicked ideas. *or* He's always got some trick or other up his sleeve.

鬼斧神工 guǐfǔ-shéngōng uncanny workmanship; superlative craftsmanship

鬼怪 guǐguài ghosts and monsters; monsters of all kinds; forces of evil: 妖魔鬼怪 yāomó-guǐguài

鬼鬼祟祟 guǐguǐsuìsuì sneaking; furtive; stealthy: 这家伙～的, 想干什么? What's that fellow up to, sneaking around like that? / 两个人～的, 不知说什么。Goodness knows what they're being so secretive about.

鬼话 guǐhuà false words; lies: 说～ tell lies

鬼话连篇 guǐhuà liánpiān a pack of lies; lies from start to finish

鬼画符 guǐhuàfú ① scrawly handwriting ② hypocritical talk

鬼魂 guǐhún ghost; spirit; apparition

鬼混 guǐhùn lead an aimless or irregular existence; fool around: 和不三不四的人～ hang around with shady characters

鬼火 guǐhuǒ popular name for 磷火 línhuǒ

鬼哭狼嚎 guǐkū-lánghao wail like ghosts and howl like wolves; let loose wild shrieks and howls

鬼脸 guǐliǎn ① funny face; wry face; grimace: 做～ make a wry face; make faces; make grimaces ② a mask used as a toy

鬼魅 guǐmèi *formal* ghosts and goblins; forces of evil

鬼门关 guǐménguān the gate of hell—a danger spot; a trying moment: 穷人进了收租院, 就象进了～。For the poor peasants, to enter that rent-collection courtyard was like entering the gate of hell.

鬼迷心窍 guǐ mí xīnqiào be possessed; be obsessed

鬼神 guǐshén ghosts and gods; spirits; supernatural beings

鬼使神差 guǐshǐ-shénchāi doings of ghosts and gods—unexpected happenings; a curious coincidence

鬼胎 guǐtāi sinister design; ulterior motive; dark scheme: 怀鬼胎 huái guǐtāi

鬼剃头 guǐtìtóu popular name for 斑秃 bāntū

鬼头鬼脑 guǐtóu-guǐnǎo thievish; stealthy; furtive: 有两个人～地从山洞里钻了出来。Two suspicious-looking people sneaked out of the cave. / ～的! 走开! Get out of here! Peeping and prying like that!

鬼物 guǐwù ghost; spirit; apparition

鬼鲉 guǐyóu devil stinger; lumpfish

鬼蜮 guǐyù evil spirit; demon; treacherous person

鬼蜮伎俩 guǐyù jìliǎng a devilish stratagem; evil tactics; dirty underhanded tricks

鬼针草 guǐzhēncǎo *bot.* beggar-ticks (*Bidens bipinnata*)

鬼主意 guǐzhǔyì evil plan; wicked idea: 打～ form an evil plan

鬼子 guǐzi devil (a term of abuse for foreign invaders)

鬼子姜 guǐzijiāng popular name for 菊芋 júyù

晷 guǐ ① *formal* a shadow cast by the sun—time: 余晷 yúguǐ ② sundial: 日晷 rìguǐ

簋 guǐ *archaeol.* a round-mouthed food vessel with two or four loop handles

guì

刿（劌） guì *arch.* cut off; chop off

刽子手 guìzishǒu ① executioner; headsman ② slaughterer; butcher

刿(劌) guì *arch.* stab; cut

柜(櫃) guì ① cupboard; cabinet: 碗柜 wǎnguì / 衣柜 yīguì ② cashier's office in a shop; shop cashier: 现款都交了～了。The cash has all been handed in to the cashier.

柜房 guìfáng cashier's office in a shop; shop cashier

柜上 guìshang cashier's office in a shop; shop cashier

柜台 guìtái counter; bar ——see also 站柜台 zhàn guìtái

柜子 guìzi cupboard; cabinet

贵 guì ① expensive; costly; dear: 这本书不～。This book is not expensive. / 丝绸比棉布～。Silk is more expensive than cotton. / 我买～了。I paid too much for it. ② highly valued; valuable: 兵～精，不～多。Troops are valued for their quality, not their number. ③ of high rank; noble: ～妇人 a noble lady ④ *honor.* your: ～国 your country / 您～姓? May I ask your name? *or* What's your name, please? ⑤ (Guì) short for 贵州 Guìzhōu

贵宾 guìbīn honoured guest; distinguished guest

贵宾席 guìbīnxí seats for distinguished guests; distinguished visitors' gallery

贵宾休息室 guìbīn xiūxishì reserved lounge (for honoured guests)

贵处 guìchù *honor.* your native place; your home town: 请问～。May I ask where you come from?

贵妃 guìfēi highest-ranking imperial concubine: 杨～ Lady Yang

贵干 guìgàn *pol.* honourable business; noble errand: 有何～? What honourable business (*or* noble errand) brings you here?

贵庚 guìgēng *honor.* your honourable age: ～多少? May I ask your age?

贵金属 guìjīnshǔ noble (*or* precious) metal

贵客 guìkè honoured guest

贵人 guìrén ① a high official ② a high-ranking imperial concubine

贵人多忘事 guìrén duō wàng shì ① a man of your eminence has a short memory (said with good-natured sarcasm); important people have short memories: 你是"～", 哪里还能记得我呀? The higher the rank, the worse the memory. How could you remember me?

贵阳 Guìyáng Guiyang (capital of Guizhou Province)

贵重 guìzhòng valuable; precious: ～物品 valuables / ～药品 costly (*or* expensive) medicines / 他送了一份儿～的礼物。He gave a valuable present.

贵州 Guìzhōu Guizhou (Province)

贵胄 guìzhòu descendants of feudal rulers or aristocrats

贵族 guìzú noble; aristocrat: 封建～ feudal nobles / 精神～ intellectual aristocrats / ～老爷式的态度 an aristocratic attitude

桂¹ guì ① cassia ② laurel; bay tree ③ sweet-scented osmanthus

桂² Guì ① (also 桂江 Guì Jiāng) a river in Guangxi ② another name for 广西 Guǎngxī ③ a surname

桂冠 guìguān laurel (as an emblem of victory or distinction): 该队以七战七胜的成绩摘取了本届篮球大赛的～。With seven wins and no losses, the team won the championship of the basketball tournament.

桂冠诗人 guìguān shīrén poet laureate

桂花 guìhuā *bot.* sweet-scented osmanthus

桂花酒 guìhuājiǔ wine fermented with osmanthus flowers

桂皮 guìpí ① cassia-bark tree; Chinese cinnamon tree ② cassia; cassia bark; Chinese cinnamon

桂圆 guìyuán longan: ～肉 dried longan pulp

桂枝 guìzhī *Chin. med.* cassia twig

桧(檜) guì *bot.* Chinese juniper

跪 guì kneel: ～下 kneel down; go (*or* get) down on one's knees / ～着祈祷 be kneeling in prayer / 他的腿都～麻了。His legs were numb from kneeling. / ～一条腿 go down on one knee

跪拜 guìbài worship on bended knees; kowtow: 行～礼 perform the kowtow; perform the prostration ceremony

跪倒 guìdǎo throw oneself on one's knees; prostrate oneself; grovel: ～在敌人脚下的可耻叛徒 a shameless renegade who prostrated himself before the enemy / 双膝～在地 get down on one's knees

跪射 guìshè *mil.* kneeling fire

跪姿 guìzī kneeling position: ～射击 shoot from a kneeling position

鲹(鯵) guì minnow

鳜 guì mandarin fish

gǔn

衮(袞) gǔn ceremonial dress for royalty: 衮服 gǔnfú

衮服 gǔnfú imperial robe

衮衮 gǔngǔn *arch.* ① continual ② numerous

衮衮诸公 gǔngǔn zhūgōng ① high-ranking officials; government dignitaries ② *humor.* Your Excellencies

绲 gǔn ① ribbon; band; tape ② string; cord ③ bind; trim: 袖口上～一条边儿 bind the cuffs / 用红绲子在领口上～一道边儿 bind the collar with a red silk ribbon / 裙子～上花边 trim the skirt with lace

绲边 gǔnbiān (also 绲条 gǔntiáo) an embroidered border

辊 gǔn *mech.* roller

辊筒印花 gǔntǒng yìnhuā *text.* roller printing

滚(滾) gǔn ① roll; trundle: 一个球在地上～。A ball is rolling on the ground. / 一块石头从山坡上～下来。A stone came rolling down the slope. / ～铁环 trundle a hoop / 从马背上～下来 tumble from a horse / 汗珠不停地从她脸上～下来。Drops of sweat coursed (*or* trickled) down her face. ② get away; beat it: ～出去! Get out of here! / 你给我～! Get lost! ③ boil: 水～了。The water is boiling. ④ same as 绲 gǔn③

滚边 gǔnbiān same as 绲边 gǔnbiān

滚槽机 gǔncáojī *mech.* channelling machine

滚齿机 gǔnchǐjī *mech.* gear-hobbing machine; hobbing machine

滚蛋 gǔndàn *offens.* beat it; scram: 滚你的蛋吧! Get lost!

滚刀 gǔndāo *mech.* hobbing cutter; hob

滚刀肉 gǔndāoròu *dial.* unreasonable trouble-maker; nuisance

滚动 gǔndòng roll; trundle

滚动摩擦 gǔndòng mócā *phys.* rolling friction

滚动轴承　gǔndòng zhóuchéng　*mech.*　rolling bearing

滚翻　gǔnfān　*sports*　roll: 侧～ sideward roll

滚瓜烂熟　gǔnguālànshú　(recite, etc.) fluently; (know sth.) by heart: 背得～ have memorized sth. thoroughly; have (*or* know) sth. off pat

滚瓜溜圆　gǔnguā liūyuán　(of animals) fat and round; roly-poly

滚滚　gǔngǔn　roll; billow; surge: 不尽长江～来。(杜甫) The Long River rolls on, forever, wave after wave. / ～的浓烟 billowing smoke / 历史车轮～向前。The wheel of history rolls on.

滚开¹　gǔnkāi　boiling (water, etc.)

滚开²　gǔnkāi　*offens.*　beat it; scram: ～，要不我揍你! Beat it, or I'll hit you! / 这儿没你的事儿，～! You're not wanted here, so scram!

滚雷　gǔnléi　*mil.*　rolling mine

滚轮　gǔnlún　*sports*　gyro wheel; hoop

滚热　gǔnrè　piping hot; burning hot; boiling hot: 刚出锅的～的汤 boiling hot soup just from the pot / 他脑袋儿，一定在发高烧。His forehead feels scalding hot; he must be running a very high fever.

滚水　gǔnshuǐ　boiling water

滚水坝　gǔnshuǐbà　*water conservancy*　overflow dam

滚烫　gǔntàng　boiling hot; burning hot

滚筒　gǔntǒng　cylinder; roll

滚筒印刷机　gǔntǒng yìnshuājī　cylinder press

滚雪球　gǔn xuěqiú　(of a business, project, etc.) get bigger and bigger as it proceeds; snowball: 放高利贷是～，连本带利，越滚越多。When practising usury, the capital and interest can have a snowball effect. / 他的买卖近来像～似的，越做越大。His business has snowballed recently.

滚圆　gǔnyuán　round as a ball: 腰身～的母牛 a round-bellied cow / 她的两只眼睛睁得～～的。She opened her eyes wide and round.

滚轧　gǔnzhá　*mech.*　rolling: ～机 rolling mill

滚针轴承　gǔnzhēn zhóuchéng　needle bearing

滚珠　gǔnzhū　*mech.*　ball

滚珠轴承　gǔnzhū zhóuchéng　ball bearing

滚柱轴承　gǔnzhù zhóuchéng　roller bearing

滚子链　gǔnziliàn　roller chain

碌（礅）

gǔn　① roller: 石～ stone roller ② level (ground, etc.) with a roller: ～地 roll the ground

碌子　gǔnzi　① stone roller ② roller

gùn

棍¹

gùn　rod; stick: 木～ a wooden stick / 小～儿 a small stick

棍²

gùn　scoundrel; rascal: 恶棍 ègùn

棍棒　gùnbàng　① club; cudgel; bludgeon ② a stick or staff used in gymnastics

棍子　gùnzi　rod; stick ——see also 打棍子 dǎ gùnzi

guō

过（過）

Guō　a surname ——see also 过 guò;

guo

郭

guō　① the outer wall of a city: 东～ the east wall of a city ② (Guō) a surname

埚（堝）

guō　see 坩埚 gānguō

聒

guō　noisy: 聒耳 guō'ěr

聒耳　guō'ěr　grate on one's ears: 蝉声～。The shrilling of the cicadas grated on my ears.

聒噪　guōzào　*dial.*　noisy; clamorous

锅（鍋）

guō　① pot, pan, boiler, cauldron, etc.: 两口大～ two cauldrons / 炒菜～ wok ② bowl (of a pipe, etc.): 烟锅 yānguō

锅巴　guōbā　crust of cooked rice; rice crust

锅铲　guōchǎn　slice (a kitchen utensil)

锅盖　guōgài　the lid of a cooking pot

锅炉　guōlú　boiler: 火管～ fire tube boiler / 水管～ water tube boiler / ～给水 boiler feedwater

锅炉防垢剂　guōlú fánggòujì　boiler compound

锅炉房　guōlúfáng　boiler room

锅台　guōtái　the top of a kitchen range: 围着～转 be tied to the kitchen sink / 我不想当家庭妇女，一辈子围着～转。I don't want to be a housewife slaving away at a hot stove all my life.

锅贴儿　guōtiēr　lightly fried dumpling

锅驼机　guōtuójī　portable steam engine; locomobile

锅烟子　guōyānzi　soot on the bottom of a pan

锅子　guōzi　① bowl (of a pipe, etc.) ② chafing dish: 涮锅子 shuànguōzi

蝈（蟈）

guō　see below

蝈蝈儿　guōguor　katydid; long-horned grasshopper

guó

国（國、囯）

guó　① country; nation; state: 大～ a big country / 强～ a powerful nation / 诸侯～ feudal states / 此河流经数～。That river flows through several countries. / 保家卫～ protect our homes and defend our country / 利～利民 benefit both the country and the people; good for the country and good for the people ② of the state; national: 国花 guóhuā ③ of our country; Chinese: 国画 guóhuà ④ (Guó) a surname

国宝　guóbǎo　national treasure: 熊猫号称是中国的～。The Giant Panda is known as the national treasure of China.

国本　guóběn　the foundation of a nation

国宾　guóbīn　state guest

国宾馆　guóbīnguǎn　state guesthouse: 总统夫妇当晚在钓鱼台～下榻。The President and the First Lady stayed at Diaoyutai State Guesthouse that night.

国柄　guóbǐng　state power

国策　guócè　the basic policy of a state; national policy

国产　guóchǎn　made in our country; made in China: ～远洋货轮 Chinese-built oceangoing freighter / ～影片 a homemade film

国耻　guóchǐ　national humiliation: 洗雪～ wipe out a national humiliation

国粹　guócuì　the quintessence of Chinese culture

国都　guódū　national capital; capital: 北京是中华人民共和国的～。Beijing is the capital of the People's Republic of China.

国度　guódù　country; state; nation

国法　guófǎ　the law of the land; national law; law: ～难容 punishable by law

国防　guófáng　national defence: 巩固～ strengthen the national defence / 建设强大的～ build up a strong national defence / ～力量 defence capability

国防部　guófángbù　the Ministry of National Defence

国防军　guófángjūn　national defence troops (*or* forces)

国防前哨　guófáng qiánshào　national defence outpost

国防委员会 guófáng wěiyuánhuì the National Defence Council

国防线 guófángxiàn national defence line

国防支出 guófáng zhīchū expenditure on national defence; defence spending

国父 guófù father of a republic (formerly an epithet for 孙中山 Dr. Sun Yat-sen)

国歌 guógē national anthem: 中国～叫《义勇军进行曲》. The Chinese national anthem is called *March of the Volunteers*.

国格 guógé national prestige: 不做有损～的事 will do nothing that would undermine national prestige

国故 guógù the national heritage (referring to developments in the field of classical studies): 整理～ reorganize the national heritage (as Hu Shi 胡适 and others tried to do in the 1920s)

国号 guóhào the title of a reigning dynasty (e.g. 元 Yuan, 明 Ming, 清 Qing, etc.)

国后岛 Guóhòudǎo Kunashiri

国花 guóhuā national flower (as an emblem)

国画 guóhuà traditional Chinese painting: ～家 a painter in the traditional Chinese style

国徽 guóhuī national emblem

国会 guóhuì parliament; (in the U.S.) Congress; (in Japan) the Diet

国货 guóhuò China-made goods; Chinese goods

国籍 guójí nationality; citizenship: 你是哪国～? What's your nationality? / 他是中国～。 He has Chinese nationality (*or* is of Chinese nationality). / 选择～ choose one's nationality / 保留中国～ retain one's Chinese citizenship / ～不明的飞机 an unidentified aircraft

国计民生 guójì-mínshēng the national economy and the people's livelihood: 轻工业和农业关系～极大。 Light industry and agriculture are of vital importance to the nation's economy and the people's livelihood.

国际 guójì international: ～地位 international status (*or* standing) / ～合作 international cooperation / ～问题 international problem; foreign relations issue / ～形势 the international (*or* world) situation / ～影响 international repercussions; impact abroad / 带有～性 have an international character

国际奥林匹克委员会 Guójì Àolínpǐkè Wěiyuánhuì the International Olympic Committee (IOC)

国际博览会 guójì bólǎnhuì international fair

国际裁判 guójì cáipàn international referee

国际单位制 guójì dānwèizhì international system of units

国际地球物理年 guójìdìqiúwùlǐnián international geophysical year

国际儿童节 Guójì Értóngjié International Children's Day (June 1)

国际法 guójìfǎ short for 国际公法 guójì gōngfǎ

国际法院 Guójì Fǎyuàn the International Court of Justice; the World Court

国际妇女节 Guójì Fùnǚjié International Women's Day (March 8)

国际歌 Guójìgē *The Internationale*

国际公法 guójì gōngfǎ (public) international law; the law of nations

国际公制 guójì gōngzhì the metric system

国际共产主义运动 guójì gòngchǎnzhǔyì yùndòng the international communist movement

国际共管 guójì gòngguǎn condominium

国际关系 guójì guānxi international relations

国际惯例 guójì guànlì international practice

国际航道 guójì hángdào international waterway (*or* sea-lane)

国际化 guójìhuà internationalize

国际货币 guójì huòbì convertible foreign exchange; international currency

国际机场 guójì jīchǎng international airport

国际劳动节 Guójì Láodòngjié International Labour Day; May Day (May 1)

国际联盟 Guójì Liánméng the League of Nations (1920–1946)

国际列车 guójì lièchē international train

国际贸易 guójì màoyì international trade (*or* commerce); world trade

国际日期变更线 guójì rìqī biàngēngxiàn international date line

国际社会 guójì shèhuì international community

国际市场 guójì shìchǎng international market: 打入～ get into the international market

国际事务 guójì shìwù international (*or* world) affairs

国际收支 guójì shōuzhī balance of (international) payments: ～不平衡 disequilibrium of balance of payments / ～逆差 international payments deficit; unfavourable balance of payments / ～顺差 international payments surplus; favourable balance of payments / ～危机 international payments crisis

国际水域 guójì shuǐyù international waters

国际私法 guójì sīfǎ private international law

国际象棋 guójì xiàngqí chess

国际音标 guójì yīnbiāo the International Phonetic Symbols (*or* Alphabet)

国际友人 guójì yǒurén foreign friends

国际舆论 guójì yúlùn world (public) opinion

国际争端 guójì zhēngduān international dispute

国际制 guójìzhì short for 国际单位制 guójì dānwèizhì

国际主义 guójìzhǔyì internationalism: ～义务 international duty / ～者 internationalist

国际纵队 Guójì Zòngduì the International Brigade (in the Spanish civil war of 1936–1939)

国家 guójiā country; nation; state: 社会主义～ a socialist country / 那次会议有五个～的代表出席。 Five nations were represented at the conference. / 在我国, 母亲和儿童受～的保护。 In our country, mothers and children are protected by the state. / ～至上。 The state above all. *or* The state is supreme.

国家裁判 guójiā cáipàn state (*or* national) referee

国家大事 guójiā dàshì national (*or* state) affairs

国家典礼 guójiā diǎnlǐ state functions

国家队 guójiāduì national team

国家法 guójiāfǎ constitutional law; the law of the state

国家副主席 guójiā fùzhǔxí (Chinese) vice-president

国家机关 guójiā jīguān state organs; government offices: ～工作人员 personnel of organs of state; state personnel

国家机器 guójiā jīqì state apparatus (*or* machinery)

国家将兴, 必有祯祥; 国家将亡, 必有妖孽 guójiā jiāng xīng, bì yǒu zhēnxiáng; guójiā jiāng wáng, bì yǒu yāoniè when a country is about to flourish, there are bound to be omens of good; when it is about to perish, there are bound to be omens of evil fortune

国家决算 guójiā juésuàn final accounts of state revenue and expenditure; final state accounts

国家领导人 guójiā lǐngdǎorén state leaders

国家垄断资本主义 guójiā lǒngduàn zīběnzhǔyì state monopoly capitalism

国家权力 guójiā quánlì state power: ～机关 organs of state power

国家所有制 guójiā suǒyǒuzhì state ownership

国家兴亡, 匹夫有责 guójiā xīngwáng, pǐfū yǒu zé every man has a share of responsibility for the fate of his country

国家学说 guójiā xuéshuō theory of the state

国家银行 guójiā yínháng state bank

国家预算　guójiā yùsuàn　state budget

国家元首　guójiā yuánshǒu　head of state

国家政权　guójiā zhèngquán　state power

国家职能　guójiā zhínéng　functions and powers of the state

国家主席　guójiā zhǔxí　(Chinese) president

国家资本主义　guójiā zīběnzhǔyì　state capitalism

国交　guójiāo　diplomatic relations

国教　guójiào　state religion

国界　guójiè　national boundaries

国境　guójìng　national territory: 偷越～ cross the border illegally

国境线　guójìngxiàn　the boundary (line) of a country: 划定～ fix the boundaries of a country

国舅　guójiù　the emperor's maternal uncle or brother-in-law

国君　guójūn　monarch

国库　guókù　national (or state) treasury; exchequer: 充实～ augment the national treasury / ～空虚。The national treasury is depleted.

国库券　guókùquàn　State treasury bond; treasury bill

国力　guólì　national power (or strength, might): ～雄厚 have solid national strength

国立　guólì　state-maintained; state-run: ～大学 national university

国联　Guólián　short for 国际联盟 Guójì Liánméng

国门　guómén　formal the gateway of a country (fig.): 御敌于～之外 turn the enemy back at the border / 这是我第一次跨出～，踏上异国土地。This is the first time I have left my country and set foot on foreign soil.

国民　guómín　a member of a nation; national; the people of a nation

国民党　Guómíndǎng　the Kuomintang (KMT)

国民经济　guómín jīngjì　national economy

国民生产总值　guómín shēngchǎn zǒngzhí　gross national product (GNP)

国民收入　guómín shōurù　national income

国母　guómǔ　① empress dowager ② the first lady

国难　guónàn　national crisis (esp. as brought on by foreign aggression): ～当头。A national crisis is imminent. / 共赴～ unite to meet the national crisis

国内　guónèi　internal; domestic; home: ～市场 domestic (or home) market / ～贸易 domestic trade / ～新闻 home news / ～革命战争 revolutionary civil war / ～形势 the domestic situation; internal conditions / ～外形势 the situation at home and abroad

国破家亡　guópò-jiāwáng　country conquered and family ruined

国旗　guóqí　national flag

国情　guóqíng　the condition (or state) of a country; national conditions

国情咨文　guóqíng zīwén　(in the U.S.) State of the Union Message

国庆　guóqìng　(also 国庆节 guóqìngjié) National Day (in China observed on October 1)

国人　guórén　formal compatriots; fellow countrymen; countrymen: ～皆曰可杀。The whole country says that the man deserves death.

国色　guósè　liter. reigning beauty; a woman of matchless beauty

国色天香　guósè-tiānxiāng　ethereal colour and celestial fragrance (said of the peony or a beautiful woman)

国殇　guóshāng　formal one who dies for his country; a martyr to the national cause

国史　guóshǐ　① national or dynastic history ② (in former times) official historian; historiographer

国事　guóshì　national (or state) affairs

国事访问　guóshì fǎngwèn　state visit

国是　guóshì　formal affairs of state; affairs of national interest; matters of national importance: 共商～ hold discussions on affairs of state

国手　guóshǒu　national champion (in chess, etc.); grand master

国书　guóshū　letter of credence; credentials: 这位新任驻华大使向中华人民共和国政府主席递交～。The new ambassador to China presented his credentials to the President of the People's Republic of China.

国术　guóshù　traditional Chinese martial arts

国泰民安　guótài-mín'ān　the country is prosperous and the people live in peace: 风调雨顺，～。The elements were propitious, the country prospered and the people were at peace.

国体　guótǐ　① state system: ～问题就是社会各阶级在国家中的地位问题。The question of the state system is a question of the status of the various social classes within the state. ② national prestige: 有辱～ bring disgrace to national prestige

国土　guótǔ　territory; land: 神圣～ our sacred land / 捍卫每一寸～ defend every inch of our territory

国外　guówài　external; overseas; abroad: ～事务 external affairs / ～来信 letter from abroad / ～市场 overseas (or foreign) market / ～投资 investment in foreign countries

国王　guówáng　king

国威　guówēi　national prestige

国文　guówén　old national language (i.e. Chinese, esp. written Chinese)

国务　guówù　state affairs

国务会议　guówù huìyì　state conference

国务卿　guówùqīng　(in the U. S.) Secretary of State

国务委员　guówù wěiyuán　a member of the State Council; State Councillor

国务院　guówùyuàn　① the State Council ② (in the U.S.) the State Department

国玺　guóxǐ　① imperial seal ② national seal

国学　guóxué　Chinese national culture

国宴　guóyàn　state banquet

国药　guóyào　traditional Chinese medicines

国营　guóyíng　state-operated; state-run: ～工商业 state-operated industry and commerce / ～牌价 state-set prices

国营经济　guóyíng jīngjì　state sector of the economy; state-owned economy

国营农场　guóyíng nóngchǎng　state farm

国营企业　guóyíng qǐyè　state enterprise

国用　guóyòng　national expenditures

国优　guóyōu　(of a product) national best

国有　guóyǒu　belonging to the nation (or the state); state-owned: 土地～ nationalization of land / 将私营企业收归～ bring private enterprises under state control

国有化　guóyǒuhuà　convert to national ownership; nationalize

国语　guóyǔ　① national language ② old name for 普通话 pǔtōnghuà ③ old Chinese as taught in school

国乐　guóyuè　traditional Chinese music

国运　guóyùn　the fortunes or destiny of a nation: ～昌盛 a nation growing in prosperity

国葬　guózàng　state funeral: 举行～ hold a state funeral for sb.

国贼　guózéi　a national traitor

国债　guózhài　national debt

国丈　guózhàng　the emperor's father-in-law

国子监　guózǐjiàn　the Imperial College (the highest educational administration in feudal China)

掴（摑）

guó variant pronunciation for 掴 guāi

guǒ

帼（幗） guó see 巾帼 jīnguó

腘（膕） guó *physiol.* the back of the knee

腘窝 guówō *physiol.* the hollow of the knee

果[1] guǒ ① fruit: 水果 shuǐguǒ ② result; consequence: 结果 jiéguǒ

果[2] guǒ resolute; determined: 果敢 guǒgǎn

果[3] guǒ ① *adv.* really; as expected; sure enough: ～不出所料 just as one expected ② *conj.* if indeed; if really: ～能如此 if things can really turn out that way; if that is so

果报 guǒbào *Buddhism* retribution

果不其然 guǒ bù qí rán just as expected; sure enough: 他经常酒后开车, 早晚得出事。～! He often drove when drunk, sooner or later I knew something would happen. Wasn't I right?

果冻 guǒdòng jelly

果断 guǒduàn resolute; decisive; determined: 办事～ handle affairs in a decisive manner / ～地作出决定 resolutely make a decision / 采取～措施 take decisive measures

果脯 guǒfǔ preserved fruit; candied fruit

果腹 guǒfù *formal* fill the stomach; satisfy one's hunger: 食不～ not have enough food in one's belly; be starving

果敢 guǒgǎn courageous and resolute; resolute and daring: 采取～的行动 take resolute action / 她～地跳入水中, 救起溺水的孩子。Without hesitation, she leapt into the water and saved the drowning child.

果盒 guǒhé a compartmentalized box for holding assorted fruits and candies

果酱 guǒjiàng jam (as made of preserves)

果决 guǒjué decisive; resolute

果料儿 guǒliàor raisins, kernels, melon seeds, etc. used in making cakes, buns, etc.: ～面包 raisin bread

果木 guǒmù fruit tree

果木园 guǒmùyuán orchard

果农 guǒnóng fruit grower

果盘 guǒpán ① fruit bowl; fruit tray ② *dial.* same as 果盒 guǒhé

果皮 guǒpí the skin of fruit; peel; rind

果皮箱 guǒpíxiāng litterbin

果品 guǒpǐn fruit: 干鲜～ fresh and dried fruit

果然 guǒrán ① *adv.* really; as expected; sure enough: ～你说对了。As expected, what you said proved to be correct. / 他说要下雪, ～就下了。He said it would snow, and sure enough it did. / ～名不虚传。A really well-deserved reputation. ② *conj.* if indeed; if really: 事情～是那样, 那就好办了。If that's really the way things are, there should be no difficulty.

果仁儿 guǒrénr ① kernel ② shelled peanut; peanut kernel

果肉 guǒròu the flesh of fruit; pulp

果实 guǒshí ① fruit: ～累累 fruit growing in close clusters; fruit hanging heavy on the trees ② gains; fruits: 劳动～ fruits of labour / 胜利～ fruits of victory / 保卫革命～ guard the gains of the revolution

果树 guǒshù fruit tree: ～栽培 fruit growing; pomiculture

果糖 guǒtáng *chem.* fructose; levulose

果园 guǒyuán orchard

果真 guǒzhēn ① *adv.* really; as expected; sure enough: 说来, 他～来了。He came just as expected. / 这一回男排～夺到了冠军。The men's volleyball team did win the title this time. ② *conj.* if indeed; if really: ～如此, 我就放心了。If this is really true, it'll take a load off my mind.

果汁 guǒzhī fruit juice

果枝 guǒzhī ① fruit-bearing shoot; fruit branch ② boll-bearing branch (of the cotton plant)

果子 guǒzi ① fruit ② same as 馃子 guǒzi

果子酱 guǒzijiàng same as 果酱 guǒjiàng

果子酒 guǒzijiǔ fruit wine

果子狸 guǒzilí another name for 花面狸 huāmiànlí

果子露 guǒzilù fruit syrup

馃 guǒ see below

馃子 guǒzi ① a kind of fried dough; puffed fritter ② *dial.* pastry

椁（槨） guǒ outer coffin: 棺椁 guānguǒ

裹 guǒ ① bind; wrap: 把伤口～好 bind up (or bandage) the wound / 头上～着毛巾 have one's head wrapped in a towel; wear a towel turban / 我～了一条毯子。I wrapped a blanket around myself. ② carry off: 匪军撤退时, ～走了几个村子里的人。The bandit troops carried off some villagers when they pulled out. ③ *dial.* suck (milk): 小孩儿一生下来就会～奶。Babies can suck milk as soon as they are born.

裹脚 guǒjiǎo foot-binding (a vile feudal practice which crippled women both physically and spiritually)

裹脚 guǒjiao (also 裹脚布 guǒjiaobù) bandages used in binding women's feet in feudal China

裹腿 guǒtui puttee; leggings

裹挟 guǒxié ① (of circumstances, trends, etc.) sweep sb. along ② same as 裹胁 guǒxié

裹胁 guǒxié force to take part (in bad things); coerce: 把敌军中被～的人争取过来 win over those who joined the enemy army under duress

裹足不前 guǒ zú bù qián hesitate to move forward

guò

过（過） guò ① cross; pass: 长征途中, 红军爬雪山, ～草地。On the Long March, the Red Army climbed snow-topped mountains and plodded through grasslands. / 野营部队要从咱们村～。The troops will be passing through our village on their camping trip. / 我接～这位大师手中的指挥棒, 开始了我的指挥生涯。I took up the baton from the master and began my conducting career. ② spend (time); pass (time): 假期～得怎样? How did you spend your holiday? / 日子越来越好～了。Life is getting better and better. / 我们今年春节是在工地上～的。This year we spent the Spring Festival at the construction site. / 退休工人～着幸福的晚年。The retired workers have a happy old age. / ～生日 celebrate one's birthday ③ go beyond (a certain point of time): ～了好几个月我才收到他的信。Several months passed before I heard from him. / ～了夏至, 天就开始变短。The days get shorter after the Summer Solstice. / 我～两天再来。I'll come again in a couple of days. ④ undergo a process; go through; go over: ～了筛子又～箩 sifted again and again; carefully screened / 咱们把这篇稿子再～一遍。Let's go over the draft once again. ⑤ exceed; go beyond: 亩产～千斤。The yield is over 1,000 *jin* per *mu*. / 树长得～了房。The tree has grown taller than the house. / 小心别坐～了站。Be

sure you don't go past your station. / 雪深～膝。The snow is more than knee-deep. ⑥ *adv.* too; unduly; excessively: 雨水～多 excessive rainfall; too much rain / ～早 too early; premature / ～长 too long; unduly long ⑦ *chem. phys.* per-; super-; over-: ～氧化物 peroxide / ～熔 superfusion ⑧ fault; mistake: 苟有～,人必知之。(《论语》) Whenever I make a mistake, other people are sure to notice it. ⑨ (used after a verb plus 得 or 不 to indicate winning or deserving): 要说跑,咱们谁也比不～他。None of us can run as fast as he can. / 这样的大学生,我们信得～。We have faith in college students of this sort. / 小伙子们干起活来,个个赛(得)～小老虎。The lads threw themselves into the work with more vigour than young tigers. ——see also guō; guo

过(過)

guo *part.* ① (used after a verb to indicate the completion of an action): 我吃～午饭就去。I'll go right after lunch. / 桃花都已经开～了。The peach blossoms are over. ② (used after a verb or an adjective to indicate a past action or state): 你去～韶山吗? Have you ever been to Shaoshan? / 我以前没看～这个戏。I've never seen this opera before. / 没见～的大旱 an unprecedented drought / 解放战争时期他打～仗,负～伤。He fought in the War of Liberation and was wounded in action. / 他年轻的时候胖～。He used to be fat in his youth. ——see also guō; guò

过儿 guòr *m. dial.* time: 衣服漂了仨～了。The clothes have been rinsed three times. / 我又重新读了一～。I have read it once more.

过半 guòbàn more than half: 敌兵伤亡～。Over half the enemy soldiers were wounded or killed.

过半数 guòbànshù more than half; majority: 这个工厂的职工是妇女。More than half the workers and staff members in this mill are women. / ～的同志赞成第一个方案。The majority of the comrades were in favour of the first plan.

过磅 guòbàng weigh (on the scales): 你的行李在机场得～。You must have your luggage weighed at the airport.

过饱和 guòbǎohé *chem.* supersaturation; oversaturation: ～溶液 supersaturated solution

过不去 guòbuqù ① cannot get through; be unable to get by: 前面正在修路,～。As the road ahead is under repair, you can't get through. / 这条路给水淹了,～。The road is impassable because of flooding. ② be hard on; make it difficult for; embarrass: 人家批评你,并不是跟你～。People didn't mean to be hard on you when they criticized you. / 请放心,他不会跟你～的。You can rest assured that he won't make things difficult for you. / 他在班上受到老师的批评,觉得脸上～。He felt embarrassed when the teacher criticized him in class. ③ feel sorry: 费了你这么多时间,我心里真～。I'm sorry for having taken up so much of your time.

过不着 guòbuzháo not be on familiar terms

过场 guòchǎng ① *theat.* interlude ② *theat.* cross the stage ③ see 走过场 zǒu guòchǎng

过程 guòchéng course; process: 在讨论～中 in the course of the discussion / 缩短制作～ shorten the process of manufacture / 思想转变要有个～。Changing one's ideology is quite a long process.

过秤 guòchèng weigh (on the steelyard): 他们把摘下的水果过了过秤。They weighed the fruit they had picked.

过从 guòcóng *formal* have friendly intercourse; associate: ～甚密 be in close association with sb.

过错 guòcuò fault; mistake: 这不是你一个人的～,我也有责任。It's not all your fault. I'm also responsible.

过道 guòdào passageway; corridor

过得去 guòdeqù ① be able to pass; can get through:

这条胡同儿很宽,汽车～。The lane is wide enough for a car to get through. ② passable; tolerable; so-so; not too bad: 我身体还～。My health is not too bad. / 他的生活还～。He makes a fairly comfortable living. / 干工作可不能满足于～。No one should be satisfied with just doing a passable job. ③ (used in a rhetorical question) feel at ease: 叫你一趟一趟地跑,我怎么～呢? I'm terribly sorry to have kept you on the go like this.

过得着 guòdezháo be on intimate terms

过冬 guòdōng pass the winter; winter: 把羊群赶到山坳里去～ herd the sheep into the valley for the winter / 这种鸟在哪儿～? Where do these birds winter?

过冬作物 guòdōng zuòwù same as 越冬作物 yuèdōng zuòwù

过度 guòdù excessive; undue; over-: 饮酒～对身体有害。Excessive drinking is harmful to the health. / ～兴奋 be overexcited / ～疲劳 be overtired / 劳累～ be overworked

过渡 guòdù transition; interim: ～措施 interim measure / 从社会主义～到共产主义 transition from socialism to communism

过渡内阁 guòdù nèigé caretaker cabinet or government

过渡时期 guòdù shíqī transition period

过房 guòfáng *dial.* ① adopt a young relative ② have one's child adopted by a relative

过访 guòfǎng *formal* pay a visit

过费 guòfèi *dial.* go to undue expense

过分 guòfèn excessive; undue; over-: ～的要求 excessive demands / ～强调 put undue stress on; overemphasize / 做得太～ go too far; overdo sth. / ～谦虚,就显得虚伪了。Modesty carried too far is little short of hypocrisy. / 说他骄傲自大,一点儿也不～。It is no exaggeration to say that he is conceited.

过福 guòfú *dial.* enjoy too much ease and comfort

过关 guòguān ① pass a barrier; go through an ordeal ② pass a test; reach a standard: 过技术关 be technically up to standard; be technically proficient / 这项新产品的质量已经～。The quality of this new product is up to standard. / 粮食问题还没有～。The problem of adequate grain production has not been solved yet. / 这次考试我没有很好准备,恐怕过不了关。I'm not well prepared for the exam. I'm afraid I won't be able to pass.

过关思想 guòguān sīxiǎng attitude of just getting by (*or* scraping past)

过河拆桥 guò hé chāi qiáo pull down the bridge after crossing the river—drop one's benefactor once his help is not needed; kick down the ladder

过后 guòhòu afterwards; later: 他起初同意,～又翻悔了。At first he agreed, but later he backed out. / 我先去通知了他,～才来通知你的。I first went to tell him, and then came to tell you.

过户 guòhù *leg.* transfer ownership; change the name of the owner in a register: 车辆转让必须到市公安局办理～手续。If you want to transfer ownership of a vehicle, you must go to the municipal public security bureau to do the required paper work.

过话 guòhuà *dial.* ① exchange words; talk with one another: 我跟他不在一个单位,所以很少～。We don't work in the same outfit, and we haven't talked much. ② send word; pass on a message: 请你替我过个话,就说我明天不去找他了。Would you mind giving him a message? Just say I won't call on him tomorrow.

过活 guòhuó make a living; live: 解放前他父亲靠拉洋车～。Before liberation his father made a living by pulling a rickshaw. / 我一家五口就靠我的工资～。My family of five relies solely on my salary.

过火 guòhuǒ go too far; go to extremes; overdo: ～的

行动 excesses / 这话说得太～了。It's going too far to say that.

过激 guòjī too drastic; extremist: ～的言论 extremist opinions

过继 guòjì ① adopt a young relative ② have one's child adopted by a relative

过家家 guòjiājiā *dial.* play house (a children's game)

过奖 guòjiǎng *pol.* overpraise; give undeserved compliment: 您的英语说得真好。——您～了。You speak very good English. ——Thank you. You flatter me.

过街老鼠 guò jiē lǎoshǔ a rat crossing the street—a person or thing that provokes a hue and cry ——see also 老鼠过街，人人喊打 lǎoshǔ guò jiē, rénrén hǎn dǎ

过街楼 guòjiēlóu an overhead building projection spanning a lane

过节 guòjié celebrate a festival: ～后咱们就开始做新的工作。After the Festival, we'll start doing new work.

过劲儿 guòjìnr go beyond the limit; overdo: 饿～了往往吃不下。Often one can't eat for being overhungry.

过境 guòjìng pass through the territory of a country; be in transit

过境贸易 guòjìng màoyì transit trade

过境签证 guòjìng qiānzhèng transit visa

过境权 guòjìngquán right of passage

过境税 guòjìngshuì transit duty

过客 guòkè passing traveller; transient guest: 匆匆来去的～ travellers coming and going hurriedly

过来 guòlái come over; come up: 快～! Come over here, quick! / 有个人～向我打听去火车站的路。A man came up and asked me the way to the railway station. / 你能不能过这边儿来一下儿? Could you come over for a while? / 他是从旧社会～的人，什么苦都吃过。He's a veteran of the old society. He's been through all kinds of hardships.

过来 ·guò·lái ① (used after a verb plus 得 or 不 to indicate the sufficiency or insufficiency of time, capability or quantity): 你一个人忙得～吗? Can you manage by yourself? / 参考书太多，简直看不～。There are just too many reference books. I simply can't read them all. / 孩子多了照顾不～。If you have too many children, you won't be able to take good care of them all. ② (used after a verb to indicate motion towards the speaker): 一队士兵正朝我们走～。A contingent of soldiers was marching towards us. / 捷报从四面八方飞～。News of victory kept pouring in from all directions. / 把被敌人占领的阵地夺～ recapture the position seized by the enemy ③ (used after a verb to indicate turning around towards the speaker): 他转过脸来，我才认出是位老同学。He turned around, and then I recognized him as a former classmate of mine. / 把柴火翻～晒晒。Turn the firewood over and sun it. / 请你转～让我量量胸围。Please turn round and let me measure your chest. ④ (used after a verb to indicate a return to the normal state): 醒～ wake up; sober up; come to / 他的坏习惯一定得改～。His bad habits must be changed. / 他终于觉悟～了。At last he saw the light. / 他真固执，简直劝不～。He's really stubborn and simply can't be persuaded. / 爬到山顶，大家都累得喘不过气来。When we reached the mountain peak, we were all out of breath.

过来人 guò·láirén a person who has had the experience: 作为～，我可以讲讲我的体会。As one who has had experience in this respect, let me tell you how I feel about it. / 要知水深浅，须问～。He knows the water best who has waded through it.

过冷 guòlěng *phys.* super-cooling

过礼 guòlǐ present betrothal gifts to the bride's family before marriage

过梁 guòliáng lintel

过量 guòliàng excessive; over-: 饮食～ excessive eating and drinking / 这种药千万不能服～。Whatever happens, never take an overdose of this medicine.

过磷酸钙 guòlínsuāngài calcium superphosphate

过路 guòlù pass by on one's way: 我是个～的人，对这儿的情况完全不了解。I'm only a passerby and know nothing at all about this place.

过路财神 guòlù cáishén a temporary God of Wealth—a person temporarily handling large sums of money

过虑 guòlǜ be overanxious; worry overmuch; worry unnecessarily: 问题会得到解决的，你不必～。The problem will be solved. You needn't be overanxious. / 孩子不会出什么事的，你也太～了。No harm will come to the child. You worry too much.

过滤 guòlǜ filter; filtrate

过滤器 guòlǜqì filter

过滤嘴 guòlǜzuǐ filter tip (of a cigarette)

过门 guòmén (of a woman) go over to a man's house —get married

过门儿 guòménr *mus.* ① opening bars ② short interlude between verses

过敏 guòmǐn ① *med.* allergy: 皮肤～ skin allergy / 他对鸡蛋(青霉素)～。He is allergic to eggs (penicillin). ② see 神经过敏 shénjīng guòmǐn

过敏性反应 guòmǐnxìng fǎnyìng *med.* allergic reaction

过目 guòmù look over (papers, lists, etc.) so as to check or approve: 名单已经排好，请您～。Here's the list for you to go over. / 帐算好了，你要过过目吗? The accounts have been worked out. Do you want to have a look?

过目不忘 guòmù bù wàng learn sth. by heart after reading it once; have a photographic (*or* very retentive) memory

过目成诵 guòmù chéng sòng be able to recite sth. after reading it once; have a photographic (*or* very retentive) memory

过年 guònián celebrate the New Year or the Spring Festival; spend the New Year or the Spring Festival: 他今年回家～。He'll be home for the New Year holiday. / 快～了。It'll soon be New Year.

过年 guònian *inf.* next year: 这孩子～该上学了。The boy's going to start school next year.

过期 guòqī exceed the time limit; be overdue: 你借的书已经～。The book you borrowed is overdue. / ～作废 become invalid after the specified date

过期胶卷 guòqī jiāojuǎn expired film

过期提单 guòqī tídān stale bill of lading

过期杂志 guòqī zázhì back number of a magazine

过谦 guòqiān too modest: 这件事你办最合适，不必～了。You are the best person for the job. Don't be so modest.

过去 guòqù (in or of) the past; formerly; previously: ～我没见过他。I have never seen him before. / 这个地方～流行的一些疾病已经基本消除。Diseases formerly prevalent here have been mostly eradicated. / ～的荒山坡如今成了果园。The once desolate slopes have been turned into orchards. / 他比～胖多了。He's much fatter than he used to be. / 回顾～，展望未来 review the past and look forward to the future

过去 guò·qù go over; pass by: 你在这里等着，我～看看。You wait here, I'll go over and see. / 一辆公共汽车刚～。A bus has just passed by. / 暑假很快就要～了。Summer vacation is almost over. / 半小时～了，我一道题也没做出来。After half an hour, I hadn't even finished one problem.

过去 ·guò·qù ① (used after a verb to indicate motion away from the speaker): 把车开～。Drive the car over (there). / 一只燕子飞～了。A swallow flew past. ② (used after a verb to indicate turning away from the

speaker): 先别把这一页翻～。 Don't turn over the page yet. ③ (used after a verb to indicate a departure from the normal state): 病人晕～了。 The patient has fainted. ④ (used after a verb to indicate acceptability): 企图蒙混～ try to get by under false pretences / 老太太脑子很清楚，你休想骗～。 The old lady is sharp-witted. You won't fool her. ⑤ (used after an adjective plus 得 or 不 to indicate superiority or inferiority): 鸡蛋还能硬得过石头去! How can an egg be harder than a stone?

过去了 guò·qùle *euph.* pass away; die: 他祖父昨晚～。 His grandfather died last night.

过热 guòrè overheated: 经济～ overheated economic growth

过人 guòrén surpass; excel: 精力～ surpass many others in energy / 勇气～ excel in courage / ～的记忆力 a remarkable memory / ～之处 the things one excels in; one's forte

过日子 guò rìzi live; get along: 勤俭～ live industriously and frugally / 挺会～ can manage to get along quite well / 小两口儿和和气气地～。 The young couple get along harmoniously together. *or* The young couple live in harmony.

过筛 guòshāi sift out

过甚 guòshèn exaggerate; overstate

过甚其词 guòshèn qí cí give an exaggerated account; overstate the case

过剩 guòshèng excess; surplus: 生产～ overproduction / 资本～ surplus of capital / 商品～ a glut of goods

过失 guòshī ① fault; slip; error: 那算不上什么错误，只是一种～罢了。 That wasn't really a mistake; it was only a slip. ② *leg.* negligence

过失犯罪 guòshī fànzuì *leg.* offence through negligence; unpremeditated crime

过失杀人 guòshī shārén *leg.* manslaughter

过时 guòshí out-of-date; outmoded; obsolete; antiquated; out of fashion: ～的设备 outmoded (*or* obsolete) equipment / 这种观点早就～了。 That kind of viewpoint has long been considered antiquated.

过时不候 guòshí bù hòu no waiting after the set time: 校车六点开车，～。 The school bus leaves at six sharp and won't wait.

过世 guòshì die; pass away

过手 guòshǒu take in and give out (money, etc.); receive and distribute; handle: 银钱～，当面点清。 Count the money on the spot. / 他～信件千千万，但没有错过一件。 He handled thousands and thousands of letters without making a single mistake.

过熟林 guòshúlín overmature forest

过数 guòshù take a count; count: 这是付给你的三万元，请你过数。 This is your 30,000 *yuan.* Please count it.

过堂 guòtáng *old* appear in court to be tried

过堂风 guòtángfēng wind coming through a passageway; draught

过厅 guòtīng hallway in an old Chinese house

过头 guòtóu go beyond the limit; overdo: 菜煮～了。 The food is overcooked. / 批评他是可以的，不过你说得～了。 It was all right to criticize him, but you overdid it. / 聪明～ be too clever by half

过屠门而大嚼 guò túmén ér dà jué start munching when passing the butcher's—feed on illusions

过往 guòwǎng ① come and go: ～的行人 pedestrian traffic / ～的车辆 vehicular traffic ② have friendly intercourse with; associate with: 他们俩是老同学，～很密。 The two of them have been friends since school days and see much of each other.

过问 guòwèn concern oneself with; take an interest in; bother about: 亲自～ take up a matter personally; take a personal interest in a matter / 无人～ not be attended to by anybody; be nobody's business / 这事你不必～了。 You needn't bother about this.

过午 guòwǔ afternoon: 他不在家，请你～再来吧。 He's not at home. Please come again in the afternoon.

过五关，斩六将 guò wǔ guān, zhǎn liù jiàng force five passes and slay six captains—win glory in battle; surmount numerous difficulties

过细 guòxì meticulous; careful: ～地做工作 work carefully; work with meticulous care / 他～地检查了所有的安全设备。 He closely examined all the safety equipment.

过眼云烟 guò yǎn yúnyān as transient as a fleeting cloud

过夜 guòyè ① pass the night; put up for the night; stay overnight: 附近的旅馆都客满，只好到朋友家～。 All the hotels in the area are full. We'll have to go spend the night in a friend's home. ② of the previous night

过意不去 guòyìbùqù feel apologetic; feel sorry: 这事给你添了不少麻烦，真～。 I'm very sorry to have put you to so much trouble.

过瘾 guòyǐn satisfy a craving; enjoy oneself to the full; do sth. to one's heart's content: 今天我一口气游了两千米，真～。 Today I really swam to my heart's content. I did 2,000 metres at a stretch. / 这段唱腔听起来很～。 This aria is a joy to hear.

过硬 guòyìng have a perfect mastery of sth.; be really up to the mark; be able to pass the stiffest test: ～的操作技术 a perfect mastery of operational technique / 苦练～的本领 train hard to perfect one's skill

过犹不及 guò yóu bù jí going too far is as bad as not going far enough

过于 guòyú *adv.* too; unduly; excessively: ～劳累 overtired / 你不必～为我们担心。 You needn't worry too much about us.

过鱼孔 guòyúkǒng *fishery* fish pass; fish way

过誉 guòyù *pol.* overpraise; unearned praise: 您如此～，叫我感到不安。 I am embarrassed by such unearned praise.

过逾 guòyú go beyond what is acceptable or necessary: 小心没～。 I couldn't have been too careful.

过云雨 guòyúnyǔ a passing shower

过载 guòzài ① transship ② overload

过帐 guòzhàng transfer items (as from a daybook to a ledger); post

过重 guòzhòng (of luggage, letters, etc.) overweight: 这个包裹～一公斤。 This parcel is overweight by one kilo. / ～加费 overweight charge

H

hā

哈¹　hā　① breathe out (with the mouth open): 眼镜上～点儿气再擦。Breathe on your glasses before wiping them. ② *onom.* (usu. reduplicated) the sound of laughing: ～～大笑 laugh heartily; roar with laughter ③ *interj.* (usu. reduplicated, expressing self-pride or satisfaction): ～～, 我猜着了。Aha, I've got (*or* guessed) it. / ～～, 小鬼, 这下子可跑不了啦。Aha, you can't get away from me this time, you little devil.

哈²**(毈)**　hā　see 哈腰 hāyāo
——see also hǎ; hà

哈巴罗夫斯克(伯力)　Hābāluófūsīkè　(Bólì)　Khabarovsk (Boli)

哈尔滨　Hā'ěrbīn　Harbin (capital of Heilongjiang Province)

哈哈镜　hāhājìng　distorting mirror

哈哈　hāhā　see 打哈哈 dǎ hāhā

哈哈儿　hāhar　*dial.* a ridiculous thing; a laughing matter: 瞧～ enjoy watching other people make fools of themselves / 他那件丢人的事成了～了。That disgraceful affair has made him a laughing stock.

哈吉　hājí　*Islam* haji (a title of honour for a Moslem who has made a pilgrimage to Mecca)

哈喇子　hālázi　*dial.* dribble; drivel; drool: 流～ slobber / 宝宝流～, 围嘴儿都湿了。The baby has slobbered its bib.

哈喇¹　hāla　*inf.* rancid: 这大油～了。The lard has gone rancid.

哈喇²　hāla　*old* kill; put sb. to death

哈雷彗星　Hāléi Huìxīng　Halley's Comet; the Halley Comet

哈里发　hālǐfā　*Islam* caliph

哈密瓜　hāmìguā　Hami melon (a variety of muskmelon)

哈乃斐派　Hānǎifěipài　*Islam* the Hanafite school

哈尼族　Hānízú　the Hani nationality or the Hanis, inhabiting Yunnan Province

哈欠　hāqian　yawn: 他太困了, ～连天的。He kept yawning for he was too sleepy.

哈萨克斯坦　Hāsàkèsītǎn　Kazakhstan

哈萨克族　Hāsàkèzú　the Kazak (Kazakh) nationality, or the Kazaks (Kazakhs), distributed over the Xinjiang Uygur Autonomous Region and the Gansu and Qinghai Provinces

哈腰　hāyāo　*inf.* ① bend one's back; stoop: 我一～把钢笔掉在地上了。As I bent over, my fountain pen fell to the ground. ② bow slightly: 点头哈腰 diǎntóu-hāyāo

铪　hā　*chem.* hafnium (Hf)

há

蛤　há　see below ——see also gé

蛤蟆　háma　① frog ② toad

蛤蟆夯　hámahāng　a kind of ramming machine; load rammer

hǎ

哈　hǎ　① *dial.* scold: 我～了他一顿。I gave him a good scolding (*or* lecturing). ② (Hǎ) a surname ——see also hā; hà

哈巴狗　hǎbagǒu　① Pekinese (a breed of dog) ② toady; sycophant

哈达　hǎdá　*hada*, a piece of silk (usu. white in colour) used as a greeting gift among the Zang and Monggol nationalities: 献～ present a *hada*

hà

哈　hà　see below ——see also hā; hǎ

哈什蚂　hàshimǎ　Chinese forest frog (*Rana temporaria chensinensis*)

哈什蚂油　hàshimǎyóu　*Chin. med.* the dried oviduct fat of the forest frog

hāi

咳(咍)　hāi　*interj.* (expressing sadness, regret or surprise): ～, 我怎么这么糊涂! Dammit! How stupid I was! / ～, 真有这种怪事儿! What! That's really strange! ——see also ké

咳声叹气　hāishēng-tànqì　heave deep sighs; sigh in despair; moan and groan

嗨　hāi　see below

嗨哟　hāiyō　*interj.* heave ho; yo-heave-ho; yo-ho

hái

还(還)　hái　*adv.* ① still; yet: 夜深了, 他～在学习。It was late at night and he was still studying. / ～有一些具体问题要解决。Some specific problems have yet to be solved. / 我们～没有开始。We haven't started yet. / 她有三十好几了, ～显得那么年轻。She still looks so young though she is well over thirty. ② even more; still more: 今年的收成比去年～要好。This

year's harvest is even better than last year's. ③ also; too; as well; in addition: 我们不但要提高产量，一要保证质量。We want not only to increase the quantity of products, but also to ensure the quality. / 这本书我一想看一遍。I want to read the book once more. ④ passably; fairly: 屋子不大，收拾得倒一干净。The room is small, but it's kept quite tidy. / 这张画儿画得一可以。The painting wasn't done too badly. or This painting's not too bad. ⑤ even: 你跑那么快一赶不上他，何况我呢? If a good runner like you can't catch up with him, how can I? ⑥ (used for emphasis): 这一了得! This is the limit! or This is simply atrocious! / 那一用说! That goes without saying. / 你小时候，我一抱过你呢! I used to carry you in my arms when you were a small kid. ⑦ (expressing realization or discovery): 他一真有办法。You've got to admit he's resourceful. or He really is resourceful. / 下这么大的雨，没想到你一真准时到了。I didn't expect you'd arrive on time as it's raining so hard. ——see also huán

还好 háihǎo ① not bad; passable: 你今天感觉怎么样?——一。How are you feeling today?——Not so bad. / 你最近很忙吧?——一。Are you very busy these days?——So so. / 不想一，一想就生气。It's all right if I don't think about it, but whenever I do, I always get angry. ② fortunately; luckily: 一，这场大水没有把堤坝冲坏。Fortunately, the flood did not break the dyke. / 一，电话总算打通了。I was fortunate enough to get through finally.

还是 háishi ① *adv.* still; yet: 废物一可以利用。Waste materials can still be made use of. / 这次一他做我们的向导。He is still our guide for this trip. / 她一会来的。She may come yet. / 尽管旱情严重，今年的小麦一丰收了。Despite the serious drought, the wheat harvest this year was good. ② *adv.* (expressing a preference for an alternative): 天冷了，你一多穿点儿吧。It's getting cold, you'd better put on more clothes. / 一你来吧，我在家等你。It would be better for you to come; I'll be at home waiting for you. / 一坐飞机快。It's much faster to travel by plane after all. ③ *adv.* (expressing realization or discovery): 这个人一真了不起。This chap is really great. / 一利害的人有办法。It's the pushing type that gets on. / 我没想到这事儿一真难办。I didn't expect it to be so difficult. ④ *conj.* or: 你去，一他去? Are you going or is he? / 先去上海一先去西安没有最后定。We haven't decided yet whether we go to Shanghai or Xi'an first. ⑤ *conj.* no matter what, how etc.; whether...or...; regardless of: 无论唱歌一跳舞，她都行。Singing or dancing, she is good at them all. / 不管刮风一下雨，他天天准时到校。He goes to school on time everyday no matter whether it rains or blows.

孩

hái child: 小孩儿 xiǎoháir / 女孩 nǚhái

孩儿 hái'ér *old* ① (parents addressing their children) my child; my son ② self reference when talking to one's parents

孩儿参 hái'érshēn *Chin. med.* caryophyllaceous ginseng (*Pseudostellaria heterophylla*)

孩提 háití *formal* early childhood; infancy: 我在故乡度过了自己的一时代。I spent my childhood in my hometown.

孩童 háitóng child

孩子 háizi ① child: 男一 boy / 女一 girl ② son or daughter; children: 她有两个一。She has two children.

孩子话 háizihuà silly childish talk: 别说一了! Don't say such silly childish things!

孩子气 háiziqì childish: 你已经十六啦，别这么一! You shouldn't be so childish, you're sixteen now! / 他一脸的一。He still looks so childish.

孩子头 háizitóu ① a person who is very popular with children ② leader of a group of children

骸

hái ① bones of the body; skeleton: 四肢百一 all the limbs and bones ② body: 形骸 xínghái

骸骨 háigǔ bones of the dead

hǎi

海

hǎi ① sea or big lake: 大一 the sea / 洱一 Erhai Lake (in Yunnan Province) ② a great number of people or things coming together: 人海 rénhǎi / 林海 línhǎi ③ extra large; of great capacity: 海碗 hǎiwǎn ④ *dial.* (usu. followed by 了 or 啦) countless: 广场上的人可一啦! There were countless people in the square. ⑤ *dial.* randomly or aimlessly: 一骂 shout at no one in particular / 一找 look high and low (for sth.) / 他有钱就一吃一喝。Whenever he has some money, he squanders it on food and drink. ⑥ (Hǎi) a surname

海岸 hǎi'àn seacoast; coast; seashore

海岸炮 hǎi'ànpào coast gun: 一兵 coast (or seacoast) artillery / 一台 coast battery

海岸平原 hǎi'àn píngyuán coastal plain

海岸线 hǎi'ànxiàn coastline

海拔 hǎibá height above sea level; elevation: 一四千米 4,000 metres above sea level; at an elevation of 4,000 metres

海百合 hǎibǎihé *zool.* sea lily; crinoid

海报 hǎibào playbill: 贴一 put up a playbill / 电影一 a film bill

海豹 hǎibào seal

海笔 hǎibǐ same as 海鳃 hǎisāi

海滨 hǎibīn seashore; seaside: 一疗养院 a seaside sanatorium / 一风景游览区 a seashore scenic and tourist area

海波 hǎibō common name for 大苏打 dàsūdá

海舶 hǎibó a seagoing ship

海菜 hǎicài edible seaweed

海产 hǎichǎn marine products

海昌蓝 hǎichānglán *text.* hydron blue

海潮 hǎicháo (sea) tide

海程 hǎichéng distance travelled by sea; voyage

海船 hǎichuán seagoing vessel

海错 hǎicuò *formal* seafood ——see also 山珍海错 shānzhēn-hǎicuò

海带 hǎidài kelp

海胆 hǎidǎn sea urchin

海岛 hǎidǎo island (in the sea)

海岛棉 hǎidǎomián sea island cotton

海盗 hǎidào pirate; sea rover: 一行为 piracy / 这一海域经常有一出没。That sea is infested with pirates.

海盗船 hǎidàochuán pirate (ship); sea rover

海堤 hǎidī sea wall

海底 hǎidǐ the bottom of the sea; seabed; sea floor

海底采矿 hǎidǐ cǎikuàng undersea mining; offshore mining

海底电报 hǎidǐ diànbào submarine telegraph; cablegram

海底电缆 hǎidǐ diànlǎn submarine cable

海底勘察 hǎidǐ kānchá submarine exploration

海底矿 hǎidǐkuàng submarine mine

海底捞月 hǎidǐ lāo yuè try to fish out the moon from the bottom of the sea—strive for the impossible or illusory: 一一场空 as futile as fishing for the moon in the sea

海底捞针 hǎidǐ lāo zhēn fish for a needle in the ocean; look for a needle in a haystack: 要在茫茫人海中找到他，就像一一样难。Trying to find him in such a huge crowd of people is as difficult as looking for a needle

in a haystack.

海底山　hǎidǐshān　seamount

海底水雷　hǎidǐ shuǐléi　ground mine (or torpedo)

海底峡谷　hǎidǐ xiágǔ　submarine canyon

海底油田　hǎidǐ yóutián　offshore oilfield

海底资源　hǎidǐ zīyuán　seabed resources; submarine resources

海地　Hǎidì　Haiti

海地人　Hǎidìrén　Haitian

海防　hǎifáng　coast defence: ～前哨 outpost of coastal defence / ～前线 coastal front

海防部队　hǎifáng bùduì　coastal defence force

海防艇　hǎifángtǐng　coastal defence boat

海风　hǎifēng　sea breeze; sea wind

海港　hǎigǎng　seaport; harbour: ～设备 harbour installations

海沟　hǎigōu　(oceanic) trench

海狗　hǎigǒu　fur seal; ursine seal

海关　hǎiguān　customhouse; customs

海关检查　hǎiguān jiǎnchá　customs inspection (or examination): 通过～ go through customs / ～站 customs inspection post

海关检疫　hǎiguān jiǎnyì　customs quarantine control

海关手续　hǎiguān shǒuxù　customs formalities

海关税则　hǎiguān shuìzé　customs tariff

海龟　hǎiguī　green turtle (Chelonia mydas)

海涵　hǎihán　pol.　be magnanimous enough to forgive or tolerate (sb.'s errors or shortcomings): 招待不周, 还望～。Please forgive us if we have not looked after you well. or Please forgive us for our poor hospitality.

海魂衫　hǎihúnshān　sailor's striped shirt

海货　hǎihuò　marine products

海脊　hǎijǐ　(also 海岭 hǎilǐng) submarine ridge

海鲫　hǎijì　Japanese seaperch

海疆　hǎijiāng　coastal areas and territorial seas

海椒　hǎijiāo　dial.　hot pepper; chilli

海角　hǎijiǎo　cape; promontory

海角天涯　hǎijiǎo-tiānyá　same as 天涯海角 tiānyá-hǎijiǎo

海进　hǎijìn　geol.　transgression

海禁　hǎijìn　ban on maritime trade or intercourse with foreign countries (as during the Ming and Qing dynasties)

海景　hǎijǐng　seascape

海鸠　hǎijiū　guillemot

海军　hǎijūn　navy

海军航空兵　hǎijūn hángkōngbīng　naval air force

海军基地　hǎijūnjīdì　naval base

海军陆战队　hǎijūn lùzhànduì　marine corps; marines

海军呢　hǎijūnní　navy cloth

海军武官　hǎijūn wǔguān　diplomacy　naval attaché

海军学校　hǎijūn xuéxiào　naval academy

海口¹　hǎikǒu　seaport

海口²　hǎikǒu　(usu. used in) 夸～ boast about what one can do; talk big

海口³　Hǎikǒu　Haikou (capital of Hainan Province)

海枯石烂　hǎikū-shílàn　(even if) the seas run dry and the rocks crumble: ～心不变。The seas may run dry and the rocks may crumble, but our hearts will always remain loyal.

海葵　hǎikuí　zool.　sea anemone

海阔天空　hǎikuò-tiānkōng　as boundless as the sea and the sky; unrestrained and far-ranging: ～地聊个没完 have a rambling chat about everything under the sun / ～地谈一通, 不解决任何实际问题 indulge in far-ranging rambling discourse without solving any practical problems

海蓝　hǎilán　sea green; sea blue

海蓝宝石　hǎilán bǎoshí　aquamarine

海狸　hǎilí　old name for 河狸 hélí

海狸鼠　hǎilíshǔ　coypu; nutria

海里　hǎilǐ　nautical mile; sea mile

海力司粗呢　hǎilìsī cūní　Harris tweed

海蛎子　hǎilìzi　another name for 牡蛎 mǔlì

海量　hǎiliàng　① pol.　magnanimity: 对不住的地方, 望您～包涵。I hope you will be magnanimous enough to excuse any incorrect behaviour on my part. ② great capacity for liquor: 您是～, 再来一杯。Have another one. You can hold your liquor.

海流　hǎiliú　ocean current

海龙　hǎilóng　① inf.　sea otter ② pipefish

海路　hǎilù　sea route; sea-lane; seaway: 走～ travel by sea

海绿石　hǎilùshí　glauconite

海轮　hǎilún　seagoing (or oceangoing) vessel

海螺　hǎiluó　conch

海洛因　hǎiluòyīn　heroin

海马　hǎimǎ　sea horse

海鳗　hǎimán　conger pike

海米　hǎimǐ　dried shrimps

海绵　hǎimián　① sponge ② foam rubber or plastic; sponge

海绵垫　hǎimiándiàn　foam rubber cushion

海绵球拍　hǎimián qiúpāi　foam-rubber (or sponge) table-tennis bat: 正(反)贴～ outward (inward) pimpled rubber bat

海绵田　hǎimiántián　mellow-soil field; spongy soil

海绵铁　hǎimiántiě　sponge iron

海面　hǎimiàn　sea surface

海南　Hǎinán　Hainan (Province)

海难　hǎinàn　perils of the sea

海内　hǎinèi　within the four seas; throughout the country: 他的书画～知名。He's known throughout the country for his calligraphy and painting.

海内存知己, 天涯若比邻　hǎinèi cún zhījǐ, tiānyá ruò bǐlín　if in this world an understanding friend survives, then the ends of the earth seem like next door; a bosom friend afar brings a distant land near

海鲇　hǎinián　sea catfish

海牛　hǎiniú　manatee; sea cow

海鸥　hǎi'ōu　sea gull

海派　hǎipài　the Shanghai school of Beijing opera (opp. the Beijing school)

海盘车　hǎipánchē　zool.　starfish

海泡石　hǎipàoshí　sepiolite; sea-foam (a mineral)

海盆　hǎipén　ocean basin

海螵蛸　hǎipiāoxiāo　Chin. med.　cuttlebone

海平面　hǎipíngmiàn　sea level

海侵　hǎiqīn　same as 海进 hǎijìn

海区　hǎiqū　mil.　sea area

海群生　hǎiqúnshēng　pharm.　hetrazan

海鳃　hǎisāi　zool.　sea pen; sea feather

海扇　hǎishàn　another name for 扇贝 shànbèi

海商法　hǎishāngfǎ　maritime law

海上　hǎishàng　at sea; on the sea: ～风暴 a storm at sea / ～作业 operation on the sea / ～空间 air space above the sea / ～霸权 maritime (or naval) hegemony

海上保险　hǎishàng bǎoxiǎn　marine (or maritime) insurance

海上补给　hǎishàng bǔjǐ　sealift; seaborne supply

海上封锁　hǎishàng fēngsuǒ　naval blockade

海上交通　hǎishàng jiāotōng　maritime traffic: ～线 sea route; sea-lane

海上遇险信号　hǎishàng yùxiǎn xìnhào　signal of distress; GMDSS

海上运输　hǎishàng yùnshū　marine transportation

海蛇　hǎishé　sea snake

海参　hǎishēn　sea cucumber; sea slug; trepang

海参崴　Hǎishēnwǎi　Haishenwai (Chinese name for 符拉

迪沃斯托克 Fúlādíwòsītuōkè）

海狮 hǎishī sea lion

海蚀 hǎishí be washed and eroded by sea water

海蚀洞 hǎishídòng sea cave

海市蜃楼 hǎishì shènlóu ① mirage ② illusion

海事 hǎishì maritime affairs

海事法庭 hǎishì fǎtíng admiralty court; maritime court

海誓山盟 hǎishì-shānméng (make) a solemn pledge of love

海水 hǎishuǐ seawater; brine; the sea

海水不可斗量 hǎishuǐ bùkě dǒu liáng the sea cannot be measured with a bushel—great minds cannot be fathomed

海水工业 hǎishuǐ gōngyè marine industry

海水浴 hǎishuǐyù seawater bath; sea bathing

海损 hǎisǔn com. average: 共同（单独）～ general (particular) average /～理算 average adjustment

海獭 hǎitǎ sea otter

海滩 hǎitān seabeach; beach: 孩子们喜欢在～上玩耍。 Children love playing on the beach.

海棠 hǎitáng Chinese flowering crabapple

海塘 hǎitáng seawall

海桐花 hǎitónghuā tobira

海图 hǎitú sea (or marine, nautical) chart: ～室 chart room (or house)

海涂 hǎitú tidal land

海退 hǎituì geol. regression

海豚 hǎitún dolphin

海豚泳 hǎitúnyǒng sports dolphin butterfly; dolphin fishtail; dolphin

海外 hǎiwài overseas; abroad: 扬名～ known the world over / 中国丝绸畅销～。 Chinese silk is sold all over the world. / 他在～住了几十年。 He lived abroad for scores of years. / ～华侨 overseas Chinese; Chinese nationals residing abroad / ～侨胞 countrymen residing abroad

海外版 hǎiwàibǎn overseas edition: 《人民日报》～ the overseas edition of Renmin Ribao

海外关系 hǎiwài guānxi relatives abroad

海外奇谈 hǎiwài qítán a strange story from over the seas; a traveller's tale; a tall story

海湾 hǎiwān bay; gulf

海碗 hǎiwǎn a very big bowl

海王星 Hǎiwángxīng Neptune

海味 hǎiwèi choice seafood: 山珍海味 shānzhēn-hǎiwèi

海峡 hǎixiá strait; channel: 台湾～ the Taiwan Straits / 英吉利～ the English Channel

海峡群岛 Hǎixiá Qúndǎo the Channel Islands

海鲜 hǎixiān seafood

海相 hǎixiàng geol. marine (or sea) facies

海相沉积 hǎixiàng chénjī geol. marine deposit

海象 hǎixiàng walrus; morse

海啸 hǎixiào tsunami; seismic sea wave

海蟹 hǎixiè sea crab

海星 hǎixīng starfish: sea star

海熊 hǎixióng fur seal; ursine seal

海寻 hǎixún nautical fathom

海牙 Hǎiyá The Hague

海盐 hǎiyán sea salt

海蜒 hǎiyán dried anchovy

海晏河清 hǎiyàn-héqīng same as 河清海晏 héqīng-hǎiyàn

海燕 hǎiyàn (storm) petrel

海洋 hǎiyáng seas and oceans; ocean

海洋动物 hǎiyáng dòngwù marine animal

海洋法 hǎiyángfǎ law of the sea

海洋工程 hǎiyáng gōngchéng oceanics industries

海洋公约 hǎiyáng gōngyuē maritime convention

海洋环境 hǎiyáng huánjìng marine environment: ～污染损害 marine environmental pollution damage

海洋气象船 hǎiyáng qìxiàngchuán ocean weather ship

海洋气象学 hǎiyáng qìxiàngxué marine meteorology

海洋权 hǎiyángquán marine rights

海洋生物 hǎiyáng shēngwù marine organisms: ～学 marine biology

海洋石油 hǎiyáng shíyóu offshore oil: ～采油平台 offshore oil extraction platform / ～勘探 offshore oil exploration / ～资源 offshore petroleum resources / ～钻井船 offshore oil drilling rig / ～钻井平台 offshore oil drilling platform

海洋特别保护区 hǎiyáng tèbié bǎohùqū special marine protection area; special marine reserve

海洋性冰川 hǎiyángxìng bīngchuān marine glacier

海洋性气候 hǎiyángxìng qìhòu maritime (or marine) climate

海洋学 hǎiyángxué oceanography; oceanology

海洋渔业 hǎiyáng yúyè sea fishery

海洋资源 hǎiyáng zīyuán marine resources

海洋自然资源保护区 hǎiyáng zìrán zīyuán bǎohùqū marine nature conservation area; marine nature reserve

海涌 hǎiyǒng swell

海鱼 hǎiyú sea fish

海隅 hǎiyú formal coastal areas; coastland

海域 hǎiyù sea area; maritime space: 南海～ Nanhai Sea waters

海员 hǎiyuán seaman; sailor; mariner: ～俱乐部 seamen's club / ～用语 nautical expression

海月水母 hǎiyuè shuǐmǔ zool. aurelia

海运 hǎiyùn sea transportation; ocean shipping

海葬 hǎizàng sea-burial

海枣 hǎizǎo bot. date palm; date

海藻 hǎizǎo marine alga; seaweed

海战 hǎizhàn sea warfare; naval battle

海蜇 hǎizhé jellyfish

海震 hǎizhèn geol. seaquake

海蜘蛛 hǎizhīzhū sea spider

海猪 hǎizhū common name for 海豚 hǎitún

海子 hǎizi dial. lake

胲 hǎi chem. hydroxylamine

醢 hǎi formal ① fish or meat paste ② cut sb. into small pieces (a form of punishment in ancient China)

hài

亥 hài the last of the twelve Earthly Branches （地支）——see also 干支 gān-zhī

亥时 hàishí the period of the day from 9 p.m. to 11 p.m.

骇 hài be astonished; be shocked: 惊骇 jīnghài

骇怪 hàiguài be shocked; be astonished

骇惧 hàijù be frightened; be terrified

骇然 hàirán gasping with astonishment; struck dumb with amazement

骇人听闻 hài rén tīngwén shocking; appalling: ～的暴行 horrifying atrocities / ～的纵火事件 a shocking case of arson

骇异 hàiyì be shocked; be astonished

害 hài ① evil; harm; calamity: ～多利少 more disadvantages than advantages; more harm than good ② harmful; destructive; injurious: 害鸟 hàiniǎo ③ do harm to; impair; cause trouble to: 你把地址搞错了，～得我白

跑一趟。You gave me the wrong address and made me go all that way for nothing. ④ kill; murder: 遇害 yùhài ⑤ contract (an illness); suffer from: 害病 hàibìng ⑥ feel (ashamed, afraid, etc.): 害羞 hàixiū

害病 hàibìng　fall ill: 害了一场大病 have been seriously ill

害虫 hàichóng　injurious (or destructive) insect; pest

害处 hàichu　harm: 吸烟过多对身体有~。Excessive smoking is harmful to one's health. / 田鼠对庄稼~很大。Field mice can do a lot of damage to crops.

害肚子 hàidùzi　dial. suffer from diarrhoea; have loose bowels

害口 hàikǒu　dial. suffer from morning sickness

害命 hàimìng　murder

害鸟 hàiniǎo　harmful (or destructive) bird

害怕 hàipà　be afraid; be scared: 没有什么可~的。There's nothing to be afraid of. / ~得要命 be scared to death; be mortally afraid

害群之马 hài qún zhī mǎ　an evil member of the herd; one who brings disgrace on his group; a black sheep

害人不浅 hài rén bù qiǎn　no small harm is done; do people great harm

害人虫 hàirénchóng　an evil creature; pest; vermin

害臊 hàisào　inf. feel ashamed; be bashful; be shy: 替他~ be ashamed of him / 真不~。You've got some nerve!

害兽 hàishòu　harmful (or destructive) animal

害喜 hàixǐ　suffer from morning sickness

害羞 hàixiū　be bashful; be shy: 她是第一次当众讲话,有些~。This was the first time she had spoken before many people, so she was a bit shy.

害眼 hàiyǎn　have eye trouble

害月子 hàiyuèzi　dial. suffer from morning sickness

氦 hài　chem. helium (He)

嗐 hài　interj. (expressing regret or sadness): ~,想不到他病得这么重。Oh, I didn't know he was so seriously ill.

hān

猂 hān　dial. elk; moose

顸 hān　dial. thick: 这线太~了,有细的吗? This thread is too thick. Have you got anything finer? / 他的胳膊真~。He has thick and muscular arms.

蚶 hān　zool. blood clam

蚶子 hānzi　zool. blood clam

酣 hān　(drink, etc.) to one's heart's content: ~歌 sing to one's heart's content

酣畅 hānchàng　① merry and lively (with drinking) ② sound (sleep) ③ with ease and verve; fully: 笔墨~ write with ease and verve

酣畅淋漓 hānchàng línlí　heartily; to one's heart's content: 这首诗~地抒发了作者的革命豪情。This poem fully expresses the author's revolutionary fervour.

酣梦 hānmèng　a sweet dream

酣眠 hānmián　sleep soundly; be fast asleep

酣然 hānrán　① merrily (drunk) ② sound (asleep)

酣熟 hānshú　sleep soundly

酣睡 hānshuì　sleep soundly; be fast asleep: 闹钟的响声将我从~中惊醒。The alarm clock roused me from my deep sleep.

酣甜 hāntián　(of sleep or dream) sweet: 睡得很~ have a sweet sleep

酣饮 hānyǐn　drink to the full; carouse

酣战 hānzhàn　hard-fought battle: 两军~ two armies locked in fierce battle

酣醉 hānzuì　be dead drunk

憨 hān　① foolish; silly: 憨痴 hānchī ② straightforward; naive; ingenuous: 憨直 hānzhí

憨痴 hānchī　idiotic

憨厚 hān·hòu　straightforward and good-natured; simple and honest

憨实 hānshí　simple and honest; straightforward and good-natured

憨态可掬 hāntài kě jū　charmingly naive

憨笑 hānxiào　smile fatuously; simper

憨直 hānzhí　honest and straightforward: 为人~ be honest and straightforward towards others

憨子 hānzi　dial. fool; blockhead; simpleton

鼾 hān　snore: 打鼾 dǎhān

鼾声 hānshēng　sound of snoring: 从屋里传来连续不断的~。The continuous sound of snoring was heard from the room.

鼾声如雷 hānshēng rú léi　snore thunderously

鼾睡 hānshuì　sound, snoring sleep

hán

汗 hán　see 可汗 kèhán ——see also hàn

含 hán　① keep in the mouth: 嘴里~着止咳糖 with a cough drop in one's mouth / 此丸宜~服。This pill is to be sucked, not swallowed. ② contain: ~多种矿物 contain several kinds of minerals / ~泪 with tears in one's eyes / ~硫污水 sulphur bearing waste water / 这种梨~的水分很多。These pears are very juicy. / ~沙量 silt content ③ nurse; cherish; harbour: 含恨 hánhèn

含苞 hánbāo　formal in bud

含苞待放 hánbāo dài fàng　a bud just ready to burst

含垢忍辱 hángòu-rěnrǔ　endure contempt and insults; bear shame and humiliation

含恨 hánhèn　nurse a grievance or hatred

含糊 hánhu　(also 含胡 hánhú) ① ambiguous; vague: 他的话很~,不明白是什么意思。He was rather vague. I don't know what he really meant. / 他含糊糊地说了半天,也没说清。He talked on and on beating about the bush and never made himself clear. / 在原则问题上不能~。One must not be vague on matters of principle. ② careless; perfunctory: 这事一点儿也不能~。We'll have to handle the matter with meticulous care. ③ see 不含糊 bùhánhu

含糊其词 hánhu qí cí　talk ambiguously; equivocate: ~的答复 an equivocally worded reply

含混 hánhùn　indistinct; ambiguous: 言词~,令人费解 speak so ambiguously as to be barely intelligible / 发音~不清 unclear articulation

含量 hánliàng　content: 牛奶的乳糖~ the lactose content of the milk

含怒 hánnù　be in anger

含情脉脉 hánqíng mòmò　(soft eyes) exuding tenderness and love

含沙射影 hán shā shè yǐng　innuendo; insinuations: 采用~的卑劣手法 resort to insinuation / ~,恶语中伤 vilify sb. by insinuation

含漱剂 hánshùjì　pharm. gargle

含水 hánshuǐ　containing water or moisture

含水层 hánshuǐcéng *geol.* water-bearing stratum; aquifer

含水率 hánshuǐlǜ moisture content

含笑 hánxiào have a smile on one's face: ～点头 nod with a smile

含辛茹苦 hánxīn-rúkǔ endure suffering; bear hardships

含羞 hánxiū with a shy look; bashfully

含羞草 hánxiūcǎo *bot.* sensitive plant

含蓄 hánxù ① contain; embody ② implicit; veiled: ～的批评 implicit criticism / 这首诗简短而～。The poem is brief and pregnant with meaning. ③ reserved: 他是个很～的人。He is a very reserved person.

含血喷人 hán xuè pēn rén make slanderous accusations; make vicious attacks

含饴弄孙 hán yí nòng sūn play with grandchildren with candy in mouth—enjoy happy old age

含义 hányì meaning; implication: 这个词用在不同场合有不同的～。The meaning of this word varies with different contexts. / 这句话～深刻。This remark has profound implications.

含英咀华 hányīng-jǔhuá relish the joys of literature

含油层 hányóucéng *petroleum* oil-bearing formation (*or* stratum)

含冤 hányuān suffer a wrong: ～死去 die uncleared of a false charge

含怨 hányuàn bear a grudge; nurse a grievance

邯 hán short for 邯郸 Hándān, a city in Hebei Province

邯郸学步 Hándān xué bù learn the Handan walk—in trying to acquire a new trick, lose the ability one already has (from the parable in the Zhuang Zi《庄子》about the young boy of the state of Yan 燕, who went to Handan, capital of the state of Zhao 赵, to learn the Handan way of walking but who, before mastering what the Handan people had to teach him, forgot his own way of walking and had to crawl all the way back home)

函（圅） hán ① *formal* case; envelope: 镜～ a case for a mirror / 这部《全唐诗》分成十二～。This set of *Complete Tang Poems* is in twelve cases. ② letter: 来函 láihán

函大 hándà short for 函授大学 hánshòu dàxué

函电 hándiàn letters and cables

函牍 hándú *formal* letters; correspondence

函复 hánfù reply by letter; write a letter in reply

函告 hángào inform by letter

函购 hángòu purchase by mail; mail order: ～部 mail-order department

函件 hánjiàn letters; correspondence

函授 hánshòu teach by correspondence; give a correspondence course: ～部 correspondence department (of a school)

函授大学 hánshòu dàxué correspondence university

函授学校 hánshòu xuéxiào correspondence school

函数 hánshù *math.* function

函索 hánsuǒ request by letter: 备有目录，～即寄。A catalogue is available on request.

涵 hán ① contain: 海涵 hǎihán ② culvert: 桥涵 qiáohán

涵洞 hándòng culvert

涵管 hánguǎn ① pipes for making culverts ② pipe-shaped culvert

涵容 hánróng *formal pol.* excuse; forgive; bear with: 不周之处，尚望～。We hope you will excuse us if we have been a poor host.

涵蓄 hánxù same as 含蓄 hánxù

涵养 hányǎng ① ability to control oneself; self-restraint: 他从不发火，很有～。He has self-control and never loses his temper. ② conserve: 用造林来～水源 conserve water through afforestation

涵义 hányì same as 含义 hányì

涵闸 hánzhá culverts and water gates

焓 hán *phys.* enthalpy; total heat

琀 hán *archaeol.* a jade piece put in the mouth of the dead upon burial

寒 hán ① cold: ～夜 a cold night / 受了一点～ catch a slight cold ② tremble (with fear): 胆寒 dǎnhán ③ poor; needy: 贫寒 pínhán ④ *hum.* my: 寒舍 hánshè

寒痹 hánbì *Chin. med.* arthritis (aggravated by cold)

寒蝉 hánchán a cicada in cold weather (which can no longer make any noise or can only make a very low noise): ～凄切，对长亭晚，骤雨初歇。(柳永) A cold cicada sadly droning—I face the post-pavilion at twilight, When the shower has just stopped. ——see also 噤若寒蝉 jìn ruò hánchán

寒潮 háncháo *meteorol.* cold wave

寒碜 hánchen (also 寒伧 hánchen) *inf.* ① ugly; unsightly: 长得不～ not bad-looking / 穿得～死了 be distastefully dressed ② shabby; disgraceful: 这有什么～。There's nothing to be ashamed of. / 你说出这样的话来也不嫌～! Aren't you ashamed of yourself for saying such a thing? / 穷并不～。Being poor is no disgrace. / 你画得多好，相比之下，我画的就显得～了。Your beautiful drawing puts mine to shame. ③ ridicule; make fun of: 叫人～了一顿 be ridiculed by sb. / 不知道他这么说是赞赏她还是～她。I couldn't tell whether he was praising her or ridiculing her.

寒窗 hánchuāng a cold window—the difficulties of a poor student

寒带 hándài frigid zone

寒冬腊月 hándōng-làyuè severe winter; dead of winter

寒风 hánfēng cold wind: ～凛冽 a piercing wind / ～刺骨。The cold wind chilled one to the bone.

寒光 hánguāng ① pallid light (of the moon) ② dazzling gleam (of a sword)

寒悸 hánjì *dial.* shiver (with cold or fear)

寒假 hánjià winter vacation

寒噤 hánjìn shiver (with cold or fear): 他打了个～。A shiver ran over his body. *or* A chill shot through him.

寒荆 hánjīng *old hum.* my wife

寒苦 hánkǔ destitute; poverty-stricken

寒来暑往 hánlái-shǔwǎng as summer goes and winter comes—as time passes; with the passage of time

寒冷 hánlěng cold: 气候～。The climate is cold. / 一、二月是北京最～的月份。January and February are the coldest months in Beijing.

寒冽 hánliè *formal* cold; frigid: 雪后～。It was bitterly cold after the snow.

寒流 hánliú *meteorol.* cold current

寒露 Hánlù ① Cold Dew—the 17th of the 24 solar terms ② the day marking the beginning of the 17th solar term (Oct. 8 or 9, which sees the first leaves falling from the trees) ——see also 节气 jiéqì, 二十四节气 èrshí sì jiéqì

寒毛 hánmáo fine hair on the human body: 吓得我～直竖。My hair stood on end with fright.

寒门 hánmén *formal* ① a poor and humble family ② *hum.* my family

寒漠 hánmò *geog.* cold desert

寒气 hánqì cold air; cold draught; cold: ～逼人。There is a nip in the air.

寒峭 hánqiào *formal* chilly

寒秋 hánqiū　late autumn: 独立～, 湘江北去, 橘子洲头。(毛泽东) Alone I stand in the autumn cold On the tip of Orange Island, The Xiang flowing northward.

寒热 hánrè　*Chin. med.*　chills and fever: ～往来 alternating spells of fever and chill / 发～ have (*or* run) a fever; have (*or* run) a temperature

寒色 hánsè　cool colour

寒森森 hánsēnsēn　chilly

寒舍 hánshè　*hum.*　my humble home (*or* abode)

寒食 Hánshí　Cold Food Festival (the day before Qingming 清明 when people ate cold food only)

寒士 hánshì　*formal*　a poor scholar

寒暑 hánshǔ　① cold and heat ② winter and summer—a year: 经历了几十个～ after scores of years

寒暑表 hánshǔbiǎo　thermometer

寒丝丝 hánsīsī　a bit chilly

寒素 hánsù　*formal*　① impoverished; poor: 家世～ come of an impoverished (*or* poor) family ② poor people ③ simple; plain; crude

寒酸 hánsuān　(usu. of a poor scholar) shabby and miserable: 一副～相 look shabby and miserable

寒腿 hántuǐ　*inf.*　rheumatism in the legs

寒微 hánwēi　(also 寒贱 hánjiàn) of low station; of humble origin

寒武纪 Hánwǔjì　*geol.*　the Cambrian Period

寒心 hánxīn　① be bitterly disappointed: 令人～ bitterly disappointing ② be afraid; fear

寒暄 hánxuān　exchange of conventional greetings; exchange of amenities (*or* compliments): 他们～了几句就转入正题。After exchanging a few words of greetings they got down to business.

寒鸦 hányā　jackdaw

寒衣 hányī　winter clothing

寒意 hányì　a nip (*or* chill) in the air: 初春季节仍有～。It's spring but there's still a chill in the air.

寒战 hánzhàn　(also 寒颤 hánzhàn) shiver (with cold or fear): 迎面吹来一阵冷风, 她禁不住打了个～。She couldn't help shivering in the face of a gust of cold wind.

寒症 hánzhèng　*Chin. med.*　symptoms caused by cold factors (e. g. chill, slow pulse, etc.)

韩 (韓)
Hán　a surname

韩国 Hánguó　The Republic of Korea

hǎn

罕
hǎn　rarely; seldom: 希罕 xīhan

罕百理派 Hǎnbǎilǐpài　*Islam*　the Hanbalite school

罕觏 hǎngòu　*formal*　rarely seen

罕见 hǎnjiàn　seldom seen; rare: 一场～的洪水 an exceptionally serious flood

罕事 hǎnshì　a rare event

罕闻 hǎnwén　seldom heard of

罕物 hǎnwù　a rare thing: 拜送～ present sb. with a rare and valuable thing

罕有 hǎnyǒu　very rare

喊
hǎn　① shout; cry out; yell: ～口号 shout slogans / 把嗓子～哑了 shout oneself hoarse / "站住!"他大～一声。"Halt!" he cried. / ～救命 cry "Help! Help!" ② call (a person): 你走以前～他一声。Give him a shout before you go.

喊话 hǎnhuà　① propaganda directed to the enemy at the front line: 对敌人～ shout propaganda at enemy troops across the lines ② communicate by tele-equipment: 向团部～ establish radio contact with the regimental headquarters

喊叫 hǎnjiào　shout; cry out: 他疼得大声～。He screamed with pain.

喊门 hǎnmén　call at the door

喊嗓子 hǎn sǎngzi　① shout ② train (*or* exercise) one's voice (as opera singers do in an open space early in the morning)

喊冤叫屈 hǎnyuān-jiàoqū　cry out about one's grievances; complain loudly about an alleged injustice

铪
hǎn　*chem.*　hahnium (Ha)

hàn

汉¹ (漢)
Hàn　① the Han Dynasty (206 B.C.–A.D. 220) ② the Han nationality: 汉人 Hànrén ③ Chinese (language): ～英词典 a Chinese-English dictionary ④ (hàn) man: 老汉 lǎohàn / 大汉 dàhàn

汉² (漢)
hàn　the Milky Way: 银汉 yínhàn

汉白玉 hànbáiyù　white marble

汉堡包 hànbǎobāo　hamburger

汉奸 hànjiān　traitor (to China): ～卖国贼 traitor and collaborator

汉剧 hànjù　(also 汉调 hàndiào) Hubei opera

汉民 Hànmín　*inf.*　the Han nationality

汉人 Hànrén　① the Hans; the Han people ② people of the Han Dynasty

汉学 Hànxué　① the Han school of classical philology ② Sinology: ～家 Sinologist

汉语 Hànyǔ　Chinese (language)

汉语拼音方案 Hànyǔ Pīnyīn Fāng'àn　the Scheme for the Chinese Phonetic Alphabet

汉语拼音字母 Hànyǔ pīnyīn zìmǔ　the Chinese phonetic alphabet

汉字 Hànzì　Chinese character: ～改革 reform of Chinese characters / ～简化方案 the Scheme for Simplifying Chinese Characters / ～注音 phonetic annotation of Chinese characters

汉子 hànzi　① man; fellow ② *dial.*　husband

汉族 Hànzú　the Han nationality, China's main nationality, or the Hans, distributed all over the country

汗
hàn　sweat; perspiration: ～如雨下 dripping with perspiration ——see also hán

汗斑 hànbān　① sweat stain ② same as 花斑癣 huābānxuǎn

汗背心 hànbèixīn　sleeveless undershirt; vest; singlet

汗褂儿 hànguàr　*inf.*　undershirt

汗碱 hànjiǎn　sweat stain

汗脚 hànjiǎo　feet that sweat easily; sweaty feet

汗津津 hànjīnjīn　*dial.*　sweaty; moist with sweat

汗孔 hànkǒng　*physiol.*　pore

汗淋淋 hànlínlín　dripping with perspiration; soaked with sweat

汗流浃背 hàn liú jiā bèi　sweat streaming down and drenching one's back; soaked with sweat: 他大惊失色, ～。He turned pale with fright and sweat broke out all over his body.

汗马功劳 hàn mǎ gōngláo　① distinctions won in battle; war exploits: 立下了～ win glory in battle; perform deeds of valour in battle ② one's contributions in work; render great services: 她为女排夺得冠军立下了～。She distinguished herself in winning the championship for the woman's volleyball team.

汗漫 hànmàn　*formal*　wide-ranging; wide of the mark:

〜之言 a rambling talk

汗毛 hànmáo　fine hair on the human body

汗牛充栋 hàn niú chōng dòng　enough books to make the pack-ox sweat or to fill a house to the rafters—an immense collection of books

汗青 hànqīng　① sweating green bamboo strips—completion of a literary undertaking (reference to the ancient practice of drying green bamboo strips on the fire before writing on them) ② historical records; chronicles; annals: 人生自古谁无死，留取丹心照〜。(文天祥) Everyone must die, Let me but leave a loyal heart shining in the pages of history.

汗衫 hànshān　① undershirt; T-shirt ② *dial.* shirt

汗水 hànshuǐ　sweat (esp. in large amounts): 〜湿透了他的衣衫。His shirt was soaked through with sweat.

汗褟儿 hàntār　*dial.* singlet

汗腺 hànxiàn　sweat gland

汗颜 hànyán　*formal* blush with shame; feel deeply ashamed

汗液 hànyè　sweat; perspiration

汗珠子 hànzhūzi　beads of sweat

汗渍 hànzì　① sweat stain ② be soaked with sweat

扦[1] hàn　same as 捍 hàn

扦[2] hàn　see below

芞格 hàngé　*formal* mutually conflict: 〜不入 incompatible with; out of tune with

旱 hàn　① dry spell; drought: 庄稼都〜了。All the crops dried up. ② dryland: 旱稻 hàndào ③ on land: 旱路 hànlù

旱魃 hànbá　the demon of drought: 〜为虐。The demon of drought stalked the land. *or* There was a severe drought.

旱冰场 hànbīngchǎng　roller rink

旱冰鞋 hànbīngxié　roller skates

旱船 hànchuán　land boat, a model boat used as a stage prop in some folk dances

旱道 hàndào　*dial.* overland route

旱稻 hàndào　upland rice; dry rice

旱地 hàndì　nonirrigated farmland; dry land: 〜耕作 dry farming

旱季 hànjì　dry season

旱金莲 hànjīnlián　(also 旱莲花 hànliánhuā) *bot.* nasturtium

旱井 hànjǐng　① water-retention well ② dry well (used to store vegetables in winter)

旱涝保收 hàn-lào bǎo shōu　ensure stable yields despite drought or excessive rain

旱柳 hànliǔ　dryland willow (*salix matsudana*)

旱路 hànlù　overland route: 走〜 travel by land

旱年 hànnián　year of drought

旱桥 hànqiáo　viaduct; overpass; flyover

旱情 hànqíng　damage to crops by drought; ravages of a drought: 〜严重 be afflicted with a severe drought / 〜缓和了。The drought has become less serious.

旱伞 hànsǎn　*dial.* parasol

旱生动物 hànshēng dòngwù　xerophilous animal

旱生植物 hànshēng zhíwù　xerophyte

旱獭 hàntǎ　marmot

旱田 hàntián　dry farmland; dry land

旱象 hànxiàng　signs of drought: 普降喜雨，〜解除。A welcome rain fell, ending all signs of drought.

旱鸭子 hànyāzi　① ducks raised on dry land as opposed to ducks raised by rivers and ponds ② non-swimmer

旱烟 hànyān　tobacco (smoked in a long-stemmed Chinese pipe): 〜袋 long-stemmed Chinese pipe

旱灾 hànzāi　drought

悍 hàn　① brave; bold: 一员〜将 a brave warrior ② fierce; ferocious: 凶悍 xiōnghàn

悍妇 hànfù　a shrewish woman; shrew

悍然 hànrán　outrageously; brazenly; flagrantly: 〜入侵 outrageously invade / 〜撕毁协议 flagrantly scrap an agreement

悍然不顾 hànrán bù gù　in flagrant disregard of; in defiance of: 〜人民群众的反对 in flagrant disregard of the opposition of the masses / 〜世界舆论的谴责 in defiance of condemnation by world public opinion

捍(扞) hàn　defend; guard: 捍卫 hànwèi

捍蔽 hànbì　*formal* protect; guard

捍拒 hànjù　*formal* resist; fight back

捍卫 hànwèi　defend; guard; protect: 〜祖国 defend one's motherland / 〜国家主权 uphold state sovereignty / 〜民族经济权益 protect national economic rights and interests

捍御 hànyù　*formal* defend; guard; protect

焊(銲、釬) hàn　weld; solder: 把断了的车轴〜起来 weld the pieces of the broken axle

焊缝 hànfèng　welding seam; weld line

焊工 hàngōng　① welding; soldering ② welder; solderer

焊接 hànjiē　weld; solder: 电弧〜 (electric) arc welding / 〜钢管 welded steel pipe

焊料 hànliào　solder

焊枪 hànqiāng　welding torch; (welding) blowpipe

焊条 hàntiáo　welding rod

焊锡 hànxī　soldering tin; tin solder

焊液 hànyè　welding fluid; soldering fluid

焊油 hànyóu　soldering paste

菡 hàn　see below

菡萏 hàndàn　*formal* lotus

颔 hàn　*formal* ① chin ② nod

颔首 hànshǒu　*formal* nod: 〜微笑 nod smilingly / 〜致意 nod in greeting

憾 hàn　regret: 死而无〜 die without regret

憾事 hànshì　a matter for regret: 行前未及告别，至今引为〜。I didn't find time to say good-bye to you before I left. I regret it to this day.

撼 hàn　shake: 摇撼 yáohàn / 震撼 zhènhàn

撼动 hàndòng　shake; vibrate

撼天动地 hàntiān-dòngdì　shake heaven and earth

翰 hàn　*formal* ① writing brush: 挥翰 huīhàn ② writing: 华翰 huáhàn

翰林 hànlín　member of the Imperial Academy

翰林院 hànlínyuàn　the Imperial Academy (in feudal China)

翰墨 hànmò　*formal* brush and ink—writing, painting, or calligraphy: 少陵〜无形画，韩干丹青不语诗。(苏轼) Shaoling's writings are pictures without forms; Han Gan's paintings are unspoken poems.

瀚 hàn　*formal* vast: 浩瀚 hàohàn

瀚海 hànhǎi　*formal* big desert

hāng

夯(砼) hāng　① rammer; tamper ② ram; tamp; pound: 把土〜实 ram the earth ③ *dial.* strike

heavily ④ *dial.* carry sth. heavy on one's shoulder

夯歌　hānggē　rammers' work chant

夯具　hāngjù　rammer; tamper

夯土机　hāngtǔjī　rammer; tamper

háng

行　háng　① line; row: 第三～ the third line／排成两～ fall into two lines／杨柳成～ lined with rows of willows ② seniority among brothers and sisters: 你～几？—我～三。Where do you come among your brothers and sisters? —I'm the third. ③ trade; profession; line of business: 他干哪～? What's his line? ／干一～爱一～ love whatever job one takes up ④ business firm: 拍卖行 pāimàiháng／银行 yínháng ⑤ *m.*: 一～树 a row of trees／四～诗句 four lines of verse ——see also xíng

行帮　hángbāng　*old* trade association

行辈　hángbèi　seniority in the family or clan; position in the family hierarchy: 他～比我大。He ranks as my senior in the clan.

行车　hángchē　*dial.* overhead travelling crane; shop traveller

行当　hángdang　① *inf.* trade; profession; line of business: 干我们这个～, 吃不得苦可不行。People of our profession must endure a lot of hardships. ② type of role (in traditional Chinese operas)

行道　hángdao　*dial.* trade; profession

行东　hángdōng　owner of a trading company or a workshop

行贩　hángfàn　pedlar

行规　hángguī　*old* guild regulations

行行出状元　hángháng chū zhuàngyuán　every profession produces its own leading authority

行话　hánghuà　professional jargon; cant

行会　hánghuì　*old* guild: ～制度 the guild system

行货　hánghuò　crudely-made articles

行纪　hángjì　*old* ① middleman ② broker house

行家　hángjia　① expert; connoisseur: 老～ an old hand ② *dial.* (used in the affirmative) be expert at sth.: 你对吃挺～嘛! You are quite a connoisseur of food!

行间　hángjiān　① *formal* in the ranks ② between lines: 字里行间 zìlǐ-hángjiān ③ between rows: 栽种向日葵～的距离要宽。Leave a wide space between the rows when planting sunflowers.

行距　hángjù　*agric.* row spacing

行款　hángkuǎn　form and arrangement of lines in calligraphy or printing; make-up

行列　hángliè　ranks: 排成整齐的～ be drawn up in orderly ranks／参加革命～ join the ranks of the revolution

行列式　hánglièshì　*math.* determinant

行频　hángpín　*TV* line frequency

行情　hángqíng　quotations (on the market); prices: ～见涨。A rising market is expected.

行情表　hángqíngbiǎo　quotations list

行市　hángshi　quotations (on the market); prices: 一天一个～。The prices change from day to day.

行手　hángshǒu　*dial.* expert; connoisseur

行伍　hángwǔ　*old* the ranks: ～出身 rise from the ranks／投身～ join the army

行业　hángyè　trade; profession; industry

行业语　hángyèyǔ　professional jargon; cant

行佣　hángyòng　*dial.* commission; brokerage; middleman's fee

行院　hángyuàn　houses of prostitutes or actresses in the Jin and Yuan Dynasties

行栈　hángzhàn　broker's storehouse

行长　hángzhǎng　president (of a bank)

吭　háng　throat: 引吭高歌 yǐn háng gāo gē ——see also kēng

杭　Háng　① short for 杭州 Hángzhōu ② a surname

杭纺　hángfǎng　a silk fabric produced in Hangzhou

杭育　hángyō　*interj.* heave ho; yo-heave-ho; yo-ho: 拉纤的船夫在河岸上一步步挣扎着前进, 一面有节奏地齐声哼着"～! ～!" As they inched forward, step by step, on the banks of the river, the boat-pullers kept up a constant rhythmical "Heave ho! Heave ho!"

杭州　Hángzhōu　Hangzhou (capital of Zhejiang Province)

珩　háng　see below ——see also héng

珩床　hángchuáng　*mech.* honing machine

珩磨　hángmó　*mech.* honing

绗　háng　sew with long stitches: ～被子 sew on the quilt cover with long stitches

航　háng　① boat; ship ② navigate (by water or air): 民航 mínháng／首航 shǒuháng

航班　hángbān　scheduled flight; flight number

航标　hángbiāo　navigation mark

航测　hángcè　short for 航空测量 hángkōng cèliáng

航程　hángchéng　voyage; passage; range: ～记录器 odograph

航船　hángchuán　boat that plies regularly between inland towns

航次　hángcì　① the sequence of voyages or flights; voyage or flight number ② the number of voyages or flights made

航道　hángdào　channel; lane; course: 主～ the main channel

航海　hánghǎi　navigation: ～仪器 nautical instrument／～用语 nautical term

航海法规　hánghǎi fǎguī　navigation law

航海罗盘　hánghǎi luópán　mariner's compass

航海日志　hánghǎi rìzhì　logbook; log

航海天文历　hánghǎi tiānwénlì　nautical almanac

航海天文学　hánghǎi tiānwénxué　nautical astronomy

航迹　hángjì　*aviation* flight path; track

航空　hángkōng　aviation: ～发动机 aero-engine; aircraft engine／～工程 aeronautical engineering／～货运 airfreight／～机械员 aircraft mechanic／～联运 through air transport／～汽油 aviation gasoline／～器材 air material／～燃料 aviation (or aircraft) fuel／～通信 air communications／～运输 air transportation

航空版　hángkōngbǎn　airmail edition

航空保险　hángkōng bǎoxiǎn　aviation insurance

航空标塔　hángkōng biāotǎ　airway beacon

航空兵　hángkōngbīng　① air arm ② airman: ～部队 air unit

航空病　hángkōngbìng　airsickness

航空测量　hángkōng cèliáng　aerial survey

航空磁测　hángkōng cícè　aeromagnetic survey

航空地图　hángkōng dìtú　aeronautical chart; aerial map

航空电子学　hángkōng diànzǐxué　avionics

航空法　hángkōngfǎ　air law

航空港　hángkōnggǎng　air harbour

航空公司　hángkōng gōngsī　airline company; airways

航空力学　hángkōng lìxué　aeromechanics

航空模型　hángkōng móxíng　model airplane

航空母舰 hángkōngmǔjiàn aircraft carrier
航空气象台 hángkōng qìxiàngtái air weather station; aeronautical meteorological station
航空气象学 hángkōng qìxiàngxué aeronautical meteorology
航空器 hángkōngqì air vehicle; aircraft
航空日志 hángkōng rìzhì aircraft logbook
航空探矿 hángkōng tànkuàng mineral exploration aviation; aerial prospecting
航空体育运动 hángkōng tǐyù yùndòng air sports; flying sports
航空天文历 hángkōng tiānwénlì air almanac
航空协定 hángkōng xiédìng air transport agreement
航空信 hángkōngxìn airmail letter; air letter; airmail
航空学 hángkōngxué aeronautics; aviation
航空学校 hángkōng xuéxiào aviation (or flying) school
航空学院 hángkōng xuéyuàn aeronautical engineering institute
航空照相 hángkōng zhàoxiàng aerial photography: ～机 aerocamera; aerial camera
航路 hánglù air or sea route: ～标志 route markings
航模 hángmó ① short for 航空模型 hángkōng móxíng ② model of a ship
航速 hángsù speed of a ship or plane
航天 hángtiān spaceflight: ～技术 space technology / ～通信 space communication (SPACECOM)
航天舱 hángtiāncāng space capsule
航天飞机 hángtiān fēijī space shuttle
航天器 hángtiānqì spacecraft; space vehicle
航天站 hángtiānzhàn spaceport
航图 hángtú chart
航务 hángwù navigational matters
航线 hángxiàn air or shipping line; route; course: 内河～ inland navigation line
航向 hángxiàng course (of a ship or plane): 改变～ change course / ～指示器 direction (or heading) indicator
航行 hángxíng ① navigate by water; sail: 内河～ inland navigation ② navigate by air; fly: 空中～ aerial navigation
航行半径 hángxíng bànjìng navigation radius
航行灯 hángxíngdēng navigation light
航行权 hángxíngquán right of navigation
航运 hángyùn shipping
航运保险 hángyùn bǎoxiǎn shipping insurance
航运公司 hángyùn gōngsī shipping company

颃
háng see 颉颃 xiéháng

hàng

沆
hàng formal a vast expanse of water
沆瀣 hàngxiè formal evening mist
沆瀣一气 hàngxiè yī qì ① be congenial to each other ② act in collusion with; wallow in the mire with

巷
hàng tunnel ——see also xiàng
巷道 hàngdào min. tunnel: ～掘进机 tunnelling machine

hāo

蒿
hāo wormwood artemisia

蒿莱 hāolái overgrowth of weeds
蒿目 hāomù gaze into the distance
蒿目时艰 hāomù shíjiān watch the country's ills with deep concern
蒿子 hāozi wormwood; artemisia
蒿子杆儿 hāozigǎnr crown daisy chrysanthemum (as a vegetable)

薅
hāo ① pull up (weeds, etc.) ② dial. pull; tug; drag
薅草 hāocǎo weeding
薅锄 hāochú weeding hoe

嚆
hāo see below
嚆矢 hāoshǐ formal ① an arrow with a whistle attached ② forerunner; harbinger; precursor

háo

号(號)
háo ① howl; yell: 怒号 nùháo ② wail: 哀号 āiháo ——see also hào
号叫 háojiào howl; yell: 他疼得～起来。He yelled (or cried out) with pain. / 救火车～着开来了。The fire engine came with its siren screaming.
号哭 háokū wail: 一个妇女在一座墓前～。A woman was weeping and wailing at a grave.
号丧 háosāng howl at a funeral
号丧 háosang dial. offens. howl as if at a funeral
号啕 háotáo (also 号咷 háotáo) cry loudly; wail: ～大哭 cry loudly; weep and wail

蚝(蠔)
háo oyster
蚝豉 háochǐ dried oyster meat
蚝油 háoyóu oyster sauce

毫
háo ① fine long hair: 羊毫笔 yánghǎobǐ ② writing brush: 挥毫 huīháo ③ one of the two or three loops on a steelyard for hanging from the user's hand: 头(二)～ first (second) loop ④ adv. (used in the negative) in the least; at all: ～不足怪 not at all surprising / ～不动摇 not waver in the least; be unswerving / ～无道理 utterly unjustifiable; for no reason whatsoever / ～无顾虑 free from all inhibitions ⑤ milli-: 毫米 háomǐ ⑥ hao, a unit of length (= 1/3 decimillimetre) ⑦ hao, a unit of weight (= 0.005 grams) ⑧ dial. same as 角 jiǎo⑦
毫安 háo'ān elec. milliampere: ～表 milliammeter
毫巴 háobā meteorol. millibar
毫不利己，专门利人 háo bù lì jǐ, zhuānmén lì rén utter devotion to others without any thought of self
毫法 háofǎ elec. millifarad
毫发 háofà formal (usu. used in the negative) a hair; the least bit; the slightest: ～不差 not deviate a hair's breadth; be perfectly accurate
毫发不爽 háofà bù shuǎng not deviating a hair's breadth; without the slightest error
毫伏 háofú elec. millivolt: ～计 millivoltmeter
毫克 háokè milligram (mg.)
毫厘 háolí the least bit; an iota: ～不差 without the slightest error; just right
毫毛 háomáo soft hair on the body: 那些诬蔑无损于我们一根～。Those slanders can't harm a single hair of our head. / 谁敢动他一根～? Who would dare touch a hair of his?
毫米 háomǐ millimetre (mm.): ～波 millimetre wave
毫秒 háomiǎo millisecond
毫末 háomò formal the tip of a hair——an extremely

small thing ——see also 合抱之木, 生于毫末 hébào zhī mù, shēng yú háomò

毫升 háoshēng　millilitre (ml.)

毫微法 háowēifǎ　*elec.*　millimicrofarad

毫微米 háowēimǐ　millimicron (m μ)

毫微秒 háowēimiǎo　nanosecond; millimicrosecond

毫无二致 háo wú èr zhì　without the slightest difference; just the same; identical: 在这一点上, 他们～。On this point they are entirely at one.

毫洋 háoyáng　formerly the basic monetary unit of Guangdong and Guangxi Provinces

毫针 háozhēn　filiform needle in acupuncture; acupuncture needle

毫子 háozi　① a former silver coin of Guangdong and Guangxi Provinces (in denominations of 1, 2, and 5 *jiao*) ② same as 毫 háo⑥⑦

嗥（嘷） háo　(of a jackal or wolf) howl

貉 háo　see below ——see also hé

貉绒 háoróng　racoon dog fur

貉子 háozi　racoon dog

豪 háo　① a person of extraordinary powers or endowments: 文豪 wénháo ② bold and unconstrained; forthright; unrestrained: 豪迈 háomài ③ despotic; bullying: 土豪 tǔháo

豪宕 háodàng　*formal*　bold and unconstrained

豪夺 háoduó　secure (sb.'s belongings, right, etc.) by force ——see also 巧取豪夺 qiǎoqǔ-háoduó

豪放 háofàng　① bold and unconstrained: 性情～ a bold and uninhibited character ② powerful and free (said of a vigorous and sprightly style of the *ci*, such as is characteristic of Su Shi 苏轼 and Xin Qiji 辛弃疾): 苏轼创立了与传统的婉约词派相对立的～派。Su Shi founded the powerful and free school of *ci* writing as opposed to the traditional subtle and concise school.

豪放不羁 háofàng bùjī　bold and uninhibited

豪富 háofù　① powerful and wealthy ② the rich and powerful

豪贵 háoguì　① powerful and wealthy ② the rich and powerful

豪横 háohèng　despotic; bullying

豪横 háoheng　*dial.*　firm; staunch; unyielding

豪华 háohuá　luxurious; sumptuous; splendid: ～的生活 a life of luxury; luxurious living / ～的住宅 a magnificent house / ～的陈设 sumptuous furnishings / ～的饭店 a luxury hotel / ～型汽车 a de luxe model of a car

豪杰 háojié　person of exceptional ability; hero: 江山如画, 一时多少～!（苏轼）The River and the mountains make a vivid picture——What a host of heroes once were!

豪举 háojǔ　① a bold move ② a munificent act

豪客 háokè　*formal*　robber; bandit

豪兰岛和贝克岛 Háolándǎo hé Bèikèdǎo　Howland Island and Baker Island

豪迈 háomài　bold and generous; heroic: ～的誓言 a bold pledge / ～的气概 heroic spirit / ～地说 say with pride / 以～的步伐跨入新的一年 stride into the new year with pride and confidence / 李白才气～, 全以神运。Li Bai's talent is bold and unrestrained, impelled entirely by the spirit.

豪门 háomén　rich and powerful family; wealthy and influential clan: ～大族 powerful families and great clans / ～子弟 sons of the rich

豪奴 háonú　a servant of a powerful family who takes advantage of his master's power to bully people

豪气 háoqì　heroism; heroic spirit

豪强 háoqiáng　① despotic; tyrannical ② despot; bully

豪情 háoqíng　lofty sentiments

豪情满怀 háoqíng mǎnhuái　full of pride and enthusiasm; full of spirit

豪情壮志 háoqíng-zhuàngzhì　lofty sentiments and high aspirations

豪商 háoshāng　a wealthy and powerful merchant

豪绅 háoshēn　despotic gentry

豪爽 háoshuǎng　bold and uninhibited

豪侠 háoxiá　① gallant ② a gallant man

豪兴 háoxìng　exuberant spirits; exhilaration; keen interest: 虽到老年, 他仍吟诗作画, ～不减。As an old man, he continued to compose verses and paint pictures, his exuberant spirits undiminished.

豪言壮语 háoyán-zhuàngyǔ　brave words; proud words

豪饮 háoyǐn　drink with abandon; drink heavily

豪雨 háoyǔ　torrential rain

豪语 háoyǔ　brave words; bold promise

豪猪 háozhū　porcupine

豪壮 háozhuàng　grand and heroic: ～的事业 a grand and heroic cause / ～的声音 a firm, strong voice

壕（濠） háo　① moat: 城壕 chéngháo ② trench: 防空壕 fángkōngháo

壕沟 háogōu　① *mil.*　trench ② ditch

壕堑 háoqiàn　same as 堑壕 qiànháo

嚎 háo　① howl: 一声长～ give a long howl ② same as 号 háo②

嚎啕 háotáo　(also 嚎咷 háotáo) same as 号啕 háotáo

hǎo

好 hǎo　① good; fine; nice: ～人 a nice person / 天气真～。The weather's really nice. / 祖国的～儿子 a worthy (*or* fine) son of our country / 庄稼长得真～。The crops are doing well. ② friendly; kind: ～朋友 a good (*or* great) friend / 他们对我真～。They are really kind to me. / 这两个孩子又～了。The two children are friends again. ③ be in good health; get well: 我的病～了。I'm well (*or* all right) now. / 你～哇! How are you? ④ be ready; done: 饭～了。The food (*or* rice) is ready. ⑤ (used after verbs to indicate finishing or finishing satisfactorily): 这件事他做不～。He can't do that job well. / 我把他的病治～了。I cured his illness. / 坐～吧, 要开会了。Take your seats, please. The meeting is going to begin. ⑥ *adv.*　(used before verbs) be good to; be easy to: ～喝 good to drink / 这个问题～回答。This question is easy to answer. / 这本书可不～买。This book is not easily available. / 暖瓶放在这儿～拿。It's handy to have the thermos here. ⑦ *interj.*　(used at the beginning of a sentence or clause, to express agreement, disapproval, surprise, etc.): ～, 就这么办。O.K., it's settled. / ～了, 不要再说了。All right, no need to say any more. / ～, 这下可麻烦了。Well, we're in for trouble now. / ～! 那得多少钱! Gosh! How much money will that cost! / 我一看, ～, 都走了。I took a look, gosh, everybody has left. ⑧ *adv.*　the better to; in order to; so that: 今儿早点睡, 明儿～早起赶火车。Let's turn in early, so as to get up early tomorrow to catch the train. / 把她的地址告诉我, 我～找她。Tell me her address so that I can go and see her. ⑨ *adv.*　(used before adjectives with exclamatory force) very; quite; so: 今天～冷。Today is quite cold. / 你～大胆子! You are so daring. / ～大的工程! What a huge project! ⑩ *adv.*　(used before adjectives in the same way as 多) to what extent; how: 火车站离这儿～远? How far is the railway station from here? ⑪ *adv.*　(used before

indefinite numbers) quite a few: ～几个 quite a few／～几天 quite a few days／～半天 quite a while ⑫ *dial.* may; can; should: 我～进来吗? May I come in?／时间不早了，你～走了。It's getting late. You ought to get going. ——see also hào

好儿 hǎor *inf.* ① favour; kindness: 人家过去对咱有过～，咱不能忘恩负义。They have been kind to us, and we must be grateful to them. ② benefit; advantage: 这事要是让他知道了，还会有你的～? If he gets to know about it, you'll get into trouble, won't you? ③ good wishes; regards: 见着你母亲，给我带个～。Give my regards to your mother.

好办 hǎobàn easy to handle: 这事不～。This is no easy matter. *or* This is rather a headache.／这件事～。That can be easily arranged.

好比 hǎobǐ can be compared to; may be likened to; be just like: 军民关系～鱼和水的关系。The relationship between the army and the people is like that between fish and water. *or* The people are to the army what water is to fish.

好不 hǎobù *adv.* (used with exclamatory force) very; quite; so: 人来人往，～热闹! What a busy place, with so many people coming and going.／他们见了面，～欢喜。How happy they were to see each other.

好不容易 hǎobùróngyi (also 好容易 hǎoróngyi) not at all easy; very difficult: 你～来一次，多待一会儿再走。It's not at all easy for you to come. Stay a little longer before you go.／这本书我～才买到。I just managed to get hold of a copy of this book.／他们～才找到我这儿。They had a hard tfme trying to find my place.

好丑 hǎochǒu *dial.* ① good and bad; what's good and what's bad: 不识～ can't tell good from bad; not know what's good for one ② in any case; at any rate; anyhow: 不管发生了什么事，你～得去一趟。You've got to go there, whatever happens.

好处 hǎochu ① good; benefit; advantage: 计划生育～多。Family planning has many advantages.／你每天做点户外运动会有～。Some outdoor exercises every day will do you good. ② gain; profit: 他从这里捞不到任何～。He can gain nothing from this.／别上他的当! 他给你这点～是为了拉拢你。Don't fall into his trap. He's given you this to win you over.

好处费 hǎochufèi pickings

好歹 hǎodǎi ① (hǎo-dǎi) good and bad; what's good and what's bad: 不知好歹 bù zhī hǎo-dǎi ② mishap; disaster: 万一她有个～，这可怎么办? What if something should happen to her? ③ *adv.* in any case; at any rate; anyhow: ～试试看。Let's try, anyhow.／他要是在这里，～也能拿主意。If he were here he would give us some advice. ④ *adv.* no matter in what way; anyhow: 别再做什么了，～吃点儿就得了。Don't cook us anything more. We'll have whatever there is.

好端端 hǎoduānduān in perfectly good condition; when everything is all right: ～的，怎么生起气来了? Why are you angry when everything is perfectly all right?／～的一个图书馆搞得乱七八糟! A smooth-running library thrown out of gear!

好多 hǎoduō ① a good many; a good deal; a lot of: 还有～问题没解决。There are still lots of problems to be solved.／她上街买了～东西。She went shopping and bought quite a few things. ② *dial.* how many; how much: 今天到会的人有～? How many came to the meeting today?

好感 hǎogǎn good opinion; favourable impression: 对他有～ be well disposed towards him; have a good opinion of him／给人～ make a good impression on people

好钢用在刀刃上 hǎogāng yòng zài dāorènshang use the best steel to make the knife's edge—use material where it is needed most; use the best material at the key point

好过 hǎoguò ① have an easy time; be in easy circumstances: 这几年她家的日子越来越～了。Her family have had an easier and easier time these last few years.／日子很不～ have a very hard time ② feel well: 他吃了药，觉得～一点儿了。He felt a bit better after taking the medicine.

好汉 hǎohàn brave man; true man; hero

好汉不吃眼前亏 hǎohàn bù chī yǎnqiánkuī a wise man will not fight when the odds are obviously against him; a wise man doesn't fight against impossible odds: 别惹他们。这一帮人不好惹，～。Don't get on the wrong side of them. People like that can be nasty if you annoy them. Only a fool goes looking for trouble.

好汉不提当年勇 hǎohàn bù tí dāngniányǒng a hero is silent about his past glories

好汉做事好汉当 hǎohàn zuòshì hǎohàn dāng a true man has the courage to accept the consequences of his own actions: ～，我死就死，决不连累旁人! Come what may, I'll brace myself and face the music. I'd rather die than implicate others!

好好儿 hǎohāor ① in perfectly good condition; when everything is all right: 电话刚才还是～的，怎么就坏了? Why isn't the phone working now? It was all right a moment ago.／他的一支笔，叫他给弄折了。He broke a perfectly good pen.／那棵百年的老树，至今还长得～的。That hundred-year-old tree is still growing well.／你～地跟他说，别生气。Talk to him nicely. Don't get angry. ② all out; to one's heart's content: ～想一想。Think it over carefully.／把这房间～打扫一下。Give the room a thorough cleaning.／我得～谢谢他。I'll really have to thank him.／咱俩一聊一聊。Let's have a good talk.

好好先生 hǎohǎoxiānsheng one who tries not to offend anybody; Mr. Agreeable; Mr. Goody-goody

好话 hǎohuà ① a good word; word of praise: 给他说句～ put in a good word for him／不要听了一些～就沾沾自喜。Don't become complacent when you hear a few words of praise.／当领导的，～、坏话都要听。A leader should listen to unpleasant words as well as pleasant words. ② fine words

好话说尽，坏事做绝 hǎohuà shuōjìn, huàishì zuòjué say every fine word and do every foul deed

好几 hǎojǐ (a little more than 几 "several") ① (in addition to a multiple of ten) and quite a few: 她今年已经三十～了。She's well over thirty this year. ② (before a measure word, a time word, and the numerals 百, 千, 万, etc.) quite a few; a good few: 我已经去过～次了。I've already been there a good few times.／咱们～年没见了。We haven't seen each other for quite a few years.／昨天来了～百人。Several hundred people came yesterday.

好家伙 hǎojiāhuo *interj.* good god; good lord; good heavens: ～，他们一天足足走了一百里! Good lord, they walked a hundred *li* in a day!

好价 hǎojià a good (selling) price: 他卖猪仔得了个～，满心喜欢。He is quite satisfied with the good price he got for selling piglings.

好景不长 hǎojǐng bù cháng good times don't last long

好久 hǎojiǔ ① a long time: ～以前 a long time ago; long ago／～没见。I haven't seen you for a long time. ② *dial.* how long: 你学英语学了～了? How long have you been learning English?

好看 hǎokàn ① good-looking; nice: 这花布做裙子一定很～。This piece of cotton print would surely make a very beautiful skirt.／你戴那顶帽子很～。That hat looks nice on you. ② interesting: 这本小说很～。This novel is very interesting. ③ honoured; proud: 儿子立了功，我这做娘的脸上也～。My son has won distinction;

as his mother, I share the honour. ④ in an embarrassing situation; on the spot: 等着吧, 有他的～。You can be sure he'll soon find himself on the spot. / 让我上台表演, 这不是要我的～吗? Me, on the stage? Do you want me to make a fool of myself?

好赖 hǎolài same as 好歹 hǎodǎi①③④

好了疮疤忘了疼 hǎole chuāngbā wàngle téng forget the pain once the wound is healed—forget the bitter past when released from one's suffering

好脸 hǎoliǎn inf. (usu. used in the negative) a smiling face: 他一听我是问他借钱, 马上就没～给我看了。He pulled a long face as soon as he learnt I wanted to borrow money from him.

好男不跟女斗 hǎonán bù gēn nǚ dòu a gentleman doesn't fight women

好孬 hǎonāo dial. ① good and bad; what's good and what's bad ② in any case; whatever happens; at all events: 你既然来了, 我～也不能让你走。Now that you're here, I will on no account let you go.

好评 hǎopíng favourable comment; high opinion: 对他颇有～ have a rather high opinion of him / 博得读者～ be well received by the readers

好气儿 hǎoqìr inf. (usu. used in the negative) good humour; good temper: 老头儿一见儿子抽烟喝酒就没～。Seeing his son smoking and drinking would get the old man into a bad mood.

好球 hǎoqiú well played (or shot); good shot; bravo

好人 hǎorén ① a good (or fine) person: 他是个～。He's a good man. ② a healthy person: 他身体不好, 别把他当～使。He's in poor health; don't work him as you would a healthy person. ③ a soft person who tries to get along with everyone (often at the expense of principle): 她只想做个～, 连说句话也怕得罪人。She's out to please everyone, and she takes care that whatever she says offends no one.

好人好事 hǎorén-hǎoshì good people and good deeds; fine people and fine deeds

好人家 hǎorénjiā ① a decent family; a respectable family ② a woman from a respectable family; a respectable woman ③ dial. a wealthy family; a well-to-do family

好人主义 hǎorénzhǔyì seeking good relations with all and sundry at the expense of principle

好日子 hǎorìzi ① auspicious day: 他们拣个～开张。They chose an auspicious day to start the business. ② wedding day: 今天是他们的～。Today is their wedding day. ③ good days; happy life: 过～ live a happy life; live well; live in happiness

好商量 hǎoshāngliang can be settled through discussion: 这事～。That can be settled through discussion.

好生 hǎoshēng ① adv. quite; exceedingly: ～奇怪! What an exceedingly strange thing! / 这个人～面熟。That person looks quite familiar. ② dial. carefully; properly: ～想一想。Think it over carefully. / ～拿着。Mind how you carry it.

好声好气 hǎoshēng-hǎoqì inf. in a kindly manner; gently: 他说话从来不～, 总是板着脸训人。He never has a kind word for anyone, and is always pulling a long face and lecturing others.

好使 hǎoshǐ be convenient to use; work well: 这把剪刀不～。This pair of scissors doesn't work well. / 这架录音机很～。This tape recorder is very reliable. / 这支笔挺～。This pen writes very well. / 你脑子～。You have a quick mind.

好事 hǎoshì ① good deed; good turn: 为群众做～ do people good turns ② an act of charity; good works ③ formal happy event; joyous occasion ——see also hǎoshì

好事不出门, 恶事传千里 hǎoshì bù chūmén, èshì chuán qiānlǐ good news never goes beyond the gate, while bad news spreads far and wide

好事多磨 hǎoshì duō mó ① the road to happiness is strewn with setbacks ② the course of true love never did run smooth

好手 hǎoshǒu good hand; past master: 做针线活儿, 她可是把～。She is adept at needlework.

好受 hǎoshòu feel better; feel more comfortable: 我吃了药以后～多了。I felt much better after taking the medicine. / 白天太热, 夜里还～点。It's terribly hot during the day but a bit better at night. / 你别说了, 他心里正不～呢! Don't say anything more; he's feeling bad enough as it is.

好说 hǎoshuō ① pol. (used in answer to praises or thanks): ～, ～! 您太夸奖了。It's very good of you to say so, but I don't deserve such praise. or You flatter me. I wish I could deserve such compliments. ② no problem: 关于费用问题, ～。The expenses are no problem.

好说歹说 hǎoshuō-dǎishuō try every possible way to persuade sb.: 我～, 他总算答应了。He agreed, but only after I had pleaded with him in every way I could.

好说话儿 hǎoshuōhuàr good-natured; open to persuasion: 王大爷～, 求求他准行。Uncle Wang is very obliging. He's sure to help if you ask him.

好死 hǎosǐ natural death: 他这人不得～! May he die a violent death!

好死不如赖活 hǎosǐ bùrú làihuó even a good death is not like a wretched existence

好似 hǎosì seem; be like: 大坝～铜墙铁壁, 顶住了洪水的冲击。Like an iron bastion, the dam withstood the rushing floodwaters.

好天儿 hǎotiānr fine day; lovely weather: 这些衣服～要拿出去晒晒。These clothes should be put out to air on a sunny day. / 要是这些云散去, 下午就是～。If those clouds drift away, we'll have a fine afternoon.

好听 hǎotīng pleasant to hear: ～的话 fine words / 这支歌很～。This is a very pleasant song. / 他说的比唱的还～。His glib talk sounds as sweet as a song.

好玩儿 hǎowánr amusing; interesting: 颐和园～极了。The Summer Palace is a most delightful place. / 这小娃娃挺～。The baby is very cute. / 这可不是～的! This is no joking matter.

好闻 hǎowén smell good; smell sweet: 茉莉花挺～。Jasmine flowers smell sweet.

好戏 hǎoxì ① good play ② great fun (used sarcastically): 这回可有～看了! We're going to see some fun! / ～还在后头呢! The worst is yet to come!

好像 hǎoxiàng adv. seem; be like: ～要下雪。It looks like snow. / ～谁也没听见铃响。No one seems to have heard the bell. / 他们～是多年的老朋友了。They seem to have been close friends for many years. / 她们俩处得～亲姐妹一样。The two of them were as intimate as sisters. / 这个人我～是在哪儿见过。I seem to have met this man before.

好笑 hǎoxiào laughable; funny; ridiculous: 有什么～的? What's so funny? / 又好气又～ be annoying and amusing at the same time

好些个 hǎoxiēge (also 好些 hǎoxiē) quite a lot; a good deal of: 他有～朋友。He has quite a lot of friends.

好心 hǎoxīn good intention: 一片～ with the best of intentions / ～没好报 get no thanks for one's good intentions

好心当作驴肝肺 hǎoxīn dàngzuò lǘgānfèi take an honest man's heart for a donkey's liver and lungs—take sb.'s goodwill for ill intent

好性儿 hǎoxìngr good-natured

好样儿的 hǎoyàngrde inf. (of a man or woman) fine example; great fellow: 你们个个都抢重活儿干, 真是～!

Each one of you wanted to do the hardest job. That's the stuff! /是～，就站出来说吧! If you are man enough, come out with what you have to say!

好一个 hǎoyīge (also 好个 hǎoge) what a (used in praise or in condemnation): ～幽雅去处! What a quiet, elegant spot! /～投手，一人得了40分! What a shooter! He scored 40 points all by himself. /～守门员，从他手里漏过了七个球! What a great goalkeeper! He let the other team score seven goals. /～正人君子! An honourable man, indeed!

好意 hǎoyì good intention; kindness: ～相劝 give well-intentioned advice /谢谢您的～。 Thank you for your kindness.

好意思 hǎoyìsi how can one have the face (or nerve) to do sth.: 人家请我喝酒，我～不喝吗? When he offered me a drink, how could I have the face to refuse it? /做了这种事，亏他还～说呢! Fancy his doing that sort of thing and then having the nerve to talk about it!

好在 hǎozài adv. fortunately; luckily: ～他伤势不重。 Luckily he was not very seriously wounded. /我可以再去一趟，～路不远。 Luckily it's not very far. I can easily go there again.

好转 hǎozhuǎn take a turn for the better; take a favourable turn; improve: 形势～。 The situation took a favourable turn. /病情～。 The patient is on the mend.

好自为之 hǎo zì wéi zhī look out for yourself: 有这样的机会不容易，希望你～。 An opportunity like this is not easy to come by, so I hope you'll make best use of it.

好走 hǎozǒu dial. goodbye

郝 Hǎo a surname

hào

号¹（號） hào ① name: 国号 guóhào /绰号 chuòhào ② assumed name; alternative name; literary name; sobriquet: 苏轼字子瞻，～东坡。 Su Shi, styled Zizhan, was also known by his literary name Dongpo ("Eastern Slope"). /吴镇（元画家）字仲圭，～梅花道人。 Wu Zhen (a Yuan painter), whose courtesy name was Zhonggui, had the sobriquet "Taoist of the Plum Blossom." ③ business house: 银号 yínhào ④ mark; sign; signal: 问号 wènhào / 暗号 ànhào ⑤ number: 五～楼 Building No. 5 ⑥ size: 大（中，小）～ large (medium, small) size /这鞋小了两～。 These shoes are two sizes too small. ⑦ date: 今天几～? —十三～。 What date is it today? —The 13th. ⑧ personnel: 病号 bìnghào ⑨ m. ⓐ (for workmen): 今天有一百多～人出工。 Over a hundred people went to work today. ⓑ (for business deals): 一会儿工夫就做了几～买卖。 Several deals were clinched in a short time. ⓒ kind; sort: 这～生意不能做。 You can't do this kind of business. /这～人甭理他。 Don't bother with such a person. ⑩ make a mark on: 把你要的东西都～一～。 Have all the items you want marked. ⑪ examine (the pulse): 号脉 hàomài

号²（號） hào ① order: 发号施令 fāhào-shīlìng ② any brass-wind instrument: 军号 jūnhào / 小号 xiǎohào ③ anything used as a horn: 螺号 luóhào ④ bugle call; any call made on a bugle: 起床号 qǐchuánghào —— see also hào

号兵 hàobīng bugler; trumpeter

号称 hàochēng ① be known as: 四川～天府之国。 Sichuan is known as a land of plenty. ② claim to be: ～五十万大军 an army claiming to be half a million strong / 一切～强大的反动派 all allegedly powerful reactionaries

号灯 hàodēng signal lamp

号房 hàofáng old ① janitor's room; reception office ② janitor ③ dormitory for candidates of the imperial examination

号角 hàojiǎo ① bugle; horn ② bugle call: 吹响战斗的～ sound a bugle call for battle /吹响了向科学技术现代化进军的～ sound the clarion call to march towards the modernization of science and technology

号坎儿 hàokǎnr old numbered singlet worn by coolies

号令 hàolìng verbal command; order

号码 hàomǎ number: 电话～ telephone number

号码机 hàomǎjī numbering machine

号脉 hàomài Chin. med. feel the pulse

号牌 hàopái numberplate

号炮 hàopào signal gun

号手 hàoshǒu bugler; trumpeter

号头 hàotóu inf. number

号外 hàowài extra (of a newspaper)

号衣 hàoyī old livery or army uniform

号召 hàozhào call; appeal: 响应党的～ respond to the Party's call /～人们参军 call on the people to enlist

号召书 hàozhàoshū appeal

号志灯 hàozhìdēng red signal lamp used by railworkers

号子¹ hàozi dial. mark; sign; signal

号子² hàozi a work song sung to synchronize movements, with one person leading

好 hào ① like; love; be fond of: ～说话 like to talk /～表现 like to show off /～跳舞 love dancing /～喝酒 be fond of drinking /～管闲事 meddlesome; officious ② be liable to: ～晕船 be liable to seasickness; be a bad sailor /～伤风 be subject to colds; catch cold easily —— see also hǎo

好吃 hàochī enjoy eating good food

好吃懒做 hàochī-lǎnzuò be fond of eating and averse to work; be gluttonous and lazy

好大喜功 hàodà-xǐgōng crave for greatness and success; have a fondness for the grandiose

好读书 hàodúshū love to read books; be fond of reading books; be addicted to study: ～，不求甚解; 每有会意，便欣然忘食。（陶潜） He delights in study but does not seek abstruse explanations. Whenever there is something of which he apprehends the meaning, then in his happiness he forgets to eat.

好高务远 hàogāo-wùyuǎn (also 好高骛远 hàogāo-wùyuǎn) reach for what is beyond one's grasp; aim too high

好客 hàokè be hospitable; keep open house: 他这个人热情～。 He is a good-natured and hospitable man.

好奇 hàoqí be curious; be full of curiosity: 孩子们都很～。 Children are very curious.

好奇心 hàoqíxīn curiosity

好强 hàoqiáng eager to do well in everything

好色 hàosè love woman's beauty; be fond of women: ～即淫，知情更淫。（《红楼梦》） To be moved by woman's beauty is itself a kind of lust. To experience loving feelings is, even more assuredly, a kind of lust.

好色之徒 hàosè zhī tú lecher; libertine

好尚 hàoshàng one's likes or preferences; what is valued or held in esteem

好胜 hàoshèng love to outshine others; seek to do others down

好事 hàoshì meddlesome; officious —— see also hǎoshì

好事者 hàoshìzhě busybody: 此皆向壁虚构，～为之也。 These were all fabrications by people who had nothing better to do.

好事之徒 hàoshì zhī tú　busybody

好为人师 hào wéi rén shī　like to lecture people; be given to laying down the law: 人之患在~。《孟子》) The trouble with people is that they are too eager to assume the role of teacher.

好恶 hào-wù　likes and dislikes; taste: 人各有~。Everyone has his likes and dislikes. / 翻译时不应根据自己的~改变原文意思。In doing translation, one should not alter the meaning of the original to suit one's own taste.

好学 hàoxué　be fond of learning; be eager to learn: 聪明~ be intelligent and fond of learning / 日知其所亡，月无忘其所能，可谓~也已矣。《论语》) A man can, indeed, be said to be eager to learn who is conscious, in the course of a day, of what he lacks and who never forgets, in the course of a month, what he has mastered.

好逸恶劳 hàoyì-wùláo　love ease and hate work

好战 hàozhàn　bellicose; warlike: ~分子 bellicose (or warlike) elements

好整以暇 hào zhěng yǐ xiá　remain calm and composed while handling pressing affairs

昊
hào　formal ① vast and boundless ② sky; heaven

耗[1]
hào　① consume; cost: 这汽车~油。This car uses a lot of petrol. / ~了不少粮食 have consumed much grain / 锅里的水快~干了。The pot is boiling dry. ② waste time; dawdle: 别~着了，快走吧。Stop dawdling and get going.

耗[2]
hào　bad news: 噩耗 èhào

耗电量 hàodiànliàng　power consumption

耗费 hàofèi　consume; expend: ~时间、金钱 expend time and money

耗竭 hàojié　exhaust; use up: 人力~ be drained of manpower

耗尽 hàojìn　exhaust; use up: ~心血 exhaust all one's energies / ~体力 use up all one's strength

耗能 hàonéng　consume energy

耗散 hàosàn　phys. dissipation: 功率~ power dissipation

耗损 hàosǔn　consume; waste; lose: 减少水果在运输中的~ reduce the wastage of fruit in transit

耗资 hàozī　cost (a large sum of money): ~百万 cost a million yuan

耗子 hàozi　dial. mouse; rat

耗子药 hàoziyào　ratsbane

浩
hào　① great; vast; grand: 浩繁 hàofán ② many; much: 浩博 hàobó

浩博 hàobó　extensive; wide-embracing

浩大 hàodà　very great; huge; vast: ~的工程 a huge (or vast) project

浩荡 hàodàng　vast and mighty: ~的长江 the mighty Changjiang River / 东风~。The east wind blows with mighty power.

浩繁 hàofán　vast and numerous: ~的开支 heavy expenditure

浩瀚 hàohàn　formal vast: ~的沙漠 a vast expanse of desert / 典籍~ a vast accumulation of ancient literature / ~的大海 a boundless sea

浩浩荡荡 hàohàodàngdàng　vast and mighty: ~的革命大军 an enormous and powerful revolutionary army; mighty revolutionary contingents / 石油工人~开进了新油田。Oil workers gathered in force at the new oil field.

浩劫 hàojié　great calamity; catastrophe: 空前~ an un-heard-of calamity

浩茫 hàománg　formal vast; extensive; boundless

浩淼 hàomiǎo　(of water) extending into the distance; vast: 烟波浩淼 yānbō hàomiǎo

浩渺 hàomiǎo　same as 浩淼 hàomiǎo

浩气 hàoqì　noble spirit: ~长存 a noble spirit that will never perish

浩然之气 hàorán zhī qì　noble spirit; moral force

浩如烟海 hào rú yānhǎi　vast as the open sea—a tremendous amount (of literature, data, etc.)

浩叹 hàotàn　① heave a deep sigh; sigh deeply ② be greatly touched

浩特 hàotè　Mongolian for "village" or "town" (as in 呼和~, or Huhhot, lit. "green city", capital of the Inner Mongolian Autonomous Region)

皓（皜）
hào　① white: 皓齿 hàochǐ ② bright; luminous: 皓月当空 hàoyuè dāngkōng

皓白 hàobái　white; pure white

皓齿 hàochǐ　white teeth ——see also 明眸皓齿 míngmóu-hàochǐ

皓矾 hàofán　chem. zinc sulphate

皓首 hàoshǒu　formal hoary head: ~穷经 continue to study even in old age

皓月当空 hàoyuè dāngkōng　a bright moon hung in the sky

hē

诃[1]
hē　same as 呵[2] hē

诃[2]
hē　see below

诃子 hēzǐ　bot. myrobalan (Terminalia chebula)

呵[1]
hē　breathe out (with the mouth open): ~一口气 give a puff / 他一边写，一边~手。As he wrote, he kept breathing on his hands to warm them.

呵[2]（訶）
hē　scold: 呵责 hēzé

呵斥 hēchì　(also 呵叱 hēchì) berate; excoriate

呵呵 hēhē　onom. the sound of laughing: ~大笑 laugh loudly; roar with laughter

呵喝 hēhè　formal shout (as a warning or reprimand)

呵护 hēhù　formal bless

呵欠 hēqiàn　yawn

呵责 hēzé　berate; excoriate

喝[1]（飲）
hē　① drink: ~茶 drink tea / ~汤 drink soup ② drink alcoholic liquor: 爱~两盅 be fond of drinking / ~醉了 be drunk

喝[2]
hē　same as 嗬 hē ——see also hè

喝叱 hēchì　(also 喝斥 hēchì) berate; excoriate

喝墨水 hē mòshuǐ　drink ink—go to school: 他没喝过几年墨水。He's had only a few years of school.

喝水不忘掘井人 hēshuǐ bùwàng juéjǐngrén　when you drink the water, think of those who dug the well

喝西北风 hē xīběifēng　drink the northwest wind—live on air; have nothing to eat

嗬（呵）
hē　interj. ah; oh: ~，这小伙子真棒! Oh, what a fine young chap! / ~，真了不得了! Oh, how terrible! / ~，怎么这么贵! Wow, how expensive!

hé

禾 hé standing grain (esp. rice)
禾本科 héběnkē *bot.* the grass family
禾草类 hécǎolèi *bot.* grass
禾场 héchǎng *dial.* threshing floor
禾苗 hémiáo seedlings of cereal crops

合[1] hé ① close; shut: 把书～上 close the book / 笑得～不上嘴 grin from ear to ear ② join; combine: 合办 hébàn ③ whole: ～村 the whole village ④ suit; agree: ～胃口 suit one's taste; be to one's taste / 正～我意。It suits me fine. ⑤ be equal to; add up to: 一公顷～十五市亩。A hectare is equal to 15 *mu*. / 这件上衣连工带料～多少钱? How much will this coat cost, including material and tailoring? ⑥ *formal* proper: 理～声明。I deem it appropriate to make a statement. ⑦ *m.* passage at arms; round; bout ⑧ *meteorol.* conjunction

合[2] hé *mus.* a note of the scale in *gongchepu* (工尺谱), corresponding to 5 in numbered musical notation
——see also gě

合办 hébàn operate or run jointly: ～企业 a joint enterprise; a joint venture
合瓣 hébàn *bot.* sympetalous; gamopetalous: ～花 sympetalous flower / ～花类 metachlamydeae; sympetalae
合抱 hébào (of a tree, etc.) so big that one can just get one's arms around: 院中有树一株，围可～。In the yard there is a tree so big that a man can barely put his arms around it.
合抱之木, 生于毫末 hébào zhī mù, shēngyú háomò a tree that can fill the span of a man's arms grows from a downy tip; great oaks from little acorns grow
合璧 hébì (of two different things) combine harmoniously; match well: 中西～ a good combination of Chinese and Western elements
合编 hébiān ① compile in collaboration with: 这本书是他们两位～的。They are the two joint compilers of this book. ② merge and reorganize (army units, etc.): 两支军队～后, 兵力达万人。A merging of the two army units brought the strength up to 10,000 men.
合并 hébìng ① merge; amalgamate: 五个组～为两个组了。The five groups have merged into two. / 这家公司是由几家小公司～起来组成的。This firm is an amalgamation of several small ones. / 这三个提议～讨论。The three proposals will be discussed together. ② (of an illness) be complicated by another illness
合并症 hébìngzhèng *med.* complication
合不来 hébùlái not get along well; be incompatible
合不着 hébuzháo *dial.* not worthwhile: 跑那么远去看场戏, ～。It's not worth it to go all that way to watch a performance.
合唱 héchàng chorus: 混声～ mixed chorus
合唱曲 héchàngqǔ (music for) chorus
合唱团 héchàngtuán chorus (a group of singers): ～指挥 chorus master
合成 héchéng ① compose; compound: 由两部分～ be composed of two parts / 力的～ composition of forces ② *chem.* synthetize; synthesize
合成氨 héchéng'ān *chem.* synthetic ammonia
合成词 héchéngcí *gram.* compound word
合成革 héchénggé synthetic leather
合成结晶牛胰岛素 héchéng jiéjīng niúyídǎosù synthetic crystalline bovine insulin
合成酶 héchéngméi *biochem.* synzyme
合成树脂 héchéng shùzhī synthetic resin
合成洗涤剂 héchéng xǐdíjì synthetic detergent
合成纤维 héchéng xiānwéi synthetic fibre
合成橡胶 héchéng xiàngjiāo synthetic rubber
合当 hédāng *old* be fated: 林冲～有事。《水浒》 Lin Chong was fated for trouble.
合得来 hédelái get along well; be compatible
合得着 hédezháo *dial.* worthwhile: 买这件衣服吧, 价廉物美, ～。You should buy this coat. It's of good quality and well worth the price.
合订本 hédìngběn one-volume edition; bound volume: 《毛泽东选集》～ one-volume edition of the *Selected Works of Mao Zedong* / 《红旗》～ a bound volume of *Hongqi* / 《人民日报》～ a file of *Renmin Ribao*
合度 hédù right; proper; appropriate: 长短～ of the right length / 身材修短～ of trim build
合二而一 hé èr ér yī *philos.* two combine into one
合法 héfǎ legal; lawful; legitimate; rightful: 唯一～政府 the sole legal government / ～地位 legal status / ～斗争 legal struggle / ～继承人 rightful heir / ～权利 legitimate right; lawful right / ～权益 legitimate rights and interests / ～收入 lawfully earned income / ～途径 legal means
合法化 héfǎhuà legalize; legitimize
合肥 Héféi Hefei (capital of Anhui Province)
合该 hégāi should; ought to: ～如此。It should be so. / ～你这病要好了。You ought to get well again soon.
合格 hégé qualified; up to standard: ～的司机 a qualified driver / 产品～。The product is up to standard. / 我们保证质量～。We can vouch for the quality.
合格证 hégézhèng certificate of inspection; certificate of quality
合共 hégòng *adv.* altogether; in all; all told
合股 hégǔ ① pool capital; form a partnership ② *text.* plying: ～线 ply (*or* plied) yarn
合乎 héhū conform with (*or* to); correspond to; accord with; tally with: ～人民的利益 conform with the interests of the people / ～实际 conform to the actual situation / ～历史发展的规律 be in conformity with the law of historical development / ～情理 stand to reason; be reasonable; be sensible / ～事实 tally with the facts / ～广大群众的需要 meet the needs of the broad masses / ～规格 up to the specifications / ～逻辑 logical
合欢 héhuān ① conjoined happiness—sexual pairing ② *bot.* silk tree
合伙 héhuǒ form a partnership: ～经营 run a business in partnership / 两人～买下了这家公司。The two of them formed a partnership and bought the company.
合击 héjī make a joint attack on: 分进～ concerted attack by converging columns
合计 héjì amount to; add up to; total: 这两项开支～一千元。The cost of the two items amounts to 1,000 *yuan*. / 把这一栏的数字～一下。Add up the figures in this column.
合计 héji ① think over; figure out: 他心里老～这件事。He kept thinking it over. ② consult: 大家～～该怎么办。Let's put our heads together and see what's to be done.
合剂 héjì *pharm.* mixture
合家 héjiā the whole family: ～团圆 a reunion of the whole family
合家欢 héjiāhuān *dial.* a family group photo
合脚 héjiǎo (of shoes or socks) fit
合金 héjīn alloy: 二元(三元)～ binary (ternary) alloy
合金钢 héjīngāng alloy steel: 高～ high-alloy steel
合金元素 héjīn yuánsù alloying element
合卺 héjǐn *formal* (of bride and bridegroom) drink

the nuptial cup—go through the marriage ceremony

合刊 hékān combined issue (of a periodical)

合口[1] hékǒu (of a wound) heal up

合口[2] hékǒu (of a dish) be to one's taste: 你做的菜很～。 The dishes you make are very much to my taste.

合口呼 hékǒuhū *phonet.* a class of syllables with u as the final 韵母 or a final beginning with u (e.g. 关 guān) ——see also 四呼 sìhū

合饹 héle same as 饸饹 héle

合理 hélǐ rational; reasonable; equitable: 收费～ reasonable charges / 时间安排～ a well worked out timetable / ～分工 rational division of labour / ～利用资源 put resources to rational use; make rational use of resources / ～的价格 a reasonable (*or* equitable) price / ～解决两国之间的争端 equitable settlement of the issues between the two countries / ～轮作 proper rotation of crops / ～施肥 apply fertilizer rationally

合理化 hélǐhuà rationalize: ～建议 rationalization proposal

合力 hélì ① join forces; pool efforts: ～修建水库 pool efforts to build a reservoir / 只要大家同心～，任务一定能完成。 We are sure to accomplish the task as long as we unite and make a common effort. ② *phys.* resultant of forces

合流 héliú ① flowing together; confluence: 永定河和大清河在天津附近～。 The Yongding and Daqing rivers meet near Tianjin. ② collaborate; work hand in glove with sb. ③ different schools (of thought, art, etc.) merge into one

合流河 héliúhé confluent

合龙 hélóng ① closure (of a dam, dyke, etc.) ② join the two sections of a bridge, etc.

合拢 hélǒng close up; join together

合霉素 héméisù *pharm.* syntomycin

合谋 hémóu ① conspire; plot together; connive ② *leg.* conspiracy

合拍 hépāi in time; in step; in harmony: 与时代潮流～ in step with the trend of the times

合浦珠还 Hépǔ zhū huán (also 合浦还珠 Hépǔ huán zhū) pearls returned to Hepu (said of the regaining of sth. lost or the return of sb. after a long absence; from the story that in Hepu, a pearl-producing area in what is now Guangdong and Guangxi, the pearls disappeared when the administration was corrupt, but reappeared with the improvement of the administration)

合情合理 héqíng-hélǐ fair and reasonable; fair and sensible: 这个建议～。 The proposal is fair and reasonable.

合群 héqún ① get on well with others; be sociable ② be gregarious

合扇 héshàn *dial.* hinge

合身 héshēn fit: 这件上衣很～。 This jacket fits well.

合十 héshí put the palms together before one (a Buddhist greeting)

合时 héshí fashionable; in vogue: 穿戴～ dress fashionably

合适 héshì (also 合式 héshì) suitable; appropriate; becoming; right: 这双鞋我穿着正～。 These shoes fit me beautifully. / 星期五对我最～。 Friday suits me best. / 你这样说不～。 It's not right (*or* suitable) for you to say so. / 这个词用在这里不～。 This isn't the right word to use here.

合算 hésuàn ① paying; worthwhile ② reckon up

合题 hétí *philos.* synthesis

合同 hétong contract: 订立～ conclude (*or* make) a contract / 撕毁～ tear up a contract / ～期限 contract period

合同工 hétonggōng contract worker

合同医院 hétong yīyuàn assigned hospital (to which people from a given organization or area go for treatment)

合同制 hétongzhì contract system

合围 héwéi ① surround ② same as 合抱 hébào

合眼 héyǎn close one's eyes; sleep: 他昨晚一夜没～。 He didn't get a wink of sleep last night.

合演 héyǎn appear in the same play, dance, etc.; co-star

合叶 héyè (also 合页 héyè) hinge

合宜 héyí suitable; appropriate; becoming; right: 他担任这个工作倒很～。 He's just the right man for the job.

合议庭 héyìtíng *leg.* collegiate bench (of judges, or of a judge and people's assessors); collegial panel: 由审判员一人，人民陪审员二人组成的～ a collegial panel composed of one judge and two people's assessors

合议制 héyìzhì *leg.* collegiate system (a judicial system according to which justice is administered by a collegiate bench of judges, or by a judge and people's assessors)

合意 héyì suit; be to one's liking (*or* taste): 这个合你的意吗? Does this suit you? / 你说的正合我意。 You took the very words out of my mouth.

合营 héyíng jointly owned; jointly operated ——see also 公私合营 gōng-sī héyíng

合影 héyǐng ① take a group photo (*or* picture): ～留念 have a group photo taken to mark the occasion ② group photo (*or* picture)

合用 héyòng ① share: 两家～一个厨房。 Two families share a kitchen. ② of use: 绳子太短，不～。 The rope is too short to be of any use.

合约 héyuē contract

合葬 hézàng (of husband and wife) be buried in the same grave

合掌 hézhǎng put the palms together before one (a Buddhist greeting)

合帐 hézhàng *inf.* make up accounts; figure out accounts

合辙 hézhé ① in rhyme ② in agreement: 两人一说就～。 The moment they started talking they found themselves in complete agreement.

合着 hézhe *dial.* (expressing surprised discovery) so: 我白说了半天，～你没在听。 So I've been wasting my breath as you weren't listening. / ～你的病是假装的。 So you are pretending to be sick.

合著 hézhù write in collaboration with; coauthor

合资 hézī pool capital; enter into partnership

合资经营 hézī jīngyíng jointly owned; jointly operated: 中外～企业 a Chinese-foreign joint venture / ～各方 parties to a venture

合子 hézǐ *biol.* zygote

合子 hézi ① a kind of meat pie ② same as 盒子 hézi

合奏 hézòu instrumental ensemble

合作 hézuò cooperate; collaborate; work together: 互相～ cooperate with each other / 这幅画是他们～的。 This painting is their joint work. / 南南～ South-South cooperation

合作化 hézuòhuà (a movement to) organize cooperatives: 农业～ cooperative transformation of agriculture

合作经营 hézuò jīngyíng jointly operated; cooperative management; cooperative business operation: ～企业 a cooperatively managed enterprise

合作社 hézuòshè cooperative; co-op

合作医疗 hézuò yīliáo cooperative medical service

纟 hé see 回纥 Huíhé ——see also gē

何 hé *formal* ① what; which; how; why: ～人 who / ～时 what time; when / ～处 what place; where /

~往 whither / 从~而来? Where from? / ~济于事? Of what avail is it? / 有~不可? Why not? ② (Hé) a surname

何必 hébì *adv.* there is no need; why: ~去那么早。There is no need to go so early. / 开个玩笑嘛, ~当真呢! I was only joking. Why take it so seriously? / 为了这点小事生气, ~呢? What's the point of getting angry about such a trivial matter?

何不 hébù *adv.* why not: ~早说? Why didn't you say so earlier?

何曾 hécéng *adv.* (used in rhetorical questions) did ever: 我~说过此话? When did I ever say that? *or* I never said that.

何尝 hécháng *adv.* (used in rhetorical questions) ever so: 我~不想去, 只是没工夫罢了。Not that I don't want to go; I just haven't got the time. / 他这样的态度, ~有解决问题的诚意呢? If that's his attitude, how can you say he sincerely wants the question settled? / 我知道你心里难受, 我又~不难受呢? I know you feel bad, and don't think I feel any better.

何啻 héchì *formal* (used in rhetorical questions) can it be any less than...: 今昔对比, ~天壤之别? There's a world of difference between the past and the present.

何等 héděng ① what kind: 你知道他是~人物? Do you know what kind of person he is? ② *adv.* (used in exclamations) what; how: 他们生活得~幸福! How happily they are living! *or* What a happy life they are leading! / 这是~高超的技术! What consummate skill!

何妨 héfáng *adv.* why not; might as well: ~一试? Why not have a try? *or* You might as well have a try. / 人少不热闹, ~多请些人? The more the merrier—why not invite some more people?

何干 hégān (used in rhetorical questions) what connection: 此事与你~? What has that got to do with you?

何故 hégù why: 不知~。I don't know why.

何苦 hékǔ *adv.* why bother; is it worth the trouble: 你~在这些小事上伤脑筋? Why bother your head about such trifles? / 冒着这么大的雨去看电影, ~呢? Going to the movies in this rain—is it worth it? 你这是~ (来)? Why are you doing this (and making yourself suffer)?

何况 hékuàng *conj.* ① much less; let alone: 这根木头连小伙子都抬不动, ~老人呢? The log is too heavy even for a young fellow to lift, let alone an old man. ② moreover; besides; in addition: 我不喜欢那所房子, ~价钱也太高。I don't like the house, and moreover, the price is too high. / 这鞋太贵, ~尺码也太小。These shoes are expensive—besides, they're too small.

何乐而不为 hé lè ér bù wéi why not do it; one would be only too glad to do it: 养猪对集体对个人都有利, ~? Pig-breeding is beneficial to both the collective and the individual. Why not go ahead with it?

何其 héqí *adv.* (used in exclamations to express disapproval) what; how: ~愚蠢! What a fool! / ~荒唐! How absurd!

何其相似乃尔 héqí xiāngsì nǎi'ěr *derog.* what a striking likeness (or similarity)

何去何从 héqù-hécóng what course to follow: ~, 速宜抉择。What course to follow—that is a question you must quickly decide for yourselves.

何如 hérú ① how about: 请君一试, ~? How about you having a try? ② wouldn't it be better: 与其强攻, ~智取。It would be better to use strategy than to attack by force.

何首乌 héshǒuwū *Chin. med.* the tuber of multiflower knotweed (*Polygonum multiflorum*)

何谓 héwèi *formal* what is meant by; what is the meaning of: ~灵感? What is meant by inspiration? /

此~也? What does it mean? *or* What do you mean?

何消 héxiāo *adv.* (used in rhetorical questions) what is the need: ~说, 我明天一定会来的。Assuredly, I'll come tomorrow.

何须 héxū *adv.* (used in rhetorical questions) what is the need: ~这样慌张? What's the need for all this hurry? / 室雅~大, 花香不在多。An elegant chamber wouldn't lay claim to largeness, Fragrant flowers are of their number careless.

何许 héxǔ *formal* what kind of; what: ~人 what sort of person

何以 héyǐ *formal* how; why: ~自解? How are you to explain yourself? / ~见得? What makes you think so?

何在 hézài *formal* where: 困难~? Wherein lies the difficulty? / 原因~? What is the reason for it?

何止 hézhǐ far more than: 例子~这些。There are far more instances than we have just enumerated.

何足挂齿 hé zú guàchǐ not worth mentioning; don't mention it: 区区小事, ~。Such a trifle is not worth mentioning.

河

hé ① river ② the Milky Way system ③ (Hé) the Huanghe River; the Yellow River

河岸 hé'àn river bank

河浜 hébāng *dial.* creek; streamlet

河北 Héběi Hebei (Province)

河北梆子 Héběi bāngzi Hebei clapper opera ——see also 梆子腔 bāngziqiāng

河汊子 héchàzi a branch of a river

河川 héchuān rivers and creeks

河床 héchuáng (also 河槽 hécáo; 河身 héshēn) riverbed

河道 hédào river course

河堤 hédī river embankment

河东狮吼 Hé dōng shī hǒu the roar of the lioness from the east side of the River (said of sb.'s dominating wife in a temper)

河防 héfáng flood-prevention work done on rivers, esp. the Huanghe River

河港 hégǎng river port

河工 hégōng ① river conservancy works (esp. for the Huanghe River) ② river conservancy workers

河沟 hégōu brook; stream

河谷 hégǔ river valley

河汉 héhàn *liter.* the River of Stars—the Milky Way: 清浅望~, 低昂看北斗。(储光羲) I gaze on the River of Stars so clear, Watch the Dipper rise and sink.

河汉斯言 héhàn sī yán take these as farfetched words (as far-off as the Milky Way): 幸毋~。I hope you will not take this as wild talk.

河口 hékǒu river mouth; stream outlet: ~湾 estuary

河狸 hélí beaver

河流 héliú rivers

河流沉积 héliú chénjī fluvial (or fluviatile) deposit

河流袭夺 héliú xíduó *geol.* river capture; river piracy

河马 hémǎ hippopotamus; hippo; river horse

河鳗 hémán river eel

河南 Hénán Henan (Province)

河南梆子 Hénán bāngzi Henan clapper opera (another name for 豫剧 yùjù) ——see also 梆子腔 bāngziqiāng

河南坠子 Hénán zhuìzi ballad singing to the accompaniment of the *zhuiqin* (坠琴), popular in Henan Province

河泥 héní river silt; river mud

河清海晏 héqīng-hǎiyàn the Yellow River is clear and the sea is calm—the world is at peace

河曲 héqū bend (of a river); meander

河渠 héqú rivers and canals; waterways: ~纵横 be crisscrossed by rivers and canals

河山 héshān rivers and mountains; land; territory

河滩地　hétāndì　flood land

河塘　hétáng　river embankment

河套　hétào　① the bend of a river ② (Hétào) the Great Bend of the Huanghe River

河套地区　Hétào Dìqū　the Hetao area (at the top of the Great Bend of the Huanghe River in the Nei Monggol Autonomous Region and Ningxia)

河豚　hétún　globefish; balloonfish; puffer

河外星云　héwài xīngyún　(also 河外星系 héwàixīngxì) *meteorol.* extragalactic nebula

河网　héwǎng　a network of waterways: ～化 build a network of waterways

河西走廊　Héxī Zǒuláng　the Hexi (*or* Gansu) Corridor (in northwestern Gansu, so called because it lies to the west of the Yellow River)

河蟹　héxiè　river crab

河沿　héyán　river bank; riverside

河鱼　héyú　freshwater fish

河源　héyuán　river head (*or* source)

河岳　héyuè　rivers and mountains; land; territory

河运　héyùn　river transport

和¹（龢）　hé　① gentle; mild; kind: 温和 wēnhé ② harmonious; on good terms: ～为贵。 Harmony is what matters. ③ peace: 讲和 jiǎnghé ④ *sports* draw; tie: 那盘棋～了。 That game of chess ended in a draw. ⑤ (Hé) a surname

和²　hé　① together with: 和衣 héyī ② *prep.* (indicating relationship, comparison, etc.): ～这件事没有关系 have nothing to do with the matter; bear no relation to it / 他～我一样高。 He's the same height as I. ③ *conj.* and: 工人～农民 workers and peasants / 你～我 you and I ④ *math.* sum: 两数之～ the sum of the two numbers

和³　Hé　Japan: 汉～词典 a Chinese-Japanese dictionary
——see also hè; hú; huó; huò

和蔼　hé'ǎi　kindly; affable; amiable: 态度～ amiable

和蔼可亲　hé'ǎi kěqīn　affable; amiable; genial

和畅　héchàng　(of a wind) gentle and pleasant: 惠风～ a gentle and pleasant breeze

和道　hédao　*dial.* gentle; kind; polite; amiable

和风　héfēng　① soft (*or* gentle) breeze: ～拂面 a gentle breeze caressing one's face / ～丽日 a gentle breeze and a bright sun; fine weather ② *meteorol.* moderate breeze

和风细雨　héfēng-xìyǔ　like a gentle breeze and light rain—in a gentle and mild way: ～地开展批评和自我批评 make criticism and self-criticism in the manner of "a gentle breeze and a mild rain"

和服　héfú　kimono

和光同尘　héguāng tóngchén　soften one's glare and move along old ruts—swim with the tide

和好　héhǎo　become reconciled: 他们吵过架，现在～了。 They had a quarrel but have made it up now. / ～如初 be on good terms again; restore good relations

和合　héhé　*formal* harmonious

和合二仙　Hé-Hé èr xiān　the twin genii He-He (the gods of harmonious union whose pictures used to be displayed at marriage ceremonies)

和缓　héhuǎn　① gentle; mild: 水流～ gentle flow of a stream / 态度～ adopt a mild attitude ② ease up; relax: ～一下气氛 relieve the tension a little

和会　héhuì　peace conference

和奸　héjiān　commit adultery

和解　héjiě　become reconciled: 两国开始对话，表示愿意～。 The two countries started to hold dialogues and

showed a willingness to conciliate. / 采取～的态度 adopt a conciliatory attitude

和局　héjú　drawn game; draw; tie: 三盘棋却有两盘是～。 Two of the three chess games ended in draws.

和乐　hélè　happy and harmonious

和美　héměi　harmonious: 小两口儿日子过得挺～。 The young couple are living together in perfect harmony. / 和和美美地过日子 live happily together

和睦　hémù　harmony; concord; amity: ～相处 live in harmony / 民族～ national concord / 家庭～ family harmony; domestic peace / 友好～关系 friendly and harmonious relations

和暖　hénuǎn　pleasantly warm; genial: 天气～ warm, genial weather / ～的阳光 genial sunshine

和盘托出　hé pán tuōchū　reveal everything; hold nothing back: 把自己的想法～ reveal everything on one's mind

和平　hépíng　① peace: ～倡议 peace proposals / ～环境 peaceful environment / ～利用原子能 peaceful utilization of atomic energy; use of atomic energy for peaceful purposes / ～解决边界争端 peaceful settlement of a boundary dispute ② mild: 药性～。 The medicine is mild.

和平队　Hépíngduì　Peace Corps

和平鸽　hépínggē　dove of peace

和平攻势　hépíng gōngshì　peace offensive

和平共处　hépíng gòngchǔ　peaceful coexistence

和平共处五项原则　hépíng gòngchǔ wǔxiàng yuánzé　the Five Principles of Peaceful Coexistence (mutual respect for territorial integrity and sovereignty, mutual non-aggression, non-interference in each other's internal affairs, equality and mutual benefit, and peaceful coexistence)

和平过渡　hépíng guòdù　peaceful transition

和平竞赛　hépíng jìngsài　peaceful competition

和平谈判　hépíng tánpàn　peace negotiations; peace talks

和平演变　hépíng yǎnbiàn　peaceful evolution (from socialism back to capitalism)

和平中立政策　hépíng zhōnglì zhèngcè　policy of peace and neutrality

和平主义　hépíngzhǔyì　pacifism: ～者 pacifist

和棋　héqí　a draw in chess or other board games

和气　héqi　① gentle; friendly; polite; amiable: 对人～ be friendly to people / 他们彼此很～。 They are very friendly with each other. / 说话～ speak politely (*or* gently); be soft-spoken / 和和气气 polite and amiable ② harmony; friendship: 咱们别为那件小事儿伤了～。 Don't let that unpleasantness end our friendship.

和气生财　héqi shēngcái　amiability begets riches (a motto for businessmen): 买卖买卖，～。 Do business with a smile, and you'll make a pile.

和洽　héqià　harmonious; on friendly terms: 相处～ live in harmony

和亲　héqīn　(of some feudal dynasties) attempt to cement relations with rulers of minority nationalities in the border areas by marrying daughters of the Han imperial family to them

和软　héruǎn　gentle; soft; mild: ～的语气 a mild tone

和善　héshàn　kind and gentle; genial

和尚　héshang　Buddhist monk

和尚打伞，无法无天　héshang dǎsǎn, wúfǎ-wútiān　like a Buddhist monk holding an umbrella, no hair (law) nor Heaven—defy laws human and divine; be absolutely lawless; run wild (a pun on the homophones 发 "hair" and 法 "law," a Buddhist monk having a shaven head)

和尚头　héshangtóu　*inf.* shaven head: 剃个～ have one's head shaved

和声　héshēng　*mus.* harmony

和事老　héshìlǎo　peacemaker (esp. one who is more

concerned with stopping the bickering than settling the issue)

和数 héshù *math.* sum

和顺 héshùn gentle and amiable: 性情～ of gentle and amiable disposition

和谈 hétán short for 和平谈判 hépíng tánpàn

和头 hétóu both ends of a coffin or the front of a coffin

和婉 héwǎn (of speech) mild and roundabout; tactful

和文 héwén Japanese (language)

和弦 héxián *mus.* chord

和祥 héxiáng kindly; affable; amiable: 面貌～ a kindly face

和谐 héxié harmonious: 音调～ in perfect harmony; melodious; tuneful / 颜色搭配得很～。The colours match quite well. / ～的气氛 a harmonious atmosphere

和煦 héxù pleasantly warm; genial: ～的阳光 genial sunshine / 春风～。The spring breeze is warm and gentle.

和颜悦色 héyán-yuèsè have a kind face; have a genial expression

和衣 héyī (sleep) with one's clothes on: ～而卧 sleep with one's clothes on

和议 héyì peace talks: ～成功 reach a peace agreement

和易 héyì unassuming; amiable: ～近人 amiable and easy of approach

和约 héyuē peace treaty

和悦 héyuè kindly; affable; amiable

和衷共济 hézhōng-gòngjì work together with one accord (in time of difficulty)

劾 tánhé hé expose sb.'s misdeeds or crimes: 弹劾 tánhé

饸 hé see below

饸饹 héle a kind of noodles made from buckwheat, sorghum flour, etc.

曷 hé *formal* ① how; why ② when

阂 hé cut off from; not in communication with: 隔阂 géhé

荷 hé lotus ——see also hè

荷包 hé·bāo ① small bag (for carrying money and odds and ends); pouch ② pocket (in a garment)

荷包蛋 hé·bāodàn poached or fried eggs

荷尔蒙 hé'ěrméng hormone (old name for 激素 jīsù)

荷花 héhuā lotus

荷兰 Hélán the Netherlands (Holland)

荷兰牛 hélánniú Holstein (cattle)

荷兰人 Hélánrén the Dutch; Dutchman

荷兰水 hélánshuǐ *dial.* aerated water; soda water

荷兰语 Hélányǔ Dutch (language)

荷兰猪 hélánzhū guinea pig; cavy

荷叶 héyè lotus leaf

核[1] hé ① pit; stone: 桃～ peach-pit; peach-stone / 无～蜜桔 pipless tangerine / 无～葡萄干 seedless raisins ② nucleus: 细胞核 xìbāohé ③ atomic nucleus

核[2]（覈） hé examine; check: 核准 hézhǔn ——see also hú

核保护伞 hébǎohùsǎn nuclear umbrella

核爆炸 hébàozhà nuclear explosion

核查 héchá examine and verify; check

核磁共振 hé cí gòngzhèn nuclear magnetic resonance

核打击力量 hédǎjī lìliàng nuclear strike capability (or force)

核大国 hédàguó nuclear power

核蛋白 hédànbái *biochem.* nucleoprotein

核弹头 hédàntóu nuclear warhead

核导弹 hédǎodàn nuclear missile

核电站 hédiànzhàn nuclear power plant

核定 hédìng check and ratify; appraise and decide

核动力 hédònglì nuclear power

核对 héduì check: ～数字 check figures / ～帐单 check a bill / ～事实 check the facts

核讹诈 hé'ézhà nuclear blackmail

核发 héfā approve and issue (a driving license, etc.)

核反应 héfǎnyìng nuclear reaction

核反应堆 héfǎnyìngduī nuclear reactor

核辐射 héfúshè nuclear radiation

核苷 hégān *biochem.* nucleoside: ～酸 nucleotide

核果 héguǒ *bot.* drupe

核黄素 héhuángsù riboflavin; lactoflavin

核火箭 héhuǒjiàn nuclear rocket

核计 héjì assess; calculate: ～成本 assess the cost

核减 héjiǎn examine (a budget, etc.) and make cuts

核聚变 héjùbiàn nuclear fusion

核扩散 hékuòsàn nuclear proliferation

核裂变 hélièbiàn nuclear fission

核垄断 hélǒngduàn nuclear monopoly

核能 héněng (also 核子能 hézǐnéng) nuclear energy

核潜艇 héqiántǐng nuclear-powered submarine

核燃料 héránliào nuclear fuel

核仁 hérén ① *biol.* nucleolus ② kernel (of a fruit-stone)

核实 héshí verify; check: ～的产量 verified output / 请把这些数字～一下。Please check these figures.

核试验 héshìyàn nuclear test: 大气层 (高空，地下)～ atmospheric (high-altitude, underground) nuclear test

核素 hésù ① *chem.* nuclein ② *phys.* nuclide

核酸 hésuān *biochem.* nucleic acid: ～酶 nuclease / ～内切酶 endonuclease

核算 hésuàn ① examine and calculate; assess: ～生产成本 work out the costs of production ② business accounting

核算单位 hésuàn dānwèi accounting unit: 基本～ basic accounting unit / 独立～ independent accounting unit

核糖 hétáng *biochem.* ribose

核糖核酸 hétáng hésuān *biochem.* ribonucleic acid; RNA: 脱氧～ deoxyribonucleic acid; DNA / 信息～ messenger ribonucleic acid; m-RNA

核桃 hétao walnut

核桃仁 hétaorén walnut meat

核威慑力量 héwēishè lìliàng nuclear deterrent (power)

核威胁 héwēixié nuclear threat

核微粒沾染 héwēilì zhānrǎn contamination from nuclear fallout

核武库 héwǔkù nuclear arsenal

核武器 héwǔqì nuclear weapon: ～储备 stockpiling of nuclear weapons; nuclear weapons stockpile

核销 héxiāo cancel after verification

核心 héxīn nucleus; core; kernel: 领导～ the core of leadership / ～力量 force at the core / ～人物 key person; key figure / 起～作用 play a key role / 抓住问题的～ get to the heart of the matter / 辩证法的～ the kernel of dialectics

核心家庭 héxīn jiātíng nuclear family

核战争 hézhànzhēng nuclear war (or warfare)

核装置 hézhuāngzhì nuclear device

核准 hézhǔn examine and approve; check and approve: 经主管部门～后，发给营业执照。Business licences shall be issued after examination and approval by the department concerned.

核子 hézǐ *phys.* nucleon

核子学 hézǐxué　nucleonics

盍（盇） hé　*formal*　why not: ～往视之? Why not go and see it?

涸 hé　*formal*　dry up: 干涸 gānhé
涸竭 héjié　dried up; exhausted
涸泽而渔 hé zé ér yú　same as 竭泽而渔 jié zé ér yú
涸辙之鲋 hé zhé zhī fù　a fish stranded in a dry rut—in a desperate situation

盒 hé　box; case: 一～火柴 a box of matches
盒饭 héfàn　box lunch
盒式磁带 héshìcídài　cassette tape
盒子 hézi　① box; case; casket ② same as 盒子枪 héziqiāng
盒子枪 héziqiāng　(also 盒子炮 hézipào) *dial.* Mauser pistol

颌 hé　jaw: 上（下）～ the upper (lower) jaw ——see also gé
颌针鱼 hézhēnyú　needlefish

阖（阁） hé　*formal*　① entire; whole: ～城 the whole town ② shut; close: ～户 close the door
阖府 héfǔ　(also 阖第 hédì) *honor.* your whole family: 敬请～光临。The presence of your whole family is cordially requested.
阖家 héjiā　the whole family
阖眼 héyǎn　close one's eyes

貉 hé　racoon dog ——see also háo

翮 hé　① shaft of a feather; quill ② *formal* wing (of a bird): 振～高飞 flap the wings and soar high into the sky

hè

吓（嚇） hè　① threaten; intimidate ② *interj.* (showing disapproval): ～, 怎么能干这种事? Tut-tut, how could you do that? ——see also xià

和 hè　① join in the singing: 一唱百和 yī chàng bǎi hè ② compose a poem in reply: 奉～一首 write a poem in reply (to one sent by a friend, etc., using the same rhyme sequence) ——see also hé; hú; huó; huò

贺 hè　① congratulate: 道贺 dàohè ② (Hè) a surname
贺匾 hèbiǎn　congratulatory plaque
贺词 hècí　speech (*or* message) of congratulation; congratulations; greetings: 致～ give a speech of congratulation
贺电 hèdiàn　message of congratulation; congratulatory telegram: 发～ send a congratulatory telegram
贺兰石 hèlánshí　Helan jade
贺礼 hèlǐ　congratulatory gift
贺联 hèlián　congratulatory couplet (written on scrolls, etc.)
贺年 hènián　extend New Year greetings or pay a New Year call
贺年片 hèniánpiàn　New Year card
贺喜 hèxǐ　congratulate sb. on a happy occasion (e.g. a wedding, the birth of a child, etc.); offer congratulations
贺信 hèxìn　(also 贺函 hèhán) congratulatory letter; letter of congratulation

贺仪 hèyí　*formal* congratulatory gift (usu. a gift of money)
贺幛 hèzhàng　congratulatory silk scroll

荷 hè　*formal*　① carry on one's shoulder or back: ～锄 carry a hoe on one's shoulder ② burden; responsibility: 重荷 zhònghè ③ (usu. used in letter writing) grateful; obliged: 无任感～。I'll be very much obliged. / 请早日示复为～。An early reply will be appreciated. ——see also hé
荷负 hèfù　*formal*　bear; shoulder
荷枪实弹 hèqiāng-shídàn　(of soldiers or policemen) carry loaded rifles—ready for an emergency
荷载 hèzài　load
荷重 hèzhòng　the weight a building can bear; load

喝 hè　shout loudly: 大～一声 give a loud shout ——see also hē
喝彩 hècǎi　acclaim; cheer; shout "bravo!": 齐声～ cheer in chorus; cheer with one accord / 博得全场～ bring the house down
喝倒彩 hè dàocǎi　make catcalls; hoot; boo: 观众～, 这位喜剧演员下了场。The comedian left the stage because of the catcalls of the audience.
喝道 hèdào　(of yamen runners, lictors, etc. in former times) clear the road for the official appearing in public by going in front shouting to the crowd to give way
喝令 hèlìng　shout an order (*or* command)
喝六呼么 hèliù-hūyāo　same as 呼么喝六 hūyāo-hèliù
喝问 hèwèn　shout a question to

褐 hè　① *formal*　coarse cloth or clothing ② brown
褐斑病 hèbānbìng　*bot.* brown spot
褐煤 hèméi　(also 褐炭 hètàn) brown coal; lignite
褐色土 hèsètǔ　drab soil
褐铁矿 hètiěkuàng　brown iron ore; limonite
褐藻 hèzǎo　brown alga

赫[1] hè　① conspicuous; grand: 显赫 xiǎnhè ② (Hè) a surname
赫[2] hè　short for 赫兹 hèzī
赫赫 hèhè　illustrious; very impressive: ～战功 illustrious military exploits; brilliant military success
赫赫有名 hèhè yǒumíng　distinguished; illustrious: ～的人物 an illustrious personage
赫然 hèrán　① impressively; awesomely: 一只猛虎～出现在山坡上。To his consternation, a fierce tiger suddenly appeared on the mountain slope. ② terribly (angry): ～震怒 get into a terrible temper; fly into a violent rage
赫哲族 Hèzhézú　the Hezhen (Hoche) nationality, or the Hezhens (Hoches), inhabiting Heilongjiang Province
赫兹 hèzī　*elec.* hertz

鹤 hè　crane
鹤发鸡皮 hèfà-jīpí　white hair and wrinkled skin—aged
鹤发童颜 hèfà-tóngyán　white hair and ruddy complexion—healthy in old age; hale and hearty
鹤立鸡群 hè lì jīqún　like a crane standing among chickens—stand head and shoulders above others
鹤嘴镐 hèzuǐgǎo　pick; pickaxe; mattock

壑 hè　gully; big pool: 千山万～ innumerable mountains and valleys

hēi

黑 hēi ① black: 〜发 black hair ② dark: 〜屋子 a dark room / 天〜了。 It's dark. ③ secret; shady: 〜交易 shady deal ④ wicked; sinister: 黑心 hēixīn ⑤ reactionary ⑥ (Hēi) short for 黑龙江 Hēilóngjiāng②

黑暗 hēi'àn dark: 山洞里一片〜。 It's all darkness in the cave. / 〜统治 dark rule; reactionary rule / 〜面 a dark aspect; the seamy side / 〜势力 forces of darkness; reactionary forces

黑白 hēi-bái ① black and white: 〜花儿 a black-and-white pattern ② right and wrong: 颠倒黑白 diāndǎo hēi-bái

黑白电视 hēibái diànshì black-and-white television

黑白分明 hēi-bái fēnmíng with black and white sharply contrasted; in sharp contrast: 两种态度，〜。 The two attitudes stand in sharp contrast.

黑白片儿 hēibáipiānr inf. black-and-white film

黑白片 hēibáipiàn black-and-white film

黑斑病 hēibānbìng bot. black spot

黑板 hēibǎn blackboard

黑板报 hēibǎnbào blackboard newspaper; blackboard bulletine

黑板擦 hēibǎncā (blackboard) eraser

黑帮 hēibāng reactionary gang; sinister gang; cabal

黑不溜秋 hēibuliūqiū dial. swarthy: 他长得〜的。 He is dark and swarthy. / 这件上衣〜的，一点也不好看。 This jacket is too dark and doesn't look nice at all.

黑潮 hēicháo geog. black stream; Kuroshio; Japan Current (or Stream)

黑沉沉 hēichēnchēn (of the sky) gloomy; overcast

黑道 hēidào ① dark road: 拿着电筒，省得走〜。 Take a torch, or you'll be groping your way in the dark. ② dark deeds (as of robbers)

黑道日子 hēidàorìzi an unlucky day

黑灯瞎火 hēidēng-xiāhuǒ inf. dark; unlighted: 〜的，小心别走错路了。 It's dark outside. Mind you don't get lost.

黑地 hēidì unregistered land

黑点 hēidiǎn stain; blemish; smirch

黑店 hēidiàn old an inn run by brigands

黑貂 hēidiāo sable: 〜皮 sable fur

黑鲷 hēidiāo black porgy

黑洞洞 hēidōngdōng pitch-dark

黑洞 hēidòng astron. black hole; collapsar

黑豆 hēidòu black soya bean

黑非洲 Hēi Fēizhōu Black Africa

黑粉病 hēifěnbìng same as 黑穗病 hēisuìbìng

黑粪 hēifèn med. melaena

黑钙土 hēigàitǔ same as 黑土 hēitǔ①

黑更半夜 hēigēng-bànyè inf. in the dead of night; in the still of the night; in the middle of the night: 〜的，我到哪儿去找住处? Where can I find a place to sleep at this time of night? / 〜的，来找我干吗! What an unearthly time of night to come calling!

黑咕隆咚 hēigulōngdōng inf. very dark; pitch-dark: 天还〜的，他就起来了。 He got up when it was still pitch-dark.

黑管 hēiguǎn popular name for 单簧管 dānhuángguǎn

黑光 hēiguāng black light

黑海 Hēihǎi the Black Sea

黑黑实实 hēiheishíshí (of a person) dark and sturdy

黑糊糊 hēihūhū (also 黑忽忽 hēihūhū; 黑乎乎 hēihūhū) ① black; blackened: 满手油泥，〜的 hands dirty with grease / 墙熏得〜的。 The wall was blackened by smoke. ② rather dark; dusky: 屋子里〜的。 It's rather dark in the room. ③ indistinctly observable in the distance: 远处是一片〜的树林。 A dark mass of trees loomed in the distance.

黑户 hēihù ① unregistered household; unregistered resident ② a shop without a license; an illegal shop

黑话 hēihuà ① (bandits') argot; (thieves') cant ② double-talk; malicious words

黑鲩 hēihuàn another name for 青鱼 qīngyú

黑会 hēihuì a clandestine meeting

黑货 hēihuò smuggled goods; contraband

黑间 hēijiān dial. night

黑胶布 hēijiāobù elec. black tape; friction tape

黑胶绸 hēijiāochóu a rust-coloured variety of summer silk; gambiered Guangdong silk

黑颈鹤 hēijǐnghè black-necked crane

黑牢 hēiláo dark prison cell

黑里康大号 hēilǐkāng dàhào mus. helicon

黑里俏 hēilǐqiào a dark beauty

黑溜溜 hēiliūliū black and bright: 〜的眼珠 black and sparkling eyes

黑瘤 hēiliú med. melanoma

黑龙江 Hēilóngjiāng ① the Heilongjiang River ② Heilongjiang (Province)

黑麦 hēimài rye

黑眉乌嘴 hēiméi-wūzuǐ black and dirty; filthy: 〜的茶壶 a filthy teapot

黑霉 hēiméi black mould

黑面包 hēimiànbāo black bread; brown bread; rye bread

黑名单 hēimíngdān blacklist: 上了〜 be blacklisted

黑木耳 hēimù'ěr same as 木耳 mù'ěr

黑幕 hēimù inside story of a plot, shady deal, etc.: 揭穿〜 expose a sinister project; tell the inside story of a plot, etc.

黑啤酒 hēipíjiǔ dark beer; black beer; stout

黑钱 hēiqián ill-gotten money

黑枪 hēiqiāng ① illegally possessed firearms ② a shot fired from a hiding-place: 打〜 fire shots from a hiding-place; snipe

黑黢黢 hēiqūqū (also 黑漆漆 hēiqīqī) pitch-dark: 〜的夜晚 a pitch-dark night

黑热病 hēirèbìng kala-azar

黑人 Hēirén Black people; Black: 美国〜 Afro-American; Black American

黑人 hēirén unregistered resident

黑色 hēisè black (colour)

黑色火药 hēisè huǒyào black powder

黑色金属 hēisè jīnshǔ ferrous metal

黑色人种 Hēisè Rénzhǒng the black race

黑色素 hēisèsù biochem. melanin

黑色幽默 hēisè yōumò black humour

黑纱 hēishā black armband

黑社会 hēishèhuì the underworld

黑市 hēishì black market

黑市票 hēishìpiào scalping ticket

黑手 hēishǒu a vicious person manipulating sb. or sth. from behind the scenes; evil backstage manipulator

黑手党 Hēishǒudǎng Mafia

黑死病 hēisǐbìng the plague

黑穗病 hēisuìbìng agric. smut

黑索金 hēisuǒjīn hexogen; cyclonite; RDX

黑糖 hēitáng dial. brown sugar

黑桃 hēitáo spade (in cards)

黑陶 hēitáo black pottery (of a late Neolithic culture)

黑陶文化 hēitáo wénhuà the black pottery culture (another name for 龙山文化 Lóngshān wénhuà)

黑体 hēitǐ ① phys. blackbody ② print. boldface: 〜字 boldface type

黑天 hēitiān night; nightfall: 我等她等到〜，也没见她

来。I waited until after dark, but she didn't show up.

黑天白日 hēitiān-báirì (also 黑间白日 hēijiān-báirì) day and night; night and day: 来来往往的车辆吵得人～不得安宁。The noise of the traffic disturbed us day and night.

黑甜乡 hēitiánxiāng land of dark sweetness—sound sleep

黑帖 hēitiě same as 无名帖 wúmíngtiě

黑铁皮 hēitiěpí black sheet (iron)

黑头 hēitóu black-face role—the painted-face role in traditional opera whose make-up is largely in black (e.g. the role of Lord Bao 包公, the greatest judge in Chinese fiction and drama): 裘盛戎以演～著称。Qiu Shengrong was famous for his renderings of the black-face role.

黑土 hēitǔ ① chernozem; black earth ② opium

黑钨矿 hēiwūkuàng wolframite

黑瞎子 hēixiāzi dial. black bear

黑匣子 hēixiázi black box

黑下 hēixia dial. night

黑线 hēixiàn black line (used during the "Cultural Revolution" to refer to things counterrevolutionary)

黑心 hēixīn black heart; evil mind

黑信 hēixìn inf. poison-pen letter

黑猩猩 hēixīngxing chimpanzee

黑熊 hēixióng black bear

黑魆魆 hēixūxū dark

黑压压 hēiyāyā (also 黑鸦鸦 hēiyāyā) a dense or dark mass of: 广场上～地挤满了人。The square was thronged with a dense crowd. / 远处～的一片，看不清是些什么东西。One couldn't make out what the dark mass was from a distance.

黑眼镜 hēiyǎnjìng sunglasses

黑眼珠 hēiyǎnzhū iris

黑曜岩 hēiyàoyán obsidian

黑夜 hēiyè night: 他们昨天～到了上海。They arrived in Shanghai last night. / ～笼罩着大地。Night enshrouded the earth.

黑影儿 hēiyǐngr a dark shadow; shadow: 他一回头，只见有个～一晃而过。He turned round and saw a shadow flit by.

黑油油 hēiyōuyōu jet-black; shiny black: ～的头发 shiny black hair

黑黝黝 hēiyōuyōu ① same as 黑油油 hēiyōuyōu ② dim; dark: 四周～的。It's dark all around.

黑鱼 hēiyú snakeheaded fish; snakehead

黑云 hēiyún black clouds; dark clouds: ～翻墨未遮山，白雨跳珠乱入船。(苏轼) Black clouds—spilled ink half blotting out the hills; Pale rain—bouncing beads that splatter in the boat.

黑云母 hēiyúnmǔ black mica; biotite

黑运 hēiyùn bad luck: 走～ have bad luck; be out of luck

黑枣 hēizǎo dateplum persimmon (Diospyros lotus)

黑种 Hēizhǒng the black race

黑竹 hēizhú same as 紫竹 zǐzhú

黑子 hēizǐ ① formal black mole (on the skin) ② astron. sunspot

嘿（嗨） hēi interj. hey; why: ～, 我说的你听见没有? Hey! Did you hear what I said? / ～! 快走吧! Hey, hurry up! / ～, 咱们生产的机器可真不错呀! Hey, the machine we made is really not bad. / ～, 下雪了! Why, it's snowing! / ～, 真没想到! Well, what do you know?

hén

痕 hén mark; trace: 刀痕 dāohén

痕迹 hénjì mark; trace; vestige: 轮子的～ wheel tracks / 旧社会的～ vestiges of the old sociey / 罪犯没有留下任何作案的～。The criminal didn't leave behind any trace of his crime.

痕量 hénliàng (also 痕迹量 hénjìliàng) chem. trace: ～元素 trace elements / ～杂质 trace impurity

hěn

很 hěn adv. very; very much; quite: 我家离学校～近。I live quite near the school. / 这故事发生在～久～久以前。The story took place a long long time ago. / 这几天热得～。It's been very hot these last few days. / 他这个人好得～。He's a very good man. / 我近来身体不～好。I don't feel quite well thesse days. / 他觉得～不好受。He felt very bad. / 现在他口袋里～有几个钱。He's made himself quite a nice little pile. / ～满意 feel very satisfied; feel quite pleased / ～有道理 contain much truth; be quite correct

狠[1] hěn ① ruthless; relentless: 比豺狼还～ more savage than a wolf ② harden (the heart); suppress (one's feelings): 狠心[1] hěnxīn ③ firm; resolute; severe: 我把他～～打了一顿。I gave him a good beating. / ～批了他一顿。He was severely criticized. / ～～打击歪风邪气 take vigorous measures to counter evil trends

狠[2] hěn same as 很 hěn

狠毒 hěndú vicious; venomous: 用心～ with vicious intent

狠命 hěnmìng dial. go all out

狠心[1] hěnxīn harden one's heart; make a painful decision: 我一～, 打了他一顿。I hardened my heart and gave him a beating. / 我狠不下心去。I can't make such a painful decision.

狠心[2] hěnxīn cruel; heartless; callous: 你真～。You are being rather callous.

hèn

恨 hèn ① hate: 她～你就因为你说了那句话。She hates you for saying that. ② regret: 遗恨 yíhèn

恨不得 hènbude (also 恨不能 hènbuneng) one wishes one could; one would if one could; be dying to: 我～立刻就去。I wish I could go immediately. / 我～立刻就认识他。I'm dying to meet him.

恨事 hènshì a matter for regret

恨铁不成钢 hèn tiě bù chéng gāng wish that iron could turn straight into steel—be anxious for sb. to improve

恨小非君子，无毒不丈夫 hèn xiǎo fēi jūnzǐ, wú dú bù zhàngfū a man with little power of hatred is no man at all; every real man has his venom

恨之入骨 hèn zhī rùgǔ hate sb. to the marrow of one's bones; bear a bitter hatred for sb.; bitterly hate

hēng

亨 hēng go smoothly: 亨通 hēngtōng

亨利 hēnglǐ *elec.* henry: 微~ microhenry

亨通 hēngtōng go smoothly; be prosperous: 万事~。 Everything is going smoothly.

哼

hēng ① groan; snort: 痛得直~~ groan with pain / 轻蔑地~了一声 give a snort of contempt ② hum; croon: 他一边走，一边~着曲子。 He was humming a tune as he walked along. / ~着歌儿哄孩子睡觉 croon the baby to sleep ——see also hng

哼哧 hēngchī *onom.* puff hard: 他跑得~~地直喘。 He was puffing and blowing from running.

哼哈二将 Hēng-Hā èr jiàng ① the Marshals Heng and Ha (two fierce-looking divinities guarding a temple gate; Heng, or the "Snorter," ejecting two rays of light from his nostrils; Ha, or the "Blower," blowing a great gust of yellow gas out of his mouth) ② a pair of fierce men serving one master or acting in collusion with each other

哼儿哈儿 hēngrhār *onom.* hem and haw: 他总是~的，就是不说句痛快话。 He hemmed and hawed but wouldn't say anything definite.

哼哼唧唧 hēngheng jī mumble: 他~的叫人心烦。 His mumbling is so annoying.

哼唧 hēngji mutter; hum

哼唷 hēngyō *interj.* heave ho; yo-heave-ho; yo-ho

脬

hēng　see 膨脬 pénghēng

héng

姮

héng　see below

姮娥 Héng'é another name for 嫦娥 Cháng'é

恒（恆）

héng ① permanent; lasting: 永恒 yǒnghéng ② perseverance: 有恒 yǒuhéng ③ usual; common; constant: 恒言 héngyán

恒产 héngchǎn real estate; immovable property; immovables

恒齿 héngchǐ (also 恒牙 héngyá) permanent tooth

恒等 héngděng *math.* identically equal; identical: ~式 identical equation; identity

恒定 héngdìng constant

恒河沙数 Hénghé shā shù as numerous as the sands of the Ganges; innumerable; countless

恒久 héngjiǔ permanent; lasting; enduring

恒量 héngliàng *phys.* constant

恒流调节器 héngliú tiáojiéqì *elec.* constant current regulator

恒山 Héngshān Mount Heng (in Shanxi Province) ——see also 五岳 Wǔyuè

恒湿 héngshī constant humidity: ~器 humidistat

恒温 héngwēn constant temperature: ~器 thermostat

恒温动物 héngwēn dòngwù homoiothermal (or warm-blooded) animal

恒心 héngxīn perseverance; constancy of purpose: 你要是没有~可学不好。 Unless you persevere with a subject you can't hope to master it.

恒星 héngxīng *astron.* (fixed) star

恒星年 héngxīngnián *astron.* sidereal year

恒星日 héngxīngrì *astron.* sidereal day

恒星时 héngxīngshí *astron.* sidereal time

恒星天文学 héngxīng tiānwénxué *astron.* stellar astronomy

恒星物理学 héngxīng wùlǐxué *astron.* stellar physics

恒星系 héngxīngxì *astron.* stellar system; galaxy

恒星月 héngxīngyuè *astron.* sidereal month

恒星云 héngxīngyún *astron.* star cloud

恒性 héngxìng perseverance; persistence: 他干什么都没个~。 He lacks perseverance in whatever he does.

恒压器 héngyāqì barostat

恒言 héngyán common saying

珩

héng the top gem of a girdle-pendant (as worn by aristocrats and high officials in ancient China) ——see also háng

桁

héng *archit.* purlin

桁架 héngjià *archit.* truss: ~桥 truss bridge

桁条 héngtiáo *archit.* purlin

鸻

héng *zool.* plover: 金~ golden plover

横

héng ① horizontal; transverse: ~线 a horizontal line ② from east to west or from west to east: 横贯 héngguàn ③ crosswise; sideways: 中文也能~着写。 Chinese can also be written across the page. / 一棵倒了的树~在马路上。 A fallen tree lay across the road. / 他~在长沙发上看报。 He reclined on the settee reading the newspaper. / 车间里~挂着一幅大标语。 A huge streamer was hung across the workshop. ④ at a right angle to: 横剖面 héngpōumiàn ⑤ place sth. crosswise or horizontally: 把扁担~过来。 Put the carrying pole in a horizontal position. / 把这个桌子~过来。 Turn this table and place it crosswise. / ~刀跃马 gallop ahead with sword drawn ⑥ unrestrained; turbulent: 蔓草~生 overgrown with creepers / 老泪~流 tears flowing from aged eyes ⑦ (meaning much the same as 横 hèng①, limited to use in idiomatic expressions) violent; fierce; flagrant: 横行霸道 héngxíng-bàdào ⑧ horizontal stroke (in a Chinese character) ⑨ *adv. dial.* in any case; anyway: 我~不那么办！ I'm not going to do that anyway. ⑩ *adv. dial.* most likely; probably: 今天下雨，他~不来了。 It's raining today; he most likely won't come. ——see also hèng

横波 héngbō *phys.* transverse wave

横冲直撞 héngchōng-zhízhuàng push one's way by shoving or bumping; jostle and elbow one's way; dash around madly; barge about; charge about

横穿 héngchuān cross: ~马路 cross a street

横档 héngdàng crosspiece (of a table, etc.)

横倒竖歪 héngdǎo-shùwāi in disorder; higgledy-piggledy

横笛 héngdí bamboo flute

横渡 héngdù cross a river, etc.: ~太平洋的飞行 a trans-Pacific flight

横断面 héngduànmiàn same as 横剖面 héngpōumiàn

横队 héngduì rank; row: 排成三列~ line up three deep

横幅 héngfú ① horizontal scroll of painting or calligraphy ② banner; streamer: 欢迎群众举着~标语。 The welcoming crowd carried banners with slogans on them.

横格纸 hénggézhǐ lined paper

横膈膜 hénggémó *physiol.* diaphragm

横亘 hénggèn lie across; span: 一座雄伟的大桥~在江上。 A magnificent bridge spans the river.

横贯 héngguàn pass through from east to west or from west to east; traverse: 黄河~本省。 The Yellow River flows through this province from west to east. / 这条铁路~五省。 The railway traverses five provinces.

横巷 hénghàng *min.* crosscut

横祸 hénghuò unexpected calamity; sudden misfortune

横加 héngjiā do sth. to sb. unreasonably, forcibly, wilfully, etc.: ~指责 make unwarranted charges / ~干涉 flagrantly interfere / ~阻挠 wilfully obstruct

横结肠 héngjiécháng *physiol.* transverse colon

横跨 héngkuà stretch over or across: 一道彩虹~天际。

A rainbow arched across the sky. /～长江的大桥 a gigantic bridge spanning the Changjiang River

横梁 héngliáng ① *archit.* crossbeam ② cross member (of a car)

横眉 héngméi frown in anger; scowl

横眉冷对千夫指,俯首甘为孺子牛 héngméi lěng duì qiānfū zhǐ, fǔshǒu gān wéi rúzǐniú fierce-browed, I coolly defy a thousand pointing fingers; head bowed, like a willing ox I serve the children

横眉怒目 héngméi-nùmù with frowning brows and angry eyes; darting fierce looks of hate

横眉竖眼 héngméi-shùyǎn glare in anger

横拍握法 héngpāi wòfǎ *table tennis* tennis grip; handshake grip

横批 héngpī a horizontal scroll bearing an inscription (usu. hung over a door and flanked by two vertical scrolls forming a couplet)

横披 héngpī a horizontal wall inscription; a horizontal hanging scroll

横剖面 héngpōumiàn cross (or transverse) section

横七竖八 héngqī-shùbā in disorder; at sixes and sevens; higgledy-piggledy: 满院子～的绳子上,晒着各家的破衣破裤。Lines are strung across here and there on which the families have hung out their old and tattered clothes and bedding to dry. / 屋子里～地堆放着许多杂物。The room was cluttered with all sorts of things.

横切 héngqiē crosscut

横切面 héngqiēmiàn same as 横剖面 héngpōumiàn

横肉 héngròu (usu. used in) 一脸～ look ugly and ferocious

横扫 héngsǎo sweep across or over; sweep away: 飓风从西北方向～过来。The hurricane swept over in a southeasterly direction. /（七百里驱十五日,赣水苍茫闽山碧,～千军如卷席。(毛泽东) In fifteen days we have marched seven hundred *li* Crossing misty Gan waters and green Fujian hills, Rolling back the enemy as we would a mat.

横生 héngshēng ① grow wild: 蔓草～ be overgrown with weeds ② be overflowing with; be full of: 妙趣横生 miàoqù héngshēng ③ happen unexpectedly: ～是非 a dispute unexpectedly broke out

横生枝节 héngshēng zhījié raise unexpected difficulties; deliberately complicate an issue

横是 héngshi *dial.* probably; most likely: ～要下雨了。It will probably rain. / 太晚了,他～不会来了。He isn't likely to come now; it's too late. / 他～快八十了吧？He's getting on for eighty, I suppose?

横竖 héngshu *adv. inf.* in any case; anyway: ～我要去的,不用给他打电话了。No need to ring him up. I'll be going there anyway.

横顺 héngshùn *dial.* in any case; anyway: 我妈说我不能去参加那个晚会,可我～是去定了。My mother says I can't go to the party but I'm going anyway.

横说竖说 héngshuō-shùshuō say again and again (in persuasion or explanation): 我～,他就是不答应。I bent over backwards trying to persuade him, but he still refused.

横躺竖卧 héngtǎng-shùwò (of a number of persons) lie about in disorder

横挑鼻子竖挑眼 héng tiāo bízi shù tiāo yǎn *inf.* find fault in a petty manner; pick holes in sth.; nitpick

横尾翼 héngwěiyì *aviation* tail plane; horizontal stabilizer

横纹肌 héngwénjī striated muscle

横向 héngxiàng horizontal; crosswise: 发展沿海开放城市同内地的～经济联合 expand the horizontal economic collaboration (or ties) of the open coastal cities with the interior areas

横心 héngxīn steel one's heart; become desperate: 横下一条心 resolve to do sth. in desperation

横行 héngxíng run wild; run amuck; be on a rampage: 盗匪～。Banditry was rife.

横行霸道 héngxíng-bàdào ride roughshod over; trample on; tyrannize; domineer: ～,为所欲为 act like an overlord and do whatever one wishes

横行无忌 héngxíng wújì run wild; run amuck

横行一时 héngxíng yīshí run wild for a time

横许 héngxǔ *dial.* probably; most likely

横溢 héngyì ① (of a river) overflow; be in flood: 江河～ turbulent waters overflowing their banks ② (of talent, enthusiasm, etc.) brimming; overflowing; abundant: 才气～ brimming with talent / 热情～ overflowing with enthusiasm

横征暴敛 héngzhēng-bàoliǎn extort excessive (or heavy) taxes and levies; levy exorbitant taxes: 利用独裁权力～ use one's dictatorial powers to extort taxes and levies

横直 héngzhí *dial.* in any case; anyway

横轴 héngzhóu *mech.* cross axle (or shaft)

横坐标 héngzuòbiāo *math.* abscissa

衡

héng ① the graduated arm of a steelyard ② weighing apparatus ③ weigh; measure; judge: 衡量 héng·liáng

衡量 héng·liáng weigh; measure; judge: 用政治标准来～ measure sth. or judge sb. by political criteria / 请你～一下这件事该怎么办。Will you please consider what to do about it?

衡量得失 héng·liáng déshī weigh up the gains and losses

衡器 héngqì weighing apparatus

衡情度理 héngqíng-duólǐ considering the circumstances and judging by common sense; all things considered

衡山 Héngshān Mount Heng (in Hunan Province) ——see also 五岳 Wǔyuè

蘅

héng see 杜蘅 dùhéng

hèng

横

hèng ① harsh and unreasonable; perverse: ～话 harsh, unreasonable words ② unexpected: 横事 hèngshì ——see also héng

横暴 hèngbào perverse and violent

横财 hèngcái ill-gotten wealth (or gains): 发～ get rich by foul means

横蛮 hèngmán rude and unreasonable: 他是个～不讲理的人。He's a most rude and unreasonable man.

横逆 hèngnì *formal* a perverse and unreasonable manner; an outrageous manner: 待我以～ treat me in an outrageous manner

横事 hèngshì an untoward accident

横死 hèngsǐ die a violent death; meet with a sudden death

横议 hèngyì *formal* comment without reserve; make unbridled criticism

横恣 hèngzì *formal* perverse and wanton

hm

噷

hm *interj.* (expressing disapproval or reproach) humph: ～,别提了。Humph, don't bring that up. / ～,算了吧。Humph, forget about it.

hng

哼 hng *interj.* (expressing disapproval or suspicion) humph: ～，谁信你的! Humph! Who believes what you say? ——see also hēng

hōng

轰[1]**(轟)** hōng ① *onom.* bang; boom: ～的一声，敌人的碉堡给炸飞了。The enemy pillbox was blown up with a bang. / ～! ～! ～! 一连串爆破声震撼山谷。Boom! Boom! Boom! A series of explosions shook the valley. ② rumble; bombard; explode: 雷～电闪。Thunder rumbled and lightning flashed. / 万炮齐～ten thousand cannons booming

轰[2]**(轟、揈)** hōng shoo away; drive off: ～麻雀 shoo away the sparrows / ～下台 hoot sb. off the platform; oust sb. from office or power / 把他～出去。Throw him out.

轰动 hōngdòng cause a sensation; make a stir: ～全国 cause a sensation throughout the country / 全场～make a stir in the audience (*or* in the hall)

轰动一时 hōngdòng yīshí create a furore; make a great stir; cause a great sensation: ～的谋杀案 a sensational murder case / 这部电影曾～。The film was a great hit.

轰赶 hōnggǎn shoo away; drive off: ～鸡 shoo the chickens away / ～苍蝇 whisk the flies off

轰轰 hōnghōng *onom.* rumble; boom; buzz: 火车～地响。The train thundered along. / 蝇子～地乱飞。Flies buzzed around the room.

轰轰烈烈 hōnghōnglièliè on a grand and spectacular scale; vigorous; dynamic: ～的群众运动 vigorous mass movements / 老一辈的人们完全不能设想的变革，都～地出现了。Transformations utterly inconceivable to people of the older generation have come into being amid fire and thunder.

轰击 hōngjī ① shell; bombard: ～敌人阵地 shell enemy positions ② *phys.* bombard: 中子～neutron bombardment

轰隆 hōnglōng *onom.* rumble; roll: 雷声～～地响。Thunder rumbled. / ～的机器声 the hum of machines

轰鸣 hōngmíng thunder; roar: 马达～。Motors roared. / 雷声～。There was a peal of thunder.

轰然 hōngrán with a loud crash (*or* bang)

轰响 hōngxiǎng roar; rumble: 大炮～。The cannons roared. / 货车～着开过去了。The lorry roared past.

轰炸 hōngzhà attack with bombs; bomb: ～陆地目标 bomb targets on the ground / 昨天有五架敌机前来～。Five enemy planes came to bomb us yesterday. / 二次世界大战期间，伦敦多次遭到～。London was bombed many times during World War Ⅱ.

轰炸机 hōngzhàjī bomber
轰炸瞄准具 hōngzhà miáozhǔnjù bombsight
轰炸误差 hōngzhà wùchā bombing error

哄 hōng ① *onom.* roars of laughter ② hubbub ——see also hǒng; hòng

哄传 hōngchuán (of rumours) circulate widely: 这个消息很快就～开了。It was not long before the news was widely circulated.

哄动 hōngdòng same as 轰动 hōngdòng
哄闹 hōngnào (of a crowd of people) make a lot of noise; make a racket

哄抢 hōngqiǎng (of a crowd of people) make a mad rush for; make a scramble for (public property, goods, etc.)

哄然 hōngrán boisterous; uproarious: ～大笑 burst into uproarious laughter / 舆论～。There was a public outcry.

哄抬 hōngtái drive up (prices)

哄堂大笑 hōngtáng dàxiào the whole room rocking with laughter: 引起听众～make the audience roar with laughter / 众人听了，～起来。The whole party exploded in fits of mirth.

哄笑 hōngxiào (of a crowd of people) break into loud laughter; roar with laughter

訇 hōng ① *formal* loud noise: ～然 with a loud crash ② see 阿訇 āhōng

烘 hōng ① dry or warm by the fire: ～手 warm one's hands at the fire / 把湿衣服～一～ dry wet clothes by the fire / ～面包 bake bread ② set off: 烘托 hōngtuō

烘焙 hōngbèi cure (tea or tobacco leaves)
烘衬 hōngchèn same as 烘托 hōngtuō
烘干 hōnggān ① dry over heat: 把湿衣服～ dry wet clothes over the fire ② *chem.* stoving
烘缸 hōnggāng dryer
烘烘 hōnghōng *onom.* the sound of a roaring fire
烘烤 hōngkǎo toast; bake: ～面包 bake bread / 大家围着火堆，～着冻得发僵的手。Everybody sat round the fire, warming their frozen hands.
烘篮 hōnglán a hand-held basketwork brazier
烘笼 hōnglóng ① a basketwork frame put over an oven or brazier for drying clothes ② *dial.* a hand-held basketwork brazier
烘漆 hōngqī baking finish; stoving finish
烘丝机 hōngsījī cut-tobacco drier
烘托 hōngtuō ① (in Chinese painting) add shading around an object to make it stand out ② set off by contrast; throw into sharp relief: ～出音乐的主题 set off the *leitmotiv* by contrast
烘箱 hōngxiāng oven
烘相器 hōngxiàngqì *photog.* print drier
烘云托月 hōngyún-tuōyuè paint clouds to set off the moon; provide a foil for a character or incident in a literary work: 收到了～的艺术效果 achieve the artistic effect of prominence through contrast

薨 hōng (of feudal lords or high officials) die; pass away

hóng

弘 hóng ① great; grand; magnificent ② enlarge; expand

弘论 hónglùn same as 宏论 hónglùn
弘扬 hóngyáng carry forward; develop; enhance: ～五四精神 carry forward the spirit of the May 4th Movement
弘愿 hóngyuàn same as 宏愿 hóngyuàn
弘旨 hóngzhǐ same as 宏旨 hóngzhǐ

红 hóng ① red: ～墙绿瓦 a red ochre wall with green tiles / 他的眼睛都熬～了。His eyes become bloodshot from lack of sleep. / 脸上一阵白一阵～flush and turn pale by turns ② revolutionary; red: ～五月 the red month of May ③ red cloth, bunting,

etc. used on festive occasions: 披红 pīhóng ④ symbol of success: 他是个很～的歌星。He's a very popular singer. ⑤ bonus; dividend: 分红 fēnhóng ——see also gōng

红案 hóng'àn red (chopping) board—cooking that deals with dishes, both meat and vegetable ——see also 白案 bái'àn

红白喜事 hóng-bái xǐshì weddings and funerals: 什么～，讨媳妇，死了人，大办其酒席，实在可以不必。When people wear red or white, that is, at weddings or funerals, the practice of giving lavish feasts can well be dispensed with.

红斑 hóngbān *med.* erythema

红斑狼疮 hóngbān lángchuāng lupus erythematosus

红榜 hóngbǎng honour roll (*or* board)

红包 hóngbāo a red paper envelope containing money as a gift, tip, or bonus

红宝石 hóngbǎoshí ruby

红不棱登 hóngbulēngdēng *inf.* (disagreeably) reddish in colour: 这件兰布大褂染得不好，太阳一晒显得～的。This blue jacket was badly dyed and has turned reddish after exposure to the sun.

红菜汤 hóngcàitāng borsch

红菜头 hóngcàitóu beetroot

红茶 hóngchá black tea

红场 Hóngchǎng Red Square (in Moscow)

红潮 hóngcháo ① blush; flush: 人家一夸，她脸上就泛起～。She blushes when praised. ② *biol.* red tide; red water

红尘 hóngchén the world of mortals; human society

红赤赤 hóngchīchī very red: 他通宵没睡，眼睛熬得～的。He stayed up all night and his eyes are bloodshot.

红绸舞 hóngchóuwǔ red silk dance

红丹 hóngdān *chem.* red lead; minium

红丹漆 hóngdānqī red lead paint

红蛋 hóngdàn red eggs (eggs dyed red on the happy occasion of the birth of a child and given as gifts to friends and relatives)

红得发紫 hóngde fā zǐ (of a person) extremely popular: 三十年代他～，战后就默默无闻了。He reached the height of his popularity in the thirties, and was all but forgotten after the war.

红灯区 hóngdēngqū red-light district

红电气石 hóngdiànqìshí *min.* rubellite

红定 hóngdìng betrothal gifts (from the bridegroom to the bride's family)

红豆 hóngdòu red bean (*Abrus precatorius,* Indian licorice or paternoster pea, a shrub famous for its red seeds which were used as love tokens, hence the variant name 相思子"lovesickness seeds"): ～生南国，春来发几枝。愿君多采撷，此物最相思。(王维) The red bean grows in southern lands. With spring its slender tendrils twine. Gather for me some more, I pray, Of fond remembrance 'tis the sign.

红矾 hóngfán *dial.* (white) arsenic

红粉 hóngfěn rouge and powder—women

红封 hóngfēng same as 红包 hóngbāo

红汞 hónggǒng *pharm.* mercurochrome

红骨顶 hónggǔdǐng *zool.* moorhen

红光满面 hóngguāng mǎnmiàn one's face glowing with health; in the pink

红果 hóngguǒ *dial.* the fruit of large Chinese hawthorn; haw

红海 Hónghǎi the Red Sea

红鹤 hónghè ibis

红红绿绿 hónghónglǜlǜ in gay colours: 孩子们穿得～的过新年。Children were gaily dressed on New Year's Day.

红狐 hónghú red fox

红花 hónghuā *Chin. med.* safflower

红花草 hónghuācǎo another name for 紫云英 zǐyúnyīng

红货 hónghuò *old* pearls and jewels; jewelry

红火 hónghuo *dial.* flourishing; prosperous: 石榴花越开越～。The pomegranate flowers were more and more flourishing. / 他们的日子越过越～。Their days are becoming better and better. / 晚会开得很～。The evening party was a great success.

红极一时 hóng jí yīshí be well-known for a time; enjoy popularity for a time

红脚鹬 hóngjiǎoyù redshank

红教 Hóngjiào the Red Sect (the prevailing Lamaist cult in Tibet in the 8th and 9th centuries; so called from the colour of its vestments)

红净 hóngjìng red-face role—the painted-face role in traditional opera whose make-up is largely in red (e.g. the role of Lord Guan 关公, grandest of the heroes of the chivalrous Three Kingdoms period)

红角 hóngjué a very popular actor or actress

红军 Hóngjūn ① (short for 中国工农红军) the Chinese Workers' and Peasants' Red Army (1928—1937); the Red Army ② Red Army man ③ Soviet Union army before 1946

红利 hónglì bonus; extra dividend

红脸 hóngliǎn ① blush: 这小孩跟生人说话爱～。This child often blushes when speaking to strangers. ② flush with anger; get angry: 他俩从来没有红过脸。There has never been a cross word between the two of them. ③ red face, face painting in Beijing opera, etc., traditionally for the heroic or the honest ——see also 唱红脸 chàng hóngliǎn

红粮 hóngliáng *dial.* kaoliang; Chinese sorghum

红磷 hónglín red phosphorus

红铃虫 hónglíngchóng pink bollworm

红领巾 hónglǐngjīn ① red scarf (worn by Young Pioneers) ② Young Pioneer

红领章 hónglǐngzhāng red collar tab (as formerly on PLA uniforms)

红柳 hóngliǔ another name for 柽柳 chēngliǔ

红绿灯 hónglǜdēng traffic light; traffic signal

红麻 hóngmá *bot.* bluish dogbane (*Apocynum venetum*)

红麻料儿 hóngmáliàor another name for 朱雀 zhūquè

红帽子 hóngmàozi ① red cap (anyone branded a Communist or a Communist sympathiser before Liberation was said to be wearing a red cap) ② (railway) porter; redcap

红媒 hóngméi matchmaker; go-between

红煤 hóngméi *dial.* anthracite

红霉素 hóngméisù erythromycin

红焖 hóngmèn stew in soy sauce: ～鸡 stewed chicken

红米 hóngmǐ red rice

红棉 hóngmián same as 木棉 mùmián

红模子 hóngmúzi a sheet of paper with red characters printed on it, to be traced over with a brush by children learning calligraphy

红木 hóngmù padauk; mahogany: ～家具 mahogany furniture

红男绿女 hóngnán-lǜnǚ gaily dressed young men and women

红娘 Hóngniáng ① the maid in the play the *Western Chamber* (《西厢记》), whose good offices help bring about the union of the lovers, her mistress Yingying (莺莺) and Student Zhang (张生) ② go-between; matchmaker

红娘鱼 hóngniángyú sea robin; red gurnard

红牌 hóngpái *sports* red card

红喷喷 hóngpēnpēn reddish; with a red tint: ～的苹果 red apples / 姑娘脸颊～的, 挂着微笑。The girl had rosy cheeks, brightened by a smile.

红砒 hóngpī another name for 砒霜 pīshuāng

红皮书 hóngpíshū red paper; red book

红扑扑 hóngpūpū flushed: 喝了几杯酒, 脸上～的。After a few drinks his face flushed.

红旗 hóngqí red flag or banner (often as a symbol of the proletarian revolution or of an advanced unit): 在～下长大 be brought up under the red flag; grow up in socialist society / 工业战线上的一面～ a red banner (*or* pacesetter) on the industrial front

红旗单位 hóngqí dānwèi red-banner unit; advanced unit

红旗手 hóngqíshǒu red-banner pacesetter; advanced worker

红曲 hóngqū red colouring agent for food, also used as a Chinese medicine

红壤 hóngrǎng (also 红土 hóngtǔ) red soil (or earth)

红人 hóngrén a favourite with sb. in power; fair-haired boy: 部长的～ a favourite with the Minister

红润 hóngrùn ruddy; rosy: 脸色～ ruddy complexion; rosy cheeks

红三叶 hóngsānyè red clover

红色 hóngsè ① red ② revolutionary; red: ～政权 red political power

红杉 hóngshān Chinese larch

红烧 hóngshāo braise in soy sauce: ～肉 pork braised in brown sauce; red-cooked pork

红苕 hóngsháo *dial.* sweet potato

红生 hóngshēng same as 红净 hóngjìng

红十字会 Hóngshízìhuì the Red Cross

红薯 hóngshǔ common name for 甘薯 gānshǔ

红树 hóngshù mangrove

红松 hóngsōng Korean pine

红糖 hóngtáng brown sugar

红桃 hóngtáo heart (in cards)

红陶 hóngtáo red pottery; terra-cotta

红藤 hóngténg Sargent gloryvine (*Sargentodoxa cuneata*)

红彤彤 hóngtōngtōng (also 红通通 hóngtōngtōng) bright red; glowing: ～的火苗 glowing red flames / 他脸儿晒得～的。His face is aglow from exposure to the sun.

红铜 hóngtóng same as 紫铜 zǐtóng

红外激射 hóngwàijīshè *phys.* iraser

红外线 hóngwàixiàn (also 红外光 hóngwàiguāng) infrared ray

红外线辐射 hóngwàixiàn fúshè infrared radiation

红外线扫描装置 hóngwàixiàn sǎomiáo zhuāngzhì infrared scanner

红外线探测器 hóngwàixiàn tàncèqì infrared detector

红外线照相 hóngwàixiàn zhàoxiàng infrared photography

红卫兵 Hóngwèibīng ① the Red Guards (an organization during the "Cultural Revolution") ② Red Guard

红细胞 hóngxìbāo red blood cell; erythrocyte: ～计数 red cell count

红线 hóngxiàn red line (used during the "Cultural Revolution" to refer to things revolutionary): 贯穿全书的一条～ a red thread running through the book

红小兵 Hóngxiǎobīng ① the Little Red Guards (a school children's organization during the "Cultural Revolution") ② Little Red Guard

红小豆 hóngxiǎodòu red bean

红心 hóngxīn a red heart—a heart loyal to the cause of proletarian revolution: 一颗～为人民 with a red heart always loyal to the people

红锌矿 hóngxīnkuàng zincite

红新月会 Hóngxīnyuèhuì the Red Crescent

红星 hóngxīng red star (a symbol of the proletarian revolution): ～帽徽 red star cap insignia (of PLA soldiers)

红学 Hóngxué studies of the *Hongloumeng* (《红楼梦》, *A Dream of Red Mansions*); *Hongloumeng* scholarship; Red-ology: ～家 *Hongloumeng* scholar

红血球 hóngxuèqiú red blood cell; erythrocyte

红颜 hóngyán *liter.* a pretty face—a beautiful woman: 一朝春尽～老, 花落人亡两不知。(《红楼梦》) The day that spring takes wing and beauty fades, Who will care for the fallen blossom or dead maid?

红颜薄命 hóngyán bómìng beautiful women suffer unhappy fates

红眼 hóngyǎn ① become infuriated; see red: 别再跟他闹了, 再闹, 他可要～了。Don't tease him any more or he'll see red in a minute. ② *dial.* be envious; be jealous of: 一见别人收入比他多, 他就～。He is always jealous of people who earn more than he does.

红眼病 hóngyǎnbìng ① popular name for 结膜炎 jiémóyán ② envy; jealousy

红艳艳 hóngyànyàn brilliant red: ～的杜鹃花 bright red azaleas

红药水 hóngyàoshuǐ mercurochrome

红叶 hóngyè red autumnal leaves (of the maple, etc.)

红衣主教 hóngyī zhǔjiào *Catholicism* cardinal

红缨枪 hóngyīngqiāng red-tasselled spear

红鱼 hóngyú (red) snapper

红运 hóngyùn good luck: 走～ have a spate of good luck

红晕 hóngyùn blush; flush: 脸上泛出～ one's face blushing scarlet

红糟 hóngzāo red wine dregs (used as seasonings)

红枣 hóngzǎo red date

红藻 hóngzǎo red alga

红涨 hóngzhàng (of one's face) be swelled with blood: 他～着脸, 不知说什么好。He flushed and could think of nothing to say.

红蜘蛛 hóngzhīzhū *dial.* red spider (mite); spider mite

红肿 hóngzhǒng red and swollen

红柱石 hóngzhùshí *geol.* andalusite

红装 hóngzhuāng (also 红妆 hóngzhuāng) *liter.* ① gay feminine attire: 只恐夜深花睡去, 高烧银烛照～。(苏轼) My only fear is that in the depth of night the flowers will go to sleep, So aloft I burn a silver candle to light their red raiment. ② young woman

红装素裹 hóngzhuāng sùguǒ clad in white, adorned in red (said of a sunlit snow scene): 须晴日, 看～, 分外妖娆。(毛泽东) On a fine day, the land, Clad in white, adorned in red, Grows more enchanting.

宏

宏 hóng great; grand; magnificent: 宽宏 kuānhóng

宏博 hóngbó extensive; wide: 知识～ have extensive knowledge; erudite

宏敞 hóngchǎng (of a building, etc.) spacious; grand

宏大 hóngdà grand; great: 规模～ on a grand scale / ～的计划 a great plan / ～的志愿 great aspirations / 一支～的马克思主义理论队伍 a mighty contingent of Marxist theoretical workers / 建设～的科学技术队伍 build a mammoth force of scientific and technical personnel

宏放 hóngfàng *formal* broad-minded; unprejudiced

宏富 hóngfù abundant; rich: 学识～ very learned / 内容～ rich in content

宏观 hóngguān ① *phys.* macroscopic ② macro-: ～经济效益 macroeconomic results / 越是搞活经济, 越要重视～调节。The more the economy is enlivened, the

more attention we should pay to macroeconomic regulation./把～管理和微观搞活结合起来。Combine macro-control and micro-flexibility.

宏观结构 hóngguān jiégòu　macrostructure

宏观经济学 hóngguān jīngjìxué　macroeconomics

宏观世界 hóngguān shìjiè　macrocosm

宏阔 hóngkuò　vast; broad: ～的天空 vast expanse of sky

宏朗 hónglǎng　loud and clear; sonorous

宏丽 hónglì　magnificent; grand; majestic

宏论 hónglùn　informed opinion; intelligent view

宏谟 hóngmó　*formal.* a grand plan; a great project

宏图 hóngtú　great plan; grand prospect: 发展国民经济的～ great plans for developing the national economy

宏伟 hóngwěi　magnificent; grand: ～的人民大会堂 the magnificent Great Hall of the People / ～的前景 grand prospects / 一项～壮丽的事业 a magnificent undertaking

宏愿 hóngyuàn　great aspirations; noble ambition: 改造自然的～ the great aspirations to reshape nature / 中国女排实现了三连冠的～。The Chinese women's volleyball team realized their great ambition of winning the world championship three times in succession.

宏旨 hóngzhǐ　main theme; leading idea of an article

闳
泓 hóng　*formal* ① gate of a lane ② great; grand

hóng　*formal* ① (of water) deep ② *m.*: 一～清泉 a clear spring / 一～秋水 an expanse of limpid water in autumn

洪 hóng　① big; vast: 洪亮 hóngliàng ② flood: 防洪 fánghóng ③ (Hóng) a surname

洪帮 Hóngbāng　the *Hong* Gang (formerly, a secret society)

洪波 hóngbō　(also 洪涛 hóngtāo) big waves

洪大 hóngdà　loud: ～的回声 resounding echoes

洪都拉斯 Hóngdūlāsī　Honduras

洪都拉斯人 Hóngdūlāsīrén　Honduran

洪恩 hóng'ēn　great kindness; great favour

洪泛区 hóngfànqū　floodplain; flooded area

洪峰 hóngfēng　flood peak

洪福 hóngfú　great blessing

洪福齐天 hóngfú qítiān　limitless blessing

洪荒 hónghuāng　chaotic state—primeval times: ～时代 primeval ages; remote antiquity

洪亮 hóngliàng　loud and clear; sonorous: 嗓音～ a sonorous voice

洪量 hóngliàng　① magnanimity; generosity ② great capacity for liquor

洪流 hóngliú　mighty torrent; powerful current: 木筏顺着～远下。The mighty torrent carried the raft far downstream. / 时代的～ the powerful current of the times

洪炉 hónglú　great furnace: 在革命的～里锻炼成长 be tempered in the mighty furnace of revolution

洪脉 hóngmài　*Chin. med.* pulse beating like waves; full pulse

洪水 hóngshuǐ　flood; floodwater: ～位 flood level

洪水猛兽 hóngshuǐ-měngshòu　fierce floods and savage beasts—great scourges

洪灾 hóngzāi　a big flood; inundation

洪钟 hóngzhōng　*formal* large bell: 声如～ have a stentorian (*or* sonorous) voice

虹 hóng　rainbow

虹彩 hóngcǎi　old name for 虹膜 hóngmó

虹膜 hóngmó　*physiol.* iris

虹膜炎 hóngmóyán　iritis

虹吸管 hóngxīguǎn　siphon

虹吸现象 hóngxī xiànxiàng　siphonage

虹雉 hóngzhì　monal

虹鳟 hóngzūn　rainbow trout

䏠 hóng　stingray

鸿 hóng　① swan goose ② *formal* letter: 来鸿 láihóng ③ great; grand: 鸿图 hóngtú

鸿博 hóngbó　*formal* erudite; learned: ～之士 an erudite person; a man of learning

鸿福 hóngfú　same as 洪福 hóngfú

鸿沟 hónggōu　wide gap; chasm; gulf

鸿鹄 hónghú　① swan ② a person of noble aspirations; a person with lofty ideals

鸿鹄之志 hónghú zhī zhì　lofty ambition; high aspirations

鸿基 hóngjī　foundation for a great undertaking

鸿毛 hóngmáo　*liter.* goose feather—something very light or insignificant: 轻于鸿毛 qīngyú hóngmáo

鸿门宴 Hóngmén yàn　Hongmen feast—a meeting contrived as a trap (originally a feast held at Hongmen by Xiang Yu 项羽 for his rival Liu Bang 刘邦, at which an attempt was made on Liu's life)

鸿蒙 hóngméng　(in ancient thought) the vital principle in nature before creation; the primeval atmosphere of nature: 超～混希夷(柳宗元) transcend the primeval atmosphere of nature and blend with the inaudible and the unseen

鸿篇巨制 hóngpiān-jùzhì　a monumental work

鸿儒 hóngrú　*formal* an erudite person; a learned scholar: 谈笑有～，往来无白丁。(刘禹锡) Within, the laugh of cultured wit, where no gross soul intrudes.

鸿图 hóngtú　same as 宏图 hóngtú

鸿雁 hóngyàn　swan goose

鸿运 hóngyùn　good luck

鸿爪 hóngzhǎo　see 雪泥鸿爪 xuění hóngzhǎo

蕻 hóng　see 雪里蕻 xuělǐhóng ——see also hòng

黉(黌) hóng　*arch.* school

黉门 hóngmén　*arch.* school

黉宇 hóngyǔ　*arch.* school building

hǒng

哄 hǒng　① fool; humbug: 你这是～我，我不信。You're kidding me; I don't believe it. ② keep (esp. a child) in good humour; coax: ～孩子 keep a child in good humour——see also hōng; hòng

哄逗 hǒngdòu　keep (esp. a child) in good humour; coax: 她很会～孩子。She knows how to handle children. *or* She has a way with children.

哄弄 hǒng·nòng　*dial.* cheat; humbug; hoodwink

哄骗 hǒngpiàn　cheat; humbug; hoodwink: 他编了一套假话来～人。He made up a string of lies to hoodwink people.

哄劝 hǒngquàn　coax: ～孩子吃药 coax a child to take medicine

hòng

讧 hòng　see 内讧 nèihòng

哄(鬨) hòng　uproar; horseplay: 起哄 qǐhòng

——see also hōng; hǒng

哄场 hòngchǎng make catcalls; hoot; boo

蕻 hòng ① *formal* luxuriant; flourishing ② *dial.* stem of some vegetables ——see also hóng

hōu

齁[1] hōu see 齁声 hōushēng

齁[2] hōu ① sickeningly sweet or salty: 这个菜咸得～人。 This dish is much too salty. ② *dial.* (usu. implying disapproval) very; awfully: ～苦 very bitter / 天气～热。 It's awfully hot.

齁齁 hōuhōu *onom.* the sound of snoring: ～熟睡 snore in deep slumber / 鼻息～ snore loudly

齁声 hōushēng the sound of snoring; snore

hóu

侯 hóu ① marquis: 侯爵 hóujué ② a nobleman or a high official: 侯门似海 hóumén sì hǎi ③ (Hóu) a surname

侯爵 hóujué marquis

侯爵夫人 hóujué fūren marquise

侯门似海 hóumén sì hǎi the gate of a noble house is like the sea—impassable to the common man

喉 hóu larynx; throat

喉擦音 hóucāyīn *phonet.* guttural fricative

喉急 hóují *dial.* feel anxious; feel worried

喉结 hóujié *physiol.* Adam's apple

喉镜 hóujìng *med.* laryngoscope: ～检查 laryngoscopy

喉咙 hóulóng throat: ～痛 have a sore throat / 他～叫哑了。 He shouted himself hoarse. / 我渴得～里冒烟。 My throat feels parched.

喉塞音 hóusèyīn *phonet.* glottal stop

喉痧 hóushā *Chin. med.* scarlet fever

喉舌 hóushé mouthpiece: 人民的～ the mouthpiece of the people

喉头 hóutóu larynx; throat

喉炎 hóuyán laryngitis

猴 hóu ① monkey ② *dial.* naughty (boy) ③ *dial.* squat on the heels like a monkey

猴急 hóují same as 喉急 hóují

猴儿精 hóurjīng *dial.* astute; shrewd: 这家伙～～的。 That fellow is very shrewd.

猴面包树 hóumiànbāoshù *bot.* monkey-bread tree; baobab

猴年马月 hóunián-mǎyuè same as 驴年马月 lúnián-mǎyuè

猴皮筋儿 hóupíjīnr (also 猴儿筋 hóurjīn) *inf.* rubber band

猴手猴脚 hóushǒu-hóujiǎo be careless (in handling things); not be steady; act rashly

猴头 hóutóu *bot.* hedgehog hydnum (Hydnum erinaceus)

猴戏 hóuxì a show by a performing monkey; monkey show: 要～ give a monkey show

猴子 hóuzi monkey

瘊 hóu see below

瘊子 hóuzi common name for 疣 yóu

篌 hóu see 箜篌 kōnghóu

糇（餱） hóu *formal* solid food; field rations

骺 hóu see 骨骺 gǔhóu

hǒu

吼 hǒu roar; howl: 狮～ the roar of a lion / 汽笛长～了一声。 The siren sounded loud and long. / 远方传来大炮的～声。 Guns rumbled in the distance. / 示威群众愤怒的～声 the angry shouts of the demonstrators

吼叫 hǒujiào roar; howl; shout: 伤员痛楚地～。 The wounded soldier shouted in pain. / 狂风～着穿过树林。 The wind howled through the trees.

吼鸣 hǒumíng roar; rumble; thunder: 马达～。 Motors roared. / 雷声～。 Thunder rumbled.

hòu

后[1]**（後）** hòu ① behind; back; rear: 村前村～ in front of and behind the village / 屋～ behind (or at the back of) a house ② after; afterwards; later: 课～ after class ③ last: ～五名 the last five (persons) ④ offspring: 无后 wúhòu

后[2] hòu empress; queen

后半场 hòubànchǎng same as 下半场 xiàbànchǎng

后半晌 hòubànshǎng *dial.* afternoon

后半生 hòubànshēng (also 后半辈子 hòubànbèizi) the latter half of one's life

后半天 hòubàntiān afternoon

后半叶 hòubànyè latter half of a century: 十九世纪～ the latter half of 19th century

后半夜 hòubànyè the second half of the night; the small hours

后备 hòubèi reserve: 留有～ keep sth. in reserve / ～力量 reserve forces / ～基金 reserve fund

后备部队 hòubèi bùduì *mil.* reserve units

后备军 hòubèijūn ① reserves ② reserve force: 产业～ industrial reserve army; industrial reserve; reserve army of labour

后背 hòubèi ① back (of the body): 他～上长了个疮。 He has a boil on his back. ② *dial.* at the back; in the rear: 从～袭击敌人 attack the enemy from the rear

后辈 hòubèi ① younger generation; juniors ② posterity

后边 hòubian same as 后面 hòumian

后步 hòubù room for manoeuvre: 留～ leave sufficient room for manoeuvre

后尘 hòuchén *formal* dust kicked up by sb. walking in front: 步人后尘 bù rén hòuchén

后沉 hòuchén (of a car) more heavily loaded in the rear (than in the front)

后处理 hòuchǔlǐ ① *chem.* aftertreatment ② *text.* finishing

后代 hòudài ① later periods (in history); later ages ② later generations; descendants; posterity: 为～着想 for the sake of future generations; in the interest of future generations ③ *biol.* progeny

后灯 hòudēng taillight (of a car); tail lamp

后爹 hòudiē *inf.* stepfather

后盾 hòudùn backing; backup force: 坚强的～ powerful backing

后发制人 hòu fā zhì rén　gain mastery by striking only after the enemy has struck

后方 hòufāng　① rear: ～工作 rear-area work; work in the rear／～勤务 rear service; logistics (service)／～医院 base (or rear) hospital ② behind

后妃 hòufēi　empress and imperial concubines

后夫 hòufū　second husband

后福 hòufú　① future blessings ② blessings in one's old age

后父 hòufù　stepfather

后儿个 hòurge (also 后儿 hòur) inf. day after tomorrow

后跟 hòugēn　heel (of a shoe or sock)

后宫 hòugōng　① imperial harem; palace of imperial concubines ② imperial concubines

后顾 hòugù　① turn back (to take care of sth.): 无暇～ have no time to look after things one has left behind ② look back (on the past): ～与前瞻 look back to the past and ahead into the future

后顾之忧 hòugù zhī yōu　fear of disturbance in the rear; trouble back at home: 安稳坐占，毫无～ entrench oneself securely without any fear of attacks from behind／孩子有人照管，父母上班没有～。With the baby well cared for, the parents will be free of worries at work.

后滚翻 hòugǔnfān sports backward roll

后果 hòuguǒ　consequence; aftermath: 承担～ accept the consequences／～不堪设想 The consequences would be too ghastly to contemplate. or The consequences would be disastrous.／检查制度不严，会造成严重的～。A lax checking system may have serious consequences.

后汉 Hòu Hàn　① the Later Han (another name for 东汉 Dōng Hàn) ② the Later Han Dynasty (947-950), one of the Five Dynasties (五代)

后花园 hòuhuāyuán　back garden

后话 hòuhuà　part of a story to be recounted later; part of a story that is to come: 这是～，暂且不提。That's what happened later, so no more of it now.

后患 hòuhuàn　future trouble: 根除～ dig up the root of (or remove the cause of) future trouble

后患无穷 hòuhuàn wúqióng　no end of trouble for the future

后悔 hòuhuǐ　regret; repent: ～不已 be overcome with regret／我很～当初没有听他的话。I regret that I didn't heed his advice.

后悔莫及 hòuhuǐ mò jí　too late to repent: 你会感到～。You will find it too late for regrets.

后悔药 hòuhuǐyào　see 吃后悔药 chī hòuhuǐyào

后会有期 hòuhuì yǒu qī　we'll meet again some day: ～，请多保重。We shall meet again. Till then take good care of yourself.

后婚儿 hòuhūnr　a remarried woman

后脊梁 hòujǐliang　same as 脊梁 jǐliang

后记 hòujì　postscript (added to a finished book, etc.)

后继 hòujì　succeed; carry on: 前赴后继 qiánfù-hòujì

后继无人 hòujì wú rén　leave no successor (to carry on a tradition, transmit an art or craft, etc.)

后继有人 hòujì yǒu rén　there is no lack of successors; there's another generation to carry on

后脚 hòujiǎo　① the rear foot (in walking): 前脚一滑，～也站不稳。As the front foot slipped, the rear foot became unsteady. ② (used after 前脚) close behind: 我前脚到车站，他～就赶到了。Immediately after I got to the station, he arrived.／我前脚走，他～到，两人没能碰面。He got there just after I had left, so we missed each other.

后襟 hòujīn　the back of a Chinese robe or jacket

后进 hòujìn　① lagging behind; less advanced; backward: 见～就帮 ready to help those who lag behind／

～赶先进 the less advanced striving to catch up with the more advanced ② juniors

后劲 hòujìn　① delayed effect; aftereffect: 这酒～大。This wine has a strong delayed effect. ② reserve strength; stamina: 他干活有～。He has staying power when he's doing a job.／长跑运动员～得足。Long-distance runners require plenty of stamina.

后晋 Hòu Jìn　the Later Jin Dynasty (936-947), one of the Five Dynasties

后景 hòujǐng　background (of a picture)

后空翻 hòukōngfān sports backward somersault

后昆 hòukūn formal descendants; children

后来 hòulái　afterwards; later: ～怎么样？ What happened afterwards?／～的情况好多了。Things got much better later on.

后来居上 hòu lái jū shàng　the latecomers surpass the old-timers

后来人 hòuláirén　successors: 革命自有～。There is no lack of successors to carry on the revolutionary cause.

后浪推前浪 hòulàng tuī qiánlàng　the waves behind drive on those before: 长江～，一代更比一代强。As in the Changjiang River the waves behind drive on those before, so each new generation excels the last one.

后脸儿 hòuliǎnr dial. the back; the reverse side

后梁 Hòu Liáng　the Later Liang Dynasty (907-923), one of the Five Dynasties

后路 hòulù　① communication lines to the rear; route of retreat: 抄～ attack from the rear／切断敌人～ cut off the enemy's route of retreat ② room for manoeuvre; a way of escape: 留后路 liú hòulù

后掠角 hòuluèjiǎo aviation sweep angle; sweepback

后掠翼 hòuluèyì aviation swept-back wing

后轮 hòulún　rear wheel

后妈 hòumā inf. stepmother

后门 hòumén　① back door (or gate): 大院的～ the back gate of a compound ② backdoor (or backstairs) influence: 开后门 kāi hòumén／走后门 zǒu hòumén

后面 hòumian　① at the back; in the rear; behind: ～还有座位。There are vacant seats at the back. ② later: 这个问题我～还要讲。I'll come back to this question later.

后母 hòumǔ　stepmother

后脑 hòunǎo　hindbrain; rhombencephalon

后脑勺子 hòunǎosháozi (also 后脑勺儿 hòunǎosháor) dial. the back of the head

后年 hòunián　the year after next

后娘 hòuniáng inf. stepmother

后怕 hòupà　fear after the event: 事过之后，我倒真有些～。After it was all over, I became really scared.

后排 hòupái　back row: ～座位 back row seats

后妻 hòuqī　second wife

后期 hòuqī　later stage; later period: 解放战争～ the later stage of the War of Liberation／十九世纪四十年代～ the late 1840s

后起 hòuqǐ　(of people of talent) of new arrivals; of the younger generation: ～的乒坛好手 the younger generation of crack table-tennis players／～的青年作家 budding young writers

后起之秀 hòuqǐ zhī xiù　an up-and-coming youngster; a promising young person

后桥 hòuqiáo　rear (or back) axle (of a car): ～壳 rear axle housing

后勤 hòuqín　rear service; logistics: ～部 rear-service department; logistics department (or command)／～部队 rear-service units; rear services／～机关 rear-service establishments／～基地 logistics base; rear supply base／～人员 rear-service personnel／～支援 logistic support

后人 hòurén　① later generations ② posterity; descen-

dants

后任 hòurèn successor (to a post)

后三角队形 hòusānjiǎo duìxíng *mil.* V formation

后厦 hòushà back veranda

后晌 hòushǎng *dial.* afternoon

后晌 hòushang *dial.* evening: ～饭 supper

后身 hòushēn ① the back of a person: 我只看见个～, 认不清是谁。 I couldn't make out who he was as I only saw his back. ② the back of a garment: 这件衬衫的～太长了。 The back of the shirt is too long. ③ the back of a building: 房～有几棵树。 There are several trees at the back of the house. ④ reincarnation: 她相信那只猫是她去世的姑母的～。 She believes that the cat is a reincarnation of her dead aunt. ⑤ sth. deriving from an earlier form; descendant: 国民党是同盟会的～。 The Kuomintang is the descendant of the Tongmenghui.

后生 hòu·shēng *dial.* ① young man; lad ② having a youthful appearance: 他长得～, 看不出是四十岁的人。 He's forty but looks much younger.

后生可畏 hòushēng kěwèi a youth is to be regarded with respect: ～, 焉知来者之不如今也? (《论语》) It is fitting that we should hold the young in awe. How do we know that the generations to come will not be the equal of the present?

后生女 hòushēngnǚ *dial.* a young woman

后生子 hòushēngzǐ *dial.* a young man

后世 hòushì ① later ages: 《诗经》对～的文学有很大的影响。 The Book of Songs had great influence on the literature of later ages. ② later generations: ～子孙 descendants; posterity

后事 hòushì ① (usu. used in traditional novels) what happened afterwards: 欲知～如何, 且听下回分解。 If you want to know what happened afterwards, read the next chapter. ② funeral affairs

后视镜 hòushìjìng rearview (*or* rear-vision) mirror (as inside a car)

后视图 hòushìtú *mech.* back view; rearview

后手 hòushǒu ① *old* successor ② defensive position (in chess): 这一着儿一走错, 就变成～了。 By this false move you've forced yourself into the defensive. ③ room for manoeuvre; a way of escape

后首 hòushǒu *dial.* afterwards; later

后熟作用 hòushú zuòyòng *agric.* afterripening

后嗣 hòusì descendants

后送 hòusòng *mil.* evacuation

后台 hòutái ① backstage ② backstage supporter; behind-the-scenes backer: ～很硬 have very strong backing

后台老板 hòutái lǎobǎn backstage boss; backstage supporter; behind-the-scenes backer

后唐 Hòu Táng the Later Tang Dynasty (923-936), one of the Five Dynasties

后天[1] hòutiān (also 后日 hòurì) day after tomorrow

后天[2] hòutiān postnatal; acquired: 知识是～获得的, 不是先天就有的。 Knowledge is acquired, not innate.

后天免疫 hòutiān miǎnyì same as 获得性免疫 huòdéxìng miǎnyì

后天免疫缺损综合症 hòutiān miǎnyì quēsǔn zōnghézhèng acquired immunodeficiency syndrome; acquired immune deficiency syndrome (Aids)

后头 hòutou ① at the back; in the rear; behind ② later; future: 吃苦还在～呢。 The worst is yet to come.

后图 hòutú *formal* future plan

后土 hòutǔ Earth (personified); All-producing Earth: 皇天淫溢而秋霖兮, ～何时而得干?(《楚辞·九辩》) High Heaven overflows, and the autumn rains are here, And it seems that Earth will never be dry again.

后腿 hòutuǐ hind legs

后退 hòutuì draw back; fall back; retreat: 主动～, 以便歼灭更多敌人 retreat on one's own initiative in order to wipe out more enemy troops / 遇到困难决不～ never shrink from difficulties

后卫 hòuwèi ① *mil.* rear guard: ～战斗 rear-guard action ② *football* full back; defender: 左后卫 zuǒhòuwèi/右后卫 yòuhòuwèi ③ *basketball* guard

后项 hòuxiàng *math.* consequent

后效 hòuxiào see 以观后效 yǐ guān hòuxiào

后行 hòuxíng carry out as a second step; carry out later: 先行登记姓名, ～分配住房。 Let's enter everyone's name first, then we'll allot the rooms.

后续 hòuxù ① follow-up: ～部队 follow-up units / ～会议 follow-up meeting ② *dial.* remarry after the death of one's wife

后悬 hòuxuán rear overhang (of a car)

后学 hòuxué a young or junior scholar or student (often used as a modest term referring to oneself when addressing an elder)

后仰壳 hòuyǎngke *dial.* (usu. used in) 摔了个～ fall flat on one's back

后腰 hòuyāo *inf.* the small of the back

后遗症 hòuyízhèng ① sequelae: 脑震荡～ sequelae of cerebral concussion ② aftereffect; aftermath

后尾儿 hòuyǐr *inf.* the rear part; behind: 他走得很慢, 落在～了。 He was very slow and fell behind.

后裔 hòuyì descendant (of a dead person); offspring

后影 hòuyǐng the shape of a person or thing as seen from the back: 看～像是小李。 From the back view I thought he must be Xiǎo Lǐ.

后援 hòuyuán reinforcements; backup force; backing

后院 hòuyuàn backyard

后帐 hòuzhàng accounts kept secret

后者 hòuzhě the latter

后肢 hòuzhī hind legs (of an animal)

后周 Hòu Zhōu the Later Zhou Dynasty (951-960), one of the Five Dynasties

后轴 hòuzhóu rear axle

后缀 hòuzhuì suffix

后坐力 hòuzuòlì recoil

后座议员 hòuzuò yìyuán backbencher

厚 hòu ① thick: ～木板 a thick plank / ～棉衣 a heavy padded coat / 一尺～的雪 snow one *chì* deep ② deep; profound: 交情很～ profound friendship ③ kind; magnanimous: 忠厚 zhōnghòu ④ large; generous: 厚利 hòulì ⑤ rich or strong in flavour: 酒味很～。 The wine tastes strong. ⑥ favour; stress: 厚此薄彼 hòu cǐ bó bǐ

厚爱 hòu'ài *pol.* your kind thought; your kindness: 承蒙～, 赠我画册, 十分感谢。 Thank you for your kindness in giving me this lovely collection of paintings.

厚薄 hòubó thickness: ～合适。 It's just the right thickness.

厚薄规 hòubóguī *mech.* feeler (gauge)

厚此薄彼 hòu cǐ bó bǐ favour one and be prejudiced against the other; favour one and discriminate against the other

厚待 hòudài treat sb. kindly

厚道 hòudao honest and kind

厚度 hòudù thickness

厚墩墩 hòudūndūn very thick: ～的棉大衣 a heavy padded overcoat

厚恩 hòu'ēn *pol.* your great kindness

厚非 hòufēi see 未可厚非 wèikě hòufēi

厚古薄今 hòu gǔ bó jīn stress the past, not the present

厚今薄古 hòu jīn bó gǔ stress the present, not the past

厚金 hòujīn handsome reward; liberal remuneration

厚礼 hòulǐ generous gifts

厚利 hòulì large profits

厚脸皮 hòuliǎnpí (also 厚脸 hòuliǎn) thick-skinned; brazen; cheeky: 厚着脸皮说 have the nerve to say

厚禄 hòulù handsome salary; high government pay

厚朴 hòupò *Chin. med.* the bark of official magnolia (*Magnolia officinalis*)

厚漆 hòuqī paste paint

厚实 hòushi ① *inf.* thick: 这布挺～。This cloth is very thick. / ～的被褥 thick, heavy quilts and mattresses ② *dial.* abundant; rich: 储备～ abundant reserves / 家底～ a family with substantial resources

厚望 hòuwàng great expectations: 不负～ live up to sb.'s expectations; not let sb. down / 寄予～ place high hopes on

厚味 hòuwèi savoury; rich (*or* greasy) food

厚谢 hòuxiè give sb. a rich reward: 事成之后，必当～。When the thing is done, there will be a rich reward for you.

厚颜无耻 hòuyán-wúchǐ impudent; brazen; shameless

厚谊 hòuyì profound friendship

厚意 hòuyì kind thought; kindness: 多谢你的～。Thank you for your kindness.

厚遇 hòuyù excellent pay and conditions; high wages and good benefits

厚葬 hòuzàng ① bury with full honours ② a lavish funeral

厚重 hòuzhòng ① thick and heavy ② rich and generous: ～的礼物 generous gifts ③ *formal* kind and dignified

近 hòu see 邂逅 xièhòu

候[1] hòu ① wait; await: 请稍～一会儿。Please wait a moment. / ～领 to be kept until claimed ② inquire after: 问候 wènhòu

候[2] hòu ① time; season: 时候 shíhòu ② condition; state: 症候 zhènghou

候补 hòubǔ be a candidate (for a vacancy); be an alternate: 中共中央政治局～委员 an alternate member of the Political Bureau of the Central Committee of the CPC

候场 hòuchǎng (of an actor or actress) wait to go on stage; wait in the wings

候车 hòuchē wait for a train, bus, etc.

候车室 hòuchēshì waiting room (in a railway or bus station)

候光 hòuguāng *pol. formal* await the honour of your presence (at a dinner party, etc.)

候机室 hòujīshì airport lounge or waiting room

候教 hòujiào *pol.* await your instructions: 本星期日下午在舍下～。I'll be expecting you at my place this coming Sunday afternoon.

候鸟 hòuniǎo migratory bird; migrant

候审 hòushěn *leg.* await trial

候选人 hòuxuǎnrén candidate: 提出～ nominate candidates / ～名单 list of candidates / ～资格 qualifications for standing for election

候诊 hòuzhěn wait to see the doctor

候诊室 hòuzhěnshì waiting room (in a hospital)

堠 hòu watchtower in ancient times

鲎[1]（鱟） hòu *zool.* king (*or* horseshoe) crab

鲎[2]（鱟） hòu *dial.* rainbow

鲎虫 hòuchóng apus

乎[1] hū *part. formal* (expressing doubt): 成败之机，其在斯～? Does not success or failure hinge on this?

乎[2] hū ① (verb suffix): 超～寻常 be out of the ordinary ② (suffix of an adjective or adverb): 巍巍～ towering; lofty / 确～重要 very important indeed

乎[3] hū *interj. formal* Oh; O: 天～! Oh, my God!

恗（幠） hū *dial.* cover: 小苗都快让草～住了，赶快锄吧。Let's start hoeing at once. The young shoots are almost choked by the weeds.

呼[1] hū ① breathe out; exhale: ～出二氧化碳 exhale carbon dioxide ② shout; cry out: ～口号 shout slogans ③ call: 直～其名 address sb. disrespectfully (by name) ④ bleep; page: 有人在～我。Somebody is paging me. / ～一下王大夫! Call Dr. Wang on his bleeper!

呼[2] hū *onom.*: 北风～～地吹。A north wind is whistling.

呼哧 hūchī (also 呼蚩 hūchī) *onom.* the sound of panting: ～～直喘 puff and blow

呼叱 hūchì (also 呼斥 hūchì) berate; excoriate; shout at (sb.)

呼嗒 hū·dā same as 忽搭 hū·dā

呼风唤雨 hūfēng-huànyǔ summon wind and rain—exercise magic powers; stir up trouble: ～，驾雾腾云 command the wind and rain, ride on the mists and clouds / ～，推波助澜 stir up trouble and make things worse

呼喊 hūhǎn call out; shout: 大声～ shout at the top of one's voice

呼号 hūháo wail; cry out in distress

呼号 hūhào ① call sign; call letters ② catchword (of an organization)

呼和浩特 Hūhéhàotè Huhhot (Huhehot) (capital of the Nei Monggol Autonomous Region)

呼吼 hūhǒu whistle; roar: 北风～。The north wind howled.

呼唤 hūhuàn call; shout to: 我们在门外～了半天，他才开门。We called at the door for a long time before he opened it. / 祖国在～我们! Our country is calling us.

呼饥号寒 hūjī-háohán same as 啼饥号寒 tíjī-háohán

呼叫 hūjiào ① call out; shout ② *telecommunications* call: ～灯 calling lamp / ～信号 calling signal

呼救 hūjiù call for help; send out GMDSS signals

呼拉圈 hūlāquān hula hoop

呼啦 hūlā (also 呼喇 hūlā) *onom.* the sound of flapping: 风卷红旗～～地响。The red flags are flapping in the wind.

呼噜 hūlū (also 呼噜噜 hūlūlū) *onom.*: 他喉咙里～～地响。He's a bit wheezy.

呼噜 hūlu *inf.* snore: 打～ snore

呼朋引类 hūpéng-yǐnlèi gang up: ～，聚众闹事 gang up to make trouble

呼扇 hū·shān *inf.* ① shake: 过木桥时，木板直～。The planks shook as I crossed the wooden bridge. ② fan: 他摘下草帽不停地～。He took off his straw hat and fanned himself with it.

呼哨 hūshào whistle: 打～ give a whistle

呼声 hūshēng cry; voice: 群众的～ the voice of the masses / 世界舆论的强大～ the powerful voice of

world opinion / 在几个候选人中, 他的～最高。He is the most likely of all the candidates.

呼天抢地 hūtiān-qiāngdì lament to heaven and knock one's head on earth—utter cries of anguish

呼吸 hūxī breathe; respire: ～新鲜空气 have a breath of fresh air / ～急促 be short of breath / ～困难 breathe with difficulty; lose one's breath / 停止～ stop breathing; die

呼吸道 hūxīdào respiratory tract

呼吸率 hūxīlǜ respiratory rate

呼吸器 hūxīqì respirator

呼吸器官 hūxī qìguān respiratory apparatus

呼吸系统 hūxī xìtǒng respiratory system

呼吸相通 hū xī xiāngtōng share the same sentiments and fate; be bound together by common interests

呼啸 hūxiào whistle; scream; whizz: 子弹～而过。A bullet whizzed past. / 寒风～。A cold wind is whistling.

呼延 Hūyán a two-character surname

呼幺喝六 hūyāo-hèliù ① shout for numbers in throwing dice—noisy shouting in gambling ② *dial.* shouting right and left—arrogant

呼应 hūyìng echo; work in concert with: 互相～ echo each other

呼吁 hūyù appeal; call on: ～团结 appeal for unity

呼吁书 hūyùshū letter of appeal; appeal

呼噪 hūzào noisy shouting

呼之即来, 挥之即去 hū zhī jí lái, huī zhī jí qù have sb. at one's beck and call

呼之欲出 hū zhī yù chū (of lifelike figures in pictures or vivid characters in novels) ready to come out at one's call—be vividly portrayed

忽[1] hū neglect; overlook; ignore: 忽视 hūshì

忽[2] hū *adv.* suddenly; all of a sudden: ～见前面一个人影。All of a sudden, I saw a figure in front of me.

忽布 hūbù hops (a transliteration, also called 啤酒花 píjiǔhuā)

忽搭 hū·dā *onom.* the sound of flapping: 我们听见那面旗子被风吹得～～响。We heard the flag flapping in the wind.

忽地 hūdì *adv.* suddenly; all of a sudden: 灯～灭了。The light suddenly went out.

忽而 hū'ér *adv.* now..., now...: ～哭, ～笑 cry and laugh by turns / ～主张这个, ～主张那个 advocate one thing today and another tomorrow

忽忽 hūhū *adv.* (used in describing the passing of time) fast; quickly: 离开北京, ～又是一年。A year has slipped by since I left Beijing.

忽…忽… hū…hū… now…, now…: 情绪忽高忽低 be in high spirits one moment and in low spirits the next; be subject to sudden changes of mood / 天气忽冷忽热。The weather is cold one minute and hot the next. / 镜头忽远忽近。Sometimes there are long shots, sometimes close-ups. / 灯光忽明忽暗。The lights keep flickering.

忽略 hūlüè neglect; overlook; lose sight of: 我们～了一个重要的细节。We overlooked an important detail. / 我们在注意主要矛盾的同时, 不可～次要矛盾。While paying attention to the main contradiction, we should not neglect the secondary ones.

忽然 hūrán *adv.* suddenly; all of a sudden: 他正要出去, ～下起大雨来了。It suddenly started pouring just as he was going out.

忽闪 hūshǎn (of a light) flash

忽闪 hūshan (of the eyes, etc.) sparkle; flash: 小姑娘～着大眼睛看着妈妈。The little girl stared at her mother, her big eyes flashing.

忽视 hūshì ignore; overlook; neglect: 不可～的力量 a force not to be ignored; a force to be reckoned with / 不应～困难。We should not overlook the difficulties. / 不要强调一面而～另一面。Don't stress one aspect to the neglect of another.

忽悠 hūyou *dial.* flicker: 渔船上的灯火～～的。Lights flickered on the fishing boats. / 大旗叫风吹得直～。The flag fluttered in the wind.

忽左忽右 hūzuǒ-hūyòu suddenly left, suddenly right—now one extreme, now the other

烀 hū stew in shallow water

溿 hū see below

溿浴 hūyù *dial.* have (*or* take) a bath; bathe

惚 hū see 恍惚 huǎng·hū

糊 hū plaster: 用灰把墙缝～上 plaster up cracks in the wall / ～一层泥 spread a layer of mud ——see also hú; hù

hú

囫 hú see below

囫囵 húlún whole: ～吞下 swallow sth. whole

囫囵个儿 húlúngèr *dial.* ① whole: 这孩子没一条～的裤子, 全都破了。The boy doesn't have a single pair of untorn trousers. ② sleep with one's clothes on: 他太累了, 顾不上脱衣服就～睡了。He was so tired that he went to bed without taking his clothes off.

囫囵觉 húlúnjiào uninterrupted sleep; a good night's sleep: 他最近太忙, 几乎没睡过一个～。He has been very busy lately and has hardly had a single good night's rest.

囫囵吞枣 húlún tūn zǎo swallow a date whole—lap up information without digesting it; read without understanding: 读这份材料要细嚼慢咽, 不能～。You must read the texts carefully, and not gloss over them without properly digesting them.

和 hú complete a set in mahjong ——see also hé; hè; huó; huò

狐 hú fox

狐步 húbù foxtrot (a ballroom dance)

狐臭 húchòu (also 狐臊 húsāo) body odour; bromhidrosis

狐蝠 húfú fox bat

狐假虎威 hú jiǎ hǔ wēi the fox borrows the tiger's fierceness (by walking in the latter's company)—bully people by flaunting one's powerful connections

狐狸 hú·li fox

狐狸精 húlijīng fox spirit—a seductive woman

狐狸尾巴 hú·li wěiba fox's tail—something that gives away a person's real character or evil intentions; cloven hoof: ～总是要露出来的。A fox cannot hide its tail. *or* The devil can't hide his cloven hoof. / 抓住阴谋家的～ seize hold of the evidence which gives the conspirator away

狐埋狐搰 hú mái hú hú (like) the fox burying and digging up—hesitant; indecisive

狐媚 húmèi bewitch by cajolery; entice by flattery

狐裘 húqiú fox-fur robe

狐群狗党 húqún-gǒudǎng (also 狐朋狗党 húpéng-gǒudǎng) a pack of rogues; a gang of scoundrels

狐死首丘 hú sǐ shǒu qiū a fox dies with its face towards

its den (said of sb. longing for home or mindful of his origin)

狐仙 húxiān fairy fox

狐疑 húyí doubt; suspicion: 满腹～ be full of misgivings; be very suspicious

弧 hú ① *math.* arc ② *arch.* bow

弧度 húdù *math.* radian

弧光 húguāng arc light; arc: ～灯 arc lamp; arc light

弧菌 hújūn vibrio

弧圈球 húquānqiú *table tennis* lòop drive

弧线 húxiàn pitch arc

弧形 húxíng arc; curve: ～闸门 radial gate

胡[1] hú ① non-Han nationalities living in the north and west in ancient times ② introduced from the northern and western nationalities or from abroad: 胡萝卜 húluóbo ③ (Hú) a surname

胡[2] hú *adv.* recklessly; wantonly; outrageously: ～编 cook up; concoct

胡[3] hú *formal* why: ～不归? Why not return?

胡[4] (鬍) hú moustache, beard or whiskers: 胡须 húxū

胡扯 húchě talk nonsense; chatter idly: ～! Nonsense! *or* That's a lie! / 别～了，快干活吧。 Stop chattering and get on with your work. / 这纯粹是～。 This is sheer nonsense.

胡臭 húchòu same as 狐臭 húchòu

胡吹 húchuī boast outrageously; talk big

胡达 Húdá *Islam* Khudā (Persian for Allah)

胡蝶 húdié same as 蝴蝶 húdié

胡豆 húdòu another name for 蚕豆 cándòu

胡匪 húfěi *dial.* bandit

胡蜂 húfēng wasp; hornet

胡搞 húgǎo ① mess things up; meddle with sth. ② carry on an affair with sb.; be promiscuous

胡瓜 húguā another name for 黄瓜 huángguā

胡话 húhuà ravings; wild talk: 烧得直说～ be delirious from fever

胡笳 hújiā Tartar reed flute (a reed instrument like the flute, used by the northern tribes in ancient times); nomad flute; nomad pipes: 夜听～折杨柳，教人气尽忆长安。（王翰） By night we listened to nomad flutes play "Break Willow Branch, Farewell," It made a man's bold spirit fail, think back upon Chang'an (In Tang times it was a custom to break a willow twig and present it to a departing friend.) / 蔡琰《～十八拍》 Cai Yan's *Eighteen Songs Accompanied by the Tartar Reed Flute* (an eighteen-stanza suite)

胡椒 hújiāo pepper

胡椒鲷 hújiāodiāo *zool.* grunt (*Plectorhynchus cinctus*)

胡搅 hújiǎo ① pester sb.; be mischievous ② argue tediously and vexatiously; wrangle

胡搅蛮缠 hújiǎo-mánchán argue tediously and vexatiously; plague sb. with unreasonable demands

胡来 húlái ① mess things up; fool with sth.: 你要是不会修就别～。 If you don't know how to repair it, don't fool with it (*or* mess it up). ② run wild; act irresponsibly or recklessly: 他溜冰溜到了冰层很薄的地方，真是～。 It was reckless of him to skate out onto the thin ice. / 车还没有停你就往下跳，真是～。 You were very foolhardy to jump off the bus while it was still moving.

胡噜 húlu *dial.* ① rub: 孩子的头碰疼了，你给他～～。 The child's knocked his head against something. Rub it for him. / 他用手巾～了一把脸就上工了。 He gave his face a quick rub with a towel and went off to work. ② sweep (away); scrape together: 把瓜子壳～到簸箕里 sweep the melon-seed shells into a dustpan / 把剥好的豆子～到一堆儿 scrape the hulled beans together

胡乱 húluàn carelessly; casually; at random: ～吃了点饭 eat a hasty meal; grab a quick bite / ～写了几行 scribble a few lines / ～猜测 make wild guesses

胡萝卜 húluóbo carrot

胡萝卜素 húluóbosù *biochem.* carotene

胡闹 húnào run wild; be mischievous; make trouble: 他喝酒喝多了就～。 When he drinks too much he makes trouble. / 我们在谈正经事. 你别～。 We're discussing something serious, Don't talk nonsense.

胡琴 húqin *huqin*, a general term for certain two-stringed bowed instruments, such as *erhu* (二胡), *jinghu* (京胡), etc.

胡说 húshuō ① talk nonsense; drivel: 你再～，我从此不理你。 If you utter any more nonsense, I'm not going to pay any attention to you. ② nonsense

胡说八道 húshuō-bādào talk nonsense; sheer nonsense; rubbish: 你要是～我就不听。 If you're going to talk nonsense, I won't listen. / 这部电视剧是～。 This TV drama is nonsense.

胡思乱想 húsī-luànxiǎng go off into flights of fancy; give way to foolish fancies; let one's imagination run away with one: 无根据地～ disregard reality and indulge in flights of fancy / 他拿着《红楼梦》在那儿～。 A copy of *A Dream of Red Mansions* in his hand, he gave free play to his imagination.

胡荽 hú·suī another name for 芫荽 yán·suī

胡桃 hútáo another name for 核桃 hétao

胡同 hú·tòng lane; alley

胡涂 hútu same as 糊涂 hútu

胡颓子 hútuízi *bot.* thorny elaeagnus (*Elaeagnus pungens*)

胡须 húxū beard, moustache or whiskers

胡言乱语 húyán-luànyǔ talk nonsense; rave

胡杨 húyáng *bot.* diversiform-leaved poplar (*Popular diversifolia*)

胡枝子 húzhīzi *bot.* shrub lespedeza (*Lespedeza bicolor*)

胡诌 húzhōu fabricate wild tales; cook up: ～了一大堆理由 cook up a lot of excuses

胡子 húzi ① beard, moustache or whiskers ② same as 胡匪 húfěi

胡子拉碴 húzilāchā a stubbly beard; a bristly unshaven chin

胡作非为 húzuò-fēiwéi act wildly in defiance of the law or public opinion; commit all kinds of outrages; run amuck

壶 (壺) hú ① kettle; pot: ～里是开水 There's boiled water in the pot. ② bottle; flask: 行军壶 xíngjūnhú

核 hú see below——see also hé

核儿 húr *inf.* ① stone; pit; core: 杏～ apricot stone / 梨～ pear core ② sth. resembling a fruit stone: 煤～ partly-burnt coals or briquets; cinders

斛 hú a dry measure used in former times, originally equal to 10 *dou* (斗), later 5 *dou*

湖 hú ① lake ② (Hú) a name referring to the provinces of Hunan and Hubei ③ (Hú) short for 湖洲 Huzhou (a city in Zhejiang Province famous for its writing brushes and silk)

湖北 Húběi Hubei (Province)

湖笔 húbǐ writing brush produced in Huzhou (湖州),

Zhejiang Province

湖滨 húbīn lakeside

湖光山色 húguāng-shānsè a beautiful scenery of lakes and mountains: 园内轩窗四启,〔庄徵君〕看着～,真如仙境。(《儒林外史》) Zhuang's house had large windows on every side from which he could enjoy the lakeside scenery, as enchanting as fairyland.

湖广 Húguǎng ① a province of the Yuan Dynasty, covering what is now Hubei, Hunan, Guangdong and Guangxi ② a province of the Ming Dynasty, covering what is now Hubei and Hunan

湖南 Húnán Hunan (Province)

湖泊 húpō lakes

湖色 húsè light green

湖田 hútián land reclaimed from a lake; shoaly land

湖心亭 húxīntíng a pavilion in the middle of a lake; mid-lake pavilion

湖鸭 húyā duck

湖羊 húyáng a breed of sheep found in Zhejiang and Jiangsu, famous for its soft wool

湖泽 húzé lakes and marshes

湖沼学 húzhǎoxué limnology

湖绉 húzhòu a kind of silk fabric produced in Huzhou (湖州), Zhejiang Province

葫 hú see below

葫芦 húlu bottle gourd; calabash: 拿～装酒 have a gourd filled with wine / 他的～里到底卖的是什么药? What has he got up his sleeve?

葫蔓藤 húmànténg another name for 钩吻 gōuwěn

猢 hú see below

猢狲 húsūn macaque; monkey

鹕 hú gruel; porridge; congee; mush

鹕口 húkǒu keep body and soul together; eke out one's livelihood: 干些零活～ eke out a living by doing odd jobs

鹄 hú swan ——see also gǔ

鹄候 húhòu formal await respectfully; expect: ～回音。 I am awaiting your reply.

鹄立 húlì formal stand erect

鹄望 húwàng formal eagerly look forward to

搰 hú arch. dig up

煳 hú (of food) burnt: 饭～了。 The rice is burnt.

煳锅 húguō burnt in a pot: 肉都～了。 The meat is burnt.

瑚 hú see 珊瑚 shānhú

鹕 hú see 鹈鹕 tíhú

糊[1] hú ① same as 煳 hú ② stick with paste; paste: ～窗户 paste a sheet of paper over a lattice window or seal with paper the cracks around a window

糊[2] hú same as 煳 hú ——see also hū, hù

糊糊 húhu dial. ① mush; paste ② trouble: 你们这么闹下去会闹下～的。 You'll get into trouble if you go on like this.

糊精 hújīng chem. dextrin; artificial gum

糊口 húkǒu same as 鹕口 húkǒu

糊里糊涂 húlihútū muddle-headed; mixed up: 他觉得自己有点～。 He felt rather confused. / 我～地跑到这儿。 Somehow I stumbled here in a daze. / 这个人～的, 管帐不行。 That chap's no good for book-keeping; he's so

muddle-headed.

糊料 húliào thickener

糊涂 hútu ① muddled; confused; bewildered: ～观念 a muddled idea / 他越想越～。 The more he thought the more confused he became. / 我真～, 把信忘在家里了。 How careless of me to have left the letter at home. ② dial. blurred; indistinct ——see also 装糊涂 zhuāng hútu

糊涂虫 hútuchóng blunderer; bungler

糊涂帐 hútuzhàng chaotic accounts; a mess

糊嘴 húzuǐ same as 鹕口 húkǒu

槲 hú bot. Mongolian oak (Quercus dentata)

槲寄生 hújìshēng bot. mistletoe (Viscum coloratum)

槲栎 húlì bot. oriental white oak (Quercus aliena)

衚 hú see below

衚衕 hútòng same as 胡同 hútòng

蝴 hú see below

蝴蝶 húdié butterfly

蝴蝶花 húdiéhuā fringed iris

蝴蝶结 húdiéjié bowknot; bow

醐 hú see 醍醐 tíhú

觳 hú see below

觳觫 húsù formal shiver out of fear

hǔ

虎[1] hǔ ① tiger: 幼～ a tiger cub ② brave; vigorous: 虎将 hǔjiàng ③ dial. look ferocious: 他突然～起脸对我吼起来。 He suddenly turned ferocious and shouted at me.

虎[2] hǔ same as 唬 hǔ ——see also hù

虎背熊腰 hǔbèi-xióngyāo have a back like a tiger's and a waist like a bear's—tough and stocky

虎贲 hǔbēn knight; warrior

虎彪彪 hǔbiāobiāo strong and vigorous; strapping: ～的青年战士 a strapping young soldier

虎伥 hǔchāng same as 伥 chāng

虎耳草 hǔ'ěrcǎo bot. saxifrage

虎伏 hǔfú old name for 滚轮 gǔnlún

虎符 hǔfú a tiger-shaped tally issued to generals as imperial authorization for troop movement in ancient China

虎骨酒 hǔgǔjiǔ tiger-bone liquor

虎虎有生气 hǔhǔ yǒu shēngqì be full of vim and vigour

虎将 hǔjiàng a brave general

虎劲 hǔjìn dauntless drive; dash: 有一股子～ be full of drive and daring; have plenty of dash

虎踞龙盘 hǔjù-lóngpán same as 龙盘虎踞 lóngpán-hǔjù

虎口[1] hǔkǒu tiger's mouth—jaws of death: 把同志救出～ save one's comrade from the jaws of death

虎口[2] hǔkǒu part of the hand between the thumb and the index finger

虎口拔牙 hǔkǒu báyá pull a tooth from the tiger's mouth—dare the greatest danger

虎口余生 hǔkǒu yúshēng be saved from the tiger's mouth—have a narrow escape from death; be snatched from the jaws of death

虎狼 hǔláng tiger and wolf—cruel and ruthless: ～之性 voracious and wolfish nature / ～之国 a nation of savages

虎列拉 hǔlièlā　cholera (a transliteration, also called 霍乱 huòluàn)

虎里虎气 hǔlǐhǔqì　(usu. of a young man) strong and vigorous; strapping

虎魄 hǔpò　same as 琥珀 hǔpò

虎钳 hǔqián　vice: 台～ bench vice / 万能～ universal vice / ～口 vice jaw

虎鲨 hǔshā　bullhead shark

虎视眈眈 hǔ shì dāndān　glare like a tiger eyeing its prey; eye covetously or menacingly

虎势 hǔshi　*dial.*　strong: 这小伙子膀大腰粗的，长得真～。 The young man is strongly built, with broad shoulders and thick waist.

虎头虎脑 hǔtóuhǔnǎo　(usu. of a boy) looking strong and good-natured: 你儿子长得～，非常可爱。 Your son's a lovely boy, so strong and good-natured.

虎头牌 hǔtóupái　a wooden board with a tiger-head design hung outside a *yamen* in the Qing Dynasty as a sign of authority

虎头蛇尾 hǔtóu-shéwěi　a tiger's head and a snake's tail—a fine start and a poor finish; in like a lion, out like a lamb

虎威 hǔwēi　(of a military officer) valiant and awe-inspiring

虎尾春冰 hǔwěi-chūnbīng　(like) treading on the tail of a tiger or walking on the ice in springtime—in a precarious position

虎穴 hǔxué　tiger's den—a danger spot: ～追踪 track the tiger to its lair

虎牙 hǔyá　*inf.*　protruding canine teeth

虎跃龙腾 hǔyuè-lóngténg　same as 龙腾虎跃 lóngténg-hǔyuè

虎杖 hǔzhàng　*Chin. med.*　giant knotweed (Polygonum cuspidatum)

浒 hǔ　waterside: 《水～传》 (name of a novel) Water Margin; Outlaws of the Marsh

唬(虎) hǔ　*inf.*　bluff: 你别～人。 Quit bluffing. / 她没被～住。 She wasn't intimidated.

琥 hǔ　see below

琥珀 hǔpò　amber: ～油 amber oil

hù

户 hù　① door: 足不出～ never step out of doors; confine oneself within doors ② household; family: 全村共三十～。 There are thirty households in the village. / 无房～ residents who do not have their own living quarters / ③ family status: 门当户对 méndāng-hùduì ④ (bank) account: 开户 kāihù

户部 Hùbù　the Board of Revenue ——see also 六部 Liùbù

户籍 hùjí　① census register; household register ② registered permanent residence

户籍警 hùjíjǐng　policeman in charge of household registration

户均 hùjūn　per household; per family: ～收入 per household income; average family income

户口 hùkǒu　① number of households and total population ② registered permanent residence: 他在北京没～。 He's an unregistered resident in Beijing.

户口簿 hùkǒubù　(also 户口本 hùkǒuběn) (permanent) residence booklet

户口清册 hùkǒu qīngcè　census record

户枢不蠹 hùshū bù dù　a door-hinge never becomes wormeaten—constant activity staves off decay ——see also 流水不腐，户枢不蠹 liúshuǐ bù fǔ, hùshū bù dù

户头 hùtóu　(bank) account: 开～ open an account

户外 hùwài　outdoor: ～运动 outdoor games; outdoor sports

户限为穿 hùxiàn wéi chuān　a threshold worn low by visitors—an endless flow of visitors

户牖 hùyǒu　*formal*　door and window

户长 hùzhǎng　*dial.*　head of a household

户主 hùzhǔ　head of a household

互 hù　*adv.*　mutually; each other: ～不干涉内政 noninterference in each other's internal affairs / ～为条件 mutually conditional; interdependent / ～通情报 exchange information; keep each other informed / ～派常驻使节 exchange resident envoys; mutually accredit resident envoys

互不侵犯条约 hù bù qīnfàn tiáoyuē　nonaggression treaty (or pact)

互导 hùdǎo　*elec.*　mutual conductance; transconductance

互访 hùfǎng　exchange visits: 两国体育代表团的～ exchange of sports delegations between two countries

互感应 hùgǎnyìng　(also 互感 hùgǎn) *elec.*　mutual inductance

互…互… hù…hù…　mutual; each other: 互勉互助 encourage and help each other / 互教互学 teach and learn from each other; teach each other / 互帮互学 help each other and learn from each other / 互谅互让 mutual understanding and (mutual) accommodation

互换 hùhuàn　exchange: ～批准书 exchange instruments of ratification / ～记者 exchange correspondents

互惠 hùhuì　mutually beneficial; reciprocal: 在～的基础上 on a mutually beneficial basis / 贸易～ reciprocity in trade

互惠待遇 hùhuì dàiyù　reciprocal treatment

互惠关税 hùhuì guānshuì　mutually preferential tariff

互惠条约 hùhuì tiáoyuē　reciprocal treaty

互见 hùjiàn　① cross-reference ② (of two contrasting things) exist side by side: 瑕瑜互见 xiá-yú hù jiàn

互利 hùlì　mutually beneficial; of mutual benefit

互让 hùràng　yield to each other; give in to each other

互生 hùshēng　*bot.*　alternate: ～叶 alternate leaf

互市 hùshì　frontier trade

互通有无 hù tōng yǒu-wú　each supplies what the other needs; supply (or meet) each other's needs: ～, 调剂余缺 each making up the other's deficiency from his own surplus

互为因果 hù wéi yīn guǒ　interact as both cause and effect

互相 hùxiāng　*adv.*　mutually; each other: ～依存 depend on each other for existence; be interdependent / ～排斥 be mutually exclusive / ～配合 work in coordination / ～利用 each using the other for his own ends / ～掣肘 hold each other back / ～勾结 work in collusion

互训 hùxùn　mutual glossing

互助 hùzhù　help each other: ～合作 mutual aid and cooperation

互助组 hùzhùzǔ　① mutual aid group: 学习～ mutual help study group ② mutual aid team (an elementary form of organization in China's agricultural cooperation): 临时～ temporary mutual aid team / 常年～ all-the-year-roud mutual aid team

沪(滬) Hù　another name for 上海 Shànghǎi: ～宁线 the Shanghai-Nanjing Railway

沪剧 hùjù　Shanghai opera

护（護）

hù ① protect; guard; shield: ～厂 guard a factory / 在敌机扫射时，她用自己的身子～住伤员。 She shielded the wounded soldier from the strafing of the enemy plane with her own body. ② be partial to; shield from censure: 别～着自己的孩子。 Don't be partial to your own child.

护岸 hù'àn　bank revetment

护岸林 hù'ànlín　protective belt (of trees) along an embankment

护壁 hùbì　another name for 墙裙 qiángqún

护庇 hùbì　inf. shield; put under one's protection; take under one's wing

护兵 hùbīng　(an official's) bodyguard; guard

护城河 hùchénghé　city moat

护持 hùchí　shield and sustain

护犊子 hù dúzi　inf. derog. shield the shortcomings or faults of one's child; be partial to one's child

护短 hùduǎn　shield a shortcoming or fault: 做母亲的对孩子～没什么好处。 It does no good to a child to have his faults shielded by his mother.

护耳 hù'ěr　earflaps; earmuffs

护发素 hùfàsù　hair conditioner

护封 hùfēng　book jacket; jacket

护肤霜 hùfūshuāng　face cream

护航 hùháng　escort; convoy: 由五艘军舰～ be convoyed by five warships; have an escort of five warships / ～部队 escort force / ～飞机 escort aircraft / ～舰 convoy ship; escort vessel

护肩 hùjiān　dial. shoulder pad (or padding)

护壳 hùké　mech. protective case (or shell)

护理 hùlǐ　nurse; tend and protect: ～伤病员 nurse the sick and the wounded / 精心～小麦越冬 take good care of the wheat through the winter

护理人员 hùlǐ rényuán　nursing staff

护林 hùlín　protect a forest

护路 hùlù　① patrol and guard a road or railway ② road maintenance

护路林 hùlùlín　protective belt (of trees) along a road

护面 hùmiàn　sports mask

护目镜 hùmùjìng　goggles

护坡 hùpō　water conservancy, transportation slope protection

护青 hùqīng　dial. keep watch over the ripening crops

护秋 hùqiū　keep watch over the autumn harvest

护身符 hùshēnfú　① amulet; protective talisman ② (also 护符 hùfú) a person or thing that protects one from punishment or censure; shield

护士 hùshi　(hospital) nurse

护士学校 hùshi xuéxiào　nurses' school

护士长 hùshizhǎng　head nurse

护手盘 hùshǒupán　sports hand guard

护守 hùshǒu　guard; defend

护送 hùsòng　escort; convoy: ～伤员去后方医院 escort wounded men to a rear hospital / ～救灾物资 convoy vehicles bringing relief to a disaster-stricken area

护腿 hùtuǐ　sports shinguard

护卫 hùwèi　① protect; guard: 他在保卫人员的～下离开了机场。 He left the airport under the protection of the security guards. ② bodyguard

护卫舰 hùwèijiàn　escort vessel; corvette

护卫艇 hùwèitǐng　another name for 炮艇 pàotǐng

护膝 hùxī　sports kneepad; kneecap

护胸 hùxiōng　sports chest protector

护袖 hùxiù　dial. oversleeve

护养 hùyǎng　① cultivate; nurse; rear: ～秧苗 cultivate seedlings; nurse young plants / ～仔猪 rear (or look after) piglets ② maintain: ～公路 maintain a highway

护照 hùzhào　passport: 外交～ diplomatic passport / 公

务～ service passport

护罩 hùzhào　guard shield; hood shield

怙

hù　formal rely on: 失怙 shīhù

怙恶不悛 hù è bù quān　be steeped in evil and refuse to repent; remain impenitent: ～，继续做坏事 remain impenitent and keep up one's evildoing / ～的罪犯 an incorrigible criminal

怙恃 hùshì　formal ① rely on ② parents

戽

hù　① bailing bucket ② bail: ～水灌田 bail water to irrigate fields

戽斗 hùdǒu　bailing bucket

虎

hù　see below ——see also hǔ

虎不拉 hùbùlǎ　dial. shrike

祜

hù　formal blessing; bliss

笏

hù　a tablet held before the breast by officials when received in audience by the emperor

扈

hù　① formal retinue ② (Hù) a surname

扈从 hùcóng　formal retinue; retainer

瓠

hù　see below

瓠子 hùzi　bot. a kind of edible gourd

糊

hù　paste: 辣椒～ chilli paste / 玉米～ (cornmeal) mush ——see also hū; hú

糊弄 hùnong　dial. ① fool; deceive; palm sth. off on: 你别～我。 Don't try to fool me. ② go through the motions; be slipshod in work: 这可是细活，不能瞎～。 This is a delicate job. It mustn't be done carelessly.

糊弄局 hùnongjú　dial. muddle through one's work

huā

化

huā　spend; expend: ～钱 spend money; cost money / ～工夫 spend time; take time ——see also huà

化子 huāzi　same as 花子 huāzi

花[1]

huā　① flower; blossom; bloom: 一朵～ a flower ② anything resembling a flower: 火花 huǒhuā / 雪花 xuěhuā ③ fireworks: 放～ let off fireworks ④ pattern; design: 白底红～ red flowers on a white background / 她织的～儿真好看。 The pattern she knitted is really beautiful. / 这被面的～儿很大方。 The design on this quilt cover is quite elegant. ⑤ multicoloured; coloured; variegated: ～衣服 bright-coloured clothes / ～蝴蝶 variegated butterfly / 小～狗 spotted puppy / 布染～了。 The cloth is dyed unevenly. ⑥ flower-decorated; coloured: 花篮 huālán ⑦ blurred; dim: 看书看得眼睛都～了 read until the print looks blurred ⑧ fancy; florid; flowery; showy: 你的字太～了。 Your handwriting is too fancy. ⑨ cream; essence: 文艺之～ the cream of literature and art ⑩ used metaphorically for women: 姊妹花 zǐmèihuā ⑪ used metaphorically for courtesans or prostitutes: 寻花问柳 xúnhuā-wènliǔ ⑫ cotton: 轧花 yàhuā ⑬ smallpox: 出花 chūhuā / 种花 zhònghuā[2] ⑭ wound: 挂花 guàhuā ⑮ (Huā) a surname

花[2]

huā　spend; expend: ～不少钱 spend a lot of money / 很～时间 take a lot of time; be time-consuming

花把势 huābǎshì　(also 花把式 huābǎshì) florist; gardener

花白　huābái　(of hair or beard) grey; grizzled: 头发～ with grey (*or* grizzled) hair; grey-haired

花斑　huābān　piebald: ～马 a piebald horse

花斑癣　huābānxuǎn　*med.* tinea versicolour

花瓣　huābàn　petal

花苞　huābāo　(flower) bud

花被　huābèi　*bot.* perianth; floral envelope

花绷子　huābēngzi　embroidery frame

花边　huābiān　① decorative border: 瓶口上有一道～。 There is a floral border round the mouth of the vase. ② lace: ～装饰 lace trimmings / 在衣服上镶一条～ trim a dress with lace ③ *print.* fancy borders in printing

花边新闻　huābiān xīnwén　titbits (of news); interesting sidelights

花布　huābù　cotton print; print

花不棱登　huābulēngdēng　extravagantly fancy; loud; flashy; gaudy: 这件衣服～的，我不喜欢。 This dress is too fancy (*or* loud) for me.

花菜　huācài　*dial.* cauliflower

花草　huācǎo　① flowers and plants ② *dial.* Chinese milk vetch

花插　huāchā　any container for cut flowers

花插　huācha　crisscross

花茶　huāchá　scented tea: 茉莉～ jasmine tea

花厂　huāchǎng　*old* flower shop; florist's

花车　huāchē　festooned vehicle

花池子　huāchízi　flower bed

花虫　huāchóng　*dial.* pink bollworm

花丛　huācóng　flowering shrubs; flowers in clusters

花大姐　huādàjiě　*zool.* potato ladybird

花搭着　huādazhe　interspersed; diversified: 细粮粗粮～吃 diversify one's diet by eating both fine and coarse grain

花旦　huādàn　one of the main divisions of the *dan* or female role in traditional opera (traditionally the role for a woman of questionable morals, notably a coquettish maidservant or an amorous young woman, bold, seductive, and charming; great emphasis being placed on acting)

花灯　huādēng　festive lantern (as displayed on the Lantern Festival)

花灯戏　huādēngxì　local opera popular in Yunnan and Sichuan Provinces

花点子　huādiǎnzi　*inf.* deceit; artifice

花钿　huādiàn　woman's head ornament

花雕　huādiāo　high-grade Shaoxing (绍兴) wine

花儿洞子　huārdòngzi　a hothouse half underground for growing flowers

花缎　huāduàn　figured satin; brocade

花朵　huāduǒ　flower: 盛开的～ flowers in full bloom / 儿童是祖国的～。 Children are the flowers of our country.

花萼　huā'è　calyx

花儿　huā'ér　a kind of folk song, popular in Gansu, Qinghai, and Ningxia

花房　huāfáng　greenhouse

花肥　huāféi　fertilizers for potted flowers

花费　huāfèi　spend; expend; cost: ～金钱 spend money (on a project, etc.) / ～时间 spend time; take time / ～心血 take pains

花费　huāfei　money spent; expenditure; expenses: 这笔～我担负不了。 I can't afford the expense.

花粉　huāfěn　*bot.* pollen: ～管 pollen tube

花粉食品　huāfěn shípǐn　pollen food

花岗岩　huāgāngyán　(also 花岗石 huāgāngshí) ① granite ② incorrigibly obstinate: ～脑袋 a granite-like skull; ossified thinking

花岗岩化　huāgāngyánhuà　*geol.* granitize

花格窗　huāgéchuāng　lattice window

花梗　huāgěng　pedicel

花骨朵　huāgūduo　common name for 花蕾 huālěi

花鼓　huāgǔ　flower-drum, a folk dance popular in the Changjiang valley

花鼓戏　huāgǔxì　flower-drum opera, popular in Hunan, Hubei and Anhui

花冠[1]　huāguān　corolla: 合瓣～ gamopetalous corolla / 离瓣～ choripetalous corolla

花冠[2]　huāguān　an ornamental crown worn by a bride on her wedding day in former times

花棍舞　huāgùnwǔ　same as 霸王鞭 bàwángbiān[2]

花好月圆　huāhǎo-yuèyuán　(usu. used as a congratulatory message for sb.'s marriage) blooming flowers and full moon—perfect conjugal bliss

花红[1]　huāhóng　*bot.* Chinese pear-leaved crabapple

花红[2]　huāhóng　① gift for a wedding, etc. ② bonus

花红柳绿　huāhóng-liǔlǜ　red flowers and green willows—a beautiful spring scene

花候　huāhòu　*bot.* flowering season

花花肠子　huāhua chángzi　*dial.* ① cunning; trickery; deceit: 一肚子～ be full of cunning ② a cunning person

花花公子　huāhuā gōngzǐ　playboy; dandy; coxcomb; fop

花花绿绿　huāhuālǜlǜ　brightly coloured; colourful: 穿得～的 be colourfully dressed / ～的招贴画 poster in colour

花花世界　huāhuā shìjiè　the dazzling human world with its myriad temptations; this mortal world: 大都市这～使他感到眼花缭乱。 He was dazzled by the gaiety and splendour of the metropolis.

花环　huāhuán　garland; floral hoop

花卉　huāhuì　① flowers and plants ② painting of flowers and plants in traditional Chinese style: ～画 flower-and-plant painting

花会　huāhuì　flower fair

花鸡　huājī　bramble finch; brambling

花甲　huājiǎ　a cycle of sixty years: ～之年 sixty (years of age) / 年逾～ over sixty years old

花架子　huājiàzi　showy postures of martial arts—a thing that is showy but of no practical use: 要练好基本功，别尽学～。 You should spend time on basic training, not on those flourishes.

花剑　huājiàn　*sports* foil: ～运动员 foil fencer; foilsman

花键　huājiàn　*mech.* spline: ～轴 spline shaft / ～座 splined hub

花匠　huājiàng　gardener

花椒　huājiāo　Chinese prickly ash

花轿　huājiào　bridal sedan chair

花秸　huājiē　chopped straw

花街柳巷　huājiē-liǔxiàng　streets of ill repute; red-light district

花镜　huājìng　presbyopic glasses

花酒　huājiǔ　a dinner party with singsong girls in attendance

花卷　huājuǎn　fancy-shaped (*or* plaited, twisted) steamed roll; steamed twisted roll

花魁　huākuí　the queen of flowers—an epithet for the plum blossom or a famous courtesan: 《卖油郎独占～》 "The Oil Vendor Wins the Hand of the Flower Queen" (a story)

花篮　huālán　① a basket of flowers ② gaily decorated basket

花蕾　huālěi　(flower) bud

花里胡哨　huālihúshào　① gaudy; garish; showy: 穿得～的 be gaudily dressed ② without solid worth: 他吹得～的，不能信。 Don't believe his florid words.

花鲢　huālián　variegated carp

花脸　huāliǎn　flowery-face role—a popular name for 净[2]

jīng (so called from the elaborate facial painting)

花柳病 huāliǔbìng venereal disease (V. D.)

花露 huālù (medicinal) liquid distilled from honeysuckle flowers or lotus leaves

花露水 huālùshuǐ toilet water

花榈木 huālúmù (also 花梨 huālí) rosewood

花蜜 huāmì *bot.* nectar

花面狸 huāmiànlí masked civet; gem-faced civet

花苗 huāmiáo flower seedling

花名册 huāmíngcè register (of names); membership roster; muster roll

花明柳暗 huāmíng-liǔ'àn same as 柳暗花明 liǔ'àn-huāmíng

花木 huāmù flowers and trees (in parks or gardens)

花呢 huāní fancy suiting

花鸟 huāniǎo painting of flowers and birds in traditional Chinese style: ～画 flower-and-bird painting

花农 huānóng flower grower

花盘 huāpán ① *bot.* flower disc ② *mech.* disc chuck; faceplate

花炮 huāpào fireworks and firecrackers: 放～ let off fireworks

花盆 huāpén flowerpot

花瓶 huāpíng ① flower vase; vase ② a woman employed for her beauty only, usu. installed as secretary in an office for decorative purposes ③ a woman who only knows how to make herself up and can do no useful work

花圃 huāpǔ flower nursery

花期 huāqī florescence

花旗 huāqí *old* star-spangled banner—the United States

花前月下 huāqián-yuèxià amidst flowers and in the moonlight—an ideal setting for amorous dalliance

花枪 huāqiāng ① a short spear used in ancient times ② trickery: 要～ play tricks

花腔 huāqiāng ① florid ornamentation in Chinese opera singing; *coloratura* ② guileful talk: 要～ speak guilefully

花腔女高音 huāqiāng nǚgāoyīn *coloratura soprano; coloratura*

花墙 huāqiáng lattice wall

花青 huāqīng *chem.* cyanine: ～染料 cyanine dyes

花青素 huāqīngsù *chem.* anthocyanidin

花圈 huāquān (floral) wreath

花拳绣腿 huāquán-xiùtuǐ showy but not practical martial arts; any showy but not practical skill

花容月貌 huāróng-yuèmào flower-like features and moonlike face—a great beauty

花蕊 huāruǐ stamen or pistil

花色 huāsè ① design and colour: 这布的～很好看。This cloth is beautiful in both design and colour. ② (of merchandise) variety of designs, sizes, colours, etc.: 新的～ latest designs / ～繁多 a great variety

花色品种 huāsè pǐnzhǒng variety of colours and designs: 增加～ increase the variety of colours and designs

花纱布 huāshābù a collective name for cotton, cotton yarn and cloth

花衫 huāshān a *dan* or female role in traditional opera, combining the vivacious *huadan* (花旦) and the sedate *qingyi* (青衣) and stressing both acting and singing

花哨 huāshao ① garish; gaudy: 她打扮得太～。She was gaudily dressed. ② full of flourishes; flowery: 他鼓点子敲得又响亮又～。He beat the drum loudly and with a lot of flourishes.

花生 huāshēng peanut; groundnut

花生饼 huāshēngbǐng *agric.* peanut cake

花生豆儿 huāshēngdòur *dial.* shelled peanut; peanut kernel

花生黑斑病 huāshēng hēibānbìng cercospora black spot of peanut

花生酱 huāshēngjiàng peanut butter

花生米 huāshēngmǐ (also 花生仁 huāshēngrén) shelled peanut; peanut kernel

花生糖 huāshēngtáng peanut brittle

花生油 huāshēngyóu peanut oil

花市 huāshì flower market

花饰 huāshì ornamental design

花鼠 huāshǔ Siberian chipmunk; chipmunk

花束 huāshù a bunch of flowers; bouquet

花说柳说 huāshuō-liǔshuō *dial.* use flatteries; use sweet and insincere words

花丝 huāsī ① *bot.* filament ② *arts & crafts* filigree

花坛 huātán (raised) flower bed; flower terrace

花天酒地 huātiān-jiǔdì indulge in dissipation; lead a life of debauchery

花厅 huātīng reception room or parlour (usu. in a garden or side courtyard)

花筒 huātǒng tube-shaped fireworks

花团锦簇 huātuán-jǐncù bouquets of flowers and piles of silks—rich multi-coloured decorations: 打扮得～ be splendidly dressed / ～，挤了一厅的人。(《红楼梦》) The hall was packed with people, gay with flowers and silks. / 那第七篇文字，做的～一般。(《儒林外史》) Thus he wrote seven excellent examination papers.

花托 huātuō *bot.* receptacle

花纹 huāwén decorative pattern; figure: 各种～的地毯 carpets of different patterns / 这些瓷盘的～很别致。These porcelain plates have rather original designs on them. / ～玻璃 figured glass

花坞 huāwù sunken flower-bed

花线 huāxiàn ① coloured thread ② *elec.* flexible cord; flex

花香鸟语 huāxiāng-niǎoyǔ same as 鸟语花香 niǎoyǔ-huāxiāng

花消 huāxiao (also 花销 huāxiao) *inf.* cost; expense: 他抽烟喝酒的～大。He spends a lot on smoking and drinking.

花鞋 huāxié embroidered shoes

花须 huāxū *inf.* stamen or pistil

花序 huāxù *bot.* inflorescence

花絮 huāxù titbits (of news); interesting sidelights: 运动会～ sidelights on the sports meet

花薰 huāxūn *arts & crafts* a jade vessel for perfuming; jade perfumer

花押 huāyā *old* a cursive hand signature on documents, contracts, etc.

花芽 huāyá (flower) bud

花言巧语 huāyán-qiǎoyǔ sweet words; fine words; flattery; blandishments: 他们的一切～都是骗人的。All their fine words are nothing but humbug.

花眼 huāyǎn ① presbyopia ② be dazzled: 挑来挑去挑～了 be dazzled by so many varieties to choose from

花样 huāyàng ① decorative pattern; variety: ～繁多 a great variety ② trick: 玩～ play tricks / 他又在闹什么新～。I wonder what he's up to now.

花样翻新 huāyàng fānxīn ① innovations in pattern or design ② old things in a new guise

花样滑冰 huāyàng huábīng figure skating: 单人～ single skating; solo-skating / 双人～ pair skating; pairs

花样滑水 huāyàng huáshuǐ figure water skiing; acrobatic water skiing

花样游泳 huāyàng yóuyǒng water ballet; synchronized swimming

花儿样子 huāryàngzi a flower pattern to do embroi

dery work on

花药 huāyào *bot.* anther

花椰菜 huāyēcài cauliflower

花叶病 huāyèbìng *agric.* mosaic (disease): 甜菜~ beet mosaic

花园 huāyuán (also 花园子 huāyuánzi) flower garden; garden

花帐 huāzhàng padded accounts or bills: 开~ make out a padded account; pad accounts

花招 huāzhāo (also 花着 huāzhāo) ① showy movement in *wushu* (武术); flourish ② trick; game ——see also 耍花招 shuǎ huāzhāo

花朝 huāzhāo birthday of flowers (on the 15th of the 2nd lunar month)

花朝月夕 huāzhāo-yuèxī (also 花晨月夕 huāchén-yuèxī) ① a fine day and a beautiful scene ② the 15th of the 2nd lunar month and the 15th of the 8th lunar month

花儿针 huārzhēn fine needle for embroidery

花枝招展 huāzhī zhāozhǎn (of women) be gorgeously dressed: 打扮得~的 freshly made up and as pretty as a flower

花轴 huāzhóu (also 花茎 huājīng) *bot.* floral axis

花烛 huāzhú candles with dragon and phoenix patterns used in the bridal chamber on the wedding night: ~之夜 the wedding night

花烛夫妻 huāzhú fūqī legally married man and wife; husband and wife by the first marriage

花柱 huāzhù *bot.* style

花砖 huāzhuān ornamental slab for paving the floor

花子儿 huāzǐr ① flower seeds ② *dial.* cottonseed

花子 huāzi beggar

哗 (嘩)

huá *onom.*: 铁门~的一声拉上了。The iron gate was pulled to with a clang. / 溪水~地流。The stream went gurgling on. ——see also huá

哗啦 huālā (also 哗啦啦 huālālā) *onom*: 风吹得树叶~~地响。The leaves rustled in the wind. / 墙~一声倒了。The wall fell with a crash. / 雨~~地下个不停。The rain kept pouring down.

huá

划¹

huá paddle; row: ~船 paddle (or row) a boat

划²

huá be to one's profit; pay: 划得来 huádelái

划³ (劃)

huá scratch; cut the surface of: ~玻璃 cut a piece of glass / ~火柴 strike a match / 她手~破了。Her hands were scratched. / 几道闪电~破长空。Flashes of lightning streaked across the sky. ——see also huà; huai

划不来 huábulái (also 划不着 huábuzháo) be not worth it; do not pay: 这么好的地,种饲料~。It doesn't pay to grow feed crops on such good soil.

划得来 huádelái (also 划得着 huádezháo) be worth it; pay: 还是买质量好的东西~。It always pays to buy good quality products (or goods).

划拉 huála *dial.* ① brush away ② scrawl; scribble: 他在纸上随便~了几个字。He scribbled a few words on the paper.

划拳 huáquán play the finger-guessing game (a game played at a dinner party by two persons, both of whom open certain fingers of the right hand and name the number they are supposed to have spread out, the game recommencing if both players guess wrong and the loser taking a drink if one guesses right)

划水 huáshuǐ strike water with one's arms in swimming

划算 huásuàn ① calculate; weigh: 下星期要花多少钱我得~一下。I must calculate how much money I'll spend next week. / ~来,~去 carefully weigh the pros and cons ② be to one's profit; pay: ~不~,不能只从本单位的利益考虑。One mustn't consider whether or not it pays simply from the standpoint of one's own unit.

划艇 huátǐng canoe: ~运动 canoeing

划子 huázi small rowboat

华¹ (華)

huá ① magnificent; splendid: 华丽 huálì / 光华 guānghuá ② prosperous; flourishing: 繁华 fánhuá / 荣华 rónghuá ③ best part; cream: 精华 jīnghuá ④ flashy; extravagant: 奢华 shēhuá / 浮华 fúhuá ⑤ grizzled; grey: 华发 huáfà ⑥ *honor. formal* your: 华翰 huáhàn ⑦ *meteorol.* corona

华² (華)

Huá ① China: 华北 Huáběi ② Chinese (language): ~俄词典 a Chinese-Russian dictionary ——see also Huà

华北 Huáběi North China (Hebei, Shanxi, the Municipalities of Beijing and Tianjin)

华表 huábiǎo ornamental columns erected in front of palaces, tombs, etc.

华彩乐段 huácǎi yuèduàn *mus. cadenza*

华达呢 huádání gabardine

华诞 huádàn *honor. formal* your birthday

华灯 huádēng colourfully decorated lantern; light: ~初上 when the evening lights are lit

华东 Huádōng East China (Shandong, Jiangsu, Zhejiang, Anhui, Jiangxi, Fujian, Taiwan and Shanghai Municipality)

华而不实 huá ér bù shí flashy and without substance; superficially clever

华尔街 Huá'ěrjiē Wall Street: ~财阀 Wall Street magnates

华尔兹 huá'ěrzī waltz

华发 huáfà *liter.* grey hair: 故国神游,多情应笑我,早生~。(苏轼) As my spirit wanders to the ancient kingdom, You may well laugh at me for being so sentimental And growing grey hair so soon!

华盖 huágài ① canopy (as over an imperial carriage) ② ancient name for a certain star considered unlucky

华工 huágōng *old* overseas Chinese labourers

华贵 huáguì ① luxurious; sumptuous; costly: ~的地毯 luxurious carpet ② wealthy: ~之家 a wealthy family

华翰 huáhàn *honor. formal* your esteemed letter

华居 huájū *honor. formal* your magnificent mansion

华里 huálǐ *li*, a unit of distance (=½ kilometre)

华丽 huálì magnificent; resplendent; gorgeous: ~的宫殿 a magnificent palace / 服饰~ gorgeously dressed and richly ornamented / ~的词藻 flowery language

华美 huáměi magnificent; resplendent; gorgeous

华南 Huánán South China (Guangdong and Guangxi)

华年 huánián *liter.* youth; tender years: 锦瑟无端五十弦,一弦一柱思~。(李商隐) Vain are the jewelled zither's fifty strings: Each string, each stop, bears thought of vanished things.

华侨 huáqiáo overseas Chinese

华人 huárén Chinese: 美籍~ an American Chinese

华沙条约 Huáshā Tiáoyuē the Warsaw Treaty (1955): ~组织 the Warsaw Treaty Organization

华氏温度计 huáshìwēndùjì the Fahrenheit thermometer

华西 Huáxī West China (Sichuan)

华夏 Huáxià archaic name for 中国 Zhōngguó

华夏系构造 Huáxiàxì gòuzào *geol.* Cathaysian (structural) system

华裔 Huáyì foreign citizen of Chinese origin: ~美国人 an American of Chinese descent

华语 Huáyǔ Chinese (language)

华章 huázhāng *honor. liter.* your beautiful writing; your brilliant work: 三十一年还旧国, 落花时节读～。(毛泽东) Back in the old capital after thirty-one years, At the season of falling flowers I read your polished lines.

华中 Huázhōng Central China (Hunan and Hubei)

华胄[1] huázhòu *formal* descendants of a nobleman

华胄[2] huázhòu *formal* Chinese people

华滋 huázī *liter.* luxuriant; flourishing: 庭中有奇树, 绿叶发～。(《古诗十九首》) In the garden a strange tree grows, From green leaves a shower of blossoms bursting.

哗 (嘩、譁)

huá noise; clamour: 喧哗 xuānhuá ——see also huā

哗变 huábiàn mutiny

哗然 huárán in an uproar; in commotion: 举座～。The audience burst into an uproar. / 舆论～。There was a public outcry.

哗笑 huáxiào uproarious laughter

哗众取宠 huá zhòng qǔ chǒng try to please the public with claptrap: 无实事求是之意, 有～之心 have no intention of seeking truth from facts, but only a desire to curry favour by claptrap

铧 (鏵)

huá ploughshare: 双～犁 double-shared plough; double-furrow plough

滑

huá ① slippery; smooth: 又圆又～的小石子 smooth, round pebbles / 路～。The road is slippery. ② slip; slide: ～倒 slip and fall / 在错误的道路上越～越远 slide further and further down the wrong road ③ cunning; crafty; slippery: 又奸又～ mean and crafty

滑板 huábǎn ① *mech.* slide ② *table tennis* feint play ③ skateboard

滑冰 huábīng ice-skating; skating

滑冰场 huábīngchǎng skating rink

滑不唧溜 huábujīliū *dial.* slippery: 刚下过雨, 地下～的。The road was slippery after the rain.

滑车神经 huáchē shénjīng *physiol.* trochlear nerve

滑道 huádào chute; slide

滑动 huádòng *phys.* slide

滑动摩擦 huádòng mócā *phys.* sliding friction

滑动轴承 huádòng zhóuchéng *mech.* sliding bearing

滑竿 huágān a kind of litter

滑旱冰 huáhànbīng roller-skate

滑稽 huáji ① funny; amusing; comical: 这个丑角的表演非常～。The clown gave a very funny performance. / 他样子很～。He is funny-looking. ② comic talk

滑稽戏 huájixì farce

滑交 huájiāo slip and fall

滑精 huájīng *Chin. med.* involuntary emission; spermatorrhoea

滑溜 huáliū *sauté* with starchy sauce: ～里脊 *sauté* fillet with thick gravy

滑溜 huáliu *inf.* slick; smooth; slippery: 这块绸子摸着挺～。This piece of silk feels very smooth.

滑轮 huálún (also 滑车 huáchē) pulley; block

滑轮组 huálúnzǔ assembly pulley

滑脉 huámài *Chin. med.* smooth pulse

滑面 huámiàn *mech.* sliding surface; slide face

滑膜 huámó *physiol.* synovial membrane; synovium

滑膜炎 huámóyán synovitis

滑腻 huání (of the skin) satiny; velvety; creamy

滑坡 huápō ① landslide; landslip ② be on the slippery slope; decline; come down; drop: 财政收入连续两年～。State revenue declined for two years in succession.

滑润 huárùn smooth; well-lubricated

滑石 huáshí talcum; talc

滑石粉 huáshífěn talcum powder

滑爽 huáshuǎng (of textiles) smooth

滑水 huáshuǐ *sports* water skiing

滑膛枪 huátángqiāng smoothbore (gun); musket

滑梯 huátī (children's) slide

滑天下之大稽 huá tiānxià zhī dàjī be the biggest joke in the world; be the laughingstock of the world; be the object of universal ridicule

滑头 huátóu ① slippery fellow; sly customer ② slippery; shifty; slick

滑头滑脑 huátóu-huánǎo crafty; artful; slick

滑翔 huáxiáng glide

滑翔机 huáxiángjī glider; sailplane

滑行 huáxíng slide; coast: 冰上～ slide on the ice / 下坡 coast down a slope / 飞机在跑道上～。The plane taxied along the runway.

滑雪 huáxuě *sports* skiing: ～板 skis / ～鞋 ski boots / ～杖 ski pole; ski stick

滑音 huáyīn ①*phonet.* glide ② *mus.* portamento

滑脂枪 huázhīqiāng *mech.* grease gun

猾

huá cunning; crafty; sly: ～吏 a cunning and unscrupulous official

huà

化[1]

huà ① change; turn; transform: ～害为利 turn harm into good; turn a disadvantage into an advantage / ～公为私 appropriate public property ② convert; influence: 感化 gǎnhuà ③ melt; dissolve: 雪～了。The snow has melted. / 他把药片用水～开。He dissolved the pills in water. ④ digest: 化食 huàshí ⑤ burn up: 焚化 fénhuà ⑥ *religion* die: 坐化 zuòhuà ⑦ short for 化学 huàxué ⑧ (verb suffix) -ize; -ify: 绿化 lǜhuà

化[2]

huà (of Buddhist monks or Taoist priests) beg alms: 化斋 huàzhāi ——see also huā

化悲痛为力量 huà bēitòng wéi lìliang turn grief into strength (usu. used in a memorial speech)

化除 huàchú eliminate; dispel; remove: ～成见 dispel prejudices

化冻 huàdòng thaw; melt: 冰冻的食品必须化了冻才能煮。Frozen food must be thawed before cooking. / 湖上的冰已经～了。The ice on the lake has melted.

化肥 huàféi short for 化学肥料 huàxué féiliào

化粪池 huàfènchí septic tank

化腐朽为神奇 huà fǔxiǔ wéi shénqí turn the foul and rotten into the rare and ethereal—① turn bad into good ② change waste material into things of value

化干戈为玉帛 huà gāngē wéi yùbó turn hostility into friendship; bury the hatchet

化工 huàgōng short for 化学工业 huàxué gōngyè

化工厂 huàgōngchǎng chemical plant

化工原料 huàgōng yuánliào industrial chemicals

化合 huàhé *chem.* chemical combination: ～反应 combination reaction

化合价 huàhéjià *chem.* valence

化合物 huàhéwù chemical compound

化境 huàjìng sublimity; perfection: 这幅山水画已臻～。This landscape painting is a consummate work of art.

化疗 huàliáo short for 化学疗法 huàxué liáofǎ

化名 huàmíng ① use an assumed name ② assumed name; alias

化募 huàmù (of Buddhist monks or Taoist priests) collect alms

化脓 huànóng fester; suppurate: 伤口～了。The wound is festering.

化身 huàshēn incarnation; embodiment: 智慧和勇敢的～ the embodiment of wisdom and courage / 魔鬼的～ the devil incarnate / 这部小说的主人公正是作者自己的～。The hero of this novel is a portrait of the author himself.

化石 huàshí fossil: 整理～ dress fossils / 标准～ index fossil / 指相～ facies fossil / 微体～ microfossil / ～作用 fossilization

化食 huàshí help (or aid) digestion

化痰 huàtán reduce phlegm: ～止咳 reduce phlegm and relieve coughing

化铁炉 huàtiělú metall. cupola furnace

化外 huàwài outside the pale of civilization

化为乌有 huà wéi wūyǒu melt into thin air; vanish; come to naught

化纤 huàxiān short for 化学纤维 huàxué xiānwéi

化险为夷 huà xiǎn wéi yí turn danger into safety; head off a disaster

化学 huàxué ① chemistry: 应用～ applied chemistry / 理论～ theoretical chemistry ② inf. celluloid: 这把梳子是～的。This comb is made from celluloid.

化学变化 huàxué biànhuà chemical change
化学成分 huàxué chéngfen chemical composition
化学当量 huàxué dāngliàng chemical equivalent
化学反应 huàxué fǎnyìng chemical reaction
化学方程式 huàxué fāngchéngshì chemical equation
化学肥料 huàxué féiliào chemical fertilizer
化学符号 huàxué fúhào chemical symbol
化学工业 huàxué gōngyè chemical industry
化学疗法 huàxué liáofǎ chemotherapy
化学试剂 huàxué shìjì chemical reagent
化学武器 huàxué wǔqì chemical weapons
化学纤维 huàxué xiānwéi chemical fibre
化学性质 huàxué xìngzhì chemical property
化学元素 huàxué yuánsù chemical element
化学战争 huàxué zhànzhēng chemical warfare
化学作用 huàxué zuòyòng chemical action

化验 huàyàn chemical examination; laboratory test: ～单 laboratory test report / ～室 laboratory / ～员 laboratory technician (or assistant)

化油器 huàyóuqì mech. carburettor

化缘 huàyuán (of Buddhist monks or Taoist priests) beg alms

化雨春风 huàyǔ chūnfēng same as 春风化雨 chūnfēng huàyǔ

化斋 huàzhāi (of Buddhist monks or Taoist priests) beg a vegetarian meal

化整为零 huà zhěng wéi líng break up the whole into parts

化妆 huàzhuāng ① (of actors) make up ② put on makeup; make up: 年轻妇女多喜欢～。Most young ladies like to use makeup.

化妆品 huàzhuāngpǐn cosmetics

化妆室 huàzhuāngshì ① dressing room ② dial. lavatory; toilet; W.C.

化装 huàzhuāng ① (of actors) make up ② disguise oneself: ～侦察 go reconnoitring in disguise / 他～成商人,混过了封锁线。He disguised himself as a merchant and managed to pass through the blockade line.

化装师 huàzhuāngshī makeup man
化装室 huàzhuāngshì dressing room
化装舞会 huàzhuāng wǔhuì fancy dress ball; masked ball; masquerade

划¹(劃)
huà ① delimit; differentiate: ～界 delimit a boundary / ～成分 determine class status / ～为右派 be branded as a Rightist ② transfer; assign: ～款 transfer money / 他把试验田～给这个小组负责。He assigned the experimental plot to that group. ③ plan: 筹划 chóuhuà

划²(劃)
huà same as 画² huà
——see also huá; huai

划拨 huàbō ① transfer; 这笔款子由银行～。The money will be transferred through the bank. ② assign; allocate: 把节余的钢材～给农具厂。Allocate the spare steel to the Farm Tools Factory.

划策 huàcè plan; scheme

划等号 huà děnghào equate one thing with another: 弃权票不能和反对票～。An abstention is not equivalent to a negative vote.

划定 huàdìng delimit; designate: ～捕鱼区 delimit fishing areas / ～边界 delimit a boundary line / 在～的区域内游泳 swim in the designated areas

划分 huàfēn ① divide: ～行政区域 divide a country into administrative areas / 帝国主义～势力范围的斗争 a struggle among the imperialists to carve out spheres of influence ② differentiate: ～阶级成分 determine class status

划归 huàguī put under (sb.'s administration, etc.); incorporate into: 这个企业已～地方管理。The enterprise has been put under local administration. / 一九五五年撤消了热河省,辖区分别～河北、辽宁二省和内蒙古自治区。In 1955 Rehe Province was abolished and the area previously under its jurisdiction was divided and incorporated into the provinces of Hebei and Liaoning and the Inner Mongolian Autonomous Region.

划价 huàjià have a prescription priced (in a hospital dispensary)

划框框 huà kuàngkuang set limits; place restrictions

划清 huàqīng draw a clear line of demarcation; make a clear distinction: ～是非 make a clear distinction between right and wrong / ～政策界限 draw distinctions in accordance with the policy / 跟他～界线 make a clean break with him

划时代 huàshídài epoch-making: 具有～的意义 have epoch-making significance / ～的宣言 a declaration that is a landmark in history; an epoch-making declaration

划一 huàyī ① standardized; uniform: ～的模式 a uniform model ② standardize: ～这本词典的体例 standardize the layout of the dictionary

划一不二 huà yī bù èr fixed; unalterable; rigid: 价钱～ fixed price (not subject to bargaining) / 写文章没有～的公式。There's no hard and fast rule for writing.

华(華)
Huà ① see below ② a surname
——see also huá

华山 Huàshān Mount Hua (in Shaanxi Province)
——see also 五岳 Wǔyuè

话
huà ① word; talk: 说几句～ say a few words / ～不能这么说。I wouldn't say that. ② talk about; speak about: 话别 huàbié

话把儿 huàbàr same as 话柄 huàbǐng

话本 huàběn printed versions of the prompt-books used by popular storytellers in Song and Yuan times (salient features of huaben stories: use of the vernacular larded with the stock expressions of professional storytellers; liberal admixture of colloquialisms and archaisms; frequent inclusion of rhymed passages, idioms, or poems for narrative or descriptive purposes; a routine preamble before the feature story): 《清平山堂～》Colloquial Stories Published by the Qingpingshan Studio

话别 huàbié say a few parting words; say good-bye: 他

们在车站～。They said their good-byes at the station.

话柄 huàbǐng subject for ridicule; handle: 留下了～ leave behind a subject for ridicule

话不投机半句多 huà bù tóujī bàn jù duō if there's no common ground, a single word is a waste of breath: 有时我也同他说几句，结果总是～，只得又停下来。Occasionally I addressed a remark to him, but invariably gave up after a few words, realizing that we had nothing in common. ——see also 酒逢知己千杯少，话不投机半句多 jiǔ féng zhījǐ qiān bēi shǎo, huà bù tóujī bàn jù duō

话茬儿 huàchár (also 话碴儿 huàchár) dial. ① thread of discourse: 接上～ take up the thread of a conversation ② tone of one's speech: 听他的～，这件事不好办。From what he says, that can't be easily done. ③ a cause for dispute; quarrel: 他正找不到～呢，别惹他。He's trying to pick a quarrel, so it's better to leave him alone.

话到舌边留半句 huà dào shé biān liú bàn jù hold back part of what you have to say when you're about to say it

话锋 huàfēng thread of discourse; topic of conversation: 把～一转 switch the conversation to some other subject

话家常 huà jiācháng chitchat; exchange small talk

话旧 huàjiù talk over old times; reminisce

话剧 huàjù modern drama; stage play

话剧团 huàjùtuán modern drama troupe; theatrical company

话里有话 huàlǐ yǒu huà the words mean more than they say; there's more to it than meets the ear

话篓子 huàlǒuzi dial. chatterbox

话说 huàshuō it is told that ... (an opening phrase used in traditional stories and novels): ～故宋绍兴年间，临安虽然是个建都之地，富庶之乡，其中乞丐的依然不少。《今古奇观·金玉奴棒打薄情郎》It is told that in the Shaoxing reign period of the Song Dynasty, although Lin'an had been made the capital city and was a wealthy and populous district, still the great number of beggars had not diminished.

话题 huàtí subject of a talk; topic of conversation: 他见有人进来，马上转了～。He changed the subject as soon as he saw someone coming in.

话筒 huàtǒng ① microphone ② telephone transmitter ③ megaphone

话头 huàtóu thread of discourse: 打断～ interrupt sb.; cut sb. short / 拾起～ take up the thread of a conversation / 他知道越解释越糟，马上拨转～谈别的了。Knowing that any explanation would only make matters worse, he hastened to change the subject.

话务员 huàwùyuán *(telephone) operator

话匣子 huàxiázi dial. ① gramophone ② radio receiving set ③ chatterbox: 这人是个～。That fellow is a chatterbox. / 他打开～就没个完。Once he opens his mouth, he never stops.

话音 huàyīn ① one's voice in speech: ～儿未落 when one has hardly finished speaking ② inf. tone; implication: 听他的～儿，准是另有打算。His tone suggests that he has something else in mind.

话语 huàyǔ what one says; words: 他～不多，可句句中听。His words are few, but everything he says makes good sense.

画[1]（畫） huà ① draw; paint: ～一个圈 draw (or describe) a circle / ～一张草图 make a sketch ② drawing; painting; picture: 一张～ a picture ③ be decorated with paintings or pictures: 画屏 huàpíng

画[2]（畫、劃） huà ① draw; mark; sign: ～

线 draw a line ② stroke (of a Chinese character): "人"字有两～。The character 人 is made up of two strokes. ③ dial. horizontal stroke (in Chinese characters): 一～ a horizontal stroke

画板 huàbǎn drawing board

画报 huàbào illustrated magazine or newspaper; pictorial

画笔 huàbǐ painting brush; brush

画饼 huàbǐng a painted cake; pie in the sky: 他的希望成了～。His hope came to nothing.

画饼充饥 huà bǐng chōngjī draw cakes to allay hunger—feed on illusions

画布 huàbù canvas (for painting)

画册 huàcè an album of paintings; picture album

画策 huàcè same as 划策 huàcè

画到 huàdào sign in; check in

画地为牢 huà dì wéi láo draw a circle on the ground to serve as a prison—restrict sb.'s activities to a designated area or sphere

画栋雕梁 huàdòng-diāoliáng same as 雕梁画栋 diāoliáng-huàdòng

画法 huàfǎ technique of painting or drawing: ～新颖 a novel technique in painting or drawing

画舫 huàfǎng gaily-painted pleasure-boat

画符 huàfú Taoism draw magic figures or incantations

画幅 huàfú ① picture; painting: 美丽的田野是天然的～。The beautiful open country is a painting done by nature. ② size of a picture: ～虽然不大，所表现的天地却十分广阔。The picture is small but it shows broad vistas.

画稿[1] huàgǎo (of a person in charge) put one's signature to an official document to indicate approval

画稿[2] huàgǎo rough sketch (for a painting)

画舸 huàgě formal gaily-painted pleasure-boat

画工 huàgōng artisan-painter

画供 huàgòng sign a written confession to a crime

画画儿 huàhuàr draw a picture

画虎类狗 huà hǔ lèi gǒu (also 画虎不成反类犬 huà hǔ bù chéng fǎn lèi quǎn) try to draw a tiger and end up with the likeness of a dog—attempt sth. over-ambitious and end in failure

画家 huàjiā painter; artist

画架 huàjià easel

画匠 huàjiàng ① artisan-painter ② inferior painter

画境 huàjìng picturesque scene: 如入～ feel as though one were in a landscape painting

画具 huàjù painter's paraphernalia

画卷 huàjuàn ① picture scroll ② magnificent scenery or stirring battle scene

画绢 huàjuàn silk for drawing on; drawing silk

画刊 huàkān ① pictorial section of a newspaper ② pictorial

画廊 huàláng ① painted corridor ② (picture) gallery

画龙点睛 huà lóng diǎn jīng bring a picture of a dragon to life by putting in the pupils of its eyes—add the touch that brings a work of art to life; add the finishing touch; add an apt word to clinch the point

画眉[1] huàméi zool. a kind of thrush

画眉[2] huàméi blacken eyebrows; draw eyebrows

画面 huàmiàn ① general appearance of a picture; tableau ② film frame

画皮 huàpí disguise or mask of an evildoer: 剥～ rip off sb.'s mask

画片 huàpiàn a miniature reproduction of a painting

画屏 huàpíng painted screen

画谱 huàpǔ ① same as 画帖 huàtiè ② a book on the art of drawing or painting

画圈儿 huàquānr inf. draw a circle round one's name

on a document submitted for approval to show that one has read it

画蛇添足 huà shé tiān zú　draw a snake and add feet to it—ruin the effect by adding sth. superfluous

画师 huàshī　① painter; artist ② artisan-painter

画十字 huà shízì　① mark a cross (on a document in place of a signature by sb. who cannot write) ② cross oneself

画室 huàshì　studio

画坛 huàtán　art circle

画帖 huàtiè　a book of model paintings or drawings

画图 huàtú　① draw designs, maps, etc. ② picture (fig.): 这些诗篇构成了一幅农村生活多彩的～。These poems give a colourful picture of country life.

画外音 huàwàiyīn　*film* offscreen voice

画像 huàxiàng　① draw a portrait; portray: 给孩子画个像 draw a portrait of the child／让人～ sit for one's portrait ② portrait; portrayal: 巨幅～ a huge portrait

画像石 huàxiàngshí　stone relief (on ancient Chinese tombs, shrines, etc.)

画行 huàxíng　(of a person in charge) write the character 行 on a document to show one's approval

画押 huàyā　make one's cross (*or* mark); sign

画页 huàyè　page with illustrations (in a book or magazine); plate

画一 huàyī　same as 划一 huàyī

画院 huàyuàn　imperial art academy, notably that of the reign of the Emperor Huizong (徽宗) of the Song Dynasty, whose paintings were characterized by delicate brushwork and close attention to detail

画展 huàzhǎn　art exhibition; exhibition of paintings

画知 huàzhī　write the character 知 ("know") under one's name on an invitation list to indicate that one has been informed of the invitation

画轴 huàzhóu　painted scroll; scroll painting: 山水～ a scroll of landscape painting

画字 huàzì　*dial.* make one's cross; sign

桦(樺)
huà　*bot.* birch

huái

怀(懷)
huái　① bosom: 小孩儿在妈妈的～里睡着了。The baby fell asleep in its mother's arms. ② mind: 襟怀 jīnhuái ③ keep in mind; cherish: ～着真诚的愿望 cherish sincere hopes／～着深厚的感情 with deep feelings／少～大志 harbour lofty ambition when still young ④ think of; yearn for: ～友 think of a friend／～乡 yearn for one's native place; be homesick ⑤ conceive (a child): ～了孩子 become pregnant; be with child

怀抱 huáibào　① hold or carry in the arms: ～着婴儿 carry a baby in one's arms ② bosom: 她把孩子搂在～里。She held the child to her bosom. ／回到祖国的～ return to the embrace of one's homeland ③ cherish: ～远大的理想 cherish lofty ideals

怀表 huáibiǎo　pocket watch

怀才不遇 huái cái bù yù　have unrecognized talents

怀春 huáichūn　*formal* harbour the amorous thoughts of spring—(of a young girl) have thoughts of love

怀古 huáigǔ　recall antiquity; meditate on the past (often used in titles of poems which are reflections on historical events): ～诗 a poem recalling antiquity／苏东坡《赤壁～》Su Dongpo's "Recalling Antiquity at the Red Cliff" *or* "Meditations on the Red Cliff"／～之幽情 nostalgic musings over the past

怀鬼胎 huái guǐtāi　have evil intentions; harbour sinis-

ter designs

怀恨 huáihèn　nurse hatred; harbour resentment: ～在心 nurse a hatred

怀旧 huáijiù　remember past times or old acquaintances (usu. with kindly thoughts)、

怀恋 huáiliàn　think fondly of (past times, old friends, etc.); look back nostalgically: 他深深地～童年的生活。He felt a great nostalgia for his childhood.

怀念 huáiniàn　cherish the memory of; think of: ～革命先烈 cherish the memory of revolutionary martyrs／～远方的友人 think of an absent friend who is far away／～故乡 yearn for one's hometown

怀柔 huáiróu　(of feudal rulers) make a show of conciliation in order to bring other nationalities or states under control: ～政策 policy of control through conciliation; policy of mollification

怀胎 huáitāi　be (*or* become) pregnant

怀想 huáixiǎng　think about with affection (a faraway person, place, etc.); yearn for

怀疑 huáiyí　doubt; suspect: 引起～ raise doubts; arouse suspicion／消除～ dispel doubts; clear up suspicion／受到～ come under suspicion／～他的动机 suspect his motives／持～态度 take a sceptical attitude／他这话很叫人～。What he said is extremely doubtful. ／我～他今天来不了。I doubt if he'll come today. ／你～谁作的案? Whom do you suspect of the crime?

怀疑论 huáiyílùn　*philos.* scepticism

怀孕 huáiyùn　(also 怀妊 huáirèn) be pregnant: ～五个月了 be five months pregnant; be five months gone／～期 period of pregnancy; gestation period

徊
huái　see 徘徊 páihuái

淮
huái　the Huaihe River

淮北 Huáiběi　the area north of the Huaihe River; specifically, northern Anhui Province

淮海战役 Huái-Hǎi Zhànyì　the Huai-Hai Campaign (Nov. 6, 1948-Jan. 10, 1949), the second of the three decisive campaigns in the Chinese People's War of Liberation

淮剧 huáijù　Huai opera, popular in northern Jiangsu Province

淮南 Huáinán　the area south of the Huaihe River and north of the Changjiang River; specifically, central Anhui Province

槐
huái　Chinese scholartree

槐角 huáijiǎo　*Chin. med.* the pod of Chinese scholartree

槐米 huáimǐ　*Chin. med.* flower buds of Chinese scholartree

踝
huái　ankle

踝骨 huáigǔ　anklebone

huài

坏(壞)
huài　① bad; harmful: ～习惯 bad habit／～透了 downright bad; rotten to the core／～天气 foul weather／～书 a harmful book ② become or make bad; ruin; spoil: 鱼～了。The fish has gone bad. ／身体～ be in poor health／他胃口～了。He has lost his appetite. ／看小字会看～眼睛的。Small type hurts the eyes. ／雹子把庄稼砸～了。The hail damaged the crop. ／肚子吃～了 have an upset stomach ③ (used after certain verbs or adjectives) extremely: 吓～了 be badly scared／气～了 be beside oneself with rage／乐～了 be

wild with joy / 累～了 be dead tired; be dog-tired ④ evil idea; dirty trick: 使坏 shǐhuài

坏包儿 huàibāor *inf.* rascal; rogue

坏处 huàichu harm; disadvantage: 一点～也没有。 There's no harm in it at all. *or* There's nothing bad about it. / 从～着想, 往好处努力。 Prepare for the worst; strive for the best.

坏蛋 huàidàn *inf.* bad egg; scoundrel; bastard

坏东西 huàidōngxi bastard; scoundrel; rogue

坏分子 huàifènzǐ *leg.* bad element; evildoer

坏话 huàihuà ① malicious remarks; vicious talk: 讲别人～ speak ill of others ② unpleasant words: 好话～都要让人讲完。 One should let others finish what they have to say whether it sounds pleasant or unpleasant. / 好话～都要听。 You should listen to criticisms as well as praises.

坏疽 huàijū *med.* gangrene

坏人 huàirén bad person; evildoer; scoundrel

坏事 huàishì ① bad thing; evil deed: 向坏人～作斗争 struggle against evildoers and evil deeds ② ruin sth.; make things worse: 急躁只能～。 Impetuosity will only make things worse. / ～了! Something terrible has happened. / 他太粗心了, 结果坏了事。 He was so careless that he made a hash of it.

坏水儿 huàishuǐr *inf.* wicked idea: 一肚子～ be full of wicked ideas

坏死 huàisǐ *med.* necrosis: 局部～ local necrosis / 牙～ dental necrosis

坏心眼儿 huàixīnyǎnr *inf.* evil intention; ill will: 他没有～, 完全是为了你好。 He meant no harm, what he did was for your benefit.

坏血病 huàixuèbìng scurvy

坏帐 huàizhàng a bad debt

huai

划 (劃)　huai see 刮划 bāihuai ——see also huá; huà

huān

欢 (歡、懽)　huān ① joyous; merry; jubilant: 联欢 liánhuān ② *dial.* vigorously; with great drive; in full swing: 这些小青年干得可～呢! How vigorously these lads work! / 春耕闹得正～。 Spring ploughing is in full swing. / 雨越下越～。 It's raining harder and harder. / 火着得很～。 The fire is burning cheerfully.

欢蹦乱跳 huānbèng-luàntiào healthy-looking and vivacious: 幼儿园里的孩子个个都是～的。 The children in the kindergarten were healthy and lively. / 小马驹和小牛犊围着饲养员～。 The colts and calves are gambolling round the stockman.

欢忭 huānbiàn *formal* happy; joyous; gay

欢畅 huānchàng thoroughly delighted; elated

欢唱 huānchàng sing merrily

欢度 huāndù spend (an occasion) joyfully: ～佳节 celebrate a festival with jubilation

欢呼 huānhū hail; cheer; acclaim: 人们在街道两旁列队, 向归来的英雄们～。 The people lined the streets to hail the returning heroes. / ～胜利 hail the victory / 长时间的～ prolonged cheers (*or* ovation) / 他在一片～声中走上讲台。 He stepped on the platform amidst loud cheers.

欢聚 huānjù happy get-together; happy reunion: 春节到了, 全家老小～在一起。 The whole family got together happily for the Spring Festival.

欢聚一堂 huānjù yī táng happily gather under the same roof: 不同国度、不同肤色的运动员～。 Athletes from different lands and of different colours were gathered happily together.

欢快 huānkuài cheerful and light-hearted; lively: ～的心情 in a cheerful mood / ～的曲调 a lively melody / 随着音乐～地起舞 dance cheerfully to the music

欢乐 huānlè happy; joyous; gay: ～的人群 happy crowds / ～的景象 a scene of great joy / 给节日增添～气氛 add to the gaiety of the festival

欢洽 huānqià friendly; congenial: 两人谈得十分～。 The two of them talked very congenially.

欢庆 huānqìng celebrate joyously: ～五一 celebrate May Day

欢声雷动 huānshēng léidòng cheers resound like peals of thunder: 全场～。 The audience broke into deafening cheers.

欢声笑语 huānshēng-xiàoyǔ happy laughters and cheerful voices

欢实 huānshi *dial.* lively; full of vigour: 孩子们多～啊! How lively the children are!

欢送 huānsòng see off; send off: 热烈～毕业生到祖国需要的地方去 give a warm send-off to graduates going to where the country needs them / ～会 farewell meeting; send-off meeting / ～仪式 seeing-off ceremony

欢腾 huānténg great rejoicing; jubilation: 喜讯传来, 举国～。 There was nationwide rejoicing at the good news. / 广场上一片～。 The square was astir with jubilant crowds.

欢天喜地 huāntiān-xǐdì with boundless joy; wild with joy; overjoyed: ～地迎接国庆 greet National Day with boundless joy

欢慰 huānwèi be gratified: 得知我们的建议已被采纳, 甚感～。 We are gratified to learn that our suggestion has been accepted.

欢喜 huānxǐ ① joyful; happy; delighted: 满心～ be filled with joy / 欢欢喜喜过春节 spend a joyful Spring Festival ② like; be fond of; delight in: 她～拉手风琴。 She likes to play the accordion.

欢笑 huānxiào laugh heartily

欢心 huānxīn favour; liking; love: 想博取～ try to win sb.'s favour

欢欣鼓舞 huānxīn-gǔwǔ be filled with exultation; be elated: 捷报传来, 全国人民无不～。 The good tidings filled the whole nation with joy. *or* The good tidings elated the whole nation. / ～地跨入了新的一年 stride into the new year in high spirits

欢宴 huānyàn entertain sb. to dinner on some happy occasion

欢迎 huānyíng ① welcome; greet: ～大家批评 Criticisms are welcome. / 我们受到了非常热烈的～。 We received a very warm welcome. / ～您到北京来! Welcome to Beijing! / 到机场～贵宾 meet distinguished guests at the airport / ～老王给我们唱个歌! Let's ask Lao Wang to sing us a song! / ～词 welcoming speech; address of welcome / ～会 a party (*or* meeting) to welcome sb. ② be well received: 这部电影深受群众～。 The film has been well received by the people.

欢娱 huānyú *formal* happy; joyous; gay

欢悦 huānyuè happy; joyous

欢跃 huānyuè jump for joy

獾 (貛)　huān *zool.* badger

獾油 huānyóu badger fat (for treating burns)

huán

还(還) huánxiāng ① go (or come) back: 还乡 huánxiāng ② give back; return; repay: 这几本是到期要~的书。These books are due for return. / 下个月~你钱。I'll pay you back next month. ③ give or do sth. in return: 还价 huánjià ——see also hái

还本 huánběn　repayment of principal (or capital): ~付息 repay capital with interest

还魂 huánhún　① revive after death; return from the grave ② *dial.* reprocessed: ~纸 reprocessed paper

还击 huánjī　① fight back; return fire; counterattack: 进行自卫~ fight in self-defence / ~敌人 hit back at the enemy ② *fencing* riposte

还价 huánjià　counter-offer; counter-bid

还口 huánkǒu　answer back; retort: 打不还手, 骂不~ not hit back when beaten, and not answer back when insulted

还礼 huánlǐ　① return a salute ② *dial.* send a present in return; present a gift in return

还清 huánqīng　pay off: ~债务 pay off one's debts

还情 huánqíng　repay a favour

还手 huánshǒu　strike (or hit) back

还俗 huánsú　(of Buddhist monks and nuns or Taoist priests) resume secular life

还席 huánxí　give a return dinner

还乡 huánxiāng　return to one's native place

还乡团 huánxiāngtuán　home-going legions (armed bands formed of landlords and local tyrants who fled from the Liberated Areas to the Kuomintang areas during the People's War of Liberation); landlords' restitution corps

还醒 huánxǐng　revive; regain consciousness; come to; come round

还阳 huányáng　return to life from the nether world; revive after death

还原 huányuán　① return to the original condition or shape; restore ② *chem.* reduction: ~剂 reducing agent; reductant / ~酶 reductase

还原焰 huányuányàn　same as 内焰 nèiyàn

还愿 huányuàn　① redeem a vow to a god ② fulfil one's promise: 说话要算数, 不能光许愿不~。You should do what you say; you can't go on making promises and not keeping them.

还债 huánzhài　pay one's debt; repay a debt

还帐 huánzhàng　pay one's debt; settle accounts

还嘴 huánzuǐ　*inf.* answer (or talk) back; retort: 不许和奶奶~, 这不礼貌。Don't answer back to your grandmother; it's not polite.

环(環) huán　① ring; hoop: 在窗帘上缝几个~儿。Sew a few rings on the curtain. ② link: 一~套一~ all linked with one another; wheels within wheels / 最薄弱的一~ the weakest link ③ surround; encircle; hem in: ~滁, 皆山也。(欧阳修) Chuzhou is surrounded by mountains. ④ *sports* ring: 命中九~ hit the nine-point ring / 在射箭中取得三百四十二~的成绩 score 342 points in archery

环靶 huánbǎ　*sports* round target

环保 huánbǎo　short for 环境保护 huánjìng bǎohù

环抱 huánbào　surround; encircle; hem in: 群山~的村庄 a village nestling among the hills

环城 huánchéng　around the city: ~赛跑 round-the-city race / ~公路 ring road; belt highway; beltway

环带[1] huándài　*zool.* clitellum

环带[2] huándài　a ring of light

环肥燕瘦 Huán féi Yàn shòu　Yang Yuhuan (杨玉环) was plump while Zhao Feiyan (赵飞燕) was slender (both being reigning beauties)—each beautiful woman is beautiful in her own way; each literary or artistic work has its distinctive features

环顾 huángù　*formal* look about (or round): ~四周 look all round / ~国际局势 take stock of the world situation

环海 huánhǎi　be surrounded by sea

环礁 huánjiāo　*geol.* atoll

环节 huánjié　① link; sector: 减少~, 提高效率 reduce the number of intermediate links and raise efficiency / 不少~上存在着问题。Problems exist in many sectors. / 主要~ a key link / 生产~ links in the production chain ② *zool.* segment

环节动物 huánjié dòngwù　annelid

环颈雉 huánjǐngzhì　*zool.* ring-necked pheasant

环境 huánjìng　environment; surroundings; circumstances: 换换~ have a change of environment / 为~所迫 be forced by circumstances / 在艰苦的~中成长 grow up under tough conditions / ~顺利 under favourable circumstances / 如~许可 if circumstances permit / 创造适宜的经济和社会~ create a favourable economic and social environment / 改善投资~ improve the investment environment

环境保护 huánjìng bǎohù　environmental protection

环境监测系统 huánjìng jiāncè xìtǒng　environmental monitoring system

环境卫生 huánjìng wèishēng　environmental sanitation; general sanitation

环境污染 huánjìng wūrǎn　pollution of the environment; environmental pollution

环流 huánliú　*meteorol.* circulation

环球 huánqiú　① round the world: ~旅行 travel round the world; a round-the-world tour ② the earth; the whole world

环绕 huánrào　surround; encircle; revolve around: 大院的四周, 绿树~。The compound is surrounded by trees. / 月亮~着地球转动。The moon revolves around the earth. / ~着中心任务 centre around the main task

环绕速度 huánrào sùdù　*astron.* circular (or orbital) velocity; first cosmic velocity ——see also 宇宙速度 yǔzhòu sùdù

环山 huánshān　① around a mountain: ~公路 a road circumscribing (or going around) a mountain ② be surrounded by mountains: 这村子四面~。The village is surrounded (or hemmed in) by mountains. or There are mountains all round the village.

环蛇 huánshé　krait

环食 huánshí　*astron.* annular eclipse (of the sun)

环视 huánshì　look around: 我~车站四周, 那位朋友毫无踪影。I looked around the station but couldn't see my friend anywhere.

环烃 huántīng　*chem.* cyclic hydrocarbon

环烷 huánwán　*chem.* cycloalkanes; cycloparaffin; naphthene

环卫 huánwèi　① short for 环境卫生 huánjìng wèishēng ② *formal* imperial guards; guards

环行 huánxíng　going in a ring: ~一周 make a circuit / ~公共汽车 bus with a circular route / ~公路 ring road; belt highway; beltway / ~铁路 circuit railway; belt line

环形 huánxíng　annular; ringlike

环形山 huánxíngshān　*astron.* ring structure; lunar crater

环氧树脂 huányǎng shùzhī　*chem.* epoxy resin

环游 huányóu　tour around (a place): ~世界 take a round-the-world tour

环宇 huányǔ　same as 寰宇 huányǔ

环子 huánzi　ring; link

桓　Huán　a surname

锾　huán　a unit of weight used in ancient China, equal to six *liang* (两)

寰　huán　extensive region: 人寰 rénhuán
寰球　huánqiú　the earth; the whole world
寰宇　huányǔ　*formal* the earth; the whole world

圜　huán　see 转圜 zhuǎnhuán

缳　huán　*formal* ① noose: 投缳 tóuhuán ② strangle

鹮　huán　*zool.* ibis

鬟　huán　bun (of hair): 云鬟 yúnhuán

huǎn

缓　huǎn　① slow; unhurried: ～流 flow slowly ② delay; postpone; put off: ～办 postpone doing sth. / 这事～几天再说。Let's put it off for a couple of days. ③ not tense; relaxed ④ recuperate; revive; come to: 过了好一阵他才～过来。It was a long time before he came to. / 这场及时雨使受旱的禾苗都～过来了。The timely rain revived the drought-stricken crops. / ～过劲儿来 feel refreshed after a breathing spell
缓兵之计　huǎn bīng zhī jì　measures to stave off an attack; a stratagem to gain a respite: 这不过是～而已。These are nothing but stalling tactics.
缓不济急　huǎn bù jì jí　slow action cannot save a critical situation
缓步　huǎnbù　walk unhurriedly
缓冲　huǎnchōng　① buffer; cushion: 弹性～ elastic buffer / 起～的作用 produce a cushioning effect; absorb the shock / ～的余地 leeway; room for manoeuvre ② *chem.* buffer: ～剂 buffer
缓冲地带　huǎnchōng dìdài　buffer zone
缓冲国　huǎnchōngguó　buffer state
缓冲器　huǎnchōngqì　*mech.* buffer; bumper
缓和　huǎnhé　① relax; ease up; mitigate; alleviate: 风势渐趋～。The wind is subsiding. / ～矛盾 mitigate (*or* alleviate) a contradiction ② *détente*: 两国关系出现了一定程度的～。Some relaxation of tensions has been brought about between the two countries.
缓和剂　huǎnhéjì　*phys.* moderator
缓急　huǎnjí　① pressing or otherwise; of greater or lesser urgency: 轻重缓急 qīngzhòng-huǎnjí ② emergency
缓急相助　huǎnjí xiāng zhù　help each other in time of need
缓颊　huǎnjiá　*formal* intercede for sb.; put in a good word for sb.
缓建　huǎnjiàn　postpone construction
缓缰　huǎnjiāng　slacken the reins
缓解　huǎnjiě　relieve; alleviate; ease: ～疼痛 relieve (*or* ease) the pain / ～住房 (供应) 紧张情况 alleviate (*or* ease) the housing (food) shortage
缓慢　huǎnmàn　slow: 动作～ slow in action; slowmoving / 进展～ make slow progress
缓辔　huǎnpèi　slacken the reins: ～徐行 amble along
缓坡　huǎnpō　gentle slope
缓期　huǎnqī　postpone a deadline; suspend: ～付款 delay (*or* defer) payment / 判处死刑，～二年执行 condemned to death with the sentence suspended for two years; sentenced to death with a two-year reprieve

缓气　huǎnqì　get a breathing space; have a respite; take a breather: 他实在太忙了，连缓口气的工夫都没有。He was so busy that he didn't even have a chance to take a breather. / 我跑不动了，让我缓缓气。I'm shagged out! Let me get my breath back.
缓图　huǎntú　plan slowly and carefully
缓限　huǎnxiàn　postpone a deadline; suspend
缓行　huǎnxíng　① walk or drive slowly ② postpone implementation
缓刑　huǎnxíng　*leg.* temporary suspension of the execution of a sentence; reprieve; probation: ～二年 two years' probation
缓醒　huǎnxǐng　*dial.* revive; regain consciousness; come to; come round
缓役　huǎnyì　*mil.* deferment (of service)
缓征　huǎnzhēng　postpone the imposition of a tax or levy

huàn

幻　huàn　① unreal; imaginary; illusory: 虚幻 xūhuàn ② magical; changeable: 变幻 biànhuàn
幻灯　huàndēng　① slide show: 放～ show slides / 看～ watch a slide show ② slide projector
幻灯机　huàndēngjī　slide projector; epidiascope
幻灯片　huàndēngpiàn　(lantern) slide
幻化　huànhuà　magically change: 雪后的山谷～成一个奇特的琉璃世界。The snow changed the valley into a strange glazed world.
幻景　huànjǐng　illusion; mirage
幻境　huànjìng　dreamland; fairyland
幻觉　huànjué　hallucination; illusion
幻梦　huànmèng　illusion; dream
幻灭　huànmiè　vanish into thin air: 他的希望～了。His hopes were dashed.
幻视　huànshì　*med.* photism
幻术　huànshù　magic; conjuring
幻听　huàntīng　*med.* phonism
幻想　huànxiǎng　① imagine; dream: 自古以来，人们就～能在天空飞行。People have dreamed of flying ever since ancient times. ② illusion; fancy; fantasy: 抱有～ cherish illusions / 丢掉～ cast away illusions / 沉湎于～ indulge in fantasy; be lost in reverie / 生活在～的世界里 live in a world of fantasy
幻想曲　huànxiǎngqǔ　*mus.* fantasia: 《韩德尔主题～》 *Fantasia on a Theme of Handel*
幻象　huànxiàng　mirage; phantom; phantasm
幻影　huànyǐng　unreal image

奂 (奂)　huàn　*formal* ① abundant; plentiful ② bright-coloured

宦　huàn　① official: 宦海 huànhǎi ② be an official; fill an office: 仕宦 shìhuàn ③ eunuch ④ (Huàn) a surname
宦场　huànchǎng　officialdom; official circles
宦官　huànguān　eunuch
宦海　huànhǎi　officialdom; official circles: ～沉浮 the ups and downs in officialdom; the vicissitudes of an official career
宦门　huànmén　an official family: ～公子 son of an official family
宦囊　huànnáng　*formal* personal savings from an official career
宦途　huàntú　*formal* official career
宦游　huànyóu　*formal* go from place to place seeking official posts: ～四方 wander about seeking office

浣（澣）

huàn ① wash: ～衣 wash clothes ② any of the three ten-day divisions of a month: 上～ the first ten days of a month

浣熊 huànxióng racoon

涣

huàn melt; vanish

涣涣 huànhuàn *formal* (of flood) overflowing

涣然 huànrán (of misgivings, doubts, etc.) melt away; disappear; vanish

涣然冰释 huànrán bīngshì melt away; disappear; vanish: 他的疑虑～。All his misgivings vanished.

涣散 huànsàn lax; slack: 纪律～ be lax in discipline / ～斗志 sap sb.'s morale (or fighting will)

换

huàn ① exchange; barter; trade: 以兽皮～工业品 exchange (or barter) furs for industrial products / 用鲜血～来的教训 a lesson paid for in blood ② change: ～衣服 change one's clothes / 他～工作了吗? Has he changed his job? / ～乘火车 change to a train / 出去走一下，～～脑筋。Let's go for a walk and give our minds a rest. ③ exchange; convert: 把美元～成人民币 convert (or change) U. S. dollars into *Renminbi*

换班 huànbān ① change shifts: 日班和夜班的工人正在～。Daytime and nighttime workers are changing shifts now. ② relieve a person on duty ③ *mil.* changing of the guard

换边 huànbiān *sports.* change sides

换步 huànbù *mil.* change step

换茬 huànchá *agric.* change of crops

换车 huànchē change trains or buses: 从学校回家一路上要换四趟车。I have to change buses four times going home from school.

换代 huàndài replace; regenerate: 产品更新～ replace the older generations of products by new ones

换挡 huàndǎng *mech.* shift gears

换发球 huànfāqiú *sports.* change of service

换防 huànfáng *mil.* relieve a garrison

换房 huànfáng exchange houses: ～站 housing exchange office

换俘协定 huànfú xiédìng agreement for exchange of prisoners; cartel

换岗 huàngǎng relieve a sentry (or guard)

换个儿 huàngèr *inf.* change places: 咱们换个个儿，你就能瞧清楚点儿了。If we change places you'll be able to see better. / 这两个抽屉大小不一样，不能～。The two drawers are not the same size, so they are not exchangeable.

换工 huàngōng exchange labour

换货 huànhuò exchange goods; barter: ～和付款协定 goods exchange and payments agreement / ～协定 barter agreement

换机放映 huàn jī fàngyìng *film* changeover

换季 huànjì change garments according to the season; wear different clothes for a new season

换肩 huànjiān shift the carrying pole onto the other shoulder

换句话说 huàn jù huà shuō in other words

换毛 huànmáo moult: 雏燕在什么时候第一次～? When do the young swallows have their first moult?

换能器 huànnéngqì *phys.* transducer

换谱 huànpǔ same as 换帖 huàntiě

换气 huànqì take a breath (in swimming)

换气扇 huànqìshàn ventilation fan

换钱 huànqián ① change money (or bills) ② sell: 废铁也可以～。Scrap iron can be sold for money.

换亲 huànqīn (of two families) take each other's daughters as daughters-in-law

换取 huànqǔ exchange (or barter) sth. for; get in re-turn: 用工业品～农产品 exchange (or barter) industrial products for farm produce / ～外汇 gain foreign exchange / 以较小的代价～更大的收益 get greater gains at smaller cost

换人 huànrén *sports* substitution (of players)

换算 huànsuàn conversion: ～表 conversion table

换汤不换药 huàn tāng bù huàn yào the same medicine with a different name—the same old stuff with a different label; a change in form but not in content (or essence)

换帖 huàntiě exchange cards with personal and family details when becoming sworn brothers: ～弟兄 sworn brothers

换文 huànwén exchange of notes (or letters): 建立外交关系的～ an exchange of notes on the establishment of diplomatic relations

换洗 huànxǐ change clothes (for washing): 带一套～衣服。Take along a change of clothes.

换心 huànxīn *dial.* intimate; understanding: ～朋友 bosom friend; intimate friend

换牙 huànyá (of a child) grow permanent teeth

换言之 huànyánzhī *formal* in other words

换样 huànyàng vary: 顿顿吃面条，就不能换个样儿? Can't we vary our diet a bit instead of having noodles all the time?

换药 huànyào change bandage; use fresh dressing for a wound

换羽 huànyǔ moult

换约 huànyuē exchange of notes (or letters)

换装站 huànzhuāngzhàn *railway* transshipment station

唤

huàn call out: 呼唤 hūhuàn

唤起 huànqǐ ① arouse: ～民众 arouse the masses of the people ② call; recall: 有必要～人们注意这个事实。It is necessary to call attention to this fact. / ～对往事的回忆 evoke past memories

唤醒 huànxǐng wake up; awaken: 他睡得正香,我不愿～他。I didn't want to wake him from his sound sleep. / ～人民 arouse the people

焕

huàn shining; glowing

焕发 huànfā shine; glow; irradiate: ～精神,努力工作 call forth all one's vigour and work with redoubled efforts / 老干部～出革命青春。Old cadres still radiate the revolutionary vigour of their youth.

焕然一新 huànrán yī xīn take on an entirely new look (or aspect); look brand-new: 自从有了中国共产党,中国革命的面目就～了。With the birth of the Communist Party of China, the face of the Chinese revolution took on an altogether new aspect. / 这个老港经过改造和建设, 面貌～。After renovation and reconstruction the old port has changed beyond recognition.

患

huàn ① trouble; peril; disaster: 水患 shuǐhuàn ② anxiety; worry: 不～人之不己知,～其不能也。(《论语》) It is not the failure of others to appreciate your abilities that should trouble you, but rather your own lack of them. ③ contract; suffer from: ～肝炎 contract (or have) hepatitis

患病 huànbìng suffer from an illness; fall ill; be ill

患处 huànchù affected part (of a patient's body)

患得患失 huàndé-huànshī worry about personal gains and losses; be swayed by considerations of loss and gain

患难 huànnàn trials and tribulations; adversity; trouble: 可与共～,不可与共安乐 can share distress with others, but not happiness

患难夫妻 huànnàn fūqī husband and wife who have

gone through difficult times together

患难与共 huànnàn yǔ gòng　go through thick and thin together; share weal and woe

患难之交 huànnàn zhī jiāo　friends in adversity; tested friends

患者 huànzhě　sufferer; patient: 结核病〜 a person suffering from tuberculosis; a TB patient

瘓 huàn　see 瘫瘓 tānhuàn

豢 huàn　see below

豢养 huànyǎng　feed; groom; keep: 反动政府〜的走狗 running dogs kept by a reactionary government

漶 huàn　see 漫漶 mànhuàn

鲩 huàn　another name for 草鱼 cǎoyú

攌 huàn　formal　wear; put on

攌甲执兵 huànjiǎ zhíbīng　put on one's armour and take up arms

huāng

肓 huāng　see 病入膏肓 bìng rù gāohuāng

荒 huāng　① waste: 地〜了。 The land lies waste. ② desolate; barren: 荒村 huāngcūn ③ famine; crop failure: 荒年 huāngnián ④ wasteland; uncultivated land: 垦荒 kěnhuāng ⑤ neglect; be out of practice: 别把功课〜了。 Don't neglect your lessons. / 好久不下棋，〜了。 It's a long time since I played chess. I'm out of practice. / 他的英语〜掉了。 His English is rusty. ⑥ shortage; scarcity: 房荒 fánghuāng ⑦ unreasonable: 荒谬 huāngmiù ⑧ dial.　uncertain: 荒信 huāngxìn ⑨ formal　give way to; indulge: 荒淫 huāngyín ⑩ roughly processed; crude: 荒子 huāngzi

荒草 huāngcǎo　weeds

荒村 huāngcūn　a deserted village

荒诞 huāngdàn　fantastic; absurd; incredible: 〜的想法 a fantastic idea / 〜的情节 an incredible plot

荒诞不经 huāngdàn bù jīng　preposterous; fantastic; absurd:《聊斋志异》所记鬼怪故事诚属〜，然而却能引人入胜，多年来为无数读者所喜爱。 Though admittedly wild and fanciful, the ghost stories of the *Liao Zhai Zhi Yi* have a beauty that has captivated countless readers over the years.

荒诞无稽 huāngdàn wújī　fantastic; absurd; incredible: 〜之谈 a tall story; a preposterous statement

荒岛 huāngdǎo　a desert (or uninhabited) island

荒地 huāngdì　wasteland; uncultivated (or undeveloped) land

荒废 huāngfèi　① leave uncultivated; lie waste: 我们村里没有一亩地是〜的。 Not a single *mu* of land in our village lies waste. ② fall into disuse (or disrepair): 〜了的水渠又利用起来了。 The irrigation canals that fell into disrepair are in use again. / 这所别墅〜已久。 This villa has long fallen into disuse. ③ waste (time): 她一边说话一边干活，不肯〜半点功夫。 She worked while she chatted, not wasting a single moment. ④ neglect; be out of practice: 〜学业 neglect one's studies

荒古 huānggǔ　remote antiquity

荒秽 huānghuì　formal　lie waste; go out of cultivation: 晨兴理〜，带月荷锄归。(陶潜) At dawn, I rise and go out to weed the field; Shouldering the hoe, I walk home with the moon.

荒火 huānghuǒ　prairie fire; bush fire

荒货 huānghuò　dial.　junk: 〜店 junk shop

荒瘠 huāngjǐ　wild and barren; desolate and infertile

荒寂 huāngjì　desolate and still; bleak and quiet

荒郊 huāngjiāo　desolate place outside a town; wilderness

荒凉 huāngliáng　bleak and desolate; wild: 一片〜 a scene of desolation / 过去这里是〜的穷山沟。 This used to be a bleak and barren gully. / 〜的景色 wild scenery

荒乱 huāngluàn　in great disorder; in turmoil

荒谬 huāngmiù　absurd; preposterous: 〜的说法 an absurd formulation

荒谬绝伦 huāngmiù juélún　utterly absurd; absolutely preposterous: 这种评论〜。 This comment is absolutely preposterous.

荒漠 huāngmò　① desolate and boundless: 〜的草原 desolate and boundless grasslands ② bleak and boundless desert; wilderness

荒年 huāngnián　famine (or lean) year

荒僻 huāngpì　desolate and out-of-the-way: 〜的山区 a desolate mountain area

荒弃 huāngqì　leave uncultivated; lie waste: 这个村里没有〜的土地。 No land in the village lies waste.

荒歉 huāngqiàn　crop failure; famine

荒山 huāngshān　a barren hill

荒时暴月 huāngshí-bàoyuè　a time of dearth; a lean year; hard times: 〜，他们就向亲友乞哀告怜。 In hard times, they piteously beg help from relatives and friends.

荒疏 huāngshū　out of practice; rusty: 好多年不拉提琴了，现在都已〜了。 I'm out of practice since I haven't played the violin for many years. / 因为长期居住国外，我的汉语有点〜了。 My Chinese is a little rusty after a long residence abroad.

荒数 huāngshù　dial.　an approximate number

荒唐 huāngtáng　① absurd; fantastic; preposterous: 〜可笑 ridiculous; absurd / 〜透顶 absolutely ridiculous; preposterous ② dissipated; loose; intemperate

荒无人烟 huāng wú rényān　desolate and uninhabited: 〜的地带 a region with no sign of human habitation

荒芜 huāngwú　lie waste; go out of cultivation: 由于连年战乱，百姓流离，田园〜。 Owing to long years of war, people left their homes and the land was allowed to lie waste.

荒信 huāngxìn　dial.　unconfirmed news

荒墟 huāngxū　wasteland; ruins

荒野 huāngyě　wilderness; the wilds

荒淫 huāngyín　dissolute; licentious; debauched

荒淫无耻 huāngyín wúchǐ　shamelessly dissipated: 过着〜的生活 lead a life of shameless dissipation

荒原 huāngyuán　wasteland; wilderness

荒置 huāngzhì　throw sth. aside (as useless); discard

荒子 huāngzi　mech.　blank

慌 huāng　flurried; flustered; confused: 沉住气，别〜! Keep calm! Don't panic! / 〜了手脚 be alarmed and confused; be flustered / 〜作一团 be thrown into utter confusion

慌 ·huang　inf.　(used after 得 as a complement) awfully; unbearably: 心里闷得〜 be bored beyond endurance / 累得〜 be tired out; be dog-tired; be played out

慌乱 huāngluàn　flurried; alarmed and bewildered: 作好充分准备，免得临时〜 make ample preparations so as not to be in a rush at the last moment

慌忙 huāngmáng　in a great rush; in a flurry; hurriedly: 〜赶到现场 rush to the spot / 〜起身迎客 hurriedly rise to greet one's guest

慌神儿 huāngshénr　dial.　be scared out of one's wits

慌手慌脚 huāngshǒu-huāngjiǎo in a rush; in a flurry
慌张 huāngzhāng flurried; flustered; confused: 神色～ look flurried (or flustered) / 为什么这样慌慌张张的? Why are you so flustered?

huáng

皇 huáng ① *formal* grand; magnificent: 堂皇 tánghuáng ② emperor; sovereign: 女皇 nǚhuáng
皇朝 huángcháo feudal dynasty
皇储 huángchǔ crown prince; designated heir to the throne
皇带鱼 huángdàiyú oarfish
皇帝 huángdì emperor
皇甫 Huángfǔ a two-character surname
皇宫 huánggōng (imperial) palace
皇冠 huángguān imperial crown
皇后 huánghòu empress
皇皇[1] huánghuáng same as 惶惶 huánghuáng
皇皇[2] huánghuáng grand: ～巨著 a monumental work
皇家 huángjiā imperial family (or house): ～卫队 imperial guards
皇历 huángli *inf.* almanac
皇陵 huánglíng imperial mausoleum
皇亲国戚 huángqīn-guóqī relatives of the emperor
皇权 huángquán imperial power (or authority)
皇上 huángshàng ① the emperor; the throne; the reigning sovereign ② Your Majesty or His Majesty
皇室 huángshì imperial family (or house)
皇太后 huángtàihòu empress dowager
皇太子 huángtàizǐ crown prince
皇天 huángtiān Heaven (personified); High Heaven: ～无亲, 惟德是辅。《书经》High Heaven has no affections and helps only the virtuous.
皇天不负苦心人 huángtiān bù fù kǔ xīn rén Providence doesn't let down a man who does his best
皇天后土 huángtiān-hòutǔ Heaven and Earth (personified and apostrophized, esp. when speaking a vow): ～, 实鉴此心。背义忘恩, 天人共戮。All-ruling Heaven, All-producing Earth, witness my determination, and may god and man jointly scourge me should I fail my duty or forget my obligation.
皇族 huángzú people of imperial lineage; imperial kinsmen

黄[1] huáng ① yellow; sallow: ～沙 yellow sands / 脸色发～ a sallow face ② (Huáng) (short for 黄河) the Huanghe River: 治～ harness the Huanghe River ③ (Huáng) a surname

黄[2] huáng *inf.* fizzle out; fail; come to nothing; fall through: 那笔买卖～了。The deal is off.
黄包车 huángbāochē *dial.* rickshaw
黄骠马 huángbiāomǎ a horse with a yellow coat marked with white spots
黄病 huángbìng *inf. med.* jaundice
黄檗 huángbò (also 黄柏 huángbò) *Chin. med.* the bark of a cork tree (*Phellodendron*)
黄菜 huángcài *dial.* dishes made from scrambled eggs
黄灿灿 huángcàncàn bright yellow; golden: ～的稻子 golden rice
黄刺玫 huángcìméi yellow rose (*Rosa xanthina*)
黄丹 huángdān common name for 铅丹 qiāndān
黄疸 huángdǎn *med.* jaundice: 肝原性～ hepatogenous jaundice / 阻塞性～ obstructive jaundice / ～指数 icterus index

黄道 huángdào *astron.* ecliptic: ～光 zodiacal light / ～星座 zodiacal constellation / ～座标 ecliptic coordinates
黄道带 huángdàodài zodiac
黄道吉日 huángdào jírì (also 黄道日 huángdàorì) a propitious (or auspicious) date; a lucky day: 挑个～娶亲 choose an auspicious day for wedding
黄道十二宫 huángdào shíèrgōng the 12 signs of the zodiac; zodiacal signs
黄澄澄 huángdēngdēng glistening yellow; golden: ～的麦穗儿 golden ears of wheat
黄鲷 huángdiāo yellow porgy
黄碘 huángdiǎn same as 碘仿 diǎnfǎng
黄豆 huángdòu soya bean; soybean
黄泛区 Huángfànqū areas formerly flooded by the Huanghe River; the Huanghe River Inundated Area
黄蜂 huángfēng wasp
黄姑鱼 huánggūyú spotted maigre
黄骨髓 huánggǔsuǐ yellow marrow
黄瓜 huángguā cucumber
黄瓜香 huángguāxiāng another name for 地榆 dìyú
黄冠 huángguān ① yellow hat worn by a Taoist priest ② Taoist priest
黄海 Huánghǎi the Huanghai Sea; the Yellow Sea
黄河 Huánghé the Huanghe River; the Yellow River
黄河象 Huánghéxiàng *palaeontology* Huanghe River stegodon
黄褐色 huánghèsè yellowish-brown; tawny
黄花 huánghuā ① chrysanthemum ② day lily ③ *inf.* virgin
黄花菜 huánghuācài day lily
黄花地丁 huánghuā dìdīng another name for 蒲公英 púgōngyīng
黄花苜蓿 huánghuā mùxu *bot.* (California) bur clover
黄花女儿 huánghuānǚr virgin; maiden
黄花鱼 huánghuāyú yellow croaker
黄昏 huánghūn dusk
黄鹡鸰 huángjílíng yellow wagtail
黄酱 huángjiàng salted and fermented soya paste
黄教 Huángjiào the Yellow Sect (a sect of Lamaism in Tibet, founded by Zong Kaba or Tsong-kha-pa 宗喀巴 in the 15th century; so called from the colour of its vestments)
黄巾起义 Huángjīn Qǐyì *hist.* the Yellow Turbans Uprising (a large-scale peasant uprising at the close of the Eastern Han Dynasty)
黄金 huángjīn gold: ～储备 gold reserve (or stock) ～价格 price of gold; gold rate / ～市场 gold market / ～总库 gold pool
黄金分割 huángjīn fēngē *math.* golden section
黄金时代 huángjīn shídài golden age: 唐朝是诗的～。The Tang Dynasty is the golden age of Chinese poetry.
黄金时间 huángjīn shíjiān prime time; peak viewing time: ～的广告费是很贵的。Prime-time advertising rates are very high.
黄金树 huángjīnshù another name for 梓树 ānshù
黄荆 huángjīng *bot.* five-leaved chaste tree (*Vitex negundo*)
黄猄 huángjīng muntjac
黄精 huángjīng *Chin. med.* sealwort (*Polygonatum sibiricum*)
黄酒 huángjiǔ yellow rice or millet wine; Shaoxing (绍兴) wine
黄口小儿 huángkǒu xiǎo'ér baby—an ignorant youth
黄蜡蜡 huánglàlā wax yellow; waxen; sallow: ～的脸 a sallow face
黄蜡 huánglà common name for 蜂蜡 fēnglà
黄鹂 huánglí oriole: 黑枕～ black-naped oriole
黄历 huánglì same as 皇历 huángli

黄连　huánglián　*Chin. med.*　the rhizome of Chinese goldthread (*Coptis chinensis*)

黄连木　huángliánmù　*bot.*　Chinese pistache

黄粱美梦　huángliáng měimèng　Golden Millet Dream (from the story of a poor scholar who dreamt he had become an official but awoke to find the pot of millet still cooking on the fire)—pipe dream

黄磷　huánglín　*chem.*　yellow phosphorus

黄龙　Huánglóng　see 直捣黄龙 zhídǎo Huánglóng

黄栌　huánglú　smoke tree (*Cotinus coggygria*)

黄麻　huángmá　*bot.*　(roundpod) jute: ～袋 gunnysack; gunny-bag; gunny / ～袋布 gunny (cloth)

黄毛丫头　huángmáo yātou　a chit of a girl; a silly little girl

黄梅季　huángméijì　(also 黄梅天 huángméitiān) the rainy season, usu. in April and May, in the middle and lower reaches of the Changjiang River

黄梅戏　huángméixì　a form of regional drama popular in central Anhui Province

黄梅雨　huángméiyǔ　intermittent drizzles in the rainy season in the middle and lower reaches of the Changjiang River

黄米　huángmǐ　glutinous millet

黄明胶　huángmíngjiāo　*Chin. med.*　oxhide gelatin

黄鸟　huángniǎo　common name for 金丝雀 jīnsīquè

黄牛　huángniú　① ox; cattle ② *dial.*　scalper of tickets, etc.

黄牌　huángpái　*sports*　yellow card

黄袍加身　huángpáo jiā shēn　be draped with the imperial yellow robe by one's supporters—be acclaimed emperor; seize political power after a coup

黄皮寡瘦　huángpí-guǎshòu　*dial.*　sallow and emaciated; lean and haggard

黄皮书　huángpíshū　popular name for 检疫证明书 jiǎnyì zhèngmíngshū

黄皮子　huángpízi　*dial.*　yellow weasel

黄埔军官学校　Huángpǔ Jūnguān Xuéxiào　the Huangpu (Whampoa) Military Academy (established by Sun Yat-sen in 1924)

黄芪　huángqí　*Chin. med.*　the root of membranous milk vetch (*Astragalus membranaceus*)

黄芩　huángqín　*Chin. med.*　the root of large-flowered skullcap (*Scutellaria baicalensis*)

黄曲霉毒素　huángqūméi dúsù　aflatoxin: ～中毒 aflatoxicosis

黄泉　huángquán　the Yellow Springs—the world of the dead; the underworld; the nether world: 命赴～ go to the Yellow Springs—die / 上穷碧落下～，两处茫茫皆不见。(白居易) Above, he searched the Green Void, below, the Yellow Springs; But he failed, in either place, to find the one he looked for.

黄雀　huángquè　siskin

黄壤　huángrǎng　yellow earth; yellow soil

黄热病　huángrèbìng　yellow fever

黄色　huángsè　① yellow ② decadent; obscene; pornographic: ～电影 pornographic movie; sex film / ～书刊 pornographic books and periodicals / ～小说 pornographic novel / ～新闻 yellow journalism / ～音乐 decadent music

黄色工会　huángsè gōnghuì　yellow union; scab union

黄色人种　Huángsè rénzhǒng　the yellow race

黄色炸药　huángsè zhàyào　① trinitrotoluene (TNT) ② common name for 苦味酸 kǔwèisuān

黄鳝　huángshàn　ricefield eel; finless eel

黄熟　huángshú　*agric.*　yellow maturity

黄鼠　huángshǔ　ground squirrel; suslik

黄鼠狼　huángshǔláng　another name for 黄鼬 huángyòu

黄鼠狼给鸡拜年，没安好心　huángshǔláng gěi jī bàinián, méi ān hǎoxīn　the weasel goes to pay his respects to the hen—not with the best of intentions

黄水疮　huángshuǐchuāng　common name for 脓疱病 nóngpàobìng

黄汤　huángtāng　*offens.*　yellow stuff (referring to yellow rice or millet wine): 你少灌点儿～吧! Don't get drunk with so much of this yellow stuff!

黄糖　huángtáng　*dial.*　brown sugar

黄体　huángtǐ　*physiol.*　corpus luteum

黄体酮　huángtǐtóng　*pharm.*　progesterone

黄铁矿　huángtiěkuàng　pyrite

黄铜　huángtóng　brass: ～管 brass pipe (*or* tube)

黄铜矿　huángtóngkuàng　chalcopyrite

黄土　huángtǔ　*geog.*　loess

黄土高原　huángtǔ gāoyuán　loess plateau

黄萎病　huángwěibìng　*agric.*　verticillium wilt: 棉～ verticillium wilt of cotton

黄癣　huángxuǎn　*med.*　favus

黄烟　huángyān　*dial.*　tobacco (smoked in a long-stemmed Chinese pipe)

黄羊　huángyáng　Mongolian gazelle

黄杨　huángyáng　*bot.*　Chinese littleleaf box

黄莺　huángyīng　same as 黄鹂 huánglí

黄油　huángyóu　① *chem.*　grease: ～枪 grease gun ② butter

黄鼬　huángyòu　yellow weasel

黄鱼　huángyú　① yellow croaker ② (in former times) extra passengers which sailors or drivers pick up for extra money to fill their own pockets

黄玉　huángyù　topaz (a mineral)

黄种　Huángzhǒng　the yellow race

凰　huáng　see 凤凰 fènghuáng

隍　huáng　dry moat outside a city wall

惶　huáng　fear; anxiety; trepidation: 惊惶 jīnghuáng

惶惶　huánghuáng　in a state of anxiety; on tenterhooks; alarmed

惶惶不可终日　huánghuáng bùkě zhōng rì　be in a constant state of anxiety; be on tenterhooks

惶惑　huánghuò　perplexed and alarmed; apprehensive: ～不安 perplexed and uneasy

惶遽　huángjù　*formal*　frightened; scared: 神色～ look scared

惶恐　huángkǒng　terrified: ～万状 be seized with fear; be frightened out of one's senses

惶恐不安　huángkǒng bù'ān　in a state of alarm (*or* trepidation)

惶悚　huángsǒng　*formal*　terrified

徨　huáng　see 彷徨 pánghuáng

遑　huáng　*formal*　leisure: 不～ have no time; be too busy

遑遑　huánghuáng　*formal*　in a hurry; hastily

煌　huáng　bright; brilliant: 辉煌 huīhuáng

煌斑岩　huángbānyán　*geol.*　lamprophyre

煌煌　huánghuáng　bright; brilliant: 明星～的天空 a starlit sky

潢¹　huáng　*formal*　pool; pond

潢²　huáng　see 装潢 zhuānghuáng

璜　huáng　*formal*　semi-annular jade pendant

蝗　huáng　locust

蝗虫　huángchóng　locust

蝗蝻 huángnǎn　the nymph of a locust
蝗灾 huángzāi　plague of locusts

篁 huáng　*formal* ① bamboo grove: 幽篁 yōuhuáng ② bamboo: 修～ tall bamboos

磺 huáng　sulphur: 硫磺 liúhuáng
磺胺 huáng'àn　*pharm.* sulphanilamide (SN): ～醋酰 sulphacetamide (SA) / ～胍 sulphaguanidine (SG) / ～嘧啶 sulphadiazine (SD) /～噻唑 sulphathiazole (ST) /～异噁唑 sulphafurazole; gantrisin
磺化 huánghuà　sulphonate: ～剂 sulphonating agent
磺酸盐 huángsuānyán　*chem.* sulphonate
磺酰胺 huángxiān'àn　*chem.* sulphonic acid amide

蟥 huáng　see 蚂蟥 mǎhuáng

簧 huáng　① *mus.* reed ② spring: 闹钟的～断了。The main spring of the alarm clock is broken.
簧风琴 huángfēngqín　reed organ; harmonium
簧片 huángpiàn　*mus.* reed
簧乐器 huángyuèqì　reed instrument

鳇 huáng　huso sturgeon

huǎng

恍 huǎng　① all of a sudden; suddenly ② (used together with 如, 若, etc.) seem; as if: ～如梦境 as if in a dream
恍惚 huǎnghū　(also 恍忽 huǎnghū) ① in a trance; absentminded: 精神～ be in a trance ② dimly; faintly; seemingly: 我～听见他进屋去了。I was faintly aware that he entered the room.
恍然大悟 huǎngrán dàwù　suddenly see the light; suddenly realize what has happened: 经他一指点，我才～，原来是我错了。When he dropped the hint, it suddenly dawned on me that I was wrong.
恍如隔世 huǎng rú géshì　there seems to be an interval of a whole generation (said on finding things greatly changed)

晃 huǎng　① dazzle: 明晃晃 mínghuǎnghuǎng ② flash past: 窗外有个人影儿一～就不见了。A figure flashed past the window.——see also huàng
晃眼 huǎngyǎn　① dazzle: 亮得～ be dazzlingly bright / 汽车车灯晃了我的眼，我看不清路了。I was dazzled by the car's headlights and couldn't see the road. ② twinkling: 一～十年过去了。Ten years have passed in a twinkling.

谎 huǎng　lie; falsehood: 撒谎 sāhuǎng
谎报 huǎngbào　lie about sth.; give false information; start a *canard*: ～年龄 lie about one's age
谎报军情 huǎngbào jūnqíng　make a false report about the (military) situation
谎称 huǎngchēng　falsely claim to be; pretend to be: 他～自己是记者，混了进来。He pretended to be a reporter and managed to get in.
谎话 huǎnghuà　lie; falsehood: 说～ tell a lie; lie / ～连篇 a pack of lies
谎价 huǎngjià　boosted price
谎骗 huǎngpiàn　deceive; cheat; dupe
谎言 huǎngyán　lie; falsehood: 墨写的～掩盖不了血写的事实。Lies written in ink cannot cover up facts recorded in blood.

幌 huǎng　*formal* heavy curtain
幌子 huǎngzi　① shop sign; signboard ② pretence; cover; front: 打着"援助"的～ under the pretence of aid; in the guise of aid / 骗人的～ a facade; a front

huàng

晃 (提) huàng　shake; sway: 他～～手说："不去了"。With a sweep of his hand he said, "I won't go." / 他一朗读就爱～脑袋。He has a habit of swaying his head when he reads aloud. ——see also huǎng
晃荡 huàngdang　rock; shake; sway: 小船在江面上～。The small boat is rocking on the river. / 桶里水很满，一～就出来了。The bucket was so full that it overflowed at the slightest motion. / 风吹得马灯不停地～。The barn lantern kept swaying in the wind.
晃动 huàngdòng　rock; sway: 别～这船。Don't rock the boat. / 车轮有点～。The wheels wobble a bit.
晃梯 huàngtī　*acrob.* balancing on an upright ladder
晃摇 huàngyáo　rock; sway
晃悠 huàngyou　shake from side to side; wobble; stagger: 树枝在风中来回～。The branches of the trees are swaying in the wind. / 他晃晃悠悠地往前走。He was staggering along.

huī

灰 huī　① ash: 烧成～ be burnt to ashes ② dust: 积了厚厚的一层～ accumulate a thick layer of dust / 看你弄了一脸的～。Look at your face! It's all covered with dust. ③ lime; (lime) mortar: ～墙 plastered wall / 和～ mix mortar ④ grey: ～马 a grey horse ⑤ disheartened; discouraged: 心灰意懒 xīnhuī-yìlǎn
灰暗 huī'àn　murky grey; gloomy: ～的天空 a gloomy (or murky grey) sky / 他脸色～，象有什么大病。His face is grey and he looks very ill.
灰白 huībái　greyish white; ashen; pale: ～的鬓发 greying temples / 脸色～ look pale
灰不喇唧 huībulājī　(also 灰不溜丢 huībuliūdiū) *dial.* dull grey: 这条裤子怎么变得这么～的了。How did this pair of trousers get so faded?
灰尘 huīchén　dust; dirt: 大风过后，桌上落了一层～。After the wind, there was a layer of dust on the desk. / 掸掉桌上的～ dust the table
灰尘肺 huīchénfèi　same as 尘肺 chénfèi
灰沉沉 huīchénchén　gloomy; leaden: 天空～的 a gloomy sky; a leaden sky
灰飞烟灭 huīfēi-yānmiè　flying ashes and smouldering smoke: 羽扇纶巾，谈笑间，强虏～。(苏轼) Holding a feather fan and wearing a silk kerchief, Amidst talk and laughter, He reduced his strong enemy to flying ashes and smouldering smoke.
灰分 huīfēn　*min.* ash content
灰姑娘 Huīgūniang　Cinderella
灰鹤 huīhè　grey crane
灰黄霉素 huīhuángméisù　*pharm.* griseofulvin
灰浆 huījiāng　*archit.* mortar
灰烬 huījìn　ashes: 化为～ be reduced to ashes
灰口铁 huīkǒutiě　(also 灰铁 huītiě) grey (pig) iron
灰溜溜 huīliūliū　① dull grey ② gloomy; dejected; crestfallen: 他看起来有点～的样子。He looked a little crestfallen (or depressed). / 老李，别那么～的。Cheer up, Lao Li.
灰蒙蒙 huīmēngmēng　dusky; overcast: ～的夜色 a

dusky night scene / 天色～的。The sky was overcast.

灰锰氧 huīměngyǎng common name for 高锰酸钾 gāoměngsuānjiǎ

灰泥 huīní *archit.* plaster

灰雀 huīquè bullfinch

灰壤 huīrǎng *agric.* podzol

灰色 huīsè ① grey; ashy: 一件～上衣 a grey jacket ② pessimistic; gloomy: ～人生观 a pessimistic (*or* grey) outlook on life / ～的作品 a literary work pessimistic in tone ③ obscure; ambiguous

灰沙 huīshā dust and sand

灰沙燕 huīshāyàn sand martin

灰鼠 huīshǔ squirrel

灰头土脸儿 huītóu-tǔliǎnr *dial.* ① head and face covered with dust ② dejected; despondent; depressed

灰土 huītǔ dust

灰心 huīxīn lose heart; be discouraged: 这个队一场都没赢，队长都感到～了。The team had won no games and the captain lost heart. / 成功不骄傲，失败不～。When you succeed don't get conceited; when you fail don't be dejected.

灰心丧气 huīxīn-sàngqì be disheartened; get discouraged; lose heart: 他一遇上困难就～。He's easily disheartened by difficulties.

灰指甲 huīzhǐjia common name for 甲癣 jiǎxuǎn

灰质 huīzhì *physiol.* grey matter

灰子 huīzi *dial.* opium

诙 huī *formal* ① banter; crack jokes ② ridicule; laugh at

诙谐 huīxié humorous; jocular: 谈吐～ be witty in conversation

诙谐曲 huīxiéqǔ *mus.* humoresque

诙嘲 huīzhāo *formal* ① humorous; jocular ② banter; crack jokes

恢 huī extensive; vast: 恢恢 huīhuī

恢诞 huīdàn *formal* (of a speech, article, etc.) exaggerated; fantastic; absurd; incredible

恢复 huīfù ① resume; renew: ～邦交 resume diplomatic relations / ～正常 return to normal / ～行使主权 resume the exercise of sovereignty (over a place) ② recover; regain: 他的身体～了没有? Is he fully recovered? / ～镇静 regain one's composure / ～知觉 recover consciousness; come to ③ restore; reinstate; rehabilitate: ～民族权利 restoration of national rights / ～名誉 rehabilitation (of a person's reputation) / ～失地 restore lost land; recover lost territory / ～组织生活 be allowed to resume Party activities; be reinstated as a Party member

恢复期 huīfùqī *med.* convalescence

恢弘 huīhóng (also 恢宏 huīhóng) *formal* ① broad; extensive; magnanimous: 气度～ broad-minded; magnanimous ② develop; carry on (*or* forward)

恢恢 huīhuī *formal* extensive; vast

恢廓 huīkuò *formal* ① large-minded: ～的胸襟 broad-mindedness ② expand; spread; extend; develop

咴 huī see below

咴儿咴儿 huīrhuīr *onom.* neigh; whinny

挥 huī ① wave; wield: 他把手一～，上马驰骋而去。With a wave of his hand, he mounted the horse and galloped away. / ～刀 wield a sword / ～笔 wield the brush; put pen to paper ② wipe off: 挥泪 huīlèi ③ command (an army): 指挥 zhǐhuī ④ scatter; disperse: 发挥 fāhuī

挥斥 huīchì *formal* bold and unrestrained; untrammelled: 恰同学少年，风华正茂; 书生意气，～方遒。(毛泽

东) Young we were, schoolmates, At life's full flowering; Filled with student enthusiasm Boldly we cast all restraints aside.

挥动 huīdòng brandish; wave: ～大棒 brandish a big stick / ～旗子 wave a flag / ～拳头 shake one's fist

挥发 huīfā volatilize: 瓶盖没拧紧，里面的酒精都～光了。Because the top is loose, the alcohol inside has volatilized. / ～性 volatility

挥发油 huīfāyóu volatile oil

挥戈 huīgē brandish one's weapons: ～东进 march eastward

挥汗如雨 huīhàn rú yǔ dripping with sweat

挥翰 huīhàn *formal* wield one's writing brush; write (with a brush)

挥毫 huīháo *formal* wield one's writing brush; write or draw a picture (with a brush)

挥霍 huīhuò spend freely; squander: ～浪费 spend extravagantly; wantonly squander / ～无度 spend without restraint

挥金如土 huī jīn rú tǔ throw money about like dirt; spend money like water

挥泪 huīlèi wipe away tears; wipe one's eyes: ～而别 take a tearful leave

挥洒 huīsǎ ① sprinkle (water); shed (tears) ② write or paint freely and easily: ～自如 write or paint with facility

挥师 huīshī command an army: ～北上 command an army to march north

挥手 huīshǒu wave one's hand; wave: ～致意 wave greetings to; wave to sb. in acknowledgment / ～告别 wave farewell; wave good-bye to sb.

挥舞 huīwǔ wave; wield; brandish: ～花束表示欢迎 wave bouquets in welcome / ～指挥棒 brandish the baton—order sb. about / ～核武器 brandish nuclear weapons

晖 huī sunshine; sunlight: 朝晖 zhāohuī

晖映 huīyìng same as 辉映 huīyìng

辉(煇) huī ① brightness; splendour: 光辉 guānghuī ② shine: 与日月同～ shine for ever like the sun and the moon

辉长岩 huīchángyán *geol.* gabbro

辉光 huīguāng *elec.* glow: ～灯 glow lamp / ～放电 glow discharge / ～放电管 glow discharge tube

辉煌 huīhuáng brilliant; splendid; glorious: ～的战果 a brilliant military victory / ～的文化 splendid civilization / ～的一生 a glorious life

辉绿岩 huīlǜyán *geol.* diabase

辉钼矿 huīmùkuàng molybdenite

辉砷钴矿 huīshēngǔkuàng cobaltite

辉石 huīshí *geol.* pyroxene; augite

辉锑矿 huītīkuàng stibnite

辉铜矿 huītóngkuàng chalcocite

辉耀 huīyào shine; illuminate

辉银矿 huīyínkuàng argentite

辉映 huīyìng shine; reflect: 交相辉映 jiāo xiāng huīyìng

翬 huī ① *formal* fly ② a kind of pheasant known for beautiful plumes (mentioned in ancient texts)

麾 huī *formal* ① standard of a commander (used in ancient times) ② command: ～军前进 command an army to march forward

麾下 huīxià *formal* ① under sb.'s command ② (a respectful title) general; commander

徽[1] huī ① emblem; badge; insignia: 国徽 guóhuī

② fine: glorious: 徽号 huīhào

徽² Huī short for 徽州 Huizhou (a prefecture including modern Shexian 歙县 in Anhui Province, famous as a producer of inksticks)

徽调 huīdiào ① the Anhui musical style (i.e, the musical style of Anhui opera 徽剧, which spread from Anhui to Beijing in the 18th century and played a part in the development of the musical style of Beijing opera) ② old name for 徽剧 huījù

徽号 huīhào title of honour; good name

徽记 huījì sign; mark

徽剧 huījù Anhui opera (popular in Jiangsu, Zhejiang, and Jiangxi as well as Anhui)

徽墨 huīmò Huizhou inkstick (originally produced in Huizhou 徽州, a prefecture in modern Anhui Province, considered the best of its kind)

徽章 huīzhāng badge; insignia

隳（堕） huī formal destroy; ruin

huí

回¹（囘、囬、迴、廻） huí circle; wind: 巡回 xún huí

回²（囘、囬、廻） huí ① return; go back: ～家 go back home / ～到原地 return to where one came from / ～到生产第一线 go back to one's post on the production front ② turn round: ～过身来 turn round ③ answer; reply: 回信 huíxìn ④ report back (to one's superior): 回禀 huíbǐng ⑤ decline (an invitation, etc.); refuse; cancel; dismiss ⑥ m. chapter: 这部小说共一百一十二～. This novel has 112 chapters. ⑦ m. time; occasion: 来过一～ have been here once / 有一～我在路上碰到他. Once, I ran into him in the street. / 完全是两～事 two entirely different matters

回³（囘、囬） Huí the Hui nationality see also 回族 Huízú

回拜 huíbài pay a return visit

回报 huíbào ① report back on what has been done ② repay; requite; reciprocate: ～他的盛情 repay him for his hospitality or kindness ③ retaliate; get one's own back

回避 huíbì ① evade; dodge; avoid (meeting sb.): ～要害问题 evade (or sidestep) the crucial question / ～困难 dodge difficulties / 他～我的问题, 不作答复。He avoided answering my questions. ② leg. withdraw: 如果审判员是案件的当事人, 应当自行～. If the judge is a party to the case, he should withdraw of his own accord.

回禀 huíbǐng report back (to one's superior)

回波 huíbō electron. echo: ～脉冲 echo pulse

回驳 huíbó refute: 当面～ refute sb. immediately to his face

回采 huícǎi min. stoping; extraction: ～工作面 stope / ～率 percentage of recovery; recovery / ～损失 mining loss

回肠¹ huícháng physiol. ileum

回肠² huícháng formal worried; agitated; anxious

回肠荡气 huícháng-dàngqì (of music, poems, etc.) soul-stirring; thrilling; inspiring

回肠九转 huícháng jiǔ zhuàn with anxiety gnawing at one's heart; weighed down with grief

回潮 huícháo ① (of dried things) get damp again ② resurgence; reversion: 思想～ an ideological relapse

(or retrogression) / 农村迷信活动有所～。There is a revival of superstitious practices in the countryside.

回潮率 huícháolù text. (moisture) regain

回嗔作喜 huíchēn-zuòxǐ cease to be angry and begin to smile; one's angry face relaxes into a smile

回程 huíchéng ① return trip ② mech. return (or back) stroke

回春 huíchūn ① return of spring: 大地回春 dàdì huíchūn ② bring back to life: ～灵药 a miraculous cure; a wonderful remedy

回答 huídá answer; reply; response: 请～我的问题。Answer my question, please. / 从理论上～了这个问题 furnish a theoretical answer to this question / 他的～是 "我不知道"。"I don't know" was his reply. / 事实是对造谣者最有力的～. Facts are the most powerful rebuff to rumourmongers.

回单 huídān a short note acknowledging receipt of sth.; receipt

回荡 huídàng resound; reverberate: 欢呼声在山谷间～. Shouts of joy reverberated in the valleys. / 她美妙的歌声依然～在我的耳际. Her beautiful songs still ring in my ears.

回电 huídiàn ① wire back: 请即～. Wire reply immediately. ② a telegram in reply

回跌 huídiē (of prices) go down after a rise

回动 huídòng mech. reverse: ～机构 reversing mechanism / ～弹簧 return spring

回访 huífǎng pay a return visit

回风道 huífēngdào min. air return way

回奉 huífèng same as 回敬 huíjìng

回复 huífù ① reply (to a letter) ② return to normal state

回顾 huígù look back; review: ～长征 look back on the Long March / ～近年来两国的友好关系 review the friendly relations between the two countries in recent years / 一九九一年的～ 1991 in retrospect

回顾展 huígùzhǎn retrospective exhibition: 中国电影～ a retrospective exhibition of Chinese films

回光返照 huíguāng fǎnzhào ① the last radiance of the setting sun ② momentary recovery of consciousness just before death; a sudden spurt of activity prior to collapse

回归¹ huíguī statistics regression

回归² huíguī ① return: ～故里 return to one's homeland ② draw back; fall back; retreat

回归带 huíguīdài same as 热带 rèdài

回归年 huíguīnián astron. tropical year; solar year

回归热 huíguīrè med. relapsing fever

回归线 huíguīxiàn geog. tropic: 南回归线 nánhuíguīxiàn / 北回归线 běihuíguīxiàn

回锅 huíguō ① heat up (a cooked dish) ② cook again

回锅肉 huíguōròu twice-cooked pork (often with chilli seasoning)

回航 huíháng return to base or port

回合 huíhé round; bout: 他在第二个～中被击倒。He was knocked out in the second round. / 第一个～的胜利 a first-round victory

回纥 Huíhé (also 回鹘 Huíhú) Huihe (Ouigour), an ancient nationality in China

回护 huíhù give unprincipled protection to; be partial to; shield

回话 huíhuà reply; answer: 请你给他带个～. Please take a message to him by way of reply. / 后天给你～. I'll give you an answer the day after tomorrow.

回还 huíhuán return; go back

回环 huíhuán winding

回黄转绿 huíhuáng-zhuǎnlù leaves turning from green to yellow and from yellow to green—the succession of the seasons; the vicissitudes of life

回回 Huíhui *old* the Huis; the Hui people

回火 huíhuǒ *mech.* tempering: ～脆性 temper brittleness

回击 huíjī fight back; return fire; counterattack: 给以有力的～ strike a powerful counterblow; hit back hard

回见 huíjiàn *inf.* see you later (*or* again); cheerio

回交 huíjiāo *biol.* backcross

回教 Huíjiào Islam

回敬 huíjìng ① return a compliment; do or give sth. in return: ～一杯 drink a toast in return ② give sb. tit for tat: 他先动手，我～了他一拳。He hit me first, and I hit him back.

回绝 huíjué decline; refuse: 一口～ flatly refuse / 她婉言～了他的邀请。She declined his invitation politely.

回空 huíkōng (of vehicles and ships) make the return trip empty (without passengers or cargo)

回口 huíkǒu *dial.* answer back; retort

回扣 huíkòu sales commission

回来 huílái return; come back; be back: 他马上就～。He'll be back in a minute.

回来 ·huílái (used after a verb) back (here): 跑～ run back / 把借出去的书要～。Recall the books on loan. / 可把你盼～了。Thank heavens, you're finally back.

回廊 huíláng winding corridor

回老家 huí lǎojiā *inf.* meet one's maker; die: 送他～! Kill him! *or* Bump him off!

回礼 huílǐ ① return a salute ② send a present in return; present a gift in return: 他送了礼给我，我得回他一份礼。He sent me a gift; I should give him something in return.

回历 Huílì the Moslem Calendar

回笼 huílóng ① steam again: 把凉馒头回回笼。Heat up the cold steamed buns. ② withdrawal (of currency) from circulation

回笼觉 huílóngjiào fall asleep again after waking up in the morning

回炉 huílú ① melt down: 废铁～ melt down scrap iron; use scrap iron for smelting ② bake (cakes, etc.) again

回路 huílù *elec.* return circuit; return; loop: ～增益 loop gain

回禄 Huílù *formal* God of fire: ～之灾 fire (as a disaster); conflagration

回落 huíluò (of water levels, prices, etc.) fall after a rise

回马枪 huímǎqiāng back thrust: 杀他个～ give sb. a back thrust; swing round and catch sb. off guard

回门 huímén the bride visits her parents with her husband for the first time after the wedding

回民 Huímín the Huis; the Hui people

回眸 huímóu *liter.* (of a woman) glance back: ～一笑百媚生，六宫粉黛无颜色。(白居易) Glancing back and smiling, she revealed a hundred charms. All the powdered ladies of the six palaces at once seemed dull and colourless.

回暖 huínuǎn get warm again after a cold spell

回棋 huíqí same as 悔棋 huíqí

回青 huíqīng *dial.* (of winter crops or transplanted seedlings) turn green

回请 huíqǐng return hospitality; give a return banquet

回去 ·huíqù return; go back; be back: 他明天回杭州去。He will return to Hangzhou tomorrow. / 他离开家乡十年，从未～过。He has never been back to his birthplace since he left it ten years ago. / 天太晚了，你今天回不去了。It's too late; you can't go back home.

回去 ·huíqù (used after a verb) back (there): 请把这封信给他退～。Please return the letter to him. / 昨天我是走～的。I went back on foot yesterday.

回扫 huísǎo *electron.* flyback

回升 huíshēng rise again (after a fall); pick up: 气温～。The temperature has gone up again. / 指数～。The index is picking up. / 价格又～了。Prices rose again.

回生[1] huíshēng bring back to life: 起死回生 qǐsǐ-huíshēng

回生[2] huíshēng forget through lack of practice; get rusty: 几年不用，我的法语又～了。I haven't used my French for years and it's getting rusty.

回声 huíshēng echo: 孩子们在山洞里高声喊叫，听听～。The children shouted loudly in the cave so that they could hear the echoes of their voices.

回师 huíshī (of troops) move back: 出敌不意，红军～遵义。The Red Army swung back to Zunyi, taking the enemy by surprise.

回收 huíshōu retrieve; recover; reclaim: ～贵重金属 retrieve rare metals / 发射和～卫星 launch and retrieve satellites / 余热～ recovery of waste heat

回收率 huíshōulǜ rate of recovery (*or* reclamation)

回收塔 huíshōutǎ *chem.* recovery tower

回收站 huíshōuzhàn (waste materials) collection depot

回收装置 huíshōu zhuāngzhì retrieving device

回手 huíshǒu ① turn round and stretch out one's hand: 他走出了屋子，～把门带上。He went out of the room and closed the door behind him. ② hit back; return a blow

回首 huíshǒu ① turn one's head; turn round ② *formal* look back; recollect: ～往事 recall the past

回书 huíshū *formal* a letter in reply

回赎 huíshú redeem

回水 huíshuǐ water conservancy backwater

回苏灵 huísūlíng *pharm.* dimefline

回溯 huísù recall; look back upon: ～革命战争的岁月 look back upon the years of revolutionary war

回天乏术 huí tiān fá shù unable to save the situation

回天之力 huí tiān zhī lì power capable of saving a desperate situation; tremendous power

回填 huítián *archit.* backfill: ～土 backfill

回条 huítiáo a short note acknowledging receipt of sth.; receipt

回帖 huítiě *old* a money order receipt to be signed and returned to the sender

回头[1] huítóu ① turn one's head; turn round: 他～往后看。He turned his head and looked back. / 干了多年的行政工作，回过头来再教书，对我来说，相当困难。After long years of administrative work, it would be difficult for me to switch back to teaching. ② repent: 及早～ repent before it is too late

回头[2] huítóu *inf.* later: ～再谈。We'll talk it over later.

回头见 huítóujiàn *inf.* see you later (*or* again); cheerio

回头路 huítóulù the road back to one's former position; the road of retrogression: 走～ take the road back; backtrack

回头人 huítóurén *dial.* widow

回头是岸 huítóu shì àn turn the head and the shore is at hand——repent and be saved: 劝说他发出善心，～ try to persuade him to show kindness of heart and turn from his evil ways ——see also 苦海无边，回头是岸 kǔhǎi wú biān, huítóu shì àn

回味 huíwèi ① aftertaste ② call sth. to mind and ponder over it: ～他说的话 ponder over what he has said

回戏 huíxì cancel a performance (of a traditional opera)

回乡 huíxiāng return to one's home village: ～探亲 go home to visit one's family and relatives / ～知识青年 a school graduate who returns to work in his or her home village

回翔 huíxiáng circle round; wheel

回响 huíxiǎng reverberate; echo; resound: 雷声在山谷里激起了～。Thunder reverberated in the valley. / 他的

亲切教导仍在我的耳边～。His earnest instructions still ring in my ears.

回想 huíxiǎng　think back; recollect; recall: 这首歌使我～起在中国的留学生活。The song brought back to my mind the days when I was studying in China. / 他确切的话我已～不起来了。I can no longer recall his exact words.

回销 huíxiāo　same as 返销 fǎnxiāo

回心转意 huíxīn-zhuǎnyì　change one's mind; come around; have a change of heart: 我晓得, 这不过是你的气话, 你会～的。I know you're talking in anger and you'll come round.

回信 huíxìn　① write in reply; write back: 我回了他一封信。I wrote him a reply. / 望早日～。I'm looking forward to hearing from you soon. ② a letter in reply ③ a verbal message in reply; reply: 事情办妥了, 我给你个～儿。I'll let you know when I'm through with it.

回形针 huíxíngzhēn　same as 曲别针 qūbiézhēn

回修 huíxiū　return sth. for repairs

回旋 huíxuán　① circle round: 飞机在上空～。The aeroplane is circling overhead. ② (room for) manoeuvre

回旋加速器 huíxuán jiāsùqì　phys.　cyclotron

回旋曲 huíxuánqǔ　mus.　rondo

回旋余地 huíxuán yúdì　room for freedom of action; room for manoeuvre; leeway; latitude: 留点儿～, 别把话说死了。Don't make it so definite—allow a little latitude. / 这件事还有～。The whole thing is not final. or It's still possible to make changes.

回忆 huíyì　call (or bring) to mind; recollect; recall: 他的脸我还认得, 可是他的名字我却～不起来了。I remember his face, but I can't call his name to mind. / 战争年代的～ reminiscences of the war years / 童年的～ recollections of childhood; childhood memories

回忆对比 huíyì duìbǐ　recall the past and contrast it with the present

回忆录 huíyìlù　reminiscences; memoirs; recollections

回音 huíyīn　① echo ② reply: 立候～ hoping for an immediate reply / 我去过三封信, 但一直没有～。I've written him three letters but haven't heard anything from him yet. ③ mus.　turn: 逆～ inverted turn

回音壁 huíyīnbì　the Echo Wall (in the Temple of Heaven in Beijing)

回应 huíyìng　answer; respond: 我在窗外喊他, 他没～。I called to him at the window but he didn't answer.

回佣 huíyòng　dial.　sales commission

回游 huíyóu　same as 洄游 huíyóu

回赠 huízèng　send a present in return; present a gift in return

回涨 huízhǎng　(of water levels, prices, etc.) rise again after a fall: 物价～。Prices are rising again.

回执 huízhí　a short note acknowledging receipt of sth.; receipt

回注 huízhù　petroleum　recycle

回柱 huízhù　min.　prop drawing: ～机 prop drawer; post puller

回转 huízhuǎn　turn round: ～马头 turn the horse round

回转半径 huízhuǎn bànjìng　navigation　radius of gyration

回转工作台 huízhuǎn gōngzuòtái　mech.　rotary table

回转炉 huízhuǎnlú　metall.　rotary furnace

回转式钻床 huízhuǎnshì zuànchuáng　rotary drill

回转体 huízhuǎntǐ　math.　solid of revolution

回转仪 huízhuǎnyí　astron.　gyroscope; gyro

回族 Huízú　the Hui nationality, or the Huis, mainly distributed over the Ningxia Hui Autonomous Region, Gansu, Henan, Hebei, Qinghai, Shandong, Yunnan, Anhui, the Xinjiang Uygur Autonomous Region, Liaoning, Beijing and Tianjin

回嘴 huízuǐ　answer (or talk) back; retort

洄
huí　formal　(of water) whirl

洄游 huíyóu　zool.　migration: 索饵～ feeding migration / 产卵～ spawning migration

茴
huí　see below

茴香 huíxiāng　bot.　① fennel: ～油 fennel oil ② dial.　aniseed: ～豆 beans flavoured with aniseed

蛔（蚘、蛕）
huí　see below

蛔虫 huíchóng　roundworm; ascarid: ～病 roundworm disease; ascariasis

huǐ

悔
huǐ　regret; repent: ～之晚矣 too late to repent / ～不该听信了他的话。I shouldn't have believed him.

悔不当初 huǐ bù dāngchū　regret having done sth.: 早知今日, ～。If I'd known then what was going to happen, I wouldn't have done as I did.

悔改 huǐgǎi　repent and mend one's ways: 毫无～之意 have no intention of mending one's ways; show no sign of repentance / 表示愿意～ show willingness to mend one's way

悔过 huǐguò　repent one's error; be repentant: 有～表示 show signs of repentance / 诚恳～ sincerely repent one's error; show sincere repentance / ～书 a written statement of repentance

悔过自新 huǐguò zìxīn　repent and turn over a new leaf; repent and make a fresh start: 停止作恶, ～ stop doing evil, repent and start anew

悔恨 huǐhèn　regret deeply; be bitterly remorseful: ～终身 eternal regret

悔婚 huǐhūn　break a pledge of marriage; break off an engagement

悔棋 huǐqí　retract a false move in a chess game

悔悟 huǐwù　realize one's error and show repentance

悔之无及 huǐ zhī wújí　too late to repent; too late for regrets: 再要推延, 就会～了。With further delay it will be too late to repent.

悔罪 huǐzuì　show repentance; show penitence: 确有～表现 show real repentance

毁¹
huǐ　① destroy; ruin; damage: 森林为大火所～。The forest was destroyed by fire. / 这场雹子把庄稼～了。The hailstorm ruined the crops. / 她的一生给～了。She was ruined for life. ② dial.　(of clothes) refashion; make over: 把这件大褂给孩子们～两件上衣。Make two children's jackets out of this gown.

毁²（燬）
huǐ　burn up: 烧毁 shāohuǐ

毁³（譭）
huǐ　defame; slander: 毁谤 huǐbàng

毁谤 huǐbàng　slander; malign; calumniate: 这纯系～。This is slander, pure and simple. / 敌人对鲁迅的～, 更坚定了他的战斗意志。The enemy's calumnies made Lu Xun all the more determined to go on fighting.

毁害 huǐhài　destroy; damage

毁坏 huǐhuài　destroy; damage: 气旋～了好几十户人家。The cyclone destroyed dozens of houses. / 洪水～了铁路。The flood damaged the railway. / ～名誉 ruin sb.'s reputation

毁家纾难 huǐjiā shūnàn　give the family fortune to the state in a time of crisis

毁灭 huǐmiè　destroy; exterminate: 旧唐山在1976年的一场地震中～。The old city of Tangshan was destroyed

in an earthquake in 1976. / 给侵略者以～性打击 deal the aggressors a crushing (*or* devastating) blow

毁弃 huǐqì　scrap; annul: 敌军逃跑时沿途～了许多武器。 The fleeing enemy abandoned and destroyed many weapons along the road. / 邮电工作人员私自开拆或者隐匿、～邮件、电报的, 处二年以下有期徒刑或者拘役。 Postal and telecommunications personnel who open, conceal or destroy mail or telegrams of their own accord are to be sentenced to not more than two years of fixed-term imprisonment or criminal detention.

毁容 huǐróng　disfigure one's face

毁伤 huǐshāng　injure; hurt; damage

毁损 huǐsǔn　damage; impair: 很多古代建筑遭到～。 Many ancient buildings have been damaged.

毁于一旦 huǐyú yīdàn　be destroyed in one day; be destroyed in a moment / 十年心血～! The fruits of ten years' labours destroyed in one day!

毁誉 huǐ-yù　praise or blame; praise or condemnation: 不计～ be indifferent to people's praise or blame / ～不一。 Evaluations differ widely.

毁誉参半 huǐ-yù cānbàn　be as much censured as praised; get both praise and blame; find a mixed reception

毁约 huǐyuē　① break one's promise ② scrap a contract or treaty

毁訾 huǐzǐ　*formal* slander; malign; calumniate

huì

汇[1]（滙、匯）huì　converge: ～成巨流 converge into a mighty torrent

汇[2]（滙、匯、彙）huì　① gather together: ～印成书 have (articles on a given subject) collected and published in book form ② things collected; assemblage; collection: 词汇 cíhuì

汇[3]（滙、匯）huì　remit: 给家里～点钱 remit money to one's family; send some money home

汇报 huìbào　report; give an account of: ～调查结果 report the findings of an investigation / 我把生产情况一一向厂长作了～。 I've made a report to the director on every aspect of our production. / ～会 a report-back meeting

汇报演出 huìbào yǎnchū　report-back performance (as given by a dramatic troupe back from a tour in the countryside or abroad)

汇编 huìbiān　compilation; collection; corpus: 资料～工作 compilation of reference material / 文件～ a collection of documents / 语言学研究资料～ a corpus of philological data

汇兑 huìduì　remittance: 国内～ domestic remittance / ～网 remittance network

汇费 huìfèi　(also 汇水 huìshuǐ) remittance fee

汇合 huìhé　converge; join: 这两条河在什么地方～? Where do the two rivers join? / ～成一支巨大的力量 unite to form a gigantic force / 五条支流的～口 the confluence of five tributaries

汇集 huìjí　① collect; compile: ～材料 collect all relevant data / ～经济信息 collect economic information ② come together; converge; assemble: 游行队伍从四面八方～到天安门广场上。 The paraders converged on Tian'anmen Square from all directions.

汇寄 huìjì　remit: 通过邮局～款项 remit (*or* send) money by post / 你需要钱我～给你。 If you need money I'll send it.

汇聚 huìjù　same as 会聚 huìjù

汇款 huìkuǎn　① remit money; make a remittance: 他到银行～去了。 He went to the bank to remit some money. / ～单 money order / ～人 remitter ② remittance: 收到一笔～ receive a remittance / 邮政～ postal remittance

汇流 huìliú　converge; flow together

汇流点 huìliúdiǎn　*geol.* confluence

汇流条 huìliútiáo　*elec.* busbar

汇拢 huìlǒng　① come together; gather; assemble ② collect; compile

汇率 huìlǜ　(also 汇价 huìjià) exchange rate: 固定～ fixed (exchange) rate / 浮动～ floating (exchange) rate / 中心～ central rate

汇票 huìpiào　draft; bill of exchange; money order: 银行～ bank draft / 邮政～ postal money order

汇算 huìsuàn　settle accounts; wind up an account

汇演 huìyǎn　same as 会演 huìyǎn

汇总 huìzǒng　gather; collect; pool: 把材料～上报 collect data for the higher level; present an itemized report to the higher level

卉 huì　(various kinds of) grass: 奇花异卉 qíhuā-yìhuì

会[1]（會）huì　① get together; assemble: 聚会 jùhuì ② meet; see: 昨天我没有～着他。 I didn't see him yesterday. ③ meeting; gathering; party; get-together; conference: 晚上有个全组～。 There's going to be a meeting of the whole group tonight. ④ association; society; union: 帮会 bānghuì ⑤ a temple fair: 庙会 miàohuì ⑥ an association of worshippers: 香会 xiānghuì ⑦ a revolving credit association (an association of people who regularly contribute to a common fund and draw from it by turns) ⑧ chief city; capital: 都会 dūhuì ⑨ opportunity; occasion: 适逢其会 shì féng qí huì ⑩ *formal* happen to: ～有客来。 A guest happened to be in the house.

会[2]（會）huì　① understand; grasp: 误会 wùhuì ② know: 我～英语, 不～日语。 I know English but don't know Japanese. / 他还～两出京戏。 He's able to sing a few airs of Beijing Opera. ③ can; be able to: ～滑冰 can skate / 这孩子刚～走路, 还不大～说话。 The baby has just learnt to walk but hasn't learnt to speak yet. ④ be good at; be skilful in: ～修各种钟表 be skilled in repairing all kinds of clocks and watches / 很～这一套 be a past master of this sort of game ⑤ be likely to; be sure to: 他～在家吗? Is he likely to be at home? / 他～来的。 He's sure to come. / 没想到～这么顺利。 I didn't expect things would go off so smoothly.

会[3]（會）huì　pay (*or* foot) a bill: 饭钱我～过了。 I've paid for the meal.

会[4]（會）huì　*inf.* a moment: 一会儿 yīhuìr —see also kuài

会儿 huìr　*inf.* moment: 等～。 Wait a moment. / 用不了多大～。 It won't be a minute. *or* It won't take long.

会标 huìbiāo　emblem of a sports meet, etc.

会餐 huìcān　dine together; have a dinner party

会操 huìcāo　hold a grand parade; hold a joint drill exercise

会场 huìchǎng　meeting-place; conference (*or* assembly) hall

会钞 huìchāo　same as 会帐 huìzhàng

会道门 huì-dàomén　superstitious sects and secret societies: 反动～ reactionary secret societies

会费 huìfèi　membership dues

会馆 huìguǎn　*old* guild hall; provincial or county guild

会合 huìhé　join; meet; converge; assemble: 成千上万的村民在水坝工地～。Thousands of villagers assembled at the dam site. / 两军～后继续前进。The two armies joined forces and marched on. / 黄浦江在吴淞口与长江～。The Huangpu River joins the Yangtze at Wusong Estuary. / 你先走，到了那儿我们再和你～。You go first and we'll join you there.

会合点 huìhédiǎn　*mil.* meeting point; rallying point; rendezvous

会话 huìhuà　conversation (as in a language course)

会徽 huìhuī　emblem of a sports meet, etc.

会集 huìjí　same as 汇集 huìjí

会籍 huìjí　membership (of an association)

会见 huìjiàn　meet with (esp. a foreign visitor)

会聚 huìjù　assemble; flock together: 游园群众～于各个公园，欢庆五一节。Holidaymakers flocked to the parks to celebrate May Day.

会聚透镜 huìjù tòujìng　*phys.* convergent lens

会刊 huìkān　① proceedings of a conference, etc. ② the journal of an association, society, etc.

会考 huìkǎo　general examination (an examination for the graduating students of all schools in a locality)

会客 huìkè　receive a visitor (or guest): 厂长正在～，请别打扰。The director is receiving guests. Please don't disturb him. / ～时间 the time for receiving visitors; visiting hours / 现在开会，不～。No visitors. Meeting in progress.

会客室 huìkèshì　reception room

会盟 huìméng　meetings of sovereigns or their deputies in ancient China to form alliances

会面 huìmiàn　meet: 我约定了星期天和他～。I have an appointment to meet him on Sunday. / 我和他才会过一次面。I met him only once.

会期 huìqī　① the time fixed for a conference; the date (or time) of a meeting ② the duration of a meeting: ～定为三天。The meeting is scheduled to last three days.

会齐 huìqí　get together; assemble: 明晨七时在门口～。We'll assemble at the gate at 7 o'clock tomorrow morning.

会旗 huìqí　the banner of a meeting

会签 huìqiān　(of two or more than two units) jointly sign an official document

会商 huìshāng　hold a conference or consultation: ～解决办法 consult to find a solution

会审 huìshěn　① joint hearing (or trial) ② make a joint checkup: ～施工图纸 have a joint checkup on the blueprints for a project

会师 huìshī　join forces; effect a junction

会试 huìshì　metropolitan examination (under the Ming-Qing civil service examination system, the examination for the selection of *jinshi* 进士 out of *juren* 举人, held triennially in Beijing, the national capital)

会水 huìshuǐ　know how to swim

会说 huìshuō　have the gift of the gab; be a glib talker

会所 huìsuǒ　the office of an association

会谈 huìtán　talks: 双边～ bilateral talks / ～纪要 minutes of talks; notes on talks; summary of a conversation

会堂 huìtáng　assembly hall; hall: 人民大会堂 Rénmín Dàhuìtáng

会通 huìtōng　same as 融会贯通 rónghuì guàntōng

会同 huìtóng　(handle an affair) jointly with other organizations concerned: 这件事由计委～经委审批。This matter is subject to joint examination and approval by the Planning Commission and the Economic Commission.

会务 huìwù　administrative matters concerning a meeting

会悟 huìwù　*formal* understand; comprehend

会晤 huìwù　meet: 两国外长定期～。The foreign ministers of the two countries meet regularly.

会衔 huìxián　(of two or more than two units) jointly sign an official document

会心 huìxīn　understanding; knowing: ～的微笑 an understanding smile / 露出～的表情 with a knowing look

会穴 huìxué　*Chin. med.* crossing point (a point where two or more channels cross each other)

会演 huìyǎn　joint performance (by a number of theatrical troupes, etc.): 文艺～ theatrical festival

会厌 huìyàn　*physiol.* epiglottis

会议 huìyì　① meeting; conference: 正式～ official meeting / 全体～ plenary session / ～地点 meeting-place; venue / ～日程表 the daily agenda of a conference / ～室 meeting (or conference) room; council chamber / ～厅 conference (or assembly) hall ② council; congress: 部长会议 bùzhǎng huìyì

会意[1] huìyì　*linguis.* associative compounds, one of the six categories of Chinese characters (六书), which are formed by combining two or more elements, each with a meaning of its own, to create a new meaning, e.g. 信, a character made up of 人 (man) and 言 (word), meaning a message or something that can be believed or trusted

会意[2] huìyì　same as 会心 huìxīn

会阴 huìyīn　*physiol.* perineum

会员 huìyuán　member: 工会～ a member of the trade union / 正式～ full (or full-fledged) member / ～人数 membership

会员国 huìyuánguó　member state (or nation)

会员证 huìyuánzhèng　membership card

会员资格 huìyuán zīgé　the status of a member; membership

会战 huìzhàn　① *mil.* meet for a decisive battle ② launch a mass campaign; join in a battle: ～海河工地 join in the battle to harness the Haihe River / 石油大～ a great battle for oil (as when the Daqing Oil Field was being opened up)

会章 huìzhāng　① the constitution (or statutes) of an association, society, etc. ② the emblem of an association, society, etc.

会长 huìzhǎng　the president of an association or society

会帐 huìzhàng　pay (or foot) a bill

会诊 huìzhěn　*med.* consultation of doctors; (group) consultation: 中西医～ hold group consultations of doctors practising Chinese and Western medicine / 几位大夫对这个病人进行了～。Several doctors consulted about the case.

会址 huìzhǐ　① the site of an association or society ② the site of a conference or meeting

会众 huìzhòng　① participants in a meeting ② members of a superstitious sect or secret society

会子 huìzi　a while: 说～话儿 talk for a while

讳（諱）

huì　① avoid as taboo: 直言不讳 zhíyán bù huì ② forbidden word; taboo: 犯了他的～了。Something was said that happened to be taboo with him. ③ the name, regarded as taboo, of a deceased emperor or head of a family

讳疾忌医 huìjí-jìyī　hide one's sickness for fear of treatment—conceal one's fault for fear of criticism

讳忌 huìjì　same as 忌讳 jìhuì

讳莫如深 huì mò rú shēn　closely guard a secret; not breathe a word to a soul; not utter a single word about sth.

讳饰 huìshì　avoid mentioning; cover up; conceal

讳言 huìyán　dare not or would not speak up: 毫不～ make no attempt to conceal the truth; confess freely

诲

huì　teach; instruct: 教诲 jiàohuì

诲人不倦 huì rén bù juàn　be tireless in teaching; teach with tireless zeal: ～的教师 an indefatigable teacher / 学而不厌，～ have never grown tired of learning nor wearied of teaching others what one has learnt

诲淫诲盗 huìyín-huìdào　propagate sex and violence; stir up the base passions

荟 (薈)

huì　formal　luxuriant growth (of plants)

荟萃 huìcuì　(of distinguished people or exquisite objects) gather together; assemble: ～一堂 gather together in one hall

荟集 huìjí　gather; assemble; collect

绘 (繪)

huì　paint; draw: 描绘 miáohuì

绘画 huìhuà　drawing; painting

绘声绘色 huìshēng-huìsè　(also 绘声绘影 huìshēng-huìyǐng; 绘影绘声 huìyǐng-huìshēng) vivid; lively: ～的描述 a vivid description (or portrayal)

绘图 huìtú　same as 制图 zhìtú

绘图板 huìtúbǎn　drawing board

绘制 huìzhì　draw (a design, etc.): ～图表 draw up a table / ～了新农村的宏伟图景 draw up a grand plan for a new countryside

恚

huì　formal　anger

恚愤 huìfèn　formal　be indignant

恚恨 huìhèn　formal　hate

恚怒 huìnù　formal　be enraged

烩 (燴)

huì　① braise: ～虾仁 braised shrimp meat ② cook (rice or shredded pancakes) with meat, vegetables and water

贿

huì　① formal　wealth ② bribe: 受贿 shòuhuì / 行贿 xínghuì

贿赂 huìlù　① bribe ② bribery

贿赂公行 huìlù gōng xíng　practise open bribery; corruption is rife

贿买 huìmǎi　buy over; suborn

贿通 huìtōng　buy over; buy off; bribe

贿选 huìxuǎn　practise bribery at an election; get elected by bribery

彗 (篲)

huì　formal　broom

彗尾 huìwěi　the tail of a comet

彗星 huìxīng　comet

晦

huì　① the last day of a lunar month ② dark; obscure; gloomy ③ night

晦暗 huì'àn　dark and gloomy

晦迹 huìjì　formal　live in seclusion; withdraw from society and live in solitude

晦明 huìmíng　formal　night and day; gloomy and bright

晦冥 huìmíng　(also 晦暝 huìmíng) dark and gloomy

晦气 huìqì　unlucky: 碰到这种事真是～! What rotten luck to have this happen to me!

晦涩 huìsè　(of literary writing, music, etc.) hard to understand; obscure: 文辞～ obscure language (in poetry, drama, etc.)

晦朔 huìshuò　formal　from the last day of a lunar month to the first day of the next one

秽 (穢)

huì　① dirty: 污秽 wūhuì ② ugly; abominable: 秽行 huìxíng

秽德 huìdé　formal　immoral conduct; abominable behaviour

秽迹 huìjì　formal　dirty business; scandalous affair

秽乱 huìluàn　(sexually) promiscuous; licentious

秽气 huìqì　stink; bad (or offensive) smell: ～冲天 stink to high heaven

秽土 huìtǔ　rubbish; refuse; dirt

秽闻 huìwén　formal　ill repute (referring to sexual behaviour); reputation for immorality

秽亵 huìxiè　formal　① filthy; foul ② obscene; salacious; bawdy

秽行 huìxíng　formal　debauched behaviour; immoral conduct

秽语 huìyǔ　obscene words; lewd speech

秽浊 huìzhuó　foul; filthy; dirty

惠

huì　① favour; kindness; benefit: 受惠 shòuhuì ② pol.　kind; gracious: 惠书 huìshū ③ (Huì) a surname

惠存 huìcún　pol.　please keep (this photograph, book, etc. as a souvenir); to so-and-so

惠而不费 huì ér bù fèi　beneficial and not costly

惠风 huìfēng　gentle breeze; soft breeze

惠顾 huìgù　pol.　your patronage: 欢迎～。(used by shopkeepers) Your patronage is solicited.

惠鉴 huìjiàn　pol.　be kind enough to read (the following letter)

惠临 huìlín　pol.　your gracious presence: 敬请～。Your presence is requested.

惠书 huìshū　pol.　your kind letter

惠允 huìyǔn　pol.　be kind enough to allow one (to do sth.)

惠泽 huìzé　formal　kindness; favour

喙

huì　formal　① beak or snout: 长～ a long beak ② mouth: 百喙莫辩 bǎi huì mò biàn

殨 (潰)

huì　festering: ～脓 suppuration

慧

huì　intelligent; bright: 智慧 zhìhuì

慧黠 huìxiá　formal　clever and artful; shrewd

慧心 huìxīn　wisdom

慧眼 huìyǎn　① Buddhism　a mind which perceives both past and future ② mental discernment (or perception); insight; acumen: 独具～ have exceptional insight

蕙

huì　bot.　orchid

蕙兰 huìlán　a species of orchid

蕙心 huìxīn　formal　pure heart of a woman

蟪

huì　see below

蟪蛄 huìgū　a kind of cicada

hūn

昏

hūn　① dusk: 晨～ at dawn and dusk ② dark; dim: 天昏地暗 tiānhūn-dì'àn ③ confused; muddled: 昏头昏脑 hūntóu-hūnnǎo ④ lose consciousness; faint: ～倒 fall into a swoon; go off into a faint; fall unconscious

昏暗 hūn'àn　dim; dusky: ～的灯光 a dim light / 太阳下山了，屋里渐渐～起来。The sun was setting, and the room was getting darker and darker.

昏沉 hūnchén　① murky: 暮色～ murky twilight ② dazed; befuddled: 我昨晚没睡好，头脑昏昏沉沉的。I feel

in a daze because I didn't sleep well last night.

昏黑 hūnhēi　dusky; dark

昏花 hūnhuā　dim-sighted: 老眼昏花 lǎoyǎn hūnhuā

昏话 hūnhuà　preposterous speech; ravings

昏黄 hūnhuáng　pale yellow; faint; dim: 月色～ faint moonlight ／～的灯光 a dim light

昏昏欲睡 hūnhūn yù shuì　drowsy; sleepy: 这出戏太沉闷, 观众都～。This dull play is sending the audience to sleep.

昏厥 hūnjué　faint; swoon: ～过去 fall into a coma; faint away

昏君 hūnjūn　a fatuous and self-indulgent ruler

昏聩 hūnkuì (also 昏愦 hūnkuì) decrepit and muddleheaded: ～无能 muddleheaded and incompetent

昏乱 hūnluàn　① dazed and confused; befuddled ② *formal* benighted and disorderly

昏迷 hūnmí　stupor; coma: 处于～状态 be in a state of unconsciousness; be in a coma ／ 她～过去了。She went into a coma. ／～不醒 remain unconscious

昏睡 hūnshuì　lethargic sleep; lethargy

昏死 hūnsǐ　faint; fall into a coma

昏天黑地 hūntiān-hēidì　① heaven and earth in darkness: 到了晚上, ～的, 就更不好走了。Night fell and, as darkness closed in, the going became even harder. ② be in a state of delirium; lose consciousness: 当时我流血过多, 觉得～的。I blacked out through loss of blood. ／ 我只觉得一阵～, 随即失去了知觉。Suddenly everything went black and I lost consciousness. ③ dissipated: 过着荒淫无耻、～的生活 lead an immoral life, given to dissipation and sensuality ④ dark rule and social disorder: 当时军阀混战, 盗贼横行, 真是～。Ridden with warlordism and banditry, the country was then in a dark, troubled period of its history.

昏头昏脑 hūntóu-hūnnǎo (also 昏头胀脑 hūntóu-zhàngnǎo) dizzy; muddle-headed; absent-minded

昏头转向 hūntóu zhuànxiàng　same as 晕头转向 yūntóu zhuànxiàng

昏星 hūnxīng　evening star

昏眩 hūnxuàn　dizzy; giddy: 一阵～ a spell of giddiness

昏庸 hūnyōng　fatuous; muddleheaded; stupid: 老朽～ senile and fatuous

荤 hūn　① meat or fish: 三～一素 three meat dishes and one vegetable dish ／ 她不吃～。She doesn't eat meat. or She's a vegetarian. ② strong-smelling vegetables forbidden to Buddhist vegetarians, such as onions, leeks, garlic, etc.

荤菜 hūncài　meat dish

荤腥 hūnxīng　meat or fish

荤油 hūnyóu　lard

惛 hūn　*formal* slow-witted; muddled

婚 hūn　① wed; marry: 未婚 wèihūn ② marriage; wedding: 婚姻 hūnyīn

婚假 hūnjià　marriage leave

婚嫁 hūnjià　marriage

婚礼 hūnlǐ　wedding ceremony; wedding: 星期天举行～。The wedding will take place on Sunday.

婚龄 hūnlíng　(legally) marriageable age: 法定～ legally marriageable age

婚配 hūnpèi　married: 子女两人, 均未～。Both son and daughter are unmarried.

婚期 hūnqī　wedding day

婚娶 hūnqǔ　(of a man) get married; take a wife

婚生子女 hūnshēng zǐnǚ　*leg.* children born in wedlock; legitimate children

婚事 hūnshì　marriage; wedding: 操办～ prepare a wedding

婚书 hūnshū　*old* marriage certificate

婚外恋 hūnwàiliàn　an extramarital affair

婚姻 hūnyīn　marriage; matrimony: ～自由 freedom of marriage ／～纠纷 matrimonial dispute

婚姻法 hūnyīnfǎ　marriage law

婚姻介绍所 hūnyīn jièshàosuǒ　matrimonial agency

婚姻状况 hūnyīn zhuàngkuàng　marital status

婚育期 hūnyùqī　marriageable and child-bearing age: 进入～ reach the marriageable and child-bearing age.

婚约 hūnyuē　marriage contract; engagement: 解除～ break off one's engagement

阍 hūn　*formal* ① tend or guard a gate: 司阍 sīhūn ② palace gate

阍者 hūnzhě　*formal* gatekeeper; janitor

hún

浑 hún　① muddy; turbid: 水～得很。The water is very muddy. ② foolish; stupid ③ simple and natural; unsophisticated: 浑朴 húnpǔ ④ whole; all over: 浑身 húnshēn

浑蛋 húndàn　*offens.* blackguard; wretch; scoundrel; bastard; skunk

浑厚 húnhòu　① simple and honest ② (of writing, painting, etc.) simple and vigorous: 笔力～ (of handwriting) bold and vigorous strokes ／ 他的声音～洪亮。He has a deep and rich voice.

浑话 húnhuà　impudent remark

浑浑噩噩 húnhún-è'è　muddle-headed and ignorant

浑家 húnjiā　*old* my wife

浑金璞玉 húnjīn-púyù　same as 璞玉浑金 púyù-húnjīn

浑朴 húnpǔ　simple and natural; unsophisticated

浑球儿 húnqiúr　*dial.* blackguard; wretch; scoundrel; bastard; skunk

浑然一体 húnrán yìtǐ　one integrated mass; a unified entity; an integral whole

浑人 húnrén　an unreasonable person

浑身 húnshēn　from head to foot; all over: 吓得～发抖 tremble all over with fear ／～疼痛 aching all over ／～是劲 brimming with energy; bursting with energy

浑身是胆 húnshēn shì dǎn　be every inch a hero; be the embodiment of valour

浑水摸鱼 húnshuǐ mō yú　fish in troubled waters: 挑拨离间, 制造混乱, 以便～ sow discord and create confusion so as to fish in troubled waters

浑说 húnshuō　talk nonsense; drivel

浑似 húnsì (also 浑如 húnrú) just like

浑天仪 húntiānyí　*astron.* ① armillary sphere ② celestial globe

浑象 húnxiàng　*astron.* celestial globe

浑仪 húnyí　*astron.* armillary sphere

浑圆 húnyuán　perfectly round: ～的珍珠 a perfectly round pearl ／～的月亮 full moon

浑浊 húnzhuó　muddy; turbid: ～的水 turbid water ／～的空气 foul (or stale) air

珲 hún　*formal* a kind of jade

混 hún　same as 浑 hún①② ——see also hùn

混蛋 húndàn　same as 浑蛋 húndàn

混球儿 húnqiúr　same as 浑球儿 húnqiúr

混水摸鱼 húnshuǐ mō yú　same as 浑水摸鱼 húnshuǐ mō yú

锟 hún　see below

锟饨 húntun　*won ton*; dumpling soup

魂 hún ① soul: 灵魂 línghún ② mood; spirit: 神魂 shénhún ③ the lofty spirit of a nation: 民族~ national spirit

魂不附体 hún bù fù tǐ　feel as if one's soul had left one's body: 吓得~ be scared out of one's wits

魂不守舍 hún bù shǒu shè　be scared out of one's wits; have lost one's mind

魂飞魄散 húnfēi-pòsàn　be scared out of one's wits; be half dead with fright

魂灵 húnlíng　*inf.* soul

魂魄 húnpò　soul

hùn

诨 hùn　joke; jest: 打诨 dǎhùn

诨名 hùnmíng　(also 诨号 hùnhào) nickname

混 hùn ① mix; confuse: ~在一起 mix things up / 这是两码事，不要搞~了。They're two entirely different matters; don't mix them up. ② pass for; pass off as: 混充 hùnchōng ③ muddle along; drift along: 连口饭都~不上 can hardly make a living / 我是~一天算一天。I just manage to get by from day to day. ④ get along with sb.: 同他们~得很熟 be quite familiar with them ⑤ thoughtlessly; recklessly; irresponsibly: ~出主意 put forward irresponsible suggestions ——see also hún

混充 hùnchōng　pass oneself off as; palm sth. off as

混沌 hùndùn ① Chaos (the primeval state of the universe according to folklore): ~初开 when earth was first separated from heaven ② ignorant; simple-minded; muddle-headed

混饭吃 hùnfànchī　engage in a job for the sake of making a living (without having any real interest in it): 这种工作还有什么意思呢？我只是在那儿混碗饭吃。What interest could there possibly be in such a job? I'm just working there for the sake of making a living.

混纺 hùnfǎng　*text.* blending: ~织物 blend fabric / ~毛线 blended wool

混合 hùnhé　mix; blend; mingle: 客货~列车 mixed train

混合编队 hùnhé biānduì　*mil.* composite formation

混合面 hùnhémiàn　flour mixed with adulterants (sold in the occupied areas during the War of Resistance Against Japan)

混合器 hùnhéqì　*chem.* mixer

混合色 hùnhésè　secondary colour

混合授粉 hùnhé shòufěn　*agric.* mixed pollination

混合双打 hùnhé shuāngdǎ　*sports* mixed doubles

混合物 hùnhéwù　mixture

混合岩 hùnhéyán　*geol.* migmatite

混混儿 hùnhùnr　*dial.* rascal; scoundrel

混迹 hùnjì　*formal* unworthily occupy a place among: ~于上层社会 unworthily move in the highest circles of society

混交林 hùnjiāolín　mixed forest

混进 hùnjìn　(also 混入 hùnrù) infiltrate; sneak into; worm one's way into: 他随着人流~会场。He mixed with the crowd and gate-crashed the meeting.

混乱 hùnluàn　confusion; chaos: 敌军陷于~。The enemy were thrown into confusion. / 思想~ ideological confusion / 交通~ chaotic traffic conditions / 语言造成的~严重影响人们的生活。The confusions created by language deeply affect men's lives. / 管理~ bad management

混名 hùnmíng　(also 混号 hùnhào) nickname

混凝剂 hùnníngjì　*chem.* coagulant

混凝土 hùnníngtǔ　concrete: ~搅拌机 concrete mixer / ~结构 concrete structure / ~振捣器 (concrete) vibrator

混频管 hùnpínguǎn　*electron.* mixer tube

混日子 hùnrìzi　drift along aimlessly

混世魔王 hùn shì mówáng　world-wrecking demon king —an evil man who disturbs the peace of the world; human fiend; devil incarnate: 我有一个孽根祸胎，是家里的"~"。(《红楼梦》) I have a little monster of a son who tyrannizes over all the rest of this household.

混事 hùnshì　work just to keep alive

混同 hùntóng　confuse; mix up: 不要把诗和词~起来。Don't confuse poetry of regular metre with poetry with irregular metre.

混为一谈 hùn wéi yī tán　lump (or jumble) together; confuse sth. with sth. else: 把正义战争与非正义战争~ lump together just wars and unjust wars

混响 hùnxiǎng　*phys.* reverberation

混淆 hùnxiáo　obscure; blur; confuse; mix up: ~敌友 confuse friend with foe / ~两类不同性质的矛盾 mix up the two different types of contradictions

混淆黑白 hùnxiáo hēi-bái　mix up black and white; confound right and wrong: 颠倒是非，~ confound right and wrong and turn things upside down

混淆是非 hùnxiáo shì-fēi　confuse right and wrong

混淆视听 hùnxiáo shì-tīng　mislead the public; confuse public opinion

混血儿 hùnxuè'ér　a person of mixed blood; half-breed

混一 hùnyī　amalgamation

混杂 hùnzá　mix; mingle: 不要把不同的种子~在一起。Don't mix up different kinds of seeds.

混战 hùnzhàn　tangled warfare: 军阀~ tangled warfare among warlords; tangled fighting between warlords / 球门前一场~，球被捅进了球门。In a scramble in front of the goal, the ball was kicked in.

混帐 hùnzhàng　*offens.* scoundrel; bastard; son of a bitch

混帐话 hùnzhànghuà　impudent remark

混浊 hùnzhuó　muddy; turbid: ~的水 turbid water / ~的空气 foul (or stale) air / 两眼~ bleary-eyed / 小便~ cloudy urine

混子 hùnzi　charlatan; fake

溷 hùn　*formal* ① confused; chaotic ② lavatory; toilet

溷厕 hùncè　*formal* lavatory; toilet

溷浊 hùnzhuó　same as 混浊 hùnzhuó

huō

耠 huō　hoeing

耠子 huōzi　a hoeing implement

劐 huō　*inf.* ① slit or cut with a knife: 把鱼肚子~开 slit open the fish ② hoeing

嚄 huō　*interj.* (expressing surprise): ~! 好大的鱼! Oh! What a big fish! ——see also ǒ

豁[1] huō　slit; break; crack: 墙上~了一个口子。There is a breach in the wall.

豁[2] huō　give up; sacrifice: ~出三天时间，也要把它做好。Even if it takes us three whole days, we must get the job done.
——see also huò

豁出去 huōchuqu　go ahead regardless; be ready to risk everything: 我们~了，决心跟他们干到底。We are re-

solved to fight it out with them at all costs.

豁口 huōkǒu　opening; break; breach: 城墙～ an opening in the city wall

豁命 huōmìng　same as 拼命 pīnmìng

豁子 huōzi　*dial.* ① opening; break; breach ② a harelipped person

豁嘴 huōzuǐ　① *inf.* harelip ② a harelipped person

攉 huō　shovel coal, ore, etc. from one place to another: ～煤工人 coal shoveller

huó

和 huó　mix (powder) with water, etc.: ～点儿灰泥把洞堵上。 Prepare some plaster to fill the hole. —see also hé, hè, hú, huò

和面 huómiàn　knead dough

和面机 huómiànjī　flour-mixing machine

活[1] huó　① live: 她～到八十岁。 She lived to be eighty. / 鱼在水里才能～。 Fish can only live in water. ② alive; living: 在他～着的时候 during his lifetime / ～老虎 a live tiger ③ save (the life of a person): ～人无算 (of a good doctor, etc.) save countless lives ④ vivid; lively: 把这个角色演～了 give a vivid portrayal of the character / 把经济搞～ reinvigorate the economy / 脑子很～ have a quick mind / 把会开得～点 make the meeting more lively ⑤ movable; moving: 活结 huójié ⑥ *adv.* exactly; simply: 活像 huóxiàng

活[2] huó　① work: 我的～儿干完了。 I have finished the work. ② product: 这批～儿做得好。 This batch of products is well made.

活靶 huóbǎ　*mil.* manoeuvring target

活靶子 huóbǎzi　a live target

活版 huóbǎn (also 活字版 huózìbǎn) *print.* typography; letterpress

活版印刷 huóbǎn yìnshuā　typographic printing; typography; letterpress printing: ～机 letterpress (printing) machine

活瓣 huóbàn　*physiol.* valve

活宝 huóbǎo　a bit of a clown; a funny fellow

活报剧 huóbàojù　living newspaper; skit; street performance

活蹦乱跳 huóbèng-luàntiào　skip and jump about; gambol; frolic: 孩子们在雪地里～。 The children were frolicking happily in the snow.

活便 huóbian　*inf.* ① dexterous; nimble; agile: 手脚～ dexterous and quick in action ② convenient: 两个门都打开，进出～一点。 It's more convenient for people coming in and out of the building to have both doors open.

活茬 huóchá　*inf.* farm work

活到老, 学到老 huó dào lǎo, xué dào lǎo　one is never too old to learn; keep on learning as long as you live

活地狱 huódìyù　hell on earth

活动 huó·dòng　① move about; exercise: 站起来～～ stand up and move about / ～一下筋骨 limber up the joints; limber oneself up ② shaky; unsteady: 这把椅子直～。 The chair is rickety. / 这颗牙～了。 This tooth's loose. ③ movable; mobile; flexible: 口气有点～ sound less adamant; begin to relent a little ④ activity; manoeuvre: 政治～ political activities / 从事科学～ go in for scientific pursuits / 游击队在敌人后方～。 The guerrilla forces were operating behind the enemy lines. / ～余地 room for manoeuvre ⑤ use personal influence or irregular means: 替他～～ put in a word for him; use

one's influence on his behalf ⑥ *psychol.* behaviour

活动坝 huódòngbà　*water conservancy* movable dam

活动扳手 huódòng bānshǒu　*mech.* adjustable spanner (or wrench)

活动房屋 huódòng fángwū　movable house

活动家 huódòngjiā　activist; public figure

活动桥 huódòngqiáo　movable bridge

活动资本 huódòng zīběn　liquid capital

活度 huódù　*chem.* activity: ～系数 activity coefficient

活泛 huófan　*inf.* flexible: 办事别那么死板, 心眼放～点。 Don't be so rigid. Be more flexible.

活佛 huófó　① Living Buddha ② (in Lamaism) a Buddha incarnate

活该 huógāi　*inf.* it serves sb. right: ～, 谁叫你不听我的话。 It serves you right. You should have listened to me. / 罚了他五块钱, ～。 They fined him five *yuan*. It serves him right. / 这家伙落得如此下场, ～。 The fellow got what he deserved.

活荷载 huóhèzài　*transportation archit.* live load

活化 huóhuà　*chem.* activation: ～剂 activator / ～吸附 activation adorption

活话 huóhuà　indefinite words; vague promise: 他说了个～, 说可能下星期日再来。 He vaguely said that he might come next Sunday.

活活 huóhuó　while still alive: ～烧死 be burnt alive / ～打死 be beaten to death / ～气死 die from anger

活火山 huóhuǒshān　active volcano

活计 huóji　① handicraft work; manual labour: 针线～ needlework / 把～统一安排一下。 Make an overall arrangement of the work. ② handiwork; work: 她拿着～给大家看。 She showed her work to everybody.

活检 huójiǎn　short for 活组织检查 huózǔzhī jiǎnchá

活见鬼 huójiànguǐ　sheer nonsense; utterly impossible; simply absurd

活教材 huójiàocái　persons or things that can serve to educate people

活结 huójié　a knot that can be undone by a pull; slipknot

活局子 huójúzi　*dial.* swindle; trap

活口 huókǒu　① a survivor of a murder attempt ② a prisoner who can furnish information ③ keep body and soul together; eke out an existence ④ flexible tone; flexible words

活扣 huókòu　*inf.* a knot that can be undone by a pull; slipknot

活力 huólì　vigour; vitality; energy: 他是个小伙子, 充满～。 He is a young lad with plenty of vigour.

活灵活现 huólíng-huóxiàn (also 活龙活现 huólóng-huóxiàn) vivid; lifelike: 说得～ give a vivid description; make it come to life

活溜 huóliu　*dial.* ① shaky; unsteady ② nimble; agile; quick

活路 huólù　① means of subsistence; way out: 旧社会哪有咱穷人的～。 What way out was there for us poor folk in the old society? ② workable method

活路 huólu　physical labour

活络 huóluò　*dial.* ① loose: 牙齿有点～。 The tooth has become a bit loose. ② noncommittal; indefinite: 他说得很～。 He was rather noncommittal.

活埋 huómái　bury alive

活门 huómén　*mech.* valve

活命 huómìng　① earn a bare living; scrape along; eke out an existence: 过去他靠卖艺～。 In the old days he scraped along as a street entertainer. ② *formal* save sb.'s life: ～之恩 indebtedness to sb. for saving one's life ③ life

活泼 huópo　① lively; vivacious; vivid: 天真～的孩子 lively children / 文字～ written in a lively style ② *chem.* reactive

活菩萨　huópúsà　living Bodhisattva—an epithet for a person who is full of compassion for the needy and the suffering

活期　huóqī　'current: ～储蓄 current deposit; demand deposit／～存款帐户 current account

活气　huóqì　lively atmosphere: 大地充满了一片春耕的～。The land is alive with spring sowing activities.

活钱儿　huóqiánr　inf.　① ready money; cash ② extra income

活塞　huósāi　mech.　piston: ～杆 piston rod／～圈 piston ring

活神仙　huóshén·xiān　living immortal —an epithet for a man noted for his longevity or supposed to have clairvoyance

活生生　huóshēngshēng　① real; living: ～的例子 a living example／这篇小说里的人物都是～的,有血有肉的。The characters in the novel are all vividly portrayed. ② while still alive: 万恶的封建礼教把这个年轻的妇女～地折磨死了。The barbarous feudal ethical code literally snuffed out her young life.

活食　huóshí　living food (for animals)

活受罪　huóshòuzuì　inf.　suffer a living hell; have a hell of a life: 听那又臭又长的报告, 简直是～。It was a real torture to listen to that long-winded dull speech.

活水　huóshuǐ　flowing water; running water

活死人　huósǐrén　dial. offens.　a living corpse—a slow-witted, clumsy person

活似　huósì　same as 活像 huóxiàng

活体检查　huótǐ jiǎnchá　same as 活组织检查 huózǔzhī jiǎnchá

活体解剖　huótǐ jiěpōu　vivisection

活头儿　huótour　will to live; interest in life: 那还有什么～? What's there to live for?

活脱儿　huótuōr　inf.　bear a remarkable resemblance; be strikingly alike: 他长得～是他爸爸。He's the very spit (or image) of his father.

活现　huóxiàn　appear vividly; come alive: 黄继光的英雄形象又～在我们眼前。The heroic image of Huang Jiguang once again appeared vividly in our mind's eye.

活像　huóxiàng　look exactly like; be the spit and image of; be an exact replica of: 这孩子长得～他父亲。The child is the very spit (or image) of his father.

活性　huóxìng　chem.　active; activated

活性染料　huóxìng rǎnliào　reactive dyes

活性炭　huóxìngtàn　chem.　active (or activated) carbon

活血　huóxuè　Chin. med.　invigorate the circulation of blood

活阎王　huóyánwang　devil incarnate; tyrannical ruler

活页　huóyè　loose-leaf: ～笔记本 loose-leaf notebook／～夹 loose-leaf binder; spring binder／～文选 loose-leaf selections／～纸 paper for a loose-leaf notebook

活用　huóyòng　apply flexibly; apply with imagination and ingenuity

活跃　huóyuè　① brisk; active; dynamic: 市场～。Business is brisk.／听到这消息, 大家顿时一起来。Everybody got excited at the news.／这些青年的思想很～。These young people have active minds.／她是工会的～分子。She's active in the trade union. ② enliven; animate; invigorate: ～文娱生活 liven up cultural and recreational activities／～会场气氛 enliven the atmosphere of the meeting／～城乡物资交流 stimulate the interchange of urban and rural products／～经济 revitalize the economy

活捉　huózhuō　capture alive

活字　huózì　print.　type; letter: ～盘 type case; letter board

活字典　huózìdiǎn　a walking dictionary

活字合金　huózì héjīn　same as 铅字合金 qiānzì héjīn

活组织检查　huózǔzhī jiǎnchá　med.　biopsy

活罪　huózuì　① living hell; untold suffering ② living punishment: 死罪已免, ～难饶。Your life is spared but not your living punishment.

huǒ

火　huǒ　① fire: 这屋里有～。There's a fire in the room. ② firearms; ammunition: 军火 jūnhuǒ ③ Chin. med.　internal heat—one of the six causes of disease: 败火 bàihuǒ ④ fiery; flaming: 火红 huǒhóng ⑤ urgent; pressing: 火速 huǒsù ⑥ anger; temper: 心头～起 flare up in anger／你怎么这么大的～儿? Why are you in such a temper?／他～儿了。He flared up. ⑦ same as 伙 huǒ

火把　huǒbǎ　torch

火伴　huǒbàn　same as 伙伴 huǒbàn

火棒　huǒbàng　lighted torch (used in acrobatics)

火暴[1]　huǒbào　(also 火爆 huǒbào) dial. fiery; irritable: ～性子 a hot temper

火暴[2]　huǒbào　(also 火爆 huǒbào) dial. vigorous; exuberant; lively: 牡丹开得真～。The peonies are in full bloom.／这出戏的场面很～。The play is full of action and excitement.

火并　huǒbìng　open fight between factions: 军阀内部的～ an open factional fight within the warlords

火柴　huǒchái　match: 划根～ strike a match／～盒 matchbox

火场　huǒchǎng　the scene of a fire

火车　huǒchē　train: 乘～ go by train／～票 railway ticket／～时刻表 railway timetable; train schedule／～司机 engine driver; (locomotive) engineer／～站 railway station

火车轮渡　huǒchē lúndù　train ferry

火车头　huǒchētóu　(railway) engine; locomotive: 面向～的座位 a seat facing the engine／革命是历史的～。Revolutions are the locomotives of history.

火车座　huǒchēzuò　booth (in a restaurant)

火成岩　huǒchéngyán　geol.　igneous rock

火炽　huǒchì　white-hot (fig.): 球赛到了最～的阶段。The match has reached a white-hot stage.

火刀　huǒdāo　dial.　same as 火镰 huǒlián

火法冶金　huǒfǎ yějīn　metall.　pyrometallurgy

火夫　huǒfū　old　① stoker; fireman ② mess cook

火攻　huǒgōng　fire attack (using fire as a weapon against enemy personnel and installations)

火罐儿　huǒguànr　Chin. med.　cupping jar (or glass)

火光　huǒguāng　flame; blaze: ～冲天。The flames lit up the sky.

火锅　huǒguō　chafing dish

火海　huǒhǎi　a sea of flames: 阵地上成了一片～。The battlefield became a sea of flames.

火海刀山　huǒhǎi-dāoshān　same as 刀山火海 dāoshān-huǒhǎi

火红　huǒhóng　red as fire; fiery; flaming: ～的太阳 a flaming sun／医生摸了摸病人～发烫的脸颊。The doctor felt the patient's fiery cheek.／～的战旗 a flame-red battle flag／～的青春 flaming youth

火候　huǒhou　① duration and degree of heating, cooking, smelting, etc.: 炒菜掌握～很重要。Heat control is very important in stir-frying.／烧窑得看～。In operating a kiln you must pay attention to temperature control.／这鸭子烤得～正好。This roast duck is done to a turn. ② level of attainment: 他的书法到～了。He has matured as a calligrapher. ③ a crucial moment: 正在战斗的～上, 援军赶到了。Reinforcements rushed up at the crucial moment of the battle.

火狐　huǒhú　red fox

火花　huǒhuā　spark: ～四溅 sparks flying off in all directions / 生命的～ the sparks of life—exuberant vitality

火花塞　huǒhuāsāi　*mech.* sparking plug; spark plug; ignition plug

火化　huǒhuà　cremate

火鸡　huǒjī　turkey

火急　huǒjí　urgent; pressing: 十万火急 shíwàn huǒjí

火剪　huǒjiǎn　① fire-tongs; tongs ② curling tongs; curling irons

火碱　huǒjiǎn　caustic soda

火箭　huǒjiàn　rocket: 发射～ fire (*or* launch) a rocket / ～部队 rocket troops / ～发射场 rocket launching site / ～发射台 rocket launching pad; rocket mount / ～技术 rocketry / 水下～ submarine rocket

火箭弹　huǒjiàndàn　rocket projectile; rocket shell

火箭炮　huǒjiànpào　rocket gun

火箭筒　huǒjiàntǒng　rocket launcher (*or* projector); bazooka

火井　huǒjǐng　*dial.* gas well

火警　huǒjǐng　fire alarm

火酒　huǒjiǔ　*dial.* alcohol

火炬　huǒjù　torch: ～赛跑 torch race / ～游行 torchlight parade

火炕　huǒkàng　heated *kang;* heated brick bed

火坑　huǒkēng　fiery pit; pit of hell; abyss of suffering: 跳出～ escape from the living hell

火筷子　huǒkuàizi　fire-tongs; tongs

火辣辣　huǒlālā　burning: ～的太阳 a scorching sun / 疼得～的 a searing pain / 脸上觉得～的 feel one's cheeks burning (as with shame) / 心里～的 burning with anxiety

火老鸦　huǒlǎoyā　*dial.* leaping flames (of raging fire)

火力　huǒlì　*mil.* firepower; fire: 发扬～ make full use of firepower / ～点 firing point / ～控制 control of fire / ～配系 organization of fire; fire system / ～突击 fire assault / ～圈 field of fire / ～网 network of fire; fire net / ～掩护 fire cover / ～侦察 reconnaissance by firing (to observe enemy reactions) / ～支援 support fire; fire support

火力发电　huǒlì fādiàn　thermal power generation: ～厂 thermal power plant

火镰　huǒlián　steel (for flint)

火烈鸟　huǒlièniǎo　flamingo

火流星　huǒliúxīng　*astron.* bolide; fireball

火龙　huǒlóng　① fiery dragon—a procession of lanterns or torches ② *dial.* an air channel from a brick kitchen stove to a chimney; flue

火笼　huǒlóng　*dial.* hand-held bamboo basket brazier

火炉　huǒlú　(also 火炉子 huǒlúzi) (heating) stove

火轮　huǒlún　(also 火轮船 huǒlúnchuán) *old* steam boat

火冒三丈　huǒ mào sān zhàng　fly into a rage; flare up

火帽　huǒmào　*mil.* detonating cap; percussion cap

火煤　huǒméi　(also 火媒 huǒméi) kindling

火棉　huǒmián　guncotton; pyroxylin

火苗　huǒmiáo　(also 火苗子 huǒmiáozi) a tongue of flame; flame: ～蹿上来了。The flames leapt up.

火捻　huǒniǎn　① kindling ② fuse

火炮　huǒpào　cannon; gun

火盆　huǒpén　fire pan; brazier

火拼　huǒpīn　same as 火并 huǒbìng

火漆　huǒqī　sealing wax

火气　huǒqì　① *Chin. med.* internal heat (as a cause of disease) ② anger; temper: ～很大 have a bad temper / 压不住心头的～ can hardly contain one's anger; cannot hold back one's rage

火器　huǒqì　*mil.* firearm

火钳　huǒqián　same as 火剪 huǒjiǎn①

火枪　huǒqiāng　firelock

火墙　huǒqiáng　a wall with flues for space heating

火情　huǒqíng　the condition of a fire

火热　huǒrè　① burning hot; fervent; fiery: ～的太阳 a burning sun / ～的心 a fervent heart / ～的斗争 fiery struggles ② intimate: 打得火热 dǎde huǒrè

火绒　huǒróng　tinder

火肉　huǒròu　*dial.* ham

火伞高张　huǒsǎn gāo zhāng　a fully spread umbrella of fire—scorching sunlight in summer

火色　huǒsè　*dial.* condition of fire (as for cooking); strength of fire: 看～ see if the fire is good enough / 拿稳了～ make sure that the fire is just right

火山　huǒshān　volcano: ～喷发 volcanic eruption / ～灰 volcanic ash / ～口 crater / ～砾 lapillus / ～作用 volcanism

火山岛　huǒshāndǎo　volcanic island

火山地震　huǒshān dìzhèn　volcanic earthquake

火山学　huǒshānxué　volcanology

火伤　huǒshāng　burn (caused by fire)

火上加油　huǒ shàng jiā yóu　(also 火上浇油 huǒ shàng jiāo yóu) pour oil on the flames; add fuel to the flames: 她听了这些话，像是～。These words only added fuel to the flames of her anger.

火烧　huǒshāo　destroy by fire; burn:《～圆明园》*The Burning of Yuanmingyuan* (a film)

火烧　huǒshao　baked wheaten cake

火烧火燎　huǒshāo-huǒliǎo　① feeling terribly hot: 他身上每处伤口都疼得～。His every wound began to burn like fire. ② restless with anxiety: 孩子有病，妈妈急得～的。The mother was filled with anxiety about her child's illness.

火烧眉毛　huǒ shāo méimao　the fire is singeing the eyebrows—a desperate situation: ～的事儿 a matter of the utmost urgency

火烧油层　huǒshāo yóucéng　*petroleum* combustion (of oil) in situ

火烧云　huǒshāoyún　red clouds (at sunset or sunrise)

火舌　huǒshé　tongues of fire: 房子起了火，～正在吞没屋顶。The flames were licking the roof of the burning building.

火绳　huǒshéng　a rope of plaited plants burnt as a mosquito repellent

火石　huǒshí　flint

火势　huǒshì　the intensity of a fire: ～很猛。The fire burned fiercely.

火势　huǒshi　lively; flourishing; prosperous: 这晚会开得真～。The party was a great success. / 他俩的小日子过得挺～。The young couple are quite happy.

火树银花　huǒshù-yínhuā　fiery trees and silver flowers—dazzling displays of fireworks and lanterns (on a festival night): ～不夜天。弟兄姊妹舞翩跹。(柳亚子) Displays of fiery trees and silver flowers, a night without darkness. Brothers and sisters skip by gracefully in dance.

火速　huǒsù　at top speed; posthaste: ～增援 rush up reinforcements / 任务十分紧急，必须～完成。It's an urgent task and must be completed at once. / 警察～赶到现场。The police rushed to the scene.

火炭　huǒtàn　burning charcoal or faggot

火烫　huǒtàng　① burning hot ② curl hair with iron tongs

火头　huǒtóu　① flame: 油灯的～儿太小。The flame of the lamp is too low. ② duration and degree of heating, cooking, smelting, etc.: ～儿不到，饼就烙不好。You can't bake a cake properly if the fire is not right. ③ same as 火主 huǒzhǔ ④ anger: 你先把～压一压，别着急。Don't fly off the handle. Calm down.

火头军 huǒtóujūn *humor.* army cook

火头上 huǒtóushang the height of anger: 他正在～, 听不进你的解释。He's mad and won't listen to your explanation.

火腿 huǒtuǐ ham

火腿蛋 huǒtuǐdàn ham and egg

火网 huǒwǎng *mil.* network of fire; fire net

火匣子 huǒxiázi *dial.* cheap small coffin

火险 huǒxiǎn fire insurance

火线 huǒxiàn ① battle (*or* firing, front) line: ～入党 join the Party at the battlefront / 轻伤不下～ refuse to leave the front because of minor wounds / ～抢救 frontline first aid ② *elect.* live wire

火硝 huǒxiāo common name for 硝酸钾 xiāosuānjiǎ

火星[1] Huǒxīng Mars

火星[2] huǒxīng spark: 铁锤打在石头上, 迸出不少～。Sparks flew up when the hammer struck the rock. / 他气得两眼直冒～。His eyes flashed with anger.

火星卫星 Huǒxīng wèixīng Martian satellite

火性 huǒxìng *inf.* bad temper; hot temper

火眼 huǒyǎn *med.* pinkeye

火眼金睛 huǒyǎn-jīnjīng fiery eyes and diamond pupils—discerning eyes: ～识真假。Fiery eyes and diamond pupils are able to discern truth and falsehood.

火焰 huǒyàn flame

火焰光谱 huǒyàn guāngpǔ flame spectrum

火焰喷射器 huǒyàn pēnshèqì flamethrower

火药 huǒyào gunpowder; powder: ～库 powder magazine / ～桶 powder keg

火药味 huǒyàowèi the smell of gunpowder (fig.): 他的发言～很浓。He made a very aggressive speech. / 这是一篇充满～的声明。This statement has a strong smell of gunpowder.

火印 huǒyìn a mark burned on bamboo or wooden articles; brand

火油 huǒyóu *dial.* kerosene

火源 huǒyuán burning things which may cause a fire disaster

火灾 huǒzāi fire (as a disaster); conflagration

火葬 huǒzàng cremation

火葬场 huǒzàngchǎng crematorium; crematory

火躁 huǒzào *dial.* irascible; irritable

火蜘蛛 huǒzhīzhū *dial.* two-spotted spider mite

火纸 huǒzhǐ (also 火硝纸 huǒxiāozhǐ) touch paper

火中取栗 huǒzhōng qǔ lì pull sb.'s chestnuts out of the fire; be a cat's-paw

火种 huǒzhǒng ① kindling material; kindling; tinder ② live cinders kept for starting a new fire: 革命的～ sparks of revolution; seeds of revolution

火烛 huǒzhú things that may cause a fire: 小心～! Be careful about fires!

火主 huǒzhǔ the owner of the house where a fire started; the person responsible for the starting of a fire

火柱 huǒzhù a column of flame

火箸 huǒzhù *dial.* fire-tongs; tongs

火砖 huǒzhuān refractory brick; firebrick

伙[1]（火） huǒ mess; board; meals: 包伙 bāohuǒ / 入伙 rùhuǒ

伙[2]（火、夥） huǒ ① partner; mate: 同伙 tónghuǒ ② partnership; company: 合伙 héhuǒ / 拆伙 chāihuǒ ③ *m.* group; crowd; band: 三个一群, 五个一～ in small groups; in knots; in twos and threes / 一～强盗 a band of robbers ④ combine; join: ～买 club together to buy sth. / ～着用 share in the use of sth.

伙伴 huǒbàn partner; companion: 我小时候的～ a childhood pal of mine / 贸易～ trade partner

伙犯 huǒfàn accomplice

伙房 huǒfáng kitchen (in a school, factory, etc.)

伙夫 huǒfū *old* mess cook

伙计 huǒji ① partner ② *inf.* fellow; mate: 他是我的老～。He's an old pal of mine. / ～, 上哪儿去? Where are you going, mate? ③ *old* salesman; salesclerk; shop assistant; farm labourer

伙食 huǒ·shí mess; food; meals: 管理～ handle messing arrangements / 我们学校的～不好。The food at our school is no good. / ～补助 food allowance / ～费 money spent on meals; board expenses / ～节余 mess savings

伙食科 huǒshíkē catering office

伙食团 huǒshítuán mess

伙同 huǒtóng in league with; in collusion with

伙友 huǒyǒu partners and friends

钬 huǒ *chem.* holmium (Ho)

夥[1] huǒ *formal* much; a great deal; many; numerous: 获益甚～ have derived much benefit

夥[2] huǒ same as 伙[2]

huò

或 huò ① *adv.* perhaps; maybe; probably: 代表团明晨～可到达。The delegation may arrive tomorrow morning. ② *conj.* or; either... or...: 这块地可以种高粱～玉米。We can grow sorghum or maize on this plot. ③ *conj.* no matter what, how, etc.: 无论唱～跳, 她都行。She is good at both singing and dancing. ④ *formal* someone; some people: ～曰 someone says; some say ⑤ *adv. formal* (usu. used in the negative) a little; a bit; slightly: 不可～缓 brook no delay

或然 huòrán probable

或然率 huòránlǜ old name for 概率 gàilǜ

或许 huòxǔ *adv.* perhaps; maybe: 他～没有赶上火车。Perhaps he has missed the train. / 她～能来。She might be able to come.

或则 huòzé *conj.* or; either...or...: ～你来, ～我去, 请你决定。Either you come or I go, you just say the word.

或者 huòzhě ① *adv.* perhaps; maybe: 快点走, ～还赶得上他。Hurry up, we may catch up with him yet. / 这个建议对于改进工作～有点好处。This suggestion may help to improve our work. ② *conj.* or; either... or...: 请你把这本书交给小王～小李。Please give this book to either Xiao Wang or Xiao Li. ③ *conj.* no matter what, how, etc.: 不论大事～小事, 大家都愿意找他商量。Everybody likes to consult with him about their problems no matter what kind of problem it is.

和[1] huò mix; blend: 豆沙里～点儿糖 mix a little sugar into the bean paste / 油和水～不到一块儿。Oil and water do not mix.

和[2] huò *m.* a washing (of clothes); a decocting (of medicinal herbs): 衣裳已经洗了三～。The clothes have been rinsed three times. / 二～药 second decoction (of medicinal herbs)

——see also hé; hè; hú; huó

和弄 huònong *dial.* ① stir; agitate; mix ② instigate; incite; sow discord

和稀泥 huò xīní try to mediate differences at the sacrifice of principle; try to smooth things over

货 huò ① money: 通货 tōnghuò ② goods; com-

modity: 中国～ Chinese goods ③ *offens.* 蠢货 chǔnhuò ④ *formal* sell: ～卖 sell commodities

货币 huòbì money; currency: 储备～ reserve currency / 周转～ vehicle currency / 自由兑换～ convertible currency

货币贬值 huòbì biǎnzhí ① (currency) devaluation ② (currency) depreciation

货币单位 huòbì dānwèi monetary unit

货币地租 huòbì dìzū money rent

货币工资 huòbì gōngzī money wages

货币回笼 huòbì huílóng withdrawal of currency from circulation

货币交换 huòbì jiāohuàn exchange through money

货币流通量 huòbì liútōngliàng currency (*or* money) in circulation; money supply

货币平价 huòbì píngjià currency parity; par value of currency

货币升值 huòbì shēngzhí ① (currency) revaluation ② (currency) appreciation

货币危机 huòbì wēijī monetary crisis

货币政策 huòbì zhèngcè monetary policy

货币资本 huòbì zīběn money-capital

货舱 huòcāng (cargo) hold; cargo bay (of a plane)

货场 huòchǎng goods (*or* freight) yard

货车 huòchē ① goods train; freight train ② goods van (*or* wagon); freight car (*or* wagon) ③ lorry; truck

货船 huòchuán freighter; cargo ship; cargo vessel: 定期～ cargo liner

货单 huòdān manifest; waybill; shipping list

货到付款 huò dào fù kuǎn cash on delivery (COD)

货店 huòdiàn *dial.* shop; store

货柜 huòguì ① counter; bar ② another name for 集装箱 jízhuāngxiāng

货机 huòjī cargo aircraft (*or* plane); air freighter

货价 huòjià commodity price; price of goods

货架子 huòjiàzi goods shelves: ～上摆满各种商品。The shelves are stocked full.

货款 huòkuǎn money for buying or selling goods; payment for goods

货郎 huòláng itinerant pedlar; street vendor

货郎担 huòlángdàn street vendor's load (carried on a shoulder pole)

货轮 huòlún freighter; cargo ship; cargo vessel

货品 huòpǐn kinds or types of goods

货色 huòsè ① goods: ～齐全。Goods of every description are available. / 上等～ first-class goods; quality goods ② *derog.* stuff; trash; rubbish: 那本杂志登的尽是这种～。That magazine is nothing but a load of such trash. / 那是小报上的～。That's just tabloid rubbish.

货摊 huòtān stall; stand

货物 huòwù goods; commodity; merchandise

货箱 huòxiāng packing box

货样 huòyàng sample goods; sample

货源 huòyuán source of goods; supply of goods: ～充足 an ample supply of goods / 开辟～ find (*or* open up) new sources of goods

货运 huòyùn freight transport: ～业务 cargo service

货运单 huòyùndān waybill

货运费 huòyùnfèi shipping cost; freight (charges)

货运量 huòyùnliàng volume of goods transported; volume of rail freight; volume of road haulage

货运列车 huòyùn lièchē goods train; freight train

货运周转量 huòyùn zhōuzhuǎnliàng rotation volume of goods (*or* freight) transport

货栈 huòzhàn warehouse

货真价实 huòzhēn-jiàshí ① genuine goods at a fair price ② through and through; out-and-out; dyed-in-the-wool: ～的骗子 an out-and-out swindler / ～的伪君子 a dyed-in-the-wool hypocrite

货殖 huòzhí *arch.* engage in trade

货主 huòzhǔ owner of cargo

获¹（獲） huò ① capture; catch: 捕获 bǔhuò ② obtain; win; reap: ～一等奖 win the first prize

获²（穫） huò reap; harvest; gather in: 收获 shōuhuò

获得 huòdé gain; obtain; acquire; win; achieve: ～第一名 win first place; get a first; win a championship / ～解放 achieve emancipation; win liberation / ～独立 gain independence / ～巨大的成绩 achieve great success / ～知识 acquire knowledge / ～好评 win acclaim; earn favourable comment

获得性 huòdéxìng *biol.* acquired character

获得性免疫 huòdéxìng miǎnyì *med.* acquired immunity

获奖 huòjiǎng win a prize; be awarded a prize: ～作品 an award-winning work / 这部影片获奥斯卡奖。The film won an Oscar.

获救 huòjiù be rescued

获利 huòlì make a profit; reap profits

获取 huòqǔ procure; obtain; gain; reap: ～暴利 reap staggering (*or* colossal) profits

获胜 huòshèng win victory; be victorious; triumph: 革命人民的斗争必将～。The struggles of the revolutionary people will surely triumph. / 甲队以五比二～。Team A won the match five to two.

获释 huòshì be released (from prison)

获悉 huòxī (also 获知 huòzhī) *formal* learn (of an event)

获致 huòzhì gain; obtain; acquire; achieve

获准 huòzhǔn get (*or* obtain) permission

祸（禍） huò ① misfortune; disaster; calamity: 惹祸 rěhuò ② bring disaster upon; ruin: 祸国殃民 huòguó-yāngmín

祸不单行 huò bù dān xíng misfortunes never come singly; it never rains but it pours

祸不旋踵 huò bù xuánzhǒng trouble is not far off; disaster looms ahead

祸从口出 huò cóng kǒu chū trouble comes out of the mouth (i.e. from a loose tongue)

祸从天降 huò cóng tiān jiàng a disaster descends from heaven (i.e. befalls sb. unexpectedly)

祸端 huòduān *formal* the source of the disaster; the cause of ruin

祸福无门 huò fú wú mén fortune or misfortune knows no doors—they are invited in

祸根 huògēn the root of the trouble; the cause of ruin; bane: 埋下～ lay up trouble for the future

祸国殃民 huòguó-yāngmín bring calamity to the country and the people: 一小撮～的民族败类 dregs of the nation who wreck the country and ruin the people

祸害 huòhài ① disaster; curse; scourge: 黄河在历史上经常引起～。Throughout the ages the Huanghe River was a scourge of the nation. ② damage; destroy: 防止野猪～庄稼。Don't let the boars damage the crops.

祸患 huòhuàn disaster; calamity

祸乱 huòluàn disastrous disorder; turmoil; social upheaval

祸起萧墙 huò qǐ xiāoqiáng trouble arises behind the walls of the home—trouble arises within the family; there is internal strife afoot

祸事 huòshì disaster; calamity; mishap

祸首 huòshǒu chief culprit (*or* offender)

祸水 huòshuǐ a person (esp. a woman) who is the source of trouble

祸胎 huòtāi the root of the trouble; the cause of the

disaster

祸兮福所倚, 福兮祸所伏 huò xī fú suǒ yǐ, fú xī huò suǒ fú good fortune lieth within bad, bad fortune lurketh within good

祸心 huòxīn evil intent: 包藏祸心 bāocáng huòxīn

祸殃 huòyāng disaster; calamity; catastrophe

祸种 huòzhǒng the root of the trouble; the cause of ruin; bane

惑 huò ① be puzzled; be bewildered: 智者不～。The wise are free from perplexities. ② delude; mislead: 造谣惑众 zàoyáo huòzhòng

惑乱 huòluàn delude and confuse: ～人心 confuse and poison people's minds／～军心 undermine the morale of an army

霍 huò ① suddenly; quickly ② (Huò) a surname

霍地 huòdì *adv.* suddenly: ～立起身来 suddenly stand up; spring to one's feet

霍霍 huòhuò ① *onom.*: ～的磨刀声 the scrape, scrape of a sword being sharpened ② flash: 电光～。The lightning flashed.

霍乱 huòluàn ① cholera ② *Chin. med.* acute gastroenteritis

霍然 huòrán ① *adv.* suddenly; quickly: 手电筒～一亮。Suddenly somebody flashed an electric torch. ② *formal* (of an illness) be cured quickly: 数日之后, 定当～。You will be restored to health in a matter of days.

霍闪 huòshǎn *dial.* lightning

豁 huò ① clear; open; open-minded; generous: 显豁 xiǎnhuò ② exempt; remit: 豁免 huòmiǎn ——see also huō

豁达 huòdá sanguine; optimistic

豁达大度 huòdá dàdù open-minded and magnanimous

豁朗 huòlǎng high-spirited; broad-minded

豁亮 huòliàng ① roomy and bright: 这屋子又干净, 又～。The room is clean, bright and spacious. ② sonorous; resonant: 嗓音～ have a sonorous voice

豁免 huòmiǎn exempt (from taxes or from customs inspection, etc.); remit: ～捐税 exempt sb. from taxes; remit taxes

豁然贯通 huòrán guàntōng suddenly see the whole thing in a clear light

豁然开朗 huòrán kāilǎng ① see 开朗 kāilǎng[1] ② suddenly see the light; be suddenly enlightened

藿 huò *formal* leaves of pulse plants

藿香 huòxiāng *Chin. med.* wrinkled giant hyssop (*Agastache rugosa*)

镬 huò ① *dial.* pot ② cauldron

镬子 huòzi *dial.* pot

嚯 huò ① *interj.* (indicating surprise or wonder) wow; gee: ～, 那么大! Good Heavens! That big!／～, 怎么这么贵! Wow! How come it is so expensive! ② *onom.* ho-ho: ～～一笑 give a hearty laugh

蠖 huò see 尺蠖 chǐhuò

J

jī

几[1] jī *a small table*: 茶几 chájī

几[2] (幾) jī *adv. formal* nearly; almost; practically: 到会者～三千人。 Nearly 3,000 people came to the meeting.
　　——see also jǐ

几乎 jīhū (also 几几乎 jījīhū) *adv.* almost; nearly; practically: 他～一夜没睡。 He lay awake almost the whole night. / 我在物理学方面的知识,～等于零。 My knowledge of physics is practically nil. / 你比我～高了一头。 You're nearly a head taller than I. / 故乡变化太大了,我～认不出来了。 My home town had changed so much that I could hardly recognize it. / 我脚下一滑,～(没)摔倒。 I slipped and nearly fell. / 不是你提醒我, 我～忘了。 It would have slipped my mind if you hadn't reminded me of it.

几近 jījìn be close to; be on the verge of: 这种动物已～灭绝。 This species of animal is on the verge of extinction.

几率 jīlǜ same as 概率 gàilǜ

几维鸟 jīwéiniǎo kiwi

讥 (譏) jī ridicule; mock; satirize: 反唇相讥 fǎn chún xiāng jī

讥嘲 jīcháo ridicule; satirize

讥刺 jīcì *formal* ridicule; satirize

讥讽 jīfěng ridicule; satirize: 这是～,不是善意的批评。 This is sarcasm, not constructive criticism.

讥诮 jīqiào *formal* sneer at; deride: 他为人孤傲, 常冷言冷语～他人。 He is cold and aloof, and he often makes derisive, sarcastic remarks about people.

讥笑 jīxiào ridicule; jeer; sneer at; deride: 他毫不理睬某些人的～,继续进行试验。 Completely ignoring some people's sneers, he went on with his experiments. / 他们～她穿得破旧。 They sneered at her old, worn-out clothes.

击 (擊) jī ① beat; hit; strike: ～鼓 beat a drum ② attack; assault: 游击 yóujī / 袭击 xíjī ③ come in contact with; bump into: 撞击 zhuàngjī

击败 jībài defeat; beat; vanquish: 他以三比一～了对手。 He beat his opponent 3 to 1.

击毙 jībì shoot dead: 四名匪徒被当场～。 Four bandits were shot dead on the spot.

击沉 jīchén bombard and sink; send (a ship) to the bottom: ～敌舰三艘 sink three enemy warships

击穿 jīchuān *elec.* puncture; breakdown

击发 jīfā ① pull the trigger (of a gun) ② *mil.* percussion: ～装置 percussion lock (*or* mechanism)

击毁 jīhuǐ smash; wreck; shatter; destroy: ～坦克二十四辆 destroy 24 tanks

击剑 jījiàn *sports* fencing

击节 jījié *formal* beat time: ～叹赏 show appreciation (of a poem or a piece of music) by beating time with one's hand; greatly admire

击溃 jīkuì rout; put to flight: 他们把敌军～了。 They routed the enemy.

击落 jīluò shoot down; bring down; down: ～敌机七架 bring down seven enemy planes

击破 jīpò break up; destroy; rout: 各个击破 gègè jīpò

击球 jīqiú batting (in baseball or softball): ～员 batter; batsman

击伤 jīshāng wound (a person); damage (a plane, tank, etc.)

击赏 jīshǎng *formal* applaud; admire

击水 jīshuǐ ① strike waters: 曾记否, 到中流～, 浪遏飞舟? (毛泽东) Remember still How, venturing midstream, we struck the waters And waves stayed the speeding boats? ② swim

击退 jītuì beat back; repel; repulse: ～敌军几次进攻 repulse several enemy assaults

击弦乐器 jīxián yuèqì hammered string instrument

击以猛掌 jī yǐ měngzhǎng give sb. a shove—give a sharp warning

击乐器 jīyuèqì percussion instrument

击掌 jīzhǎng clap one's hands: ～为号 signal by clapping hands

击中 jīzhòng hit the target: 他一枪～了目标。 He hit the target with one shot.

击中要害 jīzhòng yàohài hit the nail on the head; hit sb.'s vital point; hit home: 你批评得对, 击中了我的要害。 You're right in your criticism. You've pinpointed my main weakness.

叽 (嘰) jī *onom.* the sound of a bird chirping: 小鸟～～叫。 Little birds were chirping.

叽咕 jīgu talk in a low voice; whisper; mutter: 他俩叽叽咕咕地说些什么?What are those two whispering to each other about?

叽叽嘎嘎 jījīgāgā *onom.* the sound of cackling, creaking, etc.: 大家～地笑起来。 Everybody started cackling. / 这门老～响。 This door always creaks.

叽叽喳喳 jījīzhāzhā same as 唧唧喳喳 jījīzhāzhā

叽里旮旯儿 jīligālár *dial.* every nook and cranny

叽里咕噜 jīligūlū *onom.* the sound of sb. talking indistinctly or of sth. rolling around: 他们～地说了半天。 They gabbled away for a long time. / 石块～滚下山去。 Rocks went tumbling down the hill.

叽哩呱啦 jīliguālā *onom.* the sound of loud talk or chatter:他～地说个没完。 He talked loudly and endlessly.

饥[1] jī hungry; starved; famished

饥[2] (饑) jī famine; crop failure: 大～之年 a year of great famine

饥不择食 jī bù zé shí a hungry person is not picky and choosy: ～, 寒不择衣。 When one's hungry one eats what there is; when one's cold one wears what one has.

饥肠 jīcháng *liter.* empty stomach

饥肠辘辘 jīcháng lùlù one's stomach rumbling with hunger

饥饿 jī'è hungry; starved: 挣扎在～线上 struggling along on the verge of starvation

饥寒 jī-hán hunger and cold

饥寒交迫 jī-hán jiāopò suffer from hunger and cold; live in hunger and cold; be poverty-stricken: 陷入～的困难境地 suffer the terrible hardship of hunger and cold

饥荒 jīhuang ① famine; crop failure: 一九三四年中国发生过一次大～。 In 1934, there was a severe famine in China. ② *inf.* be hard up; be short of money: 解放前我家月月闹～。 Before liberation my family ran short of cash month after month. ③ *inf.* debt: 拉饥荒 lā jīhuang

饥馑 jījǐn *formal* famine; crop failure

饥渴 jīkě hunger and thirst: ～难耐 unbearable hunger and thirst

饥民 jīmín famine victim; famine refugee

圾

jī see 垃圾 lājī

芨

jī see below

芨芨草 jījīcǎo splendid achnatherum (*Achnatherum splendens*)

机（機）

jī ① machine; engine: 内燃机 nèi-ránjī / 打字机 dǎzìjī ② aircraft; aeroplane; plane: 客机 kèjī ③ crucial point: 转机 zhuǎnjī / 生机 shēngjī ④ chance; occasion; opportunity: 趁机 chènjī / 时机 shíjī ⑤ organic: 有机 yǒujī ⑥ flexible; quick-witted: 机智 jīzhì

机变 jībiàn ① flexible ② sly

机不可失，时不再来 jī bùkě shī, shí bù zài lái don't let slip an opportunity as it may never come again; opportunity knocks but once

机舱 jīcāng ① engine room (of a ship) ② passenger compartment (of an aircraft); cabin

机铲 jīchǎn mechanical shovel

机场 jīchǎng airport; airfield; aerodrome: ～标志 aerodrome markings / ～待战 ground alert / ～灯标 airport beacon

机车 jīchē locomotive; engine

机车车辆厂 jīchē chēliàngchǎng rolling stock plant

机车组 jīchēzǔ locomotive crew

机船 jīchuán **motor vessel**

机床 jīchuáng machine tool: 木工～ woodworking machine tool / 数字程序控制～ numerical controlled machine tool

机电 jīdiàn mechanical and electrical: ～设备 mechanical and electrical equipment

机动[1] jīdòng power-driven; motorized: ～车 motor-driven (*or* motor) vehicle / ～炮 mobile artillery / ～自行车 moped; autocycle

机动[2] jīdòng ① flexible; expedient; mobile: 你可以根据情况～灵活地处置。 You can deal with it flexibly as you see fit. ② in reserve; for emergency use: 拨出五十元作为～开支 allot 50 *yuan* for extras / 不要把日程排得满满的，要留些～时间。 Don't arrange such a tight schedule. Leave some time to spare.

机动力量 jīdòng lìliàng reserve force

机动粮 jīdòngliáng grain reserve for emergency use

机动性 jīdòngxìng mobility; manoeuvrability; flexibility: 这些规定并不那么死板，有一定的～。 These rules aren't totally rigid. They are flexible within certain limits.

机断 jīduàn act on one's own judgment in an emergency: ～行事 act promptly at one's own discretion

机帆船 jīfānchuán motor sailboat; motorized junk

机房 jīfáng ① generator or motor room ② engine room (of a ship)

机耕 jīgēng tractor-ploughing: ～面积 area ploughed by tractors

机耕船 jīgēngchuán boat tractor; wet-field tractor

机工 jīgōng mechanic; machinist

机构 jīgòu ① *mech.* mechanism: 传动～ transmission mechanism / 分离～ disengaging mechanism ② organization; setup: 政府～ government organization / 国家～ state institution / 外交代表～ diplomatic mission / 领事～ consular mission / 商务～ commercial organization / 国际组织～ office of international organization / 民间～ non-governmental institution / 金融～ financial setup / 权力～ organ of power / 宣传～ propaganda organ ③ the internal structure of an organization: 调整～ adjust the organizational structure / ～重叠 organizational overlapping / ～臃肿 an overstaffed organization

机关 jīguān ① *mech.* mechanism; gear: 起动～ starting gear ② machine-operated: ～布景 machine-operated stage scenery ③ office; organ; body: 你们在～坐办公室，不了解下面的生产情况。 You work in an office and don't understand conditions down below. / 领导～ leading bodies / 党政～ Party and government organizations / 文化教育～ cultural and educational institutions ④ stratagem; scheme; intrigue: 识破～ see through a trick

机关报 jīguānbào the official newspaper of a political party, a government, etc.; organ

机关干部 jīguān gànbù government functionary; office worker

机关刊物 jīguān kānwù the official publication of a party, government, etc.

机关炮 jīguānpào cannon

机关枪 jīguānqiāng machine gun

机关算尽 jīguān suànjìn (also 机关用尽 jīguān yòngjìn) use up all one's tricks; for all one's calculations and scheming: ～太聪明，反算了卿卿性命! (《红楼梦》) Too much plotting and scheming is the cause of her own undoing.

机会 jīhuì chance; opportunity: 错过（抓住）～ miss (seize) a chance / 千载一时的好～ a golden opportunity; the chance of a lifetime / 能有～见到他就好了。 It would be wonderful if I could meet him in person. / 我愿借此～向你们表示衷心的感谢。 I wish to avail myself of this opportunity to extend to you my heartfelt thanks.

机会均等 jīhuì jūnděng equal opportunities

机会主义 jīhuìzhǔyì opportunism: “左”、右倾～ Right and "Left" opportunism / ～路线 opportunist line / ～者 opportunist

机件 jījiàn *mech.* parts; works: 钟表的～ the works of a clock or watch

机井 jījǐng motor-pumped well

机警 jījǐng alert; sharp-witted; vigilant: 游击队～地监视敌人的动静。 The guerrillas kept a close watch on the movements of the enemy.

机具 jījù machines and tools: 农业～ farm implements

机库 jīkù hangar

机理 jīlǐ mechanism: 腐蚀～ corrosion mechanism / 结晶～ crystallization mechanism / 分娩～ *med.* mechanism of labour

机灵[1] jīling (also 机伶 jīling) clever; smart; sharp; intelligent: 这孩子怪～的。 This child's very smart. / 她有一双～的大眼睛。 She has large, intelligent eyes. / 这个人办事挺～。 This chap manages things quite cleverly. / 这家伙真～，只要你一点，他就都清楚了。 This chap is really sharp. He would understand everything at the slightest hint.

机灵[2]　jīling　same as 激灵 jīling

机灵鬼　jīlingguǐ　a clever person

机米　jīmǐ　① machine-processed rice ② same as 籼米 xiānmǐ

机密　jīmǐ　① secret; classified; confidential: 这个计划很～，不得向任何人泄露。 The plan is top-secret and we can't allow it to be leaked to anyone. / ～文件 classified papers; confidential documents ② sth. secret; secret: 严守国家～ strictly guard state secrets

机敏　jīmǐn　alert and resourceful: 她在紧急关头总是沉着～。 She is calm and resourceful in an emergency.

机谋　jīmóu　formal　stratagem; artifice; scheme

机能　jīnéng　physiol.　function: 心脏的～ the function of the heart / ～障碍 a functional obstruction / 他下肢瘫痪，两腿丧失～。 His lower body was paralyzed, so he lost the use of his legs.

机器　jīqì　machine: machinery; apparatus: 安装新～ install new machinery / ～造型 machine moulding / ～制造 machine building

机器翻译　jīqì fānyì　machine translation

机器脚踏车　jīqì jiǎotàchē　dial.　motocycle

机器人　jīqìrén　robot

机器油　jīqìyóu　lubricating oil; lubricant

机枪　jīqiāng　short for 机关枪 jīguānqiāng

机枪手　jīqiāngshǒu　machine gunner

机巧　jīqiǎo　adroit; ingenious: 她对记者的回答很～。 She gave the newsman an adroit reply. / 他～地避开了记者提出的这个敏感问题。 He adroitly avoided the sensitive question which the reporter raised.

机群　jīqún　a group of planes: 大～ air armada; air fleet

机上导弹　jīshàng dǎodàn　air-launched missile

机身　jīshēn　fuselage

机师　jīshī　① engineer ② dial. air pilot

机体　jītǐ　same as 有机体 yǒujītǐ

机头　jītóu　nose (of an aircraft)

机头炮　jītóupào　nose gun (of a fighter)

机尾　jīwěi　tail (of an aircraft)

机务人员　jīwù rényuán　① maintenance personnel ② ground crew

机械　jīxiè　① machinery; machine; mechanism: ～故障 mechanical failure (or breakdown) ② mechanical; inflexible; rigid: 别人的经验不能～地照搬。 Other people's experience should not be applied mechanically. / 你这样来理解他的话就太～了。 You're taking his words too literally.

机械动力学　jīxiè dònglìxué　mechanical kinetics

机械工程学　jīxiè gōngchéngxué　mechanical engineering

机械工业　jīxiè gōngyè　machine building

机械功　jīxiègōng　mechanical work

机械化　jīxièhuà　mechanize: 农业～ mechanization of agriculture; mechanization of farm work

机械化部队　jīxièhuà bùduì　mechanized force (or troops, unit)

机械加工　jīxiè jiāgōng　machining

机械论　jīxièlùn　same as 机械唯物主义 jīxièwéiwùzhǔyì

机械能　jīxiènéng　phys.　mechanical energy

机械师　jīxièshī　machinist

机械手　jīxièshǒu　mech.　manipulator: 仿效～ master-slave manipulator / 万能～ general-purpose manipulator

机械唯物主义　jīxièwéiwùzhǔyì　mechanical materialism

机械运动　jīxiè yùndòng　phys.　mechanical movement

机械制图　jīxiè zhìtú　mechanical drawing

机心[1]　jīxīn　diabolical scheme; cunning idea

机心[2]　jīxīn　inner works (of a watch, etc.)

机型　jīxíng　① type (of an aircraft) ② model (of a machine)

机要　jīyào　confidential: ～部门 departments in charge of confidential or important work / ～工作 confidential

机要秘书　jīyào mìshū　confidential secretary

机宜　jīyí　principles of action; guidelines: 面授机宜 miàn shòu jīyí

机翼　jīyì　wing (of an aircraft)

机油　jīyóu　engine oil; machine oil

机遇　jīyù　formal　favourable circumstances; opportunity: 新技术革命对我们的经济发展是一种新的～。 The new technological revolution presents new opportunities for economic growth in our country. / 他的成功是靠他的努力和一定的～。 His success was brought about by hard work and a certain amount of good luck.

机缘　jīyuán　good luck; lucky chance: ～凑巧 as luck would have it; by a lucky coincidence; by chance / 由于一个偶然的～，我和她相识了。 I met her because of a lucky coincidence.

机长　jīzhǎng　aircraft (or crew) commander

机罩　jīzhào　bonnet (of an aircraft)

机制[1]　jīzhì　machine-processed; machine-made: ～糖 machine-processed sugar / ～纸 machine-made paper

机制[2]　jīzhì　mechanism: 激发～ phys. excitation mechanism / 建立富有活力的管理体制和运行～ establish dynamic management systems and operating mechanisms

机智　jīzhì　quick-witted; resourceful: ～勇敢的侦察兵 brave and resourceful scouts / 领航员～地带领船只通过险滩。 The navigator skillfully guided the ship over the dangerous shoals.

机助翻译　jīzhù fānyì　machine-aided translation

机杼　jīzhù　liter.　① loom ② conception (of a piece of writing): 自出～ be original in conception

机子　jīzi　inf.　① loom ② a small machine (e.g. a sewing machine, a telephone) ③ trigger

机组　jīzǔ　① mech.　unit; set: 发电～ generating unit (or set) ② aircrew; flight crew

玑（璣）　jī　① liter. a pearl that is not quite round: 珠玑 zhūjī ② an ancient astronomical instrument

乱　jī　see 扶乱 fújī

肌　jī　muscle; flesh: 随意肌 suíyìjī

肌肤　jīfū　formal　(human) skin and muscle

肌肤甲错　jīfūjiǎcuò　Chin. med. scaly dry skin, a symptom of blood stasis; pellagra

肌腱　jījiàn　tendon

肌理　jīlǐ　formal　skin texture: ～细腻 fine-textured skin

肌瘤　jīliú　short for 肌肉肿瘤 jīròu zhǒngliú

肌肉　jīròu　muscle: 举重运动员～发达。 Weight lifters are muscular.

肌肉肿瘤　jīròu zhǒngliú　muscle tumor

肌肉注射　jīròu zhùshè　intramuscular injection

肌体　jītǐ　human body; organism

肌萎缩　jīwěisuō　muscular dystrophy; amyotrophy

矶（磯）　jī　a rock projecting over the water

鸡（鷄、雞）　jī　chicken: 公～ cock; rooster / 母～ hen / 雏～ chick; chicken / ～鸣而起 rise at cock-crow

鸡巴　jība　vulg.　cock (penis)

鸡蛋　jīdàn　(hen's) egg

鸡蛋糕　jīdàngāo　(sponge) cake

鸡蛋里挑骨头　jīdànlǐ tiāo gútou　look for a bone in an egg—look for a flaw where there's none to be found; find fault; nitpick

鸡蛋碰石头　jīdàn pèng shítou　(like) an egg striking a

rock—attack sb. far stronger than oneself; court destruction

鸡飞蛋打 jīfēi-dàndǎ the hen has flown away and the eggs in the coop are broken—all is lost

鸡公 jīgōng *dial.* cock; rooster

鸡冠 jīguān cockscomb

鸡冠花 jīguānhuā cockscomb (a flower)

鸡冠石 jīguānshí realgar

鸡霍乱 jīhuòluàn fowl cholera

鸡奸 jījiān sodomy; buggery

鸡口牛后 jīkǒu-niúhòu (also 鸡尸牛从 jīshī-niúcóng) see 宁为鸡口，无为牛后 nìng wéi jīkǒu, wú wéi niúhòu

鸡肋 jīlèi *liter.* chicken ribs—things of little value or interest: 味同～ taste like chicken ribs—be of little or no value

鸡零狗碎 jīlíng-gǒusuì in bits and pieces; fragmentary

鸡毛 jīmáo chicken feather

鸡毛掸子 jīmáo dǎnzi feather duster

鸡毛店 jīmáodiàn *old* a small and crude inn

鸡毛蒜皮 jīmáo-suànpí chicken feathers and garlic skins—trifles; trivialities: 你何苦为这点～的事跟他吵呢?Why quarrel with him over such a trifle?

鸡毛信 jīmáoxìn (in former times) a message with a feather attached as a sign of urgency

鸡毛帚 jīmáozhǒu *dial.* feather duster

鸡鸣狗盗 jīmíng-gǒudào (ability to) crow like a cock and snatch like a dog—get up to mean or petty tricks: ～之徒 mean people who resort to petty tricks

鸡鸣犬吠 jīmíng-quǎnfèi the crowing of cocks and the barking of dogs—country sounds

鸡内金 jīnèijīn *Chin. med.* the membrane of a chicken's gizzard

鸡皮疙瘩 jīpí gēda gooseflesh: 冻得我直起～. It was so cold I was gooseflesh all over. / 想起那可怕的情景，我浑身都起～. The thought of that horrible scene made my flesh crawl.

鸡皮鹤发 jīpí-hèfà wrinkled skin and white hair—advanced in age

鸡婆 jīpó *dial.* hen

鸡犬不惊 jī-quǎn bù jīng even fowls and dogs are not disturbed (said of excellent army discipline or of a state of peace and tranquillity)

鸡犬不留 jī-quǎn bù liú even fowls and dogs are not spared—ruthless mass slaughter

鸡犬不宁 jī-quǎn bù níng even fowls and dogs are not left in peace—general turmoil: 闹得家里～ stir the whole family into a tempest

鸡犬升天 jī-quǎn shēng tiān see 一人得道，鸡犬升天 yī rén dé dào, jī-quǎn shēng tiān

鸡犬之声相闻，老死不相往来 jī-quǎn zhī shēng xiāng wén, lǎo sǐ bù xiāng wǎnglái people do not visit each other all their lives, though the crowing of their cocks and the barking of their dogs are within hearing of each other

鸡肉 jīròu chicken (as food)

鸡头 jītóu chicken head (another name for 芡 qiàn ; so called from the appearance of the pods)

鸡头米 jītóumǐ another name for 芡实 qiànshí

鸡尾酒 jīwěijiǔ cocktail

鸡尾酒会 jīwěijiǔhuì cocktail party

鸡瘟 jīwēn chicken pest

鸡窝 jīwō chicken coop; henhouse; roost

鸡窝里飞出金凤凰 jīwōli fēichū jīnfèng·huáng a golden phoenix flying out of a henhouse—a person of humble origin rising to prominence

鸡血藤 jīxiěténg reticulate millettia (*Millettia reticulata*)

鸡心 jīxīn ① chicken's heart ② heart-shaped: ～领 V-neck ③ a heart-shaped pendant

鸡胸 jīxiōng *med.* pigeon breast; chicken breast

鸡眼 jīyǎn *med.* corn; clavus: ～膏 corn plaster

鸡杂 jīzá chicken giblets

鸡子儿 jīzǐr *dial.* (hen's) egg

鸡子 jīzi *dial.* chicken

奇

jī ① odd (number) ② *formal* a fractional amount (over that mentioned in a round number); odd lots: 五十有～ fifty odd ——see also qí

奇零 jīlíng *formal* a fractional amount (over that mentioned in a round number); odd lots

奇数 jīshù *math.* odd number

唧

jī spurt; squirt: ～了我一身水。 The water squirted all over me.

唧咕 jīgu same as 叽咕 jīgu

唧唧 jījī *onom.* the sound of insects chirping: 蟋蟀在草丛里～地叫。 Crickets are chirping in the grass.

唧唧喳喳 jījizhāzhā *onom.* the sound of birds chirping or people talking rapidly and indistinctly: 麻雀在外面～地叫。 Sparrows are twittering outside. / 别～的了，干点正经事吧。 Stop jabbering and get down to business. / 这几个女孩儿碰到一起就～说个没完。 Whenever these girls get together, they chatter away nonstop.

唧哝 jīnong talk in a low voice; whisper: 那孩子在妈妈耳边～了几句就跑出去了。 The boy whispered in his mother's ear and ran out of the room. / 别在下面～，有话站起来大声说。 Stop whispering. If you have something to say, then stand up and say it out loud.

唧筒 jītǒng pump

积(積)

jī ① amass; store up; accumulate: ～粮 store up grain / ～几十年的经验 accumulate experience over scores of years / ～小胜为大胜 Many small victories add up to a big one. ② long-standing; long-pending; age-old: 积案 jī'àn ③ *Chin. med.* indigestion (in infants and children): 这孩子有～了。 The child is suffering from indigestion. ④ *math.* product: 求～ find the product by multiplication

积案 jī'àn a long-pending case

积弊 jībì age-old malpractice; long-standing abuse: 这种迷信的风俗存在了很长的时间，～很深，改革起来比较复杂。 This form of superstition has existed for ages and is deeply rooted, so it's not so easy to bring about reform.

积不相能 jī bù xiāng néng have always been at variance; have never been on good terms; be always at loggerheads

积储 jīchǔ store up; lay up; stockpile

积存 jīcún store up; lay up; stockpile: ～的物资 goods in stock

积德 jīdé accumulate merit (by good works)

积非成是 jī fēi chéng shì same as 习非成是 xí fēi chéng shì

积肥 jīféi collect (farmyard) manure

积分 jīfēn *math.* integral: 定(不定)～ definite (indefinite) integral

积分方程 jīfēn fāngchéng integral equation

积分学 jīfēnxué integral calculus

积分仪 jīfēnyí *math.* integrator

积谷防饥 jī gǔ fáng jī store up grain against famine

积毁销骨 jī huǐ xiāo gǔ repeated calumny can bring about one's ruin

积极 jījí ① positive: 只有调动一切～因素，我们才能做好这项工作。 We can do the work well only by mobilizing all positive factors. / 对这项工程，希望大家提出～建议。 For this project, I hope that everyone will make positive suggestions. / 作出～贡献 make positive contributions ② active; energetic; vigorous: 他～工作受到奖励。 He was given an award for being a hard work-

er. / 我们要～地推进医药卫生事业。 We should take vigorous action to expand the medical and health services. / 他锻炼身体一向很～。 He has always been very keen on doing physical exercises. / 采取～措施 adopt vigorous measures

积极分子 jījífènzǐ activist; active element; enthusiast: 在建立村文化站的过程中，涌现出大批的～。 Large numbers of activists have come forward in the course of building the village cultural centre. / 体育运动的～ sport enthusiast

积极性 jījíxìng zeal; initiative; enthusiasm: 这样的天气去游泳，孩子们～并不高。 The children are not enthusiastic about swimming in such weather. / 只有让他们明白工作的重要性，才能调动他们的～。 Once you make them see the importance of their work, their enthusiasm will be aroused.

积渐 jījiàn gradually

积久 jījiǔ accumulate in the course of time: ～成习 form a habit or custom through long-repeated practice

积聚 jījù gather; accumulate; build up: 他把零用钱～起来，想买件礼物。 He saved up his pocket money in order to buy a gift. / 游击队在山上～力量，准备反攻。 The guerrilla forces were in the mountains gathering their strength and preparing for a counterattack. / 资本～ concentration of capital

积劳 jīláo formal be overworked for a very long period

积劳成疾 jīláo chéng jí fall ill from constant overwork

积累 jīlěi ① accumulate: 他在工作中～了丰富的经验。 He has accumulated a wealth of experience in his work. / 渊博的知识是一点点～起来的。 Profound knowledge is accumulated little by little. / 工厂发展生产，～资金。 The factory accumulated funds by developing production. ② econ. accumulation (for expanded reproduction): 逐年增加公共～和个人收入 increase public accumulation and personal income year by year / ～与消费 accumulation and consumption / ～率 rate of accumulation

积木 jīmù building blocks; toy bricks

积年 jīnián formal for many years: ～旧案 law cases which have piled up over the years

积年累月 jīnián-lěiyuè for years on end; year after year

积欠 jīqiàn ① have one's debts piling up: 我要尽快还清～的各种债务。 I want to clear up all my outstanding debts as soon as possible. ② outstanding debts; arrears: 还清～ clear up all outstanding debts

积善 jīshàn same as 积德 jīdé

积少成多 jī shǎo chéng duō many a little makes a mickle

积食 jīshí dial. (of children) have indigestion: 这孩子～了，不愿吃东西。 The child has indigestion and has lost his appetite.

积习 jīxí old habit; long-standing practice: ～难除。 It is difficult to get rid of deep-rooted habits. or Old habits die hard.

积蓄 jīxù ① put aside; save; accumulate: ～力量 accumulate strength ② savings: 她从不乱花钱，月月有～。 She is never extravagant and saves some money every month. / 他把～拿出来送给了这个老人。 He took out his savings and gave it all to the old man.

积雪 jīxuě accumulated snow: 路上～很深。 The roads are deep in snow.

积压 jīyā keep long in stock; overstock: 长期～的物资 materials kept too long in stock / 不要～国家资金。 Don't let state funds lie idle. / 把～的事情做完 clear off arrears of work / ～在心头的愤怒 pent-up anger / 因为质量不好，所以产品～，卖不出去。 The goods have been piling up in stock and can't be sold because of poor quality.

积羽沉舟 jī yǔ chén zhōu enough feathers can sink a boat—tiny things may gather into a mighty force; minor offences unchecked may bring disaster

积雨云 jīyǔyún meteorol. cumulonimbus

积怨 jīyuàn accumulated rancour; piled-up grievances: 他一贯欺压邻里，～甚多。 He always rode roughshod over his neighbours and incurred widespread resentment.

积云 jīyún meteorol. cumulus

积攒 jīzǎn inf. save (or collect) bit by bit: ～邮票 collect stamps / 这家业是一点一滴地～起来的。 The family fortune has been accumulated bit by bit. / 他省吃俭用，～学费。 He economized on food and clothing to save for his tuition.

积重难返 jī zhòng nán fǎn bad old practices die hard; ingrained habits are hard to change

积铢累寸 jīzhū-lěicùn save every tiny bit; accumulate bit by bit

笄 jī arch. hairpin

屐 jī ① clogs: 木屐 mùjī ② shoes in general: 草～ straw sandals

屐履 jīlǚ shoes

姬 jī ① a complimentary term for women used in ancient China ② a name used in ancient China for a concubine: ～妾 concubines / 宠～ a concubine in high favour ③ arch. a professional female singer: 歌～ singing girl; female entertainer / 舞～ a professional female dancer ④ (Jī) a surname

姬蜂 jīfēng ichneumon wasp

勋 jī achievement; accomplishment; merit

基 jī ① base; foundation: 路基 lùjī / 房基 fángjī ② basic; key; primary; cardinal: 基调 jīdiào ③ chem. radical; base; group: 自由～ free radical / 石蜡～ paraffin base

基本 jīběn ① foundation: 人民是国家的～。 The people are the foundation of a nation. ② basic; fundamental; elementary: 他们之间存在着～分歧。 Fundamental differences exist between them. / ～原则 basic principles / ～观点 basic concept / ～知识 elementary (or rudimentary) knowledge ③ main; essential: 这个车间一个技术人员也没有，不具备生产的～条件。 There's not one trained technician in the whole workshop, so it doesn't have the basic conditions necessary for production. ④ basically; in the main; on the whole; by and large: 那项工程已～完工。 The project has been basically completed. / 这部电影～上是好的。 This film is good on the whole. / 情况～属实。 It has been found to be basically true.

基本词汇 jīběn cíhuì basic vocabulary; basic word-stock

基本工资 jīběn gōngzī basic wage (or salary)

基本功 jīběngōng basic training; basic skill; essential technique: 练好～ have a thorough training in basic skills; master the basic skills: 他的语言～很扎实。 He has a solid mastery of basic language skills.

基本建设 jīběn jiànshè capital construction: ～的规模要和国力相适应。 The scale of capital construction must be suited to the overall capabilities of the nation.

基本粒子 jīběn lìzǐ phys. elementary particle

基本路线 jīběn lùxiàn basic line

基本矛盾 jīběn máodùn fundamental contradiction

基层 jīcéng basic level; primary level; grass-roots unit: 领导深入～了解情况。 The leading cadre went down to the grass-roots level to gain an understanding of the situation. / 镇人民代表大会是我国～政权组织。 The

people's congress of a town is an organization of political power at the grass-roots level in our country. /～单位 basic unit; grass-roots unit; unit at the grass-roots level /～干部 cadre at the basic (*or* grass-roots) level /～选举 elections at the basic level

基础 jīchǔ ① foundation; base; basis: 工人们正在为新校动打～。 The workmen are laying the foundations of the new school. /物质～ material base /理论～ theoretical basis /农业是国民经济的～。 Agriculture is the foundation of the national economy. /在原有的～上提高一步 make improvements on what has already been achieved /在和平共处五项原则的～上,同各国建立和发展关系 establish and develop our relations with other countries on the basis of the Five Principles of Peaceful Coexistence /他正在努力学习,为日后的研究工作打下牢固的～。 He is studying hard in order to lay a good foundation for his future research work. ② short for 经济基础 jīngjì jīchǔ

基础代谢 jīchǔ dàixiè *biol.* basal metabolism
基础工业 jīchǔ gōngyè basic industry
基础教育 jīchǔ jiàoyù elementary education
基础科学 jīchǔ kēxué basic science
基础课 jīchǔkè basic courses (of a college curriculum)
基础理论 jīchǔ lǐlùn basic theory
基础设施 jīchǔ shèshī infrastructure
基础知识 jīchǔ zhīshi rudimentary (*or* elementary) knowledge: 他对计算机缺乏起码的～。 He lacks even a rudimentary knowledge of computers.
基底细胞癌 jīdǐxìbāo'ái basal-cell carcinoma
基地 jīdì base: 爬到山顶以后,我们就下山回到～宿营。 After we had reached the top of the mountain, we returned to our base camp for the night. /商品粮～ marketable grain base /原料～ source of raw materials
基点 jīdiǎn ① centre: 建立科研～ set up scientific research centres ② basic point; starting point: 分析问题是解决问题的～。 The analysis of a problem is the starting point for its solution. /我们的方针要放在自力更生的～上。 Our policy should rest on the basis of self-reliance. ③ *surveying & drawing* base point (BP)
基调 jīdiào ① *mus.* fundamental key; main key ② keynote: 他讲话的～是团结。 The keynote of his speech was unity. /这部小说的～是健康的,鼓舞人向上的。 The main message of this novel is a healthy one—it encourages people to improve themselves. ③ *photog.* key tone
基督 Jīdū Christ
基督教 Jīdūjiào the Christian religion; Christianity
基督教女青年会 Jīdūjiào Nǚqīngniánhuì the Young Women's Christian Association (Y. W. C. A.)
基督教青年会 Jīdūjiào Qīngniánhuì the Young Men's Christian Association (Y. M. C. A.)
基督徒 Jīdūtú Christian
基尔特 jī'ěrtè guild
基肥 jīféi base manure; base fertilizer
基干 jīgàn backbone; hard core: ～民兵 primary militia; core members of the militia
基极 jījí *electron.* base
基价 jījià base price
基建 jījiàn short for 基本建设 jīběn jiànshè
基金 jījīn fund: 积累(消费)～ accumulation (consumption) fund /福利～ welfare fund /教育～ education fund /救济～ fund for relief /专用～ fund for special use
基金会 jījīnhuì foundation: 残疾人福利～ welfare foundation for the disabled
基里巴斯 Jīlǐbāsī Kiribati
基诺族 Jīnuòzú the Jino nationality, or the Jinos, inhabiting Yunnan Province
基期 jīqī *statistics* base period

基色 jīsè primary colours
基石 jīshí foundation stone; cornerstone: 剩余价值学说是马克思经济理论的～。 The doctrine of surplus value is the cornerstone of Marx's economic theory.
基数 jīshù ① *math.* cardinal number ② *statistics* base: 以一九六五年的产量为～ taking the output of 1965 as the base
基态 jītài *phys.* ground state: 原子的～ atomic ground state
基线 jīxiàn *surveying & drawing* datum line
基岩 jīyán bedrock
基业 jīyè property, inheritance, family estate, etc., considered as a foundation on which to build
基因 jīyīn *biol.* gene: 等位～ allele /显性～ dominant gene /隐性～ recessive gene /～突变 gene mutation /～型 genotype
基因工程学 jīyīn gōngchéngxué same as 遗传工程学 yíchuán gōngchéngxué
基音 jīyīn *mus.* fundamental tone
基于 jīyú *prep.* because of; in view of: ～目前这种情况,我们不得不修改原来的计划。 In view of the present situation, we'll have to revise our original plan. /～以上理由,我不赞同他的意见。 For the above-mentioned reasons, I cannot agree with him.
基准 jīzhǔn ① *surveying & drawing* datum: ～点(面,线) datum point (plane, line) ② standard; criterion
基准兵 jīzhǔnbīng *mil.* guide; base marker

犄 jī see below
犄角 jījiǎo *inf.* corner: 桌子～ the corner of a table /屋子～里有一个衣架。 A clothes tree stands in a corner of the room.
犄角 jījiao *inf.* horn: 牛～ ox horn /鹿～ antler

赍(賫) jī *formal* ① hold (in mind); harbour ② give
赍志而没 jī zhì ér mò die without fulfilling one's ambitions

稽 jī a surname

期(朞) jī *arch.* anniversary ——see also qī

缉 jī seize; arrest: 通缉 tōngjī ——see also qī
缉捕 jībǔ seize; arrest: 公安人员在～逃犯。 The police are pursuing the escaped prisoner.
缉拿 jīná seize; arrest; apprehend: ～凶手 apprehend the murderer /已将叛乱分子一一～归案。All the rebels have been brought to justice.
缉私 jīsī seize smugglers or smuggled goods; suppress smuggling
缉私船 jīsīchuán anti-smuggling patrol boat; coast guard vessel
缉私人员 jīsī rényuán anti-contraband personnel

跻(隮) jī *formal* ascend; mount: 使中国科学～于世界先进科学之列 enable China's science to rank among the world's most advanced
跻身 jīshēn ascend; mount: 中国队夺得四枚金牌,～世界四强之列。 The Chinese team captured four gold medals which put them in the ranks of the top four.

畸 jī ① lopsided; unbalanced ② irregular; abnormal: 畸形 jīxíng ③ *formal* a fractional amount (over that mentioned in a round number); odd lots: 畸零 jīlíng
畸变 jībiàn *radio* distortion
畸零 jīlíng same as 奇零 jīlíng
畸轻畸重 jīqīng-jīzhòng attach too much weight to this

and too little to that; lopsided; now too much, now too little

畸形 jīxíng ① *med.* deformity; malformation: 先天～ congenital malformation / 肢体发育～ have deformed limbs / ～儿 a congenitally deformed baby ② lopsided; unbalanced; abnormal: 这种经济～发展的现象已经纠正了。 The occurrence of that type of lopsided economic development has been checked.

箕

jī ① dustpan: 簸箕 bòji ② winnowing basket; winnowing fan ③ loop (of a fingerprint) ④ the seventh of the twenty-eight constellations (二十八宿) into which the celestial sphere was divided in ancient Chinese astronomy (consisting of four stars in the shape of a sieve in Sagittarius)

箕斗 jīdǒu *min.* skip

箕踞 jījù *arch.* sit (on the floor) with one's legs stretched out

稽¹

jī ① check; examine; investigate: 有案可稽 yǒu àn kě jī ② recriminate; argue; dispute

稽²

jī *formal* delay; procrastinate: 稽延 jīyán
——see also qǐ

稽查 jīchá ① check (to prevent smuggling, tax evasion, etc.) ② an official engaged in such work; customs officer

稽核 jīhé check; examine: ～账目 audit accounts

稽考 jīkǎo *formal* ascertain; verify: 这个名称起于何时, 已经无从～了。 The date of origin of this name is unascertainable.

稽留 jīliú *formal* delay; detain: 他因事在沪～, 不能如期归来。 He will not be able to return from Shanghai on schedule because he was detained on business.

稽留热 jīliúrè *med.* continued fever

稽延 jīyán *formal* delay; procrastinate: ～时日 be considerably delayed

齏（齏）

jī *formal* ① fine; powdery: 齏粉 jīfěn ② finely chopped ginger, garlic, etc.

齏粉 jīfěn *formal* fine powder; broken bits: 碾成～ be ground to dust

畿

jī see below

畿辅 jīfǔ *arch.* the environs of a capital

激

jī ① swash; surge; dash: 海水冲击礁石, ～起高高的浪花。 Swashing against the rocks, the breakers sent up a fountain of spray. ② arouse; stimulate; excite: ～起我们学习科学技术的热情 arouse our enthusiasm for studying science and technology / ～于义愤 be stirred by righteous indignation / ～起公愤 arouse public indignation / ～起强烈的反抗 evoke strong opposition / ～起了一场风波 cause a commotion ③ sharp; fierce; violent: 激战 jīzhàn ④ fall ill from getting wet: 他叫雨～着了。 He caught a chill from getting wet in the rain. ⑤ *dial.* chill (by putting in ice water, etc.): 把西瓜放在冷水里～一～ chill a watermelon in cold water

激昂 jī'áng excited and indignant; roused: 群情～。 Public feeling was aroused (*or* ran high). / 会场上响起～嘹亮的歌声。 The meeting hall resounded with impassioned, lusty singing.

激昂慷慨 jī'áng kāngkǎi same as 慷慨激昂 kāngkǎi jī'áng

激变 jībiàn change violently: 政局发生～, 他在这里耽不下去了。 The political situation changed drastically, and he couldn't stay here any longer.

激波 jībō *phys.* shock wave

激磁 jīcí same as 励磁 lìcí

激荡 jīdàng agitate; surge; rage: 海水～。 The sea surged. / 他的呼唤在山谷里～。 His shout echoed across the mountain valley. / 知道这消息以后, 她心潮～。 When she heard the news, her heart leapt. / 雄壮的歌声～人心。 The magnificent singing stirred people's hearts.

激动 jīdòng excite; stir; agitate: 受到这样的屈辱, 他情绪～, 气得发抖。 Being slandered that way made his blood boil, and he shook with anger. / 他获得冠军, ～得流下眼泪。 When he won the championship, he was moved to tears. / 当这～人心的消息传开以后, 全城沸腾。 When this sensational piece of news spread, the whole town was seething with excitement.

激发 jīfā ① arouse; stimulate; set off: 他的榜样～了同学们学数学的热情。 The example he set aroused other students' enthusiasm for mathematics. / 这出戏～了观众的爱国心。 This play aroused the audience's patriotism. ② *phys.* excite: 热～ thermal excitation / ～机制 excitation mechanism / ～能级 excitation level / ～态 excited state

激奋 jīfèn rouse sb. to action: 好消息传来, 人心～。 When we heard the good news, everyone felt encouraged.

激愤 jīfèn wrathful; indignant: 心情～ be filled with indignation

激光 jīguāng laser: ～波束制导武器 laser beam riding weapon / ～唱机 compact disc player / ～唱片 compact disc (CD) / ～测距仪 laser range finder / ～测云仪 laser ceilometer / ～导弹跟踪系统 laser missile tracking system / ～干涉仪 laser interferometer / ～光谱学 laser spectroscopy / ～束 laser beam / ～显微光谱分析仪 laser microspectral analyser / ～照明器 laser illuminator / ～准直仪 laser collimator

激化 jīhuà sharpen; intensify; become acute: 两国之间的矛盾进一步～。 The contradictions between the two countries are intensifying.

激活 jīhuó *phys.* activation: ～剂 activator / ～媒质 active medium / ～能 activation energy

激将法 jījiàngfǎ prodding (*or* goading) sb. into action (as by ridicule, sarcasm, etc.): 他故意说我球打得很差, 想用～使我同意和他比赛。 He tried to goad me into playing a match with him by taunting me and saying that I was a terrible player.

激进 jījìn radical: 他主张马上来个彻底改变, 我觉得这意见太～了。 He advocates making immediate drastic changes, but I think this idea is too radical.

激进派 jījìnpài radicals

激浪 jīlàng turbulent waves

激励 jīlì ① encourage; impel; urge: 同学们相互学习, 相互～。 Classmates learn from each other and encourage each other. / 用革命先烈的英雄事迹～自己 draw inspiration from the heroic deeds of the revolutionary martyrs / 为国争光的志愿～运动员刻苦训练。 The desire to win glory for their country impels the athletes to train diligently. ② *electron.* drive; excitation: ～器 driver; exciter

激烈 jīliè intense; sharp; fierce; acute: ～的争论 heated argument / 一场～的比赛 a closely fought game; a gruelling match / 争吵得很～ quarrel bitterly / 这一仗打得很～。 It was a fierce fight. / 两派爆发了～的冲突。 A fierce conflict erupted between the two factions.

激灵 jīling *dial.* give a start: 那恶梦吓得他一～就醒了。 He woke up from the bad dream with a start.

激流 jīliú torrent; rapids; turbulent current: 这里到处是～、险滩, 行船要加倍留意。 There are rapids and dangerous shoals throughout the area, so boats must be navigated with the utmost care.

激怒 jīnù enrage; infuriate; exasperate: 种族主义者的暴行～了人民。 The atrocities committed by the racists

enraged the people. / ～之下，他一甩门走了。 Infuriated, he slammed the door and left. / 他一顶嘴更把父亲～了。 His back talk further infuriated his father.

激切 jīqiè *formal* (of language) impassioned; vehement: 言辞～ impassioned language

激情 jīqíng intense emotion; fervour; passion; enthusiasm: 他们的演出充满了爱国～。 Their performance was permeated with patriotic fervour. / 他满怀～，歌唱着自己美丽的家乡。 He passionately sang a song of his beloved hometown.

激赏 jīshǎng *formal* highly appreciate; greatly admire

激素 jīsù hormone

激扬 jīyáng ① short for 激浊扬清 jīzhuó-yángqīng ② encourage; urge: ～士气 boost morale ③ inspired; excited: 会场上响起了～的欢呼声。 The assembly hall was filled with the sound of excited cheering.

激越 jīyuè intense; vehement; loud and strong: 草原上扬起清亮～的歌声。 Songs were heard ringing loud and clear over the grasslands. / 他感情～，提笔作诗。 In the grip of intense emotion, he picked up his pen and wrote a poem.

激增 jīzēng increase sharply; soar; shoot up: 化肥的产量～。 The output of chemical fertilizer has soared. / 粮食每亩产量从五百斤～至九百斤。 The per-*mu* grain yield has jumped from 500 to 900 *jin*. / 经济危机加剧，失业人数～。 With the deepening of the economic crisis, unemployment shot up.

激战 jīzhàn fierce fighting

激浊扬清 jīzhuó-yángqīng drain away the mud and bring in fresh water—drive out evil and usher in good; eliminate vice and exalt virtue

激子 jīzǐ *phys.* exciton

鏨 jī see 土鏨 tǔjī

羁（羈） jī *formal* ① bridle; headstall: 无～之马 a horse without a bridle—running wild ② control; restrain: 放荡不羁 fàngdàng bùjī ③ stay; delay; detain: 事务～身 be detained by one's duties

羁绊 jībàn *formal* trammels; fetters; yoke: 挣脱旧思想的～break the fetters of old ideas; smash the shackles of convention / 她为家务所～，未能前往。 She was tied up with housework and couldn't go.

羁勒 jīlè *formal* tie; bind up; fetter

羁留 jīliú ① stay (in a strange place); stop over: 在穗～三日 stop over in Guangzhou for three days ② keep in custody; detain

羁旅 jīlǚ *formal* stay long in a strange place; live in a strange land

羁縻 jīmí *formal* keep (vassal states, etc.) under control

羁押 jīyā *formal* detain; take into custody

jí

及[1] jí ① reach; come up to: 目力所～ as far as the eye can reach / 水深～腰。 The water came up to one's waist (*or* was waist-deep). ② in time for: 及时 jíshí

及[2] jí *conj.* and; as well as: 图书、仪器～其他 books, instruments and other things / 工人、农民～士兵 workers, peasants and soldiers / 地里种着小麦、油菜～其他作物。 The fields are under wheat, rape and other crops. / 句子的主要成分～其语法功能 major sentence elements and their grammatical functions

及第 jídì pass an imperial examination

及格 jígé pass a test, examination, etc.; pass: 他的历史课考试～了。 He passed the history test. / 中国学校一般采用百分制，六十分为～。 Most schools in China use the hundred percentage point system, with 60 percent as the passing grade.

及冠 jíguān *arch.* (of a young man) come of age

及笄 jíjī *arch.* (of a girl) reach the age of fifteen, i.e. come of age (in former times girls at fifteen began to wear their hair bound up and held in place by a pin)

及龄 jílíng reach a required age: ～儿童 children who have reached school age

及门弟子 jímén dìzǐ *formal* disciples who are directly taught by the master

及时 jíshí ① timely; in time; seasonable: 要～下种。 Sowing must be done at the right time. / 这场雪很～。 This snow has come at the right time. ② promptly; without delay: ～纠正错误 correct a mistake promptly / ～汇报 report without delay / 要～解决交通拥挤问题。 The problem of traffic congestion must be dealt with in good time. / 今晚有暴风，要～报告渔民。 Tonight there will be storm force winds. We must notify the fishermen without delay.

及时行乐 jíshí xínglè enjoy life while ye may

及时雨 jíshíyǔ timely rain—help rendered in the nick of time; timely help: 我们正缺这方面的技术，这篇介绍文章真如～一般。 We just happen to lack this type of technology right now. This introductory article has come just in the nick of time.

及物动词 jíwù dòngcí *gram.* transitive verb

及早 jízǎo at an early date; as soon as possible; before it is too late: 有病要～治。 When you are ill, see the doctor as soon as possible. / 一有消息，请～通知我。 As soon as you get any news, please let me know. / 既然知道错了，就要～回头。 Now that you know you are wrong, you should mend your ways without delay

及至 jízhì *conj.* up to; until: ～宋代，方有刻本。 Block-printed books did not appear until the Song Dynasty (960—1279). / 我们动身太迟，～赶到机场，班机已经起飞了。 We started off too late. By the time we got to the airport the plane had already taken off.

汲 jí draw (water): 从井里～水 draw water from a well

汲汲 jíjí *formal* (usu. followed by 于) anxious; avid: ～于个人名利 crave personal fame and gain

汲取 jíqǔ draw; derive: 植物通过根部～养分。 Plants assimilate nutriment through their roots. / 我们可以～其他地方的经验。 We can draw on the experience of other regions.

吉 jí ① lucky; auspicious; propitious: 万事大吉 wànshì dàjí ② (Jí) short for 吉林 Jílín ③ (Jí) a surname

吉卜赛人 Jíbǔsàirén Gypsy

吉布提 Jíbùtí Djibouti

吉布提人 Jíbùtírén Djiboutian

吉尔吉斯斯坦 Jí'ěrjísīsītǎn Kirghizstan

吉光片羽 jíguāng piàn yǔ a fragment of a highly treasured relic

吉利 jílì lucky; auspicious; propitious: 门上贴个"喜"字，取个～。 Put the character 喜 on the door for good luck.

吉林 Jílín Jilin (Province)

吉普车 jípǔchē jeep

吉期 jíqī wedding day: 什么时候请我们喝喜酒啊？～定了没有？ When will you be inviting us to your wedding? Have you set a date yet? *or* When are we going to wish you joy? Have you fixed the happy date yet?

吉庆 jíqìng an auspicious occasion; a happy occasion

吉庆有余 jíqìng yǒu yú auspicious happiness in over-

measure (*or* in superabundance)

吉人天相 jírén tiānxiàng　Heaven stands by the good man

吉日 jírì　auspicious day; lucky day

吉他 jítā　guitar

吉祥 jíxiáng　lucky; auspicious; propitious: 过年了, 按老风俗, 见面都要说一些～话。It's the lunar New Year. According to the old custom, when you meet someone, you should say a few auspicious words. / 饺子像元宝, 吃了～如意! Dumplings symbolize silver ingots. Eat them and you'll have good luck.

吉祥物 jíxiángwù　mascot

吉星高照 jíxīng gāo zhào　be blessed by a lucky star

吉凶 jí-xiōng　good or ill luck

吉凶未卜 jí-xiōng wèi bǔ　one's fate is in the balance; fate unknown: 他们在海上遇上了大风暴, 至今尚无消息, ～。They've met with a storm at sea, and we haven't had any news of them yet. Their fate is still unknown.

吉兆 jízhào　good omen; propitious sign: 今年一月份买卖就不错, 这是个～。This year began auspiciously with good trade figures for January. / 妈妈听见喜鹊在房上叫, 觉得是个～。Mother heard a magpie call from the roof and took it for a good omen.

岌

岌 jí　*formal* (of a mountain) lofty; towering

岌岌 jíjí　*formal* precarious: ～不可终日 in grave danger; in a critical condition

岌岌可危 jíjí kě wēi　in imminent danger

级

级 jí　① level; rank; grade: 各～党组织 Party organizations at all levels / 大使～会谈 talks at ambassadorial level / 甲～产品 grade A products; first-class products / 三～工 grade-3 worker / 一～战备 No. 1 alert / 七～地震 an earthquake of magnitude 7 (on the Richter scale) / 七～风 force 7 wind (on the Beaufort scale) ② any of the yearly divisions of a school course; grade; class; form: 同～不同班 be in different classes of the same grade ③ step: 石～ stone steps / 拾～而登 follow the steps up ④ *m.* (for steps, etc.): 十几～台阶 a flight of a dozen steps ⑤ *gram.* degree: 比较～ the comparative degree / 最高～ the superlative degree

级别 jíbié　rank; level; grade; scale: 外交～ diplomatic rank / 工资～ wage scale; grade on the wage scale / 她的～比我高。She is above me in rank. / 她是什么～的干部? What rank of cadre is she?

级差地租 jíchā dìzū　differential (land) rent

级间分离 jíjiān fēnlí　*space* stage separation

级联 jílián　*elec.* cascade: ～管 cascade tube

级任 jírèn　form master; teacher in charge of a grade

级数 jíshù　*math.* progression; series

极 (極)

极 jí　① the utmost point; extremity: 愚蠢之～ be the height of folly / ～而言之 talk in extreme terms ② pole: 南极 nánjí / 阴极 yīnjí / 极地 jídì ③ do one's utmost: ～一时之盛 reach a temporary magnificence ④ extreme; of the highest degree: 极度 jídù / 极量 jíliàng ⑤ *adv.* extremely; to the greatest extent; exceedingly: ～好(快、慢) extremely good (fast, slow) / ～重要 of the utmost importance / ～少数 a tiny minority; only a few; a handful / 给予～大的注意 give maximum attention to; pay very close attention to / ～少例外 with few exceptions / 这件事～能说明问题。This incident is very illustrative (of the issue in question). / 我厂～需要这种钢材。Our factory is badly in need of this kind of steel. / 这样操作机器～不安全。It's absolutely unsafe if you operate the machine this way. / 我最近忙～了。I've been extremely busy lately. / 这本书有意思～了。The book is very interesting. / 他对你的工

作满意～了。He's thoroughly satisfied with your work.

极板 jíbǎn　*elec.* plate

极地 jídì　polar region: ～航行 arctic navigation; polar air navigation

极点 jídiǎn　the limit; the extreme; the utmost: 感动到了～ be extremely moved / 蛮横无理到了～ reach the height of truculence

极度 jídù　① *adv.* extremely; exceedingly; to the utmost: 他～兴奋, 一夜没睡着。He was so elated that he couldn't sleep all night. / ～疲劳 be extremely tired; be overcome with fatigue ② the limit; the extreme; the utmost

极端 jíduān　① extreme: 对他的能力应该有个正确的估价, 不要从一个～走到另一个～。You should make a correct evaluation of his ability. Don't go from one extreme to the other. ② *adv.* extremely; exceedingly: 灾区～需要食品。The disaster area was in dire need of food. / ～仇视 show extreme hatred for / ～困难 exceedingly difficult / ～贫困 in dire poverty / ～腐败 rotten to the core / 对工作～负责任 have a boundless sense of responsibility in one's work / ～个人主义者 out-and-out egoist / ～民主化 ultra-democracy

极光 jíguāng　*astron.* aurora; polar lights ——see also 北极光 běijíguāng; 南极光 nánjíguāng

极化 jíhuà　*phys.* polarization: ～张量 polarization tensor

极口 jíkǒu　in highest terms: ～称赞 praise lavishly

极乐鸟 jílèniǎo　bird of paradise

极乐世界 jílè shìjiè　*Buddhism* the Land of Ultimate Bliss

极力 jílì　*adv.* do one's utmost; spare no effort: 我们将～避免发生事故。We'll do our utmost to avoid accidents. / ～劝阻 try very hard to dissuade sb. from doing sth. / ～吹捧 laud sb. to the skies / ～鼓吹 vigorously publicize (an erroneous theory, etc.); clamorously advocate / ～扩大 expand to the maximum / ～缩小 reduce to the minimum; minimize

极量 jíliàng　*med.* maximum dose

极目 jímù　look as far as the eye can see: ～远眺 gaze far into the distance (from a high place, as a mountaintop)

极品 jípǐn　*formal* highest grade; best quality: ～绿茶 best quality green tea / 关东人多号称～。The ginseng of northeast China is known to be the best.

极谱 jípǔ　*phys.* polarogram: ～分析 polarographic analysis / ～仪 polarograph

极其 jíqí　*adv.* most; extremely; exceedingly: 他对这个问题的看法～荒唐。His views on this subject are absolutely ridiculous. / 吸烟对身体～有害。Smoking is extremely harmful to your health. / 他的评论～深刻。His comments were most penetrating.

极圈 jíquān　polar circle ——see also 北极圈 běijíquān; 南极圈 nánjíquān

极权主义 jíquánzhǔyì　totalitarianism

极盛 jíshèng　the highest (point of development): 在古埃及文明的～时期 at the height of ancient Egyptian civilization / 在他精力～的时期 in the prime of his life / 唐朝是中国旧诗的～时期。The Tang Dynasty was the golden age of classical Chinese poetry.

极限 jíxiàn　① the limit; the maximum: 这辆卡车的载重量已达到了～。This truck has already reached the limit of its load capacity. / ～负载 *elec.* limit load / ～压力 *phys.* limiting pressure ② *math.* limit

极刑 jíxíng　capital punishment; the death penalty: 处以～ sentence sb. to death

极夜 jíyè　polar night

极右 jíyòu　ultra-Right: ～势力 ultra-Right forces

极值 jízhí　*math.* extreme value

极致 jízhì　ultimate attainment; highest achievement

极"左" jí"zuǒ" ultra-"Left": 以～的面貌出现 put on an extremely "Left" front / ～分子 ultra-"Leftist" / ～思潮 ultra-"Left" trend of thought

即¹

jí ① approach; reach; be near: 可望而不可即 kě wàng ér bùkě jí ② assume; undertake: 即位 jíwèi ③ at present; in the immediate future: 在即 zàijí ④ prompted by the occasion: 即兴 jíxìng

即²

jí *formal* ① be; mean; namely: 春节～农历新年。The Spring Festival is the lunar New Year. / 非此～彼。It must be either this or that. / 对旧中国的许多大学生来说, 毕业～失业。For many college students in old China, graduation meant unemployment. / 元代建都于大都, ～今之北京。The Yuan Dynasty established its capital in Dadu, or present-day Beijing. ② *adv.* promptly; at once: 闻过～改 correct one's mistake as soon as it is pointed out / 招之～来 be on call at any hour / 稍加修改～可发排。After a few minor revisions we can send it off to be printed. / 以上问题盼～答复。We expect prompt answers to the above questions. ③ *conj.* even; even if: ～遇困难, 亦应按期完成任务。We should fulfill the mission even if we run up against difficulties.

即便 jíbiàn *conj.* even; even if; even though: ～你有理, 也不应该发火呀! You shouldn't have lost your temper even if you were in the right.

即或 jíhuò *conj.* even; even if; even though: ～是那样, 我也不愿求人帮忙。Even should that be the case, I wouldn't ask for help.

即将 jíjiāng *adv.* be about to; be on the point of; soon: 比赛～开始。The match is about to begin. / 水电站～竣工。The hydroelectric station is nearing completion. / 国庆节～来临。It will soon be National Day. / 胜利～到来。Victory is at hand.

即景 jíjǐng *liter.* (of a literary or artistic work) be inspired by what one sees: 西湖～ glimpses of the West Lake

即景生情 jíjǐng shēng qíng the scene touches a chord in one's heart: 他～, 赋诗一首。The scene moved him to compose a poem.

即景诗 jíjǐngshī extempore verse

即刻 jíkè *adv.* at once; immediately; instantly: 警察～出发, 火速赶到出事现场。The police left immediately, and rushed to the scene of the accident.

即令 jílìng *conj.* even; even if; even though

即期 jíqī *econ.* immediate; spot: ～付现 immediate (or prompt) cash payment / ～外汇 spot exchange / ～汇价 spot rate

即日 jírì *formal* ① this or that very day: 本条例自～起施行。The regulations come into force (or go into effect) as of today. ② within the next few days: 本片～放映。The film will be shown within the next few days.

即若 jíruò *formal* even; even if; even though

即时 jíshí *adv.* immediately; forthwith

即使 jíshǐ *conj.* even; even if; even though: ～下雨我也去。I'll go anyway even if it rains. / ～条件再好, 也还要靠自己努力。No matter how favourable the conditions are, we'll still rely on our own efforts. / 今年的粮食～不能达到亩产一千斤, 也还能打个八百斤。The per *mu* yield of grain for this year can be at least eight hundred *jin*, if not one thousand. / ～跟我没有关系, 我也要管。I shall make it my business even if it has nothing to do with me.

即事 jíshì write out of inspiration

即位 jíwèi *formal* ascend the throne: 清德宗1875年～, 定年号为光绪。The Emperor Dezong of the Qing Dynasty ascended the throne in 1875, and chose the reign title of Guangxu.

即席 jíxí *formal* ① impromptu; extemporaneous: ～赋诗一首 compose a poem impromptu; improvise a poem / ～讲话 speak impromptu; make an impromptu (or extemporaneous) speech ② take one's seat (at a dinner table, etc.)

即兴 jíxìng impromptu; extemporaneous: ～之作 an improvisation

即兴曲 jíxìngqǔ *mus.* impromptu

即兴诗 jíxìngshī extempore verse

即以其人之道, 还治其人之身 jí yǐ qí rén zhī dào, huán zhì qí rén zhī shēn deal with a man as he deals with you; pay a person back in his own coin

亟

jí *formal* urgently; anxiously; earnestly: ～盼 earnestly hope / ～欲 desire most ardently; want very much / ～待解决的重大问题 important problems demanding prompt solution / ～须纠正 must be speedily put right ——see also qì

佶

jí *formal* robust and sturdy

佶屈聱牙 jíqū áoyá full of difficult, unpronounceable words: 这文章念起来～, 很不顺口。With so many unpronounceable words, the article doesn't make smooth reading.

诘

jí see below ——see also jié

诘屈聱牙 jíqū áoyá same as 佶屈聱牙 jíqū áoyá

急

jí ① impatient; anxious: ～着要出发 be impatient to set out ② worry: 你怎么来得这么晚, 真把人～死啦! Why are you so late? We were worried to death about you. ③ irritated; annoyed; nettled: 你老唠叨他, 会把他弄～的。If you keep nagging him, you'll make him very annoyed. / 我没想到他真～了。I didn't expect him to get angry. ④ fast; rapid; violent: 水流很～。The current is swift. or It's a strong current. / 雨下得正～。It's raining hard. / ～转弯 make a sharp turn ⑤ urgent; pressing: 事情很～, 必须立即处理。The matter is pressing (or urgent) and must be dealt with at once. / 他走得很～。He left in a hurry. ⑥ urgency; emergency: 应急 yìngjí ⑦ be eager to help: ～人之难 be eager to help those in need / ～病人之所急 be eager to meet the needs of the patients; put oneself in a patient's position

急巴巴 jíbābā anxious; impatient

急板 jíbǎn *mus.* presto

急变 jíbiàn a sudden turn of events; emergency or crisis

急病 jíbìng acute disease

急不可待 jí bùkě dài too impatient to wait; extremely anxious: 他一拿到信, 在路上就～地拆开看了。As soon as he was handed the letter, he anxiously ripped it open and read it right on the street.

急茬儿 jíchár *inf.* an urgent matter

急赤白脸 jíchìbáiliǎn *dial.* being very agitated and looking ugly in the face: 两个人～地吵个没完。The two never stopped quarrelling, fuming and red in the face.

急促 jícù ① hurried; rapid: ～的脚步声 hurried footsteps / ～的枪声 rapid gunfire / 呼吸～ be short of breath / 脉搏～ have a short, quick pulse ② (of time) short; pressing: 时间很～, 不要再犹豫了。Time is running short. Stop hesitating (or dithering).

急电 jídiàn urgent telegram; urgent cable

急风暴雨 jífēng-bàoyǔ violent storm; hurricane; tempest: 这场农民运动如～, 势不可挡。This peasant movement carried all before it like a hurricane.

急腹症 jífùzhèng *med.* acute abdominal disease; acute abdomen

急公好义 jígōng-hàoyì zealous for the common weal;

public-spirited: 这位老人历来～，为全村老百姓办了不少好事。This old man has always been public-spirited, and has done a lot of good things for the community.

急功近利 jígōng-jìnlì eager for instant success and quick profits: 制定政策不能～，要有长远的观点。In formulating policies, we must not be seeking short-term successes and quick profits. We should take a long-range view of things.

急管繁弦 jíguǎn-fánxián fast beat or quick rhythm in music

急急巴巴 jíjibābā hastily; in a hurry

急件 jíjiàn an urgent document or dispatch

急进 jíjìn same as 激进 jíjìn

急惊风 jíjīngfēng *Chin. med.* acute infantile convulsions

急救 jíjiù first aid; emergency treatment: 有十几个人食物中毒，立刻送医院～。Ten or so victims of food poisoning were sent to the hospital for emergency treatment.

急救包 jíjiùbāo first-aid dressing

急救人员 jíjiù rényuán first-aid personnel

急救药品 jíjiù yàopǐn first-aid medicine

急救药箱 jíjiù yàoxiāng first-aid kit

急救站 jíjiùzhàn first-aid station

急救中心 jíjiù zhōngxīn first-aid centre

急就章 jíjiùzhāng hurriedly-written essay; hasty work; improvisation

急剧 jíjù rapid; sharp; sudden: ～的变化 rapid change / ～转折 abrupt turn / 物价～上升。There was a steep rise in prices. / 气温～下降。There was a sudden drop in the temperature.

急遽 jíjù rapid; sharp; sudden: ～的敲门声把她吓了一跳。A sudden sharp knock on the door startled her.

急口令 jíkǒulìng *dial.* tongue-twister

急来抱佛脚 jí lái bào fójiǎo clasp Buddha's feet when in trouble—seek help at the last moment; make a frantic last-minute effort ——see also 平时不烧香，急来抱佛脚 píngshí bù shāoxiāng, jí lái bào fójiǎo

急流 jíliú ① torrent; rapid stream; rapids: ～滚滚 a torrent surging ahead / 闯过～险滩 sweep over rapids and shoals ② *meteorol.* jet stream; jet flow

急流勇进 jíliú yǒng jìn forge ahead against a swift current; press on in the teeth of difficulties

急流勇退 jíliú yǒng tuì resolutely retire at the height of one's official career: 尊大人精神正旺，何以就这般～? (《儒林外史》) Your father is still in his prime: why should he be so eager to retire?

急忙 jímáng in a hurry; in haste; hurriedly; hastily: 你干吗这样急急忙忙的? Why are you in such a hurry? / 他起晚了，没吃早饭就～向学校跑去。He got up late and hurriedly ran off to school without eating any breakfast.

急难 jínàn *formal* ① misfortune; grave danger ② be anxious to help (those in grave danger): 扶危～ be eager to help those in need or in danger

急迫 jípò urgent; pressing; imperative: 这是当前最～的任务。This is the most pressing task at present. / 事情很～，得赶快处理。The matter is urgent and something's got to be done about it at once.

急起直追 jíqǐ-zhízhuī rouse oneself to catch up; do one's utmost to overtake: 我们要～，迎头赶上。We must do our utmost to catch up with the foremost.

急切 jíqiè ① eager; impatient: 她用～的目光注视着我，希望得到我的同意。She looked at me intently; hoping that I would give her my consent. / 我们～地盼望他早日归来。We are eagerly awaiting his early return. ② in a hurry; in haste: ～间找不着适当的人 cannot find the right person on such short notice

急如星火 jí rú xīnghuǒ extremely pressing; most urgent; posthaste: 灾区需用医药，～。Medical aid must be sent to the stricken area posthaste

急刹车 jíshāchē ① slam the brakes on ② bring to a halt: 工程进行得很顺利，突然上面下达命令，来了个～。The project was going ahead smoothly when suddenly orders came from above to bring the whole thing to a halt.

急射 jíshè *mil.* quick fire

急速 jísù very fast; rapid: 汽车～地向前行驶。The car was running at high speed. / 他的病情～恶化。His condition rapidly worsened. / 情况～变化。The situation changed quickly.

急湍 jítuān *formal* swift (*or* rushing) current; gurgling rapids: 清流～ clear streams and gurgling rapids

急弯 jíwān sharp turn: 拐了个～ made a sharp turn / 前有～，行车小心。Sharp turn ahead. Drive carefully.

急务 jíwù urgent task: 因有～在身，不敢在此逗留。I have an urgent task to attend to, so I can't make a stop-over here.

急先锋 jíxiānfēng ① daring vanguard ② most aggressive, adventurous henchman

急行军 jíxíngjūn rapid march; forced march: 部队～，一夜走了一百里。The detachment made a rapid march of 100 *li* in one night.

急性 jíxìng acute: ～阑尾炎 acute appendicitis / ～传染病 acute infectious disease

急性病 jíxìngbìng ① *med.* acute disease ② impetuosity: 要周密计划后再开始做，不要犯～。You must plan carefully before you begin. Don't make the mistake of being too impetuous.

急性子 jíxìngzǐ *Chin. med.* the seed of garden balsam

急性子 jíxìngzi ① of impatient disposition; impetuous ② an impetuous person: 他是个～，不把这件事干完是不肯歇的。He's an impatient man. He won't rest until after he's finished the job.

急需 jíxū ① be badly in need of: ～帮助 be in need of immediate help / 提供～的资金 provide much-needed funds ② urgent need: 以应～ meet a crying need

急眼 jíyǎn *dial.* be taken aback; feel anxious: 进屋一看，孩子不见了，她～了。When she came into the room and saw that her child was nowhere to be seen, she became very anxious.

急用 jíyòng urgent need: 节约储蓄，以备～ practise economy and save money against a rainy day / 请把材料赶紧送来，有～。Please send us the material at once; it's urgently needed.

急于 jíyú eager; anxious; impatient: ～完成任务 eager to fulfil a task / ～表态 impatient to state one's position / 没准备好，就不要～开会。Don't call the meeting till we're ready.

急于求成 jíyú qiú chéng overanxious for quick results; impatient for success: 为什么有些作品不成熟呢? 因为～。Some works are immature owing to undue haste.

急躁 jízào ① irritable; irascible: 他性情～。He has an irascible temperament. / 一听说事情还没办，他就～起来。As soon as he heard that the matter hadn't been taken care of yet, he got very irritable. ② impetuous; rash; impatient: 防止～情绪 guard against impetuosity / 产生～情绪 give way to impatience / ～冒进 advance impetuously / 别～，准备好了再开始行动。Don't get impatient. Wait until everything's ready before you act.

急诊 jízhěn emergency call; emergency treatment: 这病不能耽误，上医院看～吧。This kind of illness allows no delay. Go right to hospital for emergency treatment.

急诊病人 jízhěn bìngrén emergency case

急诊室 jízhěnshì emergency room

急症 jízhèng sudden attack (of illness); acute disease; emergency case

急智　jízhì　nimbleness of mind in dealing with emergencies; quick-wittedness

急中生智　jí zhōng shēng zhì　hit upon a plan in desperation; show resourcefulness in an emergency; suddenly hit on a way out of a predicament

急骤　jízhòu　hurried; flurried: ～的脚步声 the sound of hurried footsteps

急转直下　jízhuǎn-zhíxià　(of the march of events, etc.) take a sudden turn and then develop rapidly

笈　jí　formal　book box; satchel: 负笈 fùjí

疾[1]　jí　①disease; sickness; illness: 痼疾 gùjí ② suffering; pain; difficulty: 疾苦 jíkǔ ③ hate; abhor: 疾恶如仇 jí è rú chóu

疾[2]　jí　① fast; quick: ～走 walk quickly; march swiftly ② vigorous; strong: 疾风 jífēng

疾病　jíbìng　disease; illness: 防治～ prevention and treatment of disease

疾步　jíbù　walking quickly; at a fast pace: ～上前 go forward quickly

疾恶如仇　jí è rú chóu　hate evil like an enemy: 他的绝对公正和～赢得了群众的信任和拥护。His absolute fairness and abhorrence of evil won him the confidence and support of the masses.

疾风　jífēng　① strong wind; gale ② meteorol. moderate gale

疾风扫落叶　jífēng sǎo luòyè　like a strong wind sweeping away dead leaves—carrying everything before one: 我军以～之势追击残敌。Our army routed the enemy like a strong wind sweeping away dead leaves.

疾风知劲草，烈火见真金　jífēng zhī jìngcǎo, lièhuǒ jiàn zhēnjīn　sturdy grass withstands high winds; true gold stands the test of fire—strength of character is tested in a crisis

疾患　jíhuàn　formal　illness; disease

疾苦　jíkǔ　sufferings; hardships: 关心人民的～ be concerned about the weal and woe of the people / 他总是把厂里工人的～挂在心上。He always has the well-being of the workers at heart.

疾驶　jíshǐ　(of vehicles) speed along: ～而去 speed past

疾首蹙额　jíshǒu-cù'é　with aching head and knitted brows—frowning in disgust; with abhorrence

疾言厉色　jíyán-lìsè　harsh words and stern looks: 他对人很和蔼，从不～。He is always affable and never brusque with people.

棘　jí　①sour jujube ② thorn bushes; brambles ③ zool.　spine; spina

棘轮　jílún　mech.　ratchet (wheel)

棘皮动物　jípí dòngwù　echinoderm

棘手　jíshǒu　thorny; troublesome; knotty: ～的问题 a knotty problem / 这件事情很～。This is a sticky business.

棘爪　jízhuǎ　mech.　pawl; detent: 止回～ check pawl

殛　jí　formal　kill: 雷～ be struck dead by lightning

集　jí　① gather; collect: 聚集 jùjí / ～各家之长 incorporate the strong points of different schools ② country fair; market: 这个镇每三天一个～, 今天逢～。An outdoor market is held every three days in this town, and today happens to be a market day. ③ collection; anthology: 画～ an album of paintings ④ volume; part: 这些文章分三～出版。These articles will be published in three volumes. / 这部影片分上、下两～。This film is in two parts.

集材　jícái　forestry　logging; skidding; yarding

集尘器　jíchénqì　mech.　dust arrester; dust collector; duster

集成电路　jíchéng diànlù　electron.　integrated circuit: ～晶体管 integrated circuit transistor

集大成　jí dàchéng　gather together all that is good; synthesize; be the culmination of; be a comprehensive expression of: 韩非子集法家思想之大成。In Han Fei Zi all previous teachings of the Legalist thinkers were synthesized and brought to their highest development.

集电极　jídiànjí　electron.　collecting electrode; collector

集股　jígǔ　collect capital; form a stock company

集管　jíguǎn　mech.　header

集合　jíhé　gather; assemble; muster; call together: ～! (word of command) Fall in! / 紧急～ emergency muster / ～地点 assembly place; rendezvous / 命令全排战士～. Order the whole platoon to fall in.

集合号　jíhéhào　bugle call for fall-in; assembly

集合论　jíhélùn　math.　set theory

集合名词　jíhé míngcí　gram.　collective noun

集合体　jíhétǐ　min.　aggregate

集会　jíhuì　assembly; rally; gathering; meeting: ～结社自由 freedom of assembly and association / 举行群众～ hold a mass rally

集结　jíjié　(esp. of troops) mass; concentrate; build up: ～军队 mass troops; concentrate forces / ～力量 build up strength / ～待命 assemble and await orders

集结地域　jíjié dìyù　mil.　assembly area

集解　jíjiě　(usu. used in book titles) collected explanations or commentaries: 《周易～》Collected Commentaries on the "Book of Changes"

集锦　jíjǐn　(usu. used in book titles) a collection of choice specimens: 儿童画～ outstanding examples of children's drawings

集句　jíjù　a poem made up of lines from various poets

集聚　jíjù　gather; collect; assemble: ～资金 accumulate funds

集刊　jíkān　collected papers (of an academic institution)

集流环　jíliúhuán　elec.　slip ring

集录　jílù　collect and compile

集权　jíquán　centralization of state power: 中央～的封建帝国 a centralized feudal empire

集日　jírì　market day: 镇上每逢～, 四乡农民都带着土特产前来赶集。Whenever market day comes round, the farmers of the surrounding countryside all come to town, bringing their special produce for the market.

集散地　jísàndì　collecting and distributing centre; distributing centre: 该市位居南北交通枢纽, 为各种重要物资的～. This city, situated at the transportation hub between north and south, is a distribution centre for all kinds of important goods and materials.

集市　jíshì　country fair; market

集市贸易　jíshì màoyì　country fair trade; open market

集释　jíshì　(usu. used in book titles) collected explanations: 《韩非子～》Collected Explanations of the "Han Fei Zi"

集水　jíshuǐ　water conservancy　catchment

集水面积　jíshuǐ miànjī　catchment area

集思广益　jísī-guǎngyì　draw on collective wisdom and absorb all useful ideas; pool the wisdom of the masses

集体　jítǐ　collective: ～的智慧 collective wisdom / 一个战斗的～ a militant collective / 荣立～二等功 gain a Collective Award of Merit, Second Class / ～创作 collective effort in literary or artistic creation / ～观念 collective spirit

集体化　jítǐhuà　collectivize: 农业～ the collectivization of agriculture / 走～的道路 follow (or take) the road of collectivization

集体经济 jítǐ jīngjì　collective economy

集体领导 jítǐ lǐngdǎo　collective leadership

集体农庄 jítǐ nóngzhuāng　collective farm

集体生产劳动 jítǐ shēngchǎn láodòng　collective productive labour

集体宿舍 jítǐ sùshè　dormitory

集体所有制 jítǐ suǒyǒuzhì　collective ownership

集体舞 jítǐwǔ　group dancing

集体英雄主义 jítǐyīngxióngzhǔyì　collective heroism

集体主义 jítǐzhǔyì　collectivism

集团 jítuán　group; clique; circle; bloc: 七十七国～ the Group of 77 / 统治～ the ruling clique; the ruling circle / 军事～ a military bloc / 货币～ monetary bloc / 小～ a small clique

集团购买力 jítuán gòumǎilì　the purchasing power of institutions; institutional purchases: 压缩～ cut down the purchasing power of institutions

集团军 jítuánjūn　group army; army

集训 jíxùn　assemble for training: 干部轮流～。Cadres take turns to receive training at a given place.

集训队 jíxùnduì　*sports* team of athletes in training

集腋成裘 jí yè chéng qiú　the finest fragments of fox fur, sewn together, will make a robe—many a little makes a mickle

集邮 jíyóu　stamp collecting; philately

集邮爱好者 jíyóu àihàozhě　stamp-collector; philatelist

集邮簿 jíyóubù　stamp-album

集约 jíyuē　*agric.* intensive: ～经营 intensive farming

集约化 jíyuēhuà　intensify: 渔业生产开始转向～。Fish farming is beginning to be intensified.

集运 jíyùn　transport sth. containerized

集镇 jízhèn　town; market town

集中 jízhōng　concentrate; centralize; focus; amass; put together: ～精力 concentrate one's energy / ～火力 concentrate fire (on a target) / ～目标 concentrate on the same target / 民主基础上的～，～指导下的民主 centralism on the basis of democracy and democracy under centralized guidance / ～大量财富 amass vast fortunes / ～注意力 focus one's attention on / ～群众的智慧 pool the wisdom of the masses / ～各方面的正确意见 sum up correct ideas from all quarters / ～管理 centralized management / ～指挥 centralized direction (*or* command) / 思想不～ be absent-minded

集中供热 jízhōng gōngrè　central heating

集中轰炸 jízhōng hōngzhà　mass bombing

集中营 jízhōngyíng　concentration camp

集注[1] jízhù　focus: 代表们的眼光都～在大会主席台上。All eyes at the conference were focused on the rostrum.

集注[2] jízhù　(usu. used in book titles) collected commentaries; variorum: 朱熹《四书章句～》Zhu Xi's *Collected Commentaries on the "Four Books"*

集注本 jízhùběn　variorum edition

集装箱 jízhuāngxiāng　container: ～船 container ship / ～化 containerize / ～码头 container terminal / ～运输 containerized traffic

集资 jízī　raise funds; collect money; pool resources: 这座大桥由当地农民～兴建，没花国家一分钱。This bridge was built with funds pooled by the local farmers. Not a cent of state money was spent.

集子 jízi　collection; collected works; anthology: 这个～里收有二十篇小说。This anthology consists of 20 novels.

集总 jízǒng　*elec.* lumped: ～电容 lumped capacitance

楫

jí　*formal* oar: 舟楫 zhōují

戢

jí　*formal* ① hide; conceal: ～翼 (of a bird) fold its wings ② restrain: ～怒 restrain one's anger;

become placated

辑

jí　① collect; compile; edit: 编辑 biānjí ② part; volume; division: 新闻简报第一～ Newsreel No.1 / 这部丛书分三～，每～五本。This set of books are in three parts, and each part is in five volumes.

辑录 jílù　compile: 这个集子～了这位已故作家的所有来往信件。All the letters of the late writer are compiled in this collection.

辑要 jíyào　summary; abstract

蒺

jí　see below

蒺藜 jíli　*bot.* puncture vine

嫉

jí　① be jealous; be envious ② hate

嫉妒 jídù　same as 忌妒 jìdu

嫉恨 jíhèn　envy and hate; hate out of jealousy

嫉贤妒能 jíxián-dùnéng　be envious of people of worth and ability

瘠

jí　*formal* ① lean; thin and weak ② barren; poor; lean: ～土 poor soil; lean soil; barren land

瘠薄 jíbó　barren; unproductive: 这里土地～，作物产量很低。The land here is barren and yields poorly.

瘠田 jítián　infertile land

鹡

jí　see below

鹡鸰 jílíng　wagtail

藉

jí　see 狼藉 lángjí ——see also jiè

籍

jí　① book; record: 古籍 gǔjí ② registry; roll: 户籍 hùjí ③ native place; home town; birthplace: 祖籍 zǔjí ④ membership: 党籍 dǎngjí / 国籍 guójí

籍贯 jíguàn　the place of one's birth or origin; native place

籍籍 jíjí　*liter.* ① noisy; vociferous: 人言～ a hubbub of voices ② disorderly; confused: 尸骨～ corpses lying scattered around

籍没 jímò　*formal* make a list of sb.'s property and confiscate it

jǐ

几（幾）

jǐ　① how many: ～点了? What's the time? *or* What time is it? / 你～号? What's your number? / 四乘六等于～? What's four times six? / 太平天国起义在一八～～年? In which year of the 19th century did the Taiping Revolution break out? ② a few; several; some: 说～句话 say a few words / 他过不了～天就会回来的。He'll be back in a couple of days. / ～十 tens; dozens; scores / ～万万 several hundred million; hundreds of millions / 十～岁的孩子 teenager / 二十～个人 twenty odd people / 村子很小，没有～户人家。The village is quite small, with a few households. / 来了十～二十个人。About twenty people came. ——see also jī

几儿 jǐr　*inf.* what date: 你～来的? When did you get here? / 今儿是～? What's the date today? / 我～答应过你? When did I ever promise you?

几多 jǐduō　*dial.* how many; how much: ～人? How many people? / 这袋米有～重? How much does this sack of rice weigh?

几分 jǐfēn　a bit; somewhat; rather: 有～醉意 a bit merry; a bit tipsy / 让他～ humour him a little / 她说的有～道理。There's something in what she said. / 对他的意图我有～怀疑。I'm somewhat suspicious of his intentions.

几儿个 jǐrge *inf.* when: 你们～结婚? When will you get married?

几何 jǐhé ① *formal* how much; how many: 不知尚有～ be uncertain how much is left or how many are left ② geometry

几何级数 jǐhé jíshù geometric progression; geometric series

几何体 jǐhétǐ same as 立体 ②

几何图形 jǐhé túxíng geometric figure

几何学 jǐhéxué *math.* geometry

几经 jǐjīng several times; time and again: 这堵墙已～倒塌,～修补。The wall has collapsed and been rebuilt several times. / 这件事～周折才办成。The matter was settled after a lot of bother.

几内亚 Jǐnèiyà Guinea

几内亚比绍 Jǐnèiyà-Bǐshào Guinea-Bissau

几内亚人 Jǐnèiyàrén Guinean

几起几落 jǐqǐ-jǐluò repeated rises and falls

几时 jǐshí ① what time; when: 你们～走? What time are you leaving? / 不知～咱们才能再见面! Who knows when we'll meet again? / 你们～看见他马虎过? Have you ever seen him doing anything in a casual way? ② any time; when: 你～有空～来。Come when you are free. / 你们～见到他代我问好。Please remember me to him when you meet him. / 你们～需要,我～到。I'll come whenever you need me.

几许 jǐxǔ *liter.* how much; how many: 不知～。No one can tell how much. / 满头黑发新染了～银霜。White streaks appeared in his mane of black hair.

己 jǐ ① oneself; one's own; personal: 舍～为公 make personal sacrifices for the public good ② the sixth of the ten Heavenly Stems (天干)(see also 干支 gān-zhī)

己方 jǐfāng one's own side

己任 jǐrèn *formal* one's duty: 这批青年将建设边疆引为～。These young people regard the construction of the borderland as their duty.

己所不欲,勿施于人 jǐ suǒ bù yù, wù shī yú rén do not impose on others what you yourself do not desire; do not unto others as you would not have them do unto you

纪 jǐ a surname ——see also jì

虮(蟣) jǐ see below

虮子 jǐzi the egg of a louse; nit

济(濟) jǐ see below ——see also jì

济济 jǐjǐ (of people) many; numerous: 人才济济 réncái jǐjǐ

济济一堂 jǐjǐ yītáng gather together under the same roof: 代表们～,进行了热烈的讨论。The representatives gathered together and had a lively discussion.

济南 Jǐnán Jinan (capital of Shandong Province)

挤(擠) jǐ ① squeeze; press: 把水～掉 squeeze the water out / 他无法再在厂里呆下去,他是被副厂长～走的。He was unable to continue working in this factory. He was squeezed out by the assistant manager. / ～时间 try and find time to do sth.; find time ② jostle; push against: ～进去 force (*or* elbow, shoulder, push) one's way in; squeeze in / ～上前去 push to the front / ～别～。Don't push. / 人们互相～来～去。People jostled each other. ③ crowd; pack; cram: ～做一团 pressed close together; packed like sardines / 小屋～不下那么多人。It's impossible to pack so many people into the small room. / 礼堂已经～满了。The assembly hall is filled to capacity. / 几件事～在一块儿

了。Several matters have cropped up at the same time.

挤兑 jǐduì a run on a bank

挤对 jǐduì *dial.* ① force into submission ② push aside; push out; squeeze out; elbow out ③ make fun of; poke fun at

挤咕 jǐgu *dial.* wink; blink: 我朝他～眼儿,叫他别开腔。I winked at him to keep quiet.

挤挤插插 jǐjichāchā *dial.* very crowded; packed tight; jammed together; packed like sardines: ～地坐了一屋子人。The room was packed with people. / 屋子里这么多家具,～的。The room is overfurnished.

挤眉弄眼 jǐméi-nòngyǎn make eyes; wink

挤奶 jǐnǎi milk (a cow, etc.)

挤奶机 jǐnǎijī milking machine; milker

挤压 jǐyā *metall.* extruding: ～机 extrusion press; extruder

挤牙膏 jǐyágāo squeeze toothpaste out of a tube—be forced to tell the truth bit by bit: 审问这个惯犯就跟～一样。To interrogate this hardened criminal, you have to squeeze every word out of him.

挤眼 jǐyǎn wink: 他意味深长地向她挤挤眼。He winked meaningfully to her.

给 jǐ ① supply; provide: 补给 bǔjǐ / 自给自足 zìjǐ-zìzú ② ample; well provided for: 家给人足 jiājǐ-rénzú ——see also gěi

给水 jǐshuǐ ① *archit.* watersupply: ～工程 water-supply engineering ② *mech.* feed water: 锅炉～ boiler feed water / ～器 water feeder

给养 jǐyǎng provisions; victuals: ～充足 be abundantly provisioned / ～不足 be short of provisions / 补充～ replenish the provisions

给予 jǐyǔ *formal* give; render: ～支持 give support to / ～协助 render assistance to / ～正式承认 give official recognition to / ～很高的评价 have a very high opinion of; appreciate highly / ～同情 show sympathy for / ～适当的纪律处分 take appropriate disciplinary measures against sb. / ～法律保护 give legal protection

脊 jǐ ① spine; backbone ② ridge: 山脊 shānjǐ / 屋脊 wūjǐ

脊背 jǐbèi back (of a human being or any other vertebrate)

脊梁 jǐliang *dial.* back (of the human body): 光着～ bare-backed

脊梁骨 jǐliaggǔ *dial.* backbone; spine: 断了～的癞皮狗 a mangy dog with a broken back (a term of contempt for renegades, etc.) ——see also 戳脊梁骨 chuō jǐliaggǔ

脊檩 jǐlǐn *archit.* ridgepole; ridgepiece

脊鳍 jǐqí *zool.* dorsal fin

脊神经 jǐshénjīng spinal nerve

脊髓 jǐsuǐ spinal cord

脊髓灰质炎 jǐsuǐ huīzhìyán poliomyelitis; polio

脊髓炎 jǐsuǐyán myelitis

脊索 jǐsuǒ *zool.* notochord

脊索动物 jǐsuǒ dòngwù chordate (animal)

脊瓦 jǐwǎ *archit.* ridge tile

脊柱 jǐzhù spinal column; vertebral column; backbone; spine

脊椎 jǐzhuī vertebra

脊椎动物 jǐzhuī dòngwù vertebrate

脊椎骨 jǐzhuīgǔ vertebra; spine

戟 jǐ halberd

戟指 jǐzhǐ *formal* point a finger at sb. and scold him

麂 jǐ muntjac

麂皮 jǐpí chamois (leather); chammy

麂子 jǐzi *inf.* muntjac

jì

计 jì ① count; compute; calculate; number: 数以万～ by the tens of thousands; numbering tens of thousands / 外币贷款按外币～收利息。Interest on a foreign currency loan shall be computed and charged in foreign currency. / 买进的新书，～中文三十种，外文二十种。Of the new books recently bought, there are thirty copies in Chinese and twenty in foreign languages. / 大小拖拉机～二十台。The tractors, light and heavy, numbered twenty in all. *or* There were twenty light and heavy tractors in all. ② (usu. used in the negative) haggle over: 不～个人得失 never give a thought to personal gain or loss / 工作不～时间 be ready to work longer hours than required; not mind working extra hours / 不～报酬 not be concerned about pay ③ (only used in the pattern "为……计") for the purpose of; in order to: 为长远～ from a long-term point of view / 为提高教学质量～，我们必须抓好师资培训工作。In order to improve our teaching quality, we must pay special attention to the training of teachers. ④ idea; ruse; stratagem; plan: 退敌之～ a stratagem to repulse the enemy / 作归～ plan to go home / 他们一～不成，又生一～。Their first ruse having failed, they tried another. ⑤ meter; gauge: 雨量计 yǔliàngjì / 体温计 tǐwēnjì ⑥ (Jì) a surname

计策 jìcè stratagem; plan: 定下了诱敌深入的～ make a plan to lure the enemy in

计程表 jìchéngbiǎo taximeter; meter

计程车 jìchéngchē same as 出租汽车 chūzū qìchē

计程仪 jìchéngyí *navigation* log

计酬 jìchóu work out or calculate payment: 按件～ pay by the piece / 按钟点～ pay by the hour

计出万全 jì chū wànquán make a perfectly safe plan

计划 jìhuà ① plan; project; programme: 切实可行的～ a feasible (or workable) plan / 宏伟的～ a magnificent project / 河流开发～ a river development programme / 有～地进行 proceed in a planned way / ～外的商品 goods produced over and above the plan / ～外项目 projects outside the plan ② map out; plan: ～好了再动手干。Map it out before you start. / 我们～下周出发。We plan to leave next week.

计划供应 jìhuà gōngyìng planned supply

计划经济 jìhuà jīngjì planned economy

计划生产 jìhuà shēngchǎn planned production

计划生育 jìhuà shēngyù family planning; birth control

计价 jìjià valuate: 固定资产应当以原价为准。The valuation of fixed assets shall be based on the original cost. / ～过低 undervaluation / ～过高 overvaluation

计件 jìjiàn reckon by the piece

计件工资 jìjiàn gōngzī piece rate wage

计件工作 jìjiàn gōngzuò piecework

计较 jìjiào ① haggle over; fuss about: ～小事 be too particular about trifles / 他不～个人得失。He gives no thought to personal gains or losses. ② argue; dispute: 我不同你～，等你气平了再说。I won't argue with you now. Let's talk it over when you've calmed down. ③ think over; plan: 先安排一周的活儿，以后再作～。We'll arrange a week's work first and think about the rest afterwards.

计量 jìliàng measure; calculate; estimate: 这项发明影响之大不可～。The influence of the invention is inestimable.

计量学 jìliàngxué metrology

计谋 jìmóu scheme; stratagem

计日程功 jì rì chéng gōng estimate exactly how many days are needed to complete a project; have the completion of a project in sight: 祖国的兴盛是可以～的。The day is not far off when our country will attain prosperity.

计时 jìshí reckon by time

计时工资 jìshí gōngzī payment by the hour; time wage

计时工作 jìshí gōngzuò timework

计数 jìshù count

计数器 jìshùqì counter: 盖革～ Geiger counter / 闪烁～ scintillation counter

计算 jìsuàn ① count; compute; calculate: ～出席人数 count the number of people present / ～产值 calculate the output value / 以人民币为～单位 be computed in terms of Renminbi ② consideration; planning: 做事不能没个～。We shouldn't do anything without a plan. ③ scheme; plot

计算尺 jìsuànchǐ slide rule

计算机 jìsuànjī computer; calculating machine: 机械～ mechanical computer / 电子～ electronic computer / 模拟～ analogue computer / 微型～ microcomputer / 数字控制～ digital control computer / 自动数字跟踪分析～ automatic digital tracking analyser computer / 自动程序控制～ automatic sequence-controlled calculator / 超高速巨型～ giant ultra-high-speed computer

计算机病毒 jìsuànjī bìngdú computer virus

计算机程序 jìsuànjī chéngxù computer program: ～设计 computer programming

计算机存储器 jìsuànjī cúnchǔqì computer memory; computer storage

计算机代码 jìsuànjī dàimǎ computer code

计算机断层扫描 jìsuànjī duàncéng sǎomiáo computed tomography (popularly called CT 扫描)

计算机辅助设计 jìsuànjī fǔzhù shèjì computer-aided design (CAD)

计算机辅助语言教学 jìsuànjī fǔzhù yǔyánjiàoxué computer-assisted language learning (CALL)

计算机辅助制造 jìsuànjī fǔzhù zhìzào computer-aided manufacturing (CAM)

计算机监控系统 jìsuànjī jiānkòng xìtǒng computer supervisory control system

计算机控制 jìsuànjī kòngzhì computer control

计算机排字 jìsuànjī páizì computer typesetting

计算机配置 jìsuànjī pèizhì computer configuration

计算机情报检索 jìsuànjī qíngbào jiǎnsuǒ information retrieval by computer

计算机软件 jìsuànjī ruǎnjiàn computer software

计算机网络 jìsuànjī wǎngluò computer network: ～设备 computer network facilities

计算机应用 jìsuànjī yìngyòng computer application; computer utility

计算机硬件 jìsuànjī yìngjiàn computer hardware

计算机语言 jìsuànjī yǔyán computer language

计算机站 jìsuànjīzhàn computer installation

计算机指令 jìsuànjī zhǐlìng computer instruction

计算器 jìsuànqì electronic calculator

计算语言学 jìsuàn yǔyánxué computational linguistics

计议 jìyì deliberate; talk over; consult: 二人～已定。The two of them settled on a scheme.

记 jì ① remember; bear in mind; commit to memory: ～错了 remember wrongly / ～不清 cannot recall exactly; remember only vaguely / 牢牢地～在心上 keep firmly in mind ② write (or jot, take) down; record: ～在笔记本上 write it down in a notebook / 把结果～下来 record the results / ～下电话号码 jot down the telephone number ③ notes; record: 游记 yóujì / 大事记 dàshìjì ④ mark; sign: 暗～儿 secret mark ⑤ birthmark: 他左腿有块～。There is a birthmark on his left

leg. ⑥ *dial. m.*: 一～耳光 a slap in the face

记仇 jìchóu bear grudges; harbour bitter resentment: 他可不～。He's not the sort of person to bear a grudge. / 她心胸狭隘, 好～。She is narrow-minded and tends to bear grudges.

记得 jìde remember: ～他的模样儿 remember what he looked like / 我完全记不得了。I simply don't remember it. / 我不～他有多大年纪了。I don't remember how old he is.

记分 jìfēn ① keep the score; record the points (in a game) ② register a student's marks ③ record work-points

记分牌 jìfēnpái scoreboard

记分员 jìfēnyuán scorekeeper; scorer; marker

记工 jìgōng record workpoints

记功 jìgōng cite sb. for meritorious service; record a merit: 给全体指战员～ award all the officers and men Citations for Merit / 记一等功 award sb. a Citation for Merit, First Class

记挂 jìguà *dial.* be concerned about; keep thinking about; miss: 她一心～着生病的孩子, 一下班就往家跑。She was worried about her sick child, so she hurried home immediately after work.

记过 jìguò record a demerit: 违反校规者将给予～处分。Whoever violates the school regulations will be given a demerit.

记号 jìhao mark; sign: 做个～ make a sign; mark out / 联络～ mark for contact / 我们按他在树干上做的～往前走。We followed the marks he had made on the tree trunks.

记恨 jìhèn bear grudges: 她年轻不懂事, 您别～她。She is young and ignorant, so you shouldn't bear her any grudge.

记录 jìlù ① take notes; keep the minutes; record: 把发言的主要内容～下来 note down the main points of the speeches / ～在案 place on record; as a matter of record ② minutes; notes; record: 会议～ the minutes of a meeting / 会谈～ a transcript of talks / 正式～ official records / 逐字～ verbatim record / 摘要～ summary record ③ notetaker: 这次讨论请你做～好吗? Would you take the minutes of the discussion? ④ record: 创～ set a record; chalk up a record / 世界～ world record

记录本 jìlùběn minute book

记录片儿 jìlùpiānr *inf.* documentary film; documentary

记录片 jìlùpiàn documentary film; documentary

记录员 jìlùyuán notetaker; stenographer; reporter: 逐字～ verbatim reporter

记名 jìmíng put down one's name (on a cheque, etc. to indicate responsibility or claim); sign

记名支票 jìmíng zhīpiào order cheque

记念 jìniàn same as 纪念 jìniàn

记谱法 jìpǔfǎ *mus.* musical notation

记取 jìqǔ remember; bear in mind: ～这个血的教训 bear firmly in mind this lesson learned at the cost of blood / ～正反两方面的经验 draw on experience both positive and negative

记时仪 jìshíyí *astron.* chronograph

记事 jìshì ① keep a record of events; make a memorandum: 刻木结绳～ keep records by notching wood or tying knots ② account; record of events; chronicles

记事儿 jìshìr (of a child) begin to remember things: 那时我只有五岁, 才～。I was then only five years old and had just begun to remember things.

记述 jìshù record and narrate: 该书前言～了作者生平。The preface of the book includes an account of the author's life. / 这次庆祝活动没有什么可以～的。The celebration has nothing worth recording.

记诵 jìsòng commit to memory and be able to recite; learn by heart

记性 jìxing memory: ～好 have a good memory / ～坏 have a poor (*or* short) memory

记叙 jìxù narrate: 这篇文章～了他的先进事迹。The article tells about his exemplary deeds.

记叙文 jìxùwén narrative writing

记要 jìyào same as 纪要 jìyào

记忆 jìyì ① remember; recall: 就我～所及 so far as I can remember ② memory: 你们的深情厚谊将永远留在我们的～中。Your warm friendship will always remain in our memory.

记忆力 jìyìlì the faculty of memory; memory: ～衰退 one's memory is failing / ～强(弱) have a good (poor) memory

记忆犹新 jìyì yóu xīn remain fresh in one's memory

记载 jìzǎi ① put down in writing; record: 详细地～事情经过 record the incident in detail / 有文字～的历史 recorded history ② record; account: 地方志中有关于这次旱灾的～。There is an account of this drought in the local chronicles.

记帐 jìzhàng ① keep accounts ② charge to an account: 请把这笔开支记在我帐上。Please charge the expenses to my account.

记者 jìzhě reporter; correspondent; newsman; journalist: 新华社～ Xinhua correspondent; reporter of the Xinhua News Agency / 本报～ staff reporter; staff correspondent

记者席 jìzhěxí press gallery

记者协会 jìzhě xiéhuì journalists' association

记者招待会 jìzhě zhāodàihuì press conference

记者证 jìzhězhèng press card

记住 jìzhu remember; learn by heart; bear in mind: 把这首诗～ learn the poem by heart / 你记得住这些数字吗? Can you carry all these figures in your head? / 我记不住这么多电话号码。I can't bear in mind so many telephone numbers. / 我们要～这个教训。We must keep this lesson in mind.

纪¹ jì discipline: 风纪 fēngjì / 军纪 jūnjì

纪² jì ① put down in writing; record ② age; epoch: 中世～ the Middle Ages ③ *geol.* period: 震旦～ the Sinian Period
——see also jǐ

纪纲 jìgāng *formal* ① law ② moral standard

纪检 jìjiǎn (short for 纪律检查) inspect discipline

纪录 jìlù same as 记录 jìlù

纪录片儿 jìlùpiānr same as 记录片儿 jìlùpiānr

纪录片 jìlùpiàn same as 记录片 jìlùpiàn

纪律 jìlǜ discipline: 遵守～ keep discipline; observe discipline / 劳动～ labour discipline; labour regulations / 无～现象 indiscipline / 加强～性 heighten one's sense of discipline / ～严明 highly disciplined / 给予～处分 take disciplinary measures against sb.

纪律检查委员会 jìlǜ jiǎnchá wěiyuánhuì commission for inspecting discipline

纪年 jìnián ① a way of numbering the years: 阴历用干支～。In the lunar calendar, the years are designated by the Heavenly Stems and Earthly Branches. ② chronological record of events; annals

纪念 jìniàn ① commemorate; mark: 人们集会～这位伟大的音乐家。People held a meeting to commemorate the great musician. / ～活动 commemorative activities / 举行～大会 hold a commemoration meeting / ～建军节 mark (*or* observe) Army Day ② souvenir; keepsake; memento: 留个～ keep sth. as a souvenir / 给你这张照片作个～。Have this picture for a souvenir. / 这盏油灯是我们延安生活的～。This oil lamp is a memento of our days in Yan'an. ③ commemoration day;

anniversary: 十周年～ the tenth anniversary

纪念碑 jìniànbēi　monument; memorial: 人民英雄～ the Monument to the People's Heroes / 建立革命烈士～ erect a memorial to the revolutionary martyrs

纪念册 jìniàncè　autograph book; autograph album

纪念封 jìniànfēng　(stamp collecting) commemorate envelope

纪念馆 jìniànguǎn　memorial hall; museum in memory of sb.: 鲁迅～ the Lu Xun Museum

纪念品 jìniànpǐn　souvenir; keepsake; memento

纪念日 jìniànrì　commemoration day

纪念塔 jìniàntǎ　memorial tower; monument

纪念堂 jìniàntáng　memorial hall; commemoration hall

纪念邮票 jìniàn yóupiào　commemorative stamp

纪念章 jìniànzhāng　souvenir badge

纪实 jìshí　record of actual events; on-the-spot report: 会议～ an on-the-spot report of the meeting

纪事本末体 jìshì běnmòtǐ　history presented in separate accounts of important events

纪委 jìwěi　short for 纪律检查委员会 jìlù jiǎnchá wěiyuánhuì

纪行 jìxíng　(usu. used in book titles) travel notes: 《陕北～》 *Notes On a Trip to Northern Shaanxi*

纪要 jìyào　summary of minutes; summary: 会谈～ summary of conversations (or talks) / 座谈会～ summary of a forum or panel discussion

纪元 jìyuán　① the beginning of an era (e.g. an emperor's reign) ② epoch; era: 开辟了世界历史的新～ usher in a new era in world history

纪传体 jìzhuàntǐ　history presented in a series of biographies

伎

jì　① skill; ability; trick: 故伎重演 gùjì chóngyǎn ② a professional female dancer or singer in ancient China

伎俩 jìliǎng　trick; intrigue; manoeuvre: "分而治之"是帝国主义者惯用的～。 "Divide and rule" has long been a favourite trick of the imperialists. / 玩弄卑劣的～ play a nasty trick

技

jì　skill; ability; trick: 绝技 juéjì / 一技之长 yī jì zhī cháng

技法 jìfǎ　skill and technique (in painting, sculpture, etc.)

技工 jìgōng　① short for 技术工人 jìshù gōngrén ② mechanic; technician

技击 jìjī　the art of attack and defence in *wushu*

技能 jìnéng　technical ability; mastery of a skill or technique: 生产～ skill in production

技巧 jìqiǎo　skill; technique; craftsmanship: 写作～ writing technique / 艺术～ artistry / 精湛的玉雕～ superb skill in jade carving

技巧运动 jìqiǎo yùndòng　acrobatic gymnastics

技穷 jìqióng　exhaust one's whole bag of tricks; come to the end of one's rope

技师 jìshī　technician

技术 jìshù　technology; skill; technique: 科学～ science and technology / 提高～水平 increase technical competence / ～要求很高 demand high-level technology / 重大～改革 key technological transformations / ～密集 skill-intensive; technology-intensive

技术兵种 jìshù bīngzhǒng　technical arms (or troops)

技术服务 jìshù fúwù　technical service

技术改造 jìshù gǎizào　technical transformation; technological transformation

技术革命 jìshù gémìng　technological revolution

技术革新 jìshù géxīn　technological innovation; technical innovation

技术工人 jìshù gōngrén　skilled worker

技术规范 jìshù guīfàn　technical specification; technological specification

技术鉴定 jìshù jiàndìng　technical appraisement

技术开发 jìshù kāifā　technological development

技术科学 jìshù kēxué　same as 应用科学 yìngyòng kēxué

技术力量 jìshù lìliàng　technical force; technical personnel

技术名词 jìshù míngcí　technical term

技术人员 jìshù rényuán　technical personnel (or staff)

技术手册 jìshù shǒucè　technical manual; technological manual

技术推广站 jìshù tuīguǎngzhàn　technical advice station: 农业～ agrotechnical station

技术性 jìshùxìng　technical; of a technical nature: ～问题 technical matters / 这工作～很强。 This job is highly technical.

技术学校 jìshù xuéxiào　technical school

技术研究所 jìshù yánjiūsuǒ　technological research institute

技术员 jìshùyuán　technician: 农业～ agronomist

技术知识 jìshù zhīshi　technological know-how; technical knowledge

技术职称 jìshù zhíchēng　titles for technical personnel

技术指导 jìshù zhǐdǎo　① technological (or technical) guidance ② technical adviser

技术转让 jìshù zhuǎnràng　technology transfer

技术装备 jìshù zhuāngbèi　technical equipment

技术资料 jìshù zīliào　technical data; technological data

技术咨询 jìshù zīxún　technical advice

技术作物 jìshù zuòwù　same as 经济作物 jīngjì zuòwù

技痒 jìyǎng　itch to exercise one's skill: 他看到孩子们打乒乓, 不觉～。 Seeing the children playing ping-pong, he itched to have a go.

技艺 jìyì　skill; artistry: ～精湛 highly skilled; masterly

芰

jì　an ancient name for water caltrop

系(繫)

jì　tie; fasten; do up; button up: ～鞋带 tie shoe laces / 把衣服扣子～上 button up a jacket / 把晾衣绳～在树上 fasten a clothesline between two trees / 少先队员都～着红领巾。 The Young Pioneers all wear red scarves. / 她～上围裙下厨房了。 She put on her apron and went to the kitchen. ——see also xì

系泊 jìbó　moor (a boat)

系泊浮筒 jìbó fútǒng　mooring buoy

系船索 jìchuánsuǒ　mooring rope; mooring line

系留 jìliú　moor (a balloon or airship)

系留塔 jìliútǎ　mooring mast; mooring tower

忌

jì　① be jealous of; envy: ～才 be jealous of other people's talent; resent people more able than oneself ② fear; dread; scruple: 横行无忌 héngxíng wújì ③ avoid; shun; abstain from: 孕妇～服 not to be taken by pregnant women / ～生冷 avoid cold and uncooked food / 研究问题, ～带主观性、片面性和表面性。 In studying a problem, we must shun subjectivity, one-sidedness and superficiality. ④ quit; give up: ～酒 give up alcohol; abstain from wine / ～烟 quit smoking

忌辰 jìchén　the anniversary of the death of a parent, ancestor, or anyone else held in esteem

忌惮 jìdàn　dread; fear; scruple: 她破口大骂, 毫无～。 She shouted abuse without any restraint. ——see also 肆无忌惮 sì wú jìdàn

忌妒 jìdu　be jealous (or envious) of; envy: 她～她姐姐, 因为她姐姐比她漂亮得多。 She is jealous of her sister because her sister is much prettier than herself. / 对他取得的成就我不由得感到～。 I find it hard to suppress my envy of his success.

忌恨 jìhèn　same as 嫉恨 jíhèn

忌讳 jìhuì ① taboo: 犯～ violate (or break) a taboo; offend a person's sensitivity; touch a person's sore spot ② avoid as taboo: 老张～人家叫他的外号。Lao Zhang resents being called by his nickname. ③ avoid as harmful; abstain from: 得了痢疾～吃生冷油腻。People suffering from dysentery must avoid raw, cold or greasy food.

忌刻 jìkè (also 忌克 jìkè) jealous and mean; jealous and malicious

忌口 jìkǒu avoid certain food (as when one is ill); be on a diet: 我现在～，不能吃辣的。I'm on a diet now and can't eat anything hot.

忌日 jìrì same as 忌辰 jìchén

忌嘴 jìzuǐ same as 忌口 jìkǒu

际 (際)

jì ① border; boundary; edge: 水～ the edge of a body of water; waterside ② between; among; inter-: 春夏之～ between spring and summer / 校～比赛 interschool matches; intercollegiate games ③ inside: 脑～ in one's head (or mind) ④ occasion; time: 在代表大会召开之～ on the occasion of the convening of the congress / 临别之～ at the time of parting ⑤ on the occasion of: ～此盛会 on the occasion of this grand gathering ⑥ one's lot; circumstances: 遭际 zāojì

际遇 jìyù formal favourable turns in life; spells of good or bad fortune: 他～好，很快就提升了。Fortune smiled on him and he was soon promoted.

妓

jì prostitute

妓女 jìnǚ prostitute

妓院 jìyuàn brothel

季

jì ① season: 四季 sìjì ② the yield of a product in one season; crop: 由种一～改为种两～ reap two crops a year instead of one ③ the last month of a season: 季春 jìchūn ④ the fourth or youngest among brothers: ～弟 the fourth or youngest brother ⑤ (Jì) a surname

季春 jìchūn last month of spring

季冬 jìdōng last month of winter

季度 jìdù quarter (of a year): ～报告 a quarterly report / 第一～生产指标 the production quota for the first quarter / 我这份报纸是按～订的。I subscribed to the newspaper by the quarter. / 我的房租一～一付。I pay my rent by the quarter.

季风 jìfēng (also 季候风 jìhòufēng) meteorol. monsoon

季风气候 jìfēng qìhòu monsoon climate

季风雨 jìfēngyǔ monsoon rain

季候 jìhòu dial. season

季节 jìjié season: 农忙～ a busy farming season / 收获～ harvest season; harvest time / 旅游～ tourist season

季节工 jìjiégōng seasonal worker

季节回游 jìjié huíyóu seasonal migration (of fish, etc.)

季节性 jìjiéxìng seasonal: ～工作 seasonal work; seasonal jobs

季刊 jìkān quarterly publication; quarterly

季秋 jìqiū last month of autumn

季夏 jìxià last month of summer

剂 (劑)

jì ① a pharmaceutical or other chemical preparation: 麻醉剂 mázuìjì ② m. (for herbal medicine): 一～中药 a dose of Chinese herbal medicine

剂量 jìliàng med. dosage; dose

剂型 jìxíng med. the form of a drug (e.g. liquid, powder, pill, etc.)

济 (濟)

jì ① cross a river: 同舟共济 tóng zhōu gòng jì ② aid; relieve; help: 缓不济急 huǎn bù jì jí ③ be of help; benefit: 无济于事 wú jì yú shì ——see also jǐ

济困扶危 jìkùn-fúwēi same as 扶危济困 fúwēi-jìkùn

济贫 jìpín aid the poor; relieve the poor

济世 jìshì benefit mankind; do good to society

济事 jìshì (usu. used in the negative) be of help (or use): 空谈不～。Empty talk doesn't help matters. / 光我们几个不～，要发动群众。Just the few of us are no use; we must mobilize the masses. ——see also 不济事 bùjìshì

荠 (薺)

jì see below ——see also qí

荠菜 jìcài shepherd's purse

荠苧 jìníng Chinese mosla (Mosla chinensis)

洎

jì formal up to (a point or a period of time): ～今 up to now / ～平近世 until recent times

迹 (跡、蹟)

jì ① mark; trace: 血迹 xuèjì / 足迹 zújì ② remains; ruins; vestige: 遗迹 yíjì / 陈迹 chénjì ③ an outward sign; indication: ～近剽窃 an act verging on plagiarism

迹地 jìdì slash (in forest land)

迹象 jìxiàng sign; indication: 各种～都表明形势将好转。There is every indication that the situation will take a favourable turn. or All signs point to a turn for the better. / 这是一种不寻常的～。This is an unusual sign. / 有～表明两国将改善关系。There are indications that the two countries are going to improve their relations.

既

jì ① adv. already: 漱洗～毕 having performed one's ablutions / ～得权利 vested right ② conj. since; as; now that: 他～如此坚决，我也不便多说。Since he is so determined, I consider it wise not to say any more. / ～要做，就要做好。Since you are to do it, you must do it well. / ～来了，就多呆会儿吧。As you are here, you may as well stay a little longer. ③ adv. (used correlatively with 且、又、也, etc.) both...and; as well as: 这间屋子～宽敞，又亮堂。The room is both light and spacious. / ～不实用，又不美观 neither useful nor attractive / 他～懂英语也懂日语。He knows Japanese as well as English. / 他～没来过，我也没去过。He didn't come; nor did I go. / ～深且广 wide and deep; profound and extensive / ～高且大 tall and massive ④ formal done with; finished

既成事实 jìchéng shìshí accomplished fact; fait accompli: 造成～ present a fait accompli; make sth. an accomplished fact / 承认～ accept a fait accompli

既得利益 jìdé lìyì vested interest

既得利益集团 jìdé lìyì jítuán vested interests

既定 jìdìng set; fixed; established: ～目标 set objective; fixed goal / 就按～方案办吧，不要再改了。Let's do it according to the existing plan. Don't make any further changes.

既而 jì'ér adv. formal afterwards; later; subsequently: ～雨霁，欣然登山。It stopped raining afterwards, and we started climbing up the mountain with pleasure.

既来之，则安之 jì lái zhī, zé ān zhī since you are here, you may as well stay and make the best of it

既然 jìrán conj. since; as; now that: ～如此 since it is so; such being the case; under these circumstances / 你～表示了决心，就应该见之于行动。Now that you have expressed your determination, you should act. / ～事前提醒过他们，他们就没什么可埋怨的。Since they had a fair warning, they have no reason to complain. / ～你没准备好，我们只能先走了。As you are not ready,

we must go without you.

既是 jìshì *conj.* since; as; now that: ～天气不好,那就不去了吧。Since the weather is bad, let's call off the trip. / ～他有事,我就不等了。Since he's engaged, I won't wait for him. / ～他不愿意去,那就算了吧。As he doesn't want to go, he doesn't need to.

既遂 jìsuì *leg.* accomplished offence

既往 jìwǎng ① in or of the past; formerly; previously: 一如既往 yī rú jìwǎng ② what one has done in the past: 既往不咎 jìwǎng bù jiù

既往不咎 jìwǎng bù jiù forgive sb.'s past misdeeds; not censure sb. for his past misdeeds: 过去的事情～,以后你可得注意。We'll overlook what you've done in the past but you'd better watch out in the future.

觊(覬)　jì *formal* covet

觊觎 jìyú *formal* covet; cast greedy eyes on: ～别国领土 covet another country's territory

继(繼)　jì ① continue; succeed; follow: ～踵 follow close on sb.'s heels / ～成昆铁路之后,我国西南又一条铁路建成通车了。Following the Chengdu-Kunming Railway another new railway in southwest China was completed and opened to traffic. ② *adv.* then; afterwards: 初感头晕,～又呕吐 feel dizzy and then begin to vomit

继承 jìchéng ① inherit: 夫妻有相互～遗产的权利。Husband and wife have the right to inherit each other's property. ② carry on: ～优良传统 carry forward the good traditions / ～革命事业 carry on the revolutionary cause

继承权 jìchéngquán right of succession; right of inheritance: 非婚生子女享有与婚生子女同等的～。Children born out of wedlock enjoy the same right of inheritance as children born in lawful wedlock. / 剥夺～ disinherit sb.

继承人 jìchéngrén heir; successor; inheritor: 直系～ lineal successor / 王位～ successor to the throne / 法定～ heir at law; legal heir / 那老人收养了这孩子并确定他为～。The old man adopted the boy and made him his heir.

继电器 jìdiànqì *elec.* relay

继而 jì'ér *adv.* then; afterwards

继父 jìfù stepfather

继进 jìjìn go on; continue the process

继母 jìmǔ stepmother

继女 jìnǚ stepdaughter

继配 jìpèi (also 继室 jìshì) *old* second wife (taken after the death of one's first wife)

继任 jìrèn succeed sb. in a post: ～首相 succeed sb. as prime minister

继嗣 jìsì *formal* ① adopt a son ② heir

继往开来 jìwǎng-kāilái carry forward the cause and forge ahead into the future

继位 jìwèi succeed to the throne: 乔治六世死后,伊丽莎白二世～。When George Ⅵ died, Elizabeth Ⅱ succeeded to the throne.

继武 jìwǔ *formal* follow the footsteps of; carry on the task left by one's predecessor

继续 jìxù ① continue; go on: ～工作 continue working / ～有效 remain valid; remain in force / ～执政 continue in office; remain in power / 会议～到深夜。The meeting went on till late at night. / 有些问题仍需～研究。Some problems require further study. / 他们第二天又～会谈。They resumed the talks the next day. / 大雨～了三昼夜。It rained heavily for three days and nights. ② continuation: 中国革命是伟大的十月革命的～。The Chinese revolution is a continuation of the great October Revolution.

继子 jìzǐ stepson

寄　jì ① send; post; mail: ～信 post a letter; mail a letter / ～包裹 send a parcel by post / ～钱 remit money ② entrust; deposit; place: ～希望于人民 place hopes on the people / 别～希望于他的帮助。Don't count on him to help you. ③ depend on; attach oneself to: 寄居 jìjū ④ adopted: 寄子 jìzǐ

寄存 jìcún deposit; leave with; check: 把大衣～在衣帽间 check one's overcoat at the cloakroom / 我把钥匙～在他那里了。I've entrusted the key to him. *or* I've left my key with him. / 行李～处 left-luggage office; checkroom / 自行车～处 bicycle park

寄存器 jìcúnqì *computer* register: 变址～ index register / 进位～ carry storage register

寄放 jìfàng leave with; leave in the care of: 把箱子～在朋友家里 leave a suitcase with a friend / 他把书～在哥哥家了。He left his books in his brother's keeping.

寄费 jìfèi postage

寄父 jìfù foster father

寄件人 jìjiànrén sender

寄居 jìjū live away from home: 从小～在舅父家里 live from childhood with one's uncle

寄居蟹 jìjūxiè hermit crab

寄卖 jìmài (also 寄售 jìshòu) consign for sale on commission; put up for sale in a secondhand shop: 把自行车放在委托商店里～ put a bicycle on sale in a secondhand shop

寄卖品 jìmàipǐn consignment merchandise

寄卖商店 jìmài shāngdiàn commission shop; secondhand shop

寄母 jìmǔ foster mother

寄女 jìnǚ adopted daughter

寄情 jìqíng give expression to one's feelings (usu. in writing)

寄人篱下 jì rén líxià live under another's roof; depend on sb. for a living: 他想尽快找个工作,摆脱～的生活。He was most anxious to find a job so as not to have to depend on others.

寄生 jìshēng ① *biol.* parasitism ② parasitic: 过着～生活 lead a parasitic life

寄生虫 jìshēngchóng parasite

寄生虫病 jìshēngchóngbìng parasitic disease; parasitosis

寄生虫学 jìshēngchóngxué parasitology

寄生动物 jìshēngdòngwù parasitic animal

寄生蜂 jìshēngfēng parasitic wasp

寄生振荡 jìshēng zhèndàng *elec.* parasitic oscillation

寄生植物 jìshēng zhíwù parasitic plant

寄食 jìshí live with a relative, etc. (because of one's straitened circumstances); sponge upon a relative, etc.

寄宿 jìsù ① lodge: ～在朋友家里 lodge (*or* put up) at a friend's house ② (of students) board

寄宿生 jìsùshēng resident student; boarder

寄宿学校 jìsù xuéxiào boarding school; residential college

寄托 jìtuō ① entrust to the care of sb.; leave with sb.: 把孩子～在邻居家里 entrust one's child to the care of a neighbour ② place (hope, etc.) on; find sustenance in: 精神有所～ have spiritual sustenance / 他把希望全～在儿子身上。He places all his hopes on his son.

寄信人 jìxìnrén sender

寄养 jìyǎng entrust one's child to the care of sb.; ask sb. to bring up one's child: 把孩子～在亲戚家里 leave a child in the care of a relative

寄意 jìyì send one's regards

寄予 jìyǔ ① place (hope, etc.) on: 党对青年一代～很大的希望。The Party places great hopes on the youth. ② show; give; express: ～深切的同情 show heartfelt sympathy to

寄语 jìyǔ *formal* send word: ～亲人报喜讯。Send our dear ones the happy news.

寄寓 jìyù *formal* lodge at

寄主 jìzhǔ *biol.* host (of a parasite)

寄子 jìzǐ adopted son

徛 jì *dial.* stand

寂 jì ① quiet; still; silent: ～无一人 quiet and deserted ② lonely; lonesome; solitary

寂静 jìjìng quiet; still; silent: 在～的深夜里 in the still of the night ／～的山村，顿时沸腾起来。The quiet mountain village suddenly became astir. ／一阵阵号子声，打破了森林的～。Work songs broke the silence of the forest.

寂静无哗 jìjìng wú huá silent and still; perfectly quiet

寂寥 jìliáo *liter.* still; silent; lonely; desolate: 时夜将半，四顾～。(苏轼) It was nearing midnight and all around was still. ／坐潭上，四面竹树环合，～无人。(柳宗元) I sat by the tarn, with bamboos and trees all around me, in utter silence and solitude.

寂寞 jìmò ① lonely; lonesome: 我在这里又交了新朋友，一点也不～。I don't feel lonely as I've made new friends here. ② quiet; still; silent: ～的原野 a quiet open country

寂然 jìrán *liter.* silent; still: ～无声 quiet and still

悸 jì *formal* (of the heart) throb with terror; palpitate: 惊悸 jīngjì

悸动 jìdòng palpitate from nervousness

悸栗 jìlì tremble with fear

偈 jì a Buddhist hymn ——see also jié

绩 jì ① twist hempen thread ② achievement; accomplishment; merit: 战绩 zhànjì ／功绩 gōngjì

祭 jì ① hold a memorial ceremony for ② offer a sacrifice to: ～天 offer a sacrifice to Heaven; worship Heaven ③ wield: ～起法宝 wield a magic wand

祭奠 jìdiàn hold a memorial ceremony for

祭礼 jìlǐ ① sacrificial rites ② memorial ceremony ③ sacrificial offerings

祭品 jìpǐn sacrificial offerings; oblation

祭器 jìqì sacrificial utensil

祭扫 jìsǎo offer sacrifices at and sweep (the ancestral tomb)

祭祀 jìsì offer sacrifices to gods or ancestors

祭坛 jìtán (also 祭台 jìtái) sacrificial altar

祭文 jìwén funeral oration; elegiac address

祭灶 jìzào offer sacrifices to the kitchen god on the 23rd or 24th of the 12th lunar month

蓟 jì *bot.* setose thistle

蓟马 jìmǎ *zool.* thrips: 烟～ tobacco thrips

霁（霽） jì ① cease raining or snowing; clear up after rain or snow: 雪～。It's stopped snowing and is clearing up. ② calm down after being angry: ～颜 calm down after a fit of anger; appear mollified

霁月光风 jìyuè-guāngfēng same as 光风霁月 guāngfēng-jìyuè

跽 jì *formal* kneel on the ground with the upper part of the body straight

暨 jì *formal* ① and ② up to; till: ～今 up till now

鲚（鱭） jì long-tailed anchovy; anchovy

稷 jì ① millet ② the god of grains worshipped by ancient emperors

鲫 jì crucian carp

鲫瓜子 jìguāzi *dial.* crucian carp

鲫鱼 jìyú crucian carp

髻 jì hair worn in a bun or coil

冀[1] jì *formal* hope; long for; look forward to: ～其成功 look forward to the success of sb. or sth.

冀[2] jì ① another name for 河北 Héběi ② a surname

冀望 jìwàng *formal* hope for; long for

穄 jì same as 穄子 jìzi

穄子 jìzi another name for 糜子 méizi

暨 jì black finless porpoise

鳓 jì gizzard shad

骥 jì *formal* ① a thoroughbred horse ② an able and virtuous person

jiā

加 jiā ① add; plus: 二～三等于五。Two plus three makes five. *or* Two and three is five. ② increase; augment: ～工资 increase (*or* raise) sb.'s wages ／～件衣服再出去。Put on more clothes before you go out. ／～大油门 open the throttle; step on the gas ③ put in; add; append: 汤里～点盐 put some salt in the soup ／往威士忌里～水 add water to whisky ／～注解 append notes to ④ (used in the same way as 加以 jiāyǐ, usu. after a monosyllabic adverb): 大～赞扬 praise highly; lavish praise on ／不～考虑 not consider at all ／严～处分 punish severely

加班 jiābān work overtime; work an extra shift: 今天晚上我们得加个班，不能去看电影。We've got to work overtime tonight, so we can't go to the movies.

加班费 jiābānfèi overtime pay

加班加点 jiābān-jiādiǎn work extra shifts or extra hours; put in extra hours

加倍 jiābèi double; redouble: 明年产量可能～。The output may double next year. ／今天路滑，开车要～小心。The roads are slippery today, so you'll have to be doubly careful driving the car. ／～努力 redouble one's efforts ／～警惕 redouble one's vigilance

加餐 jiācān snack: 小学生课间有～。School boys and girls have snacks between classes.

加车 jiāchē (put on) extra buses or trains

加成 jiāchéng *chem.* addition: ～化合物 additive compound; addition compound

加法 jiāfǎ *math.* addition

加封[1] jiāfēng seal up (a door, document, etc.)

加封[2] jiāfēng grant additional titles and territories (to the nobles)

加工 jiāgōng ① process: 食品～ food processing ／～中草药 process medicinal herbs ／～厂 processing factory ／粗～制成品 extensively processed products ／精～制成品 intensively processed products ② *mech.* machining; working: 冷～ cold working ／机～ machin-

ing ③ improve; polish (writings); put final touches to: 这篇文章需要～。 This article needs polishing.

加工订货 jiāgōng dìnghuò　place orders with enterprises for processing materials or supplying manufactured goods

加固 jiāgù　reinforce; consolidate: ～堤坝 reinforce dykes and dams ／～工事 improve defence works ／为了防震, 这座楼正在～。 As a precaution against earthquakes, the building is being reinforced.

加官晋爵 jiāguān-jìnjué　be promoted to a higher office and rank

加害 jiāhài　injure; do harm to: ～于人 do harm to sb.; do sb. an injury

加号 jiāhào　plus sign (＋)

加级鱼 jiājíyú　common name for 真鲷 zhēndiāo

加急电 jiājídiàn　urgent telegram; urgent cable

加紧 jiājǐn　step up; speed up; intensify: ～生产 step up production ／～准备 speed up preparation ／登山队～训练。 The mountaineering party intensified its training.

加劲 jiājìn　put more energy into; make a greater effort: 加把劲儿! Put your back into it! or Put on a spurt!

加剧 jiājù　aggravate; intensify; exacerbate: ～紧张局势 aggravate tension ／矛盾正在～。 The contradictions are sharpening. ／病势～。 The patient's condition has taken a turn for the worse.

加快 jiākuài　quicken; speed up; accelerate; pick up speed: ～步子 quicken one's steps ／农业机械化的进程 speed up farm mechanization ／火车～了速度。 The train picked up speed. ／～改革 expedite reform

加宽 jiākuān　broaden; widen: ～路面 widen the road ／适当～某些专业培养内容 appropriately broaden the training in some specialities

加勒比共同体 Jiālèbǐ Gòngtóngtǐ　the Caribbean Community (CARICOM)

加勒比海 Jiālèbǐhǎi　the Caribbean Sea

加力 jiālì　aviation thrust augmentation; afterburning: ～俯冲 afterburning dive

加料 jiāliào　① feed in raw material: 自动～ automatic feeding ② reinforced: ～药酒 reinforced tonic wine ／～狼毫 a writing brush reinforced with superfine weasel hair

加榴炮 jiāliúpào　gun-howitzer

加仑 jiālún　gallon

加码 jiāmǎ　① old raise the price of commodities; overcharge ② raise the stakes in gambling ③ raise the quota: 层层～ raise the quota at each level

加盟 jiāméng　become a member of an alliance or union

加冕 jiāmiǎn　coronation

加冕日 jiāmiǎnrì　Coronation Day

加拿大 Jiānádà　Canada

加拿大人 Jiānádàrén　Canadian

加纳 Jiānà　Ghana

加纳人 Jiānàrén　Ghanaian

加捻 jiāniǎn　text. twisting

加农炮 jiānóngpào　cannon; gun

加蓬 Jiāpéng　Gabon

加蓬人 Jiāpéngrén　Gabonese

加气 jiāqì　archit. air entrainment: ～混凝土 aerocrete ／～水泥 air entraining cement

加强 jiāqiáng　① strengthen; enhance; augment; reinforce: 同学们要～团结, 互相帮助。 We students must strengthen our unity and help each other. ／看到工作成绩, 大家信心～了。 Seeing the results of their work, everyone felt their confidence increase. ／～纪律性 strengthen discipline ／～战备 enhance combat preparedness; intensify preparations against war ／～军事力量 augment military strength ／～敌情观念 heighten one's awareness of the enemy's activities ／～控制

tighten one's control (or grip) ② reinforced: ～排(连、营) reinforced platoon (company, battalion)

加氢 jiāqīng　chem. hydrogenization; hydrogenation: ～精制 hydrofining ／～裂化 hydrocracking

加权平均值 jiāquán píngjūnzhí　math. weighted average

加热 jiārè　heating: ～炉 heating furnace ／～器 heating apparatus; heater

加入 jiārù　① add; mix; put in ② join; accede to: ～共产党 join the Communist Party ／～条约 accede to a treaty

加入国 jiārùguó　acceding (or adhering) state

加入书 jiārùshū　instrument of accession

加塞儿 jiāsāir　inf. push into a queue out of turn; jump a queue

加色法 jiāsèfǎ　additive process (in cinematography)

加上 jiāshàng　① add; give: ～种种罪名 level all sorts of charges against sb. ／给自己～新的头衔 confer a new title on oneself ② conj. moreover; in addition: 办个企业本来就不容易, ～这些没完没了的烦琐手续, 工作就更加困难了。 It isn't easy to start a business in the first place, but with all this endless red tape, it is all the more difficult. ／她住处离这里远, ～交通不便, 所以很少来。 She lives very far away, and what with transport problems, she seldom comes.

加深 jiāshēn　deepen: ～河道 deepen the channel of a river ／～理解 get a deeper understanding

加湿器 jiāshīqì　same as 空气加湿器 kōngqì jiāshīqì

加数 jiāshù　math. addend

加速 jiāsù　quicken; speed up; accelerate; expedite: ～资本周转 accelerate capital turnover ／队伍～前进。 The contingent quickened its advance. ／采取这些措施可以～工程进度。 These measures can speed up the pace of the project. ／～其灭亡 hasten the collapse (or doom) of

加速度 jiāsùdù　phys. acceleration: 重力～ acceleration of gravity

加速度计 jiāsùdùjì　accelerometer

加速器 jiāsùqì　phys. accelerator

加线 jiāxiàn　mus. ledger line; leger line

加以 jiāyǐ　① (used before a disyllabic verb to indicate that the action is directed towards sth. or sb. mentioned earlier in the sentence): 不合理的规定必须～改革。 The irrational rules must be changed. ／原计划须～修改。 It is necessary to revise the original plan. ／有问题要及时～解决。 Problems should be resolved in good time. ② conj. in addition; moreover: 这种鞋结实耐穿, ～价格便宜, 很受群众欢迎。 These shoes are very popular. They're sturdy and, what's more, they're cheap. ／我今晚不想去了, 我太累了, ～时间也太晚了。 I won't go tonight as I am tired. Besides, it's too late.

加意 jiāyì　with special care; with close attention: 对这些犯人, 你们必须～提防。 You must keep a close watch on the prisoners. ／～保护 protect with special care

加油 jiāyóu　① oil; lubricate: 这台机器该～了。 This machine needs oiling. ② refuel: 飞机要在上海降落～。 The plane will land in Shanghai for refuelling. ／空中～ in-flight (or air) refuelling ③ make an extra effort: ～干 work with added vigour ／～! ～! Come on! Come on! ／观众为运动员～。 The spectators cheered the players on.

加油车 jiāyóuchē　refuelling truck; refueller

加油飞机 jiāyóu fēijī　tanker aircraft

加油添醋 jiāyóu-tiāncù　same as 添油加醋 tiānyóu-jiācù

加油站 jiāyóuzhàn　filling (or petrol, gas) station

加枝添叶 jiāzhī-tiānyè　same as 添枝加叶 tiānzhī-jiāyè

加重 jiāzhòng　① make or become heavier; increase the weight of: ～任务 add to one's tasks ／～思想负担 add to one's worries ／～语气 say sth. with emphasis ② make or become more serious; aggravate: ～危机

夹¹（夾）

jiā ① press from both sides; place in between: 把相片～在书里 put the photos in between the leaves of a book / 用钳子把烧红的铁～住 grip a piece of red-hot iron with a pair of tongs / 用筷子～菜 pick up food with chopsticks / 他～在我们两人中间。He was sandwiched between the two of us. / 我的手指头被门～了一下。My fingers got squeezed in the door. / 鞋子～脚。The shoe pinches. ② mix; mingle; intersperse: ～在人群里 mingle with the crowd / 狂风～着暴雨 a violent wind accompanied by a torrential rain ③ clip, clamp, folder, etc.: 纸～ paper clip / 发～ hairpin / 文件～ folder

夹²（夾、挾）

jiā carry sth. under one's arm: ～着皮包 carry a briefcase under one's arm ——see also gā; jiá

夹板 jiābǎn ① boards for pressing sth. or holding things together ② *med.* splint: 上～ put (a limb, etc.) in splints / 石膏～ plaster splints

夹板气 jiābǎnqì the state of being between two fires: 婆媳不和，儿子在中间受～。When the mother quarrelled with the daughter-in-law, the son was caught between two fires.

夹层 jiācéng double layer: ～墙 a double-layered wall

夹叉射击 jiāchā shèjī *mil.* bracket

夹带 jiādài ① carry secretly; smuggle: 邮寄包裹不能～信件。Don't put letters into a parcel. ② notes smuggled into an examination hall

夹道 jiādào ① a narrow lane; passageway ② line both sides of the street: ～欢迎贵宾 line the street to welcome a distinguished guest

夹缝 jiāfèng a narrow space between two adjacent things; crack; crevice

夹攻 jiāgōng attack from both sides; converging attack; pincer attack: 受到两面～ be under a pincer attack; be caught in a two-way squeeze / 前后～ attack from the front and the rear simultaneously / 内外～ attack from both within and without

夹击 jiājī converging attack; pincer attack

夹剪 jiājiǎn tweezers; tongs

夹具 jiājù *mech.* clamping apparatus; fixture; jig

夹七夹八 jiāqī-jiābā incoherent; confused; cluttered (with irrelevant remarks): 他～地说了许多话，我也没听懂是什么意思。He rambled on at great length but I couldn't make head or tail of what he said.

夹生 jiāshēng (of food) half-cooked; (of a job) not well done; (of facts or knowledge) not quite assimilated

夹生饭 jiāshēngfàn ① half-cooked rice ② a job not thoroughly done

夹馅 jiāxiàn stuffed (pastry, etc.)

夹心 jiāxīn with filling: 果酱～糖 sweets with jam centre

夹心饼干 jiāxīn bǐnggān sandwich biscuits

夹叙夹议 jiāxù-jiāyì narration interspersed with comments: 他的游记写得～，谈了不少自己的看法。His travel sketch was written as a narrative interspersed with comments. In it he gave voice to many of his personal views.

夹杂 jiāzá be mixed up with; be mingled with: 脱粒机的轰鸣声～着年轻人的欢笑声。The droning of the threshers intermingled with youthful laughter. / 他说话～着南方口音。He speaks with a slight southern accent. / 文章里～不少生造的词语。The article is cluttered up with unclear coined expressions.

夹杂物 jiāzáwù *metall.* inclusion

夹竹桃 jiāzhútáo (sweet-scented) oleander

夹注 jiāzhù interlinear notes

夹子 jiāzi ① clip; tongs: 弹簧～ spring clip / 点心～ cake tongs / 衣服～ clothes-peg; clothespin ② folder: 文件～ folder; binder / 皮～ wallet; pocketbook

伽

jiā *phys.* gal ——see also gā; qié

伽倻琴 jiāyēqín a plucked stringed instrument, used by the Chaoxian nationality

佳

jiā good; fine; beautiful: ～景 fine landscape; beautiful view / 成绩甚～ achieve very good results

佳话 jiāhuà a deed praised far and wide; a story on everybody's lips; a much-told tale ——see also 传为佳话 chuán wéi jiāhuà

佳节 jiājié happy festival time; festival: 中秋～ the joyous Mid-Autumn Festival / 欢度国庆～ celebrate the joyous festival of National Day

佳境 jiājìng *formal* the most enjoyable or pleasant stage

佳句 jiājù beautiful line (in a poem); well-turned phrase

佳丽 jiālì *formal* ① (of looks, scenery, etc.) beautiful ② a beautiful woman

佳偶 jiā'ǒu *formal* a happily married couple

佳品 jiāpǐn excellent product; famous produce: 枸杞是滋补～。Chinese wolfberry is an excellent tonic.

佳期 jiāqī wedding (or nuptial) day

佳人 jiārén *formal* a beautiful woman; beauty

佳肴 jiāyáo delicacies: 美味～ delicious food

佳音 jiāyīn *formal* welcome news; good tidings; favourable reply: 静候～。I am awaiting the news of your success.

佳作 jiāzuò a fine piece of writing; an excellent work

迦

jiā a character used in proper names and in rendering some foreign names, as in 释迦牟尼 (Sakyamuni)

迦太基 Jiātàijī Carthage

迦太基人 Jiātàijīrén Carthaginian

茄

jiā see below ——see also qié

茄克 jiākè jacket

枷

jiā cangue

枷锁 jiāsuǒ yoke; chains; shackles; fetters: 精神～ spiritual shackles / 摆脱殖民主义的～ shake off the yoke of colonialism

浃（浹）

jiā see 汗流浃背 hàn liú jiā bèi

家

jiā ① family; household: 他全～都是工人。They're all workers in his family. / 张～和王～ the Zhangs and the Wangs ② home: 回～ go home / 不在～ not be in; be out / 上我～去吧。Come to my place. ③ a person or family engaged in a certain trade: 船家 chuánjiā ④ a specialist in a certain field: 科学家 kēxuéjiā / 画家 huàjiā ⑤ a school of thought; school: 法家 Fǎjiā ⑥ *hum.* my (used in speaking of relatives older than oneself): 家父 jiāfù ⑦ domestic; tame: 家兔 jiātù ⑧ *m.* (for families or business establishments): 两～人家 two families / 三～商店 three shops / 一～电影院 a cinema

家

.jia *inf.* ① (suffix used after certain nouns to indicate a specified kind or class of people: 女人～ women / 学生～ students / 小孩子～别插嘴！You kids shouldn't interrupt! / 现在姑娘～也会开飞机啦！Nowadays girls pilot planes, too! ② (suffix used after a man's name or designation of order of seniority to in-

dicate his wife): 秋生～ Qiusheng's wife / 老三～ Lao San's (Number Three's) wife
——see also gū; jie

家蚕 jiācán　silkworm

家产 jiāchǎn　(also 家财 jiācái) family property

家长里短 jiācháng-lǐduǎn　*dial.* domestic trivia: 谈谈～儿 have chitchat

家常 jiācháng　the daily life of a family; domestic trivia ——see also 扯家常 chě jiācháng; 话家常 huà jiācháng; 拉家常 lā jiācháng; 谈家常 tán jiācháng

家常便饭 jiācháng biànfàn　① homely food; simple meal: 在这儿吃午饭吧,～。 How about staying for lunch? Just potluck. ② common occurrence; routine; all in the day's work: 在旧社会当学徒,挨打受骂是～。 In the old society it was routine for an apprentice to be cursed and beaten. / 搬家对勘探队员来说,简直是～。 To the members of a prospecting team, moving from place to place is all in the day's work.

家常菜 jiāchángcài　home cooking

家常话 jiāchánghuà　small talk; chitchat

家丑 jiāchǒu　family scandal; the skeleton in the cupboard (or closet)

家丑不可外扬 jiāchǒu bùkě wàiyáng　the disgrace of a family should never be spread without; do not give publicity to family scandals; don't wash your dirty linen in public

家畜 jiāchù　domestic animal; livestock

家传 jiāchuán　handed down from the older generations of the family: 他们全家都爱好音乐,～的。 All of them are music lovers—it runs in the family.

家传秘方 jiāchuán mìfāng　a secret recipe handed down in the family

家祠 jiācí　ancestral temple or shrine

家慈 jiācí　*hum. formal* my mother

家当 jiādang　*inf.* family belongings; property: 我们这个润滑油厂创办的时候,全部～就是三口大锅。 When we first set up this lubricant factory, all we had was three cauldrons.

家道 jiādào　family financial situation: ～小康 be comfortably off / ～中落。 The family fortunes declined. *or* The family fortunes were at a low ebb.

家底 jiādǐ　family property accumulated over a long time; resources: ～薄 without substantial resources; not financially solid / 把咱们的～清理清理。 Let's take stock of what we've got.

家电 jiādiàn　short for 家用电器 jiāyòng diànqì

家丁 jiādīng　retainer of a big family

家法 jiāfǎ　① domestic discipline exercised by the head of a feudal household ② a rod for punishing children or servants in a feudal household ③ *old* theories and research methods handed down from master to pupil

家访 jiāfǎng　a visit to the parents of schoolchildren or young workers: 她工作认真,下课后又去～了。 She was very conscientious. After school, she went to visit her students' parents.

家风 jiāfēng　family tradition; family trait

家父 jiāfù　*hum.* my father

家鸽 jiāgē　pigeon

家馆 jiāguǎn　(also 家塾 jiāshú) family school (formerly a private school maintained by a rich family for the education of its own children and the children of its relatives)

家规 jiāguī　domestic discipline and family rules

家伙 jiāhuo　*inf.* ① tool; utensil; weapon: 不要打架,更不能动～。 You shouldn't fight, still less use weapons. / 这把～挺好使。 This is a very handy tool. ② fellow; guy: 小～ little chap; kid / 那个～是谁? Who's that fellow? / 你这～真会开玩笑。 What a joker you are! / 这～!

连结婚都不通知一声。 That devil! He never said a word about getting married. / 一帮反动～ a pack of reactionary scoundrels / 一个极端阴险的～ a most treacherous villain

家给人足 jiājǐ-rénzú　each family is provided for and every person is well-fed and well-clothed; all live in plenty

家计 jiājì　*formal* family livelihood

家家 jiājiā　every household: 这个村里～都爱养花。 In this village, every family loves growing flowers.

家家户户 jiājiā-hùhù　each and every family; every household: ～有余粮。 Every household has surplus grain. / 村里～都装上了电灯。 Electric lights have been installed in every house of the village.

家家有本难念的经 jiājiā yǒu běn nánniànde jīng　every family has some sort of trouble; every family has its own hard nut to crack

家教 jiājiào　family education; upbringing: 没有～ not properly brought up; ill-bred / ～严 be strict with one's children

家境 jiājìng　family financial situation; family circumstances: ～贫寒 with one's family in straitened circumstances / ～好 come from a well-to-do family

家居 jiājū　stay idle at home; be unemployed

家具 jiāju　furniture: 几件～ several pieces of furniture / 一套～ a set of furniture

家眷 jiājuàn　① wife and children; one's family ② wife

家口 jiākǒu　members of a family; the number of people in a family

家累 jiālěi　family burden

家里的 jiālide　(also 家里人 jiāliren) *inf.* (my) wife

家门 jiāmén　① the gate of one's house: 他父母说他要是再和那个女人鬼混就要把他赶出～。 His parents threatened to turn him out if he continued to fool around with that woman. ② *formal* one's own clan or family ③ *dial.* a member of one's own clan or family: 他是我的～堂兄弟。 He's my cousin on my father's side.

家庙 jiāmiào　same as 家祠 jiācí

家母 jiāmǔ　*hum.* my mother

家奴 jiānú　house slave

家贫如洗 jiā pín rú xǐ　utterly destitute; penniless

家破人亡 jiāpò-rénwáng　(also 家败人亡 jiābài-rénwáng) with one's family broken up, some gone away, some dead: 如果不是解放,我早已是～了。 If it were not for the liberation, my whole family would have been ruined or dead long ago.

家谱 jiāpǔ　family tree; genealogical tree; genealogy

家雀儿 jiāqiǎor　*dial.* sparrow

家禽 jiāqín　domestic fowl; poultry

家去 jiāqu　*inf.* return home; go back: ～吧,天黑了。 It's getting dark. Let's go home.

家人 jiārén　① family member ② servant

家史 jiāshǐ　family history: 老贫农血泪斑斑的～ an old poor peasant's family history of blood and tears

家世 jiāshì　*formal* a family's social standing

家事 jiāshì　family matters; domestic affairs

家室 jiāshì　① wife: 他已有～。 He is married. ② family

家什 jiāshí　*inf.* utensils, furniture, etc.: 厨房里的～擦得很干净。 The kitchen furnishings have all been wiped clean.

家书 jiāshū　① a letter home ② a letter from home

家书抵万金 jiāshū dǐ wàn jīn　a letter from home is worth ten thousand pieces of gold

家属 jiāshǔ　family members; (family) dependents: 工人～ families of workers / 军人～ armymen's families / 他的～没跟他一起来。 His family didn't come with him. / 死者及其～ the deceased and his bereaved family

家属工厂 jiāshǔ gōngchǎng　factory run by family mem-

bers of workers, cadres, armymen, etc.

家鼠 jiāshǔ　home mouse

家私 jiāsī　*inf.*　family property

家庭 jiātíng　family; household: 他有一个美满幸福的～。 He has a happy family. / 现在差不多每个～都有电冰箱了。 Now almost every household owns a fridge.

家庭背景 jiātíng bèijǐng　family background

家庭病床 jiātíng bìngchuáng　hospital bed at home (for a patient who stays at home and receives treatment from doctors who call periodically)

家庭成员 jiātíng chéngyuán　family member

家庭出身 jiātíng chūshēn　class status of one's family; family origin

家庭妇女 jiātíng fùnǚ　housewife

家庭副业 jiātíng fùyè　household sideline production

家庭观念 jiātíng guānniàn　attachment to one's family: 中国人～很重。 The Chinese have very strong feelings for family ties.

家庭教师 jiātíng jiàoshī　private teacher; tutor

家庭教育 jiātíng jiàoyù　family education; home education

家庭纠纷 jiātíng jiūfēn　family quarrel; domestic discord

家庭联产承包责任制 jiātíng liánchǎn chéngbāo zérènzhì　household contract responsibility system with remuneration linked to output

家庭生活 jiātíng shēnghuó　home life; family life

家庭作业 jiātíng zuòyè　homework

家童 jiātóng　boy servant

家徒四壁 jiā tú sì bì　have nothing but the bare walls in one's house—be utterly destitute

家兔 jiātù　rabbit

家务 jiāwù　household duties: ～劳动 housework; household chores / ～总也做不完。 Household chores never get completely finished. *or* There is no end to household chores.

家乡 jiāxiāng　hometown; native place

家乡话 jiāxiānghuà　native dialect

家小 jiāxiǎo　*inf.*　① wife and children ② wife

家信 jiāxìn　① a letter home ② a letter from home

家兄 jiāxiōng　*hum.*　my elder brother

家学 jiāxué　learning handed down in a family: ～渊源。 The family has a long tradition of learning.

家训 jiāxùn　*formal*　family precepts (*or* instructions): 《颜氏～》 *Yan Family Instructions*

家严 jiāyán　*hum. formal*　my father

家宴 jiāyàn　① family reunion feast ② family feast

家燕 jiāyàn　house swallow

家业 jiāyè　family property; property: 不要以为我们厂～大, 浪费一点不算啥。 Don't think, just because our factory is big and well-off, that we can waste things.

家蝇 jiāyíng　housefly

家用 jiāyòng　family expenses; housekeeping money: 贴补～ help out with the family expenses

家用电器 jiāyòng diànqì　electrical home appliances; electrical household appliances

家喻户晓 jiāyù-hùxiǎo　known to every household; widely known; known to all: 做到～, 人人明白 make known to every household and individual / 雷锋这个名字在中国已是～的了。 The name of Lei Feng is a household word in China.

家园 jiāyuán　home; homeland: 重建～ rebuild one's homeland; rebuild one's village or town / 重返～ return to one's homeland

家贼 jiāzéi　a thief within a house

家贼难防 jiāzéi nán fáng　a thief within a house is hard to guard against

家长 jiāzhǎng　① the head of a family; patriarch ② the parent or guardian of a child: 学校里明天开～会。 There will be a parents' meeting in our school

tomorrow.

家长式 jiāzhǎngshì　patriarchal: ～统治 paternalism; arbitrary rule as by a patriarch / 封建、～的领导 leadership characterized by feudal, patriarchal practices

家长制 jiāzhǎngzhì　patriarchal system

家长作风 jiāzhǎng zuòfēng　a high-handed way of dealing with people; patriarchal behaviour

家政 jiāzhèng　① household management ② home economics

家政学 jiāzhèngxué　home economics

家子 jiāzi　*inf.*　household; family: 这～有五口人。 There are five people in this family. / 这～的人都很勤快。 The family are all hard-working.

家族 jiāzú　clan; family

痂 jiā　scab; crust: 结痂 jiéjiā

袈 jiā　see below

袈裟 jiāshā　*kasaya*, a patchwork outer vestment worn by a Buddhist monk

笳 jiā　same as 胡笳 hújiā

跏 jiā　see below

跏趺 jiāfū　sit cross-legged (as the Buddhists do when in meditation)

筴（筴、梜） jiā　*arch.*　chopsticks

傢 jiā　see below

傢伙 jiāhuo　same as 家伙 jiāhuo

傢具 jiāju　same as 家具 jiāju

傢什 jiāshi　same as 家什 jiāshi

葭 jiā　*formal*　the young shoot of a reed

葭莩 jiāfú　*formal*　the membrane of a reed stem—a tenuous relationship: ～之亲 distant relatives

嘉 jiā　① good; fine: 嘉宾 jiābīn ② praise; commend: 精神可～ a praiseworthy spirit

嘉宾 jiābīn　honoured guest; welcome guest

嘉奖 jiājiǎng　commend; cite: 传令～全连指战员 cite the officers and men of the company for their meritorious service / 这个士兵因为作战英勇而受到～。 The soldier was cited for his bravery.

嘉奖令 jiājiǎnglìng　citation

嘉勉 jiāmiǎn　*formal*　praise and encourage

嘉许 jiāxǔ　*formal*　praise; approve

嘉言懿行 jiāyán-yìxíng　(also 嘉言善行 jiāyán-shànxíng) wise words and noble deeds

镓 jiā　*chem.*　gallium (Ga)

jiá

夹（夾、袷、袷） jiá　double-layered; lined: ～袄 lined jacket ——see also gā; jiā

荚（荚） jiá　pod: 结～ bear pods; pod

荚果 jiáguǒ　pod; legume

恝 jiá　*formal*　indifferent; unconcerned

恝然 jiárán　*formal*　indifferent; unconcerned

恝置 jiázhì　*formal*　disregard; neglect

铗（鋏） jiá　*formal*　① pincers; tongs ② sword ③ the hilt of a sword

戛(戛)

jiá *formal* knock gently; tap

戛戛 jiájiá *formal* ① difficult; hard going ② original: ～独造 have great originality

戛然 jiárán *onom. liter.* the loud cry of a bird: ～长鸣 long and loud cries

戛然而止 jiárán ér zhǐ (of a sound, etc.) cease abruptly; come to an abrupt end

蛱(蛺)

jiá see below

蛱蝶 jiádié a kind of butterfly harmful to crop plants; vanessa

颊(頰)

jiá cheek: 两～红润 with rosy cheeks / 双～凹陷 sunken (*or* hollow) cheeks

颊骨 jiágǔ cheekbone

颊囊 jiánáng *zool.* cheek pouch

jiǎ

甲¹

jiǎ ① the first of the ten Heavenly Stems (天干)(see also 干支 gān-zhǐ) ② first: ～级 first rate; Class A / 桂林山水～天下。The mountains and waters of Guilin are the finest under heaven. ③ (used for an unspecified person or thing): 某～与某乙 Mr. A and Mr. B / ～方和乙方 the first party and the second party / ～队 和乙队 team A and team B

甲²

jiǎ ① shell; carapace: 龟甲 guījiǎ ② nail: 指甲 zhǐjia ③ armour: 装甲车 zhuāngjiǎchē

甲³

jiǎ formerly, a unit of civil administration consisting of 10 households ——see also 保甲制度 bǎojiǎ zhìdù

甲板 jiǎbǎn deck

甲苯 jiǎběn *chem.* toluene; methylbenzene

甲兵 jiǎbīng *formal* ① armour and weaponry: military equipment ② soldier in armour

甲虫 jiǎchóng beetle

甲醇 jiǎchún *chem.* methyl alcohol; methanol; wood spirit; wood alcohol

甲酚 jiǎfēn *chem.* cresol

甲肝 jiǎgān short for 甲型肝炎 jiǎxíng gānyán

甲睾酮 jiǎgāotóng *pharm.* methyltestosterone

甲沟炎 jiǎgōuyán *med.* paronychia

甲骨文 jiǎgǔwén inscriptions on bones or tortoise shells of the Shang Dynasty (c. 16th-11th century B.C.)

甲基 jiǎjī methyl

甲基纤维素 jiǎjī xiānwéisù *pharm.* methylcellulose

甲克 jiǎkè same as 茄克 jiākè

甲壳 jiǎqiào crust

甲壳动物 jiǎqiào dòngwù crustacean

甲醛 jiǎquán *chem.* formaldehyde

甲醛水 jiǎquánshuǐ *chem.* formalin

甲酸 jiǎsuān *chem.* formic acid; methanoic acid

甲烷 jiǎwán methane

甲午战争 jiǎwǔ Zhànzhēng the Sino-Japanese War of 1894-1895 (launched by Japanese imperialism to annex Korea and invade China)

甲型肝炎 jiǎxíng gānyán hepatitis A

甲癣 jiǎxuǎn onychomycosis; ringworm of the nails

甲氧胺 jiǎyǎng'àn *pharm.* methoxamine

甲鱼 jiǎyú soft-shelled turtle

甲胄 jiǎzhòu *formal* armour

甲状腺 jiǎzhuàngxiàn *physiol.* thyroid gland

甲状腺功能亢进 jiǎzhuàngxiàn gōngnéng kàngjìn hyperthyroidism

甲状腺切开术 jiǎzhuàngxiàn qiēkāishù thyroidectomy

甲状腺素 jiǎzhuàngxiànsù thyroxine

甲状腺肿 jiǎzhuàngxiànzhǒng goitre

甲子 jiǎzǐ a cycle of sixty years ——see also 干支 gān-zhǐ

甲紫 jiǎzǐ gentian violet

岬

jiǎ ① (usu. used as part of a place name) cape; promontory: 成山～ Chengshanjia (in Shandong Province) ② a narrow passage between mountains

岬角 jiǎjiǎo cape; promontory

胛

jiǎ see below

胛骨 jiǎgǔ *physiol.* shoulder blade

贾

Jiǎ a surname ——see also gǔ

钾

jiǎ *chem.* potassium (K)

钾肥 jiǎféi potash fertilizer

钾碱 jiǎjiǎn potash

钾氩法 jiǎyàfǎ *archaeol.* potassium-argon dating (K-Ar)

钾盐 jiǎyán sylvite

假

jiǎ ① false; fake; sham; phoney; artificial: ～腿 artificial leg / ～民主 bogus democracy; sham democracy / ～和平 phoney peace / ～裁军 sham disarmament / ～检讨 insincere self-criticism ② if; in case suppose; assume; grant; presume ④ borrow; avail oneself of: 久～不归 keep putting off returning sth. one has borrowed; appropriate sth. borrowed for one's own use ——see also jià

假扮 jiǎbàn disguise oneself as; dress up as: 小游击队员～放牛娃, 骗过了敌人的岗哨。The boy guerrilla fighter disguised himself as a cowherd and got past the enemy sentry.

假充 jiǎchōng pretend to be; pose as: ～内行 pretend to be an expert

假传圣旨 jiǎ chuán shèngzhǐ deliver a false imperial edict—deliver a false order

假道 jiǎdào via; by way of: 代表团～欧洲去联合国。The delegation went to the United Nations via Europe.

假道学 jiǎdàoxué a sanctimonious person; hypocrite

假定 jiǎdìng ① suppose; assume; grant; presume: ～有这么一回事 suppose it really happened / ～这是真的, 也影响不了大局。Even if this is the case, it will not affect the whole situation. ② hypothesis

假发 jiǎfà wig

假分数 jiǎfēnshù *math.* improper fraction

假根 jiǎgēn *bot.* rhizoid

假公济私 jiǎ gōng jì sī use public office for private gain; jobbery

假果 jiǎguǒ *bot.* pseudocarp; spurious fruit

假花 jiǎhuā artificial flower

假话 jiǎhuà lie; falsehood: 说～ tell lies

假借 jiǎjiè ① make use of: ～外力 make use of outside forces / ～名义 under the guise of; in the name of; under false pretences ② *linguis.* phonetic loan characters, characters adopted to represent homophones, e.g. 求 qiú (fur) for 求 qiú (entreat)—one of the six categories of Chinese characters (六书)

假令 jiǎlìng *conj. formal* if; in case; in the event of

假冒 jiǎmào pass oneself off as; palm off (a fake as genuine): 谨防～。Beware of imitations.

假寐 jiǎmèi *formal* catnap; doze

假面具 jiǎmiànjù mask; false front: 他戴了个～, 我没认出他来。He was wearing a mask and I didn't recognize him. / 撕下伪君子的～ unmask a hypocrite

假面舞会 jiǎmiàn wǔhuì masked ball; masquerade

假名[1] jiǎmíng pseudonym

假名[2] jiǎmíng *kana* (Japanese syllabic script)

假模假式 jiǎmó-jiǎshì insincere; hypocritical: 她巴不得我快离开,可是还～地要留我吃饭。Actually she was anxious to see me leave, but she most insincerely asked me to stay for lunch.

假撇清 jiǎpiēqīng *dial.* pretend innocence

假漆 jiǎqī varnish

假仁假义 jiǎrén-jiǎyì pretended benevolence and righteousness; hypocrisy

假如 jiǎrú *conj.* if; supposing; in case: ～有这必要,就这么干吧。Do so, if necessary. / ～明天开会,准备工作来得及吗? Supposing we hold the meeting tomorrow, will there be enough time to prepare? / ～我忘了,请提醒我一下。Remind me in case I forget. / ～有空,我一定来。I will come provided I have the time.

假若 jiǎruò *conj.* if; supposing; in case: ～我来不了,我会通知你的。If I should be unable to come, I'll let you know. / ～情况是这样,我就同意。If that is the case, I'll agree.

假嗓子 jiǎsǎngzi *falsetto*

假山 jiǎshān rockery

假设 jiǎshè ① suppose; assume; grant; presume ② hypothesis: 科学～ a scientific hypothesis

假声 jiǎshēng *mus.* falsetto

假使 jiǎshǐ *conj.* if; in case; in the event that: ～他不同意,那就作罢。If he disagrees, let the matter drop. / ～他到这儿来,通知我一下。Let me know should he come here.

假释 jiǎshì *leg.* release on parole (*or* on probation)

假手 jiǎshǒu do sth. through sb. else; make a cat's-paw of sb.

假手于人 jiǎshǒu yú rén (achieve one's end) through the instrumentality of sb. else

假说 jiǎshuō hypothesis

假死 jiǎsǐ ① *med.* suspended animation ② *zool.* play dead; feign death; play possum

假托 jiǎtuō ① on the pretext of: 他～有病没来开会。He absented himself from the meeting on the pretext of illness. ② under sb. else's name: 这篇文章不是他写的,是别人～他的名义发表的。He didn't write the essay; somebody else did, and published it under his name. ③ by means of; through the medium of: 人们～披着羊皮的狼的故事说明要警惕伪装的敌人。The story of the wolf in sheep's clothing is a fable intended to teach people to be on guard against enemies in disguise.

假想 jiǎxiǎng ① imagination; hypothesis; supposition ② imaginary; hypothetical; fictitious: 这个故事里的人物都是～的。The characters in this story are all fictitious.

假想敌 jiǎxiǎngdí *mil.* imaginary enemy; hypothetical enemy

假象[1] jiǎxiàng (also 假相 jiǎxiàng) false appearance: 制造～ create a false impression; put up a false front / 不要被～所迷惑。Don't be misled by appearances.

假象[2] jiǎxiàng *geol.* pseudomorph

假小子 jiǎxiǎozi tomboy

假惺惺 jiǎxīngxīng hypocritically; unctuously: ～地表示愿意支持 hypocritically express willingness to support / ～地宣称 declare unctuously

假牙 jiǎyá dental prosthesis; false tooth; denture

假眼 jiǎyǎn ocular prosthesis; artificial eye; glass eye

假以辞色 jiǎ yǐ císè speak to sb. encouragingly

假意 jiǎyì ① unction; insincerity; hypocrisy ② pretend; put on: ～奉承 cheap flattery

假造 jiǎzào ① forge; counterfeit: ～证件 forge a certificate / 这张钞票是～的。This banknote is a forgery. *or* This is a forged banknote. ② invent; fabricate: ～理由

invent an excuse / ～罪名 cook up a false charge against; frame up

假正经 jiǎzhèngjing be hypocritical; pretend to be a saint

假肢 jiǎzhī artificial limb

假植 jiǎzhí *agric.* heel in

假装 jiǎzhuāng pretend; feign; simulate; make believe: 他～生病。He pretended illness. / ～不知道 feign ignorance / 孩子们～解放军攻山头。The boys played at being PLA men storming a mountain stronghold.

斝 (斚) jiǎ an ancient round-mouthed three-legged wine vessel

瘕 jiǎ a lump in the abdomen

jià

价 (價) jià ① price: 买之前,你该问问～。Before buying it you should ask the price. ② value: 等价交换 děngjià jiāohuàn ③ *chem.* valence: 氢是一～的元素。Hydrogen is a one-valence element. ——see also jie

价格 jiàgé price: 标明～ mark (goods) with a price tag; have goods clearly priced / ～管理 price control / ～政策 price policy

价格补贴 jiàgé bǔtiē price subsidies (from the state); state subsidies to off-set price

价格结构 jiàgé jiégòu price mechanism

价格体制 jiàgé tǐzhì price system: 建立合理的～ establish a rational price system

价格指数 jiàgé zhǐshù price index

价款 jiàkuǎn money paid for sth. purchased or received for sth. sold; cost

价廉物美 jiàlián-wùměi (of a commodity) cheap but good; inexpensive but elegant

价码 jiàmǎ *inf.* listed price; marked price

价目 jiàmù marked price; price

价目表 jiàmùbiǎo price list

价钱 jiàqian price: 讲～ haggle over the price; bargain / ～公道 a fair (*or* decent, reasonable) price / 西红柿什么～? How much are the tomatoes? / ～在涨。The prices are rising. / 这张书桌你是什么～买的? What price did you pay for this desk?

价值 jiàzhí ① *econ.* value: 剩余价值 shèngyú jiàzhí ② worth; value: ～五百万元的设备 five million yuan worth of equipment; equipment worth (*or* valued at) five million yuan / 毫无～ completely worthless / 这些资料对我们很有～。This data is of great value to us. / 这是一个很有～的试验。This is a worthy experiment.

价值尺度 jiàzhí chǐdù measure of value

价值观念 jiàzhí guānniàn values: 社会～ social values / 他的～跟我不一样。He has different values than I do.

价值规律 jiàzhí guīlǜ *econ.* law of value

价值连城 jiàzhí liánchéng worth several cities—invaluable; priceless

价值量 jiàzhíliàng *econ.* magnitude of value

价值形态 jiàzhí xíngtài *econ.* form of value

驾 jià ① harness; draw (a cart, etc.): ～上牲口耕地 harness cattle to plough the fields / 那匹马没～过车。That horse has never been harnessed to a cart. ② drive (a vehicle); pilot (a plane); sail (a boat) ③ *honor.* you: 劳驾 láojià / 大驾 dàjià ④ the emperor: 保驾 bǎojià / 驾崩 jiàbēng

驾崩 jiàbēng (of an emperor) pass away; die

驾临 jiàlín *pol.* your arrival; your esteemed presence:

恭候～。Your presence is requested.

驾轻就熟　jiàqīng-jiùshú　drive a light carriage on a familiar road—handle a job with ease because of previous experience; do a familiar job with ease

驾驶　jiàshǐ　drive (a vehicle); pilot (a ship or plane): ～拖拉机 drive a tractor

驾驶舱　jiàshǐcāng　*aviation* control cabin; cockpit; pilot's compartment

驾驶杆　jiàshǐgǎn　*aviation* control stick (*or* column); joystick

驾驶盘　jiàshǐpán　steering wheel

驾驶室　jiàshǐshì　driver's cab

驾驶台　jiàshǐtái　bridge (of a ship)

驾驶员　jiàshǐyuán　driver (of a vehicle); pilot (of an airplane)

驾驶执照　jiàshǐ zhízhào　driving (*or* driver's) license

驾束式导弹　jiàshùshì dǎodàn　beam rider

驾驭　jiàyù　(also 驾御 jiàyù) ① drive (a cart, horse, etc.): 这匹马不好～。This horse is hard to control. ② control; master: ～自然 tame nature / 能够～复杂的局势 be able to cope with complicated situations

驾辕　jiàyuán　pull a cart or carriage from between the shafts; be hitched up: 车太重, 得用一匹大骡子～。The cart is heavy and we need to hitch up a big mule.

架

架　jià　① frame; rack; shelf; stand: 房～ the frame of a house / 工具～ tool rack / 黄瓜～ cucumber trellis / 钢～桥 steel-framed bridge ② put up; erect: 把梯子～在墙上。Put up the ladder against the wall. / 鼻梁上～着一副眼镜。His nose was surmounted by a pair of glasses. / ～桥 put up (*or* build) a bridge / ～电话线 set up telephone lines / ～枪 stack rifles / ～起机枪 mount a machine gun ③ fend off; ward off; withstand: 他一刀砍来, 我拿枪～住。I fended off his sword thrust with my spear. ④ support; prop; help: ～着伤员走路 help a wounded soldier to walk / ～着拐走 walk on crutches / 他扭了脚脖子, 我们只得把他～回去。He sprained his ankle and had to be helped home. ⑤ kidnap; take sb. away forcibly: 强行～走 carry sb. away by force; kidnap ⑥ fight; quarrel: 打架 dǎjià ⑦ *m.* (for machines, airplanes, and instruments which rest on a tripod or stand): 一～收音机 a radio set / 几百～飞机 several hundred planes / 一～照像机 a camera / 一～钢琴 a piano

架不住　jiàbuzhù　*dial.* ① cannot sustain (the weight); cannot stand (the pressure); cannot stand up against: 他开始不想来, ～我一说, 也就来了。At first he didn't feel like coming, but I persuaded him to. / 谁也～这么大的浪费。Nobody can afford to be so extravagant. ② be no match for; cannot compete with: 主队虽然技术不错, 也～客队合作得好。The home team displayed great skill but were no match for the visitors in teamwork.

架次　jiàcì　sortie: 出动四批飞机共六十～ fly sixty sorties in four groups

架得住　jiàdezhù　*dial.* be able to bear or endure: 小学生怎么～这么多家庭作业? How can the pupils cope with so much homework?

架豆　jiàdòu　another name for 菜豆 càidòu

架空　jiàkōng　① built on stilts: 这里的竹楼都是～的。The bamboo huts here are all built on stilts. ② impracticable; unpractical: 不采取相应的措施, 计划就会～。Unless we adopt the necessary measures the plan will come to nothing. ③ make sb. a mere figurehead

架空管道　jiàkōng guǎndào　overhead pipe

架票　jiàpiào　kidnap (for ransom)

架设　jiàshè　erect (above ground or water level, as on stilts or posts): 这儿正在～一座天桥。A platform

bridge is being erected here. / 在河上～浮桥 throw a pontoon bridge across the river / ～输电线路 erect power transmission lines

架势　jiàshi　(also 架式 jiàshi) *dial.* posture; stance; manner: 摆出一副海上霸主的～ assume the posture of lord of the seas / 看他们的～, 是来碴打架的。They seem to have come only to pick a quarrel with us. / 他不会干农活, 拿起耙子来没个～。He was a poor hand at farming and held his rake clumsily.

架子　jiàzi　① frame; stand; rack; shelf: 脸盆～ washstand ② framework; skeleton; outline: 写文章要先搭好～。Make an outline before you start writing. / 把新机构的～搭起来 set up the framework of the new organization ③ airs; haughty manner: 没有～ be modest and unassuming; be easy of approach / 放下～ get down from one's high horse ④ posture; stance: 他拉开～, 打起了太极拳。He adopted a stance and began to do *Taiji* shadowboxing. ——see also 摆架子 bǎi jiàzi; 拿架子 ná jiàzi

架子车　jiàzichē　handcart

架子工　jiàzigōng　scaffolder

架子猪　jiàzizhū　feeder pig

假

假　jià　① holiday; vacation ② leave of absence; furlough: 病假 bìngjià ——see also jiǎ

假期　jiàqī　vacation; holiday; period of leave

假日　jiàrì　holiday; day off

假条　jiàtiáo　① application for leave ② leave permit: 病～ doctor's certificate (for sick leave)

嫁

嫁　jià　① (of a woman) marry: 她～了个出租车司机。She married a taxi driver. ② marry off a daughter: 她把女儿～给一个出租车司机。She married her daughter to a taxi driver. ③ shift; transfer: 转嫁 zhuǎnjià②

嫁祸于人　jià huò yú rén　shift the misfortune onto sb. else; put the blame on sb. else

嫁鸡随鸡, 嫁狗随狗　jià jī suí jī, jià gǒu suí gǒu　follow the man you marry, be he fowl or cur

嫁接　jiàjiē　*bot.* grafting

嫁奁　jiàlián　dowry; trousseau

嫁娶　jiàqǔ　marriage

嫁人　jiàrén　*inf.* (of a woman) get married; marry

嫁妆　jiàzhuang　dowry; trousseau

稼

稼　jià　① sow (grain): 稼穑 jiàsè ② cereals; crops: 庄稼 zhuāngjia

稼穑　jiàsè　*formal* sowing and reaping; farming; farm work

jiān

戋(戔)

戋(戔)　jiān　see below

戋戋　jiānjiān　*formal* small; tiny: ～之数 an insignificant amount; a very small amount; a little bit

尖

尖　jiān　① point; tip; top: 钢笔～ the point of a pen / 铅笔～ the tip of a pencil / 指～ fingertip / 塔～ the pinnacle of a pagoda ② pointed; tapering: ～下巴 a pointed chin / 把铅笔削～ sharpen a pencil ③ shrill; piercing: ～声～气 in a shrill voice / ～叫 scream ④ sharp; acute: 耳朵～ have sharp ears; be sharp-eared / 眼～ have sharp eyes; be sharp-eyed / 鼻子～ have an acute (*or* sharp) sense of smell ⑤ the best of its kind; the pick of the bunch; the cream of the crop: 全班学生中他是个～儿。He is a top-notch student in the class.

尖兵　jiānbīng　① *mil.* point ② trailblazer; pathbreaker; pioneer; vanguard: 他是开拓石油工业的～。He was a

pioneer in developing the oil industry.

尖刀 jiāndāo sharp knife; dagger: 像一把～插入敌人心脏 like a dagger stuck into the enemy's heart

尖顶 jiāndǐng pinnacle

尖端 jiānduān ① pointed end; acme; peak: 标枪的～ the point of a javelin ② most advanced; sophisticated: ～产品 highly sophisticated products

尖端放电 jiānduān fàngdiàn point discharge

尖端科学 jiānduān kēxué most advanced branches of science; frontiers of science

尖端武器 jiānduān wǔqì sophisticated weapons

尖刻 jiānkè acrimonious; caustic; biting: 说话～ speak with biting sarcasm

尖括号 jiānkuòhào angle brackets (〈　〉)

尖利 jiānlì ① sharp; keen; cutting: ～的钢刀 a sharp knife / 眼光～ sharp-eyed ② shrill; piercing: ～的叫声 a shrill cry

尖溜溜 jiānliūliū dial. sharp; pointed: ～的嗓子 a shrill voice

尖脐 jiānqí ① the narrow triangular abdomen of a male crab ② male crab

尖锐 jiānruì ① sharp-pointed ② penetrating; incisive; sharp; keen: ～的对比 a sharp contrast / ～的批评 incisive (or sharp) criticism / ～地指出 point out sharply / 他看问题很～. He sees things with a keen (or sharp) eye. ③ shrill; piercing: ～的哨声 the shrill sound of a whistle ④ intense; acute; sharp: ～的思想斗争 sharp mental conflicts / ～对立 be diametrically opposed to each other

尖锐化 jiānruìhuà sharpen; intensify; become more acute: 矛盾～了. The contradictions intensified.

尖酸 jiānsuān acrid; acrimonious; tart

尖酸刻薄 jiānsuān kèbó tart and mean; bitterly sarcastic: 这人说起话来老这么～. He is given to making scathing remarks.

尖团音 jiāntuányīn (in some dialects and in opera singing) sharp and rounded sounds (the former being a class of syllables beginning with the nonpalatals z, c, and s, e.g. 尖 ziān, 千 ciān, 先 siān, 三 sān; the latter being a class of syllables beginning with the palatals j, q, x, zh, ch, and sh, e.g. 兼 jiān, 牵 qiān, 掀 xiān, 山 shān)

尖音 jiānyīn see 尖团音 jiāntuányīn

尖子 jiānzi ① the best of its kind; the pick of the bunch; the cream of the crop: 他是班上的～. He's one of the top students in the class. ② a sudden rise in pitch (in opera singing)

尖嘴薄舌 jiānzuǐ-bóshé have a caustic and flippant tongue

尖嘴猴腮 jiānzuǐ-hóusāi have a mouth that sticks out and a chin like an ape's—have a wretched appearance

奸[1] jiān ① wicked; evil; treacherous: 奸计 jiānjì ② traitor: 汉奸 hànjiān ③ inf. self-seeking and wily: 这个人才～哪, 总想占便宜. He's a self-seeker; he's always on the make.

奸[2]（姦） jiān illicit sexual relations: 通奸 tōngjiān

奸臣 jiānchén treacherous court official

奸夫 jiānfū adulterer

奸妇 jiānfù adultress

奸宄 jiānguǐ formal evildoers; malefactors

奸猾 jiānhuá (also 奸滑 jiānhuá) treacherous; crafty; deceitful

奸计 jiānjì an evil plot

奸佞 jiānnìng formal ① crafty and fawning ② crafty sycophant

奸商 jiānshāng unscrupulous merchant; profiteer

奸污 jiānwū rape or seduce

奸细 jiānxi spy; enemy agent

奸险 jiānxiǎn wicked and crafty; treacherous; malicious

奸笑 jiānxiào sinister (or villainous) smile

奸邪 jiānxié formal ① crafty and evil; treacherous ② a crafty and evil person: 士无幸赏, 无逾行, 杀必当, 罪不赦, 则～无所容私。(《韩非子》) If men do not receive any unearned rewards nor overstep their authority, if death penalties are justly handed out and no crime goes unpunished, then evil and malicious men will find no opening to carry out their private schemes.

奸雄 jiānxióng a person who achieves high position by unscrupulous scheming; arch-careerist: 治世之能臣, 乱世之～ a capable minister in an age of tranquillity, a treacherous pretender in an age of chaos (said of men like Cao Cao 曹操)

奸淫 jiānyín ① illicit sexual relations; adultery ② rape or seduce

奸淫掳掠 jiānyín lǔlüè rape and loot: ～, 无恶不作 rape and pillage and commit all kinds of atrocities

奸贼 jiānzéi traitor; conspirator

奸诈 jiānzhà fraudulent; crafty; treacherous

间（閒） jiān ① between; among: 师生之～ between teacher and pupil / 同志之～ among comrades ② within a definite time or space: 世间 shìjiān / 晚间 wǎnjiān ③ room: 里间 lǐjiān / 衣帽间 yīmàojiān ④ m. ⓐ (for rooms): 一～卧室 a bedroom / 四～屋子 four rooms ⓑ (for room space) a section of a room or the lateral space between two pairs of pillars: 三～门面 a three-bay shop front ——see also jiàn

间冰期 jiānbīngqī geol. interglacial stage; interglacial

间不容发 jiān bù róng fà not a hair's breadth apart or away—extremely critical

间架 jiānjià ① framework of a house ② form of a Chinese character ③ structure of an essay

间量 jiānliang dial. the area of a room; floor space: 这间屋子～儿太小. This room is not spacious enough.

间奏曲 jiānzòuqǔ mus. ① entr'acte ② intermezzo

歼（殲） jiān annihilate; wipe out; destroy: ～敌五千 annihilate 5,000 enemy troops

歼击 jiānjī attack and wipe out

歼击机 jiānjījī fighter plane; fighter; pursuit plane

歼灭 jiānmiè annihilate; wipe out; destroy: ～一切敢于入侵之敌 destory any enemy that should dare to intrude / ～敌人有生力量 wipe out the enemy's effective strength / ～性的打击 a crushing blow; a smashing blow

歼灭射击 jiānmiè shèjī annihilation fire

歼灭战 jiānmièzhàn war or battle of annihilation

坚（堅） jiān ① hard; solid; firm; strong: ～冰 solid ice; hard ice / 身残志～ broken in body but firm in spirit ② a heavily fortified point; fortification; stronghold: 攻坚 gōngjiān ③ firmly; steadfastly; resolutely: ～拒 flatly refuse / ～称 state insistently; insist

坚壁 jiānbì hide supplies to prevent the enemy from seizing them; place in a cache; cache: 把粮食～起来 hide grain from the enemy

坚壁清野 jiānbì-qīngyě strengthen defence works, evacuate noncombatants, and hide provisions and livestock; strengthen the defences and clear the fields

坚不可摧 jiān bùkě cuī indestructible; impregnable; indomitable: ～的堡垒 an indestructible bulwark

坚持 jiānchí persist in; persevere in; uphold; insist on; stick to; adhere to: ～原则 adhere (or stick) to principle / ～真理 hold firmly to the truth / ～上次会议上提出的条件 insist on the terms put forward at the pre-

vious session /～已见 hold on to one's own views /～错误 persist in one's errors / 你应该～做早操。You must persevere in doing morning exercises. / 救援队希望船里的人能～到他们赶来。The rescue team hoped that the men in the boat could hold out till they arrived. / 再走十里，～得了吗? Can you hold on for another ten *li*? / 他～要走。He insisted on leaving. / 他们在阵地上～了三天三夜。They held the position for three days and nights.

坚持不懈 jiānchí bù xiè unremitting; persistent: 作～的努力 make unremitting efforts

坚持不渝 jiānchí bù yú persistent; persevering

坚定 jiāndìng ① firm; staunch; steadfast: ～的决心 strong determination /～的步伐 firm strides /～的立场 a firm stand /～的意志 constancy of purpose /～正确的政治方向 a firm and correct political orientation / 革命的～性 revolutionary steadfastness (*or* staunchness) ② strengthen: ～了攀登科学技术新高峰的决心 strengthen one's resolve to scale new heights of science and technology

坚定不移 jiāndìng bù yí firm and unshakable; unswerving; unflinching: ～的信念 an impregnable belief; an unshakable faith

坚固 jiāngù firm; solid; sturdy; strong: ～耐用 sturdy and durable /～的家具 solid furniture /～的工事 strong fortifications / 这座桥造得很～。This bridge is very solidly built.

坚固呢 jiāngùní denim

坚果 jiānguǒ *bot.* nut

坚甲利兵 jiānjiǎ-lìbīng strong armour and sharp weapons—armed might

坚决 jiānjué firm; resolute; determined: ～支持 firmly support; stand firmly by /～反对 resolutely oppose / 态度～ a determined attitude; a firm position /～完成任务! We'll carry out the task without fail! / 采取～措施 take resolute measures

坚苦 jiānkǔ steadfast and assiduous

坚苦卓绝 jiānkǔ zhuōjué showing the utmost fortitude: ～的斗争 an extremely hard and bitter struggle; a most arduous struggle /～的战斗 a hard-fought battle

坚牢 jiānláo strong; solid

坚牢度 jiānláodù *text.* fastness: 耐日光～ fastness to sunlight; sunfastness / 耐洗～ washfastness

坚强 jiānqiáng ① strong; firm; staunch: ～的意志 strong will /～的领导 firm leadership / 一个性格～的人 a person of strong character ② strengthen: ～党的组织 strengthen the Party organizations

坚忍 jiānrěn steadfast and persevering (in face of difficulties)

坚韧 jiānrèn ① tough and tensile ② firm and tenacious: 运动员在比赛中表现出～的斗志。The athletes displayed great tenacity throughout the contest.

坚韧不拔 jiānrèn bù bá firm and indomitable; persistent and dauntless: ～的革命精神 indomitable revolutionary spirit /～的毅力 an inflexible will

坚如磐石 jiān rú pánshí solid as a rock; rock-firm

坚实 jiānshí ① solid; substantial: 他做的家具相当～。The furniture he made is quite sturdy. /～的基础 a solid foundation / 迈出～的步子 make solid progress / 这条公路～平整。This is a smooth, strongly built highway. ② strong; robust: ～的年轻人 a robust young man

坚守 jiānshǒu stick to ; hold fast to; stand fast: ～岗位 stand fast at one's post /～阵地 hold fast to one's position; hold one's ground

坚挺 jiāntǐng *finance* strong: 美元～。The dollar was getting stronger /～的市场价格 a strong market / 石油价格趋向～。The oil price is tending upwards.

坚信 jiānxìn firmly believe: 他们～一定能获得胜利。

They are fully confident that they will win.

坚信不疑 jiānxìn bù yí firmly believe; have not the slightest doubt

坚毅 jiānyì firm and persistent; with unswerving determination; with inflexible will

坚硬 jiānyìng hard; solid: ～的岩石 solid rock

坚贞 jiānzhēn faithful; constant

坚贞不屈 jiānzhēn bù qū remain faithful and unyielding

坚执 jiānzhí insist on; persist in: ～已见 hold on to one's own views /～不允 refuse to give in

肩

jiān ① shoulder: ～并～ shoulder to shoulder; side by side / 耸耸～ shrug one's shoulders ② take on; undertake; shoulder; bear: 身～重任 shoulder heavy responsibilities

肩膀 jiānbǎng shoulder

肩负 jiānfù take on; undertake; shoulder; bear: 我们～人民的希望。The people place their hopes on us. /～着全体职工委托的任务 be entrusted with a mission by the whole staff /～光荣的任务 undertake a glorious task /～重荷 bear a heavy burden; shoulder heavy loads

肩胛骨 jiānjiǎgǔ *physiol.* scapula; shoulder blade

肩摩毂击 jiānmó-gǔjī shoulder to shoulder and hub to hub—crowded with people and vehicles

肩头 jiāntóu ① *formal* on the shoulders ② *dial.* shoulders

肩舆 jiānyú sedan chair

肩章 jiānzhāng ① shoulder loop; shoulder strap ② epaulet

艰(艱)

jiān difficult; hard

艰巨 jiānjù arduous; formidable: ～的工作 arduous work / 光荣而～的任务 a glorious but arduous task / 付出～的劳动 make tremendous efforts / 这个工程非常～。This is a formidable project.

艰苦 jiānkǔ arduous; difficult; hard; tough: ～的生活 hard life /～的工作 a tough job / 做～细致的思想工作 do painstaking ideological work /～创业 build an enterprise through arduous effort / 自愿到最～的地方去 volunteer to go where conditions are hardest / 艰苦的环境能磨炼人的意志。Difficult circumstances can temper one's will.

艰苦备尝 jiānkǔ bèi cháng have experienced all hardships; have suffered untold hardships

艰苦奋斗 jiānkǔ fèndòu hard struggle: 不经过～, 就不能胜利。We cannot be victorious without arduous struggle. / 永远保持～的作风 always keep to the style of hard struggle and plain living

艰苦朴素 jiānkǔ pǔsù hard work and plain living: 平生～ live simply and work hard all one's life

艰苦卓绝 jiānkǔ zhuōjué extreme hardship and difficulty: ～的斗争 an extremely hard and bitter struggle; a most arduous struggle

艰难 jiānnán difficult; hard: 行动～ walk with difficulty / 生活～ live in straitened circumstances /～的岁月 difficult days; hard times; arduous years

艰难竭蹶 jiānnán jiéjué hardship and destitution: 于～之中, 存聊到卒岁之想 hope in the midst of hardship and destitution to tide over the year

艰难困苦 jiānnán kùnkǔ difficulties and hardships: 不论多么～, 我们都要继续战斗下去。No matter what the difficulties and hardships, we will fight on.

艰难曲折 jiānnán qūzhé difficulties and setbacks: 经过无数～ experience countless difficulties and setbacks

艰难险阻 jiānnán-xiǎnzǔ difficulties and obstacles: 路上遇着了说不尽的～。We encountered untold difficulties and dangers on the way.

艰涩 jiānsè involved and abstruse; intricate and

obscure: 文词～ involved and abstruse writing

艰深 jiānshēn difficult to understand; abstruse

艰危 jiānwēi difficulties and dangers (confronting a nation)

艰险 jiānxiǎn hardships and dangers: 不避～ brave hardships and dangers

艰辛 jiānxīn hardships: 他们历尽～, 方取得胜利。They achieved success only after experiencing all kinds of hardships.

浅 (淺、濺)
jiān see below ——see also qiǎn

浅浅 jiānjiān *onom. liter.* the sound of flowing water

兼
jiān ① double; twice: 兼旬 jiānxún ② simultaneously; concurrently: 任总理～外交部长 be Premier and concurrently Minister of Foreign Affairs / ～管 be concurrently in charge of; also look after / 身～数职 hold several posts simultaneously

兼爱 jiān'ài universal love (as advocated by the ancient philosopher Mo Zi 墨子)

兼备 jiānbèi have both... and...: 德才兼备 dé-cái jiānbèi

兼并 jiānbìng annex (territory, property, etc.): 用武力～邻国领土 annex the territories of a neighbouring country by force

兼并国 jiānbìngguó annexing state

兼差 jiānchāi same as 兼职 jiānzhí

兼程 jiānchéng travel at double speed: ～前进 advance at the double / 日夜～ travel day and night

兼而有之 jiān ér yǒu zhī have both at the same time

兼顾 jiāngù give consideration to (*or* take account of) two or more things: 发展生产和改善人民生活二者必须～。Consideration must be given to both the development of production and the improvement of the people's livelihood.

兼课 jiānkè ① do some teaching in addition to one's main occupation ② hold two or more teaching jobs concurrently

兼任 jiānrèn ① hold a concurrent post: 党委副书记～英语系系主任。The deputy Party committee secretary is concurrently dean of the English Department. ② part-time

兼容 jiānróng *TV* compatible: ～制电视 compatible television

兼容并包 jiānróng-bìngbāo all-embracing; all-inclusive

兼收并蓄 jiānshōu-bìngxù incorporate things of diverse nature; take in everything: 在继承古代文化上, 我们决不能无批判地～。In inheriting our old culture, we should never swallow anything and everything uncritically.

兼祧 jiāntiāo *formal* be appointed heir to one's uncle as well as to one's father

兼听则明, 偏信则暗 jiān tīng zé míng, piān xìn zé àn listen to both sides and you will be enlightened; heed only one side and you will be benighted

兼旬 jiānxún twenty days

兼之 jiānzhī *formal* furthermore; besides; in addition; moreover

兼职 jiānzhí ①hold two or more posts concurrently: ～过多 hold too many posts at the same time ② concurrent post; part-time job: 辞去～ resign one's concurrent job

兼职教师 jiānzhí jiàoshī part-time teacher

监 (監)
jiān ① supervise; inspect; watch: 监督 jiāndū ② prison; jail: 收监 shōujiān ——see also jiàn

监测 jiāncè monitor: ～新药的副作用 monitor the side effects of new drugs / 加强环境～ intensify monitoring of the environment

监测器 jiāncèqì monitor: 污染～ contamination moni-

tor

监察 jiānchá supervise; control: 加强对行政工作人员的～ strengthen supervision over administrative personnel

监察委员会 jiānchá wěiyuánhuì control commission; supervisory committee

监察员 jiāncháyuán supervisor; controller

监场 jiānchǎng invigilate

监督 jiāndū ① supervise; superintend; control: 国家机关工作人员必须接受群众～。The personnel of organs of state must accept supervision by the masses. / 加强质量～和财务 exercise effective supervision with regard to quality and finances / 国际～ international control; international supervision ② supervisor

监督劳动 jiāndū láodòng do penal labour under surveillance

监督权 jiāndūquán authority to supervise; right of supervision

监犯 jiānfàn prisoner; convict

监工 jiāngōng ① supervise work; oversee ② overseer; supervisor

监管 jiānguǎn supervise; keep watch on: 海关对商品和货物出口执行～。The customs office supervises the export of commodities and goods. / ～人犯 supervise and control offenders

监护 jiānhù *leg.* guardianship

监护人 jiānhùrén *leg.* guardian: 责令他的～加以管教。The guardian is to be ordered to subject him to discipline.

监禁 jiānjìn take into custody; imprison; put in jail (*or* prison)

监考 jiānkǎo ① invigilate ② invigilator

监牢 jiānláo *inf.* prison; jail

监理 jiānlǐ inspect and control; manage: 交通～部门 traffic control department

监票 jiānpiào scrutinize balloting

监票人 jiānpiàorén scrutineer

监舍 jiānshè prison house

监视 jiānshì keep watch on; keep a lookout over: ～敌人的行动 keep watch on the movements of the enemy

监视居住 jiānshì jūzhù *leg.* live at home under surveillance

监视器 jiānshìqì monitor

监视哨 jiānshìshào *mil.* lookout post; lookout

监事 jiānshì supervisor: 首席～ chief supervisor / ～会 board of supervisors

监守 jiānshǒu have custody of; guard; take care of

监守自盗 jiānshǒu zì dào steal what is entrusted to one's care; embezzle; defalcate

监听 jiāntīng monitor

监听器 jiāntīngqì monitor

监听无线电台 jiāntīng wúxiàndiàntái monitoring station

监外执行 jiānwài zhíxíng *leg.* execute (a sentence) outside prison

监狱 jiānyù prison; jail

监狱长 jiānyùzhǎng warden

监证 jiānzhèng check and affirm: 承包合同需要有关部门的～。All contracts for responsibility must be checked and affirmed by departments concerned.

监制 jiānzhì supervise the manufacture of

笺¹ (箋、牋)
jiān ① writing paper: 信笺 xìnjiān ② letter

笺² (箋)
jiān *formal* annotation; commentary

笺牍 jiāndú *formal* letters; correspondence

笺札 jiānzhá *formal* letters; correspondence

笺注 jiānzhù *formal* notes and commentary on

ancient texts

渐 jiān *formal* ① soak; be saturated with ② flow into: 东～于海 flow east and empty into the sea ——see also jiàn

渐染 jiānrǎn *formal* be imperceptibly influenced

菅 jiān *bot.* villous themeda (*Themeda gigantea* var. *villosa*)

湔 jiān *formal* wash

湔洗 jiānxǐ *formal* wash

湔雪 jiānxuě *formal* wipe away (a humiliation); redress (a wrong)

犍 jiān bullock

犍牛 jiānniú bullock

缄 jiān seal; close: 信封上写着"刘～"。 On the envelope is written: "from Liu".

缄口 jiānkǒu *formal* keep one's mouth shut; hold one's tongue; say nothing

缄默 jiānmò keep silent; be reticent

煎 jiān ① fry in shallow oil without stirring: ～鸡蛋 fried eggs ② simmer in water; decoct: ～药 decoct medicinal herbs ③ *m.* (for herb medicine): 头(二)～ first (second) decoction / 吃一～药就会好的。 One decoction will put you right.

煎熬 jiān'áo suffering; torture; torment: 由于长期生病, 他受尽～。 He suffered severely from the lingering illness.

煎饼 jiānbing thin pancake made of millet flour, etc.

搛 jiān pick up with chopsticks: 请自己～菜。 Please help yourself to the food.

缣 jiān *formal* fine silk

鹣 jiān a fabulous bird with one eye and one wing (so that a pair must unite in order to fly): ～～ a pair of such birds——husband and wife

鹣鲽 jiāndié *liter.* a one-winged bird and a one-eyed fish moving in a pair—a devoted couple

鲣(鰹) jiān oceanic bonito; skipjack (tuna)

鳒 jiān spiny-rayed flounder; big-mouthed flounder

鞯(韉) jiān see 鞍鞯 ānjiān

jiǎn

拣¹(揀) jiǎn choose; select; pick out: 把最好的西红柿～出来 pick out the best tomatoes / 担子～重的挑 choose the heavy loads to carry; volunteer to undertake difficult tasks / ～要紧的说。 Say what you think is most urgent.

拣²(揀) jiǎn same as 捡 jiǎn

拣便宜 jiǎn piányi get a bargain; gain a small advantage

拣选 jiǎnxuǎn select; choose

茧¹(繭) jiǎn cocoon: 这是蚕结的～。 It's a silkworm cocoon.

茧²(繭) jiǎn same as 胼 jiǎn

茧绸 jiǎnchóu pongee

茧子¹ jiǎnzi *dial.* silkworm cocoon

茧子² jiǎnzi same as 胼子 jiǎnzi

柬 jiǎn card; note; letter: 请柬 qǐngjiǎn

柬埔寨 Jiǎnpǔzhài Cambodia

柬埔寨人 Jiǎnpǔzhàirén Cambodian

柬帖 jiǎntiě note; short letter

俭(儉) jiǎn thrifty; frugal: 省吃俭用 shěng-chī-jiǎnyòng

俭朴 jiǎnpǔ thrifty and simple; economical: 生活～ lead a thrifty and simple life / 衣着～ dress simply / 她是个～的主妇。 She is a thrifty housewife.

俭省 jiǎnshěng economical; thrifty: 过日子～ live a frugal life; live economically / 用钱～点。 Be sparing in your use of money.

俭约 jiǎnyuē *formal* thrifty; economical

筧 jiǎn bamboo water pipe

捡(撿) jiǎn pick up; collect; gather: ～麦穗 pick up ears of wheat; glean a wheat field / ～煤核儿 pick out unburnt coal from cinders / ～粪 collect manure / ～柴火 gather firewood / ～到一支钢笔 find a fountain pen / ～了一条命 barely escape death

捡了芝麻, 丢了西瓜 jiǎnle zhīma, diūle xīguā pick up the sesame seeds but overlook the watermelons—concentrate on minor matters to the neglect of major ones

捡漏 jiǎnlòu repair the leaky part of a roof; plug a leak in the roof

捡破烂儿 jiǎn pòlànr pick odds and ends from refuse heaps

捡拾压捆机 jiǎnshíyākǔnjī *agric.* pick-up bale; pick-up press

检(檢) jiǎn ① check up; inspect; examine ② restrain oneself; be careful in one's conduct: 不检 bùjiǎn ③ same as 捡 jiǎn

检波 jiǎnbō *electron.* detection: ～管 detection tube / ～器 detector

检测 jiǎncè test; examine; check up: 利用电脑装置～交通 check traffic with computerized devices

检查 jiǎnchá ① check up; inspect; examine: ～工作 check up on work / ～质量 check on the quality of sth. / ～数字有无错误 check the figures / ～护照 inspect sb.'s passport / ～行李 inspect (or examine) sb.'s luggage / ～身体 have a physical examination; have a health check; have a medical check-up / ～视力 test sb.'s eyesight / 邮件～ postal inspection / ～自己对群众的态度 examine one's attitude to the masses / 把练习～一遍再交。 Look over your exercises before handing them in. ② self-criticism: 作～ criticize oneself / 写～ write a self-criticism

检查哨 jiǎncháshào checkpost

检查团 jiǎnchátuán inspection party

检查站 jiǎncházhàn checkpoint; checkpost; inspection station

检察 jiǎnchá procuratorial work: 加强对经济犯罪行为的～工作 strengthen the procuratorial work in dealing with economic crimes

检察官 jiǎncháguān public procurator (*or* prosecutor)

检察机关 jiǎnchá jīguān procuratorial organ

检察院 jiǎncháyuàn procuratorate

检察长 jiǎncházhǎng chief procurator; public procurator-general

检点 jiǎndiǎn ① examine; check: ～一下行李, 看是不是

都齐了。Check the luggage and see if everything is there. ② be cautious (about what one says or does): 他后悔自己说话不～。He regrets his inappropriate remarks. / 言行有失～ be careless about one's words and acts; be indiscreet in one's speech and conduct / 病人对饮食要多加～。Sick people should be careful about their diet.

检定 jiǎndìng examine and determine: 药品～ test drugs

检举 jiǎnjǔ report (an offence) to the authorities; inform against (an offender); accuse: ～特务 inform against a secret agent / ～失实 accusation at variance with the facts

检举人 jiǎnjǔrén accuser

检举箱 jiǎnjǔxiāng a box for accusation letters

检举信 jiǎnjǔxìn letter of accusation; written accusation

检漏 jiǎnlòu elec. leak hunting: ～器 leak detector; leak localizer

检录 jiǎnlù call the roll of the contestants in athletic events

检视 jiǎnshì inspect

检束 jiǎnshù restrain

检索 jiǎnsuǒ refer to; look up: 资料按音序排列便于～。For convenience of reference, the materials are arranged in pinyin order. / 资料～系统 data retrieval system

检讨 jiǎntǎo ① self-criticism: 作～ make a self-criticism / ～自己的错误 examine one's mistakes / 书面～ a written self-criticism ② formal examine; inspect

检修 jiǎnxiū examine and repair; overhaul: ～汽车 overhaul a car / ～汽车引擎 overhaul the engine of a car

检验 jiǎnyàn test; examine; inspect: 严格～产品质量 strictly examine the quality of the products / ～商品 commodity inspection / 社会实践及其效果是～主观愿望或动机的标准。The criterion for judging subjective intention or motive is social practice and its effect. / 实践是～真理的唯一标准。Practice is the sole criterion for testing truth.

检验费 jiǎnyànfèi survey fees

检验员 jiǎnyànyuán inspector; inspecting officer

检疫 jiǎnyì quarantine: 卫生～ health quarantine / 动植物～ the quarantine of animals and plants / ～对象 objects subject to quarantine / ～范围 quarantine range

检疫旗 jiǎnyìqí quarantine flag; yellow flag

检疫员 jiǎnyìyuán quarantine officer

检疫站 jiǎnyìzhàn quarantine station

检疫证明书 jiǎnyì zhèngmíngshū quarantine certificate; vaccination certificate; yellow book

检阅 jiǎnyuè review (troops, etc.); inspect: ～仪仗队 review a guard of honour / 对科研新成果的一次～ a review of recent achievements in scientific research

检阅台 jiǎnyuètái reviewing stand

检字表 jiǎnzìbiǎo word index (in a dictionary)

检字法 jiǎnzìfǎ the way in which Chinese characters are arranged and are to be located (as in a dictionary); indexing system for Chinese characters

剪

jiǎn ① scissors; shears; clippers ② cut (with scissors); clip; trim: 别把头发～得太短了。Don't cut the hair too short. / 把图片从杂志上～下来 cut the pictures out of the magazine / ～指甲 trim one's nails / ～羊毛 shear a sheep ③ wipe out; exterminate: 剪除 jiǎnchú

剪报 jiǎnbào newspaper cutting (or clipping)

剪裁 jiǎncái ① cut out (a garment); tailor: ～服装 cut out dresses ② cut out unwanted material (from a piece of writing); prune: 写文章要下一番～的工夫。In writing an essay one must do a lot of pruning.

剪彩 jiǎncǎi cut the ribbon at an opening ceremony: 为展览会～ cut the ribbon at the opening of an exhibition

剪草除根 jiǎncǎo-chúgēn same as 斩草除根 zhǎncǎo-chúgēn

剪除 jiǎnchú wipe out; annihilate; exterminate

剪床 jiǎnchuáng mech. shearing machine

剪刀 jiǎndāo scissors; shears: 一把～ a pair of scissors

剪刀差 jiǎndāochā scissors movement of prices; scissors differential (or difference); price scissors: 我们对于工农业产品的交换是缩小～，而不是扩大～。In the exchange of industrial products for agricultural products, we try to narrow the price scissors, not widen them.

剪辑 jiǎnjí ① film montage; film editing ② editing and rearrangement: 话剧录音～ highlights of a live recording of a play

剪接 jiǎnjiē film montage; film editing

剪径 jiǎnjìng old waylay and rob

剪毛 jiǎnmáo animal husbandry shearing; clipping

剪票 jiǎnpiào punch a ticket

剪票铗 jiǎnpiàojiā conductor's punch

剪秋萝 jiǎnqiūluó bot. senno campion (Lychnis senno)

剪贴 jiǎntiē ① clip and paste (sth. out of a newspaper, etc.) in a scrapbook or on cards ② cutting out (as school-children's activity)

剪贴簿 jiǎntiēbù scrapbook

剪影 jiǎnyǐng ① paper-cut silhouette ② outline; sketch

剪应力 jiǎnyìnglì mech. shearing stress

剪纸 jiǎnzhǐ paper-cut; scissor-cut

剪子 jiǎnzi scissors; shears; clippers

减（减）

jiǎn ① subtract: 九～四得五。Nine minus four is five. or Four from nine is five. ② reduce; decrease; cut: 工作热情有增无～ work with ever increasing zeal

减半 jiǎnbàn reduce by half: 儿童票价～ half-price fare for children / ～征收所得税 be allowed a 50% reduction of income tax

减产 jiǎnchǎn reduction of output; drop in production: ～百分之十。Output dropped by ten per cent.

减低 jiǎndī reduce; lower; bring down; cut: ～速度 lower (or slacken) speed; slow down / 耗煤率～了百分之五。Consumption of coal went down by 5%.

减法 jiǎnfǎ subtraction

减肥 jiǎnféi reduce weight; slim: 我不敢多吃，我想～。I mustn't eat too much. I'm trying to slim. / 医生要他～。The doctor told him to reduce weight. / ～体操 slimming exercises

减号 jiǎnhào minus sign (－)

减河 jiǎnhé water conservancy distributary

减缓 jiǎnhuǎn retard; slow down: ～进程 slow down the pace (or progress)

减价 jiǎnjià reduce (or lower) the prices; mark down: ～出售 sell at a reduced prices / ～一成 be marked down by 10%

减免 jiǎnmiǎn ① mitigate or annul (a punishment) ② reduce or remit (taxation, etc.): 申请～所得税 apply for a reduction of or exemption from income tax / 成绩好的学生可以～学费。Students with high marks can enjoy a partial or total tuition waiver.

减摩 jiǎnmó mech. antifriction: ～合金 antifriction alloy (or metal) / ～轴承 antifriction bearing / ～涂层 friction coat

减轻 jiǎnqīng lighten; ease; alleviate; mitigate: ～国家的负担 lighten the burden on the state / ～劳动强度 reduce labour intensity / ～病人的痛苦 alleviate (or ease) a patient's suffering / ～处分 mitigate a punishment

减弱 jiǎnruò weaken; abate: 体力大大～ be much weakened physically / 风势～了。The wind has subsided. / 思想政治工作一刻也不能～。Ideological and political work must never for a moment be relaxed.

减色 jiǎnsè lose lustre; impair the excellence of; detract from the merit of: 音响效果不好, 使演出大为～。Poor acoustics spoilt the performance.

减色法 jiǎnsèfǎ subtractive process (in cinematography)

减杀 jiǎnshā weaken; reduce

减少 jiǎnshǎo reduce; decrease; lessen; cut down: ～非生产性开支 reduce nonproductive expenditure / 精简机构, ～层次 simplify the administrative structure and eliminate duplication / 给他～一些工作 relieve him of some of his work / 交通事故～了。There has been a decrease in traffic accidents.

减声器 jiǎnshēngqì mech. muffler

减数 jiǎnshù math. subtrahend

减数分裂 jiǎnshù fēnliè biol. meiosis

减税 jiǎnshuì tax reduction

减速 jiǎnsù slow down; decelerate; retard

减速度 jiǎnsùdù deceleration

减速副翼 jiǎnsù fùyì aviation deceleron

减速火箭 jiǎnsù huǒjiàn retro-rocket

减速剂 jiǎnsùjì phys. moderator

减速伞 jiǎnsùsǎn aviation drag (or deceleration) parachute

减速运动 jiǎnsù yùndòng phys. retarded motion

减缩 jiǎnsuō reduce; cut down; retrench: ～开支 reduce expenditure

减退 jiǎntuì drop; go down: 视力 (记忆力)～。One's eyesight (memory) is failing. / 雨后炎热～了许多。After the rain, the heat abated considerably.

减刑 jiǎnxíng leg. reduce a penalty; reduce a sentence; commute (or mitigate) a sentence

减压 jiǎnyā reduce pressure; decompress: ～器 pressure reducer; decompressor

减员 jiǎnyuán depletion of numbers (in the armed forces, etc.): 战斗～ combat depletion of strength / 非战斗～ noncombat depletion of strength / 这个单位将补充自然～约百人。About 100 persons will replace those who retire or cannot work for various reasons in this unit.

减灾 jiǎnzāi reduce natural disasters

减震 jiǎnzhèn shock absorption; damping: ～器 shock absorber; damper

减租减息 jiǎnzū-jiǎnxī reduction of rent for land and of interest on loans (the Chinese Communist Party's agrarian policy during the War of Resistance Against Japan); reduction of rent and interest

跰（繭） jiǎn callus

跰子 jiǎnzi callus

硷（礆、鹼） jiǎn same as 碱 jiǎn

裥 jiǎn dial. pleat

睑（瞼） jiǎn eyelid

睑腺炎 jiǎnxiànyán med. sty

铜 jiǎn mace

简¹ jiǎn simple; simplified; brief: 从简 cóngjiǎn

简² jiǎn ① bamboo slips (used for writing on in ancient times) ② letter: 书简 shūjiǎn

简³ jiǎn formal select; choose: 简拔 jiǎnbá

简拔 jiǎnbá formal select and promote

简报 jiǎnbào bulletin; brief report: 会议～ conference bulletin; brief reports on conference proceedings

简本 jiǎnběn concise edition

简编 jiǎnbiān (usu. used in book titles) short course; concise edition: 《中国文学史～》A Short History of Chinese Literature

简便 jiǎnbiàn simple and convenient; handy: ～的方法 a simple and convenient method; a handy way / 操作～ easy to operate / ～的手续 simple procedures

简称 jiǎnchēng ① the abbreviated form of a name; abbreviation: "鞍钢"是鞍山钢铁公司的～。"Angang" is the abbreviation for the Anshan Iron and Steel Company. ② be called sth. for short: 中国共产党党员和中国共产主义青年团团员～"党团员"。Members of the Chinese Communist Party and the Chinese Communist Youth League are called "Party and League members" for short.

简单 jiǎndān ① simple; uncomplicated: ～明了 simple and clear; concise and explicit / 这机器构造～。The machine is simple in structure. / 吃得很～ have simple food / 生活很～ lead a simple life / 事情没那么～。There is more to it. ② (usu. used in the negative) commonplace; ordinary: 她的枪法那么准,真不～。She's a marvel to be able to shoot with such accuracy. / 这家伙鬼点子特多,可不～。This fellow is no simpleton. He is full of tricks. (see also 不简单 bù jiǎndān) ③ oversimplified; casual: ～粗暴 do things in an oversimplified and crude way / 不能用～的方法去解决这个问题。This matter cannot be settled in a summary fashion. / 这篇文章我只是～地看了看。I only skimmed through this article.

简单多数 jiǎndān duōshù simple majority

简单化 jiǎndānhuà oversimplify: 看问题～ take a naïve view; oversimplify a problem

简单劳动 jiǎndān láodòng econ. simple work

简单再生产 jiǎndān zàishēngchǎn econ. simple reproduction

简短 jiǎnduǎn brief: 他的发言～有力。His speech was brief and forceful.

简而言之 jiǎn ér yán zhī in brief; in short; to put it in a nutshell

简古 jiǎngǔ formal laconic and archaic

简化 jiǎnhuà simplify: ～工序 simplify working processes / ～手续 simplify the procedure; simplify the formalities

简化汉字 jiǎnhuà Hànzì ① simplify Chinese characters (i.e. reduce the number of strokes and eliminate complicated variants) ② simplified Chinese characters

简洁 jiǎnjié succinct; terse; pithy: ～生动的语言 terse and lively language / 文笔～ written in a pithy style

简捷 jiǎnjié (also 简截 jiǎnjié) simple and direct; forthright

简介 jiǎnjiè brief introduction; synopsis; summarized account: 剧情～ the synopsis of a drama / 《天坛～》A Short Guide to the Temple of Heaven

简括 jiǎnkuò brief but comprehensive; compendious

简历 jiǎnlì biographical notes; curriculum vitae; résumé

简练 jiǎnliàn terse; succinct; pithy: 内容丰富, 文字～ rich in content and succinct in style

简陋 jiǎnlòu simple and crude: 设备～ simple and crude equipment / ～的小木屋 a crude log cabin

简略 jiǎnlüè simple (in content); brief; sketchy: 他提供的材料过于～。The material he supplied is too sketchy. / ～地拟出计划要点 sketch out the main points of the plan

简慢 jiǎnmàn negligent (in attending to one's guest)

简明 jiǎnmíng simple and clear; concise: 《～汉英词典》A Concise Chinese-English Dictionary

简明扼要 jiǎnmíng èyào　brief and to the point; concise: 讲话、演说、写文章和写决议案，都应当～。Talks, speeches, articles and resolutions should all be concise and to the point.

简明新闻 jiǎnmíng xīnwén　news in brief

简朴 jiǎnpǔ　simple and unadorned; plain: 生活～a simple and frugal life; plain living／～的语言 plain language／衣着～be simply dressed

简谱 jiǎnpǔ　*mus.* numbered musical notation

简缩 jiǎnsuō　condense; simplify; reduce

简体字 jiǎntǐzì　simplified Chinese character

简图 jiǎntú　sketch; diagram

简谐运动 jiǎnxié yùndòng　*phys.* simple harmonic motion

简写 jiǎnxiě　① write a Chinese character in simplified form ② simplify a book for beginners

简写本 jiǎnxiěběn　simplified edition

简讯 jiǎnxùn　news in brief

简要 jiǎnyào　concise and to the point; brief: ～的介绍 a brief introduction; briefing／～记录 a summary record

简仪 jiǎnyí　*astron.* abridged armilla

简易 jiǎnyì　① simple and easy: ～的办法 a simple and easy method ② simply constructed; simply equipped; unsophisticated

简易病房 jiǎnyì bìngfáng　simply equipped ward

简易读物 jiǎnyì dúwù　easy reader

简易公路 jiǎnyì gōnglù　simply-built highway

简易机场 jiǎnyì jīchǎng　airstrip

简易楼 jiǎnyìlóu　economy building

简易师范 jiǎnyì shīfàn　elementary teachers training school

简约 jiǎnyuē　brief; concise; sketchy

简则 jiǎnzé　general regulations

简章 jiǎnzhāng　general regulations

简政放权 jiǎnzhèng-fàngquán　streamline administration and institute decentralization

简直 jiǎnzhí　*adv.* simply; at all: 这消息～好得叫人不敢相信。The news is almost too good to be true.／我～不能相信自己的耳朵。I could hardly believe my ears.／天冷得～连口水都能冻起来。It was cold enough to freeze the spit in one's mouth.／我～不能想象有这种事。I simply couldn't imagine such a thing.／这个星期～没有一个好天。We've had no fine weather at all this week.／～是浪费时间。It's a sheer waste of time.／这车修理以后，～跟新车一样。When the car was repaired, it looked as good as new.

简装 jiǎnzhuāng　simple packing

谫（譾）
jiǎn　*formal* shallow

谫陋 jiǎnlòu　*formal* shallow and ignorant: 学识～be possessed of meagre knowledge

碱（鹼、堿）
jiǎn　① alkali ② soda: 洗涤～washing soda

碱地 jiǎndì　alkaline land

碱化 jiǎnhuà　alkalization; basification

碱金属 jiǎnjīnshǔ　alkali (*or* alkaline) metal

碱式盐 jiǎnshìyán　*chem.* basic salt

碱土金属 jiǎntǔ jīnshǔ　alkaline-earth metal

碱性 jiǎnxìng　basicity; alkalinity: ～染料 basic dyes／～土 alkaline soil

碱性反应 jiǎnxìng fǎnyìng　alkaline reaction

戬
jiǎn　*formal* ① wipe out; annihilate ② bliss; blessedness

翦
jiǎn　a surname

蹇
jiǎn　*formal* ① crippled ② unlucky: 命蹇 mìngjiǎn ③ donkey or inferior horse ④ (Jiǎn) a surname

謇
jiǎn　*formal* ① stuttering ② upright; honest

jiàn

见¹（見）
jiàn　① see; catch sight of: 从来没～过这种鸟。I've never seen a bird like that before.／只～一个人影闪过墙角 catch sight of sb. turning the corner ② meet with; be exposed to: 这种药怕～光。This medicine is not to be exposed to daylight.／冰～热就化。Ice melts with heat.／～困难就上，～荣誉就让 dash forward where there are difficulties to overcome and draw back when honours are to be conferred; take the difficulties for oneself and leave the honours to others ③ show evidence of; appear to be: 并不～瘦 not seem to be any thinner／～之于行动 be translated into action ④ refer to; see; *vide*: ～第三十六页 see page 36 ⑤ meet; call on; see: 待会儿～。See you later.／你～到他了没有？Did you meet him?／我不想～他。I don't wish to see him.／她今天下午要来～你。She'll call on you this afternoon. ⑥ view; opinion: 依我之～ in my opinion; to my mind

见²（見）
jiàn　*part. formal* ① (used before a verb to indicate the passive): 见笑 jiànxiào／见责 jiànzé ② (used before a verb in polite requests): 见告 jiàngào／见教 jiànjiào
——see also xiàn

见报 jiànbào　appear in the newspapers: 有关这次会议的报道明日即可～。Reports on this conference will appear in tomorrow's newspapers.

见背 jiànbèi　*formal euph.* (of one's parents) pass away: 生孩六月，慈父～。I lost my father when I was only six months old.

见不得 jiànbude　① not to be exposed to; unable to stand: ～阳光 not to be exposed to the sunlight ② not fit to be seen or revealed: 我没有做～人的事。I've done nothing I am ashamed of. ③ *dial.* cannot bear the sight of; frown upon: 她就～那个懒汉。She can't stand that sluggard.

见财起意 jiàn cái qǐ yì　entertain evil thoughts at the sight of money

见长 jiàncháng　be good at; be expert in: 她以写作～。She is good at writing. ——see also jiànzhǎng

见称 jiànchēng　*formal* noted; famous: 这个导演以执导惊险片～。This director is famous for making thrillers.

见得 jiàn·dé　(only used in the negative or in questions) seem; appear: 这片稻子不～比那片差。This plot of paddy doesn't seem to be any worse than that one.／明天不～会下雨。It doesn't look as if it's going to rain tomorrow.／怎么～他来不了？How do you know he can't come?／何以～？How so? ——see also 不见得 bùjiànde

见地 jiàndì　insight; judgment: 很有～ have keen insight; show sound judgment

见多识广 jiànduō-shíguǎng　experienced and knowledgeable: 他去过许多地方，～。He is well-travelled, and is a man of wide experience.

见方 jiànfāng　*inf.* square: 这张桌子三尺～。The table is 3 *chi* square.

见风是雨 jiàn fēng shì yǔ　take wind as the forerunner of rain—jump to hasty conclusions

见风转舵 jiàn fēng zhuǎn duò　trim one's sails

见缝插针 jiàn fèng chā zhēn stick in a pin wherever there's room—make use of every bit of time or space

见告 jiàngào *pol.* inform me: 即希～。 Hope to be informed immediately.

见怪 jiànguài mind; take offence: 菜做得不好, 请不要～。 I hope you won't mind my poor cooking. / 批评得不对, 可别～。 Don't take offence if my criticism is incorrect.

见怪不怪, 其怪自败 jiàn guài bù guài, qí guài zì bài face the fearful with no fears, and its fearfulness disappears

见鬼 jiànguǐ ① fantastic; preposterous; absurd: 种庄稼不除草不是～吗? Isn't it absurd to plant crops and not weed the fields? / 手套怎么不见了? 真～! That's funny! What have I done with my gloves? ② go to hell: 让他的那套理论～去吧! To hell with that theory of his! / 让语法学家通通～去吧! Let the grammarians go hang! / 真～, 定好了今天郊游, 怎么偏偏今天下雨! What damned bad luck that it should rain today when we have already arranged for an outing!

见好 jiànhǎo (of a patient's condition) get better; mend: 她的病～。 She's on the mend.

见后 jiànhòu see after; *vide post*

见惠 jiànhuì *pol.* be favoured with a gift

见机 jiànjī as the opportunity arises; as befits the occasion; according to circumstances

见机行事 jiànjī xíngshì act according to circumstances; do as one sees fit; use one's discretion

见教 jiànjiào *pol.* favour me with your advice; instruct me: 有何～? Is there something you want to see me about?

见解 jiànjiě view; opinion; understanding: 抱有不同～ hold different views / 一篇很有～的文章 an article with original ideas / 对这个问题他没有提出任何新的～。 He didn't put forward any new ideas on the subject. / 这只是我个人的～。 That's just my own opinion.

见景生情 jiàn jǐng shēng qíng have one's emotion aroused by the scene

见老 jiànlǎo be aged: 十年没见, 你还那个样子, 一点不～。 You haven't aged at all and still look the same as ten years ago when we last met.

见利思义 jiàn lì sī yì remember what is right at the sight of profit

见利忘义 jiàn lì wàng yì forget what is right at the sight of profit

见谅 jiànliàng *pol.* excuse me; forgive me: 务希～。 I sincerely hope you'll excuse me.

见猎心喜 jiàn liè xīn xǐ thrill to see one's favourite sport and itch to have a go

见面 jiànmiàn meet; see: 他俩经常～。 They see a lot of each other. / 思想～ each stating frankly what's on his mind / 要使产销直接～ establish direct links between the producer and the seller / 这个话剧将通过电视与观众～。 This play will be shown on the TV.

见面礼 jiànmiànlǐ a present given to sb. on first meeting him

见面熟 jiànmiànshóu *inf.* hail-fellow-well-met

见票即付 jiàn piào jí fù *com.* payable at sight; payable to bearer

见弃 jiànqì *formal* be rejected; be discarded

见前 jiànqián see before; *vide ante*

见钱眼开 jiàn qián yǎn kāi be wide-eyed at the sight of money—greedy

见轻 jiànqīng take a favourable turn: 病势～。 The patient's condition has improved.

见仁见智 jiànrén-jiànzhì different people, different views; opinions differ

见上 jiànshàng see above; *vide supra*

见世面 jiàn shìmiàn see the world; enrich one's experience: 这回到化工厂去参观, 可见了世面了。 The trip to the chemical works was a real eye-opener.

见识 jiànshi ① widen one's knowledge; enrich one's experience: 到各处走走, ～～也是好的。 It's not a bad idea to go around a bit and gain experience. ② experience; knowledge; sensibleness: 长～ widen one's knowledge; broaden one's horizons / 他～很广。 He's a man of wide experience. / 他那样对待你是不对的, 你别和他一般～。 He's behaved badly towards you, but a sensible person like you shouldn't want to take him up on it.

见树不见林 jiàn shù bù jiàn lín not see the wood for the trees

见死不救 jiàn sǐ bù jiù not try to save sb. who is in mortal danger; be impervious to other people's misfortunes or disasters

见所未见 jiàn suǒ wèi jiàn see what one has never seen before: 许多奇事, ～, 闻所未闻。 I saw and heard of many strange things of which I had hitherto been unaware.

见天 jiàntiān *inf.* everyday: 他～早上出去散步。 He goes out for a walk every morning.

见天见 jiàntiānjian *dial.* every day: 他～打太极拳。 He does *taijiquan* every day.

见外 jiànwài regard sb. as an outsider: 你我老朋友还那么客气干什么? 太～了。 Why all this formality between old friends like us? Anybody would think we were strangers! / 到了我这儿可别～。 Just make yourself at home.

见危授命 jiàn wēi shòumìng be ready to die for one's country when it is in danger

见微知著 jiàn wēi zhī zhù from the first small beginnings one can see how things will develop; from one small clue one can see what is coming

见闻 jiànwén what one sees and hears; knowledge; information: 增长～ add to one's knowledge / ～广 well-informed; knowledgeable

见物不见人 jiàn wù bù jiàn rén see things but not people; see only material factors, not human ones

见习 jiànxí learn on the job; be on probation

见习技术员 jiànxí jìshùyuán technician on probation

见习领事 jiànxí lǐngshì student consul

见习生 jiànxíshēng probationer

见习医生 jiànxí yīshēng intern

见下 jiànxià see below; *vide infra*

见贤思齐 jiàn xián sī qí when you meet someone better than yourself, turn your thoughts to becoming his equal

见效 jiànxiào become effective; produce the desired result: 这药吃下去就～。 This medicine produces an instant effect. / 这些企业投资少, ～快。 These enterprises call for small investments and yield quick returns.

见笑 jiànxiào ① laugh at (me or us): 我刚开始学, 您可别～。 Now don't laugh at me. I'm only a beginner. ② incur ridicule (by one's poor performance): 写得不好, ～, ～。 Excuse my poor writing.

见笑大方 jiànxiào dàfāng same as 贻笑大方 yíxiào dàfāng

见血封喉 jiànxuèfēnghóu *bot.* upas

见义勇为 jiàn yì yǒng wéi see what is right and have the courage to do it; be ready to take up the cudgels for a just cause

见异思迁 jiàn yì sī qiān change one's mind the moment one sees something new; be inconstant

见责 jiànzé *formal* be blamed

见长 jiànzhǎng grow perceptibly: 下了一场雨, 麦苗立刻～。 The wheat sprouts grew perceptibly after the rain. / 这孩子不～。 The child doesn't seem to be growing. ——see also jiàncháng

见证　jiànzhèng　witness; testimony: 警察找不到任何人作～。The police could find no eyewitnesses. / 历史是最好的～。History is the most telling witness.

见证人　jiànzhèngrén　eyewitness; witness: 被告的～ a witness for the defence

见罪　jiànzuì　*formal*　take offence: 招待不周，请勿～。Forgive me for my poor hospitality.

件

件　jiàn　① *m.* ⓐ (for matters in general): 一～事 a matter; a thing / 一～工作 a piece of work; a job ⓑ (for clothing, furniture, luggage, etc.): 一～大衣 an overcoat / 一～家具 a piece of furniture / 三～行李 three pieces of luggage ② single item: 工件 gōngjiàn / 零件 língjiàn ③ letter; correspondence; paper; document: 来件 láijiàn / 密件 mìjiàn

间 (閒)

间　jiàn　① space in between; opening: 无间 wújiàn ② separate: 相间 xiāngjiàn ③ sow discord: 离间 líjiàn ④ thin out (seedlings): 间苗 jiànmiáo——see also jiān

间壁　jiànbì　next door; next-door neighbour

间道　jiàndào　*formal*　bypath; shortcut

间谍　jiàndié　spy

间谍飞机　jiàndié fēijī　spy plane

间谍网　jiàndiéwǎng　espionage network

间谍卫星　jiàndié wèixīng　spy satellite

间断　jiànduàn　be disconnected; be interrupted: 他坚持锻炼，几年来从不～。He has kept up physical training for several years without interruption. / 斗争一刻也没有～过。Never for a moment has the struggle ceased.

间断性　jiànduànxìng　*philos.*　discontinuity: 不～ continuity

间隔　jiàngé　interval; intermission: 两次会议～才二十天。There was an interval of only twenty days between the two conferences. / 每两行树苗～三米。There is a space of three metres between each two rows of saplings. / 幼苗～匀整。The seedlings are evenly spaced.

间隔号　jiàngéhào　separation dot, a punctuation mark separating the day from the month, as in 一二·九运动 (the December 9th Movement), or separating the parts of a person's name, as in 诺尔曼·白求恩(Norman Bethune)

间或　jiànhuò　*adv.*　occasionally; now and then; sometimes; once in a while: 大家很安静地听着，～有人提一两个问题。Everybody listened in silent attention, with occasional questions from the floor.

间接　jiànjiē　indirect; secondhand: 这消息我是～听来的。I heard the news indirectly.

间接宾语　jiànjiē bīnyǔ　*gram.*　indirect object

间接肥料　jiànjiē féiliào　indirect fertilizer

间接接触　jiànjiē jiēchù　*med.*　mediate contacts

间接经验　jiànjiē jīngyàn　indirect experience

间接贸易　jiànjiē màoyì　indirect trade

间接税　jiànjiēshuì　indirect tax

间接推理　jiànjiē tuīlǐ　*log.*　mediate inference

间接消费　jiànjiē xiāofèi　indirect consumption

间接选举　jiànjiē xuǎnjǔ　indirect election

间接证据　jiànjiē zhèngjù　circumstantial evidence

间苗　jiànmiáo　thin out seedlings (*or* young shoots)

间日　jiànrì　*formal*　every other day

间隙　jiànxì　① interval; gap; space: 利用工作～收集些资料 find free time to gather material / 利用战斗～进行休整 rest, train and consolidate between battles ② *mech.* clearance: 齿轮～ gear clearance

间歇　jiànxiē　intermittence; intermission: ～性的精神病人 a person whose mental illness is of an intermittent nature

间歇喷泉　jiànxiē pēnquán　geyser

间歇泉　jiànxiēquán　intermittent spring

间歇热　jiànxiērè　*med.*　intermittent fever

间杂　jiànzá　be intermingled; be mixed

间作　jiànzuò　*agric.*　intercropping: 实行玉米和大豆～ intercrop maize and soya beans

饯¹ (餞)

饯　jiàn　give a farewell dinner: 饯行 jiànxíng

饯² (餞)

饯　jiàn　preserve (fruits): 蜜饯 mìjiàn

饯别　jiànbié　give a farewell dinner: ～友人 give a friend a farewell dinner

饯行　jiànxíng　give a farewell dinner: 我们将设宴为他～。We'll give a farewell dinner for him.

建¹

建　jiàn　① build; construct; erect: ～电站 build a power station / 新厂房已经～成。The new factory building has been completed. / ～桥工地 the construction site of the bridge ② establish; set up; found: ～社 set up a people's commune or a cooperative / ～新功 make new contributions ③ propose; advocate: 建议 jiànyì

建²

建　Jiàn　of Fujian Province: 建漆 Jiànqī

建材　jiàncái　short for 建筑材料 jiànzhù cáiliào

建党　jiàndǎng　①found (*or* form) a political party ② build up the Party: ～路线 line for Party building

建都　jiàndū　found a capital; make (a place) the capital: 唐代～长安。The Tang Dynasty made Chang'an its capital.

建馆　jiànguǎn　set up an embassy: 办理～事宜 arrange for the setting up of an embassy

建国　jiànguó　① found (*or* establish) a state: 像这样的大会还是～以来第一次。This congress is the first of its kind since the founding of our People's Republic. ② build up a country: ～宏图 a grand project for national reconstruction

建交　jiànjiāo　establish diplomatic relations: ～联合公报 a joint *communiqué* on the establishment of diplomatic relations

建军　jiànjūn　① found an army ② build up the Army (i.e. the Chinese People's Liberation Army): ～路线 line for army building / ～原则 principles of army building

建军节　Jiànjūnjié　same as 八一建军节 Bā Yī Jiànjūnjié

建兰　jiànlán　sword-leaved cymbidium (*Cymbidium ensifolium*)

建立　jiànlì　build; establish; set up; found: ～友好关系 build friendly relations / ～外交关系 establish diplomatic relations / ～农村根据地 build rural base areas / ～统一战线 form a united front / ～"铁人"式的工人队伍 build up contingents of workers of the "Iron Man" type / ～信心 build up one's confidence / ～功勋 perform meritorious deeds / ～合作医疗制度 set up (*or* institute) a cooperative medical service / ～良好的公共秩序 establish good public order

建漆　Jiànqī　Fujian lacquerware

建设　jiànshè　build; construct: 把我国～成为社会主义的现代化强国 build China into a powerful modern socialist country / 加强连队～ strengthen the Army at company level / 国家～ national reconstruction / 城乡～ urban and rural development / 党的～ party building / 思想～ ideological education / 组织～ organizational building / 作风～ cultivation of a fine work style / 一万多人的～大军 a work force of more than 10,000

建设性　jiànshèxìng　constructive: ～的意见 constructive suggestions / 起～的作用 play a constructive role / 这次会谈富有～。The talks were very constructive.

建树　jiànshù　*formal*　make a contribution; contribute:

对发展体育事业有所～ contribute to the development of physical culture / 人类认识史上的重大～ major attainments in the history of human knowledge / 他在任职期间毫无～。He did nothing noteworthy during his tenure.

建团 jiàntuán build up the League (i.e. the Communist Youth League)

建议 jiànyì ①propose; suggest; recommend: 他们～休会。They propose that the meeting be adjourned. / 我～你多做点户外运动。I suggest you should have more outdoor exercise. / 我建个议。I'd like to make a suggestion. ②proposal; suggestion; recommendation: 提～ offer suggestions

建造 jiànzào build; construct; make: ～房屋 build houses

建制 jiànzhì organizational system: 部队～ the organizational system of the army / ～部队 organic unit

建筑 jiànzhù ① build; construct; erect: ～桥梁 construct a bridge / ～高楼 erect a tall building / ～铁路 build a railway / 你不能把自己的幸福～在别人的痛苦上。You shouldn't build your happiness on the suffering of other people. ② building; structure; edifice: 古老的～ an ancient building / 宏伟的～ a magnificent structure ③ architecture: 他是学现代～的。His speciality is modern architecture. / ～设计 architectural design

建筑材料 jiànzhù cáiliào building materials

建筑工程学 jiànzhù gōngchéngxué architectural engineering

建筑工地 jiànzhù gōngdì building site; construction site

建筑工人 jiànzhù gōngrén building worker; builder

建筑红线 jiànzhù hóngxiàn property line

建筑群 jiànzhùqún architectural complex

建筑师 jiànzhùshī architect

建筑物 jiànzhùwù building; structure

建筑学 jiànzhùxué architecture

建筑业 jiànzhùyè building industry

剑 （劍、剱）

jiàn sword; sabre: ～柄 the handle of a sword; hilt / ～鞘 scabbard

剑拔弩张 jiànbá-nǔzhāng with swords drawn and bows bent; at daggers drawn

剑齿虎 jiànchǐhǔ palaeontology sabre-toothed tiger; machairodont

剑齿象 jiànchǐxiàng palaeontology stegodon

剑客 jiànkè chivalrous swordsman (in old novels)

剑兰 jiànlán another name for 菖兰 chānglán

剑麻 jiànmá sisal hemp

剑眉 jiànméi straight eyebrows slanting upwards and outwards; dashing eyebrows

剑术 jiànshù swordsmanship; fencing skill

剑侠 jiànxiá chivalrous swordsman (in old novels)

荐¹（薦）

jiàn recommend: 推荐 tuījiàn

荐²（薦）

jiàn formal ① grass; straw ② straw mat

荐举 jiànjǔ propose sb. for an office; recommend

荐头 jiàntóu dial. employment agent: ～行 employment agency

荐贤 jiànxián recommend men of worth

荐引 jiànyǐn formal recommend; introduce

贱（賤）

jiàn ① low-priced; inexpensive; cheap: ～卖 sell cheap ② lowly; humble: 贫贱 pínjiàn ③ low-down; base; despicable: 她很～! She's cheap! ④ hum. my: 贱内 jiànnèi

贱骨头 jiàngǔtou offens. miserable (or contemptible) wretch

贱货 jiànhuò ① cheap goods ② offens. miserable (or contemptible) wretch

贱民 jiànmín ① people of the lowest social strata ② untouchables

贱内 jiànnèi old my (humble) wife

贱人 jiànrén old offens. slut

涧

jiàn ravine; gully

舰（艦）

jiàn warship; naval vessel; man-of-war

舰队 jiànduì fleet; naval force: 东海～ the Dong Hai Sea Fleet; the East China Sea Fleet / 联合～ a combined fleet

舰对空导弹 jiàn duì kōng dǎodàn ship-to-air missile

舰首炮 jiànshǒupào bow chaser

舰艇 jiàntǐng naval ships and boats; naval vessels

舰尾炮 jiànwěipào stern chaser

舰载 jiànzài carrier-borne; carrier-based; ship-based: ～导弹 ship-based missile / ～飞机 shipboard aircraft; deck-landing aircraft

舰长 jiànzhǎng captain (of a warship)

舰只 jiànzhī warships; naval vessels: 海军～ naval vessels

监（監）

jiàn an imperial office: 钦天～ Board of Astronomy ——see also jiàn

监生 jiànshēng a student of the Imperial College (国子监) in the Ming and Qing Dynasties

健

jiàn ① healthy; strong ② strengthen; toughen; invigorate: ～胃 be good for the stomach; aid digestion / ～脾 invigorate the function of the spleen ③ be strong in; be good at: 健谈 jiàntán

健步 jiànbù walk with vigorous strides: ～登上主席台 mount the rostrum in vigorous strides

健步如飞 jiànbù rú fēi walk as if on wings; walk fast and vigorously

健存 jiàncún same as 健在 jiànzài

健儿 jiàn'ér ① valiant fighter ② good athlete: 乒坛～ skilful ping-pong players

健将 jiànjiàng master sportsman, top-notch player: 运动～ master of sports; master sportsman / 足球～ top-notch footballer

健康 jiànkāng ① health; physique: ～状况 state of health; physical condition / 人民的～水平有了很大提高。The general level of the people's health has markedly improved. ②healthy; sound: 身体～ be in good health / 为朋友们的～干杯! Let's drink a toast to our friends' health! / 祝你～! I wish you good health. / 运动正在～地发展。The movement is developing healthily. / 情况基本上是～的。The situation is basically sound.

健康证明书 jiànkāng zhèngmíngshū health certificate

健美 jiànměi strong and handsome; vigorous and graceful: ～的体操表演 a vigorous and graceful performance of callisthenics

健美运动 jiànměi yùndòng bodybuilding

健全 jiànquán ① sound; perfect: 身心～ sound in mind and body / 头脑～的人 a person in his or her right mind ② strengthen; amplify; perfect: ～合理的规章制度 amplify necessary rules and regulations / ～民主集中制 strengthen democratic centralism / 社会主义法制正在逐步～。The socialist legal system is being gradually perfected.

健身房 jiànshēnfáng gymnasium; gym

健谈 jiàntán be a good talker; be a brilliant conversationalist

健忘 jiànwàng forgetful; having a bad memory

健忘症 jiànwàngzhèng amnesia

健旺 jiànwàng healthy and vigorous

健在 jiànzài *formal* (of a person of advanced age) be still living and in good health: 她本人已年过七十，而她的父母还～。 She is over seventy and her parents are still alive.

健壮 jiànzhuàng healthy and strong; robust: ～的小伙子 a robust young man / 像马一样～ as strong as a horse

谏

jiàn *formal* remonstrate with (one's superior or friend); expostulate with; admonish: ～止 plead with sb. not to do sth.; admonish against sth.

谏诤 jiànzhèng *formal* criticize sb.'s faults frankly

渐

jiàn *adv.* gradually; by degrees: 天气～冷。 The weather is getting cold. ——see also jiān

渐变 jiànbiàn gradual change

渐次 jiàncì *formal* gradually; one after another

渐渐 jiànjiàn *adv.* gradually; by degrees; little by little: 天气～转暖。 The weather is getting warm. / 路上的行人～少了。 The number of pedestrians gradually dwindled. / 雨～小了。 The rain is beginning to let up. / ～地，我们就跟他熟起来了。 Little by little, we began to get to know him.

渐进 jiànjìn advance gradually; progress step by step: 实现这目标是一个～过程。 The attainment of this goal is an evolutionary process.

渐入佳境 jiàn rù jiājìng (of a situation) be improving; be getting better

渐缩管 jiànsuōguǎn *mech.* reducing pipe

渐显 jiànxiǎn *film.* fade in

渐新世 Jiànxīnshì *geol.* the Oligocene Epoch

渐隐 jiànyǐn *film.* fade out

溅（濺）

jiàn splash; spatter: ～一身泥 be spattered with mud / 钢花四～ sparks of molten steel flying in all directions

溅落 jiànluò (of a space vehicle, etc.) splash down

溅落点 jiànluòdiǎn splash point

践（踐）

jiàn ① trample; tread ② act on; carry out: 实践 shíjiàn

践诺 jiànnuò (also 践言 jiànyán) keep one's promise (or word)

践踏 jiàntà tread on; trample underfoot: 请勿～草地。 Keep off the grass. / 肆意～别国主权 wantonly trample on the sovereignty of other countries / 这是对国际关系准则的～。 This is a flagrant violation of the principles of international relations.

践约 jiànyuē keep a promise; keep an appointment

腱

jiàn *physiol.* tendon

腱鞘 jiànqiào *physiol.* tendon sheath

腱鞘炎 jiànqiàoyán *med.* tenosynovitis

腱子 jiànzi (beef or mutton) shank

键

jiàn shuttlecock

键子 jiànzi shuttlecock: 踢～ kick the shuttlecock (as a game)

鉴（鑒、鑑）

jiàn ① mirror (made of bronze or brass in ancient times): 以铜为～，可整衣冠。以古为～，可知兴替。(唐太宗) By using a mirror of brass you may see to adjust your cap; by using antiquity as a mirror, you may learn to foresee the rise and fall of empires. ② reflect; mirror: 水清可～。 The water is so clear that you can see your reflection in it. ③ warning; object lesson: 殷鉴 yīnjiàn ④ inspect; scruti-

nize; examine: 鉴定 jiàndìng ⑤ *pol.* (usu. used in the opening phrase in letters): 某先生台～。 Dear Mr. so-and-so: May I draw your attention to the following.

鉴别 jiànbié distinguish; differentiate; discriminate: 他可以～这块宝石是不是真的。 He can judge whether the stone is genuine. / 有比较才能～。 Only by comparing can one distinguish. / 要能～书的好坏。 You should discriminate good books from bad. / ～文物 make an appraisal of a cultural relic

鉴别器 jiànbiéqì *elec.* discriminator

鉴定 jiàndìng ① appraisal (of a person's strong and weak points): 毕业～ graduation appraisal ② appraise; identify; authenticate; determine: ～产品质量 appraise the quality of a product / ～文物年代 determine the date of a cultural relic / 这种产品已通过～。 This product has been tested and appraised. / 人民是最好的～人。 The people are the best judges. ③ *leg.* expert evaluation: ～人 expert witness

鉴戒 jiànjiè warning; object lesson: 我们应当把这次挫折引为～。 We should take warning from this setback.

鉴赏 jiànshǎng appreciate: ～能力 ability to appreciate (painting, music, etc.); connoisseurship / 对音乐颇有～力 have a good ear for music / 对文学有～力 have a discriminating taste in literature

鉴往知来 jiànwǎng-zhīlái predict the future by reviewing the past

鉴于 jiànyú in view of; seeing that: ～情况紧急，我们立即作出决定。 We made up our minds at once in view of the urgency of the case. / ～上述情况，我们提出以下建议。 In view of the above-mentioned facts, we wish to make the following proposals. / ～这几个学生基础太差，所以进行了额外辅导。 Extra coaching had been given to these students because they had too poor a start.

键

jiàn ① *mech.* key: 轴～ shaft key ② key (of a typewriter, piano, etc.) ③ *chem.* bond ④ *formal* bolt (of a door)

键槽 jiàncáo *mech.* keyway; key slot; key seat

键盘 jiànpán keyboard; fingerboard

键盘乐器 jiànpán yuèqì keyboard instrument

槛（檻）

jiàn ① banisters; balustrade ② cage: 兽～ a cage for animals / ～车 prisoners' van (used in ancient times) ——see also kǎn

僭

jiàn *formal* overstep one's authority

僭越 jiànyuè *formal* overstep one's authority

箭

jiàn arrow

箭靶子 jiànbǎzi target for archery

箭步 jiànbù a sudden big stride forward: 他一个～蹿上前去。 He leapt up with a big stride.

箭垛子 jiànduǒzi ① battlements ② target for archery

箭杆 jiàngǎn arrow shaft

箭楼 jiànlóu an embrasured watchtower over a city gate

箭石 jiànshí *palaeontology* belemnite

箭筒 jiàntǒng quiver (for arrows)

箭头 jiàntóu ① arrowhead ② arrow (as a sign)

箭在弦上，不得不发 jiàn zài xián shàng, bùdé bù fā an arrow fitted to the bowstring cannot avoid being discharged—one cannot but go ahead; one has reached the point of no return

箭猪 jiànzhū porcupine

箭镞 jiànzú metal arrowhead

jiāng

江 jiāng ① river ② (Jiāng) the Changjiang River ③(Jiāng) a surname

江北 Jiāngběi north of the River—a region including parts of Jiangsu and Anhui which are north of the Changjiang (Yangtze)

江河日下 jiānghé rì xià go from bad to worse; be on the decline

江河行地 jiānghé xíng dì rivers run their courses across the land—unalterable

江湖 jiānghú rivers and lakes—all corners of the country; the wide world: 自叙少小时欢乐事，今漂沦憔悴，转徙于～间。(白居易) She told me of the pleasures of her youth and said now that her beauty had faded she was drifting from place to place, by rivers and lakes. / 流落～ live a vagabond life

江湖 jiāng·hú rivers and lakes—people wandering from place to place and living by their wits, e. g. fortune-tellers, quack doctors, itinerant entertainers, etc., considered as a social group: 为因学得一家道术，善能呼风唤雨，驾雾腾云，～上都称贫道做"入云龙"。(《水浒》) Among the rivers and lakes I am known as the "Cloud-soaring Dragon" because of my studies as a Taoist adept, which enable me to summon the wind and rain and to ride the clouds and the mist.

江湖好汉 jiānghú hǎohàn a good fellow of the rivers and lakes; a bravo of river and lake: 结交～ make friends with the good fellows of the rivers and lakes

江湖骗子 jiānghú piànzi swindler; charlatan

江湖气 jiānghúqì derog. worldly-wise; slippery; sleek

江湖医生 jiānghú yīshēng quack; mountebank

江湖艺人 jiānghú yìrén itinerant entertainer

江郎才尽 Jiāngláng cái jìn a Jianglang depleted of his talents—a writer written out (originally said of Jiang Yan 江淹 of the Southern Dynasties period, who showed brilliance as a poet at an early age and became widely known as Jianglang, or young Jiang, but who produced nothing of note in his later years, esp. after rising to high office)

江蓠 jiānglí ① *Gracilaria confervoides* ② a fragrant plant mentioned in ancient texts

江轮 jiānglún river steamer

江米 jiāngmǐ polished glutinous rice

江米酒 jiāngmǐjiǔ fermented glutinous rice

江南 jiāngnán south of the River—a region in the lower Changjiang (Yangtze) valley, including southern Jiangsu and Anhui and northern Zhejiang (much celebrated in poetry for its beauties and joys): ～好。(白居易) It's good to be in the South. / 人人尽说～好。(韦庄) Everyone is full of praise for the beauty of the South.

江山 jiāngshān ① rivers and mountains; land; landscape: ～如画 a picturesque landscape; beautiful scenery ②country; state power: 保卫人民的～ safeguard the people's state power

江山易改，本性难移 jiāngshān yì gǎi, běnxìng nán yí it's easy to change rivers and mountains but hard to change a person's nature

江苏 Jiāngsū Jiangsu (Province)

江天 jiāngtiān *liter.* the sky over the river: 对萧萧暮雨洒～，一番洗清秋。(柳永) Facing me, the blustering evening rain besprinkles the sky over the river, Washing the cool autumn air once more.

江豚 jiāngtún (also 江猪 jiāngzhū) black finless porpoise

江西 Jiāngxī Jiangxi (Province)

江洋大盗 jiāngyáng dàdào a great robber

江珧 jiāngyáo *zool.* pen shell

江珧柱 jiāngyáozhù the dried adductor of a pen shell

将(將) jiāng ①*formal* support; take; bring: ～幼弟而归 bring home one's little brother / 相～而去 go off supporting each other ② take care of (one's health): 将养 jiāngyǎng ③ do sth.; handle (a matter): 慎重～事 handle a matter with care ④ *Chinese chess* check: ～! Check! / 他连～我三次。 He checked me three times in a row. ⑤ put sb. on the spot: 我们这一问可把他～住了。 Our question certainly put him on the spot. ⑥ incite sb. to action; challenge; prod: 他已拿定主意不参加比赛了，你再～他也没用。 It's no use egging him on; he's made up his mind not to join in the tournament. ⑦ *prep.* with; by means of; by: ～开水沏茶 make tea with boiling water ⑧ *prep.* (used in the same way as 把²): ～他请来 invite him to come over / ～革命进行到底 Carry the revolution through to the end. ⑨ *adv.* be going to; be about to; will; shall: 船～启碇。 The ship is about to weigh anchor. / 我们～制定一个长远规划。 We are going to draw up a long-range plan. / 天～黄昏。 It's almost dusk. ⑩ *adv.* certainly; no doubt: 如不刻苦钻研，则～一事无成。 You will certainly achieve nothing unless you study assiduously. ⑪ *part. dial.* (used between a verb and its complement of direction): 唱～起来 start to sing / 传～出去 (of news, etc.) spread abroad / 赶～上去 hurry to catch up / 打～起来 start to fight ——see also jiàng

将才 jiāngcái *adv.* just now; a moment ago: 他～还在这儿。 He was here a moment ago.

将次 jiāngcì *formal* be going to; will; shall

将错就错 jiāng cuò jiù cuò leave a mistake uncorrected and make the best of it

将功补过 jiāng gōng bǔ guò make amends for one's faults by good deeds

将功赎罪 jiāng gōng shú zuì atone for a crime by good deeds; expiate one's guilt by good deeds: 凡是已经做过坏事的人们，赶快停止作恶，悔过自新，我们准其～。 Those who have been doing evil should immediately stop, repent and start anew and we will give them a chance to make amends for their crimes by good deeds.

将功折罪 jiāng gōng zhé zuì same as 将功赎罪 jiāng gōng shú zuì

将计就计 jiāng jì jiù jì meet plot with plot; turn sb.'s trick against him; beat sb. at his own game

将将 jiāngjiāng *adv.* just; barely; only: 这间屋子～能容十个人。 The room can barely hold ten people. / 这块布～够给孩子做件上衣。 This piece of cloth is just enough to make a jacket for the child.

将近 jiāngjìn *adv.* close to; nearly; almost: ～一百人 close to a hundred people / ～完成 almost completed / 这个国家有～四千年有记载的历史。 This country has nearly 4,000 years of recorded history.

将就 jiāngjiu make do with; make the best of; put up with: 这件大衣稍微短一点，你～着穿吧。 This coat may be a bit too short for you, but perhaps you could make do with it. / 没有什么再好的工作了，你就～点吧。 There is no better job, so make the best of it. / 哄着他点儿，～～他吧。 Humour him a little and bear with him.

将军 jiāngjūn ① general ② *Chinese chess* check: 他将了我两次军。 He checked me twice in a row. ③ put sb. on the spot; embarrass; challenge: 他们要我唱歌，这可将了我一军。 They embarrassed me by calling on me to sing.

将来 jiānglái future: 在不远的～ in the not too distant

future; before long / 在可以预见的～ in the foreseeable future

将息 jiāngxī rest; recuperate

将心比心 jiāng xīn bǐ xīn put oneself in sb.'s shoes; think of others; be empathic

将心换心 jiāng xīn huàn xīn to win other people's hearts by one's sincerity

将信将疑 jiāngxìn-jiāngyí half believing, half doubting: 对他的话～ take him half seriously and half sceptically; only half believe what he says

将养 jiāngyǎng rest; recuperate: 医生说你再～一个礼拜就可以好了。The doctor says you ought to be well again after another week's rest.

将要 jiāngyào *adv.* be going to; will; shall: 他～到西藏去工作。He's going to work in Xizang.

将欲取之，必先与之 jiāng yù qǔ zhī, bì xiān yǔ zhī give in order to take

姜¹(薑) jiāng ginger

姜² Jiāng a surname

姜还是老的辣 jiāng háishi lǎode là old ginger is hotter than new—veterans are abler than recruits

姜黄 jiānghuáng *bot.* turmeric

姜片虫 jiāngpiànchóng fasciolopsis: ～病 fasciolopsiasis

姜汤 jiāngtāng ginger tea

豇 jiāng see below

豇豆 jiāngdòu cowpea

浆(漿) jiāng ① thick liquid: 糖浆 tángjiāng / 纸浆 zhǐjiāng ② starch: ～衣服 starch clothes ——see also jiàng

浆板 jiāngbǎn *papermaking* pulp board

浆度 jiāngdù *papermaking* degree of beating (in making pulp)

浆果 jiāngguǒ *bot.* berry

浆纱 jiāngshā *text.* sizing

浆洗 jiāngxǐ wash and starch

浆纸机 jiāngzhǐjī *papermaking* coating machine

僵¹(殭) jiāng stiff; numb: 他的脚冻～了。His feet were numb with cold.

僵² jiāng ① deadlocked: 他把事情搞～了。He's brought things to a deadlock. ② *dial.* stop smiling; look serious: 他～着脸。He kept a straight face. *or* He pulled a long face.

僵持 jiāngchí (of both parties) refuse to budge: 双方～好久。For quite some time, neither party was willing to budge from its original position. / 谈判处于～状态。The negotiations are now in a stalemate.

僵化 jiānghuà become rigid; ossify; stereotyped: 思想～a rigid (*or* ossified) way of thinking; stereotyped thinking / 冲破～的经济体制 break down the rigid economic structures

僵局 jiāngjú deadlock; impasse; stalemate: 打破～break a deadlock

僵尸 jiāngshī corpse: 政治～ a political mummy

僵死 jiāngsǐ dead; ossified

僵硬 jiāngyìng ① stiff: 觉得四肢～ feel stiff in the limbs ② rigid; inflexible: ～的公式 a rigid formula / 工作方法太～ work in a mechanical way / 政策～ an inflexible policy

缰(韁) jiāng reins; halter

缰绳 jiāngsheng reins; halter

鰔(鱂) jiāng killifish

礓 jiāng see below

礓磋 jiāngcā a flight of steps

疆 jiāng boundary; border

疆场 jiāngchǎng battlefield

疆界 jiāngjiè boundary; border

疆土 jiāngtǔ territory

疆域 jiāngyù territory; domain

jiǎng

讲(講) jiǎng ① speak; say; tell: ～英语 speak English / ～故事 tell stories / ～几句话 say a few words / ～几点意见 make a few remarks / ～的是一套，做的是另一套 say one thing and do another ②explain; make clear; interpret: 把道理～清楚 state the reasons clearly / 我来～～今天开会的目的。Let me explain the purpose of today's meeting. / 这本书是～气象的。This is a book about meteorology. ③ discuss; negotiate: ～条件 negotiate the terms; insist on the fulfilment of certain conditions ④ stress; pay attention to; be particular about: ～卫生 pay attention to hygiene / ～质量 stress quality / ～排场 go in for ostentation and extravagance; go in for showy display; be ostentatious / 不～情面 have no consideration for anyone's sensibilities ⑤ as far as sth. is concerned; when it comes to; as to; as regards: ～干劲，她比谁都足。When it comes to drive, she's got more than any of us. / ～能力，她不如你。As to ability, she is not your match.

讲法 jiǎngfa ① the way of saying a thing; wording: 这个意见你如果换一个～就不会惹他生气了。If you had put your idea in a different way, he wouldn't have been offended. / 这个字有几个～。This word may be interpreted in different ways. ② statement; version; argument: 按他的～办吧。Do as he says.

讲稿 jiǎnggǎo the draft or text of a speech; lecture notes

讲和 jiǎnghé make peace; settle a dispute; become reconciled: 现在我们不能跟他们～。We cannot make peace with them now. / 这次停战将为～铺平道路。The truce will pave the way for peace.

讲话 jiǎnghuà ① speak; talk; address: 对着话筒～ speak into a microphone / 他在会上讲了话。He spoke at the meeting. *or* He addressed the meeting. ② speech; talk: 鼓舞人心的～ an inspiring speech ③ talks (used in titles of books that set out basic information): 《语法修辞～》 *Talks on Grammar and Rhetoric*

讲价 jiǎngjià (also 讲价钱 jiǎng jiàqian) ① haggle over the price; bargain ② negotiate the terms; insist on the fulfilment of certain conditions

讲解 jiǎngjiě explain: 他指着示意图给来宾～远景规划。Pointing at a sketch map, he explained the long-term plan to the visitors.

讲解员 jiǎngjiěyuán guide; announcer; narrator; commentator

讲究 jiǎngjiu ① be particular about; pay attention to; stress; strive for: 她太～吃穿。She is too fastidious about her food and clothing. / ～卫生, 减少疾病 pay attention to hygiene and reduce the incidence of disease / ～实际效果 stress practical results / 写文章一定要～逻辑。In writing one must have regard for logic. ② exquisite; tasteful: 宾馆布置得很～。The guesthouse is tastefully furnished. ③careful study: 翻译技巧大有～。The art of translation calls for careful study.

or Translation is quite an art./其中大有～。There's an art to it.

讲课 jiǎngkè　teach; lecture: 他讲数学课。He gives lessons in mathematics. /～时数 teaching hours

讲理 jiǎnglǐ　① reason with sb.; argue: 咱们跟他～去。Let's go and argue it out with him. ② listen (or be amenable) to reason; be reasonable; be sensible: 这人没法跟他～。He is utterly unreasonable. or He is impervious to reason.

讲明 jiǎngmíng　explain; make clear; state explicitly: ～立场 explain (or state) one's stand /向群众～党的政策 make the Party's policies clear to the masses

讲评 jiǎngpíng　comment on and appraise: ～学生的作业 comment on the students' work

讲情 jiǎngqíng　intercede; plead for sb.: 为他～ plead for him /向他为我～ intercede with him for me

讲求 jiǎngqiú　be particular about; pay attention to; stress; strive for: ～效率 strive for efficiency /～实效 lay stress on practical results

讲师 jiǎngshī　lecturer

讲授 jiǎngshòu　lecture; instruct; teach: 他～哲学。He teaches philosophy. /～提纲 an outline for a lecture; teaching notes

讲述 jiǎngshù　tell about; give an account of; narrate; relate: 故事～两姐妹在恋爱和婚姻中的遭遇。The story tells about the fortunes of two sisters in love and marriage.

讲台 jiǎngtái　platform; dais; rostrum

讲坛 jiǎngtán　① (speaker's) platform; rostrum ② forum (for public discussion)

讲堂 jiǎngtáng　lecture room; classroom

讲题 jiǎngtí　topic of a lecture

讲习 jiǎngxí　lecture and study

讲习班 jiǎngxíbān　study group

讲习所 jiǎngxísuǒ　institute (for instruction or training)

讲学 jiǎngxué　give lectures; discourse on an academic subject: 应邀来华～ be invited to give lectures in China

讲演 jiǎngyǎn　① give a speech or lecture ② speech; lecture: 他的～你听了没有? Did you attend his lecture?

讲义 jiǎngyì　(mimeographed or printed) teaching materials

讲座 jiǎngzuò　a course of lectures: 英语广播～ English lessons over the radio; English by radio

奖(獎)

jiǎng　① encourage; praise; reward: 有功者～。Those who have gained merit will be rewarded. /～勤罚懒, ～优罚劣 reward the diligent and good and punish the lazy and bad ② award; prize; reward: 得～win a prize /一等～ first prize

奖杯 jiǎngbēi　cup (as a prize)

奖惩 jiǎng-chéng　rewards and punishments; rewards and penalties

奖金 jiǎngjīn　money award; bonus; premium

奖励 jiǎnglì　encourage and reward; award; reward: ～模范工作者 give awards to model workers / 精神～ moral encouragement / 物质～ material reward /～发明创造 encourage innovations by giving awards

奖牌 jiǎngpái　medal: ～获得者 medalist

奖品 jiǎngpǐn　prize; award; trophy

奖旗 jiǎngqí　banner (as an award)

奖券 jiǎngquàn　lottery ticket

奖赏 jiǎngshǎng　award; reward: 他因学习成绩优秀而受到～。He was awarded a prize for excellence in his studies.

奖售 jiǎngshòu　encourage sales to the state

奖许 jiǎngxǔ　praise; give encouragement to

奖学金 jiǎngxuéjīn　scholarship; exhibition

奖掖 jiǎngyè　formal　reward and promote; encourage by promoting and rewarding

奖章 jiǎngzhāng　medal; decoration

奖状 jiǎngzhuàng　certificate of merit

桨(槳)

jiǎng　oar

蒋(蔣)

jiǎng　a surname

耩

jiǎng　sow with a drill

耩子 jiǎngzi　dial.　drill

膙

jiǎng　see below

膙子 jiǎngzi　callosity; callus

jiàng

匠

jiàng　craftsman; artisan: 铁匠 tiějiàng / 石匠 shíjiàng

匠气 jiàngqì　unimaginative craftsmanship

匠人 jiàngrén　artisan; craftsman

匠心 jiàngxīn　formal　ingenuity; craftsmanship

匠心独运 jiàngxīn dú yùn　consummate craftsmanship

降

jiàng　① fall; drop: 温度～到摄氏零下十度。The temperature dropped to minus ten degrees centigrade. ② lower; reduce; cut down: 把价钱～下来 lower the price ——see also xiáng

降半旗 jiàng bànqí　same as 下半旗 xià bànqí

降低 jiàngdī　reduce; cut down; drop: 气温～了。The temperature dropped. /～半个音。make the note a semitone lower /～生产成本 reduce production costs; lower production costs /～定额 reduce the quota (or norm) /～原料消耗 cut down the consumption of raw materials /价格～了，但质量并未～。The price is lower, but the quality is the same.

降调 jiàngdiào　phonet.　falling tune; falling tone

降格 jiànggé　lower one's standard or status: 两国关系～ lower the level of diplomatic relations between two countries

降格以求 jiànggé yǐ qiú　fall back on sth. inferior to what one hoped for; settle for a second best

降号 jiànghào　mus.　flat (b)

降级 jiàngjí　reduce to a lower rank; demote: 这个军官因行为不端而被～。The officer was demoted for misconduct. ② send (a student) to a lower grade

降价 jiàngjià　reduce (or lower) the prices

降临 jiànglín　formal　befall; arrive; come: 灾难～了。A disaster has befallen us. /夜色～。Night fell.

降落 jiàngluò　descend; land: 大型飞机的起飞和～ the take-off and landing of big aircraft

降落场 jiàngluòchǎng　landing field

降落伞 jiàngluòsǎn　parachute

降旗 jiàngqí　lower a flag

降生 jiàngshēng　formal　(of the founder of a religion, etc.) be born

降水 jiàngshuǐ　meteorol.　precipitation

降水量 jiàngshuǐliàng　meteorol.　precipitation: 南方的年～比北方大。The annual precipitation is greater in the south than in the north.

降温 jiàngwēn　① lower the temperature (as in a workshop) ② meteorol.　drop in temperature

降心相从 jiàng xīn xiàng cóng　obey others against one's will

降压 jiàngyā　elec.　step-down: ～变电站 step-down substation /～变压器 step-down transformer

降压片 jiàngyāpiàn　pharm.　hypertension pill

降雨 jiàngyǔ a fall of rain; rainfall
降雨量 jiàngyǔliàng rainfall: 年～ annual rainfall
降旨 jiàngzhǐ issue an imperial edict

绛 jiàng deep red; crimson
绛紫 jiàngzǐ dark reddish purple

将(將) jiàng ① general: 上将 shàngjiàng ② commander in chief, the chief piece in Chinese chess ③ *formal* command; lead: ～兵 command troops —see also jiāng
将材 jiàngcái (also 将才 jiàngcái) a man with military talent; a man born to command troops
将官 jiàngguān general
将官 jiàngguan *inf.* high-ranking military officer
将领 jiànglǐng high-ranking military officer; general
将令 jiànglìng *old* military orders
将门 jiàngmén the family of a general
将门有将 jiàngmén yǒu jiàng the family of a general is bound to produce more generals
将门无犬子 jiàngmén wú quǎnzǐ a general's family will not produce a mongrel of a son
将士 jiàngshì *formal* officers and men
将帅 jiàngshuài commander-in-chief
将校 jiàngxiào generals and field officers; high-ranking officers
将相 jiàngxiàng *old* generals and ministers of state
将在外，君命有所不受 jiàng zài wài, jūn mìng yǒu suǒ bù shòu a general in the field is not bound by orders from his sovereign
将指 jiàngzhǐ *formal* ① middle finger ② big toe
将佐 jiàngzuǒ a high-ranking officer

浆(漿) jiàng same as 糨 jiàng

犟 jiàng *dial.* ① trap; snare: 装～捉鸟 set a trap to catch birds ② catch in a trap; trap

强(強、彊) jiàng stubborn; unyielding —see also qiáng; qiǎng
强嘴 jiàngzuǐ reply defiantly; answer back; talk back

酱(醬) jiàng ① a thick sauce made from soya beans, flour, etc. ② cooked or pickled in soy sauce ③ sauce; paste; jam: 苹果～ apple jam
酱菜 jiàngcài vegetables pickled in soy sauce; pickles
酱豆腐 jiàngdòufu fermented bean curd
酱缸 jiànggāng jar for making or keeping thick soya bean sauce
酱肉 jiàngròu pork cooked in soy sauce; braised pork seasoned with soy sauce
酱色 jiàngsè dark reddish brown
酱油 jiàngyóu soy sauce; soy
酱园 jiàngyuán (also 酱坊 jiàngfāng) a shop making and selling sauce, pickles, etc.; sauce and pickle shop
酱紫 jiàngzǐ dark reddish purple

犟(勥) jiàng obstinate; stubborn; self-willed: 这人真～。He is a pigheaded (*or* bullheaded) person. *or* He is as stubborn as a mule.
犟劲 jiàngjìn obstinacy; stubbornness
犟嘴 jiàngzuǐ same as 强嘴 jiàngzuǐ

糨(糡) jiàng thick: 粥熬得太～了。The porridge is too thick.
糨糊 jiànghu paste
糨子 jiàngzi *inf.* paste: 打～ make paste

jiāo

芄 jiāo 见 "秦芄" qínjiāo

交[1] jiāo ① hand over; give up; deliver: ～还 give back; return / ～活 turn over a finished item (*or* product) / ～公粮 deliver tax grain to the state / ～会费 pay membership dues / 把任务～给我们实验室吧。Assign the task to our laboratory. ② (of places or periods of time) meet; join: 井冈山位于四县之～。The Jinggang Mountains stand where the boundaries of four counties meet. / 春夏之～ when spring is changing into summer ③ reach (a certain hour or season): ～冬以后 when winter has set in / 明天就～夏至了。Tomorrow will be the Summer Solstice. / ～了好运气 have good luck ④ cross; intersect: 这两条直线～于P点。The two lines intersect at P. ⑤ associate with: ～朋友 make friends ⑥ friend; acquaintance; friendship; relationship: 知交 zhījiāo / 邦交 bāngjiāo ⑦ have sexual intercourse ⑧ mate; breed: 杂交 zájiāo ⑨ mutual; reciprocal; each other: 交换 jiāohuàn ⑩ together; simultaneous: 饥寒交迫 jī-hán jiāopò ⑪ business transaction; deal; bargain: 成交 chéngjiāo

交[2] **(跤)** jiāo fall: 他脚一滑, 摔了一大～。He slipped and fell heavily.
交白卷 jiāo báijuàn ① hand in a blank examination paper ② completely fail to accomplish a task: 咱们得把情况摸清楚, 要不回去就得～。We must find out exactly how things stand here, or we'll have nothing to report.
交班 jiāobān hand over to the next shift
交保 jiāobǎo release on bail: ～释放 release on bail
交杯酒 jiāobēijiǔ drink the nuptial cup (part of an old-fashioned marriage ceremony, in which the bride and the bridegroom drink out of goblets tied together by red thread, exchanging cups and drinking again)
交臂失之 jiāo bì shī zhī same as 失之交臂 shī zhī jiāo bì
交兵 jiāobīng *formal* (of two or more parties) be at war; wage war
交叉 jiāochā ① intersect; cross; crisscross: 两条铁路在此～。The two railways cross here. ② overlapping: 两个提案中～的部分 the overlapping parts of the two proposals ③ alternate; stagger: ～进行 do alternately
交叉点 jiāochādiǎn intersection
交叉感染 jiāochā gǎnrǎn cross infection
交叉汇率 jiāochā huìlǜ cross rate
交叉火力 jiāochā huǒlì *mil.* cross fire
交差 jiāochāi report to the leadership after accomplishing a task: 你不开收据, 我们回去怎么～? If you don't give us a receipt, how are we going to account for it?
交出 jiāochū surrender; hand over: ～武器 surrender one's weapons
交存 jiāocún deposit; hand in for safekeeping: ～批准书 deposit instruments of ratification
交错 jiāocuò ① interlock; crisscross: 沟渠～。Ditches and canals crisscross. ② *mech.* staggered: ～气缸 staggered cylinder
交代 jiāodài (also 交待 jiāodài) ① hand over: ～工作 hand over work to one's successor; brief one's successor on handing over work ② explain; make clear; brief; tell: ～政策 explain policy / ～任务 assign and explain a task; brief sb. on his task / 作者对此未作进一步～。The author makes no further reference to this. / 政委一再～我们要保护群众的利益。The political commissar

repeatedly told us to protect the interests of the masses. ③ account for; justify oneself: 这个问题你怎么～? How are you going to account for this? / ～不过去 be unable to justify an action ④ confess: ～罪行 confess a crime / 彻底～ make a clean breast of

交道 jiāodao　see 打交道 dǎ jiāodao

交底 jiāodǐ　tell sb. what one's real intentions are; put all one's cards on the table

交点 jiāodiǎn　① *math.* point of intersection ② *astron.* node: ～月 nodical month

交锋 jiāofēng　cross swords; engage in a battle or contest: 敌人不敢和我们正面～. The enemy didn't dare to risk a frontal engagement with us. / 第一次大～ the first great trial of strength / 思想～ confrontation of ideas / 这两支足球队将在明天～. The two football teams will face each other tomorrow.

交付 jiāofù　① pay: ～租金 pay rent ② hand over; deliver; consign: ～表决 put to the vote / 新建的楼房已经～使用。 The new building has been made available to the users.

交感神经 jiāogǎn shénjīng　*physiol.* sympathetic nerve

交割 jiāogē　complete a business transaction: 此项货款业已～。 The money for this consignment has already been paid.

交工 jiāogōng　hand over a completed project

交公 jiāogōng　hand over to the collective or the state

交媾 jiāogòu　sexual intercourse; copulation

交关 jiāoguān　① have to do with; involve: 性命交关 xìngmìng jiāoguān ② *dial.* very; extremely: 今年冬天～冷。 This is an extremely cold winter. ③ *dial.* very many: 公园里人～。 The park is very crowded.

交好 jiāohǎo　(of people or states) be on friendly terms

交互 jiāohù　① each other; mutual: 学生～批改作业。 Students corrected each other's papers. / ～校订译文 check each other's translations ② alternately; in turn: 两种策略～使用 use the two tactics alternately / 他两手～地抓住野藤爬上崖顶。 Holding on to the creepers, he climbed hand over hand to the top of the cliff.

交欢 jiāohuān　*formal* be on friendly terms

交还 jiāohuán　give back; return: 他把书～给图书馆了。 He has returned the book to the library. / 联合王国政府将于1997年7月1日将香港～给中华人民共和国。 The Government of the United Kingdom will restore Hong Kong to the People's Republic of China with effect from 1 July 1997。

交换 jiāohuàn　exchange; swop: ～意见 exchange views; compare notes / ～场地 *sports* change of courts, goals or ends / ～文本 exchange of texts (*or* copies) / ～战俘 exchange of prisoners of war / 用小麦～大米 barter wheat for rice

交换齿轮 jiāohuàn chǐlún　change gear

交换价值 jiāohuàn jiàzhí　*econ.* exchange value

交换器 jiāohuànqì　*elec.* converter

交火 jiāohuǒ　exchange shots; fight

交货 jiāohuò　delivery: 即期～ prompt delivery / 近期～ near delivery / 远期～ forward delivery / 分批～ delivery by instalments; partial delivery / 仓库～ *ex* warehouse / 船上～ *ex* ship / 铁路旁～ *ex* rail

交货港 jiāohuògǎng　port of delivery

交货期 jiāohuòqī　date of delivery

交货收据 jiāohuò shōujù　delivery receipt

交集 jiāojí　(of different feelings) be mixed; occur simultaneously ——see also 百感交集 bǎi gǎn jiāojí; 悲喜交集 bēi-xǐ jiāojí

交际 jiāojì　social intercourse; communication: 语言是人们～的工具。 Language is the means by which people communicate with each other. / 她～很广。 She has a large circle of acquaintances. / 她善于～, 认识不少人。 She is very good at socializing (*or* is a good mix-er) and knows quite a few people.

交际花 jiāojìhuā　social butterfly; society woman

交际舞 jiāojìwǔ　(also 交谊舞 jiāoyìwǔ) ballroom dancing; social dancing

交加 jiāojiā　*formal* (of two things) accompany each other; occur simultaneously: 雷电～ lightning accompanied by peals of thunder; there was thunder and lightning / 风雪～ a raging snowstorm / 悔恨～ regret mingled with self-reproach / 贫病～ be plagued by both poverty and illness / 拳足～ give sb. both punches and kicks; cuff and kick; beat up

交角 jiāojiǎo　*math.* angle of intersection

交接 jiāojiē　① join; connect: 夏秋～的季节 when summer is changing into autumn ② hand over and take over: 保证顺利～ ensure a smooth transfer / ～战俘 delivery and reception of prisoners of war / ～班 relief of a shift / ～手续(仪式) handing over procedure (ceremony) ③ associate with: 他所～的朋友 the people he associates with; the friends he has made

交睫 jiāojié　close eyes: 目不交睫 mù bù jiāojié

交界 jiāojiè　(of two or more places) have a common boundary: 三省～的地方 a place where three provinces meet; the juncture of three provinces / 江苏北面与山东～。 Jiangsu is bounded on the north by Shandong.

交颈 jiāojǐng　neck to neck——fondle and kiss: ～鸳鸯 a pair of mandarin ducks crossing their necks

交卷 jiāojuàn　① hand in an examination paper ② fulfil one's task; carry out an assignment

交口 jiāokǒu　① with one voice ② converse; talk

交口称誉 jiāokǒu chēngyù　unanimously praise

交困 jiāokùn　beset by troubles ——see also 内外交困 nèi-wài jiāokùn

交流 jiāoliú　exchange; interflow; interchange: ～经验 exchange experience; draw on each other's experience / 城乡物资～ flow of goods and materials between city and country / 国际文化～ international cultural exchange / 经济和技术～ economic and technical interchange

交流电 jiāoliúdiàn　alternating current (AC)

交流发电机 jiāoliú fādiànjī　alternating current generator; alternator

交纳 jiāonà　pay (to the state or an organization); hand in: ～会费 pay membership dues / 照章～税款 pay customs duty according to the regulation / ～公粮 deliver tax grain to the state

交配 jiāopèi　mating; copulation

交配期 jiāopèiqī　mating season

交迫 jiāopò　hard pressed on both sides ——see also 饥寒交迫 jī-hán jiāopò; 贫病交迫 pín-bìng jiāopò

交情 jiāoqing　friendship; friendly relations: 老～ long-standing friendship / 讲～ do things for the sake of friendship / 他们两人～不错。 The two of them are on very good terms. / 他这么办事, 一点～都不讲。 It's very unfriendly of him to act the way he did. ——see also 套交情 tào jiāoqing

交融 jiāoróng　blend; mingle ——see also 水乳交融 shuǐ-rǔ jiāoróng

交涉 jiāoshè　negotiate; make representations: 办～ carry on negotiations with; take up a matter with / 口头～ verbal representations / 向有关方面进行过多次～ have made many representations to the quarters concerned; have more than once approached the departments concerned / 经过～, 问题解决了。 The problem was solved through negotiations.

交手 jiāoshǒu　fight hand to hand; be engaged in a hand-to-hand fight; come to grips: 一言不合, 两人交起手来。 The two came to grips after an exchange of hot words. / 听说你棋下得不错, 很想什么时候和你交交手。 I hear you are very good at chess. I'd like to play with you sometime.

交售 jiāoshòu sell (to the state): 踊跃向国家～油菜籽 enthusiastically sell rapeseed to the state

交谈 jiāotán talk with each other; converse; chat: 自由～ a freewheeling conversation / 他们就广泛的问题进行了友好的～。They had a friendly conversation on a wide range of subjects. / 和外国朋友进行亲切的～ have cordial conversations with foreign friends

交替 jiāotì ① supersede; replace: 新旧～。The new replaces the old. / 新旧体制的～ in the transition from the old structure to the new ② alternately; in turn: ～演奏两国乐曲 play music of the two countries alternately

交通 jiāotōng ① be connected; be linked: 阡陌～。Linking paths lead everywhere. ② traffic; communications: 公路～ highway traffic / 陆上～ land traffic / 市区～ urban traffic / ～便利 have transport facilities / 妨碍～ interfere with the traffic ③ liaison; liaison man: ～员 liaison man; underground messenger

交通安全 jiāotōng ānquán traffic safety

交通标线 jiāotōng biāoxiàn traffic marking

交通标志 jiāotōng biāozhì traffic sign

交通部 jiāotōngbù the Ministry of Communications

交通车 jiāotōngchē special bus (service)

交通干线 jiāotōng gànxiàn main line of communication; main communications artery

交通高峰 jiāotōng gāofēng traffic peak; rush hour; peak hour

交通工具 jiāotōng gōngjù means of transportation

交通管理 jiāotōng guǎnlǐ traffic control

交通规则 jiāotōng guīzé traffic regulations

交通壕 jiāotōngháo mil. communication trench

交通警 jiāotōngjǐng traffic police

交通量 jiāotōngliàng volume of traffic

交通事故 jiāotōng shìgù traffic (or road) accident

交通网 jiāotōngwǎng network of communication lines

交通线 jiāotōngxiàn communication lines; communication routes

交通信号 jiāotōng xìnhào traffic signal

交通要道 jiāotōng yàodào vital communication line

交通运输 jiāotōng yùnshū communications and transportation

交通阻塞 jiāotōng zǔsè traffic jam (or block)

交头接耳 jiāotóu-jiē'ěr speak in each other's ears; whisper to each other

交往 jiāowǎng association; contact: 我和他～，得益不少。I have gained a lot by associating with him. / 在同各国人民的～中，我们学习到不少有用的东西。In our contacts with people of other countries, we have learned many useful things. / 两人～甚密。The two of them often got together / 他不大和人～。He is unsociable.

交尾 jiāowěi mating; pairing; coupling

交恶 jiāowù fall foul of each other; become enemies: 自此两人～。After that they grew to hate each other.

交相辉映 jiāo xiāng huīyìng enhance each other's beauty: 湖光山色，～。The lake and the hills enhance each other's beauty.

交响曲 jiāoxiǎngqǔ mus. symphony

交响诗 jiāoxiǎngshī mus. symphonic poem; tone poem

交响乐 jiāoxiǎngyuè mus. symphony; symphonic music

交响乐队 jiāoxiǎngyuèduì symphony orchestra; philharmonic orchestra

交卸 jiāoxiè old hand over office to a successor

交心 jiāoxīn lay one's heart bare; open one's heart to: 互相～ have a heart-to-heart talk

交验 jiāoyàn hand over for examination or checking: 必须向海关～许可证。The licence must be produced for the customs office to examine.

交椅 jiāoyǐ ① an ancient folding chair ② armchair: 坐第二把～ occupy the second highest post; be second in command

交易 jiāoyì business; deal; trade; transaction: 现款～ cash transaction / 赊帐～ credit transaction / 期货～ dealing in futures / ～额 volume of trade / 做成一笔～ make a deal / 肮脏的政治～ a dirty political deal / 决不拿原则做～ never barter away principles

交易所 jiāoyìsuǒ exchange

交谊 jiāoyì formal friendship; friendly relations

交游 jiāoyóu formal make friends: ～甚广 have a large circle of friends

交运 jiāoyùn be in luck

交战 jiāozhàn be at war; fight; wage war: ～状态 state of war; belligerency / ～行为 belligerent act / ～的一方 a belligerent / ～双方 the two belligerent parties

交战国 jiāozhànguó belligerent countries (or states, nations)

交战团体 jiāozhàn tuántǐ belligerent community; party to a war

交帐 jiāozhàng ① hand over the accounts ② account for: 把小孩冻坏了，我们怎么向他母亲～? If the child catches a chill, what are we going to say to its mother?

交织 jiāozhī interweave; intertwine; mingle: 用羊毛和蚕丝～ interweave wool with silk / 惊异和喜悦的感情～在一起。Joy mingled with surprise.

交嘴雀 jiāozuǐquè crossbill

郊 jiāo suburbs; outskirts: 京～ the suburbs of Beijing / 西～ the western suburbs

郊区 jiāoqū suburban district; suburbs; outskirts

郊外 jiāowài the countryside around a city; outskirts

郊游 jiāoyóu outing; excursion

菱 jiāo formal hay

菱白 jiāobái (also 菱瓜 jiāoguā) bot. wild rice stem

浇¹(澆) jiāo ① pour liquid on; sprinkle water on: 大雨～得他全身都湿透了。He was drenched with rain. ② irrigate; water: ～花 water flowers / ～地 irrigate the fields ③ print. cast: ～铅字 type casting; type founding

浇²(澆) jiāo formal degenerate; depraved

浇版 jiāobǎn print. casting: ～机 casting machine

浇薄 jiāobó formal (of customs, morals, etc.) degenerate; depraved: 世风～。Morals and manners have become degenerate. / 人情～。Human relationships are tenuous.

浇灌 jiāoguàn ① water; irrigate ② pour: ～混凝土 pour concrete

浇口 jiāokǒu metall. runner

浇冷水 jiāo lěngshuǐ same as 泼冷水 pō lěngshuǐ

浇头 jiāotou dial. gravy with meat or vegetables poured over rice or noodles

浇注 jiāozhù ① pour (melted metal, cement mixed with water, etc.) into a mould ② devote (one's energies, etc.) to: 他把全部心血都～在事业上。He put his heart and soul into advancing the cause.

浇铸 jiāozhù metall. casting; pouring: ～机 casting machine

娇(嬌) jiāo ① tender; lovely; charming: 江山如此多～，引无数英雄竞折腰。(毛泽东) This land so rich in beauty, Has made countless heroes bow in homage. / 嫩红～绿 tender blossoms and delicate leaves ② fragile; frail; delicate: 这孩子身体太～。The

child's health is fragile. ② squeamish; finicky: 她才走几里地就叫苦，未免太～了。 She started grumbling after walking only a few *li*. She's really too soft. ④ pamper; spoil: 别把你的小女儿～坏了! Don't pamper your little daughter.

娇嗔 jiāochēn　grumble in a flirtish manner

娇痴 jiāochī　lovely and innocent

娇滴滴 jiāodīdī　delicately pretty; affectedly sweet: ～的声音 a sweet and charming voice

娇儿 jiāo'ér　a darling son

娇惯 jiāoguàn　pamper; coddle; spoil: ～孩子 pamper a child

娇贵 jiāogui　① spoiled; coddled ② delicate and fragile: 仪表～，要小心轻放。 The apparatus is fragile and should be handled with care.

娇憨 jiāohān　lovely and innocent

娇客 jiāokè　① son-in-law ② a pampered person

娇媚 jiāomèi　① coquettish ② sweet and charming

娇嫩 jiāonèn　① tender and lovely ② fragile; delicate: ～的幼苗 delicate seedlings / ～的身子 delicate health

娇娘 jiāoniáng　a beautiful young woman

娇女 jiāonǚ　a beloved daughter

娇妻 jiāoqī　a beloved wife; a pretty young wife

娇气 jiāoqi　① fragile; delicate: 这种菜太～，我们这儿种不了。 This kind of vegetable's too delicate to grow here. / 你的身子也太～了，淋这么几滴雨就感冒。 You're really too delicate, catching cold from just a few drops of rain. ② squeamish; finicky: 粗粮细粮一样吃，别那么～。 Coarse grain is just as good as fine. Don't be so finicky. / 去掉～ get rid of squeamishness

娇娆 jiāoráo　enchantingly beautiful

娇柔 jiāoróu　gentle and demure

娇生惯养 jiāoshēng-guànyǎng　have been delicately brought up; be pampered and spoiled: 她自幼～，未受过一日委屈。 She's always lived in comfort, never had to put up with a single day's bad treatment. / 她不是小姐堆里～出来的人。 She isn't one of those aristocratic young ladies who've been pampered and spoiled all their lives.

娇娃 jiāowá　*old* a pretty girl

娇小 jiāoxiǎo　petite; delicate: ～的女孩子 a cute little girl

娇小玲珑 jiāoxiǎo línglóng　delicate and exquisite; petite and dainty: 这姑娘长得～。 She is a dainty little girl.

娇羞 jiāoxiū　coy

娇艳 jiāoyàn　delicate and charming; tender and beautiful: ～的桃花 delicate and charming peach blossoms

娇养 jiāoyǎng　pamper (a child); spoil: 她从小～。 She has been pampered and spoiled since her childhood.

娇纵 jiāozòng　indulge (a child); pamper; spoil

骄(驕)
jiāo　① proud; arrogant; conceited: 骄傲 jiāo'ào ② *liter.* fierce; intense: 骄阳 jiāoyáng

骄傲 jiāo'ào　① arrogant; conceited: 我们永远不能～，不能翘尾巴。 We should never become arrogant and cocky. ② be proud; take pride in: 老科学家为青年同志的成就感到～。 The old scientist takes pride in the achievements of his young colleagues. ③ pride: 民族的～ the pride of the nation

骄傲自大 jiāo'ào zìdà　self-important; conceited and arrogant

骄傲自满 jiāo'ào zìmǎn　conceited and self-satisfied; arrogant and complacent

骄兵必败 jiāobīng bì bài　an army puffed up with pride is bound to lose

骄横 jiāohèng　arrogant and imperious; overbearing

骄横跋扈 jiāohèng báhù　arrogant and overbearing; lordly and imperious

骄矜 jiāojīn　*formal* self-important; proud; haughty: 他为人谦逊，毫无～之态。 He is modest, and never puts on airs.

骄慢 jiāomàn　arrogant; haughty

骄气 jiāoqì　overbearing airs; arrogance

骄奢淫逸 jiāoshē-yínyì　lordly, luxury-loving, loose-living and idle; wallowing in luxury and pleasure; extravagant and dissipated

骄阳 jiāoyáng　*liter.* blazing sun: ～似火 a scorching sun beating down

骄子 jiāozǐ　favourite son (usu. fig.): 天之骄子 tiān zhī jiāozǐ

骄纵 jiāozòng　arrogant and wilful

姣
jiāo　*liter.* handsome; beautiful-looking

姣好 jiāohǎo　*liter.* beautiful and charming

胶(膠)
jiāo　① glue; gum ② stick with glue; glue ③ gluey; sticky; gummy ④ rubber

胶版 jiāobǎn　offset plate

胶版打样机 jiāobǎn dǎyàngjī　offset proof press

胶版印刷 jiāobǎn yìnshuā　offset printing; offset lithography; offset: ～机 offset press; offset (printing) machine

胶版纸 jiāobǎnzhǐ　offset paper

胶布 jiāobù　① rubberized fabric ② *inf.* adhesive plaster

胶布带 jiāobùdài　*elec.* rubberized tape; adhesive tape

胶合 jiāohé　glue together; veneer

胶合板 jiāohébǎn　plywood; veneer board

胶结 jiāojié　glued; cemented

胶结材料 jiāojié cáiliào　cementing material

胶结剂 jiāojiéjì　cementing agent

胶卷 jiāojuǎn　roll film; film

胶料 jiāoliào　*chem.* sizing material; size

胶轮 jiāolún　rubber tyre: ～大车 rubber-tyred cart

胶木 jiāomù　bakelite

胶囊 jiāonáng　capsule

胶泥 jiāoní　① clay ② *chem.* daub

胶粘 jiāonián　*dial.* sticky; glutinous

胶粘剂 jiāoniánjì　adhesive

胶凝作用 jiāoníng zuòyòng　*chem.* gelation

胶皮 jiāopí　① (vulcanized) rubber ② *dial.* rickshaw

胶片 jiāopiàn　film: 正色～ orthochromatic film / 缩微～ microfiche

胶乳 jiāorǔ　*chem.* latex: 硫化～ vulcanized latex; vultex

胶水 jiāoshuǐ　mucilage; glue

胶态 jiāotài　*phys.* colloidal state: ～发射药 colloidal propellant / ～悬浮 colloidal suspension / ～运动 colloidal movement

胶体 jiāotǐ　*chem.* colloid

胶体化学 jiāotǐ huàxué　colloid chemistry

胶体溶液 jiāotǐ róngyè　another name for 溶胶 róngjiāo

胶鞋 jiāoxié　① rubber overshoes; galoshes; rubbers ② rubber-soled shoes; tennis shoes; sneakers

胶靴 jiāoxuē　high rubber overshoes; galoshes

胶印 jiāoyìn　short for 胶版印刷 jiāobǎn yìnshuā

胶柱鼓瑟 jiāo zhù gǔ sè　play the *se* (an ancient zither-like instrument) with the pegs glued—stubbornly stick to old ways in the face of changed circumstances

胶着 jiāozhuó　deadlocked; stalemated: ～状态 deadlock; stalemate; impasse

教
jiāo　teach; instruct: 她～我们做实验。 She taught us how to conduct experiments. ——see also jiào

教书 jiāoshū　teach school; teach: 在小学～ teach in a primary school

教书匠 jiāoshūjiàng　*derog.* pedagogue

教书先生 jiāoshū xiānsheng　school teacher

教书育人　jiāoshū-yùrén　impart knowledge and educate people

教学　jiāoxué　teach school; teach

蛟

蛟　jiāo　same as 蛟龙 jiāolóng

蛟龙　jiāolóng　flood dragon, a mythical creature capable of invoking storms and floods

焦

焦　jiāo　① burnt; scorched; charred: 饼烤～了。 The pancake is burnt. / 树被烧～了。 The trees are charred. ② coke: 炼焦 liànjiāo　③ worried; anxious: 心焦 xīnjiāo　④ (Jiāo) a surname

焦比　jiāobǐ　*metall.*　coke ratio

焦点　jiāodiǎn　① *phys.* focal point; focus: 主～ prime (*or* principal) focus / 虚～ virtual focus ② central issue; point at issue: 这就是问题的～。 That is the heart of the matter. / 争论的～ the point at issue

焦耳　jiāo'ěr　*phys.*　joule

焦黑　jiāohēi　burned black

焦化　jiāohuà　*chem.*　coking: 延迟～ delayed coking

焦黄　jiāohuáng　sallow; brown: 脸色～ a sallow face / 把馒头烤得～ toast a steamed bun brown

焦急　jiāojí　anxious; worried: 你不必为钱～。 You need not worry yourself about money. / 大家都在～地等着他。 Everyone is waiting anxiously for him.

焦痂　jiāojiā　*med.*　eschar

焦距　jiāojù　*phys.*　focal distance; focal length

焦渴　jiāokě　terribly thirsty; parched

焦枯　jiāokū　shrivelled; dried up; withered

焦雷　jiāoléi　a clap of thunder

焦虑　jiāolù　feel anxious; have worries and misgivings: 我为她的健康感到～。 I am anxious about her health.

焦煤　jiāoméi　coking coal

焦炭　jiāotàn　coke

焦头烂额　jiāotóu-làn'é　in a sorry plight; in a terrible fix: 麻烦事一大堆, 弄得他～。 He was in a sorry plight, weighed down by numerous troublesome problems. / 敌军被打得～, 狼狈逃窜。 Badly battered, the enemy fled in utter confusion.

焦土　jiāotǔ　scorched earth—ravages of war

焦土政策　jiāotǔ zhèngcè　scorched earth policy

焦心　jiāoxīn　*dial.*　feel terribly worried

焦油　jiāoyóu　*chem.*　tar

焦枣　jiāozǎo　fire-dried stoned dates

焦躁　jiāozào　restless with anxiety; impatient: 克服～情绪 curb one's impatience

焦炙　jiāozhì　terribly worried; burning with anxiety; on pins and needles

焦灼　jiāozhuó　*formal*　deeply worried; very anxious

椒

椒　jiāo　any of several hot spice plants: 辣椒 làjiāo / 胡椒 hújiāo

椒房　jiāofáng　pepper rooms—private apartments of the empress (so called from the pepper-mud mixture painted on the walls to preserve warmth and provide a pleasant aroma for the rooms)

椒盐　jiāoyán　a condiment made of roast prickly ash and salt; spiced salt

鲛

鲛　jiāo　shark

蕉

蕉　jiāo　any of several broadleaf plants: 香蕉 xiāngjiāo / 美人蕉 měirénjiāo

蕉麻　jiāomá　abaca; Manila hemp

礁

礁　jiāo　reef

礁石　jiāoshí　reef; rock

鹪

鹪　jiāo　see below

鹪鹩　jiāoliáo　wren

鹪莺　jiāoyīng　wren warbler

jiáo

矫(矯)

矫　jiáo　see below ——see also jiǎo

矫情　jiáoqing　*dial.*　argumentative; contentious; unreasonable ——see also jiǎoqíng

嚼

嚼　jiáo　masticate; chew; munch: 吃东西好好～, 容易消化。 If you chew your food properly it is easier to digest. ——see also jiào; jué

嚼裹儿　jiáoguor　same as 缴裹儿 jiǎoguor

嚼舌　jiáoshé　(also 嚼舌头 jiáoshétou; 嚼舌根 jiáoshégēn) ① wag one's tongue; chatter; gossip: 别在背后～。 Don't gossip behind people's backs. ② argue meaninglessly; squabble: 没功夫跟你～。 I've got no time to argue with you.

嚼烟　jiáoyān　chewing tobacco

嚼子　jiáozi　bit (of a bridle)

jiǎo

角[1]

角　jiǎo　① horn: 牛～ ox horn ② bugle; horn: 号角 hàojiǎo　③ sth. in the shape of a horn: 菱角 língjiǎo　④ cape; promontory; headland: 好望～ the Cape of Good Hope ⑤ corner: 桌子～儿 the corner of a table / 信息～ information corner (a section in a newspaper giving various kinds of information) / 英语～ English corner (a designated spot, esp. in a park, where students gather and talk in English) ⑥ *math.* angle: 三十度的～ an angle of 30 degrees ⑦ *m.* quarter: 一～饼 a quarter of a pancake ⑧ the first of the twenty-eight constellations (二十八宿) into which the celestial sphere was divided in ancient Chinese astronomy (consisting of four stars in the shape of a cross in Virgo)

角[2]

角　jiǎo　*jiao*, a fractional unit of money in China (=1／10 of a *yuan* or 10 *fen*)

角[3]

角　jiǎo　same as 饺 jiǎo ——see also jué

角暗里　jiǎo'ànli　*dial.*　in a corner; in a remote place

角尺　jiǎochǐ　angle square

角动量　jiǎodòngliàng　*phys.*　angular momentum

角度　jiǎodù　① *math.* angle: 撑条和横梁之间～太大。 The brace is at too big an angle with the beam. ② point of view; angle: 从各个～来研究问题 examine the matter from various angles

角度计　jiǎodùjì　goniometer; angle gauge

角钢　jiǎogāng　angle iron

角弓反张　jiǎogōng fǎnzhāng　*med.*　opisthotonos

角规　jiǎoguī　angle gauge

角砾岩　jiǎolìyán　breccia

角楼　jiǎolóu　a watchtower at a corner of a city wall; corner tower; turret

角落　jiǎoluò　corner; nook: 在院子的一个～里 in a corner of the courtyard / 找遍每一个～ search every nook and cranny; search high and low / 躲在阴暗的～里搞阴谋诡计 plot in a dark corner / 喜讯传遍了祖国的各个～。 The good news spread to every corner of the country.

角马　jiǎomǎ　gnu

角门　jiǎomén　side gate

角膜 jiǎomó *physiol.* cornea

角膜混浊 jiǎomó hùnzhuó opacity of the cornea

角膜炎 jiǎomóyán keratitis

角膜移植术 jiǎomó yízhíshù corneal transplantation; keratoplasty

角票 jiǎopiào *inf.* banknotes of one, two, or five *jiao* denominations

角球 jiǎoqiú *football* corner (kick)

角鲨 jiǎoshā spiny dogfish

角闪石 jiǎoshǎnshí hornblende

角速度 jiǎosùdù *phys.* angular velocity

角铁 jiǎotiě same as 角钢 jiǎogāng

角岩 jiǎoyán hornstone

角页岩 jiǎoyèyán hornfels

角质 jiǎozhì *biol.* cutin: ～层 cuticle (of plants)

角雉 jiǎozhì *zool.* tragopan

角柱体 jiǎozhùtǐ prism

角锥体 jiǎozhuītǐ pyramid

角子 jiǎozi *dial.* silver coin (of small denominations, used in the old days)

侥（僥）

jiǎo see below

侥幸 jiǎoxìng lucky; by luck; by a fluke: ～取胜 gain victory by sheer good luck; win by a fluke / ～心理 the idea of leaving things to chance; trusting to luck

佼

jiǎo *formal* handsome; beautiful

佼佼 jiǎojiǎo *formal* above average; outstanding: ～者 an outstanding figure; a giant among dwarfs

狡

jiǎo crafty; foxy; cunning

狡辩 jiǎobiàn quibble; indulge in sophistry: 任何～都不能掩盖事实真相。No amount of sophistry can cover up the truth.

狡猾 jiǎohuá sly; crafty; cunning; tricky

狡计 jiǎojì crafty trick; ruse

狡狯 jiǎokuài *formal* deceitful; crafty

狡赖 jiǎolài deny (by resorting to sophistry): 证据确凿，不容～。It's no use denying it; the evidence is conclusive.

狡兔三窟 jiǎotù sān kū a wily hare has three burrows—a crafty person has more than one hideout

狡黠 jiǎoxiá *formal* sly; crafty; cunning

狡诈 jiǎozhà deceitful; crafty; cunning

绞

jiǎo ① twist; wring; entangle: 把几股铁丝～在一起 twist several strands of wire together / 把衣服～干 wring out wet clothes / 心如刀～ feel as if a knife were being twisted in one's heart / 许多问题～在一起，闹不清楚。With so many things mixed up it's hard to make out what's what. ② wind: ～动辘轳 wind a windlass ③ hang by the neck ④ *mech.* bore with a reamer; ream: ～孔 ream a hole ⑤ *m.* skein; hank: 一～毛线 a skein of woollen yarn

绞肠痧 jiǎochángshā *Chin. med.* dry cholera

绞车 jiǎochē winch; windlass

绞刀 jiǎodāo *mech.* reamer

绞架 jiǎojià gallows

绞尽脑汁 jiǎojìn nǎozhī rack one's brains

绞盘 jiǎopán capstan

绞肉机 jiǎoròujī meat mincer; mincing machine

绞杀 jiǎoshā strangle

绞纱 jiǎoshā *text.* skein: ～染色 skein dyeing

绞索 jiǎosuǒ (the hangman's) noose

绞痛 jiǎotòng *med.* angina: 肚子～ abdominal angina; colic

绞刑 jiǎoxíng death by hanging: ～架 gallows

饺

jiǎo dumpling: 水饺 shuǐjiǎo

饺子 jiǎozi dumpling (with meat and vegetable stuffing): ～皮 dumpling wrapper / ～馅 filling for dumplings; stuffing

皎

jiǎo clear and bright: ～月当空。A bright moon hung in the sky.

皎皎 jiǎojiǎo very clear and bright; glistening white

皎皎者易污 jiǎojiǎozhě yì wū the immaculate stains easily; the immaculate is easily sullied

皎洁 jiǎojié (of moonlight) bright and clear

铰

jiǎo *inf.* ① cut with scissors: ～一件男衬衣 cut out a shirt / ～成两半 cut in two; cut into halves; cut in half ② same as 绞 jiǎo④

铰接 jiǎojiē *mech.* join with a hinge; articulate: ～式大客车 articulated bus

铰链 jiǎoliàn hinge: ～接合 hinge joint

脚（腳）

jiǎo ① foot: 看他那两只～。Look at his two feet. ② base; foot: 墙脚 qiángjiǎo / 山脚 shānjiǎo ③ *dial.* dregs; residue: 茶～ leftover tea and tea leaves ——see also jué

脚板 jiǎobǎn *dial.* sole (of the foot)

脚背 jiǎobèi instep

脚本 jiǎoběn script; scenario: 电影～ film script

脚脖子 jiǎobózi *dial.* ankle

脚步 jiǎobù step; pace: 加快～ quicken one's pace / 放轻～ walk softly / ～声 footfall; footsteps

脚灯 jiǎodēng *theat.* footlights

脚蹬子 jiǎodēngzi pedal; treadle

脚底板 jiǎodǐbǎn *dial.* sole (of the foot)

脚垫 jiǎodiàn callus on the sole (of the foot)

脚夫 jiǎofū *old* ① porter ② one who hires out his donkey or horse to riders and leads or follows it on foot

脚杆 jiǎogǎn *dial.* leg

脚跟 jiǎogēn (also 脚根 jiǎogēn) heel

脚行 jiǎoháng *old* a business concern operating a porters' service

脚后跟 jiǎohòugēn heel

脚迹 jiǎojì footprint; footmark; track

脚尖 jiǎojiān the tip of a toe; tiptoe: 踮着～走 walk on tiptoe

脚劲 jiǎojìn *dial.* strength of one's legs

脚扣 jiǎokòu foot clasp (for climbing posts)

脚力 jiǎolì ① strength of one's legs: 他一天能走一百里，～真好。He's really got strong legs to be able to walk 100 *li* a day. ② *old* porter ③ *old* payment to a porter

脚镣 jiǎoliào fetters; shackles

脚炉 jiǎolú foot warmer; foot stove

脚门 jiǎomén same as 角门 jiǎomén

脚面 jiǎomiàn instep

脚盆 jiǎopén a basin for washing feet

脚蹼 jiǎopǔ flippers

脚气 jiǎoqì ① *med.* beriberi ② *inf.* athlete's foot

脚钱 jiǎoqian *old* payment to a porter

脚手架 jiǎoshǒujià scaffold; scaffolding

脚踏板 jiǎotàbǎn treadle (of a sewing machine, etc.)

脚踏车 jiǎotàchē *dial.* bicycle

脚踏两只船 jiǎo tà liǎngzhī chuán straddle two boats—have a foot in either camp

脚踏实地 jiǎo tà shídì have one's feet planted on solid ground—earnest and down-to-earth: 既要有远大的理想，又要～地干 have both an ambitious goal and a down-to-earth style of work / ～，埋头苦干，循序前进 work in a down-to-earth manner and advance step by step

脚踏脱粒机 jiǎotà tuōlìjī pedal thresher

脚腕子　jiǎowànzi　(also 脚腕儿 jiǎowànr) ankle

脚下　jiǎoxià ① underfoot ② *dial.* the present moment ③ *dial.* near at hand

脚心　jiǎoxīn　the underside of the arch (of the foot); arch

脚癣　jiǎoxuǎn　ringworm of the foot; tinea pedis; athlete's foot

脚丫子　jiǎoyāzi　(also 脚鸭子 jiǎoyāzi) *dial.* foot

脚印　jiǎoyìn　footprint; footmark; track: 侦察兵在雪地上发现了可疑的～ The scouts discovered suspicious footprints in the snow. / 踏着革命前辈的～前进 follow in the footsteps of the older generation of revolutionaries

脚闸　jiǎozhá　(on a bicycle) backpedalling brake; coaster brake

脚掌　jiǎozhǎng　sole (of the foot)

脚爪　jiǎozhǎo　*dial.* claw; paw; talon

脚正不怕鞋歪　jiǎo zhèng bù pà xié wāi　a straight foot is not afraid of a crooked shoe—an upright man fears no gossip

脚指甲　jiǎozhǐjia　toenail

脚指头　jiǎozhǐtou　*inf.* toe

脚趾　jiǎozhǐ　toe

脚注　jiǎozhù　footnote

脚镯　jiǎozhuó　ankle bangle

矫¹(矯)　jiǎo　rectify; straighten out; correct: 矫正 jiǎozhèng

矫²(矯)　jiǎo　strong; brave: ～若游龙 as powerful as a flying dragon; as strong and brave as a lion

矫³(矯)　jiǎo　pretend; feign; dissemble: ～命 counterfeit an order; issue false orders ——see also jiáo

矫健　jiǎojiàn　strong and vigorous: ～的步伐 vigorous strides

矫捷　jiǎojié　vigorous and nimble; brisk

矫情　jiǎoqíng　*formal* be affectedly unconventional ——see also jiáoqing

矫揉造作　jiǎoróu zàozuò　affected; artificial: ～的姿态 affected manners

矫饰　jiǎoshì　feign in order to conceal sth.; dissemble: 这篇文章语言质朴, 毫无～。This article is written in a simple style, free from any kind of affectation.

矫枉过正　jiǎo wǎng guò zhèng　exceed the proper limits in righting a wrong; overcorrect

矫形　jiǎoxíng　*med.* orthopaedics

矫形术　jiǎoxíngshù　orthopaedics

矫形外科　jiǎoxíng wàikē　orthopaedic surgery

矫形医生　jiǎoxíng yīshēng　orthopaedist

矫正　jiǎozhèng　correct; put right; rectify: ～发音 correct sb.'s pronunciation mistakes / ～偏差 correct a deviation / ～口吃 correct a stammer / ～视力 correct defects of vision / ～生产关系中各种阻碍生产力发展的东西 rectify those aspects of the relations of production that impede the expansion of productive forces

矫直机　jiǎozhíjī　*metall.* straightening machine; straightener

搅(攪)　jiǎo ① stir; mix: 把粥～一～ give the porridge a stir ② disturb; annoy: 她在工作, 别～她。She's working. Don't disturb her.

搅拌　jiǎobàn　stir; agitate; mix: 把农药和种子～在一起 mix insect powder with seed

搅拌机　jiǎobànjī　mixer

搅拌器　jiǎobànqì　stirrer; agitator

搅动　jiǎodòng　mix; stir: 拿棍子～灰浆 stir the plaster with a stick

搅浑　jiǎohún　stir and make muddy; deliberately create confusion ——see also 把水搅浑 bǎ shuǐ jiǎohún

搅混　jiǎohun　*inf.* mix; blend; mingle: 歌声和笑声～成一片。Singing and laughing were mingled together.

搅和　jiǎohuo　*inf.* ① mix; blend; mingle: 这是两码事, 别～在一起。They are two different matters. Don't mix them up. / 惊奇和喜悦的心情～在一起 feel a mixture of joy and surprise ② mess up; spoil: 事情都让他～糟了。He's messed everything up. *or* He's made a mess of everything.

搅局　jiǎojú　upset a scheme or plan

搅乱　jiǎoluàn　confuse; throw into disorder: 警惕敌人～我们的阵线 be on the alert and not let the enemy create confusion in our ranks / 这消息～了她的心。The news disturbed her very much.

搅扰　jiǎorǎo　disturb; annoy; bother: 你姐姐在做功课, 别去～。Your sister is doing her homework. Don't disturb her. / 对不起, ～了。Sorry to have bothered you.

湫　jiǎo　*formal* low-lying ——see also qiū

湫隘　jiǎo'ài　*formal* narrow and low-lying

剿(勦)　jiǎo　send armed forces to suppress; put down ——see also chāo

剿除　jiǎochú　exterminate; wipe out

剿匪　jiǎofěi　suppress bandits

剿灭　jiǎomiè　exterminate; wipe out: 土匪都～了。The bandits were all wiped out.

傲　jiǎo　see below

傲倖　jiǎoxìng　same as 侥幸 jiǎoxìng

徼　jiǎo ① *formal* pray for ② see below ——see also jiào

徼倖　jiǎoxìng　same as 侥幸 jiǎoxìng

缴　jiǎo ① pay; hand over; hand in: ～税 pay taxes ② capture: 他们～了三挺机枪。They captured three machine guns.

缴裹儿　jiǎo·guǒr　*dial.* living expenses: 挣的钱不够～ not earn enough to make both ends meet

缴获　jiǎohuò　capture; seize: ～很多战利品 seize a lot of booty / 一切～要归公。Turn in everything captured.

缴纳　jiǎonà　same as "交纳" jiāonà

缴枪不杀　jiǎoqiāng bù shā　lay down your arms and we'll spare your lives

缴销　jiǎoxiāo　hand in for cancellation: ～营业执照 hand in the business licence for cancellation

缴械　jiǎoxiè ① disarm: 他从后面悄悄爬过来, 缴了那人的械。He crept up from behind and managed to disarm the man. ② surrender one's weapons; lay down one's arms: ～投降 lay down one's arms and surrender

jiào

叫¹(呌)　jiào ① cry; shout: 大～一声 give a loud cry; shout; cry out loudly / 汽笛在～。The steam whistle is blowing. ② call; greet: 外边有人～你。Somebody outside is calling you. / 你的电话～通了。Your call has been put through. / 这孩子腼腆, 不爱～人。The child is shy and doesn't like to greet people. ③ hire; order: ～个出租汽车 hire (*or* call) a taxi / ～二百斤煤 order 200 *jin* of coal ④ name; call: 人们～他小张。People call him Xiao Zhang. / 他～什么名儿？What's his name? / 这棉花长得真～棒。That's what I call a really good crop of cotton. / 这能～虚心接受批评

么? Can this be called readiness to accept criticism? ⑤ *dial.* male (animal): 叫驴 jiàolǘ

叫²(呌) jiào ① ask; order: ～他进来吗? Shall I ask him (to come) in? / 医生～她卧床休息。The doctor ordered her to stay in bed. ② permit; allow: 他哥哥不～他去。His brother did not allow him to go. ③ *prep.* (used in a passive sentence to introduce the doer of the action): ～你猜着了。You've guessed right. / 你～雨淋湿了吗? Did you get wet?

叫板 jiàobǎn (in traditional opera) call for music (a signal given by an actor, just before breaking into song, for the musicians to set their musical instruments for accompaniment, by sustaining the last word he has spoken almost to a musical pitch)

叫菜 jiàocài choose dishes from a menu; order dishes (in a restaurant)

叫哥哥 jiàogēge *dial.* katydid; long-horned grasshopper

叫喊 jiàohǎn shout; yell; howl: 高声～ shout at the top of one's voice / 他把嗓子都～哑了。He shouted himself hoarse.

叫好 jiàohǎo applaud; shout "bravo!"; shout "well done!"

叫号 jiàohào call out the numbers (of waiting patients, etc.): 该我了,在叫我的号了。It's my turn, my number is being called.

叫花子 jiàohuāzi (also 叫化子 jiàohuāzi) *inf.* beggar

叫花子鸡 jiàohuāzijī beggar's chicken (a whole chicken roasted in caked mud)

叫唤 jiàohuan ① cry out; call out: 疼得直～ cry out with pain / 咬紧牙关,一声也不～ clench one's teeth and not utter a sound ② (of animals, birds, insects, etc.) cry; call: 小鸟儿在树上叽叽喳喳地～。Birds are chirping in the tree.

叫鸡 jiàojī *dial.* cock

叫绝 jiàojué shout "bravo!"; applaud ——see also 拍案叫绝 pāi àn jiàojué

叫苦 jiàokǔ complain of hardship or suffering; moan and groan: 她总是抢重活儿干,从来不～不叫累。She always grabs the heaviest jobs and never complains of hardship or fatigue. / 暗暗～ groan inwardly

叫苦不迭 jiàokǔ bùdié complain incessantly; pour out endless grievances

叫苦连天 jiàokǔ liántiān complain to high heaven; complain bitterly

叫驴 jiàolǘ jackass

叫骂 jiàomà shout curses: 他在一片～声中跑掉了。He ran off amid shouts of cursing.

叫卖 jiàomài cry one's wares; peddle; hawk: 沿街～ hawk one's wares in the streets

叫门 jiàomén call at the door to be let in

叫名 jiàomíng *dial.* ① name ② nominal; in name; titular: 这孩子～十岁,其实还不到九岁。The child is said to be ten, but actually he's not nine yet.

叫牌 jiàopái make a bid at bridge; bid: 你～了没有? Have you bid yet? / 该谁～? Whose call is it?

叫屈 jiàoqū complain of being wronged; protest against an injustice

叫嚷 jiàorǎng shout; howl; clamour

叫嚣 jiàoxiāo clamour; raise a hue and cry: 发出战争～ clamour for war / 大肆～ raise a terrific hue and cry; raise a hullabaloo

叫醒 jiàoxǐng wake up; awaken

叫阵 jiàozhèn challenge an opponent to a fight when two armies meet

叫子 jiàozi *dial.* whistle

叫座 jiàozuò draw a large audience; draw well; appeal to the audience; be a box-office success: 这出戏很～。

The play is a great box-office success.

叫做 jiàozuò (also 叫作 jiàozuò) be called; be known as: 这种机器～起重机。This machine is called a crane. / 我们的工作方法～"从群众中来,到群众中去。" Our method of work may be described as "from the masses, to the masses." / 你这～自作自受,没人可怜你。This is what I call stewing in your own juice. Nobody feels sorry for you.

觉(覺) jiào sleep: 一～醒来 wake from one's sleep ——see also jué

校 jiào ① check; proofread; collate: ～长条样 read galley proofs / 四～ the fourth proof; proofread for the fourth time ② same as 较¹ jiào ——see also xiào

校场 jiàochǎng *old* drill ground

校雠 jiàochóu *formal* collate

校点 jiàodiǎn check (against the authoritative text) and punctuate

校订 jiàodìng check against the authoritative text

校对 jiàoduì ① proofread; proof ② proofreader ③ check against a standard; calibrate: 一切计量器都必须～合格才可以出厂。All measuring instruments must be calibrated before leaving the factory.

校对符号 jiàoduì fúhào proofreader's mark

校改 jiàogǎi read and correct proofs

校勘 jiàokān collate

校勘学 jiàokānxué textual criticism

校样 jiàoyàng proof sheet; proof: 已看完～ have read the proofs / 付印～ final proof / 长条～ galley proof

校阅 jiàoyuè read and revise

校正 jiàozhèng proofread and correct; rectify: ～错字 correct misprints

校准 jiàozhǔn *mech.* calibration: 方位～ bearing calibration / ～器 calibrator

较¹ jiào ① compare; contrast: 相较 xiāngjiào ② *prep.* (used to compare a difference in degree): 工作～前更为努力 work even harder than before ③ *adv.* comparatively; relatively; fairly; quite; rather: ～好 fairly good; quite good / ～差 relatively poor / 有～大的进步 have made considerable progress ④ *formal* dispute: 锱铢必较 zīzhū bì jiào

较² jiào *formal* clear; obvious; marked: 二者～然不同。There is a marked difference between the two.

较比 jiàobǐ *adv. dial.* comparatively; relatively; fairly; quite

较场 jiàochǎng same as 校场 jiàochǎng

较劲 jiàojìn *dial.* match strength: 较一较劲儿 have a trial of strength

较量 jiàoliàng ① measure one's strength with; have a contest; have a trial (*or* test) of strength: 经过反复的～ after repeated trials of strength ② haggle; argue; dispute

较为 jiàowéi *adv.* comparatively; relatively; fairly: 这本书～便宜。This book is comparatively cheap.

较真 jiàozhēn *dial.* serious; earnest: 他工作顶～儿的。He is a conscientious worker. / 谁都知道他爱混闹,没人跟他～儿。He's known for his horseplay—no one takes it seriously.

较著 jiàozhù see 彰明较著 zhāngmíng jiàozhù

轿(轎) jiào sedan (chair): 花轿 huājiào

轿车 jiàochē ① *old* (horse-drawn) carriage ② bus or car: 大～ bus; coach / 小～ car; limousine; sedan

轿夫 jiàofū *old* sedan-chair bearer

轿子 jiàozi　sedan (chair)——see also 抬轿子 tái jiàozi

教[1] jiào　① teach; instruct: 受～于名师 be taught by a great master / ～子务农 encourage one's children to go in for farming ② religion: 信～ believe in a religion; be religious

教[2] jiào　same as 叫[2] jiào
——see also jiāo

教案[1] jiào'àn　teaching plan; lesson plan

教案[2] jiào'àn　hist. missionary case (an incident involving foreign missionaries)

教本 jiàoběn　textbook

教鞭 jiàobiān　(teacher's) pointer

教材 jiàocái　teaching material

教程 jiàochéng　① course of study ② (published) lectures:《近代史～》A Course in Modern History

教导 jiàodǎo　① instruct; teach; give guidance: 在党的～下 guided by the Party ② teaching; guidance: 师长的～记心间 bear in mind the teacher's instructions

教导员 jiàodǎoyuán　(battalion) political instructor

教范 jiàofàn　mil. manual: 兵器～ a manual of arms; manual

教父 jiàofù　godfather

教改 jiàogǎi　short for 教学改革 jiàoxué gǎigé

教工 jiàogōng　teaching and administrative staff (of a school)

教官 jiàoguān　old drillmaster; instructor

教规 jiàoguī　rules of a religion; canon

教化 jiàohuà　formal enlighten by education

教皇 jiàohuáng　pope; pontiff

教皇通谕 jiàohuáng tōngyù　Papal Encyclical

教会 jiàohuì　(the Christian) church

教会学校 jiàohuì xuéxiào　missionary school

教诲 jiàohuì　formal teaching; instruction: 谆谆～ earnest teachings

教具 jiàojù　teaching aid

教科书 jiàokēshū　textbook

教练 jiàoliàn　① train; drill; coach: 持枪～ drill with weapons / 徒手～ drill without weapons ② coach; instructor; trainer: 足球～ football coach / ～兼队员 playing coach / 主～ head coach

教练车 jiàoliànchē　learner-driven vehicle

教练船 jiàoliànchuán　training ship

教练弹 jiàoliàndàn　practice projectile; dummy projectile; dummy

教练机 jiàoliànjī　trainer aircraft; trainer

教练员 jiàoliànyuán　coach; instructor; trainer

教龄 jiàolíng　length of service as a teacher: 有四十年～的教员 a teacher of 40 years' standing

教门 jiàomén　inf. Islam

教母 jiàomǔ　godmother

教派 jiàopài　religious sect; denomination

教区 jiàoqū　parish; diocese

教权主义 jiàoquán zhǔyì　clericalism

教师 jiàoshī　teacher; schoolteacher

教士 jiàoshì　priest; clergyman; Christian missionary

教室 jiàoshì　classroom; schoolroom

教授 jiàoshòu　① professor ② instruct; teach: ～历史 teach history

教授法 jiàoshòufǎ　teaching methods; pedagogics

教唆 jiàosuō　instigate; abet; put sb. up to sth. : 谁～他们这样做的呢? Who instigated them to do this? / ～不满十八岁的人犯罪的，应当从重处罚。One who instigates a person under the age of eighteen to commit a crime shall be given a heavier punishment.

教唆犯 jiàosuōfàn　abettor; instigater

教唆罪 jiàosuōzuì　guilt of instigation to a crime

教堂 jiàotáng　church; cathedral

教条 jiàotiáo　dogma; doctrine; creed; tenet: 马克思主义不是～而是行动的指南。Marxism is not a dogma, but a guide to action.

教条主义 jiàotiáozhǔyì　dogmatism; doctrinairism: ～者 dogmatist; doctrinaire

教廷 jiàotíng　the Vatican; the Holy See

教廷大使 jiàotíng dàshǐ　nuncio

教廷公使 jiàotíng gōngshǐ　internuncio

教头 jiàotóu　① old chief military instructor ② inf. coach; instructor; trainer

教徒 jiàotú　believer (or follower) of a religion

教务 jiàowù　educational administration

教务处 jiàowùchù　Dean's Office

教务长 jiàowùzhǎng　Dean of Studies

教习 jiàoxí　old teacher; instructor

教学 jiàoxué　① teaching; education: ～内容 content of courses ② teaching and studying ③ teacher and student——see also 教学 jiàoxué

教学大纲 jiàoxué dàgāng　teaching programme; syllabus

教学法 jiàoxuéfǎ　teaching methods; pedagogics

教学方针 jiàoxué fāngzhēn　principles of teaching

教学改革 jiàoxué gǎigé　transformation of education; reform in education; educational reform

教学相长 jiào-xué xiāng zhǎng　teaching benefits teacher and student alike; teaching benefits teachers as well as students

教训 jiàoxun　① lesson; moral: 血的～ a lesson paid for with blood; lesson written in blood / 吸取～ draw a lesson (or moral) from sth. ; take warning from sth. / 要牢记历史的～。We must keep these lessons of history firmly in mind. ② chide; teach sb. a lesson; give sb. a talking-to; lecture sb. (for wrongdoing, etc.): 他～了儿子一顿。He gave his son a lecture.

教研室 jiàoyánshì　teaching and research section

教研组 jiàoyánzǔ　teaching and research group

教养 jiàoyǎng　① bring up; train; educate ② breeding; upbringing; education; culture: 他是个很有～的人。He is a man of fine breeding. / 他家的孩子都很有～。All his children are well brought up. / 这人一点～都没有。He is a most ill-bred man.

教养员 jiàoyǎngyuán　kindergarten teacher

教义 jiàoyì　religious doctrine; creed

教益 jiàoyì　formal benefit gained from sb.'s wisdom; enlightenment

教友 jiàoyǒu　member of a church; fellow believer

教友会 jiàoyǒuhuì　the Society of Friends; the Quakers

教育 jiàoyù　① education: ～必须为无产阶级政治服务，必须同生产劳动相结合。Education must serve proletarian politics and be combined with productive labour. / 他受过大学～。He has had a college education. / 他没受过什么～。He didn't receive much education. ② teach; educate; inculcate: 她～孩子懂礼貌。She teaches her children to have good manners. / 那本书起了巨大的～作用。That book has played a great educative role.

教育程度 jiàoyù chéngdù　level of education

教育方针 jiàoyù fāngzhēn　policy for education; educational policy: 我们的～, 应该使受教育者在德育、智育、体育几方面都得到发展，成为有社会主义觉悟的有文化的劳动者。Our educational policy must enable everyone who receives an education to develop morally, intellectually and physically and become a worker with both socialist consciousness and culture.

教育革命 jiàoyù gémìng　revolution in education

教育家 jiàoyùjiā　educationist; educator

教育界 jiàoyùjiè　educational circles

教育心理学 jiàoyù xīnlǐxué　educational psychology

教育学 jiàoyùxué　pedagogy; pedagogics; education

教育制度　jiàoyù zhìdù　system of education

教员　jiàoyuán　teacher; instructor: 汉语～a teacher of Chinese

教员休息室　jiàoyuán xiūxishì　staff room; common room

教泽　jiàozé　*formal* the enlightening influence of a teacher

教长　jiàozhǎng　*religion* imam; dean: 坎特伯雷～ Dean of Canterbury

教长国　jiàozhǎngguó　*Islam* imamate

教正　jiàozhèng　*pol.* give comments and criticisms (used when presenting sb. with a piece of one's work): 送上拙著一册, 敬希～。Here's a copy of my humble work. I hope you'll be kind enough to give your valuable criticisms.

教职员　jiào-zhíyuán　teaching and administrative staff

教主　jiàozhǔ　the founder of a religion

窨

jiào　① cellar or pit for storing things: 这个～是用来储存蔬菜的。This cellar is used for storing vegetables. ② store sth. in a cellar or pit

窨藏　jiàocáng　store sth. in a cellar or pit

窨肥　jiàoféi　*dial.* make compost

酵

jiào　ferment; leaven

酵母　jiàomǔ　yeast

酵母菌　jiàomǔjūn　saccharomycete

酵素　jiàosù　*chem.* ferment; enzyme

酵子　jiàozi　*dial.* leavening dough

噍

jiào　*formal* chew; eat

噍类　jiàolèi　*formal* living human beings: 玉石俱焚, 民无～。The place was razed to the ground with not a single human being left alive.

徼

jiào　*formal* ① frontier; border ② inspect
——see also jiǎo

藠

jiào　see below

藠头　jiàotou　Chinese onion (*Allium chinense*)

醮

jiào　① Taoist sacrificial ceremony: 打醮 dǎjiào ② libation at an ancient wedding ceremony: 再醮 zàijiào

嚼

jiào　see 倒嚼 dǎojiào ——see also jiáo ; jué

jiē

节(節)

jiē　see below ——see also jié

节骨眼　jiēguyǎn　*dial.* critical juncture; vital link: 就在这个～上, 援军赶到了。/ 你回来得正是～上! You've come back in the nick of time! / 思想工作要做到～儿上。To help a person ideologically, you must put your finger on the right spot. *or* Ideological work must go straight to the point.

节子　jiēzi　knot (in wood)

阶(階、堦)

jiē　① steps; stairs: 台阶 táijiē ② rank: 军阶 jūnjiē / 官阶 guānjiē

阶层　jiēcéng　(social) stratum: 社会～ social stratum / 特权～ privileged stratum

阶地　jiēdì　*geog.* terrace

阶段　jiēduàn　① stage; phase: 过渡～ transitional stage / 战役的最后～ the final phase of the campaign ② *min.* level: ～高度 level interval

阶级　jiējí　① *formal* steps; stairs ② *old* rank ③ (so-cial) class

阶级报复　jiējí bàofu　class vengeance

阶级本能　jiējí běnnéng　class instinct

阶级本质　jiējí běnzhì　class nature

阶级成分　jiējí chéngfen　class status

阶级斗争　jiējí dòuzhēng　class struggle

阶级队伍　jiējí duìwu　class ranks

阶级分化　jiējí fēnhuà　class polarization

阶级分析　jiējí fēnxi　class analysis

阶级感情　jiējí gǎnqíng　class feeling

阶级根源　jiējí gēnyuán　class origin

阶级观点　jiējí guāndiǎn　class viewpoint

阶级教育　jiējí jiàoyù　class education

阶级觉悟　jiējí juéwù　class consciousness

阶级烙印　jiējí làoyìn　brand of a class

阶级立场　jiējí lìchǎng　class stand

阶级路线　jiējí lùxiàn　class line

阶级矛盾　jiējí máodùn　class contradictions

阶级社会　jiējí shèhuì　class society

阶级性　jiējíxìng　class character; class nature

阶级异己分子　jiējíyìjǐfènzi　alien-class element; individual from an alien class

阶级阵线　jiējí zhènxiàn　class alignment

阶梯　jiētī　a flight of stairs; ladder: 进身的～ stepping stone

阶梯教室　jiētī jiàoshì　lecture theatre

阶下囚　jiēxiàqiú　prisoner; captive

疖(癤)

jiē　furuncle; boil

疖子　jiēzi　furuncle; boil

皆

jiē　*formal* all; each and every: 人人～知。It is known to all. *or* It is public knowledge.

皆大欢喜　jiē dà huānxǐ　everybody is happy; to the satisfaction of all

皆伐　jiēfá　*forestry* clear felling

结

jiē　bear (fruit); form (seed): 这些花～子儿了。These flowers have gone to seed. ——see also jié

结巴　jiēba　① stammer; stutter ② stammerer; stutterer

结巴颏子　jiēbakēzi　*dial.* stammerer; stutterer

结果　jiēguǒ　bear fruit; fructify: 这棵树去年结了好多果儿。This tree bore a lot of fruit last year. ——see also 结果 jiéguǒ

结实　jiēshi　① solid; sturdy; durable: 一双～的鞋子 a durable pair of shoes / 这张桌子很～。This is a very solid table. / 拴～点儿。Tie it fast. ② strong; sturdy; tough: 个子不高但是长得很～ short but sturdy

接

jiē　① come into contact with; come close to: 邻接 línjiē ② connect; join; put together; continue: ～电线 connect wires / ～关系 establish contact (as in underground work) / ～线头 tie broken threads; join two threads together / 线太短, ～不上。The line is too short to make a connection. / 请～286分机。Put me through to Extension 286, please. / ～下页 continued next page / 起来发言的人一个～一个。People got up to speak one after another. ③ catch; take hold of: ～球 catch a ball ④ receive: ～到一封信 receive a letter / ～电话 answer the phone ⑤ meet; welcome: 到车站～人 go to the station to meet sb. ⑥ take over: ～工作 take over a job / 把艰苦奋斗的传统～过来, 传下去 take over and carry forward the tradition of hard struggle

接班　jiēbān　take one's turn on duty; take over from; succeed; carry on: 谁接你的班? Who comes on duty after you? *or* Who takes over from you? / 接好革命的班 be worthy successors to the revolution

接班人　jiēbānrén　successor: 培养革命事业的～ train successors to the cause of revolution

接茬儿 jiēchár (also 接碴儿 jiēchár) dial. ① pick up the thread of a conversation; chime in: 他几次跟我说到老王的事, 我都没～。 He brought up Lao Wang's affair several times but I avoided the subject. ② after that; and then: 随后他们～商量晚上开会的事。 After that they began to discuss the meeting to be held in the evening.

接产 jiēchǎn ① practise midwifery ② deliver animals of their young

接触 jiēchù ① come into contact with; get in touch with: 她的手～了硫酸, 烧伤了。 Her hand came into contact with sulphuric acid and was burned. / 代表团～了各界人士。 The delegation met with people from all walks of life. / ～资产阶级生活方式 be exposed to the bourgeois way of life ② engage: 与敌人～ engage the enemy / 小规模～ a minor (or small-scale) engagement / 双方武装力量已脱离～。 The armed forces of the two sides have disengaged. ③ elec. contact: ～不良 loose (or poor) contact / ～故障 contact fault

接触传染 jiēchù chuánrǎn med. contagion

接触炉 jiēchùlú chem. contact furnace

接触眼镜 jiēchù yǎnjìng contact lens

接待 jiēdài receive; admit: ～外宾 receive foreign guests / 受到亲切～ be accorded a cordial reception / 博物馆从上午九点到下午五点～观众。 The museum is open from 9 a.m. to 5 p.m. / 这饭店可以～八百位客人。 This hotel can accommodate 800 guests.

接待单位 jiēdài dānwèi host organization

接待人员 jiēdài rényuán reception personnel

接待日 jiēdàirì reception day (a day when a responsible person of an organization receives visitors to answer questions)

接待室 jiēdàishì reception room

接待站 jiēdàizhàn reception centre

接敌 jiēdí mil. close (or contact) with the enemy: ～队形 approach formation

接地 jiēdì ① elec. ground connection; grounding; earthing: ～线 ground wire; earth lead ② aviation touchdown; ground contact: ～迎角 landing angle

接点 jiēdiǎn elec. contact

接二连三 jiē'èr-liánsān one after another; in quick succession: 捷报～地传来。 Reports of victory came in one after another.

接防 jiēfáng relieve a garrison; relieve: ～部队 relieving unit

接风 jiēfēng give a dinner of welcome (to a visitor from afar)

接羔 jiēgāo animal husbandry deliver lambs: ～房 lamb-delivery room / ～季节 lambing season

接骨 jiēgǔ set a (broken) bone; set a fracture

接管 jiēguǎn take over control; take over: ～产业 take over the estate / 在他～之前, 那个部门是一团糟。 The department was in utter chaos until he took charge.

接合 jiēhé mech. joint: 气密～ airtight joint / 水密～ watertight joint / 螺栓～ bolted joint / ～器 adapter

接合点 jiēhédiǎn mil. junction point

接火 jiēhuǒ inf. ① start to exchange fire: 先头部队跟敌人～了。 The advanced detachment has started to exchange fire with the enemy. ② elec. energize: 电灯安好了, 可还没～呢。 The lights have been fixed, but not yet connected to the mains.

接济 jiējì give material assistance to; give financial help to: 他在困难的日子里生活靠朋友～。 In his difficult days, he relied on friends for financial assistance.

接驾 jiējià welcome the emperor

接见 jiējiàn receive sb.; grant an interview to: ～外宾 receive foreign guests / ～记者 give an interview to reporters

接界 jiējiè same as 交界 jiāojiè

接近 jiējìn be close to; near; approach: ～国际水平 approach the international level / 他们俩的意见很～。 The two of them have almost identical views. or The two of them see pretty well eye to eye. / 该项工程～完成。 The project is nearing completion. / 比分很～。 It was a close game. / 这个人不容易～。 That chap's rather standoffish. / 我舰飞速地～敌舰, 开炮射击。 Our warships quickly closed in on (or closed with) the enemy vessel and opened fire.

接境 jiējìng border on; share a common border

接客 jiēkè ① (of a hotel, etc.) receive lodgers or guests ② (of a prostitute) receive or sleep with a patron

接力 jiēlì work by relays

接力棒 jiēlìbàng relay baton

接力赛跑 jiēlì sàipǎo relay race; relay

接连 jiēlián adv. on end; in a row; in succession: ～好几天 for days on end / ～三小时 for three hours at a stretch / ～提出许多问题 raise one question after another / 短期内～打几仗 fight successive battles in a short time / ～不断地传来好消息。 Glad tidings came in rapid succession.

接龙 jiēlóng (in cards or dominoes) build up a sequence

接木 jiēmù bot. grafting

接目镜 jiēmùjìng eyepiece; ocular

接纳 jiēnà admit (into an organization): ～新会员 admit new members / ～某国加入联合国 admit a state to membership in the United Nations

接片 jiēpiàn splicing (of pieces of film): ～机 splicer

接气 jiēqì coherent: 这一段跟上一段不太～。 This paragraph doesn't quite hang together with the preceding one.

接洽 jiēqià take up a matter with; arrange (business, etc.) with; consult with: 请同有关部门～。 Please take up the matter with the department concerned. / 他来～工作。 He's here to talk business. or He's here on business. / 明天去参观展览会, 我们正在～车辆。 We are arranging transport for our visit to the exhibition tomorrow.

接壤 jiērǎng formal border on; be contiguous to; be bounded by: 法国和瑞士～。 France borders on Switzerland. / ～地区 contiguous areas

接任 jiērèn take over a job; replace; succeed: 他的职务已由另一同志～。 His job has been taken over by another comrade. / 她将～校长。 She will replace the present chancellor.

接生 jiēshēng deliver a child; practise midwifery

接生婆 jiēshēngpó old midwife

接生员 jiēshēngyuán midwife

接事 jiēshì take over a job

接收 jiēshōu ① receive: ～礼物 receive gifts ② radio receive: ～无线电信号 receive radio signals / ～机 receiver / ～天线 receiving antenna; receiving aerial ③ take over (property, etc.); expropriate: ～敌军的武器装备 take over the enemy's arms and equipment / 我们把他们的房子～过来了。 We've taken over their house. ④ admit: ～新会员 recruit new members

接手 jiēshǒu ① take over (duties, etc.): 这项工作我刚～, 还不熟悉。 I'm new to the job; in fact, I've just taken over. ② baseball, softball catcher

接受 jiēshòu accept: ～邀请 accept an invitation / ～辞职 accept a resignation / ～任务 accept an assignment / ～意见 take sb.'s advice / ～马克思主义 embrace Marxism / 容易～新思想 be readily receptive to new ideas / ～教训 learn (or draw) a lesson / ～考验 face up to a test / ～群众的监督 subject oneself to supervision by the masses / ～贿赂 accept (or take) bribes / 附保留～ acceptance under reserve

接受国　jiēshòuguó　accepting state; receiving state

接受书　jiēshòushū　instrument of acceptance

接受条款　jiēshòu tiáokuǎn　acceptance clause

接穗　jiēsuì　*bot.* scion

接谈　jiētán　receive sb. to discuss things: 来访者由你负责。 You'll receive and talk with all visitors (who come with requests, questions, etc.)

接替　jiētì　take over; replace: 已经派人来～他的工作。 A new person has been appointed to take over his work. / 他～他父亲任商行经理。 He succeeded his father as manager of the firm.

接通　jiētōng　put through: 电话～了吗? Have you got through?

接头　jiētóu　① connect; join; joint ② *text.* piecing; tying-in ③ *inf.* contact; get in touch with; meet: 我找谁～? Who shall I get in touch with? / 货已到上海, 正在～。 The goods are already at Shanghai and contacts are being made. / ～地点 contact point; rendezvous ④ have knowledge of; know about: 这事我不～。 I know nothing about it.

接头儿　jiētóur　connection; joint; junction: 这根带子有个～。 There's a joint in the band. / 四通～ *mech.* four-way connection / 万向～ *mech.* universal joint

接吻　jiēwěn　kiss

接物镜　jiēwùjìng　objective lens; objective

接线　jiēxiàn　*elec.* wiring: ～图 wiring diagram; connection diagram / ～箱 junction box / ～柱 terminal; binding post

接线生　jiēxiànshēng　*old* switch board operator

接续　jiēxù　continue; follow: 此段应～前页末行。 This paragraph should follow the last line of the previous page.

接应　jiēyìng　① come to sb.'s aid; coordinate with; reinforce: 一排冲上去了, 二排随后～。 Platoon One charged and was soon followed by Platoon Two. ② supply: 水泥一时～不上。 Cement was in short supply at the time.

接援　jiēyuán　*mil.* reinforce

接着　jiēzhe　① catch: 给你一个苹果, ～! Here's an apple for you. Catch! ② follow; carry on: 一个～一个 one after another / 你说完了, 我～说几句。 I'll add a few words when you finish. / ～干吧。 Carry on with your work. / 土改以后～就搞合作化。 The land reform was followed by agricultural cooperation. / 我～刚才的讲下去。 I'll continue from where I left off a moment ago. ③ after that; and then: ～我们又讨论了明年的计划。 Next (*or* Then, After that), we discussed plans for the following year.

接枝　jiēzhī　*bot.* grafting

接旨　jiēzhǐ　receive an imperial edict

接踵　jiēzhǒng　*formal* following on sb.'s heels

接踵而来　jiēzhǒng ér lái　(also 接踵而至 jiēzhǒng ér zhì) follow hard at heel: 来访者～。 Visitors came one after another. / 水旱灾害～。 Flood and drought came one after the other.

接种　jiēzhòng　have an inoculation; inoculate: ～防霍乱疫苗 inoculate sb. against cholera / ～牛痘疫苗 be vaccinated

秸（稭）

jiē stalks left after threshing; straw: 秫秸 shújiē / 麦秸 màijiē

秸秆　jiēgǎn　straw: ～肥 compost made of stalks

揭

jiē　① tear off; take off: 把墙上那幅画～下来。 Take that picture off the wall. ② uncover; lift (the lid, etc.) ③ expose; show up; bring to light: ～矛盾, 找差距 expose contradictions and find out where one is lagging behind / 把他的罪行～透 thoroughly expose his crimes ④ *formal* raise; hoist: ～竿为旗 raise a bamboo pole to serve as a standard of revolt

揭不开锅　jiēbukāiguō　*inf.* have nothing in the pot; have nothing to eat; go hungry

揭穿　jiēchuān　expose; lay bare; show up: ～谎言 expose a lie / ～假面具 tear the mask off sb.'s face; unmask sb. / ～骗局 show up the fraud / ～阴谋 lay bare an evil plot / 他们的一切好话都已被他们自己的行为～。 All their fine words have been belied by their own deeds.

揭疮疤　jiē chuāngbā　pull the scab right off sb.'s sore; touch sb.'s sore spot; touch sb. on the raw: 揭别人的疮疤, 不管关系怎么深, 都是不好的。 No matter how intimate you are with people, you shouldn't prod their old wounds.

揭底　jiēdǐ　reveal the inside story: 揭了他的老底 exposed his old secret; dragged the skeleton out of his closet

揭短　jiēduǎn　rake up sb.'s faults, shortcomings or weaknesses

揭发　jiēfā　expose; unmask; bring to light: ～检举反革命分子 expose and denounce counterrevolutionaries / 根据已经～的材料 according to facts already revealed / 我们～自己工作中的错误, 目的是为了改正。 We expose mistakes in our work in order to correct them.

揭盖子　jiēgàizi　take the lid off sth.; bring sth. into the open

揭竿而起　jiē gān ér qǐ　raise the standard of revolt; start an uprising; rise in rebellion: 公元前209年, 陈胜、吴广～, 领导了中国历史上第一次农民大起义。 In 209 B. C. Chen Sheng and Wu Guang raised the standard of revolt and led China's first great peasant uprising.

揭开　jiēkāi　uncover; reveal; open: ～宇宙的奥秘 reveal the secrets of the universe / ～两国关系史上的新篇章 open a new chapter in the annals of relations between the two countries / ～新民主主义革命的序幕 raise the curtain on the New-Democratic Revolution

揭露　jiēlù　expose; unmask; ferret out: ～阴谋 expose the plot / ～其真面目 expose sb.'s true colours; show sb. up for what he is / ～钻进党内的野心家、阴谋家 unmask the careerists and conspirators who have sneaked into the Party / ～暗藏的敌特分子 ferret out hidden enemy agents / ～矛盾, 分析矛盾, 正确处理矛盾 expose contradictions, analyse them and handle them correctly

揭幕　jiēmù　unveil (a monument, etc.); inaugurate: 市长为展览会～。 The mayor inaugurated the exhibition.

揭幕式　jiēmùshì　unveiling ceremony

揭破　jiēpò　expose; lay bare

揭示　jiēshì　① announce; promulgate ② reveal; bring to light: 马克思主义～了人类社会发展的客观规律。 Marxism brought to light the objective laws governing the development of human society. / 小说作者深刻地～了人物的内心世界。 The novelist subtly delineates the inner world of his characters.

揭帖　jiētiě　*old* notice, poster

揭晓　jiēxiǎo　announce; make known; publish: 选举结果已经～。 The result of the election has been published.

嗟

jiē, also juē *formal* sigh; lament: 悲～ sigh in sorrow

嗟悔无及　jiēhuǐ wújí　too late for regrets and lamentations

嗟来之食　jiē lái zhī shí　food handed out in contempt; handouts

街

jiē　① street ② *dial.* country fair; market: 赶～ go to a fair; go to market

街道　jiēdào　① street ② residential district; neighbourhood

街道办事处　jiēdào bànshìchù　subdistrict office

街道工厂　jiēdào gōngchǎng　neighbourhood factory

街道居民委员会　jiēdào jūmín wěiyuánhuì　neighbourhood committee; residents' committee

街坊　jiēfang　*inf.* neighbour: 我们是～。We are neighbours.

街坊四邻　jiēfang sìlín　*inf.* neighbours; neighbourhood: ～都知道你。Everyone in this neighbourhood knows you.

街垒　jiēlěi　street barricade

街门　jiēmén　a gate or door facing the street

街面儿上　jiēmiànrshang　*inf.* ① (activities, etc.) in the street: 镇子不大, ～倒挺热闹。Small as the town is, it has a busy street. *or* Though small, the town boasts a busy street. ② neighbourhood: ～都知道他会修收音机。Everybody in the neighbourhood knows he can repair radios.

街市　jiēshì　downtown streets

街谈巷议　jiētán-xiàngyì　street gossip; the talk of the town: 我会到各方面的人, 听到许多的～。I met all sorts of people and picked up a good deal of gossip.

街头　jiētóu　street corner; street: 流落～ tramp the streets; be down and out in a city / 涌上～ pour into the streets

街头剧　jiētóujù　street-corner skit; street performance

街头诗　jiētóushī　poems stuck on street walls or handed out as leaflets, usu. reflecting the problems of the times

街头巷尾　jiētóu-xiàngwěi　streets and lanes: ～, 到处都是欢乐的人群。There are happy crowds in all the streets and lanes. / ～议论纷纷。You hear the affair discussed on the street corners everywhere and by everybody.

街心公园　jiēxīn gōngyuán　parks at the intersections

嗒　jiē　see below

嗒嗒　jiējiē　*onom. liter.* ① harmonious sounds: 钟鼓～。Bells and drums resounded. ② the sounds of birds: 鸡鸣～。A cock was crowing.

jié

孑　jié　*formal* lonely; all alone: 孑然　jiérán

孑孓　jiéjué　wiggler; wriggler

孑然　jiérán　solitary; lonely; alone:

孑然一身　jiérán yīshēn　all alone in the world

孑身　jiéshēn　*formal* all by oneself; all alone

孑遗　jiéyí　*formal* the few survivors (of a disaster, massacre etc.)

节(節)　jié　① joint; node; knot: 竹～ bamboo joint / ～材 nodal wood ② division; part: 音节 yīnjié ③ *m.* section; length: 一～铁管 a length of iron pipe / 两～课 two periods; two classes / 八～车厢 eight railway coaches / 第一章第二～ Chapter One, Section Two ④ festival; red-letter day; holiday: 过节 guòjié ⑤ abridge: 节译 jiéyì ⑥ economize; save: ～电 economize on electricity / ～煤 economize on coal; save coal ⑦ item: 细节 xìjié ⑧ moral integrity; chastity: 气节 qìjié ⑨ *navigation* knot: 现在船的速度是十八～。The ship is making 18 knots. ——see also jiē

节哀　jié'āi　*formal* restrain one's grief (used in offering one's condolences): 令堂天年有限, 过伤无益, 且自～。Your mother was bound by her allotted life span. You must restrain your grief; excessive mourning won't do you any good.

节本　jiéběn　abridged edition; abbreviated version

节操　jiécāo　*formal* high moral principle; moral integrity

节假日　jiéjiàrì　festivals and holidays

节俭　jiéjiǎn　thrifty; frugal: 提倡～ encourage frugality / 她是个很～的主妇。She is a very thrifty housewife.

节减　jiéjiǎn　save and economize: ～经费 cut the expenses

节节　jiéjié　successively; steadily: ～胜利 win many victories in succession; go from victory to victory / ～败退 retreat in defeat again and again; keep on retreating / ～产量～上升。Production rose steadily.

节劳　jiéláo　don't overwork yourself; take things easy

节理　jiélǐ　*geog.* joint: 倾向(走向)～ dip (strike) joint

节烈　jiéliè　(of a woman, esp. a widow) rigorously chaste

节令　jiélìng　climate and other natural phenomena of a season: ～不等人。Don't miss the right season in farming. *or* The seasons wait for no man. / 七月是西瓜上市的～。Watermelons are in season in July. / 今年冬天～不正。We are having unseasonable winter weather. / 中秋节吃点月饼, 应应～。Let's eat moon cakes at the Mid-Autumn Festival, as befits the occasion.

节流　jiéliú　① reduce expenditure: 开源节流 kāiyuán jiéliú ② *mech.* throttle: 全～ full throttle

节录　jiélù　extract; excerpt: 我从收音机里听到过这本小说的～。I have heard excerpts from the novel on the radio.

节律　jiélǜ　the rhythm and pace of moving things

节略　jiélüè　*diplomacy* memorandum; aide-mémoire

节目　jiémù　programme; item (on a programme); number: 晚会的～ 安排得不够紧凑。The programme for the evening party was not well organized. / 下一个～ the next item (or number)

节目单　jiémùdān　programme; playbill

节目主持人　jiémù zhǔchírén　host (of a radio or TV show); compère; master of ceremonies

节能　jiénéng　save energy

节拍　jiépāi　*mus.* metre

节拍器　jiépāiqì　*mus.* metronome

节气　jiéqì　① solar term or period (one of the 24 periods, of approximately 15 days each, into which the lunar year is divided, corresponding to the day on which the sun enters the lst or 15th degree of one of the 12 zodiacal signs; each period being given an appropriate name indicating the obvious changes in nature at the time it comes round) ② the day marking the beginning of a solar term (e.g. , Feb. 3, 4, or 5 is the day marking the beginning of the lst solar term "Beginning of Spring" 立春) ——see also 二十四节气 èrshí sì jiéqì

节日　jiérì　festival; red-letter day; holiday: 庆祝～ celebrate (or observe) a festival / ～气氛 festive air / 致以～的祝贺 extend holiday greetings / 穿上～的盛装 in one's holiday best; in gala dress

节省　jiéshěng　economize; save; use sparingly; cut down on: ～时间 save time / ～篇幅 save space / ～人力物力 use manpower and material resources sparingly / 财政的支出, 应该根据～的方针。Thrift should be the guiding principle in our government expenditure.

节食　jiéshí　be moderate in eating and drinking; be (or go) on a diet: 她要保持身材苗条就不得不～。She has to diet to stay slim.

节外生枝　jié wài shēng zhī　① side issues or new problems crop up unexpectedly ② raise obstacles; deliberately complicate an issue: 快要达成协议时, 对方又～。An agreement was about to be reached when the other side raised new issues (or caused complications).

节下　jiéxia　*inf.* the coming festival: ～我需要点钱用。I need some money for the coming festival.

节衣缩食 jiéyī-suōshí　economize on food and clothing; live frugally: 他们～, 但是仍然供不起儿子上学。They scraped and saved, but still couldn't pay for their son's education.

节译 jiéyì　abridged translation

节余 jiéyú　① save: 就这一项, 我们～了一万余元。We saved over ten thousand *yuan* on this item alone. ② surplus (as a result of economizing)

节育 jiéyù　birth control

节育环 jiéyùhuán　intrauterine device (IUD); the loop

节育手术 jiéyù shǒushù　birth control surgery

节约 jiéyuē　practise thrift; economize; save: ～原料 economize on raw materials / ～人力物力 economize on manpower and material resources / ～用电 economize on electricity / ～粮食 save on food / ～开支 cut down expenses; retrench (expenditure) / 厉行～ practise strict economy

节肢动物 jiézhī dòngwù　arthropod

节制 jiézhì　① control; check; be moderate in: ～饮食 be moderate in eating and drinking; be (*or* go) on a diet ② temperance; abstinence

节制闸 jiézhìzhá　*water conservancy* check gate

节奏 jiézòu　① rhythm: ～明快 lively rhythm / 有～地鼓掌 clap hands rhythmically ② tempo: 生活～ the tempo of life

讦 jié　*formal* expose sb.'s past misdeeds: 攻讦 gōngjié

劫[1]（刧、刼、刦）　jié　① rob; plunder; raid: 打劫 dǎjié ② coerce; compel: 劫持 jiéchí

劫[2]　jié　calamity; disaster; misfortune: 浩劫 hàojié

劫持 jiéchí　kidnap; hold under duress; hijack: ～飞机（船舰、火车、汽车）hijack an aeroplane (a ship, a train, a motor vehicle) / ～者 hijacker

劫夺 jiéduó　seize (a person or his property) by force

劫富济贫 jiéfù-jìpín　rob the rich to give to the poor

劫后余烬 jié hòu yújìn　signs (*or* indications) of disaster

劫后余生 jié hòu yúshēng　be a survivor of a disaster

劫机 jiéjī　hijack a plane

劫掠 jiélüè　plunder; loot

劫数 jiéshù　inexorable doom; predestined fate

劫营 jiéyíng　raid the enemy camp

劫狱 jiéyù　break into a jail and rescue a prisoner: 他是聚众～的首要分子。He is the ringleader in the prison raid.

杰（傑）　jié　① outstanding; prominent: 杰作 jiézuò ② outstanding person; hero: 豪杰 háojié

杰出 jiéchū　outstanding; remarkable; prominent: ～贡献 a brilliant contribution / ～的共产主义战士 an outstanding Communist fighter / ～的政治家 a prominent politician / ～的画家 an outstanding painter

杰作 jiézuò　masterpiece

诘 jié　*formal* closely question; interrogate: 反诘 fǎnjié / 盘诘 pánjié ——see also jí

诘问 jiéwèn　*formal* closely question; interrogate; crossexamine

诘责 jiézé　*formal* censure; rebuke; denounce

洁（潔）　jié　clean: 整洁 zhěngjié

洁白 jiébái　spotlessly white; pure white: ～的桌布 a spotlessly white tablecloth / ～的心灵 a pure mind

洁净 jiéjìng　clean; spotless: 他房间里的东西都收拾得很～。He kept everything clean in his room.

洁癖 jiépǐ　an unhealthy obsession with cleanliness; mysophobia

洁身自好 jié shēn zì hào　① refuse to be contaminated by evil influence; preserve one's purity ② mind one's own business in order to keep out of trouble

洁治 jiézhì　*dentistry* scaling

拮 jié　see below

拮据 jiéjū　in straitened circumstances; short of money; hard up

结 jié　① tie; knit; knot; weave: ～网 weave a net ② knot: 我解不开这个～。I can't untie this knot. ③ congeal; form; forge; cement: 牛奶上面～了一层皮。A skin has formed on the milk. / ～下深厚的友谊 forge a profound friendship ④ settle; conclude: 这不～了吗? That's that! ⑤ written guarantee; affidavit: 具结 jùjié ⑥ *electron.* junction: p-n～ p-n junction / 生长～ grown junction ⑦ *physiol.* node: 淋巴结 línbājié ——see also jiē

结案 jié'àn　wind up a case

结疤 jiébā　become scarred

结拜 jiébài　become sworn brothers or sisters

结伴 jiébàn　go with: ～而行 go or travel in a group

结冰 jiébīng　freeze; ice up; ice over

结彩 jiécǎi　adorn (*or* decorate) with festoons: 这店新开张, 门口结了彩。The shop is newly opened and the shop front is decorated with festoons. ——see also 张灯结彩 zhāngdēng-jiécǎi

结草衔环 jiécǎo-xiánhuán　pay a debt of gratitude

结肠 jiécháng　*physiol.* colon

结肠炎 jiéchángyán　colitis

结成 jiéchéng　form: ～同盟 form an alliance; become allies / ～最广泛的统一战线 form the broadest united front / ～一定的生产关系 enter into definite relations of production / ～一伙 gang up; band together

结仇 jiéchóu　start a feud; become enemies

结存 jiécún　① cash on hand; balance: 现金～ cash balance / 银行存款～ bank balance / 财政年度年终～ balance at the end of a fiscal year ② goods on hand; inventory

结党营私 jiédǎng-yíngsī　form a clique to pursue selfish interests; band together for selfish purposes

结缔组织 jiédì zǔzhī　*physiol.* connective tissue

结发 jiéfà　① *arch.* bind up one's hair——come of age ② *old* first wife

结发夫妻 jiéfà fūqī　husband and wife by the first marriage

结构 jiégòu　① structure; composition; construction: 经济～ economic structure / 所有制～ the structure of ownership / 产品～ product mix / 产业～ the structure of production; industrial set-up / 进口～ import mix / 原子～ atomic structure / 这篇文章～严密。This article is compact and well organized. ② *archit.* structure; construction: 钢～ steel structure / 钢筋混凝土～ reinforced concrete structure / 铆合（焊接）～ riveted (welded) construction ③ *geol.* texture: 斑状～ porphyritic texture / 致密～ compact texture

结构钢 jiégòugāng　structural steel

结构力学 jiégòu lìxué　structural mechanics

结构式 jiégòushì　*chem.* structural formula

结构图 jiégòutú　structural drawing

结构心理学 jiégòu xīnlǐxué　structural psychology

结构语言学 jiégòu yǔyánxué　structural linguistics

结构主义 jiégòuzhǔyì　structuralism

结构主义学派 jiégòuzhǔyì xuépài　structuralists

结构主义语法 jiégòuzhǔyì yǔfǎ　structural grammar

结关 jiéguān　customs clearance

结棍 jiégùn　*dial.* ① sturdy: 他个子小, 可长得很～。He is small but sturdy. ② terrible; formidable: 他这一交跌得真～。He had a terrible fall.

结果[1] jiéguǒ result; outcome: 必然～ inevitable result / 会谈的～ the outcome of the talks / 这样瞎吵下去不会有什么。 Squabbling like this won't get you anywhere. / 经过一番争论，他还是让步了。 After a heated argument he finally gave in.

结果[2] jiēguǒ old kill; finish off ——seel also 结果 jiéguǒ

结合 jiéhé ① combine; unite; integrate; link: 把革命精神和科学态度～起来 combine revolutionary spirit with a scientific approach / 理论与实践相～ combine theory with practice / ～具体情况进行处理 deal with sth. in the light of specific conditions / 知识分子必须与工农群众相～。 Intellectuals must integrate with the masses of workers and peasants. ② be united in wedlock

结合膜 jiéhémó same as 结膜 jiémó

结合能 jiéhénéng phys. binding energy

结核 jiéhé ① med. tubercle ② med. tuberculosis: 肺结核 fèijiéhé ③ min. nodule: 锰～ manganese nodule

结核病 jiéhébìng tuberculosis: ～院 tuberculosis hospital; tuberculosis sanatorium

结核杆菌 jiéhé gǎnjūn tubercle bacillus

结核菌素 jiéhéjūnsù tuberculin

结喉 jiéhóu physiol. Adam's apple

结汇 jiéhuì settlement of exchange

结婚 jiéhūn marry; get married; be married: 她～了吗？ Is she married? / 她跟谁～了？ Who did she marry? / 她是什么时候结的婚？ When did she get married? / 她结过两次婚了。 She's been married twice.

结婚登记 jiéhūn dēngjì marriage registration

结婚证书 jiéhūn zhèngshū marriage certificate; marriage lines

结集 jiéjí ① concentrate; mass: ～兵力 concentrate troops ② collect articles, etc. into a volume: ～付印 compile a collection of writings and send it to the press

结痂 jiéjiā form a scab; crust

结交 jiéjiāo make friends with; associate with: 他～的朋友大多是青年工人。 He associates mostly with young workers.

结节 jiéjié biol. tubercle; node

结节虫 jiéjiéchóng nodular worm

结晶 jiéjīng ① crystallize ② crystal: 盐～ salt crystals / ～岩石 crystalline rock / ～水 water of crystallization; crystal water ③ crystallization: 智慧的～ a crystallization of wisdom / 劳动的～ the fruit of labour

结晶化学 jiéjīng huàxué crystal chemistry

结晶学 jiéjīngxué crystallography

结局 jiéjú final result; outcome; ending: 小说的～ the ending of a novel / 这是逆历史潮流而动的人的必然～。 This is the inescapable fate of those who go against the current of history. / 这事情最后～如何？ What was the final upshot of that affair?

结块 jiékuài agglomerate; curdle

结蜡 jiélà paraffin (or wax) precipitation (in oil refining): ～事故 paraffin trouble

结缡 jiélí formal (of a woman, or of a man and a woman) marry

结论 jiélùn ① log. conclusion (of a syllogism) ② con-clusion; verdict: 得出～ draw (or come to, reach) a conclusion / 不要忙于下～。 Don't jump to conclusions. / 对某人的历史作～ reach a conclusion on sb.'s personal history; pass (official) judgment on sb.'s history / 这是否可行，还不能下～。 Whether this is feasible is still an open question.

结盟 jiéméng form an alliance; ally; align

结膜 jiémó physiol. conjunctiva

结膜炎 jiémóyán conjunctivitis

结幕 jiémù last act; final act; ending; final result; grand finale

结欠 jiéqiàn balance due

结亲 jiéqīn ① inf. marry; get married ② (of two families) become related by marriage

结清 jiéqīng settle; square up: ～帐目 square accounts (with sb.) / ～债务 settle a debt by payment

结球甘蓝 jiéqiú gānlán cabbage

结舌 jiéshé be tongue-tied; be at a loss for words: 瞠目结舌 chēngmù-jiéshé / 张口结舌 zhāngkǒu-jiéshé

结社 jiéshè form an association

结社自由 jiéshè zìyóu freedom of association

结绳 jiéshéng tie knots: ～记事 keep records by tying knots (in primitive times before the invention of writing)

结石 jiéshí med. stone; calculus: 排出～ discharge of stones; pass stones

结识 jiéshí get acquainted with sb.; get to know sb.: ～了很多新朋友 have made a lot of new friends / 有幸～了一位大人物 have the honour of making the acquaintance of a VIP

结束 jiéshù end; finish; conclude; wind up; close: ～讲话 wind up a speech / ～战争状态 terminate the state of war / 代表团～了对我国的访问。 The delegation has concluded its visit to China. / 主席宣布讨论～。 The chairman declared the discussion closed. / 会议下午五时～。 The meeting ended at 5 p. m. / 斗争远远没有～。 The struggle is far from over. / 演出到此～。 That's the end of our performance. / 招待会到此～。 The reception is over. (said by the host)

结束语 jiéshùyǔ concluding remarks

结素 jiésù short for 结核菌素 jiéhéjūnsù

结算 jiésuàn settle accounts; close (or wind up) an account: 用人民币计价～ use Renminbi for quoting prices and settling accounts / 记帐～ settlement on account

结为 jiéwéi enter into a specified relationship: ～夫妻 become husband and wife

结尾 jiéwěi ① ending; winding-up stage: ～工程 the winding-up work of a project / 文章的～很有力量。 The article has a forceful ending. ② mus. coda

结业 jiéyè complete a course; wind up one's studies

结义 jiéyì become sworn brothers or sisters: 桃园三～ the sworn brotherhood of the three Shu Han (蜀汉) heroes in the Peach Garden (i.e. of Liu Bei 刘备, Guan Yu 关羽, and Zhang Fei 张飞)

结余 jiéyú cash surplus; surplus; balance

结语 jiéyǔ same as 结束语 jiéshùyǔ

结冤 jiéyuān same as 结仇 jiéchóu

结缘 jiéyuán form ties (of affection, friendship, etc.); become attached to: 他从小就和音乐结了缘。 He developed a liking for music even as a boy.

结怨 jiéyuàn contract enmity; incur hatred

结扎 jiézā med. ligation; ligature: ～血管 ligature (or tie up) blood vessels / 输卵管～术 ligation of oviduct / 输精管～术 vasoligation

结帐 jiézhàng settle (or square) accounts; balance the books

结子 jiézi knot

桔 jié see below ——see also jú

桔槔 jiégāo well sweep; sweep

桔梗 jiégěng Chin. med. the root of balloonflower (Platycodon grandiflorum)

桀 Jié the name of the last ruler of the Xia Dynasty (c.21st-c.16th century B.C.), traditionally considered a tyrant

桀骜不驯 jié'ào bù xún stubborn and intractable; obstinate and unruly

桀犬吠尧 Jié quǎn fèi Yáo the tyrant Jie's cur yapping

at the sage-king Yao—the underling of an evil man will attack whoever he is told to attack

桀纣 Jié-Zhòu Jie and Zhou, last rulers of the Xia and Shang Dynasties respectively (used as bywords for tyranny)

捷[1]（捷） jié prompt; nimble; quick: 敏捷 mǐnjié

捷[2]（捷） jié victory; triumph: 连战皆～ win a series of victories

捷报 jiébào news of victory; report of a success

捷报频传 jiébào pínchuán news of victory keeps pouring in

捷径 jiéjìng shortcut: 走～ take a shortcut

捷克 Jiékè Czech

捷克人 Jiékèrén Czech

捷克语 Jiékèyǔ Czech (language)

捷足先登 jiézú xiān dēng the swift-footed arrive first; the early bird catches the worm: 二班～，把最艰巨的任务抢走了。Squad Two grabbed the most difficult task before the others had a chance to.

婕 jié see below

婕妤 jiéyú favoured beauty (a title conferred upon an accomplished imperial concubine)

偈 jié arch. brave; martial——see also jì

睫 jié eyelash; lash: 交睫 jiāojié

睫毛 jiémáo eyelash; lash

睫毛油 jiémáoyóu mascara

竭 jié exhaust; use up: 衰竭 shuāijié

竭诚 jiéchéng wholeheartedly; with all one's heart: ～拥护 give wholehearted support

竭尽 jiéjìn use up; exhaust: ～造谣诬蔑之能事 stop at nothing in spreading lies and slanders

竭尽全力 jiéjìn quánlì spare no effort; do one's utmost; do all one can

竭蹶 jiéjué formal destitute; impoverished: 艰难竭蹶 jiānnán jiéjué

竭力 jiélì adv. do one's utmost; use every ounce of one's energy; try by every possible means: ～支持 give all-out support / ～反对 actively oppose / ～鼓吹 boost with all one's might; energetically advocate / ～抗拒 stubbornly resist / 我将～帮助你。I'll do my utmost to assist you.

竭泽而渔 jié zé ér yú drain the pond to get all the fish; kill the goose that lays the golden eggs

截 jié ① cut; sever: ～成两段 cut in two ② m. section; chunk; length: 一～儿木头 a log ③ stop; check; stem: 把惊马～住 stop a bolting horse / ～球 intercept a pass ④ by (a specified time); up to: 截至 jiézhì

截长补短 jié cháng bǔ duǎn take from the long to add to the short; draw on the strength of each to offset the weakness of the other

截断 jiéduàn ① cut off; block: ～敌人的退路 cut off the enemy's retreat / ～河流 dam a river ② cut short; interrupt: 电话铃声～了他的话。He was interrupted by the telephone.

截获 jiéhuò intercept and capture: 游击队～了敌人一辆卡车。The guerrillas intercepted and captured an enemy truck.

截击 jiéjī intercept: ～敌增援部队 intercept the enemy's reinforcements

截击导弹 jiéjī dǎodàn interceptor (or interception) missile

截击机 jiéjījī interceptor

截流 jiéliú dam a river

截流井 jiéliújǐng catch basin

截留 jiéliú intercept and hold on to; retain for one's own use; withhold: ～国家收入 withhold state funds / ～上交利润 retain profits which ought to be turned over to the state / 不准～国家木材。Intercepting and holding on to state timber is not allowed. / 不得～师范毕业生分配做其他工作。Graduates from normal schools should not be assigned to other jobs than teaching.

截煤机 jiéméijī min. coalcutter; cutter

截门 jiémén pipe valve

截面 jiémiàn section: 横～ cross section / 正～ normal section

截取 jiéqǔ cut off a section of sth.

截然 jiérán sharply; completely: ～对立 be diametrically opposed / 同他们以前的谈话～相反 completely contradict their previous statement / 两者不能～分开。No hard and fast line can be drawn between the two.

截然不同 jiérán bù tóng completely different; different as black and white; poles apart: 孩子的世界，与成人～。The child's world is completely different from that of a fully grown man.

截瘫 jiétān med. paraplegia

截肢 jiézhī med. amputation

截止 jiézhǐ ① end; close: 登记已经～了。Registration has closed. / 申请到本月二十日～。The 20th of this month is the closing day for applications. / ～日期 closing date ② elec. cut-off: ～电平 cut-off level

截至 jiézhì by (a specified time); up to: ～本月底 by the end of this month / ～目前为止 up to now

碣 jié stone tablet: 墓～ tombstone

羯[1] jié see 羯羊 jiéyáng

羯[2] Jié Jie (Chieh), an ancient nationality in China

羯鼓 jiégǔ a kind of drum used in ancient China

羯羊 jiéyáng wether

jiě

姐 jiě ① elder sister; sister ② a general term for young women

姐儿 jiěr dial. ① sisters (including the person spoken to or about): 你们～几个? How many sisters are there in your family? ② brothers and sisters

姐夫 jiěfu elder sister's husband; brother-in-law

姐姐 jiějie elder sister; sister

姐妹 jiěmèi ① sisters: 她没有～，只有一个哥哥。She has a brother but no sisters. / 她们～俩都是先进生产者。Both sisters are advanced workers. ② brothers and sisters: 你们～几个? How many brothers and sisters are there in your family?

姐妹城 jiěmèichéng sister cities

姐妹学校 jiěmèi xuéxiào sister schools; sister universities

姐儿们 jiěrmen inf. sisters

姐丈 jiězhàng elder sister's husband; brother-in-law

媎 jiě see 媎驰 āijiě

解（解） jiě ① separate; divide: 溶解 róngjiě / 瓦解 wǎjiě ② untie; undo: ～缆 untie the mooring

rope / ～鞋带 undo shoelaces ③ allay; dispel; dismiss: ～油腻 cut the grease of a rich meal (as with a cup of tea, etc.) ④ explain; interpret; solve: 此字作何～? What does this word mean? / 新～ a new interpretation ⑤ understand; comprehend: 令人不～ puzzling; incomprehensible ⑥ relieve oneself: 小解 xiǎojiě / 大解 dàjiě ⑦ *math.* solution: 求解 qiújiě ——see also jiè; xiè

解饱 jiěbǎo *dial.* (of food) satisfy hunger

解表 jiěbiǎo *Chin. med.* induce sweat; diaphoresis: ～药 diaphoretic

解馋 jiěchán satisfy a craving for good food

解嘲 jiěcháo try to explain things away when ridiculed ——see also 聊以解嘲 liáo yǐ jiěcháo; 自我解嘲 zìwǒ jiěcháo

解酲 jiěchéng *formal* neutralize the effect of alcoholic drinks

解除 jiěchú remove; relieve; get rid of: ～职务 remove sb. from his post; relieve sb. of his office / ～合同 rescind a contract; terminate a contract / ～武装 disarm / ～禁令 lift a ban / ～婚约 renounce an engagement / ～思想负担 have a load taken off one's mind; be relieved of a mental burden / ～顾虑 free one's mind of apprehensions / 旱象已经～. The dry spell is over.

解除警报 jiěchú jǐngbào ① sound the all-clear ② all-clear

解答 jiědá answer; explain: ～疑难问题 answer difficult questions / 习题的～ key to an exercise

解冻 jiědòng ① thaw; unfreeze: ～季节 thawing season / 两国关系～ a thawing of the relations between the two countries ② unfreeze (funds, assets, etc.)

解毒 jiědú ① *med.* detoxify; detoxicate ② *Chin. med.* relieve internal heat or fever: ～药 antidote

解饿 jiě'è satisfy one's hunger

解乏 jiěfá ① recover from fatigue: 他得好好睡一觉, 才能～. He needs a good long sleep to get over his fatigue. / 烫烫脚～. Bathe your feet in hot water and you won't feel so tired. ② refreshing

解法 jiěfǎ *math.* solution

解放 jiěfàng ① liberate; emancipate: 革命就是～生产力. Revolution means liberating the productive forces. / 无产阶级只有～全人类, 才能最后～自己. Only by emancipating all mankind can the proletariat achieve its own final emancipation. / 和平～北平 the peaceful liberation of Beiping / 民族～运动 the national liberation movement / 妇女～ the emancipation of women ② Liberation (signifying the termination of Kuomintang rule in mainland China in 1949): ～前中国人民受帝国主义、封建主义、官僚资本主义的压迫. ～后劳动人民成了国家的主人. Before Liberation, the Chinese people were oppressed by imperialism, feudalism and bureaucrat-capitalism; after Liberation, the labouring people have become the masters of the country. / 故事描写～前四川农村的社会状况. The story depicts the social conditions in pre-Liberation rural Sichuan. / 该书论述～初期华北农民生活. The book is a study of peasant life in north China in the early post-Liberation period (or in the years just following Liberation).

解放脚 jiěfàngjiǎo liberated feet—half-bound feet; bound feet unbound

解放军 jiěfàngjūn ① liberation army ② short for 中国人民解放军 Zhōngguó Rénmín Jiěfàngjūn ③ PLA man

解放区 jiěfàngqū liberated area

解放思想 jiěfàng sīxiǎng emancipate the mind; free oneself from old ideas

解放战争 jiěfàng zhànzhēng ① war of liberation ② China's War of Liberation (1945-1949)

解雇 jiěgù discharge; dismiss; fire

解恨 jiěhèn vent one's hatred; have one's hatred slaked: 这坏蛋打他一顿也不～. Thrashing this scoun-

drel wouldn't be enough to slake our hatred for him.

解惑 jiěhuò *formal* resolve (*or* remove, dispel) doubts: 师者, 所以传道授业～也. (韩愈) It takes a teacher to transmit wisdom, impart knowledge, and resolve doubts.

解甲归田 jiě jiǎ guī tián take off one's armour and return to the land; be demobilized

解禁 jiějìn lift a ban

解痉 jiějìng *Chin. med.* spasmolysis

解酒 jiějiǔ neutralize the effect of alcoholic drinks

解救 jiějiù save; rescue; deliver: 把农奴从苦难的深渊中～出来 deliver the serfs from the abyss of misery / 通货膨胀政策～不了经济危机. Inflationary policies are no remedy for an economic crisis.

解聚 jiějù *chem.* depolymerization

解决 jiějué ① solve; resolve; settle: ～争端 settle a dispute / ～困难 overcome a difficulty; find a way out of a difficulty / ～问题 solve a problem; settle a question (*or* an issue); work out a solution / 很快地～战斗 bring a battle to a quick decision / 不同质的矛盾, 只有用不同质的方法才能～. Qualitatively different contradictions can only be resolved by qualitatively different methods. ② dispose of; finish off: 这一仗把敌人完全～了. In that battle we finished off all the enemy troops.

解开 jiěkāi untie; undo: ～头巾 untie a kerchief / ～上衣 unbutton one's jacket / ～这个谜 find a clue to the mystery / ～疑团 clear up suspicions / ～疙瘩 get rid of a hang-up

解渴 jiěkě quench one's thirst: 这西瓜真～. This watermelon really quenches your thirst. / 他喝了一大杯水才解了渴. He satisfied his thirst by drinking a large glass of water.

解扣 jiěkòu *elec.* trip: 自动～ automatic trip

解扣儿 jiěkòur ① unbutton ② remove doubts, ill will, etc.

解理 jiělǐ *geol.* cleavage

解铃还是系铃人 jiělíng háishì xìlíngrén (also 解铃系铃 jiělíng xìlíng) let him who tied the bell on the tiger take it off—whoever started the trouble should end it

解码 jiěmǎ decipher; decode

解闷 jiěmèn divert oneself (from boredom)

解囊 jiěnáng *formal* open one's purse (to help sb. with money) ——see also 解囊相助 jiěnáng xiāng zhù; 慷慨解囊 kāngkǎi jiěnáng

解囊相助 jiěnáng xiāng zhù help sb. generously with money

解聘 jiěpìn dismiss an employee (usu. at the expiration of a contract)

解剖 jiěpōu dissect: 我们上生物课时～了一只青蛙. We dissected a frog in biology class. / 严于～自己 be strict in dissecting oneself ideologically; be strict in appraising oneself

解剖刀 jiěpōudāo scalpel

解剖麻雀 jiěpōu máquè dissect a sparrow—analyze a typical case

解剖学 jiěpōuxué anatomy

解气 jiěqì vent one's spleen; work off one's anger

解劝 jiěquàn soothe; mollify; comfort: 你去～几句, 叫他别生气了. Say something to mollify his anger. / 经过同志们一～, 他们俩又和好了. Their comrades helped them patch up their quarrel.

解热 jiěrè allay a fever

解人 jiěrén *formal* a person of great intelligence and understanding

解散 jiěsàn ① dismiss: 队伍～后, 战士们都在操场上休息. After they were dismissed, the soldiers had a rest on the drill ground. / ～! (word of command) Dismiss! ② dissolve; disband: ～组织 disband an organization

解事 jiěshì be experienced and understanding

解释 jiěshì explain; expound; interpret: ～一个新词 explain a new word / ～法律 interpret laws / 河水的流动可以用重力原理来～。 The flow of water in a river is explained by the principle of gravity. / 对这件事你作何～? How do you account for this? / 这些事实不能有别的～。 The facts admit of no other explanation. / 这是误会,～一下就行了。 This is a misunderstanding. A little explanation will clear it up. / 你应该虚心听取同志们的批评,不要老是～。 You should listen carefully to the criticism of the comrades and not keep trying to explain things away. / 对本协定这一上遇有分岐,应以中文本为准。 In case there is any divergence of interpretation of this agreement, the Chinese text shall prevail.

解释权 jiěshìquán right to interpret

解释性 jiěshìxìng explanatory; interpretative: ～保留 interpretative reservation / ～备忘录 explanatory memorandum / ～规定 interpretative provision / ～声明 interpretative declaration (or statement) / ～条款 interpretation (or interpretative) clause / 投票之前,中国代表作了～发言。 Before casting his vote, the Chinese representative made an explanatory statement.

解手[1] jiěshǒu relieve oneself; go to the toilet (or lavatory)

解手[2] jiěshǒu formal part company

解说 jiěshuō explain orally; comment: 向观众～这种卡车的构造和性能 explain to the visitors the structure and performance of this type of truck

解说词 jiěshuōcí (oral) commentary; (written) caption

解说员 jiěshuōyuán announcer; narrator; commentator

解溲 jiěsōu same as 解手[1] jiěshǒu

解题 jiětí solve a (mathematical, etc.) problem

解体 jiětǐ disintegrate: 原始社会的～ the disintegration of primitive society

解脱 jiětuō ① free (or extricate) oneself: 从困境中～出来 extricate oneself from a predicament / 从世间烦恼中～出来 free oneself from worldly worries / 他认为死是最轻松的～。 He thought death is the easiest way out. / 陷入不可～的危机 land oneself in an inextricable crisis ② absolve; exonerate

解围 jiěwéi ① force an enemy to raise a siege; rescue sb. from a siege ② help sb. out of a predicament; save sb. from embarrassment: 他们拿我开玩笑,你怎么不来给我～? Why didn't you come to my rescue when they were making fun of me?

解悟 jiěwù come to understand

解析几何学 jiěxī jǐhéxué analytic geometry

解析数论 jiěxī shùlùn math. analytic theory of numbers

解严 jiěyán declare martial law ended; lift a curfew

解衣 jiěyī undress

解衣推食 jiěyī-tuīshí doff one's own garments to clothe sb. else and give him the food from one's own plate—treat sb. with great kindness

解颐 jiěyí formal break into a smile

解忧 jiěyōu allay sorrow; assuage grief: 何以～, 惟有杜康。(曹操) Sorrows naught allays, Save the cup, since ancient days.

解约 jiěyuē terminate an agreement; cancel (or rescind) a contract

解职 jiězhí dismiss from office; discharge; relieve sb. of his post

jiè

介[1] jiè be situated between; interpose: 这座山～于两县之间。 The mountain lies between two counties.

介[2] jiè ① armour: 介胄 jièzhòu ② shell 介壳 jièqiào

介[3] jiè formal upright: 耿介 gěngjiè

介[4] jiè m. formal (now usu. used in) 一～书生 a mere scholar / 一～武夫 a plain soldier

介词 jiècí gram. preposition

介弟 jièdì honor. formal your (younger) brother

介电常数 jièdiàn chángshù dielectric constant

介夫 jièfū formal men in armour; ancient warriors

介壳 jièqiào shell (of oysters, snails, etc.)

介壳虫 jièqiàochóng scale insect

介入 jièrù intervene; interpose; get involved: 不～无原则争论 not get involved in unprincipled disputes / ～两国之间的纷争 be involved in the disputes and conflicts between two countries

介绍 jièshào ① introduce; present: 让我～一下, 这就是张同志。 Allow me to introduce Comrade Zhang. / 作自我～ introduce oneself / ～对象 introduce sb. to a potential marriage partner; find sb. a boy or girl friend / 这种灭虫方法是去年才～到我们县来的。 This method of pest control was introduced into our county only last year. ② recommend; suggest: 申请入党, 必须有正式党员二人负责～。 An applicant for Party membership must be recommended by two full Party members. / 我给你～一本书。 I'll recommend you a book. / 因为有张先生的～, 我给了他这份工作。 I gave him the job on Mr. Zhang's recommendation. ③ let know; brief: ～情况 brief sb. on the situation; put sb. in the picture; fill sb. in / ～经验 pass on experience

介绍人 jièshàorén ① one who introduces or recommends sb.; sponsor: 他们二人是我的入党～。 They are the two comrades who recommended me for Party membership. or The two of them were my sponsors when I applied for Party membership. ② matchmaker

介绍信 jièshàoxìn letter of introduction; reference

介形虫 jièxíngchóng mussel-shrimp

介意 jièyì (also 介怀 jièhuái) (usu. used in the negative) take offence; mind: 我是开玩笑, 你可别～呀。 I was only joking. I hope you won't take offence. / 即使有些批评过头了, 他也不～。 He didn't mind even when some criticisms were excessive.

介音 jièyīn phonet. the medial or semivowel of a final ——see also 韵母 yùnmǔ

介质 jièzhì phys. medium: 工作～ actuating medium

介胄 jièzhòu formal armour: ～之士 men in armour; ancient warriors

介子 jièzǐ phys. meson; mesotron

芥 jiè mustard ——see also gài

芥菜 jiècài leaf mustard ——see also gàicài

芥菜疙瘩 jiècài gēda rutabaga

芥蒂 jièdì formal ill feeling; unpleasantness; grudge: 心存～ bear a grudge

芥末 jièmo mustard

芥子 jièzǐ mustard seed

芥子气 jièzǐqì chem. mustard gas

戒 jiè ① guard against: ～浮夸 avoid boasting and exaggeration ② exhort; admonish; warn: 引以为戒 yǐn yǐ wéi jiè ③ give up; drop; stop: ～荤腥 go on a vegetarian diet ④ Buddhist monastic discipline: 受戒 shòujiè ⑤ (finger) ring: 钻～ diamond ring

戒备 jièbèi guard; take precautions; be on the alert: 处于～状态 be on the alert

戒备森严 jièbèi sēnyán tight security is in force

戒尺 jièchǐ teacher's ruler for beating pupils

戒除 jièchú　give up; drop; stop: ～恶习 give up a bad habit

戒刀 jièdāo　Buddhist monk's knife

戒牒 jièdié　same as 度牒 dùdié

戒忌 jièjì　① taboos; don'ts ② be wary of violating a taboo

戒骄戒躁 jièjiāo-jièzào　guard against arrogance and rashness; be on one's guard against conceit and impetuosity: ～，永远保持谦虚进取的精神 guard against conceit and rashness, always remain modest and keep forging ahead

戒酒 jièjiǔ　give up drinking; swear off drinking

戒惧 jièjù　be frightened and watchful

戒律 jièlǜ　religious discipline; commandment

戒条 jiètiáo　same as 戒律 jièlǜ

戒心 jièxīn　vigilance; wariness: 对某人怀有～ be on one's guard against someone; keep a wary eye on someone

戒烟 jièyān　give up smoking; swear off smoking: 抽一枝烟吧?—谢谢，我～了。Cigarette? —No thanks, I've sworn off smoking. / ～糖(茶) habit-breaking candy (tea) for smokers

戒严 jièyán　enforce martial law; impose a curfew; cordon off an area: 宣布～ proclaim martial law / 警察在车站～，搜捕逃犯。The police cordoned off the railway station to search for the escape prisoner.

戒严令 jièyánlìng　proclamation of martial law

戒指 jièzhi　(finger) ring: 戴～wear a ring / 订婚～ engagement ring / 结婚～ wedding ring / 钻石～ diamond ring

届（屆） jiè　① fall due ② m. (for meetings, graduating classes, etc.): 第五～全国人民代表大会 the Fifth National People's Congress

届满 jièmǎn　at the expiration of one's term of office: 任期～。The term of office has expired.

届期 jièqī　when the day comes; on the appointed date

届时 jièshí　when the time comes; at the appointed time; on the occasion: 大桥下月竣工，～将举行通车典礼。There will be an opening ceremony next month when the bridge is completed. / ～务请出席。Your presence is requested for the occasion.

疥 jiè　scabies

疥虫 jièchóng　med. sarcoptic mite

疥疮 jièchuāng　scabies

疥蛤蟆 jièháma　toad

疥螨 jièmǎn　itch mite

疥癣 jièxuǎn　mange: 羊～ sheep scab

诫 jiè　① warn; admonish: 告诫 gàojiè ② commandment: 十～ the Ten Commandments

界 jiè　① boundary: 山西和陕西以黄河为～。The boundary between Shanxi and Shaanxi is the Huanghe River. ② scope; extent: 眼界 yǎnjiè / 外界 wàijiè ③ circles: 新闻界 xīnwénjiè ④ primary division; kingdom: 动(植、矿)物～ the animal (vegetable, mineral) kingdom ⑤ geol. erathem: 古生界 Gǔshēngjiè ⑥ math. bound: 上(下)～ upper(lower) bound

界碑 jièbēi　boundary tablet; boundary marker

界尺 jièchǐ　ungraduated ruler

界河 jièhé　boundary river

界内球 jiènèiqiú　sports in bounds; in

界石 jièshí　boundary stone or tablet

界说 jièshuō　old definition

界外球 jièwàiqiú　sports out-of-bounds; out

界限 jièxiàn　① demarcation line; dividing line; limits; bounds: 划清～ draw a clear line of demarcation / 打破行业～，实行大协作 break the bounds of different trades and go in for extensive coordination / 注意决定事物质量的数量～ pay attention to the quantitative limits that determine the qualities of things ② limit; end

界线 jièxiàn　① boundary line ② same as 界限 jièxiàn①

界桩 jièzhuāng　boundary marker

借¹ jiè　① borrow: 跟人～钱 borrow money from sb. / 从图书馆～书 borrow a book from the library ② lend: 把自行车～给我骑一下好吗? Could you lend me your bicycle?

借²（藉） jiè　① make use of; take advantage of (an opportunity, etc.): 火～风势，越烧越旺。Fanned by the wind, the fire burned more and more furiously. / 部队～着月光急速前进。The troops marched swiftly forward by the light of the moon. / ～这次大会的东风 make the most of the favourable situation brought about by the congress / 我愿～此机会向大家表示感谢。I wish to take this opportunity to thank you all. ② use as a pretext: ～"援助"之名，行掠夺之实 use "aid" as a pretext for plunder

借词 jiècí　linguis. loanword; loan

借贷 jièdài　① borrow or lend money ② debit and credit sides

借贷资本 jièdài zīběn　loan capital

借刀杀人 jiè dāo shā rén　kill sb. by another's hand; make use of one person to get rid of another

借调 jièdiào　temporarily transfer; loan: 他～到旅行社去工作了。He's on loan to the Travel Service.

借读 jièdú　study at a school on a temporary basis

借端 jièduān　use as a pretext: ～生事 find an excuse to make trouble; avail oneself of a pretext to stir up trouble

借方 jièfāng　bookkeeping debit side; debit

借风使船 jiè fēng shǐ chuán　sail the boat with the help of the wind—achieve one's purpose through the agency of sb. else

借古讽今 jiè gǔ fěng jīn　use the past to disparage the present

借故 jiègù　find an excuse: ～推托 find an excuse to refuse / 他～走了。He found an excuse and left.

借光 jièguāng　pol. excuse me: ～, ～! Would you mind stepping to one side, please. or Out of the way, please. / ～, 去百货大楼怎么走啊? Excuse me, but can you direct me to the Department Store?

借花献佛 jiè huā xiàn fó　present Buddha with flowers given by another—make a gift of sth. given by another

借火 jièhuǒ　ask for a light: 劳驾, 借个火儿。Excuse me. Would you mind giving me a light?

借鉴 jièjiàn　(also 借镜 jièjìng) use for reference; draw lessons from; draw on the experience of: 他们的做法有许多值得我们～的地方。There's much in their method that we can make use of. / ～外国的经验 use the experience of other countries for reference

借酒浇愁 jiè jiǔ jiāo chóu　drown one's sorrows in liquor

借据 jièjù　receipt for a loan (IOU)

借口 jièkǒu　① use as an excuse (or pretext): 他～另有约会, 提前走了。He left early, on the pretext of having another appointment. / 别拿忙做～而放松学习。Don't slacken your study on the excuse of being too busy. ② excuse; pretext: 找～ find an excuse (or pretext) / 制造～ invent an excuse; cook up a pretext

借款 jièkuǎn　① borrow or lend money; ask for or offer a loan ② loan

借尸还魂 jiè shī huán hún　(of a dead person's soul) find reincarnation in another's corpse—(of sth. evil) revive in a new guise

借书处　jièshūchù　loan desk (of a library)

借书证　jièshūzhèng　library card

借水行舟　jiè shuǐ xíng zhōu　sail the boat with the help of the current—achieve one's purpose through the agency of sb. else

借宿　jièsù　stay overnight at sb. else's place; put up for the night: 勘探队员在牧民家里～了一夜。Members of the prospecting team put up for one night in the homes of the herdsmen.

借题发挥　jiè tí fāhuī　make use of the subject under discussion to put over one's own ideas; seize on an incident to exaggerate matters

借条　jiètiáo　receipt for a loan (IOU)

借位　jièwèi　borrow ten (in subtraction)

借问　jièwèn　pol.　may I ask

借以　jièyǐ　so as to; for the purpose of; by way of: 试举数例,～说明问题的严重性。Let me give a few examples to show how serious the problem is.

借用　jièyòng　① borrow; have the loan of: ～一下你的铅笔。May I use your pencil? ② use sth. for another purpose: ～一句古诗表达自己的心情 quote a line from classical poetry to express one's feelings

借债　jièzhài　borrow money; raise (or contract) a loan: ～度日 live by borrowing

借支　jièzhī　ask for an advance on one's pay

借重　jièzhòng　rely on for support; enlist sb.'s help: 以后要～您的地方还多着呢。We'll need a lot more of your help in the future.

借住　jièzhù　stay at sb. else's place: 下周四我们能在你那里～一晚吗? Can you put us up next Thursday night?

借助　jièzhù　have the aid of; draw support from: ～望远镜观察天体 observe the celestial bodies with the aid of a telescope

借箸代筹　jiè zhù dài chóu　plan for others

蚧　jiè　see 蛤蚧 géjiè

解 (解)　jiè　send under guard: 犯人已～到县里了。The prisoner has been sent to the county seat under guard. ——see also jiě; xiè

解差　jièchāi　(also 解子 jièzi) old　guards escorting prisoners

解送　jièsòng　send under guard

解元　jièyuán　the first on the list of successful candidates who passed the provincial imperial examination

褯　jiè　see below

褯子　dial.　diaper

藉　jiè　① formal　mat; mattress ② place sth. underneath: 枕藉 zhěnjiè ③ same as 借² jiè ——see also jí

jie

价 (價)　jie　part. dial.　① (added to negative adverbs to form an emphatic statement): 不 (甭、别)～。No! ② (added to certain adverbs as a suffix): 震天～响 make a thunderous noise／成天～忙 be busy all day long ——see also jià

家　jie　same as 价 jie② ——see also jiā; jia

jīn

巾　jīn　a piece of cloth (as used for a towel, scarf, kerchief, etc.): 毛巾 máojīn／浴巾 yùjīn

巾帼　jīnguó　① ancient woman's headdress ② woman

巾帼英雄　jīnguó yīngxióng　a heroic woman; heroine

今　jīn　① modern; present-day: 今人 jīnrén ② now; the present: 从～以后 from now on; henceforth／～胜于昔。The present is superior to the past. ③ of today; of this year: ～冬 this (coming) winter

今儿　jīnr　(also 今儿个 jīnrge) dial.　today

今草　jīncǎo　a type of cursive hand (草书)

今晨　jīnchén　this morning

今番　jīnfān　this time

今非昔比　jīn fēi xī bǐ　no comparison between past and present; the past cannot be compared with the present

今后　jīnhòu　from now on; in the days to come; henceforth; hereafter; in future: ～的十年内 in the next decade; in the coming ten years／～的任务 the tasks ahead／希望～两国人民之间有更多的交往。We hope from now on there will be more exchanges between our two peoples.

今年　jīnnián　this year

今人　jīnrén　moderns; contemporaries; people of our era

今日　jīnrì　① this day; today ② present; now: ～中国 China now; China today

今生　jīnshēng　this life

今世　jīnshì　① this life ② this age; the contemporary age

今是昨非　jīnshì-zuófēi　today right, yesterday wrong (i.e. what I do today is right, what I did yesterday was wrong; said of repentance and reformation): 悟已往之不谏, 知来者之可追; 实迷途其未远, 觉今是而昨非。(陶潜) I realize that there's no remedying the past But I know that there's hope in the future. After all I have not gone far on the wrong road And I am aware that what I do today is right, yesterday wrong.

今岁　jīnsuì　this year

今天　jīntiān　① this day; today: ～是星期天。Today is Sunday.／我～有客人来。I'm expecting company today.／～上午 (下午) this morning (afternoon)／一年前的～ a year ago today ② the present time or age; today: ～的青年有不同的道德观念。Young people today (or of today) have different moral values.

今晚　jīnwǎn　this evening; tonight

今文　jīnwén　modern script (another name for 隶书 lìshū used in the Han Dynasty)

今夕　jīnxī　formal　this evening; tonight

今昔　jīn-xī　the present and the past; today and yesterday: 西安的～ Xi'an past and present; Xi'an yesterday and today

今昔对比　jīn-xī duìbǐ　contrast the past with the present: ～, 忆苦思甜 recall one's suffering in the old society and contrast it with one's happiness in the new

今宵　jīnxiāo　formal　tonight: ～酒醒何处?—杨柳岸、晓风、残月。(柳永) Where shall I be when I wake up from my drink tonight?—Willow banks, the breeze at dawn, and the waning moon.

今夜　jīnyè　this evening; tonight

今译　jīnyì　modern translation; modern-language version: 古诗～ ancient poems rendered into modern Chinese

今音　jīnyīn　modern (as distinct from classical) pronunciation of Chinese characters

今朝 jīnzhāo ① *dial.* today ② the present; now: 数风流人物，还看今朝。(毛泽东) For truly great men Look to this age alone.

今朝有酒今朝醉 jīnzhāo yǒu jiǔ jīnzhāo zuì drink today while drink you may: ～，明日愁来明日愁。(罗隐) Drink today while drink you may. You ne'er may drink another day. As for what sorrow may come tomorrow, Why, let it be tomorrow's sorrow!

斤¹(觔) jīn *jin*, currently called 市斤 shìjīn, a traditional unit of weight ——see also 市斤 shìjīn

斤² jīn a tool used for felling trees in ancient times

斤斗 jīndǒu *dial.* ① fall ② somersault

斤斤 jīnjīn be particular (about small matters): ～于表面形式 be particular about matters of form

斤斤计较 jīnjīn jìjiào haggle over every ounce; be calculating: ～个人得失 be preoccupied with one's personal gains and losses

斤两 jīnliǎng weight: ～不足 short weight; underweight / 他的话很有～。What he said should not be taken lightly. or What he said carried a lot of weight.

金¹ jīn ① metals: 五金 wǔjīn ② money: 现金 xiànjīn ③ ancient metal percussion instruments: 鸣金收兵 míngjīn shōubīng ④ *chem.* gold (Au) ⑤ golden: 红底～字 golden characters on a red background ⑥ highly respected; precious: 金口玉言 jīnkǒu yùyán ⑦ (Jīn) a surname

金² Jīn the Jin Dynasty (1115—1234)

金榜 jīnbǎng a list of successful candidates in the imperial examinations: ～题名 succeed in the imperial examinations

金本位 jīnběnwèi *econ.* gold standard

金笔 jīnbǐ (quality) fountain pen

金币 jīnbì gold coin

金碧辉煌 jīnbì huīhuáng (of a building, etc.) looking splendid in green and gold; resplendent and magnificent

金碧山水 jīnbì shānshuǐ gold-and-green landscape (a coloured landscape done in golds, blues, and greens)

金伯利岩 jīnbólìyán kimberlite

金箔 jīnbó goldleaf; gold foil

金不换 jīnbuhuàn not to be exchanged even for gold; invaluable; priceless ——see also 浪子回头 làngzǐ huítóu

金灿灿 jīncàncàn glittering: ～的阳光洒满大地。The sun's golden rays lit up the earth.

金蝉脱壳 jīnchán tuō qiào slip out of a predicament like a cicada sloughing its skin; escape by cunning manoeuvring

金城汤池 jīnchéng-tāngchí ramparts of metal and a moat of boiling water—an impregnable fortress

金翅雀 jīnchìquè greenfinch

金疮 jīnchuāng *Chin. med.* metal-inflicted wound; incised wound

金额 jīn'é *formal* amount (*or* sum) of money

金风 jīnfēng *formal* autumn wind

金刚 Jīngāng Buddha's warrior attendant

金刚努目 Jīngāng nǔmù (also 金刚怒目 Jīngāng nùmù) glare like a temple door-god—be fierce of visage

金刚砂 jīngāngshā emery; corundum; carborundum: ～磨床 emery grinder

金刚石 jīngāngshí diamond

金刚石婚 jīngāngshíhūn diamond wedding

金刚钻 jīngāngzuàn diamond: ～钻头 diamond bit

金糕 jīngāo haw jelly

金戈铁马 jīngē-tiěmǎ golden spears and armoured horses—war or warriors: 想当年～，气吞万里如虎。(辛弃疾) He has been thinking of those years, When, amidst golden spears and armoured horses, His inhalations engulfed all the ten thousand *li* like a tiger's.

金工 jīngōng metalworking; metal processing: ～机械 metalworking machinery

金箍棒 jīngūbàng golden cudgel (a weapon used by the Monkey King in the novel *Pilgrimage to the West* 《西游记》)

金鼓齐鸣 jīngǔ qí míng all the gongs and drums are beating

金光 jīnguāng golden light (*or* ray): 万道～ myriad golden rays / ～闪闪 glittering; glistening

金光大道 jīnguāng dàdào golden road; bright broad highway: 社会主义的～ the golden road of socialism

金龟 jīnguī tortoise

金龟子 jīnguīzǐ scarab

金合欢 jīnhéhuān sponge tree

金衡 jīnhéng troy weight; troy

金红 jīnhóng golden red

金红石 jīnhóngshí rutile

金花菜 jīnhuācài (California) bur clover

金煌煌 jīnhuānghuāng (also 金晃晃 jīnhuǎnghuāng) golden: ～的琉璃瓦 golden glazed tiles

金黄 jīnhuáng golden yellow; golden: 菜花一片～ a vast stretch of golden rape flowers

金汇兑本位 jīnhuìduì běnwèi *econ.* gold exchange standard

金婚 jīnhūn golden wedding

金鸡 jīnjī golden pheasant

金鸡独立 jīnjī dú lì standing on one leg like a cock (a posture in Chinese boxing)

金鸡纳树 jīnjīnàshù cinchona

金鸡纳霜 jīnjīnàshuāng quinine

金橘 jīnjú kumquat

金科玉律 jīnkē-yùlǜ golden rule and precious precept: 奉为～ accept as an infallible law

金壳郎 jīnkéláng *dial.* scarab

金口玉言 jīnkǒu-yùyán a golden mouth and pearly words—precious words; utterances that carry great weight

金库 jīnkù national (*or* state) treasury; exchequer

金块 jīnkuài gold bullion

金兰之交 jīn lán zhī jiāo intimate friendship; sworn brotherhood

金莲 jīnlián lily feet (formerly, men's laudatory term for women's bound feet) ——see also 三寸金莲 sāncùn jīnlián

金缕玉衣 jīnlǚ yùyī *archaeol.* jade clothes sewn with gold thread

金绿宝石 jīnlǜ bǎoshí chrysoberyl

金銮殿 jīnluándiàn the Hall of Golden Chimes (a popular name for the emperor's audience hall, e.g. the Hall of Great Harmony 太和殿 in the Imperial Palace)

金霉素 jīnméisù aureomycin

金门岛 Jīnméndǎo Jinmen (Quemoy) Islands

金迷纸醉 jīnmí-zhǐzuì same as 纸醉金迷 zhǐzuì-jīnmí

金木水火土 jīn-mù-shuǐ-huǒ-tǔ metal, wood, water, fire and earth—the five elements of Chinese philosophy ——see also 五行 wǔxíng

金牛座 jīnniúzuò *astron.* Taurus

金瓯 jīnōu golden goblet—national territory

金瓯无缺 jīnōu wú quē territorial integrity unimpaired

金牌 jīnpái gold medal

金漆 jīnqī gold lacquer: ～镶嵌制品 inlaid gold lacquerware

金器 jīnqì gold vessel

金钱 jīnqián money

金钱豹　jīnqiánbào　leopard

金枪鱼　jīnqiāngyú　tuna

金融　jīnróng　finance; banking: ～货币危机 financial and monetary crises / ～机构 banking institution / ～机关 financial institution

金融寡头　jīnróng guǎtóu　financial oligarch (*or* magnate)

金融界　jīnróngjiè　financial circles

金融巨头　jīnróng jùtóu　financial magnate; shark of high finance; financial tycoon

金融市场　jīnróng shìchǎng　money (*or* financial) market

金融体制　jīnróng tǐzhì　banking system

金融中心　jīnróng zhōngxīn　financial (*or* banking) centre

金融资本　jīnróng zīběn　financial capital

金嗓子　jīnsǎngzi　golden voice—beautiful voice

金色　jīnsè　golden: ～的朝阳 golden rays of the morning sun; golden dawn

金石　jīnshí　① *formal* metal and stone—a symbol of hardness and strength: 精诚所至，金石为开 jīngchéng suǒ zhì, jīnshí wéi kāi ② inscriptions on ancient bronzes and stone tablets

金石学　jīnshíxué　the study of inscriptions on ancient bronzes and stone tablets; epigraphy

金属　jīnshǔ　metal

金属工艺品　jīnshǔ gōngyìpǐn　metal handicrafts

金属加工　jīnshǔ jiāgōng　metal processing; metalworking

金属结构　jīnshǔ jiégòu　metal structure

金属模　jīnshǔmó　metal pattern

金属疲劳　jīnshǔ pīláo　metal fatigue

金属探伤　jīnshǔ tànshāng　metal defect detection; crack detection: ～器 flaw detector

金属陶瓷　jīnshǔ táocí　cermet

金属涂料　jīnshǔ túliào　metallic paint

金属性　jīnshǔxìng　metallicity

金丝猴　jīnsīhóu　golden monkey; snub-nosed monkey

金丝雀　jīnsīquè　canary

金丝镶嵌　jīnsī xiāngqiàn　gold filigree

金丝燕　jīnsīyàn　esculent swift

金丝枣　jīnsīzǎo　a variety of the Chinese date

金粟兰　jīnsùlán　zhulan tree

金汤　jīntāng　short for 金城汤池 jīnchéng-tāngchí ——see also 固若金汤 gù ruò jīntāng

金条　jīntiáo　gold bar

金童玉女　jīntóng-yùnǚ　the Golden Boy and the Jade Maiden (attendants of the Taoist immortals)

金文　jīnwén　inscriptions on ancient bronze objects

金乌　jīnwū　*liter.* the Golden Crow—the sun: ～西坠。The sun is sinking in the west.

金线鱼　jīnxiànyú　red coat, golden thread

金相学　jīnxiàngxué　metallography

金小蜂　jīnxiǎofēng　tiny golden wasp; ptermalid

金星[1]　Jīnxīng　Venus

金星[2]　jīnxīng　① golden star (an object or figure) ② flashes of light that one seems to see (as from dizziness or a blow on the head): 冒金星 mào jīnxīng

金钥匙　jīnyàoshi　golden key—the best solution to a problem: 自学是打开知识宝库的一把～。Self-study is the golden key to the treasure-trove of knowledge.

金要足赤，人要完人　jīn yào zú chì, rén yào wánrén　gold must be pure and man must be perfect—perfectionism

金银财宝　jīnyíncáibǎo　gold, silver, treasures, and jewels—riches

金银花　jīnyínhuā　honeysuckle

金银花露　jīnyínhuālù　*Chin. med.* distilled liquid of honeysuckle

金樱子　jīnyīngzǐ　*Chin. med.* the fruit of Cherokee rose (*Rosa laevigata*)

金鱼　jīnyú　goldfish

金鱼虫　jīnyúchóng　another name for 水蚤 shuǐzǎo

金鱼缸　jīnyúgāng　goldfish bowl; goldfish basin

金鱼藻　jīnyúzǎo　hornwort (*Ceratophyllum demersum*)

金玉　jīnyù　*formal* gold and jade—valuable; precious

金玉良言　jīnyù liángyán　golden sayings; invaluable advice

金玉满堂　jīnyù mǎntáng　a hall filled with gold and jade— wealthy; learned

金玉其外，败絮其中　jīnyù qí wài, bàixù qí zhōng　rubbish coated in gold and jade; fair without, foul within

金元　jīnyuán　gold dollar; U. S. dollar

金圆券　jīnyuánquàn　gold *yuan* notes (issued by the Kuomintang government in 1948)

金云母　jīnyúnmǔ　phlogopite

金盏花　jīnzhǎnhuā　pot marigold (*Calendula officinalis*)

金针　jīnzhēn　① acupuncture needle ② dried day lily flower

金针菜　jīnzhēncài　day lily

金针虫　jīnzhēnchóng　wireworm

金枝玉叶　jīnzhī-yùyè　golden branches and jade leaves —people of imperial lineage; royalty: 学生家道贫寒; 岂敢与～为偶! I am a poor student from a low family. How could I dare become the spouse of royalty?

金字塔　jīnzìtǎ　pyramid

金字招牌　jīnzì zhāopai　a gold-lettered signboard—a vainglorious title

金子　jīnzi　gold

津[1]　jīn　① saliva: 生～止渴 help produce saliva and slake thirst ② sweat: 遍体生～ perspire all over ③ moist; damp

津[2]　jīn　① ferry crossing; ford: 要津 yàojīn ② (Jīn) short for 天津 Tiānjīn

津巴布韦　Jīnbābùwéi　Zimbabwe

津逮　jīndài　*formal* ① access to by way of a ferry crossing ② a gateway to (learning)

津渡　jīndù　*formal* ferry crossing

津筏　jīnfá　*formal* ① ferry raft ② a way or path to sth. (fig.)

津津乐道　jīnjīn lè dào　take delight in talking about; dwell upon with great relish

津津有味　jīnjīn yǒu wèi　with relish; with gusto; with keen pleasure: 吃得～ eat with great relish / 讲得～ talk with gusto / 这个故事他们听得～。They listened to the story with great interest.

津梁　jīnliáng　*formal* bridge and ford—help; aid

津贴　jīntiē　① financial aid; subsidy; allowance: 学校从政府领～。The school receives aid from the government. / 出差～ travel subsistence allowance / 伙食～ food allowance / 生活～ living allowance / 岗位～ subsidies appropriate to particular jobs ② give financial aid; subsidize

津要　jīnyào　*formal* ① key place ② key post

津液　jīnyè　① *Chin. med.* body fluid ② saliva

衿　jīn　① same as 襟 jīn ② *formal* girdle

矜　jīn　① pity; sympathize with: 矜恤 jīnxù ② self-important; conceited: 骄矜 jiāojīn ③ restrained; reserved: 矜重 jīnzhòng

矜持　jīnchí　restrained; reserved: 举止～ have a reserved manner

矜贵　jīnguì　*formal* ① self-important; conceited: 恃才～ be proud of one's ability ② precious; valuable: 此书刊印精美，且为海内孤本，弥足～。Beautifully produced and being the only copy extant, this book is to be highly treasured.

矜夸　jīnkuā　conceited and boastful

矜悯　jīnmǐn　*formal* take pity on; have compassion for

矜恤 jīnxù　show sympathy and consideration for

矜重 jīnzhòng　reserved and dignified

筋(觔)
jīn ① muscle ② *inf.* tendon; sinew ③ *inf.* veins that stand out under the skin: 青筋 qīngjīn ④ anything resembling a tendon or vein: 叶～ ribs of a leaf / 这菜～多嚼不烂。The greens are full of fibres that you can't chew. / 芹菜太老，有很多～。This celery is too old; it's very stringy.

筋斗 jīndǒu　*dial.* ① somersault: 翻～ turn a somersault ② fall; tumble (over): 摔了个～ fall; have a fall; tumble over

筋骨 jīngǔ　bones and muscles—physique: 武术可以锻炼～。Practising *wushu* strengthens the physique.

筋节 jīnjié　muscles and joints—vital links in a speech or essay

筋疲力尽 jīnpí-lìjìn (also 筋疲力竭 jīnpí-lìjié) exhausted; played out; worn out; tired out; all in; dead-beat; dog-tired

筋肉 jīnròu　muscles

禁
jīn ① bear; stand; endure: 这布～洗吗？Will this cloth stand a lot of washing? / 这鞋～穿。These shoes are durable. / 黑颜色～脏。Black colour doesn't show dirt easily. ② contain (*or* restrain) oneself: 不禁 bùjīn——see also jìn

禁不起 jīnbuqǐ　be unable to stand (tests, trials, etc.): ～严峻考验 fail to stand rigorous tests

禁不住 jīnbuzhù ① be unable to bear or endure: 这种植物～冻。This plant can't stand frost. / 你怎么这样～批评？How is it that you can't stand a little bit of criticism? ② can't help (doing sth.); can't refrain from: ～笑了起来 can't help laughing; burst out laughing / ～掉下了眼泪 can't hold back one's tears

禁得起 jīndeqǐ　be able to stand (tests, trials, etc.): ～艰苦环境的考验 be able to stand the test of hardships

禁得住 jīndezhù　be able to bear or endure: 这把椅子～我坐吗？Will this chair hold me? / 河上的冰已经～人走了。The ice on the river is thick enough to walk on. / 这座桥～多重？How much weight will the bridge hold?

禁受 jīnshòu　bear; stand; endure: 这些建筑～了时间的考验。These buildings have stood the test of time.

襟
jīn ① front of a garment ② brothers-in-law whose wives are sisters: ～兄 husband of one's wife's elder sister; brother-in-law

襟怀 jīnhuái　*formal* bosom; (breadth of) mind

襟怀坦白 jīnhuái tǎnbái　open-hearted and aboveboard; honest and straightforward

襟翼 jīnyì　*aviation* (wing) flap

jǐn

仅(僅)
jǐn *adv.* only; merely; alone: ～次于 second only to / ～一人缺席。Only one is absent. / ～该市一地死于吸烟者已达数千人。Smoking has caused thousands of deaths in this city alone. ——see also jìn

仅供参考 jǐn gōng cānkǎo　just for reference; for reference only

仅见 jǐnjiàn　rarely seen: 世所～ have no parallel anywhere

仅仅 jǐnjǐn　*adv.* only; merely; alone: 这～是开始。This is only the beginning. / 他解这道题～用了十分钟。It took him only ten minutes to solve the problem. / 她～是个孩子。She was merely a child. / 这座桥～半年就完工了。This bridge was built in the short space of six months.

仅只 jǐnzhǐ　*adv.* only; merely: 这～是个时间问题。It is merely a question of time.

尽¹(盡)
jǐn ① *adv.* to the greatest extent: ～早 as early as possible; at the earliest possible date ② be within the limits of : ～着三天把事情办好。Get the job done in three days at the outside. / ～着一百块钱花。Don't spend more than 100 *yuan*. ③ give priority to: ～着年纪大的坐。Let the older people sit down first. ④ *adv.* (used before a noun of locality) furthest; extreme: ～北边 the northernmost end, etc. / ～底下 at the very bottom / 他家住在村子～西头。He lives at the western end of the village.

尽²(盡)
jǐn *dial.* keep on doing sth.: 他衣服都叫汗湿透了，还～着干呢。He was wet through with sweat, but he kept on working. / 这些日子～下雨。We're having an awful lot of rain these days. ——see also jìn

尽管 jǐnguǎn ① *adv.* feel free to; not hesitate to: 有什么问题～问。If you have any questions, don't hesitate to ask them. / 你～拿吧。You're welcome to it. *or* Take as much as you like. / 工作有我们，你～放心吧。Don't worry. We'll attend to the work. ② *adv. dial.* always; all the time ③ *conj.* though; even though; in spite of; despite: ～旱情严重，今年的小麦还是丰收了。Despite the serious drought, the wheat harvest this year was good. / 他～身体不好，仍然坚持工作。Though he's not in good health, he still keeps on working. / 我喜欢这个工作，～报酬很低。I like the job, even though it's badly paid.

尽可能 jǐnkěnéng　*adv.* as far as possible; to the best of one's ability: ～早点儿来 come as early as possible / 我～做好。I'll do it to the best of my ability. / 革命的政治内容和～完美的艺术形式的统一 the unity of revolutionary political content and the highest possible perfection of artistic form / 我国的艰巨的社会主义建设事业，需要～多的知识分子为它服务。China needs the services of as many intellectuals as possible for the colossal task of building socialism.

尽快 jǐnkuài　*adv.* as quickly (*or* soon, early) as possible: 请～答复。Please reply at your earliest convenience.

尽量 jǐnliàng　*adv.* to the best of one's ability; as far as possible: ～采用先进技术 make the widest possible use of advanced technology / 请大家～发表意见。Please voice your opinions as fully as possible. / 把你知道的～报告给大家。Tell us as much as you know. ——see also jìnliàng

尽让 jǐnràng　*dial.* let others take precedence

尽先 jǐnxiān　*adv.* give first priority to: ～照顾孩子们 look after the children first / ～生产这种农具 give first priority to producing this kind of farm tool / 我们都饿坏了，得～解决吃饭问题。We are starving—see to our meals first.

尽自 jǐnzi　*dial.* always; all the time: 别～诉苦。Stop complaining all the time. / 他不说话，～笑。He didn't say anything, but kept smiling.

卺
jǐn *formal* nuptial wine cup: 合卺 héjǐn

紧(緊)
jǐn ① tight; taut; close: 把绳子拉～ pull the rope taut / 把螺丝拧～ tighten the screw / ～握手中枪 hold the gun tight in one's hands / 这双鞋太～。These shoes are too tight. *or* These shoes pinch. / 他住在我的～隔壁。He lives right next door to me. / 日程安排得很～。The programme is packed. / 一个胜利～接着一个胜利。One victory followed another in quick succession. / 全国人民团结～。The whole nation is closely

united. ② tighten: ～一～背包带 tighten the knapsack straps ③ urgent; pressing; tense: 任务～。The task is urgent. / 风声～。Things are tense. / 雨下得正～。It was raining hard. / 枪声越来越～。The firing got heavier and heavier. / 这篇报告厂里催得很～。The factory leadership are pressing us to hand in this report. ④ strict; stringent: 管得～ exercise strict control; be strict with ⑤ hard up; short of money: 手头～ be short of money; be hard up / 银根～。Money is tight.

紧巴巴 jǐnbābā ① tight: 我这条裤子穿着～的。My trousers are too tight. ② hard up; short of money: 日子过得～的 be in financial straits / 手头～的 be short of money; be hard up

紧绷绷 jǐnbēngbēng ① tightly drawn: 皮带系得～的 with a belt fastened tight ② (of one's facial expression) taut: 他脸～的, 像很生气的样子。He had a taut expression on his face, apparently very angry.

紧逼 jǐnbī press hard; close in on: 步步～ press on at every stage

紧凑 jǐncòu compact; terse; well-knit: 这个工厂布局～。The factory is compactly laid out. / 影片情节～。The film has a well-knit plot. / 会议开得很～。It was a well-organized meeting. / 活动安排得很～ have a tight schedule

紧跟 jǐngēn follow closely; keep in step with: ～时代的步伐 keep in step with the times / ～形势 keep abreast of the situation

紧箍咒 jǐngūzhòu the Incantation of the Golden Hoop (originally used by the Monk in the novel *Pilgrimage to the West* 《西游记》 to keep the Monkey King under control)——inhibition

紧急 jǐnjí urgent; pressing; critical: 发出～呼吁 issue an urgent appeal / 情况～。The situation is critical. / ～行动起来 act promptly; take immediate action / ～任务 an urgent task

紧急出口 jǐnjí chūkǒu emergency exit

紧急措施 jǐnjí cuòshī emergency measures

紧急法令 jǐnjí fǎlìng emergency act

紧急会议 jǐnjí huìyì emergency meeting

紧急集合 jǐnjí jíhé emergency muster

紧急警报 jǐnjí jǐngbào emergency (air-raid) alarm

紧急起飞 jǐnjí qǐfēi scramble

紧急信号 jǐnjí xìnhào emergency (or distress) signal

紧急闸 jǐnjízhá emergency brake

紧急状态 jǐnjí zhuàngtài state of emergency

紧急着陆 jǐnjí zhuólù emergency landing

紧紧 jǐnjǐn closely; firmly; tightly: ～相连 closely linked / ～盯着 watch closely; stare fixedly; gaze steadfastly / ～依靠群众 rely firmly on the masses / 两人～握手。They clasped hands tightly. / 门关得～的。The door was shut tight. / 他～抓住这个贼, 不让他跑掉。He grasped the thief firmly to stop him running away.

紧邻 jǐnlín close neighbour; next-door neighbour

紧锣密鼓 jǐnluó-mìgǔ a wild beating of gongs and drums—an intense publicity campaign (usu. in preparation for some sinister undertaking)

紧密 jǐnmì ① close together; inseparable: ～团结 be closely united / ～合作 close cooperation / ～联系 close contact / 学习理论要～结合实际。Theoretical study must be closely integrated with practice. ② rapid and intense: 枪声～。There was rapid, intense firing.

紧迫 jǐnpò pressing; urgent; imminent: 时间～ be pressed for time / 我有更～的事情要做。I have more pressing things to attend to. / 形势很～。The situation is critical.

紧迫感 jǐnpògǎn a feeling of urgency; a sense of urgency

紧俏 jǐnqiào (of consumer goods) in great demand but short supply

紧缺 jǐnquē in short supply; badly needed: ～商品 goods in short supply / ～人才 badly-needed professionals

紧身儿 jǐnshēnr close-fitting undergarment

紧缩 jǐnsuō reduce; retrench; tighten: ～编制 reduce staff / ～开支 cut down expenses; retrench; curtail outlay / ～贷款 decrease credit / ～包围圈 tighten the ring of encirclement

紧要 jǐnyào critical; crucial; vital: ～关头 critical moment (*or* juncture); crucial moment / 这一点十分～。That's an extremely important point. *or* That's a vital point.

紧张 jǐnzhāng ① nervous; keyed up: 神情～ look nervous / 慢慢讲, 别～。Speak slowly and don't be nervous. / 试验到了关键时刻, 大家都～起来。Everybody was keyed up as the experiment reached a crucial point. ② tense; intense; strained: ～局势 a tense situation / ～气氛 a tense atmosphere / ～的战斗 intense fighting / 两国关系～。Relations between the two countries are strained. / ～而有秩序的工作 intense but orderly work / 团结～的集体生活 a collective life marked by solidarity and activity / 这场比赛真～! What an exciting game! / 工程正在～地进行。Construction was in full swing. / 日程安排得太～ It's rather a tight schedule. / 缓和交通运输的～状况 relieve the pressure on transport ③ in short supply; tight: 这几天鸡蛋供应有点～。Eggs have been in rather short supply for the last few days. *or* There's been rather a shortage of eggs lately. / 这里只有一口井, 用水比较～。There's only one well here and water is in great demand. / 目前这里住房相当～。Accommodation here is pretty tight at present.

紧着 jǐnzhe *inf.* speed up; press on with; hurry: 时间不多了, 咱们～干吧。There's not much time left. Let's hurry.

紧追 jǐnzhuī in hot pursuit: 小偷往街上跑, 警察在后面～。The thief ran down the street with a policeman in hot pursuit.

紧自 jǐnzi *dial.* always; all the time: 她的心～扑通扑通地跳。Her heart kept beating violently.

堇

堇 jǐn see below

堇菜 jǐncài *bot.* violet

堇青石 jǐnqīngshí cordierite

堇色 jǐnsè violet (colour)

锦

锦 jǐn ① brocade ② bright and beautiful: ～霞 rosetinted clouds

锦标 jǐnbiāo prize; trophy; title

锦标赛 jǐnbiāosài championship contest; championships: 世界乒乓球～ the World Table Tennis Championships

锦标主义 jǐnbiāozhǔyì cups and medals mania

锦簇花团 jǐncù-huātuán same as 花团锦簇 huātuán-jǐncù

锦缎 jǐnduàn brocade

锦鸡 jǐnjī golden pheasant

锦葵 jǐnkuí *bot.* high mallow

锦纶 jǐnlún polyamide fibre

锦囊佳句 jǐnnáng jiājù embroidered bag verses—fine verses (from the peculiar habit of the Tang poet Li He 李贺, who would often go out riding, and while on horseback would jot down single lines on scraps of paper as some idea struck him and drop the scraps into an embroidered bag for later assemblage into a finished poem)

锦囊妙计 jǐnnáng miàojì instructions for dealing with an emergency; wise counsel

锦旗 jǐnqí silk banner (as an award or a gift)

锦上添花 jǐn shàng tiān huā add flowers to the bro-

cade—make what is good still better

锦心绣口 jǐnxīn-xiùkǒu (also 锦心绣腹 jǐnxīn-xiùfù) beautiful writing

锦绣 jǐnxiù as beautiful as brocade; beautiful; splendid

锦绣河山 jǐnxiù héshān a land of splendours; a land of charm and beauty; a beautiful land

锦绣前程 jǐnxiù qiánchéng a glorious future

锦衣卫 jǐnyīwèi the Embroidered-Uniform Guard (a Ming Dynasty star chamber)

锦衣玉食 jǐnyī-yùshí live in luxury

谨 jǐn ① careful; cautious; circumspect: ～记在心 bear in mind / ～守规则 strictly adhere to the rules ② solemnly; sincerely: ～致谢意。Please accept my sincere thanks. / 我～代表全体职工, 向你们表示热烈的欢迎。On behalf of the staff and workers, I wish to extend to you our warmest welcome.

谨饬 jǐnchì *formal* prudent; careful; cautious; circumspect

谨防 jǐnfáng guard against; beware of: ～扒手。Beware of pickpockets. / ～假冒。Beware of imitations.

谨上 jǐnshàng (also 谨启 jǐnqǐ) (used after the signature in a formal letter) yours respectfully

谨慎 jǐnshèn prudent; careful; cautious; circumspect: 说话～ be guarded in one's speech / ～从事 act with caution

谨小慎微 jǐnxiǎo-shènwēi overcautious in small matters; overcautious

谨严 jǐnyán careful and precise: 治学～ careful and exact scholarship / 文章结构～。The article is compact and carefully constructed.

谨言慎行 jǐnyán-shènxíng speak and act cautiously; be discreet in word and deed

馑 jǐn see 饥馑 jǐjǐn

槿 jǐn see 木槿 mùjǐn

jǐn

仅(僅) jǐn *adv. formal* nearly; approximately: 士卒～万人。The soldiers numbered nearly 10,000. ——see also jìn

尽(盡) jǐn ① exhausted; finished: 想～各种方法 try all possible means ② to the utmost; to the limit: 尽善尽美 jìnshàn-jìnměi ③ use up; exhaust: 一饮而～ empty a glass at one gulp; drain the cup with one gulp ④ try one's best; put to the best use: ～最大努力 do one's best; exert one's utmost effort / 为建设社会主义～一分力量 do one's bit in building socialism ⑤ all; exhaustive: 不可～信 not to be believed word for word; to be taken with a grain of salt / ～收眼底 have a panoramic view ——see also jìn

尽瘁 jìncuì *formal* do one's utmost; spare no effort; do all one can

尽欢 jìnhuān enjoy oneself to the full: ～而散 (of a party) break up after everyone has enjoyed himself to the full

尽力 jìnlì *adv.* do all one can; try one's best: 我们一定～支援。We'll do our best to help.

尽力而为 jìnlì ér wéi do one's best; do everything in one's power

尽量 jìnliàng (drink or eat) to the full ——see also jǐnliàng

尽其所有 jìn qí suǒyǒu give everything one has; give one's all

尽其在我 jìn qí zài wǒ do one's utmost; do all one can

尽情 jìnqíng *adv.* to one's heart's content; as much as one likes: ～欢呼 cheer heartily / ～歌唱 sing to one's heart's content

尽然 jìnrán (usu. used in the negative) entirely so: 也不～ not exactly so; not exactly the case

尽人皆知 jìn rén jiē zhī be known to all; be common knowledge

尽人事 jìn rénshì do what one can (to save a dying person, etc.); do all that is humanly possible (though with little hope of success)

尽日 jìnrì *formal* the whole day; all day; all day long

尽如人意 jìn rú rényì just as one wishes; entirely satisfactory: 哪能事事～? How can you expect everything to turn out just as you wish?

尽善尽美 jìnshàn-jìnměi the acme of perfection; perfect

尽是 jìnshì full of; all; without exception: 这儿原来～石头。This place used to be full of boulders. / 这里展出的～新产品。All the exhibits here are new products. / 一路上～去参加庆祝活动的人群。There was a continuous stream of people going to the celebrations.

尽数 jìnshù total number; whole amount: 所借图书已～归还。All the books we borrowed have been returned. / 将所欠款项～归还 pay the debt in full

尽态极妍 jìntài-jíyán beauty shown to the best advantage

尽头 jìntóu end: 路的～ the end of the road / 学问是没有～的。There is no limit to knowledge.

尽孝 jìnxiào fulfil one's duty to one's parents; display filial piety towards one's parents

尽心 jìnxīn with all one's heart: 医护人员为照看受伤的工人真是尽了心。The doctors and nurses did their utmost to tend the injured workers. / 这些年青人干活可～呢。These young people are really conscientious in their work.

尽心竭力 jìnxīn-jiélì (do sth.) with all one's heart and all one's might

尽信书不如无书 jìn xìn shū bù rú wú shū to believe everything in books is worse than to have no books at all

尽兴 jìnxìng to one's heart's content; enjoy oneself to the full: ～而归 return after thoroughly enjoying oneself

尽义务 jìn yìwù ① do one's duty; fulfil one's obligation: 尽公民的义务 do one's duty as a citizen ② work for no reward

尽责 jìnzé do one's duty; discharge one's responsibility

尽职 jìnzhí fulfil one's duty: 他工作一向很～。He has always been a conscientious worker.

尽忠 jìnzhōng ① be utterly loyal ② be faithful unto death

进(進) jìn ① advance; move forward; move ahead: 向前～ move forward ② enter; come or go into; get into: ～屋 enter a house or room / ～大学 enter college / ～工厂当学徒 start work in a factory as an apprentice / ～医院 be sent to hospital; be hospitalized / ～请～! Come in! ③ receive; admit: 我们单位～了一个新打字员。Our unit has taken on a new typist. ④ eat; drink; take: 进餐 jìncān ⑤ submit; present: ～一言 give a word of advice ⑥ (used after a verb) into; in: 走～车间 walk into the workshop / 把子弹压～弹匣 press the cartridges into the magazine / 住～新楼 move into a new building ⑦ any of the several rows of houses within an old-style residential compound ⑧ *sports* score a goal: ～了! It's in! *or* Goal! / 这球没～。He's missed it.

进逼 jìnbī close in on; advance on; press on towards

进兵 jìnbīng dispatch troops to attack (a place); (of

troops) march on (a place)

进步 jìnbù ① advance; progress; improve: 世界是在～的。The world is progressing. *or* The world moves ahead. / 两国关系向前进了一步。The relationship between the two nations has moved a step forward. / 今年我们农场各方面的工作都有了很大的～。Great advances have been made in every field of work on our farm this year. / 你的发音很有～。Your pronunciation has greatly improved. ② (politically) progressive: 思想～ have progressive ideas / ～人士 progressive personages / ～势力 progressive forces

进餐 jìncān *formal* have a meal: 共进午餐 have lunch together

进场 jìnchǎng ① march into the arena ② *aviation* approach: ～失败 missed approach

进城 jìnchéng ① go into town; go to town ② enter the big cities (to live and work): ～以后他仍旧保持着艰苦朴素的作风。After he came into the city, he still kept up his style of hard work and plain living.

进程 jìnchéng course; process; progress: 历史～ the course of history

进尺 jìnchǐ *min.* footage: 掘进 (凿岩, 开拓)～ drifting (drilling, tunnelling) footage

进出 jìnchū ① pass in and out: 这儿进进出出的人真多。What a lot of people are coming in and out of here. / 车辆由此～。Vehicles this way! / 保障资金在香港特别行政区流动和～的自由 safeguard the free flow of capital within, into and out of the Hong Kong Special Administrative Region ② (business) turnover: 这个商店每天有好几千元的～。This store has a daily turnover of several thousand *yuan*.

进出口[1] jìnchūkǒu exits and entrances; exit

进出口[2] jìnchūkǒu imports and exports: ～公司 import and export corporation / ～商品 import and export commodities

进出口贸易 jìnchūkǒu màoyì import and export trade; foreign trade

进刀 jìndāo *mech.* feed: ～装置 feed arrangement; feed gear; feeder

进德修业 jìndé-xiūyè improve one's virtue and refine one's achievements: 君子～, 欲及时也。(《周易》) The superior man improves his virtue and refines his achievements, in the hope that he will be ready if the chance offers.

进抵 jìndǐ (of troops) reach (a place)

进度 jìndù ① rate of progress (*or* advance): 加快～ quicken the pace (*or* tempo) ② planned speed; schedule: 我们已按照～完成了这道工序。We have finished this part of the process according to plan.

进度表 jìndùbiǎo progress chart

进而 jìn'ér *conj.* and then; after that: 我们工厂准备首先实现半自动化, ～实现完全自动化。Our factory plans first to achieve semiautomation and then proceed to complete automation.

进发 jìnfā set out; start: 列车向北京～。The train started for Beijing.

进犯 jìnfàn intrude into; invade: 打败～的敌人 beat back the invading enemy / 全歼～之敌 wipe out all the invading enemy

进风井 jìnfēngjǐng *min.* downcast (shaft)

进攻 jìngōng attack; assault; offensive: 做好～准备 get ready to take the offensive / 发起全面～ launch an all-out offensive

进攻性武器 jìngōngxìng wǔqì offensive weapon

进贡 jìngòng ① pay tribute (to a suzerain or emperor) ② grease (*or* oil) sb.'s palm

进化 jìnhuà evolution: 人是从类人猿～而来的。Man evolved from the anthropoid ape.

进化论 jìnhuàlùn the theory of evolution; evolutionism

进货 jìnhuò stock (a shop) with goods; lay in a stock of merchandise; replenish one's stock: 这家商店进了一批货。The shop laid in a new stock of goods.

进击 jìnjī advance on (the enemy)

进见 jìnjiàn call on (sb. holding high office); have an audience with

进爵 jìnjué *formal* be promoted to a higher rank

进军 jìnjūn march; advance: 向西北～ march into the Northwest / 吹响～的号角 sound the bugle to advance; sound the advance / 向科学技术现代化～ march towards the modernization of science and technology / 号召向沙漠～ a call to conquer the desert

进军号 jìnjūnhào bugle to advance

进口[1] jìnkǒu ① entrance ② *mech.* inlet: 鼓风～ blast inlet

进口[2] jìnkǒu ① enter port ② import

进口壁垒 jìnkǒu bìlěi import barrier

进口补贴 jìnkǒu bǔtiē import subsidy

进口港 jìnkǒugǎng port of entry

进口货 jìnkǒuhuò imported goods; imports

进口检疫 jìnkǒu jiǎnyì import quarantine

进口商 jìnkǒushāng importer

进口税 jìnkǒushuì import duties

进口限额 jìnkǒu xiàn'é import quota

进口许可证 jìnkǒu xǔkězhèng import license

进款 jìnkuǎn *inf.* income; receipts

进来 jìn·lái come (*or* get) in; enter: 让他～。Let him in. / 进屋来吧, 外面太冷了。Do come in, it's cold outside. / 门是关着的, 谁也进不来。The door is closed, no one can get in.

进来 ·jìn·lái (used after a verb) in (here): 她气喘吁吁地走～, 浑身湿透了。She came in panting and soaked to the skin. / 从窗口飞～一只燕子。A swallow flew in through the window. / 卡车开得～开不～? Can the truck drive in? / 有个人从外面跑进教室来。A man came running into the classroom.

进汽 jìnqì *mech.* admission: 高压～ high pressure admission

进取 jìnqǔ keep forging ahead; be eager to make progress; be enterprising: 永远保持谦虚和～的精神 always remain modest and keep forging ahead

进取心 jìnqǔxīn enterprising spirit; initiative; gumption; push

进去 jìn·qù go in; get in; enter: 你～看看, 我在门口等着。Go in and have a look, and I'll wait for you at the gate. / 明天我进城去。I'll go to town tomorrow. / 洞口太小, 我进不去。The opening of the cave is too small; I can't get in.

进去 ·jìn·qù (used after a verb) in (there): 把桌子搬～ move the table in / 冲～ rush in / 从旁门走进几个人去了。Some people went in through the side door. / 胡同太窄, 救护车开不～。The lane is too narrow for the ambulance to drive in. / 他对批评听不～。He turns a deaf ear to criticism.

进入 jìnrù enter; get into: ～阵地 get into position / ～决赛阶段 enter the finals / 运动已～高潮。The movement has reached a high tide. / 中国社会主义建设～了新的发展时期。China has entered a new stage of development in socialist construction.

进入角色 jìnrù juésè get inside the character that one is playing; enter into the spirit of a character; live one's part

进身之阶 jìnshēn zhī jiē stepping-stone (in one's official career)

进深 jìnshen the depth or length of a house, yard or room

进食 jìnshí take food; have one's meal

进士 jìnshì a successful candidate in the highest imperial examinations

进水闸 jìnshuǐzhá intake work; intake

进退 jìn-tuì ① advance and retreat: ～自如 free to advance or retreat (in a battle or game); have room for manoeuvre ② sense of propriety: 不知进退 bù zhī jìn-tuì

进退两难 jìn-tuì liǎng nán find it difficult to advance or to retreat—be in a dilemma

进退失据 jìn-tuì shī jù in a hopeless position

进退维谷 jìn-tuì wéi gǔ in a dilemma; between the devil and the deep blue sea

进位 jìnwèi math. carry (a number, as in adding)

进献 jìnxiàn offer or present (to one's superior)

进香 jìnxiāng offer incense in a temple; worship in a temple

进项 jìnxiang income; receipts

进行 jìnxíng ① be in progress; be underway; go on: 工作～得怎么样? How are you getting on with your work? / 勘探工作已经在～。 Prospecting is already in progress. / 手术～了六个小时。 The operation lasted six hours. / 大会明天继续～。 The conference continues tomorrow. ② carry on; carry out; conduct: 对党员～党的优良传统教育 educate Party members in the Party's fine tradition / ～一场激烈的争论 carry on a spirited debate / ～实地调查 make on-the-spot investigations / ～科学实验 engage in scientific experiment / ～改革的探索和试验 conduct exploratory and pilot reforms / ～表决 put a question to the vote / ～英勇斗争 wage a heroic struggle / ～亲切的谈话 have a cordial conversation / ～侵略 commit aggression / ～抵抗 put up a resistance / ～经济封锁 impose (or enforce) an economic blockade ③ be on the march; march; advance

进行曲 jìnxíngqǔ mus. march

进修 jìnxiū engage in advanced studies; take a refresher course: 出国～ go abroad for advanced studies / 教师的业务～ teachers' vocational studies

进修班 jìnxiūbān class for advanced studies

进修生 jìnxiūshēng graduate student

进言 jìnyán offer a piece of advice or an opinion: 大胆～ make so bold as to offer an opinion / 我向您进一言。 Let me give you a piece of advice.

进谒 jìnyè formal call on (a superior)

进一步 jìnyíbù go a step further; further: ～发展我们两国之间的友好合作关系 further develop the friendly relations and cooperation between our two countries / ～加强我军的革命化和现代化 take further steps to revolutionize and modernize our armed forces / 有了～的了解 have a better understanding / ～改善 make further improvements / ～开放 open the door wider

进益 jìnyì formal progress (in study, etc.)

进展 jìnzhǎn make progress; make headway: ～神速 advance at a miraculous pace / 工程～很顺利。 The project is making good progress. or Construction is proceeding smoothly. / 事情～如何? How are things going? / 谈判毫无～。 The talks have made no headway.

进占 jìnzhàn march on and take (a place)

进站 jìnzhàn (of a train) get into (or draw into, pull into) a station: 火车正在～，我们快点儿还来得及。 The train is just getting into (or drawing into, pulling into) the station. If we hurry we can catch it.

进帐 jìnzhàng income; receipts

进驻 jìnzhù enter and be stationed in; enter and garrison: 部队已～该市。 Troops have been garrisoned in that city.

近 jìn ① near; close: 歌声由远而～。 The singing came closer and closer. / 离国庆节很～了。 National Day is drawing near. or It'll soon be National Day. / ～百年史 the history of the last hundred years / ～在眼前 right before one's eyes; imminent ② approaching; approximately; close to: 年～六十 approaching sixty;

getting on for sixty / 观众～万人。 There were nearly 10,000 spectators. ③ intimate; closely related: 两家走得挺～。 The two families are on intimate terms. ④ easy to understand: 浅近 qiǎnjìn

近便 jìnbian close and convenient: 咱们找个～的饭馆吃点吧。 Let's have a snack at the nearest restaurant. / 来回挺～的,不用搭车。 It's no distance at all. There's no need to take a bus.

近臣 jìnchén courtier

近程 jìnchéng short range: ～雷达 short-range radar

近处 jìnchù vicinity; neighbourhood: ～一个饭馆也没有。 There are no restaurants nearby.

近刺 jìncì mil. short thrust; short lunge

近代 jìndài modern times: ～史 modern history

近道 jìndào shortcut

近地点 jìndìdiǎn astron. perigee

近东 jìndōng the Near East

近古 jìngǔ the age of recent antiquity (in Chinese history, the period from the 9th to the mid-19th century)

近海 jìnhǎi coastal waters; inshore; offshore: 我国～有丰富的水产资源。 Our country has rich offshore aquatic resources. / ～渔业 inshore fishing

近乎 jìnhu ① close to; little short of: ～荒谬的论点 an argument little short of being ridiculous; an argument bordering on the absurd / 他已～破产。 He is on the verge of bankruptcy. ② dial. intimate; friendly: 他们关系一直很～。 They have been intimate friends. ——see also 拉近乎 lā jìnhu; 套近乎 tào jìnhu

近郊 jìnjiāo outskirts of a city; suburbs; environs

近景 jìnjǐng photog. close shot

近况 jìnkuàng recent developments; how things stand: 中东～ recent developments in the Middle East / 多日不见来信,不知～如何? I haven't heard from you for a long time. How are things with you?

近来 jìnlái recently; of late; lately: ～她身体很不好。 Recently she has been rather unwell.

近邻 jìnlín near neighbour: 他家和我家是～。 His family and mine are close neighbours.

近路 jìnlù shortcut: 走～ take a shortcut

近年 jìnnián recent years: ～来 in recent years

近旁 jìnpáng nearby; near: 屋子～ near the house

近迫作业 jìnpò zuòyè mil. construction under fire; sapping

近期 jìnqī in the near future: ～内无大雨。 There won't be heavy rain in the coming few days. / ～预报 short-term forecast / ～目标 immediate objective

近前 jìnqián dial. nearby; near

近亲 jìnqīn close relative; near relation

近亲繁殖 jìnqīn fánzhí inbreeding

近亲婚姻 jìnqīn hūnyīn consanguineous marriage

近人 jìnrén ① a person of modern times or alive at present ② one's close associate

近日 jìnrì ① recently; in the past few days: ～未曾见到他。 I haven't seen him recently. ② within the next few days: 这项工程～即将完工。 The project will be completed within the next few days.

近日点 jìnrìdiǎn astron. perihelion

近世 jìnshì modern times

近视 jìnshì myopia; nearsightedness; shortsightedness: 她稍微有点～。 She is slightly myopic. or She is a bit nearsighted. / 政治上的～ political myopia

近视眼 jìnshìyǎn myopia; nearsightedness; shortsightedness: 他是～。 He is myopic (or nearsighted).

近视眼镜 jìnshì yǎnjìng spectacles for nearsighted person

近水楼台 jìn shuǐ lóutái waterside pavilion—a favourable position

近水楼台先得月 jìn shuǐ lóutái xiān dé yuè a waterside pavilion gets the moonlight first—a person in a favour-

able position gains special advantages

近似 jìnsì　approximate; similar: 这两幅画有些～。These two paintings are somewhat similar. / 游击队采用～木马计的方法夺取了敌人的据点。The guerrillas captured the enemy stronghold by a method similar to the Trojan horse stratagem.

近似读数 jìnsì dúshù　approximate reading

近似计算 jìnsì jìsuàn　approximate calculation

近似商 jìnsìshāng　approximate quotient

近似值 jìnsìzhí　approximate value

近岁 jìnsuì　*formal*　recent years

近体诗 jìntǐshī　"modern style" poetry, referring to innovations in classical poetry during the Tang Dynasty (618–907), marked by strict tonal patterns and rhyme schemes

近卫军 jìnwèijūn　*mil.*　guards (in European countries): 青年～ Youth Guards (in the former Soviet Union)

近义词 jìnyìcí　near synonym

近因 jìnyīn　immediate cause

近于 jìnyú　bordering on; little short of: ～荒唐 little short of preposterous; bordering on the absurd

近月点 jìnyuèdiǎn　*space*　perilune

近在咫尺 jìn zài zhǐchǐ　close at hand; well within reach

近战 jìnzhàn　fighting at close quarters; close combat

近朱者赤, 近墨者黑 jìnzhūzhě chì, jìnmòzhě hēi　he who stays near vermilion gets stained red, and he who stays near ink gets stained black—one takes on the colour of one's company

近作 jìnzuò　recent writings (of an author)

妗 jìn　see below

妗母 jìnmǔ　*dial.*　wife of one's mother's brother; aunt

妗子 jìnzi　*inf.*　① wife of one's mother's brother; aunt ② wife of one's wife's brother

劲 (勁、劤) jìn　① strength; energy: 他～儿大。He has great strength. / 这酒～大。This liquor is quite strong. / 我烧是退了, 可身上还是没～儿。My temperature is down, but I'm still feeling weak. ② vigour; spirit; drive; zeal: 保持革命战争时期的那么一股～ maintain the same vigour as in the years of revolutionary war / 扎扎实实埋头苦干的～儿 down-to-earth and hardworking spirit / 要鼓实～, 不要鼓虚～。We should encourage genuine enthusiasm, not sham enthusiasm. / 他跟我别着～哪! 能听我的吗? How can you expect him to listen to me, when he's still in a huff with me? ③ air; manner; expression: 你这骄傲～儿得好好改改。You've got to get rid of your arrogant ways. / 瞧他那高兴～儿。See how happy he looks. ④ interest; relish; gusto: 打扑克没～, 咱们去游泳吧。Playing cards is no fun; let's go swimming. ——see also jìng

劲头 jìntóu　*inf.*　① strength; energy ② vigour; spirit; drive; zeal: 工作有～ be full of drive in one's work / 小伙子们～十足。The young fellows are all enthusiasm.

荩¹ (藎) jìn　same as 荩草 jìncǎo

荩² (藎) jìn　*formal*　loyal; faithful; staunch: ～臣 a loyal minister; a loyal subject

荩草 jìncǎo　hispid arthraxon (*Arthraxon hispidus*)

浸¹ jìn　soak; steep; immerse: 把衣服放在肥皂水里～一会儿再洗。Soak the clothes in soapy water for a while before you wash them. / 他的衣服让汗～湿了。His clothes were soaked with sweat.

浸² (寖) jìn　*formal*　gradually; increasingly: 友情～厚。Friendship gradually deepened.

浸沉 jìnchén　soak; immerse

浸膏 jìngāo　*pharm.*　extract

浸剂 jìnjì　*pharm.*　infusion

浸礼 jìnlǐ　*Christianity*　baptism; immersion

浸礼会 jìnlǐhuì　the Baptist Church; the Baptists

浸泡 jìnpào　soak; immerse: ～棉籽 soak cottonseed

浸染 jìnrǎn　① be contaminated; be gradually influenced ② soak; infiltrate ③ dip-dye

浸软 jìnruǎn　macerate

浸润 jìnrùn　① soak; infiltrate: 春雨～着田野。The spring rain is soaking into the fields. ② *med.* infiltration

浸润之谮 jìnrùn zhī zèn　insidious slander which gradually soaks into the mind: ～, 肤受之诉, 不行焉, 可谓明也已矣。(《论语》) When a man is not influenced by slanders which are assiduously repeated or by complaints for which he feels a direct sympathy, he can be said to be perspicacious.

浸透 jìntòu　soak; saturate; steep; infuse: 汗水～了他的衣裳。His clothes were soaked with sweat. / 他伤口出的血～了绷带。The blood from his wound has soaked right through the bandage. / 他满脑子～了邪念。His mind is saturated with evil thoughts.

浸种 jìnzhǒng　seed soaking (in water)

浸渍 jìnzì　soak; ret; macerate: 亚麻～ flax retting / ～剂 soaker / ～液 maceration extract

烬 (燼) jìn　cinder: 灰烬 huījìn / 余烬 yújìn

晋¹ (晉) jìn　① enter; advance: 晋见 jìnjiàn ② promote: 加官晋爵 jiāguān-jìnjué

晋² (晉) Jìn　① a state in the Zhou Dynasty, occupying parts of what is now Shanxi, Shaanxi, Hebei, and Henan ② the Jin Dynasty (265–420) (see also 西晋 Xī Jìn; 东晋 Dōng Jìn) ③ another name for 山西 Shānxī

晋级 jìnjí　*formal*　rise in rank; be promoted

晋见 jìnjiàn　call on (sb. holding high office); have an audience with

晋剧 jìnjù　Shanxi opera ——see also 梆子腔 bāngzi-qiāng

晋升 jìnshēng　*formal*　promote to a higher office

晋谒 jìnyè　*formal*　call on (sb. holding high office); have an audience with

赆 (贐、賮) jìn　*formal*　a parting gift

赆仪 jìnyí　*formal*　farewell presents

靳 jìn　① *formal*　be stingy; grudge ② (Jìn) a surname

缙 jìn　*formal*　red silk

缙绅 jìnshēn　(in former times) government official; government official in retirement

禁 jìn　① prohibit; forbid; ban: 严禁 yánjìn ② imprison; detain: 监禁 jiānjìn ③ what is forbidden by law or custom; a taboo: 入国问禁 rù guó wèn jìn ④ forbidden area: 宫禁 gōngjìn ——see also jīn

禁闭 jìnbì　confinement (as a punishment): 关～ be placed in confinement

禁城 jìnchéng　the forbidden city—the imperial palace

禁地 jìndì　forbidden area; restricted area; out-of-bounds area

禁赌 jìndǔ　ban gambling

禁锢 jìngù　① debar from holding office (in feudal times) ② keep in custody; imprison ③ confine: 历代封建统治阶级都力图用礼教把妇女～起来。All through the feudal ages the ruling class did their best to shackle women with Confucian ethics.

禁忌 jìnjì ① taboo ② avoid; abstain from: ～辛辣油腻 abstain from peppery or greasy food ③ *med.* contraindication

禁绝 jìnjué totally prohibit; completely ban

禁军 jìnjūn imperial guards

禁例 jìnlì prohibitory regulations; prohibitions

禁猎 jìnliè prohibit hunting: ～期 a period when hunting is prohibited / ～区 an area where hunting is prohibited

禁令 jìnlìng prohibition; ban

禁脔 jìnluán a chunk of meat for one's exclusive consumption; one's exclusive domain: 视为～ regard as one's exclusive domain

禁区 jìnqū ① forbidden zone; restricted zone: 空中～ *mil.* restricted airspace / 针灸～ forbidden zone of acupuncture / 那里是～,不准过去。You can't go there. That place is out-of-bounds. ② (wildlife or plant) preserve; reserve; natural park ③ *football* penalty area ④ *basketball* restricted area

禁食 jìnshí fast: 穆斯林在斋月的时候要～。Muslims fast during the festival of Ramadan. / 她在开刀前得～一天。She had to fast for one day before her operation.

禁食疗法 jìnshí liáofǎ fasting treatment; starvation cure

禁书 jìnshū banned book

禁卫军 jìnwèijūn imperial guards

禁烟 jìnyān ban on opium-smoking and the opium trade

禁渔 jìnyú prohibit fishing: ～季 closed fishing season / ～区 forbidden fishing zone

禁欲 jìnyù be ascetic

禁欲主义 jìnyùzhǔyì asceticism

禁苑 jìnyuàn imperial park

禁运 jìnyùn embargo: 战时～品 contraband of war / 实行～ lay (or put, place) an embargo on (sth.) / 解除～ lift (or remove) the embargo on (sth.) / 属～之列 under an embargo

禁运品 jìnyùnpǐn contraband

禁止 jìnzhǐ prohibit; ban; forbid: 中国政府一贯主张全面～和彻底销毁核武器。The Chinese Government has consistently stood for the complete prohibition and thorough destruction of nuclear weapons. / 医生～他抽烟。The doctor forbids him to smoke. / ～砍伐树木。Felling trees is forbidden. / ～入内。No admittance. / 停车。No parking. / ～通行。No thoroughfare. or Closed to traffic. / ～倒垃圾。No garbage here. / ～招贴。Post no bills. / ～拍照。Cameras are forbidden.

禁制品 jìnzhìpǐn articles the manufacture of which is prohibited except by special permit; banned products

禁子 jìnzi (also 禁卒 jìnzú) *old* jailer

禁阻 jìnzǔ prohibit; ban; forbid; prevent; stop

觐 jìn ① present oneself before (a monarch) ② go on a pilgrimage

觐见 jìnjiàn present oneself before (a monarch); go to court; have an audience with

噤 jìn ① *formal* keep silent ② shiver: 寒噤 hánjìn

噤若寒蝉 jìn ruò hánchán as silent as a cicada in cold weather—keep quiet out of fear

jīng

泾（涇） Jīng (or 泾河 Jīnghé) a river rising in Ningxia and flowing into central Shaanxi where it empties into the Weihe (渭河)

泾渭不分 Jīng-Wèi bù fēn fail to distinguish between the good and the bad ——see also 泾渭分明 Jīng-Wèi fēnmíng

泾渭分明 Jīng-Wèi fēnmíng as different as the waters of the Jinghe and the Weihe—entirely different

京¹ jīng ① the capital of a country: 进～ go to the capital ② (Jīng) short for 北京 Běijīng

京² jīng ten million (an ancient numeral)

京白 jīngbái parts in Beijing opera spoken in Beijing dialect

京城 jīngchéng *old* the capital of a country

京都 jīngdū *old* the capital of a country

京官 jīngguān *old* officials with posts in the capital

京胡 jīnghú *jinghu*, a two-stringed bowed instrument with a high register; Beijing opera fiddle

京花 jīnghuā another name for 绢花 juànhuā

京华 jīnghuá *formal* the capital of a country: 誉满～。His fame resounded throughout the capital. /《～烟云》 *Passing Scenes in Beijing*

京畿 jīngjī *formal* the capital city and its environs

京剧 jīngjù Beijing opera

京派 jīngpài the Beijing school of Beijing opera (opp. 海派 hǎipài)

京腔 jīngqiāng *old* Beijing accent: 撇～ affect a Beijing accent

京师 jīngshī *formal* the capital of a country: ～大学堂 the Imperial University (the predecessor of Beijing University 北京大学)

京戏 jīngxì *inf.* Beijing opera

京油子 jīngyóuzi *old* Beijing sharper (from the traditional belief that the Beijing people are oily-tongued): 十个～说不过一个卫嘴子。Ten Beijing sharpers cannot talk down one Tianjin wrangler (a saying).

京韵大鼓 jīngyùn dàgǔ story-telling in Beijing dialect with drum accompaniment

京族 Jīngzú the Jing (Ching) nationality, or the Jings (Chings), inhabiting the Guangxi Zhuang Autonomous Region

茎（莖） jīng ① stem (of a plant); stalk ② a thing like a stem or stalk: 刀～ the handle of a knife / 剑～ the hilt of a sword ③ *m. formal* (for long, narrow things): 数～小草 a few small blades of grass / 数～白发 a few white hairs

经¹（經） jīng ① *text.* warp ② *Chin. med.* channels ③ *geog.* longitude: 东经 dōngjīng / 西经 xījīng ④ manage; deal in; engage in: 经商 jīngshāng ⑤ constant; regular: 经常 jīngcháng ⑥ scripture; sutra; canon; classic:《孝～》 *The Classic of Filial Piety* /《金刚～》 *The Diamond Sutra* ⑦ menses; menstruation ⑧ (Jīng) a surname

经²（經） jīng ① pass through; undergo; experience: 赴沪途中～宁而未停留。I passed through Nanjing on my way to Shanghai, but I didn't stay there. / ～卡拉奇回国 return home via (or by way of) Karachi / 我这辈子可～了不少事。I have seen quite a lot in my life. ② *prep.* as a result of; after; through: ～商定 it has been decided through consultation that / ～某人建议 upon sb.'s proposal / ～检查,产品质量合格。Examination confirmed that the quality of the products was up to specification. ③ stand; bear; endure: ～得起时间的考验 can stand the test of time / ～不起资产阶级糖衣炮弹的袭击 cannot withstand the sugarcoated bullets of the bourgeoisie ——see also jìng

经办 jīngbàn handle; deal with: 这件事是他～的。He

managed that affair.

经闭 jīngbì *Chin. med.* amenorrhoea

经编 jīngbiān *text.* warp knitting: ～针织物 warpknitted fabric

经产妇 jīngchǎnfù multipara

经常 jīngcháng ① day-to-day; everyday; daily: ～工作 day-to-day work / ～开支 running expenses ② *adv.* frequently; constantly; regularly; often: 领导干部一定要～关心群众疾苦。Leading cadres must always have the well-being of the masses at heart. / 这类问题是～发生的。This kind of problem frequently crops up. *or* This sort of thing is a common occurrence. / 他～上图书馆去。He goes to the library regularly. / ～化 become a regular practice; make a practice of it

经典 jīngdiǎn ① classics ② scriptures: 佛教～ Buddhist scriptures ③ classical: 马列主义～著作 Marxist-Leninist classics; classical works of Marxism-Leninism

经典力学 jīngdiǎn lìxué *phys.* classical mechanics

经典作家 jīngdiǎn zuòjiā author of a classic; classic

经度 jīngdù longitude

经断 jīngduàn *Chin. med.* menopause

经费 jīngfèi funds; outlay: ～不足 be short of funds

经风雨，见世面 jīng fēngyǔ, jiàn shìmiàn face the world and brave the storm; see life and stand its tests

经管 jīngguǎn be in charge of: ～财务 be in charge of financial affairs

经过 jīngguò ① pass; go through; undergo: 这汽车～动物园吗? Does this bus pass the Zoo? / ～长期磨练 undergo a long process of tempering ② *prep.* as a result of; after; through: ～充分讨论, 大家取得了一致意见。After thorough discussion unanimity was achieved. / ～抢救, 病人脱离了危险。The patient is out of danger after emergency treatment. ③ process; course: 事件的全部～ the whole course of the incident; the whole process from beginning to end / 事情的～是这样的。This is how it happened.

经互会 jīnghùhuì short for 经济互助委员会 Jīngjì Hùzhù Wěiyuánhuì

经籍 jīngjí *formal* ① Confucian classics ② books generally (with special reference to ancient texts)

经纪 jīngjì ① manage (a business) ② manager; broker

经纪人 jīngjìrén broker; middleman; agent: 房地产～ estate agent / 外汇～ foreign exchange broker

经济 jīngjì ① economy: 发展社会主义～ develop the socialist economy / 混合～ mixed economy / ～部门 branches of the economy; economic departments / ～地位 economic status; economic position / ～犯罪行为 economic crimes / ～封锁 economic blockade / ～平衡 economic equilibrium / ～失调 dislocation of the economy / ～信息 economic information ② of industrial or economic value; economic: 经济植物 jīngjì zhíwù ③ financial condition; income: ～宽裕 well-off; well-to-do / ～拮据 be hard up ④ economical; thrifty: ～实惠 economical and practical / ～地使用 use economically / 不～ costing too much; uneconomical ⑤ *formal* govern the country

经济舱 jīngjìcāng economy class

经济承包责任制 jīngjì chéngbāo zérènzhì economic responsibility system with contracted jobs

经济成分 jīngjì chéngfen sector of the economy; economic sector: 发展多种～ develop diverse sectors of the economy

经济地理学 jīngjì dìlǐxué economic geography

经济法规 jīngjì fǎguī laws and regulations pertaining to the economy; economic statutes

经济法庭 jīngjì fǎtíng economic tribunal

经济复苏 jīngjì fùsū economic resurgence; economic recovery

经济杠杆 jīngjì gànggǎn economic lever

经济合同 jīngjì hétong economic contract: ～仲裁委员会 economic contract arbitration committee

经济核算 jīngjì hésuàn economic accounting; business accounting: ～单位 business accounting unit

经济互助委员会 Jīngjì Hùzhù Wěiyuánhuì the Council of Mutual Economic Assistance (CMEA); Comecon (now dissolved)

经济环境 jīngjì huánjìng economic environment: 治理～ improve the economic environment

经济基础 jīngjì jīchǔ economic base; economic basis

经济技术开发区 jīngjì jìshù kāifāqū economic and technological development zone

经济开放区 jīngjì kāifàngqū open economic region

经济恐慌 jīngjì kǒnghuāng economic crisis

经济昆虫 jīngjì kūnchóng economic insects

经济立法 jīngjì lìfǎ economic legislation

经济联合体 jīngjì liánhétǐ economic association

经济林 jīngjìlín economic forest

经济命脉 jīngjì mìngmài economic lifeline; economic arteries; key branches of the economy

经济模式 jīngjì móshì economic mould

经济实体 jīngjì shítǐ economic entity: 所有企业都应办成自主经营的～。All enterprises should be turned into economic entities operating independently.

经济特区 jīngjì tèqū special economic zone

经济体制 jīngjì tǐzhì economic structure: ～改革 reform of the economic structure; economic restructuring / 集中统一的～ a unified and centralized economic structure

经济危机 jīngjì wēijī economic crisis: ～周期 economic crisis cycle

经济萧条 jīngjì xiāotiáo economic depression (*or* slump)

经济效益 jīngjì xiàoyì economic performance; economic results; economic effectiveness; economic benefit: 提高～ improve economic performance

经济学 jīngjìxué economics: ～家 economist

经济援助 jīngjì yuánzhù economic aid

经济杂交 jīngjì zájiāo *animal husbandry* commercial crossbreeding

经济植物 jīngjì zhíwù economic plants

经济制裁 jīngjì zhìcái economic sanctions

经济制度 jīngjì zhìdù economic system

经济秩序 jīngjì zhìxù economic order: 整顿～ rectify the economic order / 新的国际～ new international economic order

经济主义 jīngjìzhǔyì economism

经济作物 jīngjì zuòwù industrial crop; cash crop

经久 jīngjiǔ ① prolonged ② durable: ～耐用 durable; able to stand wear and tear

经久不息 jīngjiǔ bù xī prolonged: ～的掌声 prolonged applause

经理 jīnglǐ ① handle; manage ② manager; director

经历 jīnglì ① go through; undergo; experience: 现代科学技术正在～着一场伟大的革命。Modern science and technology are undergoing a great revolution. ② experience: 我们两国人民过去都有遭受帝国主义压迫的共同～。Our two peoples share the same experience of having been oppressed by imperialism in the past. / 他这人～多, 见识广。He's a man of wide knowledge and experience. / 个人～ personal experiences / 生活～ life experience

经略 jīnglüè *formal* plan and control (politically or militarily)

经纶 jīnglún *formal* statecraft; statesmanship: 大展～ put one's statecraft to full use; turn one's statesmanship to full account

经络 jīngluò *Chin. med.* main and collateral channels, regarded as a network of passages, through which vital

energy circulates and along which the acupuncture points are distributed

经脉　jīngmài　Chin. med.　passages through which vital energy circulates, regulating bodily functions

经密　jīngmì　text.　warp density; ends per inch

经年累月　jīngnián-lěiyuè　for years and years; year in year out

经期　jīngqī　(menstrual) period

经纱　jīngshā　text.　① warp ② end

经商　jīngshāng　engage in trade; be in business

经史子集　jīng-shǐ-zǐ-jí　classical works, historical works, philosophical works, and belles-lettres—the four traditional divisions of a Chinese library

经始　jīngshǐ　mil.　laying out the ground plan of a fortified work; tracing: ～线 trace

经手　jīngshǒu　handle; deal with: ～公款 handle public money / 这件事是他～的。He's the one who handled this matter. / ～人 person handling a transaction, particular job, etc.

经受　jīngshòu　undergo; experience; withstand; stand; weather: ～挫折 go through setbacks / ～各种考验 experience all sorts of trials; stand up to all tests; withstand all trials and tribulations / 这些花～不住寒气。These flowers cannot stand the cold.

经售　jīngshòu　sell on commission; deal in; distribute; sell: 这农村商店～邮票。The village shop sells postage stamps. / ～处 agency

经书　jīngshū　Confucian classics

经天纬地　jīngtiān-wěidì　have heaven and earth under one's control—have great ability

经停　jīngtíng　stop over: ～香港的飞机航班 air services with stops at Hong Kong

经痛　jīngtòng　same as 痛经 tòngjīng

经外奇穴　jīngwài qíxué　Chin. med.　extra nerve points, i. e. points not mentioned in the ancient medical classics

经纬度　jīngwěidù　geog.　latitude and longitude

经纬仪　jīngwěiyí　theodolite; transit: ～测量 transit survey

经线　jīngxiàn　① text.　warp ② meridian (line)

经销　jīngxiāo　same as 经售 jīngshòu

经心　jīngxīn　careful; mindful; conscientious: ～搜集各种资料 take great care to collect all kinds of data / 干什么工作都要～。One should be conscientious in any kind of work. / 你看宝玉何尝肯念书?他若一～，无有不能的。(《红楼梦》) Baoyu never showed any inclination to study, yet he'd only to glance at a book to master it.

经学　jīngxué　study of Confucian classics

经血　jīngxuè　Chin. med.　menses; menstruation

经验　jīngyàn　① experience: ～丰富 have rich experience; be very experienced / ～不足 lack experience; not be sufficiently experienced / 直接 (间接) ～ direct (indirect) experience ② go through; experience: 我从来没～过这样的艰难。I have never experienced such hardships.

经验批判主义　jīngyànpīpànzhǔyì　empirio-criticism (another name for 马赫主义 Mǎhèzhǔyì)

经验之谈　jīngyàn zhī tán　the wise remark of an experienced person; remark made by one who has had experience

经验主义　jīngyànzhǔyì　empiricism: ～者 empiricist

经意　jīngyì　careful; mindful

经营　jīngyíng　manage; operate; run; engage in: 统一 (分散) ～ unified (decentralized) management / ～少量家庭副业 engage in limited household side-line production / 发展多种～ promote a diversified economy / ～范围 the scope of operation / ～方式 the form of operation / 改善～ improve management and administration / ～管理良好 soundly managed / ～管理落后 backward operation and management

经营权　jīngyíngquán　power of management; managerial authority: 实行所有权与～分离 separate ownership from managerial authority

经由　jīngyóu　via; by way of: ～武汉去重庆 be bound for Chongqing via Wuhan

经院哲学　jīngyuàn zhéxué　scholasticism

经轴　jīngzhóu　text.　warp beam

经传　jīngzhuàn　① Confucian classics and commentaries on them; Confucian canon ② classical works; classics——see also 不见经传 bùjiàn jīngzhuàn

荆

荆　jīng　① chaste tree; vitex ② (Jīng) a surname

荆钗布裙　jīngchāi-bùqún　thornwood hairpins and hemp skirts—the plain, simple dress of a poor woman

荆棘　jīngjí　thistles and thorns; brambles; thorny undergrowth: ～丛生 overgrown with brambles

荆棘载途　jīngjí zài tú　a path overgrown with brambles—a path beset with difficulties

荆芥　jīngjiè　Chin. med.　jingjie (Schizonepeta tenuifolia)

荆条　jīngtiáo　twigs of the chaste tree (used for weaving baskets, etc.)

旌

旌　jīng　① an ancient type of banner hoisted on a featherdecked mast ② same as 旌表 jīngbiǎo

旌表　jīngbiǎo　(of an emperor) confer honours on the virtuous and the worthy (e. g. a loyal subject, a filial son, or a virtuous widow, usu. by ordering monuments erected to them)

旌旗　jīngqí　banners and flags

惊 (驚)

惊　jīng　① start; be frightened: 听到大坝出现险情，她心里一～。She started at the news that the dyke was in danger. / ～呆了 be stupefied ② surprise; shock; alarm: 惊动 jīngdòng ③ shy; stampede: 马～了。The horse shied. / 大雷雨～了牛群。The thunderstorm stampeded the cattle.

惊诧　jīngchà　surprised; amazed; astonished

惊动　jīngdòng　alarm; alert; disturb: 枪声～了森林中的鸟兽。The report of a gun startled the birds and animals in the forest. / 注意隐蔽，不要～敌人。Take good cover and don't alert the enemy. / 别为这么点儿小事～他。Don't trouble him about such a trifling matter.

惊愕　jīng'è　formal　stunned; stupefied

惊风　jīngfēng　Chin. med.　infantile convulsions: 急～ acute infantile convulsions

惊弓之鸟　jīng gōng zhī niǎo　a bird that starts at the mere twang of a bow-string—a badly frightened person

惊骇　jīnghài　formal　frightened; panic-stricken

惊呼　jīnghū　cry out in alarm: 他～："大事不好!" He cried out in alarm: "Oh, calamity!"

惊慌　jīnghuāng　(also 惊惶 jīnghuáng) alarmed; scared; panic-stricken: ～不安 jittery; nervy / ～的神色 frightened looks / 没有半点～ not in the least scared / ～地叫了起来 cry out in alarm / 不必～。Don't panic. or There's no cause for alarm.

惊慌失措　jīnghuāng shīcuò　frightened out of one's wits; seized with panic; panic-stricken

惊魂　jīnghún　the state of being frightened: ～稍定 barely recovered from a fright

惊魂未定　jīnghún wèi dìng　not yet recovered from a fright; still badly shaken

惊悸　jīngjì　formal　palpitate with fear

惊叫　jīngjiào　cry in fear; scream

惊厥　jīngjué　① faint from fear ② med.　convulsions

惊恐　jīngkǒng　alarmed and panicky; terrified; panic-stricken; seized with terror: ～失色 pale with fear

惊恐万状　jīngkǒng wànzhuàng　in a great panic; con-

vulsed with fear

惊雷 jīngléi　a sudden clap of thunder (often fig.)

惊梦 jīngmèng　wake from a dream with a start:《游园～》 *A Garden Stroll and a Dream Interrupted* (a *kunqu* drama)

惊奇 jīngqí　wonder; be surprised; be amazed: 孩子睁大眼睛，～地望着魔术师。The child stared with wonder at the magician.

惊扰 jīngrǎo　alarm; agitate

惊人 jīngrén　astonishing; amazing; alarming: ～的成就 astonishing (*or* amazing) achievements / ～的毅力 amazing willpower / 交通事故多得～。There is a horrifying number of traffic accidents. / 语不～死不休。(杜甫) If my lines don't startle others, in death I'll find no rest.

惊人之笔 jīngrén zhī bǐ　telling phrases

惊人之举 jīngrén zhī jǔ　masterstroke; *coup de maître*

惊叹 jīngtàn　wonder at; marvel at; exclaim (with admiration): 这些精美的牙雕，使大家～不已。The exquisite ivory carvings won everybody's admiration.

惊叹号 jīngtànhào　exclamation mark (!)

惊堂木 jīngtángmù　(also 惊堂板 jīngtángbǎn) (in former times) a wooden block used by a magistrate to strike the table in calling for attention or order

惊涛骇浪 jīngtāo-hàilàng　(often fig.) terrifying waves; a stormy sea: 充满～的一生 a life full of hazards

惊天动地 jīngtiān-dòngdì　shaking heaven and earth; earth-shaking; world-shaking: ～的伟业 a magnificent and earth-shaking feat

惊悉 jīngxī　be shocked to learn: ～某人不幸逝世 be distressed to learn of the passing away of sb.

惊喜 jīngxǐ　pleasantly surprised: ～地叫了起来 call out in happy astonishment

惊吓 jīngxià　frighten; scare: 这孩子受了～，睡得不安稳。The child has had a shock and isn't sleeping well.

惊险 jīngxiǎn　alarmingly dangerous; breathtaking; thrilling: ～动作 astounding feat / ～的表演 breathtaking performance / ～的场面 thrilling scene

惊险小说 jīngxiǎn xiǎoshuō　thriller

惊心动魄 jīngxīn-dòngpò　soul-stirring; profoundly affecting: ～的革命运动 stirring revolutionary movements

惊醒 jīngxǐng　① wake up with a start ② rouse suddenly from sleep; awaken: 一声巨响把他从睡梦中～。He was awakened by a terrific bang.

惊醒 jīngxing　sleep lightly; be a light sleeper: 他睡觉很～，有点响动都知道。He's a very light sleeper; any little noise disturbs him. / 睡觉～着点，有什么情况就叫我们。Sleep with your eyes half open, and call us should there be anything amiss.

惊讶 jīngyà　surprised; amazed; astonished; astounded: 他的无知令人～。His ignorance is astonishing.

惊疑 jīngyí　surprised and bewildered

惊异 jīngyì　surprised; amazed; astonished; astounded

惊蛰 jīngzhé　① the Waking of Insects—the 3rd of the 24 solar terms ② the day marking the beginning of the 3rd solar term (March 5, 6, or 7, when creation stirs after the winter sleep)——see also 节气 jiéqì，二十四节气 èrshí sì jiéqì

猄 jīng　see 黄猄 huángjīng

菁 jīng　see below

菁华 jīnghuá　essence; cream; quintessence

菁菁 jīngjīng　*liter.* lush; luxuriant

晶 jīng　① brilliant; glittering: 晶莹 jīngyíng ② quartz; (rock) crystal: 茶晶 chájīng ③ any crystalline substance: 晶体 jīngtǐ

晶格 jīnggé　*phys.* (crystal) lattice: 面心～ face-centred lattice / 体心～ body-centred lattice

晶粒 jīnglì　*phys.* crystalline grain; grain

晶石 jīngshí　spar

晶体 jīngtǐ　crystal

晶体点阵 jīngtǐdiǎnzhèn　same as 空间点阵 kōngjiāndiǎnzhèn

晶体发生学 jīngtǐfāshēngxué　crystallogeny

晶体管 jīngtǐguǎn　transistor: 硅～ silicon transistor / 锗～ germanium transistor / ～收音机 transistor radio

晶体学 jīngtǐxué　crystallography

晶莹 jīngyíng　sparkling and crystal-clear; glittering and translucent: 草上的露珠～发亮。The grass glistened with dewdrops. / 她有一颗～的心。She has a pure crystal-like heart.

晶状体 jīngzhuàngtǐ　*physiol.* crystalline lens

腈 jīng　*chem.* nitrile

腈纶 jīnglún　acrylic fibres

粳（粳、秔） jīng　same as 粳稻 jīngdào

粳稻 jīngdào　round-grained nonglutinous rice; *japonica* rice

粳米 jīngmǐ　polished round-grained nonglutinous rice

睛 jīng　eyeball: 定睛 dìngjīng

精 jīng　① refined; picked; choice: 精盐 jīngyán ② essence; extract: 杏仁儿～ almond extract ③ perfect; excellent: 精良 jīngliáng / 精彩 jīngcǎi ④ meticulous; fine; precise: 那个裁缝的手工很～。That tailor does skilful work. / 这花瓶工艺很～。This vase is a piece of exquisite workmanship. / ～修钟表 do a good job of repairing clocks and watches / ～收细打 careful reaping and threshing ⑤ smart; sharp; clever; shrewd: 这小鬼真～。That's a really smart kid. / 他做生意很～。He is a shrewd businessman. / 小算盘打得～ be selfish and calculating ⑥ skilled; conversant; proficient: ～于绘画 skilled in painting ⑦ energy; spirit: 精疲力竭 jīngpí-lìjié ⑧ sperm; semen; seed: 受精 shòujīng ⑨ *Chin. med.* the fundamental substance which maintains the functioning of the body; essence of life ⑩ goblin; spirit; demon: 狐狸精 húlíjīng ⑪ *dial.* (used before certain adjectives) extremely; very: 精湿 jīngshī

精白 jīngbái　pure white; spotlessly white: ～米 polished white rice

精薄 jīngbáo　*dial.* very thin: ～的被子 a very thin quilt

精兵 jīngbīng　picked troops; crack troops

精兵简政 jīngbīng-jiǎnzhèng　better troops and simpler administration; better staff and simpler administration; streamlined administration

精彩 jīngcǎi　brilliant; splendid; wonderful: ～的表演 a brilliant performance / 发言中最～的地方 most interesting parts of a speech / 这场球打得真～。This is an exciting game.

精巢 jīngcháo　*physiol.* spermary; testis; testicle

精诚 jīngchéng　*formal* absolute sincerity; good faith: ～合作 sincerely cooperate

精诚所至，金石为开 jīngchéng suǒ zhì, jīnshí wéi kāi　complete sincerity can affect even metal and stone

精虫 jīngchóng　*physiol.* spermatozoon

精粹 jīngcuì　succinct; pithy; terse

精打光 jīngdǎguāng　*dial.* with nothing left: 一锅饭吃得个～。Not a grain of rice was left after the meal.

精打细算 jīngdǎ-xìsuàn　careful calculation and strict budgeting: 对人力物力的使用要～。We must be meticulous in planning the use of men and material.

精当 jīngdàng　precise and appropriate: 用词～ precise

and appropriate wording; masterly choice of words

精到 jīngdào precise and penetrating

精雕细刻 jīngdiāo-xìkè (also 精雕细镂 jīngdiāo-xìlòu) work at sth. with the care and precision of a sculptor; work at sth. with great care

精豆子 jīngdòuzi *dial.* a bright and clever child

精读 jīngdú ① read carefully and thoroughly ② intensive reading

精度 jīngdù (short for 精密度) precision: 这台机床的～达到国家标准。The precision of this lathe is up to state requirements. / 高～ high precision

精干 jīnggàn ① (of a body of troops, etc.) small in number but highly trained; crack: 一支～的小分队 a small detachment of picked troops ② keen-witted and capable: 队长虽然年轻, 但很～。Young as he is, the team leader is very capable.

精耕细作 jīnggēng-xìzuò intensive and meticulous farming; intensive cultivation

精怪 jīngguài goblins; spirits; demons

精光 jīngguāng ① with nothing left: 票不到一个钟头就卖得～。All the tickets sold out in an hour. / 把衣服脱个～ strip off one's clothes / 刚插的秧苗被洪水冲得～。Every one of the newly planted seedlings was washed away by the flood. ② bright and clean; shiny: 锅擦得～发亮。The pot was polished to a high shine.

精悍 jīnghàn ① capable and vigorous ② pithy and poignant

精华 jīnghuá cream; essence; quintessence: 我国民族文化的～ the cream of our national culture / 去其糟粕, 取其～ discard the dross and select the essence

精加工 jīngjiāgōng *mech.* finish machining; precision work

精荚 jīngjiá *zool.* spermatophore

精简 jīngjiǎn retrench; simplify; cut; reduce: ～节约 simplify administration and practise economy / ～开支 cut expenses; retrench / ～会议 cut (the number of) meetings to a minimum / ～编制 reduce the staff / ～机构 simplify (or streamline) the administrative structure / ～报表 reduce the number of forms; cut down paper work / 国家机关都必须实行～的原则。Every organ of state must apply the principle of efficient and simple administration.

精矿 jīngkuàng *min.* concentrate

精力 jīnglì energy; vigour; vim: 把毕生～献给共产主义事业 devote the energies of a lifetime to the cause of communism / 集中～解决主要矛盾 concentrate one's effort on solving the main contradiction

精力充沛 jīnglì chōngpèi full of vim and vigour; vigorous; energetic

精练 jīngliàn concise; succinct; terse: 语言～ succinct language

精炼 jīngliàn ① *metall.* refine; purify: 火法～ fire refining / 真空～ vacuum refining ② same as 精练 jīngliàn

精良 jīngliáng excellent; superior; of the best quality: 制作～ of excellent workmanship / 装备～ well-equipped

精量播种 jīngliàngbōzhòng *agric.* precision drilling: ～机 precision (seed) planter; precision (seed) drill

精灵 jīnglíng ① spirit; demon ② *dial.* (of a child) clever; smart; intelligent

精馏 jīngliú *chem.* rectification: ～酒精 rectified alcohol / ～塔 rectifying (or fractionating) tower

精美 jīngměi exquisite; elegant: ～的刺绣 elegant embroidery / 包装～ beautifully packaged / ～的食品 delicacies

精密 jīngmì ① precise; accurate: ～的观察 accurate (or close) observation ② precision: ～机床 precision machine tool / ～仪器 precision instrument / ～铸造 precision casting

精密度 jīngmìdù precision: 机床的～ the precision of lathes

精妙 jīngmiào exquisite: 书法～ write a beautiful hand / ～的手工艺品 exquisite handicrafts

精明 jīngmíng astute; shrewd; sagacious: ～的政治家 an astute statesman / ～的小伙子 a bright young fellow / 你骗不了他; 他～着呢, 不会上当。You can't fool him; he's much too clever for that.

精明强干 jīngmíng qiánggàn intelligent and capable; able and efficient

精囊 jīngnáng *physiol.* seminal vesicle

精疲力竭 jīngpí-lìjié (also 精疲力尽 jīngpí-lìjìn) exhausted; worn out; tired out; spent

精辟 jīngpì penetrating; incisive: 进行～的分析 make a penetrating analysis / ～的论述 a brilliant exposition

精品 jīngpǐn ① fine works (of art): 艺术～ art treasures ② quality goods; articles of fine quality

精巧 jīngqiǎo exquisite; ingenious: ～的牙雕 exquisite ivory carving / 构造～ ingeniously constructed

精确 jīngquè accurate; exact; precise: ～的统计 accurate statistics / 下一个～的定义 give a precise definition / 这个回答大致不差, 但不～。This answer is only approximate, not exact.

精肉 jīngròu *dial.* lean meat

精锐 jīngruì crack; picked: ～部队 crack troops; picked troops

精深 jīngshēn profound: ～的理论 a comprehensive and profound theory

精神 jīngshén ① spirit; mind; consciousness: 国际主义～ the spirit of internationalism / 崇高的～ noble spirit / 作好～准备 be mentally prepared / 给予～上的支持 give moral support / ～上的负担 a load on one's mind / ～支柱 spiritual (or ideological) prop / ～财富 spiritual wealth / ～空虚 be spiritually barren ② essence; gist; spirit: 传达文件的～ convey (or pass on) the gist of a document / 领会社论的～ try to understand the thrust of an editorial / 贯彻代表大会的～ act in the spirit of the congress / 译者没有体会原文的～。The translator failed to capture the spirit of the original. / 他们想从她那儿打听上头的～。They tried to sound her out about the intentions of the higher-ups.

精神 jīngshen ① vigour; vitality; drive: ～饱满 full of vigour (or vitality); energetic / 没有～ listless; languid / 振作～ bestir oneself; summon up one's energy; get up steam ② lively; spirited; vigorous; smart: 他穿上军装显得格外～。The army uniform made him look especially impressive. / 那孩子大大的眼睛, 怪～的。That child with the big eyes is certainly full of life. / 这孩子长得多～! What a cute child!

精神病 jīngshénbìng mental disease; mental disorder; psychosis: ～人 a mental patient / ～学 psychiatry / ～医生 psychiatrist / ～院 psychiatric hospital; mental home (or hospital, institution)

精神错乱 jīngshén cuòluàn mentally deranged; insane

精神抖擞 jīngshén dǒusǒu full of energy (or vitality); vigorous: ～地迈着大步 walk with long, vigorous strides

精神分裂症 jīngshén fēnlièzhèng schizophrenia

精神分析 jīngshén fēnxi psychoanalysis: ～学家 psychoanalyst

精神鼓励 jīngshén gǔlì moral encouragement

精神贵族 jīngshén guìzú intellectual aristocrats

精神焕发 jīngshén huànfā be in high spirits; one's spirits rise: ～地继续向前行进 continue one's advance in a mood of keen exhilaration

精神枷锁 jīngshén jiāsuǒ spiritual (or mental) shackles

精神疗法 jīngshén liáofǎ psychotherapy

精神面貌 jīngshén miànmào mental attitude; mental outlook

精神生活 jīngshén shēnghuó cultural life

精神食粮 jīngshén shíliáng nourishment for the mind; spiritual food

精神世界 jīngshén shìjiè inner world; mental world

精神衰弱 jīngshén shuāiruò psychasthenia

精神头儿 jīngshéntóur *inf.* vigour; energy; vim: 瞧他～多足! How energetic he is!

精神文明 jīngshén wénmíng spiritual civilization: 促进社会主义物质文明和～的建设 promote the construction of socialist material and spiritual civilization

精神污染 jīngshén wūrǎn spiritual contamination; cultural contamination; ideological pollution

精神状态 jīngshén zhuàngtài state of mind; mental outlook

精审 jīngshěn *formal* (of writings, plans, opinions, etc.) accurate and comprehensive; carefully thought-out

精湿 jīngshī *dial.* soaking wet: 他的衣服被雨淋得～。His clothes were soaked with rain.

精瘦 jīngshòu *dial.* very lean: 浑身～ all skin and bone

精梳 jīngshū *text.* combing: ～机 comber / ～毛纺 worsted spinning / ～纱 combed yarn

精饲料 jīngsìliào concentrated feed; concentrate

精髓 jīngsuǐ marrow; pith; quintessence: 马克思主义的～ the quintessence of Marxism

精通 jīngtōng be proficient in; have a good command of; master: ～业务 be proficient in professional work / ～英语 have a good command of English / 各级领导干部要努力使自己成为～政治工作和业务工作的专家。Leading cadres at all levels must strive hard to become expert in both political and vocational work.

精微 jīngwēi profound and subtle: 探索宇宙的～ explore the mysteries of the universe

精卫填海 jīngwèi tián hǎi the mythical bird *jingwei* trying to fill up the sea with pebbles—dogged determination to achieve one's purpose

精细 jīngxì meticulous; fine; careful: 手工十分～ show fine workmanship / ～的计算 careful calculation / 考虑问题很～ think matters over carefully; be circumspect / 这件上衣做工～。This jacket is well-tailored.

精心 jīngxīn meticulously; painstakingly; elaborately: ～护理 nurse with the best of care / ～设计，～施工 be meticulous in design and construction; painstakingly design and carefully construct / ～策划的阴谋 a carefully calculated plot; an elaborately planned conspiracy / ～炮制 elaborately cook up

精选 jīngxuǎn ① *min.* concentration ② carefully chosen; choice: 用～的原料制成 made of choice material

精研 jīngyán make a detailed (*or* intensive) study

精盐 jīngyán refined salt; table salt

精液 jīngyè *physiol.* seminal fluid; semen

精一 jīngyī *formal* single-minded; concentrated

精义 jīngyì essential ideas; essentials: 《英语语法～》 *Essentials of English Grammar*

精益求精 jīng yì qiú jīng constantly improve sth.; keep improving: 对技术～ be constantly improving (*or* perfecting) one's skill

精英 jīngyīng essence; cream; flower: 周代青铜器是我国古代艺术的～。Zhou bronzes are the finest specimens of ancient Chinese art. / 当代青年的～ the flower of modern youth / 象棋～ chess master

精轧 jīngzhá *metall.* finish rolling: ～机 finishing mill; finisher

精湛 jīngzhàn consummate; exquisite: ～的技巧 consummate skill; superb technique / 工艺～ exquisite workmanship; perfect craftsmanship

精整 jīngzhěng *metall.* finishing

精制 jīngzhì make with extra care; refine: ～品 highly finished products; superfines

精致 jīngzhì fine; exquisite; delicate: ～的丝织品 fine silks / ～的烟盒 an exquisite cigarette case

精忠 jīngzhōng utterly (*or* unreservedly) loyal

精忠报国 jīngzhōng bàoguó serve one's country with unreserved loyalty

精装 jīngzhuāng (of books) clothbound; hardback; hardcover

精装本 jīngzhuāngběn *de luxe* edition

精壮 jīngzhuàng able-bodied; strong

精子 jīngzǐ *physiol.* sperm; spermatozoon

兢

jīng see below

兢兢业业 jīngjīngyèyè cautious and conscientious: 多少年来，他工作一直～。He'd been doing his job conscientiously for many years.

鲸

jīng whale: 雌～ cow whale / 雄～ bull whale / 幼～ whale calf

鲸波 jīngbō ocean waves

鲸目动物 jīngmù dòngwù cetacean

鲸吞 jīngtūn swallow like a whale; annex (territory) ——see also 蚕食鲸吞 cánshí-jīngtūn

鲸须 jīngxū baleen; whalebone

鲸油 jīngyóu whale oil; blubber: 割～ flench

鲸鱼 jīngyú whale

鲸仔 jīngzǎi whale calf

鼱

jīng see 鼩鼱 qújīng

jǐng

井¹

jǐng ① well: 一口～ a well / 打～ sink a well; drill a well ② sth. in the shape of a well: 油井 yóujǐng ③ the twenty-second of the twenty-eight constellations (二十八宿) into which the celestial sphere was divided in ancient Chinese astronomy (consisting of eight stars in Gemini)

井²

jǐng neat; orderly: 井然 jǐngrán

井壁 jǐngbì *petroleum* the wall of an oil well: ～取心 sidewall coring / ～取样 wall sampling

井场 jǐngchǎng *petroleum* well site

井底 jǐngdǐ ① the bottom of a well ② *min.* shaft bottom; pit bottom: ～车场 shaft station / ～矿仓 shaft pocket

井底之蛙 jǐngdǐ zhī wā a frog in a well—a person with a very limited outlook —— see also 井蛙 jǐngwā

井冈山 Jǐnggāngshān the Jinggang Mountains

井灌 jǐngguàn well irrigation

井架 jǐngjià ① *petroleum* derrick: 轻便～ portable derrick (*or* mast) ② *min.* headframe; headgear; pitheadframe

井井有条 jǐngjǐng yǒu tiáo in perfect order; shipshape; methodical: ～地工作 work methodically / 各种仪器、工具摆得～。All the instruments and tools are kept in perfect order. / 他当过机关干部，喜欢把什么都弄得～的。He had once been an office worker and liked everything to be shipshape and orderly.

井口 jǐngkǒu ① the mouth of a well ② *min.* pithead ③ *petroleum* wellhead: ～气 wellhead gas; casinghead gas / ～装置 wellhead assembly

井喷 jǐngpēn *petroleum* blowout

井然 jǐngrán *formal* orderly; neat and tidy; shipshape; methodical: 秩序～ in good order

井然有序 jǐngrán yǒu xù in good order; orderly; me-

thodical

井绳 jǐngshéng　a rope for drawing water from a well

井水不犯河水 jǐngshuǐ bù fàn héshuǐ　well water does not intrude into river water——I'll mind my own business, you mind yours

井台 jǐngtái　a raised platform around a well

井田制 jǐngtiánzhì　the well-field system (a farming system supposed to have existed in the feudal period, according to which arable lands in a fief were divided into units of nine squares of 100 *mu* each, like the Chinese character for a "well" 井; the eight outer squares were dealt out to eight peasant families as their private fields, on which they worked and from the produce of which they derived their sole means of support; and the eight families tilled together the central square of the "well," which was the public field, its yearly yield going to the granary of the feudal lord, the hereditary master of the land)

井筒 jǐngtǒng　*min.* pit shaft: ～隔间 shaft compartment／～掘进 shaft excavation

井蛙 jǐngwā　well frog—a person with a very limited outlook: ～之见 a very limited outlook; a very narrow-minded view／～不可语于海者,拘于虚也。《庄子》 You can't discuss the ocean with a well frog—he's limited by the space he lives in.

井下 jǐngxià　in the pit; under the shaft: ～作业 operation in the pit; underpit operation／他在～工作。He works at (or down) the pit.

井斜 jǐngxié　*petroleum* well deflection; well deviation: 第一口井～是1.7度。The first well had a deviation of 1.7 degrees from the vertical.

井盐 jǐngyán　well salt

阱(穽) jǐng　trap; pitfall; pit: 陷阱 xiànjǐng

刭(剄) jǐng　*formal* cut the throat: 自刭 zìjǐng

胼 jǐng　*chem.* hydrazine

颈(頸) jǐng　neck——see also gěng

颈动脉 jǐngdòngmài　carotid
颈项 jǐngxiàng　neck
颈椎 jǐngzhuī　cervical vertebra
颈子 jǐngzi　neck

景[1] jǐng　① view; scenery; scene: 雪～ a snow scene／西湖十～ the ten sights of the West Lake ② situation; condition: 背景 bèijǐng／晚景 wǎnjǐng ③ scenery (of a play or film): 换～ change of scenery ④ scene (of a play): 第三幕第一～ Act III, scene 1 ⑤ (Jǐng) a surname

景[2] jǐng　admire; revere; respect: 景慕 jǐngmù

景德镇 Jǐngdézhèn　Jingdezhen (a town in Jiangxi Province, one of China's leading porcelain-manufacturing centres)

景观 jǐngguān　landscape: 自然～ natural landscape／岩溶～ karst landscape

景教 Jǐngjiào　Nestorianism: 大秦～流行中国碑 the Nestorian Tablet (the oldest relic of Christianity in China, first set up in a Nestorian church in the Tang capital at Chang'an in 781, unearthed in 1625)

景况 jǐngkuàng　situation; circumstances: 她家的～越来越好了。Things are getting easier and easier for her family.

景慕 jǐngmù　*formal* esteem; revere; admire
景片 jǐngpiàn　a piece of (stage) scenery; flat
景颇族 Jǐngpōzú　the Jingpo (Chingpaw) nationality, or the Jingpos (Chingpaws), inhabiting Yunnan Province

景气 jǐngqì　prosperity; boom ——see also 不景气 bùjǐngqì

景色 jǐngsè　scenery; view; scene; landscape: 深秋～ a late autumn scene／南方～ southern landscape／海上看日出,～特别美丽。At sea one can get a particularly beautiful view of the sunrise.

景深 jǐngshēn　*photog.* depth of field
景泰蓝 jǐngtàilán　*cloisonné* enamel; cloisonné
景天 jǐngtiān　*bot.* red-spotted stonecrop (Sedum erythrostictum)

景物 jǐngwù　scenery: 站在山上眺望山下的～ stand on the top of the hill looking down at the scenery below

景象 jǐngxiàng　scene; sight; picture: 一派丰收～ one vast panorama of bumper crops／呈现出一片团结战斗的～ present a scene of unity and militancy

景仰 jǐngyǎng　respect and admire; hold in deep respect: 怀着无限～的心情 with boundless respect and admiration

景遇 jǐngyù　*formal* circumstances; one's lot

景致 jǐngzhì　view; scenery; scene: 从塔顶可以看到全城的～。The tower commands a view of the whole town.／一下雪,这里的～就更美了。This place looks even more beautiful after a fall of snow.

儆 jǐng　warn; admonish: 惩一儆百 chéng yī jǐng bǎi
儆戒 jǐngjiè　warn; admonish; exhort

憬 jǐng　*formal* awake; come to understand
憬然 jǐngrán　*formal* awake; aware
憬悟 jǐngwù　wake up to reality; come to see the truth, one's error, etc.

警 jǐng　① alert; vigilant: 警戒 jǐngjiè／机警 jǐng ② warn; alarm: 警告 jǐnggào ③ alarm: 火警 huǒjǐng ④ short for 警察 jǐngchá

警报 jǐngbào　alarm; warning; alert: 拉～ sound the alarm (or siren)／台风～ a typhoon warning／战斗～ combat alert

警报器 jǐngbàoqì　siren; alarm

警备 jǐngbèi　guard; garrison: ～森严 be heavily guarded／～区 garrison command／～司令部 garrison headquarters

警策 jǐngcè　*formal* ① whip a horse on ② pithy; aphoristic: ～之言 pithy sayings

警察 jǐngchá　police; policeman: 女～ policewoman
警察局 jǐngchájú　police headquarters; police station
警车 jǐngchē　police car; police van
警笛 jǐngdí　① police whistle ② siren
警服 jǐngfú　police uniform

警告 jǐnggào　① warn; caution; admonish: 我～你,你再这样就没你的好。I'm warning you, if you do that again there'll be trouble.／对敌人的军事挑衅提出严重～ issue a serious warning to the enemy against their military provocations／我们一再～他不要跟那种人来往。We repeatedly admonished him not to associate with that sort of people. ② warning (as a disciplinary measure): 给予～处分 give sb. a disciplinary warning

警告信号 jǐnggào xìnhào　*transportation* warning signal

警官 jǐngguān　police officer
警棍 jǐnggùn　policeman's baton; truncheon

警戒 jǐngjiè　① warn; admonish ② be on the alert against; guard against; keep a close watch on: 采取～措施 take precautionary measures／沿公路放出～ post guards along the highway／～部队 outpost troops; security force (or detachment)

警戒色 jǐngjièsè　*zool.* warning (or aposematic) coloration

警戒水位 jǐngjiè shuǐwèi　warning water level; warning stage

警戒线 jǐngjièxiàn　cordon; security line

警句 jǐngjù　aphorism; epigram

警觉 jǐngjué　vigilance; alertness: 引起～ arouse vigilance / 政治～性 political alertness / 海防战士～地注视着出现在海面上的黑点。The coastal guard kept a watchful eye on the black spot that had appeared out at sea.

警铃 jǐnglíng　alarm bell

警犬 jǐngquǎn　police dog

警世 jǐngshì　warn or admonish the world: 冯梦龙《～通言》Feng Menglong's *Comprehensive Words to Admonish the World* (a collection of stories)

警探 jǐngtàn　police detective

警惕 jǐngtì　be on guard against; watch out for; be vigilant: 这个人搞阴谋, 你得～。Be on your guard against his tricks. / 要特别～个人野心家和阴谋家。We must especially watch out for careerists and conspirators. / ～地守卫着大桥 vigilantly guard the bridge / 保持高度～ maintain sharp vigilance / 丧失～ drop one's guard; be off one's guard / ～性 vigilance

警亭 jǐngtíng　police box

警卫 jǐngwèi　(security) guard: 执行～任务 be on guard duty / ～人员 security personnel / ～室 guardroom / ～团 guards regiment / ～员 bodyguard

警务 jǐngwù　police affairs; police service

警醒 jǐngxǐng ① same as 惊醒 jǐngxǐng ② (also 警省 jǐngxǐng) watchful; alert

警钟 jǐngzhōng　alarm bell; tocsin ——see also 敲警钟 qiāo jǐngzhōng

jìng

劲 (勁) jìng　strong; powerful; sturdy: ～松 sturdy pines —— see also jìn

劲吹 jìngchuī　(of the wind) blow hard: 北风～。A north wind was blowing hard.

劲敌 jìngdí　formidable adversary; strong opponent (*or* contender)

劲风 jìngfēng　a strong wind

劲旅 jìnglǚ　*formal* strong contingent; crack force: 这个厂的篮球队可算是全市的一支～。This factory's basketball team is one of the strongest in the city.

净¹ (淨、凈) jìng ① clean: ～水 clean water / 擦～ wipe sth. clean / 这件褂子没洗～。This jacket hasn't been properly washed. ② make clean: ～一～桌面儿。Clean the top of the table. ③ (used after a verb) finished; with nothing left: 钱都用～了。The money is all used up. / 把药喝～。Drink your medicine up. ④ net: ～收入 net income / ～出口 net export / ～进口 net import ⑤ *adv.* all; all the time: ～说不干 all talk, no action / 他～说瞎话。He lies all the time. / 别～打岔。Don't keep interrupting. / 别～装穷。Don't keep pretending to be so poor. / 这几天～刮大风。It's been very windy these last few days. / 屋子里～是土。There is dirt everywhere in the room. ⑥ *adv.* only; merely; nothing but: ～吃肉不行。It's not good to eat only meat. / 他～说好听的。He talks about nothing but pleasant things.

净² (淨、凈) jìng　painted-face role (one of the four main roles in traditional opera, the other three being 生 shēng, 旦 dàn, and 丑 chǒu, so called from the variety of intricate and startling patterns in brilliant colours painted on the faces of the players; the *jing* or painted-face actor represents a man of virile or rough character, who may be a warrior, a general, a minister, a brigand, or a demon, singing and speaking in a full raucous voice rising to protracted enunciation of tremendous volume)

净产值 jìngchǎnzhí　net output value

净高 jìnggāo　*archit.* clear height

净荷载 jìnghèzài　net load

净化 jìnghuà　purify: ～空气 purify the air / ～废水 purify liquid waste / ～灵魂 purify one's soul / ～塔 purifying column

净价 jìngjià　net price

净街 jìngjiē　clear the streets of people and traffic

净尽 jìngjìn　completely used up; with nothing left: 消灭～ utterly annihilate

净角 jìngjué　same as 净² jìng

净利 jìnglì　net profit

净面 jìngmiàn　wash one's face

净身 jìngshēn　(of a man) be castrated

净手 jìngshǒu ① *dial.* wash one's hands ② *euph.* relieve oneself

净水厂 jìngshuǐchǎng　water treatment plant

净桶 jìngtǒng　*euph.* nightstool; closestool; commode

净土 jìngtǔ　the Pure Land (a paradise into which anyone is reborn who calls on the name of the Buddha Amitabha with sincere devotion and in which one can attain final Enlightenment)

净土宗 jìngtǔzōng　the Pure Land Sect (which emphasizes salvation by faith in Amitabha)

净余 jìngyú　net balance; remainder; surplus: 除去开支, ～二百元。After deducting expenses, we have 200 *yuan* left.

净增 jìngzēng　net increase; net growth: 人口～率 net growth rate of population

净值 jìngzhí　net worth; net value: 出口～ net export value / 进口～ net import value

净重 jìngzhòng　net weight

净赚 jìngzhuàn　make a net profit of; clear: 他的买卖每月～一万元。His business clears ten thousand *yuan* a month.

径¹ (徑、逕) jìng ① footpath; path; track: 山～ a mountain path ② way; means: 捷径 jiéjìng ③ *adv.* straight; directly; straightaway: ～行办理 deal with the matter straightaway / ～回广州 go straight back to Guangzhou / 来稿请～寄编辑部。Please send your contributions directly to the editorial department.

径² (徑) jìng　(short for 直径) diameter: 口径 kǒujìng / 半径 bànjìng

径迹 jìngjì　*phys.* track: 蜕变～ decay track / ～起点 track origin

径流 jìngliú　runoff: 地表～ surface runoff / 地下～ groundwater runoff

径情直遂 jìng qíng zhí suì　as smoothly as one would wish: 战胜困难的过程往往不是～的。The process of overcoming a difficulty is usually not as direct and smooth as one would wish. / 事物是往返曲折的, 不是～的。Events have their twists and turns and do not follow a straight line.

径赛 jìngsài　*sports* track: ～项目 track events

径庭 jìngtíng　*formal* very unlike: 大相径庭 dà xiāng jìngtíng

径向 jìngxiàng　*phys.* radial: ～间隙 radial clearance / ～轴承 radial bearing

径直 jìngzhí　*adv.* straight; directly; straightaway: 登山队～向主峰进发。The mountaineers made straight for the summit. / 飞机将～飞往昆明。The plane will fly nonstop to Kunming. / ～写下去吧, 等写完了再修改。

Just go on writing and do the polishing when you've finished.

径自 jìngzì *adv.* without leave; without consulting anyone: 会没开完，他～走了。He left abruptly in the middle of the meeting.

经(經)

jīng *text.* warping ——see also jīng

胫(脛)

jīng *physiol.* shin

胫骨 jìnggǔ shin bone; tibia

痉(痙)

jīng see below

痉病 jìngbìng *Chin. med.* febrile disease with symptoms such as convulsions, opisthotonos, trismus, etc.

痉挛 jìngluán convulsion; spasm: 食管～ spasm of the esophagus; esophagospasm

竞(競)

jìng ① compete; contend; vie: 鹰击长空，鱼翔浅底，万类霜天～自由。(毛泽东) Eagles cleave the air, Fish glide in the limpid deep; Under freezing skies a million creatures contend in freedom. ② *formal* strong; forceful

竞渡 jìngdù ① boat race: 龙舟～ dragon boat regatta ② swimming race

竞技 jìngjì sports; athletics: ～场 arena

竞技状态 jìngjì zhuàngtài form (of an athlete): ～好 in good form; in top form / ～不好 not in good form; out of form; off one's game

竞赛 jìngsài contest; competition; emulation; race: 社会主义劳动～ socialist labour emulation drive / 体育～ athletic contest (*or* competition) / 军备～ arms (*or* armament) race

竞相 jìngxiāng compete; vie: 两国正在～部署中程导弹。The two powers are competing in the deployment of intermediate-range missiles. / ～效尤 vie with each other in following a bad example

竞选 jìngxuǎn enter into an election contest; campaign for (office); run for: ～总统 run for the presidency / ～活动 electioneering / ～演说 election speech / ～运动 election campaign

竞争 jìngzhēng compete: 市场～ competition for markets / 自由～ free competition / ～能力 competitive power / ～优势 competitive edge / 富有～力 (of a price, product, etc.) highly competitive

竞争价格 jìngzhēng jiàgé competitive price

竞争性 jìngzhēngxìng competitiveness: ～贬值 competitive depreciation (*or* devaluation)

竞走 jìngzǒu heel-and-toe walking race

竟¹

jìng ① finish; complete: 未～之业 unaccomplished cause; unfinished task ② throughout; whole: ～夜 the whole night; throughout the night ③ *formal* in the end; eventually: 有志者事竟成 yǒuzhìzhě shì jìng chéng

竟²

jìng *adv.* ① unexpectedly; actually: 这么陡的峭壁，谁知他～爬上去了。Who would have expected that he could climb up that steep cliff? ② go so far as to; go to the length of; have the impudence (*or* effrontery) to

竟敢 jìnggǎn actually dare; have the audacity; have the impertinence: 你～跟我讲这种话！How dare you say that to me! / 敌人～如此嚣张，我们不能不予以回击。When the enemy is on the rampage like this, we've got to hit back.

竟然 jìngrán *adv.* ① unexpectedly; to one's surprise; actually: 这样宏伟的建筑，～只用十个月的时间就完成了。To think that such a magnificent building was completed in ten months! / 想不到他们～把一座荒山变

成了花果山。Who would have thought that they could turn a barren hill into an orchard? ② go so far as to; go to the impudence (*or* effrontery) to: ～不顾事实 go so far as to disregard the facts

竟日 jìngrì the whole day; all day long: 盘恒～ linger about all day long

竟至 jìngzhì *adv.* actually go so far as to: ～如此之多 actually so much (*or* so many)

竟自 jìngzì *adv.* unexpectedly; to one's surprise; actually: 虽然没有人教他，他摸索了一段时间，～学会了。Though nobody taught him, he learnt it all by himself through trial and error.

敬

jìng ① respect: 致敬 zhìjìng ② respectfully: 敬请 jìngqǐng ③ offer politely: ～茶 serve tea (to a guest) / ～烟 offer a cigarette (to a guest) / ～你一杯! To your health!

敬爱 jìng'ài respect and love: ～的领袖 esteemed (*or* respected) and beloved leader; beloved leader

敬辞 jìngcí term of respect; polite expression

敬而远之 jìng ér yuǎn zhī stay at a respectful distance from sb.

敬奉 jìngfèng ① piously worship ② offer respectfully; present politely

敬服 jìngfú respect and admire

敬告 jìnggào *pol.* beg to inform: ～读者 notice to readers

敬鬼神而远之 jìng guǐshén ér yuǎn zhī keep one's distance from the gods and spirits while showing them respect—stay at a respectful distance from sb.

敬贺 jìnghè *pol.* congratulate with respect; send respectful greetings to

敬候 jìnghòu *pol.* await respectfully: ～佳音。We are waiting to hear the good news.

敬酒 jìngjiǔ propose a toast; toast

敬酒不吃吃罚酒 jìngjiǔ bù chī chī fájiǔ refuse a toast only to drink a forfeit—submit to sb.'s pressure after first turning down his request; be constrained to do what one at first refused to

敬老爱幼 jìnglǎo-àiyòu respect the aged and cherish the young

敬老院 jìnglǎoyuàn home of respect for the aged; old folks' home

敬老尊贤 jìnglǎo-zūnxián respect the aged and honour the worthy

敬礼 jìnglǐ ① salute; give a salute ② *pol.* (used at the end of a letter): 此致～ salutations; with high respect; with best wishes

敬慕 jìngmù respect and admire

敬佩 jìngpèi esteem; admire: 我对他的文才非常～。I have the highest esteem for his literary ability. / 大家以～的目光望着他。Everybody looked at him admiringly.

敬启者 jìngqǐzhě I beg to state; I wish to inform you (stock opening phrase in a letter)

敬请 jìngqǐng *pol.* invite respectfully: ～光临。Your presence is cordially requested. / ～斧正。Will you be kind enough to correct and improve my poor work? / ～指教。Kindly give me your advice.

敬若神明 jìng ruò shénmíng same as 奉若神明 fèng ruò shénmíng

敬上 jìngshàng (also 敬启 jìngqǐ) (used after the signature in a letter to one's senior or superior) yours respectfully; yours sincerely

敬挽 jìngwǎn (used on funeral scrolls) with deep condolences from sb.

敬畏 jìngwèi hold in awe and veneration; revere

敬谢不敏 jìng xiè bù mǐn I beg to be excused; I'm sorry but I can't do it

敬仰 jìngyǎng revere; venerate: 深受人民的爱戴和～ command deep love and reverence among the people

敬意 jìngyì .respect; tribute: 表示衷心的～ extend one's heartfelt respects; pay sincere tribute / 顺致崇高的～。I avail myself of this opportunity to express to Your Excellency the assurances of my high consideration. or Please accept, Your Excellency, the assurances of my high consideration. / 不成～ just a small token of my regard (said when presenting a gift)

敬赠 jìngzèng (used when sending a gift) with compliments: 某某～ with compliments from so-and-so / 作者～ with the author's compliments

敬重 jìngzhòng deeply respect; revere; honour: 大家都十分～这位老红军战士。We all have great respect for the veteran Red Army man.

敬祝 jìngzhù pol. (used at the end of a letter) I wish you: ～身体健康。I wish you the best of health.

靓 jìng formal dress up; make up ——see also liàng

靓妆 jìngzhuāng formal (of a woman) gorgeously dressed

靖 jìng ① quiet; peaceful; tranquil: 安靖 ānjìng① ② formal make tranquil; pacify: ～乱 quell (or put down) a rebellion / ～边 pacify the border region

境 jìng ① border; boundary: 在本省～内 within the boundaries of this province ② place; area; territory: 敌～ enemy territory ③ condition; situation; circumstances: 困境 kùnjìng

境地 jìngdì condition; circumstances: 处于狼狈的～ be in a sorry plight; be in a predicament / 陷入完全孤立的～ land oneself in utter isolation

境界 jìngjiè ① boundary ② extent reached; plane attained; state; realm: 理想～ ideal state; ideal / 他的诗有时达到了晚清诗人的～。His poetry sometimes rises to the level of the late Qing poets.

境况 jìngkuàng (financial) condition; circumstances: ～不佳 in straitened circumstances / ～不错 be well-off; be comfortably off

境域 jìngyù ① condition; circumstances ② area; realm: 大同～ the realm of Great Harmony

境遇 jìngyù circumstances; one's lot: 极困难的～ extremely adverse circumstances / 悲惨的～ a hard lot

静（靜） jìng still; quiet; calm: ～～地躺着 lie motionless / 海浪～下来了。The sea is now calm. / 请～一～。Please be quiet.

静场 jìngchǎng still the theatre (i.e. see to it that the audience leave the theatre after the end of a performance or show)

静电 jìngdiàn static electricity: ～除尘器 electrostatic precipitator / ～纺纱 electrostatic spinning / ～感应 electrostatic induction / ～荷 electrostatic charge / ～计 electrometer / ～学 electrostatics / ～印刷 xerography

静观 jìngguān watch quietly: ～默察 sit back and watch

静荷载 jìnghèzài archit. dead load

静街 jìngjiē same as 净街 jìngjiē

静力学 jìnglìxué phys. statics: 气体～ aerostatics

静脉 jìngmài phisiol. vein

静脉点滴 jìngmài diǎndī intravenous drip

静脉曲张 jìngmài qūzhāng varix; varicosity

静脉炎 jìngmàiyán phlebitis

静脉注射 jìngmài zhùshè intravenous injection

静谧 jìngmì formal quiet; still; tranquil

静默 jìngmò ① become silent: 会场上又是一阵～。Another spell of silence fell upon the meeting room. ② mourn in silence; observe silence: 为悼念革命先烈, 全体起立,～致哀。All rose in silent tribute to the memory of the revolutionary martyrs.

静穆 jìngmù solemn and quiet

静悄悄 jìngqiāoqiāo very quiet: 屋子里～的。It was very quiet in the room.

静态 jìngtài phys. static state: ～电阻 static resistance / ～平衡 static equilibrium / ～特性 static characteristic

静物 jìngwù still life: ～写生 paint still life

静物画 jìngwùhuà still-life picture; still life

静养 jìngyǎng rest quietly to recuperate; convalesce: 希望你安心～。I hope you'll set aside your worries and have a good rest.

静园 jìngyuán stilling the park (i.e. time for visitors to leave the park after it closes for the day)

静止 jìngzhǐ static; motionless; at a standstill: 相对～的状态 a state of relative rest / 生活永远不是～的。Life is never at a standstill. / 形而上学宇宙观用孤立的、～的和片面的观点去看世界。The metaphysical world outlook sees things as isolated, static and one-sided.

静坐 jìngzuò ① sit quietly ② sit still as a form of therapy ③ sit-down; sit-in: ～罢工 sit-down (strike) / ～示威 sit-in (demonstration); sit-down (protest)

镜 jìng ① looking glass; mirror: 湖平如～。The lake is as smooth as a mirror. ② lens; glass: 放大镜 fàngdàjìng / 墨镜 mòjìng

镜花水月 jìnghuā-shuǐyuè flowers in a mirror or the moon in the water—an illusion

镜框 jìngkuàng ① picture frame ② spectacles frame

镜片 jìngpiàn lens

镜台 jìngtái dressing table

镜头 jìngtóu ① camera lens: 远摄～ telephoto lens / 可变焦距～ zoom lens / 长焦距～ telelens; long focus lens ② shot; scene: 特写～ close-up (shot) / 伪装～ process shot

镜匣 jìngxiá a wooden case with a looking glass and other toilet articles; dressing case

镜像 jìngxiàng phys. mirror image

镜鱼 jìngyú same as 鲳鱼 chāngyú

镜子 jìngzi ① mirror; looking glass ② inf. glasses; spectacles

jiǒng

坰 jiōng formal outermost suburbs

扃 jiōng formal ① a bolt or hook for fastening a door from outside ② shut a door

jiǒng

迥 jiǒng formal widely different: 他病前病后～若两人。He doesn't look like the same person after his illness.

迥别 jiǒngbié totally different

迥然 jiǒngrán far apart; widely different

迥然不同 jiǒngrán bù tóng utterly different; not in the least alike

迥异 jiǒngyì totally different: 他们二人性情～。They are diametrically opposed in temperament.

炯 jiǒng see below

炯炯 jiǒngjiǒng *formal* (of eyes) bright; shining: 他的一双眼睛～发光。 He has a pair of bright piercing eyes.

炯炯有神 jiǒngjiǒng yǒu shén (of eyes) bright and piercing: 他矮而且瘦,可是目光～。 He was short and thin, with, however, a pair of gleaming, penetrating eyes.

窘 jiǒng ① in straitened circumstances; hard up: 他一度生活很～。 He was rather hard up for a time. ② awkward; embarrassed; ill at ease: 他唱着唱着走了调,～得不敢往台下看。 He began to sing out of tune and he was too embarrassed to look at the audience. ③ embarrass; disconcert: 这个问题～得他无言可答。 The question embarrassed him so much that he was quite at a loss for an answer.

窘促 jiǒngcù *formal* ① poverty-stricken ② hard pressed; embarrassed; in a predicament

窘境 jiǒngjìng awkward situation; predicament; plight

窘况 jiǒngkuàng awkward situation; predicament; plight

窘迫 jiǒngpò ① poverty-stricken; very poor: 生活～ live in poverty ② hard pressed; embarrassed; in a predicament: 处境～ find oneself in a predicament

窘态 jiǒngtài an embarrassed look: ～百出 be most embarrassed; to one's great embarrassment

窘相 jiǒngxiàng an embarrassed look

jiū

纠[1] jiū entangle: 纠缠 jiūchán

纠[2] jiū gather together: 纠合 jiūhé

纠[3] jiū correct; rectify: 有错必纠 yǒu cuò bì jiū

纠察 jiūchá ① maintain order at a public gathering ② picket: ～队 pickets / ～线 picket line

纠缠 jiūchán ① get entangled; be in a tangle: 防止在枝节问题上～不休 avoid endless quibbling over side issues / 完成侦察任务要紧,不要与敌人～。 Be sure to accomplish your scouting mission; don't get tied down by the enemy. ② nag; worry; pester: 他忙着呢,别～他了。 He's busy. Stop pestering him.

纠缠不清 jiūchán bù qīng too tangled up to unravel: 问题～。 The problem has been made very complicated.

纠纷 jiūfēn dispute; issue: 无原则～ an unprincipled dispute / 国与国之间的～ disputes between countries / 调解～ mediate an issue / 挑起～ stir up trouble

纠葛 jiūgé entanglement; dispute: 他们之间发生了一点～。 There's a dispute between them.

纠合 jiūhé *derog.* gather together: ～一伙流氓 get together (*or* round up) a bunch of hoodlums / ～党羽,图谋不轨 gather together one's followers for criminal purposes

纠集 jiūjí *derog.* get together; muster: ～一批打手 gather together a bunch of thugs / ～残部 muster the remaining forces

纠结 jiūjié intertwine; entangle

纠偏 jiūpiān rectify a deviation; correct an error

纠正 jiūzhèng correct; put right; redress: ～错误 correct a mistake; redress an error / ～姿势 correct sb.'s posture / ～不正之风 check unhealthy tendencies / 问题处理不当的,应予～。 Cases which have not been handled properly should be put right.

究 jiū ① study carefully; go into; investigate: ～其根源 trace sth. to its source ② *adv. formal* actually; really; after all: ～应如何办理? How should this really be dealt with? / ～系何因,尚待深查。 The actual cause awaits further investigation.

究办 jiūbàn investigate and deal with: 依法～ investigate and deal with according to law

究诘 jiūjié *formal* interrogate; cross-examine

究竟 jiūjìng ① outcome; what actually happened: 大家都想知道个～。 Everybody wants to know what actually happened. / 不管什么事,他总爱问个～。 He always likes to get to the heart of a matter, whatever it may be. ② *adv.* (used in questions to press for an exact answer) actually; exactly: 明天的会～谁去参加? Who is actually going to the meeting tomorrow? / 你们～要什么? What exactly do you want? / 这一～是什么意思? Whatever does this mean? / 他～上哪儿去了? Where on earth is he? ③ *adv.* after all; anyway; finally: 他～经验丰富,让他负责这项工作最合适。 After all, he is very experienced, so it is only suitable to put him in charge of the job. / 他～是你弟弟。 Anyway he is your younger brother.

鸠 jiū turtledove: 绿～ green pigeon

鸠合 jiūhé same as 纠合 jiūhé

鸠集 jiūjí same as 纠集 jiūjí

鸠形鹄面 jiūxíng-húmiàn gaunt and emaciated

赳 jiū see below

赳赳 jiūjiū valiant; gallant

赳赳武夫 jiūjiū wǔfū a stalwart, martial man

阄（鬮） jiū lot: 抓阄儿 zhuājiūr / 拈阄儿 niānjiūr

揪 jiū ① hold tight; seize: 他～着绳子不撒手。 He held tightly to the rope and wouldn't let go. / 他～着他的领子打他。 He seized him by the collar and hit him. / ～住一个小偷 grab a thief / 他承认了错误,就不要再～住不放。 Now that he has admitted his mistake, we should not keep picking on him. ② pull; tug; drag: ～花 pluck flowers / 别那么使劲～绳子。 Don't pull so hard at the rope.

揪辫子 jiū biànzi seize sb.'s queue—seize upon sb.'s mistakes or shortcomings; capitalize on sb.'s vulnerable point

揪出 jiūchū uncover; ferret out: ～幕后操纵者 uncover (*or* ferret out) the wirepuller

揪揪 jiūjiu *dial.* creased; crumpled: 衣服还～着呢,得熨一下。 The dress is full of creases and needs to be ironed.

揪痧 jiūshā *Chin. med.* a popular treatment for sunstroke or other febrile diseases by repeatedly pinching the patient's neck, etc. to achieve congestion

揪心 jiūxīn *dial.* ① anxious; worried: 小杨到现在还没有回来,真叫人～。 Xiao Yang's still not back. I'm really getting worried. ② heartrending; agonizing; gnawing: 伤口痛得～。 There was a gnawing pain from the wound.

啾 jiū see below

啾唧 jiūjī *onom.* the chirping of birds or insects

啾啾 jiūjiū *onom.* ① the chirping of birds ② a piteous cry

鬏 jiū bun; knot; chignon: 她头上梳了一个～儿。 She does her hair up in a knot.

jiǔ

九 jiǔ ① nine: ～车间 No. 9 Workshop / ～连 the

Ninth Company ② each of the nine nine-day periods beginning from the day after the Winter Solstice ③ many; numerous: 三弯～转 many twists and turns / ～曲桥 a zigzag bridge

九重霄 jiǔchóngxiāo　same as 重霄 chóngxiāo

九二〇 jiǔèrlíng　*biochem.*　gibberellin

九宫 jiǔgōng　same as 宫调 gōngdiào

九宫格儿 jiǔgōnggér　squared paper for practising Chinese calligraphy

九归 jiǔguī　rules for doing division with a one-digit divisor on the abacus

九级风 jiǔjífēng　*meteorol.*　force 9 wind; strong gale

九节狸 jiǔjiélí　zibet; large Indian civet

九斤黄鸡 jiǔjīnhuángjī　(also 九斤黄 jiǔjīnhuáng) a breed of Chinese chicken famous for its meat and size

九九表 jiǔjiǔbiǎo　multiplication table

九九归一 jiǔ jiǔ guī yī　when all is said and done; in the last analysis; after all: ～, 还是他的话对. All things considered, what he says is right.

九流三教 jiǔliú sānjiào　same as 三教九流 sānjiào jiǔliú

九牛二虎之力 jiǔ niú èr hǔ zhī lì　the strength of nine bulls and two tigers—tremendous effort: 费了～ strain oneself to the limit; use every ounce of one's strength; make herculean efforts

九牛一毛 jiǔ niú yī máo　a single hair out of nine ox hides—a drop in the ocean

九泉 jiǔquán　*liter.* the Nine Springs—the nether world; grave: 含笑于～ rest happy in one's grave

九泉之下 jiǔquán zhī xià　down in the Nine Springs—in the nether regions; after death: 兄弟同气连枝, 假如不和不睦, 那爹娘在～, 心上必然不乐. (《今古奇观》) If brothers, who are like branches from the same tree, should fail to live in perfect accord with each other, their parents who now dwell below in the Nine Springs must surely feel sorrow in their hearts.

九死一生 jiǔ sǐ yī shēng　a narrow escape from death; survival after many hazards

九天 jiǔtiān　*liter.* the highest heavens; heaven: 飞流直下三千尺, 疑是银河落～. (李白) Down it cascades a sheer three thousand feet—As if the Silver River [i.e. the Milky Way] were falling from Heaven!

九头鸟 jiǔtóuniǎo　① nine-headed bird (a fabulous bird whose appearance was formerly regarded as a bad omen) ② a crafty fellow

九尾狐 jiǔwěihú　nine-tailed fox—a crafty and villainous person

九五之尊 jiǔ wǔ zhī zūn　the imperial throne

九霄云外 jiǔxiāo yúnwài　beyond the highest heavens—far, far away: 把个人安危抛到～ cast personal safety to the winds; disregard one's safety / 他把那事丢到了～了. He has forgotten completely about it. / 匡超人此时恍若亲见瑶宫仙子, 月下嫦娥, 那魂灵都飘在～去了. (《儒林外史》) Kuang felt that he was gazing at a goddess and his spirit had flown to heaven.

九一八事变 Jiǔ Yībā Shìbiàn　the September 18th Incident (the seizure of Shenyang in 1931 by the Japanese invaders, as a step towards their occupation of the entire Northeast)

九一四 jiǔyīsì　*pharm.* "914" or neosalvarsan (a modification of 六〇六 liùlíngliù)

九音锣 jiǔyīnluó　nine-toned gong (another name for 云锣 yúnluó)

九月 jiǔyuè　① September ② the ninth month of the lunar year; the ninth moon

九州 jiǔzhōu　① the nine divisions of China in remote antiquity ② a poetic name for China: ～生气恃风雷. (龚自珍) Only in wind and thunder can the country show its vitality. ③ (Jiǔzhōu) Kyushu

九族 jiǔzú　the nine degrees of kindred (construed as either the nine generations from one's great-great-grandfather down to one's great-great-grandson; or four generations of one's paternal relations, three generations of one's maternal relations, and two generations of one's wife's relations)

久 jiǔ　① for a long time; long: 我们～不见面了. We haven't seen each other for a long time. / 很～以前 long ago ② of a specified duration: 两个月之～ for as long as two months / 来了有多～? How long have you been here?

久别重逢 jiǔ bié chóngféng　meet again after a long separation; reunite after a long parting

久病成医 jiǔ bìng chéng yī　prolonged illness makes a doctor of a patient

久病床前无孝子 jiǔ bìng chuángqián wú xiàozǐ　in cases of chronic sickness, there are no dutiful children at the bedside

久等 jiǔděng　wait for a long time: 对不起, 让你～了. Sorry to have kept you waiting.

久而久之 jiǔ ér jiǔ zhī　in the course of time; with the lapse of time; as time passes: 只要你注意搜集, ～, 资料就丰富了. If you keep on collecting, in time you'll have a wealth of data.

久旱逢甘雨 jiǔ hàn féng gānyǔ　have a welcome rain after a long drought—have a long-felt need satisfied

久航高度 jiǔháng gāodù　*aviation* altitude for maximum endurance

久航速度 jiǔháng sùdù　*aviation* speed for maximum endurance

久后 jiǔhòu　long afterwards; in the future

久假不归 jiǔ jiǎ bù guī　put off indefinitely returning sth. one has borrowed; appropriate sth. borrowed

久久 jiǔjiǔ　for a long, long time: 老乡们把医疗队送到村口, ～不肯回去. The villagers stood for a long time at the edge of the village waving good-bye to the medical team. / 他知道这消息后心里很难过, ～不能平静. He was deeply grieved to learn the news, and it was a long time before he calmed down. / 他的话～地回响在我的耳边. His words were still ringing in my ears long after he said them.

久留 jiǔliú　stay long: 有要事在身, 不敢～. I can't stay long because I have some important business to attend to.

久违 jiǔwéi　*pol.* how long it is since we last met; I haven't seen you for ages

久闻大名 jiǔ wén dàmíng　I've long heard about your great name (used when meeting sb. for the first time) ——see also 如雷贯耳 rú léi guàn ěr

久仰 jiǔyǎng　*pol.* I've heard about you for a long time (used when meeting sb. for the first time); I've long been looking forward to meeting you; I'm very pleased to meet you

久已 jiǔyǐ　for a long time; long since: ～忘怀 long since forgotten / ～不在人世 long since dead

久远 jiǔyuǎn　far back; ages ago; remote: 年代～ of the remote past; age-old; time-honoured

玖[1]　jiǔ　nine (used for the numeral 九 on cheques, etc., to avoid mistakes or alterations)

玖[2]　jiǔ　a black jade-like stone

灸　jiǔ　*Chin. med.*　moxibustion

韭(韮)　jiǔ　fragrant-flowered garlic; (Chinese) chives: 青～ young chives; chive seedlings

韭菜 jiǔcài　fragrant-flowered garlic; (Chinese) chives

韭黄 jiǔhuáng　hotbed chives

酒 jiǔ alcoholic drink; wine; liquor; spirits

酒吧间 jiǔbājiān bar; barroom

酒保 jiǔbǎo *old* bartender; barkeeper

酒不醉人人自醉 jiǔ bù zuì rén rén zì zuì liquor does not intoxicate, one intoxicates oneself

酒菜 jiǔcài ① food and drink ② food to go with wine or liquor

酒厂 jiǔchǎng brewery; winery; distillery

酒池肉林 jiǔchí-ròulín lakes of wine and forests of meat—unbridled debauchery and licentiousness (from the legend that Zhou Xin 纣辛, the cruel and infamous last ruler of the Shang Dynasty, had a lake of wine made at his palace, caused the trees to be hung with meats, and set men and women, naked, to chase each other before his eyes)

酒刺 jiǔcì acne

酒德 jiǔdé propriety in drinking: 没有～ offend propriety in drinking

酒店 jiǔdiàn ① wineshop; public house ② hotel (used in names of hotels)

酒饭 jiǔfàn food and drink

酒疯 jiǔfēng the silly behaviour of a person when drunk; a drunken fit: 发酒疯 fā jiǔfēng / 撒酒疯 sā jiǔfēng

酒逢知己千杯少,话不投机半句多 jiǔ féng zhījǐ qiān bēi shǎo, huà bù tóujī bàn jù duō for a congenial friend a thousand toasts are too few; in a disagreeable conversation one word more is too many

酒馆 jiǔguǎn public house; pub

酒鬼 jiǔguǐ ① *offens.* drunkard; sot ② winebibber; toper

酒酣 jiǔhān *formal* the drinking is at its height: ～，临邛令前奏琴曰：“窃闻长卿好之，愿以自娱。”(《史记》) When the drinking was at its height the magistrate came forward with a lute and, presenting it to Xiangru, said, "I have heard that you are fond of this instrument. I wonder if you could be persuaded to amuse yourself with a selection?"

酒酣耳热 jiǔhān-ěrrè warmed with wine; mellow with drink: ～，仰而赋诗。Warmed with the wine, the company fell to composing poems.

酒后 jiǔhòu after drinking; under the influence of wine (*or* alcohol): ～戏笑之言 some remarks made in jest after drinking; a few jesting remarks made under the influence of wine / ～失态 forget oneself after a few drinks / ～失言 make an indiscreet remark under the influence of alcohol

酒后开车 jiǔhòu kāichē driving a car under the influence of alcohol; drunk driving

酒后吐真言 jiǔhòu tǔ zhēnyán wine in, truth out

酒壶 jiǔhú wine pot; flagon

酒花 jiǔhuā *bot.* hops

酒会 jiǔhuì cocktail party

酒家 jiǔjiā ① *old* wineshop; tavern: 借问～何处有, 牧童遥指杏花村。(杜牧) "Pardon," he says, "can you tell me a place where wine is served?" "There's Apricot Village in the distance," says a little buffalo-tender. ② restaurant (used in names of restaurants): 广东～ Guangdong Restaurant ③ same as 酒保 jiǔbǎo

酒浆 jiǔjiāng *formal* wine

酒窖 jiǔjiào wine cellar

酒精 jiǔjīng ethyl alcohol; alcohol

酒精比重计 jiǔjīng bǐzhòngjì spirit gauge

酒精灯 jiǔjīngdēng spirit lamp; alcohol burner

酒精炉 jiǔjīnglú alcohol heater

酒精中毒 jiǔjīng zhòngdú alcoholism

酒具 jiǔjù drinking set

酒帘 jiǔlián (in former times) a wineshop sign in the form of a streamer

酒量 jiǔliàng capacity for liquor: 他～很大。He's a heavy drinker. *or* He can hold a lot of liquor. / ～不济 have little capacity for wine; not be a good drinker

酒令 jiǔlìng drinkers' wager game

酒楼 jiǔlóu restaurant (used in names of restaurants): 广东～ Guangdong Restaurant

酒母 jiǔmǔ distiller's yeast

酒囊饭袋 jiǔnáng-fàndài wine skin and rice bag—a good-for-nothing

酒酿 jiǔniàng (also 酒娘 jiǔniáng) fermented glutinous rice

酒器 jiǔqì drinking vessel

酒钱 jiǔqian tips

酒曲 jiǔqū distiller's yeast

酒肉朋友 jiǔròu péngyou wine-and-meat friends; fair-weather friends

酒色 jiǔ-sè wine and women—sensual pursuits: 沉湎～ abandon oneself to wine and women; indulge in sensual pursuits / ～过度 be dissipated in wine and sex

酒色财气 jiǔ-sè-cái-qì wine, women, wealth, and temper—generally considered to be the four archevils of life

酒色之徒 jiǔ-sè zhī tú debauchee; libertine

酒石酸 jiǔshísuān tartaric acid: ～锑钾 antimony potassium tartrate

酒食 jiǔshí food and drink

酒肆 jiǔsì *formal* wineshop; public house

酒提 jiǔtí wine dipper

酒徒 jiǔtú winebibber; toper

酒望 jiǔwàng same as 酒帘 jiǔlián

酒窝 jiǔwō (also 酒涡 jiǔwō) dimple: 她笑起来脸上有个～。She has a dimple in her cheek when she smiles.

酒席 jiǔxí feast; banquet

酒醒 jiǔxǐng awake from a drunken sleep (*or* a drunken stupor)

酒兴 jiǔxìng elation caused by intoxicants; rapture with wine: ～正浓 be buoyant with drunken elation

酒性 jiǔxìng alcoholic strength: 他～发作了。He is feeling the effects of the wine.

酒筵 jiǔyán feast; banquet

酒宴 jiǔyàn feast; banquet

酒药 jiǔyào yeast for brewing rice wine or fermenting glutinous rice

酒靥 jiǔyè *dial.* dimple

酒意 jiǔyì a tipsy feeling: 已有几分～ be slightly tipsy; be mellow

酒糟 jiǔzāo distillers' grains

酒糟鼻 jiǔzāobí acne rosacea; brandy nose

酒盅 jiǔzhōng (also 酒钟 jiǔzhōng) a small handleless wine cup

酒足饭饱 jiǔzú-fànbǎo have drunk and eaten to one's heart's content

酒醉 jiǔzuì be drunk: ～失言 make an indiscreet remark under the influence of alcohol

jiù

旧(舊) jiù ① past; bygone; old: ～社会 the old society / ～时代 former times / ～思想 old way of thinking; timeworn ideas / ～的传统观念 outdated conventional ideas ② used; worn; old: ～衣服 used (*or* old) clothes / 买～的 buy sth. secondhand / 你的鞋～了, 买一双新的吧。Your shoes are worn. Buy a new pair. ③ former; onetime: 旧都 jiùdū ④ old friendship; old friend: 故旧 gùjiù

旧案 jiù'àn ① a court case of long standing: 积年～都已经清理完毕。Court cases of many years' standing

have now been cleared. ② old regulations; former practice

旧病 jiùbìng　old (or chronic) complaint

旧病复发 jiùbìng fù fā　① have a recurrence of an old illness; have an attack of a recurrent sickness; have a relapse ② relapse into one's old bad habits; slip back into one's bad old ways: 他发过誓不再偷了, 可不久又～, 走上了犯罪道路。 He swore that he would never steal again, but soon relapsed into a life of crime.

旧部 jiùbù　former subordinates

旧地 jiùdì　a once visited place

旧地重游 jiùdì chóng yóu　revisit a once familiar place

旧调重弹 jiùdiào chóng tán　same as 老调重弹 lǎodiào chóng tán

旧都 jiùdū　former capital

旧恶 jiù'è　old grievance; old wrong: 不念旧恶 bù niàn jiù'è

旧故 jiùgù　old acquaintance; old friend

旧观 jiùguān　former appearance; former state: 迥非～ entirely different from what it used to be / 工厂由于实行了科学管理而一改～。 With scientific management, the factory has taken on a completely new look. / 北京许多古建筑已经修缮一新, 恢复了～。 Many old buildings in Beijing have been renovated and restored to their former glory (or splendour).

旧国 jiùguó　liter. former capital; old capital: 三十一年还～, 落花时节读华章。(毛泽东) Back in the old capital after thirty-one years, At the season of falling flowers I read your polished lines.

旧好 jiùhǎo　formal ① old friendship: 重修旧好 chóng xiū jiùhǎo ② old friend

旧恨新仇 jiùhèn-xīnchóu　new hatred piled on old

旧货 jiùhuò　secondhand goods; junk: 我买的是～。 I bought it secondhand.

旧货店 jiùhuòdiàn　secondhand shop; junk shop

旧货市场 jiùhuò shìchǎng　flea market

旧疾 jiùjí　old (or chronic) complaint

旧交 jiùjiāo　old acquaintance; old friend

旧教 jiùjiào　Catholicism

旧金山 jiùjīnshān　San Francisco

旧居 jiùjū　former residence; old home

旧历 jiùlì　the old Chinese calendar; the lunar calendar

旧历年 jiùlìnián　the lunar New Year

旧梦重温 jiùmèng chóng wēn　same as 重温旧梦 chóng wēn jiùmèng

旧民主主义革命 jiùmínzhǔzhǔyì gémìng　democratic revolution of the old type

旧年 jiùnián　① the lunar New Year: 很多中国人还是过～。 Many Chinese still celebrate the lunar New Year. ② dial. last year

旧瓶装新酒 jiùpíng zhuāng xīnjiǔ　new wine in old bottles——new content in old form

旧情 jiùqíng　old or former friendship; former affection

旧日 jiùrì　former days; old days

旧诗 jiùshī　old-style poetry; classical poetry ——see also 古体诗 gǔtǐshī; 近体诗 jìntǐshī

旧石器时代 jiùshíqì shídài　the Old Stone Age; the Paleolithic Period

旧时 jiùshí　old times; old days

旧式 jiùshì　old type; old style: ～文人 old-type scholars / ～婚姻 old-style marriage

旧事 jiùshì　an old matter or affair; a past event: ～重提 bring up a matter of the past /《城南～》 Reminiscences of Old Peking (a film)

旧书 jiùshū　① secondhand book; used (or old) book ② ancient book; ancient text

旧书店 jiùshūdiàn　secondhand bookstore

旧俗 jiùsú　old customs: 破～, 立新风 do away with old customs and introduce new ones

旧闻 jiùwén　old lore

旧物 jiùwù　① past heritage ② lost territory ——see also 光复旧物 guāngfù jiùwù

旧学 jiùxué　old Chinese learning (as distinct from the new or Western learning)

旧业 jiùyè　① old trade or profession: 重操旧业 chóng cāo jiùyè ② ancestral estate; family fortune: ～荡然无存 a goodly family fortune all dissipated

旧雨 jiùyǔ　liter. old friend: ～重逢 the meeting of old friends / ～新知 friends old and new

旧怨 jiùyuàn　old grievance: 不记～ nurse no old grievances; forgive and forget

旧约 jiùyuē　the Old Testament

旧址 jiùzhǐ　site (of a former organization, building, etc.): 农会～ the site of the former peasant association / 这是我们机关的～。 Here's where our organization used to be.

旧制 jiùzhì　① old system ② the old system of weights and measures (opp. the metric system)

臼 jiù　① mortar: 石～ stone mortar ② any mortar-shaped thing ③ joint (of bones): 脱臼 tuōjiù

臼齿 jiùchǐ　molar

疚 jiù　formal　remorse: 内疚 nèijiù

咎 jiù　① fault; blame: 归咎 guījiù ② censure; punish; blame: 既往不咎 jìwǎng bù jiù ③ bad fortune: 休咎 xiūjiù

咎由自取 jiù yóu zì qǔ　have only oneself to blame

柩 jiù　a coffin with a corpse in it: 灵柩 língjiù

柩车 jiùchē　hearse

柏 jiù　Chinese tallow tree

救 jiù　① rescue; save: 他跳进急流, 把孩子～了出来。 He jumped into the torrent and rescued the child from drowning. / ～溺水儿童 save a drowning child ② save sb. from; relieve (distress, etc.): 救亡 jiùwáng / 救灾 jiùzāi

救兵 jiùbīng　relief troops; reinforcements: 搬～ call in reinforcements

救场 jiùchǎng　go on stage as a last-minute understudy

救国 jiùguó　save the nation: 上中学时, 他就参加了抗日～运动。 As a middle-school student he joined in the movement to resist Japanese aggression and save the country.

救护 jiùhù　relieve a sick or injured person; give first-aid; rescue: ～伤员 give first-aid to the wounded / 奋勇～战友 valiantly go to the rescue of one's comrade-in-arms

救护车 jiùhùchē　ambulance

救护船 jiùhùchuán　ambulance ship

救护队 jiùhùduì　ambulance corps

救护飞机 jiùhù fēijī　ambulance aircraft

救护所 jiùhùsuǒ　medical aid station (or point)

救护站 jiùhùzhàn　first-aid station

救荒 jiùhuāng　send relief to a famine area; help to tide over a crop failure: 生产～ tide over a crop failure by production

救活 jiùhuó　bring sb. back to life; resuscitate: 他们把一个几乎淹死了的人～了。 They resuscitated a man who had almost drowned. / ～了一个工厂 save a factory from bankruptcy

救火 jiùhuǒ　fight a fire; try to put out a fire: 消防队员正在～。 The firemen are fighting the fire.

救火车 jiùhuǒchē　fire engine

救火队 jiùhuǒduì　fire brigade: ～员 fireman; fire fighter

救急 jiùjí help sb. to cope with an emergency; help meet an urgent need: 你们支援我们这些材料,可真～了。You gave us this material just when we needed it most.

救济 jiùjì extend relief to; relieve the distress of: ～难民 give relief to refugees / ～灾区人民 provide relief to the people in a disaster area / 社会～事业 social relief facilities / ～和善后工作 relief and rehabilitation operations / ～费 relief fund / ～粮 relief grain; relief food

救驾 jiùjià *humor.* come to the rescue of the emperor—come to the rescue

救苦救难 jiùkǔ-jiùnàn help the needy and relieve the distressed: ～的观世音 the benevolent Goddess of Mercy

救命 jiùmìng save sb.'s life: ～! Help!

救命稻草 jiùmìng dàocǎo a straw to clutch at

救命恩人 jiùmìng ēnrén saviour

救难 jiùnàn help out of distress

救难船 jiùnànchuán rescue boat

救人一命胜造七级浮屠 jiù rén yī mìng shèng zào qī jí fútú saving one life is better than building a seven-tiered pagoda

救生 jiùshēng save life (esp. through the prevention of drowning): ～设备 lifesaving appliance; life preserver

救生带 jiùshēngdài life belt

救生圈 jiùshēngquān life buoy

救生艇 jiùshēngtǐng lifeboat

救生衣 jiùshēngyī life jacket

救生员 jiùshēngyuán lifeguard; lifesaver

救世军 Jiùshìjūn the Salvation Army (a Christian organization)

救世主 jiùshìzhǔ the Saviour; the Redeemer

救死 jiùsǐ rescue the dying

救死扶伤 jiùsǐ-fúshāng heal the wounded and rescue the dying: ～,实行革命的人道主义。Heal the wounded, rescue the dying, practise revolutionary humanitarianism.

救亡 jiùwáng save the nation from extinction: ～图存 save the nation from doom and ensure its survival

救亡运动 jiùwáng yùndòng national salvation movement

救险车 jiùxiǎnchē wrecking truck; wrecking car

救星 jiùxīng liberator; emancipator; saviour

救药 jiùyào (usu. used in the negative) cure; remedy: 不可救药 bùkě jiùyào

救应 jiùyìng aid and support; reinforce

救援 jiùyuán rescue; come to sb.'s help

救灾 jiùzāi provide disaster relief; send relief to a disaster area; help the people tide over a natural disaster

救治 jiùzhì bring a patient out of danger; treat and cure: 大批医务人员奔赴灾区～伤病员。Large numbers of medical workers hurried to the disaster area to give treatment to the sick and wounded.

救助 jiùzhù help sb. in danger or difficulty; succour

厩(廄、廏) jiù stable; cattle-shed; pen

厩肥 jiùféi barnyard manure

就¹ jiù ① come near; move towards: 大家～拢来烤火取暖。They all gathered round the fire to get warm. / 我们～着路灯下棋。We played chess by the light of a street lamp. / 你～着桌子吃西瓜。Eat your watermelon over the table. ② undertake; engage in; enter upon: 就业 jiùyè / 就职 jiùzhí ③ accomplish; make: 这个鼎是青铜铸～的。This tripod is made of bronze. ④ take advantage of; accomodate oneself to: 我们～这个机会谈谈。We'll take this opportunity to have a talk. / 我反正有空,～你的时间吧。Make it anytime that suits you; I'm free anyway. / 只好～这块料子做了。We'll

have to make do with this little piece of material. ⑤ be eaten with; go with: 炒鸡蛋～饭 have some scrambled eggs to go with the rice / 他用花生～酒。He has peanuts with his drinks. ⑥ *prep.* with regard to; concerning; on: ～我所知 so far as I know / 双方～共同关心的问题进行了会谈。The two sides held talks on questions of common interest.

就² jiù *adv.* ① at once; right away: 我～来。I'll come right away. / 我这～去。I'll be going right away. / 一会儿～得。It'll be ready in a minute. ② as early as; already: 今天我七点钟～来了。I was here as early as 7 o'clock today. / 我星期一～给你钱。I'll pay you right on Monday. ③ as soon as; right after: 他每天下了课～回家。He comes home every day right after class. / 我吃了饭～出去了。As soon as I finished eating, I went out. / 我一见他～生气。As soon as I see him, I get angry. / 说干～干 act without delay ④ in that case; then: 不经过艰苦奋斗,～不能胜利。We cannot be victorious without arduous struggle. / 要是你来,我～高兴了。If you come, (then) I'll be very happy. ⑤ as much as; as many as: 光衬衫他～有二十件。He has as many as 20 shirts. / 光回收废品一项,他们～给国家节约了二万元。Just by collecting scrap, they saved as much as 20,000 *yuan* for the state. ⑥ (used between two identical elements to express resignation): 丢了～丢了吧,以后小心点。If it's lost, it's lost. Just be more careful from now on. ⑦ to begin with; as is expected: 我～料到他会等我们的。I knew he'd be waiting for us. / 我本来～不懂法语。I never said I knew any French. ⑧ only; merely; just: ～这一本了,看完请马上还。This is the only copy left. Please return it as soon as you finish reading it. / 我～去过一次上海。I've been to Shanghai only once. / 我们～等你的决定了。We're merely waiting for your decision. / 我～要几张纸。I just want a few sheets of paper. ⑨ just; simply: 我～不信我们妇女干不了这一行。I just wouldn't believe that we women couldn't do this sort of work. / 我不知道为什么,我～不喜欢他。I don't know why, I just don't like him. ⑩ exactly; precisely: 你～是我要找的那个人。You are precisely the person I'm looking for. / 医务室～在这儿。This is where the clinic is.

就³ jiù *conj.* even if: 你～不说,我也会知道的。Even if you won't tell me, I'll know anyway. / 你～生气也没用。Even if you get angry, it won't help.

就伴 jiùbàn keep sb. company; accompany sb.: 你一个人在家多闷得慌,我来和你～吧。Don't you feel bored staying at home all alone? Let me come and keep you company. / 她们俩～去了广州。The two of them went to Guangzhou together.

就便 jiùbiàn at sb.'s convenience; while you're at it: ～也替我买一本。While you're at it (*or* about it), buy me a copy too.

就餐 jiùcān *formal* have a meal; eat; dine: 客队在第一食堂～。The visiting team are to dine in the No.1 dining-hall.

就此 jiùcǐ at this point; here and now; thus: 讨论～结束。The discussion was thus brought to a close. / 工作虽然有了一点成绩,但不能～松懈下来。It's true that we have accomplished something, but this doesn't mean we can let up now.

就道 jiùdào *formal* set out on a journey; start off (*or* out): 束装～ pack up and start out / 来电一再催促立即～。Telegrams kept arriving urging me to start out at once.

就地 jiùdì on the spot: ～解决问题 settle the problem on the spot / 将敌人～歼灭 wipe out the enemy on the spot / ～免职 relieve sb. of his post then and there

就地取材 jiùdì qǔcái obtain materials from local sources; use local materials; draw on local resources

就地视察 jiùdì shìchá on-site-inspection

就地正法 jiùdì zhèngfǎ execute (a criminal) on the spot

就读 jiùdú *formal* attend school: 他早年～于师范学校。He attended a normal school in his early years.

就范 jiùfàn submit; give in: 迫使～ compel sb. to submit / 不肯～ refuse to submit to control; refuse to give in

就合 jiùhe *dial.* accommodate oneself to; yield to

就教 jiùjiào go to sb. for advice or instructions

就近 jiùjìn (do or get sth.) nearby; in the neighbourhood; without having to go far: ～找个住处 find accommodation in the neighbourhood

就里 jiùlǐ inside information; inside story: 不知～ not be in the know

就木 jiùmù *formal* enter the coffin—die ——see also 行将就木 xíngjiāng jiùmù

就擒 jiùqín be seized; be captured: 束手就擒 shùshǒu jiùqín

就寝 jiùqǐn retire for the night; go to bed

就让 jiùràng *inf.* even if: ～他来，也晚了。Even if he comes it will be too late.

就任 jiùrèn take up one's post; take office

就势 jiùshì making use of momentum: 对手扑过来，我一把他摔倒在地。As my opponent threw himself at me, I made use of his momentum to fling him to the ground.

就事 jiùshì *old* take up an office; assume a post

就事论事 jiù shì lùn shì consider sth. in isolation or out of context; deal with a matter on its merits: 我不清楚这件事的背景，只能～地谈谈。I don't know the whole background, so I can only judge the case as it stands.

就是[1] jiùshì ① (used, usu. with 了, at the end of a sentence to give force to the statement): 他想要点儿钱～了。He wants some money, that's all. / 你说～了。Just say it! / 放心吧，我照办～了。Don't worry. I promise to do just as you say. ② yes, that's right; exactly; precisely: 这是不是你说的那个?— ～。Is that what you were talking about?—Yes, that's it. / ～嘛，我也是这么想的。Precisely. That's just what I had in mind. ③ same as 就[2] jiù⑧⑨

就是[2] jiùshì *conj.* (used correlatively with 也) even if: 你～不愿意去，也得打个电话。Even if you don't want to go, you still have to make a phone call.

就是说 jiùshìshuō that is to say; in other words; namely

就手 jiùshǒu while you're at it: 你～把这个也洗洗。Please wash this too while you are washing the other things. / 你～把我的信件也带来吧。Please get my mail as well while you're at it. / ～把门关上。Close the door behind you.

就算 jiùsuàn *conj. inf.* even if; granted that: ～你工作干得不错，也不应该骄傲吧。Granted you have not done badly, still there is no reason to be conceited.

就位 jiùwèi take one's place

就席 jiùxí take one's seat (at a banquet, etc.); be seated at the table

就绪 jiùxù be in order; be ready: 一切都已～。Everything is ready (or in order). / 准备工作已经大致～。The preparations are more or less completed.

就学 jiùxué go to school; attend school

就要 jiùyào *adv.* be about to; be going to; be on the point of: 火车～开了。The train is about to start. *or* The train is starting in a minute.

就业 jiùyè obtain employment; take up an occupation; get a job: 充分～ full employment / ～不足 underemployment

就医 jiùyī seek medical advice; go to a doctor

就义 jiùyì be executed for championing a just cause; die a martyr

就诊 jiùzhěn seek medical advice; go to a doctor

就枕 jiùzhěn *formal* go to bed

就正 jiùzhèng solicit comments (on one's writing): ～于读者 request (*or* invite) the readers to offer their criticisms

就职 jiùzhí assume office: 宣誓～ take the oath of office; be sworn in

就职典礼 jiùzhí diǎnlǐ inaugural ceremony; inauguration

就职演说 jiùzhí yǎnshuō inaugural speech

就中 jiùzhōng ① between them: ～调停 mediate between them ② among them: 这件事他们三个人都知道，～老王知道得最清楚。The three of them all know about it, and of the three Lao Wang knows most.

就座 jiùzuò (also 就坐 jiùzuò) take one's seat; be seated: 在主席台前列～的有… seated in the front row on the rostrum were… / 贵宾们依次～。The honoured guests took their seats in due order.

舅

舅 jiù ① mother's brother; uncle ② wife's brother; brother-in-law ③ *formal* husband's father

舅父 jiùfù mother's brother; uncle

舅姑 jiù-gū *formal* husband's parents; parents-in-law

舅舅 jiùjiu *inf.* mother's brother; uncle

舅妈 jiùmā *inf.* wife of mother's brother; aunt

舅母 jiùmu wife of mother's brother; aunt

舅嫂 jiùsǎo *inf.* wife of wife's brother; sister-in-law

舅子 jiùzi *inf.* wife's brother; brother-in-law

鹫

鹫 jiù vulture

jū

车(車)

车(車) jū chariot, one of the pieces in Chinese chess ——see also chē

拘

拘 jū ① arrest; detain: 昨天晚上闹事的足球迷给～起来了。The football fans who made trouble last night were detained. ② restrain; restrict; constrain: 拘谨 jūjǐn ③ inflexible: 拘泥 jū·nì ④ limit: 不拘 bùjū

拘板 jūbǎn *dial.* stiff; formal: 他待人接物有些～。He has a rather stiff manner. / 自己人随便谈话，不必这么～。You're among friends, don't be so formal.

拘捕 jūbǔ arrest; take into custody

拘传 jūchuán *leg.* summon sb. for detention: 人民法院对被告人可以～。The people's courts may summon a defendant for detention.

拘管 jūguǎn keep in custody

拘谨 jūjǐn overcautious; reserved: 初次见面时，他有些～，不大爱说话。At the first meeting he was rather reserved and withdrawn.

拘禁 jūjìn take into custody; detain

拘礼 jūlǐ be punctilious; stand on ceremony: 熟不～ too familiar with each other to stand on ceremony

拘留 jūliú detain; hold in custody; intern

拘留所 jūliúsuǒ house of detention; lockup

拘留证 jūliúzhèng detention warrant

拘挛 jūluán ① cramps; spasms ② *formal* rigidly adhere to: ～章句 insist on a textual interpretation

拘挛儿 jūluānr *dial.* (of hands and feet) frozen stiff; numb with cold: 我的手都冻～了。My hands are frozen stiff.

拘拿 jū·ná arrest; take into custody

拘泥 jū·nì be a stickler for (form, etc.); rigidly adhere to (formalities, etc.): ～于形式 rigidly adhere to form; be formalistic / ～于细节 be very punctilious / ～成说 rigidly adhere to accepted theories

拘票 jūpiào arrest warrant; warrant

拘牵 jūqiān *formal* restrain; confine

拘守 jūshǒu ① hold fast to; stick to: ～成规 hold fast to convention / ～绳墨 stick to the rules ② *formal* imprison

拘束 jūshù ① restrain; restrict: 不要～孩子们的正当活动。Don't restrict the proper activities of children. ② constrained; awkward; ill at ease: 在生人面前显得～ look ill at ease in the presence of strangers / 不要～。Make yourself at home.

拘系 jūxì take into custody; detain

拘押 jūyā take into custody; detain

拘役 jūyì *leg.* criminal detention: ～的期限为十五日以上, 六个月以下。The term of criminal detention is not less than fifteen days and not more than six months.

拘囿 jūyòu rigidly adhere to

拘执 jūzhí rigid; inflexible: 这些事儿可以变通着办, 不要过于～。We should be flexible in dealing with these matters, and not be so rigid.

狙 jū ① a kind of monkey mentioned in ancient texts ② *formal* watch for

狙击 jūjī snipe

狙击手 jūjīshǒu sniper

狙击战 jūjīzhàn sniping action

居 jū ① reside; dwell; live: 侨居 qiáojū ② residence; house: 故居 gùjū / 迁居 qiānjū ③ be (in a certain position); occupy (a place): ～世界首位 occupy first place in the world; rank first in the world / 身～要职 hold an important post ④ claim; assert: 自居 zìjū ⑤ store up; lay by: 居奇 jūqí ⑥ stay put; be at a standstill: 岁月不居 suìyuè bù jū ⑦ restaurant (usu. used in names of restaurants): 同和～ the Tonghe Restaurant / 沙锅～ Casseroles ⑧ (Jū) a surname

居安思危 jū ān sī wēi think of danger in times of safety; be vigilant in peace time

居多 jūduō be in the majority: 我们球队里北方人～。Most of the players in our team are northerners.

居高临下 jū gāo lín xià occupy a commanding position (*or* height)

居功 jūgōng claim credit for oneself

居功自傲 jūgōng zì'ào become arrogant because of one's achievements; claim credit and put on airs

居官 jūguān *formal* hold office; be in office: ～多年 have a long official career

居积 jūjī *formal* accumulate (wealth): ～致富 amass a fortune

居家 jūjiā live at home; run a household: ～过日子 keep house (economically and efficiently)

居间 jūjiān (mediate) between two parties: ～调停 mediate between two parties; act as mediator

居间人 jūjiānrén intermediary; mediator

居里 jūlǐ *phys.* curie

居留 jūliú reside: 在国外～ reside abroad / 长期～ permanent residence

居留权 jūliúquán right of residence

居留证 jūliúzhèng residence permit

居民 jūmín resident; inhabitant: 城镇～ residents in cities and towns; urban residents

居民点 jūmíndiǎn residential area

居民委员会 jūmín wěiyuánhuì neighbourhood (*or* residents') committee

居奇 jūqí hoard and speculate: 囤积居奇 túnjī jūqí

居然 jūrán *adv.* ① unexpectedly; actually; to one's surprise: 真没想到他～会做出这种事来。Who would have thought he could do such a thing? / 你怎么～相信这种谣言? How could you believe such a rumour? ② go so far as to: ～当面撒谎 go so far as to tell a bare-

faced lie ③ *formal* obviously: ～可知 abundantly clear

居丧 jūsāng *formal* be in mourning

居士 jūshì ① lay Buddhist ② retired scholar: 六一～ Retired Scholar Liuyi (a sobriquet of Ouyang Xiu 欧阳修)

居室 jūshì ① room: 三～ a three-room flat ② *dial.* house ③ *formal* (of husband and wife) live together: 男女～, 人之大伦也。(《孟子》) A man and woman living together is the most important of human relationships.

居首 jūshǒu occupy first place; rank first: 这个县的工农业总产值在全省中～。This county ranks first in the province in the total value of industrial and agricultural production.

居孀 jūshuāng *formal* remain a widow; live in widowhood

居停 jūtíng ① stop and stay (at a place when travelling) ② *formal* (originally 居停主人) landlord; host

居心 jūxīn harbour (evil) intentions: 他们～何在? What are they up to?

居心不良 jūxīn bù liáng harbour evil intentions

居心叵测 jūxīn pǒ cè with hidden intent; with ulterior motives

居于 jūyú occupy (a certain position): ～领导地位的干部 cadres in leading positions

居中 jūzhōng ① (mediate) between two parties: ～斡旋 mediate between disputants ② be placed in the middle: 小标题一律～。Subheads should be placed in the middle of the column. *or* Centre the subheads. / 两旁是对联, ～是一幅山水画。On either side is a couplet scroll, and in the middle is a landscape painting.

居住 jūzhù live; reside; dwell: 他家一直～在乡下。His family have always lived in the country. / 苗族～地区 a region inhabited by the Miao nationality / ～条件 housing conditions

居住面积 jūzhù miànjī living space; floor space

居住期限 jūzhù qīxiàn length of residence

居住证 jūzhùzhèng residence permit

驹 jū ① colt ② foal: 怀～ be in (*or* with) foal / 小驴～儿 foal

驹子 jūzi foal

疽 jū *Chin. med.* subcutaneous ulcer; deep-rooted ulcer

掬(匊) jū hold with both hands: 以手～水 scoop up some water with one's hands

据 jū see 拮据 jiéjū ——see also jù

琚 jū ① a jade pendant ② (Jū) a surname

锔(锯) jū mend (crockery) with cramps: ～碗(缸) mend a bowl (jar) with cramps ——see also jú

锔碗儿的 jūwǎnrde crockery mender

锔子 jūzi a cramp used in mending crockery

趄 jū see 趔趄 zìjū ——see also qiè

睢 jū used as a personal name in ancient times: 范～ (a statesman of the Warring States period)

睢鸠 jūjiū a waterfowl mentioned in ancient texts

裾 jū *formal* ① the full front of a Chinese gown ② the full front and back of a Chinese gown

裾礁 jūjiāo fringing reef; shore reef

鞠[1] jū ① *formal* rear; bring up: 鞠养 jūyǎng ②

(jū) a surname

鞠²

jū　a ball used in play in ancient times: 蹴~ kick a ball

鞠躬¹　jūgōng　bow: ~致谢 bow one's thanks / 行个~礼 salute by making a bow / 深深地鞠一个躬 make a deep bow; bow low

鞠躬²　jūgōng　*formal* in a discreet and scrupulous manner: 入公门, ~如也, 如不容。(《论语》) On going through the outer gates to his lord's court, he drew himself in, as though the entrance was too small to admit him.

鞠躬尽瘁　jūgōng jìn cuì　bend oneself to a task and exert oneself to the utmost; spare no effort in the performance of one's duty

鞠躬尽瘁, 死而后已　jūgōng jìn cuì, sǐ érhòu yǐ　bend one's back to the task until one's dying day; give one's all till one's heart stops beating

鞠养　jūyǎng　*formal* rear; bring up

jú

局¹

jú　① chessboard: 棋局 qíjú ② game; set; innings: 第一~ (in table tennis, etc.) the first game; the first set; (in shuttlecock, baseball and softball) the first innings / 下一~棋 play a game of chess ③ situation; state of affairs: 战局 zhànjú / 全局 quánjú ④ largeness or smallness of mind; extent of one's tolerance of others: 器局 qìjú ⑤ gathering: 赌局 dǔjú ⑥ ruse; trap: 骗局 piànjú ⑦ limit; confine: 局限 júxiàn

局²

jú　① part; portion: 局部 júbù ② bureau; office: 教育~ bureau of education / 邮政~ post office ③ (used in shop names) shop: 书局 shūjú

局部　júbù　part: ~必须服从全局。The part must be subordinated to the whole. / 不能只顾~和眼前。One mustn't be concerned only with the partial and the immediate. / ~地区 some areas; parts of an area / ~利益 partial and local interests

局部麻醉　júbù mázuì　local anaesthesia

局部战争　júbù zhànzhēng　local war; partial war

局促　júcù　① narrow; cramped: 这地方~, 走动不便。This place is rather cramped; there's little room for free movement. ② *dial.* (of time) short: 三天太~, 恐怕办不成。I'm afraid three days is not long enough for us to get it done. ③ feel or show constraint

局促不安　júcù bù'ān　ill at ease: 他跟不认识的人在一起感到~。He was ill at ease with people whom he didn't know.

局度　júdù　*formal* tolerance; forbearance: 有~ be large-minded; be tolerant

局量　júliàng　*formal* tolerance

局麻　júmá　short for 局部麻醉 júbù mázuì

局面　júmiàn　① aspect; phase; situation: 出现了崭新的~。Things have taken on a new aspect. / 打开~ open up a new prospect; make a breakthrough ② *dial.* scope; scale: 这家商店~虽不大, 货色倒齐全。Though this store is not very large, goods of every description are available here.

局内人　júnèirén　a person in the know; insider

局骗　júpiàn　swindle

局势　júshì　situation: 国际~ the international situation / 紧张~ a tense situation; tension

局外人　júwàirén　a person not in the know; outsider: ~不得而知 unknown to an outsider

局限　júxiàn　limit; confine: 颇有~ be rather limited (in outlook, etc.); have many limitations / 由于时代和阶级

地位的~ owing to the limitations of the times and one's class status / 他的报告不~于教学法问题。His talk wasn't confined to teaching methods.

局限性　júxiànxìng　limitations

局子　júzi　*inf.* police station

侷

jú　see below

侷促　júcù　same as 局促 júcù

桔

jú　a popular form for 橘 jú ——see also jié

菊

jú　chrysanthemum

菊花　júhuā　chrysanthemum

菊科　júkē　*bot.* the composite family

菊石　júshí　ammonite

菊芋　júyù　*bot.* Jerusalem artichoke

焗

jú　*dial.* ① steam food in a sealed container: 全~鸡 a whole steamed chicken ② feel smothered; be stifling

焗油　júyóu　① treatment of the hair with a cream to make it soft and shiny ② hair treatment cream

锔

jú　*chem.* curium (Cm) ——see also jū

橘

jú　tangerine

橘柑　júgān　*dial.* tangerine

橘红　júhóng　① tangerine (colour); reddish orange ② *Chin. med.* dried tangerine peel

橘黄　júhuáng　orange (colour)

橘络　júluò　*Chin. med.* tangerine pith

橘汁　júzhī　orange juice

橘子　júzi　tangerine

jǔ

沮

jǔ　① *formal* stop; prevent: ~其成行 stop sb. from going ② turn gloomy; turn glum: 沮丧 jǔsàng

沮遏　jǔ'è　*formal* prevent

沮丧　jǔsàng　① dejected; depressed; dispirited; disheartened: 敌人士气~。The enemy's morale is low. ② depress; dispirit; dishearten: ~敌人的精神 demoralize the enemy

咀

jǔ　chew: 含英咀华 hányīng-jǔhuá ——see also zuǐ

咀嚼　jǔjué　① masticate; chew ② mull over; ruminate; chew the cud: 演员对每句台词都要反复吟咏、~, 才能进入角色。An actor must rehearse his lines again and again, chewing on them so to speak, before he can hope to get inside the character that he is playing.

举 (擧、舉)

jǔ　① lift; raise; hold up: 他把孩子~了起来。He lifted the child up. / 他~起棍子, 打了下来。Raising his staff, he chopped down. / ~枪瞄准 level one's gun at the target ② act; deed; move: 国家安危, 系于此~。The entire safety of our country depends upon this one move. ③ start: 举义 jǔyì ④ elect; choose: 我们~他当主席。We elected him as chairman. ⑤ cite; enumerate: 我可以~出好几件事来说明。I can cite quite a few instances to illustrate. / 你能~出什么理由来吗? Can you give any reason for it? ⑥ *formal* whole; entire: 举座 jǔzuò ⑦ *formal* give birth to (a child): ~一男 give birth to a boy ⑧ (short for 举人 jǔrén): 中~ pass the *juren* examination

举哀　jǔ'āi　① wail in mourning ② go into mourning: 宣布全国~三天 declare three days national mourning

举案齐眉 jǔ àn qí méi　holding the tray level with the brows—husband and wife treating each other with courtesy

举办 jǔbàn　conduct; hold; run: ～训练班 conduct a training course／～学习班 run a study class／～展览会 hold (*or* put on) an exhibition／～音乐会 give a concert

举报 jǔbào　report (an offender); inform against

举杯 jǔbēi　raise one's glass (to propose a toast)

举兵 jǔbīng　*formal* call out the troops: ～起义 call out the troops in revolt

举不胜举 jǔ bùshèng jǔ　too numerous to mention

举步 jǔbù　*formal* take a step: ～向前 take a step forward／～维艰 have difficulty in taking a step

举措 jǔcuò　move; act

举措失当 jǔcuò shīdàng　make an ill-advised move: 敌军调动慌忙，～。The enemy manoeuvred his troops in a disorderly way and made false moves.

举动 jǔdòng　movement; move; act; activity: 轻率的～ a rash act／他年迈体衰，～越来越慢慢。He's old and infirm, and his movements are getting slower and slower.／你有什么～要先告诉我一声。Let me know before you make a move.

举发 jǔfā　report (an offender); inform against

举凡 jǔfán　*formal* ranging from...to...; all...such as

举国 jǔguó　the whole nation: ～欢腾 The whole nation is jubilant.／得到～一致的支持 enjoy nationwide support／～一致的愿望 the unanimous aspiration of the nation

举国上下 jǔguó shàngxià　the whole nation from top to bottom; from the leaders of the nation to all the people: ～团结一致。There is solid unity throughout the nation.

举火 jǔhuǒ　*formal* ① light a fire: ～为号 light a beacon ② light a kitchen fire; light a stove

举家 jǔjiā　the whole family: ～老小 the whole family, old and young

举架 jǔjià　*dial.* the height of a house: 这间房子～矮。This house is quite low.

举荐 jǔjiàn　recommend (a person)

举例 jǔlì　give an example: 举个例 give an example／～说明 illustrate with examples

举目 jǔmù　*formal* raise the eyes; look: ～四望 look round／～远眺 look into the distance

举目无亲 jǔmù wú qīn　be away from all one's kin; be a stranger in a strange land; have no one to turn to (for help)

举棋不定 jǔ qí bù dìng　hesitate about (*or* over) what move to make; be unable to make up one's mind; vacillate; shilly-shally: 接受好还是不接受好，他～。He vacillated between accepting and not accepting.

举人 jǔrén　a successful candidate in the imperial examinations at the provincial level in the Ming and Qing dynasties

举世 jǔshì　throughout the world; universally: ～皆知 known to all／～公认 universally acknowledged

举世闻名 jǔshì wénmíng　of world renown; world-famous

举世无双 jǔshì wúshuāng　unrivalled; matchless

举世瞩目 jǔshì zhǔmù　attract worldwide attention; become the focus of world attention

举事 jǔshì　*formal* stage an uprising; rise in insurrection

举手 jǔshǒu　raise (*or* put up) one's hand or hands: 赞成的请～。Those in favour please put up their hands.／举起手来! Hands up!／～表决 vote by a show of hands

举手礼 jǔshǒulǐ　hand salute

举坛 jǔtán　weight-lifting circles

举头 jǔtóu　raise the head: ～望明月，低头思故乡。(李

白) Raising my head, I look at the bright moon; Bending my head, I think of my old home.

举行 jǔxíng　hold (a meeting, ceremony, etc.): ～会谈 hold talks／～宴会 give (*or* host) a banquet／～罢工 stage a strike／大会在人民大会堂～。The congress took place (*or* was held) in the Great Hall of the People.／你们几时～婚礼? When are you going to have your wedding?

举一反三 jǔ yī fǎn sān　draw inferences about other cases from one instance

举一赅百 jǔ yī gāi bǎi　same as 举一反三 jǔ yī fǎn sān

举义 jǔyì　*formal* start a revolt; rise in revolt

举债 jǔzhài　*formal* borrow money; raise (*or* contract) a loan

举止 jǔzhǐ　bearing; manner; mien: ～庄重 deport oneself in a dignified manner; carry oneself with dignity／～大方 have poise; have an easy manner; be gentle of mien

举踵 jǔzhǒng　*formal* be on tiptoe

举重 jǔzhòng　weight lifting: ～运动员 weight lifter

举子 jǔzǐ　a candidate for the imperial examinations

举足轻重 jǔ zú qīngzhòng　hold the balance; prove decisive: 一支～的力量 a decisive force／处于～的地位 occupy a pivotal position

举坐 jǔzuò　(also 举座 jǔzuò) all those present: ～惊慌失色。All those present turned pale with fright.

枸

jǔ　see below——see also gōu; gǒu

枸橼 jǔyuán　citron

枸橼酸 jǔyuánsuān　citric acid

枸橼酸钠 jǔyuánsuānnà　sodium citrate

矩(榘)

jǔ　① carpenter's square; square: 矩尺 jǔchǐ ② rules; regulations: 循规蹈矩 xúnguī-dǎojǔ ③ *phys.* moment: 力矩 lìjǔ

矩臂 jǔbì　*phys.* moment arm

矩尺 jǔchǐ　carpenter's square

矩形 jǔxíng　rectangle

矩矱 jǔyuē　*formal* rules; regulations

矩阵 jǔzhèn　*math.* matrix

蒟

jǔ　see below

蒟酱 jǔjiàng　betel pepper

蒟蒻 jǔruò　another name for 魔芋 móyù

龃

jǔ　see below

龃龉 jǔyǔ　*formal* the upper and lower teeth not meeting properly—disagreement; discord: 双方发生～。The two parties quarrelled.

榉(櫸)

jǔ　see 山毛榉 shānmáojǔ

踽

jǔ　see below

踽踽 jǔjǔ　*formal* (walk) alone: ～独行 walk alone; walk in solitude

jù

巨(鉅)

jù　huge; tremendous; gigantic: ～幅标语 a huge poster／～型运输机 a giant transport plane／为数甚～ a huge sum

巨变 jùbiàn　a great change; a tremendous change: 山村～ tremendous changes in a mountain village

巨擘 jùbò　① thumb ② authority in a certain field: 医界～ a leading medical authority

巨大 jùdà　huge; tremendous; enormous; gigantic; immense: ～的胜利 a tremendous victory／～的力量

tremendous force; immense strength / ～的工程 a giant project / ～的规模 a massive scale / 做出～的努力 make gigantic efforts

巨额 jù'é　a huge amount; a huge sum: 积累了～财富 have accumulated a huge amount of wealth / ～投资 huge investments / ～利润 enormous profits / ～赤字 huge financial deficits

巨富 jùfù　① immense wealth ② a man of immense wealth; multimillionaire: 美国石油～ a U. S. oil tycoon

巨祸 jùhuò　a great calamity

巨奸 jùjiān　*formal* a very treacherous person

巨奸大猾 jùjiān-dàhuá　*formal* an arrant swindler

巨匠 jùjiàng　*formal* great master; consummate craftsman; giant: 文坛～ a literary giant

巨款 jùkuǎn　a huge sum of money

巨流 jùliú　a mighty current (fig.): 汇成一股～ converge into a mighty current

巨轮 jùlún　① a large wheel (fig.): 历史的～是拖不回来的。 The wheel of history cannot be turned back. ② a large ship: 远洋～ a large oceangoing ship

巨人 jùrén　giant; colossus

巨人症 jùrénzhèng　gigantism

巨石文化 jùshí wénhuà　*archaeol.* megalithic culture

巨头 jùtóu　magnate; tycoon: 金融～ financial magnate; shark of high finance; financial tycoon / 三（四）～ the Big Three (Four)

巨万 jùwàn　*formal* millions; myriads; a huge amount (of money): 耗资～ cost huge sums of money

巨细 jù-xì　big and small: 事无～ all matters, big and small / ～毕究 let nothing pass unnoticed

巨星 jùxīng　*astron.* giant star; giant

巨著 jùzhù　monumental work: 历史～ a magnum opus of historic significance

巨子 jùzǐ　magnate; tycoon; giant: 实业界～ a business tycoon / 文坛～ a literary giant

句　jù　① sentence: 这～我不懂。 I don't understand this sentence. / 我来说几～。 Let me say a few words. ② *m.* sentence: 一～话 a sentence / 两～诗 two lines of verse / 我一～话也没说。 I didn't say a word. / 他说的一～实话也没有。 There's not a word of truth in what he says.

句读 jùdòu　the period and the comma; sentences and phrases

句法 jùfǎ　① sentence structure ② *gram.* syntax

句号 jùhào　full stop; full point; period (。) (.)

句型 jùxíng　sentence pattern

句子 jùzi　sentence

句子成分 jùzi chéngfen　sentence element; member of a sentence

诅　jù　*formal* (used in rhetorical questions): ～料天气骤寒。 Who could have expected that the weather would turn cold suddenly?

拒　jù　① resist; repel: ～敌 resist the enemy; keep the enemy at bay ② refuse; reject: ～不接受 refuse to accept

拒捕 jùbǔ　resist arrest

拒付 jùfù　refuse payment; dishonour (a cheque)

拒谏饰非 jùjiàn-shìfēi　reject representations and gloss over errors; reject criticisms and whitewash one's mistakes

拒绝 jùjué　① refuse: ～参加 refuse to participate / ～发表意见 refuse to comment ② reject; turn down; decline: ～无理要求 turn down (*or* reject) unreasonable demands / ～别人的批评 reject other people's criticism

拒人于千里之外 jù rén yú qiānlǐ zhī wài　keep people at a distance of 1,000 *li*—be arrogant and unapproachable

苣　jù　see 莴苣 wō·jù ——see also qǔ

具¹　jù　① utensil; tool; implement: 农具 nóngjù / 雨具 yǔjù ② *m. formal* (for coffins, dead bodies, and certain instruments or machines): 一～尸体 a corpse / 座钟一～ a desk clock

具²　jù　① possess; have: 初～规模 begin to take shape ② *formal* provide; furnish: 谨～薄礼 allow me to present to you this trifling gift

具保 jùbǎo　*old.* sign a guarantee

具备 jùbèi　possess; have; be provided with: 申请贷款者应～上述条件。 Those who ask for loans should satisfy the conditions listed above. / ～党员条件 be qualified for Party membership

具结 jùjié　*old* sign an undertaking: ～领回失物 sign a receipt for restored lost property / ～悔过 make a statement of repentance / ～释放 enter into a bond and be released

具名 jùmíng　put one's name to a document, etc.; affix one's signature

具体 jùtǐ　concrete; specific; particular: ～政策 specific policies / 对于～情况作～的分析 make a concrete analysis of concrete conditions / 她谈得非常～。 She spoke in very concrete terms. / ～日期未定。 No exact date has been set. / 方案尚待～化。 Details of the plan have yet to be worked out.

具体而微 jùtǐ ér wēi　small but complete; miniature

具体劳动 jùtǐ láodòng　*econ.* concrete labour

具文 jùwén　mere formality; dead letter: 一纸～ a mere scrap of paper

具有 jùyǒu　have (sth. immaterial); possess: 这场运动～深远的历史意义。 The present movement has profound historical significance. / 我们的军队～一往无前的精神。 Our army is imbued with an indomitable spirit. / 建设～中国特色的社会主义 build a socialism with Chinese characteristics

炬　jù　① torch: 火炬 huǒjù ② fire: 付之一炬 fù zhī yī jù

钜¹　jù　*formal* ① hard iron ② hook

钜²　jù　same as 巨 jù

俱　jù　*formal* all; complete: 罪证～在。 All the evidence of the crime is available.

俱乐部 jùlèbù　club

俱全 jùquán　complete in all varieties: 样样～。 Everything necessary is available.

剧¹ (劇)　jù　theatrical work; drama; play; opera: 这个～是谁主演的？ Who is the leading actor in the play?

剧² (劇)　jù　acute; severe; intense: 产量～增 a sharp increase in output

剧本 jùběn　① drama; play ② script; scenario; libretto: 分镜头～ shooting script / ～创作 play writing; script writing

剧变 jùbiàn　a violent (*or* drastic) change

剧场 jùchǎng　theatre

剧跌 jùdiē　(of prices, output, etc.) drop sharply

剧毒 jùdú　hypertoxic

剧烈 jùliè　violent; acute; severe; fierce: ～运动 strenuous exercise / ～的对抗 acute antagonism / ～的社会变动 radical social changes

剧目　jùmù　a list of plays or operas

剧评　jùpíng　a review of a play or opera; dramatic criticism

剧情　jùqíng　the story (or plot) of a play or opera: ～简介 synopsis

剧坛　jùtán　theatrical circles

剧痛　jùtòng　a severe pain

剧团　jùtuán　theatrical company; opera troupe; troupe

剧务　jùwù　① stage management ② stage manager

剧院　jùyuàn　theatre

剧照　jùzhào　stage photo; still

剧中人　jùzhōngrén　characters in a play or opera; *dramatis personae*

剧终　jùzhōng　the end; curtain

剧种　jùzhǒng　type (*or* genre) of drama

剧作　jùzuò　drama; play

剧作家　jùzuòjiā　playwright; dramatist

倨
jù　*formal*　haughty; arrogant: 前倨后恭 qián jù hòu gōng

倨傲　jù'ào　haughty; arrogant

惧（懼）
jù　fear; dread: 毫无所～ not cowed in the least; fearless

惧内　jùnèi　*formal*　henpecked

惧怕　jùpà　fear; dread

惧色　jùsè　a look of fear: 面无～ look undaunted

据（據）
jù　① occupy; seize: 盘据 pánjù ② rely on; depend on: ～险固守 take advantage of a natural barrier to put up a strong defence ③ *prep.* according to; on the grounds of: ～报道 according to (press) reports; it is reported that / ～我看 as I see it; in my opinion / ～我所知 as far as I know / 只有充分了解具体情况，才能～以定出正确的政策。Correct policies can be formulated only on the basis of a thorough understanding of the actual situation. ④ evidence; certificate: 证据 zhèngjù ——see also jū

据称　jùchēng　it is said; they say; allegedly

据传　jùchuán　a story is going around that; rumour has it that

据此　jùcǐ　on these grounds; in view of the above; accordingly

据点　jùdiǎn　strongpoint; fortified point; stronghold

据理力争　jù lǐ lìzhēng　argue strongly on just grounds

据实　jùshí　according to the facts; according to the actual situation: ～汇报 report the facts; give a factual report; make a truthful report

据守　jùshǒu　guard; be entrenched in: ～交通要道 guard vital lines of communication; be entrenched in communication centres / 掘壕～ dig in; entrench oneself

据说　jùshuō　it is said; they say; allegedly: ～他在那里干得不错。They say he is doing quite well there. / 这场事故～是由于疏忽造成的。The accident was allegedly due to negligence.

据为己有　jù wéi jǐ yǒu　take forcible possession of; appropriate

据悉　jùxī　it is reported: ～，他将于明天辞职。He is reportedly going to resign tomorrow.

距¹
jù　① distance: 行距 hángjù ② be apart (*or* away) from; be at a distance from: 天津～北京约有一百二十公里。Tianjin is about 120 km from Beijing. / 飞机于～地面1,000米处爆炸。The plane blew up 1,000 m above the ground. / ～今已有十年。That was ten years ago.

距²
jù　spur (of a cock, etc.)

距离　jùlí　① distance: 保持一个～ keep one's distance;

keep at a distance ② be apart (*or* away) from; be at a distance from: ～车站十五里 15 *li* from the station / 他的看法和你有～。His opinion differs from yours. / 我们的工作～要求还很远。Our work falls far short of the expected standard.

飓
jù　see below

飓风　jùfēng　hurricane

窭（窶）
jù　*formal*　poverty

锯
jù　① saw: 一把～ a saw ② cut with a saw; saw: ～木头 saw wood

锯齿　jùchǐ　sawtooth

锯齿草　jùchǐcǎo　popular name for 蓍 shī

锯床　jùchuáng　sawing machine: 圆盘～ circular sawing machine

锯鳞鱼　jùlínyú　big-eyed soldierfish

锯末　jùmò　sawdust

锯木厂　jùmùchǎng　sawmill; lumber-mill

锯条　jùtiáo　saw blade

锯屑　jùxiè　sawdust

锯子　jùzi　*dial.*　saw

聚
jù　assemble; gather; get together: 大家～在一起商量商量。Let's get together and talk it over. / 咱们找个地方～～。Let's find a place to have a get-together.

聚氨酯　jù'ānzhǐ　(also 聚氨基甲酸酯 jù'ānjījiǎsuānzhǐ) polyurethane

聚宝盆　jùbǎopén　treasure bowl—a place rich in natural resources; cornucopia

聚苯乙烯　jùběnyǐxī　polystyrene

聚变　jùbiàn　*phys.*　fusion: 核～ nuclear fusion / 受控～ controlled fussion

聚变反应堆　jùbiàn fǎnyìngduī　*phys.*　fusion reactor

聚丙烯　jùbǐngxī　polypropylene

聚丙烯腈　jùbǐngxījīng　polyacrylonitrile

聚餐　jùcān　dine together (usu. on festive occasions); have a dinner party

聚赌　jùdǔ　get together to gamble

聚光灯　jùguāngdēng　spotlight

聚光镜　jùguāngjìng　condensing lens

聚合　jùhé　① get together ② *chem.*　polymerization: 定向～ stereoregular (*or* stereotactic) polymerization / ～反应 polyreaction

聚合物　jùhéwù　*chem.*　polymer: 工程～ engineering polymers

聚花果　jùhuāguǒ　collective fruit

聚会　jùhuì　① get together; meet: 老战友～在一起，格外亲热。The meeting of the old comrades-in-arms was extremely cordial. ② get-together: 他们每隔两个月搞一次～。They have a get-together every two months.

聚积　jùjī　accumulate; collect; build up: ～军事力量 build up military forces

聚集　jùjí　gather; assemble; collect: 机场上～着数千人，为代表团送行。Thousands of people gathered at the airport to see the delegation off.

聚甲醛　jùjiǎquán　polyformaldehyde

聚歼　jùjiān　round up and annihilate; annihilate *en masse*

聚焦　jùjiāo　*phys.*　focusing: 指向～ directional focusing

聚精会神　jùjīng-huìshén　concentrate one's attention; be all attention: ～地工作 concentrate on one's work; be intent on one's work / ～地听 listen with rapt attention

聚居　jùjū　inhabit a region (as an ethnic group); live in a compact community: 少数民族～的地区 regions where minority nationalities live in compact communi-

ties

聚居点 jùjūdiǎn　settlement

聚敛 jùliǎn　amass wealth by heavy taxation

聚拢 jùlǒng　gather together

聚氯乙烯 jùlǜyǐxī　polyvinyl chloride (PVC)

聚落 jùluò　settlement; village

聚齐 jùqí　gather (at an appointed place); assemble: 参观的人明天早上八点在展览馆门前～。Visitors will assemble at the gate of the exhibition hall at eight tomorrow morning.

聚醛树脂 jùquánshùzhī　aldehyde resin

聚伞花序 jùsǎn huāxù　*bot.* cyme

聚沙成塔 jù shā chéng tǎ　many grains of sand piled up will make a pagoda—many a little makes a mickle

聚首 jùshǒu　*formal* gather; meet: ～一堂 gather together

聚四氟乙烯 jùsìfúyǐxī　polytetrafluoroethylene (PTFE)

聚讼纷纭 jùsòng fēnyún　argue back and forth without coming to an agreement; opinions differ widely; a welter of conflicting opinions

聚碳酸脂 jùtànsuānzhī　polycarbonate

聚蚊成雷 jù wén chéng léi　a swarm of mosquitoes makes a noise like thunder—popular report is formidable

聚酰胺 jùxiān'àn　polyamide: ～塑料 polyamide plastics

聚星 jùxīng　*astron.* multiple star

聚乙烯 jùyǐxī　polyethylene; polythene

聚乙烯醇 jùyǐxīchún　polyvinyl alcohol

聚酯 jùzhǐ　polyester: ～塑料 polyester plastics

聚众 jùzhòng　assemble a crowd; gather a mob: ～闹事 assemble a crowd to make trouble / ～斗殴 gather a mob to have brawls / ～赌博 organize gambling parties

踞

jù　① crouch; squat ② sit ③ occupy: 盘踞 pánjù

踞守 jùshǒu　same as 据守 jùshǒu

遽

jù　① hurriedly; hastily: ～下结论 pass judgment hastily ② frightened; alarmed: 惶遽 huángjù

遽然 jùrán　*formal* suddenly; abruptly: ～变色 suddenly change countenance

屦（屨）

jù　straw sandals

juān

涓

juān　*formal* a tiny stream: 涓滴 juāndī

涓埃 juān'āi　*formal* insignificant; negligible: 略尽～之力 make what little contribution one can; do one's bit

涓滴 juāndī　a tiny drop; dribble; driblet

涓滴归公 juāndī guī gōng　every bit goes to the public treasury; turn in every cent of public money

涓涓 juānjuān　*liter.* trickling sluggishly: ～流水 a sluggish trickle of water

捐

juān　① relinquish; abandon: 捐生 juānshēng ② contribute; donate; subscribe: 我向基金会～了一笔钱。I have donated some money to the foundation. ③ tax: 车～ a tax on cars, etc.

捐款 juānkuǎn　① contribute money ② contribution; donation; subscription

捐弃 juānqì　*formal* relinquish; abandon: ～前嫌 bury old grudges

捐躯 juānqū　sacrifice one's life; lay down one's life

捐生 juānshēng　sacrifice one's life

捐输 juānshū　*formal* contribute (to an organization); donate; present

捐税 juānshuì　taxes and levies

捐献 juānxiàn　contribute (to an organization); donate; present: 他把全部藏书～给图书馆。He presented his whole collection of books to the library.

捐赠 juānzèng　contribute (as a gift); donate; present: 向图书馆～图书 present books to a library / 他～了一万元给那家医院。He made a donation of 10,000 *yuan* to that hospital.

捐助 juānzhù　offer (financial or material assistance); contribute; donate

娟

juān　*formal* beautiful; graceful: 婵娟 chánjuān

娟娟 juānjuān　*liter.* beautiful; graceful: ～明月 the beautiful moon

娟秀 juānxiù　*formal* beautiful; graceful: 字迹～ beautiful handwriting; a graceful hand

圈

juān　① shut in a pen; pen in: 把羊群～起来 herd the sheep into the pens / 别老～在书房里。Don't shut yourself up in your study. ② *inf.* lock up; put in jail: 犯人都～起来了。The prisoners were locked up. ——see also juàn; quān

鹃

juān　see 杜鹃 dùjuān

镌（鐫）

juān　*formal* engrave: ～碑 engrave a stone tablet

镌刻 juānkè　*formal* engrave

蠲

juān　① *formal* exempt from ② *old* store up

蠲除 juānchú　*formal* remove; abolish

蠲免 juānmiǎn　*formal* exempt from (an obligation)

juǎn

卷¹（捲）

juǎn　① roll up: 把竹帘子～起来 roll up the bamboo screen / ～起袖子就干 roll up one's sleeves and pitch in ② sweep off; carry along: 一个大浪把小船～走了。A huge wave swept the boat away. / 汽车飞驰而过，～起一阵尘土。A car sped past, raising a cloud of dust. ③ cylindrical mass of sth.; roll: 把书裹成一个～儿寄出去。Roll up the book and take it to the post. ④ curler: 她顶着一脑袋的～儿就出去了。She went out with her hair in curlers. ⑤ *m.* roll; spool; reel: 一～手纸 a roll of toilet paper / 一～软片 a roll of film / 一～铺盖 a roll of bedding

卷²（餐）

juǎn　roll (a food): 花卷 huājuǎn ——see also juàn

卷笔刀 juǎnbǐdāo　pencil sharpener

卷层云 juǎncéngyún　*meteorol.* cirrostratus

卷尺 juǎnchǐ　tape measure; band tape: 布～ cloth (or linen) tape / 钢～ steel tape

卷发 juǎnfà　curly hair; wavy hair

卷发器 juǎnfàqì　curler

卷积云 juǎnjīyún　*meteorol.* cirrocumulus

卷铺盖 juǎn pūgài　① pack up and quit ② get the sack

卷曲机 juǎnqūjī　*text.* crimping machine

卷染机 juǎnrǎnjī　*text.* dye jigger

卷绕 juǎnrào　*text.* winding: ～机 take-up machine

卷刃 juǎnrèn　(of a knife blade) be turned (*or* twisted): 你把我的刀拿去干什么啦? 都卷了刃儿了! What have you been doing to my knife? The blade's all turned.

卷入 juǎnrù　be drawn into; be involved in: ～漩涡 be drawn into a whirlpool / ～一场纠纷 be involved in a dispute

卷舌辅音 juǎnshéfǔyīn　*phonet.* retroflex consonant

卷舌元音　juǎnshéyuányīn　*phonet.*　retroflex vowel
卷逃　juǎntáo　abscond with valuables
卷筒　juǎntǒng　reel
卷筒纸　juǎntǒngzhǐ　web: ～印刷机 web press
卷土重来　juǎn tǔ chóng lái　stage a comeback
卷尾猴　juǎnwěihóu　(weeping) capuchin; weeping monkey
卷心菜　juǎnxīncài　*dial.*　cabbage
卷须　juǎnxū　*bot.*　tendril
卷烟　juǎnyān　① cigarette ② cigar
卷烟纸　juǎnyānzhǐ　cigarette paper
卷扬机　juǎnyángjī　hoist; hoister
卷叶蛾　juǎnyè'é　(also 卷叶虫 juǎnyèchóng) leaf roller
卷云　juǎnyún　*meteorol.*　cirrus
卷轴　juǎnzhóu　reel: 天线～ aerial reel ——see also juànzhóu
卷子　juǎnzi　steamed roll ——see also juànzi

juàn

卷　juàn　① book: 手不释卷 shǒu bù shì juàn ② chapter, section, or volume; fascicle; *juan* (a rather ambiguous unit of book-division; for ancient texts, a *juan* of which usu. contains less than a volume, "fascicle" or the romanized form is to be preferred): 古书的数量论～。Ancient texts are counted in *juan*. / 佛经一千零三十一部, 共三千四百七十四～。In all there are 1,031 Buddhist texts in 3,474 fascicles. / 吾家藏书一万～。In my house I have a collection of 10,000 *juan* of books. / 这个图书馆藏书十万～。This library has 100,000 volumes. / 《新大英百科全书》共三十～。The *New Encyclopaedia Britannica* is complete in 30 volumes. ③ examination paper: 交卷 jiāojuàn ④ file; dossier: 查～ look through the files ——see also juàn
卷帙　juànzhì　*formal*　books; volumes; tomes: 唐人诗集各注, ～浩繁, 购置维艰。Collections of Tang poems, together with notes and commentaries, are a vast literature, hardly accessible to the average reader.
卷轴　juànzhóu　*formal*　scroll ——see also juǎnzhóu
卷子　juànzi　① examination paper: 看～ mark examination papers ② a handwritten copy in scroll form ——see also juǎnzi
卷宗　juànzōng　① folder ② file; dossier

倦　juàn　weary; tired: 疲倦 píjuàn
倦怠　juàndài　languid; sluggish: 神色～ a languid look
倦容　juànróng　a tired look: 面有～ look tired
倦色　juànsè　a tired look
倦意　juànyì　a feeling of tiredness: 他滔滔不绝地讲, 好像毫无～。He talked on and on, apparently not feeling in the least tired.
倦游　juànyóu　*formal*　weary of wandering and sightseeing: ～归来 be back home, sated, from pleasure excursions

绢　juàn　thin, tough silk
绢本　juànběn　silk scroll
绢纺　juànfǎng　silk spinning
绢花　juànhuā　silk flower
绢画　juànhuà　classical Chinese painting on silk
绢丝　juànsī　spun silk (yarn): ～纺绸 spun silk pongee / ～织物 spun silk fabric
绢网印花　juànwǎng yìnhuā　*text.*　screen printing: ～法 silk-screen process
绢子　juànzi　*dial.*　handkerchief

隽(儁)　juàn　*formal*　meaningful

隽永　juànyǒng　*formal*　meaningful: 语颇～, 耐人寻味。The remarks are meaningful and thought-provoking.

狷(獧)　juàn　*formal*　① impetuous; rash ② upright; incorruptible
狷急　juànjí　*formal*　impetuous; rash
狷介　juànjiè　*formal*　upright; incorruptible

眷¹　juàn　family dependant: 女眷 nǚjuàn

眷²(睠)　juàn　*formal*　have tender feeling for: 眷顾 juàngù
眷爱　juàn'ài　regard with affection; love
眷顾　juàngù　*formal*　regard with tenderness; be concerned about
眷眷　juànjuàn　*formal*　longingly; yearningly: 纷进拜兮堂前, 目～兮琼筵。(王维) In a swirl they come forward and bow there before the hall, Eyes filled with love-longing toward the sacred mats like jade.
眷恋　juànliàn　*formal*　be sentimentally attached to (a person or place)
眷念　juànniàn　*formal*　think fondly of; feel nostalgic about
眷属　juànshǔ　family dependants
眷注　juànzhù　*formal*　give tender devotion to; show loving solicitude about: 深承～。I am most grateful to you for your great solicitude.

圈　juàn　pen; fold; sty: 把羊轰到～里去 Put the flock in the fold. ——see also juàn; quān
圈肥　juànféi　barnyard manure

juē

嗟　juē　a variant pronunciation for 嗟 jiē

撅¹　juē　stick up: ～着尾巴 sticking up the tail / ～嘴 pout (one's lips)

撅²(捒)　juē　*inf.*　break (sth. long and narrow); snap: 把树枝～成两段 break the twig in two

噘　juē　same as 撅¹ juē, limited to use in 噘嘴 "pout (one's lips)"

jué

孑　jué　see 孑孓 jiéjué

决¹(決)　jué　① decide; determine: 表决 biǎojué ② *adv.* (used before a negative) definitely; certainly; under any circumstances: ～非恶意 be entirely without malice; bear no ill will whatsoever / ～不退让 will under no circumstances give in / 不达目的～不罢休。We'll never give up until the goal is reached. ③ execute a person: 枪决 qiāngjué

决²(決)　jué　(of a dyke, etc.) be breached; burst: 溃决 kuìjué
决策　juécè　① make policy; make a strategic decision: 运筹～ devise strategies ② policy decision; decision of strategic importance: 战略～ strategic decision
决策机构　juécè jīgòu　policy-making body
决策人　juécèrén　policy-maker
决出　juéchū　contest (prizes); fight for: 今天将～三块金

牌。Three golds will be contested and awarded today.

决堤 juédī　breach (*or* burst) a dyke

决定 juédìng　① decide; resolve; make up one's mind: 领导～派她出国。The leadership decided to send her abroad. / 理事会～下届友好邀请赛在北京举行。The Council resolved that the next friendship invitational tournament should be held in Beijing. / 一时～不了 cannot make up one's mind for the moment; be unable to come to a decision for the moment ② decision; resolution: 通过一项～ pass a resolution ③ determine; decide: 存在～意识。Man's social being determines his consciousness. / ④ decisive: ～因素 decisive factor; determinant

决定论 juédìnglùn　*philos.* determinism

决定权 juédìngquán　power to make decisions: 有最后～ have the final say

决定性 juédìngxìng　decisiveness: ～的胜利 a decisive victory / 起～作用 play a decisive part (*or* role)

决斗 juédòu　① duel ② decisive struggle

决断 juéduàn　① make a decision ② resolve; decisiveness; resolution: 他很有～。He shows great resolve. / 你要有～, 你认为怎么办好就怎么办。You must be resolute and do what you think best.

决计 juéjì　① have decided; have made up one's mind: 我～把工作搞完再走。I have decided to get the work done before I leave. ② definitely; certainly: 那样办～没错儿。We definitely can't go wrong if we do it that way. *or* There is absolutely nothing wrong with doing it that way.

决绝 juéjué　break off relations

决口 juékǒu　(of a dyke, etc.) be breached; burst: 河～了。The river burst its banks.

决裂 juéliè　break with; rupture: 这样她就和我～了, 彼此再没有见面。With that she broke off with me, and we were never to see each other again. / 与旧世界～ break with the old world / 和封建主义的传统～ break with the feudal tradition

决然 juérán　*adv. formal* ① resolutely; determinedly: ～返回 turn back resolutely ② definitely; unquestionably; undoubtedly: 那～不是我的错。That's definitely not my fault. / 搞阴谋的人～没有好下场。Those who engage in conspiracies are bound to come to no good end.

决撒 juésā　*old* break with; rupture

决赛 juésài　*sports* finals

决胜 juéshèng　decide the issue of the battle; determine the victory

决胜局 juéshèngjú　*sports* deciding game (*or* set)

决死 juésǐ　life-and-death: ～的斗争 a life-and-death struggle; a last-ditch fight

决算 juésuàn　final accounts; final accounting of revenue and expenditure

决心 juéxīn　determination; resolution: 下定～ make up one's mind; be resolute; be determined / 有～, 有信心 have both determination and confidence / ～改正错误 be determined to correct one's mistake

决心书 juéxīnshū　written pledge; statement of one's determination

决一雌雄 jué yī cí-xióng　fight to see who is the stronger; fight it out

决一胜负 jué yī shèng-fù　fight it out

决一死战 jué yī sǐzhàn　fight to the death; fight to a finish

决疑 juéyí　resolve doubts

决议 juéyì　resolution: ～草案 a draft resolution

决意 juéyì　have one's mind made up; be determined: 他～要走。He's made up his mind to quit.

决战 juézhàn　decisive battle; decisive engagement

诀[1]　jué　① rhymed formula: 口诀 kǒujué ② knack; tricks of the trade: 秘诀 mìjué

诀[2]　jué　bid farewell; part: 永诀 yǒngjué

诀别 juébié　bid farewell; part (usu. with the implication that there is little likelihood of meeting again)

诀窍 juéqiào　secret of success; key to success; tricks of the trade; knack: 炒菜的～主要是拿准火候儿。By and large, the key to success in stir-frying is proper control of time and temperature. / 你这么快就做得了, 有什么～啊? You finished your job really fast. What's the secret of it? / 你掌握了～就容易了。It's easy once you've got the knack of it. *or* It's simple if you know the trick.

诀要 juéyào　same as 诀窍 juéqiào

抉　jué　*formal* pick out; single out: 抉择 juézé

抉择 juézé　*formal* choose: 作出～ make one's choice

抉摘 juézhāi　*formal* ① choose ② expose and censure: ～弊端 expose and censure malpractices

角[1]　jué　① role; part; character: 他在这出戏里演哪个～儿? What's his role in this play? ② type of role (in traditional Chinese drama): 丑角 chǒujué ③ actor or actress: 名～ a famous actor or actress

角[2]　jué　contend; wrestle: 口角 kǒujué

角[3]　jué　an ancient three-legged wine cup

角[4]　jué　a note of the ancient Chinese five-tone scale, corresponding to 3 in numbered musical notation

——see also jiǎo

角斗 juédòu　wrestle

角斗场 juédòuchǎng　wrestling ring

角力 juélì　have a trial of strength; wrestle

角色 juésè　① role; part: 她在这部电影里演哪个～? What part does she play in that film? / 扮演了不光彩的～ play a contemptible role ② type of role (in traditional Chinese drama)

角逐 juézhú　contend; tussle; enter into rivalry

珏　jué　penannular jade ring (worn as an ornament in ancient China)

玦(瑴)　jué　*formal* two pieces of jade put together

觉(覺)　jué　① sense; feel: 下过这场雪, 就～出冷来了。After the snow it is really cold. / 身上～着不舒服 not feel well ② wake (up); awake: 如梦初～ as if waking from a dream ③ become aware; become awakened: 他的意思你还没～出来吗? Haven't you figured out what he meant yet? ——see also jiào

觉察 juéchá　detect; become aware of; perceive: 敌人没有～出我侦察排的行动。The enemy didn't detect our scouting platoon's movements. / 她～到这里面有问题。She sensed there was something wrong.

觉得 juéde　① feel: 一点儿也不～累 not feel tired at all ② think; feel: 我～应该先跟他商量一下。I think we should consult him first. / 我～他这几天情绪不好。I have a feeling that he's been in low spirits these last few days. / 你～这个计划怎么样? What do you think of the plan?

觉乎 jué·hū　*inf.* feel

觉悟 juéwù　① consciousness; awareness; understanding: 阶级～ class consciousness ② come to under-

stand; become aware of; become politically awakened: ～了的人民 an awakened people／他～到了改造世界观的重要性。He has come to see the importance of remoulding his world outlook.

觉醒 juéxǐng　awaken

绝

绝 jué　① cut off; sever: ～其后路 cut off his retreat／掌声不～ prolonged applause　② exhausted; used up; finished: 法子都想～了。All possible ways have been tried. *or* All possibilities have been exhausted.　③ desperate; hopeless: 绝境 juéjìng　④ unique; superb; matchless: 她发的那球真～。Her serve was a beauty.　⑤ *adv.* extremely; most: ～大的错误 an egregious error; a grievous fault／～大多数 most; the overwhelming majority／～好的机会 an excellent opportunity　⑥ *adv.* (used before a negative) absolutely; in the least; by any means; on any account: ～无此意 have absolutely no such intentions／～非偶然 by no means fortuitous／～不可粗心大意 must on no account be negligent　⑦ leaving no leeway; making no allowance; uncompromising: 他尽管不同意，但是没把话说～。He disagreed, but he didn't say anything definitive.　⑧ short for 绝句 juéjù: 五绝 wǔjué／七绝 qījué

绝版 juébǎn　out of print

绝笔 juébǐ　① last words written before one's death　② the last work of an author or painter

绝壁 juébì　precipice

绝产 juéchǎn　① same as 绝收 juéshōu　② property left without an inheritor

绝唱 juéchàng　the peak of poetic perfection: 堪称千古～ rank as a poetic masterpiece through the ages

绝处逢生 juéchù féng shēng　be unexpectedly rescued from a desperate situation

绝代 juédài　*formal* unique among one's contemporaries; peerless: 才华～ unrivalled talent／～佳人 a woman of matchless beauty

绝倒 juédǎo　*formal* shake one's sides; roar with laughter: 令人～ sidesplitting

绝地 juédì　① a danger spot: 这里左边是悬崖，右边是深沟，真是个～。A precipice on the left side and a deep gully on the right—a veritable danger spot.　② hopeless situation; dead end; impasse: 陷于～ come to a dead end

绝顶 juédǐng　① extremely; utterly: ～聪明 extremely intelligent／～愚蠢的行为 the height of folly　② *formal* peak; summit: 会当凌～，一览众山小。(杜甫) The time will come when I pass up to its very summit, And see in one encompassing vision how tiny all other mountains are.

绝对 juéduì　① absolute: ～多数 absolute majority; overwhelming majority／～优势 absolute predominance; overwhelming superiority／防止思想上的～化 avoid thinking in terms of absolutes　② *adv.* absolutely; perfectly; definitely: ～可靠 absolutely reliable／你～不能去。You absolutely can't go.／我～有把握。I'm absolutely sure.／这事～保密。This must be kept absolutely secret. *or* This is strictly confidential.／那事～真实。That story is definitely true.

绝对地租 juéduì dìzū　absolute rent

绝对高度 juéduì gāodù　absolute altitude

绝对观念 juéduì guānniàn　*philos.* absolute idea

绝对量度 juéduì liángdù　*phys.* absolute measurement

绝对零度 juéduì língdù　*phys.* absolute zero

绝对贫困化 juéduì pínkùnhuà　absolute impoverishment

绝对平均主义 juéduì píngjūnzhǔyì　absolute equalitarianism

绝对湿度 juéduì shīdù　*meteorol.* absolute humidity

绝对温度 juéduì wēndù　*phys.* absolute temperature

绝对音乐 juéduì yīnyuè　absolute music

绝对真理 juéduì zhēnlǐ　*philos.* absolute truth

绝对值 juéduìzhí　*math.* absolute value

绝对主义 juéduìzhǔyì　*philos.* absolutism

绝后 juéhòu　① without offspring (*or* issue)　② never to be seen again: 空前绝后 kōngqián-juéhòu

绝户 juéhu　① without offspring (*or* issue)　② a childless person

绝技 juéjì　unique skill; consummate skill

绝迹 juéjì　disappear; vanish; be stamped out: 血吸虫病在我们县已经～。Schistosomiasis has been stamped out in our county.／猛犸在史前时期就～了。Mammoths became extinct in prehistoric times.

绝交 juéjiāo　break off relations (as between friends or countries)

绝经 juéjīng　menopause

绝境 juéjìng　① isolated condition　② hopeless situation; impasse; blind alley; *cul-de-sac*: 濒于～ face an impasse

绝句 juéjù　*jueju,* a poem of four lines, each containing five or seven characters, with a strict tonal pattern and rhyme scheme; quatrain: 五言～ a pentasyllabic quatrain／七言～ a heptasyllabic quatrain

绝口 juékǒu　① (only used after 不) stop talking: 骂不～ heap endless abuse upon; pour out unceasing abuse　② keep one's mouth shut: ～不提 never say a single word about; avoid all mention of

绝粒 juélì　*formal* ① go without food; fast　② run out of food

绝路 juélù　① block the way out; leave no way out: 这个办法要是还不行，那可就绝了路了。If this proves to be no solution, then there can be no solution.　② road to ruin; blind alley; dead end; impasse: 自寻～ court destruction; bring ruin upon oneself／走上～ come to a dead end (*or* impasse)

绝伦 juélún　*formal* unsurpassed; unequalled; peerless; matchless: 精美～ exquisite beyond compare; superb

绝密 juémì　top-secret; strictly confidential: ～文件 top-secret papers／～情报 top-secret information

绝妙 juémiào　extremely clever; ingenious; excellent; perfect: ～的一招 a masterstroke／～的讽刺 a supreme (*or* perfect) irony

绝命书 juémìngshū　① suicide note　② note written on the eve of one's execution

绝情 juéqíng　heartless; cruel: ～忘义 ungrateful and heartless／夫妻之间不要说这种～的话。It's not for a husband or wife to make such heartless (*or* cruel) remarks.

绝然 juérán　*adv.* absolutely; perfectly; completely: ～不同 be totally different; have nothing in common

绝热 juérè　*phys.* heat insulation: ～材料 heat-insulating material／～冷却 adiabatic cooling／～曲线 adiabatic curve; adiabatics／～压缩 adiabatic compression

绝色 juésè　*formal* (of a woman) exceedingly beautiful; of unrivalled beauty

绝食 juéshí　go on a hunger strike; fast

绝收 juéshōu　total crop failure

绝嗣 juésì　*formal* without offspring (*or* issue)

绝望 juéwàng　give up all hope; despair: ～情绪 feeling of despair／～的挣扎 desperate struggle

绝无仅有 juéwújǐnyǒu　the only one of its kind; unique

绝响 juéxiǎng　*formal* lost art; inimitable art

绝续 jué-xù　continue or discontinue; survive or perish ——see also 存亡绝续 cún-wáng jué-xù

绝学 juéxué　a lost body of knowledge

绝艺 juéyì　consummate art or skill

绝育 juéyù　*med.* sterilization

绝域 juéyù　*formal* a distant and inaccessible land

绝缘 juéyuán　① cut all ties with sth.: 我与酒～了。I

have stopped drinking. ② *elec.* insulation: 〜材料 insulating material; insulant / 〜体 insulator / 〜线 covered wire / 〜纸 insulating paper / 〜子 insulator

绝早 juézǎo　extremely early

绝招 juézhāo　(also 绝着 juézhāo) ① unique skill ② unexpected tricky move (as a last resort)

绝症 juézhèng　incurable disease; fatal illness

绝种 juézhǒng　(of a species) become extinct; die out

倔 jué　same as 倔 juè, limited to use in 倔强 jué-jiàng ——see also juè

倔强 juéjiàng　stubborn; unbending

掘 jué　dig: 〜井 dig a well

掘进 juéjìn　*min.* driving; tunnelling: 平巷〜 drifting / 快速〜 quick tunnelling / 全断面〜 full-face tunnelling

掘墓人 juémùrén　gravedigger

掘土机 juétǔjī　excavator; power shovel

崛 jué　*formal* rise abruptly

崛起 juéqǐ　*formal* ① (of a mountain, etc.) rise abruptly; suddenly appear on the horizon ② rise to prominence: 太平军〜于广西金田村。 The Taipings rose in revolt at Jintian Village, Guangxi. / 吴淞口畔,一座新的钢铁城正在〜。 At Wusong a new city of steel is emerging on the horizon.

觖 jué　*formal* dissatisfied

觖望 juéwàng　*formal* dissatisfied and resentful

厥[1] jué　faint; lose consciousness; fall into a coma: 昏厥 hūnjué

厥[2] jué　*formal* his or her; its; their: 〜后 thereafter / 〜父 his or her father

谲 jué　*formal* cheat; swindle: 诡谲 guǐjué

谲诈 juézhà　cunning; crafty

蕨 jué　brake (fern)

蕨类植物 juélèi zhíwù　pteridophyte

獗 jué　see 猖獗 chāngjué

橛(橜) jué　a short wooden stake; wooden pin; peg

橛子 juézi　a short wooden stake; wooden pin; peg

噱 jué　*formal* loud laughter: 可发一〜 make one laugh out loud ——see also xué

爵[1] jué　the rank of nobility; peerage: 封〜 confer a title (of nobility) upon

爵[2] jué　an ancient wine vessel with three legs and a loop handle

爵禄 juélù　*formal* ranks and stipends; titles and stipends; dignities and emoluments: 明主之为官职〜也,所以进贤才劝有功也。《韩非子》 The enlightened ruler assigns posts and hands out titles and stipends as a means of promoting men of worth and talent and encouraging men of achievement. / 财贿不以动其心,〜不以移其志。 Rich bribes serve not to move him, nor do dignities and emoluments deflect his purpose.

爵士 juéshì　① knight ② Sir: 约翰·史密斯〜 Sir John Smith

爵士音乐 juéshì yīnyuè　*jazz*

爵位 juéwèi　the rank (*or* title) of nobility

蹶(蹷) jué　① fall ② suffer a setback: 一蹶不振 yī jué bù zhèn ——see also juě

矍 jué　*formal* look around in alarm

矍铄 juéshuò　*formal* hale and hearty

嚼 jué　same as 嚼 jiáo, limited to use in 咀嚼 jǔjué and 过屠门而大嚼 guò túmén ér dà jué ——see also jiáo; jiào

攫 jué　seize; grab: 〜为己有 seize possession of; appropriate

攫取 juéqǔ　seize; grab: 〜别国的资源 grab the resources of other countries / 〜暴利 rake in exorbitant profits

镢(钁) jué　*dial.* pick; pickaxe

镢头 juétou　*dial.* pick; pickaxe

juě

蹶 juě　see below ——see also jué

蹶子 juězi　see 尥蹶子 liào juězi

juè

倔 juè　gruff; surly: 这老头儿脾气〜。 That old man is rather surly. ——see also jué

倔巴 juèba　*dial.* gruff; surly: 这家伙有点〜。 This guy is rather surly.

倔头 juètóu　a stubborn and surly person; a difficult customer

倔头倔脑 juètóu-juènǎo　blunt of manner and gruff of speech

jūn

军 jūn　① armed forces; army; troops: 日〜 Japanese troops ② army (consisting of two or more divisions): 第一〜 the First Army / 全歼敌人一个〜 wipe out an enemy army / 〜以上干部 cadres including and above the level of army commander; cadres of army level and above

军备 jūnbèi　armament; arms: 〜控制 arms control / 〜限制 arms limitation

军备竞赛 jūnbèi jìngsài　armament (*or* arms) race

军部 jūnbù　army headquarters

军操 jūncāo　military drill

军车 jūnchē　military vehicle

军刀 jūndāo　soldier's sword; sabre

军地两用人才 jūn-dì liǎngyòng réncái　PLA men trained to be competent for both military and civilian services

军队 jūnduì　armed forces; army; troops

军队标号 jūnduì biāohào　military symbols

军阀 jūnfá　warlord: 〜战争 war among warlords / 〜作风 warlord ways; warlord style

军阀主义 jūnfázhǔyì　warlordism

军法 jūnfǎ　military criminal code; military law: 〜从事 punish by military law

军法审判 jūnfǎ shěnpàn　court-martial

军方 jūnfāng　the military

军费 jūnfèi　military expenditure

军分区 jūnfēnqū　military subarea

军风纪 jūnfēngjì　soldier's bearing and discipline

军服 jūnfú　military (or army) uniform; uniform

军服呢 jūnfúní　army coating

军港 jūngǎng　naval port

军歌 jūngē　army song

军工 jūngōng　① (short for 军事工业) war industry: ～生产 war production ② (short for 军事工程) military project

军功 jūngōng　military merit; military exploit

军功章 jūngōngzhāng　medal for military merit

军官 jūnguān　officer

军管 jūnguǎn　short for 军事管制 jūnshì guǎnzhì

军管会 jūnguǎnhuì　short for 军事管制委员会 jūnshì guǎnzhì wěiyuánhuì

军棍 jūngùn　(in former times) a cane for corporal punishment in the army

军国主义 jūnguózhǔyì　militarism: ～者 militarist

军国主义化 jūnguózhǔyìhuà　militarization

军号 jūnhào　bugle

军徽 jūnhuī　army emblem

军婚 jūnhūn　marriage with one or both partners in military service

军火 jūnhuǒ　munitions; arms and ammunition: ～工业 munitions industry; armament industry / ～舰 ammunition ship

军火库 jūnhuǒkù　arsenal

军火商 jūnhuǒshāng　munitions merchant; arms dealer; merchant of death

军机 jūnjī　① military plan: 贻误～ delay or frustrate the fulfilment of a military plan ② military secret: 泄漏～ leak a military secret

军籍 jūnjí　military status; one's name on the army roll: 保留～ retain one's military status / 开除～ strike sb.'s name off the army roll; discharge sb. from the army

军纪 jūnjì　military discipline

军舰 jūnjiàn　warship; naval vessel

军阶 jūnjiē　(military) rank; grade

军界 jūnjiè　military circles; the military

军垦 jūnkěn　reclamation of wasteland by an army unit

军垦农场 jūnkěn nóngchǎng　army reclamation farm; army farm

军礼 jūnlǐ　military salute

军力 jūnlì　military strength

军粮 jūnliáng　army provisions; grain for the army

军粮库 jūnliángkù　military grain depot; army granary

军龄 jūnlíng　length of military service: 他的～比我长。 He has served in the army longer than I have.

军令 jūnlìng　military orders: 颁布～ issue a military order

军令如山 jūnlìng rú shān　military orders are like mountains (i.e. are unalterable and must be obeyed)

军令状 jūnlìngzhuàng　① (in old novels and dramas) a military pledge (an agreement made between an army officer and his superior that the officer would be severely punished if he could not successfully carry out a special mission, which, unlike a regular commission, is usually taken by the officer on his own initiative): 立下～ write a military pledge ② a promise to get a job done, failing which one is willing to accept a severe penalty

军旅 jūnlǚ　formal armies; troops: ～生涯 life in the army; soldiering / ～之事 military matters

军马 jūnmǎ　army horse

军马场 jūnmǎchǎng　army horse-breeding farm; army horse ranch

军帽 jūnmào　army cap; service cap

军民 jūn-mín　the army and the people; soldiers and civilians; military and civilian: ～关系 the relations between the army and the people; army-people relations / ～联防 army-civilian joint defence / ～鱼水情。 The army and the people are as close to each other as fish and water.

军品 jūnpǐn　military products

军旗 jūnqí　army flag; colours; ensign

军旗礼 jūnqílǐ　colours salute

军情 jūnqíng　military (or war) situation: 刺探～ spy out military secrets; gather military intelligence

军区 jūnqū　military region; (military) area command: 各大～ the greater military areas / ～司令部 the headquarters of a military area command

军权 jūnquán　military leadership; military power

军犬 jūnquǎn　a police dog used for military purposes

军人 jūnrén　soldier; serviceman; armyman: ～大会 soldiers conference (of a company)

军容 jūnróng　soldier's discipline, appearance and bearing: 整饬～ strengthen army discipline and maintain required standards for appearance and bearing

军师 jūnshī　old war counsellor; military adviser

军士 jūnshì　noncommissioned officer (NCO)

军事 jūnshì　① military affairs ② military: ～表演 display of military skills / ～部署 military deployment; disposition of military forces / ～分界线 military demarcation line / ～路线 military line / ～设施 military installations / ～素质 military qualities; fighting capability / ～训练 military training / ～演习 military manoeuvre; war exercise / ～优势 military superiority

军事法庭 jūnshì fǎtíng　military tribunal (or court)

军事工业 jūnshì gōngyè　war industry

军事管制 jūnshì guǎnzhì　military control

军事管制委员会 jūnshì guǎnzhì wěiyuánhuì　military control commission

军事化 jūnshìhuà　militarize; place on a war footing: 参加野营的学生过着～的生活。 The students who went camping followed a military routine.

军事基地 jūnshì jīdì　military base

军事家 jūnshìjiā　strategist

军事科学 jūnshì kēxué　military science

军事体育 jūnshì tǐyù　military sports

军事条令 jūnshì tiáolìng　military manuals

军事学 jūnshìxué　military science: ～家 military scientist

军事学院 jūnshì xuéyuàn　military academy (or institute)

军属 jūnshǔ　(short for 军人家属) soldier's dependants; armyman's family

军统 jūntǒng　(short for 军事委员会调查统计局) the Bureau of Investigation and Statistics of the Military Council (one of the Kuomintang's huge secret service agencies)

军团 jūntuán　army group

军威 jūnwēi　military might: ～大振。 The might of the army was made felt.

军委 jūnwěi　(short for 中国共产党中央军事委员会) the Military Commission of the Central Committee of the Communist Party of China

军务 jūnwù　military affairs; military task: ～繁忙 be busy with military affairs

军衔 jūnxián　military rank ～制度 system of military ranks

军饷 jūnxiǎng　old soldier's pay and provisions

军校 jūnxiào　(short for 军事学校) military school; military academy

军械 jūnxiè　ordnance; armament: ～员 armourer

军械处 jūnxièchù　ordnance department

军械库 jūnxièkù　ordnance depot; arms depot; armoury

军心 jūnxīn　soldiers' morale: 动摇～ shake the army's morale / ～大振。 The morale of the troops has been

greatly raised.

军需 jūnxū ① military supplies ② *old* quartermaster

军需库 jūnxūkù military supply depot

军需品 jūnxūpǐn military supplies; military stores

军训 jūnxùn (short for 军事训练) military training

军衣 jūnyī military (or army) uniform; uniform

军医 jūnyī medical officer; military surgeon

军营 jūnyíng military camp; barracks

军用 jūnyòng for military use; military: ～地图 military map / ～飞机 warplane; military aircraft / ～机场 military airfield / ～列车 military train / ～物资 military supplies; *matériel*

军邮 jūnyóu army postal service; army post (or mail)

军援 jūnyuán (short for 军事援助) military aid

军乐 jūnyuè martial (or military) music

军乐队 jūnyuèduì military band

军运 jūnyùn military transportation

军长 jūnzhǎng army commander

军政 jūnzhèng ① military affairs and politics ② military administration ③ army and government: ～当局 civil and military authorities / ～关系 the relations between the army and the government

军政府 jūnzhèngfǔ military government

军职 jūnzhí official post in the army; military appointment

军中无戏言 jūn zhōng wú xìyán there is no room for levity in the army

军种 jūnzhǒng (armed) services

军装 jūnzhuāng military (or army) uniform; uniform

均

jūn ① equal; even: 人口分布不～。The population is unevenly distributed. ② *adv.* without exception; all: 各项准备工作～已就绪。All the preparatory work has been completed.

均等 jūnděng equal; impartial; fair: 机会～ equal opportunity

均分 jūnfēn divide equally; share out equally: 这批建筑材料由三个单位～。This lot of building materials will be shared out equally among three units.

均衡 jūnhéng balance; equilibrium: 走钢丝的演员举着一把伞，保持身体的～。The tightrope walker kept her balance by holding up an umbrella. / 国民经济的～发展 the balanced (or harmonious) development of the national economy / 矛盾双方达到某种暂时的～。A certain temporary parity has been attained between the two sides of the contradiction.

均衡论 jūnhénglùn *philos.* the theory of equilibrium

均热 jūnrè *metall.* soaking: ～炉 soaking pit

均势 jūnshì balance of power; equilibrium of forces; equilibrium; parity: 保持 (打破)～ keep (upset) the balance of power

均摊 jūntān share equally: ～费用 share the expenses equally

均相 jūnxiàng *chem.* homogeneous phase: ～催化剂 homogeneous catalyst

均一 jūnyī even; uniform; homogeneous

均一性 jūnyīxìng *chem.* homogeneity

均匀 jūnyún even; well-distributed: ～的呼吸 even breathing / ～撒播 even broadcasting of seeds / 今年的雨水很～。Rainfall has been fairly well-distributed this year.

均匀混合物 jūnyún hùnhéwù *chem.* homogeneous mixture

均沾 jūnzhān share (profits, benefits, etc.) equally: 利益～ an equal share of profits

君

jūn ① monarch; sovereign; supreme ruler ② *formal* (used as a title) Mr.: 张～ Mr. Zhang / 张刘二～ Messrs. Zhang and Liu / 诸～ gentlemen (used in

addressing a group) ③ *formal* (used in direct address) you; sir: 祝～早安。Good morning, sir. / 劝～莫惜金缕衣，劝～惜取少年时。(杜秋娘) I adjure you, sir, not to prize your coat of gold thread; I adjure you, sir, to prize the time of youth.

君迁子 jūnqiānzǐ *Chin. med.* the fruit of date plum (*Diospyros lotus*)

君权 jūnquán monarchical power; royal prerogative

君王 jūnwáng monarch; sovereign; emperor: 天生丽质难自弃，一朝选在～侧。(白居易) Too fairly formed for loneliness, one day She stood selected for the monarch's side.

君主 jūnzhǔ monarch; sovereign

君主国 jūnzhǔguó monarchical state; monarchy

君主立宪 jūnzhǔ lìxiàn constitutional monarchy

君主制 jūnzhǔzhì monarchy

君主专制 jūnzhǔ zhuānzhì autocratic monarchy; absolute monarchy

君子 jūnzǐ a man of noble character; a man of virtue; gentleman (originally a Confucianist term, meaning an ideal man whose character embodies the virtue of benevolence and whose acts are in accordance with the rites and rightness, opp. 小人 xiǎorén): ～喻于义，小人喻于利。《论语》The gentleman understands what is moral. The small man understands what is profitable.

君子国 jūnzǐguó the Land of Gentlemen (an imaginary land free from deceit and avarice)

君子兰 jūnzǐlán scarlet kafirlily (*Clivia miniata*)

君子协定 jūnzǐ xiédìng gentlemen's agreement

君子之交淡如水 jūnzǐ zhī jiāo dàn rú shuǐ the friendship of a gentleman is insipid as water: 君子之交淡若水，小人之交甘若醴；君子淡以亲，小人甘以绝。《庄子》The friendship of a gentleman is insipid as water; that of a petty man, sweet as rich wine. But the insipidity of the gentleman leads to affection, while the sweetness of the petty man leads to revulsion.

龟(龜)

jūn see below ——see also guī

龟裂 jūnliè ① (of parched earth) be full of cracks: 长期干旱，田地～。There has been no rain for a long time and the earth is full of cracks. ② (of skin) chap

钧

jūn ① an ancient unit of weight (equal to 30 jīn) ② *formal* honor. (said to one's seniors or superiors) you; your: 钧命 jūnmìng

钧安 jūn'ān *formal* may you enjoy repose (a complimentary close in a letter to one's senior or superior)

钧鉴 jūnjiàn *formal* I beg to inform you (a salutation in a letter to one's senior or superior)

钧命 jūnmìng *formal* your instructions

钧启 jūnqǐ *formal* to be opened by (written after the name of the addressee on the envelope of a letter to one's senior or superior)

钧谕 jūnyù *formal* your instructions

钧座 jūnzuò *formal* Your Excellency; Your Honour

菌

jūn ① fungus ② bacterium ——see also jùn

菌肥 jūnféi short for 细菌肥料 xìjūn féiliào

菌核 jūnhé sclerotium

菌落 jūnluò colony (of bacteria)

菌苗 jūnmiáo *med.* bacterial vaccine; vaccine

菌丝 jūnsī *bot.* hypha

菌血症 jūnxuèzhèng bacteraemia

鲀

jūn see below

鲀裂 jūnliè *formal* (of skin) chap

麇(麏)

jūn *arch.* river deer ——see also qún

jùn

俊¹（儁）

jùn handsome; pretty: 这小伙子长得挺～的。That lad is very handsome. / 这孩子长得多～哪! What a pretty little child!

俊²（隽、儁）

jùn of outstanding talent: 俊杰 jùnjié

俊杰 jùnjié a person of outstanding talent; hero
俊美 jùnměi pretty
俊气 jùnqi pretty: 那个小姑娘长得挺～。That little girl is very pretty.
俊俏 jùnqiào *inf.* pretty and charming
俊秀 jùnxiù pretty; of delicate beauty
俊雅 jùnyǎ *formal* refined and elegant

郡

jùn *hist.* prefecture
郡县制 jùnxiànzhì the system of prefectures and counties (a system of local administration which took shape during the Spring and Autumn Period and the Qin Dynasty)

浚（濬）

jùn dredge: ～渠 dredge a canal
浚泥船 jùnníchuán dredger

峻

jùn ① (of mountains) high: ～岭 a lofty mountain range ② harsh; severe; stern: 严峻 yánjùn
峻急 jùnjí *formal* ① (of currents) flowing swiftly ② intolerant and impetuous
峻拒 jùnjù *formal* refuse sternly
峻峭 jùnqiào high and steep

骏

jùn fine horse; steed
骏马 jùnmǎ fine horse; steed

菌

jùn mushroom ——see also jūn
菌子 jùnzi *dial.* mushroom

竣

jùn complete; finish: 告竣 gàojùn
竣工 jùngōng (of a project) be completed: 这座大楼已提前～。The building has been completed ahead of schedule.
竣事 jùnshì (of a task) be completed

K

kā

咖 kā see below ——see also gā
咖啡 kāfēi coffee
咖啡馆 kāfēiguǎn coffee house; café
咖啡色 kāfēisè coffee (colour)
咖啡因 kāfēiyīn (also 咖啡碱 kāfēijiǎn) *pharm.* caffeine

喀 kā *onom.* noise made in coughing or vomiting
喀嚓 kāchā *onom.* a cracking or snapping sound: 〜一声，树枝断了。The branch broke with a snap. *or* The branch snapped.
喀尔巴阡山 Kā'ěrbāqiānshān the Carpathians
喀麦隆 Kāmàilóng Cameroon
喀麦隆人 Kāmàilóngrén Cameroonian
喀秋莎 kāqiūshā katyusha rocket launcher
喀斯特 kāsītè *geol. karst*: 〜地形 *karst* topography

撠 kā *inf.* scrape with a knife: 〜铅笔 sharpen a pencil
撠吃 kāchi (also 撠哧 kāchi) *inf.* scrape with a knife: 我们应该先把门上的油漆〜掉。We ought to scrape the old paint off the door first.

kǎ

卡[1] kǎ ① block; check: 〜住通往海港的公路 block the road to the seaport / 会计及时〜住了这笔不必要的开支。The accountant checked this unnecessary spending in good time. ② clutch; choke: 〜脖子 seige sb. by the throat
卡[2] kǎ ① short for 卡路里 kǎlùlǐ ② short for 卡片 kǎpiàn ——see also qiǎ
卡巴迪 kǎbādí *sports* kabaddi
卡巴胂 kǎbāshèn *pharm.* carbarsone
卡宾枪 kǎbīnqiāng carbine
卡车 kǎchē lorry; truck
卡尺 kǎchǐ short for 游标卡尺 yóubiāo kǎchǐ
卡介苗 kǎjièmiáo *pharm.* BCG vaccine (Bacille Calmette-Guérin)
卡拉 OK kǎlā'ōukēi karaoke
卡路里 kǎlùlǐ *phys.* calorie
卡那霉素 kǎnàméisù *pharm.* kanamycin
卡片 kǎpiàn card: 借书〜 library card / 〜目录 card catalogue / 〜索引 card index
卡片柜 kǎpiànguì card cabinet
卡其 kǎqí *text.* khaki
卡钳 kǎqián *mech.* callipers: 内外〜 combination callipers
卡曲 kǎqū (also 卡装 kǎzhuāng) car coat (a translitera-tion)

卡他 kǎtā *med.* catarrh
卡塔尔 Kǎtǎ'ěr Qatar
卡塔尔人 Kǎtǎ'ěrrén Qatari
卡特尔 kǎtè'ěr *econ.* cartel
卡通 kǎtōng ① caricature; cartoon ② another name for 动画片 dònghuàpiàn

佧 kǎ see below
佧佤族 Kǎwǎzú old name for 佤族 Wǎzú

咔 kǎ see below
咔叽 kǎjī same as 卡其 kǎqí
咔唑 kǎzuò *chem.* carbazole

喀 kǎ cough up: 把鱼刺〜出来 cough up a fish-bone ——see also gē; lo; luò
喀痰 kǎtán cough up phlegm
喀血 kǎxiě *med.* spit blood; haemoptysis

胩 kǎ *chem.* carbylamine; isocyanide

kāi

开[1]（開）kāi ① open: 〜锁 open a lock; unlock / 门〜了。The door opened. ② make an opening; open up: 墙上〜了个窗口。A window was made in the wall. / 〜了三千亩水稻田。3,000 *mu* of paddy fields were opened up. ③ open out; come loose: 花都〜了。The flowers are all open. / 扣儿〜了。The knot has come untied. / 两块木板没粘好，又〜了。The two pieces of wood were not glued together properly. They have come loose again. ④ (of a frozen river) thaw out: 等河〜了坐船走。Wait until the river is open and then go by boat. ⑤ lift (a ban, restriction, etc.): 开禁 kāijìn ⑥ start or operate (a machine, car, ship, plane, etc.); turn on (a light, radio, T.V., etc.): 〜机器 operate a machine / 〜汽车 drive a car / 〜飞机 fly (*or* pilot) an airplane / 〜灯 turn on a light / 把汽船〜到对岸去。Steer the motorboat over to the opposite bank. ⑦ (of a train, bus, ship, etc.) leave; start: 火车几点〜? What time does the train leave? / 校车快〜了。The school bus is about to start. ⑧ (of troops) set out; move: 昨天〜来了两团人，今天又〜走了。Two regiments came yesterday and set off today. / 部队正往前线〜去。The troops are moving to the front. ⑨ start or run (a factory, school, store, etc.); set up: 〜工厂 set up a factory / 〜茶馆 run a teahouse / 他〜了一个饭馆。He has opened a restaurant. / 百货店就〜在十字路口。The department store is located at the intersection. ⑩ begin; start: 开拍 kāipāi ⑪ hold (a meeting, exhibition, etc.): 〜运动会 hold an athletic meet / 〜舞会 give a dance / 舞会〜了一夜。The dance lasted all night. ⑫ make a list of; write out: 把你需要的东西〜个单子。Make a list of the things you need. / 〜一张支票 write out a cheque / 〜介绍信 write a letter of introduction ⑬ pay

(wages, fares, etc.): 〜工资 pay wages ⑭ *dial.* fire (an employee): 过去资本家随便〜掉我们工人。In the past the capitalists could fire us workers at will. ⑮ boil: 水〜了。The water is boiling. ⑯ *inf.* eat up: 他把包子都〜了。He ate up all the stuffed buns. ⑰ (used to express a ratio between two things considered as parts of a whole which is 10): 二八〜 2:8 / 大家认为他的功过是三七〜。The general assessment of his work is 70% achievements and 30% mistakes. ⑱ *print.* division of standard size printing paper: 四开 sìkāi / 八开 bākāi

开²(開)
开(開)

kāi carat: 十四〜金 14-carat gold

kāi ① (indicating separation or dissemination) open; apart; away; widely: 躲〜! Get out of the way! / 站〜! Stand aside! / 把门推〜。Push the door open. / 把书翻〜。Open the book. / 消息传〜了。The news has got about. / 这支歌儿流行〜了。The song has become very popular. / 流行性感冒在这里蔓延〜了。The flu has spread throughout this area. / 我好不容易把他俩劝〜了。It wasn't easy for me to keep the two of them from quarreling. ② (indicating the beginning and continuation of an action): 一见到亲人他就哭〜了。He began to cry the moment he saw his own people. / 冻得他哆嗦〜了。He was shivering with cold. / 下了两天雨，天就冷〜了。After two days of rain, the cold weather set in. ③ (indicating capacity): 天安门广场站得〜五十万人。Tian'anmen Square can hold 500,000 people. / 这儿放不〜四张床。There isn't enough room for four beds here. / 这间屋子大，五十个人也坐〜了。This room is big enough to seat 50 people.

开拔 kāibá (of troops) set out; move: 第三天拂晓前，部队〜了。On the third day the troops set out before dawn.

开办 kāibàn start or run (a factory, school, store, etc.); set up: 〜训练班 start a training course

开本 kāiběn *print.* format; book size: 八〜 octavo / 十六〜 16 mo / 三十二〜 32 mo

开笔 kāibǐ ① write (esp. poetry) for the first time; start writing one's first work: 他一〜就做的同光体。He started right off writing poetry in the style of the Tongzhi (同治) and Guangxu (光绪) periods. ② start practising calligraphy for the year

开标 kāibiāo open sealed tenders

开采 kāicǎi mine; extract; exploit: 〜煤炭 mine coal / 〜石油 recover petroleum / 〜天然气 tap (or extract) natural gas

开仓济贫 kāicāng-jìpín *old* open the granaries to relieve the poor

开衩 kāichà make a slit or vent (at the sides or back of a garment); slit: 你的上衣开不开衩？Do you want a slit made in your coat? / 她的长连衣裙中国式样，〜开到膝部。Her long dress was slit up to the knee in Chinese style.

开场 kāichǎng (of a performance, etc.) begin; start: 他们到剧院时，戏已经〜了。The play had already begun when they got to the theatre. / 主席简洁有力的发言，给会议做了个很好的〜。The meeting got off to a good start with a short and forceful speech by the chairman.

开场白 kāichǎngbái ① prologue (of a play) ② opening (or introductory) remarks

开敞 kāichǎng open wide: 〜着大门 leave the door wide open

开畅 kāichàng free from worry; happy

开车 kāichē ① drive or start a car, train, etc.: 〜的时候精神要集中。You should concentrate when driving. / 快〜了，大家上车吧。The bus is about to leave. Hurry up, everybody. ② set a machine going

开诚布公 kāichéng-bùgōng frank and sincere; open-hearted: 〜地谈一谈 speak frankly and sincerely / 我希望大家〜，把问题摆到桌面上谈清楚。I hope that we can all be perfectly honest about the matter and put all our cards on the table for a frank discussion.

开诚相见 kāichéng xiāngjiàn deal with sb. in all sincerity; treat sb. open-heartedly; be frank and open

开秤 kāichèng (of a purchasing station) start purchasing seasonal commodities

开初 kāichū *dial.* at first; at the outset

开除 kāichú expel; discharge: 〜出党 expel from the Party / 〜学籍 expel from school / 〜公职 discharge sb. from public employment; take sb.'s name off the books

开锄 kāichú begin tilling land for the year

开船 kāichuán set sail; sail: 〜时间 sailing time; hour of sailing

开创 kāichuàng start; initiate: 〜新局面 create a new situation; open up a new prospect / 十月革命〜了人类历史的新纪元。The October Revolution ushered in a new epoch in human history. / 〜社会新风尚 initiate a new social custom

开春 kāichūn beginning of spring (usu. referring to the first month of the lunar year)

开打 kāidǎ acrobatic fighting in Chinese opera

开裆裤 kāidāngkù open-seat (or split) pants (for children)

开刀 kāidāo ① *old* behead; decapitate: 〜问斩 execution by decapitation ② *inf.* perform or have an operation; operate or be operated on: 给病人〜 operate on a patient / 他得了阑尾炎，〜了。He had an operation for appendicitis. ③ make sb. the first target of attack: 拿某人〜 make an example of sb.

开导 kāidǎo help sb. to see what is right or sensible; help sb. to straighten out his wrong or muddled thinking; enlighten: 他一时想不通，你〜〜他好吗？He hasn't come round yet. Could you try and straighten him out? / 孩子有缺点，要耐心〜。The child has some faults; try to bring him along patiently.

开倒车 kāi dàochē back the car—turn back the clock: 开历史倒车 try to reverse the trend of history; try to turn back the wheel of history

开道 kāidào ① clear the way: 鸣锣开道 míngluó-kāidào ② *dial.* make way

开地 kāidì ① turn up the soil; plough; till ② *dial.* open up (or reclaim) wasteland

开吊 kāidiào *old* hold funeral rites

开动 kāidòng ① start; set in motion: 火车〜了。The train was starting. / 〜机器 start a machine / 〜宣传机器 set the propaganda machine in motion / 〜脑筋 use one's brains ② move; march: 队伍休息了一会儿又〜了。The troops were on the move again after a short rest.

开冻 kāidòng thaw; unfreeze

开端 kāiduān beginning; start: 良好的〜 a good beginning / 两国关系新的〜 a new turn in the relations between the two countries

开恩 kāi'ēn show mercy; bestow favours

开发 kāifā develop; open up; exploit: 〜山区 develop mountain areas / 〜新产品 develop new products / 〜油田 open up oilfields / 〜自然资源 exploit natural resources / 〜合作 cooperation in development / 智力〜 tapping intellectual resources

开饭 kāifàn serve a meal: 〜了。The meal's ready. or Time to eat! / 食堂什么时候〜？When does the cafeteria serve meals?

开方¹ kāifāng (also 开方子 kāifāngzi) write out a prescription

开方² kāifāng *math.* extraction of a root; evolution

开房间 kāi fángjiān *dial.* rent a room in a hotel (esp.

for a secret liaison)

开放 kāifàng ① (of flowers) come into bloom ② lift a ban, restriction, etc. ③ open to traffic or public use: 新建的港口已向外轮～。 The new port has been opened to foreign ships. ④ be open (to the public): 星期日图书馆照常～。 The library is open on Sundays as well as on weekdays. ⑤ be open (to the outside world): ～政策 the policy of opening to the outside world; the open policy

开放城市 kāifàng chéngshì a city open to foreigners; open city

开放骨折 kāifàng gǔzhé *med.* open (or compound) fracture

开缝 kāifèng crack; fracture

开赴 kāifù move (or march) to; be bound for: ～前线 march to the front / 劳动大军即将～建设工地。 A contingent of workers is heading for the construction site.

开革 kāigé *old* expel; discharge

开工 kāigōng ① (of a factory, etc.) go into operation: ～不足 be operating under capacity / 新厂～了。 The new factory has gone into operation. ② (of work on a construction project, etc.) start: 水库工程～了。 Construction of the reservoir has started.

开工率 kāigōnglǜ utilization of capacity

开沟机 kāigōujī ditching machine; trench digger

开关 kāiguān *elec.* switch: 分档～ step switch / 通断～ on-off switch / ～厂 switchgear plant

开关灯头 kāiguān dēngtóu switch socket

开锅 kāiguō *inf.* (of a pot) boil

开国 kāiguó found a state: ～大典 founding ceremony (of a state) / ～元勋 founders of a state

开航 kāiháng ① become open for navigation: 又一条新航线～了。 Another new air route has been opened up. / 运河～了。 The canal is now open. ② set sail: 去武汉的船上午八点～。 The boat for Wuhan sails at 8 a. m. / ～日 sailing day

开合桥 kāihéqiáo bascule bridge; folding bridge

开河[1] kāihé (of a frozen river) thaw out

开河[2] kāihé construct a canal

开后门 kāi hòumén open the "backdoor"—give sb. special advantage or privilege: 利用职权～ abusing one's powers to secure advantages for others

开户 kāihù open (or establish) an account (with a bank)

开花 kāihuā ① blossom; bloom: 木兰要～了。 The magnolias are beginning to blossom. / 二踢脚在空中开了花。 The double-bang firecracker exploded in the air. ② split (like a flower blooming): 这只鞋～儿了。 The shoe has split open. ③ feel happy or smile happily: 心里乐开了花 burst with joy; feel elated ④ (of an experience) spread over; (of an undertaking) rise; spring up

开花结果 kāihuā-jiéguǒ blossom and bear fruit—yield positive results

开花馒头 kāihuā mántou split-top steamed bun

开花期 kāihuāqī *bot.* florescence

开化 kāihuà ① become civilized ② *dial.* thaw; unfreeze

开怀 kāihuái to one's heart's content: ～畅饮 drink (alcohol) to one's heart's content; go on a drinking spree / ～大笑 laugh heartily

开怀儿 kāihuáir *inf.* (of a woman) give birth to the first baby: 没开过怀儿 has never given birth to a baby

开荒 kāihuāng open up (or reclaim) wasteland

开会 kāihuì hold or attend a meeting: 我要～去。 I'm going to a meeting. / 他正在～。 He's at a meeting. / 现在～。 Let's start the meeting. / 我们昨天开了个会。 We had a meeting yesterday.

开荤 kāihūn (esp. of a person with a religious belief) begin or resume a meat diet; end a meatless diet

开火 kāihuǒ open fire: 准备～! (word of command) Ready, fire! / 前线～了。 Fighting has started at the frontlines.

开伙 kāihuǒ ① run a mess or cafeteria ② provide food

开豁 kāihuò ① open and clear: 雾气一散, 四处都显得十分～。 With the lifting of the mist, the view opened up. ② with one's mental outlook broadened: 听了报告, 他的心里更～了。 After hearing the report, his mind opened up. or The report widened his horizons.

开价 kāijià state or quote a price

开架 kāijià open shelves (as in a supermarket, from which customers select goods)

开架式 kāijiàshì open shelves (a system of library management which permits readers open access to bookshelves)

开间 kāijiān ① *dial.* the standard width of a room in an old-style house (about 10 *chi*, the length of a purlin): 单～ a house about 10 *chi* wide / 双～ a one-room house about 20 *chi* wide ② *dial.* width of a room: 这间屋子～很大。 The room is quite wide. ③ *archit.* bay

开讲 kāijiǎng begin lecturing or story-telling

开奖 kāijiǎng draw lottery in public and announce winner

开胶 kāijiāo come unglued; come unstuck

开戒 kāijiè break an abstinence (from smoking, drinking, etc.)

开禁 kāijìn lift a ban

开局 kāijú opening (of a chess game, etc.)

开具 kāijù *formal* write out (a certificate, etc.): ～清单 write out a detailed list / 由所在单位～证明。 A certificate is to be provided by the organization one belongs to.

开卷 kāijuàn ① *formal* open a book; read ② (of examinations) open-book: ～考试 an open-book examination

开卷有益 kāijuàn yǒuyì reading is always profitable

开掘 kāijué dig: ～运河 dig a canal / ～新的矿井 open up a new mine

开课 kāikè ① school begins; begin classes: 学校九月一日～。 School will begin on September 1st. ② (chiefly in college) give a course; teach a subject: 开一门光合作用课 give a course in photosynthesis / 朱教授这学期给研究生～。 Professor Zhu will teach a course for graduate students this term. / 你下学期开什么课? Which subjects are you going to teach next term? or What courses are you offering next term?

开垦 kāikěn open up (or reclaim) wasteland; bring under cultivation: ～荒山 bring barren hills under cultivation

开口 kāikǒu ① open one's mouth; start to talk: 难以～ find it difficult to bring the matter up / 没等我～, 他就抢先替我说了。 Before I could open my mouth, he hastened to speak on my behalf (or he went ahead and said it for me). ② put the first edge on a knife

开口闭口 kāikǒu-bìkǒu every time one opens one's mouth; whenever one speaks

开口呼 kāikǒuhū *phonet.* a class of syllables with sounds other than i, u, and ü as the final 韵母 or as the beginning of the final (e.g. 肝 gān) ——see also 四呼 sìhū

开口跳 kāikǒutiào another name for 武丑 wǔchǒu

开口销 kāikǒuxiāo split pin

开口子 kāi kǒuzi ① (of a dyke) break; burst ② (of the skin) chap: 天气干冷, 我的手都开了口子了。 The cold, dry weather made my hands get chapped.

开快车 kāi kuàichē step on the gas; speed up the work

开矿 kāikuàng open up a mine; exploit a mine

开阔　kāikuò　① open; wide: ～的广场 an open square / ～的原野 wide open fields / ～的天空 the wide open sky / ～的前额 a broad forehead ② tolerant; broad-minded: 他是一个思想～而又活泼愉快的人。He's a broad-minded, energetic and cheerful person. ③ widen: ～路面 widen a road

开阔地　kāikuòdì　*mil.*　open terrain; open ground; unenclosed ground

开阔眼界　kāikuò yǎnjiè　broaden one's outlook (*or* horizons)

开朗　kāilǎng　① open and clear: 我们在密林中穿行，约数百米，便豁然～。We pushed ourselves through the thick forest for a few hundred metres and then reached an open space. / 早晨还是阴沉沉的，到午后才逐渐～起来。It was cloudy in the morning and began to clear up in the afternoon. ② sanguine; optimistic: 性情～ of a sanguine disposition; always cheerful / 今晚上她的心情似乎特别～。Tonight she seems to be in an especially cheerful mood.

开犁　kāilí　① start the year's ploughing ② same as 开墒 kāishāng

开例　kāilì　create a precedent: 如果从你这里～，以后事情就不好办了。If we allow you to set this precedent, it will create difficulties for us afterwards.

开镰　kāilián　start harvesting (with sickles)

开脸　kāiliǎn　① *old* (of a girl on the eve of marriage) remove the fine hairs on the face and neck and tidy up hairline at temples ② carve the face of a statue

开列　kāiliè　draw up (a list); list: ～如下 as listed below / ～名单 draw up (*or* make out) a name list / 按照～的项目进行 work through the list of assignments

开裂　kāiliè　crack; fracture: 湖面上的冰～了。The ice on the lake fractured.

开溜　kāiliū　*dial.*　sneak away; slink off; make oneself scarce

开耧　kāilóu　start to use the seed-plough—start the year's sowing

开路　kāilù　① open a way; blaze a trail: 逢山～，遇水搭桥 cut paths through the mountains and build bridges across the rivers / 我在前面～，你们跟紧我。I'll be in front blazing the trail, you follow close behind. ② *elec.* open circuit

开路先锋　kāilù xiānfēng　pathbreaker; trail-blazer; pioneer

开绿灯　kāi lǜdēng　give the green light; give the go-ahead

开锣　kāiluó　strike up the band—start an operatic performance: ～戏 the first item on an operatic programme / 我们进了剧院，离～的时候还早。We got to the theatre long before the performance started.

开曼群岛　Kāimàn Qúndǎo　Cayman Islands

开毛机　kāimáojī　*text.*　wool opener

开门　kāimén　① open the door: 有人敲门，快～去。Somebody's knocking at the door. Quick, go and open it. / ～整风 open-door rectification of the work style (of the Communist Party) / ～办学 open-door schooling ② (of a store) begin a day's business

开门红　kāiménhóng　make a good beginning; get off to a good start

开门见山　kāimén jiàn shān　come straight to the point: 他说话喜欢～，不绕弯子。He likes to speak candidly, and not beat about the bush. / 这篇文章～，一落笔就点明了主题。This essay comes straight to the point right at the beginning.

开门七件事　kāimén qījiànshì　the seven necessities of life (i.e. firing, rice, oil, salt, soy, vinegar, and tea)

开门揖盗　kāimén yī dào　open the door to robbers—invite disaster by letting in evildoers

开蒙　kāiméng　① start schooling: 他六岁开的蒙。He started schooling at six. ② teach beginner: 请王老师给他～。We will ask Mr. Wang to be his first teacher.

开棉机　kāimiánjī　*text.*　opener: 棉箱～ hopper opener / 豪猪～ porcupine opener

开明　kāimíng　enlightened: ～人士 enlightened persons

开明绅士　kāimíng shēnshì　the enlightened gentry (individual landlords and rich peasants with democratic leanings who, influenced by the CCP's education and its policy of unity, favoured resistance against Japan, supported democracy and reduction of land rent and loan interest during the War of Resistance Against Japan, and in the War of Liberation approved of the land reform)

开幕　kāimù　① the curtain rises: 戏已经～了。The opera has begun. ② (of a meeting, exhibition, etc.) open; inaugurate: 展览会明天～。The exhibition will open tomorrow. / 大会今天上午～了。The conference was inaugurated this morning.

开幕词　kāimùcí　opening speech (*or* address): 致～ deliver an opening speech

开幕式　kāimùshì　opening ceremony: 奥林匹克运动会昨天举行了～。The opening ceremony of the Olympic Games was held yesterday.

开年　kāinián　① the beginning of the year ② *dial.* next year

开拍　kāipāi　start shooting (a film)

开盘　kāipán　*econ.*　give the opening quotation (on the exchange): ～汇率 opening exchange rate / ～价格 opening price; opening quotation

开炮　kāipào　① open fire with artillery; fire: 向敌人猛烈～ fiercely open fire on the enemy ② fire criticism at sb. or sth.: 他在会上对这种现象又开了炮。At the meeting he unleashed a great deal of criticism against this trend.

开坯　kāipī　*metall.*　cogging; blooming: ～机 cogging mill; bloomer

开辟　kāipì　① open up; start: ～航线 open an air or sea route / ～专栏 start a special column (in a newspaper, etc.) / ～财源 tap new financial resources / ～革命根据地 set up a revolutionary base / ～各种商品流通渠道 explore more avenues for commodity circulation / ～光辉灿烂的未来 open up the way to a bright future / 中国共产党的诞生，～了中国历史的新时代。The birth of the Communist Party of China ushered in a new epoch in Chinese history. ② short for 开天辟地 kāitiān-pìdì

开篇　kāipiān　introductory song in *tanci* (弹词)

开瓢儿　kāipiáor　*dial.*　have a cut in one's head

开票　kāipiào　① open the ballot box and count the ballots ② make out an invoice, receipt, voucher, etc.

开屏　kāipíng　(of a peacock) spread its tail; display its fine tail feathers

开启　kāiqǐ　open: 这种灭火器的开关能自动～。The switch on this kind of fire extinguisher opens up automatically.

开枪　kāiqiāng　fire with a rifle, pistol, etc.; shoot: ～射击 open fire / ～还击 return fire

开腔　kāiqiāng　begin to speak; open one's mouth: 他半天不～。For a long time he didn't utter a word. *or* He kept silent for a long while. / 大家都还没说话，他先～了。He opened his mouth first, before anyone else had spoken.

开窍　kāiqiào　① have one's ideas straightened out: 他一听这么说，就～了。He straightened his ideas out as soon as the matter was explained to him. ② (of a child) begin to know things ③ *dial.* open one's eyes; widen one's view (*or* horizons); broaden one's mind

开球　kāiqiú　kick off (in soccer)

开缺　kāiquē　*old* (of an official) quit a post and thus leave it vacant

开刃儿 kāirènr sharpen a new knife or a new pair of scissors before use

开山 kāishān ① cut into a mountain (for quarrying, etc.): 〜劈岭 open up a mountain ② unseal a closed mountain for a period of time ③ *Buddhism* build the first temple on a famous mountain

开山 kāi·shān same as 开山祖师 kāishān zǔshī

开山祖师 kāishān zǔshī (also 开山老祖 kāishān lǎozǔ) builder of the first temple on a famous mountain—the founder of a religious sect, a school of thought, etc.

开墒 kāishāng plough the first furrow as a guideline

开设 kāishè ① open (a shop, factory, etc.); set up: 〜店铺 set up a store ② offer (a course in college, etc.): 〜音乐欣赏课 give (*or* offer) a course in music appreciation

开始 kāishǐ ① begin; start: 阅兵式〜了。 The military review has begun. / 今天从第五课〜。 Today we'll begin with Lesson 5. / 〜讨论实质性问题 come to substantive questions / 〜生效 take effect; come into effect (*or* force) ② initial stage; beginning; outset: 一种新的工作，〜总会遇到一些困难。 You always run into some difficulties at the beginning of any new job.

开市 kāishì ① (of a shop) reopen after a cessation of business ② conduct the first transaction of a day's business

开释 kāishì release (a prisoner)

开首 kāishǒu *dial.* beginning; outset

开水 kāishuǐ ① boiling water ② boiled water

开司米 kāisīmǐ (also 开士米 kāishìmǐ) cashmere

开台 kāitái begin a theatrical performance: 戏已〜。 The performance has begun.

开台锣鼓 kāitái luógǔ a flourish of gongs and drums introducing a theatrical performance—prelude

开膛 kāitáng cut open the chest (of a pig, chicken, etc.); draw: 杀猪〜 slit a pig's throat and cut open its chest

开天窗 kāi tiānchuāng ① syphilis nose start festering ② put in a blank in a publication to show that sth. has been censored

开天辟地 kāitiān-pìdì the creation of heaven and earth—the beginning of history: 中国产生了共产党，这是〜的大事变。(毛泽东) In China, the Communist Party was born. This was an epoch-making event. / 〜君真健，说项依刘我大难。(柳亚子) You excel as the maker of a new epoch! Hard it was for me to laud Light in dark times.

开庭 kāitíng *leg.* open a court session; call the court to order: 〜审理 hold a hearing / 下月〜。 The court sits next month.

开通 kāitōng remove obstacles from; dredge; clear: 河道 dredge a river / 坚冰已经打破，航道已经〜。 The ice has been broken and the river route is open. / 〜风气 heighten the general mood of society

开通 kāitong open-minded; liberal; enlightened: 老大爷上夜校以后，脑筋更〜了。 After attending evening classes Grandpa became more open-minded.

开头 kāitóu ① begin; start: 我们的学习刚〜。 We've only just begun our study. / 请你先开个头儿。 Would you make a start? ② beginning; start: 这篇文章〜讲了我国当前的形势。 The article begins with an account of the current situation in our country. / 你一〜就错了。 You've been wrong from the start. / 〜我们都在一起，后来就分开了。 At first we were all together, then later on we separated.

开脱 kāituō absolve; exonerate: 〜罪责 absolve sb. from guilt or blame / 替某人〜 plead for sb.

开拓 kāituò ① open up: 在荒原上〜出大片农田 open up large areas of wasteland and turn them into farmland / 为发展石油工业〜一条道路 open up a path for

the development of the oil industry ② *min.* developing; opening: 〜巷道 development opening / 〜进尺 tunnelling footage

开拓者 kāituòzhě pioneer

开挖 kāiwā excavate: 〜机械 excavating machinery

开外 kāiwài over; above: 他看起来有四十〜。 He looks over forty. / 东西相距六十里〜 over sixty *li* from east to west / 漫天大雾，五步〜，什么都看不见。 A dense fog obscured everything beyond a distance of 5 steps.

开玩笑 kāi wánxiào crack a joke; joke; make fun of: 他是跟你〜呢，你别当真。 He was only joking. Don't take it seriously. / 这可不是〜的事情。 This is no joking matter. / 他跟你开几句玩笑，你就生气了? Why get angry? He's only teasing. / 人家正烦着呢，你开什么玩笑。 I'm in no mood for your fooling.

开往 kāiwǎng (of a train, ship, etc.) leave for; be bound for: 〜广州的特快 the Guangzhou express

开胃 kāiwèi ① whet (*or* stimulate) the appetite: 这药吃了能〜。 This medicine will improve your appetite. ② *dial.* amuse oneself at sb.'s expense; make fun of sb.

开戏 kāixì start a performance; raise the curtain

开线 kāixiàn burst at the seams; come unsewn: 衣服开了线。 A seam in the clothing came apart.

开销 kāi·xiāo ① pay expenses: 我带的钱够一路〜的。 I've brought enough money with me to cover the expenses of the trip. ② expense: 日常的〜 daily expenses; running expenses / 住在这儿〜不大。 Living is cheap here.

开小差 kāi xiǎochāi ① (of a soldier) desert ② be absent-minded; be woolgathering: 他一开会思想就〜。 His mind wanders whenever he attends a meeting.

开心 kāixīn ① happy; joyous; elated: 他们去长城玩得很〜。 They went on a trip to the Great Wall and enjoyed themselves very much. ② amuse oneself at sb.'s expense; make fun of sb.: 别拿这老汉〜了。 Don't amuse yourself at the old man's expense. / 他有一点儿结巴，别的孩子就拿他〜。 Because he stammerd slightly, the other boys made fun of him.

开心果 kāixīnguǒ pistachio

开心丸儿 kāixīnwánr same as 宽心丸儿 kuānxīnwánr

开行 kāixíng (of a boat or vehicle) start: 火车已经〜，站上欢送的人们还在挥手致意。 The train had started and the people on the platform were waving their hands.

开学 kāixué school opens; term begins: 九月一日〜。 The term will begin on September 1. / 开了学大家都要忙了。 Everybody will be busy when the new term begins.

开学典礼 kāixué diǎnlǐ school-opening ceremony

开言 kāiyán *old* begin talking

开颜 kāiyán smile; beam: 剧团进山寨，男女老少笑〜。 Men and women, old and young, beamed with joy when the opera troupe entered the mountain village. / 更喜岷山千里雪，三军过后尽〜。(毛泽东) Minshan's thousand *li* of snow joyously crossed, The three Armies march on, each face glowing.

开眼 kāiyǎn (also 开眼界 kāi yǎnjiè) open one's eyes; widen one's view (*or* horizons); broaden one's mind: 这个展览会真叫人〜。 The exhibition is a real eye-opener.

开演 kāiyǎn (of a play, movie, etc.) begin: 今晚节目七点三十分〜。 The performance begins at 7:30 this evening.

开洋 kāiyáng *dial.* dried, shelled shrimps (usu. larger ones)

开洋荤 kāi yánghūn *dial.* have a new experience; see or eat sth. for the first time

开业 kāiyè ① (of a shop, etc.) start business: 这家铺子

明天～。The store will open for business tomorrow. ② (of a lawyer, doctor, etc.) open a private practice

开夜车 kāi yèchē work late into the night; put in extra time at night; burn the midnight oil

开音节 kāiyīnjié *phonet.* open syllable

开映 kāiyìng (of a film show) begin

开元音 kāiyuányīn *phonet.* open vowel

开源节流 kāiyuán jiéliú increase income and reduce expenditure; tap new sources of supply and reduce consumption

开云见日 kāi yún jiàn rì the clouds disperse and the sun shines forth—① darkness recedes and light dawns ② all misunderstanding has been dispelled

开凿 kāizáo cut (a canal, tunnel, etc.): 在山岩上～渠道 hew a channel through stony mountains

开闸 kāizhá open a sluice gate

开斋 kāizhāi ① resume a meat diet ② *Islam* come to the end of Ramadan

开斋节 kāizhāijié *Islam* Lesser Bairam; the Festival of Fast-breaking

开展 kāizhǎn ① develop; launch; unfold: ～体育活动 develop an athletics program / ～劳动竞赛 launch an emulation drive / ～增产节约运动 launch a movement for increasing production and practising economy / ～批评与自我批评 carry out criticism and self-criticism ② development: 整风运动推动了工作的～。The rectification campaign gave impetus to work performance. ③ open-minded; politically progressive: 他思想很～。He is very open-minded. / 政治上不～ lagging behind in political understanding; slow in political progress

开战 kāizhàn ① make war; open hostilities ② battle (against nature, conservative forces, etc.): 向穷山恶水～ battle against barren hills and untamed rivers

开战理由 kāizhàn lǐyóu *casus belli*

开绽 kāizhàn come unsewn: 鞋后跟～了。The shoe has split at the heel.

开张[1] kāizhāng ① open a business; begin doing business: 那家新粮店～了。The new grain store has opened for business. ② conduct the first transaction of a day's business ③ (of certain activities) begin; start

开张[2] kāizhāng *formal* ① be open (to the outside world) ② grand and wide: 气势～ grand and imposing

开仗 kāizhàng make war; open hostilities

开帐 kāizhàng ① make out a bill ② pay the bill (at a restaurant, hotel, etc.)

开征 kāizhēng begin to levy (*or* collect) taxes

开支 kāizhī ① pay (expenses): 这笔钱厂里不能～。The factory shouldn't foot this bill. ② expenses; expenditure; spending: 节省～ cut down expenses; retrench / 军费～ military spending ③ *dial.* pay wages or salaries: 我们每月五号～。We get our pay on the 5th of every month.

开宗明义 kāizōng-míngyì make clear the purpose and theme from the very beginning: ～第一章 in the first place; first of all

开足马力 kāizú mǎlì put into high gear; go full steam ahead; with the throttle wide open: 这条船～，向前行驶。The ship was moving full steam ahead. / 我们的车开足了马力。We were stepping on it. / 有些企业由于原料不足不能～生产。Some enterprises cannot operate at full capacity because of insufficient raw materials.

开钻 kāizuàn *petroleum* spud in

开罪 kāizuì offend; displease

揩 kāi wipe: ～汗 wipe off sweat / 把桌子～干净 wipe the table clean

揩拭 kāishì clean; wipe

揩油 kāiyóu get petty advantages at the expense of other people or the state; scrounge

锎 kāi *chem.* californium (Cf)

kǎi

凯（凱） kǎi triumphant (strains); victorious: 奏凯 zòukǎi

凯风 kǎifēng *formal* a south wind

凯歌 kǎigē a song of triumph; paean: 高唱～而归 return amidst songs of triumph

凯旋 kǎixuán triumphant return: 大军～归来。The army returned in triumph.

凯旋门 ① kǎixuánmén triumphal arch ② Kǎixuánmén *Arc de Triomphe* (in Paris); Arch of Triumph

剀（剴） kǎi see below

剀切 kǎiqiè *formal* ① true and pertinent: ～详明 true and clear in every detail ② earnest and sincere: ～教导 teach earnestly

铠（鎧） kǎi (a suit of) armour: 铁铠 tiěkǎi

铠甲 kǎijiǎ (a suit of) armour

铠装 kǎizhuāng *elec.* armour: ～电缆 armoured cable

慨[1] kǎi ① indignant: 愤慨 fènkǎi ② generous: 慨允 kǎiyǔn

慨[2]（嘅） kǎi sigh with emotion: 感慨 gǎnkǎi

慨诺 kǎinuò generously promise; readily consent

慨然 kǎirán ① with deep feeling: ～长叹 heave a sigh of regret ② generously: ～相赠 give (as a present) generously

慨叹 kǎitàn sigh with regret

慨允 kǎiyǔn readily consent; kindly promise

楷 kǎi ① model; pattern: 楷模 kǎimó ② (in Chinese calligraphy) regular script: 大楷 dàkǎi

楷范 kǎifàn *formal* model; paragon

楷模 kǎimó model; paragon; example

楷书 kǎishū (in Chinese calligraphy) regular script

楷体 kǎitǐ ① same as 楷书 kǎishū ② block letter

kài

忾（愾） kài *formal* hatred: 敌忾 díkài

欬 kài *formal* cough

欬唾成珠 kàituò chéng zhū cough out pearls—① each word a gem when one talks ② words flow from the mouth as from the pen of a master

kān

刊（栞） kān ① print; publish: 创刊 chuàngkān / 停刊 tíngkān ② periodical; publication: 报刊 bàokān / 周刊 zhōukān ③ delete or correct: 刊误 kānwù

刊布 kānbù *formal* publish (in print)

刊登 kāndēng publish in a newspaper or magazine; carry: ～广告 print an advertisement; advertise / 今天的《中国日报》～了两封读者来信。Two letters to the editor were published in today's *China Daily*.

刊刻 kānkè inscribe

刊落　kānluò　*formal*　strike out; delete

刊谬补缺　kānmiù-bǔquē　errata and supplements

刊头　kāntóu　masthead of a newspaper or magazine

刊物　kānwù　publication: 定期～ periodical (publication) / 内部～ restricted publication

刊误　kānwù　correct errors in printing

刊误表　kānwùbiǎo　errata; corrigenda

刊行　kānxíng　print and publish

刊印　kānyìn　① cut blocks and print ② compose and print

刊载　kānzǎi　publish (in a newspaper or magazine); carry: 报纸上～了几篇有关激光技术的文章。The newspaper carried a few articles about laser technology.

看

kān　① look after; take care of; tend: ～孩子 look after children / ～瓜 keep watch in the melon fields / ～牛 tend cattle / 他病很重, 得有人～着。He is seriously ill and needs someone to look after him. / 她一个人～两台机器。She minds two machines all by herself. ② keep under surveillance; keep an eye on: ～住他, 别让这坏家伙跑了! Keep an eye on that rascal. Don't let him run away. / 家里把他～得很严。His family keeps a strict watch over him. / 这场比赛你要～住对方中锋。Your job in this match is to mark the opponent's centre. ——see also kàn

看财奴　kāncáinú　same as 守财奴 shǒucáinú

看场　kānchǎng　guard the threshing floor (during the harvest season): 麦收季节要派人～。We should send someone to guard the threshing floor during the wheat harvest season.

看管　kānguǎn　① look after; attend to: 我去买票, 你～一下行李。You look after the luggage while I go to buy the tickets. ② guard; watch: ～犯人 guard prisoners / 对于精神病人应严加～。Mental patients should be subjected to strict surveillance.

看护　kānhù　① nurse: ～病人 nurse the sick / 他伤得很重, 要细心～。He's seriously wounded and needs careful nursing. ② *old*　a hospital nurse

看家　kānjiā　① look after the house; mind the house: 我明天出差, 你好好看看家。I'm going away on a business trip tomorrow. You stay home and mind the house. ② outstanding (ability); special (skill): ～的武艺 one's outstanding skill in martial arts

看家本领　kānjiā běnlǐng　one's special skill; one's stock-in-trade

看家狗　kānjiāgǒu　*old*　watchdog—a person who takes care of the affairs and property of a landlord, high official, etc.

看家戏　kānjiāxì　the most successful repertoire (of an actor or actress): 这位演员的～是猴戏。This actor specializes in playing the role of the Monkey King.

看门　kānmén　① guard the entrance; act as doorkeeper ② look after the house

看青　kānqīng　keep watch over the ripening crops

看守　kānshǒu　① watch; guard: ～仓库 guard a storehouse / ～犯人 guard prisoners ② jailer; warder

看守内阁　kānshǒu nèigé　caretaker cabinet

看守所　kānshǒusuǒ　lockup for prisoners awaiting trial; detention house

看押　kānyā　take into custody; detain: ～俘虏 detain prisoners / 把犯罪分子～起来 take the criminal into custody

勘

kān　① read and correct the text of; collate: 校勘 jiàokān ② investigate; survey: 勘察 kānchá

勘测　kāncè　survey

勘察　kānchá　(also 勘查 kānchá) ① reconnoitre (an area for engineering or other purposes) ② *geol.* prospecting

勘探　kāntàn　exploration; prospecting: 磁法～ magnetic prospecting / ～地震学 exploration seismology / ～队 prospecting team

勘误　kānwù　correct errors in printing

勘误表　kānwùbiǎo　errata; corrigenda

勘验　kānyàn　(of judicial workers) examine on the spot; hold an inquest

龛（龕）

kān　niche; shrine: 佛龛 fókān

龛影　kānyǐng　*med.*　niche (shown in an X-ray photograph)

堪

kān　① may; can: ～称佳作 may be rated as a good piece of writing or a fine work of art / ～当重任 be capable of shouldering important tasks; can hold a post of great responsibility ② bear; endure: 不堪一击 bùkān yī jī

堪达罕　kāndáhǎn　*dial.*　elk; moose

堪舆　kānyú　*formal*　the location of a house or tomb, supposed to have an influence on the fortune of a family; geomantic omen

戡

kān　suppress: ～平叛乱 suppress (or put down) a rebellion

戡乱　kānluàn　suppress (or put down) a rebellion

kǎn

坎¹

kǎn　bank; ridge: 田～儿 a raised path through fields

坎²（埳）

kǎn　*formal*　pit; hole

坎儿　kǎnr　*dial.*　insinuating language; professional jargon

坎肩儿　kǎnjiānr　sleeveless jacket (usu. padded or lined)

坎儿井　kǎnrjǐng　an irrigation system of wells connected by underground channels used in Xinjiang; karez

坎坷　kǎnkě　① bumpy; rough: ～不平的道路 a rough and bumpy road ② *formal*　full of frustrations: ～一生 a lifetime of frustrations

坎壈　kǎnlǎn　*formal*　meeting hard luck; full of frustrations

坎土曼　kǎntǔmàn　a kind of mattock used by the Uygur nationality

坎子　kǎnzi　mound; rise

侃

kǎn　① upright and outspoken ② amiable; pleasant ③ *inf.*　chat idly; gossip

侃儿　kǎnr　same as 坎儿 kǎnr

侃大山　kǎndàshān　*dial.*　chat idly; gossip

侃侃　kǎnkǎn　*formal*　with assurance and composure: ～而谈 speak with fervour and assurance

砍

kǎn　① cut; chop; hack: 把树枝～下来 cut (or lop) off a branch / ～柴 cut firewood / 把树～倒 fell a tree / 这篇稿子太长, 得～去一半。The manuscript is too long and should be cut down by half. ② *dial.* throw sth. at: 拿砖头～狗 throw a brick at a dog

砍大山　kǎndàshān　same as 侃大山 kǎndàshān

砍刀　kǎndāo　chopper

砍伐　kǎnfá　fell (trees): ～森林 cut down trees in a forest; lumber

砍头　kǎntóu　chop off the head; behead

砍头疮　kǎntóuchuāng　(also 砍头痈 kǎntóuyōng) a kind of malignant boil or carbuncle on the neck

砍砸器 kǎnzáqì *archaeol.* chopper; chopping tool

莰 kǎn *chem.* camphane; bornane

槛(檻) kǎn threshold: 门槛 ménkǎn ——see also jiàn

kàn

看 kàn ① see; look at; watch: ～电影 see a film; go to the movies / ～戏 go to the theatre; see a play or an opera / ～电视 watch TV / ～球赛 watch a ball game ② read (silently): ～报 read a newspaper / ～书 read (a book) ③ think; consider: 你～她这个人可靠吗? Do you think she's reliable? / 你对这件事怎么～? What's your view on this matter? / 比较全面地～问题 try and look at (or approach) problems from all angles / ～清形势 make a correct appraisal of the situation ④ look upon; regard: 把人民的利益～得高于一切 put the interests of the people above all else ⑤ see or consult (a doctor); treat (a patient or an illness): 李大夫把她的肺炎～好了。Dr. Li has cured her of pneumonia. / 有病就该去～。You ought to go and see a doctor when you are ill. ⑥ look after: 衣帽自～。Take care of your own hats and coats. ⑦ call on; visit; see: 我明天去～他。I'll go and see him tomorrow. / 有空我来～你。I'll drop in on you when I have time. ⑧ depend on: 明天是不是打场,得～天气。Whether we'll do the threshing tomorrow will depend on the weather. ⑨ mind; watch out: 别跑这么快!～摔着! Don't run so fast! Mind you don't fall. ⑩ (used after a reduplicated verb or a verb phrase) try and see (what happens): 试试～ have a try / 等一等～ wait and see / 尝尝～。Just taste this. ⑪ (used in exclamations to express surprise or rebuke, esp. in the phrase 看你 or 你看你): 你～你! 怎么满头大汗啊! Look at yourself! How come you're bathed in sweat! / ～你,水都烧干了。Look what you've done! The water has all boiled away. ——see also kān

看扁 kànbiǎn *inf.* (usu. followed by 了) underestimate (a person): 别把人～了。Don't underestimate people.

看病 kànbìng ① (of a doctor) see a patient: 大夫出去～去了。The doctor has gone out to see a patient. / 王大夫～很认真。Dr. Wang handles his cases with great care. / 哪位大夫给你看的病? Who is your doctor? ② (of a patient) see or consult a doctor: 明天我要～去。I'm going to see a doctor tomorrow.

看不过去 kànbuguòqù (also 看不过 kànbuguò) *inf.* cannot stand by and watch: 他这么虐待老人,真叫人～。Nobody can stand his cruelty towards his own old parents.

看不起 kànbuqǐ *inf.* look down on; scorn; despise: 别～这本小字典,它真能帮助我们解决问题。Don't look down on this little dictionary. It really solves our problems. / 你别看他不起,人家可是位大诗人呢! Don't look down on him. He's actually a fine poet. / 他太骄傲了,总～别人。He is very proud and always holds others in contempt.

看菜吃饭,量体裁衣 kàn cài chīfàn, liàng tǐ cáiyī fit the appetite to the dishes and the dress (or clothes) to the figure—act according to actual circumstances: 俗话说:"～。" 我们无论做什么事都要看情形办理。There is a proverb: "Fit the appetite to the dishes and the dress to the figure". Whatever we do must be done according to actual circumstances.

看茶 kànchá *old* (said to a servant) bring a cup of tea to the guest: 来客了,老王,～! There's a guest, Lao Wang. Bring some tea, please.

看成 kànchéng ① take sb. or sth. for; look upon as; regard as: 你把我～什么人了? What do you take me for? / 我把十块的票子～五块的了。I mistook the ten-*yuan* bill for a five-*yuan* one. ② be able to see or watch: 我有会,电影没～。I had a meeting and wasn't able to see the film.

看承 kànchéng *formal* look after; attend to

看出 kànchū make out; see: ～问题在哪里 see where the trouble is / 看不出真假 cannot tell whether it is genuine or fake / 我没～他的用意。I failed to see his intention. / 看不出来,你还会弹钢琴。I never expected that you could play the piano. / 我一眼就～是他。I recognized him at first glance.

看穿 kànchuān see through: 小张一眼就～了他的诡计。Xiao Zhang saw through his trick right off.

看待 kàndài look on (or upon); regard; treat: 我把他当朋友～。I look on him as a friend. / 矛盾要分主次,不能一律～。We should distinguish between major and minor contradictions and not treat them all alike. / 奴隶主根本不把奴隶当人～。Slave owners never regarded (or treated) their slaves as human beings. / 人家怎样～我我不管。I don't care what other people think about me.

看到 kàndào catch sight of; see: 拐个弯儿就可以～村子了。The village will come into view at the next turn. / 我们满意地～,两国的友好关系有了进一步的发展。We notice with gratification that the friendly relations between our two countries have further developed. / 我们在困难的时候,要～成绩,要～光明,要提高我们的勇气。In times of difficulty we must not lose sight of our achievements, must see the bright future and must pluck up our courage. / 我明天就走,这次演出我看不到了。I'll leave tomorrow. I won't be able to see the performance.

看得过去 kàndeguòqù (also 看得过儿 kàndeguòr) *inf.* passable; just presentable: 这手工做得不算很精细,但还～。The workmanship is not too fine, but it's passable.

看得起 kàndeqǐ *inf.* have a good opinion of; think highly of: 没有什么人～他。Few people think highly of him. / 承蒙他～,请我帮他解答几个问题。He respected me enough to ask my help in answering several questions. / 送这么点儿礼物,人家～吗? If we send such a small gift, will they scorn us?

看低 kàndī *inf.* look down on; belittle

看跌 kàndiē (of market prices) be expected to fall: 这两天香港股票行情～。Stock market quotations in Hong Kong are expected to fall in the next few days.

看法 kànfǎ ① a way of looking at a thing; view: 对这个问题有两种不同的～。There are two different views on this question. ② an unfavourable or a critical view of sb.: 我对一个候选人有～。I'm critical of one of the candidates.

看风色 kàn fēngsè (also 看风头 kàn fēngtóu; 看风向 kàn fēngxiàng) see which way the wind blows; see how things stand

看风使舵 kàn fēng shǐ duò *derog.* steer according to the wind; trim one's sails: 他这人善于～,所以官运亨通。He was good at trimming his sails, so he had had a successful career as an official.

看风水 kàn fēngshuǐ practise geomancy for selecting a site for a tomb, house, etc.

看顾 kàngù look after; take care of: 这位护士～病人很周到。The nurse is very attentive towards her patients.

看官 kànguān (used in old novels to address readers) gentle readers; dear readers: 列位～,欲知后事如何,且听下回分解。Dear readers, if you want to know what

happens next, read the next chapter.

看惯 kànguàn be accustomed to the sight of; get used to the sight of: 这种服装～了也还不错。This kind of clothes looks OK after you get used to it. / 你看得惯他这样发脾气吗? Can you put up with his bad temper? / 这种浪费现象我们可看不惯。We hate to see such waste. / 我可看不惯你这么娇惯孩子。I don't approve of your spoiling the child like that. / 她这种打扮我可看不惯。I can't stand the way she dresses.

看好 kànhǎo have a good prospect (of winning, gaining, etc.): 赛前人们普遍～辽宁队。Before the match most people expected the Liaoning team would win. / 今年的西瓜市场～。The prospects of this year's watermelon market are good.

看见 kànjian catch sight of; see: 你～老张了吗? Did you see Lao Zhang? / 我看了好半天, 可是什么也没～。I looked for a while but didn't see anything. / 他们航行了二十天才～陆地。They sighted land after being at sea for twenty days. / 黑板上的字你看得见吗? Can you see the words on the blackboard?

看开 kànkāi accept (or resign oneself to) an unpleasant fact or situation: 伯母去世, 你要～些, 不要过分悲伤。Auntie has passed away. Try to resign yourself to that fact and don't grieve too much.

看来 kànlái it seems (or appears); it looks as if: 这活儿～今天可以做完。It looks as if we'll be able to finish this job today. / ～他还没有拿定主意。Evidently he has not made up his mind yet.

看破 kànpò see through: ～那些卑劣勾当 see through those base tricks

看破红尘 kànpò hóngchén see through the vanity of the world; be disillusioned with the mortal world

看齐 kànqí ① dress: 向右(左)～! (word of command) Dress right (left), dress! ② keep up with; emulate: 向先进工作者～ emulate the advanced workers

看起来 kànqilai it seems (or appears); it looks as if: ～要下雪。It looks like snow. / 他～很凶, 其实心眼儿挺好的。He looks fierce, but in fact he's kindhearted.

看轻 kànqīng underestimate; look down on: 我们不应～自己的力量。We must not underestimate our own strength.

看热闹 kàn rènao watch the excitement; watch the fun: 咱们上庙会～去吧。Let's go to the temple fair and have some fun. / 大伙儿在会上争得不可开交, 他却在一旁～。Everybody at the meeting was arguing excitedly while he stood by and watched the fun.

看人下菜碟儿 kàn rén xià càidiér decide on the dishes according to the guest—treat a person according to his social standing; be snobbish

看上 kàn·shàng (also 看上眼 kàn·shàngyǎn) take a fancy to; settle on: 他～了一位漂亮的姑娘。He's taken a fancy to a pretty girl.

看死 kànsǐ take a static view of people; form an unchangeable opinion of a person

看台 kàntái bleachers; stands

看透 kàntòu ① understand thoroughly: 这一着棋我看不透。I don't quite understand this move. ② see through: 这个人我～了, 没有什么真才实学。I've seen through him; he's not a man of real learning.

看头 kàntou inf. sth. worth seeing or reading: 这个展览会没什么～。There is nothing much to see in the exhibition. / 这部小说很有～。This novel is well worth reading.

看图识字 kàn tú shí zì learn to read with the aid of pictures

看望 kàn·wàng call on; visit; see: ～老战友 call on an old comrade-in-arms / 这位老人很孤单, 没有人来～。The old man is lonely, and never has any visitors.

看相 kànxiàng read fortune (by face, palm lines, etc.)

看笑话 kàn xiàohua amuse oneself by watching other people make fools of themselves; watch the fun; have a good laugh at: 别吵了, 让人家～。Stop squabbling, will you? People will laugh at us. / 他们一直等着看我们的笑话, 可到头来让人笑话的是他们自己。They had been waiting to have a good laugh at us, but in the end, the joke was on them.

看样子 kàn yàngzi same as 看来 kànlái

看医生 kàn yīshēng see a doctor; consult a doctor

看涨 kànzhǎng (of market prices) be expected to rise

看着办 kànzhebàn do as one sees fit: 需要买点什么, 你～吧。You may buy whatever you need, as you see fit.

看中 kànzhòng take a fancy to; settle on: 这些布你～了哪块?—我一块都看不中。Which of these materials have you settled on?—None of them catch my fancy. / 人家姑娘是博士学位, 不见得看得中我。The young lady has a Ph. D. degree. It's unlikely that she'll take a fancy to me.

看重 kànzhòng regard as important; value; set store by: 不要只～书本知识, 还要在实践中学习。We must not consider that book knowledge alone is important; we should also learn through practice. / 我非常～我们之间的友谊。I value our friendship highly.

看朱成碧 kàn zhū chéng bì take red for green—be dazzled or confused

看做 kànzuò (also 看作 kànzuò) look upon as; regard as: 你把次要问题～主要问题了。You have taken a minor question for a major one. / 他把别人的困难～是自己的困难。He looks upon the problems of other people as his own.

看座 kànzuò old (said to a servant, waiter, etc.) find a seat for the guest

阚 Kàn a surname

瞰[1] kàn look down from a height; overlook: 鸟瞰 niǎokàn

瞰[2]（矙） kàn formal peep; spy

kāng

康[1] kāng ① well-being; health: 健康 jiànkāng ② (Kāng) a surname

康[2] kāng same as 糠 kāng

康拜因 kāngbàiyīn combine (harvester)

康采恩 kāngcǎi'ēn econ. concern

康复 kāngfù restored to health; recovered: 病体～ be restored to health / 祝您早日～。Hope you'll soon be well again. or I wish you a speedy recovery.

康健 kāngjiàn healthy; in good health

康乐 kānglè happy and peaceful

康乐球 kānglèqiú caroms

康耐馨 kāngnàixīn carnation (a transliteration)

康宁 kāngníng formal healthy and free from worry

康泰 kāngtài formal healthy and well

康铜 kāngtóng constantan

康庄大道 kāngzhuāng dàdào broad road; main road: 走社会主义～ take the broad road of socialism

慷（忼） kāng see below

慷慨 kāngkǎi ① vehement; fervent: ～陈词 present one's views vehemently / ～的歌声 fervent singing ② generous; liberal: ～的援助 generous aid / 他为人～大方。He is generous and free-handed. / 他真～, 一下子

借给我五百块钱。He is really generous. He lent me 500 *yuan* right off.

慷慨悲歌 kāngkǎi bēigē　sing with solemn fervour

慷慨激昂 kāngkǎi jī'áng　impassioned; vehement: 他讲得↗，非常感人。His impassioned speech was very moving.

慷慨解囊 kāngkǎi jiěnáng　help sb. generously with money; give generously (of one's money)

慷慨就义 kāngkǎi jiùyì　go to one's death like a hero; die a martyr's death

慷他人之慨 kāng tārén zhī kǎi　be generous at other people's expense; be liberal with other people's possessions

榔 kāng　see 榔榔 láng·kāng

糠 (穅) kāng　① chaff; bran; husk ② (usu. of a radish) spongy: 这萝卜↗了。This radish has gone spongy.

糠秕 kāngbǐ　① chaff ② worthless stuff

糠菜半年粮 kāngcài bànnián liáng　eat chaff and herbs for half the year—lead a life of semistarvation

糠醛 kāngquán　*chem.* furfural: ↗树脂 furfural resin

糠油 kāngyóu　oil extracted from rice husks

鱇 kāng　see 鮟鱇 ānkāng

káng

扛 káng　carry on the shoulder; shoulder: ↗着锄头 carry a hoe on one's shoulder / ↗枪 shoulder a gun; bear arms—see also gāng

扛长活 káng chánghuó　(also 扛长工 káng chánggōng) work as a farm labourer on a yearly basis

扛大个儿 káng dàgèr　*dial.* work as a porter: ↗的 porter

扛竿 kánggān　acrobatics on a bamboo pole

扛活 kánghuó　(also 扛大活 káng dàhuó) work as a farm labourer

kàng

亢 kàng　① high: 高亢 gāokàng ② haughty: 不亢不卑 bùkàng-bùbēi ③ excessive; extreme: 亢旱 kànghàn ④ the second of the twenty-eight constellations (二十八宿) into which the celestial sphere was divided in ancient Chinese astronomy (consisting of four stars in the shape of a bent bow in Virgo)

亢奋 kàngfèn　extremely excited; stimulated

亢旱 kànghàn　severe drought

亢进 kàngjìn　*med.* hyperfunction: 甲状腺机能↗ hyperthyroidism

亢直 kàngzhí　*formal* upright and outspoken; upright and unyielding

伉 kàng　*formal* ① (of a married couple) fit for each other; equal ② high; mighty

伉俪 kànglì　*formal* married couple; husband and wife: ↗之情 affection between husband and wife

抗 kàng　① resist; combat; fight: 喝点儿酒↗↗风寒。Have a drink. It's good for preventing colds. / 这羽绒服能挡风↗冻。This down jacket can resist wind and cold. / 我↗了他几句。I said a few words to him in retort. ② refuse; defy: 违抗 wéikàng ③ contend with;

be a match for: 分庭抗礼 fēntíng-kànglǐ

抗癌 kàng'ái　anticancer: ↗药 anticancer drugs

抗暴 kàngbào　fight against violent repression

抗爆 kàngbào　*chem.* antiknock: ↗剂 antiknock (agent) / ↗汽油 antiknock gasoline

抗辩 kàngbiàn　① contradict ② *leg.* counterplea; demurrer

抗病 kàngbìng　*agric.* disease-resistant: ↗性 disease resistance

抗磁性 kàngcíxìng　diamagnetism

抗大 Kàngdà　(short for 中国人民抗日军政大学) the Chinese People's Anti-Japanese Military and Political College (set up in Yan'an during the War of Resistance Against Japan)

抗倒伏 kàng dǎofú　*agric.* resistant to lodging; lodging-resistant

抗毒素 kàngdúsù　*med.* antitoxin

抗毒血清 kàngdú xuèqīng　antitoxin serum

抗旱 kànghàn　fight (*or* combat) a drought: ↗措施 drought-relief measures / ↗品种 drought-resistant variety / ↗保丰收 fight the drought to ensure a harvest / 这个新品种↗性很好。This new variety has a very good resistance to drought.

抗衡 kànghéng　contend with; match

抗洪 kànghóng　fight (*or* combat) a flood

抗坏血酸 kànghuàixuèsuān　ascorbic acid; vitamin C

抗击 kàngjī　resist and fight back: ↗侵略者 resist the aggressors

抗剪强度 kàngjiǎn qiángdù　*mech.* shearing strength

抗拒 kàngjù　resist; defy: ↗逮捕 resist arrest / 人的衰老死亡是不可↗的。Old age and death are inevitable.

抗捐 kàngjuān　refuse to pay levies and taxes

抗菌素 kàngjūnsù　*pharm.* antibiotic

抗拉强度 kànglā qiángdù　*mech.* tensile strength

抗老剂 kànglǎojì　*chem.* antiager

抗粮 kàngliáng　resist the grain levy

抗美援朝战争 Kàng Měi Yuán Cháo Zhànzhēng　the War to Resist U. S. Aggression and Aid Korea (1950-1953)

抗命 kàngmìng　defy orders; disobey

抗热合金 kàngrè héjīn　heat-resisting alloy

抗日战争 Kàng Rì Zhànzhēng　the War of Resistance Against Japan (1937-1945)

抗渗 kàngshèn　*water conservancy* impervious: ↗试验 impermeability test

抗生菌肥 kàngshēngjūnféi　antibiotic fertilizer

抗生素 kàngshēngsù　old name for 抗菌素 kàngjūnsù

抗属 kàngshǔ　family dependents of military personel in the liberated areas during the War of Resistance Against Japan (1937-1945)

抗霜 kàngshuāng　frost-resistant

抗水性 kàngshuǐxìng　water-resistance; water-resisting property

抗税 kàngshuì　refuse to pay taxes

抗诉 kàngsù　*leg.* protest: ↗书 written protest / ↗案件 protested case

抗体 kàngtǐ　*med.* antibody

抗弯强度 kàngwān qiángdù　*mech.* bending strength

抗压强度 kàngyā qiángdù　*mech.* compressive strength (*or* resistance)

抗药性 kàngyàoxìng　*med.* resistance to the action of a drug: 产生↗ become drug-fast (*or* drug-resistant)

抗议 kàngyì　protest: 我↗！I protest! / 提出↗ lodge a protest / ↗集会 a protest rally

抗议照会 kàngyì zhàohuì　note of protest

抗御 kàngyù　resist and guard against: ↗外侮 resist foreign aggression

抗原 kàngyuán　*med.* antigen

抗灾 kàngzāi　fight natural calamities

抗战[1] kàngzhàn　war of resistance against aggression

抗战[2] Kàngzhàn short for 抗日战争 Kàng Rì Zhànzhēng

抗张强度 kàngzhāng qiángdù same as 抗拉强度 kànglā qiángdù

抗震 kàngzhèn ① anti-seismic capability: ～结构 anti-seismic structure ② take precautions against an earthquake; fight an earthquake: ～救灾工作 earthquake relief work ③ same as 抗爆 kàngbào

抗争 kàngzhēng take a stand against; resist: 以理～ fight sb. with rational arguments

炕 kàng ① kang; a heatable brick bed ② dial. bake or dry by the heat of a fire: 把湿麦子摊在炕上～干 spread the wet wheat on a heated kang to dry / 白薯还在～着呢。The sweet potatoes are still baking.

炕单儿 kàngdānr bed sheet

炕洞 kàngdòng the flue of a kang

炕头 kàngtóu inf. ① the warmer end of a kang ② the edge of a kang

炕席 kàngxí a kang mat

炕沿 kàngyán inf. the edge of a kang

炕桌儿 kàngzhuōr a small, short-legged table for use on a kang; a kang table

钪 kàng chem. scandium (Sc)

kāo

尻 kāo arch. buttocks; bottom

kǎo

考[1]（攷） kǎo ① give or take an examination, test or quiz: ～大学 take a college entrance examination / 我～～你。I'll give you a quiz. or Let me quiz you. / 你的数学～得怎么样? How did you do in the maths test (or quiz)? / ～上大学 be admitted to a university ② check; inspect: 考勤 kǎoqín ③ study; investigate; verify: 待考 dàikǎo ④ (formerly often used in titles of research papers) study; investigation:《宋元戏曲～》"A Study of Song and Yuan Drama" /《毛诗古音～》"Investigations on the Sounds in Mao's Version of The Book of Songs"

考[2] kǎo formal one's deceased father: 先考 xiānkǎo

考妣 kǎobǐ formal one's late parents

考查 kǎochá examine or check (against a certain standard): ～学生成绩 check students' work / ～计划完成的情况 check on the progress of a project

考察 kǎochá ① inspect; make an on-the-spot investigation: ～水利工程 investigate a water conservancy project / ～地形 investigate the terrain / 出国～ go abroad on a tour of investigation / 科学～ a scientific investigation / ～团 an investigation (or observation) group ② observe and study: 在日常工作中～和识别干部 test and judge cadres in day-to-day work / ～组 a study group

考场 kǎochǎng an examination hall or room

考茨基主义 Kǎocíjīzhǔyì Kautzkyism

考订 kǎodìng examine and correct; do textual research

考分 kǎofēn marks (in a test); grades

考古 kǎogǔ ① engage in archaeological studies ② archaeology

考古学 kǎogǔxué archaeology: ～家 archaeologist

考官 kǎoguān examiner (for imperial examinations)

考核 kǎohé examine; check; assess (sb.'s proficiency): 定期～ a routine check / ～干部 check on cadres / 技术～制度业已建立。A system to assess technical proficiency has been established. / ～飞行 test flight; check out flight

考绩 kǎojī assess the work of an employee

考究 kǎojiu ① observe and study; investigate: 这问题很值得～。We need to go into the matter seriously. or This problem merits serious attention. ② be particular about; pay attention to; strive for: 穿衣服不必过于～。One need not be overly particular about dress. ③ exquisite; fine: 用料～ use choice materials / 这本画册装订得很～。This album is beautifully bound. / 这条裤子剪裁漂亮, 做工～。This pair of pants is handsomely cut and well made.

考据 kǎojù textual criticism; textual research

考卷 kǎojuàn examination paper

考克 kǎokè cock (a transliteration, also called 旋塞 xuánsāi)

考课 kǎokè assess the service of an official

考虑 kǎolǜ think over; consider: 让我～一下再答复你。Let me think it over before I give you an answer. / 这方面的情况你～了吗? Have you taken this aspect of the matter into account? / 计划～不周。The plan has not been carefully thought out. / 不～个人得失 disregard personal gains and losses / 给予同情的～ give sympathetic consideration to / 我正～去呢。I'm considering going. / 你～谁担任这个工作合适? Who do you think is more suitable for the job?

考期 kǎoqī date of an examination

考勤 kǎoqín check on work attendance: ～簿 attendance record

考取 kǎoqǔ pass an entrance examination; be admitted to school or college (after an examination): 他～了师范大学。He's been admitted to a normal university. / 他今年没～, 打算明年再考。He failed the entrance examination this year, and will try again next year.

考生 kǎoshēng a candidate for an entrance examination; examinee

考试 kǎoshì ① take an examination: 你们什么时候～? When will you have the exam? ② examination; test: 期中～ mid-term exam / 期末～ final (or end-of-term) exam / 他顺利地通过了～。He's successfully passed the exam. / 他这次～的成绩很好。He got excellent grades in this exam.

考释 kǎoshì make philological studies of ancient texts

考题 kǎotí examination questions; examination paper: 出～ prepare an examination paper; set examination questions

考问 kǎowèn examine orally; question

考验 kǎoyàn test; trial: 经受了严峻的～ have stood a severe test / 久经～的革命战士 a tried revolutionary fighter / 这场战争～了他。The war tempered him. / 她还不打算跟我结婚, 说还要～～我。She's not ready to marry me yet. She says she wants to test me some more.

考语 kǎoyǔ old written comments on the work, etc. of public officials

考证 kǎozhèng make textual criticism; do textual research

考中 kǎozhòng pass an examination or test

拷 kǎo flog; beat; torture: 拷打 kǎodǎ

拷贝 kǎobèi film copy

拷贝纸 kǎobèizhǐ copy (or copying) paper

拷绸 kǎochóu another name for 黑胶绸 hēijiāochóu

拷打 kǎodǎ flog; beat; torture

拷花 kǎohuā text. embossing: ～布 embossed cloth

拷掠 kǎolüè formal flog; beat; torture

拷纱　kǎoshā　same as 香云纱 xiāngyúnshā

拷问　kǎowèn　torture sb. during interrogation; interrogate with torture

烤

kǎo ① bake; roast; toast: ～白薯 baked sweet potatoes／～馒头 toasted steamed buns／把湿衣裳～干 dry wet clothes by a fire／在火边～～脚 toast (or warm) one's feet by a fire ② scorching: 这炉子太～人。This stove is really scorching.／太阳～得大地火辣辣的。The earth, scorched by the sun, was burning hot.

烤电　kǎodiàn　med. diathermy

烤火　kǎohuǒ　warm oneself by a fire: 围炉～ sit around a fire

烤蓝　kǎolán　give a protective coating to metal objects

烤炉　kǎolú　oven

烤面包　kǎomiànbāo　toast: 一片～ a slice of toast

烤肉　kǎoròu　roast meat; roast

烤肉叉　kǎoròuchā　spit; skewer

烤箱　kǎoxiāng　oven

烤鸭　kǎoyā　roast duck: 北京～ roast Beijing duck

烤烟　kǎoyān　flue-cured tobacco

栲

kǎo bot. evergreen chinquapin (Castanopsis)

栲胶　kǎojiāo　tannin extract

栲栳　kǎolǎo　round-bottomed wicker basket

箸

kǎo see below

笭笭　kǎolǎo　same as 栲栳 kǎolǎo

kào

铐

kào ① handcuffs ② put handcuffs on; handcuff: 把犯人～起来。Handcuff the criminal.

犒

kào reward with food and drink: ～师 reward an army with food and drink

犒劳　kào·láo　reward with food and drink: ～解放军 reward the PLA soldiers with food and drink／吃～ enjoy rewarded food and drink

犒赏　kàoshǎng　reward a victorious army, etc. with bounties

靠¹

kào ① lean against; lean on: 扁担～在门背后。The shoulder pole is standing behind the door.／把梯子～在墙上 lean a ladder against a wall ② stand by the side of; get near; come up to: 车辆一律～右走。All vehicles should keep to the right.／船已经～码头了。The ship has docked.／疗养院～海。The sanatorium stands by the sea.／他已是～五十的人了。He's already close on fifty. ③ depend on; rely on: 他家里～他维持生活。His family depended on him for support. ④ trust: 可靠 kěkào

靠²

kào (in traditional opera) stage armour (made of silk and embroidered back and front): 扎～ wear stage armour

靠岸　kào'àn　pull in to shore; draw alongside

靠把　kàobǎ　(in traditional opera) wearing or featuring stage armour: ～武生 wusheng actors wearing stage armour／～戏 military plays featuring warriors or high-ranking generals in full armour

靠背¹　kàobèi　back (of a chair)

靠背²　kàobèi　same as 靠把 kàobǎ

靠背轮　kàobèilún　popular name for 离合器 líhéqì

靠背椅　kàobèiyǐ　chair

靠边　kàobiān ① keep to the side: ～！～！Make way! Move aside! or Mind your backs, please!／行人～走。Pedestrians keep to the side of the road. ② (be forced to) step down from one's post ③ dial. reasonable; sensible: 这话说得还～儿。That sounds more like it.

靠边儿站　kàobiānrzhàn ① stand aside; step aside; get out of the way ② (be forced to) step down from one's post

靠不住　kàobuzhù　unreliable; undependable; untrustworthy: 这话～。This story cannot be relied upon.／他的好朋友原来～。His best friend proved to be untrustworthy.

靠得住　kàodezhù　reliable; dependable; trustworthy: 这消息～吗? Is the information reliable?／这个投资～。This is a solid investment.

靠垫　kàodiàn　cushion (for leaning on)

靠耩　kàojiǎng　(also 靠耧 kàolóu) extend the sowing area (by ploughing the edges of the field)

靠近　kàojìn ① be close to; be near: ～我们厂有一家百货公司。There's a department store near our factory.／两人坐得十分～。The two of them sat quite close together. ② draw near; approach: 轮船慢慢地～码头。The ship is gradually nearing the dock.／～些。Come closer.

靠拢　kàolǒng　draw close; close up: 向前～! (word of command) Close ranks!

靠模　kàomú　mech. profiling; modelling: ～铣床 profiling (or copying) milling machine／～车床 copying lathe

靠旗　kàoqí　(in traditional opera) armour flags (the four triangular flags, made of silk and embroidered, strapped over the back of a warrior outside of his coat of mail)

靠山　kào·shān　backer; patron; backing

靠山吃山，靠水吃水　kào shān chī shān, kào shuǐ chī shuǐ　those living on a mountain live off the mountain, those living near the water live off the water—make use of local resources

靠实　kào·shí　dial. ① indeed; really: 他～累了。He is very tired indeed. ② dependable; reliable; trustworthy: 你得找个～的人来办这事。You have to find someone dependable to handle this matter. ③ feel relieved; be at ease: 知道你平安到达我心里才～了。I was relieved to hear you had arrived safely.

靠手　kàoshǒu　armrest

靠头　kàotou　sth. or sb. to fall back on: 生活有了～ have an assured livelihood

靠枕　kàozhěn　back cushion

靠准　kàozhǔn　dial. reliable; dependable; trustworthy: 这消息不～。This information is not reliable.／他很～，这事可全交给他。He is very dependable, so you can let him handle the whole matter.

kē

坷

kē see below ——see also kě

坷拉　kēla　(also 坷垃 kēla) dial. a clod of earth: 打～ break clods

苛

kē harsh; severe; exacting: 他待人太～。He treats people ungenerously.／对方提出的条件太～了。The terms advanced by the other party are too harsh.

苛察　kēchá　formal meticulously faultfinding

苛待　kēdài　treat (inferiors) harshly

苛捐杂税　kējuān-zāshuì　exorbitant taxes and levies

苛刻　kēkè　harsh; severe; exacting: 这个条件太～，接受不了。The terms are too harsh. We cannot accept them.

苛求　kēqiú　make excessive demands; be overcritical:

他的汉语底子差，对他不能～。He has a poor grounding in Chinese, so don't make excessive demands of him.

苛细 kēxì *formal* severe and exacting

苛性 kēxìng *chem.* causticity

苛性钾 kēxìngjiǎ *chem.* caustic potash

苛性碱 kēxìngjiǎn *chem.* caustic alkali

苛性钠 kēxìngnà *chem.* caustic soda

苛杂 kēzá exorbitant taxes and levies

苛责 kēzé criticize severely; excoriate

苛政 kēzhèng harsh (*or* oppressive) government; tyranny

苛政猛于虎 kēzhèng měngyú hǔ tyranny is fiercer than a tiger

珂 kē *formal* ① a jade-like stone ② an ornament on a bridle

珂罗版 kēluóbǎn (also 珂珴版 kēluóbǎn) collotype: ～印刷 collotype printing

柯 kē ① *formal* stalk or branch ② *formal* axe-handle; helve ③ (Kē) a surname

柯尔克孜族 Kē'ěrkèzīzú the Kirgiz (Khalkha) nationality, or the Khalkhas, inhabiting the Xinjiang Uygur Autonomous Region

轲 kē used in names, as in 孟轲

科[1] kē ① a branch of academic or vocational study: 文科 wénkē / 理科 lǐkē ② a division or subdivision of an administrative unit, etc.; section; department: 我们～只有八个人。There are only eight people in our section. ③ *biol.* family: 猫～动物 animals of the cat family / 松～ the coniferous tree family

科[2] kē *formal* impose a punishment; pass a sentence: ～以罚金 impose a fine on sb.; fine

科[3] kē stage directions in classical Chinese drama: 笑～ (*laughs*)

科白 kēbái actions and spoken parts in classical Chinese drama

科班 kēbān ① old-type opera school ② regular professional training

科班出身 kēbān chūshēn be a professional by training

科场 kēchǎng imperial examination hall

科处 kēchǔ impose a punishment; pass a sentence: ～徒刑 sentence sb. to imprisonment

科第 kēdì grade the candidates in the imperial examinations

科斗 kēdǒu tadpole

科斗文 kēdǒuwén (also 科斗字 kēdǒuzì) tadpole character (an ancient form of Chinese script, so called from its resemblance to tadpoles swimming about in water)

科罚 kēfá *formal* impose a punishment; punish

科幻 kēhuàn (short for 科学幻想) science fiction: ～小说 science fiction (novel) / ～片儿 science fiction film

科技 kējì (short for 科学技术) science and technology: ～大学 university of science and technology / ～界 scientific and technological circles / ～术语 scientific and technical terminology / ～情报 scientific and technological information

科教片儿 kējiàopiānr *inf.* popular science film; science and educational film

科教片 kējiàopiàn short for 科学教育影片 kēxué jiàoyù yīngpiàn

科举 kējǔ (also 科甲 kējiǎ) imperial examinations: ～制度 imperial examination system

科摩罗 Kēmóluó the Comoros

科目 kēmù ① subject (in a curriculum); course ② headings in an account book

科派 kēpài *formal* apportion levies officially

科普 kēpǔ (short for 科学普及) popular science: ～读物 popular science books; popular science

科室 kēshì administrative or technical offices: ～人员 office staff; administrative personnel

科特迪瓦 Kētèdíwǎ Côte d'Ivoire

科头跣足 kētóu-xiǎnzú *formal* bareheaded and barefooted

科威特 Kēwēitè Kuwait

科威特人 Kēwēitèrén Kuwaiti

科学 kēxué ① science; scientific knowledge: 自然～ natural science / ～工作者 scientific worker; scientist / ～实验 scientific experiment / ～文献 scientific literature / ～研究 scientific research / ～仪器 scientific instruments (*or* apparatus) ② scientific: 这种工作方法不～。This working method is not scientific. / ～种田 scientific farming

科学共产主义 kēxuégòngchǎnzhǔyì scientific communism

科学家 kēxuéjiā scientist

科学技术 kēxuéjìshù science and technology: ～是第一生产力。Science and technology are the primary productive forces.

科学教育影片 kēxué jiàoyù yīngpiàn popular science film; science and educational film

科学社会主义 kēxuéshèhuìzhǔyì scientific socialism

科学院 kēxuéyuàn ① academy of sciences ② short for 中国科学院 Zhōngguó Kēxuéyuàn

科研 kēyán (short for 科学研究) scientific research: ～机构 scientific research institution / ～考察船 research ship / ～人员 scientific research personnel

科员 kēyuán a member of an administrative section; section member

科长 kēzhǎng section chief

疴 kē *formal* illness: 沉疴 chénkē

砢 kē see below

砢碜 kēchen same as 寒碜 hánchen

钶 kē *chem.* columbium (Cb)

棵 kē *m.* (usu. for plants): 一～树 a tree / 一～大白菜 a (head of) Chinese cabbage

棵儿 kēr size (of plants): 这棵花～小。This flower is quite small. / 拣～大的白菜拔。Pick and pull out the bigger cabbages.

棵子 kēzi *dial.* stalk; stem: 玉米的～长得很高。Corn stalks grow very tall.

颏 kē chin

颏勒嗉 kēlesù *dial.* Adam's apple

窠 kē nest; burrow: 鸟在树上做～。Birds make their nests in trees.

窠臼 kējiù *formal* set pattern (usu. of writing or artistic creation): 摆脱前人的～，独创一格 break free of conventions and create a style of one's own

稞 kē see below

稞麦 kēmài same as 青稞 qīngkē

颗 kē *m.* (usu. for anything small and roundish): 一～珠子 a pearl / 一～黄豆 a soya bean / 他脸上的汗珠子一～～往下掉。Beads of sweat were dripping down from his face.

颗粒 kēlì ① anything small and roundish (as a bean,

pearl, etc.); pellet: 这些珍珠的～大小很整齐。These pearls are uniform in size. / 这个玉米棒子上有多少～? How many grains are there on this corncob? ② a grain (of rice, wheat, etc.): ～归仓 every grain to the granary / ～无收 total crop failure

颗粒肥料 kēlì féiliào　granulated fertilizer; pellet fertilizer

颗粒物质 kēlì wùzhì　particulate matter

颗粒细胞 kēlì xìbāo　granular cell

榼
kē　an ancient wine vessel

磕(搕)
kē　① knock (against sth. hard): 牙～掉了一颗 have one's tooth knocked out / 摔了一跤，脸上～破了皮 fall and graze one's face / 碗边儿～掉了一块。The edge of the bowl was chipped. / 他脑门儿上～了个包。He got a bump on his forehead. ② knock sth. out of a vessel, container, etc.: ～烟袋锅儿 knock the ashes out of a pipe; empty out a pipe

磕巴 kēba　inf.　stutter; stammer: 他说话有点～。He speaks with a slight stutter. or He stammers slightly.

磕打 kēda　knock sth. out of a vessel, container, etc.; knock out: 把鞋拿到外边去～～吧! Take your shoes outside and knock the dirt out of them.

磕磕绊绊 kēkebànbàn　① (of a road) bumpy; rough ② (of a person) limping

磕磕撞撞 kēkezhuàngzhuàng　walk unsteadily (when drunk or in a hurry); stumble or stagger along; reel

磕碰 kēpèng　① knock against; collide with; bump against: 这箱瓷器一路上磕磕碰碰的，碎了不少。This box of porcelain has been bumped about all the way here and quite a few pieces got broken. / 搪瓷的比瓷的禁得起～。Enamelware can withstand jostling better than chinaware. / 凳子放在门口，走路的时候总是～。The stool is placed in front of the door, so people often bump against it when walking by. ② clash; squabble: 几家住一个院子难免有些～。With several families living in a siheyuan, there will inevitably be some minor squabbles.

磕碰儿 kēpèngr　dial.　① crack (in cups, etc.) caused by knocking ② setback; reverse

磕头 kētóu　kowtow

磕头虫 kētóuchóng　same as 叩头虫 kòutóuchóng

磕头碰脑 kētóu-pèngnǎo　bump against things on every side (as in a room full of furniture); push and bump against one another (as in a crowd): 一大群人～地挤在一起看热闹。A large crowd of people are pushing and jostling each other, trying to get a look at the excitement.

磕膝盖 kēxīgài　dial.　knee

瞌
kē　see below

瞌睡 kēshuì　sleepy; drowsy: 一宿没睡，白天～得很。I'm terribly sleepy today, I didn't sleep a wink last night.

瞌睡虫 kēshuìchóng　① sleep-inducing insect (mentioned in traditional stories) ② a sleepy person

蝌
kē　see below

蝌蚪 kēdǒu　tadpole

蝌蚪文 kēdǒuwén　same as 科斗文 kēdǒuwén

蝌子 kēzi　inf.　tadpole

髁
kē　condyle

kě

壳(殻)
ké　① inf.　shell: 鸡蛋～儿 egg shell / 核

桃～儿 walnut shell / 子弹～儿 bullet shell ② mech. housing; casing; case: 拼合～ split housing / 涡轮～ turbine casing / 护～ protective case ——see also qiào

壳郎猪 kélangzhū　dial.　feeder pig

咳
ké　cough: ～得很厉害 cough badly; have a bad cough / 她～了一晚上。She coughed the whole night. / 他～了一声，清了清嗓子。He coughed in order to clear his throat. ——see also hāi

咳嗽 késou　cough: 感冒了就容易～。A cold can easily cause a cough. / 他听到轻轻的一声～。He heard a quiet cough.

咳嗽糖浆 késou tángjiāng　cough syrup

搕
ké　dial.　① get stuck; wedge: 抽屉～住了，拉不开。The drawer's stuck. It won't open. / 这双鞋太小，穿着～脚。This pair of shoes is too small. They cramp my feet. ② create difficulties; make things difficult: ～人 make things difficult for sb.

kě

可¹
kě　① approve: 许可 xǔkě / 认可 rènkě ② can; may: 今秋～望丰收。We can expect a good harvest this autumn. / 这篇文章～长～短，你看着办吧。You can make this article either long or short, as you see fit. ③ need (doing); be worth (doing): 没有什么～担心的。There is nothing to worry about. / 北京～游览的地方不少。There are quite a few places worth visiting in Beijing. ④ formal　about: 重～千斤 weigh about 1,000 jin / 年～二十 be aged about 20

可²
kě　① conj.　but; yet; however: 劳动很艰苦，～大家干劲十足。It was hard work, but everybody went at it with a will. / 文字虽短，～内容不错。It's a short piece of writing, but it's meaningful in content. / 我嘴里不说，心里～高兴极啦。I said nothing, but felt extremely happy inside. ② adv. inf.　(used for emphasis): 他～没说过这话。He never said that. / 我跑得～不快。I'm by no means a fast runner. / 他汉语说得～好啦! He speaks excellent Chinese. / ～别忘了。Mind you don't forget it. or Be sure to remember it. / 你～来了! So you're here at last! / 你～不能粗心大意啊。You'd better not be careless. ③ adv.　(used in a rhetorical question for emphasis): 都这么说，～谁见过呢? So they say, but who has ever actually seen it? ④ adv. (used in a question for emphasis): 一向～好? Have you been all right? / 这话～是真的? Is that really true? / 你～曾跟他谈过这个问题? Did you ever talk it over with him?

可³
kě　fit; suit: 可心 kěxīn / 可口 kěkǒu ——see also kè

可爱 kě'ài　lovable; likable; lovely: ～的祖国 my beloved country / 多么～的孩子! What a cute child! / 这花儿真～。What a lovely flower! / 湖水清得～。The lake is beautifully clear.

可悲 kěbēi　sad; lamentable: 她的后半生实在太～了。The latter half of her life was really too sad. / 一个人要是一味追求物质享受，那是～的。It's really sad if a person seeks nothing but material pleasures.

可比价格 kěbǐ jiàgé　same as 不变价格 bùbiàn jiàgé

可鄙 kěbǐ　contemptible; despicable; mean: 行为～ act in a contemptible way

可变 kěbiàn　variable

可变电容器 kěbiàn diànróngqì　variable capacitor (or condenser)

可变资本 kěbiàn zīběn *econ.* variable capital

可怖 kěbù horrible; frightful

可不 kěbu (also 可不是 kěbushì; 可不是吗 kěbushìma) *inf.* exactly; right; that's just the way it is: 咱们该去看看老赵了。一一，好久没去了。We should go to see Lao Zhao. —Right! It's been a long time since we last visited him. / 这孩子真聪明。一一，这回又是全班第一。The child is really smart.—You've said it. She's top of her class again. / 我说他们俩不般配，一一，上个月吹了。I said the two of them weren't right for each other, didn't I? They broke up last month.

可采储量 kěcǎi chǔliàng recoverable reserves (of petroleum)

可操左券 kě cāo zuǒquàn be sure to succeed; be certain of success

可拆 kěchāi removable; detachable: 一装置 detachable device

可拆砂箱 kěchāi shāxiāng *mech.* snap flask

可乘之机 kě chéng zhī jī an opportunity that can be exploited: 不要给敌人以一。Don't give the enemy a chance.

可耻 kěchǐ shameful; disgraceful; ignominious: 一的行为 shameful behaviour / 一的失败 ignominious defeat / 以爱学习为光荣，以不学习为一。It is praiseworthy to love study, and shameful to neglect it. / 人穷并不一。Being poor is nothing to be ashamed of.

可待因 kědàiyīn *pharm.* codeine

可的松 kědìsōng *pharm.* cortisone

可读性 kědúxìng readability

可锻性 kěduànxìng *metall.* malleability; forgeability

可锻铸铁 kěduàn zhùtiě *metall.* malleable (cast) iron

可兑换 kěduìhuàn convertible: 一货币 convertible currency (or money)

可纺性 kěfǎngxìng *text.* spinnability

可歌可泣 kěgē-kěqì move one to song and tears: 一的英雄事迹 heroic and moving deeds / 这部记录片记下了一百多年来我国人民一的革命斗争历史。This documentary film records the history of the Chinese people's epic revolutionary struggle during the last hundred years and more.

可耕地 kěgēngdì arable land; cultivable land

可观 kěguān ① worth seeing: 这出戏大有一。This play is well worth seeing. ② considerable; impressive; sizable: 这个数目相当一。This is a considerable figure.

可贵 kěguì valuable; praiseworthy; commendable: 一的品质 fine qualities / 这种积极性和热情是很一的。Such initiative and enthusiasm are highly commendable. / 她的一之处在于坚持真理。Her finest quality lies in upholding the truth. / 时间是最一的。Time is of the essence.

可好 kěhǎo as luck would have it; by a happy coincidence: 我正想找他来帮忙，一他来了。I was just about to seek his help when he turned up.

可恨 kěhèn hateful; detestable; abominable: 他这人真一，老在背后说别人的坏话。He's a most hateful person, always saying nasty things behind people's back. / 这邮局把我的包裹弄丢了，太一了。The post office lost my parcel. It's awfully annoying.

可加工性 kějiāgōngxìng *mech.* machinability

可嘉 kějiā praiseworthy; commendable

可见 kějiàn *conj.* it is thus clear (or evident, obvious) that; it shows; that proves; so: 师部连夜召开会议，一军情十分紧急。The division headquarters held a meeting all through the night, so it is evident that the military situation is critical.

可见度 kějiàndù visibility

可见光 kějiànguāng *phys.* visible light

可脚 kějiǎo (of a shoe or sock) fit well

可敬 kějìng worthy of respect; respected: 他是位一的老师。He is a respected teacher.

可卡因 kěkǎyīn *pharm.* cocaine

可靠 kěkào reliable; dependable; trustworthy: 一消息 reliable information / 一的同盟军 dependable allies / 一性 reliability / 这个人很一。This person is reliable (or trustworthy).

可可 kěkě cocoa

可可儿的 kěkěrde *dial.* by chance; fortunately; as chance would have it: 我刚出门，一就遇着下雨。As luck would have it, it started to rain as soon as I went out.

可控硅 kěkòngguī (also 可控硅整流器 kěkòngguī zhěngliúqì) silicon controlled rectifier (SCR); thyristor

可口 kěkǒu good to eat; nice; tasty; palatable: 这菜很一。This dish is very tasty.

可口可乐 Kěkǒu Kělè Coca-Cola; coke

可兰经 Kělánjīng same as 古兰经 Gǔlánjīng

可乐 kělè ① laughable; funny; amusing: 那猴子的怪样真一。The monkey's antics are really amusing. ② cola (a type of non-alcoholic drink)

可怜 kělián ① pitiful; pitiable; poor: 装出一付一相 put on a pitiable look / 他这付样子真一。He looks so pitiful. / 这个一的老头儿最近死了老伴儿。The poor old man lost his wife recently. ② have pity on; pity: 他这是自作自受，没人一他。Nobody feels sorry for him; he's got what he deserves. / 你一一我，借我点钱吧。Have a heart and lend me some money. ③ (of quantity or quality) meagre; wretched; miserable; pitiful: 这一带雨水少得一。There's terribly little rainfall in this area. or The rainfall is pitifully low in this area. / 他们每星期给他的工钱少得一。They paid him a miserable weekly wage. / 他竟然无知到这样一的程度! I never realized that he was so pitifully (or pathetically) ignorant. / 音乐会上她的钢琴演奏太一了。Her performance on the piano was pitiful (or pitiable) at the concert.

可怜巴巴 kěliánbābā pitiable; pathetic

可怜虫 kěliánchóng a pitiful creature; wretch

可怜见 kěliánjiàn pitiable; poor; pathetic; miserable

可裂变物质 kělièbiàn wùzhì *phys.* fissile (or fissionable) material

可恼 kěnǎo annoying; irritating

可能 kěnéng ① possible; probable; likely: 唯一一的解释 the only possible explanation / 在一的条件下给予照顾 give all the preferential treatment possible under the conditions / 提前一个月交工是完全一的。It's entirely possible to complete the project and hand it over one month ahead of time. / 没有知识分子的参加，革命的胜利是不一的。Without the participation of the intellectuals victory in the revolution is impossible. ② *adv.* probably; maybe: 他一不知道。He probably doesn't know. / 她今天一会再来的。Maybe she'll pop in again today. / 问题一会得到解决。The problem may be settled. / 一要下雪了。It looks like snow. / 很一他已经到家了。He's most likely already home by now. / 他不一这么快到家。He couldn't have got home so soon. ③ possibility: 事情发展有两种一。The matter may develop in two possible directions.

可能性 kěnéngxìng possibility: 这种一不大。The possibility is very small. or There isn't much possibility of that happening.

可逆 kěnì reversible

可逆反应 kěnì fǎnyìng *chem.* reversible reaction

可怕 kěpà fearful; frightful; terrible; terrifying: 做了一个一的梦 had a terrible dream / 真一! 他自杀了! How dreadful! He committed suicide. / 困难再大也没什么一的。However great the difficulties, there's nothing to be afraid of.

可欺 kěqī ① gullible; easily duped ② easily cowed or bullied

可气　kěqì　annoying; exasperating: 这孩子刚换的衣服就弄脏了，真～！ The child just changed his clothes and now he's got them dirty again. How annoying!

可巧　kěqiǎo　as luck would have it; by a happy coincidence: 大家正念叨他，～他来了。 We were just talking about him when he turned up.

可亲　kěqīn　amiable; affable; genial

可取　kěqǔ　desirable: 他的意见没什么～的。 There is nothing desirable in his suggestion. / 这个方案有～之处。 This plan has something to recommend it.

可燃性　kěránxìng　chem. combustibility; flammability

可人　kěrén　formal ① a person with admirable qualities ② likable; satisfying; agreeable: 风味～ agreeable taste

可溶性　kěróngxìng　chem. solubility

可身　kěshēn　dial. (of clothing) be a good fit; fit nicely: 这件大衣穿着真～。 The overcoat is a good fit.

可视电话　kěshì diànhuà　videophone; viewphone; picture telephone

可是　kěshì　① conj. but; yet; however: 他们劳动了一天，虽然很累，～都很愉快。 They were tired out after the day's work, but they all felt happy. / 他嘴里不说，心里～想着呢! He wouldn't say it, but he sure was thinking it! / 她飞速驶往机场，～还是误了飞机。 She drove very fast to the airport, yet she missed the plane. / 我的房间是小，～却很舒适。 My room is small; however (or even so), it's very comfortable. ② adv. (used for emphasis): 他～没说过这话。 He never said that. / 说话～要算数的。 You can never go back on your word. / 这鱼～新鲜的。 The fish is really fresh.

可塑性　kěsùxìng　plasticity

可塑性炸药　kěsùxìng zhàyào　plastic explosive

可叹　kětàn　what a pity; regrettable

可体　kětǐ　be a good fit; fit nicely

可望而不可即　kě wàng ér bùkě jí　within sight but beyond reach—unattainable; inaccessible

可谓　kěwèi　formal one may well say; it may be said; it may be called: 老师对他的教育挽救～仁至义尽。 One may well say that the teacher has done his very best to educate and save him. / ～神速 may well be termed lightning speed

可恶　kěwù　hateful; abominable; detestable: 这些棉铃虫真～! What a curse those bollworms are! / 他那样对待她，太～了。 It's hateful of him to treat her that way.

可惜　kěxī　it's a pity; it's too bad: ～我去晚了一步，最精彩的节目已经演过了。 What a pity I was just too late for the best item on the programme. / 他写的诗不少，～大部分都散失了。 He wrote quite a few poems, but it's a pity that most of them were lost. / 这手套还没破，扔了多～。 The gloves aren't worn out yet. It would be a pity to throw them away. / 半途而废，实在太～了! It's really a shame to give it up when we're already halfway there.

可喜　kěxǐ　gratifying; heartening: ～的成就 gratifying achievements / 取得了～的进展 have made encouraging progress

可想而知　kě xiǎng ér zhī　one can well imagine: 大家都不愿意接近他，他的为人～。 Everybody stays away from him. You can imagine what he is that way.

可笑　kěxiào　laughable; ridiculous; ludicrous; funny: ～不自量 ridiculously overrate oneself; make oneself ridiculous by overestimating one's ability / 他说的话我觉得很～。 What he said struck me as funny. / 六十多岁的人了，还跳霹雳舞，简直～! It's simply ridiculous for a man over 60 to do break dance.

可心　kěxīn　satisfying; to the satisfaction (or liking) of: 这件衣服买得挺～的，既合身，又便宜。 I'm satisfied with my clothing purchase. It's a good fit and cheap too. / 这回倒可了他的心了。 It suited him perfectly this

time. / 他是我们的～人。 He is the person we really like.

可行　kěxíng　feasible: 我看这个办法是～的。 I think this method is workable. / 是否～，请斟酌。 Please consider whether or not this is feasible.

可疑　kěyí　suspicious; dubious; questionable: ～分子 a suspect; a suspicious character / 这案子有些～之处。 There are some questionable points in this case.

可以[1]　kěyǐ　① can; may: 这间屋子～住四个人。 This room can accommodate four people. / 这片麦子已经熟了，～割了。 This field of wheat is ripe and can be gathered in. / 棉花～织布。 Cotton can be woven into cloth. / 你～走了。 You may go. / 问题一定会搞清楚的，你～放心。 Don't worry. Things will be straightened out in the end. ② be worth (doing): 这个问题很～研究一番。 This question is worth looking into. / 这个展览我觉得倒还～一看，可他说不值得看。 I think the exhibition is worth a visit, but he doesn't think so.

可以[2]　kěyǐ　inf. ① passable; pretty good; not bad: 这篇文章写得还～。 This article is pretty good. / 她的英语还～。 Her English is not at all bad. ② terrible; awful: 他今天忙得真～。 He's awfully busy today. / 你这张嘴真～! What a sharp tongue you've got!

可意　kěyì　gratifying; satisfactory: 这间房子你住得～吗? Are you satisfied with your room?

可有可无　kěyǒu-kěwú　not essential; not indispensable

可遇不可求　kě yù bùkě qiú　sth. that can only be found by accident, and not through seeking

可造之才　kě zào zhī cái　a person suitable for training; a promising (or hopeful) young person; a person with great potentialities

可憎　kězēng　hateful; detestable; abominable

可着　kězhe　inf. manage to make do: ～劲儿干 work to the best of one's ability / 你就～这块布裁吧。 You'll have to make do with this piece of cloth.

可支配收入　kězhīpèi shōurù　econ. disposable income

可知性　kězhīxìng　philos. knowability: 世界～ knowability of the universe

坷

坷　kě　see 坎坷 kǎnkě ——see also kē

渴

渴　kě　① thirsty: 我有点～了。 I'm getting a little thirsty. / ～死了 be dying of thirst / 这里有开水，～了请随便喝。 Here's some boiled water. Have some whenever you're thirsty. ② yearningly: 渴念 kěniàn

渴慕　kěmù　think of sb. with respect; admire: 我们怀着～的心情访问了这位著名学者。 With deep admiration we called on the famous scholar.

渴念　kěniàn　long for; yearn for; miss sb. very much

渴盼　kěpàn　eagerly look forward to; earnestly hope

渴求　kěqiú　eagerly desire; crave for: ～进步 earnestly strive for progress

渴望　kěwàng　thirst for; long for; yearn for: ～参加解放军 long to join the PLA / ～自由 long for freedom / 她～着和这位作家见见面。 She's yearning to meet this writer in person.

渴想　kěxiǎng　long for; miss sb. very much

渴仰　kěyǎng　admire; look up to

kè

可　kè　see below ——see also kě

可汗　kèhán　khan

克[1]

克　kè　① can; be able to: 弗～如愿 could not have it as one wished / ～享 be able to enjoy; be in good health ② restrain: 克己 kèjǐ

克²(剋、尅)　kè ① overcome; subdue; capture (a city, etc.): 连～名城 capture one important city after another ② digest: 克食 kèshí

克³(剋、尅)　kè set a time limit: 克期 kèqī

克⁴　kè gram (g.)

克⁵　kè ① a Tibetan unit of volume or dry measure (holding about 25 *jin* of barley) ② a Tibetan unit of land area equal to about 1 *mu*

克当量　kèdāngliàng *chem.* gram equivalent

克敌制胜　kèdí zhìshèng vanquish (*or* conquer) the enemy and win victory

克分子　kèfēnzǐ *chem.* gram molecule

克分子浓度　kèfēnzǐ nóngdù *chem.* molarity

克分子体积　kèfēnzǐ tǐjī *chem.* gram molecular volume

克服　kèfú ① surmount; overcome; conquer: ～缺点 overcome one's shortcomings / ～困难 surmount a difficulty / ～私心杂念 overcome selfish considerations / ～官僚主义 get rid of bureaucracy / ～片面性 eliminate one-sidedness / ～恐惧心理 conquer one's fear ② *inf.* put up with (hardships, inconveniences, etc.): 这儿生活条件不太好，咱们先～点吧。The living conditions here are not very good, but let's put up with them for a while.

克复　kèfù retake; recapture; recover: ～失地 recover lost territory

克格勃　Kègébó KGB (the former Soviet State Security Committee)

克化　kèhuà *dial.* digest (food)

克己　kèjǐ ① restrain oneself ② *old* sell at reduced profit (claimed by a store) ③ be thrifty; be frugal

克己奉公　kèjǐ-fènggōng be wholeheartedly devoted to public duty; work selflessly for the public interest

克卡　kèkǎ *phys.* gram calorie

克扣　kèkòu embezzle part of what should be issued: ～军饷 pocket a portion of the soldiers' pay

克拉　kèlā carat

克郎球　kèlángqiú (also 克郎棋 kèlángqí) same as 康乐球 kānglèqiú

克厘米　kèlímǐ *phys.* gram-centimetre

克里奥尔语　Kèlǐ'ào'ěryǔ Creole (language)

克里姆林宫　Kèlǐmǔlíngōng the Kremlin

克罗的亚共和国　Kèluódìyà Gònghéguó Republic of Croatia

克罗马努人　Kèluómǎnǔrén Cro-Magnon man (an Upper Palaeolithic species of man)

克罗米　kèluómǐ same as 铬 gè

克期　kèqī set a date; set a time limit: ～完工 set a date for completing the work

克勤克俭　kèqín-kèjiǎn be industrious and frugal; be hard-working and thrifty

克丘亚语　Kèqiūyàyǔ Quechua (language)

克日　kèrì set a date; set a time limit

克山病　kèshānbìng Keshan disease

克绍箕裘　kè shào jīqiú follow in the footsteps of one's father; carry on what one's father started

克什米尔　Kèshímǐ'ěr Kashmir

克食　kèshí help digestion

克丝钳　kèsīqián combination pliers; cutting pliers

克汀病　kètīngbìng cretinism

克原子　kèyuánzǐ *chem.* gram atom

克制　kèzhì restrain; exercise restraint: ～自己的感情 restrain one's passion / 他非常生气，难以～。He was so angry that he could hardly restrain himself. / 他在处理这个问题时表现出很大的～。He showed great re-

straint in handling this matter.

刻　kè ① carve; engrave; cut: ～图章 engrave a seal / ～蜡版 cut stencils / 他那满脸的皱纹好像～出来的。The wrinkles covering his face seemed to be engraved. ② quarter (of an hour): 五点一～ a quarter past five ③ moment: 顷刻 qǐngkè / 此刻 cǐkè ④ unkind; harsh: 苛刻 kēkè ⑤ in the highest degree: 深刻 shēnkè ⑥ same as 克³ kè

刻板　kèbǎn ① cut blocks for printing; carve printing blocks ② mechanical; stiff; inflexible: ～地照抄 copy mechanically

刻版　kèbǎn cut blocks for printing; carve printing blocks

刻版印刷　kèbǎn yìnshuā block printing

刻本　kèběn block-printed edition: 宋～ a Song Dynasty block-printed edition

刻薄　kèbó unkind; harsh; mean: 说～话 speak unkindly; make caustic remarks / 待人～ treat people meanly / 他为人～，人缘儿很坏。He's mean and extremely unpopular.

刻不容缓　kè bùróng huǎn brook no delay; demand immediate attention; be of great urgency: 大大加快我国国民经济发展的步伐，是～的。Greatly accelerating the development of our national economy is a task which brooks no delay.

刻刀　kèdāo burin; graver

刻毒　kèdú venomous; spiteful: ～的语言 venomed remarks

刻度　kèdù graduation (on a vessel or instrument): ～盘 graduated disc; dial / ～瓶 graduated bottle

刻骨　kègǔ deeply ingrained; deep-rooted: ～仇恨 inveterate hatred; deep-seated hatred

刻骨铭心　kègǔ-míngxīn be engraved on one's bones and heart—be remembered with deep gratitude

刻鹄类鹜　kè hú lèi wù try to carve a swan and at least you'll get a duck—aim reasonably high and you won't fall far short

刻花　kèhuā engraved designs; carved designs

刻画　kèhuà depict; portray: 鲁迅生动地～了阿Q这个形象。Lu Xun vividly portrayed the character of Ah Q.

刻苦　kèkǔ ① assiduous; hardworking; painstaking: ～学习 study hard / ～钻研 study assiduously / ～耐劳 bear hardships and work hard / 他们练球的时候可～啦。The players really apply themselves when they practise. ② simple and frugal: 生活～ lead a simple and frugal life

刻期　kèqī same as 克期 kèqī

刻日　kèrì same as 克日 kèrì

刻丝　kèsī same as 缂丝 kèsī

刻下　kèxià *adv.* at present; at the moment: 因为～有事，暂时不能离开上海。I can't leave Shanghai just yet because at present I still have some business to take care of.

刻意　kèyì be painstaking; be meticulous about; sedulously strive: ～加工 make painstaking refinements / ～修饰 be very meticulous about clothes or makeup

刻意求工　kèyì qiú gōng sedulously strive for perfection; be a scrupulous craftsman

刻舟求剑　kè zhōu qiú jiàn nick the boat to seek the sword (make a notch on the side of a moving boat to show where to look for the sword which has dropped overboard)—take measures without regard to changes in circumstances

刻字　kèzì carve (*or* engrave) characters on a seal, slabstone, etc.

刻字社　kèzìshè seal-engraving shop

客　kè ① visitor; guest: 家里来～了。We have a

guest at home. / 他是哪村来的～? Which village does the guest come from? ② traveller; passenger: 客舱 kècāng / 客车 kèchē ③ travelling merchant: 珠宝～ jeweller ④ customer: 乘客 chéngkè / 房客 fángkè ⑤ settle or live in a strange place; be a stranger: 客居 kèjū ⑥ a person engaged in some particular pursuit: 政客 zhèngkè / 刺客 cìkè ⑦ objective: 客观 kèguān ⑧ *m. dial.* portion (of food, drink, etc.): 三～冰激凌 three servings of ice cream; three ice creams

客帮 kèbāng *old* pedlars coming in throngs from outside the district

客舱 kècāng passenger cabin

客车 kèchē ① passenger train: 350次列车是～还是货车? Is train No. 350 a passenger train or a cargo train? ② bus: 你坐大～还是小面包车? Are you going to take a bus, or a minibus?

客船 kèchuán passenger ship (*or* boat): 定期～ liner

客串 kèchuàn (of an amateur singer, actor, etc.) play a part in a professional performance; be a guest performer

客地 kèdì a place far away from home; an alien land

客店 kèdiàn inn

客队 kèduì *sports* visiting team

客饭 kèfàn ① a meal specially prepared for visitors at a cafeteria ② set meal; table d'hôte

客房 kèfáng guest room

客观 kèguān objective: ～存在 objective reality (*or* fact, existence) / ～事物 objective things (*or* reality); objectively existing things / ～条件 objective conditions / ～性 objectivity / ～形势 objective situation / 他看问题比较～。 He looks at problems objectively. / ～地讲 objectively speaking; objectively

客观规律 kèguān guīlǜ objective law or principle: 掌握～ master objective laws

客观实在 kèguān shízài objective reality

客观世界 kèguān shìjiè objective world: 认识～ understand the objective world

客观唯心主义 kèguānwéixīnzhǔyì objective idealism

客观真理 kèguān zhēnlǐ objective truth

客观主义 kèguānzhǔyì objectivism

客官 kèguān *old* a form of address to a customer at a shop or to a guest at a hotel

客户 kèhù customer: 国内外～ domestic and foreign customers

客货船 kè-huòchuán passenger-cargo vessel

客机 kèjī passenger plane; airliner

客籍 kèjí ① a settler from another province ② the province into which settlers move

客家 Kèjiā the Hakkas

客家话 Kèjiāhuà Hakka (dialect)

客居 kèjū live in a place other than one's hometown; stay in a strange land

客来客往 kèlái-kèwǎng customers come and go—be thronged with customers

客流 kèliú the flow of passengers

客轮 kèlún passenger ship or liner

客满 kèmǎn ① (of a theatre, cinema, etc.) have a full house; house full ② no vacancy (in a hotel)

客票 kèpiào passenger ticket

客气 kèqi ① polite; courteous: 他对人很～。 He is very polite to people. / 你怎么净说 ～话。 What are you making so many polite remarks for? ② modest: 您太～了。 You are being too modest. *or* You are too kind. ③ make polite remarks or act politely; be polite; be courteous: 别～。 (to a guest) Please don't stand on ceremony. *or* Make yourself at home. (to the host) Please don't bother. / 双方～了一番, 就开始谈正事。 After some polite exchanges (*or* a few words of courtesy), they got down to business.

客卿 kèqīng a person from one feudal state serving in the court of another

客人 kèren ① visitor; guest ② guest (at a hotel, etc.); traveller ③ same as 客商 kèshāng

客商 kèshāng travelling trader

客室 kèshì (also 客屋 kèwū) guest room

客死 kèsǐ *formal* die in a strange land; die abroad

客随主便 kè suí zhǔ biàn a guest should suit the convenience of the host or hostess

客岁 kèsuì *formal* last year

客堂 kètáng *dial.* drawing room; parlour

客套 kètào ① polite formula; civilities: 我们是老朋友, 用不着讲～。 As old friends we don't need to stand on ceremony. / 他们见了面从来没有任何～。 There were never any formalities when they met. ② make polite remarks; exchange greetings: 他们～了几句, 就坐下了。 After an exchange of greetings, they took their seats.

客套话 kètàohuà polite expressions or formulas (such as 劳驾 láojià, 借光 jièguāng, 慢走 mànzǒu, 留步 liúbù, etc.)

客体 kètǐ *philos.* object

客厅 kètīng drawing room; parlour; living room; sitting room

客土 kètǔ ① soil moved in to improve the original ② *formal* foreign land; strange land: 侨居～ live in a foreign land

客位 kèwèi seats reserved for guests or passengers

客星 kèxīng *arch.* nova and comet

客姓 kèxìng a surname different from that of most of the families in a village (e.g. the surname Zhang 张 or Li 李 in Wang Family Village 王家庄)

客寓 kèyù ① inn ② live in a place other than one's hometown; stay in a strange land

客运 kèyùn passenger transport; passenger traffic

客运列车 kèyùn lièchē passenger train

客栈 kèzhàn inn

客座教授 kèzuò jiàoshòu guest professor; visiting professor

恪 kè *formal* scrupulous and respectful: ～遵 obey (orders, rules, etc.) with respect

恪守 kèshǒu *formal* scrupulously abide by (a treaty, promise, etc.): ～中立 observe a strict neutrality

恪守不渝 kèshǒu bù yú strictly abide by (a promise, agreement, etc.)

课[1] kè ① class: 一节物理～ a class in physics; a physics class / 我们星期六下午没～。 We don't have any classes on Saturday afternoon. ② subject; course: 这学期共有五门～。 We have five courses this term. ③ lesson: 第一～ Lesson One / 这本教科书共有二十五～。 This textbook contains 25 lessons. / 这～书比较难。 This lesson is rather difficult. ④ a division or subdivision of certain administrative units; section: 秘书～ secretariat / 会计～ accounting section

课[2] kè ① *old* tax: 完粮交～ pay the grain tax ② levy; collect; impose: ～以罚款 impose a fine on sb.; fine sb.

课[3] kè a session at divination: 占课 zhānkè

课本 kèběn textbook

课表 kèbiǎo (also 课程表 kèchéngbiǎo) school timetable; class schedule

课程 kèchéng course; curriculum: 这学期我们的～很多。 We are taking a lot of courses this term. / 我们的～安排得很紧。 We have a heavy course-load.

课间 kèjiān break (between classes)

课间餐 kèjiāncān a break-time snack (for pupils)

课间操 kèjiāncāo　setting-up exercises during the break between classes

课卷 kèjuàn　written homework

课时 kèshí　class hour; period: 每周授课十六～ teach 16 periods a week

课室 kèshì　classroom; schoolroom

课税 kèshuì　① levy (or collect) taxes ② taxes

课堂 kètáng　classroom; schoolroom: ～教学 classroom instruction (or teaching) / ～讨论 classroom discussion / ～作业 classwork

课题 kètí　① a question for study or discussion: 我们现在研究的～是光合作用。Our current research topic is photosynthesis. ② problem; task: 如何教育好独生子女，这给我们提出了新的～。How to educate an only child is a new problem before us.

课外 kèwài　extracurricular; outside class; after school: ～辅导 instruction after class / ～活动 extracurricular activities / ～阅读 outside reading / ～作业 homework / 这个问题留到～去讨论吧。Leave this question for discussion outside class.

课文 kèwén　text (of a lesson)

课业 kèyè　lessons; schoolwork: 要好好用功，不可荒废～。Study hard and never neglect schoolwork.

课余 kèyú　after school; after class: 利用～时间进行义务劳动 do voluntary labour after school

课桌 kèzhuō　(school) desk

氪 kè　chem. krypton (Kr)

骒 kè　see below

骒马 kèmǎ　mare

缂 kè　see below

缂丝 kèsī　arts & crafts　a type of weaving done in fine silks and gold thread by the tapestry method

锞 kè　a small ingot of gold or silver: 金～ a gold ingot

锞子 kèzi　a small ingot of gold or silver: 银～ a silver ingot

嗑（龄） kè　crack sth. between the teeth: ～瓜子儿 crack melon seeds / 老鼠把箱子～破了。A rat has eaten a hole in the box.

溘 kè　formal　suddenly: ～逝 pass away; die

溘然长逝 kèrán chángshì　pass away; die

kēi

剋（尅） kēi　inf.　scold or beat: 老师～了他一顿。The teacher gave him a good scolding.

剋架 kēijià　dial.　come to blows; fight; scuffle

kěn

肯 kěn　① agree; consent: 我劝说了半天，他才～了。He did not agree until I had talked to him for a long time. ② be willing to; be ready to: ～干 be willing to do hard work / ～虚心接受意见 be ready to listen to criticism with an open mind / 青年人最～学习。Young people are most eager to learn. / 只要你～下功夫，总可以学会的。As long as you are willing to work hard, you will learn how to do it. / 他～不～来？— 。— ～。Is he willing to come? — Yes. / 你～安静一会儿吗？Can't you be quiet for a moment? / 他对工作向来不～马虎。He's always meticulous with his work. ③ dial.　often or tending to: 这几天～下雨。It's been raining these past few days.

肯定 kěndìng　① affirm; confirm; approve; regard as positive: ～十月革命的伟大意义 affirm the great significance of the October Revolution / ～成绩 affirm the achievements / 对于我们的工作的看法，～一切或者否定一切，都是片面性的。In the appraisal of our work, it is one-sided to affirm everything or to negate everything. / 他的设计得到了总工程师的～。His design was approved by the chief engineer. ② positive; affirmative: ～的判断 a positive assessment / 他的回答是～的。His answer is in the affirmative. ③ definite; sure: 请给我一个～的答复。Please give me a definite answer. / 他今天来不来，我不能 ～。I'm not sure whether he will come today. / 他～敌人要逃跑。He was sure that the enemy would try to get away. ④ adv.　certainly; undoubtedly; definitely: ～按时送到 guarantee punctual delivery / 情况～是对我们有利的。The situation is undoubtedly in our favour.

肯尼亚 Kěnníyà　Kenya

肯尼亚人 Kěnníyàrén　Kenyan

肯綮 kěnqìng　formal　bone joints—most important juncture; key points

垦（墾） kěn　cultivate (land); reclaim (wasteland): ～了三亩地 have cultivated 3 mu of land

垦荒 kěnhuāng　reclaim wasteland; bring wasteland under cultivation; open up virgin soil

垦区 kěnqū　reclamation area

垦殖 kěnzhí　reclaim and cultivate wasteland

恳（懇） kěn　① earnestly; sincerely: 勤恳 qínkěn ② request; beseech; entreat: 敬～ respectfully request

恳辞 kěncí　sincerely decline; earnestly beg off

恳切 kěnqiè　earnest; sincere: ～的要求 an earnest request / ～的态度 a sincere attitude / 言词～ speak in an earnest tone / 我～希望你能帮助我。I sincerely hope you'll help me. / 他的话很十分～。He spoke with total sincerity. / 她～地向他解释。She gave him a sincere explanation.

恳请 kěnqǐng　earnestly request: ～协助。Your assistance is earnestly requested. / ～出席会议。We earnestly request your presence at the meeting.

恳求 kěnqiú　implore; entreat; beseech: ～宽恕 implore forgiveness / ～的目光 an imploring look

恳谈 kěntán　talk sincerely; have a heart-to-heart conversation

恳托 kěntuō　make a sincere request; earnestly ask

恳挚 kěnzhì　formal　earnest; sincere: 情意～ show sincere feeling / 词意～动人 express oneself in moving words

啃（齦） kěn　gnaw; nibble: ～骨头 gnaw a bone / ～老玉米 nibble at an ear of corn / ～书本 delve into books / 《资本论》我～了两年才掌握它的基本观点。I wrestled with The Capital for two years before I could grasp its basic concepts.

kèn

掯 kèn　see 勒掯 lēikèn

kēng

坑 kēng ① hole; pit; hollow: 挖一个～ dig a pit / 留神,那儿有个～儿。Mind the hole over there. ② tunnel; pit: 坑道 kēngdào / 矿坑 kuàngkēng ③ arch. bury alive: ～杀 execute sb. by burying him alive ④ entrap; cheat: 坑害 kēnghài

坑道 kēngdào ① min. gallery ② mil. tunnel: ～工事 tunnel defences (or fortifications) / ～战 tunnel warfare

坑害 kēnghài lead into a trap; entrap

坑井 kēngjǐng a mine pit

坑坑洼洼 kēngkengwāwā full of bumps and hollows; bumpy; rough: 一路上～的。The road was bumpy and rough the whole way.

坑蒙拐骗 kēng-mēng-guǎi-piàn swindle

坑木 kēngmù min. pit prop; mine timber

坑骗 kēngpiàn entrap; cheat

坑人 kēngrén ① entrap; cheat: 这家商店净～。That store is a racket. ② dial. be upset (by a heavy loss)

坑子 kēngzi inf. hole; pit; hollow

吭 kēng utter a sound or a word: 他坐在那儿一声不～。He sat there without saying a word. / 这么半天,他连～都没～一声。For a long time he didn't even utter a sound. ——see also háng

吭哧 kēngchi ① puff and blow: 他背起麻包～～地走了。He heaved the sack on his back and staggered off, puffing and blowing from the strain. ② work hard; toil: 她～了半天才把文章写出来。She toiled a long time over her article. ③ hum and haw: 他～了好一会儿才说出来。He hummed and hawed for quite a while before he finally came out with it.

吭气 kēngqì same as 吭声 kēngshēng

吭声 kēngshēng utter a sound or a word: 你为什么不～? Why do you keep silent? / 没人敢～。No one dared to speak. / 他受了很多累,可是从来不～。He'd been put to a lot of trouble but never complained.

阬 kēng formal same as 坑 kēng

砼(硁、硻) kēng formal the sound of striking stones

硁硁 kēngkēng formal shallow and obstinate

铿(鏗) kēng onom. the sound of clanging or clattering: 拖拉机走在路上～～地响。Tractors clattered along the road.

铿锵 kēngqiāng (of sound produced by the gong, piano, cymbals, etc.) rhythmic and sonorous: 音调～ a rhythmic and sonorous tune / 钢琴声～悦耳。The piano produced a sonorous and pleasant melody. / 这首诗读起来～有力。This poem is rhythmic and forceful.

铿然 kēngrán formal loud and clear: 溪水奔流,～有声。The brook rushed on, rippling and bickering.

kōng

空 kōng ① empty; hollow; void: ～箱子 an empty box / 把抽屉腾～ empty out a drawer / 这棵树被虫子蛀～了。This tree has been eaten hollow by worms. / 屋里～～的,一个人也没有。The room is empty; there's no one inside. or There isn't a single soul in the house. / 书已销售一～。All the books have been sold out. ② sky; air: 晴空 qíngkōng ③ for nothing; in vain: ～跑一趟 make a journey for nothing / ～忙 make fruitless efforts / 说了半天是～欢喜一阵。We spoke too soon, only to have our hopes dashed to pieces. ——see also kòng

空靶 kōngbǎ air (or aerial, airborne) target

空包弹 kōngbāodàn mil. blank cartridge

空舱费 kōngcāngfèi transportation dead freight

空肠 kōngcháng physiol. jejunum

空城计 kōngchéngjì the stratagem of the empty city ——presenting a bold front to conceal a weak defence

空挡 kōngdǎng mech. neutral gear

空荡荡 kōngdàngdàng empty; deserted: 农忙季节,人都下地了,村子里显得～的。In the busy season the village looked deserted when all the peasants had gone to the fields.

空洞[1] kōngdòng cavity: 肺～ pulmonary cavity

空洞[2] kōngdòng empty; hollow; devoid of content: ～的理论 an empty theory / ～的词句 empty phraseology; empty rhetoric / 这篇文章写得空空洞洞,没有什么内容。The article is empty and hollow, devoid of substance.

空洞无物 kōngdòng wú wù utter lack of substance; devoid of content: ～的八股调 a piece of stereotyped writing devoid of content

空对地导弹 kōng duì dì dǎodàn air-to-ground guided missile

空对空导弹 kōng duì kōng dǎodàn air-to-air guided missile

空乏 kōngfá poverty-striken; destitute

空翻 kōngfān sports somersault; flip: 后～ backward somersault; backflip

空泛 kōngfàn vague and general; not specific: ～的议论 vague and general opinions; generalities / 这篇评论语言干瘪,内容～。The review is dull and devoid of content.

空防 kōngfáng air defence

空腹 kōngfù on an empty stomach: ～抽血 a blood test taken on an empty stomach / 此药需～服用。This medicine is to be taken on an empty stomach.

空谷足音 kōnggǔ zúyīn the sound of footsteps in a deserted valley——unexpected good news

空喊 kōnghǎn loud empty talk: 光～,没有实际行动,什么事情都办不成。Loud empty talk without action would get us nowhere.

空耗 kōnghào waste: ～时间 waste time

空话 kōnghuà empty talk; idle talk; hollow words: 说～ indulge in idle talk / ～连篇 pages and pages of empty verbiage

空怀 kōnghuái animal husbandry nonpregnant; barren

空幻 kōnghuàn visionary; illusory

空际 kōngjì in the sky; in the air: 掌声和欢呼声洋溢～。Clapping and cheering filled the air.

空寂 kōngjì quiet and deserted

空架子 kōngjiàzi a mere skeleton (usu. referring to a piece of writing, an organization, etc.); a bare outline

空间 kōngjiān space: ～技术 space technology / ～科学 space science

空间点阵 kōngjiān diǎnzhèn phys. space lattice; crystal lattice

空间天文学 kōngjiān tiānwénxué space astronomy

空间站 kōngjiānzhàn space station

空间知觉 kōngjiān zhījué psychol. space perception

空降 kōngjiàng land from the air; be airborne: ～地点 landing area

空降兵 kōngjiàngbīng airborne forces; paratroops

空姐 kōngjiě short for 空中小姐 kōngzhōng xiǎojiě

空军 kōngjūn air force: ～部队 air (force) unit / ～基地

air base / ～司令部 general headquarters of the air force; air command / ～司令员 commander of the air force／～武官 air *attaché*

空空如也 kōngkōng rú yě　absolutely empty: 有些人喜欢夸夸其谈，其实肚子里却是～。Some people have a glib tongue but an empty head.

空口 kōngkǒu　eat dishes without rice or wine; eat rice or drink wine with nothing to go with it: 别～吃饭不吃菜呀。Don't only eat rice. Help yourself to what you like.

空口说白话 kōngkǒu shuō báihuà　make empty promises; pay mere lip service

空口无凭 kōngkǒu wú píng　a mere verbal statement is no guarantee: ～，立字为证。Word of mouth being no guarantee, a written statement is hereby given.

空旷 kōngkuàng　open; spacious: ～的原野 an expanse of open country; champaign / 砍掉了这棵树，院里显着～点儿。After cutting down the tree the courtyard seems much more spacious.

空阔 kōngkuò　open; spacious: 水天～ a vast expanse of water and sky / 高原上，到处都是一样的～，一样的爽朗。On the highland plateau, the view is expansive and clear in all directions.

空廓 kōngkuò　open; spacious: 四望～ spacious and open on all sides

空灵 kōnglíng　free and natural; unconventionally graceful

空论 kōnglùn　empty talk: 切不可只发～。Don't just make a lot of empty remarks.

空落落 kōngluōluò　empty and desolate: 落了叶子的树林子～的。The leafless forest looked desolate. / 孩子们离家后她心里觉得～的。After the children left home, she felt very lonely.

空门 kōngmén　Buddhism

空濛 kōngméng　*liter.* hazy; misty: 山色～。The hills were shrouded in mist.

空名 kōngmíng　① empty title; empty name ② undeserved reputation

空难 kōngnàn　air disaster; aviation accident; aeroplane crash

空气 kōngqì　① air: 湿～ moist air / 山上～稀薄。Up in the mountains the air is thin. ② atmosphere: 会场上～紧张。A tense atmosphere pervaded the meeting. / 这里的政治～很浓厚。People here take a great interest in politics.

空气锤 kōngqìchuí　pneumatic hammer; air hammer

空气弹道 kōngqì dàndào　aeroballistic (*or* atmospheric) trajectory

空气加湿器 kōngqì jiāshīqì　humidifier

空气冷却 kōngqì lěngquè　air-cooling

空气力学 kōngqì lìxué　aeromechanics

空气调节 kōngqì tiáojié　air-conditioning

空气调节器 kōngqì tiáojiéqì　air conditioner

空气压缩机 kōngqì yāsuōjī　air compressor

空气浴 kōngqìyù　air bath

空前 kōngqián　unprecedented: ～的规模 an unprecedented scale / ～的灾难 an unprecedented catastrophe / 中国石油工业正以～的速度向前发展。China's oil industry is developing at an unprecedented rate. / 我们的国家现在是～统一的。Never before has our country been as united as it is today. / 工人的劳动积极性～高涨。The workers' enthusiasm for their work is reaching an all-time high.

空前绝后 kōngqián-juéhòu　unprecedented and unrepeatable; unique: 第一次世界大战在历史上是空前的，但不是绝后的战争。World War I was first of its kind in history, but not the last.

空勤 kōngqín　air duty: ～人员 aircrew; aircraft crew; flight crew

空阒 kōngqù　*formal* empty and quiet: ～的古寺 a quiet ancient temple

空身 kōngshēn　carry no luggage; carry nothing

空手 kōngshǒu　empty-handed: 他想去买激光唱片的，结果～而还。He went to buy some compact discs but came back empty-handed. / 你去看你岳母，可不能空着手去。You can't go to see your mother-in-law without taking a gift.

空疏 kōngshū　*formal* (of learning, writing, etc.) empty; lacking in substance

空谈 kōngtán　① indulge in empty talk ② empty talk; idle talk; prattle

空谈主义 kōngtánzhǔyì　phrase-mongering

空调 kōngtiáo　short for 空气调节 kōngqì tiáojié or 空气调节器 kōngqì tiáojiéqì

空桐树 kōngtóngshù　same as 珙桐 gǒngtóng

空头 kōngtóu　① (on the stock exchange) bear; short-seller ② nominal; phony: ～文学家 phony writer / ～政治家 armchair politician / ～人情 nominal friendship or lip service; empty favour

空头支票 kōngtóu zhīpiào　① dud (*or* rubber) cheque; bad cheque ② empty promise; lip service: 他这回又给我开了张～。His promises turned out to be empty again this time.

空投 kōngtóu　air-drop; paradrop: ～包 parapack / ～场 dropping ground / ～救灾物资 air-drop relief supplies (to a stricken area) / ～伞 aerial delivery parachute / ～特务 air-dropped agent

空文 kōngwén　ineffective law, rule, etc. ——see also 一纸空文 yī zhǐ kōngwén

空吸 kōngxī　*phys.* suction

空袭 kōngxí　make an air attack (*or* raid): 对敌军阵地进行～ make an air raid on the enemy position / 这座城市遭到～。The city was attacked from the air. / 其后的三天，～的次数增加了。In the next three days the air attacks increased.

空袭警报 kōngxí jǐngbào　air raid alarm: ～器 air raid siren

空想 kōngxiǎng　① indulge in fantasy; daydream: 别～了，还是从实际出发吧。Stop daydreaming. Be realistic. / ～家 dreamer; visionary ② unrealistic thought; fantasy; daydream: 离开了客观现实的想象就成为～。An imagination which is divorced from objective reality can only produce empty fantasies.

空想社会主义 kōngxiǎngshèhuìzhǔyì　utopian socialism: ～者 utopian socialist

空心 kōngxīn　(of trees, vegetables, etc.) become hollow inside: 这棵柳树空了心了。The willow tree has become hollow inside. / 大白菜空了心了。The cabbages have gone spongy. ——see also kòngxīn

空心菜 kōngxīncài　another name for 蕹菜 wèngcài

空心长丝 kōngxīn chángsī　*chem. fibre* hollow filament

空心面 kōngxīnmiàn　macaroni

空心砖 kōngxīnzhuān　hollow brick

空虚 kōngxū　hollow; void: 生活～ lead a life devoid of meaning / 思想～ lack mental or spiritual ballast; be spiritually barren / 敌人后方～。The enemy rear is weakly defended.

空穴 kōngxué　*electron.* hole

空穴来风 kōngxué lái fēng　an empty hole invites the wind—weakness lends wings to rumours

空言无补 kōngyán wǔbǔ　empty talk is of no avail

空邮 kōngyóu　send a letter, etc. by airmail

空域 kōngyù　airspace: 战斗～ combat airspace

空运 kōngyùn　transport by air; airlift: ～救灾物资 airlift relief supplies (to a stricken area)

空运货物 kōngyùn huòwù　airfreight; air cargo

空战 kōngzhàn　air battle; aerial combat

空中 kōngzhōng　in the sky; in the air; aerial; overhead:

~补给 air-supply; air-resupply / ~待战 air alert / ~加油 air refueling; inflight refueling / ~禁区 restricted airspace / ~警戒 air alert / ~摄影 aerophotography / ~掩护 air umbrella; air cover / ~侦察 aerial reconnaissance / ~走廊 air corridor; air lane

空中飞人 kōngzhōng fēirén *acrob.* flying trapeze
空中客车 kōngzhōng kèchē airbus
空中楼阁 kōngzhōng lóugé castles in the air
空中小姐 kōngzhōng xiǎojiě air hostess
空重 kōngzhòng *transportation* empty weight
空钟 kōngzhōng *inf.* diabolo
空竹 kōngzhú diabolo: 抖~ play with a diabolo
空转 kōngzhuàn ① (of a motor, etc.) idle; race: 不要让马达~。Don't race your motor. ② (of a wheel) turn without moving forward; spin

倥 kōng see below ——see also kǒng
倥侗 kōngtóng *formal* benighted; unenlightened

箜 kōng see below
箜篌 kōnghóu an ancient plucked stringed instrument

kǒng

孔 kǒng ① hole; opening; aperture: 钥匙~ keyhole / 这座石桥有七个~。This stone bridge has seven arches. ② *m.* (for cave-dwellings): 一~土窑 a cave-dwelling ③ (Kǒng) a surname
孔道 kǒngdào a narrow passage providing the only means of access to a certain place; pass
孔洞 kǒngdòng opening or hole in a utensil, etc.
孔方兄 kǒngfāngxiōng *humor. derog.* Brother Square Hole—money (so called from the appearance of a former coin which was pierced with a square hole)
孔家店 Kǒngjiādiàn *derog.* Confucius and Sons—Confucianism as official Chinese ideology: 打倒~! Down with Confucius and Sons! (a popular slogan among intellectuals during the May 4th Movement, 1919)
孔径 kǒngjìng ① *phys.* aperture ② *mech.* bore diameter
孔孟之道 Kǒng-Mèng zhī dào the doctrine of Confucius and Mencius
孔庙 Kǒngmiào Confucian temple
孔雀 kǒngquè peacock
孔雀绿 kǒngquèlǜ peacock green; malachite green
孔雀石 kǒngquèshí malachite (a mineral)
孔隙 kǒngxì small opening; hole
孔隙度 kǒngxìdù *geol.* porosity
孔型 kǒngxíng *metall.* pass
孔穴 kǒngxué hole; cavity

恐 kǒng ① fear; dread: 惊恐 jīngkǒng ② terrify; intimidate: 恐吓 kǒnghè ③ *formal* fear; dread; be afraid of: 窃~我躬不阅。I am afraid my body cannot hold up much longer. ④ *adv.* perhaps; probably; maybe: 消息~不可靠。I'm afraid the information is not reliable. / ~另有原因。There may be some other reason behind it.
恐怖 kǒngbù terror; horror: ~分子 terrorist / ~手段 terrorism / ~电影(小说) horror film (fiction) / ~统治 reign of terror / ~的经历 a terrifying experience / ~的神色 a terrified look / ~的景象 a terrifying sight / 她看见这蛇,~地缩成一团。She recoiled in horror (or terror) from the snake. / 战争的~ the horrors of war
恐怖症 kǒngbùzhèng *med.* phobia
恐怖主义 kǒngbùzhǔyì terrorism
恐高症 kǒnggāozhèng acrophobia

恐吓 kǒnghè threaten; intimidate: ~信 blackmailing letter; threatening letter / 恐怖分子~说要杀死人质。The terrorists threatened to kill the hostages.
恐慌 kǒnghuāng panic: ~万状 panic-stricken / 使敌人感到~ throw the enemy into a panic; strike terror into the enemy / 地震在全市引起了~。The earthquake caused a panic in the city.
恐惧 kǒngjù fear; dread: ~不安 be frightened and restless / 他有~对手的心理。He regarded his opponent with some apprehension. / 深夜呼啸的风声使她非常~。The howling of the night wind frightened her very much. / 火山的轰鸣引起了当地居民的~。The rumble of the volcano caused terror among the natives.
恐龙 kǒnglóng dinosaur
恐怕 kǒngpà ① fear; dread; be afraid of: 他~迟到,一早就起来了。He got up earlier for fear of being late. ② *adv.* perhaps; probably; maybe: 他走了~有十来天了。It's been almost ten days since he left. / ~要下雨。It looks like rain. / ~他不会同意。I'm afraid he won't agree. / 这样做,~不行。I'm afraid this won't do.
恐慑 kǒngshè *formal* fear; dread
恐水病 kǒngshuǐbìng same as 狂犬病 kuángquǎnbìng

倥 kǒng see below ——see also kōng
倥偬 kǒngzǒng *formal* ① pressing; urgent: 戎马倥偬 róngmǎ kǒngzǒng ② poverty-stricken; destitute

kòng

空 kòng ① leave empty or blank: 请把前面一排座位~出来。Please leave the front row of seats vacant. / 每段开头要~两格。Leave two blank spaces at the beginning of each paragraph. ② unoccupied; vacant: ~房 a vacant room / 车厢里~得很。There are many vacant seats in the carriage. ③ empty space: 各行之间多留点~儿。Leave a little more space between the rows. ④ free time; spare time: 有~儿到我这儿来。Come over when you have time. / 今天没~,改日再谈吧。I'm busy today. Let's talk about it some other day. ⑤ same as 控³ ——see also kōng
空白 kòngbái blank space: 版面上那块~可以补一篇短文。We can fill up that space with a short article. / 填补科学技术上的~ fill the gaps in science and technology / ~表格 blank form / ~支票 blank cheque
空白点 kòngbáidiǎn blank spot; gap; blank: 过去这个地区的煤炭工业是个~。Coal mining used to be nonexistent in this area.
空当子 kòngdāngzi (also 空当儿 kòngdāngr) *inf.* space; interval; gap: 从一个~挤过去 squeeze through a gap / 趁这~,我去把报纸拿来。I'll go and fetch the newspapers during this break. / 书架上摆满了书,没有~。The bookshelves are packed with books; there's no extra space.
空地 kòngdì vacant lot; open ground; open space: 咱们把砖卸在那边~上吧。Let's leave the bricks on that patch of open ground over there.
空额 kòng'é vacancy: ~已经补上了。The vacancy has already been filled. ——see also 吃空额 chī kòng'é
空格 kònggé blank space (on a form)
空缺 kòngquē vacant position; vacancy: 主任的~谁来补? Who will fill in for the director?
空隙 kòngxì space; gap; interval: 铁轨接头的地方都有一定的~。There is a specified gap at every rail joint. / 战士们利用战斗~加固工事。The soldiers strengthened defensive works in the intervals of fighting.
空暇 kòngxiá free time; spare time; leisure: 小王一有~就背英文单词。Whenever he has a bit of spare time,

Xiao Wang uses it to memorize English words.

空闲 kòngxián ① idle; free: 我们车间里的机器没有一台是～的。 None of the machines in our workshop are idle. / 等你～的时候，咱俩谈谈心。 The next time you're free, let's have a heart-to-heart talk. ② free time; spare time; leisure: 战士们一有～就练习投弹。 The soldiers practise grenade-throwing whenever they have some spare time.

空心 kòngxīn on an empty stomach: 别喝～酒。 Don't drink on an empty stomach. / 这剂药～吃。 This dose of medicine should be taken on an empty stomach. ——see also kōngxīn

空余 kòngyú free; vacant; unoccupied: ～的时间 free time; spare time / ～的房间 unoccupied room

空子 kòngzi ① unoccupied place or time; gap; opening: 那孩子找了个～往里挤。 The child found a gap and squeezed in. / 抽个～到我们这里来。 Do find time to come visit us. ② chance or opportunity (for doing sth. bad): 他专门找～说风凉话。 He uses every opportunity to make sarcastic comments. ——see also 钻空子 zuān kòngzi

控[1] kòng accuse; charge: 指控 zhǐkòng

控[2] kòng control; dominate: 遥控 yáokòng

控[3] kòng ① keep part of the body in a certain position unsupported: 我的腿都～肿了。 My lower leg got swollen from keeping it in one place for too long a time. / 枕头掉了，我～着脑袋睡着。 After the pillow fell off, I kept sleeping with my head unsupported. ② turn a container upside down to let the liquid trickle out: 把瓶子先 一～一～再装油。 Turn the bottle upside down to empty it before you fill it with oil.

控告 kònggào charge; accuse; complain: 向法院提出～ file charges in court / 向国家机关提出～ lodge complaints with organs of state / ～某人的罪行 accuse sb. of a crime

控股公司 kònggǔ gōngsī *econ.* holding company

控诉 kòngsù accuse; denounce: ～旧社会的罪恶 condemn the evils of the old society / ～帝国主义的侵略罪行 denounce the imperialists' criminal act of aggression / 这位老人的家史就是对旧社会的血和泪的。 The old man's family history is a blood-and-tear indictment against the old society. / ～会 an accusation meeting (usu. held on a large scale for people to criticize the old society, bad elements, etc.) / ～人 accuser

控制 kòngzhì control; dominate; command: ～人口增长 control population growth / ～货币发行 control monetary issue / ～局面 have the situation under control / ～险要 command a strategic position / 她～不住自己的感情。 She lost control of her emotions. / ～地面沉降 bring surface subsidence under control / ～产量，提高质量 restrict the output and improve the quality / 他发起脾气来自己也不能够～。 He can't control himself when he loses his temper.

控制联想 kòngzhì liánxiǎng *psychol.* controlled association

控制论 kòngzhìlùn *math.* cybernetics

控制数字 kòngzhì shùzì *econ.* control figure

控制台 kòngzhìtái *automation* console

kōu

芤 kōu *arch.* onion; scallion

芤脉 kōumài *Chin. med.* hollow pulse

抠（摳） kōu ① dig or dig out with a finger or sth. pointed; scratch: 在墙上～个洞 drill a hole in the wall / 把掉在缝里的豆粒～出来 dig out the beans from the crevices ② carve; cut: 在镜框边上～点花儿 carve a design on a picture frame ③ delve into; study meticulously: 这本书用不着一字一句地～。 You needn't puzzle over every single word or phrase in the book. ④ *dial.* stingy; miserly: 这人真 ～! How stingy he is!

抠门儿 kōuménr *dial.* stingy; miserly

抠搜 kōusou *inf.* ① dig or dig out with a finger or sth. pointed; scratch ② be stingy: 他真～，像个守财奴。 He is stingy—just like a miser. ③ move slowly; dawdle: 你这么抠抠搜搜的，什么时候才办完? If you go dawdling like this, when will you ever be able to finish?

抠唆 kōusuo (also 抠挲 kōusuo) same as 抠搜 kōusou

抠字眼儿 kōu zìyǎnr pay too much attention to wording or find fault with the choice of words

眍（瞘） kōu (of the eyes) sink in; become sunken: 她病了一场，眼睛都～进去了。 Her illness made her look sunken-eyed.

眍䁖 kōulou same as 眍 kōu

kǒu

口 kǒu ① mouth (of a human being or animal): 口述 kǒushù ② opening; entrance; mouth: 瓶～ the mouth of a bottle / 碗～ the rim of a bowl / 胡同～儿 the entrance of an alley / 信箱的～儿 the slit of a letter box ③ a gateway of the Great Wall (usu. used as part of a place name): 张家～ Zhangjiakou (in Hebei Province) ④ cut; hole: 衣服撕了个～儿。 A hole was torn in the jacket. / 茶碗缺了个～儿。 The rim of the teacup is chipped. ⑤ the edge of a knife, etc.: 刀卷～了。 The edge of the knife is turned. ⑥ the age of a draft animal: 六岁～ six years of age / 这匹马～还轻。 This horse is still young. ⑦ a number of government organs; departments: 文教～ departments of cultural and educational affairs ⑧ *m.* (for family members, pigs, knives, etc.): 一家五～人 a family of five / 三～猪 three pigs / 一～钢刀 a knife / 一～井 a well / 被狗咬了一～ get bitten by a dog / 他说一～漂亮的北京话。 He speaks excellent Beijing dialect. / 吸一～～气 take a breath

口岸 kǒu'àn port: 通商～ trading port / 入境～ port of entry

口白 kǒubái spoken parts in an opera

口碑 kǒubēi public praise

口碑载道 kǒubēi zài dào be praised everywhere

口北 Kǒuběi area north of Zhangjiakou (张家口), including the northern part of Hebei Province and the central part of the Inner Mongolia Autonomous Region

口才 kǒucái eloquence: 他很有～。 He is an eloquent speaker.

口沉 kǒuchén *dial.* ① salty ② be fond of salty food

口称 kǒuchēng call oneself; claim to be; profess

口吃 kǒuchī stutter; stammer: 他说话有点～。 He speaks with a slight stutter.

口齿 kǒuchǐ ① enunciation: ～清楚 have clear enunciation ② ability to speak: ～伶俐 be fluent and eloquent

口臭 kǒuchòu bad breath; halitosis

口传 kǒuchuán instruct orally: ～技艺 pass on one's special skill orally / 民间艺人大都用～的方法来教徒弟。 Most folk artists teach their apprentices by oral in-

struction.

口传心授 kǒuchuán-xīnshòu　oral teaching inspires true understanding

口疮 kǒuchuāng　aphtha

口袋 kǒudài　pocket

口袋 kǒudai　bag; sack: 纸～儿 paper bag ／ 面～ flour sack

口对口复苏 kǒu duì kǒu fùsū　*med.*　mouth-to-mouth resuscitation

口对口呼吸 kǒu duì kǒu hūxī　*med.*　mouth-to-mouth breathing

口耳之学 kǒu ěr zhī xué　knowledge from hearsay; second-hand knowledge

口风 kǒu·fēng　one's intention or view as revealed in what one says: 先探探他的～。Sound him out first.

口服[1] kǒufú　profess to be convinced: 心服口服 xīnfú-kǒufú

口服[2] kǒufú　take orally: 不得～ not to be taken oràlly ／ ～避孕药 oral contraceptive; the pill

口服心不服 kǒufú xīn bùfú　pretend to be convinced

口服液 kǒufúyè　oral liquid

口福 kǒufú　*humor.*　gourmet's luck; the luck to get sth. very nice to eat: 我们今天～可不浅。We've really lucked out today in the food department.

口腹 kǒufù　food: 不贪～ not indulge one's appetite

口腹之欲 kǒufù zhī yù　the desire for good food

口感 kǒugǎn　texture (of foods): 这种面条吃起来～好。These noodles have a nice chewy texture.

口供 kǒugòng　a statement made by the accused under examination

口过 kǒuguò　make a slip of the tongue

口号 kǒuhào　slogan; watchword: 呼～ shout slogans ／ 提出～ put forward a slogan ／ 标语～ posters and slogans

口红 kǒuhóng　lipstick

口惠 kǒuhuì　lip service; empty promise

口惠而实不至 kǒuhuì ér shí bù zhì　make a promise and not keep it; pay lip service

口技 kǒujì　vocal mimicry; vocal imitation

口角 kǒujiǎo　corner of the mouth: ～流涎 slobber ——see also kǒujué

口角春风 kǒujiǎo chūnfēng　make favourable remarks about sb.; put in a good word for sb.

口角生风 kǒujiǎo shēngfēng　speak fluently

口角炎 kǒujiǎoyán　*med.*　perlèche

口紧 kǒujǐn　closemouthed; tight-lipped

口径 kǒujìng　① bore; calibre: ～155 毫米的大炮 155mm. gun ② requirements; specifications; line of action: ～不合 not meet the requirements ／对～ arrange to give the same story; give the same account by arrangement ／ 咱俩说话～要一致。We two must speak along the same lines. *or* We two must have the same approach in speaking about this.

口诀 kǒujué　a pithy mnemonic formula (often in rhyme); mnemonic rhyme: 珠算～ abacus rhymes

口角 kǒujué　quarrel; bicker; wrangle: 这对小夫妻常常发生～。The young couple often bicker with one another. ——see also kǒujiǎo

口渴 kǒukě　thirsty

口口声声 kǒukǒushēngshēng　say again and again; keep on saying: 他～说不知道。He kept on pleading ignorance. ／ 他～称我是他的老前辈。He always addresses me as his senior.

口快 kǒukuài　① outspoken; plain-spoken ② thoughtless in speech; quick with one's tongue

口粮 kǒuliáng　grain ration

口令 kǒulìng　① word of command ② password; watchword; countersign: ～问答 challenge and reply

口蜜腹剑 kǒumì-fùjiàn　honey-mouthed and dagger-hearted; honey on one's lips and murder in one's heart; hypocritical and malignant

口蘑 kǒumó　a kind of dried mushroom (from Zhangjiakou 张家口)

口沫 kǒumò　saliva; spittle

口气 kǒu·qì　① tone; note: 严肃的～ a serious tone ／ 改变～ change one's tone ／ 他说话有埋怨的～。There was a note of complaint in what he said. ／ ～强硬的声明 a strongly worded statement ② manner of speaking: 他的～真不小。He talked big. ／ 总经理的话～很硬。The general manager spoke with firmness. ③ what is actually meant; implication: 听他的～，好像感到为难。Judging by the way he spoke, he seemed to be in an awkward situation. ——see also 探口气 tàn kǒuqi

口器 kǒuqì　mouthparts (of an insect)

口腔 kǒuqiāng　*physiol.*　oral cavity: ～卫生 oral hygiene

口腔学 kǒuqiāngxué　stomatology

口腔医院 kǒuqiāng yīyuàn　stomatological hospital

口琴 kǒuqín　mouth organ; harmonica

口轻[1] kǒuqīng　① not too salty: 我喜欢吃～的，请你少放点盐。I prefer food that's not too salty. Please don't put too much salt in it. ② be fond of food that is not too salty: 他～。He's fond of food that is not too salty.

口轻[2] kǒuqīng　(also 口小 kǒuxiǎo) (of a horse, donkey, etc.) young: ～的骡子 young mules

口若悬河 kǒu ruò xuán hé　let loose a flood of eloquence; be eloquent; speak volubly: 这人～，一说就是一大套。It seemed as if his flow of words would never stop.

口哨儿 kǒushàor　whistling sound made through rounded lips: 吹～ whistle

口舌 kǒushé　① dispute or misunderstanding caused by gossip: ～是非 disputes and quarrels ② talking round: 费了很大的～才把他说服。It took a lot of talking to convince him. ／ 不必费～了。You might as well save your breath.

口实 kǒushí　*formal*　a cause for gossip; handle: 贻人口实 yí rén kǒushí

口试 kǒushì　oral examination; oral test

口是心非 kǒushì-xīnfēi　say yes and mean no; say one thing and mean another

口授 kǒushòu　① teach or instruct orally: 我国许多地方戏曲都是由民间艺人世代～而保存下来的。Many of our local operas were preserved by folk artists who passed them down from generation to generation by word of mouth. ② dictate: 他写的这封信是他父亲～的。The letter he wrote was dictated by his father.

口述 kǒushù　give an oral account: ～全部经过 give an oral account of what happened from beginning to end

口水 kǒushuǐ　saliva: 流～ slobber ／ 他见了这些吃的直流～。His mouth watered at the sight of all the food.

口说无凭 kǒu shuō wú píng　verbal statements are no guarantee: ～，立此为据。Verbal statements being no guarantee, a written agreement is hereby made.

口算 kǒusuàn　do a sum orally

口蹄疫 kǒutíyì　*animal husbandry*　foot-and-mouth disease

口条 kǒutiáo　pig's or ox's tongue (as food)

口头 kǒutóu　oral: ～通知 notify orally ／ ～革命派 a revolutionary in word; a vocal revolutionary ／ ～上赞成，实际上反对 agree in words but oppose in deeds ／ ～表决 voice vote; vote by "yes" and "no" ／ ～汇报 oral report ／ ～声明 oral statement

口头 kǒutou　*dial.*　flavour; taste (of fruit)

口头禅 kǒutóuchán　pet phrase

口头交 kǒutóujiāo　an casual acquaintance

口头文学 kǒutóu wénxué　folk tales, ballads, etc. handed down orally; oral literature

口头语 kǒutóuyǔ pet phrase: "研究研究"这几个字几乎成了他的～。These words "We'll think it over" have become his pet phrase.

口外 Kǒuwài same as 口北 Kǒuběi

口腕 kǒuwàn *zool.* oral arm

口味 kǒuwèi ① a person's taste: 合～ suit one's taste / 不合～ not be to one's taste / 各人～不同。Tastes differ. / 京剧最合我的～。Beijing opera suits my taste best. ② the flavour or taste of food: 这菜～不错。This dish is tasty. / 这些菜都是湖南～。These are all Hunanese dishes.

口吻 kǒuwěn ① *zool.* muzzle; snout ② tone; note: 玩笑的～ jocular tone / 以教训人的～ in a lecturing tone

口误 kǒuwù ① make a slip of the tongue ② a slip of the tongue; an oral slip

口涎 kǒuxián saliva

口香糖 kǒuxiāngtáng chewing gum

口信 kǒuxìn oral message: 请你给我家捎个～, 说我今晚不回家了。Please tell my family that I'm not going home tonight.

口形 kǒuxíng *phonet.* degree of lip-rounding

口型 kǒuxíng the shape of the mouth as one speaks or produces a sound

口血未干 kǒu xuè wèi gān before the blood of the sacrifice is dry on one's lips—before the ink is dry

口炎 kǒuyán *med.* stomatitis

口眼㖞斜 kǒuyǎn wāixié *Chin. med.* facial paralysis

口译 kǒuyì oral interpretation

口音 kǒuyīn *phonet.* oral speech sounds

口音 kǒuyin ① voice: 她一听是她儿子的～, 就赶紧出来了。Recognizing her son's voice, she hurried out. ② accent: 说话带广东～ speak with a Guangdong accent

口语 kǒuyǔ ① spoken language ② *formal* slander; calumny

口谕 kǒuyù *old* verbal instructions (from one's superior)

口燥唇干 kǒuzào-chúngān (talk until) the lips are dry and the mouth is parched

口占 kǒuzhàn *formal* ① dictate ② improvise (a poem): ～一绝 improvise a *jueju* (or quatrain)

口罩 kǒuzhào gauze mask (worn over nose and mouth); surgical mask

口重 kǒuzhòng ① salty: 我爱吃～的。I like salty dishes. ② be fond of salty food: 我～。I'm fond of salty food.

口诛笔伐 kǒuzhū-bǐfá condemn both in speech and in writing

口子[1] kǒuzi *inf.* ① *m.* person: 你们家有几～? How many people are there in your family? ② my husband or my wife: 我们那～整天很忙。My husband (*or.* My wife) is busy all day long.

口子[2] kǒuzi opening; hole; cut; tear: 我手上拉的～快好了。The cut on my hand is nearly healed. / 袖子撕了个～。There is a tear in the sleeve. / 水渠开了～。The canal has burst its banks (*or* sprung a leak). / 可不能开这个～啊! Let's not set such a precedent!

kòu

叩[1](敂) kòu knock: ～门 knock at a door

叩[2] kòu ① kowtow ② *formal* inquire; ask: ～其姓名 ask sb.'s name

叩拜 kòubài kowtow

叩齿 kòuchǐ clicking the teeth (a method of dental care)

叩打 kòudǎ knock; tap; rap: 他用铅笔轻轻～着桌子。He tapped the table with his pencil.

叩阍 kòuhūn *formal* lodge a complaint with the imperial court

叩见 kòujiàn *formal* visit (one's superior); call on (one's superior)

叩首 kòushǒu kowtow

叩头 kòutóu kowtow

叩头虫 kòutóuchóng click beetle; snapping beetle

叩问 kòuwèn *formal* make inquiries

叩谢 kòuxiè kowtow in thanks; offer earnest thanks

叩诊 kòuzhěn *med.* percussion: ～锤 percussion hammer

扣[1] kòu ① button up; buckle: 把衣服～上 button (up) one's coat / 把皮带～上 buckle a belt / 把门～上 latch the door / ～扣子 do up the buttons ② place a cup, bowl, etc. upside down; cover with an inverted cup, bowl, etc.: 把缸～过来。Turn the vat upside down. / 用碗把菜～上, 免得凉了。Cover the food with a bowl to keep it from getting cold. ③ detain; take into custody; arrest: 把可疑分子～起来 detain a suspect / 他违反交通规则, 交通警～了他的自行车。The policeman took away his bike because he had violated traffic regulations. ④ deduct: ～工资 deduct a part of sb.'s pay ⑤ give a discount: 打九～ give a 10 per cent discount ⑥ smash or spike (a ball): ～球 smash a ball ⑦ knot: 绳～儿 a knot (in a rope) / 系个～儿 tie (*or* make) a knot ⑧ circle of thread (on a screw): 拧了三～ drive in a screw in three twists

扣[2](鈕) kòu button; buckle: 上衣掉了个～儿。I lost a button off my coat. / 带金属～儿的皮带 a belt with a metal buckle

扣除 kòuchú deduct: ～各种费用后, 收入超过万元。After deducting costs, the proceeds still exceeded 10,000 yuan. / 从工资里～房租 deduct rent from wages

扣篮 kòulán *basketball* dunk shot; over-the-rim shot

扣留 kòuliú detain; hold in custody; arrest: 把走私犯～起来 detain the smuggler / ～驾驶执照 suspend a driving licence

扣帽子 kòu màozi put a (political) label on sb.: 批评要以理服人, 不要乱～。When criticizing people, we must try to convince them through reasoning, not just put labels on them.

扣襻 kòupàn button loop

扣人心弦 kòu rén xīnxián exciting; thrilling; breathtaking: 一场～的比赛 an exciting match

扣杀 kòushā smash or spike (a ball): 闪电般的～ lightning smashes / 大板～ overpowering smashes (in table-tennis)

扣头 kòutou discount (the amount of money taken off)

扣压 kòuyā withhold; pigeonhole: ～稿件 withhold a manuscript from publication

扣押 kòuyā ① detain; hold in custody: 被告在～中。The accused is in custody. / ～人质 hold sb. hostage ② *leg.* distrain; seize

扣眼 kòuyǎn buttonhole

扣子 kòuzi ① knot ② button ③ an abrupt break in a story to create suspense; a point of high suspense

寇 kòu ① bandit; invader; enemy: 海～ pirate / 敌～ the (invading) enemy ② invade: 入寇 rùkòu ③ (Kòu) a surname

寇仇 kòuchóu enemy; foe

筘(簆) kòu *text.* reed

蔻 kòu see below

蔻丹 kòudān nail polish (from "Cutex")

蔻蔻　kòukòu　same as 可可 kěkě

kū

刳　kū　*formal* hollow out: ～木为舟 hollow out a tree trunk and make it into a canoe; make a canoe out of a tree trunk

砝　kū　see below
砝砝　kūkū　*formal* diligent; industrious; assiduous

枯　kū　① (of a plant, etc.) withered: ～草 withered grass / ～叶 dead leaves ② (of a well, river, etc.) dried up: 枯井　kūjǐng　③ dull; uninteresting: 枯坐　kūzuò
枯饼　kūbǐng　*agric.* oil cake
枯草热　kūcǎorè　*med.* hay fever
枯肠　kūcháng　*liter.* impoverished mind: 搜索枯肠 sōusuǒ kūcháng
枯干　kūgān　dried-up; withered; wizened
枯槁　kūgǎo　① (of a plant, etc.) withered ② haggard: 形容～ look haggard
枯骨　kūgǔ　(also 枯骸 kūhái) dry bones (of a person long dead)
枯涸　kūhé　(of the source of a river) dry up
枯黄　kūhuáng　withered and yellow: 树叶逐渐～了。The leaves are beginning to turn yellow.
枯瘠　kūjí　emaciated; skinny
枯寂　kūjì　bored and lonely: 他们人多，虽然在沙漠中行进，也不感到～。They travelled in a large group, so they didn't feel bored or lonely while passing through the desert.
枯焦　kūjiāo　dried-up; withered; shrivelled
枯竭　kūjié　dried up; exhausted: 水源～。The source has dried up. / 财源～。Financial resources were exhausted. / 他天天讲故事，来源好像永远不会～。He tells stories every day. It's as if he has an inexhaustible supply of them.
枯井　kūjǐng　a dry well
枯窘　kūjiǒng　*formal* dried up: 文思～ the source of one's inspiration has dried up; be devoid of inspiration; run out of ideas to write about
枯木逢春　kūmù féng chūn　spring comes to the withered tree—get a new lease of life
枯木朽株　kūmù xiǔzhū　a withered tree—① a senile or sick person ② a declining power
枯涩　kūsè　dull and heavy: 文字～ a dull and heavy style (of writing)
枯瘦　kūshòu　emaciated; skinny: ～如柴 skinny; be all skin and bones
枯水　kūshuǐ　low water
枯水期　kūshuǐqī　dry season
枯萎　kūwěi　withered: 这花已经～了。The flower has withered.
枯朽　kūxiǔ　dry and decayed; rotten
枯哑　kūyǎ　hoarse; husky; raucous: ～的声音 a husky voice
枯叶蛾　kūyè'é　lappet moth
枯燥　kūzào　dry and dull; uninteresting: 这本书那么～，谁高兴看呢? This book is so dull. Who would ever want to read it?
枯燥无味　kūzào wúwèi　dry as dust; dry and dull: 群众不欢迎他们的～的宣传。The masses don't think much of their dry and dull propaganda.
枯痔法　kūzhìfǎ　*Chin. med.* necrosis therapy of haemorrhoids
枯皱　kūzhòu　wizened and wrinkly
枯坐　kūzuò　sit in boredom; sit idle

哭　kū　cry; weep: ～了起来 burst into tears /《～任弼时同志》"Lament for Comrade Ren Bishi"
哭鼻子　kūbízi　*inf.* snivel: 输了可别～啊。If you lose, don't go and start snivelling.
哭哭啼啼　kūkutítí　weep and wail
哭泣　kūqì　cry; weep; sob
哭穷　kūqióng　go about telling people how hard up one is; complain of being hard up
哭丧棒　kūsāngbàng　(in former times) a staff used by the son of the deceased in a funeral procession
哭丧着脸　kūsangzheliǎn　put on (or wear) a long face; go around with a long face: 想开点，别整天～。Cheer up. Don't go around with such a sad look on your face all the time.
哭诉　kūsù　complain tearfully; accuse while weeping; sob out
哭天抹泪　kūtiān-mǒlèi　*derog.* wailing and whining; crying piteously
哭笑不得　kūxiào bude　not know whether to laugh or to cry; find sth. both funny and annoying

窟　kū　① hole; cave: 石窟　shíkū　② den: 赌窟 dǔkū
窟窿　kūlong　① hole; cavity: 耗子～ mouse-hole / 鞋底磨了个～ have worn a hole in the sole of one's shoe ② deficit; debt: 填窟窿　tián kūlong
窟窿眼儿　kūlongyǎnr　small hole: 这块木头上有好些虫蛀的～。There're a lot of worm-holes on this piece of wood.
窟臀　kūtún　*dial.* buttocks
窟宅　kūzhái　bandits' lair

骷　kū　see below
骷髅　kūlóu　① human skeleton ② human skull; death's-head

kǔ

苦　kǔ　① bitter: 这药～极了。This medicine tastes very bitter. ② hardship; suffering; pain: ～日子 hard times / 勘探队员以～为乐，以～为荣。The prospectors feel it a joy and an honour to work under hard conditions. / 她～了一辈子，也没～出头。She never knew anything but hardship her whole life. ③ cause sb. suffering; give sb. a hard time: 这事可～了他了。This matter really gave him a hard time. ④ suffer from; be troubled by: ～旱 suffer from drought ⑤ painstakingly; doing one's utmost: ～劝 earnestly advise (or exhort) / 刚才你妹妹找你找～了。Your sister was knocking herself out looking for you. ⑥ *dial.* cut off too much or be worn out: 指甲剪得太～ trim one's nails too short / 树枝修得太～了。The trees are overpruned. / 这双鞋穿得太～了，不能修理了。This pair of shoes is worn out beyond repair.
苦熬　kǔ'áo　go through years of suffering and hardship
苦差　kǔchāi　a hard and unprofitable job
苦楚　kǔchǔ　suffering; misery; distress
苦处　kǔchu　suffering; hardship; difficulty: 你可不知道我当童养媳那时的～。You don't know how I suffered as a child bride.
苦大仇深　kǔdà-chóushēn　have suffered bitterly and nurse deep hatred: ～的老工人 old workers who suffered bitterly in the old society and have deep class hatred
苦胆　kǔdǎn　common name for 胆囊 dǎnnáng
苦迭打　kǔdiédǎ　coup d'état (a transliteration, now usu.

replaced by 政变　zhèngbiàn)

苦恶鸟　kǔ'èniǎo　white-breasted water rail

苦干　kǔgàn　work hard: 〜精神 the spirit of hard work／〜加巧干 work hard and skilfully; work hard and use one's brain

苦工　kǔgōng　① hard (manual) work; hard labour ② a person doing hard (manual) work

苦功　kǔgōng　hard work; painstaking effort: 语言这东西, 不是随便可以学好的, 非下〜不可。 The mastery of language is not easy and requires painstaking effort.／下〜学习 study hard

苦瓜　kǔguā　① bot. balsam pear ② bitter gourd (fig.): 咱们俩是一根藤上的〜。 We are two bitter gourds on the same vine—we both suffered the same hard lot in the old society.

苦果　kǔguǒ　a bitter pill (to swallow)

苦海　kǔhǎi　sea of bitterness; abyss of misery: 解放前的上海是冒险家的乐园, 劳动人民的〜。 Preliberation Shanghai was paradise for the adventurers but hell for the working people.／脱离〜 get out of the abyss of misery

苦海无边, 回头是岸　kǔhǎi wú biān, huítóu shì àn　the sea of bitterness has no bounds, repent and the shore is at hand

苦害　kǔhài　dial. harm; damage

苦寒　kǔhán　bitter cold

苦活儿　kǔhuór　a hard and unprofitable job

苦尽甘来　kǔjìn-gānlái　the bitterness ends and the sweetness begins: 直到解放, 他们才〜。 Only with liberation did their misery end and their happiness begin.

苦境　kǔjìng　hard and difficult circumstances; morass

苦口　kǔkǒu　① (admonish) in earnest: 〜相劝 earnestly advise (or exhort) ② bitter to the taste

苦口婆心　kǔkǒu-póxīn　(admonish) earnestly and maternally

苦苦　kǔkǔ　strenuously; hard; persistently: 〜思索 think hard

苦苦哀求　kǔkǔ āiqiú　entreat piteously; implore urgently

苦剌吧唧　kǔlabājī　inf. bitter: 这根黄瓜〜的, 不好吃。 This cucumber tastes bitter and is not good to eat.

苦劳　kǔláo　credit for hard work (opp. good work): 他没有功劳也有〜。 Give him credit for hard work, if not for good work.

苦乐　kǔ-lè　comfort and discomfort; joy and sorrow: 〜不均 an inequitable distribution of the work load

苦力　kǔlì　coolie

苦楝子　kǔliànzǐ　Chin. med. chinaberry

苦闷　kǔmèn　depressed; dejected; feeling low: 没有人理解她, 她感到很〜。 She was in a depressed state because no one understood her.

苦命　kǔmìng　cruel fate; ill-fated life: 〜人 a luckless person

苦难　kǔnàn　suffering; misery; distress: 帝国主义的战争使人民遭受了巨大的〜。 Wars launched by imperialism have caused the people untold suffering.／〜的深渊 the abyss of misery／〜的年代 an era of suffering／〜的家史 the tragic history of one's family

苦难深重　kǔnàn shēnzhòng　be in deep distress; be in the depth of misery: 新中国成立了, 〜的中国人民终于见到了光明。 When the New China was founded, the deeply distressed Chinese people finally saw the light of their bright future.

苦恼　kǔnǎo　vexed; worried: 受到一点挫折用不着〜。 You shouldn't get frustrated just because of a few setbacks.／这个问题使人非常〜。 This problem is extremely vexing.

苦肉计　kǔròujì　the ruse of self-injury (inflicting an injury on oneself to win the confidence of the enemy)

苦涩　kǔsè　① bitter and astringent ② pained; agonized;

anguished: 〜的表情 a pained look／他〜地笑了笑。 He forced a smile.

苦水　kǔshuǐ　① bitter water ② gastric secretion, etc. rising to the mouth ③ suffering (in the old society): 她是在〜里泡大的。 She grew up amidst suffering. ——see also 吐苦水 tǔ kǔshuǐ

苦思　kǔsī　think hard; cudgel one's brains

苦思冥想　kǔsī-míngxiǎng　think long and hard; cudgel (or rack) one's brains (to evolve an idea): 他〜了半天, 还是拿不出什么主意来。 He racked his brains for a long time, but couldn't come up with any ideas.

苦痛　kǔtòng　pain; suffering; agony

苦头　kǔtóu　bitter taste: 这个井里的水带点〜儿。 Water from this well has a slightly bitter taste.

苦头　kǔ·tóu　suffering: 他在敌人的监狱里吃尽了〜。 He endured untold sufferings in the enemy prison.／你不听我的话, 早晚要吃〜的。 If you turn a deaf ear to my advice, you'll have to pay for it sooner or later.

苦味酸　kǔwèisuān　chem. picric acid: 〜盐 picrate

苦夏　kǔxià　loss of appetite and weight in summer

苦想　kǔxiǎng　think hard

苦笑　kǔxiào　force a smile; make a wry smile

苦心　kǔxīn　trouble taken; pains: 一片〜 troubles and pains taken for a good cause／〜钻研 do painstaking research

苦心孤诣　kǔxīn gūyì　make extraordinarily painstaking efforts

苦心经营　kǔxīn jīngyíng　take great pains to build up (an enterprise, etc.)

苦辛　kǔxīn　toil; hardship

苦行　kǔxíng　religion ascetic practices

苦行主义　kǔxíngzhǔyì　asceticism

苦役　kǔyì　leg. hard labour; penal servitude

苦于　kǔyú　① suffer from (a disadvantage): 〜不识字 be handicapped by illiteracy／〜时间紧 be hard pressed for time ② be harder than; be worse off than: 半自耕农, 其生活〜自耕农。 The semi-owner peasants were worse off than the owner-peasants.

苦雨　kǔyǔ　too much rain

苦战　kǔzhàn　① hard fighting; bitter battle ② wage an arduous struggle; struggle hard: 大家决心〜二年, 改变这个山区的面貌。 We are determined to carry on a bitter struggle to transform the mountain area in two years.

苦中作乐　kǔ zhōng zuòlè　seek joy amidst sorrow; try to enjoy oneself despite one's suffering

苦衷　kǔzhōng　difficulties that one is reluctant to discuss or mention: 应该体谅他的〜。 Allowance must be made for his difficulties.／难言的〜 sth. which is too embarrassing or painful to talk about

苦竹　kǔzhú　bot. bitter bamboo (Pleioblastus amarus)

苦主　kǔzhǔ　the family of the victim in a murder case

kù

库　kù　warehouse; storehouse: 材料〜 warehouse for raw materials

库藏　kùcáng　have in storage: 图书馆〜图书三十万册。 There are 300,000 books in the library. ——see also kùzàng

库存　kùcún　stock; reserve: 有大量〜 have a large stock of goods／〜物资 goods kept in stock; reserve of materials

库房　kùfáng　storehouse; storeroom

库克群岛　Kùkè Qúndǎo　the Cook Islands

库雷蚊　kùléiwén　same as 库蚊 kùwén

库仑　kùlún　elec. coulomb

库仑定律 Kùlúndìnglǜ *elec.* Coulomb's law

库伦 kùlún (Mongolian) enclosed pasture (usu. used as part of a place name)

库券 kùquàn short for 国库券 guókùquàn

库容 kùróng storage capacity (of a reservoir, warehouse, etc.)

库蚊 kùwén *zool.* culex

库藏 kùzàng *formal* warehouse; storehouse; depository ——see also kùcáng

绔 kù see 纨绔 wánkù

袴 kù same as 裤 kù

裤 kù trousers; pants: 长裤 chángkù／短裤 duǎnkù

裤衩 kùchǎ underpants; undershorts

裤裆 kùdāng crotch (of trousers)

裤兜 kùdōu trouser pocket

裤缝 kùfèng seams of a trouser leg

裤管 kùguǎn (also 裤脚管 kùjiǎoguǎn) *dial.* trouser legs

裤脚 kùjiǎo ① bottom of a trouser leg ② *dial.* trouser legs

裤筒 kùtǒng *dial.* trouser legs

裤头 kùtóu *dial.* underpants; undershorts

裤腿 kùtuǐ trouser legs

裤线 kùxiàn creases (of trousers)

裤腰 kùyāo waist of trousers

裤腰带 kùyāodài waist belt; band; girdle

裤子 kùzi trousers; pants

詟(嚳) Kù a legendary ruler of remote antiquity

酷 kù ① cruel; oppressive: 残酷 cánkù ② very; extremely: 酷寒 kùhán／酷似 kùsì

酷爱 kù'ài ardently love

酷寒 kùhán bitter cold

酷好 kùhào have a deep love for (art, music, etc.); be very keen on

酷吏 kùlì an oppressive (feudal) official

酷烈 kùliè *formal* ① cruel; fierce: ～的太阳 the scorching sun／～的苦难 severe sufferings ② (of fragrance) very strong

酷虐 kùnüè cruel and ferocious; ruthless; savage

酷热 kùrè (of weather) extremely hot: 天气～ sweltering hot weather／这是一个～的夏天。It was an extremely hot summer.

酷暑 kùshǔ the intense heat of summer; high summer

酷似 kùsì be the very image of; be exactly like

酷肖 kùxiào closely resemble; be the very image of; be exactly like

酷刑 kùxíng cruel (*or* savage) torture

kuā

夸(誇) kuā ① exaggerate; overstate; boast: 她把一点小事～得比天还大。She's made a mountain out of a molehill. ② praise: 人人都～她机灵。Everyone praised her for her cleverness.／成绩不～跑不了,缺点不找不得了。Merits uncited will not vanish; shortcomings undiscovered may prove disastrous.

夸大 kuādà exaggerate; overstate; magnify: ～困难 exaggerate the difficulties／～敌情 overestimate the enemy／原来的数字被～了。The original figures were inflated.

夸大其词 kuādà qí cí make an overstatement; exagger-

ate: 对已经取得的成绩不要～。We shouldn't overstate our past achievements.

夸诞 kuādàn *formal* exaggerating to an incredible extent; boastful

夸奖 kuā·jiǎng praise; commend: 老师～他进步快。The teacher praised him for his rapid progress.

夸克 kuākè *phys.* quark

夸口 kuākǒu boast; brag; talk big

夸夸其谈 kuākuā qí tán indulge in exaggeration; indulge in verbiage

夸示 kuāshì lavish praise on oneself; boast

夸饰 kuāshì give an exaggerated account

夸脱 kuātuō quart

夸许 kuāxǔ speak favourably of; praise; commend

夸耀 kuāyào brag about; show off; flaunt: 她从不～自己。She never brags.／～自己的见识 show off one's knowledge and experience

夸赞 kuāzàn speak highly of; commend; praise

夸张 kuāzhāng ① exaggerate; overstate: 你这样说未免太～了。I'm afraid you've been exaggerating. *or* I'm afraid you've overstated the case.／～的语言 inflated language; exaggerations／艺术～ artistic exaggeration ② hyperbole

夸嘴 kuāzuǐ *inf.* boast; brag; talk big

kuǎ

侉(咵) kuǎ *dial.* ① (speak) with an accent (esp. a provincial accent) ② big and clumsy; unwieldy: 几年不见,长成个～大个儿了。Haven't seen you for several years, you've grown up into a strapping young man.／这个箱子太～了,携带不方便。The suitcase is too big and clumsy to carry.

侉子 kuǎzi *dial.* a person who speaks with an accent

垮 kuǎ collapse; fall; break down: 这堵墙要～了。The wall's going to collapse.／我身体结实,累不～。I'm very strong; no amount of hard work can wear me down.／洪水冲～了堤坝。The flood waters burst the dyke.

垮台 kuǎtái fall from power; collapse: 与人民为敌的人总是要～的。Those who oppose the people will surely come to grief.

kuà

挎 kuà ① carry on the arm: ～着个篮子 with a basket on one's arm／～着胳膊 arm in arm ② carry sth. over one's shoulder or around one's neck or at one's side: ～着照相机 have a camera slung over one's shoulder

挎包 kuàbāo satchel

挎兜 kuàdōu satchel

挎斗 kuàdōu sidecar

胯 kuà hip

胯骨 kuàgǔ common name for 髋骨 kuāngǔ

跨 kuà ① stride (forward or sideways): ～进大门 step into a doorway／向前～一步 take a step forward／～过小沟 stride over a ditch／欢欣鼓舞地～入了新的一年 stride into the new year in high spirits ② bestride; straddle: ～上战马 mount (*or* bestride) a war-horse ③ cut across; go beyond: 亚洲地～寒、温、热三带。Asia extends across the frigid, temperate and tropical zones./

组织～地区的商品供应 organize transregional commodity supplies

跨度 kuàdù *archit.* span

跨国公司 kuàguó gōngsī transnational corporation

跨栏赛跑 kuàlán sàipǎo *sports* hurdle race; the hurdles

跨年度 kuàniándù go beyond the year: ～预算 a budget to be carried over to the next year

跨线桥 kuàxiànqiáo flyover; overpass

跨院儿 kuàyuànr side courtyard

跨越 kuàyuè stride across; leap over; cut across; span: ～几个历史阶段 span several historical stages of development / ～障碍 surmount an obstacle

kuǎi

扣¹（擓） kuǎi *dial.* scratch: ～痒痒 scratch an itch

扣²（擓） kuǎi *dial.* carry on the arm: ～着小竹篮 with a small bamboo basket on one's arm

扣³（擓） kuǎi *dial.* ladle out; spoon up (*or* out); scoop up: ～水 ladle out water / ～一勺儿白面 take a scoopful of flour

蒯 kuǎi ① wool grass ② (Kuǎi) a surname

蒯草 kuǎicǎo *bot.* wool grass

kuài

会（會） kuài see below ——see also huì

会计 kuàijì ① accounting ② bookkeeper; accountant

会计年度 kuàijì niándù fiscal (*or* financial) year

会计师 kuàijìshī certified accountant; chief accountant; treasurer

快 kuài ① fast; quick; rapid; swift: 请别说得那么～。Please don't speak so fast. / 我的表～五分。My watch is five minutes fast. / 他学东西～。He learns quickly. / 他进步很～。He has made rapid progress. / ～马 a swift horse ② speed: 这车能跑多～? How fast can this car go? ③ hurry up; make haste: ～上车吧! Hurry up and get on the bus! / ～点儿, 车要赶不上了! Come on, or we'll miss the bus! / ～跟我走。Quick, come with me. ④ *adv.* soon; before long: 他～回来了。He'll be back soon. / 这学期～结束了。The term will be over before long. / 火车～开了。The train is about to leave. / ～吃午饭了。It's almost time for lunch. / 天～黑了。It's getting dark. / ～半夜了。It's going on midnight. / ～三十岁的人还没有个对象! The man's going on thirty but still doesn't have a girl friend! / 我来了～两年了。I've been here for nearly two years. / 春节～到了。The Spring Festival is drawing near. ⑤ quick-witted; nimble; clever: 他脑子～。He's quick-witted. *or* He has a quick mind. ⑥ (of a knife, sword, etc.) sharp: ～刀 a sharp knife ⑦ straight-forward; forthright; plainspoken: 快人快语 kuàirén-kuàiyǔ ⑧ pleased; happy; gratified: 不快 bùkuài / 大快人心 dà kuài rénxīn ⑨ a *yamen* runner or officer charged with making arrests: 捕快 bǔkuài

快板 kuàibǎn *mus.* allegro

快板儿 kuàibǎnr *kuaibanr*, rhythmic comic talk or monologue to the accompaniment of bamboo clappers; clapper talk

快板儿书 kuàibǎnrshū rhymed story recited to the rhythm of bamboo clappers

快报 kuàibào wall bulletin; bulletin

快步 kuàibù ① walk at a quick pace ② *mil.* half step; trot

快步流星 kuàibù liúxīng same as 大步流星 dàbù liúxīng

快步舞 kuàibùwǔ quickstep

快餐 kuàicān quick meal; fast food; snack: ～部 quick-lunch counter; snack counter

快车 kuàichē express train or bus

快车道 kuàichēdào fast traffic lane (on a street)

快当 kuàidang quick; prompt: 她做起事来又细心又～。She's quick and careful.

快刀斩乱麻 kuàidāo zhǎn luànmá cut a tangled skein of jute with a sharp knife; cut the Gordian knot: 当地群众都主张～, 以迅雷不及掩耳的手段把这伙刑事犯罪分子逮捕起来。The people here urge the authorities to be swift and resolute and arrest those criminals at once.

快递 kuàidì express delivery: ～邮件 express mail

快干 kuàigān quick-drying: ～漆 quick-drying paint

快感 kuàigǎn pleasant sensation; delight: 觉着一阵～ experience a sensation of pleasure

快攻 kuàigōng quick attack (in ball games): 打～ use the strategy of quick attack

快活 kuàihuo happy; merry; cheerful: 日子过得挺～ live a happy life / 孩子们～地打雪仗。The children were enjoying a snowball fight.

快件 kuàijiàn express mail, package, etc.

快乐 kuàilè happy; joyful; cheerful: ～的微笑 a happy smile / ～的童年生活 a happy childhood / 节日过得很～。The festival was spent joyfully. / 小鸟在树上～地歌唱。A little bird was singing happily in the tree.

快马加鞭 kuàimǎ jiā biān spur on the flying horse——at top speed; posthaste; whip and spur: 这项工作必须～地进行。This work must be carried out at top speed.

快慢 kuài-màn speed: 这些按钮是管～的。These buttons control the speed. / 这条轮船的～怎么样? What's the speed of this steamer? *or* How fast can this steamer sail?

快慢针 kuài-mànzhēn regulator (in a clock or watch)

快门 kuàimén (camera) shutter: ～开关 shutter release

快人 kuàirén *formal* a straight person

快人快语 kuàirén-kuàiyǔ straight talk from a straight person

快事 kuàishì a happening that gives great satisfaction or pleasure; delight: 引～为 recall (an event) with great satisfaction / 生平一大～ one of the most delightful experiences in one's life

快手 kuàishǒu quick worker; deft hand

快书 kuàishū quick-patter (rhythmic storytelling accompanied by bamboo or copper clappers): 山东～ Shandong clapper ballad

快速 kuàisù fast; quick; high-speed: ～部队 mobile force (*or* troops, units) / ～掘进 high-speed drivage / ～切削 high-speed cutting / ～炼钢 high-speed steelmaking / ～行军 forced march

快艇 kuàitǐng speedboat; motor boat; mosquito boat

快慰 kuàiwèi feel pleased with and derive comfort from sth.; be pleased: 我们都为她的进步感到～。We are all pleased with the progress she has made.

快信 kuàixìn express letter

快婿 kuàixù a good son-in-law ——see also 乘龙快婿 chénglóng kuàixù

快讯 kuàixùn newsflash; flash

快要 kuàiyào *adv.* soon; before long: 新年～到了。It'll soon be the New Year. / 酒～喝完了, 再去拿些来。Wine is about to run out. Go and get some more.

快意 kuàiyì pleased; satisfied; comfortable: 微风吹来, 我感到十分～。A gentle breeze was blowing, and I felt refreshed.

快硬水泥 kuàiyìng shuǐní *archit.* quick-hardening cement

快鱼 kuàiyú same as 鲙鱼 kuàiyú

快照 kuàizhào snapshot

快中子 kuàizhōngzǐ *phys.* fast (*or* high-speed) neutron

快嘴 kuàizuǐ ① one who readily voices his thoughts; one who is quick to articulate his ideas; a straight person ② one who has a loose tongue

块（塊） kuài ① piece; lump; chunk: 糖～儿 hard candy (*or* fruit drops) or lumps of sugar / 把肉切成～儿 cut the meat into cubes ② *m.* piece; lump: 两～肥皂 two cakes of soap / 一～面包 a piece or hunk of bread / 一～手表 a wrist watch / 一～试验田 an experimental plot (of land) / 一～桌布 a table cloth / 一～云彩 a cloud / 一～黑疤 a black scar ③ *m. inf.* (for gold or silver dollars, Renminbi, and certain paper money): 两～银洋 two silver dollars / 三～钱 three *yuan* / 一千～港币 1,000 Hong Kong dollars

块儿 kuàir *dial.* place: 我在这～工作好几年了。I've been working here for quite a few years now. / 你哪～摔疼了? Where were you hurt?

块儿八毛 kuàirbāmáo a *yuan* or slightly less

块根 kuàigēn *bot.* root tuber

块规 kuàiguī *mech.* slip gauge; gauge block

块茎 kuàijīng *bot.* stem tuber

块垒 kuàilěi *formal* ① indignation ② gloom; depression

块煤 kuàiméi lump coal

块头 kuàitóu *dial.* (physical) build: 他的～很大。He's a big burly man.

侩（儈） kuài *formal* middleman: 驵侩 zǎngkuài

邻（鄶） Kuài see 自邻以下 zì Kuài yǐ xià

浍（澮） kuài *formal* ditch in the fields

哙（噲） kuài *formal* swallow

狯（獪） kuài see 狡狯 jiǎokuài

脍（膾） kuài *formal* ① meat chopped into small pieces; minced meat ② chop meat or fish into small pieces

脍炙人口 kuàizhì rénkǒu (of a piece of good writing, etc.) win universal praise; enjoy great popularity: 一首～的唐诗 an oft-quoted and widely loved Tang poem

筷 kuài chopsticks: 牙～ ivory chopsticks

筷子 kuàizi chopsticks: 竹～ bamboo chopsticks

鲙（鱠） kuài see below

鲙鱼 kuàiyú Chinese herring

kuān

宽（寬） kuān ① wide; broad: ～肩膀 broad-shouldered / ～边草帽 broad-brimmed straw hat / 眼界～ have a broad outlook / 这条马路很～。This road is very wide. ② width; breadth: 这条河有一里～。This river is one *li* wide. ③ relax; relieve: 听说他的病情并不严重，我们的心就～多了。We were greatly relieved to learn that his condition was not serious. / 把心放～一点。Relax, don't worry so much. *or* Don't take it too

hard. ④ extend: 限期能再～几天吗? Can the deadline be extended a few more days? ⑤ generous; lenient: 从宽 cóngkuān ⑥ comfortably off; well-off: 他手头比过去～多了。He's much better off than before.

宽畅 kuānchàng free from worry; happy

宽敞 kuānchang spacious; roomy; commodious: ～的房子 a commodious house / 新建的厂房又高大又～。The newly-built factory building is tall and spacious.

宽绰 kuānchuo ① spacious; commodious: 这间屋子很～。The room is spacious. ② relaxed; relieved: 听了他的话，我心里～多了。When I heard him say that, I felt greatly relieved. *or* I felt a big load taken off my mind when I heard what he said. ③ comfortably off; well-off

宽打窄用 kuāndǎ-zhǎiyòng budget liberally and spend sparingly

宽大 kuāndà ① spacious; roomy: ～的候车室 a spacious waiting room (for bus, train, etc.) / ～的窗户 a big, wide window / 他身上穿着显得过分～的军衣。He's wearing an oversized army uniform. ② lenient; magnanimous: 受到～处理 be dealt with leniently; be accorded lenient treatment; receive clemency / 实行镇压与～相结合的政策 adopt a policy of combining suppression with leniency (towards criminals) ③ show leniency (towards an offender)

宽大为怀 kuāndà wéi huái be magnanimous (with an offender); be lenient

宽待 kuāndài treat with leniency; be lenient in dealing with: ～俘虏 give lenient treatment to prisoners of war; treat prisoners of war leniently

宽贷 kuāndài pardon; forgive

宽度 kuāndù width; breadth: 这料子的～是多少? What is the width of this material?

宽泛 kuānfàn (of meaning) wide in range: 这个词的涵义很～。This word has many different meanings.

宽广 kuānguǎng broad; extensive; vast: ～的田野 a broad expanse of country / 心胸～ broad-minded

宽轨 kuānguǐ broad gauge: ～铁路 broad-gauge railway

宽宏大量 kuānhóng dàliàng large-minded; magnanimous

宽洪 kuānhóng ① resonant (voice) ② large-minded; magnanimous

宽厚 kuānhòu ① thick and broad: ～的胸膛 a big and strong chest ② tolerant and generous; honest and kind: 待人～ be generous towards others

宽怀 kuānhuái set one's mind at rest; be at ease; rest assured; feel relieved: 你～吧，这病过几天就会好的。Don't you worry. You'll be all right in a couple of days.

宽假 kuānjiǎ *formal* pardon; forgive

宽解 kuānjiě ease sb.'s anxiety; ease sb. of his trouble: 我生气的时候，妈妈总能设法～我。When I'm angry, my mother can always think of a way to calm me down.

宽旷 kuānkuàng extensive; vast: ～的草原 extensive grasslands

宽阔 kuānkuò broad; wide: ～的林荫道 a broad (*or* wide) avenue / ～的大厅 a spacious hall / ～的胸怀 broad-mindedness / 人们的眼界～了，信心也就增强了。When people's minds are broadened, their confidence is also strengthened.

宽谅 kuānliàng excuse; forgive

宽猛相济 kuān-měng xiāng jì (of a ruler) alternate leniency with severity; use hard and soft tactics in turn

宽免 kuānmiǎn ① exempt (from taxation) ② pardon (an offence)

宽饶 kuānráo forgive; show mercy; give quarter

宽容 kuānróng tolerant; lenient

宽舒 kuānshū ① happy; entirely free from worry: 心境～ have ease of mind; feel happy ② spacious and comfortable

宽恕 kuānshù forgive: 请求～ ask for forgiveness / 立功

赎罪，以求得人民～ perform meritorious service to atone for one's crimes and obtain clemency from the people

宽松 kuānsong *inf.* ① (of clothes) loose and comfortable ② not crowded: 这个车厢比较～。This carriage is not so crowded. ③ feel relieved; be free from worry ④ comfortably off; ample; easy: 手头～ be in easy circumstances; be quite well-off at the moment / 在经济环境还不～的条件下进行改革 undertake the reform in a still stringent economic environment

宽慰 kuānwèi comfort; console: 你去～她几句。Go and say something to comfort her. / 这样一想，我心里才～了些。This thought brought me a little comfort.

宽狭 kuānxiá *formal* width; breadth; size

宽限 kuānxiàn extend a time limit: ～期 days of grace; grace period / ～一星期 give a week's grace / 请～几天。Please extend the deadline a few days.

宽心 kuānxīn feel relieved: 说几句～话 say a few reassuring words / 请喝杯茶，宽宽心。Please have a cup of tea and relax yourself.

宽心丸儿 kuānxīnwánr anxiety-relief pills—words that set sb.'s mind at ease; reassuring words: 吃了～ be reassured

宽衣 kuānyī *pol.* take off your coat: 天气热，请～。It's hot. Do take your coat off.

宽银幕电影 kuānyínmù diànyǐng wide-screen film

宽宥 kuānyòu *formal* pardon; forgive

宽余 kuānyú ① spacious and comfortable ② same as 宽裕 kuānyù

宽裕 kuānyù well-to-do; comfortably off; ample: 经济～ in easy circumstances; well-off / 时间很～。There's plenty of time yet.

宽窄 kuānzhǎi width; breadth; size: 这块布做窗帘，～正合适。This piece of cloth is just the right size for a curtain.

宽展 kuānzhǎn *dial.* ① happy; entirely free from worry ② broad; wide

宽纵 kuānzòng indulge: 不要～自己。Don't be so self-indulgent.

髋（髖） kuān see below

髋骨 kuāngǔ *physiol.* hipbone; innominate bone

kuǎn

款¹（欵） kuǎn ① sincere: 款曲 kuǎnqū ② receive with hospitality; entertain: ～客 entertain guests

款²（欵） kuǎn ① section of an article in a legal document, etc.; paragraph: 根据该条约的第六条第二～ according to Article 6, Section 2 of the Treaty ② a sum of money; fund: 公款 gōngkuǎn ③ the name of sender or recipient inscribed on a painting or a piece of calligraphy presented as a gift: 上款 shàngkuǎn

款³（欵） kuǎn *formal* knock: 款门 kuǎnmén

款⁴（欵） kuǎn *formal* leisurely; slow: 款步 kuǎnbù

款步 kuǎnbù *formal* walk with deliberate steps

款待 kuǎndài treat cordially; entertain: ～客人 entertain guests / 感谢你对我们的盛情～。Thank you for the hospitality you have shown us.

款冬 kuǎndōng *bot.* coltsfoot

款额 kuǎn'é an amount of money

款款 kuǎnkuǎn *formal* ① sincere; faithful ② slowly; leisurely: ～而行 walk slowly (*or* leisurely) / 点水蜻

蜓～飞。(杜甫) The dragonfly takes its sip of water, and flits away.

款留 kuǎnliú cordially urge (a guest) to stay

款门 kuǎnmén *formal* knock on a door

款洽 kuǎnqià *formal* cordial and harmonious

款曲 kuǎnqū heartfelt feelings: 互通～ express feelings of mutual affection or friendship

款式 kuǎnshì pattern; style; design: 这些上衣的～都不错。The styles of these coats are good. / 这套家具～新颖。This set of furniture is of a brand-new design.

款项 kuǎnxiàng ① a sum of money; fund ② sections and items (in a legal document, etc.)

款识 kuǎnzhì inscriptions (on bronzes, etc.)

款子 kuǎnzi *inf.* a sum of money: 很大一笔～ a huge sum of money / 一笔汇来的～ a remittance

kuāng

匡 kuāng ① *formal* rectify; correct: ～谬 correct mistakes ② *formal* assist; save: ～我不逮 help me to overcome my shortcomings ③ *dial.* roughly estimate: ～一～ make a guess; give a rough estimate ④ (Kuāng) a surname

匡复 kuāngfù save the state

匡计 kuāngjì calculate roughly; estimate

匡救 kuāngjiù deliver sb. (from evil); rescue; save

匡算 kuāngsuàn roughly estimate

匡正 kuāngzhèng rectify; correct: ～时弊 correct the maladies of the times

匡助 kuāngzhù help; assist

诓 kuāng deceive; hoax: 我哪能～你？How could I deceive you?

诓骗 kuāngpiàn (also 诓哄 kuānghǒng) deceive; hoax; dupe

哐 kuāng *onom.* crash; bang: ～的一声，脸盆掉在地上了。The basin fell with a crash.

哐啷 kuānglāng *onom.* crash: ～一声把门关上 bang the door shut

筐 kuāng basket

筐子 kuāngzi a small basket

kuáng

狂 kuáng ① mad; crazy: 发狂 fākuáng ② violent: 雨骤风～。The wind blew hard and the rain came down in sheets. / 股票价格～跌。The stocks slumped. ③ wild; unrestrained: 狂奔 kuángbēn ④ arrogant; overbearing: 这个人～得很。That person is very arrogant.

狂傲 kuáng'ào wildly arrogant; presumptuous

狂暴 kuángbào violent; wild: ～的山洪 raging mountain torrents

狂悖 kuángbèi *formal* arrogant and unreasonable; presumptuous

狂奔 kuángbēn run wildly; run like mad: 他在街上～而去。He ran wildly down the street. / ～的马 a bolting horse

狂飙 kuángbiāo hurricane

狂飙运动 Kuángbiāo Yùndōng *Sturm und Drang*; Storm and Stress (a German literary movement of the latter part of the 18th century)

狂草 kuángcǎo wild cursive hand (an erratic type of cursive hand 草书, the characters often being illegible)

狂放　kuángfàng　unruly or unrestrained

狂吠　kuángfèi　bark furiously; howl

狂奋　kuángfèn　wildly excited; elated

狂风　kuángfēng　① *meteorol.* whole gale ② fierce wind: 〜呼啸。The wind howled.

狂风暴雨　kuángfēng-bàoyǔ　violent storms: 他们向敌人展开了〜似的攻击。They launched a furious whirlwind attack on the enemy.

狂风恶浪　kuángfēng-èlàng　violent winds and fierce waves—grave perils; great hazards

狂轰滥炸　kuánghōng-lànzhà　wanton and indiscriminate bombing

狂欢　kuánghuān　revelry; carnival: 〜节 carnival / 〜之夜 a night of revelry

狂澜　kuánglán　raging waves: 力挽狂澜 lì wǎn kuánglán

狂怒　kuángnù　furious; mad with rage

狂气　kuángqì　arrogance; conceit

狂犬病　kuángquǎnbìng　hydrophobia; rabies

狂热　kuángrè　fanaticism: 〜的军备竞赛 feverish armament race / 〜的信徒 a fanatical follower; fanatic; zealot / 〜性 fanaticism

狂人　kuángrén　① madman; maniac: 帝国主义战争〜 imperialist war maniacs ② an extremely arrogant person

狂人呓语　kuángrén yìyǔ　ravings of a madman

狂妄　kuángwàng　wildly arrogant; presumptuous: 〜的野心 a wild ambition / 他太〜了。He is too arrogant.

狂妄自大　kuángwàng zìdà　arrogant and conceited

狂喜　kuángxǐ　wild with joy: 他们相见时〜地拥抱起来。When they met, they hugged each other in an ecstasy of delight.

狂笑　kuángxiào　laugh wildly; laugh boisterously

狂言　kuángyán　ravings; wild language: 口出〜 talk wildly

狂恣　kuángzì　*formal* unbridled

诳

诳　kuáng　see below

诳骗　kuángpiàn　deceive; hoax; dupe

诳语　kuángyǔ　(also 诳话 kuánghuà) lies; falsehood

鵟

鵟　kuáng　*zool.* buzzard

kuàng

邝(鄺)

邝　Kuàng　a surname

圹(壙)

圹　kuàng　① open grave; coffin pit: 圹穴 kuàngxué ② *formal* open country; champaign

圹埌　kuànglàng　*formal* (of an open country) boundless

圹穴　kuàngxué　open grave; coffin pit

纩(纊)

纩　kuàng　*formal* silk floss; silk wadding

况¹(況)

况　kuàng　① condition; situation: 情况 qíngkuàng ② compare: 比〜 draw an analogy / 以古〜今 draw parallels from history ③ (Kuàng) a surname

况²(況)

况　kuàng　*conj.* *formal* ① moreover; besides ② much less; let alone

况兼　kuàngjiān　*conj.* *formal* moreover; besides; in addition

况且　kuàngqiě　*conj.* moreover; besides; in addition: 这房子太贵，〜地点也不适中。The price is too high, and moreover, the house isn't in a suitable position. / 上海地方那么大，〜你又不知道他的地址，一下子怎么能找到他呢? Shanghai is so big. Besides, you don't have his address. How do you expect to find him so quickly?

旷(曠)

旷　kuàng　① vast; spacious: 野〜天低树，江清月近人。(孟浩然) Wilds so vast, the sky stoop to the trees; The river so clear, moon close to man. ② free from worries and petty ideas: 心旷神怡 xīnkuàng-shényí ③ neglect or waste: 〜日废时 waste time ④ loose-fitting: 螺丝〜了。The screw has come loose. / 这身衣服她穿着太〜了。The dress sits loosely (or is too loose-fitting) on her.

旷达　kuàngdá　*formal* broad-minded; bighearted

旷代　kuàngdài　*formal* unequalled by contemporaries: 〜文豪 a literary giant unequalled by his contemporaries; an unrivalled great writer

旷废　kuàngfèi　neglect or waste: 〜学业 neglect one's studies

旷费　kuàngfèi　waste: 〜时间 waste one's time

旷夫　kuàngfū　*liter.* an unmarried man (opp. 怨女 yuànnǚ)

旷工　kuànggōng　stay away from (or miss) work without leave or good reason

旷古　kuànggǔ　from time immemorial

旷古未闻　kuànggǔ wèi wén　unheard-of; unprecedented

旷课　kuàngkè　be absent from school without leave; cut school: 旷一堂课 cut a class

旷朗　kuànglǎng　(of a room) bright and spacious

旷日持久　kuàngrì chíjiǔ　long-drawn-out; protracted; prolonged: 〜的谈判 long-drawn-out negotiations / 〜的战争 a long-drawn-out war

旷世　kuàngshì　*formal* unequalled in one's time; unrivalled; unique: 〜功勋 unique deeds / 〜之才 a man of brilliance unequalled in his time

旷野　kuàngyě　wilderness

旷远　kuàngyuǎn　① vast and extending far into the distance: 江面浩渺〜。The river is a vast expanse of water extending far into the distance. ② far back; ages ago; remote: 年代〜 of the remote past; age-old

旷职　kuàngzhí　be absent from duty without leave or good reason

矿(礦、鑛)

矿　kuàng　① ore (or mineral) deposit: 报〜 report where deposits are found ② ore: 这里新发现了一种〜。A kind of ore has been discovered here recently. ③ mine: 他在〜上工作。He works at the mine.

矿藏　kuàngcáng　mineral resources: 中国〜丰富。China is rich in mineral resources. / 〜量 (ore) reserves

矿层　kuàngcéng　ore bed; ore horizon; seam

矿产　kuàngchǎn　mineral products; minerals

矿车　kuàngchē　mine car; tub; tram

矿尘　kuàngchén　mine dust

矿床　kuàngchuáng　mineral (or ore) deposit; deposit: 金属〜 metalliferous deposit / 层状〜 bedded deposit

矿灯　kuàngdēng　miner's lamp

矿工　kuànggōng　miner

矿浆　kuàngjiāng　ore pulp; pulp

矿井　kuàngjǐng　mine shaft or pit: 〜火灾 mine-shaft fire

矿坑　kuàngkēng　(mining) pit

矿脉　kuàngmài　mineral ore; mineral vein; lode

矿棉　kuàngmián　mineral wool

矿苗　kuàngmiáo　outcropping; outcrop; crop

矿泥　kuàngní　sludge; slime; slurry

矿区　kuàngqū　mining area: 〜铁路 mine railway

矿泉　kuàngquán　mineral spring: 〜水 mineral water

矿砂　kuàngshā　ore in sand form

矿山　kuàngshān　mine (with its accompanying shafts, buildings, etc.): 〜地压 rock pressure / 〜工程图 mine map / 〜机械 mining machinery / 〜救护 mine rescue /

～运输 mine haul (*or* haulage); pit haulage

矿石 kuàngshí ore

矿石机 kuàngshíjī common name for 矿石收音机 kuàngshí shōuyīnjī

矿石收音机 kuàngshí shōuyīnjī crystal radio receiver (*or* set)

矿体 kuàngtǐ same as 矿床 kuàngchuáng

矿田 kuàngtián ore field

矿物 kuàngwù mineral: 伴生～ associated mineral / ～界 mineral kingdom

矿物学 kuàngwùxué mineralogy

矿物油 kuàngwùyóu mineral oil

矿盐 kuàngyán same as 岩盐 yányán

矿样 kuàngyàng sample ore

矿业 kuàngyè mining industry

矿渣 kuàngzhā slag: ～水泥 slag cement / ～砖 slag brick

矿脂 kuàngzhī another name for 凡士林 fánshìlín

矿质肥料 kuàngzhì féiliào mineral fertilizer

矿柱 kuàngzhù (ore) pillar

贶 kuàng *formal* present as a gift; grant

框 kuàng ① frame; circle; case: 给照片配个～儿 have a photo framed ② draw a frame round: 用红线把标题～起来 frame the heading in red / 报上登载了～有黑边的烈士遗像。The newspaper carried the martyr's photo framed in black. ③ restrict; restrain; bind: 不能～得太死 not make rigid restrictions

框架 kuàngjià frame; framework: 窗户的～ a window frame / 计划商品经济的～ the framework for a planned commodity economy

框框 kuàngkuang ① frame; circle: 他拿红铅笔在图片四周画了个～。He drew a circle around the picture with a red pencil. ② restriction; convention; set pattern: 突破旧～的限制 throw convention to the winds

框子 kuàngzi frame; rim: 眼镜～ rims (of spectacles)

眶 kuàng eye socket: 眼眶 yǎnkuàng

kuī

亏（虧） kuī ① lose (money, etc.); have a deficit: 做生意～了 have lost money in business / ～了二百元 have a deficit of 200 *yuan* ② deficient; short: ～什么就买什么。Buy what you're short of. / ～你十块钱。I owe you 10 *yuan*. ③ treat unfairly: 你放心吧，～不了你。Don't worry, we won't be unfair to you. / 人不～地，地不～人。The land won't fail people as long as people don't fail the land. ④ *adv.* fortunately; luckily; thanks to: ～他提醒了我，要不我早忘了。Luckily he reminded me; otherwise I'd have forgotten all about it. ⑤ (used to show approval): 这么大年纪，～你还能走那么多路。It is remarkable that you should have walked such a long distance at your age. ⑥ (used to show sarcasm): ～他说得出口! And he had the nerve to say so! / ～你还是个大学生呢，连这个都不懂。For a college student, you ought to know better than that! ⑦ (of the moon) wane: 月满则～。《史记》When the moon reaches the full, it begins to wane.

亏本 kuīběn lose money in business; lose one's capital: ～生意 a losing proposition

亏仓 kuīcāng broken stowage

亏产 kuīchǎn fail to fulfil a production target (*or* quota)

亏秤 kuīchèng give short weight

亏待 kuīdài treat unfairly; treat shabbily: 我可从来没～过你。I've never treated you unfairly.

亏得 kuīde *adv.* ① fortunately; luckily; thanks to: ～大家帮忙，我们才按时把这活干完。Thanks to everybody's help, we finished the job on time. ② (used to show sarcasm): ～你长这么大，那么点事儿都不懂。Fancy a big boy like you not understanding such a simple thing! / 这么热天还穿毛衣，真～你。How can you wear a woollen sweater on such a hot day!

亏短 kuīduǎn insufficient; deficient

亏乏 kuīfá short (of supplies); deficient

亏负 kuīfù let sb. suffer; let sb. down: 他没有～你的地方。He didn't let you down in any way.

亏耗 kuīhào loss by a natural process: 货物在运输中的～ losses incurred in the course of transportation

亏空 kuīkong ① loss money in business; be in debt: 公司今年～不少。The corporation lost a lot of money this year. ② debt; deficit: 弥补～ meet (*or* make up) a deficit; make up (for) a loss / 过日子要是精打细算，就拉不了～。If you plan your budget carefully, you won't get into debt.

亏累 kuīlěi show repeated deficits

亏欠 kuīqiàn have a deficit; be in arrears

亏弱 kuīruò weak; debilitated

亏折 kuīshé lose money in business; lose one's capital

亏蚀 kuīshí ① eclipse of the sun or moon ② lose money in business; lose one's capital ③ loss; wear and tear

亏损 kuīsǔn ① loss; deficit: 企业～ loss incurred in an enterprise ② general debility: 久病而～ be in general debility after a long illness

亏心 kuīxīn have a guilty conscience: ～事 a deed that troubles (*or* weighs on) one's conscience / 你说这话，不～吗? Doesn't your conscience trouble you for saying that?

岿（巋） kuī see below

岿然 kuīrán *formal* towering; lofty: ～屹立 stand towering like a giant

岿然不动 kuīrán bù dòng steadfastly stand one's ground: 敌军围困万千重，我自～。(毛泽东) The foe encircles us thousands strong, Steadfastly we stand our ground.

岿巍 kuīwēi *formal* towering; lofty

盔 kuī helmet: 钢盔 gāngkuī

盔甲 kuījiǎ a suit of armour

窥（闚） kuī peep; spy: 窥视 kuīshì

窥测 kuīcè spy out: ～时机 bide one's time

窥测方向 kuīcè fāngxiàng see how the land lies; see which way the wind blows: ～，以求一逞 spy out the land in order to accomplish one's schemes; see which way the wind blows in order to achieve one's evil ends

窥察 kuīchá spy upon; pry about

窥见 kuījiàn get (*or* catch) a glimpse of; detect: 从他这首诗里可以～他的胸怀。From his poem we can get a hint of his breadth of mind.

窥器 kuīqì *med.* speculum

窥视 kuīshì peep at; spy on: 他发现一个形迹可疑的人向屋内～。He spotted a suspicious character peeping into the house.

窥伺 kuīsì *derog.* lie in wait for; be on watch for

窥探 kuītàn spy upon; pry about: ～军事机密 pry into military secrets

窥听 kuītīng eavesdrop

窥望 kuīwàng peep at; spy on

kuí

奎 kuí ① the fifteenth of the twenty-eight constellations （二十八宿） into which the celestial sphere was divided in ancient Chinese astronomy (consisting of sixteen stars, said to be like a person striding, in Pisces) ② (Kuí) a surname

奎宁 kuíníng *pharm.* quinine

隗 Kuí a surname——see also Wěi

逵 kuí *formal* thoroughfare

馗 kuí same as 逵 kuí

揆 kuí *formal* ① conjecture; guess; estimate: ～其本意, 或非如此。That presumably was not his original intention. ② principle; standard

揆度 kuíduó *formal* estimate; conjecture

揆情度理 kuíqíng-duólǐ considering the circumstances and judging by common sense

葵 kuí certain herbaceous plants with big flowers: 向日葵 xiàngrìkuí

葵花 kuíhuā sunflower

葵花子 kuíhuāzǐ sunflower seeds

葵扇 kuíshàn palm-leaf fan

喹 kuí see below

喹啉 kuílín *chem.* quinoline

暌 kuí separate: 暌离 kuílí

暌隔 kuígé *formal* be parted; be apart

暌离 kuílí (also 暌别 kuíbié) *formal* (of friends) leave each other; part

暌违 kuíwéi *formal* (used in letters) separate; part: ～数载。It's years since we parted.

魁 kuí ① chief; head: 罪魁 zuìkuí ② of stalwart build: 魁梧 kuíwú ③ same as 魁星 kuíxīng

魁岸 kuí'àn *formal* big and tall; stalwart

魁首 kuíshǒu (also 魁元 kuíyuán) a person who is head and shoulders above others; the brightest and best: 文章～ outstanding writer of the day

魁伟 kuíwěi big and tall; stalwart

魁梧 kuíwú big and tall; stalwart: ～的身躯 be of great stature / 身量～ of great height and powerful build; tall and sturdy

魁星 kuíxīng the four stars in the bowl of the Big Dipper, or the one at the tip of the bowl

睽 kuí ① same as 暌 kuí ② *formal* go against; run counter to

睽睽 kuíkuí stare; gaze: 众目睽睽 zhòng mù kuíkuí

睽异 kuíyì (of views) be in disagreement

蝰 kuí see below

蝰蛇 kuíshé viper

kuǐ

傀 kuǐ see below

傀儡 kuǐlěi puppet: 殖民主义者及其～ colonialists and their stooges (*or* puppets) / ～政府 puppet govern-

ment / ～政权 puppet regime

傀儡戏 kuǐlěixì same as 木偶戏 mù'ǒuxì

跬 kuǐ *formal* half a step: ～步 take a small step

kuì

匮 kuì *formal* deficient: 匮乏 kuìfá

匮乏 kuìfá (also 匮缺 kuìquē) *formal* short (of supplies); deficient: 物资～ short of supplies / 极度～ a serious shortage in the supply / 人口的激增引起资源的～。The rapid increase in population caused a shortage of natural resources.

匮竭 kuìjié exhausted

溃 kuì ① (of a dyke or dam) burst: 溃决 kuìjué ② break through (an encirclement): 溃围 kuìwéi ③ be defeated; be routed: 击溃 jīkuì ④ fester; ulcerate: 溃烂 kuìlàn

溃败 kuìbài be defeated; be routed

溃兵 kuìbīng a routed army

溃不成军 kuì bù chéng jūn (of troops) be utterly routed; break and scatter

溃窜 kuìcuàn (of troops) be defeated and dispersed; flee helter-skelter

溃决 kuìjué (also 溃堤 kuìdī) (of flood waters) burst (a dyke, dam, etc.): 大坝～成灾。The dam broke and caused a flood.

溃军 kuìjūn a routed army

溃烂 kuìlàn fester; ulcerate

溃灭 kuìmiè (of a regime, etc.) crumble and fall

溃散 kuìsàn (of troops) be defeated and dispersed

溃逃 kuìtáo escape in disorder; fly pell-mell; flee helter-skelter

溃退 kuìtuì beat a precipitate retreat

溃围 kuìwéi *formal* break through an encirclement: ～南奔 break through the encirclement and head south

溃疡 kuìyáng *med.* ulcer

馈（餽） kuì make a present of: ～以鲜果 make a present of fresh fruit

馈电 kuìdiàn *elec.* feed: 交叉～ cross feed / ～线 feed line; feeder

馈遗 kuìwèi present (a gift); make a present of sth.

馈献 kuìxiàn present (a gift) to one's senior or superior

馈赠 kuìzèng (also 馈送 kuìsòng) present (a gift); make a present of sth.

愦 kuì muddled; dazed and confused; befuddled: 昏愦 hūnkuì

愦乱 kuìluàn dazed and confused; befuddled

喟 kuì *formal* sigh: 喟叹 kuìtàn

喟然长叹 kuìrán chángtàn *formal* sigh deeply; heave a deep sigh

喟叹 kuìtàn *formal* sigh with deep feeling

蒉 kuì *formal* straw sack for holding earth

愧（媿） kuì ashamed; conscience-stricken: ～无以报。I feel ashamed of my inability to repay your favour. / ～不敢当。I really don't deserve such an honour. *or* You flatter me.

愧汗 kuìhàn *formal* sweat with shame—feel ashamed to the utmost degree

愧恨 kuìhèn ashamed and remorseful; remorseful: ～交

集 be overcome with shame and remorse / 内心深自～ feel bitterly remorseful

愧悔 kuǐhuǐ　ashamed and regretful

愧疚 kuǐjiù　*formal*　feel remorseful and uneasy; be conscience-stricken

愧赧 kuǐnǎn　blush from shame

愧恧 kuǐnǜ　*formal*　be ashamed

愧色 kuǐsè　a look (*or* an expression) of shame: 面有～ look ashamed / 毫无～ look unashamed (*or* unabashed)

愧痛 kuǐtòng　feel ashamed and agonized; feel agonized out of shame

愧怍 kuǐzuò　*formal*　feel ashamed

聩 kuì　*formal*　deaf; hard of hearing: 振聋发聩 zhènlóng-fākuì

篑 kuì　*formal*　basket for holding earth: 功亏一篑 gōng kuī yī kuì

kūn

坤 kūn　female; feminine: ～鞋 woman's shoes / ～包 lady's handbag

坤表 kūnbiǎo　woman's watch

坤角儿 kūnjuér　(also 坤伶 kūnlíng) *old*　actress

坤宅 kūnzhái　*old*　the bride's side; the wife's family

昆 kūn　① elder brother: 昆仲 kūnzhòng ② *formal* offspring: 后昆 hòukūn

昆布 kūnbù　*Chin. med.*　kelp

昆虫 kūnchóng　insect: 传病～ insect vector

昆虫学 kūnchóngxué　entomology: ～家 entomologist

昆弟 kūndì　elder and younger brothers; brothers

昆季 kūnjì　elder and younger brothers; brothers

昆仑 Kūnlún　the Kunlun Mountains

昆明 Kūnmíng　Kunming (the capital of Yunnan Province)

昆腔 kūnqiāng　melodies which originated in Kunshan (昆山), Jiangsu Province, in the Ming Dynasty; melodies for *Kunqu* opera

昆曲 kūnqǔ　① *Kunqu* opera ② melodies for *Kunqu* opera

昆仲 kūnzhòng　elder and younger brothers; brothers

堃 kūn　usu. used in a person's name

裈(**裩**、**裙**)　kūn　*arch.*　trousers

崑 kūn　see below

崑崟 Kūnlún　old form for 昆仑 Kūnlún

琨 kūn　*formal*　a kind of jade

髡(**髠**)　kūn　shave a man's head (as a punishment in ancient times)

醌 kūn　*chem.*　quinone

鲲 kūn　enormous legendary fish, which could change into a roc

鲲鹏 kūnpéng　roc (an enormous legendary bird transformed from a gigantic fish)

kǔn

捆(**綑**)　kǔn　① tie; bind; bundle up: ～行李 tie up one's baggage / ～谷草 bundle up millet stalks / 把他～起来 tie him up / ～住手脚 bound hand and foot ② m. bundle: 一～柴禾 a bundle of firewood

捆绑 kǔnbǎng　tie up (usu. a person); truss up; bind

捆扎 kǔnzā　tie up; bundle up: 一定要把这批货物～好了。Be sure to bundle the goods up firmly.

阃 kǔn　*formal*　① threshold ② women's quarters

悃 kǔn　*formal*　sincere

悃愊 kǔnbì　*formal*　complete sincerity

悃诚 kǔnchéng　sincerity

壸(**壼**)　kǔn　*arch.*　an alley inside the imperial palace

kùn

困[1]　kùn　① be stranded; be hard pressed: ～于异乡 be left stranded in a foreign land / ～于酒色 be addicted to wine and women / 为病所～ be afflicted with illness ② surround; pin down: 把敌人～死在据点里 bottle up the enemy in his stronghold ③ tired: 困乏 kùnfá

困[2]（**睏**）　kùn　① sleepy: 你～了就睡吧。Go to bed if you feel sleepy. / 孩子们～得眼睛都睁不开了。The children were so sleepy that they could hardly keep their eyes open. ② *dial.* sleep: 天不早了，快点～吧。It's getting late. Hurry up and get yourself to bed.

困惫 kùnbèi　*formal*　tired out; exhausted: ～不堪 be in a state of utter exhaustion; be dog-tired

困处 kùnchǔ　① difficult position; predicament; straits ② be stranded in; be in a fix: ～一隅 find oneself in a tight corner; fall into dire straits

困顿 kùndùn　① tired out; exhausted ② be in financial straits

困厄 kùn'è　dire straits; distress

困乏 kùnfá　① tired; fatigued ② *formal* financially difficult; straitened economically

困惑 kùnhuò　perplexed; puzzled: ～的神色 a perplexed look / ～不解 feel puzzled

困觉 kùnjiào　*dial.*　sleep

困境 kùnjìng　difficult position; predicament; straits: 处于～ be in a difficult position / 陷于～ fall into dire straits; find oneself in a tight corner; land oneself in a fix / 摆脱～ extricate oneself from a difficult position

困窘 kùnjiǒng　① in straitened circumstances; in a difficult position; embarrassed ② poverty-stricken; destitute

困居 kùnjū　be stranded; be hard pressed: ～异国 be left stranded in a foreign land

困倦 kùnjuàn　sleepy: 昨晚没有睡好，现在感到十分～。I feel very sleepy because I didn't sleep well last night.

困苦 kùnkǔ　(live) in privation: 艰难～ difficulties and hardships / 在那战争的岁月里，他们的生活相当～。They suffered a lot of privations during the war.

困累 kùnlèi　tired; fatigued

困难 kùnnan　① difficulty: 情况十分～。Conditions are very difficult. / 山上空气稀薄，呼吸很～。Up in the

mountains the air is thin and breathing is difficult. / ～ 重重 be beset with difficulties ② financial difficulties; straitened circumstances: 生活～ live in straitened circumstances / ～户 families with financial (*or* material) difficulties / 他三岁时死了父亲，家里更～了。The boy's family has been much worse off since his father died when he was three.

困恼 kùnnǎo ① be vexed; be worried ② vexation; worry

困迫 kùnpò hard pressed; embarrassed; in a predicament

困穷 kùnqióng poverty-stricken; destitute

困扰 kùnrǎo perplex; puzzle: 为一个难题所～ be puzzled by a difficult question

困人 kùnrén (of weather) oppressive; close

困守 kùnshǒu defend against a siege; stand a siege: ～孤城 be entrenched in a beseiged city

困兽犹斗 kùnshòu yóu dòu cornered beasts will still fight; beasts at bay will fight back

困学 kùnxué *formal* study assiduously

kuò

扩(擴) kuò expand; enlarge; extend: 扩大 kuòdà

扩编 kuòbiān enlarge the establishment of an army unit

扩充 kuòchōng expand; strengthen; augment: ～实力 expand (military or political) forces / ～军备 engage in arms expansion / ～设备 augment the equipment

扩大 kuòdà enlarge; expand; extend: ～战果 exploit a victory / ～眼界 widen one's outlook; broaden one's horizons / ～政治影响 extend political influence / ～集体福利事业 extend collective welfare undertakings; increase collective welfare facilities / ～耕地面积 expand the area under cultivation / 不断～企业的公共积累 steadily add to the accumulation fund of an enterprise / ～经营范围 expand business scope / ～相互间的经济技术合作 extend mutual economic and technological cooperation

扩大化 kuòdàhuà broaden the scope; magnify: 不把敌我矛盾～ not magnify the contradictions between ourselves and the enemy / 使错误没有～ keep mistakes within bounds

扩大会议 kuòdà huìyì enlarged meeting (*or* session, conference)

扩大再生产 kuòdà zàishēngchǎn reproduction on an extended scale; extended (*or* expanded) reproduction

扩建 kuòjiàn extend (a factory, mine, etc.): ～码头 extend a wharf

扩建工程 kuòjiàn gōngchéng extension (project)

扩军 kuòjūn engage in arms expansion: ～备战 engage in arms expansion and war preparations

扩孔 kuòkǒng *mech.* reaming: ～钻头 reaming bit; reamer bit

扩散 kuòsàn spread; diffuse: ～谣言 spread rumours / ～影响 extend influence / 不让废气～ prevent the diffusion of waste gas / 病菌～ proliferation of germs

扩胸器 kuòxiōngqì chest expander; chest developer

扩音器 kuòyīnqì ① megaphone ② audio amplifier

扩印 kuòyìn make enlargements from a 135 (esp. colour) film

扩展 kuòzhǎn expand; spread; extend; develop: 五年内全省林地将～到一千万亩。The forest land of the province will be expanded to ten million *mu* within five years.

扩张 kuòzhāng ① expand; enlarge; extend; spread: 对外～ expansionism; foreign aggrandizement / ～野心 expansionist ambitions ② *med.* dilate: 血管～ blood vessel dilatation

扩张器 kuòzhāngqì *med.* dilator

扩张战果 kuòzhāng zhànguǒ *mil.* exploitation of success

扩张主义 kuòzhāngzhǔyì expansionism: ～分子 expansionist

括 kuò ① draw together (muscles, etc.); contract: 括约肌 kuòyuējī ② include: 概括 gàikuò

括号 kuòhào brackets (〔 〕, ( ), 〈 〉)

括弧 kuòhú parentheses

括约肌 kuòyuējī *physiol.* sphincter

括注 kuòzhù an explanatory note in brackets

蛞 kuò see below

蛞蝼 kuòlóu *arch.* mole cricket

蛞蝓 kuòyú *zool.* slug

阔(闊) kuò ① wide; broad; vast: 辽阔 liáokuò ② wealthy; rich: 他～起来了。He's getting rich.

阔别 kuòbié long separated; long parted: ～多年的战友 long-separated comrades-in-arms / 我们已～多年了。We've been apart for many years now.

阔步 kuòbù take big strides: ～前进 advance with giant strides

阔绰 kuòchuò ostentatious; liberal with money: ～的生活 an extravagant life / 他的日子过得很～。He leads an extravagant life.

阔幅平布 kuòfú píngbù sheeting: 本色～ grey sheeting

阔老 kuòlǎo (also 阔佬 kuòlǎo) a rich (old) man

阔气 kuòqi luxurious; extravagant; lavish: 花钱～ spend lavishly / 摆～ display (*or* parade) one's wealth

阔人 kuòrén a rich man

阔少 kuòshào a rich man's son

阔叶树 kuòyèshù broadleaf tree

廓 kuò ① wide; extensive: 寥廓 liáokuò ② outline: 耳廓 ěrkuò

廓落 kuòluò *formal* spacious and still

廓清 kuòqīng sweep away; clean up

廓张 kuòzhāng *formal* expand; enlarge; extend; spread

L

lā

拉[1] lā ① pull; draw; tug; drag: ～弓 draw a bow / ～风箱 work the bellows / 把车～过来. Pull the cart over here. / 马～农具 horse-drawn farm implements / 他把我～到一边. He drew me aside. ② transport by vehicle; haul: 套车去～肥料 get a cart ready to haul back the fertilizer ③ move (troops to a place): 把二班～到桥头 move Squad Two to the bridge ④ play (certain musical instruments): ～小提琴(手风琴) play the violin (accordion) ⑤ drag out; draw out; space out: ～长声音说话 drawl ⑥ give (or lend) a helping hand; help: 他犯了错误, 要～他一把. He's made mistakes and we must help him. ⑦ drag in; implicate: 这是你自己做的事, 为什么要～上别人? It was all your own doing. Why drag in others? ⑧ draw in; win over; canvass: ～一派打一派 draw in one faction and hit out at another / ～选票 canvass votes; canvass ⑨ dial. chat: 拉话 lāhuà ⑩ press; pressgang: ～壮丁 grab sb. for military service; forcibly conscript; pressgang ⑪ table tennis lift

拉[2] lā inf. empty the bowels: 又～又吐 suffer from vomiting and diarrhoea

——see also lá; lǎ; là

拉拔 lābá mech. drawing

拉巴 lāba dial. ① take great pains to bring up (a child) ② help; support; promote

拉帮结伙 lābāng-jiéhuǒ recruit people to form a faction; gang up; band together

拉鼻儿 lābír inf. sound a siren

拉场子 lā chǎngzi perform in the open at fairs or in marketplaces

拉扯 lāche inf. ① drag; pull: 别～, 让我走. Don't hold me back. Let me go. ② take great pains to bring up (a child): 你妈把你～到这么大可真不容易啊. It wasn't at all easy for your mother to bring you up. ③ help; support; promote: 师傅见他有出息, 愿意特别～他一把. His instructor finds him promising and is willing to give him special help. ④ gang up with; rope in ⑤ implicate; drag in: 干吗把我～进去? Why drag me in? ⑥ chat: 他心里有事, 无心跟我～. He had something on his mind and was in no mood to chat with me.

拉出去 lāchuqu pull out; drag out: 把他～枪毙! Lead him off to execution!

拉床 lāchuáng mech. broaching machine

拉大 lādà dial. bring up (a child): 他母亲很不容易地把他～. Her mother brought him up under difficult conditions.

拉大片 lā dàpiàn same as 拉洋片 lā yángpiàn

拉大旗作虎皮 lā dàqí zuò hǔpí use a great banner (of revolution, etc.) as a tiger-skin—deck oneself out and intimidate people

拉刀 lādāo mech. broach

拉倒 lādǎo inf. forget about it; leave it at that; drop it: 你不同意, 就～. Since you don't agree let's forget about it.

拉德 lādé rad (a unit of absorbed radiation dose)

拉丁美洲 Lādīng Měizhōu Latin America

拉丁文 Lādīngwén Latin (language)

拉丁字母 Lādīng zìmǔ the Latin alphabet; the Roman alphabet

拉肚子 lā dùzi inf. suffer from diarrhoea; have loose bowels

拉队伍 lā duìwǔ raise a force or contingent; form a band

拉夫 lāfū pressgang; press people into service

拉幅机 lāfújī text. stenter; tenter

拉杆 lāgān mech. pull rod; drag link; draw bar; tension link

拉杆天线 lāgān tiānxiàn telescopic antenna

拉呱儿 lāguǎr dial. chat

拉关系 lā guānxi derog. try to establish a relationship with sb.; cotton up to: 拉亲戚关系 claim kinship / ～, 走后门 use personal connections and get in through the back door

拉管 lāguǎn popular name for 长号 chánghào

拉后腿 lā hòutuǐ hold sb. back; be a drag on sb.; be a hindrance to sb.: 我要参军, 决不让家里的人～. I want to join the army, and won't let my family hold me back.

拉祜族 Lāhùzú the Lahu nationality, or the Lahus, inhabiting Yunnan Province

拉花 lāhuā garland: 纸～ festoon; paper garland

拉话 lāhuà dial. make conversation; chat

拉簧 lāhuáng mech. extension spring

拉魂腔 lāhúnqiāng another name for 泗州戏 sìzhōuxì

拉火绳 lāhuǒshéng mil. lanyard

拉饥荒 lā jīhuang inf. be in debt; get into debt

拉家常 lā jiācháng talk about everyday matters; engage in small talk; chitchat

拉家带口 lājiā-dàikǒu be burdened with a family

拉架 lājià try to stop people from fighting each other: 他们又打起来了, 你去拉拉架. They're fighting again. Go and stop them.

拉交情 lā jiāoqing derog. try to form ties with; cotton up to

拉脚 lājiǎo transport persons or goods by cart

拉近乎 lā jìnhu same as 套近乎 tào jìnhu

拉锯 lājù ① work a two-handed saw ② be locked in a seesaw struggle: ～地带 area which frequently changes hands in a war; scene of a seesaw battle

拉锯战 lājùzhàn seesaw battle

拉开 lā·kāi ① pull open; draw back: ～抽屉 pull the drawer open / ～窗帘 draw back the curtain / ～枪栓 pull back the bolt (of a rifle) / ～架式 get into a ready position (to fight) / ～战幕 start a competition (or match) / ～嗓门就唱 start singing when asked to without making a fuss ② increase the distance between; space out: 不要～距离! Close up! / 比分逐渐～了. The gap between the scores gradually widened. / 把比分～到十六比八 pull away to 16—8; increase the lead to 16 —8 / ～档次 widen the difference between different

grades／同类商品的质量差价没有～。There are inadequate price differentials for a given product with diverse quality.

拉客 lākè ① (of inns, small restaurants, etc.) solicit guests or diners ② (of taxi drivers, pedicab riders, etc.) take on passengers ③ (of prostitutes) solicit patrons

拉亏空 lā kuīkong be in debt; get into debt

拉拉扯扯 lālāchěchě ① pull (or drag) sb. about ② exchange flattery and favours; scratch each other's backs: 吃吃喝喝，～ wining and dining and flattering each other

拉拉队 lālāduì cheering squad; rooters

拉力 lālì pulling force: ～试验 pull (or tension) test

拉力器 lālìqì chest-developer; chest-expander

拉力赛 lālìsài *sports* rally

拉练 lāliàn camp and field training

拉链 lāliàn zip fastener; zipper

拉拢 lālong draw sb. over to one's side; win over; rope in: ～一些人，排挤一些人 drawing some people in and pushing others out／不要受坏人～。Don't get roped in by bad people.

拉马克学说 Lāmǎkè xuéshuō *biol.* Lamarckism

拉买卖 lā mǎimai canvass business orders; drum up trade

拉美 Lāměi short for 拉丁美洲 Lādīng Měizhōu

拉门 lāmén sliding door

拉面 lāmiàn *dial.* same as 抻面 chēnmiàn

拉模 lāmú *mech.* drawing die

拉皮条 lā pítiáo *dial.* act as a procurer or pimp

拉平 lāpíng bring to the same level; even up: 双方比分渐渐～。The score gradually evened up.

拉纤 lāqiàn ① tow (a boat) ② act as go-between

拉绒 lāróng woven nap; pile

拉萨 Lāsà Lasa (Lhasa, capital of the Tibet Autonomous Region)

拉山头 lā shāntóu form a faction

拉屎 lāshǐ *inf.* have a bowel movement; shit

拉手 lāshǒu shake hands

拉手 lāshou handle (of a door, window, drawer, etc.)

拉丝 lāsī same as 拔丝 básī①

拉锁儿 lāsuǒr zip fastener; zipper

拉套 lātào ① (of an extra animal) help pull a cart ② *dial.* help others

拉条 lātiáo *mech.* brace; stay: 斜～ batter brace／链～ chain stay

拉脱维亚 Lātuōwéiyà Latvia

拉网 lāwǎng ① draw in (or up) the net; haul in the net ② close in on (besieged forces)

拉稀 lāxī *inf.* have loose bowels; have diarrhoea

拉下脸 lāxialiǎn ① look displeased; pull a long face; put on a stern expression: 他听了这句话，立刻～来。When he heard this, his expression became stern immediately. ② *inf.* not spare sb.'s sensibilities: 他办事大公无私，对谁都能～来。He is perfectly fair and impartial and never tries to spare anybody's feelings.／拉不下脸 be afraid of hurting sb.'s feelings

拉下马 lāxiamǎ pull sb. off the horse—force sb. out of his position ——see also 舍得一身剐，敢把皇帝拉下马 shěde yīshēn guǎ, gǎn bǎ huángdì lāxiamǎ

拉下水 lāxiashuǐ pull sb. into the water—get sb. involved in one's scheme; drag sb. into the mire; make an accomplice of sb.; corrupt sb.

拉闲篇 lā xiánpiān same as 扯闲篇 chě xiánpiān

拉线 lāxiàn act as go-between

拉线开关 lāxiàn kāiguān pullswitch

拉削 lāxiāo *mech.* broaching

拉延 lāyán *mech.* draw (a wire, tube, etc.)

拉秧 lāyāng uproot plants after their edible portions have been harvested

拉洋片 lā yángpiàn give peep shows accompanied by singing commentary

拉杂 lāzá rambling; jumbled; ill-organized: 这篇文章写得太～。This article is very badly organized.／我拉拉杂杂就谈这些吧。I think I'll stop my rambling talk here.

拉帐 lāzhàng be in debt; get into debt

拉制 lāzhì same as 拉延 lāyán

垃 lā see below

垃圾 lājī rubbish; garbage; refuse: ～处理 garbage disposal／焚化～ refuse incineration

垃圾堆 lājīduī rubbish heap; refuse dump; garbage heap: 把它扔到～里去。Throw it on the rubbish heap.／被扫进了历史的～ be swept onto the rubbish heap of history

垃圾箱 lājīxiāng dustbin; ash can; garbage can

啦 lā see 哩哩啦啦 līlilālā ——see also la

喇 lā see 呼喇 hūlā 哇喇 wālā ——see also lá; lǎ

邋 lā see below

邋遢 lā·ta *inf.* slovenly; sloppy: 你怎么这样～？How did you ever get so sloppy?

lá

晃 lá see 旮晃儿 gālár

拉(剌) lá slash; slit; cut; make a gash in: 把这块皮子～开 slit the leather／手上～了个口子 cut one's hand; get a cut in the hand ——see also lā; lǎ; là

砬 lá see 石砬子 shílázi

喇 lá see 哈喇子 hālázi ——see also lā; lǎ

lǎ

拉 lǎ see 半拉 bànlǎ; 虎不拉 hùbulǎ ——see also lā; lá; là

喇 lǎ see below ——see also lā; lá

喇叭 lǎba ① popular name for 唢呐 suǒnà ② brass-wind instruments in general or any of these instruments ③ loudspeaker; horn (in a car)

喇叭花 lǎbahuā (white-edged) morning glory

喇叭裤 lǎbakù flared trousers; bell-bottoms

喇叭筒 lǎbatǒng megaphone

喇嘛 lǎma lama

喇嘛教 lǎmajiào Lamaism

喇嘛庙 lǎmamiào lamasery

là

拉 là see below ——see also lā; lá; lǎ

拉拉蛄 làlagǔ same as 蝲蝲蛄 làlagǔ

剌 là *formal* perverse; disagreeable: 乖剌 guāilà

落 là ① leave out; be missing: 这里～了两个字。

Two words are missing here. ② leave behind; forget to bring: 我忙着出来，把书～在家里了。 I was in a hurry and left my book at home. ③ lag (*or* fall, drop) behind: ～下很远 fall (*or* be left) far behind / 谁也不愿意～在后面。 No one likes to lag behind. / 他～了一个星期的课。 He's a whole week behind with his lessons. *or* He missed a week's lessons. ——see also lào; luò

腊（臘、臈）

là ① an ancient sacrifice which took place each (lunar) year shortly after the winter solstice ② the twelfth lunar month: ～尽冬残。 The year is drawing to a close. ③ cured (fish, meat, etc., generally done in the twelfth lunar month) ——see also xī

腊八 Làbā the eighth day of the twelfth lunar month (marked by eating *laba* porridge)

腊八粥 làbāzhōu *laba* porridge (rice porridge with beans, nuts and dried fruit eaten on the eighth day of the twelfth lunar month)

腊肠 làcháng sausage

腊梅 làméi winter sweet (an ornamental shrub bearing sweet yellow flowers in winter)

腊肉 làròu cured meat; bacon

腊味 làwèi cured meat, fish, etc.

腊月 làyuè the twelfth month of the lunar year; the twelfth moon

辣

là ① peppery; hot: 这个辣椒～不～? Is this pepper hot? / 我爱吃～的。 I like hot foods. ② (of smell or taste) burn; bite; sting: 切葱头～眼睛。 When you slice an onion it makes your eyes sting. / ～得舌头发麻。 The hot taste burns the tongue. ③ vicious; ruthless: 心毒手～ vicious and ruthless / 口甜心～ sweet words but a wicked heart

辣根 làgēn horseradish

辣乎乎 làhūhū peppery; hot: 鱼香肉丝～的。 Fish-flavoured pork has a hot taste. / 他想起自己的错误, 心里不由得一阵～地发烧。 A feeling of shame came over him as he recalled the mistakes he had made.

辣酱 làjiàng thick chilli sauce

辣酱油 làjiàngyóu pungent sauce (similar to Worcestershire sauce)

辣椒 làjiāo hot pepper; chilli

辣椒粉 làjiāofěn chilli powder

辣椒油 làjiāoyóu chilli oil

辣手 làshǒu ① ruthless method; vicious device ② *dial.* vicious; ruthless ③ *inf.* thorny; troublesome; knotty: 这件事真～。 That's really a knotty problem. *or* That's a real hot potato.

辣丝丝 làsīsī a little hot

辣酥酥 làsūsū a little hot

辣子 làzi *inf.* hot pepper; cayenne pepper; chilli

蜡（蠟）

là ① wax ② candle: 点一支～ light a candle

蜡版 làbǎn mimeograph stencil (already cut)

蜡版术 làbǎnshù cerography

蜡笔 làbǐ wax crayon

蜡笔画 làbǐhuà crayon drawing

蜡虫 làchóng wax insect

蜡防印花法 làfáng yìnhuāfǎ batik

蜡光纸 làguāngzhǐ glazed paper

蜡果 làguǒ wax fruit

蜡花 làhuā snuff

蜡黄 làhuáng wax yellow; waxen; sallow: 面色～ have a sallow complexion

蜡炬 làjù *liter.* candle: 春蚕到死丝方尽, ～成灰泪始干。(李商隐) The spring silkworm will only end his thread when death befalls; The candle will drip with tears until it turns to ashes.

蜡克 làkè lacquer (a transliteration, also called 清喷漆 qīngpēnqī)

蜡泪 làlèi drips from a burning candle; wax guttering

蜡疗 làliáo wax therapy

蜡皮 làpí *Chin. med.* wax coating for a big pill

蜡扦 làqiān candlestick

蜡染 làrǎn *text.* wax printing; batik

蜡人 làrén wax figure; waxwork

蜡台 làtái candlestick

蜡丸 làwán a wax-coated pill

蜡像 làxiàng wax figure; waxwork: ～陈列馆 waxworks museum; waxworks

蜡印 làyìn wax seal: 打上～ affix a wax seal (to a contract, etc.)

蜡纸 làzhǐ ① wax paper ② stencil paper; stencil: 刻～ cut a stencil

蜡烛 làzhú (wax) candle

蜡嘴雀 làzuǐquè hawfinch

瘌

là see below

瘌痢 làlì *dial.* favus of the scalp

瘌痢头 làlìtóu *dial.* a person affected with favus on the scalp

蝲

là see below

蝲蛄 làgǔ crayfish

蝲蝲蛄 làlagǔ mole cricket

鯻

là grunt; tigerfish

鬎

là see below

鬎鬎 làlì same as 瘌痢 làlì

鑞（鎯）

là solder

la

啦

la *part.* (a fusion of 了 and 啊): 他早来～! Why, he's been here a long time! / 二组跟我们挑战～。 Look! Group B has sent us a challenge. / 这回我可亲眼看见～! This time I've actually seen it for myself. / 她真来～? Has she really come? ——see also lā

鞡

la see 靰鞡 wùla

lái

来¹（來）

lái ① come (to): 老赵已经～了。 Lao Zhao has already come. / 老郑明天～北京。 Lao Zheng is coming to Beijing tomorrow. / 他今天～过两次。 He came twice today. / 客人～了。 The guests are here. / ～客人了。 We have a guest. / 昨天～过三个朋友。 I had three friends over yesterday. / 你～啦! Hello! *or* So you're here already. / 远处～了一条小船。 A small boat came into view in the distance. / 开春以后, 农忙季节～了。 When spring came round, the farming season began. / 这事儿怎么～的? How did it come about? / 问题～了。 A problem has come up. ② cause to come; send here; bring: 他～过两封信。 He's sent me two letters. / 我们可以～两个人帮忙。 We can send two people over to help. / 他刚才～了一个电话。 He gave me a call just now. / ～个糖醋鱼。 A sweet-and-sour fish, please (said at a restaurant). ③ (used as a substitute for some other verb): 你歇歇, 让我～吧。 You take a

rest. Let me do it. / 慢慢儿～, 别忙。 Take it easy. No hurry. / 我自己～吧, 别客气。 Please don't bother. I'll do it myself. / 你拿那个, 这个我自己～。 You take that one, and I'll take this one. / 你～块糖。 Have some candy. / 咱们～一盘棋好吗? Let's have a game of chess, OK? / 我们打篮球, 你～不～? We're going to play basketball. Will you join in? / 再一～个! Encore! ④ (used with 得 or 不, indicating possibility or impossibility, capability or incapability): 上海话我说不～。 I don't speak Shanghai dialect. / 这个歌我唱得～。 I can sing this song. / 这道题我做不～。 I can't do this problem. / 西餐我吃得～。 Western food suits me all right. / 我吃不～四川菜。 I can't get used to Sichuan cuisine. ⑤ (used before a verb, indicating an intended or suggested action): 你去打水, 我～生炉子。 You get some water and I'll light the stove. / 我～问你。 Let me ask you. / 我～说两句。 Let me say a few words. / 大家～想办法。 Let's think of a way (to solve the problem). or Let's put our heads together and see how to do it. ⑥ (used after a verb or verbal expression) come in order to: 我们支援你们～了。 We've come to help you out. / 我们道喜～了。 We've come to congratulate you. / 他回家探亲～了。 He's come home to see his parents. ⑦ (used between a verbal expression and a verb or between two verbal expressions) in order to: 大家想办法～解决。 Let's think of a way to solve the problem. / 我们得尽一切力量～完成计划。 We must do all we can to implement the plan. / 你又能用什么理由～说服他呢? And what arguments can you use to convince him? ⑧ same as 来着 láizhe ⑨ future; coming; next: 来年 láinián ⑩ (used after a time expression, indicating a period of time that extends from the past up to the present): 一年～ during the past year / 这三年～ over the last three years / 几天～ for the last few days / 两千年～ over the past 2,000 years ⑪ (used after a round number or after a numeral plus a measure) approximately; about; around: 二十～个 about 20 / 十～个人 about 10 people / 四十～岁 about 40 years old / 十～块钱 over 10 yuan / 两米～高 about two metres high / 六尺～长 about six chi long / 七斤～重 weigh about seven jin / 三里～地 a distance of about three li / 百十～里地 a distance of about 100 li ⑫ (used after the numerals 一, 二, and 三, indicating points in an explanation or argument): 我不要, 一～我不喜欢, 二～我也没钱。 I don't want it. In the first place, I don't like it; in the second place, I don't have the money. / 他这次进城, 一～是汇报工作, 二～是修理机器, 三～是采购图书。 He's in town this time to do three things: first, to report on his work; second, to have a machine repaired; and third, to purchase books. ⑬ (Lái) a surname

来²(來) lái (used as a syllable filler in folk ballads): 正月里～是新春, 家家户户点红灯。 The first month is the beginning of spring; every house has a red lantern alight.

来(來) ·lái ① (used after a verb, indicating motion towards the speaker) hither; here: 出～ come out / 上～ come up / 回～ come back / 上楼～ come upstairs / 回家～ come home / 把车开～。 Bring the car over. / 把报纸拿～。 Bring me the newspaper. / 他给我送～一部汉英词典。 He sent me a Chinese-English dictionary. / 我借了几本小说～。 I've brought some novels I borrowed. / 前面走～一群学生。 A group of students is heading towards us. ② (used after a verb, indicating completeness or finality): 一觉醒～ wake up after a sound sleep / 信笔写～ write down one's ideas as they come to mind ③ (used in certain stock

phrases which serve as sentence openings or parenthetical remarks, having the force of "when one comes to"): 算～时间已经不短了, 快有十年了。 When you come to think of it, it's been quite a while—almost ten years. / 想～你是早有准备的了。 I suppose you've been well prepared all along. / 他的话听～很有道理。 What he says sounds quite true. / 这个人看～年纪不小了。 That man looks well along in years.

来宾 láibīn guest; visitor: 接待～ receive guests

来宾席 láibīnxí seats for guests

来不得 láibude won't do; be impermissible: 这是一个科学问题, ～半点虚伪。 This is a matter of science, which permits no dishonesty.

来不及 láibují there's not enough time (to do sth.); it's too late (to do sth.): 今天我们～去看他了。 There's no time for us to go and see him today. / 写信已经～了, 还是给他打个电报吧。 It's too late to reach him by letter. Better send a telegram.

来朝 láicháo come to court; come to pay tribute (to the emperor): 岁岁～ come to pay tribute year after year ——see also láizhāo

来潮 láicháo the tide comes in

来到 láidào arrive; come: 雨季～了。 The rainy season has set in. / 你们终于～了。 So here you are at last.

来得¹ láide inf. competent; equal to: 样样农活她都～。 She can cope with any kind of farmwork. / 他说话结结巴巴, 笔底下倒还～。 He speaks with a stammer, but he writes well.

来得² láide inf. emerge (from a comparison) as; come out as: 海水比淡水重, 因此压力也～大。 Sea water is heavier than freshwater, so its pressure is greater, too.

来得及 láidejí there's still time; be able to do sth. in time; be able to make it: 赶快去, 还～。 Go at once while there's still time. / 春耕前把拖拉机修好, ～吗? Can you get the tractor repaired in time for the spring ploughing? / 我把车开快点还～。 We can make it if I drive a bit faster.

来得容易去得快 láide róngyì qùde kuài easy come, easy go

来电 láidiàn ① incoming telegram; your telegram; your message: 三月十七日～悉。 Your message of March 17 received. ② send a telegram here: 请～告知。 Please inform me by telegram.

来而不往非礼也 lái ér bù wǎng fēi lǐ yě it is impolite not to reciprocate—one should return as good as one receives

来犯 láifàn come to attack us; invade our territory: 坚决消灭敢于～之敌。 Resolutely wipe out any enemy that dares to invade our territory.

来访 láifǎng come to visit; come to call: 认真对待人民群众来信～ treat seriously the letters the people send in and the complaints they make when they call

来复枪 láifùqiāng rifle

来复线 láifùxiàn rifling

来稿 láigǎo incoming manuscript; your manuscript

来归 láiguī ① come over and pledge allegiance ② arch. (of a woman) join a man in marriage

来函 láihán formal incoming letter; your letter

来亨鸡 láihēngjī Leghorn

来鸿 láihóng formal a letter from faraway: 海外～ a letter from abroad

来回 láihuí ① make a round trip; make a return journey; go to a place and come back: 从车间到我们宿舍～有一里地。 It's one li from the workshop to our quarters and back. / ～有多远? How far is it there and back? ② a round trip: 一天打两个～ make two round trips in one day ③ back and forth; to and fro: 织布机上梭子～地飞动。 The shuttle flies back and forth on

the loom. / 在房间里~走动 pace up and down the room / ~摇摆 oscillate; vacillate

来回飞行 láihuí fēixíng round-trip flight

来回来去 láihuí-láiqù back and forth; over and over again: ~地跑了好多趟 run back and forth many times / ~地说 say sth. over and over again; repeat again and again

来回票 láihuípiào round-trip ticket; return ticket

来火 láihuǒ flare up; get angry

来件 láijiàn communication or parcel received

来劲 láijìn *dial.* ① full of enthusiasm; in high spirits: 他越干越~儿。The longer he worked at it, the more enthusiastic he became. ② exhilarating; exciting; thrilling: 这样伟大的工程, 可真~! What a magnificent project! How thrilling! ③ jest with; annoy; offend: 你别跟我~。I won't stand any nonsense from you.

来客 láikè guest; visitor

来历 láilì origin; source; antecedents; background; past history: 查明~ trace to the source; ascertain a person's antecedents / 提起这把手术刀可大有~。Talking of this scalpel, there is a long history to it.

来历不明 láilì bùmíng (of things) of unknown origin; (of persons) of dubious background or of questionable antecedents

来料加工 láiliào jiāgōng process materials supplied by customers; accept customers' materials for processing; customers' own materials made up (notice outside tailor's shop)

来临 láilín arrive; come; approach: 每当春天~, 这里是一片绿油油的庄稼。When spring comes, this place is an expanse of lush green crops.

来龙去脉 láilóng-qùmài origin and development; the entire process: 请你把事情的~给我们讲一遍。Please tell us the whole story from beginning to end.

来路 láilù incoming road; approach: 六连挡住了敌人的~。Company Six blocked the enemy's path of approach.

来路 láilu origin; antecedents: ~不正 (of things) of questionable origin; (of persons) of dubious background / ~不明的飞机 unidentified aircraft

来路货 láilùhuò *dial.* imported goods

来年 láinián the coming year; next year

…来…去 …lái…qù (used with two identical or synonymous verbs) back and forth; over and over again: 飞来飞去 fly back and forth / 挑来挑去 pick and choose / 考虑来考虑去 turn sth. over and over again in one's mind / 翻来覆去睡不着 toss and turn in bed

来人 láirén bearer; messenger: 收条请交~带回。Please give the receipt to the bearer.

来人儿 láirénr *old* middleman

来日 láirì the days to come; the future

来日方长 láirì fāng cháng there will be ample (*or* plenty of) time; there will be time for that

来神 láishén *inf.* full of enthusiasm; in high spirits: 他越说越~。His spirits rose as he spoke.

来生 láishēng next life; afterlife

来使 láishǐ an envoy from another country or state: 两国交兵, 不斩~。When two states are at war, the envoys are never executed (an old maxim).

来示 láishì *formal* incoming letter; your letter

来世 láishì next life; afterlife

来势 láishì the force with which sth. breaks out; oncoming force: 这场雨~很猛。The rainstorm broke with tremendous force. / ~汹汹 bear down menacingly

来事 láishì ① *dial.* deal with people: 这人挺会~儿。He knows how to make friends with the right people. ② *dial.* (usu. used in the negative) be all right; will do: 这样做不~。That won't do. ③ *formal* future events: 知~ can foretell the future

来书 láishū *formal* ① send a letter here ② your letter

来苏 láisū *pharm.* lysol (a transliteration)

来头 láitou ① connections; backing: 这个人~不小。This guy has powerful backing. ② the motive behind (sb.'s words, etc.); cause: 他这些话有~, 是冲着我们说的。He didn't say all that without cause; it was directed against us. ③ the force with which sth. breaks out ④ interest; fun: 下棋没什么~儿, 不如去打乒乓球。Playing chess is no fun. It'd be better to go and play table tennis.

来往 láiwǎng come and go: ~于津沪之间 travel between Tianjin and Shanghai / 街上~的人很多。There are many people coming and going on the streets. / 翻修路面, 禁止车辆~。Road Under Repair. No thoroughfare. (*or* No Through Traffic.) / ~的信件 correspondence

来往 láiwang ① dealings; contact; intercourse: 我跟他从来没有任何~。I've never had any dealings with him. ② have contact or dealings: 我跟他~过, 但不很熟。I've had dealings with him, but I don't know him very well.

来文 láiwén document received

来项 láixiang income; receipts

来信 láixìn ① send a letter here: 到了那里就~。Write to us as soon as you get there. / 他好久没~了。I haven't heard from him for a long time. ② incoming letter; your letter: 十日~收到。I have received your letter of the 10th. / 人民~ letters from the people

来意 láiyì one's purpose in coming: 说明~ make clear what one has come for

来由 láiyóu reason; cause: 没~ without rhyme or reason / 他讲了他学针灸的~。He explained how he came to study acupuncture.

来源 láiyuán ① source; origin: 经济~ source of income / 税收~ source of revenue ② (followed by 于) originate; stem from: 知识~于实践。Knowledge stems from practice (or experience).

来札 láizhá *formal* incoming letter; your letter

来朝 láizhāo *formal* tomorrow ——see also láicháo

来者 láizhě ① the things to come or the generations to come: 往者不可谏, ~犹可追。(《论语》) What is past is beyond help; what is to come is not yet lost. / 后生可畏, 焉知~之不如今也? (《论语》) It is fitting that we should hold the young in awe. How do we know that the generations to come will not be the equal of the present? ② any person or thing that comes or has come: 来者不拒 láizhě bù jù

来者不拒 láizhě bù jù refuse nobody; refuse nobody's request or offer

来者不善, 善者不来 láizhě bù shàn, shànzhě bù lái ① he who has come is surely strong or he'd never have come along ② he who has come, comes with ill intent, certainly not on virtue bent

来着 láizhe *part.* (used at the end of affirmative sentences or special questions, indicating a past action or state): 你刚才说什么~? What were you saying just now? / 他去年冬天还回家~。He was home only last winter. / 我进来的时候, 他在这儿站着~。When I came in, he was standing here.

来之不易 lái zhī bù yì not easily come by; hard-earned: 我们的胜利~。Our victory was hard-won. / 每一粒粮食都~。Every single grain is the result of toil.

来兹 láizī *formal* the coming year; the future: 展望~ look towards the future

来踪去迹 láizōng-qùjì traces of sb.'s movements; traces of sb.'s whereabouts

莱(萊) lái ① same as 藜 lí ② *arch.* fields lying fallow in rotation

莱菔　láifú　radish
莱菔子　láifúzǐ　*Chin. med.*　radish seed
莱诺铸排机　láinuò zhùpáijī　linotype
莱塞　láisài　laser (a transliteration)
莱氏体　láishìtǐ　*mech.*　ledeburite
莱索托　Láisuǒtuō　Lesotho
莱索托人　Láisuǒtuōrén　Mosotho (sing.); Basotho (pl.)

徕（徕、倈）　lái　see 招徕 zhāolái

楝（楝）　lái　same as 楝木 láimù

楝木　láimù　large-leaved dogwood (*Cornus macrophylla*)

铼（錸）　lái　*chem.*　rhenium (Re)

lài

赉（賚）　lài　*formal*　grant; bestow; confer: 赏赉 shǎnglài

睐（睞）　lài　*formal*　① squint ② look at: 青睐 qīnglài

赖[1]　lài　① rely; depend: ～以生存的条件 conditions on which persons or things rely (*or* depend) for existence ② rascally; shameless: 赖皮 làipí ③ hang on in a place; drag out one's stay in a place; hold on to a place: 不容许侵略者～在别国的领土上。 The aggressors must not be allowed to hold on to the territories of other countries. / ～着不走 hang on and refuse to clear out ④ deny one's error or responsibility; go back on one's word: ～是～不掉的。 It's no good trying to deny it. *or* You simply can't deny it. ⑤ blame sb. wrongly; put the blame on sb. else: 自己错了还～别人，这就不对了。 It's not right to blame others for one's own mistake. ⑥ *inf.*　blame: 这事全～我。 I'm entirely to blame for that. ⑦ (Lài) a surname

赖[2]　lài　*inf.*　no good; poor: 好的～的我都能吃。 I can eat anything, good or bad.

赖床　làichuáng　be feeling too lazy to get out of bed
赖婚　làihūn　repudiate a marriage contract
赖皮　làipí　rascally; shameless; unreasonable: 耍～ act shamelessly
赖学　làixué　*dial.*　play truant; cut class
赖债　làizhài　repudiate a debt
赖帐　làizhàng　① repudiate a debt ② go back on one's word

濑　lài　*formal*　rapids

癞　lài　① leprosy ② *dial.*　favus of the scalp
癞瓜　làiguā　*dial.*　another name for 苦瓜 kǔguā
癞蛤蟆　làiháma　toad
癞蛤蟆想吃天鹅肉　làiháma xiǎng chī tiān'éròu　a toad lusting after a swan's flesh—aspiring after sth. one is not worthy of
癞皮狗　làipígǒu　① mangy dog ② loathsome creature
癞子　làizi　*dial.*　① favus ② a person affected with favus of the scalp

籁　lài　① an ancient musical pipe ② sound; noise: 万籁俱寂 wànlài jù jì

lán

兰（蘭）　lán　① same as 兰花 lánhuā ② same as 兰草 láncǎo ③ (used in ancient texts) lily magnolia: ～桨 magnolia oars
兰草　láncǎo　fragrant thoroughwort (*Eupatorium fortunei*)
兰摧玉折　láncuī-yùzhé　the orchid has withered and the jade is broken—a worthy person has died young
兰闺　lánguī　boudoir
兰花　lánhuā　cymbidium; orchid
兰花指　lánhuāzhǐ　orchid fingers—a lady's hand gesture with the tips of the thumb and the forefinger touching and the other three fingers raised (usu. made on the stage to show delicacy and grace)
兰盆　lánpén　① short for 盂兰盆会 yúlánpénhuì ② *old* bathtub
兰谱　lánpǔ　genealogical records exchanged by those who have sworn brotherhood
兰室　lánshì　boudoir
兰章　lánzhāng　*formal pol.*　your beautiful writings
兰州　Lánzhōu　Lanzhou (capital of Gansu Province)

岚　lán　*liter.*　haze; vapour; mist: 晓～ morning mists

拦（攔）　lán　bar; block; hold back: 别～着我，我一定得走。 Don't stop me; I must go. / 他刚要说，我把他给～住了。 He was just about to speak when I stopped him. / 一道河～住了我们的去路。 A river blocked our way.
拦挡　lándǎng　block; obstruct: ～住敌人的去路 block the enemy's way
拦道木　lándàomù　road fence; roadblock
拦柜　lánguì　counter
拦河坝　lánhébà　a dam across a river; dam
拦洪坝　lánhóngbà　a dam for holding back floodwater; a dam for flood control
拦击　lánjī　① intercept and attack ② *table tennis* volley
拦劫　lánjié　waylay and rob; mug
拦截　lánjié　intercept: ～增援的敌人 intercept enemy reinforcements
拦路　lánlù　block the way: ～抢劫 waylay; hold up
拦路虎　lánlùhǔ　a road-blocking tiger—obstacle; hindrance: 读科技书籍时，专门术语对我是个～。 In reading books on science and technology, I have trouble with technical terms.
拦网　lánwǎng　*volleyball* block
拦污栅　lánwūzhà　*water conservancy* trashrack
拦蓄　lánxù　retain (water); impound: ～洪水 impound floodwater
拦腰　lányāo　(hold) by the waist; (cut across) in the middle: ～抱住 seize sb. by the waist (*or* round the middle) from behind / 大坝把河水～截断。 The dam cut the river in the middle.
拦鱼栅　lányúzhà　fish screen
拦阻　lánzǔ　block; hold back; obstruct

栏（欄）　lán　① fence; railing; balustrade; hurdle: 桥～ the railing of a bridge ② pen; shed: 牛栏 niúlán ③ column (of a page or of a table, or in a newspaper): 左～ the left column / 那条新闻占了两～。 That news takes up two columns. / 体育～ sports column / 把这一～数字加起来。 Add up this column of figures.
栏杆　lángān　railing; banisters; balustrade: 桥～ the

railing of a bridge

栏柜　lánguì　same as 拦柜 lánguì

栏目　lánmù　the heading or title of a column (in a magazine, etc.)

婪　lán　see 贪婪 tānlán

阑[1]　lán　① same as 栏 lán① ② same as 拦 lán

阑[2]　lán　*liter.* (of time) late: 岁～ late in the year

阑干　lángān　① *liter.* across; crisscross: 北斗～。The Dipper lies across the sky. / 夜深忽梦少年事, 梦啼妆泪红～。(白居易) Late at night, dreaming of her girlhood, She cries in her sleep, staining her rouged cheeks with tears. ② same as 栏杆 lángān

阑入　lánrù　*formal* ① enter a place that is forbidden to one ② bring in extraneous matters

阑珊　lánshān　*liter.* coming to an end; waning: 意兴～。One's interest is flagging.

阑尾　lánwěi　*physiol.* appendix

阑尾炎　lánwěiyán　appendicitis

阑尾切除术　lánwěi qiēchúshù　appendectomy

蓝 (藍)　lán　① blue ② indigo plant ③ (Lán) a surname

蓝宝石　lánbǎoshí　sapphire

蓝本　lánběn　① writing upon which later work is based; chief source ② original version (of a literary work)

蓝点鲅　lándiǎnbà　another name for 鲅 bà

蓝靛　lándiàn　indigo

蓝矾　lánfán　*chem.* blue vitriol; cupric sulphate

蓝晶晶　lánjīngjīng　(of water, precious stones, etc.) bright blue

蓝晶石　lánjīngshí　*min.* kyanite; disthene

蓝鲸　lánjīng　blue whale

蓝领工人　lánlǐng gōngrén　blue-collar worker

蓝缕　lánlǚ　same as 褴褛 lánlǚ

蓝皮书　lánpíshū　blue book

蓝青官话　lánqīngguānhuà　*old* blue and green Mandarin—Mandarin spoken with a provincial accent

蓝田人　Lántiánrén　Lantian Man (*Sinanthropus lantienensis*), primitive man of about 600,000 years ago whose fossil remains were found in Lantian, Shaanxi Province, in 1964

蓝田猿人　Lántián yuánrén　same as 蓝田人 Lántiánrén

蓝铜矿　lántóngkuàng　azurite; chessylite

蓝图　lántú　blueprint: 绘制～ design a blueprint / 新图书馆的～ the blueprints of a new library / 国家建设的～ a blueprint for national reconstruction

蓝藻　lánzǎo　blue green algae

谰　lán　*formal* calumniate; slander

谰言　lányán　calumny; slander: 无耻～ shameless slander

澜　lán　billows; waves: 微～ ripples

褴 (襤)　lán　see below

褴褛　lánlǚ　ragged; shabby

篮 (籃)　lán　① basket ② *basketball* goal; basket: 投篮 tóulán

篮板　lánbǎn　*basketball* backboard; bank

篮板球　lánbǎnqiú　*basketball* rebound: 控制～ control the rebounds / 抓住～投篮入网 grab the rebound and sink a basket

篮球　lánqiú　basketball: 打～ play basketball / ～队 basketball team

篮球场　lánqiúchǎng　basketball court

篮球架　lánqiújià　basketball stands

篮圈　lánquān　*basketball* ring; hoop

篮子　lánzi　basket

斓　lán　see 斑斓 bānlán

镧　lán　*chem.* lanthanum (La)

lǎn

览 (覽)　lǎn　① look at; see; view: 游览 yóulǎn ② read: 阅览 yuèlǎn

览古　lǎngǔ　*formal* visit historic sites: 洛阳～ a tour of the historic sites in Luoyang

览胜　lǎnshèng　*formal* visit scenic spots: 《泰山～》 "Splendours of Mt. Tai"

揽 (攬)　lǎn　① pull sb. into one's arms; take into one's arms: 母亲把孩子～在怀里。The mother clasped the child to her bosom. ② fasten with a rope, etc.: 用绳子～上 tie a rope around sth. ③ take on; take upon oneself; canvass: 他把责任都～到自己身上。He took all the responsibility on himself. / ～买卖 canvass business orders ④ grasp; monopolize: ～权 arrogate power to oneself

揽笔　lǎnbǐ　*formal* take up one's pen; write

揽承　lǎnchéng　agree (*or* contract) to do a job

揽活　lǎnhuó　take on work

揽总　lǎnzǒng　assume overall responsibility; take on everything

缆 (纜)　lǎn　① hawser; mooring rope; cable: 解～ cast off; set sail / 新船砍～下水。The new ship cut her cable and slipped into the water. ② thick rope; cable: 电缆 diànlǎn ③ fasten (a boat) with a rope or cable: ～舟 moor a boat

缆车　lǎnchē　cable car

缆车铁道　lǎnchē tiědào　cable railway

缆道　lǎndào　cableway

缆索　lǎnsuǒ　thick rope; cable

缆索铁道　lǎnsuǒ tiědào　funicular railway; funicular

榄 (欖)　lǎn　see 橄榄 gǎnlǎn

罱　lǎn　① a kind of net used for fishing or for dredging up river sludge, etc. ② dredge up: ～河泥 dredge up sludge from a river

罱泥船　lǎnníchuán　a boat used in collecting river sludge for fertilizer

灆 (灠)　lǎn　① mix (raw fish, meat, or vegetables) with salt or other seasonings ② soak (a persimmon) in hot water or limewater to take away its harsh, puckery taste

懒 (懶)　lǎn　① lazy; indolent; slothful: 你未免太～点儿了吧。Aren't you being a bit too lazy? / 你越不做事越～。The less you do the lazier you get. ② sluggish; languid: 发懒 fālǎn

懒虫　lǎnchóng　*inf.* lazybones

懒怠　lǎndai　① lazy; indolent ② too lazy to: 我这两天身体不太好, 话也～说了。I haven't felt too well for the last couple of days, and I don't have the energy to talk.

懒得　lǎnde　not feel like (doing sth.); not be in the mood to; be disinclined to: 天太热, 我～出去。It's too hot. I don't feel like going out.

懒惰　lǎnduò　lazy

懒骨头　lǎngǔtou　*inf.*　lazybones

懒汉　lǎnhàn　sluggard; idler; lazybones

懒汉鞋　lǎnhànxié　Chinese cloth shoes with elasticated gussets (making them easy to slip on and off)

懒猴　lǎnhóu　slender loris; loris

懒散　lǎnsǎn　sluggish; negligent; indolent: 不要这样～，振作起来。Don't be so sluggish. Pull yourself together.

懒洋洋　lǎnyāngyāng　languid; listless: 每到炎热的夏天，我就有点～的。I always feel rather listless on hot summer days.

懒腰　lǎnyāo　see 伸懒腰　shēn lǎnyāo

壖（壖）　lǎn　see 坎壈　kǎnlǎn

làn

烂（爛）
làn　① soft; mashed; pappy: 牛肉烧得很～。The beef is very tender. *or* The beef melts in your mouth. / 豆子煮～了。The beans are now soft enough to eat. ② rot; fester: 阴雨天要防止～秧。In wet weather we must prevent the seedlings from rotting. / 苹果都～了。The apples are all rotten. / 伤口～了。The wound is festering. ③ worn-out: 衣服穿～了。The clothes are worn-out. / ～纸片 scraps of paper ④ messy: 烂帐 lànzhàng①

烂肠瘟　lànchángwēn　*dial.*　rinderpest; cattle plague

烂糊　lànhu　(of food) mashed; pulpy: 老年人爱吃～面。Old people like noodles cooked to a pulp.

烂漫　lànmàn　① bright-coloured; brilliant: 山花～ bright mountain flowers in full bloom ② unaffected; natural: 天真烂漫　tiǎnzhēn lànmàn

烂熳　lànmàn　same as 烂漫　lànmàn

烂泥　lànní　mud; slush: 汽车陷在～里了。The car is stuck in the mud. / ～塘 a muddy pond

烂舌头　làn shétou　(also 烂舌根　làn shégēn)　*inf.*　① tell tales; be fond of gossip ② talebearer; gossip; scandalmonger

烂熟　lànshú　① thoroughly cooked ② know sth. thoroughly: 台词背得～ learn one's lines thoroughly

烂摊子　làntānzi　a shambles; an awful mess: 那个厂是个～。That factory's affairs are in a terrible mess. / 新任首相得忙于收拾前任首相留下来的～。The new prime minister will have a hard time clearing up the mess left by his predecessor.

烂帐　lànzhàng　① messy accounts: 真是一本～。The accounts are all in a mess. ② uncollectable debts

烂醉　lànzuì　dead drunk: 喝得～ be dead drunk / ～如泥 be dead drunk; be as drunk as a lord

滥（濫）
làn　① overflow; flood ② excessive; indiscriminate: ～施轰炸 indiscriminate bombing; wanton bombing / ～发钞票 issue banknotes recklessly; inflate the paper currency / ～发奖金 distribute bonuses indiscriminately

滥调　làndiào　hackneyed tune; worn-out theme

滥伐　lànfá　severe deforestation; denudation

滥交　lànjiāo　choose friends indiscriminately

滥觞　lànshāng　*formal*　origin; beginning

滥诉　lànsù　indiscriminate lawsuits

滥套子　làntàozi　clichés; hackneyed phrases

滥用　lànyòng　abuse; misuse; use indiscriminately: ～经费 squander funds / 不要～成语典故。We should not use proverbs and allusions indiscriminately.

滥用职权　lànyòng zhíquán　abuse one's power; abuse one's authority or position

滥竽充数　lànyú chōng shù　pass oneself off as one of the players in an ensemble—be there just to make up the number (used of incompetent people or inferior goods)

lāng

啷
lāng　see 当啷　dānglāng; 哐啷　kuānglāng

láng

郎
láng　① an official title in imperial times ② (used in forming nouns designating certain classes of persons): 放牛～ cowherd / 货郎 huòláng / 女郎 nǚláng ③ (used by a woman in addressing her husband or lover) my darling ④ (Láng) a surname —see also 榔 láng

郎才女貌　lángcái-nǚmào　a brilliant young scholar and a beautiful woman—a fine couple

郎当[1]　lángdāng　same as 锒铛　lángdāng

郎当[2]　lángdāng　① (of clothes) loose-hanging; ill-fitting; untidy: 衣裤～ be shabbily dressed ② discouraged; dejected ③ down-and-out

郎舅　lángjiù　a man and his wife's brother: 他们俩是～。Those two are brothers-in-law.

郎君　lángjūn　*old*　(used in addressing one's husband) you

郎猫　lángmāo　*inf.*　tomcat

郎中　lángzhōng　*dial.*　a physician trained in herbal medicine; doctor: 江湖～ quack doctor; mountebank

狼
láng　wolf

狼把草　lángbǎcǎo　bur beggar-ticks

狼狈　lángbèi　in a difficult position; in a tight corner: ～逃窜 flee in panic; flee helter-skelter / 陷于～境地 find oneself in a fix; be caught in a dilemma (*or* quandary) / 显出一副～相 cut a sorry figure / 傀儡政权的处境极为孤立和～。The puppet regime was extremely isolated and in dire straits. / 打得敌人十分～。The enemy was badly battered.

狼狈不堪　lángbèi bùkān　in an extremely awkward position; in a sorry plight; in sore straits

狼狈为奸　lángbèi wéi jiān　act in collusion (*or* cahoots) with each other

狼狈周章　lángbèi zhōuzhāng　terror-stricken; panic-stricken: 我军行动神速，致使敌军措手不及，～。Our lightning speed knocked the enemy completely off balance and struck fear into its heart.

狼奔豕突　lángbēn-shǐtū　run like wolves and rush like boars—tear about like wild beasts

狼疮　lángchuāng　*med.*　lupus

狼毒　lángdú　*Chin. med.*　the root of langdu (*Euphorbia fisheriana*)

狼狗　lánggǒu　wolfhound

狼顾　lánggù　look back from time to time as a wolf does—be very nervous or suspicious: 左右～ look back right and left suspiciously

狼毫　lángháo　a writing brush made of weasel's hair

狼嗥　lángháo　the howl of a wolf

狼獾　lánghuān　glutton

狼藉　lángjí　(also 狼籍　lángjí)　*formal*　in disorder; scattered about in a mess: 杯盘狼藉　bēi-pán lángjí

狼贪　lángtān　greedy as a wolf; insatiably avaricious; rapacious

狼头　lángtou　same as 榔头　lángtou

狼吞虎咽　lángtūn-hǔyàn　wolf down; gobble up: 他端起

碗来，～地吃着，觉得又香又甜。He took the mess and wolfed it down, finding it sweet and good.

狼尾草 lángwěicǎo *bot.* Chinese pennisetum (*Pennisetum alopecuroides*)

狼心狗肺 lángxīn-gǒufèi rapacious as a wolf and savage as a cur; cruel and unscrupulous; brutal and cold-blooded; heartless and ungrateful

狼牙 lángyá ① wolf's fang ② *bot.* cryptotaeneous cinquefoil (*Potentilla cryptotaeniae*)

狼牙棒 lángyábàng wolf-teeth club (a club with spikes on one end and a long handle on the other, formerly used as a weapon)

狼烟 lángyān the smoke of wolves' dung burnt at border posts in ancient China to signal alarm

狼烟四起 lángyān sì qǐ smoke signals rising on all sides—war alarms raised everywhere

狼子野心 lángzǐ yěxīn a wolf cub with a savage heart —have a wolfish nature; be full of wild ambitions

廊 láng porch; corridor; veranda: 回廊 huíláng / 走廊 zǒuláng

廊庙 lángmiào *formal* imperial court
廊檐 lángyán the eaves of a veranda
廊腰 lángyāo the corner of a corridor
廊子 lángzi porch; corridor; veranda

琅(瑯) láng see below
琅玕 lánggān *liter.* a pearl-like stone
琅嬛 lánghuán *liter.* the place where the Lord of Heaven（天帝）stores his books
琅琅 lángláng *onom.* a tinkling or jingling sound; the sound of reading aloud

榔 láng see below
榔槺 láng·kāng bulky; cumbersome: 这个大铁箱太～，不便携带。This trunk is too cumbersome to carry.

榔头 lángtou hammer

锒 láng see below
锒铛 lángdāng ① *formal* iron chains ② *onom.* a clanking or clanging sound: 铁索～ iron chains clanking
锒铛入狱 lángdāng rùyù be put in chains and thrown into prison

锒 láng see below
锒头 lángtou hammer

螂(蜋) láng see 螳螂 tángláng; 蜣螂 qiāngláng; 蟑螂 zhāngláng; 屹螂 gèláng

lǎng

朗 lǎng ① light; bright: 晴朗 qínglǎng ② loud and clear: 朗诵 lǎngsòng
朗读 lǎngdú read aloud; read loudly and clearly
朗朗 lǎnglǎng *onom.* the sound of reading aloud: 书声～ reading aloud in a clear voice
朗姆酒 lǎngmǔjiǔ rum (a transliteration)
朗声 lǎngshēng in a clear loud voice: ～大笑 laugh loudly
朗爽 lǎngshuǎng hearty: ～的笑声 hearty laughter
朗诵 lǎngsòng read aloud with expression; recite; declaim: ～诗歌 recite poems

làng

郎 làng see 屎壳郎 shǐkelàng ——see also láng

浪 làng ① wave; billow; breaker: ～很大。The waves are very high. / 白～滔天 white breakers leaping skywards ② unrestrained; dissolute: 放浪 fànglàng ③ *dial.* stroll; roam

浪潮 làngcháo (fig.) tide; wave: 革命的～ the tide of revolution / 罢工～ a wave of strikes
浪船 làngchuán swingboat
浪荡 làngdàng ① loiter about; loaf about ② dissolute; dissipated
浪费 làngfèi waste; squander; be extravagant: ～时间 waste time; fritter away one's time / ～人力物力 waste manpower and material resources / 你太～了。You are too extravagant. / 你这样花钱是～。Spending money as you do is a waste. / 反对～，提倡节约 combat waste and encourage economy
浪花 lànghuā ① the foam of breaking waves: ～四溅 the waves breaking and foaming ② episodes in one's life: 生活的～ life's little episodes
浪迹 làngjì wander about; roam about: ～江湖 wander from place to place / ～天涯 rove all over the world
浪漫 làngmàn ① romantic:《梁山伯与祝英台》是个很～的爱情故事。Liang Shanbo and Zhu Yingtai is a very romantic love story. ② unconventional; bohemian; loose: 她的生活很～。She leads a loose life.
浪漫史 làngmànshǐ romance: 他们俩的～在中学时代就开始了。Their romance began in middle school.
浪漫主义 làngmànzhǔyì romanticism: ～作家(诗人) a romantic writer (poet) / ～诗歌 romantic poetry / 李白的诗篇～色彩浓厚。Li Bai's poetry contains a strong element of romanticism.
浪漫主义运动 Làngmànzhǔyì Yùndòng the Romantic Movement (in western Europe in the early 19th century)
浪木 làngmù swing log (used for physical exercise)
浪桥 làngqiáo same as 浪木 làngmù
浪人 làngrén ① wanderer; vagrant ② ronin (in Japan)
浪头 làngtou *inf.* ① wave: 风大，～高。The wind is strong and the waves are high. ② trend: 赶浪头 gǎn làngtou
浪涌 làngyǒng *elec.* surge: ～放电器 surge arrester
浪游 làngyóu travel about without any definite destination: ～四方 travel from place to place
浪语 làngyǔ ① obscene words; lewd talk ② nonsensical talk; nonsense; rubbish ③ make irresponsible remarks; gossip
浪子 làngzǐ prodigal; loafer; wastrel
浪子回头 làngzǐ huítóu return of the prodigal son: ～金不换。A prodigal who returns is more precious than gold.

莨 làng see below ——see also liáng
莨菪 làngdàng *bot.* (black) henbane

垠 làng see 圹垠 kuànglàng

lāo

捞(撈) lāo ① scoop up from a liquid; dredge up; fish for; drag for: ～鱼 fish with a net; net

fish / 在河里～水草 dredge up water plants from the river / 他在水里～什么? What is he fishing for in the water? / 把面～出来。 Take the noodles out of the water. / ② get by improper means: ～外快 make extra money / 他～了一大笔钱。 He made a killing. / 他一分钱也没～着。 He didn't make a single penny. / 他们能从这里～到什么好处呢? What good can they get out of this?

捞本 lāoběn win back lost wagers; recoup one's losses; recoup oneself

捞稻草 lāo dàocǎo (try to) take advantage of sth.; (try to) make capital of sth.: 休想在这件事上～。 Don't imagine you can get anything out of it. / 捞救命稻草 clutch at a straw

捞饭 lāofàn rice boiled, strained and then steamed

捞摸 lāomo inf. feel about in water—try to gain some unfair advantage

捞钱 lāoqián make money (by quick or improper means)

捞取 lāoqǔ ① scoop up from a liquid ② fish for; gain: ～政治资本 fish for political capital; seek political advantage

捞一把 lāo yībǎ reap some profit; gain some advantage

捞油水 lāo yóushui derog. make a side profit; get a squeeze

捞着 lāozháo get the opportunity (of doing sth.): 那天的电影, 我没～看。 I missed the film the other day.

láo

牢 láo ① formal an enclosure for animals; pen; fold: 豕～ pigpen ② arch. sacrificial animal: 太～ sacrificial ox ③ prison; jail: 坐牢 zuòláo ④ firm; fast; durable: 绳子没系～。 The rope hasn't been tied fast.

牢不可破 láo bùkě pò unbreakable; indestructible: ～的友谊 unbreakable friendship

牢房 láofáng prison cell

牢固 láogù firm; secure: 地基很～。 The foundations are very firm.

牢记 láojì keep firmly in mind; remember well: 老师的教导我～在心。 I always bear in mind my teacher's instructions.

牢监 láojiān prison; jail

牢靠 láokao ① firm; strong; sturdy: 这堵墙不太～。 This wall is not very strong. ② dependable; reliable: 办事～ dependable (or reliable) in handling matters

牢牢 láoláo firmly; safely: 这一点你必须～记住。 You must keep this firmly in mind. / 政权～掌握在人民手里。 Power rests firmly in the hands of the people.

牢笼 láolóng ① cage (fig.); bonds: 冲破旧思想的～ shake off the bonds of old ideas ② trap; snare: 陷入～ fall into a trap; be entrapped ③ entrap; ensnare ④ confine; restrain: 为旧思想所～ be shackled by old ideas

牢骚 láo·sāo ① complaint; grumble: 他老发～。 He's always grumbling. ② complain; grumble: 他～了半天。 He grumbled for a long time. / ～太盛防肠断, 风物长宜放眼量。 (毛泽东) Beware of heartbreak with grievance overfull, Range far your eye over long vistas.

牢什子 láoshízi same as 劳什子 láoshízi

牢实 láo·shí firm and solid; secure and steady: 基础～ a firm and secure foundation

牢头 láotóu old jailer

牢稳 láowěn safe; reliable: 重要文件放在保险柜里比较～。 It's safer to keep important papers in a strongbox.

牢稳 láowen (of objects) stable; secure; firm: 梯子靠这儿比较～。 The ladder will be more secure here.

牢狱 láoyù prison; jail

劳(勞) láo ① work; labour: 操劳 cāoláo ② pol. (used in asking a favour of sb.) put sb. to the trouble of: ～你帮个忙。 Will you please do me a favour (or give me a hand)? ③ fatigue; toil: 积劳成疾 jī láo chéng jí ④ meritorious deed; service: 汗马之～ distinctions won in battle; war exploits ⑤ express one's appreciation (to the performer of a task); reward: 犒劳 kào·láo ⑥ (Láo) a surname

劳保 láobǎo ① (short for 劳动保险) labour insurance: 吃～ live on labour insurance allowances ② (short for 劳动保护) labour safety: ～设施 labour safety devices

劳步 láobù pol. thanks for coming

劳瘁 láocuì formal exhausted from excessive work; worn-out: 不辞～ not mind hard work

劳动 láodòng ① work; labour: ～创造世界。 Labour creates the world. / 大家的～热情很高。 Everyone worked with great enthusiasm. ② physical labour; manual labour: ～锻炼 temper oneself through manual labour ③ do physical labour: 他～去了。 He's gone out to do physical labour.

劳动 láodong pol. cause sb. trouble (by asking a favour): ～您跑一趟。 May I trouble you to make a trip? / 不敢～您的大驾。 I don't dare to trouble you.

劳动保护 láodòng bǎohù labour safety: ～设施 labour safety devices

劳动保险 láodòng bǎoxiǎn labour insurance: ～条例 labour insurance regulations

劳动布 láodòngbù denim

劳动定额 láodòng dìng'é work norm; production quota

劳动对象 láodòng duìxiàng subject of labour

劳动法 láodòngfǎ labour law

劳动改造 láodòng gǎizào reform (of criminals) through labour

劳动观点 láodòng guāndiǎn labour viewpoint (i.e. to view labour, esp. manual labour, with respect); attitude towards labour: 树立～ form a correct attitude towards labour / 增强～ improve one's attitude towards labour

劳动号子 láodòng hàozi work song (sung to synchronize movements with one person leading)

劳动化 láodònghuà (of intellectuals) integrate oneself with the working people

劳动教养 láodòng jiàoyǎng reeducation (of juvenile delinquents, etc.) through labour

劳动节 Láodòngjié Labour Day (May 1)

劳动竞赛 láodòng jìngsài labour emulation; emulation drive; emulation campaign: 开展～ start a labour emulation campaign

劳动力 láodònglì ① labour (or work) force; labour: ～调配 allocation of the labour force / ～不足 short of manpower; shorthanded ② capacity for physical labour: 丧失～ lose one's ability to work; be rendered unfit for physical labour; be incapacitated; be disabled ③ able-bodied person: 强劳动力 qiáng láodònglì

劳动密集型 láodòng mìjíxíng labour-intensive: ～产品 labour-intensive products

劳动模范 láodòng mófàn model worker

劳动强度 láodòng qiángdù labour intensity

劳动权 láodòngquán the right to work

劳动人民 láodòng rénmín labouring people; working people

劳动日 láodòngrì workday; working day

劳动生产率 láodòng shēngchǎnlǜ labour productivity; productivity

劳动手段 láodòng shǒuduàn means (or instruments) of labour

劳动英雄 láodòng yīngxióng labour hero

劳动者 láodòngzhě labourer; worker

劳动资料 láodòng zīliào means (or instruments) of labour

劳顿 láodùn *formal* fatigued; wearied: 旅途～ fatigued by a journey; travel-worn

劳而无功 láo ér wú gōng work hard but to no avail; work fruitlessly

劳乏 láofá tired; weary

劳方 láofāng labour (as opposed to capital or management): ～与资方 labour and capital

劳改 láogǎi short for 劳动改造 láodòng gǎizào

劳改队 láogǎiduì a group sentenced to reform through labour

劳改犯 láogǎifàn a prisoner serving a sentence of reform through labour

劳改农场 láogǎi nóngchǎng reform-through-labour farm

劳工 láogōng *old* labourer; worker: ～运动 labour movement

劳绩 láojì merits and accomplishments

劳驾 láojià *pol.* excuse me; may I trouble you...; would you please... : ～，把那本书递给我。 May I trouble you to pass that book, please? / ～替我捎个信儿。 Would you mind taking a message for me? / 劳您驾，替我写封信吧! Would you be kind enough to write a letter for me? / ～，挪挪窝儿行吗? Excuse me, would you move over a bit? / ～，请让让路。 Excuse me.

劳教 láojiào short for 劳动教养 láodòng jiàoyǎng

劳教人员 láojiào rényuán a person subjected to reeducation in a reform school

劳金 láojīn *old* money given for work; pay

劳军 láojūn take greetings and gifts to army units

劳苦 láokǔ toil; hard work: 不辞～ spare no pains / ～大众 toiling masses; labouring people

劳苦功高 láokǔ gōng gāo have worked hard and performed a valuable service

劳累 láolèi tired; run-down; overworked

劳力 láolì ① labour; labour force: ～可能紧张一些，但我们一定努力完成任务。 We may be a little short of labour, but we'll do our best to fulfil the task. / 合理安排～ rational allocation of labour ② labour with one's strength; work with one's brawn

劳碌 láolù work hard; toil: 母亲操持家务，～一生。 My mother worked hard as a housewife all her life. / 家庭妇女大都是个～命。 Most housewives are condemned to a life of hard toil.

劳民伤财 láomín-shāngcái exhaust the people and drain the treasury; waste money and manpower

劳模 láomó short for 劳动模范 láodòng mófàn

劳伤 láoshāng *Chin. med.* internal lesion caused by overexertion

劳神 láoshén be a tax on (one's mind); bother; trouble: 你现在身体不好，不要过于～。 You're in poor health, so don't overtax yourself. / ～替我照顾一下孩子。 (a polite request) Please keep an eye on my child.

劳师 láoshī *formal* take greetings and gifts to army units

劳师动众 láoshī-dòngzhòng mobilize too many troops—drag in lots of people (to do sth.)

劳师远征 láoshī yuǎnzhēng tire the troops on a long expedition

劳什子 láoshízi *dial.* nuisance

劳损 láosǔn *med.* strain: 肌腱～ muscular strain

劳务 láowù labour services: ～输出 export of labour services / ～费 service charge / ～人员 contract workers (sent abroad) / ～合作 labour cooperation

劳心 láoxīn work with one's mind or brains

劳心者治人,劳力者治于人 láoxīnzhě zhì rén, láolìzhě zhìyú rén those who work with their brains rule and those who work with their brawn are ruled

劳燕分飞 láo-yàn fēn fēi the shrike and the swallow flying in different directions—part from each other

劳役 láoyì ① penal servitude; forced labour ② corvée

劳役地租 láoyì dìzū rent paid in labour; labour rent

劳逸 láoyì work and rest

劳逸不均 láoyì bù jūn uneven allocation of work

劳逸结合 láoyì jiéhé strike a proper balance between work and rest; alternate work with rest and recreation

劳资 láo-zī labour and capital: ～关系 relationship between labour and capital; labour-capital relationship / ～两利 be of benefit to both labour and capital / ～纠纷 labour trouble / ～争议 labour dispute

劳作 láozuò ① (formerly a school subject) manual work ② do manual labour: 他们在田间～。 They are working in the fields.

唠(嘮) láo see below——see also lào

唠叨 láodao be garrulous; chatter: 人老了，就爱～。 As one grows old, one tends to be garrulous. / 唠唠叨叨说个不停 chatter interminably

崂(嶗) Láo used in 崂山 (also written 劳山, a mountain in Shandong Province)

痨(癆) láo consumptive disease; tuberculosis; consumption: 肺痨 fèiláo

痨病 láobìng *Chin. med.* tuberculosis; TB

铹(鐒) láo *chem.* lawrencium (Lw)

醪 láo *formal* ① wine with dregs; undecanted wine ② mellow wine

醪糟 láozāo fermented glutinous rice

lǎo

老 lǎo ① old (not young): ～妇人 an old woman / ～马 an old horse / ～树 an old tree / 他父亲很～了。 His father is very old. / 我～了,走路走不快了。 I'm getting old and can't walk very fast. / 他六十多岁了,可是一点也不显～。 He's over sixty, but he doesn't look old at all. ② old people; a venerable old man: 敬～ show respect for the aged / 徐～ our revered Comrade Xu ③ *inf. euph.* (followed by 了; usu. of an old person) pass away; die: 隔壁前天～了人了。 One of our next-door neighbours (presumably an old person) died the day before yesterday. ④ experienced; veteran: ～作家 a veteran writer ⑤ old (not new): ～朋友 an old friend / ～部下 a former subordinate / ～机器 an old machine / ～地方 the same old place / ～习惯 an old habit / 一首～歌 an old song / 这种纸烟牌子很～了。 This is a very old brand of cigarettes. / 这所房子太～了。 This house is too old. ⑥ (of vegetables) overgrown: 菠菜不收就～了。 The spinach will be overgrown if we don't get it in now. ⑦ (of food) tough; overdone; well-done: 牛肉太～。 The beef is too tough. / 我喜欢吃～一点的牛排。 I like steak quite well-done. / 鸡蛋煮～了。 The eggs have been boiled hard. / 青菜不要炒得太～。 Don't overcook the greens. ⑧ (of certain colours) dark: ～绿(红) dark green (red) / 这件上衣颜色太～了。 This jacket is too dark. ⑨ *adv.* for a long time: ～没见你啊。 I haven't seen you for ages. / 这屋子～不住人,有股霉味儿。 This room has been left vacant for a long time, so there is a mouldy smell. ⑩ *adv.* always; all the time: 他～跟我借钱。 He's always borrowing money from me. / 他～那么干。 He does it all the time. ⑪ *adv.* very: ～早 very early / ～远 far

away / ～长的胡子 a very long beard / 太阳已经～高了。 The sun is already high. ⑫ *inf.* last born; youngest: ～闺女 the youngest daughter / ～儿子 the youngest son ⑬ (used as a prefix) ⓐ (in terms of address before the surnames of acquaintances or friends to indicate intimacy or informality): ～王 Lao Wang / ～李 Lao Li ⓑ (in kinship terms before numerals to indicate order of seniority): ～大 number one (among sons, daughters, brothers, or sisters) / ～二 number two / ～三 number three / ～幺 the youngest ⓒ (in certain names of animals and plants): 老虎 lǎohǔ / 老玉米 lǎoyùmi ⑭ (Lǎo) a surname

老八板儿 lǎobābǎnr *dial.* ① conservative ② diehard

老八辈子 lǎobābèizi old-fashioned; outdated: 这是～的话了，没人听了。 Such ideas are outdated, and no one would take them seriously.

老百姓 lǎobǎixìng *inf.* common people; ordinary people; civilians: 这些活报剧～很欢迎。 These skits are popular with the man in the street. / 既当官又当～ remain one of the common people while serving as an official

老板 lǎobǎn (also 老闆 lǎobǎn) shopkeeper; proprietor; boss

老板娘 lǎobǎnniáng shopkeeper's wife; proprietress

老半天 lǎobàntiān *inf.* a long time: 我等你～了。 I've been waiting for you for an awfully long time.

老伴儿 lǎobànr *inf.* (of an old married couple) husband or wife: 我的～ my old man or woman

老蚌生珠 lǎo bàng shēng zhū an old oyster yielding a pearl——have a son born in one's old age

老鸨 lǎobǎo (also 老鸨子 lǎobǎozi) a woman running a brothel; procuress; madam

老辈 lǎobèi one's elders; old folks

老本 lǎoběn principal; capital: 把～输光 lose one's last stakes ——see also 吃老本 chī lǎoběn

老鼻子 lǎobízi *dial.* (followed by 了) an awful lot: 昨天游园的人可～了。 There were an awful lot of people in the park yesterday.

老表 lǎobiǎo ① a male cousin (on the maternal side or on the paternal aunt's side) ② *dial.* a polite form of address to a male stranger

老兵 lǎobīng old soldier; army veteran

老病 lǎobìng ① chronic illness; old trouble ② old and sick; ageing and declining: 名岂文章著, 官应～休。(杜甫) How should I look for fame to what I have written? In age and sickness, how continue to serve?

老伯 lǎobó uncle (used in addressing a friend of one's father or the father of one's friend)

老伯伯 lǎobóbo *honor.* granddad

老布 lǎobù *dial.* handwoven (*or* handloomed) cloth; homespun cloth

老财 lǎocái *dial.* moneybags; landlord: 地主～ landlord

老巢 lǎocháo nest; den; lair: 直捣土匪～ swoop down on the bandits' den

老成 lǎochéng experienced; steady

老成持重 lǎochéng chízhòng experienced and prudent: 他～, 不大随便发表意见。 He was experienced and reserved and did not give his views on anything without due thought.

老成凋谢 lǎochéng diāoxiè a grand old man has passed away

老处女 lǎochǔnǚ old maid; spinster

老粗 lǎocū (often used in self-deprecation) an uneducated person; a rough and ready chap

老搭档 lǎodādàng old partner; old workmate

老大 lǎodà ① *formal* old (in age): 少小离家～回, 乡音无改鬓毛衰。(贺知章) I left home young. I return old, Speaking as then, but with hair grown thin. ②

number one (in order of seniority, i.e. the eldest son, daughter, brother, or sister) ③ *dial.* the captain of a boat ④ *adv.* greatly; very: 心里～不高兴 feel very annoyed

老大不小 lǎodàbùxiǎo have grown up and be no longer a child: 你也～的了，该懂点事了。 You are no longer a child and should show some sense.

老大哥 lǎodàgē elder brother (a respectful form of address for a man older than oneself)

老大姐 lǎodàjiě elder sister (a respectful form of address for a woman older than oneself)

老大难 lǎo-dà-nán long-standing, big and difficult (problem): ～单位 a unit with serious and long-standing problems / ～的技术问题 a knotty technical problem of long standing

老大娘 lǎodàniáng *inf.* (a polite form of address to an old woman, esp. a stranger) aunty; granny

老大爷 lǎodàye *inf.* (a polite form of address to an old man, esp. a stranger) uncle; grandpa

老旦 lǎodàn the role of an old woman in traditional opera

老当益壮 lǎo dāng yì zhuàng old but vigorous

老道 lǎodào *inf.* Taoist priest

老到 lǎodao *dial.* experienced; mature

老等 lǎoděng ① wait for a long time: 你快去吧，别让她在那儿～。 You'd better hurry up and not keep her waiting. ② *inf.* heron

老底 lǎodǐ sb.'s past; sb.'s unsavoury background: 揭～ dredge up some embarrassing facts about sb.'s past; drag the skeleton out of sb.'s closet

老弟 lǎodì (a familiar form of address to a man much younger than oneself) young man; young fellow; my boy

老叼 lǎodiāo *inf.* crane (a machine)

老调 lǎodiào hackneyed theme; platitude

老调重弹 lǎodiào chóng tán harp on the same string; play the same old tune

老掉牙 lǎodiàoyá very old; out of date; obsolete; antediluvian: 这部机器已经～了。 This machine is completely obsolete.

老东西 lǎodōngxi *offens.* old silly thing; old fool

老豆腐 lǎodòufu processed bean curd

老而弥笃 lǎo ér mí dǔ the older one gets, the deeper one's love

老佛爷 lǎofóye ① old Buddha (popular name for Buddha) ② (in Manchu usage) a title of respect for the queen mother or the emperor's father

老夫 lǎofū *old* I (used by an old man)

老夫子 lǎofūzǐ a bookish man

老赶 lǎogǎn *dial.* ① inexperienced in the ways of the world; green; raw: 你怎么这么～，连这个也不懂 How can you be so green as to know nothing about such things? ② greenhorn; fool; blockhead: 你拿我当～? Do you take me for a fool?

老干部 lǎogànbù veteran cadre

老疙瘩 lǎogēda *dial.* one's youngest child: 她是我们家的～。 She's the baby of our family.

老哥 lǎogē (a term of address used among friends) my elder brother

老公 lǎogōng *dial.* husband

老公 lǎogong *inf.* eunuch

老公公 lǎogōnggong *dial.* ① grandpa (used by children in addressing an old man) ② husband's father; father-in-law

老古董 lǎogǔdǒng old fogey; fuddy-duddy

老骨头 lǎogútou *inf.* old bones——an old person's physical condition; an old person (used disrespectfully or jocularly)

老鸹 lǎo·guā *inf.* crow

老光 lǎoguāng presbyopic: ～眼 presbyopia / ～眼镜 presbyopic glasses

老规矩 lǎoguīju old rules and regulations; convention; established custom or practice: 时代变了, 那一套～不行了。 Times have changed, and the old way of doing things is no good any more. / 照～办事 do things in the same old way

老憨 lǎohān old fogey

老汉 lǎohàn ① old man ② I (used by an old man)

老好人 lǎohǎorén inf. a benign and uncontentious person who is indifferent to matters of principle; one who tries never to offend anybody

老狐狸 lǎohúli old fox; crafty scoundrel

老虎 lǎohǔ tiger

老虎凳 lǎohǔdèng rack (an instrument of torture)

老虎屁股摸不得 lǎohǔ pìgu mōbude like a tiger whose backside no one dares to touch—not to be provoked

老虎钳 lǎohǔqián ① vise ② pincer pliers

老虎头上蹭痒 lǎohǔ tóushang cèng yǎng scratch oneself against a tiger's head—court disaster

老花 lǎohuā presbyopic

老花镜 lǎohuājìng presbyopic glasses

老花眼 lǎohuāyǎn presbyopia

老化 lǎohuà ① chem. ageing ② (of cadres) become old: 干部～问题 the problem of cadres becoming old and losing efficiency ③ (of knowledge, etc.) become outdated

老话 lǎohuà ① old saying; saying; adage: 中国有句～: 世上无难事, 只怕有心人。 There is an old Chinese saying: nothing in the world is difficult for one who sets his mind on it. ② remarks about the old days: 咱们谈的这些～, 年轻人都不大明白了。 What we are saying about the old days is incomprehensible to young people.

老皇历 lǎohuánglì last year's calendar—ancient history; obsolete practice

老黄牛 lǎohuángniú willing ox—a person who is diligent and conscientious in serving the people

老火 lǎohuǒ dial. ① serious; critical ② difficult to do; tough

老鸡头 lǎojītóu another name for 鸡头 jītóu

老几 lǎojǐ ① order of seniority among brothers or sisters: 你是～? Where do you come in the family? or Are you the oldest, the second or what? ② (used in rhetorical questions to express disparagement): 你算～? Who do you think you are? / 我算～? Who am I? or I'm a nobody.

老骥伏枥, 志在千里 lǎojì fú lì, zhì zài qiānlǐ an old steed in the stable still aspires to gallop a thousand li—an old hero still cherishes high aspirations

老家 lǎojiā native place; old home: 我～在山东。 My old home is in Shandong. ——see also 回老家 huí lǎojiā

老奸巨滑 lǎojiān-jùhuá a past master of machination and manoeuvre; a crafty old scoundrel; a wily old fox; an old hand at trickery and deception

老茧 lǎojiǎn (also 老趼 lǎojiǎn) callosity; callus

老江湖 lǎojiānghu old a well-travelled, worldly-wise person; a person who has seen much of the world

老将 lǎojiàng veteran; old-timer

老将出马, 一个顶俩 lǎojiàng chūmǎ, yīge dǐng liǎ when a veteran goes into action, he can do the job of two

老交情 lǎojiāoqing long-standing friendship; an old friend

老街坊 lǎojiēfang inf. old neighbour

老街旧邻 lǎojiē-jiùlín inf. old neighbour

老解放区 lǎojiěfàngqū old liberated area

老景 lǎojǐng life and circumstances in old age: ～堪怜 have a miserable old age

老境 lǎojìng ① old age: 渐入～ be getting on in years ② life and circumstances in old age: ～凄凉 have a neglected old age

老酒 lǎojiǔ dial. wine (esp. Shaoxing rice wine)

老辣 lǎolà shrewd and ruthless

老来俏 lǎoláiqiào inf. an elderly woman who tries to make herself attractive

老来少 lǎoláishào ① an old person having a young heart; a person old in age but young in spirit ② dial. tricolour amaranth

老老实实 lǎolǎoshíshí honestly; conscientiously; in earnest: 我们应该是～地办事; 在世界上要办成几件事, 没有老实态度是根本不行的。 We should do things honestly, for without an honest attitude it is absolutely impossible to accomplish anything in this world. / 我们必须拜他们做老师, 恭恭敬敬地学, ～地学。 We must learn from them respectfully and conscientiously, esteeming them as teachers. / 马克思列宁主义是科学, 科学是～的学问, 任何一点调皮都是不行的。 Marxism-Leninism is a science, and science means honest, solid knowledge; it permits no playing of tricks.

老老 lǎolao same as 姥姥 lǎolao

老泪纵横 lǎolèi zònghéng (of an old person) be in tears

老例 lǎolì old practice; old custom

老脸 lǎoliǎn ① old face (used by an old person in speaking of his dignity or self-respect): 你叫我这～往哪儿搁? How could I ever face people again? ② a thick-skinned person

老脸皮 lǎoliǎnpí a thick-skinned person

老练 lǎoliàn seasoned; experienced: 他比起过去来已经～得多了。 He's much more experienced and capable now than before. / 她办事很～。 She is experienced and works with a sure hand.

老林 lǎolín virgin forest

老伶工 lǎolínggōng old old skilled actor

老路 lǎolù old road; beaten track: 咱们还是走那条～回家吧。 Let's go home the usual way. / 走～ follow the beaten track; slip back into the old rut

老妈子 lǎomāzi (also 老妈儿 lǎomār) old amah; maidservant

老马识途 lǎomǎ shí tú an old horse knows the way; an old hand is a good guide

老迈 lǎomài aged; senile

老毛病 lǎomáobing inf. old trouble; old weakness: 我有个～, 一到冬天就咳。 My cough is an old trouble. I get it every winter. / 粗心大意是他的～。 Carelessness is an old weakness of his.

老耄 lǎomào formal senile; decrepit

老米 lǎomǐ old, stale rice

老面皮 lǎomiànpí same as 老脸皮 lǎoliǎnpí

老谋深算 lǎomóu-shēnsuàn circumspect and far-seeing; experienced and astute

老衲 lǎonà formal old monk

老奶奶 lǎonǎinai ① paternal great grandmother ② old granny (used by children in addressing an old woman)

老脑筋 lǎonǎojin old (or outmoded) way of thinking: 你这～也该换换了。 It's high time you got rid of your old way of thinking.

老年 lǎonián old age

老年人 lǎoniánrén old people; the old; the aged

老年学 lǎoniánxué gerontology

老年医学 lǎoniányīxué geriatrics

老年间 lǎoniánjiān former times; ancient times

老娘 lǎoniáng ① old mother ② I, your old mother (used by a harridan to refer to herself)

老娘 lǎoniang old inf. ① midwife ② dial. maternal grandmother

老娘们儿 lǎoniángmenr dial. ① a married woman ②

derog. woman ③ wife

老牛破车 lǎoniú-pòchē an old ox pulling a rickety cart —making slow progress

老牛舐犊 lǎoniú shì dú an old cow licking her calf—a parent doting on his or her child

老农 lǎonóng old farmer; experienced peasant

老牌 lǎopái old brand: ～帝国主义 old-line imperialism / ～特务 an old hand at espionage

老派 lǎopài ① old-fashioned; conservative ② an old-fashioned person; conservative

老婆婆 lǎopópo *dial.* ① granny (used by children in addressing an old woman) ② husband's mother; mother-in-law

老婆儿 lǎopór old woman (with overtones of intimacy)

老婆子 lǎopózi ① old biddy ② my old woman

老婆 lǎopo *inf.* wife

老圃 lǎopǔ *formal* expert vegetable grower

老气 lǎoqì ① mature and steady: 他年纪虽小却很～。He's old for his years. ② (of clothes) dark and old-fashioned

老气横秋 lǎoqì héngqiū ① arrogant on account of one's seniority ② lacking in youthful vigour

老前辈 lǎoqiánbèi one's senior; one's elder: 革命～ a veteran of the revolution

老枪 lǎoqiāng an inveterate smoker (esp. an opium smoker)

老亲 lǎoqīn ① old parents ② old relatives: ～旧邻 old relatives and neighbours

老区 lǎoqū short for 老解放区 lǎojiěfàngqū

老拳 lǎoquán fist (as used in hitting sb.): 饱以老拳 bǎo yǐ lǎoquán

老人 lǎo·rén ① old man or woman; the aged; the old ② one's aged parents or grandparents

老人斑 lǎorénbān (also 老年斑 lǎoniánbān) senile plaque

老人星 Lǎorénxīng Canopus

老人政治 lǎorén zhèngzhì gerontocracy

老人家 lǎorenjia *inf.* ① a respectful form of address to an old person: 您～今年多大年纪了？How old are you, granddad (*or* grandma)? ② parent: ～都好吗?How are your parents?

老弱 lǎo-ruò ① the old and the young ② the old and the weak

老弱病残 lǎo-ruò-bìng-cán the old, weak, sick and disabled

老弱残兵 lǎoruò-cánbīng old, weak and wounded troops; those who on account of old age, illness, etc. are no longer active or efficient

老少 lǎo-shào old and young: 这种杂志～咸宜。This magazine suits the taste of both old and young.

老少爷们 lǎoshàoyémen *dial.* elders and brethren

老身 lǎoshēn *old* I (used by an old woman)

老生 lǎoshēng one of the main divisions of the male role in traditional opera (the *laosheng* actor is always bearded and represents a man of maturity and integrity, e.g. a middle-aged scholar, a magistrate, a statesman, etc.)

老生常谈 lǎoshēng chángtán commonplace; platitude; truism

老师 lǎoshī teacher (sometimes used as a form of address)

老师傅 lǎoshīfu master craftsman; experienced worker

老实 lǎoshi ① honest; frank: 做～人, 说～话, 办～事 be an honest person, honest in word and honest in deed / ～说, 我很不赞成这个意见。To be frank, I don't like the idea at all. / ～回答我的问题。Give me a straight answer. / ～交待 come clean; own up; make a clean breast of ② well-behaved; good: 放～点! Behave your-

self! *or* None of your tricks! / 这孩子可～了。The child is as good as gold. ③ *euph.* simpleminded; naive; easily taken in

老实巴交 lǎoshibājiāo *dial.* soft-spoken and timid

老式 lǎoshì old style: ～家具 old-fashioned furniture

老是 lǎoshì *adv.* always; all the time: 他～犯错误。He is always making mistakes.

老视眼 lǎoshìyǎn presbyopia

老手 lǎoshǒu old hand; old stager; veteran: 干这一行他是～。He is an old hand at the trade. / 谈判～ veteran negotiator

老鼠 lǎo·shǔ mouse; rat

老鼠过街, 人人喊打 lǎo·shǔ guò jiē, rénrén hǎn dǎ a rat running across the street, with everybody shouting, "Kill it!" (said of a person or thing hated by everyone)

老死不相往来 lǎo sǐ bù xiāng wǎnglái grow old and die without having had any dealings with each other—never be in contact with each other

老宋体 lǎosòngtǐ same as 宋体字 sòngtǐzì (opp. 仿宋体 fǎngsòngtǐ)

老太婆 lǎotàipó old woman

老太太 lǎotàitai ① old lady; (in direct address) Venerable Madam ② (a polite term) your mother; his mother; my mother or grandmother

老太爷 lǎotàiyé ① elderly gentleman; (in direct address) Venerable Sir ② (a polite term) your father; his father; my father or grandfather

老态龙钟 lǎotài lóngzhōng senile; doddering

老饕 lǎotāo *formal* voracious eater; glutton; gourmand

老套 lǎotào old stuff; old ways: 报纸要办得生动, 切忌死板～。A newspaper should be lively and should avoid hackneyed stuff.

老套子 lǎotàozi out-of-date practices; outmoded ways of doing things

老天爷 lǎotiānyé (used in exclamations) God; Heavens: 我的～! My goodness! *or* Good Heavens! *or* Good Gracious!

老头儿 lǎotóur old man; old chap

老头儿鱼 lǎotóuryú popular name for 鮟鱇 ānkāng

老头子 lǎotóuzi ① old fogey; old codger ② my old man

老外 lǎowài *inf.* ① layman ② foreigner

老顽固 lǎowán·gù old stick-in-the-mud; old diehard; old fogey

老王卖瓜, 自卖自夸 Lǎo Wáng mài guā, zì mài zì kuā Lao Wang selling melons praises his own goods —praise one's own work or wares

老翁 lǎowēng *formal* old man; greybeard

老挝 Lǎowō Laos

老挝人 Lǎowōrén Laotian

老挝语 Lǎowōyǔ Laotian (language)

老倭瓜 lǎowōgua *dial.* pumpkin

老乡 lǎoxiāng ① fellow-townsman; fellow-villager ② a friendly form of address to a man in the countryside

老相 lǎo·xiàng looking older than one's age

老小 lǎo·xiǎo grown-ups and children; one's family: 全村～ the whole village, old and young / 一家～ the whole family

老兄 lǎoxiōng (a familiar form of address between male friends) brother; man; old chap

老羞成怒 lǎo xiū chéng nù fly into a rage out of shame; be shamed into anger

老朽 lǎoxiǔ ① decrepit and behind the times; 昏庸～ old and stupid / ～无能 old and useless ② *hum.* I (used by an old man)

老学究 lǎoxuéjiū old pedant

老鸦 lǎoyā *dial.* crow

老腌瓜 lǎoyānguā *dial.* snake melon

老眼光 lǎoyǎnguāng　old ways of looking at things; old views: 不能以～看新事物。One mustn't judge new things by old standards. / 你这是拿～看人，他跟以前不一样了。You are judging him by what he used to be. He's changed.

老眼昏花 lǎoyǎn hūnhuā　dim-sighted from old age

老爷儿 lǎoyér　*dial.*　the sun

老爷们儿 lǎoyémenr　*dial.*　① man ② husband

老爷爷 lǎoyéye　① great grandfather ② grandpa (used by children in addressing an old man)

老爷子 lǎoyézi　*dial.*　① a polite form of address to an old man ② my (old) father; your (old) father

老爷 lǎoye　① master; bureaucrat; lord: 做官当～ act as lords and masters / 采取～式的态度 adopt a bureaucratic attitude ② *old* a respectful address to a master by a servant ③ same as 姥爷 lǎoye

老爷兵 lǎoyebīng　pampered soldier

老一辈 lǎoyībèi　older generation: ～无产阶级革命家 proletarian revolutionaries of the older generation; veteran proletarian revolutionaries

老一套 lǎoyītào　the same old stuff; the same old story: 他们的所谓新建议无非是～。Their so-called new proposal is nothing but the same old stuff. / 改变～的做法 change outmoded methods

老鹰 lǎoyīng　black-eared kite; hawk; eagle

老油条 lǎoyóutiáo　same as 老油子 lǎoyóuzi

老油子 lǎoyóuzi　wily old bird; old campaigner

老于世故 lǎoyú shìgù　versed in the ways of the world; worldly-wise

老玉米 lǎoyùmi　*inf.*　① maize; Indian corn; corn ② ear of maize (or corn)

老妪 lǎoyù　*formal*　old woman

老妪能解 lǎoyù néng jiě　(of writing) intelligible to old women—easy to understand

老丈 lǎozhàng　*formal*　old gentleman

老丈人 lǎozhàngren　father-in-law

老帐 lǎozhàng　old debts; long-standing debts: ～未清又欠新帐。While old debts are still unpaid, new ones are incurred.——see also 翻老帐 fān lǎozhàng

老者 lǎozhě　old man

老着脸皮 lǎozhe liǎnpí　unabashedly; unblushingly

老主顾 lǎozhǔgù　old customer; old client

老资格 lǎozīgé　old-timer; veteran: ～的外交家 a veteran diplomat / 摆～ flaunt one's seniority; put on the airs of a veteran

老子 lǎozi　*inf.*　① father: ～英雄儿好汉 the father a hero, the son a brave man; like father, like son ② I, your father (said in anger or in fun): ～不吃你这一套! I'll have none of your nonsense!

老子天下第一 lǎozi tiānxià dìyī　think oneself the most important person in the world

老字号 lǎozìhào　an old name in business —an old firm or shop

老总 lǎozǒng　① an old form of address to a soldier ② used after a surname as an affectionate form of address to a general or high-ranking commander of the PLA

老祖宗 lǎozǔzōng　ancestor; forefather

佬
　lǎo　*derog.*　man; guy; fellow: 乡巴佬儿 xiāngbālǎor

姥
　lǎo　see below ——see also mǔ

姥姥 lǎolao　① *dial.* (maternal) grandmother; grandma ② *dial.* midwife

姥爷 lǎoye　*dial.*　(maternal) grandfather; grandpa

栳
　lǎo　see 栲栳 kǎolǎo

铑
　lǎo　*chem.*　rhodium (Rh)

筶
　lǎo　see 筶筶 kǎolǎo

潦
　lǎo　*formal*　① heavy rains ② puddles on roads ——see also liáo

lào

涝(澇)
　lào　waterlogging (of land or crops): 庄稼～了。The crops were waterlogged.

涝洼地 làowādì　waterlogged lowland

涝灾 làozāi　damage or crop failure caused by waterlogging

烙
　lào　① brand; iron: 给马～上印记 brand a horse / ～衣服 iron clothes ② bake in a pan: ～两张饼 bake a couple of cakes ——see also luò

烙饼 làobǐng　a kind of pancake

烙铁 làotie　① flatiron; iron ② soldering iron

烙印 làoyìn　① brand (on cattle; often fig.): 他的作品都有鲜明的时代～。His works all bear a marked brand of the times. / 打上阶级的～ be stamped with the brand of a class ② brand (cattle; often fig.): 这个教训已经～在我的心头，永远不会忘记。This lesson is branded on my mind for ever.

唠(嘮)
　lào　*dial.*　talk; chat ——see also láo

落
　lào　same as 落 luò①②⑥⑨⑩, confined to use in the following ——see also là; luò

落儿 làor　*inf.*　(used after 有 or 没有) means of support: 有～ be well-off / 没～ be poor

落汗 làohàn　*inf.*　stop sweating: 咱们歇一会儿，等落了汗再接着干。Let's take a rest and go on with our work when we've stopped sweating.

落好儿 làohǎor　make a good impression on others; get favourable comments

落价 làojià　fall (or drop) in price; go down in price

落炕 làokàng　*dial.*　stay in bed with illness; be laid up

落色 làoshǎi　discolour; fade

落枕 làozhěn　have a stiff neck (caused by cold or an awkward sleeping posture)

落子[1] làozi　*dial.*　① a class of popular songs such as 莲花落 liánhuālào ② old name for 评剧 píngjù

落子[2] làozi　same as 落儿 làor

耢(耮)
　lào　① a kind of farm tool used to level land ② level land with this kind of tool

酪
　lào　① junket ② thick fruit juice; fruit jelly: 红果～ haw jelly ③ sweet paste made from crushed nuts; sweet nut paste: 核桃～ walnut cream

酪氨酸 lào'ānsuān　*chem.*　tyrosine

酪素 làosù　*chem.*　casein: ～胶 casein glue

酪酸 làosuān　*inf.*　butyric acid

lē

肋
　lē　see below ——see also lèi

肋脦 lēde or lēte　*dial.*　(of clothes) untidy

lè

仂 lè *formal* remainder

仂语 lèyǔ word group; phrase

乐(樂)

lè ① happy; cheerful; joyful: 我心里～开了花。My heart swelled with happiness (*or* was filled with joy). ② be glad to; find pleasure in; enjoy: 幸灾乐祸 xìngzāi-lèhuò ③ *inf.* laugh; be amused: 他说的笑话把大家逗～了。His joke amused everyone. / 你～什么呀? What are you laughing at? *or* What's the joke? ——see also yuè

乐儿 lèr same as 乐子 lèzi

乐不可支 lè bùkě zhī overwhelmed with joy; overjoyed

乐不思蜀 lè bù sī Shǔ so happy as to forget home and duty

乐此不疲 lè cǐ bù pí always enjoy it; never be bored with it: 二十年前他对编词典发生了兴趣, 从此～。He began to be interested in dictionary-making 20 years ago, and since then has worked at it gladly and never tired.

乐得 lèdé readily take the opportunity to; be only too glad to: 既然如此, 我们～在这儿多待几天。In that case, we'll be only too glad to spend a few more days here.

乐而不淫 lè ér bù yín joy without wantonness

乐观 lèguān optimistic; hopeful; sanguine: ～的看法 an optimistic view / ～的报道 a sanguine report / 对前途很～ be optimistic about the future / 事情的发展是很可～的。The prospects are very bright.

乐观主义 lèguānzhǔyì optimism: ～者 optimist

乐果 lèguǒ Rogor (an insecticide)

乐呵呵 lèhēhē buoyant; happy and gay: 他成天～的。He's always cheerful and gay.

乐和 lèhe *dial.* happy: 日子过得挺～ lead a happy life / 人们辛苦了一年, 春节的时候都愿意～～。After a hard year's work, people want to have a good time during the Spring Festival.

乐极生悲 lè jí shēng bēi extreme joy begets sorrow: ～, 否极泰来。When joy reaches its height, it is sorrow's turn; when ill luck reaches its limit, good luck comes in.

乐趣 lèqù delight; pleasure; joy: 生活中的～ joys of life / 要在工作中找到～, 得先把工作做好。Joy in work comes from mastery of work.

乐融融 lèróngróng happy and harmonious: 今年又是大丰收, 家家户户～。There is another bumper harvest this year, and every family is as happy as can be.

乐善好施 lèshàn-hàoshī be given to doing charitable work

乐事 lèshì pleasure; delight: 以助人为～ find pleasure in helping others

乐陶陶 lètáotáo *liter.* (usu. used in rhymes) cheerful; happy; joyful: 船家生活～, 赶潮撒网月儿高。Happy is the life of a boatman—Out fishing when the tide's in and the moon's high.

乐天 lètiān carefree; happy-go-lucky

乐天派 lètiānpài optimist; a happy-go-lucky person

乐天知命 lètiān-zhīmìng submit to the will of Heaven and be content with one's lot

乐土 lètǔ land of happiness; paradise: 逝将去女, 适彼～。(《诗经》) At last we are going to leave you And go to that happy land.

乐业 lèyè work in peace and contentment ——see also 安居乐业 ānjū-lèyè

乐意 lèyì ① be willing to; be ready to: ～帮忙 be willing to help ② pleased; happy: 他听了这话有点不～。

He seemed somewhat displeased with that remark.

乐于 lèyú be happy to; take delight in: ～助人 be ready to help others

乐园 lèyuán paradise; playground; amusement park: 人间～ earthly paradise; paradise on earth / 儿童～ children's playground; children's amusement park / 上海在解放前是冒险家的～。Before liberation, Shanghai was a paradise for adventurers.

乐滋滋 lèzīzī *inf.* contented; pleased: 他听了这话心里～的。He was quite pleased to hear this.

乐子 lèzi *dial.* ① fun; pleasure: 闲得没事干, 出去找个～。Since we have nothing better to do, let's go out and have some fun. ② a laughable matter: 你丢脸, 人家瞧～。You make a fool of yourself and others laugh at you.

芳

lè see 萝芳 luólè

勒[1]

lè ① rein in: ～马 rein in the horse ② force; coerce: ～交 force sb. to hand sth. over

勒[2]

lè *formal* carve; engrave: ～碑 carve on a stone tablet

勒[3]

lè short for 勒克司 lèkèsī ——see also lēi

勒逼 lèbī force; coerce: 债主～她父亲立即还债。The usurer forced her father to pay back the debt at once.

勒克司 lèkèsī *phys.* lux; metre-candle

勒令 lèlìng compel (by legal authority); order: ～交出赃物 order sb. to surrender stolen goods / ～退学 order a student to leave school

勒派 lèpài force sb. to pay levies or do corvée labour

勒索 lèsuǒ extort; blackmail: ～钱财 extort money from sb.

鳓

lè Chinese herring

le

了

le *part.* ① (used after a verb to indicate the completion of an action, at a point in the past or before the beginning of another action): 我吃～三碗饭。I ate three bowls of rice. / 水位低～两米。The water level fell by two metres. / 我教～三十年的书。I taught for 30 years. / 你先去, 我下～班就去。You go ahead. I'll go right after work. ② (used at the end of a sentence, usu. after 了 for completed action, to indicate that something has taken place): 我吃了三碗饭～。I have eaten three bowls of rice. / 我等了半天～, 他还没来。I've been waiting a long time, but he still hasn't turned up. / 我教书教了三十年～。I've been teaching for 30 years. / 我上星期从图书馆借了一本小说, 已经看了一半～。I borrowed a novel from the library last week and have already read half of it. ③ (used at the end of a sentence to indicate a change of situation or state, whether actual or envisaged): 他胖～。He's got fat. / 东西贵～。Things have gone up. *or* Things are expensive now. / 下雨～。It's raining. / 他不是我的英语老师～。He's no longer my English teacher. / 今天去不成～。We can't go today. (Before the situation had changed, we thought we could go.) / 我喝了五杯～, 不能再喝～。I have drunk five glasses and can't drink any more. / 你早来一天就见着他～。You would have seen him if you'd come a day sooner. ④ (used after an adjective, with or without 太 "too", to express an excessive degree, i.e. to indicate that something has gone to the

extreme): 这种工作太累~。This job is too fatiguing. / 他现在太老~, 不能工作了。He's too old now, he can't work any more. / 袖子长~。The sleeves are too long. / 汤咸~。The soup is too salty. ⑤ (used in commands or requests in response to a changed situation): 吃饭~! Let's eat now! / 别说话~! Stop talking! / 走~, 走~, 不能再等~! Let's go. We can't wait any longer. ——see also liǎo

㴂 le see 饸饹 héle

lēi

勒 lēi tie or strap sth. tight: 带子太松了, 再~一~。The strap is too loose. Tighten it up a bit. / 背包带太紧, ~得慌。The pack straps are too tight. They cut into the flesh. / ~紧裤带 tighten the belt ——see also lè

勒脚 lēijiǎo *archit.* plinth
勒掯 lēikèn *dial.* force sb. to do sth.; make things difficult for sb.

léi

累(纍) léi see below ——see also lěi; lèi
累累[1] léiléi *formal* haggard; gaunt: ~若丧家之狗 wretched as a stray cur ——see also lěiléi
累累[2] léiléi *formal* clusters of; heaps of: 果实~ fruit growing in close clusters; fruit hanging heavy on the trees ——see also lěiléi
累坠 léizhui same as 累赘 léizhui
累赘 léizhui ① burdensome; cumbersome ② wordy; verbose: 这个句子太~。That's a clumsy, involved sentence. ③ encumbrance; burden; nuisance: 行李带得多了, 是个~。Too much luggage is a nuisance.

雷 léi ① thunder: 打~了。It's thundering. ② mine: 布雷 bùléi ③ (Léi) a surname
雷暴 léibào *meteorol.* thunderstorm
雷暴雨 léibàoyǔ thunderstorm rain
雷池 Léichí a river in ancient China (now confined to use in 不敢越雷池一步 bùgǎn yuè Léichí yī bù)
雷达 léidá radar: ~兵 radar operator; radarman / ~测距 radar ranging / ~干扰 radar jamming / ~跟踪 radar tracking / ~导航 radar navigation / ~截面 radar cross section (RCS) / ~探测区 radar coverage / ~信标 racon; radar beacon / ~荧光屏 radar screen / ~员 radar operator; radarman / 超视距~ over-the-horizon radar / 成像~ image radar / 跟踪~ tracking radar / 机载~ airborne radar / 全景~ panoramic radar / 搜索~ surveillance radar / 相控阵~ phased array radar / 预警~ early-warning radar / 作战~ battle managing radar
雷打不动 léi dǎ bù dòng not to be shaken by thunder —(of an arrangement or plan) not to be altered under any circumstances
雷电 léidiàn thunder and lightning: ~交作 lightning accompanied by peals of thunder
雷电计 léidiànjì ceraunograph
雷动 léidòng thunderous: 欢声(掌声)~ thunderous cheers (applause)
雷公 Léigōng Thunder God
雷公打豆腐, 拣软的欺 Léigōng dǎ dòufu, jiǎn ruǎnde qī the God of Thunder strikes the bean curd—bullies pick on the soft and weak

雷汞 léigǒng *chem.* mercury fulminate
雷管 léiguǎn detonator; detonating cap; blasting cap; primer: 电~ electric detonator
雷害 léihài damage to crops caused by thunder
雷击 léijī be struck by lightning
雷厉风行 léilì-fēngxíng with the power of a thunderbolt and the speed of lightning—(carry out orders, policies, etc.) vigorously and speedily; vigorously and resolutely: ~地开展一个反对贪污浪费的斗争 launch a vigorous, resolute struggle against corruption and waste
雷米封 léimǐfēng *pharm.* rimifon
雷鸣 léimíng ① thunder: ~电闪。It's thundering and lightning. ② thunderous: ~般的掌声 thunderous applause
雷鸟 léiniǎo white partridge
雷诺数 léinuòshù *phys.* Reynolds number
雷声 léishēng thunderclap; thunder: ~隆隆 the rumble (*or* roll) of thunder
雷声大, 雨点小 léishēng dà, yǔdiǎn xiǎo loud thunder but small raindrops—much said but little done; much talk, little action
雷酸汞 léisuāngǒng same as 雷汞 léigǒng
雷霆 léitíng ① thunderclap; thunderbolt ② thunder-like power or rage; wrath: 大发雷霆 dà fā léitíng
雷霆万钧 léitíng wàn jūn as powerful as a thunderbolt: 以~之力 with the force of a thunderbolt
雷同 léitóng ① echoing what others have said ② duplicate; identical
雷丸 léiwán *Chin. med.* stone-like omphalia (*Omphalia lapidescens*)
雷雨 léiyǔ thunderstorm
雷雨云 léiyǔyún *meteorol.* thundercloud
雷阵雨 léizhènyǔ thunder shower

嫘 léi used in persons' names, as in 嫘祖 (wife of the legendary 黄帝 Yellow Emperor and reputed discoverer of sericulture)

缧 léi see below
缧绁 léixiè *formal* bonds

擂 léi ① pestle; pound ② beat (a drum) ——see also lèi
擂钵 léibō mortar (a vessel)

镭 léi *chem.* radium (Ra)
镭疗 léiliáo radium therapy
镭射气 léishèqì *chem.* radium emanation

纍 léi *formal* ① rope ② twine; bind

羸 léi *formal* thin; skinny
羸惫 léibèi *formal* tired out; exhausted
羸顿 léidùn *formal* ① feeble and wasted ② tired out; exhausted
羸弱 léiruò *formal* thin and weak; frail

罍 léi an ancient urn-shaped wine-vessel

lěi

耒 lěi ① a fork-like farm tool used in ancient China ② the handle of the farm tool: 耒耜 lěisì
耒耜 lěisì a plough-like farm tool used in ancient China

诔 lěi ① pronounce a eulogy over the dead ② funeral eulogy; dirge

垒[1]（壘）　lěi　build by piling up bricks, stones, earth, etc.: ～一道墙 build a wall／～猪圈 build a pigsty

垒[2]（壘）　lěi　① rampart ② *baseball, softball* base

垒球　lěiqiú　softball: ～棒 softball bat

累[1]（纍）　lěi　① pile up; accumulate: 日积月累 rìjī-yuèlěi　② continuous; repeated; running:／～戒不改 refuse to mend one's ways despite repeated warnings ③ same as 垒[1] lěi

累[2]　lěi　involve: 连累 liánlěi
——see also lěi; lèi

累次　lěicì　time and again; repeatedly

累代　lěidài　for many generations; generation after generation

累牍连篇　lěidú-liánpiān　same as 连篇累牍 liánpiān-lěidú

累犯　lěifàn　① recidivism ② recidivist

累积　lěijī　accumulate: 头八个月完成的工程量一累起来，已达到全年任务的百分之九十。The work done in the first eight months amounts to ninety per cent of the year's quota.

累及　lěijí　implicate; involve; drag in: ～无辜 involve the innocent

累计　lěijì　① add up: 全年实现利润一为二十二万三千元。Profits for the whole year add up to 223,000 *yuan*. ② accumulative total; grand total

累见不鲜　lěi jiàn bù xiān　same as 屡见不鲜 lǚ jiàn bù xiān

累教不改　lěi jiào bù gǎi　same as 屡教不改 lǚ jiào bù gǎi

累进　lěijìn　progression: ～率 graduated rates／～税 progressive tax; progressive taxation

累累　lěilěi　① again and again; many times ② innumerable; countless: 罪行～ have a long criminal record; have committed countless crimes——see also léiléi

累卵　lěiluǎn　a stack of eggs—liable to collapse any moment; precarious——see also 危如累卵 wēi rú lěiluǎn

累年　lěinián　for years in succession; year after year: ～丰收 have bumper harvests year after year

累日　lěirì　*formal* for days (in succession): ～不适 have been unwell for days／奋战～ carry on the fight for several days running

累时　lěishí　*formal* for a long time

累世　lěishì　for many generations; generation after generation

累月经年　lěiyuè-jīngnián　same as 经年累月 jīngnián-lěiyuè

磊　lěi　see below

磊落　lěiluò　open and upright: 胸怀～ openhearted and upright

蕾　lěi　flower bud; bud

蕾铃　lěilíng　cotton buds and bolls

儡　lěi　see 傀儡 kuǐlěi

lèi

肋　lèi　① rib ② costal region: 两～ both sides of the chest／左（右）～ left (right) side of the chest——see also lē

肋骨　lèigǔ　rib

肋骨切除术　lèigǔ qiēchúshù　costectomy

肋间肌　lèijiānjī　intercostal muscle

肋膜　lèimó　pleura

肋膜炎　lèimóyán　pleurisy

肋木　lèimù　*sports* stall bars

肋条　lèi·tiáo　*dial.* ① rib ② pork ribs; spareribs

肋窝　lèiwō　armpit

泪（淚）　lèi　tear; teardrop: 欲哭无～ in tearless grief

泪痕　lèihén　tear stains: 满脸～ a face bathed in tears／～斑斑 tear-stained

泪花　lèihuā　tears in one's eyes: 她眼里闪烁着喜悦的～。Her eyes glistened with tears of joy.

泪人儿　lèirénr　in tears; all tears: 她哭得成了个～了。She was all tears.

泪如泉涌　lèi rú quán yǒng　tears welling up in one's eyes; tears gushing from one's eyes

泪如雨下　lèi rú yǔ xià　tears falling like rain

泪水　lèishuǐ　tear; teardrop

泪汪汪　lèiwāngwāng　(eyes) brimming with tears

泪腺　lèixiàn　lachrymal gland

泪腺炎　lèixiànyán　dacryoadenitis

泪眼　lèiyǎn　tearful eyes: ～模糊 eyes blurred by tears

泪液　lèiyè　tear

泪盈盈　lèiyíngyíng　brimming with tears; tearful: 她两眼～的。Her eyes were brimming with tears.

泪珠　lèizhū　teardrop

类（類）　lèi　① kind; type; class; category: 这是另一～问题。This is a problem of another kind. ② resemble; be similar to: 类似 lèisì

类比　lèibǐ　analogy: 作历史的～ draw a historical analogy

类别　lèibié　classification; category: 土壤的～ classification of soil／属于不同的～ belong to different categories

类地行星　lèidì xíngxīng　*astron.* terrestrial planet

类毒素　lèidúsù　*med.* toxoid

类风湿性关节炎　lèifēngshīxìng guānjiéyán　rheumatoid arthritis

类乎　lèihu　seem; be like: 这个故事很离奇，～神话。This fantastic story sounds like a fairy tale.

类木行星　lèimù xíngxīng　*astron.* Jovian planet

类人猿　lèirényuán　anthropoid (ape)

类书　lèishū　a class of works combining to some extent the characteristics of encyclopaedias and concordances (embracing the whole field of literature, methodically arranged according to subjects, and each heading giving extracts from former works on the subject in question; e.g.《太平御览》*The Taiping Reign-Period Imperial Encyclopaedia*）

类似　lèisì　similar (to); analogous (to): 保证不再发生～事件 guarantee against the occurrence of similar incidents／我见过很多～这样的例子。I have seen many instances similar to this.

类同　lèitóng　roughly the same; alike; similar: 样式～ similar in style

类推　lèituī　analogize; reason by analogy: 照此～ on the analogy of this／其余～ reason out the rest by analogy

类星体　lèixīngtǐ　*astron.* quasi-stellar object

类型　lèixíng　type; category

类型学　lèixíngxué　typology

类型语言学　lèixíng yǔyánxué　typological linguistics; linguistic typology

累　lèi　① tired; weary; fatigued: 我～了，想去睡觉了。I'm tired and I want to go to sleep.／不怕苦，不怕～

fear neither hardship nor fatigue ② tire; wear out; strain: 这个活儿真～人。This work really makes you tired. / 我怕出去那么一趟会把我～坏了。I'm afraid that trip will tire me out too much. / 看小字～眼睛。Reading small print strains the eyes. / 这件事别人做不了，还得～你。Since no one else can do it, I have to bother you. ③ work hard; toil: 你～了一天，该休息了。You've been working hard all day. You need a rest. ——see also lèi; lěi

累活 lèihuó　tiring work; strenuous work; heavy work

累死累活 lèisǐ-lèihuó　tire oneself out with backbreaking toil; work oneself to death

酹

lèi　*formal*　pour a libation 一尊还～江月。(苏轼) With a cup of wine, let me yet pour a libation to the moon on the river.

擂

lèi　a platform for martial contests; arena: 打擂 dǎlèi ——see also léi

擂台 lèitái　a platform for martial contests; ring; arena: 摆～ give an open challenge

---

lei

嘞

lei　*part.*　(used in the same way as 喽 lou②, with a little more airy effect): 好～，我就去。All right, I'll go. / 雨不下了，走～! It has stopped raining. Shall we go?

---

léng

棱(稜)

léng　① arris; edge: 桌子～儿 edges of a table / 见～见角 angular ② corrugation; ridge: 搓板的～儿 ridges of a washboard

棱缝 léng·fèng　*dial.*　loophole; opportunity
棱角 léngjiǎo　① edges and corners ② edge; pointedness: 你对他的批评很有～。Your criticism of him was pointed. / 他是个有～的人。He has a forceful personality. / 不露～ keep a low profile / 不要把～磨掉。Don't draw in your horns.
棱镜 léngjìng　*phys.*　prism: ～分光 prismatic decomposition
棱台 léngtái　short for 棱锥台 léngzhuītái
棱线 léngxiàn　*mil.*　crest line
棱柱体 léngzhùtǐ　*math.*　prism
棱锥台 léngzhuītái　*math.*　frustum of a pyramid
棱锥体 léngzhuītǐ　*math.*　pyramid

楞

léng　same as 棱 léng

---

lěng

冷

lěng　① cold: 今天真～。It's really cold today. / ～天 the cold season; cold days / 你～不～?Do you feel cold? ② *dial.* (of food) cool: 太烫了，一下再吃。It's too hot. Let it cool off before you eat it. ③ cold in manner; frosty: 他待人很～。He is very cold towards people. / 他～～地说了声"好吧"。He said coldly, "All right!" ④ unfrequented; deserted; out-of-the-way: 冷清清 lěngqīngqīng ⑤ strange; rare: 冷字 lěngzì ⑥ receiving little attention; unwelcomed: 冷货 lěnghuò ⑦ shot from hiding: 冷枪 lěngqiāng ⑧ (Lěng) a surname

冷拔 lěngbá　*mech.*　cold-drawing

冷板凳 lěngbǎndèng　cold bench—an indifferent post or a cold reception ——see also 坐冷板凳 zuò lěngbǎndèng
冷冰冰 lěngbīngbīng　① cold in manner; frosty: ～的脸色 a cold expression; frosty looks / ～的态度 an icy manner / 对人～的 be cold towards people ② (of objects) ice-cold; icy: 她的手～的。Her hands are icy.
冷不丁 lěngbudīng　*dial.*　suddenly; unexpectedly: 汽车～地停住了。The car came to a sudden stop. or The car suddenly pulled up.
冷不防 lěngbufáng　suddenly; unexpectedly; without warning: ～，他打了我一下。Suddenly, without warning, he gave me a blow. / 打他一个～ take him unawares; catch him off guard
冷布 lěngbù　(cotton) gauze
冷菜 lěngcài　cold dish
冷餐 lěngcān　buffet: ～招待会 buffet reception
冷藏 lěngcáng　refrigeration; cold storage
冷藏车 lěngcángchē　(on a railway train) refrigerator car (*or* van)
冷藏库 lěngcángkù　cold storage; freezer
冷藏汽车 lěngcáng qìchē　cold storage truck
冷藏室 lěngcángshì　refrigerating compartment (in a refrigerator)
冷藏箱 lěngcángxiāng　refrigerator; fridge
冷场 lěngchǎng　① awkward silence on the stage when an actor enters late or forgets his lines ② awkward silence at a meeting
冷嘲热讽 lěngcháo-rèfěng　with freezing irony and burning satire; with biting sarcasm: 鲁迅用～的杂文形式与黑暗统治势力作战。Lu Xun used burning satire and freezing irony, cast in the form of essays, to do battle against the rule of the forces of darkness.
冷处理 lěngchǔlǐ　*mech.*　cold treatment
冷床 lěngchuáng　*agric.*　cold bed; cold frame
冷脆 lěngcuì　*metall.*　cold-short
冷待 lěngdài　treat coldly; cold-shoulder; slight
冷淡 lěngdàn　① cheerless; desolate ② cold; indifferent: 反应～ a cold response / 对倡议表示～ show indifference towards a proposal / ～的态度 a frigid manner ③ treat coldly; cold-shoulder; slight: 他强打着精神说话，怕～了朋友。He forced himself to perk up and make conversation so that his friend wouldn't feel he'd been given the cold shoulder.
冷调 lěngdiào　cool colour-tone (as in painting); cool tone
冷碟儿 lěngdiér　*dial.*　cold dish; *hors d'œuvres*
冷丁 lěngdīng　same as 冷不丁 lěngbudīng
冷冻 lěngdòng　freeze: ～精液 frozen semen / ～厂 cold storage plant
冷冻干燥 lěngdòng gānzào　freeze-dry
冷冻机 lěngdòngjī　refrigerator; freezer
冷冻剂 lěngdòngjì　refrigerant
冷冻室 lěngdòngshì　freezer compartment (in a refrigerator); freezer
冷锻 lěngduàn　*mech.*　cold forging; cold hammering
冷风 lěngfēng　cold wind—rumour; gossip: 吹～ spread rumour (*or* gossip)
冷锋 lěngfēng　(also 冷锋面 lěngfēngmiàn) *meteorol.* cold front
冷敷 lěngfū　*med.*　cold compress
冷宫 lěnggōng　① cold palace—a place to which disfavoured queens and concubines were banished ② limbo ——see also 打入冷宫 dǎrù lěnggōng
冷孤丁 lěnggūdīng　same as 冷不丁 lěngbudīng
冷光 lěngguāng　*phys.*　cold light
冷害 lěnghài　damage to plants caused by a sudden drop in temperature
冷汗 lěnghàn　cold sweat: 出～ be in a cold sweat;

break out in a cold sweat

冷焊 lěnghàn *mech.* cold welding

冷荤 lěnghūn cold meat; cold buffet

冷货 lěnghuò goods not much in demand; dull goods

冷寂 lěngjì cold and still: ～的秋夜 a cold and still autumn night

冷加工 lěngjiāgōng *mech.* cold working

冷箭 lěngjiàn an arrow shot from hiding; sniper's shot ——see also 放冷箭 fàng lěngjiàn

冷噤 lěngjìn same as 寒噤 hánjìn

冷静 lěngjìng ① sober; calm; 头脑～ sober-minded; level-headed; cool-headed / 保持～ keep calm / 请你～一点儿。Please calm down. / 他的话使我～下来。His words sobered me. ② *dial.* (of a place) quiet: 这个地方很～。This place is very quiet.

冷觉 lěngjué sensation of cold; sense of cold

冷峻 lěngjùn grave and stern: 面色～ a grave and stern face

冷库 lěngkù same as 冷藏库 lěngcángkù

冷酷 lěngkù unfeeling; callous; grim: ～的人 a callous person / ～的现实 grim reality

冷酷无情 lěngkù wúqíng unfeeling; cold-blooded

冷拉 lěnglā same as 冷拔 lěngbá

冷冷清清 lěnglěngqīngqīng cold and cheerless; desolate: 对待同志要满腔热忱，不能～，漠不关心。We should be warm towards our comrades, not cold and indifferent. / 不要只靠少数人～地做工作。Do not rely on a mere handful of people working in quiet isolation. / 会议开得～。The meeting was very dull.

冷脸子 lěngliǎnzi *dial.* cold face; severe expression

冷落 lěngluò ① unfrequented; desolate: 狭窄～的胡同 an unfrequented narrow alley ② treat coldly; cold-shoulder; leave out in the cold: ～了客人 leave a guest out in the cold

冷铆 lěngmǎo *mech.* cold riveting

冷门 lěngmén ① a profession, trade or branch of learning that receives little attention ② an unexpected winner; dark horse: 那次比赛出了个～。The contest produced an unexpected winner. ——see also 爆冷门 bào lěngmén

冷门货 lěngménhuò same as 冷货 lěnghuò

冷漠 lěngmò cold and detached; unconcerned; indifferent: ～的态度 an indifferent attitude / 他对人向来～。He is always unconcerned about others.

冷凝 lěngníng *phys.* condensation

冷凝点 lěngníngdiǎn condensation point

冷凝器 lěngníngqì condenser

冷凝物 lěngníngwù condensate

冷暖 lěngnuǎn changes in temperature—daily life: 注意～ be careful about changes of temperature; take care of oneself / 把群众的～时刻挂在心上 always be concerned with the well-being of the masses

冷暖自知 lěngnuǎn zìzhī one knows whether it's cold or warm without being told—one knows best by personal experience

冷盘 lěngpán cold dish; hors d'oeuvres

冷僻 lěngpì ① deserted; out-of-the-way ② rare; unfamiliar: ～的字眼 rarely used words / ～的典故 unfamiliar allusions

冷气 lěngqì air conditioning: 这个剧院有～设备。The theatre is air-conditioned

冷气机 lěngqìjī air conditioner

冷气团 lěngqìtuán cold air mass

冷枪 lěngqiāng sniper's shot ——see also 打冷枪 dǎ lěngqiāng

冷峭 lěngqiào ① biting cold ② scathing (remarks)

冷清清 lěngqīngqīng cold and cheerless; desolate; lonely; deserted: ～的小巷 a deserted lane / ～的月色 cold and cheerless moonlight / 通跨院儿的月亮门～地开着。

A moon gate, forlorn and uninviting, opened into a side yard.

冷清 lěngqīng cold and cheerless; desolate; lonely; deserted: ～的秋夜 a cold and cheerless autumn night / 这里很～。It's very quiet here. / 他一个人住着很～。He's very lonely living all by himself.

冷泉 lěngquán cold spring

冷却 lěngquè become or make cool

冷却导管 lěngquè dǎoguǎn cooling duct

冷却剂 lěngquèjì coolant; cooler

冷却塔 lěngquètǎ cooling tower

冷然 lěngrán ① cold: ～一笑 give a cold smile ② unexpectedly; suddenly: ～一声惨叫 suddenly give a piteous cry

冷热病 lěngrèbìng ① *dial.* malaria ② capricious changes in mood; sudden waxing and waning of enthusiasm: 他的～又犯了。He's in one of his moods again.

冷若冰霜 lěng ruò bīngshuāng (usu. of women) as cold as ice; have an icy (or chilly) manner

冷色 lěngsè cool colour

冷涩 lěngsè ① (of water or air) chilly: ～的空气 chilly air ② cold and dull: ～的目光 cold and dull eyes ③ (of sound) dull: ～的声音 a dull voice ④ obscure and rarely used: ～的字眼 words which are rarely used and hard to understand

冷森森 lěngsēnsēn chilly; chilling: 山洞里～的。It's very chilly inside the cave.

冷杉 lěngshān fir

冷食 lěngshí cold drinks and snacks: ～部 cold drink and snack counter

冷霜 lěngshuāng cold cream

冷水 lěngshuǐ ① cold water: ～浴 cold bath ② unboiled water: 喝～容易得病。If you drink unboiled water, you're likely to get sick. ——see also 泼冷水 pō lěngshuǐ

冷水浇头 lěngshuǐ jiāo tóu splashing the head with cold water—a rude shock; a bitter disappointment

冷丝丝 lěngsīsī a bit chilly: 晚风吹来，身上～的。The night wind was blowing, and I felt a bit chilly.

冷飕飕 lěngsōusōu (of wind) chilling; chilly: 北风～地迎面吹来。The north wind blew cold in my face.

冷烫 lěngtàng cold wave (in the hair): ～精 cold wave agent

冷线 lěngxiàn cold line

冷笑 lěngxiào sneer; laugh grimly; grin with dissatisfaction, helplessness, bitterness, etc.

冷心肠 lěngxīncháng coldhearted; heartless

冷性肥料 lěngxìng féiliào cold manure

冷血动物 lěngxuè dòngwù ① cold-blooded animal; poikilothermal animal ② an unfeeling person; a coldhearted person

冷言冷语 lěngyán-lěngyǔ sarcastic comments; ironical remarks: ～敲打人 irritate people with sarcastic remarks

冷眼 lěngyǎn ① (with) a cold eye; (with) cool detachment: 他坐在墙角里，～观察来客的言谈举止。He sat in a corner, watching with a cold eye how the guests were conducting themselves. ② cold shoulder: ～相待 give sb. the cold shoulder

冷眼旁观 lěngyǎn pángguān look on with a cold eye

冷饮 lěngyǐn cold drink

冷遇 lěngyù cold reception; cold shoulder: 遭到～ be given the cold shoulder; be left out in the cold

冷錾 lěngzàn *mech.* cold chisel

冷轧 lěngzhá *metall.* cold rolling: ～钢 cold-rolled steel / ～机 cold-rolling mill

冷战 lěngzhàn cold war

冷战 lěngzhan *inf.* shiver: 打～ shiver with cold

冷铸 lěngzhù *metall.* chill casting

冷字　lěngzì　a rarely used word; an unfamiliar word
冷子　lěngzi　*dial.* hail; hailstone

lèng

愣　lèng ① dumbfounded; stupefied; dazed: 他一问, 大家都～了。When he asked the question, everybody was dumbfounded. / 听到这消息, 他～住了。He was struck dumb by the news. / 他～了半天没说话。For a long while he was in a daze, saying not a word. ② *inf.* rash; blunt; brusque: 他很～。He has a very blunt manner. / 他说话很～。He speaks very bluntly. / 一小子 a rash (*or* brusque) young fellow; a young hothead ③ *inf.* forcefully insist on sth. without proof or basis: 我告诉他不能去, 可是他～去。I told him he couldn't go, but he just went. / 明知不对, 他～那么说。He knew it was wrong, but he still went ahead and said it. / 我～饿着, 也不愿意吃这个。I would rather be hungry than eat this.

愣干　lènggàn　*inf.* do things recklessly (*or* rashly); persist in going one's own way: 要遵守操作规程, 不能～。You've got to observe the working regulations. You can't do things any way you like.

愣劲儿　lèngjìnr　*dial.* dash; pep; vigour: 这些小伙子真有股子～。These boys are really full of pep.

愣神儿　lèngshénr　*dial.* stare blankly; be in a daze: 他站在一旁～, 不知道想些什么。He stood by staring blankly, lost in thought.

愣是　lèngshì　*dial.* insist on sth. without good reason: 不叫他去, 他～要去。We didn't want him to go, but he insisted on going.

愣说　lèngshuō　*inf.* insist; allege; assert: 是他自己拿的, 他～他没拿。He took it himself, but he insisted that he didn't.

愣头愣脑　lèngtóu-lèngnǎo　rash; impetuous; reckless

愣头儿青　lèngtóurqīng　*dial.* rash (*or* brusque) fellow; hothead

愣着　lèngzhe　not moving; in a daze: 快干吧, 别～。Get to work quickly, don't just stand there.

愣怔　lèngzheng　same as 睖睁 lèngzheng

睖　lèng　see below

睖睁　lèngzheng　stare blankly; be in a daze

lí

哩　lí　see below ——see also lǐ; li; yīnglǐ

哩哩啦啦　lǐlilālā　*inf.* scattered; sporadic: ～下了一天雨。It rained on and off all day. / 跟上队伍, 不要～的。Close up, don't straggle along. / 客人～的直到中午还没到齐。The guests came in dribs and drabs; not until after 12 o'clock were they all present.

哩哩罗罗　lǐliluōluō　*inf.* verbose and unclear in speech; rambling and indistinct: 他～说了半天, 没有一句要紧的话。He gibbered away for a long time, but said nothing of importance.

lí

丽（麗）　lí ① used in 丽水 (a county in Zhejiang Province) ② used in 高丽 Gāolí ——see also lì

厘（釐）　lí ① centi-: 厘米 límǐ / 厘升 líshēng /

厘克　líkè ② *li*, also called 市厘 shìlí, traditional units of measures of length, area and weight, each equal to 0.1 *fen* 市分 or 10 *hao* 市毫 (see also 市厘 shìlí) ③ *li*, a unit of Chinese currency, equal to 0.1 *fen* 分 or 0.001 *yuan*: 三元五角六分四～3.564 *yuan* ④ a unit of interest rate, equal to 0.1% monthly interest, or 1% annual interest: 月利率五～七 0.57% monthly interest / 年利率七～二 7.2% annual interest ⑤ a very small amount; a fraction; the least: 分厘 fēnlí ⑥ *formal* regulate; rectify: 厘定 líding

厘定　líding　*formal* collate and stipulate (rules and regulations, etc.)

厘革　lígé　*formal* rectify and reform: ～旧制 reform the outdated institutions

厘金　líjīn　a former provincial transit duty (usu. transliterated as *likin*)

厘克　líkè　centigram (cg.)

厘米　límǐ　centimetre (cm.)

厘米波　límǐbō　*elec.* centimetre wave

厘米克秒单位　límǐ-kè-miǎo dānwèi　centimetre-gram-second unit (CGS unit)

厘升　líshēng　centilitre (cl.)

厘正　lízhèng　correct; revise: ～税则 revise the tax regulations

离（離）　lí ① leave; part from; be away from: ～京赴穗 leave Beijing for Guangzhou / 她～家已经三年了。She's been away from home for three years. ② from (in giving distances): 车站～这儿三里地。The railway station is three *li* from here. / ～国庆节只有十天了。National Day is only ten days away. ③ without; independent of: 发展工业～不了钢铁。Industry cannot develop without steel. / 他～不了酒。He can't stay away from the bottle.

离岸价格　lí'àn jiàgé　*econ.* free on board (FOB)

离瓣花冠　líbàn huāguān　*bot.* a floral corolla divided into distinct petals

离瓣花类　líbàn huālèi　*bot.* choripetalae

离别　líbié　part (for a longish period); leave; bid farewell: 我～故乡已经两年了。It's two years since I left my hometown.

离不开人　líbukāirén　must be guarded or looked after all the time: 他的病很重, 身边～。He is very ill, and needs someone to watch over him all the time.

离不开身　líbukāishēn　be fully occupied or be very much needed and unable to leave for a moment: 这孩子淘得要命, 大人一会儿也～。The child is too naughty to be left alone even for a little while.

离愁　líchóu　*liter.* the sorrow of parting; the pain of separation: 剪不断, 理还乱, 是～, 别是一般滋味在心头。(李煜) Cut—still unsevered; Unravelled—still entangled—The sorrows of parting—A strange taste that lingers in the heart.

离地间隙　lídì jiànxì　road (*or* ground) clearance (of a car)

离队　líduì　leave the ranks; leave one's post: 擅自～ leave one's post without permission

离格儿　lígér　go beyond what is proper; be out of place

离宫　lígōng　a temporary abode for an emperor on progresses

离轨　líguǐ　leave the right or normal track; stray or deviate from the right path

离合　lí-hé　separation and reunion: 悲欢离合 bēi-huān-lí-hé

离合器　líhéqì　*mech.* clutch

离婚　líhūn　divorce: 他们～了。They divorced (*or* divorced each other). / 她跟他～了。She divorced him. / 她已经离过三次婚了。She has been divorced three times. / ～程序 divorce proceedings / ～证明书 divorce

certificate

离间 líjiàn　sow discord; drive a wedge between; set one party against another

离解 líjiě　*chem.* dissociation

离经叛道 líjīng-pàndào　depart from the classics and rebel against orthodoxy

离境 líjìng　leave a country or place

离境签证 líjìng qiānzhèng　exit visa

离开 líkāi　leave; depart from; deviate from: 他已经～北京了。He has left Beijing. / 小孩儿离不开母亲。Children cannot do without their mothers. / ～本题 stray from the subject; digress / 离不开手儿 be too busy with the job on hand; have one's hands full

离离 lílí　*liter.* luxuriant

离乱 líluàn　separation and war: 八年～ eight years of separation and war

离谱 lípǔ　go beyond what is proper; be out of place: 你开的价太～了。The price you ask is unreasonable.

离奇 líqí　strange; odd; fantastic; bizarre: ～的故事 a strange story / ～的谎言 a fantastic lie / 这事儿很～。This is a very odd business.

离弃 líqì　abandon; desert; forsake

离情别绪 líqíng-biéxù　sad feelings at parting

离去角 líqùjiǎo　angle of departure (of a car)

离群索居 líqún-suǒjū　live in solitude; live all alone

离任 lírèn　leave one's post: ～回国 leave one's post for home / 即将～的大使 the outgoing ambassador

离散 lísàn　(of relatives) be dispersed; be scattered about; be separated from one another: 解放前～了的母女终于重新团聚了。Mother and daughter who were separated from each other before liberation have at long last been reunited.

离世 líshì　① cut oneself off from the world; keep aloof from worldly affairs ② *euph.* depart this life; pass away

离索 lísuǒ　*formal* desolate and lonely

离题 lítí　digress from the subject; stray from the point: 发言不要～。Please keep to the subject.

离析 líxī　*formal* ① disintegrate ② analyse

离弦走板 líxián-zǒubǎn　off the standard; off the beam

离乡背井 líxiāng-bèijǐng　same as 背井离乡 bèijǐng-líxiāng

离心 líxīn　① be at odds with the community or the leadership ② centrifugal: ～倾向 a centrifugal tendency / ～作用 centrifugal effects

离心泵 líxīnbèng　centrifugal pump

离心机 líxīnjī　centrifugal machine; centrifuge

离心离德 líxīn-lídé　torn by dissension and discord

离心力 líxīnlì　*phys.* centrifugal force

离休 líxiū　(of veteran cadres) retire: ～干部 retired veteran cadres

离异 líyì　*formal* divorce

离辙 lízhé　*inf.* off the track—off the beam; off the point

离职 lízhí　① leave one's job temporarily: ～学习 leave one's job and join a study group ② leave office; resign

离中趋势 lízhōng qūshì　*statistics* dispersion

离子 lízǐ　*phys.* ion: 阴～ anion / 阳～ cation / 氩～ argon ion

离子泵 lízǐbèng　ionic pump

离子交换 lízǐ jiāohuàn　*chem.* ion exchange

离子交换剂 lízǐ jiāohuànjì　ion exchanger

离子交换树脂 lízǐ jiāohuàn shùzhī　ion exchange resin

离子束 lízǐshù　ion beam

离子淌度 lízǐ tǎngdù　ionic mobility

离子雾 lízǐwù　ion-atmosphere

狸 lí　racoon dog

狸猫 límāo　leopard cat

狸藻 lízǎo　*bot.* bladderwort (*Utricularia vulgaris*)

狸子 lízi　leopard cat

骊（驪） lí　*formal* black horse

梨（棃） lí　pear

梨膏 lígāo　pear syrup (for the relief of coughs)

梨花大鼓 líhuā dàgǔ　castanets *dagu* (a form of *dagu* characterized by the use for accompaniment, besides the drum, of a pair of brass castanets shaped like 犁铧 líhuā "ploughshares," from which derives the homophone 梨花 líhuā "pear flowers")

梨涡 líwō　*liter.* dimple (of a female)

梨园 Líyuán　*old* the Pear Garden—the theatre; the theatre world (originally the name of a college of dramatics founded by imperial decree in the Tang Dynasty)

梨园子弟 Líyuán zǐdì　*old* students of the Pear Garden —operatic actors

梨枣 lízǎo　pear and date—printing blocks (which were usu. made of the wood of pear or date trees): 付之～ send to the press

梨子 lízi　pear

犁（犂） lí　① plough ② work with a plough; plough: 地已经～了两遍。The fields have been ploughed twice.

犁壁 líbì　same as 犁镜 líjìng

犁底层 lídǐcéng　*agric.* plough sole; plough pan

犁铧 líhuā　ploughshare; share

犁镜 líjìng　mouldboard

犁牛 líniú　*dial.* farm cattle

犁庭扫穴 lítíng-sǎoxué　(also 犁庭扫闾 lítíng-sǎolǘ) plough up the courtyard and destroy the hide-outs —annihilate the enemy

犁头 lítóu　① ploughshare ② *dial.* plough

犁杖 lízhang　*dial.* plough

喱 lí　see 咖喱 gālí

鹂（鸝） lí　see 黄鹂 huánglí

漓¹ lí　see 淋漓 línlí

漓²（灘） Lí　a river (also called 漓江) in Guangxi Province

蓠（蘺） lí　see 江蓠 jiānglí

缡（褵） lí　*arch.* bridal veil

嫠 lí　see below

嫠妇 lífù　*formal* widow

犛 lí　yak

犛牛 líniú　yak

黎 lí　① *formal* multitude; host ② (Lí) a surname

黎巴嫩 Líbānèn　Lebanon

黎巴嫩人 Líbānènrén　Lebanese

黎黑 líhēi　*formal* (of complexion) dark

黎民 límín　*formal* the common people; the multitude

黎明 límíng　dawn; daybreak

黎庶 líshù　*formal* the common people; the multitude

黎族 Lízú　the Li nationality, or the Lis, inhabiting Hainan Province

鲡（鱺） lí　see 鳗鲡 mánlí

罹 lí　*formal* suffer from; meet with: ～病 suffer

from a disease; fall ill /～祸 suffer misfortune

罹难 línàn *formal* ① die in a disaster or an accident ② be murdered

篱¹
lí　see 笊篱 zhàoli

篱²（籬）
lí　hedge; fence: 树～ hedge; hedge-row

篱笆 líba　bamboo or twig fence: ～墙 wattled wall

篱落 líluò *formal* bamboo or twig fence

篱墙 líqiáng　wattled wall

藜
lí　lamb's-quarters

藜藿 líhuò *formal* coarse food: ～之羹 coarse food

藜芦 lílú　black false hellebore

黧
lí　see below

黧黑 líhēi *formal* (of complexion) dark

蠡
lí *formal* ① calabash shell serving as a dipper; dipper ② seashell ——see also lǐ

蠡测 lícè　short for 以蠡测海 yǐ lí cè hǎi ——see also 管窥蠡测 guǎnkuī-lícè

lǐ

礼（禮）
lǐ ① ceremony; rite: 婚礼 hūnlǐ ② courtesy; etiquette; manners: 失礼 shīlǐ ③ gift; present: 这份儿～很重。This is a generous gift.

礼拜 lǐbài ① religious service: 做～ go to church; be at church ② *inf.* week: 下～ next week ③ *inf.* day of the week: 今天～几？What day is it today? ④ *inf.* Sunday: 今儿个～。Today is Sunday.

礼拜二 lǐbài'èr *inf.* Tuesday

礼拜六 lǐbàiliù *inf.* Saturday

礼拜日 lǐbàirì *inf.* Sunday

礼拜三 lǐbàisān *inf.* Wednesday

礼拜四 lǐbàisì *inf.* Thursday

礼拜寺 lǐbàisì　another name for 清真寺 qīngzhēnsì

礼拜堂 lǐbàitáng　church

礼拜天 lǐbàitiān *inf.* Sunday

礼拜五 lǐbàiwǔ *inf.* Friday

礼拜一 lǐbàiyī *inf.* Monday

礼宾司 Lǐbīnsī　the Department of Protocol; the Protocol Department: ～司长 Director of the Protocol Department; Chief of Protocol

礼部 Lǐbù　the Board of Rites ——see also 六部 Liùbù

礼成 lǐchéng　ceremony is over (said by the master of ceremonies)

礼单 lǐdān　a list of presents

礼多人不怪 lǐ duō rén bù guài　nobody will blame you for being too polite

礼法 lǐfǎ　rules of etiquette; the proprieties

礼服 lǐfú　ceremonial robe or dress; full dress; formal attire

礼服呢 lǐfúní　another name for 直贡呢 zhígòngní

礼花 lǐhuā　fireworks display: 每逢国庆节晚上都要放～。We always have a fireworks display on the evening of National Day.

礼记 Lǐjì　*The Book of Rites* ——see also 五经 wǔjīng

礼教 lǐjiào　the Confucian or feudal ethical code: 吃人的～ cannibalistic feudal ethics (a watchword of the iconoclasts during the May Fourth Movement)

礼节 lǐjié　courtesy; etiquette; protocol; ceremony: ～性拜访 a courtesy call / 社交～ social etiquette / 中国有许多～跟外国不同。Much of Chinese etiquette is different from that of other countries.

礼金 lǐjīn　a gift of money

礼路儿 lǐlùr *dial.* manners; etiquette

礼帽 lǐmào　a hat that goes with formal dress: 大～ top hat

礼貌 lǐmào ① courtesy; politeness; manners: 有～ be courteous; be polite / 没～ have no manners; be impolite ② courteous; polite: 我觉得这么早就走不大～。I don't think it'd be polite for us to leave so soon. / ～语言 polite language

礼炮 lǐpào　salvo; (gun) salute: 鸣～二十一响。A 21-gun salute was fired.

礼品 lǐpǐn　gift; present

礼品部 lǐpǐnbù　gift and souvenir department or counter (in a shop)

礼聘 lǐpìn　invite sb. cordially; enlist the service of sb. with rich gifts

礼器 lǐqì　sacrificial vessel

礼轻人意重 lǐ qīng rényì zhòng　the gift is trifling but the feeling is profound; it's nothing much, but it's the thought that counts

礼让 lǐràng　give precedence to sb. out of courtesy or thoughtfulness; comity: 国际～ the comity of nations / 中速行驶, 安全～。Drive at moderate speed; yield right of way for safety's sake.

礼尚往来 lǐ shàng wǎnglái ① courtesy demands reciprocity ② deal with a man as he deals with you; pay a man back in his own coin; give as good as one gets

礼数 lǐshù *inf.* courtesy; etiquette: 不懂～ have no manners

礼俗 lǐsú　etiquette and custom

礼堂 lǐtáng　assembly hall; auditorium

礼物 lǐwù　gift; present: 他送了一份很重的～。He gave a generous present. / 一定得送他们点儿～才好。We must send them some sort of gift. / 谢谢您圣诞节的～。Thank you for your Christmas gift.

礼贤下士 lǐxián-xiàshì (of a ruler or a high minister) treat worthy men with courtesy

礼仪 lǐyí　ceremony and propriety: 中国向被称为～之邦。China has long been known as the "land of ceremony and propriety."

礼义廉耻 lǐ-yì-lián-chǐ　propriety, righteousness, honesty, and a sense of shame (formerly upheld as 四维 the "four social bonds")

礼遇 lǐyù　courteous reception: 受到～ be accorded a courteous reception

李
lǐ ① plum ② (Lǐ) a surname

李代桃僵 lǐ dài táo jiāng ① substitute one thing for another; substitute oneself for another person ② sacrifice oneself for another person; bear the blame for another person's mistake

李逵 Lǐ Kuí　one of the Mount Liang heroes (梁山好汉) in *Water Margin* (《水浒传》), nicknamed the "Black Whirlwind" (黑旋风), coarse and ferocious, impetuous and violent in temper, but straightforward and honest, sincere to his friends, devoted to his mother, and faithful to the sworn brotherhood

李自成起义 Lǐ Zìchéng Qǐyì　the Li Zicheng Rebellion (1644), which terminated the Ming Dynasty

李子 lǐzi　plum

里¹（裏、裡）
lǐ ① lining; inside (of clothing): 衣服～儿 the lining of a garment / 这面是～儿, 那面是面儿。This is the inside, that is the outside. ② inner: 里间 lǐjiān

里²
lǐ ① neighbourhood: 邻里 línlǐ ② native place: 故里 gùlǐ ③ (Lǐ) a surname

里[3] lǐ *m. li*, currently called 市里 shìlǐ, a traditional unit of length ——see also 市里 shìlǐ

里（裏、裡） lǐ ① in; inside: 往～走 go inside / 手～ in one's hands / 皮箱～ in (or inside) the suitcase ② (used after 这, 那, 哪, etc. to indicate a place): 这～ here / 那～ there / 县～发的通知 a circular issued by the county authorities / 家～没人。There is no one at home.

里边 lǐbian inside; in; within: 他们都在～。They are all inside. / ～有很多人。There are a lot of people inside. / 这所房子～还没完工。The inside of this house isn't finished yet. / 他一年～没有请过一次假。He has not once asked for leave during the whole year. / 这～有问题。There is something wrong here. or Something is wrong here. / ～请! Come on in, please!

里程 lǐchéng ① mileage ② course of development; course: 革命的～ the course of the revolution

里程碑 lǐchéngbēi milestone: 历史的～ a milestone in history

里程标 lǐchéngbiāo milepost

里程表 lǐchéngbiǎo odometer

里出外进 lǐchū-wàijìn irregular; uneven: 他的牙长得～的。His teeth are uneven.

里带 lǐdài *inf.* inner tube (of a tyre)

里勾外联 lǐgōu-wàilián in collusion with forces within and without

里海 Lǐhǎi the Caspian Sea

里急后重 lǐjí-hòuzhòng *med.* tenesmus

里脊 lǐji tenderloin

里间 lǐjiān inner room

里拉 lǐlā lira (Italian monetary unit)

里里外外 lǐlǐwàiwài inside and outside: 屋子～都打扫得很干净。The house has been given a thorough cleaning inside and out. / ～一把手 competent in all one does, both inside and outside the house

里弄 lǐlòng *dial.* lanes and alleys; neighbourhood: 担任～工作 work on the neighbourhood committee

里面 lǐmiàn inside; interior: 宿舍～清洁豁亮。It's clean and bright inside the dormitory.

里圈 lǐquān *sports* inner lane (of a running track)

里三层外三层 lǐsāncéng-wàisāncéng crowds of people: 街上狂欢的人～，把交通都堵塞了。Crowds of merry-makers jammed the streets, and no cars could pass.

里手[1] lǐshǒu the left-hand side (of a running vehicle or machine)

里手[2] lǐshǒu expert; old hand

里首 lǐshǒu *dial.* inside; interior

里通外国 lǐ tōng wàiguó have (or maintain) illicit relations with a foreign country

里头 lǐtou inside; interior: 炉子～的煤已经烧得很红了。The coal inside the stove is glowing red.

里外 lǐ-wài ① inside and outside: ～受敌 face opposition within and without ② (used after round numbers) about; or so; or thereabouts: 她看上去, 不过三十岁。She appears to be about thirty.

里外里 lǐwàilǐ *dial.* ① adding the two sums; taken all together: 我省下了五块, 家里又寄来十块, ～有十五块。I've saved up five yuan, and my family has sent me ten yuan, so all together I have fifteen yuan. ② no matter how you figure it out; either way: 三个人干五天跟五个人干三天, ～是一样。Three people working five days or five people working three days—either way it's all the same.

里屋 lǐwū same as 里间 lǐjiān

里弦 lǐxián the thicker inner string on the *huqin* (胡琴)

里巷 lǐxiàng lanes and alleys

里应外合 lǐyìng-wàihé act from inside in coordination with forces attacking from outside; collaborate from within with forces from without

里证 lǐzhèng *Chin. med.* interior symptom-complex; diseases caused by the endogenous factors involving serious disorders in the internal organs

里子 lǐzi lining: 棉袄～ the lining of a cotton-padded jacket

俚 lǐ vulgar; rustic; unrefined

俚歌 lǐgē a rustic song

俚曲 lǐqǔ popular music; pop

俚俗 lǐsú vulgar; rustic; unrefined

俚语 lǐyǔ slang

浬 lǐ also hǎilǐ old form for 海里 hǎilǐ

哩 lǐ also yīnglǐ old form for 英里 yīnglǐ ——see also lī; li

娌 lǐ see 妯娌 zhóuli

逦（邐） lǐ see 迤逦 yǐlǐ

理 lǐ ① texture; grain (in wood, skin, etc.): 木～ the grain of wood ② reason; logic; truth: 是他没～。He's the one who's been unreasonable. / 他讲的句句是～。There is truth in every word he says. ③ natural science (esp. physics): ～学院 college of science ④ manage; run: ～家 keep house; manage family affairs / 有要事待～ have important business to attend to ⑤ put in order; tidy up: 把书～一～。Put the books in order. / 把房间～一～。Straighten up the room. ⑥ (usu. used in the negative) pay attention to; make a gesture or speak to: 别～那条狗。Don't pay any attention to that dog. / 他想跟我讲话, 我没～他。I ignored him when he tried to talk to me.

理财 lǐcái manage money matters; conduct financial transactions

理财家 lǐcáijiā financier

理睬 lǐcǎi (usu. used in the negative) pay attention to; show interest in: 没人～这事。Nobody pays any attention to this matter. / 不予～ ignore; turn a deaf ear to; pay no heed to

理舱费 lǐcāngfèi stowage charges

理当 lǐdāng ought to; should: ～如此。That's just as it should be. or It's only right and proper.

理短 lǐduǎn be in the wrong; have no justification

理发 lǐfà ① (of men) get a haircut; (of women) go to the hairdresser's: 我去理个发。(of men) I'm going to get a haircut. or (of women) I'm going to the hairdresser's (or going to have my hair done). ② give a haircut; do sb.'s hair: 我每月给他理一次发。I give him a haircut once a month.

理发馆 lǐfàguǎn barbershop; barber's; hairdresser's

理发师 lǐfàshī barber; hairdresser

理发员 lǐfàyuán barber; hairdresser

理该 lǐgāi same as 理当 lǐdāng

理工 lǐ-gōng science and engineering: ～科大学 college (or university) of science and engineering

理合 lǐhé *old* (used in official documents) ought to; should

理化 lǐ-huà physics and chemistry

理会 lǐhuì ① understand; comprehend: 不难～ not difficult to understand ② (usu. used in the negative) take notice of; pay attention to: 叫了他好几声, 他都没～。We called him several times, but he took no notice of us. / 我没～那件事。I didn't pay any attention to that. ③ *old* argue; debate ④ *old* take care of; deal with

理货　ľīhuò　freight forwarding; customs brokerage

理货单　ľīhuòdān　tally sheet

理货员　ľīhuòyuán　tallyman; tally clerk

理解　ľījiě　understand; comprehend: 你的意思我完全～。I understand you completely. or I see perfectly well what you mean. / 加深～ deepen one's comprehension; acquire a better understanding / 不可～ incomprehensible; beyond one's comprehension

理解力　ľījiělì　faculty of understanding; understanding; comprehension: ～强 have good understanding (or comprehension)

理科　ľīkē　① science (as a field of study) ② science department in a college

理亏　ľīkuī　be in the wrong: 自知～ know that one is in the wrong; realize that justice is not on one's side

理亏心虚　ľīkuī-xīnxū　feel that one is not on solid ground

理疗　ľīliáo　physiotherapy: ～科医生 physiotherapist

理路　ľīlù　① line of reasoning: 这篇文章～不清。This article doesn't have a clear line of reasoning (or lacks coherence). ② dial. reason; sense: 他每句话都在～上, 使人听了不能不心服。Everything he says is reasonable and convincing.

理论　ľīlùn　① theory; principle: 学习马列主义～ study Marxist-Leninist theory / 别空谈～。Don't just talk about abstract principles. / 你的意见～上我同意, 但实际上恐怕行不通。In theory, I agree with you, but I feel that your ideas would not work in practice. / ～和实践相结合 the integration of theory and practice / ～联系实际 unite theory with practice / ～脱离实际 theory divorced from practice / ～根据 theoretical foundation / ～水平 theoretical level / 《词典学的～与实际》Lexicography: Principles and Practice ② old argue; debate: 我得跟他～。I have to argue this out with him.

理论家　ľīlùnjiā　theoretician; theorist

理气　ľīqì　Chin. med. regulating the flow of vital energy and removing obstruction to it: ～止痛药 medicines for regulating the flow of vital energy and assuaging the pain caused by functional disorder of various organs

理屈　ľīqū　be in the wrong; have a weak case: 他觉得自己有点～, 没再说下去。He felt he had a rather weak case, and said nothing more.

理屈词穷　ľīqū-cíqióng　fall silent on finding oneself bested in argument; be unable to advance any further arguments

理事　ľīshì　member of an executive council or of a board of directors; director; manager

理事国　ľīshìguó　a member of the UN Security Council

理事会　ľīshìhuì　executive council; board of directors

理事长　ľīshìzhǎng　chairman of a board of directors or of an executive council

理顺　ľīshùn　straighten out; sort out: 把事情～ straighten out one's affairs / ～经济关系 straighten out economic relationships

理所当然　ľī suǒ dāngrán　of course; as a matter of course; naturally: 他们的荒谬提案～地被否决了。Of course their absurd proposal was rejected. / 有的人安于现状, 把这一切看成～的了。Some people are resigned to the present state of affairs and regard it as a matter of course. / 他把帮助别人当做自己～的义务。He considered helping other people his natural duty.

理想　ľīxiǎng　① an ideal: 他的～很高。He has high ideals. / 你～中的丈夫是个什么样的人? What's your ideal of what a husband should be? / 在现实面前, 他的～都破灭了。All his ideals were destroyed by actualities. ② be ideal: 天气很～。The weather is ideal. / 他找到了一个～的伴侣。He found an ideal companion. / 他考得不够～。He didn't do too well in the exam.

理想国　ľīxiǎngguó　an ideal state; utopia

理想气体　ľīxiǎng qìtǐ　phys. ideal gas

理想主义　ľīxiǎngzhǔyì　idealism

理性　ľīxìng　① rational ② the rational faculty; reason: 失去～ lose one's reason

理性认识　ľīxìng rènshi　philos. rational cognition; rational knowledge

理学　ľīxué　① a rationalistic Confucian philosophical school that developed during the Song and Ming Dynasties, known to the West as Neo-Confucianism ② natural science: ～博士 Doctor of Science (D. Sc.) / ～硕士 Master of Science (M. Sc.)

理学士　ľīxuéshì　Bachelor of Science (B. Sc.)

理血　ľīxuè　Chin. med. regulating blood condition, including its generation, circulation and removal of stasis

理应　ľīyīng　ought to; should: 他有困难, 我们～帮助。He's in difficulties, and we ought to help him.

理由　ľīyóu　reason; ground; argument: 有充分～相信 have every reason to believe / 没有～抱怨 have no grounds for complaint / 他提出的～不能成立。His argument is untenable. / 他想找～为自己的错误辩解。He tried to find an excuse for his error. / 这些要求毫无～。These demands have neither rhyme nor reason.

理喻　ľīyù　reason with sb.: 不可理喻 bùkě ľīyù

理直气壮　ľīzhí-qìzhuàng　with justice on one's side, one is bold and assured: ～地回答 reply with perfect assurance / ～地予以驳斥 justly and forcefully refute / 我们～, 难道让他欺侮不成! We have justice on our side, so there's no fear of his getting the better of us!

理智　ľīzhì　① reason; intellect: 丧失～ lose one's reason; lose one's senses / 碰到严重事情的时候, 他的～总控制不住感情。When confronted with a serious matter, his reason always gives way to emotion. ② rational: ～点儿 Do try to be rational.

理中　ľīzhōng　Chin. med. regulating the functions of the stomach and spleen

锂
ľī　chem. lithium (Li)

锂云母　ľīyúnmǔ　lepidolite; lithia mica

鲤
ľī　carp

鲤鱼　ľīyú　carp

鲤鱼钳　ľīyúqián　slip-joint pliers

醴
ľī　formal sweet wine

鳢
ľī　murrel; snakehead

蠡
ľī　① used in persons' names, as in 范～ ② (Lǐ) (also 蠡县 Lǐxiàn) a county in Hebei Province ——see also ľí

ľī

力
ľì　① phys. force ② power; strength; ability: 人力 rénlì / 理解力 ľījiělì ③ physical strength: ～大无比 of prodigious strength ④ do all one can; make every effort: ～谏 try all one can to remonstrate

力巴　ľìba　dial. ① not adept; awkward; clumsy ② (also 力巴头 ľìbatóu) layman

力避　ľìbì　try hard to avoid or avert: ～嫌疑 try hard to avoid suspicion

力臂　ľìbì　phys. arm of force

力不从心　ľì bù cóng xīn　ability falling short of one's wishes; unable to do as much as one would like to

力不能支　ľì bùnéng zhī　unable to stand the strain any

longer; too weak to stay on one's feet

力不胜任 lì bù shèngrèn be unequal to one's task; incompetent

力场 lìchǎng *phys.* field of force

力持 lìchí insist on; uphold: ～异议 insist on one's dissenting views / ～正义 uphold justice

力畜 lìchù draught animal; beast of burden

力促 lìcù make every effort to promote: ～此事成功 try hard to make it a success

力点 lìdiǎn *phys.* force (on a lever)

力度 lìdù *mus.* dynamics

力疾从公 lì jí cóng gōng attend to one's duties in spite of illness

力竭声嘶 lìjié-shēngsī same as 声嘶力竭 shēngsī-lìjié

力戒 lìjiè strictly avoid; do everything possible to avoid; guard against: ～临战分散兵力 strictly avoid the dispersal of forces before an engagement / ～浪费 do everything possible to avoid waste / ～骄傲 guard against arrogance

力矩 lìjǔ *phys.* moment of force; moment: 合～ resultant moment

力量 lìliang ① physical strength: 这一脚～很大。This is a powerful kick. ② power; force; strength: 我一定尽我的～帮忙。I'll certainly do everything in my power to help. / 不要过低估计敌人的～。Don't underestimate the strength of the enemy. / 依靠群众的～ rely on the strength of the masses / 增强国防～ build up defence capability / 世界上没有任何～可以阻止历史车轮的前进。No force on earth can hold back the wheel of history. ③ potency; efficacy; strength: 这种农药的～大。This pesticide is strong.

力谋 lìmóu try hard to; strive to: ～缓和国际紧张局势 strive for a relaxation of international tension

力偶 lì'ǒu *phys.* couple

力排众议 lì pái zhòngyì prevail over all dissenting views; override all objections

力气 lìqi physical strength; effort: 他的～不小。He has great strength. / 他连上楼的～都没有。He hasn't even the strength to walk upstairs. / 不费～是什么都学不好的。You can't learn anything without making an effort.

力气活 lìqihuó heavy work; strenuous work

力钱 lìqian *dial. old* payment to a porter

力求 lìqiú make every effort to; do one's best to; strive to: 文字～精练。Strive to be concise in writing. / 我们～取得一致意见。We'll do our best to reach a consensus.

力士 lìshì a man of great strength; strong man

力所能及 lì suǒ néng jí in one's power: 在～的范围内 within one's power / 退休老工人主动为集体做些～的工作。The retired workers volunteered to do everything they could for the collective.

力透纸背 lì tòu zhǐbèi (of handwriting or calligraphy) vigorous; powerful; forceful

力图 lìtú try hard to; strive to: ～否认 try hard to deny / ～摆脱困境 strive to get out of a predicament / 敌军～挽回败局。The enemy made a desperate attempt to avert defeat.

力挽狂澜 lì wǎn kuánglán do one's utmost to stem a raging tide or save a desperate situation; make vigorous efforts to turn the tide

力线 lìxiàn *phys.* line of force

力行 lìxíng be diligent in action; practise with earnestness

力学[1] lìxué mechanics: 波动～ wave mechanics / 断裂～ fracture mechanics / 生物～ biomechanics

力学[2] lìxué *formal* study hard: ～不倦 be tireless in studying

力战 lìzhàn fight with all one's might

力争 lìzhēng ① work hard for; do all one can to: ～主

动 do all one can to gain the initiative / ～更大的丰收 work hard for a still bigger harvest / ～少花钱,多办事 strive by every means to spend less and accomplish more ② argue strongly; contend vigorously

力争上游 lìzhēng shàngyóu aim high; strive for first place

力证 lìzhèng strong evidence; convincing proof

力租 lìzū common name for 劳役地租 láoyì dìzū

历[1]**（歷）** lì ① go through; undergo; experience: 历尽 lìjìn ② all previous (occasions, sessions, etc.): 历年 lìnián / 历届 lìjiè ③ covering all; one by one: ～访各有关部门 have visited the departments concerned one by one

历[2]**（厤、曆、歷）** lì calendar: 阴历 yīnlì / 日历 rìlì

历本 lìběn *dial.* almanac

历朝 lìcháo ① successive dynasties; past dynasties ② the successive reigns of a dynasty

历程 lìchéng course: 回顾我们党的战斗～ look back on the course of the struggle of our Party

历次 lìcì all previous (occasions, etc.): 解放后～政治运动 the various political movements since liberation / 在～比赛中她都取得了优异的成绩。She has done well in all past contests.

历代 lìdài successive dynasties; past dynasties: ～封建王朝 the feudal dynasties of past ages / ～名画 famous paintings through the ages

历法 lìfǎ calendric system; calendar: 这国的～跟别国不一样。This country has a different calendar.

历届 lìjiè all previous (sessions, governments, etc.): ～全国人民代表大会 all the previous National People's Congresses / ～毕业生 graduates of all previous years

历尽 lìjìn have gone through a lof of: ～艰辛 have gone through all kinds of hardships and difficulties / ～沧桑 have experienced various vicissitudes of life

历久 lìjiǔ for a long time

历来 lìlái *adv.* always; constantly; all through the ages: ～认为 have invariably insisted; have consistently held; have always maintained / 这些岛屿～都是中国的领土。These islands have been Chinese territory from time immemorial.

历来如此 lìlái rúcǐ this has always been the case

历历 lìlì distinctly; clearly: 往事～在心头。Past events remain fresh in my memory. / 湖水清澈,游鱼～可数。The water of the lake was so clear that every fish could be seen distinctly.

历历在目 lìlì zài mù come clearly into view; leap up before the eyes: 追忆往事,～。As I look back, scenes of the past leap before my eyes. / 回想起来,震后情景依然～。In my mind's eye I can still see the sight of horror after the earthquake.

历练 lìliàn experience and training

历乱 lìluàn *formal* mixed and disorderly; chaotic: ～的脚步声 a flurry of footsteps

历年[1] lìnián over the years: ～的积蓄 savings over the years

历年[2] lìnián calendar year

历任 lìrèn ① have successively held the posts of; have served successively as: 他～连长、营长、团长、师长等职。He successively held the posts of company, battalion, regiment and division commander. ② successive: 这家公司的～经理 the successive managers of this company

历时 lìshí last (a period of time); take (a period of time): 手术～三个小时。The operation took three hours. / ～八年的抗日战争 the eight-year-long War of Resistance Against Japan

历史 lìshǐ ① history: 人民群众是～的创造者。The masses of the people are the makers of history. / 中国～悠久。China has a long history. / ～上有很多像这样的例子。There are many such examples in history. / 这件事早已成为～了。That's past history already. / 五四运动具有重大的～意义。The May Fourth Movement was of historic significance. / 全然不顾～事实 in utter disregard of historical fact / ～地看问题 look at the problem historically / 创～最高水平 hit an all-time high / ～上的今天 today in history / ～上遗留下来的问题 a problem (or issue) left over by history (or from the past); a legacy from the past ② history (as a course of study): 他是研究～的。His field is history. ③ personal records: ～清白 have a clean personal record / 隐瞒自己的～ conceal one's past record / ～问题 questions of a political nature in one's personal history

历史比较语言学 lìshǐ bǐjiào yǔyánxué historical comparative linguistics

历史博物馆 lìshǐ bówùguǎn history (or historical) museum

历史潮流 lìshǐ cháoliú the tide of history; historical trend

历史地图 lìshǐ dìtú historical map or atlas

历史观 lìshǐguān view (or conception) of history

历史剧 lìshǐjù historical play

历史人物 lìshǐ rénwù historical personage; historical figure

历史唯物论 lìshǐwéiwùlùn historical materialism

历史唯物主义 lìshǐwéiwùzhǔyì historical materialism

历史唯心论 lìshǐwéixīnlùn historical idealism

历史唯心主义 lìshǐwéixīnzhǔyì historical idealism

历史小说 lìshǐ xiǎoshuō historical novel

历史性 lìshǐxìng historic; of historic significance: ～胜利 a historic victory

历史学家 lìshǐxuéjiā historian

历史循环论 lìshǐ xúnhuánlùn historicism

历史遗产 lìshǐ yíchǎn legacy of history; historical heritage

历书 lìshū almanac

历数 lìshǔ count one by one; enumerate: ～侵略者的罪行 enumerate the crimes of the aggressors

历险 lìxiǎn experience dangers or adventures

历元 lìyuán *astron.* epoch

历月 lìyuè *astron.* calendar month

立 lì ① stand: 他在那儿～了半天了。He has stood there for quite a while. ② set or stand sth. up; erect: 别横着放，～着放。Don't lay it down, stand it up. / 把梯子～起来。Set up the ladder. / 把伞～在门后头。Stand the umbrella behind the door. / ～碑 set up (or erect) a monument / ～界桩 erect boundary markers ③ upright; vertical; erect: 立柜 lìguì ④ establish; found; set up: 这是谁～的规矩? Who established this rule? / ～标兵 make sb. the pacesetter; set up a model; set a good example ⑤ draw up; conclude: ～合同 conclude (or sign) a contract / ～章程 draw up rules and regulations / ～遗嘱 make a will ⑥ *formal* ascend the throne: 文帝初～，大赦天下。When Emperor Wen first came to the throne, a general amnesty was proclaimed to the empire. ⑦ appoint; designate: ～皇太子 designate a crown prince / 吕太后～诸吕为王。Empress Lu set up members of her family as kings. ⑧ exist; live: 过去这块地不～一苗。In the past nothing could grow on this tract of land. ⑨ *adv.* immediately; instantaneously: ～见功效 produce immediate results; feel the effect immediately

立案 lì'àn ① register; put on record ② *leg.* place a case on file for investigation and prosecution: 对该案予以～受理。This case should be put on file for investigation and prosecution.

立场 lìchǎng position; stand; standpoint: 阐明我们对这一问题的～ make clear our position on this question / 马克思主义的～、观点和方法 the Marxist stand, viewpoint and method / 站在党的～ keep to the stand of the Party / 丧失～ depart from the correct stand / ～坚定 be steadfast in one's stand; take a firm stand

立春 Lìchūn ① the Beginning of Spring—the 1st of the 24 solar terms ② the day marking the beginning of the 1st solar term (Feb. 3, 4, or 5) ——see also 节气 jiéqì; 二十四节气 èrshí sì jiéqì

立此存照 lì cǐ cún zhào a contract (or an agreement, etc.) is hereby concluded and to be filed for future reference

立党为公 lì dǎng wèi gōng build a party serving the interests of the people

立德粉 lìdéfěn *chem.* lithopone

立等 lìděng wait for sth. to be done immediately: ～回信 wait for an immediate reply / 本店设有快修部，～可取。We have a quick repair service where repairs can be done on the spot.

立地 lìdì *adv.* on the spot; immediately

立定 lìdìng halt: ～! (word of command) Halt!

立定跳远 lìdìng tiàoyuǎn standing long jump

立冬 Lìdōng ① the Beginning of Winter—the 19th of the 24 solar terms ② the day marking the beginning of the 19th solar term (Nov. 7 or 8) ——see also 节气 jiéqì; 二十四节气 èrshí sì jiéqì

立法 lìfǎ make (or enact) laws; legislate: 经济～ economic legislation / 行政～ administrative legislation

立法机关 lìfǎ jīguān legislative body; legislature

立法权 lìfǎquán legislative power: 全国人民代表大会行使国家～。The National People's Congress exercises the legislative power of the state.

立方 lìfāng ① *math.* cube: 二的～ the cube of 2; 2^3 ② short for 立方体 lìfāngtǐ ③ *m.* cubic metre; stere: 一～土 one cubic metre of earth

立方根 lìfānggēn *math.* cube root

立方厘米 lìfāng límǐ cubic centimetre

立方米 lìfāngmǐ cubic metre

立方体 lìfāngtǐ cube

立竿见影 lì gān jiàn yǐng set up a pole and you see its shadow—produce instant results

立功 lìgōng render meritorious service; do a deed of merit; win honour; make contributions: 立大功 render outstanding service / 立新功 make new contributions / 立一等功 win a first class merit citation / 立集体三等功 be awarded a class three collective commendation / ～者受奖。Those who render meritorious service receive awards.

立功奖状 lìgōng jiǎngzhuàng certificate for meritorious service; certificate of merit

立功赎罪 lìgōng shúzuì do good deeds to atone for one's crimes

立柜 lìguì clothes closet; wardrobe; hanging cupboard

立国 lìguó found a state; build up a nation: 工农业乃～之本。Agriculture and industry are the base on which to build up the nation.

立候 lìhòu *formal* wait for sth. to be done immediately: ～回音 An immediate reply is requested. or Awaiting your prompt reply.

立户 lìhù ① register for a household residence card; register for permanent residence ② (less common than 立户头) open an account with the bank

立即 lìjí *adv.* immediately; at once; promptly: 有要事相商, 请你～回厂。There is something important to discuss. Please return to the factory immediately. / 种了树应该～浇水。Trees should be watered right after they are planted. / 判处死刑, ～执行 be sentenced to death

and executed immediately / 接到命令必须～无条件执行。When you receive orders you must obey them promptly without question.

立交 lìjiāo short for 立体交叉 lìtǐ jiāochā

立交桥 lìjiāoqiáo ① overpass; flyover ② motorway interchange

立脚点 lìjiǎodiǎn same as 立足点 lìzúdiǎn

立井 lìjǐng same as 竖井 shùjǐng

立决 lìjué summary execution

立克次体 lìkècìshǐtǐ *med.* rickettsia

立刻 lìkè *adv.* immediately; at once; right away: 我～就去。I'll go right away. / 铃声一响，教室里～安静下来。As soon as the bell rang, the classroom quieted down at once. / 他～作了回答。He answered immediately.

立论 lìlùn ① set forth one's views; present one's arguments ② argument; position; line of reasoning

立马 lìmǎ ① *formal* pull up a horse: ～横刀 on horseback with sword drawn ② *dial.* immediately; at once; right away: 我～就去。I'll go immediately.

立眉瞪眼 lìméi-dèngyǎn (also 立眉竖眼 lìméi-shùyǎn) get angry; lose one's temper: 你为什么动不动就～? Why do you lose your temper so easily?

立米 lìmǐ short for 立方米 lìfāngmǐ

立面图 lìmiàntú *archit.* elevation (drawing)

立契 lìqì conclude a contract (*or* an agreement)

立秋 Lìqiū ① the Beginning of Autumn—the 13th of the 24 solar terms ② the day marking the beginning of the 13th solar term (Aug. 7, 8, or 9) ——see also 节气 jiéqì; 二十四节气 èrshí sì jiéqì

立绒 lìróng cut velvet

立射 lìshè *mil.* fire from a standing position

立身处世 lìshēn-chǔshì the way one conducts oneself in society

立时 lìshí same as 立刻 lìkè

立式 lìshì vertical; upright: ～车床 vertical lathe / ～钻床 upright drill; vertical drill

立誓 lìshì take an oath; vow

立嗣 lìsì adopt an heir

立陶宛 Lìtáowǎn Lithuania

立体 lìtǐ ① three-dimensional; stereoscopic ② *math.* solid

立体电影 lìtǐ diànyǐng stereoscopic film; three-dimensional (*or* 3-D) film; cinerama: ～院 stereoscopic cinema

立体感 lìtǐgǎn three-dimensional effect

立体化学 lìtǐ huàxué stereochemistry

立体几何 lìtǐ jǐhé solid geometry

立体交叉 lìtǐ jiāochā grade separation

立体角 lìtǐjiǎo *math.* solid angle

立体模型 lìtǐ móxíng space model

立体派 lìtǐpài cubism

立体声 lìtǐshēng stereophony; stereo: ～唱机 stereo record-player; stereo / ～唱片 stereo record / ～磁带 stereotape / ～收录机 stereo radio-tape recorder; stereo tape recorder; stereo / ～音响设备 stereo component system; stereo

立体图 lìtǐtú hologram

立体图像 lìtǐ túxiàng stereopicture

立体显微镜 lìtǐ xiǎnwēijìng stereoscopic microscope; stereomicroscope

立体战争 lìtǐ zhànzhēng three-dimensional warfare; triphibious warfare

立体照相机 lìtǐ zhàoxiàngjī stereoscopic camera; stereo camera

立夏 Lìxià ① the Beginning of Summer—the 7th of the 24 solar terms ② the day marking the beginning of the 7th solar term (May 5, 6, or 7) ——see also 节气 jiéqì; 二十四节气 èrshí sì jiéqì

立宪 lìxiàn constitutionalism: 君主～ constitutional monarchy / ～政体 constitutional government; constitutionalism

立像 lìxiàng standing statue

立效 lìxiào ① have immediate effect; be instantly effective ② *formal* render meritorious service

立言 lìyán expound one's ideas in writing; achieve glory by writing

立意 lìyì ① be determined; make up one's mind ② conception; approach: 这幅画～新颖。This painting shows an interesting new approach.

立于不败之地 lì yú bù bài zhī dì establish oneself in an unassailable position; be in an impregnable position; be invincible: 不论时局发展的情况如何，我们均须作持久打算，才能～。No matter how the situation develops, we must always calculate on a long-term basis, if our position is to be invincible.

立约 lìyuē conclude a treaty; draw up an agreement (*or* a contract)

立帐 lìzhàng open an account

立正 lìzhèng stand at attention: ～! (word of command) Attention!

立志 lìzhì resolve; be determined: ～改革 be determined to carry out reforms; be resolved to institute reforms / 他～要当一名宇航员。He is determined to become an astronaut.

立轴 lìzhóu ① vertical scroll of painting or calligraphy; wall scroll ② *mech.* vertical shaft; upright shaft

立传 lìzhuàn write a biography

立锥之地 lì zhuī zhī dì (usu. used in the negative with 无) land just enough to stick an awl into: 无～ have not even enough land to stick an awl into—very poor / 贫无～ so poor as to have not even a pin-point (*or* speck) of land—utterly destitute

立姿 lìzī *mil.* standing position

立字 lìzì sign an agreement, a contract, a receipt, etc.

立足 lìzú ① have a foothold somewhere ② base oneself upon: ～于独立自主和自力更生 be based on independence and self-reliance / ～基层，面向群众 have one's feet firmly planted at the grass roots and keep in view the broad masses of the people

立足点 lìzúdiǎn ① foothold; footing: 找不到～ be unable to find a foothold ② standpoint; stand: 把～移到人民群众这边来 change one's stand to that of the masses; move one's feet over to the side of the masses

立足之地 lìzú zhī dì foothold; footing: 在社会上获得～ gain a place in society

厉（厲）

lì ① strict; rigorous: ～禁 strictly forbid ② stern; severe: 厉声 lìshēng ③ (Lì) a surname

厉兵秣马 lìbīng-mòmǎ same as 秣马厉兵 mòmǎ-lìbīng

厉鬼 lìguǐ an evil spirit

厉害 lìhai same as 利害 lìhai

厉色 lìsè a stern countenance

厉声 lìshēng in a stern voice

厉行 lìxíng strictly enforce; rigorously enforce; make great efforts to carry out: ～节约 practise strict economy

吏

lì *old* ① a government clerk ② official; mandarin

吏部 Lìbù the Board of Civil Office ——see also 六部 Liùbù

吏治 lìzhì *old* the administration of local officials: 澄清～ bring order into the local administration

沥（瀝）

lì ① drip; trickle: ～血 drip blood ② drop: 余沥 yúlì

沥涝 lìlào waterlogging: ～成灾。 Waterlogging has

caused serious damage.

沥沥 *onom.* the sound of wind or of flowing waters

沥青 lìqīng pitch; asphalt; bitumen: 天然～ natural asphalt; natural bitumen / ～混凝土 bituminous concrete; asphalt concrete / ～基原油 asphalt-base crude oil / ～路 bituminous road; asphalt road / ～煤 pitch coal / ～油毡 asphalt felt / ～油纸 asphalt paper / ～铀矿 uraninite

沥水 lìshuǐ waterlogging caused by excessive rainfall

丽¹(麗)

lì beautiful: 美丽 měilì

丽²(麗)

lì *formal* depend on; attach oneself to: 附丽 fùlì
——see also lí

丽人 lìrén *formal* a beautiful woman; a beauty

丽日 lìrì *formal* bright sun

丽质 lìzhì beauty (of a woman): 天生～ natural beauty

励(勵)

lì encourage: 勉励 miǎnlì

励磁 lìcí *phys.* excitation

励磁机 lìcíjī exciter

励精图治 lì jīng tú zhì (usu. of a ruler or prime minister) exert oneself to make the country prosperous

励志 lìzhì be determined to fulfil one's aspirations

利

lì ① sharp: ～爪 sharp claws ② favourable; smooth: 顺利 shùnlì ③ advantage; benefit: 有利有弊 yǒulì-yǒubì ④ profit; interest: 连本带利 lián běn dài lì profit as well as capital ⑤ do good to; benefit: ～己～人 benefit other people as well as oneself

利比里亚 Lìbǐlǐyà Liberia

利比里亚人 Lìbǐlǐyàrén Liberian

利比亚 Lìbǐyà Libya

利比亚人 Lìbǐyàrén Libyan

利弊 lì-bì advantages and disadvantages; pros and cons: 各有～ there are both advantages and disadvantages

利导 lìdǎo see 因势利导 yīn shì lìdǎo

利钝 lì-dùn ① sharp or blunt ② smooth going or rough: 成败利钝 chéng-bài lì-dùn

利多卡因 lìduōkǎyīn *pharm.* lidocaine

利福霉素 lìfúméisù *pharm.* rifamycin

利福平 lìfúpíng *pharm.* rifampin (RFP)

利改税 lì gǎi shuì tax payments (made by state-owned enterprises) instead of profit deliveries to the state

利滚利 lì gǔn lì at compound interest

利害 lì-hài advantages and disadvantages; gains and losses: 不计～ regardless of gains or losses / ～冲突 conflict of interests / 有共同的～关系 have common interests / 他不知道～。 He doesn't realize what the consequences will be.

利害 lìhai ① (of a wild animal or of one's temper, words, etc.) fierce; terrible: 老虎比狮子还～。 Tigers are even fiercer than lions. / 那些话很～。 Those are very sharp words. / 他这张嘴很～了。 He has a sharp tongue. ② (of a person) strict; stern; harsh: 我们老师很～。 Our teacher is very strict. / 他的样子很～。 His appearance is very stern. / 我要给他点～。 I'll teach him a lesson. ③ (of illness, heat, cold, etc.) intense; severe; terrible: 他病得很～。 He is seriously ill. / 这几天热得很～。 It's been terribly hot these few days. / 这种烟太～。 This kind of tobacco is too strong. / 这着棋十分～。 That's a devastating (chess) move.

利害攸关 lì-hài yōu guān concern sb.'s vital interests

利己主义 lìjǐzhǔyì egoism

利口 lìkǒu ① a glib tongue ② tasty and refreshing: 这几样凉菜, 吃起来挺～。 These cold dishes are quite tasty and refreshing.

利令智昏 lì lìng zhì hūn be blinded by lust for gain

利禄 lìlù *formal* rank and wealth: 功名利禄 gōngmíng-lìlù

利率 lìlǜ rate of interest; interest rate

利落 lìluo ① agile; nimble; dexterous: 动作～ agile movements / 手脚～ dexterous; deft / 说话不～ speak slowly and indistinctly ② neat; orderly: 他做事干净～。 He is a neat worker. ③ settled; finished: 事情已经办～了。 The matter is all settled.

利眠宁 lìmiánníng *pharm.* librium

利尿 lìniào diuresis

利尿剂 lìniàojì diuretic

利器 lìqì ① a sharp weapon ② good tool; efficient instrument

利钱 lìqian interest (on an investment): 付～ pay interest

利权 lìquán economic rights (esp. of a country): ～外溢 lose economic rights to foreigners

利刃 lìrèn a sharp sword

利润 lìrùn profit

利润留成 lìrùn liúchéng retained profits

利润率 lìrùnlǜ profit margin

利润税 lìrùnshuì profits tax

利市 lìshì ① *formal* profits: ～三倍 threefold profits ② *dial.* a good market: 发个～ find a good market ③ *dial.* lucky

利索 lìsuo same as 利落 lìluo

利他主义 lìtāzhǔyì altruism

利息 lìxī interest (on an investment): ～很高。 The interest is very high. / ～回扣 interest rebate

利血平 lìxuèpíng *pharm.* reserpine

利益 lìyì interest; benefit; profit: 为大多数人谋～ work for the interests of the vast majority of people / 使人民群众得到～ benefit the masses of the people

利用 lìyòng ① use; utilize; make use of: ～废料 make use of scrap material; turn scrap material to good account / 充分～最新科学技术成就 make full use of the latest achievements in science and technology / 他常～假日为周围群众做好事。 On holidays he often gives a helping hand to people in the neighbourhood. ② take advantage of; exploit. ～职权 take advantage of one's position and power; exploit one's office / 受人～ be made use of; be a cat's-paw / 互相～ each using the other for his own ends

利用率 lìyònglǜ utilization ratio

利用系数 lìyòng xìshù utilization coefficient; utilization factor

利诱 lìyòu lure by promise of gain

利于 lìyú be of advantage to; benefit

利欲熏心 lìyù xūn xīn be obsessed with the desire for gain; be overcome by covetousness; be blinded by greed

呖(嚦)

lì see below

呖呖 lìlì *onom. liter.* the warble of birds: 莺声～。 The orioles are warbling.

戾

lì ① crime; sin: 罪戾 zuìlì ② perverse; unreasonable: 乖戾 guāilì

例

lì ① example; instance: 举例 jǔlì ② precedent: 破例 pòlì / 援例 yuánlì ③ case; instance: 患这种病的三十三～中, 二十一～有显著好转。 Out of the 33 cases of this disease, 21 showed marked progress. ④ rule; regulation: 旧～ an old rule / 不在此～。 That is an exception. ⑤ regular; routine: 例会 lìhuì

例规 lìguī ① convention; usual practice ② rules; regulations

例会 lìhuì regular meeting

例假 lìjià ① official holiday; legal holiday ② *euph.* menstrual period; period: 她来～的时候总是不大舒服。 She always feels unwell at the start of her period.

例句 lìjù illustrative sentence; example sentence

例如 lìrú for instance; for example (e.g.); such as: 田径 运动的项目很多,～跳高、跳远、百米赛跑等。There are many track-and-field events, such as the high jump, the long jump, the 100-metre dash, etc.

例题 lìtí a problem designed to illustrate a principle or method (as in a mathematics book); example

例外 lìwài ① be an exception: 世界各国都有环保问题, 中国也不～。The problem of environmental protection affects all countries, and China is no exception. / 大家 都得遵守规定,谁也不能～。Everyone must obey the rules—no exceptions are made. ② exception: 什么事都 有～。There's an exception to everything. / 那是～。 That's an exception.

例行公事 lìxíng gōngshì ① routine; routine business ② mere formality

例言 lìyán introductory remarks; notes on the use of a book

例语 lìyǔ illustrative phrase; example word or phrase

例证 lìzhèng illustration; example; case in point

例子 lìzi *inf.* example; case; instance: 你给我举个～。 Give me an example.

隶(隸、隸) lì ① be subordinate to; be under: 隶属 lìshǔ ② a person in servitude: 奴隶 núlì ③ same as 隶书 lìshū

隶书 lìshū official script, an ancient style of calligraphy current in the Han Dynasty (206 B.C.–A.D. 220), simpli- fied from *xiaozhuan* (小篆)

隶属 lìshǔ be subordinate to; be under the jurisdiction or command of: 这支部队～市警备区。This unit is under the command of the municipal garrison. / 直辖市 是直接～国务院的市。A province-level municipality is under the direct control of the State Council.

枥(櫪) lì *formal* manger

疬(癧) lì *formal* ① pestilence; plague ② sore; ulcer

疠(癘) lì see 瘰疬 luǒlì

栎(櫟) lì oak (*Quercus*) ——see also yuè

荔 lì see below

荔枝 lìzhī litchi; lichee

俐 lì see 伶俐 líng·lì; 伶牙俐齿 língyá-lìchǐ

郦(酈) lì a surname

俪(儷) lì ① paired; parallel: 俪句 lìjù ② hus- band and wife; married couple: 伉俪 kànglì

俪辞 lìcí a form of literary writing marked by antith- eses

俪句 lìjù parallel sentences

俪影 lìyǐng a photograph of a couple

俪语 lìyǔ same as 俪辞 lìcí

轹(轢) lì *formal* ① (of a cart) run over ② bully; oppress

莉 lì see 茉莉 mòlì

莅(蒞、涖) lì *formal* arrive; be present:

～场 be present on the occasion / ～会 be present at a meeting

莅临 lìlín *formal* arrive; be present: 敬请～指导。Your presence and guidance are requested.

砺(礪) lì *formal* ① whetstone ② whet; sharpen

砺石 lìshí *formal* whetstone

鬲(鬴、鬶) lì an ancient cooking tripod with hollow legs

栗¹ lì ① chestnut ② (Lì) a surname

栗²(慄) lì tremble; shudder: 战栗 zhànlì

栗暴 lìbào (also 栗凿 lìzáo) a knock on the head with the knuckles

栗钙土 lìgàitǔ chestnut soil

栗然 lìrán trembling; shuddering

栗色 lìsè chestnut colour; maroon

栗子 lìzi chestnut

猁 lì see 猞猁 shēlì

砾(礫) lì gravel; shingle: 砂砾 shālì

砾石 lìshí gravel: ～混凝土 gravel concrete / ～路 gravel road

砾岩 lìyán *geol.* conglomerate

粒 lì ① grain; granule; pellet: 砂～儿 grains of sand / 盐～儿 grains of salt / 豆～儿 beans ② m. (for grain- like things): 一～砂 a grain of sand / 一～米 a grain of rice / 三～子弹 three bullets / 每服五～。Dosage: 5 pills each time.

粒度 lìdù *metall.* size

粒肥 lìféi short for 颗粒肥料 kēlì féiliào

粒选 lìxuǎn grain-by-grain seed selection

粒雪 lìxuě granular snow; firn; *névé*

粒状 lìzhuàng granular: ～物 granules

粒子 lìzǐ *phys.* particle: ～加速器 particle accelerator / ～束 particle beam

粒子 lìzi grain; granule; pellet

笠 lì a large bamboo or straw hat with a conical crown and broad brim: 斗笠 dǒulì

唳 lì *onom. liter.* the cry of a crane, wild goose, etc.

蛎(蠣) lì see 牡蛎 mǔlì

粝(糲、糳) lì *formal* unpolished rice; brown rice

粝粱 lìliáng *formal* coarse food

詈 lì *formal* scold; curse

詈骂 lìmà *formal* scold; abuse: 互相～ hurl abuse at each other

霳(靂) lì see 霹雳 pīlì

痢 lì dysentery

痢疾 lìji dysentery

痢特灵 lìtèlíng *pharm.* furazolidone

傈 lì see below

傈僳族 Lìsùzú the Lisu nationality, or the Lisus, in- habiting Yunnan Province

髟

lí　see 鬎髟 làlí

lī

哩

lī　*part. dial.* ① (same as 呢, confined to use in declarative sentences): 天还早着~! It's still early. ② (same as 啦, used in enumerating items): 历史~, 地理~, 哲学~, 各种参考书都在书架上放着。History, geography, philosophy—you'll find all sorts of reference books on the shelves. ——see also lǐ; lǐ; yīnglǐ

蜊

lí　see 蛤蜊 géli

璃(瓈)

lí　see 玻璃 bōli; 琉璃 liúli

liǎ

俩(倆)

liǎ　*inf.* ① (a fusion of 两 and 个) two: 咱~ we two; both of us; the two of us / 这种冰棍儿一块钱~。You can get two of these popsicles for a *yuan*. ② some; several: 给他~钱儿。Give him some money. / 那么多事情, 这么~人干不了。There's so much to do that these few people can hardly cope. or There's too much work here for so few people. ——see also liǎng

lián

连¹

lián　① link; join; connect: 把这两条电线~起来。Connect these two electric wires. / 把零散的土地~成一片 join together scattered pieces of land / 这两句话~不起来。The two sentences are disconnected. or The two sentences don't hang together. ② *adv.* continuously; in succession; one after another: 他~说了三个钟头。He spoke continuously for three hours. / 他~着三天没来。He hasn't come for three days in a row. / ~发三封电报 send three telegrams in succession / ~挫强手 defeat strong opponents one after another / ~战皆捷 win a series of victories; win battle after battle ③ *prep.* including: ~你一共十个人。There are ten people, including you. ④ *mil.* company: 一营有三个~。A battalion has three companies. ⑤ (Lián) a surname

连²

lián　*prep.* (used correlatively with 也, 都, etc.) even: ~我都知道。Even I know. / 他~报也看不懂。He can't even read a newspaper. / 他~看都没看。He didn't even look.

连本带利　lián běn dài lì　both principal and interest; profit as well as capital

连比　liánbǐ　*math.* continued proportion (e.g. 1:3:9=27:81)

连鬓胡子　liánbìnhúzi　*inf.* whiskers; full beard

连茬　liánchá　same as 连作 liánzuò

连词　liáncí　*gram.* conjunction

连带　liándài　related: 人的作风和思想是有~关系的。A person's work style is related to his ideology.

连…带…　lián…dài…　① (indicating the inclusion of two items): 连吃带住一个月八十块钱 eighty *yuan* per month including room and board / 连老带小一共二十三个人。There are altogether 23, including the old people and children. ② (indicating the simultaneous

occurrence of two actions): 连说带比划 talking and gesticulating / 连蹦带跳 hopping and skipping / 连打带骂 beating and cursing

连带责任　liándài zérèn　*leg.* joint liability

连裆裤　liándāngkù　child's pants with no slit in the seat ——see also 穿连裆裤 chuān liándāngkù

连队　liánduì　*mil.* company

连发　liánfā　*mil.* running fire: ~枪 repeating rifle; magazine gun / ~射击 burst (of fire) / ~武器 repeating firearms

连分数　liánfēnshù　*math.* continued fraction

连杆　liángǎn　*mech.* connecting rod

连根拔　liángēnbá　tear up by the roots; uproot

连亘　liángèn　(of mountain ranges) continue; extend: 山岭~ a continuous stretch of mountains

连拱坝　liángǒngbà　multiple-arch dam; multi-arch dam

连拱桥　liángǒngqiáo　multiple-arch bridge; multi-arch bridge

连贯　liánguàn　link up; piece together; hang together; be coherent: 长江大桥把南北交通~起来了。The Changjiang bridges link up the communication lines between north and south. / 把各种材料~起来考虑 piece together various kinds of data and ponder over them / 文章写得很不~。This article is rather incoherent. / 上下句意思要~。Two consecutive sentences must hang together.

连贯性　liánguànxìng　coherence; continuity

连锅端　liánguōduān　take all the pots and pans—take or get rid of the whole lot: 伪军据点被游击队~了。The stronghold of the puppet regime's troops was completely destroyed by the guerrillas.

连环　liánhuán　a chain of rings

连环保　liánhuánbǎo　collective responsibility (an old system by which each household of a district was made responsible for any infringement of the law in the whole district)

连环画　liánhuánhuà　a book (usu. for children) with a story told in pictures; picture-story book

连环计　liánhuánjì　a set of interlocking stratagems; a series of stratagems

连环图画　liánhuán túhuà　comic strips; comics

连击　liánjī　*sports* double hit (in table tennis); double contact (in volleyball)

连枷　liánjiā　flail

连脚裤　liánjiǎokù　infant's pants with bootees attached

连接　liánjiē　join; link: 把两条铁路~起来 link up the two railway lines / ~不断的山岭 a continuous range of mountains

连接号　liánjiēhào　hyphen (-)

连接线　liánjiēxiàn　*mus.* tie

连结　liánjié　same as 连接 liánjiē

连襟　liánjīn　husbands of sisters: 他们是~。Their wives are sisters. or They are brothers-in-law.

连裤袜　liánkùwà　panty hose

连累　lián·lěi　implicate; involve; get sb. into trouble

连类　liánlèi　sort out and classify

连理枝　liánlǐzhī　two trees with branches interlocked—a loving couple ——see also 比翼鸟 bǐyìniǎo

连连　liánlián　*adv.* repeatedly; again and again: ~点头 nod again and again (to show agreement, etc.) / 演出结束, 观众~叫好。At the end of the performance, the audience applauded again and again.

连忙　liánmáng　*adv.* hastily; hurriedly; promptly: 他~道歉。He hastened to apologize. / 听见有人叫唤, 他~去开门。Hearing someone calling him, he hurriedly went to open the door.

连袂　liánmèi　*formal.* ① same as 联袂 liánmèi ② same as 连襟 liánjīn

连绵　liánmián　continuous; unbroken; uninterrupted: 阴

雨～。 There was an unbroken spell of wet weather. / ～起伏的山峦 rolling hills

连年 liánnián in successive years; in consecutive years; for years running; for years on end: 战胜～干旱 conquer successive years of drought / ～丰收 reap rich harvests for many years running / 产量～上升。 Output increases year after year.

连皮 liánpí (weight of goods) including the packing; gross (weight): ～三十斤。 It weighs 30 *jin*, including the packing. *or* The gross weight is 30 *jin*.

连翩 liánpiān same as 联翩 liánpiān

连篇 liánpiān ① throughout a piece of writing; page after page: 空话～ pages and pages of empty verbiage ② one article after another; a multitude of articles

连篇累牍 liánpiān-lěidú lengthy and tedious; at great length: ～地发表文章 publish one article after another

连谱号 liánpǔhào *mus.* accolade; brace

连翘 liánqiáo *Chin. med.* the capsule of weeping forsythia (*Forsythia suspensa*)

连任 liánrèn be reappointed or reelected consecutively; renew one's term of office: ～党支部书记 be reelected secretary of the Party branch / ～部长 be reappointed minister / ～总统 be reelected president

连日 liánrì for days on end; day after day: ～来 for the last few days / ～刮大风。 The wind blew hard for several days running.

连射 liánshè *mil.* running fire

连声 liánshēng say repeatedly: ～称谢 say "thanks" repeatedly; thank sb. profusely / ～称赞 be profuse in one's praise

连史纸 liánshǐzhǐ a fine paper made from bamboo (produced in Jiangxi Province)

连锁 liánsuǒ linked together

连锁反应 liánsuǒ fǎnyìng chain reaction

连台本戏 liántái běnxì a serialized theatrical performance

连体婴 liántǐyīng same as 联体婴 liántǐyīng

连天 liántiān ① for several days in a row; for days on end: ～连夜 for days and nights / ～阴雨。 It was cloudy and drizzly for days on end. ② continuously; incessantly: 叫苦连天 jiàokǔ liántiān ③ (of a mountain, horizon, flames, etc.) touch the sky: 高峰～ skyscraping peaks / 炮火～。 Gunfire licked the heavens. / 杀声～ air-rending battle cries / 天连水, 水～。 The sky and the water seem to merge.

连同 liántóng *conj.* together with; along with: 图纸～清单一并送去。 Send the blueprints along with the inventory.

连谓式 liánwèishì *gram.* sentence with consecutive predicates

连写 liánxiě (in Chinese phonetic transcription) write the two or more syllables of a word together (e.g. rénmín for 人民, tuōlājī for 拖拉机)

连续 liánxù *adv.* continuously; successively; in a row: ～作战 continuous fighting; successive battles; consecutive operations / ～爆破 continuous demolition / ～十五年丰收 reap bumper harvests for fifteen years in succession / ～工作八小时 work eight hours at a stretch / ～六年未出事故。 There have been no accidents for six years running.

连续光谱 liánxù guǎngpǔ *phys.* continuous spectrum

连续航次 liánxù hángcì consecutive voyages

连续剧 liánxùjù serial

连续性 liánxùxìng continuity; continuance: 保持政策的～ maintain the continuity of a policy

连选连任 liánxuǎn-liánrèn be reelected and serve another term

连夜 liányè ① the same night; that very night; all through the night: 我们～开车, 赶回来了。 We drove

far into the night and rushed back. / 他们～立起了井架。 They got the derrick into place before the night was out. ② for nights on end

连衣裙 liányīqún a woman's dress; dress

连阴天 liányīntiān cloudy weather for several days running

连阴雨 liányīnyǔ an unbroken spell of wet weather

连用 liányòng use consecutively; use together: 这两个词不能～。 These two words do not go together.

连载 liánzǎi publish in instalments; serialize: 长篇～ serial (of a novel, etc.)

连长 liánzhǎng company commander

连种 liánzhòng same as 连作 liánzuò

连轴转 liánzhóuzhuàn work day and night; work round the clock

连珠 liánzhū like a chain of pearls or a string of beads —in rapid succession: ～似的机枪声 a continuous rattle of machine-gun fire / 捷报～似的传来。 One piece of good news followed another.

连珠炮 liánzhūpào continuous firing; drumfire: 说话像～ chatter away like a machine gun / 像～似地向他提问 bombard him with questions; fire questions at him

连属 liánzhǔ join; link

连缀 liánzhuì ① join together; put together: 孤立地看, 每一个情节都很平淡, ～在一起, 就有趣了。 When taken separately, each of the episodes is rather dull, but when linked together, they're very interesting. ② *phonet.* cluster: 辅音～ consonant cluster

连字号 liánzìhào hyphen (-)

连奏 liánzòu *mus.* *legato*

连坐 liánzuò (in former times) be punished for being related to or friendly with sb. who has committed an offence

连作 liánzuò *agric.* continuous cropping

奁 (匲、匳、匲、籢) lián a toilet case used by women in ancient China

帘[1] lián flag as a shop sign: 酒帘 jiǔlián

帘[2] (簾) lián (hanging) screen; curtain: 窗帘 chuānglián

帘布 liánbù cord fabric (in tyres)

帘幕 liánmù heavy curtain: ～低垂。 The curtain hung low.

帘栅管 liánshānguǎn *electron.* screen-grid tube

帘栅极 liánshānjí *electron.* screen grid

帘子 liánzi *inf.* (hanging) screen; curtain: 竹～ a bamboo screen or curtain / 窗～ a window curtain

帘子布 liánzibù same as 帘布 liánbù

怜 (憐) lián ① sympathize with; pity: 同病相怜 tóng bìng xiāng lián ② love: 怜爱 lián'ài

怜爱 lián'ài love tenderly; have tender affection for: 这小姑娘惹人～。 The little girl is so lovable.

怜悯 liánmǐn pity; take pity on; have compassion for

怜贫惜老 liánpín-xīlǎo feel compassion for the aged and the poor

怜惜 liánxī take pity on; have pity for: 决不～恶人。 We should never take pity on evil people.

怜香惜玉 liánxiāng-xīyù show pity and tenderness to women

怜恤 liánxù *formal* take pity on; have compassion for

涟 lián *formal* ① ripples ② continuous flow (of tears): 泣涕～～ tears flowing continuously

涟洏 lián'ér *formal* weeping copiously

涟漪 liányī *liter.* wimpled waves; ripples

莲 lián lotus: 采～ pick lotus

莲步 liánbù *liler.* lily steps—a beautiful woman's graceful way of walking: ～半折小弓弓，莺啭一声娇滴滴。(《京本通俗小说·碾玉观音》) Her bound feet in small bow-like shoes walk with lily steps. Like the trills of an oriole is her voice, sweet and charming.

莲花 liánhuā lotus flower; lotus

莲花落 liánhuālào a popular song sung to the accompaniment of the castanets (so called from the refrain 莲花落，落莲花 "And so fall the lotus flowers")

莲花纹 liánhuāwén lotus design

莲灰 liánhuī pale pinkish grey

莲藕 lián'ǒu the lotus plant, or esp. its root: 种植～ plant lotuses / ～同根 the lotus stems spring from the selfsame root—inseparable

莲蓬 liánpeng seedpod of the lotus

莲蓬头 liánpengtóu *dial.* shower nozzle

莲蓬子儿 liánpengzǐr ① lotus seed ② a thing shaped like a lotus seed

莲肉 liánròu lotus-seed kernel

莲台 liántái a Buddha's seat in the form of a lotus flower; lotus throne

莲心 liánxīn the heart of a lotus seed

莲子 liánzǐ lotus seed

莲座 liánzuò same as 莲台 liántái

联 (聯) lián ① ally oneself with; unite; join: 联盟 liánméng ② antithetical couplet: 对联 duìlián

联邦 liánbāng federation; union; commonwealth

联邦调查局 Liánbāng Diàochájú the (U.S.) Federal Bureau of Investigation (FBI)

联邦共和国 liánbāng gònghéguó federal republic; federated republic

联邦制 liánbāngzhì federal system; federalism

联苯胺 liánběn'àn *chem.* benzidine

联播 liánbō radio hookup; broadcast over a radio network: 新闻～ news hookup / ～节目时间 network time

联产承包责任制 liánchǎn chéngbāo zérènzhì a system of contracted responsibility linking remuneration to output; a contract system with remuneration linked to output

联产计酬 liánchǎn jìchóu payment linked to output

联大 Liándà short for 联合国大会 Liánhéguó Dàhuì

联单 liándān receipts or other documents in duplicate

联电 liándiàn a joint circular telegram

联队 liánduì *mil.* wing (of an air force)

联防 liánfáng ① joint defence; joint command of defence forces: 军民～ joint defence by army and militia; army-civilian defence ② *sports* joint defence

联管节 liánguǎnjié *mech.* pipe union; pipe coupling; union joint

联管箱 liánguǎnxiāng *mech.* header: 汽锅～ boiler header

联贯 liánguàn same as 连贯 liánguàn

联合 liánhé ① unite; ally: 全世界无产者，～起来! Workers of all countries, unite! / ～一切可能～的力量 ally oneself with all forces that can be allied with ② joint; combined: ～举办 jointly organize or sponsor / ～进攻 launch a combined (*or* concerted) attack ③ combination; alliance; union; coalition: 各派大～ a grand alliance of all groups / 专业性的生产～ a combination of specialized productive undertakings ④ *physiol.* symphysis: 耻骨～ symphysis pubis

联合兵种 liánhé bīngzhǒng *mil.* combined arms

联合采煤机 liánhé cǎiméijī cutter-loader; combine

联合词组 liánhé cízǔ *gram.* coordinative word group

联合公报 liánhé gōngbào joint *communiqué*

联合国 Liánhéguó the United Nations (U.N.)

联合国安全理事会 Liánhéguó Ānquán Lǐshìhuì the United Nations Security Council

联合国大会 Liánhéguó Dàhuì the United Nations General Assembly

联合国秘书处 Liánhéguó Mìshūchù the United Nations Secretariat

联合国宪章 Liánhéguó Xiànzhāng the United Nations Charter

联合会 liánhéhuì federation; union: 妇女～ women's federation / 学生～ students' union

联合机 liánhéjī combine

联合经营 liánhé jīngyíng joint venture

联合企业 liánhé qǐyè an incorporated business enterprise: 农工～ agribusiness

联合声明 liánhé shēngmíng joint statement

联合收割机 liánhé shōugējī combine (harvester)

联合体 liánhétǐ an organic whole; association: 农工商～ an association of agricultural, industrial and commercial units; an agricultural-industrial-commercial association

联合王国 Liánhé Wángguó the United Kingdom

联合行动 liánhé xíngdòng joint action; concerted action

联合宣言 liánhé xuānyán joint declaration

联合演习 liánhé yǎnxí *mil.* joint manoeuvre; joint exercise

联合战线 liánhé zhànxiàn united front

联合政府 liánhé zhèngfǔ coalition government

联合作战 liánhé zuòzhàn *mil.* combined operations

联欢 liánhuān have a social gathering; have a get-together: 节日～ gala celebrations / 军民～ get-together of soldiers and civilians

联欢会 liánhuānhuì get-together; party

联欢节 liánhuānjié festival; carnival; fiesta

联欢晚会 liánhuān wǎnhuì (evening) party

联接 liánjiē ① same as 连接 liánjiē ② *elec.* connection; strapping

联结 liánjié join; connect; link; bind: 画一条直线把这两点～起来。Draw a line to join the two points. / 锦州是～东北和华北的战略要地。Jinzhou is a strategic place connecting the Northeast and North China. / 共同的目标把我们紧紧～在一起。A common goal has bound us closely together. / ～两国人民的友谊纽带 the ties of friendship that join the two peoples

联句 liánjù do linking verses (a literary pastime in which two or more persons each chant one or two lines of poetry, so that the lines in sequence make up an entire poem)

联军 liánjūn allied forces; united army

联立方程 liánlì fāngchéng *math.* simultaneous equations

联络 liánluò ① start or keep up personal relations; make or maintain contact or liaison: 你可以用电话跟他～。You could maintain contact with him by telephone. / 多多～ Let's get in touch more often. / ～感情 start or keep up a friendship; strengthen the bonds of friendship ② contact (between people); liaison: 失掉～ lose contact

联络部 liánluòbù liaison department

联络处 liánluòchù liaison office

联络官 liánluòguān liaison officer

联络网 liánluòwǎng liaison net

联络员 liánluòyuán liaison man

联络站 liánluòzhàn liaison station

联袂 liánmèi *formal* go, come, etc. together: ～而往 go together / ～而至 arrive together

联盟 liánméng alliance; coalition; league; union: 工农～ alliance of the workers and peasants; worker-peasant alliance

联绵　liánmián　same as 连绵 liánmián

联绵字　liánmiánzì　a compound word consisting of two characters; binome: 双声～ an alliterative compound (*or* binome, e.g. 伶俐 líng·lì) / 叠韵～ a rhyming compound (*or* binome, e.g. 阑干 lángān)

联名　liánmíng　jointly signed; jointly: ～发起 jointly initiate; jointly sponsor / ～上书 submit a joint letter

联翩　liánpiān　in close succession; together: ～而至 come in close succession; arrive one after another

联赛　liánsài　*sports* league matches: 足球～ league football matches

联锁机构　liánsuǒ jīgòu　*mech.* interlocking mechanism

联体婴　liántǐyīng　Siamese twins

联席会议　liánxí huìyì　joint conference; joint meeting

联系　liánxì　① contact; touch; connection; relation: 失去～ lose contact / 取得～ get in touch with; establish contact with / 保持～ keep in contact (*or* touch) with / 有广泛的社会～ have wide social connections / 巩固党和群众的～ strengthen the ties between the Party and the masses / 事物的内(外)部～ the internal (external) relations of things ② integrate; relate; link; get in touch with: 理论～实际 integrate theory with practice; apply theory to reality / 密切～群众 maintain close ties with the masses / 把两件事一起来看就清楚了。 Relate the two problems to each other and you'll understand them clearly. / 看电影的问题, 找俱乐部～。 As for movies, please get in touch with the club. / 跟我随时～。 Keep in touch with me. / 中国的前途是同世界的前途紧密地～在一起的。 The future of China is closely linked with that of the whole world.

联想　liánxiǎng　connect with mentally; associate with: 提起大夫, 小孩儿就～到打针、疼。 Children always associate the doctor with injections and pain.

联谊　liányì　keep up a friendship; strengthen the bonds of friendship: ～会 get-together; party

联姻　liányīn　*formal* (of two families) be related by marriage; form an alliance by marriage

联营　liányíng　(short for 联合经营) joint venture: ～公司 integrated company

联运　liányùn　through transport; through traffic: 国际铁路～ international railway through transport / 火车汽车～ train-and-bus coordinated transport

联运票　liányùnpiào　through ticket

联运提单　liányùn tídān　through bill of lading

联轴节　liánzhóujié　*mech.* shaft coupling; coupling: 刚性～ rigid coupling / 挠性～ flexible coupling / 万向～ universal coupling

联属　liánzhǔ　same as 连属 liánzhǔ

联装炮　liánzhuāngpào　multiple gun

裢　lián　see 褡裢 dālian

廉(廉)　lián　① honest and clean: 清廉 qīnglián / 廉耻 liánchǐ ② low-priced; inexpensive; cheap: 价廉物美 jiàlián-wùměi ③ (Lián) a surname

廉耻　liánchǐ　integrity and a sense of honour: 不知～ have no sense of shame; be shameless

廉价　liánjià　low-priced; cheap: ～书 a cheap book / ～买进 buy cheap / ～出售 sell at a low price; sell cheap / ～劳动力 cheap labour / ～品 cheap goods; bargain

廉价部　liánjiàbù　bargain counter

廉洁　liánjié　honest and clean; incorruptible: ～政府 an honest and clean government

廉洁奉公　liánjié fènggōng　be honest in performing one's official duties

廉明　liánmíng　(of officials) upright and incorruptible

廉正　liánzhèng　upright and honest

廉政　liánzhèng　honest and clean government: ～建设 building an honest and clean government

廉直　liánzhí　same as 廉正 liánzhèng

鲢　lián　silver carp

鲢鱼　liányú　silver carp

臁　lián　*physiol.* shank

臁疮　liánchuāng　ulcer on the shank

镰(鐮)　lián　sickle

镰刀　liándāo　sickle

镰鱼　liányú　Moorish idol (a fish)

蠊　lián　see 蜚蠊 fěilián

liǎn

敛(斂)　liǎn　① hold back; restrain: 敛足 liǎnzú ② collect: 敛钱 liǎnqián

敛步　liǎnbù　check one's steps; hold back from going

敛财　liǎncái　accumulate wealth by unfair means

敛迹　liǎnjì　temporarily desist from one's evil ways; lie low

敛钱　liǎnqián　*inf.* collect money; raise money

敛衽　liǎnrèn　*formal* straighten one's lapels (to show respect)

敛容　liǎnróng　*formal* assume a serious expression

敛足　liǎnzú　*formal* check one's steps; hold back from going

琏　liǎn　a vessel used to hold grain at the imperial sacrifice

脸(臉)　liǎn　① face (of people or animals): 洗～ wash one's face ② the front part of sth.: 门脸儿 ménliǎnr ③ face (fig.): ～上下不来 haven't the face to do sth. ④ facial expression; face: 把～一变 get angry

脸大　liǎndà　① (usu. of a woman) be bold; be immodest ② have prestige; command respect

脸蛋儿　liǎndànr　(usu. children's) cheeks; face: 小姑娘的～红得像苹果。 The little girl's rosy cheeks are like apples.

脸红　liǎnhóng　① blush (with shame or embarrassment) ② flush with anger; get excited; get worked up

脸红脖子粗　liǎn hóng bózi cū　get red in the face from anger or excitement; flush with agitation: 争得～ get red in the face in the heat of the argument / 大家～, 闹得不可开交。 Red in the face, cords standing out in their necks, they kept up an ear-splitting clamour.

脸颊　liǎnjiá　cheeks; face: 红润的～ ruddy cheeks / 泪珠儿顺着她的～直往下淌。 Tears streamed down her cheeks.

脸孔　liǎnkǒng　same as 面孔 miànkǒng

脸面　liǎnmiàn　① face (lit.) ② face; self-respect; sb.'s feelings: 看我的～, 不要生他的气了。 For my sake, don't get angry with him. / 不顾～ have no regard for face

脸嫩　liǎnnèn　be bashful; be shy

脸盘儿　liǎnpánr　(also 脸庞儿 liǎnpángr) the cast of one's face: 大～ a big face / 方～ a square face

脸盆　liǎnpén　washbasin; washbowl

脸盆架　liǎnpénjià　washstand

脸皮　liǎnpí　face (fig.); cheek: ～厚 thick-skinned; shameless / ～薄 thin-skinned; shy; sensitive / 居然有～说出这种话来 have the cheek (*or* nerve) to say such things / 撕破～ put aside all considerations of face

脸谱　liǎnpǔ　types of facial makeup in operas

脸容　liǎnróng　facial features; face: 俊俏的～ a pretty

and charming face / ～憔悴 have a pallid look; look haggard

脸软 liǎnruǎn softhearted; good-natured; disinclined to hurt others' feelings

脸色 liǎnsè ①complexion; look: ～红润 a ruddy complexion / 他这几天～不好。He doesn't look well these days. ② facial expression: 一看他的～, 我就知道有了好消息。I could see from the expression on his face that there was good news. / 奴才看主子的～行事。The flunkey adjusts his behaviour to his master's expression.

脸上无光 liǎnshang wú guāng have lost face

脸水 liǎnshuǐ water for washing the face

脸膛儿 liǎntángr dial. face: 四方～ a square face / ～晒得黑黑的 have a sunburnt face

脸相 liǎnxiàng appearance; looks; facial expression: ～端正 have regular features / 他露出一副凶神恶煞的～。A fiendish look appeared on his face.

脸小 liǎnxiǎo ① (usu. of a woman) be bashful; be shy ②have little or no prestige; be a nobody: 我知道我的～, 说话也不顶用。I know I'm just a nobody; my words carry no weight.

脸形 liǎnxíng (also 脸型 liǎnxíng) the shape of one's face; facial features: ～端正 have regular features / ～瘦长 a thin and long face / 圆圆的～ a full (or round) face

liàn

练 (練)
liàn ① white silk: 江平如～。The river lies as smooth as silk. ② boil and scour raw silk: 练漂 liànpiǎo ③ practise; train; drill: 我得先～～才能跟你赛。I need to practise a little more before I can take you on. / ～工夫 practise one's skill / ～气功 do breathing exercises / ～字 practise calligraphy / ～钢琴 practise the piano / ～跑 practise running / ～单杠 train (or practise) on the horizontal bar / ～节目 rehearse / ～好本领 perfect one's skill / ～好身体 do exercises to build up one's physique (or health) ④experienced; skilled; seasoned: 老练 lǎoliàn

练笔 liànbǐ ① practise writing ② practise calligraphy

练兵 liànbīng train troops; drill soldiers

练兵场 liànbīngchǎng drill ground; parade ground

练操 liàncāo (of troops, etc.) drill

练达 liàndá formal experienced and worldly-wise

练队 liànduì drill in formation; drill for a parade

练功 liàngōng do exercises in gymnastics, wushu, acrobatics, etc.; practise one's skill

练漂 liànpiǎo text. scouring and bleaching

练球 liànqiú practise a ball game: 主队和客队在一起～。The home team and the visitors are practising together. / 赛前～ warm-up (before a match)

练鹊 liànquè long-tailed flycatcher

练手 liànshǒu try one's hand (at some skill); practise one's skill

练武 liànwǔ ① learn or practise martial arts ② learn or practise military skills

练习 liànxí ① practise: 要多～～。You must practise some more. / ～讲英语 practise speaking English / ～写文章 practise writing / ～射击 practise marksmanship / 写字得经常～才能写好。Chinese calligraphy requires constant practice before you can master the art. ② exercise (in a book): 做～ do exercises / 交～ hand in exercises / 算术～ arithmetic exercises

练习本 liànxíběn (also 练习簿 liànxíbù) exercise-book

练习曲 liànxíqǔ mus. étude

练习题 liànxítí exercise problems; exercises

炼 (煉、鍊)
liàn ① smelt; refine:～铅 smelt lead / ～糖 refine sugar ② temper (a metal) with fire ③ weigh one's word; seek the right phrase: 炼句 liànjù

炼丹 liàndān (try to) make pills of immortality (as a Taoist practice)

炼钢 liàngāng make steel; smelt steel

炼钢厂 liàngāngchǎng steel mill; steelworks

炼钢工人 liàngāng gōngrén steelworker

炼钢炉 liàngānglú steelmaking furnace; steel-smelting furnace

炼焦 liànjiāo make coke; coke

炼焦厂 liànjiāochǎng coking plant; cokery

炼焦炉 liànjiāolú coke oven: ～煤气 coke-oven gas

炼焦煤 liànjiāoméi coking coal

炼金术 liànjīnshù alchemy

炼句 liànjù try to find the best turn of phrase; polish and repolish a sentence

炼乳 liànrǔ condensed milk

炼铁 liàntiě smelt iron

炼铁厂 liàntiěchǎng ironworks

炼铁炉 liàntiělú iron-smelting furnace; blast furnace

炼油 liànyóu ① refine oil ② extract oil by heat: 炼猪油 boil down fat to get lard ③ heat edible oil

炼油厂 liànyóuchǎng (oil) refinery

炼狱 liànyù Catholicism purgatory

炼制 liànzhì refine: 石油～ petroleum refining

炼字 liànzì cudgel one's brains for the right word; try to find the exact word

恋 (戀)
liàn ① love (one of the opposite sex):相～ be in love with each other ②long for; feel attached to: ～家 reluctant to be away from home; be tied to home

恋爱 liàn'ài ① romantic love; love affair: 谈～ be in love; have a love affair ② be in love; have a courtship: 他们两个人在～呢。They are falling in love. / 他们没～就结婚了。They had no courtship, they just got married.

恋歌 liàngē love song

恋旧 liànjiù ① yearn for one's native place; be filled with nostalgia ② same as 怀旧 huáijiù

恋恋不舍 liànliàn bù shě be reluctant to part from; hate to see sb. go: 老人～, 把他们一直送到门外。The old man hated (or couldn't bear) to see them go. He accompanied them to outside the door.

恋慕 liànmù have tender feelings towards; adore

恋情 liànqíng romantic love

恋人 liànrén sweetheart; loved one; girlfriend or boyfriend

恋栈 liànzhàn derog. (of an official) be loath to give up his post (as a horse is loath to leave its stable)

殓 (殮)
liàn put a body into a coffin; encoffin: 入殓 rùliàn

殓衣 liànyī graveclothes

链 (鍊)
liàn ① chain: 铁链 tiěliàn ② cable length (1/10 of a nautical mile)

链扳手 liànbānshǒu chain wrench

链钩 liàngōu chain hook; sling

链轨 liànguǐ caterpillar track (of a tractor)

链锯 liànjù chain saw

链轮 liànlún chain wheel; sprocket (wheel)

链霉素 liànméisù pharm. streptomycin

链球 liànqiú sports hammer: 掷～ hammer throw

链球菌 liànqiújūn streptococcus

链上取代 liànshàng qǔdài　*chem.*　chain substitution

链式反应 liànshì fǎnyìng　*chem.*　chain reaction

链套 liàntào　chain case (of a bicycle)

链条 liàntiáo　① chain ② roller chain (of a bicycle); chain

链烃 liàntīng　*chem.*　chain hydrocarbon

链罩 liànzhào　chain guard (of a bicycle); chain cover

链子 liànzi　① chain: 铁～ iron chain ② *inf.* roller chain (of a bicycle); chain

楝

楝 liàn　chinaberry

楝树 liànshù　chinaberry

潋(潋)

liàn　see below

潋滟 liànyàn　*liter.*　① overflowing; inundating ② billowing; rippling:波光～柳条柔。(欧阳修) The bright ripples spread; the willow twigs hang soft.

liáng

良

liáng　① good; fine: 优良 yōuliáng ② good people: 除暴安良 chúbào-ānliáng ③ *adv. formal* very; very much: 获益～多 benefit a great deal

良材 liángcái　① good timber ② able person

良策 liángcè　good plan; sound strategy

良辰美景 liángchén-měijǐng　a fine moment and a beautiful scene

良导体 liángdǎotǐ　*phys.*　good conductor

良方 liángfāng　① effective prescription; good recipe ② good plan; sound strategy

良港 liánggǎng　a good harbour:青岛三面环海，背靠崂山，是个天然～。Surrounded on three sides by the sea, with Mt. Lao as the backdrop, Qingdao is a fine natural harbour.

良工 liánggōng　a skilled worker

良好 liánghǎo　good; well:～的开端 a good beginning /～的习惯 good habits /～的愿望 good intentions /～的比赛风格 fine sportsmanship / 为双方会谈创造～的气氛 create a favourable atmosphere for bilateral talks / 打下～的基础 lay a sound foundation / 水稻长势～。The rice is coming on splendidly./手术经过～。The operation came off well. / 财政贸易情况～。Finance and trade are in a good state./自我感觉～ feel fine

良机 liángjī　*formal* good (*or* golden) opportunity: 莫失～。Don't let this good opportunity slip.

良家 liángjiā　*old* a respectable family: ～妇女 a woman from a respectable family; a respectable woman

良将 liángjiàng　a good general; an able general

良久 liángjiǔ　*formal* a good while; a long time

良马 liángmǎ　a fine horse

良民 liángmín　*old* good citizen; law-abiding people

良能 liángnéng　intuitive ability; inborn ability

良朋 liángpéng　good friend

良人 liángrén　*arch.* my goodman; my husband

良师 liángshī　good teacher

良师益友 liángshī-yìyǒu　good teacher and helpful friend

良田 liángtián　good farmland; fertile farmland

良图 liángtú　*formal* ① plan deliberately ② good plan; sound strategy

良心 liángxīn　conscience: 有～ have a conscience; be good-hearted / 没～ conscienceless; heartless; ungrateful /～上感到不安 have an uneasy conscience; feel the pricks of conscience /～发现。The conscience is moved./说句～话 to be fair; in all fairness /他昧着～做事。He's doing this against his conscience./凭～吧。All right, do it according to your conscience.

良性 liángxìng　*med.*　benign: 那个肿瘤检查出来是～的。The tumour proved benign.

良性循环 liángxìng xúnhuán　a virtuous circle: 国民经济的～ a virtuous circle in the national economy

良性肿瘤 liángxìng zhǒngliú　benign tumour

良药 liángyào　good medicine (usu. fig.): 对症～ the right remedy

良药苦口 liángyào kǔ kǒu　good medicine tastes bitter: ～利于病，忠言逆耳利于行。Just as bitter medicine cures sickness, unpalatable advice benefits conduct.

良医 liángyī　a skilful doctor

良友 liángyǒu　good friend

良莠不齐 liáng-yǒu bù qí　the good and the bad are intermingled

良缘 liángyuán　a good match; a happy match:喜结～ make a good match

良知 liángzhī　intuitive knowledge; innate knowledge

良种 liángzhǒng　① (fine) improved variety:水稻～ improved varieties of rice ② fine breed: ～马 a horse of fine breed

良种场 liángzhǒngchǎng　seed multiplication farm

凉(凉)

liáng　① cool; cold: ～风 cool breeze / 天气忽然～了。The weather has suddenly got cold./饭～了。The food's got cold. ② discouraged; disappointed: 一听这消息他就～了半截。His heart sank at the news. ——see also liàng

凉白开 liángbáikāi　*inf.*　cold boiled water

凉拌 liángbàn　(of food) cold and dressed with sauce: ～生菜 tossed salad /～面 cold noodles in sauce

凉冰冰 liángbīngbīng　chilly; ice-cold; icy:我挨了浇，一身湿衣服，～的怪不好受。I've got drenched, and I feel chilly with the wet clothes on.

凉不丝儿 liángbusīr　*inf.*　cool: 大热天喝碗～的绿豆汤真舒服。There's nothing like a bowl of cool mung bean tea in hot weather.

凉菜 liángcài　cold dish

凉床 liángchuáng　bamboo couch (for summer use)

凉碟 liángdié　cold dish

凉粉 liángfěn　bean-starch noodles

凉糕 liánggāo　cake made of glutinous rice, served cold

凉快 liángkuai　① nice and cool; pleasantly cool: 这里～，坐下来歇会儿。It's nice and cool here. Let's sit down and have a rest. ② cool oneself; cool off: 咱们到树荫下面去～一下吧! Let's sit in the shade and cool off a bit.

凉帽 liángmào　summer hat; sun hat; straw hat

凉面 liángmiàn　cold noodles in sauce

凉棚 liángpéng　mat-awning; mat shelter ——see also 搭凉棚 dā liángpéng

凉气 liángqì　cold air; chilly air:～袭人。The cold air chills one to the core. / 站在峭壁顶上朝下望，不由人倒抽一口～。It took my breath away to look down from the brink of the precipice.

凉伞 liángsǎn　sunshade; parasol

凉森森 liángsēnsēn　piercingly cold: 一阵山风掠过，～的。A gust of mountain air swept by, sending chills down the spine.

凉薯 liángshǔ　*dial.*　yam bean

凉爽 liángshuǎng　nice and cool; pleasantly cool: ～的秋天 pleasantly cool autumn days

凉水 liángshuǐ　① cold water ② unboiled water

凉丝丝 liángsīsī　coolish; rather cool; a bit cool

凉飕飕 liángsōusōu　(of wind) chilly; chill

凉台 liángtái　balcony; veranda

凉亭 liángtíng　wayside pavilion; summer house; kiosk

凉席 liángxí　summer sleeping mat (of woven split bamboo, etc.)

凉鞋 liángxié　sandals

凉药 liángyào *Chin. med.* medicine of a cold nature (for reducing fever or inflammation); antipyretic

凉意 liángyì a slight chill in the air: 立秋过后，早晚有些～了。After the Beginning of Autumn there is a slight chill in the air in the mornings and evenings.

莨

liáng see 薯莨 shǔliáng ——see also làng

莨绸 liángchóu another name for 黑胶绸 hēijiāochóu

梁¹（樑）

liáng ① roof beam: 架～ set a roof beam in place ② bridge: 桥梁 qiáoliáng ③ ridge: 山梁 shānliáng／鼻梁 bíliáng

梁²

Liáng ① a state during the Warring States period ② the Liang Dynasty (502–557), one of the Southern Dynasties ③ short for 后梁 Hòu Liáng ④ a surname

梁龙 liánglóng diplodocus (a dinosaur)

梁桥 liángqiáo beam bridge

梁上君子 liángshàng jūnzǐ gentleman on the beam—burglar; thief

椋

liáng see below

椋鸟 liángniǎo starling

量

liáng ① measure: ～地 measure land; measure a piece of ground／用斗～米 mete out rice with a *dou* measure／～身材 take sb.'s measurements／～尺寸 take sb.'s measurements／～体温 take sb.'s temperature ② (·liáng) appraise; evaluate; estimate: 打量 dǎliang／估量 gūliang ——see also liàng

量杯 liángbēi measuring glass; graduate

量度 liángdù measurement

量规 liángguī gauge

量角器 liángjiǎoqì protractor

量具 liángjù measuring tool

量瓶 liángpíng measuring (or graduated, volumetric) flask

量热器 liángrèqì calorimeter

量日仪 liángrìyí heliometer

量筒 liángtǒng graduated (or volumetric, measuring) cylinder; graduate

量图仪 liángtúyí map measurer

量雪尺 liángxuěchǐ snow scale

量雪器 liángxuěqì snow gauge

量油尺 liángyóuchǐ oil dip rod; dipstick

量雨筒 liángyǔtǒng precipitation gauge

粱

liáng ① a fine strain of millet ② fine grain; choice food: 膏粱 gāoliáng

粱肉 liángròu *formal* choice food

粮（糧）

liáng ①grain; food; provisions: ～棉双丰收 a bumper harvest of grain and cotton ② grain tax paid in kind: 公粮 gōngliáng

粮仓 liángcāng ① granary; garner ② granary (fig.); rice bowl: 东北是祖国的～。The Northeast is the granary of the country.

粮草 liángcǎo army provisions; rations and forage (or fodder)

粮店 liángdiàn grain shop

粮行 liánghāng *old* wholesale grain store

粮户 liánghù *dial.* landlord

粮荒 liánghuāng grain shortage; food scarcity

粮库 liángkù grain depot

粮秣 liángmò army provisions; rations and forage; grain and fodder

粮秣库 liángmòkù ration depot

粮票 liángpiào food coupon; grain coupon

粮食 liángshi grain; cereals; food

粮食产量 liángshi chǎnliàng grain yield

粮食储备 liángshi chǔbèi grain reserves; grain stock

粮食定量 liángshi dìngliàng monthly quota of food grain for an individual

粮食供应 liángshi gōngyìng staple food supply

粮食加工 liángshi jiāgōng grain processing

粮食配给 liángshi pèijǐ grain ration

粮食作物 liángshi zuòwù cereal crops; grain crops

粮税 liángshuì grain tax

粮饷 liángxiǎng *old* provisions and funds for troops

粮栈 liángzhàn wholesale grain store; grain depot

粮站 liángzhàn grain distribution station; grain supply centre

liǎng

两¹（兩）

liǎng ① (used before measure words and before 半，千，万，and 亿) two: ～匹马 two horses／～个半月 two and a half months／～千元 two thousand *yuan*／～亿～千万 two hundred and twenty million ② both (sides); either (side): ～利 benefit both; be good for both sides／～不吃亏。Neither side suffers any loss. ③ a few; some: 我想讲～句。I'd like to say a few words.／这事过～天再说。Let's leave it for a couple of days.

两²（兩）

liǎng ① *liang,* currently called 市两 shìliǎng, a traditional unit of weight (see also 市两 shìliǎng①) ② *old liang,* currently called 旧市两 (see also 市两 shìliǎng②) ③ (in former times) tael, a unit of weight for silver

两败俱伤 liǎng bài jù shāng both sides suffer (or lose); neither side gains

两半儿 liǎngbànr two halves; in half; in two: 碟子摔成～了。The dish is broken in two.／把苹果切成～ cut an apple in half

两边 liǎngbiān ① both sides; both directions; both places: 沟的～种着豆子。Beans were grown on both sides of the ditch.／这张纸～长短不齐。The two edges of this piece of paper aren't even in length.／人群向～散开。The crowd dispersed in both directions.／老大娘常常～走动，看望两个孙女儿。Grandma is always going back and forth, visiting her two granddaughters. ② both parties; both sides: ～讨好 try to please both sides／～都说好了，明儿下午赛球。The two teams have agreed to play the match tomorrow afternoon.

两边倒 liǎngbiāndǎo lean now to one side, now to the other; waver: 墙上一棵草，风吹～。A tuft of grass atop the wall sways right and left in the wind (a saying).

两便 liǎngbiàn be convenient to both; make things easy for both: 您甭等我了，咱们～。Please don't wait for me. That might be more convenient for both of us.

两鬓斑白 liǎng bìn bānbái greying at the temples

两鬓苍苍 liǎng bìn cāngcāng greying at the temples

两不找 liǎng bù zhǎo that's just right (i.e. the exact amount in payment for sth.)

两曹 liǎngcáo *formal* same as 两造 liǎngzào①

两重 liǎngchóng double; dual; twofold: ～意义 a double meaning／～任务 a two-fold task／新旧社会～天。The old and new societies are two different worlds.

两重性 liǎngchóngxìng same as 二重性 èrchóngxìng

两次三番 liǎngcì-sānfān again and again; time and again; over and over again

两次运球 liǎngcì yùnqiú *basketball* double dribble

两党制 liǎngdǎngzhì two-party system; bipartisan system

两抵 liǎngdǐ balance or cancel each other: 收支～。Income and expenditure balance each other. or The account balances out.

两点论 liǎngdiǎnlùn the doctrine that everything has two aspects (in accordance with the Marxist law that "one divides into two")

两耳不闻窗外事 liǎng ěr bù wén chuāngwài shì both ears shut to what goes on outside the window: ～，一心只读圣贤书。Both ears are shut to what goes on outside the window; the whole mind is concentrated on the sages' books (said, usu. disapprovingly, of one who is absorbed in study and oblivious of his surroundings).

两分法 liǎngfēnfǎ application of the Marxist law that "one divides into two"

两公婆 liǎnggōngpó *dial.* husband and wife; a married couple

两广 Liǎng Guǎng the Two Guangs—Guangdong and Guangxi Provinces

两汉 Liǎng Hàn the Two Hans—the Western and the Eastern Han Dynasties

两湖 Liǎng Hú the Two Hus—Hubei and Hunan Provinces

两虎相斗，必有一伤 liǎng hǔ xiāng dòu, bì yǒu yī shāng when two tigers fight, one is bound to get hurt

两回事 liǎnghuíshì two entirely different things; two different matters: 严格要求和求全责备是～。Being strict and being a nitpicker are two entirely different things.

两极 liǎngjí ①the two poles of the earth ②*phys.* the two poles (of a magnet or an electric battery)③two opposing extremes

两极分化 liǎngjí fēnhuà polarize: 贫富～ the polarity between rich and poor

两脚规 liǎngjiǎoguī ① compasses ② dividers

两晋 Liǎng Jìn the Two Jins—the Western and the Eastern Jin Dynasties

两可 liǎngkě both will do; either will do; could go either way: 我去不去～。It's all right with me whether I go or not./成不成还在～。Whether it will succeed or not—it could go either way.

两可之间 liǎngkě zhījiān ① either will do; not know which to choose ②both are possible; maybe, maybe not

两口子 liǎngkǒuzi (also 两口儿 liǎngkǒur) *inf.* husband and wife; couple: 他们～都工作。Both he and his wife work.

两码事 liǎngmǎshì same as 两回事 liǎnghuíshì

两面 liǎngmiàn ① two sides; both sides; two aspects; both aspects: 这张纸～都写满了字。Both sides of the paper were covered with writing. / 左右～都是高山。There are high mountains to the right and left. / 问题的～我们都要看到。We should see both aspects of the problem. ② having a dual (*or* double) character; dual; double: ～手法 double-faced tactics; double-dealing; double game

两面光 liǎngmiànguāng (try to) please both parties

两面夹攻 liǎngmiàn jiāgōng close in from both sides; make a pincer attack: 受到～ be under a pincer attack; be caught in a two-way squeeze; be caught in cross fire

两面派 liǎngmiànpài double-dealer: 耍～ resort to double-dealing; be double-faced

两面三刀 liǎngmiàn-sāndāo double-dealing; double cross

两面性 liǎngmiànxìng dual nature; duplicity; ambivalence

两难 liǎngnán face a difficult choice; be in a dilemma: 去也不好，不去也不好，真是～。I'm in a dilemma as to whether to go or not.

两旁 liǎngpáng both sides; either side: 马路～都种着树。There are trees on either side of the road./大街～挤满了欢迎的人群。The streets were lined with welcoming crowds.

两栖 liǎngqī amphibious

两栖部队 liǎngqī bùduì amphibious forces; amphibious units

两栖动物 liǎngqī dòngwù amphibious animal; amphibian

两栖植物 liǎngqī zhíwù amphibious plant; amphibian

两栖作战 liǎngqī zuòzhàn amphibious warfare; amphibious operations: ～舰艇 amphibious (warfare) vessel

两歧 liǎngqí *formal* (of two things) not tally; be inconsistent

两讫 liǎngqì (business Chinese) the goods are delivered and the bill is cleared

两全 liǎngquán be satisfactory to both parties; have regard for both sides: ～的办法 measures satisfactory to both sides (*or* in both respects)/忠孝不能～。It is impossible to be a loyal subject and a filial son at the same time.

两全其美 liǎng quán qí měi satisfy both sides; satisfy rival claims

两审终审制 liǎngshěnzhōngshěnzhì *leg.* the system of the court of second instance being the court of last instance

两世为人 liǎng shì wéi rén barely escape with one's life; be lucky to have escaped death

两手 liǎngshǒu dual tactics: 作～准备 prepare oneself for both eventualities

两条腿走路 liǎng tiáo tuǐ zǒulù walking on two legs (a series of policies for balancing the relations between industry and agriculture, heavy and light industry, central and local government enterprises, etc.):贯彻执行一整套～的方针 implement a whole set of policies known as "walking on two legs"

两条心 liǎng tiáo xīn in fundamental disagreement; not of one mind

两跳 liǎngtiào *table tennis* double bounce

两头 liǎngtóu ① both ends; either end:大人坐在当间儿，孩子们坐在～儿。The grown-ups sat in the middle, the children at both ends. / ～尖 pointed at both ends / ～儿跑 go back and forth between two places ② both parties; both sides: ～都满意。Both sides are satisfied./～说情 intercede between two parties / ～为难 find it hard to please either party; find it difficult to satisfy two conflicting demands

两头落空 liǎngtóu luòkōng fall between two stools

两头小，中间大 liǎngtóu xiǎo, zhōngjiān dà small at both ends and big in the middle; a few at each extreme and many in between; a few advanced, a few backward, but the majority middling

两下里 liǎngxiàli (also 两下 liǎngxià) both parties; both sides: 这办法对集体对个人～都有好处。This practice benefits both the collective and the individual./～都没意见。Neither of them has any objection.

两下子 liǎngxiàzi ① a few times: 轻轻敲了～ give a couple of raps (on sth.) ② a few tricks of the trade: 要做好工作, 光靠这～是不够的。If we are to do good work, we can't rely on just these few tricks of the trade./你真有～! You really are smart!

两相情愿 liǎng xiāng qíngyuàn by mutual consent; both parties being willing

两厢 liǎngxiāng ① wing-rooms on either side of a one-storey house ② both sides: 站立～ stand on either side

两相 liǎngxiāng *elec.* two-phase: ～电动机 two-phase motor

两小无猜 liǎng xiǎo wú cāi (of a little boy and a little

girl) be innocent playmates

两性 liǎngxìng ① both sexes ② *chem.* amphiprotic; amphoteric

两性关系 liǎngxìng guānxi sexual relations

两性花 liǎngxìnghuā hermaphrodite flower

两性化合物 liǎngxìng huàhéwù amphoteric compound

两性胶体 liǎngxìng jiāotǐ amphoteric colloid; ampholytoid

两性人 liǎngxìngrén bisexual person; hermaphrodite

两性生殖 liǎngxìng shēngzhí bisexual reproduction

两袖清风 liǎng xiù qīngfēng (of an official) have clean hands; remain uncorrupted

两样 liǎngyàng different: 他跟别人～。He is different from other people. / ～做法.两种结果。Two different methods, two different results. / 有什么～? What's the difference?

两姨 liǎngyí maternal cousins: ～兄弟 male maternal cousins / ～姐妹 female maternal cousins

两姨亲 liǎngyíqīn maternal cousins

两翼 liǎngyì ① both wings: 鸟的～ both wings of a bird / 飞机的～ both wings of an airplane ② *mil.* both wings; both flanks: ～包抄 double envelopment

两用 liǎngyòng dual purpose: ～炉子 dual-purpose stove / ～雨衣 reversible raincoat

两用衫 liǎngyòngshān same as 春秋衫 chūnqiūshān

两院制 liǎngyuànzhì two-chamber system; bicameral system; bicameralism

两造 liǎngzào ① *leg.* both parties in a lawsuit; both plaintiff and defendant ② *dial.* two crops: 改一年～为一年三造 change from two crops a year to three

俩(倆)

liǎng see 伎俩 jìliǎng ——see also liǎ

唡(啢)

liǎng, also yīngliǎng old form for 英两 yīngliǎng

蝈(蝈)

liǎng see 蝈蝈 wǎngliǎng

蛃(蛃)

liǎng see 魍魉 wǎngliǎng

liàng

亮

liàng ① bright; light: 屋里很～。The room is very bright. / 那个电灯很～。That electric light is very bright. / 天～了。It's light already. / 地板擦得真～。The floor has been scrubbed clean and shiny. ② shine: 屋子里一着灯光。Lights were shining in the room. / 他把手电筒～了一下。He flashed the torch on for a second. ③ loud and clear: 她的嗓子真～。She has a resonant voice. ④ make one's voice loud and clear: 一起嗓子lift one's voice ⑤ enlightened: 你这一说，我心里头～了。I find what you say most enlightening. ⑥ show; reveal: ～刀 pull out a knife / 他把工作证～了一下就进去了。He showed his identity card and went in. / 你真有本事就～几手儿。If you are really good at this, show us. / ～思想 lay bare one's innermost thoughts / ～观点 declare one's position; air one's views

亮儿 liàngr *inf.* ① light (opp. darkness): 远处有一点～。A light gleamed in the distance. ② light (a lamp, candle, etc.): 拿个～来。Bring a light.

亮底 liàngdǐ reveal the whole story; disclose one's plan, stand, views, etc.; put one's cards on the table

亮度 liàngdù *phys.* brightness; brilliance: 星的～ the brightness of a star / 荧光屏～ screen brilliance

亮光 liàngguāng light (opp. darkness): 一道～ a shaft of light

亮光光 liàngguāngguāng shining: 一把～的剑 a shining sword

亮光漆 liàngguāngqī lacquer polish

亮晃晃 liànghuǎnghuǎng dazzling; brilliant; glittering: ～的阳光 brilliant sunshine / ～的金表 a glittering gold watch

亮节高风 liàngjié-gāofēng same as 高风亮节 gāofēng-liàngjié

亮晶晶 liàngjīngjīng glittering; sparkling; glistening: ～的星星 glittering stars / ～的露珠 glistening dewdrops

亮蓝 liànglán light blue: ～的裙子 a light blue skirt

亮牌 liàngpái lay one's cards on the table; have a showdown

亮闪闪 liàngshǎnshǎn sparkling; glittering: ～的眼睛 sparkling eyes

亮台 liàngtái same as 晾台[2] liàngtái

亮堂堂 liàngtāngtāng brightly lit; well lit; brilliant: 电灯把礼堂照得～的。Electric lights lit up the assembly hall.

亮堂 liàngtang ① light; bright: 这屋子又宽敞又～。The room is light and spacious. ② (of voice) loud and clear: 嗓门～ have a resonant voice / ～ clear; enlightened: 经过反复讨论，大家心里更～了。After repeated discussions, we had a much better understanding of the whole thing.

亮相 liàngxiàng ① (in Beijing opera, dancing, etc.) strike a pose on the stage ② declare one's position; state one's views

亮眼人 liàngyǎnrén the bright-eyed ones (blind people's term for those who can see)

亮铮铮 liàngzhēngzhēng shining; gleaming: 一辆～的新自行车 a shiny new bicycle / 一把～的剑 a gleaming sword

亮子 liàngzi transom (window); fanlight

悢

liàng *formal* sad

悢悢 liàngliàng *formal* ① sad ② think fondly of; feel nostalgic about

凉(涼)

liàng let sth. cool: ～一会儿再吃。Let it cool off a bit before you eat it. ——see also liáng

谅[1]

liàng forgive; understand: 本着互～互让的精神 in the spirit of mutual understanding and mutual accommodation

谅[2]

liàng I think; I suppose; I expect: 前信～已收到。I expect you have received my last letter. / ～他也不会这样做。I don't think he'd do that. / ～必如此。I think it must be so. *or* Presumably it is so. / ～不见怪。I trust that you will not blame me.

谅察 liàngchá (used in letters) ask for your understanding and forgiveness

谅解 liàngjiě understand; make allowance for: 他很～你的苦衷。He understands your difficulties. / 你们应当互相～，搞好关系。You should try to understand each other and be good friends. / 达成～ reach an understanding

辆(輛)

liàng *m.* (for vehicles): 一～公共汽车 a bus / 三～大车 three carts

晾

liàng ① dry in the air; air: 草垫子该～一～了。The straw mattress needs to be aired. ② dry in the sun; sun: ～衣服 sun clothes; hang the wash out to dry / 海滩上～着渔网。Fishnets are spread out on the beach to dry. ③ neglect sb.: 我不喜欢玩儿牌。他们每次玩儿的时候都把我～在一边儿。As I didn't like cards I was

left out in the cold every time they played. ④ same as 凉 liàng

晾干 liànggān dry by airing: 把衣服拿出去〜。Hang the clothes out to dry. / 草药已经〜了。The medicinal herbs are dry now.

晾台[1] liàngtái sun terrace (for drying clothes)

晾台[2] liàngtái cut the ground from under sb.'s feet; let sb. down: 她觉得他不来是晾了她的台。She felt let down because he didn't come.

晾烟 liàngyān ① air-curing of tobacco leaves ② air-cured tobacco

晾衣绳 liàngyīshéng clothesline

量 liàng ① capacity for tolerance or for taking food or drink: 饭量 fànliàng / 气量 qìliàng ② quantity; amount; volume: 出口〜 the volume of exports ③ estimate; measure: 量力 liànglì ——see also liáng

量变 liàngbiàn *philos.* quantitative change

量才录用 liàng cái lùyòng give sb. work suited to his abilities; assign jobs to people according to their abilities

量词 liàngcí *gram.* measure word (as 个, 只, 次, 阵); classifier

量纲 liànggāng *phys.* dimension: 〜分析 dimensional analysis

量力 liànglì estimate one's own strength or ability (and act accordingly)

量力而行 liànglì ér xíng do what one is capable of; act according to one's capability

量入为出 liàng rù wéi chū keep expenditures below income; live within one's means; cut one's coat according to one's cloth

量体裁衣 liàng tǐ cái yī cut the garment according to the figure——act according to actual circumstances

量刑 liàngxíng *leg.* measurement of penalty

量子 liàngzǐ *phys.* quantum: 光〜 light quantum

量子化学 liàngzǐ huàxué quantum chemistry

量子力学 liàngzǐ lìxué quantum mechanics

量子论 liàngzǐlùn quantum theory

量子生物学 liàngzǐ shēngwùxué quantum biology

嘹 liàng see 嘹嘹 liáoliàng

靓 liàng *dial.* beautiful; pretty; handsome ——see also jìng

靓女 liàngnǚ *dial.* a pretty girl

靓仔 liàngzǎi *dial.* a handsome young man

踉 liàng see below

踉跄 liàngqiàng (also 踉蹡 liàngqiàng) stagger: 那个醉汉跟跟跄跄地在路上走着。The drunk man staggered along the road.

liáo

撩 liáo ① raise or lift up (a part of sth. which is hanging): 〜起帘子 raise the curtains / 〜裙子 lift (or hold up) the hem of one's skirt ② sprinkle (with one's hand): 先〜些水再扫地。Sprinkle some water on the floor before sweeping it. ——see also liáo

liáo

辽[1]**（遼）** liáo distant; faraway: 辽远 liáoyuǎn

辽[2]**（遼）** Liáo ① the Liao Dynasty (907-1125) ② short for 辽宁 Liáoníng

辽东 Liáodōng the area east of the Liao River, coextensive with eastern and southern Liaoning Province: 〜半岛 the Liaodong Peninsula

辽阔 liáokuò vast; extensive: 〜的土地 a vast expanse of land; vast territory / 我国幅员〜。Our country has a vast territory.

辽宁 Liáoníng Liaoning (Province)

辽沈战役 Liáo-Shěn Zhànyì the Liaoxi-Shenyang Campaign (Sept. 12-Nov. 2, 1948), the first of the three decisive campaigns of the War of Liberation

辽西 Liáoxī the area west of the Liao River, coextensive with western Liaoning Province

辽远 liáoyuǎn distant; faraway: 〜的边疆 distant frontier regions / 但见一行大雁正飞向〜的天空。A column of wild geese was seen flying into the distant sky.

疗（療） liáo treat; cure: 医疗 yīliáo / 治疗 zhìliáo

疗程 liáochéng course (or period) of treatment

疗法 liáofǎ therapy; treatment: 化学〜 chemotherapy / 新针〜 new acupuncture therapy / 电休克〜 shock treatment

疗饥 liáojī *formal* stay (or appease) one's hunger

疗效 liáoxiào curative effect: 青霉素对肺炎有显著的〜。Penicillin is particularly effective against pneumonia.

疗养 liáoyǎng recuperate; convalesce

疗养院 liáoyǎngyuàn sanatorium; convalescent hospital (or home)

聊[1] liáo ① merely; just: 〜表谢意 just a token of gratitude; just to show my appreciation ② a little; slightly: 聊胜于无 liáo shèngyú wú

聊[2] liáo *inf.* chat; gab: 晚饭后咱们〜〜。Let's have a chat after supper. / 你们在〜些什么？What are you folks gabbing about?

聊备一格 liáo bèi yī gé may serve as a specimen

聊复尔耳 liáo fù ěr ěr (also 聊复尔尔 liáo fù ěr ěr) *formal* just as a matter of form; just from a sense of good form

聊赖 liáolài see 无聊赖 wú liáolài; 百无聊赖 bǎi wú liáolài

聊且 liáoqiě tentatively; for the moment

聊生 liáoshēng *formal* (usu. used in the negative) earn a livelihood: 无所〜 be unable to earn a livelihood

聊胜于无 liáo shèngyú wú better than nothing

聊天儿 liáotiānr *inf.* chat; gab: 我们聊了半天天儿。We chatted for a long time.

聊以解嘲 liáo yǐ jiěcháo make a feeble attempt to explain things away when ridiculed; in a feeble attempt to silence jeers

聊以塞责 liáo yǐ sèzé just to meet the bare requirements

聊以自慰 liáo yǐ zì wèi just to console oneself

聊以卒岁 liáo yǐ zú suì just to tide over the year

寥 liáo ① few; scanty: 寥落 liáoluò ② silent; deserted: 寂寥 jìliáo

寥寂 liáojī same as 寂寥 jìliáo

寥廓 liáokuò *formal* boundless; vast: 〜的天空 the boundless sky

寥寥 liáoliáo very few

寥寥可数 liáoliáo kě shǔ very few: 到会者〜。Very few people came to the meeting.

寥寥无几 liáoliáo wú jǐ　very few: 号召自愿参加，但响应者～。A call for volunteers was sent out, but very few people responded.

寥落 liáoluò　few and far between; sparse; scattered: 疏星～ only a few solitary stars twinkling in the sky／～古行宫，宫花寂寞红。(元稹) A deserted old travelling palace, Flowers in utter loneliness blush.

寥若晨星 liáo ruò chénxīng　as sparse as the morning stars; few and far between

僚　liáo　① official: 官僚 guānliáo ② an associate in office: 同僚 tóngliáo

僚机 liáojī　mil.　① wing plane; wingman ② wingman

僚舰 liáojiàn　mil.　consort

僚属 liáoshǔ　old　officials under sb. in authority; subordinates; staff

僚友 liáoyǒu　old　colleagues (in the same government office)

僚佐 liáozuǒ　old　assistants in a government office

寮　liáo　dial.　small house; hut: 僧～ a monk's cell (or hut)／茶～酒肆 teahouses and wineshops

寮棚 liáopéng　shed; hut

撩　liáo　① tease; tantalize ② provoke; stir up ——see also liào

撩拨 liáobō　① tease; banter ② incite; provoke

撩动 liáodòng　provoke; stir up: ～心弦 tug at one's heartstrings; be heart-stirring

撩逗 liáodòu　tease; provoke: 他这两天好像心情不好，你别去～他。He seems very moody these days. Don't tease him.

撩乱 liáoluàn　same as 缭乱 liáoluàn

撩惹 liáorě　provoke; incite

撩人 liáorén　stirring; exciting; teasing: 春色～。Spring's hues are teasing.

嘹　liáo　see below

嘹亮 liáoliàng　resonant; loud and clear: 歌声～。The singing is loud and clear.／～的号角 a clarion call

嘹喨 liáoliàng　same as 嘹亮 liáoliàng

獠　liáo　see below

獠牙 liáoyá　long, sharp, protruding teeth

缭　liáo　① entangled: 缭乱 liáoluàn ② sew with slanting stitches: ～贴边 stitch a hem; hem

缭乱 liáoluàn　formal　confused; in a turmoil: 心绪～ in a confused state of mind

缭绕 liáorào　curl up; wind around: 炊烟～ smoke curling up from kitchen chimneys／歌声～。The song lingered in the air.

嫽　liáo　arch.　fine; happy; glorious

潦　liáo　see below ——see also lǎo

潦草 liáocǎo　① (of handwriting) hasty and careless; illegible: 字迹～。The writing is illegible. ② sloppy; slovenly: 干活儿～ work in a slipshod way／～塞责 do one's duty perfunctorily

潦倒 liáodǎo　be frustrated; be down on one's luck

燎　liáo　burn ——see also liǎo

燎泡 liáopào　(also 燎浆泡 liáojiāngpào) blister raised by a burn or scald

燎原 liáoyuán　set the prairie ablaze: 革命的烈火已成～之势。The flames of revolution are spreading far and wide.

燎原烈火 liáoyuán lièhuǒ　a blazing prairie fire

鹩　liáo　see below

鹩哥 liáogē　hill myna

liǎo

了¹　liǎo　① finish; conclude; settle; dispose of: 这事情还没～哇。This matter hasn't been settled yet.／帐也～了，我的心事也～了。The debt is settled, and my worry is over.／好吧！这事儿就这样～啦。All right, so that's that. ② (used after a verb plus 得 or 不) to a finish: 办得～ can manage it／受不～ cannot stand it／你骗不～我。You can't fool me.／你来得～来不～？Will you be able to come? ③ formal　(not) in the least: ～不相涉 have nothing at all to do with it

了²**(瞭)**　liǎo　know clearly; understand: 明了 míngliǎo^① ——see also le

了不得 liǎobude　① wonderful; terrific: 他真～。He's really terrific.／一件～的大事 a matter of the utmost importance ② (used as complement after 得) extremely; awfully; terribly: 高兴得～ be extremely happy／怕得～ be very much afraid／好(坏)得～ be awfully good (bad) ③ terrible; awful: 可～，他昏过去了！Good God! He's fainted.／危险是有的，但并不是那么～。There was danger, but it wasn't so serious.

了不起 liǎobuqǐ　amazing; terrific; extraordinary: ～的成就 an amazing achievement／他真～。He's really terrific.／没什么～。There's nothing so terrific.／有些人出了一点力就觉得～。There are people who swell with pride whenever they make some small contribution.

了当 liǎodàng　① frank; straightforward; forthright: 说话脆快～ be outspoken／～地说 not to mince matters ② settled; in order: 收拾～ have got everything ready; have put everything in order ③ old　handle; manage: 自能～得来 can certainly manage it

了得 liǎode　(used, usu. after 还, in exclamations) horrible; terrible: 哎呀！这还～! Oh! How outrageous (or terrible, awful)!／过去要是遇到这样的大旱，那还～! How terrible such a drought would have been in the past!

了结 liǎojié　finish; settle; wind up; bring to an end: ～一场纠纷 settle a dispute; end a conflict

了解 liǎojiě　① understand; comprehend: 我完全～你。I understand you perfectly.／我很～你的困难。I very much understand your difficulty.／他根本不～实际情况。He doesn't understand the facts at all.／他对工人的生活和工作情况很～。He has an intimate understanding of how the workers live and work. ② find out; acquaint oneself with: 你去～一下。Go and find out.／你去～～大伙儿有什么意见再做决定。Try to find out their views before making a decision.／我们必须设法～全部情况。We must try to find out about the whole situation.／～国内外科技发展情况 keep abreast of current developments in science and technology at home and abroad ③ understanding; comprehension: 我对市场经济的～很差。My understanding of market economy is very limited.／增进两国人民之间的～ promote understanding between the two peoples

了局 liǎojú　① end: 这就是故事的～。This is how the story ends. ② solution; settlement: 拖下去不是个～。Putting things off is no solution.

了了 liǎoliǎo　formal　① know clearly: 心中～ be perfectly clear about sth. ② intelligent; clever: 小时～，大未必佳。A clever child may not distinguish himself when grown up.

了却 liǎoquè　settle; solve: 这就〜了我的一桩心事。 That settled a matter which had been weighing on my mind.

了然 liǎorán　understand; be clear: 真相如何，我也不大〜。 I don't have a clear picture of the real situation either.

了如指掌 liǎo rú zhǐ zhǎng　know sth. like the palm of one's hand; have sth. at one's fingertips: 他对这一带的地形〜。 He knows the terrain of this locality like the back of his hand.

了事 liǎoshì　dispose of a matter; finish up sth.; get sth. over: 这样就算〜了吗? Do you consider this done? / 应付〜 deal with sth. in a perfunctory way

了手 liǎoshǒu　dial. be over and done with

了无惧色 liǎo wú jùsè　not show a trace of fear; look completely undaunted

了悟 liǎowù　understand; realize

了愿 liǎoyuàn　fulfil a wish, promise, or vow

了帐 liǎozhàng　settle a debt or an account

钌 liǎo　chem. ruthenium (Ru) ——see also liào

蓼 liǎo　knotweed

蓼科 liǎokē　bot. Polygonaceae

蓼蓝 liǎolán　indigo plant

燎 liǎo　singe ——see also liào

liào

尥 liào　see below

尥蹶子 liào juězi　(of mules, horses, etc.) give a backward kick

钌 liào　see below ——see also liǎo

钌铞儿 liàodiàor　hasp and staple

料[1] liào　suppose; expect; anticipate: 〜他不敢。 I don't think he dare. / 〜定敌军会有行动 anticipate movements on the part of the enemy

料[2] liào　① material; stuff: 〜备足了没有? Have we got enough material? ② (grain) feed: 多给牲口加点〜。 Put more grain in the fodder. ③ makings; material: 我不是唱歌的〜。 I haven't got the makings of a singer. / 瞧他那块〜想当教授。 Even an oaf like him thinks he can be a professor. ④ opaque coloured glassware ⑤ m. (for pills of Chinese medicine) prescription:配一〜药 make up one prescription of pills

料车 liàochē　skip car; skip

料到 liàodào　foresee; expect: 没〜他会来。 We didn't expect him to come. / 我们克服了许多没有〜的困难。 We overcame many unforeseen difficulties.

料斗 liàodǒu　① feed container ② (charging) hopper

料豆儿 liàodòur　beans used as livestock feed

料度 liàoduó　surmise; estimate

料货 liàohuò　glassware

料及 liàojí　formal expect; foresee: 中途大雨，原未〜。 Unexpectedly, a rainstorm overtook us before we reached our destination.

料酒 liàojiǔ　cooking wine

料理 liàolǐ　arrange; manage; attend to; take care of: 〜家务 manage household affairs / 孩子们已能自己〜生活。 The children can take care of themselves now.

料理后事 liàolǐ hòushì　make arrangements for a funeral

料器 liàoqì　glassware

料峭 liàoqiào　liter. chilly: 春寒〜。 There is a chill in the air in early spring.

料事如神 liào shì rú shén　predict like a prophet; foretell with miraculous accuracy

料想 liàoxiǎng　expect; think; presume: 真是〜不到的事情! Who would have thought that would happen! / 他〜领导一定能批准他的请求。 He fully expected that the leadership would grant his request.

料子 liàozi　① material for making clothes ② dial. woollen fabric: 〜裤 trousers made of woollen fabric / 〜服 suits of woollen cloth ③ wood; timber ④ inf. makings; material: 他是教书的〜。 He's excellent teacher material. ⑤ dial. heroin

撂 (撩) liào　inf. ① put down; leave behind: 把帘子〜下来。 Let down the curtain. / 他把东西都〜在地下了。 He put everything down on the floor. / 听说有急诊，医生〜下筷子就走。 Hearing that there was an emergency case, the doctor put down his chopsticks and left at once. / 我不能把我的事〜下就跟你走。 I can't just drop my work and go with you. / 咱们把她〜下的活儿干完吧。 Let's finish off the work she has left behind. ② throw down; knock down; shoot down: 一枪就〜倒一个敌人 hit an enemy soldier with each shot ③ throw away; cast aside; abandon

撂荒 liàohuāng　dial. let a piece of farmland go to waste

撂交 liàojiāo　dial. trip and fall

撂手 liàoshǒu　lay aside what one is doing: 〜不管 wash one's hands of the matter

撂挑子 liào tiāozi　put down the load—give up one's responsibilities; quit one's job: 不该挨了批评就〜。 It's bad to quit one's job just because one's been criticized.

廖 Liào　a surname

瞭 liào　watch from a height or a distance

瞭望 liàowàng　watch from a height or a distance; keep a lookout: 用望远镜〜敌军阵地 look at the enemy's position through field glasses

瞭望哨 liàowàngshào　lookout post

瞭望台 liàowàngtái　observation tower; lookout tower

镣 liào　fetters: 脚镣 jiǎoliào

镣铐 liàokào　fetters and handcuffs; shackles; irons; chains: 戴上〜 be shackled; be in chains

liē

咧 liē　see below ——see also liě; lie

咧咧 liēliē　see 大大咧咧 dàdaliēliē; 骂骂咧咧 màmaliēliē

咧咧 liēlie　dial. ① talk nonsense; blabber: 你瞎〜什么? What are you blabbering about? ② (of a child) cry: 那个小孩儿老〜。 That child is always crying.

liě

咧 liě　see below ——see also liē; lie

咧嘴 liězuǐ　draw back the corners of the mouth; grin: 疼得直〜 grin with pain / 他咧着嘴笑。 His face broadened into a grin. / 他尝了一口，直〜。 He made a face when he tasted it.

裂 liě　inf. (of two pieces joined together) come

apart; open up: 衣服没扣好，～着怀 with one's coat or shirt unbuttoned ——see also　liě

liè

列 liè ①arrange; set out: ～出理由 set out one's reasons (for sth.) / ～表 arrange (facts, figures, etc.) in tables or columns; tabulate ② list; enter in a list: 代表姓名～后。Listed below are the names of the delegates. / ～入议程 be placed on the agenda / ～为甲等 be classified as first-rate; be rated as class A ③ row; file; rank: 前列 qiánliè ④ *m.* (for a series or row of things): 一～火车 a train ⑤ kind; sort: 不在讨论之～ not among the subjects to be discussed ⑥ various; each and every: 列国 lièguó

列兵 lièbīng *mil.* private

列车 lièchē train: 旅客～ passenger train / 直达～ through train / 15次～ No.15 train

列车调度员 lièchē diàodùyuán train dispatcher

列车时刻表 lièchē shíkèbiǎo train schedule; timetable

列车员 lièchēyuán attendant (on a train)

列车运行图 lièchē yùnxíngtú train schedule; timetable

列车长 lièchēzhǎng head of a train crew

列当 lièdāng *bot.* broomrape

列岛 lièdǎo a chain of islands; archipelago

列队 lièduì line up: ～欢迎 line up to welcome sb.

列国 lièguó the various countries, states, or kingdoms: ～相争 kingdoms warring against each other / 《东周～志》 *Chronicles of the States of the Eastern Zhou*

列举 lièjǔ enumerate; list: ～大量事实 cite numerous facts / 计划中～了各种具体办法。Various concrete measures were enumerated in the plan.

列宁主义 Lièníngzhǔyì Leninism

列强 lièqiáng *old* the Great Powers: 打倒～! Down with the imperialist Powers!

列氏温度计 lièshìwēndùjì the Réaumur thermometer

列位 lièwèi all of you; gentlemen; ladies and gentlemen: ～来宾 all of you honoured guests

列席 lièxí attend (a meeting) as an observer or a nonvoting delegate; attend without voting rights

列席代表 lièxí dàibiǎo delegate without the right to vote; nonvoting delegate

列支敦士登 Lièzhīdūnshìdēng Liechtenstein

列支敦士登人 Lièzhīdūnshìdēngrén Liechtensteiner

列传 lièzhuàn biographies (a section in dynastic histories, dealing with a variety of famous individuals and also with the affairs of the various non-Han peoples): 《李将军～》"The Biography of General Li Guang" / 《匈奴～》"An Account of the Xiongnu"

列祖列宗 lièzǔ-lièzōng successive generations of ancestors

劣 liè bad; inferior; of low quality: 优劣 yōu-liè

劣等 lièděng of inferior quality; low-grade; poor: ～产品 poor quality products; products of inferior quality / ～人种 an inferior race (a racist term)

劣根性 liègēnxìng deep-rooted bad habits; an inherent weakness

劣弧 lièhú *math.* minor arc

劣货 lièhuò poor quality goods; goods of inferior quality

劣迹 lièjì misdeed; evil doing

劣迹昭彰 lièjì zhāozhāng have a notorious record

劣马 lièmǎ ① inferior horse; nag ② vicious horse; fiery steed

劣绅 lièshēn evil gentry

劣势 lièshì inferior position; unfavourable situation: 处于～ be in an inferior position

劣质 lièzhì of poor (*or* low) quality; inferior: ～煤 inferior coal; faulty coal

劣种 lièzhǒng inferior strain (*or* breed, stock)

冽 liè *formal* cold: 凛冽 lǐnliè

洌 liè *formal* (of water or wine) clear: 泉香而酒～。The spring water is sweet, and the wine made with it is clear and smooth to the palate.

埒 liè *arch.* equal; alike: 二人才力相～。The two are much alike in ability. / 邯郸郭纵以铁冶成业，与王者～富。《史记》Guo Zong of Handan made a business of smelting iron, and his wealth equalled that of the ruler of a kingdom.

烈 liè strong; violent; intense: ～酒 a strong drink; hard liquor / 两国之间的争夺愈演愈～。The rivalry between the two countries is becoming increasingly acute. ② staunch; upright; stern: 刚烈 gāngliè ③ sacrificing oneself for a just cause: 先烈 xiānliè ④ achievements: 功烈 gōngliè

烈度 lièdù (short for 地震烈度) earthquake intensity

烈风 lièfēng *meteorol.* strong gale

烈火 lièhuǒ raging fire; raging flames: 熊熊的～ a raging fire

烈火见真金 lièhuǒ jiàn zhēnjīn pure gold proves its worth in a blazing fire—people of worth show their mettle during trials and tribulations ——see also 疾风知劲草 jífēng zhī jìngcǎo

烈女 liènǚ (in former times) a paragon of chastity (a woman who dies in defence of her chastity or who prefers to die rather than remarry, or marry after the death of her betrothed)

烈日 lièrì burning sun; scorching sun: ～当空 with the scorching sun directly overhead

烈士 lièshì ① martyr: 革命～ a revolutionary martyr ② (in former times) a man of high endeavour; hero

烈士纪念碑 lièshì jìniànbēi a monument to revolutionary martyrs

烈士陵园 lièshì língyuán revolutionary martyrs' cemetery; martyrs' park

烈士墓 lièshìmù the tomb of a revolutionary martyr

烈士暮年，壮心不已 lièshì mùnián, zhuàngxīn bùyǐ the heart of a hero in his old age is as stout as ever; a noble-hearted man retains his high aspirations even in old age

烈属 lièshǔ members of a revolutionary martyr's family

烈暑 lièshǔ hot summer weather

烈性 lièxìng ① spirited: ～汉子 a man of character ② strong: ～酒 a strong (*or* stiff) drink; hard liquor; spirits / ～毒药 deadly poison / ～炸药 high explosive

烈性子 lièxìngzi ① fiery disposition ② spitfire

烈焰 lièyàn raging flames; a roaring blaze

䴕 liè woodpecker

捩 liè twist; turn: 转捩点 zhuǎnlièdiǎn

捩转 lièzhuǎn turn round: ～车身 turn the car round

猎(獵) liè hunt: ～虎 tiger hunting

猎豹 lièbào cheetah

猎捕 lièbǔ hunt

猎场 lièchǎng hunting ground; hunting field

猎刀 lièdāo hunting knife

猎狗 liègǒu hunting dog; hound

猎户 lièhù hunter; huntsman

猎户座 Lièhùzuò *astron.* Orion

猎获　lièhuò　capture or kill in hunting; bag: ～两三只野兔 bag a couple of hares / ～一头幼象 trap a young elephant

猎获物　lièhuòwù　bag

猎猎　lièliè　*onom. liter.* the sound of the wind or a fluttering flag

猎奇　lièqí　hunt for novelty; seek novelty

猎潜艇　lièqiántǐng　submarine chaser

猎枪　lièqiāng　shotgun; fowling piece; hunting rifle

猎取　lièqǔ　① hunt: 原始社会的人用粗糙的石器～野兽。Primitive man hunted wild animals with crude stone implements. ② pursue; seek; hunt for: ～个人名利 pursue personal fame and gain / ～廉价的声誉 make a bid for cheap popularity

猎犬　lièquǎn　hunting dog; hound

猎人　lièrén　hunter; huntsman

猎杀　lièshā　hunt and kill: ～珍奇动物是违法的。It's illegal to hunt and kill rare animals.

猎手　lièshǒu　hunter

猎艳　lièyàn　*formal* ① rack one's brains for ornate diction ② chase after pretty women

猎鹰　lièyīng　falcon

猎装　lièzhuāng　hunting suit; hunting outfit

裂　liè　split; crack; rend: 杯子～了。The cup's cracked. / 地都干～了。The earth was so dry that it cracked. / 他的手冻～了。His hands are chapped by the cold. / ～成两半 split in two ——see also　liě

裂变　lièbiàn　*phys.* fission

裂变产物　lièbiàn chǎnwù　fission product

裂变武器　lièbiàn wǔqì　the fission type of weapon

裂齿　lièchǐ　carnassial tooth (of certain carnivores)

裂唇　lièchún　same as 唇裂　chúnliè

裂缝　lièfèng　① crack; split: 墙上裂了一道缝。The wall has cracked. ② rift; crevice; crack; fissure: 墙上有一道～。There is a crack in the wall.

裂谷　liègǔ　*geol.* rift valley

裂果　lièguǒ　*bot.* dehiscent fruit

裂痕　lièhén　rift; crack; fissure: 这块玻璃有一道～。There is a crack in the glass. / 他们之间一度有过～。There was once a rift between them.

裂化　lièhuà　cracking (in the distillation of petroleum)

裂化炉　lièhuàlú　cracking still (*or* furnace, heater)

裂化气　lièhuàqì　cracked gas

裂解　lièjiě　*chem.* splitting decomposition; splitting

裂解作用　lièjiě zuòyòng　*chem.* splitting action

裂开　lièkāi　crack open; split open: 盒子掉在地上～了。The box fell on the ground and cracked open. / 木板干得～了。The board was so dry that it split open.

裂口　lièkǒu　① crack; split: 堤上～了。The dike has cracked. / 他的手冻得～了。His hands are chapped by the cold. ② breach; gap; crack; split: 堤上的～越来越大。The crack in the dike is getting wider. ③ vent (of a volcano)

裂口火山锥　lièkǒu huǒshānzhuī　breached cone

裂片　lièpiàn　*bot.* lobe (of a leaf)

裂纹　lièwén　① crack (the sides being still together): 窗户上有一道～, 是踢球踢的。The window has a crack in it where the ball hit it. ② crackle (on pottery, porcelain, etc.)

裂璺　lièwèn　same as 裂纹　lièwén①

裂隙　lièxì　crack; crevice; fracture

裂隙水　lièxìshuǐ　crevice water

裂罅　lièxià　*formal* crack; split; rift; crevice

裂殖菌　lièzhíjūn　schizomycete

趔　liè　see below

趔趄　lièqie　stagger; reel: 他～着走进屋来。He staggered into the room. / 他打了个～, 摔倒了。He reeled

and fell.

蹑　liè　*formal* ① overstep; go beyond; skip over ② trample

蹑等　lièděng　*formal* skip over the normal steps; not follow the proper order: ～求进 try to advance by skipping necessary steps

蹑级　lièjí　same as 蹑等　lièděng

蹑进　lièjìn　*formal* advance by skipping necessary steps

鬣　liè　mane

鬣狗　liègǒu　hyena; striped hyena

鬣羚　lièlíng　serow

lie

咧　lie　*part. dial.* (used in the same way as 了, 啦, and 哩) ——see also　liē; liě

līn

拎　līn　*dial.* carry; lift: 他～着桶去打水。He was carrying a bucket to fetch water.

拎包　līnbāo　*dial.* handbag; shopping bag; bag

lín

邻 (鄰、隣)　lín　① neighbour: 近邻 jìnlín ② neighbouring; near; adjacent: ～县 a neighbouring county / ～座 an adjacent seat

邻邦　línbāng　neighbouring country: 我们两国历来是友好的～。Our two countries have always been good neighbours.

邻国　línguó　neighbouring country

邻家　línjiā　next-door family; next-door (*or* close) neighbour

邻角　línjiǎo　*math.* adjacent angles

邻接　línjiē　border on; be next to; be contiguous to; adjoin: 西班牙～法国西南部。Spain borders on the southwest of France. / 化肥厂～农机厂。The chemical fertilizer plant adjoins the farm machinery plant.

邻近　línjìn　① be near; be close to; be adjacent to: 我国东部跟朝鲜接壤, 跟日本～。In the east, our country adjoins Korea and is close to Japan. ② neighbourhood; vicinity: ～没有医院。There's no hospital in the neighbourhood. / 学校～有商店。There's a shop in the vicinity of the school.

邻居　línjū　neighbour

邻里　línlǐ　① neighbourhood: ～服务所 a neighbourhood service centre ② people of the neighbourhood; neighbours

邻人　línrén　neighbour

邻舍　línshè　*dial.* neighbour

邻位　línwèi　*chem.* ortho-position: ～化合物 ortho-compound

林　lín　① forest; woods; grove: 松～ pine forest ② a group of persons or things: 艺林 yìlín ③ forestry: 农林 nónglín ④ (Lín) a surname

林薄　línbó　*formal* a dense growth of plants and trees

林产　línchǎn　forest products

林场　línchǎng　forestry centre (including tree nurseries,

lumber camps, etc.); tree farm

林带 líndài　forest belt: 防沙～ a sand-break forest belt

林地 líndì　forest land; woodland; timberland

林分 línfēn　*forestry* standing forest; stand

林冠 línguān　*forestry* crown canopy; crown cover

林海 línhǎi　immense forest

林壑 línhè　woods and ravines; forests and dales: 环滁皆山也。其西南诸峰，～尤美。(欧阳修) All around Chu are mountains. The ranges towards the southwest are particularly lovely with their woods and ravines.

林可菌素 línkějūnsù　*pharm.* lincomycin

林垦 línkěn　forestry and land reclamation

林立 línlì　(of masts, smokestacks, derricks, tall buildings, etc.) stand (in great numbers) like a forest: 港口樯桅～。There is a forest of masts in the harbour.

林林总总 línlínzǒngzǒng　numerous; multitudinous: 中国不患无实行家, 盖～者皆是也。(孙中山) China does not suffer from a lack of men of action; on the contrary, there are multitudes of them.

林龄 línlíng　*forestry* age of stand

林莽 línmǎng　jungle

林木 línmù　① forest; woods: ～葱郁 densely wooded ② forest tree

林农 línnóng　forest farmer; forester

林檎 línqín　another name for 花红[1] huāhóng

林区 línqū　forest zone; forest region; forest

林泉 línquán　*formal* forests and streams—mountain retreat; a place for a recluse: 甘老～ be content to grow old among the forests and streams—be content to live out one's days in retirement

林薮 línsǒu　*formal* woods and marshes

林涛 líntāo　the soughing of the wind in forest trees

林网 línwǎng　crisscross forest belts

林下 línxià　*formal* a sylvan life—retirement from official life: 退隐～ retire from official life / 优游～ live happily in retirement

林业 línyè　forestry

林业工人 línyè gōngrén　forest worker; forester

林狸 línyì　*zool.* lynx

林荫道 línyīndào　(also 林荫路 línyīnlù) boulevard; avenue

林苑 línyuàn　hunting park (for emperors)

林子 línzi　*inf.* woods; grove; forest

临(臨)

lín　① face; overlook: ～街的窗子 a window overlooking the street / 这所房子～河。This house looks out on a river. / 东～大海 border on the sea in the east ② arrive; be present: 亲临 qīnlín ③ *prep.* on the point of; just before; be about to: ～睡 just before going to bed; at bedtime / 这本书是我～离开北京时买的。I bought this book just before I left Beijing. ④ copy (a model of calligraphy or painting): ～画 copy a painting / ～帖 practise calligraphy after a model

临本 línběn　copy (of a painting, etc.)

临别 línbié　at parting; just before parting: ～合影 have a group photo taken just before parting / 作为～纪念 as a parting souvenir

临别赠言 línbié zèngyán　words of advice at parting; parting advice

临产 línchǎn　about to give birth; parturient

临产阵痛 línchǎn zhèntòng　labour pains; birth pangs

临场 línchǎng　① when attending an examination; when participating in a contest: ～要沉着, 不要慌。Keep calm during the exam. Don't panic. ② come personally to the site or spot: ～指导 come personally to give on-the-spot guidance

临池 línchí　*formal* at the pond—practising calligraphy (from the story of the Han Dynasty calligrapher Zhang Zhi 张芝 who practised calligraphy on the edge of a pond and washed his inkslab in the pond water until the whole pond was blackened)

临床 línchuáng　clinical: ～检查 clinical examination / ～教学 clinical instruction / ～经验 clinical experience / ～诊断 clinical (*or* bedside) diagnosis

临床表现 línchuáng biǎoxiàn　clinical manifestation

临床学 línchuángxué　clinical medicine

临床医生 línchuáng yīshēng　clinician

临床应用 línchuáng yìngyòng　clinical practice

临到 líndào　① just before; on the point of: ～开会, 她还在准备发言。She was still preparing her speech when the meeting began. ② befall; happen to: 这事如果～你的头上, 你怎么办? What would you do if it happened to you?

临风 línfēng　*formal* facing (*or* against) the wind

临机 línjī　face an emergency: ～应变 make changes as the situation demands; act according to circumstances; be prepared for all contingencies / ～立断 make a quick decision as the situation demands

临界 línjiè　*phys.* critical

临界点 línjièdiǎn　critical point

临界角 línjièjiǎo　critical angle

临界态 línjiètài　critical state

临界体积 línjiè tǐjī　critical size

临界温度 línjiè wēndù　critical temperature

临近 línjìn　close to; close on: ～黎明 close on daybreak / ～太湖的一所疗养院 a sanatorium close by Taihu Lake

临渴掘井 lín kě jué jǐng　not dig a well until one is thirsty—start acting too late; make an eleventh-hour attempt

临了 línliǎo　(also 临末了儿 línmòliǎor) *inf.* finally; in the end: 人人都想去, ～只好由组长决定。Everyone wanted to go. In the end the group leader had to decide.

临门 línmén　① come to the house: 贵客～。A distinguished guest came to the house. ② facing the goal: ～一脚 (in football) shooting (at the goal) after breaking through the opponent's defence; go for the goal

临摹 línmó　copy (a model of calligraphy or painting)

临难 línnàn　*formal* face danger or disaster: ～毋苟免。Don't shirk dangers.

临盆 línpén　be giving birth to a child; be confined; be in labour

临氢重整 línqīngchóngzhěng　*chem.* hydroforming: ～汽油 hydroformer gasoline

临蓐 línrù　be confined; be in labour

临深履薄 línshēn-lǚbó　as if on the brink of a chasm, as if treading on thin ice—with caution and care

临时 línshí　① at the time when sth. is needed or is expected to happen: 你现在不准备, ～怎么办呢? If you don't prepare now, what will you do when the time comes? / 事先作好准备, 免得～忙乱。Arrange everything in advance so that you won't be in a rush at the last moment. / 我们只是～帮帮忙。We just help when we are needed. ② temporarily; for the time being: 我们～就用这个办法吧。Let's use this method temporarily. / ～凑合 make do for the moment ③ temporary; provisional: ～办法 a temporary solution (*or* arrangement); makeshift measures / ～工作人员 a temporary member of the staff / ～舞台 a makeshift stage / ～协议 a provisional (*or* interim) agreement / ～议程 a provisional agenda

临时抱佛脚 línshí bào fójiǎo　embrace Buddha's feet in one's hour of need—seek help at the last moment; make a frantic last-minute effort

临时代办 línshí dàibàn　*chargé d'affaires ad interim*

临时动议 línshí dòngyì　extempore motion

临时法庭 línshí fǎtíng　provisional court

临时费用 línshí fèiyòng interim (*or* incidental) expenses

临时工 línshígōng casual labourer; temporary worker

临时户口 línshí hùkǒu temporary residence permit

临时证书 línshí zhèngshū (in diplomacy) temporary credentials (*or* papers)

临时政府 línshí zhèngfǔ provisional (*or* interim) government

临时主席 línshí zhǔxí interim chairman

临死 línsǐ on one's deathbed

临眺 líntiào *formal* ascend a height and enjoy a distant view

临头 líntóu befall; happen: 大祸临头 dàhuò líntóu

临完 línwán finally; in the end

临危 línwēi ① be dying (from illness) ② face death or deadly peril

临危不惧 línwēi bù jù face danger fearlessly; betray no fear in face of danger

临危授命 línwēi shòumìng be ready to give one's life in times of national danger

临行 línxíng before leaving; on the eve of departure: 代表团在～前举行了一次答谢宴会。The delegation gave a return banquet before leaving for home. / ～匆匆，不及告别。I left in such a hurry that I didn't have time to say goodbye.

临刑 línxíng just before execution

临幸 línxìng (of the emperor) visit (a place)

临渊羡鱼 lín yuān xiàn yú stand by a pond longing for fish: ～，不如退而结网。《汉书》Better go back and make a net than stand by the pond longing for fish.

临月 línyuè about to give birth

临战 línzhàn just before a battle: 进入～状态 be combat-ready

临阵 línzhèn ① just before going into battle; at a critical juncture ② at the front; on the battlefield: ～指挥 direct military operations at the front lines / 他有～经验。He's seen some action.

临阵磨枪 línzhèn mó qiāng sharpen one's spear just before going into battle—start to prepare at the last moment

临阵脱逃 línzhèn tuōtáo desert on the eve of a battle; sneak away at a critical juncture

临终 línzhōng approaching one's end; immediately before one's death; on one's deathbed

临终遗言 línzhōng yíyán deathbed testament; last words

淋
lín pour; drench: 他的衣服让雨～湿了。His clothes were drenched by the rain. / 日晒雨～ sun-scorched and rain-drenched; exposed to the elements——see also lìn

淋巴 línbā lymph

淋巴结 línbājié lymph node (*or* gland)

淋巴结炎 línbājiéyán lymphnoditis

淋巴球 línbāqiú lymphocyte

淋巴肉瘤 línbā ròuliú lymphosarcoma

淋巴液 línbāyè same as 淋巴 línbā

淋漓 línlí ① dripping wet: 大汗～ dripping with sweat / 鲜血～ dripping with blood ② (of a piece of writing or a speech) free from inhibition: 痛快～ impassioned and forceful

淋漓尽致 línlí jìn zhì vividly and incisively; in great detail: 刻画得～ portray most vividly / 揭露得～ make a telling exposure / 他这番表演，真可谓～。He put on an act, which showed him up completely.

淋淋 línlín dripping wet: 湿～的衣服 dripping wet clothes

淋洗 línxǐ drip washing

淋雨 línyǔ get wet in the rain

淋浴 línyù shower bath; shower: 洗～ take (*or* have) a shower

啉
lín see 喹啉 kuílín

琳
lín *formal* beautiful jade

琳琅 línláng beautiful jade; gem

琳琅满目 línláng mǎnmù a superb collection of beautiful things; a feast for the eyes: 展品～，美不胜收。One is dazzled by the endless array of beautiful exhibits. *or* The exhibition is a feast for the eyes.

嶙
lín see below

嶙嶙 línlín *liter.* (of water, stone, etc.) clear; crystalline: ～碧波 clear, blue ripples

遴
lín choose or select (a person) carefully

遴选 línxuǎn *formal* select sb. for a post; select; choose: ～接班人 select a successor

嶙
lín see below

嶙嶙 línlín same as 嶙峋 línxún

嶙峋 línxún *formal* ① (of mountain rocks, cliffs, etc.) jagged; rugged; craggy: 怪石～ jagged rocks of grotesque shapes / ～的山峦 craggy hills ② (of a person) bony; thin: 瘦骨～ be terribly emaciated

霖
lín continuous heavy rain: 秋～ autumn rains

霖雨 línyǔ continuous heavy rain

嶙
lín see below

嶙嶙 línlín *onom. liter.* the sound made by a running cart, chariot, etc.: 车～，马萧萧，行人弓箭各在腰。(杜甫) Chariots rumbling, horses neighing; Soldiers on the march, each with a bow and arrow at the waist.

璘
lín the lustre of jade

磷（燐）
lín *chem.* phosphorus (P)

磷肥 línféi phosphate fertilizer

磷光 línguāng phosphorescence

磷光体 línguāngtǐ phosphor

磷火 línhuǒ phosphorescent light; will-o'-the-wisp; jack-o'-lantern

磷矿粉 línkuàngfěn ground phosphate rock

磷磷 línlín same as 嶙嶙 línlín

磷燃烧弹 línránshāodàn phosphorous bomb

磷酸 línsuān phosphoric acid

磷酸铵 línsuān'ǎn ammonium phosphate

磷酸钙 línsuāngài calcium phosphate

磷酸盐 línsuānyán phosphate

磷细菌 línxìjūn phosphobacteria

磷虾 línxiā euphausiid shrimp

磷脂 línzhī phosphatide

磷脂酸 línzhīsuān phosphatidic acid

鳞
lín scale (of fish, etc.)

鳞比 línbǐ (of buildings) like fish scales; in tight rows; row upon row: 大街两旁商店～。The street was lined with shops.

鳞波 línbō *liter.* ripples

鳞翅目 línchìmù *zool.* Lepidoptera

鳞次栉比 líncì-zhìbǐ (of buildings) like fish scales and comb teeth; in tight rows; row upon row: 江岸新建的仓库～。Row upon row of newly built warehouses line the waterfront.

鳞甲 línjiǎ scale and shell (of reptiles and arthropods)

鳞介 línjiè *formal* aquatic animals

鳞茎 línjīng *bot.* bulb

鳞鳞 línlín *formal* ① numerous as fish scales: 强敌～

large numbers of formidable enemies ② resembling scales; scaly: ～的白云 layers of white clouds / 湖上金光～。The lake glistens with ripples.

鳞片 línpiàn　① scale (on fish or insects' wings) ② bud scale

鳞伤 línshāng　cuts and bruises all over the body: 遍体鳞伤 biàntǐ línshāng

鳞屑 línxiè　scales of skin that peel off

鳞爪 línzhǎo　*formal* scales and claws—small bits; fragments; odd scraps:《羊城～》"Titbits from the City of Rams" (i.e. Guangzhou)

麟（麐） lín　*formal* (Chinese) unicorn

麟凤龟龙 lín-fèng-guī-lóng　the unicorn, the phoenix, the tortoise, and the dragon (formerly called the "four spiritually endowed beings")—worthy men

麟角凤嘴 línjiǎo-fèngzuǐ　the unicorn's horn and the phoenix's beak—rare treasures

lǐn

凛（凜） lǐn　① cold: 凛冽 lǐnliè ② strict; stern; severe: ～遵 strictly abide by ③ afraid; apprehensive: ～于远行 be afraid of going on a long journey

凛冽 lǐnliè　piercingly cold: 北风～，大雪纷飞。The north wind was blowing cold; the snowflakes were flying.

凛凛 lǐnlǐn　① cold: 寒风～。A cold wind chills. / ～岁云暮，蝼蛄夕鸣悲。《古诗十九首》Cold, cold the year draws to its end, The crickets and grasshoppers make a doleful chirping. ② stern; awe-inspiring: 威风凛凛 wēifēng lǐnlǐn

凛然 lǐnrán　stern; awe-inspiring: 正气～ awe-inspiring righteousness / 态度～ stern in manner / 一副～不可侵犯的样子 look stern and forbidding

凛若冰霜 lǐn ruò bīngshuāng　look severe; have a forbidding manner

廪（廩） lǐn　*formal* granary: 仓廪 cānglǐn

廪生 lǐnshēng　(during the Ming and Qing Dynasties) a *xiucai* living on a government stipend; a salaried *xiucai*

檩（檁） lǐn　purlin

檩条 lǐntiáo　purlin

檩子 lǐnzi　*dial.* purlin

lìn

吝 lìn　stingy; mean; closefisted: 悭吝 qiānlìn

吝啬 lìnsè　stingy; niggardly; miserly; mean

吝啬鬼 lìnsèguǐ　miser; niggard; skinflint

吝惜 lìnxī　grudge; stint: 不～自己的力量 spare no effort; stint no effort / 不～钱财 spare no expense

赁 lìn　rent; hire: ～一辆车 hire a car / 房屋出～ house to let

赁费 lìnfèi　rental fee; rent

赁金 lìnjīn　rental fee; rent

淋 lìn　strain; filter: 用纱布把药～一下 strain the herbal medicine with a piece of gauze ——see also lín

淋病 lìnbìng　gonorrhoea

淋溶 lìnróng　*geol.* leaching; eluviation

淋溶层 lìnróngcéng　leached horizon; eluvial horizon;

eluvium

蔺 lìn　① see 马蔺 mǎlìn ② (Lìn) a surname

膦 lìn　*chem.* phosphine

蹸 lìn　see 蹂蹸 róulìn

líng

〇 líng　(same as 零, usu. used in numbers) zero: 三～六号 No. 306 (number three-oh-six) / 一九九～年 1990 (nineteen ninety)

伶 líng　*old* actor: 名～ a famous actor / 坤～ actress

伶仃 língdīng　left alone without help; lonely: 孤苦伶仃 gūkǔ-língdīng

伶俐 línglì　clever; bright; quick-witted: 口齿～ be clever and fluent / 这孩子真～! What a clever child!

伶俜 língpīng　*liter.* lonely

伶人 língrén　*old* actor

伶牙俐齿 língyá-lìchǐ　have the gift of the gab; have a glib tongue; have a ready tongue

灵（靈、灵） líng　① quick; clever; sharp: 他耳朵很～。He has sharp ears. *or* His hearing is very good. / 他脑子很～。His mind is very sharp. / 这个孩子～极了。This is a very alert child. / 资金周转不～。The capital turnover is not quick enough. ② spirit; intelligence: 英灵 yīnglíng ③ fairy; sprite; elf: 灵怪 língguài ④ efficacious; effective: 这个药真～。This medicine is very effective. / 我们试了一下，果然很～。We tried it out and it really worked. ⑤ (remains) of the deceased; bier: ～前摆着花圈。Wreaths were laid in front of the coffin.

灵便 língbian　① nimble; agile: 他虽然上了年纪，手脚倒还～。Though getting on in years, he is still nimble. / 老大爷耳朵不～，请你说话大声点。Speak louder, please. Grandpa is hard of hearing. ② easy to handle; handy: 这把钳子使着真～。This pair of pliers is really handy.

灵车 língchē　hearse

灵榇 língchèn　same as 灵柩 língjiù

灵床 língchuáng　① bier ② a bed kept as it was when the person was alive

灵丹妙药 língdān-miàoyào　(also 灵丹圣药 língdān-shèngyào) a magic (*or* wonder) drug; a miraculous cure; panacea

灵幡 língfān　funeral banner

灵府 língfǔ　*formal* the mind; the faculties

灵感 línggǎn　inspiration (for creative work): 中国画家的～来源于大自然。Chinese painters' inspiration comes from nature.

灵怪 língguài　① gods and spirits ② mystical; strange; unusual

灵光 língguāng　① a divine light ② halo (round the head of a god) ③ *dial.* excellent; wonderful: 他的羽毛球打得真～。He plays badminton very well.

灵盒 línghé　cinerary casket

灵魂 línghún　soul: ～不灭论 the theory of the immortality of the soul / 纯洁的～ an unblemished soul / 金钱能腐蚀～。Money can deprave the soul. / 失掉一个人的～ lose one's soul / 出卖～ sell one's soul / 教师是人类～的工程师。A teacher is an architect of man's soul. / 简练含蓄是中国诗的～。Brevity and suggestiveness are the soul of Chinese poetry.

灵魂深处 línghún shēnchù in one's innermost soul; in the depth of one's soul

灵活 línghuó ① nimble; agile; quick: 手脚～ dexterous and quick in action / 脑筋～ be quick-witted; have a supple mind ② flexible; elastic: ～机动的战略战术 flexible strategy and tactics / ～多样的经营方式 flexible and diversified forms of operation

灵活性 línghuóxìng flexibility; elasticity; mobility

灵机 língjī sudden inspiration; brainwave

灵机一动 língjī yī dòng have a brainwave: 她～, 想出了个好办法。 She had a brainwave and found a good solution.

灵柩 língjiù a coffin containing a corpse; bier

灵快 língkuài nimble; agile

灵猫 língmāo civet (cat): 大～ zibet

灵敏 língmǐn sensitive; keen; agile; acute: 嗅觉～ have an acute sense of smell / 动作～ be quick in one's movements / 这架仪器很～。 This instrument is highly sensitive.

灵敏度 língmǐndù sensitivity

灵牌 língpái spirit tablet

灵巧 língqiǎo dexterous; nimble; skilful; ingenious: 一双～的手 a pair of clever hands / 她的体操动作准确而～。 Her movements in callisthenics were precise and nimble. / 他的心思挺～, 会捏各种泥人儿。 He showed great ingenuity in moulding various types of clay figurines.

灵寝 língqǐn a place where a coffin containing a corpse is kept

灵台 língtái ① *formal* the mind; the heart ② a platform on which a coffin or a cinerary casket is placed

灵堂 língtáng mourning hall

灵通 língtōng ① having quick access to information; well-informed: 他消息特别～。 He is well-informed. ② *dial.* be of use (*or* help)

灵透 língtou *dial.* clever

灵位 língwèi same as 灵牌 língpái

灵物 língwù spiritual beings; supernatural beings

灵犀 língxī magic horn (i.e. rhinoceros horn with its threadlike white core, mentioned in old texts as having a high sensibility): 身无彩凤双飞翼, 心有～一点通。 (李商隐) For bodies no fluttering side by side of splendid phoenix wings, Between hearts the one minute thread from root to tip of the magic horn. (The second line is often quoted as meaning a meeting of minds.)

灵效 língxiào (usu. of drugs) effective; efficacious

灵性 língxìng intelligence (of animals): 这匹马很有～, 能领会主人的意图。 This horse is very intelligent. He can sense what his master wants.

灵秀 língxiù (of scenery) beautiful

灵验 língyàn ① efficacious; effective: 这种药非常～。 This medicine is highly efficacious. ② (of a prediction, etc.) accurate; right: 天气预报果然～。 The weather forecast turned out to be accurate.

灵长目 língzhǎngmù *zool. Primates*: ～动物 primate

灵芝 língzhī magic fungus—glossy ganoderma (*Ganoderma lucidum*; used in medicine; formerly credited with miraculous powers and considered a symbol of good luck)

苓 líng see 茯苓 fúlíng

吟 líng see 嘌吟 piàolíng

图 líng see below

图圄 língyǔ (also 图圉 língyǔ) *formal* jail; prison: 身陷～ be behind prison bars; be thrown into prison

泠 líng *liter.* cool: ～风 a cool breeze

泠泠 línglíng *liter.* ① cool ② (of sound) clear and far-reaching

玲 líng see below

玲玲 línglíng *onom. liter.* the tinkling of pieces of jade

玲珑 línglóng ① (of things) ingeniously and delicately wrought; exquisite: 小巧玲珑 xiǎoqiǎo línglóng ② (of people) clever and nimble: 娇小玲珑 jiāoxiǎo línglóng

玲珑剔透 línglóng tītòu exquisitely carved; beautifully wrought: ～的玉石雕刻 exquisitely wrought jade carvings

瓴 líng *formal* water jar: 高屋建瓴 gāowū jiàn líng

凌¹(淩) líng ① insult: 盛气凌人 shèngqì líng rén ② approach: 凌晨 língchén ③ rise high; tower aloft: 凌空 língkōng ④ (Líng) a surname

凌² líng *dial.* ice (esp. in blocks or cone-shaped): 冰凌 bīnglíng

凌波 língbō *liter.* ① dashing waves ② like treading the waves (said of a beautiful woman's graceful way of walking): ～微步 walk with dainty steps

凌晨 língchén in the small hours; before dawn: 七月三日～ in the small hours of July 3 / 火车将于明日～四时半到达。 The train arrives at half past four tomorrow morning.

凌迟 língchí (in imperial times) the punishment of dismemberment and the lingering death (for heinous crimes): ～处死 execute by the slow process

凌泽 língduó *dial.* icicle

凌驾 língjià place oneself above; override: 决不能把个人～于群众之上。 One must never place oneself above the masses. / 救人的念头～一切, 他转身向大火中冲去。 The idea of saving people's lives was paramount. He turned round and rushed into the blaze.

凌空 língkōng be high up in the air; soar or tower aloft: 大桥～飞架两山之间。 High up in the air, a bridge spans the valley. / 飞机～而过。 The plane streaked across the sky. / 雪花～飞舞。 Snowflakes were flying in the sky.

凌厉 línglì swift and fierce: 攻势～ a swift and fierce attack / 朔风～。 A north wind was blowing hard.

凌轹 línglì *formal* oppress: ～百姓 oppress the people

凌乱 língluàn in disorder; in a mess: ～不堪 in a fearful mess; in a state of utter confusion / 头发～ with hair dishevelled / 楼上传来～的脚步声。 A flurry of footsteps could be heard in the room above. / 我歌月徘徊, 我舞影～。 (李白) I sing and the moon rambles; I dance and the shadow runs helter-skelter.

凌虐 língnüè *formal* maltreat; tyrannize over

凌日 língrì *astron.* transit: 金星～ transit of Venus

凌辱 língrǔ insult; humiliate: 受到～ be humiliated; suffer humiliation

凌替 língtì same as 陵替 língtì

凌霄 língxiāo ① *formal* reach up to heaven: 浩气～ a noble spirit reaching up to heaven ② same as 凌霄花 língxiāohuā

凌霄花 língxiāohuā Chinese trumpet creeper (*Campsis grandiflora*)

凌虚 língxū *formal* reach up to heaven: ～飞翔 soar aloft

凌汛 língxùn spring flood caused by melting river ice

凌夷 língyí *formal* decline; be on the wane

凌云 língyún reach the clouds; soar to the skies: 久有～志, 重上井冈山。 (毛泽东) I have long aspired to reach for the clouds And I again ascend Jinggangshan.

凌杂 língzá in disorder; in disarray

凌锥　língzhuī　*dial.* icicle

铃　líng ① bell: ～响了。The bell is ringing. ② a thing like a bell: 哑铃 yǎlíng / 棉铃 miánlíng ③ short for 蕾铃 lěilíng

铃钹　língbó　bell cymbals
铃铛　língdang　small bell
铃鼓　línggǔ　*mus.* tambourine
铃兰　línglán　lily of the valley

鸰　líng　see 鹡鸰 jīlíng

陵　líng ① hill; mound ② tomb; mausoleum: 谒～ pay homage at sb.'s mausoleum

陵迟　língchí　same as 凌迟 língchí
陵谷　línggǔ　hills and valleys: ～变迁 vicissitudes; ups and downs
陵轹　línglì　same as 凌轹 línglì
陵墓　língmù　mausoleum; tomb
陵寝　língqǐn　*formal* emperor's or king's resting place; mausoleum
陵替　língtì　*formal* ① (of law and order) break down ② decline: 家道～。The family fortunes were declining.
陵夷　língyí　same as 凌夷 língyí
陵园　língyuán　funerary park; cemetery

羚　líng ① antelope; gazelle ② antelope's horn

羚牛　língniú　takin
羚羊　língyáng　antelope; gazelle: 大～ oryx
羚羊角　língyángjiǎo　antelope's horn (used in medicine)

聆　líng　*formal* listen; hear: 亲聆 qīnlíng

聆教　língjiào　hear your words of wisdom (used in letters)
聆取　língqǔ　*formal* listen to (advice, etc.)
聆听　língtīng　*formal* listen (respectfully): ～教导 listen to sb.'s instructions

菱　líng　ling; waternut; water caltrop (*Trapa natans*)

菱角　língjiao　ling; waternut; water caltrop (*Trapa natans*)
菱镁矿　língměikuàng　magnesite
菱铁矿　língtiěkuàng　siderite
菱锌矿　língxīnkuàng　smithsonite
菱形　língxíng　diamond; rhombus; lozenge
菱形队形　língxíng duìxíng　*mil.* diamond formation
菱形六面体　língxíng liùmiàntǐ　rhombohedron

棂(欞、櫺)　líng　(window) lattice; latticework: 窗棂 chuānglíng

蛉　líng　see 白蛉 báilíng

翎　líng　plume; tail feather; quill: 孔雀～ peacock plumes; peacock feathers

翎毛　língmáo ① plume ② a type of classical Chinese painting featuring birds and animals
翎子　língzi ① peacock feathers worn at the back of a mandarin's hat ② long pheasant tail feathers worn on warriors' helmets in traditional operas

绫　líng　a silk fabric resembling satin but thinner; twill-weave silk

绫罗绸缎　líng-luó-chóu-duàn　silks and satins
绫子　língzi　same as 绫 líng

零1　líng ① fragmentary; fractional: 这种纸都是一本一本的，没有～的。This kind of paper comes in pads;

there are no individual sheets. / 可以买成套的，也可以买～的。One can buy sets as well as odd-lot pieces. ② fragment; fraction: 把～儿去了，就要个整数儿。Round off that fraction to a whole number. / 年纪六十有～ a little over sixty years old ③ (in expressions of time, age, money, weight, etc., used between two different denominations, even when these are consecutive if the excess is to be emphasized): 一年～三天 one year and three days / 一岁～五个月 one year and five months old / 五点～一分 5: 01 (five oh one) / 五点～十分 5: 10 (five ten) / 三块～五分 ￥3.05 (three *yuan* and five *fen*) / 二十斤～一两 twenty *jin* and one *liang* / 一尺～一点儿 one *chi* plus something ④ (used in a number to indicate the absence of a unit, representing a final or a medial zero) ⓐ (representing a final or a medial zero in serial numbers or in designations of years, in which each digit is spoken separately; now usu. replaced by 〇): 二～五号 or 二〇五号 No. 205 (number two-oh-five) / 一九八～年 or 一九八〇年 (the year) 1980 (nineteen eighty) ⓑ (representing a medial zero in ordinary numbers): 一百～八 108 (one hundred and eight) / 一千～八 1008 (one thousand and eight) / 一万～八十 10080 (ten thousand and eighty) (as in the last two examples, one 零 will suffice for two or more medial zeroes running together) ⑤ the number or figure 〇; nought; zero; nil: 一减一等于～。One minus one equals zero. *or* One minus one leaves nought (*or* zero). / 我考得太坏，得了个～。I failed miserably in the examination; I got a zero. / 我在这方面的知识几乎等于～。My knowledge of the subject is practically nil. / 上半场的比分是二比～。The score at half-time was two-nil (*or* two-nothing). / ～比～ no score; love all ⑥ the lowest point on a thermometer; zero: ～上（下）五度 five degrees above (below) zero / 摄氏～下十度 10 degrees below zero centigrade; minus 10 degrees centigrade

零2　líng　withered: 凋零 diāolíng

零吃　língchī　*inf.* between-meal nibbles; snacks
零打碎敲　língdǎ-suìqiāo　same as 零敲碎打 língqiāo-suìdǎ
零蛋　língdàn　*humor.* duck's egg—nought; zero: 我考试得了个～。I got a duck's egg (i.e. a zero) in the exam.
零点　língdiǎn　00:00 hour; zero hour; midnight: ～三十分 00:30; zero hour thirty; midnight thirty / 中国第三次人口普查是在 1982 年 7 月 1 日～开始的。China's third national census was taken as of 00:00 hours 1 July 1982.
零点方案　língdiǎn fāng'àn　zero option
零点人口增长　língdiǎn rénkǒu zēngzhǎng　zero population growth
零丁　língdīng　same as 伶仃 língdīng
零度　língdù　zero degrees: 今天的温度是～。Today's temperature is zero. / 气温降到了～。The (atmospheric) temperature has fallen to zero. / 这儿的温度常常到～以下。The temperature here often goes below zero.
零工　línggōng ① odd job; short-term hired labour: 打～ do odd jobs ② odd-job man; casual labourer
零花　línghuā ① spend money on minor purchases: 你留着这点钱在路上～吧! Keep this money for incidental expenses on the way. ② *inf.* pocket money: 妈妈给了他五块钱做～。Mother gave him five *yuan* as pocket money.
零活儿　línghuór　odd jobs: 他给这块儿的人做点～。He does odd jobs for people around here.
零件　língjiàn ① part (of a machine): 这个马达少了一个～。This motor has a part missing. ② spare parts; spares
零乱　língluàn　same as 凌乱 língluàn

零落 língluò ① (of plants) withered; stripped of leaves: 草木～。The grass is withered and the trees are bare. /～残红似胭脂颜色。(李清照) Fallen and withered blossoms, their colour red as rouge. ② desolate; wretched; in reduced circumstances: 一片凄凉～的景象 a desolate scene / 妾貌虽不逮桃李，而一过之。(皇甫枚《飞烟传》) Though my face cannot be compared with peach blossoms, I have suffered a fate much more wretched. ③ scattered; sporadic: ～枪声此起彼伏。Scattered reports of gunfire (or Sporadic shooting) could be heard. / 村庄零零落落地散布在河边。There are scattered villages along the river.

零卖 língmài ① sell retail; retail: 他们只批发，不～。They do only wholesale, they don't sell retail. ② sell by the piece or in small quantities: 这些茶具成套出售，不～。These tea things are sold by the set, not separately.

零七八碎 língqībāsuì ① scattered and disorderly: ～的东西放满了一屋子。The room is cluttered up with all kinds of things. ② miscellaneous trifles; odds and ends: 整天忙些个～儿 fuss over trifles all day long / 桌上放着好些～儿。There were various odds and ends lying about on the table.

零钱 língqián ① small change: 我要换点～。I want to exchange this for some small change. / 您能给我换十块钱的～吗? Could you give me (small) change for a ten-yuan note? ② pocket money

零敲碎打 língqiāo-suìdǎ do sth. bit by bit, off and on; adopt a piecemeal approach: 把这事一气儿解决了吧，别～了。Let's settle the matter at one stroke, not piecemeal. or Let's do this at one go, not bit by bit.

零散 língsǎn scattered: 桌子上～地放着几本书。Several books lie scattered on the desk. / 把～的情况凑到一块儿 piece together scraps of information

零时 língshí same as 零点 língdiǎn

零声母 língshēngmǔ phonet. zero initial ——see also 声母 shēngmǔ

零食 língshí between-meal nibbles; snacks: 他喜欢吃～。He likes to eat between meals.

零售 língshòu ① sell retail; retail ② sell by the piece or in small quantities: 这套家具不能～。We can't sell this set of furniture by the piece. / 服务台～报刊，还能代订。The service counter sells single issues of newspapers and magazines, and also takes subscriptions.

零售店 língshòudiàn retail shop (or store)

零售额 língshòu'é turnover (from retail trade)

零售价格 língshòu jiàgé retail price

零售商 língshòushāng retail trader (or dealer); retailer

零售网 língshòuwǎng retail network

零售总额 língshòu zǒng'é total volume of retail sales

零数 língshù the remaining sum beyond the round figure; remainder; fractional amount

零碎 língsuì ① scrappy; fragmentary; piecemeal: ～活儿 odd jobs / 这些～东西很占地方。These odds and ends take up a lot of space. / 我们收集的材料零碎碎用处不大。The material we have collected is too fragmentary to be of much use. / 我还有点儿～事情没有办完。I still have some miscellaneous items to take care of. ② odds and ends; oddments; bits and pieces: 她正在拾掇～儿。She is tidying up the odds and ends.

零头 língtóu ① the remaining sum beyond the round figure: 咱们别争那几块钱～了，干脆二百五十块整数儿好吗? Let's not haggle over the odd few yuan. Shall we settle at a round figure of ¥250? / 这个袋子装一百斤，剩下四斤～怎么办? This bag holds 100 jin. What shall we do with the odd four jin? /～不算，我们花了二十元。We spent 20 yuan, not counting the small change. ② remnant (of cloth): 一块～布 a remnant

零星 língxīng ① fragmentary; odd; piecemeal: ～材料 fragmentary material /～土地 odd pieces of land / 一些零零星星的消息 some odd scraps of news ② scattered; sporadic: ～小雨 occasional drizzles; scattered showers /～战斗 sporadic fighting /～的枪声 scattered reports of gunfire; sporadic shooting / 草地上零零星星地点缀着一些小花。The lawn is dotted with little flowers.

零讯 língxùn scraps of news (often used as a column title)

零用 língyòng ① spend money on minor purchases ② pocket money

零用费 língyòngfèi petty cash

零用钱 língyòngqián pocket money

零用帐 língyòngzhàng petty cash book; petty cash account

零杂 língzá ① odds and ends; oddments; bits and pieces: 把那些小～儿收拾起来。Clear away those odds and ends. ② odd jobs: 打～ do odd jobs

零指数 língzhǐshù math. zero exponent

零族 língzú chem. zero group

零嘴 língzuǐ dial. between-meal nibbles; snacks

龄

líng ① age; years: 年龄 niánlíng ② length of time; duration: 工龄 gōnglíng

鲮

líng see below

鲮鲤 línglǐ pangolin

鲮鱼 língyú dace

líng

令

líng m. ream (of paper) ——see also lìng

岭(嶺)

líng ① mountain; ridge: 翻山越岭 fānshān-yuèlǐng ② mountain range: 大(小)兴安～ the Greater (Lesser) Xing'an Mountains ③ short for 五岭 Wǔlǐng

岭南 Lǐngnán south of the Five Ridges (五岭) ——the area covering Guangdong and Guangxi

领

líng ① neck: 引领而望 yǐnlǐng ér wàng ② collar; neckband: 把大衣～儿翻起来 turn up one's coat collar / 尖～儿 V-shaped collar ③ outline; main point: 要领 yàolǐng ④ m. (for mats): 一～席 a mat ⑤ lead; usher: ～兵打仗 lead troops into battle / 把客人～到餐厅去 usher the guests into the dining hall /～我们参观学校 show us round the school ⑥ have jurisdiction over; be in possession of; be in sb.'s possession: 占领 zhànlǐng / 领土 lǐngtǔ ⑦ receive; draw; get: ～奖 receive a prize (or an award) /～养老金 draw one's pension / 学习材料已经～到了。We have already got our study material. ⑧ understand; comprehend; grasp: 领会 lǐnghuì

领班 lǐngbān ① head a work group ② gaffer; foreman

领唱 lǐngchàng ① lead a chorus ② leading singer (of a chorus)

领带 lǐngdài necktie; tie: 打～ tie the necktie / 把～解下来 untie (or remove) the necktie / 穿衬衫系～ wear a shirt and tie

领带扣针 lǐngdài kòuzhēn tiepin

领带卡 lǐngdàiqiǎ (also 领带夹 lǐngdàijiā) tie clasp; tie clip

领导 lǐngdǎo ① lead; exercise leadership: 在党的～下 under the leadership of the Communist Party / 担任～工作 shoulder the responsibility of leadership; hold a leading position ② leadership; leader: 他是我们厂的～。He's a leading cadre of our factory. / 这个错误由我们～上负责。We of the leadership must accept re-

sponsibility for this mistake.

领导班子 lǐngdǎo bānzi　leading group

领导地位 lǐngdǎo dìwèi　a position of leadership; status as a leader

领导方法 lǐngdǎo fāngfǎ　method of leadership

领导干部 lǐngdǎo gànbù　leading cadre

领导骨干 lǐngdǎo gǔgàn　the backbone (*or* mainstay, key members) of the leadership

领导核心 lǐngdǎo héxīn　leading nucleus (*or* core)

领导机关 lǐngdǎo jīguān　leading body

领导权 lǐngdǎoquán　leadership; authority; overall control

领导人 lǐngdǎorén　leader

领导水平 lǐngdǎo shuǐpíng　the level of leadership

领导同志 lǐngdǎo tóngzhì　leading comrade

领导小组 lǐngdǎo xiǎozǔ　leading group

领导艺术 lǐngdǎo yìshù　the art of leadership

领导者 lǐngdǎozhě　leader

领导作风 lǐngdǎo zuòfēng　the work style of the leadership; leadership style

领导作用 lǐngdǎo zuòyòng　leading role

领道 lǐngdào　*inf.* lead the way: 得找个人给我们～。We must find a guide to show us the way.

领地 lǐngdì　① manor (of a feudal lord); domain ② territory

领读 lǐngdú　lead (a class, group, etc.) in reading aloud

领队 lǐngduì　① lead a group: 我们这次远足谁～? Who's going to lead us on the hike? ② the leader of a group, sports team, etc.

领队机 lǐngduìjī　*mil.* lead aircraft

领港 lǐnggǎng　① pilot a ship into or out of a harbour; pilot ② (harbour) pilot

领钩 lǐnggōu　hook and eye on the collar

领海 lǐnghǎi　territorial waters; territorial sea: ～范围 extent of territorial waters / ～宽度 breadth (*or* extent) of the territorial sea / ～线 boundary line of territorial waters

领航 lǐngháng　① navigate; pilot ② navigator; pilot

领航飞机 lǐngháng fēijī　pathfinder aircraft

领航员 lǐnghángyuán　navigator; pilot

领会 lǐnghuì　understand; comprehend; grasp: ～文件的精神 grasp the essence of a document / 我还没有～你的意思。I still don't see your point.

领江 lǐngjiāng　① navigate a ship on a river ② river pilot

领教 lǐngjiào　① *pol.* (lit. "receive instructions," used to express thanks for sb.'s advice or performance): 你说得很对,～～! You're quite right. Thanks for your advice. / 请你弹一个曲子, 让我们～一下。Could you oblige us by playing a tune? ② ask sb.'s advice or opinion: 有点儿小事向您～。I'd like to ask you for advice about a small matter. / 你有什么新的看法?我想～～。Have you some new ideas on the subject? If so, I'd very much like to hear them. / 不敢～。I beg to differ. ③ (used ironically): 他们的伎俩, 我们早就～过了。We've encountered their tricks before. / 我叫你～～我的厉害! See how I'm going to teach you a lesson!

领结 lǐngjié　bow tie

领巾 lǐngjīn　scarf; neckerchief ——see also 红领巾 hóng-lǐngjīn

领空 lǐngkōng　territorial sky (*or* air); territorial air space

领口 lǐngkǒu　① collarband; neckband: 这件毛衣～太小。The neckband of the sweater is too small. ② the place where the two ends of a collar meet: 她～上别着一个宝石别针。She wore a jewelled brooch at the neck of her dress.

领扣 lǐngkòu　collar button; collar stud

领款 lǐngkuǎn　receive funds; draw money

领款人 lǐngkuǎnrén　payee

领路 lǐnglù　lead the way: 我在前面～。I'll be in front leading the way.

领略 lǐnglüè　have a taste of; understand; appreciate: ～川菜风味 taste Sichuan dishes / ～塞外风光 see and appreciate the scenery north of the Great Wall

领命 lǐngmìng　receive orders; take orders

领情 lǐngqíng　feel grateful to sb.; appreciate the kindness: 同志们的好意, 我十分～。I'm very grateful to you comrades for your kindness. / 您的心意我～, 但是礼物不能收。I appreciate your kindness, but I can't accept your gift.

领取 lǐngqǔ　receive; draw; get: ～工资 draw (*or* collect) one's pay / ～办公用品 get office supplies / ～出入证 receive one's pass

领事 lǐngshì　*diplomacy* consul: 副～ vice-consul / 代理～ pro-consul

领事裁判权 lǐngshì cáipànquán　consular jurisdiction

领事处 lǐngshìchù　(also 领事部 lǐngshìbù) consular section

领事馆 lǐngshìguǎn　consulate

领事条例 lǐngshì tiáolì　consular act

领事团 lǐngshìtuán　consular corps (c.c.)

领事委任书 lǐngshì wěirènshū　certificate of appointment of consul; consular commission

领事协定 lǐngshì xiédìng　consular agreement

领事证书 lǐngshì zhèngshū　exequatur

领受 lǐngshòu　accept (kindness, etc.); receive: 她怀着激动的心情～了同志们的慰问。She was deeply moved by her comrades' comforting words.

领属 lǐngshǔ　possess and control; have dominion over

领水 lǐngshuǐ　① inland waters ② territorial waters

领水员 lǐngshuǐyuán　navigator; pilot

领头 lǐngtóu　*inf.* take the lead; be the first to do sth.: 我领个头, 大家跟着一起唱吧。I'll lead off, if everyone will join in. / 队伍由三个举红旗的青年～。At the head of the procession were three young men holding red flags. / ～的一架敌机被打下来了。The leading enemy plane was shot down.

领土 lǐngtǔ　territory: 台湾是中国～。Taiwan is Chinese territory.

领土不可侵犯性 lǐngtǔ bùkěqīnfànxìng　territorial inviolability

领土扩张 lǐngtǔ kuòzhāng　territorial expansion; territorial aggrandizement

领土完整 lǐngtǔ wánzhěng　territorial integrity

领土要求 lǐngtǔ yāoqiú　territorial claim

领舞 lǐngwǔ　① lead a dancer ② leading dancer

领悟 lǐngwù　comprehend; grasp

领洗 lǐngxǐ　receive baptism; be baptized

领先 lǐngxiān　be in the lead; lead: 她～登上了山顶。She was the first to reach the top of the hill. / 客队～五分。The visiting team led by five points. / 前半场球赛二比一, 上海队～。The score at half-time stood at 2:1 in favour of the Shanghai Team.

领衔 lǐngxián　head the list of signers (of a document); be the first on a name list: 最近两部影片由他～主演。He has starred in two recent films.

领袖 lǐngxiù　leader

领袖欲 lǐngxiùyù　the desire to be a leader

领养 lǐngyǎng　adopt (a child)

领有 lǐngyǒu　possess; own

领域 lǐngyù　① territory; domain; realm ② field; sphere; domain; realm: 上层建筑～ the realm of the superstructure / 社会科学～ the domain of the social sciences / 意识形态～ the ideological sphere

领章 lǐngzhāng　collar badge; collar insignia

领主 lǐngzhǔ　feudal lord; suzerain

领子　lǐngzi　collar
领罪　lǐngzuì　admit one's guilt; plead guilty

líng

另　líng ① *adv.* ⓐ in addition; besides: 买一打，～送半打。If you buy a dozen, you get a half dozen free in addition. /～有多少？How many more are there? ⓑ in place of that: 我们得～想办法。We have to try and find some other way. /全文～发。The full text will be dispatched separately. /～有打算 have other plans /～搞一套 go one's own way; do what suits oneself /～立户头 open another (*or* separate) bank account ② (used with nouns) different; other: 那是～一回事。That's another matter. /从一个极端跳到一个极端 jump from one extreme to another /～纸抄寄 copied on a separate sheet

另案　líng'àn　a separate case: 作～处理 to be handled as a separate case
另册　língcè　the other register (opp. 正册 zhèngcè), a Qing Dynasty census book for listing disreputable people: 打入～ list sb. as an undesirable
另当别论　líng dāng bié lùn　should be regarded as a different matter
另函　línghán　① a separate letter ② write another letter
另寄　língjì　(also 另邮 língyóu) post (*or* mail) separately; post (*or* mail) under separate cover
另起炉灶　líng qǐ lúzào　set up another kitchen—make a fresh start; start all over again
另请高明　líng qǐng gāomíng　find someone better qualified (than myself): 这事我恐怕干不了，你还是～吧。I'm afraid I'm not equal to the job. You'd better try and find someone better qualified.
另外　língwài　① *adv.* ⓐ in addition; besides: 我虽然有一个，可是我还想～买一个。Even though I already have one, I want to buy another one besides. ⓑ in place of that: 我今天有事，咱们～再找时间谈吧。I've got some things to attend to today. Shall we find another time to talk? ② (used with nouns) different; other: 我还要跟你谈～一件事情。There's another thing I want to talk over with you. /～两个人我不认识。I don't know the other two people. ③ *conj.* in addition; besides: 这篇文章我改动了几处，～又补充了一小段。I made a few changes in this article. I also supplemented it with one short paragraph.
另行　língxíng　(do sth.) separately: ～安排 make separate arrangements /～通知 issue a separate notice /会议改期，时间～通知。The meeting is postponed till further notice.
另选　língxuǎn　select sb. or sth. else
另眼看待　líng yǎn kàndài　look at sb. with quite different eyes—regard sb. with favour; treat sb. with favour; give sb. special treatment
另眼相看　líng yǎn xiāng kàn　① regard (*or* look up to) sb. with special respect; give sb. special treatment ② view sb. in a new, more favourable light; see sb. in a new light
另议　língyì　discuss or negotiate separately

令¹　líng ① order; command: ～即返家 order sb. to return home at once ② order; command; decree: 下令 xiàlíng ③ cause sb. to: ～人深思 set sb. thinking; provide food for thought /～人鼓舞 encouraging; heartening; inspiring /～人满意 satisfying; satisfying /～人肃然起敬 awe-inspiring ④ drinking game: 酒令 jiǔlíng ⑤ an ancient official title: 县令 xiànlíng

令²　líng　season: 当令 dānglìng /夏令 xiàlíng
令³　líng ① *formal* good; excellent: 令名 língmíng ② *honor.* your (used before certain relationship terms when referring to a member of a friend's family): ～兄 your elder brother /～妹 your younger sister
令⁴　líng　short for 小令 xiǎolíng (usu. used in tune titles): 《叨叨～》"Chattering Song" /《如梦～》"Like a Dream"
——see also líng

令爱　líng'ài　(also 令媛 língài) *honor.* your daughter
令出如山　líng chū rú shān　orders are like a mountain (i.e. compel obedience)
令德　língdé　*formal* excellent virtue
令箭　língjiàn　an arrow-shaped token of authority (used formerly in the army)
令箭荷花　língjiàn héhuā　*bot.* nopalxochia
令阃　língkǔn　*old honor.* your wife
令郎　línglǎng　*honor.* your son
令名　língmíng　*formal* good name; good reputation
令旗　língqí　flag of command (used formerly in the army)
令亲　língqīn　*honor.* your relative
令人齿冷　líng rén chǐlěng　arouse scorn
令人发指　líng rén fàzhǐ　get one's hackles up; make one bristle with anger
令人喷饭　líng rén pēnfàn　side-splitting; screamingly funny
令人捧腹　líng rén pěngfù　set people roaring with laughter; make one burst out laughing
令人神往　líng rén shénwǎng　fire one's imagination; have a strong appeal for one
令人作呕　líng rén zuò'ǒu　make one sick; nauseating; revolting: 她那装模作样劲儿真～。Her affectations make you sick. /～地吹捧 nauseatingly extol
令堂　língtáng　*honor.* your mother
令闻　língwén　*formal* good name; good reputation
令行禁止　líng xíng jìn zhǐ　any order will be carried out, any prohibition will be heeded
令尊　língzūn　*honor.* your father

liū

溜¹　liū ① slide; glide: 从山坡上～下来 slide down a slope ② smooth: 滑溜 huáliu ③ sneak off; slip away: 从后门～出去 slip out through the back door /他跟谁也没说就～了。He sneaked off without telling anyone.
溜²　liū　same as 熘 liū
——see also liù

溜边　liūbiān　*inf.* keep to the edge (of a road, river, etc.)
溜冰　liūbīng　① skate ② *dial.* roller-skate; go roller-skating
溜冰场　liūbīngchǎng　skating rink
溜槽　liūcáo　chute
溜达　liūda　*inf.* stroll; saunter; go for a walk: 他在河边来回～。He sauntered up and down the river bank. /吃完饭出去～～吧。Let's go for a stroll after the meal.
溜工　liūgōng　sneak away during work hours
溜沟子　liūgōuzi　*dial.* lick sb.'s boots; toady to; fawn
溜光　liūguāng　*dial.* ① very smooth; sleek; glossy: 他的头发梳得～。His hair is combed sleek. ② totally bare; not a bit left: 山上的树砍得～。The trees were all cut down, leaving the mountain totally bare. *or* The

mountain was totally deforested.

溜号 liūhào *dial.* sneak away; slink off

溜滑 liūhuá *dial.* ① slippery: 小心点儿, 这道儿～～的。Be careful, the road is slippery. ② sly; slippery: 这个人～～的。He's a slippery character.

溜肩膀 liūjiānbǎng ① sloping shoulders ② *dial.* lacking a proper sense of responsibility; irresponsible

溜溜转 liūliūzhuàn (of a round object) turn round and round

溜门撬锁 liūmén-qiàosuǒ be a sneak thief

溜平 liūpíng *dial.* smooth and level: 这块板子刨得～。This board has been planed smooth.

溜索 liūsuǒ overhead cable

溜须拍马 liūxū-pāimǎ smooth sb.'s beard and pat his horse's hindquarters—lick sb.'s boots; toady to; fawn on

溜圆 liūyuán *dial.* perfectly round: 他制作了一个～的象牙球。He made a perfectly round ivory ball.

溜之大吉 liū zhī dàjí sneak away; slink off; make oneself scarce

溜之乎也 liū zhī hū yě same as 溜之大吉 liū zhī dàjí

熘（溜）
liū *sauté* (with thick gravy); quick-fry: ～肝尖 liver *sauté* / ～鱼片 fish slices *sauté*

liú

刘（劉）
Liú a surname

刘海儿 Liú Hǎir a fairy boy popularly represented as wearing his hair in bangs, resting on foot on a toad, and holding in his hand a waving fillet or ribbon on which five gold cash are strung

刘海儿 liúhǎir bang; fringe: 她留着～。She wears her hair in bangs.

刘寄奴 liújìnú another name for 千里光 qiānlǐguāng (originally the name of the first ruler of the Liu Song Dynasty, one of the Southern Dynasties in the early fifth century, who reportedly used the plant as a dressing for his wounds)

浏（瀏）
liú *formal* (of water) clear; limpid

浏览 liúlǎn glance over; skim through; browse: 这本书我只～过一遍。I've only skimmed through (*or* glanced over) the book. / ～各种报章杂志 browse among newspapers and magazines

流
liú ① (of liquid) flow: 水～得很快。The water is flowing very fast. / 这条河向北～。This river flows in a northerly direction. / 农村人口～入城市 the flow of rural population into urban areas / 伤口～脓。The wound is festering. / ～汗 perspire; sweat / ～鼻涕 have a runny nose / ～泪 shed tears / ～涎 water at the mouth; slaver; slobber ② moving from place to place; drifting; wandering: 流民 liúmín / 流通 liútōng ③ spread; circulate: 流传 liúchuán ④ change for the worse; degenerate: 流于形式 liúyú xíngshì ⑤ banish; send into exile: 流放 liúfàng ⑥ stream of water: 中流 zhōngliú / 河流 héliú ⑦ sth. resembling a stream of water; current: 气流 qìliú / 电流 diànliú ⑧ class; rate; grade: 一～作家 a first-class writer / 一～～作品 a first-rate (literary) work / 考茨基之～ Kautsky and his like (*or* ilk)

流辈 liúbèi *formal* people of the same generation or class

流弊 liúbì corrupt practices; abuses

流别 liúbié ① river branch; tributary ② types or genres (of literature): 文章～ different types or genres of literature

流播 liúbō *formal* spread; circulate

流布 liúbù spread; disseminate

流产 liúchǎn ① (of a woman) have a miscarriage; miscarry: 她上月～了。She had a miscarriage last month. / 她～过几次。She has had several miscarriages. ② (of a plan, etc.) miscarry; fall through: 他们的计划～了。Their project miscarried. / ～政变 an abortive coup

流畅 liúchàng (of writing) easy and smooth: 文笔～ write with ease and grace / 这篇文章读起来很～。The essay reads very smoothly.

流程 liúchéng ① a distance travelled by a stream of water ② technological process ③ *min.* circuit: 破碎～ crushing circuit / 浮选～ flotation circuit

流程图 liúchéngtú flow chart; flow diagram

流传 liúchuán spread; circulate; hand down: 群众中广泛～着这位战斗英雄的事迹。Stories of the combat hero's exploits spread far and wide among the masses. / 古代～下来的寓言 fables handed down from ancient times

流窜 liúcuàn flee hither and thither: ～在山区的残匪不久都被消灭了。The remaining bandits who fled to the hills were soon wiped out.

流窜犯 liúcuànfàn criminal on the run

流弹 liúdàn stray bullet

流荡 liúdàng ① flow; float: 空气里～着一股香味。A pleasant smell wafted through the air. ② roam about; rove

流动 liúdòng ① (of water, air, etc.) flow; circulate: 溪水缓缓地～。The brook flowed sluggishly. ② go from place to place; be on the move; be mobile: 放映队常年在农村～。Film projection teams are always on the move in the countryside. / 促进人才的合理～ facilitate a rational flow of trained personnel

流动电影放映队 liúdòng diànyǐng fàngyìngduì mobile film projection team; mobile cinema team

流动红旗 liúdòng hóngqí mobile red banner (awarded to a team, workshop, etc. for outstanding performance and kept by it until another unit proves more deserving)

流动货车 liúdòng huòchē shop-on-wheels

流动人口 liúdòng rénkǒu floating (*or* transient) population

流动商店 liúdòng shāngdiàn mobile shop

流动哨 liúdòngshào person (*or* soldier) on patrol duty; patrol

流动图书馆 liúdòng túshūguǎn travelling library

流动性 liúdòngxìng mobility; fluidity

流动资本 liúdòng zīběn circulating capital; floating capital; working capital

流动资产 liúdòng zīchǎn current assets; liquid assets; floating assets

流动资金 liúdòng zījīn (also 流动基金 liúdòng jījīn) circulating fund; operating fund; revolving fund

流毒 liúdú ① exert a pernicious (*or* baneful) influence: ～甚广 exert a widespread pernicious influence ② pernicious (*or* baneful) influence: 肃清～ liquidate a pernicious influence / 封建礼教的～ the baneful influence of the feudal ethical code

流芳 liúfāng *formal* leave a good name

流芳百世 liúfāng bǎishì leave a good name for a hundred generations; leave a good name to posterity; win immortal fame; leave one's mark on history

流放[1] liúfàng banish; send into exile

流放[2] liúfàng float (logs) downstream

流风余韵 liúfēng-yúyùn the lingering influence of former worthies

流感 liúgǎn short for 流行性感冒 liúxíngxìng gǎnmào

流光 liúguāng *liter.* time: ～易逝。Time flies.

流滑 liúhuá ① fluent: 他说的北京话地道～。He speaks

Beijing dialect idiomatically and fluently. ② crafty; slippery

流火 liúhuǒ ① *dial.* filariasis ② *Chin. med.* erysipelas on the leg

流箭 liújiàn stray arrow

流金铄石 liújīn-shuòshí same as 铄石流金 shuòshí-liújīn

流浸膏 liújìngāo liquid extract (prepared from medicinal herbs)

流寇 liúkòu ① roving bandits ② roving rebel bands

流览 liúlǎn same as 浏览 liúlǎn

流浪 liúlàng roam about; lead a vagrant life: ～街头 roam the streets

流浪儿 liúlàng'ér waif; street urchin

流浪汉 liúlànghàn tramp; vagrant

流离 liúlí *formal* wander about as a refugee or vagrant

流离失所 liúlí shīsuǒ become destitute and homeless; wander about homeless: 解放前遇到荒年就有千千万万的农民～。Before liberation famine forced thousands upon thousands of peasants to wander about as refugees.

流丽 liúlì (of writing or calligraphy) fluent and elegant

流利 liúlì fluent; smooth: 她说一口～的英语。She speaks fluent English. / 文章写得～。The article reads smoothly. / 这枝笔书写～。This pen writes smoothly.

流里流气 liúliliúqì rascally

流连 liúlián be reluctant to leave; linger on

流连忘返 liúlián wàng fǎn enjoy oneself so much as to forget to go home; linger on with no thought of leaving; cannot tear oneself away: 展品琳琅满目, 令人～。The exhibition is absolutely fascinating—you can't tear yourself away.

流量 liúliàng volume of flow; rate of flow; flow; discharge: 管道～ flow of a pipe / 河道～ discharge of a river / 交通～ traffic flow / 渡槽的～为十五至十八秒立方米。The aqueduct has a flow capacity of 15 to 18 cubic metres per second.

流量计 liúliàngjì flowmeter

流露 liúlù show unintentionally (one's thoughts or feelings); reveal; betray: 她不大～自己的感情。She seldom shows her emotions. / 他的许多诗篇都～出对祖国的热爱。Many of his poems reveal his ardent love for his country. / 真情～ a revelation of one's true feelings

流落 liúluò wander about destitute

流落江湖 liúluò jiānghú live a vagabond life

流落他乡 liúluò tāxiāng lead a wretched life far from home; be stranded in a strange land

流氓 liúmáng ① rogue; hoodlum; hooligan; gangster ② immoral (*or* indecent) behaviour; hooliganism; indecency: 耍流氓 shuǎ liúmáng

流氓集团 liúmáng jítuán gang of hooligans (*or* hoodlums); criminal gang

流氓无产者 liúmáng wúchǎnzhě *lumpen*-proletariat

流氓习气 liúmáng xíqì hooliganism

流氓行为 liúmáng xíngwéi indecent behaviour; hooliganism

流眄 liúmiǎn *liter.* give a sidelong glance; ogle: 瞬美目以～, 含言笑而不分。(陶潜) A swift glance from her lovely sparkling eyes—Uncertain whether to speak or smile.

流民 liúmín refugee

流明 liúmíng *phys.* lumen

流脑 liúnǎo short for 流行性脑脊髓膜炎 liúxíngxìng nǎojǐsuǐmóyán

流年 liúnián ① *liter.* fleeting time: 似水流年 sì shuǐ liúnián ② (in fortune-telling) prediction of a person's luck in a given year

流年不利 liúnián bù lì an unlucky year

流派 liúpài school; sect: 学术～ schools of thought

流盼 liúpàn *liter.* ① amorous glances ② cast amorous glances at; make sheep's eyes at

流配 liúpèi banish; exile

流品 liúpǐn *formal* family status; social status: 不入～ be of no standing in society

流气 liú·qì ① rascally: 他这个人很～。He's a regular rascal. ② rascally behaviour; hooliganism

流人 liúrén *formal* ① a person who lives in exile; exile ② refugee

流散 liúsàn scatter; drift: 敦煌经卷现已大多～国外。Most of the Dunhuang MSS are now scattered in various foreign countries.

流散人口 liúsàn rénkǒu drifting population

流沙 liúshā shifting sands; drifting sands; quicksand

流生 liúshēng school dropout

流失 liúshī ① run off; be washed away: 黄金储备～ be a drain on gold reserves / 堵住管道的漏洞, 不让石油～ stop up the leaks in the pipe so that no oil will seep through ② (of students) drop out

流食 liúshí liquid food

流矢 liúshǐ stray arrow

流驶 liúshǐ (of time) pass; elapse: 时间不停地～。Time marches on.

流势 liúshì the force and velocity of a current

流逝 liúshì (of time) pass; elapse: 时光～。Time passes. / 随着时间的～, 人们就会把这件事全忘了。With the passage of time, the whole thing will be forgotten.

流水 liúshuǐ ① flowing water (often fig.): 思君如～, 何有穷已时。(徐干) My thoughts of you are like flowing water; Will they ever have an end? ② turnover (in business): 本月做了十五万元的～。We have had a turnover of ￥150,000 this month. *or* We have turned over ￥150,000 this month.

流水不腐, 户枢不蠹 liúshuǐ bù fǔ, hùshū bù dù running water is never stale and a door-hinge never gets worm-eaten

流水号 liúshuǐhào serial number

流水席 liúshuǐxí feast at which guests are served as they come

流水线 liúshuǐxiàn assembly line

流水帐 liúshuǐzhàng day-to-day (bookkeeping) account; current account

流水作业 liúshuǐ zuòyè flow process; assembly line method; conveyer system

流苏 liúsū tassels

流俗 liúsú *derog.* prevalent custom; current fashion

流速 liúsù ① *mech.* velocity of flow ② *water conservancy* current velocity

流速仪 liúsùyí current meter (for use in water conservancy)

流淌 liútǎng (of liquid) flow

流体 liútǐ fluid

流体动力学 liútǐ dònglìxué hydrokinetics; hydrodynamics

流体静力学 liútǐ jìnglìxué hydrostatics

流体力学 liútǐ lìxué hydromechanics; fluid mechanics

流体压力计 liútǐ yālìjì manometer

流铁槽 liútiěcáo *metall.* iron runner

流通 liútōng (of air, money, commodities, etc.) circulate: 打开窗户使室内空气～ open the windows to increase the circulation of air in the room / 货币(商品)～ the circulation of money (commodities)

流通费用 liútōng fèiyòng circulation costs

流通管 liútōngguǎn *mech.* runner pipe

流通货币 liútōng huòbì currency

流通券 liútōngquàn (in former times) paper money issued by a provincial bank to be circulated in a given area

流通手段 liútōng shǒuduàn medium (*or* means) of cir-

culation

流通资金 liútōng zījīn (also 流通基金 liútōng jījīn) same as 流动资金 liúdòng zījīn

流亡 liúwáng be forced to leave one's native land; go into exile: 孙中山曾长期～海外。Sun Yat-sen spent long years in exile abroad.

流亡政府 liúwáng zhèngfǔ government-in-exile

流网 liúwǎng *fishery* drift net

流纹岩 liúwényán rhyolite

流徙 liúxǐ wander about

流线型 liúxiànxíng streamlined: ～汽车 streamlined car

流向 liúxiàng ① the direction of a current ② the direction of the flow of personnel, commodities, etc.

流泻 liúxiè (of liquid or light) pour out; gush out: 泉水从岩石里～出来。The spring water gushes out from the rock crevices. / 我拉开了窗帘，明亮的阳光～进来。When I opened the curtains, bright sunshine poured in. / 诗人的激情从笔端全盘～出来。The poem is an outpouring of the poet's overflowing heart.

流星[1] liúxīng meteor; shooting star

流星[2] liúxīng ① an ancient weapon, composed of two iron balls fixed on a long iron chain ② (in acrobatics) meteors: 火～ fire-meteors / 水～ water-meteors

流星尘 liúxīngchén meteoric dust

流星防护 liúxīng fánghù *space* meteoroid protection

流星群 liúxīngqún meteor stream; meteor swarm

流星雨 liúxīngyǔ meteor (or meteoric) shower

流刑 liúxíng (in former times) the punishment of banishment

流行 liúxíng popular; prevalent; fashionable; in vogue: 这首民歌在陕北很～。This folk song is very popular in northern Shaanxi. / 这种发型很～。This kind of hairdo is very popular. / 这是当时～的论调。This argument was prevalent at the time. / 现在～这种鞋。Shoes like these are in vogue just now. / 现在～一种很奇怪的病。There's a very strange disease spreading around just now.

流行病 liúxíngbìng epidemic disease

流行病学 liúxíngbìngxué epidemiology

流行歌曲 liúxíng gēqǔ pop song; pop music; pop

流行色 liúxíngsè fashionable colour

流行性 liúxíngxìng epidemic

流行性感冒 liúxíngxìng gǎnmào influenza; flu

流行性脑脊髓膜炎 liúxíngxìng nǎojǐsuǐmóyán epidemic cerebrospinal meningitis

流行性腮腺炎 liúxíngxìng sāixiànyán mumps

流行性乙型脑炎 liúxíngxìng yǐxíngnǎoyán epidemic encephalitis B

流血 liúxuè lose blood; shed blood; draw blood; bleed: 你的鼻子～了。Your nose is bleeding. / 他流了很多血。He lost a lot of blood. / 拔这个牙会～吗? Will pulling my tooth out draw blood? / 为革命流尽最后一滴血 shed the last drop of one's blood for the revolution / 政治是不～的战争，战争是～的政治。Politics is war without bloodshed while war is politics with bloodshed. / ～的斗争 a sanguinary struggle / 不～的政变 a bloodless coup

流言 liúyán rumour; gossip

流言飞语 liúyán-fēiyǔ (also 流言蜚语 liúyán-fēiyǔ) rumours and slanders

流言止于智者 liúyán zhǐ yú zhìzhě rumours find no credence with a wise man

流于形式 liúyú xíngshì become a mere formality

流域 liúyù river valley; river basin; drainage area: 黄河～ the Huanghe River (or Yellow River) valley (or basin) / ～面积 drainage area

流贼 liúzéi roving bandits

流质 liúzhì (or 流质膳食 liúzhì shànshí) liquid diet (for patients): 半～ semiliquid

流转 liúzhuǎn ① wander about; roam; be on the move: ～四方 wander all over the country ② (of goods or capital) circulate

留（霤）

留 liú ① remain; stay: 你～在原地。Stay where you are. / 会后你～一下。Will you please remain after the meeting. / 他～在农村工作了。He stayed on in the countryside to work. ② reside in a foreign country to study: ～日 study in Japan / ～美 study in the U.S. ③ ask sb. to stay; keep sb. where he is: 他们一定要～我们吃午饭。They pressed us to stay for lunch. / 那我就不～你了。In that case I won't keep you any longer. ④ pay attention to: 留心 liúxīn ⑤ reserve; keep; save: ～座位 reserve a seat for sb. / 把钱～起来，以后用。Save the money for use later on. / ～着这个有什么用? What's the use of keeping this? / 三块钱给你两块，我～一块。Here's three *yuan*. I give you two and I keep one. / 这本书是我给你～着的。I've kept this book for you. ⑥ let grow; grow: ～胡子 grow a beard (or moustache) / ～小辫儿 wear plaits (or braids); wear one's hair in plaits (or braids) / ～短头发 wear one's hair short; have short hair; have bobbed hair ⑦ accept (sth. given); take: 礼物先～下来。Let's accept the gift first. / 我们的邻居想把五只小猫都给我们，我们只～了一只。Our neighbours wanted to give us all of their five kittens, but we only took one. ⑧ leave behind: 给她～个条。Leave a note for her. / 请他～个地址。Ask him to leave his address. / 他把孩子～在家里了。He left the children at home. / 他死后～下三个孩子。He died and left three children. / 他父亲死后给他～下一所房子。His father died and left him a house. / 祖先～给了我们丰富的文化遗产。Our forefathers have left us a rich cultural heritage. / 这次参观给我们～下了深刻的印象。The visit made a deep impression on us.

留班 liúbān *inf.* (of pupils, etc.) fail to go up to the next grade (or year); repeat the year's work; stay behind

留别 liúbié *formal* give sb. a parting gift or write a poem for him when taking leave of him

留别纪念 liúbié jìniàn souvenir; keepsake

留步 liúbù *pol.* (said by departing guest to host) don't bother to see me out; don't bother to come any further

留成 liúchéng retain a portion (of earnings, profits, etc.): 利润（外汇）～ retain a portion of the profits (foreign exchange) brought in / ～利润（外汇）retained profits (foreign exchange)

留传 liúchuán hand down (to descendants)

留存 liúcún ① preserve; keep: 此稿～ keep this copy on file ② remain; be extant

留待 liúdài wait till later: 那件事可以～明天再定。The matter can wait until tomorrow.

留党察看 liúdǎng chákàn be placed on probation within the Party (as an inner-Party disciplinary measure)

留得青山在，不怕没柴烧 liúdé qīngshān zài, bù pà méi chái shāo (also 留得青山在，不愁没柴烧 liúdé qīngshān zài, bù chóu méi chái shāo) as long as the green hills last, there'll always be wood to burn

留地步 liú dìbu same as 留余地 liú yúdì

留点 liúdiǎn *astron.* stationary point

留饭 liúfàn ① keep or save food for sb.: 我今天回来晚，给我留点儿饭。I'll be home rather late this evening, so save some food for me, please. ② ask sb. to stay for a meal: 表姐定要～，情意难却。My cousin pressed me to stay for supper, and I found it hard to refuse.

留后路 liú hòulù keep a way open for retreat; leave a way out: 给自己留条后路 leave oneself a way out; leave oneself an option

留后手 liú hòushǒu leave room for manoeuvre

留话 liúhuà leave a message; leave word: 他给你留了个话儿。He left a message for you. / 我留了话了，叫他一回来就给我来个电话。I left word for him to call me as soon as he gets back.

留级 liújí (of pupils, etc.) fail to go up to the next grade (*or* year); repeat the year's work; stay behind

留局候领 liújú hòulǐng (in postal service) *poste restante*; general delivery

留空 liúkòng leave a blank; leave a space in writing

留兰香 liúlánxiāng spearmint

留连 liúlián same as 流连 liúlián

留恋 liúliàn ① be reluctant to leave (a place); can't bear to part (from sb. or with sth.): 临毕业时，同学们对学校都十分～。As their graduation day drew near, the students felt reluctant to leave their school. ② recall with nostalgia: ～过去 yearn for the past

留量 liúliàng *mech.* allowance: 机械加工～ stock allowance

留门 liúmén leave a door unlocked or unbolted (in expectation of sb. during the night)

留难 liúnàn make things difficult for sb.; put obstacles in sb.'s way: 他故意～。He's being difficult on purpose.

留尼汪岛 Liúníwāngdǎo Réunion

留念 liúniàn accept or keep as a souvenir: 照相～ have a photo taken as a memento / 某某先生～ To Mr. so-and-so (an inscription for a gift)

留鸟 liúniǎo resident (bird)

留情 liúqíng show mercy or forgiveness: 对敌人毫不～ show the enemy no mercy; give the enemy no quarter

留任 liúrèn retain a post; remain (*or* continue) in office

留神 liúshén be careful; take care: 你留点儿神。Be careful. / 过马路要～。Be careful when you cross the street. / ～，汽车来了！Mind the car! / ～摔下来。Take care you don't fall over. / 你～这个人。Watch this person. / 打字时一不～，就会出错。When you type, you'll make mistakes unless you give your whole attention to it.

留声机 liúshēngjī gramophone; phonograph

留守 liúshǒu ① act for the emperor during his absence from the capital ② stay behind to take care of things; stay behind for garrison or liaison duty (after the main force has left)

留守处 liúshǒuchù rear office

留守人员 liúshǒu rényuán rear personnel

留宿 liúsù ① put up a guest for the night ② stay overnight; put up for the night

留题 liútí write down comments, impressions, etc. (as at a place of resort)

留头 liútóu let the hair grow

留尾巴 liúwěiba leave loose ends: 他做事老留个尾巴让我来收拾。He always leaves some loose ends for me to clear up for him. / 问题现在不能做出决定，留个尾巴吧。Leave the matter open. We can't make a final decision now.

留校 liúxiào remain at a school or university after graduation as a faculty member

留心 liúxīn be careful; take care: 他开车非常～。He is very careful when he's driving. / ～别写错了。Mind you don't write it wrong. / ～听讲 listen attentively to a lecture / ～看门 watch the door closely / 他很～股票的行情。He watches the stock market very closely.

留学 liúxué study abroad: 他想～。He wants to study abroad. / 他～美国已经三年了。He's been studying in the United States for three years.

留学生 liúxuéshēng student studying abroad; returned student

留言 liúyán leave one's comments; leave a message

留言簿 liúyánbù visitors' book

留洋 liúyáng *old* study abroad

留一手 liú yīshǒu hold back a trick or two (in teaching a trade or skill)

留意 liúyì be careful; look out; keep one's eyes open: 这是个细致活，稍不～就会出错。This is a delicate job. If you let your mind wander for a single moment, you'll do it wrong. / 你去买东西的时候替我留点儿意，看有没有这种毛巾。When you go shopping, please look and see if there are any towels like this.

留影 liúyǐng ① take a photo as a memento; have a picture taken as a souvenir ② a picture taken as a souvenir

留用 liúyòng continue to employ; keep on

留用人员 liúyòng rényuán personnel (of the old regime) who were kept on after liberation

留余地 liú yúdì allow for unforeseen circumstances; leave some leeway: 咱们订计划时要留有余地。When drawing up a plan, we should allow for unforeseen circumstances.

留针 liúzhēn let the acupuncture needle remain at a certain point for a designated period of time (in order to enhance the effect of the treatment)

留职 liúzhí retain one's post: ～察看 retain one's post on probation (as a disciplinary measure) / ～停薪 retain one's post with salaries suspended during a long leave of absence

留滞 liúzhì *formal* be detained; be held up: ～他乡 be held up in a place far away from home

留置 liúzhì *formal* keep somewhere: 书籍数册，临行时～案头。I left behind a few books on the desk. / ～部分兵力 keep part of the troops in reserve

留置权 liúzhìquán *leg.* lien: 对船货有～ have a lien on the cargo

留种 liúzhǒng reserve seed for planting; have seed stock

留种地 liúzhǒngdì seed-breeding field

留驻 liúzhù remain stationed

琉（瑠） liú see below

琉璃 liúli coloured glaze

琉璃塔 liúlìtǎ glazed pagoda

琉璃瓦 liúliwǎ glazed tile

琉球群岛 Liúqiú Qúndǎo the Ryukyu Islands

硫 liú *chem.* sulphur (S)

硫胺素 liú'ànsù thiamin(e)

硫代硫酸钠 liúdàiliúsuānnà sodium thiosulphate

硫分 liúfèn *min.* sulphur content

硫华 liúhuá *chem.* sublimed sulphur

硫化 liúhuà *chem.* vulcanize

硫化汞 liúhuàgǒng mercuric sulphide

硫化剂 liúhuàjì vulcanized agent; curing agent

硫化氢 liúhuàqīng hydrogen sulphide

硫化染料 liúhuà rǎnliào sulphur dyes

硫化物 liúhuàwù sulphide

硫化橡胶 liúhuà xiàngjiāo vulcanized rubber; vulcanizate

硫磺 liúhuáng (also 硫黄 liúhuáng) common name for 硫 liú

硫磺泉 liúhuángquán sulphur spring

硫苦 liúkǔ *chem.* magnesium sulphate

硫塑料 liúsùliào thioplast

硫酸 liúsuān sulphuric acid

硫酸铵 liúsuān'ǎn ammonium sulphate

硫酸盐 liúsuānyán sulphate (e.g. 硫酸铜 cupric sulphate)

旒 liú *arch.* ① streamer; pennant ② jade pendants on a crown

馏 liú distil ——see also liù
馏出油 liúchūyóu distillate oil
馏份 liúfèn *chem.* fraction; cut: 轻 (重)～ light (heavy) fraction (*or* cut)

榴 liú pomegranate
榴弹 liúdàn high explosive shell
榴弹炮 liúdànpào howitzer
榴火 liúhuǒ *liter.* the fiery red of pomegranate blossoms
榴莲 liúlián durian
榴霰弹 liúsǎndàn shrapnel; canister (shot); case shot

飗 liú see 飗飗 sōuliú

瘤 liú tumour
瘤胃 liúwèi rumen
瘤胃臌胀 liúwèi gǔzhàng bloat
瘤子 liúzi *inf.* tumour

镏 liú see below ——see also liù
镏金 liújīn gold-plating: ～银器 gilded silverware

鹠 liú see 鸺鹠 xiūliú

鎏 liú ① *formal* fine gold ② same as 镏 liú

liǔ

柳 liǔ ① willow ② the twenty-fourth of the twenty-eight constellations (二十八宿) into which the celestial sphere was divided in ancient Chinese astronomy (consisting of eight stars in Hydra) ③ (Liǔ) a surname
柳安 liǔ'ān *bot.* lauan
柳暗花明 liǔ'àn-huāmíng dark willows and blooming flowers—a beauteous scene; a new vista ——see also 山穷水尽 shānqióng-shuǐjìn
柳编 liǔbiān wickerwork
柳斗 liǔdǒu round-bottomed wicker basket
柳拐子病 liǔguǎizibìng another name for 大骨节病 dàgǔjiébìng
柳罐 liǔguàn wicker bucket
柳江人 Liǔjiāngrén Liujiang man, a type of primitive man whose fossilized remains were found in 1958 at Liujiang, Guangxi Zhuang Autonomous Region
柳毛子 liǔmáozi *dial.* ① clumps of willow trees ② willow catkins
柳眉 liǔméi (also 柳叶眉 liǔyèméi) arched eyebrows (of a woman)
柳琴 liǔqín a plucked stringed instrument
柳杉 liǔshān cryptomeria
柳体 Liǔtǐ the Liu style (a calligraphic style created by Liu Gongquan 柳公权 of the Tang Dynasty)
柳条 liǔtiáo willow twig; osier; wicker
柳条筐 liǔtiáokuāng wicker basket
柳条帽 liǔtiáomào wicker safety helmet
柳条箱 liǔtiáoxiāng wicker suitcase (*or* trunk)
柳条制品 liǔtiáo zhìpǐn wickerwork; wicker
柳巷花街 liǔxiàng-huājiē same as 花街柳巷 huājiē-liǔxiàng
柳絮 liǔxù willow catkins
柳腰 liǔyāo willowy (*or* slender) waist
柳阴 liǔyīn the shade of a willow tree
柳莺 liǔyīng willow warbler: 黄腰～ yellow-rumped willow warbler
柳子[1] liǔzi clumps of willow trees

柳子[2] liǔzi major tunes used in 柳子戏 liǔzixì
柳子戏 liǔzixì a local opera popular in western Shandong, northern Jiangsu and eastern Henan

绺 liǔ *m.* (for thread, hair, etc.) tuft; lock; skein: 一～丝线 a skein of silk thread / 一～头发 a lock (*or* tuft, wisp) of hair

liù

六[1] liù six: ～个班 six classes / ～班 the sixth class; class 6 / 棉纺～厂 No. 6 Cotton Textile Mill
六[2] liù *mus.* a note of the scale in *gongchepu* (工尺谱), corresponding to 5 in numbered musical notation
六边形 liùbiānxíng hexagon
六部 Liùbù the Six Boards (which formed the central government in imperial times; i.e., in order of importance, 吏部 Lìbù, 户部 Hùbù, 礼部 Lǐbù, 兵部 Bīngbù, 刑部 Xíngbù, and 工部 Gōngbù)
六朝 Liù Cháo the Six Dynasties—the six dynasties between the downfall of the Han in 220 and the reunification of China in 589 which had for their capital what is now Nanjing (i.e. the Wu 吴, the Eastern Jin 东晋, the Song 宋, the Qi 齐, the Liang 梁, and the Chen 陈)
六朝金粉 Liù Cháo jīnfěn the gaiety and splendour of Six Dynasties aristocratic life
六朝文 Liù Cháo wén Six Dynasties prose
六畜 liùchù the six domestic animals (pig, ox, goat, horse, fowl and dog)
六畜兴旺 liùchù xīngwàng the domestic animals are all thriving
六分仪 liùfēnyí sextant
六腑 liùfǔ *Chin. med.* the six hollow organs (gallbladder, stomach, large intestine, small intestine, bladder and *sanjiao* 三焦)
六根 liùgēn (in Buddhism) the six roots of sensation—eye, ear, nose, tongue, body and mind: ～清净 be free from human desires and passions
六谷 liùgǔ *dial.* maize; corn: ～粉 maize flour; cornmeal
六合 liùhé *formal* the six directions—north, south, east, west, up and down; the world; the universe: ～同春。Spring is everywhere.
六级风 liùjífēng *meteorol.* force 6 wind; strong breeze
六甲 liùjiǎ see 身怀六甲 shēn huái liùjiǎ
六角车床 liùjiǎo chēchuáng turret lathe
六角形 liùjiǎoxíng hexagon
六经辨证 liùjīng biànzhèng *Chin. med.* analysing and differentiating febrile diseases in accordance with the theory of six pairs of channels
六〇六 liùlíngliù "606" or salvarsan (a remedy for syphilis commonly employed until the advent of antibiotics)
六六六 liùliùliù BHC (benzene hexachloride)
六面体 liùmiàntǐ hexahedron
六气 liùqì *Chin. med.* the six factors in nature (wind, cold, summer heat, humidity, dryness and fire)
六亲 liùqīn the six relations (father, mother, elder brothers, younger brothers, wife, children); one's kin
六亲不认 liùqīn bù rèn disown all one's relatives and friends
六亲无靠 liùqīn wú kào have no relatives or friends to depend on
六神无主 liù shén wú zhǔ all six vital organs failing to work properly—distracted; out of one's wits; at a loss what to do

六十四开 liùshí sì kāi *print.* sixty-fourmo; 64 mo

六书 liùshū the six scripts—the six categories of Chinese characters (i.e. 指事 zhǐshì, 象形 xiàngxíng, 形声 xíngshēng, 会意 huìyì, 转注 zhuǎnzhù, and 假借 jiǎjiè)

六仙桌 liùxiānzhuō six immortals table (a square table smaller than 八仙桌 bāxiānzhuō and larger than 四仙桌 sìxiānzhuō)

六弦琴 liùxiánqín guitar

六一国际儿童节 Liù Yī Guójì Értóngjié International Children's Day (June 1)

六艺 liùyì ① the six arts (i.e. rites 礼, music 乐, archery 射, charioteering 御, reading and writing 书, and arithmetic 数, the mastery of which was required of ancient scholars) ② the six classics (i.e. *The Book of Songs* 《诗》, *The Book of History* 《书》, *The Book of Rites* 《礼》, *The Book of Music* 《乐》, *The Book of Changes* 《易》, and *The Spring and Autumn Annals* 《春秋》)

六淫 liùyín *Chin. med.* the six external factors which cause diseases; the excessive or untimely working of the six natural factors (wind, cold, summer heat, humidity, dryness and fire)

六月 liùyuè ① June ② the sixth month of the lunar year; the sixth moon

六指儿 liùzhǐr ① a six-fingered hand ② a person with a six-fingered hand

陆（陸） liù six (used for the numeral 六 on cheques, etc. to avoid mistakes or alterations) ——see also lù

溜[1] liù ① swift current: 河里～很大。The river has a strong current. ② line; column; row: 一～平房 a row of one-storeyed houses / 一～松树 a row of pines ③ surroundings; neighbourhood: 这～儿果木树很多。There are plenty of fruit trees round our way.

溜[2]（霤） liù ① rainwater from the roof ② eaves gutter

溜[3] liù *dial.* fill (a crevice, fissure, etc.) ——see also liū

溜子 liùzi *min.* scraper-trough conveyer

碌 liù see below ——see also lù

碌碡 liùzhou stone roller (for threshing grain, levelling a threshing floor, etc.)

遛 liù ① saunter; stroll: 出去～～。Let's go for a stroll. / ～大街 stroll around the streets; go window-shopping ② walk (an animal): ～狗 walk a dog

遛达 liùda same as 溜达 liūda

遛马 liùmǎ walk a horse

遛鸟 liùniǎo (of bird keepers) take caged birds out into the country (to eat insects or to listen to and learn the songs of their kind who are free to roam the skies)

遛弯儿 liùwānr *dial.* take a walk; go for a stroll: 我晚饭后到公园遛了个弯儿。I went for a stroll in the park after supper.

遛早儿 liùzǎor *dial.* take a morning stroll

馏 liù heat up in a steamer: 把凉馒头～一～ heat up the cold steamed bread ——see also liú

鎦 liù see below ——see also liú

鎦子 liùzi *dial.* (finger) ring

鷚 liù pipit: 树～ tree pipit

蹓 liù saunter; stroll: 到公园去～一～ go for a stroll in the park / ～大街 stroll around the streets; go window-shopping

蹓达 liùda same as 溜达 liūda

lo

咯 lo *part.* (used at the end of a sentence to indicate obviousness, slightly stronger than 了 le): 当然～ of course; needless to say ——see also gē; kǎ; luò

lōng

隆 lōng see 黑咕隆咚 hēigulōngdōng ——see also lóng

lóng

龙（龍） lóng ① dragon ② the dragon as the symbol of the emperor; of the emperor: ～床 the emperor's bed / ～袍 imperial robe ③ a huge extinct reptile: 恐龙 kǒnglóng ④ (Lóng) a surname

龙船 lóngchuán dragon boat (a dragon-shaped racing boat)

龙胆 lóngdǎn *bot.* rough gentian (*Gentiana scabra*)

龙胆紫 lóngdǎnzǐ gentian violet

龙灯 lóngdēng dragon lantern

龙洞 lóngdòng dragon's cave—stalactite cave

龙飞凤舞 lóngfēi-fèngwǔ like dragons flying and phoenixes dancing—lively and vigorous flourishes in calligraphy; a flamboyant style of calligraphy

龙凤呈祥 lóng fèng chéng xiáng the dragon and the phoenix bringing prosperity—excellent good fortune

龙肝凤胆 lónggān-fèngdǎn (also 龙肝凤髓 lónggān-fèngsuǐ) rare delicacies

龙宫 lónggōng the palace of the Dragon King

龙骨 lónggǔ ① a bird's sternum ② *Chin. med.* fossil fragments ③ keel

龙骨车 lónggǔchē dragon-bone water lift; square-pallet chain-pump

龙睛鱼 lóngjīngyú dragon-eyes (a species of goldfish with prominent eyes and a large tail)

龙井 lóngjǐng Dragon Well tea (a famous green tea produced in Hangzhou, Zhejiang Province)

龙驹 lóngjū *formal* dragon colt—a brilliant young man

龙驹凤雏 lóngjū-fèngchú dragon colt or young phoenix—a brilliant young man: 北静王见他语言清朗, 谈吐有致, 一面又向贾政笑道: "令郎真乃～, 非小王在世翁前唐突, 将来'雏凤清于老凤声', 未可量也。"《红楼梦》The clarity and fluency of Baoyu's answers made the prince turn to observe to Jia Zheng, "Your son is truly a dragon colt or a young phoenix. May I venture to predict that in time to come this young phoenix may even surpass the old one?"

龙卷 lóngjuǎn *meteorol.* spout

龙卷风 lóngjuǎnfēng tornado

龙口夺粮 lóngkǒu duó liáng snatch food from the dragon's mouth—speed up the summer harvesting before the storm breaks

龙葵 lóngkuí *bot.* black nightshade

龙马精神 lóngmǎ jīngshén the spirit of a dragon horse

(usu. said in praise of a vigorous old age)

龙门刨 lóngménbào (also 龙门刨床 lóngmén bàochuáng) double housing planer

龙门吊 lóngméndiào another name for 龙门起重机 lóngmén qǐzhòngjī

龙门起重机 lóngmén qǐzhòngjī gantry crane

龙门石窟 Lóngmén Shíkū the Longmen Grottoes (in Luoyang, Henan Province)

龙门铣床 lóngmén xǐchuáng planer-type milling machine

龙脑 lóngnǎo chem. borneol; borneo camphor

龙盘虎踞 lóngpán-hǔjù a coiling dragon and a crouching tiger—a forbidding strategic point (usu. referring to the city of Nanjing)

龙山文化 Lóngshān wénhuà the Longshan culture (a late Neolithic culture characterized by a burnished black pottery; named after Longshan, Shandong Province, where remains were first found in 1928)

龙舌兰 lóngshélán century plant

龙蛇 lóng-shé dragons and snakes—flourishes in calligraphy ——see also 笔走龙蛇 bǐ zǒu lóng-shé

龙蛇混杂 lóng-shé hùnzá dragons and snakes jumbled together—good and bad people mixed up

龙生九子 lóng shēng jiǔ zǐ the dragon had nine sons and each of them was different from the others —brothers born of the same parents differ from each other (from an old story)

龙生龙，凤生凤 lóng shēng lóng, fèng shēng fèng dragons beget dragons, phoenixes beget phoenixes—each after its own kind

龙虱 lóngshī predacious diving beetle

龙潭虎穴 lóngtán-hǔxué a dragon's pool and a tiger's den— a danger spot

龙套 lóngtào ① costume with dragon designs, worn by groups of soldiers or attendants in traditional opera ② actor playing a walk-on part in traditional opera; utility man ——see also 跑龙套 pǎo lóngtào

龙腾虎跃 lóngténg-hǔyuè dragons rising and tigers leaping—a scene of bustling activity

龙头 lóngtóu ① tap; faucet; cock ② dial. handlebar (of a bicycle)

龙头鱼 lóngtóuyú Bombay duck

龙王 Lóngwáng the Dragon King (the God of Rain in Chinese mythology)

龙虾 lóngxiā lobster

龙涎香 lóngxiánxiāng ambergris

龙骧虎步 lóngxiāng-hǔbù (also 龙行虎步 lóngxíng-hǔbù) dragon-like prancing and tiger-like pacing—majestic gait; imposing air

龙须菜 lóngxūcài dial. asparagus

龙须草 lóngxūcǎo Chinese alpine rush (Eulaliopsis binata)

龙须面 lóngxūmiàn dragon whiskers noodles—long, thin noodles

龙血树 lóngxuèshù dragon tree (Dracaena draco)

龙牙草 lóngyácǎo hairyvein agrimony (Agrimonia pilosa)

龙颜 lóngyán imperial countenance: ～大悦。 The imperial countenance shows great pleasure. or The emperor looks greatly pleased.

龙眼 lóngyǎn bot. longan

龙洋 lóngyáng dragon dollar (a silver dollar with the emblem of a coiled dragon, minted towards the end of the Qing Dynasty)

龙吟虎啸 lóngyín-hǔxiào dragons singing and tigers roaring (said of the howling of the wind, the roaring of waves, etc.)

龙爪槐 lóngzhǎohuái Chinese pagoda tree

龙争虎斗 lóngzhēng-hǔdòu fighting between a tiger and

a dragon—a fierce struggle between well-matched opponents; a contest between giants

龙钟 lóngzhōng formal decrepit; senile: 老态龙钟 lǎotài lóngzhōng

龙舟 lóngzhōu dragon boat: ～竞渡 dragon-boat regatta; dragon-boat race

泷（瀧） lóng dial. rapids (often used as part of a place name): 七里～ (a place in Zhejiang Province) ——see also shuāng

茏（蘢） lóng see below

茏葱 lóngcōng verdant; luxuriantly green

咙（嚨） lóng see 喉咙 hóulóng

珑（瓏） lóng see below

珑璁 lóngcōng ① onom. liter. the tinkling sound of metal striking against metal or of jade striking against jade ② same as 茏葱 lóngcōng

珑玲 lónglíng liter. ① onom. the tinkling sound of metal striking against metal or of jade striking against jade ② bright; shining

昽（曨） lóng see 曚昽 ménglóng

栊（櫳、欚） lóng formal ① window: 帘～ a curtained window ② a cage for animals

胧（朧） lóng see 朦胧 ménglóng

眬（矓） lóng see 曚眬 ménglóng

砻（礱） lóng ① rice huller ② hull (rice)

砻谷机 lónggǔjī rice huller

砻糠 lóngkāng rice chaff

聋（聾） lóng deaf; hard of hearing: 他耳朵～。 He is deaf.

聋聩 lóngkuì formal ① deaf ② ignorant

聋哑 lóngyǎ deaf and dumb; deaf-mute

聋哑人 lóngyǎrén deaf-mute

聋哑学校 lóngyǎ xuéxiào school for deaf-mutes

聋哑症 lóngyǎzhèng deaf-mutism

聋子 lóngzi a deaf person

笼（籠） lóng ① cage; coop: 鸟～ birdcage / 鸡～ chicken coop ② basket; container ③ (food) steamer: 一～肉包子 a steamerful of meat-filled buns ——see also lǒng

笼鸟 lóngniǎo cage bird

笼屉 lóngtì bamboo or wooden utensil for steaming food (composed of several tiers); food steamer

笼头 lóngtou headstall; halter

笼养 lóngyǎng raise (poultry) in coops, cages, etc.

笼子 lóngzi ① cage; coop ② basket; container ——see also lǒngzi

笼嘴 lóngzui muzzle (put over the mouth of an animal)

隆 lóng ① grand: 隆重 lóngzhòng ② prosperous; thriving: 兴隆 xīnglóng ③ intense; deep: ～情厚谊 profound sentiments of friendship ④ swell; bulge: 隆起 lóngqǐ ——see also lōng

隆冬 lóngdōng midwinter; the depth of winter

隆隆 lónglóng onom. rumble; boom: 雷声～。 The thunder rumbled. / 炮声～。 The guns boomed.

隆起 lóngqǐ swell; bulge: 他碰得前额～一个大包。 He got a bad bump on his forehead.

隆盛 lóngshèng ① abundant; flourishing; prosperous:

国势～。The country is prospering. ② grand; magnificent: ～的仪式 a grand ceremony

隆暑 lóngshǔ　midsummer; the height of summer

隆替 lóng-tì　*formal*　rise and fall (of a dynasty, nation, etc.): 国运～ ups and downs in the fortunes of a nation

隆头鱼 lóngtóuyú　wrasse

隆重 lóngzhòng　grand; solemn; ceremonious: ～的典礼 a grand ceremony / 受到～的接待 be accorded a grand reception; be given a red carpet reception / 代表大会于昨日～开幕。The congress was solemnly opened yesterday.

隆准 lóngzhǔn　*formal*　a prominent nose

癃 lóng ① *arch.* infirmity ② *arch.* bent with age; hunchbacked ③ same as 癃闭 lóngbì

癃闭 lóngbì　*Chin. med.*　retention of urine; difficulty in urination

窿 lóng　*dial.*　gallery (in a mine)

lǒng

陇（隴） Lǒng　another name for 甘肃 Gānsù

陇剧 lǒngjù　Gansu opera

垄（壟、壠） lǒng ① ridge (in a field): 土改前我家房无一间,地无一～。Before the land reform my family hadn't a single room or a strip of land. ② raised path between fields ③ a thing like a ridge: 瓦垄 wǎlǒng

垄断 lǒngduàn　monopolize: ～市场 monopolize (*or* corner) the market

垄断集团 lǒngduàn jítuán　monopoly group

垄断价格 lǒngduàn jiàgé　monopoly price

垄断利润 lǒngduàn lìrùn　monopolist profits

垄断资本 lǒngduàn zīběn　monopoly capital

垄断资本主义 lǒngduànzīběnzhǔyì　monopoly capitalism

垄断资产阶级 lǒngduànzīchǎnjiējí　monopoly capitalist class

垄沟 lǒnggōu　field ditch; furrow

垄作 lǒngzuò　*agric.*　ridge culture

拢（攏） lǒng ① approach; reach: 我们快～工地了。We are almost on the worksite now. ② add up; sum up: 把帐～一～ sum up the accounts ③ hold (*or* gather) together: 把所有的书都～在一块。Gather all the books together. / 用绳子把柴火～住。Tie the firewood in a bundle. / 她把孩子～在怀里。She held her child in her arms. ④ (used after verbs) bring together: 他笑得嘴都合不～了。He grinned from ear to ear. / 他们谈不～。They talk but never get close to each other. ⑤ comb (hair): 我来给你～一～头发。Let me comb your hair.

拢岸 lǒng'àn　(of a ship) come alongside the shore

拢共 lǒnggòng　altogether; all told; in all: 买这么多东西,～才花了十块钱。It cost ten *yuan* altogether to buy this many things.

拢头 lǒngtóu　comb hair

拢子 lǒngzi　a fine-toothed comb

拢总 lǒngzǒng　same as 拢共 lǒnggòng

笼（籠） lǒng ① envelop; cover: ～着手 put each hand in the opposite sleeve / 烟～雾罩 be enveloped (*or* hidden) in mist ② a large box or chest; trunk ——see also lóng

笼火 lǒnghuǒ　light a coal fire with firewood; make a fire

笼络 lǒngluò　win sb. over by any means; draw over; rope in: 他很会～人。He is very good at buying people's support.

笼络人心 lǒngluò rénxīn　cultivate people's good will (by dispensing charity, favours, etc.)

笼统 lǒngtǒng　general; sweeping: 他的话说得很～。He spoke in very general terms. / 这么说未免太～了。That statement is rather too sweeping. / 他只是笼笼统统地解释了一下。He only tried to explain in generalities.

笼罩 lǒngzhào　envelop; shroud: 晨雾～在湖面上。The lake is shrouded in morning mist. / 会场上～着一种悲痛的气氛。A cloud of gloom hung over the meeting.

笼子 lǒngzi　a large box or chest; trunk ——see also lóngzi

lòng

弄 lòng　*dial.*　(usu. used in names of lanes) lane; alley; alleyway ——see also nòng

弄堂 lòngtáng　*dial.*　lane; alley; alleyway

lōu

搂（摟） lōu ① gather up; rake together: ～柴火 rake up twigs, dead leaves, etc. (for fuel) ② hold up; tuck up: ～起袖子 tuck up one's sleeves ③ squeeze (money); extort: ～钱 extort money ④ *dial.* pull: ～扳机 pull a trigger ——see also lǒu

搂草机 lōucǎojī　rake

搂火 lōuhuǒ　*inf.*　pull a trigger

搂揽 lōulǎn　take on everything; monopolize: ～当地的茶叶生意 monopolize the local tea business

搂头 lōutóu　*dial.*　head-on; directly

搂头盖脸 lōutóu-gàiliǎn　same as 劈头盖脸 pītóu-gàiliǎn

䁖（瞜） lōu　*dial.*　look: 让我～一眼。Let me have a look.

lóu

娄（婁） lóu ① *dial.* weak (physically): 他的身体可～啦。He's very weak. ② *dial.* (of melons, gourds, etc.) overripe and unfit to eat ③ the sixteenth of the twenty-eight constellations（二十八宿）into which the celestial sphere was divided in ancient Chinese astronomy (consisting of three stars in the shape of an isosceles triangle in Aries) ④ (Lóu) a surname

娄子 lóuzi　*inf.*　trouble; blunder: 惹～ stir up trouble ——see also 出娄子 chū lóuzi; 捅娄子 tǒng lóuzi

偻（僂） lóu ① see 佝偻病 gōulóubìng ② see 偻㑩 lóuluo ——see also lǚ

偻㑩 lóuluo　① the rank and file of a band of outlaws ② underling; lackey

喽（嘍） lóu　see below ——see also lou

喽啰 lóuluo　① the rank and file of a band of outlaws ② underling; lackey

楼（樓） lóu ① a storied building; tower: 教室～ classroom building / 黄鹤～ Yellow Crane Tower ② storey; floor: 一～ (British) ground floor; (Amer-

ican) first floor / 二～ (British) first floor; (American) second floor ③ superstructure: 城楼 chénglóu ④ (used in shop names): 萃华楼 Cuihualou (the name of a restaurant) ⑤ (Lóu) a surname

楼板 lóubǎn　floor; floorslab

楼层 lóucéng　storey; floor: 每个～都有消火栓。 On every floor there is a fire hydrant.

楼船 lóuchuán　towered ship (used in ancient times)

楼道 lóudào　corridor; passageway

楼房 lóufáng　a building of two or more storeys

楼面 lóumiàn　*archit.* floor: ～面积 floor area

楼上 lóushàng　upstairs: ～住的是一位退休老工人。 A retired worker lives upstairs.

楼台 lóutái　① *liter.* a high building; tower ② *dial.* balcony

楼堂馆所 lóu-táng-guǎn-suǒ　office buildings, large halls and guest houses

楼梯 lóutī　stairs; staircase; stairway: 一层～ a flight of stairs / 上(下)～ go up (down) by the stairway / ～平台 landing (of stairs)

楼下 lóuxià　downstairs: 他住在～。 He lives downstairs. / 他住在我～。 He lives on the floor below me. / ～有人叫你。 Somebody is calling you downstairs. / ～的房间 a downstairs room; a room on the floor below

蝼（螻）　lóu　mole cricket

蝼蛄 lóugū　mole cricket

蝼蚁 lóuyǐ　① mole crickets and ants ② nobodies; nonentities: ～尚且偷生，何况人乎? Even the lowly cricket and ant cling to life, let alone a human being.

耧（耬）　lóu　an animal-drawn seed plough; drill barrow; drill

耧播 lóubō　sow with a drill

耧车 lóuchē　old name for 耧 lóu

髅（髏）　lóu　see 髑髅 dúlóu; 骷髅 kūlóu

lǒu

搂（摟）　lǒu　① hold in one's arms; hug; embrace: 她把孩子～在怀里。 She held the child in her arms. ② *m.* 两～粗的大树 a tree two arm-spans around ——see also lōu

搂抱 lǒubào　hug; embrace; cuddle: 小姑娘亲热地～着小猫。 The little girl cuddled her pet cat.

篓（簍）　lǒu　basket: 字纸篓 zìzhǐlǒu

篓子 lǒuzi　basket

lòu

陋　lòu　① plain; ugly: 丑陋 chǒulòu ② (of a dwelling-place) humble; mean: ～室 a humble room / ～巷 a mean alley ③ vulgar; corrupt; undesirable: 陋习 lòuxí ④ (of knowledge) scanty; limited; shallow: 浅陋 qiǎnlòu

陋规 lòuguī　objectionable practices

陋见 lòujiàn　shallow (*or* superficial) views

陋俗 lòusú　undesirable customs

陋习 lòuxí　corrupt customs; bad habits

漏　lòu　① leak: 水壶～了。 The kettle is leaking. / ～雨了。 The rain is leaking in. / 油箱～油。 The tank is leaking petrol. ② water clock; hourglass: ～尽更残。

The night is waning. ③ divulge; leak: 你千万不能把这个消息～出去。 You absolutely must not let this news leak out. ④ be missing; leave out by mistake: ～了一行。 A line is missing. / 这一项可千万不能～掉。 Be sure not to leave out this item. / 他抄～了三个字。 When he made the copy, he left out three words by mistake.

漏报 lòubào　fail to report sth.; fail to declare (dutiable goods)

漏疮 lòuchuāng　anal fistula

漏电 lòudiàn　leak electricity

漏洞 lòudòng　① leak: 检查一下管道有没有～。 Check and see if there is any leak in the pipe. ② flaw; hole; loophole: 严格制度，堵塞～。 Tighten the rules and stop up all loopholes. / 他的话里有许多～。 What he says is full of holes.

漏洞百出 lòudòng bǎi chū　full of loopholes: 他的话前后矛盾，～。 His argument is full of holes.

漏兜 lòudōu　*dial.* spill the beans

漏斗 lòudǒu　funnel

漏风 lòufēng　① leak air; not be airtight: 这个风箱～。 This bellows is not airtight. ② speak indistinctly through having one or more front teeth missing ③ (of information, secrets) leak out

漏缝 lòufèng　crack; leak: 壶底有道～。 There is a crack in the bottom of the kettle.

漏鼓 lòugǔ　a drum used to beat the watches

漏光 lòuguāng　leak light: 这个照相机～。 The camera has a light leak.

漏壶 lòuhú　(also 漏刻 lòukè) water clock; clepsydra; hourglass

漏划 lòuhuà　escape being classified as a landlord or rich peasant, etc.: ～地主 a landlord who escaped being classified as such

漏孔 lòukǒng　small opening; hole

漏落 lòuluò　(also 漏脱 lòutuō) leave out by mistake; miss out

漏勺 lòusháo　strainer; colander

漏税 lòushuì　evade payment of a tax; evade taxation

漏网 lòuwǎng　slip through the net; escape unpunished: 决不让一个犯罪分子～。 Don't let a single criminal escape. / 四面包围敌人，力求全歼，不使～。 Encircle the enemy forces completely, strive to wipe them out thoroughly, and do not let any escape from the net.

漏网之鱼 lòuwǎng zhī yú　a fish that has slipped through the net—fugitive; runaway

漏泄 lòuxiè　① (of water, light, etc.) leak out; filter: 阳光从枝叶的缝隙中～下来。 Sunbeams filtered through the foliage. ② let out; leak; divulge; give away: 一定有人～试题了。 Somebody must have leaked out the exam questions.

漏泄春光 lòuxiè chūnguāng　give a hint of spring—leak out news or secrets

漏夜 lòuyè　in the dead of night

漏卮 lòuzhī　*formal* a leaky wine cup—the loss of economic rights to foreigners

漏子 lòuzi　① *inf.* funnel ② flaw; hole; loophole

漏嘴 lòuzuǐ　let slip a remark; make a slip of the tongue ——see also 说漏嘴 shuōlòuzuǐ

瘘（瘻、瘺）　lòu　see below

瘘管 lòuguǎn　fistula

镂（鏤）　lòu　engrave; carve

镂骨铭心 lòugǔ-míngxīn　same as 刻骨铭心 kègǔ-míngxīn

镂花 lòuhuā　ornamental engraving

镂刻 lòukè　① carve; engrave: ～花纹 engrave designs ② impress deeply (on the mind); engrave: 这番情景将永远～在她的心中。 The scene would always be en-

graved on her memory.

镂空 lòukōng pierced work; reticulated work; open-work; fretwork: 〜的象牙球 a pierced ivory ball /〜套瓶 a vase enclosed in a reticulated envelope (the whole fired in one piece)

露

lòu *inf.* same as 露² lù, limited to use in the following ——see also lù

露白 lòubái show money or valuables one carries unintentionally

露丑 lòuchǒu make a fool of oneself in public

露底 lòudǐ let the secret out

露风 lòufēng divulge a secret; leak out information

露富 lòufù show one's wealth

露脸 lòuliǎn become known (by doing sth.); be successful; shine: 那次讲演他很〜。 He made himself known when he made that speech. / 今天下午排球比赛他可〜了。 He really shone in this afternoon's volleyball match.

露马脚 lòu mǎjiǎo give oneself away; let the cat out of the bag

露面 lòumiàn show one's face; make (*or* put in) an appearance; appear or reappear on public occasions: 他整天没〜儿。 He didn't show up for a whole day. / 他没有开完会, 只是开始的时候露了一面儿。 He didn't stay for the whole meeting; he just put in an appearance at the beginning.

露苗 lòumiáo same as 出苗 chūmiáo

露怯 lòuqiè *dial.* display one's ignorance; make a fool of oneself

露头 lòutóu ① show one's head ② appear; emerge: 太阳刚〜, 我们就起来了。 The sun had hardly appeared when we got up. ——see also lùtóu

露馅儿 lòuxiànr let the cat out of the bag; give the game away; spill the beans: 别再保密了, 你的话已经〜了。 Don't try to keep it a secret any longer. You've already given the game away.

露相 lòuxiàng *dial.* show one's true colours

露一手 lòu yìshǒu make an exhibition of one's abilities or skills; show off: 我来做鱼, 给你们〜。 Let me cook the fish and have a chance to show off.

lou

喽（嘍）

lou *part.* (used like 了 le) ① (after a verb to indicate the completion of an envisaged action): 我吃〜饭就走。 I'll go as soon as I've eaten. / 他要知道〜一定很高兴。 I'm sure he'll be glad to hear it. ② (at the end of a sentence to call attention to a new situation): 钟停〜! The clock has stopped, you know! / 起床〜。 Look, it's time to get up. ——see also lóu

lū

噜

lū see below

噜苏 lū·sū *dial.* ① long-winded; wordy ② over-elaborate; troublesome

撸

lū *dial.* ① rub one's palm along (sth. long): 把树枝上的叶子〜下来 strip a twig of its leaves ② dismiss (a person from his post) ③ dress down: 挨了一顿〜 get a dressing-down

撸子 lūzi *dial.* a small pistol

lú

卢（盧）

Lú a surname

卢比 lúbǐ rupee

卢布 lúbù rouble

卢瑟福 Lúsèfú *phys.* rutherford

卢森堡 Lúsēnbǎo Luxembourg

卢森堡人 Lúsēnbǎorén Luxembourger

卢旺达 Lúwàngdá Rwanda

卢旺达人 Lúwàngdárén Rwandese

庐（廬）

lú hut; cottage: 茅庐 máolú

庐山真面目 Lúshān zhēnmiànmù the true face of Lushan—the truth about a person or a matter: 不识〜, 只缘身在此山中。 (苏轼) I can't tell the true shape of Lushan Because I myself am in the mountain. (often quoted to mean that the truth is incomprehensible to one too deeply involved to be objective)

庐舍 lúshè *formal* house; farmhouse

芦（蘆）

lú reed ——see also lù

芦柴 lúchái reed stems

芦荡 lúdàng reed marshes

芦丁 lúdīng *pharm.* rutin

芦蓬 lúfèi *dial.* reed mat

芦根 lúgēn *Chin. med.* reed rhizome

芦沟桥事变 Lúgōuqiáo Shìbiàn the Lugouqiao Incident, the incident staged at Lugouqiao near Beiping (now Beijing) on July 7, 1937 by the Japanese imperialists in their attempt to annex the whole of China, which marked the beginning of their all-out war of aggression against China

芦花 lúhuā reed catkins

芦荟 lúhuì *bot.* aloe

芦笙 lúshēng a reed-pipe wind instrument, used by the Miao, Yao and Dong nationalities

芦笋 lúsǔn common name for 石刁柏 shídiāobǎi

芦苇 lúwěi reed

芦苇荡 lúwěidàng reed marshes

芦席 lúxí reed mat

炉（爐、鑪）

lú ① stove; oven; furnace: 新出〜的烧饼 baked sesame buns fresh out of the oven ② *m. metall.* heat: 一〜钢 a heat of steel

炉箅子 lúbìzi fire grate

炉衬 lúchèn (furnace) lining: 〜寿命 lining durability

炉顶 lúdǐng *metall.* furnace top; furnace roof

炉甘石 lúgānshí *Chin. med.* calamine

炉灰 lúhuī stove ashes

炉火纯青 lúhuǒ chúnqīng the stove fire (for making pills of immortality) begins to glow a pure blue—attain a high degree of perfection: 他画山水的技巧达到了〜的地步。 He attained the acme of perfection in landscape painting.

炉坑 lúkēng space for collecting ashes in a stove

炉料 lúliào *metall.* furnace charge; furnace burden

炉龄 lúlíng *metall.* furnace life

炉门 lúmén the draft of a stove

炉盘 lúpán stone or metal plate for standing a stove on as a precaution against fire

炉前工 lúqiángōng blast-furnace man; furnaceman

炉桥 lúqiáo *dial.* grate

炉身 lúshēn *metall.* (furnace) shaft; furnace stack

炉台 lútái stove top

炉膛 lútáng the chamber of a stove or furnace

炉条 lútiáo fire bars; grate

炉温　lúwēn　*metall.*　furnace temperature

炉灶　lúzào　kitchen range; cooking range

炉渣　lúzhā　slag; cinder

炉子　lúzi　stove; oven; furnace: 生～ light a stove

垆¹（壚）　lú　black earth: ～土 black earth

垆²（壚、鑪）　lú　an earthen stand for wine jars; wineshop: 酒～ wineshop

垆邸　lúdǐ　*formal*　wineshop

垆坶　lúmǔ　old name for 壤土 rǎngtǔ

垆埴　lúzhí　black clay

胪（臚）　lú　*formal*　set out; display; exhibit

胪陈　lúchén　*formal*　(used in old-style documents or letters) narrate in detail; state

胪欢　lúhuān　*formal*　express joy: 万众～。 There was universal rejoicing.

胪列　lúliè　*formal*　enumerate; list

栌（櫨）　lú　see 黄栌 huánglú

鸬（鸕）　lú　see below

鸬鹚　lúcí　cormorant

铲（鑪）　lú　*chem.*　rutherfordium (Rf)

颅（顱）　lú　cranium; skull

颅骨　lúgǔ　cranial bones

颅腔　lúqiāng　cranial cavity

舻（艫）　lú　bow (of a ship): 舳舻 zhúlú

鲈（鱸）　lú　perch

lǔ

芦（蘆）　lǔ　see 油葫芦 yóuhúlú ——see also lú

卤（鹵、滷）　lǔ　① bittern ② *chem.* halogen ③ stew (whole chickens or ducks, large cuts of meat, etc.) in soy sauce: ～鸡 pot-stewed chicken ④ thick gravy used as a sauce for noodles, etc.: 打～ make such gravy ⑤ a thick infusion: 茶卤儿 chálǔr

卤菜　lǔcài　pot-stewed meat or fowl

卤化　lǔhuà　*chem.*　halogenate

卤化物　lǔhuàwù　halogenide; halide

卤莽　lǔmǎng　same as 鲁莽 lǔmǎng

卤水　lǔshuǐ　① bittern ② brine

卤素　lǔsù　*chem.*　halogen

卤味　lǔwèi　pot-stewed fowl, meat, etc. served cold

卤虾　lǔxiā　salted shrimp gravy

卤虾油　lǔxiāyóu　shrimp sauce

卤质　lǔzhì　alkali (found in soils)

卤族　lǔzú　*chem.*　halogen family

虏（虜）　lǔ　① take prisoner ② captive; prisoner of war ③ *arch.* slave ④ *arch. derog.* enemy: 谈笑间，强～灰飞烟灭。（苏轼）Amidst talk and laughter, He reduced his strong enemy to flying ashes and smouldering smoke.

虏获　lǔhuò　capture (men and arms)

掳（擄）　lǔ　carry off; capture

掳掠　lǔlüè　pillage; loot

掳人勒赎　lǔrén lèshú　hold captives for ransom

鲁¹　lǔ　① stupid; dull: 愚鲁 yúlǔ ② rash; rough; rude: 粗鲁 cūlǔ

鲁²　Lǔ　① one of the warring states into which China was divided during the Eastern Zhou period (770-256 B.C.), located in the southern portion of modern Shandong Province ② another name for 山东 Shāndōng ③ a surname

鲁班　Lǔ Bān　a master craftsman of the Spring and Autumn period (770-476 B.C.), since deified as the patron saint of carpenters

鲁班尺　lǔbānchǐ　carpenter's square

鲁菜　lǔcài　Shandong food; Shandong cuisine

鲁钝　lǔdùn　dull-witted; obtuse; stupid

鲁莽　lǔmǎng　crude and rash; rash: ～行事 act rashly; act without thought / 对待思想上的毛病决不能采取～的态度。 In treating an ideological malady, one must never be crude.

鲁莽灭裂　lǔmǎng-mièliè　rash and careless: ～的干法 rash and foolhardy conduct

鲁米那　lǔmǐnà　*pharm.*　luminal (a transliteration)

鲁鱼亥豕　lǔ-yú hài-shǐ　confusion of 鲁 with 鱼 and of 亥 with 豕 —clerical or typographical errors made through confusing similar characters

橹¹（櫓、艣、艪）　lǔ　scull; sweep

橹²　lǔ　*arch.*　a big shield

镥　lǔ　*chem.*　lutecium; lutetium (Lu)

lù

陆（陸）　lù　① land: 水陆 shuǐ-lù ② (Lù) a surname ——see also liù

陆半球　lùbànqiú　the continental hemisphere; the land hemisphere

陆稻　lùdào　dryland rice; upland rice; dry rice

陆地　lùdì　dry land; land

陆地棉　lùdìmián　upland cotton

陆风　lùfēng　*meteorol.*　land breeze

陆海空　lù-hǎi-kōng　land, sea, and air: ～三军 the army, the navy, and the air force; the armed forces

陆架　lùjià　same as 大陆架 dàlùjià

陆军　lùjūn　ground force; land force; army

陆军武官　lùjūn wǔguān　military attaché

陆离　lùlí　varicoloured: 光怪陆离 guāngguài-lùlí

陆连岛　lùliándǎo　land-tied island; tombolo

陆龙卷　lùlóngjuǎn　*meteorol.*　tornado; landspout

陆路　lùlù　land route: 走～ travel by land / ～交通 overland communication; land communication

陆棚　lùpéng　same as 大陆架 dàlùjià

陆生动物　lùshēng dòngwù　terrestrial animal

陆台　lùtái　tableland; table

陆相　lùxiàng　*geol.*　land facies

陆相沉积　lùxiàng chénjī　*geol.*　continental deposit

陆续　lùxù　*adv.*　one after another; in succession: 代表们～到达。 The delegates arrived one after another.

陆运　lùyùn　land transportation

陆战队　lùzhànduì　marine corps; marines

录（録）　lù　① record; write down; copy: 抄录 chāolù / 记录 jìlù ② choose; employ; hire: 录用 lùyòng ③ tape-record: 报告已经 ～下来了。 The speech has been tape-recorded. / 你给我～盘磁带，好吗? Would you please copy a tape for me? ④ record;

register; collection: 语录 yǔlù ／回忆录 huíyìlù

录放 lù-fàng　record and play back

录供 lùgòng　*leg.*　take down a confession or testimony during an interrogation

录取 lùqǔ　enroll; recruit; admit: ～新生五百名 enroll 500 students

录取通知书 lùqǔ tōngzhīshū　admission notice

录事 lùshì　*old*　copyist

录像 lùxiàng　to videotape; to video: 他为婚礼录了像。 He videotaped (*or* videoed) the wedding ceremony.

录像带 lùxiàngdài　① videotape ② video cassette ③ a videotape recording

录像机 lùxiàngjī　video recorder; videotape recorder; video

录音 lùyīn　① tape-record (sound); record; tape: 我去～去。 I'm going to do some recording. ／他的讲话已经录了音。 His speech has been recorded. ② sound-recording: 磁带～ tape recording ／放～ play back the recording

录音报告 lùyīn bàogào　tape-recorded speech

录音打字 lùyīn dǎzì　audiotyping

录音带 lùyīndài　magnetic tape; tape

录音机 lùyīnjī　tape recorder; cassette recorder; recorder

录音胶片 lùyīn jiāopiàn　recording film

录音摄影机 lùyīn shèyǐngjī　sound camera

录音室 lùyīnshì　recording room

录用 lùyòng　employ; take sb. on the staff: 这家公司从几百名应试者中～了五人。 The company took on five out of several hundred candidates.

赂

赂 lù　*formal*　give costly presents; bribe: 贿赂 huìlù

赂遗 lùwèi　*formal*　① give costly presents; bribe ② costly presents given as bribes; bribes: 广收～ take bribes from many people

鹿

鹿 lù　deer: 公～ stag; buck／母～ doe／小～ fawn

鹿角 lùjiǎo　① deerhorn; antler ② another name for 鹿砦 lùzhài

鹿角菜 lùjiǎocài　*bot.*　siliquose pelvetia (*Pelvetia siliquosa*)

鹿角胶 lùjiǎojiāo　*Chin. med.*　deerhorn glue

鹿圈 lùjuàn　deer enclosure; deer pen

鹿皮 lùpí　deerskin

鹿茸 lùróng　*Chin. med.*　pilose antler (of a young stag)

鹿肉 lùròu　venison

鹿死谁手 lù sǐ shuí shǒu　at whose hand will the deer die—who will win the prize; who will gain supremacy: 不知～。 It's hard to tell who will emerge victor.

鹿苑 lùyuàn　deer park

鹿砦 lùzhài　(also 鹿寨 lùzhài) *mil.*　abatis

绿

绿 lù　same as 绿 lǜ, limited to use in the following ——see also lǜ

绿林 lùlín　the greenwood—brigands; outlaws

绿林好汉 lùlín hǎohàn　greenwood hero—brigand; outlaw

绿林起义 Lùlín Qǐyì　the Lulin Uprising (A.D.17)

绿营 lùyíng　(in the Qing Dynasty) green camps (i. e. Chinese troops identified by green banners, as distinguished from Manchu troops identified by white, yellow, red, and blue banners)

禄

禄 lù　official's salary in feudal China; emolument: 俸禄 fēnglù

禄蠹 lùdù　*formal*　sinecurist

禄位 lùwèi　official rank and salary

碌

碌 lù　① (of a person) commonplace; mediocre: 庸碌 yōnglù ② busy: 忙碌 mánglù ——see also liù

碌碌 lùlù　① mediocre; commonplace: 碌碌无能 lùlù wúnéng ② busy with miscellaneous work: ～半生 plod away for half a lifetime

碌碌无能 lùlù wúnéng　devoid of ability; incompetent; mediocre

碌碌无为 lùlù wúwéi　lead a vain and humdrum life

路

路 lù　① road; path; way: 新开～ a new road／上山的～ a path up the mountain ② journey; distance: ～很远。 It's a long way.／一小时走二十里～ cover 20 *li* an hour ③ way; means: 我实在没～可走了。 I'm really at a dead end. ④ sequence; line; logic: 思路 sīlù ⑤ region; district: 外～人 nonlocal people／南～货 southern products ⑥ route: 三～进军 advance along three routes／七～公共汽车 No. 7 bus ⑦ sort; grade; class: 这一～人 this sort of people／哪一～病？ What kind of disease is this？／纸有好几～。 There are several kinds of paper.／二三～角色 a second- or third-class role ⑧ (Lù) a surname

路拌 lùbàn　road mix

路拌路面 lùbàn lùmiàn　road-mixed pavement

路毙 lùbì　same as 路倒儿 lùdǎor

路标 lùbiāo　① road sign ② *mil.*　route marking; route sign

路不拾遗 lù bù shí yí　same as 道不拾遗 dào bù shí yí

路程 lùchéng　distance travelled; journey: 三天～ a three days' journey／走了五百里的～ have covered a distance of 500 *li*

路单 lùdān　① same as 路条 lùtiáo ② the transport record of a lorry

路倒儿 lùdǎor　the body of a person who has dropped dead by the roadside

路道 lùdào　*dial.*　① way; approach: 他人倒聪明，就是～没有走对。 He's quite intelligent, but he doesn't have a correct approach to things. ② behaviour: 此人～不正。 The person's behaviour is questionable.

路德宗 Lùdézōng　Lutheranism; the Lutheran Church

路灯 lùdēng　street lamp; road lamp

路堤 lùdī　embankment

路段 lùduàn　a section of a highway or railway

路费 lùfèi　travelling expenses

路风 lùfēng　work style of the railway workers; quality of the railway service

路轨 lùguǐ　① rail ② track

路过 lùguò　pass by or through (a place): 他每次～总要来看望他的老战友。 Every time he passes by, he drops in to see his old comrades-in-arms.／从天津到上海，～济南 pass through Jinan en route from Tianjin to Shanghai

路基 lùjī　roadbed; bed

路祭 lùjì　(in former times) offer sacrifices by the roadside as a funeral procession passes

路见不平，拔刀相助 lù jiàn bù píng, bá dāo xiāng zhù　see injustice on the road and draw one's sword to help the victim—take up the cudgels for the injured party: 他生得膂力过人，武艺出众，一生豪侠好义，真正～。（《初刻拍案惊奇》） He had remarkable strength, excelled in military arts, and had always championed those in distress.

路劫 lùjié　highway robbery; holdup; mugging

路警 lùjǐng　railway police

路径 lùjìng　① route; way: ～不熟 not know one's way around ② method; ways and means: 成功的～ the road to success

路局 lùjú　railway administration; road bureau

路口 lùkǒu　crossing; intersection

路矿 lùkuàng　railways and mines

路面 lùmiàn　road surface; pavement: 柔(刚)性～ flexible (rigid) pavement

路牌 lùpái　street nameplate

路卡 lùqiǎ　an outpost of the tax office

路签 lùqiān　train-staff; staff

路堑 lùqiàn　cutting (for a railway or highway)

路人 lùrén　passerby; stranger: 视同路人 shì tóng lùrén

路容 lùróng　the appearance of a street (with regard to the road surface, greenery, etc.)

路上 lùshang　① on the road: ～停着一辆车。There is a car parking on the road. ② on the way; en route: ～不要耽搁。Don't waste any time on the way. / 我在回来的～碰见了他。I came across him on my way back. / 由于～的种种耽搁，我们比原计划迟到了两天。Owing to various delays en route, we arrived two days behind schedule. / ～要用的东西放在这个包里。Put the things you'll need for the journey in this bag.

路数 lùshù　① same as 路子 lùzi ② a movement in martial arts: 击剑的～ thrusts in fencing ③ exact details; inside story

路条 lùtiáo　travel permit; pass

路头 lùtou　inf. ① road; way: 你对这一带的～熟不熟? Do you know the way around here? ② social connections; pull: ～多 have many social connections; have a lot of pull

路途 lùtú　① road; way: 他熟悉这一带的～。He knows the roads in this district quite well. ② way; journey: ～遥远 a long way to go; far away

路线 lùxiàn　① route; itinerary: 旅行的～ the route of a journey / 按规定的～进行越野比赛 run the cross-country race over a set course ② line: ～错误 errors of line

路线斗争 lùxiàn dòuzhēng　struggle between two lines; two-line struggle: ～觉悟 political awareness of the two-line struggle

路遥知马力, 日久见人心 lù yáo zhī mǎlì, rìjiǔ jiàn rénxīn　as distance tests a horse's strength, so time reveals a person's heart

路椅 lùyǐ　roadside bench

路引 lùyǐn　old　pass; travel permit

路障 lùzhàng　roadblock; barricade: 设置～ set up roadblocks (or barricades)

路政 lùzhèng　road administration

路子 lùzi　① way; approach; means: 寻找解决问题的～ seek ways to solve the problem / ～不对等于白费劲儿。A wrong approach means a waste of effort. ② social connections; pull: ～宽 have many social connections; have a lot of pull / 找～ try to secure help from potential backers

漉　lù　seep through; filter

漉网 lùwǎng　vat-net (used in paper making)

辘　lù　see below

辘轳 lùlu　well-pulley; windlass; winch

辘辘 lù-lù　onom. the rumbling sound of cart wheels: 牛车发出笨重的～声。The ox cart rumbled down the road.

戮¹　lù　kill; slay: 杀戮 shālù

戮²(勠)　lù　formal　unite; join

戮力 lùlì　formal　join forces; join hands: 天下共苦秦久矣, 相与～击秦。(《史记》) The world suffered long under Qin till all the states joined forces to attack it.

戮力同心 lùlì tóngxīn　unite in a concerted effort; make concerted efforts

璐　lù　formal　fine jade

簏　lù　① bamboo trunk ② bamboo basket

簏籔 lùsù　liter.　hanging down; drooping

鹭　lù　egret; heron: 牛背～ cattle egret / 池～ pond heron

鹭鸶 lùsī　egret

麓　lù　formal　the foot of a hill or mountain: 华山北～ at the northern foot of Huashan Mountain

露¹　lù　① dew ② beverage distilled from flowers, fruit or leaves; syrup: 果子露 guǒzilù

露²　lù　show; reveal; betray: ～出原形 reveal one's true colours; betray oneself / 她脸上～出了笑容。A smile appeared on her face.
——see also lòu

露布 lùbù　① arch. war proclamation ② arch. announcement of victory ③ an unsealed imperial edict or memorial to the throne ④ dial. notice; bulletin; playbill

露地 lùdì　① formal　open country ② an open or uncovered vegetable plot: ～育苗 raise seedlings on open plots ③ (of roots, etc.) show above the ground

露点 lùdiǎn　dew point: 温度～差 dew-point deficit

露点湿度表 lùdiǎn shīdùbiǎo　dew-point hygrometer

露骨 lùgǔ　thinly veiled; undisguised; barefaced: 说得十分～ speak undisguisedly; speak in no equivocal terms / ～地干涉别国内政 flagrantly interfere in the internal affairs of another country

露光计 lùguāngjì　photog. exposure meter

露脊鲸 lùjǐjīng　right whale

露酒 lùjiǔ　alcoholic drink mixed with fruit juice

露水 lùshuǐ　inf. dew

露水夫妻 lùshuǐ fūqī　man and woman living together without being married

露水珠儿 lùshuǐzhūr　inf. dewdrop

露宿 lùsù　sleep in the open: ～街头 sleep in the street

露宿风餐 lùsù-fēngcān　same as 风餐露宿 fēngcān-lùsù

露台 lùtái　dial. flat roof (for drying clothes, etc.)

露天 lùtiān　in the open (air); outdoors: 今晚电影在～演。The film will be shown in the open air tonight.

露天电影 lùtiān diànyǐng　open-air cinema

露天堆栈 lùtiān duīzhàn　open-air repository; open-air depot

露天剧场 lùtiān jùchǎng　open-air theatre

露天开采 lùtiān kāicǎi　opencast mining

露天矿 lùtiānkuàng　opencut; opencast; open-pit; strip mine

露天煤矿 lùtiān méikuàng　opencut coal mine

露头 lùtóu　min. outcrop; outcropping ——see also lòutóu

露头角 lù tóujiǎo　(of a young person) beginning to show ability or talent; budding

露演 lùyǎn　(of a play) be staged: 下月将有一出新戏～。A new play will be staged next month.

露营 lùyíng　camp (out); encamp; bivouac

露珠 lùzhū　dewdrop

lu

轳(轤)　lu　see 辘轳 lùlu

碌　lu　see 碌碡 pǔlu

lǘ

驴(驢) lǘ donkey; ass

驴唇不对马嘴 lǘchún bù duì mǎzuǐ donkeys' lips don't match horses' jaws—incongruous; irrelevant: 这个比方有点～。 The analogy is rather farfetched. / 他的回答～。 His answer is irrelevant. *or* His answer is beside the point.

驴打滚 lǘdǎgǔn a form of usury in the old society, the borrower having to pay interest on interest; snowballing usury

驴肝肺 lǘgānfèi see 好心当作驴肝肺 hǎoxīn dàngzuò lǘgānfèi

驴脸 lǘliǎn *derog.* a donkey's face—a long face

驴骡 lǘluó hinny

驴鸣犬吠 lǘmíng-quǎnfèi asses braying and dogs barking—a poor style of writing

驴年马月 lǘnián-mǎyuè year of the donkey and month of the horse—a time that will never come (as there is no such year or month in the Chinese calendar)

驴皮胶 lǘpíjiāo *Chin. med.* donkey-hide gelatin

驴皮影 lǘpíyǐng *dial.* leather-silhouette show; shadow play

驴子 lǘzi *dial.* donkey; ass

闾 lǘ ① the gate of (*or* entrance to) an alley: 倚～而望 waiting at the entrance to the alley (for the return of one's son) ② alleys and lanes; neighbourhood ③ a neighbourhood of 25 families in ancient China

闾里 lǘlǐ *formal* native village; home town

闾巷 lǘxiàng *formal* alley; lane; alleyway

闾阎 lǘyán *arch.* a neighbourhood of commoners; the common people

闾左 lǘzuǒ *arch.* a poor neighbourhood; poor people: 陈胜、吴广起于～。 Chen Sheng and Wu Guang rose up from squalid poverty.

桐 lǘ see 棕榈 zōnglǘ

lǚ

吕 lǚ ① see 律吕 lǜlǚ ② (Lǚ) a surname

吕剧 lǚjù Lü opera (of Shandong Province)

吕宋 Lǚsòng Luzon

吕宋烟 lǚsòngyān Luzon cigar; cigar

侣 lǚ companion; associate: 伴侣 bànlǚ / 情侣 qínglǚ

侣伴 lǚbàn same as 伴侣 bànlǚ

旅¹ lǚ ① travel; stay away from home: 旅居 lǚjū ② same as 稆 lǚ

旅² lǚ ① *mil.* brigade ② troops; force: 军～之事 military affairs ③ together: 旅进旅退 lǚjìn-lǚtuì

旅伴 lǚbàn travelling companion; fellow traveller

旅差费 lǚchāifèi travelling expenses on a business trip

旅程 lǚchéng route; itinerary; journey: 登上～ start on a journey

旅次 lǚcì a stopping place on one's journey

旅店 lǚdiàn inn

旅费 lǚfèi travelling expenses

旅馆 lǚguǎn inn; hotel

旅进旅退 lǚjìn-lǚtuì always follow the steps of others, forward or backward—have no views of one's own

旅居 lǚjū live away from one's native place; sojourn: ～海外的侨胞 Chinese nationals residing abroad / 这几张照片是我～成都时照的。 These pictures were taken during my residence in Chengdu.

旅客 lǚkè hotel guest; traveller; passenger: 过往～ travellers passing through; transients

旅客登记簿 lǚkè dēngjìbù hotel register

旅社 lǚshè hotel (often used in hotel names)

旅舍 lǚshè *formal* hotel

旅途 lǚtú journey; trip: ～见闻 what one sees and hears during a trip; traveller's notes / 祝你～愉快。 Have a pleasant journey. *or* Bon voyage.

旅行 lǚxíng travel; journey; tour: 他去～去了。 He's going travelling. / 今年夏天我们要去中国～。 This summer we're going to take a trip to China. / 作长途～ make a long journey / 组织外国留学生到南方～ arrange a tour to the South for foreign students

旅行包 lǚxíngbāo travelling bag

旅行车 lǚxíngchē station wagon

旅行袋 lǚxíngdài travelling bag

旅行剪 lǚxíngjiǎn folding scissors

旅行闹钟 lǚxíng nàozhōng travelling clock

旅行社 lǚxíngshè travel service; travel agency

旅行团 lǚxíngtuán touring party

旅行证 lǚxíngzhèng travel certificate

旅行支票 lǚxíng zhīpiào traveller's cheque

旅行指南 lǚxíng zhǐnán guidebook

旅游 lǚyóu tour; tourism

旅游鞋 lǚyóuxié sneakers; walking shoes

旅游业 lǚyóuyè tourist industry; tourism

旅长 lǚzhǎng brigade commander

旅资 lǚzī travelling expenses

捋 lǚ smooth out with the fingers; stroke: ～胡子 stroke one's beard / 把纸～平 smooth out a piece of paper ——see also luō

铝 lǚ *chem.* aluminium (Al)

铝箔 lǚbó aluminium foil

铝合金 lǚhéjīn aluminium alloy

铝胶 lǚjiāo alumina gel

铝热剂 lǚrèjì thermite: ～燃烧弹 thermite bomb

铝土矿 lǚtǔkuàng bauxite

稆(穭) lǚ self-sown: ～生 self-sown

偻¹(僂) lǚ *formal* hunchbacked; bent: 伛偻 yǔlǚ

偻²(僂) lǚ *formal* instantly; directly; at once: 不能一～指 unable to point out straight away ——see also lóu

屡(屢) lǚ *adv.* time and again; repeatedly: ～战～胜 have fought many battles and won every one of them; score one victory after another / ～遭打击 repeatedly came under attack

屡次 lǚcì *adv.* time and again; repeatedly: 他～打破全国纪录。 He repeatedly broke the national record. / 我～告诉过你，你总是不听。 I've told you time and again, but you never listened.

屡次三番 lǚcì-sānfān again and again; over and over again; many times: 我～提醒他要谨慎。 I've reminded him over and over again that he should be cautious.

屡见不鲜 lǚ jiàn bù xiān common occurrence; nothing new: 考试作弊～。 Cheating in examinations is a matter of common occurrence.

屡教不改 lǚ jiào bù gǎi refuse to mend one's ways despite repeated disciplinary action

屡屡 lǚlǚ *adv.* time and again; repeatedly: 他写这篇回忆录的时候，～搁笔沉思。While writing his reminiscences, again and again he laid down his pen and fell into meditation.

屡试不爽 lǚ shì bù shuǎng put to repeated tests and proved right: 这种新杀虫药效果良好，～。This new insecticide has proved effective every time it's been used.

缕（縷）

lǚ ① thread: 千丝万缕 qiānsīwànlǚ ② detailed; in detail: 缕陈 lǚchén ③ *m.* wisp; strand; lock: 一～烟 a wisp (or curl) of smoke / 一～麻 a strand of hemp / 一～头发 a lock of hair

缕陈 lǚchén *formal* state in detail (esp. when reporting to a superior)

缕缕 lǚlǚ continuously: 村中炊烟～上升。Wisps of smoke rose continuously from the village chimneys.

缕述 lǚshù state in detail; give all the details; go into details (or particulars): 为了节省篇幅，恕不一一～。For economy of space, I shall not go into details.

缕析 lǚxī make a detailed analysis: 条分缕析 tiáofēnlǚxī

褛（褸）

lǚ see 褴褛 lánlǚ

膂

lǚ *formal* backbone

膂力 lǚlì muscular strength; physical strength; brawn

膂力过人 lǚlì guòrén possessing extraordinary muscular (or physical) strength

履

lǚ ① shoe: 革履 gélǚ ② tread on; walk on: 履险如夷 lǚ xiǎn rú yí ③ footstep: 步履 bùlǚ ④ carry out; honour; fulfil: 履约 lǚyuē

履穿踵决 lǚchuān-zhǒngjué shoes worn-out and heels chapped—wretchedly poor

履带 lǚdài caterpillar tread; track: ～式拖拉机 caterpillar (or crawler) tractor

履端 lǚduān *formal* ① the beginning of the year; the first day of the first lunar month ② the beginning of an emperor's reign ③ beginning

履历 lǚlì ① one's personal record (of education, work experience, and attainments); antecedents ② (British) *curriculum vitae* (cv); (American) *résumé*

履历表 lǚlìbiǎo (British) *curriculum vitae* (cv); (American) *résumé*

履险如夷 lǚ xiǎn rú yí go over a dangerous pass as if walking on level ground—cope with a crisis without difficulty

履新 lǚxīn *formal* ① celebrate the New Year ② take up a new post

履行 lǚxíng perform; fulfil; carry out: ～诺言 keep one's word; fulfil (or carry out) one's promise / ～合同 fulfil a contract / ～手续 go through the procedures / ～职责 do one's duty

履约 lǚyuē *formal* keep a promise, pledge, agreement, appointment, etc.

lǜ

律

lǜ ① law; statute; rule: 定律 dìnglǜ / 规律 guīlǜ ② pitch-pipes used in ancient music ③ short for 律诗 lǜshī ④ *formal* restrain; keep under control: ～己甚严 be strict with oneself; exercise strict self-discipline

律动 lǜdòng regular movements: 心脏的～ regular heartbeats

律令 lǜlìng laws and decrees; laws and statutes

律吕 lǜlǚ ① a series of 12 bamboo pitch-pipes used in ancient music (the odd-numbered ones being called lǜ 律，the even-numbered ones lǚ 吕) ② *mus.* temperament

律师 lǜshī lawyer; (British) barrister; (British) solicitor; (American) attorney: 我想请个～来打这场官司。I'm trying to employ a lawyer to handle the case.

律师事务所 lǜshī shìwùsuǒ lawyer's office

律诗 lǜshī regulated verse (a poem of eight lines of five or seven characters or syllables—each line set down in accordance with a strict tonal pattern and rhyme scheme—with parallel structure in the middle, or second and third, couplets): 五言～ pentasyllabic (or five-syllable) regulated verse / 七言～ septasyllabic (or seven-syllable) regulated verse

虑（慮）

lǜ ① consider; ponder; think over: 考虑 kǎolǜ ② concern; be anxious; worry: 不足为～ give no cause for anxiety

率

lǜ rate; proportion; ratio: 人口增长～ the rate of population growth / 圆周～ the ratio of the circumference of a circle to its diameter ——see also shuài

绿

lǜ green: ～叶 green leaves / 书皮儿是～的。The book cover is green. ——see also lù

绿宝石 lǜbǎoshí emerald

绿茶 lǜchá green tea

绿葱葱 lǜcōngcōng green and luxuriant

绿灯 lǜdēng ① green light (a traffic signal) ② green light (fig.): 开绿灯 kāi lǜdēng

绿地 lǜdì greenery patches (in a town or city)

绿豆 lǜdòu mung bean; green gram

绿豆糕 lǜdòugāo a pastry made of mung bean flour

绿豆芽 lǜdòuyá mung bean sprouts

绿矾 lǜfán *chem.* green vitriol

绿肥 lǜféi green manure

绿肥作物 lǜféi zuòwù green manure crop

绿化 lǜhuà make (a place) green by planting trees, flowers, etc.; afforest: ～山区 afforest the mountain district / ～城市 plant trees in and around the city / 植树造林，～祖国。Plant trees everywhere and make the country green.

绿化地带 lǜhuà dìdài greenbelt

绿蓝色 lǜlánsè turquoise (blue)

绿篱 lǜlí hedgerow; hedge

绿帘石 lǜliánshí epidote

绿帽子 lǜmàozi (also 绿头巾 lǜtóujīn) a green hat or turban—the state of being a cuckold: 戴～ be a cuckold

绿内障 lǜnèizhàng another name for 青光眼 qīngguāngyǎn

绿泥石 lǜníshí chlorite

绿茸茸 lǜróngróng lush green: ～的稻田 a lush green rice paddy

绿色 lǜsè green colour

绿色革命 lǜsè gémìng the Green Revolution

绿色食品 lǜsè shípǐn green food

绿色植物 lǜsè zhíwù green plants

绿生生 lǜshēngshēng fresh and green: ～的菠菜 fresh, green spinach

绿水青山 lǜshuǐ-qīngshān same as 青山绿水 qīngshān-lǜshuǐ

绿松石 lǜsōngshí turquoise

绿头鸭 lǜtóuyā mallard

绿茵 lǜyīn ① a carpet of green grass; greensward ② (used in) ～场 football field

绿茵茵 lǜyīnyīn green; verdant: ～的草原 verdant grasslands

绿荫 lǜyìn green shade (of trees): ～蔽日。The greenery shut out the sun.

绿莹莹 lǜyíngyíng glittering green: ～的宝石 a glittering green stone／秧苗在雨中显得～的。In the rain the rice seedlings were a glistening green.

绿油油 lǜyōuyōu fresh green: ～的麦苗 fresh green wheat seedlings／我们所到之处，都是～的田野。We passed miles and miles of fresh green countryside.

绿藻 lǜzǎo green alga

绿洲 lǜzhōu oasis

绿柱石 lǜzhùshí beryl

氯

lǜ *chem.* chlorine (Cl)

氯丙嗪 lǜbǐngqín chlorpromazine; wintermine

氯丁橡胶 lǜdīng xiàngjiāo chloroprene rubber

氯仿 lǜfǎng *chem.* chloroform

氯化铵 lǜhuà'ǎn ammonium chloride

氯化钾 lǜhuàjiǎ potassium chloride

氯化钠 lǜhuànà sodium chloride

氯化物 lǜhuàwù chloride (e.g. 氯化钠 sodium chloride)

氯喹 lǜkuí *pharm.* chloroquine

氯磷定 lǜlíndìng *pharm.* pyraloxime methylchloride

氯纶 lǜlún *text.* polyvinyl chloride fibre

氯霉素 lǜméisù chloromycetin; chloramphenicol

氯气 lǜqì chlorine

氯噻酮 lǜsāitóng *pharm.* chlorthalidone

氯酸 lǜsuān chloric acid

氯酸钾 lǜsuānjiǎ potassium chlorate

葎

lǜ see below

葎草 lǜcǎo scandent hop (*Humulus scandens*)

滤（濾）

lǜ strain; filter: 咖啡得～一～。The coffee must be strained.／把水～一下再喝。Filter the water before you drink it.

滤波器 lǜbōqì *elec.* wave filter: 带通～ band-pass filter／高通～ high-pass filter

滤过性病毒 lǜguòxìng bìngdú filterable virus

滤器 lǜqì filter: 粗～ strainer

滤色镜 lǜsèjìng *photog.* (colour) filter

滤液 lǜyè filtrate

滤纸 lǜzhǐ filter paper: 定量（定性）～ quantitative (qualitative) filter paper

luán

峦（巒）

luán *formal* ① low but steep and pointed hill ② mountains in a range

娈（孌）

luán *liter.* pretty; handsome

娈童 luántóng ① a handsome boy ② kept man; gigolo

孪（孿）

luán *formal* twin: ～子 twin boys

孪生 luánshēng twin: ～姐妹 twin sisters／～兄弟 twin brothers／～子 twin boys

栾（欒）

luán ① goldenrain tree ② (Luán) a surname

挛（攣）

luán contraction: 痉挛 jìngluán

挛缩 luánsuō contracture

鸾（鸞）

luán a fabulous bird related to the phoenix

鸾凤 luánfèng ① a married couple ② distinguished talents

鸾凤和鸣 luánfèng hé míng be blessed with conjugal felicity; be a happy couple

鸾飘凤泊 luánpiāo-fèngbó ① free and powerful calligraphic style ② husband and wife separated ③ men of worth neglected

鸾翔凤集 luánxiáng-fèngjí a gathering of talented men

鸾翔凤翥 luánxiáng-fèngzhù flamboyant calligraphy

脔（臠）

luán *formal* a small slice of meat

脔割 luángē *formal* slice up; carve up

圞（圝、圞）

luán see 团圞 tuánluán

銮（鑾）

luán a small tinkling bell

銮驾 luánjià imperial carriage

銮铃 luánlíng tinkling bells on a carriage

銮舆 luányú imperial carriage

luǎn

卵

luǎn ovum; egg; spawn

卵白 luǎnbái white of an egg; albumen

卵巢 luǎncháo ovary

卵黄 luǎnhuáng yolk

卵磷脂 luǎnlínzhī lecithin

卵生 luǎnshēng oviparity

卵生动物 luǎnshēng dòngwù oviparous animal; ovipara

卵石 luǎnshí cobble; pebble; shingle

卵胎生 luǎntāishēng ovoviviparity

卵胎生动物 luǎntāishēng dòngwù ovoviviparous animal; ovovivipara

卵细胞 luǎnxìbāo egg cell; ovum

卵翼 luǎnyì *derog.* cover with wings as in brooding; shield: 在某人～之下 under the aegis of sb.; be shielded by sb.

卵用鸡 luǎnyòngjī a chicken raised for egg production (e.g. 来亨鸡 the Leghorn chicken); layer

卵子 luǎnzǐ ovum; egg

luàn

乱（亂）

luàn ① in disorder; in a mess; in confusion: 车站很～。The station was in a state of disorder.／屋里很～，请你把它收拾一下。The room is in a mess; please tidy it up.／线～了。The thread is tangled.／这篇稿子太～，是不是重抄一下？The manuscript's too messy. How about copying it out?／这里太～，找个安静点儿的地方谈谈。It's too noisy here; let's find a quieter place to chat. ② disorder; upheaval; riot; unrest; turmoil: 安史之～ The Rebellion of An Lushan and Shi Siming (755-763) ③ throw into disorder; confuse; mix up: 君其遗之女乐，以～其政。（《韩非子》）You might send him some women musicians to throw his rule into disorder. ④ in a confused state of mind; in a turmoil: 我心里很～。My mind is in a turmoil. ⑤ indiscriminate; random; arbitrary: 各种木料～堆在一起。Logs and planks of all shapes and sizes were jumbled together.／他在墙上～写。He scribbled on the wall.／～跑 run all over the place; dash about／～花钱 spend money extravagantly／～讲一气 speak indiscreetly; make irresponsible remarks／～作决定 make an arbitrary decision／给人～扣帽子 slap political labels on people right and left／～搞男女关系 en-

gage in improper sexual relationships ⑥ illicit sexual relationships: 太子爽知之，念后数恶己无已时，欲与～以止其口。《史记》Crown Prince Shuang knew what the queen was planning and considered that there would be no end to her slanders if he did not do something. He therefore decided to commit adultery with her in order to silence her.

乱兵 luànbīng ① mutinous soldiers ② totally undisciplined troops

乱臣 luànchén treacherous minister; rebellious subject

乱臣贼子 luànchén-zéizǐ rebellious subjects and undutiful sons; traitors and usurpers; disloyal followers: 孔子成《春秋》，而～惧。《孟子》Confucius completed the *Spring and Autumn Annals* and struck terror into the hearts of rebellious subjects and undutiful sons.

乱点鸳鸯 luàn diǎn yuān·yāng ① misarrangement of matches through wrong identification of couples ② misarrangement of personnel

乱纷纷 luànfēnfēn disorderly; confused; chaotic: ～的人群 a tumultuous crowd / 他心里～的。He's rather disturbed.

乱坟岗 luànféngāng unmarked common graves; unmarked burial-mounds

乱哄哄 luànhōnghōng in noisy disorder; in a hubbub; tumultuous; in an uproar: 大家听到这个消息，～地议论起来。The news set them arguing heatedly among themselves.

乱乎 luànhu (also 乱糊 luànhu) *inf.* in confusion; in chaos: 这里已经够～的了，你别再来添乱啦。Things here are in a mess already. Don't make it worse.

乱来 luànlái act foolishly or recklessly

乱了营 luànle yíng *dial.* be thrown into confusion; be in disarray

乱离 luànlí be separated by war; be rendered homeless by war

乱伦 luànlún commit incest

乱麻麻 luànmāmā in a mess; very confused

乱蓬蓬 luànpēngpēng dishevelled; tangled; jumbled: ～的头发 dishevelled hair; tangled hair / ～的茅草 a jumbled mass of reeds

乱七八糟 luànqībāzāo at sixes and sevens; in great disorder; in an awful mess: 他的屋子～的。His room was in great disorder. / 我心里～的，这会儿不想吃。I don't feel like eating—my mind's in a whirl. / 学校办得～。The school is being run in a chaotic manner.

乱世 luànshì troubled times; turbulent days

乱世英雄 luànshì yīngxióng heroes in times of disorder

乱说 luànshuō speak carelessly or foolishly; talk in a scatterbrained way; talk nonsense; make irresponsible remarks: 别～。Don't talk nonsense. / 当面不说，背后～ gossip behind people's backs but say nothing to their faces

乱说乱动 luànshuō-luàndòng talk and act in a wholly irresponsible way; be unruly in word and deed

乱弹 luàntán a general name for opera styles other than 昆腔 kūnqiāng and 弋阳腔 yìyángqiāng during the Qianlong and Jiaqing periods of the Qing Dynasty (e.g. the clapper opera 梆子腔 was called *luantan*)

乱弹琴 luàntánqín act or talk like a fool; talk nonsense: 这简直是～。That's a lot of nonsense. *or* It's downright nonsense.

乱套 luàntào *dial.* muddle things up; turn things upside down: 要是各行其是，那就～了。If everyone acts as he pleases, everything will be in a muddle.

乱腾腾 luàntēngtēng confused; upset: 心里～的 feel all hot and bothered

乱腾 luànteng confused; disorderly; restless

乱杂 luànzá same as 杂乱 záluàn

乱葬岗子 luànzànggǎngzi unmarked common graves; unmarked burial-mounds

乱糟糟 luànzāozāo ① chaotic; in a mess: 屋子里～的。The room is in a mess. ② confused; perturbed: 心里～的 feel very perturbed

乱真 luànzhēn ① (of fakes) look genuine: 他临摹的画足以～。The copy he made of the painting can pass for an authentic. ② *phys.* spurious: ～放电 spurious discharge / ～脉冲 spurious pulse

乱子 luànzi disturbance; trouble; disorder

lüè

掠 lüè ① plunder; pillage; sack: 我国许多珍贵文物被帝国主义～走了。Many of our cultural treasures have been plundered by imperialists. ② sweep past; brush past; graze; skim over: 凉风～面。A cool breeze brushed my face. / 探照灯～过夜空。The searchlights swept the night sky. / 燕子～水而过。The swallows skimmed over the water. / 她嘴角上～过一丝微笑。A faint smile flickered across her lips. ③ beat (with a stick or whip): 拷掠 kǎolüè

掠地飞行 lüèdì fēixíng minimum-altitude flight; treetop flight; hedgehopping

掠夺 lüèduó plunder; rob; pillage: 帝国主义～成性。Imperialism is predatory by nature. / ～别国领土 seize the territory of another country

掠美 lüèměi (also 掠人之美 lüè rén zhī měi) claim credit due to others: 这是她的高见，我不敢～。It was her idea. I can't claim credit for it.

掠取 lüèqǔ seize; grab; plunder: ～别国的资源 plunder the resources of other countries

略¹(畧) lüè ① brief; sketchy: ～述大意 give a brief account / 这个提纲写得太～了。This outline is rather too rough. / ～读 a cursory reading ② *adv.* slightly; a little; somewhat: ～加修改 make some slight changes; edit slightly / ～有所闻 have heard a little about the matter / ～有出入 vary slightly; there's a slight discrepancy ③ summary; brief account; outline: 史略 shǐlüè / 事略 shìlüè ④ omit; delete; leave out: ～去不提 make no mention of; leave out altogether / ～去细节 leave out the details

略²(畧) lüè strategy; plan; scheme: 方略 fānglüè / 策略 cèlüè

略³(畧) lüè capture; seize: 侵略 qīnlüè / 攻城略地 gōngchéng-lüèdì

略称 lüèchēng abbreviation; shortened form

略见一斑 lüè jiàn yī bān catch a glimpse of; get a rough idea of

略略 lüèlüè *adv.* slightly; briefly: 关于那个问题他只～说了几句。He touched only briefly on that question. / 微风吹来，湖面上～起了点波纹。The lake rippled gently in the breeze.

略胜一筹 lüè shèng yī chóu a notch (*or* cut) above; slightly better

略识之无 lüè shí zhī-wú know only a few simple characters

略图 lüètú sketch map; sketch

略微 lüèwēi *adv.* slightly; a little; somewhat: ～有点感冒 have a slight cold; have a touch of flu / 我脸擦破了，～流了点血。I got a scratch on my face and it bled a little.

略为 lüèwéi *adv.* slightly; a little; somewhat: 她～定了定神。She calmed down a little.

略语 lüèyǔ abbreviation; shortening (e.g. 土改 for 土地改革,扫盲 for 扫除文盲,沧桑 for 沧海桑田)

略知一二 lüè zhī yī-èr have only a smattering of; know only a little

lūn

抡(掄) lūn brandish; swing: ～刀 brandish a sword／～起大铁锤 swing a sledgehammer ——see also lún

lún

仑(侖) lún formal logical sequence; coherence

伦(倫) lún ① human relations (esp. as conceived by feudal ethics): 天伦 tiānlún ② logic; order: 伦次 lúncì ③ peer; match: 绝伦 juélún

伦巴 lúnbā rumba (a dance)

伦比 lúnbǐ formal rival; equal: 史无～ unrivalled (or peerless, unequalled) in history

伦常 lúncháng feudal order of importance or seniority in human relationships

伦次 lúncì coherence; logical sequence: 文笔错杂,毫无～。The writing is tangled, utterly lacking in coherence.

伦敦 Lúndūn London

伦理 lúnlǐ ethics; moral principles

伦理学 lúnlǐxué ethics

伦琴 lúnqín phys. röntgen (or roentgen)

伦琴射线 lúnqín shèxiàn phys. röntgen (or roentgen) rays

论(論) Lún (short for 论语) The Analects of Confucius; The Analects: 上（下）～ The Analects Part One (Two) ——see also lùn

论语 Lúnyǔ The Analects of Confucius; The Analects ——see also 四书 sìshū

沦(淪) lún ① sink: 沉沦 chénlún ② fall; be reduced to: ～于敌手 fall into enemy hands／～为殖民地 be reduced to the status of a colony

沦肌浃髓 lúnjī-jiāsuǐ to the marrow

沦落 lúnluò fall low; come down in the world; be reduced to poverty

沦落街头 lúnluò jiētóu be driven onto the streets (to become a tramp, beggar, etc.); be reduced to beggary, vagrancy, etc.

沦灭 lúnmiè be ruined; be destroyed

沦没 lúnmò ① sink; submerge ② (of humans) die

沦丧 lúnsàng be lost; be ruined: 道德～ decay of morals

沦亡 lúnwáng (of a country) be annexed (or subjugated)

沦陷 lúnxiàn ① (of territory, etc.) be occupied by the enemy; fall into enemy hands ② formal submerge; inundate; flood; drown

沦陷区 lúnxiànqū enemy-occupied area (i.e. an area occupied by the Japanese during the War of Resistance Against Japan)

囵(圇) lún see 囫囵 húlún

纶(綸) lún ① black silk ribbon ② fishing

line ③ synthetic fibre: 锦纶 jǐnlún／涤纶 dílún ——see also guān

纶音 lúnyīn formal imperial edict

岩(崙) lún see 崑岩 Kūnlún

抡(掄) lún formal choose; select: ～才 select men of ability ——see also lūn

轮(輪) lún ① wheel: 十～卡车 ten-wheel truck ② sth. resembling a wheel; disc; ring: 光～ halo ③ steamboat; steamer: 江轮 jiānglún／巨轮 jùlún ④ take turns: 下一个就～到你了。It will be your turn next.／今天～到我值班。It's my turn to be on duty today.／一个人～一天 each person on duty by turns for a day ⑤ m. ⓐ (for the sun, the moon, etc.): 一～红日 a red sun／一～明月 a bright moon ⓑ round: 第一～比赛 the first round of the match／新的一～会谈 a new round of talks

轮班 lúnbān in shifts; in relays; in rotation: ～护理病人 take turns tending the sick

轮拨儿 lúnbōr dial. in shifts; in relays; in rotation: ～守夜 take turns keeping watch at night

轮唱 lúnchàng mus. round

轮齿 lúnchǐ teeth of a cogwheel

轮虫 lúnchóng wheel animalcule; rotifer

轮船 lúnchuán steamer; steamship; steamboat

轮次 lúncì ① order of turns ② number of turns or rounds

轮带 lúndài common name for 轮胎 lúntāi

轮渡 lúndù (steam) ferry

轮番 lúnfān take turns: 我们～给锅炉添煤。We took turns stoking the furnaces.／～轰炸 bomb in waves

轮辐 lúnfú spoke

轮箍 lúngū tyre

轮毂 lúngǔ (wheel) hub; (wheel) boss; nave

轮换 lúnhuàn rotate; take turns: 我们～着照料他。We take turns looking after him.

轮回 lúnhuí Buddhism samsara; transmigration

轮机 lúnjī ① (short for 涡轮机) turbine: 燃气～ combustion gas turbine／冲压空气～ ram-air turbine ② motorship engine; engine

轮机室 lúnjīshì engine room

轮机员 lúnjīyuán engineer

轮机长 lúnjīzhǎng chief engineer

轮奸 lúnjiān (of two or more men) rape a woman in turn; gang-rape

轮距 lúnjù track; tread

轮空 lúnkōng sports bye: 他在第一轮比赛中～。He drew a bye in the first round of the tournament.

轮廓 lúnkuò outline; contour; rough sketch: 先画个～,再画细部。Draw an outline before you fill in the details.／夜幕降临了,但厂房还能看见个～。Night fell, but the outline of the factory buildings was still discernible. or The factory buildings were silhouetted against the growing darkness.／听了汇报后,新来的经理对这个公司的情况有了个～。After hearing the reports from below, the newly-appointed manager got a general picture of the situation in the company.

轮流 lúnliú take turns; do sth. in turn: 我们大家～,好不好?How about our taking turns?／我们～到医院去看他。We'll take turns going to the hospital to see him.／他俩～值夜班。They work on night shifts in turn.

轮牧 lúnmù rotation grazing

轮批 lúnpī take turns in batches; do sth. batch by batch

轮生 lúnshēng bot. verticillate: ～叶 verticillate leaves

轮式拖拉机 lúnshì tuōlājī wheeled tractor

轮胎 lúntāi tyre: 防滑～ antiskid tyre; nonskid tyre／双

层～ two ply tyre／翻制～ retreaded tyre

轮胎帘子线 lúntāi liánzǐxiàn　tyre cord

轮胎压力计 lúntāi yālìjì　tyre pressure gauge

轮替 lúntì　rotate; take turns: ～着休息 have days off by turns

轮辋 lúnwǎng　rim (of a wheel)

轮休 lúnxiū　① (of land) lie fallow in rotation ② have holidays by turns; rotate days off; stagger holidays

轮训 lúnxùn　training in rotation

轮训班 lúnxùnbān　a training class operating on a rotating basis

轮椅 lúnyǐ　wheelchair

轮栽 lúnzāi　same as 轮作 lúnzuò

轮值 lúnzhí　on duty by turns

轮种 lúnzhòng　same as 轮作 lúnzuò

轮轴 lúnzhóu　① *phys.* wheel and axle ② wheel axle

轮转 lúnzhuàn　rotate

轮转印刷机 lúnzhuàn yìnshuājī　rotary press

轮子 lúnzi　wheel

轮作 lúnzuò　crop rotation: 粮棉～ rotation of cereal crops and cotton

lùn

论（論）
lùn　① discuss; talk about; discourse: 讨论 tǎolùn／辩论 biànlùn　② view; opinion; statement: 高论 gāolùn／立论 lìlùn　③ dissertation; essay: 《实践～》 On Practice ④ theory: 进化论 jìnhuàlùn／唯物论 wéiwùlùn　⑤ mention; regard; consider: 别论 biélùn　⑥ decide on; determine: 按质～价 determine the price according to the quality ⑦ *prep.* by (a certain unit of measure); according to (a certain system or principle): 鸡蛋～斤卖。Eggs are sold by the *jin.*／～小时给钱 pay by the hour／～业务, 她比组里其他同志要强些。So far as professional proficiency goes, she is better than the other members of the group.——see also Lún

论辩 lùnbiàn　argue; debate: ～有力。The argument is strong.

论处 lùnchǔ　decide on sb.'s punishment; punish: 以违反纪律～ be punished for a breach of discipline

论敌 lùndí　one's opponent in a debate

论点 lùndiǎn　argument; thesis: 这篇文章～鲜明。The argument set forth in the article is clear-cut.

论调 lùndiào　*derog.* view; argument: 这种～是错误的。Such views are erroneous.／荒谬的～ an absurd argument

论断 lùnduàn　inference; judgment; thesis: 作出～ draw an inference

论功行赏 lùn gōng xíng shǎng　dispense rewards or honours according to merit; give people awards according to their contributions

论据 lùnjù　grounds of argument; argument: ～不足 insufficient grounds／有力的～ strong argument; valid reasons

论理[1] lùnlǐ　reason (with sb.): 我要跟他～。I'll try and reason with him.

论理[2] lùnlǐ　① normally; as things should be: ～她早可以退休了, 可是她仍然坚持工作。She really ought to have retired long ago, but she's still working. ② logic: 合乎～ be logical; stand to reason

论理学 lùnlǐxué　old name for 逻辑学 luójíxué

论列 lùnliè　discuss point by point

论难 lùnnàn　argue; wrangle: 两个学派各执一说, 互相～。The two schools of thought wrangled, each sticking to its guns.

论述 lùnshù　discuss; expound: 第一章～数学的基本原理。The first chapter discusses the fundamentals of mathematics.／本文准备就以下三个问题分别加以～。This paper will take up the following three questions one by one.／精辟的～ a brilliant exposition

论说[1] lùnshuō　exposition and argumentation

论说[2] lùnshuō　*inf.* normally; as things should be: ～这个会他应该参加, 不知道为什么没有来? Normally he ought to have attended the meeting. I wonder why he didn't come.

论说文 lùnshuōwén　argumentation

论坛 lùntán　forum; tribune: 这是最近～上引起剧烈争论的问题。This question has caused heated controversy in recent forums of public opinion.

论题 lùntí　*log.* proposition

论文 lùnwén　thesis; dissertation; treatise; paper: 学术～ an academic thesis (or paper)／科学～ a scientific treatise

论文答辩 lùnwén dábiàn　thesis defence: 我明天～。I'm going to defend my thesis tomorrow.

论战 lùnzhàn　polemic; debate: 展开～ launch a debate

论争 lùnzhēng　argument; debate; controversy: ～的焦点 the point in controversy; the point at issue

论证 lùnzhèng　① demonstration; proof: 无可辩驳的～ irrefutable proof ② expound and prove: 文章～了改革的必要性。The article proves the necessity of the reform. ③ grounds of argument

论著 lùnzhù　treatise; work; book

论资排辈 lùnzī-páibèi　arrange in order of seniority; give top priority to seniority in promotion

论罪 lùnzuì　decide on the nature of the guilt: 按贪污～ be found guilty of corruption

luō

捋
luō　rub one's palm along (sth. long): ～起袖子 push up one's sleeve／～掉树枝上的叶子 strip a twig of its leaves ——see also lǚ

捋胳膊 luō gēbo　push up one's sleeve and show the arm

捋虎须 luō hǔxū　stroke the tiger's whiskers—do sth. very daring; run great risks

啰（囉）
luō　see below ——see also luó; luo

啰唆 luōsuo　(also 啰嗦 luōsuo) ① talkative; long-winded; wordy: 他说话太～。He's far too long-winded.／他啰啰嗦嗦地说了半天, 还是没把问题说清楚。He talked on and on but didn't make himself clear.／我再～几句。Let me say just another word or two. *or* Bear with me a little longer.／我告诉过你不能去, 你怎么还跟我～? I told you you're not going, why do you have to ask over and over again? ② fussy ③ over-elaborate; troublesome: 这些手续真～。All these formalities are overelaborate.／这真是件～事儿! This is really a troublesome matter!

luó

罗[1]（羅）
luó　① a net for catching birds: 罗网 luówǎng　② catch (birds) with a net: 门可罗雀 mén kě luó què　③ collect; gather together: 搜罗 sōuluó　④ display; spread out: 星罗棋布 xīngluó-qíbù　⑤ sieve; sifter: 把面过一次～。Sift the flour through a sieve. ⑥ sieve; sift: ～面 sift flour／把面再～一过儿。Sift the flour over again. ⑦ a kind of silk gauze ⑧ (Luó) a surname

罗²(羅)　luó　*m.*　twelve dozen; a gross

罗拜　luóbài　*formal*　(of a group of people) surround and kneel before

罗布　luóbù　spread out (over a large area): 营地上帐篷～。Tents are spread out over the campsite.

罗布麻　luóbùmá　bluish dogbane (*Apocynum venetum*)

罗刹　luóchà　(in Hindu mythology) rakshas or rakshasa (a demon)

罗得西亚　Luódéxīyà　Rhodesia

罗浮宫　Luófú Gōng　the Louvre (in Paris)

罗锅　luóguō　arched: ～桥 arch bridge

罗锅儿　luóguōr　① hunchbacked; humpbacked ② hunchback; humpback

罗锅　luóguo　bend (the back): ～着腰坐在炕上 sit hunched up on the *kang*

罗汉　luóhàn　① *Buddhism* arhat, arahat, or arahant (a perfected person who has achieved nirvana 涅槃 and freed himself from the bonds of desire) ② (in Chinese Buddhism) one of the *arhats* often depicted on the walls of temples in groups of 16 or 18 (or even 500), representing close disciples of the Buddha who were entrusted by him to remain in the world and not to enter nirvana until Maitreya (弥勒) appeared as Buddha and brought in a new system

罗汉病　luóhànbìng　*dial.*　snail fever; schistosomiasis

罗汉豆　luóhàndòu　*dial.*　broad bean

罗汉果　luóhànguǒ　mangosteen

罗汉松　luóhànsōng　yew podocarpus

罗经　luójīng　compass: 电～ gyrocompass / 磁～ magnetic compass / 航海～ mariner's compass

罗掘　luójué　(short for 罗雀掘鼠) (originally in a beleaguered city) net birds and dig out rats—contrive ways and means to live when in straits; try very hard to scrape up money

罗掘俱穷　luójué jù qióng　all sources of money and material exhausted

罗口　luókǒu　rib cuff or rib collar; rib top (of socks)

罗口灯泡　luókǒu dēngpào　same as 螺口灯泡 luókǒu dēngpào

罗口灯头　luókǒu dēngtóu　same as 螺口灯头 luókǒu dēngtóu

罗拉　luólā　① *mech.*　roller ② roller on a loom

罗勒　luólè　*bot.*　sweet basil

罗列　luóliè　① spread out; set out: 厂房～在山坡上。Factory buildings spread out over the hillside. ② enumerate: 光～事实还不够，必须加以分析。It's not enough just to enumerate the facts. You've got to analyse them, too.

罗马法　Luómǎfǎ　Roman law

罗马公教　Luómǎ gōngjiào　another name for 天主教 Tiānzhǔjiào

罗马教廷　Luómǎ jiàotíng　same as 教廷 jiàotíng

罗马尼亚　Luómǎníyà　Romania

罗马尼亚人　Luómǎníyàrén　Romanian

罗马尼亚语　Luómǎníyàyǔ　Romanian (language)

罗马数字　Luómǎ shùzì　Roman numerals

罗马语族　Luómǎ yǔzú　*linguis.*　the Romance group of languages; Romance languages

罗曼蒂克　luómàndìkè　romantic (a transliteration)

罗曼司　luómànsī　romance (a transliteration): 他跟他表妹有过一段～。He had a romance with his cousin.

罗盘　luópán　compass

罗圈　luóquān　the round frame of a sieve

罗圈腿　luóquāntuǐ　① bowlegs; bandy legs ② bowlegged; bandy-legged

罗圈儿揖　luóquānryī　bows made (with hands clasped) to people on all sides

罗圈椅　luóquānyǐ　(or 罗圈椅子 luóquānyǐzi) an easy chair

罗裙　luóqún　a skirt of thin silk; silk skirt

罗扇　luóshàn　silk gauze fan

罗宋汤　luósòngtāng　Russian beef soup; borscht or borsch (罗宋 being the old transliteration of "Russia")

罗网　luówǎng　net; trap

罗望子　luówàngzǐ　*bot.*　tamarind

罗帷　luówéi　a gauze curtain

罗纹　luówén　same as 螺纹 luówén①

罗纹机　luówénjī　rib knitting machine; ribber

罗纹鸭　luówényā　falcated teal; falcated duck

罗衣　luóyī　a garment of thin silk

罗唣　luózào　same as 啰唣 luózào

罗织　luózhī　*formal*　frame sb. up: ～诬陷 frame sb. up

罗织罪名　luózhī zuìmíng　cook up charges; frame a case against sb.

罗致　luózhì　enlist the services of; secure sb. in one's employment; collect; gather together

罗致人才　luózhì réncái　enlist the services of able people

视(覼)　luó　see below

视缕　luólǚ　*formal*　narrate in detail

啰(囉)　luó　see below——see also luō; luo

啰唣　luózào　*old*　quarrelsome; argumentative

胴(腡)　luó　fingerprint

萝(蘿)　luó　trailing plants: 藤萝 téngluó

萝卜　luóbo　radish

萝卜干儿　luóbogānr　dried radish

萝芙木　luófúmù　*bot.*　devilpepper

萝芳　luólè　same as 罗勒 luólè

猡(玀)　luó　see 猪猡 zhūluó

逻(邏)　luó　patrol: 巡逻 xúnluó

逻辑　luóji　logic: 研究～ study logic / ～上的错误 an error in logic / 城里人的～ the logic of city dwellers / 生活的～ the logic of life / 这句话不合～。This statement is illogical.

逻辑电路　luóji diànlù　logical circuit

逻辑思维　luóji sīwéi　logical thinking

逻辑学　luójixué　logic: ～家 logician

逻辑主语　luóji zhǔyǔ　*gram.*　logical subject

逻骑　luóqí　mounted patrol

逻卒　luózú　soldiers on patrol; patrolmen

椤(欏)　luó　see 桫椤 suōluó

锣(鑼)　luó　gong

锣槌　luóchuí　(gong) hammer

锣鼓　luógǔ　① gong and drum ② traditional percussion instruments ③ ensemble of such instruments with gongs and drums playing the main part

锣鼓喧天　luógǔ xuāntiān　a deafening sound of gongs and drums

箩(籮)　luó　a square-bottomed bamboo basket

箩筐　luókuāng　a large bamboo or wicker basket

骡(騾)　luó　mule

骡马店　luómǎdiàn　an inn with sheds for carts and animals

骡子　luózi　mule

螺　luó　① spiral shell; snail ② whorl (in finger-

print)

螺钿 luódiàn (also 螺甸 luódiàn) mother-of-pearl inlay: ～漆盘 lacquer tray inlaid with mother-of-pearl

螺钉 luódīng screw: 木～ wood screw; screwnail / 十字槽～ Phillips screw

螺号 luóhào conch; shell trumpet

螺距 luójù mech. (screw) pitch; thread pitch

螺口灯泡 luókǒu dēngpào screw-socket bulb; screw bulb

螺口灯头 luókǒu dēngtóu screw socket

螺母 luómǔ (also 螺帽 luómào) mech. (screw) nut: ～垫圈 nut collar

螺栓 luóshuān mech. (screw) bolt: 连接～ binder bolt; connecting bolt / 地脚～ foundation bolt

螺丝 luósī inf. screw

螺丝板牙 luósī bǎnyá screw die; threading die

螺丝刀 luósīdāo screwdriver

螺丝钉 luósīdīng inf. screw

螺丝攻 luósīgōng same as 丝锥 sīzhuī

螺丝扣 luósīkòu inf. thread (of a screw)

螺丝帽 luósīmào same as 螺母 luómǔ

螺丝母 luósīmǔ inf. (screw) nut

螺丝起子 luósīqǐzi screwdriver

螺蛳 luósi spiral shell; snail

螺纹 luówén ① whorl (in fingerprint) ② mech. thread (of a screw): 公制～ metric thread / 惠氏～ Whitworth thread

螺纹刀具 luówén dāojù threading tool; screw tool

螺旋 luóxuán ① spiral; helix ② phys. screw

螺旋桨 luóxuánjiǎng (also 螺旋推进器 luóxuán tuījìnqì) (screw) propeller; screw: 飞机～ airscrew; aircraft propeller

螺旋桨调速器 luóxuánjiǎng tiáosùqì propeller governor

螺旋桨叶 luóxuánjiǎngyè propeller blade

螺旋式 luóxuánshì spiral: ～发展 spiral development; developing in spirals / ～军备竞赛 arms race spiral / ～通货膨胀 inflation spiral; spiralling inflation

螺旋体 luóxuántǐ bacteriol. spirochaeta

螺旋线 luóxuánxiàn helix; helical line; spiral

螺旋钻 luóxuánzuàn spiral drill; (screw) auger

luǒ

裸（躶、赢） luǒ bare; naked; exposed

裸鲤 luǒlǐ naked carp

裸露 luǒlù uncovered; exposed: ～的煤层 exposed coal seam

裸麦 luǒmài naked barley; highland barley

裸体 luǒtǐ naked; nude: 一张～的照片 a photograph (or picture) of a nude

裸体画 luǒtǐhuà . a painting of a nude (esp. a nude woman)

裸体像 luǒtǐxiàng a nude figure or statue; nude

裸线 luǒxiàn bare wire

裸装货 luǒzhuānghuò nude cargo

裸子植物 luǒzǐ zhíwù gymnosperm

瘰 luǒ see below

瘰疬 luǒlì med. scrofula

luò

荦（犖） luò formal prominent; outstanding: 卓荦 zhuóluò

荦荦 luòluò formal conspicuous; apparent; obvious

荦荦大端 luòluò dàduān (also 荦荦大者 luòluò dàzhě) major items; salient points

洛 Luò (also 洛河) ① a river in Shaanxi Province ② a river in Henan Province

洛氏硬度 Luòshì yìngdù phys. Rockwell hardness

洛阳纸贵 Luòyáng zhǐ guì paper is dear in Luoyang (said of the wide circulation of a popular work; from the story of Zuo Si 左思 in the Jin Dynasty, whose long work, the "Three Capitals Rhapsody"《三都赋》was copied by so many people as to cause a paper shortage in Luoyang)

咯 luò see 吡咯 bǐluò ——see also gē; kǎ; lo

络 luò ① sth. resembling a net: 橘络 júluò ② Chin. med. subsidiary channels in the human body through which vital energy, blood and nutriment circulate: 经络 jīngluò ③ hold sth. in place with a net: 她头上～着一个发网。She kept her hair in place with a net. ④ twine; wind: ～纱 winding yarn; spooling

络合 luòhé chem. complexing: ～物 complex compound

络离子 luòlízǐ chem. complex ion

络脉 luòmài Chin. med. collaterals which connect channels; branches of channels

络腮胡子 luòsāihúzi whiskers; full beard

络纱 luòshā text. doff: ～工 doffer / ～机 doffer

络筒机 luòtǒngjī text. (high speed) cone winder; winding machine; winder

络盐 luòyán chem. complex salt

络绎不绝 luòyì bù jué in an endless stream: 参观展览会的人～。A continuous flow of visitors came to the exhibition. / 一夜人声杂沓, 语笑喧阗, 爆竹起火, ～。(《红楼梦》) The babel of talk and laughter, punctuated by the explosion of firecrackers, went on without intermission the whole night long.

骆 luò ① a white horse with a black mane (mentioned in ancient texts) ② (Luò) a surname

骆驼 luòtuo camel

骆驼刺 luòtuocì (also 骆驼草 luòtuocǎo) camel thorn

骆驼队 luòtuoduì camel train; caravan

骆驼绒 luòtuoróng camel hair cloth

烙 luò see 炮烙 páoluò ——see also lào

珞 luò see below

珞巴族 Luòbāzú the Lhoba (Lopa) nationality, or the Lhobas (Lopas), inhabiting the Xizang Autonomous Region

落 luò ① fall; drop: 有些棉桃～在地上了。Some cotton bolls have fallen on the ground. ② go down; set: 潮水～了。The tide is low (or out). / 太阳～山了。The sun has set. ③ lower: 把帘子～下来 lower the blinds ④ decline; come down; sink: ～到这步田地 come to such a pass ⑤ lag behind; fall behind: 落伍 luòwǔ ⑥ leave behind; stay behind: 不～痕迹 leave no trace ⑦ whereabouts: 下落 xiàluò ⑧ settlement: 村落 cūnluò ⑨ fall onto; rest with: 这项任务～在我们肩上了。The task was put on our shoulders. / 政权～在人民手里了。Political power passed into the hands of the people. ⑩ get; have; receive: ～褒贬 be criticized; lay oneself open to censure / 就这么办吧, 我不怕～埋怨。Let's do it that way, then. I don't mind taking the blame. ⑪ put pen to paper; write down: 落款 luòkuǎn ——see also là; lào

落榜 luòbǎng fail in an entrance examination; fail as a

candidate

落笔 luòbǐ put pen to paper; start to write or draw: 写文章时，～之前要很好构思。 When you write you should think it all out before you put pen to paper.

落膘 luòbiāo (of livestock) become thin

落泊 luòbó (also 落魄 luòbó) *formal* ① be in dire straits; be down and out ② untrammelled by convention; casual; unconventional

落不是 luò bùshi be blamed: 我为他们忙乎了一上午，反倒落了一身不是。 I ran around for them the whole morning, and got blamed for it.

落槽 luòcáo ① low water ② family fortunes declining ③ tenon in mortise—settled; at rest: 事情没办好，心里总是不～。 As long as the matter goes unsettled, I won't be able to put my mind at rest.

落草[1] luòcǎo take to the greenwood; take to the heather; become an outlaw

落草[2] luòcǎo *dial.* (of a baby) be born

落差 luòchā ① drop in elevation (between two points in a stream) ② head drop (in hydroelectric power plants)

落潮 luòcháo ebb tide

落成 luòchéng (of a building, etc.) be completed: 大桥已经～，日内就可以正式通车。 The bridge has been completed and will be open to traffic in a few days.

落成典礼 luòchéng diǎnlǐ inauguration ceremony (for a building, etc.)

落锤 luòchuí *mech.* drop hammer

落得 luòde get; end in: ～一场空 come to nothing; end up in smoke / 搞阴谋诡计的人，必然要～可耻的下场。 Plotters come to no good end.

落底 luòdǐ ① *dial.* the end of a year or month: 一月～要进行大扫除。 We shall have a thorough cleaning at the end of January. ② feel at ease; have one's mind set at rest: 事情办成了，咱们的心也就～了。 The matter was settled, and our minds were set at rest.

落地 luòdì ① fall to the ground: 人头～ be killed or beheaded ② (of a baby) be born: 呱呱～ come into the world with a cry; be born

落地窗 luòdìchuāng French window

落地灯 luòdìdēng floor lamp; standard lamp

落地生根 luòdìshēnggēn air plant; life plant

落地式电扇 luòdìshì diànshàn (also 落地扇 luòdìshàn) standard fan

落地式收音机 luòdìshì shōuyīnjī console (radio) set

落第 luòdì fail in an imperial examination

落点 luòdiǎn ① *sports* placement (of a ball): ～准 accuracy in placement ② *mil.* point of fall

落顶 luòdǐng *min.* caving

落发 luòfà take the tonsure—become a Buddhist monk or nun: ～为僧 become a Buddhist monk

落果 luòguǒ *agric.* premature drop

落后 luòhòu ① be behind; fall behind; lag behind: 要是我们不努力，就要～了。 If we don't work hard, we'll fall behind. / 我们的工作～了。 We've fallen behind in our work. / 谁也不甘心～。 Nobody is willing to be left behind. / 他们的空军比我们～五年。 Their air force is five years behind ours. / 他的思想～于时代。 His thoughts are behind the times. / 上半场主队～一分。 The home team trailed by one point at half time. ② backward; behind the times: 他的思想很～。 His thoughts are very backward (*or* are far behind the times). / 改变山区一面貌 put an end to the backwardness of the mountainous areas / ～的生产工具 backward production tools / ～地区 backward areas; less developed areas

落后分子 luòhòu fènzǐ backward elements

落户 luòhù settle: 在农村～ settle in the countryside / 他是十年前在这里落的户。 He settled down here ten years ago.

落花流水 luòhuā-liúshuǐ like fallen flowers carried away by flowing water—in a sorry plight: 敌人被打得～。 The enemy was utterly routed. / 把几千年封建地主的特权打得个～。 The privileges which the feudal landlords had enjoyed for thousands of years were shattered to pieces.

落花有意，流水无情 luòhuā yǒu yì, liúshuǐ wú qíng the waterside flower pining for love sheds petals, while the heartless brook babbles on—unrequited love

落花生 luòhuāshēng peanut; groundnut

落荒 luòhuāng *old* take to the wilds—be defeated and flee the battlefield; take to flight (usu. followed by 而逃 *or* 而走): 扈成见局面不好，投马～而走，弃家逃命。《水浒》 Hu Cheng, seeing the outlook was evil for him, turned his horse and went off alone into the wilderness, and left his home and escaped for his life.

落籍 luòjí ① take up permanent residence (in a new place); settle: 她的父母在五十年代就迁到新疆～了。 Her parents moved to Xinjiang in the fifties and settled down there. ② *formal* remove sb.'s name from the rolls; take sb.'s name off the books; expunge sb.'s name from a list

落价 luòjià fall (*or* drop) in price: 收音机～了。 The price of radios has gone down.

落角 luòjiǎo *mil.* angle of fall

落脚[1] luòjiǎo stay (for a time); stop over; put up: 找个地方～ find a place to stay / 在客店～ put up at an inn

落脚[2] luòjiǎo same as 下脚[2] xiàjiǎo

落脚处 luòjiǎochù temporary lodging

落井下石 luò jǐng xià shí drop stones on someone who has fallen into a well—hit a person when he's down

落空 luòkōng come to nothing; fail; fall through: 希望～ fail to attain one's hope / 这事有～的危险。 There is a danger that nothing will come of it.

落款 luòkuǎn write the names of the sender and the recipient on a painting, gift or letter; inscribe (a gift, etc.)

落雷 luòléi same as 霹雳 pīlì

落泪 luòlèi shed tears; weep

落铃 luòlíng *agric.* shedding (*or* premature dropping) of cotton bolls

落令 luòlìng be out of season

落落大方 luòluò dàfāng natural and at ease

落落寡合 luòluò guǎ hé standoffish; unsociable; aloof: 他性情孤傲，～。 He is proud and arrogant, holding himself aloof from the others.

落寞 luòmò (also 落漠, 落莫 luòmò) lonely; desolate

落墨 luòmò put pen to paper; start to write or draw

落幕 luòmù the curtain falls; lower the curtain

落难 luònàn meet with misfortune; be in distress

落魄 luòpò (*or* luòtuò) *formal* ① in dire straits; down and out ② untrammelled by convention; casual; unconventional

落日 luòrì the setting sun

落腮胡子 luòsāihúzi same as 络腮胡子 luòsāihúzi

落纱 luòshā *text.* doff: ～工 doffer / ～机 doffer

落生 luòshēng *dial.* (of a baby) be born

落实 luòshí ① practicable; workable: 生产计划要订得～。 Production plans must be practicable. ② fix (*or* decide) in advance; ascertain; make sure: 交货时间还没有最后～。 The date of delivery hasn't been fixed yet. / 去颐和园的人数要～一下。 Make sure how many are going to the Summer Palace. ③ carry out; fulfil; implement; put into effect: ～政策 implement a policy / 把任务～到每个基层 fulfil a task down to every grass-roots organization ④ *dial.* feel at ease: 心里总是不～ just can't set one's mind at ease

落市 luòshì be out of season

落水 luòshuǐ ① fall into water: 打救～儿童 save a

drowning child ② fall into evil ways

落水狗 luòshuǐgǒu   dog in the water—a bad person who is down: 打落水狗 dǎ luòshuǐgǒu

落水管 luòshuǐguǎn   same as 水落管 shuǐluòguǎn

落俗 luòsú   show poor taste

落汤鸡 luòtāngjī   (of a person) like a drenched chicken; like a drowned rat; soaked through; drenched and bedraggled

落套 luòtào   (of literary works) conform to a conventional pattern; get into a rut

落体 luòtǐ   *phys.* falling body: 自由～ freely falling body

落托 luòtuō   same as 落拓 luòtuò

落拓 luòtuò   (also 落魄 luòtuò) *formal* ① in dire straits; down and out ② untrammelled by convention; casual; unconventional

落拓不羁 luòtuò bùjī   unconventional and uninhibited

落网 luòwǎng   (of a criminal) fall into the net—be caught; be captured: 主犯已经～。The chief criminal has been caught.

落伍 luòwǔ   ① fall behind the ranks; straggle; drop behind; drop out: 在革命急速发展的时候, 总不免有人要～的。When the revolution is developing rapidly, some people are bound to fall behind. ② out of date; behind the times; backward: 他的思想～了。His way of thinking is out of date (*or* behind the times).

落霞 luòxiá   sunset clouds: ～与孤鹜齐飞, 秋水共长天一色。(王勃) Sunset clouds fly with the solitary wild duck; Autumnal waters merge with the limitless sky.

落线 luòxiàn   *mil.* line of fall

落选 luòxuǎn   fail to be chosen (*or* elected); lose an election

落叶 luòyè   ① fallen leaves ② *bot.* deciduous leaf

落叶归根 luòyè guī gēn   same as 叶落归根 yè luò guī gēn

落叶树 luòyèshù   deciduous tree

落叶松 luòyèsōng   larch

落音 luòyīn   (of talking or singing) stop: 他的话刚～, 你就进来了。You came in just as he stopped talking.

落英 luòyīng   *liter.* ① fallen or falling flowers ② new-bloomed flowers

落英缤纷 luòyīng bīnfēn   petals falling in riotous profusion: 芳草鲜美, ～。(陶渊明) On scented grasses fresh and pleasing to the eye lay fallen blossoms in gay profusion

落帐 luòzhàng   make an entry in an account book; enter sth. in an account

落照 luòzhào   the glow of the setting sun

落职 luòzhí   remove from office; demote

落座 luòzuò   take a seat (in restaurants, theatres, etc.): 各位观众请～, 节目就要开始了。Will all spectators be seated. The performance is going to start.

攞   luǒ   ① pile up; stack up: 把砖一～起来 stack up the bricks / 他屋里的书一直～到屋顶。The books in his room piled up to the ceiling. ② *m.* pile; stack: 一～砖 a pile of bricks / 一～书 a stack of books / 一～碗 a pile of bowls

luo

偻（儸）   luo   see 偻偻 lóuluo

啰（囉）   luo   see 喽啰 lóuluo ——see also luǒ; luó

M

m̄

姆
姆 m̄ see below ——see also mǔ
姆妈 m̄mā *dial.* ① ma; mum; mummy; mother ② wife of father's elder brother; aunt ③ aunt (an affectionate or respectful form of address for an elderly woman); auntie; aunty: 高家～ Auntie Gao

ḿ

呒(嘸)
呒(嘸) ḿ *dial.* not have; be without
呒没 ḿméi *dial.* ① not have; there is not; be without: 房间里～人。There isn't anyone in the room. ② not: 我～去。I didn't go.
呒啥 ḿshà *dial.* ① nothing: 他的报告里～新内容。He says nothing new in that report. ② not: 这部电影～好看。This film isn't interesting.

嗯
嗯 m̌ *interj.* (used to show doubt): ～, 你说什么? Eh? What did you say? *or* Pardon? / ～, 是真的吗? Oh, really? *or* What? Is that true? ——see also m̀

m̀

嗯
嗯 m̀ *interj.* (used to respond): ～, 我知道了。Um-hum (*or* Uh-huh, Yes), I see. ——see also m̌

mā

妈
妈 mā ① *inf.* ma; mum; mummy; mother: 我～让你去。Mother wants you to go to her. / ～, 再见。Goodbye, Mum! ② a form of address for a married woman one generation one's senior: 姑妈 gūmā ③ (used in an exclamation): 我的～呀! 钱包丢了。Oh dear! I've lost my purse. ④ *old* a middle-aged or old maidservant (called together with her surname): 王～ Nanny Wang
妈妈 māmā *inf.* ma; mum; mummy; mother

抹¹
抹¹ mā wipe: ～桌子 wipe a table clean / ～一把脸 wipe one's face

抹²(㧍)
抹²(㧍) mā rub sth. down; slip sth. off: 把帽子～下来 slip one's cap off ——see also mǒ; mò
抹布 mābù rag (to wipe things with)
抹搭 mādā *dial.* (of eyelids) half close; droop: ～着眼皮 half close one's eyes
抹脸 māliǎn *inf.* be strict with sb. all of a sudden: 抹不下脸来 find it difficult to be strict with sb. (for fear of hurting his feelings)
抹澡 māzǎo *dial.* rub oneself down with a wet towel; take a sponge bath

麻
麻 mā see below ——see also má
麻麻黑 māmahēi *dial.* (it is) dusk: 天～了, 屋里逐渐模糊起来。As dusk fell, the room got dimmer and dimmer.
麻麻亮 māmaliàng *dial.* (it is) just dawning; (day is) just beginning to break; just getting light: 天～ at the crack of dawn

摩
摩 mā see below ——see also mó
摩挲 māsa ① gently stroke; smooth sth. out with one's hands: 你把这件衣服上的褶子～～。Smooth the wrinkles out of this shirt, please. / 他向后～头发。He smoothed his hair back. / 她肚子疼, 你给她～～肚子。She's got a stomachache. Massage her stomach for her. ② *dial.* do sth. in a careless and quick way: 你让他洗把脸, 他好歹一～。When you tell him to wash his face, he just gives it a wipe. ③ coax; humour: 你是怎么把他给～顺了的? How did you get him to quiet down? ——see also mósuō

嬷
嬷 mā see below
嬷嬷 māma *dial.* ① a form of address for an elderly woman ② wet nurse

má

吗
吗 má *dial.* what: 要～有～。You can have whatever you want. / 你说～? What did you say? / ～事? What's the matter? *or* What's going on? ——see also mǎ; ma

麻¹(蔴)
麻¹(蔴) má ① general name for hemp, flax, etc. ② fibre of hemp, flax, etc. for textile materials: 这块手绢是～的。This handkerchief is linen. ③ sesame: ～糖 sesame candy

麻²
麻² má ① rough; coarse: 这种纸一面光, 一面～。This paper is smooth on one side and rough on the other. ② pocked; pockmarked; pitted; spotty: 得了天花, 脸就～了。Smallpox will leave pockmarks on the face. / 铸件上有～点。There are pits in the casting. ③ (Má) a surname

麻³
麻³ má ① feeling pins and needles; tingling; numb: 她坐得太久, 腿都～了。She'd been sitting so long that she felt pins and needles in her legs. / 针灸大夫问病人～不～。The acupuncturist asked the patient if he felt a tingling sensation. / 辣得舌头发～。The hot taste burns the tongue. / 他手指头都冻～了。The cold numbed his fingers. ② short for 麻醉 mázuì ——see also mā

麻包　mábāo　gunnybag; gunnysack; burlap sack; sack

麻痹　mábì　① *med.* paralysis: 面部神经～ facial paralysis ② benumb; lull; blunt: ～人们的斗志 lull (*or* blunt) people's fighting will ③ lower one's guard; slacken one's vigilance: ～粗心是产生事故的原因。 Carelessness is the cause of accidents. / 思想～ a slackening of vigilance; a decline in alertness

麻痹大意　mábì dàyì　lower one's guard and become careless; be off one's guard

麻布　mábù　① gunny (cloth); sackcloth; burlap; hessian ② linen

麻袋　mádài　gunnybag; gunnysack; burlap sack: ～片 a piece of gunnysacking

麻捣　mádǎo　*formal* hemp; hair

麻刀　mádao　*archit.* hemp; hair: ～灰泥 hemp-fibred plaster

麻烦　máfan　① troublesome; inconvenient: 这事要是太～, 你就别管了。Don't bother if it's too much trouble. —一一点也不～。No trouble at all. / 这下可～了, 我把钥匙锁在屋里了。What a nuisance. I've locked my key in the room. / ～的事情, 我经历过不少。As for troubles and predicaments, I've been through quite a few. / 手续很～。It's rather troublesome to go through all these formalities. / ～还在后头呢! There will be more trouble to come. / 服务周到, 不怕～ spare no pains to give good service / 自找～ ask for trouble ② put sb. to trouble; trouble sb.; bother: 对不起, 太～你了。Sorry to have put you to so much trouble. / 这点小事不要去～他了。Don't bother him with such trifles. ——see also 捣麻烦 dǎo máfan

麻纺　máfǎng　the spinning of jute, hemp or flax

麻风¹　máfēng　*med.* leprosy: ～病人 leper

麻花¹　máhuā　fried dough twist

麻花²　máhuā　*dial.* (of clothes) wearing thin; worn out: 两只袖子都～了。The sleeves are wearing thin.

麻花钻　máhuāzuàn　*mech.* (fluted) twist drill

麻黄　máhuáng　*bot.* Chinese ephedra (*Ephedra sinica*); mahuang

麻黄碱　máhuángjiǎn　*pharm.* ephedrine

麻将　májiàng　mahjong: ～牌 mahjong pieces; mahjong tiles / 打～ play mahjong

麻酱　májiàng　sesame paste

麻辣辣　málàlà　(of a pain) searing

麻利　máli　① quick and neat; dexterous; deft: 干活～ work dexterously; be a quick and neat worker / 她手脚～, 不一会儿一桌酒菜就端上来了。She was very quick and efficient, and in a minute, a lavish dinner was ready to be served. ② *dial.* quick; fast: 厂里开会, 叫你～回去。You've been asked to return quickly to attend a meeting in the factory.

麻脸　máliǎn　a pockmarked face

麻乱　máluàn　confused (state of mind); in a turmoil: ～的情绪 anxious state of mind / 他的心里～极了。His mind was in a turmoil.

麻密　mámì　thick; dense: 脸上皱纹～ a face full of wrinkles / ～的枪声 sound of intensive gunfire

麻木　mámù　① numb: 他手脚～了。Both his hands and feet have gone numb. ② apathetic; insensitive; lifeless: ～地生活 lead an empty life / 他年龄不大, 思想却近乎～。Though he is not old, his mind is already deadened.

麻木不仁　mámù bùrén　apathetic; insensitive; unfeeling: 对同志对人民要满腔热忱, 而不应该漠不关心, ～。We should feel warmth towards our comrades and the people, and not be uncaring and indifferent.

麻婆豆腐　mápó dòufu　pockmarked grandma's beancurd (stir-fried beancurd in hot sauce; the recipe is attributed to a certain pockmarked old woman)

麻雀　máquè　(house) sparrow

麻雀虽小, 五脏俱全　máquè suī xiǎo, wǔzàng jù quán　the sparrow may be small but it has all the vital organs—small but complete

麻雀战　máquèzhàn　sparrow warfare (as a form of guerrilla warfare)

麻纱　máshā　① yarn of ramie, flax, etc. ② cambric; haircords

麻绳　máshéng　rope made of hemp, flax, jute, etc.

麻酥酥　másūsū　slightly numb; tingling: 脚在冷水里冻得～的。The cold water gave my feet a tingling feeling.

麻线　máxiàn　flaxen thread; linen thread

麻药　máyào　anaesthetic: 上～ apply an anaesthetic; administer anaesthesia

麻油　máyóu　sesame oil

麻疹　mázhěn　measles: 出～ have measles

麻织品　mázhīpǐn　fabrics of flax, hemp, etc.; linen fabrics

麻子　mázi　① pockmarks: 他脸上有几点～。He's got a few pockmarks on his face. ② a person with a pock-marked face

麻醉　mázuì　① *med.* anaesthesia; narcosis: 全身(局部、脊髓)～ general (local, spinal) anaesthesia ② *med.* anaesthetize: 病人已经～过了, 您可以动手术了。The patient has been anaesthetized and you can operate now. ③ corrupt (sb.'s mind); poison: 用海淫海盗的电影～青年人 poison young people's minds with films full of sex and violence

麻醉剂　mázuìjì　anaesthetic; narcotic

麻醉品　mázuìpǐn　narcotic; drug

麻醉师　mázuìshī　anaesthetist

麻　　mǎ　see below

麻痹　mǎbì　same as 麻痹 mábì

麻风　mǎfēng　same as 麻风 máfēng

麻疹　mǎzhěn　same as 麻疹 mázhěn

mǎ

马(馬)　mǎ　① horse ② horse, one of the pieces in Chinese chess ③ big; large: 马蜂 mǎfēng ④ (Mǎ) a surname

马鞍　mǎ'ān　(also 马鞍子 mǎ'ānzi) saddle

马鞍形　mǎ'ānxíng　the shape of a saddle—a falling-off between two peak periods: 由于这次事故, 我厂生产一度出现了～。As a result of the accident, there was a temporary falling-off (*or* drop) in production at our factory.

马帮　mǎbāng　a train of horses carrying goods; caravan

马宝　mǎbǎo　*Chin. med.* bezoar of a horse

马鼻疽　mǎbíjū　*animal husbandry* glanders

马鞭　mǎbiān　horsewhip

马弁　mǎbiàn　*old* (officer's) bodyguard

马表　mǎbiǎo　stopwatch

马鳖　mǎbiē　common name for 水蛭 shuǐzhì

马不停蹄　mǎ bù tíng tí　a horse galloping—without a stop; nonstop: 部队～地赶到了目的地。The troops rushed to their destination without a single halt. / 我接到电报就赶来了, 一路上可是～啊! I hurried here as soon as I got your telegram and didn't waste a single minute on the way.

马车　mǎchē　① (horse-drawn) carriage ② cart

马齿徒增　mǎchǐ tú zēng　just like a horse increasing its number of teeth with the years—grow old with nothing accomplished (used in self-depreciation)

马齿苋　mǎchǐxiàn　*bot.* purslane

马刺　mǎcì　spur

马达 mǎdá common name for 电动机 diàndòngjī

马达加斯加 Mǎdájiāsījiā Madagascar

马达加斯加人 Mǎdájiāsījiārén Madagascan

马达加斯加语 Mǎdájiāsījiāyǔ Malagasy (language)

马大哈 mǎdàhā ① careless; forgetful: 他可真够～的了, 自己丢了表, 居然不知道。How careless he is! He even doesn't know that he's lost his watch. ② a careless person; scatterbrain: 他是个～, 老忘锁门。He's such a scatterbrain that he always forgets to lock the door.

马刀 mǎdāo sabre

马到成功 mǎ dào chénggōng be victorious the moment the battle steeds arrive—win success immediately upon arrival; gain an immediate victory; win instant success: 祝你～! I wish you instant success!

马灯 mǎdēng barn lantern; lantern

马镫 mǎdèng stirrup

马店 mǎdiàn an inn with a stable (catering to caravan merchants)

马丁炉 mǎdīnglú metall. Martin furnace; open-hearth furnace; open hearth

马兜铃 mǎdōulíng bot. birthwort

马队 mǎduì ① a train of horses carrying goods; caravan ② a contingent of mounted troops; cavalry

马尔代夫 Mǎ'ěrdàifū Maldives

马尔代夫人 Mǎ'ěrdàifūrén Maldivian

马尔加什语 Mǎ'ěrjiāshíyǔ Malagasy (language)

马尔萨斯人口论 Mǎ'ěrsàsī rénkǒulùn Malthusian theory of population

马尔萨斯主义 Mǎ'ěrsàsīzhǔyì Malthusianism

马尔维纳斯群岛 Mǎ'ěrwéinàsī Qúndǎo Islas Malvinas; the Falkland Islands

马耳他 Mǎ'ěrtā Malta

马耳他人 Mǎ'ěrtārén Maltese

马耳他语 Mǎ'ěrtāyǔ Maltese (language)

马贩子 mǎfànzi horse dealer; coper

马粪纸 mǎfènzhǐ strawboard

马蜂 mǎfēng common name for 胡蜂 húfēng

马蜂窝 mǎfēngwō hornet's nest ——see also 捅马蜂窝 tǒng mǎfēngwō

马夫 mǎfū old groom

马竿 mǎgān blindman's stick; white stick

马革裹尸 mǎgé guǒ shī be wrapped in horsehide after death—die on the battlefield: 青山处处埋忠骨, 何必～还? There are green hills everywhere to bury loyal bones, Why wrap the corpse in horsehide and bring it back?

马褂 mǎguà mandarin jacket (worn over a gown)

马关条约 Mǎguān Tiáoyuē the Treaty of Shimonoseki (1895)

马锅头 mǎguōtóu leader of a caravan

马海毛 mǎhǎimáo text. mohair

马号[1] mǎhào public stable

马号[2] mǎhào long-tubed bugle (used by cavalry)

马赫数 mǎhèshù (also 马赫 mǎhè) phys. Mach number; Mach

马赫主义 Mǎhèzhǔyì philos. Machism: ～者 Machist

马后炮 mǎhòupào (a Chinese chess term used figuratively to mean) belated action or advice; belated effort: 切记不要使问题成了堆, 才来一个总结, 放～。Make sure that you don't wait until problems pile up before making a reckoning—that would be firing belated shots. / 我这个建议也许是～。It's probably already too late for my suggestion to do any good. / 事情都做完了, 你才说要帮忙, 这不是～吗? You come and offer to help when the work's all done. Isn't that a bit late?

马虎 mǎhu (also 马糊 mǎhu) careless; casual: ～了事 get sth. done in a slapdash manner / 他这个人做事比较～。He's a rather careless fellow. / 这是件大事, 不能～过去。This is a serious matter. It shouldn't be handled in just any old way.

马甲 mǎjiǎ dial. a sleeveless garment

马鲛鱼 mǎjiāoyú same as 鲅鱼 bàyú

马脚 mǎjiǎo sth. that gives the game away ——see also 露马脚 lòu mǎjiǎo

马厩 mǎjiù stable

马驹子 mǎjūzi inf. foal; colt or filly

马克 mǎkè ① mark (German monetary unit) ② markka

马克思列宁主义 Mǎkèsī-Lièníngzhǔyì Marxism-Leninism: ～者 Marxist-Leninist

马克思主义 Mǎkèsīzhǔyì Marxism: ～哲学 Marxist philosophy / ～者 Marxist / ～政治经济学 Marxist political economy

马口铁 mǎkǒutiě tinplate; galvanized iron

马裤 mǎkù riding breeches

马裤呢 mǎkùní text. whipcord

马拉犁 mǎlālí agric. horse-drawn plough

马拉松 mǎlāsōng marathon: ～赛跑 marathon race; marathon / 一场毫无结果的～式的谈判 a marathon negotiation that produces no results / ～演说 a marathon speech

马拉维 Mǎlāwéi Malawi

马拉维人 Mǎlāwéirén Malawian

马来半岛 Mǎlái Bàndǎo the Malay Peninsula

马来西亚 Mǎláixīyà Malaysia

马来西亚人 Mǎláixīyàrén Malaysian

马来语 Mǎláiyǔ Malay (language)

马蓝 mǎlán bot. acanthaceous indigo (Strobilanthes cusia)

马里 Mǎlǐ Mali

马里人 Mǎlǐrén Malian

马力 mǎlì phys. horsepower (h.p.): ～小时 horsepower-hour (hp-hr)

马立克派 Mǎlìkèpài Islam the Malikite school (or sect)

马列主义 Mǎ-Lièzhǔyì short for 马克思列宁主义 Mǎkèsī-Lièníngzhǔyì

马蔺 mǎlìn bot. Chinese small iris (Iris pallasii var. chinensis)

马铃薯 mǎlíngshǔ potato: ～晚疫病 late blight of potato

马六甲海峡 Mǎliùjiǎ Hǎixiá the Strait of Malacca

马鹿 mǎlù zool. red deer

马路 mǎlù road; street; avenue: 逛～ stroll around the streets; go window-shopping

马路新闻 mǎlù xīnwén street-gossip; hearsay

马骡 mǎluó zool. mule

马马虎虎 mǎmǎhūhū ① careless; casual: 他的信我只是～地看了一下。I merely glanced over his letter. / 产品出厂要严格检查, ～可不行。Products must be strictly, not carelessly, inspected before they leave the factory. / 你最近工作有些～。You've been slack in your work recently. ② not very good; just passable; so-so; fair; not so bad: 这种牌子的香烟怎么样? ——～, 你来一支试试。How's this brand of cigarettes? —Not so bad. Try one. / 你的游泳技术怎么样? ——～, 游不远。Are you a good swimmer? —Just so-so. I can't swim far.

马面鲀 mǎmiàntún zool. black scraper

马奶 mǎnǎi mare's milk

马尼拉麻 mǎnílámá another name for 蕉麻 jiāomá

马趴 mǎpā (usu. used in) 摔了个大～ fall flat on one's face

马匹 mǎpǐ horses

马屁 mǎpì see 拍马屁 pāi mǎpì

马屁精 mǎpìjīng sycophant; flatterer

马其顿共和国 Mǎqídùn Gònghéguó Republic of Mace-

donia

马前卒 mǎqiánzú　pawn; cat's-paw

马钱子 mǎqiánzǐ　*bot.*　vomiting nut; nux vomica

马枪 mǎqiāng　carbine

马球 mǎqiú　*sports*　equestrian polo; polo

马赛克 mǎsàikè　*archit.*　mosaic: ～铺面 mosaic pavement

马上 mǎshàng　*adv.*　① at once; immediately; straight away; right away: 我们～动手。We'll start working straight away. / 你～就走吗? Are you leaving right away? / 我～就回来。I won't be a minute. or I'll be back in a minute. / 演出～就要开始了。The performance will begin in a minute. / ～集合! Fall in immediately! ② in the near future; soon: 工作没有结束,他～还不会走。The work isn't finished yet, so he won't be leaving anytime soon. / ～就要高考了。The college entrance examinations are coming up soon.

马勺 mǎsháo　ladle

马绍尔群岛 Mǎshào'ěr Qúndǎo　the Marshall Islands

马首是瞻 mǎshǒu shì zhān　(usu. used in) 唯某某之～ take the head of sb.'s horse as guide—follow sb.'s lead

马术 mǎshù　horsemanship

马提尼克 Mǎtíníkè　Martinique

马蹄 mǎtí　① horse's hoof: ～声 hoofbeat; clatter of a horse's hoofs; clip-clop ② *dial.*　water chestnut

马蹄表 mǎtíbiǎo　round or hoof-shaped desk clock, usu. an alarm clock

马蹄螺 mǎtíluó　top shell

马蹄铁 mǎtítiě　① horseshoe ② U-shaped magnet; horseshoe magnet

马蹄形 mǎtíxíng　the shape of a hoof; U-shaped

马桶 mǎtǒng　(also 马子 mǎzi) ① nightstool; closestool; commode; chamber pot ② toilet

马头琴 mǎtóuqín　a bowed stringed instrument with a scroll carved like a horse's head, used by the Mongolians

马尾松 mǎwěisōng　masson pine

马戏 mǎxì　circus: ～团 circus troupe

马熊 mǎxióng　same as 棕熊 zōngxióng

马靴 mǎxuē　riding boots

马仰人翻 mǎyǎng-rénfān　same as 人仰马翻 rényǎng-mǎfān

马缨丹 mǎyīngdān　*bot.*　lantana

马缨花 mǎyīnghuā　another name for 合欢 héhuān②

马蝇 mǎyíng　horse botfly

马约特岛 Mǎyuētèdǎo　Mayotte

马扎 mǎzhá　(also 马劄 mǎzhá) campstool; folding stool

马掌 mǎzhǎng　① cutin skin of a horse's hoof ② horseshoe

马桩 mǎzhuāng　hitching post

马子 mǎzi　*dial.*　① nightstool; closestool; commode; chamber pot ② bandit; brigand

马鬃 mǎzōng　horse's mane

马祖岛 Mǎzǔdǎo　Mazu Island

吗　mǎ　see below ——see also mā; ma

吗啡 mǎfēi　morphine

犸　mǎ　see 猛犸 měngmǎ

玛　mǎ　see below

玛瑙 mǎnǎo　agate

玛雅人 Mǎyǎrén　Maya

玛雅文化 Mǎyǎ wénhuà　the Mayan Culture

玛祖卡 mǎzǔkǎ　*mus.*　mazurka

码¹　mǎ　① a sign or thing indicating number: 页码 yèmǎ　② an instrument used to indicate number:

砝码 fǎmǎ　③ *m.*　(used to indicate the same thing or the same kind): 这是两～事。They are two different matters. / 你们说的是一～事。You were talking about the same thing.

码²　mǎ　*inf.*　pile up; stack: ～砖 stack bricks / 把这些报纸～齐了。Put these newspapers in a neat pile.

码³　mǎ　yard (yd.)

码垛 mǎduò　pile up neatly; stack

码放 mǎfàng　put or keep things in good order

码头 mǎtou　① wharf; dock; quay; pier ② *dial.*　port city; commercial and transportation centre: 水陆～ a port city where land and water transport service is highly developed ——see also 跑码头 pǎo mǎtou

码头费 mǎtoufèi　wharfage; dockage

码头工人 mǎtou gōngrén　docker; stevedore; longshoreman

码头交货 mǎtou jiāohuò　ex wharf (or pier, quay)

码子 mǎzi　① numeral ② counter; chip ③ *old* (in financial circles) cash under one's control

蚂　mǎ　see below ——see also mà

蚂蜂 mǎfēng　same as 马蜂 mǎfēng

蚂蟥 mǎhuáng　leech

蚂蚁 mǎyǐ　ant

蚂蚁搬泰山 mǎyǐ bān Tàishān　ants can move Mount Taishan—the united efforts of the masses can accomplish mighty projects

蚂蚁啃骨头 mǎyǐ kěn gútou　ants gnawing at a bone—a concentration of small machines on a big job; plod away at a big job bit by bit

蚂蚁缘槐 mǎyǐ yuán huái　ants on the locust tree—little people inflated with pride

mà

骂（罵）　mà　① verbally abuse; curse; swear; call names: ～人 swear (at people) / ～人话 abusive language; swearwords; curse / 他～我是笨蛋。He called me an idiot. ② condemn; rebuke; reprove; scold: 这样铺张浪费, 没有一个人不～。Such extravagance is an object of general condemnation. / 把孩子～了一顿 give one's child a scolding (or dressing down) / 他爹～他不长进。His father blamed him for not striving to make progress.

骂架 màjià　quarrel; wrangle; have a row

骂街 màjiē　shout abuses in public; call people names in public ——see also 泼妇骂街 pōfù màjiē

骂骂咧咧 màmaliēliē　intersperse one's talk with curses; be foul-mouthed; be grumbling and swearing

骂名 màmíng　bad name; infamy: 留下千古～ earn oneself eternal infamy

蚂　mà　see below ——see also mǎ

蚂蚱 màzha　*dial.*　locust

ma

吗（么）　ma　*part.*　① (used at the end of a question): 下午有会～? Is there a meeting this afternoon? / 你找我有事～? Is there something you want to see me about? / 明天他来～? Will he come tomorrow? ② (used to form a pause in a sentence before introducing the theme of what one is going to say): 特殊情

况～, 还得特殊对待。Special cases, of course, need special consideration. / 这件事～, 其实也不能怪他。This matter, actually, is not his fault. ③ (used at the end of a rhetorical question): 你发这么大脾气像话～? Aren't you ashamed of flying into such a rage? / 你难道没看见我正忙着～? Don't you see I'm busy at the moment? / 这不是很明白的么～? Isn't this perfectly clear? ——see also má; mà

嘛（么）

ma *part.* ① (indicating that sth. is obvious): 这也不能怪他, 头一回做～。He's not to blame. After all, it was the first time he'd done it. / 这件事他是知道的～。He's well aware of it. / 他本来就不愿意去～, 就不要勉强他了。He just doesn't want to go. Don't force him. / 有意见就提～, 你怎么不提呀? If you have any suggestions to make, by all means make them. What are you keeping quiet for? ② (expressing a hope or giving advice): 喂, 汽车开慢点～! Hey, don't drive so fast! / 既然你忙, 就别去～。Since you are busy, don't go then. ③ (used to form a pause in a sentence, calling listener's attention): 这个问题～, 很简单。As for this problem, it's really quite simple. / 不让他去～, 他有意见; 让他去～, 他又不去了。If you don't let him go, he'll complain; but if you ask him to go, then he'll refuse to. / 好～, 那就快找他去吧。O. K. Go to him at once.

蟆（蟇）

ma see 蛤蟆 háma

mái

埋

mái ① cover up (with earth, snow, etc.); bury: 雪把这口井～起来了。The well is buried in snow. / ～地雷 lay a mine ② *inf.* bury (a dead person): 莫扎特是～在穷人的乱葬岗子上的。Mozart was buried in an unmarked pauper's grave. ——see also mán

埋藏 máicáng lie hidden in the earth; bury: 这一带地下～着丰富的矿产。There are rich mineral deposits in this region. / 奴隶们～在心底的仇恨像火山一样爆发出来了。The slaves' hatred, which had lain buried deep in their hearts, erupted like a volcano. / 他向她倾诉～在心底的感情。He revealed his innermost feelings to her. / 他是个直爽人, 从来不把自己想说的话～在心里。He's a straightforward person. If there is something he wants to say, he'll always say it.

埋伏 máifu ① lie in ambush; ambush: 设下～ lay an ambush / ～了一部分兵力 have part of the troops wait in ambush / 中～ fall into an ambush / 游击队～在青纱帐里。The guerrillas lay in ambush behind a green curtain of tall crops. ② hide; lie low ——see also 打埋伏 dǎ máifu

埋名 máimíng conceal one's identity; keep one's identity hidden; live incognito

埋没 máimò ① cover up (with earth, snow, etc.); bury: 泥石流～了整个村庄。The mud-rock flow submerged the whole village. ② neglect; stifle: ～人才 stifle real talents / 瞧, 这儿有重要的资料, 差点给～了。Look, here's some important source material we almost overlooked. / 他总是担心自己那点功劳被～了。He was always afraid that his bit of contribution would be overlooked.

埋设 máishè fit sth. underground: ～地雷 lay a mine

埋汰 máitai *dial.* ① dirty: 看你那股～劲, 不许你进屋。Look, how dirty you are! You can't go inside. / 把脸涂得埋埋汰汰的 have one's face smeared; smear one's face ② insult or ridicule: ～人 insult or make fun of sb.

埋头 máitóu immerse oneself in; be engrossed in: ～读书 bury oneself in one's studies / ～业务 engross oneself in vocational work

埋头苦干 máitóu kǔgàn quietly immerse oneself in hard work; quietly put one's shoulder to the wheel: 我就喜欢你们这股扎扎实实～的劲儿。I like your down-to-earth and hardworking spirit.

埋头铆钉 máitóu mǎodīng countersunk rivet

埋线疗法 máixiàn liáofǎ *Chin. med.* catgut embedding therapy (embedding a piece of catgut in a selected point to produce protracted stimulation)

埋葬 máizàng bury (a dead person): 这里～着一位伟人。A great man is buried here. *or* Here lies a great man.

霾

mái *meteorol.* haze: 阴霾 yīnmái

mǎi

买（買）

mǎi buy; purchase: 我家～了台彩电。We've bought a colour TV set. / 这是人家送的, 不是～的。It is a present, not a purchase. / ～东西 buy things; go shopping / 太贵了, ～不起。It's too expensive. I can't afford it. / 三块钱～两个。Three *yuan* will buy two pieces.

买办 mǎibàn comprador

买办资产阶级 mǎibàn zīchǎnjiējí comprador bourgeoisie

买椟还珠 mǎi dú huán zhū keep the glittering casket and give back the pearls—show lack of judgment; make the wrong choice

买方 mǎifāng the buying party (of a contract, etc.); buyer: ～市场 a buyer's market

买关节 mǎi guānjié get round (law, rules, etc.) by bribery; offer bribes to facilitate one's operations

买好 mǎihǎo try to win sb.'s favour; ingratiate oneself with; play up to: 他使出浑身的解数向她～。He did all he could do to win her favour.

买价 mǎijià buying price

买空仓 mǎi kōngcāng same as 放青苗 fàng qīngmiáo

买空卖空 mǎikōng-màikōng speculate (in stocks, etc.)

买路钱 mǎilùqián ① paper money thrown on the road during a funeral procession ② toll money (formerly asked for by highwaymen)

买麻藤 mǎimáténg *bot.* sweetberry jointfir (*Gnetum montanum*)

买卖公平 mǎi-mài gōngpíng be fair in buying and selling; buy and sell at reasonable prices

买卖婚姻 mǎimài hūnyīn mercenary marriage

买卖 mǎimai ① buying and selling; business; deal; transaction: 做成一笔～ make a deal / ～兴隆。Business is brisk. / 今天～怎么样? How was business today? ② (private) shop: 他原先在城里有个～。He used to have a shop in the city.

买卖人 mǎimàirén *inf.* businessman; trader; merchant

买面子 mǎi miànzi have regard for sb.'s face; defer to sb.: 不是我不买你的面子, 实在这事不好办。I'd be happy to defer to your wishes, but there's really nothing I can do about it. / 他买我的面子准同意。He's sure to agree for my sake.

买通 mǎitōng bribe; buy over; buy off: ～官府 bribe the local authorities (in old times)

买帐 mǎizhàng (usu. used in the negative) acknowledge the superiority or seniority of; show respect for: 他越是神气, 我们越不买他的帐。The more airs he gives himself, the less respect we'll show him. / 你摆架子, 人家就不买你的帐。If you put on airs, people just won't go for it.

买主 mǎizhǔ buyer; customer

荬(蕒) mǎi see 苣荬菜 qǔmaicài

mài

迈¹(邁) mài step; stride: ～过门槛 step over the threshold / ～着矫健的步伐 walk with vigorous strides / ～开双脚，走向基层。 Get yourself moving and go down to the grass roots.

迈²(邁) mài advanced in years; old: 年迈 niánmài

迈³(邁) mài ① mile (a transliteration): 这卡车一小时走七十～。 This truck can go 70 miles per hour (mph). ② mistakenly used by some drivers for kilometre

迈步 màibù take a step; make a step; step forward: ～走向讲台 step up to the platform / 迈出第一步 make the first step

迈方步 mài fāngbù walk with measured steps; stride leisurely forward

迈进 màijìn stride forward; forge ahead; advance with big strides: 朝着四个现代化的宏伟目标～ stride forward towards the great goal of the four modernizations / 他在学习上又～了一步。 He made further progress in his studies.

麦(麥) mài ① general name for wheat, barley, etc. ② wheat ③ (Mài) a surname

麦茬 màichá wheat stubble: ～白薯 sweet potatoes grown after the wheat harvest / ～地 a field of wheat stubble (ready for growing other crops)

麦地那 Màidìnà Medina

麦冬 màidōng Chin. med. the tuber of dwarf lilyturf (Ophiopogon japonicus)

麦蛾 mài'é gelechiid (moth)

麦尔登呢 mài'ěrdēngní melton (cloth)

麦麸 màifū wheat bran

麦秆虫 màigǎnchóng skeleton shrimp

麦红吸浆虫 màihóngxījiāngchóng wheat midge

麦加 Màijiā Mecca

麦角 màijiǎo pharm. ergot

麦秸 màijiē wheat straw

麦秸画 màijiēhuà woven straw patchwork

麦精 màijīng malt extract: ～鱼肝油 cod-liver oil with malt extract

麦克风 màikèfēng microphone (a transliteration); mike

麦浪 màilàng rippling wheat; billowing wheat fields: ～翻滚。 The wheat bent before the wind in swaying billows. / ～起伏。 The wheat was rippling in the wind.

麦粒肿 màilìzhǒng med. sty

麦芒 màimáng awn of wheat ——see also 针尖对麦芒 zhēnjiān duì màimáng

麦门冬 màiméndōng same as 麦冬 màidōng

麦苗 màimiáo wheat seedling

麦片 màipiàn oatmeal: ～粥 oatmeal porridge; oatmeal

麦淇淋 màiqílín margarine (a transliteration, also called 人造黄油 rénzào huángyóu)

麦秋 màiqiū wheat harvest season: ～假 wheat harvest vacation (for village schools)

麦乳精 màirǔjīng extract of malt and milk

麦收 màishōu wheat harvest

麦穗 màisuì ear of wheat; wheat head

麦芽 màiyá malt

麦芽糖 màiyátáng malt sugar; maltose

麦蚜 màiyá (also 麦蚜虫 màiyáchóng) wheat aphid

麦子 màizi wheat

卖(賣) mài ① sell: 把余粮～给国家 sell surplus grain to the state / ～文为生 write for a living / 这套剪纸～多少钱? What does this set of paper-cut sell for? / 大伏天西瓜～得快。 Watermelons sell fast during the dog days. / 他的画～不出去。 He can't sell off his paintings. ② betray (one's country or friends): 这件事我只跟你说，你可别把我给～了。 I'm telling this only to you. Don't give me away. ③ exert to the utmost; not spare: 卖劲儿 màijìnr ④ show off: 卖弄 màinong ⑤ m. old one dish: 一～炒腰花 a dish of stir-fried pork kidneys

卖卜 màibǔ practise divination for a living; be a fortune-teller

卖不动 màibudòng not sell well; be unsalable: 这种次货～。 This kind of inferior goods doesn't sell.

卖唱 màichàng sing for a living

卖大户 mài dàhù (also 卖大号 mài dàhào) (of a shop) profiteer by selling goods in great demand to individual buyers in batches

卖呆 màidāi ① pretend to be naive or stupid; feign stupidity ② dial. (of a woman) stand idly at the gate and watch what's going on in the street

卖恩 mài'ēn do sb. a favour for an ulterior motive

卖儿鬻女 mài'ér-yùnǚ sell one's children

卖方 màifāng the selling party (of a contract, etc.); seller: ～市场 a seller's market

卖功 màigōng brag; boast of one's contribution

卖狗皮膏药 mài gǒupí gāoyào sell quack remedies; practise quackery; palm things off on people

卖乖 màiguāi show off one's cleverness: 得了便宜～ pretend innocence and disinterest after succeeding in gaining some advantages; swagger and brag after having gained some advantages

卖关子 mài guānzi (stop a story at a climax to) keep the listeners in suspense; keep people guessing: 结果怎么样呢? 快说吧，别～了。 How did it end? Come on! Don't keep us guessing.

卖官鬻爵 màiguān-yùjué sell official posts and titles

卖国 màiguó betray one's country; turn traitor to one's country: ～集团 traitorous clique / ～条约 traitorous treaty / ～行为 treasonable act / ～主义 national betrayal

卖国求荣 màiguó qiú róng seek power and wealth by betraying one's country; turn traitor for personal gain

卖国贼 màiguózéi traitor (to one's country)

卖好 màihǎo curry favour with; ingratiate oneself with; play up to; fawn on: 谁有钱有势，他就向谁～。 He would fawn on anyone of wealth and position.

卖价 màijià selling price

卖劲儿 màijìnr exert all one's strength; spare no effort: 姑娘们干活真～。 The girls are really going all out in their work. / 你不必太～，要注意身体。 Don't work too hard. Take good care of yourself.

卖老 màilǎo flaunt one's seniority; put on the airs of a veteran

卖力 màilì exert all one's strength; spare no effort; do all one can: 他干活一向很～。 He is always hardworking.

卖力气 mài lìqi ① exert all one's strength; exert oneself to the utmost; do one's very best: 他做事很～。 He always does his very best. / 我再～也不容易讨她的好。 She is hard to please no matter how hard I try. ② live by the sweat of one's brow; make a living by manual labour

卖名 màimíng capitalize on one's reputation or prestige

卖命 màimìng ① work oneself to the bone for sb.: 地主逼着长工们为他～。 The landlord forced the farm labourers to work themselves to the bone. ② die (unworthily) for: 这些士兵没有一个愿意为侵略战争～。 None of these soldiers wanted to die in a war of aggression.

卖弄 màinong show off; parade: ～学问 show off one's learning; parade one's knowledge / ～小聪明 show off one's smartness / ～风骚 play the coquette / 别再在大伙儿跟前～了! Stop showing off in front of everybody.

卖破绽 mài pòzhàn old (in a fight or combat) feign an opening in order to hoodwink the opponent

卖钱 màiqián sell for money: 这东西卖不了几个钱。 You can't get much for this if you sell it.

卖俏 màiqiào play the coquette; coquette; flirt

卖人情 mài rénqíng show favours for one's own ends; win gratitude by favours

卖舌 màishé make sensational statements for the sake of publicity

卖身 màishēn ① sell oneself or a member of one's family: ～契 an indenture by which one sells oneself or a member of one's family ② inf. sell one's body; sell one's soul

卖身投靠 màishēn tóukào barter away one's honour for sb.'s patronage; basely offer to serve some reactionary bigwig

卖相 màixiàng dial. ① outward appearance; exterior; surface ② demeanour; bearing; manner: ～十足 have poise

卖笑 màixiào (of a prostitute or a singing girl) show a smiling face and flirt

卖艺 màiyì make a living as a performer: 在街头～ be a street-performer

卖淫 màiyín be a prostitute

卖友 màiyǒu betray one's friend

卖主 màizhǔ seller

卖嘴 màizuǐ show off verbal skill; indulge in clever talk

卖座 màizuò (of a theatre, etc.) draw large audiences; (of a restaurant, teahouse, etc.) attract large numbers of customers: 那出戏可～啦。 That play drew large audiences. or That play was a great draw.

脉(脈、衇) mài ① arteries and veins ② pulse: 病人的～很弱。 The patient's pulse was weak. ③ vein (of a leaf, etc.): 叶脉 yèmài / 翅脉 chìmài ④ sth. linking up to form a blood-vessel-like network: 矿脉 kuàngmài / 山脉 shānmài ——see also mò

脉搏 màibó pulse: 他的～每分钟一百次。 His pulse was one hundred beats per minute. / 这部小说把握了我们时代的～。 The novel throbs with the pulse of our times.

脉搏计 màibójì sphygmometer

脉冲 màichōng phys. pulse: ～发生器 pulser / ～计数器 pulse counter / ～雷达 pulse radar / ～信号 pulse signal

脉冲星 màichōngxīng astron. pulsar

脉动 màidòng phys. pulsation: ～式喷气发动机 pulse-jet engine

脉动电流 màidòng diànliú (also 脉冲电流 màichōng diànliú) pulsating current

脉动星 màidòngxīng astron. pulsating star

脉管炎 màiguǎnyán med. vasculitis

脉络 màiluò ① Chin. med. general name for arteries and veins ② veins (of a leaf, etc.) ③ train (or thread) of thought; sequence of ideas: 这篇文章结构严谨,～分明。 This article is closely knit and presents its ideas in a clear, logical way.

脉石 màishí gangue (a mineral); veinstone: ～矿物 gangue mineral

脉息 màixī pulse: ～微弱 have a weak pulse / 文学应与时代共～。 Literature should beat with the pulse of the times.

脉象 màixiàng Chin. med. pulse condition; type of pulse

脉泽 màizé phys. maser

脉诊 màizhěn Chin. med. diagnosis by feeling the pulse

mān

颟(顢) mān see below

颟顸 mānhan muddleheaded and careless: ～无能 careless and incompetent / 那人太～,什么事都做不好。 That man is so muddleheaded and careless that he can't do anything right.

mán

埋 mán see below ——see also mái

埋怨 mányuàn blame; complain; grumble: 她总是～自己不好,从不抱怨别人。 She always puts the blame on herself, and never on others. / 这台录音机是他搞坏的,却～上我了。 He's the one who broke the recorder, but he blames me for it. / 这场球打输了,大家找找原因,不要互相～。 Instead of blaming one another for losing the game, let's find out what exactly went wrong. / 他的话里有～情绪。 There was a note of complaint in what he said. / 他干什么总是～来～去的。 He can't do anything without grumbling about it.

蛮(蠻) mán ① rough; fierce; reckless; unreasoning: 野蛮 yěmán ② (Mán) an ancient name for the tribes in the south ③ dial. quite; pretty: 这电影～好。 This is quite a good film. or This is a pretty good film.

蛮不讲理 mán bù jiǎnglǐ be impervious to reason; persist in being unreasonable; wilful; obstinate: 他脾气很坏,而且～。 He's bad-tempered and wilful. / 跟这种～的人争辩没有用。 It's no use trying to reason with such an obstinate person.

蛮缠 mánchán see 胡搅蛮缠 hújiǎo-mánchán

蛮干 mángàn act rashly; act recklessly; be foolhardy: 要苦干加巧干,不要～。 We should work hard and intelligently, not blindly. / 不采取安全措施就下矿井,那纯粹是～。 It's downright foolhardy to go down the pit without taking safety measures. / 他明知干不成还要去试,真是～。 He was foolhardy to try, when he knew he'd fail.

蛮横 mánhèng rude and unreasonable; arbitrary; peremptory: ～的态度 an unreasonable attitude / ～地拒绝合理建议 arbitrarily reject reasonable proposals / 他太～,没法跟人合作。 He's much too peremptory to cooperate with others.

蛮横无理 mánhèng wúlǐ rude and unreasonable; arbitrary; peremptory: ～的要求 peremptory demands

蛮劲 mánjìn sheer animal strength

谩 mán deceive; hoodwink ——see also màn

谩语 mányǔ deceitful words; lies

蔓 mán see below ——see also màn; wàn

蔓菁 mánjing same as 芜菁 wújīng

馒 mán see below

馒头 mántou steamed bun; steamed bread

瞒（瞞）

mán hide the truth from: 他怕妻子着急，把病情～着不说。He didn't let his wife know about his illness for fear she'd worry. / 不～你说 to tell you the truth / 这件事不能再～着他了。We cannot keep him in the dark about this any longer. / 她～了两岁。She pretended to be two years younger. / 你干的丑事～得住吗?Did you think you could cover up such a disgraceful affair? / 什么事也～不过她的眼睛。Nothing could escape her notice.

瞒哄 mánhǒng deceive; pull the wool over sb.'s eyes: ～领导 hide the truth from the leadership

瞒上欺下 mán shàng qī xià deceive those above and bully those below

瞒天过海 mán tiān guò hǎi cross the sea by a trick—practise deception

鳗

mán eel

鳗鲡 mánlí eel

mǎn

满（滿）

mǎn ① full; filled; packed: ～～一卡车煤 a full truckload of coal / 这两个抽屉都～了。Both drawers are full. / 屋里坐～了人。The room was packed with people. / 果树～山坡。The slope was covered with fruit trees. / 欢声笑语～山村。The mountain village rang with cheers and laughter. / 话不能说得太～、太绝。One shouldn't speak in absolute terms, leaving no room for compromise. / 一头大汗 one's face streaming with sweat / ～脑子封建思想 be steeped in feudal ideology ② fill: 再给你～上一杯。Let me fill your glass once more. ③ expire; reach the limit: 年～十八的公民 citizens who have reached the age of 18 / 他的服役期还没～。His term of military service hasn't expired yet. / 她学徒还不～一年。It isn't a year yet since she became an apprentice. / 假期已～。The holidays are over. ④ adv. completely; entirely; perfectly: ～有信心 be fully confident / ～不是那么回事。That wasn't the way it was at all. / 我～以为他会同意的。I had counted on him to agree with me. ⑤ adv. quite; very: 这首歌～好听。This song is quite pleasant. / 您说的～对。What you've said is quite right. / 节目倒也～不错。The performances were pretty good. ⑥ satisfied: 不满 bùmǎn ⑦ complacent; conceited: 自满 zìmǎn ⑧ (Mǎn) the Man nationality (see also 满族 Mǎnzú) ⑨ (Mǎn) a surname

满不在乎 mǎn bù zàihu not worry at all; not care in the least; give (or take) no heed: 别人都替他着急，他却～。Everybody was anxious about him, but he wasn't worried at all. / 他表面上装出一副～的样子，内心却是恐慌的。Although feigning complete indifference, he was actually terrified.

满城风雨 mǎn chéng fēngyǔ (become) the talk of the town: 这件丑闻闹得～。The scandal has created a sensation.

满打满算 mǎndǎ-mǎnsuàn reckoning in every item (of income or expenditure); at the very most: 这项工程～有一百吨水泥就足够了。We need 100 tons of cement at most for this project.

满登登 mǎndēngdēng (also 满满登登 mǎnmandēngdēng) inf. full: 粮仓里装得～的。The grainary was stuffed full of grain.

满额 mǎn'é fulfil the (enrolment, etc.) quota: 我校今年招生已经～。Our school has already fulfilled its enrolment quota for this year.

满分 mǎnfēn full marks: 他考试得了～。He got full marks in his examination. / 体操比赛的～是十分。The highest possible score in a gymnastics event is ten points.

满服 mǎnfú (also 满孝 mǎnxiào) be at the expiration of a mourning period

满腹经纶 mǎn fù jīnglún be possessed of learning and ability

满腹牢骚 mǎn fù láosāo full of grievances; full of resentment; full of grumbles

满贯 mǎnguàn ① reach the limit ② (in mahjong, card games, etc.) perfect score; slam: (in bridge) 小（大）～ little or small (grand) slam

满怀[1] mǎnhuái ① have one's heart filled with; be imbued with: ～胜利的信心 fully confident of victory; with full confidence in victory / ～着对战友的深情 imbued with ardent love for one's comrade-in-arms / ～着对敌人的深仇大恨 burning with bitter hatred for the enemy / 我们对灾民～同情。We're filled with sympathy for the victims of the natural disaster. ② (usu. used in) 撞了个～ bump right into sb.

满怀[2] mǎnhuái (of sheep, cattle, etc.) bear a full crop of young

满坑满谷 mǎnkēng-mǎngǔ in every valley and ravine—in large numbers; in great abundance; in plenty

满口 mǎnkǒu (speak) unreservedly or profusely; be full of: ～称赞 praise profusely; be full of praises / ～答应 readily promise / ～谎言 spout lies / ～脏话 pour out dirty words

满脸花 mǎnliǎnhuā a bloody nose and a swollen face; badly battered

满满当当 mǎnmandāngdāng inf. full to the brim: 他吃了～三碗饭。He ate three full bowls of rice. / 挑着～的两桶水 carry (or tote) two brimming buckets of water / 厩肥～地装了一大车。The cart was piled high with barnyard manure.

满门 mǎnmén the whole family: ～抄斩 (in feudal China) execution of the entire family

满面 mǎnmiàn have one's face covered with: 泪流～ tears streaming down one's cheeks / ～笑容 grinning from ear to ear; be all smiles / ～红光 glowing with health

满面春风 mǎnmiàn chūnfēng beaming with satisfaction; radiant with happiness

满目 mǎnmù meet the eye on every side: ～荒凉。A scene of desolation met the eye on every side.

满目疮痍 mǎnmù chuāngyí same as 疮痍满目 chuāngyí mǎnmù

满期 mǎnqī expire: 租约～ the expiration of a lease / 进修～ complete a refresher course

满腔 mǎnqiāng have one's bosom filled with: ～仇恨 burning with hatred / ～怒火 filled with rage / ～的热血已经沸腾。Our blood is boiling.

满腔热忱 mǎnqiāng rèchén filled with ardour and sincerity: ～地接待顾客 willingly wait on customers / ～地提出建议 propose in all earnestness

满腔热情 mǎnqiāng rèqíng full of enthusiasm; wholehearted: 她～地投入工作。She enthusiastically threw herself into the work. / 老王总是～地为大家服务。Lao Wang is always ready to help people out wholeheartedly.

满山遍野 mǎnshān-biànyě same as 漫山遍野 mànshān-biànyě

满身 mǎnshēn have one's body covered with; be covered all over with: ～油泥 covered all over with grime / ～是汗 sweat all over; be soaked with sweat / 他～都长了疙瘩。There were swellings all over his body.

满师 mǎnshī (of an apprentice) finish serving one's time; serve out one's apprenticeship: 学徒三年～。The apprenticeship requires three years of service.

满堂彩 mǎntángcǎi (usu. used in) 得了个～ bring the house down

满堂灌 mǎntángguàn (of a teacher) cram students; spoonfeed

满堂红[1] mǎntánghóng all-round victory; success in every field: 今年我们厂是～,各项指标都提前完成了。 Our factory has had all-round success this year. All our targets have been fulfilled ahead of schedule.

满堂红[2] mǎntánghóng common name for 紫薇 zǐwēi

满天 mǎntiān all over the sky: 乌云～。 The sky is overcast with dark clouds. / 鹅毛大雪～飞。 The snow is falling thick and heavy.

满天星斗 mǎntiān xīngdǒu a star-studded sky

满-通古斯语族 Mǎn-Tōnggǔsī yǔzú linguis. the Manchu-Tungusic group

满心 mǎnxīn have one's heart filled with: ～欢喜 be filled with joy

满眼 mǎnyǎn ① have one's eyes filled with: 他一连两夜没有睡,～都是血丝。 He didn't get any sleep for two successive nights, so his eyes were all bloodshot. ② meet the eye on every side: ～的山花 mountain flowers greeting the eye everywhere

满意 mǎnyì satisfied; pleased; content: 双方对会谈的结果表示～。 Both sides expressed satisfaction with the results of the talks. / 大家对他的工作很～。 Everyone was pleased with his work. / 我妻子不～我给她照的像。 My wife isn't satisfied with the photo I took of her. / 他给了我一个～的答复。 He gave me a satisfactory reply. / 她～地笑了。 She smiled with contentment.

满员 mǎnyuán ① mil. be at full strength: 保证主力部队经常～ ensure that the main forces are always kept at full strength ② (of a train, etc.) have all seats taken: 二号车厢已经～。 No. 2 carriage is full.

满园春色 mǎnyuán chūnsè same as 春色满园 chūnsè mǎnyuán

满月[1] mǎnyuè a baby's completion of its first month of life: 孩子明天就～了。 The baby will be a month old tomorrow.

满月[2] mǎnyuè full moon

满载 mǎnzài be loaded to capacity; be fully loaded; be laden with: 一辆～木材的卡车 a truck fully loaded with timber / 一艘～煤炭的货船 a freighter laden with coal / 医疗队～着非洲人民的友谊回到北京。 The medical team returned to Beijing bringing with it the friendship of the African people.

满载而归 mǎnzài ér guī come back with fruitful results; return from a rewarding journey

满招损,谦受益 mǎn zhāo sǔn, qiān shòu yì haughtiness invites disaster, humility receives benefit

满洲 Mǎnzhōu Manchuria (old name for 东北 Dōngběi)

满足 mǎnzú ① satisfied; content; contented: ～于现状 be satisfied with the existing state of affairs; be content with things as they are / 不～于已经取得的成绩 not rest content with one's achievements; not rest on one's laurels / 能有这样的工作条件,我已经很～了。 I'm very much satisfied with such good working conditions. / 学习的敌人是自己的～。 Complacency is the enemy of study. ② satisfy; meet (needs, demands, etc.): ～人民的需要 satisfy (or meet) the needs of the people / 我们将尽可能地～你们的要求。 We'll do our best to meet your demands.

满族 Mǎnzú the Manchu nationality, or the Manchus, mainly distributed over the provinces of Liaoning, Heilongjiang, Jilin and Hebei, the municipality of Beijing and the Inner Mongolia Autonomous Region

满座 mǎnzuò have a capacity audience; have a full house: 这个剧演了一个月,场场～。 The play ran for a month to capacity audiences. / 今晚电影将～。 The film will be shown to a full house tonight.

螨(蟎) mǎn zool. mite

màn

曼 màn ① graceful: 轻歌曼舞 qīnggē-mànwǔ ② prolonged; long-drawn-out: 曼延 mànyán

曼丁哥语 Māndīnggēyǔ Mande; Mandingo

曼妙 mànmiào liter. (of dancing) lithe and graceful

曼声 mànshēng (sing or recite in) lengthened sounds: ～吟诵 recite in slow, measured tones / ～而歌 drawl out a song / ～低语 murmur slowly / 她一面走,一面～地唱着。 She sang lazily as she strolled along.

曼陀林 màntuólín mus. mandolin

曼陀罗 màntuóluó bot. datura

曼延 mànyán draw out (in length); stretch: ～曲折的羊肠小道 a winding footpath stretching into the distance

谩 màn disrespectful; rude ——see also mán

谩骂 mànmà hurl invectives; fling abuse; rail: ～决不是战斗。 To hurl abuse is no way to fight.

漫 màn ① overflow; brim over; flood; inundate: 池塘的水～出来了。 The pool overflowed its banks. / 水不深,只～过我脚面。 The water wasn't deep. It only came up to my ankles. ② be all over the place; be everywhere: ～江碧透。 The whole stream was emerald green. / 山头上忽然～起好大的云雾。 The hilltops were suddenly covered in thick mist. ③ free; unrestrained; casual: ～无目标 aimless; at random / ～无限制 without any limit; with no restrictions whatsoever

漫儿 mànr the side of a copper coin without words on it

漫笔 mànbǐ (usu. used as title of an essay) literary notes: 灯下～ (literary) notes by the lamp—illuminating (literary) notes

漫不经心 màn bù jīngxīn careless; casual; negligent: ～地说 speak in an offhand way / 看他那～的样子,能把事情办好么? He looks as if he couldn't care less, so I doubt he'll do a good job. / "嗨,好吧。"他～地回答着。 "Oh, all right," he answered indifferently.

漫步 mànbù stroll; ramble; roam: ～街头 stroll along the street

漫长 màncháng very long; endless: ～的海岸线 a long coastline / 在～的岁月中 during the long years; over the years√ 中国的革命走过了～而曲折的道路。 The Chinese revolution has followed a long and tortuous course.

漫道 màndào do not say or talk: ～如此。 Do not talk like that. / 雄关～真如铁,而今迈步从头越。(毛泽东) Idle boast the strong pass is a wall of iron, With firm strides we are crossing its summit.

漫反射 mànfǎnshè phys. diffuse reflection

漫灌 mànguàn ① flood irrigation ② (of a flood) overflow (into an area)

漫画 mànhuà caricature; cartoon

漫话 mànhuà chat freely; have an informal discussion

漫漶 mànhuàn (of pictures, writing, etc.) blurred; indistinct; illegible: 字迹～。 The words have become illegible.

漫卷 mànjuǎn (of banners) flutter (or wave) freely: 六盘山上高峰,红旗～西风。(毛泽东) High on the crest of Mount Liupan Red banners wave freely in the west wind.

漫骂 mànmà use bad language against sb.; fling abuse

漫漫 mànmàn very long; boundless: ～长夜 endless night / 四野都是一眼望不到头的～白雪。 A boundless

expanse of snow stretched out as far as the eye could see.

漫灭 mànmiè　wear away; efface; obliterate

漫坡 mànpō　a gentle slope

漫山遍野 mànshān-biànyě　all over the mountains and plains; over hill and dale: 战士们～地奔跑，去占领这个高地。 The soldiers began swarming across the countryside trying to occupy the height.

漫射 mànshè　*phys.* diffusion: ～光 diffused light / ～体 diffuser

漫说 mànshuō　same as 慢说 mànshuō

漫谈 màntán　(have an) informal discussion: ～国际形势 have a free discussion about the world situation / 听完报告咱们～一下吧。 After we've heard the report, we'll talk about it.

漫天 màntiān　① filling the whole sky; all over the sky: ～大雾 a dense fog obscuring the sky / ～大雪 whirling snow / 黄土～。 A cloud of loess filled the whole sky. ② boundless; limitless: ～大谎 a monstrous lie

漫天要价 màntiān yàojià　ask (*or* demand) an exorbitant price: ～，就地还钱。 The seller can ask a sky-high price; the buyer can make a rock-bottom offer.

漫无边际 màn wú biānjì　① boundless: ～的海洋 the boundless sea ② straying far from the subject; rambling; discursive: ～的长篇大论 a long-winded speech or article; a long rambling talk

漫无止境 màn wú zhǐjìng　know no bounds; be without limit: 一个人的欲望是～的。 A man's desires know no bounds.

漫延 mànyán　same as 蔓延 mànyán

漫野 mànyě　all over the plains

漫溢 mànyì　overflow; flood; brim over: 洪流～。 The floodwaters were overflowing.

漫游 mànyóu　go on a pleasure trip; roam; wander: ～西湖 go boating on or roam around the West Lake

蔓

màn　see below——see also　mán; wàn

蔓生植物 mànshēng zhíwù　trailing plant

蔓延 mànyán　spread; extend: 火势～很快。 The fire spread quickly. / 控制流行性感冒的～ keep flu from spreading

慢[1]

màn　① slow: 反应～ be slow to react / 他看书看得～。 He reads slowly. / 他跑得～。 He's a slow runner. / 病人恢复得很～。 The patient is making a slow recovery. / 火车～～地驶进了车站。 Slowly the train pulled into the station. / 公共汽车到站时～了下来。 The bus slowed down as it approached the stop. / 我的表～五分钟。 My watch is five minutes slow. / 这钟一天～十秒。 This clock loses 10 seconds a day. / 他～～会想通的。 He'll come round by and by. / 行 Drive Slow (highway sign) ② (used in imperative sentences, alone or before verbs): 我这就给她打电话去。一～! 等票子拿到了再打。 I'm going to ring her right away.—Just a moment! Not until we get the tickets. / 你～点儿吃。 Don't rush through your meal. / ～～来，别着急。 Take your time and don't worry. / 这事～点儿告诉他，等两天再说。 Don't tell him the news just now; wait a couple of days.

慢[2]

màn　supercilious; rude: 傲慢 àomàn

慢藏诲盗 màncáng-huìdào　failure to put things away properly is inviting theft

慢车 mànchē　slow train

慢车道 mànchēdào　slow (traffic) lane (on a street); inside lane

慢道 màndào　same as 漫道 màndào

慢工出细活 màngōng chū xìhuó　slow work yields fine products

慢火 mànhuǒ　slow fire; gentle heat

慢镜头 mànjìngtóu　*film* slow motion

慢慢腾腾 mànmantēngtēng　(also 慢慢吞吞 mànmantūntūn) loiteringly slow: 这样～地走，什么时候才能到啊? If we walk at this snail's pace, when will we ever get there?

慢坡 mànpō　a gentle slope

慢说 mànshuō　*conj.* let alone; to say nothing of: 这种动物，～国内少有，在全世界也不多。 This kind of animal is rare anywhere in the world, let alone China. / 他讲故事，～孩子，连大人都爱听。 Even the adults like to listen to his stories, to say nothing of the children.

慢腾腾 màntēngtēng　(also 慢吞吞 màntūntūn) at a leisurely pace; unhurriedly; sluggishly: 你这么～的，什么时候能做完哪? When will you ever finish the job if you go on at this pace? / 他干什么都是～的。 He always works at a leisurely pace, no matter what he does. / 说话～ speak slowly

慢条斯理 màntiáosīlǐ　slowly; leisurely; unhurriedly: 他说话做事总是～的。 He always speaks slowly and acts unhurriedly.

慢性· mànxìng　① chronic: ～支气管炎 chronic bronchitis ② slow (in taking effect): ～毒药 slow poison

慢性病 mànxìngbìng　*med.* chronic disease

慢性子 mànxìngzi　① phlegmatic temperament ② slowpoke; slowcoach

慢悠悠 mànyōuyōu　(also 慢慢悠悠 mànmanyōuyōu) unhurried; leisurely: ～地走着 walk leisurely

慢中子 mànzhōngzǐ　*phys.* slow neutron; low-speed neutron

慢走 mànzǒu　① don't go yet; stay; wait a minute ② *pol.* (said by the host or hostess to a guest at departure) good-bye; take care

墁

màn　pave floor with bricks, stones, etc.

幔

màn　curtain; screen: 布～ cotton curtain / 窗～ window curtain

幔帷 mànwéi　heavy curtain

幔帐 mànzhàng　curtain; screen; canopy

幔子 mànzi　*dial.* curtain; screen

缦

màn　*formal* plain silk fabrics

嫚

màn　*formal* scorn; humiliate

嫚骂 mànmà　hurl invectives; fling abuse; rail

熳

màn　see 烂熳 lànmàn

镘 (槾)

màn　*arch.* trowel

máng

牤 (牪)

máng　see below

牤牛 māngniú　*dial.* bull

máng

忙

máng　① busy; fully occupied: 我这会儿～得很。 I'm very busy just now. / 她～了一整天，为这些报告打字。 She was busy all day typing the reports. / 这两天～不～?—得团团转。 Are you busy these days?—Yes, I'm running round in circles. / 她正～着做饭呢。 She's busying herself preparing the meal. / 你在～什么呢?——开会。 What are you busy with?—Attending

meetings. / 我一个人～不过来。 I can't manage all this by myself. / 不要～于小事而忽略大事。 Don't immerse yourself in minor matters to the neglect of major ones. / ～完一天工作 have finished up a long day's work ② hurry; hasten; make haste: 他～从里屋出来。 He came hurrying out of the inner room. / 你～什么，再坐一会儿吧。 What's the hurry? Stay a bit longer. / 别～于下结论。 Don't jump to conclusions.

忙乎 mánɡhu　be busy; bustle about: ～了一天 have been busy all day

忙活[1] mánɡhuó　be busy with sth.: 这几天正～。 I've been very busy with my work these last few days. / 你忙什么活？ What are you busy with?

忙活[2] mánɡhuó　an urgent piece of work; an urgent job: 这是件～，要先做。 This is an urgent piece of work. Do it first.

忙活 mánɡhuo　*dial.*　be busy; bustle about: 他们俩已经～了一上午了。 The two of them have been busy the whole morning.

忙里偷闲 mánɡlǐ tōuxián　snatch a little leisure from a busy life

忙碌 mánɡlù　be busy; bustle about: 为了全厂工人的生活，她成天～不停。 She's busy all day looking after the daily life of the workers in the factory. / 她一天到晚忙忙碌碌，真不知道她究竟忙些什么。 She's kept busy all day long, but I've no idea what she was busying herself with. / 忙忙碌碌 as busy as a bee

忙乱 mánɡluàn　be in a rush and a muddle; tackle a job in a hasty and disorderly manner: 要克服～现象。 Don't work in a rush and get into a muddle. / 最近会议多，头绪多，太～了。 Recently there have been so many meetings to be attended and so many things to be taken care of. Everything seems to be in a muddle.

忙忙叨叨 mánɡmanɡdāodāo　busy and flustered

忙人 mánɡrén　busy person: 他是个大～，哪有功夫上这儿来。 He's a busy man and certainly doesn't have the time to come here.

芒 mánɡ　awn; beard; arista

芒刺在背 mánɡcì zài bèi　feel prickles down one's back—feel nervous and uneasy

芒果 mánɡɡuǒ　same as 杧果 mánɡɡuǒ

芒硝 mánɡxiāo　*chem.*　mirabilite; Glauber's salt

芒种 Mánɡzhònɡ　① Grain in Beard—the 9th of the 24 solar terms ② the day marking the beginning of the 9th solar term (June 5, 6, or 7, which marks the end of the grain-growing season and reminds the farmer that it is the last chance for sowing): 过了～，不可强种。 Once the time of Grain in Beard passes, it will be no use planting. (a proverb) —— see also 节气 jiéqì; 二十四节气 èrshí sì jiéqì

杧 mánɡ　see below

杧果 mánɡɡuǒ　*bot.*　mango

盲 mánɡ　blind: 色盲 sèmánɡ

盲肠 mánɡchánɡ　*physiol.*　caecum

盲肠炎 mánɡchánɡyán　popular name for 阑尾炎 lánwěiyán

盲椿象 mánɡchūnxiànɡ　*zool.*　plant bug

盲从 mánɡcónɡ　follow blindly

盲点 mánɡdiǎn　*physiol.*　blind spot; scotoma

盲动 mánɡdònɡ　act blindly; act rashly

盲动主义 mánɡdònɡzhǔyì　putschism

盲干 mánɡɡàn　act aimlessly or rashly: 这样一味～，结果非碰壁不可。 Such rashness is bound to land you in great difficulties.

盲井 mánɡjǐnɡ　same as 暗井 ànjǐnɡ

盲流 mánɡliú　unchecked flow of population (from the countryside to the cities)

盲鳗 mánɡmán　hagfish

盲目 mánɡmù　blind: ～崇拜 worship blindly / ～服从 obey blindly / ～乐观 be unrealistically optimistic / 人口的～增长 unchecked growth of the population

盲目飞行 mánɡmù fēixínɡ　blind flight; instrument flying

盲目轰炸 mánɡmù hōnɡzhà　blind bombing

盲目性 mánɡmùxìnɡ　blindness (in action): 去掉～，养成分析的习惯。 Stop acting blindly and cultivate the habit of analysis.

盲目着陆 mánɡmù zhuólù　blind landing

盲棋 mánɡqí　blind chess (a chess game played by one person without looking at the chessboard against a number of individual opponents)

盲区 mánɡqū　*radio*　blind area

盲人 mánɡrén　a blind person

盲人摸象 mánɡrén mō xiànɡ　a group of blind men trying to size up an elephant, each mistaking the part he touches for the whole animal—take a part for the whole

盲人瞎马 mánɡrén xiāmǎ　a blind man on a blind horse—rushing headlong to disaster; in for trouble

盲鼠 mánɡshǔ　same as 鼢鼠 fénshǔ

盲文 mánɡwén　① braille ② braille publication

盲哑教育 mánɡ-yǎ jiàoyù　education for the blind and the deaf-mute

盲字 mánɡzì　braille

氓 mánɡ　see 流氓 liúmánɡ ——see also ménɡ

茫 mánɡ　① boundless and indistinct: 白茫茫 báimánɡmánɡ ② ignorant; in the dark: 迷茫 mímánɡ[2]

茫茫 mánɡmánɡ　boundless and indistinct; vast: ～大海 a vast sea / ～草原 the boundless grasslands / ～一片白雾 a vast expanse of fog / 前途～ bleak prospects / 天苍苍，野～，风吹草低见牛羊。《敕勒歌》 The sky is blue, blue: And the steppe wide, wide: Over grass that the wind has battered low, Sheep and oxen roam.

茫昧 mánɡmèi　*formal*　① dim; gloomy; blurred ② confused; uncomprehending; ignorant

茫然 mánɡrán　① boundless and indistinct; vast: 纵一苇之所如，凌万顷之～。(苏轼) We let our boat float along, sailing over the vast expanse. ② ignorant; in the dark; at a loss: ～无知 be utterly ignorant; be in the dark / ～不知所措 be at a loss what to do; be at sea / 显出～的神情 look blank; wear a blank expression ③ frustrated; disappointed: 她坐车走了，我～若失地站在那里。 She got on the bus and was gone, leaving me standing there with a feeling of loss.

茫无头绪 mánɡ wú tóuxù　not know how to go about things; be in a hopeless muddle

铓 mánɡ　see 锋铓 fēnɡmánɡ

碒 mánɡ　see below

碒硝 mánɡxiāo　*chem.*　mirabilite; Glauber's salt

mǎnɡ

莽[1] mǎnɡ　① rank grass: 草莽 cǎomǎnɡ ② *formal*　big; large; huge

莽[2] mǎnɡ　rash: 鲁莽 lǔmánɡ

莽苍 mǎnɡcānɡ　(of scenery) blurred; misty: 烟雨莽苍苍，龟蛇锁大江。(毛泽东) Blurred in the thick haze of the misty rain Tortoise and Snake hold the great river locked.

莽汉　mǎnghàn　(also 莽夫 mǎngfū) a boorish fellow; boor

莽莽　mǎngmǎng　① (of plant growth) lush; rank ② (of fields, plains, etc.) vast; boundless

莽原　mǎngyuán　wilderness overgrown with grass

莽撞　mǎngzhuàng　crude and impetuous; rash: ～的小伙子 a young harum-scarum / 他说话太～。It was rash for him to talk like that. / 要小心行事，不要～。Be careful and don't act rashly. / 恕我～。Forgive me for my bluntness.

漭　mǎng　see below

漭漭　mǎngmǎng　liter. vast; boundless

蟒　mǎng　① boa; python ② short for 蟒袍 mǎngpáo

蟒袍　mǎngpáo　official robe worn by ministers during Ming and Qing Dynasties, with gold designs of pythons

蟒蛇　mǎngshé　boa; python

māo

猫 (貓)

māo　① cat: 雄～ tomcat / 小～ kitten ② dial. hide oneself: 他一听我们到来，就赶紧～起来了。As soon as he heard us coming, he quickly hid himself somewhere. ——see also máo

猫哭老鼠　māo kū lǎoshǔ　(usu. used in) ～——假慈悲 the cat weeping over the dead mouse—shed crocodile tears

猫头鹰　māotóuyīng　owl

猫熊　māoxióng　panda; giant panda

猫眼　māoyǎn　dial. peephole (fixed in a door); spyhole

猫眼石　māoyǎnshí　cat's eye (a mineral)

猫鱼　māoyú　small fish for feeding cats

máo

毛[1]

máo　① hair; feather; down: 这马长得一身好～。The horse has a fine coat of hair. / 桃子的皮上有细～。A peach has downy skin. ② wool: ～袜 woollen stockings / 这件夹克衫是棉的还是～的? Is this jacket cotton or woollen? ③ mildew; mould: 长毛 zhǎngmáo ④ semifinished: 毛坯 máopī ⑤ gross: 毛利 máolì ⑥ little; small: ～贼 petty thief; pilferer ⑦ inf. (of currency) be no longer worth its face value; depreciate: 钱～了。Money has gone down in value. ⑧ (Máo) a surname

毛[2]

máo　① careless; crude; rash: ～头～脑 rash; impetuous ② panicky; scared; flurried: 这下可把他吓了。This really made him scared. / 她一考试就～。She panics whenever she takes an exam. ③ dial. get angry; lose one's temper: 你可别再说他了，再说，他就要～了。Don't scold him any more or he'll get angry.

毛[3]

máo　inf. mao, a fractional unit of money in China (=1/10 yuan 元 or 10 fen 分): 一～钱 one mao / 这支笔几～钱?—四～。How much is this pen?—Four mao.

毛白杨　máobáiyáng　bot. Chinese white poplar

毛笔　máobǐ　writing brush

毛边纸　máobiānzhǐ　(also 毛边 máobiān) writing paper made from bamboo

毛病　máobing　① trouble; mishap; breakdown: 这架收音机有点～。There's something wrong with the radio. ② defect; shortcoming; fault; mistake: 克服工作作风上的～ overcome defects in one's work style / 犯了主观主义的～ make the mistake of being subjective; commit the error of subjectivism / 他的～是性急。He's impetuous—that's the trouble with him. ③ bad habit; shortcoming: 他抽烟的～总也改不了。He'll never give up his bad habit of smoking. ④ dial. illness: 孩子有～，不要让他受凉了。The child is ill. Don't let him catch a chill. / 他胃有～。He has stomach trouble. / 她有头疼的～。She suffers from headaches. ——see also 出毛病 chū máobìng

毛玻璃　máobōli　frosted glass; ground glass

毛布　máobù　coarse cotton cloth; coarse calico

毛糙　máocao　crude; coarse; careless: 这活做得太～。That's rather crude work. / 你做事怎么这么～? How could you be so careless?

毛虫　máochóng　(also 毛毛虫 máomaochóng) caterpillar

毛刺　máocì　mech. burr

毛地黄　máodìhuáng　pharm. digitalis

毛豆　máodòu　young (or fresh) soya bean

毛发　máofà　hair (on the human body and head)

毛纺　máofǎng　wool spinning: 粗梳～ woollen spinning / 精梳～ worsted spinning / ～厂 woollen mill

毛感　máogǎn　the feel of wool: 这料子～强。This cloth feels very much like wool.

毛葛　máogé　text. poplin

毛茛　máogèn　bot. buttercup

毛估　máogū　roughly estimate

毛骨悚然　máogǔ sǒngrán　with one's hair standing on end—absolutely terrified: 令人～ send cold shivers down one's spine; make sb.'s hair stand on end; be bloodcurdling

毛孩子　máoháizi　inf. a small child; a mere child

毛蚶　máohān　dial. blood clam

毛烘烘　máohōnghōng　hairy; furry

毛活　máohuó　inf. knitting work

毛姜　máojiāng　dial. Jarusalem artichoke

毛巾　máojīn　towel: ～布 towelling / ～架 towel rail or rack

毛焦火辣　máojiāo-huǒlà　burning with impatience; in a nervous state

毛巾被　máojīnbèi　(also 毛巾毯 máojīntǎn) towelling coverlet

毛举细故　máo jǔ xì gù　(also 毛举细务 máo jǔ xì wù) bring up trifling matters

毛孔　máokǒng　physiol. pore

毛口　máokǒu　mech. burr: 去～ burring

毛裤　máokù　long woollen underwear; woollen pants

毛拉　máolā　Islam maula; mullah

毛梾　máolái　bot. long-petioled dogwood (Cornus walteri)

毛蓝　máolán　darkish blue: ～土布 dyed (or blue) nankeen

毛里求斯　Máolǐqiúsī　Mauritius

毛里求斯人　Máolǐqiúsīrén　Mauritian

毛里塔尼亚　Máolǐtǎníyà　Mauritania

毛里塔尼亚人　Máolǐtǎníyàrén　Mauritanian

毛利　máolì　gross profit

毛料　máoliào　woollen cloth; woollens

毛驴　máolǘ　donkey

毛毛　máomao　dial. baby

毛毛腾腾　máomaotēngtēng　dial. flurried and excited; flustered

毛毛雨　máomaoyǔ　drizzle

毛南族　Máonánzú　the Maonan nationality, or the Maonans, inhabiting the Guangxi Zhuang Autonomous Region

毛呢　máoní　woollen cloth (for heavy clothing); heavy

woollen cloth; wool coating or suiting

毛坯 máopī ① semifinished product ② *mech.* blank

毛皮 máopí fur; pelt: ～兽 fur-bearing animal / ～大衣 a fur coat

毛票 máopiào *inf.* banknotes of one, two or five *jiao* (角) denominations

毛钱儿 máoqiánr *old* coins of one or two *jiao* (角) denominations

毛渠 máoqú sublateral canal; sublateral

毛茸茸 máoróngróng hairy; downy: ～的胸脯 a hairy chest / ～的小鸭子 a downy little duck

毛瑟枪 máosèqiāng Mauser

毛纱 máoshā *text.* wool yarn: 粗纺～ woollen yarn / 精纺～ worsted yarn

毛石 máoshí *archit.* rubble: ～混凝土 rubble concrete

毛手毛脚 máoshǒu-máojiǎo careless (in handling things): 看他那～的样子,能干得了什么? He's so careless and sloppy—how can he accomplish anything? / 他～地把杯子打了。 He clumsily knocked over his cup and broke it.

毛丝 máosī *text.* broken filament

毛遂自荐 Máo Suì zì jiàn offer one's services as Mao Sui (of the Warring States Period) did—volunteer one's services

毛笋 máosǔn the shoot of *mao* bamboo (毛竹)

毛毯 máotǎn woollen blanket

毛桃 máotáo wild peach

毛细管 máoxìguǎn capillary

毛细管水 máoxìguǎnshuǐ *agric.* capillary

毛细现象 máoxì xiànxiàng *phys.* capillarity

毛细血管 máoxì xuèguǎn *physiol.* blood capillary

毛虾 máoxiā shrimp

毛线 máoxiàn knitting wool: ～针 knitting needle / 打～ do knitting work

毛象 máoxiàng another name for 猛犸 měngmǎ

毛丫头 máoyātou *inf.* a chit of a girl

毛样 máoyàng *print.* galley proof

毛腰 máoyāo *dial.* arch one's back: 他毛着腰悄悄地溜过窗口。 He bent over and slipped by the window.

毛衣 máoyī woollen sweater; sweater; woolly

毛蚴 máoyòu *zool.* miracidium

毛躁 máozao ① short-tempered; irritable: 他的脾气很～。 He has a short temper. ② rash and careless: 他这个人做事从来就是毛毛躁躁的。 He always does things in a careless way.

毛泽东思想 Máo Zédōng Sīxiǎng Mao Zedong Thought

毛毡 máozhān felt

毛织品 máozhīpǐn ① wool fabric; woollens ② woollen knitwear

毛痣 máozhì hairy nevus; pilose nevus

毛重 máozhòng gross weight

毛猪 máozhū *com.* a live pig

毛竹 máozhú *mao* bamboo

毛子 máozi ① *old derog.* Westerner ② *old dial.* bandit ③ *dial.* a tuft of fine hair

矛 máo lance; pike; spear

矛盾 máodùn ① *philos. log.* contradiction: ～的普遍性 (特殊性) the universality (particularity) of contradiction / 主要 (非主要)～ principal (nonprincipal) contradiction / ～的主要 (次要) 方面 the principal (secondary) aspect of a contradiction / ～的同一性 (斗争性) the identity (struggle) of opposites / 对抗性 (非对抗性)～ antagonistic (nonantagonistic) contradiction / ～的转化 the transformation of a contradiction ② problem; conflict; contradiction: 双方发生～已有多年。 The two sides have been in conflict for years. / 他俩在闹～。 The two of them have fallen out. / ～百出 full of contradictions / ～上交 pass on problems to a higher

level instead of solving them oneself ③ contradict: 他说的话前后～。 He was contradicting himself in what he said. ④ contradictory: 这两种意见并不～。 These two views are not contradictory (*or* mutually exclusive)./ 他的心情很～。 His feelings were mixed.

矛盾律 máodùnlǜ *log.* the law of contradiction

矛头 máotóu spearhead: ～所向 the target of attack / 漫画家把讽刺的～指向官僚主义。 The cartoonist directed his satire at the bureaucracy.

茅 máo ① *bot.* cogongrass ② (Máo) a surname

茅草 máocǎo *bot.* cogongrass

茅草棚 máocǎopéng (also 茅棚 máopéng) thatched shed; thatched shack

茅房 máofáng *inf.* latrine; outhouse

茅膏菜 máogāocài *bot.* sundew

茅坑 máokēng ① *inf.* latrine pit ② *dial.* latrine; outhouse

茅庐 máolú thatched cottage ——see also 初出茅庐 chū chū máolú

茅塞顿开 máo sè dùn kāi same as 顿开茅塞 dùn kāi máo sè

茅舍 máoshè *liter.* thatched cottage

茅厕 máosi *inf.* latrine; outhouse

茅台酒 máotáijiǔ *Maotai* (a famous Chinese spirit)

茅屋 máowū thatched cottage

牦 (犛) máo see below

牦牛 máoniú yak

旄 máo ancient flag with yak's tail

猫 (貓) máo see below ——see also māo

猫腰 máoyāo same as 毛腰 máoyāo

锚 máo anchor

锚地 máodì anchorage

锚雷 máoléi *mil.* mooring mine; moored buoyant mine

锚爪 máozhuǎ fluke (of an anchor)

髦 máo ① *arch.* bangs (of a child) ② see 时髦 shímáo

蝥 máo see 斑蝥 bānmáo

蟊 máo an insect destructive to the roots of seedlings

蟊贼 máozéi a person harmful to the country and people; pest

mǎo

冇 mǎo *dial.* not have; there is not; be without

卯[1] mǎo the fourth of the twelve Earthly Branches (地支) ——see also 干支 gān-zhī

卯[2] mǎo mortise

卯时 mǎoshí the period of the day from 5 a. m. to 7 a. m.

卯榫 mǎosǔn mortise and tenon

卯眼 mǎoyǎn mortise

昴 mǎo the eighteenth of the twenty-eight constellations (二十八宿) into which the celestial sphere was divided in ancient Chinese astronomy (consisting

of seven stars in Pleiades)

铆

铆　mǎo　① fasten with a rivet; rivet ② *mech.* riveting: 风动~ pneumatic riveting / 对接~ butt riveting / 搭接~ lap riveting

铆钉　mǎodīng　rivet: ~距 rivet pitch / 开口~ bifurcated rivet

铆钉枪　mǎodīngqiāng　riveting gun

铆工　mǎogōng　① riveting ② riveter

铆机　mǎojī　riveter: 风动~ pneumatic riveter / 水力~ hydraulic riveter

铆接　mǎojiē　riveting; rivet joint

铆劲儿　mǎojìnr　① *inf.* make a sudden all-out effort: 几个人一~，就把大石头撬下坡去了。With a sudden thrust, they sent the boulder rolling down the hillside. ② *dial.* have a trial of strength; compete; contest: 他跟我铆上劲儿了。He's trying to get the upper hand of me.

mào

茂¹

茂　mào　① luxuriant; exuberant; profuse: 繁茂 fánmào ② rich and splendid: 情文并~ excellent in both content and language

茂²

茂　mào　*chem.* cyclopentadiene

茂林修竹　màolín-xiūzhú　thick forest of trees and tall bamboos

茂密　màomì　(of grass or trees) dense; thick: ~的森林 a dense forest / 山上的野菊生得十分~。The wild chrysanthemums are growing thickly on the hillsides.

茂盛　màoshèng　(of plants) luxuriant; exuberant; flourishing: 庄稼长得很~。The crops are growing luxuriantly. / 枝叶~ an exuberant growth of branches and leaves / 丁香花开得正~。The lilacs are blooming luxuriantly.

冒

冒　mào　① emit; send out (*or* up, forth); give off: ~泡 send up bubbles; be bubbling / 水壶正~着气。The kettle is giving off steam. / 泥浆从地下~出来。Mud oozed from underground. / 错误思想总是要~出来的。Wrong ideas are bound to manifest themselves. ② risk; brave: 小李~着生命危险抢救国家财产。Xiao Li risked his life to save state property. / 卡车~着敌机的轰炸扫射向前急驶。Braving the bombing and strafing of enemy planes, the truck sped ahead. / ~着风浪出海 put to sea in spite of wind and wave; venture out on a stormy sea / ~风险 run risks ③ boldly; rashly: ~猜一下 make a bold guess; venture a guess / 看见那人好象是老李，我~喊一声。As he looked very much like Lao Li, I made bold as to call out to him. ④ falsely (claim, etc.); fraudulently: ~认 lay a false claim to / 那人~称是部长的亲戚。The man falsely claimed to be a relative of the minister. ⑤ (Mào) a surname

冒充　màochōng　pretend to be (sb. or sth. else); pass (sb. or sth.) off as: ~内行 pretend to be an expert; pose as an expert / 他~记者。He passed himself off as a journalist. / 用次品~正品 pass off defective goods as certified goods

冒顶　màodǐng　*min.* roof fall: 工作面~ face fall / 大~ bulk caving

冒渎　màodú　*formal* bother or annoy a superior

冒犯　màofàn　offend; affront: 谁知道这一句话竟~了他？Who would have thought that the remark would offend him? / ~禁令 violate a prohibition / ~尊严 offend sb's dignity

冒功　màogōng　claim the credit for oneself

冒汗　màohàn　perspire; sweat: 他急得直~。He was so worried that he kept sweating. / 他脑门上直~。Sweat kept oozing out from his forehead.

冒号　màohào　colon (:)

冒坏　màohuài　(also 冒坏水儿 màohuàishuǐr) *dial.* be up to mischief; play a dirty trick

冒火　màohuǒ　burn with anger; get angry; flare up: 有话好好说，冒什么火! If you have something to say, then say it. No reason to get angry. / 一提起这事，他就~。A mere mention of the matter would make him angry.

冒尖儿　màojiānr　① be piled high above the brim: 筐里的土豆装得~了。The basket is piled high with potatoes. ② be a little over; be a little more than: 十斤刚~ a little over ten *jin* / 弟弟十岁刚~。My brother is just over ten years old. ③ stand out; be conspicuous: 怕~ be afraid of becoming too conspicuous / 她就爱~。She likes to be in the limelight. *or* She's too pushing. ④ begin to crop up: 问题一~，就及时采取了措施。Proper measures were taken as soon as the problem cropped up.

冒金星　mào jīnxīng　see stars: 我一头撞在门上，眼前直~。I banged my head on the door and saw stars.

冒进　màojìn　prematurely advance; advance rashly

冒口　màokǒu　*mech.* rising head; riser

冒领　màolǐng　falsely claim as one's own: 虚报~ fraudulent applications and claims / 他~了汇给我的钱。He falsely collected the money remitted to me.

冒昧　màomèi　*hum.* make bold; venture; take the liberty: ~地给你写信。I'm taking the liberty of writing to you. / 我可以~地提一个问题吗? May I venture to ask a question? / 这么晚了还来打搅您，真是太~了。Is it too presumptuous of me to come and disturb you at this late hour?

冒昧陈辞　màomèi chén cí　*hum.* make bold to express my views; venture an opinion

冒名　màomíng　go under sb. else's name; assume another's name

冒名顶替　màomíng dǐngtì　take another's place by assuming his name

冒牌　màopái　falsely use a well-known trade mark; be an imitation; be a fake: ~货 an imitation (of a well-known trade mark); pirated goods / ~医生 a quack doctor / ~社会主义 bogus (*or* sham) socialism

冒失　màoshi　rash; abrupt: 说话~ speak without due consideration / 这样冒冒失失去找他可不好。It's not appropriate to drop in on him so casually. / 他干什么事都不惜力气，就是有点~。He goes all out in whatever he does even to the point of being a little reckless.

冒失鬼　màoshiguǐ　harum-scarum

冒天下之大不韪　mào tiānxià zhī dà bùwěi　defy world opinion; risk universal condemnation; fly in the face of the will of the people

冒头　màotóu　begin to crop up: 不良倾向一~就要抓住它。Watch out for harmful tendencies and deal with them the moment they crop up.

冒险　màoxiǎn　take a risk; take chances: 戴上安全帽再下去，不要~。Wear your safety helmet when you go down. Don't take any chances. / 小分队~穿过敌人的封锁线。The detachment ventured a thrust through the enemy blockade. / 犯不上为这件事去冒那么大的险。It's not worthwhile taking such a big risk over this job. / 军事~ military adventure / ~政策 adventurist policy

冒险家　màoxiǎnjiā　adventurer

冒险主义　màoxiǎnzhǔyì　adventurism: ~者 adventurist

冒烟　màoyān　① (of smoke) rise: 烟囱正冒着烟。Smoke was rising from the chimney. ② *dial.* get angry; flare up

冒雨　màoyǔ　braving the rain; in spite of the rain

贸 mào trade: 外贸 wàimào

贸然 màorán (also 贸贸然 màomàorán) adv. rashly; hastily; without careful consideration: ～下结论 draw a hasty conclusion; jump to a conclusion / ～同意 agree without careful consideration / ～从事 act rashly / 我考虑再三，总觉得这事～不得。 I've given the matter much thought and am convinced that we shouldn't be too hasty.

贸易 màoyì trade: 和别国进行～ trade with foreign countries; do business with other countries / ～中心 trade centre

贸易差额 màoyì chā'é balance of trade

贸易额 màoyì'é volume of trade; turnover

贸易风 màoyìfēng another name for 信风 xìnfēng

贸易伙伴 màoyì huǒbàn trade partner

贸易逆差 màoyì nìchā unfavourable balance of trade

贸易顺差 màoyì shùnchā favourable balance of trade

贸易往来 màoyì wǎnglái trade contacts; commercial intercourse

贸易协定 màoyì xiédìng trade agreement

贸易议定书 màoyì yìdìngshū trade protocol

耄 mào formal ① octogenarian ② advanced in years: 老耄 lǎomào

耄耋 màodié advanced in years: ～之年 old age (esp. from 70 to 90)

袤 mào see 广袤 guǎngmào

帽 mào ① headgear; hat; cap: 草帽 cǎomào ② cap-like cover for sth.: 笔帽 bǐmào

帽耳 mào'ěr earflaps (of a cap)

帽徽 màohuī (also 帽章 màozhāng) insignia (or badge) on a cap

帽盔儿 màokuīr skullcap

帽舌 màoshé peak (of a cap); visor

帽檐 màoyán (also 帽沿 màoyán) the brim of a hat

帽子 màozi ① headgear; hat; cap: 戴上(摘下)～ put on (take off) a hat or cap ② label; tag; brand: 摘掉文盲的～ rid oneself of the label of "illiterate" / 大庆油田的胜利建成使我国甩掉了"贫油"的～。 The successful opening of the Daqing oilfield took the "oil-poor" label off China. ——see also 戴帽子 dài màozi; 扣帽子 kòu màozi

瑁 mào see 玳瑁 dàimào

瞀 mào formal ① dizzy; dazzled ② confused ③ ignorant

貌 mào looks; appearance: 美貌 měimào

貌不惊人 mào bù jīngrén be unprepossessing (or unimposing) in appearance; be of undistinguished appearance

貌合神离 màohé-shénlí (of two persons or parties) seemingly in harmony but actually at variance

貌似 màosì seem to be; appear to be: ～公允 be seemingly just and sound (or fair and equitable)

貌似公正 màosì gōngzhèng pretend to be just and fair; put on an appearance of impartiality

貌似强大 màosì qiángdà be seemingly powerful; be outwardly strong

貌似有理 màosì yǒulǐ be apparently reasonable (but actually not reasonable)

懋 mào ① formal diligent ② same as 茂¹ mào

me

么¹(麽、末) me suf.: 什么 shénme / 多么 duōme / 怎么 zěnme / 这么 zhème

么²(麽) me (used as a syllable inserted in a line of a song for balance): 五月的花儿红呀～红似火。 Red as fire are the flowers that bloom in May.

méi

没¹ méi inf. ① not have; there is not; be without: 他还～女朋友。 He doesn't have a girlfriend yet. / 这儿～人。 There's nobody here. / 她～钱了。 She has no more money. / 我的钢笔～水了。 My pen has run dry. / 票卖～了。 The tickets are all sold out. / 用～了。 It's all used up. ② be not so... as: 我～你高。 I'm not so tall as you. / 谁都～他会说话。 No one is as eloquent as he is. ③ less than; not more than: 他去了～多大工夫。 He wasn't gone for long. / 我家里～多大地方。 There isn't much space in my home.

没² méi adv. inf. have not or did not: 他来～来? 一还～来呢。 Has he come yet?—Not yet. / 她三天～来了。 She hasn't been here for three days. / 你买了吗? 一～买。 Did you buy it?—No, I didn't. / 银行昨天～开门。 The bank was closed yesterday. ——see also mò

没词儿 méicír inf. ① can find nothing to say ② be at a loss for words; be stuck for an answer: 刚说了几句，他就～了。 After uttering a few sentences, he got stuck.

没错儿 méicuòr ① I'm quite sure; you can rest assured: ～，准是小王告诉他的。 I'm quite sure it was Xiao Wang who told him about it. / ～，就是他干的。 There's no doubt about it. He's the one that did it. / 电影七点的，是吗?一～。 The film begins at seven, doesn't it?—Yes, that's right. ② can't go wrong: 照说明书做，准保～。 Just follow the directions. You can't go wrong.

没大没小 méidà-méixiǎo show no respect for one's elders: 这孩子真～的，在爷爷面前也这么说话! The child really has no manners. Talking like that in front of his grandpa!

没法儿 méifǎr ① dial. most unlikely; absolutely impossible: 哼，～是他干的。 Humph, it's most unlikely that he should have done it. / 你～不知道。 You certainly know it. ② dial. beyond comparison: 今晚这场戏，～那么好的了。 The performance tonight was terrific. ③ same as 没法子 méi fǎzi

没法子 méi fǎzi can do nothing about it; can't help it; there is no way out: 我当时手头紧，～，只好卖书。 I was hard up then, and had to sell off my books.

没骨头 méi gútou weak-kneed; spineless

没关系 méi guānxi it doesn't matter; it's nothing; that's all right; never mind: 他来不来都～。 It doesn't matter whether he comes or not. / 对不起，挡你道了。一～。 Excuse me for getting in your way.—That's all right. / 如果他有事，我在这儿多等一会儿，～。 If he's busy, I don't mind waiting here a while longer.

没好气儿 méi hǎoqìr be angry; be in a bad temper: 他一听这话就～。 He got angry as soon as he heard this.

没精打采 méijīng-dǎcǎi listless; in low spirits; out of sorts; lackadaisical: 他～地坐在地上，低着头，不吱声。 He sat on the ground listlessly with his head hanging and said nothing.

没救 méijiù　incurable; incorrigible; beyond remedy or hope: 得了这种癌症是～的。The cancer is incurable. / 医生认为这个病人～了。The doctor considered the patient's case hopeless. / 他撒谎成性，～了。He's a hopeless (or incorrigible) liar.

没脸 méiliǎn　feel ashamed; feel embarassed: ～见人 be too ashamed (or embarassed) to face anyone

没…没… méi…méi…　① (used before two synonyms to emphasize the sense of "without"): 没皮没脸 have no sense of shame / 没羞没臊 shameless; have no sense of shame ② (used before two antonyms to indicate that no distinction is made): 没老没少 overfamiliar (between old and young) / 没深没浅 have no sense of propriety

没门儿 méiménr　dial. ① have no access to sth.; have no means of doing sth.: 你能给我们弄几张戏票吗？——我可～。Can you get us some tickets for the performance?—You're asking the wrong person. ② no go; nothing doing: 他想拉拢我？～! He wants to rope me in? Not a chance! / 你别想蒙我。～! You can't fool me. No way!

没命 méimìng　① lose one's life; die: 要不是医生及时赶到，这小孩就～了。The child would have died if the doctor hadn't come just in time. ② recklessly; desperately; like mad; for all one's worth: 敌兵～地逃跑。The enemy soldiers ran off as fast as their legs could carry them. / 他白天黑夜～地干。He worked day and night like mad.

没跑儿 méipǎor　beyond doubt; undoubtedly: 这次你输定了，～! You're sure to lose this time.

没谱儿 méipǔr　dial. be unsure; have no idea: 这炉子一个月要烧多少煤，我可～。I have no idea how much coal this stove will consume each month. / 下一步该怎么走还～呢。We have no plan yet as to our next move. / 这个计划行不行，他心里～。He's not too sure whether the plan will work.

没轻没重 méiqīng-méizhòng　(speak) tactlessly or indiscreetly

没趣 méiqù　feel put out; feel snubbed: 没有人理他，他觉得～，只好走了。Very much put out by their indifference, he slunk off. / 咱们别理他，给他个～。Let's pay no attention to him. Just ignore him.

没商量儿 méishāngliangr　irretrievable; irredeemable; irrevocable: 这是最后决定，～。The decision is final and irrevocable. / 你一点儿不让步，这事～了。If you refuse to make any concessions, the deal is off.

没什么 méishénme　it doesn't matter; it's nothing; that's all right; never mind: 你怎么了？——～，有点头疼。What's the matter with you?—Just a bit of a headache; nothing serious. / 住二层当然很好，住五层也～。It's good, of course, to live on the first floor; but the fourth floor would be all right too.

没事儿 méishìr　① have nothing to do; be free; be at a loose end: 今晚～，我想去看电影。I've got nothing to do this evening. I think I'll go to the film. / 我今天一天都～。I'm free all day today. ② it doesn't matter; it's nothing; that's all right; never mind: 哼，踩了你的脚了。——～。Sorry to have stepped on your toe.—That's all right. / 他刚才还头疼来着，现在～了。He was having a headache a moment ago, but he's all right now. / 外边乱哄哄的，出了什么事儿？——～，就几个孩子起哄。What's all that noise outside?—It's nothing. Only some kids making a row.

没事人 méishìrén　not care in the least; give (or take) no heed; be indifferent: 你怎么批评他，他还像个～似的。However much you criticize him, he still looks unconcerned. / 喝了一瓶酒，他跟～似的。After drinking a whole bottle, he didn't even turn a hair.

没事找事 méishì zhǎoshì　① ask for trouble; ask for it ② try hard to find fault; cavil

没挑儿 méitiāor　faultless; perfect: 要说她的工作那是～了。Her work is beyond reproach. / 他的英语真～。He speaks perfect English.

没头没脑 méitóu-méinǎo　without rhyme or reason; abrupt: 他一到就～地把我们批评了一顿。No sooner had he stepped in the door than he began criticizing us, for no reason at all.

没完 méiwán　have not finished with sb. (in quarrelling): 你等着吧，这事儿～! Just wait. You haven't seen the end of this yet! / 我跟他～! I haven't finished with him yet! or I'll never let him off!

没完没了 méiwán-méiliǎo　endless; without end: 她这么～地唠叨，真是烦死人了。Her endless chattering is really driving me up the wall.

没戏 méixì　dial. hopeless: 去黄山旅游的事～了。Our trip to Huangshan Mountain is off. / 他俩谈得怎样了？——～! How is their talk going? — Nothing will come of it!

没想儿 méixiǎngr　inf. hopeless: 指挥病倒，这场演出恐怕～了。I'm afraid the performance's off because the conductor's ill.

没心没肺 méixīn-méifèi　① simple-minded ② scatter-brained

没羞 méixiū　have no shame; be unabashed: 那么大的小子还哭，真～。Tut, tut! Such a big boy crying.

没样儿 méiyàngr　have no manners; be ill-mannered

没意思 méiyìsi　① bored: 一个人待在家里实在～。I'm bored stiff staying at home all alone. ② boring; uninteresting: 这本书～。This book is boring. ③ (of people) petty: 这个人～。He's a petty person.

没影儿 méiyǐngr　① disappear without a trace: 一转眼，他怎么就～? How could he disappear in just the blink of an eye? / 他早就忘得～了。He's clean forgotten it. ② groundless; unfounded; fantastic: 这都是～的事，你怎么就相信了? This is all nonsense. How can you take it so seriously?

没有[1] méi·yǒu　① not have; there is not; be without: 我～多余的录音带。I don't have cassettes to spare. / 他在文学方面～什么培养前途。He has no potential for a career in literature. / 电影票早～了。Tickets for the film were sold out quite a while ago. / 屋里～人。There isn't anyone in the room. / 你说的这种事我们那儿是～的。That kind of thing never happens at our place. / ～矛盾，就～世界。Without contradiction nothing would exist. / ～哪个说过这样的话。No one ever said that. ② be not so …as: 我弟弟～他聪明。My younger brother is not so clever as he. / 谁都跑得～他快。No one can run as fast as he. / 这项试验～我们预料的那样顺利。The experiment didn't go as smoothly as we had expected. ③ less than; not more than: 他来了还～三天就走了。He was here less than three days. / 这间屋子～十平方米。This room is not more than 10 metres square.

没有[2] méi·yǒu　adv. have not or did not: 他回来～?——还～呢。Has he come back yet?—No, not yet. / 衣服还～干。The clothes aren't dry yet. / 我～着急，只是有点担心。I'm not upset, but I'm a bit worried. / 你看见他了～?——～。Did you see him?—No, I didn't. / ～经过专业训练的业余歌唱家 an untrained amateur singer

没有的话 méi·yǒudehuà　it's not true; nothing of the sort

没有的事儿 méi·yǒudeshìr　nothing of the sort; it's impossible

没有说的 méi·yǒushuōde　① really good: 这小伙子思想好、劳动好，真是～。He's good in ideology and in work, a really fine young chap. / 论这些产品的质量，那是～。As for the quality of these products, it's excellent. ② there's no need to say any more about it; it goes without saying: ～，这是我们应尽的责任。It goes without

saying that we should do it; it's our duty. ③ there's no need arguing; indisputable: 这车你们使了三天了，今天该我们使了，～。You've been using that cart for three days. Now it's our turn today. Let's stop arguing about that.

没有种 méiyǒuzhǒng （also 没种 méizhǒng） *inf.* gutless; cowardly

没辙 méizhé *inf.* can find no way out; be at the end of one's rope: 她这么对付我，我完全～了。The way she's been treating me—I really can't take it any more. ／下一步该怎么办，我～了。I have no idea what to do next.

没治 méizhì *inf.* ① incurable; beyond hope: 这个人算是～了，不管怎么劝他就是不听。That man is really hopeless. He is deaf to all advice. ／这台机器坏了，～了。This machine is beyond repair. ② excellent; beyond description: 他的表演真～了。His performance was first-rate indeed. ③ cannot do anything with sb.: 我真拿他～。I simply can't do anything with him.

玫 méi　see below

玫瑰 méigui　rugosa rose; rose

玫瑰红 méiguihóng　rose-red

枚 méi　*m.* (for small-piece things): 三～纪念章 three souvenir badges ／一～古币 an ancient coin ／两～邮票 two stamps

眉 méi　① eyebrow; brow ② the top margin of a page: 书眉 shūméi

眉笔 méibǐ　eyebrow pencil

眉端 méiduān　① the space between the eyebrows: 愁上～ be with a worried frown; have a worried look ② the top of a page; top margin

眉飞色舞 méifēi-sèwǔ　with dancing eyebrows and radiant face—enraptured; exultant: 小王听得～。A look of delight came into Xiao Wang's face as he listened. ／说起拿乒乓球冠军的事，他就～。His face lights up whenever he speaks of the table tennis championship he's won.

眉峰 méifēng　brows

眉高眼低 méigāo-yǎndī　an expression on the face: 看人～行事 take one's cue from sb.

眉急 méijí　short for 燃眉之急 rán méi zhī jí

眉尖 méijiān　brows: ～微微一皱 knit the brows a little

眉睫 méijié　(as close to the eye as) the eyebrows and eyelashes: 祸在～ in imminent danger

眉开眼笑 méikāi-yǎnxiào　be all smiles; beam with joy: 他听到这好消息，顿时～起来。He was all smiles the moment he heard the good news.

眉来眼去 méilái-yǎnqù　make eyes at each other; exchange amorous glances; flirt with each other: 两人～，以目送情。The two of them exchanged amorous glances and clearly made known their passions.

眉棱骨 méilénggǔ　superciliary ridge

眉毛 méimao　eyebrow; brow

眉毛胡子一把抓 méimao húzi yībǎzhuā　try to grasp the eyebrows and the beard all at once—try to attend to big and small matters all at once

眉目 méimù　① features; looks: ～清秀 have delicate features ② logic (of writing); sequence of ideas: 这篇文章～清楚。The article is clear and well-organized.

眉目 méimu　prospect of a solution; sign of a positive outcome: 你托我办的事已经有点～了。About that job you asked me to do, I'm beginning to get somewhere with it. *or* I'm getting on with what you asked me to do. ／计划有了～。The plan is beginning to take shape.

眉目不清 méimù bù qīng　(of writing) not well organized

眉目传情 méi-mù chuán qíng　flash amorous glances; make eyes at sb.

眉批 méipī　notes and commentary at the top of a page

眉清目秀 méiqīng-mùxiù　have delicate features; have finely chiselled features: 那孩子生得～，十分俊雅。The boy was remarkably handsome, with finely chiselled features.

眉梢 méishāo　the tip of the brow: ～间露出忧郁的神色 a melancholy cast between the brows

眉头 méitóu　brows: ～紧锁 frown severely

眉头一皱，计上心来 méitóu yī zhòu, jì shàng xīn lái　knit the brows and a plan (*or* stratagem) comes to one's mind: 他寻思了半天，～。He thought to himself for a while. He knit his brows heavily and at last a plan was born in his heart.

眉心 méixīn　the space between the eyebrows

眉眼 méiyǎn　appearance; looks: 小姑娘～长得很俊。The little girl is very pretty.

眉眼高低 méiyǎn gāo-dī　an expression on the face: 你这人真不识～，谁都看得出她正发愁呢。You should learn to read a person's thoughts from his face. Anyone can see she's worrying about something.

眉宇 méiyǔ　*liter.* forehead

眉月 méiyuè　eyebrow-shaped moon—the crescent moon; crescent

莓（苺） méi　certain kinds of berries: 草莓 cǎoméi

梅（楳、槑） méi　① plum ② (Méi) a surname

梅毒 méidú　*med.* syphilis

梅红色 méihóngsè　plum (colour)

梅花 méihuā　① plum blossom ② *dial.* wintersweet

梅花大鼓 méihuā dàgǔ　a variation of 大鼓 dàgǔ②

梅花鹿 méihuālù　sika (deer)

梅天 méitiān　same as 黄梅季 huángméijì

梅童鱼 méitóngyú　baby croaker

梅雨 méiyǔ　same as 黄梅雨 huángméiyǔ

梅子 méizi　plum

湄 méi　river bank

嵋 méi　see 峨嵋 Éméi

猸 méi　see below

猸子 méizi　common name for 蟹獴 xièměng

媒 méi　① matchmaker; go-between: 做媒 zuòméi ② intermediary: 触媒 chùméi

媒介 méijiè　intermediary; medium; vehicle: 空气是传播声音的～。Air is a medium of sound. ／传染疾病的～ vehicle of disease; vector ／新闻～ news media

媒婆 méipó　a woman matchmaker

媒染 méirǎn　mordant dyeing: ～染料 mordant dye

媒染剂 méirǎnjì　*chem.* mordant

媒人 méirén　matchmaker; go-between

媒妁 méishuò　*formal* matchmaker

媒妁之言 méishuò zhī yán　the good offices of a matchmaker——see also 父母之命，媒妁之言 fùmǔ zhī mìng, méishuò zhī yán

媒质 méizhì　*phys.* medium: 吸收～ absorbing medium

煤 méi　coal: 炉子上添点～。Put some coal on the fire. ／一块烧红的～ a live (*or* hot) coal

煤仓 méicāng　coal bunker

煤层 méicéng　coal seam; coal bed

煤铲 méichǎn　coal shovel

煤场 méichǎng　coal yard

煤尘　méichén　coal dust: ～爆炸 coal-dust explosion

煤斗　méidǒu　coal scuttle; scuttle

煤毒　méidú　carbon monoxide poisoning; gas poisoning

煤酚皂溶液　méifēnzào　róngyè　*pharm.* cresol and soap solution; saponated cresol solution; lysol

煤矸石　méigānshí　gangue

煤耗　méihào　coal consumption

煤核儿　méihúr　partly-burnt briquet; coal cinder

煤化　méihuà　carbonize

煤灰　méihuī　coal ash

煤焦油　méijiāoyóu　(also 煤溚 méitǎ, 煤黑油 méihēiyóu) coal tar

煤精　méijīng　(also 煤玉 méiyù) black amber; jet

煤矿　méikuàng　coal mine; colliery: ～工人 coal miner

煤末子　méimòzi　coal dust

煤气　méiqì　coal gas; gas: 你们家烧～吗? Do you use a gas stove at home? / ～设备 gas fittings / ～中毒 carbon monoxide poisoning; gas poisoning / ～贮罐 gas (storage) holder

煤气表　méiqìbiǎo　gas meter

煤气厂　méiqìchǎng　gasworks; gashouse

煤气灯　méiqìdēng　gas lamp; gas light

煤气管　méiqìguǎn　gas pipe

煤气机　méiqìjī　gas engine

煤气炉　méiqìlú　gas stove; gas furnace

煤气灶　méiqìzào　gas range; gas cooker

煤气总管　méiqì zǒngguǎn　gas main

煤球　méiqiú　(egg-shaped) briquet

煤炱　méitái　coal soot; soot

煤炭　méitàn　coal: ～工业 coal industry

煤田　méitián　coalfield: ～地质学 coal geology

煤系　méixì　*geol.* coal measures

煤烟　méiyān　① smoke from burning coal ② (also 煤烟子 méiyānzi) coal soot; soot

煤烟污染　méiyān wūrǎn　coal-smoke pollution

煤窑　méiyáo　coalpit

煤油　méiyóu　kerosene; paraffin

煤油灯　méiyóudēng　kerosene lamp

煤油炉　méiyóulú　kerosene stove

煤渣　méizhā　coal cinder: ～路 cinder road / ～跑道 cinder track

煤砟子　méizhǎzi　a small piece of coal

煤砖　méizhuān　(brick-shaped) briquet

楣　méi　lintel (of a door): 门楣 ménméi

酶　méi　*biochem.* enzyme; ferment: 消化～ digestive ferment

酶原　méiyuán　*biochem.* zymogen; fermentogen

鹛　méi　*zool.* babbler: 钩嘴～ scimitar babbler

镅　méi　*chem.* americium (Am)

霉[1](黴)　méi　mould; mildew

霉[2]　méi　become mildewy; go mouldy: 这块饼～了。The cake is mouldy. / 箱子里有股～味。The inside of the trunk has a mildewy smell.

霉变　méibiàn　become mildewy; go mouldy

霉病　méibìng　*agric.* mildew

霉蠹　méidù　(of books) get mildewed and worm-eaten

霉菌　méijūn　*bacteriol.* mould

霉菌病　méijūnbìng　mycosis

霉烂　méilàn　mildew and rot: ～食品 mildewy and rotten food

霉天　méitiān　early summer rains ——see also 黄梅季 huángméijì

霉头　méitóu　*dial.* bad luck ——see also 触霉头 chù

méitóu

霉雨　méiyǔ　same as 黄梅雨 huángméiyǔ

穈(穈、藦)　méi　see below ——see also mí

穈子　méizi　*bot.* broom corn millet

měi

每　měi　① every; each; per: ～星期五 every Friday / 节约～一分钱 save every penny / ～四小时服一次 to be taken once every four hours / ～两周开一次会 hold a meeting every other week / ～人一张票 a ticket for each person / ～时～刻 all the time; at all times / 以～小时四十公里的速度行驶 drive at (a speed of) forty kilometres an hour / ～年的平均产量 average yearly yield; average output *per annum* ② *adv.* on each occasion; each time: ～到上海, 我总要去逛一下城隍庙。I invariably visit the Town God's Temple when I go to Shanghai. / ～逢春节, 我都要去看老师。I always go to see my teachers during the Spring Festival. / ～当我见到这位满头白发的老人, 我就想起我的父亲。Whenever I see this old white-haired gentleman, I think of my father. ③ *adv.* often: 春秋佳日, ～作郊游。We often go for an outing in the country on fine days in spring and autumn.

每逢佳节倍思亲　měiféng jiājié bèi sī qīn　on festive occasions more than ever we think of our dear ones far away

每况愈下　měi kuàng yù xià　steadily deteriorate; go from bad to worse: 他的病情～, 治不好了。His condition is getting steadily worse, and there is no hope of recovery.

每每　měiměi　*adv.* often: 他们常在一起, ～一谈就是半天。They often got together, and when they did, they'd chat for hours.

每下愈况　měi xià yù kuàng　same as 每况愈下 měi kuàng yù xià

美[1]　měi　① beautiful; pretty: 她长得很～。She's very pretty. / 风景多～啊! What beautiful scenery! ② beautify; prettify: 美容 měiróng ③ very satisfactory; good: ～酒 good wine / 这鱼的味道很～。The fish tastes quite good. / ～～地吃了一顿 have had an excellent dinner / 日子过得挺～ live quite happily ④ *dial.* be pleased with oneself: 夸了他两句, 他就～得不得了。Just a few words of praise made him exceedingly pleased with himself.

美[2]　Měi　① short for 美洲 Měizhōu ② short for 美国 Měiguó

美不胜收　měi bùshèng shōu　so many beautiful things that one simply can't take them all in; more beauty than one can take in: 展览会上的工艺品, 琳琅满目, ～。We were dazzled by the endless array of beautiful handiwork exhibits which were more than the eye could take in.

美餐　měicān　① tasty food; table delicacies ② eat and drink one's fill; have an excellent dinner

美差　měichāi　a cushy job; a pleasant task: 你去桂林开会, 这可是一趟～! What a pleasant assignment you've got going to Guilin for the conference!

美钞　měichāo　U. S. banknote; greenback

美称　měichēng　laudatory title; good name: 四川向有天府之国的～。Sichuan has always enjoyed the reputation of being "Nature's storehouse".

美传　měichuán　a story passed on with approval

美德　měidé　virtue; moral excellence: 艰苦朴素是我们

的传统～。Hard work and plain living are traditional virtues of ours.

美吨 mĕidūn　short ton

美感 mĕigǎn　aesthetic feeling; aesthetic perception; sense of beauty: 舒伯特的艺术歌曲给人以～。Art songs by Schubert give one sensuous pleasure.

美工 mĕigōng　*film* ① art designing ② art designer

美观 mĕiguān　pleasing to the eye; beautiful; artistic: 房间布置得很～。The room is artistically decorated. / 这些花布设计得～大方。The design of the cotton print is artistic and in good taste.

美国 Mĕiguó　the United States (U. S. A)

美国佬 Mĕiguólǎo　*inf.* Yankee (U. S. citizen)

美国人 Mĕiguórén　American

美好 mĕihǎo　fine; happy; glorious: ～的日子 happy days; a happy life / ～的将来 a glorious future / ～的回忆 happy memories / ～的远景 magnificent prospects / 致以～的祝愿 with best wishes

美化 mĕihuà　beautify; prettify; embellish: ～环境 beautify the environment / 竭力～自己 try hard to prettify oneself / ～精神生活和物质生活 enrich one's cultural and material life

美金 mĕijīn　same as 美元 mĕiyuán

美劲儿 mĕijìnr　*inf.* ① outward expression of joy or delight: 瞧他这～。Look how delighted he is. ② joy; delight: 工作之后, 听点儿好音乐, 那个～就别提啦。What a delight it is to listen to some good music after work.

美景 mĕijǐng　beautiful scenery (*or* landscape): 西湖～ the enchanting scenery of the West Lake

美拉尼西亚 Mĕilāníxīyà　Melanesia

美利奴羊 mĕilìnúyáng　Merino (sheep)

美丽 mĕilì　beautiful: ～富饶的国家 a beautiful and richly-endowed country / ～的小姑娘 a pretty little girl / 让我们的青春更～! Let's make the days of our youth as beautiful as can be!

美轮美奂 mĕilún-mĕihuàn　a magnificent mansion

美满 mĕimǎn　happy; perfectly satisfactory: 生活～ lead a happy life / ～婚姻 a happy marriage; conjugal happiness / ～幸福的家庭 a happy family

美貌 mĕimào　① good looks ② pretty; beautiful: ～的年轻女子 a beautiful young lady

美梦 mĕimèng　fond dream

美妙 mĕimiào　beautiful; splendid; wonderful: ～的青春 the wonderful days of one's youth / ～的诗句 beautiful verse / 歌声是多么的～! What beautiful singing! / 那家公司的经济情况很不～。The financial situation of that company is anything but good.

美名 mĕimíng　good name; good reputation: 英雄～天下扬。A hero's good name spreads far and wide.

美男子 mĕinánzǐ　a handsome man

美尼尔氏症 mĕiní'ěrshìzhèng　*med.* Ménière's syndrome (*or* disease)

美女 mĕinǚ　a beautiful woman

美其名曰 mĕi qí míng yuē　call it by the fine-sounding name of; describe it euphemistically as

美气 mĕiqì　*dial.* comfortable; easy: 日子过得很～。We're leading a very comfortable life.

美缺 mĕiquē　an ideal vacancy; a well-paid post

美人 mĕirén　a beautiful woman; beauty

美人计 mĕirénjì　beauty trap: 定下～ set a beauty trap

美人蕉 mĕirénjiāo　*bot.* canna; Indian shot

美容 mĕiróng　improve (esp. a woman's) looks: ～院 beauty parlour; beauty shop / ～手术 cosmetic surgery / 她今天去做～了。She went to the beauty parlour today.

美容术 mĕiróngshù　cosmetology; beauty treatment

美食 mĕishí　good food; table delicacies

美食家 mĕishíjiā　gourmet

美术 mĕishù　① the fine arts; art: 工艺～ industrial arts; arts and crafts / ～工作者 art worker; artist / ～人型 artist figurine ② painting

美术革 mĕishùgé　fancy leather

美术馆 mĕishùguǎn　art gallery

美术家 mĕishùjiā　artist

美术明信片 mĕishù míngxìnpiàn　picture (*or* pictorial) postcard

美术片 mĕishùpiàn　*film* cartoons, puppet films, etc.

美术设计 mĕishù shèjì　artistic design

美术字 mĕishùzì　artistic calligraphy; art lettering

美谈 mĕitán　a story passed on with approval ——see also 传为美谈 chuán wéi mĕitán

美味 mĕiwèi　① delicious food; delicacy ② delicious; dainty: ～小吃 dainty snacks

美学 mĕixué　aesthetics

美言 mĕiyán　put in a good word for sb.: 请帮我在他面前～几句。Please put in a good word for me when you're with him.

美艳 mĕiyàn　beautiful and voluptuous; gorgeous; glamorous

美意 mĕiyì　good intention; kindness: 谢谢您的～。Thank you for your kindness.

美育 mĕiyù　aesthetic education; art education

美誉 mĕiyù　good name; good reputation

美元 mĕiyuán　(also 美圆 mĕiyuán) American dollar; U. S. dollar ($)

美展 mĕizhǎn　(short for 美术作品展览) art exhibition

美中不足 mĕi zhōng bù zú　a blemish in an otherwise perfect thing; a blemish in a thing of beauty: 这本小说很好, ～的是结尾太冗长了。This is a good novel, except for the long and tedious ending.

美洲 Mĕizhōu　America

美洲虎 mĕizhōuhǔ　jaguar

美洲狮 mĕizhōushī　cougar; puma

美滋滋 mĕizīzī　very pleased with oneself: 他被选中当队长, 心里～的。He was very pleased at being chosen to captain the team.

浼

mĕi　*formal* ① contaminate ② entrust (a person) to do sth.

镁

mĕi　*chem.* magnesium (Mg)

镁光 mĕiguāng　magnesium light: ～照明弹 magnesium flare

镁砂 mĕishā　*metall.* magnesia; magnesite

镁砖 mĕizhuān　*metall.* magnesia brick

mèi

妹

mèi　younger sister; sister: 兄～ brother and sister / 她是我小～。She's my youngest sister.

妹夫 mèifu　(also 妹丈 mèizhàng) younger sister's husband; brother-in-law

妹妹 mèimei　younger sister; sister

妹婿 mèixù　*formal* younger sister's husband; brother-in-law

妹子 mèizi　*dial.* ① younger sister; sister ② a young girl

袂

mèi　*formal* sleeve: 分袂 fēnmèi

昧

mèi　① have hazy notions about; be ignorant of: 愚昧 yúmèi ② hide; conceal: ～着良心 (do evil) against one's conscience

昧爽 mèishuǎng　*formal* dawn; daybreak

昧心 mèixīn　(do evil) against one's conscience: ～钱

money obtained by dishonest means

昧于 mèiyú　be ignorant of; fail to understand: 〜事实 be ignorant of the facts; be unaware of the truth / 〜事理 lack common sense

寐 mèi　*formal* sleep: 喜而不〜 too happy and excited to fall asleep

媚 mèi　① fawn on; curry favour with; flatter; toady to: 谄媚 chǎnmèi　② charming; fascinating; enchanting: 〜人的景色 enchanting scenery

媚敌 mèidí　curry favour with (*or* toady to) the enemy

媚骨 mèigǔ　obsequiousness: 没有丝毫的奴颜与〜 be free from all sycophancy or obsequiousness

媚世 mèishì　① try to please the public; play to the gallery

媚态 mèitài　① obsequiousness　② (also 媚气 mèi-qì) feminine charms

媚外 mèiwài　fawn on (*or* toady to) foreign powers: 崇洋媚外 chóngyáng mèiwài

媚笑 mèixiào　a bewitching smile; an ingratiating smile

媚眼 mèiyǎn　seductive eyes: 抛〜 (esp. of a woman) make eyes at sb.; throw amorous glances at sb.

魅 mèi　evil spirit; demon

魅力 mèilì　glamour; charm; enchantment; fascination: 艺术〜 artistic charm / 音乐的〜 the magic of music / 他是个很有〜的男人。He's a very attractive man.

mēn

闷 mēn　① stuffy; close: 开开窗吧，屋里太〜了。Open the windows. It's too stuffy in here. / 我觉得胸口〜得慌。I feel like I can't breathe. / 这天儿真〜。It is very oppressive today.　② cover tightly: 〜一会儿，茶味儿就出来了。Let the tea draw for a while and the flavour will come out.　③ *dial.* (of a sound) muffled: 说话〜声〜气的 speak in a muffled voice; won't come out with a clear statement　④ keep silent; say nothing: 你有什么事就说吧，别〜在心里。Speak out. Don't just brood over things.　⑤ shut oneself or sb. indoors: 别老〜在屋里看书，出来活动活动。Don't shut yourself indoors reading all day long. Come outside and stretch your legs.——see also mèn

闷气 mēnqì　stuffy; close——see also mènqì

闷热 mēnrè　hot and suffocating; sultry; muggy: 我看快下雨了，天这么〜。I think it's going to rain—it's so sultry.

闷声不响 mēnshēng bù xiǎng　remain silent: 她〜只管干活。She kept silent, concentrating on her work.

闷头儿 mēntóur　(work hard) quietly or silently: 〜干 work doggedly in silence; plod away silently

mén

门(門) mén　① door; gate; entrance: 校〜 school gate / 炉〜儿 a stove door / 柜〜儿 a cabinet door / 请走南〜。Please use the south entrance. / 这扇〜关不上。The door won't shut. / 到会议厅得穿过好几道〜。You have to pass through several doors to get to the conference hall.　② valve; switch: 气门 qìmén① / 电门 diànmén　③ way to do sth.; knack: 我到钢厂劳动了一段时间，对炼钢摸着点〜儿了。After working in the steel mill for a while I got an inkling of how steel is made.　④ family: 张〜王氏 Mrs. Zhang, *née* Wang　⑤

(religious) sect; school (of thought): 佛门 fómén　⑥ relating to the teacher: 同门 tóngmén　⑦ class; category: 分门别类 fēnmén-biélèi　⑧ *biol.* phylum: 亚〜 subphylum /脊椎动物〜 Vertebrata　⑨ *computer* gate: "与"〜 AND gate / "非"〜 NOT gate　⑩ *m.* ⓐ (for subjects of study, etc.): 两〜功课 two subjects; two courses / 这〜学问 this subject of study / 你选了几〜课? How many courses did you select? / 掌握三〜技术 master three skills　ⓑ (for cannons): 一〜大炮 a piece of artillery; a cannon; a gun　ⓒ (for a marriage): 一〜亲事 a marriage　ⓓ (for relatives): 一〜亲戚 a set of relatives　⑪ (Mén) a surname

门巴族 Ménbāzú　the Moinba (Monba) nationality, or the Moinbas (Monbas), inhabiting the Xizang Autonomous Region

门把 ménbà　door knob; door handle

门板 ménbǎn　① door plank　② shutter: 上〜儿 put up the shutters

门鼻儿 ménbír　bolt staple

门钹 ménbó　gate cymbal (nailed onto old-fashioned gates, with a ring-shaped knocker attached to it)

门插关儿 ménchāguānr　(door) bolt

门齿 ménchǐ　front tooth; incisor

门刺 méncì　*formal* visiting card; calling card

门当户对 méndāng-hùduì　be well-matched in social and economic status (for marriage): 这两家〜。The two families are fairly well matched in social status.

门道 mén·dào　gateway; doorway

门道 méndao　*inf.* ① way to do sth.; knack: 治疗这种病，他们医院已经研究出〜来了。Their hospital has found the way to cure this disease. / 技术革新的〜很多。There are all sorts of possibilities for technical innovation.　② social connections; contacts: 他这个人〜很粗。He's a very well-connected man.

门第 méndì　family status: 诗书〜 an intellectual family

门吊 méndiào　*mech.* gantry crane

门吊儿 méndiàor　hasp and staple

门丁 méndīng　*old* doorman; gatekeeper

门洞儿 méndòngr　gateway; doorway

门阀 ménfá　a family of power and influence (in feudal China)

门房 ménfáng　① gate house; janitor's room; porter's lodge　② gatekeeper; doorman; janitor; porter

门风 ménfēng　ethics and moral standards that a family or a clan keeps

门缝 ménfèng　a crack between a door and its frame or between two doors

门岗 méngǎng　gate sentry

门户 ménhù　① door: 〜紧闭 with the doors tightly shut / 小心〜 Watch the door and beware of intruders.　② gateway; important passageway: 天津港是北京通往海洋的〜。The port of Tianjin is Beijing's gateway to the sea.　③ faction; sect: 门户之见 ménhù zhī jiàn　④ family: 兄弟分居，自立〜。The brothers have set up their own homes.　⑤ family status: 〜相当 families well-matched in social status

门户开放政策 ménhù kāifàng zhèngcè　*hist.* Open Door policy (U. S. policy towards China, 1899)

门户之见 ménhù zhī jiàn　sectarian bias; sectarianism

门环子 ménhuánzi　knocker

门禁 ménjìn　entrance guard: 〜森严 with the entrances heavily guarded

门警 ménjǐng　police guard at an entrance

门径 ménjìng　access; key; way: 经过反复实验，他终于找到了节省原料的〜。Through repeated experiments he at last found the way to save raw materials.

门静脉 ménjìngmài　*physiol.* portal vein

门槛 ménkǎn　(also 门坎 ménkǎn) ① threshold　② *dial.* way to do sth.; knack: 你不懂〜。You don't

know the tricks. / 他～精，不会上当。He's too sharp to be taken in.

门可罗雀 mén kě luó què you can catch sparrows on the doorstep—visitors are few and far between

门客 ménkè a hanger-on of an aristocrat

门口 ménkǒu entrance; doorway: 在～等候 wait at the door (or gate) / 走过学校～ walk past the school entrance / 把客人送到～ see the guest to the door

门框 ménkuàng doorframe

门廊 ménláng *archit.* porch; portico

门类 ménlèi class; kind; category: 基础科学和技术科学这两大～ the two major departments of basic and technical sciences

门里出身 ménli chūshēn *dial.* born in a family with a certain traditional skill

门帘 ménlián (also 门帘子 ménliánzi) door curtain; *portière*

门联 ménlián scrolls pasted on either side of the door forming a couplet; gatepost couplet

门脸儿 ménliǎnr *dial.* ① the vicinity of a city gate ② the facade of a shop; shop front

门铃 ménlíng doorbell

门楼 ménlóu an arch over a gateway

门路 ménlu ① way to do sth.; knack: 摸到一些～ have learned the ropes; know one's way around / 广开生产～ tap new sources of production / 广开就业～ create job opportunities on an extensive scale ② social connections (for securing jobs, etc.); pull: 找～ solicit help from potential backers / 办这种事，他有～。He knows the right places to go to get this kind of job done.

门罗主义 Ménluózhǔyì Monroe Doctrine (1823)

门脉 ménmài short for 门静脉 ménjìngmài

门楣 ménméi ① lintel (of a door) ② family status: 辱没～ bring disgrace to one's family

门面 ménmian ① the facade of a shop; shop front: 三间～ a three-bay shop front / 这家店铺～很大。The shop puts on a very prosperous front.② appearance; facade: 支撑～ keep up appearances; put up a front ——see also 摆门面 bǎi ménmian; 装门面 zhuāng ménmian

门面话 ménmianhuà formal and insincere remarks; lip service

门钮 ménniǔ door knob; door handle

门牌 ménpái ① (house) number plate ② street number; house number: 你家～几号? What's the street number of your house?

门票 ménpiào entrance ticket; admission ticket: 不收～ admission free / ～一元 one *yuan* for each ticket

门桥 ménqiáo *mil.* raft of pontoons; boat raft

门球 ménqiú *sports* croquet

门人 ménrén ① pupil; disciple; follower ② a hanger-on of an aristocrat

门扇 ménshàn door leaf

门神 ménshén door-god (whose pictures were often pasted on the front door of a house as a talisman in old China)

门生 ménshēng pupil; disciple; follower

门市 ménshì retail sales: ～部 retail department; sales department; salesroom / 快过年了，所以～很好。Spring Festival is coming, so retail sales are brisk.

门闩 ménshuān (door) bolt; (door) bar

门厅 méntīng *archit.* entrance hall; vestibule

门庭 méntíng ① courtyard ② family status

门庭若市 mén-tíng ruò shì the courtyard is as crowded as a marketplace—① a much visited house ② the shop is doing booming business

门徒 méntú disciple; follower; adherent

门外汉 ménwàihàn layman; the uninitiated: 对于美术，我是个～。Where the fine arts are concerned, I am only a layman.

门卫 ménwèi entrance guard

门下 ménxià same as 门人 ménrén

门牙 ményá front tooth; incisor

门诊 ménzhěn outpatient service: ～时间 consulting hours

门诊病人 ménzhěn bìngrén outpatient; clinic patient

门诊部 ménzhěnbù clinic; outpatient department

门柱 ménzhù doorpost

扪 mén *formal* touch; stroke

扪心自问 ménxīn zìwèn examine or search one's conscience: ～，我从来没有亏待过你。I have searched my conscience, and believe I have never mistreated you.

扪诊 ménzhěn *med.* palpation

钔 mén *chem.* mendelevium (Md)

mèn

闷 mèn ① bored; depressed; in low spirits: 你一个人在这儿多～得慌，跟我们出去走走吧! Don't you feel bored staying here all alone? Why not come out with us for a walk? ② tightly closed; sealed: ～屋子住着憋气。I feel suffocated in a tightly closed room. ——see also mēn

闷沉沉 mènchénchén depressed; gloomy

闷棍 mèngùn see 打闷棍 dǎ mèngùn

闷葫芦 mènhúlu enigma; puzzle; riddle: 这几句没头没脑的话真把人装进～里了。These abrupt remarks were really a puzzle to everyone.

闷葫芦罐儿 mènhúluguànr *inf.* earthenware money box; piggy bank

闷酒 mènjiǔ drinks taken alone to drown one's sorrows

闷倦 mènjuàn bored and listless

闷雷 mènléi ① muffled thunder ② unpleasant surprise; shock

闷闷不乐 mènmèn bù lè depressed; in low spirits: 她～，满腹心事。She was in low spirits and laden with anxiety.

闷气 mènqì the sulks: 生～ be sulky; be in the sulks ——see also mēnqì

闷香 mènxiāng narcotic incense burned to paralyse victims

闷子车 mènzichē (also 闷罐车 mènguànchē) boxcar

焖 mèn boil in a covered pot over a slow fire; braise: ～饭 cook rice over a slow fire / ～牛肉 braised beef

懑(懑) mèn see 愤懑 fènmèn

men

们 men *suf.* ① (used after a personal pronoun or a noun referring to a person to form a plural): 同志～ comrades / 女士～，先生～ ladies and gentlemen / 工人～ workers ② (used in personification after a noun referring to a thing or an animal to form a plural): 满天的星星～眨着眼睛。All the stars were blinking their eyes. / 奶奶管我们叫小燕子～。Grandma calls us "little swallows". ③ (used after the name of a person to mean people of the same kind, or to mean

his or her associates): 希特勒～ the Hitlers / 张刚～打了一天夯。 Zhang Gang and his fellows have been ramming the earth all day.

měng

蒙¹（矇）
méng ① cheat; deceive; dupe: 你～我! You're kidding me! / 一张假票子把他～了。 He was taken in by a forged note. / 欺上～下 deceive one's superiors and dupe one's subordinates ② make a wild guess: ～对了 make a lucky guess

蒙²
méng unconscious; senseless: 给打～了 be knocked senseless / 他觉得脑袋发～。 He felt his head swimming. / 老师一问到这个问题, 她就～了。 Her teacher's question baffled her.
——see also méng; Měng

蒙蒙黑 méngmēnghēi dusk; twilight
蒙蒙亮 méngméngliàng first glimmer of dawn; daybreak: 天～他就起床了。 He got up at the crack of dawn.
蒙骗 méngpiàn deceive; cheat; hoodwink; delude: ～顾客 cheat customers
蒙头转向 méngtóu zhuànxiàng lose one's bearings; be utterly confused: 情况这样复杂, 我都有点儿～了。 In all this mass of facts, I've rather lost my bearings.

méng

氓（吂）
méng arch. the common people
——see also máng

虻（蝱）
méng horsefly; gadfly: 牛虻 niúméng

萌¹
méng sprout; shoot forth; bud; germinate

萌²
méng same as 氓 méng

萌动 méngdòng ① (of plants) sprout; shoot forth; germinate; bud ② start: 春意～。 The breath of spring stirs.
萌发 méngfā bot. sprout; shoot forth; bud; germinate: 茶树修剪后又～新枝。 The tea plants sprouted new buds after the pruning.
萌生 méngshēng formal come into being; arise: 她的心底～出一个强烈的愿望。 There arose a strong desire in her heart.
萌芽 méngyá ① sprout; shoot forth; bud; germinate ② rudiment; shoot; seed; germ: 资本主义的～ the seeds of capitalism / 处于～状态 in the embryonic stage; in the bud
萌兆 méngzhào formal omen; presage; harbinger
萌苗 méngzhuó formal sprout; germinate

蒙
méng ① cover: ～上一层灰尘 be covered with a layer of dust / 她们头上都～着白毛巾。 They all covered their heads with white towels. / ～住眼睛 be blindfolded / ～头睡大觉 tuck oneself in and sleep like a log ② receive; meet with: ～大力协助, 十分感谢。 Thank you very much for your kind help. ③ ignorant; illiterate: 启蒙 qǐméng ——see also měng; Měng
蒙蔽 méngbì hoodwink; deceive; hide the truth from; pull the wool over sb.'s eyes: ～一部分群众 hoodwink part of the masses / 不要被花言巧语所～。 Don't let yourself be fooled by honeyed words. / ～是长久不了的。 No deception can last long.

蒙导法 méngdǎofǎ biol. mentor method
蒙垢 ménggòu formal be subjected to humiliation; be humiliated
蒙馆 méngguǎn (also 蒙塾 méngshú) old a private school
蒙汗药 ménghànyào a narcotic believed to have been used by highwaymen, etc. to drug their victims; knockout drops
蒙哄 ménghǒng deceive; hoodwink; swindle; cheat
蒙混 ménghùn deceive or mislead people
蒙混过关 ménghùn guòguān get by under false pretences
蒙眬 ménglóng half asleep; drowsy; somnolent: 睡眼～ eyes heavy with sleep; drowsy / ～睡去 doze off / ～中他仿佛听见有人敲门。 While he was half asleep, he seemed to hear a knock on the door.
蒙昧 méngmèi ① barbaric; uncivilized; uncultured: ～时代 age of barbarism ② ignorant; benighted; unenlightened
蒙昧无知 méngmèi wúzhī unenlightened; benighted; childishly ignorant
蒙昧主义 méngmèizhǔyì obscurantism
蒙蒙 méngméng drizzly; misty: ～细雨 a fine drizzle / 烟雾～ misty
蒙难 méngnàn (of a revolutionary) be confronted by danger; fall into the clutches of the enemy
蒙皮 méngpí envelope (of an aerostat); covering; skin
蒙受 méngshòu suffer; sustain: ～耻辱 be subjected to humiliation; be humiliated / ～生命财产的巨大损失 suffer a tremendous loss of lives and property
蒙太奇 méngtàiqí film montage
蒙特塞拉特岛 Méngtèsèlātèdǎo Montserrat
蒙脱石 méngtuōshí montmorillonite
蒙学 méngxué same as 蒙馆 méngguǎn
蒙药 méngyào common name for 麻醉剂 mázuìjì
蒙冤 méngyuān be wronged; suffer an injustice
蒙在鼓里 méng zài gǔlǐ be kept inside a drum—be kept in the dark: 这事儿早就传扬开了, 只有他还～。 The news has already got abroad only he himself is still completely in the dark.
蒙子 méngzi watch glass; crystal

盟
méng ① alliance: 结盟 jiéméng ② league (an administrative division of the Nei Monggol Autonomous Region, corresponding to a prefecture) ③ sworn (brothers): 盟兄弟 méngxiōngdì
盟邦 méngbāng an allied country; ally
盟国 méngguó an allied country; ally
盟军 méngjūn allied forces
盟誓 méngshì ① formal an oath of alliance; a treaty of alliance ② inf. take an oath; make a pledge: 对天～ swear by Heaven / 盟个誓 take an oath / 盟过誓 have made a pledge
盟兄弟 méngxiōngdì sworn brothers
盟友 méngyǒu ally
盟员 méngyuán a member of an alliance (or league)
盟约 méngyuē an oath of alliance; a treaty of alliance
盟主 méngzhǔ the leader (or chief) of an alliance

甍
méng formal ridge (of a roof)

濛
méng see below
濛濛 méngméng same as 蒙蒙 méngméng

檬
méng see 柠檬 níngméng

矇
méng see below
矇眬 ménglóng formal (of sunlight) dim

朦　méng　see below

朦胧　ménglóng　① (of moonlight) dim; hazy: 月色～ hazy moonlight ② obscure; dim; hazy: ～的景色 a hazy view / 烟雾～ misty / 暮色～ in the gloaming / 他年轻时有过～的人道主义思想。When he was young, he had hazy notions of humanitarianism.

朦胧诗　ménglóngshī　obscure poems

矇　méng　see below

矇胧　ménglóng　same as 蒙眬 ménglóng

艨　méng　see below

艨艟　méngchōng　arch. war vessel

měng

勐　měng　formal brave

猛　měng　① fierce; violent; energetic; vigorous: ～虎 a fierce tiger / 炮火很～。There was heavy gunfire. / 用力过～ use too much strength; overexert oneself / 在背上击一～掌 give sb. a powerful shove in the back ② adv. suddenly; abruptly: ～吃一惊 be startled / 河水～涨。The river suddenly rose. / 产量～增 a sharp increase in output / 物价～涨 (跌) a sharp rise (fall) in prices / 他正要睡去，～听得门响。He was about to go to bed when there was a sudden knock at the door. ③ adv. vigorously; with sudden force: ～干 work with vim and vigour / 他一脚～射，球破门而入。He sent the ball into the net with a powerful kick. / ～冲～打 fiercely charge and attack

猛不防　měngbùfáng　by surprise; unexpectedly; unawares: ～后面有人推了他一下。Suddenly someone gave him a push from behind.

猛地　měngde　adv. suddenly; abruptly: ～往前一跳 suddenly jump forward

猛孤丁地　měnggūdīngde　dial. suddenly; abruptly: 火车～停住了。The train came to an abrupt halt.

猛将　měngjiàng　a valiant general

猛进　měngjìn　push ahead vigorously; advance in quick and big strides: 祝你学业～! I wish you a rapid progress in your studies.

猛劲儿　měngjìnr　inf. ① a spurt of energy; dash: 她一个～，就超过了跑在前面的人。Putting on a spurt, she overtook all the other runners. / 搬重东西要用～。To lift heavy things, you need to use a sudden jerk of strength. ② great vigour: 这小伙子干活有股子～。This young chap works with vim and vigour.

猛力　měnglì　with sudden force: ～扣杀 smash (a ball) with all one's strength / 把手榴弹～一甩 throw a grenade with all one's might / ～一拉 pull with a jerk

猛厉　měnglì　fierce; vigorous; violent: 朔风～。There was a fierce north wind.

猛烈　měngliè　fierce; vigorous; violent: 发动～的进攻 wage a vigorous offensive / ～的炮火 heavy shellfire / 这里气候寒冷，风势～。It's bitter cold and violently windy here.

猛犸　měngmǎ　palaeontol. mammoth

猛禽　měngqín　bird of prey

猛然　měngrán　adv. suddenly; abruptly: 我～想起来了。In a flash I remembered. / ～一拉 pull with a jerk / ～回头 hastily turn one's head

猛士　měngshì　a brave warrior: 安得～兮守四方? (刘邦) Where will I find brave men to guard the four corners of my land?

猛兽　měngshòu　beast of prey

猛醒　měngxǐng　(also 猛省 měngxǐng) suddenly wake up (to the truth)

猛鸷　měngzhì　hawk; eagle

猛子　měngzi　see 扎猛子 zhā měngzi

蒙

蒙　Měng　the Monggol nationality ——see also 蒙古族 Měnggǔzú[①] ——see also méng; mēng

蒙古　Měnggǔ　Mongolia ——see also 内蒙古 Nèi Měnggǔ

蒙古包　Měnggǔbāo　yurt

蒙古人　Měnggǔrén　Mongolian; Mongol

蒙古人种　Měnggǔ rénzhǒng　same as 黄种 Huángzhǒng

蒙古语　Měnggǔyǔ　Mongolian (language); Mongol (language)

蒙古语族　Měnggǔ yǔzú　linguis. the Mongolian group

蒙古族　Měnggǔzú　① the Mongolian nationality, or the Mongolians (or Mongols), distributed over the Inner Mongolia, Xinjiang and Ningxia Autonomous Regions, and Jilin, Liaoning, Heilongjiang, Gansu, Qinghai, Hebei and Henan Provinces ② the Mongolians (or Mongols) of Mongolia

蒙栎　měnglì　bot. Mongolian oak (Quercus mongolica)

锰

锰　měng　chem. manganese (Mn)

锰钢　měnggāng　manganese steel

锰结核　měngjiéhé　geol. manganese nodule

锰铁　měngtiě　ferromanganese

蜢

蜢　měng　see 蚱蜢 zhàměng

獴

獴　měng　zool. mongoose

蠓

蠓　měng　zool. midge; biting midge

懵 (懞)

懵　měng　muddled; ignorant: ～然无知 be totally ignorant

懵懂　měngdǒng　muddled; ignorant

mèng

孟　mèng　① the first month of a season: 孟春 mèngchūn ② the eldest among brothers ③ (Mèng) a surname

孟春　mèngchūn　the first month of spring

孟德尔主义　Mèngdé'ěrzhǔyì　biol. Mendelism

孟冬　mèngdōng　the first month of winter

孟加拉　Mèngjiālā　Bengal

孟加拉国　Mèngjiālāguó　Bangladesh

孟加拉人　Mèngjiālārén　Bengalese; Bengali

孟加拉湾　Mèngjiālāwān　the Bay of Bengal

孟加拉语　Mèngjiālāyǔ　Bengali (language)

孟浪　mènglàng　rash; impetuous; impulsive: 不可～行事。Don't act rashly.

孟秋　mèngqiū　the first month of autumn

孟什维克　Mèngshíwéikè　Menshevik

孟什维主义　Mèngshíwéizhǔyì　Menshevism

孟夏　mèngxià　the first month of summer

孟子　Mèngzǐ　Mencius ——see also 四书 sìshū

梦 (夢)

梦　mèng　① dream: 昨晚我做了个可怕的～。I had a terrible dream last night. ② fancy; illusion: 痴人说梦 chīrén shuō mèng

梦笔生花　mèng bǐ shēng huā　dream that one's brush is blooming—begin to show one's literary brilliance

梦话　mènghuà　① words uttered in one's sleep; somniloquy: 昨晚我听见你说～。I heard you talk in your sleep last night. ② daydream; nonsense: 六个月就能编

一本词典? 这简直是在说~! To compile a dictionary within 6 months—that's just daydreaming!

梦幻 mènghuàn illusion; dream; reverie: ~一般的境界 a dreamlike world; dreamland / 舒曼的《~曲》 Träumerei ("Reverie") by Schumann

梦幻泡影 mènghuàn-pàoyǐng pipe dream; bubble; illusion: 一切希望都成了~. All my hopes have come to nothing.

梦见 mèngjian see in a dream; dream about: 他~自己又回到了部队. He dreamt that he was back in the army. / 我~我母亲了. I saw my mother in my dream.

梦境 mèngjìng dreamland; dreamworld; dream: 乍到桂林, 我如入~一般. On arriving in Guilin, I felt as if I were in a dreamland.

梦寐 mèngmèi dream; sleep: ~难忘 be unable to forget sth. even in one's dreams

梦寐以求 mèngmèi yǐ qiú crave sth. so that one even dreams about it; long (or yearn) for sth. day and night

梦乡 mèngxiāng dreamland: 他太累了, 一躺下就进入了~. He was so tired that as soon as his head hit the pillow, he went off to dreamland.

梦想 mèngxiǎng ① vain hope; wishful thinking: 他以为她会嫁给自己的, 这只是~而已. His belief that she will marry him is only wishful thinking. ② vainly hope; dream of: 他居然得了冠军, 这是连他自己都~不到的事. His winning of the championship was something he'd never dreamt of before.

梦魇 mèngyǎn nightmare

梦遗 mèngyí med. nocturnal emission; wet dream

梦呓 mèngyì ① sleeptalking; somniloquy ② rigmarole

梦游症 mèngyóuzhèng (also 梦行症 mèngxíngzhèng) somnambulism; sleepwalking

mī

咪

mī see below

咪咪 mīmī onom. mew; miaow: 小猫一饿就~叫. The kittens mewed when they were hungry.

眯 (瞇)

mī ① narrow (one's eyes): ~着眼睛笑 narrow one's eyes into a smile / ~着眼睛瞧 squint at ② dial. take a nap: ~一会儿 take a short nap; have forty winks—see also mǐ

眯盹儿 mīdǔnr dial. doze off; take a nap

眯缝 mīfeng narrow (one's eyes): 他不说话, 只是~着眼睛笑. He didn't say anything, but only narrowed his eyes into a smile.

mí

弥 (彌)

mí ① full; overflowing: 弥漫 mímàn ② cover; fill: 弥缝 míféng ③ adv. formal more; still more; even more: 仰之~高, 钻之~坚.《论语》 The more I look up at it the higher it appears. The more I bore into it the harder it becomes.

弥补 míbǔ make up; remedy; make good: ~损失 make up for (or make good) a loss / ~缺陷 remedy a defect / 无法~的损失 an irreparable loss / ~赤字 make up (or meet) a deficit / 学习别人的优点, ~自己的不足 learn from other people's strong points to counteract one's own weaknesses

弥封 míféng seal the examinee's name on an exam paper so as to prevent fraudulence

弥缝 míféng plug up holes—gloss over faults

弥合 míhé close; bridge: ~裂痕 close a rift

弥勒 Mílè Maitreya (a Bodhisattva 菩萨 usu. represented as a very stout monk with a broad smile on his face and with his naked breast and paunch exposed to view)

弥留 míliú formal be dying

弥留之际 míliú zhī jì on one's deathbed

弥漫 mímàn fill the air; spread all over the place: 春意~。 Spring is very much in the air. / 风雪~ be in a blinding snowstorm

弥撒 mísa Catholicism Mass: 望~ attend Mass; go to Mass

弥撒曲 mísaqǔ mus. mass

弥散 mísàn spread or diffuse in all directions

弥天大谎 mítiān dàhuǎng monstrous lie; outrageous lie

弥天大罪 mítiān dàzuì monstrous crime; heinous crime

迷

mí ① be confused; be lost: ~了方向 lose one's bearings; get lost ② be fascinated by; be crazy about: 小伙子们~上了霹雳舞. The youngsters became crazy about break dance. ③ fan; enthusiast; fiend: 足球~ a soccer fan (or enthusiast) ④ confuse; perplex; fascinate; enchant: 景色~人. The scenery is of enchanting beauty. / 他让金钱~住了心窍. He was obssessed by lust for money.

迷宫 mígōng labyrinth; maze

迷航 míháng (of a plane, ship, etc.) drift off course; lose one's course; get lost

迷糊 míhu ① misted; blurred; dimmed: 这么多花布我都看~了. I was simply dazzled by all these cotton prints. ② dazed; confused: 睡~了 be dazed with sleep / 喝酒喝~了 get tipsy / 把人给弄~了 make one feel muddled / 我刚合上眼就迷迷糊糊地睡着了. I dozed off as soon as I closed my eyes. ③ muddleheaded: 他这个人有点~. He's somewhat muddleheaded.

迷魂汤 míhúntāng (also 迷魂药 míhúnyào) ① sth. intended to turn sb.'s head; magic potion ② flattery——see also 灌迷魂汤 guàn míhúntāng

迷魂阵 míhúnzhèn a scheme for confusing or bewildering sb.; maze; trap: 摆~ lay out a scheme to bewitch sb.; set a trap

迷惑 míhuo puzzle; confuse; perplex; baffle: 感到~不解 feel puzzled; feel perplexed / ~敌人 confuse the enemy / 不要被假象所~. Don't be misled by false appearances.

迷津 míjīn miss the ferry—stray from the right path: 指破~ point out where sb. has gone astray

迷离 mílí blurred; misted: 睡眼~ eyes dim with sleep

迷离扑朔 mílí pūshuò same as 扑朔迷离 pūshuò mílí

迷离惝恍 mílí tǎnghuǎng indistinct; blurred

迷恋 míliàn be infatuated with; madly cling to: ~纸醉金迷的生活 be infatuated with (or be addicted to) a life of luxury and dissipation

迷路[1] mílù ① lose one's way; get lost: 天太黑, 我迷了路. I lost my way because it was too dark. ② go astray

迷路[2] mílù same as 内耳 nèi'ěr

迷乱 míluàn dazed and confused; befuddled

迷漫 mímàn boundless and indistinct; vast and hazy: 烟雾~ be enveloped in mist; be covered in thick mist

迷茫 mímáng ① vast and hazy: 大雪纷飞, 原野一片~. The vast plain was obscured by the falling flakes of snow. ② confused; perplexed; dazed: 他脸上显出~的神情. There was a confused look on his face.

迷梦 mímèng pipe dream; fond illusion

迷迷怔怔 mímízhēngzhēng dazed; confused: 睡得~的 be dazed with sleep

迷你裙 mínǐqún miniskirt

迷失 míshī lose (one's way, etc.)

迷失方向 míshī fāngxiàng lose one's bearings; get lost

迷途 mítú ① lose one's way ② wrong path: 走入～ go astray

迷途知返 mítú zhī fǎn recover one's bearings and return to the fold; realize one's errors and mend one's ways

迷惘 míwǎng be perplexed; be at a loss: ～的神色 a perplexed look

迷雾 míwù ① dense fog ② anything that misleads people

迷信 míxìn ① superstition; superstitious belief; blind faith; blind worship ② have blind faith in; make a fetish of: ～权威 have blind faith in authority

迷走神经 mízǒu shénjīng *physiol.* vagus (nerve)

谜 mí ① riddle; conundrum: 猜谜儿 cāimèir ② enigma; mystery; puzzle: 他的死因现在还是一个～。 The cause of his death remains a mystery to this day.

谜底 mídǐ ① answer (*or* solution) to a riddle ② truth: 揭开～ find out the truth (of a matter)

谜面 mímiàn (the version of a) riddle; conundrum

谜团 mítuán doubts and suspicions: 揭开～ resolve doubts

谜语 míyǔ riddle; conundrum

眯(瞇) mí (of dust, etc.) get into one's eye: 沙子～了眼。 The dust has got into my eye. ——see also mī

猕(獼) mí see below

猕猴 míhóu macaque; rhesus monkey

猕猴桃 míhóutáo *bot.* yangtao (*Actinidia chinensis*)

醚 mí *chem.* ether

糜 mí ① gruel or paste: 肉糜 ròumí ② rotten: 糜烂 mílàn ③ spend extravagantly; waste: 糜费 mífèi ④ (Mí) a surname ——see also méi

糜费 mífèi spend extravagantly; waste: ～钱财 waste money / 节约开支，防止～ cut down expenses and avoid waste

糜烂 mílàn ① rotten to the core; dissipated; debauched: 生活～ lead a dissipated (*or* fast) life ② *med.* erosion

糜烂性毒剂 mílànxìng dújì *mil.* vesicant agent; blister agent

麋 mí elk

麋羚 mílíng hartebeest

麋鹿 mílù mi-lu; David's deer

靡 mí spend extravagantly; waste: 奢靡 shēmí ——see also mǐ

靡费 mífèi same as 糜费 mífèi

蘪 mí see 荼蘪 túmí

醾(醿、酉麋) mí see 酴醾 túmí

mǐ

米[1] mǐ ① (husked) rice ② shelled or husked seed: 高粱米 gāoliangmǐ / 花生米 huāshēngmǐ ③ (Mǐ) a surname

米[2] mǐ metre

米波 mǐbō *radio* metric wave

米醋 mǐcù rice vinegar

米饭 mǐfàn (cooked) rice

米粉 mǐfěn ① ground rice; rice flour ② rice-flour noodles

米粉肉 mǐfěnròu steamed rice flour pork

米泔水 mǐgānshuǐ water in which rice has been washed

米黄 mǐhuáng cream-coloured

米酒 mǐjiǔ rice wine

米糠 mǐkāng rice bran

米粒 mǐlì grain of rice

米粮川 mǐliángchuān rich rice-producing area: 昔日穷山沟，今日～。 The barren gully of yesterday has become a granary.

米面 mǐmiàn ① rice and wheat flour ② ground rice; rice flour ③ *dial.* rice-flour noodles

米色 mǐsè cream-coloured

米汤 mǐtang ① water in which rice has been cooked ② thin rice or millet gruel; rice water

米突 mǐtū old name for 米[2] mǐ

米线 mǐxiàn *dial.* rice-flour noodles

米象 mǐxiàng *zool.* rice weevil

米制 mǐzhì same as 国际公制 guójì gōngzhì

米珠薪桂 mǐzhū-xīnguì rice is as precious as pearls and firewood as costly as cassia—exorbitantly high cost of living

米烛光 mǐzhúguāng *phys.* metre-candle; lux

米蛀虫 mǐzhùchóng ① rice worm ② rice profiteer

弭 mǐ *formal* put an end to; stop; suppress; remove: 消弭 xiāomǐ

弭谤 mǐbàng *formal* stop a slander

弭兵 mǐbīng (also 弭战 mǐzhàn) *formal* stop a war; have a truce

弭除 mǐchú eliminate; dispel; remove; clear up: ～成见 dispel prejudices

弭患 mǐhuàn *formal* remove the source of trouble

弭乱 mǐluàn put down a rebellion or stop a civil war

脒 mǐ *chem.* amidine

敉 mǐ *formal* soothe; pacify

敉平 mǐpíng *formal* put down (a rebellion); quell; suppress

靡[1] mǐ *formal* blown away by the wind: 披靡 pīmǐ

靡[2] mǐ *formal* not have; there is not; be without: ～日不思 not a day passes without one's thinking of sth. or sb. ——see also mí

靡丽 mǐlì *formal* ① magnificent; resplendent ② luxurious; extravagant

靡靡之音 mǐmǐ zhī yīn decadent music

mì

汨 Mì short for 汨罗 Mìluó

汨罗 Mìluó name of a river, rising in Jiangxi Province and running into Hunan

泌 mì secrete: 分泌 fēnmì ——see also bì

泌尿科 mìniàokē *med.* urological department

泌尿器官 mìniào qìguān *physiol.* urinary organs

宓 mì ① *formal* tranquil; quiet ② (Mì) a surname

觅（覓） mì look for; hunt for; seek: 鸟雀经常在这里～食。Birds often look for food here.

觅句 mìjù seek a telling line (for a poem)

觅取 mìqǔ look for; hunt for; seek

秘（祕） mì ① secret; mysterious: 诡秘 guǐmì ② keep sth. secret; hold sth. back: 秘而不宣 mì ér bù xuān ——see also bì

秘奥 mì'ào profound mystery

秘宝 mìbǎo a rare treasure

秘本 mìběn treasured private copy of a rare book

秘传 mìchuán hand down (a recipe, formula, etc.) from generation to generation in the family as a closely guarded secret

秘而不宣 mì ér bù xuān keep sth. secret; not let anyone in on a secret

秘方 mìfāng secret recipe

秘结 mìjié constipated; costive

秘诀 mìjué secret (of success): 成功的～ the secret of (or key to) one's success

秘密 mìmì ① secret; clandestine; confidential: ～会议 secret meeting; closed-door session /～活动 clandestine activities /～文件 secret papers; confidential document /～报告 a secret report ② sth. secret: 探索海底的～ explore the secrets of the ocean bed / 军事～ a military secret

秘密警察 mìmì jǐngchá secret police

秘史 mìshǐ secret history (as of a feudal dynasty); inside story

秘事 mìshì a private affair; secret

秘书 mìshū secretary

秘书处 mìshūchù secretariat

秘书长 mìshūzhǎng secretary-general

密 mì ① close; dense; thick: 这两行苗栽得太～了。These two rows of seedlings are planted too close together. /～不透风 airtight / 枪声很～。There was the sound of intensive gunfire. ② intimate; close: 亲密 qīnmì ③ fine; meticulous: 周密 zhōumì ④ secret: ～通声息 secretly communicate with each other ⑤ text. density: 经密 jīngmì / 纬密 wěimì

密报 mìbào ① secretly report; inform against sb. ② a secret report

密闭 mìbì airtight; hermetic: ～容器 airtight container; hermetically-sealed chamber

密布 mìbù be densely covered: 阴云～。The sky was overcast. or Dark clouds were gathering. / 礁石～ be thick with reefs

密电 mìdiàn ① secretly telegraph sb. ② cipher telegram

密电码 mìdiànmǎ cipher code

密度 mìdù ① density; thickness: 兵力～ density of troops / 火力～ density (or volume) of fire / 果树的～不宜太大。Fruit trees should not be planted too close together. ② phys. density

密度计 mìdùjì densimeter

密封 mìfēng ① seal up: ～的文件 sealed documents ② seal airtight; seal hermetically: ～的容器 airtight container; hermetically-sealed chamber /～保存 preserve sth. by sealing it airtight

密封舱 mìfēngcāng sealed cabin; airtight cabin

密封垫圈 mìfēng diànquān mech. sealing washer

密封机身 mìfēng jīshēn closed fuselage

密封压盖 mìfēng yāgài mech. sealing gland

密告 mìgào secretly report; inform against sb.

密集 mìjí concentrated; crowded together: 人口～ densely populated; thickly populated / 对敌人进行～包围 closely surround the enemy

密集队形 mìjí duìxíng close formation; tight formation

密集轰炸 mìjí hōngzhà mass bombing

密集炮火 mìjí pàohuǒ intensive bombardment; concentrated fire; massed fire; drumfire

密件 mìjiàn a confidential paper or letter; classified matter; classified material

密克罗尼西亚 Mìkèluóníxīyà Micronesia

密林 mìlín thick (or dense) forest

密令 mìlìng ① give a secret order or instructions ② secret order or instructions

密锣紧鼓 mìluó-jǐngǔ same as 紧锣密鼓 jǐnluó-mìgǔ

密码 mìmǎ cipher; cipher code; secret code

密码电报 mìmǎ diànbào cipher telegram

密码机 mìmǎjī cipher machine; cryptograph

密码术 mìmǎshù cryptography; cryptology

密码员 mìmǎyuán cryptographer

密码子 mìmǎzi biol. codon

密密层层 mìmìcéngcéng packed closely layer upon layer (or ring upon ring); dense; thick: ～的人群 a dense crowd

密密丛丛 mìmìcóngcóng (of grass or trees) dense; thick: ～的森林 a dense forest

密密麻麻 mìmìmámá inf. close and numerous; thickly dotted: 笔记本上写满了～的小字。The notebook was filled with small, closely-written characters.

密密匝匝 mìmìzāzā same as 密匝匝 mìzāzā

密谋 mìmóu conspire; plot; scheme: ～叛变 conspire to defect /～政变 plot a coup

密切 mìqiè ① close; intimate: ～配合 act in close coordination /～相关 be closely related /～联系群众 maintain close ties with the masses / 双方关系很～。They two are very close to each other. or They two are on intimate terms. ② build (or forge, establish) close links (between two parties): 进一步～两国的关系 build closer relations between the two countries ③ careful; intent; close: ～注视 pay close attention to; watch closely

密商 mìshāng hold private counsel; hold secret talks

密使 mìshǐ secret emissary; secret envoy

密室 mìshì a room used for secret purposes: 策划于～ plot behind closed doors

密实 mìshi closely knit; dense; thick: 这件棉衣针脚做得真～。This padded jacket is sewn tightly with small stitches. or The stitches on this padded jacket are small and close.

密谈 mìtán have a secret (or confidential, private) talk; talk behind closed doors

密探 mìtàn secret agent; spy

密陀僧 mìtuósēng chem. litharge; yellow lead

密位 mìwèi mil. mil

密纹唱片 mìwén chàngpiàn long-playing record; microgroove record

密西西比河 Mìxīxībǐhé the Mississippi

密写情报 mìxiě qíngbào intelligence written in invisible ink, etc.

密信 mìxìn secret letter; confidential letter

密友 mìyǒu close (or fast) friend; bosom friend

密语通信 mìyǔ tōngxìn crypto-communication

密约 mìyuē secret agreement; secret treaty

密云不雨 mì yún bù yǔ dense clouds but no rain ——trouble is brewing

密匝匝 mìzāzā inf. thick; dense

密植 mìzhí agric. close planting: 合理～ rational close planting

幂（冪） mì ① math. power ② formal cloth cover

幂级数 mìjíshù math. power series

谧 mì *formal*　quiet; still; tranquil: 安谧 ānmì

谧静 mìjìng *formal*　quiet; still; tranquil

蜜 mì ① honey: 蜂蜜 fēngmì ② honey-like thing: 糖蜜 tángmì ③ honeyed; sweet: 甜蜜 tiánmì

蜜虫 mìchóng *dial.*　aphid; aphis

蜜蜂 mìfēng　honeybee; bee

蜜柑 mìgān　mandarin orange; tangerine orange

蜜饯 mìjiàn　candied fruit; preserved fruit

蜜橘 mìjú　tangerine

蜜蜡 mìlà　beeswax

蜜里调油 mì lǐ tiáo yóu　like honey mixed with oil——be deeply attached to each other

蜜色 mìsè　light yellow

蜜甜 mìtián　as sweet as honey; very sweet

蜜丸子 mìwánzi *Chin. med.*　a bolus made of powdered Chinese medicine and honey

蜜腺 mìxiàn *bot.*　nectary

蜜源 mìyuán　nectar source

蜜源区 mìyuánqū　(bee) pasture

蜜源植物 mìyuán zhíwù　nectariferous (*or* bee, honey) plant

蜜月 mìyuè　honeymoon: 度～ spend (*or* be on) one's honeymoon; honeymoon

蜜枣 mìzǎo　candied date or jujube

蜜渍 mìzì　candied; preserved in sugar

嘧 mì　see below

嘧啶 mìdìng *chem.*　pyrimidine

mián

眠 mián ① sleep: 不～之夜 a sleepless night; a white night ② *zool.* dormancy: 冬眠 dōngmián

眠尔通 mián'ěrtōng *pharm.*　miltown

绵(綿) mián ① silk floss: 丝绵 sīmián ② continuous: 连绵 liánmián ③ soft: 软绵绵 ruǎnmiánmián①

绵白糖 miánbáitáng　fine white sugar

绵薄 miánbó *hum.*　(my) meagre strength; humble effort: 愿尽～。I'll do what little I can.

绵长 miáncháng　(of time) very long: 福寿～。I wish you a happy and long life (said to an elderly person).

绵绸 miánchóu　fabric made from waste silk

绵亘 miángèn　(of mountains, etc.) stretch in an unbroken chain: 大别山～在河南、安徽和湖北三省的边界上。The Dabie Mountains stretch along the borders of Henan, Anhui and Hubei.

绵里藏针 mián lǐ cáng zhēn　a needle hidden in silk floss —a ruthless character behind a gentle appearance; an iron hand in a velvet glove

绵力 miánlì　same as 绵薄 miánbó

绵联 miánlián　same as 连绵 liánmián

绵马 miánmǎ　another name for 羊齿 yángchǐ

绵密 miánmì　meticulous; detailed; circumspect

绵绵 miánmián　continuous; unbroken: 秋雨～。The autumn rain goes on and on.

绵邈 miánmiǎo *formal*　faraway; remote: 年代～ of the remote past; age-old / 道路～ a long journey; a long way to go

绵软 miánruǎn ① soft: ～的羊毛 soft wool ② weak: 觉得浑身～ feel weak all over

绵延 miányán　be continuous; stretch long and unbroken: ～千里的山脉 mountains extending (*or* stretching) a thousand *li* / 第二次世界大战后，局部战争一直～不断。Local wars have been going on continual-

ly ever since the end of World War II.

绵羊 miányáng　sheep

绵纸 miánzhǐ　tissue paper

绵子 miánzi *dial.*　silk floss; silk wadding

棉 mián ① general name for cotton and kapok ② cotton: ～纺织品 cotton textiles ③ cotton-padded; quilted: ～大衣 cotton-padded overcoat

棉袄 mián'ǎo　cotton-padded (*or* quilted) jacket

棉包 miánbāo　a bale of cotton

棉被 miánbèi　a quilt with cotton wadding; cotton-wedded quilt

棉布 miánbù　cotton cloth; cotton

棉纺 miánfǎng　cotton spinning

棉纺厂 miánfǎngchǎng　cotton mill

棉凫 miánfú *zool.*　cotton teal

棉红铃虫 miánhónglíngchóng　pink bollworm

棉红蜘蛛 miánhóngzhīzhū　two-spotted spider mite

棉猴儿 miánhóur　hooded cotton-padded coat; (knee-length) parka; anorak

棉花 miánhua　cotton

棉花签 miánhuaqiān　(cotton) swab

棉花蛆 miánhuaqū *dial.*　pink bollworm

棉花胎 miánhuatāi *dial.*　a cotton wadding (for a quilt, etc.)

棉花套子 miánhuatàozi *dial.*　a cotton wadding (for a quilt)

棉卷 miánjuǎn *text.*　lap

棉枯萎病 miánkūwěibìng　fusarium wilt of cotton

棉裤 miánkù　cotton-padded trousers

棉铃 miánlíng　cotton boll

棉铃虫 miánlíngchóng　bollworm

棉毛机 miánmáojī　interlock (knitting) machine

棉毛裤 miánmáokù　cotton (interlock) trousers (worn as underwear)

棉毛衫 miánmáoshān　cotton (interlock) jersey (worn as underwear)

棉毛衫布 miánmáoshānbù　cotton interlock (fabric)

棉农 miánnóng　cotton grower

棉袍子 miánpáozi (*also* 棉袍儿 miánpáor)　cotton-padded robe

棉绒 miánróng　cotton velvet

棉纱 miánshā　cotton yarn

棉纱头 miánshātóu　(cotton) waste

棉毯 miántǎn　cotton blanket

棉桃 miántáo　cotton boll

棉套 miántào　a cotton-padded covering for keeping sth. warm

棉田 miántián　cotton field

棉条 miántiáo *text.*　sliver

棉条桶 miántiáotǒng *text.*　sliver can

棉线 miánxiàn　cotton thread; cotton

棉鞋 miánxié　cotton-padded shoes

棉絮 miánxù ① cotton fibre ② a cotton wadding (for a quilt, etc.)

棉蚜虫 miányáchóng　cotton aphid

棉衣 miányī　cotton-padded clothes

棉织品 miánzhīpǐn　cotton goods; cotton textiles; cotton fabrics

棉籽 miánzǐ　cottonseed

棉籽饼 miánzǐbǐng　cottonseed cake

棉籽绒 miánzǐróng　(cotton) linters

棉籽油 miánzǐyóu　cottonseed oil

miǎn

免 miǎn ① excuse sb. from sth.; exempt; dispense

with: ～试 be excused from an examination / ～服兵役 be exempt from military service / 互相～办签证协议 mutual exemption of visas agreement / 这些手续就～了。We'll dispense with the formalities. ② remove from office; dismiss; relieve: 他已被～去教育部长的职务。He has been removed from his post as minister of education. / 他工作太多, 得给他～掉几项。He's got too much to do. He should be relieved of some of his jobs. ③ avoid; avert; escape: ～于受灾 avert a disaster ④ be not allowed: 闲人～进。No admittance except on business.

免不得 miǎnbude be unavoidable; be bound to be: 在这个问题上他们的看法分歧很大, ～有一场争论。Their views differ greatly on this question, so a dispute is unavoidable.

免不了 miǎnbuliǎo be unavoidable; be bound to be: 在前进的道路上, ～会有困难。There are bound to be difficulties in the course of our advance. / 这件事如果处理不当, ～人家会有意见。If it is not handled properly, popular complaints will be unavoidable.

免除 miǎnchú ① prevent; avoid: 兴修水利, ～水旱灾害 build irrigation works to prevent droughts and floods / 参加集体生产劳动, 可以帮助干部～官僚主义。Participation in collective productive labour helps cadres to avoid bureaucracy. ② remit; excuse; exempt; relieve: ～债务 remit a debt / ～一项任务 excuse sb. from a task; relieve sb. of a task / ～处罚 be exempt from (criminal) punishment

免得 miǎnde conj. so as not to; so as to avoid: 多问几句, ～走错路。Make some more inquiries so that you won't go the wrong way. / 我再说明一下, ～引起误会。To avoid any misunderstanding, let me explain once again. / 你要是能去最好, ～他跑一趟。It would be best if you could go. It would save him a trip.

免费 miǎnfèi free of charge; free; gratis: ～医疗 free medical care / ～入场 admission free; be admitted gratis

免冠 miǎnguān ① take one's hat off (in salutation) ② without a hat on; bareheaded: 半身～正面相片 a half-length, bareheaded, full-faced photo

免开尊口 miǎn kāi zūnkǒu please keep your mouth shut (i.e. not broach the ticklish topic): 这事让她出面, 你就～! You'd better keep your honourable mouth shut in this matter and leave it to her.

免票 miǎnpiào ① free pass; free ticket ② free of charge: 身高不满一米的儿童～。Children under a metre in height free of charge.

免税 miǎnshuì ① exempt from taxation ② tax-free; duty-free: ～货物 duty-free goods

免税商店 miǎnshuì shāngdiàn duty-free shop

免刑 miǎnxíng leg. exempt from punishment

免修 miǎnxiū be excused from a college course

免验 miǎnyàn exempt from customs examination: ～放行 pass without examination (P. W. E.)

免验证 miǎnyànzhèng laissez-passer

免役 miǎnyì exempt from military service

免疫 miǎnyì med. immunity (from disease)

免疫性 miǎnyìxìng med. immunity

免予起诉 miǎn yǔ qǐsù leg. exempt from prosecution: ～决定书 decision to exempt from prosecution

免战牌 miǎnzhànpái a sign used in ancient times to show refusal to fight ——see also 挂免战牌 guà miǎnzhànpái

免征 miǎnzhēng exempt from taxation

免职 miǎnzhí remove sb. from office; relieve sb. of his post

免罪 miǎnzuì exempt from punishment

勉 miǎn ① exert oneself; strive: 奋勉 fènmiǎn ②

encourage; urge; exhort: 互～ encourage one another / 自～ spur oneself on ③ strive to do what is beyond one's power: 勉强 miǎnqiǎng

勉力 miǎnlì exert oneself; try hard; make great efforts: ～为之 exert oneself to the utmost; do one's best

勉励 miǎnlì encourage; urge: 同志们～她努力取得更大的成绩。Her comrades encouraged her to do still better. / 他～学生努力学习。He urged his students to work hard.

勉强 miǎnqiǎng ① manage with an effort; do with difficulty: 病人～喝了点粥。With an effort the patient ate some gruel. or The patient forced himself to take a few mouthful of gruel. ② reluctant; grudging: ～协助 (许诺) give reluctant assistance (a reluctant promise) / ～同意 reluctantly agree / ～地笑了笑 force a smile / 他接受了我们的建议, 但是很～。He accepted our suggestion, but rather grudgingly. ③ force sb. to do sth.: 要是他不愿意去, 就不要～他。If he doesn't want to go, don't force him to. ④ inadequate; unconvincing; strained; farfetched: 你的理由很～。The reason you give is rather unconvincing. ⑤ barely enough: 草料～够牲口吃一天。There's just enough cattle fodder for one day's feed. / 他的身高也许～能达到参军的标准。He might be just tall enough to join the army. / ～的多数 a bare majority / ～维持生活 eke out a bare living; scrape along

勉为其难 miǎn wéi qí nán undertake to do a difficult job as best one can; agree to do what one knows is beyond one's ability or power

眄 miǎn a variant pronunciation for 眄 miàn

娩(挽) miǎn childbirth; delivery; parturition: 分娩 fēnmiǎn

冕 miǎn crown (worn by an emperor, etc.): 加冕 jiāmiǎn

湎 miǎn see 沉湎 chénmiǎn

缅 miǎn remote; far back

缅甸 Miǎndiàn Myanmar; Burma

缅甸人 Miǎndiànrén Myanmese; Burmese

缅甸语 Miǎndiànyǔ Myanmese (language); Burmese

缅怀 miǎnhuái cherish the memory of; recall: ～革命先烈 cherish the memory of our revolutionary martyrs / ～往事 recall past events

缅邈 miǎnmiǎo formal remote; far back

缅茄 miǎnqié bot. Shan pahudia (Pahudia xylocarpa)

缅想 miǎnxiǎng think of (past events); recall

腼 miǎn see below

腼腆 miǎn·tiǎn shy; bashful: 这孩子见了生人有点～。The child is shy with strangers.

鮸 miǎn slate cod croaker

miàn

面¹(靣) miàn ① face: ～带笑容 with a smile on one's face / ～无惧色 not look at all afraid / 看在我的～上, 饶了他这一回吧。Please let him off this time just for my sake. ② face (a certain direction): 这房子～南坐北。The house faces south. ③ surface; top; face: 钟～ clock face; dial / ～儿磨得很光。The surface has been polished shining bright. ④ side: 这种纸一～

光。This kind of paper is smooth on one side. / 这本书有多少～? How many pages are there in this book? ⑤ the right side; cover; outside: 书～儿 the cover of a book / 夹袄的～儿 the outside of a lined jacket / 这块布做里儿，那块布做～儿。Use this piece of cloth for the lining and use that piece for the outside. ⑥ *math.* surface: 立方体有六～。A cube has six surfaces. ⑦ an entire area (as opposed to particular points): 部长下去蹲点了，～上的工作他让我来抓。The minister has gone to work at a grass-roots unit and has left me in charge of the ministry. ⑧ extent; range; scale; scope: 知识～广(窄) have a wide (narrow) range of knowledge / 这次讨论涉及的～很广。The discussion covered a wide range of topics. ⑨ personally; directly: ～告 tell sb. personally ⑩ *suf.* (to a noun of locality): 前面 qiánmian / 外面 wàimian ⑪ *m.* (for flat things): 一～镜子 a mirror / 两～旗子 two flags

面²(麵、麪)
miàn ① wheat flour; flour: 大米～ rice flour ② powder: 药～儿 medicinal powder / 胡椒～儿 ground pepper ③ noodles: 一碗～ a bowl of noodles ④ *dial.* soft and floury: 这块白薯真～。This sweet potato is soft and floury.

面包 miànbāo bread

面包车 miànbāochē popular name for 旅行车 lǔxíngchē

面包房 miànbāofáng bakery

面包干 miànbāogān rusk

面包果 miànbāoguǒ *bot.* breadfruit

面包渣儿 miànbāozhār breadcrumbs; crumbs

面禀 miànbǐng report (to one's superior) in person

面不改色 miàn bù gǎisè not change colour; remain calm; without turning a hair; without batting an eyelid: ～心不跳 remain absolutely calm

面茶 miànchá seasoned millet mush

面陈 miànchén tell or explain in person

面呈 miànchéng submit in person

面斥 miànchì give sb. a talking-to; reprove

面辞 miàncí go to say good-bye to sb.; take leave of sb.

面从后言 miàncóng-hòuyán say yes to sb.'s face but begin to carp the moment his back is turned

面对 miànduì face; confront: ～现实 face reality; be realistic / ～危险情况，镇定自若 remain calm in the face of danger / ～这一派大好形势，怎能不欢欣鼓舞? Who wouldn't be happy to see such a good situation?

面对面 miàn duì miàn facing each other; face-to-face; vis-à-vis: ～地坐着 sit face-to-face; sit vis-à-vis / ～的斗争 a face-to-face struggle; direct confrontation

面额 miàn'é ① *econ.* denomination: 各种～的纸币 banknotes of different denominations / ～为五元和十元的人民币 Renminbi in 5- and 10-*yuan* notes ② forehead

面肥 miànféi ① leavening dough; leaven ② *agric.* topdressing

面粉 miànfěn wheat flour; flour

面粉厂 miànfěnchǎng flour mill

面革 miàngé upper leather

面和心不和 miàn hé xīn bùhé remain friendly in appearance but estranged at heart

面红耳赤 miànhóng-ěrchì be red in the face; be flushed: 争得～ argue until everyone is red in the face; have a heated argument / 羞得～ blush with shame or shyness

面糊 miànhù paste

面糊 miànhu *dial.* soft and floury: 面条煮得太～了。The noodles are cooked almost to a pulp.

面黄肌瘦 miànhuáng-jīshòu sallow and emaciated; lean and haggard

面积 miànjī area: 我国～约为九百六十万平方公里。The area of China is about 9.6 million square kilometres. /

棉花种植～ the acreage under cotton / 展览会～为三千平方米。The exhibition covers a floor space of 3,000 square metres.

面颊 miànjiá cheek

面交 miànjiāo deliver personally; hand-deliver

面巾 miànjīn *dial.* towel

面巾纸 miànjīnzhǐ face tissues

面筋 miànjin gluten

面具 miànjù mask: 防毒～ gas mask

面孔 miànkǒng face: 和蔼(严肃)的～ a kind (stern) face / 板起～ put on a stern expression / 装出一副救世主的～ assume the guise of a saviour

面料 miànliào material for making the outside (of a garment)

面临 miànlín be faced with; be confronted with; be up against: ～一场严重的危机 be faced with a serious crisis / 我们正～一场新的斗争。A new struggle lies ahead of us. / 我们～的问题和困难还很多。We still face a great many problems and difficulties.

面聆 miànlíng hear sb.'s words of wisdom in person

面貌 miànmào ① face; features: 他俩的～十分相似。The two of them look very much alike. ② appearance (of things); look; aspect: 精神～ mental outlook (*or* attitude) / ～一新 take on a new look (*or* aspect) / 改变了中国的～ have changed the face of China / 一个国家的社会经济～ the social and economic physiognomy of a country

面面俱到 miànmiàn jù dào attend to each and every aspect of a matter: 文章因篇幅有限，不可能讲得～。Limitation of space forbids full treatment of the subject. / 我没看到的，你都看到了，真是～。You can see all the things that I can't, you don't miss a thing.

面面相觑 miàn miàn xiāng qù look at each other in blank dismay; gaze at each other in speechless despair

面膜 miànmó face-pack; mask

面目 miànmù ① face; features; visage: ～清秀 of fine and delicate features ② appearance (of things); look; aspect ③ self-respect; honour; sense of shame; face: 愧无～见人 feel too ashamed to face people

面目可憎 miànmù kě zēng repulsive in appearance

面目全非 miànmù quán fēi be changed beyond recognition: 照那样改动，～，就不是原来的《茶馆》了。If the play is changed the way like that, it will be completely disfigured and no longer recognizable as the original *Teahouse*.

面目一新 miànmù yī xīn take on an entirely new look; present a completely new appearance; assume a new aspect: 这个工厂经过改建，已经～了。The factory has taken on an entirely new look after being reconstructed. / 马克思列宁主义的普遍真理一经和中国革命的具体实践相结合，就使中国革命的面目为之一新。(毛泽东) As soon as it was linked with the concrete practice of the Chinese revolution, the universal truth of Marxism-Leninism gave an entirely new complexion to the Chinese revolution.

面目狰狞 miànmù zhēngníng ferocious features; a vile visage

面嫩 miànnèn ① look younger than one's age ② shy; bashful; sensitive

面庞 miànpáng contours of the face; face: 圆圆的～ a round face

面盆¹ miànpén *dial.* washbasin; washbowl

面盆² miànpén bowl for kneading dough

面皮¹ miànpí face; cheek

面皮² miànpí wrapper (of dumpling)

面洽 miànqià discuss with sb. face to face; take up a matter with sb. personally: 有关事宜，请找张同志。For particulars, please go and see Comrade Zhang.

面前 miànqián in (the) face of; in front of; before: 在事

实～ in the face of the truth / 任务摆在我们～。The task is laid before us. / 我们～困难还多, 不可忽视。There are still many difficulties ahead which we must not overlook.

面罄 miànqìng *formal* explain in detail personally

面人儿 miànrénr dough figurine

面容 miànróng facial features; face: ～消瘦 look emaciated

面如死灰 miàn rú sǐhuī look like dying embers—be deathly pale due to fright or poor health

面如土色 miàn rú tǔsè look ashen; look pale: 吓得～ turn pale with fright

面软 miànruǎn thin-skinned; shy; sensitive

面色 miànsè ① complexion: ～苍白 look pale / ～红润 have rosy cheeks; be ruddy-cheeked ② facial expression: ～忧郁 have a melancholy look; look worried

面纱 miànshā veil

面善 miànshàn ① look familiar: 他很～。He looks familiar to me. ② affable; amiable: ～心慈 affable and kind-hearted

面商 miànshāng discuss with sb. face to face; consult personally

面神经 miànshénjīng *physiol.* facial nerve

面生 miànshēng look unfamiliar: 这个人～得很。I don't think I've seen this person before.

面试 miànshì interview

面食 miànshi cooked wheaten food

面首 miànshǒu *old* a kept man of a noblewoman; a noblewoman's gigolo

面授机宜 miàn shòu jīyí personally instruct sb. on the line of action to pursue; give a confidential briefing; brief sb. on how to act

面熟 miànshú look familiar: 这人看着～, 就是想不起来是谁。That person looks familiar but I simply can't place him.

面塑 miànsù *arts & crafts* dough modelling

面谈 miàntán speak to sb. face to face; take up a matter with sb. personally

面汤[1] miàntāng *dial.* hot water for washing face

面汤[2] miàntāng water in which noodles have been boiled

面汤 miàntang *dial.* noodles in soup

面条 miàntiáo noodles

面团 miàntuán dough

面无人色 miàn wú rénsè look ghastly pale: 他惊恐得～, 象僵了似的。His face was ghastly and he seemed paralysed.

面线 miànxiàn upper thread

面向 miànxiàng ① turn one's face to; turn in the direction of; face: ～党旗严宣誓 stand facing the Party flag and make a solemn vow ② be geared to the needs of; cater to: ～四个现代化 be geared to the needs of the four modernizations / ～基层 cater to (*or* meet) the needs of grass-roots units / ～出口 be export-oriented

面相 miànxiang *dial.* facial features; looks; appearance

面谢 miànxiè thank sb. in person

面议 miànyì negotiate face to face; take up a matter with sb. personally

面有菜色 miàn yǒu càisè look famished

面有难色 miàn yǒu nánsè show signs of reluctance or embarrassment

面谕 miànyù (of superiors or elders) instruct or tell sb. in person

面誉背毁 miànyù-bèihuǐ praise sb. to his face and abuse him behind his back; praise openly and slander secretly

面罩 miànzhào face guard

面值 miànzhí ① par value; face value; nominal value ② denomination

面砖 miànzhuān *archit.* face brick

面子[1] miànzi ① outer part; outside; face: 大衣的～ the outside of an overcoat ② reputation; prestige; face: 保全～ save face / 撕破～ cast aside all considerations of face; not spare sb.'s sensibilities / 有～ enjoy due respect / 给～ show due respect for sb.'s feelings ③ feelings; sensibilities: 给某人留～ spare sb.'s feelings / 不顾～ have no consideration for sb.'s feelings ——see also 驳面子 bó miànzi; 买面子 mǎi miànzi

面子[2] miànzi *inf.* powder: 药～ medicinal powder

眄

miàn, also miǎn *formal* give a sidelong glance

眄视 miànshì *formal* give a sidelong glance

miāo

喵

miāo *onom.* mew; miaow

miáo

苗

miáo ① young plant; seedling: 麦～儿 wheat seedling / 这孩子看来是个游泳的好～～。The girl is showing great promise as a swimmer. ② the young of some animals: 鱼苗 yúmiáo ③ vaccine: 卡介苗 kǎjièmiáo ④ sth. resembling a young plant: 火苗 huǒmiáo ⑤ (Miáo) a surname

苗儿 miáor *dial.* symptom of a trend; suggestion of a new development

苗床 miáochuáng seedbed

苗而不秀 miáo ér bù xiù put forth shoots that fail to flower—show great potentialities but fail to fulfil them: ～者有矣夫! 秀而不实者有矣夫!《论语》 There are, are there not, young plants that fail to produce blossoms, and blossoms that fail to produce fruit?

苗木 miáomù *forestry* nursery stock

苗圃 miáopǔ nursery (of young plants)

苗期 miáoqī *agric.* seedling stage

苗条 miáotiao (of a woman) slender; slim: 身材～ have a slim figure

苗头 miáotou symptom of a trend; suggestion of a new development: 要注意不良倾向的～。Watch out for symptoms of unhealthy tendencies. / 他一看～不对就溜了。He slipped off when he saw what was going to happen.

苗裔 miáoyì *formal* progeny; descendants; offspring

苗子 miáozi ① *dial.* young plant; seedling ② young successor ③ *dial.* symptom of a trend; suggestion of a new development

苗族 Miáozú the Miao nationality, or the Miaos, distributed over Guizhou, Hunan, Yunnan, the Guangxi Zhuang Autonomous Region, Sichuan and Guangdong

描

miáo ① trace; copy: ～图样 trace designs; copy designs ② touch up; retouch: ～眉 pencil (*or* paint) one's eyebrows / 练毛笔字, 一笔是一笔, 不要～。In practising Chinese calligraphy, write with a sure hand — don't retouch.

描红 miáohóng trace in black ink over characters printed in red (in learning to write with a brush)

描画 miáohuà draw; paint; depict; describe: ～出美好的前景 paint a bright future / 漓江美景难以用语言

来～。The beauty of the scenery along the Lijiang River defies description.

描绘　miáohuì　depict; describe; portray: 这幅画～了西湖的景色。The painting gives a view of the West Lake. / 这部小说生动地～了青年建设边疆的战斗生活。The novel vividly depicts the life and struggle of young people in reconstructing a frontier region.

描金　miáojīn　*arts & crafts*　trace a design in gold

描摹　miáomó　depict; portray; delineate

描述　miáoshù　describe: 详细～事情的经过 describe what happened in great detail / 当时的感受实在难以～。It's really hard to describe how I was feeling at that moment.

描图　miáotú　tracing: ～员 tracer / ～纸 tracing paper

描写　miáoxiě　describe; depict; portray: ～一位优秀画家的成长过程 describe how he grew up to be an outstanding painter / 这段～非常生动。This description is very vivid.

描写语言学派　miáoxiě yǔyánxuépài　descriptivists

瞄　miáo　concentrate one's gaze on; take aim: ～得准,打得狠 take good aim and hit hard

瞄准　miáozhǔn　take aim; aim; train on; lay; sight: 练习～ practise aiming / ～靶心 aim at the bull's-eye / 把高射炮～敌机 train the antiaircraft guns on the enemy planes

瞄准环　miáozhǔnhuán　ring sight

瞄准具　miáozhǔnjù　sighting device; (gun) sight

瞄准手　miáozhǔnshǒu　layer; pointer

鹋　miáo　see 鸸鹋 érmiáo

miǎo

杪　miǎo　① the tip of a twig: 树杪 shùmiǎo ② end (of a year, month or season): 岁杪 suìmiǎo

秒　miǎo　second (=1/60 of a minute)

秒表　miǎobiǎo　stopwatch; chronograph

秒差距　miǎochājù　*astron.* parsec

秒立方米　miǎolìfāngmǐ　*water conservancy* cubic metre per second

秒针　miǎozhēn　second hand (of a clock or watch)

眇　miǎo　*formal* ① blind: ～一目 be blind in one eye ② very small: 眇小 miǎoxiǎo

眇小　miǎoxiǎo　*formal* very small; tiny; insignificant

渺　miǎo　① (of an expanse of water) vast: 浩渺 hàomiǎo ② distant and indistinct; vague: ～无人迹 remote and uninhabited / ～若烟云 as vague as mist ③ tiny; insignificant: ～不足道 insignificant; negligible; not worth mentioning

渺茫　miǎománg　① distant and indistinct; vague: 他走后音信～。We haven't heard from him since he left. ② uncertain: 前途～ have an uncertain future / 希望～ have slim hopes (of success)

渺无人烟　miǎo wú rényān　uninhabited; without a trace of human habitation

渺无音信　miǎo wú yīnxìn　there has been no news whatsoever about sb.; never been heard of since

渺小　miǎoxiǎo　tiny; negligible; insignificant; paltry: 个人的力量是～的。The strength of an individual is insignificant. / 人和大海相比是何等的～。How insignificant man is beside the great ocean!

渺远　miǎoyuǎn　faraway; distant; remote

淼　miǎo　*formal* (of an expanse of water) vast: 浩淼 hàomiǎo

淼茫　miǎománg　(of an expanse of water) stretch as far as the eye can see

缈　miǎo　see 缥缈 piāomiǎo

邈　miǎo　*formal* faraway; remote: 绵邈 miánmiǎo

邈远　miǎoyuǎn　faraway; distant; remote

藐　miǎo　① small; petty: 藐小 miǎoxiǎo ② slight; despise: 言者谆谆，听者藐藐 yánzhě zhūnzhūn, tīngzhě miǎomiǎo

藐视　miǎoshì　despise; look down upon: 在战略上我们要～一切敌人，在战术上我们要重视一切敌人。Strategically we should despise all our enemies, but tactically we should take them all seriously.

藐小　miǎoxiǎo　tiny; negligible; insignificant; paltry

miào

妙　miào　① wonderful; excellent; fine: ～极了! Wonderful! / 这主意真～。That's an excellent idea. ② ingenious; clever; subtle: 深得其中之～ have got the trick of it; fully appreciate its subtlety / 他回答得很～。He made a clever answer.

妙不可言　miào bùkě yán　too wonderful for words; most intriguing

妙计　miàojì　(also 妙策 miàocè) an excellent plan; a brilliant scheme: 想出一条～ hit upon an excellent idea

妙境　miàojìng　fairyland; wonderland

妙句　miàojù　a beautiful sentence; a well-turned phrase

妙诀　miàojué　a clever way; an ingenious method

妙龄　miàolíng　youthfulness (of a girl): ～少女 a young lady / 正当～ be in the bloom of (a girl's) youth

妙论　miàolùn　an ingenious remark; a very clever remark

妙品　miàopǐn　① fine quality goods: 调味～ best-quality condiment ② fine work of art

妙棋　miàoqí　a clever (chess) move

妙趣横生　miàoqù héngshēng　full of wit and humour; very witty

妙手回春　miàoshǒu huí chūn　(of a doctor) effect a miraculous cure and bring the dying back to life

妙手空空　miàoshǒu kōngkōng　① petty (*or* sneak) thief; pilferer ② not own a thing in the world; not have a thing to one's name

妙算　miàosuàn　wonderful foresight; accurate calculations: 神机妙算　shénjī-miàosuàn

妙药　miàoyào　efficacious medicine; wonder drug

妙用　miàoyòng　magical effect: 小小银针，大有～。A tiny acupuncture needle can work wonders.

妙语　miàoyǔ　witty remark; witticism: 妙人～ a clever person and his clever remarks / ～如珠 a stream of witticism / ～惊人 an unsurpassed beauty of expression

妙语解颐　miàoyǔ jiěyí　witty remarks that make people laugh; wisecracks that really tickle

妙语双关　miàoyǔ shuāngguān　a very clever pun

妙在不言中　miào zài bù yán zhōng　the charm lies in what is left unsaid

庙（廟）　miào　① temple; shrine;· ② temple fair: 赶～ go to the fair

庙号　miàohào　temple title (a title, usu. with a *zu* 祖

"founder" or a *zong* 宗 "ancestor", given to an emperor posthumously when his spirit tablet was established in the imperial ancestral temple 太庙; e.g. Han Gaozu or Emperor Gaozu of the Han Dynasty 汉高祖, Song Huizong or Emperor Huizong of the Song Dynasty 宋徽宗)

庙会 miàohuì　temple fair; fair

庙堂 miàotáng　① the Imperial Ancestral Temple ② imperial court

庙宇 miàoyǔ　temple

庙祝 miàozhù　temple attendant in charge of incense and religious service; acolyte

缪

Miào　a surname ——see also miù; móu

miē

乜

miē　see below

乜斜 miēxie　① squint: 他～着眼睛，眼角挂着讥诮的微笑。He squinted with a sneering look in the corner of his eye.② (of eyes) half-closed: ～的睡眼 half-closed eyes heavy with sleep

咩（哶）

miē　*onom.*　baa; bleat

miè

灭（滅）

miè　① (of a light, fire, etc.) go out: 火～了。The fire has gone out./灯突然～了。All of a sudden the lights went out. ② extinguish; put out; turn off: 消防队很快把火～了。The fire brigade soon put out the fire./请把烟～了。Please stub out (*or* extinguish) your cigarette./节约用电，人走灯～。Save electricity—turn off the lights when you leave. ③ submerge; drown: 灭顶 mièdǐng ④ destroy; exterminate; wipe out: ～蝇 kill flies

灭茬 mièchá　*agric.*　clean stubble (fields): ～机 stubble cleaner

灭虫宁 mièchóngníng　*pharm.*　bephenium

灭此朝食 miè cǐ zhāo shí　will not have breakfast until the enemy is wiped out—be anxious to finish off the enemy immediately

灭滴灵 mièdīlíng　*pharm.*　metronidazole; flagyl

灭顶 mièdǐng　be drowned

灭顶之灾 mièdǐng zhī zāi　getting drowned

灭火 mièhuǒ　① put out a fire; extinguish a fire ② cut out an engine

灭火剂 mièhuǒjì　fire-extinguishing chemical (*or* agent)

灭火器 mièhuǒqì　fire extinguisher

灭迹 mièjì　destroy the evidence (of one's evildoing)

灭绝 mièjué　① become extinct: 现已～的动物 extinct animals ② completely lose

灭绝人性 mièjué rénxìng　inhuman; savage; cannibalistic: ～的暴行 inhuman atrocities

灭口 mièkǒu　do away with a witness or accomplice: 杀人～ silence a witness by killing him; kill sb. to prevent him from disclosing a secrect

灭门 mièmén　exterminate an entire family

灭绦灵 miètāolíng　*pharm.*　niclosamide

灭亡 mièwáng　be destroyed; become extinct; die out: 逃脱不了～的命运 be doomed to destruction／汉朝的～使中国陷入了分裂的局面。The downfall of the Han Dynasty brought China national disunity.

灭种 mièzhǒng　① exterminate a race; commit genocide ② same as 绝种 juézhǒng

灭族 mièzú　extermination of an entire family (a punishment in ancient China)

蔑 ¹

miè　*formal*　① slight; disdain: 轻蔑 qīngmiè ② nothing; none: ～以复加 in the extreme

蔑 ²（衊）

miè　see 诬蔑 wūmiè

蔑视 mièshì　despise; show contempt for; scorn: ～某人 hold sb. in contempt／～妇女 look down upon women

蔑视法庭 mièshì fǎtíng　*leg.*　contempt of court

篾

miè　① thin bamboo strip ② the rind of reed or sorghum

篾黄 mièhuáng　the inner skin of a bamboo stem

篾匠 mièjiàng　a craftsman who makes articles from bamboo strips

篾片 mièpiàn　① thin bamboo strip ② *old*　hanger-on; sycophant

篾青 mièqīng　the outer cuticle of a bamboo stem

篾条 miètiáo　bamboo strip

篾席 mièxí　a mat made of thin bamboo strips

mín

民

mín　① the people: 人民 rénmín ② a member of a nationality: 回民 Huímín ③ a person of a certain occupation: 农民 nóngmín／牧民 mùmín ④ of the people; folk: 民歌 míngē ⑤ civilian: 军民 jūn-mín

民办 mínbàn　be run by the local people: ～公助 be run by the local people and subsidized by the state／～小学 a primary school run by the local people

民变 mínbiàn　mass uprising; popular revolt

民兵 mínbīng　① people's militia; militia: ～师 a contingent of the people's militia ② militiaman: 女～ militiawoman

民不聊生 mín bù liáo shēng　the people have no means of livelihood; the masses live in dire poverty; the people are destitute: 军阀混战，～。Incessant fighting among the warlords made life impossible for the people.

民不畏死，奈何以死惧之 mín bù wèi sǐ, nàihé yǐ sǐ jù zhī　the people have no fear of death, why threaten them with it?

民船 mínchuán　a junk or small boat for civilian use

民法 mínfǎ　civil law

民法典 mínfǎdiǎn　civil code

民防 mínfáng　civil defence

民房 mínfáng　a house owned by a citizen; a private house

民愤 mínfèn　popular indignation; the people's wrath: ～极大 have earned the bitter hatred of the people; have incurred the greatest popular indignation／激起～ arouse popular indignation

民风 mínfēng　folkways; local traits

民夫 mínfū　*old*　conscripted labourer

民负 mínfù　burden (of texation, etc.) on the people

民富国强 mínfù-guóqiáng　the people live in plenty and the country is strong

民歌 míngē　folk song

民工 míngōng　a labourer working on a public project

民国 Mínguó　the Republic of China (1912-1949)

民航 mínháng　short for 民用航空 mínyòng hángkōng

民航机 mínhángjī　civil aircraft; civil airplane

民间 mínjiān　① among the people; popular; folk: ～验方 folk remedy; folk recipe／这个故事长久地在～流传。For generations the story has circulated among the people. ② nongovernmental; people-to-people: ～来往

nongovernmental contact; people-to-people exchange / ～组织 a nongovernmental organization / ～协定 nongovernmental agreement

民间传说 mínjiān chuánshuō popular legend; folk legend; folklore

民间故事 mínjiān gùshi folktale; folk story

民间疾苦 mínjiān jíkǔ hardships of the people

民间诗人 mínjiān shīrén folk bard

民间文学 mínjiān wénxué folk literature

民间舞蹈 mínjiān wǔdǎo folk dance

民间艺术 mínjiān yìshù folk art

民间音乐 mínjiān yīnyuè folk music

民警 mínjǐng people's police; people's policeman: 女～ people's policewoman

民居 mínjū local-style dwelling houses

民康物阜 mínkāng-wùfù products abound and the people live in peace

民力 mínlì financial resources of the people

民氓 mínméng (also 民氓 mínméng) the masses of the people; the common people

民命 mínmìng the life of the people

民瘼 mínmò *formal* hardships of the people

民品 mínpǐn civilian products

民气 mínqì the people's morale; popular morale

民情 mínqíng ① condition of the people: 熟悉地理～ be familiar with the place and the people ② feelings of the people; public feeling: 不了解～ fail to keep abreast of public feeling

民穷财尽 mínqióng-cáijìn the people are impoverished and the nation's resources exhausted; the people are destitute and the national economy is in dire straits

民权 mínquán civil rights; civil liberties; democratic rights

民权主义 mínquánzhǔyì the Principle of Democracy ——see also 三民主义 sānmínzhǔyì

民生 mínshēng the people's livelihood

民生凋敝 mínshēng diāobì the people live in destitution: ～、民怨沸腾、民变峰起的严重危机 a grave crisis of mass impoverishment, seething discontent and widespread revolt

民生主义 mínshēngzhǔyì the Principle of the People's Livelihood ——see also 三民主义 sānmínzhǔyì

民食 mínshí foodstuff for the people; provisions for the people

民事 mínshì *leg.* relating to civil law; civil: ～管辖权 civil jurisdiction / ～纠纷 civil litigation / ～责任 civil liability

民事案件 mínshì ànjiàn *leg.* civil case

民事法庭 mínshì fǎtíng civil court

民事审判庭 mínshì shěnpàntíng *leg.* the civil division of a people's court; civil court

民事诉讼 mínshì sùsòng *leg.* civil action (*or* process, lawsuit)

民俗 mínsú folk custom; folkways

民俗学 mínsúxué folklore

民庭 míntíng short for 民事法庭 mínshì fǎtíng

民团 míntuán civil corps (formerly, reactionary local armed forces organized by landlords)

民为邦本，本固邦宁 mín wéi bāng běn, běn gù bāng níng the people are the root of a country; when the root is firm, the country is tranquil

民校 mínxiào ① sparetime school for adults ② school run by the local people

民心 mínxīn popular feelings; common aspiration of the people: 深得～ enjoy the ardent support of the people

民心所向 mínxīn suǒ xiàng where the popular will inclines; (what conforms to) the common aspiration of the people

民选 mínxuǎn elected by the people

民谚 mínyàn common proverb

民谣 mínyáo folk rhyme (esp. of the topical and political type)

民以食为天 mín yǐ shí wéi tiān the masses regard food as their heaven (i.e. as their prime want)

民意 mínyì the will of the people; popular will: ～测验 public opinion poll; poll

民用 mínyòng for civil use; civil: ～产品 products for civil use

民用航空 mínyòng hángkōng civil aviation

民用机场 mínyòng jīchǎng civil airport

民怨沸腾 mínyuàn fèiténg the people are boiling with resentment; seething popular discontent: 军阀混战，～。 Warlords fought one another and popular grievances ran high.

民乐 mínyuè music, esp. folk music, for traditional instruments: ～合奏 ensemble of traditional instruments

民乐队 mínyuèduì traditional instruments orchestra

民运 mínyùn ① civil transport ② the army's propaganda and organizational work among the civilians during the revolutionary wars led by the Chinese Communist Party ③ mass movement; mass campaign

民贼 mínzéi traitor to the people

民宅 mínzhái a private (*or* civilian) residence

民政 mínzhèng civil administration

民政机关 mínzhèng jīguān civil administration organ

民脂民膏 mínzhī-míngāo flesh and blood of the people: 反动政府搜刮～。 The reactionary government fed on the flesh and blood of the people.

民众 mínzhòng the masses of the people; the common people; the populace

民众团体 mínzhòng tuántǐ people's organization; mass organization

民主 mínzhǔ ① democracy; democratic rights ② democratic: 他作风～。 He has a democratic workstyle.

民主党 Mínzhǔdǎng the Democratic Party (in U. S.)

民主党派 mínzhǔ dǎngpài democratic parties (political parties that have accepted the leadership of the Chinese Communist Party and joined the revolutionary united front)

民主改革 mínzhǔ gǎigé democratic reform

民主革命 mínzhǔ gémìng democratic revolution

民主共和国 mínzhǔ gònghéguó democratic republic

民主集中制 mínzhǔjízhōngzhì democratic centralism (the organizational principle of the Party and state, namely, centralism on the basis of democracy and democracy under centralized guidance)

民主人士 mínzhǔ rénshì democratic personages

民主生活 mínzhǔ shēnghuó democratic life: 坚持正常的～ maintain the normal practice of democracy

民主协商 mínzhǔ xiéshāng democratic consultation

民族 mínzú nation; nationality; ethnic group: 国内各～的团结 the unity of our various nationalities / ～复兴 revival of nationhood; national rejuvenation / ～败类 scum of a nation / ～大家庭 the great family of nationalities / ～动乱 ethnic unrest / ～独立 national independence / ～革命 national revolution / ～利己主义 national egoism / ～民主革命 national-democratic revolution / ～歧视 ethnic discrimination / ～统一战线 national united front / ～投降主义 national capitulationism / ～虚无主义 national nihilism / ～学 ethnology / ～意识 national consciousness / ～杂居地区 multinational area / ～政策 policy towards nationalities / ～自信心 national confidence / ～自尊心 national pride / ～自尊严 national dignity

民族共同语 mínzú gòngtóngyǔ common national language

民族解放运动　mínzú jiěfàng yùndòng　national liberation movement

民族区域自治　mínzú qūyù zìzhì　regional autonomy of minority nationalities; regional national autonomy

民族同化　mínzú tónghuà　national assimilation

民族文化宫　Mínzú Wénhuàgōng　the Cultural Palace of the Nationalities (in Beijing)

民族形式　mínzú xíngshì　national style; national form

民族英雄　mínzú yīngxióng　national hero

民族主义　mínzúzhǔyì　① nationalism ② the Principle of Nationalism (see also 三民主义 sānmínzhǔyì)

民族资产阶级　mínzú zīchǎnjiējí　national bourgeoisie

民族自决　mínzú zìjué　national self-determination

民族自治　mínzú zìzhì　autonomy of minority nationalities: ～地方 autonomous minority nationality area

旻　mín　liter. ① autumn ② the sky: 苍～ the blue sky

缗（緡）　mín　string for stringing up cash in ancient times

mǐn

皿　mǐn　see 器皿 qìmǐn

闵　mǐn　① same as 悯 mǐn ② (Mǐn) a surname

泯　mǐn　vanish; die out: 永存不～ be everlasting; be immortal / 良心未～ still have some conscience; not be devoid of conscience

泯灭　mǐnmiè　die out; disappear; vanish: 难以～的印象 an indelible impression

泯没　mǐnmò　vanish; sink into oblivion; become lost: 烈士的功绩永远不会～。 The contributions of the revolutionary martyrs will never be forgotten.

抿[1]　mǐn　smooth (hair, etc.) with a wet brush: ～了～头发 give a few touches to one's hair (with a brush)

抿[2]　mǐn　① close lightly; furl; tuck: ～着嘴笑 smile with closed lips; compress one's lips to smile / 水鸟儿一～翅膀，钻入水中。 The water bird tucked its wings and dived into the water. ② sip: ～一口酒 take a sip of wine

抿子　mǐnzi　a small hairbrush (used by a woman)

黾（黽）　mǐn　see below

黾勉　mǐnmiǎn　formal exert oneself; try hard; strive: ～从事 exert oneself to the utmost; do one's best

闽　Mǐn　another name for 福建 Fújiàn

悯　mǐn　① commiserate; pity: 其情可～。 His case deserves sympathy. ② formal sorrow

悯恻　mǐncè　formal feel compassion for; pity

悯惜　mǐnxī　take pity on; have pity for

悯恤　mǐnxù　feel compassion for; pity

敏　mǐn　quick; nimble; agile: ～于应对 quick at repartee

敏感　mǐngǎn　sensitive; susceptible: 政治～性 political sensitivity / 他对机器里不正常的声音非常～。 His ears are highly sensitive to any unusual noise in the machine. / 他是一个对语言十分～的人。 He has a tremendous feeling for language. / 手指尖特别～。 The tips of the fingers are particularly sensitive. / ～的问题 a sensitive issue

敏感度　mǐngǎndù　susceptibility

敏感元件　mǐngǎn yuánjiàn　radio sensitive element; sensor

敏化　mǐnhuà　phys. sensibilization; sensitization: ～剂 sensitizer / ～纸 sensitized paper

敏慧　mǐnhuì　bright; intelligent

敏捷　mǐnjié　quick; nimble; agile: 动作～ be quick in movement / 守门员～地跃向右方，救出了险球。 The goal-keeper lept nimbly to the right and saved the goal. / 干这个工作需要思想～。 The job requires an agile mind.

敏锐　mǐnruì　sharp; acute; keen: 目光～ have sharp eyes; be sharp-eyed / 听觉～ have good (or sharp) ears / 嗅觉～ have a keen sense of smell / ～的政治眼光 keen political insight

鳘　mǐn　common name for 鳁｜miǎn

míng

名　míng　① name: 一种～为九二〇的生长激素 a growth hormone known as 920 / 他～叫张南。 His name is Zhang Nan. or He is called Zhang Nan. ② given name: 这位同志姓李～大刚。 This comrade's surname is Li and his given name, Dagang. ③ excuse; false prentences: 以出差为～游山玩水 take a pleasure trip in the guise of a business trip ④ fame; reputation; renown: 不为～，不为利 seek neither fame nor gain / ～闻中外 be well-known both at home and abroad ⑤ famous; celebrated; well-known; noted: ～厨师 a famous chef / ～诗人 a noted poet / ～教授 a well-known (or prominent) professor ⑥ express; describe: 不可名状 bùkě míngzhuàng ⑦ m. (for people): 十二～学生 twelve students

名不副实　míng bù fù shí　(also 名不符实 míng bù fú shí) the name falls short of the reality, be sth. more in name than in reality; be unworthy of the name or title: 一个～的军事学家 not a military expert in the real sense of the term

名不虚传　míng bù xūchuán　have a well-deserved reputation; deserve the reputation one enjoys; live up to one's reputation

名册　míngcè　(also 名籍 míngjí) register; roll: 学生～ students' register; students' roll / 部队～ muster roll / 工作人员～ personnel roll

名产　míngchǎn　famous product: 织锦是杭州的～。 Brocade is a famous product of Hangzhou.

名称　míngchēng　name (of a thing or organization)

名城　míngchéng　a famous city: 历史～ a city famous for its historical associations

名垂青史　míng chuí qīngshǐ　go down in history; be crowned with eternal glory

名词　míngcí　① gram. noun; substantive ② term; phrase: 化学～ chemical term ③ log. name

名次　míngcì　position in a name list; place in a competition: 我们参加这次运动会不是为了争～。 We haven't come to this sports meet just to compete for places. / 按比赛成绩排列～ arrange the names of contestants in the order of their results

名刺　míngcì　visiting card; calling card

名存实亡　míngcún-shíwáng　cease to exist except in name only; exist in name only

名单　míngdān　name list: 入伍～ list of recruits

名额　míng'é　the number of people assigned or allowed; quota of people: 代表～ the number of de-

puties to be elected or sent / 招生～ the number of students to be enrolled; planned enrolment figure / 今年的征兵～已满。 This year's enlistment quota has already been filled. / 由于～有限，这次参观不能人人都去。 Since the number of people allowed is limited, not everyone can go on this visit.

名分 míngfèn a person's status

名副其实 míng fù qí shí (also 名符其实 míng fú qí shí) the name matches the reality; be sth. in reality as well as in name; be worthy of the name: 一个～的共产党员 a Party member in the real sense of the term / 建设起一个崭新的强盛的～的人民共和国 build a new powerful and prosperous people's republic worthy of the name / 这真是～的奇迹。 That's a veritable miracle.

名贵 míngguì famous and precious; rare: ～药材 rare medicinal herbs / ～的字画 priceless scrolls of calligraphy and painting

名过其实 míng guò qí shí be sth. more in name than in reality; have an undeserved reputation

名讳 mínghuì old name of one's elders and betters or of a respected person

名家 Míngjiā the School of Logicians (in the Spring and Autumn and Warring States Periods, 770–221 B.C.)

名家 míngjiā a person of academic or artistic distinction; famous expert; master

名缰利锁 míngjiāng-lìsuǒ the fetters of fame and wealth

名将 míngjiàng famous general; great soldier: 足球～ a football hero (or star)

名教 míngjiào the Confucian ethical code

名句 míngjù a well-known phrase; a much quoted line

名款 míngkuǎn the name of the painter or writer inscribed on a painting or a piece of calligraphy

名利 mínglì fame and gain; fame and wealth: ～思想 desire for personal fame and gain / 不求～ not seek fame and gain

名利场 mínglìchǎng Vanity Fair

名利双收 mínglì shuāng shōu gain both fame and wealth

名列前茅 míng liè qiánmáo be among the best of the successful candidates

名流 míngliú distinguished personages; celebrities

名落孙山 míng luò Sūn Shān fall behind Sun Shan (who was last on the list of successful candidates)—fail in a competitive examination

名门 míngmén an old and well-known family; a distinguished family; an illustrious family: ～闺秀 daughter of an illustrious family

名目 míngmù names of things; items

名目繁多 míngmù fánduō a multitude of names (or items); names of every description: 解放前，苛捐杂税，～。 Before liberation there were exorbitant taxes and levies of every sort under the sun.

名牌 míngpái ① famous brand: 优质～商品 famous-brand quality products / ～香烟 a famous brand of cigarettes / 创～ establish a brand / ～产品 best brands of products / ～大学 a prestigious university ② nameplate; name tag

名片 míngpiàn visiting card; calling card: 留下～ leave one's card

名气 míngqì inf. reputation; fame; name: 有点～ enjoy some reputation; be quite well-known; have made a name for oneself / 他是一位很有～的医生。 He is a very famous doctor. / 她在我们这儿还小有～呢! She's quite popular here.

名人 míngrén famous person; eminent person; celebrity; notable: ～墨迹 original work by a famous calligrapher or painter / 文化界～ celebrities in cultural circles

名山大川 míngshān-dàchuān famous mountains and great rivers

名山事业 míngshān shìyè commitment to literature

名声 míngshēng reputation; repute; renown: ～很坏 have an unsavoury reputation; be held in ill repute; be notorious / 享有好～ enjoy a good reputation; be held in high repute

名胜 míngshèng a place famous for its scenery or historical relics; scenic spot

名胜古迹 míngshèng-gǔjī places of historic interest and scenic beauty; scenic spots and historical sites

名师出高徒 míngshī chū gāotú a great teacher produces a brilliant student

名士 míngshì old ① a person with a literary reputation ② a celebrity with no official post

名士派 míngshìpài an unconventional and self-indulgent old-style intellectual

名士气 míngshìqì scholar's eccentricities

名世 míngshì formal well known to one's contemporaries

名手 míngshǒu a famous artist, player, etc.

名数 míngshù ① math. concrete number ② numeral-classifier compound (as 三斤，四尺二寸)

名堂 míngtang ① variety; item: 别看他们只是个业余文工团，演出的～可多啦! It's true they're only an amateur troupe, but they have an amazingly large repertoire. / 这个坏家伙又在搞什么～? What's that villain up to now? / 办婚事吗，别搞那么多～。 Don't make too much of a do of the wedding party. ② result; achievement: 依靠集体力量，一定能搞出～来。 As long as we rely on collective effort we can certainly achieve something. / 问了他半天也没问出个～。 I questioned him for a long time but couldn't get anything out of him. ③ what lies behind sth.; reason: 敌军突然撤走了，这里面有什么～? What's behind the enemy's sudden retreat? / 墙角上的砖这么砌是有～的。 There's a reason for laying the corner bricks this way.

名头 míngtou dial. reputation; repute; renown

名望 míngwàng fame and prestige; good reputation; renown: 有～的大夫 a famous doctor

名位 míngwèi fame and position

名物 míngwù the name and description of a thing

名下 míngxià under sb.'s name; belonging or related to sb.: 这笔帐就记在我～吧。 Charge these expenses to my account. / 这事怎么搞到我～来了? How could it be my fault? or How could it have anything to do with me?

名下无虚 míngxià wú xū deserve the reputation one enjoys; live up to one's reputation

名学 míngxué old name for 逻辑学 luójixué

名言 míngyán well-known saying; celebrated dictum; famous remark

名义 míngyì ① name: 以革命的～ in the name of the revolution / 以会议执行主席的～ in one's capacity as executive chairman of the conference ② (usu. followed by 上) nominal; titular; in name: ～上裁军，实际上扩军 disarmament in name, armament in reality / 他只是～上的队长罢了。 He was the captain of the team in name only.

名义工资 míngyì gōngzī econ. nominal wages

名义汇价 míngyì huìjià econ. nominal rate (of exchange)

名优 míngyōu a famous actor or actress

名优产品 míng yōu chǎnpǐn famous quality products

名誉 míngyù ① fame; reputation: ～和地位 fame and position / ～好 have a good reputation; be of high repute; be held in high esteem ② honorary: ～会员 honorary member / ～主席 honorary chairman; honorary president

名噪一时 míng zào yī shí enjoy fleeting fame

名正言顺 míngzhèng-yánshùn the name is correct and what is said accords with reason—perfectly justifiable; fitting and proper: 名不正则言不顺, 言不顺则事不成。《论语》 If names be not correct, language accords not with truth. If language accords not with truth, affairs cannot achieve success.

名著 míngzhù famous book; famous work: 文学～ a famous literary work; a literary masterpiece

名状 míngzhuàng (usu. used in the negative) give the right name for; describe: 难以～的奇花异草 exotic flowers and rare plants that words fail to describe

名字 míngzi ① name or given name: 您叫什么～? What's your name? or May I know your name? ② name (of a thing): 这种花的～很特别。 This flower has a peculiar name.

名作 míngzuò (literary) masterpiece

明[1] míng ① bright; brilliant; light: ～月 a bright moon / 天已微～。 Day is breaking. ② clear; distinct: 真理愈辩愈～。 The more truth is debated, the clearer it becomes. / ～心迹 make one's intention clear; lay bare one's true feelings / 问～来意 ask what sb. has come for ③ open; overt; explicit: 有不同意见～着说。 Those who differ should air their views openly. ④ sharp-eyed; clear-sighted: 眼明手快 yǎnmíng-shǒukuài ⑤ aboveboard; honest: 明人不做暗事 míngrén bù zuò ànshì ⑥ sight: 失明 shīmíng ⑦ understand; know: ～是非 know the difference between right and wrong; know right from wrong

明[2] míng immediately following in time: ～春 next spring / ～晚 tomorrow evening

明[3] Míng ① the Ming Dynasty (1368–1644) ② a surname

明儿 míngr inf. ① tomorrow: ～见。 See you tomorrow. ② one of these days; some day: ～你长大了, 也开拖拉机好不好? What about you becoming a tractor driver too when you grow up?

明暗 míng-àn light and shade

明暗对照法 míng-àn duìzhàofǎ arts chiaroscuro

明摆着 míngbǎizhe obvious; clear; plain: 这不是～的事儿吗? Isn't this obvious? or Isn't it as clear as daylight?

明白 míngbai ① clear; obvious; plain: 他讲得～易懂。 He spoke clearly and simply. / 这个问题很～。 The matter is quite clear. ② open; unequivocal; explicit: 有意见就～提出来。 If you have any opinions, state them openly. / 你还是跟他讲～了好。 It would be best to be frank with him. / 他～表示不赞成这个提议。 He stated clearly that he didn't agree with the proposal. ③ sensible; reasonable: 明白人 míngbairén ④ understand; realize; know: ～事理 know what's what; have good sense / 我不～你的意思。 I don't see what you mean. / 我忽然～了。 The truth suddenly dawned on me.

明白人 míngbairén a perceptive person; a sensible person: 他是个～, 不会干什么傻事。 He is too sensible to do anything foolish.

明辨是非 míng biàn shìfēi make a clear distinction between right and wrong

明察暗访 míngchá-ànfǎng observe publicly and investigate privately—conduct a thorough investigation

明察秋毫 míng chá qiūháo have eyes sharp enough to perceive an animal's autumn hair—be perceptive of the minutest detail

明察秋毫之末, 而不见舆薪 míng chá qiūháo zhī mò, ér bù jiàn yú xīn be sharp-sighted enough to perceive the tip of an animal's autumn hair but unable to see a cartload of firewood—see the minute details but miss the major issue

明畅 míngchàng clear and lucid; lucid and smooth: 译文～。 The translation is clear and lucid.

明澈 míngchè bright and limpid; transparent: ～的眼睛 bright and limpid eyes / 湖水～如镜。 The lake is like a mirror.

明处 míngchù ① where there is light: 你把相片拿到～来, 让大家看个清楚。 Bring the photo to the light so we can see it better. ② in the open; in public: 有话说在～。 If you've got anything to say, say it openly. / 敌军在～, 游击队在暗处。 The guerrillas were acting under cover while the enemy troops were in the open.

明达 míngdá sensible; understanding: ～公正 sensible and fairminded

明打明 míngdǎmíng dial. clear; obvious; plain

明德 míngdé illustrious virtue; highest virtue: 大学之道, 在明～, 在新民, 在止于至善。《大学》 What the Great Learning teaches is to illustrate illustrious virtue, to renovate the people, and to rest in the highest excellence.

明灯 míngdēng bright lamp (fig.); beacon

明兜 míngdōu patch pocket

明断 míngduàn formal pass (fair) judgment

明矾 míngfán (also 明石 míngshí) alum

明矾石 míngfánshí alumstone; alunite

明沟 mínggōu open drain

明河 mínghé formal the Milky Way

明后天 mínghòutiān tomorrow or the day after tomorrow

明晃晃 mínghuǎnghuǎng gleaming; shining: ～的刺刀 gleaming bayonets

明慧 mínghuì formal intelligent; bright; clever

明火 mínghuǒ ① flame ② carry torches (esp. in a robbery)

明火执仗 mínghuǒ-zhízhàng carry torches and weapons (in a robbery)—do evil openly

明鉴 míngjiàn ① a bright mirror; a clear mirror ② pol. your brilliant idea; your penetrating judgment

明胶 míngjiāo gelatin

明教 míngjiào pol. (usu. used in a letter) your brilliant idea; your advice

明净 míngjìng bright and clean; clear and bright: ～的橱窗 a bright and clean shop window / 北京秋天的天空分外～。 In Beijing the autumn sky is especially clear and bright.

明镜 míngjìng a bright mirror; a clear mirror: 湖水清澈, 犹如～。 The lake is bright and clear like a mirror.

明镜高悬 míngjìng gāo xuán a clear mirror hung on high—an impartial and perspicacious judge

明决 míngjué clear and decided; decisive

明快 míngkuài ① lucid and lively; sprightly: ～的笔调 a lucid and lively style / 节奏～ with sprightly rhythm ② straightforward; forthright: ～的性格 a forthright character ③ dial. bright

明来暗往 mínglái-ànwǎng have overt and covert contacts with sb.

明朗 mínglǎng ① bright and clear: ～的月色 bright moonlight / ～的天空 a clear sky ② clear; obvious: 局势逐渐～。 The situation is becoming clear. / 态度～ take a clear-cut position; adopt an unequivocal attitude / 听了报告, 他心里～了。 The speech helped him to straighten out his thinking. ③ forthright; bright and cheerful: ～的性格 an open and forthright character / 这幅画色调～。 This picture is painted in bright, warm colours.

明理 mínglǐ ① sensible; reasonable: ～的人 a sensible person ② an obvious truth or fact

明丽 mínglì bright and beautiful: ～的秋色 a bright and

beautiful autumn scene

明亮 míngliàng ① well-lit; bright: 宽敞而～的教室 a bright and spacious classroom / 会议大厅里灯光～。 The conference hall is brightly lit. ② bright; shining: ～的眼睛 bright eyes ③ become clear: 听了同志们这番解释，老张心里～了。 The comrades' explanation helped Lao Zhang to straighten out his thinking.

明了 míngliǎo ① understand; be clear about: 你的意思我～。 I understand what you mean. / 不～实际情况，就不能做出正确的判断。 You can't form a correct judgment without a clear understanding of the actual situation. ② clear; plain: 简单～ simple and clear; concise and explicit

明令 mínglìng explicit order; formal decree; public proclamation: ～取谛 proscribe by formal decree / ～嘉奖 issue a commendation; mention in a citation

明码 míngmǎ ① plain code: ～电报 plain code telegram / 用～发报 send a telegram in plain code ② with the price clearly marked: ～售货 put goods on sale with the prices clearly marked; sell at marked prices

明媒正娶 míngméi-zhèngqǔ be legally and formally married

明媚 míngmèi bright and beautiful; radiant and enchanting: ～的阳光 bright and beautiful sunshine / ～的早晨 a glorious morning / 河山～ a land of enchanting beauty

明灭 míngmiè now in view, now hidden; appearing and vanishing: 星光～。 The stars twinkled in the sky. / 小山重叠金～, 鬓云欲度香腮雪。 (温庭筠) The manifold hills look golden and dark upon the panelled screen, Her cloudy hair droops over the snow of her fragrant cheeks.

明明 míngmíng *adv.* obviously; plainly; undoubtedly: 这事～是他干的嘛! This is obviously his doing. or There can be no doubt that it was he who did it. / ～是他的过错, 你为什么要怪我? Why do you blame me when it's obviously his fault?

明眸皓齿 míngmóu-hàochǐ (of a beautiful woman) have bright eyes and white teeth

明目张胆 míngmù-zhāngdǎn brazenly; flagrantly: ～地进行武装干涉 brazenly commit armed intervention

明年 míngnián next year

明盘 míngpán *old com.* negotiated price

明器 míngqì funerary objects (used in ancient China); burial objects

明前 míngqián a kind of green tea picked before Pure Brightness (清明 around April 5)

明枪暗箭 míngqiāng-ànjiàn spear thrusts in the open and arrows shot from hiding—both open and covert attacks

明枪易躲, 暗箭难防 míngqiāng yì duǒ, ànjiàn nán fáng it is easy to dodge a spear thrust in the open, but difficult to guard against an arrow shot from hiding

明确 míngquè ① clear and definite; clear-cut; explicit; unequivocal: 目的～ have a clear aim / ～的立场 a clear-cut stand / ～的答复 a definite answer / 用～的语言 use unequivocal terms / 宪法～规定了公民的权利和义务。 The Constitution clearly defines the rights and duties of citizens. ② make clear; make definite; clarify: 这篇社论进一步～了当前的中心任务。 The editorial further defined the key task for the present period. / ～学习的目的 be clear about the purpose of one's study / 需要～几个基本观念。 Several basic concepts need to be clarified.

明人不做暗事 míngrén bù zuò ànshì an honest man does nothing underhand

明日 míngrì ① tomorrow ② the near future

明日黄花 míngrì huánghuā chrysanthemums after the Double Ninth Festival—things that are stale and no longer of interest

明睿 míngruì *formal* wise and farsighted

明升暗降 míngshēng-ànjiàng a promotion in appearance but a demotion in fact: 使某人～ kick sb. upstairs

明示 míngshì explicitly instruct; clearly indicate

明誓 míngshì same as 盟誓 méngshì②

明说 míngshuō speak frankly; speak openly: 我对你～了吧。 I'll be frank with you. / 他嘴里虽没～, 心里却有想法。 He didn't say anything definitely, although he had ideas of his own. / 这事不便～。 We'd better not state it so explicitly.

明太鱼 míngtàiyú walleye pollack

明堂 míngtáng (also 明唐 míngtáng) *dial.* ① threshing ground ② courtyard; yard; compound

明天 míngtiān ① tomorrow ② the near future: 光辉灿烂的～ a bright future

明文 míngwén (of laws, regulations, etc.) proclaimed in writing: ～规定 stipulate in explicit terms; expressly provide

明晰 míngxī distinct; clear: 雷达荧光屏上出现了～的图像。 A distinct blip appeared on the radar screen.

明细帐 míngxìzhàng subsidiary ledger

明虾 míngxiā same as 对虾 duìxiā

明显 míngxiǎn clear; obvious; evident; distinct: ～的优势 clear superiority / ～的改进 distinct improvement / ～的成效 tangible result / ～目标。 The target is quite clear. / 这很～是一个借口。 This is evidently a pretext.

明线 míngxiàn *electron.* open-wire line; open wire: ～载波设备 open-wire carrier equipment

明效 míngxiào obvious results; telling (*or* marked) effects

明效大验 míngxiào-dàyàn clinching proof of effectiveness; telling (*or* marked) effects

明信片 míngxìnpiàn postcard

明星 míngxīng ① *arch.* Venus ② a famous performer; star: 电影～ a film (*or* movie) star / 足球～ a football star / 全～队 an all-star team ③ *old* society lady; social butterfly

明修栈道, 暗渡陈仓 míng xiū zhàndào, àn dù Chéncāng pretend to advance along one path while secretly going along another; do one thing under cover of another

明眼人 míngyǎnrén a person with a discerning eye; a person of good sense

明一套, 暗一套 míng yī tào, àn yī tào act one way in the open and another way in secret

明莹 míngyíng sparkling and crystal-clear; glittering and translucent: ～的金钢钻 a sparkling diamond

明于知人, 昧于知已 míng yú zhī rén, mèi yú zhī jǐ have a good knowledge of others but a poor knowledge of oneself; understand others but not oneself

明喻 míngyù simile

明早 míngzǎo *dial.* ① tomorrow morning ② tomorrow

明哲保身 míng zhé bǎo shēn be worldly-wise and play safe

明争暗斗 míngzhēng-àndòu both open strife and veiled struggle; overt contention and covert struggle

明正典刑 míng zhèng diǎnxíng carry out a death sentence according to the law

明证 míngzhèng clear proof: 西沙群岛自古即为我国领土, 这些文物就是～。 These cultural relics are clear proof that the Xisha Islands have been China's territory since ancient times.

明知 míngzhī know perfectly well; be fully aware: 你～他不愿意参加, 为什么还要勉强他? You know quite well that he doesn't want to join us. Why do you force him to?

明知故犯 míngzhī-gùfàn knowingly violate (discipline,

etc.); deliberately break (a rule, etc.); do sth. one knows is wrong

明知故问 míngzhī-gùwèn　ask while knowing the answer

明知山有虎，偏向虎山行 míngzhī shān yǒu hǔ, piān xiàng hǔ shān xíng　go deep into the mountains, knowing well that there are tigers there—go on undeterred by the dangers ahead

明志 míngzhì　show one's high ideals

明智 míngzhì　sensible; sagacious; wise: 表现出～的态度 show a sensible attitude / 他这样决定是～的。 It was wise of him to make that decision.

明珠 míngzhū　bright pearl; jewel

明珠暗投 míngzhū àn tóu　a bright pearl cast into darkness— ① a person of talent or a thing of value unrecognized ② a good person fallen among bad company

明珠弹雀 míngzhū tán què　shoot a pearl at the sparrow—the loss outweighs the gain; the game is not worth the candle

明子 míngzi　pine torch

鸣

míng　① (of birds, animals or insects) cry: 鸡～ the crow of a cock / 秋虫夜～ autumn insects chirping at night / 两个黄鹂～翠柳。(杜甫) A pair of orioles sing amid the willows green. ② make a sound; ring: 我耳～。My ears are ringing. / ～笛 blow a whistle / ～鼓 beat a drum / ～礼炮二十一响 fire a 21-gun salute / 钟～三下。The clock struck three. ③ express; voice; air: 鸣冤 míngyuān

鸣不平 míng bùpíng　complain of unfairness; cry out against injustice

鸣镝 míngdí　whistling (or twanging) arrow (used in ancient times)

鸣放 míngfàng　① fire a shot ② air one's views (through meetings, newspapers and other media)

鸣鼓而攻之 míng gǔ ér gōng zhī　beat the drum and launch the attack—make a scathing indictment

鸣金收兵 míng jīn shōubīng　beat the gong and recall the troops—call off a battle

鸣锣开道 míngluó-kāidào　beat gongs to clear the way (for officials in feudal times)—prepare the public for a coming event; pave the way for sth.

鸣枪示警 míngqiāng shìjǐng　fire a warning shot

鸣禽 míngqín　songbird; singing bird

鸣谢 míngxiè　express one's thanks formally: ～启事 a notice expressing one's thanks to benefactors (mentioned in the notice)

鸣冤 míngyuān　voice grievances; complain of unfairness

鸣冤叫屈 míngyuān-jiàoqū　complain and call for redress; voice grievances

鸣啭 míngzhuàn　formal (of birds) twitter; sing

茗

míng　① tender tea leaves ② tea: 香茗 xiāngmíng

冥

míng　① dark; obscure: 晦冥 huìmíng ② deep; profound: 冥想 míngxiǎng ③ dull; stupid: 冥顽 míngwán ④ underworld; the nether world: 冥府 míngfǔ

冥钞 míngchāo　paper made to resemble bank notes and burned for the dead

冥府 míngfǔ　the nether world

冥器 míngqì　same as 明器 míngqì

冥寿 míngshòu　birthday anniversary of the dead

冥思苦想 míngsī-kǔxiǎng　same as 苦思冥想 kǔsī-míngxiǎng

冥顽 míngwán　formal thickheaded; stupid

冥顽不灵 míngwán bùlíng　dull and stupid; impenetrably thickheaded

冥王星 Míngwángxīng　Pluto

冥想 míngxiǎng　deep thought; meditation: 歌声把我带到对草原的～中去了。 On hearing the song, I fell into a reverie about the grasslands.

铭

míng　① inscription: 墓志铭 mùzhìmíng ② engrave: 铭刻 míngkè

铭感 mínggǎn　formal be deeply grateful: ～终身 remain deeply grateful for the rest of one's life

铭记 míngjì　① bear firmly in mind; always remember: ～在心 always bear in mind / 您对我们的恩情，我们将永远～不忘。We'll never forget the kindness you've shown us. ② inscription; epigraph

铭刻 míngkè　① inscription: 古代～ ancient inscription ② be engraved on one's mind; be always remembered: 周总理的光辉形象永远～在人民的心中。 The shining image of Premier Zhou Enlai is indelibly engraved on the memory of the Chinese people.

铭刻学 míngkèxué　epigraphy

铭牌 míngpái　mech. data plate; nameplate

铭文 míngwén　inscription; epigraph

铭心 míngxīn　be engraved on one's heart—be remembered with gratitude

铭诸肺腑 míng zhū fèifǔ　be engraved on one's mind (or memory); be borne firmly in mind

溟

míng　formal sea: 东～ the east sea

暝

míng　formal ① (of the sun) set; (of the sky) grow dark: 日将～。 The sun is setting. / 天将～。 Dusk has fallen. ② dusk; evening twilight

瞑

míng　see below

瞑目 míngmù　close one's eyes in death—die content: 死不瞑目 sǐ bù míngmù

瞑眩 míngxuàn　Chin. med. dizziness, nausea, etc. as a side effect of drugs

螟

míng　snout moth's larva

螟虫 míngchóng　snout moth's larva

螟蛾 míng'é　snout moth

螟蛉 mínglíng　① corn earworm ② adopted son

mǐng

酩

mǐng　see below

酩酊 mǐngdǐng　be dead drunk

酩酊大醉 mǐngdǐng dà zuì　be dead drunk

mìng

命¹

mìng　① life: ～在旦夕 be on the verge of death; be dying ② lot; fate; destiny: 他认为自己受苦是～苦。 He thought he had suffered because of his cruel fate. / ～好 be born under a lucky star

命²

mìng　① order; command: ～其速归。 Order him to return immediately. ② order; commandation: 奉命 fèngmìng ③ assign (a name, title, etc.): 命名 mìngmíng

命案 mìng'àn　a case involving the killing of a person; homicide case

命笔 mìngbǐ　formal take up one's pen; set pen to paper: 欣然～ gladly set pen to paper; be happy to start writing

命不该绝 mìng bùgāi jué　not be destined to die (said of

a person who has had a narrow escape)

命定 mìngdìng be determined by fate; be predestined

命根子 mìnggēnzi one's very life; lifeblood: 孙子是她的〜。 Her grandson is the very apple of her eye.

命蹇 mìngjiǎn *formal* suffer many a setback during one's life; have a hapless fate

命令 mìnglìng ① order; command: 连长〜一排担任警戒。 The company commander ordered the first platoon to keep watch. ② order; commandation: 下〜 issue an order / 服从〜 obey orders / 〜式的口气 a commanding tone

命令句 mìnglìngjù *gram.* imperative sentence

命令主义 mìnglìngzhǔyì commandism

命脉 mìngmài lifeblood; lifeline: 经济〜 economic lifelines / 水利是农业的〜。 Irrigation is the lifeblood of agriculture.

命门 mìngmén *Chin. med.* the gate of vitality, the area between the kidneys, generally regarded as the source of vitality, the function of which is to promote respiration, digestion, reproduction and the metabolism of body fluid

命名 mìngmíng name (sb. or sth.): 以白求恩医生〜的医院 a hospital named after Dr. Norman Bethune / 〜典礼 (大会) a naming ceremony / 这条水渠被〜为"红旗渠"。 The canal was named the Red Flag Canal.

命名法 mìngmíngfǎ nomenclature

命数 mìngshù destiny; fate; lot

命数法 mìngshùfǎ *math.* numeration

命题[1] mìngtí assign a topic; set a question: 〜作文 assign a subject for composition

命题[2] mìngtí ① *math.* proposition: 〜演算 propositional calculus ② *log.* proposition

命途多舛 mìngtú duō chuǎn suffer many a setback during one's life

命运 mìngyùn destiny; fate; lot: 悲惨的〜 a tragic lot / 国家的前途和〜 the future and destiny of the state

命中 mìngzhòng hit the target (*or* mark); score a hit: 她第一枪就〜靶心。 Her first shot hit the bull's-eye. / 〜目标 hit the target (*or* mark) / 〜率 percentage of hits / 〜偏差 deviation of impact

miù

谬 miù wrong; false; erroneous; mistaken: 荒谬 huāngmiù

谬爱 miù'ài *pol.* undeserved kindness

谬传 miùchuán a false report

谬见 miùjiàn ① a wrong view ② *hum.* my humble opinion

谬奖 miùjiǎng *pol.* overpraise (me)

谬论 miùlùn fallacy; false (*or* absurd) theory; falsehood: 驳斥〜 refute a fallacy / 散布〜 spread absurd theories

谬托 miùtuō pass oneself off as

谬误 miùwù falsehood; error; mistake: 真理是在同〜作斗争中间发展起来的。 Truth develops through its struggle against falsehood.

谬悠 miùyōu *formal* fantastic; absurd

谬种 miùzhǒng ① error; fallacy ② *offens.* scoundrel

谬种流传 miùzhǒng liúchuán the dissemination of error: 〜，误人不浅。 The dissemination of error does people great harm.

缪 miù see 纰缪 pīmiù ——see also Miào; móu

mō

摸 mō ① feel; stroke; touch: 你〜〜刀口，看看快不快。 You feel the edge of the knife and see whether it is sharp. / 这衣料〜着很软。 The material feels soft. / 她轻轻地〜了〜孩子的头。 She gently stroked the child's head. ② feel for; grope for; fumble: 在黑暗中〜着下楼 grope one's way down the stairs in the dark / 〜敌人岗哨 steal up to an enemy sentinel in the dark and get rid of him / 他在口袋里〜了半天，〜出一张纸条来。 He felt in his pocket for a while and finally produced a slip of paper. / 他从床底下〜出一双鞋来。 He fished out a pair of shoes from under the bed. ③ try to find out; feel out; sound out: 你去〜〜他对这个问题的看法。 Go and sound him out on this matter. / 〜清敌情 find out about the enemy's situation / 〜出一套种植水稻的好经验 gain good experience in growing rice

摸底 mōdǐ ① know the real situation: 这事我不〜，你可以问问别人。 I don't know much about this business. Please ask someone else. / 大家的想法，他都〜。 He knows quite well what is in everybody's mind. ② try to find out the real intention or situation; sound sb. out: 他是想摸我们的底。 He was trying to feel us out.

摸黑儿 mōhēir *inf.* grope one's way on a dark night: 〜赶路 press on with the journey at night / 起早〜地干work from morning till night

摸门儿 mōménr *inf.* learn the ropes; get the hang of sth.: 这事初看起来不容易，可是过了几个星期你就能摸着门儿了。 It may seem difficult at first, but you'll get the hang of it after a few weeks.

摸哨 mōshào steal up to an enemy sentinel in the dark and get rid of him

摸索 mōsuo ① grope; feel about; fumble: 在黑暗中〜前进 grope (*or* fumble) one's way in the dark ② try to find out: 〜种花生的规律 try to find out the secret of peanut growing

摸头 mōtóu get to know sth.; begin to understand

摸透 mōtòu get to know sb. or sth. very well: 〜了这台车床的脾气 get to know the lathe very well / 〜某人的脾气 get to know sb. inside out

摸瞎 mōxiā same as 摸黑儿 mōhēir

mó

无(無) mó see 南无 nāmó ——see also wú

谟 mó *formal* plan: 宏谟 hóngmó

馍(饃、饝) mó (also 馍馍 mómo) *dial.* steamed bun; steamed bread

麽 mó see 幺麽 yāomó

摹 mó copy; trace: 临摹 línmó

摹本 móběn facsimile; copy

摹仿 mófǎng (also 摹效 móxiào) same as 模仿 mófǎng

摹绘 móhuì *formal* draw; paint; depict; describe

摹刻 mókè ① carve a reproduction of an inscription or painting ② a carved reproduction of an inscription or painting

摹拟 mónǐ same as 模拟 mónǐ

摹写 móxiě ① copy; imitate ② describe; depict: 〜人物情状 depict characters in various situations

摹印 móyìn ① copy and print ② a style of characters

or lettering on ancient imperial seals

摹状 mózhuàng depict; portray; delineate

模 mó ① pattern; standard: 楷模 kǎimó ② imitate: 模仿 mófǎng ③ short for 模范 mófàn ——see also mú

模本 móběn calligraphy or painting model

模范 mófàn an exemplary person or thing; model; fine example: 劳动～ model worker /～共青团员 model member of the Communist Youth League /～作用 exemplary role /～事迹 exemplary deeds /～地执行党的路线和政策 carry out the Party's line and policies in an exemplary way

模仿 mófǎng (also 模效 móxiào) imitate; copy; model oneself on: ～动物的叫声 imitate the cries of animals / 这部机器是～上海的一种新产品制造的。 This machine is modelled on one recently made in Shanghai. /～鲁迅的笔调 imitate Lu Xun's style / 儿童的～能力特强。 Children are very imitative.

模糊 móhu (also 模胡 móhu) ① blurred; indistinct; dim; vague: 字迹～了。 The writing was blurred. / 我模模糊糊看见远处有个人影在跑动。 I saw indistinctly someone running in the distance. /～的景物 a hazy scene / 只有些～的印象 have only a vague idea of sth. / 她对这个问题还有一些～认识。 She still has some confused ideas about that question. ② blur; obscure; confuse; mix up: 泪水～了他的双眼。 Tears blurred his eyes. or His eyes were dim with tears. /～两者之间的界限 obscure the distinction between the two things

模棱两可 móléng liǎngkě equivocal; ambiguous: 采取～的态度 take an equivocal attitude

模拟 mónǐ imitate; simulate: ～考试 a mock examination or test / 经过电子技术处理～立体声 (of a record, etc.) be electronically reprocessed to simulate stereo

模拟飞行 mónǐ fēixíng mil. simulated flight

模拟计算机 mónǐ jìsuànjī analogue computer

模拟人像 mónǐ rénxiàng effigy

模拟试验 mónǐ shìyàn a simulated test

模拟通信 mónǐ tōngxìn analogue communication

模数 móshù (also 模量 móliàng) phys. modulus: 弹性～ modulus of elasticity

模特儿 mótèr model

模型 móxíng ① model: 宇宙飞船～ a spaceship model / 原尺寸～ mock-up ② mould; matrix; pattern: ～板 mould plate

模型展品 móxíng zhǎnpǐn scale model; replica

膜 mó ① membrane: 细胞膜 xìbāomó ② film; thin coating: 纸浆表面结了一层～。 A thin film formed on the surface of the pulp.

膜拜 móbài prostrate oneself (before an idol or person); worship: 顶礼膜拜 dǐnglǐ-móbài

膜翅目 móchìmù zool. Hymenoptera

膜法 mófǎ environ. protec. membrane method

膜片 mópiàn diaphragm

摩 mó ① rub; scrape; touch: 按摩 ànmó ② mull over; study: 揣摩 chuǎimó ——see also mā

摩擦 mócā ① rub: 轴颈在轴承上～。 The journal rubs against the bearing surface. ② phys. friction: ～生热。 Friction generates heat. ③ clash (between two parties); friction: 制造～ create friction / 与某人发生～ have a brush with sb. / 工作中的～ conflicts in work

摩擦力 mócālì phys. frictional force; friction

摩擦抛光 mócā pāoguāng mech. burnishing

摩擦音 mócāyīn phonet. fricative

摩擦桩 mócāzhuāng archit. friction pile

摩登 módēng modern; fashionable: ～家具 fashionable furniture /～女郎 a fashionable girl

摩电灯 módiàndēng dynamo-powered lamp (on a bicycle, etc.)

摩顶放踵 módǐng-fàngzhǒng wear the whole body smooth from head to foot—serve the interests of others at great self-sacrifice

摩尔 mó'ěr phys. mole

摩尔多瓦 Mó'ěrduōwǎ Moldova

摩尔根主义 Mó'ěrgēnzhǔyì biol. Morganism

摩肩接踵 mójiān-jiēzhǒng jostle each other in a crowd: 那天街上人特别多，真是～，川流不息。 That day the street was jam-packed with people coming and going all the time.

摩厉以须 mólì yǐ xū sharpen one's sword in preparation—get ready for action

摩洛哥 Móluògē Morocco

摩洛哥人 Móluògērén Moroccan

摩纳哥 Mónàgē Monaco

摩纳哥人 Mónàgērén Monacan

摩拳擦掌 móquán-cāzhǎng rub one's fists and palms—be eager for a fight; be itching to have a go: 战士们一个个～，准备战斗。 The soldiers were rolling up their sleeves for the battle.

摩丝 mósī styling mousse; mousse

摩挲 mósuō stroke; caress ——see also māsa

摩天 mótiān skyscraping: ～岭 a mountain ridge towering into the sky; a towering mountain ridge; a cloud-capped mountain /～大楼 skyscraper / 峻岭～。 The high mountains seem to scrape the sky.

摩托 mótuō motor

摩托车 mótuōchē motorcycle; motor bicycle; motorbike

摩托船 mótuōchuán (also 摩托艇 mótuōtǐng) same as 汽艇 qìtǐng

摩托化部队 mótuōhuà bùduì motorized troops

磨 mó ① rub; wear: 他的脚上～了泡。 His feet were blistered from the rubbing. / 没关系，就～破了一点皮。 Nothing serious. Just a graze. / 袜子～破了。 The socks are worn into holes. / 鞋跟～平了。 The heels of the shoes are worn down. / 我劝了他半天，嘴皮都快～破了。 I talked till my jaws ached, trying to bring him around. ② grind; polish: ～剪子 grind scissors; sharpen scissors /～大理石 polish marble /～墨 rub an ink stick against an inkstone; make ink for writing with a brush ③ wear down; wear out: 他被这场病～得不成样子。 The illness has worn him down to a mere shadow of his former self. ④ trouble; pester; worry: 这孩子可真～人。 What a little torment that child is. / 他不答应，你就跟他～。 If he doesn't agree, just keep on at him until he does. ⑤ obliterate; die out: 百世不～ will endure for centuries ⑥ dawdle; waste time: 快走吧，别再～时间了。 Stop dawdling and get going. ——see also mò

磨版机 móbǎnjī print. graining machine

磨擦 mócā same as 摩擦 mócā

磨蹭 móceng ① rub (lightly); stroke (gently): 他右脚轻轻地在地上～着。 He was scraping his right foot lightly on the floor. ② move slowly; dawdle: 他的腿好多了，可以一个人扶着向前～。 His leg is getting better and he can slowly move forward supporting himself on something. / 你这么磨磨蹭蹭的，什么时间才完得了呀？ If you go on dawdling like this, when will you ever be able to finish? / 别～了，快走吧。 Stop dawdling and get going. ③ pester; nag: 我跟爸爸～了半天，他才答应明天带我到动物园玩去。 I kept on at my father untill he promised to take me to the zoo tomorrow.

磨杵成针 mó chǔ chéng zhēn see 只要工夫深，铁杵磨成针 zhǐyào gōngfu shēn, tiěchǔ móchéng zhēn

磨穿铁砚 móchuān tiěyàn wear out an iron inkslab

—study assiduously

磨床 móchuáng　*mech.*　grinding machine; grinder: 内圆～ internal grinder / 外圆～ cylindrical grinder

磨刀不误砍柴工 mó dāo bù wù kǎncháigōng　sharpening the axe won't interfere with the cutting of firewood

磨刀霍霍 mó dāo huòhuò　sharpening one's sword; sabre-rattling: 小弟闻姐来，～向猪羊。《木兰诗》When her little brother heard that his sister had come, He sharpened his knife and darted like a flash towards the pigs and sheep.

磨刀石 módāoshí　whetstone; grindstone

磨电灯 módiàndēng　same as 摩电灯 módiàndēng

磨革 mógé　buff (leather): ～机 buffing machine

磨工 mógōng　*mech.*　① grinding work: ～车间 grindery ② grinder

磨工夫 mó gōngfu　consume time: 这活最～。This is a time-consuming job.

磨光 móguāng　polish: ～机 polishing machine; glazing machine

磨光玻璃 móguāng bōli　polished glass

磨耗 móhào　wear and tear

磨砺 mólì　go through the mill; steel oneself; harden oneself; discipline oneself

磨练 móliàn　put oneself through the mill; temper oneself; steel oneself: 困难能～我们的意志。Difficulties can temper our willpower.

磨料 móliào　abrasive; abradant

磨灭 mómiè　wear away; efface; obliterate: 留下难以～的印象 leave an indelible impression / 年深月久，碑文已经～。The inscription on the tablet has worn away with the passage of time.

磨木机 mómùjī　*paper making* (wood) grinder: 链式～ caterpillar grinder / 袋式～ pocket grinder

磨难 mónàn　tribulation; hardship; suffering: 历经～ have gone through all kinds of hardships

磨砂玻璃 móshā bōli　same as 毛玻璃 máobōli

磨砂灯泡 móshā dēngpào　frosted bulb

磨舌头 mó shétou　*dial.*　indulge in idle talk; argue pointlessly

磨蚀 móshí　*geol.*　abrasion

磨损 mósǔn　wear and tear: 这台机器基本上没有什么～。The machine shows scarcely any sign of wear and tear.

磨损留量 mósǔn liúliàng　*mech.*　wear allowance

磨洗 móxǐ　wear away; corrode; erode: 碑文经受了岁月的～。The inscription on the stone had been worn away over the years.

磨削 móxiāo　*mech.*　grinding: ～裕量 grinding tolerance

磨牙 móyá　① grind one's teeth (in sleep) ② *dial.* indulge in idle talk; argue pointlessly: 你别跟他～了。Don't waste your time arguing with him.

磨洋工 mó yánggōng　dawdle over one's work; loaf on the job; lie down on the job: 别～了，快把活干完。Stop dawdling and finish your work.

磨嘴皮子 mó zuǐpízi　(also 磨嘴 mózuǐ)　*dial.*　① jabber; blah-blah: 成天～不干活，还能建设好社会主义? How can you build socialism if you just blah-blah and don't do a stroke of work? ② do a lot of talking: 这可是～的事。It'll take a hell of a lot of talking to settle this. / 我跟他磨了半天嘴皮子，也没能把他说服。I failed to bring him around though I talked myself hoarse. ③ indulge in idle talk; argue pointlessly: 我没功夫跟他～。I can't afford to waste my time arguing with him.

蘑 mó　mushroom: 鲜～ fresh mushrooms

蘑菇[1] mógu　mushroom

蘑菇[2] mógu　① worry; pester; keep on at: 你别跟我～了，我还有急事呢。Don't pester me. I've got something

urgent to attend to. ② dawdle; dillydally: 你再这样～就赶不上火车了。If you go on dawdling like this, you'll miss the train. ——see also 泡蘑菇 pào mógu

蘑菇云 móguyún　mushroom cloud (esp. from nuclear explosion)

蘑菇战术 mógu zhànshù　*mil.*　the tactics of "wear and tear" (wearing the enemy down and then wiping them out)

魔 mó　① evil spirit; demon; devil; monster: 恶魔 èmó　② magic; mystic: 魔力 mólì

魔法 mófǎ　sorcery; witchcraft

魔怪 móguài　demons and monsters; fiends

魔鬼 móguǐ　devil; demon; monster

魔君 mójūn　a brutal person

魔窟 mókū　den of monsters

魔力 mólì　magical power; magic; charm

魔难 mónàn　same as 磨难 mónàn

魔术 móshù　magic; conjuring; sleight of hand: ～演员 magician; conjurer

魔术师 móshùshī　magician

魔王 mówáng　① Prince of the Devils; erlking ② tyrant; despot; fiend

魔影 móyǐng　spectre: 内战的～正威胁着那个国家。The spectre of civil war was haunting the country.

魔芋 móyù　*Amorphophallus rivieri*

魔掌 mózhǎng　devil's clutches; evil hands: 逃出敌人的～ escape from the clutches of the enemy

魔杖 mózhàng　magic wand

魔爪 mózhǎo　devil's talons; claws; tentacles: 斩断侵略者的～ cut off the tentacles of the aggressors

mǒ

抹 mǒ　① put on; apply; smear; plaster: ～点雪花膏 put on a little vanishing cream / 面包上～点果酱 spread some jam on a piece of bread / ～药膏 apply ointment / 你～浆糊，我来贴布告。You smear the wall with paste and I'll stick the notice on it. ② wipe: ～眼泪 wipe one's eyes; be weeping / 用手把嘴一～ wipe one's mouth with the back of the hand ③ cross (or strike, blot) out; erase: 把这一行字～了。Cross out this line. / ～掉磁带上的录音 erase the recording from a tape ——see also mā; mò

抹鼻子 mǒ bízi　*dial.*　cry; weep

抹脖子 mǒ bózi　cut one's own throat; commit suicide

抹刀 mǒdāo　trowel

抹黑 mǒhēi　blacken sb.'s name; throw mud at; bring shame on; discredit: 他的所作所为简直是在给我们集体脸上～。What he did is simply bringing shame on our collective.

抹零 mǒlíng　not count the small change (in a payment)

抹杀 mǒshā　(also 抹煞 mǒshā) blot out; obliterate; write off: ～成绩 obliterate achievements / 历史事实是～不了的。The facts of history cannot be denied.

抹稀泥 mǒ xīní　*dial.*　try to mediate differences at the sacrifice of principle; try to gloss things over

抹香鲸 mǒxiāngjīng　sperm whale

抹一鼻子灰 mǒ yī bízi huī　same as 碰一鼻子灰 pèng yī bízi huī

抹子 mǒzi　trowel

mò

万 mò　see below ——see also wàn

万俟 Mòqí a two-character surname

末[1] mò ① tip; end: 秋毫之末 qiūháo zhī mò ② nonessentials; minor details: 本末倒置 běn-mò dàozhì ③ end; last stage: 明～农民起义 the peasant uprisings towards the end of the Ming Dynasty / 一学期的最～一天 the last day of a school term ④ powder; dust: 茶叶～儿 broken tea leaves; tea dust / 把药研成～儿 grind medicinal herbs into powder

末[2] mò the role of a middle-aged man in traditional operas

末班车 mòbānchē ① last bus ② inf. last chance or turn

末代 mòdài the last reign of a dynasty: ～皇帝 the last emperor (of a dynasty)

末伏 mòfú ① the last or third fu—the third hottest period of the year (10 days) ② the first day of the last or third fu (falling in early or mid August) ——see also 三伏 sānfú

末后 mòhòu last; finally; in the end

末技 mòjì a trifling skill; an insignificant stunt

末减 mòjiǎn formal leniently convict sb.; lighten a punishment

末节 mòjié minor details; nonessentials: 细枝末节 xìzhī-mòjié

末了 mòliǎo (also 末末了儿 mòmòliǎor) last; finally; in the end: 第五行～的那个字我不认识。I don't know the last word of the fifth line. / 他～还是同意了大家的意见。In the end he agreed with the others.

末流 mòliú ① the later and decadent stage of a school of thought, literature, etc. ② inferior; low-grade: ～演员 a minor actor or actress

末路 mòlù dead end; impasse: 英雄～ a hero in dire straits

末年 mònián last years of a dynasty or reign: 明朝～ the last years of the Ming Dynasty (1368–1644)

末期 mòqī last phase; final phase; last stage: 七十年代～ in the late seventies / 第二次世界大战～ the last stage of the Second World War

末日 mòrì ① Christianity doomsday; Day of Judgment; Judgment Day: ～审判 Last Judgment ② end; doom: 封建王朝的～ the end of a feudal dynasty

末梢 mòshāo tip; end: 鞭子的～ the tip of a whip / 五月～ the end of May / 她在辫子的～打了个花结。She tied a ribbon bowknot at the tip end of her plait.

末梢神经 mòshāo shénjīng physiol. nerve ending

末世 mòshì last phase (of an age): 封建～ the last years of feudalism

末俗 mòsú decadent customs and practices of troubled times

末尾 mòwěi ① end: 信的～ at the end of the letter / 排队排在～ stand at the end of a queue / 一切结论产生于调查情况的～, 而不是在它的先头。Conclusions invariably come after investigation, and not before. ② mus. fine; end

末席 mòxí the least prominent seat at a dinner table

末屑 mòxiè bits; scraps; crumbs: 面包～ crumbs (of bread)

末药 mòyào same as 没药 mòyào

末业 mòyè (in ancient times) industry and commerce

末叶 mòyè last years (of a century or dynasty): 十九世纪～ the end of the 19th century; the late 19th century / 清朝～ the last years of the Qing Dynasty

末议 mòyì formal hum. my view

末子 mòzi powder; dust: 煤～ coal dust

没[1] mò ① sink; submerge: 潜水艇很快就～入水中。It was not long before the submarine submerged. ② overflow; rise beyond: 洪水几乎～过了大坝。The flood nearly overflowed the dam. / 水深～顶。The water goes above a man's head. / 雪深～膝。The snow was knee-deep. ③ disappear; hide: 出没 chūmò ④ confiscate; take possession of: 没收 mòshōu ⑤ till the end: 没世 mòshì ⑥ same as 殁 mò

没[2] mò see 没奈何 mònàihé ——see also méi

没齿不忘 mò chǐ bù wàng (also 没世不忘 mòshì bù wàng) will never forget to the end of one's days; remember for the rest of one's life

没骨画 mògǔhuà boneless painting (i.e. painting without outline but with forms achieved by washes of ink and colour)

没落 mòluò decline; wane: 他出生在一个～的封建家庭里。He was born in a declining feudal family. / 这个文学流派从此日趋～。This school of literature has since been on the wane.

没奈何 mònàihé be utterly helpless; have no way out; have no alternative: 等了他好久也没来, ～我只好一个人去了。I waited for a long time, but he didn't show up, so I had to go alone.

没世 mòshì all one's life; lifelong

没收 mòshōu confiscate; expropriate: ～官僚资本 confiscate bureaucrat capital / ～违禁物品 confiscate contraband

没药 mòyào Chin. med. myrrh

沫 mò foam; froth: 啤酒～ froth on beer; the head on a glass of beer / 肥皂～ soapsuds; lather / 有的啤酒～儿比较多。Some beer has more froth than others.

沫子 mòzi foam; froth

茉 mò see below

茉莉 mòli bot. jasmine

茉莉花茶 mòli huāchá jasmine tea

抹 mò ① daub; plaster: ～墙 plaster a wall; daub plaster on a wall ② skirt; bypass: ～过林子 skirt the edge of the forest ——see also mā; mǒ

抹不开 mòbukāi same as 磨不开 mòbukāi

抹得开 mòdekāi same as 磨得开 mòdekāi

抹灰 mòhuī archit. plastering: ～工 plasterer

抹头 mòtóu turn round; face about

抹胸 mòxiōng an undergarment covering the chest and abdomen

殁 mò formal die: 病～ die of illness

陌 mò ① a path between fields (running east and west): 阡陌 qiānmò ② road: 陌头 mòtóu

陌路 mòlù (also 陌路人 mòlùrén) formal stranger (whom one passes in the street): 视同～ treat like a stranger; cut sb. dead

陌生 mòshēng strange; unfamiliar: ～人 stranger / 对这些年青人来说, 养鹿是一件～的事情。Breeding deer was something completely new for these young people. / 尽管我们初次见面, 但并不感到～。Although this was only our first meeting, we didn't feel like strangers. / 在会场上我看到许多～的面孔。I saw many unfamiliar faces at the meeting.

陌头 mòtóu roadside: ～杨柳 roadside willows

脉（脈） mò see below ——see also mài

脉脉 mòmò affectionate; loving; amorous: 她～地注视

着远去的儿子。She followed with loving eyes the departing figure of her son.

莫

mò ① *formal* no one; nothing; none: ～之能御。No one (*or* Nothing) can resist it. ② *adv.* no; not: ～知所措 not know what to do; be at a loss / ～性急。Don't be impatient. *or* Take it easy. / ～道昆明湖水浅, 观鱼胜过富春江。(毛泽东) Do not say the waters of Kunming Lake are too shallow, For watching fish they are better than Fuchun River. ③ (Mò) a surname

莫不 mòbù there's no one who doesn't *or* isn't: 胜利的消息传来, 各族人民～为之欢欣鼓舞。People of all nationalities were jubilant on hearing the news of victory. / ～为之感动。There was no one who was unmoved.

莫不是 mòbushì same as 莫非 mòfēi

莫测高深 mò cè gāoshēn unfathomable; enigmatic

莫此为甚 mò cǐ wéi shèn a more flagrant instance has yet to be found

莫大 mòdà greatest; utmost: 感到～的光荣 feel greatly honoured / ～的幸福 the greatest happiness / ～的侮辱 a gross insult / ～的愤慨 the utmost indignation

莫非 mòfēi *adv.* can it be that; is it possible that: 今天她没来, ～又生了病不成?She is absent today. Can she be ill again? / 听你的意思, ～是我错了? Do you mean to say that I'm in the wrong?

莫过于 mòguòyú nothing is more...than: 最大的幸福～此。There's no greater happiness than this. / 我国古代的伟大建筑, 恐怕～万里长城了。Of all the ancient Chinese buildings, the Great Wall is perhaps the greatest.

莫霍界面 mòhuò jièmiàn *geol.* Moho discontinuity; Moho

莫可名状 mòkě míng zhuàng same as 不可名状 bùkě míng zhuàng

莫可指数 mòkě zhǐ shù beyond counting on one's fingers—countless; innumerable

莫名 mòmíng beyond description; indescribable; nameless: 一种～的紧张 a nameless nervousness / ～所以 be unable to make head or tail of sth.; be baffled / 感谢～ many thanks

莫名其妙 mòmíng qí miào (also 莫明其妙 mòmíng qí miào) ① be unable to make head or tail of sth.; be baffled: 他为什么讲这番话, 真叫人～。It is quite baffling why he should have made such remarks. / 大家想不到他这句话是什么意思, 都～地望着他。Nobody could make out what he meant and they all looked at him with puzzled expressions. ② without rhyme or reason; inexplicable; odd: 她～地哭了起来。Quite unaccountably she burst out crying.

莫逆 mònì very friendly; intimate: 他们二人最称～。The two of them have become the best of friends.

莫逆之交 mònì zhī jiāo bosom friends

莫如 mòrú (also 莫若 mòruò) would be better; might as well: 与其你去, ～他来。It would be better for him to come than for you to go. / 她想既然来了, ～跟着进去看看。Now that she'd come to the place, she thought she might as well go in with the others to have a look.

莫桑比克 Mòsāngbǐkè Mozambique

莫桑比克人 Mòsāngbǐkèrén Mozambican

莫信直中直, 须防仁不仁 mò xìn zhí zhōng zhí, xū fáng rén bù rén don't believe the honesty of the honest, be wary of the unkindness of the kind

莫须有 mòxūyǒu unwarranted; groundless; fabricated; trumped-up: ～的罪名 a fabricated charge; an unwarranted charge

莫予毒也 mò yú dú yě same as 人莫予毒 rén mò yú dú

莫衷一是 mò zhōng yī shì unable to agree or decide which is right ——see also 众说纷纭 zhòng shuō fēnyún

秣

mò ① fodder: 粮秣 liángmò ② feed animals: see below

秣马厉兵 mòmǎ-lìbīng (also 秣马利兵 mòmǎ-lìbīng) feed the horses and sharpen the weapons—make preparations for war; prepare for battle

漠

mò ① desert: 沙漠 shāmò ② indifferent; unconcerned: 冷漠 lěngmò

漠不关心 mò bù guānxīn indifferent; unconcerned: 官长必须爱护士兵, 不能～。Officers must cherish their men and must not be indifferent to their well-being.

漠漠 mòmò ① misty; foggy: 湖面升起一层～的烟雾。A thick mist rose over the lake. ② vast and lonely: 黄沙～ a vast stretch of yellow sand / 平林～烟如织。(李白) Silent planes of woods woven in mist.

漠然 mòrán indifferent; apathetic; unconcerned: 这个作家对批评意见处之～。The writer was indifferent to criticism.

漠然置之 mòrán zhì zhī remain indifferent towards sth.; look on with unconcern

漠视 mòshì treat with indifference; ignore; overlook; pay no attention to: 不能～群众的意见。The masses' opinions must not be treated with indifference.

寞

mò lonely; deserted: 寂寞 jìmò

蓦

mò *adv.* suddenly

蓦地 mòdì *adv.* suddenly; unexpectedly; all of a sudden: 黑暗里～窜出个人来。Suddenly, somebody ran out of the darkness. / 傍晚～刮起了大风。As dusk fell, a gale suddenly started blowing.

蓦然 mòrán *adv.* suddenly: ～想起 suddenly remember

瘼

mò see 民瘼 mínmò

墨¹

mò ① China (*or* Chinese) ink; ink stick: ～太稠了。The ink is too thick. ② pigment; ink: 油墨 yóumò ③ handwriting or painting: 遗墨 yímò ④ learning: 胸无点墨 xiōng wú diǎn mò ⑤ black; pitch-dark: 墨黑 mòhēi ⑥ *formal* corruption; graft; embezzlement: 墨吏 mòlì ⑦ tabooing the face (a punishment in ancient China) (see also 五刑 wǔxíng) ⑧ (Mò) short for 墨家 Mòjiā ⑨ (Mò) a surname

墨²

Mò short for 墨西哥 Mòxīgē

墨宝 mòbǎo ① treasured scrolls of calligraphy or painting ② *pol.* your beautiful handwriting

墨笔 mòbǐ same as 毛笔 máobǐ

墨斗 mòdǒu carpenter's ink marker

墨斗鱼 mòdǒuyú popular name for 乌贼 wūzéi

墨海 mòhǎi a big basin-like inkstone

墨盒 mòhé (also 墨盒子 mòhézi) ink box (for Chinese calligraphy or painting)

墨黑 mòhēi pitch-dark: 一个～的夜晚 one pitch-dark night

墨迹 mòjì ① ink marks; ink stains: 他衬衫上有～。There were ink stains on his shirt. ② sb.'s writing or painting: 这是鲁迅的～。This is Lu Xun's calligraphy.

墨迹未干 mòjì wèi gān before the ink is dry: 协议～, 他们就把它撕毁了。They tore up the agreement before the ink was hardly dry.

墨家 Mòjiā Mohist School (a school of thought in the Spring and Autumn and Warring States Periods, 770–221 B.C.): ～学说 Mohism

墨晶 mòjīng smoky quartz

墨镜 mòjìng sunglasses

墨客 mòkè *formal* literary men; men of letters

墨吏 mòlì *formal* corrupt officials

墨绿 mòlù blackish green

墨囊 mònáng ink sac (of a cuttlefish)

墨守成规 mò shǒu chéngguī stick to convention; stay in a rut

墨水 mòshuǐ ① prepared Chinese ink ② ink: 红 (蓝) ～ red (blue) ink ③ book learning: 他肚子里还有点儿～。 He's something of a scholar.

墨水池 mòshuǐchí inkwell

墨水瓶 mòshuǐpíng ink bottle

墨水台 mòshuǐtái inkstand

墨西哥 Mòxīgē Mexico

墨西哥人 Mòxīgērén Mexican

墨西哥湾 Mòxīgēwān the Gulf of Mexico

墨西哥湾流 Mòxīgēwānliú the Gulf Stream

墨线 mòxiàn ① the line in a carpenter's ink marker ② a line made by a carpenter's ink marker

墨刑 mòxíng tabooing the face (a punishment in ancient China) ——see also 五刑 wǔxíng

墨鸦 mòyā *dial.* cormorant

墨鱼 mòyú popular name for 乌贼 wūzéi

墨汁 mòzhī prepared Chinese ink

墨渍 mòzì ink blot; ink spot

默 mò ① silent; tacit: ～不作声 keep silent ② write from memory: ～生字 write out the new words from memory

默哀 mò'āi stand in silent tribute: 全体起立～。 All rose and stood in silent tribute. / ～三分钟 observe three minutes' silence

默察 mòchá watch quietly

默祷 mòdǎo pray in silence; say a silent prayer

默悼 mòdào pay a silent tribute of memory (to the dead)

默读 mòdú read silently

默记 mòjì make a mental note; learn by heart; commit to memory

默默 mòmò quiet; silent: ～无言 without saying a word; silently / 一连几天, 她总是这么～的, 不理人。 She's been like that for days, silent and unapproachable. / 他～地发誓要继承革命先烈的遗志。 He vowed to himself that he would carry forward the cause left behind by the revolutionary martyrs.

默默无闻 mòmò wú wén unknown to the public; without attracting public attention: 一生～ remain in obscurity all one's life / ～地工作 work quietly and never show off

默念 mòniàn ① read silently ② think back; recollect; recall: ～童年情景, 如在昨日。 My childhood days passed through my mind as if they were yesterday.

默契 mòqì ① tacit agreement; tacit understanding: 互相～ have a perfect mutual understanding in doing sth.; coordinate by tacit agreement / 这对双打选手配合～。 This pair of doubles played in perfect unison. ② secret agreement: 关于这个问题双方曾有～。 The two sides had a secret agreement on this question.

默然 mòrán silent; speechless: ～无语 fall silent; be speechless / 二人～相对。 The two of them sat face to face in silence.

默认 mòrèn give tacit consent to; tacitly approve; acquiesce in: ～现状 give tacit consent to the *status quo*

默书 mòshū write out a text from memory

默诵 mòsòng ① read silently ② read silently to oneself from memory

默算 mòsuàn ① do mental arithmetic; do sums in one's heart ② calculate; figure; plan

默想 mòxiǎng think deeply; ponder over; reflect on

默写 mòxiě write from memory: 她把这一课的生词～了一遍。 She wrote out from memory the new words in the lesson.

默许 mòxǔ tacitly consent to; acquiesce in

默志 mòzhì (also 默识 mòzhì) make a mental note; learn by heart; commit to memory

默坐 mòzuò sit quietly

磨 mò ① mill; millstones: 电～ electric mill ② grind; mill: ～麦子 grind wheat / ～面 mill flour ③ turn round: 把大车～过来。 Turn the cart round. / 我几次三番劝他, 他还是～不过来。 I had talked to him again and again, but he simply wouldn't come round. ——see also mó

磨不开 mòbukāi ① feel embarrassed; be put out: 本想说他两句, 又怕他脸上～。 I hesitated to criticize him for fear of making him uncomfortable. ② unable to act impartially for fear of offending sb.; afraid of impairing personal relations: 他有错误, 就该批评, 有什么～的? If he's made mistakes, you should criticize him and not let personal considerations get in your way. ③ *dial.* not be convinced; not come round

磨得开 mòdekāi ① not feel embarrassed; be at ease: 你这样说他, 他脸上～吗? Don't you think your sharp criticism would embarrass him? ② not find it embarrassing (to do sth.): 你不答应她的请求, 你～吗? Don't you find it difficult to refuse her request? ③ *dial.* be convinced; come round

磨豆腐 mòdòufu ① grind soya beans to make bean curd ② *dial.* say sth. over and over again; repeat again and again

磨坊 mòfáng (also 磨房 mòfáng) mill

磨面机 mòmiànjī flour-milling machine

磨盘 mòpán ① nether (or lower) millstone ② *dial.* mill; millstones

磨棚 mòpéng grinding shed; mill shed

磨扇 mòshàn upper and lower millstones

磨子 mòzi *dial.* mill; millstones

貘（獏） mò *zool.* tapir

糖 mò same as 耢 lào①

mōu

哞 mōu *onom.* (the sound made by an ox) moo; low; bellow

móu

牟 móu ① try to gain; obtain; seek: 牟利 móulì ② (Móu) a surname

牟利 móulì seek private (or selfish) interests; seek personal gain

牟取 móuqǔ try to gain; seek; obtain: ～暴利 seek exorbitant profits; reap staggering (or colossal) profits

侔 móu *formal* equal; match: 彼此相～ match each other

谋 móu ① stratagem; plan; scheme; 计谋 jìmóu ② work for; seek: 为人民～福利 work for the interests of the people / ～独立, 求解放 seek independence and liberation ③ consult: 不谋而合 bù móu ér hé

谋财害命 móucái-hàimìng murder sb. for his money

谋臣 móuchén emperor's counsellor

谋刺 móucì plot to assassinate

谋反 móufǎn conspire against the state; plot a rebellion

谋国 móuguó *formal* work for the interests of one's country

谋害 móuhài ① plot to murder ② plot a frame-up against

谋和 móuhé sue for peace

谋划 móuhuà plan; scheme; try to find a solution

谋虑 móulǜ consider carefully; contemplate; deliberate

谋略 móulüè astuteness and resourcefulness; strategy: 此人颇有～。He is a man of resource and astuteness.

谋面 móumiàn *formal* meet each other or be acquainted with sb.: 我与此人素未～。I never had the pleasure of meeting him.

谋篇 móupiān *formal* plan a composition

谋求 móuqiú seek; strive for; be in quest of: ～两国关系正常化 seek normalization of relations between the two countries / ～独立 strive for independence / ～解决办法 try to find a solution / ～职业 try to find a job; look for a job

谋取 móuqǔ try to gain; seek; obtain: 不能为了～暂时的利益而牺牲原则。We mustn't seek temporary gain at the expense of principle.

谋杀 móushā murder

谋生 móushēng (also 谋食 móushí) seek a livelihood; make a living: ～的手段 a means of life

谋士 móushì adviser; counsellor

谋事 móushì ① plan matters: ～不密 leave loopholes in a plan ② *old* look for a job

谋事在人,成事在天 móu shì zài rén, chéng shì zài tiān the planning lies with man, the outcome with Heaven; man proposes, God disposes

谋算 móusuàn ① plan; scheme; try to find a solution ② scheme against sb. or for sth.; plot ③ calculate; plan: 很有～ be very calculating

谋议 móuyì *formal* plan; scheme

谋主 móuzhǔ arch-plotter; ringleader

眸 móu pupil (of the eye); eye: 凝眸 níngmóu

眸子 móuzi pupil (of the eye); eye

蛑 móu see 蝤蛑 yóumóu

缪 móu see 绸缪 chóumóu; 未雨绸缪 wèi yǔ chóumóu ——see also Miào; miù

mǒu

某 mǒu ① certain; some: ～日 at a certain date / 张～ a certain person called Zhang / 解放军～部 a certain unit of the PLA / 在四川～地 somewhere in Sichuan Province / ～些农产品 certain agricultural products / 在～种程度上 to some (*or* a certain) extent / 在～种意义上 in a sense / 他老说～～～是他的朋友。He's always saying that so-and-so is a friend of his. ② (referring to oneself): 我李～不是干这种事的人。Yours truly is not the sort of person to do a thing like that.

某某 mǒumǒu so-and-so: ～同志 Comrade so-and-so / ～学校 a certain school / ～人 someone

某人 mǒurén ① a certain person; someone ② (referring to oneself): 我王～从来不说假话。As for me, I've never told lies.

mú

模 mú mould; matrix; pattern: 铜模 tóngmú ——see also mó

模板 múbǎn ① *archit.* shuttering; formwork ② *mech.* pattern plate

模具 mújù mould; matrix; pattern; die

模压 múyà mould pressing: ～胶底皮鞋 leather shoes with moulded-on rubber soles

模压机 múyàjī moulding press

模样 múyàng ① appearance; look: 他老多了,～变得都认不出来了。He's aged a lot and his appearance is beyond recognition. / 那人是什么～?What did that person look like? / 这孩子的～像他妈妈。The child takes after his mother. / 这姑娘～儿真不错。The young lady is quite pretty. ② (indicating a rough estimate of time or age): 我等了有半小时～。I waited for about half an hour. / 那男的有三十岁～。The man was around thirty.

模子 múzi mould; matrix; pattern; die: 一个～里铸出来的 made out of the same mould; as like as two peas

mǔ

母 mǔ ① mother: ～女 mother and daughter / 老～ one's old mother ② one's female elders: 伯母 bómǔ / 祖母 zǔmǔ ③ female (animal): ～象 female (*or* cow) elephant / 你的狗是公的还是～的?Is your dog a he or a she? / ～狼 she-wolf ④ nut (so called because of the female screw thread): 螺母 luómǔ ⑤ origin; parent: 母公司 mǔgōngsī

母爱 mǔ'ài mother love; maternal love

母本 mǔběn *bot.* female parent: ～植株 maternal plant

母畜 mǔchù mother of a domestic animal; dam

母党 mǔdǎng mother's kinsfolk

母蜂 mǔfēng queen bee

母公司 mǔgōngsī parent company

母狗 mǔgǒu female dog; bitch

母机 mǔjī ① machine tool ② mother aircraft; launching aircraft

母鸡 mǔjī hen

母舰 mǔjiàn mother ship

母老虎 mǔlǎohǔ ① tigress ② vixen; shrew; termagant

母马 mǔmǎ female horse; mare

母牛 mǔniú cow

母亲 mǔqīn mother

母权制 mǔquánzhì matriarchy

母乳 mǔrǔ breast milk; mother's milk: ～喂养 breast-feeding

母山羊 mǔshānyáng she-goat; nanny goat

母狮 mǔshī lioness

母体 mǔtǐ *zool.* the mother's body; the (female) parent

母系 mǔxì ① maternal: ～亲属 maternal relatives ② matrilineal; matriarchal: ～社会 matrilineal society / ～氏族制 matriarchy

母线 mǔxiàn ① *elec.* bus; bus bar ② *math.* generatrix; generator

母校 mǔxiào one's old school; Alma Mater

母性 mǔxìng maternal instinct

母羊 mǔyáng ewe

母夜叉 mǔyè·chā an ugly and fierce woman; an ugly shrew

母液 mǔyè *chem.* mother liquor; mother solution

母音　mǔyīn　*phonet.* vowel
母语　mǔyǔ　① mother tongue ② parent language; linguistic parent
母株　mǔzhū　*bot.* maternal plant; mother plant
母猪　mǔzhū　female pig; sow
母子　mǔzǐ　mother and son: ～候车室 waiting room (as in a railway station) for mothers with babies

亩（畮）　mǔ *mu*, currently called 市亩 shìmǔ, a traditional unit of area: ～产量 per *mu* yield ——see also 市亩 shìmǔ

牡　mǔ (opp. 牝 pìn) male (of some birds and animals): ～牛 bull / ～雉 male pheasant
牡丹　mǔdān　tree peony; peony
牡蛎　mǔlì　oyster

拇　mǔ　see below
拇战　mǔzhàn　finger-guessing game—a drinking game at feasts
拇指　mǔzhǐ　① thumb ② big toe

姆　mǔ　see 保姆 bǎomǔ ——see also m̄
姆夫蒂　mǔfūdì　*Islam* mufti
姆欧　mǔ'ōu　*elec.* mho

坶　mǔ　see 垆坶 lúmǔ

姥　mǔ　*formal* an old woman ——see also lǎo

畮　mǔ, also yīngmǔ old form for 英亩 yīngmǔ

mù

木[1]　mù　① tree: 树木 shùmù ② timber; wood: 松～ pinewood ③ made of wood; wooden: ～制家具 wooden furniture / ～箱 wooden box / ～桥 wooden bridge ④ coffin: 棺木 guānmù

木[2]　mù　① simple; plain: 木讷 mùnè ② numb; wooden: 两脚都冻～了。Both feet were numb with cold. / 舌头～了，什么味儿也尝不出来。My tongue has lost all its sense of taste.
木板　mùbǎn　plank; board
木板床　mùbǎnchuáng　plank bed
木版　mùbǎn　*print.* block
木版画　mùbǎnhuà　woodcut; wood engraving
木版印花　mùbǎn yìnhuā　*text.* block printing
木版印刷　mùbǎn yìnshuā　block printing
木本水源　mùběn-shuǐyuán　the root of a tree and the source of a stream—the root of a matter
木本植物　mùběn zhíwù　*bot.* xylophyta; woody plant
木笔　mùbǐ　another name for 木兰 mùlán
木菠萝　mùbōluó　*bot.* jackfruit
木材　mùcái　wood; timber; lumber: ～防腐 wood preservation
木材厂　mùcáichǎng　timber mill
木柴　mùchái　firewood
木醇　mùchún　another name for 甲醇 jiǎchún
木醋酸　mùcùsuān　*chem.* pyroligneous acid
木雕　mùdiāo　wood carving
木雕泥塑　mùdiāo-nísù　like an idol carved in wood or moulded in clay; as wooden as a dummy: 那黛玉倚着床栏杆，两手抱着膝，眼睛含着泪，好似～的一般。《红楼梦》She sat, motionless as a statue, leaning against the back of the bed, her hands clasped about her knees, her eyes full of tears.

木牍　mùdú　*archaeol.* inscribed wooden tablet
木蠹蛾　mùdù'é　wood moth; carpenter moth
木耳　mù'ěr　an edible fungus (*Auricularia auricula-judae*)
木筏　mùfá　(also 木筏子 mùfázi) raft
木芙蓉　mùfúróng　(also 木莲 mùlián) *bot.* cotton rose (*Hibiscus mutabilis*)
木工　mùgōng　① woodwork; carpentry ② woodworker; carpenter
木工机械　mùgōng jīxiè　woodworking machinery
木瓜　mùguā　① *bot.* Chinese flowering quince ② *dial.* papaya
木管乐器　mùguǎn yuèqì　woodwind instrument; woodwind
木化石　mùhuàshí　(also 木变石 mùbiànshí) petrified wood; woodstone
木屐　mùjī　clogs
木简　mùjiǎn　*archaeol.* inscribed wooden slip
木浆　mùjiāng　*paper making* wood pulp: 化学～ chemical wood pulp
木僵　mùjiāng　numb; stiff
木强　mùjiàng　*formal* upright; unyielding: ～敦厚 upright and honest
木匠　mùjiàng　carpenter
木焦油　mùjiāoyóu　*chem.* wood tar
木结构　mùjiégòu　*archit.* timber structure; wood construction
木槿　mùjǐn　*bot.* rose of Sharon
木精　mùjīng　another name for 甲醇 jiǎchún
木刻　mùkè　woodcut; wood engraving
木刻术　mùkèshù　xylography
木兰　mùlán　*bot.* lily magnolia
木立　mùlì　stand motionless
木料　mùliào　timber; lumber
木马　mùmǎ　① *sports* vaulting horse; pommelled horse ② (children's) hobbyhorse; rocking horse
木马计　mùmǎjì　the stratagem of the Trojan horse; Trojan horse
木棉　mùmián　silk cotton; kapok
木乃伊　mùnǎiyī　mummy
木讷　mùnè　*formal* simple and slow (of speech): ～寡言 simple and reticent
木牛流马　mùniú liúmǎ　Wooden Ox and Gliding Horse —picturesque names of Zhuge Liang's (诸葛亮) army service wheelbarrows
木偶　mù'ǒu　① puppet; marionette ② wooden image; carved figure: 像～地站着 stand as still as a carved figure
木偶片　mù'ǒupiàn　puppet film
木偶戏　mù'ǒuxì　(also 木偶剧 mù'ǒujù) puppet show; puppet play
木排　mùpái　raft
木片　mùpiàn　wood chip
木器　mùqì　wooden furniture; wooden articles
木琴　mùqín　*mus.* xylophone
木然　mùrán　stupefied: 神情～ look stupefied
木人石心　mùrén-shíxīn　a body of wood and a heart of stone—insusceptible; unfeeling
木石　mùshí　a lifeless thing; a senseless being: ～心肠 heartless; unfeeling
木梳　mùshū　wooden comb
木薯　mùshǔ　*bot.* cassava
木栓　mùshuān　*bot.* phellem; cork
木丝　mùsī　wood wool
木丝板　mùsībǎn　*archit.* wood wool board
木炭　mùtàn　charcoal
木炭画　mùtànhuà　charcoal drawing
木通　mùtōng　*bot.* akebi
木头木脑　mùtóumùnǎo　wooden-headed; dull-witted

木头 mùtou *inf.* wood; log; timber: 一块～ a piece of wood / ～桌子 a wooden table

木头人儿 mùtourénr woodenhead; blockhead; slow coach

木屋 mùwū log cabin

木犀 mùxī (also 木樨 mùxī) ① *bot.* sweet-scented osmanthus ② egg beaten and then cooked: ～饭 fried rice with scrambled eggs / ～肉 pork fried with scrambled eggs / ～汤 eggdrop soup

木锨 mùxiān wooden winnowing spade

木星 Mùxīng Jupiter

木已成舟 mù yǐ chéng zhōu the wood is already made into a boat—what is done cannot be undone

木偶 mùyǒng *archaeol.* wooden figurine (used as a burial object)

木鱼 mùyú wooden fish (a percussion instrument made of a hollow wooden block, originally used by Buddhist priests to beat rhythm when chanting scriptures)

木贼 mùzéi *bot.* scouring rush

木质部 mùzhìbù *bot.* xylem

目 mù ①eye: 注目 zhùmù ② *formal* look; regard: ～为奇迹 regard as a miracle ③ item: 项目 xiàngmù ④ *biol.* order: 亚～ suborder ⑤ a list of things; catalogue; table of contents: 书目 shūmù

目标 mùbiāo ① objective; target: 发现～ find the target / 攻击～ target (or objective) of attack / 军事～ military objective; military target ② goal; aim; objective: 共同～ a common goal (or objective) / 我的生活～是当一名小提琴手。 My goal in life is to be a violinist.

目不见睫 mù bù jiàn jié the eye can't see its lashes—lack self-knowledge

目不交睫 mù bù jiāo jié not sleep a wink

目不窥园 mù bù kuī yuán never take a peep into the garden—bury oneself in one's studies

目不忍睹 mù bùrěn dǔ cannot bear to look at

目不识丁 mù bù shí dīng not know one's ABC; be totally illiterate

目不暇接 mù bù xiá jiē (also 目不暇给 mù bù xiá jǐ) the eye cannot take it all in; too many things for the eye to take in

目不邪视 mù bù xié shì not cast sidelong glances—① be upright and proper ②cold and detatched; unconcerned; indifferent

目不斜视 mù bù xié shì not look sideways; refuse to be distracted

目不转睛 mù bù zhuǎn jīng look with fixed gaze; regard with rapt attention: 歌唱演员们～地望着指挥。The singers kept their eyes fixed on the conductor. / 雷达兵～地注视着荧光屏。The radarman's eyes were glued to the screen.

目测 mùcè range estimation

目次 mùcì table of contents; contents

目瞪口呆 mùdèng-kǒudāi gaping; dumbstruck; stupefied: 吓得～ be struck dumb with fear

目的 mùdì purpose; aim; goal; objective; end: ～明确 have a definite purpose / ～与手段 ends and means / 怀着不可告人的～ harbour evil intentions; have ulterior motives / 共产党的最终～是实现共产主义。The ultimate aim of the Communist Party is the realization of communism. / 我们的～一定能够达到。Our goal can certainly be attained.

目的地 mùdìdì destination

目的港 mùdìgǎng port of destination

目的论 mùdìlùn *philos.* teleology

目睹 mùdǔ see with one's own eyes; witness: 整个事件我都亲眼～。 I saw the incident from beginning to end with my own eyes.

目光 mùguāng ① sight; vision; view: ～锐利 sharpeyed; sharp-sighted / ～远大 farsighted; farseeing ② gaze; look: ～炯炯 flashing eyes / 两人的～碰到一起。 Their eyes met.

目光短浅 mùguāng duǎnqiǎn short-sighted

目光如豆 mùguāng rú dòu vision as narrow as a bean—of narrow vision; short-sighted

目光如炬 mùguāng rú jù ① eyes blazing like torches—blazing with anger ②looking ahead with wisdom; far-sighted

目击 mùjī see with one's own eyes; witness: ～其事 witness the event / ～者 eyewitness; witness

目见 mùjiàn see for oneself: 耳闻不如目见 ěrwén bùrú mùjiàn

目镜 mùjìng *phys.* eyepiece; ocular

目空一切 mù kōng yīqiè consider everybody and everything beneath one's notice; be supercilious

目力 mùlì same as 视力 shìlì

目录 mùlù ① catalogue; list: 图书～ library catalogue / 出口商品～ a catalogue of export commodities; export list ② table of contents; contents

目录学 mùlùxué bibliography (as a science)

目迷五色 mù mí wǔsè dazzled by a riot of colour—bewildered by a complicated situation

目前 mùqián at present; at the moment: ～形势 the present (or current) situation / ～的生产能力 existing production capacity / 到～为止 up till the present moment; up till now; so far; to date / ～我还不能给你肯定的答复。 I can't give you a definite answer at the moment.

目视飞行 mùshì fēixíng *aviation* visual flight

目送 mùsòng follow sb. with one's eyes; watch sb. go; gaze after: 她～着他的背影远去。 She gazed affectionately after his receding figure.

目无法纪 mù wú fǎjì disregard (or flout) law and discipline; show contempt for the law

目无全牛 mù wú quánniú (of an experienced butcher) see an ox not as whole (but only as parts to be cut)—be supremely skilled

目无余子 mù wú yúzǐ as if other people didn't exist; supercilious

目无组织 mù wú zǔzhī disregard organizational discipline; defy the leadership of one's organization

目无尊长 mù wú zūnzhǎng with no regard for one's elders and betters

目下 mùxià at present; now: ～较忙, 过几天再来看你。 I'm busy at the moment. I'll see you again in a couple of days.

目眩 mùxuàn dizzy; dazzled: 灯光强烈, 令人～。 The light is too dazzling.

目语 mùyǔ communicate with the eyes

目指气使 mùzhǐ-qìshǐ order people about by a glare; be insufferably arrogant

目中无人 mù zhōng wú rén consider everyone beneath one's notice; be supercilious; be overweening: 你看她神气的, 简直是～。 Just look at the airs she's giving herself, looking down her nose at everybody.

仫 mù see below

仫佬族 Mùlǎozú the Mulam (Mulao) nationality, or the Mulams (Mulaos), inhabiting the Guangxi Zhuang Autonomous Region

沐 mù wash one's hair: 栉风沐雨 zhìfēng-mùyǔ

沐猴而冠 mùhóu ér guàn a monkey with a hat on—a worthless person in imposing attire

沐雨栉风 mùyǔ-zhìfēng same as 栉风沐雨 zhìfēng-mùyǔ

沐浴 mùyù ① have (or take) a bath; bathe; im-

merse: 百里油田～着金色的朝晖。The vast oilfield was bathed in the golden rays of the morning sun. ╱ 他们～在青春的欢乐里。They revelled in the joy of youth.

苜 mù see below

苜蓿 mùxu *bot.* lucerne; alfalfa

牧 mù tend (sheep, cattle, etc.); herd: ～马 herd horses ╱ ～羊 tend sheep

牧草 mùcǎo herbage; forage grass

牧场 mùchǎng (also 牧地 mùdì) grazing land; pastureland; pasture

牧放 mùfàng herd; tend; put out to pasture

牧歌 mùgē ① pastoral song; pastoral ② *mus.* madrigal

牧工 mùgōng hired herdsman

牧马人 mùmǎrén herdsman (of horses)

牧民 mùmín herdsman

牧区 mùqū ① pastureland; pasture ② pastoral area

牧犬 mùquǎn shepherd dog; sheep dog

牧人 mùrén herdsman

牧师 mùshī *Christianity* pastor; minister; clergyman

牧竖 mùshù *formal* shepherd boy; buffalo boy

牧童 mùtóng shepherd boy; buffalo boy

牧畜 mùxù same as 畜牧 xùmù

牧羊人 mùyángrén shepherd

牧业 mùyè animal (or livestock) husbandry; stock raising; livestock farming

牧主 mùzhǔ herd owner (who owns livestock and pastures and hires herdsmen)

钼 mù *chem.* molybdenum (Mo)

钼钢 mùgāng molybdenum steel

钼酸 mùsuān molybdic acid

钼酸铵 mùsuān'ǎn ammonium molybdate

募 mù ① raise; collect: ～款 raise money (or fund) ② enlist; recruit: ～兵 recruit soldiers

募兵制 mùbīngzhì mercenary system

募股 mùgǔ raise capital by floating shares

募化 mùhuà (of Buddhist monks or Taoist priests) collect alms

募集 mùjí raise; collect: ～资金 raise a fund

募捐 mùjuān solicit contributions; collect donations

墓 mù grave; tomb; mausoleum: 马克思～ Marx's grave ╱ 列宁～ the Lenin Mausoleum

墓碑 mùbēi (also 墓表 mùbiǎo) tombstone; gravestone

墓道 mùdào ① path leading to a grave; tomb passage ② aisle leading to the coffin chamber of an ancient tomb

墓地 mùdì graveyard; burial ground; cemetery

墓木已拱 mùmù yǐ gǒng the trees at the grave can fill an arm-span now —the man is dead and gone

墓室 mùshì coffin chamber

墓穴 mùxué coffin pit; open grave

墓茔 mùyíng same as 坟茔 fényíng

墓园 mùyuán same as 陵园 língyuán

墓葬 mùzàng *archaeol.* grave: ～群 graves

墓志 mùzhì inscription on the memorial tablet within a tomb

墓志铭 mùzhìmíng inscription on the memorial tablet within a tomb; epitaph: 韩愈的《柳子厚～》 Han Yu's "Inscription on Liu Zihou's Tomb Tablet" (*or* "Epitaph for Liu Zihou")

幕 mù ① tent: 帐幕 zhàngmù ② curtain; screen: ～启。The curtain rises. ╱ ～落。The curtain falls. *or* Curtain. ③ act (of a play): 第一～ the first act; Act 1 ╱

一出三～五场的话剧 a play in three acts and five scenes ╱ 长征时的情景一～一～地重现在我眼前。Scene after scene of the Long March reappeared before my eyes. ④ office of a commanding general in ancient China: 幕府 mùfǔ

幕宾 mùbīn (also 幕客 mùkè) ① same as 幕僚 mùliáo ② same as 幕友 mùyǒu

幕布 mùbù ① (theatre) curtain ② (cinema) screen

幕府 mùfǔ office of a commanding general in ancient China

幕后 mùhòu behind the scenes; backstage: ～操纵 pull strings (or wires) behind the scenes ╱ ～活动 behind-the-scenes activities; backstage manoeuvring ╱ ～交易 behind-the-scenes deal; backstage deal ╱ ～人物 wire-puller; backstage manipulator

幕间休息 mùjiān xiūxi interval (in a play, etc.); intermission

幕僚 mùliáo ① aides and staff ② assistant to a ranking official or general in old China

幕天席地 mùtiān-xídì have the sky as one's tent and the earth as one's mat—① take one's ease out in the open air ② have great breadth of view

幕友 mùyǒu a private assistant attending to legal, fiscal or secretarial duties in a local *yamen;* private adviser

睦 mù peaceful; harmonious: 婆媳不～ mother-in-law and daughter-in-law not getting along well

睦邻 mùlín good-neighbourliness: ～关系 good-neighbourly relations ╱ ～政策 good-neighbour policy

慕 mù admire; yearn for: 爱慕 àimù

慕光性 mùguāngxìng same as 趋光性 qūguāngxìng

慕名 mùmíng out of admiration for a famous person

慕尼黑 Mùníhēi Munich

慕尼黑协定 Mùníhēi Xiédìng the Munich Agreement (1938)

慕尼黑阴谋 Mùníhēi yīnmóu the Munich conspiracy

慕容 Mùróng a two-character surname

暮 mù ① dusk; evening; sunset: 薄暮 bómù ② towards the end; late: 岁暮 suìmù

暮霭 mù'ǎi evening mist: 晚霞渐渐暗淡，～沉沉，野旷天低。The sunset grew darker and darker; the evening mist became heavier. The vast fields were dim as far as the eye could see.

暮齿 mùchǐ *formal* old age; one's later (or remaining) years

暮春 mùchūn late spring (the third month of the lunar year)

暮鼓晨钟 mùgǔ-chénzhōng the evening drum and the morning bell (in a monastery)—exhortations to virtue and purity

暮景 mùjǐng ① sunset scene; twilight ② life in old age; evening of one's life

暮年 mùnián declining years; old age; evening of one's life

暮气 mùqì lethargy; apathy

暮气沉沉 mùqì chénchén lethargic; apathetic; lifeless

暮秋 mùqiū late autumn (the ninth month of the lunar year)

暮色 mùsè dusk; twilight; gloaming

暮色苍茫 mùsè cāngmáng deepening dusk; spreading shades of dusk: ～看劲松，乱云飞渡仍从容。(毛泽东) Amid the growing shades of dusk stand sturdy pines, Riotous clouds sweep past, swift and tranquil.

暮世 mùshì modern times

暮岁 mùsuì ① towards the end of the year ② old age; one's later (or remaining) years

暮云春树 mùyún-chūnshù sunset clouds and spring trees—longings for a faraway friend (from Du Fu's 杜甫 lines reminiscing about Li Bai 李白: 渭北春天树, 江东日暮云。 Spring trees in Weibei [where Du was], Sunset clouds over Jingdong [where Li was].)

穆 mù ①solemn; reverent: 肃穆 sùmù ② (Mù) a surname

穆罕默德 Mùhǎnmòdé *Islam* Mohammed (c. 570–632), founder of Islam

穆民 mùmín believers in Islam

穆斯林 Mùsīlín Moslem; Muslim

N

ń

嗯(唔)

ń   a variant pronunciation for 嗯 ńg

ň

嗯(吽)

ň   a variant pronunciation for 嗯 ňg

ǹ

嗯(呃)

ǹ   a variant pronunciation for 嗯 ǹg

nā

那

Nā   a surname ——see also nà

南

nā   see below ——see also nán

南无 nāmó *Buddhism* (expressing one's devotion to Buddha or Buddhism): ～阿弥陀佛! I devote myself to *Amitabha!*

ná

拿(拏)

ná   ① hold; take: ～去。Take it. / ～来。Bring it here. / 她手里～着一把扇子。 She's holding a fan in her hand. / 把这些东西～走。Take these things away. / 不～枪的敌人 enemies without guns ② seize; capture: ～下敌人的碉堡 capture the enemy's blockhouse / 他们～住三个匪徒。They captured three bandits. ③ have a firm grasp of; be able to do; be sure of: ～不准 not be sure; feel uncertain / 这事你～得稳吗? Are you sure of it? ④ put sb. in a difficult position: 这件事你～不住人。I don't think you can make things difficult by not doing the job. / 他说不干了，想～我一把。He said he wasn't going to do it and tried to put me in an awkward position. ⑤ (of a chemical agent, etc.) turn sth. bad: 这块木头让药水～白了。The chemical agent has bleached the wooden block. ⑥ *prep. inf.* by means of; with; by: ～尺量 measure with a ruler / ～事实证明 prove with facts; cite facts to prove / ～这个标准去衡量 judge by this standard / ～几句话来概括 to sum up in a few words / 我们不能～原则作交易。We cannot barter away our principles. / 你～什么谢我? How would you show your gratitude to me? ⑦ *prep. inf.* (used in the same way as 把² bǎ): 不能～工作当儿戏。You shouldn't treat your work as a trifling matter. / 她要是一定要走, 你又能～她怎么样? If she insists

on leaving, what can you do about it? / 别～我开玩笑。Don't make fun of me. *or* Don't crack jokes at my expense. / 我简直～他没办法。I simply can't do anything with him. ⑧ *prep. inf.* (used with 来说, 来讲, 来看, etc.) as regards; as to: ～产品质量来讲 as to the quality of the products / ～英语水平来看, 她比组里其他人要强些。So far as English proficiency goes, she is better than the other members of the group.

拿办 nábàn   apprehend and punish by law; arrest and bring to justice

拿不出去 nábuchūqù (also 拿不出手 nábuchūshǒu) not be presentable: 我这笔字～。My handwriting is not presentable.

拿不起来 nábuqǐlái   cannot manage: 这样的工作他～。He cannot manage this kind of work.

拿大 nádà   *dial.* give oneself airs; put on airs

拿大顶 ná dàdǐng (also 拿顶 nádǐng) stand on one's hands

拿大头 ná dàtóu   ① take the lion's share ② take sb. for a sucker; cheat sb. out of his money; fleece sb.: 我买这台录音机让人～了。I've been had over this recorder I've bought.

拿刀动杖 nádāo-dòngzhàng take up swords and cudgels; start a fight with weapons

拿得起, 放得下 nádeqǐ, fàngdexià can take it up or put it down—be adaptable to circumstances

拿得起来 nádeqǐlái   can manage; can do: 样样农活她都～。She can do every kind of farm work.

拿定主意 ná dìng zhǔyì   make up one's mind: 我还没～。I haven't made up my mind yet. / 她一直拿不定主意。She's been wavering all along.

拿获 náhuò   apprehend (a criminal): 凶手被当场～。The murderer was seized on the spot (*or* was caught red-handed).

拿架子 ná jiàzi   put on airs; assume great airs; throw one's weight around: 你拿什么架子? 没有你, 别人也干得了。Who do you think you are to put on such airs? They can manage perfectly well without you.

拿捏 nánie   *dial.*   ① be affectedly bashful: 有话快说, ～个什么劲儿! Out with it. Why be so shy and hesitant? ② make things difficult for; put pressure on; threaten: 我就做错过那么一次, 你就老用这个来～我。That's the only mistake I made and you are always using it against me.

拿腔拿调 náqiāng-nádiào   speak with an affected tone of voice

拿腔作势 náqiāng-zuòshì (also 拿班作势 nábān-zuòshì) be affected or pretentious; act affectedly; strike a pose

拿乔 náqiáo   strike a pose to impress people

拿权 náquán   wield power; be in the saddle

拿人 nárén   make things difficult for others; raise difficulties: 你这不是故意～吗? Aren't you being difficult on purpose?

拿事 náshì   have the power to do sth. or to decide what to do: 父母都出门了, 家里连个～的人也没有。The parents are away; no one in the family can make a decision.

拿手 náshǒu　adept; expert; good at: 剪纸她很～。 She's good at making paper-cuts. / ～菜 a cook's best dishes; dishes one is particularly good at making

拿手好戏 náshǒu hǎoxì　① the play that an actor does best: 《贵妃醉酒》是她的～。 *The Drunken Beauty* was the play she did best. ② one's speciality; one's forte: 游泳是她的～。 Swimming is her forte. / 挑拨离间是他的～。 He makes a speciality of sowing discord. *or* He is a past master at sowing discord.

拿糖 nátáng　*dial.*　strike a pose to impress people

拿问 náwèn　*old*　detain for interrogation

拿印把子 ná yìnbàzi　(also 拿印把儿 náyìnbàr) hold the seal of authority—be in an important position; be in power

拿着鸡毛当令箭 názhe jīmáo dàng lìngjiàn　take a chicken feather for a warrant to issue orders—treat one's superior's casual remark as an order and make a big fuss about it

拿主意 ná zhǔyi　make a decision; decide: 究竟去不去, 你自己～吧。 You'd better decide for yourself whether to go or not.

拿总儿 názǒngr　*inf.*　exercise overall control

锛
nǎ　*chem.*　neptunium (Np)

nǎ

哪[1] (那)
nǎ　① (used in questions) which; what: 我们这里有两位姓张的, 您要找的是～一位? We've got two Zhangs here. Which one do you want to see? / 你学的是～国语言? What foreign language are you studying? ② (used in statements to indicate sth. indefinite) whichever; any that: ～天有空就请过来。 Come over any time you are free. / 你最喜欢～件就拿～件。 Take whichever you like best.

哪[2] (那)
nǎ　*adv.*　(used in rhetorical questions to express negation): 没有革命前辈的流血牺牲, ～有今天的幸福生活? Without the sacrifices of the revolutionaries of the older generation, how could we have such a happy life today? / ～有这样的事? Nothing of the sort (*or* kind) !
──see also na; né

哪儿 nǎr　*inf.*　① where: 他上～去啦? Where has he gone? / 这本书, 你是～捡来的? Where did you pick up this book? ② wherever; anywhere: 昨天你没有上～去过吗? Did you go anywhere yesterday? / ～需要, 我就上～去。 I'll go wherever I'm needed. / 他是～都找不到他。 He is nowhere to be found. ③ (used in rhetorical questions to express negation): 我～知道他不吃牛肉。 How was I to know he didn't eat beef? / 这么多的词儿, 我～记得住。 How could I remember all those words?

哪儿的话 nǎrdehuà　*pol.*　what are you saying; you shouldn't say that: 太麻烦您了。——～。 Sorry to have caused you so much trouble. —You shouldn't say that.

哪个 nǎge　① which: 你们是～班的? Which class are you in? ② *dial.*　who: ～在打电话? Who's using the telephone?

哪会儿 nǎhuìr　(also 哪会子 nǎhuìzi) *adv.*　① when: 你这篇文章～才能脱稿? When can you get the draft ready? / 你是～从广州回来的? When did you get back from Guangzhou? ② whenever; any time: 你要～来就～来。 Come any time you like. / 趁天好把毛料衣服统统拿出去晒晒, 说不定～天要变。 Put all your woollen clothes out to air when it's fine. Who knows, the weather may change any time.

哪里 nǎli　① where: 你到～去? Where are you going? /

你是～人? Where are you from? / 你～不舒服? What is the trouble with you? *or* Where do you feel the pain? ② wherever; where: ～最艰苦就在～干 go and work where the work is hardest / ～有压迫, ～就有反抗。 Where there is oppression, there is resistance. ③ (used in rhetorical questions to express negation): 我～知道他会改变主意的? How could I know that he should change his mind? ④ *hum.*　(used as a polite reply to a compliment): 你对我们帮助很大。——～, ～。 You gave us a lot of help. —It was nothing. / 你的英语说得真好。——～, ～。 You speak very good English. —I'm flattered.

哪门子 nǎménzi　*dial.*　(used to emphasize a rhetorical question): 好好儿的, 你哭～? Everything is all right. What on earth are you crying for? / 他说的是～事呀! What the hell is he talking about?

哪能 nǎnéng　(used in rhetorical questions to express negation) how can; how could: 我～干那种缺德事儿呢。 How could I play that sort of mean trick? It's the last thing I would do in the world ! / 你可别涮我。——～呢? Don't you fool me ! —How could I? / 你答应了的事～反悔? How can you go back on your promise?

哪怕 nǎpà　*conj.*　even; even if; even though; no matter how: ～天气不好也要去。 We'll go even if it rains. / ～是一粒米也不应该浪费。 We should not waste even a single grain of rice. / ～是再大的困难我们也能克服。 However great the difficulties may be, we can overcome them.

哪些 nǎxiē　which (ones); who; what: ～是你的? Which ones are yours? / ～人出席这次会议? Who will attend the meeting? / 你们讨论了～问题? What problems did you discuss? / 你到过～地方? What places have you been to?

哪样 nǎyàng　① what kind; what: 你要～颜色的? What colour do you want? ② whatever kind; whatever: 我们这儿的毛线颜色齐全, 你要～的就有～的。 We have knitting wool in a variety of colours. You can have whatever colour you want.

哪知 nǎzhī　who would have thought: ～他会出这样的丑? Who would have thought he could make such a fool of himself?

nà

那[1]
nà　that: ～老头儿 that old man / ～时候 at that time / ～两棵树 those two trees / ～是我的错。 That was my fault. / ～是谁? Who is that? / ～是1958年的事。 That was in 1958. / 我们说这道～的, 不知不觉已到凌晨。 We talked about this and that, and without our realizing it, it was almost dawn.

那[2]
nà　*conj.*　then; in that case: 你要想跟我们一块走, ～就得快点。 If you're coming with us, you must hurry. / ～我们就不再等了。 In that case, we won't wait any longer.
──see also Nà

那儿 nàr　*inf.*　① same as 那里 nàli ② (used after 打, 从, 由) that time; then: 打～起, 她就用心念书了。 She's been studying hard since then.

那程子 nàchéngzi　*dial.*　those days; that period: ～我很忙, 没有工夫来看你。 I was terribly busy those days and couldn't find time to come to see you.

那达慕 nàdámù　Nadam Fair, a Mongolian traditional fair

那当儿 nàdāngr　at that time; in those days

那个 nàge　① that (one): ～孩子 that child / ～根本谈不到。 That's out of the question. / ～你甭担心。 Don't

you worry about that. ② *inf.* (used before a verb or adjective with exclamatory force): 瞧他们干得～欢哪! See how they're throwing themselves into their work! / 他～高兴劲儿啊，就别提了! There is no need to tell how happy he was. ③ *inf.* (used euphemistically as a predicative adjective): 你刚才的脾气也太～了。The way you lost your temper was a little—you know what I mean.

那会儿 nàhuìr (also 那会子 nàhuìzi) *inf.* at that time; then: 到～钢的产量将大大增加。By that time the steel output will have greatly increased. / ～我们还是新手。At that time we were greenhorns. / 傍晚～下了一阵小雨。Toward evening, there came a drizzly rain.

那里 nàli that place; there: 我刚从～回来。I've just come from there. *or* I've just been there. / ～的气候怎么样? What's the weather like there? / ～出产香蕉。That place abounds in bananas. / 这星期天，老张～有个聚会。There'll be a get-together at Lao Zhang's place this coming Sunday.

那么 nàme (also 那末 nàme) ① *adv.* like that; in that way; so: 你不该～做。You shouldn't have done that. *or* You oughtn't to have acted the way you did. / 她不好意思～说。It embarrassed her to say that. / 你～喜欢它，就送给你作个纪念吧。As you like it so much, take it as a keepsake. / 说说容易，做起来可并不～容易。It's easier said than done. / 问题没有他所想像的～复杂。The problem is not as complicated as he imagined. ② (used before numerals to indicate approximation) a-bout; or so: 估计得走～三、四个钟头才能到。I think it will take three or four hours to get there. / 再有～三几十个麻袋就够了。Another thirty sacks or so will probably be enough. ③ *conj.* (used to connect a clause expressing a logical consequence to a conditional clause) then; in that case: 既然这样不行，～你打算怎么办呢? Since that's impossible, what are you going to do? / 如果你们都要去，～我就一个人留下吧。If you all want to go, then I'll stay home alone.

那么点儿 nàmediǎnr so little; so few: ～活儿，一天就可以干完了。We can finish that little bit of work in a day. / ～书，一个箱子就装下了。Those few books can be packed in one box.

那么些 nàmexiē so much; so many: 她一个人照料～孩子，真不容易。She looks after all those kids by herself. That's not so easy. / ～书，一个星期哪儿看得完? So many books! How can I finish them all in just a week?

那么着 nàmezhe do that; do so: 他～是为了集体。He did it for the collective. / 你再～，我可要恼了。If you do that again, I'll get angry. / 你帮病人翻个身，～他也许会舒服点儿。If you help the patient to turn over, he may feel a bit better.

那摩温 nàmówēn *old* number one; foreman

那时 nàshí at that time; then; in those days: ～正是冬天。It was wintertime then. / ～是旧社会，哪有咱穷人说话的地方? In the old society where could we poor people dare to open our mouths?

那些 nàxiē those: ～苹果 those apples / ～饭店都是最近几年盖的。Those hotels were all built in recent years. / 奶奶爱把～事儿讲给孩子们听。Grandma liked telling those stories to the kids.

那样 nàyàng of that kind; like that; such; so: 他不像你～仔细。He's not so careful as you are. / ～儿也好，先试试再说。All right, let's try it out. / 这点小事你怎么就急得～儿了? Why let such trifles worry you so much? / 别这样～的了，你还是亲自去一趟的好。No more shilly-shallying. Better go and see to it yourself.

那早晚 nàzǎowǎn (also 那咱 nàzan) *inf.* at that time; then

那阵儿 nàzhènr (also 那阵子 nàzhènzi) *inf.* during that period (of time); in those days; then: 大伙儿开

会～, 你上哪儿去了? Where were you when we were all at the meeting? / ～, 天天下雨。There was an unbroken spell of wet weather those days.

呐 nà see below

呐喊 nàhǎn shout loudly; cry out: ～助威 shout encouragement; cheer

纳[1] nà ① receive; admit: 闭门不～ refuse to admit; shut sb. out ② accept: 采纳 cǎinà ③ enjoy: 纳凉 nàliáng ④ pay; offer: 交纳 jiāonà / 纳税 nàshuì

纳[2] nà sew close stitches (over a patch, etc.): ～鞋底子 stitch soles (of cloth shoes)

纳彩 nàcǎi (of the bridegroom-to-be's family) present gifts to the girl's family at time of betrothal

纳粹 Nàcuì Nazi: ～分子 Nazi

纳粹主义 Nàcuìzhǔyì Nazism

纳呆 nàdāi *Chin. med.* indigestion and loss of appetite

纳福 nàfú (usu. of elderly people) enjoy a life of ease and comfort

纳贡 nàgòng pay tribute (to a suzerain or emperor)

纳罕 nàhǎn be surprised; marvel: 朋友们都～我为什么近来沉默寡言。My friends wondered why I had been so reticent recently.

纳贿 nàhuì ① take bribes ② offer bribes

纳谏 nàjiàn *formal* (of a sovereign, an elder or superior) accept an admonition; accept advice

纳款 nàkuǎn *formal* surrender and pledge allegiance

纳凉 nàliáng enjoy the cool (in the open air)

纳闷儿 nàmènr *inf.* feel puzzled; be perplexed; wonder: 他怎么还没给我回电呢? 真叫人～。I wonder why he hasn't wired back yet. / 家里一个人也没有, 他心里很～。He was surprised to find nobody at home.

纳米比亚 Nàmǐbǐyà Namibia

纳聘 nàpìn same as 纳彩 nàcǎi

纳妾 nàqiè (also 纳小 nàxiǎo) take a concubine

纳入 nàrù bring (*or* channel) into: ～正轨 put sth. on the right course / ～国家计划 bring sth. into line with the state plan / 把整个国民经济～有计划、按比例、高速度发展的社会主义轨道 bring the country's entire economy into the orbit of planned, proportionate and high-speed socialist development

纳纱制品 nàshā zhìpǐn *arts & crafts* petit-point articles

纳税 nàshuì pay taxes: ～人 taxpayer / ～年度 tax year / ～凭证 tax payment receipt

纳头 nàtóu *old* bow one's head (in greeting): ～便拜 kneel down and kowtow at once

纳西族 Nàxīzú the Naxi (Nahsi) nationality, or the Naxis (Nahsis), inhabiting Yunnan Province

纳降 nàxiáng accept the enemy's surrender

纳新 nàxīn take in the fresh—take in new Party members: ～对象 a candidate for Party membership; prospective Party member

肭 nà see 腽肭 wànà; 腽肭兽 wànàshòu

衲 nà ① patch up ② patchwork vestment worn by a Buddhist monk

钠 nà *chem.* sodium (Na)

钠长石 nàchángshí albite (a mineral)

钠钙玻璃 nàgàibōli (also 钠玻璃 nàbōli) soda-lime glass

娜 nà used in feminine names ——see also nuó

捺 nà ① press down; restrain: ～着性子 control one's temper / 勉强～住心头的怒火 barely manage to

restrain one's anger ② right-falling stroke (in Chinese characters)

na

哪（呐） na *part.* (used in the same way as 啊 a, only after words ending with consonant n): 谢谢您～! Thank you! / 我没留神～! I wasn't noticing. / 加油干～! Speed up! *or* Come on! ——see also nǎ; né

nǎi

乃（迺、廼） nǎi *formal* ① be: 此～我国特产。This is a special product of China. / 失败～成功之母。Failure is the mother of success. ② so; therefore: 因山势高峻,～在山腰休息片时。It was a steep climb, so we rested for a while halfway up the hill. ③ only then: 惟虚心～能进步。You can make progress only if you are modest. / 今～知之。I didn't know it until now. ④ you; your: ～父 your father

乃尔 nǎi'ěr *formal* like this; to such an extent: 何其相似乃尔 héqí xiāngsì nǎi'ěr

乃是 nǎishì *formal* be: 人民群众～真正的英雄。The masses of the people are the true heroes.

乃至 nǎizhì *formal* and even: 中国革命的胜利, 对全中国～全世界都具有伟大的历史意义。The victory of the Chinese revolution had great historical significance for China and the world.

芋 nǎi see 芋芋 yùnǎi

奶（嬭） nǎi ① breasts (of a female mammal); mammae ② milk ③ suckle; breast-feed: ～孩子 suckle (*or* breast-feed) a baby / 他是奶妈～大的。He was breast-fed by a wet nurse.

奶茶 nǎichá tea with milk

奶疮 nǎichuāng common name for 乳腺炎 rǔxiànyán

奶粉 nǎifěn milk powder; powdered milk; dried milk: 冲一杯～ make a cup of milk with milk powder

奶糕 nǎigāo a baby food made of rice-flour, sugar, etc.

奶积 nǎijī *Chin. med.* indigestion of suckling babies due to improper breast-feeding

奶酒 nǎijiǔ same as 奶子酒 nǎizijiǔ

奶酪 nǎilào cheese

奶妈 nǎimā (also 奶母 nǎimǔ) wet nurse

奶毛 nǎimáo foetal hair

奶名 nǎimíng a child's pet name; infant name

奶奶 nǎinai *inf.* ① (paternal) grandmother; grandma ② a respectful form of address for an old woman ③ *dial.* young mistress of the house

奶娘 nǎiniáng *dial.* wet nurse

奶牛 nǎiniú milch cow; milk cow; cow

奶皮 nǎipí skin formed on boiled milk

奶品 nǎipǐn milk products; dairy products

奶瓶 nǎipíng feeding bottle; nursing bottle; (baby's) bottle

奶水 nǎishuǐ *inf.* milk: 她～足不足? Has she got enough milk to nurse her baby?

奶糖 nǎitáng toffee

奶头 nǎitóu *inf.* ① nipple; teat ② nipple (of a feeding bottle)

奶牙 nǎiyá common name for 乳齿 rǔchǐ

奶羊 nǎiyáng milch goat

奶油 nǎiyóu cream: ～分离器 cream separator

奶罩 nǎizhào brassiere; bra

奶汁 nǎizhī milk

奶子 nǎizi ① *inf.* milk ② *dial.* breasts ③ *dial.* wet nurse

奶子酒 nǎizijiǔ fermented (cow's or mare's) milk (used by Mongolians as an alcoholic drink)

奶嘴 nǎizuǐ nipple (of a feeding bottle)

氖 nǎi *chem.* neon (Ne)

氖灯 nǎidēng neon lamp; neon light; neon

氖管 nǎiguǎn neon tube

氖气 nǎiqì common name for 氖 nǎi

哪（那） nǎi a variant pronunciation for 哪 nǎ in colloquial speech

nài

奈 nài ① what; how; but: ～援军不至 but unfortunately the reinforcements didn't arrive ② bear; endure: ～不过 unable to bear it

奈何 nàihé .① (used in a rhetorical question) what alternative is there; what's to be done: 徒唤～ utter bootless cries / 没～ have no way out; have no choice; there is no alternative ② *formal* how; why: 民不畏死, 奈何以死惧之 mín bù wèi sǐ, nàihé yǐ sǐ jù zhī ③ do sth. to (a person); cope with; deal with: 其奈我何? What can they do to me? / 谁也～他不得。Nobody could do anything against him.

柰 nài a kind of apple

柰子 nàizi a kind of apple

耐 nài be able to bear or endure: ～穿 can stand wear and tear; be endurable / 这种料子很～洗。This material washes well. / 他再也～不住性子了。He could no longer hold back his anger.

耐波力 nàibōlì seakeeping qualities (of a vessel)

耐烦 nàifán be patient: 显出不～的样子 show signs of impatience / 谁～你的絮叨? Who can bear the endless chatter of yours?

耐寒 nàihán cold-resistant: 耐严寒 resistant to low temperature / ～性 cold resistance; winterhardiness

耐旱 nàihàn drought-enduring

耐旱植物 nàihàn zhíwù drought-enduring plant

耐火 nàihuǒ fire-resistant; refractory: ～衬砌 refractory lining

耐火材料 nàihuǒ cáiliào refractory (material); fireproof material

耐火黏土 nàihuǒ niántǔ (also 耐火土 nàihuǒtǔ) refractory clay

耐火水泥 nàihuǒ shuǐní refractory cement

耐火砖 nàihuǒzhuān refractory brick; firebrick

耐久 nàijiǔ lasting long; durable: ～力 durability; endurance

耐苦 nàikǔ able to endure hardships

耐劳 nàiláo able to stand hard work; able to endure heavy labour

耐力 nàilì endurance; staying power; stamina

耐磨 nàimó (of metals) wear-resisting; wearproof: ～性 wearability; wear resistance

耐磨合金钢 nàimó héjīngāng wear-resisting alloy steel

耐磨硬度 nàimó yìngdù abrasion hardness

耐热 nàirè heat-resisting; heatproof: ～性 heat resistance

耐热合金 nàirè héjīn heat-resisting alloy

耐人寻味 nài rén xúnwèi afford food for thought: 他的话是很～的。What he says gives one much food for

thought. / 语颇隽永，～。The remarks are meaningful and thought-provoking.

耐蚀钢　nàishígāng　corrosion-resisting steel

耐受　nàishòu　bear; stand; endure

耐水作物　nàishuǐ zuòwù　water-tolerant crop

耐酸　nàisuān　acidproof; acid-resisting: ～缸器 acid-proof stoneware / ～混凝土 acid-resisting concrete

耐心　nàixīn　patient: ～等待 wait patiently / 她做任何事都～得很。She does everything patiently. ② patience: 失去～ lose one's patience; be out of patience

耐心烦　nàixīnfán　inf.　patience: 伺候病人没有～可不行。It needs great patience to nurse the sick.

耐性　nàixìng　patience; endurance

耐印力　nàiyìnlì　print.　pressrun

耐用　nàiyòng　durable: ～物品 durable goods; durables / 这种地毯经久～。This kind of carpet is highly resistant to (or stands any amount of) wear and tear.

萘　nài　chem.　naphthalene

萘酚　nàifēn　naphthol

萘乙酸　nàiyǐsuān　methyl α-naphthyl acetate

褦　nài　see below

褦襶　nàidài　formal　(of a person) not sensible; lacking good sense: ～子 a stupid and dull person

鼐　nài　formal　a big tripod

nān

囡（囝）　nān　dial.　child: 男小～ a little boy / 女小～ a little girl

囡囝　nānnān　dial.　little darling (used as a term of endearment for a child or a baby)

nán

男¹　nán　① man; male: ～病房 men's ward / ～护士 male nurse / ～主人公 hero / ～学生 boy student / ～佣人 manservant ② son; boy: 长～ one's eldest son

男²　nán　baron: 男爵 nánjué

男扮女装　nán bàn nǚzhuāng　a man disguised as a woman

男傧相　nánbīnxiàng　best man

男厕所　náncèsuǒ　① men's lavatory (or toilet, room) ② (used to indicate a lavatory) Gentlemen; Men; Gents

男盗女娼　nándào-nǚchāng　behave like thieves and whores; be out-and-out scoundrels: 他满嘴仁义道德，满肚子～。All his talk is of humanity, justice and morality, while in his heart there is nothing but greed and lust.

男低音　nándīyīn　mus.　bass

男儿　nán'ér　man: 好～ a fine man / ～本色 the manliness of a man

男方　nánfāng　the bridegroom's or husband's side

男高音　nángāoyīn　mus.　tenor

男耕女织　nángēng-nǚzhī　men plough the fields and women weave——an agricultural community's ideal of peace and order

男孩儿　nánháir　(also 男孩子 nánháizi) ① boy ② son: 她有一个～。She's got a son (or boy).

男家　nánjiā　the bridegroom's or husband's family

男角　nánjué　male role (in a play, film, etc.)

男爵　nánjué　baron

男爵夫人　nánjué fūren　baroness

男男女女　nánnánnǚnǚ　men and women: 全村～都投入了抗旱斗争。The whole village, men and women alike, joined in fighting the drought.

男女　nán-nǚ　① men and women: ～青年 young men and women / ～同工同酬。Men and women get equal pay for equal work. ② dial.　sons and daughters

男女关系　nán-nǚ guānxi　relations between the two sexes: 不正当的～ illicit sexual relations

男女老少　nán-nǚ-lǎo-shào　men and women, old and young

男女平等　nán-nǚ píngděng　equality of men and women; equality of the sexes

男朋友　nánpéngyou　boyfriend

男人　nánrén　① man ② menfolk

男人　nánren　inf.　husband

男生　nánshēng　man student; boy student; schoolboy

男声　nánshēng　mus.　male voice: ～合唱 men's chorus; male chorus

男士　nánshì　humor.　man; gentleman: 下一场舞，由女士们邀请～们跳。The next will be a ladies' invitation dance.

男相　nánxiàng　(of a female) look or behave like a man: 她长得有些～。She looks quite masculine.

男性　nánxìng　① the male sex ② man

男中音　nánzhōngyīn　mus.　baritone

男装　nánzhuāng　menswear; men's clothing: 有些女客穿着～。Some of the women were dressed up in men's clothes.

男子　nánzǐ　man; male: ～单（双）打 men's singles (doubles) / ～团体赛 men's team event

男子汉　nánzǐhàn　a manly man; man: 不像个～ not manly; not man enough / ～，大丈夫，一人做事一人当。A man should have the courage to take the blame for what he does.

南　nán　① south: 城～ south of the city / ～屋 a room with a northern exposure ② (Nán) a surname ——see also nā

南半球　nánbànqiú　the Southern Hemisphere

南梆子　nánbāngzi　a variety of 西皮 xipi tune (in Beijing opera)

南北　nán-běi　① north and south: ～合击 make a joint attack from north and south / 大江～一片丰收景象。Scenes of a bumper harvest greet the eye on both sides of the Changjiang River. ② from north to south: 这个水库～足有五公里。This reservoir extends a good five km. from north to south.

南北朝　Nán-Běi Cháo　the Northern and Southern Dynasties (420-589)

南北对话　Nán-Běi duìhuà　North-South dialogue (i.e. dialogue between developed countries in the Northern Hemisphere and developing countries in the Southern Hemisphere)

南边　nánbian　① south; the southern side ② inf.　the southern part of the country, esp. the area south of the Changjiang River; the South

南部　nánbù　southern part; south: 广州位于广东省～。Guangzhou is in the south of Guangdong Province. / ～非洲 southern Africa

南昌　Nánchāng　Nanchang (capital of Jiangxi Province)

南昌起义　Nánchāng Qǐyì　same as 八一南昌起义 Bā Yī Nánchāng Qǐyì

南朝　Nán Cháo　the Southern Dynasties (420-589), namely, the Song Dynasty (宋, 420-479), the Qi Dynasty (齐, 479-502), the Liang Dynasty (梁, 502-557) and the Chen Dynasty (陈, 557-589)

南斗　nándǒu　the Southern Dipper (common name for 斗 dǒu⑤)

南方 nánfāng ① south ② the southern part of the country, esp. the area south of the Changjiang River; the South: 住在～ live in the South / ～风味 southern style; southern flavour / ～话 southern dialect / ～人 Southerner

南方古猿 nánfāng gǔyuán Australopithecus

南非 nánfēi South Africa

南风 nánfēng south wind

南瓜 nánguā pumpkin; cushaw

南国 nánguó *liter.* the southern part of the country; the South: ～风光 southern scenery / 红豆生～, 春来发几枝。(王维) The red bean grows in southern lands. With spring its slender tendrils twine.

南海 Nánhǎi the Nanhai Sea; the South China Sea

南寒带 nánhándài the south frigid zone

南胡 nánhú another name for *erhu* (二胡), a two-stringed bowed instrument

南回归线 nánhuíguīxiàn the Tropic of Capricorn

南货 nánhuò delicacies from south China (such as dried bamboo shoots, etc.)

南极 nánjí ① the South Pole; the Antarctic Pole ② the south magnetic pole

南极光 nánjíguāng *astron.* southern lights; aurora australis

南极圈 Nánjíquān the Antarctic Circle

南极虾 nánjíxiā another name for 磷虾 línxiā

南极洲 Nánjízhōu the Antarctic Continent; Antarctica

南京 Nánjīng Nanjing (capital of Jiangsu Province)

南京条约 Nánjīng Tiáoyuē the Treaty of Nanjing (1842)

南柯一梦 Nánkē yī mèng a Nanke dream—a fond dream; an illusory joy (from a Tang romance in which a disappointed scholar and military man in one of his drunken stupors dreamed that he became the governor of Nanke and attained great fame and success, only to fall from his pinnacle of power in the end)

南来北往 nánlái-běiwǎng going north and south (said of heavy traffic or a bustling crowd)

南美洲 Nán Měizhōu South America

南面[1] nánmiàn face south—be a ruler (from the fact that the emperor sat facing south when holding court): ～称孤 face south and call oneself the Lonely One—become a ruler ——see also 北面① běimiàn

南面[2] nánmiàn south; the southern side

南南合作 Nán-Nán hézuò South-South cooperation (i. e. cooperation among developing countries in the Southern Hemisphere)

南泥湾精神 Nánníwān jīngshén the spirit of Nanniwan (the spirit of arduous struggle shown by the Eighth Route Armymen who became self-sufficient in food and clothing by reclaiming barren land in Nanniwan, Shaanxi Province, during the War of Resistance Against Japan)

南宁 Nánníng Nanning (capital of Guangxi Zhuang Autonomous Region)

南欧 Nán Ōu Southern Europe

南齐 Nán Qí the Southern Qi Dynasty (479-502), one of the Southern Dynasties

南腔北调 nánqiāng-běidiào (speak with) a mixed accent: 他说话～。He speaks with a mixture of accents.

南曲 nánqǔ ① southern tunes (tunes and melodies popular in the South during the Song, Yuan and Ming Dynasties) ② opera sung in southern tunes

南沙群岛 Nánshā Qúndǎo the Nansha Islands

南式 nánshì (of) southern style: ～糕点 southern-style pastry

南斯拉夫 Nánsīlāfū Yugoslavia

南斯拉夫人 Nánsīlāfūrén Yugoslav

南宋 Nán Sòng the Southern Song Dynasty (1127-1279)

南天极 nántiānjí *astron.* south pole; south celestial pole

南天竹 nántiānzhú *bot.* nandina

南纬 nánwěi south (or southern) latitude

南味 nánwèi of southern taste and flavour or food of southern taste and flavour

南温带 nánwēndài the south temperate zone

南戏 nánxì southern drama (a form of drama that emerged in the Wenzhou area in southern China during the early Southern Song Dynasty)

南下 nánxià go down south: 大军～ large contingents of the army advancing south

南亚 Nán Yà South Asia

南亚次大陆 Nán Yà Cìdàlù the South Asian Subcontinent

南洋 Nányáng ① a general name used towards the end of the Qing Dynasty for the coastal provinces of Jiangsu, Zhejiang, Fujian and Guangdong ② an old name for the Malay Archipelago, the Malay Peninsula and Indonesia or for southeast Asia

南音 nányīn southern music—① a kind of ballad singing accompanied by dulcimer, *pipa* (琵琶), *dongxiao* (洞箫), etc., popular in the Zhujiang (Pearl River) Delta ② a type of classical music popular in Fujian Province

南猿 nányuán another name for 南方古猿 nánfāng gǔyuán

南辕北辙 nányuán-běizhé try to go south by driving the chariot north—act in a way that defeats one's purpose

南乐 nányuè same as 南音 nányīn②

南岳 Nán Yuè the Southern Mountain (another name for 衡山 Mount Heng in Hunan Province) ——see also 五岳 Wǔ Yuè

南诏 Nánzhào Nanzhao (Nanchao), a local regime in ancient China

南针 nánzhēn ① compass ② a guide (to action)

南征北战 nánzhēng-běizhàn fight north and south; campaign all across the country: 这是一支解放战争中经过～的英雄连队。This is a heroic company which fought on many fronts in the Liberation War.

南竹 nánzhú same as 毛竹 máozhú

难 (難)

nán ① difficult; hard; troublesome: 很～想像 it's hard to imagine / 这道题～解。This problem is hard to solve. / 山路～走。Mountain paths are hard to travel. / 说起来容易, 做起来～。It's easier said than done. ② put sb. into a difficult position: 这问题一下子把我～住了。The question put me on the spot. ③ hardly possible: 难免 nánmiǎn / 难说 nánshuō ④ bad; unpleasant: 难吃 nánchī / 难看 nánkàn ——see also nàn

难熬 nán'áo hard to bear: 饥饿～ can hardly bear (or stand) the hunger

难保 nánbǎo ① there is no guarantee; one cannot say for sure; it's hard to say: ～不出问题。There's no guarantee that there won't be any trouble. / 今天～不下雨。You can't say for sure that it won't rain today. ② difficult to preserve, protect, defend, etc.: 地位～。One's position is untenable. / 性命～。One's life is in danger.

难缠 nánchán (of a person) unreasonable and hard to deal with

难产 nánchǎn ① *med.* difficult labour; dystocia ② (of a literary work, plan, etc.) be difficult of fulfilment; be slow in coming

难吃 nánchī taste bad; be unpalatable

难处 nánchǔ hard to get along (or on) with: 他只是脾气暴躁些, 并不～。He's a bit quick-tempered, but not difficult to get along with.

难处 nánchu difficulty; trouble: 他有他的～。He has his

difficulties. / 你有什么～尽管告诉我们。 Please tell us whatever troubles you have.

难当 nándāng ① find it hard to shoulder (a responsibility, etc.): ～重任 can hardly shoulder responsibilities ② hard to endure; unbearable; insufferable: 羞愧～ be mortally ashamed

难倒 nándǎo　daunt; baffle; beat: 这个问题可把我～了。 This problem baffles (or beats) me. / 什么困难也难不倒他。 No difficulty can daunt him.

难道 nándào　*adv.* (used to give force to a rhetorical question): ～你忘了自己的诺言吗? Can you have forgotten your promise? / 这一点儿困难～我们还不能克服吗? Can't we overcome even such small difficulties? / 这～还不明白吗? Isn't this perfectly clear? / ～就罢了不成? How can we let the matter rest here?

难得 nándé ① hard to come by; rare: ～的好机会 a rare chance / 这种草药很～。 This medicinal herb is hard to come by. / 他在一年之内两次打破世界纪录, 是十分～的。 He's performed the rare feat of breaking a world record twice in one year. / 像他这样的人很～。 There aren't many like him. ② seldom; rarely: 我们～见面, 你多待一会儿吧。 Can't you stay a bit longer? We so seldom have a chance to get together. / 她千年～看书。 She seldom, if ever, reads a book.

难点 nándiǎn a difficult point; difficulty; a hard nut to crack

难度 nándù degree of difficulty; difficulty: 这个杂技动作～很大。 This acrobatic feat is extremely difficult.

难分难解 nánfēn-nánjiě same as 难解难分 nánjiě-nánfēn

难割难舍 nángē-nánshě find it hard to part with (a person, place, etc.); be loath to tear oneself away

难怪 nánguài ① no wonder: ～找不到人, 都开会去了。 No wonder you can't find anybody here; they're all away at a meeting. / 你吃得这么多, ～睡不好觉。 It's no wonder you can't sleep well when you eat so much. ② understandable; pardonable: 他不大了解情况, 搞错了也～。 You can hardly blame him for the mistake he made; he didn't know much about the situation.

难关 nánguān difficulty; crisis: 渡过～ tide over a difficulty (or crisis) / 攻克技术～ break down a technical barrier; resolve key technical problems

难过 nánguò ① have a hard time: 父亲失业, 我们日子很～。 We had a hard time when father lost his job. ② feel sorry; feel bad; be grieved: 他听到老师去世的消息, 非常～。 He was deeply grieved to learn that his teacher had died.

难乎为继 nán hū wéi jì hard to carry on or keep up: 尽管我们极为节省, 生活仍～。 Though extremely frugal, we still found it hard to make both ends meet. / 不从根本上改变管理的状况, 工业和其他部门的发展也～。 Without a thorough change in management, it will be difficult for industry and other sectors of our economy to move ahead.

难解难分 nánjiě-nánfēn ① be inextricably involved (in a dispute); be locked together (in a struggle): 两军厮杀, ～。 The two opposing armies are locked in battle. ② be sentimentally attached to each other; can't bear to part

难堪 nánkān ① intolerable; unbearable: ～的话 annoying remarks / 天气闷热～。 It was terribly hot and sultry. ② embarrassed: 感到～ feel very much embarrassed / 处于～的境地 be in an extremely awkward (or miserable) situation

难看 nánkàn ① ugly; unsightly: 这座楼房真～。 This building is ugly. / 他听到这个消息, 脸色变得很～。When he heard the news, his face took on a ghastly expression. ② shameful; embarrassing: 咱们在音乐会上要是演奏不好, 那就太～了。 It would be a shame if we put on a bad performance at the concert.

难免 nánmiǎn hard to avoid: 犯错误是～的, 你认真改了就好了。 Mistakes are hard to avoid, but if you correct them conscientiously, things will be all right. / 人们的看法有时～带片面性。 Sometimes people can't help being onesided in their views. / 由于缺乏经验, 工作中有时～要走弯路。 Owing to lack of experience, we sometimes can't avoid taking a roundabout course in our work.

难耐 nánnài hard to bear; unbearable: ～的不眠之夜 a tormenting sleepless night

难能可贵 nán néng kěguì difficult of attainment, hence worthy of esteem; deserving praise for one's excellent performance or behaviour; estimable; commendable

难人 nánrén ① difficult; delicate; ticklish: 这种～的事, 我办不了。 I cannot handle such a ticklish matter. ② a person handling a delicate matter: 有麻烦我们帮助你, 决不叫你做～。 We'll stand by you in case of trouble, and will never leave you holding the bag.

难色 nánsè a reluctant or embarrassed expression: 面有难色 miàn yǒu nánsè

难上难 nánshàngnán (also 难上加难 nán shàng jiā nán) extremely difficult; all the more difficult

难舍难分 nánshě-nánfēn (also 难分难舍 nánfēn-nánshě) loath to part from each other: 两人依依惜别, ～。 The two of them could hardly tear themselves away from each other.

难事 nánshì a difficult matter; sth. not easy to manage

难受 nánshòu ① feel unwell; feel ill; suffer pain: 浑身疼得～ be aching all over / 胃里～ feel queasy ② feel unhappy; feel bad: 他知道事情做错了, 心里很～。 He felt bad when he realized his error.

难说 nánshuō it's hard to say; you never can tell: 他什么时候回来还很～。 No one can tell when he will return. / 很～谁对谁不对。 It's pretty hard to say who's in the right and who's in the wrong.

难说话儿 nánshuōhuàr be difficult to talk with or deal with: 你那位上司真～。 That boss of yours is really a difficult person.

难题 nántí a difficult problem; a hard nut to crack; poser: 出～ set difficult questions / 在这样干旱的地区种水稻可是一个～。 How to grow rice in such a dry area is a difficult problem.

难听 nántīng ① unpleasant to hear: 这个曲子真～。 This tune is not very pleasing to the ear. ② offensive; coarse: 你怎么骂人, 多～! Why do you swear? It's really bad. / 她在背后说了你很多～话。 She said a lot of mean things about you behind your back. ③ scandalous: 这事情说出去多～。 The story will create a scandal once it gets out.

难忘 nánwàng unforgettable; memorable: ～的一课 an unforgettable lesson / ～的岁月 memorable years / 当时的情景令人～。 It was so impressive that it always remained fresh in my memory.

难为情 nánwéiqíng ① abashed; embarrassed: 试验不成功, 也别～。 Don't feel ashamed if your experiment isn't a success. / 他听别人这样夸他, 感到很～。 He was very embarrassed to hear people speak so highly of him. ② embarrassing; disconcerting: 答应吧, 办不到; 不答应吧, 又有点～。 It is not feasible to comply, but a bit embarrassing to refuse.

难为 nánwei ① embarrass; press: 她不会唱歌, 就别～她了。 She can't sing. So don't press her to. ② be a tough job to: 一个人拉扯大五六个孩子, 真～了她。 It was quite a job for her to bring up half a dozen children all by herself. ③ *pol.* (used to thank sb. for doing a favour): 机票也替我们买好了, 真～你了。 It was really very kind of you to get the plane tickets for us.

难闻 nánwén smell unpleasant; smell bad

难兄难弟 nánxiōng-nándì two of a kind; birds of a

feather ——see also nànxiōng-nàndì

难言之隐 nán yán zhī yǐn sth. which it would be awkward to disclose; sth. embarrassing to mention; a painful topic: 他似有～. He seemed too embarrassed to say what was on his mind.

难以 nányǐ hard to; difficult to: ～捉摸 difficult to pin down; elusive; unintelligible / ～想像 unimaginable / ～形容 indescribable; beyond description / ～预料 hard to predict (or forecast) / ～置信 hard to believe

难以为继 nán yǐ wéi jì same as 难乎为继 nán hū wéi jì

难于 nányú hard to; difficult to: 时间太短, 工程～完成. It's hard to finish the project in such a short time.

难字 nánzì uncommon word; rarely used word

喃

nán see below

喃喃 nánnán onom. mutter; murmur: ～自语 mutter to oneself

楠(枬)

nán see below

楠木 nánmù bot. nanmu (Phoebe nanmu)

楠竹 nánzhú another name for 毛竹 máozhú

nǎn

赧(赦)

nǎn blushing; shamefaced

赧红 nǎnhóng (of one's face) blush for shame; crimson from shame

赧愧 nǎnkuì formal ashamed

赧赧 nǎnnǎn blushing; shamefaced

赧然 nǎnrán formal. blushing; shamefaced

赧颜 nǎnyán formal. blush; be shamefaced

腩

nǎn see 牛腩 niúnǎn

蝻

nǎn the nymph of a locust

蝻子 nǎnzi the nymph of a locust

nàn

难(難)

nàn ① calamity; adversity; misfortune; trouble: 一方有～, 八方支援。When trouble occurs at one spot, help comes from all quarters. / 多灾多～ be dogged by misfortunes ② take to task; blame: 非难 fēinàn ——see also nán

难胞 nànbāo fellow countrymen in distress

难民 nànmín refugee: ～收容所 a haven or shelter for refugees / ～营 refugee camp

难侨 nànqiáo fellow countrymen in distress overseas

难兄难弟 nànxiōng-nàndì fellow sufferers ——see also nánxiōng-nándì

难友 nànyǒu fellow sufferer

nāng

囊

nāng see below ——see also náng

囊揣 nāngchuǎi ① old weak; cowardly; feeble ② same as 囊腩 nāngchuǎi

囊腩 nāngchuǎi the flabby meat from a sow's belly

囔

nāng see below

囔囔 nāngnāng speak in a low voice; murmur

náng

囊

náng ① bag; pocket: 药～ medicine bag / 背～ knapsack ② anything shaped like a bag: 胆囊 dǎnnáng ——see also nāng

囊虫 nángchóng cysticercus: ～病 cysticercosis

囊空如洗 náng kōng rú xǐ with empty pockets; penniless; broke

囊括 nángkuò ① include; embrace: ～四海 bring the whole country under imperial rule ② sports win all: ～锦标赛上的全部四块金牌 pocket all the four gold medals at the championships

囊生 nángshēng Tibetan household slave (or bondman, bondwoman)

囊尾蚴 nángwěiyòu another name for 囊虫 nángchóng

囊中物 nángzhōngwù sth. which is in the bag—sth. certain of attainment

囊肿 nángzhǒng med. cyst

馕

náng a kind of crusty pancake (staple food of the Uygur and Kazak nationalities) ——see also nǎng

nǎng

曩

nǎng formal former; past: ～者 in former times; formerly; in the past

曩昔 nǎngxī (also 曩日 nǎngrì, 曩时 nǎngshí) formal former times; olden days; days begone: 追思～ be reminiscent of the olden times; recall the past

攮

nǎng stab

攮子 nǎngzi dagger

饢

nǎng cram food into one's mouth ——see also náng

nàng

齉

nàng snuffling: 受了凉, 鼻子发～ snuffle with a cold

齉鼻儿 nàngbír ① snuffle; speak through the nose: 他感冒了, 说话有点～. He had a cold and spoke with a slight snuffle. ② a person who speaks with a twang

nāo

孬

nāo dial. ① bad ② cowardly

孬种 nāozhǒng dial. coward

náo

呶

náo talk noisily

呶呶不休 náonáo bù xiū formal talk on and on tediously

挠(撓)

náo ① scratch: ～痒痒 scratch an itch ② hinder: 阻挠 zǔnáo ③ yield; flinch: 不屈不挠 bùqū-bùnáo

挠度　náodù　*archit.*　deflection

挠钩　náogōu　long-handled hook

挠头　náotóu　① scratch one's head ② difficult to tackle: 这可是件～的事。This is a knotty problem.

挠性　náoxìng　*phys.*　flexibility

挠秧　náoyāng　weed rice fields and loosen the soil around the seedlings

硇(硇、硇)　náo　see below

硇砂　náoshā　*chem.*　sal ammoniac

硇洲　Náozhōu　an island in Guangdong Province

铙(鐃)　náo　① cymbals ② an ancient percussion instrument resembling an inverted tongueless bell, sounded by a hammer

铙钹　náobó　big cymbals

蛲(蟯)　náo　see below

蛲虫　náochóng　pinworm

蛲虫病　náochóngbìng　enterobiasis

猱　náo　a kind of monkey mentioned in ancient literature

猱犬　náoquǎn　dhole; red dog

猱升　náoshēng　*formal*　climb a tree as nimbly as a monkey

náo

恼(惱)　náo　① angry; irritated; annoyed: 再说我可要～了。I'll be angry with you if you go on talking like that. ② unhappy; worried: 烦恼 fánnǎo

恼恨　nǎohèn　resent; hate: 他的批评是为你好, 你可别～他。You shouldn't resent his criticism. He meant well.

恼火　nǎohuǒ　annoyed; irritated; vexed: 对于他那种听不进批评的态度, 我们感到～。We're annoyed at his not listening to criticism.

恼怒　nǎonù　angry; indignant; furious

恼人　nǎorén　irritating; annoying: 这件事真～。It's really irritating./春色～。Spring's hues are teasing.

恼羞成怒　nǎo-xiū chéng nù　fly into a rage from shame; be shamed into anger

脑(腦)　náo　① brain: 用～过度 overtax one's brain ② brains; mind; head: 动手动～ use one's hands and brains ③ essence: 樟脑 zhāngnǎo

脑儿　nǎor　① animal brains (as food): 猪～ pig's brains ② brain-like jellied food: 豆腐脑儿 dòufunǎor

脑充血　nǎochōngxuè　*med.*　encephalemia

脑袋　nǎodai　*inf.*　① head ② brains; mind

脑袋瓜子　nǎodaiguāzi　(also 脑袋瓜儿 nǎodaiguār) *dial.*　① head ② brains; mind: 他的～好使。He's very clever. *or* He's got a clever mind.

脑电波　nǎodiànbō　*physiol.*　brain wave

脑电图　nǎodiàntú　*med.*　electroencephalogram (EEG)

脑动脉　nǎodòngmài　*physiol.*　cerebral artery

脑瓜子　nǎoguāzi　(also 脑瓜儿 nǎoguār) *dial.*　head

脑海　nǎohǎi　brain; mind: 多年前的旧事又重现在他的～里。Memories of things long past flashed across his mind.

脑积水　nǎojīshuǐ　*med.*　hydrocephalus

脑脊髓炎　nǎojǐsuǐyán　*med.*　encephalomyelitis

脑脊液　nǎojǐyè　*physiol.*　cerebrospinal fluid (CSF)

脑际　nǎojì　mind; memory: 突然一个念头浮上～。An idea flashed across my mind.

脑浆　nǎojiāng　brains: ～迸裂 have one's brains dashed out

脑筋　nǎojīn　① brains; mind; head: 动～ use one's brains (*or* head)/你问老杨去。他～好, 记得清。Ask Lao Yang, he has a good memory. ② way of thinking; ideas: 旧～ a person who clings to old-fashioned ideas; an old fogey

脑壳　nǎoké　① skull ② *dial.*　head

脑力　nǎolì　mental power; intelligence

脑力劳动　nǎolì láodòng　mental work: 逐步消灭～和体力劳动的差别 gradually eliminate the distinction between mental and manual labour

脑力劳动者　nǎolì láodòngzhě　mental worker; brain worker

脑颅　nǎolú　brainpan; cranium

脑满肠肥　nǎomǎn-chángféi　heavy-jowled and potbellied (said of the idle rich)

脑门子　nǎoménzi　(also 脑门儿 nǎoménr) *inf.*　forehead; brow

脑膜　nǎomó　*physiol.*　meninx

脑膜炎　nǎomóyán　*med.*　meningitis

脑贫血　nǎopínxuè　*med.*　cerebral anaemia

脑桥　nǎoqiáo　*physiol.*　pons

脑上体　nǎoshàngtǐ　*physiol.*　pineal body

脑勺子　nǎosháozi　*dial.*　the back of the head

脑神经　nǎoshénjīng　*physiol.*　cranial nerve

脑室　nǎoshì　*physiol.*　ventricles of the brain

脑室造影　nǎoshì zàoyǐng　*med.*　ventriculography

脑髓　nǎosuǐ　brains

脑下垂体　nǎoxiàchuítǐ　*physiol.*　pituitary body; pituitary gland; hypophysis

脑血管造影　nǎoxuèguǎn zàoyǐng　*med.*　cerebral angiography

脑炎　nǎoyán　*med.*　encephalitis; cerebritis: 流行性乙型～ epidemic encephalitis B

脑溢血　nǎoyìxuè　*med.*　cerebral haemorrhage

脑震荡　nǎozhèndàng　*med.*　cerebral concussion; concussion

脑汁　nǎozhī　brains: 绞尽脑汁 jiǎojìn nǎozhī

脑子　nǎozi　① *inf.*　brain ② brains; mind; head: 没～ have no brains/～灵活 quick-witted/问题是复杂的, 我们的～也要复杂一点。The problems are complicated, and our brains must be a little complicated, too.

瑙　nǎo　see 玛瑙 mǎnǎo

瑙鲁　Nǎolǔ　Nauru

瑙鲁人　Nǎolǔrén　Nauruan

nào

闹(鬧)　nào　① noisy: 这屋里太～。This room is too noisy. ② make a noise; stir up trouble: 叫孩子们别～了。Tell the children to stop making a noise (*or* fooling around). / 又哭又～ make a tearful scene / 孙悟空大～天宫。The Monkey King caused havoc in Heaven./她这个人呀, 为一点小事就能找你～一通。She always makes a great fuss over a trifle. / ～名誉地位 be out for fame and position ③ give vent (to one's anger, resentment, etc.): 闹脾气 nào píqi / 闹情绪 nào qíngxù ④ suffer from; be troubled by: ～眼睛 have eye trouble / ～嗓子 have a sore throat / ～虫灾 suffer from insect pests / ～矛盾 be at loggerheads / ～分裂 engage in splittism / 你最近瘦了, 怎么～的? How come you look so thin these days? ⑤ go in for; do; make: ～生产 go in for production / 把问题～清楚再发言。Don't speak until you've got the thing clear in your mind.

闹别扭　nào bièniu　be difficult with sb.; be at odds with sb.: 两口子又在～了。The couple are at odds with each

other again.

闹病 nàobìng　fall ill; be ill: 这孩子体弱, 爱～。The child is weak and sickly.

闹不清 nàobuqīng　cannot tell; be unclear about: 我也～这里谁是负责人。I'm not clear either who's in charge here.

闹场 nàochǎng　a flourish of gongs and drums introducing a theatrical performance

闹洞房 nào dòngfáng　same as 闹房 nàofáng

闹独立性 nào dúlìxìng　assert one's independence —refuse to obey the leadership

闹肚子 nào dùzi　*inf.* have diarrhoea; be suffering from loose bowels

闹翻 nàofān　fall out with sb.: 他俩为了一点小事儿就～了。They fell out with each other over some little thing.

闹翻身 nàofānshēn　fight for emancipation: 共产党领导咱穷人～。The Communist Party led us poor people in our struggle for emancipation.

闹翻天 nàofāntiān　raise hell; raise a rumpus

闹房 nàofáng　(of friends and relatives) banter or tease the newlyweds on wedding night

闹风潮 nào fēngcháo　carry on agitation; stage strikes, demonstrations, etc.

闹革命 nào gémìng　carry out revolution; make revolution; rise in revolution

闹鬼 nàoguǐ　① be haunted ② play tricks behind sb.'s back; use underhand means

闹哄哄 nàohōnghōng　clamorous; noisy: 这里～的, 我们另找个地方谈吧。It's too noisy here, so let's find another place to talk.

闹哄 nàohong　① make a noise; make a fuss ② (of a group of people) bustle about

闹荒 nàohuāng　(of peasants in former times) start famine riots

闹饥荒 nào jīhuang　① suffer from famine ② *dial.* be hard up; be short of money: 快到发工资那几天他就～。He's always hard up before payday.

闹架 nàojià　*dial.* fall out and come to blows; quarrel and fight

闹剧 nàojù　farce

闹乱子 nào luànzi　cause trouble: 我担心他们再这么闹下去会闹出乱子来。I'm afraid there will be trouble if they go on like that.

闹猛 nào·měng　*dial.* bustling with noise and excitement; full of bustling activity; lively

闹脾气 nào píqi　vent one's spleen; lose one's temper; be in a tantrum

闹气 nàoqì　*dial.* be cross with sb.

闹情绪 nào qíngxù　be disgruntled; be in low spirits: 为这件事他闹了好几天情绪。He has been unhappy about this for quite a few days.

闹嚷嚷 nàorāngrāng　noisy: 外面～的, 什么事呀? What's all that noise about outside?

闹嚷 nào·rǎng　clamour; make a racket; kick up a row

闹热 nàorè　*dial.* lively; bustling with noise and excitement

闹市 nàoshì　busy streets; busy shopping centre; downtown area

闹事 nàoshì　create a disturbance; make trouble: 上街～ take to the streets and make trouble

闹腾 nàoteng　① make a noise; kick up a row ② talk and laugh boisterously

闹天儿 nàotiānr　*dial.* have bad weather: 一连好几天都～ have an unbroken spell of bad weather

闹戏 nàoxì　an old-style comic opera

闹笑话 nào xiàohuà　make a fool of oneself; make a stupid mistake: 不懂装懂就会～。If you pretend to know what you don't know, you'll only make a fool of

yourself.

闹心 nàoxīn　*dial.* ① be vexed; be annoyed ② feel sick; feel queasy

闹新房 nào xīnfáng　same as 闹房 nàofáng

闹性子 nào xìngzi　lose one's temper; be in a tantrum

闹玄虚 nào xuánxū　purposely make a mystery of simple things; be deliberately mystifying

闹羊花 nàoyánghuā　another name for 羊踯躅 yángzhízhú

闹意见 nào yìjiàn　be on bad terms because of a difference of opinion; be at odds

闹意气 nào yìqì　feel resentful because something is not to one's liking; sulk: 你有意见就提出来, 不要～。If you have any complaint, don't just sulk; speak up.

闹盈盈 nàoyíngyíng　bustling with noise and excitement; full of bustling activity

闹灾 nàozāi　be hit by a calamity

闹仗 nàozhàng　*dial.* ① have a quarrel; have a row ② come to blows; fight; scuffle

闹着玩儿 nàozhewánr　be joking: 他是跟你～的, 你别当真。He was joking. Don't take it seriously. / 这可不是～的事。This is no joking matter (*or* no joke).

闹中取静 nào zhōng qǔ jìng　seek peace and quiet in noisy surroundings

闹钟 nàozhōng　alarm clock

闹嘴 nàozuǐ　*dial.* quarrel; bicker: 他们俩怎么又～啦? Why are they bickering again?

淖

淖 nào　*formal* mire

淖尔 nào'ěr　nur (the Mongolian for "lake"; usu. used as part of a place name): 罗布～ (same as 罗布泊) Lop Nur

né

哪

哪 né　limited to use in 哪吒 Né·zhā (Nata, a divine warrior in the *Journey to the West*《西游记》and the *Investiture of the Gods*《封神演义》) ——see also nǎ; na

nè

讷

讷 nè　*formal* slow (of speech): ～于言而敏于行 slow of speech but quick in action

讷讷 nènè　*formal* slow of speech; faltering in speech

那

那 nè　a variant pronunciation for 那 nà in colloquial speech

ne

呢 (吶)

呢 (吶) ne　*part.* ① (used at the end of a special, alternative, or rhetorical question): 你刚才到哪儿去了～? Where were you just now? / 我错在哪儿～? What have I done wrong? / 他们两人都有任务了, 我～? They've both got something to do. What about me? / 你对这件事是赞成～, 还是反对～? Are you for or against this? / 你到底认不认得她～? Do you or don't you know her? / 我怎么能不记得～? How could I forget this? / 这点子事, 何必大惊小怪～? Why get so excited over a little thing like this? ② (used at the end of a declarative sentence to reinforce the assertion): 远得很, 有好几千里地～。It's a long way off—thousands of *li* away. ③

(used at the end of a declarative sentence to indicate the continuation of an action or a state): 老张，有人找你～. Lao Zhang, somebody is looking for you. / 他还在生气～. He's still angry. ④ (used to mark a pause): 如今～,可比以往任何时候都要强. As for the present, things are far better than at any time in the past. / 不下雨～,就去；下雨～,就不去. If it doesn't rain, we'll go. If it does rain, then we won't go. ——see also ní

něi

哪(那)

哪(那) něi　a variant pronunciation for 哪 nǎ in colloquial speech

馁

馁 něi ① hungry; famished: 冻馁 dòngněi ② disheartened; dispirited: 气馁 qìněi ③ formal (of fish) putrid

馁怯 něiqiè　lose heart; lose courage; lose one's nerve

nèi

内

内 nèi ① (used as a noun) inside; inner part or side: 入～ go inside; enter / 请勿入～. No admittance. / 共十人,儿童包括在～. Altogether ten, children included. / ～附照片. Photos enclosed. ② (used after a noun to indicate place, time, scope or limits) within; in; inside: 校～ in the school / 墙～ within the walls / 本月～ within the month / 最近几天～ within these few days; in a few days / 市～交通 urban traffic / 党～思想斗争 inner-Party ideological struggle ③ (used before a noun or verb in forming a compound word) inner; internal: 内室 nèishì / 内伤 nèishāng / 内分泌 nèifēnmì ④ one's wife or her relatives: 内人 nèirén / 内弟 nèidì

内白 nèibái　words spoken by an actor from offstage

内宾 nèibīn　Chinese guest (as distinguished from 外宾 foreign guest)

内部 nèibù ① inside; interior; within: 在工人阶级～ within the working class / 在人民～ among the people themselves / ～装修 interior decorations / ～联系 internal relations / 事物的～规律性 inherent laws of a thing / 堡垒是最容易从～攻破的. The easiest way to capture a fortress is from within. ② inside; restricted: ～消息 inside information / ～刊物 restricted publication

内查外调 nèichá-wàidiào　make investigations both within and without

内场 nèichǎng　sports (baseball, softball) infield

内场手 nèichǎngshǒu　infielder

内臣 nèichén ① chamberlain ② eunuch

内城 nèichéng　inner city

内出血 nèichūxuè　med. internal haemorrhage (or bleeding)

内当家 nèidāngjiā　dial. ① wife ② the wife of one's master, employer or landlord

内地 nèidì　inland; interior; hinterland: ～城市 inland city / 我国的～ the interior of our country

内弟 nèidì　wife's younger brother; brother-in-law

内电阻 nèidiànzǔ　elec. internal resistance

内定 nèidìng　(of an official appointment) decided at the higher level but not officially announced: 听说他已～为下一任部长. It is said that he has been designated as the incoming minister.

内毒素 nèidúsù　med. endotoxin

内耳 nèi'ěr　internal ear; inner ear

内耳眩晕综合症 nèi'ěr xuànyùn zōnghézhèng　med. Ménière's syndrome; Ménière's disease

内耳炎 nèi'ěryán　med. otitis interna

内犯 nèifàn　formal enemy intrusion or invasion

内分泌 nèifēnmì　physiol. endocrine; internal secretion: ～系统 endocrine system

内分泌失调 nèifēnmì shītiáo　med. endocrine imbalance; endocrinopathy

内分泌腺 nèifēnmìxiàn　physiol. endocrine glands

内封 nèifēng　title page

内锋 nèifēng　sports inside forward: 左内锋 zuǒnèifēng

内服 nèifú　taken by the mouth; oral: ～药,每日三次,每次一片 an oral dose of 1 tablet, 3 times a day

内阁 nèigé　cabinet: 改组～ cabinet reshuffle / ～大臣 cabinet minister

内功 nèigōng　(wushu 武术 or qigong 气功) exercises to benefit the internal organs

内骨骼 nèigǔgé　endoskeleton

内顾 nèigù　formal look after home or domestic affairs

内顾之忧 nèigù zhī yōu　domestic worries; trouble at home

内果皮 nèiguǒpí　bot. endocarp

内海 nèihǎi ① inland sea ② continental sea

内涵 nèihán　log. intension; connotation

内行 nèiháng ① be expert at; be adept in; know the ins and outs of: 对养蚕很～ be expert at silkworm breeding / 种稻子很～ know a lot about growing rice ② an expert; a dab hand; master: 充～ pose as an expert / 要说木匠活呀,他可是～. When it comes to carpentry, he is quite a dab hand.

内耗 nèihào ①energy consumed by a machine without getting any work done ② losses suffered in internal strife

内河 nèihé　inland river (or waters, waterway): ～航行权 inland navigation rights / ～运输 inland water transport

内核 nèihé　the crux of a matter

内讧 nèihòng　(also 内哄 nèihòng) internal conflict; internal strife; internal dissension

内画壶 nèihuàhú　a bottle with painted designs inside

内踝 nèihuái　the medial part of the ankle (where the lower end of the tibia is)

内急 nèijí　have to go to the toilet

内寄生 nèijìshēng　biol. endoparasitism

内寄生物 nèijìshēngwù　biol. endoparasite

内奸 nèijiān　a secret enemy agent within one's ranks; a hidden traitor

内间 nèijiān　dial. inner room

内艰 nèijiān　formal mother's funeral

内监 nèijiàn　eunuch

内角 nèijiǎo　math. interior angle; internal angle

内接多边形 nèijiēduōbiānxíng　math. inscribed polygon

内接形 nèijiēxíng　math. inscribed figure

内景 nèijǐng　indoor setting; indoor scene; interior

内径 nèijìng　internal diameter; inside (or inner) diameter (ID): ～千分尺 inside micrometer

内径规 nèijìngguī　internal gauge

内疚 nèijiù　compunction; guilty conscience: ～于心 feel compunction; have qualms of conscience; be conscience-stricken / 她托我的事没办成,我感到～. I feel terribly bad for failing to do what she asked me to.

内聚力 nèijùlì　phys. cohesive force; cohesion

内眷 nèijuàn　female members of a family

内卡钳 nèikǎqián　mech. inside callipers

内科 nèikē　(department of) internal medicine: ～病房 medical ward / ～医生 physician / 你看～还是外科? Do you want to see a physician or a surgeon?

内窥镜 nèikuījìng　med. endoscope: ～检查 endoscopy

内涝 nèilào　waterlogging

内里 nèilǐ　dial. the inside: 这件事儿～颇有一些曲折. There are still quite a few complications in this matter.

内力　nèilì　*phys.* internal force

内流河　nèiliúhé　continental river

内陆　nèilù　inland; interior; hinterland

内陆国　nèilùguó　landlocked country

内陆海　nèilùhǎi　inland sea

内陆河　nèilùhé　continental river

内陆湖　nèilùhú　inland lake

内陆盆地　nèilù péndì　interior (*or* inland) basin

内乱　nèiluàn　civil strife; internal disorder

内蒙古　Nèi Měnggǔ　Inner Mongolia

内蒙古自治区　Nèi Měnggǔ Zìzhìqū　the Inner Mongolia Autonomous Region

内幕　nèimù　what goes on behind the scenes; inside story: ～消息 inside information

内难　nèinàn　domestic calamity; internal trouble

内能　nèinéng　*phys.* internal energy; intrinsic energy

内胚层　nèipēicéng　(*also* 内胚叶 nèipēiyè) endoderm; entoderm

内切圆　nèiqiēyuán　*math.* inscribed circle (of a triangle); incircle

内亲　nèiqīn　relatives on one's wife's side; (a man's) in-laws

内勤　nèiqín　① internal or office work (as distinguished from work carried on mainly outside the office) ② office staff

内情　nèiqíng　inside information (*or* story): 了解～ be an insider; be in the know

内燃机　nèiránjī　*mech.* internal-combustion engine

内燃机车　nèirán jīchē　diesel locomotive

内热　nèirè　*Chin. med.* internal heat—disorders due to predominance of the yang (阳)

内人　nèiren　*old* my wife

内容　nèiróng　content; substance: ～和形式的统一 unity of content and form / 他的演说毫无～. His speech lacked substance (*or* content). / 这本书～丰富. This book has substantial content. / 这次谈话的～牵涉面很广. The talk covered a lot of ground.

内容提要　nèiróng tíyào　synopsis; résumé

内伤　nèishāng　① *med.* internal injury ② *Chin. med.* disorder of internal organs caused by improper diet, fatigue, emotional strains, sexual excess, etc.

内室　nèishì　inner room; bedroom

内水　nèishuǐ　inland waters

内胎　nèitāi　inner tube (of a tyre)

内廷　nèitíng　inner chambers in an imperial palace; imperial residence

内外　nèi-wài　① inside and outside; domestic and foreign: 长城～ both sides of the Great Wall / ～反动势力 domestic and foreign reactionary forces ② around; about: 五十年～ in about fifty years

内外夹攻　nèi-wài jiāgōng　attack from both within and without: 造成～的形势 form a pincer movement from inside and out

内外交困　nèi-wài jiāo kùn　beset with difficulties both at home and abroad

内外有别　nèi-wài yǒu bié　keep inside information from outsiders or foreigners

内务　nèiwù　① internal affairs ② daily routine tasks to keep the barracks, etc. clean and tidy: ～条令 routine service regulations (for barracks)

内务部　nèiwùbù　Ministry of Internal Affairs

内吸磷　nèixīlín　*agric.* demeton

内线　nèixiàn　① planted agent ② *mil.* interior lines: ～作战 fight (*or* operate) on interior lines ③ inside (telephone) connections: ～自动电话机 interphone

内详　nèixiáng　name and address of sender enclosed

内向　nèixiàng　*psychol.* introversion: 性格～ be introverted by nature; be an introvert

内项　nèixiàng　*math.* the second or third term (in a proportion of four terms); mean

内销　nèixiāo　sold inside the country; for the domestic market: 出口转～ exportable goods put on the domestic market; exportable goods sold on home market

内斜视　nèixiéshì　*med.* esotropia; cross-eye

内心　nèixīn　① heart; innermost being: ～深处 in one's heart of hearts / 出自～的感谢 heartfelt thanks / 他～很矛盾. He is torn by conflicting thoughts. / 影片展示了一个坚强的革命战士的～世界。The film reveals the inner world of a staunch revolutionary fighter. ② *math.* incentre (of a triangle)

内省　nèixǐng　introspection: ～心理学 introspective psychology

内兄　nèixiōng　wife's elder brother; brother-in-law

内秀　nèixiù　be intelligent without seeming so

内焰　nèiyàn　*chem.* inner flame

内衣　nèiyī　underwear; underclothes

内因　nèiyīn　*philos.* internal cause: 唯物辩证法认为，外因通过～而起作用。Materialist dialectics holds that external causes become operative through internal causes.

内应　nèiyìng　a person operating from within in coordination with outside forces; a planted agent; a plant

内应力　nèiyìnglì　*mech.* internal stress

内忧外患　nèiyōu-wàihuàn　domestic trouble and foreign invasion; internal disturbance and foreign aggression

内在　nèizài　inherent; intrinsic; internal; inner: ～规律 inherent law / ～联系 inner link; internal relations / ～矛盾 inner (*or* inherent) contradictions / ～美 inner beauty / ～因素 internal factor

内在论　nèizàilùn　*philos.* immanentism

内脏　nèizàng　internal organs; viscera

内宅　nèizhái　inner chambers (for the womenfolk of a household)

内债　nèizhài　internal debt; domestic loan

内战　nèizhàn　civil war

内掌柜的　nèizhǎngguìde　wife of a shopkeeper

内障　nèizhàng　cataract or glaucoma

内争　nèizhēng　internal strife

内政　nèizhèng　internal (*or* domestic, home) affairs: 互不干涉～ noninterference in each other's internal affairs

内侄　nèizhí　son of wife's brother; nephew

内侄女　nèizhí nǚ　daughter of wife's brother; niece

内痔　nèizhì　*med.* internal piles; internal haemorrhoids

内中　nèizhōng　the inside: 你不晓得～的奥秘. You don't know the inside story.

内助　nèizhù　*formal* wife (considered as a helpful companion)

内子　nèizǐ　*formal* my wife

内阻　nèizǔ　*elec.* internal resistance; inherent resistance

那

那　nèi　a variant pronunciation for 那 nà in colloquial speech

nèn

恁　nèn　*dial.* ① such; so: ～大胆! How reckless! *or* What audacity! / 我要不了～些. I don't need so much. ② that: ～时节 at that time

恁般　nènbān　*dial.* so; such; like that

恁地　nèndì　*dial.* so; like that; (in) that way: 不要～说. Don't say so. *or* Don't put it that way.

嫩

嫩　nèn　① tender; delicate: ～叶 tender leaves / 这

肉炒得很～. This stir-fried meat is very tender. / 小孩子肉皮儿～。 Young children have delicate skin. / 脸皮～ shy; bashful ② light: 嫩绿 nènlǜ ③ inexperienced; unskilled: ～手 a raw hand; a new hand

嫩寒 nènhán *formal* slightly cold; chilly

嫩红 nènhóng pink; apricot pink

嫩黄 nènhuáng light yellow

嫩绿 nènlǜ light green; soft green

嫩气 nènqi ① delicate (*or* dainty) looks; youthfulness ② dainty-looking; youthful-looking

嫩晴 nènqíng *formal* fine (weather) after a long spell of rainy weather

嫩弱 nènruò delicate; frail

嫩色 nènsè light colour; soft colour; pastel shade

嫩生生 nènshēngshēng very tender; very delicate: 一片～的秧苗 a stretch of tender green rice shoots

néng

能 néng ① ability; capability; skill: 技能 jìnéng / 无能 wúnéng ② *phys.* energy ③ able; capable: 她可～呢, 穿的衣服都是自己做的。 She's very capable. She makes all the clothes she wears. ④ can; be able to; be capable of: 她一分钟～打七十个字。 She can type 70 words a minute. / 他好多了, ～下床了。 He's much better and can get up now. / 我干这个工作～行吗? Am I really fit for the job? ⑤ (expressing possibility) can; possibly: 天这么晚了, 他～来吗? It's already very late. Can he possibly come tonight? / 这件事她～一点也不知道吗? Could she know nothing of it? *or* Could she be completely in the dark? ⑥ (used between 不…不 to express obligation, certainty or great probability): 不能不 bùnéngbù ⑦ (usu. used negatively or interrogatively) may; can; have the permission to: 这儿～停车吗?—这儿不～. Can we park here?—No. Parking is not allowed here.

能动 néngdòng active; dynamic: 人的～作用 man's initiative (*or* dynamic role) / 从感性认识到理性认识之的飞跃 the active leap from perceptual to rational knowledge / ～地争取胜利 play a dynamic role in striving for victory

能动性 néngdòngxìng dynamic role; activity; initiative: 自觉的～ (man's) conscious dynamic role

能干 nénggàn able; capable; competent: 他是个很～的人。 He is a man of great ability. / 这些女电工真～。 These women electricians really know their job.

能工巧匠 nénggōng-qiǎojiàng skilful craftsman; skilled artisan; dab hand

能攻能守 nénggōng-néngshǒu be able to take the offensive as well as hold one's ground: 这个队～. The team is good at both attack and defence.

能够 nénggòu can; be able to; be capable of: ～独立工作 be able to work on one's own / 他～说三种外国语。 He can speak three foreign languages. / 这河的下游～行驶轮船。 The lower reaches of the river are navigable for steamers. / 明天的晚会, 家属也～参加。 You can also bring family members to tomorrow's party.

能官能民 néngguān-néngmín be ready to serve as an official or to be one of the common people

能耗 nénghào energy consumption

能级 néngjí *phys.* energy level: 费密～ Fermi level / 基态～ ground state level

能见度 néngjiàndù visibility: 地面～ ground visibility

能力 nénglì ability; capacity; capability: ～强 have great ability; be very capable / 培养学生的推理～ develop the students' reasoning capacity / 分析问题和解决问题的～ ability to analyse and solve problems / 他

经验丰富, 有～担当这项工作. He is very experienced and has the ability to take on this responsibility.

能量 néngliàng ① *phys.* energy: ～转化 conversion of energy / ～交换 energy exchange ② capabilities: 他们人数很少, ～很大。 Though few in number, they have enormous capacity for manoeuvre.

能量守恒律 néngliàng shǒuhénglǜ the law of conservation of energy

能耐 néngnai *inf.* ability; capability; skill: 她真有～, 一个人管这么多台机器。 She shows great skill in minding so many machines all by herself. / 我有什么～呀, 全靠各位撑腰呢! What could I do without you people backing me up?

能屈能伸 néngqū-néngshēn be able to stoop or to stand; submit or assert oneself as the occasion requires; be adaptable to circumstances: 大丈夫～。 A man among men is he who knows when to eat humble pie and when to hold his head high.

能人 néngrén able person

能人背后有能人 néngrén bèihòu yǒu néngrén for every able person there is always one still abler

能上能下 néngshàng-néngxià be ready to work either at the top or at the grass roots; be ready to accept a higher or a lower post: 干部要～. A cadre should be ready to take a lower as well as a higher post.

能事 néngshì (usu. used in combination with 尽 jìn) what one is particularly good at: 竭尽挑拨离间之～ stop at nothing to sow discord

能手 néngshǒu dab; expert; crackajack: 木刻～ a dab at wood engraving / 技术革新～ a crackajack at technical innovation / 解决复杂问题的～ a trouble-shooter / 她是插秧～。 She is a good hand at transplanting rice.

能说会道 néngshuō-huìdào have the gift of the gab; be a glib talker: 他以～闻名于工商界。 He earned a reputation in business circles for having a ready and eloquent tongue.

能为 néngwéi *dial.* ability; capability; skill

能文能武 néngwén-néngwǔ be versed in both polite letters and martial arts; be able to wield both the pen and the sword

能源 néngyuán the sources of energy; energy resources; energy: ～危机 energy crisis / ～工业 energy industry / 可再生～ renewable sources of energy

能愿动词 néngyuàn dòngcí *gram.* modal verb

能者多劳 néngzhě duōláo able people should do more work (said when asking sb. to perform a service or do extra work); the abler one is, the more one should do: 俗话说"～." 经理见你这样能干, 就什么都交给你了。 As the saying goes, "The abler a man is, the busier he gets." It's because you're so capable that the manager leaves everything to you.

能者为师 néngzhě wéi shī let those who know teach

ňg

嗯 (唔) ňg, also ň *interj.* (used in questioning): ～, 你说什么? Eh? What did you say? ——see also ňg; ňg

ňg

嗯 (唔) ňg, also ň *interj.* (used to show surprise or disapproval): ～, 怎么又不见了? Hey! It's gone again. / ～! 你怎么还没去? What! Haven't you started yet? ——see also ňg; ňg

ňg

嗯（呷） ňg, also ň *interj.* (used to express agreement or assent) m-hm; uh-huh: 你有空吧？—～。Are you free?—M-hm. ／他～了一声，就走了。He merely said "Uh-huh" and went away. ——see also ńg; ňg

ní

妮 ní see below
妮子 nízi (also 妮儿 nír) *dial.* girl; lass

ní

尼 ní Buddhist nun
尼安德特人 Ní'āndétèrén Neanderthal man (a Palaeolithic species of man)
尼庵 ní'ān Buddhist nunnery
尼泊尔 Níbó'ěr Nepal
尼泊尔人 Níbó'ěrrén Nepalese
尼泊尔语 Níbó'ěryǔ Nepali
尼格罗-澳大利亚人种 Nígéluó-Àodàlìyà rénzhǒng Negro-Australoid (one of the three major races of mankind)
尼姑 nígū Buddhist nun
尼古丁 nígǔdīng nicotine
尼加拉瓜 Níjiālāguā Nicaragua
尼加拉瓜人 Níjiālāguārén Nicaraguan
尼龙 nílóng nylon: ～丝 nylon yarn ／～袜 nylon socks
尼罗河 Níluóhé the Nile
尼日尔 Nírì'ěr Niger
尼日尔人 Nírì'ěrrén Nigerois
尼日利亚 Nírìlìyà Nigeria
尼日利亚人 Nírìlìyàrén Nigerian
尼亚加拉瀑布 Níyàjiālā Pùbù Niagara Falls

泥

泥 ní ① mud; mire ② sth. like paste or pulp: 土豆～ mashed potato ／苹果～ applesauce ——see also nì
泥巴 níbā *dial.* mud; mire
泥肥 níféi *agric.* sludge (used as manure)
泥封 nífēng *metall.* lute
泥工 nígōng *dial.* bricklayer; tiler; plasterer
泥垢 nígòu dirt; grime: 他满脸～。His face was covered with dirt.
泥滑 níhuá muddy and slippery: 爬上～的陡坡 clamber up the slippery muddy slope
泥灰岩 níhuīyán *geol.* marl
泥浆 níjiāng slurry; mud: 钻井～ drilling mud ／～泵 slurry (*or* mud, slush) pump ／～工 mudman
泥金 níjīn coating material made of powdered gold or other metals; golden paint: ～佛像 a gilded Buddha
泥坑 níkēng mud pit; mire; morass: 陷入～ get stuck in the mud; be bogged down in a quagmire
泥疗 níliáo *med.* mud therapy
泥煤 níméi same as 泥炭 nítàn
泥淖 nínào mire; bog; morass
泥泞 nínìng ① muddy; miry: ～的道路 a muddy road ／雨后道路～。The road is muddy after the rain. ② mire; mud: 陷入～ get stuck in the mire
泥牛入海 níniú rù hǎi like clay oxen entering the sea

——never to be heard of again; gone forever
泥盆纪 Nípénjì the Devonian period (the 4th period of the Palaeozoic era, 350,000,000-400,000,000 years ago)
泥盆系 Nípénxì the Devonian system
泥菩萨过河，自身难保 nípúsà guò hé, zìshēn nánbǎo like a clay idol fording a river—hardly able to save oneself (let alone anyone else)
泥鳅 níqiu loach
泥人 nírén clay figurine: 彩塑～ painted clay figurine
泥沙 níshā silt
泥沙俱下 ní-shā jù xià mud and sand are carried along—there is a mingling of good and bad: 在革命高潮时期，各种人都来参加，未免～，鱼龙混杂。At the high tide of the revolution, people of all descriptions flocked to join in; so inevitably the waters were muddied and the bad became mixed with the good.
泥石流 níshíliú *geol.* mud-rock flow
泥水匠 níshuǐjiàng bricklayer; tiler; plasterer
泥塑 nísù clay sculpture
泥塑木雕 nísù-mùdiāo same as 木雕泥塑 mùdiāo-nísù
泥胎 nítāi an unpainted clay idol
泥胎儿 nítāir unfired pottery
泥潭 nítán mire; morass; quagmire
泥炭 nítàn peat
泥塘 nítáng mire; bog; morass
泥土 nítǔ ① earth; soil: 春天的原野散发着～的芳香。In spring the fields give off the aroma of the earth. ② clay
泥腿子 nítuǐzi bumpkin; clodhopper
泥洼 níwā marsh; mire
泥瓦匠 níwǎjiàng bricklayer; tiler; plasterer
泥丸 níwán small clay ball
泥岩 níyán *geol.* mudstone
泥俑 níyǒng clay figure buried with the dead; funerary clay figure; earthen figurine
泥沼 nízhǎo mire; swamp; morass; slough
泥足巨人 nízú jùrén a colossus with feet of clay: 列宁把帝国主义比做～。Lenin likened imperialism to a colossus with feet of clay.
泥醉 nízuì dead drunk

呢 ní (cloth made of) wool; woollen cloth (for heavy clothing); heavy woollen cloth; wool coating or suiting: 格子～ woollen check ／厚～大衣 heavy woollen overcoat ——see also ne
呢喃 nínán (of swallows) twitter
呢绒 níróng woollen goods; wool fabric
呢子 nízi woollen cloth (for heavy clothing); heavy woollen cloth; wool coating or suiting

怩 ní see 忸怩 niǔní

倪 ní ① beginning; origin: 端倪 duānní ② (Ní) a surname

铌 ní *chem.* niobium (Nb)
铌铁矿 nítiěkuàng columbite

霓（蜺） ní *meteorol.* secondary rainbow
霓虹灯 níhóngdēng neon lamp; neon light; neon

鲵 ní salamander (an amphibian)

nǐ

拟（擬） nǐ ① draw up; design; devise; draft: ～个计划 devise a plan ／～一个方案 draw up a plan ②

intend; plan: ～于下月前往青岛 plan to go to Qingdao next month ③ imitate: 模拟 mónǐ

拟订 nǐdìng (also 拟定 nǐdìng) draw up; draft; work out: ～计划 draw up a plan; draft a plan / ～具体办法 work out specific measures / ～城市建设规划 map out a programme for municipal construction

拟稿 nǐgǎo prepare a draft; make a draft: 秘书拟了一个稿儿。 The secretary made a draft. / 这一套规章是校长亲自拟的稿。 The principal himself drafted this set of rules.

拟古 nǐgǔ model one's literary or artistic style on that of the ancients: ～之作 a work modelled after the ancients

拟人 nǐrén personification: 使之～化 personify sth.

拟态 nǐtài zool. mimicry; imitation

拟议 nǐyì ① proposal; recommendation: 事实证明他的～是正确的。 Facts show that his recommendations were sound. ② draw up; draft: 小组一致通过了她所～的意见书。 The group unanimously adopted the proposal she drew up.

拟于不伦 nǐyú bùlún draw inapt parallels

拟作 nǐzuò a work done in the manner of a certain author

你 nǐ ① you (second person singular): ～爸爸 your father / ～带了多少钱? How much money do you have on you? ② you (second person plural): ～方 your side; you / ～校 your school ③ (referring to any person) you; one; anyone: 碰到这么一个人,～有什么办法? What can you do with a person like that? ④ (used coordinately with 我 or 他 in parallel structures to indicate several or many people behaving the same way): 三个人～看看我,我看看～,谁也不说话。 The three of them kept looking at one another without saying a word. / ～一言,我一语,大家谈得很热闹。 A lively conversation went on with everybody joining in.

你好 nǐhǎo how are you; hello (a common form of greeting, used at any time of the day, requiring the same phrase as an answer; also used at the beginning of informal letters)

你们 nǐmen ① you (second person plural): 这就是～的责任所在。 This is where your responsibility lies. / ～干护士工作的实在是够辛苦的。 You nurses are really doing very hard work. ② inf. (used in the same way as 你①②): ～奶奶多大岁数了? How old is your grandma? / ～组最近情况怎么样? How is your group getting along these days?

你死我活 nǐsǐ-wǒhuó life-and-death; mortal: ～的斗争 a life-and-death struggle / 拼个～ fight to the bitter end

你追我赶 nǐzhuī-wǒgǎn try to overtake each other in friendly emulation

你走你的阳关道,我过我的独木桥 nǐ zǒu nǐde yángguāndào, wǒ guò wǒde dúmùqiáo you take the open road, I'll cross the log bridge—you go your way, I'll go mine

旎 nǐ see 旖旎 yǐnǐ

nì

泥 nì ① cover or daub with plaster, putty, etc.; putty; plaster: ～墙 cover the crevices in a wall with mud or plaster / 把窗玻璃用油灰～上 fix a windowpane with putty ② stubborn; bigoted; obstinate: 拘泥 jū·nì ——see also ní

泥古 nìgǔ have bigoted belief in the ancients; obstinately follow ancient ways: ～不化 stick to ancient ways to the letter

泥子 nìzi putty

逆 nì ① contrary; counter; inverse; converse: ～反应 inverse reaction; back reaction ② go against; disobey; defy: ～时代潮流而动 go against the trend of the times ③ traitorous; rebellious: ～贼 rebel; traitor / ～臣 traitorous vassal ④ beforehand; in advance: 逆料 nìliào

逆差 nìchā adverse balance of trade; trade deficit: 国际收支～ an adverse (or unfavourable) balance of international payments

逆产 nìchǎn a traitor's property

逆颤音 nìchànyīn mus. inverted trill

逆定理 nìdìnglǐ math. converse theorem

逆耳 nì'ěr grate on the ear; be unpleasant to the ear: ～之言 words or advice unpleasant to hear

逆风 nìfēng ① go against the wind: ～行舟 sail against the wind / ～飞行 make a head-wind flight ② contrary wind; head wind

逆光 nìguāng photog. backlighting

逆火 nìhuǒ (of an internal-combustion engine) backfire: ～式超音速轰炸机 Backfire bomber; Backfire

逆经 nìjīng med. vicarious menstruation

逆境 nìjìng adverse circumstances; adversity: 身处～ be in adverse circumstances

逆来顺受 nì lái shùn shòu meekly submit to oppression, maltreatment, etc.; resign oneself to adversity: 他一辈子老实、无能,对环境的压迫～。 All his life he had been simple, ineffective, docilely accepting the worst his environment had given him.

逆料 nìliào anticipate; foresee: 事态的发展不难～。 The course of events can be foreseen. / 月底能否成行尚难～。 It's still hard to say whether we can leave before the end of the month.

逆流 nìliú ① go against the current: ～而上 sail against the current ② adverse current; countercurrent: 一股反社会主义的～ an adverse current against socialism

逆旅 nìlǚ formal inn; hotel: 宿于～ stay at an inn

逆伦 nìlún formal the violation of proper human relationships (e.g. parricide)

逆事 nìshì ① untoward incidents; mishaps ② rebellious acts

逆水 nìshuǐ (of a boat, etc.) go against the current

逆水行舟 nìshuǐ xíng zhōu a boat sailing against the current: 学如～,不进则退。 Study is like sailing against the current: either you keep forging ahead or you keep falling behind.

逆温 nìwēn meteorol. (temperature) inversion

逆温层 nìwēncéng meteorol. inversion layer

逆行 nìxíng ① (of vehicles) go in a direction not allowed by traffic regulations; go in the wrong direction ② astron. retrograde motion

逆运 nìyùn adversity; misfortune; ill luck

逆证 nìzhèng Chin. med. a severe case with unfavourable prognosis

逆转 nìzhuǎn take a turn for the worse; reverse; deteriorate: 形势突然～。 The situation suddenly deteriorated. / 历史潮流不可～。 It is impossible to reverse the trend of history.

逆子 nìzǐ unfilial son

昵(暱) nì close; intimate: 亲昵 qīnnì

昵称 nìchēng a term of endearment; pet name

匿 nì hide; conceal: 隐匿 yǐnnì

匿报 nìbào withhold information: ～实情 withhold information on the actual situation

匿藏 nìcáng conceal; hide; go into hiding

匿伏 nìfú be in hiding; lurk

匿迹　nìjì　go into hiding; stay in concealment: ～海外 go into hiding abroad; lie low abroad

匿名　nìmíng　anonymous

匿名信　nìmíngxìn　an anonymous letter

匿笑　nìxiào　laugh secretly; laugh up one's sleeve

匿影藏形　nìyǐng-cángxíng　hide from public notice; conceal one's identity; lie low

溺

nì ① drown: ～死 be drowned ② be addicted to: ～于酒色 be given over to wine and woman

溺爱　nì'ài　spoil (a child); dote on (a child)

溺水　nìshuǐ　drowning; sinking: 抢救～儿童 rescue the drowning child／～身亡 be drowned

溺婴　nìyīng　infanticide by drowning

溺职　nìzhí　neglect of duty; dereliction

睨

nì formal look askance: ～视 look sideways; cast a sidelong glance

腻

nì ① greasy; oily: 这炖肉有点～。 This stew is a bit greasy. ／汤太～了。 The soup is too oily. ② be bored with; be tired of: 这些话我都听～了。 I'm tired of listening to all this. ③ meticulous: 细腻 xìnì ④ sticky; grimy: 擦碗布拈手都～了。 The dish towel has got grimy. ⑤ intimate: ～友 a very close friend ⑥ dirt; grime: 尘～ dirt

腻虫　nìchóng　common name for 蚜虫 yáchóng

腻烦　nìfan　inf. ① be bored; be fed up: 这本书我看了多少遍都不觉得～。 I never get bored reading and re-reading this book. ② loathe; hate: 我最～说大话的人。 I can't stand people who brag.

腻人　nìrén　① be boring or tedious: 他老重复那几个笑话，真～。 It's really boring to listen to his same old jokes. ② (of food that is too greasy or sweet) make one sick

腻味　nìwei　dial. ①be bored; be fed up: 这套节目真叫人～。 This programme is really boring. ② hate; loathe: 我最～肥肉，从来不吃。 I hate fatty pork and never eat any.

niān

拈

niān pick up (with the thumb and one or two fingers): 从罐子里～出一块糖 take a candy from the jar

拈花惹草　niānhuā-rěcǎo　toy with flowers and grass —dally with women; philander

拈阄儿　niānjiūr　draw lots

拈轻怕重　niānqīng-pàzhòng　prefer the light to the heavy—pick easy jobs and shirk hard ones

拈香　niānxiāng　offer incense at a temple

蔫

niān ① fade; wither; shrivel up; droop: 菠菜～了。 The spinach is shrivelled up. ／花儿晒～了。 The flowers drooped in the heat of the sun. ② listless; spiritless; droopy: 这孩子有点～，怕是病了。 The child looks a bit listless. I'm afraid he's not well.

蔫巴　niānba　inf. fading; withering; shrivelling: 稻秧都～了。 The rice seedlings were all shrivelled up. ／听说自己落榜，他耷拉下脑袋，～了。 When he heard that he had failed the exam, he hung his head, looking crestfallen.

蔫不唧儿　niānbujīr　dial. ① listless; droopy; sluggish ② quiet: 别看他平时～的，打起仗来可像个小老虎。 Although he is usually rather quiet, he fights like a tiger in battle. ／我还想跟他说话，没想到他一～地走了。 When I turned to speak to him, he'd gone without my noticing.

蔫不溜　niānbuliū　(also 蔫不出溜 niānbuchūliū; 蔫不悄儿 niānbuqiāor) dial. quiet; silent

蔫不声　niānbushēng　quiet; silent

蔫呼呼　niānhūhū　weak-willed and indecisive

蔫儿坏　niānrhuài　dial. be inwardly vicious; behave in an underhand way: 这人瞧着挺老实的，其实～。 He looks honest, but he is really crooked.

蔫蔫　niānniān　dial. ① quiet; silent ② listless; droopy; sluggish

蔫儿淘　niānrtáo　dial. (of a child) playfully artful; mischievous in a quiet or covert way

蔫头耷脑　niāntóu-dānǎo　with head hanging—dejected; listless; droopy

nián

年（季）

nián ① year: 三～ three years／～复一～ year after year; year in year out ② annual; yearly: ～产量 annual output; annual yield ③ age: ～过六十 over sixty (years old) ④ a period in one's life: 童年 tóngnián／老年 lǎonián ⑤ a period in history: 近～来 in recent years／明朝初～ at the beginning of the Ming Dynasty ⑥ harvest: 丰年 fēngnián ⑦ New Year: 拜年 bàinián ⑧ of or for New Year: 年货 niánhuò ⑨ (Nián) a surname

年报　niánbào　① annual (a book or magazine, often used in titles): 《文学～》 Literary Annual／《燕京史学～》 Yanjing Annual of Historical Studies or Yanjing Historical Annual ② annual report

年辈　niánbèi　one's age and generation

年表　niánbiǎo　chronological table

年菜　niáncài　dishes prepared for the lunar New Year (or Spring Festival)

年成　niáncheng　the year's harvest: 好～ a good harvest／～不好 a lean year

年齿　niánchǐ　formal age: ～尚幼 still young in age

年初　niánchū　the beginning of the year: 去年～ at the beginning of last year

年代　niándài　① age; years; time: 战争～ during the war years／～不详 without date; sine anno／～久了，石碑上的字迹已经模糊了。 The inscriptions on the stone tablet have become blurred with the passage of time.／展出的古代文物都标明了～。 The antiques on display are all marked with dates. ② a decade of a century: 八十～ the eighties／二十世纪九十～ the 1990's

年底　niándǐ　the end of the year

年度　niándù　year (a yearly period fixed for a certain purpose): 财政～ financial year; fiscal year／～计划 annual plan

年饭　niánfàn　same as 年夜饭 niányèfàn

年份　niánfèn　① a particular year: 这两笔开支不在一个～。 These two expenditures were not incurred in the same year. ② age; time: 这件瓷器的～比那件久。 This piece of porcelain is older than that one.

年俸　niánfèng　annual salary; yearly pay

年富力强　niánfù-lìqiáng　in the prime of life; in one's prime: ～的干部 young and energetic cadres

年高德劭　niángāo-déshào　of venerable age and eminent virtue; of advanced years and known integrity; venerable

年糕　niángāo　New Year cake (made of glutinous rice flour)

年根　niángēn　dial. the end of the year

年庚　niángēng　the time (year, month, day and hour) of a person's birth; date of birth

年关　niánguān　the end of the year (formerly time for settling accounts): 在旧社会，～是穷人的鬼门关。 In the

old society the end of the year was a terrible time for the poor.

年光 niánguāng ① time; years ② the year's harvest

年号 niánhào reign title (a designation for the years when an emperor was on the throne, e.g. Kaiyuan 开元, the title of the second of the three reign periods of Emperor Xuanzong of the Tang Dynasty 唐玄宗; the Ming and Qing emperors, who as a rule used just one reign title throughout the years when they were in power, are sometimes referred to by the titles of their reign periods instead of their temple titles 庙号, e.g. Emperor Shengzu of the Qing Dynasty 清圣祖, better known as Emperor Kangxi 康熙 after the title of his single reign period)

年华 niánhuá time; years: 虚度年华 xūdù niánhuá

年画 niánhuà New Year (or Spring Festival) pictures

年会 niánhuì annual meeting

年货 niánhuò special purchases for the Spring Festival: 办～ do Spring Festival shopping

年级 niánjí grade; year: 大学三～学生 third year university student / 小学一～学生 first grade primary school pupil

年集 niánjí country fair (or market) at the end of the lunar year

年纪 niánjì age: ～轻 young / 你多大～了? How old are you?

年假 niánjià ① New Year holidays ② winter vacation

年间 niánjiān certain period (of a dynasty or reign): 光绪～ in the period of Emperor Guangxu

年鉴 niánjiàn yearbook; almanac: 《中国～》(1990 年) *China Yearbook 1990*

年节 niánjié the lunar New Year Festival; the Spring Festival

年金 niánjīn annuity

年馑 niánjǐn *dial.* famine (or lean) year

年景 niánjǐng ① the year's harvest: 在正常～下 in normal harvest years ② holiday atmosphere of the Spring Festival

年久日深 niánjiǔ-rìshēn (also 年久月深 niánjiǔ-yuèshēn) same as 年深日久 niánshēn-rìjiǔ

年均 niánjūn annual average: 他们农场养的鸡每只～产蛋240个。The hens raised on their farm each average 240 eggs a year.

年来 niánlái in the past year; in recent years

年历 niánlì a calendar with the whole year printed on one sheet; single-page calendar

年利 niánlì annual interest: ～率 annual interest rate

年龄 niánlíng age: 他参军还不够～。He is too young to join the army. / 从马的牙齿可以看出它的～。You can tell a horse's age from its teeth. / ～不饶人。Age will show itself. *or* Age will tell.

年轮 niánlún *bot.* annual ring; growth ring

年迈 niánmài old; aged: ～力衰 old and infirm; senile

年貌 nián-mào age and appearance: 两人～相当。The two are well matched in age and appearance.

年末 niánmò the end of the year

年年 niánnián every year; year after year

年谱 niánpǔ chronological life: 《汤显祖～》 *Chronological Life of Tang Xianzu*

年青 niánqīng young

年轻 niánqīng young: ～人 young people / ～力壮 young and vigorous / ～一代 the younger (or rising) generation / 干部要～化。Let the age of our government officials be younger in average.

年少 niánshào ① young ② youngster; a young man: 翩翩～ an elegant young man

年深日久 niánshēn-rìjiǔ (also 年深月久 niánshēn-yuèjiǔ) with the passage of time; as the years go by: 河里的泥沙淤积在这里,～便成了沙洲。The bar was formed by

the mud and sand deposited here over a long period of time.

年时 niánshí ① *dial.* years; a long time ② *formal* former years

年时 niánshi *dial.* last year: 他们是～才结的婚。They got married only last year.

年事 niánshì *formal* age (of a person): ～已高 be advanced in years

年岁 niánsuì ① age: 上了～的人 a person who is getting on in years ② years: 因为～久远, 当时的具体情况已记不清了。As it happened so many years ago, I don't remember the details.

年头 niántóu ① year: 他到武汉已经三个～了。It's three years since he came to Wuhan. ② years; a long time: 她干这一行有～了。She has been doing this sort of work for years. / 这些树不够～, 还没成材呢。These trees need more time to grow into useful timber. ③ days; times: 那～ in those days ④ harvest: 今年～真好。This year's harvest is very good indeed.

年尾 niánwěi the end of the year

年息 niánxī annual interest

年下 niánxià *inf.* the lunar New Year (i.e. the first half of the first month)

年限 niánxiàn fixed number of years: 学习～ the number of years set for a course (of study) / 工具使用～ the service life of a tool

年薪 niánxīn annual salary; yearly pay

年夜 niányè the lunar New Year's Eve

年夜饭 niányèfàn family reunion dinner on the lunar New Year's Eve

年幼 niányòu young; under age: ～无知 young and ignorant

年月 niányue ① days; years ② *inf.* times: 太平～ peaceful times

年长 niánzhǎng older in age; senior

年终 niánzhōng the end of the year; year-end: ～结帐 year-end settlement of accounts / ～评比 year-end appraisal of work

年资 niánzī age and years of service; seniority

年尊 niánzūn older in age; advanced in age

粘 nián same as 黏 nián ——see also zhān

鮎(鯰) nián catfish

鮎鱼 niányú catfish

黏 nián sticky; glutinous: 这浆糊不～。This paste is not sticky enough.

黏儿 niánr *dial.* gum; resin

黏巴 niánba (also 黏巴巴的 niánbābāde) sticky; gluey; gummy: 手上有点儿～。My hand is somewhat sticky.

黏虫 niánchóng armyworm

黏度 niándù *chem.* viscosity: 恩氏～ Engler viscosity

黏度计 niándùjì viscosimeter

黏附 niánfù adhere: ～力 adhesion / ～体 adherend

黏糕 niángāo same as 年糕 niángāo

黏合 niánhé *chem.* bind; bond; adhere

黏合剂 niánhéjì binder; adhesive; bonding agent

黏糊 niánhu (also 黏糊糊儿的 niánhūhūrde) ① sticky; glutinous: 粥熬得怪～的。The rice gruel is well cooked. ② languid; slow-moving

黏胶 niánjiāo *chem.* viscose

黏胶长丝 niánjiāo chángsī viscose filament yarn

黏胶短纤维 niánjiāo duǎnxiānwéi viscose staple fibre

黏胶丝 niánjiāosī viscose

黏胶纤维 niánjiāoxiānwéi viscose fibre

黏结 niánjié cohere: ～力 cohesion; cohesive force / ～性 cohesiveness

黏菌 niánjūn *bacteriol.* slime mould; slime fungus

黏米　niánmǐ　① glutinous rice ② *dial.* broomcorn millet

黏膜　niánmó　*physiol.* mucous membrane; mucosa

黏膜炎　niánmóyán　*med.* mucositis

黏土　niántǔ　clay: 耐火～ refractory clay / ～矿物 clay mineral / ～岩 clay rock

黏涎子　niánxiánzi　*dial.* slaver; slobber

黏涎　niánxian　*dial.* tedious; dull

黏性　niánxìng　stickiness; viscidity; viscosity

黏性油　niánxìngyóu　viscous oil

黏液　niányè　*physiol.* mucus

黏液性水肿　niányèxìng shuǐzhǒng　*med.* myxoedema

黏着　niánzhuó　stick together; adhere

黏着语　niánzhuóyǔ　*linguis.* agglutinative language

niǎn

捻 (撚)　niǎn　① twist with the fingers: ～线 twist thread / 把油灯～大些 turn up the wick (of a lamp) ② sth. made by twisting: 灯～儿 lampwick

捻度　niǎndù　*text.* number of turns (*or* twists); twist

捻军　Niǎnjūn　the Nian Army (the Torch Bearers, a peasant army that rose against the Qing Dynasty, 1852–1868)

捻捻转儿　niǎnnianzhuànr　a wooden or plastic top set in motion by hand

捻线机　niǎnxiànjī　*text.* twisting frame

捻针　niǎnzhēn　*Chin. med.* twirling or rotating of the acupuncture needle

捻子　niǎnzi　spill (for lighting candles, lamps, etc.); wick

辇　niǎn　① a man-drawn carriage used in ancient times ② imperial carriage

碾 (輾)　niǎn　① roller and millstone; stone roller ② grind or husk with a roller: ～米 husk rice / ～得粉碎 be crushed to powder; be crushed to pieces; be pulverized / ～平 flatten or level (with a roller); roll out

碾场　niǎnchǎng　*dial.* thresh or husk grain on a threshing ground

碾槌　niǎnchuí　pestle

碾坊　niǎnfáng　(also 碾房 niǎnfáng) grain mill

碾滚子　niǎngǔnzi　stone roller (for grinding or husking grain on a millstone)

碾米厂　niǎnmǐchǎng　rice-hulling mill

碾米机　niǎnmǐjī　rice mill (a machine)

碾盘　niǎnpán　a millstone upon which a stone roller is used

碾碎　niǎnsuì　pulverize

碾砣　niǎntuó　same as 碾滚子 niǎngǔnzi

碾子　niǎnzi　roller and millstone; roller

撵　niǎn　① drive out; oust: 把人～走 drive sb. away / ～下台 oust from a leading position ② *dial.* catch up: 我～不上他。I couldn't catch up with him.

niàn

廿　niàn　twenty

念[1]　niàn　① think of; miss: 我们老～着你。We miss you very much. ② thought; idea: 杂念 zániàn

念[2] (唸)　niàn　① read aloud: 她把上级的指示～给大家听。She read out the directive from the higher authorities. ② attend school: 他～过中学。He has been to middle school.

念[3]　niàn　twenty (used for the numeral 廿 on cheques, etc. to avoid mistakes or alterations)

念白　niànbái　spoken parts of a Chinese opera

念叨　niàndao　(also 念道 niàndao) ① talk about again and again in recollection or anticipation; be always talking about: 他就是我们常常～的张大伯。This is the Uncle Zhang we're always talking about. ② *dial.* talk over; discuss: 我有个事儿跟大家～～。I've got something to talk over with you.

念佛　niànfó　chant the name of Buddha; pray to Buddha: 吃素～ be a reverent Buddhist and practise vegetarianism

念经　niànjīng　recite or chant scriptures

念旧　niànjiù　keep old friendships in mind; remember old friends

念念不忘　niànniàn bù wàng　bear in mind constantly

念念有词　niànniàn yǒu cí　① mutter incantations ② mumble

念书　niànshū　① read ② study

念诵　niànsòng　read aloud; chant: ～诗文 read aloud poems and essays

念诵　niànsong　talk about (in recollection or anticipation): 老太太方才还在～呢，可巧你就来了。Granny was just talking about you a minute ago, and here you are now.

念头　niàntou　thought; idea; intention: 当时他心中只有一个～，就是为祖国增光。At that time he had only one thing in mind: to win credit for his country. / 你最好放弃这个～。You'd better give up the idea.

念物　niànwù　souvenir; keepsake; memento

念心儿　niànxinr　*dial.* souvenir; keepsake; memento: 把这支钢笔送给你，做个～吧! Keep this pen as a souvenir.

念咒　niànzhòu　chant incantations

念珠　niànzhū　beads; rosary

念兹在兹　niàn zī zài zī　bear in mind always; have sth. or sb. constantly in one's mind

埝　niàn　a low bank between fields: 打～ build banks between fields

niáng

娘 (孃)　niáng　① ma; mum; mother: 爹～ father and mother ② a form of address for an elderly married woman: 婶～ wife of one's father's younger brother; aunt ③ a young woman: 渔～ a young fisherwoman

娘儿　niángr　*inf.* (followed by a numeral-classifier compound) mother and son or daughter; aunt and niece or nephew: ～俩 mother and son or daughter / ～三个合计了好半天，也想不出个主意来。The mother and her two children discussed it for quite some time but still couldn't make up their minds.

娘家　niángjia　a married woman's parents' home

娘舅　niángjiù　*dial.* brother of one's mother; uncle

娘儿们　niángrmen　① *inf.* mother and son or daughter ② *dial.* the womenfolk: 咱～不比男的差。We womenfolk are just as good as the men. ③ *dial.* wife

娘娘　niángniang　① (used in speaking to or of an empress or an imperial concubine): (太监)万岁爷有

旨, 宣贵妃杨～上殿。(洪昇《长生殿》) (Eunuch speaking) His Majesty orders Lady Yang to approach. / (宫女)镜奁齐备, 请～理妆。(同上) (Maid speaking) All is ready for your toilet, my lady (or for Your Ladyship's toilet). / 正宫～ emperor's wife; empress ② a name for certain guardian goddesses: 子孙～ Our Lady of Many Children or Goddess of Fertility (a patroness of marriage and giver of sons) / ～庙 Temple of the Goddess of Fertility

娘亲 niángqīn　mother

娘胎 niángtāi　mother's womb: 出了～ be born / 从～带来的记 a birthmark

娘姨 niángyí　*dial.* maidservant

娘子 niáng·zǐ　① *dial.* a form of address for one's wife ② *old* a polite form of address for a young woman

娘子军 niáng·zǐjūn　a detachment of women; any contingent entirely made up of women

niàng

酿(釀)　niàng　① make (wine); brew (beer): 酿酒 niàngjiǔ ② make (honey): 蜜蜂会～蜜。Bees make honey. ③ lead to; result in: ～祸 lead to disaster ④ wine: 佳～ good wine

酿成 niàngchéng　lead to; bring on; breed: 主观主义的批评往往～无原则的纠纷。Subjective criticism often breeds unprincipled disputes. / 小错不改往往～大错。Small mistakes left uncorrected will lead to big ones.

酿酒 niàngjiǔ　make wine; brew beer: ～业 wine-making industry

酿酒厂 niàngjiǔchǎng　winery; brewery

酿酶 niàngméi　*chem.* zymase

酿母菌 niàngmǔjūn　another name for 酵母 jiàomǔ

酿热物 niàngrèwù　ferment material

酿造 niàngzào　make (wine, vinegar, etc.); brew (beer, etc.)

niǎo

鸟(鳥)　niǎo　bird ——see also diǎo

鸟儿 niǎor　a small bird; birdie

鸟粪 niǎofèn　① birds' droppings ② guano

鸟粪层 niǎofèncéng　guano

鸟害 niǎohài　bird pest

鸟喙 niǎohuì　beak; bill

鸟尽弓藏 niǎojìn gōngcáng　cast aside the bow once the birds are all killed—cast sb. aside when he has served his purpose

鸟瞰 niǎokàn　① get a bird's-eye view: ～全城 get a bird's-eye view of the city ② a general survey of a subject; bird's-eye view: 古代史～ a general survey of ancient history

鸟瞰图 niǎokàntú　a bird's-eye view; an aerial view: 市区市郊～ a bird's-eye view of the city and its suburbs

鸟类 niǎolèi　birds (of any kind)

鸟类学 niǎolèixué　ornithology

鸟笼 niǎolóng　birdcage

鸟枪 niǎoqiāng　① fowling piece ② air gun

鸟兽 niǎo·shòu　birds and beasts; fur and feather

鸟兽散 niǎo·shòu sàn　see 作鸟兽散 zuò niǎo·shòu sàn

鸟窝 niǎowō　(bird's) nest

鸟语花香 niǎoyǔ·huāxiāng　birds sing and flowers give forth fragrance (as on a fine spring day)

鸟篆 niǎozhuàn　bird script, an ancient form of Chinese written characters, resembling birds' footprints

鸟嘴 niǎozuǐ　beak; bill

茑　niǎo　a kind of creeping plant

茑萝 niǎoluó　*bot.* cypress vine (*Quamoclit pennata*)

袅(嫋)　niǎo　slender and delicate

袅袅 niǎoniǎo　① curl upwards: 炊烟～。Smoke is curling upward from kitchen chimneys. ② wave in the wind: 垂杨～。Drooping willows are dancing in the wind. ③ linger: 余音～。The music lingered in the air long after the performance ended.

袅袅婷婷 niǎoniǎotíngtíng　*liter.* (of a girl or young woman) lithe, slim and supple; lissom and graceful

袅娜 niǎonuó　*liter.* ① (of plants) soft and slender: 春风吹拂着～的柳丝。The slender willow twigs were swaying gently in the spring breeze. ② (of a female figure) delicate and graceful; willowy: 解舞腰肢娇又软, 千般～, 万般旖旎, 似垂柳晚风前。(王实甫《西厢记》) Her dancing waist, how soft and supple! A thousand graces and ten thousand charms she has, Like a drooping willow before the evening breeze.

niào

尿(溺)　niào　① urine ② urinate; make water; piss: 这孩子～了我一身。The baby has wetted my clothes. ——see also suī

尿崩症 niàobēngzhèng　*med.* diabetes insipidus

尿闭 niàobì　*med.* anuria

尿布 niàobù　diaper; napkin; nappy

尿床 niàochuáng　bed-wetting: 这孩子又～了。The child wetted the bed again.

尿胆素 niàodǎnsù　*med.* urobilin: ～原 urobilinogen

尿道 niàodào　*physiol.* urethra: ～造影 urethrography

尿道炎 niàodàoyán　*med.* urethritis

尿毒症 niàodúzhèng　*med.* uraemia

尿肥 niàoféi　urine used as manure

尿炕 niàokàng　wet the *kang;* wet the bed

尿盆 niàopén　chamber pot; urinal

尿频 niàopín　*med.* frequent micturition

尿少症 niàoshǎozhèng　*med.* oliguria

尿失禁 niàoshījìn　*med.* urinary incontinence; incontinence of urine

尿素 niàosù　*chem.* urea; carbamide

尿素脱蜡 niàosù tuōlà　*petroleum* urea dewaxing

尿酸 niàosuān　*chem.* uric acid

尿血 niàoxiě　*med.* haematuria

尿潴留 niàozhūliú　*med.* retention of urine

脲　niào　same as 尿素 niàosù

脲醛塑料 niàoquán sùliào　*chem.* urea-formaldehyde plastics

niē

捏(揑)　niē　① hold between the finger and thumb; pinch: ～着鼻子 stop one's nose with the fingers / 把米里的虫子～出来 pick the worms out of the rice ② knead with the fingers; mould: ～泥人儿 mould clay figurines / ～饺子 make dumplings ③ fabricate; make up: ～报 fake a report

捏把汗 niē bǎ hàn　(also 捏一把汗 niē yìbǎ hàn) be breathless with anxiety or tension; be keyed up; be on edge: 看着他们表演杂技, 我们都捏一把汗。We were breathless as we watched the acrobats. / 他在第一次登

台之前着实捏了把汗呢。He was all keyed up before making his first stage appearance. / 她捏着一把汗等待发榜。She was on edge while waiting for her exam results.

捏咕 niēgu *inf.* ① play with; fiddle with ② order about; manipulate ③ discuss in private

捏合 niēhé ① put together; bring together: 他俩结婚缺乏感情基础，是双方家长硬把他们～在一起的。Their marriage was not a love match; it was their parents who brought them together against their wishes. ② *old* fabricate; concoct; fake

捏合机 niēhéjī *chem. fibre* kneading machine

捏积 niējī *Chin. med.* a method of treating children's digestive disorders by kneading or massaging the muscles along the spine; chiropractic

捏弄 niēnong ① play with; fiddle with: 她一边说话，一边～着毛衣上的纽扣。As she talked, she fiddled with the buttons on her sweater. ② order about; manipulate: 我们不能由着别人～。We shouldn't allow ourselves to be ordered about. ③ discuss in private: 这事他俩一一～就那么办了。The two of them discussed the matter in private and then got it all settled.

捏造 niēzào fabricate; concoct; fake; trump up: ～事实 invent a story; make up a story / ～罪名 trump up charges / ～数字 conjure up figures / 纯属～。That's sheer fabrication.

捏闸 niēzhá apply the handbrake

nié

茶 nié tired; listless; lethargic: 发～ look listless

niè

陧（陧） niè see 杌陧 wùniè

聂（聶） Niè a surname

涅 niè *formal* ① alunite ② dye sth. black

涅白 nièbái opaque white

涅槃 nièpán *Buddhism* nirvana

臬 niè *formal* ① target ② gnomon; style (of a sundial in ancient times) ③ standard; criterion

啮（齧、囓） niè (of rodents) gnaw; nibble

啮齿动物 nièchǐ dòngwù rodent

啮齿目 nièchǐmù *zool.* Rodentia

啮合 nièhé ① clench the teeth ② (of gears) mesh; engage: 这个小齿轮和另外两个齿轮相～。The pinion meshes with two other gear wheels. / 这两个齿轮～在一起。The two cogwheels are engaged.

嗫（囁） niè see below

嗫嚅 nièrú *formal* speak haltingly

镊（鑷） niè ① tweezers ② pick up sth. with tweezers

镊子 nièzi tweezers: 一把～ a pair of tweezers

镍 niè *chem.* nickel (Ni): ～箔 nickel foil

镍币 nièbì nickel coin; nickel

镍钢 niègāng nickel steel

镍黄铁矿 nièhuángtiěkuàng pentlandite (a mineral)

颞（顳） niè see below

颞骨 niègǔ *physiol.* temporal bone

颞颥 nièrú *physiol.* temple

蹑（躡） niè ① lighten one's steps; walk on tiptoe: 他～着脚走出病房。He tiptoed out of the ward. ② follow: 蹑踪 nièzōng ③ *formal* tread; step on; trample

蹑悄悄 nièqiāoqiāo softly; quietly: 她～地拉开门闩，没有惊动任何人。She unfastened the latch quietly without disturbing anybody.

蹑手蹑脚 nièshǒu-nièjiǎo walk gingerly; walk on tiptoe: 她～地脸也没洗就溜出门去了。Without stopping to wash, she tiptoed out of the house. / 他～摸上楼来。With light steps and soft movements of his hands he felt his way up the stairs.

蹑踪 nièzōng *formal* follow the trail of; track

蹑足 nièzú ① walk with light steps: 他～走到门口。He tiptoed to the door. ② *formal* participate in; join: ～其间 join a profession; follow a trade; associate with a certain type of people

蹑足潜踪 nièzú-qiánzōng walk stealthily

孽（孼） niè evil; sin: 作孽 zuòniè / 妖孽 yāoniè

孽报 nièbào same as 业报 yèbào

孽海 nièhǎi same as 业海 yèhǎi

孽障 nièzhàng same as 业障 yèzhàng

孽种 nièzhǒng ① *old* the bane of one's existence ② *offens.* (said to one's descendant) vile spawn; bastard

孽子 nièzǐ ① *old* son of a concubine ② an unfilial son; an unworthy descendant

蘖 niè *bot.* tiller: 分蘖 fēnniè

蘖枝 nièzhī branch stem

nín

您 nín *honor.* you: 老师，～早! Good morning, sir! *or* Good morning, ma'am!

níng

宁（寧、甯） níng ① peaceful; tranquil: 宁静 níngjìng ② (Níng) short for 宁夏回族自治区 Níngxià Huízú Zìzhìqū ③ (Níng) another name for 南京 Nánjīng: 沪～线 the Shanghai-Nanjing Railway ——see also nìng

宁靖 níngjìng *formal* stable; tranquil; in peace

宁静 níngjìng peaceful; tranquil; quiet; calm: ～的夜晚 a tranquil night / 心里渐渐～下来 calm down gradually

宁日 níngrì peaceful days

宁帖 níngtiē (of state of mind) tranquil; calm

宁夏 Níngxià Ningxia

宁夏回族自治区 Níngxià Huízú Zìzhìqū the Ningxia Hui Autonomous Region

宁馨儿 níngxīn'ér *formal* a lovely child

拧（擰） níng ① twist; wring: ～麻绳 twist hemp into rope / 把衣服～干 wring out wet clothes ② pinch; tweak: ～了他一把 give him a pinch ——see also nǐng; nìng

拧成一股绳 níngchéng yī gǔ shéng twist into a rope——stick together; make joint efforts: 只要大伙儿～，没有克服不了的困难。As long as we are united, there is no difficulty we cannot overcome.

咛（嚀）　níng　see 叮咛 dīngníng

苧（薴）　níng　*chem.* limonene

狞（獰）　níng　(of facial expression) ferocious; hideous: 狰狞 zhēngníng

狞恶　níng'è　fierce; ferocious: ～的嘴脸 ferocious features

狞视　níngshì　stare fiercely at; fix one's sinister eyes on

狞笑　níngxiào　grin hideously

柠（檸）　níng　see below

柠檬　níngméng　lemon: ～糖 lemon drops / ～汁 lemon juice

柠檬黄　níngménghuáng　citrine; lemon-coloured

柠檬水　níngméngshuǐ　lemonade; lemon squash

柠檬素　níngméngsù　*chem.* citrin; vitamin P

柠檬酸　níngméngsuān　*chem.* citric acid

聍（聹）　níng　see 耵聍 dīngníng

凝　níng　① congeal; coagulate; curdle; condense: 他的衬衣都被血～住了。His shirt was congealed with blood. / 用鲜血～成的战斗友谊 militant friendship cemented with blood ② with fixed attention: 凝思 níngsī

凝点　níngdiǎn　*phys.* condensation point

凝冻　níngdòng　freeze: 河水～。The river is frozen.

凝固　nínggù　solidify: 蛋白质遇热会～。Protein becomes solid when heated.

凝固点　nínggùdiǎn　*phys.* solidifying point

凝固汽油　nínggù qìyóu　napalm

凝固汽油弹　nínggù qìyóudàn　napalm bomb

凝固浴　nínggùyù　*text.* coagulating bath

凝华　nínghuá　*phys.* sublimate: ～核 sublimation nucleus

凝灰岩　nínghuīyán　*geol.* tuff

凝集　níngjí　(of fluids or gases) agglutinate

凝集素　níngjísù　*chem.* agglutinin

凝寂　níngjì　deep silence or stillness: 在那～的夜晚 in the deep stillness of the night

凝结　níngjié　congeal; coagulate; curdle; condense: 湖面上～了一层薄冰。A thin layer of ice formed over the lake. / 我的每一点进步都～着老师们的心血。Every bit of the progress I have made in my studies is the result of my teachers' patient guidance.

凝结剂　níngjiéjì　*chem.* coagulant

凝结力　níngjiélì　coagulability

凝结尾迹　níngjié wěijì　contrail; condensation trail; vapour trail

凝结物　níngjiéwù　coagulum

凝聚　níngjù　① (of vapour) condense; (of fluids) coagulate or curdle: 荷叶上～着晶莹的露珠。Glistening dewdrops have formed on the lotus leaves. / 南京长江大桥～着中国工人阶级的高度智慧。The Changjiang River Bridge at Nanjing is an embodiment of the superb wisdom of the Chinese working class. ② *chem.* coacervation

凝聚层　níngjùcéng　coacervate

凝聚力　níngjùlì　① *phys.* cohesive force; cohesion ② cohesion (fig.): 增强中华民族的～ increase the cohesion of the Chinese nation

凝练　níngliàn　(of writing) concise; condensed; compact

凝眸　níngmóu　*liter.* fix (or focus) one's eyes on; look with a fixed gaze: ～远望 gaze into the distance

凝神　níngshén　with fixed (or concentrated, rapt) attention: ～谛听 listen with rapt attention; listen attentively

凝视　níngshì　gaze fixedly; stare: 我久久地～着那尊铜像。I fixed my eyes on the bronze statue for a long time.

凝思　níngsī　be lost in thought; meditate

凝听　níngtīng　listen attentively (or intently) listen with rapt attention

凝望　níngwàng　gaze or stare at: 他～着她那逐渐远去的身影。He couldn't tear his eyes away from her receding figure.

凝析油　níngxīyóu　*petroleum* condensate

凝想　níngxiǎng　be lost in thought; meditate

凝血酶　níngxuèméi　thrombin; thrombase

凝血药　níngxuèyào　*med.* coagulant

凝脂　níngzhī　*liter.* congealed fat (said of a woman's skin): 肤如～ smooth, soft and glossy skin

凝滞　níngzhì　stagnant; unmoving; sluggish: ～的目光 dull, staring eyes

凝重　níngzhòng　① dignified; imposing: 神情～ look dignified ② (of sound or voice) deep and forceful: 他的声音～有力。He has a deep, powerful voice. ③ deep; dense; thick: ～的乌云 heavy (or thick) black clouds

nǐng

拧（擰）　nǐng　① twist; screw: ～开瓶盖 screw (or twist) the cap off a bottle / ～上盖子 screw a lid on / ～紧螺丝 tighten up a screw ② wrong; mistaken: 他想说"小题大做"，说～了，说成"大题小做"。He meant to say "make a mountain out of a molehill," but he got it the wrong way round and said "make a molehill out of a mountain". ③ differ; disagree; be at cross-purposes: 两个人越说越～。The more they talked, the more they disagreed. ——see also níng; nìng

拧咕　nǐnggu　*inf.* ① twisted; screwed; awry; askew: 把袜子穿～了 wear one's stockings askew ② (also 拧股 nǐnggu) disagree; be at odds; be at cross-purposes: 他俩老～着，整天吵嘴。They two are often at odds and are bickering all the time. ③ twist; turn; twiddle: 那孩子把这台收音机给～坏了。The boy twiddled with the knobs until the radio broke down.

nìng

宁¹（寧、甯）　nìng　① *adv.* would rather: 我～死也不投降。I would rather die than surrender. ② *formal* could there be: 山之险峻，～有逾此? Could there be a mountain more precipitous than this?

宁²（甯）　Nìng　a surname
——see also nìng

宁教我负天下人，休教天下人负我　nìng jiào wǒ fù tiānxià rén, xiū jiào tiānxià rén fù wǒ　I would rather betray the world than let the world betray me (a saying attributed to Cao Cao 曹操)

宁可　nìngkě　*adv.* would rather: ～站着死，绝不跪着生 would rather die on one's feet than live on one's knees / 他～放弃休假，也要把工作做完。He would rather give up his holidays than not finish his work. / ～小心一点的好。Better safe than sorry. / 与其你去，～我去。Better I go than you.

宁肯　nìngkěn　*adv.* would rather

宁缺毋滥　nìng quē wú làn　rather go without than have something shoddy—put quality before quantity

宁死不屈　nìng sǐ bù qū　rather die than submit (or surrender)

宁为鸡口，无为牛后　nìng wéi jīkǒu, wú wéi niúhòu　better

be a bird's beak than a cow's rump; better be a dog's head than a lion's tail; better to reign in hell than serve in heaven

宁为太平犬, 莫作乱离人　nìng wéi tàipíng quǎn, mò zuò luànlí rén　rather be a dog in times of peace than be a human in times of war

宁为玉碎, 不为瓦全　nìng wéi yù suì, bù wéi wǎ quán　rather be a broken piece of jade than a whole tile—better to die in glory than live in dishonour: 万一失败, 那就"~"。 In the event that we fail we'd rather fall to pieces like broken jade than remain intact as a worthless tile.

宁愿　nìngyuàn　*adv.*　would rather

佞　nìng　① given to flattery: ~人 sycophant; toady ② witty; wise: 不佞 bùnìng

佞臣　nìngchén　a sycophantic official or courtier

泞(濘)　nìng　muddy; miry

泞滑　nìnghuá　muddy and slippery

拧(擰)　nìng　*dial.*　pigheaded; stubborn ——see also níng; nǐng

niū

妞　niū　*inf.*　girl: 他家有两个~儿, 大~十岁, 小~才两岁。 They've got two girls. The elder one is ten, and the younger just two.

妞妞　niūniū　*dial.*　a little girl

niú

牛　niú　① ox; cattle: 母~ cow / 公~ bull / 小~ calf ② stubborn or arrogant: 牛脾气 niúpíqi / 牛气 niúqi ③ the ninth of the twenty-eight constellations (二十八宿) into which the celestial sphere was divided in ancient Chinese astronomy (consisting of six stars, three in Aries and three in Sagittarius) ④ (Niú) a surname

牛蒡　niúbàng　*bot.*　great burdock (*Arctium lappa*)

牛蒡子　niúbàngzǐ　*Chin. med.*　the achene of great burdock

牛鼻子　niúbízi　the nose (*or* muzzle) of an ox: 牵牛要牵~。 We must lead an ox by the halter.

牛脖子　niúbózi　*dial.*　stubbornness; obstinacy; bull-headedness

牛不喝水强按头　niú bù hēshuǐ qiáng àn tóu　try to make an ox drink by forcing his head into the water—try to impose one's will on sb.

牛车　niúchē　ox cart; bullock cart

牛刀小试　niúdāo xiǎo shì　a master hand's first small display

牛痘　niúdòu　① cowpox ② smallpox pustule; vaccine pustule: 种~ give or get smallpox vaccination

牛痘苗　niúdòumiáo　(bovine) vaccine

牛犊　niúdú　calf

牛顿　niúdùn　*phys.*　newton (the standard metre-kilogram-second unit of force, named after Sir Isaac Newton)

牛顿望远镜　niúdùn wàngyuǎnjìng　Newtonian telescope

牛轭　niú'è　oxbow; yoke

牛轭湖　niú'èhú　*geog.*　oxbow lake

牛耳　niú'ěr　see 执牛耳 zhí niú'ěr

牛肺疫　niúfèiyì　pleuropneumonia (of cattle)

牛粪　niúfèn　cow dung

牛倌　niúguān　cowherd; cowhand; oxherd; herd-boy

牛鬼蛇神　niúguǐ-shéshén　monsters and demons—forces of evil; evil people of all descriptions

牛黄　niúhuáng　*Chin. med.*　bezoar

牛角　niújiǎo　ox horn: ~画 horn mosaic / ~制品 hornware

牛角尖　niújiǎojiān　the tip of a horn—an insignificant or insoluble problem ——see also 钻牛角尖 zuān niújiǎojiān

牛劲　niújìn　① great strength; tremendous effort: 他费了~才把门打开。 He had to exert all his strength to open the door. ② stubbornness; obstinacy; tenacity: 这小伙子有股子~, 干一件事就非干到底不行。 The lad is strong-willed; once he starts doing something, he won't leave off until he's finished it.

牛栏　niúlán　cattle pen

牛郎　niúláng　① old herd-boy; cowherd; oxherd ② (Niúláng) the Herd-boy (see 牛郎织女 Niúláng Zhīnǚ②)

牛郎星　Niúlángxīng　common name for 牵牛星 Qiānniúxīng

牛郎织女　Niúláng Zhīnǚ　① the Herd-boy and the Weaving-girl (two lovers in mythology, identified with the stars Altair and Vega, who are separated by the River of Heaven, or the Milky Way, and are permitted to meet only once a year, on the seventh day of the seventh lunar month, when magpies form a bridge for them to pass over the barrier) ② husband and wife forced to live in different parts of the country

牛马　niúmǎ　oxen and horses—beasts of burden: 在旧社会, 劳动人民过的是~不如的生活。 In the old society the labouring people lived worse than beasts of burden.

牛毛　niúmáo　ox hair: ~细雨 drizzle

牛毛雨　niúmáoyǔ　drizzle

牛虻　niúméng　gadfly

牛奶　niúnǎi　milk

牛奶场　niúnǎichǎng　dairy

牛奶糖　niúnǎitáng　toffee

牛腩　niúnǎn　*dial.*　sirloin; tenderloin

牛年马月　niúnián-mǎyuè　same as 驴年马月 lǘnián-mǎyuè

牛排　niúpái　beefsteak

牛棚　niúpéng　cowshed

牛皮　niúpí　① cowhide; oxhide ② tough; tensile; pliable: 牛皮糖 niúpítáng ③ bragging: ~大王 braggart ——see also 吹牛皮 chuī niúpí

牛皮糖　niúpítáng　a sticky candy

牛皮癣　niúpíxuǎn　*med.*　psoriasis

牛皮纸　niúpízhǐ　kraft (paper)

牛脾气　niúpíqi　stubbornness; obstinacy; bullheadedness

牛气　niúqi　*dial.*　arrogant; overbearing

牛肉　niúròu　beef: ~汁 beef extract

牛舌鱼　niúshéyú　tonguefish; tongue sole

牛虱　niúshī　ox louse

牛溲马勃　niúsōu-mǎbó　cheap but useful things

牛头刨　niútóubào　(also 牛头刨床 niútóu bàochuáng) shaping machine; shaper

牛头不对马嘴　niútóu bù duì mǎzuǐ　horses' jaws don't match cows' heads—incongruous; irrelevant: 他的回答简直是~。 His answer is completely off the point.

牛头马面　Niútóu Mǎmiàn　Ox Head and Horse Face (two demon attendants of the King of Hell)

牛蛙　niúwā　bullfrog

牛尾　niúwěi　oxtail: ~汤 oxtail soup

牛尾鱼　niúwěiyú　flathead

牛瘟　niúwēn　rinderpest; cattle plague

牛膝　niúxī　*Chin. med.*　the root of bidentate achyran-

thes (*Achyranthes bidentata*)

牛性　niúxìng　(also 牛心 niúxīn) same as 牛脾气 niúpíqi

牛鞅　niúyàng　(also 牛鞅子 niúyàngzi) martingale for an ox

牛饮　niúyǐn　drink gallons

牛虻　niúyíng　common name for 牛虻 niúméng

牛油　niúyóu　butter

牛崽裤　niúzǎikù　(also 牛仔裤 niúzǎikù) jeans

niǔ

忸　niǔ　see below

忸怩　niǔní　blushing; bashful

忸怩作态　niǔní zuòtài　behave coyly; be affectedly shy: 我讨厌她的～。I'm sick of her affected manners.

扭　niǔ　① turn round: 他～过头来看了一下。He looked over his shoulder. ② twist; wrench: 把树枝子～断 twist a twig and break it / 用力把门～开 wrench the door open ③ sprain; wrench: ～了筋 wrench a tendon; sprain a muscle / ～了腰 sprain one's back ④ roll; swing: 他走路一～一～的。He walks with a rolling gait. ⑤ seize; grapple with: 两人～在一起。The two were grappling with each other.

扭摆　niǔbǎi　(of one's body) sway: 她～着腰肢走过来。She walked over swaying her hips.

扭秤　niǔchèng　*phys.*　torsion balance

扭打　niǔdǎ　wrestle; grapple

扭搭　niǔda　*inf.*　walk with a swing; have a rolling gait

扭动　niǔdòng　sway; writhe: 她走起路来～着腰肢。She walks with a swaying motion. / 他的身体痛苦地～着。He was writhing in pain.

扭股儿糖　niǔgǔrtáng　Chinese maltose candy, usually with two or three strands twisted together; twisted malt candy

扭角羚　niǔjiǎolíng　another name for 羚牛 língniú

扭结　niǔjié　twist together; tangle up

扭亏为盈　niǔ kuī wéi yíng　turn losses into profits; turn an unfavourable balance into a favourable one

扭亏增盈　niǔ kuī zēng yíng　make up deficits and increase surpluses; eliminate losses and increase profits

扭力　niǔlì　*phys.*　twisting (*or* torsional, torque) force

扭力天平　niǔlì tiānpíng　torsion balance

扭捏　niǔnie　① walk affectedly with a swing ② be affectedly bashful: 有话快说，别扭捏捏的。Out with it. Don't be bashful. / 她～了好半天才说出话来。She affected embarrassment for quite a while before she spoke.

扭曲　niǔqū　twist; distort: 地震发生后，铁路～得很厉害。The railroad was twisted out of shape after the earthquake.

扭伤　niǔshāng　sprain; wrench: ～手腕 sprain one's wrist

扭送　niǔsòng　(of civilians) seize (a criminal, etc.) and deliver him to (the police): 把违法犯罪分子～公安部门 seize the offender and hand him over to the public security authorities

扭头　niǔtóu　① turn one's head away; turn away: 她扭过头去，不理我。She turned away and cut me dead. ② turn (round): 他二话没说，～就走。He just turned and walked off, without saying another word.

扭秧歌　niǔ yāngge　do the *yangko* dance

扭转　niǔzhuǎn　① turn round: 他～身子，向车间走去。He turned round and made for the workshop. ② turn back; reverse: ～局势 turn the tide; reverse a trend / ～被动局面 put an end to a passive state of affairs; regain the initiative / 妄图～历史车轮 vainly attempt to turn back the wheel of history

扭转乾坤　niǔzhuǎn qiánkūn　bring about a radical change in the situation; reverse the course of events

纽　niǔ　① handle; knob: 秤纽 chèngniǔ / 印纽 yìnniǔ ② button: 衣～ button ③ bond; tie: 纽带 niǔdài

纽埃岛　Niǔ'āidǎo　Niue Island

纽带　niǔdài　link; tie; bond: 友谊的～ ties of friendship / 商业是工农业之间的重要～。Trade is an important link between industry and agriculture.

纽扣　niǔkòu　button: 钉～ sew a button on

纽襻　niǔpàn　button loop

纽眼　niǔyǎn　*dial.*　buttonhole

纽约　Niǔyuē　New York

纽约市　Niǔyuēshì　New York City

纽约州　Niǔyuēzhōu　New York State

纽子　niǔzi　button

狃　niǔ　be bound by; be constrained by: ～于习俗 be bound by custom

钮　niǔ　① same as 纽 niǔ ② see 电钮 diànniǔ ③ (Niǔ) a surname

niù

拗（㧱）　niù　stubborn; obstinate; difficult: 这老头子脾气很～。He is a difficult old fellow. ——see also ǎo; ào

拗不过　niùbuguò　be unable to dissuade; fail to talk sb. out of doing sth.: 他这个人脾气犟，你可～他。He is very obstinate; you won't be able to make him change his mind. / 我～她，只好同意了。I had to comply after all my attempts to dissuade her had failed.

nóng

农（農、辳）　nóng　① agriculture; farming: 务～ go in for agriculture ② peasant; farmer: 菜农 càinóng / 贫农 pínnóng

农产　nóngchǎn　① agricultural production: ～区 agrarian area; rural district ② agricultural products; farm produce: 这地区有丰富的～。This district abounds in farm produce.

农产品　nóngchǎnpǐn　agricultural products; farm produce

农场　nóngchǎng　farm: 国营～ state farm

农村　nóngcūn　rural area; countryside; village: ～集市 village fair; rural market / ～经济 rural economy

农村电气化　nóngcūn diànqìhuà　electrification of the countryside; rural electrification

农贷　nóngdài　agricultural loans (*or* credits)

农夫　nóngfū　*old*　farmer

农妇　nóngfù　*old*　peasant woman

农工　nónggōng　① peasants and workers: 扶助～ help the peasants and workers ② short for 农业工人 nóngyè gōngrén

农户　nónghù　peasant household

农会　nónghuì　short for 农民协会 nóngmín xiéhuì

农活　nónghuó　farm work

农机　nóngjī　agricultural machinery; farm machinery

农家[1]　nóngjiā　peasant family

农家[2]　Nóngjiā　the School of Agriculturists (a school of thought in the Spring and Autumn and Warring States Periods, 770-221 B.C.)

农家肥 nóngjiāféi (also 农家肥料 nóngjiā féiliào) farm manure; farmyard manure

农具 nóngjù farm implements; farm tools

农垦 nóngkěn (short for 农业垦殖) land reclamation and cultivation

农历 nónglì the traditional Chinese calendar; the lunar calendar

农林牧副渔 nóng-lín-mù-fù-yú farming, forestry, animal husbandry, sideline production and fishery

农忙 nóngmáng busy season (in farming)

农贸市场 nóngmào shìchǎng a market of farm produce (in urban areas)

农民 nóngmín peasant; peasantry: 〜阶级 the peasantry

农民起义 nóngmín qǐyì peasant uprising; peasant revolt

农民协会 nóngmín xiéhuì peasant association (a mass organization led by the Chinese Communist Party during the Democratic Revolution)

农民运动讲习所 Nóngmín Yùndòng Jiǎngxísuǒ the Peasant Movement Institute (directed by Comrade Mao Zedong in Guangzhou and later in Wuchang to train cadres for the peasant movement in the First Revolutionary Civil War, 1924-1927)

农民战争 nóngmín zhànzhēng peasant war

农奴 nóngnú serf: 〜制度 serf system; serfdom

农奴主 nóngnúzhǔ serf owner

农女 nóngnǚ peasant girl; peasant woman

农渠 nóngqú field ditch

农人 nóngrén farmer

农桑 nóngsāng farming and sericulture

农舍 nóngshè farmhouse; cottage

农时 nóngshí farming season: 不违〜 do farm work in the right season

农事 nóngshì farm work; farming: 〜繁忙 busy with farm work

农田 nóngtián farmland; cropland; cultivated land: 〜基本建设 capital construction on farmland; farmland capital construction

农田水利 nóngtián shuǐlì irrigation and water conservancy: 〜建设 construction of water conservancy works

农隙 nóngxì formal slack season (in farming)

农闲 nóngxián slack season (in farming)

农协 nóngxié same as 农会 nónghuì

农械 nóngxiè farm chemical apparatus (e.g. sprayer, duster)

农学 nóngxué agronomy; agriculture: 〜家 agronomist

农谚 nóngyàn farmer's proverb; farmer's saying

农药 nóngyào agricultural chemical; farm chemical; pesticide: 打〜 apply farm chemical or pesticide / 〜污染 pesticide pollution

农业 nóngyè agriculture; farming: 〜机械 agricultural machinery; farm machinery / 〜人口 people engaged in agriculture; agricultural population / 〜投入 agricultural input

农业八字宪法 nóngyè bā zì xiànfǎ the Eight-Point Charter for Agriculture (土 soil improvement, 肥 rational application of fertilizer, 水 water conservancy, 种 improved seed strains, 密 rational close planting, 保 plant protection, 管 field management and 工 improvement of farm implements)

农业地质学 nóngyè dìzhìxué agrogeology

农业工程学 nóngyè gōngchéngxué agricultural engineering

农业工人 nóngyè gōngrén agricultural labourer; farm labourer; farm worker

农业国 nóngyèguó an agricultural country

农业合作化 nóngyè hézuòhuà cooperative transformation of agriculture; agricultural cooperative (or coop-eration) movement

农业化学 nóngyè huàxué agricultural chemistry; agrochemistry

农业集体化 nóngyè jítǐhuà the collectivization of agriculture

农业技术 nóngyè jìshù agricultural technology; agrotechnique: 〜改造 the technical transformation of agriculture / 〜员 agrotechnician / 〜站 agrotechnical station

农业气象学 nóngyè qìxiàngxué agricultural meteorology; agrometeorology

农业生产合作社 nóngyè shēngchǎn hézuòshè agricultural producers' cooperative

农业生物学 nóngyè shēngwùxué agrobiology

农业税 nóngyèshuì agricultural tax

农业土壤学 nóngyè tǔrǎngxué agrology

农业中学 nóngyè zhōngxué secondary school of agriculture

农艺师 nóngyìshī agronomist

农艺学 nóngyìxué agronomy

农友 nóngyǒu fellow peasant; fellow farmer (a term of address used in the early days of the Democratic Revolution)

农作物 nóngzuòwù crops

侬(儂) nóng ① dial. you ② (used in old poems) I

侬人 Nóngrén the Zhuangs (壮族) inhabiting the region where Yunnan and Guangxi meet

浓(濃) nóng ① dense; thick; concentrated: 〜烟 dense smoke; thick smoke / 〜墨 thick, dark ink / 〜茶 strong tea / 〜硫酸 concentrated sulphuric acid / 〜云密布 overcast with heavy clouds ② (of degree or extent) great; strong: 兴趣很〜 take a great interest in sth. / 玫瑰花香味很〜。 The rose has a heavy fragrance. / 这幅画颜色太〜。 The painting is too heavily coloured.

浓春 nóngchūn late spring

浓淡 nóngdàn deep or light—shade of colour: 〜适宜 neither too deep nor too pale; just the right shade of colour

浓度 nóngdù consistency; concentration; density: 矿浆〜 pulp density / 当量〜 equivalent concentration

浓厚 nónghòu ① dense; thick: 〜的云层 thick clouds ② strong; pronounced: 〜的地方色彩 pronounced (or marked) local colour / 〜的封建意识 a strong feudal mentality / 会议充满着〜的火药味。 The meeting smelt strongly of gunpowder. / 孩子们对踢足球的兴趣十分〜。 The children take a great interest in football.

浓积云 nóngjīyún meteorol. cumulus congestus

浓烈 nóngliè strong; thick; heavy: 香气〜 heavily scented / 〜的色彩 rich, strong colours / 〜的乡土气息 marked local colour

浓眉 nóngméi heavy (or bushy, thick) eyebrows: 〜大眼 heavy features

浓密 nóngmì dense; thick: 〜的枝叶 thick foliage / 头发〜 thick hair

浓缩 nóngsuō chem. concentrate; enrich: 〜物 concentrate / 〜铀 enriched uranium

浓香 nóngxiāng ① giving off a strong fragrance: 〜的茅台酒 Maotai with its rich distinctive fragrance ② a strong fragrance: 〜袭人。 A strong fragrance assailed one's nose.

浓艳 nóngyàn rich and gaudy: 色彩〜 in gaudy colours

浓荫 nóngyìn dense leafy shade: 在一棵老橡树的〜下 in (or under) the thick leafy shade of an old oak tree / 〜蔽日。 The thick foliage seemed to blot out the sun.

浓郁[1] nóngyù (of perfume, fragrance, etc.) strong; rich:

桂花发出～的香味。Osmanthus blossoms give off (*or* exhale) a rich perfume.

浓郁[2] nóngyù ① dense; thick: ～的松林 a dense pine forest ② strong; rich: 色彩～ in strong colours / 这部小说具有～的乡土气息。 The novel has a strong flavour of rural life. / 表现～的兴趣 show a great interest in sth.

浓重 nóngzhòng dense; thick; strong: 烟雾越发～了。The smoke-laden fog became thicker still. / 他画的花卉，设色十分～。His paintings of flowers are distinguished by their rich colours.

浓妆 nóngzhuāng heavy makeup and gaudy dress

浓妆艳抹 nóngzhuāng-yànmǒ richly attired and heavily made-up

浓浊 nóngzhuó ① (of smoke, fog, etc.) thick and filthy; heavy and foul: ～的烟雾笼罩全城。 A thick smog hung low over the town. ② (of voice) low and hoarse

哝 (噥) nóng see below

哝哝 nóngnong talk in undertones; murmur

脓 (膿) nóng pus

脓包 nóngbāo ① *med.* pustule ② a worthless fellow; good-for-nothing

脓疮 nóngchuāng running sore

脓尿 nóngniào *med.* pyuria

脓疱病 nóngpàobìng *med.* impetigo

脓胸 nóngxiōng *med.* pyothorax

脓肿 nóngzhǒng *med.* abscess: 肝～ liver abscess / 阑尾～ appendicular abscess

秾 (穠) nóng *formal* luxuriant; gorgeously blooming: 夭桃秾李 yāotáo-nónglǐ

秾艳 nóngyàn bright-coloured and beautiful; gorgeous

nòng

弄 nòng ① play with; fool with: 小孩儿爱～沙土。 Children like to play with sand. / 你别～闹钟了。 Stop fooling with that alarm clock. ② do; manage; handle; get sb. or sth. into a specified condition: ～饭 prepare a meal; cook / 我来不及了，你帮我～～吧。 I haven't got enough time. Will you please do it for me? / 他这一说反把我～糊涂了。 His explanation only made me feel more puzzled than ever. / 他把衣服～脏了。 He got his clothes dirty. / 有些问题还需要～清楚。 Certain questions have yet to be clarified. / ～得不好，就会前功尽弃。 If we don't do a good job now, all the work we've done will be wasted. ③ get; fetch: 你去～点水来。 Go and get some water. ④ play: ～手段 play tricks ——see also lòng

弄臣 nòngchén a favourite courtier

弄错 nòngcuò make a mistake; misunderstand: 你～了。 You've got it wrong.

弄鬼 nòngguǐ *dial.* play the devil—play tricks; hatch a plot

弄好 nònghǎo ① do well: 把事情～ do a good job ② finish doing sth.: 计划～了没有? Is the plan ready?

弄坏 nònghuài ruin; put out of order; make a mess of: 把事情～ make a mess of things

弄假 nòngjiǎ practise fraud; resort to trickery

弄假成真 nòng jiǎ chéng zhēn what was make-believe has become reality; what was said in fun is fulfilled in earnest

弄僵 nòngjiāng bring to a deadlock; deadlock

弄巧成拙 nòng qiǎo chéng zhuō try to be clever only to end up with a blunder; outsmart oneself

弄清 nòngqīng make clear; clarify; gain a clear idea of; understand fully: ～问题所在 get to the heart of the problem; clarify the point at issue / ～情况 gain a clear idea of the situation; find out the real situation / ～事实 set the facts straight / ～是非 thrash out the rights and wrongs; distinguish right from wrong

弄权 nòngquán manipulate power for personal ends

弄死 nòngsǐ put to death; kill

弄通 nòngtōng get a good grasp of: 认真看书学习，～马克思主义的基本原理。 Read and study conscientiously and get a good grasp of the basic principles of Marxism.

弄瓦 nòngwǎ *formal* play with a tile—a daughter is born (from the custom in early ages of giving a curved tile, used as a weight for the spindle and constituting the emblem of the female, to a baby girl to play with)

弄虚作假 nòngxū-zuòjiǎ practise fraud; employ trickery; resort to deception: ～，骗取荣誉 seek honour through fraud and deception

弄糟 nòngzāo make a mess of; mess up; bungle; spoil: 他一插手，就把事情全都～了。 His meddling made a mess of everything.

弄璋 nòngzhāng *formal* play with a jade tablet—a son is born (from the custom in early ages of giving a jade tablet, the emblem of male supremacy, to a baby boy to play with)

nòu

耨 (鎒) nòu *formal* ① weeding hoe ② weeding

nú

奴 nú ① bondservant; slave: 女～ a slave girl; a woman slave ② *old* I; me (self-reference of girls) ③ enslave: 奴役 núyì

奴婢 núbì slave girls and maidservants

奴才 núcai flunkey; lackey: 帝国主义的～ a lackey of imperialism / ～相 servile behaviour; servility; shameless fawning

奴佛卡因 núfókǎyīn same as 普鲁卡因 pǔlǔkǎyīn

奴化 núhuà enslave: ～教育 education aimed at enslavement / ～政策 policy of enslavement

奴家 nújiā *old* I; me (self-reference of girls)

奴隶 núlì slave: ～起义 slave uprising / ～占有制度 slave-owning system

奴隶社会 núlìshèhuì slave society

奴隶主 núlìzhǔ slave owner; slaveholder

奴隶主义 núlìzhǔyì slavishness; slavish mentality

奴仆 núpú servant; lackey

奴使 núshǐ *formal* enslave; keep in bondage

奴性 núxìng servility; slavishness

奴颜婢膝 núyán-bìxī subservient; servile: 他们对外～，甘心卖国求荣。 They bow and scrape like slaves to the foreigners, willing to sell the country for their own selfish ends.

奴颜媚骨 núyán-mèigǔ bowing and scraping; sycophancy and obsequiousness: 鲁迅在反动统治阶级面前没有丝毫的～。 Lu Xun was free from all sycophancy or obsequiousness in the face of the reactionary ruling class.

奴役 núyì enslave; keep in bondage: 反抗～和压迫 resist enslavement and oppression / 剥削阶级用种种手段来～劳动人民。 The exploiting classes try every

means to keep the toiling masses in slavery.

孥 nú *formal* ① sons and daughters; children ② wife and children

驽 nú *formal* ① an inferior horse; jade ② (of a person) dull; incompetent: ～才 a person of puny intelligence; dullard

驽钝 núdùn *formal* dull; stupid

驽马 númǎ *formal* an inferior horse; jade

驽马千里，功在不舍 númǎ qiānlǐ, gōng zài bù shě if a nag travels a thousand *li*, it's only through perseverance

驽骀 nútái *formal* ① an inferior horse ② a mediocre person

nǔ

努[1] (呶、努) nǔ ① put forth (one's strength); exert (one's effort): ～劲儿 put forth all one's strength ② injure oneself through overexertion: 箱子太沉，你别扛，看～着。 Don't carry that heavy trunk, or you'll strain yourself.

努[2] (拗、呶、努、) nǔ protrude; bulge: ～着眼睛 with bulging eyes / 小姑娘把嘴一～，不高兴了。 The little girl pursed her lips to show her dislike.

努力 nǔlì make great efforts; try hard; exert oneself: ～工作 work hard / ～发展生产 actively expand production / 为实现科学技术现代化而～奋斗 exert oneself in the struggle for the modernization of science and technology / 尽最大～ do one's utmost; do the best one can / 大家再努一把力。 Let's make still greater efforts. / 学好一门外语要作出极大的～。 It takes great effort to master a foreign language. / ～办好广播，为全中国人民和全世界人民服务。 Strive to do broadcasting work well and serve the people of China and the world.

努嘴 nǔzuǐ pout one's lips as a signal: 我向他努努嘴，让他先说。 I pouted my lips at him, hinting that he should speak first.

弩 nǔ crossbow: 万～齐发。 All the crossbows shot at once.

弩弓 nǔgōng crossbow

弩机 nǔjī the trigger mechanism of a crossbow

弩箭 nǔjiàn arrows shot from a crossbow; crossbow arrows

胬 nǔ see below

胬肉 nǔròu a triangular mass of mucous membrane growing from the inner corner of the eye

胬肉攀睛 nǔròu pān jīng *Chin. med.* pterygium

nù

怒 nù ① anger; rage; fury: ～骂 curse furiously / 我一～之下狠狠地打了他一记耳光。 In a fit of anger I gave him a heavy slap on the cheek. ② forceful; vigorous; dynamic: 怒放 nùfàng

怒不可遏 nù bùkě è be beside oneself with anger; be in a towering rage; boil with rage: 对待儿童如此残忍真使我～。 It made my blood boil to see such cruelty to children.

怒潮 nùcháo ① (tidal) bore ② angry tide; raging tide:

革命～汹涌澎湃。 The raging tide of revolution surges forward.

怒斥 nùchì angrily rebuke; indignantly denounce

怒冲冲 nùchōngchōng in a rage; furiously: 他把门一摔，～地走了。 He slammed the door and left in a huff.

怒发冲冠 nùfà chōng guān bristle with anger; be in a towering rage (*or* passion)

怒放 nùfàng in full bloom: 山花～。 The mountain flowers are in full bloom.

怒号 nùháo howl; roar: 狂风～。 A violent wind is howling.

怒吼 nùhǒu roar; howl: 雄狮～。 The lion roared. / 狂风呼啸，大海～。 The wind howled and the sea roared. / 示威群众的～震天动地。 The angry shouts of the demonstrators rent the air.

怒火 nùhuǒ flames of fury; fury: 满腔～ be filled with fury / 压不住心头的～ be unable to restrain one's fury; be unable to control one's anger

怒火中烧 nùhuǒ zhōng shāo be burning with anger (*or* wrath)

怒目 nùmù ① stare with anger: ～而视 stare angrily; look daggers at; glare at; glower at ② glaring eyes; a fierce stare

怒目横眉 nùmù-héngméi same as 横眉怒目 héngméi-nùmù

怒气 nùqì anger; rage; fury: ～冲冲 in a great rage / ～冲天 be in a towering rage (*or* passion); give way to unbridled fury; be boiling with rage

怒容 nùróng an angry look: ～满面 a face contorted with anger; looking very angry

怒色 nùsè an angry look: 面带～ wear an angry look

怒视 nùshì glare at; glower at; scowl at

怒涛 nùtāo furious (*or* raging) billows: ～澎湃 billows raging with great fury

怒形于色 nù xíng yú sè betray one's anger; look angry

怒族 Nùzú the Nu nationality, or the Nus, inhabiting Yunnan Province

nǚ

女 nǚ ① woman; female: ～教师 woman teacher / ～医生 woman doctor / ～售货员 saleswoman / ～运动员 sportswoman / ～民兵 militiawoman / ～演员 actress / ～英雄 heroine / ～飞行员 aviatrix / ～职工 women staff members and women workers / ～学生 girl student ② daughter; girl: 儿女 ér-nǚ ③ the tenth of the twenty-eight constellations (二十八宿) into which the celestial sphere was divided in ancient Chinese astronomy (consisting of four stars in the shape of a sieve in Aquarius)

女扮男装 nǚ bàn nánzhuāng a woman disguised as a man

女傧相 nǚbīnxiàng bridesmaid

女厕所 nǚcèsuǒ ① women's lavatory (*or* toilet); ladies' room ② (used as a sign for a public toilet) Ladies; Women

女车 nǚchē woman's bicycle; lady's bicycle

女大十八变 nǚ dà shíbā biàn there is no telling what a girl will look like when she grows up

女低音 nǚdīyīn *mus.* alto

女弟 nǚdì *formal* younger sister

女儿 nǚ'ér daughter; girl

女儿寡 nǚ'érguǎ same as 望门寡 wàngménguǎ

女儿酒 nǚ'érjiǔ *dial.* daughter's wine—wine made at a daughter's birth and kept underground until her wedding feast

女方 nǚfāng the bride's side; the wife's side

女服务员 nǚfúwùyuán stewardess; waitress; woman attendant

女高音 nǚgāoyīn *mus.* soprano

女工[1] nǚgōng woman worker

女工[2] nǚgōng (also 女红 nǚgōng) needlework

女公子 nǚgōngzǐ *honor.* (sb. else's) daughter; daughter of a famous personality

女孩儿 nǚháir (also 女孩子 nǚháizi) ① girl ② daughter

女皇 nǚhuáng empress

女家 nǚjiā the bride's side; the wife's family

女监 nǚjiān (also 女牢 nǚláo) prison for women criminals

女将 nǚjiàng ① woman general ② a female dab, expert or mastermind

女界 nǚjiè the feminine world

女眷 nǚjuàn the womenfolk of a family

女角 nǚjué a female role (in a play, film, etc.)

女郎 nǚláng a young woman; maiden; girl

女伶 nǚlíng *old* actress

女流 nǚliú *derog.* the weaker sex

女萝 nǚluó another name for 松萝 sōngluó

女朋友 nǚpéngyou girlfriend

女气 nǚqì effeminate

女强人 nǚqiángrén a strong woman; a woman of exceptional ability

女墙 nǚqiáng (also 女儿墙 nǚ'érqiáng) parapet wall; parapet

女青年会 Nǚqīngniánhuì YWCA (short for 基督教女青年会 Jīdūjiào Nǚqīngniánhuì)

女权 nǚquán women's rights

女人 nǚrén woman; womenfolk

女人 nǚren *inf.* wife

女色 nǚsè woman's beauty; feminine charms; woman as a sexual partner: 好～ be fond of women / 不近～ be sexually continent / 年三十未尝近～ be 30 years old already without ever having had relations with a woman

女神 nǚshén goddess

女生 nǚshēng woman student; girl student; schoolgirl

女声 nǚshēng *mus.* female voice: ～合唱 women's chorus; female chorus

女史 nǚshǐ *old* a woman of learning; a woman scholar

女士 nǚshì (a polite term for a woman, married or unmarried) lady; madam: ～们, 先生们! Ladies and gentlemen!

女侍 nǚshì ① *old* waitress; woman attendant ② maidservant; maid

女娲 Nǚwā a creator-goddess who patched with stone blocks the holes in the sky made by Gonggong 共工, the Spirit of Water, in a conflict with Zhuanxu 颛顼, the Spirit of Fire

女王 nǚwáng queen

女巫 nǚwū witch; sorceress

女性 nǚxìng ① the female sex ② woman: 新～ modern women; emancipated women

女兄 nǚxiōng *formal* elder sister

女修道院 nǚxiūdàoyuàn convent

女婿 nǚxu ① son-in-law ② *inf.* husband

女优 nǚyōu *old* actress

女招待 nǚzhāodài *old* waitress

女贞 nǚzhēn *bot.* glossy privet (*Ligustrum lucidum*)

女贞子 nǚzhēnzǐ *Chin. med.* the fruit of glossy privet

女真 Nǚzhēn Nüzhen (Nuchen), an ancient nationality in China, ancestors of the Manchus 满族, who founded the Jin Dynasty (金代 1115–1234)

女中音 nǚzhōngyīn *mus.* mezzo-soprano

女主角 nǚzhǔjué feminine lead; leading lady

女主人 nǚzhǔrén hostess

女装 nǚzhuāng ① women's clothing; women's costume ——see also 男扮女装 nán bàn nǚzhuāng

女子 nǚzǐ woman; female: ～单(双)打 women's singles (doubles) / ～团体赛 women's team event

钕

nǚ *chem.* neodymium (Nd)

nù

衄(鼾)

nù *formal* ① nosebleed: 鼻衄 bínù ② be defeated in battle: 败～ be defeated

恧

nù *formal* be ashamed: 愧恧 kuìnù

nuǎn

暖(煖、煗、暱)

nuǎn ① warm; genial: 天～了. It's getting warm. ② warm up: ～一～手 warm one's hands / 雪里送炭～人心. Sending charcoal in snowy weather warms the heart.

暖调 nuǎndiào *arts* warm colour tone; warm tone

暖房[1] nuǎnfáng ① go to the bridal chamber on the eve of a wedding to offer congratulations ② call on sb. who has moved into a new home to congratulate him

暖房[2] nuǎnfáng *dial.* greenhouse; hothouse

暖锋 nuǎnfēng (also 暖锋面 nuǎnfēngmiàn) *meteorol.* warm front

暖阁 nuǎngé a partitioned-off section of a large room with a heating stove

暖锅 nuǎnguō *dial.* chafing dish

暖烘烘 nuǎnhōnghōng nice and warm

暖呼呼 nuǎnhūhū warm; nice and warm: ～的南风 the nice and warm southerly wind / 听了这番话, 我们大家心里～的. The words warmed our hearts.

暖壶 nuǎnhú ① thermos flask; thermos bottle ② a teapot or waterpot with a cosy ③ a metal or earthen hot-water bottle

暖和 nuǎnhuo ① (of weather, environment, etc.) warm; nice and warm: 炉子一着, 屋子就～了. The room became warm when the fire got going. ② warm up: 屋里有火, 快进来～～吧! There is a fire in here; come in and warm yourself up.

暖帘 nuǎnlián quilted door curtain

暖流 nuǎnliú ① *geog. meteorol.* warm current ② warm feeling: 听了她的一番劝慰, 一股～涌上我的心头。Her soothing words left me with a glow in my heart.

暖瓶 nuǎnpíng *dial.* thermos flask; thermos bottle

暖气 nuǎnqì ① steam or water heat; central heating ② central heating equipment ③ a warm gas; warm air

暖气片 nuǎnqìpiàn heating radiator; radiator

暖气团 nuǎnqìtuán *meteorol.* warm air mass

暖融融 nuǎnróngróng nice and warm

暖色 nuǎnsè warm colour

暖寿 nuǎnshòu celebrations on the eve of a birthday

暖水瓶 nuǎnshuǐpíng thermos flask; thermos bottle

暖袖 nuǎnxiù lengthened section of the sleeves of a padded coat to keep the hands warm in winter

暖洋洋 nuǎnyángyáng warm: ～的春风 a warm spring breeze

nüè

疟(瘧)

nüè malaria; ague ——see also yào

疟涤平 nüèdípíng　another name for 阿的平 ādípíng
疟疾 nüèji　malaria; ague: 恶性～ pernicious malaria
疟蚊 nüèwén　another name for 按蚊 ànwén
疟原虫 nüèyuánchóng　plasmodium; malarial parasite

虐 nüè　cruel; tyrannical: 暴虐 bàonüè
虐待 nüèdài　maltreat; ill-treat; tyrannize: ～俘虏是违反政策的。 Any maltreatment of prisoners of war is against our policy.
虐杀 nüèshā　cause sb.'s death by maltreating him; kill sb. with maltreatment
虐政 nüèzhèng　tyrannical government; tyranny

nuó

挪 nuó　move; shift: 劳驾把桌子～到那边儿去。 Move the table over there, please. / 会议～到下周了。 The meeting has been put off till next week.
挪蹭 nuóceng　inf. move slowly; dawdle
挪动 nuódòng　move; shift: 往前～几步 move a few steps forward / 把车上东西捆好，免得车开快的时候～。 Fasten the load down to keep it from shifting at high speed. / 他的脚像是钉在地上，一步也～不得。 His feet seemed nailed to the ground and he couldn't move a step.
挪借 nuójiè　borrow money for a short time; get a short-term loan
挪威 Nuówēi　Norway
挪威人 Nuówēirén　Norwegian
挪威语 Nuówēiyǔ　Norwegian (language)
挪窝儿 nuówōr　dial. ① move to another place: 这炉子真碍事，给它挪个窝儿。 The stove's in the way; let's move it to some other place. / 我不喜欢这儿的工作，我想挪个窝儿试试。 I don't like the job I'm doing here. I'm thinking of going to another place and trying another job. ② move house; move
挪用 nuóyòng　① divert (funds): 不得～基本建设资金。 The fund earmarked for capital construction is not to be diverted to any other purpose. ② misappropriate; embezzle: ～公款 misappropriation (or embezzlement) of public funds

娜 nuó　see 婀娜 ēnuó; 袅娜 niǎonuó ——see also nà

傩(儺) nuó　exorcise
傩神 nuóshén　a god which is supposed to drive away pestilence
傩戏 nuóxì　① a kind of Anhui provincial drama featuring masked dancing ② a provincial opera popular in the mountainous districts in western Hubei

nuò

诺 nuò　① promise: 许诺 xǔnuò ② yes: ～～连声 keep on saying "yes"
诺贝尔奖金 Nuòbèi'ěr jiǎngjīn　Nobel prize
诺尔 nuò'ěr　same as 淖尔 nào'ěr
诺福克岛 Nuòfúkèdǎo　Norfolk Island
诺亚方舟 Nuòyà fāngzhōu　Noah's Ark
诺言 nuòyán　promise: 履行～ fulfil one's promise; keep one's word / 违背～ break one's promise; go back on one's promise

喏 nuò　interj. dial. (used to call attention to sth.): ～，这不就是你的那把雨伞? There! Isn't that your umbrella? / ～，～，要这样挖才挖得快。 Look, dig this way and you can dig faster.

搦 nuò　formal ① hold in the hand: ～管 hold a writingbrush; take up the pen ② provoke: 搦战 nuòzhàn
搦战 nuòzhàn　old provoke sb. into fighting; challenge to a fight

锘 nuò　chem. nobelium (No)

懦 nuò　cowardly; weak: 怯懦 qiènuò
懦夫 nuòfū　coward; craven; weakling: ～懒汉思想 the coward's and sluggard's way of thinking
懦弱 nuòruò　cowardly; weak: 性情～ chicken-hearted; weak-kneed

糯(糯、稬) nuò　glutinous (cereal)
糯稻 nuòdào　glutinous rice
糯米 nuòmǐ　polished glutinous rice
糯米酒 nuòmǐjiǔ　glutinous rice wine

O

ō

喔 ō *interj.* (expressing sudden realization): ～，原来是你干的! Oh, so it was you who did it ! / ～，你也这么想! Oh, so you feel the same way ! ——see also wō

喔唷 ōyō *interj.* ① (expressing surprise) oh: ～，这么大的雹子! Oh, what big hailstones! ② (expressing pain) oh; ouch: ～，好疼! Ouch, it hurts!

噢 ō same as 喔 ō

ó

哦 ó *interj.* (expressing doubt): ～，是这样的吗? Oh? Is that so? / ～! 会有这样的事? What! How can that be? ——see also é; ǒ

ǒ

嚄 ǒ *interj.* (expressing surprise): ～! 他竟会说出这样的话来? Oh, could he really have said such a thing? / ～! 亩产都超千斤了? What! The per-*mu* yield has topped 1,000 *jin*? ——see also huò

ò

哦(喔) ò *interj.* (expressing realization, understanding, etc.): ～，我懂了。 Oh! I see. *or* Oh! Now I understand. / ～，我想起来了。 Ah, I've got it. / ～! 你是老王的弟弟。 Ah, so you're Lao Wang's brother. ——see also é; ó

ōu

区(區) Ōu a surname ——see also qū

讴(謳) ōu ① sing ② folk songs; ballads

讴歌 ōugē *formal* sing the praises of; celebrate in song; eulogize

讴吟 ōuyín *formal* sing; chant

沤(漚) ōu bubbles on water; froth ——see also òu

欧¹(歐) Ōu a surname

欧²(歐) Ōu short for 欧洲 Ōuzhōu

欧³(歐) ōu short for 欧姆 ōumǔ

欧化 ōuhuà Europeanize; westernize

欧椋鸟 ōuliángniǎo *zool.* starling

欧罗巴人种 Ōuluóbā rénzhǒng the Caucasoid race; the white race

欧姆 ōumǔ *phys.* ohm

欧姆表 ōumǔbiǎo ohmmeter

欧姆定律 Ōumǔ dìnglǜ Ohm's Law

欧佩克 Ōupèikè OPEC (transliteration for 石油输出国组织 Shíyóu Shūchūguó Zǔzhī)

欧鸲 ōuqú *zool.* robin; redbreast

欧氏管 ōushìguǎn Eustachian tube; auditory canal (named after B. Eustachio, Italian anatomist)

欧体 Ōutǐ the Ouyang style (a calligraphic style created by Ouyang Xun 欧阳询 of the Tang Dynasty)

欧西 Ōuxī *old* Europe: ～各国 the European countries

欧亚大陆 Ōu-Yà dàlù Eurasia

欧阳 Ōuyáng a two-character surname

欧洲 Ōuzhōu Europe

欧洲经济共同体 Ōuzhōu Jīngjì Gòngtóngtǐ the European Economic Community (E.E.C.)

欧洲美元 Ōuzhōu měiyuán Eurodollar

瓯¹(甌) ōu *dial.* bowl; cup

瓯²(甌) Ōu another name for 温州 Wenzhou (a city in Zhejiang Province)

瓯剧 ōujù Wenzhou opera (a local opera popular in Wenzhou of Zhejiang Province and also in the northeastern part of Fujian Province)

瓯绣 ōuxiù Wenzhou embroidery

殴(毆) ōu beat up; hit: ～伤 beat and injure; injure by beating / 他挨了流氓一顿痛～。 He got beaten up by some hooligans.

殴打 ōudǎ beat up; hit: 互相～ come to blows; exchange blows / 被～致死 be beaten to death

殴斗 ōudòu have a fist fight; have fisticuffs

殴辱 ōurǔ insult and beat up

殴杀 ōushā beat to death

鸥(鷗) ōu gull: 海鸥 hǎi'ōu

ǒu

呕(嘔) ǒu vomit; throw up

呕吐 ǒutù vomit; throw up; be sick: ～不止 keep vomiting

呕心 ǒuxīn exert one's utmost effort (in creative work): ～之作 a work embodying one's utmost effort

呕心沥血 ǒuxīn-lìxuè shed one's heart's blood; take infinite pains; work one's heart out

呕血 ǒuxuè *med.* haematemesis; spitting blood

偶[1]　ǒu　image; idol: 木偶 mù'ǒu

偶[2]　ǒu　① even (number); in pairs: 无独有偶 wúdú-yǒu'ǒu ② mate; spouse: 择偶 zé'ǒu

偶[3]　ǒu　*adv.*　① by chance; by accident: 旅途～遇故友 chance to meet an old friend while travelling ② once in a while; occasionally: 偶一 ǒuyī

偶氮基　ǒudànjī　*chem.*　azo group; azo radical

偶氮染料　ǒudàn rǎnliào　*chem.*　azo dyes

偶尔　ǒu'ěr　*adv.*　once in a while; occasionally: 我们～见面。We see each other once in a long while. / 她擅长山水画,～也画画油画。She is especially good at traditional Chinese landscape painting, but occasionally she does oils too.

偶发　ǒufā　accidental; chance; fortuitous: ～事件 a chance occurrence

偶犯　ǒufàn　casual offence

偶感　ǒugǎn　① random thoughts (often used in titles of articles): 《参观鲁迅故居～》 "Random Thoughts on a Visit to Lu Xun's Former Residence" ② suddenly feel; occasionally feel: 昨日～不适。I happened to be ill yesterday.

偶合　ǒuhé　coincidence: 他们在这一点上见解一致完全是～。It is a mere coincidence that they see eye to eye on this point.

偶或　ǒuhuò　*adv.*　occasionally; now and then; sometimes; once in a while

偶然　ǒurán　① accidental; fortuitous; chance: ～事故 an accident / ～现象 accidental (*or* fortuitous) phenomena / ～误差 accidental error ② *adv.* accidentally; by accident; by chance: ～遇见一位老朋友 run into an old acquaintance; come across an old friend; meet an old friend by chance ③ *adv.* once in a while; occasionally: 他不经常来,～来一次。He does not come very often; he comes once in a while.

偶然性　ǒuránxìng　*philos.*　contingency; fortuity; chance

偶数　ǒushù　*math.*　even number

偶数页　ǒushùyè　*print.*　even page

偶蹄动物　ǒutídòngwù　even-toed mammal; artiodactyl

偶蹄目　ǒutímù　*zool.*　artiodactyla

偶像　ǒuxiàng　image; idol: ～崇拜 idolatry / ～化 idolize

偶一　ǒuyī　on a rare occasion; occasionally; once in a while: ～不慎 careless for once

偶一为之　ǒuyī wéi zhī　do sth. once in a while; do sth. accidentally or by way of exception

耦　ǒu　① *formal* (of two persons) plough side by side ② same as 偶[2] ǒu

耦合　ǒuhé　*phys.*　coupling: 机械～ mechanical coupling / ～电路 coupled (*or* coupling) circuit / ～系数 coupling coefficient

藕（蕅）　ǒu　lotus root: 糖醋～片 sliced lotus root cooked in sweet and sour sauce

藕断丝连　ǒuduàn-sīlián　the lotus root snaps but its fibres stay joined—(of lovers, etc.) still in contact though apparently separated; separated but still in each other's thoughts

藕粉　ǒufěn　① lotus root starch ② lotus root paste (a semifluid food): 冲两碗～ prepare two bowls of lotus root paste

藕荷　ǒuhé　(also 藕合 ǒuhé) pale pinkish purple

藕灰　ǒuhuī　pale pinkish grey

藕节儿　ǒujiér　joints of a lotus root

藕煤　ǒuméi　*dial.*　honeycomb briquet

藕色　ǒusè　pale pinkish grey

òu

沤（漚）　òu　soak; steep; macerate ——see also ōu

沤肥　òuféi　① make compost ② wet compost; waterlogged compost

沤麻　òumá　ret flax or hemp

沤田　òutián　a waterlogged plot or field

怄（慪、呕）　òu　*dial.*　① be irritated; be annoyed ② irritate; annoy: 你是故意～我。You are purposely annoying me.

怄气　òuqì　be difficult and sulky: 怄了一肚子气 have a bellyful of repressed grievances / 不要～。Don't sulk.

P

pā

趴 pā ① lie on one's stomach; lie prone: ～在地上打靶 lie on the ground for target practice ② bend over; lean on: 他正～在桌子上画图。 He was bending over the desk, drawing.

趴伏 pāfú lie on one's stomach; lie prone: ～地上纹丝不动 lie prone on the ground stock-still

趴架 pājià (of houses) collapse; topple down

趴窝 pāwō *dial.* ① (of a hen) be sitting ② (of a female animal) lie on the ground ready to give birth ③ (of a person) be broken in health: 他累～了。 He's utterly worn-out. ④ (of a machine, vehicle, etc.) break down; be out of order

派 pā see below ——see also pài

派司 pāsi *dial.* pass: 没有～怕进不去。 Without a pass, you won't be able to get in, I'm afraid.

啪 pā *onom.* (the sound of clapping, slapping, a gunshot, etc.): ～的一声, 瓶塞飞出来了。 The cork popped and flew out of the bottle. / ～～两声枪响。 Bang, bang, went the gun.

啪嚓 pāchā *onom.* (the sound of sth. crashing, hitting the ground, etc.): ～一声, 碗掉在地上碎了。 The bowl dropped and broke with a crash.

啪嗒 pādā *onom.* patter: ～～的脚步声 pattering footsteps / 打字机～～地响着。 The typewriter was clattering away. / 雨点打在窗户上～～直响。 The rain went pitter-pattering against the windows.

啪唧 pāji *onom.*: 那孩子光着脚～～地跑。 The boy pattered along barefoot.

葩 pā *formal* flower: 一朵艺术上的奇～ a wonderful work of art

pá

扒 pá ① gather up; rake up: 把枯树叶～在一起 rake together the dead leaves ② stew; braise: ～羊肉 stewed mutton / ～鸡 braised chicken ③ *dial.* scratch: ～痒 scratch an itch ——see also bā

扒灰 páhuī same as 爬灰 páhuī

扒拉 pála *dial.* rake rice into one's mouth with chopsticks: 他～了两口饭就跑出去了。 He whisked a few mouthfuls of rice into his mouth and ran out. ——see also bāla

扒犁 páli *dial.* sledge; sleigh

扒搂 pálou *dial.* gather up; rake up

扒窃 páqiè pick people's pockets

扒手 páshǒu pickpocket

杷 pá see 枇杷 pípa

爬 pá ① crawl; creep: 蛇正往洞里～。 The snake is crawling into a hole. / 这小孩会～了。 The baby can crawl now. / 有一条虫子在你背上～。 There is a worm creeping up your back. ② climb; clamber; scramble: ～树(绳, 山) climb a tree (rope, mountain) / 山崖陡峭, 要手足并用, 才～得上去。 The cliff is very steep. You'll have to clamber with both hands and feet to get to its top. / 墙上～满了常春藤。 The wall is covered all over with ivy.

爬虫 páchóng old name for 爬行动物 páxíng dòngwù

爬竿 págān *sports* ① pole-climbing ② climbing pole

爬高 págāo ① climb: 蹬梯子～ climb a ladder ② same as 爬升 páshēng

爬格子 pá gézi *inf.* crawl over squared or lined paper—write (esp. in order to make a living)

爬灰 páhuī *inf.* scratching in the ashes—incest committed with one's daughter-in-law

爬景天 pájǐngtiān another name for 垂盆草 chuípéncǎo

爬犁 páli *dial.* sledge; sleigh

爬罗剔抉 páluó-tījué collect and select

爬搔 pásāo scratch (with fingernails): 他不停地在背上～。 He kept scratching his back.

爬山虎 páshānhǔ ① *bot.* Boston ivy ② *dial.* a sedan chair or litter to carry a person up a mountain

爬升 páshēng (of an airplane, rocket, etc.) ascend; climb; gain altitude: 客机开始～。 The airliner began to gain altitude.

爬梳 páshū *formal* comb; tidy up

爬行 páxíng crawl; creep: 跟在别人后面一步一步地～ trail behind others at a snail's pace

爬行动物 páxíng dòngwù *zool.* reptile

爬泳 páyǒng *sports* the crawl

耙(钯) pá ① rake: 木～ wooden rake ② make smooth with a rake; rake: 把地～平 rake the soil level / 把稻草～拢成堆 rake up the straw into a pile ——see also bà

耙子 pázi rake

琶 pá see 琵琶 pípa

琶音 páyīn *mus.* arpeggio

弄 pá see below

弄手 páshǒu pickpocket

筢 pá bamboo rake

筢子 pázi bamboo rake

pà

怕 pà ① fear; dread; be afraid of: ～蛇 be afraid of snakes / 很～艾滋病传染 be in great fear of AIDS infection / 一不～苦, 二不～死 fear neither hardship nor death / 我很～在人前讲话。 I feel nervous speaking in public. / ～有什么用? What's the use of being afraid?

② cannot stand; will be affected by: 这种蓝布～晒 This blue cloth will discolour through exposure to the sun. / 这种表不～水。 This kind of watch is waterproof. ③ (expressing supposition, judgment, estimation, etc.) I am afraid (that); I suppose; perhaps: 事情～不那么简单。 I am afraid things are not that simple. / 这生意～赚不了多少钱。 This doesn't seem a very profitable business, I'm afraid./ 这个瓜～有十几斤吧。 This melon weighs more than ten *jin*, I should think. ④ be afraid something might happen; feel anxious about; feel concerned for or about: 他～迟到，六点就动身了。He started out at six for fear of being late./ ～要下雨了，你最好带着伞。 It looks like rain, so better take your umbrella with you. / 现在的女孩子大都～胖。 Most girls are afraid of being overweight.

怕老婆 pà lǎopo　be henpecked
怕人 pàrén ① dread to meet people; be shy: 这孩子有点～。 The child is a bit shy. / 企鹅不～。 Penguins are not afraid of people. ② frightening; terrifying; horrible: 山洞里黑得～。 It's frighteningly dark inside the cave.
怕三怕四 pàsān-pàsì　have all sorts of misgivings; be apprehensive of this and that
怕生 pàshēng　(of a child) be shy with strangers
怕事 pàshì　be afraid of getting into trouble: 胆小～ timid and overcautious
怕是 pàshì　*dial.* I guess; I suppose; perhaps; maybe: 你～有点不舒服吧? You're feeling a bit unwell, aren't you?
怕死鬼 pàsǐguǐ　coward
怕头 pàtou　sth. to be afraid of: 有啥～? What's there to be afraid of? / 没有什么～。 There's nothing to be afraid of.
怕羞 pàxiū　coy; shy; bashful: 这女孩子～。 She is a bashful girl.

帕
帕 pà　handkerchief or kerchief
帕米尔高原 Pàmǐ'ěr Gāoyuán　the Pamirs

pāi

拍
拍 pāi ① clap; pat; beat: ～～他的肩膀 pat him on the shoulder / ～掉身上的土 pat one's clothes to get the dust off / ～桌子大骂 strike the table and pour out a stream of abuse / ～球 bounce a ball / ～～翅膀 flap wings; beat wings / 惊涛～岸 mighty waves beating the shore ② bat; racket: 乒乓球～ ping-pong bat / 网球～ tennis racket / 苍蝇～儿 flyswatter ③ *mus.* beat; time: 一小节四～ four beats in (*or* to) a bar / 这歌是几～的?—是4/4～的。 What time is the song in?—It's in four-four time. ④ take (a picture); shoot: ～电影 shoot (*or* make) a film / 这部小说已～成电影了。 This novel has been made into a film. / 今天天气不好，外景～不成了。 We can't shoot the outdoor scenes in this foul weather. ⑤ send (a telegram, etc.): ～电报 send a telegram ⑥ *inf.* flatter; fawn on: 一不会吹，二不会～ not be given to bragging or toadying
拍案 pāi'àn　strike (*or* bang) the table (in anger, surprise, admiration, etc.)
拍案而起 pāi'àn ér qǐ　smite the table and rise to one's feet in anger
拍案叫绝 pāi'àn jiào jué　thump the table and shout "bravo!": 精彩的表演令人～。 We were overwhelmed with admiration for the superb performance.
拍巴掌 pāi bāzhang　*inf.* clap one's hands
拍板[1] pāibǎn　clappers
拍板[2] pāibǎn ① beat time with clappers: 你来唱，我

来～。 I'll beat time while you sing. ② rap the gavel ③ have the final say; give the final verdict: 这事儿得由厂长来～。 The factory director has the final say in this matter.
拍板成交 pāibǎn chéngjiāo　strike a bargain; clinch a deal
拍打 pāida　pat; slap: ～身上的雪 pat (*or* beat) the snow off one's clothes / 把地毯～一下 beat the carpet; give the carpet a beating / 波浪～着船舷 waves lapping against the sides of the boat
拍发 pāifā　send (a telegram): ～消息 cable a dispatch or report
拍号 pāihào　*mus.* time signature
拍击 pāijī　(of waves) beat; run against: 巨浪～着礁石。 Huge waves dashed against the rocks.
拍节器 pāijiéqì　*mus.* metronome
拍马屁 pāi mǎpì　(also 拍马 pāimǎ) *inf.* lick sb.'s boots; flatter; soft-soap; play up to; fawn on: 他不是那种～的人。 He is no toady (*or* flatterer).
拍卖 pāimài ① auction: ～商 auctioneer / 交拍卖行～ come under the hammer ② selling off goods at reduced prices; sale
拍摄 pāishè　take (a picture); shoot: ～一张照片 take a photo / ～特写镜头 shoot a close-up / 把舞剧～成电影 film a dance drama / 在～外景 be on location
拍手 pāishǒu　clap one's hands; applaud: ～叫好 clap and shout "bravo!"
拍手称快 pāishǒu chēngkuài　clap in high glee; clap and cheer (as on being avenged): 正义得到伸张，人民～。 Justice prevailing at last, people clapped their hands with joy.
拍戏 pāixì　make a film; shoot a scene: 明天拍"记者招待会"这场戏。 Tomorrow we're going to film the press conference scene. / 去电影厂～ go to the film studio for the shooting of a scene
拍照 pāizhào　take a picture or have a picture taken; photograph: 我拍了十几张照。 I took about a dozen pictures. *or* I had a dozen pictures taken.
拍纸簿 pāizhǐbù　(writing) pad
拍子 pāizi ① bat; racket: 羽毛球(网球)～ badminton (tennis) racket ② *mus.* beat; time: 打～ beat time / 二 (三，四)～ duple (triple, quadruple) time / 单 (复)～ simple (compound) time

pái

排[1]
排 pái ① arrange; put in order: ～座位 arrange seats / 把课桌椅～整齐 put the desks and chairs in order / 节目单已～好。 The programme has been arranged. ② row; line: 前排 qiánpái ③ *m.* row; line: 一～椅子 a row (*or* line) of chairs ④ *mil.* platoon ⑤ rehearse: 剧团正在～一出历史剧。 The troupe is rehearsing (for) a historical play.

排[2]
排 pái　raft: 竹排 zhúpái / 木排 mùpái

排[3]
排 pái ① exclude; eject; discharge: ～脓 discharge pus / 把水～出去 drain the water away ② push: ～门而出 push the door open and go straight out

排[4]
排 pái　pie: 苹果～ apple pie
——see also pǎi

排奡 pái'ào　*formal* (of writings) vigorous and forceful
排班 páibān　arrange in order of shifts, runs, or classes and grades
排版 páibǎn　*print.* composing; typesetting: 机器～

machine composition / 照相～ photocomposition; phototypesetting; photoset / 程控～ programmed composition / 自动～ automatic typesetting; automatic composition

排比 páibǐ　parallelism

排笔 páibǐ　a broad brush comprising a row of pen-shaped brushes (for whitewashing, painting, picture colouring, etc.)

排叉儿 páichàr　(also 排权儿 páichàr, 排岔儿 páichàr) a thin and crisp fried cake

排场 páichang　① ostentation and extravagance; pomp and ceremony: 讲～ go in for ostentation and extravagance ② ostentatious and extravagant; sumptuous; lavish: 他们的婚礼办得可～了。 Their wedding was a most ostentatious and extravagant affair.

排斥 páichì　repel; exclude; reject: 同种电荷互相～。 Two like electric charges repel one another.

排斥异己 páichì yǐjǐ　discriminate against those who hold different views; exclude outsiders

排除 páichú　get rid of; remove; eliminate: ～路上积水 drain the flooded streets / ～障碍 remove (or get over) an obstacle / ～故障 fix a breakdown / ～私心杂念 get rid of selfish ideas / ～一切疑虑 remove all doubts / ～外来干扰 eliminate (or overcome) outside interference / 不能～这种可能性 cannot rule out this possibility

排除万难 páichú wàn nán　surmount every difficulty; conquer all obstacles: 全体人民团结起来, 共同努力, 一定能够～, 达到胜利的目的。 When the entire people are united in a common effort, they can certainly surmount difficulty and win victory.

排挡 páidǎng　gear (of a car, tractor, etc.)

排队 páiduì　form a line; line up; queue up: ～买票 line up for tickets / ～上车 queue up for a bus / ～前进 march in a column / 把问题按轻重缓急排排队 arrange the problems in order of importance and urgency

排筏 páifá　bamboo or timber raft

排放[1] páifàng　place (things) in proper order: 书桌上～着台灯、文具和工具书。 The reference books, stationery and reading lamp are arranged in proper order on the desk.

排放[2] páifàng　discharge; let out; drain off: ～废气 discharge used steam or gas

排风扇 páifēngshàn　ventilating fan

排骨 páigǔ　spareribs

排灌 páiguàn　irrigation and drainage: ～设备 irrigation and drainage equipment / ～网 irrigation and drainage network / ～站 irrigation and drainage pumping station

排行 páiháng　seniority among brothers and sisters: 他～第三。 He's the third child of the family.

排号 páihào　① row number (of seats in a theatre, etc.) ② *inf.* arrange in numerical order ③ *dial.* line up; queue up

排洪 páihóng　drain off floodwaters

排挤 páijǐ　push aside; push out; squeeze out; elbow out: 拉拢一些人, ～一些人 draw some in, push others out / 互相～ each trying to squeeze the other out

排解 páijiě　① mediate; reconcile: ～纠纷 mediate a dispute; reconcile a quarrel ② same as 排遣 páiqiǎn

排涝 páilào　drain flooded (or waterlogged) fields

排雷 páiléi　*mil.* removal of mines; mine clearance

排立 páilì　stand in a line; line up: 群众～在马路两侧迎贵宾。 People lined the streets to welcome the distinguished guests.

排练 páiliàn　rehearse: ～节目 have a rehearsal / 音乐会的节目正在作最后一次～。 They are having the final rehearsal for the concert.

排列 páiliè　① arrange; range; put in order: ～成行 arrange in a row (or line, column) / ～成四路纵队 form a column of fours / 按字母顺序～ arrange in alphabetical order ② *math.* permutation: ～组合 permutations and combinations

排律 páilǜ　an extended form of regulated verse (i.e. a poem in regulated verse 律诗, usu. pentasyllabic, with the middle couplets multiplied)

排卵 páiluǎn　*physiol.* ovulate

排卵期 páiluǎnqī　period of ovulation

排难解纷 páinàn-jiěfēn　mediate a dispute; pour oil on troubled waters

排尿 páiniào　urinate; micturate

排尿困难 páiniào kùnnan　*med.* dysuria

排炮[1] páipào　① (artillery) salvo; volley of guns ② successive blastings (in mining, tunnelling, etc.)

排炮[2] páipào　remove or defuse a dud, or a charge of explosive that fails to explode when it should

排气 páiqì　*mech.* exhaust

排气管 páiqìguǎn　exhaust pipe

排遣 páiqiǎn　divert oneself (from loneliness or boredom): 他闲得无聊, 只好去看场电影～～。 As time lay heavily on his hands, he went to the cinema to divert himself.

排枪 páiqiāng　volley of rifle fire

排球 páiqiú　volleyball (the game or the ball)

排沙简金 pái shā jiǎn jīn　same as 披沙拣金 pī shā jiǎn jīn

排山倒海 páishān-dǎohǎi　topple the mountains and overturn the seas: 以～之势 with the momentum of an avalanche; with the force of a landslide and the power of a tidal wave

排射 páishè　volley (of fire)

排笙 páishēng　*mus.* a reed pipe wind instrument with a keyboard

排水 páishuǐ　① drain off (or away) water ② drainage: ～工程 drainage works

排水沟渠 páishuǐ gōuqú　escape canal

排水管 páishuǐguǎn　drain pipe

排水管道 páishuǐ guǎndào　drainage pipeline

排水量 páishuǐliàng　① displacement: ～两万二千吨的远洋轮船 an ocean-going liner of 22,000 tons displacement ② discharge capacity (of a spillway, etc.)

排他性 páitāxìng　exclusiveness: ～集团 exclusive bloc / ～条约 exclusive multilateral treaty; exclusive treaty

排闼直入 pái tà zhí rù　push the door open and stride in

排调 páitiáo　*formal* tease and ridicule

排头 páitóu　the person at the head of a procession or formation; file leader: 向～看齐! Keep level with your file leader!

排头兵 páitóubīng　① the soldier at the head of a formation ② pacesetter; pacemaker

排外 páiwài　exclusive; antiforeign: 盲目～ blind opposition to everything foreign

排外心理 páiwài xīnlǐ　xenophobia

排外主义 páiwàizhǔyì　exclusivism; exclusionism; antiforeignism

排尾 páiwěi　the last person in a row, procession or formation; the person at the end of a row, etc.

排戏 páixì　rehearse a play: 排一出新戏 rehearse a new play

排险 páixiǎn　eliminate a danger

排箫 páixiāo　*mus.* panpipes; Pan's pipes

排泄 páixiè　① drain rainwater, waste water, etc.: ～不畅 drainage difficulty ② excrete: ～粪便 excrete faeces and urine / 皮肤通过毛孔～汗液 Sweat is excreted through the pores of the skin.

排泄器官 páixiè qìguān　excretory organs

排泄物 páixièwù　excreta; excrement

排演 páiyǎn　rehearse

排椅 páiyǐ　seats in a row

排印 páiyìn typesetting and printing: 在～中 in the typesetting and printing stage / 赶紧把这本书～出来。Rush the book into print.

排忧解难 páiyōu-jiěnàn relieve sb. of worries and help solve his problems: 帮助乡镇企业～ help township enterprises allay their worries and tide over their difficulties

排运 páiyùn rafting

排长 páizhǎng platoon leader

排中律 páizhōnglǜ *log.* the law of excluded middle

排钟 páizhōng *mus.* chimes

排字 páizì composing; typesetting: ～车间 composing room / ～工人 typesetter; compositor / ～机 typesetter; composing machine / ～架 composing frame / ～手托 composing stick

徘 pái see below

徘徊 páihuái ① pace up and down ② hesitate; waver ③ *econ.* fluctuate: 经济增长～在3.3-3.5%之间。Economic growth ranged between 3.3% and 3.5%.

徘徊歧路 páihuái qílù hesitate at the crossroads

牌 pái ① plate; tablet: 车～儿 number plate (on a vehicle) / (衣帽间等的)号码～ check ② brand; make: 你用什么～的肥皂? What brand of soap do you use? / 你的汽车是什么～的? What make is your car? ③ cards, dominoes, etc.: 一副扑克～ a pack of playing cards / 手里有一副好～ have a good hand / 该你出～了! It's your turn. or Play your card!

牌匾 páibiǎn an inscribed board (fixed to a wall or the lintel of a door); tablet; plaque

牌额 páí'é a horizontal inscribed board

牌坊 páifāng memorial archway (*or* gateway)

牌号 páihào ① the name of a shop; shop sign ② trademark

牌价 páijià ① list price; posted price: 按～打八折出售 goods sold at a discount of 20% off the list prices ② (market) quotation: 外汇～ (foreign) exchange quotations / 开盘～ an opening quotation / 收盘～ a closing quotation

牌九 páijiǔ *paijiu*, a kind of Chinese dominoes: 推～ play *paijiu*; play a game of Chinese dominoes

牌局 páijú a game at dominoes, mahjong, or cards; a gambling game

牌楼 páilou ① *pailou*, decorated archway ② temporary ceremonial gateway

牌示 páishì *old* . public notice; bulletin

牌位 páiwèi memorial tablet (used in ancestral worship)

牌照 páizhào license plate; license tag; license certificate; license

牌子 páizi ① plate; sign: 存车～ tally (for parking a bicycle) ② brand; trademark: 老～ old brand; well-known brand

pǎi

迫(廹) pǎi see below ——see also pò

迫击炮 pǎijīpào *mil.* mortar: ～弹 mortar projectile; mortar shell

排 pǎi see below ——see also pái

排子车 pǎizichē a large handcart

pài

派 pài ① *formal* tributary; river branch: 茫茫九～流中国。(毛泽东) Wide, wide flow the nine streams through the land. ② political group, school of thought or art, etc.: 国会议员在这个问题上分成两～。The Congressmen were divided into two opposing groups over this issue. / 很多学者都是这一～。Many scholars belong to this school. / 他的唱腔自成一～。He was unique in his style of singing. / 他是个乐天～。He is an optimist. ③ style; manner and air: 气派 qìpài ④ *m.* ⓐ (for political groups, schools of thought or art, etc.): 三～学者 scholars of three different schools / 各～政治力量 the different political forces (*or* groups) ⓑ (used with the numeral 一, for scene, atmosphere, speech, etc.): 一～深秋景色 a late autumn scene / 一～北国风光 an expanse of typical northern scenery / 一～生机勃勃的新气象 a new and dynamic atmosphere / 形势一～大好 an all-pervading excellent situation / 一～胡言! A pack of nonsense! / 一～谎言! A pack of lies! ⑤ send; dispatch; assign; appoint: ～代表团出席大会 send a delegation to the conference / ～他担任车间主任 appoint him head of the workshop / ～兵 dispatch troops / ～工作 set sb. a task / ～勤务 assign fatigue duties ——see also pā

派别 pàibié group; sect; school; faction: 清教徒是十六、十七世纪英国新教徒中的一个～。The Puritans were a sect of English Protestants in the 16th and 17th centuries.

派不是 pài bùshi put (*or* lay) the blame on sb.: 他自己不认错, 还派别人的不是。Instead of admitting his mistakes, he shifted the blame onto others.

派差 pàichāi send on a public errand

派出机构 pàichū jīgòu agency: 地区一级是省的～。The organ of state power at the prefectural level is an agency of the provincial authorities.

派出所 pàichūsuǒ local police station; police substation

派饭 pàifàn meals in peasant homes arranged for cadres, students, etc. temporarily staying at a village; arranged meals: 吃～ board with different peasant families by arrangement

派购 pàigòu (of the state) prescribe purchases (of farm produce); fix quantities for state purchase

派活 pàihuó assign sb. a task (usu. manual work): 今天派我什么活儿? What work do you assign me today?

派款 pàikuǎn impose levies of money

派力斯呢 pàilìsīní *text.* palace

派令 pàilìng order of appointment

派遣 pàiqiǎn send; dispatch: ～代表团 send a delegation / ～驻外全权代表 dispatch a plenipotentiary to a foreign country / ～医疗队 send a medical team

派遣国 pàiqiǎnguó the sending state; the accrediting state

派生 pàishēng derive: 由此～出来的问题 the questions derived therefrom

派生词 pàishēngcí *gram.* derivative

派头 pàitóu style; manner: 他～真不小! He certainly puts on quite a show!

派系 pàixì groups or factions (within a political party, etc.): ～之争 factional strife

派性 pàixìng factionalism: 进行秘密的～活动 engage in secret factionalist activities

派用场 pài yòngchǎng put to use; turn to account: 这东西将来好派大用场。It can be turned to good account in future. / 这东西我派不上用场了。I have no use for it

any more.

派驻 pàizhù ① post; station: 在边境～重兵 station large numbers of troops along the border ／ ～国外 be posted abroad ／ ～北京的外国记者 foreign correspondents resident in Beijing ② *diplomacy* accredit to: ～联合国的代表 a representative accredited to the United Nations

哌 pài　see below

哌嗪 pàiqín　*chem.* piperazine

蒎 pài　*chem.* pinane

湃 pài　see 滂湃 pāngpài; 澎湃 péngpài

pān

潘 Pān　a surname

攀 pān ① climb; clamber: ～着绳子往上爬 climb up a rope hand over hand ② seek connections in high places: 高攀 gāopān ③ involve; implicate: 乱咬乱～ make wild charges, while under interrogation, to implicate others

攀比 pānbǐ　cite the cases of others in support of one's own claim

攀缠 pānchán　climb and intertwine: 墙上～着两种藤蔓。Two vines intertwined over the wall.

攀扯 pānchě　implicate (sb. in a crime)

攀登 pāndēng　climb; clamber; scale: ～峭壁 climb up a cliff ／ ～科学技术新高峰 scale new heights in science and technology

攀登架 pāndēngjià　jungle gym (a playground apparatus for children to climb on)

攀附 pānfù ① (of a plant) climb (a support): 藤蔓～树木 vines climbing trees ② seek connections with (people of power and influence): ～权贵 seek connections with those in power

攀高 pāngāo ① climb to a higher point ② *dial.* make friends or claim ties of kinship with someone of a higher social position

攀高枝儿 pān gāozhīr　make friends or claim ties of kinship with someone of a higher social position

攀交 pānjiāo　make friends with people of a higher social position

攀龙附凤 pānlóng-fùfèng　play up to people of power and influence; put oneself under the patronage of a bigwig

攀亲 pānqīn ① claim kinship ② *dial.* arrange a match

攀亲道故 pānqīn-dàogù　claim ties of blood or friendship

攀禽 pānqín　*zool.* scansorial birds

攀雀 pānquè　*zool.* penduline tit

攀谈 pāntán　engage in small talk; have a chat: 两人边喝茶边～，十分投机。They had a most congenial chat over tea.

攀缘 pānyuán　(also 攀援 pānyuán) ① climb; clamber: ～而上 climb up ② climb the social ladder through pull

攀缘植物 pānyuán zhíwù　*bot.* climber; climbing plant

攀越 pānyuè　climb up and over; scale; surmount: ～险峰 scale a perilous peak

攀折 pānzhé　pull down and break off (twigs, etc.): 请勿～花木。Please don't pick the flowers.

攀枝花 pānzhīhuā　same as 木棉 mùmián

pán

爿 pán　*dial.* ① slit bamboo or chopped wood ② *m.* (used for shops, factories, etc.): 一～水果店 a fruit shop ／ 两～咖啡馆 two cafés

胖 pán　*formal* easy and comfortable: 心广体胖 xīnguǎng-tǐpán ——see also pàng

盘（盤） pán ① an ancient washbasin ② a rather flat receptacle, as a tray, plate, dish, etc.: 茶盘 chápán ／ 棋盘 qípán ／ 磨盘 mòpán ③ market quotation; current price: 开盘 kāipán ④ coil (up); wind; twist: 把绳子～起来 coil up the rope ／ 把头发～成一个髻 comb one's hair into a coil or bun ／ 莫干山上下十八～。There are 18 hairpin bends on the way up the Mogan Mountain. ⑤ build (by laying bricks, stones, etc.): ～炕 build a *kang* ／ ～灶 build a brick cooking range ⑥ check; examine; interrogate: 盘问 pánwèn ／ 盘帐 pánzhàng ⑦ transfer the ownership of; make over to sb. else: 把整个厂连同设备～给人家 transfer the ownership of the factory with all its equipment to another person ⑧ carry; transport: 从仓库往外头～东西 carry things out of the warehouse ⑨ *m.* ⓐ (for dishes, millstones, etc.): 一～磨 a pair of millstones ／ 四～菜 four dishes ／ 一～电线 a coil of wire ／ 一～蚊香 a coil of mosquito-repellent incense ⓑ *sports* game; set: 下一～棋 play a game of chess ／ 以六比零胜了这一～ win the set in six straight games ⑩ (Pán) a surname

盘剥 pánbō　practise usury: 重利～ lend money at usurious rates; exploit by practising usury

盘儿菜 pánrcài　ready-to-cook dish of meat, vegetables, etc. (sold at the food market)

盘查 pánchá　(also 盘察 pánchá) interrogate and examine: 加设岗哨，～行人。More sentries were posted to interrogate and examine the passersby.

盘缠 pánchán　same as 盘绕 pánrào

盘缠 pánchan　*inf.* money for the journey; travelling expenses

盘秤 pánchèng　a steelyard with a pan

盘存 páncún　take inventory: 商品～ inventory of merchandise

盘道 pándào　winding mountain paths; bends

盘点 pándiǎn　check; make an inventory of: ～存货 take stock

盘店 pándiàn　transfer the ownership of a shop with its merchandise and equipment to another person; transfer a business

盘杠子 pán gàngzi　exercise on a horizontal bar

盘根错节 pángēn-cuòjié　with twisted roots and gnarled branches——complicated and difficult to deal with; deep-rooted

盘根究底 pángēn-jiūdǐ　get to the heart of a matter; get to the bottom of things; inquire deeply into sth.: 她～问个没完。She asked about everything in great detail.

盘古 Pán Gǔ　Pan Gu, creator of the universe in Chinese mythology: 自从～开天地 since Pan Gu separated heaven and earth; since the beginning of the world

盘管 pánguǎn　*mech.* coil (pipe)

盘桓 pánhuán ① *formal* stay; linger: ～终日 linger about all day long ／ 我们在杭州～了几天，游览了各处名胜。We spent a few days sightseeing in Hangzhou. ② winding; coiling: 她梳了个～髻。She wore her hair in a coil. ③ wind round and round; spiral up or down

盘簧 pánhuáng　*mech.* coil spring

盘货 pánhuò　make an inventory of stock on hand; take stock: 今日～, 停业半天。Closed for half a day for stocktaking.

盘获 pánhuò　capture (robbers or booty) through interrogation and investigation

盘诘 pánjié　cross-examine; interrogate: ～行迹可疑的人 interrogate suspicious-looking persons

盘踞 pánjù　(also 盘据 pánjù) illegally or forcibly occupy; be entrenched: 我军一举歼灭了～海岛的敌人。At one stroke our troops wiped out the enemy who were entrenched on the island.

盘空 pánkōng　circle or whirl in the air

盘库 pánkù　make an inventory of goods in a warehouse

盘马弯弓 pán mǎ wān gōng　ride round and round bending one's bow—assume an impressive posture but take no action

盘尼西林 pánníxīlín　penicillin (a transliteration, also called 青霉素 qīngméisù)

盘弄 pánnòng　play with; fiddle with; fondle

盘曲 pánqū　*formal* winding; curling; coiled; tortuous

盘绕 pánrào　twine; coil; spiral; wreathe: 长长的藤葛～在树身上。Long vines twine round the tree.

盘山 pánshān　winding up a mountain: ～小道 a winding mountain path

盘跚 pánshān　same as 蹒跚 pánshān

盘石 pánshí　same as 磐石 pánshí

盘算 pánsuan　calculate; figure; plan: 我们～了一下, 产量将增加百分之五。We figured that the output would increase by five per cent.

盘梯 pántī　winding staircase; spiral staircase

盘条 pántiáo　*metall.* wire rod

盘头 pántóu　① hair worn in a bun or coil: 梳着～ wear one's hair in a bun or coil ② *old* turban

盘腿 pántuǐ　cross one's legs: ～坐在炕上 sit cross-legged on a kang

盘陀 pántuó　*formal* ① rocky; uneven; rough; jagged ② winding: ～路 a winding road

盘问 pánwèn　cross-examine; interrogate

盘膝 pánxī　cross one's legs: ～而坐 sit cross-legged

盘香 pánxiāng　incense coil

盘旋 pánxuán　① spiral; circle; wheel: 车队沿山路～而上。The motorcade spiralled up the mountain. / 雄鹰在空中～。Eagles were wheeling in the air. / 这件事在我脑子里～了好久。I've been turning this over in my mind for a long while. ② linger; stay: 他在暖房里～了半天才离开。He lingered in the greenhouse for some time before he left.

盘牙 pányá　*dial.* molar

盘羊 pányáng　*zool.* argali

盘运 pányùn　carry; transport

盘帐 pánzhàng　check (or audit, examine) accounts

盘子 pánzi　① tray; plate; dish ② *old* the market rate

盘坐 pánzuò　sit cross-legged

槃 pán　① see 涅槃 nièpán ② same as 盘 pán①②④

槃根错节 pángēn-cuòjié　same as 盘根错节 pángēn-cuòjié

磐 pán　huge rock

磐石 pánshí　huge rock: ～般的团结 rocklike unity; monolithic unity

磐石之固 pánshí zhī gù　the firmness of a rock

蹒（蹣） pán　see below

蹒跚 pánshān　walk haltingly; limp; hobble

蟠 pán　coil; curl: 一条蟒蛇～在大树根部。A boa lay coiled at the foot of the tree.

蟠踞 pánjù　same as 盘踞 pánjù

蟠桃 pántáo　① flat peach ② peach of immortality in Chinese mythology

pàn

判 pàn　① distinguish; discriminate: 判别 pànbié ② obviously (different): 判然 pànrán / 判若两人 pàn ruò liǎng rén ③ judge; decide: ～卷子 mark examination papers ④ sentence; condemn: ～五年徒刑 be sentenced to five years' imprisonment

判案 pàn'àn　decide a case

判别 pànbié　differentiate; distinguish: ～真假 distinguish the true from the false / 这两个品种不难～。These two varieties are not difficult to differentiate.

判别式 pànbiéshì　*math.* discriminant

判处 pànchǔ　sentence (sb.) to; condemn (sb.) to: 罪犯被～死刑。The criminal was sentenced (or condemned) to death.

判词 pàncí　*leg.* court verdict

判定 pàndìng　judge; decide; determine

判断 pànduàn　① judge; decide; determine: ～是非 judge (or decide) what is right and what is wrong / ～情况 assess (or size up) the situation / 你～得很正确。Your judgment is sound. / 你～错了。You used bad judgment. / 正确的～来源于周密的调查研究。Correct judgments stem from thorough investigation and study. ② *log.* judgment

判断词 pànduàncí　*gram.* a grammatical term for the character 是 used as a link word to form a compound predicate with a noun or pronoun

判断力 pànduànlì　the ability to judge correctly; judgment: 他～强 (差)。He is a man of good (weak) judgment.

判官 pànguān　a judge in Hades

判据 pànjù　*phys.* criterion

判决 pànjué　*leg.* pass judgment; pronounce (judgment): ～有罪 (无罪) pronounce sb. guilty (not guilty)

判决书 pànjuéshū　*leg.* court verdict; written judgment

判例 pànlì　*leg.* legal precedent; judicial precedent: 国际法～ cases in international law / ～法 case law

判明 pànmíng　clearly distinguish; ascertain: ～是非 clearly distinguish right from wrong / ～真相 ascertain the facts / ～责任 establish responsibility (for what has happened)

判然 pànrán　(of differences) noticeable; marked; striking: ～不同 be markedly different / 山南山北气温～不同。There are marked differences in temperature between regions to the north of the mountains and those to the south.

判若两人 pàn ruò liǎng rén　have become quite a different person; no longer be one's old self

判若云泥 pàn ruò yún-ní　(also 判若天渊 pàn ruò tiānyuān) be as far removed as is heaven from earth; be poles apart

判刑 pànxíng　pass a sentence on; sentence sb. to: 判死刑 pass a death sentence on sb. / 他被判了五年刑。He has been sentenced to five years' imprisonment.

判罪 pànzuì　declare guilty; convict

泮 pàn　① *formal* dissolve; melt ② an ancient institution of higher learning

叛 pàn　betray; rebel against: ～匪 rebels / ～贼 traitor

叛变 pànbiàn　betray one's country, party, etc.; turn

traitor; turn renegade: ～投敌 turn traitor and go over to the enemy

叛党 pàndǎng　turn renegade, esp. from the Communist Party; betray one's party; turn traitor to one's party

叛国 pànguó　betray one's country; commit treason: ～罪 high treason

叛军 pànjūn　rebel army; rebel forces; insurgent troops

叛离 pànlí　betray; desert; defect from; turn renegade

叛乱 pànluàn　armed rebellion: 煽动～ incite people to rise in rebellion / 镇压反革命～ suppress (or put down) a counterrevolutionary rebellion

叛卖 pànmài　betray; sell out: ～祖国 betray one's country / ～活动 traitorous activity; acts of treason

叛逆 pànnì　① rebel against; revolt against ② rebel: 封建礼教的～ a rebel against feudal ethics

叛逃 pàntáo　desert and flee one's country; defect: ～者 defector; deserter

叛徒 pàntú　traitor; renegade; turncoat

盼 pàn　① hope for; long for; expect: ～解放 long for liberation / ～复。I await your reply. ② look: 左顾右盼 zuǒgù-yòupàn

盼顾 pàngù　look around; look left and right: 引领～ crane one's neck to look around

盼念 pànniàn　look forward to seeing; long to see: 你母亲正日夜～着你呢! Your mother misses you terribly and is longing to see you.

盼头 pàntou　sth. hoped for and likely to happen; good prospects: 这事有～了。This business is looking hopeful now. or Things are looking up.

盼望 pànwàng　hope for; long for; look forward to: ～生活改善 long for better living conditions / 我们都～有这么一天。We're all looking forward to the day.

袢 pàn　① same as 襻 pàn ② see 袷袢 qiāpàn

畔 pàn　① side; bank: 河～ river bank; riverside / 湖～ the shore of a lake ② the border of a field

鋬 pàn　handle (of a utensil)

襻 pàn　① a loop for fastening a button: 纽襻 niǔpàn ② sth. shaped like a button loop or used for a similar purpose: 鞋～儿 shoe strap / 篮子～儿 the handle of a basket ③ fasten with a rope, string, etc.; tie: 用绳子～上 fasten with a rope / ～上几针 put in a few stitches

pāng

乒 pāng　onom. a loud sudden noise made by gunfire, door-slamming, breaking of things, etc.; bang; pop; slam; crash: 门～地一声关上了。The door slammed (or banged) shut. / 听到～～两声枪响。I heard two bangs of a gun.

滂 pāng　formal (of water) rushing; gushing; pouring

滂湃 pāngpài　(of water) roaring and rushing

滂沛 pāngpèi　formal ① (of water) surging; rushing ② (of rain) torrential; pouring; pelting: 大雨～。The rain was pelting down. ③ powerful; of great momentum: 文辞～ powerful writing

滂沱 pāngtuó　torrential: 大雨～。It's raining in torrents. / 涕泗～ let loose a flood of tears

膀(胮) pāng　swelling: ～肿 swollen; bloated

————see also bǎng; páng

páng

彷(徬) páng　see below

彷徨 pánghuáng　walk back and forth, not knowing which way to go; hesitate

彷徨歧途 pánghuáng qítú　hesitate at the crossroads

庞¹(龐、厐) páng　① huge ② innumerable and disordered

庞²(龐) Páng　a surname

庞³(龐) páng　the cast of one's face: 面庞 miànpáng

庞大 pángdà　huge; enormous; colossal; gigantic: 机构～ an unwieldy organization / 开支～ an enormous expenditure / ～的正规军 a massive regular army / ～的计划 a grandiose plan

庞然大物 pángrán dàwù　huge monster; colossus; giant: 帝国主义看起来是个～,其实是纸老虎。Imperialism, which looks like a huge monster, is really a paper tiger.

庞杂 pángzá　numerous and jumbled: 议论～ numerous and jumbled views / 机构～ cumbersome administrative structure

旁 páng　① side: 马路两～ both sides of the street / 站在路～ stand by the roadside ② other; else: 还有～的建议吗? Any other suggestions? / 他没说～的话。He didn't say anything else. / ～的还要什么? Do you want anything else? ③ lateral radical of a Chinese character (e.g. 亻, 氵, etc.)

旁白 pángbái　aside (in a play)

旁边 pángbiān　side: 我坐在他～。I sat by his side. / ～有一棵树。There is a tree nearby.

旁薄 pángbó　(also 旁礴 pángbó) same as 磅礴 pángbó

旁侧 pángcè　side

旁观 pángguān　look on; be an onlooker: ～者 onlooker; bystander; spectator

旁观者清 pángguānzhě qīng　the spectator sees most clearly; the onlooker sees the game best

旁皇 pánghuáng　same as 彷徨 pánghuáng

旁及 pángjí　take up (along with sth. more important): 他专攻历史,～考古。He is an historian, but also takes an interest in archaeology.

旁路 pánglù　elec. bypass: ～电容器 bypass capacitor

旁落 pángluò　(of power, etc.) pass into others' hands: 大权旁落 dàquán pángluò

旁门 pángmén　side door

旁门左道 pángmén-zuǒdào　same as 左道旁门 zuǒdào-pángmén

旁敲侧击 pángqiāo-cèjī　attack by innuendo; make oblique references

旁人 pángrén　other people: 这个错误由我一人负责,跟～不相干。I alone should be held responsible for the mistake; no one else has anything to do with it.

旁若无人 páng ruò wú rén　act as if there was no one else present—self-assured or supercilious

旁听 pángtīng　be a visitor at a meeting, in a school class, etc.: 我明天上午～你的课可以吗? May I sit in on your lecture tomorrow morning?

旁听生 pángtīngshēng　auditor

旁听席 pángtīngxí　visitors' seats; public gallery (at a Congressional session, etc.)

旁通管 pángtōngguǎn　mech. bypass pipe

旁系亲属　pángxì qīnshǔ　collateral relatives (or kinsmen); collaterals

旁压力　pángyālì　phys.　lateral pressure

旁征博引　pángzhēng-bóyǐn　quote copiously to support one's thesis; be well documented

旁证　pángzhèng　circumstantial evidence; collateral evidence

旁支　pángzhī　collateral branch (of a family)

膀　páng　see below —— see also bǎng; pāng

膀胱　pángguāng　(urinary) bladder

膀胱镜　pángguāngjìng　med.　cystoscope

膀胱炎　pángguāngyán　med.　cystitis

膀胱造影　pángguāng zàoyǐng　med.　cystography

磅　páng　see below —— see also bàng

磅礴　pángbó　boundless; majestic: 五岭逶迤腾细浪,乌蒙～走泥丸。(毛泽东) The Five Ridges wind like gentle ripples And the majestic Wumeng roll by, globules of clay.

螃　páng　see below

螃蟹　pángxiè　crab

鳉　páng　see below

鳉鲅　pángpí　bitterling (a fish)

pǎng

嗙　pǎng　dial.　brag; boast: 胡吹乱～ boast outrageously; talk big

耪　pǎng　loosen soil with a hoe: ～地 hoe the field

pàng

胖(胖)　pàng　fat; stout; plump: 他～起来了。He's getting fat. or He's putting on weight. —— see also pán

胖大海　pàngdàhǎi　Chin. med.　the seed of boat-fruited sterculia (Sterculia scaphigera)

胖墩儿　pàngdūnr　inf.　(esp. referring to children) roly-poly; fatty

胖鼓鼓　pànggūgū　fat; plump; full; bulging: ～的脸蛋儿 a chubby face / 豆荚长得～的。The pods are already full (or have grown very full).

胖乎乎　pànghūhū　(of children) plump; chubby; pudgy: 这个小孩的脸蛋～的。This child has plump (or chubby) cheeks. / 婴儿～的小手 a baby's pudgy fingers

胖头鱼　pàngtóuyú　same as 鳙鱼 yōngyú

胖子　pàngzi　a fat person; fatty

pāo

抛(抛)　pāo　① throw; toss; fling: ～球 throw (or toss) a ball / ～出一项欺骗性的提案 dish out (or trot out) a phoney proposal ② leave behind; cast aside: 跑到第三圈, 他已经把别人远远地～在后面了。On the third lap he left the other runners far behind. / ～进历史的垃圾堆 be relegated to the garbage heap of history ③ same as 抛售 pāoshòu

抛费　pāofèi　dial.　spoil; waste; ruin

抛光　pāoguāng　mech.　polishing; buffing: 摩擦～ bur-

nishing / ～剂 polishing compound; polish / ～轮 polishing wheel; buff

抛荒　pāohuāng　① (of cultivated land) go out of cultivation; lie waste ② (of one's studies) be neglected; (of one's professional knowledge or ability) be wasted through disuse; get rusty

抛离　pāolí　abandon; leave behind: ～亲生骨肉 abandon one's own flesh and blood

抛锚　pāomáo　① drop anchor; cast anchor ② (of vehicles) break down: 汽车中途～了。The car broke down on the way.

抛弃　pāoqì　abandon; forsake; cast aside: ～妻儿 abandon one's wife and kids / 被人民所～ be abandoned (or spurned) by the people / 我们决不会～真正的朋友。We shall never forsake (or desert) our true friends.

抛却　pāoquè　cast aside; throw away: ～不切实际的幻想 cast away unrealistic notions (or fanciful ideas)

抛洒　pāosǎ　(also 抛撒 pāosǎ) spill; shed; scatter: 饭粒～满地。Grains of cooked rice were scattered all over the floor. / ～一腔热血 shed one's blood (for a just cause)

抛舍　pāoshě　abandon; forsake; cast aside

抛射　pāoshè　project; catapult; launch

抛射体　pāoshètǐ　phys.　projectile

抛售　pāoshòu　sell (goods, shares, etc.) in big quantities, usu. in anticipation of or in order to bring about a fall in price

抛头颅,洒热血　pāo tóulú, sǎ rèxuè　shed one's blood and lay down one's life (for a just cause)

抛头露面　pāotóu-lùmiàn　derog.　reveal one's head and show one's face (formerly said of a woman showing herself in public, which was considered unbecoming; now said of sb. blatantly seeking publicity)

抛物线　pāowùxiàn　math.　parabola

抛掷　pāozhì　formal　throw; cast

抛砖引玉　pāozhuān-yǐnyù　cast a brick to attract jade—offer a few commonplace remarks by way of introduction so that others may come up with valuable opinions

泡¹　pāo　① sth. puffy and soft: 豆腐～儿 beancurd puff ② spongy: 这木料发～。This wood is spongy.

泡²　pāo　dial.　(used as part of a place name) a small lake

泡³　pāo　m.　(for number of excretions; slightly vulgar): 撒两～尿 piss twice / 拉一～屎 have a shit —— see also pào

泡货　pāohuò　dial.　light but bulky goods

泡桐　pāotóng　bot.　paulownia

泡子　pāozi　dial.　a small lake —— see also pàozi

脬　pāo　① see 尿脬 suīpāo ② same as 泡³ pāo

páo

刨　páo　① dig; excavate: ～个坑 dig a hole (or pit) / ～地 dig the ground / ～白薯 dig (up) sweet potatoes / 把树根～出来 dig up the roots of the tree ② inf. (used with 去, 掉 or 了 as complement) exclude; subtract; not count: 十五天～去五天, 只剩下十天了。Fifteen minus five—there are only ten days to go now. —— see also bào

刨除　páochú　exclude; subtract; not count

刨分　páofēn　deduct marks (or points) (for errors in a student's work): 他拼错了两个词, 刨了四分。He got

four marks deducted for two spelling mistakes.

刨根儿 páogēnr　get to the root (*or* bottom) of the matter

刨根问底 páogēn-wèndǐ　get to the root (*or* bottom) of things: 他这人就爱～。He's never satisfied until he gets to the bottom of things.

刨煤机 páoméijī　coal plough

庖 páo　*formal*　① kitchen: 庖厨 páochú ② cook: 名～ a famous *chef*

庖厨 páochú　*formal*　kitchen

庖代 páodài　*formal*　same as 代庖 dàipáo

庖丁 páodīng　*formal*　cook

庖人 páorén　*formal*　cook

咆 páo　*formal*　(of beasts of prey) roar; howl

咆哮 páoxiào　① (of beasts of prey) roar; howl ② (of humans) roar with rage: ～如雷 be in a thundering rage ③ (of torrents) roar on; thunder away: 黄河～。The Huanghe River roars on.

狍(麅) páo　*zool.*　roe deer

狍子 páozi　*zool.*　roe deer

炮 páo　*Chin. med.*　prepare herbal medicine by roasting or parching (in a pan): ～姜 roasted ginger ——see also bāo; pào

炮格 páogé　same as 炮烙 páoluò

炮炼 páoliàn　*Chin. med.*　parch and refine medicinal herbs

炮烙 páoluò　the hot pillar (an ancient instrument of torture)

炮炙 páozhì　same as 炮制 páozhì①

炮制 páozhì　① *Chin. med.* the process of preparing Chinese medicine, as by parching, roasting, baking, steaming, soaking, simmering, etc. ② *derog.* concoct; cook up: ～反动纲领 concoct a reactionary programme

袍 páo　robe; gown

袍哥 páogē　*old*　(a member of) a reactionary gang in southwest China before liberation

袍笏登场 páohù dēngchǎng　dress up and go on stage (said contemptuously of an official or a political puppet taking office)

袍泽 páozé　*formal*　fellow officers

袍罩儿 páozhàor　same as 罩袍 zhàopáo

袍子 páozi　robe; gown: 皮～ fur robe

跑 páo　(of animals) paw (the ground) ——see also pǎo

pǎo

跑 pǎo　① run: 他～得很快。He can run very fast. /～上前去迎接客人 run forward to meet the guests / 每天早晨练慢～ do jogging every morning / 火车在飞～。The train is racing along. ② run a race: ～百米 run (*or* take part in) the 100-metre dash / ～接力赛的第一棒 run the first leg of the relay / ～第二 run second ③ run away; escape; flee: 别让坏蛋～了。See that the scoundrel doesn't escape. / 暴风雨快来了,你还是赶紧～吧! A storm is coming up. You'd better cut and run. ④ *dial.* walk; stroll: 他们通常吃过晚饭出去～～路。They usually go for a stroll after supper. / 我们～了五里路。We walked five *li*. ⑤ run about doing sth.; run errands: ～材料 run about collecting material / 我～了好几家商店,才找到那种扳手。I had to run

around to several shops to get that wrench. / 你这辆卡车一天能～几个来回? How many round trips can your truck make in a day? ⑥ (of a liquid or gas) leak or evaporate: 哎哟,水管子～水了。Oh, the pipe leaks! / 车胎～气了。The tyre is flat. / 汽油～了半瓶。Half the bottle of gasoline has evaporated. ⑦ (used as complement to a verb) away; off: 一枪把鸟儿都吓～了。The shot scared away the birds. / 桌上的纸叫风给刮～了。The paper blew off the table. ——see also páo

跑表 pǎobiǎo　stopwatch

跑步 pǎobù　① run; march at the double: ～走! (word of command) At the double, quick march! / ～前进! (word of command) Double time! ② jogging (a form of physical exercise)

跑车[1] pǎochē　① racing bicycle ② a trolley for conveying logs in a forest

跑车[2] pǎochē　① *inf.* (of train conductors) be on the job ② (of trolleys for hoisting coal in a mine) accidentally slide down

跑驰 pǎochi　*inf.*　run errands; be on the run; hurry here and there: 他白～了一整天,什么事也没办成。He was on the run the whole day, but all for nothing. / 我可没时间替你去～。I've no time to run errands for you.

跑单帮 pǎo dānbāng　travel around trading on one's own

跑刀 pǎodāo　race skates

跑道 pǎodào　① runway (on an airfield) ② *sports* track: 煤渣～ cinder track / 渣土～ cinder and dirt track / 塑料～ plastic track

跑道儿 pǎodàor　same as 跑腿儿 pǎotuǐr

跑电 pǎodiàn　leakage of electricity

跑肚 pǎodù　have loose bowels

跑反 pǎofǎn　*dial.*　flee from war or banditry

跑光 pǎoguāng　*photog.*　(of a film) be exposed to light accidentally

跑旱船 pǎo hànchuán　boat that runs on land (a folk dance performed by a girl gliding about with a cloth boat and a man making rowing movements with an oar, singing a rude ditty as they dance)

跑合儿 pǎohér　*old*　act as go-between in a business deal; bring two parties together to make a deal

跑江湖 pǎo jiānghú　wander about, making a living as a street-performer (e.g. an acrobat, fortune-teller, physiognomist, etc.)

跑街 pǎojiē　*dial.*　① act as a travelling agent or salesman ② a travelling agent or salesman

跑警报 pǎo jǐngbào　run for shelter during an air raid

跑了和尚跑不了庙 pǎole héshang pǎobuliǎo miào　the monk may run away, but the temple can't run with him—a fugitive must belong to some place that can provide clues: 他一家子在这儿,他的房子、地在这儿,他跑?～。Escape? But his house and property can't escape. "The monk may run away, but the temple can't run with him."

跑垒 pǎolěi　*sports*　baserunning: ～员 base runner

跑龙套 pǎo lóngtào　play a walk-on part; play a bit role

跑马 pǎomǎ　① have a ride on a horse ② horse racing

跑马场 pǎomǎchǎng　racecourse; the turf

跑码头 pǎo mǎtou　travel from port to port as a trader; be a travelling merchant

跑买卖 pǎo mǎimai　be a commercial traveller: 他跑过几年买卖。He was a commercial traveller for a couple of years.

跑面 pǎomiàn　(of a cadre sent from a leading government organ) travel around taking general charge of an entire area at the grass-roots level (opp. 蹲点 dūndiǎn)

跑跑颠颠 pǎopǎodiāndiān　bustle about; be on the go: 老大娘在服务站成天～的,给大伙办事。The old lady is bustling about every day at the neighbourhood service

centre, helping people do all sorts of things.

跑跑跳跳　pǎopǎotiàotiào　skip along: 小姑娘～的上街去。The little girl skipped down the street.

跑坡　pǎopō　slip down a (mountain) slope

跑情况　pǎo qíngkuàng　*inf.* run about gathering information

跑墒　pǎoshāng　*agric.* loss of moisture in soil (through evaporation): 使用塑料薄膜覆盖，可以防止～。Plastic sheeting is used to cover the soil to prevent loss of moisture.

跑生意　pǎo shēngyi　same as 跑买卖 pǎo mǎimai

跑堂儿的　pǎotángrde　*old* waiter (in a wineshop, small restaurant, etc.)

跑题　pǎotí　digress from the subject; stray from the point

跑腿儿　pǎotuǐr　*inf.* run errands; do legwork: 我没干多少，就是跑跑腿儿。I didn't do much, just a bit of running around.

跑腿子　pǎotuǐzi　*dial.* bachelor

跑外　pǎowài　act as a travelling agent or salesman: ～的 a travelling agent or salesman

跑鞋　pǎoxié　track shoes (either with spikes for use outdoors or with rubber soles for use indoors)

跑圆场　pǎo yuánchǎng　(of traditional opera singers or actors) walk in circles on the stage at a heel-and-toe pace (a gesture of travelling a long distance in haste)

跑帐　pǎozhàng　*old* (of a shop assistant) run around collecting credits

跑辙　pǎozhé　*dial.* run off the track—digress from the subject; stray from the point

pào

泡　pào　① bubble: 肥皂～儿 soap bubbles / 冒～儿 send up bubbles; rise in bubbles ② sth. shaped like a bubble: 手上起了～ get (*or* raise) blisters on one's palm ③ steep; soak: 把种子放在温水里～一下 steep the seeds in lukewarm water / 他是在苦水里～大的。He was brought up in bitter misery. ④ dawdle: 别～时间了，快把工作做完! Stop dawdling and finish your work! ——see also pāo

泡病号　pào bìnghào　shun work on pretence of illness

泡菜　pàocài　pickled vegetables; pickles

泡茶　pàochá　make tea

泡饭　pàofàn　① soak cooked rice in soup or water ② cooked rice reheated in boiling water; gruel from re-cooked rice

泡沸石　pàofèishí　zeolite (a mineral)

泡蘑菇　pào mógu　① play for time; use delaying tactics; stall: 别～了，咱们赶紧干吧。No more dilly-dallying. Let's get going. ② importune; pester: 别跟我～了，我们不能为你破例。Stop pestering me. I can't make an exception for you.

泡沫　pàomò　foam; froth: 啤酒～ head (on a glass of newly poured beer)

泡沫玻璃　pàomò bōli　foam glass; foamed glass

泡沫混凝土　pàomò hùnníngtǔ　foam concrete

泡沫灭火器　pàomò mièhuǒqì　foam extinguisher

泡沫塑料　pàomò sùliào　foamed plastics

泡沫橡胶　pàomò xiàngjiāo　foam rubber; froth rubber

泡泡纱　pàopàoshā　*text.* seersucker

泡泡糖　pàopàotáng　bubble gum; chewing gum

泡汤　pàotāng　*dial.* ① fall flat; fall through: 这样一来，这个月的计划就要～了。In that case, this month's plan is bound to fall through. ② dawdle; dilly-dally

泡漩　pàoxuán　whirlpool

泡影　pàoyǐng　visionary hope, plan, scheme, etc.; bubble: 化为泡影 huà wéi pàoyǐng

泡罩塔　pàozhàotǎ　*chem.* bubble-cap tower (*or* column)

泡子　pàozi　*inf.* bulb; light bulb ——see also pàozi

炮（砲、礮）　pào　① big gun; cannon; artillery piece ② bombard (the earliest kind of cannon throwing stone balls) ③ firecracker: 鞭炮 biānpào ④ a blasthole filled with dynamite ⑤ cannon, one of the pieces in Chinese chess ——see also bāo; páo

炮兵　pàobīng　artillery; artillerymen: ～部队 artillery (troops) / ～连 battery / ～阵地 artillery position; gun emplacement

炮车　pàochē　gun carriage

炮铳　pàochong　*dial.* firecracker

炮打灯儿　pàodǎdēngr　*dial.* illuminant firecracker

炮弹　pàodàn　① (artillery) shell ② *old* cannon ball

炮轰　pàohōng　(of artillery) bombard; shell: 午夜开始～敌军防线。The artillery started bombarding the enemy lines at midnight.

炮灰　pàohuī　cannon fodder: 战争贩子们视士兵为～。In the eyes of the warmongers, soldiers are nothing but cannon fodder.

炮火　pàohuǒ　artillery fire; gunfire: 部队在猛烈的～掩护下向前推进。The troops advanced under cover of a heavy artillery bombardment. / 掩护～ (artillery) fire cover / ～支援 artillery support / ～准备 artillery preparation

炮击　pàojī　bombard; shell

炮架　pàojià　gun carriage; gun mount

炮舰　pàojiàn　gunboat

炮舰外交　pàojiàn wàijiāo　gunboat diplomacy

炮舰政策　pàojiàn zhèngcè　gunboat policy

炮口　pàokǒu　gun muzzle; cannon's mouth: ～焰 muzzle flash

炮楼　pàolóu　*mil.* blockhouse

炮钎　pàoqiān　rock drill

炮声　pàoshēng　report (of a big gun): ～隆隆。Cannons boomed.

炮手　pàoshǒu　gunner; artilleryman

炮栓　pàoshuān　breechblock (of a big gun)

炮塔　pàotǎ　gun turret; turret

炮台　pàotái　a fortification with built-in cannons; battery

炮膛　pàotáng　bore (of a big gun)

炮艇　pàotǐng　gunboat

炮筒　pàotǒng　barrel (of a big gun)

炮筒子　pàotǒngzi　a person who shoots off his mouth

炮尾　pàowěi　gun breech

炮位　pàowèi　emplacement

炮眼　pàoyǎn　① porthole; embrasure ② blasthole; dynamite hole; borehole

炮衣　pàoyī　gun cover

炮战　pàozhàn　artillery action (*or* engagement)

炮仗　pàozhang　firecracker

炮子儿　pàozǐr　*inf.* ① small shell ② bullet

炮座　pàozuò　gun platform

疱（皰）　pào　blister; bleb

疱疹　pàozhěn　① bleb ② herpes: 带状～ herpes zoster; zoster

疱疹净　pàozhěnjìng　*pharm.* idoxuridine

pēi

呸　pēi　*interj.* (used to express disdain, annoyance or stern disapproval) pah; bah; pooh: ～! 胡

说八道! Bah! That's nonsense! / ～! 我才不信呢! Pooh! I don't believe that!

胚(肧)　pēi　biol. embryo

胚层　pēicéng　biol. germinal layer: 内～ entoderm / 外～ ectoderm / 中～ mesoderm

胚根　pēigēn　bot. radicle

胚囊　pēináng　biol. embryo sac

胚盘　pēipán　zool. blastodisc; germinal disc

胚乳　pēirǔ　bot. endosperm

胚胎　pēitāi　① zool. embryo: ～移植 embryo transfer; embryonic implantation ② the beginning or rudimentary stage (of anything)

胚胎学　pēitāixué　embryology

胚芽　pēiyá　① bot. plumule ② an undeveloped thing; the bud: 矛盾的～ a contradiction in the bud

胚叶　pēiyè　same as 胚层 pēicéng

胚轴　pēizhóu　bot. plumular axis

胚珠　pēizhū　bot. ovule

胚子　pēizi　① silkworm embryo ② egg (fig.); person: 他是个坏～。He's a bad egg. / 好～ a good egg

pēi

陪　péi　accompany; keep sb. company: 我～你到农场去。I'll accompany you to the farm. / ～外宾参观工厂 show foreign visitors round a factory / ～病人 look after a patient

陪伴　péibàn　accompany; keep sb. company: 老太太要找个人～。The old lady wants someone to keep her company. or The old lady wants to find a companion.

陪绑　péibǎng　① be taken to the execution ground together with those to be executed as a form of intimidation ② (of an innocent person) be criticized or punished together with the guilty

陪衬　péichèn　① serve as a contrast or foil; set off: 红旗在雪山的～下, 显得分外鲜艳。The red flags stood out in sharp relief against the snow mountains. ② foil; setoff

陪床　péichuáng　(of an inpatient's family member, etc.) stay in the ward to look after the patient night and day

陪吊　péidiào　old　a person employed to help with the reception of mourners at a funeral

陪都　péidū　an alternate or secondary capital; a provisional capital (e.g. Chongqing after the fall of Nanjing during the Anti-Japanese War)

陪房　péifáng　old　a maidservant that follows the bride to her husband's house as her personal maid

陪祭　péijì　a person who helps with the officiation of funeral rites

陪嫁　péijià　dial. dowry

陪客　péikè　a guest invited to a dinner party to help entertain the guest of honour

陪奁　péilián　dial. dowry

陪审　péishěn　leg.　① act (or serve) as an assessor (in a law case) ② serve on a jury

陪审团　péishěntuán　jury

陪审席　péishěnxí　jury box

陪审员　péishěnyuán　juror; juryman

陪审制　péishěnzhì　jury system

陪侍　péishì　old　stand at sb.'s side in attendance

陪送　péisong　inf.　① give as a dowry; dower ② dowry

陪同　péitóng　① accompany: ～前往参观 accompany sb. on a visit / 外宾们由协会主任～, 观看了演出。The foreign guests, accompanied by the chairman of the association, attended a performance. ② a responsible official accompanying an important visitor or visiting delegation

陪同人员　péitóng rényuán　entourage: 女王及其～ the Queen and her entourage

陪同团　péitóngtuán　hosting team; receptionist committee: ～团长 head of a hosting team; chairman of a receptionist committee

陪葬　péizàng　① (of a wife, concubine or slave) be buried alive with the dead ② (of figurines or objects) be buried with the dead ③ (of a wife or concubine after her death) be buried by the side of her husband's grave

陪葬品　péizàngpǐn　(also 陪葬物 péizàngwù) funerary objects, figurines, etc.

陪住　péizhù　(of an inpatient's family member, etc.) sleep in the ward to tend the patient

培　péi　① bank up with earth; earth up ② foster; train: ～干 train cadres

培土　péitǔ　agric. hill up; earth up: 在玉米根部多培点儿土 earth up the maize

培修　péixiū　repair and reinforce (earthwork): ～堤坝 repair (or reinforce) the dykes and dams

培训　péixùn　train (personnel): ～医务工作者 train medical personnel / ～导游人员 train tourist guides / 在职～ on-the-job training / 短期强化～ short-term intensified training

培训班　péixùnbān　training course: 暑期～ a summer vacation training course; summer school / 秘书人员～ a course for secretarial training; secretarial course

培养　péiyǎng　① cultivate (plants); culture (microorganisms): ～花卉 cultivate flowers and plants / 细菌～ the culture of bacteria ② foster, train, or develop (a certain spirit, ability, etc.) in sb.: 从小～好习惯 develop good habits from childhood days / ～对阅读的兴趣 develop an interest in reading / ～积极分子 foster activists / ～学生自学能力 train the students to study on their own / 在老师的～教育下 be nurtured and educated by the teachers / ～和造就革命事业接班人 train and bring up successors for the revolutionary cause

培养基　péiyǎngjī　biol. culture medium

培养瓶　péiyǎngpíng　culture bottle

培壅　péiyōng　formal　① earth up (flowers, crops, etc.) ② cultivate; foster; train; develop

培育　péiyù　① help (young plants) grow by labour and care; cultivate; breed: ～小麦新品种 breed new varieties of wheat / ～树苗 grow saplings / 她这些花是从育种开始辛勤～出来的。She cultivated these flowers from seeds. ② nurture and educate; bring up; rear: 为建设社会主义～一代新人 rear (or bring up) a new generation of builders of socialism / 孩子们在父母和老师的～下健康成长。Nurtured and educated by their parents and teachers, the children are growing up healthy and strong.

培植　péizhí　① cultivate (plants): ～中草药 cultivate medicinal herbs / 寒冬腊月也可以吃到温室里～的许多新鲜蔬菜。Even in the coldest month of the year, we can still get plenty of vegetables fresh from the greenhouse. ② foster; train: ～人才 train competent personnel / ～良好的队风 foster a fine team spirit / ～私人势力 build up one's personal influence

培种　péizhǒng　cultivate (plants): ～芦笋 cultivate asparagus

赔　péi　① make good a loss; compensate; pay for; indemnify: 玻璃是我打碎的, 由我来～。I broke the glass, so I'll pay for it. ② lose money in business; stand a loss: 去年我们～的钱, 这一笔生意全赚回来了。We have retrieved in this bargain all the money we lost last year. / 你算算咱们是～是赚。Balance the

accounts and see if we have made any money.

赔本 péiběn　sustain losses in business; run a business at a loss: ～生意 a business run at a loss

赔补 péibǔ　make good a loss; make up a deficit

赔不是 péi bùshi　apologize: 是你错怪了她，你该给她赔个不是。You should apologize to her for blaming her wrongly.

赔不起 péibuqǐ　be unable to make good a loss: 这本书要是丢了，你可～。If ever this book got lost, you would never be able to make good the loss.

赔偿 péicháng　① make good a loss; compensate; indemnify: ～损失 compensate (or pay) for a loss / 照价～ compensate according to the cost / 保留要求～的权利 reserve the right to demand compensation for the losses / 对工伤的工人给予～ compensate workers for on-the-job injuries / 对遇难者亲属承担经济上的～ undertake to indemnify the victim's family ② reparations (of a defeated state for war damage): 战争～ war reparations; war indemnity / 实物～ reparations in kind / ～协定 reparations agreement

赔偿费 péichángfèi　(also 赔偿金 péichángjīn) leg. (compensatory) damages

赔错 péicuò　acknowledge a mistake; apologize for one's wrongdoing: 我向您～来啦。I've come especially to apologize to you.

赔垫 péidiàn　pay for sb. (usu. a large sum of money): 钱数太大，我可～不起。I can't pay so much money for you.

赔话 péihuà　say a word in apology

赔款 péikuǎn　① pay an indemnity; pay reparations: 割地～ cede territories and pay reparations ② indemnity; reparations: 庚子～ the Boxer Indemnity

赔了夫人又折兵 péile fūrén yòu zhé bīng　give one's enemy a wife and lose one's soldiers as well—pay a double penalty (for attempting to gain an unfair advantage); instead of making a gain, suffer a double loss

赔累 péilěi　lose money in business and run into debt

赔礼 péilǐ　make (or offer) an apology; apologize: ～道歉 make a formal apology

赔钱 péiqián　① sustain economic losses; lose money in business: ～的买卖 a business run at a loss ② pay for a loss; pay damages

赔情 péiqíng　dial. apologize (for a wrong done to sb.); ask forgiveness for one's wrongdoing

赔贴 péitiē　pay subsidies

赔小心 péi xiǎoxīn　behave with great caution; act warily: 老板动不动就生气，在他面前说话，要赔点儿小心才好。Our boss is easily offended, so be careful how you speak to him.

赔笑 péixiào　(also 赔笑脸 péi xiàoliǎn) smile obsequiously, apologetically or appeasingly; smile an apologetic or obsequious smile

赔帐 péizhàng　① pay for the loss of cash or goods entrusted to one ② dial. lose money in business

赔罪 péizuì　apologize (for a wrong done to sb.); ask forgiveness for one's wrongdoing

锫 péi　chem. berkelium (Bk)

裴 Péi　a surname

pèi

沛 pèi　copious; abundant: ～然降雨。A copious rain began to fall.

佩[1]（珮） pèi　an ornament worn as a pendant

at the waist in ancient times: 玉～ jade pendant

佩[2] pèi　① wear (at the waist, etc.): ～玉 wear a jade pendant at one's waist / ～腰～手枪 carry a pistol in one's belt ② admire: 他的国际主义精神十分可～。His internationalist spirit is altogether admirable.

佩带 pèidài　wear (at the waist, on the breast, etc.): ～徽章 (肩章, 臂章) wear a badge (shoulder loops, an armlet) / 胸前～奖章 wear a medal on one's breast / 腰间～军刀 wear a sabre at one's waist

佩刀 pèidāo　① wear a sword at the waist ② a sword worn at the waist

佩服 pèifu　esteem; admire: 他机智勇敢，令人～。One must admire his resourcefulness and courage. / 大家对他的高超演技～得不得了。Everyone was filled with admiration at his wonderful acting. / 我从心底里～她。I admire her from the bottom of my heart.

佩剑 pèijiàn　sports sabre: ～运动员 sabre fencer; sabreur

帔 pèi　a short embroidered cape (worn over a woman's shoulders)

配 pèi　① join in marriage: 英雄～模范，真是美满姻缘。A model worker married to a hero—this is really a good match. ② mate (animals): 公驴～母马 a male donkey mated with a mare / ～马 mate horses ③ mix according to a fixed ratio; compound: ～颜色 mix colours (on a palette) / 药～齐了。The prescription has been made up. / 这个食谱～得好。This is a well-combined diet. ④ distribute according to plan; apportion: 配售 pèishòu ⑤ find sth. to fit or replace sth. else: ～钥匙 have a key made to fit a lock / ～眼镜 have one's eyesight tested for glasses / ～零件 replace parts ⑥ subordinate; supplementary; supporting: 配角 pèijué ⑦ match; harmonize with; be in harmony with: 颜色不～。Those colours don't match. / 粉红和浅蓝～在一起挺好看。Pink and light blue go well together. / 她的衬衣和裙子～不到一起。Her blouse doesn't match her skirt. / 给一首老乐曲～上新歌词 set new words to an old tune / 这段唱腔要用笛子来～。This passage is to be sung to the accompaniment of a bamboo flute. ⑧ deserve; be qualified; suit: 只有他们这样的人，才～称为先进工作者。Only people like them deserve the name of advanced workers. / 她不～当代表。She is not qualified to be a representative. ⑨ exile; banish: 发配 fāpèi

配备 pèibèi　① provide (manpower or equipment); equip; fit out: 给老中医～助手 provide assistants to veteran practitioners of traditional Chinese medicine / 给图书馆～上计算机 equip the library with computers / 这些舰艇～有大口径炮。These ships are fitted with large-calibre guns. / 这个项目～的技术力量不足。The project is not sufficiently provided with technical personnel. / 这趟列车～的服务人员不够。This train is under-manned. ② dispose (troops, etc.); deploy: 按地形～火力 dispose fire-power according to terrain / 从敌军～弱的地方插进去 thrust in where the enemy deployment is weak ③ outfit; equipment: 现代化的～ modern equipment / 成套的～ a complete outfit

配菜 pèicài　① garnish food ② garnishes: 这个鱼就用黄瓜片作～。Garnish the fish with cucumber slices.

配餐 pèicān　assorted foods for a meal

配餐室 pèicānshì　pantry

配搭 pèidā　supplement; match; accompany: 这出戏的配角儿～得很整齐。The minor roles of the play are competently filled.

配搭儿 pèidār　adjunct; supplement

配电 pèidiàn　elec. (power) distribution: ～线路 dis-

tribution line

配电盘 pèidiànpán *elec.* distributor

配电网 pèidiànwǎng *elec.* distribution network

配殿 pèidiàn side hall in a palace or temple

配对[1] pèiduì pair; match: 这两只手套不～儿。These two gloves don't match (*or* aren't a pair). / 请你再给我找一只一模一样的花瓶，配成一对儿。Please find me another vase exactly like this one to make a pair.

配对[2] pèiduì *inf.* (of animals) mate; pair: 现在正是鸽子～的好时候。It's high time to pair (*or* mate) the doves.

配额 pèi'é quota: 出口～ export quota

配方[1] pèifāng fill (*or* make up) a prescription

配方[2] pèifāng ① a formula for compounding a chemical or metallurgical product: 制皂～ a formula for making soap ② prescription

配房 pèifáng wing (of a house)

配购 pèigòu buy rations

配合 pèihé coordinate; cooperate; concert: ～作战 coordination of military operations / ～行动 take concerted action / 起～作用 play a supporting role / ～中心工作组织活动 coordinate activities with the central task / 治疗过程中，病人和大夫～得很好。The patient cooperated very well with the doctors during the treatment. ——see also pèihe

配合饲料 pèihé sìliào mixed feed; compound feed

配合 pèihe be harmoniously combined or arranged: 瞧她的绣品，深浅颜色多么～! What a wonderful combination of shades of colour you find in her embroidery! ——see also pèihé

配给 pèijǐ ration: ～证 ration card (*or* book) / ～制 ration system; rationing

配件 pèijiàn ① parts, fittings, or accessories: 合页之类门窗～ door and window fittings such as hinges / 管子～ pipe fittings ② replacement

配角[1] pèijué appear with another leading player; co-star with sb.

配角[2] pèijué supporting role; supporting actor: 在该片中演～ play a supporting role in the film / 当总经理的～ play second fiddle to the general manager

配军 pèijūn *old* an exile

配料 pèiliào ① mix ingredients according to a recipe; get materials ready (for the manufacture of sth.) in the right proportion ② *metall.* burden: 高炉～ blast-furnace burden / ～表 burden sheet / ～计算 burden calculation

配尼西林 pèiníxīlín penicillin (a transliteration, also called 青霉素 qīng méisù)

配偶 pèi'ǒu *formal* spouse: 外交官及其～ diplomats and their spouses

配器 pèiqì *mus.* orchestration

配曲 pèiqǔ set to music

配色 pèisè mix colours in the right proportion

配色 pèishǎi *inf.* match colours; harmonize colours: 室内装饰的～ the matching of colours in interior decoration

配售 pèishòu ration (at state price): 下个月起汽油实行～。Gasoline will be rationed from next month.

配属 pèishǔ *mil.* place part of one's troops temporarily under the command of a subordinate officer

配水闸 pèishuǐzhá *water conservancy* distribution structure

配糖物 pèitángwù (also 配糖体 pèitángtǐ) old name for 甙 dài

配套 pèitào form a complete set or system: 就地生产，就地～ manufacture complete sets of equipment locally / 大小沟渠要～。There must be a complete network of irrigation canals and ditches.

配套成龙 pèitào-chénglóng same as 成龙配套 chéng-

lóng-pèitào

配套工程 pèitào gōngchéng ① auxiliary project ② *water conservancy* conveyance system

配套器材 pèitào qìcái necessary accessories

配伍 pèiwǔ *med.* compatibility of medicines: ～禁忌 incompatibility

配戏 pèixì play a minor part (to support a leading actor): 他有幸为梅兰芳配过戏。He had the honour of playing a supporting role in an opera starring Mei Lanfang.

配系 pèixì *mil.* system of disposition

配烟 pèiyān tobacco blending

配药 pèiyào ① (of a pharmacist) make up a prescription; dispense a prescription ② have a prescription made up: 拿这张方子到中药房去配三副药。Have three doses of this prescription made up at the Chinese pharmacy.

配页 pèiyè *print.* gather (leaves of a book) in proper sequence for binding

配音 pèiyīn dub (a film, etc.): 用汉语给外国电影～ dub foreign films in Chinese

配音演员 pèiyīn yǎnyuán dubber

配乐 pèiyuè ① select passages to serve as background music (for a film, play, radio programme, etc.) ② dub in background music: ～诗朗诵 a poem recital dubbed in with background music

配乐广播 pèiyuè guǎngbō dubbed-in radio programme

配制 pèizhì compound; make up: ～药剂 compound medicines

配置 pèizhì dispose (troops, etc.); deploy: ～兵力 dispose forces / 纵深～ disposition in depth / 生产力的合理～ a rational distribution of productive forces

配种 pèizhǒng *animal husbandry* breeding: ～率 breeding rate / ～站 breeding station

配子 pèizǐ *biol.* gamete

配子体 pèizǐtǐ *bot.* gametophyte

斾（斾） pèi *formal* ① an ancient swallow-tailed flag ② banners and flags

辔 pèi bridle: 鞍～ saddle and bridle

辔头 pèitóu bridle

霈 pèi *formal* ① a heavy rain: 甘～ a timely (*or* welcome) rain ② rain profusely: ～然下雨。It was raining heavily.

pēn

喷 pēn ① spurt; spout; gush: 喷泉向空中～水。The fountain spurted water into the air. / 石油从井口～了出来。Oil gushed from the well. / 火山不住地～出熔岩。The volcano kept throwing up streams of lava. ② spray; sprinkle: 给花～点水 sprinkle some water on the flowers / 往果树上～农药 spray fruit trees with insecticide ——see also pèn

喷薄 pēnbó gushing; spurting

喷薄欲出 pēnbó yù chū (of the sun) emerge in all its splendour: ～的一轮红日 the emerging sun with all its shimmering rays

喷出岩 pēnchūyán *geol.* extrusive rock; extrusive

喷灯 pēndēng blowtorch; blowlamp

喷发 pēnfā erupt; throw out: 火山～ volcanic eruption

喷发胶 pēnfàjiāo hair spray

喷饭 pēnfàn laugh so hard as to spew one's food; split one's sides with laughter: 令人喷饭 lìng rén pēnfàn

喷放 pēnfàng spurt; spout: 烟火在夜空中～出五彩缤纷

的火花。Fireworks shot into the night sky, sending out colourful sparks.

喷粉器　pēnfěnqì　*agric.*　duster

喷粪　pēnfèn　*offens.*　use abusive language: 满嘴～ shout filthy abuses; use foul language

喷灌　pēnguàn　sprinkling irrigation; spray irrigation

喷灌器　pēnguànqì　sprinkler

喷壶　pēnhú　watering can; sprinkling can

喷火器　pēnhuǒqì　*mil.*　flamethrower

喷溅　pēnjiàn　(of a liquid when being squeezed out) splash; spatter

喷浆　pēnjiāng　*archit.*　① whitewashing ② guniting

喷漆　pēnqī　spray paint; spray lacquer: ～枪 paint spray gun; airbrush

喷气发动机　pēnqì fādòngjī　jet engine

喷气式　pēnqìshì　jet-propelled

喷气式飞机　pēnqìshì fēijī　jet plane; jet aircraft; jet

喷气织机　pēnqì zhījī　air-jet loom

喷枪　pēnqiāng　spray gun; airbrush

喷泉　pēnquán　fountain

喷洒　pēnsǎ　spray; sprinkle: ～农药 spray insecticide

喷射　pēnshè　spray; spurt; jet: ～火焰 spurt flames

喷水池　pēnshuǐchí　(artificial) fountain

喷丝头　pēnsītóu　*text.*　spinning jet; spinning nozzle: ～牵伸 spinneret draft / ～组件 spinneret assembly

喷腾　pēnténg　(of water, flames, smoke, steam, etc.) spurt up; shoot up

喷嚏　pēntì　sneeze

喷桶　pēntǒng　*dial.*　watering can; sprinkling can

喷头　pēntóu　① shower nozzle ② sprinkler head

喷吐　pēntǔ　shoot out (flames, light, gas, etc.)

喷雾　pēnwù　spray; atomize

喷雾器　pēnwùqì　sprayer; atomizer

喷泻　pēnxiè　(of a liquid) shoot out; gush forth

喷云吐雾　pēnyún-tǔwù　① (of a smoker) puff away ② (of a chimney, etc.) belch out smoke

喷子　pēnzi　sprayer; spraying apparatus

喷嘴　pēnzuǐ　spray nozzle; spray head

pén

盆　pén　① basin; tub; pot: 大大小小的～儿一大摞 a pile of pots and basins of all sizes ② *m.* (for things held in a basin, tub, or pot): 几～花 a few pots of flowers / 一～热水 a basin of hot water

盆菜　péncài　*dial.*　ready-to-cook dish of meat, vegetables, etc. (sold at a food market)

盆地　péndì　*geog.*　basin: 柴达木～ the Qaidam Basin / 准噶尔～ the Junggar Basin

盆花　pénhuā　potted flower

盆景　pénjǐng　potted landscape; miniature trees and rockery

盆盆罐罐　pénpénguànguàn　pots and pans—household utensils

盆腔　pénqiāng　*physiol.*　pelvic cavity

盆腔炎　pénqiāngyán　*med.*　pelvic infection

盆汤　péntāng　(also 盆塘 péntáng) bathtub cubicle; bathhouse cubicle

盆浴　pényù　tub bath; tub

盆栽　pénzāi　① grown (*or* cultivated) in a pot: ～葡萄 a grapevine cultivated in a pot ② potted flowers or miniature trees

pèn

喷　pèn　*inf.*　① in season: 西瓜正在～儿上。Watermelons are in season now. ② *m.* crop: 头～儿棉花 the first crop of cotton ——see also pēn

喷红　pènhóng　crimson: 她羞得满脸～。Her face crimsoned from shame.

喷香　pènxiāng　fragrant; delicious: 饭菜～。The dishes smell delicious.

pēng

怦　pēng　(of the heart) thumping; pit-a-pat: 他的心激动得～～直跳。His heart was thumping with excitement. / ～然心动 one's heart goes pit-a-pat

抨　pēng　*formal*　impeach

抨击　pēngjī　attack (in speech or writing); assail (with words); lash out at

抨弹　pēngtán　same as 抨击 pēngjī

砰　pēng　*onom.*　the sound of sth. falling heavily on the ground or striking against sth. else: ～的一声, 门关上了。The door banged shut. / ～一声, 木板倒下来了。The plank fell on the ground with a thump.

砰然　pēngrán　with a bang; with a thump

烹　pēng　① boil; cook in water; brew (tea, coffee, etc.) ② fry quickly in hot oil and stir in sauce: ～对虾 quick-fried prawns in brown sauce

烹饪　pēngrèn　cooking; culinary art: 擅长～ be good at cooking; be a good cook

烹饪法　pēngrènfǎ　① cuisine; cookery ② recipe (for cooking)

烹调　pēngtiáo　cook (dishes): 中国式～ Chinese cooking; Chinese cuisine

péng

朋　péng　① friend: 良～ good friend / 宾～满座。There was a houseful of guests. *or* Visitors filled all the seats. ② *formal* gang up: 朋比为奸 péngbǐ wéi jiān ③ *formal* rival; equal: 硕大无朋 shuòdà wú péng

朋辈　péngbèi　*formal*　friends

朋比为奸　péngbǐ wéi jiān　act in collusion; conspire; collude; gang up

朋侪　péngchái　(also 朋俦 péngchóu) *formal*　friends; companions

朋党　péngdǎng　clique; cabal

朋僚　péngliáo　*formal*　① colleagues ② friends

朋友　péngyou　① friend: 广交～ make many friends ② boyfriend or girlfriend: 他有～了。He has got a girlfriend now.

棚　péng　① canopy or awning of reed mats, etc. ② shed; shack: 牲口～ livestock shed / 自行车～ bicycle shed

棚车　péngchē　① *railway* box wagon; boxcar ② covered truck

棚户　pénghù　*dial.*　slum-dwellers; shack-dwellers

棚圈　péngjuàn　covered pen (for animals)

棚寮　péngliáo　*dial.*　shack; shanty

棚子 péngzi *inf.* shed; shack: 草～ straw mat shed / 马～ horse shed

彭 Péng a surname

蓬 péng ① *bot.* fleabane ② fluffy; dishevelled: ～着头 with dishevelled hair ③ *m.* (for twiggy, leafy plants) clump; cluster: 一～竹子 a clump of bamboo

蓬荜增辉 péngbì zēng huī lustre lent to a humble house (said in thanks for a visit or a gift such as a scroll)

蓬勃 péngbó vigorous; flourishing; full of vitality: ～发展的社会主义建设事业 flourishing socialist construction / 新生事物～兴起。New things are springing up vigorously.

蓬蒿 pénghāo *dial.* crowndaisy chrysanthemum

蓬户 pénghù *formal* a wicker door—a humble house

蓬莱 Pénglái a fabled abode of immortals: ～仙境 fairyland

蓬乱 péngluàn (of grasses, hair, etc.) fluffy and disorderly

蓬门荜户 péngmén-bìhù (a house with) a wicker door—a humble abode

蓬蓬 péngpéng (of grasses, shrubs, hair, beard, etc.) thick and disorderly

蓬松 péngsōng fluffy; puffy: ～的头发 fluffy hair

蓬头垢面 péngtóu-gòumiàn with dishevelled hair and a dirty face; unkempt

硼 péng *chem.* boron (B)

硼砂 péngshā borax; sodium borate: ～玻璃 borax glass

硼酸 péngsuān boric acid

硼酸盐 péngsuānyán borate

鹏 péng roc

鹏程万里 péngchéng wànlǐ (make) a roc's flight of 10,000 *li*—have a bright future

澎 péng splash; spatter: ～了一身水 be splashed all over with water

澎湖列岛 Pénghú Lièdǎo the Penghu Islands; the Penghus; (European name) the Pescadores

澎湃 péngpài surge: 大海中波涛～。Waves surge in the sea.

篷 péng ① covering or awning on a car, boat, etc. ② sail (of a boat): 扯起～来 hoist the sails

篷布 péngbù tarpaulin: 用～把货物盖上 cover the goods with a tarpaulin

篷车 péngchē same as 棚车 péngchē

篷帐 péngzhàng tent

篷子 péngzi awning (for protection from the sun, rain, wind, etc.)

膨 péng see below

膨大 péngdà expand; inflate

膨大海 péngdàhǎi same as 胖大海 pàngdàhǎi

膨脝 pénghēng ① *formal* potbellied ② *dial.* bulky; unwieldy

膨化 pénghuà (of rice, corn, etc.) popped: ～玉米 popcorn

膨体纱 péngtǐshā *text.* bulk yarn

膨胀 péngzhàng expand; swell; dilate; inflate: 金属受了热就会～。Metals expand when they are heated. / 消费～ inflated consumption; over-expanded consumption / ～性 expansibility

膨胀计 péngzhàngjì *phys.* dilatometer

膨胀系数 péngzhàng xìshù *phys.* coefficient of expansion (or dilatation)

蟛 péng see below

蟛蜞 péngqí amphibious crab; brackish-water crab

鬅 péng (of hair) fluffy

鬅松 péngsōng (of hair) fluffy

鬅头 péngtóu with dishevelled hair: ～散发 with hair dishevelled; with hair in disarray

péng

捧 péng ① hold or carry in both hands: ～着一个西瓜 hold a watermelon in both hands / 她双手～着孩子的脸。She cupped the child's face in her hands. / 他～起水来喝了一大口。He scooped up some water with his hands and took a big mouthful. ② *m.* a double handful: 一～枣儿 a double handful of dates ③ boost; exalt; extol; flatter: 把某人～上天 praise sb. to the skies

捧场 pěngchǎng ① be a member of a *claque* ② boost; sing the praises of; flatter: 无原则的～ unprincipled praise

捧臭脚 pěng chòujiǎo *inf.* lick one's feet; bootlick —toady to sb.

捧读 pěngdú *formal pol.* have the pleasure of reading (your work)

捧腹 pěngfù split (*or* shake, burst) one's sides with laughter: 令人捧腹 lìng rén pěngfù

捧腹大笑 pěngfù dàxiào be convulsed with laughter; split one's sides with laughter

捧哏 pěnggén (of the supporting performer of a comic dialogue 相声) play the fool to help make people laugh

捧角 pěngjué try to build up an actor

pèng

碰（拍、踫） pèng ① touch; bump: 这件精密仪器，你可别～。Mind you don't touch this precision instrument. / 把墨水瓶一～翻了 knock the inkbottle over / 头～在门上 bump one's head against the door ② meet; run into: 在街上～到一个熟人 run into an acquaintance in the street / ～到困难 run up against difficulties / 河没挖多深就～上了流沙。Before we'd got very far in digging the canal, we met with quicksand. / 我没～着他。I didn't see him. ③ take one's chance: ～～机会 take a chance

碰杯 pèngbēi clink glasses

碰壁 pèngbì run up against a stone wall; be rebuffed: 到处～ run into snags and be foiled everywhere / 凭主观办事一定～。If you do things subjectively, you'll just run into a stone wall.

碰钉子 pèng dīngzi meet with a rebuff; hit (*or* strike, run against) a snag: 如果我是你，我就不去碰这个钉子。If I were you, I wouldn't run my head against a brick wall. / 我碰的钉子，吃的苦头，比你多得多！I've run up against many more obstacles and suffered a lot more than you! / 碰了个软钉子 be mildly rebuffed

碰顶 pèngdǐng *dial.* at most; at best

碰簧锁 pènghuángsuǒ same as 碰锁 pèngsuǒ

碰见 pèngjiàn meet unexpectedly; run into: 你猜我昨晚在首都体育馆～谁了？Who do you think I ran into at the Capital Stadium last night?

碰铃 pènglíng a pair of hand-held bells played by striking together (used as a percussion instrument in tradi-

tional opera, etc.)

碰面 pèngmiàn meet: 明天我们还在这儿～。Let's meet here again tomorrow.

碰碰车 pèngpèngchē bumper car

碰碰船 pèngpèngchuán bumper boat

碰巧 pèngqiǎo by chance; by coincidence: 我～也在那儿。I happened to be there too. *or* It just so happened that I was there too. / 正要送孩子上县医院，～医疗队到村里来了。They were going to send the child to the county hospital when a medical team arrived in the village.

碰锁 pèngsuǒ spring lock

碰头 pèngtóu meet and discuss; put (our, your, or their) heads together: 决定下次～的时间 decide on the time of the next meeting / 他们一～，很快就把问题解决了。They put their heads together and promptly solved the problem.

碰头会 pèngtóuhuì brief meeting (mainly to exchange information)

碰一鼻子灰 pèng yī bízi huī be snubbed; meet with a rebuff: 她怕～。话到了嘴边，她又把它吞了下去。She was afraid of being snubbed, so she swallowed the words that came to her lips.

碰硬 pèngyìng boldly confront or challenge a powerful opponent; try to remove a formidable obstacle

碰撞 pèngzhuàng ① collide; run into: 一辆卡车从后～了我们的汽车。A lorry ran into our car from behind. ② offend; affront *phys.* collision; impact: 核～ nuclear collision / ～负载 impact load

pī

丕 pī *formal* big; great: ～绩 great achievements

批[1] pī ① slap: 批颊 pījiá ② scrape; pare; cut into slices: 片～ slicing ③ criticize; refute: ～深～透 criticize penetratingly and thoroughly / 真理是～不倒的。Truth cannot be overthrown by criticism. ④ write instructions or comments on (a report from a subordinate, etc.): ～文件 write instructions on documents

批[2] pī ① wholesale: ～购 buy goods wholesale ② *m.* batch; lot; group: 新到的一一～化肥 a new lot of chemical fertilizer / 一大～积极分子 large numbers of activists / 出动多～飞机 dispatch wave after wave of planes

批[3] pī *inf.* fibres of cotton, flax, etc. ready to be drawn and twisted

批驳 pībó ① veto an opinion or a request from a subordinate body ② refute; criticize; rebut: 逐点予以～ refute point by point

批次 pīcì batch (of aircraft, etc.)

批答 pīdá *formal* give an official, written reply to a subordinate body

批点 pīdiǎn mark words and phrases for special attention with dots or small circles and write comments

批斗 pīdòu criticize and denounce sb. (at a public meeting)

批发 pīfā ① wholesale: ～价格 wholesale price ② (of an official document) be authorized for dispatch: 那份电报是由副部长～的。That telegram was authorized for dispatch by the vice-minister.

批发部 pīfābù wholesale department

批复 pīfù give an official, written reply to a subordinate body

批改 pīgǎi correct: ～作业 correct students' papers

批号 pīhào lot number; batch number

批颊 pījiá *formal* slap sb.'s face; box sb.'s ear

批件 pījiàn an official, written reply to a subordinate body

批量 pīliàng ① (produce) in batches: ～生产 batch process; batch production ② batch; lot: ～小 small lots (*or* batches) / 大～生产 mass production

批判 pīpàn ① criticize: ～错误路线 criticize the erroneous line / ～会 criticism meeting; criticism session / ～文章 critical article ② critique: 《哥达纲领～》 *Critique of the Gotha Programme*

批判地 pīpànde critically; discriminatingly: ～吸收 critically assimilate; assimilate with discrimination

批判现实主义 pīpànxiànshízhǔyì critical realism

批评 pīpíng ① criticize: ～缺点和错误 criticize shortcomings and mistakes ② criticism: ～与自我～ criticism and self-criticism / 党内～ inner-Party criticism / 马克思主义不怕～。Marxism fears no criticism.

批示 pīshì ① write instructions or comments on a report, memorandum, etc. submitted by a subordinate ② written instructions or comments on a report, memorandum, etc. submitted by a subordinate

批条 pītiáo a note bearing a superior's instructions or comments

批语 pīyǔ ① remarks on a piece of writing ② same as 批示 pīshì②

批阅 pīyuè read over (official papers); read and amend or comment on (writings, texts, etc.)

批注 pīzhù ① annotate and comment on ② annotations and commentaries; marginalia

批转 pīzhuǎn write instructions or comments on a report submitted by a subordinate and refer it to those concerned

批准 pīzhǔn ratify; approve; sanction: ～条约 ratify a treaty / 大会～了他的报告。The congress approved his report. / 党委～了他们的请求。The Party committee granted their request. / 计划须经～。The plan is subject to ratification (*or* approval).

批准书 pīzhǔnshū instrument of ratification: 互换～ the exchange of instruments of ratification / 本条约自互换～之日起生效。The present treaty shall come into force on the date of exchange of instruments.

纰 pī (of cloth, thread, etc.) become unwoven or untwisted; be spoilt: 线～了。The thread came untwisted.

纰漏 pīlòu a careless mistake; a small accident; slip: 出了～ made a small error; made a slip

纰缪 pīmiù *formal* error; mistake

坯（坏） pī ① a base ready to be machined into a finished product; blank; clay mould: 景泰蓝花瓶的铜～ copper base for a *cloisonné* flower vase ② unburnt brick; earthen brick; adobe ③ *dial.* semifinished product: 面～儿 cooked plain noodles; cooked but unseasoned noodles

坯布 pībù *text.* unbleached and undyed cloth; grey cloth; grey

坯革 pīgé crust leather

坯件 pījiàn *mech.* blank: 螺栓～ bolt blank

坯子 pīzi ① same as 坯 pī① ② same as 坯 pī③

狉 pī see below

狉狉 pīpī *formal* (of hordes of wild animals) roam from place to place

披 pī ① drape over one's shoulders; wrap around: ～着大衣 have an overcoat draped over one's

shoulders / ～上衣服 throw on some clothing / ～上节日的盛装 be colourfully decorated for the festival / 一只～着羊皮的狼 a wolf in sheep's clothing / ～着合法的外衣,干着非法的勾当 carry on illegal activities under the cloak of legality / 一伙～着马列主义外衣的政治骗子 a bunch of political swindlers who deck themselves out as Marxist-Leninists ② open; unroll; spread out: ～卷 open a book ③ split open; crack: 这根竹竿～了。The bamboo pole has split.

披读 pīdú open (a book) and read

披发左衽 pīfà-zuǒrèn wear one's hair down and fold one's clothes to the left (in the fashion of the non-Han peoples)

披风 pīfēng cloak

披拂 pīfú formal ① wave; sway: 微风吹来, 枝叶～。The trees are swaying in the light breeze. ② (of a breeze) blow gently: 春风～。A gentle spring breeze is blowing.

披肝沥胆 pīgān-lìdǎn open one's heart; be open and sincere; be loyal and faithful

披挂 pīguà ① put on a suit of armour: ～上阵 buckle on one's armour and go into battle ② a suit of armour

披红 pīhóng drape a band of red silk over sb.'s shoulders (on a festive occasion or as a token of honour)

披红戴花 pīhóng-dàihuā have red silk draped over one's shoulders and a big red flower pinned on one's breast (as a token of honour)

披坚执锐 pījiān-zhíruì buckle on one's armour and take up weapons—go forth to battle

披肩 pījiān ① cape ② shawl

披荆斩棘 pījīng-zhǎnjí break through brambles and thorns—hack one's way through difficulties

披览 pīlǎn formal open (a book) and read; peruse: ～群书 read extensively

披沥 pīlì formal open one's heart: ～陈辞 state one's views openheartedly

披露 pīlù ① publish; announce: 这一消息已在报上～。The news has been published in the press. / 要求不～姓名 wish to remain anonymous ② reveal; show; disclose: ～肝胆 open one's heart; be openhearted

披麻带孝 pīmá-dàixiào wear the hemp garments of mourning

披靡 pīmǐ ① (of grass, etc.) be swept by the wind ② be routed; flee: 所向披靡 suǒ xiàng pīmǐ

披散 pīsan (of hair, mane, etc.) hang down loosely

披沙拣金 pī shā jiǎn jīn sort out the fine gold from the sand—extract the essentials from a mass of material

披厦 pīshà (also 披屋 pīwū) outhouse

披剃 pītì put on the cassock and take the tonsure—become a Buddhist monk or nun

披头散发 pītóu-sǎnfà with hair dishevelled; with hair in disarray; unkempt

披星戴月 pīxīng-dàiyuè under the canopy of the moon and the stars—travel by night; work from before dawn till after dark

披阅 pīyuè open and read (a book); peruse: ～群书 peruse books of all sorts; read widely

砒 pī arsenic

砒霜 pīshuāng (white) arsenic

劈 pī ① split; chop; cleave: ～木柴 chop wood; split logs / ～成两半 cleave sth. in two / 这块木头好～。This log splits easily. ② right against (one's face, etc.): 大浪朝我们～面打来。Huge waves came crashing almost on top of us. ③ (of lightning) strike: 老树让雷～了。The old tree was struck by lightning. ④ mech. wedge ——see also pǐ

劈波斩浪 pībō-zhǎnlàng cleave through the waves

劈刺 pīcì mil. sabre or bayonet fighting: ～训练 bayonet drill

劈刀 pīdāo ① chopper ② mil. sabre fighting

劈风斩浪 pīfēng-zhǎnlàng brave the wind and the waves—slash one's way through difficulties

劈理 pīlǐ min. cleavage

劈里啪啦 pīlipālā onom. the successive sounds of crackling, etc.: 鞭 炮～地 响。The firecrackers were crackling and spluttering. / 敌人～乱打了一阵枪, 就跑了。The enemy fired off a few random shots and fled.

劈脸 pīliǎn right in the face: ～就是一巴掌 slap sb. on the face / 一块石头～向他打来。A stone came hurtling towards his face.

劈啪 pīpā onom. the sound of crackling, etc.: 把鞭子抽得～响 crack a whip / 孩子们劈劈啪啪地鼓起掌来。The children began to clap their hands.

劈杀 pīshā (usu. of a man on horseback) slash at sb. (with a sword)

劈山 pīshān level off hilltops; blast cliffs: ～造田 level off hilltops and turn them into flat fields / ～筑路 blast cliffs to build highways or railways / ～引水 cleave hills and lead in water; cut through mountains to bring in water

劈手 pīshǒu make a sudden snatch: ～夺过枪来 snatch a gun away from sb.

劈头 pītóu ① straight on the head; right in the face: ～一拳 hit sb. right on the head / 他走出门口～撞上了老王。As he reached the door, he bumped straight into Lao Wang. ② at the very start: 他一进门～就问:"准备好了吗?" The moment he entered the room he asked, "Is everything ready?"

劈头盖脸 pītóu-gàiliǎn right in the face: 倾盆大雨～地浇了下来。The rain came pelting down. / 记者们～向他提出许多问题。The reporters fired a volley of questions at him.

劈胸 pīxiōng right against the chest: ～一把抓住 grasp sb. by the front of his coat

噼 pī see below

噼里啪啦 pīlipālā same as 劈里啪啦 pīlipālā

噼啪 pīpā same as 劈啪 pīpā

霹 pī see below

霹雷 pīléi inf. thunderbolt; thunderclap

霹雳 pīlì thunderbolt; thunderclap

霹雳舞 pīlìwǔ breakdance

pí

皮 pí ① skin; rind; peel: 香蕉～ banana skin / 土豆～ potato peel / 西瓜～ watermelon rind / 荞麦～ buckwheat husk / 擦破一块～ scrape a bit of skin off ② leather; hide; fur: ～靴 leather boots / ～大衣 fur coat ③ cover; wrapper: 包袱～儿 cloth-wrapper ④ surface: 飘在水～儿上 float on the surface of the water ⑤ a broad, flat piece (of some thin material); sheet: 白铁～ galvanized iron sheet; tinplate ⑥ become soft and soggy: 花生～了。The peanuts aren't crisp any more. ⑦ naughty: 这孩子真～! What a naughty child! ⑧ case-hardened: 他老挨剋, 都～了。He gets scolded so often that he no longer cares. ⑨ rubber: 皮筋儿 píjīnr ⑩ (Pí) a surname

皮袄 pí'ǎo fur-lined jacket

皮包 píbāo leather handbag; briefcase; portfolio

皮包公司 píbāo gōngsī briefcase company—an inadequately financed company, not credit-worthy; a fly-by-night company

皮包骨头 pí bāo gútou skinny: 瘦得～ be a bag of bones; be all skin and bones

皮鞭 píbiān leather-thonged whip

皮层 pícéng ① *biol.* cortex ② short for 大脑皮层 dànǎo pícéng

皮尺 píchǐ tape measure; tape

皮带 pídài ① leather belt ② *mech.* (driving) belt: 交叉～ cross belt / 三角～ triangle belt / ～车床 belt-driven lathe / ～传动 belt transmission / ～运输机 belt conveyer

皮带轮 pídàilún (belt) pulley

皮蛋 pídàn same as 松花 sōnghuā

皮垫圈 pídiànquān *mech.* leather washer; leather packing collar

皮筏 pífá skin raft

皮肤 pífū skin

皮肤病 pífūbìng skin disease; dermatosis

皮肤病学 pífūbìngxué dermatology

皮肤科 pífūkē *med.* dermatological department; dermatology: ～医生 dermatologist

皮肤针 pífūzhēn *Chin. med.* ① cutaneous acupuncture (performed with five or seven needles tied vertically to the end of a stick and tapped lightly at the skin surface of the affected area) ② needles used in cutaneous acupuncture

皮肤真菌病 pífūzhēnjūnbìng *med.* dermatomycosis

皮傅 pífù *formal* give a strained, superficial interpretation

皮革 pígé leather; hide

皮辊花 pígǔnhuā *text.* lap waste

皮猴儿 píhóur hooded fur overcoat; fur parka; fur anorak

皮花 píhuā same as 皮棉 pímián

皮划艇 píhuátǐng *sports* canoeing (including kayaking): ～运动员 canoeist

皮黄 píhuáng (also 皮簧 píhuáng) ① short for *xipi* (西皮) and *erhuang* (二黄), two chief types of music in traditional opera ② Beijing opera

皮货 píhuò furs; peltry: ～商 fur dealer; furrier

皮夹子 píjiāzi (also 皮夹儿 píjiār) wallet; pocketbook

皮匠 píjiang ① cobbler ② tanner

皮胶 píjiāo hide glue

皮筋儿 píjīnr *inf.* rubber band ——see also 跳皮筋儿 tiào píjīnr

皮开肉绽 píkāi-ròuzhàn the skin torn and the flesh gaping: 被打得～ be bruised and lacerated (from flogging)

皮里阳秋 pí lǐ yángqiū criticism kept to oneself: ～的笔法 making well-covered or implicit remarks

皮脸 píliǎn *dial.* ① naughty ② shameless

皮毛 pímáo ① fur: 貂皮是一种极贵重的～。Marten is one of the most expensive furs. ② smattering; superficial knowledge: 略知～ have only a superficial knowledge (of a subject)

皮棉 pímián ginned cotton; lint (cotton)

皮面 pímiàn ① outer skin; surface; outside ② leather cover

皮囊 pínáng ① leather bag ② *derog.* the human body

皮内针 pínèizhēn *Chin. med.* intradermal needling (acupuncture by embedding the needle subcutaneously for one or several days)

皮钱儿 píqiánr same as 皮垫圈 pídiànquān

皮球 píqiú rubber ball; ball ——see also 踢皮球 tī píqiú

皮褥子 pírùzi fur-lined mattress

皮实 píshi ① sturdy: 这孩子真～，轻易不闹病。He's a sturdy child. He hardly ever gets ill. ② durable

皮糖 pítáng a sticky candy

皮特克恩岛 Pítèkè'ēndǎo Pitcairn Island

皮条 pítiáo ① leather strap ② see 拉皮条 lā pítiáo

皮条纤 pítiáoqiàn procurer; pimp

皮艇 pítǐng ① *sports* kayaking: ～运动员 kayaker ② kayak

皮统子 pítǒngzi (also 皮桶子 pítǒngzi, 皮桶儿 pítǒngr) fur lining (for a jacket or an overcoat)

皮下注射 píxià zhùshè *med.* subcutaneous (or hypodermic) injection

皮下组织 píxià zǔzhī *physiol.* subcutaneous tissue

皮线 píxiàn rubber-insulated wire; rubber-covered wire

皮箱 píxiāng leather suitcase; leather trunk

皮相 píxiàng skin-deep; superficial

皮相之谈 píxiàng zhī tán superficial talk

皮硝 píxiāo common name for 朴硝 pòxiāo

皮笑肉不笑 pí xiào ròu bù xiào put on a false smile; smile hypocritically

皮鞋 píxié leather shoes

皮鞋油 píxiéyóu shoe polish

皮靴 píxuē leather boots

皮炎 píyán *med.* dermatitis

皮衣 píyī ① fur clothing ② leather clothing

皮影戏 píyǐngxì leather-silhouette show; shadow play

皮张 pízhāng hide; pelt

皮掌儿 pízhǎngr outsole

皮疹 pízhěn *med.* rash

皮之不存,毛将焉附 pí zhī bù cún, máo jiāng yān fù with the skin gone, what can the hair adhere to—a thing cannot exist without its basis

皮脂腺 pízhīxiàn *physiol.* sebaceous glands

皮纸 pízhǐ tough paper made from bast fibre of the mulberry or paper mulberry, etc.

皮质 pízhì ① *physiol.* cortex ② short for 大脑皮层 dànǎo pícéng

皮重 pízhòng tare

皮子 pízi ① leather; hide ② fur

枇

枇 pí see below

枇杷 pípa loquat (the tree and its fruit)

毗(毘)

毗(毘) pí *formal* ① adjoin; be adjacent to ② assist

毗连 pílián (also 毗邻 pílín) adjoin; border on; be adjacent to: 江苏北部同山东～。Northern Jiangsu borders on Shandong. / ～地区 contiguous zone / ～国 contiguous state / ～性 contiguity

铍

铍 pí *chem.* beryllium (Be)

疲

疲 pí tired; weary; exhausted

疲惫 píbèi ① tired out; exhausted: ～不堪 be in a state of utter exhaustion; be dog-tired ② tire sb. out: 目的是～敌军。The purpose was to tire out the enemy.

疲敝 píbì (of manpower, resources, etc.) be running low; become inadequate

疲顿 pídùn *formal* be tired out

疲乏 pífá same as 疲劳 píláo①②

疲竭 píjié *formal* be completely exhausted

疲倦 píjuàn tired and sleepy: 他连坐了两天火车,显得很～。He looked quite worn-out after two days' train journey. / 同错误思想作不～的斗争 wage a tireless struggle against erroneous ideas

疲劳 píláo ① tired; fatigued; weary: 感到～ feel tired / 身心～ be weary in body and mind ② fatigue: 肌肉～ muscular fatigue / 精神～ mental fatigue ③ *mech.* weakening of material subjected to stress; fatigue: 金属～ metal fatigue / 弹性～ elastic fatigue / ～强度 fatigue strength / ～试验 fatigue test

疲癃 pílóng *formal* old and infirm

疲软 píruǎn ① fatigued and weak: 两腿～ be weak in the legs ② *econ.* weaken; slump: 最近,那个国家的货币在外汇市场上显得～。The currency of that country

is weakening on foreign exchanges.

疲弱 píruò　tired and weak; frail and fatigued: 他拖着～的双腿缓慢地往前走。He dragged his tired legs slowly along. / 身体～不堪 be extremely weak and exhausted

疲塌 píta　(also 疲沓 píta) slack; negligent: 工作～ be slack at one's work

疲于奔命 píyú bēnmìng　be tired out by too much running around; be kept constantly on the run; be weighed down with work: 使之～ tire sb. out by keeping him on the run

蚍 pí　see below
蚍蜉 pífú　ant
蚍蜉撼大树 pífú hàn dàshù　an ant trying to topple a giant tree—ridiculously overrate oneself

啤 pí　see below
啤酒 píjiǔ　beer: 生～ draught beer / 黑～ porter; brown ale; stout
啤酒厂 píjiǔchǎng　brewery
啤酒花 píjiǔhuā　*bot.* hops

琵 pí　see below
琵琶 pípa　*pipa*, a plucked string instrument with a fretted fingerboard

脾 pí　spleen
脾寒 píhán　*dial.* malaria; ague
脾气 píqi　① temperament; disposition: ～很好 have a good temper / 摸熟机器的～ get to know the characteristics of a machine ② bad temper: ～大 hot-tempered / 发～ lose one's temper; flare up
脾切除 píqiēchú　*med.* splenectomy
脾胃 píwèi　taste: 不合～ not suit one's taste; not be to one's liking
脾胃相投 píwèi xiāng tóu　have similar tastes; have similar likes and dislikes
脾性 píxìng　*dial.* temperament; disposition; nature; habits and characteristics: 一个人有一个人的～。People differ in temperament.
脾脏 pízàng　spleen
脾肿大 pízhǒngdà　*med.* splenomegaly

裨 pí　*formal* secondary; minor ——see also bì
裨将 píjiàng　subordinate or lower-ranking general in ancient China

鲅 pí　see 鳑鲅 pángpí

蜱 pí　*zool.* tick

罴(羆) pí　same as 棕熊 zōngxióng

貔 pí　*formal* a mythical bearlike wild animal
貔虎 píhǔ　brave troops
貔貅 píxiū　*formal* ① a mythical wild animal ② brave troops
貔子 pízi　*dial.* yellow weasel

鼙 pí　a small drum used in the army in ancient China
鼙鼓 pígǔ　big and small drums used in the army in ancient China—military affairs; warfare

pǐ

匹[1] pǐ　① be equal to; be a match for: 世无其～

matchless; peerless ② single; one: 单枪匹马 dānqiāng-pǐmǎ

匹[2] pǐ　*m.* (for horses, mules, etc.): 两～骡子 two mules / 三～马 three horses

匹[3]**(疋)** pǐ　*m.* (for rolls of cloth or silk): 一～布 a bolt of cloth

匹敌 pǐdí　be equal to; be well matched: 双方实力～。The two sides are well matched.
匹夫 pǐfū　① an ordinary man ② an ignorant person
匹夫匹妇 pǐfū-pǐfù　common people; ordinary people
匹夫之勇 pǐfū zhī yǒng　reckless courage; foolhardiness
匹拉米洞 pǐlāmǐdòng　another name for 氨基比林 ān-jībǐlín
匹练 pǐliàn　an unrolled bolt of white silk (often used as a metaphor for waterfalls)
匹马单枪 pǐmǎ-dānqiāng　same as 单枪匹马 dānqiāng-pǐmǎ
匹配 pǐpèi　① *formal* mate; marry ② *elec.* matching: 阻抗～ impedance matching / ～变压器 matching transformer
匹染 pǐrǎn　*text.* piece dyeing: ～色布 piece-dyed cloth
匹头 pǐtou　*dial.* piece goods (*or* fabrics)

圮 pǐ　*formal* collapse; fall apart; be destroyed: 倾圮 qīngpǐ

伾 pǐ　see below
伾离 pǐlí　*formal* ① (of husband and wife) be separated ② divorce one's spouse, esp. forsake one's wife

否 pǐ　① bad; wicked; evil ② censure: 臧否 zāngpǐ ——see also fǒu
否极泰来 pǐ jí tài lái　out of the depth of misfortune comes bliss; the extreme of adversity is the beginning of prosperity

痞 pǐ　① a lump in the abdomen ② ruffian; riffraff
痞块 pǐkuài　(also 痞积 pǐjī) *Chin. med.* a lump in the abdomen
痞子 pǐzi　ruffian; riffraff

劈 pǐ　① divide; split: 把绳子～成三股 split the rope into three strands ② break off; strip off: ～白菜帮子 strip the outer leaves off cabbages ③ split one's legs or fingers extremely wide apart ——see also pī
劈叉 pǐchà　do the splits
劈柴 pǐ·chái　kindling; firewood
劈帐 pǐzhàng　share out proceeds according to a certain rate

擗 pǐ　① break off: ～棒子 pick corn ② *formal* beat one's breast
擗踊 pǐyǒng　*formal* beat one's breast and stamp one's feet (in sorrow)

癖 pǐ　addiction; a weakness for: 嗜酒成～ be addicted to drinking
癖好 pǐhào　a favourite hobby; a fondness for: 他有集邮的～。His favourite hobby is stamp collecting.
癖习 pǐxí　an old habit
癖性 pǐxìng　natural inclination; proclivity; propensity

pì

屁 pì ① wind (from bowels): 放屁 fàngpì① ② *inf.* nonsense; shit; rubbish: 这个电影好极了。一好个～! This film is really good.—Shit!

屁股 pìgu ① *inf.* buttocks (of humans); bottom; behind; backside: 拍拍～就走了 leave without a word of explanation; leave things in a mess ② rump (of animals); haunch; hindquarters ③ end; butt: 香烟～ cigarette butt

屁股蛋儿 pìgudànr (also 屁股蛋子 pìgudànzi) *dial.* buttocks; bottom; behind; backside

屁股蹲儿 pìgudūnr *dial.* (usu. used in) 摔了个～ fall on one's bottom (or behind)

屁滚尿流 pìgǔn-niàoliú (usu. used in) 吓得～ be scared shitless; be frightened out of one's wits (or life); piss in one's pants (in terror)

屁话 pìhuà shit; nonsense; rubbish

屁事 pìshì a trifling matter; a mere nothing; nothing worth speaking of: 你爱怎么着就怎么着，关我～! Do as you please. I don't care a damn.

辟[1]（闢） pì ① open up (territory, land, etc.); break (ground): 新～一座果园 lay out a new orchard / 另～专栏 start a new column (in a newspaper, etc.) ② penetrating; incisive: 精辟 jīngpì ③ refute; repudiate: 辟谣 pìyáo

辟[2] pì *formal* law: 大辟 dàpì
——see also bì

辟谣 pìyáo refute a rumour; deny a rumour; give the lie to a rumour

媲 pì be equal to; be a match for

媲美 pìměi compare favourably with; rival

睥 pì a variant pronunciation for 睥 bì

僻 pì ① out-of-the-way; secluded: ～巷 side lane / ～处一隅 live in a remote corner ② eccentric: 怪僻 guàipì ③ rare: ～字 rare word

僻径 pìjìng a desolate and out-of-the-way path

僻静 pìjìng secluded; lonely: ～的地方 a secluded place

僻陋 pìlòu (of an area) remote and desolate

僻壤 pìrǎng an out-of-the-way place

僻性 pìxìng eccentric character

僻远 pìyuǎn remote and out-of-the-way

譬 pì example; analogy

譬解 pìjiě try to persuade; try to talk sb. round: 我从各方面去～他。 I tried every way to talk him round.

譬如 pìrú for example; for instance; such as

譬若 pìruò *formal* for example; for instance; such as

譬喻 pìyù metaphor; simile; analogy; figure of speech

鷿 pì see below

鷿鷈 pìtī *zool.* grebe

piān

片 piān same as 片 piān①, limited to use in 片子 piānzi, 相片儿 xiàngpiānr, etc. ——see also piàn

片子 piānzi ① a roll of film ② film; movie ③ gramophone record; disc ④ the negative of a roentgeno-

gram ——see also piànzi

扁 piān see below ——see also biǎn

扁舟 piānzhōu *formal* small boat; skiff: 一叶～ a small boat

偏[1] piān ① inclined to one side; slanting; leaning: 正东～北 east by north / 中间～右 (take a position) right of centre / 这一枪打～了。 That shot missed. / 这个指标～低。 The target is on the low side. ② partial; prejudiced: 偏爱 piān'ài ③ *pol.* (used to indicate one has already had one's tea, meal, etc.): 谢谢，我已经先～了，您请自己吃吧。 Thank you, I've eaten already. You go ahead.

偏[2] piān *adv.* wilfully; insistently; persistently: 他为什么～要那样做? Why must he do it that way? / 他～不听。 He simply wouldn't listen. / 不该她去，她～要去。 She was not supposed to go but she insisted on going.

偏爱 piān'ài have partiality for sth.; show favouritism to sb.

偏安 piān'ān (of a feudal regime) be content to retain sovereignty over a part of the country

偏安一隅 piān'ān yī yú be content to exercise sovereignty over only a part of the country

偏才 piāncái ① cleverness in trivial matters; cleverness in a petty way ② cleverness in a limited way; skill in a certain aspect

偏差 piānchā deviation; error: ～减为一毫米。 The deviation is reduced to one millimetre. / 纠正执行政策中的～ correct any deviations made in implementing a policy / 认识上的～ a wrong way of looking at things; an error in judgment

偏殿 piāndiàn side hall in a palace or temple

偏方 piānfāng *Chin. med.* folk prescription

偏房 piānfáng ① wing-room; wing ② concubine

偏废 piānfèi do one thing and neglect another; emphasize one thing at the expense of another: 不可偏废 bùkě piānfèi

偏锋 piānfēng ① slanting strokes in calligraphy ② an indirect approach to a subject

偏光 piānguāng same as 偏振光 piānzhènguāng

偏光镜 piānguāngjìng same as 偏振光镜 piānzhènguāngjìng

偏航 piānháng going off course; off-course; yaw

偏好 piānhǎo *dial.* it so happened that; as luck would have it: 你告诉我他到外地去了，可～我昨天看到他了。 You told me he was out of town, but as it happened, I saw him yesterday.

偏好 piānhào have a special fondness for sth.; have a partiality for sth.: 他对臭豆腐有特别的～。 He has a partiality for strong-smelling preserved bean curd.

偏护 piānhù be partial to and side with: 不～任何一方 show no partiality to either side; be impartial; be unbiased

偏畸 piānjī *formal* unjust; unfair; partial

偏激 piānjī extreme: 意见～ hold extreme views / 他这个人比较～。 He tends to go to extremes.

偏见 piānjiàn prejudice; bias: 我对他没有～。 I've no prejudice against him.

偏口鱼 piānkǒuyú same as 比目鱼 bǐmùyú

偏枯 piānkū ① *Chin. med.* hemiplegia ② lopsided (development)

偏劳 piānláo *pol.* (used when asking sb. for help or thanking sb. for his help): 谢谢您，多～了。 Thanks for all your trouble. / 请你～吧。 Can I trouble you to do it?

偏离 piānlí deviate; diverge: 船～了航线。 The ship

drifted off its course. / ～正确路线, 革命就会受到挫折。 A departure from the correct line will bring setbacks to the revolution.

偏门 piānmén ① side door ② crooked ways or means

偏旁 piānpáng character components or basic structural parts of Chinese characters (as 亻 in 住, 囗 in 固, 匚 in �, 令 in 拎, etc.)

偏裨 piānpí deputies or assistants to army generals in ancient times; high-ranking army officers

偏僻 piānpì remote; out-of-the-way: ～的山区 a remote mountainous district / 地点～。 It is an out-of-the-way place.

偏偏 piānpiān adv. ① wilfully; insistently; persistently: 我们劝他不要那样做, 可他～不听。 We tried to talk him out of it, but he just wouldn't listen. ② contrary to expectations: 他来找我, ～我出差了。 I happened to be away on business when he came to see me. / 事情的发展～同他的愿望相反。 Things turned out just the opposite to what he wanted. ③ only; alone: 干吗～问他? Why ask him, of all people? / 你为什么～不提这一点呢? Why did you choose to omit this point?

偏颇 piānpō formal biased; partial

偏巧 piānqiǎo it so happened that; as luck would have it: 我们正找她, ～她来了。 We were looking for her when she turned up. / 我找他两次, ～都不在家。 I called at his house twice, but he happened to be out each time.

偏衫 piānshān Buddhist vestment draped over the left shoulder

偏生 piānshēng dial. ① wilfully; insistently; persistently ② contrary to expectations

偏师 piānshī ① wing or flank of an army ② auxiliary force

偏食 piānshí ① astron. partial eclipse: 日～ partial solar eclipse / 月～ partial lunar eclipse ② partiality for a limited variety of food; a one-sided diet

偏私 piānsī favouritism; partiality; bias

偏瘫 piāntān med. hemiplegia

偏袒 piāntǎn be partial to and side with; give unprincipled protection to

偏疼 piānténg inf. favour one (child, etc.) more than the others

偏题 piāntí a catch (or tricky) question (in an examination)

偏听偏信 piāntīng-piānxìn heed and trust only one side; listen only to one side; be biased

偏头痛 piāntóutòng med. migraine

偏西 piānxī (of the sun) move towards the west: 太阳～了。 The sun is to the west. / 等太阳～再赶路。 Let's wait until the sun begins to move towards the west and then continue on our way.

偏狭 piānxiá biased and narrow-minded

偏向 piānxiàng ① erroneous tendency; deviation: 纠正～ correct a deviation / 反对单纯追求数量的～ oppose the tendency to concentrate on quantity alone ② be partial to; give unprincipled support or protection to

偏心 piānxīn ① partiality; bias: 她对小儿子有点儿～。 She makes rather a favourite of her youngest son. / 他丝毫不～。 He is free from any bias. or He's absolutely impartial. ② mech. eccentric: ～凸轮 eccentric cam

偏心轮 piānxīnlún mech. eccentric wheel; eccentric

偏压 piānyā elec. bias voltage; bias: 截止～ cut-off bias / ～电池 bias battery

偏远 piānyuǎn remote; faraway: ～地区 remote districts

偏振 piānzhèn phys. polarization: 光的～ polarization of light

偏振光 piānzhènguāng phys. polarized light

偏振光镜 piānzhènguāngjìng polariscope

偏振光显微镜 piānzhènguāng xiǎnwēijìng polarizing microscope

偏正词组 piānzhèng cízǔ gram. word group consisting of a modifier and the word it modifies

偏执 piānzhí stubbornly biased

偏重 piānzhòng stress one aspect at the expense of another: 学习只～记忆而忽视理解是不行的。 In studying one shouldn't stress memorization at the expense of comprehension.

偏转 piānzhuǎn phys. deflection

偏坠 piānzhuì Chin. med. swelling and hanging down of either of the testes (caused by orchitis, hernia, etc.)

犏
piān see below

犏牛 piānniú pien niu (offspring of a bull and a female yak)

翩
piān formal fly swiftly

翩翩 piānpiān ① lightly (dance, flutter, etc.): 蝴蝶在花丛中～飞舞。 Butterflies are fluttering among the flowers. ② formal elegant: ～少年 an elegant young man

翩然 piānrán formal lightly; trippingly: ～而至 come tripping down

翩若惊鸿 piān ruò jīnghóng (of a beautiful woman) tripping lightly like a startled swan

翩跹 piānxiān liter. lightly; trippingly: ～起舞 dance with quick, light steps; dance trippingly

篇
piān ① a piece of writing: 篇章 piānzhāng ② sheet (of paper, etc.): 歌～儿 song sheet / 单～儿油印材料 mimeographed sheets ③ m. (for paper, book leaves, articles, etc.) sheet; leaf; piece: 三～儿纸 three sheets (or pieces) of paper / 一～文章 a piece of writing; an article / 这本书缺了一～儿。 One leaf is missing from this book.

篇幅 piānfu ① length (of a piece of writing): 这篇文章～不太长。 This article is not very long. ② space (on a printed page): ～有限 have limited space / 报纸用大量～报道了这次会议的情况。 The press gave the conference wide coverage.

篇目 piānmù table of contents; contents; list of articles

篇什 piānshí poems

篇页 piānyè leaves and pages

篇章 piānzhāng sections and chapters; writings: ～结构 structure of an article; composition / 在民族解放斗争的史册上写下灿烂的～ add an illustrious chapter to the annals of national liberation struggles

篇子 piānzi same as 篇 piān②

pián

便
pián see below —— see also biàn

便便 piánpián bulging; swelling: 大腹便便 dàfù piánpián

便宜 piányi ① cheap: ～货 goods sold at bargain prices / 价钱相当～。 It's a real bargain. or It's quite cheap. ② unmerited advantages; unearned gains: 讨便宜 tǎo piányi / 占便宜 zhàn piányi ③ let sb. off lightly: 这次～了他。 This time we have let him off lightly. —— see also biànyí

骈
pián ① a pair of horses going side by side; a team of two horses ② parallel; antithetical: ～句 parallel sentences

骈比 piánbǐ formal next to each other; side by side

骈肩 piánjiān formal shoulders against shoulders—a

jostling crowd

骈俪 piánlì art of parallelism

骈四俪六 piánsì-lìliù parallel construction of pairs of four- and six-character sentences (which is characteristic of parallel prose 骈文)——see also 四六体 sìliùtǐ

骈体 piántǐ parallel style (a peculiarly artificial prose style much cultivated during the Six Dynasties 六朝, characterized by parallel construction of pairs of sentences and counterbalancing of tonal patterns without the use of rhyme)

骈阗 piántián (also 骈填 piántián, 骈田 piántián) *formal* close together; side by side: 人烟辐辏，车马～。People are clustered together like the spokes of a wheel; carts and horses are everywhere, side by side.

骈文 piánwén parallel prose (prose written in the parallel style 骈体)

骈枝 piánzhī *formal* ① double toe or finger ② superfluous: ～机构 superfluous structure

胼 pián see below

胼手胝足 piánshǒu-zhīzú callused hands and feet—a life of toil

胼胝 piánzhī callosity; callus

胼胝体 piánzhītǐ *physiol.* corpus callosum

蹁 pián *liter.* limping

蹁跹 piánxiān *liter.* whirling about (in dancing): 须臾客去，予亦就睡。梦一道士，羽衣～，过临皋之下。(苏轼《后赤壁赋》) Later, when my friends had left and I was in bed, I dreamed I saw a Taoist priest in flowing feathery garments pass my house at Lingao.

piǎn

谝 piǎn *dial.* show off: ～能 show off (one's abilities, skills, etc.)

piàn

片 piàn ① a flat, thin piece; slice; flake: 布～ small pieces of cloth / 牛肉～ slices of beef / 玻璃～ bits and pieces of glass / 碎纸～ scraps of paper ② part of a place: 区西那一～归他管。The western part of this district is in his charge. ③ cut into slices: ～肉片儿 slice meat / ～鱼片儿 flake a fish ④ incomplete; fragmentary; partial; brief: 片言 piànyán ⑤ *m.* ⓐ (for slices, tablets, etc.): 一～面包 a slice of bread / 两～安眠药 two sleeping tablets ⓑ (for a stretch of land, a water surface, etc.): 一～土地 a stretch of land / 一～草地 a tract of meadow / 一～汪洋 a vast sheet (*or* an expanse) of water ⓒ (used with the numeral 一, for scene, atmosphere, sound, feeling, etc.): 一～丰收景象 a vast countryside bringing in bumper crops / 一～欢腾 a scene of great rejoicing / 一～脚步声 a patter of footsteps / 一～真心 in all sincerity ——see also piān

片段 piànduàn part; passage; extract; fragment: 谈话的～ parts (*or* snatches) of a conversation / 小说的一些～ certain passages of a novel / 生活的～ an episode of sb.'s life; a slice of life

片断 piànduàn ① same as 片段 piànduàn ② fragmentary; incomplete: ～的消息 bits of information / ～的回忆 fragments of one's reminiscences

片盒 piànhé film magazine

片簧 piànhuáng *mech.* leaf spring: 多～ multiple leaf spring

片儿会 piànrhuì neighbourhood meeting

片剂 piànjì *Pharm.* tablet

片甲不存 piàn jiǎ bù cún (also 片甲不留 piàn jiǎ bù liú) not a single armoured warrior remains—the army is completely wiped out: 杀得敌人～ wipe out the enemy to a man

片假名 piànjiǎmíng *katakana* (one of the written varieties of 假名[2] jiǎmíng, the other being 平假名 píngjiǎmíng)

片刻 piànkè a short while; an instant; a moment: 稍待～ wait a little while

片孔 piànkǒng film perforation; perforation

片流 piànliú *phys.* laminar flow

片麻岩 piànmáyán *geol.* gneiss

片面 piànmiàn ① unilateral: ～宣布 declare unilaterally / ～撕毁协议 unilaterally tear up an agreement / ～之词 an account given by one party only; one party's version of an event, etc.; one person's word against another's ② one-sided: ～观点 a lopsided (*or* one-sided) view / ～地看问题 take a one-sided approach to problems / ～强调 put undue emphasis on

片面性 piànmiànxìng one-sidedness: 对人（事，形势）的看法有～ see only one side of a person (thing, situation)

片盘 piànpán film spool; bobbin

片晌 piànshǎng *dial.* a short while; a little while; a moment

片石 piànshí slabstone; flagstone

片时 piànshí a short while; a moment

片梭织机 piànsuōzhījī *text.* gripper loom

片儿汤 piànrtāng soup with small slices of dough cooked in it

片头 piàntóu titles (in a film or a TV programme); credits

片瓦无存 piàn wǎ wú cún not a single tile remains—be razed to the ground

片言 piànyán a few words; a phrase or two: ～可决 can be settled in a few words

片言只语 piànyán-zhīyǔ (also 片言只字 piànyán-zhīzì) (in) only a few words: 断章取义地挑出～ quote a phrase or two out of context

片岩 piànyán *geol.* schist

片艳纸 piànyànzhǐ a machine-glazed paper (glossy on one side)

片纸只字 piànzhǐ-zhīzì fragments of writing: 档案中并无～提及此事。There is no reference at all to this case in the files.

片子 piànzi ① a flat, thin piece; slice; flake; scrap: 铁～ small pieces of sheetiron ② visiting card ——see also piānzi

骗[1] piàn ① deceive; fool; hoodwink: 受～ be taken in; be deceived / 这种花招～不了人。Nobody will be fooled by such tricks. ② cheat; swindle: ～钱 cheat sb. out of his money

骗[2]（騗） piàn swing (*or* leap) into the saddle; mount a horse

骗局 piànjú fraud; hoax; swindle: 政治～ a political fraud / 和平～ peace hoax (*or* fraud) / 揭穿～ expose a fraud / 事实证明，这不过是个大～。Facts show that this is nothing but a swindle.

骗马 piànmǎ swing (*or* leap) into the saddle; mount a horse

骗取 piànqǔ gain sth. by cheating; cheat (*or* trick, swindle) sb. out of sth.; defraud: ～财物 defraud sb. of his money and belongings / ～信任 worm one's way into sb.'s confidence / ～支持 fool sb. into giving his support / ～选票 wangle votes / 弄虚作假，～荣誉 seek

honour through fraud and deception

骗人 piànrén deceive people: ～的空话 deceitful empty talk / ～的幌子 a camouflage; a smokescreen / ～的勾当 a fraudulent practice (or deal) / 他们的一切花言巧语都是～的。 All their fine words are nothing but humbug.

骗术 piànshù deceitful trick; ruse; hoax: 施行～ perpetrate a fraud

骗腿儿 piàntuǐr dial. swing one's leg sideways: 他一～跳上自行车就走了。 He swung into the saddle of his bike and rode off.

骗子 piànzi swindler; impostor; cheat; trickster: 政治～ a political swindler

骗子手 piànzishǒu dial. swindler; impostor; cheat; trickster

piāo

剽 piāo ① rob ② nimble; swift
剽悍 piāohàn agile and brave; quick and fierce
剽掠 piāoluè plunder; loot
剽窃 piāoqiè plagiarize; lift: 从别人的著作中成段地进行～ lift whole passages from another author's books / ～行为 plagiarism; plagiary / ～者 plagiarist
剽袭 piāoxí plagiarize; lift

漂 piāo float; drift: 树叶在水上～着。 Leaves were floating on the water. / 小船顺流～去。 The boat drifted down the stream. ——see also piǎo; piào
漂儿 piāor dial. float (on a fishing line); fishing float
漂泊 piāobó lead a wandering life; drift: ～异乡 wander aimlessly in a strange land
漂浮 piāofú ① float: 湖面上～着几只小船。 A few boats are floating on the lake. ② float or hover before the eyes or in the mind ③ (of style of work) superficial; showy
漂海 piāohǎi travel far across the sea
漂砾 piāolì geol. erratic; erratic boulder
漂流 piāoliú ① be driven by the current; drift about ② same as 漂泊 piāobó
漂萍 piāopíng liter. floating about like duckweed
漂洋过海 piāoyáng-guòhǎi travel far across the ocean (or sea)
漂移 piāoyí ① drift ② electron. drift: ～晶体管 drift transistor
漂游 piāoyóu lead a wandering life; drift: 四处～ wander from place to place
漂悠 piāoyou float slowly and gently: 小船顺水～而下。 A small boat was floating gently down the stream.

缥 piāo see below ——see also piǎo
缥缈 piāomiǎo dimly discernible; misty: 虚无缥缈 xūwú-piāomiǎo

飘(飃) piāo wave to and fro; float (in the air); flutter: 红旗～～。 Red flags are fluttering. / 稻花～香。 The air was heavy with the aroma of the paddy fields. / 外面～着小雪。 Outside it was snowing slightly. / 随风～来一阵阵花香。 The scent of the flowers was wafted to us by the breeze.
飘泊 piāobó same as 漂泊 piāobó
飘尘 piāochén airborne dust
飘带 piāo·dài streamer; ribbon
飘荡 piāodàng ① drift; float; wave; flutter: 小船随波～。 The boat was drifting with the tide. / 彩旗在风中～。 Coloured flags were flapping in the wind. / 小岛上～着军民的欢笑声。 The tiny island rang with the joyous

laughter of the local inhabitants and PLA men. / 梦幻般的华尔兹舞曲在夜空中～。 Dreamy waltz music was floating in the night air. ② lead a wanderer's life; drift: 弃家避难, 四处～ flee from home and wander about seeking refuge
飘动 piāodòng float (in the air or upon the waves); flutter; drift
飘浮 piāofú same as 漂浮 piāofú
飘海 piāohǎi same as 漂海 piāohǎi
飘忽 piāohū ① (of clouds, etc.) move swiftly; fleet ② mobile; uncertain: ～不定 drift from place to place
飘零 piāolíng ① fading and falling; whirling and scattering: 黄叶～。 Brown leaves came whirling down. / 雪花～。 Snowflakes came flying down. ② wandering; adrift; homeless: ～一身 a solitary wanderer
飘流 piāoliú same as 漂流 piāoliú
飘落 piāoluò (also 飘降 piāojiàng) drift and fall slowly; descend slowly and lightly: 伞兵徐徐～。 The paratroopers descended slowly through the air.
飘渺 piāomiǎo same as 缥缈 piāomiǎo
飘蓬 piāopéng drift about; wander about
飘飘然 piāopiāorán smug; self-satisfied; complacent: 一听到恭维话, 他就感觉～。 The least bit of praise goes to his head.
飘然 piāorán floating in the air: 浮云～而过。 Fleecy clouds floated past. / 一对白天鹅～落在湖面上。 A pair of white swans glided down on to the surface of the lake.
飘洒 piāosǎ float in the air; drift with the wind: 天空～着雪花。 Snowflakes were swirling in the air.
飘洒 piāosa free and easy: 她那一手字写得好～! What a graceful, facile hand she writes!
飘散 piāosàn (of smoke, mist, etc.) drift away
飘舞 piāowǔ wave in the wind: 东风吹拂, 柳条迎风～。 Gently blows the east wind, setting the willow branches a-dancing. / 到处～着彩旗。 Everywhere coloured banners are fluttering.
飘扬 piāoyáng (also 飘飏 piāoyáng) wave; flutter; fly: 五星红旗迎风～。 The five-star red flag is fluttering in the wind.
飘洋过海 piāoyáng-guòhǎi same as 漂洋过海 piāo yáng-guòhǎi
飘摇 piāoyáo (also 飘飖 piāoyáo) sway in the wind
飘移 piāoyí drift
飘逸 piāoyì formal possessing natural grace; elegant: 神采～ have an elegant bearing / 子美不能为太白之～, 太白不能为子美之沉郁。 (严羽) Tu Fu is incapable of Li Po's flowing grace; Li Po is incapable of Tu Fu's profound pathos.
飘溢 piāoyì drift about: 公园里～着花香。 In the park the fragrance of flowers drifted about in the air.
飘悠 piāoyou drift leisurely: 小船在水里慢慢地～着。 A small boat drifted slowly and leisurely on the water. / 几片树叶飘飘悠悠地落下来。 A few leaves fell floating to the ground.

螵 piāo see below
螵蛸 piāoxiāo the egg capsule of a mantis

piáo

朴 Piáo a surname ——see also pō; pò; pǔ
嫖(闝) piáo visit prostitutes; go whoring: 吃喝～赌 wining and dining and whoring and gambling / ～妓 visit prostitutes
嫖客 piáokè brothel (or whorehouse) frequenter;

whoremonger; whoremaster

瓢　piáo　gourd ladle; wooden dipper
瓢虫　piáochóng　ladybug; ladybird
瓢泼大雨　piáopō dàyǔ　heavy rain; torrential rain; downpour

藻　piáo　*dial.*　duckweed

piǎo

殍　piǎo　① die of hunger ② bodies of the starved
漂　piǎo　① bleach: ～过的布特别白。Cloth becomes much whiter when bleached. ② rinse: 把衣服～干净 give the clothes a good rinse ——see also piāo; piào
漂白　piǎobái　bleach: ～棉布 bleached cotton cloth / ～机 bleaching machine; bleacher / ～率 bleachability
漂白粉　piǎobáifěn　bleaching powder
漂染　piǎorǎn　bleaching and dyeing
漂洗　piǎoxǐ　rinse
漂洗槽　piǎoxǐcáo　*chem.*　potcher
缥　piǎo　*formal*　① pale green ② pale green silk ——see also piāo
瞟　piǎo　look sidelong (*or* askance) at; glance sideways at: ～了他一眼 cast a sidelong glance at him / 她一面喝茶，一面用眼～他。As she sipped her tea, she shot him glances.

piào

票　piào　① ticket: 火车～ train ticket / 凭～入场。Admission by ticket only. ② ballot: 全～一致通过 passed by unanimous vote ③ bank note; bill: 零～儿 notes of small denominations; change ④ a person held for ransom by kidnappers; hostage: 赎～儿 ransom a kidnapped person ⑤ amateur performance (of Beijing opera, etc.): 玩儿票 wánrpiào ⑥ *m. dial.* 一～货 a shipment of goods / 一～买卖 a business transaction
票额　piào'é　the sum stated on a cheque or bill; denomination; face value: 大～钞票 notes of large denominations / 这套纪念邮票包括一角、两角、一元三种～。This set of commemorative stamps is issued in denominations of 10 *fen*, 20 *fen* and 1 *yuan*.
票房¹　piàofáng　*inf.*　booking office (at a railway station, airport, etc.); box office (at a theatre, stadium, etc.)
票房²　piàofáng　a club for amateur performers of Beijing opera, etc.
票房价值　piàofáng jiàzhí　box-office value: 这部影片的～很高。The film was a box-office success.
票根　piàogēn　counterfoil or stub (of a cheque, postal order, receipt, etc.); stub (of a ticket)
票匦　piàoguǐ　ballot box
票号　piàohào　draft bank (a banking institution of 19th-century Shanxi merchants, which dealt in drafts, or bills of exchange, payable in the towns and cities of the country in which they did business)
票价　piàojià　the price of a ticket; admission fee; entrance fee: ～五元。Admission five *yuan*.
票据　piàojù　① bill; note: 应收(应付)～ bills receivable (payable) / 即期～ a demand note / 流通～ negotiable

instruments; negotiable papers / 到期未付 ～ overdue bill ② voucher; receipt
票据交换所　piàojù jiāohuànsuǒ　clearinghouse
票面　piàomiàn　face (*or* par, nominal) value: 各种～的邮票 stamps of various denominations
票面价值　piàomiàn jiàzhí　face value; par (value)
票箱　piàoxiāng　ballot box
票选　piàoxuǎn　elect (*or* vote) by ballot; vote for sb.
票友　piàoyǒu　amateur performer (of Beijing opera, etc.)
票证　piàozhèng　coupons
票庄　piàozhuāng　same as　票号　piàohào
票子　piàozi　bank note; paper money; bill: 一大摞 ～ a thick stack of bank notes

漂　piào　*dial.*　come to nothing; fall through ——see also piāo; piǎo
漂亮　piàoliang　① handsome; good-looking; pretty; beautiful: ～的小伙子 a handsome young man / ～的小姑娘 a pretty little girl / ～的衣服 pretty dresses; fine clothes / 打扮得漂漂亮亮的 be smartly dressed / ～的色彩 beautiful colours ② remarkable; brilliant; splendid; beautiful: 打一个～仗 fight a fine battle; win a brilliant victory / 普通话说得很～ speak beautiful standard Chinese / 守门员这个球救得真～。The goalie made a beautiful save.
漂亮话　piàolianghuà　fine words; high-sounding words: 说～没用，干出来才算。It's not high-sounding words but actual deeds that really count.

骠　piào　*formal*　① (of horses) galloping; fast ② brave; valiant

嘌　piào　*formal*　fast; speedy
嘌呤　piàolíng　*chem.*　purine

piē

气　piē　*chem.*　protium (H¹)
撇¹　piē　cast aside; throw overboard; neglect: 不能只抓一头，把别的事都～在一旁。We should not just concentrate on one thing to the neglect of everything else. / 对犯错误的同志要帮助，不能～下不管。We should help a comrade who has committed mistakes, and not ignore him.
撇²　piē　skim: ～油 skim off the grease / ～沫儿 skim off the scum ——see also piě
撇开　piē·kāi　leave aside; bypass: ～这个问题 bypass this issue / 咱们把次要问题～不谈了吧。Let's leave aside questions of minor importance.
撇弃　piēqì　cast away; abandon; discard
撇清　piēqīng　whitewash oneself; plead innocence
撇脱　piētuō　*dial.*　① simple and direct; convenient ② frank; straightforward
瞥　piē　① shoot a glance at; dart a look at: 他刚要插嘴，妈妈～了他一眼。He was going to butt in when his mother darted a look of disapproval at him. ② a quick glance; a glimpse: 一瞥 yīpiē
瞥见　piējiàn　get a glimpse of; catch sight of: 在大街上无意中～了一位多年不见的老友。In the street I caught sight of an old friend whom I had not seen for years.
瞥视　piēshì　cast a quick glance at: 她～了在场的每个人一眼。She cast a quick glance at everyone present.
瞥眼　piēyǎn　*formal*　in the twinkling of an eye; in an

instant; in a flash

piě

苤 piě see below
苤蓝 piělán *bot.* kohlrabi (the plant and its edible bulblike stem)

撇 piě ① throw; fling; cast: ～手榴弹 throw hand grenades ② left-falling stroke (in Chinese calligraphy) ③ *m.* (for things resembling the left-falling stroke): 两～浓眉，一双大眼 two bushy brows over a pair of big eyes / 两～小胡子 two thin strokes of moustache ——see also piè

撇嘴 piězuǐ curl one's lip (in contempt, disbelief or disappointment); twitch one's mouth: 这女孩儿～要哭。The girl's mouth began to twitch; she was on the verge of tears. / 他撇了撇嘴，轻蔑地一笑。He curled his lips into a contemptuous smile (*or* a sneer).

pīn

拼¹（拚） pīn piece together; join together: 把两块木板～起来 join the two boards together
拼²（拚） pīn be ready to risk one's life (in fighting, work, etc.); go all out in work: ～到底 fight to the bitter end / 不畏强手，敢打敢～ not fear a strong opponent but dare to stand up to him
拼版 pīnbǎn *print.* makeup
拼搏 pīnbó struggle hard; exert oneself to the utmost; go all out: 勇于～ have the courage to struggle against tremendous odds / ～精神 the spirit of hard struggle
拼刺 pīncì ① bayonet drill; bayonet practice ② bayonet charge: 和敌人～ fight it out with the enemy with bayonets
拼刺刀 pīn cìdāo same as 拼刺 pīncì②
拼凑 pīncòu piece together; knock together; rig up: 她把零碎花布～起来，给小囡女做了一件褂子。She pieced together odds and ends of coloured cloth and made a jacket for her little girl. / ～一个反革命集团 knock together a counterrevolutionary clique
拼攒 pīncuán assemble (spare parts): ～一辆小汽车 assemble parts into a car
拼接 pīnjiē piece together; join together
拼劲儿 pīnjìnr energy and determination: 他很有～。He has a lot of drive.
拼力 pīnlì go all out; do one's utmost: ～夺取金牌 go all out to win the gold medal
拼命 pīnmìng ① risk one's life; defy death; go all out regardless of danger to one's life: ～精神 the death-defying spirit / 被围困的敌人摆出一副～的架势。The encircled enemy seemed to be getting ready for a last-ditch stand. ② exerting the utmost strength; for all one is worth; with all one's might; desperately: ～奔跑 run for all one is worth / ～工作 work with all one's might / ～获取利润 do one's utmost to get as much profit as possible
拼盘 pīnpán assorted cold dishes; *hors d'oeuvres*
拼死 pīnsǐ risk one's life; defy death; fight desperately: ～挣扎 wage a desperate struggle
拼死拼活 pīnsǐ-pīnhuó ① put up a life-and-death fight ② exerting one's utmost; for all one is worth; desperately
拼图游戏 pīntú yóuxì jigsaw puzzle

拼写 pīnxiě spell; transliterate: 照汉语拼音方案～汉字 transliterate Chinese characters into the Chinese Phonetic Alphabet / ～测验 spelling quiz / ～法 spelling; orthography
拼音 pīnyīn ① combine sounds into syllables ② spell; phoneticize
拼音文字 pīnyīn wénzì alphabetic (system of) writing
拼音字母 pīnyīn zìmǔ phonetic alphabet; phonetic letters
拼装 pīnzhuāng assemble; fit together

姘

姘 pīn have illicit relations with
姘夫 pīnfū (man) lover; paramour
姘妇 pīnfù kept woman; mistress; paramour
姘居 pīnjū live illicitly as husband and wife; cohabit
姘识 pīnshí *formal* become lover and mistress
姘头 pīntou paramour

pín

贫¹ pín ① poor; impoverished: ～富不均 unequal distribution of wealth ② inadequate; deficient: 贫油 pínyóu
贫² pín garrulous; loquacious: 他的嘴真～。He is really too garrulous.
贫病交迫 pín-bìng jiāopò suffer from both poverty and sickness; be plagued by poverty and ill health
贫齿动物 pínchǐ dòngwù edentate animal; edentate
贫道 píndào *hum.* I—a poor cleric (a form of self-address used by Taoist priests)
贫乏 pínfá ① poor; needy; impoverished ② wretchedly lacking: 煤炭资源～的省份 provinces poor in coal deposits / 经验～ lack experience / 语言～ flat, monotonous language
贫雇农 píngùnóng poor peasants and farm labourers
贫骨头 píngǔtou *dial.* ① a person keen on petty gain ② a stingy person; niggard ③ an idle chatterer; windbag
贫寒 pínhán poor; poverty-stricken: ～人家 an impoverished family
贫化 pínhuà *min.* dilution: 矿石～ ore dilution
贫瘠 pínjí barren; infertile; poor: ～的土壤 poor soil; impoverished soil
贫贱 pínjiàn poor and lowly; in straitened and humble circumstances
贫贱之交 pínjiàn zhī jiāo friends that have seen poverty together; friends in days of poverty
贫贱之交不可忘 pínjiàn zhī jiāo bùkě wàng a man should not forget the friends he made when he was poor
贫窭 pínjù *formal* poverty-stricken; in straits
贫苦 pínkǔ poor; poverty-stricken; badly off: ～无告 miserably poor and friendless
贫矿 pínkuàng lean ore: 贫红铁矿 low-grade red iron ore
贫困 pínkùn impoverished; in pinching poverty; in straitened circumstances: 生活～ live in poverty / ～化 pauperization
贫民 pínmín poor people; paupers: 城市～ the urban poor
贫民窟 pínmínkū slum
贫民区 pínmínqū slum area; slum district
贫农 pínnóng poor peasant
贫农团 pínnóngtuán *hist.* the poor peasant league
贫气¹ pínqi stingy; niggardly
贫气² pínqi annoyingly garrulous

贫穷　pínqióng　poor; needy; impoverished

贫弱　pínruò　(of a country) poor and weak

贫僧　pínsēng　*hum.* I—a poor cleric (a form of self-address used by Buddhist monks)

贫下中农　pínxiàzhōngnóng　poor and lower-middle peasants: ～协会 poor and lower-middle peasants' association

贫血　pínxuè　*med.* anaemia: 再生障碍性～ aplastic anaemia

贫油　pínyóu　oil-poor: ～国 an oil-poor country

贫嘴　pínzuǐ　garrulous; loquacious

贫嘴薄舌　pínzuǐ-bóshé　be garrulous and sharp-tongued

频

频　pín　① frequently; repeatedly: ～来～往 have frequent contacts with each other ② *phys.* frequency: 高频 gāopín

频传　pínchuán　(of good news, etc.) keep pouring in: 喜讯～。Good news kept pouring in.

频次　píncì　frequency; rate of recurrence

频带　píndài　*phys.* frequency band

频道　píndào　(TV) frequency channel; channel: 这个电视台现有三个～。This TV station has three channels. / 换到二～ switch to Channel 2

频繁　pínfán　frequently; often: 两国人民之间交往～。There are frequent contacts between the people of the two countries. / 交通事故日益～。Traffic accidents are happening with increasing frequency.

频率　pínlǜ　① *phys.* frequency: ～范围 frequency range ② rate of recurrence; frequency

频年　pínnián　for years running; year after year: ～荒歉 had repeated crop failures for years running

频频　pínpín　again and again; repeatedly: ～举杯 propose repeated toasts ; drink toast after toast / ～招手 wave one's hand again and again / ～点头称是 nod approval repeatedly

频仍　pínréng　*formal* frequent: 外患～ be subject to repeated foreign aggression

频数　pínshuò　*formal* frequent and successive: 病人腹泻～。The patient suffered from frequent, successive bowel movements (*or* from acute diarrhoea).

嫔(嬪)

嫔(嬪)　pín　*formal* ① a concubine of an emperor ② a woman attendant at court

蘋

蘋　pín　*bot.* clover fern

颦

颦　pín　*formal* knit the brows: 学西施之～眉 imitate the beauty Xishi in knitting her brows — only to make oneself uglier

pǐn

品

品　pǐn　① article; product: 商品 shāngpǐn / 农产品 nóngchǎnpǐn ② grade; class; rank: ～之最上者 of the very best kind ③ character; quality: 人品 rénpǐn / 品德 pǐndé ④ taste sth. with discrimination; sample; savour: ～茶 sample tea / 这个人究竟怎么样，你慢慢就～出来了。By and by you'll be able to figure out what sort of person he actually is.

品尝　pǐncháng　taste; sample; savour: ～我们的家乡风味 try our local delicacies

品德　pǐndé　moral character

品第　pǐndì　*formal* ① appraise; rate; grade ② position; status; grade; rank

品格　pǐngé　① one's moral character ② quality and style (of literary or artistic works)

品红　pǐnhóng　① magenta; fuchsine (a dye) ② purplish red

品级　pǐnjí　① official rank in feudal times ② grade (of products, commodities, etc.): 这种茶～高。It's a high-grade tea.

品鉴　pǐnjiàn　judge; appraise

品节　pǐnjié　moral integrity

品蓝　pǐnlán　reddish blue

品类　pǐnlèi　category; class

品绿　pǐnlǜ　malachite green; bamboo green

品貌　pǐnmào　① looks; appearance: ～俊俏 handsome and charming ② character and looks; personality and appearance: ～兼优的女郎 a pretty girl of good character

品名　pǐnmíng　the name of an article; the name or description of a commodity

品茗　pǐnmíng　sip tea (to judge its quality); sample tea

品目　pǐnmù　the names or descriptions of goods: ～繁多 a wide variety of goods

品评　pǐnpíng　judge; appraise; comment on

品题　pǐntí　*formal* appraise (a person, a piece of writing, etc.)

品头论足　pǐntóu-lùnzú　① make frivolous remarks about a woman's appearance ② find fault; be overcritical

品脱　pǐntuō　pint

品位　pǐnwèi　*min.* grade: 这片矿脉中的铁矿石，平均～高达百分之六十。The iron ore in this vein has an average grade of 60%.

品味　pǐnwèi　taste; sample; savour: 请各位～一下我厂新出的特级啤酒。Gentlemen, please sample this top-grade beer, our new product. / 我品了品味儿，觉得挺不错。I tasted it and found it quite good.

品系　pǐnxì　*biol.* strain

品行　pǐnxíng　moral conduct; behaviour: ～端正 having good conduct; well-behaved / ～不端 having bad conduct; ill-behaved

品性　pǐnxìng　one's nature and moral character: ～高洁 of noble nature and unsullied character

品学兼优　pǐn-xué jiān yōu　be a good student of good character; be a student of good character and fine scholarship

品议　pǐnyì　same as 品评 pǐnpíng

品月　pǐnyuè　pale blue

品藻　pǐnzǎo　*formal* make a critical appraisal of (a person)

品质　pǐnzhì　① character; intrinsic quality: 道德～ moral character / 学习他的优秀～ learn from his fine qualities ② quality (of commodities, etc.): ～优良 of the best quality / ～证明书 certificate of quality

品质因数　pǐnzhì yīnshù　*elec.* quality factor

品种　pǐnzhǒng　① *biol.* breed; strain; variety: 羊的优良～ improved breeds of sheep / 小麦优良～ improved strains of wheat ② variety; assortment: 货物～齐全 have a good assortment of goods

pìn

牝

牝　pìn　(opp. 牡 mǔ) female (of some birds and animals): ～马 mare / ～牛 cow / ～鸡 hen

牝鸡司晨　pìnjī sīchén　a hen heralding the break of day —a woman ruling the roost

牝牡骊黄　pìn-mǔ lí-huáng　a question of a yellow mare or a black stallion—a question of outward appearance (i.e. not one of intrinsic worth)

聘

聘　pìn　① engage (a teacher, etc.): ～某人为顾问 engage sb. as a consultant / 受～为访问教授 be engaged as a visiting professor / 被～为名誉会长 be in-

vited to be honorary chairman ② *formal* visit a state as an envoy: ～使往来 an exchange of state visits ③ betroth ④ *inf.* be married off; get married: 张家快～姑娘了。The Zhangs will soon marry their daughter off.

聘金 pìnjīn betrothal money for the bride's family

聘礼 pìnlǐ betrothal gifts (from the bridegroom's to the bride's family); bride-price: 过～ send betrothal gifts over to the bride's family

聘请 pìnqǐng engage; invite: ～一位工程师担任技校兼职教师 get an engineer to act as a part-time teacher in the technical school

聘任 pìnrèn engage sb. as; appoint sb. to a position: 听说他已被～为该医院院长。It's said that he's been appointed the Director of the hospital.

聘书 pìnshū letter of appointment; contract

聘问 pìnwèn *formal* visit a state as an envoy: ～邻国 visit a neighbouring state as an envoy

聘用 pìnyòng employ; engage; appoint to a position

pīng

乒 pīng ① *onom.*: ～的一声枪响 the crack of a rifle or pistol ② short for 乒乓球 pīngpāngqiú

乒乓 pīngpāng ① *onom.*: 雹子打在屋顶上～乱响。Hailstones were rattling on the roofs. ② table tennis; ping-pong

乒乓球 pīngpāngqiú ① table tennis; ping-pong ② table tennis ball; ping-pong ball: ～拍 table tennis bat / ～台 table tennis table / ～网 table tennis net

乒赛 pīngsài table tennis match or tournament

乒坛 pīngtán the table tennis circles

傳 pīng see 伶傳 língpīng

娉 pīng see below

娉娉袅袅 pīngpīngniǎoniǎo *liter.* (of a woman) slim and supple; light and playsome: ～十三余，豆蔻梢头二月初。(杜牧) She is slim and supple and not yet fourteen, The young spring-tip of a cardamom spray.

娉婷 pīngtíng *liter.* (of a woman) have a graceful demeanour

píng

平 píng ① flat; level; even; smooth: 桌面不～。The table is not level. / 把纸铺～ smooth out the paper / 让病人躺～ help the patient to lie stretched out ② make level or even; level: 把地～一～ level the ground / 与……在同一水平; be on a par; equal: 水涨得～了河岸。The water rose until it was level with the banks. / ～世界纪录 equal a world record ④ make the same score; tie; draw: 双方打成十五～。The two teams tied at 15-15. / 这场足球最后踢～了。The football game ended in a draw. / 场上比分是七～。The score is now seven all. ⑤ equal; fair; impartial: 平分 píngfēn ⑥ calm; peaceful; quiet: 经他一解释，老太太的气也就～了。His explanation soothed the old woman's anger. / ～民愤 assuage popular indignation / 为民～愤 redress the grievances of the people ⑦ put down; suppress: ～叛 put down a rebellion ⑧ average; common: 平日 píngrì ⑨ short for 平声 píngshēng ⑩ (Píng) a surname

平安 píng'ān safe and sound; without mishap; well: ～到达目的地 arrive safe and sound; arrive without mishap / 全家～。The whole family is well. / 一路～! Have

a good trip! or Bon voyage!

平安无事 píng'ān wú shì all is well

平安险 píng'ānxiǎn *com.* free of particular average (F.P.A.)

平白 píngbái for no reason; gratuitously: ～挨一顿骂 get a scolding for no reason at all

平白无故 píngbái wúgù for no apparent reason: 昨天他发了好大一顿脾气，还～地骂了我了。Yesterday he worked himself up into a real frenzy and tore me off a strip for no reason at all.

平板 píngbǎn dull and stereotyped; flat: 文章写得太～。The article is written in a flat style.

平板玻璃 píngbǎn bōli plate glass

平板车 píngbǎnchē flatbed tricycle; flatbed

平版 píngbǎn *print.* planographic plate: ～印刷 planographic printing; planography

平辈 píngbèi persons of the same generation

平布 píngbù *text.* plain cloth

平步青云 píngbù qīngyún rapidly go up in the world; have a meteoric rise

平舱费 píngcāngfèi trimming charges

平槽 píngcáo (of a river) rise as high as the banks; be level with the banks: 雨下得河面都平了槽。It rained so heavily that the river rose as high as the banks.

平产 píngchǎn show no increases in output

平常 píngcháng ① ordinary; common: 这种现象很～。This sort of thing is quite a common occurrence. ② generally; usually; ordinarily; as a rule: ～我很少进城。I don't go to town much as a rule. / 这个词儿～很少用。This word is seldom used on ordinary occasions.

平车 píngchē ① *railway* flatcar; platform wagon; platform car ② flatbed cart

平畴 píngchóu *formal* level farmland; well-cultivated land

平川 píngchuān level land; flat, open country; plain: 山区和～ plains and mountain areas

平旦 píngdàn *formal* dawn; daybreak

平淡 píngdàn flat; insipid; prosaic; pedestrian: ～无味的谈话 an insipid (*or* a dull) conversation

平淡无奇 píngdàn wú qí commonplace; prosaic; pedestrian: ～的文章 a pedestrian piece of writing

平等 píngděng equality: 男女～ equality between the sexes / ～互利 equality and mutual benefit / ～协商 consultation on the basis of equality / ～待遇 equal treatment / ～待人 treat others as equals / 在～的基础上 on an equal footing / 各国主权～ sovereign equality of all nations

平籴 píngdí (of local authorities in old China) buy in grain in good years so as to sell it at fair prices in famine years

平底船 píngdǐchuán flat-bottomed boat; flatboat; punt; junk

平地 píngdì ① level the land (*or* ground); rake the soil smooth: 他一气儿平了十四亩地。He levelled 14 *mu* of land at one go. ② level ground; flat ground

平地风波 píngdì fēngbō a sudden storm on a calm sea—unforeseen trouble

平地机 píngdìjī ① *agric.* land leveller; grader ② road grader

平地楼台 píngdì lóutái (also 平地起楼台 píngdì qǐ lóutái) high buildings rise from the ground—start from scratch

平地木 píngdìmù same as 紫金牛 zǐjīnniú

平地一声雷 píngdì yī shēng léi a sudden clap of thunder—a sudden rise in fame and position; an unexpected happy event

平电 píngdiàn ordinary telegram

平调[1] píng-diào see 一平二调 yī píng èr diào

平调[2] píngdiào a Hebei provincial opera (popular in

Handan 邯郸 and other districts)

平定 píngdìng ① calm down: 他的情绪逐渐～下来。He gradually calmed down. ② suppress; put down: ～叛乱 put down a rebellion

平峒 píngdòng *min.* adit; tunnel

平凡 píngfán ordinary; common: 在～的岗位上做出不～的成绩 achieve extraordinary successes at an ordinary post

平反 píngfǎn redress (a mishandled case); rehabilitate: 宣布给某人～ announce sb.'s rehabilitation

平泛 píngfàn (of writings) flat and superficial

平方 píngfāng ① *math.* the second power (of a quantity); square: 三的～是九。The square of 3 is 9. ② square metre (sq. m.): 那间房有十二～。The room has a floor space of 12 sq. m.

平方根 píngfānggēn *math.* square root: 九的～是三。The square root of 9 is 3.

平方公里 píngfāng gōnglǐ square kilometre (sq. km.)

平方米 píngfāngmǐ square metre (sq. m.)

平房 píngfáng ① single-storey house; one-storey house ② *dial.* a house with a flat plastered roof

平分 píngfēn divide equally; give or take equal shares; share alike: 两人～ go halves; go fifty-fifty / ～土地 equal distribution of land / ～兵力 divide one's forces evenly

平分秋色 píngfēn qiūsè (of two parties) have equal shares (of honour, power, glory, etc.)

平分线 píngfēnxiàn *math.* bisector

平伏 píngfú ① calm down; subside; be pacified: 她的心情久久不能～下来。For quite a long while she couldn't calm down. ② lie prostrate; lie flat

平服 píngfú be convinced

平复 píng·fù ① calm down; subside; be pacified: 风浪渐渐地～了。The storm gradually subsided. / 事态～。The situation has quietened. ② be cured; be healed: 伤口～了。The wound is healed.

平光 píngguāng zero diopter; plain glass: ～眼镜 plain glass spectacles

平巷 pínghàng *min.* drift; level

平和 pínghé gentle; mild; moderate; placid: 性情～ be of gentle (or mild) disposition / ～的语气 a mild (or placid) tone / 这种药药性～。This medicine is quite mild.

平衡 pínghéng ① balance; equilibrium: 收支～ balance between income and expenditure / 失去～ lose one's balance; be in a state of imbalance / 保持～ maintain one's equilibrium; keep one's balance / 在大国之间搞～ balance between big powers ② bring into or keep in equilibrium; balance: 逐渐在全国～工业布局 gradually distribute industry evenly all over the country / 咱们组的计划还要跟别的组～一下。We'll have to fit in our plan with those of the other groups.

平衡常数 pínghéng chángshù *chem.* equilibrium constant

平衡价格 pínghéng jiàgé equilibrium price

平衡觉 pínghéngjué *physiol.* sense of equilibrium

平衡力 pínghénglì equilibrant

平衡木 pínghéngmù *sports* balance beam

平衡器 pínghéngqì *mech.* balancer

平滑 pínghuá level and smooth; smooth

平滑肌 pínghuájī *physiol.* smooth muscle; involuntary muscle

平话 pínghuà ① a style of storytelling popular in the Song Dynasty (960-1279) ② popular stories

平缓 pínghuǎn ① (of the terrain, flow of water, etc.) gentle; smooth: 地势～。The terrain slopes gently. / 水流～。The water flows gently. ② mild; placid; gentle: ～的语调 a mild tone

平毁 pínghuǐ demolish; raze: ～壕沟 fill in trenches / ～

敌人留下的碉堡 raze the fortifications evacuated by the enemy

平假名 píngjiǎmíng *hiragana* (one of the written varieties of 假名² jiǎmíng, the other being 片假名 piànjiǎmíng)

平价 píngjià ① stabilize prices ② stabilized (or normalized, moderate) prices ③ par; parity: 汇兑～ par of exchange / 铸币～ specie par / 固定～ fixed parity

平角 píngjiǎo straight angle; an angle of 180°

平金 píngjīn embroidery done with golden or silver thread coiled evenly into gorgeous designs on satin

平靖 píngjìng ① pacify; tranquillize ② tranquil; quiet

平静 píngjìng calm; quiet; tranquil: ～的夜晚 a quiet night / ～的海面 a calm sea / 他很激动, 心情久久不能～。He was very excited, and it was long before he calmed down.

平居 píngjū *formal* on ordinary days; ordinarily; usually

平局 píngjú draw; tie: 比赛最后打成～。The game ended in a draw. / 场上屡次出现～。The score was tied again and again. / 扳成～ equalize the score

平均 píngjūn ① average; mean: ～寿命 average life span; life expectancy / ～速度 average speed; mean velocity / ～亩产量 per *mu* yield / 按人口～计算收入 per capita income / ～每年增长百分之五 increase by an average of 5% a year ② equally; share and share alike: ～分摊 share out equally

平均利润 píngjūn lìrùn *econ.* average profit

平均律 píngjūnlǜ *mus.* equal temperament: 十二～ twelve-tone equal temperament

平均数 píngjūnshù average; mean

平均值 píngjūnzhí average value; mean value; mean

平均主义 píngjūnzhǔyì equalitarianism; egalitarianism

平康 píngkāng ① peaceful and prosperous ② *arch.* brothel (from Pingkang Lane 平康坊, a gay quarter in Chang'an 长安 in the Tang Dynasty): 流落～ be driven to prostitution; become a prostitute

平空 píngkōng same as 凭空 píngkōng

平口钳 píngkǒuqián flat-nose pliers

平旷 píngkuàng *formal* (of land, fields, etc.) open and flat

平列 pínglliè place side by side; place on a par with each other: 不能把客观原因与主观原因～起来分析。We should not put subjective reasons on a par with objective reasons in our analysis.

平流 píngliú *meteor.* advection

平流层 píngliúcéng stratosphere

平炉 pínglú *metall.* open-hearth furnace; open hearth; Martin furnace: ～钢 open-hearth steel / ～利用系数 capacity factor of an open-hearth furnace / ～炼钢法 open-hearth process

平乱 píngluàn put down a revolt; suppress a rebellion

平落 píngluò (of prices) drop to normal

平脉 píngmài *Chin. med.* normal pulse

平米 píngmǐ square metre (short for 平方米): 这间房该有十六～吧? This room has a floor space of about 16 square metres, I suppose?

平面 píngmiàn *math.* plane

平面波 píngmiànbō *phys.* plane wave

平面几何 píngmiàn jǐhé plane geometry

平面交叉 píngmiàn jiāochā *transportation* grade crossing; level crossing

平面镜 píngmiànjìng *phys.* plane mirror

平面磨床 píngmiàn móchuáng surface grinding machine

平面图 píngmiàntú ① plan ② plane figure

平民 píngmín the common people; the populace

平明 píngmíng *formal* dawn; daybreak

平年 píngnián ① non-leap year; common year ② average year (in crop yield)

平平 píngpíng average; mediocre; indifferent: 成绩～。 The results are about up to the average.

平平当当 píngpíngdāngdāng done smoothly; without a hitch

平铺直叙 píngpū-zhíxù ① tell in a simple, straightforward way ② speak or write in a dull, flat style

平起平坐 píngqǐ-píngzuò sit as equals at the same table; be on an equal footing

平权 píngquán (enjoy) equal rights: 男女～ equal rights for men and women

平日 píngrì on ordinary days; ordinarily; usually

平绒 píngróng *text.* velveteen

平上去入 píng-shǎng-qù-rù the level, rising, falling and entering tones—the four tones (四声) in classical Chinese pronunciation

平射 píngshè *mil.* flat (trajectory) fire

平射炮 píngshèpào flat fire gun; flat trajectory gun

平身 píngshēn ① stand up after kowtowing ② stand up (said by an emperor to a kowtowing subject)

平生 píngshēng ① all one's life; one's whole life: ～的志愿 one's lifelong aspiration (*or* wish) ② usually: 她～是很艰苦朴素的。 She usually lives simply (*or* frugally) and works hard.

平声 píngshēng level tone (the first of the four tones in classical Chinese pronunciation, which has evolved into the high and level tone 阴平 and the rising tone 阳平 in modern standard pronunciation) ——see also 四声 sìshēng

平时 píngshí ① at ordinary times; in normal times: 他～住在厂里, 星期六才回家。 Ordinarily he sleeps at the factory and goes home only on Saturdays. ② in peacetime: ～多流汗, 战时少流血。 Losing more sweat in peacetime (training, etc.) means shedding less blood in war. / ～编制 peacetime establishment; peace organization (*or* footing) / ～兵力 peacetime strength

平时不烧香, 急来抱佛脚 píngshí bù shāoxiāng, jí lái bào fójiǎo never burn incense when all is well but clasp Buddha's feet when in distress; do nothing until the last minute

平实 píngshí simple and unadorned; natural ——see also píngshi

平实 píngshi *dial.* (of land, ground, etc.) level; even; smooth ——see also píngshí

平世 píngshì *formal* times of peace and tranquillity

平视 píngshì look squarely (*or* directly); look straight ahead: 立正时两眼要～。 Keep your eyes straight when standing at attention.

平手 píngshǒu draw: 两队打了个～。 The two teams drew.

平水期 píngshuǐqī the period when a river is at its normal level

平顺 píngshùn smooth-going; plain sailing

平素 píngsù usually: 他～就不爱说话。 He's usually very quiet. *or* He is a man of few words.

平台 píngtái ① terrace ② a house with a flat plastered roof ③ a movable platform

平坦 píngtǎn (of land, etc.) level; even; smooth: 地势～ smooth terrain / 革命的道路决不是～的。 The road of revolution is by no means smooth.

平添 píngtiān add or give as an effect or a result: 这个新建的公园给市民～许多乐趣。 The new park is an important addition to the amenities of the town.

平粜 píngtiào (of local authorities in old China) sell the grain stored in granaries at fair prices in famine years

平头 píngtóu ① crew cut: 理～ have a crew cut / 留着～ wear one's hair in a crew cut ② (used to express round numbers) full; round; complete: ～二十年 a full 20 years / ～一打 a round dozen

平头数 píngtóushù *dial.* round figure (numbers given in tens, hundreds, thousands, etc.)

平头正脸 píngtóu-zhèngliǎn have regular features

平妥 píngtuǒ plain, smooth and apt: 这篇文章措词～。 This article is plainly and aptly worded.

平纹 píngwén *text.* plain weave: ～织物 plain cloth

平稳 píngwěn smooth and steady; smooth; stable: 我们的飞机飞得很～。 We had a smooth flight. / 机器运转～。 The machine runs smoothly. / 物价～。 Prices are stable. / 病人的血压～。 The patient's blood pressure is stable.

平芜 píngwú *formal* open grassland

平西 píngxī (of the sun) be setting: 太阳已经～了, 还这么热。 It's almost sunset, but it's still so hot.

平昔 píngxī in the past: 我～对语法很少研究, 现在开始感到一点兴趣了。 I didn't go in for grammar seriously, but now I'm beginning to take an interest in it.

平息 píngxī ① calm down; quiet down; subside: 一场风波～了。 The tumult has subsided. *or* The trouble is over. / 他的怒气～了。 His anger has cooled. ② put down (a rebellion, etc.); suppress: ～暴乱 put down a riot

平心而论 píngxīn ér lùn in all fairness; to give sb. his due: ～, 这出戏还算不错。 In all fairness, it's not a bad play. / ～, 他工作还是比较认真的。 To give him his due, he is quite a conscientious worker.

平心静气 píngxīn-jìngqì calmly; dispassionately: ～地讨论 calmly discuss

平信 píngxìn ① ordinary mail ② surface mail

平行 píngxíng ① of equal rank; on an equal footing; parallel: ～机关 units (*or* organizations) of equal rank; parallel organizations ② parallel: ～线 parallel lines ③ simultaneous; concurrent: ～主权 concurrent sovereignty / ～领土管辖权 concurrent territorial jurisdiction / 就各种问题举行～的会谈 hold simultaneous talks on different subjects

平行六面体 píngxíng liùmiàntǐ *math.* parallelepiped

平行脉 píngxíngmài *bot.* parallel veins

平行四边形 píngxíng sìbiānxíng *math.* parallelogram

平行作业 píngxíng zuòyè parallel operations; simultaneous operations

平衍 píngyǎn *formal* open and flat: 土地～, 一望无际 a vast expanse of flat, open country stretching to the horizon

平野 píngyě open country: 星垂～阔, 月涌大江流。(杜甫) Stars drawn low by the vastness of the plain, The moon rushing forward in the river's flow.

平一 píngyī *formal* put down rebellions and unify the land: 秦始皇～宇内。 The First Emperor of Qin quenched numerous uprisings and unified the whole of China.

平移 píngyí *phys.* translation: ～运动 translational motion

平议 píngyì ① pass a fair judgment on ② *formal* appraise sth. through discussion

平抑 píngyì stabilize: ～物价 stabilize prices; keep down prices

平易 píngyì ① unassuming; amiable ② (of a piece of writing) easy; plain

平易近人 píngyì jìn rén amiable and easy of approach: 没料到这么大干部竟如此～。 It was quite out of my expectation to find such a high-ranking official so kindly and approachable.

平庸 píngyōng mediocre; indifferent; commonplace: ～的作家 a mediocre writer / 才能～ of limited ability

平鱼 píngyú another name for 鲳鱼 chāngyú

平原 píngyuán plain; flatlands

平月 píngyuè February of a non-leap year

平匀 píngyún regular and steady; even and regular: 呼

吸～ even and regular breathing

平允 píngyǔn *formal* fair and just; equitable: 年终奖分配得很～。The year-end bonuses were distributed in an equitable manner.

平仄 píng-zè ① level and oblique tones ② tonal patterns in classical Chinese poetry

平展 píngzhǎn ① (of land, etc.) open and flat ② well smoothed out; unruffled; unwrinkled

平章 píngzhāng *formal* ① regulate; settle: ～国事 settle state affairs ② comment on; pass judgment on

平整 píngzhěng ① level (land): 他们～土地三万余亩。They levelled over 30,000 *mu* of land. ② neat; smooth; level

平正 píngzheng straight and even: 他砌的砖又～又密合。The bricks he lays are fitted evenly and closely together.

平治 píngzhì *formal* ① put in order; bring under control: ～水土 harnessing of rivers and conservation of soil; water and soil conservation ② reign of peace

平装 píngzhuāng paperback; paper-cover; paperbound: ～本 paperback (book); paperbound edition

平装开关 píngzhuāng kāiguān *elec.* flush switch

平足 píngzú flatfoot

冯

píng ① cross (a stream, etc.) on foot: 冯河 pínghé ② same as 憑 (凭) in ancient Chinese ——see also Féng

冯河 pínghé *formal* wade a river; ford a stream

评

píng ① comment; criticize; review: 博得好～ receive favourable comments; be well received ② judge; appraise: 你来～ ～谁说得对。Now you be the judge and say which of us is right. / 被～为劳动模范 be chosen as a model worker

评比 píngbǐ appraise through comparison; compare and assess: ～产品质量 compare and appraise the quality of different products; make a public appraisal of the quality of different products

评点 píngdiǎn prepare commentaries and punctuation for a literary work

评定 píngdìng pass judgment on; evaluate; assess: ～训练成绩 evaluate the results of training / ～技术职称 grade technical personnel and give them appropriate titles

评断 píngduàn judge; arbitrate: ～是非 judge between right and wrong; arbitrate a dispute

评分 píngfēn give a mark; mark (students' papers, etc.); score: 裁判给他评多少分? What did the judges score him?

评工 pínggōng evaluate sb.'s work: ～记分 evaluate (a commune member's) work and allot workpoints; calculate workpoints on the basis of work done

评功 pínggōng appraise sb.'s merits: ～授奖大会 a meeting to announce commendations and issue awards

评功摆好 pínggōng-bǎihǎo enumerate sb.'s merits; speak of sb. in glowing terms

评估 pínggū assess: 资产～ property assessment

评话 pínghuà ① same as 平话 pínghuà ② professional storytelling in a local dialect: 苏州～ storytelling in Suzhou dialect

评级 píngjí ① grade (cadres, workers, etc.) according to work ② grade (products) according to quality

评价 píngjià appraise; evaluate: 用马克思主义的观点历史人物 appraise (*or* evaluate) historical figures from a Marxist viewpoint / 高度～ set a high value on; speak highly of; highly appraise

评奖 píngjiǎng decide on awards through discussion

评介 píngjiè review (a new book, etc.): 新书～ book review

评剧 píngjù *pingju*, a local opera of north and north-east China

评卷 píngjuàn mark examination papers

评理 pínglǐ ① judge between right and wrong; decide which side is right: 谁是谁非, 让大家来评个理。Let others judge who is right and who is wrong. ② reason things out; have it out: 咱们得找他评评理。Let's go and have it out with him.

评论 pínglùn ① comment on; discuss: 请党外群众参加～党员 ask non-Party people to join in the appraisal of Party members ② comment; commentary; review: 小～ short comments / 《湘江～》 *Xiangjiang Review*

评论家 pínglùnjiā critic; reviewer

评论员 pínglùnyuán commentator

评脉 píngmài *dial.* feel the pulse

评判 píngpàn pass judgment on; judge: ～胜负 decide who is the winner; judge between contestants / ～优劣 judge which is superior

评判员 píngpànyuán judge (in sports or speech contests, etc.); adjudicator (in musical contests, etc.)

评审 píngshěn examine and appraise: ～文艺作品 make a critical examination and appraisal of literary works

评书 píngshū storytelling (by a professional storyteller)

评述 píngshù commentary

评说 píngshuō comment on; appraise; evaluate

评弹 píngtán storytelling and ballad singing in Suzhou dialect

评头论足 píngtóu-lùnzú same as 品头论足 pǐntóu-lùnzú

评戏 píngxì same as 评剧 píngjù

评薪 píngxīn discuss and determine a person's wage-grade

评选 píngxuǎn choose through public appraisal: 被～为先进工作者 be chosen as an advanced worker

评议 píngyì appraise sth. through discussion; deliberate (a question) in a formal meeting

评语 píngyǔ comment; remark

评阅 píngyuè read and appraise (sb.'s writing, etc.)

评骘 píngzhì *formal* pass judgment on; evaluate; assess: ～书画 pass judgment on paintings and calligraphic works

评注 píngzhù ① make commentary and annotation ② notes and commentary

评传 píngzhuàn critical biography: 《昭明太子～》 *A Critical Biography of Crown Prince Zhaoming*

坪

píng level ground: 草坪 cǎopíng / 停机坪 tíngjīpíng

坪坝 píngbà *dial.* a level open space

苹(蘋)

píng see below

苹果 píngguǒ apple (the tree and its fruit): ～脯 preserved apple / ～干 dried apple slices / ～酱 apple jam / ～酒 cider; applejack / ～园 apple orchard

苹果绿 píngguǒlǜ apple green

凭¹(憑、凴)

píng ① lean on; lean against: ～几 lean on a small table ② rely on; depend on: ～我们的双手重建家园 rebuild our home town with our own hands ③ evidence; proof: 口说无凭 kǒu shuō wú píng ④ go by; base on; take as the basis: ～党性办事 act with Party spirit / ～良心说 in all fairness / ～票入场。Admission by ticket only. / ～票付款 payable to bearer / 你～什么得出这个结论? What do you base this conclusion on? / 你不能～他嘴上说的就算数。You can't take him at his word.

凭²(憑、凴)

píng *conj.* no matter (what, how, etc.): ～你跑多快, 我也赶得上。I'll catch up with

you no matter how fast you run.

凭单 píngdān　a certificate for drawing money, goods, etc.; voucher

凭吊 píngdiào　visit (a historical site, etc.) and ponder on the past: ～古战场 pay a visit to an ancient battleground

凭借 píngjiè　rely on; depend on: ～自己的力量 rely on one's own strength / ～想像力 draw on one's imagination / 人类的思维是～语言来进行的。Man thinks in words.

凭据 píngjù　evidence; proof

凭靠 píngkào　rely on; depend on

凭空 píngkōng　out of the void; out of thin air; without foundation; groundless: 他这种看法决不是～产生的。His view is by no means without foundation.

凭空捏造 píngkōng niēzào　make something out of nothing; fabricate: 这完全是～。This is a sheer fabrication.

凭栏 pínglán　lean on a railing: ～远眺 lean on the railing and gaze into the distance

凭陵 pínglíng　formal ① encroach on ② rely on; depend on

凭恃 píngshì　rely on; depend on: ～天险 rely on natural barriers for defence

凭眺 píngtiào　gaze from a high place into the distance; enjoy a distant view from a height

凭险 píngxiǎn　rely on natural barriers: ～据守 hold fast to natural barriers as defences / ～抵抗 make use of a strategic vantage point to fight back

凭信 píngxìn　trust; believe: 不足～ not to be trusted; not trustworthy

凭依 píngyī　base oneself on; rely on; have something to go by: 无所～ have nothing to go by

凭倚 píngyǐ　lean against

凭仗 píngzhàng　rely on; depend on: 他们～着顽强不屈的精神克服了重重困难。They overcame all kinds of difficulties by dint of an indomitable spirit.

凭照 píngzhào　certificate; permit; licence

凭证 píngzhèng　proof; evidence; certificate; voucher: 完税～ tax payment receipt / 没有足够～定他的罪。There isn't enough evidence to prove him guilty.

枰　píng　formal chessboard

屏　píng　① screen: 画屏 huàpíng ② a set of vertically hung scrolls: 四扇～儿 a set of four scrolls ③ shield sb. or sth.; screen ——see also bǐng

屏蔽 píngbì　① screen; shield: 两条林带～着农田。Two forest belts screen the farmland from the wind. ② protective screen: 东海岛是广州湾的～。Donghai Island provides a protective screen for Guangzhou Bay. ③ phys. screen: ～电缆 screened cable / ～天线 screened antenna

屏藩 píngfān　formal ① surrounding territories (which protect as with a screen) ② protect; shield

屏风 píngfēng　screen

屏极 píngjí　electron. plate: ～电路 plate circuit

屏门 píngmén　screen door (between the outer and inner courtyards of an old-style Chinese residence)

屏幕 píngmù　electron. screen: 电视～ telescreen; screen

屏条 píngtiáo　a set of vertically hung scrolls (usu. four in a row) of painting or calligraphy; a set of wall scrolls

屏障 píngzhàng　① protective screen: 燕山是北京的天然～。The Yanshan Hills provide a natural defence for Beijing. ② provide a protective screen for: ～中原 provide a protective screen for the Central Plains

瓶（缾）　píng　① bottle; vase; jar; flask: ～～罐罐摆了一桌子。The table was littered with bottles, flasks, jars, cans, and what not. ② m. the quantity contained in a bottle, vase, jar or flask: 两～牛奶 two bottles of milk / 一～草莓酱 a jar of strawberry jam

瓶胆 píngdǎn　glass liner (of a thermos flask)

瓶装 píngzhuāng　bottled: ～奶粉 bottled milk powder / ～液化气 bottled gas (or liquefied petroleum gas)

瓶子 píngzi　bottle; vase; jar; flask

萍（蓱）　píng　bot. duckweed

萍泊 píngbó　(also 萍漂 píngpiāo) formal wander about like duckweed; lead a wandering life

萍寄 píngjì　formal wander about, staying briefly first here, then there

萍水相逢 píng-shuǐ xiāngféng　(of strangers) meet by chance like patches of drifting duckweed: 我们虽然～, 可是我觉得你和我很谈得来。Although we have only met by chance, I find we have a lot in common.

萍踪 píngzōng　formal tracks (or whereabouts) of a wanderer

萍踪浪迹 píngzōng-làngjì　leaving no traces like duckweed and waves (said of persons who wander from place to place)

鲆　píng　zool. left-eyed flounder

pō

朴　pō　see below ——see also Piáo; pò; pǔ

朴刀 pōdāo　a sword with a long blade and a short hilt wielded with both hands

钋　pō　chem. polonium (Po)

泊（�）　pō　lake: 罗布～ Lop Nur ——see also bó

坡　pō　① slope: 北～很陡。The northern slope is very steep. / 平～ a slight (or gentle, gradual) slope ② sloping; slanting: 把板子～着放 put the board on a slant / 坑边挖得太陡了, 再～一点。The sides of the pit are too steep. Slope them a bit.

坡岸 pō'àn　a sloping bank

坡地 pōdì　hillside fields; sloping fields; land on the slopes: ～梯田化 terracing of the land on the slopes

坡度 pōdù　the degree of an incline; slope; gradient: 有三十来度～的一段山路 a mountain path with a slope of about 30 degrees

泼¹（潑）　pō　sprinkle; splash; spill: 先～点儿水再扫。Sprinkle some water before you sweep. / 互相～水 splash water on each other / 这孩子把汤～了一地。The boy spilt the soup on the floor. / 别把脏水～到院子里。Don't throw the slops in the yard.

泼²（潑）　pō　① rude and unreasonable; shrewish: 泼妇 pōfù ② dial. bold and vigorous; daring and resolute: 她干事儿可～了。She is bold and resolute in her work.

泼妇 pōfù　shrew; vixen; virago: ～骂街 like a shrew shouting abuse in the street

泼剌 pōlà　onom. the sound made by fish jumping in the water; splash; splosh

泼辣 pōla　① rude and unreasonable; shrewish ② pungent; forceful: 文章写得很～。The article is written in a

pungent style. ③ bold and vigorous; daring and resolute: 她工作很～。 She is bold and vigorous in her
work.

泼冷水 pō lěngshuǐ pour (*or* throw) cold water on;
dampen the enthusiasm (*or* spirits) of

泼墨 pōmò splash-ink, a technique of Chinese ink-
painting: ～山水 splashed-ink landscape

泼水节 Pōshuǐjié the Water-Splashing (*or* Water-
Sprinkling) Festival of the Dais (傣族) and some other
minority nationalities

颇¹ pō *formal* inclined to one side; oblique: 偏
颇 piānpō

颇² pō *adv. formal* quite; rather; considerably:
～佳 quite good / ～影响～大 exert a considerable influence / ～为费解 rather difficult to understand / ～不以
为然 highly disapprove of sth. / 他说的～有道理。 There
is a lot of sense in what he says.

pó

婆 pó ① an old woman ② a woman in a certain
occupation: 媒婆 méipó / 收生婆 shōushēngpó ③ husband's mother; mother-in-law

婆家 pójiā (also 婆婆家 pópojiā) husband's family

婆罗门 Póluómén Brahman

婆罗门教 Póluóménjiào Brahmanism

婆母 pómǔ husband's mother; mother-in-law

婆娘 póniáng *dial.* ① a young married woman ②
wife

婆婆 pópo ① husband's mother; mother-in-law ②
dial. grandmother

婆婆妈妈 pópomāmā ① like an old woman; old-
womanish: 你快点儿吧，别这么～的了。 Hurry up!
Don't fuss like an old woman. ② sentimental; mawkish;
maudlin: 他就是这么～的，动不动就掉眼泪。 He's such a
sissy he easily breaks down and cries.

婆婆嘴 pópozuǐ ① an old woman's toothless jaw; a
nagging tongue ② a garrulous person

婆娑 pósuō whirling; dancing: 杨柳～。 The willows
dance in the breeze.

婆娑起舞 pósuō qǐ wǔ start dancing; begin to trip a
measure

婆媳 pó-xí mother-in-law and daughter-in-law

婆姨 póyí *dial.* ① a young married woman ② wife

婆子 pózi ① *derog.* woman ② *inf.* wife ③ a middle-aged or oldish woman servant

鄱 pó (used in place names): ～阳湖 Poyang
Lake (in Jiangxi Province)

皤 pó *formal* ① white: 白发～然 white-haired
② (of the belly) big: ～其腹 be potbellied

pǒ

叵 pǒ *formal* impossible

叵测 pǒcè *derog.* unfathomable; unpredictable: 世路
窄狭，人心～。 Life's path is narrow and men's hearts
are hard to fathom.

叵罗 pǒluó a shallow wine vessel used in ancient
times

叵耐 pǒnài (also 叵奈 pǒnài) *old* be intolerable

钷 pǒ *chem.* promethium (Pm)

筥 pǒ see below

筥箩 pǒluo a shallow basket made of wicker or thin
bamboo strips

pò

朴 pò *bot.* Chinese hackberry (*Celtis sinensis*)
——see also Piáo; pō; pǔ

朴硝 pòxiāo mirabilite; Glauber's salt

迫 (廹) pò ① compel; force; press: 被～拿起
武器 be compelled to take up arms / ～敌投降 force
the enemy to surrender / ～于形势 under the stress of
circumstances; under the pressure of events / 为饥寒
所～ be driven (to do sth.) by cold and hunger ② urgent; pressing: 从容不迫 cóngróng bù pò ③ approach;
go towards (*or* near): 迫近 pòjìn ——see also pǎi

迫不得已 pòbùdéyǐ have no alternative (but to); be
forced (*or* driven, compelled) to; (do sth.) against
one's will

迫不及待 pò bù jí dài unable to hold oneself back; too
impatient to wait: 他们都～地想知道发生了什么事。
They were too impatient to know what had happened.

迫促 pòcù ① short; pressing: 呼吸～ be short of breath /
时间～，我们必须马上动手。 As time is running short,
we must start work at once. ② urge; press; bring
pressure on (sb. to do sth.): 在人们的～下，她才把这件
事应承下来。 She was pressurized into agreeing to do
it.

迫害 pòhài persecute: 政治～ political persecution / 遭
受～ suffer persecution; be subjected to persecution

迫降 pòjiàng forced landing; distress landing ——see
also pòxiáng

迫近 pòjìn approach; get close to; draw near: ～敌人据
点 close in on the enemy stronghold / ～胜利 be nearing victory; come in sight of victory / 行期～。 The day
of departure is drawing near. / 年关～。 The end of the
year is approaching when accounts must be settled.

迫临 pòlín come near to; come in sight of; be imminent; be impending: ～决战。 A decisive battle is impending (*or* is imminent).

迫令 pòlìng force sb. to (do sth.): 被～停业三个月 be
forced to shut down for 3 months

迫切 pòqiè urgent; pressing; imperative: ～的需要 an
urgent need; a crying need / ～的心情 eager desire;
eagerness / ～性 urgency

迫使 pòshǐ force; compel: ～飞机降落 force the plane
down / ～敌人缴械投降 force the enemy to hand over
their weapons and surrender / ～对方处于守势 force
(*or* drive) one's opponent into a defensive position / 形
势～他们采取这项政策。 Circumstances compelled
them to adopt that policy. / 事态的发展～他重新考虑自
己的决定。 The march of events compelled him to reconsider his decision.

迫视 pòshì look at from close-up; watch intently

迫降 pòxiáng force sb. to surrender ——see also
pòjiàng

迫在眉睫 pò zài méijié ① extremely urgent ② imminent

珀 pò ——see 琥珀 hǔpò

破 pò ① broken; damaged; torn; worn-out: ～碗 a
broken bowl / ～衣服 worn-out (*or* ragged, tattered)

clothes / ～房子 a dilapidated (or tumbledown) house / 我的手～了。I've cut my hand. ② break; split; cleave; cut: 一～两半 break (or split) into two / ～开西瓜 cut up the watermelon / 把十元的票子～开 break a ten-*yuan* note ③ get rid of; destroy; break with: 大～天命观 eradicate the concept of the mandate of heaven / ～旧俗, 立新风 break with outmoded customs and establish new ones / ～记录 break a record ④ defeat; capture (a city, etc.): 大～敌军 inflict a crushing defeat on the enemy / 城～之日 the day the city fell ⑤ expose the truth of; lay bare: 看破 kànpò ⑥ paltry; lousy: 这支～笔真气人! This lousy pen really drives me mad! / 这点～事两分钟就办完了。To settle a simple matter like this won't take more than two minutes.

破案 pò'àn solve (or clear up) a case; crack a criminal case

破壁 pòbì dilapidated walls

破壁飞去 pò bì fēi qù break the wall and fly away—rise from obscurity to eminence (an allusion to the dragons reputedly painted on a temple wall by Zhang Sengyou 张僧繇 of the Liang Dynasty, which broke away from the wall and flew off into the sky the moment the pupils of their eyes were put in)

破败 pòbài ruined; dilapidated; tumbledown: 那所房子已经～不堪。The house is dilapidated.

破冰船 pòbīngchuán icebreaker: 原子～ atomic icebreaker

破擦音 pòcāyīn old name for 塞擦音 sècāyīn

破财 pòcái suffer unexpected personal financial losses; lose money

破产 pòchǎn ① bankruptcy: 宣告～ declare bankruptcy / 银行～ bank failure ② go bankrupt; go broke; become insolvent: 他的公司彻底～了。His company has gone broke. / ～地主 bankrupt landlords / ～农民 impoverished peasants ③ come to naught; fall through; be bankrupt: 他们的阴谋～了。Their plot has fallen through.

破钞 pòchāo same as 破费 pòfèi

破除 pòchú do away with; get rid of; eradicate; break with: ～迷信 do away with superstitions or blind faith; topple old idols / ～情面 not spare anybody's feelings

破读 pòdú split reading—the way in which a character is pronounced when it has a meaning or function other than its usual one (e.g. zhǎng for the verb meaning of "grow" is a "split reading" of 长, which is usually pronounced cháng for the adjective meaning of "long")

破读字 pòdúzì a character not pronounced in the usual way because of a different meaning or function (e.g. 长 zhǎng as a verb "grow", opp. 长 cháng as an adjective "long")

破费 pòfèi pol. spend money; go to some expense: 你何必这么～呢? Why must you go to this expense? / 不要多～, 随便吃点就行了。Don't go to any expense. I'll enjoy whatever there is to eat. / 让你～了。You really shouldn't have spent all this money (said when receiving a gift or a treat).

破釜沉舟 pòfǔ-chénzhōu break the cauldrons and sink the boats (after crossing)—cut off all means of retreat; burn one's boats

破格 pògé break a rule; make an exception: ～提升 break a rule to promote sb. / ～接待 break protocol to honour sb.

破瓜 pòguā (of a girl) reach 16 years of age; be 16 years old

破关斩将 pòguān-zhǎnjiàng (also 破五关斩六将 pò wǔ guān-zhǎn liù jiàng) break through numerous strategic passes and kill many defending generals—overcome a lot of difficulties and vanquish many opponents

破罐破摔 pòguàn pò shuāi smash a pot to pieces just because it's cracked—write off one's situation as hopeless and act recklessly

破坏 pòhuài ① destroy; wreck: ～桥梁 destroy a bridge / 战争～了很多城市。The war wrecked many towns and cities. ② do great damage to; disrupt; sabotage: ～生产 sabotage production / ～团结 disrupt unity; undermine unity / ～边境现状 disrupt the status quo along the boundary line / ～名誉 damage sb.'s reputation / ～社会秩序 undermine social order / ～人权 violate human rights / ～和平 breach of the peace / 警惕敌人的～活动。Guard against enemy sabotage. ③ change (a social system, custom, etc.) completely or violently: ～旧世界, 建设新世界。Destroy the old world and build a new one. ④ violate (an agreement, regulation, etc.); break: ～停战协定 violate an armistice agreement ⑤ decompose; destroy (the composition of a substance): 维生素 C 受热过度就会被～。Vitamin C is destroyed when overheated.

破坏分子 pòhuàifènzǐ saboteur

破坏力 pòhuàilì destructive power: 这种炸弹的～极大。This kind of bomb has immense destructive power.

破坏性 pòhuàixìng destructiveness

破货 pòhuò loose woman

破获 pòhuò unearth; uncover: ～一个特务组织 unearth (or uncover) a spy ring / ～一起凶杀案 crack a murder case

破击 pòjī mil. attack and destroy; wreck; sabotage: ～敌人的交通线 wreck the enemy's communication lines

破解 pòjiě analyse and explain

破戒 pòjiè ① break a religious precept ② break one's vow of abstinence

破镜重圆 pòjìng chóng yuán a broken mirror joined together—reunion of husband and wife after an enforced separation or rupture

破旧 pòjiù old and shabby; worn-out; dilapidated: 戴一顶～的草帽 wear a shabby straw hat / ～的家具 old, disreputable furniture

破旧立新 pòjiù-lìxīn destroy the old and establish the new

破句 pòjù pause or mark pauses in reading at the wrong place

破口 pòkǒu ① a cut (on one's hand, etc.); a break (in a hedge, etc.); a breach (in a wall, etc.); a tear (in one's clothes, etc.) ② get a cut, break, breach, tear, etc.: 手上破了个口儿 got a cut on one's hand / 袖子破了个口儿 got a tear in one's sleeve / 鞋底破了个口儿 got a hole in the sole of one's shoe ③ see 破口大骂 pòkǒu dàmà

破口大骂 pòkǒu dàmà shout abuse; let loose a torrent of abuse

破烂 pòlàn ① tattered; ragged; worn-out: 一家～的小工厂 s small run-down factory / 穿得～不堪 be dressed in rags (or tatters) ② inf. junk; scrap: 捡～ search a garbage heap for odds and ends

破烂货 pòlànhuò worthless stuff; rubbish; trash

破浪 pòlàng cleave the waves; brave the waves: ～前进 cleave (or cut, plough) through the waves

破例 pòlì break a rule; make an exception

破脸 pòliǎn turn against (an acquaintance or associate); fall out: 老夫妇俩相亲相爱, 没有破过一回脸。The old couple love each other dearly and have never quarrelled with each other.

破裂 pòliè burst; split; rupture; crack: 血管～ rupture (or breaking) of a blood vessel / 外交关系的～ break-off (or severance, disruption) of diplomatic relations / 谈判～了。The negotiations broke down. / 他们两口子感情～了。Their marriage has broken up.

破裂摩擦音 pòliè mócāyīn old name for 塞擦音 sècāyīn

破裂音 pòlièyīn old name for 塞音 sèyīn

破落 pòluò decline (in wealth and position); fall into reduced circumstances; be reduced to poverty: ～地主家庭 an impoverished landlord family

破落户 pòluòhù a family that has gone down in the world

破谜儿 pòmèir ① *inf.* solve a riddle ② *dial.* ask a riddle

破门 pòmén ① burst (*or* force) open the door: ～而入 force open a door ② (of the Christian Church) excommunicate sb. ③ (in football, handball, ice hockey, etc.) score a goal

破灭 pòmiè be shattered; fall through; evaporate: 他的幻想～了。He was disillusioned. / 他的希望～了。His hopes were shattered.

破伤风 pòshāngfēng *med.* tetanus

破身 pòshēn lose one's virginity; have one's first sexual intercourse

破水 pòshuǐ (of a woman about to give birth) one's water breaks

破说 pòshuō *dial.* analyse and explain

破私立公 pòsī-lìgōng overcome selfishness and foster public spirit

破碎 pòsuì ① tattered; broken: ～的玻璃 broken glass / 这张帛画已经～了。This painting on silk is in tatters. ② smash (*or* break) sth. to pieces; crush: 这机器每小时可以～多少吨矿石？How many tons of ore can this machine crush in an hour?

破碎机 pòsuìjī crusher; breaker

破碎险 pòsuìxiǎn *com.* risk of breakage

破损 pòsǔn damaged; worn; torn: 这本书有几页已经～。Some pages of the book are damaged.

破题 pòtí ① the first two sentences giving the theme (originally said of an old stereotyped *bagu* 八股 essay) ② give the theme in one or two sentences

破题儿第一遭 pòtír dìyī zāo the first time one ever does sth.; the first time ever: 登台演戏我还是～。This is the first time (that) I've acted on the stage.

破体字 pòtǐzì a non-standard or corrupted form of a Chinese character

破涕为笑 pò tì wéi xiào one's tears giving way to smiles: 她～, 说: "我真傻, 怎么就没有想到这一点。" She smiled through her tears, and said, "What a silly I am not to be aware of that!" / 老妈妈看见儿子快乐的神气, ～了。When the old mama saw her son's cheerfulness, her tears changed to laughter.

破天荒 pòtiānhuāng occur for the first time; be unprecedented

破土 pòtǔ ① break ground (in starting a building project, etc.) ② start spring ploughing ③ (of a seedling) break through the soil

破网 pòwǎng score a goal

破五 pòwǔ the fifth day of the first lunar month (after which the shops are reopened and business is resumed)

破袭战 pòxízhàn sabotage operations

破相 pòxiàng (of facial features) be marred by a scar, etc.

破晓 pòxiǎo dawn; daybreak: 天将～。Day is breaking.

破鞋 pòxié loose woman

破颜 pòyán break into a smile

破衣烂衫 pòyī-lànshān ragged clothes; rags; tatters

破译 pòyì decode; decipher

破约 pòyuē break one's promise

破绽 pòzhàn ① a burst seam ② flaw; weak point: 看出～ spot sb.'s weak point

破绽百出 pòzhàn bǎi chū full of flaws (*or* holes): 他的论证～。His argument is full of holes.

破折号 pòzhéhào dash (—)

破竹之势 pòzhú zhī shì an irresistible force ——see also 势如破竹 shì rú pòzhú

粕 pò *formal* dregs of rice

魄 pò ① soul: 魂魄 húnpò ② vigour; spirit: 气魄 qìpò ——see also bó; tuò

魄力 pòlì daring and resolution; boldness: 工作有～ be bold and resolute in one's work

魄散魂飞 pòsàn-húnfēi same as 魂飞魄散 húnfēi-pòsàn

po

桲 po see 榅桲 wēnpo

pōu

剖 pōu ① cut open; rip open: 把鱼肚子～开 cut open the belly of a fish ② analyse; examine; dissect: ～释 analyse and explain

剖白 pōubái explain oneself; vindicate oneself: ～心迹 lay one's heart bare / 我想找个机会向他～几句。I must find an opportunity to explain myself to him.

剖腹藏珠 pōufù cángzhū rip (*or* cut) open the stomach to hide a pearl—die for the sake of gain

剖腹产 pōufùchǎn *med.* Caesarean birth: ～术 Caesarean section (*or* operation)

剖腹自杀 pōufù zìshā (commit) *hara-kiri*

剖解 pōujiě analyse; dissect: ～细密 make a minute analysis

剖里革 pōulǐgé split leather; split

剖露 pōulù lay bare; strip bare; reveal: ～一个人的内心世界 lay bare the inner world of a man

剖面 pōumiàn section: 横～ cross section / 纵～ longitudinal section

剖面图 pōumiàntú sectional drawing; section

剖明 pōumíng analyse and make clear: ～事理 analyse the whys and wherefores / ～心迹 lay bare the true state of one's mind

剖尸 pōushī autopsy; post-mortem examination

剖视图 pōushìtú cutaway view

剖析 pōuxī analyse; dissect: ～问题的实质 analyse the essence of the problem

剖心 pōuxīn open one's heart; lay bare one's true feelings; be completely open and sincere

póu

抔 póu *formal* hold sth. with cupped hands: 一～土 a handful of earth—a grave

掊 póu *formal* ① (of a government or officials) amass wealth by heavy taxation; exact ② dig; excavate ——see also pǒu

裒 póu *formal* ① gather; collect: ～然成集 be collected into a volume ② draw out; take out: ～多益寡 take from what is in excess to make good what is deficient

裒辑 póují *formal* collect; compile: 此书系从类书中～而成。This book is a collection of selections from various reference books.

裒敛 póuliǎn *formal* amass wealth by extortion; exploit the people: ～无厌 be insatiably avaricious in ex-

ploiting the people

pǒu

掊 pǒu *formal* ① hit; attack ② break; split ——see also póu

掊击 pǒujī attack (in speech or writing); blast; lash out at

pū

仆 pū fall forward; fall prostrate: 前仆后继 qiánpū-hòujì ——see also pú

扑(撲) pū ① throw oneself on or at; pounce on: 孩子一下子～到他妈的怀里。The child threw himself into his mother's arms. / 老虎一向山羊。The tiger sprang on the goat. / 他一下～在对手身上。He threw himself at his adversary. ② rush at; attack: 直～匪徒的巢穴 swoop down on the bandits' lair / ～蝴蝶 catch butterflies ③ throw oneself into (work, etc.): 一心～在集体事业上 devote oneself heart and soul to the cause of the collective ④ flap; flutter: 鸭子～着翅膀。The duck flapped its wings. ⑤ dab (powder, etc.): 孩子浑身都～上了爽身粉。The child was dabbed all over with talcum. ⑥ *dial.* bend over: ～在桌上看地图 bend over a map on the desk

扑鼻 pūbí assail the nostrils: 香气～。A sweet smell greeted us.

扑哧 pūchī *onom.* the sound of snorting or fizzing: ～一笑 snort with laughter; chortle; chuckle / ～一声, 瓶子打开了。The bottle opened with a fizz.

扑打 pūdǎ swat: ～蝗虫 swat locusts

扑打 pūda pat; beat: ～身上的尘土 dust one's clothes

扑灯蛾子 pūdēng'ézi *inf.* grain moth

扑跌 pūdiē ① wrestling ② fall forward: 他脚下一绊, ～在地上。He stumbled and fell forward.

扑冬 pūdōng *onom.* the sound of sth. heavy dropping on the ground; thump; thud: ～一声, 摔倒在地 fall with a thump on the ground

扑尔敏 pū'ěrmǐn *pharm.* chlorpheniramine

扑粉 pūfěn ① face powder ② talcum powder ③ apply powder: 在脸上扑点儿粉 powder one's face

扑击 pūjī ① pounce on; fall on; set on: 老鹰～鸡群。An eagle swooped down and pounced on the chickens. ② lap against; beat against: 海浪～着岸边的礁石。The sea beat against the rocky coast.

扑救 pūjiù ① put out a fire to save life and property ② (in volleyball, football, etc.) diving save

扑克 pūkè ① playing cards: 打～ play cards ② poker

扑空 pūkōng fail to get or achieve what one wants; fail to find a person where he is supposed to be; come away empty-handed: 昨天我去找他, 又～了。Yesterday I went to see him, but again he wasn't home. / 游击队已经转移, 敌人扑了个空。The guerrillas had moved away and the enemy closed in on nothing.

扑拉 pūla ① flap or spread (wings): 母鸡～着翅膀咕咕叫。The hen cackled, flapping its wings. ② pat; slap; whisk: ～～身上的雪 whisk the snow off one's clothes ③ (of tears, sweat, etc.) roll down; trickle down: 额头上的冷汗～～直往下淌。Cold sweat kept rolling from his brow.

扑棱 pūlēng *onom.* the sound of flapping of wings: ～一声, 飞起一只小鸟。There was a flutter of wings and up flew a bird.

扑棱 pūleng flap: ～着翅膀 flapping its wings

扑脸儿 pūliǎnr *inf.* blow on (or against) one's face

扑落[1] pūluò ① shake off; shake out of sth.: 把口袋里的面粉～干净。Shake all the flour out of the bag. ② *formal* scattered about

扑落[2] pūluò *dial.* plug

扑满 pūmǎn earthenware money box; piggy bank

扑面 pūmiàn blow on (or against) one's face: 春风～。The spring wind caressed our faces.

扑灭 pūmiè ① stamp out; put out; extinguish: ～火灾 put out a fire / 妄图～革命的火焰 try in vain to stamp out (or quench) the flames of revolution ② exterminate; wipe out: ～蚊蝇 wipe out mosquitoes and flies

扑热息痛 pūrèxītòng *pharm.* paracetamol

扑闪 pūshan ① blink: 她惊讶地～着她那两只大眼睛。Her big eyes blinked with astonishment. ② *dial.* flap; flutter: 小蜻蜓～～翅膀飞走了。The little dragonfly fluttered its wings and flew off.

扑朔迷离 pūshuò mílí bewildering; confusing

扑簌 pūsù (of tears) trickling down: 她眼泪扑簌簌地往下掉。Tears trickled down her cheeks.

扑腾 pūtēng *onom.* the sound of a heavy fall; flop; thump; thud: ～一声, 包掉下来了。The bundle fell with a thud. / 小王～一声, 掉下水。Xiao Wang fell with a flop into the water.

扑腾 pūteng ① move one's legs up and down in the water; flop: 他不大会游泳, 在水里尽～。He can't swim much; he just flops about in the water. / 鱼在网里直～。The fish flopped helplessly in the net. ② throb; palpitate: 他心里直～。His heart was throbbing. ③ *dial.* hustle; bustle; keep the ball rolling: 这个人挺能～。He's quite a go-getter. ④ spend freely; squander: 没有几年, 他把家产全～完了。In just a few years, he squandered all his family property.

扑通 pūtōng *onom.* the sound of sth. heavy dropping into the water or to the ground; flop; thump; splash; pit-a-pat: ～一声, 跌倒在地上 fall with a flop on the ground / ～一声, 掉进水里 fall into the water with a splash / 她的心～～地跳。Her heart went pit-a-pat.

扑翼 pūyì flapping wing: ～飞机 flapping-wing aircraft; ornithopter

铺

铺 pū ① spread; extend; unfold: ～桌布 spread a tablecloth / ～地毯 spread a rug on the floor / 运动已经全面～开。The movement is fully under way. ② pave; lay: 一条～砖的小路 a path paved with bricks / ～铁轨 lay a railway track / ～路面 surface a road ③ *m. dial.* (for 炕 kang): 一～炕 one heatable brick bed / 全家四口人睡在一～炕上。The family of four slept on one big brick bed. ——see also pù

铺摆 pū·bǎi place (goods, etc.) on display; display: 货摊上～着各色蔬菜和水果。Fruits and vegetables of all kinds are displayed at the stalls.

铺陈[1] pūchén ① spread out; arrange; decorate: ～成套餐具 spread out a dinner set on the table / 室内～讲究。The room was sumptuously furnished. ② narrate in detail; describe at great length; elaborate: ～全部经过 describe the whole process in detail

铺陈[2] pūchén *dial.* bedclothes; bedding (including pillows, mattress, mosquito net, etc.)

铺衬 pūchen small pieces of cloth used for patches

铺床 pūchuáng make the bed

铺地砖 pūdìzhuān ① floor tile; paving tile ② tile the floor

铺垫 pūdiàn ① bedding ② foreshadowing: 这一段为故事的高潮作了～。This passage foreshadows the climax of the story.

铺盖 pūgài spread (evenly) over: 把草木灰～在苗床上。Spread plant ash evenly over the seedbed.

铺盖　pūgài　bedding; bedclothes

铺盖卷儿　pūgàijuǎnr　bedding roll; bedroll; luggage roll

铺轨　pūguǐ　lay a railway track: 〜机 track-laying machine; tracklayer

铺炕　pūkàng　spread out the bedclothes on the *kang*; prepare the *kang* for sleep

铺路机　pūlùjī　paver

铺墁　pūmàn　pave the ground or floor (with tiles, bricks, etc.): 厨房和浴室的地面上都〜着地砖。The kitchen and the bathroom are paved with tiles.

铺排　pūpái　① put in order; arrange: 所有的事都〜得停停当当。Everything was well arranged. ② *dial.* be extravagant

铺平　pūpíng　① smooth out; spread sth. out smoothly: 把床单〜 smooth out the sheet ② make the ground, etc. level or even; level: 把路面〜 level the road

铺平道路　pūpíng dàolù　pave the way (for sth.): 为两国之间恢复邦交〜 pave the way for the resumption of diplomatic relations between the two countries

铺砌　pūqì　*archit.* pave

铺设　pūshè　lay; build (a road, railway, etc.): 〜双轨 lay a double-track / 〜友谊之路 open up a path of friendship

铺摊　pūtan　*dial.* spread out (paper, etc.): 他〜开宣纸, 准备作画。He spread out a sheet of *Xuan* paper and got ready to paint a picture.

铺天盖地　pūtiān-gàidì　blot out the sky and cover up the earth: 暴风雪〜而来。The blizzard blotted out the sky and the earth. / 一觉醒来, 蝗虫已〜。When people awoke after a night's sleep, they found the land swarming with locusts.

铺叙　pūxù　narrate in detail; elaborate: 〜事实 elaborate on the facts

铺展　pūzhǎn　spread out; sprawl: 蔚蓝的天空〜着一片片的白云。Fleecy clouds spread over the blue sky.

铺张　pūzhāng　① extravagant: 一次过分〜的生日宴会 a much too extravagant birthday party ② exaggeration

铺张浪费　pūzhāng làngfèi　extravagant and wasteful: 反对〜 oppose extravagance and waste

铺张扬厉　pūzhāng yánglì　① praise extravagantly ② indulge in extravagance and ostentation

潽　pū　*inf.* (of a liquid) boil and spill over: 牛奶一煮开就会〜出来。Milk spills over as soon as it comes to boiling point.

噗　pū　*onom.* puff: 〜, 一口气吹灭了蜡烛 blow out a candle with one puff / 子弹把尘土打得〜〜直冒烟。Bullets whipped up the dust.

噗嗤　pūchī　same as 扑哧 pūchī

噗咚　pūdōng　same as 扑冬 pūdōng

噗噜噜　pūlūlū　*onom.* (used to describe a flood of tears rolling down the cheeks): 听着她讲身世, 很多人的眼泪〜地直往下掉。Tears trickled down the faces of many listeners when she told her story.

噗通　pūtōng　same as 扑通 pūtōng

pú

仆(僕)　pú　servant: 男〜 manservant / 女〜 maidservant ——see also pū

仆从　púcóng　footman; retainer; henchman

仆从国　púcóngguó　vassal country

仆妇　púfù　*old* older female servant

仆仆风尘　púpú fēngchén　same as 风尘仆仆 fēngchén púpú

仆人　púrén　(domestic) servant

仆役　púyì　(domestic) servants

匍　pú　see below

匍匐　púfú　(also 匍伏 púfú) ① crawl; creep: 〜前进 crawl forward / 〜在主子脚下 crawl to one's master's feet ② (of plants) grow along the ground; creep; trail: 有些植物的茎〜在地面上。Some plants have trailing (or creeping) stems.

匍匐茎　púfújīng　*bot.* stolon

匍匐植物　púfú zhíwù　*bot.* creeper

菩　pú　see below

菩萨　púsà　① Bodhisattva: 观音〜 the Bodhisattva Guanyin ② Buddha; deity; god ③ a term applied to a kindhearted person

菩萨心肠　púsà xīncháng　the heart of a Bodhisattva—the bowels of compassion (or pity); the bowels of mercy; kindheartedness; mercifulness

菩提　pútí　bodhi, supreme wisdom or enlightenment, necessary to the attainment of Buddhahood

菩提树　pútíshù　*bot.* pipal; bo tree; bodhi tree

莆　Pú　① short for 莆田, a county in Fujian Province ② a surname

莆仙戏　púxiānxì　a Fujian local opera, popular in Putian (莆田), Xianyou (仙游) and thereabouts

脯　pú　chest; breast ——see also fǔ

脯子　púzi　breast meat (of chicken, duck, etc.): 鸡〜 chicken breast

葡　pú　grape

葡糖　pútáng　short for 葡萄糖 pútaotáng

葡萄牙　Pútáoyá　Portugal

葡萄牙人　Pútáoyárén　Portuguese

葡萄牙语　Pútáoyáyǔ　Portuguese (language)

葡萄　pútao　grape: 一串〜 a bunch (or cluster) of grapes / 〜架 grape trellis / 〜藤 grapevine / 〜园 vineyard; grapery

葡萄弹　pútaodàn　*mil.* grapeshot; grape

葡萄干　pútaogān　raisin

葡萄酒　pútaojiǔ　grape wine; wine

葡萄球菌　pútaoqiújūn　staphylococcus

葡萄胎　pútaotāi　*med.* hydatidiform mole; vesicular mole

葡萄糖　pútaotáng　glucose; grape sugar; dextrose

蒲¹　pú　*bot.* ① cattail; reed mace; club grass ② short for 菖蒲 chāngpú (as in 蒲剑 pújiàn) ③ short for 蒲葵 púkuí (as in 蒲扇 púshàn)

蒲²　Pú　① short for 蒲州, a county in Shanxi Province ② a surname

蒲棒　púbàng　the clublike flower spike of cattail (or reed mace, club grass)

蒲包　púbāo　① cattail bag; rush bag ② *old* a gift of fruit or pastries (formerly packed in a cattail bag)

蒲草　púcǎo　① the stem or leaf of cattail (or reed mace, club grass) ② *dial.* dwarf lilyturf

蒲墩儿　púdūnr　(also 蒲垫 púdiàn) cattail hassock used as a stool; a thick firm rush cushion

蒲公英　púgōngyīng　*bot.* dandelion

蒲黄　púhuáng　*Chin. med.* cattail pollen

蒲剑　pújiàn　the swordlike leaf of calamus (菖蒲) (formerly hung at the door on the 5th day of the 5th lunar month, supposedly to ward off evil spirits)

蒲节　Pújié　the Calamus Festival; the Dragon Boat Festival (the 5th day of the 5th lunar month, on which calamus leaves used to be hung at the door to ward

off evil spirits)

蒲剧 pújù (also 蒲州梆子 Púzhōu bāngzi) a local opera popular in the southern parts of Shanxi Province

蒲葵 púkuí *bot.* Chinese fan palm

蒲柳 púliǔ *bot.* big catkin willow (*Salix gracilistyla*)

蒲柳之姿 púliǔ zhī zī feel like a willow withering at the approach of autumn—suffer from poor health

蒲绒 púróng (also 蒲茸 púróng) cattail wool, used for stuffing pillows

蒲扇 púshàn Chinese fan palm fan (each made with a whole Chinese fan palm leaf)

蒲式耳 púshì'ěr bushel (=8 gallons)

蒲桃 pútao (also 蒲陶,蒲萄 pútao) same as 葡萄 pútao

蒲团 pútuán cattail hassock used for kneeling; rush hassock

蒲席 púxí cattail mat; rush mat

璞
pú uncut jade

璞玉浑金 púyù-húnjīn uncut jade and unrefined gold —unadorned beauty

镤
pú *chem.* protactinium (Pa)

pǔ

朴(樸)
pǔ simple; plain ——see also Piáo; pō; pò

朴厚 pǔhòu simple and honest: 心地～ simple-minded and kindhearted

朴陋 pǔlòu crude

朴茂 pǔmào *formal* simple and honest

朴实 pǔshí ① simple; plain: 穿着很～ be plainly dressed / 文风～ a simple style of writing ② sincere and honest; guileless: ～的工作作风 a down-to-earth style of work

朴实无华 pǔshí wú huá simple and unadorned

朴素 pǔsù ① (of colour, style, language, etc.) simple; plain: 衣着～ be simply dressed / 他的诗～而感情真挚。His poems are simple in style and imbued with true feelings. ② (of one's living) frugal; thrifty; plain and modest: 艰苦朴素 jiānkǔ pǔsù ③ naive; undeveloped: 朴素唯物主义 pǔsùwéiwùzhǔyì

朴素唯物主义 pǔsùwéiwùzhǔyì naive materialism

朴直 pǔzhí honest and straightforward: 文笔～ simple and straightforward writing

朴质 pǔzhì simple and unadorned; natural

朴拙 pǔzhuō *formal* simple and unadorned; sincere and unaffected

浦
pǔ ① (often used in place names) riverside; river mouth: 乍～ Zhapu (in Zhejiang Province) / ～口 Pukou (in Jiangsu Province) ② (Pǔ) a surname

埔
pǔ (used in place names): 黄～ Huangpu (in Guangdong Province)

圃
pǔ garden: 菜圃 càipǔ / 花圃 huāpǔ / 苗圃 miáopǔ

普
pǔ general; universal: ～天下 all over the world; everywhere in the world

普遍 pǔbiàn universal; general; widespread; common: 有～意义 be of universal significance / ～的爱国主义教育 a general education in patriotism / 我们市已经～用上了煤气灶。Gas stoves are now in common use in our city. / ～规律 universal law / ～真理 universal truth

普遍性 pǔbiànxìng universality

普遍优惠制 pǔbiànyōuhuìzhì generalized system of preferences (GSP); general preferential scheme

普查 pǔchá ① general investigation (*or* survey): 常见病～ general survey of common diseases / 人口～ census ② *geol.* reconnaissance survey

普度 pǔdù *Buddhism* deliver all from torment

普度众生 pǔdù zhòngshēng *Buddhism* deliver all living creatures from torment

普洱茶 pǔ'ěrchá Pu'er tea (produced in southwestern Yunnan)

普惠制 pǔhuìzhì short for 普遍优惠制 pǔbiànyōuhuìzhì

普及 pǔjí ① be universalized in; be made popular among; be extensively spread: 这本书已经～全国。This book has reached every part of the country. ② popularize; disseminate; spread among the people: ～与提高相结合 combine popularization with the raising of standards / ～文化科学知识 spread cultural and scientific knowledge among the people / ～中等教育 make secondary education universal / ～法律常识 popularize (*or* disseminate) an elementary knowledge of law

普及本 pǔjíběn popular edition

普及教育 pǔjí jiàoyù universal education

普降 pǔjiàng (of rain or snow) fall over a large area: 昨日华北～瑞雪。A timely snow fell all over the north China area yesterday.

普鲁本辛 pǔlǔběnxīn *pharm.* propantheline (bromide); probanthine

普鲁卡因 pǔlǔkǎyīn *pharm.* procaine

普罗 pǔluó (short for 普罗列塔利亚) proletariat: ～文学 proletarian literature

普米族 Pǔmǐzú the Pumi nationality, or the Pumis, inhabiting Yunnan Province

普什图语 Pǔshítúyǔ Pushtu

普特 pǔtè pood (a Russian measure of weight equivalent to 16.38 kg.)

普天同庆 pǔtiān tóng qìng the whole world or nation joins in the jubilation

普天之下 pǔtiān zhī xià everywhere under the sun; all under heaven

普通 pǔtōng ordinary; common; average: ～一兵 an ordinary soldier; a soldier in the ranks; a rank-and-filer / ～人 the average person; the man in the street / 这是两所～的房子。These are just two ordinary houses.

普通法 pǔtōngfǎ *leg.* common law

普通股 pǔtōnggǔ *econ.* common stock

普通话 pǔtōnghuà *putonghua*; common speech (of the Chinese language); standard Chinese pronunciation

普通税则 pǔtōng shuìzé general tariff

普通心理学 pǔtōngxīnlǐxué general psychology

普通照会 pǔtōng zhàohuì *diplomacy* verbal note

普贤 Pǔxián Samantabhadra (the Bodhisattva 菩萨 representing kindness or happiness, often found in a triad with Sakyamuni Buddha 释迦牟尼 and Manjusri 文殊; depicted seated on an elephant; the patron deity of Mt. Emei 峨嵋山 in Sichuan Province)

普选 pǔxuǎn general election: 成人～权 adult suffrage

普选制 pǔxuǎnzhì universal suffrage

普照 pǔzhào illuminate all things: 阳光～大地。The sun illuminates every corner of the land.

溥
pǔ *formal* ① broad ② common; universal ③ (Pǔ) a surname

谱
pǔ ① a register or record for easy reference (in the form of charts, tables, lists, etc.): 年谱 niánpǔ / 食谱 shípǔ ② manual; guidebook: 棋谱 qípǔ / 画谱 huàpǔ ③ music score; music: 根据这首歌的～配了一段新词。New lyrics have been composed to the music of

this song. ④ set to music; compose (music): 把毛主席的诗词～成歌曲 set Chairman Mao's poems to music ⑤ sth. to count on; a fair amount of confidence: 没谱儿 méipǔr

谱斑 pǔbān *astron.* flocculus
谱表 pǔbiǎo *mus.* stave; staff: 大～ great stave
谱牒 pǔdié *formal* same as 家谱 jiāpǔ
谱号 pǔhào *mus.* clef: 高音～ treble clef; G clef / 中音～ tenor clef; alto clef; C clef / 低音～ bass clef; F clef
谱架 pǔjià　music stand
谱曲 pǔqǔ　set (words) to music; compose music for: 这首歌是谁谱的曲? Who is the composer of the song? / 歌德的有些诗都是舒伯特谱的曲。A number of Goethe's poems were set to music by Schubert.
谱系 pǔxì　pedigree
谱写 pǔxiě　compose (music): 这支曲子是在解放战争初期～的。The tune was composed at the beginning of the War of Liberation. / 革命先烈抛头颅, 洒热血,～下可歌可泣的壮丽史诗。The revolutionary martyrs, laying down their lives for a just cause, attained the stature of epic heroes.
谱制 pǔzhì　compose: ～乐曲 compose music; set to music
谱子 pǔzi　*inf.* music score; music

琶 pǔ　see below
琶氇 pǔlu　a woolen fabric produced in Tibet for making blankets, garments, etc.

错 pǔ　*chem.* praseodymium (Pr)

蹼 pǔ　web (that connects the digits of ducks, frogs, etc.)
蹼趾 pǔzhǐ　webbed toe
蹼足 pǔzú　webfoot; palmate foot

pù

铺¹(舖) pù　shop; store
铺²(舖) pù　plank bed
铺³(舖) pù　courier station in old times, now often used in place names (as in 五里铺 Wulipu, 十里铺 Shilipu)
——see also pū
铺板 pùbǎn　bed board; bed plank
铺保 pùbǎo　guarantee for a person given by a shopkeeper; shop guarantor
铺底 pùdǐ　shop fixtures
铺户 pùhù　shop; store
铺家 pùjia　*dial.* shop; store
铺面 pùmiàn　shop front
铺面房 pùmiànfáng　shop building
铺位 pùwèi　bunk; berth
铺子 pùzi　shop; store

堡 pù　same as 铺³ pù ——see also bǎo

瀑 pù　waterfall
瀑布 pùbù　waterfall; falls; cataract

曝(暴) pù　*formal* expose to the sun: 一曝十寒 yī pù shí hán
曝露 pùlù　*formal* expose to the open air
曝气池 pùqìchí　*environ. protec.* aeration tank
曝晒 pùshài　expose to the sun

Q

qī

七 qī ① seven: ～公斤 seven kilos / ～个班 seven classes / ～班 the seventh class; class 7 / ～路公共汽车 No. 7 bus ② *old* the memorial ceremony held every seven days for a person after his death till the forty-ninth day, the seventh 七

七…八… qī…bā… (used with verbs or nouns to indicate a large amount or great disorder): 七扭八歪 crooked; uneven; irregular

七边形 qībiānxíng **heptagon**

七步之才 qī bù zhī cái seven-pace talent—literary talent in ready play (an allusion to the literary genius Cao Zhi 曹植 who on one occasion, at the bidding of his elder brother Cao Pi 曹丕, then emperor of the Wei Dynasty, composed—on pain of death in case of failure—an impromptu poem within the set time of walking seven paces)

七颠八倒 qīdiān-bādǎo at sixes and sevens; all upside down; topsy-turvy: 我父亲死了以后，家里的事～。Since my father's death all affairs at home have been in great confusion.

七姑八姨儿 qīgūbāyír *inf.* very distant relatives

七级风 qījífēng *meteorol.* force 7 wind; moderate gale

七极管 qījíguǎn *radio* heptode

七件事 qījiànshì see 开门七件事 kāimén qījiànshì

七绝 qījué (short for 七言绝句) a four-line poem with seven characters to a line and a strict tonal pattern and rhyme scheme; septasyllabic (*or* seven-syllable) quatrain ——see also 绝句 juéjù

七孔 qīkǒng same as 七窍 qīqiào

七老八十 qīlǎobāshí late seventies and early eighties—a very old person

七零八落 qīlíng-bāluò scattered here and there; in disorder: ～的几间破草房 a few ramshackle huts scattered here and there / 匪徒被打得～，四散奔逃。Badly battered, the bandits fled in disorder.

七律 qīlǜ (short for 七言律诗) an eight-line poem with seven characters to a line and a strict tonal pattern and rhyme scheme; septasyllabic (*or* seven-syllable) regulated verse ——see also 律诗 lǜshī

七拼八凑 qīpīn-bācòu throw together; piece together: knock together; rig up: 用碎布～做成一个枕套 make a pillowcase from odd pieces of cloth / 我们这个小工厂是自己动手～搞起来的。We rigged up this little factory with our own hands.

七七事变 Qī Qī Shìbiàn the July 7 Incident (of 1937) ——see also 芦沟桥事变 Lúgōuqiáo Shìbiàn

七七八八 qīqibābā *inf.* mixed; assorted; miscellaneous: ～的东西 odds and ends; a medley / ～的事情 odd jobs; miscellaneous trifles

七巧板 qīqiǎobǎn seven-piece puzzle; tangram

七窍 qīqiào the seven apertures in the human head (i.e. eyes, ears, nostrils and mouth)

七窍生烟 qīqiào shēng yān fume with anger; foam with rage; be outraged

七情 qīqíng ① the seven human emotions, namely, joy, anger, sorrow, fear, love, hate and desire ② *Chin. med.* the seven emotional factors (joy, anger, melancholy, brooding, sorrow, fear and shock, considered to be the internal factors causing diseases)

七鳃鳗 qīsāimán lamprey

七色板 qīsèbǎn spectrum board

七上八下 qīshàng-bāxià (also 七上八落 qīshàng-bāluò) seven buckets coming up and eight buckets going down—be agitated; be perturbed: 他这一阵心头如同十五个吊桶打水，～，静不下心来。He was very much upset over this. His heart was beating like fifteen buckets in a well—eight going down while seven were coming up. He couldn't calm down. / 他心里～的, 不知怎么办才好。He was so agitated that he didn't know what to do.

七十二变 qīshí èr biàn seventy-two transformations (or metamorphoses) (originally of the Monkey King in the *Pilgrimage to the West*《西游记》), —countless changes of tactics

七十二行 qīshí èr háng all sorts of occupations; every conceivable line of work

七手八脚 qīshǒu-bājiǎo with everyone lending a hand: 大伙儿一把他抬了出来。Everybody lent a hand to carry him out. / 大家～一会儿就把院子扫扫干净了。With everybody lending a hand, the courtyard was soon swept clean.

七夕 qīxī the seventh evening of the seventh month (when the Herd-boy and the Weaving-girl are supposed to meet) ——see also 牛郎织女 Niúláng Zhīnǚ

七弦琴 qīxiánqín another name for 古琴 gǔqín

七言诗 qīyánshī a poem with seven characters to a line ——see also 古体诗 gǔtǐshī; 绝句 juéjù; 律诗 lǜshī

七叶树 qīyèshù Chinese Horsechestnut (*Aesculus chinensis*)

七一 Qī Yī July 1, anniversary of the founding of the Communist Party of China (1921)

七月 qīyuè ① July ② the seventh month of the lunar year; the seventh moon

七折八扣 qīzhé-bākòu various deductions

七政仪 qīzhèngyí *astron.* orrery

七嘴八舌 qīzuǐ-bāshé seven mouths and eight tongues—with everybody trying to get a word in; all talking at once: 方案一公布, 大家就～地议论开了。The draft plan touched off a lively discussion the moment it was announced; everybody was eager to put in a word. / 人们都围了上去, ～, 他不知听谁的好。People crowded round him, all talking at once, so that he didn't know who to listen to.

沏 qī infuse (with boiling water): ～茶 infuse tea; make tea / 用开水把糖～开。Dissolve the sugar in the hot water.

妻 qī wife ——see also qì

妻弟 qīdì wife's younger brother; brother-in-law

妻儿老小 qī-ér-lǎo-xiǎo parents, wife and children—a

married man's entire family

妻舅 qījiù　wife's brother; brother-in-law

妻离子散 qīlí-zǐsàn　breaking up or scattering of one's family ——see also 天各一方 tiān gè yī fāng

妻孥 qīnú　*formal*　wife and children

妻室 qīshì　*formal*　wife

妻小 qīxiǎo　*old*　wife and children

妻子 qīzǐ　wife and children

妻子 qīzi　wife

柒　qī　seven (used for the numeral 七 on cheques, etc., to avoid mistakes or alterations)

凄[1]（淒）　qī　① chilly; cold: 风雨～～。 Cold, cold are the wind and the rain. ② bleak and desolate: 凄凉 qīliáng

凄[2]（悽）　qī　sad; wretched; miserable: 凄楚 qīchǔ

凄暗 qī'àn　cheerless and dim: ～的屋子 a dim, cheerless room

凄惨 qīcǎn　wretched; miserable; tragic: ～的声音 sad (*or* plaintive) cries / ～的景象 a heartrending sight / 生活～ lead a wretched existence; lead a miserable life

凄恻 qīcè　*formal*　grieved; sad

凄楚 qīchǔ　desolate and miserable

凄怆 qīchuàng　*formal*　wretched; sad

凄风苦雨 qīfēng-kǔyǔ　① wailing wind and weeping rain: ～，夜不能眠。 With the wind moaning and the rain pattering, I lay awake all night. ② wretched circumstances; distress

凄寒 qīhán　desolate and cold

凄惶 qī-huáng　sad and worried; sad and anxious

凄寂 qījì　① desolate and still; dreary and quiet ② desolate and lonely

凄苦 qīkǔ　miserable and sad

凄冷 qīlěng　① dreary; desolate; miserable ② cold; frigid

凄厉 qīlì　sad and shrill: ～的叫声 sad, shrill cries / 风声～。 The wind was wailing.

凄凉 qīliáng　dreary; desolate; miserable: 满目～ desolation all round / 晚景～ lead a miserable and dreary life in old age

凄迷 qīmí　*formal*　① (of scenery) dreary and hazy: 夜色～。 It was a dreary and hazy night. ② sorrowful; melancholy

凄切 qīqiè　plaintive; mournful: 寒蝉～。 It was cold and the cicadas were chirping plaintively.

凄清 qīqīng　① slightly cold; cool: ～的月光 cool moonlight ② dreary; plaintive: 琴声～。 The *qin* was producing a plaintive tune.

凄然 qīrán　*formal*　sad; mournful: ～泪下 shed tears in sadness

凄伤 qīshāng　desolate; sorrowful; grieved

凄酸 qīsuān　grieved; distressed; sorrowful: 心中一阵～ feel a twinge at one's heart

凄婉 qīwǎn　(of sound) plaintive but lovely; sadly moving: ～的笛声 the plaintive tone of a flute

凄怨 qīyuàn　sad; plaintive: ～的曲调 a plaintive tune

栖（棲）　qī　① (of birds) perch: 栖息 qīxī ② dwell; stay: 栖身 qīshēn

栖身 qīshēn　stay; sojourn: 无处～ have no place to stay

栖息 qīxī　(of birds) perch; rest: 许多水鸟在岛上～。 A great number of water fowls dwell on the island.

栖息地 qīxīdì　habitat

栖止 qīzhǐ　stay; sojourn

桤（榿）　qī　alder

桤木 qīmù　alder

萋　qī　see below

萋萋 qīqī　*liter.* luxuriant; lush 晴川历历汉阳树，芳草～鹦鹉洲。（崔颢） Clear and bright in the sunlit stream the trees of Hanyang, Fragrant grasses, lush and green, all over Parrot Isle.

戚[1]　qī　① relative: 亲戚 qīnqi ② (Qī) a surname

戚[2]（慼）　qī　sorrow; woe: 哀戚 āiqī

戚[3]（鏚）　qī　an axe-like weapon used in ancient China

戚戚 qīqī　*formal*　sad; worried; anxious: 君子坦荡荡，小人长～。（《论语》）The gentleman is easy of mind, while the small man is always full of anxiety.

戚谊 qīyì　blood ties

戚友 qīyǒu　friends and relatives

期　qī　① a period of time; phase; stage: 第一～工程 the first phase of the project / 暑期班分两～，每～三周 a summer school of two three-week sessions ② scheduled time: 到期 dàoqī / 限期 xiànqī ③ *m.* (for things scheduled by periods): 最近一～的《中国画报》 the current issue of *China Pictorial* / 短训班办了三～。 The short-term training class has been run three times. ④ make an appointment: 不期而遇 bù qī ér yù ⑤ expect: 期待 qīdài ——see also jī

期待 qīdài　expect; await; look forward to: 殷切地～你早日答复 eagerly await your early reply / 我们一直～着这一天。 We've been looking forward to this day for a long time. / 老师用～的目光望着我们。 The teacher looked at us with expectant eyes.

期汇 qīhuì　forward exchange

期货 qīhuò　*econ.* futures: ～价格 forward price / ～合同 forward contract; futures contract

期冀 qījì　*formal*　ardently hope or expect

期间 qījiān　time; period; course: 就在这～ during this time; in this very period / 会议～ in the course of the conference; during the conference / 农忙～ during busy farming seasons / 他在住院～读了很多小说。 While in hospital, he read a lot of novels.

期刊 qīkān　periodical: ～阅览室 periodical reading room

期考 qīkǎo　end-of-term examination; final (*or* terminal) examination

期满 qīmǎn　expire; run out; come to an end: 合同～ the contract expires; on the expiration of the contract / 服役～ complete one's term of (military) service

期盼 qīpàn　expect; await; look forward to

期票 qīpiào　promissory note

期期艾艾 qīqī'ài'ài　stammer; stutter: 他～地说不上话来。 He stammered and stuttered and couldn't utter a single coherent sentence.

期求 qīqiú　hope to get or obtain

期望 qīwàng　① ardently hope or expect: 党和人民在～着我们。 The Party and the people place high hopes on us. / 她～着和家人团聚。 She was looking forward to joining her family. ② expectation: 我们决不辜负祖国对我们的～。 We will never disappoint our motherland in her expectations of us.

期限 qīxiàn　allotted time; time limit; deadline: 规定一个～ set a deadline; fix a target date / ～三个月 three months as the time limit / 延长～ extend the time limit / ～快到了。 The deadline is drawing near. / 必须在规定的～内完成这项工作。 The work must be finished with-

in the allotted time.

期许 qīxǔ ardently hope or expect (usu. used of one's juniors)

期颐 qīyí a 100-year-old person; centenarian: ～之年 in one's 100th year

期于 qīyú aspire to; hope to achieve; aim at

欺 qī ① deceive: 欺瞒 qīmán ② bully; take advantage of sb.: 软弱可欺 ruǎnruò kě qī ③ take advantage of (sb.'s weakness, etc.): 他～她老实。He took advantage of her good nature.

欺负 qīfu ① bully; treat sb. high-handedly; take advantage of sb.: 大国不应当～小国。Big nations should not bully small ones. / 他老爱～弟弟。He is always bullying his younger brother. / 别瞧谁老实就～谁。Don't take advantage of a nice person when you see one. ② take advantage of (sb.'s weakness, etc.): 他们～他年幼无知。They took advantage of his youth and inexperience.

欺哄 qīhǒng cheat; deceive; fool; hoodwink

欺凌 qīlíng bully and humiliate: 受尽了～ be subjected to endless bullying and humiliation / 决不任人～ never allow oneself to be trodden upon

欺瞒 qīmán hoodwink; dupe; pull the wool over sb.'s eyes

欺蒙 qīméng deceive; cheat; dupe; defraud

欺弄 qīnòng dupe; hoodwink: 老太太受了他的～。The old woman was duped by him.

欺骗 qīpiàn deceive; cheat; dupe: ～世界舆论 befuddle world opinion / 这只能～那些不明真相的人。This can only deceive those who do not know the truth. or This can only mislead those who are not aware of the facts. / 你这是在～自己。You're deceiving yourself. / 戳穿资产阶级议会民主的～性 expose the fraudulent nature of bourgeois parliamentary democracy / 揭露两面派的～性 expose the duplicity of the double-dealers / 这是一种～。This is a kind of deception.

欺人太甚 qī rén tài shèn what a beastly bully; that's going too far; push people too hard

欺人之谈 qī rén zhī tán deceitful words; deceptive talk

欺辱 qīrǔ bully and humiliate; insult

欺软怕硬 qīruǎn-pàyìng bully the weak and fear the strong: 大家骂他不公平,～。Everybody lashed out at his unfairness, calling him a cowardly bully. / 这路人我见多了,都是软的欺,硬的怕! I've known lots like him. If you let them push you around, they will. But if you stand up to them, they turn tail soon enough.

欺上瞒下 qīshàng-mánxià deceive one's superiors and delude (or dupe) one's subordinates

欺生 qīshēng ① bully or cheat strangers: 那儿的人～,见了外地人特横。The people there are apt to cheat strangers; they're particularly rough on nonnatives. / 他们家那狗～,我一进院子它就叫。Their dog is fierce towards strangers; he barks at me whenever I enter the courtyard. ② (of horses, mules, etc.) be ungovernable by strangers: 这马～,我一靠近它就尥蹶子。This horse refuses to behave for strangers; he kicks at me whenever I approach him.

欺世盗名 qīshì-dàomíng gain fame by deceiving the public; fish for undeserved fame

欺罔 qīwǎng formal deceive; cheat

欺侮 qīwǔ bully and humiliate; treat sb. high-handedly: 他不是好～的。He is not a man to be bullied. / 书评作者的批评没有必要这样～人。The reviewer's criticism was unnecessarily insulting. / 她让人～得直哭。She was driven to tears by their bullying.

欺压 qīyā bully and oppress; ride roughshod over: ～人民 ride roughshod over the people

欺诈 qīzhà cheat; swindle: 这家商店经常～顾客。This shop often swindles customers.

缉 qī sew in close and joint stitches: ～边儿 sew the hem with close stitches ——see also jī

攲 qī formal lean to one side; slant; incline

攲侧 qīcè formal lean to one side; slant; incline

顝 (魌) qī ① (in former times) an ugly mask worn by the impersonator of a god in ceremonies to drive away pestilence ② arch. ugly

漆 qī ① lacquer; paint: ～盘 lacquer tray / 他用黑～把铁桌子漆了。He painted the iron table with black lacquer. ② coat with lacquer; paint: 把门～成深绿色 paint the door dark green / 把桌子再～一遍 give the table another coat of paint / 颜色～太深(浅) paint a colour a bit too dark (light) / ～厚(薄)些 give a thick (thin) coat of paint / ～得不匀。The paint is not evenly spread. / 我把桌子～坏了。I did a bad job of painting the table. ③ (Qī) a surname

漆包线 qībāoxiàn enamel-insulated wire

漆布 qībù varnished cloth

漆雕 qīdiāo same as 雕漆 diāoqī

漆革 qīgé patent leather

漆工 qīgōng ① lacquering; painting ② lacquerer; lacquer man; painter

漆黑 qīhēi pitch-dark; pitch-black: 那是个～的夜晚。It was a pitch-dark night. / 屋子外面～一片。Outside the house it was pitch-black. / ～的头发 jet-black hair

漆黑一团 qīhēi yī tuán ① pitch-dark—utterly hopeless: 把形势描绘成～ paint a dark picture of the situation ② be entirely ignorant of; be in the dark: 这个问题在他心中还是～。He is still completely in the dark about the matter.

漆画 qīhuà lacquer painting

漆匠 qījiang ① lacquerware worker ② lacquerer; lacquer man; painter

漆皮 qīpí ① coat of paint ② shellac

漆片 qīpiàn a coating agent which has to be dissolved in alcohol before use

漆器 qīqì lacquerware; lacquerwork

漆树 qīshù lacquer tree; varnish tree

喊 qī see below

喊哩喀喳 qīlīkāchā quick and efficient (in doing things); snappy and clear-cut (in speaking)

喊喊喳喳 qīqīchāchā onom. the sound of chatter

槭 qī maple

槭树 qīshù maple

蹊 qī see below ——see also xī

蹊跷 qīqiāo odd; strange; fishy: 这事情有点～。There is something fishy about it.

睓 qī ① (of wet things) be drying: 雨过了,太阳一晒,路上就渐渐～了。The sun came out after the rain and the road began to dry. ② absorb water with sand, etc.: 地上有水,铺上点儿沙子～一～。There are puddles on the ground; let's spread some sand over them.

qí

齐[1] (齊) qí ① neat; even; uniform: 把桌子摆～ arrange the tables in an orderly way / 剪得很～ be evenly trimmed / 这两根筷子长短不～。These two

chopsticks are not of equal (*or* uniform) length. ② be level with: 水涨得～了岸。The water has risen to the level of the river banks. / 在～腰深的水里筑坝 stand waist-deep in water building the dam ③ even up at one point or along one line: 把玉米秆～着根儿砍断 cut the cornstalks right down to the roots / ～着边儿画一道线 draw a line along the edge ④ *adv.* together; simultaneously: 男女老幼～动手。Men and women, old and young, all pitched in. / 万炮～发。All the batteries fired at once. ⑤ all ready; all present: 客人都来～了。All the guests have arrived. / 人到～了没有? Is everybody here? / 东西都预备～了。Everything has been prepared. ⑥ alike; similar: 齐心 qíxīn / 齐名 qímíng

齐²(齊)　　Qí　① the Southern Qi Dynasty (479-502), one of the Southern Dynasties ② a surname

齐备　qíbèi　complete; all ready: 实验所需的东西都已～。The things necessary for the experiment are all ready. / 万事～。Everything is ready. / 货色～。Goods of every description are available.

齐步走　qíbùzǒu　*mil.*　quick march: ～! (word of command) Quick time, march!

齐唱　qíchàng　*mus.*　singing in unison; unison

齐齿呼　qíchǐhū　*phonet.*　a class of syllables with i as the final (韵母) or a final beginning with i (e.g. 坚 jiān) ——see also 四呼 sìhū

齐楚　qíchǔ　neat and smart: 衣冠～ be smartly dressed

齐东野语　Qídōng yě yǔ　what folks say; popular report; unreliable words

齐墩果　qídūnguǒ　another name for 油橄榄 yóugǎnlǎn

齐集　qíjí　assemble; gather; collect: 五大洲的朋友～在中国的首都北京。Friends from the five continents gathered in the Chinese capital Beijing.

齐家文化　Qíjiā wénhuà　the Qijia culture, a culture of the Chalcolithic period, relics of which were first unearthed at Qijiaping, Gansu Province, in 1923

齐截　qíjie　*dial.*　① neat; even: 字写得很～。The handwriting is very neat. / 庄稼长得很～。The crops are of even height. ② complete; all in readiness: 东西都预备～了。Everything is ready. / 今天到会的人很～。We have full attendance at today's meeting.

齐理　qílǐ　*inf.*　put in order; tidy up; clear away

齐眉穗儿　qíméisuìr　bang; fringe

齐民　qímín　*formal*　the common people; the populace

齐名　qímíng　enjoy equal popularity; be equally famous: 唐代诗人中, 李白与杜甫～。Among the Tang poets, Li Bai and Du Fu enjoyed equal fame.

齐明　qímíng　*phys.*　aplanatic: ～成象 aplanatic image formation / ～点 aplanatic foci / ～镜 aplanat

齐巧　qí·qiǎo　*dial.*　by chance; fortunately; as chance would have it: 我上公园去, ～她也在那儿。She chanced to be in the park when I was there.

齐全　qíquán　complete; having everything that one expects to find; all in readiness: 尺码～ have a complete range of sizes / 登山队装备～。The mountaineers are fully equipped. / 新建的住宅设备～。The new houses have all the necessary fittings. / 这商店虽然小, 货物却很～。This store, though small, has a satisfactory variety of goods.

齐射　qíshè　*mil.*　salvo; volley

齐声　qíshēng　in chorus; in unison: ～回答 answer in chorus / ～欢呼 cheer in unison

齐刷刷　qíshuāshuā　even; uniform: ～的一片麦子 an even expanse of wheat

齐头并进　qítóu bìngjìn　advance side by side; do two or more things at once: 三路人马～。The three columns advanced simultaneously. / 这些工作要分轻重缓急, 不要～。These jobs should be arranged in order of priority and not done all at once.

齐心　qíxīn　be of one mind (*or* heart): 群众～了, 一切事情就好办了。When the masses are of one heart, everything becomes easy (*or* is easily accomplished).

齐心协力　qíxīn xiélì　work as one; make concerted efforts: 我们大家～, 一定能打败他们! If we all pull together there's no doubt we can beat them!

齐整　qízhěng　neat; orderly: 运河两旁的柳树长得很～。The canal is flanked by neat rows of willows.

齐奏　qízòu　*mus.*　playing (instruments) in unison; unison

祁　　Qí　a surname

祁红　qíhóng　keemun (a black tea produced in Qimen 祁门 county, Anhui Province)

祁剧　qíjù　a local opera of Hunan

芪　　qí　see 黄芪 huángqí

圻　　qí　*formal*　boundary

祇　　qí　*formal*　god of the earth: 神祇 shénqí

祈　　qí　① pray: 祈年 qínián ② entreat: 敬～指导。We respectfully request your guidance.

祈祷　qídǎo　pray; say one's prayers: 正在～ be at one's prayer

祈年　qínián　pray for a bumper harvest year

祈年殿　Qíniándiàn　the Hall of Prayer for Good Harvests (in Beijing)

祈请　qíqǐng　request; beseech

祈求　qíqiú　earnestly hope; pray for: ～上帝 pray to God / ～和平 pray for peace / 不能～大自然的恩赐, 而要主动索取我们所需要的一切。We must never entreat Nature to bestow favours, but must rather take the initiative to wrest everything we need from it.

祈使句　qíshǐjù　*gram.*　imperative sentence

祈望　qíwàng　hope; wish

祈雨　qíyǔ　pray for rain

其¹　　qí　① his (her, its, their): ～父 his or her father / 《战国策》取～灵快。*Intrigues of the Warring States* is noted for its agility of thought and expressiveness of style. ② he (she, it, they): 劝～戒烟 advise him or her to give up smoking / 促～早日实现 help bring it about at an early date ③ that; such: 正当～时 just at that time; at the opportune moment / 查无～事。Investigation shows that nothing of this sort has happened. ④ (referring to no definite person or thing) it: 大请～客 invite many guests to dinner; entertain lavishly / 忘～所以 forget all else

其²　　qí　*part. formal*　① (used to make a guess or a retort): ～奈我何? What can they do to me? ② (used to give an order): 子～勉之! Exert yourself to the utmost!

其³　　qí　*suffix*: 极其 jíqí

其次　qícì　① next; secondly; then: 先看生产车间, ～再参观托儿所。Let's see the workshop first and then the nursery. / 会上老孙先发言, ～是小白。Lao Sun spoke first at the meeting, followed by Xiao Bai. ② secondary: 首要的问题已经解决, ～的问题就比较好办了。The secondary problems will be taken care of easily now that the main problem has been solved. / 内容是主要的, 形式还在～。Content comes first, form second.

其后　qíhòu　later; after; afterwards

其间　qíjiān　① between or among them; of them; in it ② during this or that time

其乐无穷　qí lè wúqióng　find it a delight (*or* joy): 西湖赏

月，～。It is a delight to watch the moon rising over the West Lake.

其貌不扬 qí mào bùyáng　be unprepossessing (*or* unimposing) in appearance; be of undistinguished appearance

其实 qíshí　*adv.* actually; in fact; as a matter of fact: ～情况不是那样。Actually, that is not the case. / 这台机器看起来复杂，～不难掌握。This machine looks complicated, but it's really not difficult to operate. / 你们只知道她会说英语，～她的日语也挺好。You only know that she can speak English. As a matter of fact, her Japanese is pretty good too. / 还要讨论？～没有这个必要。Why have another discussion? I don't think there's any need for it. / 何必大家掏钱？～让我做东得了。Why go Dutch? Let me play the host.

其它 qítā　(referring to things only) other; else ——see also 其他 qítā

其他 qítā　other; else: 老李在这儿，～人呢? Lao Li's here. Where are the others? / 见到～人了吗? Did you see anybody else? / 除了小冯以外，～的人都去了。Everybody went except Xiao Feng. / 除了整地，活儿也需要人。We need people for other jobs besides levelling the land. / 还有什么～事情要我们做吗? Is there anything else you want us to do? / 我同意老王的建议，没有～意见。I agree with Lao Wang on his proposal and have nothing else to add. / 先拣重要的说，再说～。Say what you think is most important first, then go on to other things.

其味无穷 qí wèi wúqióng　have a marvellous flavour; be infinitely enjoyable

其余 qíyú　all the other (persons or things); the rest; the remainder: ～的人马上就来。The others will be here in a minute. / 这个突击队只有三名男的，～都是女同志。There are only three men in the shock team; the rest are women. / 只有一间屋子亮着灯，～都是黑的。There's a light on in only one room; the others are all dark. / 这个箱子我随身带，～的行李托运。I'll take this suitcase with me and check all the other baggage.

其中 qízhōng　among them; of them; in it: 乐在～ find pleasure in it / 我们车间有五百人，～妇女占百分之六十。There are five hundred workers in our shop, and 60 per cent of them are women. / 这篇论文我已经看过，～提出的问题值得重视。I have read that paper. The questions it raises deserve serious attention. / 饭疏食，饮水，曲肱而枕之，乐亦在～矣。《论语》In the eating of coarse rice and the drinking of water, the using of one's elbow for a pillow, joy is to be found.

奇

qí　① strange; queer; rare: 希奇 xīqí ② remarkable; wonderful: 奇书 qíshū ③ be surprised; be astonished: 惊奇 jīngqí ④ *adv.* very; extremely: ～痒 itch terribly / ～痛 have a severe pain; be extremely painful ——see also jī

奇兵 qíbīng　an army suddenly appearing from nowhere; an ingenious military move

奇才 qícái　a rare talent; genius

奇彩 qícǎi　extraordinary (*or* radiant) splendour

奇耻大辱 qíchǐ-dàrǔ　galling shame and deep humiliation; deep disgrace: 这真是～。This is really galling and humiliating.

奇功 qígōng　outstanding service: 屡建～ repeatedly perform outstanding service

奇怪 qíguài　① strange; surprising; odd: ～的声音 strange noise / ～的表情 strange expression / 一些奇奇怪怪的现象 some unusual phenomena / 萤火虫很～，身体能发光。The firefly is a strange insect that can give off light. / 陨石雨是一种自然现象，没有什么可～的。A meteorite shower is a natural phenomenon; there's

nothing strange about it. / 真～，他们至今还一无所知。It's really surprising that they should still be in the dark. / 这个问题提得很～。It's a strange question to raise. / 各有各的爱好，没什么～。Everyone has his or her own hobby. It's only natural. ② feel surprised; wonder: 他们都～你为什么要辞职。They feel surprised at your resignation. / 我～他怎么不来。I wonder why he didn't come. / 这个人虽然住我隔壁，但～的是我从未见到他。He lives right next door, but strangely enough I've never seen him. / 我们都～为什么这点小事就是办不了。We really don't understand why such a small matter is so hard to settle.

奇观 qíguān　marvellous spectacle; wonder: 自然界的～ a marvellous natural phenomenon / 世界七大～ the seven wonders of the world

奇瑰 qíguī　unusually marvellous; fascinating: ～的景象 a fascinating sight

奇诡 qíguǐ　odd; eccentric

奇花异卉 qíhuā-yìhuì　(also 奇葩异草 qípā-yìcǎo) exotic flowers and rare herbs

奇幻 qíhuàn　fantastic; visionary: ～的遐想 fantastic reveries / ～的景色 visionary, kaleidoscopic scenes

奇货可居 qíhuò kě jū　a rare commodity worth hoarding: 吕不韦贾邯郸，见而怜之，曰："此～。"《史记》Lü Buwei, in Handan on business, saw the prince and pitied him. "This rare merchandise would be a sound investment," he said.

奇祸 qíhuò　an unexpected disaster

奇计 qíjì　same as 奇谋 qímóu

奇技 qíjì　special skill or feat

奇迹 qíjì　miracle; wonder; marvel: 医学上的～ a marvel of medical science

奇景 qíjǐng　wonderful view; extraordinary sight: 冰峰～ a wonderful view of ice-capped peaks

奇绝 qíjué　*formal* unsurpassably wonderful: 怪石嶙峋，山势～ jagged grotesque rock formations lending enchantment to the mountain

奇崛 qíjué　*formal* unusual; outstanding: 文笔～ an unusual style of writing

奇门 qímén　the magic skill of being invisible

奇妙 qímiào　marvellous; wonderful; intriguing

奇谋 qímóu　a very clever strategy; an ingenius plan

奇男子 qínánzǐ　a remarkable man

奇南香 qínánxiāng　another name for 沉香 chénxiāng

奇女子 qínǚzǐ　a remarkable woman

奇葩 qípā　exotic flowers: ～斗妍 exotic flowers vying for glamour / 文苑～ exotic flowers in the garden of literature—unusual literary works

奇癖 qípǐ　an eccentric habit; a curious hobby

奇僻 qípì　① very uncommon; very rare ② exotic; bizarre

奇巧 qíqiǎo　(of art or handicraft) ingenious; exquisite

奇趣 qíqù　unusual charm

奇缺 qíquē　in great shortage

奇人 qírén　① an eccentric person; eccentric ② a person of unusual ability

奇事 qíshì　a strange affair; an unusual phenomenon

奇书 qíshū　a remarkable book

奇谈 qítán　a strange tale; an absurd argument: 海外～ strange tales from over the seas

奇谈怪论 qítán-guàilùn　a strange tale; an absurd argument

奇特 qítè　peculiar; queer; singular: 在沙漠地区常常可以看到一些～的景象。In desert areas one often sees strange mirages.

奇突 qítū　① sudden; unexpected ② peculiar; distinctive ③ protruding; projecting; sticking out

奇文 qíwén　① a remarkable piece of writing ② absurd writing

奇文共欣赏 qíwén gòng xīnshǎng (also 奇文共赏 qíwén gòng shǎng) share the pleasure of reading a rare piece of writing: ～，疑义相与析。(陶潜) A remarkable work should be shared and its subtleties discussed.

奇闻 qíwén sth. unheard-of; a thrilling, fantastic story

奇袭 qíxí surprise attack; raid

奇效 qíxiào extraordinary efficacy (of medicine)

奇形怪状 qíxíng-guàizhuàng grotesque or fantastic in shape or appearance: ～的钟乳石 stalactites of grotesque shapes

奇勋 qíxūn formal outstanding service; outstanding contribution

奇验 qíyàn ① extraordinary efficacy (of medicine) ② miraculous accuracy (in fortune-telling)

奇异 qíyì ① unusual; strange; bizarre: ～的动物 rare animals ② surprised; amazed; astonished; astounded: 他们都用～的眼光看着我。They all looked at me with astounded eyes.

奇遇 qíyù ① happy encounter; fortuitous meeting ② adventure

奇缘 qíyuán relationship entered into unexpectedly; romance

奇珍 qízhēn a rarity or curio

奇珍异宝 qízhēn-yìbǎo rare treasures

奇志 qízhì high aspirations; lofty ideal

奇装异服 qízhuāng-yìfú exotic costume; bizarre dress; outlandish clothes

歧 qí ① fork; branch: 歧路 qílù ② divergent; different: 歧义 qíyì

歧出 qíchū (of the use of words, esp. technical terms in a book, etc.) conflicting and confusing; inconsistent

歧管 qíguǎn mech. manifold

歧黄 qíhuáng Chinese medicine (from 歧伯 and 黄帝, reputed founders of Chinese medicine): ～之术 Chinese traditional medical science

歧路 qílù branch road; forked road

歧路亡羊 qílù wáng yáng a lamb going astray at a fork in the road—go astray in a complex situation

歧视 qíshì discriminate against: 种族～ racial discrimination / ～妇女 discriminate against women

歧途 qítú wrong road: 被引入～ be led astray

歧义 qíyì being capable of various interpretations; ambiguity: 有～ be open to different interpretations; be equivocal / 写文章要避免产生～。One should try to avoid ambiguity in one's writing.

歧异 qíyì difference; discrepancy

荠(薺) qí see 荸荠 bíqi ——see also jì

俟 qí see 万俟 Mòqí ——see also sì

顾 qí formal tall

顾长 qícháng formal tall: 身材～ tall in build

旂 qí ① a kind of ancient banner ② banner; flag

耆 qí over sixty years of age; very old

耆艾 qí'ài formal elderly people

耆老 qílǎo formal elderly people

耆年硕德 qínián-shuòdé of venerable age and eminent virtue; of advanced years and noble character

耆绅 qíshēn formal elderly gentlemen

耆宿 qísù formal venerable old people (of a community)

脐(臍) qí ① navel; umbilicus ② the abdomen of a crab

脐带 qídài umbilical cord

脐风 qífēng Chin. med. umbilical tetanus

淇 Qí ① (also 淇河) a river in Henan Province ② (qí) see 冰淇淋 bīngqílín

其 qí dial. beanstalk: 豆萁 dòuqí

畦 qí rectangular pieces of land in a field, separated by ridges, usu. for growing vegetables: 我们种了两～萝卜。We've grown two beds of radishes.

畦灌 qíguàn agric. border method of irrigation

畦田 qítián an embanked field

崎 qí see below

崎岖 qíqū rugged: 山路～不平。The mountain path is rugged and uneven. / 学习的道路是～不平的。The road of learning is not smooth.

骑 qí ① ride (an animal or bicycle, etc.); sit on the back of: ～马 ride a horse; be on horseback / ～车回家 go home by bicycle / 善～ excel in horsemanship; be a good rider / 这摩托车你～得怎么样? How do you get on with the motorcycle? / 车太高，我女儿～不上去。The bicycle is too high for my daughter to ride. / 坡儿太陡，车～不上去。The slope is too steep to cycle uphill. / ～在人民头上作威作福 ride roughshod over the people ② horse or horse rider: 坐骑 zuòqí ③ cavalry-man; cavalry: 铁骑 tiěqí

骑兵 qíbīng cavalryman; cavalry

骑兵部队 qíbīng bùduì mounted troops; cavalry unit

骑缝 qífèng a junction of the edges of two sheets of paper: 在单据的～上盖印 put a seal across the perforation between the two halves of a voucher

骑虎难下 qí hǔ nán xià he who rides a tiger is afraid to dismount—irrevocably but unwillingly committed; unable to extricate oneself from a difficult situation

骑虎之势 qí hǔ zhī shì a case of one riding a tiger—an awkward predicament that one can neither manage nor get rid of

骑楼 qílóu dial. (overhead) terrace: ～底 arcade

骑马订 qímǎdìng print. saddle stitching

骑马找马 qí mǎ zhǎo mǎ ① sit on one horse and look for another—hold on to one job while seeking another ② sit on the very horse one is looking for—look for sth. that's right under one's nose

骑墙 qíqiáng sit on the fence: ～派 fence-sitter

骑射 qíshè horsemanship and archery: 善～ excel in horsemanship and archery

骑士 qíshì knight; cavalier

骑手 qíshǒu a good rider; horseman

骑术 qíshù horsemanship; equestrian skill

骐 qí formal a black horse

骐骥 qíjì formal a fine horse; steed

琦 qí formal ① fine jade ② outstanding; distinguished; admirable

琪 qí formal fine jade

祺 qí formal auspicious; lucky

棋(棊、碁) qí chess or any board game: 下一盘～ play a game of chess

棋布 qíbù scattered all over like men on a chessboard; spread all over the place

棋锋 qífēng brilliance shown in playing chess: ～犀利 be a brilliant chess player

棋逢对手 qí féng duìshǒu (also 棋逢敌手 qí féng díshǒu)

meet one's match in a game of chess—be well-matched in a contest: ～难相胜，将遇良才不敢骄。When a general meets a worthy opponent, he won't dare to underestimate him. *or* When players of equal skill are matched, then victory hovers between; Perhaps your opponent's a genius, so put on your lowliest mien.

棋高一着 qí gāo yī zhāo　be superior to one's opponent (in chess or otherwise); outmatch one's opponent

棋局 qíjú　① a game of chess as it develops ② *old* chessboard

棋路 qílù　chess tactics: ～高明 brilliant chess tactics

棋迷 qímí　chess fan; chess enthusiast

棋盘 qípán　chessboard; checkerboard

棋谱 qípǔ　chess manual

棋圣 qíshèng　champion chess player; grand master

棋手 qíshǒu　chess player

棋坛 qítán　chess circles

棋艺 qíyì　skill in playing chess: ～精湛 be a chess expert

棋友 qíyǒu　fellow chess player; chess friend

棋苑 qíyuàn　chess circles

棋峙 qízhì　*formal* be locked in a stalemate; each sticks to his own stand

棋子 qízǐ　piece (in a board game); chessman

蛴（蠐）　qí　see below

蛴螬 qícáo　grub

旗¹（旂）　qí　flag; banner; standard: 旗杆上挂着一面～。A flag is attached to the pole.

旗²　qí　① of the "Eight Banners"（八旗）: 在旗 zàiqí ② banner, an administrative division of county level in the Inner Monggol Autonomous Region: 阿巴嘎～ the Abga Banner

旗杆 qígān　flagpole; flag post

旗鼓相当 qí-gǔ xiāngdāng　be matched in strength; be well-matched: 这两个队～，打得十分激烈。The two teams were well-matched and the game was hotly contested. / ～的对手 an opponent worthy of one's steel

旗号 qíhào　*derog.* banner; flag: 打着…的～ flaunt the banner of…

旗舰 qíjiàn　flagship

旗开得胜 qí kāi déshèng　win victory the moment one's standard is raised; win victory in the first battle; win speedy success: 我军在南进中～，声威大震。In its southward drive our army won victory as soon as its banner was displayed and thus gained resounding fame.

旗袍 qípáo　a close-fitting woman's dress with high neck and slit skirt; cheongsam; mandarin gown

旗人 Qírén　① a member of any one of the "Eight Banners"（八旗）during the Qing Dynasty; bannerman ② the Manchus: 他是～。He is a Manchu.

旗绳 qíshéng　halyard

旗手 qíshǒu　standard-bearer: 鲁迅是新文化运动的伟大～。Lu Xun was a great standard-bearer of the New Culture Movement.

旗鱼 qíyú　sailfish

旗语 qíyǔ　semaphore; flag signal: 打～ signal by semaphore; semaphore

旗帜 qízhì　① banner; flag: 五彩缤纷的～迎风飘扬。Colourful flags are fluttering in the breeze. / 近几年来，这个厂一直是工业战线上的一面～。In recent years, this factory has served as a banner on the industrial front. ② stand; colours

旗帜鲜明 qízhì xiānmíng　have a clear-cut stand: 我们必须坚持真理，而真理必须～。（毛泽东）We must firmly uphold the truth, and truth requires a clear-cut stand.

旗装 qízhuāng　Manchu attire

旗子 qízi　flag; banner; pennant

蜞　qí　see 蟛蜞 péngqí

綦　qí　*formal* very; extremely: 希望～切 cherish high hopes

蕲（蘄）　qí　*formal* beg; seek

蕲求 qíqiú　*formal* earnestly hope; pray for

鲯　qí　see below

鲯鳅 qíqiū　dorado; dolphinfish

鳍　qí　fin

鳍脚 qíjiǎo　clasper

鳍脚动物 qíjiǎo dòngwù　Pinnipedia; pinniped

麒　qí　see below

麒麟 qílín　*kylin*; (Chinese) unicorn

麒麟座 Qílínzuò　*astron.* Monoceros

qǐ

乞　qǐ　beg (for alms, etc.); supplicate: 行乞 xíngqǐ

乞哀告怜 qǐ'āi-gàolián　beg for mercy; piteously beg for help

乞贷 qǐdài　*formal* beg for a loan

乞丐 qǐgài　beggar

乞力马扎罗山 Qǐlìmǎzhāluóshān　Kilimanjaro

乞怜 qǐlián　beg for pity (*or* mercy)

乞灵 qǐlíng　*formal* resort to; seek help from: ～于谣言和诡辩 resort to rumourmongering and sophistry

乞盟 qǐméng　sue for peace

乞免 qǐmiǎn　beg for forgiveness: ～一死 beg for one's life

乞巧 qǐqiǎo　begging for cleverness (a women's festival formerly held on the seventh evening of the seventh month when young girls made offerings to the Weaving-girl 织女 and asked for her divine aid in perfecting their needlework skills)

乞求 qǐqiú　beg for; supplicate; implore: ～宽恕 beg for mercy (*or* pardon) / ～的目光 an imploring look / 她～他饶了自己的儿子。She implored him to spare her son.

乞师 qǐshī　*formal* ask for military help or troop reinforcement

乞食 qǐshí　beg for food

乞讨 qǐtǎo　beg; go begging: 沿街～ go begging from door to door

乞降 qǐxiáng　beg to surrender

乞援 qǐyuán　ask for assistance; beg for aid

岂（豈）　qǐ　*adv. formal* (used to ask a rhetorical question): 这样做～不更实际些? Wouldn't it be more practical to do it this way? / 一国的内政～容别国干涉? How can a country tolerate external interference in its internal affairs?

岂但 qǐdàn　*conj.* not only: 这个僻字～我们不认识，恐怕连老教授们也未必知道。Not only we don't know this obsolete character, even the old professors may not know it.

岂非 qǐfēi　*adv.* (used to ask a rhetorical question): 这样解释～自相矛盾? Wouldn't it be self-contradictory to put it that way?

岂敢 qǐgǎn　*pol.* you flatter me; I don't deserve such

praise or honour

岂能 qǐnéng (also 岂可 qǐkě) adv. (used to ask a rhetorical question): ～不辞而别? How could you leave without saying good-bye? / ～容许这种行为? How could such behaviour be tolerated?

岂有此理 qǐ yǒu cǐ lǐ preposterous; outrageous; absurd: 这个破录音机要那么多钱, 真是～! This lousy tape-recorder is outrageously expensive.

岂止 qǐzhǐ same as 岂但 qǐdàn

企 qǐ ① stand on tiptoe ② anxiously expect sth.; look forward to

企待 qǐdài expect; await; look forward to

企鹅 qǐ'é penguin

企及 qǐjí hope to reach; hope to attain ——see also 不可企及 bùkě qǐjí

企口 qǐkǒu archit. tongue-and-groove: ～接合 tongue-and-groove joint; T and G connection

企口板 qǐkǒubǎn archit. matched board

企慕 qǐmù admire; look up to

企盼 qǐpàn hope for; look forward to; long for

企求 qǐqiú desire to gain; seek for; hanker after: 他一心只想把工作做好, 从不～个人名利。 All he wanted was to do his job well; he never sought personal gain.

企图 qǐtú attempt; try; seek: 敌军～突围, 但未得逞。 The enemy failed in his attempt to effect a breakthrough. / ～掩盖事实 try to conceal the facts / ～推翻政府 seek to overthrow the government / 在这部作品中, 作者～表现的主题并不突出。 The theme which the author has intended to bring forth in the book does not stand out. / 别有～ have an ulterior motive

企望 qǐwàng hope for; look forward to: 我们都～有一个持久的和平。 We all hope for an enduring peace. / 这是我们多年所～的。 This is what we have been looking forward to for years.

企羡 qǐxiàn admire; look up to

企业 qǐyè enterprise; business: 工矿～ factories, mines and other enterprises / ～管理 business management / ～结构 the line-up of enterprises / ～自主权 the power of decision of enterprises

企业化 qǐyèhuà run an enterprise on a commercial basis

企业集团 qǐyè jítuán enterprise group

企业家 qǐyèjiā entrepreneur; big businessman

企足而待 qǐ zú ér dài same as 翘足而待 qiáo zú ér dài

启(啟、啓) qǐ ① open: ～门 open a door / 幕～。 The curtain rises. / 某某～ To be opened by so-and-so——To so-and-so (written on an envelope of a personal letter) ② start; initiate: 启行 qǐxíng ③ enlighten; awaken: 启发 qǐfā ④ formal state; inform: 某某～ by so-and-so (closing words of a letter) ⑤ formal letter; note: 谢启 xièqǐ

启禀 qǐbǐng report (to one's superior)

启程 qǐchéng set out; start on a journey: 代表团已于昨日～赴日内瓦。 The delegation left for Geneva yesterday.

启齿 qǐchǐ (also 启唇 qǐchún; 启口 qǐkǒu) open one's mouth; start to talk about sth.: 我想问他借钱, 但又觉得难以～。 I wanted to borrow money from him but found it difficult to bring the matter up.

启迪 qǐdí formal enlighten; inspire: 我从这个残疾人取得的成就中得到～。 The achievement of the disabled person was an inspiration to me.

启碇 qǐdìng weigh anchor; set sail

启动 qǐdòng start (a machine, etc.); switch on: 这车没法儿～。 The car won't start.

启发 qǐfā arouse; inspire; enlighten: ～阶级觉悟 arouse class consciousness / 他常用这种方式～我们思考问题。 He often inspires us to ponder over questions this way. / 要用～的方式讲课。 You should teach with the elicitation method. / 我从他的工作方法中得到～。 I derived inspiration from his working method. / 老科学家的报告给了我们很多～。 The old scientist's lecture greatly inspired us. / ～性报告 an enlightening lecture

启发式 qǐfāshì elicitation method (of teaching); heuristic method

启封 qǐfēng ① unseal; break (or remove) the seal ② open an envelop or wrapper

启航 qǐháng set sail; weigh anchor: 这艘货轮什么时候～? When does the freighter set sail? / 那艘货轮已～去英国了。 The freighter has set sail for England.

启蒙 qǐméng ① impart rudimentary knowledge to beginners; initiate: ～老师 the teacher who introduces one to a certain field of study / ～课本 children's primer / 我做格律诗是他启的蒙。 He was the teacher who introduced me to classical poetic composition. ② enlighten; free sb. from prejudice or superstition

启蒙运动 Qǐméng Yùndòng the Enlightenment

启明星 Qǐmíngxīng literary name for 金星 Jīnxīng

启示 qǐshì enlightenment; inspiration; revelation: 从他的经验中得到很多～ gain a good deal of enlightenment from his experience; draw great inspiration from his experience / 爱因斯坦的故事给了我很大的～。 The story of Einstein is a great inspiration to me.

启事 qǐshì notice; announcement: 征稿～ a notice inviting contributions (to a magazine, newspaper, etc.) / 寻物～ Lost / 招领～ Found

启衅 qǐxìn start a quarrel; provoke discord; provoke dispute: 两次世界大战都是德国军国主义者首先～的。 Both of the World Wars were instigated by a militarist Germany.

启行 qǐxíng set off on a journey

启颜 qǐyán (of a person's face) light up; smile; beam

启用 qǐyòng start using (an official seal, etc.)

启运 qǐyùn start shipment (of goods)

启奏 qǐzòu present a memorial to an emperor

杞 Qǐ ① a surname ② the name of an ancient kingdom

杞柳 qǐliǔ purple willow; bitter willow (Salix sinopurpurea)

杞人忧天 Qǐ rén yōu tiān like the man of Qi who feared that the sky might fall——entertain imaginary or groundless fears: 这岂不是～吗? Isn't this a case of the man of Qi worrying lest the sky fall? / 事情未必如他所说的那么可怕, 也许完全是～。 Things may not be as bad as he says. Maybe he is merely imagining things.

起¹ qǐ ① rise; get up; stand up: ～席 rise from the table / 早睡早～ early to bed and early to rise ② remove; extract; pull: ～油 remove grease stains / ～瓶塞 pull the cork from a bottle / ～钉子 draw out a nail / ～雷 clear mines / 把画～下来 take down a picture ③ appear; raise: 脚上～水泡 get blisters on one's feet ④ rise; grow: ～风了。 The wind is rising. / ～疑心 become suspicious / ～作用 take effect ⑤ draft; work out: ～稿子 work out (or make) a draft ⑥ build; set up: ～一堵墙 build a wall / ～伙 set up a mess ⑦ start; begin: 从今天～ starting from today ⑧ draw; get: ～护照 get one's passport ⑨ (used after a verb preceded by 从 or 由): 从头儿讲～ tell the story from the very beginning / 从何说～? What shall I say? or What's there to say? ⑩ prep. dial. from: ～这儿往北 go north from here ⑪ prep. dial. by: 我见他～窗外走过。 I saw him going by the window.

起² qǐ m. ① case; instance: 两～大脑炎 two

cases of cerebritis ② batch; group: 分两～出发 set out in two groups (*or* batches)

起

．．．qǐ (used after a verb) ① upwards; up: 她拿～皮包就走了。 She picked up her handbag and left. ／ 我提不～这个重箱子。 I can't lift this heavy suitcase. ／ 拿～武器 take up arms ② (preceded by 得 *or* 不) up to a certain standard: 买得(不)～ can (can't) afford to buy ／ 看得(不)～ have a high (low) opinion of

起岸 qǐ'àn bring (cargo, etc. from a ship) to land

起霸 qǐbà (in traditional operas) a series of stereotyped movements by military characters before going to action

起爆 qǐbào detonate: 准时～ detonate on time ／ ～帽 detonating cap ／ ～剂 detonating agent; primer

起笔 qǐbǐ ① the first stroke of a Chinese character ② start a stroke in writing a Chinese character: ～的时候要顿一顿。 One should pause when starting a stroke (of a Chinese character).

起兵 qǐbīng dispatch troops

起驳 qǐbó start shipment by lighter

起步 qǐbù start; move: 车子～了。 The car started. ／ 我国电视事业～虽晚，但发展速度不慢。 Although the television industry got off to a late start in China, the speed of development has not been slow. ／ 这项研究尚属刚刚～阶段。 This research programme is still in its beginning stages. ／ 沿海开放城市如何起好步? How will the open coastal cities get a good start?

起草 qǐcǎo make a draft; draft; draw up: ～文件 draft (*or* draw up) a document ／ ～人 draftsman ／ 这封信你来起个草吧。 Please make a draft copy of the letter.

起草委员会 qǐcǎo wěiyuánhuì drafting committee

起承转合 qǐ-chéng-zhuǎn-hé introduction, elucidation of the theme, transition to another viewpoint, and summing up—the four steps in composing an essay

起程 qǐchéng leave; set out; start on a journey: 日内～前往广州 leave for Guangzhou in a day or two

起初 qǐchū *adv.* originally; at first; at the outset: ～我不同意他的做法，后来才觉得他是有道理的。 At first I didn't agree with his way of doing things, but later I realized that he was right. ／ 这个工厂～很小。 The factory was originally very small. ／ ～他一个字也不认识，现在已经能够写信了。 At first he couldn't read and write, but now he can even carry on a correspondence.

起床 qǐchuáng get up; get out of bed: 他们已经～了。 They are already up. ／ 我习惯六点～。 I am in the habit of getting up at six o'clock. ／ 起了床还想睡。 After I got up I still felt like going back to sleep.

起床号 qǐchuánghào reveille: 吹～ sound the reveille

起道机 qǐdàojī *railway* track jack

起点 qǐdiǎn ① starting point: 把成绩作为继续前进的新～ take achievements as starting points for further progress ② starting point (for a race)

起点运费 qǐdiǎn yùnfèi minimum freight; minimum charge per bill of lading

起电 qǐdiàn electrification; charge: ～盘 electrophorus

起吊 qǐdiào lift by crane

起钉钳 qǐdīngqián nail puller

起碇 qǐdìng weigh anchor

起动 qǐdòng (of a train, machine, etc.) start: 我们到达车站时，火车正好～。 We arrived at the station just as the train was leaving.

起动机 qǐdòngjī starter

起端 qǐduān origin or beginning (of an event, etc.)

起飞 qǐfēi ① (of aircraft) take off: ～全重 all-up weight ② *econ.* takeoff: 经济～ economic takeoff ／ 沿海城市的经济迅速～。 The economies of the coastal cities got off to a flying start.

起伏 qǐfú rise and fall; undulate: 凝望远处山峦～ gaze at the mountain ranges rising and falling in the distance ／ 微风中麦浪～ a field of wheat undulating in the breeze ／ 心潮～ one's mind being in a tumult

起稿 qǐgǎo make a draft; draft; draw up: 报告是他起的稿。 He's the one who drafted the report.

起根 qǐgēn *inf.* from the very first; all along; at all times; always: 这桩婚事我～儿就不同意。 I was against this marriage from the start.

起更 qǐgēng begin to sound the night watches

起旱 qǐhàn *old* travel by land (usu. on foot or by old means of transport)

起航 qǐháng set sail; weigh anchor

起哄 qǐhòng ① (of a crowd of people) create a disturbance: 起什么哄啊! 都排好队一个个来。 What's all the disturbance about! Everyone line up and take turns. ② (of a crowd of people) jeer; boo and hoot; tease clamorously

起火 qǐhuǒ ① catch fire; be on fire: 房子～啦! The house is on fire! ② cook meals: 他不愿意自己～，在食堂吃。 He doesn't want to do his own cooking. So he takes his meals in the cafeteria. ③ *dial.* get angry; flare up: 你别～，听我慢慢地对你说。 Don't get all worked up. Listen while I give you the whole story.

起火 qǐhuo (also 起花 qǐhuā) a kind of firecracker

起货 qǐhuò take goods (from a warehouse); unload (from a ship, etc.)

起获 qǐhuò track down and recover stolen goods, etc.

起急 qǐjí *dial.* get impatient; lose one's patience: 和老人说话不能～。 You shouldn't lose your patience when talking to old people.

起家 qǐjiā build up; grow and thrive; make one's fortune, name, etc.: 这个大工厂是靠一台旧机床起的家。 The big factory has built itself up by starting with an old machine tool.

起见 qǐjiàn *part.* (used in the pattern 为…起见 indicating purpose): 为醒目～，请排黑体字。 In order to make it stand out clearly, please print it in boldface type.

起降 qǐ-jiàng (of aircraft) take off and land

起解 qǐjiè *old* (of a prisoner) be sent to a place under guard

起劲 qǐjìn vigorous; energetic; enthusiastic: 干得很～ work very energetically ／ 孩子们～地学骑车。 The children enthusiastically learned to ride a bicycle.

起敬 qǐjìng show respect

起居 qǐjū daily life: ～有恒有助于身体健康。 To lead a regular life is conducive to good health. ／ 孩子在托儿所饮食～都有规律。 Life in a nursery provides children with a strict daily regimen.

起居室 qǐjūshì living room; sitting room

起句 qǐjù first line of a poem

起圈 qǐjuàn remove manure from a pigsty, sheepfold, etc.

起开 qǐkai *dial.* step aside; stand aside: 你～，这个菜让我来做。 You step aside and let me cook this dish.

起课 qǐkè start session in divination by tossing coins, etc.

起来 qǐ·lái ① stand up; sit up; rise to one's feet: 你～吃药吧。 Sit up and take your medicine. ／ 有个小伙子～给老太太让了个座儿。 A youngster stood up and offered his seat to the old lady. ② get up; get out of bed: 他们一～就下地了。 They went to work in the fields as soon as they got up. ③ rise; arise; revolt: ～反抗压迫 rise against oppression ／ ～，饥寒交迫的奴隶! Arise, ye prisoners of starvation! ／ ～捍卫真理 come forward in defence of truth

起来 ·qǐ·lái (used after a verb or adjective) ① upwards; up: 拿～ pick up ／ 病人能坐～了吗? Can the patient sit

up? / 中国人民站～了。 The Chinese people have stood up. / 他把孩子抱～。 He took the child up in his arms. / 举起手来! Hands up! ② start to; become: 他忽然哭～了。 He suddenly started to cry. / 他胖～了。 He's getting fat. / 热～了。 It's getting hot. / 下起雨来了。 It's starting to rain. / 那回事情，你一提～我就生气。 Every time you (start to) mention that incident I get angry. / 他这句话使我们大笑～。 This remark of his set us roaring with laughter. ③ (indicating completeness or effectiveness): 加～ add up / 锁～ lock up / 存～ store away / 合唱团组织～了。 The chorus has been organized. / 他的名字我记不～了。 I can't remember his name. / 想～了，这是杜甫的诗句。 I've got it. It's a line from Du Fu. ④ when one comes to: 看～要下雨。 It looks like rain. / 看～是不会有什么问题的。 By the look of it there won't be any problems. / 听～颇有道理。 It sounds quite reasonable. ⑤ (forming a verbal topic): 说～容易，做～难。 It's easier said than done.

起雷 qǐléi clear or sweep mines

起立 qǐlì stand up; rise to one's feet: ～欢迎 rise to welcome sb. / 全体～! Everybody stand up!

起立表决 qǐlì biǎojué vote by sitting and standing

起灵 qǐlíng move a coffin or the ashes of the dead to a burial place

起垄 qǐlǒng *agric.* ridge: ～犁 ridging plough; ridger

起落 qǐluò rise and fall: 飞机～ the takeoff and landing of an aircraft / 心潮～ one's mind being in a tumult

起落架 qǐluòjià landing gear (of a plane); undercarriage: ～放下 gear down; landing gear lowering / ～收上 gear up; landing gear raising

起码 qǐmǎ ① minimum; rudimentary; elementary: ～的要求 minimum requirements / ～的知识 rudimentary knowledge; elementary knowledge / 国际关系中最～的准则 the most rudimentary principles governing international relations / 最～的生活必需品 the bare necessities of life ② *adv.* at least: 这项工程～要到五月才能完成。 This project can't be completed until May at the earliest. / 参加测验的～有三千人。 At least 3,000 people took the test. / 你～应该跟他打个招呼。 You should at least have let him know about it. / 这是一个革命者～应该具备的条件。 This is the very least one expects of a revolutionary. / 这一箱～二百公斤。 This box must weigh at least 200 kilos. / 饭菜不算很好，～可以这样说。 The food wasn't very good, to say the least. / 你今天动身，最～星期三才能到那里。 If you leave today, you'll get there on Wednesday at the earliest.

起毛 qǐmáo (of woollen cloth) pill: 海军呢爱～。 Navy cloth pills easily.

起锚 qǐmáo weigh anchor; set sail

起名儿 qǐmíngr give a name; name: 他们还没给孩子～呢。 They haven't given their baby a name yet.

起腻 qǐnì *inf.* ① feel sick: 我看见肥肉就～。 I feel sick whenever I see fat meat. / 他的长篇大论真叫人～。 He bored everyone with his lengthy speech. ② pester; annoy: 你少跟我～。 Stop pestering me with your silly questions. / 这孩子老爱跟人～。 What a little torment that child is!

起跑 qǐpǎo *sports* start of a race: ～线 starting line (for a race); scratch line (for a relay race) / ～信号 starting signal / 在跑道上练～ practise starts on a running track

起讫 qǐqì the beginning and the end: 本书每篇各有头尾，自成～。 Each chapter is complete in itself, having beginning and end. / 展览会的～日期为五月一日到二十日。 The exhibition lasts from May first to 20th.

起色 qǐsè improvement; pickup: 她工作最近很有～。 Recently there's been a great improvement in her work. / 在她们照顾下，他的病有了～。 Thanks to their care his health has really picked up. / 经济情况有了很

大的～。 The economy has picked up greatly.

起身 qǐshēn ① get up; get out of bed: 他每天～后就做操。 He exercises everyday after getting up. ② leave; set out; get off: 我将于下周～去重庆。 I'll leave for Chongqing next week.

起始 qǐshǐ *inf.* ① originate; stem from: 她喜欢花～于童年乡居期间。 Her interest in flowers stems from her childhood in the country. ② *adv.* at first; in the beginning: ～我不喜欢他，但很快改变了看法。 At first I didn't like him, but I soon changed my mind.

起事 qǐshì start armed struggle; rise in rebellion

起誓 qǐshì take an oath; swear: ～决不泄漏秘密。 He swore that he would not divulge the secret. / 你起个誓决不再喝酒! Swear that you'll never drink again!

起手 qǐshǒu put one's hand to; set about

起手回春 qǐshǒu huí chūn same as 妙手回春 miàoshǒu huí chūn

起首 qǐshǒu *adv.* at first; in the beginning; originally: ～我不会下棋。 I didn't know how to play chess at first.

起死回生 qǐsǐ-huíshēng (of a doctor's skill) bring the dying back to life; snatch a patient from the jaws of death; raise sb. from the dead

起诉 qǐsù bring a suit (*or* an action) against sb.; sue; prosecute: ～人 suitor; prosecutor / ～书 indictment; bill of complaint; bill of prosecution / ～意见书 opinion recommending prosecution / ～资格 standing to sue

起算 qǐsuàn reckon from (a stated point): 从现在～ reckon from the present

起跳 qǐtiào *sports* take off: ～板 take-off board / ～线 take-off line (*or* mark)

起头[1] qǐtóu start; originate: 这件事是谁起的头? Who started all this? / 我想织毛衣，可不会～。 I want to knit a sweater, but I don't know how to begin.

起头[2] qǐtóu ① at first; in the beginning: ～她答应来的，后来有别的事不能来了。 At first she promised to come but then had another engagement and couldn't make it. ② beginning: 我没听清楚，你从～儿再说一遍。 I didn't get what you said. Say it all over again from the beginning.

起网 qǐwǎng *fishery* (net) hauling: ～机 net hauler

起先 qǐxiān *adv.* at first; in the beginning: ～他反对，后来才同意了。 At first he was opposed to the idea, but later he came around.

起心 qǐxīn *derog.* cherish certain intentions: ～不良 cherish evil designs (*or* intentions)

起薪 qǐxīn probationary salary

起小儿 qǐxiǎor *dial.* since childhood: 他～身体就不好。 He's been weak in health since childhood.

起行 qǐxíng leave; set out; start on a journey: 我即将～。 I am leaving soon.

起眼 qǐyǎn (usu. used in the negative) attract attention: 不起眼 bùqǐyǎn

起夜 qǐyè get up in the night (to urinate): 少喝点水，免得～。 Don't drink so much, or you'll have to get up during the night.

起疑 qǐyí become suspicious: 他的行动令人～。 His activities aroused my suspicion.

起义 qǐyì rise in revolt; revolt: 农民～ a peasant uprising / 敌军纷纷～投诚。 Many enemy soldiers revolted and crossed over.

起义军 qǐyìjūn insurrectionary army

起意 qǐyì *derog.* conceive a design: 见财起意 jiàn cái qǐyì

起因 qǐyīn cause; origin: 事故的～ the cause of the accident

起用 qǐyòng ① reinstate (an official who has retired or been dismissed) ② call sb. to office; appoint sb. to an important position: 大胆～年轻干部 boldly place young

cadres in important positions

起源 qǐyuán ① originate; stem from: 一切知识均～于劳动。 All knowledge originates from labour. / 越剧～于浙江绍兴。 Shaoxing opera originated in the town of Shaoxing in Zhejiang Province. ② origin: 生命的～ the origin of life

起运 qǐyùn start shipment: 货物业已～。 The goods are on their way. / ～地点 starting place for shipping; place of dispatch

起赃 qǐzāng track down and recover stolen goods

起早贪黑 qǐzǎo-tānhēi (also 起早搭黑 qǐzǎo-dāhēi) start work early and knock off late; work from dawn to dusk

起重车 qǐzhòngchē derrick car

起重船 qǐzhòngchuán crane ship

起重机 qǐzhòngjī hoist; crane; derrick: ～的起重能力 the lifting (or hoisting) capacity of a crane / 龙门～ gantry crane / 塔式～ tower crane / 门式～ portal crane / 移动式转臂～ mobile jib crane

起皱 qǐzhòu wrinkle; crease; crumple: 多晒太阳皮肤就会干燥～。 Too much sun dries the skin and it begins to wrinkle. / 这种料子不～。 This material won't crease (or is crease-resistant). / 这种合成纤维折叠以后也不～。 This synthetic fabric won't crumple when folded.

起皱工艺 qǐzhòu gōngyì text. creping

起子[1] qǐzi ① bottle opener ② dial. baking powder ③ dial. screwdriver

起子[2] qǐzi m. batch; lot; group: 一～旅游者 a group of tourists

起坐间 qǐzuòjiān dial. living room; sitting room

绮

qǐ ① figured woven silk material; damask ② beautiful; gorgeous: 绮丽 qǐlì

绮丽 qǐlì beautiful; gorgeous: 春天的西湖显得格外～。 In spring the West Lake looks especially enchanting. / 生活在她面前放出～的光彩。 Life was beckoning her with its fascinating beauty.

绮年 qǐnián formal young; youthful: ～玉貌 (of a girl) young and beautiful

绮思 qǐsī formal beautiful thoughts (in literature)

稽

qǐ see below——see also jī

稽首 qǐshǒu kotow

qì

气（氣）

qì ① gas: 毒气 dúqì ② air: 这球～儿挺足。 There's sufficient air in the ball. / 自行车前带没～了。 The front tyre of the bike is flat. ③ breath: 停下来歇口～ stop and catch one's breath / 老太太已经没～了。 The old woman has stopped breathing. / 长跑运动员需要～儿长。 Long-distance runners require plenty of stamina. ④ smell; odour: 香气 xiāngqì ⑤ weather: 天气 tiānqì ⑥ airs; manner: 官气 guānqì ⑦ spirit; morale: 朝气 zhāoqì ⑧ get angry; be enraged; be annoyed: ～得直哆嗦 tremble with rage / ～哭了 be annoyed to tears / ～坏了 be beside oneself with rage / ～出一场病来 have an attack of illness caused by anger / 我～他工作太马虎。 I'm angry with him for being careless in his work. / 我不～别的，～他事先不通知我一声。 I'm annoyed with him simply because he didn't notify me beforehand. ⑨ make angry; enrage; annoy: 我故意～他一下。 I got him angry on purpose. or I was deliberately trying to annoy him. / 他就是想～～我。 He just wanted to annoy me. / 你别～我了! Stop annoying me! ⑩ bully; insult: 受气 shòuqì ⑪ Chin. med. vital energy; energy of life ⑫ Chin. med. certain symp-

toms (of diseases)

气昂昂 qì'áng'áng full of mettle; full of dash ——see also 雄赳赳，气昂昂 xióngjiūjiū, qì'áng'áng

气包子 qìbāozi inf. a person who has a quick temper or is quick to take offence

气泵 qìbèng air pump

气不打一处来 qì bù dǎ yīchù lái be filled with anger: 一看见他那流里流气的样子，我就～。 As soon as I saw him, with his cocky manner and sleazy ways, I was just filled with anger and disgust.

气不忿儿 qìbùfènr dial. ① be jealous; take other people's success badly ② unable to contain one's anger: 他这样胡搅蛮缠，我就是～。 I really can't put up with his unreasonableness.

气不过 qìbùguò cannot restrain one's anger; be beside oneself with rage: 我实在～，狠狠地说了他一顿。 I got mad and gave him a good talking-to.

气不平 qìbùpíng (also 气不公 qìbùgōng) be indignant over an injustice

气藏 qìcáng petroleum gas pool

气冲冲 qìchōngchōng furious; beside oneself with rage

气冲牛斗 qì chōng niú-dǒu anger shooting up to the skies—in a towering rage; furious

气冲霄汉 qì chōng xiāohàn dauntless; fearless

气喘 qìchuǎn asthma: 阵发性～ spasmodic asthma

气窗 qìchuāng transom (window); fanlight

气锤 qìchuí same as 空气锤 kōngqìchuí

气粗 qìcū ① rough; rude; boorish ② speak in a gruff voice

气促 qìcù gasp for breath; be out of breath

气垫 qìdiàn air cushion

气垫船 qìdiànchuán hovercraft

气顶 qìdǐng petroleum gas cap: ～驱动 gas-cap drive

气动 qìdòng pneumatic: ～工具 pneumatic tool

气度 qìdù ① bearing; manner: 相貌威武，～不凡 be extraordinarily dignified and impressive in appearance / 他下棋的时候，镇定从容，很有～。 When he plays chess, he is calm and collected. He really has presence. ② tolerance; magnanimity

气短 qìduǎn ① short of breath; panting: 快爬到山顶时，大家都感到～。 By the time we got near the top of the hill, we were all out of breath. ② discouraged; disheartened: 失败并没有使他～。 He was not discouraged by failure.

气氛 qìfēn surrounding feeling; atmosphere: 会谈是在亲切友好的～中进行的。 The talks were held in a cordial and friendly atmosphere. / 讨论会的～始终很热烈。 The atmosphere was lively throughout the discussion. / 他是在宗教～中长大的。 He was brought up in a religious atmosphere.

气愤 qìfèn indignant; furious: 对于这种蛮横态度，大家无不感到～。 Everybody was indignant at such an overbearing manner. / 他听了这种不三不四的话非常～。 On hearing these frivolous remarks he became furious.

气腹 qìfù med. ① pneumoperitoneum ② short for 人工气腹 réngōng qìfù

气概 qìgài lofty quality; mettle; spirit: 不畏强暴敢于斗争的英雄～ the heroic spirit of daring to struggle against brute force

气缸 qìgāng air cylinder; cylinder: ～套筒 cylinder sleeve

气割 qìgē mech. gas cutting

气根 qìgēn (also 气生根 qìshēnggēn) bot. aerial root

气功 qìgōng qigong, a system of deep breathing exercises: ～师 qigong master

气鼓鼓 qìgǔgǔ fuming with anger; foaming with rage; furious

气臌 qìgǔ Chin. med. distension of the abdomen caused by accumulation of gas due to dysfunction of

the spleen or to emotional factors

气管 qìguǎn windpipe; trachea: ～切开术 tracheotomy

气管炎 qìguǎnyán tracheitis

气贯长虹 qì guàn cháng hóng filled with a spirit as lofty as the rainbow spanning the sky; full of noble aspiration and daring

气焊 qìhàn gas welding

气候 qìhòu ① climate: 他离开了重庆，因为～不适应。He left Chongqing because the climate did not agree with him. ② situation; climate: 政治～ political climate

气候带 qìhòudài climate zone

气候图 qìhòutú climate chart

气候学 qìhòuxué climatology

气候志 qìhòuzhì climatography

气呼呼 qìhūhū in a huff; panting with rage: ～地离去 go off in a huff

气化 qìhuà gasify

气话 qìhuà words said in a fit of rage: 他说的是～。He just said it to vent his anger.

气急 qìjí gasp for breath; be out of breath

气急败坏 qìjí bàihuài flustered and exasperated; utterly discomfited: 他～地跑回来把发生的事情告诉我们。He ran back, panting and dismayed, to tell us what had happened.

气节 qìjié integrity; moral courage: 革命者坚贞不屈的～ the unyielding integrity of a revolutionary

气结 qìjié *formal* depressed; melancholy; gloomy

气井 qìjǐng *petroleum* gas well

气绝 qìjué stop breathing—die: 登时～身亡 die immediately

气厥 qìjué faint away; lose consciousness

气可鼓而不可泄 qì kě gǔ ér bùkě xiè morale should be boosted, not dampened

气孔 qìkǒng ① *bot.* stoma ② *zool.* spiracle ③ *metall.* gas hole ④ *archit.* air hole

气浪 qìlàng blast (of an explosion)

气瘰脖儿 qìleibór popular name for 甲状腺肿 jiǎzhuàngxiànzhǒng

气冷 qìlěng *mech.* air cooling: ～式发动机 air-cooled engine

气力 qìlì effort; energy; strength: 学习外国语要用很大的～才能学好。It takes a lot of effort to learn a foreign language well. / 我们得费很大～去完成这项工作。We'll have to exert great efforts to accomplish the task. / 他用出全身～向对手猛扑过去。He pounced on the adversary with all his strength. / 他不费什么～就办成了这事。He got it done easily. / 这事需要花费～。This will take a lot of doing.

气量 qìliàng tolerance; forbearance: ～大 broadminded; large-minded; magnanimous / ～小 narrowminded / ～大的人对这点小事是不会介意的。Broadminded people won't bother about such trifles.

气流 qìliú ① air current; airflow; airstream ② *phonet.* breath

气流纺纱 qìliú fǎngshā open-end spinning; jet spinning

气流干扰 qìliú gānrǎo interference in airflow

气流畸变 qìliú jībiàn flow distortion

气楼 qìlóu a small ventilation tower on the top of a roof

气轮机 qìlúnjī short for 燃气轮机 ránqìlúnjī

气煤 qìméi gas coal

气门 qìmén ① (air) valve of a tyre ② *zool.* spiracle; stigma

气门心 qìménxīn *inf.* ① valve inside ② valve rubber tube

气闷 qìmèn ① unhappy; worried; in low spirits ② feel suffocated (*or* oppressed)

气密 qìmì airtight; gastight; gasproof: ～接合 airtight joint / ～试验 air seal test (for an aircraft); leakage test

气囊 qìnáng ① (of birds) air sac ② gasbag (of an aerostat)

气恼 qìnǎo get angry; take offence; be ruffled: 我如果考试不及格，妈妈要～的。Mother will get angry if I don't pass the exam. / 她的话真叫我～。Her words really offended me.

气馁 qìněi become dejected; be discouraged; lose heart: 他多次遇到挫折，但从不～。He never lost heart despite repeated setbacks.

气逆 qìnì *Chin. med.* circulation of vital energy in the wrong direction

气派 qìpài imposing manner; dignified air: 那大会堂修建得好～。That meeting hall is really imposing. / 一家门面～的商店 a store that has an imposing facade / 他是个很有～的人。He has an impressive bearing.

气泡 qìpào air bubble; bubble

气喷 qìpēn *petroleum* gas blowout

气魄 qìpò ① boldness of vision; breadth of spirit; daring: 以无产阶级革命家的～ with a proletarian revolutionary's boldness of vision / 他办事很有～。He's very bold and decisive in doing things. ② imposing manner: 这首诗歌颂了黄河的伟大～。This poem praises the grandeur of the Huanghe River. / 西安大雁塔的～雄伟 The Greater Wild Goose Pagoda of Xi'an is a structure of imposing grandeur.

气枪 qìqiāng air gun; pneumatic gun

气球 qìqiú balloon: 彩色～ coloured balloon

气圈 qìquān ① *text.* balloon ② *meteorol.* aerosphere

气嗓 qìsǎng *dial.* windpipe; trachea

气色 qìsè complexion; colour: ～很好 have a rosy complexion; have a good colour / 她～不好，脸上没什么血色。She's very pale; there isn't much colour in her face. / 他休养了一段时间，～好多了。After taking time off to recuperate, he looks much healthier.

气盛 qìshèng ① overbearing; arrogant; aggressive ② (of writing) forceful; vigorous

气势 qìshì momentum; imposing manner: ～雄伟的长城 the imposing Great Wall / 排球队以不可阻挡的～，直落三局击败对手。The volleyball team overwhelmed their opponent in three straight games. / 他动不动就对别人横加指责，～逼人。He's always making unwarranted accusations against others. His manner is intolerably aggressive.

气势磅礴 qìshì pángbó of great momentum; powerful: 《黄河大合唱》～。The Yellow River Cantata is full of power and grandeur. / 民族解放运动的洪流～，奔腾向前。The tide of the national liberation movement is surging forward with great momentum.

气势汹汹 qìshì xiōngxiōng fierce; truculent; overbearing: 看起来～，实际上十分虚弱 fierce in appearance but feeble in reality

气数 qìshu destiny; fate: ～已尽 (of a dynasty or regime) be nearing its fated end

气死人 qìsǐrén driving one crazy; infuriating; exasperating: 这种事是气得死人的。That sort of thing can be very exasperating.

气态 qìtài ① *phys.* gaseous state ② *formal* manner; bearing; air

气体 qìtǐ gas: ～发生器 gas generator / ～分离器 gas separator

气体动力学 qìtǐ dònglìxué aerodynamics

气体力学 qìtǐ lìxué pneumatics

气体燃料 qìtǐ ránliào gaseous fuel

气田 qìtián gas field

气筒 qìtǒng inflator; bicycle pump

气头上 qìtóushang in a fit of anger; in a temper: 这是他～说的话，你不要在意。He said that in a fit of anger. Don't take it to heart. / 他正在～，谁的话都听不进去。

He's in a temper right now, and won't listen to anyone.

气团 qìtuán *meteorol.* air mass: 冷～ cold air mass / ～变性 air-mass modification

气吞山河 qì tūn shānhé imbued with a spirit that conquers mountains and rivers; full of daring

气味 qìwèi ① smell; odour; flavour: 有些花～浓郁。 Some flowers have strong fragrances. / ～难闻。 The smell is awful. ② *derog.* smack; taste: 这人满身的市侩～。 This man has the look of a sordid merchant written all over him. / 有沙文主义～ smack of chauvinism

气味相投 qìwèi xiāng tóu congenial to each other; be two of a kind

气温 qìwēn air temperature; atmospheric temperature

气息 qìxī ① breath ② flavour; smell: 一阵芬芳的～从花丛中吹过来。 A waft of sweet-smelling fragrance blew over from the flower bush. / 这个剧具有强烈的生活～。 The play has the rich flavour of life (*or* is imbued with a strong smack of everyday life). / 时代～ the flavour of the times

气息奄奄 qìxī yǎnyǎn be breathing feebly; be at one's last gasp; be at the point of death; be sinking fast: 老人病了半年, 现在已经是～了。 The old man has been ill for half a year and is about to breathe his last.

气象 qìxiàng ① meteorological phenomena: ～观测 meteorological observation ② meteorology ③ atmosphere; scene: 生气勃勃的新～ a new and dynamic atmosphere / 商店里很热闹, 已经有过年的～了。 The shops are very lively. They already have a New Year atmosphere.

气象火箭 qìxiàng huǒjiàn meteorological rocket

气象台 qìxiàngtái meteorological observatory

气象图 qìxiàngtú meteorological map

气象万千 qìxiàng wànqiān a scene majestic in all its variety: 远望群山, ～。 Far in the distance mountains rise range after range in all their majesty. / 予观夫巴陵胜状, 在洞庭一湖。衔远山, 吞长江, 浩浩汤汤, 横天际涯。朝晖夕阳, ～。(范仲淹) Now I have found that the finest sights of Baling are concentrated in the region of Lake Dongting. Dongting, nibbling at the distant hills and gulping down the Yangtse River, strikes all beholders as vast and infinite, presenting a scene of boundless variety.

气象卫星 qìxiàng wèixīng meteorological satellite; weather satellite

气象学 qìxiàngxué meteorology

气象预报 qìxiàng yùbào weather forecast: ～明天有雪。 The weather report forecasts snow for tomorrow.

气象员 qìxiàngyuán weatherman

气性 qìxing ① temperament; disposition ② bad temper: ～大 quick to take offence; hot-tempered

气汹汹 qìxiōngxiōng fuming with anger; foaming with rage; furious

气胸 qìxiōng *med.* ① pneumothorax ② short for 人工气胸 réngōng qìxiōng

气呼呼 qìxūxū (also 气咻咻 qìxiūxiū) panting; gasping for breath: 他慢跑了一公里, ～地直出汗。 After jogging a kilometre he was panting and sweating. / 他冲进屋去, ～地报告了这消息。 He dashed into the room and gasped out the message.

气虚 qìxū *Chin. med.* deficiency of vital energy

气旋 qìxuán *meteorol.* cyclone

气血辨证 qì-xuè biànzhèng *Chin. med.* analysing and differentiating the pathological condition according to the function of vital energy and the state of the blood

气压 qìyā atmospheric pressure; barometric pressure

气压表 qìyābiǎo barometer

气压沉箱 qìyā chénxiāng *archit.* pneumatic caisson

气眼 qìyǎn ① *archit.* air hole ② *metall.* gas hole

气焰 qìyàn *derog.* arrogance; bluster: ～万丈 be swollen with arrogance

气焰嚣张 qìyàn xiāozhāng be puffed up with pride

气宇 qìyǔ bearing; manner

气宇轩昂 qìyǔ xuān'áng ~ tall and imposing-looking: 身材高大, ～ tall and imposing-looking / 此人～, 不同流俗。 His dignified bearing marks him out from the common run of men.

气郁 qìyù *Chin. med.* obstruction of the circulation of vital energy

气运 qìyùn destiny; fate

气韵 qìyùn the spirit, character, tone, or style (in the broadest sense) of a work of art or literature: 人品既高矣, ～不得不高。(郭若虚) If a man's character is high, the tone of his work must inevitably be high. / 观画之妙, 先观～, 次观笔意、骨法、位置、傅染; 然后形似, 此六法也。(汤垕) The fine art of viewing a painting is to first look at its character; next look at its conception, brushwork, composition, and colouring; and after that at the formal likeness. These are the six methods. / "～生动" 论是中国艺术理论的基础。 The concept of "spirit-resonance life-movement" is the cornerstone of Chinese art theory.

气闸 qìzhá air (*or* pneumatic) brake

气质 qìzhì ① temperament; disposition ② qualities; makings: 他英勇无畏, 表现了革命者的～。 He is brave and fearless. He has the makings of a revolutionary.

气滞 qìzhì *Chin. med.* stagnation of the circulation of vital energy

气肿疽 qìzhǒngjū *animal husbandry* blackleg; black quarter

气壮如牛 qì zhuàng rú niú fierce as a bull: 表面上～, 实际上胆小如鼠 outwardly fierce as a bull, but inwardly timid as a mouse

气壮山河 qì zhuàng shānhé full of power and grandeur; magnificent: 一篇～的宣言 a magnificent manifesto

讫 qì ① settled; completed: 付讫 fùqì / 收讫 shōuqì ② end: 起讫 qǐqì

迄 qì ① up to; till: 迄今 qìjīn ② (used before 未 or 无) so far; all along: ～无音信。 We have received no information so far. / ～未见复。 Up to now we have received no reply.

迄今 qìjīn up to now; to this day; to date; so far: 人们～怀念着这些革命先烈。 To this day people still cherish the memory of these revolutionary martyrs. / 他的态度～并无明显的转变。 There has been no visible change in his attitude so far. / 事情～还没作出决定。 To date, the matter hasn't yet been decided.

汽 qì vapour; steam: 蒸汽 zhēngqì

汽车 qìchē automobile; motor vehicle; car: ～保险 automobile insurance / ～旅店 motor hotel; motel

汽车吊 qìchēdiào truck crane

汽车队 qìchēduì motor transport corps; fleet of cars or trucks

汽车工业 qìchē gōngyè auto industry

汽车库 qìchēkù garage

汽车制造厂 qìchē zhìzàochǎng automobile factory; motor works

汽船 qìchuán steamship; steamer

汽锤 qìchuí steam hammer: 龙门～ arch type steam hammer

汽灯 qìdēng gas lamp

汽笛 qìdí steam whistle; siren; hooter: 鸣～ sound a siren

汽缸 qìgāng *mech.* cylinder: ～组 cylinder block

汽锅 qìguō Yunnan steaming pot: ～鸡 steamed chick-

en, Yunnan style

汽化 qìhuà　vaporize: ～热 heat of vaporization

汽化器 qìhuàqì　① *mech.* carburettor: ～回火 backfiring in carburettor / ～主射口 carburettor main jet ② *chem.* vaporizer

汽机 qìjī　① another name for 蒸气机 zhēngqìjī ② short for 汽轮机 qìlúnjī

汽酒 qìjiǔ　light sparkling wine

汽轮发电机 qìlún fādiànjī　turbogenerator: 双水内冷～ turbogenerator with inner water-cooled stator and rotor

汽轮机 qìlúnjī　steam turbine

汽碾 qìniǎn　(also 汽碾子 qìniǎnzi) *mech.* steamroller

汽水 qìshuǐ　aerated water; soft drink; soda water

汽提 qìtí　*petroleum* strip: ～油 stripped oil / ～塔 stripping tower

汽艇 qìtǐng　motorboat

汽油 qìyóu　petrol; gasoline; gas: 航空～ aviation gasoline / 凝固～ napalm

弃（棄） qì　throw away; discard; abandon: 敌军～城而逃。The enemy abandoned the city and fled.

弃暗投明 qìàn-tóumíng　forsake darkness for light —leave the reactionary side and cross over to the side of progress

弃妇 qìfù　*old* an abandoned wife

弃官 qìguān　give up one's office; abandon official life

弃甲曳兵 qìjiǎ-yèbīng　(of routed troops) throw away armour and trail weapons: ～而走 flee pell-mell

弃旧图新 qìjiù-túxīn　turn over a new leaf: 我们对待在工作中犯过错误的人采取规劝态度，使之翻然改进，～。Our attitude towards any person who has made mistakes in his work should be one of persuasion in order to help him change and start afresh.

弃绝 qìjué　abandon; forsake; cast aside

弃取 qìqǔ　give up or take; abandon or adopt

弃权 qìquán　① abstain from voting: 八票赞成，三票反对，一票～ 8 votes for, 3 against, and 1 abstention ② *sports* waive the right (to play); forfeit

弃舍 qìshě　give up; abandon

弃世 qìshì　pass away; die

弃市 qìshì　(in ancient times) execution and exposure of the corpse in the marketplace; public execution: 偶语者～。People caught talking together were publicly executed (as is supposed to have been the case under the rule of the First Emperor of the Qin Dynasty).

弃邪归正 qì xié guī zhèng　same as 改邪归正 gǎi xié guī zhèng

弃养 qìyǎng　*formal euph.* lose one's parents

弃婴 qìyīng　① abandon a baby ② foundling

弃之可惜 qì zhī kěxī　hesitate to discard sth.; be unwilling to throw away ——see also 食之无味，弃之可惜 shí zhī wúwèi, qì zhī kěxī

弃之如敝屣 qì zhī rú bìxǐ　cast away like a pair of worn-out shoes

弃掷 qìzhì　cast aside; throw away

弃置 qìzhì　discard; throw aside: 这所老房子早就～不用了。This old house was abandoned long ago.

泣 qì　① weep; sob: 悲泣 bēiqì / 哭泣 kūqì ② tears: 饮泣 yǐnqì

泣不成声 qì bù chéng shēng　choke with sobs: 说到伤心处，她～。When she got to the saddest part of the story, her voice was choked with sobs.

泣诉 qìsù　accuse while weeping; accuse amid tears: 她～了这些年来所受的苦。She tearfully recounted the suffering she'd undergone in the past few years.

泣下如雨 qì xià rú yǔ　shed tears like rain; weep copious tears

妻 qì　*formal* marry a girl to a man: 以女～之 give one's daughter to sb. in marriage ——see also qī

呕 qì　*formal* repeatedly; again and again: ～来问讯 come repeatedly to ask for information ——see also jǐ

炁 qì　see 坎炁 kǎnqì

契（栔） qì　① *formal* engrave; carve ② contract; deed: 房契 fángqì ③ agree; get along well: 默契 mòqì / 投契 tóuqì

契丹 Qìdān　Qidan (Khitan), an ancient nationality in China

契合 qìhé　agree with; tally with; correspond to: 与进化论相～ agree with the theory of evolution

契机 qìjī　① *philos.* moment ② turning point; juncture: 当代青年思想变化的～ a turning point in the thinking of present-day youth

契据 qìjù　deed; contract; receipt

契友 qìyǒu　close friend; bosom friend

契约 qìyuē　contract; deed; charter

契纸 qìzhǐ　contract; deed

砌 qì　① build by laying bricks or stones: ～砖 lay bricks / ～墙 build a wall (with bricks, stones, etc.) / ～井壁 build shaft lining ② step: 雕栏玉砌 diāolán-yùqì

跂 qì　*formal* stand on tiptoe

跂望 qìwàng　*formal* stand on tiptoe to look forward to sb. or sth.

葺 qì　*formal* ① cover a roof with straw; thatch ② repair; mend: 修葺 xiūqì

碛 qì　① moraine ② desert

器（噐） qì　① implement; utensil; ware: 电器 diànqì ② organ: 生殖器 shēngzhíqì ③ capacity; talent: 器识 qìshí ④ think highly of (a person): 器重 qìzhòng

器材 qìcái　equipment; material: 照相～ photographic equipment / 线路～ line materials

器官 qìguān　organ; apparatus: 消化～ digestive organs / 呼吸～ respiratory apparatus

器件 qìjiàn　parts of an apparatus or appliance: 电子～ electronic device

器局 qìjú　*formal* intellectual and spiritual capacity

器具 qìjù　utensil; implement; appliance: 日用～ household utensils; articles of daily use

器量 qìliàng　tolerance: ～小 narrow-minded; petty

器皿 qìmǐn　household utensils; containers esp. for use in the house

器任 qìrèn　*formal* have a high regard for: 甚见～ be held in high regard

器识 qìshí　*formal* capability and judgment

器使 qìshǐ　give sb. work suited to his abilities; assign jobs to people according to their abilities

器物 qìwù　implements; utensils

器械 qìxiè　① apparatus; appliance; instrument: 体育～ sports apparatus / 光学～ optical instrument ② weapon

器械体操 qìxiè tǐcāo　gymnastics on or with apparatus

器用 qìyòng　① household utensils; articles of daily use ② *formal* a person with great potentialities

器宇 qìyǔ　*formal* bearing; deportment: ～不凡 have extraordinary poise

器宇轩昂 qìyǔ xuān'áng　have a dignified appearance

器乐 qìyuè　*mus.* instrumental music: ～曲 composi-

tion for an instrument

器质性 qìzhìxìng　organic: ～精神病 organic psychosis / ～耳聋 organic deafness

器重 qìzhòng　think highly of (one's juniors or subordinates); regard highly: 他工作能力强, 上级很～他。 He is a capable worker, and his superiors think highly of him.

憩(憇)　qì　*formal*　have a rest; rest: 小憩 xiǎoqì

憩息 qìxī　(also 憩歇 qìxiē) *formal*　have a rest; rest: 我们～片刻, 继续前进。We went on after a short rest.

qiā

揢　qiā　① pinch; nip: 你把玉米杈子～掉。Pinch off the side shoots of the maize. / 不要～花。Don't pick (*or* nip off) the flowers. / 请把烟卷～了。Stub out your cigarette, please. / 她～了我一把, 好疼。She pinched me, and it really hurt. ② clutch: 把人～死 choke sb. to death ③ *dial. m.* a handful, bunch, pinch, etc. of: 一～儿韭菜 a handful of chives

揢巴 qiāba　*dial.*　grasp with a tight fist—clamp down on; suppress; make things difficult

揢菜 qiācài　mung bean sprouts with both ends chopped off (a Chinese dish)

揢断 qiāduàn　nip off; cut off: ～电线 disconnect the wire / ～水源 cut off the water supply

揢尖儿 qiājiānr　① *agric.* topping; pinching: 地里的西红柿该～了。The tomato plants need topping now. ② oust sb. from office: 你别太突出了, 小心别人揢你的尖儿。Don't try to outshine others. They can oust you from office, mind you. ③ scrounge; squeeze

揢诀 qiājué　calculate on one's fingers (while chanting incantations)

揢丝 qiāsī　*arts & crafts*　wire inlay; filigree: 景泰蓝花瓶上的～ wire inlay on a *cloisonné* vase

揢算 qiāsuàn　count (*or* reckon) sth. on one's fingers: 他细心～第一列火车即将通过的时刻。He carefully figured out what time the first train would pass by.

揢头去尾 qiātóu-qùwěi　break off both ends; leave out the beginning and the end: 这把芹菜～剩下不多了。 With both ends chopped off, there's not much left of this bunch of celery. / 引用他这段话不能～。If you quote a passage from him, you should quote it in full, not leave out the beginning and the end.

揢腰 qiāyāo　(of a dress) have a waistline: 这连衣裙是～的。The dress has a waistline.

揢子 qiāzi　*dial. m.* a handful, bunch, pinch etc. of: 一～盐 a pinch of salt

袷　qiā　see below

袷袢 qiāpàn　Uygur or Tajik robe buttoning down the front

蕎　qiā　see 菝蕎 báqiā

qiá

拤　qiá　clutch with both hands

qiǎ

卡　qiǎ　① wedge; get stuck: 有东西～在抽屉里, 拿不出来。Something has got wedged inside the drawer, so I can't pull it out. / 鱼刺～在他的嗓子里。A fish bone sticks in his throat. ② clip; fastener: 发卡 fàqiǎ ③ checkpost: 关卡 guānqiǎ ——see also kǎ

卡脖子 qiǎ bózi　① seize sb. by the throat; grip sb.'s throat: 他正要叫喊, 那歹徒猛扑过来, 卡住他的脖子。He was about to call out when that ruffian dashed at him and gripped his throat. ② have in a stranglehold; subdue: 用经济制裁来卡别国的脖子 apply economic sanctions against another country in an attempt to force it into submission / ～旱 strangler drought—a drought that hits when grain crops are putting forth ears

卡具 qiǎjù　*mech.*　clamping apparatus; fixture

卡壳 qiǎké　① (of cartridge or shell case) jam ② get stuck; be held up; have a temporary stoppage: 双方意见分歧, 会谈卡了壳。With both sides having differences of opinion, the discussions came to a halt. / 这件事到他那里卡了壳, 没办成。The matter was held up when it passed to him, and was never brought to a conclusion.

卡口灯泡 qiǎkǒu dēngpào　bayonet-socket bulb

卡口灯头 qiǎkǒu dēngtóu　bayonet socket

卡盘 qiǎpán　*mech.*　chuck

卡子 qiǎzi　① clip; fastener: 头发～ hairpin ② checkpost

卡钻 qiǎzuàn　*petroleum*　jamming of a drilling tool; sticking of a tool

qià

洽　qià　① be in harmony; agree: 意见不～ have different opinions; not see eye to eye ② consult; arrange with: 接洽 jiēqià ③ extensive; wide: 博识洽闻 bóshí-qiàwén

洽商 qiàshāng　make arrangements with; talk over with: 这事要和他们～。You will have to talk this over with them. / 旅游团成员在一起～日程。The members of the tour group were arranging the itinerary together.

洽谈 qiàtán　consult; discuss together: 双方～了贸易事宜。Both sides held trade talks. / 一些引进项目, 正在～之中。Several programmes for importation are under discussion.

洽妥 qiàtuǒ　have made an arrangement

恰　qià　① *adv.* just; exactly: ～合时宜 just appropriate to the occasion / 左边锋疾射入网, ～在此时鸣笛终场。The outside-left sent the ball into the net with a fast shot just before the whistle blew for full time. ② appropriate; proper: 恰当 qiàdàng

恰当 qiàdàng　proper; suitable; fitting; appropriate: 提出～的口号 propose a suitable slogan / 采取～的措施 adopt appropriate measures / 这篇文章里, 有的地方用词不～。Words were used inappropriately in some parts of this essay. / 没找到～的人选来做这工作。No suitable person has been found for the job. / 这件事处理得很～。This matter was taken care of properly.

恰到好处 qià dào hǎochù　just right (for the purpose or occasion)

恰好 qiàhǎo　*adv.* just right: 您穿的尺码的鞋我们～有。We have just the size of shoes you wear. / 我们赶到电影院, 售票处～还有两张票。We got to the cinema

just in time to buy the last two tickets left at the box office. / 八个人一桌，十六个人一～坐两桌。 One table seats eight people; two tables will just do for sixteen. / 距离～是五十米。 The distance is exactly 50 metres. / 我在那儿住了～十四个月。 I lived there for 14 months to the day. / 性格～相反 just the opposite in personality / 这块布～够做一件衬衫。 This piece of cloth is just the right length for a shirt. / 警察～这时赶到。 The police arrived in the nick of time. / 我正要出去，～王先生来找我。 I was about to leave when Mr. Wang came to see me.

恰恰 qiàqià *adv.* just; exactly; precisely: 这棵大树～挡住了我的视线。 This big tree is just blocking my sight. / 试验的结果～证明你的理论是正确的。 The result of the experiment only goes to prove that your theory is correct. / 这～是我想说的话。 That's exactly what I wanted to say. / 你很忙吧?—不忙。～相反，闲得没事干。 Are you busy?—No. On the contrary, I'm just idling the hours away. / 把事情搞糟的不是别人，～就是你自己。 It was you, rather than anybody else, who made a mess of things.

恰巧 qiàqiǎo *adv.* by chance; fortunately or unfortunately: 她正愁着怎么拿行李，～来了个搬运工人。 She was worrying about how to carry her baggage when a porter came. / 路上～碰上大雨，淋得我浑身湿透。 Unfortunately I was caught in a heavy rain and got drenched from head to foot. / ～这家银行需要一个打字员。 It just so happened that the bank was seeking a typist. / 那天～我也在那里。 I happened to be there that day, too.

恰如 qiàrú just like: 晚霞～一幅图画。 The evening glow is just like a painting.

恰如其分 qiàrú qí fèn apt; appropriate; just right: ～的评价 an apt appraisal / 给予～的批评 give a balanced criticism / 对成绩和缺点作～的估计 make an appropriate estimate of the achievements and shortcomings

恰似 qiàsì just like

髂

髂 qià see below

髂骨 qiàgǔ ilium

qiān

千 qiān ① thousand ② a great amount of; a great number of: ～百条建议 lots and lots of suggestions / ～百年来的梦想 an age-old dream ③ (Qiān) a surname

千儿八百 qiānrbābǎi *inf.* a thousand or slightly less: 那东西相当贵，没个～是买不回来的。 It's quite expensive. You can't buy it for less than a thousand.

千变万化 qiānbiàn-wànhuà ever-changing: 国际形势错综复杂，～。 The international situation is complex and changeable. / 他躺在草地上望着天上～的云彩出神。 As he lay in the grass looking up at the sky, he was transfixed by the ever-changing cloud formations.

千不该万不该 qiān bùgāi wàn bùgāi really should not have (done sth.): ～，不该让他独自一人去游泳。 We really shouldn't have let him go to swim by himself.

千部一腔，千人一面 qiānbù yī qiāng, qiānrén yī miàn all of the same tone, all with the same feature—(usu. of literary compositions) stereotyped

千层饼 qiāncéngbǐng multi-layer steamed bread

千层底 qiāncéngdǐ layers of cloth firmly stitched together for soles of cloth shoes

千差万别 qiānchā-wànbié differ in thousands of ways: 各地气候～。 Climate varies from place to place. / 世界上～的事物 the immense variety of things in the world

千疮百孔 qiānchuāng-bǎikǒng same as 百孔千疮 bǎikǒng-qiānchuāng

千锤百炼 qiānchuí-bǎiliàn ① thoroughly tempered (*or* steeled); finely honed: 在艰苦环境中工作，经过～，他意志越来越坚强了。 Toughened by working under difficult conditions, his will-power became stronger. ② (of literary works) be polished again and again; be revised and rewritten many times; be a finished product

千刀万剐 qiāndāo-wànguǎ (usu. used in a curse) be hacked to pieces; be made mincemeat of

千电子伏 qiāndiànzǐfú kiloelectron-volt (KeV)

千恩万谢 qiān ēn wàn xiè express a thousand thanks; be eternally indebted

千乏 qiānfá *elec.* kilovar (KVAR)

千方百计 qiānfāng-bǎijì in a thousand and one ways; by every possible (*or* conceivable) means; by hook or by crook: ～挖掘潜力 try every possible way to tap potential / ～掩盖错误 use all one's ingenuity to cover up one's mistakes / 他～地请好大夫给妻子看病。 He is doing all he can to find good doctors to treat his wife.

千分表 qiānfēnbiǎo dial gauge; dial indicator

千分尺 qiānfēnchǐ micrometer

千夫 qiānfū *formal* numerous people

千夫所指，无病而死 qiānfū suǒ zhǐ, wú bìng ér sǐ when a thousand people point accusing fingers at a man he will die even though not ill—it is dangerous to incur public wrath

千伏 qiānfú *elec.* kilovolt (Kv.): ～安 kilovolt-ampere (KVA)

千古 qiāngǔ ① through the ages; eternity; for all time: ～遗恨 eternal regret ② (used in an elegiac couplet or on wreaths dedicated to the dead): 某某先生～! Eternal repose to Mr. So-and-so!

千古奇闻 qiāngǔ qíwén a fantastic tale

千古罪人 qiāngǔ zuìrén one who stands condemned through the ages: 如此破坏生态平衡，将成为～。 They will be condemned throughout the ages for harming the environment in such a way.

千赫 qiānhè kilohertz

千呼万唤 qiānhū-wànhuàn a thousand calls; a thousand entreaties: ～始出来，犹抱琵琶半遮面。（白居易）Only after a thousand entreaties does she appear, Her face half hidden behind the *pipa* in her arms.

千回百转 qiānhuí-bǎizhuǎn full of twists and turns: 崎岖的山路～ a rugged mountain path, twisting and turning; a tortuous mountain path

千家万户 qiānjiā-wànhù innumerable households or families; every family: 物价问题关系到～。 Commodity prices affect the livelihood of every family.

千娇百媚 qiānjiāo-bǎimèi (of a woman) bewitchingly charming

千斤 qiānjīn a thousand *jin*—very heavy; weighty: ～重担 an exceptionally heavy load or responsibility

千斤 qiānjin ① short for 千斤顶 qiānjīndǐng ② *mech.* pawl

千斤顶 qiānjīndǐng hoisting jack; jack

千金 qiānjīn ① a thousand pieces of gold; a lot of money: ～难买 not to be had even for 1,000 pieces of gold; not to be bought with money ② *honor.* daughter (other than one's own)

千金一掷 qiānjīn yī zhì same as 一掷千金 yī zhì qiānjīn

千军万马 qiānjūn-wànmǎ thousands upon thousands of men and horses—a powerful army; a mighty force

千军易得，一将难求 qiānjūn yì dé, yījiàng nán qiú simpler by far to raise a thousand troops than find a single general to lead them

千钧一发 qiānjūn yī fà a hundredweight hanging by a hair—in imminent peril: 在这～、万分危急的时候，援军到了。 In this moment of extreme crisis when everything was hanging by a single thread, the relief troops

arrived.

千钧重负 qiānjūn zhòngfù a grave responsibility

千卡 qiānkǎ *phys.* kilocalorie (Kcal.)

千克 qiānkè kilogram (kg.)

千里 qiānlǐ a thousand *li*—a long distance or a vast expanse

千里光 qiānlǐguāng *bot.* climbing groundsel (*Senecio scandens*)

千里驹 qiānlǐjū thousand-*li* colt—a son who is showing great promise

千里马 qiānlǐmǎ a horse that covers a thousand *li* a day; a winged steed

千里送鹅毛 qiānlǐ sòng émáo a goose feather sent from a thousand *li* away (*or* from afar): ～, 礼轻情意重。The gift itself may be light as a goose feather; but sent from afar, it conveys deep feeling.

千里迢迢 qiānlǐ tiáotiáo from a thousand *li* away; from afar; (come) all the way from: 我们热烈欢迎～从海外专程前来参加纪念活动的各位先生。We warmly welcome all those who made a special trip, travelling all the way across the seas to join us in the commemoration ceremonies.

千里眼 qiānlǐyǎn ① farsighted person ② *old* telescope; field glasses

千里姻缘一线牵 qiānlǐ yīnyuán yī xiàn qiān two beings destined to marry each other, though a thousand *li* apart, are tied together as if by a thread; people a thousand *li* apart may be linked by marriage

千里之堤，溃于蚁穴 qiānlǐ zhī dī, kuì yú yǐxuè one anthole may cause the collapse of a thousand-*li* dyke—slight negligence may lead to great disaster

千里之行，始于足下 qiānlǐ zhī xíng, shǐ yú zú xià a thousand-*li* journey is started by taking the first step

千虑一得 qiān lù yī dé ① see 愚者千虑，必有一得 yúzhě qiān lù, bì yǒu yī dé ② *hum.* my observations may contain a grain of truth

千虑一失 qiān lù yī shī see 智者千虑，必有一失 zhìzhě qiān lù, bì yǒu yī shī

千枚岩 qiānméiyán *geol.* phyllite

千米 qiānmǐ kilometre (km.)

千难万险 qiānnán-wànxiǎn innumerable hazards and hardships: 纵有～, 也挡不住英雄的登山队员。Even myriad hardships and hazards can't stop the dauntless mountaineers.

千篇一律 qiān piān yī lù stereotyped; following the same pattern: ～的论调 stereotyped views / 那些文章～, 没有什么新东西。Those articles repeat each other; they contain nothing new. / 这样的人物很容易演得～。This kind of character usually becomes stereotyped on the screen.

千奇百怪 qiānqí-bǎiguài all kinds of strange things; an infinite variety of fantastic phenomena: 七星岩里的石头～。There are all kinds of strange stone formations in the Seven-star Cave.

千千万万 qiānqiānwànwàn thousands upon thousands

千秋 qiānqiū ① a thousand years; centuries ② *honor.* birthday (other than one's own)

千秋万代 qiānqiū-wàndài throughout the ages; generation after generation; forever

千日红 qiānrìhóng *bot.* globe amaranth

千山万水 qiānshān-wànshuǐ same as 万水千山 wànshuǐ-qiānshān

千丝万缕 qiānsī-wànlù countless ties; a thousand and one links: 这两个国家的文化有着～的联系。There are countless cultural ties between these two countries.

千岁 qiānsuì (usu. used in traditional operas) Your (His or Her) Royal Highness

千头万绪 qiāntóu-wànxù thousands of strands and loose ends; a multitude of things: 工作～, 要理出个轻重缓急来。With thousands of tasks on our hands, we should arrange them in order of priority. / 心里～, 不知从何说起。There are so many thoughts welling up in my mind that I really don't know where to start.

千瓦 qiānwǎ *elec.* kilowatt (KW): ～小时 kilowatt-hour (KWh)

千万 qiānwàn ① ten million; millions upon millions ② *adv.* be sure to; must: 到达后～来信。Be sure to write us when you get there. / ～要小心啊! Do be careful! / 这事儿～不可掉以轻心。We must under no circumstances take this lightly. / 这种药没有医嘱不能服用, ～, ～。This kind of medicine can't be taken without doctor's orders. You must be very careful!

千辛万苦 qiānxīn-wànkǔ innumerable trials and tribulations; untold hardships: 历尽～ go through innumerable (*or* untold) hardships / 他幼年丧父, 母亲在～中把他扶养成人。His father died when he was a child, and his mother brought him up amidst innumerable hardships.

千言万语 qiānyán-wànyǔ thousands and thousands of words: 她心里有～, 可一句也说不出来。Her heart was filled with unspoken words but she failed to utter a single one. / ～也说不尽我感激之情。No words can express my gratitude to you.

千载难逢 qiān zǎi nán féng not occurring once in a thousand years; very rare: ～的机会 a golden opportunity; the chance of a lifetime

千载一时 qiān zǎi yī shí a chance that comes once in a thousand years—the chance of a lifetime; a rare opportunity: 这是～的好机会, 不能错过。This is the chance of a lifetime. Don't miss it.

千真万确 qiānzhēn-wànquè absolutely true

千周 qiānzhōu kilocycle (KC)

仟 qiān thousand (used for the numeral 千 on cheques, etc. to avoid mistakes or alterations)

阡 qiān *formal* ① a footpath between fields, running north and south ② a path leading to a grave

阡陌 qiānmò crisscross footpaths between fields: ～纵横。The paths crisscrossed in the fields. / ～交通 footpaths connecting with each other

扦 qiān ① a short slender pointed piece of metal, bamboo, etc.: 蜡扦 làqiān ② a sharp-pointed metal tube used to extract samples of grains, etc. from sacks ③ *dial.* stick in; insert: ～门 bolt a door / 请把花～在瓶子里。Please put the flowers in the vase.

扦插 qiānchā make a cuttage

扦脚 qiānjiǎo *dial.* pedicure

扦子 qiānzi ① a slender pointed piece of metal, bamboo, etc. ② a sharp-pointed metal tube used to extract samples of grains, etc. from sacks

芊 qiān see below

芊绵 qiānmián (also 芊眠 qiānmián) (of grass or trees) dense; thick

芊芊 qiānqiān *formal* luxuriant; exuberant; flourishing

迁(遷) qiān ① move: 这个工厂已～到内地。The factory has moved to the interior. ② change: 变迁 biànqiān

迁变 qiānbiàn changes; vicissitudes

迁都 qiāndū move the capital to another place: 明成祖～北京。Emperor Cheng Zu of the Ming Dynasty moved the capital to Beijing.

迁飞 qiānfēi (of birds) migrate: ～途径 flyway

迁户口 qiān hùkǒu report to the local authorities for change of domicile; change one's residence registra-

tion

迁就 qiānjiù　accommodate oneself to; yield to: ～姑息 excessively accommodating; overlenient / 他太～孩子了, 要什么就给买什么。 He gives in to the child too much. Whatever she wants, he buys for her. / 在小事情上互相～着点儿 give in a little to each other over small matters

迁居 qiānjū　change one's dwelling place; move (house): 他已～到成都。 He has moved to Chengdu. / 从城里～郊区的人越来越多。 The movement of people from the cities to the suburbs is on the increase.

迁客 qiānkè　*formal* moved-in squire (the name by which an official was formerly called by the people of a place to which he was demoted and banished)

迁离 qiānlí　move to another place

迁流 qiānliú　*formal* (of time) flow past: 岁月～。 Time flows past.

迁怒 qiānnù　vent one's anger on sb. who's not to blame; take it out on sb.: 你碰到不顺心的事也不该～于人啊。 If things haven't been going your way lately, you shouldn't take it out on others.

迁徙 qiānxǐ　move; migrate; change one's residence: 人口～ population migration / 燕子秋天往南方～。 Swallows migrate south in autumn.

迁延 qiānyán　delay; defer; procrastinate: ～时日 cause a long delay; become long-drawn-out

迁移 qiānyí　move; remove; migrate: 从城市～到农村 move from urban to rural areas

迁移性 qiānyíxìng　*zool.* animal migration

迁葬 qiānzàng　move a grave to another place

金[1]（僉）　qiān　*formal* unanimous; together: ～谋 together plan to

金[2]（僉）　qiān　same as 签 qiān

金同 qiāntóng　*formal* unanimously agree

瓩　qiānwǎ　kilowatt (KW)

钎　qiān　drill rod; drill steel; borer: 钢钎 gāngqiān

钎子 qiānzi　hammer drill (for making holes in rock); rock drill

牵（牽）　qiān　① lead along (by holding the hand, the halter, etc.); pull: ～牛下地 lead an ox to the fields / 手～手 hand in hand ② involve: 他不愿意～在这里头。 He didn't want to get involved in it.

牵鼻子 qiān bízi　lead by the nose: 你自己应该有个主意, 不能叫别人牵着鼻子走。 You should make your own decisions, and not let others to lead you by the nose.

牵缠 qiānchán　involve sb. or get sb. entangled

牵肠挂肚 qiāncháng-guàdù　feel deep anxiety; be very worried; be on tenterhooks: 好长时间收不到他的信, 叫人～的。 I haven't heard from him for ages, and I'm getting extremely anxious. / 人家～的等着, 你倒在那里玩得高兴! Here were we practically beside ourselves with anxiety, and all the time you were there enjoying yourself!

牵扯 qiānchě　involve; implicate; drag in: 这事～很多人。 A number of people have become involved in the matter.

牵掣 qiānchè　① hold up; impede: 互相～ hold each other up / 抓主要问题, 不要被枝节问题～住。 Let's focus our attention on the main problem and not get bogged down in minor issues. ② same as 牵制 qiānzhì

牵动 qiāndòng　affect; influence: ～全局 affect the situation as a whole / ～整个作战计划 affect the overall operational plan

牵挂 qiānguà　worry; care: 好好工作, 不要～家中老小。 Do your work well and don't worry about us folks at home. / 我家里都安顿好了, 没有什么～了。 I've got everything settled at home; I'm free of worries now.

牵合 qiānhé　make a match; act as go-between

牵记 qiānjì　keep thinking about; be anxious about; worry about; miss

牵就 qiānjiù　same as 迁就 qiānjiù

牵累 qiānlěi　① tie down: 受家务～ be tied down by household chores ② implicate; involve (in trouble): 他怕这事说出来会～家庭, 所以隐瞒了。 He was afraid that if he mentioned the matter it would implicate his family, so he kept it secret.

牵连 qiānlián　① involve (in trouble); implicate: 清查同这次破坏活动有～的人和事 investigate the individuals and incidents connected with the sabotage / 这个案件～了很多人。 Many people were implicated in this case. ② tie up with; integrate with

牵念 qiānniàn　worry about sb. or sth.; think constantly of

牵牛花 qiānniúhuā　(white-edged) morning glory

牵牛星 Qiānniúxīng　the Herd-boy star: 迢迢～, 皎皎河汉女。《古诗十九首》 Far away twinkles the Herd-boy star; Brightly shines the Lady of the Silver River.

牵强 qiānqiǎng　forced (interpretation, etc.); farfetched: 这些理由都很～。 These reasons are farfetched.

牵强附会 qiānqiǎng fùhuì　draw a forced analogy; make a farfetched (*or* irrelevant) comparison; give a strained interpretation: 你这样解释这篇文章太～了。 Your interpretation of this essay is much too forced.

牵切纺 qiānqiēfǎng　*text.* tow-to-yarn direct spinning

牵涉 qiānshè　involve; drag in: 这项决定～很多部门。 This decision involves many departments. / 他的发言既然～到我, 我就想讲几句。 Since he has dragged me into his speech, I'd like to say a few words.

牵伸 qiānshēn　*text.* draft; drawing

牵头 qiāntóu　take the lead; lead off; be the first to do sth.: 这件事得几个单位商量着办, 谁来～? Several units must discuss how to handle this matter. Who will lead off? / 我只是牵个头, 事情是大伙儿办的。 I took the lead, but the work was done by everyone.

牵头 qiān·tóu　① act as go-between ② go-between

牵系 qiānxì　link; join; connect

牵线 qiānxiàn　① manipulate or control (from behind the scenes) ② *inf.* act as go-between: 他们俩谈恋爱是我牵的线。 I acted as go-between for them to meet and fall in love.

牵线搭桥 qiānxiàn dāqiáo　act as go-between

牵线人 qiānxiànrén　① wire-puller ② go-between

牵一发而动全身 qiān yī fà ér dòng quánshēn　pull one hair and you move the whole body—a slight move in one part may affect the whole situation

牵引 qiānyǐn　① tow; draw: 这条线上的列车都由电力机车～。 The trains on this line are all drawn by electric locomotives. ② *med.* traction: ～器 tractor

牵引车 qiānyǐnchē　tractor; tractor truck

牵引犁 qiānyǐnlí　trailed plough

牵引力 qiānyǐnlì　*phys.* traction force; traction; pulling force

牵引能量 qiānyǐn néngliàng　haulage capacity (of a locomotive, etc.)

牵引炮 qiānyǐnpào　towed artillery

牵引式滑翔机 qiānyǐnshì huáxiángjī　towed glider

牵制 qiānzhì　(usu. used with reference to military operations) pin down; tie up; check; contain: ～敌人 pin down the enemy / 这对敌人是一种～。 This is a kind of check on the enemy. / ～行动 containing action / ～性攻击 diversionary attack

悭（慳） qiān ① see below ② be short of; lack: 缘悭一面 yuán qiān yīmiàn

悭吝 qiānlìn stingy; miserly: ～人 miser; niggard; skinflint

铅 qiān ① *chem.* lead (Pb) ② lead (in a pencil); black lead

铅白 qiānbái *chem.* white lead

铅版 qiānbǎn *print.* stereotype

铅笔 qiānbǐ pencil

铅笔刀 qiānbǐdāo a small knife for sharpening pencils; pen-knife

铅笔盒 qiānbǐhé pencil-case

铅笔画 qiānbǐhuà pencil drawing

铅笔心 qiānbǐxīn lead (in a pencil); black lead

铅玻璃 qiānbōli lead glass

铅垂线 qiānchuíxiàn *archit.* plumb line

铅锤 qiānchuí *archit.* plummet; plumb (bob)

铅丹 qiāndān *chem.* red lead; minium

铅刀一割 qiāndāo yī gē a leaden knife can cut—a mediocre person can be put to some use

铅粉 qiānfěn same as 铅白 qiānbái

铅封 qiānfēng lead sealing

铅黄 qiānhuáng lead and yellow—collation (so called from the use in former times of lead and yellow ochre for making corrections in editing)

铅球 qiānqiú *sports* shot: 推～ shot put; putting the shot / ～运动员 shot-putter

铅丝 qiānsī ① galvanized wire ② *elec.* lead wire

铅条 qiāntiáo ① *print.* slug; lead ② lead (for a propelling pencil)

铅印 qiānyìn letterpress (*or* relief, typographic) printing; stereotype

铅直 qiānzhí vertical; plumb

铅中毒 qiānzhòngdú lead poisoning; saturnism

铅坠 qiānzhuì plummet

铅子 qiānzǐ *inf.* bullet

铅字 qiānzì type; letter: 大号～ large type / ～面 typeface / ～盘 type case; letter board

铅字合金 qiānzì héjīn type metal

谦 qiān modest: 过谦 guòqiān

谦卑 qiānbēi humble; modest

谦诚 qiānchéng modest and sincere

谦辞 qiāncí self-depreciatory expression; humble words

谦恭 qiāngōng modest and courteous

谦和 qiānhé modest and amiable

谦谦君子 qiān qiān jūnzǐ a modest gentleman

谦让 qiānràng modestly decline: 您来主持这个讨论最合适，不要～了。You're just the person to chair the discussion. Don't decline out of modesty. / 客人们互相～了一下，然后落了座。The guests politely offered their seats to each other before finally settling down in them.

谦慎 qiānshèn modest and prudent

谦顺 qiānshùn modest and deferential

谦虚 qiānxū ① modest; self-effacing: 钱教授很～，从来不摆架子。Professor Qian is very modest. He never puts on airs. / 别～了，我们知道你是这方面的行家。Don't be so modest. We know you're an expert in this field. ② make modest remarks: 他～了一番，终于答应来做一次演讲。After making a few modest remarks he finally agreed to come and give a talk.

谦虚谨慎 qiānxū jǐnshèn modest and prudent: 保持～、不骄不躁的作风 remain modest, prudent and free from arrogance and rashness in one's style of work

谦逊 qiānxùn modest; unassuming: 他知识丰富，但总是保持～的态度。He's a man of great knowledge, but he always maintains an attitude of modesty.

签¹（簽） qiān ① sign; autograph: ～支票 sign a cheque ② make brief comments on a document: 看完请～个意见。After you've read it, please write down a few brief comments.

签²（簽、籤） qiān ① bamboo slips used for divination or drawing lots: 抽签 chōuqiān ② label; sticker: 标签 biāoqiān ③ a slender pointed piece of bamboo or wood: 牙签 yáqiān ④ (of sewing) tack: 把袖口～上 tack on a cuff

签呈 qiānchéng a brief document submitted to a superior; memorial

签到 qiāndào register one's attendance at a meeting or at an office; sign in: 来宾请在这儿签一下到。Guests are requested to sign in here. / 我们一到办公室就得～。We have to sign in when we arrive at the office. / ～簿 attendance book / ～处 sign-in desk

签订 qiāndìng conclude and sign (a treaty, etc.): ～条约 sign a treaty / ～合同 sign a contract / ～协定的各方 the parties signatory to the agreement

签发 qiānfā sign and issue (a document, certificate, etc.): 这种通行证由国防部负责～。The Defense Department is responsible for the signing and issuing of this type of travel permit.

签名 qiānmíng sign one's name; autograph: 她请这个电影明星在本子上签了个名。She asked the movie star to sign his autograph in her notebook. / ～盖章 sign and affix one's seal; set one's hand and seal to / 亲笔～的照片 an autographed picture / 来宾～簿 visitors' book

签名运动 qiānmíng yùndòng signature drive

签收 qiānshōu sign after receiving sth.: 挂号信须由收件人～。A receipt for a registered letter is to be signed by the recipient. *or* A registered letter must be signed for by the recipient. / 他不在，我代他～这些文件。He's not here. I'll sign for these documents on his behalf.

签署 qiānshǔ sign: 联合公报是由双方代表团长～的。The joint *communiqué* is signed by the heads of both delegations. / ～意见 write comments and sign one's name (on a document)

签筒 qiāntǒng ① a tube-like holder of lot-sticks ② a sharp-pointed metal tube used to extract samples of grains, etc. from sacks

签押 qiānyā put one's signature or seal on an official document

签证 qiānzhèng ① visa; visé: 入（出）境～ entry (exit) visa / 过境～ transit visa / 一次有效出入境～ entry-exit visa valid for a single journey / 多次往返有效的出入境～ multiple entry-exit visa / 团体～ group visa / 互免～ mutual exemption of visas ② grant a visa: ～机关 visa office

签注 qiānzhù ① attach a slip of paper to a document with comments on it; write comments on a document (for a superior to consider) ② write comments or points for attention on a certificate, book of tables, etc.

签字 qiānzì sign; affix one's signature: 本条约在～后立即生效。This treaty shall come into force upon signature. / 请作者在扉页上～ ask the author to autograph the title page / ～国 signatory state (*or* power); signatory / ～仪式 signing ceremony

签子 qiānzi *inf.* ① bamboo slips used for divination or drawing lots ② a slender pointed piece of bamboo or wood

愆 qiān *formal* ① fault; transgression: 前愆 qiánqiān ② see below

愆期 qiānqī *formal* pass the appointed time; delay

(payment, etc.)

鸽　qiān　(of birds with sharp beaks) peck at (wheat head, etc.)

骞　qiān　*formal* ① hold high up ② same as 搴 qiān

搴　qiān　*formal* ① pull out ② same as 褰 qiān

褰　qiān　*formal* lift up (skirt, bed-curtain, etc.)

韆　qiān　see 鞦韆 qiūqiān

qián

前　qián　① front: ～院 front courtyard / 楼～ in front of the building / 将军胸～戴着所有的勋章。The general was wearing all his medals on his chest. ② forward; ahead: 朝～走 go straight ahead / 往～看 look forward ③ ago; before: 这个故事发生在五百年～。The story took place 500 years ago. / 晚饭～ before supper ④ preceding: ～一阶段 the preceding stage / ～资本主义 precapitalism ⑤ former; formerly: ～校长 former principal (of a school) / 张家口是～华北察哈尔省省会。Zhangjiakou used to be the capital of Chaha'er, a sometime province in north China. ⑥ first: 这次比赛的～三名 the first three places in this competition / ～五排 the first five rows ⑦ future: 前程 qiánchéng

前半场　qiánbànchǎng　same as 上半场 shàngbànchǎng

前半晌　qiánbànshǎng　*dial.* before noon; morning

前半生　qiánbànshēng　(also 前半辈子 qiánbànbèizi) the first half of one's life

前半天　qiánbàntiān　before noon; morning

前半夜　qiánbànyè　the first half of the night (from nightfall to midnight)

前辈　qiánbèi　senior (person); elder; the older generation: 他们都是我的～。They are all my seniors. / 革命～ revolutionaries of the older generation / 在书法方面，你是我们的～。You are our venerable senior in calligraphy.

前臂　qiánbì　forearm

前边　qiánbian　same as 前面 qiánmian

前不巴村，后不巴店　qián bù bā cūn, hòu bù bā diàn　with no village ahead and no inn behind—be stranded in an uninhabited area

前不见古人，后不见来者　qián bù jiàn gǔrén, hòu bù jiàn láizhě　I look back—I do not see the ancients; I look ahead—can't see the generations to come: ～。念天地之悠悠，独怆然而涕下。(陈子昂) I look back—I do not see the ancients; I look ahead—can't see the generations to come. I brood on the endlessness of Heaven and Earth, And tears stream down—I stand alone.

前叉　qiánchā　front fork (of a bicycle)

前朝　qiáncháo　the previous dynasty or dynasties

前车之覆，后车之鉴　qiánchē zhī fù, hòuchē zhī jiàn　the overturned cart ahead is a warning to the ones behind

前车之鉴　qiánchē zhī jiàn　warning taken from the overturned cart ahead; lessons drawn from others' mistakes: 他们试验失败对我们是个～。The failure of their experiment should be a warning to us.

前尘　qiánchén　*formal* the past: 回首～ look back upon the past

前沉　qiánchén　(of a car) more heavily loaded in the front (than in the rear)

前程　qiánchéng　① future; prospect: 你的孩子又聪明又用功，一定～远大。Your son is smart and diligent; he

definitely has a bright future before him. ② *old* a desired career or a high rank (sought after by an intellectual or official)

前程似锦　qiánchéng sì jǐn　splendid prospects; a glorious future

前程万里　qiánchéng wànlǐ　bright prospects

前池　qiánchí　*water conservancy* forebay

前仇　qiánchóu　old hatred; old grievance

前此　qiáncǐ　up till now; previously

前导　qiándǎo　① lead the way; march in front; precede ② a person who leads the way; guide: 以仪仗队为～ with the guard of honour marching at the head

前敌　qiándí　front line: 身临～ come personally to the front / ～总指挥 frontline commander-in-chief

前敌委员会　qiándí wěiyuánhuì　front committee

前度刘郎　qián dù Liú Láng　the young Master Liu of those days—a person who revisits a place (from Liu Yuxi's 刘禹锡 lines 种桃道士知何处?～今又来。Where has the Taoist who planted the peach-trees gone? The young Master Liu of those days [referring to himself] has come again!)

前额　qián'é　forehead

前方　qiánfāng　① ahead: 注视着～ look (or gaze) ahead / 大副发现船的左～有鲸鱼群。The first mate sighted a herd of whales ahead to the left of the boat. ② the front: 开赴～ be dispatched to the front / 支援～ support the front

前房　qiánfáng　former wife who has died

前锋　qiánfēng　① vanguard: 部队～已到达目的地。The vanguard units have reached the destination. ② *sports* forward ③ *meteorol.* front: 冷空气的～已进入我省。The cold front has reached this province.

前夫　qiánfū　former husband (either divorced or dead); ex-husband

前赴后继　qiánfù-hòujì　advance wave upon wave

前儿个　qiánrge　(also 前儿 qiánr) *inf.* day before yesterday

前功尽弃　qiángōng jìn qì　all that has been achieved is spoiled; all one's previous efforts are wasted: 成功的希望不大，还可能～。There is small chance of success, and you risk all you have gained.

前滚翻　qiángǔnfān　*sports* forward roll

前汉　Qián Hàn　the Former Han (another name for 西汉 Xī Hàn)

前后　qiánhòu　① *part.* around (a certain time); about: 天亮～ shortly before and after daybreak / 1949 年～ round about 1949 / 春节～ around the Spring Festival ② from beginning to end (in time): 这项工程，从动工到完成，～只用了十个月。The entire project, from beginning to end, took only ten months. / 她～来过四次。She has been here four times altogether. ③ in front and behind: 房子～都有树 There are trees both in front and at the back of the house. / ～次序不要颠倒。Don't get the order mixed up. / ～受敌 be attacked by the enemy both front and back; be caught between two fires / ～左右 on all sides; all around / ～车厢都坐满了。There're no empty seats in any of the carriages. ④ people or things of the same kind in succession: ～两位主席 two successive chairmen / ～三种版本 three consecutive editions / 你～几封信都已收到。I've received all your letters.

前…后…　qián…hòu…　① (indicating one thing behind another, or one action after another): 前街后巷 front street and back lane / 前思后想 think over again and again / 前松后紧 be slack at the beginning and have to speed up towards the end / 前有大河，后有追兵。There was a great river in front of us, and pursuing troops were closing in from behind. ② (indicating backward and forward movements): 前俯后仰 bend forwards and

backwards

前后夹击 qiánhòu jiā jī make a simultaneous frontal and rear attack; attack from the front and the rear simultaneously

前后脚儿 qiánhòujiǎor *inf.* almost simultaneously; one close behind another: 他们俩～到的。They arrived at almost the same time.

前呼后拥 qiánhū-hòuyōng with attendants crowding round

前胡 qiánhú *Chin. med.* the root of purple-flowered peucedanum (*Peucedanum decursivum*)

前记 qiánjì same as 前言 qiányán

前脚 qiánjiǎo ① the forward foot in a step: 我～一滑，身体站不稳，就摔了。As soon as my front foot slipped, I lost my balance and fell over. ② (used together with 后脚) no sooner...than; the moment (when): 你～走，他后脚就来了。He arrived the moment you had left.

前襟 qiánjīn the front part of a Chinese robe or jacket

前进 qiánjìn advance; go forward; forge ahead: 列车～在京广线上。The train proceeded along the Beijing-Guangzhou track. / 我们不能停留在现有的成绩上，要继续～。We can't rest on our laurels; we must forge ahead. / 生产飞跃～。Production increases by leaps and bounds.

前景[1] qiánjǐng foreground (of a view, picture, photo, etc.)

前景[2] qiánjǐng prospect; vista; perspective: 他的发现为利用当地资源开辟了广阔的～。His discovery opened up a vast range of prospects for making use of local resources. / 大丰收的～使大家心里乐滋滋的。The prospect of a good harvest made everyone feel happy.

前臼齿 qiánjiùchǐ premolar teeth

前倨后恭 qiánjù-hòugōng first supercilious and then deferential; change from arrogance to humility

前科 qiánkē record of previous crime: 这个罪犯是有～的。This offender has a criminal record.

前空翻 qiánkōngfān *sports* forward somersault in the air

前来 qiánlái come: 今天他举行婚礼，许多同事～贺喜。Today is his wedding day and many of his colleagues came to congratulate him.

前例 qiánlì precedent: 这样处理有～可援，不算咱们独创。This is not a creation of ours. There are precedents to be cited.

前列 qiánliè front row (*or* rank); forefront; van: 主席台～ the front row on the rostrum / 年轻力壮的小伙子们站在与洪水搏斗的最～。The able-bodied young men were at the forefront in the fight against the flood.

前列腺 qiánlièxiàn prostate (gland): ～素 prostaglandin / ～肥大 hypertrophy of the prostate; prostatomegaly

前列腺炎 qiánlièxiànyán prostatitis

前烈 qiánliè *formal* ① the achievements of past worthies ② worthies of the past generations

前掠翼 qiánlüèyì buzzard-type wing (of a plane)

前轮 qiánlún front wheel (of a vehicle); nosewheel (of a plane)

前门 qiánmén front door; front gate

前门拒虎，后门进狼 qiánmén jù hǔ, hòumén jìn láng drive the tiger from the front door and let a wolf in at the back—fend off one danger only to fall a prey to another

前面 qiánmian ① in front; at the head; ahead: 在房子～ in front of the house / ～有座位。There're seats in the front rows. / 走在队伍～ march at the head of the column / ～就是宿营地。The campsite is right ahead. / ～来了一个人。A man was coming towards us. / 科学研究工作应当走在经济建设的～。Scientific research should anticipate economic construction. ② above; preceding: ～提到的原则 the above-mentioned

principle / ～的一章 the preceding chapter

前脑 qiánnǎo forebrain

前年 qiánnián the year before last

前怕狼，后怕虎 qián pà láng, hòu pà hǔ (also 前怕龙，后怕虎 qián pà lóng, hòu pà hǔ) fear wolves ahead and tigers behind—be full of fears: 我们如果～，就什么事情也做不成。We'll never get anywhere if we are plagued by all sorts of fears.

前排 qiánpái front row: ～座位 front-row seats / 在～就座 be seated in the front rows

前炮 qiánpào forward gun (on a ship); bow-piece

前仆后继 qiánpū-hòujì no sooner has one fallen than another steps into the breach: 无数革命先烈为了共产主义事业～，英勇地献出了生命。Countless revolutionary martyrs, one stepping into the breach as another fell, have fought and laid down their lives for the cause of communism.

前妻 qiánqī former wife (either divorced or dead); ex-wife

前期 qiánqī earlier stage; early days

前愆 qiánqiān *formal* past faults

前前后后 qiánqiánhòuhòu ① the whole story; the ins and outs: 一件事情的～ the ins and outs of a matter ② from beginning to end (in time): 这次旅游～共一个月。The tour took a whole month's time.

前桥 qiánqiáo front axle (of a car): ～壳 front axle housing

前清 Qián Qīng the Qing Dynasty

前情 qiánqíng ① antecedent; cause ② old friendship; former affection

前驱 qiánqū forerunner; precursor; pioneer

前驱期 qiánqūqī *med.* prodromal stage

前人 qiánrén forefathers; predecessors: ～总结的经验 experience summed up by our predecessors

前人栽树，后人乘凉 qiánrén zāi shù, hòurén chéng liáng one generation plants the trees in whose shade another generation rests—profiting by the labour of one's forefathers; sweating for the benefit of future generations

前任 qiánrèn predecessor: ～书记 former secretary / 他的～ his predecessor / ～总统 ex-president / ～首相 the former prime minister

前日 qiánrì the day before yesterday

前晌 qiánshǎng *dial.* before noon; morning

前哨 qiánshào outpost; advance guard: 与敌～接触 skirmish with the enemy's advance guards

前哨战 qiánshàozhàn *mil.* skirmish

前身 qiánshēn ① predecessor: 八路军的～是工农红军。The Eighth Route Army grew out of the Workers' and Peasants' Red Army. ② same as 前襟 qiánjīn

前生 qiánshēng (also 前世 qiánshì) previous incarnation; previous existence: 他这是～注定的。This was decided in his previous incarnation.

前失 qiánshī ① (of a horse, etc.) slip ② *formal* errors committed

前室 qiánshì same as 前妻 qiánqī

前事不忘，后事之师 qiánshì bù wàng, hòushì zhī shī past experience, if not forgotten, is a guide for the future; lessons learned from the past can guide one in the future

前视图 qiánshìtú *mech.* front view

前束 qiánshù toe-in (of a car)

前思后想 qiánsī-hòuxiǎng think over again and again

前所未闻 qián suǒ wèi wén never heard of before: ～的奇迹 an unheard-of miracle / 这样的怪事真是～。I've never heard of such a strange thing before.

前所未有 qián suǒ wèi yǒu never existed before; hitherto unknown; unprecedented: ～的盛况 an unprecedentedly grand occasion / 遇到～的困难 encounter

greater difficulties than ever / 他一人独得七块金牌，这在奥运会历史上是～的。He alone got 7 gold medals. This is unprecedented in the history of the Olympic Games.

前台 qiántái ① proscenium ② on the stage (fig.): 有人在～表演，有人在幕后指挥。Some appeared on the stage, while others pulled strings behind the scenes.

前提 qiántí ① *log.* premise: 大 (小)～ major (minor) premise ② prerequisite; presupposition: 必要的～ essential prerequisite / 矛盾的一方各以其另一方为自己存在的～。Each aspect of a contradiction presupposes the existence of the other aspect. / 这个问题的政治解决必须以撤出外国军队为～。A political settlement of this question must be predicated on the withdrawal of foreign forces.

前天 qiántiān day before yesterday: ～晚上 the night before last

前厅 qiántīng antechamber; vestibule

前庭 qiántíng *physiol.* vestibule

前庭炎 qiántíngyán vestibulitis

前头 qiántou same as 前面 qiánmian

前途 qiántú future; prospect: 你们的工作很有～。Your work has a great future. / 这个事儿没有～。This job has no future. *or* There are no prospects in this job.

前途茫茫 qiántú mángmáng have a bleak future; have gloomy prospects: 他感觉到自己～，往后的光景难混了。He felt that his future was bleak and the days ahead would be trying.

前途无量 qiántú wúliàng have boundless prospects; have unlimited possibilities

前腿 qiántuǐ foreleg

前往 qiánwǎng go to; leave for; proceed to: 代表团已动身～日内瓦。The delegation has left for Geneva. / 他们将由西安～延安。From Xi'an they will proceed to Yan'an.

前委 qiánwěi short for 前敌委员会 qiándí wěiyuánhuì

前卫 qiánwèi ① *mil.* advance guard; vanguard ② *sports* halfback: 左～ left halfback; left half

前无古人 qián wú gǔrén without parallel in history; unprecedented

前夕 qiánxī eve: 解放～ on the eve of liberation; shortly before liberation / 毕业～，学生们紧张地准备考试。As graduation day drew near, the students were all anxiously preparing for their final exams.

前贤 qiánxián *formal* former worthies

前嫌 qiánxián previous ill will; old grudge: ～尽释。All previous ill will has been removed. *or* We have agreed to bury the hatchet.

前线 qiánxiàn frontline; front: 上～ go to the front / 远离～ far from the frontline

前项 qiánxiàng *math.* antecedent

前言 qiányán preface; foreword; introduction: ～说明如何使用这本词典。The preface explains how to use the dictionary. / 宪法的～ the preamble to a constitution

前言不搭后语 qiányán bù dā hòuyǔ utter words that do not hang together; talk incoherently; babble disconnected phrases

前沿 qiányán *mil.* forward position: ～阵地 forward position / ～指挥所 forward command post

前仰后合 qiányǎng-hòuhé rock (with laughter): 笑得～ rock (or shake) with laughter; double up with mirth

前夜 qiányè same as 前夕 qiánxī

前因后果 qiányīn-hòuguǒ cause and effect; the entire process: 这件事情的～已经调查得清清楚楚。The entire matter, its cause and effect, has been fully cleared up through investigation.

前缘 qiányuán predestined ties or relationship; fore-ordained affinity: 咱俩结为夫妻，也是～。It is our fore-ordained affinity that we should become husband and wife.

前院 qiányuàn front courtyard

前站 qiánzhàn see 打前站 dǎ qiánzhàn

前兆 qiánzhào omen; forewarning; premonition: 这次地震很突然，没有任何～。The earthquake was very sudden. There'd been no warning signs whatsoever.

前哲 qiánzhé *formal* former worthies

前者 qiánzhě the former

前肢 qiánzhī forelegs (of an animal); forelimbs

前置词 qiánzhìcí another name for 介词 jiècí

前装炮 qiánzhuāngpào muzzle-loading gun; muzzle-loader

前缀 qiánzhuì prefix

前奏 qiánzòu prelude: 德国入侵波兰是第二次世界大战的～。The German invasion of Poland was a prelude to World War II.

前奏曲 qiánzòuqǔ *mus.* prelude

钤 qián ① seal; stamp ② affix a seal to: 钤印 qiányìn ③ *formal* lock

钤记 qiánjì seal or stamp of a government organization in old China

钤键 qiánjiàn *formal* ① hinge; key ② stratagem; artifice; scheme

钤印 qiányìn affix a seal to

荨 (蕁、藔) qián see below —— see also xún

荨麻 qiánmá *bot.* nettle

钳¹ (箝) qián pincers; pliers; tongs: 克丝钳 kèsīqián / 火钳 huǒqián

钳² (拑) qián ① grip (with pincers); clamp ② restrain; limit: 钳制 qiánzhì

钳工 qiángōng ① benchwork ② fitter

钳口 qiánkǒu ① force sb. into silence; prevent sb. from talking ② shut up; keep silent: ～无言 keep one's mouth shut; hold one's tongue; say nothing

钳口结舌 qiánkǒu-jiéshé keep one's mouth shut; hold one's tongue

钳形 qiánxíng pincerlike: ～攻势 a pincer movement; a two-pronged offensive / 形成～包围 form a pincerlike encirclement

钳制 qiánzhì clamp down on; suppress: ～舆论 muzzle (or gag) public opinion / 游击队从后方～住敌人的兵力。The guerrillas pinned down the enemy's armed forces from the rear.

钳爪 qiánzhuǎ chela (of a crab, lobster, etc.)

钳子 qiánzi ① pliers; pincers; forceps ② *dial.* earrings

虔 qián pious; sincere: 虔诚 qiánchéng

虔诚 qiánchéng pious; devout: ～的佛教徒 a pious adherent of Buddhism; devout Buddhist / ～地祈祷上帝 pray devoutly to God

虔敬 qiánjìng reverent: 他听布道很～。He gave reverent attention to the sermon.

虔婆 qiánpó *old* a madam (of brothel); procuress

钱¹ (錢) qián ① copper coin; cash: 铜钱 tóngqián ② money: 这个多少～? How much is this? ③ fund; sum: 这笔～是专为保健事业用的。This fund is earmarked for public health services. / 买拖拉机的～ the wherewithal to buy tractors ④ (Qián) a surname

钱² (錢) qián *qian,* currently called 市钱 shìqián, a traditional unit of weight —— see also 市钱 shìqián

钱包　qiánbāo　wallet; purse

钱币　qiánbì　coin

钱币学　qiánbìxué　numismatics

钱财　qiáncái　wealth; money: 浪费～ waste money

钱钞　qiánchāo　*old*　money

钱串子　qiánchuànzi　① cash string—money-minded: ～脑袋 a money-minded person ② *zool.*　millipede

钱褡裢　qiándālian　(also 钱褡子 qiándāzi) a money bag for carrying over the shoulder

钱谷　qiángǔ　① money and cereal ② revenue in the Qing Dynasty: ～师爷 revenue clerk

钱柜　qiánguì　money-locker; money-box; till

钱粮　qiánliáng　*old*　① land tax: 完～ pay the land tax ② same as 钱谷 qiángǔ②

钱龙　qiánlóng　*zool.*　millipede

钱迷心窍　qián mí xīnqiào　be blinded by lust for money; money-grubbing

钱能通神　qián néng tōng shén　money will move the gods; money opens the gates of heaven

钱票　qiánpiào　*inf.*　① paper money ② tickets used in cafeterias in place of cash

钱塘潮　Qiántángcháo　the Qiantang bore (in Zhejiang Province)

钱儿癣　qiánrxuǎn　*inf.*　ringworm of the body

钱庄　qiánzhuāng　old-style Chinese private bank

钱租　qiánzū　common name for 货币地租 huòbì dìzū

掮

　　qián　*dial.*　carry on the shoulder

掮客　qiánkè　broker: 房地产～ a real estate broker / 他没什么原则, 只是个政治～。He has no principles; he's just a political broker.

乾

乾　qián　male: 乾宅 qiánzhái

乾坤　qiánkūn　heaven and earth; the cosmos; the universe: 云迷世界, 雾罩～。(《西游记》) Clouds over the world; Mist shrouds the cosmos. ——see also 扭转乾坤 niǔzhuǎn qiánkūn

乾宅　qiánzhái　*old*　the bridegroom's side; the husband's family

潜(潛)

　　qián　① latent; hidden: 潜能 qiánnéng ② stealthily; secretly; on the sly: 潜入 qiánrù

潜步　qiánbù　walk stealthily; slink

潜藏　qiáncáng　hide; go into hiding

潜遁　qiándùn　abscond

潜伏　qiánfú　hide; conceal; lie low: ～特务 a hidden enemy agent / ～的疾病 an insidious disease / ～着的危机 a latent crisis / 游击小分队在预定地点～下来。The guerrilla detachment was lying low at the predetermined location.

潜伏期　qiánfúqī　*med.*　incubation period; latency period

潜航　qiánháng　(of a submarine) submerge: ～深度 submerged depth / ～速度 submerged speed

潜力　qiánlì　latent capacity; potential; potentiality: 有很大～ have great potentialities / 充分发挥～ fully bring out latent potentialities; bring the potential into full play / 挖掘～ exploit potentialities; tap potentials

潜流　qiánliú　*geol.*　undercurrent; underflow

潜能　qiánnéng　*phys.*　latent energy

潜匿　qiánnì　hide; go into hiding

潜热　qiánrè　*phys.*　latent heat

潜入　qiánrù　① slip into; sneak into; steal in: ～敌占区 slip into the enemy-occupied area / ～室内 sneak into a room ② dive (into water); submerge

潜水　qiánshuǐ　① go under water; dive: ～器 scuba / ～钟 diving bell ② *geol.*　phreatic water

潜水艇　qiánshuǐtǐng　submarine

潜水衣　qiánshuǐyī　diving suit

潜水员　qiánshuǐyuán　diver; frogman: ～病 caisson disease; decompression sickness

潜台词　qiántáicí　① unspoken words in a play left to the understanding of the audience or reader ② what is actually meant (in one's speech); implication

潜逃　qiántáo　abscond: 携公款～ abscond with public funds

潜艇　qiántǐng　submarine: ～探测器 submarine detector

潜望镜　qiánwàngjìng　periscope

潜心　qiánxīn　with great concentration: ～研究科学 apply oneself to scientific study with great concentration; devote oneself to the study of science

潜行　qiánxíng　① move under water ② move stealthily; slink

潜血　qiánxuè　*med.*　occult blood (in the faeces): ～试验 occult blood test

潜移默化　qiányí-mòhuà　exert a subtle influence on sb.'s character, thinking, etc.; imperceptibly influence: 文艺对人们的思想起着～的作用。Literature and art exert an imperceptible influence on people's thinking.

潜意识　qiányìshí　the subconscious; subconsciousness

潜隐　qiányǐn　① hide; conceal: 她淡淡地一笑, 笑里却～着悲哀。She gave a faint smile, a smile tinged with sadness. ② *formal*　withdraw from society and live in solitude; be a hermit

潜泳　qiányǒng　underwater swimming

潜鱼　qiányú　pearlfish

潜在　qiánzài　latent; potential: ～的意识 subconsciousness / 一股～的势力 a potential force (of a group of people) / 要想办法使每个人的～力量充分发挥出来。We must find a way to allow everyone to realize their potential.

潜滋暗长　qiánzī-ànzhǎng　grow and develop imperceptibly

黔1

黔　qián　*formal*　black

黔2

黔　Qián　another name for 贵州 Guìzhōu

黔黎　qiánlí　same as 黔首 qiánshǒu

黔驴技穷　Qián lú jì qióng　the (proverbial) Guizhou donkey has exhausted its tricks—at one's wit's end; at the end of one's rope

黔驴之技　Qián lú zhī jì　tricks of the (proverbial) Guizhou donkey—tricks not to be feared; cheap tricks

黔首　qiánshǒu　the common people (a term used in ancient China)

qiǎn

浅(淺)

浅　qiǎn　① shallow: ～水 shallow water; shoal water / ～～的一碗饭 a partly-filled bowl of rice / 这房子进深～。The house is not deep. ② simple; easy: 这篇课文很～。This lesson is very easy. ③ superficial: 对问题的认识很～ just have a superficial understanding of the problem / 功夫～ have superficial mastery of a skill ④ not intimate; not close: 交情很～ not on familiar terms ⑤ (of colour) light; pale: ～蓝 light blue / ～黄 pale yellow / 这种毛线色儿太～。The colour of this woollen yarn is too pale. ⑥ not long in time: 相处的日子还～ have not been together long / 他在这儿工作的日子～。He's been working here for only a short time. ——see also jiān

浅薄　qiǎnbó　shallow; superficial; meagre: 我读过他的几本书, 内容～得很。I've read some of his books —they're very shallow. / 他的历史知识很～。He has a very meagre knowledge of history. / 他这人太～, 不能领略这部小说里的深刻感情。He's too superficial to

appreciate the deep feelings in the novel.

浅尝辄止 qiǎn cháng zhé zhǐ　stop after gaining a little knowledge; be satisfied with a smattering of knowledge

浅成岩 qiǎnchéngyán *geol.* hypabyssal rock

浅淡 qiǎndàn ① (of colour) light; pale: ~的红色 pale red ② (of feeling) vague; faint: 她的声音流露出~的哀愁。There was a tinge of sadness in her voice.

浅耕 qiǎngēng　shallow ploughing

浅海 qiǎnhǎi　shallow sea; epeiric sea; epicontinental sea: ~水域 the shallow waters along the coast

浅见 qiǎnjiàn ① superficial view: ~寡闻 ignorant and ill-informed ② *hum.* humble opinion: 依我~ in my humble opinion

浅近 qiǎnjìn　simple; plain; easy to understand: 这本书写得~易懂。The language of this book is simple and easy to understand.

浅口鞋 qiǎnkǒuxié　shoes with low-cut uppers

浅陋 qiǎnlòu　meagre; mean: 学识~ have meagre knowledge

浅露 qiǎnlù　blunt (in expression): 词意~ blunt words

浅明 qiǎnmíng　simple; plain; clear; obvious: ~的道理 a plain truth

浅色 qiǎnsè　light colour: ~的女衬衣 a light-coloured blouse

浅释 qiǎnshì　(usu. used in book titles) simple explanation: 《唐诗~》*Tang Poems with Simple Explanations*

浅水池 qiǎnshuǐchí　the shallow end of a swimming pool; shallow pool

浅说 qiǎnshuō　(usu. used in titles of books and articles) elementary introduction: 《无线电~》*An Elementary Introduction to Radio*

浅滩 qiǎntān　shoal; shallows

浅谈 qiǎntán　(usu. used in titles of books and articles) brief talk: 《~被动语态》*A Brief Talk on the Passive Voice*

浅显 qiǎnxiǎn　plain; easy to read and understand: ~的道理 a plain truth / ~通俗的科学读物 simple popular scientific literature

浅鲜 qiǎnxiǎn　*formal* meagre; scanty

浅笑 qiǎnxiào　smile

浅学 qiǎnxué　having superficial knowledge; of little learning; ill-educated

浅易 qiǎnyì　simple and easy: ~读物 easy readings; easy-to-read literature

浅斟低唱 qiǎnzhēn-dīchàng　drinking leisurely and singing softly—a cultured way of enjoying oneself

浅种 qiǎnzhòng　shallow sowing

浅子 qiǎnzi　(also 浅儿 qiǎnr) a shallow container

遣 qiǎn ① send; dispatch: 派遣 pàiqiǎn ② dispel; expel: 消遣 xiāoqiǎn

遣词造句 qiǎncí-zàojù　choice of words and building of sentences; wording and phrasing

遣返 qiǎnfǎn　repatriate: ~战俘 repatriate prisoners of war

遣怀 qiǎnhuái　*formal* give vent to one's feelings (usu. in verse): 赋诗~ express oneself in verse

遣闷 qiǎnmèn　dispel boredom; divert oneself (from boredom)

遣派 qiǎnpài　same as 派遣 pàiqiǎn

遣散 qiǎnsàn　disband; dismiss; send away; lay off: 这个机构已撤消，人员已~。The agency has been disbanded, and all its employees have been sent elsewhere.

遣散费 qiǎnsànfèi　severance pay

遣戍 qiǎnshù　*formal* banish; send into exile

遣送 qiǎnsòng　send back; repatriate: 他因为没护照，被~回国。He was sent back to his country because he had no passport. / ~出境 deport

遣兴 qiǎnxìng　same as 遣怀 qiǎnhuái

遣 qiǎn　see below

遣责 qiǎnzé　condemn; denounce; censure: 世界舆论~侵略者的挑衅。World opinion condemned the aggressor's provocation. / 他做了错事，受到良心的~。He had done wrong, and his conscience plagued him for it.

缱 qiǎn　see below

缱绻 qiǎnquǎn　*liter.* deep attachment; tender affection: 欲掩香帏论~，先敛双眉愁夜短。(柳永) Before lowering the perfumed curtain to express her love, Shé knits her eyebrows, worried that the night is too short.

qiàn

欠¹ qiàn ① yawn: 哈欠 hāqian ② raise slightly (a part of the body): ~脚儿 slightly raise one's heels

欠² qiàn ① owe; be behind with: ~租 be behind with the rent / 我~他十块钱。I owe him ten *yuan*. / 我还~图书馆一本书。I still owe the library a book. ② not enough; lacking; wanting: 文字~通。The writing is not altogether grammatical. *or* The wording is somewhat awkward. / ~三天就是一个月了。It's three days short of a month. / 你这样做有点~聪明。You weren't shrewd enough in your handling of the matter. *or* It wasn't very wise of you to have done that. / 说话~考虑 be too free with one's tongue ③ *dial.* be fidgety and bungling: 他手~着呢。He always likes to fiddle with things. / 嘴~ have a loose tongue

欠安 qiàn'ān　(of an aged person or a VIP) feeling unwell; indisposed; under the weather: 爷爷今天身体~。Grandpa is not feeling very well today.

欠产 qiànchǎn　fall short of the production target; have a shortfall in output: 今年非但没超产还欠了产。Not only did we not exceed this year's production target, we even fell short of it.

欠户 qiànhù　debtor

欠火 qiànhuǒ　have not been cooked or heated long enough; undercooked: 这些馒头~。These buns haven't been steamed long enough.

欠佳 qiànjiā　not good enough; not up to the mark: 身体~ not feel well; be under the weather

欠款 qiànkuǎn ① owe a debt: 这家公司~数百万，倒闭了。This company was several million *yuan* in debt and went bankrupt. / 他欠了银行的款。He owes money to the bank. ② money that is owing; arrears; balance due: 银行限期要公司还清~。The bank demanded that the company repay its debt within the prescribed time limit.

欠情 qiànqíng　owe sb. a debt of gratitude; be indebted to sb.: 人家帮了那么些忙，也没好好谢谢，总觉得~儿。He helped us so much, and we never even thanked him properly. We feel indebted to him.

欠缺 qiànquē ① be deficient in; be short of: 我们的经验还很~。We are still lacking in experience. ② shortcoming; deficiency: 我们的工作还有很多~。There are still many shortcomings in our work.

欠伸 qiànshēn　stretch oneself and yawn

欠身 qiànshēn　raise oneself slightly; half rise from one's seat: 他~向进来的客人打招呼。He rose slightly to greet the visitor. / 主人给他端来一杯茶，他欠了欠身说：“谢谢。”His host brought him a cup of tea, and half rising from his seat, he said, "Thank you."

欠条 qiàntiáo　(also 欠据 qiànjù) a bill signed in acknowledgement of debt; IOU

欠妥 qiàntuǒ not proper: 措词～ not properly worded / 这件事你办得～。You didn't handle the matter properly.

欠息 qiànxī debit interest

欠项 qiànxiàng liabilities

欠薪 qiànxīn ① delay paying a salary: 工厂欠了我们两个月的薪 The factory still owes us two months' salary. ② back pay; overdue salaries

欠债 qiànzhài owe a debt; run into debt: 他非但没有积蓄，还欠着债呢。He not only has no savings but is also in debt. / 他欠了很多债。He is heavily in debt.

欠帐 qiànzhàng ① owe a debt; run into debt ② bills due; outstanding accounts

欠资 qiànzī postage due: ～信 postage-due letter / ～邮件 postage-due mail

欠揍 qiànzòu inf. need a spanking: 你太淘气了，真是～。You're being awfully naughty. You need a good spanking.

纤(縴) qiàn a rope for towing a boat; tow line: 拉纤 lāqiàn ——see also xiān

纤夫 qiànfū boat tracker

纤路 qiànlù towpath; towing path; track road

纤绳 qiànshéng towline; towrope

纤手 qiànshǒu old estate agent; real estate broker

芡 qiàn Gorgon euryale (Euryale ferox)

芡粉 qiànfěn ① the seed powder of Gorgon euryale ② any starch used in cooking

芡实 qiànshí Gorgon fruit

茜(蒨) qiàn ① see 茜草 qiàncǎo ② alizarin red

茜草 qiàncǎo bot. madder

茜素染料 qiànsù rǎnliào alizarin dyes

倩¹ qiàn formal pretty; handsome

倩² qiàn formal ask sb. to do sth.: ～人执笔 ask sb. to write on one's behalf

倩男倩女 qiànnán-qiànnǚ smartly dressed men and women

倩影 qiànyǐng beautiful image (of a woman); picture (of a beautiful woman)

倩装 qiànzhuāng (a woman's) beautiful dress

堑 qiàn moat; chasm: 天堑 tiānqiàn

堑壕 qiànháo mil. trench; entrenchment: ～工事 entrenchment works / ～战 trench warfare

嵌 qiàn inlay; embed; set: ～花的地面 a mosaic pavement / 桌面上～着象牙雕成的花。The table is inlaid with an ivory flower-pattern.

嵌镶 qiànxiāng same as 镶嵌 xiāngqiàn

椠 qiàn ① board for taking notes in ancient times ② block-printed edition: 宋～ a Song Dynasty block-printed edition

歉 qiàn ① apology: 道歉 dàoqiàn ② crop failure: 以丰补～ make up for a crop failure with a bumper harvest

歉忱 qiànchén formal apology; regret

歉疚 qiànjiù having a guilty conscience: 让你代我受过，甚感～。You took the blame for me, which troubles my conscience deeply.

歉年 qiànnián a lean year

歉然 qiànrán apologetic: ～一笑 give an apologetic smile

歉收 qiànshōu crop failure; poor harvest: 因遭天灾而～ have a bad harvest due to natural disaster

歉岁 qiànsuì a lean year

歉意 qiànyì apology; regret: 表示～ offer an apology; express one's regret / 谨致～。Please accept my apologies.

歉仄 qiànzè formal feel apologetic; be sorry; regret

qiāng

抢(搶) qiāng formal bump against: 呼天抢地 hūtiān-qiāngdì ——see also qiǎng

呛(嗆) qiāng choke: 吃饭吃～了 choke over one's food / 他喝得太猛，～着了。He took a big gulp and almost choked. / 他游泳时～了一口水。He choked on a mouthful of water while swimming. / 米粒～进他气管里去了。A grain of rice got stuck in his windpipe. ——see also qiàng

羌 Qiāng see 羌族 Qiāngzú

羌活 qiānghuó bot. notopterygium (Notopterygium incisium)

羌族 Qiāngzú ① the Qiang (Chiang) nationality, or the Qiangs (Chiangs), inhabiting Sichuan Province ② Qiang, an ancient nationality in China

枪¹(槍、鎗) qiāng ① rifle; gun; firearm ② a thing which is shaped or functions like a gun: 焊枪 hànqiāng ③ spear: 红缨枪 hóngyīngqiāng

枪²(槍) qiāng see 枪替 qiāngtì

枪靶 qiāngbǎ (shooting) target

枪把 qiāngbà the small of the stock; pistol grip

枪崩 qiāngbēng inf. execute by shooting

枪毙 qiāngbì execute by shooting: 这几个罪犯该～。These criminals should be shot.

枪刺 qiāngcì bayonet

枪带 qiāngdài (rifle) sling

枪弹 qiāngdàn ① cartridge ② bullet

枪法 qiāngfǎ marksmanship: 她～高明。She is a crack shot.

枪放下 qiāngfàngxià (word of command) Order arms!

枪杆 qiānggǎn (also 枪杆子 qiānggǎnzi) rifle; gun; arms: 拿起～儿上前线 take up arms and go to the front / ～子里面出政权。(毛泽东) Political power grows out of the barrel of a gun.

枪管 qiāngguǎn barrel (of a gun)

枪机 qiāngjī rifle bolt

枪架 qiāngjià rifle rack

枪决 qiāngjué execute by shooting: 死刑用～的方法执行。The death penalty is to be executed by means of shooting.

枪口 qiāngkǒu muzzle: 把～对准靶子 aim a gun at the target

枪林弹雨 qiānglín-dànyǔ a forest of guns and a hail of bullets—heavy fire: 冒着～冲锋陷阵 charge under a hail of bullets; charge under heavy fire / 新闻记者出入于～，采集前方战讯。The reporters gathered news of the front amidst heavy fire.

枪榴弹 qiāngliúdàn rifle grenade

枪炮 qiāngpào firearms; arms; guns

枪杀 qiāngshā shoot dead

枪伤 qiāngshāng bullet wound

枪上肩 qiāngshàngjiān (word of command) Shoulder arms!

枪声 qiāngshēng report of a gun; shot; crack: 听到远处

的～ hear gunshots in the distance

枪手 qiāngshǒu ① marksman; gunner ② *old* spearman

枪手 qiāngshou one who sits for an examination in place of another person

枪栓 qiāngshuān rifle bolt

枪膛 qiāngtáng bore (of a gun)

枪替 qiāngtì sit for an examination in place of another person

枪托 qiāngtuō (rifle) butt; buttstock

枪乌贼 qiāngwūzéi squid

枪械 qiāngxiè firearms

枪眼 qiāngyǎn ① embrasure; loophole ② bullet hole

枪鱼 qiāngyú marlin

枪支 qiāngzhī firearms: ～弹药 firearms and ammunition

枪子儿 qiāngzǐr *inf.* ① cartridge ② bullet; shot

戗（戧）

qiāng ① go in an opposite direction: ～辙儿走 go in a direction not allowed by traffic regulations; go in the wrong direction / 他老爱跟人～着说,叫人生气。He's always ready to argue, much to our annoyance. ② clash; be at loggerheads with: 他们说～了,吵起来啦。Their views clashed and this eventually led to a quarrel. ——see also qiàng

戗风 qiāngfēng against the wind: ～行船 sail against the wind

戗顺不吃 qiāng-shùn bù chī *dial.* yield neither to coercion nor to persuasion

戕

qiāng *formal* kill: 自戕 zìqiāng

戕害 qiānghài injure; harm

戕贼 qiāngzéi injure; undermine: ～身体 undermine (*or* ruin) one's health

斨

qiāng a kind of axe used in ancient times

腔

qiāng ① cavity (in human or animal bodies): 胸腔 xiōngqiāng ② tune; pitch: 唱走了～儿 sing out of tune ③ accent: 山东～ Shandong accent ④ speech: 开腔 kāiqiāng

腔肠动物 qiāngcháng dòngwù coelenterate

腔调 qiāngdiào ① tune: 京剧的～ tunes of Beijing opera ② *derog.* tone of voice: 他讲起话来一副十足的流氓～。He speaks like a genuine gangster. ③ accent; intonation: 听他说话的～象是河南人。Judging from his accent, he is probably from Henan.

腔骨 qiānggǔ *dial.* spinal joints of pigs, sheep, etc. (for food)

蜣

qiāng see below

蜣螂 qiānglláng dung beetle

锖（鏘）

qiāng *onom.* a clanging or clanking sound: 锣声～～。Gongs clanked.

锵

qiāng see below ——see also qiàng

锵水 qiāngshuǐ popular name for 强酸 qiángsuān

qiáng

强（強、彊）

qiáng ① strong; powerful: 身～体壮 strong and healthy / 能力很～ very capable / 责任心～ have a strong sense of responsibility / ～冷空气 a strong cold air current / 决赛时两～将有一场恶战。There'll be a fierce struggle between the two strong teams. ② by force: ～取 take by force ③ better:

我们的劳动条件一年比一年～。Our working conditions are getting better each year. ④ slightly more than; plus: 三分之一～ slightly more than one third ——see also jiàng; qiǎng

强半 qiángbàn *formal* more than half; greater part; most

强暴 qiángbào ① violent; brutal: ～的行为 an act of violence ② ferocious adversary: 不畏～ defy brute force

强大 qiángdà big and powerful; powerful; formidable: ～的人民解放军 the powerful People's Liberation Army / 阵容～的代表团 strong delegation; big high-ranking delegation / 这种植物具有～的生命力。This kind of plant has great vitality.

强盗 qiángdào robber; bandit: ～行为 banditry; robbery / ～头子 gang boss; ringleader / 法西斯～ fascist bandits

强盗逻辑 qiángdào luóji gangster logic

强的松 qiángdísōng *pharm.* prednisone

强敌 qiángdí formidable opponent or enemy

强调 qiángdiào stress; emphasize; underline: 不适当地～情况特殊 lay undue stress on special circumstances / 必须～产品质量。Emphasis must be placed on the quality of the products. / 不要～客观原因。Don't overemphasize the influence of objective forces.

强度 qiángdù intensity; strength: 钢的～ the strength of the steel / 辐射～ radiation intensity

强渡 qiángdù *mil.* fight one's way across a river; force a river: 1935 年 5 月, 红军～大渡河。The Red Army forced its way across the Dadu River in May, 1935.

强风 qiángfēng *meteorol.* strong breeze

强干 qiánggàn capable and experienced

强攻 qiánggōng take by storm; storm: ～敌人阵地 storm the enemy position

强固 qiánggù strong; solid: ～的工事 strong fortifications / 为国家工业化打下～的基础 lay a solid (*or* firm) foundation for the industrialization of the country

强国 qiángguó powerful (*or* strong) nation; power: 把我国建设成为社会主义的现代化～ build China into a modern, powerful socialist country

强悍 qiánghàn fierce; intrepid; doughty: 匈奴民族～好战, 自公元前三世纪以后, 常为中国患。The Xiongnu, a fierce and warlike people, became a constant threat to Han China after the 3rd century B. C.

强横 qiánghèng rude and unreasonable; tyrannical; surly; arrogant: 他态度～, 没法跟他讲理。He is too surly to reason with.

强化 qiánghuà strengthen; intensify; consolidate: ～国家机器 strengthen the state apparatus / ～麦乳精 fortified extract of malt and milk / 英语～训练班 an intensive English training course

强击机 qiángjījī attack plane

强记 qiángjì *formal* have a retentive memory ——see also qiǎngjì

强加 qiángjiā impose; force: 任何一方不得把自己的意志～给对方。No party may impose its will on the other party.

强加于人 qiángjiā yú rén impose (one's views, etc.) on others: 不要把你的意见～。Don't force your views on others.

强奸 qiángjiān violate (a woman); rape

强奸民意 qiángjiān mínyì defile public opinion

强碱 qiángjiǎn *chem.* alkali; strong base

强健 qiángjiàn strong and healthy: 体魄～ be physically strong; have a strong constitution

强将手下无弱兵 qiángjiàng shǒuxià wú ruòbīng there are no poor soldiers under a good general

强劲 qiángjìng powerful; forceful: ～的海风 a strong

wind from the sea

强劳动力 qiángláodònglì　an able-bodied labourer

强力霉素 qiánglìméisù　*pharm.* doxycycline

强梁 qiángliáng　brutal; tyrannical; surly: 不畏～ defy brute force

强烈 qiángliè　① strong; intense; violent: 他怀着当一个音乐家的～愿望。He has a strong desire to become a musician. ／～的求知欲 a strong thirst for knowledge ／～的仇恨 intense hatred ／～反对 strongly oppose ／～谴责 vehemently condemn ／提出～抗议 lodge a strong protest; protest strongly ／～地震 a violent earthquake ② clear-cut; distinct; striking; sharp: 这张照片黑白分明，显出～的对比。The distinction between black and white in this photo creates a sharp contrast.

强令 qiánglìng　arbitrarily give orders: ～执行 arbitrarily give orders to carry out sth.

强龙不压地头蛇 qiánglóng bù yā dìtóushé　a powerful dragon cannot crush a snake in its old haunts—even a powerful man cannot crush a local bully

强弩之末 qiángnǔ zhī mò　an arrow at the end of its flight—a spent force: ～，力不能入鲁缟。《汉书》When the arrow is spent, it cannot break fine silk.

强拍 qiángpāi　*mus.* strong beat; accented beat: 次～ subsidiary strong beat

强权 qiángquán　power; might: ～即公理—这是帝国主义的逻辑。Might is right—that is the logic of imperialism. ／～终于向正义低头。Power gave way to justice at last. ／～外交 power diplomacy ／～政治 power politics

强人 qiángrén　① strong man ② (also 强徒 qiángtú) old robber; bandit

强溶剂 qiángróngjì　*chem.* strong solvent

强身 qiángshēn　build up a good physique; improve one's health

强盛 qiángshèng　(of a country) powerful and prosperous

强手 qiángshǒu　① a very capable person ② a master player; a topnotch athlete; ace

强似 qiángsì　(also 强如 qiángrú) be better than; superior to: 今年的秋收～去年。This year's autumn harvest is better than last year's.

强酸 qiángsuān　*chem.* strong acid

强袭 qiángxí　take by storm; storm

强项[1] qiángxiàng　*formal* resolute and unbending; upright and unyielding

强项[2] qiángxiàng　*sports* strong point (of an athlete or a team)

强心剂 qiángxīnjì　cardiac stimulant; cardiotonic

强行 qiángxíng　force: ～闯入 force one's way in ／～登陆 force a landing ／～通过一项议案 force a bill through

强行军 qiángxíngjūn　forced march

强压 qiángyā　suppress; stifle: ～住心中怒火 suppress one's anger

强毅 qiángyì　resolute and steadfast; staunch

强硬 qiángyìng　strong; tough; unyielding: 措词～的声明 a strongly worded statement ／提出～抗议 lodge a strong protest ／～路线 tough line; hard line ／～的态度 an uncompromising stand ／～派 hardliner

强有力 qiángyǒulì　strong; vigorous; forceful: 采取～的行动 take vigorous action

强于 qiángyú　be better than: 我们队略～对方。Our team is slightly better than the opponent.

强占 qiángzhàn　forcibly occupy; seize

强震 qiángzhèn　*geol.* strong shock: ～区 meizoseismal area

强直 qiángzhí　*med.* rigidity

强制 qiángzhì　force; compel; coerce: ～措施 compulsory (*or* mandatory) measure ／～劳动 forced labour ／～手段 compulsory means; coercive measure ／～性规定 mandatory provision ／～性规章 peremptory regulations ／～性命令 mandatory order ／～性制裁 compulsory sanction ／～执行 enforce ／～仲裁解决 compulsory arbitral settlement ／不能～人们接受一种艺术风格或一种学派。People cannot be compelled to accept one particular style of art or school of thought. ／法院～他缴纳五百元罚款。The court compelled him to pay a 500 *yuan* fine.

强中自有强中手 qiáng zhōng zì yǒu qiáng zhōng shǒu　however strong you are, there's always someone stronger

强壮 qiángzhuàng　strong; sturdy; robust: 他身体～。He's strong and healthy.

强壮剂 qiángzhuàngjì　roborant; tonic

强子 qiángzǐ　*phys.* hadron

墙（墻、牆）　qiáng　wall

墙报 qiángbào　wall newspaper

墙壁 qiángbì　wall

墙倒众人推 qiáng dǎo zhòngrén tuī　when a wall is about to collapse, everybody gives it a shove—everybody hits a man who is down

墙根 qiánggēn　the foot of a wall

墙角 qiángjiǎo　a corner formed by two walls: ～石 cornerstone

墙脚 qiángjiǎo　① the foot of a wall ② foundation——see also 挖墙脚 wā qiángjiǎo

墙裙 qiángqún　*archit.* dado

墙头 qiángtóu　① the top of a wall ② a short, low enclosing wall

墙头草，随风倒 qiángtóucǎo, suífēngdǎo　grass atop a wall swaying in the wind—a person who follows the crowd

墙头诗 qiángtóushī　same as 街头诗 jiētóushī

墙垣 qiángyuán　*formal* wall

墙纸 qiángzhǐ　wallpaper

蔷（薔）　qiáng　see below

蔷薇 qiángwēi　rose: ～科 the rose family

嫱（嬙）　qiáng　a woman court official in ancient China

樯（檣、艢）　qiáng　*formal* mast: 帆樯 fānqiáng

qiǎng

抢[1]（搶）　qiǎng　① rob; loot: ～银行 rob a bank ② snatch; grab: 他把信～了过去。He snatched away the letter. ③ vie for; scramble for: ～球 scramble for the ball ／～干重活 vie with each other for the hardest job ／孩子们～着要排第一个。The children jostled with each other for the first place in line. ④ rush: 他～步上前接过了客人手上的行李。He rushed over and took the luggage from his guest's hands. ／我们必须～在洪水的前面把堤坝修好。We must rush to repair the dykes before the flood comes.

抢[2]（搶）　qiǎng　scrape; scratch: 把锅底～一～ scrape the bottom of the pot ／磨剪子～菜刀 sharpen scissors and kitchen knives ／他摔了一跤，膝盖上～去了一块皮。He fell and scraped his knee.——see also qiāng

抢白 qiǎngbái　tell off; dress down; rebuff: 我劝他别生气，反被他～了一顿。I tried to pacify him, but got a rebuff for my pains.

抢答 qiǎngdá　race to be the first to answer a question

抢点 qiǎngdiǎn　① (of a train, etc.) make up time (in order to keep on schedule) ② (of a football striker, etc.) race to a favourable position

抢渡 qiǎngdù　speedily cross (a river): 河水可能暴涨，得立即～。The river may suddenly rise. We must make a swift crossing immediately.

抢夺 qiǎngduó　snatch; wrest; seize: ～胜利果实 seize the fruits of victory

抢饭碗 qiǎngfànwǎn　inf. fight for a job; snatch sb. else's job: 这儿只有一个打字员的名额，有好几个人抢这饭碗呢。There is only one opening here for a typist, and quite a few people are competing for the position.

抢购 qiǎnggòu　rush to purchase (anticipating inflation or scarcity): ～风潮 panic purchasing; panic buying spree / ～面粉 rush to the store to buy flour / 谣传物价要涨，人们都去商店～。The rumour that prices were going to rise led to a rush on the shops. / 这个商店来了一批新式毛衣，一上午就被～一空。The store received a shipment of new-style sweaters, which were all sold out in one morning.

抢劫 qiǎngjié　rob; loot; plunder: 有四个人今天早上～了银行。Four men robbed the bank this morning. / 把商店～一空 ransack a store

抢截 qiǎngjié　sports intercept

抢镜头 qiǎngjìngtóu　① (of a cameraman) fight for a vantage point from which to take a news picture: 他会～，常常向报社提供精采的照片。He's good at finding the best vantage points, and often gives the newspaper its best action-shots. / 这次上山考察熊猫生活，他抢下了很多珍贵的镜头。During this expedition to study the life of the giant panda, he took a lot of valuable snapshots. ② steal the show; be fond of being in the limelight: 她就喜欢～，出风头。She loves to steal the show and be the centre of attention.

抢救 qiǎngjiù　rescue; save; salvage: ～国家财产 save state property (from a fire, flood, etc.) / ～水淹了的庄稼 salvage flooded crops / ～病人 give emergency treatment to a patient; rescue a patient / ～无效。All rescue measures proved ineffectual. / ～工作 rescue work / ～组 rescue party

抢掠 qiǎnglüè　loot; sack; plunder: 在地震灾区进行～的人将被枪决。Anyone found looting in the earthquake-stricken area will be shot. / 入侵者到处烧杀～。The invaders burned, killed and plundered wherever they went.

抢亲 qiǎngqīn　(also 抢婚 qiǎnghūn) ① a marriage ceremony in which the bridegroom pretends to kidnap his bride ② steal, kidnap or force a woman to be one's wife

抢青 qiǎngqīng　rush a harvest of ripening crops (in anticipation of bad weather)

抢墒 qiǎngshāng　hurry to sow seeds while the soil is still moist

抢时间 qiǎng shíjiān　race against time: 农活有季节性，必须～。Farm work is seasonal, so we must race against time.

抢收 qiǎngshōu　rush in the harvest; get the harvest in quickly: 天气很快会变，得赶快～。The weather is bound to change soon. We must get the harvest in quickly.

抢手 qiǎngshǒu　(of goods) in great demand: ～货 goods in great demand / 如今，高档化妆品在市场上最～。Nowadays high-grade cosmetics are the most popular items on the market.

抢先 qiǎngxiān　try to be the first to do sth.; anticipate; forestall: 部队～占了那座桥。The troops have anticipated the enemy and seized the bridge. / 一个个进来，别～。Come in one at a time. Don't rush in all at once. / 会议一开始，她就～发言。As soon as the meeting started, she rushed to speak before everyone else.

抢险 qiǎngxiǎn　rush to deal with an emergency (e.g. a breach in an embankment, a cave-in, etc.): 河堤决口后马上派出了工程队去～。The river dyke sprang a leak, and the construction brigade was immediately sent to deal with it.

抢修 qiǎngxiū　rush to repair; do rush repairs: 线路正在～，半小时后恢复供电。The line is being rush-repaired and the power supply will return to normal in half an hour.

抢运 qiǎngyùn　rush to transport

抢占 qiǎngzhàn　① race to control; seize; grab: ～制高点 race to control a commanding point ② unlawfully occupy: 这家工厂～了附近学校的一块地。The factory unlawfully built on a piece of land which belongs to a nearby school.

抢种 qiǎngzhòng　rush-plant: ～晚稻 rush-plant the late rice

抢嘴 qiǎngzuǐ　dial. ① try to get the first word in; try to be heard above the rest: 按次序发言，别～。We will take turns speaking, so don't all try to speak at once. ② rush to eat up the food

羟 (羥) qiǎng　see below

羟基 qiǎngjī　chem. hydroxyl (group): ～化物 hydroxylate

强 (強、彊) qiǎng　make an effort; strive: ～作镇静 make an effort to appear composed; try hard to keep one's composure / ～不知以为知 pretend to know what one does not know ——see also jiàng; qiáng

强逼 qiǎngbī　compel; force: 我并不想来，是被～着来的。I didn't want to come, I was forced to.

强辩 qiǎngbiàn　defend oneself by sophistry; argue against all reason; argue stubbornly or obstinately

强词夺理 qiǎngcí-duólǐ　use lame arguments; resort to sophistry; reason fallaciously: 他在人行道上骑车撞了人，还～说人家没给他让路。He hit a pedestrian while riding his bicycle on the pavement, but still he offered the lame excuse that the person didn't make way for him.

强记 qiǎngjì　force oneself to memorize; learn by rote: 这几课书我并没弄懂，考试全得靠～。I didn't understand these lessons, so I had to rely on sheer memorization to pass the exam. ——see also qiángjì

强留 qiǎngliú　force sb. to stay on: 愿意退出的决不～。Those who want to drop out are free to do so.

强迫 qiǎngpò　compel; force; coerce: ～命令 resort to coercion and commandism / ～敌机降落 compel the enemy plane to land / 不要～我同意你的意见。Don't force me to agree with you.

强求 qiǎngqiú　insist on; impose: 各地情况不同，不能～一律。No uniformity should be imposed since conditions vary from place to place.

强人所难 qiǎng rén suǒ nán　try to make sb. do what he is unwilling or unable to: 各人有各人的嗜好，不要～。Everybody's got their own interests; you mustn't try and force people into doing things they don't want to. / 他不会跳舞，你偏要拉他去跳，这不是～吗？He can't dance, but then you go and drag him onto the dance floor. Aren't you forcing him to do something against his will?

强使 qiǎngshǐ　compel; force

强笑 qiǎngxiào　① force a smile ② a forced smile

强颜欢笑 qiǎng yán huānxiào　put on an air of cheerfulness; try to look happy

强作解人 qiǎng zuò jiěrén　pretend to be in the know

襁(繦) qiǎng　see below

襁褓 qiǎngbǎo　swaddling clothes: 从～中抚育成人 bring sb. up from infancy / 我们的新计划还只是在～中呢。Our new plan is still only in its infancy.

镪 qiǎng　strings of cash ——see also qiāng

qiàng

呛(嗆) qiàng　irritate (respiratory organs): 炸辣椒的味儿～鼻子。The smell of red pepper being fried irritates the nose. / 烟把我～着了。The smoke almost choked me. ——see also qiāng

炝(熗) qiàng　① boil (meat or vegetables) in water for a while, then dress with soy, vinegar, etc. ② fry sth. quickly in hot oil, then cook it with sauce and water

戗(戧) qiàng　① archit. prop ② dial. brace; shore up: 用两根木头来～住这堵墙 brace the wall with two logs ——see also qiāng

跄(蹌) qiàng　see below

跄踉 qiàngliàng　same as 踉跄 liàngqiàng

qiāo

悄 qiāo　see below ——see also qiǎo

悄悄 qiāoqiāo　adv. quietly; on the quiet: 我～地披上大衣，带上门出去。Quietly, I put on my coat and went out, closing the door after me. / 他～儿地跟我全说了。He told me everything on the quiet.

悄悄话 qiāoqiāohuà　whisperings (esp. between husband and wife, lovers, etc.)

硗(磽、墝) qiāo　see below

硗薄 qiāobó　(also 硗确 qiāoquè; 硗瘠 qiāojí) (of land) hard and infertile; barren

雀 qiāo　see below ——see also qiǎo; què

雀子 qiāozi　freckle

跷(蹺) qiāo　① lift up (a leg); hold up (a finger): ～着腿坐着 sit with one's legs crossed / 他一起大姆指说"好，好！" He made a thumbs-up sign and said, "Good, good!" ② stand or walk on tiptoe: ～着脚走路 walk on tiptoe / 他一起脚往人群里看。He stood on tiptoe to scan the crowd. ③ stilts: 踩着～扭秧歌 do the yanko dance on stilts

跷蹊 qiāoqi　same as 蹊跷 qīqiāo

跷跷板 qiāoqiāobǎn　seesaw: 玩～ play on a seesaw

跻(躋) qiāo　same as 硗 qiāo

敲 qiāo　① knock; beat; strike: ～门 knock at the door / 钟刚～过四点。The clock has just struck four. / ～锣打鼓迎新年 usher in the new year with drums and gongs; beat drums and gongs to greet the new year ② inf. overcharge; fleece sb.: 给～去五块钱 be stung for five yuan / 他提了工资，我们～了他一顿饭。His pay has been raised, so we made him treat us to a dinner. / 这家铺子卖这些东西给我时～了我一下子。The store overcharged me for the goods.

敲边鼓 qiāo biāngǔ　speak or act to assist sb. from the sidelines; back sb. up: 你可以在会上提出这建议，我在旁边给你～。You present this proposal at the meeting and I'll back you up from the sidelines.

敲打 qiāodǎ　① beat; rap; tap: 锣鼓～得很热闹。Drums and gongs were beating boisterously. ② dial. say sth. to irritate sb.: 冷言冷语～人 irritate people with sarcastic remarks ③ pressurize and supervise sb.: 这孩子老得大人～着点，不然就不好好做功课了。The boy needs constant prodding from his parents, otherwise he won't get his homework done.

敲骨吸髓 qiāogǔ-xīsuǐ　break the bones and suck the marrow—suck the lifeblood; be a cruel, bloodsucking exploiter

敲击 qiāojī　beat; rap; tap

敲警钟 qiāo jǐngzhōng　sound the alarm bell—sound a warning: 这次事故给我们敲了警钟，今后必须严格制度。The accident sounded a warning against a relaxation of the rules.

敲门砖 qiāoménzhuān　a brick picked up to knock on the door and thrown away when it has served its purpose—a stepping-stone to success

敲丧钟 qiāo sāngzhōng　sound the funeral bell: 民族独立运动敲响了殖民主义的丧钟。The national independence movement sounded the death knell of colonialism.

敲小鼓 qiāo xiǎogǔ　beat a little drum—feel uneasy or nervous

敲诈 qiāozhà　extort; blackmail; racketeer: ～钱财 extort money / 他想利用这种丑闻～我。He tried to use the scandal to blackmail me.

敲诈勒索 qiāozhà-lèsuǒ　extort; blackmail; racketeer

敲竹杠 qiāo zhúgàng　① fleece sb.; daylight robbery: 那家饭店真是～！They really fleeced us at that hotel! ② blackmail: 他知道我们的秘密，就借此敲我们的竹杠。He knows our secret and is holding it over us.

劁 qiāo　geld; castrate: ～猪 castrate a pig

锹(鍫) qiāo　spade: 一把～ a spade / 一～煤 a shovelful of coal / 挖一～深 dig a spade's depth; dig a spit deep

缲(幧) qiāo　hem with invisible stitches: 给裙子～边 hem a skirt

橇 qiāo　sledge; sled; sleigh: 雪橇 xuěqiāo

qiáo

乔¹(喬) qiáo　① tall: 乔木 qiáomù ② (Qiáo) a surname

乔²(喬) qiáo　disguise: 乔装 qiáozhuāng

乔林 qiáolín　forestry high forest

乔模乔样 qiáomú-qiáoyàng　in an artificial or affected manner

乔木 qiáomù　arbor; tree

乔其纱 qiáoqíshā　text. georgette

乔迁 qiáoqiān　move to a better place or get a promotion

乔迁之喜 qiáoqiān zhī xǐ　congratulations on your new home

乔装 qiáozhuāng　disguise: ～成商人 disguise oneself as a merchant

乔装打扮 qiáozhuāng-dǎbàn　disguise oneself; masquerade

侨(僑) qiáo ① live abroad: 侨居 qiáojū ② a person living abroad: 华侨 huáqiáo

侨胞 qiáobāo countrymen (or nationals) residing abroad; overseas compatriots

侨汇 qiáohuì overseas remittance; immigrant remittance

侨汇券 qiáohuìquàn overseas remittance coupon

侨居 qiáojū live abroad: ～国 country of residence / 他在国外～了三十年。He lived abroad for thirty years. / 他是英国人，～中国。He is British but lives in China.

侨眷 qiáojuàn relatives of overseas Chinese who remain in the homeland

侨民 qiáomín a national of a particular country residing abroad: ～社会 foreign community

侨生 qiáoshēng ① children of overseas Chinese born abroad ② overseas Chinese studying in China

侨属 qiáoshǔ same as 侨眷 qiáojuàn

侨务 qiáowù affairs concerning nationals living abroad; overseas Chinese affairs

侨乡 qiáoxiāng village or town inhabited by relatives of overseas Chinese and returned overseas Chinese

侨资 qiáozī capital investments of overseas Chinese: ～企业 overseas Chinese enterprise

荞(蕎) qiáo see below

荞麦 qiáomài buckwheat

桥(橋) qiáo bridge: 木～ a wooden bridge / 石～ a stone bridge / 铁～ an iron bridge

桥洞 qiáodòng inf. bridge opening

桥墩 qiáodūn (bridge) pier

桥拱 qiáogǒng bridge arch

桥涵 qiáohán bridges and culverts

桥孔 qiáokǒng bridge opening

桥梁 qiáoliáng bridge: 在河上架设～ build a bridge across a river / 商业是联结生产同消费的～。Commerce is a bridge that links production with consumption. / 这本双语词典起着沟通两国文化的～作用。This bilingual dictionary serves as a bridge between the cultures of the two nations.

桥楼室 qiáolóushì bridge house

桥牌 qiáopái bridge (a card game): 打～ play bridge

桥式起重机 qiáoshì qǐzhòngjī bridge crane; overhead travelling crane

桥塔 qiáotǎ archit. bridge tower

桥台 qiáotái archit. abutment

桥头 qiáotóu either end of a bridge

桥头堡 qiáotóubǎo ① mil. bridgehead ② archit. bridge tower

桥塌 qiáotù either end of a bridge

桥支座 qiáozhīzuò bridge seat

翘(翹) qiáo ① raise (one's head): 翘首 qiáoshǒu ② become warped: 木板～了。The board has warped. ——see also qiào

翘楚 qiáochǔ formal an outstanding (or talented) person: 医中～ an eminent physician

翘棱 qiáoleng dial. become warped: 这老房子有年代了，地板都～了。This old house has stood for decades. The floor boards have all become warped with age.

翘盼 qiáopàn eagerly look forward to

翘企 qiáoqǐ formal raise one's head and stand on tiptoe—eagerly look forward to: 不胜～ look forward to sth. with eager anticipation

翘首 qiáoshǒu formal raise one's head and look: ～星空 look up at the starry sky

翘足而待 qiáozú ér dài wait on tiptoe—expect sth. to happen soon

翘足引领 qiáo zú yǐn lǐng stand on tiptoe and crane one's neck—eagerly look forward to

谯 qiáo see below

谯楼 qiáolóu formal ① watchtower ② drum tower

憔 qiáo see below

憔悴 qiáocuì wan and sallow; thin and pallid: 这姑娘脸色～，眼皮浮肿。The girl's face looks wan and sallow, and her eyelids are swollen.

樵 qiáo ① dial. firewood ② formal gather firewood

樵夫 qiáofū old woodcutter; woodman

瞧 qiáo inf. look; see: 等着～吧。Wait and see. / ～书 read a book / 东～西～ look about / 你～着办吧。You can do as you see fit. / 他～朋友去了。He went to see his friend.

瞧病 qiáobìng inf. ① (of a patient) see (or consult) a doctor ② (of a doctor) see a patient

瞧不起 qiáobuqǐ inf. look down on; despise

瞧不上眼 qiáobushàng yǎn inf. consider beneath one's notice; turn one's nose up at: 这些茶具，我一套也～。Of all these tea sets, there's not one that I consider worth a second look.

瞧得起 qiáodeqǐ inf. have a good opinion of; think highly of sb.

瞧惯 qiáoguàn same as 看惯 kànguàn

瞧哈哈儿 qiáo hāhar inf. have a good laugh over (sb.'s misfortune); gloat over

瞧见 qiáojian inf. see; catch sight of: 你在图书馆～我弟弟了吗?—没～。Did you see my brother in the library?—No, I didn't.

瞧热闹 qiáo rènao same as 看热闹 kàn rènao

瞧上 qiáoshang ① have a chance to see: 人们围着看熊猫，我挤不进去，一眼也没～。People crowded round the panda and I couldn't squeeze in, so I didn't get a chance to see it. / 那剧团已经离开这里了，我们瞧不上那出戏了。The troupe has already left here, so we've missed the chance to see the play. ② to one's liking: 你～了这姑娘，可人家不一定瞧得上你。You've taken a liking to the girl, but she won't necessarily take a liking to you.

qiǎo

巧 qiǎo ① skilful; ingenious; clever: ～匠 a skilled (or clever) workman / 他的手艺很～。His workmanship is excellent. / 你嘴～，你去说他准听。You're a clever talker and he'll listen to you if you try to persuade him. / 她真～，看见什么花就能画什么花。She's really clever—she can draw any flower that she sees. ② cunning; deceitful; artful: 花言巧语 huāyán-qiǎoyǔ ③ opportune; coincidental: 太～了，我一出家门就来了一辆出租汽车。It was most opportune that a taxi arrived just as I was leaving the house. / 你来得真～，我们今天正好包饺子。You've come just at the right time. We're just about to make jiaozi.

巧辩 qiǎobiàn argue skilfully or plausibly

巧夺天工 qiǎo duó tiāngōng wonderful workmanship (or superb craftsmanship) excelling nature

巧妇难为无米之炊 qiǎofù nán wéi wú mǐ zhī chuī the cleverest housewife can't cook a meal without rice—one can't make bricks without straw

巧妇鸟 qiǎofùniǎo wren

巧干 qiǎogàn work ingeniously; do sth. in a clever

way: 你光是苦干是达不到指标的, 得～才行。You can't meet the standards only by working hard; you have to do the work in a clever way.

巧合 qiǎohé coincidence: 他俩同年, 生日又是同一天, 真是～。What a coincidence it is that they were born in the same year and on the same day.

巧计 qiǎojì clever device; artful scheme

巧劲儿 qiǎojìnr *dial.* ① knack; trick: 常常练习, 慢慢就找着～了。Do it often, and in time you'll learn the trick. ② coincidence: 我正要去找他, 他就来了, 真是～。What a coincidence that I was just going to see him when he came.

巧克力 qiǎokèlì chocolate: 果仁～ nut chocolate / 酒心～ whisky heart chocolate / ～饼干 chocolate biscuit

巧立名目 qiǎo lì míngmù invent all sorts of excuses; concoct various pretexts: ～搜刮民财 extort people's wealth under all sorts of pretexts / ～滥发奖金 invent excuses to give out extravagant bonuses

巧妙 qiǎomiào ingenious; clever: ～的战术 ingenious tactics / 他用的方法很～。The method he uses is very clever.

巧取豪夺 qiǎoqǔ-háoduó secure (sb.'s belongings, rights, etc.) by force or trickery

巧舌如簧 qiǎoshé rú huáng have a smooth tongue like the reed of a wind instrument—have a glib tongue

巧事 qiǎoshì coincidence

巧手 qiǎoshǒu a dab (or deft) hand; being clever with one's hands; dexterity: 她是个绣花～。She's a dab hand at embroidering. / ～儿什么都会做。A deft hand can do just about anything.

巧思 qiǎosī ingenious or brilliant conception

巧黠 qiǎoxiá *formal* crafty; cunning; tricky

巧言令色 qiǎoyán-lìngsè clever talk and an ingratiating manner: ～, 鲜矣仁。《论语》Clever talk and an ingratiating manner are seldom found in a virtuous man.

巧遇 qiǎoyù encounter by chance

悄

qiāo ① silent or low-voiced: 低声～语 speak in a low voice ② *liter.* sad; worried; sorrowful: 忧心～～, 愠于群小。《诗经》My sad heart is consumed, I am harassed By a host of small men. ——see also qiǎo

悄静 qiǎojìng quiet; still; silent

悄没声儿 qiǎomoshēngr *dial.* silent or low-voiced: 她说起话来～的, 可唱起歌来是条女高音甜嗓子。Her voice is very low when she speaks, but she has a lovely soprano singing voice.

悄然 qiǎorán *liter.* ① sad; worried; sorrowful: ～泪下 shed tears in sorrow; shed sad tears ② quiet; soft: ～无声。All was quiet.

悄声 qiǎoshēng a low voice; whisper: 他～地告诉我窗外有人在偷听。He whispered to me that there was an eavesdropper outside the window.

雀

qiāo sparrow: 家雀儿 jiāqiǎor ——see also qiǎo; què

雀盲眼 qiǎomangyǎn *dial.* night blindness; nyctalopia

愀

qiǎo see below

愀然 qiǎorán *liter.* ① sorrowful-looking ② stern; grave-looking

qiào

壳(殼)

qiào shell; hard surface: 甲壳 jiǎqiào ——see also ké

壳菜 qiàocài mussel

壳斗 qiàodǒu *bot.* acorn-cup; cupule

壳质 qiàozhì *biochem.* chitin

俏

qiào ① pretty; smart-looking; handsome: 打扮得真～ be smartly dressed / 瞧她这～模样! Look how pretty she is! ② sell well; be in great demand: 俏货 qiàohuò ③ *dial.* flavour; season: ～点儿生姜 flavour (or season) food with some ginger

俏货 qiàohuò goods in great demand

俏丽 qiàolì handsome; pretty

俏皮 qiàopi ① good-looking; smart-looking: 她穿上那套新衣服, 显得很～。She looks very smart in her new dress. ② witty; clever: 他讲的话很～。What he said was very clever.

俏皮话 qiàopihuà ① witty remark; witticism; wisecrack ② sarcastic remark ③ same as 歇后语 xiēhòuyǔ

俏事 qiàoshì a paying proposition

俏式 qiàoshi *dial.* pretty and charming

俏头[1] qiàotou tricks to gain applause

俏头[2] qiàotou *dial.* flavouring; seasoning; condiment

诮(誚)

qiào *formal* censure; blame

诮呵 qiàohē blame; reproach; berate

诮让 qiàoràng *formal* condemn; denounce; censure

窍(竅)

qiào ① aperture; hole: 七窍 qīqiào ② a key to sth.: 诀窍 juéqiào

窍门 qiàomén key (to a problem); knack: 找～ try to find the key to a problem; try to get the knack of doing sth.

峭(陗)

qiào ① high and steep; precipitous: 陡峭 dǒuqiào ② severe; stern: 峭直 qiàozhí

峭拔 qiàobá ① (of a mountain) high and steep ② (of style of writing) vigorous: 笔锋～ have a vigorous style of writing

峭壁 qiàobì cliff; precipice; steep

峭寒 qiàohán (esp. of early spring) chilly

峭立 qiàolì rise steeply

峭厉 qiàolì *formal* ① (of wind, cold, etc.) bitter; sharp ② stern; severe; grim

峭直 qiàozhí *formal* upright and stern

帩

qiào see below

帩头 qiàotóu scarf used by man in ancient times to tie hair

翘(翹、翹)

qiào stick up; hold up; bend upwards; turn upwards: ～起拇指 hold up one's thumb / 你的头发～起来了, 要梳一梳。A lock of your hair is sticking up. Go and comb it. ——see also qiáo

翘板 qiàobǎn same as 跷跷板 qiāoqiāobǎn

翘辫子 qiào biànzi *humor.* kick the bucket: 袁世凯刚刚登上皇帝的宝座就～了。Yuan Shikai had just taken the throne when he kicked the bucket.

翘尾巴 qiào wěiba be cocky; get stuck-up: 别一有成绩就～。Don't get cocky when you've achieved something.

撬

qiào prize; pry: ～石头 pry (or lift) up a stone / ～起箱子盖 prize (or pry) the top off a box / 用撬杠把锁着的门～开 pry open the locked door with a crowbar

撬杠 qiàogàng (also 撬棍 qiàogùn) pinch bar; crowbar; pry

鞘

qiào sheath; scabbard: 剑～ (sword) scabbard / 刀出～ take the knife out of the sheath ——see also shāo

鞘翅　qiàochì　*zool.*　elytrum

qiē

切　qiē　① cut; slice: ～菜 cut up vegetables／～肉 slice meat／～开西瓜 cut a watermelon open／～成两半 cut sth. into halves ② *math.* tangency ——see also qiè

切变　qiēbiàn　*phys.*　shear

切布机　qiēbùjī　*paper making*　rag cutter (*or* chopper)

切菜机　qiēcàijī　vegetable-chopper; vegetable-cutter

切槽　qiēcáo　*mech.*　grooving

切齿机　qiēchǐjī　*mech.*　gear cutting machine

切除　qiēchú　excise; resect: ～脂肪瘤 resect (*or* remove) a lipoma／～扁桃腺 remove tonsils／全(部分)～ total (partial) excision

切磋　qiēcuō　learn from each other by exchanging views: 比赛后两国篮球运动员聚在一起,～球艺。The basketball players of the two countries got together and swopped pointers after the match.

切磋琢磨　qiēcuō zhuómó　carve and polish—learn from each other by exchanging views

切点　qiēdiǎn　*math.*　point of tangency; point of contact

切断　qiēduàn　cut off: ～敌人后路 cut off the enemy's retreat／～电源 cut off the electricity supply

切分音　qiēfēnyīn　*mus.*　syncopation

切腹自杀　qiēfù zìshā　commit hara-kiri; commit seppu-ku

切糕　qiēgāo　a kind of cake made of glutinous rice, sold in sliced pieces

切割　qiēgē　cut metal (by lathes, etc.)

切开　qiēkāi　*med.*　incise: ～引流 incision and drainage

切口　qiēkǒu　the side margin of a page in a book ——see also qiēkǒu

切块　qiēkuài　stripping and slicing (food)

切力　qiēlì　*phys.*　shearing force; shear: 横～ transverse shear

切面[1]　qiēmiàn　cut noodles; machine-made noodles

切面[2]　qiēmiàn　① *math.* tangent plane ② same as 剖面 pōumiàn

切片[1]　qiēpiàn　cut into slices

切片[2]　qiēpiàn　*med.*　section (of organic tissues): ～检查 section for microscopic examination

切片机　qiēpiànjī　① slicer ② *text.* chipper ③ *med.* microtome

切线　qiēxiàn　*math.*　tangent (line)

切削　qiēxiāo　*mech.*　cut: 粗～ rough cut

切纸机　qiēzhǐjī　paper cutting machine; paper cutter

qié

伽　qié　see below ——see also gā; jiā

伽蓝　qiélán　a Buddhist temple

伽南香　qiénánxiāng　another name for 沉香 chénxiāng

茄　qié　eggplant; aubergine ——see also jiā

茄泥　qiéní　mashed eggplant (a dish)

茄子　qiézi　eggplant; aubergine

qiě

且[1]　qiě　*adv.*　① just; for the time being: 你～等一下。Just wait a little while.／这事～放一下。Let the matter rest for the time being.／～不说中文期刊, 外文期刊也订了不少。Lots of periodicals in foreign languages have been subscribed to, not to mention those in Chinese. ② *dial.* for a long time: 这种钢笔～使呢。These fountain pens last a long time.／他～来不了呢。He's a long time coming. *or* It'll be a while yet before he gets here.

且[2]　qiě　*conj.*　*formal*　① even: 死～不惧, 况困难乎! Even death holds no fears for us, to say nothing of difficulties. ② both...and...: 既高～大 both tall and heavy set; both high and wide／她工作既快～好。She works quickly and well.

且慢　qiěmàn　wait a moment; not so soon; not so fast: ～, 听我把话说完。Wait a minute, let me finish what I have to say.／～高兴! 他答应我们的要求是有条件的。Don't rejoice too soon! He agreed to our request only on certain conditions.

且…且…　qiě…qiě…　*conj.*　(used with monosyllabic verbs) while; as: 他们一路上且谈且走。All the way they talked as they walked.

且说　qiěshuō　(a stock phrase used in old novels or stories to introduce a new episode) meanwhile: ～颜氏自阿寄去后, 朝夕悬挂, 常恐他消折了这些本钱, 怀着鬼胎。(《今古奇观》) Meanwhile, the widow had lived in suspense from morning until night since the old servant left. Her constant cause for worry was that he might have lost her capital.

qiè

切　qiè　① correspond to: 译文不～原意。The translation does not quite correspond to the original. ② be close to: 亲切 qīnqiè ③ eager; anxious: 心切 xīnqiè ④ be sure to: ～勿迟延。Be sure not to delay.／～不可自以为是。One should never be presumptuous and opinionated. ⑤ see 反切 fǎnqiè ——see also qiē

切齿　qièchǐ　gnash one's teeth (in hatred): ～痛恨 gnash one's teeth in hatred／令人～ make one bristle with anger

切当　qièdàng　proper; suitable; fitting; appropriate: 用词～ well-chosen wording; appropriate use of words

切肤之痛　qiè fū zhī tòng　keenly felt pain

切骨　qiègǔ　(of hatred) deep; bitter

切合　qièhé　suit; fit in with: 计划要～实际。Plans should be geared to actual circumstances.／～人民的需要 fit in with the needs of the people／～实际的办法 a practical approach

切己　qièjǐ　of immediate concern to oneself

切记　qièjì　be sure to keep in mind; must always remember: 妈妈的嘱咐, 你要～在心。You must never forget what your mother told you.／这是个大事, 马虎不得,～!～! This is a serious matter. It shouldn't be handled just any old way. Do remember that!

切忌　qièjì　must guard against; avoid by all means: ～主观片面。Be careful to avoid being subjective and one-sided. ／～生冷 cold and raw food strictly forbidden (often found in directions for prepared Chinese medicines)

切谏　qièjiàn　*formal*　remonstrate in frank terms; earnestly advise

切近　qièjìn　① close to: 这样解释比较～作者原意。This interpretation seems to be closer to the author's original meaning. ② close; near: 要实现一个崇高的目标, 必须从～处做起。To achieve a lofty goal, we must proceed from what is close at hand.

切口 qièkǒu　the secret language of underworld gangs or of certain professions ——see also qiēkǒu

切脉 qièmài　*Chin. med.*　feel the pulse

切盼 qièpàn　(also 切望 qièwàng) eagerly look forward to; wait impatiently for

切切 qièqiè　① be sure to: ～不可骄傲。Be sure not to become conceited. *or* Guard against arrogance by every means. ② eager; urgent; earnest: ～请求 urgently request ③ same as 窃窃 qièqiè

切切此布 qièqiè cǐ bù　(used at the end of a proclamation, etc.) this proclamation is hereby issued in all sincerity and earnestness; this is hereby solemnly proclaimed

切身 qièshēn　① of immediate concern to oneself or sb.: 物价影响到千家万户的～利益。Prices affect the immediate interests of every family. ② personal; first-hand: ～体验 personal experience / 他在山区工作过, 对那里缺医少药的情况有～体会。He has worked in mountainous areas before, and has first-hand knowledge of the lack of doctors and medicine there.

切实 qièshí　① feasible; practical; realistic: ～有效的办法 practical and effective measures / ～可行的计划 a feasible (or realistic) plan ② conscientious; earnest: ～改正错误 correct one's mistakes in real earnest / 切切实实地工作 do one's job conscientiously

切题 qiètí　keep to the point; be relevant to the subject: 写文章要～。When writing, keep to the subject.

切要 qièyào　highly necessary; very important

切责 qièzé　*formal*　severely rebuke; sternly condemn

切诊 qièzhěn　*Chin. med.*　pulse feeling and palpation, one of the four methods of diagnosis ——see also 四诊 sìzhěn

切中 qièzhòng　hit (the mark): 她的批评～要害。Her criticism struck home. / 文章～时弊。The article hit hard at the ills of the time.

切嘱 qièzhǔ　urge again and again; repeatedly exhort; din sth. into sb.

妾 qiè　① concubine ② a form of self-address formerly used by a wife when speaking to her husband: ～不负郎君, 郎君自负～耳!《今古奇观》I have not been untrue to you; it's you who have betrayed me!

妾身 qièshēn　same as 妾 qiè②

怯 qiè　① timid; cowardly; nervous: 胆怯 dǎnqiè ② (used by Beijing natives of people from other parts of northern China) rustic accent: 他说话真～。He speaks with a rustic accent. ③ *dial.* in poor taste; vulgar; tawdry: 这两种颜色配起来显～。These two colours look tawdry when put together.

怯步 qièbù　draw back (in fear); hang back: 殿堂幽黑阴森, 令人～。The caverous hall, dark and gloomy, was uninviting.

怯场 qièchǎng　have stage fright: 他～, 在台上一句话也说不出来。He was suffering from stage fright and could not utter a word.

怯懦 qiènuò　timid and overcautious

怯弱 qièruò　timid and weak-willed: 她生性～, 没有主见。She has a timid and weak-willed nature and has no definite views of her own.

怯生 qièshēng　*dial.*　shy with strangers: 这孩子～, 客人一抱他就哭。The baby is shy with strangers and will cry whenever a guest holds him.

怯生生 qièshēngshēng　in a timid manner

怯声怯气 qièshēng-qièqì　speak in a timid manner; speak haltingly

怯头怯脑 qiètóu-qiènǎo　uncouth; lumpish; countrified

怯阵 qièzhèn　① feel nervous when going into battle;

be battle-shy ② same as 怯场 qièchǎng

窃（竊） qiè　① steal; pilfer: 偷窃 tōuqiè ② secretly; surreptitiously; furtively: 窃笑 qièxiào ③ *formal hum.* (referring to one's views) my: ～以为 in my humble opinion; I presume

窃案 qiè'àn　larceny; burglary

窃夺 qièduó　usurp; grab

窃钩者诛, 窃国者侯 qiègōuzhě zhū, qièguózhě hóu　he who steals a belt buckle pays with his life; he who steals a state gets to be a feudal lord

窃国 qièguó　usurp state power: ～大盗 arch usurper of state power

窃据 qièjù　usurp; unjustly occupy: ～要职 usurp a high post; unjustly occupy a high post

窃密 qièmì　steal secret information; steal secrets

窃窃 qièqiè　low (voice); whispering

窃窃私议 qièqiè sīyì　exchange whispered comments

窃窃私语 qièqiè sīyǔ　talk in whispers; whisper

窃取 qièqǔ　usurp; steal; grab: ～别人的劳动果实 grab (or seize) the fruits of other people's labour

窃听 qiètīng　eavesdrop; wiretap; tap; bug: ～电话 tap a telephone / 他怕有人～, 不敢在电话里说。He was afraid of being bugged, and didn't dare to talk over the phone. / 他在窗外～屋里人谈话。He hid just outside the window and eavesdropped on the conversation going on inside the room.

窃听器 qiètīngqì　tapping device; listening-in device; bug: 装～ bug (a room, etc.) / 拆除～ debug (a room, etc.)

窃笑 qièxiào　laugh secretly; laugh up one's sleeve

窃玉偷香 qièyù-tōuxiāng　same as 偷香窃玉 tōuxiāng-qièyù

窃贼 qièzéi　thief; burglar; pilferer

挈 qiè　① take along; carry: 他～眷返回故里。He went back to his native place, taking his family along with him. ② lift; raise; take up: 提纲挈领 tígāng-qièlǐng

挈带 qièdài　take along; carry

惬（愜、匧） qiè　*formal*　be satisfied: 惬意 qièyì

惬当 qièdàng　*formal*　apt; proper; appropriate

惬怀 qièhuái　*formal*　be pleased; be satisfied

惬心 qièxīn　*formal*　be pleased; be satisfied

惬意 qièyì　be pleased; be satisfied

趄 qiè　slanting; inclined: ～坡 slope / ～着身子 (of a person) leaning sideways ——see also jū

慊 qiè　*formal*　be satisfied; be pleased

箧（篋） qiè　*formal*　small suitcase: 藤～ wicker suitcase

锲 qiè　*formal*　carve; engrave

锲而不舍 qiè ér bù shě　keep on chipping away—work with perseverance: 学习要有～的精神。Study requires perseverance.

qīn

亲（親） qīn　① parent: 双亲 shuāngqīn ② blood relation; next of kin: ～兄弟 blood brother ③ relative: 近亲 jìnqīn ④ marriage; match: 说亲 shuōqīn ⑤ bride: 迎亲 yíngqīn ⑥ close; intimate; dear: 我和大姐最～。My eldest sister is very dear to me. ⑦ in per-

son; oneself: 亲眼 qīnyǎn ⑧ kiss: 她～了～孩子的脸。 She kissed the child on the cheek. ——see also qìng

亲爱 qīn'ài dear; beloved: ～的同志们 dear comrades / ～的祖国 one's beloved country

亲本 qīnběn *biol.* parent: 轮回～ recurrent parent

亲笔 qīnbǐ ① in one's own handwriting: 这信是他～写的。This letter is in his own hand. / ～信 a personal, handwritten message or letter; an autograph letter / ～签名 one's own signature; autograph ② one's own handwriting: 这是他的～。This is his handwriting.

亲兵 qīnbīng (also 亲军 qīnjūn) *old* bodyguard (of a senior official)

亲代 qīndài *biol.* parental generation

亲丁 qīndīng blood relation

亲睹 qīndǔ see with one's own eyes; see for oneself

亲骨肉 qīngǔròu one's own flesh and blood (i.e. parents and children, brothers and sisters)

亲故 qīngù (also 亲旧 qīnjiù) relatives and old friends

亲贵 qīnguì *formal* an emperor's close relatives or favourite courtiers

亲和力 qīnhélì *chem.* affinity

亲近 qīnjìn be close to; be on intimate terms with: 这两人很～。Those two are on intimate terms. / 他对人热情诚恳, 大家都愿意～他。As he is warmhearted and sincere, everyone wants to be friends with him.

亲眷 qīnjuàn *dial.* ① one's relatives ② family dependants

亲口 qīnkǒu (say sth.) personally: 这是他～告诉我的。He told me this himself.

亲历 qīnlì *formal* have a personal experience of sth.

亲临 qīnlín come or go to a place personally: ～指导 come personally to give guidance / ～现场 be on the spot / 将军～前线指挥。The general directed the battle personally at the front.

亲聆 qīnlíng go in person to listen to (instructions): ～教诲 go in person to listen to sb.'s instructions

亲密 qīnmì close; intimate: ～的战友 a close comrade-in-arms / 他俩非常～。The two of them are on very intimate terms.

亲密无间 qīnmì wújiàn be on intimate terms

亲昵 qīnnì very intimate; affectionate: ～的称呼 an affectionate form of address

亲朋 qīnpéng relatives and friends; kith and kin: ～故旧 relatives and old acquaintances

亲戚 qīnqi relative: 我们两家是～。Our two families are relatives. / 一门～ a set of relatives

亲切 qīnqiè ① cordial; kind: ～的关怀 kind attention; loving care / ～的教导 kind guidance / ～的谈话 a cordial conversation / 他的话我们感到很～。What he said touched our hearts. ② close; intimate; dear

亲热 qīnrè affectionate; intimate; warmhearted: 我们都～地称她为大姐。We all affectionately refer to her as our elder sister. / ～地问长问短 make warmhearted inquiries (about sb.'s health, etc.)

亲人 qīnrén ① one's parents, spouse, children, etc.; one's family members: 他除母亲外, 没有别的～。His mother is the only other member of his family. ② dear ones; those dear to one: 感谢～解放军 thank our beloved Liberation Army

亲如手足 qīn rú shǒuzú (also 亲如兄弟 qīn rú xiōngdì) as close as brothers

亲如一家 qīn rú yìjiā as dear to each other as members of one family

亲善 qīnshàn close and friendly (between countries): ～关系 good will

亲身 qīnshēn personal; firsthand: ～经历 personal experience; firsthand experience

亲生 qīnshēng ① be sb.'s own child (i.e. not an adopted one): 小明是她～的。Xiao Ming is her own

child. ② one's own (children or parents): ～子女 one's own children / ～父母 one's own parents (i.e. not foster parents or stepparents)

亲事 qīnshì marriage: 他的～快成了吧? Is he going to get married soon?

亲手 qīnshǒu with one's own hands; personally; oneself: 这些是他～种的树。Those are the trees he planted with his own hands. / 你～做一做。Do it yourself.

亲疏 qīn-shū (of relatives or social connections) close or distant: 不分～ whether close or distant

亲属 qīnshǔ kinsfolk; relatives

亲随 qīnsuí *old* personal attendant or footman

亲痛仇快 qīn tòng chóu kuài (also 亲者痛, 仇者快 qīnzhě tòng, chóuzhě kuài) sadden one's own folk and gladden the enemy: 凡举事无为亲厚者所痛, 而为见仇者所快。(《后汉书》) Whatever you do, you must be sure that you do not sadden your friends and gladden your enemies.

亲王 qīnwáng prince

亲吻 qīnwěn kiss

亲信 qīnxìn ① close and trustful ② *derog.* trusted aide (*or* follower)

亲眼 qīnyǎn with one's own eyes; personally: 这是我～看见的。I saw it with my own eyes. / 我们～看到了贵国人民对中国人民的友好情谊。We have seen for ourselves how friendly the people of your country are towards the people of China.

亲友 qīnyǒu relatives and friends; kith and kin

亲鱼 qīnyú parent fish

亲缘 qīnyuán *biol.* affinity

亲征 qīnzhēng (of an emperor) personally lead a military expedition

亲政 qīnzhèng (of a sovereign) take over the reins of government upon coming of age

亲知 qīnzhī ① know by firsthand ② *formal* relatives and friends; kith and kin

亲炙 qīnzhì *formal* be personally taught or influenced by sb.; be intimate with sb.: 久仰芳名, 无由～。(《红楼梦》) I have long known of your fine reputation, but never had the chance to meet you in person.

亲自 qīnzì personally; in person; oneself: ～动手 personally take a hand in the work; do the job oneself / ～拜访 make a personal call / 你～去看看。Go and see for yourself. / 他～带领我们参观博物馆。He showed us round the museum himself.

亲族 qīnzú members of the same clan

亲嘴 qīnzuǐ kiss

侵 qīn ① invade; intrude into; infringe upon: 入侵 rùqīn ② approaching (daybreak): 侵晨 qīnchén

侵彻力 qīnchèlì penetrativeness (of a bullet)

侵晨 qīnchén approaching daybreak; towards dawn

侵夺 qīnduó seize by force

侵犯 qīnfàn encroach on; infringe (upon); violate: ～人权 infringe upon human rights / ～著作权 infringe a copyright / ～领土和主权 violate a country's territorial integrity and sovereignty / 决不允许～集体利益。No encroachment on the interests of the collective is allowed. / 公共财产不可～。Public property shall be inviolable.

侵害 qīnhài encroach on; make inroads on: 建造防护林, 减少风沙的～ build shelterbelts to reduce encroachments by sandstorms / 防止蝗虫～农作物 prevent the inroads of locusts on the crops / 同一公民权利的行为作斗争 fight against any infringement of the rights of citizens

侵凌 qīnlíng bully and humiliate

侵略 qīnlüè aggression; invasion: ～别国 commit

aggression against another country / ～国 aggressor (nation) / ～军 aggressor troops; invading army / ～行为 act of aggression; aggression / ～战争 war of aggression / ～者 aggressor; invader

侵掠 qīnlüè *formal* seize by force

侵权行为 qīnquán xíngwéi *leg.* tort

侵染 qīnrǎn (of germs, bacteria, or viruses) infect

侵扰 qīnrǎo invade and harass: ～边境 harass a country's frontiers; make border raids

侵入 qīnrù invade; intrude into; make incursions into: ～领海 intrude into a country's territorial waters / 外国资本的～ the invasion of foreign capital / 病菌已～肺部。 Germs have invaded the lungs.

侵入岩 qīnrùyán *geol.* intrusive rock; irruptive rock

侵蚀 qīnshí ① corrode; erode: 风雨的～ erosion by wind and rain / 各种酸类～金属。 Acids erode (*or* eat into) metals. / 资产阶级思想的～ the corrosive influence of bourgeois ideology / 细菌～人体。 Germs invade the human body. / ～性 corrodibility ② seize (property) in secret and bit by bit: ～公款 embezzle public funds; help oneself to public money

侵蚀土 qīnshítǔ eroded soil

侵吞 qīntūn ① embezzle; misappropriate: ～公款 embezzle public funds / ～社会财富 appropriate social property ② swallow up; annex: ～别国领土 annex another country's territory

侵袭 qīnxí make inroads on; invade and attack; hit: 台风～沿海地区。 The typhoon hit the coastal areas.

侵晓 qīnxiǎo approaching daybreak; towards dawn

侵渔 qīnyú *formal* seize by force

侵越 qīnyuè encroach on; infringe upon

侵早 qīnzǎo same as 侵晨 qīnchén

侵占 qīnzhàn ① invade and occupy: ～别国领土 invade and occupy another country's territory ② seize; embezzle: ～公有土地 seize public land / ～国家收入 embezzle state revenue

钦 qīn ① admire; respect: 钦佩 qīnpèi ② by the emperor himself: 钦定 qīndìng ③ (Qīn) a surname

钦差 qīnchāi imperial envoy; imperial commissioner

钦差大臣 qīnchāi dàchén ① imperial commissioner; imperial envoy: ～林则徐 (Imperial) Commissioner Lin Zexu ② a nickname for a representative of the higher authorities: "～" 满天飞 "imperial envoys" rushing here, there, and everywhere

钦迟 qīnchí *formal* (used in correspondence) admire; look up to with respect

钦定 qīndìng (of a book, etc.) made by imperial order: 《～四库全书总目提要》 *Analytical Catalogue of the Complete Library in Four Divisions, Made by Imperial Order*

钦服 qīnfú esteem; admire

钦敬 qīnjìng admire and respect

钦命 qīnmìng ① imperial order ② ordered by the emperor

钦慕 qīnmù admire; respect

钦佩 qīnpèi admire; esteem: 表示～ express admiration for / 他们坚持科学实验的精神令人～。 Their persistence in scientific experiment commands admiration.

钦羡 qīnxiàn admire and respect

钦仰 qīnyǎng *formal* revere; venerate; esteem

衾 qīn *formal* ① quilt: ～枕 quilt and pillow ② coverlet for the dead when encoffined

骎 qīn see below

骎骎 qīnqīn *formal* like a galloping horse: 建设事业～日上。 Reconstruction is forging ahead.

qín

芹 qín celery

芹菜 qíncài celery

芹献 qínxiàn *formal hum.* my humble gift

矜(殣) qín *arch.* shaft of a spear ——see also jīn

秦 Qín ① one of the Warring States into which China was divided during the Eastern Zhou period (770-256 B.C.), comprising parts of modern Shaanxi and Gansu ② the Qin Dynasty (221-207 B.C.) ③ a name for modern Shaanxi and Gansu (esp. the former) ④ a surname

秦川 qínchuān old name for what is now Shaanxi and Gansu provinces

秦艽 qínjiāo *bot.* large-leaved gentian (*Gentiana macrophylla*)

秦椒 qínjiāo *dial.* long and thin hot pepper

秦晋之好 Qín-Jìn zhī hǎo the amity between Qin and Jin (sealed by a marriage alliance between the two royal houses)—a marriage alliance between two families: 两家结了～。 The two families formed a marriage alliance.

秦镜高悬 Qín jìng gāo xuán same as 明镜高悬 míng jìng gāo xuán

秦楼楚馆 qínlóu-chǔguǎn towers of Qin and pavilions of Chu—quarters of pleasure; courtesans' quarters

秦皮 qínpí *Chin. med.* the bark of ash (*Fraxinus bungeana*)

秦腔 qínqiāng Shaanxi opera, popular in the northwestern provinces

秦越 qínyuè as far apart as Qin and Yue—have no dealings with each other

秦篆 qínzhuàn another name for 小篆 xiǎozhuàn

琴 qín ① general name for certain musical instruments: 小提琴 xiǎotíqín ② qin, a seven-stringed plucked instrument in some ways similar to the zither

琴拨 qínbō plectrum

琴凳 qíndèng music stool

琴剑飘零 qín-jiàn piāolíng (of a scholar) wander from place to place

琴键 qínjiàn key (on a musical instrument)

琴马 qínmǎ *mus.* bridge (of a stringed instrument)

琴鸟 qínniǎo lyrebird

琴棋书画 qín-qí-shū-huà lute-playing, chess, calligraphy, and painting—accomplishments of a scholar of the old school

琴瑟不调 qín-sè bù tiáo the *qin* and the *se* are not in harmony—discord between husband and wife; an uncongenial marriage

琴瑟和谐 qín-sè héxié the *qin* and *se* are in harmony—husband and wife living in harmony; wedded bliss

琴师 qínshī a stringed instrumentalist, esp. a *jinghu* (京胡) player, who acts as accompanist in traditional opera

琴书 qínshū story-telling, mainly in song, with dulcimer accompaniment

琴弦 qínxián string (of a musical instrument)

琴心剑胆 qínxīn-jiàndǎn the sentiments of the lute (*qin*) and the spirit of the sword—a cultivated mind animated with a chivalrous spirit

覃 Qín a surname ——see also tán

禽 qín ① birds: 家禽 jiāqín ② *formal* general name for 鸟兽 niǎo-shòu

禽龙 qínlóng iguanodon

禽兽 qínshòu birds and beasts—inhuman: ～行为 brutish acts; bestial acts

勤 qín ① diligent; industrious; hardworking: 辛勤 xīnqín ② frequent; regular; constant: 衣服要～洗～换。Clothes should be changed and washed regularly. / 夏季雨水～。Rain is frequent in summer. ③ (office, school, etc.) attendance: 值勤 zhíqín

勤奋 qínfèn diligent; assiduous; industrious: 学习～ be diligent in one's studies / 他一天到晚都在～地工作着。He buries himself in his work from morning till night.

勤工俭学 qíngōng-jiǎnxué part-work and part-study system; work-study programme

勤俭 qínjiǎn hardworking and thrifty: ～过日子 live industriously and frugally; lead an industrious and thrifty life

勤俭持家 qínjiǎn chíjiā be industrious and thrifty in running a household: 老人们都是～, 才挣来家业。Old people always have thrifty habits. That's how a family is established.

勤俭建国 qínjiǎn jiànguó build up the country through thrift and hard work

勤谨 qínjin *dial.* diligent; industrious; hardworking

勤恳 qínkěn diligent and conscientious: 勤勤恳恳地为人民服务 be diligent and conscientious in serving the people

勤苦 qínkǔ diligent; hardworking; assiduous

勤快 qínkuai *inf.* diligent; hardworking: 她真～, 一会儿也不闲着。She is diligent and keeps herself busy all the time.

勤劳 qínláo diligent; industrious; hardworking: ～勇敢的中国人民 the valiant and industrious Chinese people / ～的双手 an untiring pair of hands

勤密 qínmì frequent; regular; constant

勤勉 qínmiǎn diligent; assiduous: ～好学 diligent and eager to learn

勤娘子 qínniángzǐ popular name for 牵牛花 qiānniúhuā

勤朴 qínpǔ industrious and thrifty

勤劬 qínqú *formal* diligent; industrious; hardworking

勤王 qínwáng *formal* ① come to the rescue of the king: 发兵～ send troops to save the throne ② do one's best to serve the throne

勤务 qínwù ① (public) duties; service ② a person who does logistic duties

勤务兵 qínwùbīng orderly

勤务员 qínwùyuán ① odd-jobman (in an army unit or government office) ② (used in) 人民的～ a servant of the people

勤学苦练 qínxué-kǔliàn study diligently and train hard

勤杂工 qínzágōng odd-jobman; handyman

勤杂人员 qínzá rényuán personnel regularly doing certain odd jobs (in an army unit or government office); odd-jobmen

嗪 qín see 哌嗪 pàiqín

擒 qín capture; catch; seize: 生擒 shēngqín

擒拿 qínná arrest; capture; catch

擒贼先擒王 qín zéi xiān qín wáng to catch brigands, first catch their king: 射人先射马, ～。(杜甫) Aim at the rider's horse: the king Of brigands first to justice bring.

擒纵轮 qínzònglún *mech.* escape wheel

噙 qín hold in the mouth or the eyes: ～着烟袋 hold a pipe between one's lips / ～着眼泪 eyes brimming with tears

檎 qín see 林檎 línqín

锓 qín *formal* carve; engrave

寝(寢) qín ① sleep: 废寝忘食 fèiqín-wàngshí ② bedroom: 就寝 jiùqín ③ coffin chamber: 陵寝 língqín ④ *formal* stop; end: 其事遂～。The matter was then allowed to rest. *or* No more was heard of the matter thereafter.

寝车 qínchē sleeping car; sleeping carriage; sleeper

寝宫 qíngōng ① sleeping quarters of the emperor and empress ② coffin chamber in an imperial mausoleum

寝具 qínjù bedding

寝食 qín-shí eating and sleeping—daily life

寝食不安 qín-shí bù ān feel uneasy even when eating and sleeping; be worried waking or sleeping

寝室 qínshì room (in a dormitory)

沁 qìn ① ooze; seep; exude: 他的额上～出了汗珠。His forehead was oozing sweat. ② *dial.* let one's head droop downward; hang: 他～着头 He hung (or drooped) his head. ③ *dial.* put sth. into water

沁人心脾 qìn rén xīn-pí gladdening the heart and refreshing the mind; mentally refreshing; refreshing: 空气清新, ～。The air is pure and fresh; it seeped into my heart. / 肖邦的夜曲～。Chopin's nocturnes are heart-stirring.

沁润 qìnrùn (of liquid, aroma, etc.) soak into; permeate through; penetrate to: 春雨～着大地。The spring rain was soaking into the earth. / 股股幽香～到肺腑。Whiffs of delicate fragrance penetrated to the heart.

呫(呇、嗒) qìn ① (of a cat or dog) vomit ② *inf.* fling abuses ③ *inf.* talk nonsense: 满嘴胡～ talk sheer nonsense

撳(搇) qìn *dial.* press; push down: ～电铃 press a doorbell

撳钉 qìndīng *dial.* drawing pin; thumbtack

撳纽 qìnniǔ *dial.* snap fastener

青 qīng ① blue or green: 曲终人不见, 江山数峰～。(钱起) The song is ended, no one is to be seen, On the river the mountain peaks are so blue! ② black: 青布 qīngbù ③ green grass or young crops: 踏青 tàqīng / 看青 kānqīng ④ young (people): 青年 qīngnián ⑤ (Qīng) short for 青海 Qīnghǎi

青帮 Qīngbāng the *Qing* Gang (formerly, a secret society)

青布 qīngbù black cloth

青菜 qīngcài ① general name for 蔬菜 shūcài ② another name for 小白菜 xiǎobáicài

青草 qīngcǎo green grass

青出于蓝 qīng chūyú lán (usu. used in) ～而胜于蓝

blue comes from the indigo plant but is bluer than the plant itself—the pupil surpasses the master

青春 qīngchūn　youth; youthfulness: 把～献给祖国 dedicate one's youth to serving one's country / 充满着～的活力 be bursting with youthful vigour / 老厂恢复了～。The old factory has regained its old vigour.

青春期 qīngchūnqī　puberty

青瓷 qīngcí　celadon (ware)

青葱 qīngcōng　verdant; fresh green: ～的竹林 a verdant grove of bamboo / ～的草地 fresh green grassland / 窗外长着几棵竹子,～可爱。The bamboos just outside the window are green and lovely.

青翠 qīngcuì　verdant; fresh and green: ～的西山 the verdant green Western Hills (in Beijing) / 雨后,垂柳显得格外～。The weeping willows looked fresher and greener after the rain.

青灯 qīngdēng　*liter.*　green lamp (i.e. an oil lamp): ～照壁人初睡,冷雨敲窗被未温。(《红楼梦》) A green lamp lights the wall as sleep enfolds her, Cold rain pelts the casement and her quilt is chill.

青豆 qīngdòu　green soya bean

青肥 qīngféi　same as 绿肥 lǜféi

青冈 qīnggāng　another name for 槲栎 húlì

青工 qīnggōng　(short for 青年工人) young workers

青光眼 qīngguāngyǎn　*med.*　glaucoma

青果 qīngguǒ　*dial.*　Chinese olive

青海 Qīnghǎi　Qinghai (Province)

青蒿 qīnghāo　*bot.*　Artemisia apiacea

青红皂白 qīng-hóng-zào-bái　black and white; right and wrong——see also 不分青红皂白 bù fēn qīng-hóng-zào-bái

青花瓷 qīnghuācí　blue and white porcelain

青黄不接 qīng-huáng bù jiē　when the crop is still in the blade and the old stock is all consumed—temporary shortage: 北京的三四月份,～,蔬菜很少。There is a temporary shortage of vegetables in Beijing in March and April. / 这个系正处在～的时期,青年教师大部分都没有成长。This department is in a period of crisis right now because most of the young teachers are still inexperienced.

青灰 qīnghuī　a kind of graphite, dark blue in colour, used to line a stove or as paint

青椒 qīngjiāo　green pepper

青衿 qīngjīn　(also 青襟 qīngjīn) *old*　① young scholar's dress ② scholars; intellectuals

青筋 qīngjīn　blue veins: 他额角上暴起了～。Blue veins stood out on his temples.

青稞 qīngkē　(also 青稞麦 qīngkēmài) ① highland barley (grown in Xizang and Qinghai) ② the seed of highland barley

青睐 qīnglài　*formal*　favour; good graces: 获得某人的～ find favour in sb.'s eyes; be in sb.'s good graces

青莲色 qīngliánsè　pale purple; heliotrope

青龙 qīnglóng　the Green Dragon— ① same as 苍龙 cānglóng① ② the guardian spirit of the east in Taoism

青楼 qīnglóu　*liter.*　blue mansions—pleasure quarters; courtesans' quarters: 十年一觉扬州梦,赢得～薄幸名。(杜牧) Once waking up from my ten-year dream in Yangzhou, I've won the name of a fickle man among blue mansions.

青绿 qīnglǜ　dark green: ～的松林 a dark green pine forest

青绿山水 qīnglǜ shānshuǐ　blue-and-green landscape (a coloured landscape done in blues and greens)

青麻 qīngmá　common name for 苘麻 qīngmá

青盲 qīngmáng　*Chin. med.*　glaucoma

青梅 qīngméi　green plum

青梅竹马 qīngméi-zhúmǎ　green plums and a bamboo horse—a girl and a boy playing innocently together; a man and a woman who had an innocent affection for each other in childhood

青霉素 qīngméisù　penicillin

青面獠牙 qīngmiàn-liáoyá　green-faced and long-toothed—terrifying in appearance: 露出～的凶相 reveal the ferocious features of an ogre

青苗 qīngmiáo　young crops; green shoots of (food) grains

青年 qīngnián　youth; young people: ～时代 one's youth / ～人 young people; youth / ～学生 young students; student youth / ～一代 the younger generation / 新～ young people of the new generation / 好～ a worthy young person / ～工作 work with the youth (in order to give them guidance); youth work / ～运动 youth movement

青年会 Qīngniánhuì　short for 基督教青年会 Jīdūjiào Qīngniánhuì

青年节 Qīngniánjié　short for 五四青年节 Wǔ-Sì Qīngniánjié

青鸟 qīngniǎo　① blue bird—the bird messenger of the Queen Mother of the West (西王母) ② messenger

青盼 qīngpàn　*formal*　favour; good graces

青皮 qīngpí　*dial.*　rascal; hooligan: ～流氓 hooligan / ～光棍 ruffian

青纱帐 qīngshāzhàng　the green curtain of tall crops: 游击队利用～作掩护。The guerrillas used the green curtain of tall crops as cover.

青山 qīngshān　green hills; blue mountains

青山不老,绿水长存 qīngshān bù lǎo, lǜshuǐ cháng cún　the blue mountains do not grow old, the green waters always remain: ～。他日事成,必当厚报。(《三国演义》) As the blue mountains do not grow old and the green waters always remain, so shall I never forget. And when I have accomplished my task, you shall have no mean reward.

青山绿水 qīngshān-lǜshuǐ　blue mountains and green waters—beautiful scenery

青衫 qīngshān　black gown

青少年 qīngshàonián　teen-agers; youngsters: ～犯罪 juvenile delinquency

青史 qīngshǐ　annals of history: 永垂～ go down in the annals of history / ～留名 have a place in history

青丝[1] qīngsī　*liter.*　black hair (of a woman or girl): 一缕～ a thread of black hair

青丝[2] qīngsī　green plums cut into shreds used in pastries

青饲料 qīngsìliào　greenfeed; green fodder

青松 qīngsōng　pine

青蒜 qīngsuàn　garlic leaves

青苔 qīngtái　moss

青檀 qīngtán　*bot.*　wingceltis (Pteroceltis tatarinowii)

青天 qīngtiān　① the blue sky ② the clear sky (a respectful sobriquet for a clean and upright official): 老百姓管包公叫包～。The people called Lord Bao "Bao the Clear Sky."

青天白日 qīngtiān-báirì　① bright and sunny ② broad daylight

青天霹雳 qīngtiān pīlì　same as 晴天霹雳 qíngtiān pīlì

青田石 qīngtiánshí　stone from Qingtian county in Zhejiang Province, used to make seals

青铜 qīngtóng　bronze

青铜器 qīngtóngqì　bronze ware

青铜时代 qīngtóng shídài　the Bronze Age

青蛙 qīngwā　frog

青虾 qīngxiā　freshwater shrimp

青香薷 qīngxiāngrú　*Chin. med.*　Chinese mosla (Mosla chinensis)

青葙 qīngxiāng　*bot.*　feather cockscomb (Celosia argentea)

青葙子 qīngxiāngzǐ *Chin. med.* the seed of feather cockscomb

青眼 qīngyǎn favour; good graces

青杨 qīngyáng Cathay poplar (*Populus cathayana*)

青猺 qīngyáo another name for 花面狸 huāmiànlí

青衣 qīngyī ① black clothing ② *arch.* woman servant ③ one of the main divisions of the *dan* (旦) or female role in traditional opera (portraying faithful wives, chaste women, and maidens in distress or poverty but noble in character)

青蝇 qīngyíng greenbottle (fly)

青鱼 qīngyú black carp

青郁 qīngyù verdant and luxuriant: ～的竹林 dense bamboos

青云 qīngyún high official position or rapid official advancement: 平步青云 píngbù qīngyún

青云直上 qīngyún zhíshàng rapid advancement; a meteoric rise

青云志 qīngyúnzhì high aspirations

青贮 qīngzhù *agric.* ensiling: ～饲料 ensilage; silage

青紫 qīngzǐ ① *arch.* high rank ② same as 发绀 fāgàn

轻(輕) qīng ① of little weight; light: 油比水～。 Oil is lighter than water. / 身～如燕 (of a high jumper, gymnast, etc.) as light as a swallow ② (of load, equipment, etc.) small or simple: 轻武器 qīngwǔqì ③ small in number, degree, etc.: 他年纪很～。 He is very young. / 她的病很～。 Her illness is not at all serious. / 工作很～ have a light workload / 伤势较～ have a slight injury / 她睡觉～。 She is a light sleeper. ④ not serious; relaxing; light: 轻音乐 qīngyīnyuè ⑤ not important: 责任～ carry a light responsibility / 关系不～ have an important bearing on sth. ⑥ gentle; soft: ～～地说 speak in a soft voice; whisper / ～拿～放。 Handle gently. / 她走路脚步～。 She walks with a light step. / 病人睡着了,～点儿! Be quiet! The patient is asleep. / 我只是～～推了他一下。 I just gave him a light push. / 她～～地拍着孩子。 She was patting the baby gently. ⑦ rash: 轻信 qīngxìn ⑧ belittle; make light of: 轻财重义 qīngcái-zhòngyì

轻磅纸 qīngbàngzhǐ lightweight paper

轻便 qīngbiàn ① light; portable: ～铁道 light railway / ～桥 portable bridge / ～镗床 portable boring machine / ～自行车 lightweight bicycle; light roadster ② easy and convenient: 这种旅行包携带～。 This travelling bag is easy and convenient to carry.

轻薄 qīngbó (usu. of a man towards a woman) given to philandering; frivolous

轻财重义 qīngcái-zhòngyì value friendship more than money; be generous and charitable

轻车简从 qīngchē-jiǎncóng same as 轻装简从 qīngzhuāng-jiǎncóng

轻车熟路 qīngchē-shúlù drive in a light carriage on a familiar road—do sth. one knows well and can manage with ease

轻淡 qīngdàn ① faint; dim: ～地一笑 give a faint smile / ～的记忆 faint memories ② casual; random: 有人只是～地谈起这件事。 Someone casually mentioned it.

轻敌 qīngdí take the enemy lightly; underestimate the enemy: ～思想 tendency to take the enemy or the opponent (in a game) lightly

轻而易举 qīng ér yì jǔ easy to do: 编一本词典并不是～的事。 Compiling a dictionary is no easy task. / 我们～地就把对手打败了。 We beat our opponents hands down.

轻纺工业 qīngfǎng gōngyè textile and other light industries

轻放 qīngfàng put down gently: 易碎物品, 小心～! Fragile! Handle with care!

轻粉 qīngfěn *inf.* calomel; mercurous chloride

轻风 qīngfēng *meteorol.* light breeze

轻浮 qīngfú frivolous; flighty; light: 举止～ behave frivolously / ～的行为 frivolous conduct

轻歌曼舞 qīnggē-mànwǔ soft music and graceful dances

轻工业 qīnggōngyè light industry

轻骨头 qīnggǔtou *dial.* ① smug and bloated ② *offens.* miserable (*or* contemptible) wretch

轻核 qīnghé *phys.* light nucleus

轻忽 qīnghū neglect; overlook

轻混凝土 qīnghùnníngtǔ lightweight concrete

轻活 qīnghuó light work; soft job

轻机关枪 qīngjīguānqiāng light machine gun

轻贱 qīngjiàn ① mean and worthless ② look down upon; belittle

轻健 qīngjiàn spry and light; nimble; brisk: 步履～ walk at a brisk pace; be spry in one's steps

轻捷 qīngjié spry and light; nimble: 他跨着～的脚步回家去。 He walked home with brisk steps.

轻金属 qīngjīnshǔ light metal

轻举妄动 qīngjǔ-wàngdòng act rashly; take reckless action: 这件事非同小可, 不能～。 This is no trivial matter; make no move without careful thought.

轻看 qīngkàn look down upon; belittle

轻口薄舌 qīngkǒu-bóshé ① speak unkindly; make caustic remarks; be sharp-tongued ② make improper remarks

轻快 qīngkuài ① brisk; spry: 她迈着～的步子走向公园。 She walked at a brisk pace towards the park. / 他虽已过七十, 但步履～。 He's over 70 but still spry in his steps. ② lighthearted; lively: ～的曲调 a lively tune

轻狂 qīngkuáng extremely frivolous

轻量级 qīngliàngjí *sports* lightweight

轻慢 qīngmàn treat sb. without proper respect; slight

轻描淡写 qīngmiáo-dànxiě touch on lightly; mention casually: 要认真检查自己的错误, 不要～。 You should criticize your own mistakes earnestly, and not just touch on them lightly. / 他～地说: "打了两场球都不费力就赢了。" He said casually, "We won both games easily."

轻蔑 qīngmiè despise; scorn; disdain; be contemptuous: 她用～的目光扫了他一眼。 She cast a contemptuous glance at him.

轻暖 qīngnuǎn (of clothes) light and warm

轻诺寡信 qīngnuò-guǎxìn make promises easily but seldom keep them

轻泡货 qīngpàohuò *transportation* light cargo

轻炮兵 qīngpàobīng light artillery

轻飘 qīngpiāo light; buoyant: ～的柳絮 buoyant willow catkins

轻飘飘 qīngpiāopiāo light; buoyant: 垂柳～地摆动。 Willow branches were swaying lightly. / 她高兴地走着, 脚底下～的。 She tripped joyfully along, as if treading on air.

轻骑 qīngqí ① light cavalry ② moped

轻骑兵 qīngqíbīng light cavalry

轻巧 qīngqiǎo ① light and handy: 这录音机真～。 This is a handy tape recorder. / 她身子很～, 舞跳得好。 Her figure is slim and light, so she makes a good dancer. ② dexterous; deft: 他操纵机器动作非常～。 He operates the machine dexterously. / 她的自由体操动作～, 姿势优美。 She did her floor exercises with agility and grace. ③ simple; easy: 操作计算机看起来很容易, 其实并不～。 Operating a computer appears simple, but in fact it's not so easy. / 你说得倒～。 You talk as if it were a simple matter.

轻裘肥马 qīngqiú-féimǎ same as 肥马轻裘 féimǎ-qīngqiú

轻取 qīngqǔ win an easy victory (in a game); beat

easily; win hands down: ～第一局 win the first game easily (*or* without effort)/北京队以 5：0 客队。The Beijing team won an easy victory by beating the visiting team 5:0.

轻柔 qīngróu soft; gentle: ～的枝条 pliable twigs/～的声音 a gentle voice/第一小提琴奏出第一主题, 旋律～动听。The first violins introduced the first theme, a soft and beautiful melody.

轻软 qīngruǎn light and soft

轻纱 qīngshā fine gauze

轻伤 qīngshāng a slight (*or* minor) wound; a flesh wound: ～不下火线 not leave the frontline on account of minor wounds / ～员 ambulant patient (*or* case); walking wounded

轻生 qīngshēng make light of one's life——commit suicide

轻声[1] qīngshēng in a soft voice; softly: ～低语 speak softly; whisper

轻声[2] qīngshēng *phonet.* neutral tone: 普通话中的 "了、着、的" 等虚词和做后缀的 "子、头" 等字都念～。In *putonghua*, particles like *le, zhe,* and *de* and suffixes like *zi* and *tou* are all in the neutral tone (*or* are all toneless).

轻省 qīngsheng *dial.* ① relaxed: 如今添了个助手, 你可以稍微～点。Now that you have an assistant, you can relax a little. ② light: 这个箱子挺～。This box is very light.

轻世傲物 qīngshì-àowù full of conceit and defiant of convention

轻视 qīngshì belittle; look down on; underrate: ～妇女 look down on women / ～小学教师的作用 underestimate the role of primary school teachers

轻手轻脚 qīngshǒu-qīngjiǎo gently; softly: 护士出来进去都～的, 怕惊醒病人。The nurse moved around very softly so as not to wake the patient.

轻率 qīngshuài rash; hasty; indiscreet: ～的态度 reckless attitude / ～从事 act rashly / 你这样处理太～了。It was indiscreet of you to handle it that way.

轻水 qīngshuǐ *chem.* light water

轻松 qīngsōng light; relaxed: ～的工作 light work; soft job; cushy job / ～地打败对手 beat one's opponent with ease / 我们过了一个～愉快的暑假。We had a happy and relaxed summer vacation. / 写完了初稿, 她觉得心里～多了。After finishing the first draft, she felt more relaxed. / 扎针以后, 他的腿部有～的感觉。After the acupuncture treatment, his leg felt relieved.

轻瘫 qīngtān *med.* paresis

轻佻 qīngtiāo frivolous; flippant; giddy: 举止～ flippant (*or* skittish) behaviour

轻脱 qīngtuō frivolous; flippant; giddy

轻微 qīngwēi light; slight; trifling; to a small extent: ～的伤亡 light casualties / ～的头痛 a slight headache / ～的损失 a trifling loss / ～劳动 light labour

轻武器 qīngwǔqì light arms; small arms

轻侮 qīngwǔ slight and insult

轻闲 qīngxián ① not busy; leisurely ② easy or light (work)

轻泻剂 qīngxièjì laxative

轻信 qīngxìn be credulous; readily place trust in; readily believe: 不要～谣言。Give no credence to rumours. / 重证据, 不能～口供。Lay stress on evidence and do not readily believe confessions.

轻型 qīngxíng light-duty; light: ～机械 light-duty machinery / ～飞机 light aircraft

轻言细语 qīngyán-xìyǔ speak in a soft, gentle voice

轻飏 qīngyáng (also 轻扬 qīngyáng) lightly float or drift: 舟遥遥以～, 风飘飘而吹衣。(陶潜) Lightly floats and drifts the boat, And gently flaps my gown.

轻易 qīng·yì *adv.* ① easily: 胜利成果不是～得来的。

The fruits of victory were not easily won. ② lightly; rashly: 不要～下结论。Don't draw hasty conclusions. *or* Don't jump to conclusions. / 他不～发表意见。He does not express an opinion rashly.

轻音乐 qīngyīnyuè light music

轻盈 qīngyíng ① slim and graceful; lithe; lissom: ～的舞步 graceful steps (in dancing) / 她的自由体操动作～优美。Her movements in free gymnastics are lithe and graceful. ② lighthearted; relaxed: 笑语～ talk and laugh merrily and lightheartedly.

轻油 qīngyóu light oil

轻于鸿毛 qīng yú hóngmáo lighter than a goose feather ——see also 重于泰山, 轻于鸿毛 zhòngyú Tàishān, qīngyú hóngmáo

轻重 qīng-zhòng ① weight: 这两只箱子～不一样。These two boxes do not weigh the same. ② degree of seriousness; relative importance: 根据病情～决定病人是否住院。Whether a patient is to be hospitalized depends on how serious the case is. ③ propriety: 这个人说话不知～。That man doesn't know the proper way to talk.

轻重倒置 qīng-zhòng dàozhì put the trivial above the important; stress trifles and overlook matters of moment

轻重缓急 qīng-zhòng-huǎn-jí relative importance or urgency; order of priority: 分别～解决问题 solve problems in order of priority / 工作应分～。Work should be done in order of importance and urgency.

轻重量级 qīngzhòngliàngjí *sports* light heavyweight

轻舟 qīngzhōu *liter.* a small light boat; skiff: 两岸猿声啼不住, ～已过万重山。(李白) The screams of monkeys on either bank had scarcely ceased echoing in my ear, When my skiff had left behind it ten thousand ranges of hills.

轻装 qīngzhuāng ① light packs: ～就道 travel light / ～前进 march with light packs / ～上阵 go into battle with a light pack ② light equipment: ～部队 a lightly equipped army

轻装简从 qīngzhuāng-jiǎncóng (of an important person) travel with little luggage and few attendants——travel light

轻嘴薄舌 qīngzuǐ-bóshé (also 轻口薄舌 qīngkǒu-bóshé) have a caustic and sharp tongue

轻罪 qīngzuì *leg.* misdemeanour; minor offence (*or* crime): ～重判不对, 重罪轻判也不对。It is wrong to deal with a minor offence as if it were a major one and *vice versa.*

氢（氫）

qīng *chem.* hydrogen (H)

氢弹 qīngdàn hydrogen bomb

氢弹头 qīngdàntóu hydrogen warhead; H-warhead

氢氟酸 qīngfúsuān *chem.* hydrofluoric acid

氢化 qīnghuà *chem.* hydrogenation: ～裂解 hydrocracking / ～酶 hydrogenase / ～物 hydride

氢气 qīngqì hydrogen

氢气球 qīngqìqiú hydrogen balloon

氢氰酸 qīngqíngsuān *chem.* hydrocyanic acid

氢氧 qīngyǎng *chem.* oxyhydrogen: ～焰 oxyhydrogen flame

氢氧吹管 qīngyǎngchuīguǎn oxyhydrogen blowpipe

氢氧化物 qīngyǎnghuàwù *chem.* hydroxide (e.g. 氢氧化铵 ammonium hydroxide)

倾

qīng ① incline; lean; bend: 向左～ incline to the left / 身子向前～ bend forward; lean forward ② deviation; tendency: "左"倾 "zuǒ"qīng ③ collapse: 大厦将～ a great mansion on the point of collapse ④ overturn and pour out; empty: ～其所有 give away all one has ⑤ do all one can; use up all one's resources: ～全

力把工作做好 exert oneself to the utmost to do the work well

倾侧 qīngcè　tilt; incline; slope; slant

倾巢 qīngcháo　(of the enemy or bandits) turn out in full force (*or* strength)

倾巢出动 qīngcháo chūdòng　(of the enemy or bandits, etc.) turn out in full force (*or* strength)

倾城 qīngchéng　① the whole city or town: ～而出, 迎接国宾。The whole town turned out to welcome the state guests. ② same as 倾国倾城 qīngguó-qīngchéng

倾城倾国 qīngchéng-qīngguó　same as 倾国倾城 qīngguó-qīngchéng

倾倒 qīngdǎo　① topple and fall; topple over ② greatly admire: 为之～ be infatuated with sb.; be overwhelmed with admiration for sb.

倾倒 qīngdào　tip; dump; empty; pour out: ～垃圾 dump rubbish / 他猛一使劲儿就把一车土都～到沟里了。With a heave he emptied a wheelbarrow of earth into the ditch. / 在忆苦会上～苦水 pour out one's grievances against the old social order at a meeting to recall past sufferings

倾点 qīngdiǎn　*chem.* pour point; flow point

倾动 qīngdòng　move and win admiration: ～一时 cause a great sensation; create a furore

倾耳 qīng'ěr　prick up one's ears: ～细听 prick up one's ears and listen carefully

倾覆 qīngfù　overturn; topple; capsize

倾国倾城 qīngguó-qīngchéng　(of a woman) lovely enough to cause the fall of a city or a state; devastatingly beautiful; exceedingly beautiful: 我就是个"多愁多病的身", 你就是那"～的貌"。(《红楼梦》) I'm the one "sick with longing." And yours is the beauty which causes "cities and kingdoms to fall."

倾家荡产 qīngjiā-dàngchǎn　lose a family fortune; be reduced to poverty and ruin

倾角 qīngjiǎo　① *phys.* dip ② *math.* inclination ③ *geol.* dip angle

倾角测量仪 qīngjiǎo cèliángyí　dipmeter

倾慕 qīngmù　have a strong admiration for; adore: 彼此～ have a strong admiration for each other

倾囊相助 qīng náng xiāng zhù　empty one's purse to help; give generous financial assistance

倾佩 qīngpèi　(also 倾服 qīngfú) admire; esteem

倾盆大雨 qīngpén dàyǔ　heavy downpour; torrential rain; cloudburst: 赶上一场～ be caught in a downpour / 下起了～。The rain was pelting down. *or* It was raining cats and dogs.

倾圮 qīngpǐ　*formal* collapse; topple down

倾洒 qīngsǎ　(of snow, tears, etc.) pour down or forth: 天空～着鹅毛大雪。Big snowflakes are pouring down from the sky. / 月光～在大地上。The moonlight is pouring over the earth. / 他一腔心血都～在这部词典里。In carrying out this dictionary project he spat out, so to speak, the blood of his heart.

倾诉 qīngsù　pour out (one's heart, troubles, etc.): ～衷肠 pour out one's heart; reveal one's innermost feelings

倾谈 qīngtán　have a good, heart-to-heart talk

倾听 qīngtīng　listen attentively to; lend an attentive ear to: ～群众的意见 listen attentively to the views of the masses / 他站在小溪边～着淙淙的流水声。He stood by the stream listening to the babbling of the stream.

倾吐 qīngtǔ　say what is on one's mind without reservation: ～衷情 unbosom oneself / ～苦水 unburden oneself of one's grievances

倾箱倒箧 qīngxiāng-dǎoqiè　turn out all one's boxes and suitcases—give away all one has

倾向 qīngxiàng　① tendency; trend; inclination; deviation: 政治～ political inclination / 要注意一种～掩盖另一种～。One must be alive to the possibility that one tendency may conceal another. / 反对右的和"左"的两种～ oppose Right and "Left" deviations ② be inclined to; prefer: 这两种方案我～于第一种。Of the two plans, I prefer the first.

倾向性 qīngxiàngxìng　tendentiousness: 他的发言是有～的。His statement was frankly tendentious.

倾销 qīngxiāo　sell goods at a very low price; dump: ～货物 dump goods

倾斜 qīngxié　tilt; incline; slope; slant: 我国地势大致从西北向东南～。Generally speaking, the terrain of China slopes from northwest to southeast. / 地面微微向南～。The land inclines gently to the south. / 这墙有点～。The wall is a little out of the perpendicular.

倾斜度 qīngxiédù　gradient

倾斜角 qīngxiéjiǎo　① bank angle (of an airplane) ② same as 倾角 qīngjiǎo②③

倾斜面 qīngxiémiàn　inclined plane

倾泻 qīngxiè　come down in torrents: 山水～而下, 汇成洪流。Streams rushed down the mountain and converged to a torrent.

倾卸 qīngxiè　tip; dump; empty; pour out

倾卸汽车 qīngxiè qìchē　dump truck; tipper

倾心 qīngxīn　① admire; adore ② cordial; heart-to-heart: ～交谈 have a heart-to-heart talk

倾心吐胆 qīngxīn-tǔdǎn　pour out one's heart; unburden one's heart; unbosom oneself

倾轧 qīngyà　engage in internal strife; jostle against each other: 互相～ try to do each other down

倾注 qīngzhù　① pour into: 几股山泉～到深潭里。Several mountain streams pour into the pool. ② throw (energy, etc.) into: 把全部心血～到工作中去 throw all one's energy into one's work / 她把全部的爱～在独生子身上。She poured all her affection on her only son.

卿 qīng　① a minister or a high official in ancient times ② an emperor's form of address for a minister ③ a term of endearment formerly used between husband and wife or among close friends

卿卿我我 qīngqīng-wǒwǒ　(of lovers) whisper sweet nothings to one another; bill and coo

清¹ qīng　① unmixed; clear: ～水 clear water ② distinct; clarified: 说不～ hard to explain / 数不～ countless / 问～底细 make sure of every detail; get to the bottom of the matter ③ quiet: 冷清 lěngqīng ④ completely; thoroughly: 还清 huánqīng ⑤ settle; clear up: 帐～了吗? Has the account been settled (*or* cleared up)? ⑥ clean up; purge: ～政治, ～思想, ～组织, ～经济 clean things up in the fields of politics, ideology, organization and economy ⑦ count: ～一～行李的件数 count the pieces of luggage and see how many there are ⑧ just and honest: 清官 qīngguān ⑨ pure: 清醇 qīngchún

清² Qīng　the Qing Dynasty (1644-1911)

清白 qīngbái　① pure; clean; stainless: 历史～ have a clean personal record / ～无辜 innocent ② *dial.* clear: 他说了半天也没把问题说～。He didn't make himself clear even after repeated explanations.

清仓查库 qīngcāng-chákù　make an inventory (*or* check-up) of warehouses

清册 qīngcè　detailed list: 固定资产～ an inventory of fixed assets

清茶 qīngchá　① green tea ② tea served without refreshments

清查 qīngchá　① check: ～户口 check on household occupant; check residence cards / ～仓库 make an inventory (*or* checkup) of a warehouse ② ferret out

(counterrevolutionaries, etc.); uncover; comb out

清产核资 qīngchǎn hézī general checkup on enterprise assets

清偿 qīngcháng pay off; clear off: ～债务 pay off (or clear off) debts

清唱 qīngchàng sing opera arias (without makeup and acting)

清唱剧 qīngchàngjù *mus.* oratorio

清澈 qīngchè (also 清彻 qīngchè) limpid; clear: ～的池塘 a limpid pool / 湖水～见底。The lake water is so clear that you can see to the bottom.

清晨 qīngchén early morning

清除 qīngchú clear away; eliminate; get rid of: ～垃圾 clear away the rubbish / ～障碍 remove obstacles / 把某人～出党 clear sb. out of the Party

清楚 qīngchu ① clear; distinct: 字迹～ written in a clear hand / 发音～ a clear pronunciation / 头脑～ a clear head / 他的话说得不～。He didn't speak clearly. *or* What he said was ambiguous. / 把工作交代清～ explain one's job clearly on handing it over / 大是大非问题要彻底弄～。Major issues of principle must be thoroughly thrashed out. ② be clear about; understand: 这个问题你～不～? Do you understand this question or not? / 我真不～他为什么这样做。I really can't understand why he has done this.

清创术 qīngchuāngshù *med.* débridement

清醇 qīngchún pure (in taste or smell): 酒味～可口。The wine is pure and smooth to the palate.

清脆 qīngcuì clear and melodious: ～的歌声 clear and melodious singing

清单 qīngdān detailed list; detailed account: 货物～ a detailed list of goods; inventory / 列一个～ make a detailed list

清淡 qīngdàn ① light; weak; delicate: ～的绿茶 weak green tea / ～的花香 the delicate fragrance of flowers ② not greasy or strongly flavoured; light: ～的食物 light food ③ dull; slack: 生意～。Business is slack.

清党 qīngdǎng purge (a political party); carry out a purge

清道 qīngdào ① sweep the streets ② clear the way (for a high official in imperial times)

清道夫 qīngdàofū *old* scavenger; street cleaner; street sweeper

清点 qīngdiǎn check; make an inventory; sort and count: ～物资 make an inventory of equipment and materials / ～货物 take stock / ～战利品 check and sort out spoils of war

清炖 qīngdùn boiled in clear soup (without soy sauce): ～鸡 stewed chicken without soy sauce

清芬 qīngfēn *formal* ① delicate fragrance; faint scent ② moral integrity; nobility of character

清风 qīngfēng cool breeze; refreshing breeze: ～徐来，水波不兴。(苏轼) A cool breeze blew gently, without starting a ripple.

清福 qīngfú the happiness of a leisurely, retired life

清高 qīnggāo aloof from politics and material pursuits

清稿 qīnggǎo ① make a fair (or clean) copy ② fair (or clean) copy

清歌妙舞 qīnggē-miàowǔ clear singing, exquisite dancing: 公子王孙芳树下，～落花前。(刘希夷) You princelings, young noblemen beneath the flowering trees, Clear singing, exquisite dancing before the falling flowers.

清官 qīngguān *old* honest and upright official

清官难断家务事 qīngguān nán duàn jiāwùshì even an upright official finds it hard to settle a family quarrel

清规 qīngguī monastic rules for Buddhists

清规戒律 qīngguī jièlǜ ① regulations, taboos and commandments for Buddhists or Taoists ② restrictions and fetters: 过多的评头品足，数不尽的～ endless carping and countless taboos

清锅冷灶 qīngguō-lěngzào the pot is empty and the stove is cold—(of a house, restaurant, etc.) deserted; unfrequented

清寒 qīnghán ① poor; in straitened circumstances: 家境～ come of an impoverished (or poor) family ② cold and clear: 月色～ clear, cold moonlight

清还 qīnghuán clear up and pay back (debts, etc.)

清辉 qīnghuī (also 清晖 qīnghuī) clear and bright light (esp. of the sun or the moon): 月亮的～从窗口泻进来。The clear, bright moonlight poured in through the window.

清火 qīnghuǒ *Chin. med.* relieve inflammation or internal heat

清减 qīngjiǎn *formal* thin; emaciated

清健 qīngjiàn *formal* (of an older person) spry: 他七十多岁了，还很～。He's 70 years old, but very spry.

清剿 qīngjiǎo clean up; suppress; eliminate: ～土匪 clean up bandits; suppress bandits

清教徒 Qīngjiàotú Puritan

清洁 qīngjié clean: 整齐～ clean and tidy / 人人要注意～卫生。Everybody should pay attention to sanitation and hygiene. / ～队 cleaning squad / ～工人 sanitation worker; street cleaner

清洁提单 qīngjié tídān clean bill of lading

清结 qīngjié ① settle (or square) accounts; balance the books ② bring to an end; wind up; settle

清介 qīngjiè *formal* virtuous and upright

清劲风 qīngjìngfēng *meteorol.* fresh breeze

清净 qīngjìng peace and quiet: 怕麻烦，图～ fear trouble and seek peace and quiet

清静 qīngjìng quiet: 咱们找个～的地方谈谈。Let's find a quiet place to chat.

清君侧 qīng jūncè rid the emperor of "evil" ministers (as a pretext for staging a *coup d'état* or an armed rebellion)

清客 qīngkè hangers-on of rich and powerful families in old China

清口 qīngkǒu tasty and refreshing

清苦 qīngkǔ (esp. of scholars or teachers) poor; badly off: 生活～ live in poverty

清蜡 qīnglà *petroleum* paraffin removal

清栏 qīnglán *dial.* remove manure from a pigsty, sheepfold, etc.

清朗 qīnglǎng ① cool and bright: ～的天气 clear and bright weather ② loud and clear; resounding: ～的声音 a loud and clear sound

清冷 qīnglěng ① chilly: 一个～的秋夜 a chilly autumn night ② deserted; desolate: 夜已深了，街上十分～。It was late at night and the streets were quite deserted.

清理 qīnglǐ put in order; check up; clear; sort out: 把房间～～ put the room in order; clean up the room / ～物资 check up on equipment and materials / ～债务 clear up debts / ～仓库 take stock; make an inventory of warehouse stocks / ～档案 put the archives in order; sort out documents

清丽 qīnglì ① (of writing) lucid and elegant ② (of a scene) quiet and exquisite: ～的景色 a tranquil, exquisite scene

清廉 qīnglián honest and upright; free from corruption: ～的官吏 an honest and incorruptible official

清凉 qīngliáng cool and refreshing: ～饮料 cold drink; cooler / 你的批评对我是一服很好的～剂。Your criticism had a sobering effect on me.

清凉油 qīngliángyóu cooling ointment; essential balm

清亮 qīngliàng clear and resounding; resonant: 嗓音～ a resonant voice

清亮 qīngliang *inf.* crystal; clear; limpid

清冽 qīngliè *formal* cool; chilly

清凌凌 qīnglínglíng (also 清泠泠 qīnglínglíng) (of water) clear and rippling

清流 qīngliú ① *liter.* a clear stream: 登东皋以舒啸，临～而赋诗。(陶潜) Or climbing the east hill and whistling long Or composing verses beside the clear stream. ② *hist.* uncontaminated group—scholars who were concerned with politics but held themselves aloof from those in power (e.g. members of the Donglin Academy 东林党 in the late Ming)

清棉 qīngmián *text.* scutching: ～机 scutcher / ～间 blowing room

清明[1] qīngmíng ① clear and bright: 月色～ clear and bright moonlight ② sober and calm: 神志～ be in full possession of one's faculties ③ (of government or administration) well ordered; well regulated

清明[2] Qīngmíng ① Pure Brightness—the 5th of the 24 solar terms ② the day marking the beginning of the 5th solar term (April 4, 5, or 6; traditionally observed as a festival for worshipping at ancestral graves, technically known as "sweeping the graves" 扫墓) ——see also 节气 jiéqi, 二十四节气 èrshí sì jiéqi

清明菜 qīngmíngcài another name for 鼠麴草 shǔqūcǎo

清喷漆 qīngpēnqī *chem.* clear lacquer

清贫 qīngpín (usu. of scholars or teachers) poor; badly off: 家道～ be a person of scanty means

清平 qīngpíng peaceful; tranquil: ～世界 times of peace and prosperity

清漆 qīngqī varnish: 透明～ clear varnish / 皱纹～ shrivel varnish

清奇 qīngqí quaint and elegant

清讫 qīngqì payment received; paid

清秋 qīngqiū *liter.* clear autumn air (esp. in late autumn): ～天气，校园还是一片浓绿。It was a clear autumn day. The campus was still a mass of greenery. / 无言独上西楼，月如钩，寂寞梧桐深院锁～。(李煜) Without words, I mount alone the western chamber: The moon like a hook, The *wutong* tree solitary, A clear autumn locked up in the deep courtyard.

清癯 qīngqú *formal* thin; lean; spare: 面容～ a thin face

清趣 qīngqù simple, refined tastes

清泉 qīngquán cool spring (water)

清热法 qīngrèfǎ *Chin. med.* antipyretic method (using medicines of a cold nature to treat acute febrile diseases)

清热药 qīngrèyào antipyretic

清扫 qīngsǎo thoroughly clean up; give a thorough cleanup

清瘦 qīngshòu *euph.* thin; lean; spare: 你病后略见～。You look rather thin after your illness.

清爽 qīngshuǎng ① fresh and cool: 晚风吹来，十分～。The evening breeze is cooling and refreshing. ② relieved; relaxed: 事情解决了，我心里也～了。Now that the matter is settled, I feel relieved. ③ *dial.* clean and tidy ④ *dial.* clear: 把话讲～。Try to make yourself clearer.

清水墙 qīngshuǐqiáng *archit.* dry wall

清水衙门 qīngshuǐ yámen plain water *yamen* (formerly, a government office which handled no large sums of money and had little or no chance of graft or squeeze; now usu. used with reference to an institution with limited funds and welfare facilities)

清算 qīngsuàn ① clear (accounts); square ② settle accounts; expose and criticize: ～恶霸地主的罪恶 expose and criticize the crimes of a despotic landlord

清算协定 qīngsuàn xiédìng clearing agreement

清算银行 qīngsuàn yínháng clearing bank

清算帐户 qīngsuàn zhànghù clearing account

清谈 qīngtán ① pure conversations—intellectual discussions on lofty and nonmundane matters (engaged in by philosopher wits in Wei-Jin times 魏晋) ② idle talk; empty talk: ～不能解决问题。Idle talk solves no problems. / ～误国。Empty talk and no action will ruin the country.

清汤 qīngtāng clear soup; light soup; *consommé*

清汤寡水 qīngtāng-guǎshuǐ (of a dish) watery and tasteless; dishwater

清通 qīngtōng (of writing) clear and coherent; smooth: 文章要写得～，必须下一番苦功。If you want to write a clear and coherent essay, you have to work hard on it.

清玩 qīngwán ① an elegant, refined object for enjoyment ② admire the beauty of sth.; delight in; enjoy

清婉 qīngwǎn (of voice) clear and sweet

清晰 qīngxī distinct; clear: 她发音～。Her pronunciation is clear. / 远山的轮廓～可见。The outlines of the distant hills are clearly discernible.

清晰度 qīngxīdù ① (TV) clarity ② (sound) articulation

清洗 qīngxǐ ① rinse; wash; clean: ～炊具 clean cooking utensils ② purge; comb out: 把腐化堕落分子～出去 comb out the degenerates

清闲 qīngxián at leisure; idle: 我干这个工作几乎没有～的时候。I have very little leisure time in this job. / 他过不惯～的退休生活。He finds it difficult to get used to the idle life of retirement.

清香 qīngxiāng delicate fragrance; faint scent: 晨风吹来野花的～。The morning breeze carried with it the scent of wild flowers.

清心 qīngxīn ① empty one's mind of worries; have peace of mind ② purify the heart; have a pure heart

清心寡欲 qīngxīn-guǎyù purify one's heart and reduce the number of one's desires; be pure of heart and have few desires

清新 qīngxīn pure and fresh; fresh: 雨后空气～。The air was pure and fresh after the rain. / 画报的版面～活泼。The layout of the pictorial is fresh and lively. / 文字～ written in a refreshingly lucid style

清馨 qīngxīn *formal* delicate fragrance; faint scent

清醒 qīngxǐng ① clear-headed; sober: 保持～的头脑 keep a clear (*or* cool) head; keep sober-minded / 我们对形势要有～的估计。We should make a sober estimate of the situation. / 现实使他～过来。The reality has sobered him up. ② regain consciousness: 病人已经～过来。The patient has come to.

清秀 qīngxiù delicate and pretty: 面貌～ of fine, delicate features / 山水～ beautiful landscape

清选机 qīngxuǎnjī *agric.* cleaner

清雅 qīngyǎ elegant; refined: 风格～ in an elegant style / 此诗～脱尘，句内饱含春意。This poem is elegant and sublime, and the lines are full of vernal longings.

清样 qīngyàng *print.* final proof; foundry proof

清夜 qīngyè the stillness of night: ～自思 be deep in thought in the stillness of night

清夜扪心 qīngyè mén xīn examine one's conscience in the stillness of night

清一色 qīngyīsè ① all of one suit (in playing mahjong); flush ② all of the same colour; uniform; homogeneous: 运动员～地穿着红色运动服。The players were all dressed alike in red sports suits. / 宗派主义者爱搞所谓～。Sectarians are fond of so-called homogeneous bodies. / 这个委员会的成员是～的中年妇女。The committee consists entirely of middle-aged women.

清议 qīngyì ① *hist.* pure talk—a movement for renovation started by sincere and scholarly literati working outside the centres of power for a change in policy (e.g. the movement of the Donglin Academy 东林党 in the late Ming) ② political criticism by scholars

清逸 qīngyì fresh and refined

清音[1] qīngyīn ① a type of ballad-singing popular in Sichuan Province ② *old* band music played at weddings and funerals

清音[2] qīngyīn *phonet.* voiceless sound

清莹 qīngyíng clear and glistening; limpid and sparkling: ～的泪珠 glistening tears / ～的湖水 a limpid lake

清幽 qīngyōu (of a landscape) quiet and beautiful

清油 qīngyóu *dial.* ① edible vegetable oil ② tea-seed oil; tea oil ③ rapeseed oil; rape oil

清越 qīngyuè (of sound) clear and melodious; clear and far-reaching: 歌声～。The singing was clear and melodious. / 其声～,烈如箫管。Her voice, as beautiful as the notes of a flute, was clear and far-reaching.

清早 qīngzǎo *inf.* early in the morning; early morning: 他们一～就干活去了。They went out to work early in the morning.

清湛 qīngzhàn *formal* limpid; clear

清丈 qīngzhàng measure land carefully; take the dimensions of a field

清帐 qīngzhàng square (*or* clear) an account

清真 qīngzhēn ① *formal* simple and unadorned; plain ② Islamic; Muslim: ～食堂 Muslims' canteen / ～点心 Muslims' cakes (without pork fat)

清真教 Qīngzhēnjiào another name for 伊斯兰教 Yīsīlánjiào

清真寺 qīngzhēnsì mosque

清蒸 qīngzhēng steamed in clear soup (usu. without soy sauce): ～鱼 steamed fish

清正 qīngzhèng upright and just: 为官～ be an upright and just official; be upright in performing one's official duties

清浊 qīng-zhuó ① pure and impure; good and bad ② *phonet.* voiceless and voiced sounds

圊
圊 qīng *arch.* latrine

圊肥 qīngféi *dial.* barnyard manure

蜻
蜻 qīng see below

蜻蜓 qīngtíng dragonfly

蜻蜓点水 qīngtíng diǎn shuǐ like a dragonfly skimming the surface of the water—just touch on sth. lightly without going into it deeply: 做调查工作不能～,要深入实际。To make an investigation, one should go into matters deeply, not just scratch the surface.

鲭
鲭 qīng mackerel

qíng

勍
勍 qíng *formal* powerful: ～敌 powerful enemy

情
情 qíng ① feeling; affection; sentiment: 热情 rèqíng ② love; passion: 爱情 àiqíng ③ sexual passion; lust: 情欲 qíngyù ④ favour; kindness: 求情 qiúqíng ⑤ situation; circumstances; condition: 军情 jūnqíng

情爱 qíng'ài love (esp. between man and woman): ～甚笃 be deeply in love with each other

情报 qíngbào intelligence; information: ～机关 intelligence agency / ～人员 intelligence personnel; intelligence agent / ～系统 intelligence channel

情不可却 qíng bùkě què it would be ungracious not to accept (an invitation, etc.)

情不自禁 qíng bù zì jìn cannot refrain from; cannot help (doing sth.); be seized with a sudden impulse to: ～地流下泪来 cannot refrain from tears / ～地笑起来 can't help laughing / ～地嚷起来 shout beside oneself with excitement

情操 qíngcāo sentiment: 培养共产主义的～ foster communist values

情场 qíngchǎng the arena of love; the tournaments of love: ～得意 be lucky in love / ～失意 be frustrated in love / ～老手 womanizer

情痴 qíngchī love maniac

情敌 qíngdí rival in love

情调 qíngdiào sentiment; emotional appeal: 不健康的～ unhealthy sentimentalism / 这首曲子充满了哀伤的～。The music is full of pathos. / 这位学者的书斋～高雅。The scholar's study gives the impression of a man of simple, refined tastes.

情窦初开 qíngdòu chū kāi (of a young girl) first awakening (*or* dawning) of love

情分 qíngfen mutual affection: 朋友～ friendship / 兄弟～ fraternity; brotherhood / 两家做了几辈子邻居,素来～好。The two families have been neighbours for generations and have all along been on amicable terms.

情夫 qíngfū an illicit lover of a married woman; lover

情妇 qíngfù an illicit lover of a married man; mistress

情感 qínggǎn emotion; feeling

情歌 qínggē love song

情话 qínghuà ① *formal* intimate words; heart-to-heart talk ② lovers' prattle; whispers of love; sweet nothings: ～绵绵 whispering sweet nothings

情怀 qínghuái feelings: 抒发无产阶级的革命～ express the revolutionary thoughts and feelings of the proletariat

情急智生 qíng jí zhì shēng hit on an idea in a moment of desperation

情节 qíngjié ① plot: 这个剧本～很复杂。The play has a very complicated plot. / ～紧凑 a tightknit (*or* well-knit) plot ② circumstances: 根据～轻重,分别给予处理。Each will be dealt with according to the seriousness of his case.

情景 qíngjǐng scene; sight; circumstances: 兴奋热烈的～ an exhilarating scene / 感人的～ a moving sight

情景交融 qíng-jǐng jiāoróng (of literary works) feeling and setting happily blended

情境 qíngjìng circumstances; situation

情况 qíngkuàng ① circumstances; situation; condition; state of affairs: ～不明。The situation is not clear. / 在这种～下 under these circumstances; such being the case / 根据具体～ in accordance with specific conditions / 在许多～下 in many cases / 这种～必须改变。This state of affairs must change. / 现在～不同了。Now things are different. / 他们的～怎么样? How do matters stand with them? / 那得看～而定。That depends. *or* It all depends. ② military situation: 前线有什么～? How is the situation at the front? / 前面有～,做好战斗准备。There's enemy activity ahead. Prepare for combat.

情郎 qíngláng (girl's) lover; sweetheart

情理 qínglǐ reason; sense: 不近～ unreasonable; irrational / ～难容 incompatible with the accepted code of human conduct; contrary to reason; absurd

情侣 qínglǚ sweethearts; lovers

情面 qíngmiàn feelings; sensibilities: 留～ spare sb.'s feelings / 不顾～ have no consideration for sb.'s feelings / 对错误一定要揭发,不讲～。The mistakes must be exposed without sparing anyone's sensibilities.

情趣 qíngqù ① temperament and interest: 他们二人～相投。The two of them are temperamentally compatible (*or* congenial). ② interest; appeal: 这首诗写得很有～。This poem is very charming.

情人 qíngrén sweetheart; lover

情人眼里出西施 qíngrén yǎnli chū Xīshī a lover sees a Xishi in his beloved; in the eyes of the lover, his be-

loved is a beauty; beauty is in the eye of the beholder

情诗 qíngshī love poem

情事 qíngshì (usu. used in legal documents) the facts; the phenomena

情势 qíngshì situation; circumstances; trend of events: ～危急。The situation is critical. / 对～作出估计 size up the situation

情势不变 qíngshì bù biàn *diplomacy rebus sic stantibus*

情书 qíngshū love letter

情思 qíngsī ① tender regards; affection; goodwill ② state of mind; mood

情死 qíngsǐ die for love

情愫 qíngsù (also 情素 qíngsù) *formal* ① feeling; sentiment: 朝夕相处, 增加了他们之间的～。Thrown together, their feelings for each other grew. ② real sentiment; innermost feeling

情随事迁 qíng suí shì qiān feeling change with circumstances

情态 qíngtài spirit; mood: 生动地描绘了儿童的～ depict children's spirit vividly

情态动词 qíngtài dòngcí *gram.* modal verb

情同手足 qíng tóng shǒuzú like brothers; with brotherly love for each other: 两国人民～。Our two peoples are bound together by ties of fraternal friendship.

情投意合 qíngtóu-yìhé find each other congenial: 两人说得～, 只恨相见之晚。They found so much in common that they regretted not having met earlier.

情网 qíngwǎng snares of love: 堕入～ be caught in the snares of love

情味 qíngwèi ① sentiment; emotional appeal ② interest; flavour; overtone

情文并茂 qíng-wén bìng mào (of writing) excellent in both content and language

情见乎辞 qíng xiàn hū cí sincerity shines through the words

情形 qíngxing circumstances; situation; condition; state of affairs: 两地～大不相同。Conditions in the two places differ greatly. / 大家看了这种～, 非常气愤。People felt indignant at this state of affairs. / 这是一方面的～。This is one side of the picture.

情绪 qíngxù ① morale; feeling; mood; sentiments: ～高涨。Morale is high. / ～不高 be in low spirits / 全团战斗～高昂。The whole regiment is in fine fighting fettle. ② depression; moodiness; the sulks: 有点儿～ rather sulky

情义 qíngyì ties of friendship, comradeship, etc.: 姐姐待他很有～。His elder sister is very affectionate towards him. / 阶级～ class love

情谊 qíngyì friendly feelings; friendly sentiments: 战斗～ militant bonds of friendship / 兄弟～ brotherly affection

情意 qíngyì tender regards; affection; goodwill: 深厚的～ deep affection

情由 qíngyóu the hows and whys: 不问～ without asking about the circumstances or causes

情有可原 qíng yǒu kě yuán excusable; pardonable

情欲 qíngyù sexual passion; lust

情愿 qíngyuàn ① be willing to: 他很～付这个价钱。He's quite willing to pay the price. ② would rather; prefer: 她～粉身碎骨, 也不在敌人面前屈服。She would rather be cut to pieces than yield to the enemy.

情知 qíngzhī know perfectly well (what is going on); know for certain; be fully aware

情致 qíngzhì interest; appeal

情状 qíngzhuàng state of affairs; situation; condition

睛 qíng get; receive: 别净～现成的。You can't always have what is ready and available.

晴 qíng fine; clear: 天～了。It's clearing up.

晴好 qínghǎo warm and fine

晴和 qínghé warm and fine: 天气～。It's a fine, warm day.

晴间多云 qíng jiàn duōyún fine with occasional clouds

晴空万里 qíngkōng wànlǐ a clear and boundless sky; the vast clear skies

晴朗 qínglǎng fine; sunny: 天气～。It's a sunny day.

晴丝 qíngsī gossamer

晴天 qíngtiān fine day; sunny day

晴天霹雳 qíngtiān pīlì a bolt from the blue: 噩耗传来, 犹如～。The grievous news came as a bolt from the blue.

晴雨表 qíngyǔbiǎo weatherglass; barometer

氰 qíng *chem.* cyanogen; dicyanogen

氰钴胺 qínggǔ'àn *pharm.* cyanocobalamin; vitamin B$_{12}$

氰化 qínghuà cyaniding: ～法 cyanidation / ～物 cyanide / ～钾 potassium cyanide

氰酸 qíngsuān cyanic acid

檠（橄） qíng *formal* ① lamp stand; candlestick ② device for holding crossbow in position

擎 qíng prop up; hold up; lift up: 众擎易举 zhòng qíng yì jǔ

擎天柱 qíngtiānzhù a man in a responsible position; mainstay

黥（剠） qíng ① brand the face as a kind of punishment in ancient times ② *formal* tattoo

qǐng

苘（檾、蕡） qǐng see below

苘麻 qǐngmá *bot.* piemarker

顷[1] qǐng *qing*, currently called 市顷 shìqǐng, a traditional unit of area——see also 市顷 shìqǐng

顷[2] qǐng ① *adv. formal* just; just now: ～接来信。I have just received your letter. ② *formal* a little while: 少顷 shǎoqǐng ③ *part.* (of time) about: 光绪二十年～ about the 20th year of the Guangxu period (c. 1895)

顷刻 qǐngkè *adv.* in a moment; in an instant; instantly: ～之间 in a twinkling; in no time / ～瓦解 collapse instantly

请 qǐng ① request; ask: ～他进来。Ask him in. / ～多加指导。It is hoped you will give us guidance. / ～人来修机器 get sb. to repair the machine; get the machine repaired ② invite; engage: ～医生 send for a doctor / ～总工程师来讲课 invite the chief engineer to give a lecture ③ *pol.* please: ～坐。Won't you sit down? *or* Please be seated. / ～安静。Be quiet, please. / ～速回信。Please reply as soon as possible. ④ *old* buy holy sacrificial things, such as joss sticks, candles, paper horses and shrine of Buddha

请安 qǐng'ān ① pay respects to sb.; wish sb. good health ② *dial.* make obeisance by drooping the right arm in front of oneself and bending the left knee

请便 qǐngbiàn do as you wish; please yourself: 你要是想现在去, 那就～吧。Well, if you want to leave now, go ahead.

请春客 qǐng chūnkè give a spring party (i.e. according to old custom, treat one's friends and relatives to a feast shortly after the Spring Festival)

请调 qǐngdiào ask to be transferred to another post: ～报告 a written request for a transfer (to another post)

请功 qǐnggōng ask the higher level to record sb.'s meritorious deeds

请假 qǐngjià ask for leave: 请三天假 ask for three days' leave / 因病～一天 ask for a day's sick leave

请假条 qǐngjiàtiáo written request for leave (of absence)

请柬 qǐngjiǎn *formal* invitation card

请见 qǐngjiàn *formal* request an audience; ask for an interview

请教 qǐngjiào ask for advice; consult: 我们想～你几个问题。We wish to consult you on a few questions. / 向小麦专家～ consult a wheat expert / 虚心向群众～ learn modestly from the masses

请君入瓮 qǐng jūn rù wèng kindly step into the vat—have a taste of what you intended for others

请客 qǐngkè stand treat; invite sb. to dinner; entertain guests; give a dinner party

请命 qǐngmìng ① plead on sb.'s behalf ② *old* ask (the higher authorities) for instructions

请求 qǐngqiú ask; request: ～宽恕 ask for forgiveness / ～贷款 make a request for a loan / 答应～ compile with a request

请示 qǐngshì ask for (*or* request) instructions: 向上级～ ask the higher authorities for instructions / 事前～, 事后报告 ask for instructions beforehand and submit reports afterwards

请帖 qǐngtiě invitation card; invitation: 发～ send out invitations

请托 qǐngtuō ask sb. to do sth.; entrust

请问 qǐngwèn ① *pol.* excuse me; please: ～, 到火车站怎么走? Excuse me, but could you tell me how to get to the station? ② we should like to ask; it may be asked; one may ask: ～, 要不是改革开放, 我们的经济建设能有今天吗? I'd like to ask, without reform and the open policy, could our economic development be what it is today?

请勿 qǐngwù please don't: 本室书籍～携出室外。Please don't take the books out of this room. / ～吸烟。No smoking. / ～入内。No admittance. / ～践踏草地。Keep off the lawn.

请降 qǐngxiáng beg to surrender

请缨 qǐngyīng *formal* request a cord from the emperor (to bind the enemy)—submit a request for a military assignment: ～杀敌 request to be sent to the front; volunteer for battle

请援 qǐngyuán ask for support or aid

请愿 qǐngyuàn present a petition; petition

请愿书 qǐngyuànshū petition

请战 qǐngzhàn ask for a battle assignment

请战书 qǐngzhànshū a written request for a battle assignment

请罪 qǐngzuì admit one's error and ask for punishment; apologize

謦 qǐng see below

謦欬 qǐngkài *formal* ① cough ② make light conversation

qìng

庆(慶) qìng ① celebrate; congratulate: ～丰收 celebrate a bumper harvest ② occasion for celebra-

tion: 国庆 guóqìng ③ (Qìng) a surname

庆大霉素 qìngdàméisù gentamicin

庆典 qìngdiǎn celebration; a ceremony to celebrate: 盛大～ grand celebrations

庆父不死, 鲁难未已 Qìngfù bù sǐ, Lǔ nàn wèi yǐ until Qing Fu is dead, the crisis in (the state of) Lu will not end—there will always be trouble until the one who causes it is gone

庆功会 qìnggōnghuì victory meeting

庆贺 qìnghè congratulate; celebrate: ～胜利 celebrate the victory / ～老张得奖 congratulate Lao Zhang on winning the award

庆幸 qìngxìng rejoice: 值得～的事 a matter for rejoicing / 可～的是, 这次车祸无人死亡。Happily, no one was killed in the car accident.

庆祝 qìngzhù celebrate: ～国庆 celebrate National Day

庆祝大会 qìngzhù dàhuì celebration meeting

亲(親) qìng see below——see also qīn

亲家 qìngjia ① parents of one's daughter-in-law or son-in-law ② relatives by marriage

亲家公 qìngjiagōng son's or daughter's father-in-law

亲家母 qìngjiamǔ son's or daughter's mother-in-law

磬 qìng ① chime stone ② inverted bell (a Buddhist percussion instrument)

罄 qìng *formal* use up; exhaust: ～其所有 empty one's purse; offer all one has

罄尽 qìngjìn *formal* with nothing left; all used up

罄竹难书 qìng zhú nán shū (of crimes) too many (*or* numerous) to record

綮 qìng see 肯綮 kěnqìng

qióng

穷(窮) qióng ① poor; poverty-stricken: 他家很～。His family is very poor. ② limit; end: 技穷 jìqióng ③ thoroughly: 穷究 qióngjiū ④ extremely: 穷奢极欲 qióngshējíyù

穷棒子 qióngbàngzi ① *old derog.* a poor peasant ② a poor person with high aspirations

穷棒子精神 qióngbàngzi jīngshén the spirit of the paupers—the spirit of self-reliance, hard struggle and adherence to the socialist road under difficult conditions

穷兵黩武 qióngbīng-dúwǔ use all one's armed might to wage wars of aggression; wantonly engage in military ventures

穷愁 qióngchóu poverty-stricken and woeful

穷愁潦倒 qióngchóu liǎodǎo be penniless and frustrated

穷措大 qióngcuòdà (also 穷醋大 qióngcùdà) a miserable poor scholar

穷当益坚 qióng dāng yì jiān the greater the adversity, the stronger the will

穷冬 qióngdōng *formal* midwinter; the depth of winter

穷乏 qióngfá poor; needy; impoverished

穷根 qiónggēn the roots of poverty: 挖掉～ dig up the roots of poverty

穷根究底 qiónggēn-jiūdǐ same as 追根究底 zhuīgēn-jiūdǐ

穷光蛋 qióngguāngdàn *inf.* pauper; poor wretch

穷极无聊 qióng jí wúliáo ① be utterly bored ② absolutely senseless; disgusting

穷家富路 qióngjiā-fùlù one should be frugal at home

but well equipped for a journey

穷竭 qióngjié *formal* use up; exhaust: ～心计 rack one's brains (in scheming); tax one's ingenuity

穷尽 qióngjìn limit; end: 学问是没有～的。There is no limit to learning.

穷究 qióngjiū make a thorough (*or* exhaustive) inquiry into sth.

穷开心 qióngkāixīn ① enjoy oneself despite poverty ② seek joy amidst sorrow; try to enjoy oneself despite one's suffering

穷寇 qióngkòu hard-pressed enemy; tottering foe

穷寇勿追 qióngkòu wù zhuī don't pursue a beaten enemy

穷苦 qióngkǔ poverty-stricken; impoverished

穷匮 qióngkuì *formal* be short of; lack

穷困 qióngkùn poverty-stricken; destitute; in straitened circumstances: 陷入～的境地 be reduced to destitution

穷忙 qióngmáng ① *old* try hard to eke out a living ② be pointlessly busy; be busy for nothing

穷目 qióngmù look as far as the eye can see: ～远望 gaze into the distance

穷年累月 qióngnián-lěiyuè for years on end; year after year

穷期 qióngqī termination; end: 战斗正未有～。The struggle will go on and on.

穷人 qióngrén poor people; the poor

穷日子 qióngrìzi days of poverty; straitened circumstances: 我们要把富日子当～过。We're well off now, but we should still live as if we were poor.

穷山恶水 qióngshān-èshuǐ barren mountains and unruly rivers; barren hills and untamed rivers

穷奢极欲 qióngshē-jíyù (also 穷奢极侈 qióngshē-jíchǐ) (indulge in) luxury and extravagance; (live a life of) wanton extravagance: 过着～的生活 wallow in luxury

穷酸 qióngsuān (of a scholar) poor and pedantic

穷途 qióngtú straitened circumstances; destitution

穷途潦倒 qióngtú liǎodǎo at the end of one's tether; desperate

穷途末路 qióngtú-mòlù be in an impasse; have come to a dead end

穷乡僻壤 qióngxiāng-pìrǎng a remote, backward place; remote hinterland: 从通商口岸直至～ from the trading ports to the remote hinterland

穷相 qióngxiàng appearance or manner suggestive of abject poverty

穷形尽相 qióngxíng-jìnxiàng ① describe in minute, vivid detail ② appear in all one's ugliness

穷凶极恶 qióngxiōng-jí'è extremely vicious; utterly evil; atrocious; diabolical: ～的敌人 most vicious enemy／一副～的样子 with the look of a fiendish brute

穷原竟委 qióngyuán-jìngwěi get to the bottom of the matter; make a thorough (*or* exhaustive) inquiry into sth.

穷源溯流 qióngyuán-sùliú same as 穷原竟委 qióngyuán-jìngwěi

穷则思变 qióng zé sī biàn poverty gives rise to a desire for change

穷追猛打 qióngzhuī-měngdǎ hotly pursue and fiercely attack

穹 qióng *formal* ① vault; dome ② the sky: 苍穹 cāngqióng

穹苍 qióngcāng *formal* the vault of heaven; the firmament; the sky; the heavens

穹顶 qióngdǐng *archit.* dome

穹隆 qiónglóng *formal* vault; arched roof

穹隆构造 qiónglóng gòuzào *geol.* dome structure

穹形 qióngxíng vaulted; arched: ～的屋顶 a vaulted roof

茕（煢、惸） qióng *formal* ① solitary; alone ② dejected

茕茕 qióngqióng *formal* all alone; lonely

茕茕孑立，形影相吊 qióngqióng jié lì, xíng-yǐng xiāng diào standing all alone, body and shadow comforting each other

劳（藭） qióng see 芎劳 xiōngqióng

琼（瓊） qióng *formal* fine jade: ～阁 a jewelled palace

琼浆 qióngjiāng *liter.* jadelike wine; good wine

琼楼玉宇 qiónglóu-yùyǔ a richly decorated jade palace; a magnificent building: 我欲乘风归去，又恐～，高处不胜寒。(苏轼) I long to ride the wind and return; Yet fear that marble towers and jade houses, So high, are over-cold.

琼脂 qióngzhī agar-agar; agar: ～培养基 agar medium／～酸 agaric acid／～糖 agarose

蛩 qióng *arch.* cricket (an insect)

跫 qióng see below

跫然 qióngrán *formal* (of footsteps) pattering: 足音～ footsteps pattering

qiū

丘¹ qiū ① mound; hillock: 荒～ a barren hillock ② grave: 坟丘 fénqiū ③ same as 浮厝 fúcuò ④ (Qiū) a surname

丘²（坵） qiū *m.* plot (of paddy field): 一～田 a plot of paddy field

丘八 qiūbā *old derog.* soldier (from the two components of the character 兵)

丘陵 qiūlíng hills: ～起伏 a chain of undulating hills／～地带 hilly country; hilly land

丘墓 qiūmù *formal* grave; tomb

丘脑 qiūnǎo *physiol.* cerebral ganglion

丘鹬 qiūyù *zool.* woodcock

丘疹 qiūzhěn papule

邱 qiū ① same as 丘 qiū ② (Qiū) a surname

秋（秌） qiū ① autumn: 一九八五年～ Autumn, 1985／～雨 autumn rain ② harvest time: 麦秋 màiqiū ③ year: 千秋万代 qiānqiū-wàndài ④ a period of (usu. troubled) time: 多事之秋 duō shì zhī qiū ⑤ (Qiū) a surname

秋波 qiūbō autumn ripples—the bright and clear eyes of a beautiful woman: 送～ (of a woman) cast amorous glances; make eyes; ogle

秋播 qiūbō autumn sowing

秋地 qiūdì fields waiting for autumn sowing

秋分 Qiūfēn ① the Autumn Equinox—the 16th of the 24 solar terms ② the day marking the beginning of the 16th solar term (Sept. 22, 23, or 24)——see also 节气 jiéqi, 二十四节气 èrshí sì jiéqì

秋风 qiūfēng ① autumn wind ② see 打秋风 dǎ qiūfēng

秋风过耳 qiūfēng guò ěr like autumn wind passing by the ear—unnoticed; unheeded

秋风扫落叶 qiūfēng sǎo luòyè the autumn wind sweeping away fallen leaves—carry everything before one

秋高气爽 qiūgāo-qìshuǎng autumn (sky) high and air brisk—the autumn sky is clear and the air is bracing

(a set phrase for describing fine autumn weather): 北京已经热过了，现在正是～的好时候。Beijing has already had its heat. Now it's just the fine season of "autumn (sky) high and air brisk."

秋耕 qiūgēng　autumn ploughing

秋海棠 qiūhǎitáng　begonia

秋毫 qiūháo　autumn hair or newly-grown down—sth. so small as to be almost indiscernible: 明察秋毫 míngchá qiūháo

秋毫无犯 qiūháo wú fàn　(of highly disciplined troops) not commit the slightest offence against the civilians; not encroach on the interests of the people to the slightest degree: ～的纪律 discipline which forbids the slightest violation of the people's interests / 大军所到之处，～。Wherever the troops went, they inflicted not the slightest harm on the people.

秋毫之末 qiūháo zhī mò　the tip of an autumn hair—a minute, almost indiscernible particle

秋后的蚂蚱 qiūhòude màzha　a grasshopper at the end of autumn—nearing its end: 敌人象～, 蹦跶不了几天啦。Like a grasshopper at the end of autumn, the enemy is on his last legs.

秋后算帐 qiūhòu suànzhàng　square accounts after the autumn harvest—wait until after a political movement is over to settle accounts with the leadership or the masses

秋季 qiūjì　autumn: ～作物 autumn crops

秋景 qiūjǐng　① autumn scenery ② autumn harvest

秋空 qiūkōng　autumn sky

秋老虎 qiūlǎohǔ　a spell of hot weather after the Beginning of Autumn (立秋)

秋凉 qiūliáng　cool autumn days: 等～再去吧。Don't go there until the cool autumn days.

秋令 qiūlìng　① autumn ② autumn weather: 冬行～。The winter weather is like autumn.

秋气 qiūqì　*formal*　① cool autumn weather ② autumn thoughts; melancholy; sadness; desolation: 怀抱剧有～。A feeling of "autumnal melancholy" has suddenly possessed me.

秋千 qiūqiān　swing (a seat for swinging): 打～ have a swing

秋色 qiūsè　autumn scenery: ～宜人 charming autumn scenery

秋试 qiūshì　imperial examinations (held in autumn) at the provincial level in the Ming and Qing Dynasties

秋收 qiūshōu　① autumn harvest: 农民们都在忙着～。The farmers are all busy with autumn harvest. ② autumn crops

秋收起义 Qiūshōu Qǐyì　the Autumn Harvest Uprising (an armed uprising led by Mao Zedong in 1927 in the Hunan-Jiangxi border region, which marked the Chinese Communist Party's independent building of a revolutionary army)

秋水 qiūshuǐ　autumn waters—limpid eyes (of a woman): 望穿秋水 wàngchuān qiūshuǐ

秋水仙 qiūshuǐxiān　*bot.*　meadow saffron; autumn crocus

秋水仙素 qiūshuǐxiānsù　*pharm.*　colchicine

秋天 qiūtiān　autumn

秋闱 qiūwéi　*formal*　imperial examinations (held in autumn) at the provincial level in the Ming and Qing Dynasties

秋汛 qiūxùn　autumn floods

秋游 qiūyóu　autumn outing

秋征 qiūzhēng　collection of agricultural tax in kind after the autumn harvest

秋庄稼 qiūzhuāngjia　autumn crops

蚯　qiū　see below

蚯蚓 qiūyǐn　earthworm

湫　qiū　pond; pool ——see also jiǎo

楸　qiū　*bot.*　Chinese catalpa

鳅(鰌)　qiū　see 泥鳅 níqiu; 鱼秋鳅 qíqiu

鞦　qiū　see below

鞦韆 qiūqiān　same as 秋千 qiūqiān

qiú

仇　Qiú　a surname ——see also chóu

囚　qiú　① imprison: 被～ be thrown into prison ② prisoner; convict: 死囚 sǐqiú

囚车 qiúchē　prison van; prisoners' van

囚犯 qiúfàn　prisoner; convict

囚房 qiúfáng　prison cell

囚禁 qiújìn　(also 囚困 qiúkùn) imprison; put in jail; keep in captivity

囚牢 qiúláo　*old*　prison; jail

囚笼 qiúlóng　(wooden) prisoner's cage used in imperial China

囚室 qiúshì　prison cell

囚首垢面 qiúshǒu-gòumiàn　with unkempt hair and dirty face

囚徒 qiútú　prisoner; convict

囚衣 qiúyī　prison garb

犰　qiú　see below

犰狳 qiúyú　*zool.*　armadillo

求　qiú　① beg; request; entreat; beseech: ～你帮个忙, 行吗? May I ask you a favour? ② strive for: ～进步 strive for further progress / ～解放 strive for liberation / 生物都有～生存的本能。All living beings are endowed with an instinct for survival. ③ seek; try: ～学问 seek knowledge / 不～名利 not seek fame and gain ④ demand: 供求 gōngqiú

求爱 qiú'ài　pay court to; court; woo

求备 qiúbèi　demand perfection; nitpick

求成 qiúchéng　hope for success: 急于求成 jíyú qiúchéng

求大同, 存小异 qiú dàtóng, cún xiǎoyì　seek common ground on major issues while reserving differences on minor ones

求告 qiúgào　implore; entreat; supplicate

求告无门 qiúgào wúmén　have nowhere to turn to for help

求根 qiúgēn　*math.*　extract a root

求过于供 qiú guò yú gōng　demand exceeds supply

求和 qiúhé　① sue for peace ② (in ball games or chess) try to equalize the score; try for a draw

求婚 qiúhūn　make an offer of marriage; propose

求积仪 qiújīyí　planimeter

求见 qiújiàn　ask to see (one's superior or a VIP); request an interview; beg for an audience

求教 qiújiào　ask for advice: 登门～ call on sb. for counsel; come to seek advice / 不懂的事要向别人～。Ask other people about things that you do not know.

求解 qiújiě　find the solution (of a mathematical problem); solve a problem

求借 qiújiè　ask sb. for a loan

求救 qiújiù　ask sb. to come to the rescue; cry for help: 发出～的信号 signal an SOS; send a GMDSS

求靠 qiúkào　*dial.*　seek patronage

求偶 qiú'ǒu seek a spouse

求乞 qiúqǐ beg: 沿门～ go begging from door to door

求签 qiúqiān divine by drawing lots in a temple

求亲 qiúqīn seek a marriage alliance

求亲告友 qiúqīn-gàoyǒu ask for favours (usu. loans) from relatives and friends

求情 qiúqíng plead; intercede; ask for a favour; beg for leniency: 向他～ plead with him / 为某人～ intercede for sb.; beg (for mercy) on sb.'s behalf / ～告饶 beg for leniency and mercy

求全 qiúquán ① demand perfection ② try to round sth. off: 委曲求全 wěiqū qiú quán

求全责备 qiúquán zébèi demand perfection; nitpick: 对人不要～。Don't demand perfection of others. or Don't nitpick at others.

求饶 qiúráo beg for mercy; ask for pardon

求人 qiúrén ask sb. for help

求人不如求己 qiú rén bùrú qiú jǐ self-help is better than help from others; God helps those that help themselves

求生 qiúshēng seek survival: 动物都有～的本能。All animals have an instinct to seek survival.

求胜 qiúshèng strive for victory: ～心切 be anxious to gain victory

求实精神 qiúshí jīngshén matter-of-fact attitude; realistic approach: 把革命热情和～结合起来 combine revolutionary fervour with a realistic spirit

求田问舍 qiútián-wènshè desire nothing but a homestead—have no high aims in life

求同存异 qiú tóng cún yì seek common ground while reserving differences

求仙 qiúxiān ① seek immortality ② seek divine advice

求贤若渴 qiú xián ruò kě (of a ruler) eagerly seek after men of worth and ability

求降 qiúxiáng beg to surrender; hang out (or hoist) the white flag

求学 qiúxué ① go to school; attend school ② pursue one's studies; seek knowledge

求爷爷告奶奶 qiú yéye gào nǎinai inf. beg grandpas and entreat grandmas—go about begging for help

求医 qiúyī seek medical advice; see a doctor

求雨 qiúyǔ pray for rain

求援 qiúyuán ask for help; request reinforcements

求战 qiúzhàn ① seek battle; provoke battle: 敌军进入山口,～不得,只得退却。The enemy troops advanced into the mountain pass and then, failing to provoke battle, pulled back. ② ask to go into battle: 战士们～心切。The men are itching for action.

求证 qiúzhèng seek to prove; seek evidence or verification

求之不得 qiú zhī bù dé all one could wish for; most welcome: 这对他真是～的事情。This is just what he wants. / 这是～的好机会。This is a most welcome opportunity. / 给王师傅当徒弟,他真是～。He was only too glad to be an apprentice to Master Worker Wang.

求知 qiúzhī seek knowledge: ～欲 thirst (or craving) for knowledge

求值 qiúzhí math. evaluation

求助 qiúzhù turn to sb. for help; seek help: 他理屈词穷,只好～于诡辩。As he had a weak case and could not defend himself, he had to resort to sophistry.

虬 (虯)

qiú same as 虬龙 qiúlóng

虬龙 qiúlóng legendary small dragon with horns

虬髯 qiúrán formal curly sideburns

虬须 qiúxū formal curly beard or moustache

泅

qiú swim

泅渡 qiúdù swim across

泅水 qiúshuǐ swim

泅泳 qiúyǒng (also 泅游 qiúyóu) swim

酋

qiú ① chief of a tribe ② chieftain (of bandits, invaders, etc.): 敌酋 díqiú

酋长 qiúzhǎng ① chief of a tribe ② sheik(h); emir

酋长国 qiúzhǎngguó sheikhdom; emirate

俅

Qiú old name for 独龙族 Dúlóngzú

逑

qiú arch. spouse

屌

qiú dial. penis

赇

qiú formal bribe: 受～ accept (or take) bribes

球[1]

qiú ① sphere; globe: 球体 qiútǐ ② anything shaped like a ball: 雪球 xuěqiú ③ ball game; match: 看～去。Let's go to watch the game. ④ the globe; the earth: 地球 dìqiú

球[2] (毬)

qiú ball (used in games): 传～ pass a ball

球儿 qiúr ① a small ball ② marbles

球场 qiúchǎng a ground where ball games are played; (volleyball, basketball, tennis, badminton, etc.) court; (football, baseball, softball, etc.) field

球胆 qiúdǎn bladder (of a ball)

球队 qiúduì (ball game) team

球风 qiúfēng sportsmanship shown in ball games: 他在足球场上～一直很好。His behaviour on the football pitch has always been very sportsmanlike.

球罐 qiúguàn petroleum sphere

球果 qiúguǒ bot. cone

球茎 qiújīng bot. corm

球茎甘蓝 qiújīng gānlán bot. kohlrabi

球菌 qiújūn coccus

球类运动 qiúlèi yùndòng ball games

球路 qiúlù tactics in ball games: ～多变 play with a variety of strokes (as in tennis)

球门 qiúmén sports goal: ～柱 goalpost

球迷 qiúmí (ball game) fan: 足～ football fan

球面 qiúmiàn spherical surface

球面车床 qiúmiàn chēchuáng mech. spherical turning lathe

球面镜 qiúmiànjìng phys. spherical mirror

球面天文学 qiúmiàn tiānwénxué spherical astronomy

球磨床 qiúmóchuáng mech. ball grinder

球磨机 qiúmójī mech. ball mill

球墨铸铁 qiúmò zhùtiě metall. nodular cast iron

球拍 qiúpāi (also 球拍子 qiúpāizi) ① (tennis, badminton, etc.) racket ② (table-tennis) bat

球赛 qiúsài ball game; match

球坛 qiútán the ball-playing world; ball-playing circles; ball-players: ～盛会 a grand gathering of (table tennis, etc.) players / ～新手 a new player; a newcomer to the tournament

球体 qiútǐ spheroid

球团矿 qiútuánkuàng metall. pellet

球网 qiúwǎng net (for ball games)

球窝节 qiúwōjié mech. ball-and-socket joint

球鞋 qiúxié gym shoes; tennis shoes; sneakers

球心 qiúxīn centre of sphere

球星 qiúxīng a ball-game star; star

球形 qiúxíng spherical; globular; round

球艺 qiúyì skills in playing a ball game; ball game skills

球轴承 qiúzhóuchéng mech. ball bearing

遒
qiú *formal* powerful; forceful

遒劲 qiújìng *formal* powerful; vigorous: 笔力～ vigorous strokes in calligraphy / 苍老～的古松 a sturdy old pine tree

遒媚 qiúmèi *formal* (of calligraphy) vigorous and graceful

巯 (巰)
qiú (also 巯基 qiújī) *chem.* mercapto

裘
qiú ① *formal* fur coat: 狐裘 húqiú ② (Qiú) a surname

齅
qiù have a stuffy nose

qiǔ

糗
qiǔ *arch.* solid food (prepared for a journey)

qū

区 (區)
qū ① area; district; region: 山区 shānqū ② an administrative division: 天津市河东～ the Hedong District of Tianjin Municipality; Hedong District, Tianjin / 这个～高等院校很多。There are many institutions of higher learning in this district. ③ distinguish; classify; subdivide: 区分 qūfēn ——see also Ōu

区别 qūbié ① distinguish; differentiate; make a distinction between: 把两者～开来 differentiate one from the other / ～对待 deal with each case on its merits; deal with different things or people in different ways / ～好坏 distinguish between good and bad / 你能～普通话和北京话吗? Can you make the distinction between *putonghua* and Beijing dialect? ② difference: 这两个词在意义上没有～。There is no difference in meaning between the two words.

区分 qūfēn differentiate; distinguish: ～母牛和公牛 differentiate a cow from a bull / 你能～京剧和豫剧吗? Can you tell the difference between Beijing opera and Henan opera? / 严格～两类不同性质的矛盾 strictly distinguish between the two different types of contradictions / ～两个历史时代 mark off two historical epochs

区划 qūhuà division into districts: 行政～ administrative divisions

区间车 qūjiānchē a train or bus travelling only part of its normal route

区块 qūkuài block: 划分合作～ demarcate blocks for cooperation

区区 qūqū ① trivial; trifling: ～小事, 何足挂齿。Such a trifling thing is hardly worth mentioning. / ～之数, 不必计较。Such a trifling amount of money isn't worth bothering about. ② *humor.* my humble (or insignificant) self: 此人非他, 就是～。This person is none other than my humble self.

区时 qūshí *astron.* zone time

区域 qūyù region; area; district: ～间合作 interregional cooperation

区域会议 qūyù huìyì regional conference; local conference

区域性 qūyùxìng pertaining to a region: ～公约 regional convention or pact / ～同盟 regional alliance / ～问题 a matter of regional significance / ～战争 regional war

区长 qūzhǎng head of a district (as in a city)

曲¹
qū ① bent; curved: 弯腰～背 with one's back bent ② bend: ～肱而枕 bend one's arm and rest the head on it ③ bend (of a river, etc.): 河曲 héqū ④ wrong; unjustifiable: 是非曲直 shì-fēi qū-zhí ⑤ (Qū) a surname

曲² (麯、麴)
qū leaven; yeast
——see also qǔ

曲笔 qūbǐ ① a distortion of the facts (by an official historian) ② deliberate digression in writing

曲别针 qūbiézhēn paper clip

曲柄 qūbǐng *mech.* crank: ～摇杆机构 crank and rocker mechanism

曲柄钻 qūbǐngzuàn brace drill

曲尺 qūchǐ carpenter's square

曲拱 qūgǒng arch: ～石桥 an arched stone bridge

曲古霉素 qūgǔméisù trichomycin

曲棍球 qūgùnqiú ① field hockey; hockey ② hockey ball

曲解 qūjiě misinterpret (usu. deliberately); twist: 这话意思很明确, 不可能～。These remarks are so clear that there can be no room for misinterpretation. / 你～了他的意思。You've misrepresented his meaning.

曲尽其妙 qū jìn qí miào bring out (a quality, point, etc.) in a subtle and skilful way

曲颈甑 qūjǐngzèng *chem.* retort

曲径 qūjìng a winding path

曲径通幽 qūjìng tōng yōu a winding path leads to quiet seclusion: ～处, 禅房花木深。(常建) A winding path leads to a hidden spot, A meditation chamber deep in the flowering trees.

曲里拐弯 qūliguǎiwān *inf.* winding; zigzag: ～的胡同 a winding lane / 树林里的小路～儿的。The path zigzags through the woods.

曲流 qūliú *geol.* meander

曲率 qūlù *math.* curvature

曲率计 qūlùjì flexometer

曲霉 qūméi aspergillus

曲面 qūmiàn curved surface; camber: 内～ negative camber / 外～ positive camber

曲曲弯弯 qūqūwānwān winding; meandering: 山坳里尽是些～的羊肠小道。There are a lot of winding footpaths in the col. / 这河～地流过峡谷。The river meanders through the gorges.

曲鳝 qūshàn *inf.* earthworm

曲射 qūshè *mil.* curved fire: ～弹道 curved trajectory / ～炮 curved-fire gun

曲室 qūshì a secret chamber

曲说 qūshuō a biased statement

曲突徙薪 qūtū-xǐxīn bend the chimney and remove the fuel (to prevent a possible fire)—take precautions against a possible danger

曲线 qūxiàn ① *math.* curve ② sth., esp. a human body, or part of it having the shape of a curve: 她衣服非常合体, 显出了她身材优美的～。Her suit was so well tailored that it accentuated her graceful figure.

曲线板 qūxiànbǎn curve ruler

曲线球 qūxiànqiú *baseball softball* curve ball

曲线图 qūxiàntú diagram (of curves)

曲线运动 qūxiàn yùndòng *phys.* curvilinear motion

曲意逢迎 qūyì féngyíng go out of one's way to curry favour

曲折 qūzhé ① tortuous; winding: 沿着池塘有一条～的小路。There's a winding path following the edge of the pond. / 河道～。The river takes a winding course. / 前途是光明的, 道路是～的。The road is tortuous, but the prospects are bright. ② complicated: 这个剧本情节

很～。The play has a very complicated plot. ③ complications: 这件事情里面还有不少～。There are many complications in this matter.

曲直 qū-zhí　right and wrong: ～不分 not distinguish between right and wrong

曲衷 qūzhōng　*formal* heartfelt emotion; inner feelings

曲轴 qūzhóu　*mech.* crankshaft; bent axle: ～磨床 crankshaft grinding machine／～箱 crankcase

岖（嶇） qū　see 崎岖 qíqū

诎 qū　① *formal* shorten ② same as 屈 qū

驱（驅、敺） qū　① drive (a horse, car, etc.): 驱车 qūchē ② expel; disperse: ～云防雹 disperse clouds in order to prevent a hailstorm ③ run quickly: 驰驱 chíqū

驱策 qūcè　① drive; whip on ② order about: 任人～ allow oneself to be ordered about

驱车 qūchē　drive a vehicle: ～前往 drive (in a vehicle) to a place

驱虫药 qūchóngyào　anthelmintic; vermifuge

驱除 qūchú　drive out; get rid of; repel: ～蚊蝇 repel mosquitoes and flies

驱动 qūdòng　*mech.* drive: ～齿轮 driving gear

驱赶 qūgǎn　① drive (a cart, etc.) ② drive away; brush away: ～苍蝇 brush away flies; whisk flies off／～麻雀 shoo away sparrows

驱寒 qūhán　dispel cold; warm oneself up: 喝点酒驱驱寒 have a drink to warm oneself up

驱蛔灵 qūhuílíng　*pharm.* piperazine citrate

驱迫 qūpò　order about; force; compel

驱遣 qūqiǎn　① *formal* drive away; banish; expel ② order about; drive ③ dispel; get rid of: ～别情 dispel the sad feeling of parting

驱散 qūsàn　disperse; dispel; break up: ～人群 disperse a crowd／阳光～了薄雾。The sun dispelled the mist.

驱使 qūshǐ　① order about: 供～ be ordered about; be at sb.'s beck and call／奴隶主把奴隶当作牛马任意～。The slave owners drove their slaves as they drove their cattle. ② prompt; urge; spur on: 为好奇心所～ be prompted by curiosity

驱邪 qūxié　exorcise (*or* drive out) evil spirits

驱逐 qūzhú　drive out; expel; banish: ～侵略者 drive out the aggressors／～出境 deport; expel

驱逐机 qūzhújī　old name for 歼击机 jiānjījī

驱逐舰 qūzhújiàn　destroyer

屈 qū　① bend; bow; crook: ～臂 crook one's arm ② subdue; submit: 不屈 bùqū ③ wrong; injustice: 叫屈 jiàoqū ④ in the wrong: 理屈 lǐqū ⑤ (Qū) a surname

屈才 qūcái　do work unworthy of one's talents

屈从 qūcóng　submit; yield: ～于外来压力 yield to pressure from outside

屈打成招 qū dǎ chéng zhāo　confess to false charges under torture: 他的口供是～, 不足为证。His confession was forced out of him and can't be used as evidence.

屈服 qūfú　(also 屈伏 qūfú) subdue; submit; yield; knuckle under: ～于外界的压力 yield to pressure from outside／严刑拷打并没使她～。Torture failed to make her submit.

屈光度 qūguāngdù　dioptre

屈驾 qūjià　*pol.* condescend (*or* be kind enough) to make the journey: 明日请～来舍一叙。Would you be kind enough to visit me tomorrow?

屈节 qūjié　forfeit one's honour: ～事仇 forfeit one's honour in serving the enemy

屈就 qūjiù　*pol.* condescend to take a post offered: 要是您肯～, 那是太好了。It'd be very kind of you to con-

descend to take this post.

屈居 qūjū　be forced to accept a place or position: 他以四秒之差～第二。He was forced into second place by only four seconds.

屈理 qūlǐ　unreasonable; unfair; unjust: 不要做～的事。Don't do anything unreasonable.

屈量 qūliàng　*inf.* have not done justice to one's drinking capacity; have not drunk one's fill

屈挠 qūnáo　*formal* subdue; submit; yield; knuckle under

屈曲 qūqū　bend (*or* crook) one's arm, etc.

屈辱 qūrǔ　humiliation; mortification

屈氏体 qūshìtǐ　*metall.* troostite

屈死 qūsǐ　be wronged and driven to death; be persecuted to death

屈枉 qūwǎng　treat unjustly; wrong

屈膝 qūxī　go down on one's knees; bend one's knees

屈膝投降 qūxī tóuxiáng　go down on one's knees in surrender; knuckle under

屈心 qūxīn　*inf.* have a guilty conscience: 你做出这样的事～不～哪? Don't you feel guilty about doing this kind of thing? *or* Has your action never given you a twinge of conscience? / 这种～的事我不干。I wouldn't do a mean thing like that.

屈折语 qūzhéyǔ　*linguis.* inflexional language

屈肢葬 qūzhīzàng　*archaeol.* flexed burial

屈指 qūzhǐ　count on one's fingers: ～已经八年啦。Come to think of it, eight years have already passed.

屈指可数 qūzhǐ kě shǔ　can be counted on one's fingers —very few

屈尊 qūzūn　condescend

祛 qū　dispel; remove; drive away: 祛暑 qūshǔ

祛除 qūchú　dispel; get rid of; drive out: ～疑虑 dispel one's misgivings／～邪魔 drive out (*or* exorcize) evil spirits

祛风 qūfēng　*Chin. med.* dispel the wind; relieve rheumatic pains, colds, etc.

祛风湿药 qūfēngshīyào　medicine for rheumatism

祛暑 qūshǔ　drive away summer heat

祛痰 qūtán　make expectoration easy: ～剂 expectorant

祛疑 qūyí　*formal* remove suspicion or doubts

祛瘀活血 qūyū huóxuè　*Chin. med.* remove blood stasis and promote blood circulation

胠 qū　*formal* ① sides (from waist to arm pits) ② pry open: 胠箧 qūqiè

胠箧 qūqiè　pry open a suitcase—steal; pilfer

蛆 qū　maggot

蛆虫 qūchóng　① maggot ② a shameless (*or* base) person

焌 qū　*inf.* ① extinguish a burning object by putting it in water ② sauté vegetable

焌油 qūyóu　*dial.* heat oil and then pour it on the cooked food

䓛 qū　*chem.* chrysene

躯（軀） qū　the human body: 身躯 shēnqū

躯干 qūgàn　*physiol.* trunk; torso

躯壳 qūqiào　the body (as opposed to the soul); outer form

躯体 qūtǐ　body; stature

趋（趨） qū　① hasten; hurry along: ～前 hasten forward／疾～而过 hurry past ② tend towards; tend to become: 局势～于稳定。The situation is tend-

ing towards stability. /他们的意见～于一致。 They are reaching unanimity. ③ (of a goose or snake) pop the head and bite people

趋避 qūbì　*formal*　avoid; dodge: ～路旁 dodge to one side of the road; get out of the way

趋奉 qūfèng　(also 趋承 qūchéng) toady to; fawn on

趋附 qūfù　ingratiate oneself with; curry favour with: ～权贵 curry favour with bigwigs

趋光性 qūguāngxìng　*biol.*　phototaxis

趋候 qūhòu　(used in letters) wait on; pay one's respects to

趋利 qūlì　go after profit or gain

趋热性 qūrèxìng　*biol.*　thermotaxis

趋时 qūshí　*formal*　follow the fashion

趋势 qūshì　trend; tendency: 世界历史的总～任何人也改变不了。 No one can change the general trend of world history. /他的病有进一步恶化的～。 His condition is tending to deteriorate. /物价有上涨的～。 There is an upward trend in prices.

趋向 qūxiàng　① tend to; incline to: 财政情况日益～好转。 The financial situation is taking a favourable turn. /这个工厂的生产管理制度逐步～完善。 This factory is gradually perfecting its system of production management. ② trend; tendency; direction: 总～ general trend

趋向动词 qūxiàng dòngcí　*gram.*　directional verb

趋性 qūxìng　*biol.*　taxis

趋炎附势 qūyán-fùshì　(also 趋炎附热 qūyán-fùrè) curry favour with the powerful; play up to those in power

趋药性 qūyàoxìng　*biol.*　chemotaxis

趋之若鹜 qū zhī ruò wù　go after sth. like a flock of ducks; scramble for sth.

蛐　　qū　see below

蛐蛐儿 qūqur　*dial.*　cricket (an insect)

蛐蟮 qū·shàn　same as 曲鳝 qū·shàn

觑（覷、覰）　　qū　*inf.*　narrow (one's eyes); squint: 他～着眼睛仔细地看一幅画。 He was studying a painting with narrowed eyes. /这漂亮小伙子走过她身边，她偷偷地～了他一眼。 She gave a squint to the handsome young man as he passed by. ——see also qù

觑觑眼 qūqūyǎn　*dial.*　myopia; nearsightedness; shortsightedness

骏　　qū　black; dark: 黑骏骏 hēiqūqū

骏黑 qūhēi　pitch-black; pitch-dark: 两手净是墨，～的。 Both hands are black with ink. /山洞里～，什么也看不见。 The cave is pitch-dark. You can't see anything.

嚁　　qū　*onom.*　chirping of a cricket

qú

劬　　qú　*formal*　① fatigued ② diligent; hardworking: 勤劬 qínqú

劬劳 qúláo　*formal*　fatigued; overworked

鸲　　qú　see below

鸲鹆 qúyù　*zool.*　myna

渠[1]　　qú　① canal; ditch; channel: 水渠 shuǐqú ② *formal*　big; great: 渠魁 qúkuí

渠[2]（佢）　　qú　*dial.*　he or she

渠道 qúdào　① irrigation ditch ② medium of communication; channel: 通过外交～ through diplomatic

channels /利用多种资金～ make use of funds from various channels /商品流通～不畅。 The commodity circulation is poor.

渠灌 qúguàn　canal irrigation

渠魁 qúkuí　*old*　leader, esp. a rebel leader

渠们 qúmen　*dial.*　they or them

渠首工程 qúshǒu gōngchéng　*water conservancy* headwork

渠帅 qúshuài　same as 渠魁 qúkuí

蕖　　qú　see 芙蕖 fúqú

磲　　qú　see 砗磲 chēqú

璩　　qú　*formal*　jade earrings

瞿　　Qú　a surname

瞿麦 qúmài　*bot.*　fringed pink

朐　　qú　see below

朐鵙 qújīng　*zool.*　shrew

蘧　　qú　① see below ② (Qú) a surname

蘧然 qúrán　*formal*　pleasantly surprised; in happy astonishment

氍（毺）　　qú　see below

氍毹 qúshū　① wool carpet ② *old*　stage; arena

癯　　qú　*formal*　thin; lean: 清癯 qīngqú

衢　　qú　*formal*　thoroughfare: 通衢 tōngqú

蠼　　qú　see below

蠼螋 qúsōu　*zool.*　earwig

qǔ

曲　　qǔ　① qu, a type of verse for singing, which emerged in the Southern Song and Jin Dynasties and became popular in the Yuan Dynasty ② song; tune; melody: 高歌一～ lustily sing a song ③ music (of a song): 作曲 zuòqǔ ——see also qū

曲调 qǔdiào　tune (of a song); melody

曲高和寡 qǔgāo-hèguǎ　highbrow songs find few singers; too highbrow to be popular

曲剧 qǔjù　opera derived from ballad singing

曲牌 qǔpái　the names of the tunes to which *qu* （曲） are composed ——see also 曲 qǔ①

曲谱 qǔpǔ　① music score of Chinese operas ② a collection of tunes of *qu* （曲） ——see also 曲 qǔ①

曲式 qǔshì　*mus.*　musical form

曲艺 qǔyì　quyi, folk art forms including ballad singing, story telling, comic dialogues, clapper talks, cross talks, etc.

曲终奏雅 qǔ zhōng zòu yǎ　a grand finale

曲子 qǔzi　song; tune; melody

苣　　qǔ　see below ——see also jù

苣荬菜 qǔmaicài　endive

取　　qǔ　① take; get; fetch: 请把灯泡～下来。 Please take the bulb off. /她回去～行李去了。 She's gone back to fetch her luggage. /我来～自行车。 I came to get (or collect) my bike. /上银行～钱 go and draw some money from a bank ② aim at; seek: 取乐 qǔlè ③ adopt; assume; choose: ～慎重态度 adopt a cautious attitude /

~个吉利 for good luck

取保 qǔbǎo *leg.* get sb. to go bail for one: ~释放 be released on bail; be bailed out / 对被告人~候审 allow a defendant to obtain a guarantor and await trial out of custody

取材 qǔcái draw materials: 就地~ make use of (*or* draw on) local materials / 这本小说~于炼钢工人的生活。 This novel has drawn its material from the life of steel workers.

取长补短 qǔcháng-bǔduǎn learn from others' strong points to offset one's own weaknesses: 互相学习，~ learn from each other to make up deficiencies / 必须互相~，才能有进步。 To make any progress we must overcome our own weak points by learning from each other's strong points.

取偿 qǔcháng get reimbursement or compensation

取代 qǔdài replace; substitute for; supersede; supplant: 这家航空公司目前正在用波音747~DC 10。 The airline is currently replacing its DC10s with Boeing747s.

取代衍生物 qǔdàiyǎnshēngwù *chem.* substitution derivate

取道 qǔdào by way of; via: 代表团将~巴黎回国。 The delegation will come back to China by way of Paris.

取得 qǔdé gain; acquire; obtain: ~胜利 gain (*or* win) a victory / 通过实践~经验 gain experience through practice / ~有关方面同意 obtain the consent of those concerned / ~完全一致的意见 reach complete identity of views; reach a complete agreement of views / ~群众支持 enlist popular support / ~圆满成功 be crowned with success; achieve complete success / ~相当大的进展 make considerable headway

取灯儿 qǔdēngr *dial.* match

取缔 qǔdì outlaw; ban; suppress: ~投机倒把 ban speculation and profiteering / ~反动会道门 ban reactionary secret societies / 走私必须~。 Smuggling must be suppressed.

取而代之 qǔ ér dài zhī replace sb.; supersede sb.

取法 qǔfǎ take as one's model; follow the example of

取法乎上，仅得乎中 qǔ fǎ hū shàng, jǐn dé hū zhōng aim high or you may fall below the average

取给 qǔjǐ (usu. followed by 于) draw (supplies, etc.): 所需资金主要~于企业内部的积累。 The funds needed will mainly be drawn from accumulation within the enterprise.

取经 qǔjīng ① go on a pilgrimage for Buddhist scriptures: 《西游记》讲唐僧往西天~的故事。 The *Journey to the West* tells how the Tang monk went to the Western Heaven to acquire scriptures. ② learn from sb. else's experience: 到兄弟厂去~ go to other factories (of the same kind) to learn from their experience

取精用弘 qǔjīng-yònghóng (also 取精用宏 qǔjīng-yònghóng) select the finest from a vast quantity

取景 qǔjǐng find a view (to photograph, paint, etc.)

取景器 qǔjǐngqì viewfinder (on a camera)

取决 qǔjué (usu. followed by 于) be decided by; depend on; hinge on: 消费的增长~于生产的增长。 The increase in consumption depends on the increase in production. / 我去不去庐山~于旅费得花多少。 Whether I go to Lushan Mountain or not hinges on the cost of fare.

取快一时 qǔ kuài yīshí derive momentary pleasure

取乐 qǔlè seek pleasure; find amusement; amuse oneself; make merry: 饮酒~ drink and make merry

取力器 qǔlìqì power takeoff (of a car)

取媚 qǔmèi try to ingratiate oneself with; make up to

取名 qǔmíng give a name to or be named: 给孩子取个名儿 choose a name for a child; give a name to a child / 此处可~玫瑰园。 This place may be called Rose Garden.

取闹 qǔnào ① kick up a row; make trouble ② amuse oneself at sb.'s expense; make fun of

取暖 qǔnuǎn warm oneself (by a fire, etc.): 烤火~ warm oneself (*or* keep warm) by the fire

取譬 qǔpì cite as an example; give an analogy

取平 qǔpíng make even; even up: 墙上挂的两张画应该~。 The two pictures on the wall must be aligned.

取齐 qǔqí ① make even; even up: 先把两张纸~了再裁。 Even up the edges of the two sheets of paper before you cut them. / 去年我们队的产量不如他们，今年已经~了。 Last year our team's output was less than theirs, but this year we've caught up with them. ② assemble; meet each other: 下午三点我们在门口~。 We'll assemble at the gate at 3 o'clock in the afternoon.

取枪 qǔqiāng *mil.* take arms: ~! (word of command) Take arms!

取巧 qǔqiǎo resort to trickery to serve oneself or avoid a difficulty

取容 qǔróng try to please; ingratiate oneself with sb.

取舍 qǔ-shě accept or reject; make one's choice: 对技术资料进行分析后决定~ analyse all the technical data first and then decide what to use

取胜 qǔshèng win victory; score a success: 以多~ win victory through numerical superiority

取水口 qǔshuǐkǒu *water conservancy* water intake

取消 qǔxiāo (also 取销 qǔxiāo) cancel; call off; abolish: ~一次会议 cancel (*or* call off) a meeting / ~会员资格 deprive sb. of his membership / ~决定 rescind a decision / ~禁令 lift a ban / 被~比赛资格 be disqualified from the contest / 这个月奖金~了。 There will be no bonuses this month.

取消主义 qǔxiāozhǔyì liquidationism

取笑 qǔxiào ridicule; make fun of; poke fun at: 别~人家生理上的缺陷。 Don't make fun of someone's physical handicap. / 她的嘴真损，老~人。 She has a really sharp tongue—always ridiculing people.

取信 qǔxìn win the confidence (*or* trust) of the others

取信于民 qǔxìn yú mín win the people's confidence (*or* trust)

取样 qǔyàng take a sample: ~检查 take a sample to inspect

取悦 qǔyuè try to please; ingratiate oneself with sb.: ~于人 ingratiate oneself with sb.

取证 qǔzhèng collect evidence

取之不尽，用之不竭 qǔ zhī bù jìn, yòng zhī bù jié inexhaustible

取之于民，用之于民 qǔ zhī yú mín, yòng zhī yú mín what is taken from the people is used for the people

娶 qǔ marry (a woman): ~媳妇儿 take a wife / 三十不~ (of a man) be unmarried at thirty

娶妻 qǔqī take a wife

娶亲 qǔqīn (of a man) get married

齲 qǔ see below

齲齿 qǔchǐ ① dental caries ② decayed tooth

qù

去[1] qù ① go; go to (a place): 我~。 I'll go. / 他已经~了。 He has already gone. / 他~了三天，还没回来。 He's been away for three days, and hasn't come back yet. / 昨天已经~了三个人。 Three people went there yesterday. / 我~了好几趟，都没碰到他。 I went there several times, but never saw him. / 我要~南京了。 I'm going to Nanjing. / 我想~南京一趟。 I think I'll take a

trip to Nanjing. / 我要～车站接人。 I'm going to the staion to meet someone. ② cause to go; send there: 我给他～过两封信。 I sent him two letters. / 给她～个电话。 Give her a call. / 已经～了一个电报。 A telegram has been sent (to him). / 我们只～了个代表。 We only sent a representative. ③ remove; get rid of: ～头屑 get rid of dandruff / 汽油能～油迹。 Gas is good for taking out oil stains. / ～了皮再吃。 Peel it before you eat it. / 裙子太长了，～一寸吧。 The skirt is too long—shorten it by a *cun*. / 这句话～几个字就简洁了。 Take out one or two words and the sentence will be more concise. ④ (used before and / or after a verb) go in order to; be going to (do sth. there): 咱们～看电影。 or 咱们看电影～。 or 咱们～看电影～。 Let's go to see a movie. / 你～打水，我来生炉子。 You get some water and I'll light the stove. / 你们～研究研究，看该怎么办。 Go and make a study of it, and see what's the best thing to do. / 这件事我～办吧 Let me (go and) arrange this. / 你别管，让他自己～想办法。 Don't bother, let him figure it out for himself. ⑤ (used between two verbal expressions, and / or after the second expression) in order to (do sth. there): 她上街～买东西了。 or 她上街买东西～了。 or 她上街～买东西～了。 She went to the market to buy things. / 他回家吃饭～了。 He went home to eat. / 他提了一桶水～浇花。 He took a bucket of water to water the flowers. / 用辩证唯物主义的观点～观察事物 look at things from a dialectical-materialist point of view ⑥ *formal* be apart from in space or time: 两地相～四十里。 The two places are 40 *li* apart. / ～今五十年 50 years ago ⑦ depart from; leave: 去国 qùguó ⑧ just gone or elapsed: ～秋 last autumn / ～冬今春 last winter and this spring ⑨ short for 去声 qùshēng ⑩ *dial.* (used with 了 as an intensive complement to certain adjectives with 了) very; extremely: 他到过的地方多了～了。 He's been to a great many places. / 他家远了～了。 His home is far far away. / 那片林子可大了～了。 That's a really huge forest.

去² qù play (a part or character): 他在京剧《闹天宫》里～猴王。 He played the Monkey King in the Beijing opera *Trouble in Heaven*.

去 ·qù ① (used after verbs of motion, indicating motion away from the speaker) thither; there; away: 上楼～ go upstairs / 回家～ go home / 谁把我的笔拿～了？ Who's taken my pen away? / 信寄～了没有？ Have you sent the letter off yet? / 他从我这儿借了几本书～。 He borrowed some books from me (and took them away). ② (used after certain verbs to express the idea of detachment, separation, or loss): 把多余的枝叶剪～。 Cut off the unnecessary twigs and branches. / 这些琐碎事情占～了他不少时间。 Such small things take up a lot of his time. / 那一年，他父母都相继死～。 That year both his parents died, one after the other.

去病 qùbìng prevent or cure a disease

去处 qùchù ①place to go; whereabouts: 有谁知道他的～？ Who knows his whereabouts? ②place; site: 这是一个风景优美的～。 This is a beautiful place. / 北戴河是个避暑的好～。 Beidaihe is a nice summer resort.

去粗取精 qùcū-qǔjīng discard the dross and select the essential

去垢剂 qùgòujì detergent

去官 qùguān no longer hold an official post; leave an official post

去国 qùguó leave one's country or the capital of one's country

去火 qùhuǒ *Chin. med.* reduce internal heat; relieve inflammation or fever: 消痰～ reduce phlegm and internal heat / 你喝些绿豆汤，去去火。 You'd better have

some mung bean soup so as to reduce internal heat.

去就 qùjiù hold or not hold the post of; resign or remain in office

去留 qùliú go or remain (or stay): ～由你。 You can go or stay, as you like.

去路 qùlù the way along which one is going; outlet: 挡住敌人的～ block the enemy's way / 给洪水找到～ find an outlet for the flood

去敏灵 qùmǐnlíng *pharm.* tripelennamine

去年 qùnián last year: ～十二月 last December / ～此时 this time last year

去声 qùshēng *phonet.* ①falling tone (the third of the four tones in classical Chinese pronunciation) ②falling tone (the fourth of the four tones in modern standard Chinese pronunciation)

去世 qùshì (of grown-up people) die; pass away: 他爷爷是前年～的。 His grandfather died the year before last. / 听说你父亲上个月～了，我很难过。 I'm sorry to hear that your father passed away last month.

去势 qùshì *animal husbandry* castrate; emasculate

去暑 qùshǔ drive away summer heat

去岁 qùsuì last year

去痛定 qùtòngdìng *pharm.* piminodine esylate

去伪存真 qùwěi-cúnzhēn get rid of the false and retain the true

去污粉 qùwūfěn household cleanser; cleanser

去向 qùxiàng the direction in which sb. or sth. has gone: 不知～ be nowhere to be found / 这个人～不明。 The whereabouts of this man is unknown.

去雄 qùxióng *bot.* emasculate; castrate

去杂去劣 qùzá qùliè *agric.* roguing

去职 qùzhí no longer hold the post

阒 qù *formal* quiet; still: ～无一人。 All was quiet and not a soul was to be seen.

阒然 qùrán *formal* quiet; still: ～无声 very quiet; absolutely still / 四野～。 All was quiet on the vast expanse of open ground.

趣 qù ①interest; delight: 兴趣 xìngqù ②interesting: 有趣 yǒuqù ③bent; inclination: 志趣 zhìqù

趣话 qùhuà funny remarks; joke

趣剧 qùjù farce

趣事 qùshì an interesting episode; an amusing incident

趣味 qùwèi ① interest; delight: ～无穷 be of infinite interest; afford the greatest delight; be fascinating / 这个职业很有～。 It's a very interesting occupation. ② taste; liking; preference: ～高雅 refined taste; good taste

趣闻 qùwén interesting hearsay or news

觑（覷、覰） qù *formal* look; gaze: 面面相觑 miànmiàn xiāng qù ——see also qū

觑视 qùshì *formal* look; gaze

quān

悛 quān *formal* repent; make amends: 怙恶不悛 hù è bù quān

圈 quān ① circle; ring: 画个～儿 draw a circle / 绕跑道跑两～ run around the track twice / 这是他一千五百米赛跑的最后一～。 This is his last lap in the 1,500-metre race. / 我到外面转了～。 I've been out for a walk. / 孩子们围成一～。 The children gathered around in a circle. / 我们的飞机降落前在机场上空绕～儿。 Our plane circled the airport before landing. ②cir-

cle; group: 他不是～里人。He doesn't belong to the inner circle. *or* He's not on the inside. ③ enclose; encircle: 用篱笆把菜园～起来 enclose the vegetable garden with a fence ④mark with a circle: 把那个错字～了。Mark the wrong word with a circle. ——see also juàn; juàn

圈闭 quānbì　*petroleum* trap: 地层～ stratigraphic trap / 背斜～ anticlinal trap

圈点 quāndiǎn　①punctuate (with periods or small circles) ②mark words and phrases for special attention with dots or small circles

圈定 quāndìng　draw a circle around sth. to show approval or selection

圈梁 quānliáng　*archit.* girth

圈拢 quānlong　*dial.* ①unite; rally ②draw sb. over to one's side; rope in

圈套 quāntào　snare; trap: 设下～ set a trap for sb. / 中～ play into sb.'s hands / 他的诺言是个～,我可上不了这个当。His promises are a trap and I won't be taken in. / 她缺乏生活经验,落入了这个坏人的～。She lacked experience in life, so she fell into the snares of this scoundrel.

圈椅 quānyǐ　round-backed armchair

圈阅 quānyuè　draw a circle around one's name on a document submitted for approval to show that one has read it; tick off one's name listed on a circular, notice, etc. after reading it

圈占 quānzhàn　enclose and occupy (land); seize possession of (land)

圈子 quānzi　circle; ring: 大家围成一个～站着。They stood in a circle. / 他的生活～很小。He moves in a very small circle. ——see also 兜圈子 dōu quānzi; 绕圈子 rào quānzi

quán

权(權)

quán　① *formal* the sliding weight of a steelyard② *formal* weigh: ～其轻重 weigh the relative importance (of two or more things) ③power; authority: 企业有～自行安排某些技术改造项目。The enterprises are entitled to undertake certain projects for technological transformation. ④ right: 你有～发言。You have the right to speak. / 我们无～干涉她的婚姻自由。We don't have the right to interfere with her freedom of choice in marriage. ⑤an advantageous position: 制空权 zhìkōngquán ⑥ expediency: 权诈 quánzhà ⑦ *adv.* tentatively; for the time being: ～充 act temporarily as; serve as a stopgap for ⑧ (Quán) a surname

权变 quánbiàn　adaptability (*or* flexibility) in tactics; acting according to circumstances; tact

权便 quánbiàn　expedient

权标 quánbiāo　fasces

权柄 quánbǐng　power; authority: 掌握～ be in power; be in the saddle

权臣 quánchén　a powerful minister

权贵 quánguì　influential officials; bigwigs

权衡 quánhéng　weigh; balance: ～利弊 weigh the advantages and disadvantages; weigh the pros and cons

权衡轻重 quánhéng qīngzhòng　weigh the relative importance (of two or more things)

权奸 quánjiān　a powerful and treacherous court official

权力 quánlì　①power; authority: 一切～属于人民。All power belongs to the people. / 国家～机关 organs of state power / ～下放 transfer (*or* delegate) power to lower levels ② scope of power; extent of authority;

jurisdiction: 行使会议主席的～ exercise the functions of chairman of a conference; invoke the authority of chairman of a conference / 这是他～范围以内的事。This matter comes within his jurisdiction.

权利 quánlì　right: 劳动的～ the right to work / 受教育的～ the right to education

权略 quánlüè　(political) tactics; trickery

权门 quánmén　families of influential officials: 依附～ attach oneself to families of influential officials

权谋 quánmóu　(political) tactics; trickery

权能 quánnéng　powers and functions

权且 quánqiě　*adv.* tentatively; for the time being: ～如此办理。This is to be carried out as an interim measure. / 屋子太小,今晚～住一宿,明天再想办法。Small as this room is, let's just make do with it for the night and look for another place tomorrow.

权时 quánshí　temporary; transient

权势 quánshì　power and influence

权术 quánshù　*derog.* political trickery; shifts in politics: 玩弄～ play politics

权数 quánshù　*formal* flexible strategy

权威 quánwēi　① authority; authoritativeness: ～著作 an authoritative book / ～的植物学家 an authority on botany ②a person of authority; authority: 学术～ an academic authority / 中国近代史的～ an authority on modern Chinese history / 这部著作是物理学界的～。This is an authoritative book in the field of physics. / 他的评论听起来很有～性。His comments sound very authoritative.

权威人士 quánwēi rénshì　an authoritative person; authoritative sources

权位 quánwèi　power and position

权限 quánxiàn　limits of authority; jurisdiction; competence: 在法律规定的～内 within the limits of one's authority as prescribed by law / 确定委员会的 ～ define the competence (*or* terms of reference) of the committee / 属于自治区～以内的事务 matters that come within the jurisdiction of the autonomous region

权宜 quányí　expedient

权宜之计 quányí zhī jì　an expedient measure; makeshift (device); stopgap

权益 quányì　rights and interests: 经济～ economic rights and interests

权舆 quányú　*formal* ① sprout; germinate; shoot; bud ②beginning; outset

权欲 quányù　a lust for power

权欲熏心 quányù xūn xīn　be overcome with a lust for power

权责 quánzé　power and responsibility; rights and duties

权诈 quánzhà　trickery; craftiness

权杖 quánzhàng　staff of authority (as carried by political or religious leaders)

全

quán　① complete: 这家铺子货物的品种很～。This store has a wide assortment of goods. / 这套邮票～不～?一不～,差一张。Is this set of stamps complete?—No, it's one piece short. / 资料收集得比较～。The data collected is quite comprehensive. ② make complete; keep intact: 两全其美 liǎng quán qí měi ③ whole; entire; full; total: ～世界 the whole world / ～人类 all mankind / ～中国 the whole of China; all over China / ～(交响)曲共分四个乐章。The symphony is in 4 movements. ④ *adv.* entirely; completely: ～错了 completely wrong; all wrong / 这事～怪我。It's entirely (*or* all) my fault. / 我们一家～去了。My whole family went. / 他讲的话我～记下来了。I took down all he said. / 我什么～不要。I don't want anything. / 你把唱片～借给谁了?Who did you lend all the records to? /

不论古典音乐还是现代音乐, 我～爱听。I like listening to every kind of music, classic or modern. / 他们～不是南方人。None of them are Southerners. / 他们不～是南方人。Not all of them are Southerners. / 他～不顾妻子的反对, 每天要抽五包烟的反对, 每天要抽五包烟 He completely ignored his wife's objections and consumed 5 packs of cigarettes daily. ⑤ (Quán) a surname

全般 quánbān　whole; entire: ～工作 the entire work

全豹 quánbào　the whole picture; the overall situation: 未窥～ fail to see the whole picture; fail to grasp the overall situation ——see also 管中窥豹 guǎnzhōng kuī bào

全本 quánběn　① the staging of a complete traditional opera ② same as 足本 zúběn

全部 quánbù　whole; complete; total; all: ～情况就这样。That's all there is to it. / ～开支 total expenditure / 粮食～自给 be completely self-supporting in food grain / 为革命贡献自己的～力量 contribute one's all to the revolution / 要求赔偿～损失 demand full compensation for the loss incurred / ～歼灭入侵之敌 wipe out the invading enemy to the last man / 他们～是学生。All of them are students.

全才 quáncái　a versatile person; all-rounder: 文武～ be versed in both civil and military affairs / 他是个体育～, 网球, 篮球, 游泳, 样样来得。He's a good all-rounder who likes tennis, basketball, and swimming.

全场 quánchǎng　① the whole audience; all those present: ～爆发出一片欢呼声。The audience broke out into cheers. ② sports full-court; all-court: ～紧逼 all-court press; full-court press

全称 quánchēng　full name (of a thing)

全程 quánchéng　whole journey; whole course: 自行车比赛～一百二十公里。The whole course of the bicycle race is 120 kilometres.

全等 quánděng　math. congruent: ～形 congruent figures

全动机翼 quándòng jīyì　all-moving wing (of an aircraft)

全都 quándōu　adv. all; without exception: 村里男女老少～出来欢迎贵宾。The whole village, men and women, old and young, turned out to welcome the distinguished visitors. / 去年栽的树～活了。All the trees planted last year have survived.

全反射 quánfǎnshè　phys. total reflection

全份 quánfèn　complete set: ～表册 a complete set of lists and forms

全副 quánfù　complete; full: ～武装 fully armed; in full battle array

全国 quánguó　the whole nation (or country); nationwide; countrywide; throughout the country: ～人民 the people of the whole country; the people throughout the country; the whole nation / ～上下 the whole nation from the leadership to the masses / ～运动会 the national games / ～冠军 the national champion / 他们到～各地旅行。They travelled nationwide (or all over the country).

全国农业发展纲要 Quánguó Nóngyè Fāzhǎn Gāngyào The National Programme for Agricultural Development (1956-1967)

全国人民代表大会 Quánguó Rénmín Dàibiǎo Dàhuì the National People's Congress (NPC)

全国性 quánguóxìng　nationwide; countrywide; national: ～报纸 a national newspaper; a newspaper with a nationwide circulation

全国一盘棋 quánguó yīpánqí　coordinate all the activities of the nation like moves in a game of chess; take the whole country into account

全乎 quánhu　inf. complete: 这商店虽小, 货物倒是很～。Small as it is, the store has a wide assortment of goods.

全会 quánhuì　plenary meeting; plenary session; plenum: 十一届三中～ the Third Plenary Session of the Eleventh Central Committee (of the Chinese Communist Party)

全集 quánjí　complete works; collected works: 《鲁迅～》The Complete Works of Lu Xun / 《列宁～》The Collected Works of Lenin

全家福 quánjiāfú　dial. ① a photograph of the whole family ② hotchpotch (as a dish)

全歼 quánjiān　annihilate; wipe out: ～残敌 wipe out the remnants of the enemy forces to the last man

全景 quánjǐng　panorama; a full view; a whole scene: 西湖～ a full view of the West Lake

全景宽银幕电影 quánjǐng kuānyínmù diànyǐng cinepanoramic

全景摄影机 quánjǐng shèyǐngjī　panoramic camera

全局 quánjú　the overall situation; the situation as a whole: 影响～ affect the overall situation / 胸有～ with the situation as a whole in mind / 树立～观点 adopt an overall point of view / ～利益 interests of the whole; general interests / ～性问题 a matter of overall importance

全军 quánjūn　① the whole (or entire) army: ～指战员 the officers and men of the whole army / ～运动会 army-wide sports meet ② formal preserve military strength

全军覆没 quánjūn fùmò　the whole army overwhelmed —a complete failure: 这一仗第一师～。The First Division was practically wiped out in the battle.

全开 quánkāi　print. a standard-sized sheet: 一张～的宣传画 a full-size poster (or billboard)

全劳动力 quánláodònglì (also 全劳力 quánláolì) an able-bodied farm worker

全力 quánlì　with all one's strength; all-out; sparing no effort: ～支持 support with all one's strength; spare no effort to support; give all-out support

全力爬升 quánlì páshēng　full climb (of an aircraft)

全力以赴 quánlì yǐ fù　go all out; spare no effort

全麻 quánmá　short for 全身麻醉 quánshēn mázuì

全貌 quánmào　a complete picture; a full view: 从这里可以看到大桥的～。You can get a view of the whole bridge from here. / 弄清问题的～ try to get a complete picture of the problem

全面 quánmiàn　overall; comprehensive; all-round: ～规划 overall planning / ～总结 a comprehensive summing-up / ～经验 extensive experience / ～崩溃 a total collapse; débâcle / ～进攻 an all-out attack / ～战争 a full-scale war / ～落实党的各项政策 implement the Party's policies in an all-round way / ～地看问题 look at problems all-sidedly / ～禁止和彻底销毁核武器 complete prohibition and thorough destruction of nuclear weapons / 学生要德智体～发展。Students are expected to develop in an all-round way—morally, intellectually and physically. / ～改革 all-round reform / 有关这次会议他说得非常～。His account of the meeting was most comprehensive. / 这种看法不～。This is not an all-sided view.

全苗 quánmiáo　agric. a full stand: 保证棉花～ ensure a full stand of cotton shoots

全民 quánmín　the whole (or entire) people; all the people: ～总动员 general mobilization of the nation

全民皆兵 quánmín jiē bīng　an entire nation in arms; every citizen a soldier

全民所有制 quánmín suǒyǒuzhì　ownership by the whole people: ～企业 enterprises owned by the whole people

全名 quánmíng　① full name (of a person, i.e. family name plus given name) ② same as 全称 quánchēng

全能 quánnéng　sports all-round: ～运动员 an all-round athlete; an all-rounder / ～冠军 an all-round

champion / 获得女子～冠军 win the women's individual all-round title / 五项～运动 pentathlon / 十项～运动 decathlon

全年 quánnián annual; yearly: ～收入 annual income / ～平均温度 mean annual temperature / ～雨量 yearly rainfall

全盘 quánpán whole; all; overall: ～考虑 give overall consideration to / ～接受 give a total and uncritical acceptance to / ～否定 completely negate; totally repudiate / ～西化 wholesale Westernization / ～电气化（机械化）overall electrification (mechanization)

全票 quánpiào ① full ticket ② all the votes; a unanimous vote: 他以～当选。He was elected by a unanimous vote.

全勤 quánqín full work attendance (without a single day off during a specified period)

全球 quánqiú the whole world: ～战略 global strategy / 在～范围内 on a global scale

全权 quánquán ① full powers; plenary powers: ～证书 full powers ② full responsibility: 企业的经营管理由国家委托经理～负责。Managers will be entrusted by the state with full responsibility for the management and operation of their enterprises.

全权代表 quánquán dàibiǎo plenipotentiary

全然 quánrán adv. completely; entirely: ～不了解情况 be completely ignorant of the situation / ～不计后果 in utter disregard of the consequences / ～不顾个人安危 give no thought to one's own safety

全日制教育 quánrìzhì jiàoyù full-time schooling
全日制学校 quánrìzhì xuéxiào a full-time school
全色 quánsè photog. panchromatic: ～乳剂 panchromatic emulsion

全色胶片 quánsè jiāopiàn (or 全色片 quánsèpiàn) panchromatic film

全身 quánshēn the whole body; all over (the body): ～不适 general malaise / ～发抖 shake (or shiver) all over / ～湿透 be soaked to the skin / ～是伤 be covered with cuts and bruises / ～检查 a general physical checkup

全身麻醉 quánshēn mázuì general anesthesia
全身像 quánshēnxiàng a full-length picture
全神贯注 quánshén guànzhù concentrate one's attention on; be absorbed (or engrossed) in; be preoccupied with: ～地搞技术革新 be deeply engrossed in technical innovations / ～地考虑问题 be preoccupied with a problem / 她～地听着。She listened with rapt attention. or She was all ears. / 下棋需要～。Chess requires great concentration.

全胜 quánshèng ① complete victory: 大获～ win a complete victory ② sports win every match; be all-victorious

全盛 quánshèng (of a historical period) flourishing; in full bloom: 唐朝是律诗的～时期。Lüshi poetry was in its prime during the Tang Dynasty.

全食 quánshí astron. total eclipse: ～带 path of total eclipse; belt (or zone) of totality

全始全终 quánshǐ-quánzhōng see (or carry) sth. through; stick to sth. to the very end

全视图 quánshìtú full view; general view
全数 quánshù total number; whole amount: 我们已～付讫。We have paid the whole amount.

全速 quánsù full (or maximum, top) speed: ～前进 advance at full speed / 这车～每小时一百二十公里。The car has a maximum speed of 120 kilometres an (or per) hour.

全损 quánsǔn econ. total loss
全损险 quánsǔnxiǎn econ. total loss only (T. L. O.)
全套 quántào a complete set: ～设备 a complete set of equipment / 你这贝多芬交响曲唱片是～的吗?Are your

records of Beethoven's symphonies a complete set?

全体 quántǐ all; entire; whole: ～船员 the crew (of a ship); the ship's complement / ～演员 the entire cast / ～工作人员 the whole staff / 开～会 meet in full session; hold a plenary session / ～起立默哀。All rose to their feet in silent tribute. / ～起立，长时间鼓掌。There was a long standing ovation. / 内阁～辞职。The cabinet resigned en bloc. / 看问题，不但要看到部分，而且要看到～。In approaching a problem one should see the whole as well as the parts.

全天候 quántiānhòu all-weather: ～飞机 all-weather aircraft / ～公路 all-weather road

全托 quántuō put one's child in a boarding nursery: 你的孩子是日托还是～?Is your child in a day nursery or a boarding nursery? or Does your child board at the nursery or go home in the evening?

全托托儿所 quántuō tuǒ'érsuǒ boarding nursery
全文 quánwén full text: ～如下。The full text follows. / ～记录 verbatim record / 《人民日报》～发表了总理的讲话。Renmin Ribao published the Premier's speech in full.

全武行 quánwǔháng ① full-scale battle scenes (in traditional opera) ② gang fight; free-for-all

全息电影 quánxī diànyǐng holographic movie
全息照相 quánxī zhàoxiàng hologram: 激光～ laser hologram / ～存储器 holographic memory / ～术 holography

全线 quánxiàn ① all fronts; the entire length: 边界～ the entire length of the boundary / ～出击 launch an attack on all fronts / 敌人已～崩溃。The enemy was put to rout all along the line. ② the whole line (of a railway or highway): 这条铁路已～通车。The whole railway line has been opened to traffic.

全心全意 quánxīn-quányì whole-heartedly; heart and soul: ～为人民服务 serve the people wholeheartedly / ～投身到工作里边，你的生活就会充实和快乐。If you set your whole mind and heart on your work, your life will be full and happy.

全新 quánxīn completely new; brand-new: ～的设备 brand-new equipment

全新世 Quánxīnshì geol. the Recent Epoch
全休 quánxiū ① a complete rest: 大夫建议～一星期。The doctor prescribed a complete rest of one week. ② a long-term sick leave

全音 quányīn mus. whole tone
全音符 quányīnfú mus. whole note; semibreve
全知全能 quánzhī-quánnéng omniscient and omnipotent

全脂奶粉 quánzhī nǎifěn whole milk powder

诠

quán formal annotate; give explanatory notes
诠次 quáncì formal ① order of arrangement ② arrangement of ideas (in writing or speech): 辞无～ write or speak incoherently

诠释 quánshì annotate; give explanatory notes
诠注 quánzhù provide notes and commentary

泉

quán ① spring (a small stream): 温泉 wēnquán ② the mouth of a spring; spring ③ an ancient term for coin: ～币 ancient coin

泉华 quánhuá geol. sinter
泉水 quánshuǐ spring water; spring
泉台 quántái formal the nether world
泉下 quánxià the nether world
泉眼 quányǎn the mouth of a spring; spring
泉源 quányuán ① fountainhead; springhead; wellspring ② source: 智慧（力量）的～ source of wisdom (strength)

拳 quán ①fist: 挥～ shake one's fist / 打了一～ give a punch ② boxing; pugilism: 一套～ a shadow boxing set / 练～ practise shadow boxing ③curl; twist; bend: 老大娘～着腿坐在炕上。 The old woman sat on the *kang* with her legs curled up.

拳棒 quánbàng same as 武术 wǔshù

拳不离手，曲不离口 quán bù lí shǒu, qǔ bù lí kǒu the boxer's fist must stick to its task, and the singer's mouth no rest must ask; practice makes perfect

拳打脚踢 quándǎ-jiǎotī cuff and kick; beat up

拳击 quánjī boxing; pugilism: ～台 boxing ring / ～运动员 boxer; pugilist

拳脚 quánjiǎo Chinese boxing

拳曲 quánqū curl; twist; bend: ～的头发 curly hair

拳拳 quánquán *formal* sincere: ～之忱 sincere intention; sincerity

拳拳服膺 quánquán fúyīng ① always bear in mind ② have a sincere belief in

拳师 quánshī boxing coach; pugilist

拳术 quánshù Chinese boxing

拳坛 quántán boxing circles; the boxing world

拳套 quántào a series of skills and tricks in Chinese boxing

拳头 quántou fist: 举起～喊口号 raise one's fist and shout slogans / 医生为他清理伤口时他疼得直攥～。 He clenched his fists in agony as the doctor cleaned the wound.

拳头产品 quán·tóu chǎnpǐn competitive products

拳王 quánwáng boxing champion; lord of the ring

辁 quán *formal* ① spokeless wheel ② shallow; superficial

痊 quán fully recover from an illness

痊愈 quányù fully recover from an illness; be fully recovered: 她还没有～。 She's not recovered yet. / 希望你早日～。 I wish you a speedy recovery. / 伤口～后，他又返回了前线。 After his wound healed, he went back to the front.

铨 quán *formal* ①select; choose ②weigh; measure; judge

铨叙 quánxù *old* examine the records and qualifications of officials in making appointments

惓 quán see below

惓惓 quánquán same as 拳拳 quánquán

筌 quán *formal* a bamboo fish trap: 得鱼忘筌 dé yú wàng quán

蜷（踡） quán curl up; huddle up: 小猫在沙发上～作一团睡觉。 The kitten was sleeping curled up on the sofa.

蜷伏 quánfú curl up; huddle up; lie with the knees drawn up: 他喜欢～着睡觉。 He likes to sleep with his knees drawn up. *or* He likes to sleep curled up on his side.

蜷局 quánjú *formal* curl; coil; twist

蜷曲 quánqū curl; coil; twist: 一条蛇在草丛里～着。 A snake lay coiled in the grass. / 他把两腿～起来做了个前滚翻。 Drawing up his knees against his chest, he did a forward roll.

蜷缩 quánsuō roll up; huddle up; curl up: 刺猬一受到攻击就～成一团。 A hedgehog rolls itself into a ball when attacked.

醛 quán *chem.* aldehyde

醛酸 quánsuān *chem.* aldehydic acid

醛糖 quántáng *chem.* aldose

醛酯 quánzhǐ *chem.* aldehydo-ester

鬈 quán ①(of hair) curly; wavy: ～发 curly hair ② (of hair) beautiful

鬈曲 quánqū *text.* crimp; crinkle; curl: ～羊毛 crimpy wool; crinkled wool

颧 quán see below

颧骨 quán·gǔ cheekbone: ～突起 have prominent cheekbones

quǎn

犬 quǎn dog: 警犬 jǐngquǎn

犬齿 quǎnchǐ canine tooth

犬马之劳 quǎn-mǎ zhī láo serve like a dog or a horse: 效～ serve one's master faithfully; be at sb.'s beck and call / 若蒙不弃, 愿效～。 Should I be fortunate enough not to be rejected, I would render such humble services as I could.

犬儒 quǎnrú cynic

犬儒主义 quǎnrúzhǔyì cynicism

犬牙 quǎnyá ① canine tooth ② fang (of a dog)

犬牙交错 quǎnyá jiāocuò jigsaw-like; interlocking: 形成～的状态 form a jagged, interlocking pattern / ～的战争 a war of jigsaw pattern

犬子 quǎnzǐ *hum.* my son

畎 quǎn *formal* a field ditch

畎亩 quǎnmǔ *formal* field; farm

绻 quǎn see 缱绻 qiǎnquǎn

quàn

劝（勸） quàn ① advise; urge; try to persuade: ～他戒烟 advise him to give up (*or* quit) smoking / ～他休息 urge him to take a rest / 我～了半天, 他就是不听。 I spent a long time trying to talk him round, but he just wouldn't listen. / 我们～他别去了。 We tried to persuade him not to go. ②encourage: 劝学 quànxué ③comfort: 他心里不好受, 你去～～吧。 He's feeling bad; please go and say a few words to comfort him.

劝导 quàndǎo try to persuade; advise; induce: 耐心～ try patiently to talk sb. round / 经过同志们的～, 他终于想通了。 With the help of his comrades, he has finally straightened things out in his mind.

劝告 quàngào ① advise; urge; exhort: 我～她开车要小心。 I urged her to drive carefully. / 医生～他注意休息。 The doctor advised him to have a good rest. ② advice; exhortations: 她不顾我们的～。 She disregarded our repeated exhortations. / 小王听从了我的～, 把烟戒了。 Xiao Wang has taken my advice and given up (*or* quitted) smoking.

劝和 quànhé try to persuade two parties to become reconciled; mediate

劝化 quànhuà ① *Buddhism* urge to do good ②same as 募化 mùhuà

劝驾 quànjià urge sb. to accept an invitation or a post

劝架 quànjià try to reconcile parties to a quarrel or to stop people from fighting each other; mediate

劝解 quànjiě ① help sb. to get over his worries, etc.: 大家～了半天，她才消气了。It was some time before we succeeded in pacifying her. ② mediate; make peace between; bring people together: 他们吵架了，你去～一下。They've had a quarrel. You try and patch things up between them.

劝诫 quànjiè admonish; expostulate: 他把我当成亲兄弟一样，时时～我，帮助我。He treats me like his own brother and often gives me advice and help.

劝酒 quànjiǔ urge sb. to drink (at a banquet)

劝勉 quànmiǎn advise and encourage: 互相～ help and encourage each other

劝募 quànmù solicit contributions by persuasions

劝善 quànshàn encourage people to do good

劝说 quànshuō persuade; advise: 我们已经～过他，叫他放弃原来的计划。We've talked him out of his original plan. / 他听从了我的～。He gave in to my persuasion.

劝慰 quànwèi console; soothe

劝降 quànxiáng induce to capitulate

劝学 quànxué encourage learning

劝业场 quànyèchǎng old bazaar

劝诱 quànyòu induce; prevail upon

劝止 quànzhǐ same as 劝阻 quànzǔ

劝阻 quànzǔ dissuade sb. from; advise sb. not to: 你最好～他别那样干。You'd better try to talk him out of doing that. / 看到损害群众利益的行为，我们就要进行～。Whenever we see a person doing something antisocial, we should try to stop him.

券 quàn certificate; ticket: 入场券 rùchǎngquàn
——see also xuàn

quē

炔 quē chem. alkyne: 乙炔 yǐquē

炔雌醇 quēcíchún pharm. ethinyloestradiol

缺 quē ① be short of; lack: ～人 be short of hands / 庄稼～水～肥就长不好。Lacking manure and water, crops won't grow well. / 这种原料较～。This kind of raw material is rather scarce. / 这本书～两页。Two pages are missing from this book. / 这些条件～一不可。Not a single one of these conditions can be dispensed with. / 我们队可不能～了小林。Our team can't do without Xiao Lin. ② incomplete; imperfect: 残缺 cánquē ③ be absent: 人都到齐了，一个不～。No one is absent. Everybody's here. ④ vacancy; opening: 空缺 kòngquē

缺编 quēbiān ① understaffed: 这家医院～。The hospital is understaffed. ② same as 缺额 quē'é

缺档 quēdàng be in short supply; be out of stock

缺德 quēdé mean; wicked; rotten: 做～事 do sth. mean; play a mean trick / 他这样做可真～。It's wicked of him to act like that. / 这样对待她真～。What a rotten thing to do to her!

缺点 quēdiǎn shortcoming; defect; weakness; drawback: 克服工作中的～ overcome shortcomings in one's work / 这种药的主要～是败胃。The chief drawback of this medicine is that it spoils your appetite. / 你的～是写作业不认真。Not doing your homework carefully is your weakness. / 这本书的插图太少是一个～。One shortcoming of this book is that it has too few illustrations.

缺额 quē'é vacant position; vacancy: 他们厂按编制还有五十名～。Their factory is still 50 people short of its quota of workers.

缺乏 quēfá be short of; lack; be in want of: ～劳动力 be short of labour power / ～经验 lack experience / ～战斗力 have poor fighting capacity / ～资源 be deficient in resources / ～证据 want of proof

缺憾 quēhàn a regrettable imperfection; regret

缺货 quēhuò be in short supply; be out of stock

缺斤短两 quējīn-duǎnliǎng give short weight: 这铺子卖东西老是～。That shop always gives short weight (or short-weights its customers).

缺刻叶 quēkèyè bot. incised leaf

缺课 quēkè be absent from school; miss a class: 缺了三课 miss three lessons / 给一个因病～的学生补习功课 give extra help to a pupil who has missed some classes on account of illness

缺口 quēkǒu ① breach; gap: 篱笆上有个～。There is a gap in the fence. / 碗边儿上碰了个～儿。The bowl has a broken edge. / 从敌人的侧翼打开一个～ make a breach in the enemy's flank ② mech. notch

缺粮户 quēliánghù grain deficient household (usu. in the countryside)

缺漏 quēlòu gaps and omissions: 弥缝～ fill in gaps and supply omissions

缺略 quēlüè ① lack; be short of ② incomplete

缺门 quēmén gap (in a branch of learning, etc.): 这本书填补了词典学方面的重大～。This book fills a major gap in lexicography.

缺欠 quēqiàn ① shortcoming; defect; weakness ② lack; be short of

缺勤 quēqín absence from duty (or work): 因病～ be on sick leave

缺勤率 quēqínlǜ absence rate; absentee rate

缺如 quērú same as 阙如 quērú

缺少 quēshǎo lack; be short of; be in want of: ～零件 lack spare parts / ～人手 be short of hands; be short-handed / 不可～的条件 indispensable conditions / 这些植物～水，都死了。The plants died for want of water. / 他工作认真，但～办法。He's a concientious worker, but is not very resourceful.

缺市 quēshì in short supply

缺损 quēsǔn ① damaged; worn; torn ② med. physiological defect; physiological deficiency

缺铁性贫血 quētiěxìng pínxuè iron-deficiency anaemia

缺位 quēwèi ① (of a position) be vacant ② a vacant position; vacancy

缺席 quēxí absent (from a meeting, etc.): 因事～ be absent through being otherwise engaged / 他这学期从没～过。He has never been absent from class this term. / ～者 absentee

缺席判决 quēxí pànjué leg. judgment by default

缺席审判 quēxí shěnpàn leg. trial by default

缺席投票 quēxí tóupiào ① absentee voting: ～者 absentee (or absent) voter ② absentee vote or absentee ballot

缺陷 quēxiàn defect; drawback; flaw; blemish: 生理～ a physical defect / 这个计划有些～。The plan has some shortcomings. / 精神上有～的人不能作证人。Those with mental handicaps cannot be witnesses.

缺心眼儿 quē xīnyǎnr ① simple-minded; scatter-brained ② dull-witted; mentally deficient; retarded

缺嘴 quēzuǐ dial. ① harelip ② fail to satisfy one's appetite or hunger: 你干重活可不能缺着嘴。You're doing heavy work. You mustn't stint yourself of food.

阙 quē formal ① fault; error ② be short of; lack
——see also què

阙如 quērú formal deficient; wanting; lacking: 竟告～ be found wanting

阙疑 quēyí leave the question open

qué

瘸 qué *inf.* be lame; limp: 左腿～了 be lame in the left leg / 一步一～ walk with a limp / 他扭了脚腕子, 站起来一～着走了。 After he twisted his ankle, he got up and limped away.

瘸腿 quétuǐ *inf.* lame: ～的人 a lame person; cripple

瘸子 quézi *inf.* a lame person; cripple

què

却¹(卻) què ①step back: 退却 tuìquè ②drive back; repulse: 却敌 quèdí ③decline; refuse: 推却 tuīquè ④(used after a verb to indicate completion of an action): 冷却 lěngquè

却²(卻) què *adv.* but; yet: 她有许多话要说, 一时～什么也说不出来。 She had a lot to say, but at the time she was unable to utter a word. / 文章虽短～很有力。 The essay is short but forceful. / 这样推理很周全, ～说服不了我。 The logic is sound, and yet it does not convince me.

却病 quèbìng *formal* prevent or cure a disease

却病延年 quèbìng-yánnián prevent illness and prolong life

却步 quèbù step back (in fear or disgust); hang back: 不要因为困难而～。 Don't hang back in the face of difficulties.

却敌 quèdí repulse the enemy

却说 quèshuō we were telling you...(a stock phrase used by traditional storytellers when resuming narration where they left off): ～八戒跳下山, 寻着一条小路。依路前行, 有五六里远近, 忽见两个女怪, 在那井上打水。(《西游记》) We were telling you about Bajie, who, having bounded down the mountain, discovered a narrow path, which he followed for some five or six *li*. Suddenly he caught sight of two female fiends bailing water from a well.

却之不恭 què zhī bù gōng *pol.* (said when receiving a gift) it would be impolite to decline: ～, 受之有愧。 To decline would be disrespectful but to accept is embarrassing.

悫(愨、慤) què *formal* honest

雀 què sparrow ——see also qiāo; qiǎo

雀斑 quèbān freckle

雀鲷 quèdiāo *zool.* damselfish

雀麦 quèmài *bot.* bromegrass; brome

雀鹰 quèyīng sparrow hawk

雀跃 quèyuè jump for joy: 欢呼～ shout and jump for joy

雀噪 quèzào *derog.* enjoy loud fame: 名声～一时 enjoy fleeting fame

阕 què ① *formal* end: 乐～。 The music ended. ② a division of a *ci* poem; stanza ③ *m.* (for songs and *ci* poems): 一～词 a *ci* poem

确(確、塙、碻) què ① true; real; authentic: 正确 zhèngquè ② *adv.* really; indeed: ～有其事。 It's a fact. *or* It really happened.

确保 quèbǎo ensure; guarantee: ～安全生产 ensure safety in production / ～质量 guarantee quality / 要～

适时播种。 Be sure to do the sowing in good time. / ～不发生类似事件 ensure against the occurrence of similar incidents

确当 quèdàng fitting; proper; appropriate

确定 quèdìng ① define; fix; determine: ～会议宗旨 define the aims of the conference / ～时限 fix a time frame / ～开会的日期和地点 determine (*or* fix) the time and place for a meeting / ～政治路线 determine a political line / ～行军路线 decide the route of the march / ～作战方案 decide on a battle plan / ～候选人名单 decide on the list of candidates / ～任务 set the tasks / ～地层的年代 ascertain the ages of the strata / ～领海宽度 delimit the extent of territorial waters / 他们已经～关系了。 They've agreed to marry. ② definite: ～的答复 a definite reply / ～不移的结论 an incontestable conclusion / ～的时间 a fixed time

确乎 quèhū *adv.* really; indeed: 这办法～有效。 This method is really effective. / 他～非常聪明。 He is very clever indeed.

确乎不拔 quèhū bù bá firm and unshakable; unswerving; unflinching

确立 quèlì establish: ～社会主义制度 establish the socialist system / ～共产主义世界观 form a communist world outlook

确论 quèlùn a sound assertion; a just argument

确切 quèqiè ① definite; exact; precise: ～的日期 an exact date / ～的解释 a clear and unambiguous explanation / 下个～的定义 give a precise definition / 用词～ precise wording ②true; reliable; sure: ～的保证 a sure guarantee

确认 quèrèn affirm; confirm; acknowledge: 参加会议的各国～了这些原则。 The participating countries affirmed these principles. / 本宪法以法律的形式～了中国各族人民斗争的成果。 This Constitution affirms in legal form the achievements of the struggles of the Chinese people of all nationalities. / ～这一经济合同无效。 The economic contract was confirmed to be void. / ～条约 confirm a treaty

确实 quèshí ① true; reliable: ～的消息 reliable information / ～的数字 exact figures / 把发生的事说得确确实实 give an accurate and detailed account of what has happened ② *adv.* really; indeed: 这～是个很好的建议。 This is really a very good suggestion. / 他～来过。 Yes, he did come. / 他最近～有些进步。 He's really made some progress recently. / 你听到爆炸声了吗?——～听到了。 Did you hear the explosion?—Indeed I did.

确守 quèshǒu strictly or scrupulously abide by: ～信义 act in strict good faith

确数 quèshù exact figures; exact amount

确信 quèxìn ① firmly believe; be convinced; be sure: 我们～正义的事业一定会胜利。 We firmly believe that a just cause is bound to triumph. ② reliable information

确凿 quèzáo conclusive; authentic; irrefutable: ～的事实 irrefutable facts / 证据～, 不容抵赖。 The evidence is conclusive and brooks no denial.

确凿不移 quèzáo bù yí well established and irrefutable

确诊 quèzhěn make a definite diagnosis; diagnose: 他的病尚未～。 No diagnosis has as yet been made of his disease. / 他的病～了没有?Has his diagnosis been confirmed? / 医生～她的病是流感。 The doctor diagnosed her illness as flu.

确证 quèzhèng ①prove conclusively or positively: 我们可以～他的论断是错误的。 We can prove conclusively that his assertion is wrong. ② proof positive; conclusive or irrefutable evidence: 在～面前他不得不承认自己的罪行。 When confronted with conclusive evidence, he had to admit his guilt.

阙　què ①watchtower on either side of a palace gate ②imperial palace: 宫阙 gōngquè ——see also quē

阙文　quèwén omissions or missing parts (in a book); hiatus (in a text)

鹊　què magpie: 喜鹊 xǐquè

鹊报　quèbào the cry of the magpie—a good omen

鹊巢鸠占　què cháo jiū zhàn the turtledove occupies the magpie's nest—one person seizes another person's place, land, etc.

鹊起　quèqǐ *formal* ①act according to circumstances; do as one sees fit; use one's discretion ②(of fame) spread; rise

鹊桥　quèqiáo Magpie Bridge (the bridge formed by magpies which the Weaving-girl is supposed to cross for her annual meeting with the Herd-boy on the seventh evening of the seventh month): ～相会 magpie bridge meeting—the reunion of husband and wife or lovers after a long separation ——see also 牛郎织女 Niúláng Zhīnǚ

鹊鸲　quèqú magpie robin

榷¹　què *formal* monopoly; exclusive possession of the trade in some commodity

榷²(搉)　què discuss: 商榷 shāngquè

qūn

逡　qūn *formal* shrink from

逡巡　qūnxún *formal* hesitate to move forward; hang back: ～不前 hesitate to make a move

qún

裙(帬)　qún ①skirt: 绸～ a silk skirt ②sth. like a skirt: 围裙 wéiqún

裙钗　qúnchāi *old* petticoats and hairpins—women

裙带　qúndài ①belt (as a decoration for a skirt or dress) ②connected through one's female relatives: 通过～关系 with the help of one's female relatives; through petticoat influence

裙带风　qúndàifēng petticoat influence

裙带官　qúndàiguān an official who owes his position to petticoat influence

裙裤　qúnkù culottes

裙子　qúnzi skirt

群(羣)　qún ①crowd; group: 人群 rénqún ② *m.* (for people or animals) group; herd; flock: 一～小孩 a group of children / 一～人 a crowd of people / 一～牛 a herd of cattle / 一～羊 a flock of sheep / 一～狼 a pack of wolves / 一～蜜蜂 a swarm of bees

群策群力　qúncè-qúnlì pool the wisdom and efforts of everyone

群岛　qúndǎo archipelago

群雕　qúndiāo a group of statues

群芳　qúnfāng ① beautiful and fragrant flowers: ～竞艳 flowers vying with each other in beauty ②a group of beauties or artists: 艳压～ the queen of beauties

群芳之冠　qúnfāng zhī guàn the queen of flowers—the reigning beauty

群峰　qúnfēng connected mountain peaks: ～耸立 mountain peaks towering into the sky

群婚　qúnhūn group marriage; communal marriage

群集　qúnjí gather; assemble: 人们～在广场上。People gathered together in the public square.

群籍　qúnjí all kinds of books; a wide variety of books

群居　qúnjū living in groups; gregarious; social

群居动物　qúnjū dòngwù social animal

群居昆虫　qúnjū kūnchóng social insect

群控制　qúnkòngzhì group control

群龙无首　qún lóng wú shǒu a host of dragons without a head—a group without a leader

群落　qúnluò *biol.* community: ～交错区 ecotone

群氓　qúnméng *formal derog.* the common herd

群魔乱舞　qún mó luàn wǔ a host of demons dancing in riotous revelry—rogues of all kinds running wild

群起　qúnqǐ all rise (to do sth.): ～响应 all rise to respond

群起而攻之　qún qǐ ér gōng zhī all rise (or turn) against sb.

群青　qúnqīng *chem.* ultramarine

群轻折轴　qún qīng zhé zhóu a load of many light things can break the axle of a cart—minor offences unchecked may bring disaster

群情　qúnqíng public sentiment; feelings of the masses: ～振奋。Everyone is exhilarated. / ～激昂。Public feeling was aroused (or ran high).

群山　qúnshān connected hills or mountains: ～环绕 be surrounded by hills

群书　qúnshū all kinds of books; a wide variety of books: 博览～ be well-read

群体　qúntǐ ① *biol.* colony ② groups: 企业～ groups of enterprises

群威群胆　qúnwēi-qúndǎn mass heroism and daring: ～, 英勇杀敌 display mass heroism and daring in destroying the enemy

群小　qúnxiǎo *formal* a group of mean (or base) people

群言堂　qúnyántáng a conference hall where everyone is allowed to have his say—rule by the voice of the many: 我们提倡"～", 反对"一言堂"。We advocate "letting everyone have his say" and oppose the practice of "what I say goes." ——see also 一言堂 yīyántáng

群英会　qúnyīnghuì a gathering of heroes; a conference of outstanding workers

群众　qúnzhòng ① the masses: ～大会 mass rally / ～监督 surveillance by the masses / ～心理 mass psychology / ～意愿 the popular will ② non-Party ③ a member of the rank and file

群众工作　qúnzhòng gōngzuò mass work

群众关系　qúnzhòng guānxi one's relations (or ties) with the masses

群众观点　qúnzhòng guāndiǎn the mass viewpoint

群众路线　qúnzhòng lùxiàn the mass line: 搞什么工作都要走～。Whatever we do, we must follow the mass line.

群众团体　qúnzhòng tuántǐ mass (non-government) organization

群众性　qúnzhòngxìng of a mass character: ～体育活动 mass sports activities / 中国气象工作的一个重要特点是它的～。Mass participation is a prominent feature of meteorological work in China.

群众运动　qúnzhòng yùndòng mass movement; mass campaign: 大搞～ unfold mass movements on a large scale

群众组织　qúnzhòng zǔzhī mass (non-government) organization; people's organization

群子弹　qúnzǐdàn another name for 榴霰弹 liúxiàndàn

麇(麏)　qún *formal* flock together ——see also jūn

麇集　qúnjí *formal* swarm; flock together: ～周围 rally round

R

rán

蚺(蚦)　rán　see below

蚺蛇　ránshé　another name for 蟒蛇 mǎngshé

然　rán　① right; correct: 不以为然 bù yǐ wéi rán ② so; like that: 尽然 jìnrén ③ *conj. formal* but; nevertheless; however: 此事虽小, ～亦不可忽视。 This is a minor point, but it must not be overlooked. ④ (adverb or adjective suffix): 忽然 hūrán / 巍然 wēirán

然而　rán'ér　*conj.* but; however; yet: 试验失败了多次, ～他们并不灰心。 Time after time they failed in the experiment, but they did not lose heart. / 这篇文章写得不错, ～还可以改进。 The composition is all right, there is room for improvement, however. / 我失败了, ～还要试试。 I have failed, yet I shall try again.

然否　ránfǒu　yes or no; is that correct: 不知诸位以为～? Do you gentlemen all agree?

然后　ránhòu　*conj.* then; after that; afterwards: 贵宾们将在太原停留一天, ～飞往上海。 The distinguished guests will stay in Taiyuan for one day and then fly to Shanghai. / 我们先研究一下, ～再决定。 We'll consider the problem carefully before coming to any decision. / 我们看了一场电影, ～就回家了。 We saw a film, and after that we went home.

然诺　ránnuò　*formal* promise; pledge: 重～ be serious about making and keeping a promise; stand by one's word

然则　ránzé　*conj. formal* in that case; then: ～如之何而可? Then, what is to be done?

髯(髥)　rán　whiskers; beard: 美～ a beautiful beard

髯口　ránkou　artificial beard or whiskers worn by traditional opera actors

燃　rán　burn; ignite; light: ～灯 light a lamp / ～起一堆篝火 light a bonfire / ～起革命的烈火 spark off (*or* kindle) the flames of revolution

燃点[1]　rándiǎn　kindle; set fire to; light; ignite: ～灯笼 light a lantern / 木柴太湿, ～不着。 The wood is too wet to kindle.

燃点[2]　rándiǎn　*chem.* ignition (*or* burning, kindling) point

燃放　ránfàng　set off (fireworks, etc.): ～爆竹 set off firecrackers

燃料　ránliào　fuel: 标准～ ideal fuels / 低热值～ low-calorie fuels

燃料比　ránliàobǐ　*metall.* fuel ratio

燃料电池　ránliào diànchí　fuel cell

燃料动力工业　ránliào dònglì gōngyè　fuel and power industry

燃料库　ránliàokù　fuel depot; fuel reservoir

燃眉之急　rán méi zhī jí　as pressing as a fire singeing one's eyebrows—extremely urgent: 敌兵入侵, 边界有～。 The enemy had started to invade the land and the situation on the border was very critical. / 母亲寄来二十块钱, 解了我～。 Mother sent me twenty *yuan* saving me from going broke.

燃气轮机　ránqìlúnjī　gas turbine: ～发电厂 gas turbine power station

燃烧[1]　ránshāo　① burn; kindle: 干柴容易～。 Dry wood burns easily. / 怒火～ burning with rage / 革命的烈火在～。 The flames of revolution are raging.

燃烧[2]　ránshāo　*chem.* combustion; inflammation: ～性能 combustibility

燃烧弹　ránshāodàn　incendiary bomb

燃烧剂　ránshāojì　incendiary agent

燃烧瓶　ránshāopíng　frangible grenade; Molotov cocktail

燃烧室　ránshāoshì　*mech.* combustion chamber; blast chamber; combustor

燃油泵　rányóubèng　fuel pump

rǎn

冉(冄)　rǎn　① see below ② (Rǎn) a surname

冉冉　rǎnrǎn　*formal* ① (of hair, twigs, etc.) hang down softly ② slowly; gradually: 一轮红日～升起。 A red sun slowly rose.

苒(荏)　rǎn　see 荏苒 rěnrǎn

染　rǎn　① dye: 把一块布～成绿色 dye a piece of cloth green / 我们的战旗是烈士的鲜血～红的。 Our standard is dyed with the blood of our martyrs. ② catch (a disease); acquire (a bad habit, etc.): ～上了痢疾 have caught dysentery / ～上了赌博的恶习 have contracted the bad habit of gambling / 母亲不允许我们～上一点坏习惯。 Mother doesn't allow us to acquire any bad habits. ③ soil; contaminate: 污染 wūrǎn ④ add details to a painting, etc.: 渲染 xuànrǎn

染病　rǎnbìng　catch (*or* contract) an illness; be infected with a disease

染毒　rǎndú　*mil.* contaminate: ～区域 contamination area

染发　rǎnfà　dye the hair

染坊　rǎnfáng　dyehouse; dye-works

染缸　rǎngāng　dye vat; dyejigger

染料　rǎnliào　dyestuff; dye

染色　rǎnsè　dye; colour: ～性 dyeability

染色剂　rǎnsèjì　colouring agent

染色体　rǎnsètǐ　*biol.* chromosome

染色质　rǎnsèzhì　*biochem.* chromatin

染液　rǎnyè　dye liquor

染印法　rǎnyìnfǎ　*film* dye transfer process: ～彩色电影 colour film made by the dye transfer process

染指　rǎnzhǐ　take a share of sth. one is not entitled to; encroach on: ～别国资源 encroach on the resources of other countries / 国家神圣领土不容他人～。 Our territory is sacred and inviolable.

染指甲　rǎn zhǐjia　paint the fingernails: 染了红指甲 paint the fingernails red

染指择肥　rǎnzhǐ zéféi　dip one's finger in the pie and claim the lion's share

rāng

嚷　rāng　see below ——see also rǎng

嚷嚷　rāngrang　inf.　① make a noise; make an uproar: 谁在那儿～? Who's making all that noise over there? / 屋里一片乱～。The room was in an uproar. ② make widely known: 这件事，你可别～。Don't breathe a word about this. / 要是～出去，对咱俩都没好处。Letting this out wouldn't do either of us any good.

ráng

禳　ráng　formal　avert (a misfortune or disaster) by prayers

禳解　rángjiě　formal　avert (a misfortune or disaster) by prayers

禳　ráng　old　dirty

瓢　ráng　① pulp; flesh; pith: 橘子～ the pulp of a tangerine / 西瓜～ the pulp (or flesh) of a watermelon ② the interior part of certain things: 信瓢儿 xìnrángr ③ dial.　(of skills) not good; (of health) weak: 你赶车的技术真不～。You're not bad at cart driving. / 病后身体～ be weak after an illness

瓢口　rángkou　inf.　taste (of a watermelon, etc.)

瓢子　rángzi　pulp; flesh; pith

穰　ráng　① dial.　stalks of rice, wheat, etc. ② same as 瓢 ráng

穰穰　rángráng　formal　(of a harvest) rich; abundant: ～满家 a rich harvest of food crops; a bumper grain harvest

rǎng

壤　rǎng　① soil: 土壤 tǔrǎng ② earth: 霄壤 xiāorǎng ③ area: 接壤 jiērǎng

壤地　rǎngdì　formal　territory; land

壤界　rǎngjiè　boundary; border

壤土　rǎngtǔ　agric.　loam

攘¹　rǎng　formal　① reject; resist: 攘外 rǎngwài ② seize; grab: 攘夺 rǎngduó

攘²（纕）　rǎng　push up one's sleeves: 攘臂 rǎngbì

攘臂　rǎngbì　formal　push up one's sleeves and bare one's arms (in excitement or agitation): ～高呼 raise one's hands and shout

攘除　rǎngchú　formal　get rid of; weed out; reject: ～奸邪 get rid of crafty and evil people / ～奸凶 eliminate treacherous people

攘夺　rǎngduó　formal　seize; grab: ～政权 seize state power / ～王位 usurp the throne

攘窃　rǎngqiè　formal　usurp; steal; grab

攘攘　rǎngrǎng　formal　disorderly; confusing; chaotic: 天下～，皆为利往。All this hustle-bustle in the world is for money.

攘善　rǎngshàn　formal　claim credit due to others

攘外　rǎngwài　resist foreign aggression

嚷　rǎng　① shout; yell; make an uproar: 别～了，人家都睡了。Stop yelling, people are sleeping. / 谁在那儿～? Who's shouting over there? / 他在窗外～了几嗓子。He shouted several times outside the window. / 孩子们在院子里～些什么? What are the children yelling about in the courtyard? ② inf.　make a noise; make an uproar ③ dial.　scold; dress down; blame: 这件事让妈知道了，她又该～我了。If Mother finds out about this, she'll give me a dressing-down. ——see also rāng

嚷叫　rǎngjiào　shout; yell; make an uproar

嚷嘴　rǎngzuǐ　dial.　quarrel; bicker

ràng

让（讓）　ràng　① give way; give ground; yield; give up: 各不相～。Neither is willing to give ground. / 我～了他两步棋。I let him have the first two moves (in a chess game). / 见困难就上，见荣誉就～ dash towards difficulties and retreat from honours / 你该～着弟弟一点。You ought to humour your younger brother a little. / 谁都～他三分。Everybody has to let him have his way. / 请一一～。Please step aside. or Excuse me. / 幸亏我～得快，要不早给那辆自行车撞倒了。Luckily I dodged in time, or I'd have been knocked down by the bike. ② invite; offer: ～茶 offer sb. tea / 把客人～进里屋 invite guests into the inner room ③ let; allow; make: ～我想一想。Let me think it over. / 大夫不～她起来。The doctor told her to stay in bed. / 他～我把这个消息转告你。He told me to pass the message on to you. / 对不起，～你久等了。Sorry to have kept you waiting. / 展品不～摸。The exhibits are not to be touched. / 妈妈不～买。Mother didn't let me buy it. / 谁～你不敲门就进来的? Why didn't you knock before you came in? / 别～老王为难了。Don't embarrass Lao Wang. or Don't make things awkward for Lao Wang. ④ let sb. have sth. at a fair price: 我把激光唱机按原价～给他了。I've turned my CD player over to him at the original price. ⑤ prep.　(used in a passive sentence to introduce the doer of the action): 台布～墨水给染了。The table cloth got stained with ink. / 庄稼～大水冲跑了。The crops were washed away by the flood. / 行李～雨淋湿了。The luggage got wet in the rain. / 她～小刘给气跑了。Xiao Liu made her so angry that she left in a huff.

让步　ràngbù　make a concession; give in; give way; yield: 准备作出某些必要的～ be prepared to make some necessary concessions / 不向无理要求～ not yield to any unreasonable demand / 最大限度的～ the greatest (or maximum) concession / 两人争吵了半天，谁也不肯～。The two of them quarrelled for a long time; neither was willing to give in. / 我们应该互相都让点步。We should meet each other halfway. / ～必须是对等的。Concessions must be reciprocal. / 我已经让了一大步，还要我怎么样? I've already given in this far. What more could you want of me?

让渡　ràngdù　transfer the possession of; alienate: 资源不得～。Resources are not subject to alienation.

让价　ràngjià　(of a seller) agree to reduce the price asked

让开　ràngkai　get out of the way; step aside; make way: 车来了，快～。A car is coming. Quick, get out of the way. / 他挡着道，可又偏不～。He was blocking the road and wouldn't make way.

让路 rànglù make way for sb. or sth.; give way; give sb. the right of way: 大家让让路。Please get out of the way, everybody. / 你们的工程得给重点工程～。Your project will have to make way for the main project.

让球ràngqiú concede points (in ball games): 教练员让了小李五个球。The coach conceded Xiao Li five points.

让位ràngwèi ① resign sovereign authority; abdicate: 1796 年, 乾隆皇帝在位 60 年后～于其子。In 1796, having reigned 60 years, Emperor Qianlong voluntarily abdicated in favour of one of his sons. / 谁领导无方, 谁就得～。Those who don't have good leaders should give up their positions. ② offer (or give up) one's seat to sb.: 请为这位孕妇让个位! Please give your seat up to this pregnant lady. ③ yield to; give way to; change into: 经过大家的努力, 困难的局面终于～于顺利的局面。As a result of collective effort, the difficult situation changed into a favourable one.

让贤 ràngxián relinquish one's post in favour of sb. better qualified

让枣推梨 ràngzǎo-tuīlí offer dates and decline pears —show brotherly love

让帐 ràngzhàng (of friends eating out) insist on paying the bill

让座 ràngzuò ① offer (or give up) one's seat to sb.: 他给一位抱孩子的妇女让了座。He offered his bus seat to a woman carrying a baby. ② invite guests to be seated: 他给客人又是～, 又是让茶。He invited the guests to be seated and offered them tea.

ráo

莪（蕘） ráo formal firewood; faggot: 刍莪 chúráo

莪花 ráohuā canescent wikstroemia (Wikstroemia canescens)

饶（饒） ráo ① rich; plentiful: ～有风趣 full of wit and humour ② have mercy on; let sb. off; forgive: 下回可不能轻～了你。We won't let you off so easily next time. / 他说话不～人。He has a sharp tongue. ③ give sth. extra; let sb. have sth. into the bargain: 给你～上一个。I'll let you have one more. / 有两个人就够了, 不要把他也～在里头。Two people will be enough; there is no need to drag him along, too. ④ conj. inf. although; in spite of the fact that: 这孩子, ～怎么说他也不听。That child! Whatever you said, he simply wouldn't listen. / ～这么让着他, 他还不满意。No matter how many concessions I made, he still wasn't satisfied. ⑤ (Ráo) a surname

饶命 ráomìng spare sb.'s life: 他跪在地上, 直求～。He knelt down begging to be spared.

饶舌 ráoshé ① too talkative; garrulous ② say more than is proper; shoot off one's mouth

饶恕 ráoshù forgive; pardon: 请求～ ask for forgiveness

饶头 ráotou inf. a small item given away free (in business transactions); extra: 这个小的是个～。This little one is an extra.

饶沃 ráowò formal (of soil) fertile; rich

饶裕 ráoyù formal richly endowed; fertile; abundant

娆（嬈） ráo see 妖娆 yāoráo ——see also rǎo

桡（橈） ráo oar

桡动脉 ráodòngmài physiol. radial artery

桡骨 ráogǔ physiol. radius

rǎo

扰（擾） rǎo ① harass; trouble: 干扰 gānrǎo ② pol. trespass on sb.'s hospitality: 我～了他一顿饭。He kindly entertained me to dinner.

扰动 rǎodòng be in turmoil; be turbulent: 明朝末年, 农民纷纷起义, ～及于全国。During the last years of the Ming Dynasty, peasant uprisings broke out one after another, throwing the whole country into a turmoil.

扰害 rǎohài disturb and harm; cause trouble

扰乱 rǎoluàn harass; disturb; create confusion: ～治安 disturb public order / ～市场 disrupt the market / ～军心 undermine the morale of an army / ～思路 interrupt a train of thought / ～睡眠 disturb sb.'s sleep / ～视线 interfere with sb.'s view

扰攘 rǎorǎng hustle and bustle; noisy confusion; tumult: 下课铃一响, 教室里一片～的声音。As soon as the bell rang, the classroom was in noisy confusion.

扰扰 rǎorǎo formal disorderly; confused; chaotic: 人声～ a hubbub of voices

娆（嬈） rǎo formal harass; disturb ——see also rǎo

rào

绕（繞） rào ① wind; coil: ～线 wind thread / 把铁丝～成圈 coil wire; wind wire into a coil ② move round; circle; revolve: 地球～着太阳转。The earth moves (or revolves) round the sun. / 运动员～场一周。The athletes marched around the arena. / ～了半天, 还是没走出这个胡同。I've been walking around for a long time, but I still haven't got out of this lane. / 飞机在机场上空～圈。The plane circled over the airfield. ③ make a detour; bypass; go round: ～过暗礁 bypass hidden reefs; steer clear of submerged rocks / 货轮～过好望角, 驶入大西洋。The freighter rounded the Cape of Good Hope and sailed into the Atlantic. / 你必须明确回答这个问题, 想～是～不过去的。You must give a definite answer to the question. There's no getting round it. ④ confuse; baffle; befuddle: 你的话把他～住了。What you said confused him. / 我一时～住了, 帐目没算对。I got confused and didn't work out the accounts correctly.

绕脖子 ràobózi dial. ① beat about the bush; speak or act in a roundabout way: 你简单地说吧, 别净～。Just speak simply. Don't beat about the bush. ② involved; knotty; tricky: 这句话太～了。This sentence is too involved. / 这道题真～。This is a very tricky question.

绕道 ràodào (also 绕路 ràolù) make a detour; go by a roundabout route: 前面有个水库, 我们得～过去。There's a reservoir ahead. We'll have to make a detour. / 你不要一遇困难就～走。Don't always try to skirt round difficulties.

绕口令 ràokǒulìng tongue twister

绕梁 ràoliáng (of the sound of singing) linger; reverberate

绕圈子 rào quānzi ① circle; go round and round ② take a circuitous route; make a detour: 他想从她家门口经过, 特地绕了一个圈子。He made a detour to pass the house where she lived. ③ same as 绕弯子 rào wānzi

绕射 ráoshè　same as 衍射 yǎnshè

绕腾 ráoteng　talk in a rounabout way; beat about the bush

绕弯儿 ráowānr　① *dial.* go for a stroll (*or* walk): 他刚吃完晚饭，在院子里～。He's just had his supper and is taking a stroll in the courtyard. / 我出去绕个弯儿就回来。I'm going out for a walk and will be back soon. ② same as 绕弯子 rào wānzi

绕弯子 rào wānzi　talk in a roundabout way; beat about the bush: 有话直说，别～。If you have anything to say, say it. Don't beat about the bush.

绕行 ráoxíng　① make a detour; bypass: 道路施工, 车辆～。Detour. Road under repair. ② move round; circle

绕远儿 ráoyuǎnr　go the long way round: 那样走可就～了。If you take that route, you'll be going the long way round.

绕组 ráozǔ　*elec.* winding: 双线～ bifilar winding

绕嘴 ráozuǐ　(of a sentence, etc.) not be smooth; be difficult to articulate: 这句话很～。This sentence is a tongue twister.

rě

嗻

惹

嗻　rě　see 唱嗻 chàngrě ——see also nuò

惹　rě　① invite or ask for (sth. undesirable): ～麻烦 ask for trouble; invite trouble / 不要把他～翻了。Don't touch off his temper. ② offend; provoke; tease: 我～不起他。I cannot afford to offend him. / 我可没～他! I said nothing to provoke him. *or* I did nothing to provoke him. ③ attract; cause: ～人注意 attract attention / ～人讨厌 make a nuisance of oneself / 他的话把大家～得哈哈大笑。His words set everybody roaring with laughter.

惹草拈花 rěcǎo-niānhuā　same as 拈花惹草 niānhuā-rěcǎo

惹火烧身 rě huǒ shāo shēn　stir up a fire only to burn oneself—court disaster; ask for trouble

惹祸 rěhuò　court disaster; stir up trouble: 这都是我惹的祸。It was I who started all the trouble. / 你又在～了! 难道还没吃够苦吗? You're stirring up trouble again! Haven't you had enough yet?

惹乱子 rě luànzi　court disaster; stir up trouble

惹恼 rěnǎo　make sb. angry; offend

惹气 rěqì　get angry: 不值得为这点小事～。It's senseless to get angry over such a trifle.

惹事 rěshì　stir up trouble; make trouble: 没看见我正忙着吗?还净给我～。Can't you see how busy I am? And still all you do is make trouble for me.

惹是非 rě shìfēi　provoke a dispute; stir up trouble

惹是生非 rěshì-shēngfēi　provoke a dispute; stir up trouble: 他是一个怕～的人。He was the kind of man who would avoid becoming involved in tittle-tattle at all costs.

惹眼 rěyǎn　*dial.* conspicuous; showy

rè

热 (熱)

热　rè　① heat: 摩擦产生～。Friction produces heat. ② hot: ～水 hot water / 三伏天很～。During the dogdays it's very hot. ③ heat up; warm up; warm: 把汤～一～ heat up the soup ④ fever; temperature: 这孩子有～。The child is running a fever. ⑤ ardent; warmhearted: 亲热 qīnrè ⑥ craze; fad: 卡拉 OK～

intense popular interest in karaoke; karaoke craze / 旅游～ travel craze ⑦ envious; eager: 眼热 yǎnrè ⑧ in great demand; popular: ～货 goods in great demand; goods which sell well ⑨ thermal; thermo-: 热中子 rèzhōngzǐ / 热核 rèhé

热爱 rè'ài　ardently love; have deep love (*or* affection) for: ～自己的工作 love one's work / ～人民 have deep love for the people / 他从小就～科学。He has loved science since childhood. / ～生活 have a keen sense of the joy of life; enjoy the pleasures of life with gusto

热拔 rèbá　*mech.* hot drawing

热病 rèbìng　*Chin. med.* acute disease accompanied by fever

热补 rèbǔ　vulcanize (tyre, etc.)

热肠 rècháng　warmhearted; enthusiastic

热潮 rècháo　great mass fervour; upsurge: 生产～ a great upsurge in production / 掀起群众性体育锻炼的～ unfold a vigorous mass campaign for sports and physical training / 新生一入校就投入了学习的～。As soon as the new students entered school, they enthusiastically threw themselves into their studies.

热忱 rèchén　zeal; warmheartedness; enthusiasm and devotion: 革命～ revolutionary zeal / 对同志对人民极端的～ extreme warmheartedness towards one's comrades and the people / ～地致敬 warmly pay tribute to sb.; send warm regards to sb.

热诚 rèchéng　warm and sincere; cordial: ～欢迎 cordially welcome / ～地希望 sincerely hope / 张先生一向对人～。Mr. Zhang is always warm and sincere towards others.

热赤道 rèchìdào　thermal equator; heat equator

热处理 rèchǔlǐ　*mech.* heat (*or* thermal) treatment: ～钢 heat-treated steel

热处理炉 rèchǔlǐlú　heat-treated furnace

热脆性 rècuìxìng　*metall.* hot-shortness; red-shortness

热带 rèdài　the torrid zone; the tropics: ～风暴 tropical storm / ～气旋 tropical cyclone; tropical revolving storm / ～植物 tropical plant / ～作物 tropical crops

热带草原 rèdài cǎoyuán　savanna

热带鱼 rèdàiyú　tropical fish

热导体 rèdǎotǐ　*phys.* heat conductor

热得快 rèdekuài　immersion heater; element

热点 rèdiǎn　① hot spot: 旅游～ a tourist hot spot ② *phys.* hot spot ③ central issue; point at issue: 讨论的～ focus of discussion ④ arousing general interest: ～问题 a topic of general interest

热电 rèdiàn　*phys.* pyroelectricity; thermoelectricity

热电厂 rèdiànchǎng　heat and power plant

热电偶 rèdiàn'ǒu　thermocouple

热电体 rèdiàntǐ　pyroelectrics

热电效应 rèdiàn xiàoyìng　pyroelectric effect

热电学 rèdiànxué　pyroelectricity

热电阻 rèdiànzǔ　thermal resistance

热度 rèdù　① degree of heat; heat: 物体燃烧需要一定的～。The burning of an object requires a certain degree of heat. ② *inf.* fever; temperature: 你～降下去了吗? Has your temperature come down?

热风炉 rèfēnglú　*metall.* hot-blast stove

热敷 rèfū　*med.* hot compress

热辐射 rèfúshè　*phys.* heat (*or* thermal) radiation

热功当量 règōng dāngliàng　*phys.* mechanical equivalent of heat

热狗 règǒu　hot dog

热固塑料 règù sùliào　thermosetting plastic

热管 règuǎn　heat pipe

热锅上蚂蚁 règuōshang mǎyǐ　an ant on a hot pan—restless: 他等着选举的结果, 像～。He was waiting for the results of the elections, restless as an ant on a hot pan.

热函 rèhán　another name for 焓 hán

热合 rèhé　heat seal

热核 rèhé　thermonuclear: ～爆炸 thermonuclear explosion

热核弹头 rèhédàntóu　thermonuclear warhead

热核反应 rèhé fǎnyìng　*phys.* thermonuclear reaction: 受控～ controlled thermonuclear reaction

热核反应堆 rèhé fǎnyìngduī　*phys.* thermonuclear reactor

热核技术 rèhé jìshù　thermonucleonics

热核武器 rèhé wǔqì　thermonuclear weapon

热烘烘 rèhōnghōng　very warm: 炉火很旺, 屋里～的。 With the stove burning cheerfully, it's very warm in the room. ／天热极了, 风吹过来都使人感到～的。 It's so hot that even the wind feels hot.

热乎乎 rèhūhū　(also 热呼呼 rèhūhū)　warm: 他的手～的。 His hands are warm. ／心里感到～的 feel it heartwarming

热乎 rèhu　(also 热呼 rèhu)　same as 热和 rèhuo

热火朝天 rèhuǒ cháotiān　buzzing (or bustling) with activity; in full swing: 工地上一派～的景象。 The construction site was bustling with activity. ／劳动竞赛正搞得～。 The emulation is now in full swing.

热火 rèhuo　① showing tremendous enthusiasm; exciting: 咱们厂的社会主义劳动竞赛搞得真～。 The socialist emulation drive in our factory is really lively. ／广场上锣鼓喧天, 场面可～啦! The square, resounding with the roll and clang of music, presented a scene of noisy hilarity. ② same as 热和 rèhuo

热和 rèhuo　*inf.*　① nice and warm; warm: 饭菜还～。 The food is still warm. ／炕上真～。 The *kang* is warm and cosy. ② warm and friendly; pally; chummy; thick: 他们一见面就很～。 They chummed up with each other the moment they met. ／他们谈得很～。 They had a very agreeable chat.

热机 rèjī　*mech.*　heat engine

热寂 rèjì　*phys.*　heat death

热加工 rèjiāgōng　*metall.*　hot-working; hot work

热扩散 rèkuòsàn　*phys.*　thermal diffusion

热辣辣 rèlālā　burning hot; scorching: 太阳晒得人～的。 The sun feels scorching hot. ／他听了大家的批评, 觉得脸上～的。 After hearing everybody's criticism, he felt his cheeks burning.

热浪 rèlàng　*meteorol.*　heat wave; hot wave

热泪 rèlèi　hot tears; tears of joy, sorrow or gratitude: 她激动得两眼含着～。 She was so moved that hot tears filled her eyes.

热泪盈眶 rèlèi yíng kuàng　one's eyes brimming with tears

热力 rèlì　*mech.*　heating power

热力学 rèlìxué　thermodynamics

热恋 rèliàn　be passionately in love; be head over heels in love

热量 rèliàng　*phys.*　quantity of heat: ～单位 thermal (or heat) unit

热量计 rèliàngjì　calorimeter

热烈 rèliè　warm; enthusiastic; animated: ～的祝贺 warm congratulations ／～欢迎 warmly welcome ／～欢送 give sb. a warm send-off ／～进行～的讨论 have a lively discussion ／～欢呼代表大会的胜利召开! Warmly hail the successful convening of the Congress! ／～的掌声 warm applause ／大家对她的建议反应很～。 Everybody responded enthusiastically to her proposal. ／会上发言很～。 There was an animated discussion at the meeting.

热裂化 rèlièhuà　*petroleum*　thermal cracking

热流 rèliú　① *meteorol.* thermal current ② warm current: 我感到一股～传遍全身。 I felt a warm current coursing through my body.

热门 rèmén　arousing popular interest; popular: 赶～ follow a craze ／～学科 a popular subject of study ／～话题 a subject of great topical interest; a topical subject

热门货 rèménhuò　goods which are in great demand or sell well; hot item: 彩电供不应求, 成了～。 The supply of colour TV sets can't keep up with the demand. They've become a hot item.

热敏电阻 rèmǐn diànzǔ　*elec.*　thermal resistor; thermistor

热闹 rènao　① lively; bustling with noise and excitement: ～的菜市场 a food market bustling with activity; a busy food market ／晚会很～。 It was a very lively evening party. ／大家热热闹闹玩了个痛快。 Everyone had a terrific time. ② liven up; have a jolly time: 你说个笑话让大伙儿～～吧。 Tell us a joke to liven things up. ／那天他们聚在一起～了一番。 That day they got together and had a jolly time. ③ a scene of bustle and excitement; a thrilling sight: 节日里街上有～看。 There will be lots of fun to watch in the streets during the holidays. ——see also 看热闹 kàn rènao

热能 rènéng　*phys.*　heat (or thermal) energy

热喷喷 rèpēnpēn　steaming hot

热气 rèqì　steam; heat: 壶里开始冒～了。 The kettle's just on the boil. ／人多～高, 干劲大。 More people mean more enthusiasm and more energy.

热气腾腾 rèqì téngténg　① steaming hot: ～的馒头 steaming hot buns ② seething with activity: 春耕生产搞得～。 The spring ploughing is going full steam ahead.

热切 rèqiè　fervent; earnest: ～的愿望 earnest wish; fervent hope ／～希望各位提出宝贵意见。 We earnestly hope that you will give us your valuable criticisms and suggestions.

热情 rèqíng　① enthusiasm; zeal; warmth: 爱国～ patriotic zeal ／工作～ enthusiasm for work ／他充满～地陈述了自己的意见。 He expressed his views with a great deal of warmth. ② warm; fervent; enthusiastic; warmhearted: ～接待 warmly receive; give sb. a warm reception ／～支持这个倡议 fervently (or enthusiastically) support this proposal ／对旅客非常～ be very warm towards the passengers ／～的字句 warm words ／他十分爽直～。 He is very frank and warmhearted.

热情奔放 rèqíng bēnfàng　bubbling with enthusiasm

热情洋溢 rèqíng yángyì　permeated (or brimming) with warm feeling; glowing with enthusiasm: 一封～的感谢信 a warm letter of thanks ／～的讲话 a speech brimming with warm feeling

热丧 rèsāng　be in mourning (for the recent death of one's father or mother)

热身赛 rèshēnsài　*sports*　warm-up game

热释光 rèshìguāng　*archaeol.*　thermoluminescence (TL) (an archaeological dating technique)

热水袋 rèshuǐdài　hot-water bottle (or bag)

热水瓶 rèshuǐpíng　*inf.*　thermos bottle (or flask); thermos; vacuum bottle (or flask)

热水器 rèshuǐqì　hot water heater; geyser: 电(燃气)～ electric (gas) geyser

热塑塑料 rèsù sùliào　thermoplastic

热塑性 rèsùxìng　*chem.*　thermoplasticity

热汤面 rètāngmiàn　noodles in hot soup

热腾腾 rèténgténg　steaming hot: ～的汤面 steaming hot noodles in soup ／太阳落了山, 地上还是～的。 The sun had set, but the ground was still very hot.

热天 rètiān　hot weather; hot season; hot days

热望 rèwàng　fervently hope; ardently wish

热线[1] rèxiàn　another name for 红外线 hóngwàixiàn

热线[2] rèxiàn　hot line

热象仪 rèxiàngyí　*electron.*　thermal imaging system

热销 rèxiāo (of goods) sell well; be in great demand

热孝 rèxiào (usu. used in) ～在身 wear mourning for one's grandparents, parents, or husband

热心 rèxīn enthusiastic; ardent; earnest; warmhearted: 他对集体福利事业向来很～。He's always been enthusiastic in promoting public welfare. / ～为顾客服务 warmheartedly serve the customers / ～科学 eager to promote science / ～传授技术 make earnest efforts to pass on one's skill/ 张大妈待人真～。Aunt Zhang has a warm heart.

热心肠 rèxīncháng inf. ① warmheartedness ② a warmhearted (or sympathetic) and helpful person

热性肥料 rèxìng féiliào agric. hot manure

热学 rèxué heat (a branch of physics)

热血 rèxuè warm blood—righteous ardour: ～青年 ardent youth / 甘洒～为人民 be ready to shed one's blood for the people

热血动物 rèxuè dòngwù warm-blooded animal; warm blood

热血沸腾 rèxuè fèiténg one's blood boils; burning with righteous indignation

热压 rèyā chem. hot pressing

热罨 rèyǎn same as 热敷 rèfū

热药 rèyào Chin. med. medicines of a hot or warm nature; tonics and stimulants

热饮 rèyǐn hot drink

热源 rèyuán phys. heat source

热轧 rèzhá metall. hot-rolling: ～机 hot-rolling mill

热战 rèzhàn hot war; shooting war

热障 rèzhàng phys. heat barrier

热证 rèzhèng Chin. med. heat symptom-complex; febrile symptoms

热值 rèzhí phys. calorific value

热中 rèzhōng (also 热衷 rèzhōng) ① hanker after; crave: ～于个人名利 hanker after personal fame and gain ② be fond of; be keen on: ～于溜冰 be very fond of skating / ～于跳迪斯科 be crazy about disco dancing

热中子 rèzhōngzǐ phys. thermal neutron

rén

人 rén ① human being; person; people: 昨天有三个～来找你。Three people came to see you yesterday./ 他家有几口～? How many people are there in his family? / 今天星期天, 商店里～很多。Today is Sunday. The stores are full of people./ ～对自然界的认识 man's knowledge of nature / 团结得像一个～ (of many people) be united as one ② an adult human being: 成人 chéngrén ③ other people; other(s): 自己做错了事, 不应该怪～。When one has done something wrong one should not blame it on others. / 这个座位有～吗? Is this seat occupied (or taken)? / 我听～说你结婚了。I hear that you've got married. / 他待～诚恳。He's sincere in his dealings with people. ④ (used rhetorically in place of the first personal pronoun, often expressing displeasure): 别小看～! Don't look down on me! / 真叫～着急。It really worries me. ⑤ a person considered as a worker or employee: 我们这里正缺～。We are shorthanded at the moment. ⑥ the physical, psychological, or moral quality or condition of a given individual: 你一个～行吗? Can you manage on your own? / 他～很好。He's a very nice man. / 他～老实。He's an honest man. / 她身体不错, ～也能干。She's healthy, and capable as well. / 这两天我～不太舒服。I haven't been feeling very well lately. / 她发烧发得～都胡涂了。Her fever was so high that she got delirious. / 只要她～好, 漂亮不漂亮没关系。So long as she has a nice personal-ity, it makes no difference whether she is pretty or not. / 他～在那儿, 心可想着别的事。He was there all right, but his mind was elsewhere. ⑦ everybody; each; all: ～所共知 be known to everybody (or all) ⑧ (used as a suffix): 四川～ a native of Sichuan／工～ worker

人儿 rénr ① figurine ② dial. personality; character: 他～很不错。He's a very nice man.

人本主义 rénběnzhǔyì philos. humanism

人不犯我, 我不犯人 rén bù fàn wǒ, wǒ bù fàn rén if others let me alone, I'll let them alone: ～; 人若犯我, 我必犯人。We will not attack unless we are attacked; if we are attacked, we will certainly counterattack.

人不可以貌相 rén bùkě yǐ mào xiàng never judge a person by his appearance; you can't judge people by appearances

人不为己, 天诛地灭 rén bù wèi jǐ, tiānzhū-dìmiè unless a man looks out for himself, Heaven and Earth will destroy him; everyone for himself and the devil take the hindmost

人不知, 鬼不觉 rén bùzhī, guǐ bùjué without a soul knowing anything about it

人才 réncái (also 人材 réncái) ① a person of ability; a talented person; talent; qualified personnel: 难得的～ a person of extraordinary ability / 科技～ qualified scientists and technicians / 管理～ management personnel ② inf. handsome appearance: 有几分～ be rather good-looking

人才辈出 réncái bèichū people of talent coming forth in large numbers

人才出众 réncái chūzhòng a person of exceptional ability or striking appearance

人才荟萃 réncái huìcuì a galaxy of talent

人才济济 réncái jǐjǐ an abundance of capable people; a galaxy of talent

人才流动 réncái liúdòng flow (or mobility) of trained personnel

人才外流 réncái wàiliú brain drain

人财两空 réncái liǎng kōng lose both a person and money (as a man does when his mistress runs away from him with his money and valuables)

人潮 réncháo stream of people

人臣 rénchén minister; subject

人称 rénchēng gram. person: 第一～ the first person / 不定～ indefinite person

人称代词 rénchēng dàicí gram. personal pronoun

人次 réncì m. person-time: 参观展览会的总共约有二十万～。Admissions to the exhibition totalled about two hundred thousand.

人丛 réncóng crowd (of people)

人大 Réndà (short for 全国人民代表大会) the National People's Congress

人大常委会 Réndà Chángwěihuì the Standing Committee of the National People's Congress

人大代表 Réndà dàibiǎo a deputy to the National People's Congress

人道[1] réndào ① humanity; human sympathy ② human; humane: 战俘应受到～待遇。Prisoners of war should receive humane treatment.

人道[2] réndào euph. (usu. used in the negative) man's sexual ability: 不能～ be impotent

人道主义 réndàozhǔyì humanitarianism: ～干涉 humanitarian intervention

人地生疏 rén-dì shēngshū be unfamiliar with the place and the people; be a complete stranger

人丁 réndīng population; number of people in a family

人丁兴旺 réndīng xīngwàng have a growing family; have a flourishing population

人定胜天 rén dìng shèng tiān man can conquer nature; man will triumph over nature

人堆儿　rénduīr　*inf.*　crowd (of people)

人多势众　rén duō shì zhòng　overwhelm with numerical strength; dominate by sheer force of numbers

人多嘴杂　rén duō zuǐ zá　many people, many words; the more people, the more talk

人而无信,不知其可　rén ér wú xìn, bù zhī qí kě　if a man does not keep his word, what is he good for?

人犯　rénfàn　*old*　the accused or people implicated in a crime: 一干～ the defendants and the implicated

人贩子　rénfànzi　trader in human beings

人防　rénfáng　short for 人民防空 rénmín fángkōng

人非木石　rén fēi mù-shí　man is not made of wood or stone—man is not feelingless

人非圣贤,孰能无过　rén fēi shèngxián, shú néng wú guò　men are not saints, how can they be free from faults; to err is human

人份　rénfèn　*m.*　person-portion; person-share: 麻疹疫苗三十万～ doses of measles vaccines for 300,000 persons

人粪尿　rénfènniào　*agric.*　night soil; human wastes (*or* excrement)

人逢喜事精神爽　rén féng xǐshì jīngshén shuǎng　joy puts heart into a man

人浮于事　rén fú yú shì　more staff (*or* hands) than needed; overstaffed

人格　réngé　① personality; character; moral quality: ～高尚 have a noble character; have moral integrity ② human dignity: 污辱～ insult human dignity / 这事千真万确,我以～担保。On my honour, I swear it is true.

人格化　réngéhuà　personify

人工　réngōng　① man-made; artificial: 人工湖 réngōng-hú ② manual work; work done by hand: 抽水机坏了,只好用～车水。We had to move water by a chain pump because the electric pump had broken down. ③ manpower; man-day: 修建这条渠道不需要很多～。It won't take a lot of manpower to construct this irrigation canal. / 修这所房子用了多少～? How many man-days were put in on repairing the house?

人工繁殖　réngōng fánzhí　*agric.*　artificial propagation

人工放顶　réngōng fàngdǐng　*min.*　artificial caving

人工孵化　réngōng fūhuà　artificial incubation

人工更新　réngōng gēngxīn　*forestry*　artificial regeneration

人工合成蛋白质　réngōng héchéng dànbáizhì　synthetic protein

人工合成结晶胰岛素　réngōng héchéng jiéjīng yídǎosù　synthetic crystalline insulin

人工呼吸　réngōng hūxī　artificial respiration: 用～进行抢救 use artificial respiration to save a patient

人工湖　réngōnghú　man-made lake

人工降水　réngōng jiàngshuǐ　artificial precipitation

人工降雨　réngōng jiàngyǔ　artificial rainfall: ～装置 artificial rain device; sprinkler

人工流产　réngōng liúchǎn　induced abortion

人工免疫　réngōng miǎnyì　artificial immunization

人工气腹　réngōng qìfù　*med.*　(artificial) pneumoperitoneum

人工气胸　réngōng qìxiōng　*med.*　(artificial) pneumothorax

人工器官　réngōng qìguān　artificial organ

人工肾　réngōngshèn　artificial kidney

人工授粉　réngōng shòufěn　*agric.*　artificial pollination

人工授精　réngōng shòujīng　*animal husbandry*　artificial insemination

人工心肺机　réngōng xīnfèijī　heart-lung machine

人工选择　réngōng xuǎnzé　*biol.*　artificial selection

人工智能　réngōng zhìnéng　artificial intelligence

人公里　réngōnglǐ　*m.*　passenger-kilometre

人海　rénhǎi　a sea of faces; a huge crowd (of people):

茫茫～ a blurry sea of faces; a vast sea of people

人和　rénhé　human unity; support of the people; unity and coordination within one's own ranks: 天时不如地利,地利不如。(《孟子》) Heaven's favourable weather is less important than Earth's advantageous terrain, and Earth's advantageous terrain is less important than human unity.

人话　rénhuà　*offens.*　human speech: sensible talk: 你怎么不说～? Aren't you capable of human speech? / 他这还算～。What he says is at least human speech.

人欢马叫　rénhuān-mǎjiào　people bustling and horses neighing—a busy, prosperous country scene

人寰　rénhuán　*formal*　the human world; man's world; the world: 惨绝人寰 cǎn jué rénhuán

人祸　rénhuò　man-made calamity

人给家足　rénjǐ-jiāzú　same as 家给人足 jiājǐ-rénzú

人际关系　rénjì guānxi　interpersonal relationships

人迹　rénjì　human footmarks (*or* footprints); traces of human presence: 我在这原始森林里走了三天三夜,不见～。I walked in the primeval forest for three days and nights without seeing any traces of human presence.

人迹罕至　rénjì hǎnzhì　without human trace; uninhabited; untraversed: ～的地区 an untraversed region

人家　rénjiā　① household; family: 这个村子有百十户～。There are a hundred or so families in this village. / 那条路上找不到一家～。No house can be seen on that road. / 勤俭～ an industrious and frugal family / 清白～ a family of blameless character ② the family of a girl's *fiancé*: 她有了～儿了。She is engaged to be married.

人家　rénjia　① a person or persons other than the speaker or hearer: ～都不怕,就你怕。No one else is afraid. It's only you who are afraid. / ～能做到的,我们也能做到。What other people can do we can do, too. *or* If other people can do it, so can we. / 别叫～笑话你。Don't make the others laugh at you. / ～的事情咱们用不着管。We needn't bother about others' affairs. / 玉梅这姑娘最热心,～的事就是她自己的事。That girl Yumei is really warmhearted, she treats other people's problems as if they were her own. / ～都这么说。That's what everybody says. ② (with the person or persons referred to in a near context, roughly equivalent to the third personal pronoun): 把信给～送去。Take the letter to him (her, them). / 小高正在写工作小结呢,～哪儿有时间陪你出去? Xiao Gao is writing his work-summary, how can he have time to go out with you now? / 我问过好几个大夫,～都说这个病不要紧。I've consulted several doctors, and they all say that this illness is nothing to worry about. ③ (used before a nominal expression, usu. with liveliness of feeling): ～小王年纪也不大呀! 学习总是全班第一。That Xiao Wang is really young, but he's always the best student in his class. / 说干活,咱们可比不上～年轻的。As for work, we can't compare with those young people. ④ (used rhetorically in place of the first personal pronoun, often playfully expressing displeasure): 你走慢点儿行不行,～跟不上啊! Would you slow down? I can't keep up! / 原来是你呀,差点儿没把～吓死! Oh, it's only you! You almost scared me to death. / 你让我给你借小说,～借来了,你又不看。You had me borrow a novel for you, but after I borrowed it, you wouldn't even read it.

人尖子　rénjiānzi　(also 人尖儿 rénjiānr) an outstanding figure; a distinguished individual

人间　rénjiān　the human world; man's world; the world: ～乐园 earthly paradise; paradise on earth / ～奇迹 a man-made miracle / 此曲只应天上有,～能得几回闻? (杜甫) But this song should only belong to heaven, Among mortals how seldom can it be heard!

人间地狱　rénjiān dìyù　a hell on earth

人间天堂 rénjiān tiāntáng heaven on earth

人杰 rénjié *formal* an outstanding personality

人杰地灵 rénjié-dìlíng the greatness of a man lends glory to a place

人尽其才 rén jìn qí cái make the best possible use of men: ～, 地尽其利, 物尽其用。 Our human, land and material resources should be used to the best advantage.

人均 rénjūn per capita: ～耕地面积 per capita area of cultivated farmland / ～住房面积 the average per capita living space / ～国民收入 per capita national income / ～国民生产总值 per capita gross national product (GNP)

人君 rénjūn prince; ruler

人客 rénkè *dial.* guest: 做～ be sb.'s guest; call on sb.

人孔 rénkǒng *archit.* manhole

人口 rénkǒu ① population: ～稠密的地区 densely populated area; thickly inhabited district / ～众多 (稀少) have a very large (a sparse) population / 这个地区的～有一百三十多万。 This district has a population of more than 1.3 million. ② number of people in a family: 他们家～不多。 There aren't many people in their family.

人口爆炸 rénkǒu bàozhà population explosion

人口动态统计 rénkǒu dòngtài tǒngjì vital statistics

人口动态学 rénkǒu dòngtàixué population dynamics

人口分布 rénkǒu fēnbù population distribution

人口过剩 rénkǒu guòshèng over population

人口基数 rénkǒu jīshù population base

人口结构 rénkǒu jiégòu population structure

人口金字塔 rénkǒu jīnzìtǎ population pyramid

人口老化 rénkǒu lǎohuà aging of population

人口密度 rénkǒu mìdù density of population; population density

人口普查 rénkǒu pǔchá (population) census

人口统计 rénkǒu tǒngjì population statistics

人口统计学 rénkǒu tǒngjìxué (also 人口学 rénkǒuxué) demography

人口增长 rénkǒu zēngzhǎng population growth

人口质量 rénkǒu zhìliàng population quality

人口自然增长率 rénkǒu zìrán zēngzhǎnglǜ natural growth rate of population

人口组成 rénkǒu zǔchéng population composition

人困马乏 rénkùn-mǎfá the men weary, their steeds spent—tired out; exhausted: 在地里干了一天, 大家都～。 After a hard day's work in the fields, they were completely exhausted.

人来疯 rénláifēng *dial.* (of a child) show off his liveliness before visitors

人老珠黄不值钱 rénlǎo-zhūhuáng bù zhíqián in old age, one is like a pearl whose lustre has faded—no longer held in esteem

人类 rénlèi mankind; humanity: ～起源 the origin of mankind; the origin of the human species / ～解放事业 the emancipation of mankind / ～征服自然的斗争 man's struggle to conquer nature / ～进步 human progress

人类学 rénlèixué anthropology

人力 rénlì manpower; labour power: ～资源 human resources / 用机械代替～ replace manpower with machines / 非～所及 be beyond human power

人力车 rénlìchē ① a two-wheeled vehicle drawn or pushed by a man ② *old* rickshaw

人流 rénliú ① stream of people: 不尽的～涌向天安门广场。 An endless stream of people swarmed towards Tian'anmen Square. ② short for 人工流产 réngōng liúchǎn

人伦 rénlún human relations (according to feudal ethics)

人马 rénmǎ forces; troops: 全部～已安全渡江。 All the troops have crossed the river safely. / 大队～随后就到。 The main force will arrive soon. / 我们编辑部的～比较整齐。 Our editorial department is well-staffed.

人马座 Rénmǎzuò *astron.* Sagittarius

人满为患 rén mǎn wéihuàn overcrowded with people; overstaffed

人们 rénmen people; men; the public: 草原上的～ people of the grasslands / ～都说她能干。 People say she is very capable.

人面兽心 rénmiàn-shòuxīn the face of a man but the heart of a beast—a beast in human form

人面桃花 rénmiàn-táohuā her face and the peach-blossoms—the pinings of a lover (from Cui Hu's 崔护 quatrain: 去年今日此门中, ～相映红。人面不知何处去, 桃花依旧笑春风。 Last year, on this day, inside this door, Her face and the peach-blossoms reflected each other's redness. Where is her face now? The peach-blossoms still smile in the spring wind.)

人民 rénmín the people

人民币 rénmínbì Renminbi (RMB, Chinese monetary unit)

人民大会堂 Rénmín Dàhuìtáng the Great Hall of the People

人民代表大会 rénmín dàibiǎo dàhuì people's congress

人民法院 rénmín fǎyuàn people's court: ～院长 president of the people's court

人民防空 rénmín fángkōng people's air defence; civil air defence

人民公社 rénmín gōngshè people's commune

人民检察院 rénmín jiǎncháyuàn people's procuratorate: ～检察长 chief procurator of the people's procuratorate

人民警察 rénmín jǐngchá the people's police

人民来信 rénmín láixìn letters from the masses

人民民主专政 rénmín mínzhǔ zhuānzhèng people's democratic dictatorship

人民内部矛盾 rénmín nèibù máodùn contradictions among the people

人民陪审员 rénmín péishěnyuán *leg.* people's assessor

人民群众 rénmín qúnzhòng the masses

人民日报 Rénmín Rìbào *Renmin Ribao; The People's Daily*

人民团体 rénmín tuántǐ mass organization; people's organization

人民武装部 rénmín wǔzhuāngbù people's armed forces department (of a county, etc.)

人民性 rénmínxìng (in literary and artistic works) popular or folk character; feeling for the people; affinity to the people: 有的现代评论家认为, 李煜的词具有一定的～。 According to some modern critics, Li Yu's *ci* poems evince a certain affinity to the people.

人民英雄纪念碑 rénmín yīngxióng jìniànbēi the Monument to the People's Heros (partically referring to the one in Tian'anmen Square in Beijing)

人民战争 rénmín zhànzhēng people's war

人民阵线 rénmín zhènxiàn popular front

人民政府 rénmín zhèngfǔ the People's Government

人命 rénmìng human life: ～案子 a case of homicide or manslaughter / 一条～ a violent death

人命关天 rénmìng guān tiān a case involving human life is one of supreme importance: ～, 非同儿戏。 Taking someone's life is a serious crime, it's no joking matter.

人命危浅, 朝不虑夕 rénmìng wēi qiǎn, zhāo bù lǜ xī be sinking fast; be dying

人莫予毒 rén mò yú dú no one dare harm me—be supercilious

人怕出名猪怕壮 rén pà chūmíng zhū pà zhuàng fame

portends trouble for men just as fattening does for pigs

人配衣服马配鞍 rén pèi yīfu mǎ pèi ān clothes make the man as the saddle makes the horse; clothes make the man

人品 rénpǐn ① moral standing; moral quality; character: ～很好 be a person of excellent character ② *inf.* looks; bearing

人弃我取 rénqì-wǒqǔ I pick up what others discard—I have my own views and tastes

人强马壮 rénqiáng-mǎzhuàng both men and horses strong—① a strong, combat effective army ② a strong working force

人墙 rénqiáng *football* wall: 筑～ set a wall

人琴俱亡 rén-qín jù wáng the man and his lute are both dead (a lament for the death of a friend, originally uttered by Wang Huizhi 王徽之 of the Jin Dynasty when he took up the lute of his dead brother Wang Xianzhi 王献之 and could not make it come into tune)

人勤地不懒 rén qín dì bù lǎn where the tiller is tireless the land is fertile

人情 rénqíng ① human feelings; human sympathy; sensibilities: 他很重～，朋友的事总是愿意帮忙。 He sets a great store on friendship, and is always willing to help his friends. ② human relationships: ～之常 be natural and normal (in human relationships) ③ favour: 做个～ do sb. a favour / 空头～ an empty promise ④ gift; present ——see also 送人情 sòng rénqíng; 托人情 tuō rénqíng

人情冷暖 rénqíng lěngnuǎn social snobbery

人情练达 rénqíng liàndá experienced in the ways of the world: 世事洞明皆学问，～即文章。《红楼梦》A grasp of mundane affairs is genuine knowledge, Worldly wisdom is true learning.

人情世故 rénqíng-shìgù worldly wisdom: 不懂～ not know the ways of the world; not know how to deal with people

人情味 rénqíngwèi human touch; human interest: 他这个人，一点～都没有。 That chap! He has no human feelings whatsoever. / 这故事很有～。 The story is warmly human.

人情债 rénqíngzhài a debt of gratitude

人穷志不短 rén qióng zhì bù duǎn poor but proud; poor but ambitious

人穷志短 rén qióng zhì duǎn poverty chills ambition

人权 rénquán human rights; rights of man

人权宣言 Rénquán Xuānyán ① short for 人权与公民权宣言 Rénquán Yǔ Gōngmínquán Xuānyán ② short for 世界人权宣言 Shìjiè Rénquán Xuānyán

人权与公民权宣言 Rénquán Yǔ Gōngmínquán Xuānyán (in French history) Declaration of the Rights of Man and of the Citizen (1789)

人群 rénqún crowd; throng; multitude

人人 rénrén everybody; everyone: ～都说这孩子机灵。 Everybody says the child is smart. / ～尽说江南好。(韦庄) Everybody is full of praise for the beauty of the South.

人人自危 rénrén zì wēi everyone finds himself in danger; everyone feels insecure

人日 rénrì the day for human beings (old name for the seventh day of the first month, on which if the weather is clear and bright, it is believed that human births will be prolific during the coming year)

人山人海 rénshān-rénhǎi huge crowds of people; a sea of people: 广场上～。 The square was a sea of people.

人身 rénshēn living body of a human being; person: ～不可侵犯 inviolability of the person

人身安全 rénshēn ānquán personal safety (*or* security)

人身保护令 rénshēn bǎohùlìng habeas corpus

人身保险 rénshēn bǎoxiǎn life insurance and insurance against accidents

人身攻击 rénshēn gōngjī personal attack

人身伤害 rénshēn shānghài personal injury

人身事故 rénshēn shìgù personal injury caused by an accident

人身自由 rénshēn zìyóu freedom of person; personal freedom

人参 rénshēn ginseng

人神共愤 rén-shén gòng fèn (of a great outrage) arouse the great indignation of both men and gods

人生 rénshēng life: ～旅程 life-long journey / ～两件宝，双手和大脑。 There are two treasures in human life—hands and brains. / 他没有什么崇高的～目的。 His aim in life is quite modest. *or* He has no great ambition in life.

人生地不熟 rén shēng dì bù shú be unfamiliar with the place and the people; be a stranger in a strange place

人生观 rénshēngguān outlook on life

人生七十古来稀 rénshēng qīshí gǔlái xī man's life from of old has rarely reached seventy; men who reach the age of seventy have always been a rarity

人生如寄 rénshēng rú jì man's life is like a traveller's stay

人生如梦 rénshēng rú mèng life is but a dream

人生一世，草生一春 rén shēng yī shì, cǎo shēng yī chūn man has but one life, grass sees but one spring; life is short

人生朝露 rénshēng zhāolù life is like the morning dew

人生哲学 rénshēng zhéxué philosophy of life

人声 rénshēng voice: 远处传来～。 Voices came from afar. *or* Voices were heard in the distance.

人声鼎沸 rénshēng dǐngfèi a hubbub of voices; a babel of voices

人士 rénshì personage; public figure: 爱国～ patriotic personage / 官方～ official quarters / 体育界～ figures in the sports world / 文艺界～ people of literary and art circles

人氏 rénshì people native to a place: 你是哪里～? Where do you come from? *or* What is your native place? / 当地～ a native-born

人世 rénshì this world; the world: 不在～ be no longer living; be no longer in the land of the living / 不久于～ be dying

人世沧桑 rénshì cāngsāng tremendous changes in this world of ours

人世间 rénshìjiān this world; the world: ～有苦也有乐。 In this world, there is happiness as well as suffering.

人事 rénshì ① human affairs; occurrences in human life ② personnel matters: ～调动 transfer of personnel / ～安排 arrangement of personnel / ～更迭 change of personnel ③ ways of the world: 不懂～ not know the ways of the world ④ consciousness of the outside world: 他昏迷过去，～不知。 He fainted and lost consciousness. ⑤ what is humanly possible: 尽～ do what is humanly possible; do one's best ⑥ *euph.* sexual awareness or passion; the facts of life: 渐省～ begin to have some understanding of the facts of life ⑦ *dial.* gift

人事处 rénshìchù personnel division

人事档案 rénshì dàng'àn personal file (*or* dossier)

人事关系 rénshì guānxi organizational affiliation

人事制度 rénshì zhìdù personnel system

人手 rénshǒu manpower; hand: ～太少 short of hands; shorthanded / ～已经够了，别派人去了。 They have enough hands. Don't send any more people there.

人手一册 rén shǒu yī cè everyone has a copy: 书不多不少，刚好～。 There are just enough books for everyone to have one copy, no more, no less.

人寿保险 rénshòu bǎoxiǎn life insurance

人寿年丰 rénshòu-niánfēng the land yields good crops and the people enjoy good health

人丝斜纹绸 rénsī xiéwénchóu rayon twill

人死如灯灭 rén sǐ rú dēng miè a man dies the way a lamp goes out

人梯 réntī ① human ladder (as used in assaulting a fortress) ② a person who helps another to rise to success: 他甘当～，言传身教，培养青年一代。He is devoted to educating the younger generation, teaching by precept and example, content to be, so to speak, a rung of the human ladder.

人体 réntǐ human body: ～模型 manikin

人同此心，心同此理 rén tóng cǐ xīn, xīn tóng cǐ lǐ on this matter people feel and think alike

人头 réntóu ① the number of people: 按～分 distribute according to the number of people ② relations with people: ～熟 know a lot of people ③ dial. moral quality; character: ～儿次 be not much of a person

人头税 réntóushuì poll tax; capitation

人望 rénwàng formal prestige; popularity

人微言轻 rénwēi-yánqīng the words of the lowly carry little weight

人为 rénwéi artificial; man-made: ～疆界线 artificial boundary line / ～的障碍 an artificially imposed obstacle / 这些困难完全是～的。These difficulties were purely man-made.

人为刀俎，我为鱼肉 rén wéi dāo-zǔ, wǒ wéi yú-ròu be meat on sb.'s chopping block—be at sb.'s mercy

人为地貌 rénwéi dìmào mil. culture features

人为嬗变 rénwéi shànbiàn phys. artificial transmutation

人为万物之灵 rén wéi wànwù zhī líng man of all creatures is the one endowed with intelligence

人为财死，鸟为食亡 rén wèi cái sǐ, niǎo wèi shí wáng men will die for wealth, as birds for food

人味儿 rénwèir humanness; humanity: 他竟连点～都没有。There's really nothing human about him. / 有了这个知心朋友，他才觉出点～。Not until he had this understanding friend did he have his first taste of warm humanity.

人文科学 rénwén kēxué the humanities; humane studies

人文主义 rénwénzhǔyì humanism

人无远虑，必有近忧 rén wú yuǎnlǜ, bì yǒu jìnyōu he who gives no thought to difficulties in the future is sure to be beset by worries much closer at hand

人五人六 rénwǔrénliù be affected; strike poses

人物 rénwù ① figure; personage: 领袖～ a leading personage; a leading public figure / 英雄～ a heroic figure; a hero or heroine / 历史上的伟大～ great historic figures / 杰出的～ an outstanding personage / 他也算个～了。He's quite a distinguished individual now. ② person in literature; character: 典型～ a typical character / ～塑造 characterization

人物表 rénwùbiǎo a list of characters (in a play or novel); characters

人物画 rénwùhuà figure painting

人物像 rénwùxiàng bust (sculpture)

人像 rénxiàng portrait; image; figure

人像靶 rénxiàngbǎ silhouette target

人心 rénxīn ① popular feeling; public feeling; the will of the people: ～安定。The public is quiet. ② human feelings; human reason: 他并不是没有～的人。He's not unfeeling. ——see also 得人心 dé rénxīn

人心不古 rénxīn bù gǔ public morality is not what it used to be (i.e. has degenerated)

人心不足蛇吞象 rénxīn bù zú shé tūn xiàng a man who rests content with nothing is like a snake trying to swallow an elephant

人心隔肚皮 rénxīn gé dùpí different hearts in different breasts—it's hard to tell what's going on in the minds of other people; people should always be on guard against one another

人心惶惶 rénxīn huánghuáng popular anxiety

人心齐，泰山移 rénxīn qí, Tàishān yí the people all working with one will can move Mount Tai; a people united can move mountains

人心如面 rénxīn rú miàn men's hearts are as different as are their faces

人心丧尽 rénxīn sàngjìn lose (or forfeit) all popular sympathy

人心所向 rénxīn suǒ xiàng popular sentiment; the feelings of the people: 这是～，大势所趋。This accords with the feelings of the people and the general trend of events. / 维护安定团结是～。To maintain stability and unity is the common aspiration of people everywhere.

人心向背 rénxīn xiàng-bèi whether the people are for or against; the feelings of the people

人行道 rénxíngdào pavement; sidewalk

人行横道 rénxíng héngdào pedestrian crosswalk; pedestrian crossing; zebra crossing

人性 rénxìng human nature; humanity: 具体的～ human nature in the concrete / 超阶级的～ human nature above classes

人性 rénxing normal human feelings; reason: 不通～ unfeeling and unreasonable

人性论 rénxìnglùn the theory of human nature

人熊 rénxióng inf. brown bear

人选 rénxuǎn person selected: 物色适当～ try to find a suitable person (for a job) / 决定秘书长的～ decide who is to be secretary-general / 他是可以考虑的～。He's an eligible candidate for the job.

人烟 rényān signs of human habitation: ～稀少 be sparsely populated / 没有～ uninhabited / 几十里不见～。No trace of human habitation could be seen for dozens of li.

人烟稠密 rényān chóumì densely populated; populous

人言可畏 rényán kě wèi the voice of the people is something to fear; gossip is a fearful thing

人言啧啧 rényán zézé there is a good deal of unfavourable comment

人仰马翻 rényǎng-mǎfān men and horses thrown off their feet—badly battered; thrown into confusion

人样 rényàng ① proper human appearance; proper behaviour: 脏得不像个～ be awfully dirty / 那孩子惯得一点～都没有。That child is terribly spoiled. ② a successful person: 不混出个～来，不要回来见我。Don't come back and see me until you've got something to show for your efforts.

人要脸，树要皮 rén yào liǎn, shù yào pí face is as important to man as the bark is to the tree

人以群分 rén yǐ qún fēn see 物以类聚 wù yǐ lèi jù

人影儿 rényǐngr ① the shadow of a human figure: 窗帘上有个～。Someone's silhouette appeared on the window curtain. ② the trace of a person's presence; figure: 她看见一个～在黑暗中消失了。She caught sight of a figure disappearing into the darkness. / 我等了半天，连个～也不见。I waited a long time but not a soul turned up.

人有脸，树有皮 rén yǒu liǎn, shù yǒu pí (also 人有面，树有皮 rén yǒu miàn, shù yǒu pí) a man has a face just as a tree has bark—a man has a sense of shame

人鱼 rényú popular name for 儒艮 rúgèn

人欲 rényù formal human desires

人欲横流 rényù héngliú unbridled indulgence of human desires and passions; universal decadence

人员 rényuán personnel; staff: 全体～ the entire per-

sonnel; the whole staff / 党政工作～ Party and government personnel / 机关工作～ office workers / ～不足 understaffed; undermanned

人缘儿 rényuánr　relations with people; popularity: ～好 be very popular; enjoy great popularity / 有～ enjoy great popularity

人猿 rényuán　anthropoid (ape)

人云亦云 rén yún yì yún　echo the views of others; have no views of one's own

人造 rénzào　man-made; artificial; imitation: ～宝石 artificial jewel; imitation jewel

人造冰 rénzàobīng　artificial ice

人造地球卫星 rénzào dìqiú wèixīng　artificial earth satellite; sputnik

人造革 rénzàogé　imitation (or artificial) leather; leatherette

人造黄油 rénzào huángyóu　margarine

人造毛 rénzàomáo　artificial wool; man-made feather

人造棉 rénzàomián　artificial cotton; staple rayon

人造丝 rénzàosī　artificial silk; rayon

人造卫星 rénzào wèixīng　man-made satellite

人造纤维 rénzào xiānwéi　man-made fibre

人造橡胶 rénzào xiàngjiāo　artificial rubber; synthetic rubber

人造羊毛 rénzào yángmáo　artificial wool

人证 rénzhèng　leg. testimony of a witness

人证物证 rénzhèng wùzhèng　leg. human testimony and material evidence: ～俱在 availability of eye-witnesses and material evidence

人之常情 rén zhī chángqíng　what is natural and normal (in human relationships): 父母为儿女前途操心，乃～。 It's natural for parents to be anxious about their children's future. / 初次相会，说话不多，也是～。 To say very little at the first meeting is natural and normal.

人之将死，其言也善 rén zhī jiāng sǐ, qí yán yě shàn　good are the words of a dying man: 鸟之将死，其鸣也哀；～。《论语》 Sad is the cry of a dying bird; good are the words of a dying man.

人治 rénzhì　rule by men (opp. 法治 fǎzhì)

人质 rénzhì　hostage: 把某人作～ take (or hold) sb. hostage / 释放～ free a hostage

人中 rénzhōng　the vertical groove on the median line of the upper lip; philtrum

人种 rénzhǒng　ethnic group; race

人种学 rénzhǒngxué　ethnology

人主 rénzhǔ　formal ruler of men—sovereign; emperor

人字呢 rénzìní　text. herringbone

人自为战 rén zì wéi zhàn　each man fighting all by himself

壬 rén　the ninth of the ten Heavenly Stems (天干)——see also 干支 gān-zhī

仁[1] rén　① benevolence; kindheartedness; humanity: ～者人也。《中庸》 Benevolence is humanity. / ～心 kindheartedness ② sensitive: 麻木不仁 mámù bù rén

仁[2] rén　kernel: 坚果的～儿多半可以吃。 The kernel of a nut is usually eatable.

仁爱 rén'ài　kindheartedness; benevolence; humanity

仁慈 réncí　benevolent; merciful; kind: ～的老人 a kind old man / ～的上帝 kind and merciful God / 对敌人～就是对人民残忍。 Mercy to the enemy means cruelty to the people.

仁德 réndé　kindheartedness; benevolence; humanity

仁弟 réndì　pol. (usu. used in a letter to a male friend younger than oneself or to a former male student) my

dear friend

仁厚 rénhòu　honest and kindhearted

仁人君子 rénrén-jūnzǐ　benevolent gentlemen; public-spirited people: 倘有～知其下落者，恳请捎信张家庄张老五。 Will those gentlemen who happen to know his whereabouts kindly send a message to Zhang Laowu at Zhang Village. / 希～慷慨解囊，共襄义举。 Public-spirited people are requested to make generous contributions in support of this nonprofit undertaking.

仁人志士 rénrén-zhìshì　same as 志士仁人 zhìshì-rénrén

仁兄 rénxiōng　pol. (usu. used in a letter to a male friend) my dear friend

仁义 rényì　benevolence and uprighteousness

仁义 rényi　dial. amiable; kind; reasonable

仁义道德 rényì-dàodé　humanity, justice and virtue; virtue and morality. 他是满口～，一肚子男盗女娼。 His speech is full of virtuous phrases, but in his heart is nothing but lust and cupidity.

仁者见仁，智者见智 rénzhě jiàn rén, zhìzhě jiàn zhì　the benevolent see benevolence and the wise see wisdom—different people have different views

仁政 rénzhèng　policy of benevolence; benevolent government: 施～ apply a policy of benevolence

仁至义尽 rénzhì-yìjìn　do everything called for by humanity and duty; do what is humanly possible to help; be magnanimous

任 Rén　a surname——see also rèn

rěn

忍 rěn　① bear; endure; tolerate; put up with: 相～相安 be tolerant towards and live in peace with one another / 他～着剧痛，继续工作。 He continued to work despite the intense pain. / 你就～着点吧。 You will just have to put up with it. / ～着眼泪 hold back one's tears ② be hardhearted enough to; have the heart to: 残忍 cánrěn

忍冬 rěndōng　bot. honeysuckle

忍饥挨饿 rěnjī-ái'è　endure the torments of hunger

忍俊不禁 rěnjùn bùjīn　cannot help laughing

忍耐 rěnnài　exercise patience; exercise restraint; restrain oneself: 你还是～一点吧，否则要吃亏的。 You'd better restrain yourself a little or you'll come to grief. / 见他这样无理取闹，我再也～不住了。 Seeing him deliberately making trouble like that, I simply couldn't keep my temper under control.

忍气吞声 rěnqì-tūnshēng　swallow an insult; submit to humiliation; stifle one's indignation: ～地过日子 manage to get by swallowing insults and humiliations

忍让 rěnràng　exercise forbearance; be forbearing and conciliatory

忍辱负重 rěnrǔ-fùzhòng　endure humiliation in order to carry out an important mission

忍辱含垢 rěnrǔ-hángòu　same as 含垢忍辱 hángòu-rěnrǔ

忍受 rěnshòu　bear; endure; stand: ～艰难困苦 endure hardships / 热得难以～ unbearably hot / 他说得这样刻薄，我无法～。 His caustic remarks was beyond my endurance.

忍痛 rěntòng　very reluctantly: ～牺牲 reluctantly give up / ～离去 reluctantly part from sb.

忍痛割爱 rěntòng gē'ài　part reluctantly with what one treasures: 文章太长，最后一段你必须～。 The article is much too long, so you must cut the last section however painful it may be.

忍无可忍 rěn wú kě rěn　be driven beyond (the limits

of) forbearance; come to the end of one's patience: 他们欺人太甚，我们～。Their provocations have gone beyond the limits of forbearance. / 他～，狠狠给了那家伙一巴掌。No longer able to contain himself, he gave the scoundrel a stinging slap.

忍心 rěnxīn have the heart to; be hardhearted enough to: 他不～拒绝他们的要求。He didn't have the heart to (or couldn't bear to) turn down their request. / 你把这个家扔下不管，你好～哪! You don't care about the family anymore. How can you be so hardhearted!

忍住 rěnzhù bear; endure: ～悲痛 bear sadness / 她真想哭，但还是～了。She was on the verge of crying but then held her tears back. / 把这鸡眼切除了吧，再疼我也忍得住。Please excise the corn. I can stand the pain. / 她～手指疼痛，继续打球。She went on spiking despite the pain in her fingers. / 他痒得几乎忍不住了。The itching was almost more than he could stand. / 她忍不住掉下了眼泪。She couldn't hold back her tears. / 他忍不住大笑起来。He couldn't help bursting into laughter.

荏¹ rěn another name for 白苏 báisū

荏² rěn formal weak; weak-kneed: 色厉内荏 sèlì-nèirěn

荏苒 rěnrǎn formal (of time) elapse quickly or imperceptibly; slip by: 光阴～，转瞬又是一年。Time zipped by and the year was soon over.

荏弱 rěnruò formal weak; feeble; delicate

稔 rěn formal ① harvest: 一年两～ two crops a year ② be familiar with sb.: ～知 know sb. quite well / 素～ have long been familiar with sb.

rèn

刃(刄) rèn ① the edge of a knife, sword, etc.; blade: 这刀没～儿了。This knife is blunt. or The knife has lost its edge. ② sword; knife: 利刃 lìrèn ③ kill with a sword or knife: 手刃 shǒurèn

刃具 rènjù mech. cutting tool

刃口 rènkǒu the edge of a knife, sword, etc.

认(認) rèn ① recognize; know; make out; identify: ～笔迹 try to recognize handwriting / 自己的东西，自己来～。Come and pick out your own things. / 他的字真难～。His handwriting is barely legible. or His handwriting is hard to read. ② enter into a certain relationship with; adopt: ～师傅 apprentice oneself to sb. / ～她作闺女 adopt her as a daughter ③ admit; recognize; own: 一个不是 offer an apology; apologize ④ undertake to do sth.: ～捐五十元 undertake to contribute 50 yuan; subscribe 50 yuan / ～公债 subscribe for (government) bonds ⑤ (followed by 了) accept as unavoidable; resign oneself to: 这东西一定得买，价钱贵一点我也～了。I simply must buy it, even if I have to pay a little more for it. / 这事是我吃亏，但我也～了。I've resigned myself to losing out this time.

认出 rènchū recognize; make out; identify: ～某人 recognize (or identify) a person / 她戴着那顶帽子，我没～她来。I didn't recognize her in that hat. / 她又病又老，模样变得都认不出来了。Illness and age had changed her appearance beyond recognition. / 我认得出他的笔迹。I recognize his handwriting.

认错 rèncuò acknowledge a mistake; admit a fault; offer (or make) an apology: 他既然～了，就原谅他一次吧。Since he has made an apology, forgive him just this once. / 给你妈认个错。Go and apologize to your mother.

认得 rènde know; recognize: 这位同志你～吗? Do you know this comrade? / 这地方我已经不～了。I can no longer recognize the place. / 你～回家的路吗? Can you find your way home?

认敌为友 rèn dí wéi yǒu take a foe for a friend

认定 rèndìng ① firmly believe; maintain; hold: 马克思主义者～，矛盾存在于一切事物的发展过程中。Marxists maintain that contradiction exists in the process of development of all things. ② set one's mind on: 既然～了目标，就要坚持不懈地干下去。Now that you've set your mind on the goal, you must go through with the task.

认罚 rènfá be ready to pay the penalty

认购 rèngòu offer to buy; subscribe: ～公债 subscribe for (government) bonds

认脚 rènjiǎo dial. put the right shoe on the right foot

认可 rènkě approve: 得到领导的～ be approved by the leadership / 点头～ nod approval

认领 rènlǐng claim: 拾得钱包一个，希望失主前来～。Found a purse. Will the owner please come to claim it. / 没有人来～这个走失的孩子。No one came to claim the lost child.

认命 rènmìng accept fate; resign oneself (or be resigned) to fate: 我总是不走运，只好～了。I'm always having bad luck! I suppose I'll just have to resign myself to fate.

认亲 rènqīn ① become related by marriage ② claim a family connection

认清 rènqīng see clearly; recognize; get a clear understanding of: ～形势 get a clear understanding of the situation / ～问题的性质 grasp the nature of the problem / ～是非 make a clear distinction between right and wrong / 我认不清是谁。I couldn't see clearly who it was. / 这两个字你认得清吗? Can you make out these two characters?

认人 rènrén (of a baby) can recognize people: 这孩子才三个多月，就开始～了。The baby is only a little over 3 months and it can already recognize people.

认生 rènshēng (of a child) be shy with strangers

认识 rènshi ① know; understand; recognize: 你在哪儿～她的? Where did you get to know her? / 他不～这种草药。He doesn't recognize this kind of medical herb. / ～世界，改造世界 understand the world and change it / ～自己的错误 see (or realize) one's mistake / 正确～当前的形势 have a correct understanding of the current situation ② understanding; knowledge; cognition: 感性(理性)～ perceptual (rational) knowledge / 我们都谈了对这件事的～。We all said what we thought about the matter.

认识过程 rènshi guòchéng process of cognition

认识论 rènshilùn theory of knowledge; epistemology

认识能力 rènshi nénglì cognitive ability

认识水平 rènshi shuǐpíng level of understanding

认输 rènshū admit defeat; throw in (or up) the sponge; give up

认死理 rèn sǐlǐ (also 认死扣儿 rèn sǐkòur) stubborn; as obstinate as a mule

认头 rèntóu resign oneself to a loss

认为 rènwéi think; consider; hold; deem: 大家～这个建议是可行的。We all think (or consider) this proposal feasible. / 你～怎样? What do you think of it? / 这件事我们～有必要跟你们说清楚。We deem it necessary to make this clear to you. / 你～这是真的吗? Do you believe it to be true? / 我们～，国家不分大小，应该一律平等。We hold that all nations, big or small, should be equal. / 五四运动被～是现代中国的一场文化和思想上的启蒙运动。The May 4th Movement was regarded as one of cultural and ideological enlightenment in modern China.

认贼作父 rèn zéi zuò fù　take the foe for one's father; regard the enemy as kith and kin

认帐 rènzhàng　acknowledge a debt (*or* an account); admit what one has said or done: 错了就要～。If you're wrong, you should admit it. / 自己说的话, 怎么不～? How can you go back upon your word?

认真[1] rènzhēn　conscientious; earnest; serious: ～对待 deal seriously with / 给予～的考虑 give serious consideration to / ～的自我批评 an earnest self-criticism / 他干什么都～。He is very conscientious in whatever he does. *or* He's a conscientious worker. / 办事不～ work half-heartedly / 进行～的研究 make a serious study

认真[2] rènzhēn　take seriouly; take to heart: 我是说着玩儿的, 你怎么就认起真来了? I was only joking. Why take it seriously (*or* to heart)?

认证 rènzhèng　*leg.* ① legalize; attest; authenticate: ～签字 attest a signature / ～文件 authenticated document / ～者 authenticator ② attestation; authentication

认准 rènzhǔn　set one's mind on

认字 rènzì　know or learn how to read: 我这个旧社会的文盲, 今天也～了。I was an illiterate in the old society, but now I can read. / 这孩子才五岁, 可他已经能认不少字了。The boy is only five, but he has already learned quite a few characters.

认罪 rènzuì　admit one's guilt; plead guilty: ～悔过 plead guilty and repent

仞 rèn　an ancient measure of length equal to seven or eight *chi* (尺)

任[1] rèn　① assign sb. to a post; appoint: 新～的厂长 the newly appointed director of the factory / 被～为化学系主任 be appointed chairman of the chemistry department ② assume a post; take up a job: ～军长 hold office as an army commander ③ official post; office: ～满 expiration of one's term of office / ～内 during one's term (*or* tenure) of office ④ undertake; bear: 任劳任怨 rènláo-rènyuàn ⑤ *m.* (for the number of terms served on an official post): 他做过两～大使。He has twice been ambassador

任[2] rèn　① let; allow; give free reign to: ～其泛滥 let it (e.g. a flood, etc.) spread unchecked / ～你挑选一个。Choose any one you like. / 衣服的花色很多, ～你选择。There are clothes of all different designs and colours for you to choose from. ② *conj.* no matter (how, what, etc.): ～我们怎样劝说, 他也不听。No matter how hard we tried to persuade him, he wouldn't listen. / 东西放在家里, ～怎么也丢不了。As long as we leave these things in the house, they can't possibly get lost. / ～谁也不能违反这些规定。No one is allowed to break the regulations, whoever he is.

——see also Rén

任便 rènbiàn　as you like; as you see fit: 你来不来～。You may come or not as you see fit.

任从 rèncóng　same as 任凭 rènpíng

任达 rèndá　*formal* unconventional and unrestrained

任何 rènhé　any; whichever; whatever: 我们能战胜～困难。We can overcome any difficulty. / 没有～理由拒绝这个建议。There's no reason whatsoever to turn down this suggestion. / ～人都不应享受特权。No one should enjoy privileges. / ～一方 either party; any of the parties

任教 rènjiào　be a teacher; teach: 在一所大学～ teach at a university / 他～多年了。He has been a teacher for many years.

任咎 rènjiù　*formal* bear responsibility for a fault; put the blame on oneself

任课 rènkè　teach (at a school)

任劳任怨 rènláo-rènyuàn　work hard regardless of criticism; willingly bear the burden of office

任免 rèn-miǎn　appoint and remove (*or* dismiss): 国务院依照法律的规定～行政人员。The State Council appoints and removes administrative personnel according to the provisions of the law. / ～事项 appointments and removals

任命 rènmìng　appoint: ～某人为校长 appoint sb. president (of a university) / 他被～为驻瑞典大使。He was appointed ambassador to Sweden.

任命状 rènmìngzhuàng　letter of appointment; commission: 外交人员～ diplomatic commission

任凭 rènpíng　① allow; let (sb. do as he pleases): 要去要留, ～你自己。You may go or stay as you please. / 这事不能～他一人决定。This shouldn't be left entirely to his discretion. ② *conj.* no matter (how, what, etc.): ～问题多复杂, 我们也能搞清楚。We can solve the problem no matter how complicated it is. / ～你怎样说, 事实总是事实。Whatever you say, facts are facts. / ～什么挫折都不能使他动摇。No setbacks can make him waver. ③ *conj.* even if; even though: ～江水冷得钻心, 工人们仍然坚持下水操作。The workers still kept on working in the river even though the water was icy cold.

任凭风浪起, 稳坐钓鱼船 rènpíng fēnglàng qǐ, wěn zuò diàoyúchuán　sit tight in the fishing boat despite the rising wind and waves—hold one's ground despite pressure or opposition

任期 rènqī　term of office; tenure of office: 全国人民代表大会每届～五年。The National People's Congress is elected for a term of five years. / 主席～已满。The term of the Presidency has expired.

任其自流 rèn qí zìliú　leave sth. to take its own course

任其自然 rèn qí zìrán　give free rein to; let nature take its course

任情 rènqíng　let oneself go; to one's heart's content; as much as one likes

任人 rènrén　let people (do sth. without restrictions): 公开展览, ～参观 An open exhibition, free to all visitors

任人唯亲 rèn rén wéi qīn　appoint people by favouritism

任人唯贤 rèn rén wéi xián　appoint people on their merits; appoint people according to their ability and political integrity

任人宰割 rèn rén zǎigē　(cannot but) allow oneself to be trampled upon

任事 rènshì　① have a job; be employed ② take up a task: 他勇于～。He never hesitates to take up a task.

任率 rènshuài　*formal* simple and natural; artless

任所 rènsuǒ　office

任务 rènwu　assignment; mission; task; job: 接受～ receive (*or* accept) an assignment / 我们保证完成～。We guarantee to fulfil (*or* complete) our mission. / ～重, 时间紧。The task is hard and we are pressed for time. / 这个～就交给我吧! Give this job to me. / 担负艰巨的～ shoulder heavy responsibilities / 本校今年的招生～是五百名。This year our school must fill an enrolment quota of five hundred.

任务观点 rènwu guāndiǎn　get-it-over-and-done-with attitude; perfunctory attitude

任侠 rènxiá　*formal* be gallant and chivalrous: [灌]夫不喜文学, 好～, 已然诺。(《史记》) Guan Fu had no taste for literature but loved feats of honour and daring and was absolutely true to his word.

任性 rènxìng　wilful; self-willed; wayward; headstrong: 她是个～的孩子。She is a wilful child. / 你这个～的脾气什么时候改得了? When will you ever change your headstrong ways?

任意 rènyì wanton; arbitrary; wilful: ～诬蔑 wantonly vilify／～捏造事实 indulge in pure fabrication／～歪曲历史 wilfully distort history／～掠夺别国资源 wantonly plunder other countries' resources／～欺负别人 bully people at will

任意常数 rènyì chángshù *math.* arbitrary constant

任意球 rènyìqiú ① *football* free kick ② *handball* free throw

任用 rènyòng assign sb. to a post; appoint

任职 rènzhí hold a post; be in office: 他在外交部任过职。He once held a post in the Ministry of Foreign Affairs.／～财政部 work (*or* hold a post) in the Ministry of Finance／在～期间 during one's tenure of office

任重道远 rènzhòng-dàoyuǎn the burden is heavy and the road is long—shoulder heavy responsibilities

任纵 rènzòng *formal* self-indulgent; undisciplined

妊（姙） rèn *formal* be pregnant: ～五月 be five months pregnant

妊妇 rènfù a pregnant woman

妊娠 rènshēn gestation; pregnancy: 输卵管～ tubal pregnancy／～反应 morning sickness

妊娠期 rènshēnqī period of gestation; gestational period

纫 rèn ① thread a needle: 老太太眼花了，～不上针。The old lady's vision had become blurred, so she couldn't thread the needle. ② sew; stitch: 缝纫 féngrèn ③ *formal* (usu. used in a letter expressing one's thanks): 至～高谊。Thank you so much for your great kindness.

纫佩 rènpèi *formal* feel gratefulness and admiration towards sb.

韧（靭、靱） rèn pliable but strong; tenacious; tough: 坚韧 jiānrèn

韧带 rèndài *physiol.* ligament

韧度 rèndù tenacity

韧劲 rènjìn indomitableness; dauntlessness; tenacity

韧力 rènlì indomitable will; indomitable spirit

韧皮部 rènpíbù *bot.* bast; phloem

韧皮纤维 rènpí xiānwéi *bot.* bast fibre

韧性 rènxìng toughness; tenacity

韧 rèn see 发轫 fārèn

饪（餁） rèn see 烹饪 pēngrèn

衽（袵） rèn *formal* ① front of a garment ② a sleeping mat

衽席 rènxí *formal* ① a sleeping mat ② a sleeping place; bed

葚 rèn see 桑葚儿 sāngrènr ——see also shèn

rēng

扔 rēng ① throw; toss; cast: ～手榴弹 throw a hand grenade／～球 throw (*or* toss) a ball／敌机～了几颗炸弹。The enemy plane dropped a few bombs. ② throw away; cast aside: 把它～了吧。Throw it away.／被～进历史的垃圾堆 be relegated to (*or* tossed on to) the rubbish heap of history／这事他早就～在脖子后边了。He'd clean forgotten about it.

扔掉 rēngdiào throw away: 这条鱼都臭了，～算了。The fish smells; throw it away.

扔弃 rēngqì abandon; discard; cast aside

扔下 rēngxia abandon; put aside; leave behind: 敌人～武器逃跑了。The enemy dropped their weapons and took to their heels.／这工作我不能～不管。I can't leave the work half-finished.

réng

仍 réng ① remain: 一～其旧 remain the same ② *formal* frequent: 频仍 pínréng ③ *adv.* still; yet: ～有效力 be still effective; be still in force／～须努力 must continue to make efforts／他的病～不见好。He's not yet recovered from his illness. *or* He's shown no sign towards recovery.

仍旧 réngjiù ① remain the same: 修订版体例～。The style will still be the same for the revised edition. ② *adv.* still; yet: 他虽然遇到许多挫折，可是意志～那样坚强。His determination remains as strong as ever despite all the setbacks he has encountered.／他～是十年前的老样子。After ten years, he still looked the same.／有些问题～没有解决。Some problems remain to be solved.

仍然 réngrán *adv.* still; yet: 补一补，这件衣服～可以穿。You can still wear the clothes if you have them mended.／等了半天，她～没有到。We've been waiting a long time for her, but she still hasn't arrived.／至今我们～没有得到回音。As yet, we have received no answer.／他把信看完，～装在信封里。He put the letter back into the envelope after he'd read it.

rì

日[1] rì ① sun: 烈日 lièrì ② daytime; day: 终日 zhōngrì ③ day: 一～，老王来我家。One day, Lao Wang came to my place.／多～不见了，你好吗? Haven't seen you for a long time. How are you? ④ daily; every day; with each passing day: 产量～增。Output is going up every day.／天气～暖。It's getting warmer and warmer. ⑤ time: 春～ springtime; spring

日[2] Rì short for 日本 Rìběn

日班 rìbān day shift: 上～ be on day shift

日斑 rìbān another name for 太阳黑子 tàiyáng hēizǐ

日报 rìbào daily paper; daily: 《人民～》 *Renmin Ribao* (the *People's Daily*)／《中国～》 *China Daily*

日本 Rìběn Japan

日本海 Rìběnhǎi the Sea of Japan

日本人 Rìběnrén Japanese

日薄西山 rì bó xīshān the sun is setting beyond the western hills—declining rapidly; nearing one's end: ～，气息奄奄，人命危浅，朝不虑夕 (李密) a dying person who is sinking fast, like the sun setting beyond the western hills

日不暇给 rì bù xiá jǐ be fully occupied every day; be pressed for time

日常 rìcháng day-to-day; everyday; daily: ～工作 day-to-day work; routine duties／～事务 routine business／～生活 everyday life; daily life／～用语 words and expressions for everyday use／这些都是～必须用的东西。These are all the things needed for daily use.

日场 rìchǎng day show; daytime performance; matinée: ～电影 daytime film show／他们每星期演六个夜场，三个～。They do six evening performances and three matinées every week.

日程 rìchéng programme; schedule: 访问～ itinerary of a visit／工作～ work schedule; programme of work／～很紧 a tight (*or* crowded) schedule／提到～上来 place

(*or* put) sth. on the order of the day

日程表 rìchéngbiǎo schedule

日出 rìchū sunrise: 看～ watch (*or* see) the sunrise

日出而作，日入而息 rì chū ér zuò, rì rù ér xī begin work at sunrise and rest at sunset—life in primitive society: ～, 凿井而饮，耕田而食，帝力于我何有哉?《击壤歌》I begin work at sunrise and rest at sunset. I dig a well for water and till my field for food. What is the Emperor's virtuous power to me?

日戳 rìchuō ① date stamp; dater ② datemark

日耳曼人 Rì'ěrmànrén Germanic people

日珥 rì'ěr *astron.* prominence

日工 rìgōng ① daywork ② day labour ③ day labourer

日光 rìguāng sunlight; sunbeam

日光灯 rìguāngdēng popular name for 荧光灯 yíngguāngdēng

日光疗法 rìguāng liáofǎ heliotherapy

日光浴 rìguāngyù sunbath: ～室 solarium

日晷 rìguǐ (also 日规 rìguī) sundial

日后 rìhòu in the future; in the days to come: 这东西～可能用得着。We may find it useful in future. *or* It may come in handy someday. / 你现在不下功夫，～会吃苦头的。If you don't work hard now, you'll suffer for it later.

日积月累 rìjī-yuèlěi accumulate over a long period: 每天学一点，～也能学不少。Learn a little every day and in time you'll have learned a lot. / 能节约就节约，这样～就是一个很可观的数目。If you economize and save whenever possible, over time you'll accumulate a nice sum.

日记 rìjì diary: 记～ keep a diary / 工作～ work diary; daily account of one's work

日记本 rìjìběn diary

日记帐 rìjìzhàng journal; daybook

日间 rìjiān in the daytime; during the day: ～气温比夜间高多了。The temperature was much higher in the daytime than at night.

日间不做亏心事，半夜敲门不吃惊 rìjiān bù zuò kuīxīnshì, bànyè qiāomén bù chījīng he who has done nothing shameful by day need not be alarmed by a knock on the door at night

日见 rìjiàn with each passing day; day by day: ～好转 get better every day / ～衰败 decline day by day

日渐 rìjiàn with each passing day; day by day: ～强壮 get stronger and stronger / ～进步 make steady progress

日脚 rìjiǎo ① the light of a setting sun: ～已偏西。The sun is shining aslant from the west. ② *dial.* day; date ③ *dial.* time ④ *dial.* life; livelihood

日界线 rìjièxiàn international date line; date line

日久 rìjiǔ with the passing of time; in (the) course of time

日久见人心 rìjiǔ jiàn rénxīn time reveals a person's heart; it takes time to know a person ——see also 路遥知马力 lù yáo zhī mǎlì

日久天长 rìjiǔ-tiāncháng after a considerable period of time: 由于水的不断侵蚀，～就形成了一个大溶洞。As a result of continuous water erosion, in the course of time a huge cave was formed.

日就月将 rìjiù-yuèjiāng achieve something every day and make progress every month—many a little makes a mickle

日课 rìkè daily lessons

日来 rìlái recently; of late; in the past few days

日理万机 rì lǐ wànjī attend to numerous affairs of state every day; be occupied with a myriad of state affairs

日历 rìlì calendar

日历手表 rìlì shǒubiǎo calendar watch

日轮 rìlún the sun

日落 rìluò sunset

日冕 rìmiǎn *astron.* (solar) corona

日冕仪 rìmiǎnyí coronagraph

日暮 rìmù evening; nightfall; dusk: ～归来, 城内已万家灯火。When we returned at dusk, the lights of the city had come on.

日暮途穷 rìmù-túqióng the day is waning and the road is ending—approaching the end of one's days; be on one's last legs; be at the end of one's rope

日内 rìnèi in a few days; in a day or two; in a couple of days: 大会将于～举行。The meeting will take place in a few days. / ～将有一场暴风雨。There will be a heavy storm in a day or two.

日内瓦 Rìnèiwǎ Geneva

日期 rìqī date: 起程的～定了吗? Has the departure date been fixed? / 信上的～是六月二日。The letter is dated June 2. / 开会的～是六月二十一日到二十七日。The congress will be in session from June 21st to June 27th.

日前 rìqián a few days ago; the other day

日趋 rìqū with each passing day; gradually; day by day: 市场～繁荣。The market is becoming brisker day by day. / 环境污染问题～严重。Environmental pollution is an increasingly serious problem.

日日夜夜 rìrìyèyè day and night; night and day: 解放军战士～守卫着祖国的边疆。The PLA men guard the borders of their motherland day and night. / 在～的紧张抢修中，他一直没有休息过。During the round-the-clock rush repair job, he never took a rest.

日色 rìsè time of the day as shown by the colour of the sun: ～不早了。It is getting dark.

日上三竿 rì shàng sān gān the sun is three poles high —it's late in the morning (usu. referring to getting up late)

日射 rìshè *meteorol.* insolation

日射表 rìshèbiǎo actinometer

日射病 rìshèbìng *med.* sunstroke; insolation

日食 rìshí *astron.* solar eclipse: 日环食 annular eclipse / 日偏食 partial solar eclipse / 日全食 total solar eclipse

日坛 Rìtán the Altar to the Sun (in Beijing)

日头 rìtóu *old* ① day; date: 我也有盼着他的～。There were also days when I missed him. ② daytime; day: 半个～ half a day

日头 rìtou *dial.* the sun: ～已很高了。The sun was high in the sky.

日托 rìtuō day care: 这个托儿所只有～。This is only a day nursery. / 你的孩子是全托还是～? Does your child board at the nursery or go home in the evening?

日托托儿所 rìtuō tuō'érsuǒ day nursery

日息 rìxī per diem interest; daily interest

日下 rìxià *formal* ① at present; now ② national capital; capital

日心说 rìxīnshuō *astron.* heliocentric theory

日新月异 rìxīn-yuèyì change with each passing day: 社会主义建设使祖国面貌～。Our socialist construction is changing the face of the land day by day.

日薪 rìxīn daily wage; per diem

日夜 rì-yè day and night; night and day; round the clock: ～警惕地守卫着边疆 vigilantly guard the borders day and night / 我们厂～三班倒。Our factory operates round the clock on three shifts.

日夜商店 rìyè shāngdiàn a shop open night and day; a round-the-clock shop; a day-and-night-service shop

日以继夜 rì yǐ jì yè night and day; round the clock

日益 rìyì *adv.* increasingly; day by day: 矛盾～尖锐。The contradictions are becoming increasingly acute. / 我们的队伍～壮大。Our ranks are growing stronger day by day. / 随着生产的发展, 人民的生活～改善。With

the development of production, people's living conditions improved increasingly. / 局势～严重。 The situation has become more and more serious. / ～升级的军备竞赛 an ever-spiralling arms race

日影 rìyǐng shadows

日用 rìyòng ① daily expenses: 一部分钱做～, 其余的都储蓄起来。 Part of the money is used for daily expenses, and the rest is put in the savings bank. ② of everyday (or daily) use: ～必需品 daily necessities; household necessities / ～工业品 manufactured goods for daily use / ～器具 household utensils; articles of everyday use / ～小商品 small articles of everyday use

日用品 rìyòngpǐn articles of everyday use

日语 Rìyǔ Japanese (language)

日元 rìyuán yen (Japanese moneytary unit)

日月 rìyuè life; livelihood: 解放前的～可真不好过啊! What a hard life we had before liberation!

日月重光 rì-yuè chóng guāng the sun and the moon shining again——back to peace and prosperity after a dark period

日月经天, 江河行地 rì-yuè jīng tiān, jiāng-hé xíng dì (like) the sun and moon that move in the sky, or the rivers that flow on the earth——eternal

日月如梭 rì-yuè rú suō the sun and the moon shuttle back and forth——how time flies

日月星辰 rì-yuè-xīngchén the sun, the moon and the stars; the heavenly bodies

日晕 rìyùn *meteorol.* solar halo

日照 rìzhào sunshine: ～计 sunshine recorder / ～时间 sunshine time

日志 rìzhì daily record; journal: 工作～ daily record of work / 航海～ logbook; log

日中 rìzhōng *formal* noon; midday

日子 rìzi ① day; date: 这个～好不容易盼到了。 The day we have been looking forward to has come at long last. / 定一个～ fix a date / 街上怎么这么多人, 今天是什么～? Why are there so many people in the streets? What's the occasion? ② time: 他走了有些～了。 He's been away for some time. / 这些～我校师生在工厂实习。 The teachers and students of our school have been doing field work at a factory recently. ③ life; livelihood: 今天我们的～多幸福啊! How happy is our life today! / 勤俭过～ lead an industrious and frugal life / ～越来越不好过。 Things are getting harder and harder.

róng

戎[1] róng *formal* army; military affairs: 投笔从戎 tóu bǐ cóng róng

戎[2] Róng ① an ancient name for the tribes in the west ② a surname

戎行 rónghǎng *formal* ① army: 久历～ have stayed in the army (or led a military life) for a long time ② the ranks

戎机 róngjī *formal* ① errands of war; war: 万里赴～, 关山度若飞。(《木兰诗》) A thousand leagues she tramped on the errands of war, Frontiers and hills she crossed like a bird in flight. ② military affairs or operations

戎马 róngmǎ *formal* army horse

戎马倥偬 róngmǎ kǒngzǒng burdened with pressing military duties

戎马生涯 róngmǎ shēngyá army life; military life

戎首 róngshǒu *formal* warmonger

戎装 róngzhuāng (also 戎服 róngfú) *formal* martial attire

荣 (榮) róng ① grow luxuriantly; flourish: 春～冬枯 grow in spring and wither in winter ② prosperous; thriving; flourishing: 繁荣 fánróng ③ honour; glory: ～立一等功 be cited for meritorious service, first class / 以艰苦为～ take pride in working under difficult conditions / 为人民而死, 虽死犹～! It is a glorious thing to die for the people. ④ (Róng) a surname

荣宠 róngchǒng ① imperial favour ② gracious favour

荣达 róngdá *formal* illustrious and influential

荣光 róngguāng honour; glory

荣归 róngguī return in glory: ～故里 return in glory to one's old home after becoming famous or rich

荣华富贵 rónghuá-fùguì glory, splendour, wealth and rank; high position and great wealth: 享不尽的～ enjoy untold wealth and high honour

荣获 rónghuò get or win sth. as an honour: ～冠军 win the championship / ～一枚奖章 be awarded a medal / ～模范教师的称号 be awarded the honourable title of model teacher

荣军 róngjūn short for 荣誉军人 róngyù jūnrén

荣枯 róngkū ① (of plants) flourishing and withering ② rise and fall (or decline)

荣任 róngrèn be honoured with a post

荣辱 róng-rǔ honour or disgrace

荣辱与共 róng-rǔ yǔ gòng (of friends) share honour or disgrace, weal or woe

荣升 róngshēng be honoured by promotion to a higher post

荣幸 róngxìng be honoured: 我们应邀访问贵国, 感到非常～。 We feel greatly honoured by your invitation to visit your country. / 如蒙光临, 不胜～。 We shall be greatly honoured by your gracious presence. / 今天很～能参加你们的晚会。 It is a great honour to be with you at this evening party. / 那天, 我～地参加了国宴。 I had the honour of attending the state banquet the other day.

荣耀 róngyào honour; glory

荣膺 róngyīng *formal* be honoured with a post or decoration

荣誉 róngyù honour; credit; glory: ～感 a sense of honour / 为祖国赢得～ win honour for one's country / 爱护集体的～ cherish the good name of the collective / 应得的～ an honour that one well deserves

荣誉军人 róngyù jūnrén a disabled soldier (wounded in revolutionary war)

茸 róng ① (of grass, etc.) fine and soft; downy: 毛茸茸 máoróngróng ② young pilose antler: 鹿茸 lùróng

茸茸 róngróng (of grass, hair, etc.) fine, soft and thick; downy: 绿草～ a carpet of green·grass / 这孩子长着一头～的头发。 The boy has a head of soft, thick hair.

绒 (羢、毧) róng ① fine hair; down: 鸭绒 yāróng ② cloth with a soft nap or pile on one or either side: 丝绒 sīróng ③ fine floss for embroidery

绒布 róngbù flannelette; cotton flannel

绒花 rónghuā *arts & crafts* velvet flowers, birds, etc.

绒裤 róngkù sweat pants

绒毛 róngmáo ① fine hair; down; villus ② *text.* nap; pile

绒毛膜上皮癌 róngmáomóshàngpí'ái chorioepithelioma

绒面革 róngmiàngé suède (leather)

绒毯 róngtǎn flannelette blanket

绒头绳 róngtóushéng ① wool (for tying pigtails) ② *dial.* knitting wool

绒线 róngxiàn ① floss for embroidery ② *dial.* knit-

ting wool: ～衫 woollen sweater

绒线刺绣 róngxiàn cìxiù crewelwork

绒绣 róngxiù *arts & crafts* woollen needlepoint tapestry; woollen embroidery: ～地毯 finished needlepoint carpet

绒衣 róngyī sweat shirt

容¹

róng ① hold; contain: 这个礼堂能～一千人。 The auditorium can hold a thousand people. *or* The auditorium has a seating capacity of 1,000. / 可～水三万多立方米的蓄水池 a reservoir with a capacity of over 30,000 cubic metres / 这座大桥可～四辆卡车并列通行。 The bridge can take four lorries abreast. ② tolerate: ～人之过 to be tolerant of others' mistakes / ～不得不同意见 cannot tolerate dissenting views ③ permit; allow: 详情～后再告。 Permit me to give the details later. / 请～我考虑几天再作决定吧! Please give me a few days to consider before I make my decision. ④ *adv. formal* perhaps; probably: ～有阴谋。 There may be a plot behind it. ⑤ (Róng) a surname

容²

róng ① facial expression: 笑容 xiàoróng ② appearance; looks: 仪容 yíróng

容光 róngguāng facial expression; bearing

容光焕发 róngguāng huànfā one's face glowing with health: ～的脸颊 a striking, radiant face

容华 rónghuá *liter.* features and complexion; looks: ～绝代 of unrivalled beauty

容或 rónghuò *adv. formal* perhaps; probably; possibly: 这篇文章是根据回忆写的,与事实～有出入。 This article is based on memory, so it's possibly not altogether accurate. / 此等人物,旧小说中～有之。 You might find such characters in old novels.

容积 róngjī volume

容积吨 róngjīdūn measurement ton

容量 róngliàng capacity: 这个油箱的～为300加仑。 The tank has a capacity of 300 gallons.

容留 róngliú give shelter to; take sb. in; keep: 我们不能～他这样不老实的人。 We can't keep a dishonest man like him here.

容貌 róngmào facial features; appearance; looks: ～端庄 have a pleasant appearance / ～娇美 look sweet and charming / 她的～已大不如前了。 She had lost her looks.

容纳 róngnà hold; have a capacity of; accommodate: 会议室能～五十人。 The meeting room can hold 50 people. / 首都体育馆能～一万八千观众。 The Capital Stadium has a seating capacity of 18,000. / 他不能～不同意见。 He can't tolerate dissenting views.

容器 róngqì container; vessel

容情 róngqíng (usu. used in the negative) show mercy: 我们对坏人决不～。 We never show any mercy towards evildoers.

容人 róngrén regard people with kindly tolerance; tolerant towards others; magnanimous; broad-minded: 大量～ be magnanimous and tolerant / 他心胸狭窄,容不下人。 He is narrow-minded and intolerant.

容忍 róngrěn tolerate; put up with; condone: 我们不能～这种浪费现象。 We cannot tolerate such waste. / 采取～和克制的态度 adopt a tolerant and restrained attitude / 他的错误行为使人无法～。 No one could put up with his bad conduct any longer. *or* People find his conduct intolerable.

容色 róngsè facial expression; countenance: ～自若 keep an easy countenance; appear composed / 忧虑不安的～ a worried look

容身 róngshēn take shelter: 这种地方,简直让人无法～。 You simply can't take shelter in a place like this.

容身之地 róngshēn zhī dì a place to stay: 四海飘零,

无～。 I drifted from one place to another with nowhere to rest. / 由于游击队的骚扰,敌人在这儿没有～。 Because of the guerrillas' harassing attacks, the enemy couldn't keep its footing in this part of the country.

容受 róngshòu ① hold; contain ② endure; put up with

容恕 róngshù tolerate; forgive

容物 róngwù *formal* tolerant; forbearing; magnanimous: 不能～ be intolerant; be unforbearing

容限 róngxiàn *phys.* tolerance; allowance: 光学～ optical tolerance

容许 róngxǔ ① tolerate; permit; allow: ～新闻自由 toleration of free press / ～宗教自由 religious toleration / ～别人把话说完 allow others to finish what they want to say / 侵犯别国主权是绝不～的。 It is absolutely impermissible to encroach upon the sovereignty of a country. / 情况不～我们再等待了。 In such circumstances we can't afford to wait any longer. / 可以～你有三天的准备时间。 You'll be allowed three days to prepare. / 我们不～任何外来干涉。 We will brook no outside interference. / 原则问题决不～让步。 There should be no concessions whatsoever on matters of principle. ② *adv. formal* perhaps; possibly: 此类事件,十年前～有之。 Such things might possibly have happened ten years ago.

容许负载 róngxǔ fùzài *elec.* allowable load

容许收缩量 róngxǔ shōusuōliàng shrinkage allowance

容颜 róngyán appearance; looks

容易 róngyì ① easy: 蛙泳～。 It's easy to do breaststroke. / ～的题先做。 Do the easy problems first. / 这台机床～操作。 This lathe is easy to operate. / 说起来～做起来难。 It's easier said than done. / 这种草药很～弄到。 This medicinal herb is easy to come by. / 今天的幸福来得不～。 The present happy life didn't come about easily. ② likely; liable; apt: 他～生病。 He often gets ill. / 这～引起误会。 This is liable to cause misunderstanding. / 人们～把这两个问题混淆起来。 People are apt to confuse the two issues.

容止 róngzhǐ *formal* bearing; demeanour

容重 róngzhòng *water conservancy* unit weight

嵘 (嶸)

róng see 峥嵘 zhēngróng

溶

róng dissolve: 樟脑～于酒精而不～于水。 Camphor dissolves in alcohol, but not in water. / ～西画之长于国画之中 apply the strong points of Western painting to traditional Chinese painting

溶洞 róngdòng limestone cave

溶化 rónghuà ① dissolve: 盐在水里很快就～。 Salt dissolves quickly in water. ② same as 融化 rónghuà

溶剂 róngjì *chem.* solvent

溶胶 róngjiāo *chem.* sol

溶解 róngjiě dissolve: 这种物质在水中不会～。 This substance does not dissolve in water. / ～热 heat of solution / ～物 dissolved matter

溶解度 róngjiědù solubility

溶菌素 róngjūnsù *med.* bacteriolysin

溶煤 róngméi same as 溶剂 róngjì

溶溶 róngróng *liter.* broad: 江 水～。 The river is broad and gentle. / 月色～ a flood of moonlight

溶蚀 róngshí *geol.* corrosion

溶性油 róngxìngyóu *chem.* soluble oil

溶血 róngxuè *med.* haemolysis

溶液 róngyè (also 溶体 róngtǐ) *chem.* solution: 实在～ real solution / 当量～ normal solution

溶质 róngzhì *chem.* solute

蓉

róng ① see 芙蓉 fúróng; 苁蓉 cōngróng ② (Róng) another name for 成都 Chéngdū

熔(鎔) róng melt; fuse; smelt: ～焊 fusion welding

熔池 róngchí *metall.* (molten) bath

熔点 róngdiǎn *phys.* melting (*or* fusing, fusion) point

熔断 róngduàn *elec.* fusing: ～器 fuse (box)

熔化 rónghuà melt: 纯铁加热到摄氏1,535度就～. Pure iron melts at 1,535℃.

熔化炉 rónghuàlú melting furnace

熔化期 rónghuàqī *metall.* melting stage

熔化速率 rónghuà sùlǜ *metall.* melting rate

熔剂 róngjì *metall.* flux

熔解 róngjiě *phys.* fuse; fusion: ～热 heat of fusion

熔炼 róngliàn smelt: 闪速～ flash smelting

熔炼炉 róngliànlú smelting furnace

熔炉 rónglú ① smelting furnace ② (fig.) crucible; furnace: 革命～ the furnace of revolution

熔融 róngróng same as 熔化 rónghuà

熔融纺丝 róngróng fǎngsī *text.* melting spinning

熔融挤压法 róngróng jǐyāfǎ *chem. fibre* extrusion by melting

熔岩 róngyán *geol.* lava

熔铸 róngzhù found; cast: ～生铁 cast pig iron

熔铸工 róngzhùgōng smelter

榕 róng ① *bot.* small-fruited fig tree; banyan ② (Róng) another name for 福州 Fúzhōu

蝾(蠑) róng see below

蝾螈 róngyuán *zool.* salamander; newt

融 róng ① melt; thaw: 春雪易～. Spring snow soon melts. ② blend; fuse; be in harmony: 交融 jiāoróng ③ circulation (of money, etc.): 金融 jīnróng

融合 rónghé mix together; fuse; merge: 铜与锡的～ the fusion of copper and tin

融和 rónghé ① pleasantly warm; genial: 天气～. The weather is pleasantly warm. ② same as 融合 rónghé

融化 rónghuà (of ice, snow, etc.) melt; thaw: 湖上的冰已经～了. The ice on the lake has already melted. / 雪已开始～. The snow is beginning to thaw.

融会 rónghuì (also 融汇 rónghuì) mix together; fuse; merge

融会贯通 rónghuì guàntōng achieve mastery through a comprehensive study of the subject; gain a thorough understanding of the subject through mastery of all relevant material

融解 róngjiě melt; thaw: 山顶的积雪～了. The snow on the mountain top has melted.

融洽 róngqià harmonious; on friendly (*or* good) terms: 干群关系很～. The relations between the cadres and the masses are harmonious. / 他们俩相处得十分～. The two of them are on very good terms (*or* are getting on very well together).

融融 róngróng *formal* ① happy and harmonious: 老战友欢聚一堂, 其乐～. When old comrades-in-arms meet, their happiness knows no bounds. ② warm: 春光～. Spring fills the air with warmth.

融通 róngtōng circulate: 聚集和～资金 collect and circulate funds

rǒng

冗(宂) rǒng *formal* ① superfluous; redundant: 冗词 rǒngcí ② full of trivial details: 冗杂 rǒngzá ③ busyness: 拨冗 bōrǒng

冗笔 rǒngbǐ superfluity in writing or painting; unnecessary touches or strokes

冗长 rǒngcháng tediously long; lengthy; long-winded; prolix: ～的讲演 a long and tedious speech / 文章～有损于主题的表达. If an essay is too long, it clouds the main theme.

冗词 rǒngcí superfluous words (in a piece of writing)

冗词赘句 rǒngcí-zhuìjù redundant words and expressions

冗繁 rǒngfán (of affairs) many and diverse; miscellaneous: ～的琐事 small fussy affairs

冗员 rǒngyuán redundant personnel: 裁减～ reduce redundant personnel

冗杂 rǒngzá ① (of writing) lengthy and jumbled ② (of affairs) miscellaneous

冗赘 rǒngzhuì verbose; diffuse

氄(氃、毪) rǒng (of feathers or hair) fine and soft

氄毛 rǒngmáo fine and soft feathers: 刚孵出来的小鸡长着一身～. Newly-hatched chicks have downy feathers.

róu

柔 róu ① soft; supple; flexible: ～枝嫩叶 supple twigs and tender leaves ② soften: 柔麻 róumá ③ gentle; yielding; mild: 温柔 wēnróu

柔板 róubǎn *mus.* adagio

柔肠 róucháng soft heart: ～寸断 be broken-hearted

柔道 róudào *judo*

柔和 róuhé soft; gentle; mild: ～的光线 soft light / ～的声音 a gentle (*or* mild) voice; a soft sound / 颜色～ a soft colour / 她的性情很～. She has a very mild disposition. / 这块料子手感～. This piece of cloth feels soft.

柔滑 róuhuá soft and smooth; satiny; creamy

柔静 róujìng gentle and quiet

柔麻 róumá soften jute, hemp, etc.

柔曼 róumàn ① soft; gentle: ～的旋律 a melody of serene beauty; a lyrical tune ② soft and smooth; satiny; creamy ③ good-looking; gorgeous

柔美 róuměi soft and graceful: 音色～ sweet tone colour / ～的舞姿 graceful dance

柔媚 róumèi gentle and lovely; genial; lovable: 这姑娘天真, ～. The girl is innocent and lovable. / ～的晚霞 the soft glow of sunset

柔嫩 róunèn tender; delicate: ～的幼芽 tender sprouts / ～的柳条 delicate willow twigs

柔能克刚 róu néng kè gāng the soft can overcome the hard

柔腻 róunì tender; delicate

柔懦 róunuò timid and overcautious; weak-willed: ～的性格 have a weak character; be weak-kneed

柔情 róuqíng tender feelings; tenderness: ～蜜意 tender affection

柔情似水 róuqíng sì shuǐ tender feelings like water— be deeply attached; be passionately devoted

柔情侠骨 róuqíng-xiágǔ a tender heart and a chivalrous spirit

柔荏 róurěn *formal* weak-kneed; cowardly

柔韧 róurèn pliable and tough

柔茹刚吐 róurú-gāngtǔ bully the weak and fear the strong

柔软 róuruǎn soft; lithe: ～的垫子 a soft cushion / ～的动作 lithe movements

柔软体操 róuruǎn tǐcāo callisthenics

柔润 róurùn soft and smooth; delicate: ～的皮肤 soft complexion; delicate skin / ～的嗓音 a sweet, mellow

voice

柔弱　róuruò　weak; delicate: 身体～ in delicate health; weak; frail / 性格～ have a weak character; be meek and mild

柔术　róushù　*jujitsu*

柔顺　róushùn　gentle and agreeable; meek: 性情～ of gentle disposition; meek and mild

柔荑　róutí　*formal* ① sprout; shoot ② (of a woman's hands) slender and white ③ a woman's hands

柔荑花序　róutí huāxù　*bot.* catkin; ament

柔婉　róuwǎn　soft and mild: ～的语调 a mild tone

柔细　róuxì　soft and fine: ～的声音 a soft voice / ～的柳条 delicate willow twigs

柔心弱骨　róuxīn-ruògǔ　soft heart and weak bone—soft; mild; meek

柔鱼　róuyú　squid

柔中有刚　róu zhōng yǒu gāng　firmness cloaked beneath gentleness; an iron hand in a velvet glove

揉　róu　① rub: 别～眼睛。Don't rub your eyes. / ～一～腿 rub one's legs ② knead; roll: ～面 knead dough / 把泥～成小球 roll the earth into small balls / 把信～成一团 crumple a letter into a ball ③ *formal* bend; twist

揉搓　róucuo　① rub: 妹妹的脑门上碰了个包,让妈妈给她～。My little sister got a bump on her forehead and asked Mum to rub it for her. / 他怕～坏了课本,包了书皮。He was afraid that his textbook would get worn, so he put a cover on it. ② *dial.* torment

揉磨　róumo　*dial.* torment

糅　róu　mix; mingle: 杂糅 záróu

糅合　róuhé　form a mixture (usu. of things which don't blend well); mix: ～莎士比亚戏剧和京剧二者的艺术形式 blend the artistic form of Shakespeare with that of Beijing opera

蹂　róu　see below

蹂躏　róulìn　trample on; ravage; make havoc of; devastate: ～别国主权 trample upon the sovereignty of other countries / 在帝国主义的～下 under the heel of imperialism / 遭到～ suffer devastation, oppression, outrages, etc. / ～人权 a gross violation of human rights / ～妇女 violate a woman

鞣　róu　tan: 这皮子～得不够熟。The hide isn't properly tanned.

鞣料　róuliào　tanning material: ～浸膏 tanning extract

鞣酸　róusuān　*chem.* tannic acid; tannin

ròu

肉　ròu　① meat (esp. pork); flesh: 她不吃～。She does not eat meat. / 许多动物的～可以吃。The flesh of many animals is eatable. / 掉～ lose flesh / 身上没有～ be skinny ② pulp; flesh (of fruit): 冬瓜～厚。A white gourd is rich in pulp. ③ *dial.* not crisp; not crunchy; squashy: ～瓤西瓜 a squashy watermelon ④ *dial.* slow (in movement); sluggish: ～脾气 a phlegmatic temperament / 这个人做事真～。He does everything in such a lethargic way.

肉包子　ròubāozi　steamed bun with meat stuffing

肉饼　ròubǐng　ground-meat pie; meat pie

肉搏　·ròubó　fight hand-to-hand

肉搏战　ròubózhàn　hand-to-hand fight (*or* combat); bayonet fighting (*or* charge)

肉畜　ròuchù　livestock raised for meat

肉垂　ròuchuí　*zool.* wattle

肉苁蓉　ròucōngróng　*Chin. med.* saline cistanche (*Cistanche salsa*)

肉店　ròudiàn　butcher's (shop)

肉丁　ròudīng　diced meat: 辣子～ diced pork with hot pepper

肉冻　ròudòng　meat jelly; aspic: 鸡～ chicken in aspic

肉豆蔻　ròudòukòu　*Chin. med.* nutmeg

肉嘟嘟　ròudūdū　plump; chubby; pudgy: ～的小手 plump little hands

肉墩墩　ròudūndūn　stocky

肉感　ròugǎn　sex appeal; sexiness: 她穿起那条牛仔裤非常～。She looks very sexy in those jeans.

肉冠　ròuguān　*zool.* comb

肉桂　ròuguì　*bot.* cinnamon tree; Chinese cinnamon tree; cassia-bark tree (*Cinnamomum cassia*)

肉果　ròuguǒ　same as 肉豆蔻 ròudòukòu

肉红　ròuhóng　flesh-coloured; pale red

肉鸡　ròujī　table hen; broiler

肉酱　ròujiàng　meat pulp; minced meat

肉类加工厂　ròulèi jiāgōngchǎng　meat processing factory

肉瘤　ròuliú　*med.* sarcoma

肉麻　ròumá　nauseating; sickening; disgusting: ～的吹捧 fulsome praise / 这种话听着真～。It's sickening to hear this kind of talk.

肉糜　ròumí　*dial.* meat paste

肉末　ròumò　minced meat; ground meat

肉牛　ròuniú　store cattle; beef cattle

肉排　ròupái　steak

肉泡眼　ròupàoyǎn　eyes with fleshy eyelids; pouchy eyes

肉皮　ròupí　pork skin

肉皮儿　ròupír　*dial.* human skin; complexion: ～细嫩 soft complexion; delicate skin

肉片　ròupiàn　sliced meat

肉票　ròupiào　*old* hostage (held for ransom)

肉色　ròusè　yellowish pink; flesh-coloured; flesh-tinted: ～袜子 flesh-tinted stockings

肉身　ròushēn　*Buddhism* the mortal body

肉食　ròushí　carnivorous: ～动物 carnivorous animal; carnivore

肉食　ròushi　meat: 老太太吃素,从不碰～。The old lady is a vegetarian and never touches meat.

肉丝　ròusī　shredded meat (esp. pork): ～面 noodles with shredded pork

肉松　ròusōng　dried meat (esp. pork) floss

肉穗花序　ròusuì huāxù　*bot.* spadix

肉袒　ròutǎn　*formal* strip off the upper garments (in begging forgiveness)—make a humble apology

肉汤　ròutāng　broth

肉体　ròutǐ　the human body; the flesh: 消灭地主阶级不是～上消灭地主个人。To eliminate the landlords as a class does not mean to destroy them physically as individuals.

肉痛　ròutòng　*dial.* feel sorry; be distressed

肉头　ròutóu　*dial.* ① weak and incompetent ② foolish; stupid: 他净办这种～事! He's always doing such foolish things. ③ full of misgivings; over-cautious ④ mean; miserly

肉头　ròutou　*dial.* soft and fleshy: 这孩子的手多～! What plump little hands the child has! / 这种米做出来的饭挺～。This kind of rice is soft and plump when cooked.

肉丸子　ròuwánzi　meatball

肉馅　ròuxiàn　meat stuffing; chopped (*or* ground) meat

肉星儿　ròuxīngr　tiny bits of meat: 这菜里连个～都没有。There is not a speck of meat in this dish.

肉刑　ròuxíng　corporal punishment

肉芽 ròuyá *med.* granulation

肉眼 ròuyǎn naked eye: ～看不见细菌。Bacteria are invisible to the naked eye.

肉眼凡胎 ròuyǎn-fántāi a very mundane person; a commonplace and ignorant person

肉眼泡儿 ròuyǎnpāor eyes with fleshy eyelids; pouchy eyes

肉用鸡 ròuyòngjī same as 肉鸡 ròujī

肉欲 ròuyù *derog.* carnal desire

肉汁 ròuzhī gravy; (meat) juice

肉制品 ròuzhìpǐn meat products

肉中刺 ròuzhōngcì see 眼中钉, 肉中刺 yǎnzhōngdīng, ròuzhōngcì

肉猪 ròuzhū slaughter pig; hog

肉赘 ròuzhuì wart

rú

如[1] rú ① in compliance with; according to: 如命 rúmìng ② like; as; as if: 湖水～镜。The lake is like a mirror. / 我们的意志坚～钢。Our will is as strong as steel. / 事情并不～他们所想的那样简单。Things aren't as simple as they think. / ～上所述 as described above / ～你所说 as you've said / 十年～一日 persevere for ten years as if it were one day ③ (used in the negative) can compare with; be as good as: 不如 bùrú[1] ④ surpass; exceed: 光景一年强～一年。The situation is getting better year by year. ⑤ for instance; such as; as: 唐朝有很多大诗人，～李白、杜甫、白居易等。The Tang Dynasty produced a host of great poets, such as Li Bai, Du Fu and Bai Juyi. ⑥ *formal* go to: ～厕 go to the toilet

如[2] rú *conj.* if; in case (of); in the event of: ～处理得当，问题不难解决。The problem will not be difficult to solve, if properly handled. / ～有火警，将玻璃击碎。In case of fire, break the glass. (a notice) / ～发生此种情况，我们即诉诸法律。In that event, we would take the matter to court.

如[3] rú *formal* (adjective suffix): 侃侃～也 fervently eloquent

如臂使指 rú bì shǐ zhǐ have a perfect command of sth.

如常 rúcháng as usual: 一切～。Things are as usual. / 病人起居～了。The patient was beginning to live a normal life.

如出一口 rú chū yī kǒu as if from one mouth—with one voice; unanimously

如出一辙 rú chū yī zhé be exactly the same; be no different from each other; be cut from the same cloth

如此 rúcǐ so; such; in this way; like that: ～勇敢 so brave / ～聪明的孩子很少见。Such an intelligent child is rarely seen. / 他来得～之快，完全出乎意料。I never expected him to get here so soon. / 似乎是～。So it appears. / 原文～，未加改动。This is a faithful reproduction of the original, without any alterations. / 他的脾气向来～。He has always been so. *or* He's always like this. / 朋友之间互相帮助，理当～。Friends always help each other, and rightly so. / 事已～，后悔也是枉然。Now it's done, regrets are of no avail. *or* It's no use crying over spilt milk. / 情况就是～。That's how things stand. / 困难是很多的，虽然～，也要想法完成任务。We'll try to fulfil our task in spite of the many difficulties.

如此等等 rúcǐ děngděng and so on and so forth

如此而已 rúcǐ éryǐ that's what it all adds up to: ～，岂有他哉! And that's all there is to it!

如此这般 rúcǐ zhèbān thus and thus; thus and so: 他～嘱咐了我一番。He told me that thus and so was to be done, in such and such a manner. / 他把这计算机的功能～地跟我说了一遍。He went through all the computer's functions with me.

如次 rúcì be as follows: 其理由～。The reasons are as follows.

如弟 rúdì *old* a sworn younger brother

如堕五里雾中 rú duò wǔlǐwù zhōng as if lost in a thick fog; utterly mystified

如堕烟海 rú duò yānhǎi as if lost on a misty sea; all at sea; completely at a loss: 他们不懂得辩证法，结果～，抓不住主要矛盾。They do not know dialectics, and the result is that they are all at sea and unable to grasp the principal contradiction.

如法炮制 rú fǎ páozhì prepare herbal medicine by the prescribed method—follow a set pattern; follow suit

如夫人 rúfū·rén *old* concubine

如故 rúgù ① as before: 依然如故 yīrán rúgù ② like old friends: 一见如故 yījiàn rúgù

如果 rúguǒ *conj.* if; in case (of); in the event of: 你～要来，请事先告诉我。Let me know in advance if you're coming. / 我们～不加强学习，就会跟不上形势。We can't keep abreast of the developing situation unless we study harder. / 我明天再来，～你现在有事的话。I'll come here tomorrow if you're tied up right now. / ～不是他指引的话，我们就迷路了。If it weren't for him, we would have gone astray. / ～发生火警，拨120电话。In case of fire, dial 120. / ～下雨，联欢会将在室内举行。In the event of rain, the party will be held indoors.

如何 rúhé how; what: 词典工作进展～? How are you getting along with the dictionary work? / 此事～办理? How are we to handle this matter? / 他不知～是好。He didn't know what to do. / 这个电影你觉得～? How do you like the film? *or* What do you think of the film?

如虎添翼 rú hǔ tiān yì like a tiger that has grown wings—with might redoubled

如花似锦 rúhuā-sìjǐn like flowers and brocade— ① beautiful (scenery) ② bright (future): 前程～ have a bright (*or* glorious) future

如花似玉 rúhuā-sìyù like flowers and jade—(of a woman) young and beautiful

如火如荼 rúhuǒ-rútú like a raging fire: 全国掀起了～的改革热潮。Reform is catching on like fire throughout the country.

如获至宝 rú huò zhìbǎo as if one had found a priceless treasure: 他终于弄到了这本书，真是～。When he at last managed to get a copy of the book, he felt as if he'd found a priceless treasure.

如饥似渴 rújī-sìkě as if thirsting or hungering for sth.; with great eagerness: ～地寻求真理 seek truth with great eagerness

如箭在弦 rú jiàn zài xián same as 箭在弦上 jiàn zài xián shàng

如胶似漆 rújiāo-sìqī stick to each other like glue or lacquer; remain glued to each other; be deeply attached to each other

如今 rújīn nowadays; now: ～很少有人用毛笔了。Few people use writing brushes nowadays. / ～咱们山村也有了自己的大学生。Now our mountain village has its own college students.

如来 Rúlái Tathagata (lit. "one who has thus arrived"; one of the titles of Buddha)

如狼牧羊 rú láng mù yáng like a wolf shepherding sheep—(of an oppressive official) ride roughshod over the people

如狼似虎 rúláng-sìhǔ as ferocious as wolves and tigers; like cruel beasts of prey

如雷贯耳 rú léi guàn ěr (also 如雷灌耳 rú léi guàn ěr)

reverberate like thunder: 久闻大名,～。Your exalted name has long resounded in my ears.

如临大敌 rú lín dàdí　as if faced with a formidable foe

如临深渊,如履薄冰 rú lín shēnyuān, rú lǚ bóbīng　as though on the brink of an abyss, as though treading on thin ice—acting with extreme caution

如芒在背 rú máng zài bèi　same as 芒刺在背 mángcì zài bèi

如梦初醒 rú mèng chū xǐng　as if awakening from a dream—beginning to see the light: 一席话, 说得他～。This conversation made him suddenly see the light.

如命 rúmìng　*pol.*　in compliance with your instructions

如鸟兽散 rú niǎo-shòu sàn　scatter and flee like birds and beasts; flee helter-skelter; be utterly routed

如牛负重 rú niú fùzhòng　like an ox carrying a heavy load: 彼等债务丛集,～。Their debts piled up like loads on the backs of oxen.

如期 rúqī　as scheduled; by the scheduled time; on schedule: 会议将～召开。The conference will be convened as scheduled. / 任务已～完成。The assignment has been completed according to schedule. / 货物～运到。The goods arrived on schedule.

如其 rúqí　*conj.*　if; in case (of); in the event of:～无人接待, 你可改日再去。If nobody is there to receive you, go again another day. / 你父亲～亡故, 由你继承其钱财。In the event of your father's death, you will inherit his money.

如泣如诉 rúqì-rúsù　(of music or singing) querulous and plaintive

如日方升 rú rì fāng shēng　rising like the morning sun—have bright and boundless prospects

如日中天 rú rì zhōngtiān　like the sun at high noon—at the apex (*or* zenith) of one's power, career, etc.

如入鲍鱼之肆 rú rù bàoyú zhī sì　(usu. used in) ～, 久而不闻其臭 it's like staying in a fish market and getting used to the stink—long exposure to bad surroundings or bad company accustoms one to evil ways

如入无人之境 rú rù wú rén zhī jìng　like entering an unpeopled land—smashing all resistance; meeting no resistance

如入芝兰之室 rú rù zhīlán zhī shì　(usu. used in) ～, 久而不闻其香 it's like entering a room full of fragrant orchids and getting used to the sweet smell—associating with people of noble character accustoms one to good ways

如若 rúruò　*conj.*　if; in case (of); in the event of: ～不信, 请拭目以待。If you don't believe it, wait and see. / 此事宜立刻进行,～不然则将坐失良机。We'd better do it right now, or else we'll miss this golden opportunity.

如丧考妣 rú sàng kǎo-bǐ　(look) as if one had lost one's parents—(look) utterly wretched

如上 rúshàng　as above: ～所述 as stated (*or* mentioned) above / 为了澄清事实, 特将经过详情报告～。The above is a detailed account of what happened, given with the express purpose of setting the record straight.

如实 rúshí　go strictly by the facts: ～地反映情况 report the situation accurately; reflect things as they really are / ～汇报 give a true account of what happened; report to sb. on the actual situation

如释重负 rú shì zhòngfù　(feel) as if relieved of a heavy load: 她写完采访, 松了一口气, 觉得～。After she finished writing up the interview, she heaved a sigh as if relieved of a heavy burden.

如数家珍 rú shǔ jiāzhēn　as if enumerating one's family treasures—show thorough familiarity with a subject: 他对故宫设计讲解甚详,～。His description of the layout of the Imperial Palace was so detailed that it was as if he were enumerating the heirlooms of his own family.

如数 rúshù　exactly the number or amount: ～偿还 pay back in full / ～到齐 all present and correct

如斯 rúsī　*formal*　like that; such: ～而已。That's what it all adds up to.

如汤沃雪 rú tāng wò xuě　like melting snow with hot water—easily done

如同 rútóng　like; as: 待我们～亲人一样 treat us like their kith and kin / 大厅里亮得～白昼。It is as bright as daylight in the great hall.

如闻其声, 如见其人 rú wén qí shēng, rú jiàn qí rén　(so vividly described that) you seem to see and hear the person

如下 rúxià　as follows: 这个计划的要点～。The main points of the plan are as follows. / 全文～。The full text follows. / 发表～声明 make the following statement

如像 rúxiàng　like; as

如心 rúxīn　after one's own heart; to one's liking

如兄 rúxiōng　*old*　a sworn elder brother

如许 rúxǔ　*formal*　① so; such; in this way; like that: 泉水清～。The spring water is so clear. ② so much; so many: 枉费～工力 have wasted so much labour

如蚁附膻 rú yǐ fù shān　like ants clinging to sth. rank—swarming after unwholesome things or attaching oneself to influential people

如意[1] rúyì　find sth. satisfactory or as one wishes; be gratified: 祝万事～。May everything turn out as you wish. / 万事很难～。You can't expect everything to turn out as you wish. / 这件事可如了他的意了。This time he got exactly what he wanted.

如意[2] rúyì, *ruyi*,　an S-shaped ornamental object, usu. made of jade, formerly a symbol of good luck

如意算盘 rúyì suànpan　smug calculations; wishful thinking: 打～ indulge in wishful thinking / 打乱了他的～ upset his smug calculations

如影随形 rú yǐng suí xíng　like the shadow following the person—closely associated with each other

如鱼得水 rú yú dé shuǐ　like a stranded fish put back into water (said of one in his proper surroundings or having got a great aid)

如愿 rúyuàn　have one's wish fulfilled: 最后他得到了博士学位, 总算如了愿。He obtained a doctor's degree and thus had his wish fulfilled.

如愿以偿 rúyuàn yǐ cháng　have one's wish fulfilled; achieve (*or* obtain) what one wishes

如云 rúyún　cloudlike; many; full of: 奴仆～ full of servants / 出其东门, 有女～。(《诗经》) Through the east gate, outward bound, Cloudlike groups of maids I found.

如之奈何 rú zhī nàihé　what's to be done

如醉如痴 rúzuì-rúchī　as if intoxicated and stupefied: 他听着这慢乐章不觉心动神摇,～。As he sat listening to the slow movement, he was moved to the depth of his being, looking intoxicated and stupefied.

如坐针毡 rú zuò zhēnzhān　feel as if sitting on a bed of nails; be on pins and needles; be on tenterhooks: 他等着高考的结果,～。He was on tenterhooks, waiting for the results of the college entrance examination.

茹 rú　① *formal*　eat: ～素 be a vegetarian ② (Rú) a surname

茹苦含辛 rúkǔ-hánxīn　same as 含辛茹苦 hánxīn-rúkǔ

茹毛饮血 rúmáo-yǐnxuè　(of primitive man) eat the raw flesh of birds and beasts

铷 rú　*chem.*　rubidium (Rb)

儒 rú ① (Rú) Confucianism; Confucianist ② *old* scholar; learned man: 老～ an old scholar

儒艮 rúgèn *zool.* dugong

儒家 Rújiā the Confucianists (a school of thought in the Spring and Autumn and Warring States Periods 770–221 B.C.); the Confucian school

儒将 rújiàng scholar-general

儒林 rúlín scholars as a class; academic circles

儒略历 rúlüèlì Julian calendar

儒生 rúshēng *old* ① a Confucian scholar ② scholar; intellectual

儒术 rúshù Confucianism

儒雅 rúyǎ *formal* scholarly and refined: ～风度 a scholarly bearing

儒医 rúyī *old* scholar-physician (trained in traditional Chinese medicine)

濡 rú *formal* ① immerse; moisten: 濡笔 rúbǐ ② linger: 濡滞 rúzhì

濡笔 rúbǐ (also 濡毫 rúháo) dip a writing brush in ink

濡染 rúrǎn immerse; imbue

濡湿 rúshī soak; make wet

濡滞 rúzhì *formal* dilatory; lingering

薷 rú see 青香薷 qīngxiāngrú

嚅 rú see below

嚅嗫 rúniè same as 嗫嚅 nièrú

嚅嚅 rúrú hesitate in speech; hem and haw; mutter and mumble

孺 rú child: 妇孺 fùrú

孺慕 rúmù *formal* adore sb. as a child would its parents; hold sb. in great esteem

孺子 rúzǐ *formal* child

孺子可教 rúzǐ kě jiào you could be taught, young man; the boy is worth teaching

孺子牛 rúzǐniú a herd boy's willing ox—a servant of the people ——see also 横眉冷对千夫指，俯首甘为孺子牛 héngméi lěng duì qiānfū zhǐ, fǔshǒu gān wéi rúzǐniú

襦 rú *formal* a short jacket

蠕（蝡） rú wriggle; squirm

蠕虫 rúchóng worm; helminth

蠕虫学 rúchóngxué helminthology

蠕动 rúdòng ① wriggle; squirm ② *physiol.* peristalsis ③ *geol.* creep

蠕蠕 rúrú wriggling; squirming: ～而动 move along by wriggling

蠕形动物 rúxíng dòngwù Vermes

颥 rú see 颞颥 nièrú

rǔ

汝 rǔ *formal* you

汝辈 rǔbèi *formal* you people; you

汝曹 rǔcáo *formal* (used by a senior to a junior or subordinate) you people; you

乳 rǔ ① breast; mamma: 乳房 rǔfáng ② milk (in general): 炼乳 liànrǔ ③ any milk-like liquid: 豆乳 dòurǔ ④ give birth to: 孳乳 zīrǔ ⑤ newborn (animal); sucking: 乳猪 rǔzhū

乳白 rǔbái milky white; cream colour: ～灯泡 opal bulb／～玻璃 opal glass; opalescent glass; milk glass

乳钵 rǔbō mortar (a vessel)

乳齿 rǔchǐ milk tooth; deciduous tooth

乳蛾 rǔé *Chin. med.* acute tonsillitis

乳儿 rǔ'ér a nursing infant; suckling

乳房 rǔfáng ① breast; mamma ② udder

乳峰 rǔfēng (young women's) rounded breasts

乳腐 rǔfǔ *dial.* fermented bean curd

乳化 rǔhuà *chem.* emulsify: ～剂 emulsifying agent; emulsifier

乳化液 rǔhuàyè *chem.* emulsion: 水包油～ oil-in-water emulsion／油包水～ water-in-oil emulsion

乳化原油 rǔhuà yuányóu emulsified crude oil

乳剂 rǔjì *chem.* emulsion

乳胶 rǔjiāo *chem.* emulsion: ～漆 emulsion paint; latex

乳疽 rǔjū *Chin. med.* intramammary abscess

乳酪 rǔlào cheese

乳糜 rǔmí *physiol.* chyle: ～尿 chyluria

乳名 rǔmíng infant name; child's pet name

乳母 rǔmǔ wet nurse

乳牛 rǔniú dairy cattle; milch cow

乳牛场 rǔniúchǎng dairy farm

乳酸 rǔsuān lactic acid: ～钙 calcium lactate

乳糖 rǔtáng milk sugar; lactose: ～酶 lactase

乳头 rǔtóu ① nipple; teat; mammilla ② papilla: 视神经～ optic papilla／～状瘤 papilloma

乳腺 rǔxiàn *physiol.* mammary gland

乳腺癌 rǔxiàn'ái breast cancer

乳腺炎 rǔxiànyán mastitis

乳香 rǔxiāng *bot.* frankincense

乳臭 rǔxiù smelling of milk—childish

乳臭未干 rǔxiù wèi gān still smell of one's mother's milk—be young and inexperienced; be wet behind the ears

乳燕 rǔyàn a young swallow

乳罩 rǔzhào brassiere; bra

乳汁 rǔzhī milk (in general)

乳脂 rǔzhī butterfat

乳脂糖 rǔzhītáng toffee; taffy

乳制品 rǔzhìpǐn dairy products: ～工业 dairy industry

乳猪 rǔzhū sucking pig; suckling pig

乳浊液 rǔzhuóyè *chem.* emulsion

辱 rǔ ① disgrace; dishonour: 羞辱 xiūrǔ ② bring disgrace (or humiliation) to; insult: 折辱 zhérǔ ③ bring disgrace on; be a disgrace to: 辱没 rǔmò ④ *formal pol.* be indebted (to sb. for a kindness): ～承指教。I am very grateful to you for your advice.

辱骂 rǔmà abuse; call sb. names; hurl insults: ～和恐吓决不是战斗。(鲁迅) Hurling insults and threats is no way to fight.

辱命 rǔmìng disgrace a commission; fail to accomplish a mission: 出使～ fail to accomplish one's diplomatic mission／幸不～。I trust that you will accomplish your mission.／使于四方，不辱君命 not disgrace the commission of one's prince (or lord) when sent abroad as an envoy

辱没 rǔmò bring disgrace to; be unworthy of: ～门楣 bring disgrace to one's family／～先进集体的光荣称号 prove unworthy of the honourable title of an advanced group

擩 rǔ *dial.* put in; fill in

rù

入 rù ① go into; enter: 部队凯旋～城。The army made a triumphal entry into the city. / 长江流～东海。The Changjiang River empties into the Donghai Sea. / 时已～冬。Winter has set in. ② join; be admitted into; become a member of: 你孩子～了托儿所没有?——～了。Is your child at a nursery?—Yes, she is. ③ income: 岁入 suìrù ④ conform to; agree with: 入时 rùshí ⑤ short for 入声 rùshēng

入不敷出 rù bù fū chū income falling short of expenditure; unable to make ends meet

入仓 rùcāng be stored in a barn; be put in storage: 粮食要晒干才能～。Grain must be dried in the sun before it can be stored.

入场 rùchǎng entrance; admission: 凭票～。Admission by ticket only. / 运动员在乐曲声中列队～。The athletes marched into the arena to the sound of music.

入场券 rùchǎngquàn (admission) ticket

入超 rùchāo unfavourable balance of trade; import surplus

入党 rùdǎng join or be admitted to a political party (esp. the Chinese Communist Party): 不但组织上～, 而且思想上～ join the Party not only organizationally but also ideologically / ～申请报告 an application for Party membership

入定 rùdìng (of Buddhists) sit in meditation (a technique for mental self-discipline): 老僧～ an old monk sitting in meditation

入肚 rùdù swallow; consume: 一大碗面, 他一会儿功夫就都～了。He consumed a big bowlful of noodles in no time. / 三杯酒～, 他来了精神, 话也多了。After downing three glasses, he became lively and talkative.

入耳 rù'ěr pleasant to the ear: 不～的话 unpleasant words

入伏 rùfú the *fu* days begin; the hottest days of the year begin: 明天～。The *fu* days begin tomorrow. *or* From tomorrow we'll be having the hottest days of the year. / ～以来, 常有阵雨。Since the *fu* days began, there have been frequent showers. ——see also 三伏 sānfú

入港 rùgǎng ① *transportation* enter a port ② (of conversation) in full agreement; in perfect harmony: 二人谈得～。The two of them are deep in conversation and in perfect agreement with one another.

入彀 rùgòu *formal* ① be controlled or manipulated by sb.; play into sb.'s hands ② conform to a standard or to the normal order

入股 rùgǔ buy a share; become a shareholder

入骨 rùgǔ to the marrow: 恨之入骨 hèn zhī rùgǔ

入国问禁 rù guó wèn jìn on entering a country, inquire about its prohibitions (*or* taboos)

入黑 rùhēi towards evening; at nightfall; at dusk: ～路灯都亮了。The street lights go on at dusk.

入户 rùhù ① go to sb.'s place; call at sb.'s house ② obtain a residence permit

入画 rùhuà suitable for a painting; picturesque: 桂林山水, 处处可以～。Every bit of Guilin scenery is worth painting.

入会 rùhuì join a society, association, etc.

入伙[1] rùhuǒ join a gang; join in partnership

入伙[2] rùhuǒ have one's meals at a canteen or mess hall: 在食堂～ eat at one's mess

入籍 rùjí be naturalized: 入中国籍 be naturalized in China; become a Chinese citizen

入寂 rùjì (of Buddhist monks or nuns) pass away; die

入教 rùjiào embrace a religion

入静 rùjìng (of Taoists) sit still (a technique for achieving mental calm and conserving energy)

入境 rùjìng enter a country: ～登记 entrance registration / ～签证 entry visa / ～口岸 port of entry / 办理～手续 go through the entry formalities

入境问俗 rù jìng wèn sú on entering a country, inquire about its customs

入口[1] rùkǒu ① enter the mouth: 难于～ have a nasty taste / 此药不可～。This medicine is not to be taken orally. ② (of foreign goods or goods from another place) be transported into; import

入口[2] rùkǒu entrance: 车站～ entrance to the station

入寇 rùkòu invade (a country); intrude

入库 rùkù be put in storage; be laid up: 粮食都已～。All the grain has been put in storage. *or* All the grain is already in the granary.

入款 rùkuǎn income; receipts

入理 rùlǐ reasonable; sensible; right

入殓 rùliàn put a corpse in a coffin; encoffin

入列 rùliè *mil.* take one's place in the ranks; fall in

入门[1] rùmén ① cross the threshold; learn the rudiments of a subject: 学英语～并不难, 学好可不容易。Rudimentary English is easy to acquire, but mastery of the language is quite difficult. / 他是我的～师傅。He is the master who initiated me into the craft. / 我学桥牌还没～呢。I don't even know the ABC of bridge yet.

入门[2] rùmén (usu. used in book titles) elementary course; ABC; primer:《汉语～》*Gateway to Chinese* /《英语语法～》*Elementary English Grammar* /《摄影～》*The ABC of Photography* /《欧洲文化～》*An Introduction to European Culture*

入梦 rùmèng ① fall asleep ② (of a person) appear in one's dream

入迷 rùmí be fascinated; be enchanted: 他们的精彩表演使观众看得入了迷。The audience was fascinated by their superb performance. / 看书看～了 be engrossed in a book / 大家听他讲故事, 都听得～了。Everybody listened to his story with rapt attention.

入魔 rùmó be infatuated; be spellbound: 她做诗入了魔了。She's got poetry mania.

入木三分 rù mù sān fēn ① (of calligraphy) written in a forceful hand: 这位书法家的书法苍劲有力, ～。This calligrapher writes a forceful hand, with bold and vigorous strokes. ② penetrating; profound; keen: 这位经济学家的分析真是～。The economist's analysis was really penetrating.

入暮 rùmù towards evening; at nightfall; at dusk: ～时分 at dusk; at twilight

入侵 rùqīn invade; intrude; make an incursion; make inroads: 消灭一切敢于～的敌人 wipe out all enemies who dare to invade our country / 再次～ make another intrusion / ～飞机 an intruding aircraft / 军事～ military incursion

入情入理 rùqíng-rùlǐ fair and reasonable: 她的建议～。Her suggestion is fair and just.

入射点 rùshèdiǎn *phys.* incidence point

入射角 rùshèjiǎo *phys.* angle of incidence; incident angle

入射线 rùshèxiàn *phys.* incident ray

入神 rùshén ① be entranced; be enthralled: 他坐着听《圣母颂》入了神了。He sat entranced listening to *Ave Maria*. / 他越说越起劲, 大家越听越～。As he talked with more and more gusto, we came more and more under his spell. ② superb; marvellous: 这幅画画得真是～。This painting is really superb. *or* This is a marvellous picture.

入声 rùshēng entering tone (the fourth of the four tones in classical Chinese pronunciation, still retained

in certain dialects)

入时 rùshí *(of clothes)* fashionable; modish; *à la mode*: 打扮～ be fashionably dressed

入世不深 rù shì bù shēn lack of experience of life; not be socially experienced

入室 rùshì *formal* become well advanced in scholarship or highly proficient in a profession: ～弟子 advanced students ——see also 登堂入室 dēngtáng-rùshì

入室操戈 rùshì cāogē attack sb. with his own spear in his own house—turn sb.'s words or argument against himself

入手 rùshǒu start with; begin with; proceed from; take as the point of departure: 解决问题要从调查研究～。 To solve a problem, one has to start with investigation.

入睡 rùshuì go to sleep; fall asleep: 他晚上工作时间长了就不容易～。He can't get to sleep easily if he works long hours at night. / 吃了这种镇静剂很快就能～。You'll fall asleep soon after you take this sedative.

入土 rùtǔ be buried; be interred: 快～了 have one foot in the grave

入团 rùtuán join or be admitted to the Chinese Communist Youth League

入托 rùtuō start going to a nursery: 办理小孩～手续 enrol a child in a nursery

入微 rùwēi in every possible way; in a subtle way: 演员的表情细腻～。The actor performed with great delicacy and sensibility.

入味 rùwèi ① tasty: 菜做得很～。The dish is very tasty. ② interesting: 这出戏我们越看越～。The more we watched the play, the more it aroused our interest.

入伍 rùwǔ enlist in the armed forces; join up

入席 rùxí take one's seat at a banquet, ceremony, etc.: 主人请大家～。The host invited everyone to go in and be seated.

入乡随俗 rù xiāng suí sú same as 随乡入乡 suí xiāng rù xiāng

入选 rùxuǎn be selected; be chosen

入学 rùxué ① start school: ～年龄 school age / 我国儿童六、七岁～。In our country children start school at the age of six or seven. ② enter a school: 新生后天～。The new students will enter school the day after tomorrow. / 从～到毕业 from entrance to graduation / ～考试 entrance examination

入眼 rùyǎn pleasing to the eye: 这些衣服没有一件她看得～的。None of these clothes are to her liking. / 你这种行为真让人看不～。Your conduct is most unseemly.

入眼货 rùyǎnhuò sth. (esp. goods) pleasant to the eye or to one's liking: 现在市场繁荣，到处都有～。The market is flourishing, and there are so many things to attract the buyer.

入药 rùyào *Chin. med.* be used as medicine: 陈皮可以～。Dried tangerine peel can be used as (Chinese) medicine.

入夜 rùyè at nightfall: ～，工地上灯火通明。When night fell the construction site was ablaze with light.

入狱 rùyù be put in prison; be sent to jail

入院 rùyuàn be admitted to hospital; be hospitalized: 办理～手续 fill out forms for admittance to a hospital

入帐 rùzhàng enter an item in an account; enter into the account book

入蛰 rùzhé *(of animals)* go into hibernation

入主出奴 rùzhǔ-chūnú academic sectarianism or bigotry

入赘 rùzhuì marry into and live with one's bride's family

入座 rùzuò take one's seat (esp. at a feast)

溽 rù *formal* humid; damp

溽热 rùrè humid and hot; muggy

溽暑 rùshǔ sweltering summer weather: ～炎夏 a sweltering hot summer

缛 rù elaborate; cumbersome: 繁文缛节 fánwén-rùjié

蓐 rù *formal* straw mat or mattress: 坐蓐 zuòrù

褥 rù cotton-padded mattress: 被褥 bèirù

褥疮 rùchuāng *med.* bedsore

褥单 rùdān (also 褥单子 rùdānzi) bed sheet

褥套 rùtào ① bedding sack ② mattress cover

褥子 rùzi cotton-padded mattress

ruá

挼 ruá *dial.* ① (of paper or cloth) wrinkle; crease ② (of clothes) wear thin ——see also ruó

ruǎn

阮 ruǎn ① short for 阮咸 ruǎnxián ② (Ruǎn) a surname

阮咸 ruǎnxián *mus.* a plucked stringed instrument

朊 ruǎn another name for 蛋白质 dànbáizhì

软(輭) ruǎn ① soft; flexible; supple; pliable: ～椅 a soft chair / 柳条很～。Willow twigs are pliable. ② soft; mild; gentle: 你对他～了些。You've been a bit soft with him. / 他话说得太～了。He spoke too mildly. / 她看儿子哭了，心～了下来。When she saw her son cry, her heart softened ③ weak; feeble: 他两腿发～。His legs felt weak (*or* like jelly). / 最近以来，爷爷的身子骨儿越来越感到～了。Grandfather has been getting feebler lately. ④ poor in quality, ability, etc.: 货色～ poor-quality goods / 工夫～ inadequate skill ⑤ easily moved or influenced: 他心肠～。He is tender-hearted.

软包装 ruǎnbāozhuāng foods sold in soft packages

软币 ruǎnbì ① paper money; paper currency; note ② soft currency

软蛋 ruǎndàn ① soft-shelled egg ② *dial.* coward

软刀子 ruǎndāozi soft knife—a way of harming people imperceptibly

软钉子 ruǎndīngzi a soft nail—a mild (*or* tactful) refusal or refutation ——see also 碰钉子 pèng dīngzi

软缎 ruǎnduàn soft silk fabric in satin weave

软腭 ruǎn'è *physiol.* soft palate

软耳朵 ruǎn'ěrduo a soft ear—a credulous person

软风 ruǎnfēng *meteorol.* light air

软腐病 ruǎnfǔbìng *agric.* soft rot

软钢 ruǎngāng mild steel; soft steel

软膏 ruǎngāo ointment; paste

软骨头 ruǎngǔtou a soft bone—a weak-kneed person; a spineless person; a coward

软骨 ruǎngǔ *physiol.* cartilage

软骨病 ruǎngǔbìng osteomalacia

软骨鱼 ruǎngǔyú cartilaginous fish

软管 ruǎnguǎn flexible pipe or tube; hose: 铠装～ armoured hose

软罐头 ruǎnguàntou foods packed in carton containers

软焊 ruǎnhàn soft soldering; soldering

软化 ruǎnhuà ① soften: 使硬水～ soften hard water / 他对我态度逐渐～。He gradually softened towards me.

② win over by soft tactics: 〜政策 soft tactics ③ bate (leather)

软话 ruǎnhuà　soft words (spoken to express apology, ask pardon, show sympathy, etc.)

软和 ruǎnhuo　*inf.*　① soft: 〜的褥子 a soft mattress / 这个枕头很〜。This pillow is very soft. ② gentle; kind; soft: 给老太太说几句〜话儿 Say some kind words (*or* Say something nice) to please the old lady.

软件 ruǎnjiàn　*computer*　software

软禁 ruǎnjìn　put (*or* place) sb. under house arrest

软科学 ruǎnkēxué　soft science

软款 ruǎnkuǎn　soft; lithe

软麻工艺 ruǎnmá gōngyì　*text.*　bruising (of flax); batching (of jute)

软媚 ruǎnmèi　gentle and lovely; genial; lovable

软锰矿 ruǎnměngkuàng　pyrolusite

软绵绵 ruǎnmiánmián　① soft: 〜的枕头 a soft pillow / 这支歌〜的。This song is too sentimental. ② weak: 她病好了,但身体还是〜的。She is well now, but she still feels weak.

软磨 ruǎnmó　use soft tactics: 〜硬抗 use both hard and soft tactics

软木 ruǎnmù　cork (bark of the oak tree): 〜塞 cork (as a stopper)

软泥 ruǎnní　*geol.*　ooze

软片 ruǎnpiàn　(a roll of) film

软弱 ruǎnruò　weak; feeble; flabby: 他病后身体〜无力。His illness has left him weak. / 领导〜 weak leadership / 他太〜,不会保护自己的权利。He is too weak to defend his rights.

软弱可欺 ruǎnruò kě qī　be weak and easy to bully: 不要把我们的克制当作〜。Don't mistake our restraint for weakness.

软弱无能 ruǎnruò wúnéng　weak and incompetent; effete; ineffectual

软设备 ruǎnshèbèi　another name for 软件 ruǎnjiàn

软食 ruǎnshí　soft diet; soft food; pap

软式网球 ruǎnshì wǎngqiú　soft tennis

软水 ruǎnshuǐ　soft water

软酥酥 ruǎnsūsū　limp; weak; soft

软糖 ruǎntáng　soft sweets; jelly drops

软梯 ruǎntī　*inf.*　rope ladder

软体动物 ruǎntǐ dòngwù　mollusc

软体动物学 ruǎntǐ dòngwùxué　malacology

软通货 ruǎntōnghuò　soft currency

软卧 ruǎnwò　short for 软席卧铺 ruǎnxí wòpù

软席 ruǎnxí　soft seat or berth; cushioned seat or berth: 〜车厢 railway carriage (*or* car) with soft seats or berths

软席卧铺 ruǎnxí wòpù　sleeping carriage with soft (*or* cushioned) berths

软线 ruǎnxiàn　*elec.*　flexible cord

软性 ruǎnxìng　softness; gentleness; lightness: 〜读物 light reading

软饮料 ruǎnyǐnliào　soft drink

软硬不吃 ruǎn-yìng bù chī　yield neither to persuasion nor to coercion

软硬兼施 ruǎn-yìng jiān shī　use both hard and soft tactics; couple threats with promises; use the stick and the carrot

软语 ruǎnyǔ　soft words

软玉 ruǎnyù　nephrite (a mineral)

软玉温香 ruǎnyù-wēnxiāng　soft fragrance and warmth —feminine charm: 〜,能不动心? How could a man resist her soft fragrance and warmth?

软炸 ruǎnzhá　(in Chinese cooking) soft-fry

软脂 ruǎnzhī　*chem.*　palmitin

软脂酸 ruǎnzhīsuān　*chem.*　palmitic acid; palmic acid

软组织 ruǎnzǔzhī　*physiol.*　soft tissue

ruí

蕤　ruí　see 葳蕤 wēiruí

ruǐ

蕊（蘃、蘂）　ruǐ　stamen or pistil: 花蕊 huāruǐ

ruì

芮　Ruì　a surname

枘　ruì　tenon

枘凿 ruìzáo　same as 凿枘 záoruì

蚋（蜹）　ruì　buffalo gnat; blackfly

锐　ruì　① sharp; keen; acute: 尖锐 jiānruì ② vigour; fighting spirit: 养精蓄锐 yǎngjīng-xùruì ③ rapid; sudden: 〜进 rapid advance

锐不可当 ruì bùkě dāng　can't be held back; be irresistible: 以〜之势 with irresistible force / 我军攻势迅猛,〜。Our attack was so swift and violent that nothing could withstand it.

锐减 ruìjiǎn　sharp fall (*or* decline); sudden drop

锐角 ruìjiǎo　*math.*　acute angle

锐利 ruìlì　① sharp-edged; sharp-pointed; sharp; keen: 〜的匕首 a sharp dagger / 〜的武器 a sharp (*or* powerful) weapon / 〜的攻势 a spirited attack / 猫爪子很〜。A cat's claws are very sharp. ② penetrating; incisive; sharp; keen: 眼光〜 sharp-eyed; sharp-sighted / 〜的笔锋 a sharp pen; a vigorous style

锐敏 ruìmǐn　(of senses or insight) keen; sharp: 〜的嗅觉 a keen sense of smell / 〜的眼光 sharp-eyed; keen-sighted

锐气 ruìqì　dash; drive: 表现了青年人的〜 show the dashing spirit of young people / 这场比赛咱们一定得赢,不能挫了〜。We've got to win the game, otherwise we'll lose our momentum. / 挫敌〜 blunt the enemy's will to fight; take the edge off the enemy's spirit

锐眼 ruìyǎn　sharp eyes

锐意 ruìyì　*formal*　firm; resolute; determined; be bent on: 〜革新 be bent (*or* keen) on reform

瑞　ruì　auspicious; lucky: 祥瑞 xiángruì

瑞典 Ruìdiǎn　Sweden

瑞典人 Ruìdiǎnrén　Swede; the Swedish

瑞典语 Ruìdiǎnyǔ　Swedish (language)

瑞士 Ruìshì　Switzerland

瑞士人 Ruìshìrén　Swiss

瑞香 ruìxiāng　*bot.*　winter daphne (*Daphne odora*)

瑞雪 ruìxuě　timely snow; auspicious snow: 华北各省普降〜。Every province in North China has had an auspicious snowfall.

瑞雪兆丰年 ruìxuě zhào fēngnián　a timely snow promises a good harvest; a snow year, a rich year

瑞芝 ruìzhī　another name for 灵芝 língzhī

睿（叡）　ruì　*formal*　farsighted; having foresight

睿哲 ruìzhé　*formal*　wise and farsighted

睿智　ruìzhì　*formal*　wise and farsighted

rùn

闰　rùn　*astron.*　intercalation
闰年　rùnnián　leap (*or* intercalary) year
闰日　rùnrì　leap (*or* intercalary) day
闰月　rùnyuè　intercalary month in the lunar calendar; leap month

润　rùn　① moist; smooth; sleek: 这个条幅墨色很～. This scroll is written in dark full-bodied ink. ② moisten; lubricate: 喝点儿水～一～嗓子. Drink some water to moisten your throat. ③ embellish; touch up: 润色 rùnsè ④ profit; benefit: 利润 lìrùn
润笔　rùnbǐ　① (of a writing brush) dip in ink ② *old* remuneration for a writer, painter or calligrapher
润肠　rùncháng　*Chin. med.*　lubricate the intestines; —ease constipation
润肺　rùnfèi　*Chin. med.*　moisten the lungs—make expectoration easy
润肤露　rùnfūlù　skin lotion; skin moisturizer
润滑　rùnhuá　lubricate: ～系统 lubricating system; lubrication system
润滑油　rùnhuáyóu　lubricating oil; lubrication oil
润滑脂　rùnhuázhī　(lubricating) grease
润色　rùnsè　polish (a piece of writing, etc.); touch up: 这篇文章需要～一下. This essay needs polishing.
润湿　rùnshī　① moist; damp: ～的泥土 damp soil ② soak; infiltrate: 露水～了他的衣服. His clothes were soaked with dew.
润饰　rùnshì　same as 润色 rùnsè
润燥　rùnzào　*Chin. med.*　moisten the respiratory tract, skin, etc.
润泽　rùnzé　① moist; smooth; sleek: 这匹马全身～有光. The horse's coat was sleek and glossy. / 雨后荷花显得更加～了. After the rain the lotus flowers looked fuller. ② moisten; lubricate: 用油～轮轴 oil an axle
润资　rùnzī　same as 润笔 rùnbǐ②

ruó

捼　ruó　*formal*　crumple; rub ——see also ruá
捼搓　ruócuo　crumple; rub: 洗衣服别使劲～. Don't rub too hard when you wash your clothes (on a washboard).

ruò

若¹　ruò　*adv. formal*　(usu. used in set phrases) as if; like: 若有所失 ruò yǒu suǒ shī
若²　ruò　*conj. formal*　if: ～不刻苦钻研, 如何取得成果? How can we achieve anything if we don't work hard?
若³　ruò　*formal*　you: ～辈 you people; you
若虫　ruòchóng　*zool.*　nymph
若非　ruòfēi　*conj. formal*　if not; were it not for: ～亲身经历, 岂知其中甘苦. You cannot appreciate the difficulty except through personal experience.
若夫　ruòfū　*part. formal*　(used at the beginning of a sentence to introduce a subject or indicate a change of subject) with regard to; as for
若干　ruògān　① a certain number or amount: ～年 a number of years / ～次 several times / ～地区 certain areas ② how many; how much: 共得～? How many in all? *or* What is the sum total?
若何　ruòhé　how; what: 结果～, 还不得而知. The outcome is not known yet. *or* I'm unable to find out how things have come out.
若即若离　ruòjí-ruòlí　be neither close nor distant; maintain a lukewarm relationship; keep sb. at arm's length
若明若暗　ruòmíng-ruò'àn　have an indistinct (*or* blurred) picture of; have a hazy (*or* vague) notion about: 对情况～ have only a vague idea of the situation
若是　ruòshì　*conj.*　if: 你们～有不同意见, 请现在提出来. If you have any different ideas, please speak up now. / 我～他, 决不会那么办. If I were him, I wouldn't have done it that way.
若无其事　ruò wú qí shì　as if nothing had happened—calm; indifferent: 敌人已逼近村子, 但白求恩医生却一地抢救伤员. The enemy was approaching the village, but Dr. Bethune went on treating the wounded as if nothing were happening. / 急着等你帮忙, 你怎么还～? How can you remain indifferent when your help is urgently needed?
若要人不知, 除非己莫为　ruò yào rén bù zhī, chúfēi jǐ mò wéi　if you don't wish anyone to know what you've done, it is better not to have done it in the first place
若隐若现　ruòyǐn-ruòxiàn　appear indistinctly: 山峰在云雾中～. The mountaintops loom through the clouds.
若有所失　ruò yǒu suǒ shī　feel as if something were missing; look distracted
若有所思　ruò yǒu suǒ sī　seem lost in thought; look pensive: 他凝视着远方, ～的样子. He gazed into the distance and seemed lost in thought.

偌　ruò　*adv.*　such; so
偌大　ruòdà　*old*　of such a size; so big: ～的地方 such a big place / ～年纪 so old; so advanced in years

弱　ruò　① weak; feeble: 他身体很～. He is very weak. / 由～变强 go from weakness to strength / 他年纪虽老, 干活并不～. Old as he is, he works energetically. / 他的语法～. He's weak in grammar. 这屋光线～. The light is poor in this room. ② young: 老弱 lǎo-ruò① ③ inferior: 她的能力并不比别人～. She's no less capable than the others. / 这个队的防守～于对方. This team's defence is not as good as the opponent's ④ *formal*　lose (through death): 又～一个. Another one (usu. a celebrity) has passed away. ⑤ (following a fraction or decimal) a little less than: 三分之一～ a little less than one-third
弱不禁风　ruò bù jīn fēng　too weak to withstand a gust of wind; extremely delicate; fragile
弱不胜衣　ruò bù shèng yī　(of a woman) too frail to bear the weight of one's clothes
弱点　ruòdiǎn　weakness; weak point; failing: 性格上的～ weaknesses of character
弱冠　ruòguàn　*formal*　a young man of around twenty (an age when man in ancient China started wearing hats)
弱碱　ruòjiǎn　*chem.*　weak base
弱脉　ruòmài　*Chin. med.*　weak pulse
弱拍　ruòpāi　*mus.*　weak beat; unaccented beat
弱肉强食　ruòròu-qiángshí　the weak are the prey of the strong—the law of the jungle
弱视　ruòshì　weak-sighted
弱酸　ruòsuān　*chem.*　weak acid
弱息　ruòxī　*formal hum.*　my child
弱小　ruòxiǎo　small and weak: ～的婴儿 a small and

weak baby / ～民族 small and weak nations

弱音器 ruòyīnqì *mus.* mute; sordine

弱智 ruòzhì mentally deficient; retarded: ～儿童 a retarded child

箬 (篛)   ruò   see below

箬帽 ruòmào (also 箬笠 ruòlì) a broad-rimmed conical bamboo hat worn by peasants, fishermen, etc., as protection against sun and rain

箬竹 ruòzhú *bot.* indocalamus

爇 (焫)   ruò   *formal* light; burn: ～烛 light a candle

S

sā

仨 sā *inf.* (not used with measure words) three: 给我来～。Give me three. / 我们 (哥儿) ～ we three (brothers); the three of us

仨瓜俩枣 sāguā-liǎzǎo three melons and two dates—only a few small things; mere trifles

撒 sā ① cast; let go; let out: 撒网 sāwǎng / 把手～开 let go one's hold ② *derog.* throw off all restraint; let oneself go: 撒酒疯 sā jiǔfēng——see also sǎ

撒巴掌 sā bāzhang *dial.* let go one's hold; let go

撒旦 Sādàn *Christianity* Satan

撒刁 sādiāo act in a slick and shameless way

撒疯 sāfēng (also 撒风 sāfēng) ① behave atrociously ② vent one's anger

撒哈拉沙漠 Sāhālā Shāmò the Sahara (Desert)

撒欢儿 sāhuānr *dial.* gambol; frisk

撒谎 sāhuǎng *inf.* tell a lie; lie: 当面～ tell a barefaced lie; lie in one's teeth

撒娇 sājiāo act like a spoiled child; act spoiled

撒酒疯 sā jiǔfēng be drunk and act crazy; be roaring drunk

撒科打诨 sākē-dǎhùn same as 插科打诨 chākē-dǎhùn

撒拉族 Sālāzú the Salar (Sala) nationality, or the Salars (Salas), distributed over Qinghai and Gansu Provinces

撒赖 sālài make a scene; act shamelessly; raise hell

撒尿 sāniào *inf.* piss; pee

撒泼 sāpō be unreasonable and make a scene

撒气 sāqì ① (of a ball, tyre, etc.) leak; go soft; get a flat: 后胎～了。The back tyre has got a puncture. *or* The back tyre is flat. ② vent one's anger or ill temper: 你别拿我～嘛。Don't take it out on me.

撒手 sāshǒu let go one's hold; let go: 你拿稳，我～了。Hold it tight. I'll let go. / ～不管 wash one's hands of the business; refuse to have anything more to do with the matter

撒手锏 sāshǒujiǎn an unexpected thrust with the mace—one's trump card

撒腿 sātuǐ take to one's heels; beat it: ～就跑 make off at once; scamper

撒网 sāwǎng ① cast a net; pay out a net ② invite relatives and friends to weddings, funerals, etc. with the intention of collecting presents

撒鸭子 sāyāzi (also 撒丫子 sāyāzi) *dial.* take to one's heels; beat it: ～就跑 beat it double-quick

撒野 sāyě act wildly; behave atrociously

sǎ

洒 (灑) sǎ sprinkle; spray; spill; shed: ～农药 spray pesticide / 别把汤～了。Don't spill the soup. /

甘～热血为人民 willingly shed one's blood for the people

洒家 sǎjiā *old* (used by men) I

洒泪 sǎlèi shed tears: ～告别 take a tearful leave

洒落 sǎluò ① drip; trickle down: 一串串汗珠～在地上。Drops of sweat trickled down to the ground. ② same as 洒脱 sǎtuō

洒洒 sǎsǎ see 洋洋洒洒 yángyángsǎsǎ

洒扫 sǎsǎo sprinkle water and sweep the floor; sweep: 黎明即起，～庭除。Rise at dawn and sweep the courtyard.

洒水车 sǎshuǐchē watering car; sprinkler

洒脱 sǎtuō (of one's speech, deportment, etc.) free and easy; unrestrained

靸 sǎ *dial.* slip on cloth shoes without pulling up the heels; slip on slippers

靸鞋 sǎxié slippers

撒 sǎ ① scatter; sprinkle; spread: ～农药 dust crops with an insecticide / ～种 sow seeds ② spill; drop: 她把～在路上的麦粒儿扫到一块儿。She swept up the grains of wheat that had spilled on the ground.——see also sā

撒播 sǎbō broadcast sowing; broadcast

撒播机 sǎbōjī broadcast seeder; broadcaster

撒肥机 sǎféijī fertilizer distributor; manure spreader

撒粉 sǎfěn *agric.* dusting

撒粉器 sǎfěnqì duster

撒漫 sǎman spending freely; squandering: 他是个～的主儿。He's a spendthrift.

撒施 sǎshī *agric.* scatter or spread fertilizer over the fields; broadcast fertilizer

sà

卅 sà thirty

飒 sà see below

飒然 sàrán *formal* soughing; whistling: 有风～而至。A soughing wind sprang up.

飒飒 sàsà *onom.* sough; rustle: 秋风～。The autumn wind is soughing through the trees.

飒爽 sàshuǎng *formal* of martial bearing; valiant

飒爽英姿 sàshuǎng yīngzī same as 英姿飒爽 yīngzī sàshuǎng

脎 sà *chem.* osazone

萨 (薩) Sà a surname

萨尔瓦多 Sà'ěrwǎduō El Salvador

萨尔瓦多人 Sà'ěrwǎduōrén Salvadoran

萨克管 sàkèguǎn *mus.* saxophone

萨克号 sàkèhào *mus.* saxhorn

萨拉热窝 Sàlārèwō Sarajevo

萨摩亚 Sàmóyà Samoa

萨摩亚人 Sàmóyàrén Samoan
萨摩亚语 Sàmóyàyǔ Samoan (language)
萨其马 sàqímǎ a kind of Manchu candied fritter

sa

挲(挱) sa see 摩挲 māsa ——see also shā; suō

sāi

塞 sāi ① fill in; squeeze in; stuff: 箱子不太满, 还可以再～点东西。 There is still room in the suitcase to squeeze a few more things in. / 把窟窿～住。 Stop that hole. / 水管～住了。 The waterpipe is clogged up. ② stopper: 木～ stopper; plug; spigot ——see also sài; sè
塞尺 sāichǐ another name for 厚薄规 hòubógūi
塞规 sāiguī mech. plug gauge
塞满 sāimǎn fill up; stuff full
塞牙 sāiyá (of food) get stuck between the teeth
塞子 sāizi stopper; plug; spigot; cork

腮(顋) sāi cheek
腮帮子 sāibāngzi inf. cheek
腮颊 sāijiá cheek
腮托 sāituō mus. chin rest (of a violin or viola)
腮腺 sāixiàn physiol. parotid gland
腮腺炎 sāixiànyán med. parotitis; mumps

噻 sāi see below
噻吩 sāifēn chem. thiophene
噻唑 sāizuò chem. thiazole

鳃 sāi gill; branchia
鳃瓣 sāibàn gill lamella
鳃盖 sāigài gill cover

sài

塞 sài a place of strategic importance ——see also sāi; sè
塞尔维亚-克罗地亚语 Sài'ěrwéiyà-kèluódìyàyǔ Serbo-Croatian
塞拉利昂 Sàilālì'áng Sierra Leone
塞拉利昂人 Sàilālì'ángrén Sierra Leonian
塞内加尔 Sàinèijiā'ěr Senegal
塞内加尔人 Sàinèijiā'ěrrén Senegalese
塞浦路斯 Sàipǔlùsī Cyprus
塞浦路斯人 Sàipǔlùsīrén Cypriot
塞舌尔 Sàishé'ěr Seychelles
塞舌尔人 Sàishé'ěrrén Seychellois
塞外 Sàiwài north of the Great Wall; beyond the Great Wall: ～江南 lush southern-type fields north of the Great Wall
塞翁失马 sàiwēng shī mǎ the old frontiersman losing his horse—a blessing in disguise: ～, 安知非福。 Just like the old frontiersman losing his horse, who knows but that this may be a blessing in disguise? (a common remark on a seeming piece of bad luck; from the parable in the *Huai Nan zi* 《淮南子》 about the old frontiersman whose strayed horse returned to its master accompanied by a better horse)

赛 sài ① match; game; competition; contest: 足球～ football match (or game) ② have a competition: 咱俩～一～看。 Let's have a competition. / 要～出水平, 也要～出风格。 We must give a good account of ourselves and display fine sportsmanship as well. ③ be comparable to; surpass: 我这萝卜～梨。 These radishes of mine taste as good as pears.
赛车 sàichē sports ① cycle racing; motorcycle race; automobile race ② racing vehicle
赛过 sàiguò overtake; be better than; surpass; exceed: 此处风光～江南。 The scenery here surpasses that south of the lower reaches of the Changjiang River. / 战士们个个～小老虎。 The soldiers were all as brave as young tigers.
赛力散 sàilìsǎn agric. phenylmercuric acetate (PMA)
赛璐玢 sàilùfēn cellophane
赛璐珞 sàilùluò celluloid
赛马 sàimǎ horse racing
赛跑 sàipǎo race: 长距离～ long-distance race / 一百米～ 100-metre dash / 越野～ cross-country race
赛艇 sàitǐng sports ① rowing ② racing boat; shell

sān

三 sān ① three ② more than two; several; many: ～弯九转 (full of) twists and turns
三八妇女节 Sān Bā Fùnǚjié March 8, International Women's Day
三八红旗手 sānbā hóngqíshǒu a woman pacesetter
三八式 sānbāshì 38-rifle (a Japanese rifle made in the 38th year of Showa 昭和): 一支～ a 38-rifle / 缴获十杆～ captured ten 38-rifles
三八式干部 sānbāshì gànbù thirty-eighter (a person who joined the revolution in 1938)
三百六十行 sānbǎi liùshí háng all trades and professions; all walks of life
三板 sānbǎn another name for 舢板 shānbǎn
三胞胎 sānbāotāi triplets
三宝 sānbǎo ① three treasures; three precious things ② Buddhism Triratna; the triad of the Buddha, the dharma, and the sangha
三倍体 sānbèitǐ biol. triploid
三边形 sānbiānxíng another name for 三角形 sānjiǎoxíng
三不管 sānbùguǎn come within nobody's jurisdiction; be nobody's business
三部曲 sānbùqǔ trilogy
三彩 sāncǎi three-colour glazed pottery (esp. of the Tang Dynasty, 618-907)
三槽出钢 sāncáo chūgāng metall. three-trough steel tapping technique
三叉戟 sānchājǐ a three-pronged spear; trident
三叉戟飞机 sānchājǐ fēijī Trident
三叉神经 sānchā shénjīng physiol. trigeminal nerve
三岔路口 sānchà lùkǒu (also 三岔口 sānchàkǒu) a fork in the road; a junction of three roads
三长两短 sāncháng-liǎngduǎn unexpected misfortune; sth. unfortunate, esp. death: 万一他有个～ if anything untoward should happen to him; in case he should die
三朝元老 sān cháo yuánlǎo minister to three emperors —an official who stays in power under different regimes: 他许家是～。改朝换代, 改不了他许家的天下。 The Xus have been ranking officials in three succeeding regimes. Dynasties may change, but the Xus' power never wanes.
三重 sānchóng triple; threefold: 遭受帝国主义、封建主

义和官僚资本主义的～压迫 be subjected to a threefold oppression by imperialism, feudalism and bureaucrat-capitalism

三重唱 sānchóngchàng *mus.* (vocal) trio

三重奏 sānchóngzòu *mus.* (instrumental) trio

三春 sānchūn *formal* the three spring months

三春柳 sānchūnliǔ another name for 柽柳 chēngliǔ

三次方程 sāncì fāngchéng *math.* cubic equation

三从四德 sāncóng sìdé the three obediences and four virtues (for a woman according to Confucian ethics)—obedience to father before marriage, to husband after marriage, and to son after husband's death; morality, proper speech, modest manner, and diligent work

三寸不烂之舌 sāncùn bù làn zhī shé a little lithe tongue; an eloquent tongue; a silver tongue: 亮(诸葛亮)借一帆风, 直至江东, 凭～, 说南北两军互相吞并。(《三国演义》) I shall borrow a little boat and make a little trip over the river and trust to my little lithe tongue to set north and south at each other's throats.

三寸金莲 sāncùn jīnlián three-*cun* lily feet (formerly, men's laudatory term for women's bound feet)

三大差别 sān dà chābié the three major distinctions (between town and country, industry and agriculture, physical and mental labour)

三大殿 Sān Dà Diàn the Three Great Halls (three audience halls in the Imperial Palace: the Hall of Supreme Harmony 太和殿, which was the emperor's throne room; the Hall of Middle Harmony 中和殿; and the Hall of Protecting Harmony 保和殿)

三大法宝 sān dà fǎbǎo the three magic weapons (of the Chinese Communist Party for defeating the enemy in the new-democratic revolution), namely, the united front, armed struggle and Party building

三大纪律八项注意 sān dà jìlù bā xiàng zhùyì the Three Main Rules of Discipline and the Eight Points for Attention of the Chinese People's Liberation Army (The Three Main Rules of Discipline are: 1. Obey orders in all your actions. 2. Don't take a single needle or piece of thread from the masses. 3. Turn in everything captured. The Eight Points for Attention are: 1. Speak politely. 2. Pay fairly for what you buy. 3. Return everything you borrow. 4. Pay for anything you damage. 5. Don't hit or swear at people. 6. Don't damage crops. 7. Don't take liberties with women. 8. Don't ill-treat captives.)

三大民主 sān dà mínzhǔ democracy in the three main fields (i.e. political, economic and military democracy at the company level in the People's Liberation Army)

三大作风 sān dà zuòfēng the Party's three important styles of work (i.e. integrating theory with practice, forging close links with the masses and practising self-criticism)

三代 sāndài three generations (i.e. of father, son, and grandson)

三代 Sān Dài the Three Dynasties—the Xia, Shang, and Zhou Dynasties

三等兵 sāndǎngbīng (U. S. Army) basic private; (U. S. Navy) apprentice seaman; (U. S. Air Force) airman third class

三等秘书 sānděng mìshū *diplomacy* third secretary

三叠纪 Sāndiéjì *geol.* the Triassic Period

三叠系 Sāndiéxì *geol.* the Triassic System

三定 sāndìng the three fixed quotas (for production, purchase and marketing of grain)

三度空间 sāndù kōngjiān three-dimensional space

三段论 sānduànlùn (also 三段论法 sānduànlùnfǎ) *log.* syllogism

三对六面 sān duì liù miàn the presence of the two interested parties plus a third disinterested party as a witness

三法 sānfǎ *Chin. med.* the three therapeutic methods of traditional Chinese medicine (i. e. diaphoresis, emetic measures, purgation and diuresis)

三番五次 sānfān-wǔcì (also 三番两次 sānfān-liǎngcì) again and again; time and again; over and over again; repeatedly

三反运动 Sānfǎn Yùndòng the movement against the three evils (i.e. corruption, waste and bureaucracy within the Party, government, army and mass organizations), 1951-1952 ——see also 五反运动 Wǔfǎn Yùndòng

三方 sānfāng tripartite: ～会谈 tripartite talks

三废 sānfèi the three wastes (i. e. waste gas, waste water, and industrial residue): 从～中回收和提取大量有用物质 salvage large quantities of useful materials from the three wastes

三分 sānfēn ① 30%; a little; somewhat: 谁都怕他～。 Everybody is a little afraid of him. / ～长相, 七分打扮 three parts natural beauty, seven parts clothing and makeup ② divided into three parts; split into three

三分像人, 七分像鬼 sānfēn xiàng rén, qīfēn xiàng guǐ look more like a ghost than a human being

三伏 sānfú ① the three *fu*—the three hottest periods of the year (i. e. 初伏 chūfú, 中伏 zhōngfú, and 末伏 mòfú; altogether 30 or 40 days) ② the third *fu* (another name for 末伏 mòfú)

三副 sānfù *navigation* third mate; third officer

三纲五常 sāngāng wǔcháng the three cardinal guides (i. e. ruler guides subject, father guides son, and husband guides wife) and the five constant virtues (i. e. benevolence, righteousness, propriety, wisdom and fidelity) as specified in the feudal ethical code

三个臭皮匠, 赛过诸葛亮 sānge chòupíjiàng, sàiguò Zhūgě Liàng three cobblers with their wits combined surpass Zhuge Liang the master mind—the wisdom of the masses exceeds that of the wisest individual

三个世界 sānge shìjiè the three worlds—the first world, the second world and the third world

三更半夜 sāngēng-bànyè in the dead of night

三宫六院 sāngōng-liùyuàn the three palaces and six chambers—the imperial harem

三姑六婆 sāngū-liùpó women of dubious character making a living by dishonest means (e.g. women matchmakers, sorceresses, etc.)

三顾茅庐 sān gù máolú make three calls at the thatched cottage (as Liu Bei did when he sought the aid of Zhuge Liang, a master strategist then living in seclusion)—repeatedly request sb. to take up a responsible post

三光 sānguāng *formal* the three luminaries—the sun, moon, and stars

三光政策 sānguāng zhèngcè the policy of "burn all, kill all, loot all" (once pursued by the Japanese invaders in China)

三国 Sān Guó the Three Kingdoms (220-265)—Wei (魏, 220-265), Shu Han (蜀汉, 221-263), and Wu (吴, 222-280)

三合板 sānhébǎn three-ply board; plywood

三合会 Sānhéhuì (also 三点会 Sāndiǎnhuì) the Triad Society (an anti-Manchu secret society during the early Qing Dynasty)

三合土 sānhétǔ (also 三和土 sānhuòtǔ) a mixture of lime, clay, and sand to which water is added (used in building)

三合星 sānhéxīng *astron.* triple star

三核苷酸 sānhégānsuān *biochem.* trinucleotide

三花脸 sānhuāliǎn three-flower face (another name for

丑³ chǒu, presumably from the outline of the white patch on the face)

三化螟 sānhuàmíng *agric.* yellow rice borer

三皇五帝 Sānhuáng-Wǔdì the Three August Ones and the Five Lords (legendary rulers of remote antiquity; usu. listed as Fu Xi 伏羲, Shennong 神农, and Suiren 燧人 or Zhurong 祝融 for the Three August Ones, and Huangdi 黄帝, Zhuanxu 颛顼, Di Ku 帝喾, Di Yao 帝尧, and Di Shun 帝舜 for the Five Lords)

三级风 sānjífēng *meteorol.* force 3 wind; gentle breeze

三级火箭 sānjí huǒjiàn three-stage rocket

三级跳远 sānjí tiàoyuǎn *sports* hop, step and jump; triple jump

三极管 sānjíguǎn *radio* triode: 充气～ gas-filled triode / 晶体～ transistor

三季稻 sānjìdào triple cropping of rice

三家村 sānjiācūn a three-family village—a very small remote village

三驾马车 sānjià mǎchē ① a carriage drawn by a team of three horses ② troika; triumvirate

三尖瓣 sānjiānbàn *physiol.* tricuspid valve

三尖瓣狭窄 sānjiānbàn xiázhǎi *med.* tricuspid stenosis

三缄其口 sān jiān qí kǒu with one's lips sealed

三焦 sānjiāo *Chin. med.* the three visceral cavities housing the internal organs: ～辨证 analysing and differentiating diseases according to the pathological changes in the three visceral cavities

三角 sānjiǎo ① triangle ② *math.* trigonometry

三角板 sānjiǎobǎn set square

三角测量 sānjiǎo cèliáng triangulation; trigonometrical survey

三角鲂 sānjiǎofáng *zool.* triangular bream

三角枫 sānjiǎofēng *bot.* trident maple (*Acer buergerianum*)

三角关系 sānjiǎo guānxi triangular relationship

三角函数 sānjiǎo hánshù trigonometric function

三角肌 sānjiǎojī *physiol.* deltoid

三角巾 sānjiǎojīn sling

三角裤 sānjiǎokù panties; briefs

三角恋爱 sānjiǎo liàn'ài love triangle; eternal triangle

三角旗 sānjiǎoqí pennant; pennon

三角铁 sānjiǎotiě ① *mus.* triangle ② angle iron; L-iron

三角湾 sānjiǎowān estuary

三角形 sānjiǎoxíng triangle

三角学 sānjiǎoxué *math.* trigonometry

三角洲 sānjiǎozhōu delta

三脚架 sānjiǎojià tripod

三脚猫 sānjiǎomāo a jack of all trades

三教九流 sānjiào-jiǔliú ① the three religions (i.e. Confucianism, Taoism and Buddhism) and the nine schools of thought (i.e. the Confucians, the Taoists, the Yin-Yang, the Legalists, the Logicians, the Mohists, the Political Strategists, the Eclectics and the Agriculturists) ② various religious sects and academic schools ③ *derog.* people in various trades; people of all sorts

三节 sānjié the three festivals—the Dragon Boat Festival, the Mid-Autumn Festival and the Spring Festival

三节棍 sānjiégùn a cudgel of three linked sections; three-section cudgel

三结合 sānjiéhé three-in-one combination: 老、中、青的领导班子 a leading body composed of the old, the middle-aged and the young

三九天 sānjiǔtiān (also 三九 sānjiǔ) the third nine-day period after the winter solstice—the coldest days of winter

三句话不离本行 sānjùhuà bù lí běnháng can hardly open one's mouth without talking shop; talk shop all the time

三军 sānjūn ① the three armed services ② *old* the army

三K党 Sānkèidǎng Ku Klux Klan

三棱尺 sānléngchǐ three-square rule; triangular scale

三棱镜 sānléngjìng *phys.* (triangular) prism

三连冠 sānliánguàn win the championship three times in succession

三连音符 sānlián yīnfú *mus.* triplet

三联单 sānliándān triplicate form

三磷酸腺甙 sānlínsuānxiàndài *pharm.* adenosine triphosphate (ATP)

三令五申 sānlìng-wǔshēn repeatedly give injunctions: 县里曾～, 干什么都得按法律办事。The county repeatedly enjoined that everything must be done according to law.

三六九等 sānliùjiǔděng various grades and ranks: 车子有～, 各有各的用处。There are all kinds of vehicles; each has its own use. / 把工作分成～ regard different kinds of work as indications of rank or grade

三氯杀螨砜 sānlǜshāmǎnfēng *agric.* tetradiphon; tedion

三轮车 sānlúnchē (also 三轮儿 sānlúnr) tricycle; pedicab

三轮摩托车 sānlún mótuōchē motor tricycle

三轮汽车 sānlún qìchē three-wheeled automobile (or motorcar)

三麦 sānmài wheat, barley and highland barley

三昧 sānmèi ① *Buddhism* samadhi ② secret; knack: 深得其中～ master the secrets of an art

三民主义 sānmínzhǔyì the Three Principles of the People (i.e. Nationalism, Democracy and the People's Livelihood; put forward by Dr. Sun Yat-sen)

三明治 sānmíngzhì sandwich

三拇指 sānmuzhǐ *dial.* middle finger

三年五载 sānnián-wǔzǎi from three to five years—in a few years

三朋四友 sānpéng-sìyǒu a lot of friends

三七 sānqī *Chin. med.* pseudo-ginseng (*Panax pseudo-ginseng* var. *notoginseng*)

三亲六故 sānqīn-liùgù relatives, friends and acquaintances

三秋 sānqiū *agric.* ① the three autumn jobs (of harvesting, ploughing and sowing) ② *formal* the three autumn months ③ *formal* three years: 一日不见, 如隔三秋 yīrì bù jiàn, rú gé sānqiū

三权分立 sān quán fēn lì separation of the three powers (i.e. the legislative, executive and judicial powers)

三人成虎 sān rén chéng hǔ the testimony of three men creates a tiger in the market—repeated false reports will lead one astray

三人行, 必有我师 sān rén xíng, bì yǒu wǒ shī where there are three men walking together, one of them is bound to be able to teach me something

三三两两 sānsānliǎngliǎng in twos and threes; in knots: 旅客～在月台上等车。Passengers were waiting in knots on the platform.

三色版 sānsèbǎn *print.* three-colour halftone; three-colour block

三色版印刷 sānsèbǎn yìnshuā trichromatic printing

三色堇 sānsèjǐn *bot.* pansy

三生 sānshēng *Buddhism* the three lives—the present life, the previous life, and the next life

三生有幸 sānshēng yǒu xìng consider oneself most fortunate (to make sb.'s acquaintance, etc.)

三牲 sānshēng the three domestic animals (i. e. cattle, sheep and pigs, formerly used as sacrificial offerings)

三十二分音符 sānshí èr fēn yīnfú *mus.* demisemiquaver; thirty-second note

三十二开 sānshí èr kāi *print.* thirty-twomo; 32mo

三十六计，走为上计 sānshí liù jì, zǒu wéi shàngjì of the thirty-six strategems, the best is running away; the best thing to do now is to quit

三熟制 sānshúzhì *agric.* triple-cropping system

三水铝矿 sānshuǐlǚkuàng gibbsite

三思 sānsī think thrice—think carefully: 事关重大，请你～。It's a matter of great importance. I would advise you to think carefully.

三思而行 sānsī ér xíng (also 三思而后行 sānsī ér hòu xíng) think thrice before you act; look before you leap: 万一遇上个什么事儿，要～! If anything happens, think well before you act!

…三…四 …sān…sì ① (expressing confusion): 颠三倒四 diānsān-dǎosì / 丢三落四 diūsān-làsì ② (expressing repetition): 推三阻四 tuīsān-zǔsì

三天打鱼，两天晒网 sān tiān dǎyú, liǎng tiān shàiwǎng go fishing for three days and dry the nets for two—work by fits and starts; lack perseverance

三天两头 sāntiān-liǎngtóu *inf.* every other day; almost every day: 他～地来找她。He comes to see her almost every day.

三通 sāntōng *mech.* tee; tee joint

三通管 sāntōngguǎn three-way pipe

三同 sāntóng (of cadres) eat, live and work together (with the common people)

三头对案 sāntóu duì àn (also 三曹对案 sāncáo duì àn) the confrontation of the three parties (i.e. the plaintiff, the defendant and the witness) in court

三头六臂 sāntóu-liùbì (with) three heads and six arms—superhuman powers

三头政治 sāntóu zhèngzhì triumvirate

三推六问 sāntuī-liùwèn *old* a good many interrogations

三维空间 sānwéi kōngjiān same as 三度空间 sāndù kōngjiān

三位一体 sān wèi yī tǐ ① *Christianity* the Trinity ② three forming an organic whole; three in one; trinity

三五成群 sān-wǔ chéngqún in threes and fours; in knots: 街头巷尾人们～，议论纷纷。People were seen standing about in knots on street corners, talking and arguing.

三下五除二 sān xià wǔ chú èr three-down-five-reject-two—neat and quick (originally an abacus formula for adding three to three, meaning "rejecting two of the three to make a new five")

三夏 sānxià *agric.* ① the three summer jobs (of planting, harvesting and field management) ② *formal* the three summer months

三鲜 sānxiān three delicacies (a combination of delicacies such as sea slug, squid, shrimp, chicken, etc., used as the ingredients of a dish): ～汤 soup with three delicacies / 炒～ stir-fried three delicacies

三弦 sānxián *sanxian*, a three-stringed plucked instrument

三项全能运动 sānxiàng quánnéng yùndòng *sports* triathlon

三相 sānxiàng *elec.* three-phase

三相变压器 sānxiàng biànyāqì three-phase transformer

三硝基甲苯 sānxiāojījiǎběn *chem.* trinitrotoluene (TNT)

三心二意 sānxīn-èryì be of two minds; shilly-shally; be half-hearted: 别～了，就这样办吧。Don't shilly-shally. Just go ahead and do it. / 我做事从来不～。I'm not a person of two minds. / 为人民服务不能～。We must not serve the people half-heartedly.

三言两语 sānyán-liǎngyǔ in a few words; in one or two words: 这事不是～能说清楚的。The matter can't be explained in a few words.

三阳开泰 sān yáng kāi tài with three *yang* begins prosperity—the New Year ushers in a renewal and a change of fortune (from the *tai* hexagram 泰卦 of the *Book of Changes* 《易经》, which in calendrical lore is correlated with the first month and whose three unbroken lines, underneath three broken ones, are three strokes of *yang* 阳 "positive force"; often said as a wordplay on the homophonous *yang* 阳 and *yang* 羊 "goat")

三氧化物 sānyǎnghuàwù *chem.* trioxide (e.g. 三氧化二砷 arsenic trioxide)

三叶虫 sānyèchóng *palaeontology* trilobite

三月 sānyuè ① March ② the third month of the lunar year; the third moon

三灾八难 sānzāi-bānàn (children's) various illnesses and ailments

三藏 Sān Zàng *Buddhism Tripitaka* or *Threefold Canon* (consisting of doctrinal records, writings on discipline, and writings on metaphysics)

三战两胜 sān zhàn liǎng shèng *sports* the best of three games

三朝 sānzhāo ① the third day of marriage on which the bride goes back to her parents' home for a visit ② the third day of a newborn baby on which it is given its second bath

三支两军 sānzhī liǎngjūn three support's and two military's (support industry, support agriculture, and support the broad masses of the Left; military control and political and military training—tasks given to the PLA during the Cultural Revolution)

三只手 sānzhīshǒu *dial.* pickpocket

三趾鹑 sānzhǐchún *zool.* button quail

三自一包 sānzì yībāo more plots for private use, more free markets, more enterprises with sole responsibility for their own profit or loss, and fixing output quotas on a household basis

三足鼎立 sān zú dǐnglì same as 鼎足而立 dǐngzú ér lì

三座大山 sān zuò dàshān the three big mountains (i.e. imperialism, feudalism and bureaucrat-capitalism, which weighed down on the backs of the Chinese people before liberation)

弍 sān same as 三 sān

叁 sān three (used for the numeral 三 on cheques, etc. to avoid mistakes or alterations)

毵(毿) sān see below

毵毵 sānsān (of hair, twigs, etc.) thin and long

sǎn

伞¹(傘、繖) sǎn umbrella

伞²(傘) sǎn sth. shaped like an umbrella: 降落伞 jiàngluòsǎn

伞兵 sǎnbīng paratrooper; parachuter

伞兵部队 sǎnbīng bùduì parachute troops; paratroops

伞齿轮 sǎnchǐlún *mech.* bevel gear

伞伐 sǎnfá *forestry* shelterwood cutting

伞房花序 sǎnfáng huāxù *bot.* corymb

伞降 sǎnjiàng parachuting; chuting: 新兵已完成～训练任务。The recruits have completed their parachuting training program.

伞投 sǎntóu drop by parachute; parachute; chute: ～炸弹 parachute bomb; parabomb / ～照明弹 parachute flare

伞形花序　sǎnxíng huāxù　*bot.*　umbel

伞形科　sǎnxíngkē　*bot.*　carrot family

散　sǎn　① come loose; fall apart; not hold together: 背包～了。 The blanket roll has come loose. / 木箱～了。 The wooden box fell apart. / 麦包～了。 The sack of wheat has spilled. ② scattered: 这个村的农民住得很～。 The peasants in this village live rather far apart from one another. ③ *Chin. med.* medicine in powder form; medicinal powder ——see also sàn

散兵　sǎnbīng　*mil.*　skirmisher

散兵壕　sǎnbīnghǎo　fire trench

散兵坑　sǎnbīngkēng　foxhole; pit

散兵线　sǎnbīngxiàn　skirmish line

散兵游勇　sǎnbīng-yóuyǒng　stragglers and disbanded soldiers

散工　sǎngōng　same as 零工 línggōng ——see also 散工 sàngōng

散光　sǎnguāng　astigmatism

散光眼镜　sǎnguāng yǎnjìng　astigmatic glasses

散货　sǎnhuò　bulk cargo

散货船　sǎnhuòchuán　bulk freighter

散记　sǎnjì　random notes; sketches; sidelights: 《农村～》 *Village Sketches*

散剂　sǎnjì　*pharm.*　powder; *pulvis*

散架　sǎnjià　*inf.*　fall apart; fall to pieces: 别再装了，大车快～了。 Don't put any more on the cart, or it'll break. / 我的胳膊腿像散了架似的。 I feel as if all my limbs are falling apart (*or* are out of joint).

散居　sǎnjū　live scattered: 游击队员～在老乡家里。 The guerrillas lived scattered among the villagers.

散乱　sǎnluàn　in disorder: ～的头发 dishevelled hair / 桌子上～地放着各种文具书籍。 Books and writing materials were scattered about on the desk.

散漫　sǎnmàn　① undisciplined; lax in discipline; slack; careless and sloppy: 克服～性 overcome slackness (*or* laxness in discipline) ② unorganized; scattered: ～无组织的状态 a disorganized state of affairs

散曲　sǎnqǔ　non-dramatic songs—a verse form evolved in the Yuan Dynasty, somewhat akin to but freer than the *ci* （词）, used for lyric songs written to express the poet's own feelings and observations, in contrast to the dramatic songs （曲）introduced between parts of the prose dialogue in the Yuan drama to utter the sentiments of a certain character

散射　sǎnshè　*phys.*　scattering

散射粒子　sǎnshè lìzǐ　scattering particles

散射通信　sǎnshè tōngxìn　scatter communication

散射线　sǎnshèxiàn　scattered rays

散套　sǎntào　a sequence of *sanqu* （散曲）songs within a particular musical mode

散体　sǎntǐ　prose style free from parallelism; simple, direct prose style

散文　sǎnwén　prose

散文诗　sǎnwénshī　prose poem

散装　sǎnzhuāng　unpackaged; loose packed; in bulk: ～饼干 loose cookies / ～货物 bulk cargo; bulk freight / ～汽油 petrol (*or* gasoline) in bulk / ～水泥 bulk cement / ～运输 bulk transportation

馓　sǎn　see below

馓子　sǎnzi　*dial.*　deep-fried dough twist

氃　sǎn　see below ——see also xiàn

氃弹　sǎndàn　same as 榴霰弹 liúsǎndàn

散　sàn　① break up; disperse: 会还没有～。 The meeting is not over yet. / 大家别出～了。 Let's not get separated. / 今天星期六，早点～吧。 It's Saturday today. Let's stop a bit earlier. / 乌云～了。 Dark clouds dispersed. ② distribute; disseminate; give out: ～传单 give out handbills; distribute leaflets ③ dispel; let out: 请打开门窗～一～烟。 Please open the door and windows to let the smoke out. ④ *dial.* sack: 旧社会资本家随便～工人。 In the old days, the capitalists sacked workers at will. ——see also sǎn

散播　sànbō　disseminate; spread: ～种子 broadcast (seeds) / ～谣言 spread rumours

散布　sànbù　① spread; disseminate; distribute: ～传单 distribute leaflets / ～流言蜚语 spread slanderous rumours ② be scattered here and there: 在一望无际的原野上～着一座座井架。 Derricks are scattered here and there on the boundless plain. / 羊群～在山坡上吃草。 A flock of sheep are grazing here and there on the hillside.

散步　sànbù　take a walk; go for a walk; go for a stroll

散场　sànchǎng　(of a show, performance, etc.) be over: 电影～了。 The movie is over.

散发　sànfā　① send out; send forth; diffuse; emit: 花儿～着清香。 The flowers sent forth a delicate fragrance. ② distribute; issue; give out: ～传单 distribute leaflets / 作为正式文件～ be circulated as an official document

散工　sàngōng　same as 放工 fànggōng ——see also 散工 sǎngōng

散会　sànhuì　(of a meeting) be over; break up: 宣布～ declare the meeting over / 一直到中午才～。 The meeting didn't end until noon.

散伙　sànhuǒ　① (of a group, body or organization) dissolve; disband ② *inf.* (of lovers or a married couple) break up: 他们吵了一架，～了。 They quarrelled and broke up.

散开　sànkāi　spread out or apart; disperse; scatter: 看热闹的群众～了。 The crowd, which had gathered to watch the fun, dispersed.

散落　sànluò　① fall scattered: 花瓣～了一地。 The ground was scattered with fallen petals. ② be scattered: 草原上～着数不清的牛羊。 Countless cattle and sheep were scattered over the grasslands. ③ scatter and disappear

散闷　sànmèn　divert oneself from boredom

散热　sànrè　① dissipate heat ② radiate heat

散热管　sànrèguǎn　① cooling tube ② radiating pipe

散热片　sànrèpiàn　① cooling fin ② radiating fin (*or* rib)

散热器　sànrèqì　radiator: 管式～ tubular radiator

散失　sànshī　① scatter and disappear; be lost; be missing: 防止图书～ prevent any loss of library books / 有些古籍早已～。 Some ancient works have long been lost. / ～的工具已经找到。 The missing tools have been found. ② (of moisture, etc.) be lost; vaporize; dissipate

散水　sànshuǐ　*archit.*　apron

散摊子　sàn tānzi　(also 散摊儿 sàntānr)　*inf.*　(of a group, body or organization) dissolve; disband; break up: 他们合伙经营的铺子不久就～了。 Their partnership soon broke up.

散亡　sànwáng　(of books, etc.) be scattered and lost

散戏　sànxì　(of a show, play, opera, etc.) be over

散心　sànxīn　drive away one's cares; relieve boredom

散佚　sànyì　(also 散轶 sànyì)　be scattered and lost;

be no longer extant: 他的著作～殆尽。His writings are practically all scattered and lost. *or* Practically none of his works are still extant.

散逸 sànyì ① (of a gas, etc.) escape; leak: 气体向外～。The gas is escaping. ② *phys.* dissipation: 热～ heat dissipation ③ same as 散佚 sànyì

sāng

丧（喪、丧） sāng funeral; mourning: 治丧 zhìsāng ——see also sàng

丧服 sāngfú mourning apparel

丧家 sāngjiā family of the deceased

丧礼 sānglǐ obsequies; funeral

丧乱 sāngluàn *formal* disturbance and bloodshed; tragic disaster

丧门星 sāngménxīng ① a woman who brings ill luck to her husband's family ② anyone who brings ill luck

丧事 sāngshì funeral arrangements

丧葬 sāngzàng burial; funeral: ～费 funeral expenses

丧钟 sāngzhōng funeral bell; death knell; knell: 敲响殖民主义的～ sound the death knell of colonialism

桑 sāng ① white mulberry; mulberry (tree) ② (Sāng) a surname

桑巴 sāngbā samba (a Brazilian dance)

桑白皮 sāngbáipí *Chin. med.* the root bark of white mulberry

桑蚕 sāngcán silkworm: ～丝 mulberry silk

桑寄生 sāngjìshēng *Chin. med.* parasitic loranthus (*Loranthus parasiticus*)

桑那浴 sāngnàyù sauna bath

桑皮纸 sāngpízhǐ mulberry (bark) paper

桑葚儿 sāngrènr *inf.* mulberry (the fruit)

桑葚 sāngshèn (also 桑葚子 sāngshènzi) mulberry (the fruit)

桑树 sāngshù white mulberry; mulberry (tree)

桑榆 sāngyú *liter.* ① waning day; evening ② the west (where the sun sets): 失之东隅，收之桑榆。shī zhī dōngyú, shōu zhī sāngyú ③ the evening of life; old age

桑榆暮景 sāngyú mùjǐng the evening of life; old age

桑园 sāngyuán mulberry field

桑梓 sāngzǐ *liter.* one's native place

sǎng

搡 sǎng *dial.* push violently: 把他～了个跟头 push him over

嗓 sǎng ① throat; larynx ② voice

嗓门儿 sǎngménr voice: 提高～ raise one's voice / ～大 have a loud voice

嗓音 sǎngyīn voice: 他～洪亮。He has a resonant voice. *or* His voice carries well.

嗓子 sǎngzi ① throat; larynx: ～疼 have a sore throat ② voice: ～好 have a good voice / 他的～哑了。He's lost his voice.

嗓子眼儿 sǎngziyǎnr throat

磉 sǎng the base of a pillar; pedestal

颡 sǎng *formal* forehead

sàng

丧（喪、丧） sàng lose ——see also sāng

丧胆 sàngdǎn be terror-stricken; be smitten with fear

丧魂落魄 sànghún-luòpò (also 丧魂失魄 sànghún-shīpò) driven to distraction; shaken to the core: 吓得～ be scared out of one's wits; be frightened out of one's life

丧家之犬 sàng jiā zhī quǎn a stray cur: 惶惶如～ as scared as a stray cur; as pitiful as a lost pup

丧尽天良 sàngjìn tiānliáng utterly devoid of conscience; conscienceless; heartless

丧命 sàngmìng meet one's death; get killed

丧偶 sàng'ǒu *formal* be bereaved of one's spouse (esp. one's wife); have lost one's wife or husband

丧气 sàngqì feel disheartened; lose heart; become crestfallen: ～话 demoralizing words

丧气 sàngqi *inf.* be unlucky; be out of luck; have bad luck

丧权辱国 sàngquán-rǔguó humiliate the nation and forfeit its sovereignty; surrender a country's sovereign rights under humiliating terms: ～的条约 a treaty of national betrayal and humiliation

丧生 sàngshēng (also 丧身 sàngshēn) meet one's death; lose one's life; get killed

丧失 sàngshī lose; forfeit: ～信心 lose confidence / ～时机 miss the opportunity / ～立场 depart from the correct stand / ～会员资格 forfeit one's membership / ～领土 lose territory / ～劳动能力 lose the ability to work; be incapacitated / 睡眠和休息～了时间，却取得了明天工作的精力。Sleep and rest involve loss of time, but they provide energy for next day's work.

丧亡 sàngwáng meet one's death

丧心病狂 sàng xīn bìng kuáng frenzied; frantic; perverse: ～地进行破坏活动 carry on frenzied wrecking activities

sāo

搔 sāo scratch: ～痒 scratch oneself to relieve itching; scratch where it itches

搔到痒处 sāo dào yǎngchù scratch where it itches—hit the nail on the head

搔首 sāoshǒu scratch one's head

搔首踟蹰 sāoshǒu chíchú scratch one's head in perplexity

搔头 sāotóu ① scratch one's head (in perplexity) ② perplexing: 这案件头绪纷纭，很是～。This case is most complicated and perplexing. ③ *arch.* hairpin; hair clasp: 玉～ a jade hairpin

搔头弄姿 sāotóu-nòngzī *formal* (of a woman) stroke one's hair in coquetry; posture and preen oneself

骚¹ sāo disturb; upset: 骚乱 sāoluàn

骚² sāo ① short for 《离骚》 (*Encountering Sorrow*), a long poem by Qu Yuan (屈原), with special reference to its style or verse form ② *formal* literary writings: 骚人 sāorén ——see also 骚体 sāotǐ

骚³ sāo ① coquettish ② *dial.* male (of some domestic animals): ～马 stallion / ～驴 jackass ③ same as 臊 sāo

骚动 sāodòng ① disturbance; commotion; ferment: 那

几位工会领袖的被囚禁, 在全国范围内引起了～。The imprisonment of the union leaders caused a commotion right through the country. ② be in a tumult; become restless: 人群～起来。The crowd was in a tumult.

骚货 sāohuò *offens.* tart

骚客 sāokè *formal* poet

骚乱 sāoluàn disturbance; riot

骚扰 sāorǎo harass; molest: ～活动 harassment / 进行～破坏 carry out harassment and sabotage

骚人 sāorén *formal* poet

骚人墨客 sāorén-mòkè literary men; men of letters

骚体 sāotǐ the *Sao* style (i.e. the style of the *Li Sao* 《离骚》, characterized by the use of six-syllable couplets, the two lines of each couplet being connected by a meaningless syllable *xi* 兮, e.g.: 帝高阳之苗裔兮, 朕皇考曰伯庸 Scion of the High Lord Gao Yang, Bo Yong was my father's name)

缫(繅)

sāo reel silk from cocoons; reel ——see also 缲 qiāo

缫丝 sāosī silk reeling; filature: ～厂 reeling mill; filature / ～机 reeling machine; filature

臊

sāo the smell of urine or of the fox, skunk, etc.; foul smell ——see also sào

臊气 sāoqì foul smell; stink ——see also sàoqì

sǎo

扫(掃)

sǎo ① sweep; sweep away: ～雪 sweep away the snow / ～街 sweep the streets ② eliminate; clear away: 扫雷 sǎoléi / 扫盲 sǎománg ③ pass quickly along or over; sweep: 他向听众～了一眼。He swept his eyes over the audience. / 探照灯光～过夜空。The searchlights swept across the night sky. ④ put all together: 扫数 sǎoshù ——see also sào

扫边 sǎobiān play a minor role (in a traditional opera)

扫除 sǎochú ① cleaning; cleanup: 院子要天天～。The courtyard should be cleaned up every day. ② clear away; remove; wipe out: ～一切害虫 sweep away all pests; away with all pests / ～前进道路上的障碍 remove the obstacles on the road of advance / ～文盲 eliminate (*or* wipe out) illiteracy

扫荡 sǎodàng mop up: 粉碎敌人的～ smash the enemy's mopping-up operations

扫地 sǎodì ① sweep the floor ② (of honour, credibility, etc.) reach rock bottom; reach an all-time low; be dragged in the dust: 名誉～ be thoroughly discredited / 威信～ be shorn of one's prestige

扫地出门 sǎodì chūmén sweep the garbage out—drive out the whole family with nothing except the clothes they have on

扫地以尽 sǎodì yǐ jìn be swept clean (fig); be swept out: 他的体面威风, ～。Every bit of his dignity and prestige was swept into the dust.

扫房 sǎofáng sweep up a room

扫雷 sǎoléi mine sweeping (*or* clearance)

扫雷舰 sǎoléijiàn minesweeper

扫雷器 sǎoléiqì mine-sweeping apparatus

扫盲 sǎománg (short for 扫除文盲) eliminate (*or* wipe out) illiteracy: ～班 literacy class / ～运动 campaign to eliminate illiteracy; anti-illiteracy campaign

扫描 sǎomiáo *electron.* scanning: 行～ line scanning / 飞点～ flying-spot scanning / ～器 scanner

扫灭 sǎomiè mop up; wipe out: ～小股残敌 mop up the last few groups of the enemy

扫墓 sǎomù (also 扫坟 sǎofén) sweep a grave—pay respects to a dead person at his tomb

扫平 sǎopíng put down; crush; suppress: ～叛乱 put down a rebellion

扫清 sǎoqīng clear away; get rid of: ～官僚主义作风 do away with bureaucracy

扫清道路 sǎoqīng dàolù clear the path; pave the way

扫射 sǎoshè strafe

扫视 sǎoshì (of one's eyes or glance) sweep: 我从左到右～了一遍。My eyes swept from left to right.

扫数 sǎoshù the total number; the whole amount: ～入库 all put in storage / ～还清 all paid off

扫榻 sǎotà *formal* sweep the bed clean (in expectation of a visitor): ～以待。We are looking forward to your visit.

扫听 sǎoting *dial.* make inquiries about

扫尾 sǎowěi wind up; round off: ～工作 rounding-off work

扫兴 sǎoxìng have one's spirits dampened; feel disappointed: 真叫人～! How disappointing!

扫雪车 sǎoxuěchē snowplough

嫂

sǎo ① elder brother's wife; sister-in-law: 二～ second brother's wife / 表～ cousin's wife ② (a form of address for a married woman about one's own age) sister: 桂英～ Sister Guiying

嫂夫人 sǎofūrén *honor.* (a form of address for a friend's wife) your wife: 内子嘱笔敬问～好。My wife has asked me to send regards to yours.

嫂嫂 sǎosao *dial.* ① elder brother's wife; sister-in-law ② (a form of address for a married woman about one's own age) sister: 王家～ Sister Wang

嫂子 sǎozi *inf.* elder brother's wife; sister-in-law

sào

扫(掃)

sào see below ——see also sǎo

扫把 sàobǎ *dial.* broom

扫帚 sàozhou broom

扫帚菜 sàozhoucài common name for 地肤 dìfū

扫帚眉 sàozhouméi bushy eyebrows

扫帚星 sàozhouxīng ① common name for 彗星 huìxīng ② *offens.* a person (esp. a woman) who brings ill luck; jinx

梢

sào ① a conical shape ② same as 锥度 zhuīdù ——see also shāo

瘙

sào *arch.* scabies

瘙痒 sàoyǎng itch

臊

sào shy; bashful: ～得满脸通红 blush scarlet ——see also sāo

臊气 sàoqì *dial.* have bad luck; be out of luck; be down on one's luck ——see also sāoqì

臊子 sàozi *dial.* minced or diced meat (cooked) to be added to noodles or other food before serving: 羊肉～面 noodles with a layer of minced or diced mutton

sè

色

sè ① colour: ～香味俱佳 look good, smell good, and taste good ② look; countenance; expression: 喜色 xǐsè ③ kind; description: 各～人等 people of ev-

ery description; all kinds of people ④ scene; scenery: 景色 jǐngsè ⑤ quality (of precious metals, goods, etc.): 成色 chéngsè ⑥ feminine charms: 姿色 zīsè / 好色 hàosè——see also shǎi

色不迷人人自迷 sè bù mí rén rén zì mí lust does not blind, one blinds oneself

色彩 sècǎi ① colour; hue: ～鲜明 in bright colours; bright-coloured ② characteristic quality; flavour; colour: 地方～ local colour / 文学～ literary flavour / 感情～ emotional colouring

色层分析 sècéng fēnxi same as 色谱分析 sèpǔ fēnxi

色层谱 sècéngpǔ phys. chromatogram

色差 sèchā ① phys. chromatic aberration; chromatism ② text. off colour; off shade

色丹岛 Sèdāndǎo Shikotan

色胆 sèdǎn the lengths to which one will go for sex: ～包天 will go to any lengths for sex; be utterly reckless in sex

色淀 sèdiàn text. (colour) lake: 绯红～ crimson lake

色调 sèdiào tone; hue: 暖～ warm tones

色度计 sèdùjì phys. colorimeter: 光电～ photoelectric colorimeter

色光 sèguāng chromatic light; coloured light

色鬼 sèguǐ lecher; sex maniac: 老～ a lecherous old man; an old dirty man

色基 sèjī chem. colour base

色觉 sèjué colour vision

色觉检查表 sèjué jiǎnchábiǎo colour test cards

色拉 sèlā same as 沙拉 shālā

色厉内荏 sèlì-nèirěn fierce of mien but faint of heart; threatening in manner but cowardly at heart

色盲 sèmáng med. achromatopsia; colour blindness

色盲表 sèmángbiǎo colour test cards

色目人 Sèmùrén people of special category—one of the classes into which China's population was divided during the Yuan Dynasty, including Central Asian allies of the Mongols, mostly Uighurs and other Turks (placed next below the Mongols and above the Han Chinese)

色品 sèpǐn phys. chroma; chromaticity

色谱法 sèpǔfǎ chromatography

色谱分析 sèpǔ fēnxi chromatographic analysis

色情 sèqíng sex

色情狂 sèqíngkuáng ① erotomania; sex mania ② erotomaniac; sex maniac

色情文学 sèqíng wénxué erotica

色情作品 sèqíng zuòpǐn pornography

色球 sèqiú astron. chromosphere

色散 sèsàn phys. chromatic dispersion

色色 sèsè every kind: ～俱全。All sorts of things are kept in stock.

色授魂与 sèshòu-húnyǔ beauty yields and passion quickens

色衰爱弛 sèshuāi-àichí passion cools as beauty fades

色素 sèsù physiol. pigment

色素沉着 sèsù chénzhuó med. pigmentation

色素痣 sèsùzhì mole

色相 sèxiàng ① Buddhism form and aspect ② feminine charms: 出卖～ sell her charms ③ the colours of the spectrum—red, orange, yellow, green, blue, indigo, and violet

色艺 sèyì looks and skills (of a female entertainer): ～俱佳 be remarkable for both looks and skills

色釉 sèyòu coloured glaze

色欲 sèyù sexual urge; lust

色泽 sèzé colour and lustre: ～鲜明 bright and lustrous

色织厂 sèzhīchǎng text. yarn-dyed fabric mill

色纸 sèzhǐ coloured paper

色痣 sèzhì pigmented mole (or nevus)

涩（澀、澁） sè ① puckery; astringent: 这柿子～不～? Are these persimmons puckery? ② unsmooth; hard-going: 推子发～了,该上油了。This pair of hair-clippers doesn't work smoothly. It needs oiling. ③ hard to understand; obscure: 艰涩 jiānsè

涩脉 sèmài Chin. med. a weak, thready, uneven pulse

涩滞 sèzhì (of style of writing) not smooth

啬（嗇） sè stingy; miserly: 吝啬 lìnsè

啬刻 sèke dial. stingy; miserly

铯 sè chem. cesium (Cs)

塞 sè ——see also sāi; sài

塞擦音 sècāyīn phonet. affricate

塞音 sèyīn phonet. plosive; stop

塞责 sèzé not do one's job conscientiously; perform one's duties perfunctorily

瑟 sè mus. se, a twenty-five-stringed or sixteen-stringed plucked instrument, somewhat similar to the zither

瑟瑟 sèsè ① (of the wind) rustling ② (of a person) trembling

瑟缩 sèsuō curl up and shiver with cold; cower

穑（穡） sè see 稼穑 jiàsè

sēn

森 sēn ① full of trees: 森林 sēnlín ② formal multitudinous; in multitudes: 森罗万象 sēnluó wànxiàng ③ dark; gloomy: 阴森 yīnsēn

森林 sēnlín forest: ～抚育 tending of woods / ～火灾 forest fire / ～资源 forest reserves

森林覆被率 sēnlín fùbèilǜ percentage of forest cover

森林学 sēnlínxué forestry

森罗殿 sēnluódiàn the Hall of Darkness (another name for 阎王殿 Yánwángdiàn)

森罗万象 sēnluó wànxiàng all-embracing; all-inclusive

森然 sēnrán ① (of tall trees) dense; thick: 林木～ thickly wooded with tall trees ② awe-inspiring

森森 sēnsēn ① (of trees) dense; thick; luxuriant: 松柏～ dense pine and cypress trees ② ghastly; eerie

森严 sēnyán stern; strict; forbidding: 门禁～ with the entrance carefully guarded / 等级～ be rigidly stratified; form a strict hierarchy

森严壁垒 sēnyán bìlěi same as 壁垒森严 bìlěi sēnyán

sēng

僧 sēng Buddhist monk; monk

僧道 sēngdào Buddhist monks and Taoist priests

僧多粥少 sēngduō-zhōushǎo same as 粥少僧多 zhōushǎo-sēngduō

僧伽罗语 Sēngjiāluóyǔ Sinhalese

僧侣 sēnglǚ monks and priests; clergy

僧侣主义 sēnglǚzhǔyì philos. fideism

僧尼 sēng-ní Buddhist monks and nuns

僧人 sēngrén Buddhist monk

僧俗 sēng-sú clergy and laity

僧徒 sēngtú (also 僧众 sēngzhòng) Buddhist monks

僧院 sēngyuàn Buddhist temple; Buddhist monastery

shā

杀（殺） shā ① kill; slaughter; butcher ② fight; go into battle: ～出重围 fight one's way out of a heavy encirclement ③ weaken; reduce; abate: ～～敌人的威风 deflate the enemy's arrogance / 风势稍～。 The wind abated. ④ *dial.* smart: 碘酒涂在伤口上真～得慌。 Iodine smarts when it is put on a cut. ⑤ take off; counteract: 白菜馅里放点盐～一～水 put some salt in the chopped cabbage to draw out the water ⑥ *adv.* (used after a verb) in the extreme; exceedingly: 笑～人 absolutely ridiculous; terribly funny / 闷～人 bored to death / 气～ hopping mad

杀虫剂 shāchóngjì insecticide; pesticide

杀虫药 shāchóngyào insecticide; pesticide

杀敌 shādí fight the enemy; engage in battle: 苦练～本领 practise hard to master combat skills / 英勇～ be brave in battle; fight heroically

杀敌致果 shādí zhìguǒ (of a soldier) fight gallantly (*or* valiantly) and win glory on the battlefield

杀风景 shāfēngjǐng spoil the fun; be a wet blanket

杀害 shāhài murder; kill; slaughter: 千千万万的平民百姓在战争中惨遭～。 Thousands upon thousands of civilians were slaughtered during the wars.

杀回马枪 shā huímǎqiāng make a backward thrust at one's pursuer; give sb. a backward thrust; wheel around and hit back

杀机 shājī murderous intentions

杀鸡取卵 shā jī qǔ luǎn kill the hen to get the eggs; kill the goose that lays the golden eggs

杀鸡吓猴 shā jī xià hóu (also 杀鸡给猴看 shā jī gěi hóu kàn) kill the chicken to frighten the monkey—punish someone as a warning to others

杀鸡焉用牛刀 shā jī yān yòng niúdāo same as 割鸡焉用牛刀 gē jī yān yòng niúdāo

杀价 shājià beat a seller down: 这架收录机卖主要价250元，我～杀到200元。 The seller was asking 250 *yuan* for the tape recorder, but I beat him down to 200.

杀戒 shājiè prohibition against taking life (one of the ten Buddhist prohibitions)

杀菌 shājūn destroy harmful microorganisms; disinfect; sterilize

杀菌剂 shājūnjì germicide; bactericide

杀戮 shālù massacre; slaughter: 惨遭～ be massacred in cold blood

杀卵剂 shāluǎnjì *agric.* ovicide

杀掠 shālüè massacre and plunder

杀螨剂 shāmǎnjì *agric.* acaricide; miticide

杀气¹ shāqì an aura of death; a murderous look: 满面～ with murder in one's face

杀气² shāqì vent one's spleen: 你有委屈就说出来，不该拿我～。 Get it off your chest if you feel you've been wronged. Don't take it out on others.

杀气腾腾 shāqì téngténg murderous-looking; ferocious

杀青 shāqīng finalize a manuscript

杀人 shārén ① *leg.* homicide ② kill a person

杀人不见血 shārén bù jiàn xiě kill without spilling blood—kill by subtle means

杀人不眨眼 shārén bù zhǎyǎn kill without batting an eyelid; kill without blinking an eye: 一伙满身鲜血的～的刽子手 a gang of blood-stained executioners, who slaughter people without blinking / 他是一个～、依靠杀人起家的凶手。 He murdered without batting an eye; in fact he built his career on killing.

杀人犯 shārénfàn homicide; murderer or manslayer

杀人放火 shārén-fànghuǒ murder and arson: ～，无恶不作 commit murder, arson and every crime imaginable

杀人如麻 shārén rú má kill people like flies

杀人越货 shārén yuè huò kill a person and seize his goods; rob and kill

杀伤 shāshāng kill and wound; inflict casualties on: ～大批敌军 inflict heavy casualties on the enemy / 这种炮弹～力很强。 This is a powerful antipersonnel shell.

杀伤弹 shāshāngdàn fragmentation bomb; antipersonnel bomb

杀身成仁 shā shēn chéng rén die to achieve virtue—die for a just cause

杀身之祸 shā shēn zhī huò a fatal disaster: 遭～ meet with a fatal disaster

杀生 shāshēng *Buddhism* take animal life

杀手 shāshǒu killer

杀鼠剂 shāshǔjì rat poison; raticide

杀头 shātóu behead; decapitate

杀退 shātuì put to flight

杀一儆百 shā yī jǐng bǎi execute one as a warning to a hundred

杀婴 shāyīng infanticide

沙¹ shā ① sand; grit ② sth. resembling sand; sth. granular or powdery: 豆沙 dòushā ③ (Shā) a surname

沙² shā (of voice) hoarse; husky

沙³ shā czar or czarist; tsar or tsarist ——see also shā

沙坝 shābà sandbar

沙包 shābāo ① sand dune ② sandbag

沙暴 shābào sandstorm

沙蚕 shācán clam worm

沙场 shāchǎng battlefield; battleground: 久经～ be a seasoned soldier—be experienced

沙尘 shāchén dust and sand in the air: 卡车驶过，扬起一片～。 The lorry raised a cloud of dust as it drove by.

沙虫 shāchóng another name for 星虫 xīngchóng

沙船 shāchuán a large junk

沙袋 shādài sandbag

沙丁鱼 shādīngyú sardine

沙俄 Shā'é tsarist Russia; czarist Russia

沙发 shāfā sofa; settee: 单人～ (upholstered) armchair / 三人～ three-seater settee

沙发床 shāfāchuáng studio couch; sofa bed

沙岗 shāgāng sand hill

沙锅 shāguō earthenware pot; casserole: ～豆腐 tofu (*or* bean curd) en casserole

沙果 shāguǒ *bot.* Chinese pear-leaved crabapple

沙狐 shāhú corsac (fox)

沙獾 shāhuān another name for 猪獾 zhūhuān

沙荒 shāhuāng sandy wasteland; sandy waste

沙皇 shāhuáng tsar; czar: ～政府 the tsarist government

沙鸡 shājī sandgrouse

沙浆 shājiāng same as 砂浆 shājiāng

沙金 shājīn placer gold; alluvial gold

沙坑 shākēng ① sandpit ② *sports* jumping pit

沙拉 shālā salad

沙梨 shālí *bot.* sand pear

沙里淘金 shā lǐ táo jīn wash grains of gold out of the sands—extract the essential from a large mass of material; get small returns for great effort

沙砾 shālì grit; gravel

沙龙 shālóng salon

沙罗周期 shāluó zhōuqī *astron.* saros

沙门 shāmén (Sanskrit) sramana (an ascetic, religious

wanderer, monk, or religious mendicant); (in Chinese usage) Buddhist monk

沙门氏菌 shāménshìjūn　Salmonella

沙弥 shāmí　a Buddhist novice

沙漠 shāmò　desert

沙漠化 shāmòhuà　desert encroachment; desertification; desertization

沙盘 shāpán　*mil.*　sand table: ～作业 sand table exercise

沙碛 shāqì　*formal*　desert

沙丘 shāqiū　(sand) dune: 流动～ moving dunes

沙瓤 shāráng　mushy watermelon pulp

沙壤土 shārǎngtǔ　same as 砂壤土 shārǎngtǔ

沙沙 shāshā　*onom.*　rustle: 风吹树叶～响。The leaves rustled in the wind.

沙参 shāshēn　*Chin. med.*　the root of straight ladybell (*Adenophora stricta*)

沙滩 shātān　sand beach

沙滩椅 shātānyǐ　beach chair

沙糖 shātáng　same as 砂糖 shātáng

沙特阿拉伯 Shātè Ālābó　Saudi Arabia

沙特阿拉伯人 Shātè Ālābórén　Saudi Arabian

沙田 shātián　farmland reclaimed from sand flats; sandy land

沙土 shātǔ　same as 砂土 shātǔ

沙文主义 shāwénzhǔyì　chauvinism

沙哑 shāyǎ　hoarse; husky; raucous: 声音～ have a husky voice

沙眼 shāyǎn　trachoma

沙鱼 shāyú　① sandfish ② same as 鲨鱼 shāyú

沙浴 shāyù　① sand bath (of birds) ② *med.* sand bath

沙枣 shāzǎo　*bot.*　narrow-leaved oleaster (*Elaeagnus angustifolia*)

沙蚤 shāzǎo　sand hopper

沙洲 shāzhōu　shoal; sandbank

沙蝎 shāzhú　lugworm

沙柱 shāzhù　dust devil; sand column

沙锥 shāzhuī　*zool.*　snipe

沙子 shāzi　① sand; grit ② small grains; pellets: 铁～ iron pellets; shot

沙钻鱼 shāzuànyú　another name for 鱚 xì

沙嘴 shāzuǐ　*geol.*　sandspit

纱　shā　① yarn: 棉纱 miánshā　② gauze; sheer: 铁纱 tiěshā

纱包线 shābāoxiàn　cotton-covered wire

纱布 shābù　gauze

纱厂 shāchǎng　cotton mill

纱橱 shāchú　screen cupboard

纱窗 shāchuāng　screen window; screen

纱灯 shādēng　gauze lantern

纱锭 shādìng　*text.*　spindle

纱巾 shājīn　gauze kerchief

纱笼 shālóng　same as 莎笼 shālóng

纱罗 shāluó　*text.*　gauze

纱帽 shāmào　same as 乌纱帽 wūshāmào

纱线 shāxiàn　yarn

纱罩 shāzhào　① gauze or screen covering (over food) ② mantle (of a lamp)

杉　shā　same as 杉 shān, limited to use in the following entry words ——see also shān

杉篙 shāgāo　fir pole (used for building a scaffold or for punting a boat)

杉木 shāmù　fir wood

刹　shā　put on the brakes; stop; check: 把车～住 stop (or brake) a car / ～住歪风 check an unhealthy

tendency ——see also chà

刹把 shābǎ　*mech.*　brake crank

刹车 shāchē　① stop a vehicle by applying the brakes; put on the brakes ② stop a machine by cutting off the power; turn off a machine ③ bring to a halt: 未经批准的项目，必须立即～。All projects started without permission must be stopped immediately. ④ the brakes

砂　shā　sand; grit

砂布 shābù　emery cloth; abrasive cloth: 刚玉～ corundum cloth

砂浆 shājiāng　mortar: 石灰～ lime mortar / 水泥～ cement mortar

砂礓 shājiāng　*geol.*　conglomerate

砂矿 shākuàng　placer deposit; placer: ～开采 placer mining; alluvial mining; placering

砂砾 shālì　same as 沙砾 shālì

砂轮 shālún　*mech.*　emery wheel; grinding wheel; abrasive wheel

砂轮机 shālúnjī　grinder

砂囊 shānáng　gizzard (of birds)

砂壤土 shārǎngtǔ　sandy loam

砂糖 shātáng　granulated sugar

砂田 shātián　same as 沙田 shātián

砂土 shātǔ　sandy soil; sand

砂箱 shāxiāng　*metall.*　sandbox; moulding box

砂心 shāxīn　*metall.*　core

砂型 shāxíng　*metall.*　sand mould

砂型铸造 shāxíng zhùzào　sand casting

砂岩 shāyán　sandstone

砂眼 shāyǎn　*metall.*　sand holes; blowholes

砂样 shāyàng　*petroleum*　drilling mud cuttings

砂纸 shāzhǐ　abrasive paper; sand paper: 玻璃～ glass paper / 金刚～ emery paper

砂质岩 shāzhìyán　arenaceous rock

莎　shā　used in names of places and persons: 莎车 (a county in Xinjiang) ——see also suō

莎鸡 shājī　same as 纺织娘 fǎngzhīniáng

莎丽 shālì　sari (the robe of a Hindu woman)

莎笼 shālóng　sarong (worn by Malay men and women)

铩（鎩）　shā　① an ancient spear ② *formal* wound; injure

铩羽 shāyǔ　*formal*　with wings clipped——be frustrated

痧　shā　*Chin. med.*　acute diseases such as cholera and sunstroke

痧子 shāzi　*dial.*　measles: 出～ have measles

袈　shā　see 袈裟 jiāshā

煞　shā　① stop; halt; check; bring to a close: ～住脚 stop short / 文章写到这里还～不住。The article can't very well end here. ② tighten: ～一～腰带 tighten one's belt ③ same as 杀 shā③⑥ ——see also shà

煞笔 shābǐ　① concluding lines of an article; ending of a piece of writing ② write the final line of an article, letter, etc.

煞车[1] shāchē　firmly fasten a load (on a vehicle); lash down

煞车[2] shāchē　same as 刹车 shāchē

煞风景 shāfēngjǐng　same as 杀风景 shāfēngjǐng

煞气 shāqì　same as 杀气[2] shāqì ——see also shàqì

煞尾 shāwěi　① finish off; round off; wind up: 事情不多了，马上就可以～。There isn't much work left; we're winding up. ② final stage; end; ending: 这出戏的～很带劲。The play has a powerful ending.

鲨 shā shark

鲨鱼 shāyú · shark

shǎ

傻 (儍) shǎ ① stupid; muddleheaded: 你真～，他这点意思都听不出来。How stupid you were. You should have known what he was driving at. / 吓～了 be dumbfounded; be stunned ② think or act mechanically: 别一个劲儿～干，要讲究方法。Don't just keep slogging away. Pay attention to method.

傻瓜 shǎguā (also 傻蛋 shǎdàn) fool; blockhead; simpleton

傻呵呵 shǎhēhē simple-minded; silly; foolish: 别看他～的，心里可有数。Maybe he doesn't look very clever, but he knows what's what. / 孩子听故事听得入了神，～地瞪大了两只眼睛。The child listened to the story with rapt attention, wide-eyed and dumb with wonder.

傻乎乎 shǎhūhū simple-minded; silly; foolish: 小孩子抿了抿嘴唇，～地笑了。The child puckered up her lips and began to smile innocently.

傻话 shǎhuà stupid talk; foolish words; nonsense

傻劲儿 shǎjìnr ① stupidity; foolishness ② sheer enthusiasm; doggedness: 不能光凭～，得找窍门。Enthusiasm alone won't do. You've got to work skilfully. / 这小伙子干活有股～。That youngster works with a will.

傻乐 shǎlè dial. laugh foolishly; giggle; smirk

傻里瓜唧 shǎliguājī dial. foolish; stupid

傻冒儿 shǎmàor humor. ① fool; blockhead; idiot ② foolish; stupid

傻气 shǎqi foolish; stupid

傻头傻脑 shǎtóushǎnǎo ① foolish-looking ② muddleheaded

傻小子 shǎxiǎozi humor. silly lad

傻笑 shǎxiào laugh foolishly; giggle; smirk

傻眼 shǎyǎn inf. be dumbfounded; be stunned: 他一看考题就～了。When he saw the examination questions he got a nasty shock.

傻样 shǎyàng inf. a foolish look: 看你这～，还不快过来和大家打招呼。Don't stand there looking so foolish. Come over and say hello to everybody.

傻子 shǎzi fool; blockhead; simpleton

shà

沙 shà dial. sift; sieve; screen: 把米里的沙子～一～。Sift the rice and sort out the sand. ——see also shā

啥 shà dial. what: 你说～来着?What did you say just now? / ～地方? Where? / 有～说～ say what one has to say; come out with what one thinks; speak one's mind / 你不快走,还罗嗦个～? It's time you went. Why do you keep on chattering away? / 困难再大也没～了不起。Difficulties, no matter how great, are nothing to be afraid of.

啥味呢 shàwèiní text. cheviot

嗏 shà see below

嗏血 shàxuè same as 歃血 shàxuè

嗏喋 shàzhá liter. the sound of a school of fish or a flock of water birds feeding

厦 (廈) shà a tall building; mansion: 高楼大厦 gāolóu-dàshà ——see also xià

歃 shà formal suck

歃血 shàxuè smear the blood of a sacrifice on the mouth—an ancient form of swearing an oath

歃血为盟 shàxuè wéi méng swear an oath of alliance by smearing the mouth with the blood of a sacrifice

煞[1] shà evil spirit; goblin

煞[2] shà adv. (used before a verb or adjective) very ——see also shā

煞白 shàbái ghastly pale; deathly pale; pallid: 脸色～ look deathly pale

煞费苦心 shà fèi kǔxīn cudgel one's brains; take great pains: ～地寻找借口 cudgel one's brains to find an excuse / 他们为了攻克技术难关,可真是～。They took great pains to solve the technical problems.

煞气 shàqì (of anything with air inside) leak: 我自行车胎～了。My bicycle has a flat tyre. ——see also shāqì

煞神 shàshén demon; fiend

煞有介事 shàyǒujièshì same as 像煞有介事 xiàng shàyǒujièshì

嗄 shà formal (of the voice) hoarse

霎 shà a very short time; moment; instant: 一霎 yīshà

霎时间 shàshíjiān (also 霎时 shàshí) in a twinkling; in a split second; in a jiffy

霎眼 shàyǎn in a moment; in a twinkling

sha

挲 (挱) sha see 挓挲 zhāsha ——see also sā; suō

shāi

筛[1] (篩) shāi ① sieve; sifter; screen ② sift; sieve; screen; riddle: ～面 sieve flour; sift flour / ～煤 screen coal / ～砂砾 riddle gravel / ～煤渣 sift cinders

筛[2] (篩) shāi ① warm up wine over a fire ② pour (wine)

筛[3] (篩) shāi dial. beat (the gong)

筛法 shāifǎ math. sieve method

筛分 shāifēn screening; sieving: ～机 screening machine

筛管 shāiguǎn bot. sieve tube

筛号 shāihào screen size; screen mesh; mesh number

筛糠 shāikāng inf. shiver: 吓得直～ shiver with fear; shake in one's shoes

筛选 shāixuǎn ① same as 筛分 shāifēn ② select: 办公大楼的设计方案是从三十个不同方案中反复～出来的。The design for the office building was selected from 30 carefully screened entries.

筛子 shāizi a sieve; sifter; screen: 粗～ riddle

shǎi

色 shǎi. inf. colour: 这布掉～吗?Will this cloth

fade? ——see also sè

色子 shǎizi　dice: 掷～ play dice; throw dice

shǎi

晒（曬）
shài　① (of the sun) shine upon: 日～雨淋 be exposed to the sun and rain / 这里～得慌。There's too much sun here. ② dry in the sun; bask: ～粮食 dry grain in the sun / ～被子 air a quilt / 他的脸～黑了。His face is tanned. / 放在太阳底下～～。Leave it to dry in the sun.

晒场 shàichǎng　sunning ground (for drying grain, etc.)

晒垡 shàifá　agric. sun the earth which has been ploughed up; sun the upturned soil

晒暖儿 shàinuǎnr　dial. bask in the sun

晒坪 shàipíng　dial. sunning ground

晒台 shàitái　flat roof (for drying clothes, etc.)

晒太阳 shài tàiyang　sunbathe; bask in the sun: 让孩子们尽量多～。Take the children out to get as much sun as possible.

晒图 shàitú　make a blueprint; blueprint

晒图员 shàitúyuán　blueprinter

晒图纸 shàitúzhǐ　blueprint paper

晒烟 shàiyān　sun-cured tobacco

晒盐 shàiyán　evaporate brine in the sun to make salt

shān

山
shān　① hill; mountain: 一座高～ a high mountain ② anything resembling a mountain: 冰山 bīngshān ③ a bunch of straw in which silkworms spin cocoons: 蚕上～了。The silkworms have gone into the straw bundles to spin their cocoons. ④ gable ⑤ (Shān) a surname

山坳 shān'ào　col

山包 shānbāo　dial. a small hill

山崩 shānbēng　landslide; landslip

山崩地裂 shānbēng-dìliè　mountains collapsing and the earth cracking up (said of a cataclysm or of deafening noises)

山苍子 shāncāngzǐ　Chin. med. the fruit of a cubeb litsea tree (Litsea cubeba)

山茶 shānchá　bot. camellia

山城 shānchéng　mountain city: ～重庆 the mountain city Chongqing

山冲 shānchōng　dial. a stretch of flatland in a hilly area

山重水复 shānchóng-shuǐfù　mountains multiply and streams double back: ～疑无路, 柳暗花明又一村。(陆游) Mountains multiply, streams double back—I doubt there's even a road; Willows cluster darkly, blossoms shine—another village ahead!

山川 shānchuān　mountains and rivers—land; landscape

山鹑 shānchún　partridge

山慈姑 shāncígu　bot. edible tulip

山村 shāncūn　mountain village

山丹 shāndān　bot. morningstar lily (Lilium concolor)

山道年 shāndàonián　pharm. santonin

山地 shāndì　① mountainous region; hilly area; hilly country ② hillside field

山顶 shāndǐng　the summit (or top) of a mountain; hilltop

山顶洞人 Shāndǐngdòngrén　Upper Cave Man (a type of primitive man who lived ten to twenty thousand years ago and whose fossil remains were found in 1933 at Zhoukoudian 周口店 near Beijing)

山东 Shāndōng　Shangdong (Province)

山东梆子 Shāndōng bāngzi　Shangdong clapper opera ——see also 梆子腔 bāngziqiāng

山东快书 Shāndōng kuàishū　Shandong clapper ballad

山洞 shāndòng　cave; cavern

山豆根 shāndòugēn　bot. subprostrate sophora (Sophora subprostrata)

山风 shānfēng　meteorol. mountain breeze

山峰 shānfēng　mountain peak

山旮旯儿 shāngālár　dial. a faraway hilly area; an out-of-the-way place in the mountains; a remote mountain area

山冈 shāngāng　low hill; hillock

山高水长 shāngāo-shuǐcháng　(of nobility of character) as high as the hills and as long as the rivers—of lasting influence

山高水低 shāngāo-shuǐdī　unexpected misfortune; sth. unfortunate, esp. death: 万一有个～ in the event of sb.'s death

山高水远 shāngāo-shuǐyuǎn　① the mountains are high and the rivers far away—a long distance ② same as 山高水低 shāngāo-shuǐdī

山歌 shāngē　folk song (sung in the fields or in mountain areas during or after work)

山根 shāngēn　inf. the foot of a hill

山梗菜碱 shāngěngcàijiǎn　pharm. lobeline

山沟 shāngōu　① gully ② ravine; (mountain) valley ③ a remote mountain area

山谷 shāngǔ　mountain valley; ravine

山国 shānguó　a mountainous country; a hilly region

山河 shānhé　mountains and rivers—the land of a country: 祖国的锦绣～ our beautiful land

山和尚 shānhéshang　common name for 戴胜 dàishèng

山核桃 shānhétao　① hickory ② hickory nut

山洪 shānhóng　mountain torrents: ～暴发。Torrents of water rushed down the mountain.

山回路转 shānhuí-lùzhuǎn　same as 峰回路转 fēnghuí-lùzhuǎn

山火 shānhuǒ　mountain fire

山货 shānhuò　① mountain products (such as haws, chestnuts and walnuts) ② household utensils made of wood, bamboo, clay, etc.

山鸡 shānjī　dial. pheasant

山鸡椒 shānjījiāo　bot. cubeb litsea tree (Litsea cubeba)

山积 shānjī　formal be piled mountain high: 货物～。Merchandise is piled mountain high.

山脊 shānjǐ　ridge (of a mountain or hill)

山涧 shānjiàn　mountain stream

山椒鸟 shānjiāoniǎo　minivet

山脚 shānjiǎo　the foot of a hill

山口 shānkǒu　mountain pass; pass

山岚 shānlán　formal mountain mists

山里红 shānlǐhóng　bot. large-fruited Chinese hawthorn (Crataegus pinnatifida var. major)

山梁 shānliáng　ridge (of a mountain or hill)

山林 shānlín　mountain forest; wooded mountain: ～地区 mountain and forest region; wooded and hilly lands

山陵 shānlíng　formal ① hills ② tombs of emperors

山岭 shānlǐng　a chain of mountains

山路 shānlù　mountain path: ～崎岖不平。The mountain path is rough and rugged.

山麓 shānlù　the foot of a mountain; piedmont: ～丘陵 foothills

山峦 shānluán　a chain of mountains; a multipeaked mountain: ～起伏 undulating hills; rolling hills

山脉 shānmài　mountain range; mountain chain

山猫 shānmāo　leopard cat

山毛榉　shānmáojǔ　*bot.* beech

山门　shānmén　① the gate of a Buddhist temple ② Buddhism

山盟海誓　shānméng-hǎishì　same as 海誓山盟 hǎishì-shānméng

山民　shānmín　mountain people; hillmen

山姆大叔　Shānmǔ Dàshū　Uncle Sam

山奈　shānnài　(also 山萘 shānnài) *chem.* cyanide

山南海北　shānnán-hǎiběi　① south of the mountains and north of the seas—far away; far and wide: ～他哪儿都过过。He has travelled far and wide. / ～，到处都有勘探人员的足迹。The prospectors have left their footprints all over the land. ② discursive; rambling: 他们～地扯了一阵。They talked about everything under the sun.

山炮　shānpào　mountain gun; mountain artillery

山坡　shānpō　hillside; mountain slope; hillslope

山气　shānqì　*formal* mountain mists; mountain air: ～日夕佳，飞鸟相与还。(陶潜) The mountain air is fine at evening of the day And flying birds return together homewards.

山墙　shānqiáng　gable

山清水秀　shānqīng-shuǐxiù　(also 山明水秀 shānmíng-shuǐxiù) green hills and clear waters—picturesque scenery

山穷水尽　shānqióng-shuǐjìn　where the hills and streams end—at the end of one's rope (*or* tether, resources): ～疑无路，柳暗花明又一村。Where the hills and streams end and there seems no road beyond, Amidst shading willows and blooming flowers another village appears. (usu. said when one begins to see hope when all seems lost)

山区　shānqū　mountain area

山泉　shānquán　mountain spring

山雀　shānquè　tit

山人　shānrén　recluse; hermit (formerly often used by scholar-officials as a form of self-address)

山水　shānshuǐ　① water from a mountain: 一股～汨汨而下。A stream gurgles down the mountain. ② mountains and rivers; scenery with hills and waters: 桂林～甲天下。The scenery of Guilin is the best under heaven. ③ traditional Chinese painting of mountains and waters; landscape painting; landscape

山水画　shānshuǐhuà　mountains-and-waters painting; landscape painting; landscape

山水记　shānshuǐjì　landscape essay: 柳宗元以～著称，写景状物，多所寄托。Liu Zongyuan is famous for his landscape essays, which are descriptions of nature animated by his own emotions.

山水相连　shān-shuǐ xiānglián　be linked by common mountains and rivers: 两国～。The two countries are joined by common mountains and rivers.

山桃　shāntáo　mountain peach

山田　shāntián　hillside plot

山桐子　shāntóngzǐ　*bot.* idesia

山头　shāntóu　① hilltop; mountain top ② mountain stronghold; faction: 拉山头 lā shāntóu ③ gable

山头主义　shāntóuzhǔyì　mountain-stronghold mentality (a type of sectarianism)

山外有山　shān wài yǒu shān　there's always a mountain beyond a mountain—there's always something better; nothing can be perfect

山窝　shānwō　(also 山窝窝 shānwōwo) an out-of-the-way mountain area

山坞　shānwù　a piece of flatland in the mountains; a mountain glen; col

山西　Shānxī　Shanxi (Province)

山西梆子　Shānxī bāngzi　Shanxi clapper opera (another name for 晋剧 jìnjù)——see also 梆子腔 bāngziqiāng

山系　shānxì　*geol.* mountain system

山峡　shānxiá　gorge

山险　shānxiǎn　difficult mountain terrain

山乡　shānxiāng　mountain village; mountain area

山响　shānxiǎng　deafening; thunderous: 鼓擂得～ drums beating thunderously / 北风刮得门窗乒乒乓乓～。The doors and windows are rattling noisily in the north wind.

山魈　shānxiāo　① *zool.* mandrill (*Mandrillus sphinx*) ② mountain elf

山鸦　shānyā　chough

山崖　shānyá　cliff

山羊　shānyáng　① goat ② *sports* buck

山羊胡子　shānyáng húzi　goatee

山羊绒　shānyángróng　cashmere

山腰　shānyāo　halfway up the mountain

山肴野蔌　shānyáo-yěsù　mountain meats and wild vegetables

山摇地动　shānyáo-dìdòng　same as 地动山摇 dìdòng-shānyáo

山药　shānyao　*bot.* Chinese yam

山药蛋　shānyaodàn　*dial.* potato

山雨欲来风满楼　shānyǔ yù lái fēng mǎn lóu　the wind sweeping through the tower heralds a rising storm in the mountains; the rising wind forebodes the coming storm

山芋　shānyù　*dial.* sweet potato

山鹬　shānyù　woodcock

山岳　shānyuè　lofty mountains: ～地区 mountainous region

山岳冰川　shānyuè bīngchuān　mountain glacier; alpine glacier

山楂　shānzhā　(also 山查 shānzhā) ① (Chinese) hawthorn ② haw: ～酱 haw jelly

山楂糕　shānzhāgāo　(also 山查糕 shānzhāgāo) haw jelly cake

山寨　shānzhài　mountain fastness; a fortified mountain village

山珍海味　shānzhēn-hǎiwèi　(also 山珍海错 shānzhēn-hǎicuò) delicacies from land and sea; dainties of every kind

山中无老虎, 猴子称大王　shān zhōng wú lǎohǔ, hóuzi chēng dàwáng　when the tiger is away from the mountain, the monkey proclaims himself king

山茱萸　shānzhūyú　*Chin. med.* the fruit of medicinal cornel (*Cornus officinalis*)

山庄　shānzhuāng　① mountain villa ② mountain village

山子　shānzi　(also 山子石儿 shānzishír) *dial.* rockery

山嘴　shānzuǐ　*geol.* spur

芟　shān　① mow (grass) ② weed out; eliminate

芟除　shānchú　① mow; cut down: ～杂草 weeding ② delete: ～繁冗的词句 delete the unnecessary words and sentences

芟夷　shānyí　(also 芟荑 shānyí) *formal* ① mow (grass) ② eliminate; exterminate

杉　shān　*bot.* China fir——see also shā

删 (刪)　shān　delete; leave out: 这一段可以～去。This paragraph can be left out. / ～掉不必要的细节 cut out the unnecessary details

删除　shānchú　delete; strike (*or* cut, cross) out

删繁就简　shānfán-jiùjiǎn　simplify sth. by cutting out the superfluous

删改　shāngǎi　delete and change; revise: 稿子几经～才定下来。The draft was revised several times before it was finalized.

删节　shānjié　abridge; abbreviate: 本报略有～ slightly

abridged by our editorial staff

删节本 shānjiébèn abridged edition; abbreviated version

删节号 shānjiéhào ellipsis; suspension points; ellipsis dots (……) (…)

删略 shānlüè leave out; omit

删削 shānxuē delete; cut out; strike out

衫 shān unlined upper garment: 衬衫 chènshān / 汗衫 hànshān

苫 shān straw mat ——see also shàn

姗(姍) shān see below

姗姗 shānshān walk slowly like a woman

姗姗来迟 shānshān lái chí be slow in coming; be late

钐(釤) shān chem. samarium (Sm)

珊(珊) shān see below

珊瑚 shānhú coral

珊瑚虫 shānhúchóng coral polyp; coral insect

珊瑚岛 shānhúdǎo coral island

珊瑚礁 shānhújiāo coral reef

栅(柵) shān see below ——see also zhà

栅极 shānjí electron. grid: 抑制～ suppressor grid

舢 shān see below

舢板 shānbǎn (also 舢版 shānbǎn) sampan

扇¹(搧) shān ① fan: ～火 fan a fire / ～扇子 fan oneself; use a fan ② slap (sb. on the face): ～他一耳光 slap him on the face

扇² shān same as 煽 shān ——see also shàn

扇动 shāndòng ① flap: ～翅膀 flap the wings ② same as 煽动 shāndòng

扇风点火 shānfēng-diǎnhuǒ fan the flames; inflame and agitate people; stir up trouble

扇风耳 shānfēng'ěr protruding ears; flappy ears

扇风机 shānfēngjī ventilating fan

扇阴风, 点鬼火 shān yīnfēng, diǎn guǐhuǒ fan the winds of evil and spread the fires of turmoil—foment trouble

蹒 shān see 蹒跚 pánshān

煽 shān ① fan (a fire): 把炉火～旺点儿 fan the fire to make it burn brighter ② incite; instigate; stir up: 煽惑 shānhuò

煽动 shāndòng instigate; incite; stir up; whip up: ～暴乱 incite rebellion / ～无政府主义 incite anarchism / ～派性 whip up factionalism / ～群众闹事 stir up trouble among the masses

煽惑 shānhuò incite; agitate: ～人心 agitate people by demagogy

煽诱 shānyòu same as 煽惑 shānhuò

潸(潛) shān liter. in tears; tearful

潸然 shānrán liter. in tears; tearful: ～泪下 tears trickling down one's cheeks

潸潸 shānshān liter. in tears; tearful: 不禁～ can't keep back one's tears / 热泪～ tears streaming down one's cheeks

膻(羶) shān the smell of mutton: 这羊肉不～。 This mutton hasn't got a strong smell.

shǎn

闪 shǎn ① dodge; get out of the way: 他要打我, 我一～, 他没打着。 He wanted to hit me, but I dodged and he missed. ② twist; sprain: ～了腰 sprain one's back ③ lightning: 打闪 dǎshǎn ④ flash; sparkle; shine: 远处灯光一～。 There was a flash of light in the distance. / 灯一～就灭了。 The light flashed and then went out. / ～金光 emit golden rays / 这时我脑子里～过一个念头。 At this moment an idea flashed through my mind. ⑤ dial. leave behind: 你去的时候叫我一声, 可别把我～下。 Please call for me when you go; don't leave me behind.

闪避 shǎnbì dodge; sidestep: ～不及 too late to dodge

闪长岩 shǎnchángyán diorite

闪挫 shǎncuò Chin. med. sudden strain or contusion of a muscle; sprain

闪点 shǎndiǎn chem. flash point

闪电 shǎndiàn lightning

闪电战 shǎndiànzhàn lightning war; blitzkrieg; blitz

闪动 shǎndòng flash; twinkle; flicker: 灯光～。 Lights flashed. / 夜空中群星～。 Stars twinkled in the night sky. / 墙上有个人影在～。 The shadow of a person was flickering on the wall.

闪躲 shǎnduǒ dodge; evade

闪光 shǎnguāng ① a flash of light: 流星像一道～, 划破黑夜的长空。 With a flash, the meteor shot across the night sky. ② gleam; glisten; glitter: 露珠在晨曦中～。 Dewdrops glistened in the morning light.

闪光灯 shǎnguāngdēng ① photog. flash lamp; flashlight; photoflash ② flashlight (used for signals)

闪光同步 shǎnguāng tóngbù photog. flash synchronization

闪击 shǎnjī launch (or make) a surprise attack

闪击战 shǎnjīzhàn lightning war; blitzkrieg; blitz

闪开 shǎnkāi get out of the way; jump aside; dodge: 车来了, 快～! Look out! There's a bus coming.

闪亮 shǎnliàng sparkling; glittering; glistening: 她说话的时候, 眼眶里含着～的泪珠。 As she spoke, her eyes glistened with tears.

闪米特人 Shǎnmǐtèrén Semite

闪念 shǎnniàn an idea which flashes through one's mind

闪闪 shǎnshǎn sparkling; glistening; glittering: ～的红星 a sparkling red star / ～发光 sparkle; glitter / 天空中电光～。 Lightning flashed in the sky.

闪射 shǎnshè glitter; shine; radiate: 向四周～光芒 radiate rays of light in all directions

闪身 shǎnshēn ① dodge: 侦察兵一～机警地躲过了敌人的探照灯。 The scout dodged nimbly and evaded the enemy's searchlight. ② move sideways: ～进门 walk sideways through the door

闪失 shǎnshī mishap; accident: 要是有个～, 怎么办呢? What if anything should go wrong?

闪石 shǎnshí amphibole

闪烁 shǎnshuò ① twinkle; glimmer; glisten: 远处～着灯光。 Lights glimmered in the distance. / 她的眼睛里～着喜悦的泪花。 Her eyes glistened with tears of joy. ② evasive; vague; noncommittal: 他闪闪烁烁, 不做肯定的答复。 He hummed and hawed, giving no definite reply. or He was evasive and noncommittal.

闪烁计数器 shǎnshuò jìshùqì scintillation counter

闪烁其词 shǎnshuò qí cí speak evasively; hedge

闪现 shǎnxiàn flash before one: 英雄的形象～在我的眼前。 The image of the hero flashed before my eyes.

闪锌矿 shǎnxīnkuàng (zinc) blende; sphalerite

闪眼 shǎnyǎn *dial.* dazzling: ～的阳光 the dazzling sunlight

闪耀 shǎnyào glitter; shine; radiate: 繁星～ glittering stars / 他两眼～着刚毅的光芒。His eyes flashed with resolution. / 巴黎公社的原则～着不灭的光辉。The principles of the Paris Commune radiate with eternal light.

闪熠 shǎnyì *formal* glitter; shine; radiate: 灯火～ lights glittering

闪音 shǎnyīn *phonet.* flap

闪语族 Shǎnyǔzú the Semitic group (including Arabic, Hebrew, etc.)

闪蒸 shǎnzhēng *petroleum* flash vaporization: ～塔 flash tower

闪灼 shǎnzhuó glitter; shine; radiate: 灯烛～ lamps and candles shining brightly

陕(陝)
Shǎn short for 陕西 Shǎnxī

陕西 Shǎnxī Shaanxi (Province)

陕西梆子 Shǎnxī bāngzi Shaanxi clapper opera (another name for 秦腔 qínqiāng[①]) ——see also 梆子腔 bāngziqiāng

睒(睒)
shǎn blink; twinkle: 这孩子一～眼就不见了。The boy vanished in the twinkling of an eye.

shàn

讪
shàn ① mock; ridicule ② embarrassed; awkward; shamefaced: 脸上发～ look embarrassed

讪谤 shànbàng *formal* slander; malign; calumniate

讪脸 shànliǎn *dial.* (of children in the presence of adults) grin mischievously; grin and grimace

讪讪 shànshàn embarrassed; awkward; shamefaced: 他觉得没趣，只好～地走开了。Feeling he was not wanted, he walked away looking embarrassed.

讪笑 shànxiào ridicule; mock; deride

汕
Shàn short for 汕头 Shàntóu

汕头 Shàntóu Shantou (a city in Guangdong Province)

疝
shàn hernia: 腹股沟～ inguinal hernia / 脐～ umbilical hernia

疝带 shàndài *med.* truss

疝气 shànqì hernia

单(單)
Shàn a surname ——see also chán; dān

苫
shàn cover with a straw mat, tarpaulin, etc.: 要下雨了，快把麦子～上。Quick! Cover up the wheat. It's going to rain. ——see also shān

苫布 shànbù tarpaulin

苫席 shànxí a mat cover

扇
shàn ① fan: 电扇 diànshàn ② a sliding, hinged or detachable flat part; leaf: 八～屏风 an eight-leaf screen ③ *m.* (for doors, windows, etc.): 一～门 a door / 两～窗子 two windows

扇贝 shànbèi *zool.* scallop; fan shell

扇车 shànchē winnowing machine; winnower

扇骨子 shàngǔzi the ribs (*or* mount) of a folding fan

扇面儿 shànmiànr the covering of a fan

扇形 shànxíng ① fan-shaped: 队伍到达开阔地便成～摆开阵势。The troops fanned out as they reached open ground. ② *math.* sector

扇形齿轮 shànxíng chǐlún sector (*or* segment) gear

扇坠 shànzhuì fan pendants

扇子 shànzi fan: 一把～ a fan / 扇(shān)～ fan oneself; use a fan

掸(撣)
Shàn ① a name for the Dai nationality (傣族) used in historical works ② the Shans (of the Shan State 掸邦 in Burma) ——see also dǎn

善
shàn ① good; virtuous: 心怀不～ harbour ill intent (*or* evil intentions) ② satisfactory; good: ～策 a wise policy; the best policy ③ make a success of; perfect: 善始善终 shànshǐ-shànzhōng ④ kind; friendly: 相～ be kind and helpful to each other ⑤ be good at; be expert (*or* adept) in: 不～经营 not good at management / ～观风色 quick to see which way the wind blows—very shrewd ⑥ well: 善为说辞 shàn wèi shuōcí ⑦ be apt to: 善变 shànbiàn

善罢甘休 shànbà-gānxiū (usu. used in the negative) leave the matter at that; let it go at that: 敌人这一仗打败了，但决不会～的。The enemy will not take their defeat lying down.

善本 shànběn reliable text; good edition: ～书 rare book

善变 shànbiàn be apt to change; be changeable

善处 shànchǔ *formal* deal discreetly with; conduct oneself well

善待 shàndài treat sb. well

善感 shàngǎn (of a person) sensitive: 多愁善感 duōchóu-shàngǎn

善果 shànguǒ good fruit—the rewards of good deeds: 行善事，结～。Good deeds bear good fruit.

善后 shànhòu deal with problems arising from an accident, etc.: 处理这次火灾的～ deal with the aftermath of the fire

善举 shànjǔ *formal* a philanthropic act or project

善类 shànlèi *formal* (usu. used in the negative) good people: 此人行迹诡秘，定非～。Secretive as he is, he cannot possibly be a good man.

善良 shànliáng good and honest; kind-hearted: ～的人们 good and honest people; people of goodwill / ～愿望 the best of intentions / 心地～ kind-hearted

善邻 shànlín *formal* be a good neighbour: ～政策 good-neighbour policy

善男信女 shànnán-xìnnǚ Buddhist devotees

善人 shànrén philanthropist; charitable person; well-doer

善始善终 shànshǐ-shànzhōng start well and end well; do well from start to finish; see sth. through

善事 shànshì charitable deeds; good deeds

善忘 shànwàng be forgetful; have a short memory

善为说辞 shàn wèi shuōcí put in a good word for sb.

善心 shànxīn mercy; benevolence: 发～ show kindness

善意 shànyì goodwill; good intentions: 出于～ out of goodwill; with the best intentions / ～的批评 well-meaning criticism

善有善报，恶有恶报 shàn yǒu shànbào, è yǒu èbào good is rewarded with good, and evil with evil: ～；不是不报，时候未到；时候一到，一切都报。Good will be rewarded with good, and evil with evil; if the reward is not forthcoming, it is because the time has not yet come; when the time comes, one will get one's due reward.

善于 shànyú be good at; be adept in: ～应对 be good at repartee / ～交际 be good at socializing / 敢于斗争，～斗争 dare to struggle and know how to struggle

善战 shànzhàn be good at fighting; be skilful in battle

善终 shànzhōng ① die a natural death; die in one's bed ② end well

善自保重 shàn zì bǎozhòng take good care of yourself

善自为谋 shàn zì wéi móu　know how to look after oneself

禅(禪) shàn　abdicate——see also chán

禅让 shànràng　abdicate and hand over the crown to another person

禅位 shànwèi　abdicate the throne

骟 shàn　castrate (an animal); geld (a male animal) or spay (a female animal): ～马 castrate a horse or a castrated horse

缮 shàn　① repair; mend: 修缮 xiūshàn　② copy; write out: ～清 make a fair copy

缮发 shànfā　copy and send out: 此稿尽速～。Make a fair copy of this manuscript and send it to the press as soon as possible.

缮写 shànxiě　write out; copy

擅 shàn　① arrogate to oneself; do sth. on one's own authority: ～作主张 make a decision without authorization　② be good at; be expert in: 不～辞令 lack facility in polite or tactful speech

擅便 shànbiàn　*formal* act on one's own authority: 未敢～，呈请定夺。Not daring to presume, I beg you to render a decision.

擅长 shàncháng　be good at; be expert in; be skilled in: ～歌舞 be good at singing and dancing / 他～侧泳。He has a good sidestroke.

擅场 shàncháng　*formal* dominate the scene——be the supreme arbiter

擅离职守 shàn lí zhíshǒu　leave one's post without permission

擅利 shànlì　have a monopoly

擅美 shànměi　*formal* get all the credit: 不敢～ dare not claim all the credit for oneself

擅权 shànquán　monopolize power; have sole power; arrogate all authority to oneself

擅自 shànzì　do sth. without authorization: 不得～修改操作规程。No unauthorized changes may be made in the rules of operation. / 任何一方不得～修改合同。Neither party may unilaterally modify the contract. / ～行动 act presumptuously

擅作威福 shàn zuò wēi fú　same as 作威作福 zuòwēizuòfú

膳(饍) shàn　meals; board: 在食堂用～ have one's meals at the mess

膳费 shànfèi　board expenses

膳食 shànshí　meals; food: 流质～ liquid diet / 半流质～ semiliquid diet

膳宿 shàn-sù　board and lodging: ～自理 be responsible for one's own board and lodging

嬗 shàn　*formal* ① transmute; transform　② same as 禅 shàn

嬗变 shànbiàn　①　*formal* evolution　②　*phys.* transmutation: 自然～ natural transmutation / 感生～ induced transmutation

赡 shàn　① support; provide for: ～家养口 support a family　②　*formal* sufficient; abundant: 力不～ beyond one's strength

赡养 shànyǎng　support; provide for: ～父母 support one's parents / 子女对父母有～扶助的义务。Children have the duty to support and assist their parents.

赡养费 shànyǎngfèi　① payment for support of one's parents　②　*old* alimony

蟮 shàn　see 曲蟮 qūshàn

鳝(鱔) shàn　eel; finless eel

shāng

伤(傷) shāng　① wound; injury: 刀～ a knife wound / 浑身是～ be covered with cuts and bruises / ～好了。The wound has healed.　② injure; hurt: 被汽车撞～ be knocked down and injured by a car / 摔～ fall and hurt oneself　③ be distressed: 伤怀 shānghuái　④ get sick of sth.; develop an aversion to sth.: 这孩子吃糖吃～了。The child has got sick of eating sweets.　⑤ be harmful to; hinder: 有～国体 discredit one's country / 无～大体 not matter much

伤疤 shāngbā　scar

伤悲 shāngbēi　sad; sorrowful

伤兵 shāngbīng　wounded soldier

伤病员 shāngbìngyuán　the sick and wounded; noneffectives

伤财 shāngcái　lose money; waste money: 这会叫你又一又惹麻烦。This will mean trouble as well as a waste of money.

伤残 shāngcán　wounded and disabled

伤悼 shāngdào　mourn sorrowfully (for sb.'s death)

伤风 shāngfēng　catch cold; have a cold

伤风败俗 shāngfēng-bàisú　offend public decency; corrupt public morals

伤俘 shāngfú　① the wounded and the captured　② the wounded POWs

伤感 shānggǎn　sick at heart; sentimental

伤害 shānghài　injure; harm; hurt: 不要～益鸟。Don't harm beneficial birds. / 饮酒过多会～身体。Excessive drinking is harmful to the health. / ～自尊心 injure (*or* hurt) one's pride; hurt one's self-respect / ～民族感情 hurt national feelings

伤寒 shānghán　①　*med.* typhoid fever; typhoid　②　*Chin. med.* diseases caused by harmful cold factors; febrile diseases; fevers

伤号 shānghào　(usu. used among army personnel) the wounded

伤耗 shānghao　damage: 这筐苹果刨去～还有四十斤。There are still forty *jin* of apples in this basket after taking out the damaged ones.

伤痕 shānghén　scar; bruise

伤痕文学 shānghén wénxué　trauma literature

伤怀 shānghuái　*formal* sad; grieved; broken-hearted

伤筋动骨 shāngjīn-dònggǔ　be injured in the tendons or bones: 他虽然浑身青肿, 但并未～。Although badly bruised all over, he had broken no bones.

伤科 shāngkē　*Chin. med.* (department of) traumatology

伤口 shāngkǒu　wound; cut: 洗～ bathe a wound

伤脑筋 shāngnǎojīn　knotty; troublesome; bothersome: ～的问题 a knotty problem; a headache / 老下雨, 真～。It's a nuisance the way it keeps on raining.

伤气 shāngqì　①　*formal* feel frustrated; feel disheartened　②　*Chin. med.* sap one's vitality

伤情 shāngqíng　① the condition of an injury or wound　② sick at heart; sentimental

伤人 shāngrén　① hurt sb.'s feelings　② inflict injuries　③ injure the health: 忧能～。Anxiety can wear you out.

伤神 shāngshén　① overtax one's nerves; be nerve-racking　② sad; grieved

伤生 shāngshēng　be injurious to life

伤食 shāngshí　*Chin. med.* dyspepsia caused by excessive eating or improper diet

伤势 shāngshì the condition of an injury or wound: ～很重 be seriously injured or wounded

伤逝 shāngshì mourn the death of sb.

伤天害理 shāngtiān-hàilǐ offend against Heaven and reason—atrocious; outrageous

伤痛 shāngtòng ① grieved; distressed ② the pain of an injury or wound

伤亡 shāngwáng injuries and deaths; casualties: ～惨重 suffer heavy casualties / ～人数 the number of casualties

伤亡报告 shāngwáng bàogào *mil.* returns of losses

伤心 shāngxīn sad; grieved; broken-hearted: 伤透了心 feel extremely heartbroken / ～落泪 shed sad tears; weep in grief / 别为这事～。Don't let it grieve you. / 这么好的庄稼给雹子打了,真叫人～。It's really heartrending to see such fine crops damaged by the hailstorm. / 丈夫有泪不轻弹,只因未到～处。A man does not easily shed tears until his heart is broken.

伤心惨目 shāngxīn-cǎnmù too ghastly to look at; tragic (scene)

伤心事 shāngxīnshì a heartbreaking affair; a painful memory; an old sore

伤员 shāngyuán (usu. used among army personnel) wounded personnel; the wounded

殇(殤) shāng *formal* die young

商[1] shāng ① discuss; consult: 共～大计 discuss matters of vital importance ② trade; commerce; business: 经商 jīngshāng / 通商 tōngshāng ③ merchant; trader; businessman; dealer: 盐～ salt dealer ④ *math.* quotient

商[2] shāng *mus.* a note of the ancient Chinese five-tone scale, corresponding to 2 in numbered musical notation

商[3] Shāng ① the Shang Dynasty (c. 16th–11th century B. C.) ② a surname

商标 shāngbiāo trademark: ～注册 trademark registration

商标法 shāngbiāofǎ trademark law

商标权 shāngbiāoquán trademark rights

商埠 shāngbù *old* commercial (or trading) port

商场 shāngchǎng market; bazaar: 西单～ the Xidan Bazaar

商船 shāngchuán merchant ship; merchantman

商船队 shāngchuánduì mercantile marine; merchant marine

商店 shāngdiàn shop; store

商调 shāngdiào (of one organization) negotiate with another organization for the transfer of one of its cadres

商定 shāngdìng decide through consultation; agree: 经～ it has been decided through consultation that / 已～的条款 the provisions already agreed upon / 我们～了下次开会的日期。We agreed on a date for our next meeting. / 双方～建立大使级外交关系。The two sides have agreed to establish diplomatic relations at ambassadorial level. / 我们在～的时间碰了头。We met at the agreed time.

商队 shāngduì a company of travelling merchants; trade caravan

商兑 shāngduì *formal* consult and consider; discuss and deliberate

商法 shāngfǎ *leg.* commercial law

商贩 shāngfàn small retailer; pedlar

商港 shānggǎng commercial port

商贾 shānggǔ *formal* merchants

商行 shānghǎng trading company; commercial firm

商号 shānghào *old* shop; store; business establishment

商会 shānghuì chamber of commerce

商计 shāngjì have discussions or consultations: 决定再作～ decide to have further discussions

商检 shāngjiǎn (short for 商品检验 commodity inspection): ～局 bureau of commodity inspection

商界 shāngjiè business circles: commercial circles

商籁体 shānglàitǐ sonnet

商量 shāngliang consult; discuss; talk over: 有事同群众～。Consult the masses when matters arise. / 这事可以～着办。That can be settled through discussion. / 全世界的事应由世界各国～着办。Matters that concern the whole world should be settled through consultation among all the nations. / 咱们得找主任～一下。We ought to talk it over with the director.

商路 shānglù trade route

商旅 shānglǚ travelling merchants

商品 shāngpǐn commodity; goods; merchandise

商品拜物教 shāngpǐn bàiwùjiào commodity fetishism

商品房 shāngpǐnfáng commercial housing

商品化 shāngpǐnhuà commercialization: 技术成果～ the commercialization of technological achievements / 推行住房～ commercialize housing

商品检验 shāngpǐn jiǎnyàn commodity inspection

商品交易会 shāngpǐn jiāoyìhuì trade fair; commodities fair

商品经济 shāngpǐn jīngjì commodity economy

商品粮 shāngpǐnliáng commodity grain; marketable grain

商品流通 shāngpǐn liútōng commodity circulation

商品生产 shāngpǐn shēngchǎn commodity production

商品销售市场 shāngpǐn xiāoshòu shìchǎng outlet for goods

商品住宅 shāngpǐn zhùzhái commercial residential building

商洽 shāngqià arrange with sb.; take up (a matter) with sb.

商情 shāngqíng market conditions: ～预测 business forecasting

商榷 shāngquè discuss; deliberate: 这一点值得～。This point is open to question. / 提出几点意见,与诸位～。Here are a few points I wish to discuss with you.

商人 shāngrén businessman; merchant; trader

商数 shāngshù *math.* quotient

商谈 shāngtán exchange views; confer; discuss; negotiate: ～递交国书事宜 discuss matters relating to the presentation of credentials / 望贵方即指派代表前来～。We hope that you will appoint representatives to come here for the negotiations.

商讨 shāngtǎo discuss; deliberate over: 就发展两国关系进行有益的～ hold useful discussions on developing relations between the two countries / ～技术交流问题 discuss matters concerning technical interchange (or technological exchange)

商亭 shāngtíng kiosk; stall

商务 shāngwù commercial affairs; business affairs

商务参赞 shāngwù cānzàn commercial counsellor: ～处 commercial counsellor's office

商务代表 shāngwù dàibiǎo commercial representative; trade representative: ～处 trade representative's office; trade delegation's office

商务秘书 shāngwù mìshū commercial secretary

商务卫星 shāngwù wèixīng commercial satellite

商务专员 shāngwù zhuānyuán commercial attaché

商业 shāngyè commerce; trade; business

商业交易法 shāngyè jiāoyìfǎ law of commercial transactions

商业区 shāngyèqū business quarter; commercial district; business district

商业网 shāngyèwǎng commercial network; network of trading establishments

商业信贷 shāngyè xìndài commercial credit

商业银行 shāngyè yínháng commercial bank

商业中心 shāngyè zhōngxīn commercial centre; trading centre; shopping centre

商业周期 shāngyè zhōuqī business cycle

商业资本 shāngyè zīběn commercial capital; merchant capital

商议 shāngyì confer; discuss

商誉 shāngyù com. goodwill

商约 shāngyuē commercial treaty

商栈 shāngzhàn inn; caravansary

商酌 shāngzhuó discuss and consider; deliberate over: 这个问题尚待～。This matter needs further discussion and consideration.

觞（觴） shāng arch. wine cup; drinking vessel

墒（鷭） shāng argric. moisture in the soil: 抢～ lose no time in sowing while there is sufficient moisture in the soil

墒情 shāngqíng soil moisture content

墒土 shāngtǔ newly-tilled moist soil: 保住～ preserve the moisture in the soil

熵 shāng phys. entropy

shǎng

上 shǎng (a variant pronunciation for 上² shàng⑤) short for 上声 shǎngshēng ——see also shàng

上声 shǎngshēng a variant pronunciation for 上声 shàngshēng

垧 shǎng shang, a land measure equal to fifteen mu in most parts of the Northeast and three or five mu in the Northwest

晌 shǎng ① part of the day: 前半～儿 morning / 晚半～儿 dusk ② dial. noon: 歇～ take a midday nap or rest

晌饭 shǎngfàn dial. ① midday meal; lunch ② extra meal in the daytime during the busy farming season

晌觉 shǎngjiào dial. afternoon nap

晌午 shǎngwu inf. midday; noon: ～饭 midday meal; lunch / ～觉 afternoon nap

赏¹ shǎng ① grant (or bestow) a reward; award: 国王～给那个士兵一匹马。The king awarded the soldier a horse. ② reward; award: 领～ receive an award

赏² shǎng ① view and admire; delight in viewing; feast one's eyes on: 赏月 shǎngyuè ② recognize; appreciate: 赞赏 zànshǎng

赏赐 shǎngcì ① grant (or bestow) a reward; award: ～他很多钱 give him a lot of money as a reward ② a reward; an award: 得到许多～ be given a handsome reward

赏罚 shǎng-fá rewards and punishments: 有赏有罚 duly mete out rewards and punishments

赏罚分明 shǎng-fá fēnmíng be fair in meting out rewards and punishments; be discriminating in one's rewards and punishments

赏罚严明 shǎng-fá yánmíng be strict and fair in meting out rewards and punishments

赏封 shǎngfēng old gift money in a red packet (given to children or servants on festive occasions)

赏格 shǎnggé old the reward offered

赏光 shǎngguāng pol. (used when requesting sb. to accept an invitation): 务请～。We request the pleasure of your company.

赏鉴 shǎngjiàn appreciate and evaluate (a work of art): ～名画 appreciate and evaluate a famous painting

赏金 shǎngjīn money reward; pecuniary reward

赏赉 shǎnglài formal give a reward; bestow a favour

赏脸 shǎngliǎn pol. honour me with your presence: 我想请你跟你夫人明天吃晚饭，你肯不肯～? I'd like to invite you and your wife to dinner tomorrow. May I have the honour?

赏钱 shǎngqian tips

赏识 shǎngshí recognize the worth of; appreciate: 主编很～他这篇文章。The editor in chief thinks highly of this article of his. / 这个奴才深得其主子的～。That flunkey was in his master's good graces. / 有些艺术家死了以后才得到人们的～。Some artists did not gain recognition until after death.

赏玩 shǎngwán admire the beauty of sth.; delight in; enjoy; fondle: ～山景 enjoy mountain scenery / ～古董 fondle antiques

赏心乐事 shǎngxīn lèshì happy moods and pleasurable things

赏心悦目 shǎngxīn-yuèmù find the scenery pleasing to both the eye and the mind

赏雪 shǎngxuě enjoy a beautiful snow scene

赏月 shǎngyuè enjoy a beautiful full moon

shàng

上¹ shàng ① (used alone, esp. in contrast to 下) above: ～至司令员，下至普通战士 from the commander down to the rank and file / 这个词是旧时下对～的称呼。This word was used in the old days to address one's superiors. ② (used after a preposition) upward: 往～看 look up (at sth.) / 向～拉 pull it up / 这头朝～ this side up / 向～反映情况 report the situation to the higher-ups ③ (used before a noun) upper (in position or quality); higher; better; superior: ～半截 the upper half / 在书架的最～一层放着 lie on the top shelf / 中～水平 above the average; better than the average / 报～一级党委 report to the Party committee immediately above ④ most recent; last; former: ～次 last time / ～星期四 last Thursday / ～个世纪 the last century / ～一季度 the previous quarter / ～两批 the last two groups ⑤ first (of sth. divided into two or three parts): ～集 Volume I; Part I / 这部词典分～、中、下三册。This dictionary is in three volumes, first, second and third. / ～半学期 the first half of the term / 二十世纪～半叶 the first half of the 20th century / ～一段 the preceding (or above, foregoing) paragraph ⑥ (formerly, referring to the emperor): 上谕 shàngyù

上² shàng ① come or go up; ascend: ～山 go or climb up a mountain / ～楼 go or come upstairs; ascend the stairs / 溯流而～ sail or go upstream ② get on (a conveyance); mount; board: ～公共汽车 get on a bus / ～飞机 board a plane / ～船 go aboard a ship; go on board ③ go to; leave for: 你～哪儿? Where are you going? / 我明天～南京。I'm leaving for Nanjing tomorrow. / 我～卫生室。I'm going to the clinic. ④ forge ahead; go ahead: 快～，投篮! Go ahead. Quick! Shoot! /

见困难就～ advance where there are difficulties to overcome / 有条件要～, 没有条件创造条件也要～。 When the conditions exist, go ahead; when they don't, create them and go ahead. ⑤ (used in stage directions) appear on the stage; enter: 二战士左～。 Enter left two soldiers. ⑥ *sports* enter the court or field: 换人! 三号下, 四号～。 Substitution: Player No. 4 for No. 3. / 这一盘你～。 You play this game. ⑦ fill; supply; serve: 上水¹ shàngshuǐ / 上菜 shàngcài ⑧ place sth. in position; fix: ～刀具 fix a cutting tool / 步枪都～了刺刀。 All the rifles have bayonets fixed on them. / 我正在～螺丝呢。 I'm fixing the screws in place. ⑨ apply; paint; smear: ～药膏 apply ointment / 给门窗～漆 paint the door and windows / 给机器～油 oil (*or* grease) the machine ⑩ be put on record; be carried (in a publication): 小王的先进事迹都～了电视。 Xiao Wang's model deeds have been reported on TV. ⑪ wind; screw; tighten: 表该～了。 The watch needs winding. / 螺丝没有～紧。 The screw hasn't been tightened. ⑫ be engaged (in work, study, etc.) at a fixed time: 我今天～中班。 I'm on the middle shift today. / 她～大学了。 She's now in college. / 明天的语文课还～不～? Shall we have our Chinese lessons tomorrow or not? ⑬ up to; as many as: ～百辆小汽车 up to a hundred cars / 出席人数已～万。 There are as many as ten thousand present. *or* There is an attendance of 10,000 or so. ⑭ short for 上声 shàngshēng

上³ shàng *mus.* a note of the scale in *gongchepu* (工尺谱), corresponding to 1 in numbered musical notation

上 shàng (used as a complement to a verb) ① up: 跑～楼 run upstairs / 登～山顶 reach the summit / 爬～河堤 climb up to the top of the dyke / 飞～蓝天 soar into the sky / 踏～非洲的土地 set foot on African soil ② (indicating the attainment of an objective): 锁～门 lock the door; lock up / 买～电视机了 have bought a TV / 她当～会计了。 She's become an accountant. / 还没吃～饭呢。 I haven't eaten yet. / 你跟他接～头了吗? Have you got in touch with him? ③ (indicating that an action has started): 她爱～了我。 She's fallen in love with me. / 他俩一聊～天了。 The two of them are having a good chat. / 会还没有开, 大家就议论～了。 The meeting has not begun yet, but they are already talking about the matter. ④ (indicating an amount, value or extent reached or to be reached): 我要能在北京多住～几天才好呢! If only I could stay a few more days in Beijing! / 近来我每天只能睡～三、四小时。 I get only three or four hours of sleep daily these days. / 我们没说～几句话车就开了。 We had barely enough time to exchange a few words before the train started.

上 shang (used after a noun) ① on: 脸～ on one's face / 山顶～ at the mountaintop / 墙～ on the wall ② within (a certain area): 世界～ in the world / 课堂～ in class / 报纸～ in the newspapers / 会～ at the meeting ③ in (some aspect): 事实～ in fact / 历史～ in history / 理论～ in theory; theoretically / 在数量～占优势 excel in numbers ④ at (the age of): 他五岁～死了父亲。 His father died when he was five years old. / 张大爷六十岁～得了孙子。 Uncle Zhang got his first grandson at sixty.
──see also shǎng

上班 shàngbān go to work; start work; be on duty: 她～去了。 She's gone to work. / 下午不～。 We'll take the afternoon off. *or* No work this afternoon. / 我们每天早上八点钟～。 We start work at 8 every morning. / ～时间 work hours; office hours

上板儿 shàngbǎnr *dial.* (of a shop) put up the shutters for the night; close up

上半场 shàngbànchǎng first half (of a game, concert, etc.): ～比分多少? What was the score at half time? / ～最后一个节目 the last item of the first half of the programme

上半晌 shàngbànshǎng *inf.* morning: ～我哪儿也没去啊。 I didn't go anywhere this morning.

上半身 shàngbànshēn the upper part of the body; above the waist

上半天 shàngbàntiān morning

上半夜 shàngbànyè before midnight

上绑 shàngbǎng truss sb. up

上报¹ shàngbào appear in the newspapers: 我们厂上了报了。 The newspaper carries a story about our factory. / 那位数学家刻苦钻研的事迹昨天～了。 In yesterday's newspaper there was an article about how perseveringly that mathematician carried out his scientific research.

上报² shàngbào report to a higher body; report to the leadership: 这件事应当立即～公安部, 不容延误。 This matter should be reported, without delay, to the Ministry of Public Security.

上辈 shàngbèi ① ancestors ② the elder generation of one's family; one's elders

上辈子 shàngbèizi ① ancestors ② previous existence

上臂 shàngbì the upper arm

上边 shàngbian same as 上面 shàngmian

上膘 shàngbiāo (of animals) become fat; fatten

上表 shàngbiǎo submit a memorial to the emperor

上宾 shàngbīn distinguished guest; guest of honour: 待为～ be treated as a distinguished guest

上不着天, 下不着地 shàng bù zháo tiān, xià bù zháo dì touch neither the sky nor the ground—be suspended in midair

上菜 shàngcài serve the dishes (of food): 上了好几道菜。 Several courses were served.

上苍 shàngcāng Heaven; God

上操 shàngcāo go out to drill; be drilling

上策 shàngcè the best plan; the best way out; the best thing to do

上层 shàngcéng upper levels; upper strata: ～领导 leadership at the upper levels / ～分子 members of the upper strata; upper-class elements / ～人士 upper circles / ～小资产阶级 upper petty bourgeoisie

上层建筑 shàngcéng jiànzhù superstructure: ～领域 the realm of the superstructure / 文化艺术属于～。 Culture and art belong to the realm of the superstructure.

上层路线 shàngcéng lùxiàn the upper-level line: 走～ take the upper-level line—get things done through the personal influence of the higher-ups

上层社会 shàngcéng shèhuì upper strata of society; upper-class society

上谄下骄 shàngchǎn-xiàjiāo obsequious towards one's superiors and arrogant towards one's inferiors

上场 shàngchǎng ① appear on the stage; enter: 学生甲～。 Enter Student A. ② *sports* enter the court or field; join in a contest: 双方运动员都已经～。 Players of both teams have entered the court. / 今天该谁～? Who's playing today?

上场门 shàngchǎngmén entrance (of a stage)

上朝 shàngcháo ① go to court ② (of the sovereign) hold court

上乘 shàngchéng ① same as 大乘 dàchéng ② first-class: ～之作 first-class work

上床 shàngchuáng go to bed; get into bed

上蔟 shàngcù (of silkworms) be placed on small straw bundles to spin cocoons

上窜下跳 shàngcuān-xiàtiào run around on sinister

errands

上达 shàngdá reach the higher authorities: 下情～ make the situation at the lower levels known to the higher levels

上代 shàngdài the previous generation; former generations

上当 shàngdàng be taken in; be fooled; be duped: 这回我可不～啦! I won't be taken in this time. / 走这条路可～了, 尽是水坑。We're fools to have chosen this path; it's full of puddles. / 不要上坏人的当。Don't let yourself be fooled by evil people. / 如果我们对他们丧失警惕性, 那就会上大当。If we lower our guard against them, we'll really come to grief. / 我们不上那个当。We won't walk into that trap.

上灯 shàngdēng light the lamp; light up: ～时分 lighting-up time

上等 shàngděng first-class; first-rate; superior: ～货 first-class goods / ～料子 high-quality material

上等兵 shàngděngbīng private first class

上低音号 shàngdīyīnhào *mus.* baritone

上帝 Shàngdì ① the Lord on High (in ancient Chinese thought, a deity who watches over human society and regulates the working of the universe) ② God (in Christianity)

上第 shàngdì *formal* first-class; first-rate; superior

上吊 shàngdiào hang oneself

上调 shàngdiào ① transfer sb. to a post at a higher level ② transfer goods, funds, etc. to a unit at a higher level ——see also 上调 shàngtiáo

上冻 shàngdòng freeze: 一定要在～以前把地基打好。We've got to finish the foundations before the ground freezes.

上颚 shàng'è ① mandible (of certain arthropods) ② the upper jaw or maxilla (of vertebrates)

上方宝剑 shàngfāng bǎojiàn same as 尚方宝剑 shàngfāng bǎojiàn

上方空间 shàngfāng kōngjiān superjacent air space

上房 shàngfáng main rooms (usu. facing south, within a courtyard)

上访 shàngfǎng apply for an audience with the higher authorities to appeal for help: ～人员 visitors from the localities appealing to the higher authorities for help

上坟 shàngfén visit a grave to honour the memory of the dead

上粪 shàngfèn apply manure to the fields

上风 shàngfēng ① windward: 咱们到烟的～头去吧。Let's get to windward of the smoke. *or* Let's go upwind of the smoke. ② advantage; superior position; upper hand: 占上风 zhàn shàngfēng

上峰 shàngfēng *old* superiors; bosses: ～的命令 orders from above

上纲 shànggāng raise to the higher plane of principle: 这个问题上不了纲。That's not a matter of principle.

上岗 shànggǎng go to one's post; go on duty

上高儿 shànggāor climb to a high place: 他一～就头晕。He always feels dizzy when he climbs to a high place.

上告 shànggào ① complain to the higher authorities or appeal to a higher court ② report to one's superior

上工 shànggōng go to work; start work: 夜班十点钟～。The night shift starts at 10.

上供 shànggòng ① offer up a sacrifice; lay offerings on the altar ② give presents to the higher-ups expecting favours in return

上钩 shànggōu rise to the bait; swallow the bait; get hooked

上古 shànggǔ ancient times; remote ages

上古史 shànggǔshǐ ancient history

上官 Shàngguān a two-character surname

上光 shàngguāng ① glazing; polishing ② *photog.* ferrotyping

上光机 shàngguāngjī glazing machine; glazer

上光蜡 shàngguānglà wax polish

上轨道 shàng guǐdào get on the right track; begin to work smoothly: 生产已～。Production is proceeding smoothly.

上海 Shànghǎi Shanghai (a seaport on the coast of East China)

上好 shànghǎo first-class; best-quality; tip-top: ～烟叶 best-quality tobacco

上颌 shànghé *physiol.* the upper jaw; maxilla

上呼吸道 shànghūxīdào *physiol.* the upper respiratory tract

上呼吸道感染 shànghūxīdào gǎnrǎn infection of the upper respiratory tract

上回 shànghuí last time

上火 shànghuǒ ① *Chin. med.* suffer from excessive internal heat (with such symptoms as constipation, conjunctivitis and inflammation of the nasal and oral cavities) ② *dial.* get angry

上货 shànghuò ① get in stocks; replenish stocks ② replenish the goods shelves

上级 shàngjí ① higher level: ～党委 a Party committee of the higher level / ～机关 higher authorities; a higher body / ～领导 a leading body at a higher level ② higher authorities; one's superior: 报告～ report to the higher authorities; report to one's superior / 他是我的老～。He is my old chief.

上计 shàngjì same as 上策 shàngcè

上家 shàngjiā (in mahjong, card games, etc.) the player whose turn comes just before

上尖儿 shàngjiānr piled high

上江 Shàngjiāng the upper Changjiang region

上浆 shàngjiāng ① starching (of clothes) ② *text.* dressing (of yarn, fabrics, etc.)'

上将 shàngjiàng (U. S. & Brit. Army, U. S. Air Force, U. S. & Brit. Marine Corps) general; (U. S. & Brit. Navy) admiral; (Brit. Air Force) air chief marshal

上交 shàngjiāo hand in (*or* over) to sb. above oneself; pass on to the higher authorities

上胶 shàngjiāo *papermaking* sizing

上焦 shàngjiāo *Chin. med.* the part of the body cavity above the diaphragm housing the heart and lungs

上缴 shàngjiǎo turn over (revenues, profits, surplus materials, etc.) to the higher authorities: 多余器材应该～。Surplus equipment should be turned over to the higher authorities.

上缴利润 shàngjiǎo lìrùn that part of the profits turned over to the state

上街 shàngjiē ① go to the street; go shopping: ～看看 go window-shopping / 我陪妈妈上了一趟街。I went shopping with my mother. ② take to the streets; go on to the streets: ～游行(示威) take to the streets

上届 shàngjiè previous term or session; last: ～人大 the last People's Congress / ～毕业生 last year's graduates

上界 shàngjiè the world above; the abode of the gods

上紧 shàngjǐn *dial.* lose no time (in doing sth.); hasten; speed up: 葡萄快熟了, 得～准备收摘了。The grapes will soon be ripe. Let's speed up our preparations for the grape harvest.

上进 shàngjìn go forward; make progress: 不求～ not strive to make progress

上进心 shàngjìnxīn the desire to do better; the urge for improvement

上劲 shàngjìn energetically; with gusto; with great vigour: 越干越～儿 work with increasing vigour (*or* gusto) / 越说越～儿 get more and more excited as one

talks

上捐 shàngjuān　pay taxes

上课 shàngkè　① attend class; go to class: 你昨天怎么没来～? Why didn't you come to class yesterday? / 今天下午我们不～。 We have no classes this afternoon. ② conduct a class; give a lesson (or lecture): 学校八点开始～。 Classes begin at 8.

上空 shàngkōng　in the sky; overhead: 五星红旗在天安门广场～高高飘扬。 The Five-Star Red Flag flies high above Tian'anmen Square.

上口 shàngkǒu　① be able to read aloud fluently: 孩子们把这首诗念了又念, 现在都能琅琅～了。 The children have read the poem several times, and can all recite it quite fluently now. ② be suitable for reading aloud; make smooth reading: 这段文字太艰深, 不易～。 The passage is too difficult and doesn't lend itself to reading aloud.

上跨交叉 shàngkuà jiāochā　transportation overpass

上款 shàngkuǎn　① the name of the recipient (as inscribed on a painting or a calligraphic scroll presented as a gift) ② the name of the addressee (of a letter or package)

上蜡 shànglà　text. waxing

上来 shànglái　① begin; get started: ～先少说话。 Don't talk too much at the beginning. / 一～就没劲 be boring right from the start ② formal to sum up (the aforesaid): ～所言 to sum up the aforesaid

上来 shàng·lái　① come up: 游了半天了, 快～歇会儿吧。 You've been swimming a long time now. Come out and have a rest. / 山高了些, 恐怕她上不来。 The hill is rather high. I'm afraid she won't be able to get to the top. ② come up to a place or state regarded as higher or above: 他是刚从基层～的。 He's just come from a grass-roots unit. / 下面的意见都已经～了。 All the opinions from below have reached us. / 你什么时候上北京来玩玩呀? When will you come up to Beijing for a visit?

上来 ·shàng·lái　(used as a complement to a verb) ① up (here): 把箱子抬～ bring the trunk up / 部队分两路增援～。 Reinforcements arrived by two routes. / 他是刚从基层提拔～的干部。 He is a cadre newly promoted from a grass-roots unit. / 外国朋友围～要他们签名留念。 The foreign friends gathered around them and asked for their autographs. ② (indicating success in doing sth.): 这个问题你答得～吗? Can you answer this question? / 看他面熟, 名字可叫不～。 I know his face but I can't recall his name. / 等我爬到山顶的时候, 气都快喘不～了。 By the time I got to the top of the hill, I was quite out of breath. ③ (indicating an increase in degree): 暖气片慢慢热～了。 Little by little the radiators got warmer. / 天色黑～了。 It is getting dark.

上联 shànglián　the first line of a couplet

上梁[1] shàngliáng　put the beams in place (in building a wooden house)

上梁[2] shàngliáng　① (of bicycles) cross bar; top tube ② (of buildings) upper beam

上梁不正下梁歪 shàngliáng bù zhèng xiàliáng wāi　if the upper beam is not straight, the lower ones will go aslant—when those above behave unworthily, those below will do the same

上列 shàngliè　listed above; above-listed; the above: ～各项 the items listed above; the above-listed items

上流 shàngliú　① upper reaches (of a river) ② belonging to the upper circles; upper-class

上流社会 shàngliú shèhuì　high society; polite society

上路 shànglù　set out on a journey; start off

上马 shàngmǎ　① mount (or get on) a horse: ～! (word of command) To horse! ② start (a project, etc.): 这项工程明年～。 The project will start next year.

上门 shàngmén　① come or go to see sb.; call; drop in; visit: 他好久没～了。 It's a long time since he last called. / 我再也不上她家的门了。 I'll never go to see her again. / 送货～ deliver goods to the doorstep ② shut the door (or lock up) for the night; bolt the door ③ dial. marry into and live with one's bride's family

上门女婿 shàngmén nǚxu　dial. live-in son-in-law

上面 shàngmian　① above; over; on top of; on the surface of: 飞机在云层～飞行。 The plane flew above the clouds. / 粉墙～挂着大幅标语。 Large streamers bearing slogans were hanging on the white wall. / 你的行李袋就在我的箱子～。 Your bag is on top of my suitcase. / ～就是琉璃塔了。 Further up is the glazed-tile pagoda. / 大桥～走汽车, 下面走火车。 The upper deck of the bridge is for motor vehicles, the lower deck for trains. / 运河～架了一座桥。 A bridge has been built across the canal. ② above-mentioned; aforesaid; foregoing: ～所举的例子 the above-mentioned example / ～这几条理由 the aforesaid reasons / ～几个发言 the speeches you've just heard; the previous speeches ③ higher authorities; higher-ups: ～有指示。 There are instructions from above. ④ aspect; respect; regard: 他在外语～下了很多功夫。 He has put a lot of effort into his study of foreign languages. ⑤ the elder generation of one's family; the elders

上年 shàngnián　last year

上年纪 shàng niánji　be getting on in years; be stricken in years: 奶奶上了年纪, 腿脚不那么灵便了。 Granny is stricken in years and isn't so surefooted as before.

上盘 shàngpán　min. hanging wall

上皮 shàngpí　physiol. epithelium

上皮癌 shàngpí'ái　epithelioma

上皮组织 shàngpí zǔzhī　physiol. epithelial tissue

上品 shàngpǐn　highest grade; top grade: 茅台是酒中～。 Maotai is a top-grade spirit.

上坡路 shàngpōlù　① an uphill road; an upward slope: 他们沿着那条十分陡峭的～爬上去。 They climbed by the very steep ascent. ② upward trend; steady progress

上铺 shàngpù　upper berth

上气不接下气 shàngqì bù jiē xiàqì　gasp for breath; be out of breath

上情 shàngqíng　feelings or wishes of the higher authorities: ～下达 make the wishes of the higher authorities known to those below

上去 shàng·qù　① go up: 登着梯子～ go up (on) a ladder / 我们～看看。 Let's go up and have a look. / 那棵树你上得去吗? Can you climb that tree? / 车来了, 咱们～吧。 Here comes the bus. Let's get on. ② rise to a place or state regarded as higher or above: 生产要～, 干部要下去。 If production is to go up, cadres must go down to the grass-roots. / 过去由于规章制度不健全, 这里的工作老是上不去。 In the past, our work here could not move forward for lack of necessary rules and regulations. / 我们提的这些意见上得去吗? Could the suggestions we raised reach the higher authorities?

上去 ·shàng·qù　(used as a complement to a verb) ① up (there): 把行李搬上楼去 take the luggage upstairs / 我们连忙迎～。 We rushed up to meet them. / 帮忙把大车推上坡去 help to push the cart up the slope / 计划已经交～了。 The plan has been sent up to the higher-ups. / 把国民经济搞～ push the national economy forward ② (indicating adding or fixing): 又铺了一床褥子～ add another mattress to the bed / 螺丝拧～了。 The screws have been driven in.

上圈套儿 shàng quāntàor　fall into sb.'s trap

上染率 shàngrǎnlǜ　text. dye-uptake

上任[1] shàngrèn　take up an official post; assume office

上任[2] shàngrèn　predecessor

上人 shàngren *dial.* parents or grandparents

上色 shàngsè best-quality; top-grade: ～茶叶 top-grade tea

上色 shàngshǎi colour (a picture, map, etc.)

上山 shàngshān ① go up a hill or mountain ② *dial. euph.* die and be buried ③ *dial.* (of silkworms) be placed on small straw bundles to spin cocoons

上山下乡 shàngshān-xiàxiāng (of urban school-leavers) go and work in the countryside and mountain areas: ～的知识青年 educated urban youth working in the countryside and mountain areas

上赏 shàngshǎng the top reward

上上 shàngshàng ① the highest; the very best: ～策 the best plan ② before last: ～星期 the week before last

上上下下 shàngshàngxiàxià high and low; old and young; everybody: 荣国府～都很高兴。 All members of the Rong family, old and young, were very pleased.

上身¹ shàngshēn ① the upper part of the body: 光着～ be stripped to the waist / 他～穿一件土布衬衫。 He's wearing a shirt of handwoven cloth. ② upper outer garment; shirt; blouse; jacket: 姑娘们穿着白～, 花裙子。 The girls are wearing white blouses and bright-coloured skirts.

上身² shàngshēn start wearing: 天冷了,羽绒服该～了。 It's getting cold. We'd better start wearing our down jackets.

上升 shàngshēng ① move upward: 一缕炊烟袅袅～。 A wisp of smoke is curling up from the kitchen chimney. ② rise (to a higher point, degree, rank, etc.); ascend: 气温～。 The temperature is going up. / 生产持续～。 Production is rising steadily. / 当时资本主义还处于～时期。 At that time capitalism was still in the ascendant. / 使经验～为理论 raise experience to the level of theory / 原来的次要矛盾现在已～为主要矛盾。 What was formerly a secondary contradiction has now become the principal one.

上升角 shàngshēngjiǎo *aviation* angle of climb (or ascent)

上升气流 shàngshēng qìliú ascending air; up current

上升失速 shàngshēng shīsù *aviation* advance stall

上升转弯 shàngshēng zhuǎnwān *aviation* pull-up turn

上声 shàngshēng *phonet.* ① rising tone (the second of the four tones in classical Chinese pronunciation) ② falling-rising tone (the third of the four tones in modern standard Chinese pronunciation) ——see also 四声 sìshēng

上士 shàngshì (U. S. Army) sergeant first class; (Brit. Army) staff sergeant; (U. S. Navy) petty officer first class; (Brit. Navy) chief petty officer; (U. S. Air Force) technical sergeant; (Brit. Air Force) flight sergeant; (U. S. Marine Corps) technical sergeant or staff sergeant; (Brit. Marine Corps) colour sergeant

上市 shàngshì ① go (or appear) on the market: 西红柿大量～。 There are plenty of tomatoes on the market. / 这是刚～的苹果。 These apples have just come in. ② go to market: 我～买菜去啦。 I'm going to market.

上视图 shàngshìtú *mech.* top view

上手¹ shàngshǒu ① left-hand seat; seat of honour ② same as 上家 shàngjiā

上手² shàngshǒu (of work, etc.) get started: 今天的活一～就很顺利。 Today's work went smoothly from the outset. / 那场球一～就打得那别扭。 Everything went wrong from the beginning of that match.

上首 shàngshǒu seat of honour

上书¹ shàngshū (of an old-style private tutor) teach a new lesson

上书² shàngshū submit a written statement to a higher authority; send in a memorial: 他～宰相,陈述政见。 He presented to the Chief Minister a memorial expounding his political views.

上疏 shàngshū submit a memorial to the emperor: ～言事 submit a memorial on government policy

上述 shàngshù mentioned above; above-mentioned; aforementioned; aforesaid: 严格遵守～原则 strictly abide by the above-mentioned principles / 达到～目标 achieve the aforementioned objectives

上闩 shàngshuān fasten with a latch or bolt: 门上了闩。 The door was latched (or bolted).

上水¹ shàngshuǐ feed water to a steam engine, radiator (of an automobile), etc.: 给水箱～ fill the tank with water

上水² shàngshuǐ ① upper reaches (of a river) ② sail upstream: ～船 an upstream boat

上水 shàngshui *dial.* haslet

上水道 shàngshuǐdào water-supply line

上税 shàngshuì pay taxes

上司 shàngsi superior; boss: 顶头～ one's immediate superior

上诉 shàngsù *leg.* appeal (to a higher court): 提出～ lodge an appeal

上诉法院 shàngsù fǎyuàn court of appeal; appellate court

上诉权 shàngsùquán right of appeal

上诉人 shàngsùrén appellant

上溯 shàngsù ① go upstream ② trace back: ～到公元前一世纪 trace back to the 1st century B.C.

上算 shàngsuàn paying; worthwhile: 烧煤气比烧煤～。 It's more economical to use gas than coal.

上岁数 shàng suìshu *inf.* be getting on in years

上锁 shàngsuǒ lock: 门上了锁。 The door was locked.

上台 shàngtái ① go up onto the platform; appear on the stage: 她～演奏了两支钢琴曲子。 She went up onto the platform and played two piano pieces. ② *derog.* assume power; come (or rise) to power

上堂 shàngtáng *dial.* ① attend class; go to class ② conduct a class; give a lesson (or lecture)

上膛¹ shàngtáng *mil.* (of a gun) be loaded: 子弹上了膛。 The gun is loaded.

上膛² shàngtáng common name for 腭 è

上套 shàngtào ① harness a draught animal (to a cart, etc.) ② fall into a trap

上体 shàngtǐ *formal* the upper part of the body

上天¹ shàngtiān ① go up to the sky; fly sky-high: 我们又有一颗卫星～了。 Another of our satellites has gone up. ② *euph.* go to Heaven—die

上天² shàngtiān Heaven; Providence

上天无路,入地无门 shàngtiān wú lù, rù dì wú mén there is no road to heaven and no door into the earth—no way of escape; in desperate straits

上调 shàngtiáo raise (prices) ——see also 上调 shàngdiào

上头 shàngtóu (formerly, of a girl on her wedding day) start wearing her hair in a bun

上头 shàngtou same as 上面 shàngmian

上吐下泻 shàngtù-xiàxiè throw up on top and purge down below; suffer from vomiting and diarrhoea; have loose bowels and vomit

上味 shàngwèi the most delicious

上尉 shàngwèi (U. S. & Brit. Army, U. S. Air Force, U. S. & Brit. Marine Corps) captain; (U. S. & Brit. Navy) lieutenant; (Brit. Air Force) flight lieutenant

上文 shàngwén foregoing paragraphs or chapters; preceding part of the text: 见上 see above

上沃尔特 Shàng Wò'ěrtè the Upper Volta

上屋 shàngwū *dial.* main rooms (usu. facing south, within a courtyard)

上无片瓦,下无插针之地 shàng wú piàn wǎ, xià wú chā

zhēn zhǐ dì have neither a tile above one's head nor an inch of land beneath one's feet—be utterly destitute

上午 shàngwǔ morning; forenoon

上西天 shàngxītiān go to the Western Paradise—die

上下[1] shàngxià ① high and low: 全军～ the whole army, officers and men alike / ～通气 full communication between the higher and lower levels / ～一条心。 The leadership and the rank and file are of one mind. ② from top to bottom; up and down: ～打量 look sb. up and down; scrutinize sb. from head to foot / 这个水塔～有五十米。 The water tower is fifty metres high. ③ relative superiority or inferiority: 不相上下 bù xiāng shàngxià ④ (used after round numbers) about; or so; or thereabouts: 四十岁～ about forty years old; forty or so / 一打～ a dozen or thereabouts

上下[2] shàngxià go up or down: 山上修了公路, 汽车～很方便。 With the completion of the highway up the mountain, cars can easily go up and down.

上下其手 shàngxià qí shǒu practise fraud; manoeuvre for some evil end; get up to tricks

上下文 shàngxiàwén context: 脱离～而想判明一句话的意思有时是很困难的。 It is sometimes very difficult to tell the meaning of a sentence taken out of its context. / 根据～确定词义 tell the meaning of a word from its context

上弦[1] shàngxián tighten the spring of; wind (up): 我的钟该～了。 My clock needs winding.

上弦[2] shàngxián meteorol. first quarter (of the moon)

上弦月 shàngxiányuè the moon at the first quarter

上限 shàngxiàn the upper limit; the maximum permissible or prescribed

上香 shàngxiāng burn joss sticks (before an idol or a spirit tablet)

上相 shàngxiàng come out well in a photograph; be photogenic

上校 shàngxiào (U. S. & Brit. Army, U. S. Air Force, U. S. & Brit. Marine Corps) colonel; (U. S. & Brit. Navy) captain; (Brit. Air Force) group captain

上鞋 shàngxié same as 绱鞋 shàngxié

上心 shàngxīn dial. set one's heart on sth.

上新世 Shàngxīnshì geol. the Pliocene Epoch

上刑[1] shàngxíng put to torture; torture

上刑[2] shàngxíng formal severe punishment

上行 shàngxíng ① (of trains) going to the capital from any part of the country; up; upgoing: ～列车 up train / 在中国,～列车编号用偶数。 In China, the up trains are given even numbers. ② (of boats) going upstream; up-river: ～船 an upstream boat ③ (of documents) sent to the upper levels: ～公文 documents sent to the upper levels

上行下效 shàngxíng-xiàxiào subordinates follow the example of their superiors; those below follow the (usu. bad) example of those above; if a leader sets a bad example, it will be followed by his subordinates

上旋 shàngxuán sports top spin

上选 shàngxuǎn the choicest; the most select

上学 shàngxué go to school; attend school; be at school: 上过几年学 have been to school for a few years; have had a few years' schooling / 没有～的机会 have no chance of going to school / 这孩子～了没有? Is the child at school?

上旬 shàngxún the first ten-day period of a month

上压力 shàngyālì phys. upward pressure

上演 shàngyǎn put on the stage; perform: 国庆节将～几个新戏。 Several new plays will be performed on National Day. / 人民剧场今晚～什么节目? What's on at the People's Theatre this evening?

上衣 shàngyī upper outer garment; jacket

上议院 shàngyìyuàn upper house; (Brit.) the House of Lords: ～议员 Lords; temporal and spiritual peers of Parliament

上瘾 shàngyǐn be addicted (to sth.); get into the habit (of doing sth.): 吸毒上了瘾 be addicted to drugs; be a drug addict / 他抽烟抽上了瘾。 He's got into the habit of smoking. / 这种药吃久了会～。 This medicine is habit-forming. / 她看侦探小说看～了。 She's developed a yen for detective stories.

上映 shàngyìng show (a film); screen: 近日将有几部新片～。 A number of new films will be shown in the next few days.

上游 shàngyóu ① upper reaches (of a river): ～国家 an upstream country ② advanced position: ～无止境。 One can always aim higher.

上有天堂,下有苏杭 shàng yǒu tiāntáng, xià yǒu Sū-Háng up above there is Paradise, down here there are Suzhou and Hangzhou

上谕 shàngyù imperial edict

上元节 Shàngyuánjié the Lantern Festival (the fifteenth of the 1st month of the lunar calendar)

上灶 shàngzào do the cooking

上涨 shàngzhǎng rise; go up: 河水～。 The river has risen. / 物价～。 The prices are going up.

上帐 shàngzhàng make an entry in an account book; enter sth. in an account

上阵 shàngzhèn go into battle; take part in a match; pitch into the work: ～杀敌 go to the front to fight the enemy / 男女老少齐～。 Men and women, old and young, all pitched into the work. / 今晚比赛谁～? Who's going to play in tonight's match?

上肢 shàngzhī upper limbs

上中农 shàngzhōngnóng upper-middle peasant

上装[1] shàngzhuāng make up (for a theatrical performance)

上装[2] shàngzhuāng dial. upper outer garment; jacket

上奏 shàngzòu memorialize or petition the emperor; report to the throne

上座 shàngzuò the seat of honour

上座儿 shàngzuòr ① (of restaurants) draw customers; (of theatres, etc.) draw an audience: 戏园子里～已达八成。 The theatre is already 80% full. ② be a draw; be a box-office success: 这出戏可～了。 This play is a great draw.

尚[1]
shàng ① esteem; value; set great store by: 尚武 shàngwǔ / 崇尚 chóngshàng ② (Shàng) a surname

尚[2]
shàng ① adv. formal still; yet: ～待进一步讨论 pending further discussion / 为时～早。 It is still too early. or The time is not yet ripe. / 此事～未解决。 The matter remains to be settled. or The problem is not resolved as yet.

尚方宝剑 shàngfāng bǎojiàn the emperor's sword (the bearer of which is invested with discretionary powers)—a symbol of delegated power

尚且 shàngqiě conj. (used in the negative, followed by a negative with even greater force of denial) (not) even … (let alone …): 她站一站不起来, 更谈不上走路了。 She can't even stand on her feet, let alone walk. / 大人～举不起来, 何况小孩子。 Even grown-ups can't lift it, to say nothing of children. / 你～不行, 更不用说我了。 If you can't do it, how can I?

尚书 shàngshū ① a high official in ancient China ② minister (in the Ming and Qing Dynasties)

尚武 shàngwǔ encourage a military or martial spirit

尚武精神 shàngwǔ jīngshén a military or martial spirit

尚飨 shàngxiǎng (used at the end of an elegiac address) I beg you to partake of this sacrifice

绱（鞝）

绱 shàng　see below

绱鞋 shàngxié　sole a shoe; stitch the sole to the upper

shang

裳

裳 shang　see 衣裳 yīshang ——see also cháng

shāo

烧（燒）

烧 shāo　① burn: 干柴好～。Wood burns better (or more easily) when dry. / 这台锅炉～油。This furnace burns oil. / 咱们把这些废纸～掉吧。Let's burn up all this waste paper. / 侵略军到处～杀抢掠。The invaders burned, killed and looted wherever they went. / 把帽子～了一个洞 burn a hole in one's hat ② cook; heat: ～一点水 heat up some water / 水～开了。The water is boiling. / ～炭 make charcoal / ～砖 bake (or fire) bricks ③ stew after frying or fry after stewing: ～茄子 stewed eggplant / 洋葱～排骨 spareribs stewed in onion and sauce ④ roast: ～乳猪 roast suckling pig ⑤ run a fever; have a temperature: 病人～得厉害。The patient's running a high fever. or The patient has a high temperature. ⑥ fever: ～退了。The fever is down. ⑦ damage or injure by excessive or improper use of fertilizer: 上的肥太多，把根儿都～坏了。Overfertilization burned the roots. / 这几棵苗全～了。These seedlings are all burnt.

烧包 shāobāo　dial.　be drunken with success; have a swollen head

烧杯 shāobēi　beaker (used in the laboratory)

烧饼 shāobing　sesame seed cake

烧刀子 shāodāozi　(also 烧刀 shāodāo) dial.　spirit usu. distilled from sorghum or maize; colourless spirit

烧饭 shāofàn　dial.　do the cooking; cook food; prepare a meal

烧锅 shāoguō　(liquor) distillery

烧化 shāohuà　① cremate ② burn (paper, etc. as an offering to the dead)

烧荒 shāohuāng　burn the grass on waste land

烧毁 shāohuǐ　destroy by fire; burn up: ～秘密文件 burn up the secret documents

烧火 shāohuǒ　make a fire; light a fire; tend the kitchen fire: 我烧的火，她做的饭。She did the cooking while I lit and tended the fire.

烧鸡 shāojī　roast chicken

烧碱 shāojiǎn　chem.　caustic soda

烧结 shāojié　sintering; agglomeration; agglutination

烧结厂 shāojiéchǎng　sintering plant

烧结法 shāojiéfǎ　metall.　sintering process

烧结剂 shāojiéjì　chem.　agglutinant

烧酒 shāojiǔ　spirit usu. distilled from sorghum or maize; colourless spirit

烧烤 shāokǎo　barbecue

烧烤架 shāokǎojià　barbecue

烧蓝 shāolán　another name for 发蓝 fālán

烧料 shāoliào　imitation frosted glass (used to make lamps and handicrafts)

烧卖 shāomai　(also 烧麦 shāomai) a steamed dumpling with the dough gathered at the top

烧毛 shāomáo　text.　singeing: 煤气～ gas singeing

烧瓶 shāopíng　flask (used in the laboratory)

烧伤 shāoshāng　med.　burn (an injury): 治疗大面积～ treat extensive burns / 三度～ third-degree burns

烧香 shāoxiāng　burn joss sticks (before an idol)

烧心 shāoxīn　① med.　heartburn ② dial.　(of cabbages) turn yellow at the heart

烧心壶 shāoxīnhú　dial.　tea-urn

烧夷弹 shāoyídàn　same as 燃烧弹 ránshāodàn

烧纸 shāozhǐ　① burn paper money for the dead ② paper money burnt as an offering to the dead

烧灼 shāozhuó　burn; scorch; singe

捎

捎 shāo　take along sth. to or for sb.; bring to sb.: 请把这张报～给她。Take this paper to her, please. / 我给你孩子～来一点花生。I've brought your children some peanuts. / 一个口信 take a message to sb. / 替我给大家～个好。Please give my regards to everybody. ——see also shào

捎搭 shāodā　dial.　conveniently; in passing: 你去寄包裹时请～把这封信发了。Please post the letter for me when you go to the post office to send the parcel.

捎带 shāodài　incidentally; in passing: 你上书店的话，～给我买张世界地图。If you happen to be going to the bookshop, please get me a map of the world.

捎带脚儿 shāodàijiǎor　dial.　incidentally; in passing

捎话 shāohuà　take a message to sb.: 请你给她捎个话。Please pass on this message to her.

捎脚 shāojiǎo　pick up passengers or goods on the way; give sb. a lift

捎手 shāoshǒu　dial.　conveniently; without extra trouble: 你到车间请～把这封信交给主任。Please give this letter to the director when you go to the workshop.

梢

梢 shāo　the thin end of a twig, etc.; tip: 鞭～ whiplash / 辫～ the end of a plait ——see also sào

梢公 shāogōng　same as 艄公 shāogōng

梢头 shāotóu　① the tip of a branch: 月到柳～，人约黄昏后。（欧阳修）The moon rose to the top of the willow tree, And my love and I met after twilight. ② forestry　top log

稍

稍 shāo　adv.　a little; a bit; slightly; a trifle: ～加修改 make slight changes; make a few alterations / 这大衣～长了一点。The coat is a bit too long. / 请～等一会儿。Please wait a moment. or Just a moment, please. / ～事休息后又继续开会。The meeting continued after a short interval. ——see also shào

稍稍 shāoshāo　adv.　a little; a bit; slightly; a trifle: ～休息一下 take a brief rest; take a breather

稍胜一筹 shāo shèng yī chóu　same as 略胜一筹 lüè shèng yī chóu

稍微 shāowēi　adv.　a little; a bit; slightly; a trifle: ～搁点盐 put in a little salt / 今天～有点冷。It's rather chilly today. / ～有点惊慌 be a trifle alarmed / 这种颜色比那种～深一点。This colour is just a shade darker than that one.

稍为 shāowéi　same as 稍微 shāowēi

稍许 shāoxǔ　same as 稍微 shāowēi

稍纵即逝 shāo zòng jí shì　transient; fleeting: ～的机会 a fleeting opportunity

筲

筲 shāo　pail (usu. made of bamboo strips or wood); bucket

艄

艄 shāo　① stern ② rudder; helm: 掌～ be at the helm

艄公 shāogōng　① helmsman ② boatman

鞘

鞘 shāo　whiplash ——see also qiào

shóo

勺[1] (杓)　shóo　spoon; ladle: 一把长柄～ a ladle; a dipper

勺[2]　shóo　*shao*, later called 市勺 shìshóo, a traditional unit of capacity ——see also 市勺 shìshóo

勺子　shóozi　ladle; scoop

芍　shóo　see below

芍药　shóoyao　Chinese herbaceous peony

苕　shóo　*dial.* sweet potato ——see also tiáo

韶　shóo　*formal* splendid; beautiful

韶光　shóoguāng　*liter.* ① beautiful springtime ② glorious youth

韶华　shóohuá　same as 韶光 shóoguāng

韶山　Shóoshān　Shaoshan (a county town in Hunan Province, noted as the birthplace of Mao Zedong)

韶秀　shóoxiù　*liter.* delicate and pretty

shăo

少　shăo　① few; little; less: 以～胜多 defeat the many with the few / ～花钱, 多办事。Get more done on less money. / ～走弯路 avoid detours / ～吃多餐 have many meals but little food at each / 最近我们很～见到他。We've seen very little of him lately. / 现在我工作中困难～些了。Now I meet with fewer difficulties in my work. / 七比九～二。Seven is two less than nine. ② be short; lack: 我们还～两把椅子。We're still two chairs short. / 缺医～药 be short of doctors and medicine / 咱们～一个好的守门员。We lack a good goalkeeper. / 帐算错了, ～一块钱。This account is wrong; we're one *yuan* short. ③ lose; be missing: 看看～不～人。See if anyone is missing. / 这里肯定～了一个字。Surely, there's a word missing here. / 羊群里～了几只羊。A few sheep have been lost from the flock. ④ a little while; a moment: 请～候。Wait a moment, please. ⑤ stop; quit: ～废话! Stop talking rubbish! / ～来这一套。Cut it out. *or* Quit that! / ～给我装蒜! Stop pretending! ——see also shào

少安毋躁　shăo ān wú zào　keep calm, don't get excited; don't be impatient, wait a while

少不得　shăobude　cannot do without; cannot dispense with: 学科学, 参考书是～的。Reference books are indispensable in scientific studies. / 这事～还要麻烦您。We may have to trouble you again about this. / 办这种事可～你。We can't handle affairs of this sort without you.

少不了　shăobuliăo　① cannot do without; cannot dispense with: 这次比赛～你。We can't do without you for this match. ② be bound to; be unavoidable: 准备仓促, 演出～会有缺点。The performance has been arranged at short notice, so it's bound to have shortcomings. ③ can't be only a few or only a little; must be a lot: 困难看来～。It looks as if there are going to be a lot of difficulties.

少待　shăodài　wait a little while, please

少得了　shăodeliăo　(used in rhetorical questions) can do without; can dispense with: 今天的晚会还～你吗? You must come to the party this evening. We can't do without you.

少而精　shăo ér jīng　smaller quantity, better quality; fewer but better: 教学内容要～。Teaching content should be concise. / 办事机构要～。The executive organs should be smaller but more efficient.

少会　shăohuì　*pol.* (a form of greeting) I haven't seen you for ages; how long it is since we last met: 刘先生, ～了! 您是哪天到这儿的? Haven't seen you for ages, Mr. Liu! When did you arrive?

少见　shăojiàn　① *pol.* (a form of greeting) I haven't seen you for a long time; I have seen very little of you these days—I'm very glad to see you again ② seldom seen; infrequent; rare: 这种事情太～了! This is indeed something rare.

少见多怪　shăojiàn-duōguài　the less a man has seen the more he has to wonder at; ignorant people are easily surprised: 用不着～。There's nothing to be surprised at. / 也许是我～。Maybe it was all due to my own ignorance.

少刻　shăokè　after a little while; a moment later

少礼　shăolǐ　*pol.* ① please don't stand on ceremony ② excuse me for my lack of manners

少量　shăoliàng　a small amount; a little; a few

少慢差费　shăo-màn-chà-fèi　fewer, slower, poorer and more costly: 这种方法～。This method will get fewer and poorer results, and progress will be slower and costs higher. *or* That's an inefficient and expensive method.

少陪　shăopéi　*pol.* (an apology for taking leave of sb.) if you'll excuse me; I'm afraid I must be going now

少顷　shăoqǐng　*formal* after a short while; after a few moments; presently

少少儿的　shăoshăorde　just a little; a tiny bit

少时　shăoshí　after a little while; a moment later; soon: ～雨过天晴, 彩虹高悬。Soon the rain stopped, the sun came out, and a rainbow appeared spanning the sky.

少数　shăoshù　a small number; few; minority: ～人 a small number of people; a few people; the minority / 他们是～。They are in the minority. / ～服从多数。The minority is subordinate to the majority.

少数党　shăoshùdǎng　a minority party; minority

少数民族　shăoshù mínzú　minority nationality; ethnic minority: 搞好汉族和～的关系 foster good relations between the Han nationality and the minority nationalities / ～地区 areas inhabited by the minority nationalities; minority nationality regions / ～干部 minority nationality cadres

少许　shăoxǔ　*formal* a little; a few; a modicum

少有　shăoyǒu　rare; few and far between: 现在这种人真是～。Men like that are few and far between these days.

shào

少　shào　① young: 男女老少 nán-nǚ-lǎo-shào ② son of a rich family; young master: 阔少 kuòshào ——see also shăo

少艾　shào'ài　*formal* ① young and handsome ② a handsome young person (usu. a beautiful girl)

少白头　shàobáitóu　① be prematurely grey ② a young person with greying hair

少不更事　shào bù gēng shì　young and inexperienced; green: ～者 a greenhorn

少东家　shàodōngjia　(a form of address formerly used by an employee to his employer's son or by a tenant-peasant to his landlord's son) young master

少妇　shàofù　young married woman

少将　shàojiàng　(U.S. & Brit. Army, U.S. Air Force, U.S.

& Brit. Marine Corps) major general; (U.S. & Brit. Navy) rear admiral; (Brit. Air Force) air vice marshal

少林拳 shàolínquán　the Shaolin form of boxing (a series of movements similar to some of the *Taijiquan* movements, supposedly developed by Bodhidharma 菩提达摩, an Indian monk who settled in China about A. D. 520, for the physically degenerated monks of the Shaolin Monastery 少林寺 on Mount Song 嵩山)

少奶奶 shàonǎinai　① (a form of address formerly used by servants of the house) young mistress ② *old honor.* your or sb. else's daughter-in-law

少年 shàonián　① early youth (from about ten to sixteen): 打从～时代我们就是好朋友了。We have been close friends since early youth. ② boy or girl in early teens; juvenile: ～运动员 juvenile athletes ／ ～单打 boys' or girls' singles

少年读物 shàonián dúwù　books for young people; juvenile books

少年犯 shàoniánfàn　juvenile delinquent

少年犯罪 shàonián fànzuì　juvenile delinquency

少年宫 shàoniángōng　Children's Palace

少年老成 shàonián lǎochéng　① an old head on young shoulders; young but mature ② an old young man; a young person lacking in vigour and drive

少年先锋队 shàonián xiānfēngduì　Young Pioneers

少年之家 shàonián zhī jiā　Children's Centre; Children's Club

少女 shàonǚ　young girl

少尉 shàowèi　(U.S. & Brit. Army, U.S. Air Force, U.S. & Brit. Marine Corps) second lieutenant; (U.S. Navy) ensign; (Brit. Navy) acting sublieutenant; (Brit. Air Force) pilot officer

少先队 shàoxiānduì　short for 少年先锋队 shàonián xiānfēngduì

少先队员 shàoxiānduìyuán　Young Pioneer

少相 shàoxiang　young-looking: 他长得～，岁数儿可不小了。He looks much younger than his age.

少小 shàoxiǎo　when young: ～离家老大回，乡音无改鬓毛衰。(贺知章) I left home young. I return old, Speaking as then, but with hair grown thin.

少校 shàoxiào　(U.S. & Brit. Army, U.S. Air Force, U.S. & Brit. Marine Corps) major; (U.S. & Brit. Navy) lieutenant commander; (Brit. Air Force) squadron leader

少爷 shàoye　① (a form of address formerly used by servants of the house) young master ② *old honor.* your or sb. else's son

少爷脾气 shàoye píqi　behaviour of a spoilt boy

少长 shào-zhǎng　the youthful and the elderly

少壮 shàozhuàng　young and vigorous

少壮不努力，老大徒伤悲 shàozhuàng bù nǔlì, lǎodà tú shāngbēi　if one does not exert oneself in youth, one will regret it in old age; laziness in youth spells regret in old age

少壮派 shàozhuàngpài　the up-and-coming

邵 Shào　a surname

劭 shào　*formal* ① encourage; urge; exhort ② excellent; admirable: 年高德劭 niángāo-déshào

绍[1] shào　carry on; continue

绍[2] Shào　short for 绍兴 Shàoxīng

绍介 shàojiè　introduce

绍剧 shàojù　Shaoxing opera (a local opera popular in Shaoxing, Zhejiang Province)

绍兴 Shàoxīng　Shaoxing (a city in Zhejiang Province)

绍兴酒 shàoxīngjiǔ　(also 绍酒 shàojiǔ) Shaoxing rice wine

捎 shào　(of mules, horses, etc.) draw back a few steps; shy ——see also shāo

捎马子 shàomǎzi　*dial.* saddlebag

捎色 shàoshǎi　fade (in colour)

哨[1] shào　sentry post; post: 观察～ observation post

哨[2] shào　① (of birds) warble; chirp ② a whistle: 吹～儿 blow a whistle

哨兵 shàobīng　sentry; guard

哨岗 shàogǎng　sentry post (where a sentinel is posted)

哨卡 shàoqiǎ　a frontier sentry post or a strategic sentry post

哨所 shàosuǒ　sentry post; post: 前沿～ forward post; outpost ／ 边防～ frontier guard post

哨子 shàozi　a whistle

稍 shào　see below ——see also shāo

稍息 shàoxī　*mil.* stand at ease: ～! (word of command) At ease!

潲[1] shào　① (of rain) slant in: 东边～雨。The rain is driving (*or* slanting) in from the east. ② *dial.* sprinkle: 往菜上～水 sprinkle the vegetables with water

潲[2] shào　*dial.* swill; slops: 猪～ hogwash; swill (*or* slops) for swine

潲水 shàoshuǐ　*dial.* swill; slops; hogwash

shē

奢 shē　① luxurious; extravagant: 奢侈 shēchǐ ② excessive; inordinate; extravagant: 奢望 shēwàng

奢侈 shēchǐ　luxurious; extravagant; wasteful: 生活～ live in luxury

奢侈品 shēchǐpǐn　luxury goods; luxuries

奢侈品税 shēchǐpǐnshuì　luxury tax

奢华 shēhuá　luxurious; sumptuous; extravagant: 陈设～ be luxuriously furnished

奢靡 shēmí　extravagant and wasteful

奢求 shēqiú　extravagant claims; excessive demands; unreasonable demands

奢望 shēwàng　extravagant hopes; wild wishes: 我对此不抱～。I entertain no high hopes in this regard.

奢想 shēxiǎng　extravagant hopes; wild wishes

猞 shē　see below

猞猁 shēlì　lynx

赊 shē　buy or sell on credit

赊购 shēgòu　buy on credit

赊欠 shēqiàn　buy or sell on credit: 购买我店家具, 可以先付半数货款, ～部分在三个月内付清。You can always buy our furniture on credit if you can pay half the price now and the rest in three months.

赊销 shēxiāo　sell on credit

赊帐 shēzhàng　① a system of buying or selling on credit; the credit system: 概不～。No credit given. ② outstanding bills or accounts: 还有几笔～未清。There are some bills still outstanding (*or* unpaid). ③ have outstanding bills or accounts: 准许赊三个月的帐 allow people 3 months' credit ／ 赊了一千元的帐 have an outstanding account of 1,000 *yuan*

畲 Shē　see below

畲族 Shēzú　the She nationality, or the Shes, distributed over Fujian, Zhejiang, Jiangxi and Guangdong Provinces

畬 shē　*formal*　slash-and-burn　cultivation
——see also yú

shé

舌 shé　① tongue (of a human being or animal) ② sth. shaped like a tongue: 鞋～ the tongue of a shoe ③ the tongue of a bell; clapper

舌敝唇焦 shébì-chúnjiāo　talk till one's tongue and lips are parched; wear oneself out in pleading, expostulating, etc.

舌根 shégēn　the root of the tongue

舌根音 shégēnyīn　*phonet.*　velar (e.g. g, k, h)

舌耕 shégēng　*formal*　make a living by teaching

舌尖 shéjiān　the tip of the tongue

舌尖后音 shéjiānhòuyīn　*phonet.*　blade-palatal (e.g. zh, ch, sh, r)

舌尖前音 shéjiānqiányīn　*phonet.*　dental (e.g. z, c, s)

舌尖音 shéjiānyīn　*phonet.*　apical (including z, c, s, d, t, n, l, zh, ch, sh, r)

舌尖中音 shéjiānzhōngyīn　*phonet.*　blade-alveolar (e.g. d, t, n, l)

舌剑唇枪 shéjiàn-chúnqiāng　same as 唇枪舌剑 chúnqiāng-shéjiàn

舌面后音 shémiànhòuyīn　another name for 舌根音 shégēnyīn

舌面前音 shémiànqiányīn　*phonet.*　dorsal (e.g. j, q, x)

舌人 shérén　*arch.*　interpreter

舌鳎 shétǎ　*zool.*　tonguefish; tongue sole

舌苔 shétāi　*Chin. med.*　coating on the tongue; fur

舌头 shétou　① tongue ② an enemy soldier captured for the purpose of extracting information: 侦察兵抓了个～。The scouts took a prisoner to get information. ——see also 吐舌头 tǔ shétou

舌下神经 shéxià shénjīng　*physiol.*　hypoglossal nerve

舌下腺 shéxiàxiàn　*physiol.*　sublingual gland

舌炎 shéyán　glossitis

舌蝇 shéyíng　tsetse fly (or tzetze fly); tsetse (or tzetze)

舌战 shézhàn　① have a verbal battle with; argue heatedly with: ～群儒 have a heated dispute with a group of scholars ② a hot dispute; a verbal battle: 一场～ a heated dispute; a battle royal

舌状花 shézhuànghuā　*bot.*　ligulate flower

折 shé　① break; snap: 扁担～了。The shoulder pole broke. / 他们太使劲，把绳子拉～了。They pulled the rope so hard that it snapped. ② lose money in business ——see also zhē; zhé

折本 shéběn　lose money in business: ～生意 a losing business; a bad bargain

折秤 shéchèng　damage and loss to goods (such as vegetables, fruits, etc.) in the course of reweighing

折耗 shéhào　damage and loss (to goods during transit, storage, etc.)

折钱 shéqián　*dial.*　suffer losses in business transactions; lose money in business

佘 Shé　a surname

蛇(虵) 　shé　snake; serpent ——see also yí

蛇根草 shégēncǎo　another name for 萝芙木 luófúmù

蛇麻 shémá　another name for 啤酒花 píjiǔhuā

蛇莓 shéméi　*bot.*　mock-strawberry

蛇皮管 shépíguǎn　flexible conduit

蛇丘 shéqiū　*geol.*　esker

蛇蜕 shétuì　*Chin. med.*　snake slough

蛇纹石 shéwénshí　serpentine (a mineral)

蛇无头不行 shé wú tóu bù xíng　a snake cannot move without its head—nothing can be accomplished without a leader

蛇蝎 shéxiē　snakes and scorpions—vicious people: 毒如～ as vicious as a viper

蛇蝎心肠 shéxiē xīncháng　as venomous as snakes and scorpions

蛇行 shéxíng　*formal*　move with the body on the ground; crawl

蛇形 shéxíng　snakelike; S-shaped

蛇足 shézú　feet added to a snake by an ignorant artist—sth. superfluous ——see also 画蛇添足 huà shé tiān zú

阇 shé　see below

阇梨 shélí　Buddhist monk

shě

舍(捨) shě　① give up; abandon: ～此别无他法。There is no other way than this. *or* This is the only way. ② give alms; dispense charity ——see also shè

舍本逐末 shěběn-zhúmò　attend to trifles and neglect essentials

舍不得 shěbude　hate to part with or use; grudge; begrudge: 我～你。I hate to leave you. *or* I hate to lose you. / 他是队里的好管家，～乱花一分钱。He is our team's good manager and hates to waste a single cent. / 他～穿那套新衣服。He begrudged wearing his new suit (so that he wouldn't wear it out). *or* He was reluctant to wear his new suit.

舍得 shěde　be willing to part with; not grudge: 练字必须～下功夫。To acquire good handwriting one mustn't begrudge time spent on practice. / 你～把这本书送给他吗? Are you willing to give the book to him?

舍得一身剐，敢把皇帝拉下马 shěde yīshēn guǎ, gǎn bǎ huángdì lāxia mǎ　he who fears not being cut to pieces dares to unhorse the emperor

舍己救人 shě jǐ jiù rén　sacrifice oneself to save sb. else

舍己为人 shě jǐ wèi rén　sacrifice one's own interests for the sake of others

舍近求远 shějìn-qiúyuǎn　(also 舍近图远 shějìn-túyuǎn) seek from afar what lies close at hand; forgo what is close at hand and seek what is far afield

舍车保帅 shějū-bǎoshuài　give up a chariot to save the marshal (in Chinese chess)—make minor sacrifices to safeguard major interests

舍命 shěmìng　risk one's life; sacrifice oneself

舍命陪君子 shěmìng péi jūnzǐ　I would throw in my lot with you, sir, at the risk of my life (said jocularly when agreeing to join sb. in some activity)

舍弃 shěqì　give up; abandon: ～亲生骨肉 abandon one's own flesh and blood

舍入 shěrù　*math.*　rounding off

舍身 shěshēn　give one's life; sacrifice oneself: ～救人 give one's life to rescue sb.; sacrifice oneself to save others

舍生取义 shě shēng qǔ yì　lay down one's life for a just cause: ～，虽死何辞? Nothing shall prevent me from

dying for righteousness.

舍死忘生 shěsǐ-wàngshēng　disregard one's own safety; risk one's life

舍我其谁 shě wǒ qí shuí　if I can't do it, who can?; who but myself can do it?

shè

设 shè ① set up; establish; found: 总部～在北京。The headquarters was established in Beijing. / 指挥所～在前沿阵地上。The command post was set up in a forward position. / 部下面～六个司。Under the ministry there are six departments. / 我们这个市，下～十个区。Our municipality is divided into ten districts. ② work out: 设计 shèjì ③ *math.* given; suppose; if: ～长方形的宽是 x 米。Suppose the width of a rectangle is x metres. / ～$x=1$ Given: $x=1$ ④ *formal* if; in case: ～有困难，当助一臂之力。You can count on me to help in case of difficulty.

设备 shèbèi　equipment; installation; facilities: 冶金～ metallurgical equipment / 电气～ electric (*or* electrical) installations / 交通运输～ facilities for transport and communication / 安装暖气～ install heating equipment / 旅馆～齐全。The hotel is well appointed. / ～利用率 utilization rate of equipment and installations

设辞 shècí　*formal* excuse; pretext

设法 shèfǎ　think of a way; try; do what one can: 大家来～。Let's all try and think of a way. / 我们乐队正在～找个小提琴手。Our orchestra is trying to find a violinist.

设防 shèfáng　set up defences; fortify; garrison: 层层～ set up defences in depth / ～地带 fortified zone

设伏 shèfú　*formal* lay an ambush

设岗 shègǎng　post a sentry: 在门口设了岗，检查出入证。A sentry was posted at the entrance to check the passes.

设或 shèhuò　*conj. formal* if; suppose

设计 shèjì ① design; plan: ～一座厂房 make designs for a factory building / ～一种新机器 design a new machine / ～一座水坝 project a dam / ～版面 lay out a printed page ② work out a plan or scheme: ～陷害 plot a frame-up; frame

设计洪水 shèjì hóngshuǐ　*water conservancy* design flood

设计能力 shèjì nénglì　designed capacity

设计师 shèjìshī ① designer: 服装～ costume designer; dress designer ② architect

设计图 shèjìtú　design drawing

设计院 shèjìyuàn　designing institute

设立 shèlì　establish; set up; found: ～新的机构 set up a new organization / 一家新～的商行 a newly established business firm

设若 shèruò　*conj. formal* if; suppose; provided

设色 shèsè　fill in colours on a sketch; lay paint on (canvas); colour: ～柔和 painted in quiet colours

设身处地 shèshēn-chǔdì　put oneself in sb. else's position: 你只要～想想他的处境，就可以理解他为什么会有那种表现。If you put yourself in his place, you may realize why he acted as he did. / 乘务员要事事～为旅客着想。The attendants should look at everything from the passengers' angle and take care of their every need.

设施 shèshī　installation; facilities: 防洪～ flood control installations / 军事～ military installations / 医疗～ medical facilities / 集体福利～ collective welfare institutions / 改善教育～ improve educational facilities / 提供多种文化娱乐～。Various recreational facilities are provided.

设使 shèshǐ　*conj.* if; suppose; in case

设想 shèxiǎng ① imagine; envisage; conceive; assume: 政府～的计划 the programme envisaged by the government / 从最坏的可能来～ anticipate the worst; prepare for the worst / ～你自己处在他的境遇中会怎么办？Imagine yourself to be in his place. What would you do then? / 过去人们难以～人类竟能登上月球。It seemed inconceivable that man should land on the moon. / 这样～是合乎逻辑的。It is logical to assume that. ② tentative plan; tentative idea: 这些只是我们的初步～。Those are just our tentative ideas. ③ have consideration for: 为群众～ take the interests of the masses into consideration / 多为青少年～ give much thought to the needs of the younger generation

设宴 shèyàn　give a banquet; fête: ～招待贵宾 give a banquet in honour of the distinguished visitors; fête the distinguished guests / 设喜（寿）宴 give a wedding (birthday) feast / 设午（晚）宴 give a midday (evening) banquet

设营 shèyíng　*mil.* quarter; encamp

设营地 shèyíngdì　camp site

设营队 shèyíngduì　quartering party

设置 shèzhì ① set up; establish: ～专门机构 set up a special organization / 课程～ courses offered in a college or school; curriculum ② put up; install: 实验室里～了闭路电视。A closed circuit TV system has been installed in the laboratories. / 给会议～重重障碍 place all sorts of obstacles before the conference

设座 shèzuò　choose a place to give a banquet: 当晚总经理～国际饭店宴请外宾。In the evening the General Manager gave a banquet at the International Hotel in honour of the foreign guests.

社 shè ① an organized body; agency; society: 通讯社 tōngxùnshè / 合作社 hézuòshè / 报社 bàoshè ② (specifically) people's commune: ～办企业 commune-run enterprise ③ the god of the land, sacrifices to him or altars for such sacrifices: 春～ spring sacrifice

社会 shèhuì　society; community: 人类～ human society / 国际～ international community / ～财富 wealth of society; public wealth / ～地位 social position; social status / ～福利 social welfare; public welfare / ～环境 social environment / ～基础 social base; social basis / ～实践 social practice

社会保险 shèhuì bǎoxiǎn　social insurance

社会保障制度 shèhuì bǎozhàng zhìdù　social security system

社会党 shèhuìdǎng　Socialist Party

社会调查 shèhuì diàochá　social investigation; social survey

社会发展史 shèhuì fāzhǎnshǐ　history of social development; history of development of society

社会分工 shèhuì fēngōng　division of labour in society

社会工作 shèhuì gōngzuò　work outside one's regular job, done for the community; community work

社会关系 shèhuì guānxi ① human relations in society; social relations ② one's social connections; relatives and friends: 她有很多～在海外。Many of her relatives and friends are residing abroad.

社会化 shèhuìhuà　socialization: 促进生产的商品化～ promote the commercialization and socialization of production / 公共福利事业应该～。Public welfare services should be socialized. / ～大生产 large-scale socialized production

社会活动 shèhuì huódòng　social activities; public activities

社会经济制度 shèhuì jīngjì zhìdù　socio-economic system

社会科学 shèhuì kēxué　social sciences

社会民主党 shèhuìmínzhǔdǎng Social Democratic Party: ～人(党员) Social Democrat

社会民主主义 shèhuìmínzhǔzhǔyì social democracy

社会名流 shèhuì míngliú noted public figures

社会青年 shèhuì qīngnián unemployed youth

社会协商对话制度 shèhuì xiéshāng duìhuà zhìdù a social system of consultation and dialogue (between groups of people with varied social interests)

社会学 shèhuìxué sociology

社会学家 shèhuìxuéjiā sociologist

社会治安 shèhuì zhì'ān public order

社会制度 shèhuì zhìdù social system

社会主义 shèhuìzhǔyì socialism: ～道路 socialist road / ～建设 socialist construction / ～觉悟 socialist consciousness / ～劳动竞赛 socialist labour emulation / ～制度 socialist system

社会主义改造 shèhuìzhǔyì gǎizào socialist transformation

社会主义革命 shèhuìzhǔyì gémìng socialist revolution

社会主义教育运动 Shèhuìzhǔyì Jiàoyù Yùndòng the Socialist Education Movement (1963–1966)

社会主义经济 shèhuìzhǔyì jīngjì socialist economy: ～是公有制基础上的有计划的商品经济。The socialist economy is a planned commodity economy based on public ownership.

社会主义所有制 shèhuìzhǔyì suǒyǒuzhì socialist ownership

社会总产品 shèhuì zǒngchǎnpǐn aggregate social product

社火 shèhuǒ traditional festivities

社稷 shèjì the altars to the gods of earth and grain —the state; the country (in ancient times each state had its own altars to the gods of earth and grain, and a state remained independent only so long as its ruler was able to maintain these altars): 天子不仁, 不保四海; 诸侯不仁, 不保～。《孟子》 An Emperor cannot keep the Empire within the Four Seas unless he is benevolent; a feudal lord cannot preserve the altars to the gods of earth and grain unless he is benevolent.

社稷之臣 shèjì zhī chén a loyal servant of the dynasty's sacred altars; a bulwark of the state

社交 shèjiāo social intercourse; social contact; social life: 要为男女青年开展～活动创造条件。Opportunities should be provided for social intercourse between young men and women.

社教 Shèjiào short for 社会主义教育运动 Shèhuìzhǔyì Jiàoyù Yùndòng

社论 shèlùn editorial; leading article; leader: 一篇占有整版篇幅的～ a full-page editorial

社评 shèpíng old editorial

社区 shèqū community: ～发展 community development

社团 shètuán mass organizations

社戏 shèxì village theatrical performance given on religious festivals in old times

社员 shèyuán a member of a society, club, etc.: 合作社～ cooperative member / 摄影社～ a member of a photographers' club

舍[1] shè ① house; shed; hut: 牛～ cowshed ② hum. my place: 敝～ my place ③ hum. (used before relatives younger than or junior to oneself) my: ～弟 my younger brother / ～侄 my nephew

舍[2] shè an ancient unit of distance equal to 30 li (里)
——see also shě

舍间 shèjiān hum. my humble abode; my house; my place: 请到～去谈谈, 吃顿便饭, 如何? Would you care to come with me to my place for a chat and have something to eat?

舍监 shèjiān old the warden of a school dormitory

舍利 shèlì (also 舍利子 shèlìzǐ) Buddhism relics left after the cremation of Buddhas or saintly monks (deposited in stupas for worship)

舍利塔 shèlìtǎ a pagoda for Buddhist relics; stupa

舍亲 shèqīn hum. my relative; a relative of mine

舍下 shèxià hum. my humble abode; my house; my place: ～逼仄。My place is rather cramped.

舍营 shèyíng mil. billeting

涉 shè ① wade; ford: ～水过河 wade across a river; ford a stream ② go through; experience: 涉险 shèxiǎn ③ involve: 涉嫌 shèxián

涉笔 shèbǐ wet the brush—start writing or painting

涉笔成趣 shèbǐ chéng qù (of a writer or painter) produce good work as soon as the brush touches paper (or as soon as he sets his brush to paper)

涉及 shèjí involve; relate to; touch upon: 双方的分歧～一些重大原则性问题。The differences between the two sides involve major matters of principle. / 遗传工程～的学科和技术面很广。Genetic engineering deals with a wide range of disciplines and technologies.

涉猎 shèliè do desultory reading; read cursorily: 有的书必须精读, 有的只要稍加～即可。Some books are for intensive study and some are for cursory reading.

涉禽 shèqín zool. wading bird; wader

涉世 shèshì gain life experience: ～不深 have scanty experience of life; have seen little of the world

涉讼 shèsòng be involved in a lawsuit

涉外 shèwài concerning foreign affairs or foreign nationals: ～活动 activities involving foreign countries or nationals / ～经济法规 laws and regulations governing business relations with foreigners

涉嫌 shèxián be suspected of being involved; be a suspect: 他因～此案而被传讯。He was cited for suspected involvement in this law case. / ～人犯 suspects in a crime

涉险 shèxiǎn go through dangers

涉想 shèxiǎng formal be lost in thought; indulge in fanciful thinking

涉足 shèzú formal set foot in: ～其间 set foot there

射 shè ① shoot; fire: 能骑善～ be a good horseman as well as a crack shot; be known for one's equestrian skill and marksmanship / ～进一球 kick the ball into the goal; score a goal / 炮弹～中了敌人坦克。The shell hit the enemy tank. ② discharge in a jet; jet; spout: 喷射 pēnshè / 注射 zhùshè ③ send out (light, heat, etc.): 探照灯～出一道道强光。The searchlights projected powerful beams of light. ④ allude to sth. or sb.; insinuate: 影射 yǐngshè

射程 shèchéng range (of fire): 有效～ effective range

射弹 shèdàn projectile

射电天文学 shèdiàn tiānwénxué radio astronomy

射电望远镜 shèdiàn wàngyuǎnjìng radio telescope

射干 shègān bot. blackberry lily

射击 shèjī ① shoot; fire: 向敌人～ fire at the enemy ② sports shooting

射击场 shèjīchǎng shooting range

射击地境 shèjīdìjìng sector of fire

射击孔 shèjīkǒng embrasure

射箭 shèjiàn ① shoot an arrow ② sports archery: ～手 archer

射角 shèjiǎo angle of fire

射界 shèjiè area (or field) of fire; firing area

射精 shèjīng physiol. ejaculation

射精管 shèjīngguǎn physiol. ejaculatory ducts

射孔　shèkǒng　*petroleum*　perforation
射猎　shèliè　hunting with bow and arrow or firearms
射流　shèliú　*phys.*　efflux: ～喷口 efflux nozzle
射流技术　shèliú jìshù　fluidics
射门　shèmén　*sports*　shoot (at the goal)
射门手　shèménshǒu　goal getter
射频　shèpín　*electron.*　radio frequency
射频放大器　shèpín fàngdàqì　radio frequency amplifier
射手　shèshǒu　① shooter; marksman; archer: 机枪～ machine gunner ② goal getter
射水鱼　shèshuǐyú　archer fish
射速　shèsù　firing rate
射线　shèxiàn　*phys.*　ray
射线病　shèxiànbìng　radiation sickness
射线疗法　shèxiàn liáofǎ　radiotherapy
射影　shèyǐng　projection

赦　shè　remit (a punishment); pardon
赦令　shèlìng　order of pardon or amnesty
赦免　shèmiǎn　remit (a punishment); pardon
赦书　shèshū　written order of pardon or amnesty
赦宥　shèyòu　*formal*　remit (a punishment); pardon
赦罪　shèzuì　absolve sb. from guilt; pardon sb.

摄¹(攝)　shè　① absorb; assimilate ② take a photograph of; shoot: ～下几个珍贵的镜头 take some superb shots

摄²(攝)　shè　*formal*　conserve (one's health)

摄³(攝)　shè　act for
摄动　shèdòng　*meteorol.*　perturbation
摄理　shèlǐ　hold an office in an acting capacity
摄录机　shèlùjī　video camera recorder (VCR)
摄谱仪　shèpǔyí　*phys.*　spectrograph
摄取　shèqǔ　① absorb; assimilate; take in: ～营养 absorb nourishment ② take a photograph of; shoot: ～几个镜头 take several shots
摄生　shèshēng　*formal*　conserve one's health; keep fit
摄食　shèshí　(of animals) feed: ～行为 feeding behaviour
摄氏温度计　shèshì wēndùjì　centigrade thermometer; Celsius thermometer
摄卫　shèwèi　*formal*　conserve one's health; keep fit
摄像　shèxiàng　make a video recording (with a video camera or TV camera)
摄像机　shèxiàngjī　video camera or television camera: 录像～ video camera / 电视～ television camera; TV camera
摄行　shèxíng　*formal*　act for another
摄养　shèyǎng　*formal*　conserve one's health; keep fit
摄影　shèyǐng　① take a photograph: ～留念 have a souvenir photograph taken / 航空～ aerial photography / 红外～ infrared photography / 风景～ landscape photography / 静物～ still-life photography / 人像～ portraiture photography / 体育～ sports photography / 舞台～ stage photography / 新闻～ reportage photography ② shoot a film; film: 全景(内景, 外景)～ panoramic (interior, exterior) shooting
摄影机　shèyǐngjī　camera: 电影～ motion-picture camera; cinecamera; cinematograph / 立体～ stereoscopic camera
摄影记者　shèyǐng jìzhě　press photographer; cameraman
摄影棚　shèyǐngpéng　film studio
摄影师　shèyǐngshī　photographer; cameraman
摄影室　shèyǐngshì　photographic studio; photo studio
摄影展览　shèyǐng zhǎnlǎn　photographic exhibition; photo exhibition
摄政　shèzhèng　act as regent

摄政王　shèzhèngwáng　prince regent
摄制　shèzhì　*film*　produce: 北京电影制片厂～ produced by the Beijing Film Studio / ～组 production unit

慑(懾、慴)　shè　*formal*　fear; be awed: ～于其淫威 be cowed by his despotic power / ～于人民民主专政的强大威力 be awed by the power of the people's democratic dictatorship
慑服　shèfú　① submit in fear; succumb ② cow sb. into submission

麝　shè　① musk deer ② short for 麝香 shèxiāng
麝牛　shèniú　musk-ox
麝鼠　shèshǔ　muskrat
麝香　shèxiāng　musk

shéi

谁　shéi　a variant pronunciation for 谁 shuí

shēn

申¹　shēn　state; express; explain: 重申 chóngshēn

申²　shēn　the ninth of the twelve Earthly Branches (地支)——see also 干支 gān-zhī

申³　Shēn　① another name for 上海 Shànghǎi ② a surname
申报　shēnbào　① report to a higher body ② declare sth. (to the Customs): 出国人员必须向海关～其携带出境的外币。Travellers leaving the country must declare the amount of foreign currency they are taking with them.
申辩　shēnbiàn　defend oneself; explain oneself; argue (*or* plead) one's case: 允许～ allow sb. to argue his case / 被告有权～。The accused has the right to defend himself.
申斥　shēnchì　rebuke (usu. one's subordinates); reprimand: 小孩不听话, 不要一味～。Don't scold your children every time they don't listen to you.
申饬　shēnchì　① (also 申敕 shēnchì) *formal*　warn; admonish ② same as 申斥 shēnchì
申令　shēnlìng　issue orders: ～全国 issue orders to all parts of the country
申明　shēnmíng　declare; state; avow: ～自己的立场 state one's position / ～理由 give one's reason for doing sth. / 公开～ openly avow
申请　shēnqǐng　apply for; file an application: 向…～ make an application to; lodge (*or* file) an application with; present a petition to / ～入党 apply for Party membership / ～入(出)境签证 apply for an entry (exit) visa / ～调动工作 apply for a transfer; ask for a transfer; ask to be transferred to another job
申请国　shēnqǐngguó　applicant country
申请人　shēnqǐngrén　applicant
申请书　shēnqǐngshū　(written) application; petition
申曲　shēnqǔ　another name for 沪剧 hùjù
申时　shēnshí　the period of the day from 3 p. m. to 5 p. m.
申述　shēnshù　state; explain in detail: ～立场 state one's position / ～来意 explain the purpose of one's visit / ～自己的观点 expound one's views / 谨～如下 have the honour to state the following / 作进一步的～ make

further observations

申说　shēnshuō　state (reasons)

申诉　shēnsù　appeal: 向上级提出～ appeal to the higher authorities / 不服判决，提出～ appeal against a legal decision / 建立人民～制度 establish a people's appeals system

申讨　shēntǎo　openly condemn; denounce: ～反动派的罪行 denounce the crimes of the reactionaries

申谢　shēnxiè　acknowledge one's indebtedness; express one's gratitude

申雪　shēnxuě　① appeal for redress of a wrong ② redress a wrong: 多年的冤狱终于得到了～。The long-standing wrong was at last redressed.

申冤　shēnyuān　① redress an injustice; right a wrong ② appeal for redress of a wrong

申状　shēnzhuàng　*formal*　document submitted to a superior; memorial; petition

申奏　shēnzòu　submit a memorial to the emperor

伸　shēn　stretch; extend: ～胳臂 stretch one's arms / ～舌头 stick out one's tongue / 两臂平～ extend (or stretch, spread) one's arms horizontally / 跳水时腿要～直。When you dive you must keep your legs straight. / 不要把头～出窗外。Don't put (or stick) your head out of the window (of a bus, etc.). / 早在十九世纪，帝国主义的魔爪就～进了中国。The imperialists stretched their claws into China as early as the nineteenth century. / 他的手～得太长了。He has over-extended himself.

伸大姆哥　shēn　dàmugē　hold up one's thumb (in praise)

伸开　shēnkāi　stretch out: 把胳臂～。Stretch out your arms.

伸懒腰　shēn lǎnyāo　stretch oneself

伸眉　shēnméi　raise one's eyebrows: ～扬气 raise one's eyebrows and blow out one's breath—feel proud and elated

伸手　shēnshǒu　① stretch (or hold) out one's hand: 他～去拿碗。He reached for the bowl. ② ask for money, honour, gifts, etc.: 一见美差就～ try to seize any cushy job that comes along / 尽管遭了水灾，他们却没有向国家～要一分钱。Although hit by the flood, they did not ask for a single copper from the state. ③ have a hand in; poke one's nose into; meddle in

伸手不见五指　shēnshǒu bù jiàn wǔzhǐ　so dark that you can't see your hand in front of you; pitch-dark: 天黑得～，我深一脚浅一脚，摸索着往前走。It was pitch-dark. I stumbled along, groping my way.

伸缩　shēnsuō　① stretch out and draw back; expand and contract; lengthen and shorten: 这架照像机的镜头可以前后～。The lens of this camera can be pulled back and forth. ② flexible; elastic; adjustable: 这些规定～性很大。These regulations are quite elastic (or flexible). / 没有～余地 leave one no latitude

伸缩缝　shēnsuōfèng　*archit.*　expansion joint

伸缩三角架　shēnsuō sānjiǎojià　extension tripod

伸头探脑　shēntóu-tànnǎo　stretch one's neck to see (or find out); peep; spy

伸腿　shēntuǐ　① stretch one's legs ② step in (to gain an advantage) ③ *inf.*　kick the bucket; turn up one's toes

伸雪　shēnxuě　same as 申雪　shēnxuě

伸腰　shēnyāo　straighten one's back; straighten oneself up

伸冤　shēnyuān　same as 申冤 shēnyuān

伸展　shēnzhǎn　spread; extend; stretch: 草原一直～到遥远的天边。The prairie stretches to the distant horizon.

伸张　shēnzhāng　uphold; promote: ～正气，打击歪风 promote healthy tendencies and combat unhealthy ones

伸张正义　shēnzhāng zhèngyì　uphold justice

身　shēn　① body: ～肢 body and limbs / ～负重伤 be seriously injured (or wounded) / ～不离劳动，心不离群众 never give up manual labour and always have the masses at heart ② life: 舍身 shěshēn ③ oneself; personally: 你～为组长，应当负起责任来。As group leader, you should take charge. ④ one's moral character and conduct: 修身 xiūshēn ⑤ the main part of a structure; body: 树～ trunk / 船～ the body of a ship; hull ⑥ *m.* (for clothes) suit: 一～新衣服 a new suit

身败名裂　shēnbài-míngliè　lose all standing and reputation; bring shame and ruin upon oneself; be utterly discredited: ～，遗臭万年 bring ruin and eternal shame on oneself

身板　shēnbǎn　*dial.*　body; bodily health: ～儿挺结实 have a strong physique

身边　shēnbiān　① at (or by) one's side: 老人把全家人叫到～。The old man summoned the whole family to his side. / 他在专家～工作，进步很快。Working at the side of the experts, he has made rapid progress. ② (have sth.) on one; with one: ～没带钱 have no money on one / 她～总是带着药箱。She never goes anywhere without her medical kit.

身不由己　shēn bù yóu jǐ　involuntarily; under compulsion; in spite of oneself: 车子突然一停，他～地向前一扑。When the bus came to a sudden stop, he jerked forward involuntarily.

身材　shēncái　stature; figure: ～矮小 short and slight of stature / ～苗条 have a slender (or slim) figure / ～魁梧 of great height and powerful build; tall and sturdy

身长　shēncháng　① height (of a person) ② length (of a garment from shoulder to hemline)

身段　shēnduàn　① (woman's) figure ② (dancer's) posture

身分　shēnfen　(also 身份　shēnfen) ① status; capacity; identity: 不合～ incompatible with one's status / ～不明 of unknown identity; unidentified / 暴露～ reveal one's identity / 以官方 (私人，个人) ～发言 speak in an official (a private, a personal) capacity ② honourable position; dignity: 有失～ be beneath one's dignity / 符合其～ befitting his position ③ *dial.*　the quality of a thing

身分证　shēnfenzhèng　(also 身份证 shēnfenzhèng) identity card; identification card; ID card; ID

身高　shēngāo　height (of a person): 他～一米八。He is 180 centimetres in height.

身故　shēngù　(of a person) die: 因病～ die of an illness

身后　shēnhòu　after one's death

身怀六甲　shēn huái liùjiǎ　be with child; be pregnant

身家　shēnjiā　① oneself and one's family: ～性命 one's personal safety and that of one's family ② family background: 他～清白。He comes from a respectable family.

身价　shēnjià　① social status ② the selling price of a slave

身价百倍　shēnjià bǎi bèi　a meteoric rise in social status: 一夜之间～ have a sudden rise in social status

身教　shēnjiào　teach others by one's own example

身教胜于言教　shēnjiào shèngyú yánjiào　example is better than precept

身经百战　shēn jīng bǎi zhàn　have fought a hundred battles: ～的老战士 a veteran who has fought countless battles; a battle-tested veteran; a seasoned fighter

身历　shēnlì　experience personally: ～其境 personally go through (or experience) the situation

身量　shēnliang　*inf.*　height (of a person); stature: 她～不高。She's not tall.

身临其境 shēn lín qí jìng　be personally on the scene: 这个场面写得很生动,使人有～之感。The scene is so vividly portrayed that the reader feels as if he is participating.

身强力壮 shēnqiáng-lìzhuàng　(of a person) strong; tough; sturdy

身躯 shēnqū　body; stature: 健壮的～ a sound body／～高大 tall of stature

身上 shēnshang　① on one's body: ～穿一件白衬衫 wear a white shirt／我～不舒服。I'm not feeling well.／希望寄托在青年人～。Our hopes are placed on the young people. ② (have sth.) on one; with one: ～没带笔。I haven't got a pen with me.／～有零钱吗? Have you got any change on you?

身世 shēnshì　one's (unfortunate) life experience; one's (hard) lot: ～凄凉 have had a sad life

身手 shēnshǒu　skill; talent: ～不凡 be of no ordinary talent; display consummate skill

身首异处 shēn-shǒu yì chù　be beheaded

身受 shēnshòu　experience personally: ～其害 personally experience its baneful influence (or evil effects)

身体 shēntǐ　① body: 保持～平衡 keep one's balance ② health: 注意～ look after one's health／～非常健康 be in excellent health／她最近～怎么样? How is she these days?

身体力行 shēntǐ-lìxíng　earnestly practise what one advocates; practise what one preaches

身体素质 shēntǐ sùzhì　physique; constitution: ～好 have a strong constitution

身外之物 shēn wài zhī wù　external things; mere worldly possessions: 功名到底是～, 德行是要紧的。Fame and fortune are external things after all; it's goodness that really counts.

身无长物 shēn wú chángwù　same as 别无长物 bié wú chángwù

身先士卒 shēn xiān shìzú　lead one's men in a charge; charge at the head of one's men

身心 shēn-xīn　body and mind: ～健康 sound in body and mind; physically and mentally healthy／～受到摧残 be physically injured and mentally affected

身影 shēnyǐng　a person's silhouette; form; figure: 一个高大的～ a tall figure

身孕 shēnyùn　pregnancy: 她有了三个月的～。She is three months pregnant.

身在福中不知福 shēn zài fú zhōng bù zhī fú　not appreciate the happy life one enjoys; growing up in happiness, one often fails to appreciate what happiness really means

身正不怕影儿斜 shēn zhèng bùpà yǐngr xié　a man standing straight doesn't worry about his shadow slanting—an upright man fears no gossip

身子 shēnzi　inf. ① body: 光着～ be naked／不大舒服 not feel well ② pregnancy: 有了七个月的～ be seven months pregnant

身子骨儿 shēnzigǔr　dial. one's health; physique: 爷爷的～还挺结实。Grandpa's enjoying good health. or Grandpa's still going strong.

呻
shēn　see below

呻吟 shēnyín　groan; moan: 痛得直～ moan and groan with pain／伤员的～ the moans of the wounded

绅
shēn　① girdle (worn by ancient officials and literary men) ② gentry: 土豪劣绅 tǔháo-lièshēn

绅士 shēnshì　gentleman; gentry

绅士协定 shēnshì xiédìng　same as 君子协定 jūnzǐ xiédìng

参¹（参、蓡、葠）　shēn　ginseng

参²（参）　shēn　the twenty-first of the twenty-eight constellations (二十八宿) into which the celestial sphere was divided in ancient Chinese astronomy (consisting of seven stars in Orion)
——see also　cān; cēn

参商 shēn-shāng　liter. shen and shang (two stars that never appear in the same sky)—two friends or relatives who are separated and can never meet again or who have become estranged and irreconcilable: 人生不相见,动如参与商。今夕复何夕,共此灯烛光。(杜甫) In this life friends may meet as seldom As the stars Shen and Shang; Then what a rare night is this, The two of us sharing the same candlelight!

砷
shēn　chem. arsenic (As)

莘
shēn　see below

莘莘 shēnshēn　formal numerous: ～学子 a great number of disciples; large numbers of students ——see also　xīn

娠
shēn　see 妊娠　rènshēn

深
shēn　① deep: 一口～井 a deep well／雪～过膝 knee-deep snow／林～苔滑。The forest is thick and the moss is slippery. ② depth: 测量水～ sound (or plumb) the depth of the water／这间大厅有三米宽、五米～。This hall is 3m. wide and 5m. deep (or 3m. in width and 5m. in depth).／这山洞有多～? What is the depth of the cave? ③ hard to understand; difficult; abstruse; profound: 这本书给孩子们看太～了。The book is too difficult for children. ④ thoroughgoing; penetrating; profound: 问题想得很～ think deeply about a question／功夫～ have put in a great deal of effort ⑤ (of relations or feelings) close; intimate: 交情～ be very close; be on intimate terms／他们之间的感情已经很～了。They are already deeply in love with each other. ⑥ (of colour) dark; deep; rich: ～蓝 dark blue／～红 deep red; crimson／颜色太～。The colour is too dark (or deep). ⑦ far on in the day, night, season, etc.; late: 夜～了。It was in the dead of night (or late at night). ⑧ adv. very; greatly; deeply: ～知 know very well; be fully (or keenly) aware／～受感动 be deeply moved; be greatly touched／～感不安 be greatly disturbed; be very much worried／～表同情 show deep (or profound) sympathy／～得人心 enjoy immense popular support／～恐出事 be terribly afraid that something may go wrong

深奥 shēn'ào　abstruse; profound; recondite: ～的哲理 abstruse philosophy; a profound truth／意义～ have a profound significance

深闭固拒 shēnbì-gùjù　obstinate and perverse

深不可测 shēn bùkě cè　unfathomable; enigmatic: 她～地微微一笑。She gave an enigmatic smile.

深藏若虚 shēn cáng ruò xū　hide what one has and act as if one had nothing—be modest about one's talent or ability; not be given to boasting or showing off

深长 shēncháng　(of meaning, intention, etc.) profound

深沉 shēnchén　① deep: 暮色～。The dusk is deepening.／～的哀悼 deep grief over sb.'s death ② (of sound or voice) low-pitched; deep; dull: 大提琴～的音调 the deep notes of a cello／～的夯土声 the dull sound of earth tamping ③ undemonstrative; reserved: ～的微笑 a knowing smile; a significant smile／这人很～。He's a deep one.

深成岩 shēnchéngyán　geol. plutonic rock; plutonite

深仇大恨 shēnchóu-dàhèn　bitter and deep-seated hatred; profound hatred

深处 shēnchù　depths; recesses: 在密林～ in the depths (*or* recesses) of the forest / 在内心～ in the depth (*or* innermost recesses) of one's heart / 在灵魂～ in one's innermost soul / 在思想～ in one's heart of hearts

深度 shēndù　① degree of depth; depth: 测量河水的～ sound the depth of the river ② profundity; depth; thoroughness: 他的发言缺乏～. His speech lacks depth. / 他对这个问题有了一定～的理解 He has gained a fairly deep understanding of this problem. ③ advanced stage of development: 向生产的～和广度进军 boost production both in depth and in breadth

深度计 shēndùjì　depth gauge

深更半夜 shēngēng-bànyè　at dead of night; in the depth (*or* dead) of night; in the middle of the night: 你打哪儿来?～的! Where have you come from so late at night?

深耕 shēngēng　*agric.* deep ploughing

深沟高垒 shēngōu-gāolěi　deep trenches and high ramparts; strong defence

深广 shēnguǎng　deep and broad: 影响～ of wide and profound influence / 见识～ of wide experience and deep knowledge

深闺 shēnguī　boudoir

深海 shēnhǎi　deep sea

深海采矿 shēnhǎi cǎikuàng　deep-sea mining

深海测量 shēnhǎi cèliáng　bathymetry

深海带 shēnhǎidài　abyssal zone

深海鱼 shēnhǎiyú　deep-sea fish

深海资源 shēnhǎi zīyuán　deep-sea resources

深厚 shēnhòu　① deep; profound: ～的感情 deep (*or* profound) feelings / 结成～的友谊 establish a profound friendship ② solid; deep-seated: ～的基础 a solid foundation

深呼吸 shēnhūxī　deep breathing

深化 shēnhuà　deepen: 认识的～ deepening of cognition / 矛盾的～ intensification of a contradiction

深交 shēnjiāo　deep friendship: 他们彼此还谈得来, 虽然并没有～. They get along quite well, though they are not close friends.

深究 shēnjiū　go into (a matter) seriously; get to the bottom of (a matter): 对这些小事不必～. These are small matters and you don't have to go into them seriously.

深居简出 shēnjū-jiǎnchū　live in the seclusion of one's own home

深刻 shēnkè　deep; profound; deepgoing: ～地阐明 expound profoundly / 给某人留下～的印象 make a deep impression on sb. / 受到一次～的教育 learn a profound lesson / 一次～的革命 a deepgoing revolution

深空 shēnkōng　*phys.* deep space

深明大义 shēn míng dàyì　be deeply conscious of the righteousness of a cause; be clear on matters of principle

深谋远虑 shēnmóu-yuǎnlǜ　think deeply and plan carefully; be circumspect and far-sighted

深浅 shēnqiǎn　① depth: 你去探一下这条小河的～, 看能不能蹚水过去. Go and find out how deep the stream is and whether we can wade across. ② shade (of colour): 颜色～不同 of different shades ③ proper limits (for speech or action); sense of propriety: 说话没个～ speak without thought and often inappropriately

深切 shēnqiè　① heartfelt; deep; profound: ～的同情 deep sympathy / ～关怀 be deeply concerned about; show profound concern for / ～怀念 dearly cherish the memory of / 表示～的哀悼 express one's heartfelt condolences (to the deceased's family); express one's profound grief (at sb.'s death) ② keen; penetrating; thorough: ～地感受到 keenly realize / ～地理解 understand thoroughly

深情 shēnqíng　deep feeling; deep love: 她～地望着她母亲的遗像. She gazed with deep feeling at the portrait of her deceased mother.

深情厚谊 shēnqíng-hòuyì　profound sentiments of friendship; profound friendship

深秋 shēnqiū　late autumn

深入 shēnrù　① go deep into; penetrate into: ～实际 go deep into the realities of life / ～敌后 penetrate far behind enemy lines / ～基层 go down to the grass-roots units / ～群众 immerse oneself (*or* go deep) among the masses; go into the midst of the common people / ～农业生产第一线 go right to the front line of agricultural production / ～生活 plunge into the thick of life / ～事物本质 probe deeply into the essence of things / 诱敌～ lure the enemy in deep ② thorough; deepgoing: 做～细致的思想工作 conduct thoroughgoing and painstaking ideological work / ～进行调查研究 make a thorough investigation and study / 运动正在～发展. The movement is developing in depth.

深入浅出 shēnrù-qiǎnchū　explain the profound in simple terms

深入人心 shēnrù rénxīn　strike root in the hearts of the people

深山 shēnshān　remote mountains: ～老林 remote, thickly forested mountains

深深 shēnshēn　deeply; keenly; profoundly: ～地鞠个躬 make a deep bow / ～地吸一口气 take a deep breath / ～感到友情的温暖 keenly feel the warmth of sb.'s friendship / 在群众中～地扎下了根 strike deep root (*or* take firm root) among the masses / 她的话～地铭刻在我心上。Her advice was indelibly engraved on my mind.

深水 shēnshuǐ　deep water

深水港 shēnshuǐgǎng　deepwater port

深水码头 shēnshuǐ mǎtou　deepwater wharf

深水炸弹 shēnshuǐ zhàdàn　depth charge; depth bomb

深思 shēnsī　think deeply about; ponder deeply over: 这难道不值得～吗? Is this not worth pondering? *or* Does this not call for deep thought? / 这个问题值得我们～. This matter gives us much food for thought.

深思熟虑 shēnsī-shúlǜ　careful consideration: 这个决定是他们经过～后作出的. Their decision was made after careful consideration.

深邃 shēnsuì　① deep: ～的山谷 a deep valley ② profound; abstruse; recondite: 寓意～ have a profound message

深谈 shēntán　discuss thoroughly; go deeply into: 这个问题我没同他～. I didn't go deeply into the matter with him.

深通 shēntōng　have a thorough understanding of; be thoroughly versed in: 他～三门外语。He has a thorough command of three foreign languages.

深透 shēntòu　deep and thorough: 问题必须分析～. We must make a deep and thorough analysis of the problem.

深望 shēnwàng　*formal* sincerely wish; earnestly hope: 上述困难, ～有关部门予以妥善解决。We earnestly hope that the departments concerned will find appropriate solutions to the problems mentioned above.

深文周纳 shēnwén-zhōunà　apply the law with the utmost severity and make sb. appear guilty

深恶痛绝 shēnwù-tòngjué　hate bitterly; abhor; detest

深悉 shēnxī　know very well; understand thoroughly

深信 shēnxìn　be deeply convinced; firmly believe

深省 shēnxǐng　(also 深醒 shēnxǐng) wake up to a sharp awareness of the truth: 发人深省 fā rén shēnxǐng

深夜 shēnyè　late at night; in the small hours of the morning: 工作到～ work far into the night

深意 shēnyì　profound meaning: 领会文章的～ grasp the profound meaning of the article

深渊 shēnyuān　abyss: 苦难的～ the abyss of suffering (or misery)

深远 shēnyuǎn　profound and lasting; far-reaching: 具有～的历史意义 have profound historic significance / 影响～ have a far-reaching influence

深造 shēnzào　take a more advanced course of study or training; pursue advanced studies: 送到体育学院～ be sent to the Institute of Physical Culture for further training / 上中央民族学院～ go to the Central Nationalities Institute for advanced studies / 出国～ pursue advanced studies abroad

深宅大院 shēnzhái-dàyuàn　imposing dwellings and spacious courtyards (a compound of deep, spacious quadrangles one leading into another, usu. occupied by a single wealthy family in the old days)

深湛 shēnzhàn　profound and thorough: ～的著作 a profound work / 功夫～ consummate skill

深挚 shēnzhì　deep and sincere: ～的友谊 deep and sincere friendship; intimate friendship

深重 shēnzhòng　very grave; extremely serious: 危机～ be in the grip of a crisis

糁(糝、籸) shēn　crushed grain: 玉米～儿 crushed corn

鲹(鰺) shēn　carangid (including scads, jacks, etc.)

shén

什(甚) shén　see below——see also shí

什么 shénme　① (used before a noun or by itself) what: 你找～? What are you looking for? / 你找～人? Who are you looking for? / 你的理想是～? What is your ideal in life? / ～叫超现实主义? What is surrealism? / 她喜欢做～工作? What sort of job would she like to take? / ～时候啦? What time is it? / 你～时候去武汉? When will you leave for Wuhan? ② something; anything: 我想吃点～。I'd like to have something to eat. / 好像出了～事。It seems something is amiss. / 你读过他的～作品吗? Have you read any of his books? / 没有～, 您不必介意。Never mind, it's nothing. / 我讲不出～新鲜玩意儿。There won't be anything new in my story. ③ (used before 也 or 都) any; every: 他～都不怕。He's afraid of nothing. / 经理正忙着, ～人也不见。The manager is too busy to see anybody. / 他除了抽烟, ～嗜好也没有。He has no other addictions than smoking. / 时间比～都宝贵。Time is more precious than anything else. ④ (used correlatively with another 什么) whatever: 冰箱里有～, 咱们就吃～。We'll eat whatever we can find in the fridge. / 我有～说～, 绝对没有保留。I'll just say what's on my mind, withholding nothing. ⑤ (expressing anger, surprise, censure or negation): ～! 没有水? What! No water? / ～! 都九点了, 车还没有来! What's happened? It's 9 o'clock and the taxi isn't here yet! / 他知道～! What the hell does he know? / 你说的是～话! You're talking sheer nonsense! / 笑～? 有～可笑的? What's so funny? / 你说呀! 装～哑巴? Speak up! Stop playing dumb. / 你嚷嚷～! 有话好好儿的对她说嘛。Stop shouting! Speak to her nicely. ⑥ (expressing disapproval or disagreement): ～不懂! 装糊涂就是了。What do you mean—not understand? You're just pretending. / 年轻～呀, 我都五十多了。Young indeed! I'm past 50 already. / 给您添麻烦了! —麻烦～! Sorry to have troubled you.—It's nothing. ⑦ things like; such as; and so on; and what not: ～缝缝补补, 洗洗涮涮, 都是奶奶的事儿。In our house it's Grandma who does all the sewing, mending, washing and what not. / ～乒乓球啊, 羽毛球啊, 篮球啊, 他都会玩。He can play table tennis, badminton, volleyball, anything.

什么的 shénmede　(used after a series of items) things like that; and so on; and what not: 她做了棉衣、棉鞋～, 准备儿子下乡时穿。She made cotton-padded clothes and shoes and what not for her son to wear in the countryside. / 修个机器, 换个零件～, 他都能对付。Repairing a machine or replacing a part—he can cope with things like that all right. / 他不喜欢打篮球～, 就爱下个围棋。He doesn't go in for basketball and things like that; what he's really keen on is go.

神 shén　① god; deity; divinity: ～鬼 gods and ghosts ② supernatural; magical; miraculous: ～投手 sharpshooter (in basketball); a superb shooter or scorer ③ spirit; mind: 耗～ take up one's energy / 双目有～ have a pair of piercing eyes ④ expression; look: 眼神 yǎnshén ⑤ dial. smart; clever: 这孩子真～! What a smart child! / 这家伙～了! This fellow is incredible!

神不守舍 shén bù shǒu shè　be out of one's wits; be distracted

神不知鬼不觉 shén bù zhī guǐ bù jué　unknown to god or ghost—without anybody knowing it; with great secrecy: 她想起那天晚上, ～地, 他突然在她背后出现。She recalled that evening when he had sprung up behind her as if from nowhere.

神采 shéncǎi　demeanour; mien; countenance: 他的眼睛充满了喜悦的～。His eyes beamed with joy.

神采奕奕 shéncǎi yìyì　glowing with health and radiating vigour

神差鬼使 shénchāi-guǐshǐ　same as 鬼使神差 guǐshǐ-shénchāi

神出鬼没 shénchū-guǐmò　come and go like a shadow; appear and disappear mysteriously: 游击队在敌人后方～地活动。The guerrilla units mysteriously appeared and disappeared in operations behind enemy lines.

神道[1] shéndào　① the way of the gods ② inf. gods; deities; divinities

神道[2] shéndào　aisle leading to the coffin chamber of an ancient tomb; tomb passage

神道[3] Shéndào　Shinto (the native religion of Japan); Shintoism

神道碑 shéndàobēi　① a stone tablet guarding a tomb passage on which are engraved the deeds of the deceased ② the inscription on such a stone tablet

神风突击队 shénfēng tūjīduì　kamikaze (Japan's corps of suicide pilots in World War Ⅱ)

神甫 shénfu　(also 神父 shénfu) Father (a title of respect for a Roman Catholic priest)

神工鬼斧 shéngōng-guǐfǔ　same as 鬼斧神工 guǐfǔ-shéngōng

神怪 shén-guài　gods and spirits

神汉 shénhàn　sorcerer

神乎其神 shén hū qí shén　fantastic; wonderful; miraculous: 吹得～ laud sth. or sb. to the skies

神乎 shénhu　strange; odd; sensational; fantastic: 他越说越～。As he talked, his story became more and more fantastic.

神化 shénhuà　deify

神话 shénhuà　mythology; myth; fairy tale

神魂 shénhún　state of mind; mind: ～不安 be distracted; have the jitters

神魂不定 shénhún bù dìng　be distracted; be deeply perturbed

神魂颠倒 shénhún diāndǎo　be infatuated: 他叫那个女人给弄得～了。He lost his head over that woman.

神机妙算 shénjī-miàosuàn　a superb strategy, a miracle

of foresight; wonderful foresight in military operations, etc.: 我们敬佩老将军的～。We admired the old general for his superb strategy and wonderful foresight.

神交 shénjiāo ① friends with mutual understanding and admiration ② friendship grown out of mutual admiration without the friends ever having met

神经 shénjīng nerve: 脑(感觉, 交感)～ cranial (sensory, sympathetic) nerve / ～紧张 be nervous; be jittery / ～坚强 have strong nerves; have iron nerves / 刺激了他的～ got on his nerves; gave him the nerves

神经病 shénjīngbìng ① neuropathy ② mental disorder; nervous disorder; neurosis ③ mentally disordered; neurotic: 这家伙有点～。That chap's not quite right in the head.

神经错乱 shénjīng cuòluàn ① mental disorder ② suffer from mental disorder

神经毒气 shénjīng dúqì nerve gas

神经官能症 shénjīng guānnéngzhèng neurosis

神经过敏 shénjīng guòmǐn ① neuroticism ② neurotic; oversensitive

神经节 shénjīngjié ganglion

神经末梢 shénjīng mòshāo nerve ending

神经衰弱 shénjīng shuāiruò neurasthenia

神经索 shénjīngsuǒ nerve cord

神经痛 shénjīngtòng neuralgia

神经外科 shénjīng wàikē neurosurgery

神经系统 shénjīng xìtǒng nervous system

神经细胞 shénjīng xìbāo same as 神经元 shénjīngyuán

神经纤维 shénjīng xiānwéi nerve fibre

神经性皮炎 shénjīngxìng píyán neurodermatitis

神经炎 shénjīngyán neuritis

神经元 shénjīngyuán (also 神经原 shénjīngyuán) neuron; nerve cell

神经战 shénjīngzhàn war of nerves

神经质 shénjīngzhì nervousness

神经中枢 shénjīng zhōngshū nerve centre

神龛 shénkān a shrine for idols or ancestral tablets

神来之笔 shén lái zhī bǐ an inspired work; a stroke of genius

神力 shénlì superhuman strength; extraordinary power

神聊 shénliáo indulge in idle and empty talk: 他俩只要一见面, 就天南海北地～起来。Whenever they met, they would start chattering away about everything under the sun.

神灵 shénlíng gods; deities; divinities

神秘 shénmì mysterious; mystical: ～人物 a mysterious person; a person shrouded in mystery / 哲学并不～。Philosophy is no mystery.

神秘化 shénmìhuà make a mystery of; mystify

神秘主义 shénmìzhǔyì mysticism

神妙 shénmiào wonderful; marvellous; ingenious: ～的笔法 wonderful style of writing; ingenious brushwork

神明 shénmíng gods; deities; divinities: 我死而有知, 必当诉之～。If my spirit survives after death, I will certainly take my case to the gods.

神农 Shénnóng the Holy Farmer (a legendary ruler, the 2nd of the Three August Ones 三皇, supposed to have invented the plough and discovered the curative virtues of plants)

神女 shénnǚ ① goddess ② old euph. prostitute

神牌 shénpái same as 神位 shénwèi

神炮手 shénpàoshǒu crack gunner

神品 shénpǐn ① a sublime work (usu. said of a painting or a piece of calligraphy) ② Christianity Catholicism holy orders

神婆 shénpó dial. sorceress; witch

神祇 shénqí formal gods; deities: 上下～ the gods of Heaven and Earth

神奇 shénqí magical; mystical; miraculous: ～的效果 miraculous effect; magical effect / 这些古代传说都被人们渲染上一层～的色彩。Through the ages, these legends have acquired an element of mystery and wonder.

神气 shén·qì ① expression; air; manner: 他脸上显出得意的～. He had an air of complacency. / 他说话的～特别像他爸爸。He is very much like his father in the way he speaks. ② spirited; vigorous: 小明带上红领巾多～. Xiaoming looks quite impressive with his red scarf. ③ putting on airs; cocky; overweening: 呵! 他倒一起来了。Humph! What airs he gives himself! / 你～什么? What makes you think you're so wonderful? or You've got nothing to be cocky about.

神气活现 shénqì huóxiàn very cocky; high and mighty: 看她那个～的样子, 真叫人受不了。Look how she gives herself airs. It's really unbearable.

神气十足 shénqì shízú looking very dignified; putting on grand airs; looking triumphant: 他～地走在前边。He was proudly marching in the fore.

神器 shénqì formal ① the throne; imperial power ② a magic weapon or implement

神枪手 shénqiāngshǒu crack shot; expert marksman; sharpshooter

神情 shénqíng expression; look: 露出愉快的～ look happy; wear a happy expression / ～尴尬 look embarrassed

神曲 shénqū Chin. med. medicated leaven

神权 shénquán ① religious authority; theocracy ② rule by divine right

神人 shénrén ① spiritual being; Taoist immortal ② a man of distinguished appearance

神色 shénsè expression; look: ～不对 look queer / ～慌张 look flustered

神色自若 shénsè zìruò be perfectly calm and collected; show composure and presence of mind

神社 shénshè ① place of worship; shrine; altar ② a Shinto shrine; jinja

神神道道 shénshendàodāo dial. odd; fantastic; bizarre: 这人～的。He's very odd.

神圣 shénshèng sacred; holy: ～职责 sacred duty / ～权利 sacred right / 我国领土～不可侵犯。Our territory is sacred and inviolable.

神圣罗马帝国 Shénshèng Luómǎ Dìguó hist. the Holy Roman Empire (962-1806)

神圣同盟 Shénshèng Tóngméng hist. the Holy Alliance (1815-1830)

神思 shénsī state of mind; mental state: ～不定 be distracted / 定一定～ manage to collect oneself

神思恍惚 shénsī huǎnghū be distracted; be distraught; be in a trance

神似 shénsì be alike in spirit; be an excellent likeness: 不仅形似, 而且～ be alike not only in appearance but also in spirit / 他画的奔马, 栩栩如生, 极其～。The galloping horses he paints are extremely lifelike.

神速 shénsù marvellously quick; with amazing speed: 收效～ yield marvellously quick results / ～地向前挺进 advance with lightning speed

神算 shénsuàn miraculous foresight; marvellous prediction

神态 shéntài expression; manner; bearing; mien: ～悠闲 look perfectly relaxed / 看她的～像舞蹈演员。From the way she carries herself she must be a dancer.

神通 shéntōng magic power; remarkable ability: 大显神通 dà xiǎn shéntōng

神通广大 shéntōng guǎngdà have vast magic powers; possess unusual powers; be infinitely resourceful: 孙悟空～。Sun Wukong had vast magic powers. / 他～, 会招摇撞骗, 又和军政界有联络。He was infinitely resourceful, knew how to bluff his way, and had contacts

神童 shéntóng　child prodigy

神往 shénwǎng　be carried away; be rapt; be charmed: 令人神往 lìng rén shénwǎng

神威 shénwēi　martial prowess; invincible might: 人民军队的～ the martial prowess of the people's army

神位 shénwèi　spirit tablet

神巫 shénwū　wizard; sorcerer

神武 shénwǔ　*formal* divine and mighty (usu. said of an emperor or a great general)

神物 shénwù　*formal* ① wonder; prodigy; phenomenon ② supernatural being; deity

神悟 shénwù　*formal* divine intelligence

神仙 shénxian　① supernatural being; celestial being; immortal ② a person who has the power of clairvoyance or who is free from worldly cares

神仙葫芦 shénxian húlu　*mech.* chain block

神仙鱼 shénxianyú　angelfish

神像 shénxiàng　the picture or statue of a god or Buddha

神效 shénxiào　magical effect; miraculous effect

神学 shénxué　theology

神学博士 shénxué bóshì　Doctor of Divinity (D. D.)

神学院 shénxuéyuàn　theological seminary

神医 shényī　highly skilled doctor; miracle-working doctor

神异 shényì　① gods and spirits ② magical; mystical; miraculous

神鹰 shényīng　*zool.* condor

神勇 shényǒng　extraordinarily brave; superhumanly brave

神游 shényóu　*formal* make a spiritual tour; range in fancy: 故国～，多情应笑我，早生华发。(苏轼) As my spirit wanders to the ancient kingdom, You may well laugh at me for being so sentimental And growing grey hair so soon!

神宇 shényǔ　*formal* mien; bearing; air

神韵 shényùn　romantic charm (in literature and art)

神职人员 shénzhí rényuán　clergy; clergymen

神志 shénzhì　consciousness; senses; mind: ～清醒 be in one's right mind; remain fully conscious / ～昏迷 have lost consciousness; be in a state of delirium

神智 shénzhì　mind; intellect

神州 Shénzhōu　the Divine Land (a poetic name for China): 春风杨柳万千条，六亿～尽舜尧。(毛泽东) The spring wind blowing amid profuse willow wands, Six hundred million in this Divine Land all Yaos and Shuns.

神主 shénzhǔ　ancestral tablet

钟
shén　*chem.* arsonium

shěn

沈¹（瀋）　Shěn　short for 沈阳 Shěnyáng

沈²　Shěn　a surname

沈阳 Shěnyáng　Shenyang (Mukden, capital of Liaoning Province)

沈阳事变 Shěnyáng Shìbiàn　the Shenyang (Mukden) Incident (Sept. 18, 1931)

审¹（審）　shěn　① careful; meticulous: 审视 shěnshì ② examine; go over: ～稿 go over a manuscript or draft and give comments ③ interrogate; try: ～案 try a case

审²（審、讅）　shěn　*formal* know; be aware of: 未～其详 not know the details

审³（審）　shěn　*formal* indeed; really: ～如其言。What he says is indeed true.

审查 shěnchá　examine (plans, proposals, credentials, etc.); investigate: ～属实。The fact was established after investigation. / ～经费 check up on the funds / 报上级～批准 submit to the higher level for examination and approval / ～证书 examine credentials / ～干部 examine the cadres' personal histories

审察 shěnchá　① closely observe; closely examine ② investigate

审处 shěnchǔ　① try and punish: 交由人民法院～ hand over to the people's court for trial ② deliberate and decide

审订 shěndìng　examine and revise; revise: ～教材 revise teaching materials / 请李教授～此稿。Ask Professor Li to make a critical examination of this manuscript (or to revise this manuscript).

审定 shěndìng　examine and approve; examine and finalize: 计划已由委员会～。The plan has been examined and approved by the committee.

审读 shěndú　read and evaluate (a manuscript); read: 拼版样已经审稿人～通过。The page proofs have been read and approved by the responsible reader.

审改 shěngǎi　examine and revise (a manuscript); revise

审改本 shěngǎiběn　a draft for examination and revision (before printing)

审干 shěngàn　(short for 审查干部) examine the cadres' personal histories

审核 shěnhé　verify; check: ～预算 verify a budget / ～存货清单 check an inventory list / 这些数字必须加以～。These figures will have to be verified.

审计 shěnjì　audit: 进行～ conduct an audit / 对企业事业组织的财务收支进行～监督 supervise through auditing the revenues and expenditures of enterprises and institutions / 事前～ pre-emptive audit / 事后～ programme result audit / 效益～ effectiveness audit

审计机构 shěnjì jīgòu　auditing bodies

审计员 shěnjìyuán　auditor

审计长 shěnjìzhǎng　auditor general

审校 shěnjiào　① check and revise ② reviser

审理 shěnlǐ　*leg.* try; hear: ～案件 try a case; hear a case / ～诉讼案 adjudicate a litigation

审美 shěnměi　appreciation of the beautiful: ～能力 aesthetic judgment

审美观 shěnměiguān　aesthetic conceptions; aesthetic standards

审判 shěnpàn　bring to trial; try: 受到人民的～ be tried by the people / 由军事法庭～ be court-martialled / ～经济案件 try economic cases

审判程序 shěnpàn chéngxù　judicial procedure

审判机关 shěnpàn jīguān　judicial organ

审判权 shěnpànquán　judicial authority; jurisdiction

审判员 shěnpànyuán　judge; judicial officer

审判长 shěnpànzhǎng　presiding judge

审批 shěnpī　examine and approve; examine and give instructions: 报请上级～ submit to the higher level for examination and approval

审慎 shěnshèn　cautious; careful; circumspect: ～从事 steer a cautious course / ～地考虑问题 think over a problem carefully / 采取坚决～的方针 adopt resolute yet cautious policies / 处理这个问题必须～。The matter has to be handled with circumspection. / ～乐观 cautious optimism; guarded optimism

审时度势 shěnshí-duóshì　judge the hour and size up the

situation: 他是一位善于～、多谋善断的经理人员。He is a resourceful and resolute manager who can make a correct assessment of the situation.

审视 shěnshì　look closely at; examine closely: 他～再三, 未置可否。He examined it closely over and over again, but still declined to give any comment.

审问 shěnwèn　interrogate; question: 正在进行～。The interrogation is going on.

审讯 shěnxùn　*leg.*　① hearing: 法官对离婚案的双方当事人各给予一次～。The judge gave a hearing to both parties of the divorce case. ② interrogate; hear; try: ～俘虏 interrogate prisoners of war / 送交军事法庭～ hand over to a military tribune for interrogation

审议 shěnyì　(of a deliberative body, a committee, etc.) review; deliberate: 重新～提案 make a critical reexamination of the proposal / 提交全国人民代表大会～ submit sth. to the National People's Congress for review / 这个纲要草案已发给你们, 请～。The draft outline (of the plan) is now submitted to you for review. / 计划在～中。The project is under review. / 安理会已完毕第一项议题。The Security Council has finished reviewing item 1 of the agenda.

审议机构 shěnyì jīgòu　deliberative body

审阅 shěnyuè　examine carefully and critically: 聘请专家～稿件并提出意见 get some specialists to go over the manuscript and give comments and criticisms / 此讲话记录未经本人～。These notes of the speech have not been checked and approved by the speaker.

哂 shěn　*formal*　smile
哂纳 shěnnà　(also 哂收 shěnshōu) *pol.*　kindly accept: 区区薄礼, 聊表敬意, 务祈～。I beg you to accept this gift as a small token of my esteem.
哂笑 shěnxiào　① *formal*　laugh at; ridicule ② smile: ～不语 smile but say not a word

矧 shěn　*formal*　besides; moreover; also
谂 shěn　*formal*　① know; be aware of ② advise; urge
谂熟 shěnshú　know sth. or sb. well; be familiar with; have an intimate knowledge of

婶(嬸) shěn　① wife of father's younger brother; aunt ② a form of address for a woman about one's mother's age; aunt; auntie: 张大～ Aunt Zhang
婶母 shěnmǔ　wife of father's younger brother; aunt
婶娘 shěnniáng　*dial.*　wife of father's younger brother; aunt
婶婆 shěnpó　husband's aunt
婶婶 shěnshen　*dial.*　wife of father's younger brother; aunt
婶子 shěnzi　*inf.*　wife of father's younger brother; aunt

shèn

肾(腎) shèn　*physiol.*　kidney
肾功能试验 shèngōngnéng shìyàn　kidney function test
肾功能衰竭 shèngōngnéng shuāijié　renal failure; kidney failure
肾结石 shènjiéshí　*med.*　kidney stone; renal calculus
肾亏 shènkuī　*Chin. med.*　renal weakness
肾囊 shènnáng　*Chin. med.*　scrotum
肾上腺 shènshàngxiàn　*physiol.*　adrenal gland; adrenal
肾上腺素 shènshàngxiànsù　adrenaline
肾下垂 shènxiàchuí　nephroptosis
肾炎 shènyán　nephritis

肾移植 shènyízhí　kidney transplant; renal transplant
肾盂 shènyú　*physiol.*　renal pelvis
肾盂肾炎 shènyú shènyán　pyelonephritis
肾盂炎 shènyúyán　pyelitis
肾脏 shènzàng　kidney

甚¹ shèn　① very; extremely: 知者～少。Very few people know about it. ② more than: 他的病情恶化, 日～一日。His condition got worse and worse. *or* His condition steadily deteriorated.

甚² shèn　*dial.*　what; whatever: ～事? What is it? / 有～说～。Just say what you've got to say. / 那有～要紧? What does it matter?

甚而 shèn'ér　same as 甚至 shènzhì
甚而至于 shèn'érzhìyú　same as 甚至 shènzhì
甚高频 shèngāopín　*radio*　very high frequency (vhf)
甚或 shènhuò　*formal*　① *adv.*　even to the extent that ② *conj.*　(go) so far as to; so much so that
甚且 shènqiě　same as 甚至 shènzhì
甚为 shènwéi　very; extremely: ～痛快 find it most satisfying / 两人～亲密。They are quite intimate.
甚嚣尘上 shèn xiāo chén shàng　cause a great clamour: 所谓和战问题竟闹得～。A great clamour arose around the question of peace or war.
甚至 shènzhì　(also 甚至于 shènzhìyú) ① *adv.*　even to the extent that: 他忙得～好几夜没睡觉。He was so busy that he didn't even go to bed for several nights. ② *conj.*　(go) so far as to; so much so that: 他对同志们的批评置若罔闻, ～反唇相讥。He not only ignored the criticism of his comrades but went so far as to be sarcastic.

肿 shèn　*chem.*　arsine

渗(滲) shèn　ooze; seep: 包扎伤口的绷带上～出了血。Blood oozed out of the dressing. / 雨水都～到地里去了。The rain all seeped into the ground.
渗沟 shèngōu　sewer
渗坑 shènkēng　seepage pit
渗漏 shènlòu　seepage: ～损失 seepage loss
渗滤 shènlǜ　*chem.*　percolation filtration; percolation
渗滤白土 shènlǜ báitǔ　*petroleum*　percolation clay
渗滤器 shènlǜqì　percolator
渗入 shènrù　① permeate; seep into: ～地下 permeate the ground; seep into the ground ② *derog.*　(of influence, etc.) penetrate; infiltrate
渗色 shènsè　*text.*　bleeding
渗碳 shèntàn　*metall.*　carburization; cementation
渗碳钢 shèntàngāng　carburizing steel
渗碳体 shèntàntǐ　cementite
渗透 shèntòu　① *phys.*　osmosis ② permeate; seep: 雨水～了泥土。The rain permeated the soil. / 每一件产品都～了工人的心血。Every product embodies the painstaking effort of the workers. ③ infiltrate: 经济～ economic infiltration
渗透性 shèntòuxìng　permeability
渗透压 shèntòuyā　osmotic pressure
渗透战术 shèntòu zhànshù　infiltration tactics

葚 shèn　see 桑葚 sāngshèn ——see also rèn

慎 shèn　careful; cautious: 保守国家机密, ～之又～。One cannot be too careful in guarding state secrets. / 不～ careless
慎独 shèndú　be careful of oneself when alone—try to be blameless in one's private life
慎密 shènmì　cautious and meticulous
慎言慎行 shènyán-shènxíng　be cautious in speech and

in conduct

慎重 shènzhòng cautious; careful; prudent; discreet: 采取～的态度 adopt a prudent policy / 处理这件事必须～。The matter has to be handled with great care. / 经过～考虑，我们决定延期开会。After careful consideration we decided to postpone the meeting. / ～初战，务求必胜。Be prudent in fighting the first battle and be sure to win.

唇 shèn clam

唇景 shènjǐng same as 海市唇楼 hǎishì shènlóu

瘆（瘆） shèn horrify: ～人 making one's flesh creep; horrifying / ～得慌 be horrified

shēng

升[1]（**昇**） shēng rise; hoist; go up; ascend: 东方红，太阳～。In the east the sky is red. The sun is rising.

升[2]（**昇**、**陞**） shēng promote: ～教授 get promoted to professor / ～到领导岗位 be promoted to positions of leadership

升[3] shēng ① litre (l.): 三～啤酒 three litres of beer ② *sheng*, later called 市升 shìshēng, a tradtional unit of capacity (see also 市升 shìshēng) ③ a *sheng* measure, equal to 0.1 *dou* 斗

升班 shēngbān *inf.* go up (one grade in school)

升船机 shēngchuánjī ship lift

升调 shēngdiào *phonet.* rising tune or tone

升格 shēnggé raise; promote; upgrade: 将外交关系～大使级 upgrade diplomatic relations to ambassadorial level / 将各自外交代表由公使～为大使 raise the status of their respective diplomatic representatives from Minister to Ambassador / 整顿近几年～的结构 reorganize organs that have been upgraded in recent years

升汞 shēnggǒng *chem.* mercuric chloride

升官 shēngguān be promoted

升官发财 shēngguān-fācái win promotion and get rich; (be out for) power and money

升号 shēnghào *mus.* sharp (♯)

升华 shēnghuá ① *phys.* sublimation ② raising of things to a higher level; distillation; sublimation: 艺术是现实生活的～。Art is the distillation of life.

升华干燥 shēnghuá gānzào lyophilization

升级 shēngjí ① go up one or more grades: 连升三级 be promoted three grades in succession ② escalate: 战争～ escalation (of a war) / 个别地区的冲突还存在着～的危险。There is still a danger of escalation of some regional conflicts.

升降 shēng-jiàng go up and down

升降舵 shēngjiàngduò *aviation* elevator

升降机 shēngjiàngjī elevator; lift

升降奖惩 shēng-jiàng-jiǎng-chéng promotion and demotion, reward and punishment

升力 shēnglì *aviation* lift: ～特性 lift efficiency

升幂 shēngmì *math.* ascending power: ～级数 ascending power series

升平 shēngpíng peace: ～世界 peaceful world; peaceful life

升旗 shēngqí hoist (*or* raise) a flag: ～仪式 flag-raising ceremony

升迁 shēngqiān be transferred and promoted

升水 shēngshuǐ *econ.* premium

升水率 shēngshuǐlǜ premium rate

升堂入室 shēngtáng-rùshì pass through the hall into the inner chamber—have profound scholarship; become highly proficient

升腾 shēngténg (of flames, gas, etc.) leap up; rise: 火焰～。The flames leapt up. / 山头上～起白蒙蒙的雾气。A thick mist rose over the hilltop.

升天 shēngtiān go up to Heaven—die

升限 shēngxiàn *aviation* ceiling: ～高度 ceiling height

升学 shēngxué go to a school of a higher grade; enter a higher school

升学率 shēngxuélǜ the proportion of students entering schools of a higher grade

升压 shēngyā *elec.* step up; boost

升压变压器 shēngyā biànyāqì step-up transformer

升压器 shēngyāqì booster

升值 shēngzhí *econ.* ① revalue ② appreciate

生[1] shēng ① give birth to; bear: ～孩子 give birth to a child ② be born; come into existence: 她～下来不多日子，她妈就死了。Her mother died soon after she was born. ③ grow: ～芽 sprout ④ life; living: 一生 yīshēng / 谋生 móushēng ⑤ alive; living: 生龙活虎 shēnglóng-huóhǔ / 生擒 shēngqín ⑥ be afflicted with; get; have: ～疖子 get boils / ～冻疮 get chilblains ⑦ light (a fire): ～炉子 light a stove

生[2] shēng ① unripe; green: ～的苹果 a green apple / 这些桃子还是～的。The peaches are not ripe yet. ② raw; uncooked: ～肉 raw meat / 黄瓜可以～吃。Cucumbers can be eaten raw. ③ unprocessed; unrefined; crude: 生石膏 shēngshígāo ④ unfamiliar; unacquainted; strange: 刚到这里，工作还很～。I've only just come here. I'm still not familiar with the work. ⑤ stiff; mechanical: 生凑 shēngcòu ⑥ *adv.* (used before certain words indicating feeling or perception) very; much: ～疼 very painful

生[3] shēng ① pupil; student: 留级～ a pupil who is repeating the year's work ② intellectual; scholar: 书生 shūshēng ③ male role (one of the four main roles in traditional opera, the other three being 旦 dàn, 净 jìng, and 丑 chǒu; subdivided into 老生 lǎoshēng, 小生 xiǎoshēng, 武生 wǔshēng, etc.) ④ (noun suffix, used in names of occupations or stations of persons): 医～ doctor

生搬硬套 shēngbān-yìngtào copy mechanically, disregarding specific conditions; apply or copy mechanically

生变 shēngbiàn trouble arises: 日久～。Delay means trouble.

生病 shēngbìng fall ill

生不逢辰 shēng bù féng chén (also 生不逢时 shēng bù féng shí) be born out of one's time; be born at the wrong time

生财 shēngcái develop financial resources; make money

生财有道 shēngcái yǒu dào know how to make money; have the knack of making money

生菜 shēngcài ① romaine lettuce; cos lettuce ② lettuce

生产 shēngchǎn ① produce; manufacture: 此地～水稻和生丝。This place produces rice and raw silk. / 我们自己要多～些粮食。We must produce more food for ourselves. / 那家工厂～汽车。That factory produces (*or* manufactures) automobiles. / 新车间已投入～。The new workshop has gone into operation. / 坚守～岗位 stick to one's post on the production front / 挖掘～潜力 tap the productive potentialities / 达到～定额 meet the required production quotas ② give birth to a

child: 她快～了。She'll be having her baby soon. *or* She's expecting her baby soon.

生产成本 shēngchǎn chéngběn cost of production; manufacturing cost

生产大队 shēngchǎn dàduì production brigade

生产单位 shēngchǎn dānwèi production unit

生产队 shēngchǎnduì production team

生产方式 shēngchǎn fāngshì mode of production

生产工具 shēngchǎn gōngjù tool of production

生产关系 shēngchǎn guānxì relations of production; production relations

生产过剩 shēngchǎn guòshèng overproduction

生产合作社 shēngchǎn hézuòshè producers' cooperative

生产建设兵团 shēngchǎn jiànshè bīngtuán production and construction corps

生产劳动 shēngchǎn láodòng productive labour

生产力 shēngchǎnlì productive forces

生产率 shēngchǎnlù productivity

生产手段 shēngchǎn shǒuduàn means of production

生产要素 shēngchǎn yàosù essential factors of production (e.g. trained personnel, funds, technologies, resources, etc.)

生产责任制 shēngchǎn zérènzhì production responsibility system

生产资料 shēngchǎn zīliào means of production

生产总值 shēngchǎn zǒngzhí total output value

生辰 shēngchén birthday

生辰八字 shēngchén bāzì same as 八字 bāzì

生成 shēngchéng ① come or bring into being; generate; produce: 碳酸钙加热分解,～氧化钙和二氧化碳。The thermal decomposition of calcium carbonate produces calcium oxide and carbon dioxide. ② be born with; be gifted with: 他～的一个塌鼻子。He was born with a flat nose.

生成物 shēngchéngwù *chem.* product; resultant

生成语法 shēngchéng yǔfǎ *linguis.* generative grammar

生齿 shēngchǐ *formal* population; members of a family: ～日繁。The population is growing day by day.

生词 shēngcí words (and phrases) new and unfamiliar to the student; new words

生凑 shēngcòu mechanically put together (disconnected words and phrases); arbitrarily dish up (unrelated facts)

生存 shēngcún subsist; exist; live: 鱼离开了水是不能～的。Fish cannot live without water.

生存竞争 shēngcún jìngzhēng struggle for existence

生存空间 shēngcún kōngjiān living space

生存权 shēngcúnquán right of existence

生旦净丑 shēng-dàn-jìng-chǒu the male role, the female role, the painted-face role, and the comic role (the four main roles in traditional opera)

生地[1] shēngdì (also 生地黄 shēngdìhuáng) *Chin. med.* the dried rhizome of rehmannia (*Rehmannia glutinosa*)

生地[2] shēngdì virgin soil; uncultivated land

生动 shēngdòng lively; vivid: ～的描写 a lively description / 人民的生活是最～最丰富的文学艺术原料。The life of the people is the most vital and rich raw material for literature and art. / 影片～地反映了当代大学生的生活。The film vividly reflects the life of the present-day college students.

生动活泼 shēngdòng huópo lively; vivid and vigorous: ～的语言 vivid language / 这次会开得～。It was a lively meeting.

生端 shēngduān *formal* stir up trouble; create a disturbance: 借故～ find an excuse to make trouble; avail oneself of a pretext to stir up trouble

生而知之 shēng ér zhī zhī be born wise; be born with knowledge; have innate knowledge: 人非～者,孰能无

惑,惑而不从师,其为惑也,终不解矣。(韩愈) As men are not born wise, who can be free from ignorance? But if ignorant men do not find teachers, they remain ignorant for ever.

生法 shēngfǎ *dial.* think of a way; try; do what one can

生发油 shēngfàyóu hair oil; hair lotion

生发 shēngfā develop; grow

生番 shēngfān an aboriginal savage tribe

生分 shēngfen estranged; not as close as before: 很久不来往,就显得～了。Not having seen each other for so long, we don't feel so close any longer.

生俘 shēngfú capture alive

生父 shēngfù one's own father

生根 shēnggēn take root; strike root: 在群众中～开花 take root and blossom among the masses

生光 shēngguāng *meteorol.* third contact (of a total solar or lunar eclipse)

生花妙笔 shēnghuā miàobǐ a brilliant pen; a brilliant style of writing

生还 shēnghuán come back alive; survive: 无一～。None survived.

生荒 shēnghuāng *agric.* virgin soil; uncultivated land

生活 shēnghuó ① life: 日常～ daily life / 政治～ political life ② live: 一个人脱离了社会就不能～下去。One cannot live cut off from society. / 跟群众～在一起 live with the masses ③ livelihood: ～困难 be badly off / 关心群众的～ be concerned with the well-being of the masses / ～出路 a chance to earn a living / ～用品 articles for daily use ④ *dial.* work (of workers, peasants, or handicraftsmen): 勤勤恳恳做～ work diligently at one's job; do conscientious work

生活必需品 shēnghuó bìxūpǐn necessaries of life; daily necessities

生活补助 shēnghuó bǔzhù extra allowance for living expenses

生活方式 shēnghuó fāngshì way of life; life style

生活费 shēnghuófèi living expenses; cost of living: ～指数 cost of living index

生活福利 shēnghuó fúlì welfare; welfare benefits

生活关 shēnghuóguān the test of rigorous living conditions: 过好～ prove oneself able to lead a rigorous life; stand the test of a rigorous life

生活环境 shēnghuó huánjìng surroundings; environment

生活经验 shēnghuó jīngyàn experience of life

生活来源 shēnghuó láiyuán source of income

生活能力 shēnghuó nénglì *biol.* viability

生活水平 shēnghuó shuǐpíng living standard

生活条件 shēnghuó tiáojiàn living conditions

生活习惯 shēnghuó xíguàn habits and customs

生活细节 shēnghuó xìjié trifling matters of everyday life; domestic trivia

生活周期 shēnghuó zhōuqī *biol.* life cycle

生活资料 shēnghuó zīliào means of subsistence; means of livelihood

生活作风 shēnghuó zuòfēng behaviour; conduct

生火 shēnghuǒ make a fire; light a fire

生机 shēngjī ① lease of life: 一线～ a slim chance of survival; a gleam of hope ② life; vitality: 春天来了,田野里充满了～。Spring has come and the fields are full of life.

生机盎然 shēngjī àngrán full of life; overflowing with vigour; exuberant

生计 shēngjì means of livelihood; livelihood: 另谋～ try to find some other means of livelihood

生忌 shēngjì the birthday of a deceased person

生姜 shēngjiāng *inf.* ginger

生津 shēngjīn *Chin. med.* promote the secretion of saliva or body fluid

生境　shēngjìng　*biol.*　habitat

生就　shēngjiù　be born with; be gifted with: ～一张利嘴 have the gift of the gab

生角　shēngjué　same as 生³ shēng③ or, specifically, 老生 lǎoshēng

生客　shēngkè　an unfamiliar guest; stranger

生恐　shēngkǒng　be very much afraid; fear greatly: 他～ 掉队, 在后面紧跟。Afraid of falling behind, he was trying hard to keep up.

生拉硬拽　shēnglā-yìngzhuài　① drag sb. along against his will ② stretch the meaning

生来　shēnglái　*adv.*　from birth: 这孩子身体～就结实。The child was born strong.

生老病死　shēng-lǎo-bìng-sǐ　birth and old age, sickness and death—the lot of man

生冷　shēng-lěng　raw or cold food: 忌食～。Avoid eating anything raw or cold.

生离死别　shēnglí-sǐbié　part never to meet again; part for ever

生理　shēnglǐ　physiology: ～反应 physiological reaction / ～缺陷 physiological defect; physiological deficiency / ～作用 physiological action

生理学　shēnglǐxué　physiology

生理盐水　shēnglǐ yánshuǐ　*pharm.*　physiological saline; normal saline

生力军　shēnglìjūn　① fresh and combat-worthy troops ② fresh activists; new force: 文艺战线上的一支～ a vital new force on the art and literary front

生灵　shēnglíng　*formal*　the people

生灵涂炭　shēnglíng tútàn　the people are plunged into an abyss of misery: 战祸复发, ～。War broke out again, plunging the people into misery and suffering.

生龙活虎　shēnglóng-huóhǔ　doughty as a dragon and lively as a tiger—brimming (*or* bursting) with energy; full of vim and vigour: 小伙子们干起活来真是～。The lads work with furious energy.

生路　shēnglù　means of livelihood; way out: 另谋～ try to find another job; look for a new means of livelihood / 杀出一条～ fight one's way out (of an encirclement)

生米煮成熟饭　shēngmǐ zhǔchéng shúfàn　the rice is cooked—what's done can't be undone

生命　shēngmìng　life: ～不息, 战斗不止 fight as long as one has a breath in one's body; go on fighting till one breathes one's last / 政策和策略是党的～。Policy and tactics are the life of the Party. / 学习古人语言中有～ 的东西 learn whatever is alive in the classical Chinese language / 贪污受贿使他丧失了政治～。Corruption and bribe-taking cost him his political career.

生命力　shēngmìnglì　life-force; vitality: 具有强大的～ have great vitality

生命率　shēngmìnglù　vital rates

生命现象　shēngmìng xiànxiàng　biological phenomena: 用放射性同位素示踪技术探讨～ apply radioisotopic tracers to study biological phenomena

生命线　shēngmìngxiàn　lifeline; lifeblood: 铁路、公路是经 济繁荣的～。Railways and highways are a lifeline to a prosperous economy. / 实地勘探是地质工作的～。Fieldwork is the lifeblood of geology.

生母　shēngmǔ　one's own mother

生怕　shēngpà　be very much afraid; fear greatly: 她轻轻 地走进卧室, ～惊醒了孩子。She went into the bedroom softly so as not to wake her child (*or* lest she should wake her child).

生皮　shēngpí　rawhide; (untanned) hide

生僻　shēngpì　(of words, expressions, etc.) uncommon; rare: ～的字眼 rarely used words / ～的典故 obscure allusions

生平　shēngpíng　all one's life: ～事迹 one's life story / 作者～简介 a brief account of the author's life; a bio-

graphical note on the author / ～第一次 the first time in one's life

生漆　shēngqī　raw lacquer

生气¹　shēngqì　take offence; get angry: 她常无缘无故～。 She often gets angry over nothing. / 他还在生我的气呢。 He is still angry with me.

生气²　shēngqì　vim; vitality: 有～ energetic; dynamic; vigorous / 毫无～ lethargic / 青年是整个社会中的一部 分最积极最有～的力量。Young people are the most ac- tive and dynamic force in society. / 解放前一些濒于绝 境的工艺美术, 现在充满了～。Certain arts and crafts which were on the verge of extinction before liberation are now flourishing.

生气勃勃　shēngqì bóbó　dynamic; vigorous; full of vital- ity: 这支部队～。The unit is bursting with vitality.

生前　shēngqián　before one's death; during one's life- time: ～愿望 unrealized wish (of a person who has passed away) / ～友好 friends of the deceased

生擒　shēngqín　capture alive

生擒活捉　shēngqín-huózhuō　capture alive; take prisoner

生趣　shēngqù　joy of life; pleasures of life

生人¹　shēngrén　stranger

生人²　shēngrén　be born: 他是1949年～。He was born in 1949.

生日　shēngrì　birthday: 今天是他的～。Today is his birthday. / 过～ celebrate a birthday

生色　shēngsè　add colour to; add lustre to; give added significance to: 老师们的演出, 为英语晚会～不少。The teachers' performance made the English evening more enjoyable.

生涩　shēngsè　(of language) jerky; choppy; not smooth

生杀予夺　shēng-shā yǔ-duó　hold power over sb.'s life and property; have sb. completely in one's power

生身父母　shēngshēn fùmǔ　one's own parents

生生世世　shēngshēngshìshì　generation after generation; for generations

生石膏　shēngshígāo　plaster stone

生石灰　shēngshíhuī　quick lime

生事　shēngshì　make trouble; create a disturbance: 这人 脾气很坏, 容易～。He has a bad temper and often makes trouble.

生手　shēngshǒu　sb. new to a job

生疏　shēngshū　① not familiar: 我对这个地方并不算～。 I'm no stranger here. / 我对这项工作很～。I don't know much about the job. ② out of practice; rusty: 他的英文 有点～了。His English is getting rusty. ③ not as close as before: 多年不来往, 我们的关系～了。We haven't been in touch with each other for years, so we're not as close as we used to be.

生水　shēngshuǐ　unboiled water

生丝　shēngsī　raw silk

生死　shēng-sǐ　life and death: 一场～斗争 a life-and- death struggle

生死存亡　shēng-sǐ cún-wáng　life or death, survival or extinction: ～的斗争 a life-and-death struggle / 这个国 家到了一个～的关头。That country has reached a point where its very existence is at stake. / 执政党的党 风关系到党的～。A good work style is vital to the very existence of a party in power.

生死关头　shēng-sǐ guāntóu　a juncture when one's life is at stake; a moment when one's fate hangs in the bal- ance; a critical juncture

生死攸关　shēng-sǐ yōuguān　of vital importance: ～的问 题 a matter of life and death; a matter of vital impor- tance

生死与共　shēng-sǐ yǔ gòng　share a common destiny; go through thick and thin together: ～的战友 comrades- in-arms through thick and thin

生死之交　shēng-sǐ zhī jiāo　friends that are ready to die

for each other

生态 shēngtài organisms' habits, modes of life and relation to their environment; ecology

生态变异 shēngtài biànyì ecocline

生态灭绝 shēngtài mièjué ecocide

生态平衡 shēngtài pínghéng ecological balance

生态圈 shēngtàiquān ecosphere

生态系统 shēngtài xìtǒng ecosystem

生态型 shēngtàixíng ecotype

生态学 shēngtàixué ecology

生铁 shēngtiě pig iron

生土 shēngtǔ immature soil

生吞活剥 shēngtūn-huóbō swallow sth. raw and whole —accept sth. uncritically: 不要～地搬用外国的经验。It's no good taking over the experience of foreign countries uncritically.

生物 shēngwù living things; living beings; organisms: 超显微镜～ ultramicroscopic organisms / 浮游～ plankton / 寄生～ parasites

生物层 shēngwùcéng biosphere

生物地理学 shēngwù dìlǐxué biogeography

生物电流 shēngwù diànliú physiol. bioelectric current

生物发生律 shēngwù fāshēnglǜ biogenetic law; recapitulation theory

生物防治 shēngwù fángzhì agric. biological control

生物工程 shēngwù gōngchéng bioengineering

生物固氮 shēngwù gùdàn biological nitrogen fixation

生物合成 shēngwù héchéng biosynthesis

生物化学 shēngwù huàxué biochemistry

生物碱 shēngwùjiǎn chem. alkaloid

生物量 shēngwùliàng biomass

生物膜 shēngwùmó biomembrane

生物气候学 shēngwù qìhòuxué bioclimatology

生物区 shēngwùqū biotic division

生物圈 shēngwùquān biosphere: 人和～ Man and Biosphere (MAB)

生物群落 shēngwù qúnluò biocommunity

生物生态学 shēngwù shēngtàixué bioecology

生物体 shēngwùtǐ organism

生物武器 shēngwù wǔqì same as 细菌武器 xìjūn wǔqì

生物学 shēngwùxué biology: ～家 biologist

生物岩 shēngwùyán biogenic rock; biolith

生物遥测器 shēngwù yáocèqì biopack

生物战 shēngwùzhàn mil. biological warfare

生物制品 shēngwù zhìpǐn biological product

生物钟 shēngwùzhōng biological clock; biochronometer; living clock

生息[1] shēngxī bear interest: ～资本 interest-bearing capital

生息[2] shēngxī formal ① live; exist: 自古以来,我们的祖先就劳动、～、繁殖在这块土地上。From ancient times our forefathers have laboured, lived and multiplied on this land. ② propagate; multiply; procreate: 休养生息 xiūyǎng shēngxī

生相[1] shēngxiàng looks; features; appearance: 她～好。She is good-looking.

生相[2] shēngxiàng same as 生肖 shēngxiào

生橡胶 shēngxiàngjiāo (also 生胶 shēngjiāo) raw rubber; caoutchouc

生肖 shēngxiào any one of the names of 12 symbolic animals associated with a 12-year cycle, often used to denote the year of a person's birth (the 12 animals are: rat, ox, tiger, hare, dragon, snake, horse, sheep, monkey, cock, dog, and hog): 他～属鼠。He was born in the year of the rat (i.e. 1924, 1936, 1948, 1960, 1972, or 1984).

生效 shēngxiào go into effect; take effect; become effective: 签字后立即～ become effective immediately upon signature / 自签字之日起～ go into effect from the date of signature / 在互换批准书以后立即～ come into force immediately on exchange of the instruments of ratification / ～条款 entry-into-force clause

生性 shēngxìng natural disposition: ～活泼 have a lively disposition

生锈 shēngxiù get rusty: 经常擦油,以免～。Oil it regularly to prevent rust. / 永不～的螺丝钉 a screw that never rusts

生涯 shēngyá career; profession: 舞台～ a stage career / 操笔墨～ write for a living / 政治～ a political career

生养 shēngyǎng inf. give birth to; bear (children): 她结婚多年没有～。She's been married for years but is still childless.

生药 shēngyào crude drug; dried medicinal herbs

生药学 shēngyàoxué pharmacognosy

生业 shēngyè occupation; business: 各安～ each being content with his occupation

生疑 shēngyí be suspicious

生意 shēngyì tendency to grow; life and vitality: ～盎然 full of life / 春天的大地一片蓬勃的～。Spring has filled the earth with life and vitality.

生意 shēngyi business; trade: ～兴隆。Trade is brisk. or Business is booming.

生意经 shēngyijīng the knack of doing business; shrewd business sense

生硬 shēngyìng ① (of writing) not smooth; not polished; crude ② stiff; rigid; harsh: 态度～ be stiff in manner

生油[1] shēngyóu unboiled oil

生油[2] shēngyóu dial. peanut oil

生油层 shēngyóucéng petroleum source bed

生育 shēngyù give birth to; bear: ～子女 bear children / 不能～ be unable to have children; be sterile / 她已过了～年龄。She is past her child-bearing age.

生员 shēngyuán another name for 秀才 xiùcai①

生源说 shēngyuánshuō biol. biogenesis

生造 shēngzào coin (words and expressions): 不要～谁也不懂的词语。Do not coin words and expressions that nobody can understand.

生造词 shēngzàocí coinage

生长 shēngzhǎng ① grow: 小麦～良好。The wheat is growing well. or The wheat is doing fine. ② grow up; be brought up: 他～在武汉。He was born and brought up in Wuhan.

生长点 shēngzhǎngdiǎn bot. growing point

生长激素 shēngzhǎng jīsù growth hormone

生长率 shēngzhǎnglǜ growth rate

生长轮 shēngzhǎnglún growth ring

生长期 shēngzhǎngqī growth period; growing period

生殖 shēngzhí reproduction: 无性～ asexual reproduction / 有性～ sexual reproduction / 营养体～ vegetative reproduction

生殖洄游 shēngzhí huíyóu breeding migration (of some fish)

生殖孔 shēngzhíkǒng gonopore

生殖率 shēngzhílǜ reproduction rate

生殖泌尿系统 shēngzhí mìniào xìtǒng urogenital system

生殖器 shēngzhíqì reproductive organs; genitals

生殖系统 shēngzhí xìtǒng reproductive system

生殖腺 shēngzhíxiàn gonad

生猪 shēngzhū live pig; pig; hog; pork on the hoof

生字 shēngzì words or characters new to the student; new words or characters

生字表 shēngzìbiǎo list of new words (attached to a textbook)

声（聲）

shēng ① sound; voice: 脚步～ the sound of footsteps / 小～说话 speak in a low voice / 高～朗读 read aloud ② make a sound: 不声不响

bùshēng-bùxiǎng ③ the initial of a Chinese syllable: 声母 shēngmǔ ④ tone: 四声 sìshēng ⑤ *m.* (for sounds): 我喊了他两～。 I called to him twice. / 我听见一～炮响。 I heard the sound of a cannon going off. ⑥ reputation: 声誉 shēngyù

声辩 shēngbiàn argue; justify oneself; explain away: 为自己的行为～ try to justify oneself for one's conduct / 不容他人～ not allow others to present their arguments

声波 shēngbō *phys.* sound wave; acoustic wave

声部 shēngbù *mus.* part (in concerted music): 歌唱～分女高音、女低音、男高音、男低音 Soprano, alto, tenor and bass constitute the four vocal parts.

声称 shēngchēng profess; claim; assert: ～已打破僵局 claim to have broken the deadlock

声带 shēngdài ① *physiol.* vocal cords ② soundtrack (on a film)

声调 shēngdiào ① tone; note: ～激昂 in an impassioned tone / ～低沉 in a low, sad voice ② *phonet.* the tone of Chinese characters ——see also 四声 sìshēng

声东击西 shēng dōng jī xī make a feint to the east and attack in the west

声符 shēngfú same as 声旁 shēngpáng

声光 shēngguāng reputation; fame; prestige

声华 shēnghuá *formal* good reputation

声价 shēngjià reputation: ～甚高 (of a person) be held in high repute; be held in high esteem

声控 shēngkòng sound-activated; sound-controlled

声浪 shēnglàng ① old name for 声波 shēngbō ② voice; clamour: 抗议的～ a wave of protest

声泪俱下 shēng-lèi jù xià shedding tears while speaking; in a tearful voice: 他～地诉说了自己的不幸遭遇。 Tears streamed down his cheeks as he recounted his unhappy experience.

声门 shēngmén *physiol.* glottis

声名 shēngmíng reputation

声名狼藉 shēngmíng lángjí have a bad name; be notorious; be utterly discredited

声明 shēngmíng ① state; declare; announce: 他正式～他不是候选人。 He announced officially that he was not a candidate. / 庄严～ solemnly state / 事先～ declare beforehand ② statement; declaration: 联合～ joint statement / 中英关于香港问题的联合～ Sino-British Joint Declaration on the Question of Hong Kong

声母 shēngmǔ *phonet.* the initial of a syllable (usu. a consonant, e.g. b in 报 bào, g in 告 gào, f in 丰 fēng, and sh in 收 shōu; a small number of syllables, such as 爱 ài, 鹅 é, and 藕 ǒu, which do not begin with a consonant, are said to begin with the initial zero or the "zero initial" 零声母)

声纳 shēngnà *phys.* sonar (sound navigation and ranging)

声囊 shēngnáng vocal sac (of tailless amphibians, such as frogs)

声能学 shēngnéngxué *phys.* sonics

声旁 shēngpáng *linguis.* the phonetic element of a Chinese pictophonetic character (e.g. 青 in 情, 清, and 菁)

声频 shēngpín same as 音频 yīnpín

声谱 shēngpǔ *phys.* sound spectrum

声谱仪 shēngpǔyí sound spectrograph

声气 shēngqì ① information: 互通～ exchange information; keep in contact with each other ② *dial.* voice; tone: 小声小气地 in a low voice; in undertones

声腔 shēngqiāng operatic tunes

声强 shēngqiáng *phys.* sound intensity

声情并茂 shēng-qíng bìng mào (of a singer) be remarkable for both voice and expression

声请 shēngqǐng make a formal request

声色[1] shēng-sè voice and countenance: 不动声色 bù dòng shēng-sè

声色[2] shēng-sè *formal* beautiful sounds and sights —music and women; sensual pleasures: 后庭～，皆第一绮丽。(沈既济《枕中记》) The sounds and sights of his harem were all of the uppermost beauty.

声色俱厉 shēng-sè jù lì stern in voice and countenance

声色犬马 shēng-sè-quǎn-mǎ music and women, keeping dogs and riding horses—sensual pleasures

声势 shēngshì prestige and power; fame and influence; impetus; momentum: 造成革命～ build up a revolutionary momentum

声势浩大 shēngshì hàodà great in strength and impetus; powerful and dynamic: 他觉得他的队伍实力坚强，～。 He was confident of the unyielding strength and formidable superiority of his troops. / ～的游行 a huge and grand parade

声嘶力竭 shēngsī-lìjié be hoarse and exhausted; shout oneself hoarse; shout oneself blue in the face

声速 shēngsù *phys.* speed of sound: 这种新型战斗机的巡航速度为～的二倍。 The cruising speed of this new type of fighter is twice the speed of sound (*or* is Mach two).

声讨 shēngtǎo denounce; condemn: 愤怒～恐怖主义者的罪行 indignantly denounce the crimes of the terrorists

声讨会 shēngtǎohuì denunciation meeting

声望 shēngwàng popularity; prestige: 在群众中享有很高的～ enjoy great prestige among the masses / 他们家在城里颇有～。 Their family enjoys quite a bit of prestige among the townspeople.

声威 shēngwēi renown; prestige

声威大震 shēngwēi dàzhèn gain great fame and high prestige

声息 shēngxī ① (usu. used in the negative) sound; noise: 没有一点～。 Not a sound is heard. ② information: ～相闻 keep in touch with each other

声响 shēngxiǎng sound; noise: 这发动机～太大。 This motor makes too much noise. / 瀑布奔泻，发出巨大的～。 The waterfall came down with a rush and a roar.

声学 shēngxué acoustics: 建筑～ architectural acoustics / 几何～ ray acoustics; geometrical acoustics

声言 shēngyán profess; claim; declare: 她～从此以后决不再过问此事。 She declared that from now on she would wash her hands of this business. / 她～自己是无辜的。 She professed herself to be guiltless (*or* innocent).

声音 shēngyīn sound; voice: 震耳欲聋的～ an ear-splitting sound / 她的～很高。 She has a high-pitched voice.

声域 shēngyù register

声誉 shēngyù reputation; fame; prestige: 维护国家的～ defend the honour of one's country / 在国内外享有很高的～ enjoy great prestige both at home and abroad / 损害～ damage sb.'s reputation (*or* prestige) / 那家公司～不好。 That firm has a bad reputation.

声冤 shēngyuān voice grievances; complain and call for redress

声援 shēngyuán express support for; support: ～被压迫民族的正义斗争 support the oppressed nations in their just struggles

声乐 shēngyuè *mus.* vocal music

声韵学 shēngyùnxué same as 音韵学 yīnyùnxué

声张 shēngzhāng (usu. used in the negative) make public; disclose: 不要～。 Don't let it out. / 事情还没弄清楚，先别～。 The matter has not been clarified yet, so don't breathe a word of it to anyone for the time being.

牲 shēng ① domestic animal ② animal sacrifice: 三牲 sānshēng

牲畜 shēngchù　livestock; domestic animals

牲畜车 shēngchùchē　*railway*　livestock wagon; stock wagon; stock car

牲粉 shēngfěn　*chem.*　animal starch; glycogen

牲口 shēngkou　draught animals; beasts of burden; livestock

牲口贩子 shēngkou fànzi　cattle dealer

牲口棚 shēngkoupéng　stock barn; livestock shed

笙 shēng　*mus.*　sheng, a reed pipe wind instrument

笙歌 shēnggē　*liter.*　music and singing

甥 shēng　sister's son; nephew

甥女 shēng·nǚ　sister's daughter; niece

shéng

绳 (繩) shéng ① rope; cord; string: 一条细～ a string / 一根钢～ a steel cable / 这条～又粗又结实。 This rope is thick and strong. ② restrict; restrain: ～以纪律 enforce discipline upon sb. ③ *formal* continue

绳鞭技 shéngbiānjì　*acrob.*　(doing) tricks with a whip; (performing) feats with a whip

绳伎 shéngjì ① same as 绳技 shéngjì ② *old* female rope walker

绳技 shéngjì　*acrob.*　rope walking or dancing; tightrope walking or slack rope walking

绳锯木断 shéng jù mù duàn　a rope can cut through a log; little strokes fell great oaks

绳捆索绑 shéngkǔn-suǒbǎng　truss up; bind; tie up

绳墨 shéngmò ① carpenter's line marker ② *formal* rules and regulations: 拘守～ stick to the rules

绳趋尺步 shéngqū-chǐbù　conform to every rule and regulation; toe the line

绳索 shéngsuǒ　a thick cord; rope: 尼龙～ a rope made of nylon / 砍断旧制度套在人民身上的～ cut the bonds forced on the people by the old system

绳套 shéngtào ① loop: 绞架上的～ a hangman's noose ② lasso

绳梯 shéngtī　rope ladder

绳之以法 shéng zhī yǐ fǎ　prosecute and punish according to law; bring to justice

绳子 shéngzi　cord; rope; string

shěng

省¹ shěng ① economize; save: ～着点用 use sparingly / ～时间 save time / ～掉不少麻烦 save a lot of trouble / 能～的就～ economize wherever possible / 我一个月～不下几个钱。 I can't save much from my monthly wages. ② omit; leave out: 这两个字不能～。 These two words cannot be omitted. / ～一道工序 eliminate one step from the process ③ abbreviation (of words): "佛"是"佛陀"之～。 *Fo* is an abbreviation of *Fotuo* ("Buddha").

省² shěng ① province: 江苏～ Jiangsu Province / ～长 governor of a province / ～人民代表大会 provincial people's congress ② provincial capital: 抵～ arrive in the provincial capital

——see also xǐng

省便 shěngbiàn　convenient; timesaving or laboursaving: 用洗衣机洗衣服就～多了。 A washing machine will save us a lot of time.

省城 shěngchéng　*inf.*　provincial capital: 我上～去办点事。 I'm going to the provincial capital on business.

省吃俭用 shěngchī-jiǎnyòng　skimp and save; live frugally: 我～把他送进学校念书。 By saving on food and clothes, I managed to send him to school.

省得 shěngde　so as to save (*or* avoid): 你就住在这儿吧，～天天来回跑。 Better stay here to avoid going back and forth every day. / 到了就来信，～我挂念。 Send me a letter as soon as you arrive so that I won't worry. / 多穿点儿衣服，～冻着。 Put on more clothes, or you'll catch cold.

省份 shěngfèn　(not to be used in names of provinces) province: 台湾是中国的一个～。 Taiwan is one of China's provinces.

省会 shěnghuì　provincial capital: 湖南省的～是长沙。 Changsha is the provincial capital of Hunan.

省俭 shěngjiǎn　*dial.*　economical; frugal: 他日子过得很～。 He lived very frugally.

省界 shěngjiè　provincial boundaries

省劲 shěngjìn　same as 省力 shěnglì

省力 shěnglì　(also 省力气 shěng lìqi) save effort; save labour: 这种耕作方法～不少。 This method of farming saves a lot of labour. / 省不了多少力气 won't save much labour

省略 shěnglüè ① leave out; omit (on purpose): 这一段与主题关系不大，满可以～。 This irrelevant paragraph may well be left out. ② *gram.* be understood: 这个句子的主语～了。 The subject of the sentence is understood.

省略号 shěnglüèhào　ellipsis; suspension points; ellipsis dots (……) (...)

省略句 shěnglüèjù　*gram.*　elliptical sentence

省免 shěngmiǎn　do without; dispense with: 这些惯常的礼节就～了吧。 Let's dispense with the usual formalities.

省钱 shěngqián　save money; be economical: 每月省点钱 save some money each month

省却 shěngquè　save: 抄近路走可以～将近一公里。 Taking the short cut will save us nearly a kilometre. / 这种装置会～百分之五十的燃料。 This device will effect a saving of 50 per cent fuel. / ～不少麻烦 save a lot of trouble

省事 shěngshì　save trouble; simplify matters: 这样可以省很多事。 We can make it much simpler this way. / 在食堂里吃饭～。 It's more convenient to eat in the canteen. / 你工作要仔细，不能只图～。 You should be conscientious in your work, and not just try to save yourself trouble.

省委 shěngwěi　provincial Party committee: ～书记 secretary of a provincial Party committee / ～委员 member of a provincial Party committee

省心 shěngxīn　save worry: 孩子进了托儿所，我～多了。 Having the child in kindergarten saves me a lot of worry.

省垣 shěngyuán　*formal*　provincial capital

省治 shěngzhì　*old*　the seat of a provincial government; provincial capital

眚 shěng　*formal* ① eyes afflicted with calaract ② disaster; calamity ③ fault; error: 不以一～掩大德。 Don't allow one error to obscure great merits.

shèng

圣 (聖) shèng ① holy; sacred: 神圣 shénshèng / 圣地 shèngdì ② saint; sage: 圣贤

shèngxián ③ emperor: 圣上 shèngshàng ④ the greatest master of a certain art or skill: 诗圣 shīshèng / 棋圣 qíshèng

圣餐 shèngcān *Christianity* the Lord's Supper; the Holy Communion; Eucharist

圣诞 shèngdàn ① *old* the birthday of Confucius ② *Christianity* Christmas (the birthday of Jesus Christ): ～前夜 Christmas Eve (Dec. 24) / 恭祝～，并贺新禧 With Best Wishes for a Merry Christmas and a Happy New Year

圣诞节 Shèngdànjié ① Christmas Day (Dec. 25) ② Christmastime; Christmastide (Dec. 24-Jan. 6)

圣诞卡 shèngdànkǎ Christmas card; Xmas card

圣诞老人 Shèngdàn Lǎorén Santa Claus

圣诞树 shèngdànshù Christmas tree

圣地 shèngdì ① *religion* the Holy Land (*or* City) ② a sacred place; shrine: 延安是中国革命的～。Yan'an is a sacred place of the Chinese revolution.

圣多美和普林西比 Shèngduōměi hé Pǔlínxībǐ São Tomé and Príncipe

圣父 Shèngfù ① *Christianity* Holy Father—God ② *Roman Catholicism* Holy Father (a title of the Pope)

圣公会 Shènggōnghuì *Christianity* the Anglican Church

圣公宗 Shènggōngzōng *Christianity* Anglicanism; the Anglican Church

圣躬 shènggōng the Emperor's health; His Majesty's health: ～欠安。His Majesty is slightly indisposed.

圣赫勒拿 Shènghèlèná St. Helena

圣基茨和尼维斯 Shèngjīcí hé Níwéisī St. Kitts and Nevis

圣洁 shèngjié holy and pure

圣经 Shèngjīng the Holy Bible; the Bible; Holy Writ; the (Holy) Scriptures

圣经贤传 shèngjīng-xiánzhuàn Confucian classics

圣灵 Shènglíng *Christianity* the Holy Spirit; the Holy Ghost

圣灵节 Shènglíngjié *Christianity* Whitsunday

圣卢西亚 Shènglúxīyà Saint Lucia

圣马力诺 Shèngmǎlìnuò San Marino

圣马力诺人 Shèngmǎlìnuòrén San Marinese

圣庙 shèngmiào Confucian temple

圣明 shèngmíng august wisdom (formerly used in adulation of the emperor)

圣母 shèngmǔ ① a female deity; goddess ② *Catholicism Christianity* the (Blessed) Virgin Mary; the Madonna: ～像 Madonna / 《～颂》 *Ave Maria*

圣皮埃尔岛和密克隆群岛 Shèngpí'āi'ěrdǎo hé Mìkèlóng Qúndǎo St. Pierre and Miquelon Islands

圣人 shèngrén ① sage; wise man ② the Sage (a title of respect for Confucius)

圣人无常师 shèngrén wú cháng shī sages have no constant teachers; a sage has more than one teacher

圣上 shèngshàng Your Majesty; His Majesty

圣手 shèngshǒu a master of a certain skill

圣水 shèngshuǐ ① sacred water credited with curative or exorcising powers ② holy water for religious uses

圣体 shèngtǐ ① same as 圣躬 shènggōng ② *Christianity Catholicism* holy bread

圣文森特岛和格林纳丁斯 Shèngwénsēntèdǎo hé Gélínnàdīngsī St. Vincent and the Grenadines

圣贤 shèngxián sages and men of virtue

圣药 shèngyào efficacious medicine: 灵丹～ miraculous cure; panacea

圣谕 shèngyù imperial decree

圣战 shèngzhàn a holy war; crusade

圣旨 shèngzhǐ imperial edict: 你把他的话当成～啦? Do you take everything he says as seriously as you would an imperial edict?

圣子 Shèngzǐ *Christianity* Holy Son—Jesus Christ

胜[1]（勝） shèng ① win: 这次比赛谁～了? Who won this match? / 我队以四～两负一平的成绩获得亚军。Our team finished second with four wins, two defeats and one tie. ② defeat: 我～了他了。I defeated him. / 以少～多 use a small force to defeat a large one / 战而～之 fight to win ③ (often followed by 于, etc.) surpass; be superior to; get the better of: 事实胜于雄辩 shìshí shèngyú xióngbiàn / 聊胜于无 liáo shèngyú wú ④ superb; wonderful; lovely: 胜景 shèngjǐng

胜[2]（勝） shèng (formerly, shēng) be equal to; can bear: 力不能～ beyond one's ability

胜[3]（勝） shèng *arch.* head ornaments

胜败 shèng-bài victory or defeat; success or failure

胜败乃兵家常事 shèng-bài nǎi bīngjiā chángshì for a military commander, winning or losing a battle is a common occurrence; victory or defeat is a common thing for the soldier

胜不骄，败不馁 shèng bù jiāo, bài bù něi not made dizzy with success, nor discouraged by failure

胜朝 shèngcháo *formal* the defunct dynasty

胜地 shèngdì a famous scenic spot: 避暑～ a famous summer resort

胜负 shèng-fù victory or defeat; success or failure: 战争的～ the outcome of a war / ～未定。Victory hangs in the balance. / 这场比赛～已定。The outcome of the game is a foregone conclusion. / 比赛的～是暂时的，友谊是永久的。To win or lose in a match is temporary while friendship between the contestants is lasting.

胜过 shèngguò be better than; be superior to: 实际行动～空洞的言辞。Action speaks louder than words.

胜迹 shèngjì a famous historical site

胜景 shèngjǐng wonderful scenery

胜境 shèngjìng a scenic spot; a beautiful place: 名山～ famous mountains and scenic spots; places of scenic beauty

胜利 shènglì ① victory; triumph: 充满了～的信心 be fully confident of victory / 敢于斗争，敢于～ dare to struggle and dare to win / 祝你们取得更大的～! Wish you even greater successes! ② successful; triumphant: ～会师 triumphantly join forces / ～完成任务 successfully carry out one's task / 大会～闭幕。The conference has concluded successfully. / 沿着社会主义大道～前进 march triumphantly along the socialist road

胜利果实 shènglì guǒshí fruits of victory

胜利者 shènglìzhě victor; winner

胜券 shèngquàn confidence in victory: 操～ be sure to win

胜任 shèngrèn be competent; be qualified; be equal to: ～工作 be competent at a job; prove equal to the task

胜任愉快 shèngrèn yúkuài be fully competent; prove more than equal to the task

胜如 shèngrú same as 胜似 shèngsì

胜似 shèngsì be better than; surpass

胜诉 shèngsù win a lawsuit (*or* court case)

胜算 shèngsuàn *formal* a stratagem which ensures success: 操～ be sure of success

胜游 shèngyóu a pleasure trip

胜友 shèngyǒu *formal* good friends

胜仗 shèngzhàng a victorious battle; victory: 打～ win a battle; score a victory

乘[1] shèng historical records; annals: 史乘 shǐshèng

乘[2] shèng *arch.* a war chariot drawn by four horses: 千～之国 a state of a thousand chariots

——see also　chéng

晟　shèng　*formal*　① bright　② flourishing

盛　shèng　① flourishing; prosperous: 桃花开得很～。The peach trees are in full bloom. *or* The peach blossoms are out. ② vigorous; energetic: 火势很～。The fire is raging. / 年轻气～ young and aggressive ③ magnificent; grand: 盛举　shèngjǔ ④ abundant; plentiful: 盛意　shèngyì ⑤ popular; common; widespread: 学术气氛很～。An academic atmosphere prevails. ⑥ greatly; deeply: ～夸 praise highly ⑦ (Shèng) a surname ——see also chéng

盛产　shèngchǎn　abound in; teem with: ～煤铁 abound in coal and iron / ～石油 be rich in oil / ～鱼蟹 teem with fish and crabs

盛传　shèngchuán　be widely known; be widely rumoured

盛大　shèngdà　grand; magnificent: ～的欢迎 a rousing welcome / ～的招待会 a grand reception / ～的游行 a mammoth parade

盛典　shèngdiǎn　a grand ceremony (or occasion): 皇帝的大婚～ the grand wedding ceremony of the emperor

盛服　shèngfú　*formal*　full dress; splendid attire; rich dress

盛会　shènghuì　distinguished gathering; grand meeting: 团结友谊的～ a grand gathering of unity and friendship / 体育～ a magnificent sports meet

盛极一时　shèngjí yìshí　be in fashion (or vogue) for a time; be all the rage

盛季　shèngjì　peak period; busy season: 草莓～ strawberry season / 旅游～ tourist season

盛举　shèngjǔ　a grand occasion (or event)

盛开　shèngkāi　(of flowers) be in full bloom; flourish: 百花～。Flowers are in full bloom.

盛况　shèngkuàng　a grand occasion; a spectacular event

盛况空前　shèngkuàng kōngqián　an exceptionally (or unprecedentedly) grand occasion

盛名　shèngmíng　great reputation

盛名之下，其实难副　shèngmíng zhī xià, qí shí nán fù　a high reputation is hard to live up to

盛年　shèngnián　the more robust years of one's life; the prime of life

盛怒　shèngnù　be very angry; be in a rage: 他在～之下，做了件鲁莽的事。He did something rash in a moment of anger.

盛气凌人　shèngqì líng rén　domineering; arrogant; overbearing: ～的样子 imperious bearing

盛情　shèngqíng　great kindness; boundless hospitality: 受到～款待 be accorded lavish hospitality

盛情难却　shèngqíng nán què　it would be ungracious not to accept your kindness

盛秋　shèngqiū　the height of autumn; midautumn

盛世　shèngshì　flourishing age; heyday: 太平盛世 tàipíng shèngshì

盛事　shèngshì　a grand occasion; a great event

盛暑　shèngshǔ　sweltering summer heat; very hot weather

盛衰　shèng-shuāi　prosperity and decline; rise and fall; ups and downs

盛衰荣辱　shèng-shuāi róng-rǔ　prosperity and decline, glory and humiliation; rise and fall; ups and downs; vicissitudes of life

盛夏　shèngxià　the height of summer; midsummer

盛行　shèngxíng　be current (or rife, rampant); be in vogue

盛行一时　shèngxíng yìshí　be in vogue; prevail for a time

盛宴　shèngyàn　(also 盛筵 shèngyán) a grand banquet; a sumptuous dinner: 设～款待佳宾 give a grand banquet in honour of the distinguished guests

盛意　shèngyì　great kindness; generosity: 衷心感谢您的一片～。I heartily appreciate your great kindness to me.

盛誉　shèngyù　great fame; high reputation: 中国丝绸在世界上素有～。Chinese silk has long been famous all over the world.

盛赞　shèngzàn　highly praise; speak of sb. in glowing terms

盛馔　shèngzhuàn　a sumptuous dinner

盛装　shèngzhuāng　splendid attire; rich dress: 穿着节日的～ be dressed in one's holiday best / 天安门广场披上了节日的～。Tian'anmen Square is splendidly decorated for the festive occasion.

剩(賸)　shèng　surplus; remnant: 我只～五块钱了。I've only five *yuan* left. / ～货 surplus goods / ～菜～饭 leftovers / 所～无几。There is not much left.

剩磁　shèngcí　*phys.*　residual magnetism

剩下　shèngxia　be left (over); remain: ～多少? How much is left (over)? / ～的敌军已经被我们消灭了。We have wiped out the remaining enemy troops. / 同志们都走了，就～我一个人了。The other comrades have all gone; I'm the only one left.

剩余　shèngyú　surplus; remainder: 收支相抵，略有～。The reckoning up of revenue and expenditure shows a small surplus.

剩余产品　shèngyú chǎnpǐn　surplus products: 剩余农产品 farm surplus

剩余价值　shèngyú jiàzhí　surplus value

剩余劳动　shèngyú láodòng　surplus labour

剩余物资　shèngyú wùzī　surplus materials

shī

尸¹(屍)　shī　corpse; dead body; remains: 兽～ carcass

尸²　shī　(in ancient times) a person who sat behind the altar, acting as the deceased during the performance of sacrificial rites

尸骨　shīgǔ　(also 尸骸 shīhái) bones of the dead

尸横遍野　shī héng biànyě　a field littered with corpses

尸居余气　shī jū yúqì　be a living corpse; be at one's last gasp; be at the point of death; be as good as dead: 彼～, 不足畏也。There is little to fear from him. He is the corpse in which a little breath remains.

尸腊　shīlà　a dead body naturally dried and preserved

尸身　shīshēn　corpse; dead body; remains

尸首　shīshou　a dead body of a human being

尸体　shītǐ　corpse; carcass

尸体解剖　shītǐ jiěpōu　autopsy; postmortem (examination)

尸位　shīwèi　hold an office without doing any work: ～误国 neglect the duties of an office to the detriment of national interest

尸位素餐　shīwèi sùcān　hold an office and enjoy all the privileges without doing a stroke of work

失　shī　① lose: ～而复得 lost and found again / ～民心 lose the support of the people / 得大于～。Gains outweigh losses. / 不要～了信心。Don't lose confidence. ② miss; let slip: 良机莫～。Don't let slip this good chance. ③ not act according to; neglect; violate: 失信 shīxìn / 失敬 shījìng ④ lose control of: 失手 shīshǒu / 失禁 shījìn / 失态 shītài ⑤ err; have a slip; be defective

in: ～之于烦琐 have the defect of being too detailed ⑥ slip; mistake; defect; mishap: 唯恐有～ fear that there may be some mishap

失败 shībài ① be defeated; lose (a war, etc.): 遭到了可耻的～ meet with ignominious defeat ② fail: 这项试验～了不止一次。The experiment has failed more than once.

失败情绪 shībài qíng·xù defeatist sentiments

失败为成功之母 shībài wéi chénggōng zhī mǔ failure is the mother of success

失败主义 shībàizhǔyì defeatism

失策 shīcè ① err in tactics, scheming or planning; do sth. unwise: 这样做非常～。It was a very unwise move. ② an error (in tactics, etc.)

失察 shīchá neglect one's supervisory duties

失常 shīcháng not normal; odd: 举止～ act oddly / 精神～ be distraught; not be in one's right mind

失宠 shīchǒng derog. fall into disfavour; be out of favour; be in disgrace

失传 shīchuán not be handed down from past generations; be lost: 一种～的艺术 a lost art / 我国有些古代科学著作已经～。Some scientific books of ancient China have been lost.

失聪 shīcōng become deaf: 双耳～ become deaf in both ears

失措 shīcuò lose one's presence of mind; lose one's head: 茫然～ be at a loss what to do

失单 shīdān a list of lost or stolen articles (or property)

失当 shīdàng improper; inappropriate: 这个问题处理～。This problem was not properly handled.

失盗 shīdào be robbed or burgled: ～事件 a robbery or burglary

失道寡助 shī dào guǎ zhù an unjust cause finds scant (or little) support ——see also 得道多助，失道寡助 dé dào duō zhù, shī dào guǎ zhù

失地 shīdì lost territory: 收复～ recover lost territory

失掉 shīdiào ① lose: ～理智 lose one's senses / ～联系 lose contact with / ～权力 be stripped of power / ～民心 lose popular support ② miss: ～机会 miss a chance / ～战机 fail to grasp a good opportunity to engage the enemy

失和 shīhé fail to keep on good terms; become estranged: 弟兄俩～有好几个月了。The brothers have been estranged for months.

失怙 shīhù formal be bereaved of one's father; have lost one's father

失欢 shīhuān lose sb.'s favour

失悔 shīhuǐ regret

失魂落魄 shīhún-luòpò driven to distraction: 吓得～ be scared out of one's wits; be frightened out of one's life

失火 shīhuǒ catch fire; be on fire: 昨晚城里～。There was a fire in town last night.

失机 shījī lose the opportunity; miss the chance

失计 shījì same as 失策 shīcè

失记 shījì formal forget

失检 shījiǎn be indiscreet: 言语～ be indiscreet with one's tongue; be indiscreet in one's speech

失脚 shījiǎo lose one's footing; slip: ～跌倒 lose one's footing (or balance) and fall

失节 shījié ① forfeit one's integrity; be disloyal ② (of a woman, according to feudal morality) lose one's chastity

失禁 shījìn lose control over one's bladder or rectum functions; be unable to restrain one's natural discharges; suffer from incontinence: 大小便～ suffer from incontinence of faeces and urine; be doubly incontinent

失惊 shījīng be startled; be shocked: 她～地叫了起来。Greatly startled, she cried out.

失敬 shījìng pol. sorry I didn't recognize you; excuse me for my lack of manners

失控 shīkòng get out of control; get out of hand: 物价～ a runaway increase in prices

失口 shīkǒu make a slip of the tongue: 我～冒犯了她。I let slip some remark that offended her.

失礼 shīlǐ ① commit a breach of etiquette: 舅舅做寿，我们要是不去，人家会怪我们～的。If we don't go to our uncle's birthday party, people will consider it a breach of etiquette. ② pol. excuse me for my impropriety, lack of manners, etc.: 对不起，～了。Pardon me for my lack of manners.

失利 shīlì suffer a setback (or defeat): 军事上的～ military reverses / 在这场乒乓球比赛中我方第一盘～。Our side lost the first game of the table-tennis match.

失恋 shīliàn be disappointed in a love affair; be jilted: ～的痛苦 the bitter taste of disappointed love

失灵 shīlíng (of a machine, instrument, etc.) not work or not work properly; be out of order: 开关～了。The switch is out of order. / 他的听觉有点～了。His hearing is getting worse.

失落 shīluò lose; drop: 我实在想不起来那块头巾可能～在什么地方。Really I can't recall where I could have dropped my kerchief.

失迷 shīmí lose one's way; lose one's bearings

失密 shīmì give away official secrets due to carelessness: 怎么失的密? How did the secret leak out? / 一起后果严重的～事件 a leakage of secrets likely to entail grave consequences

失眠 shīmián (suffer from) insomnia: 病人昨夜～。The patient had a sleepless night last night. / 经常性的～对身体极为有害。A persistent insomnia is very harmful to one's health.

失明 shīmíng lose one's sight; go blind: 双目～ lose the sight of both eyes

失能性毒剂 shīnéngxìng dújì mil. incapacitating agent

失陪 shīpéi pol. excuse me, but I must be leaving now

失窃 shīqiè have things stolen; suffer loss by theft

失去 shīqù lose: ～知觉 lose consciousness / ～信心 lose confidence / ～时效 be no longer effective; cease to be in force / ～中国国籍 forfeit one's Chinese citizenship / ～控制 get out of hand; get out of control / ～妻子 be bereaved of one's wife / ～一切希望 be bereft of all hope

失却 shīquè formal lose; be bereft of

失群 shīqún stray from one's flock: 迷途～ be lost and left behind / 我好比南来雁～飞散。I am like a wild goose from the south, having strayed from its flock.

失散 shīsàn be separated from and lose touch with each other; be scattered: 解放后，他找到了～多年的姐姐。After liberation he was reunited with his sister, whom he had had no news of for years. / 手稿的后一部分～了。The last part of the manuscript is lost.

失色 shīsè ① be discoloured; lose colour: 这些壁画已年久～。These murals have been discoloured with the passage of time. ② turn pale: 众人惊愕～，无一应对。All those present turned pale and none dared to say anything in reply.

失闪 shīshan mishap; unexpected danger: 他觉得累了就停止练习，怕有～。He stopped practising when he felt tired for fear of accidents.

失身 shīshēn (of a woman) lose one's virginity or chastity

失神 shīshén ① inattentive; absent-minded: 我有点～，没有听到他最后那段讲话。I was somewhat absent-minded and missed the last part of his speech. ② out of sorts; in low spirits: ～地望着窗外发呆 stare blankly

out of the window feeling low

失慎 shīshèn ① not cautious; careless: 我一时～, 把一杯牛奶碰洒了。I inadvertently upset a glass of milk. ② *formal* cause a fire through carelessness

失声 shīshēng ① ejaculate (involuntarily); burst out: 喊叫 exclaim outright ／ ～大笑 burst out laughing; burst into laughter ② lose one's voice: 痛哭～ be choked with tears; cry oneself hoarse

失时 shīshí miss the season; let slip the opportunity: 播种不能～。Don't miss the sowing season.

失实 shīshí inconsistent with the facts; inaccurate: 传闻～。The rumour was unfounded. ／ 报道～。The report was inaccurate.

失势 shīshì lose power and influence; fall into disgrace

失事 shīshì (have an) accident: 飞机～ aviation accident; aeroplane crash

失恃 shīshì be bereaved of one's mother; have lost one's mother

失手 shīshǒu lose control of one's hand; accidentally drop sth., hurt sb., etc.: 他一～把茶杯打碎了。He accidentally dropped the cup and broke it. ／ 小王和小李练剑的时候, 小王～刺伤了小李的左臂。When Xiao Wang was practising fencing with Xiao Li, he accidentally wounded Xiao Li in the left arm.

失守 shīshǒu (of a city, etc.) fall

失水 shīshuǐ dehydration

失溲 shīsōu *Chin. med.* lose control over one's bladder functions; incontinence of urine

失速 shīsù *aviation* stall: ～滑翔 stalled glide

失算 shīsuàn miscalculate; misjudge; be injudicious: 聪明人也有～的时候。Even wise men are not free from miscalculations. *or* Even a wise man sometimes miscalculates.

失所 shīsuǒ become homeless; be displaced: ～平民 displaced civilians

失态 shītài lose control of oneself; misbehave; forget oneself: 酒后～ forget oneself in one's cups

失调 shītiáo ① imbalance; dislocation: 供求～ imbalance of supply and demand ／ 经济～ economic dislocation ／ 比例～ disproportion ／ 雨水～ abnormal rainfall ② lack of proper care (after an illness, etc.): 产后～ lack of proper care after childbirth ③ *radio* maladjustment; detuning

失望 shīwàng ① lose hope; lose heart: 他们失败多次, 但是并没有完全～。They failed time and again, but they never gave up hope. ② disappointed: 感到～ be disappointed ／ 令人～ disappointing ／ 我们对你太～了。We are utterly disappointed with (or in) you. ／ 我非常抱歉又一次叫你～, 可是我实在抽不出身来。I'm sorry to disappoint you again, but really I'll be tied up then.

失物 shīwù lost article; lost property

失物招领处 shīwù zhāolǐngchù Lost and Found Office; Lost Property Office

失误 shīwù error; fault; muff: 判断～ an error in judgment; a misjudgment ／ 接球～ muff (or fumble) a ball ／ 发球～ a serving fault ／ 经验不足, 难免会有～。Because of lack of experience, mistakes are hard to avoid.

失陷 shīxiàn (of cities, territory, etc.) fall; fall into enemy hands

失效 shīxiào ① lose efficacy; lose effectiveness; cease to be effective: 这药已～了。The medicine no longer has any effect. ／ 使水雷～ deactivate mines ② (of a treaty, an agreement, etc.) be no longer in force; become invalid: 自动～ automatically cease to be in force ／ 条约的～ voidance (or voidness) of a treaty

失笑 shīxiào laugh in spite of oneself; cannot help laughing: 哑然失笑 yǎrán shīxiào

失谐 shīxié *radio* detuning; mismatching

失信 shīxìn break one's promise; go back on one's

word

失信于民 shīxìn yú mín (of a government) lose the confidence of the people

失修 shīxiū (of houses, etc.) be in bad repair; fall into disrepair: 年久～ have long been out of repair; have been neglected for years

失学 shīxué be deprived of education; be unable to go to school; be obliged to discontinue one's studies

失血 shīxuè lose blood: ～过多 excessive loss of blood

失言 shīyán make an indiscreet remark; make a slip of the tongue: 酒后～ make an indiscreet remark under the influence of alcohol ／ 别生气, 我是一时～。Don't get sore; I didn't mean anything by that remark.

失业 shīyè lose one's job; be out of work; be unemployed

失业率 shīyèlǜ rate of unemployment

失业者 shīyèzhě the unemployed; the jobless

失仪 shīyí ① forget one's manners: 我怕喝多了酒会～。I am afraid I might forget myself in my cups. ② a breach of etiquette

失宜 shīyí *formal* inappropriate: 处置～ handle improperly

失意 shīyì have one's aspirations, plans, etc. thwarted; be frustrated; be disappointed: 情场～ be frustrated in love

失音 shīyīn *med.* aphonia; loss of voice

失迎 shīyíng *pol.* fail to meet (a guest): ～! ～! Excuse me for not meeting you at the gate. ／ 昨天～了, 很抱歉。Sorry I was out when you called yesterday.

失语症 shīyǔzhèng *med.* aphasia

失约 shīyuē fail to keep an appointment

失责 shīzé dereliction of duty

失着 shīzhāo ① make a careless (or an unwise) move ② a careless move; an unwise move

失真 shīzhēn ① (of voice, images, etc.) lack fidelity; not be true to the original ② *radio* distortion: 频率～ frequency distortion

失之东隅, 收之桑榆 shī zhī dōngyú, shōu zhī sāngyú lose in the east and gain in the west—make up on the roundabouts what one loses on the swings

失之毫厘, 谬以千里 shī zhī háolí, miù yǐ qiānlǐ same as 差之毫厘, 谬以千里 chā zhī háolí, miù yǐ qiānlǐ

失之交臂 shī zhī jiāo bì just miss the person or opportunity: 机会难得, 幸勿～。Don't let slip such a golden opportunity.

失职 shīzhí ① neglect one's duty ② dereliction of duty

失重 shīzhòng *phys.* weightlessness; zero gravity

失主 shīzhǔ owner of lost property

失踪 shīzōng (usu. of people) be missing: 伤亡之外, 尚有多人～。In addition to the killed and wounded, many are missing.

失足 shīzú ① lose one's footing; slip: ～落水 slip and fall into the water ② take a wrong step in life: ～青少年 juvenile delinquents

师¹ (師)

shī ① teacher; tutor; master: ～者, 所以传道受业解惑也。(韩愈) It takes a teacher to transmit wisdom, impart knowledge, and resolve doubts. ② model; example: 师表 shībiǎo ③ a person skilled in a certain profession: 工程师 gōngchéngshī ／ 厨师 chúshī ④ (a term of respect for a monk or nun) master; mother: 法师 fǎshī ⑤ of one's master or teacher: 师母 shīmǔ ⑥ (Shī) a surname

师² (師)

shī ① *mil.* division: 步兵～ infantry division ② troops; army: 正义之～ an army fighting for a just cause

师表 shībiǎo *formal* a person of exemplary virtue

师部 shībù *mil.* division headquarters

师承 shīchéng *formal* ① have studied under (a teacher, usu. with reference to a particular school of thought or learning); be a disciple of: 黄侃～章炳麟。 Huang Kan was a disciple of Zhang Binglin. ② transmission from master to disciple: 这些艺人各有自己的～。 These artists have inherited the traditions of their respective masters.

师出无名 shī chū wú míng dispatch troops without just cause

师道尊严 shīdào zūnyán dignity of the teaching profession

师弟 shīdì ① junior (male) fellow apprentice ② the son of one's master (younger than oneself) ③ father's (male) apprentice (younger than oneself) ④ teacher and student

师法 shīfǎ ① model oneself after (a great master); imitate ② knowledge or technique handed down by one's master

师范 shīfàn ① teacher-training; pedagogical: ～学院 teachers college; teachers training college ② short for 师范学校 shīfàn xuéxiào ③ *formal* a model to be followed

师范学校 shīfàn xuéxiào normal school

师父 shīfu ① same as 师傅 shīfu ② (a term of respect for a monk or nun) master; mother

师父领进门，修行在个人 shīfu lǐngjìn mén, xiūxíng zài gèrén the master initiates the apprentices, but their skill depends on their own efforts; the master teaches the trade, but the prentice's skill is self-made

师傅 shīfu ① master worker (a qualified worker as distinct from an apprentice) ② a respectful form of address for a skilled worker ③ *inf.* a form of address for any stranger

师公 shīgōng ① master's master ② sorcerer

师姑 shīgū a term of respect for a nun

师姐 shījiě ① senior (female) fellow apprentice ② the daughter of one's master (older than oneself) ③ father's (female) apprentice (older than oneself)

师老兵疲 shīlǎo-bīngpí an army worn-down and war-weary

师妹 shīmèi ① junior (female) fellow apprentice ② the daughter of one's master (younger than oneself) ③ father's (female) apprentice (younger than oneself)

师母 shīmǔ the wife of one's teacher or master

师娘 shīniáng *inf.* the wife of one's teacher or master

师婆 shīpó (also 师婆子 shīpózi) witch; sorceress

师生 shī-shēng teacher and student: ～关系 relations between teachers and students; teacher-student relations

师事 shīshì *formal* treat sb. with the respect due to a teacher

师徒 shī-tú master and apprentice

师团 shītuán *mil.* division

师心自用 shī xīn zì yòng be opinionated

师兄 shīxiōng ① senior (male) fellow apprentice ② the son of one's master (older than oneself) ③ father's (male) apprentice (older than oneself)

师兄弟 shīxiōngdì male apprentices of the same master; fellow apprentices

师训 shīxùn teacher's instructions: 遵从～ follow the teacher's instructions

师爷 shīye a private assistant attending to legal, fiscal or secretarial duties in a local *yamen*; private adviser

师友 shīyǒu teachers and friends

师长 shīzhǎng ① (a term of respect) teacher ② *mil.* division commander

师直为壮 shī zhí wéi zhuàng an army fighting for a just cause has high morale

师资 shīzī persons qualified to teach; teachers: ～力量 不足 shortage of teachers / 培训～ train teachers

虱 (蝨)

shī louse

虱子 shīzi louse

诗

shī poetry; verse; poem

诗歌 shīgē poems and songs; poetry: ～朗诵 recitation of poems; poetry readings

诗话 shīhuà ① poetry talks (i.e. informal remarks on poetry or poets, a literary genre very popular with the Song and Ming scholars, usu. telling why certain famous lines were written and under what circumstances): 谢榛《四溟～》 Xie Zhen's *Siming Poetry Talks* ② vernacular stories interspersed with poems

诗集 shījí collection of poems; poetry anthology

诗经 Shījīng *The Book of Songs* ——see also 五经 wǔjīng

诗句 shījù verse; line

诗剧 shījù drama in verse; poetic drama

诗礼之家 shīlǐ zhī jiā a highly cultured household; a family of scholars

诗律 shīlǜ prosody

诗篇 shīpiān ① poems: 这些～抒发了作者的革命豪情。 These poems express the revolutionary fervour of the poet. ② an inspiring story; epic: 我们时代的壮丽～ a magnificent epic of our era / 英雄的～ a heroic epic

诗情画意 shīqíng-huàyì a quality suggestive of poetry or painting; poetic charm: 她的舞姿袅娜，富有～。 She danced with poetic grace.

诗穷而后工 shī qióng érhòu gōng poverty makes for poetic excellence; only a poet in adversity is apt to develop skill

诗人 shīrén poet

诗社 shīshè poets' club

诗圣 shīshèng poet-sage (an epithet for Du Fu 杜甫)

诗史 shīshǐ ① history of poetry ② poems that can be taken as a mirror of the times the poet lived in (as Du Fu's 杜甫 usu. are)

诗书 shīshū Confucian classics: 出身～门第 come from a family of scholars

诗坛 shītán the circle of poets: 百花齐放的中国～ a hundred flowers blooming in the circle of Chinese poets / ～领袖 the dean of poets

诗仙 shīxiān poet-immortal (an epithet for Li Bai 李白)

诗兴 shīxìng urge for poetic creation; poetic inspiration; poetic mood: ～大发 feel a strong urge to write poetry; be in an exalted, poetic mood

诗意 shīyì poetic quality or flavour: 饶有～ rich in poetic flavour; very poetic

诗余 shīyú an extension or outgrowth of the *shi* 诗 or poetry in regular metre (another name for the *ci* 词 or poetry in irregular metre)

诗韵 shīyùn ① rhyme (in poetry) ② rhyming dictionary

诗章 shīzhāng poems

诗中有画，画中有诗 shī zhōng yǒu huà, huà zhōng yǒu shī there are pictures (i.e. a pictorial imagination) in poetry and poetry (i.e. a poetic imagination) in pictures; evoke painting in poetry and poetry in painting

诗宗 shīzōng the dean of poets: 一代～ the greatest poet of the time

诗作 shīzuò poetical works

狮 (獅)

shī lion: 一头雄～ a lion / 一头母～ a lioness

狮身人面像 shīshēnrénmiànxiàng sphinx

狮头鹅 shītóu'é lion-headed goose (a fine breed of goose)

狮子 shīzi lion

狮子鼻 shīzibí　pug nose

狮子搏兔 shīzi bó tù　(like) a lion pouncing on a hare —go all out even when fighting a weaker enemy or tackling a minor problem

狮子狗 shīzigǒu　pug-dog

狮子头 shīzitóu　large meatball (usu. deep-fried before being braised with vegetables)

狮子舞 shīziwǔ　lion dance (a popular folk dance)

狮子座 Shīzizuò　*astron.* Leo

鸤 shī　nuthatch (a bird)

施 shī　① bring (*or* put) into effect; execute; carry out: 略～小技 hatch a little scheme / 他们一计不成, 又～一计。 Their first ruse having failed, they tried another. ② bestow; grant; hand out: ～恩于人 bestow favours on others ③ exert; impose: ～压力 exert pressure on sb. ④ use; apply: ～底肥 apply fertilizer to the subsoil ⑤ (Shī) a surname

施放 shīfàng　discharge; fire: ～催泪弹 fire tear-gas shells / ～烟幕 lay a smokescreen

施肥 shīféi　spread manure; apply fertilizer

施工 shīgōng　carry out construction or large repairs: 加紧进行～ speed up the construction or repairs / 去年九月开始～。 Construction began last September. / 眼下有四条公路在～(中)。 Four highways are under construction. / 道路～, 车辆绕行 Detour. Road Under Repair. / ～现场 construction site / ～单位 unit in charge of construction / ～人员 builders; constructors

施工缝 shīgōngfèng　*archit.* construction joint

施工图 shīgōngtú　working drawing

施加 shījiā　exert; bring to bear on: ～压力 bring pressure to bear on sb.; put pressure on sb. / ～影响 exert one's influence on sb.

施教 shījiào　teach; educate; instruct: 因材施教 yīn cái shījiào

施礼 shīlǐ　make a bow; salute

施力点 shīlìdiǎn　*phys.* point of application

施舍 shīshě　give alms; give in charity: 乞求～ beg for alms / 靠别人～过日子 survive on handouts

施事 shīshì　*gram.* the doer of the action in a sentence; agent

施威 shīwēi　exhibit one's power; show severity

施洗 shīxǐ　*Christianity* administer baptism: 给某人～ baptize sb.

施行 shīxíng　① put (laws, rules, regulations, etc.) into force; enforce; implement: 发布～新的关税法则 promulgate and enforce new tariff laws / 本条例自公布之日起～。 These regulations come into force upon promulgation. / 去年四月十三日起～夏时制。 Summer time was enforced from April 13 last year. ② perform; administer; apply: ～急救 administer (*or* apply) first aid / ～手术 perform a surgical operation

施药 shīyào　give medicine to the poor free of charge

施医 shīyī　(also 施诊 shīzhěn) give free medical service to the poor; treat poor patients free of charge

施用 shīyòng　use; employ: ～化肥 use chemical fertilizer

施与 shīyǔ　grant (money, gifts, etc.) to sb.; bestow (favours) on sb.

施斋 shīzhāi　provide (itinerant) monks with free food

施展 shīzhǎn　put to good use; give free play to: ～本领 put one's ability (*or* talent) to good use / 把全部技术都～出来 give full play to one's technical competence / ～出种种逼利诱的伎俩 resort to all kinds of threats and inducements / ～阴谋诡计 carry out plots and schemes

施政 shīzhèng　the management of government affairs; administration: ～纲领 administrative programme / ～方针 administrative policy

施脂粉 shī zhīfěn　apply cosmetics: 薄～ apply a light make-up

施粥 shīzhōu　provide free porridge for the poor

施主 shīzhǔ　(monks' or nuns' form of address for a layman) patron

湿 (濕、溼) shī　wet; damp; humid: 小心点, 别～了衣裳。 Be careful! Don't get your clothes wet. / 别穿那双袜子, 还～着呢。 Don't wear those socks, they're still damp.

湿痹 shībì　*Chin. med.* arthritis with fixed pain caused by dampness

湿病 shībìng　*Chin. med.* diseases caused by dampness

湿答答 shīdādā　dripping wet

湿度 shīdù　humidity; moisture: 空气～ air humidity / 土壤的～ moisture content (*or* capacity) in soil

湿度表 shīdùbiǎo　humidometer

湿法冶金 shīfǎ yějīn　hydrometallurgy

湿纺 shīfǎng　*text.* wet spinning

湿乎乎 shīhūhū　(also 湿呼呼 shīhūhū) damp; moist; humid: 近来天气老是～的。 It has been rather humid these last few days. / 这条毛巾还有点～的。 This towel is still damp.

湿津津 shījīnjīn　moist with sweat; sweaty

湿淋淋 shīlínlín　dripping wet; drenched: 身上浇得～ get dripping (*or* soaking, sopping) wet; be soaked to the skin / ～的衣服 sopping wet clothes

湿漉漉 shīlùlù　(also 湿渌渌 shīlùlù) moist; damp

湿蒙蒙 shīmēngmēng　(of the air) damp; moist: 清晨有点雾, 空气～的。 It was a misty morning, and the air was moist.

湿气 shīqì　*Chin. med.* eczema or fungus infection of hand or foot

湿热 shīrè　damp and hot

湿润 shīrùn　moist: ～的土壤 damp soil / 空气～ humid air / 她眼睛～了。 Her eyes were moist with tears.

湿水货 shīshuǐhuò　water-damaged goods

湿透 shītòu　wet through; drenched: 汗水～了他的衣服。 His clothes are drenched with sweat.

湿选 shīxuǎn　*min.* wet separation

湿疹 shīzhěn　eczema

薯 shī　*bot.* alpine yarrow (*Achillea alpina*)

嘘 shī　*interj.* hush; sh: ～, 别作声! Sh! (*or* Hush!) Keep quiet! ——see also xū

鰤 (鰤) shī　yellowtail (a fish)

蝨 shī　carp louse; fish louse

shí

十 shí　① ten: ～倍 ten times; tenfold ② topmost: ～成 100 per cent

十八般武艺 shíbā bān wǔyì　skill in wielding the 18 kinds of weapons—skill in various types of combat: ～, 样样精通 be skilful in using each and every one of the 18 weapons; be versatile

十八层地狱 shíbā céng dìyù　the eighteenth hell—the lowest depths of hell ——see also 打入十八层地狱 dǎrù shíbā céng dìyù

十边地 shíbiāndì　small plots of land by the side of houses, roads, ponds, etc.

十不闲儿 shíbùxiánr　same as 什不闲儿 shíbùxiánr

十步芳草 shíbù fāngcǎo (short for 十步之内, 必有芳草) fragrant grass is to be found within ten paces—talent is close at hand

十大功劳 shídàgōngláo *Chin. med.* Chinese mahonia (*Mahonia fortunei*)

十滴水 shídīshuǐ *pharm.* "10 drops" (a popular medicine for summer ailments)

十冬腊月 shí-dōng-làyuè the tenth, eleventh and twelfth months of the lunar year; the cold months of the year

十恶不赦 shí è bù shè guilty of unpardonable evil; unpardonably wicked: 一群青面獠牙、～的人 a horde of fiendish monsters who perpetrate every conceivable crime and are unpardonably wicked

十二分 shíèrfēn more than 100 per cent; extremely: 感到～的满意 be more than satisfied / 我有～的把握。I am more than 100 per cent sure.

十二红 shíèrhóng Japanese waxwing (a bird)

十二黄 shíèrhuáng waxwing (a bird)

十二级风 shíèrjífēng *meteorol.* force 12 wind; hurricane

十二码球 shíèrmǎqiú same as 点球 diǎnqiú

十二门徒 shíèr méntú *Christianity* the 12 apostles of Jesus Christ

十二平均律 shíèr píngjūnlǜ *mus.* twelve-tone equal temperament

十二生肖 shíèr shēngxiào (also 十二属相 shíèr shǔxiang) the 12 symbolic animals associated with a 12-year cycle—see also 生肖 shēngxiào, 属相 shǔxiang

十二月 shíèryuè ① December ② the twelfth month of the lunar year; the twelfth moon

十二指肠 shíèrzhǐcháng *physiol.* duodenum

十二指肠溃疡 shíèrzhǐcháng kuìyáng duodenal ulcer

十番 shífān short for 十番锣鼓 shífān luógǔ

十番锣鼓 shífān luógǔ (also 十番乐 shífānyuè) ensemble of ten traditional percussion instruments (with a drum and gong leading)

十方 shífāng *Buddhism* the ten positions (i.e. the four cardinal points 东、西、南、北, the intermediate points 东南、西南、东北、西北, and above and below 上、下)

十分 shífēn *adv.* very; fully; utterly; extremely: ～高兴 be very pleased; be elated / ～难过 feel very sorry; feel very bad / ～宝贵 most valuable / ～有害 extremely harmful / ～注意 pay close (*or* the closest) attention to / ～仇视 harbour intense hatred for / ～猖狂 be on a rampage / ～爱惜人力物力 use manpower and material resources most sparingly

十个指头有长短 shígè zhǐtou yǒu chángduǎn the fingers are unequal in length—you can't expect everybody to be the same

十行俱下 shí háng jù xià take in ten lines at a glance—read rapidly: 他读书～。He is a rapid reader who takes in ten lines at a glance.

十级风 shíjífēng *meteorol.* force 10 wind; whole gale

十戒 shíjiè *Buddhism* the Ten Prohibitions

十诫 shíjiè *Christianity* the Ten Commandments; the Decalogue

十锦 shíjǐn same as 什锦 shíjǐn

十进对数 shíjìn duìshù another name for 常用对数 chángyòng duìshù

十进制 shíjìnzhì *math.* the decimal system

十六分音符 shíliùfēn yīnfú *mus.* semiquaver; sixteenth note

十六开 shíliù kāi *print.* sixteenmo; 16mo

十目所视, 十手所指 shí mù suǒ shì, shí shǒu suǒ zhǐ with many eyes watching and many fingers pointing—one cannot do wrong without being seen

十拿九稳 shíná-jiǔwěn (also 十成九稳 shíchéng-jiǔwěn) ninety per cent sure; practically certain; in the bag: 这事情, 我们是～了。We have the matter well in hand. /

这生意～赚钱。This is a business where we can be sure of making money.

十年动乱 shí nián dòngluàn the decade of disturbance; the ten-year upheaval (*or* turmoil); the ten chaotic years (referring to the Cultural Revolution 1966–1976)

十年寒窗 shí nián hánchuāng ten years' study at a cold window—a student's long years of hard study: ～无人问, 一举成名天下知。After ten years' hard study noticed by none, His fame fills the land once honours are won.

十年九不遇 shí nián jiǔ bù yù not occur once in ten years; be seldom seen: 今年这么大的雨量, 真是～。Such heavy rainfalls as this year's are seldom seen.

十年内战 shí nián nèizhàn the Ten-Year Civil War (referring to the Second Revolutionary Civil War 1927–1937)

十年树木, 百年树人 shínián shù mù, bǎi nián shù rén it takes ten years to grow trees, but a hundred to rear people

十全 shíquán complete; perfect: 世上没有～的人。No man is perfect.

十全十美 shíquán-shíměi be perfect in every way; be the acme of perfection; leave nothing to be desired

十三经 Shísān Jīng the Thirteen Classics (i.e. *The Book of Changes* 《易经》, *The Book of History* 《书经》, *The Book of Songs* 《诗经》, *The Ritual of Zhou* 《周礼》, *The Book of Etiquette and Ceremonial* 《仪礼》, *The Book of Rites* 《礼记》, *The Zuo Commentary* 《左传》, *The Gongyang Commentary* 《公羊传》, *The Guliang Commentary* 《谷梁传》, *The Classic of Filial Piety* 《孝经》, *The Analects* 《论语》, *The Book of Mencius* 《孟子》, and *The Literary Expositor* 《尔雅》)

十三陵 Shísānlíng the Thirteen Tombs, or the Ming Tombs (in Beijing, where 13 of the 16 Ming emperors lie buried with their empresses and concubines)

十三辙 shísānzhé the thirteen rhyme schemes (used in traditional opera)

十室九空 shí shì jiǔ kōng nine houses out of ten are stripped bare—the aftermath of war, natural calamities, etc.

十四行诗 shísìhángshī sonnet

十万八千里 shíwàn bāqiān lǐ a distance of one hundred and eight thousand *li*; poles apart: 离题～ miles away from the subject; completely off the point

十万火急 shíwàn huǒjí most urgent; posthaste; express: 这是野战军司令部拍来的～的电报。This is a signal of the utmost urgency from Field Army Headquarters. / ～ Most Urgent (formerly as a mark on dispatches)

十项全能运动 shí xiàng quánnéng yùndòng *sports* decathlon

十羊九牧 shíyáng-jiǔmù nine shepherds for ten sheep—too many bosses

十一 Shí Yī October 1, National Day of the People's Republic of China

十一级风 shíyījífēng *meteorol.* force 11 wind; storm

十一月 shíyīyuè ① November ② the eleventh month of the lunar year; the eleventh moon

十月 shíyuè ① October ② the tenth month of the lunar year; the tenth moon

十月革命 Shíyuè Gémìng the October Revolution (in Russia, 1917)

十之八九 shí zhī bā-jiǔ (also 十有八九 shí yǒu bā-jiǔ) in eight or nine cases out of ten; most likely: ～他是误会了。Most likely there is some misunderstanding on his part.

十指连心 shí zhǐ lián xīn the fingers are linked to the heart—what happens to children is of vital interest to parents

十姊妹 shízǐmèi multiflora rose (*Rosa multiflora*)

十字镐　shízìgǎo　pick; pickaxe; mattock

十字花科　shízìhuākē　*bot.* the mustard family

十字架　shízìjià　the Cross: 背上～ take up one's cross

十字街头　shízì jiētóu　crisscross streets; busy city streets

十字军　Shízìjūn　① the Crusades (11th–13th centuries) ② crusade ③ crusader

十字路口　shízì lùkǒu　crossroads; intersection: 徘徊在～ hesitate at the crossroads

十足　shízú　① pure: ～的黄金 pure gold ② 100 per cent; out-and-out; sheer; downright: 干劲～ full of energy / ～的强权政治 100% (*or* naked) power politics / ～的唯心主义 sheer idealism / ～的强盗逻辑 downright gangster logic

十足类　shízúlèi　*zool.* Decapoda; decapods

什

什　shí　① *formal* (used in fractions or multiples) ten: ～一 one tenth / ～百 tenfold or hundredfold ② assorted; varied; miscellaneous: 什物 shíwù ——see also shén

什不闲儿　shíbùxiánr　a kind of ballad-singing, accompanied by gong, drum, cymbals, etc.

什件儿　shíjiànr　① giblets: 炒～ fried giblets ② *dial.* metal decorations fixed on trunks, carriages, swords, etc.

什锦　shíjǐn　assorted; mixed: ～饼干 assorted biscuits / ～奶糖 assorted toffees

什物　shíwù　articles for daily use; odds and ends; sundries

什叶派　Shíyèpài　*Islam* Shiah; Shiites

石

石　shí　① stone; rock ② stone inscription: 金石 jīnshí ③ (Shí) a surname ——see also dàn

石斑鱼　shíbānyú　grouper (a fish)

石板　shíbǎn　① slabstone; flagstone; flag ② slate (for writing on)

石版　shíbǎn　*print.* stone plate

石碑　shíbēi　stone tablet; stele

石笔　shíbǐ　slate pencil

石壁　shíbì　cliff; precipice

石菖蒲　shíchāngpú　grass-leaved sweetflag (*Acorus gramineus*)

石沉大海　shí chén dàhǎi　like a stone dropped into the sea—disappear for ever; never to be seen or heard of again

石担　shídàn　*sports* stone barbell

石刁柏　shídiāobǎi　asparagus (*Asparagus officinalis*)

石雕　shídiāo　① stone carving ② carved stone

石碓　shíduì　a treadle-operated tilt hammer for hulling rice

石墩　shídūn　a block of stone used as a seat

石方　shífāng　cubic metre of stonework: 一百万～ one million cubic metres of stonework

石坊　shífāng　stone memorial archway (*or* gateway)

石舫　shífǎng　① stone boat (a stone boat-shaped pavilion in Chinese gardens) ② (Shífǎng) the Marble Boat (in the Summer Palace, Beijing)

石膏　shígāo　① gypsum; plaster stone ② *med.* (for a broken bone) plaster cast; cast: 他的腿上了～。 He had a plaster cast on his leg. / 她的胳臂上着～。 Her broken arm was placed in a cast.

石膏绷带　shígāo bēngdài　plaster bandage

石膏床　shígāochuáng　plaster bed

石膏夹板　shígāo jiābǎn　plaster splint

石膏像　shígāoxiàng　plaster statue; plaster figure

石工　shígōng　① masonry ② stonemason; mason

石拱桥　shígǒngqiáo　stone arch bridge

石鼓文　shígǔwén　① inscriptions on drum-shaped stone blocks of the Warring States Period (475–221 B.C.) ②

the script used for such inscriptions

石磙　shígǔn　another name for 碌碡 liùzhou

石河　shíhé　stone river; rock stream

石斛　shíhú　① noble dendrobium (*Dendrobium nobile*) ② *Chin. med.* the stem of noble dendrobium

石花菜　shíhuācài　agar (a seaweed)

石花胶　shíhuājiāo　agar-agar

石化作用　shíhuà zuòyòng　*geol.* petrifaction

石灰　shíhuī　lime: 生～ quick lime / 熟～ slaked lime

石灰华　shíhuīhuá　travertine; tufa

石灰浆　shíhuījiāng　lime white

石灰砂浆　shíhuī shājiāng　lime mortar

石灰石　shíhuīshí　limestone

石灰水　shíhuīshuǐ　limewash

石灰岩　shíhuīyán　limestone

石灰窑　shíhuīyáo　limekiln

石灰质砂岩　shíhuīzhì shāyán　calcareous sandstone

石鸡　shíjī　chukar (a partridge)

石级　shíjí　a flight of stone steps

石家庄　Shíjiāzhuāng　Shijiazhuang (capital of Hebei Province)

石匠　shíjiang　stonemason; mason

石决明　shíjuémíng　*Chin. med.* the shell of abalone or sea-ear

石坎　shíkǎn　① stone dam (for flood control) ② stone steps (carved out of a rocky mountainside)

石刻　shíkè　① carved stone ② stone inscription

石窟　shíkū　rock cave; grotto: 云岗～ the Yungang Grottoes (at Datong in Shanxi Province)

石窟寺　shíkūsì　cave temple

石块　shíkuài　stone block; rock

石硌子　shílázi　(also 石头硌子 shítoulázi) *dial.* projecting rock; crag; boulder

石蜡　shílà　paraffin wax: ～油 paraffin oil

石栗　shílì　candlenut tree

石料　shíliào　stone as material

石林　shílín　stone forest

石硫合剂　shíliú héjì　*chem.* lime sulfur

石榴　shíliu　pomegranate

石榴红　shíliuhóng　garnet (colour)

石榴裙　shíliuqún　pomegranate-red skirt—feminine charms (used esp. in the phrase): 拜倒在～下 prostrate oneself before a pomegranate-red skirt—be infatuated with a woman

石榴石　shíliushí　garnet (a mineral)

石龙子　shílóngzǐ　skink (a lizard)

石绿　shílǜ　malachite green (a green pigment made of malachite, often used in traditional Chinese painting)

石煤　shíméi　bone coal

石棉　shímián　asbestos

石棉板　shímiánbǎn　*archit.* asbestos board

石棉布　shímiánbù　asbestos cloth

石棉衬里　shímián chènlǐ　*mech.* asbestos lining

石棉瓦　shímiánwǎ　*archit.* asbestos shingle; asbestos tile

石墨　shímò　graphite

石墨铀堆　shímòyóuduī　graphite-uranium pile

石磨　shímó　millstones

石楠　shínán　Chinese photinia (*Photinia serrulata*)

石脑油　shínǎoyóu　naphtha

石女　shínǚ　a woman with a hypoplastic vagina

石破天惊　shípò-tiānjīng　heaven-shaking—(of a message, opinion, etc.) remarkably original and forceful

石器　shíqì　① stone implement; stone artifact ② stone vessel; stoneware

石器时代　Shíqì Shídài　the Stone Age

石青　shíqīng　azurite blue (a blue pigment made of azurite, often used in traditional Chinese painting)

石蕊　shíruǐ　① reindeer moss (*Cladonia rangiferina*)

② *chem.* litmus

石蕊试纸 shíruǐ shìzhǐ *chem.* litmus paper

石首鱼 shíshǒuyú sciaenoid; sciaenid

石蒜 shísuàn short-tube lycoris (*Lycoris radiata*)

石笋 shísǔn *geol.* stalagmite

石锁 shísuǒ *sports* a stone dumbbell in the form of an old-fashioned padlock

石炭 shítàn *arch.* coal

石炭纪 Shítànjì *geol.* the Carboniferous Period

石炭酸 shítànsuān *chem.* carbolic acid

石炭系 Shítànxì *geol.* the Carboniferous System

石头 shítou stone; rock: ～砌的墙 a stone wall／心里好像一块～落了地 feel as though a load has been taken off one's mind

石头子儿 shítouzǐr *inf.* cobblestone; cobble; pebble: 男孩子们爱往池塘里扔～。 The boys like to throw pebbles (*or* stones) into the pond.／一条～铺的小路 a cobbled path

石盐 shíyán same as 岩盐 yányán

石羊 shíyáng another name for 岩羊 yányáng

石印 shíyìn lithographic printing; lithography

石印机 shíyìnjī lithographic press

石印石 shíyìnshí lithographic stone

石印油画 shíyìn yóuhuà oleograph

石印纸 shíyìnzhǐ lithographic paper

石英 shíyīng quartz

石英玻璃 shíyīng bōli quartz glass

石英电子表 shíyīng diànzǐbiǎo quartz watch

石英电子钟 shíyīng diànzǐzhōng quartz clock

石英卤钨灯 shíyīng lǔwūdēng *photog.* quartz tungsten halogen lamp

石英岩 shíyīngyán quartzite

石油 shíyóu petroleum; oil

石油地质学 shíyóu dìzhìxué petroleum geology

石油工业 shíyóu gōngyè oil industry; petroleum industry

石油管路 shíyóu guǎnlù petroleum pipeline

石油化工厂 shíyóu huàgōngchǎng petrochemical works

石油化学 shíyóu huàxué petrochemistry: ～产品 petroleum chemicals

石油勘探 shíyóu kāntàn petroleum prospecting

石油沥青 shíyóu lìqīng petroleum pitch

石油美元 shíyóu měiyuán petrodollars

石油气 shíyóuqì petroleum gas

石油输出国组织 Shíyóu Shūchūguó Zǔzhī the Organization of Petroleum Exporting Countries (OPEC)

石油运移 shíyóu yùnyí oil migration

石钟乳 shízhōngrǔ same as 钟乳石 zhōngrǔshí

石竹 shízhú China pink (*Dianthus chinensis*)

石柱 shízhù stone pillar

石子儿 shízǐr cobblestone; cobble; pebble: ～路 cobblestone road; cobbled road

石作 shízuò masonry

识(識)

shí ① know: 一字不～ not know a single character—absolutely illiterate ② knowledge: 学识 xuéshí ／见多识广 jiànduō-shíguǎng ——see also zhì

识拔 shíbá recognize the worth of and promote (a person): 他善于在青年中～人才。 He is good at picking out young talent.

识辨 shíbiàn distinguish; discern

识别 shíbié distinguish; discern; spot: ～真伪 distinguish true from false; distinguish between genuine and sham／善于～干部 know how to judge cadres／～骗子 spot a swindler／～伪装的敌人 see through enemies in disguise／你能不能～远处的那些东西？ Can you distinguish the objects in the distance?

识别力 shíbiélì discernment

识大体，顾大局 shí dàtǐ, gù dàjú have the cardinal principles in mind and take the overall situation into account

识货 shíhuò know all about the goods; be able to tell good from bad; know what's what

识见 shíjiàn *formal* knowledge and insight

识荆 shíjīng *formal pol.* have the honour of making your acquaintance

识破 shípò see through; penetrate: ～骗局 see through a fraud／～敌人的伪装 penetrate the disguise of the enemy

识趣 shíqù know how to behave in a delicate situation; be sensible; be tactful

识时务者为俊杰 shí shíwù zhě wéi jùnjié whosoever understands the times is a great man; a wise man submits to circumstances

识途老马 shí tú lǎomǎ an old horse who knows the way—a person of rich experience; a wise old bird

识文断字 shíwén-duànzì be able to read; be literate

识相 shíxiàng *dial.* be sensible; be tactful: 你还是～点，赶快走吧。 You'd better be sensible and quit.

识羞 shíxiū (usu. used in the negative) have a sense of shame: 他对我撒了谎还不～。 He feels no shame for having lied to me.

识者 shízhě *formal* the knowledgeable; the discerning: 文中不当之处，有待～教正。 Infelicities of statement, if any, await correction by the knowledgeable.

识字 shízì learn to read; become literate: 他识几个字。 He can read a little.

识字班 shízìbān literacy class

识字课本 shízì kèběn reading primer; elementary reader

时(時)

shí ① a long period of time; times; days: 古时 gǔshí ② fixed time: 按时 ànshí ③ season: 四时 sìshí ／农时 nóngshí ④ time of day; hour; o'clock: 上午八～ at 8 o'clock in the morning; at 8 a.m. ⑤ current; present: 时下 shíxià ⑥ opportunity; chance: 待～而动 bide one's time ⑦ *adv.* now and then; occasionally; from time to time: ～有发生 occur from time to time ⑧ *gram.* tense: 过去～ the past tense ⑨ (Shí) a surname

时弊 shíbì ills of the times

时病 shíbìng ① ills of the times ② seasonal disease

时不可失 shí bùkě shī don't let slip an opportunity

时不时 shíbùshí *adv. dial.* often; time and again

时不我待 shí bù wǒ dài time and tide wait for no man

时差 shíchā ① differences of local time between places belonging to different time zones ② *astron.* equation of time

时差反应 shíchā fǎnyìng jet lag; jet fatigue

时常 shícháng *adv.* often; frequently: 我们～玩儿牌。 We often play cards.

时辰 shíchen ① one of the 12 two-hour periods into which the day was formerly divided before the introduction of western chronology (each being given the name of one of the 12 Earthly Branches 地支); double-hour: 约莫半个～ about an hour ② the time for sth; opportunity

时代 shídài ① times; age; era; epoch: 封建～ feudal times／五四～ the days of the May 4 Movement／电子～ the era of electronics／开创一个新～ usher in a new era／新～的凯歌 a paean of triumph to the new age ② the times; our age; the day; the present era: ～精神 the spirit of our age; the spirit of the times／反映～的面貌 reflect the features of our age／～潮流 the tendency of the day; the trend of the times／～的需要 the needs of the times ③ a period in one's life: 从青年～到老年～ from youth to old age

时调 shídiào popular tunes in a particular locality: 天津～ Tianjin tunes

时而 shí'ér *adv.* ① from time to time; sometimes: 天上～飘过几片薄薄的白云。 Every now and then fleecy clouds floated across the sky. ② (used reduplicatively) now...now...; sometimes... sometimes...: 这天气变化无常,～晴天,～下雨! What changeable weather, fine one moment, raining the next!

时分 shífēn the time of; the time when: 黄昏～ at dusk; at twilight / 深夜～ in the dead of night / 三更～ at the third watch

时乖命蹇 shíguāi-mìngjiǎn be born under an evil star; have the hand of fate against one; fall on bad times

时光 shíguāng ① time: ～不早了。 It's getting late. / ～过得真快,一晃二十年了。 How time flies! Without my knowing it, twenty years have passed. ② times; years; days: 他一生中最好的～白白浪费了。 He wasted the best years of his life.

时过境迁 shíguò-jìngqiān things have changed with the lapse of time

时号 shíhào time signal

时好 shíhào fashion; fad

时候 shíhou ① (the duration of) time: 你写这篇文章用了多少～? How much time did you spend writing this article? / 农忙的～ a busy farming season ② (a point in) time; moment: 现在是什么～了? What time is it? / 就在这～ just at this moment

时会 shíhuì the particular circumstances of the time: 迫于～ be forced by the circumstances

时或 shíhuò now and then; sometimes; at times

时机 shíjī opportunity; an opportune moment: 等待～ wait for an opportunity; bide one's time / 错过最有利的～ let slip a golden opportunity / 抓住每一个可以利用的～ seize (*or* take) every opportunity available / ～的选择 choice of the right moment; timing / ～一到 when the opportunity arises; at the opportune moment / ～不成熟。 Conditions are not yet ripe. *or* The time is not yet ripe. / ～已经成熟,可以行动了。 The time is ripe for action.

时计 shíjì *astron.* chronometer

时际 shíjì time; occasion: 节日～我们一般都在一起聚会。 We used to get together on festive days.

时价 shíjià current price; prevailing price: 本店售价略低于～。 Our listed prices are slightly lower than the current prices.

时间 shíjiān ① (the concept of) time: ～与空间 time and space ② (the duration of) time: 这项工程需要多少～? How long will it take to finish this project? / ～紧,任务重。 Time is pressing and the task heavy. / ～到了。 Time! *or* Time's up. / 办公～ office hours / 不给对手喘息的～ give your opponent no breathing space / ～掌握得好 beautiful timing ③ (a point in) time: 现在的～是四点五分。 The time now is five minutes past four. / 北京～十九点整 19 hours Beijing time

时间表 shíjiānbiǎo timetable; schedule

时间词 shíjiāncí *gram.* time word (e.g. 过去,现在,今天,明天,etc., which are basically nouns but also function adverbially)

时间性 shíjiānxìng seasonality; timeliness; topicality: 大凡农活都有～。 Farming is largely seasonal work. / 新闻报导的～强。 News reports must be timely. / 这项任务～强。 This task must be fulfilled on time.

时间知觉 shíjiān zhījué *psychol.* time perception

时艰 shíjiān *formal* a critical situation (as for a nation); troublous times: 共济～ pull together in times of trouble

时角 shíjiǎo *astron.* hour angle

时节 shíjié ① season (marked by certain weather conditions, activities, etc.): 春耕～ the season for spring ploughing / 秋收～ harvest time ② a particular time; occasion: 解放那～她才十二岁。 She was only twelve at the time of liberation.

时局 shíjú the current political situation

时刻 shíkè ① a point of time; hour; moment: 欢乐的～ a time of rejoicing / 幸福的～ a happy moment / 在此关键～ at this crucial hour / 处于重要的历史～ at a critical historical juncture / 严守～ be strictly punctual ② *adv.* constantly; always: ～准备保卫祖国 be ready to defend the country at any moment / 时时刻刻为人民利益着想 always keep the people's interests in mind

时刻表 shíkèbiǎo timetable; schedule: 火车～ railway timetable; train schedule

时来运转 shí lái yùn zhuǎn one's luck turns in the fullness of time

时令 shílìng season: ～已交初秋。 It is already early autumn.

时令 shíling *dial.* seasonal disease: 这阵子正闹～。 At this time of year, seasonal diseases are rampant.

时令病 shílìngbìng seasonal disease: 冬春之交是～流行的季节。 Seasonal diseases are prevalent when winter is changing into spring.

时令不正 shílìng bù zhèng unseasonable weather: 今年～,春旱秋涝,夏天又闹雹灾。 We have had unseasonable weather all through the year: a prolonged drought in spring, a hailstorm in summer, and continued waterlogging in autumn.

时髦 shímáo fashionable; stylish; in vogue: ～的服装 fashionable clothes / 赶～ follow the fashion

时评 shípíng news commentary; editorial

时期 shíqī a particular period: 社会主义建设～ the period of socialist construction / 抗日战争～ during the Anti-Japanese War

时起时伏 shíqǐ-shífú now rise, now fall; have ups and downs

时气 shíqi *dial.* ① a stroke of luck: 他～多好! What luck he had! ② seasonal disease

时穷节乃见 shí qióng jié nǎi jiàn integrity (*or* loyalty) shines out in time of woe

时区 shíqū time zone

时人 shírén *old* contemporaries: ～有诗为证。 There is a verse by a contemporary poet which testifies to this.

时日 shírì time: 如若假以～,试验必获成功。 Given time, the experiment is sure to yield results.

时尚 shíshàng fashion; fad

时时 shíshí *adv.* often; constantly: ～想到 often recall or think about / ～处处严格要求自己 be strict with oneself in all matters

时…时… shí…shí… *adv.* now...now...; sometimes... sometimes...: 心情时喜时忧 have changing moods, now gay, now gloomy / 镜头时远时近 sometimes long shots and sometimes close-ups

时世 shíshì times; age: 艰难～ hard times

时式 shíshì up-to-date style (of clothes, etc.); the latest fashion: ～大衣 a coat of the latest fashion

时势 shíshì the current situation; the trend of the times; the way things are going

时势造英雄 shíshì zào yīngxióng the times produce their heroes

时事 shíshì current events; current affairs: ～报告 report on current events / ～述评 current events survey / ～学习 study of current affairs

时速 shísù speed per hour: ～高达三百公里。 It has a top speed of 300 km. per hour.

时态 shítài *gram.* tense

时文 shíwén (in former times) a prescribed essay form for the civil service examinations (referring esp. to the eight-part essay 八股文)

时务 shíwù current affairs; the current situation; the

trend of the times: 不识时务　bù shí shíwù

时下　shíxià　*adv.*　at present; right now

时鲜　shíxiān　(of vegetables, fruits, fishes, etc.) in season: ～果品 fresh fruits and nuts / 新到草莓, 是上好的～货。We've got tip-top strawberries just in season.

时贤　shíxián　*formal*　contemporary worthies; contemporary scholars

时限　shíxiàn　time limit: 在规定的～内 within the prescribed time

时宪书　shíxiànshū　*old*　almanac

时效　shíxiào　① effectiveness for a given period of time ② *leg.* prescription ③ *metall.* ageing

时效硬化　shíxiào yìnghuà　*metall.*　age-hardening

时新　shíxīn　stylish; trendy: ～的式样 up-to-date style

时兴　shíxīng　(also 时行 shíxíng) fashionable; in vogue; popular: 这种式样已经不～了。This design (or style) is no longer in vogue (or is out of fashion now).

时样　shíyàng　same as 时式 shíshì

时宜　shíyí　what is appropriate to the occasion: 不合时宜　bùhé shíyí

时移俗易　shíyí-súyì　customs change with the times

时疫　shíyì　epidemic

时运　shíyùn　luck; fortune

时运不济　shíyùn bùjì　have bad luck; be down on one's luck: 她跟着丈夫离开了家乡, 后来～, 他又病死了。She left home to go with her husband, but as ill luck would have it he fell sick and died.

时针　shízhēn　① hands of a clock or watch ② hour hand (of a clock or watch)

时政　shízhèng　*old*　the political situation of the time

时值　shízhí　*mus.*　duration; value

时至今日　shí zhì jīnrì　at this late hour; even to this day: ～, 回想起来, 仍然难过。Even now the thought of it agonizes me.

时钟　shízhōng　clock

时装　shízhuāng　① fashionable dress; the latest fashion ② contemporary costume

时装表演　shízhuāng biǎoyǎn　fashion show; modelling: ～队 modelling team

时装模特儿　shízhuāng mótèr　fashion model

时装设计师　shízhuāng shèjìshī　fashion designer

实 (實)

shí　① solid: 里面是～的。It's solid. / 地基要砸～。The foundations must be tamped solid. ② true; real; actual: ～利 actual (or tangible) benefits / ～有其事。It's a fact. ③ reality; fact: 名不副实 míng bù fú shí ④ fruit; seed: 开花结～ blossom and bear fruit

实报实销　shíbào-shíxiāo　reimburse the amount actually spent; be reimbursed for what one spends

实逼处此　shí bī chǔ cǐ　be forced to do so by the circumstances; there's no alternative under the circumstances

实诚　shícheng　*inf.*　honest; trustworthy: ～话 honest words / 这个人～, 答应了的事不会做不到的。He's an honest man, and can be trusted to do what he promised.

实词　shící　*gram.*　notional word

实打实　shí dǎ shí　real; true; honest; genuine: ～的本领 real skill; genuine skill / ～地说吧 to tell the truth; honestly

实弹　shídàn　① (of a gun or cannon) be loaded: 荷枪～ carry a loaded rifle ② *mil.* live shell; live ammunition: ～射击 live firing; firing practice; range practice / ～演习 practice with live ammunition

实地　shídì　on the spot: ～考察 on-the-spot investigation / ～了解施工情况 learn on the spot how construction is proceeding

实繁有徒　shí fán yǒu tú　there is no lack of people of that ilk

实感　shígǎn　thoughts and feelings acquired from personal experience; true feelings

实干　shígàn　get right on the job; do solid work

实干家　shígànjiā　man of action

实话　shíhuà　truth: 说～ tell the truth

实话实说　shíhuà-shíshuō　speak frankly; talk straight; not mince matters

实惠　shíhuì　① material benefit: 从中得到～ really benefit from it / 这几年人民得到的～最多。In recent years the people have received greater material benefits than ever before. ② substantial; solid: 让顾客吃到经济～的饭菜 serve the customers inexpensive but substantial meals

实际　shíjì　① reality; practice: 理论和～ theory and practice / 客观～ objective reality / 切合当地～ suit the local conditions / 从～出发 proceed from actual conditions; be realistic / ～上 in fact; in practice; in reality; actually / 思想落后于～的事是常有的。It often happens that thinking lags behind reality. / 青年人一接触生活～, 理想往往就会破灭。Young people's idealism is often destroyed when they experience life's practicalities. ② practical; realistic: ～经验 practical experience / 你这种想法不～。This idea of yours is unrealistic. / 把革命气概和～精神结合起来 combine revolutionary sweep with practicality ③ real; actual; concrete: ～的例子 a concrete instance / ～情况 the actual situation; reality / ～生活水平 the real standard of living / ～收入 real income

实际工资　shíjì gōngzī　real wages

实际汇价　shíjì huìjià　effective exchange rate

实际控制线　shíjì kòngzhìxiàn　*mil.*　line of actual control

实绩　shíjì　actual results; tangible achievements: 这本文集是他近年来创作上的～。These collected writings embody the fruits of his creative labours in recent years. / 他为官三年, 无～可言。He had nothing tangible to show for his three years of office.

实价　shíjià　actual price

实践　shíjiàn　① practice: 学习语言需要大量～。It requires much practice to learn a language. ② put into practice; carry out; live up to: ～诺言 keep one's word; make good one's promise / ～自己的主张 put one's ideas into practice

实践出真知　shíjiàn chū zhēnzhī　genuine knowledge comes from practice

实践性　shíjiànxìng　practicality; practicalness

实据　shíjù　substantial evidence; substantial proof: 查无实据 chá wú shíjù

实况　shíkuàng　what is actually happening: 电视转播群众大会～ televise a mass rally; live telecast of a mass rally

实况录音　shíkuàng lùyīn　on-the-spot recording; live recording

实况转播　shíkuàng zhuǎnbō　televise live; live broadcast; live telecast

实力　shílì　actual strength; strength: 国家经济～ national economic strength / 国防～ national defence capabilities / 军事～ military strength / ～相当 match each other in strength; be well matched in strength

实力地位　shílì dìwèi　position of strength

实力政策　shílì zhèngcè　policy of force

实例　shílì　living example; example: 用～说明 illustrate with examples

实录　shílù　① *formal* a faithful record: 这本日记是他晚年生活的～。This diary is a faithful record of his declining years. ② veritable records (a type of annalistic history narrating the events of an emperor's reign): 韩愈《顺宗～》 Han Yu's *Veritable Records of Shunzong*

实脉　shímài　*Chin. med.*　forceful pulse

实模铸造法　shímúzhùzàofǎ　*metall.*　cavityless casting

实情 shíqíng the true state of affairs; the actual situation; truth: 你得讲～。You must tell the truth.

实情实理 shíqíng-shílǐ the actual situation and the real reason: 他说的都是～。What he says is perfectly true and reasonable.

实权 shíquán real power

实生苗 shíshēngmiáo *agric.* seedling

实施 shíshī put into effect; implement; carry out: 九年制义务教育正在逐步～。The system of nine-year compulsory education is being implemented. / 协定的条款正在付诸～。The provisions of the agreement are being put into effect. / 检查政策的～情况 check up on the implementation of the policy / 监督宪法的～ supervise the enforcement of the constitution

实事 shíshì practical things: 只说空话, 不干～ indulge in empty talk and do nothing practical / 为人民做～ do practical things for the people

实事求是 shíshì qiú shì seek truth from facts; be practical and realistic: ～的态度 a realistic approach / ～的工作作风 a practical and realistic style of work / ～的批评 criticism based on facts / ～地拟定生产指标 set realistic production targets

实数 shíshù ① the actual amount or number ② *math.* real number

实说 shíshuō to tell the truth; frankly speaking; frankly: ～了吧, 我根本就不同意你的意见。Frankly, I don't agree with you at all.

实体 shítǐ ① *philos.* substance ② entity: 一个独立的政治～ an independent political entity

实体法 shítǐfǎ *leg.* substantive law

实物 shíwù ① material object; object: 纪念馆展出了许多图片和～。The memorial hall displays many photographs and objects. ② goods or produce instead of money: 以～代替 in kind

实物地租 shíwù dìzū rent in kind

实物工资 shíwù gōngzī wages in kind

实物幻灯机 shíwù huàndēngjī epidiascope

实物交易 shíwù jiāoyì barter

实物税 shíwùshuì tax paid in kind

实习 shíxí (of students or trainees) practise (what has been learnt in class); exercise one's skill in; do fieldwork: 在中学～ do practice teaching at a middle school / 去煤矿～ go on a field trip to a coal mine / 进行护理～ do practice nursing

实习工厂 shíxí gōngchǎng a factory for training students in practical skills

实习教师 shíxí jiàoshī student teacher; trainee teacher

实习生 shíxíshēng trainee

实习医生 shíxí yīshēng intern

实现 shíxiàn realize; fulfil; carry out; bring about: ～自己的理想 realize one's ideal / ～自己的诺言 fulfil one's promises / ～计划 realize a plan / ～改革 bring about a reform / ～祖国统一 reunify the motherland / ～农业、工业、国防和科学技术的现代化 accomplish the modernization of agriculture, industry, national defence, and science and technology / 他的夙愿～了。His long-cherished wish has come true. / 她～了当演员的愿望。She realized her intention of becoming an actress.

实像 shíxiàng *phys.* real image

实效 shíxiào actual effect; substantial results: 讲求～ strive for substantial results / 注重～ emphasize practical results / 如果这方法确有～, 就应该推广。If the method proves to be really effective, it should be popularized.

实心 shíxīn ① sincere; honest: ～话 words spoken from one's heart ② solid: 这种车胎是～的。These tyres are solid.

实心球 shíxīnqiú *sports* medicine ball

实心实意 shíxīn-shíyì honest and sincere

实心眼儿 shíxīnyǎnr ① honest and serious-minded ② an honest and serious-minded person

实行 shíxíng put into practice (*or* effect); carry out; practise; implement: ～精兵简政的政策 put into effect the policy of better staff and simpler administration / ～经济改革 carry out economic reforms / ～八小时工作制 institute an eight-hour (working) day / ～科学种田 farm scientifically / 对反动分子～专政 exercise dictatorship over the reactionaries / ～民主 practise democracy / ～集体领导 exercise collective leadership

实性人 shíxìngrén an honest and sincere person

实学 shíxué real learning; sound scholarship: 有虚名而无～ have a false reputation and no real learning

实言 shíyán truth: ～相告 to tell you the truth

实验 shíyàn experiment; test: 做～ do (*or* carry out) an experiment; make a test

实验动物 shíyàn dòngwù animal used as a subject of experiment

实验室 shíyànshì laboratory

实验心理学 shíyàn xīnlǐxué experimental psychology

实验员 shíyànyuán laboratory technician

实业 shíyè industry and commerce; a large-scale industry or business

实业家 shíyèjiā industrialist

实益 shíyì real benefit

实用 shíyòng practical; pragmatic; functional: 既美观, 又～ not only beautiful, but also practical (*or* useful)

实用美术 shíyòng měishù applied fine arts

实用文 shíyòngwén *old* practical writing (as in official documents, notices, receipts, etc.)

实用学 shíyòngxué pragmatics

实用主义 shíyòngzhǔyì *philos.* pragmatism: ～者 pragmatist

实在 shízài ① true; real; honest; dependable: ～的本事 real ability / 心眼儿～ honest; trustworthy / 他这个人可～了。He is an honest and truly dependable man. ② *adv.* indeed; really; honestly: ～太好了。Very good indeed. / 我～不知道。Honestly I don't know. / ～抱歉! I'm really sorry! ③ *adv.* in fact; as a matter of fact: 他装懂, ～并没懂。He pretends to understand, but as a matter of fact he doesn't.

实在 shízai *dial.* (of work) well-done; done carefully: 工作做得很～。The work is well-done.

实在论 shízàilùn *philos.* realism

实则 shízé *adv.* actually; in fact; in reality

实战 shízhàn actual combat: 从～需要出发 proceed from the needs of actual combat / ～训练 exercises under battle conditions

实战演习 shízhàn yǎnxí combat exercise with live ammunition

实证 shízhèng authentic proof; substantial evidence

实证主义 shízhèngzhǔyì *philos.* positivism: ～者 positivist

实症 shízhèng *Chin. med.* a case of a physically strong patient running a high fever or suffering from such disorders as stasis of blood, constipation, etc.

实至名归 shí zhì míng guī fame follows merit

实质 shízhì substance; essence: 问题的～ the crux of the matter; the central point at issue / ～上 in substance; in essence; essentially; virtually

实质性 shízhìxìng substantive; substantial: ～条款 substantive provision / 取得～进展 make substantial progress

实字 shízì full word; content word

实足 shízú full; solid: 这袋麦子～一百斤。This sack of wheat is a full 100 *jin.* / 我～等了两个钟头。I waited for two solid hours.

实足年龄 shízú niánlíng exact age (i.e. age in completed years)

拾¹

shí ① pick up (from the ground); collect: ～到一个钱包 picked up a purse / ～柴 collect firewood / ～麦穗儿 glean (stray ears of) wheat ② tidy up; put in order: 收拾 shōushi

拾²

shí ten (used for the numeral 十 on cheques, banknotes, etc. to avoid mistakes or alterations)

拾掇 shíduo ① tidy up; put in order: 我们把屋子～一下。Let's tidy up the room. ② repair; fix: 这机器有点毛病，你给～一下好吗？Something is wrong with the machine. Will you help me fix it? ③ *inf.* settle with; punish

拾荒 shíhuāng glean and collect scraps (to eke out an existence)

拾金不昧 shí jīn bù mèi not pocket the money one picks up

拾零 shílíng (usu. used in headlines) news in brief; tit-bits; sidelights

拾取 shíqǔ pick up; collect: 在海滩上～贝壳 collect shells on the beach

拾人牙慧 shí rén yáhuì pick up phrases from sb. and pass them off as one's own

拾物 shíwù a lost article found

拾物招领处 shíwù zhāolǐngchù Lost and Found Office; Lost Property Office

拾遗 shíyí ① appropriate lost property: 路不拾遗 lù bù shíyí ② make good omissions (often used in book titles): 《本草纲目～》Supplementary Amplifications of the "Compendium of Materia Medica"

拾遗补阙 shíyí-bǔquē make good omissions and deficiencies

拾音器 shíyīnqì *elec.* pickup; adapter

食¹

shí ① eat: 多～蔬菜。Eat plenty of vegetables. ② meal; food: 丰衣足食 fēngyī-zúshí ③ food for animals; feed: 小猫出去找～儿了。The kittens are out looking for food. / 鸡～没剩多少了。There is only a little feed left for the chickens. ④ for cooking; edible: 食油 shíyóu

食²（蚀）

shí eclipse: 日食 rìshí / 月全食 yuèquánshí ——see also sì

食变星 shíbiànxīng *astron.* eclipsing variable
食不甘味 shí bù gān wèi eat without relish: 寝不安席，～ sleep fitfully and eat without relish
食不果腹 shí bù guǒfù have not enough food in one's belly; go hungry
食不厌精，脍不厌细 shí bù yàn jīng, kuài bù yàn xì eat no rice but is of the finest quality, nor meat but is finely minced—be very particular about one's food
食草动物 shícǎodòngwù herbivorous animal; herbivore
食虫动物 shíchóngdòngwù insectivorous animal; insectivore
食虫植物 shíchóngzhíwù insectivorous plant; insectivore
食道 shídào same as 食管 shíguǎn
食而不化 shí ér bù huà eat without digesting—read without understanding
食而不知其味 shí ér bù zhī qí wèi eat without knowing the taste of what one is eating—read without understanding
食饵 shíěr (fish) bait
食粪 shífèn coprophagy
食粪动物 shífèndòngwù coprophagous animal
食腐动物 shífǔdòngwù saprophagous animal; scavenger; saprozoic
食古不化 shí gǔ bù huà swallow ancient learning with-

out digesting it
食管 shíguǎn *physiol.* esophagus
食管癌 shíguǎn'ái cancer of the esophagus
食管炎 shíguǎnyán esophagitis
食火鸡 shíhuǒjī cassowary
食积 shíjī *Chin. med.* dyspepsia; indigestion
食既 shíjì *astron.* the second contact of a total eclipse; the beginning of totality ——see also 食相 shíxiàng
食具 shíjù eating utensils; tableware
食客 shíkè ① a person sponging on an aristocrat; a hanger-on of an aristocrat ② a customer of a restaurant
食粮 shíliáng grain; food: ～供应 food supplies / 精神～ spiritual food
食量 shíliàng capacity for eating; appetite: ～大（小）have a big (small) appetite
食疗 shíliáo food therapy; diet therapy
食料 shíliào food materials
食糜 shímí chyme (the pulp to which the food is reduced in the stomach)
食品 shípǐn foodstuff; food; provisions: 罐头～ tinned (or canned) food / ～保藏 food preservation / ～部 food department / ～厂 bakery and confectionery; food products factory / ～工业 food industry / ～公司 food company / ～加工 food processing / ～商店 provisions shop / ～质量管理 quality control of food
食品规则 Shípǐn Guīzé Codex Alimentarius (the code of laws governing food standards, food hygiene, additives, etc.)
食谱 shípǔ cookbook; recipes
食亲财黑 shí qīn cái hēi *dial.* selfish and greedy
食人俗 shírénsú cannibalism
食肉动物 shíròudòngwù carnivorous animal; carnivore
食肉寝皮 shíròu-qǐnpí (want to) eat sb.'s flesh and sleep on his skin—(want to) see the person one hates destroyed
食肉植物 shíròuzhíwù carnivorous plant; insectivorous plant; insectivore
食色性也 shí-sè xìng yě appetite for food and sex is nature
食少事烦 shíshǎo-shífán eat too little and does too much—cannot last long
食甚 shíshèn *astron.* the maximum phase of an eclipse; the middle of a total eclipse ——see also 食相 shíxiàng
食双星 shíshuāngxīng another name for 食变星 shíbiànxīng
食宿 shísù board and lodging
食堂 shítáng dining room; mess hall; canteen
食糖 shítáng sugar
食蚊鱼 shíwényú mosquito fish
食物 shíwù food; eatables; edibles
食物链 shíwùliàn food chain
食物摄入 shíwù shèrù *zool.* food intake
食物污染 shíwù wūrǎn food pollution
食物中毒 shíwù zhòngdú food poisoning
食相 shíxiàng *astron.* the phases of an eclipse: 日（月）全食时，有五个～：初亏、食既、食甚、生光、复圆。A total solar (lunar) eclipse goes through five phases: the first contact, the second contact, the middle or maximum phase, the third contact, and the fourth contact. / 日（月）偏食时，有三个～：初亏、食甚、复圆。A partial solar (lunar) eclipse goes through three phases: the first contact, the maximum phase, and the last contact.
食性 shíxìng *zool.* feeding habits; eating patterns
食血动物 shíxuèdòngwù sanguivorous (or haematophagous) animal
食言 shíyán go back on one's word; break one's prom-

ise: 你放心, 他从不～。 I assure you he is as good as his word.

食言而肥 shíyán ér féi　fail to make good one's promise; break faith with sb.

食盐 shíyán　table salt; salt

食蚁兽 shíyǐshòu　anteater

食用 shíyòng　① used for food ② edible: ～植物 edible plants／～植物油 edible vegetable oil

食用色素 shíyòng sèsù　food colouring

食油 shíyóu　edible oil; cooking oil

食欲 shíyù　appetite: 促进～ stimulate (or whet) the appetite; be appetizing

食欲不振 shíyù bù zhèn　① have a jaded appetite; have a poor appetite ② med. anorexia

食之无味, 弃之可惜 shí zhī wúwèi, qì zhī kěxī　hardly worth eating but not bad enough to throw away

食指 shízhǐ　① index finger; forefinger ② formal mouths to feed (in a family): ～众多, 入不敷出 have a large family to support and can hardly make both ends meet

食治 shízhì　food therapy; diet therapy

食茱萸 shízhūyú　ailanthus prickly ash (Zanthoxylum ailanthoides)

食租衣税 shízū-yīshuì　(of officials) live on taxes and levies

蚀 shí　① lose: 亏蚀 kuīshí ② erode; corrode: 锈能～铁。 Rust corrodes iron. ③ same as 食² shí

蚀本 shíběn　lose one's capital

蚀本生意 shíběn shēngyi　a business running at a loss; a losing proposition; an unprofitable venture (or undertaking)

蚀财 shícái　lose money or property

蚀耗 shíhào　loss; wear and tear

蚀刻 shíkè　etching: ～法 etching／～玻璃 etched glass

焻 shí　see below

焻器 shíqì　stoneware

鲥(鰣) shí　hilsa herring; reeves shad

鲥鱼 shíyú　hilsa herring; reeves shad

shǐ

史 shǐ　① history: 国际关系～ history of international relations ② official historian in ancient China ③ (Shǐ) a surname

史不绝书 shǐ bù jué shū　history is full of such instances

史册 shǐcè　(also 史策 shǐcè) history; annals: 在民族解放斗争～上写下灿烂的篇章 add an illustrious page to the annals of national liberation struggles

史抄 shǐchāo　extracts from history

史官 shǐguān　official historian in ancient China; historiographer

史馆 shǐguǎn　historiographers' office in ancient China

史话 shǐhuà　stories about historical events: 《淮海战役～》Stories of the Huai-Hai Campaign

史籍 shǐjí　same as 史书 shǐshū

史记 Shǐjì　Records of the Historian (written by Sima Qian 司马迁 of the Han Dynasty)

史迹 shǐjì　historical site or relics

史剧 shǐjù　historical play

史料 shǐliào　historical data; historical materials

史略 shǐlüè　outline history; a brief history: 《中国小说～》A Brief History of Chinese Fiction

史评 shǐpíng　commentary on historical events or historical records

史前 shǐqián　prehistoric: ～时代 prehistoric age (or times)

史前考古学 shǐqián kǎogǔxué　prehistoric archaeology

史前学 shǐqiánxué　prehistory

史乘 shǐshèng　history; annals

史诗 shǐshī　epic

史实 shǐshí　historical facts: 这些故事大多有～根据。 Most of these stories are founded on historical facts.

史事 shǐshì　historical events

史书 shǐshū　history; historical records: 据～记载 according to historical records

史无前例 shǐ wú qiánlì　without precedent in history; unprecedented: ～的壮举 an unprecedented feat

史学 shǐxué　the science of history; historical science; historiography: ～家 historian; historiographer

矢¹ shǐ　arrow: 飞～ flying arrow

矢² shǐ　vow; swear: 矢志不移 shǐzhì bù yí

矢³ shǐ　faeces: 遗矢 yíshǐ

矢车菊 shǐchējú　bot. cornflower (Centaurea cyanus)

矢口 shǐkǒu　state categorically; insist emphatically; assert positively

矢口否认 shǐkǒu fǒurèn　flatly deny

矢口狡赖 shǐkǒu jiǎolài　quibble and prevaricate, refusing to admit one's guilt; persistently quibble and deny one's errors

矢量 shǐliàng　math. phys. vector: 切变～ shear vector／风～ wind vector／～分析 vector analysis

矢石 shǐ-shí　arrows and stones (ancient weapons): ～如雨 a rain of arrows and stones／亲冒～ brave the arrows and stones

矢志 shǐzhì　pledge one's devotion (to a cause): ～于科学 pledge to devote one's life to the advancement of science

矢志不移 shǐzhì bù yí　(also 矢志不渝 shǐzhì bù yú) vow to adhere to one's chosen course

豕 shǐ　formal pig

豕突狼奔 shǐtū-lángbēn　same as 狼奔豕突 lángbēn-shǐtū

使¹ shǐ　① send; tell sb. to do sth: ～人去打听消息 send sb. to make inquiries ② use; employ; apply: ～化肥 use chemical fertilizer／这支笔很好～。 This pen writes well.／把词典借我～～。 Please lend me your dictionary.／我们早就～上电脑了。 We've been using computers for quite a long time.／心往一处想, 劲往一处～ with everyone's thoughts and efforts directed towards one goal ③ make; cause; enable: 要～群众满意 see that the masses are satisfied／～革命遭到巨大损失 cause enormous losses to the revolution／～青少年在德、智、体几方面都得到发展 enable the youth to develop morally, intellectually and physically／修改原计划～之适合于新的情况 revise the original plan so as to gear it to the needs of the new situation／帮助同志克服缺点, ～他们能够大踏步前进 help comrades to overcome their shortcomings so that they can advance with great strides／他的话并不～人感到意外。 What he said was not surprising. ④ if; supposing: 纵使 zòngshǐ

使² shǐ　envoy; messenger: 出使 chūshǐ

使绊儿 shǐbànr　(also 使绊子 shǐbànzi) ① trip sb. up in wrestling ② injure sb. by underhand methods: 他当面说得好听, 背后会给你～。 He will say nice things to your face and then give you a stab in the back.

使不得 shǐbude　① cannot be used; useless; unserviceable: 这笔尖坏了, ～了。 This nib's broken—it can't be used. ② be impermissible; be undesirable: 你病刚好,

干这种重活可～。You've just been ill, you mustn't do such heavy work.

使不惯 shǐbuguàn　not used to using: 我～刀叉。I'm not used to using a knife and fork.

使不了 shǐbuliǎo　cannot use; unable to use: 这玩艺儿我～。I can't use this gadget. / 有一点儿就行，～这许多。A little will do—that's too much for us.

使臣 shǐchén　*old*　special envoy; ambassador-at-large

使出 shǐchū　use; exert: ～全副本领 use all one's resources / ～最后一点力气 expend one's last bit of strength

使出浑身解数 shǐchū húnshēn xièshù　use all one's skill; do all that one is capable of

使得[1] shǐde　① can be used; be usable: 这个汽筒～使不得? Does this pump work all right? ② be workable; be feasible: 这个主意倒还～。That's rather a good idea. / 你不去如何～? It won't do if you don't go.

使得[2] shǐde　make; cause; render: ～家喻户晓 make it known to everyone / 过度紧张的工作～他更加消瘦了。He became even thinner because of overwork.

使馆 shǐguǎn　diplomatic mission; embassy: ～工作人员 the staff of a diplomatic mission; embassy personnel / ～馆长 head of a diplomatic mission / ～馆舍 premises of a diplomatic mission; chancellery / ～区 diplomatic quarter

使坏 shǐhuài　(also 使坏水儿 shǐhuàishuǐr)　*inf.*　be up to mischief; play a dirty trick

使唤 shǐhuan　① order about: 爱～人 be in the habit of ordering people about; be bossy ② *inf.* use; handle: 这些新式农具～起来很方便。These new farm implements are easy to use (*or* handle). / 这匹马不听生人～。This horse won't obey a stranger.

使唤丫头 shǐhuan yātou　slave girl; a young maidservant

使节 shǐjié　diplomatic envoy; envoy: 各国驻华～ diplomatic envoys to China / 特别～ envoy extraordinary / ～旅行 diplomatic tour

使劲 shǐjìn　exert all one's strength: ～干活 work hard / ～蹬车 pedal (a bicycle) furiously / ～划桨 strain at the oars / 有使不完的劲 have inexhaustible energy / 再使把劲 put in more effort; put on another spurt

使君子 shǐjūnzǐ　*Chin. med.*　the fruit of Rangoon creeper (*Quisqualis indica*)

使力 shǐlì　exert all one's strength

使领馆 shǐ-lǐngguǎn　diplomatic and consular missions; embassies and consulates

使命 shǐmìng　mission: 历史～ historical mission

使女 shǐnǚ　maidservant; housemaid; chambermaid; maid

使气 shǐqì　lose one's temper; get angry

使钱 shǐqián　spend money; use money: 很会～ spend (*or* use) one's money wisely; turn one's money to good account / 甭想～买通我。Don't think you can buy me over. / 有使不完的钱 be rolling in money

使徒 shǐtú　*Christianity*　apostle

使团 shǐtuán　diplomatic mission; diplomatic corps: ～长 Dean of the Diplomatic Corps; Doyen of the Diplomatic Mission

使性子 shǐ xìngzi　get angry; lose one's temper

使眼色 shǐ yǎnsè　tip sb. the wink; wink

使役 shǐyì　work (an animal): 注意牲口的～和繁殖。Attention must be paid to the proper use and the breeding of animals.

使用 shǐyòng　use; employ; apply: ～汉语作为民族共同语 use Chinese as a common national language / 禁止～核武器 ban the use of nuclear weapons / 灵活地～兵力 flexible employment of forces / 善于识别人和～人 know how to judge men and use men / ～种种手段 resort to every possible means / ～起来很方便 be easy to use (*or* apply, operate) / 新机器已经开始～。The new machine has been put into operation.

使用额 shǐyòng'é　the amount of disbursement: 国民收入～ the volume of disbursement of the national income

使用价值 shǐyòng jiàzhí　*econ.*　use value

使用率 shǐyònglǜ　rate of utilization

使用面积 shǐyòng miànjī　usable floor area

使用权 shǐyòngquán　*leg.*　right of use; right to use a thing

使用寿命 shǐyòng shòumìng　service life (of machines, etc.)

使用说明书 shǐyòng shuōmíngshū　operation instructions; user's manual

使者 shǐzhě　emissary; envoy; messenger: 他是一位和平～。He is an ambassador of peace.

始

shǐ　① begin; start: 不知～于何时 not know exactly when this came into being ② *adv. formal* only then; not... until: 群众大会结束后，广场～能通行。Traffic cannot pass through the square until the mass meeting is over. / 坚持学习，～能不断进步。Steady progress can only be the result of persistent study. *or* Only persistent study yields steady progress.

始创 shǐchuàng　initiate; originate

始而 shǐ'ér　*adv.*　at first; originally; at the start: ～不解，继而恍然。At first I didn't catch on; then I suddenly saw the light.

始料 shǐliào　originally expected: ～所不及 unexpected; unforeseen

始乱终弃 shǐluàn-zhōngqì　(of a man) seduce and then abandon: 始乱之，终弃之，固其宜矣。愚不敢恨。必也君乱之，君终之，君之惠也。则殁身之誓，其有终矣。(元稹《莺莺传》) Those whom a man leads astray, he will in the end abandon. It must be so, and I will not reproach you. You deigned to corrupt me and now you deign to leave me. That is all. And your vows of "faithfulness till death"—they too are cancelled.

始末 shǐ-mò　beginning and end—the whole story: 事情的～ the whole story

始新世 Shǐxīnshì　*geog.*　the Eocene Epoch

始业 shǐyè　the beginning of the school year: 秋季～。The school year begins in autumn.

始终 shǐzhōng　from beginning to end; from start to finish; all along; throughout: 会谈～在友好的气氛中进行。The talks proceeded in a friendly atmosphere from beginning to end. / 手术过程中病人～是清醒的。The patient remained conscious throughout the operation.

始终不懈 shǐzhōng bù xiè　unremitting; untiring

始终不渝 shǐzhōng bù yú　unswerving; consistent; steadfast: ～地支援各国人民的正义斗争 steadfastly support and aid the just struggles of the people of all countries / 对党对人民忠心耿耿～ remain loyal and devoted to the Party and the people to the end of one's life

始终如一 shǐzhōng rú yī　constant; consistent: ～地站在革命人民一边 consistently side with the revolutionary people

始祖 shǐzǔ　first ancestor; earliest ancestor

始祖鸟 shǐzǔniǎo　*palaeontology*　archaeopteryx

始作俑者 shǐ zuò yǒng zhě　*humor.*　the man who first made tomb figures—the creator of a bad precedent (from Confucius' condemnation of the use of tomb figures because of their resemblance to men: 始作俑者，其无后乎? Didn't the man who first made tomb figures die without leaving an heir?)

驶

shǐ　① sail; drive: ～入港口 sail into the harbour / 火车～出车站。The train pulled out of the station. ② (of a vehicle, etc.) speed: 疾～而过 speed by;

fly past

屎 shǐ ① excrement; faeces; dung; droppings: 鸡～ chicken droppings / 牛～ cow dung ② secretion (of the eye, ear, etc.): 耳屎 ěrshǐ

屎壳郎 shǐkelàng *dial.* dung beetle

shì

士 shì ① bachelor (in ancient China) ② a social stratum in ancient China, between senior officials (大夫) and the common people (庶民) ③ scholar ④ soldier; armyman: 士兵 shìbīng ⑤ noncommissioned officer: 上士 shàngshì / 下士 xiàshì ⑥ a person trained in a certain field: 护士 hùshi ⑦ (commendable) person: 勇士 yǒngshì ⑧ bodyguard, one of the pieces in Chinese chess

士兵 shìbīng rank-and-file soldiers; privates

士大夫 shìdàfū scholar-officials (in imperial times)

士林 shìlín *formal* scholars as a class; literati

士敏土 shìmǐntǔ cement (a transliteration)

士女 shìnǚ ① young men and women ② same as 仕女 shìnǚ②

士气 shìqì morale: 鼓舞～ boost morale / ～低落 sagging morale / 部队战士～高昂。The morale of the troops is high.

士人 shìrén *old* scholar

士绅 shìshēn gentry

士为知己者用,女为悦己者容 shì wèi zhījǐzhě yòng, nǚ wèi yuèjǐzhě róng a gentleman acts on behalf of an understanding friend, as a woman makes herself beautiful for her lover

士卒 shìzú soldiers; privates

氏 shì ① family; clan: 张～兄弟 the Zhang brothers ② (used after a married woman's maiden name): 李王～ Mrs. Li, *née* Wang ③ (used after the surname of a famous person): 《吕～春秋》 *Master Lü's Spring and Autumn Annals* / 摄～温度计 Celsius thermometer ——see also zhī

氏族 shìzú clan: ～公社 clan commune / ～社会 clan society / ～制度 clan system

市 shì ① market: 米～ rice market ② buy or sell: 市惠 shìhuì ③ city; municipality: 天津～ the City of Tianjin; Tianjin municipality / ～内交通 city traffic / ～中心 the heart of the city; city centre; downtown ④ pertaining to the traditional Chinese system of weights and measures: 市尺 shìchǐ / 市斤 shìjīn

市曹 shìcáo *formal* ① business section (of a city); shopping centre ② official in charge of shops and stores ③ place for public execution

市廛 shìchán *formal* stores in a market or street; market; business centre

市场 shìchǎng marketplace; market; bazaar: 国内外～ domestic and foreign markets / ～供应充足。There is an ample supply of commodities. / ～繁荣。The market is brisk. / ～混乱。The market is in a chaotic state. / ～价格 market price / ～行情 market quotation / ～机制 market mechanism / ～经济 market-oriented economy / ～调节 regulation by market forces / ～业务 marketing functions / ～竞争日益加剧 increasingly intense market competition / 这种错误理论在群众中的～越来越小。This erroneous theory finds less and less support among the people.

市秤 shìchèng the traditional Chinese scale of weights

市尺 shìchǐ *chi*, a traditional unit of length, equivalent to 0.333 metre (米) or 1.094 feet (英尺)

市寸 shìcùn *cun*, a traditional unit of length, equal to 0.1 *chi* (市尺), and equivalent to 3.333 centimetres (厘米) or 1.312 inches (英寸)

市撮 shìcuō *cuo*, a traditional unit of capacity, equal to 0.001 *sheng* (市升), and equivalent to 1 millilitre (毫升) or 0.002 pint (品脱)

市石 shìdàn *dan*, a traditional unit of capacity, (esp. for grain), equal to 100 *sheng* (市升), and equivalent to 100 litres (升) or 176 pints (品脱)

市担 shìdàn *dan*, a traditional unit of weight, equal to 100 *jin* (市斤), and equivalent to 50 kilograms (公斤) or 110.25 pounds (磅)

市斗 shìdǒu *dou*, a traditional unit of capacity, equal to 10 *sheng* (市升), and equivalent to 10 litres (升) or 17.60 pints (品脱) or 2.2 gallons (加仑)

市恩 shì'ēn *formal* try to win favour; ingratiate oneself with

市分 shìfēn ① *fen*, a traditional unit of length, equal to 0.01 *chi* (市尺), and equivalent to 0.333 centimetre (厘米) or 0.131 inch (英寸) ② *fen*, a traditional unit of weight, equal to 0.001 *jin* (市斤), and equivalent to 0.5 gram (克) or 0.175 ounce (盎司) ③ *fen*, a traditional unit of area, equal to 0.1 *mu* (市亩), and equivalent to 0.667 are (公亩) or 79.73 square yards (平方码)

市合 shìgě *ge*, a traditional unit of capacity, equal to 0.1 *sheng* (市升), and equivalent to 0.1 litre (升) or 0.176 pint (品脱)

市毫 shìháo ① *hao*, a traditional unit of length, equal to 0.0001 *chi* (市尺), and equivalent to 0.0333 millimetre (毫米) or 0.0013 inch (英寸) ② *hao*, a traditional unit of weight, equal to 0.00001 *jin* (市斤), and equivalent to 5 milligrams (毫克) or 0.075 grain (谷)

市花 shìhuā city flower: 牡丹是洛阳的～。The peony is the city flower of Luoyang.

市惠 shìhuì *formal* curry favour: ～于人 curry favour with other people

市集 shìjí ① fair ② small town

市价 shìjià market price; ruling price

市郊 shìjiāo suburb; outskirts

市斤 shìjīn *jin*, a traditional unit of weight (each containing 10 *liang* 市两 or 16 old *liang* 旧市两 and equivalent to 0.5 kilogram 公斤 or 1.102 pounds 磅)

市井 shìjǐng *formal* marketplace; town

市井小人 shìjǐng xiǎorén *derog.* philistine

市井之徒 shìjǐng zhī tú *derog.* philistine

市侩 shìkuài sordid merchant: ～习气 sordid merchants' ways; philistinism

市厘 shìlí ① *li*, a traditional unit of length, equal to 0.001 *chi* (市尺), and equivalent to 0.333 millimetre (毫米) or 0.013 inch (英寸) ② *li*, a traditional unit of weight, equal to 0.0001 *jin* (市斤), and equivalent to 5 centigrams (厘克) or 0.771 grain (谷) ③ *li*, a traditional unit of area, equal to 0.01 *mu* (市亩), and equivalent to 0.667 square metre (平方米) or 0.797 square yard (平方码)

市里 shìlǐ *li*, a traditional unit of length, equal to 150 *zhang* (市丈), and equivalent to 0.5 kilometre (公里) or 0.311 mile (英里)

市立 shìlì municipal: ～学校 municipal school / ～医院 city hospital

市两 shìliǎng ① *liang*, a traditional unit of weight, equal to 0.1 *jin* (市斤), and equivalent to 50 grams (克) or 1.763 ounces (盎司) ② old *liang* (旧市两), equal to 0.0625 *jin* (as 16 old *liang* make 1 *jin*), and equivalent to 31.25 grams (克) or 1.102 ounces (盎司)

市面 shìmiàn market conditions; the state of trade; business: ～繁荣。Trade is flourishing. *or* Business is

brisk. /～萧条。Business is slack.

市民 shìmín　city residents; townspeople; urban inhabitants

市亩 shìmǔ. *mu*, a traditional unit of area, equal to 60 square *zhang* (平方市丈), and equivalent to 6.667 ares (公亩) or 0.165 acre (英亩)

市内电话 shìnèi diànhuà　local telephone service; local (phone) call

市钱 shìqián　*qian*, a traditional unit of weight, equal to 0.01 *jin* (市斤), and equivalent to 5 grams (克) or 0.176 ounce (盎司)

市顷 shìqǐng　*qing*, a traditional unit of area, equal to 100 *mu* (市亩), and equivalent to 6.667 hectares (公顷) or 16.474 acres (英亩)

市区 shìqū　city proper; urban district

市容 shìróng　the appearance of a city: 保持～整洁 keep the city clean and tidy /参观～ go sight-seeing in the city; have a look around the city

市勺 shìsháo　*shao*, a traditional unit of capacity, equal to 0.01 *sheng* (市升), and equivalent to 1 centilitre (厘升) or 0.018 pint (品脱)

市升 shìshēng　*sheng*, a traditional unit of capacity, equivalent to 1 litre (升) or 1.76 pints (品脱) or 0.22 gallon (加仑)

市声 shìshēng　the bustling noise of a market

市丝 shìsī　① *si*, a traditional unit of length, equal to 0.00001 *chi* (市尺), and equivalent to 3.333 microns (微米) ② *si*, a traditional unit of weight, equal to 0.000001 *jin* (市斤), and equivalent to 0.5 milligram (毫克) or 0.0075 grain (谷)

市肆 shìsì　*formal* shops; stores

市委 shìwěi　municipal Party committee

市用制 shìyòngzhì　another name for 市制 shìzhì

市长 shìzhǎng　mayor

市丈 shìzhàng　*zhang*, a traditional unit of length, equal to 10 *chi* (市尺), and equivalent to 3.333 metres (米) or 3.65 yards (码)

市招 shìzhāo　signboard; shop sign

市镇 shìzhèn　small towns; towns

市政 shìzhèng　municipal administration: ～当局 municipal authorities

市政工程 shìzhèng gōngchéng　municipal works; municipal engineering

市制 shìzhì　the traditional Chinese system of weights and measures (with *chi* 市尺 as its basic unit of length, *jin* 市斤 as its basic unit of weight, and *sheng* 市升 as its basic unit of capacity)

示 shì　show; notify; instruct: 盼速～知。I hope you will notify me soon. /～悉。Your letter has been received.

示波管 shìbōguǎn　*electron.* oscilloscope tube

示波器 shìbōqì　*electron.* oscillograph; oscilloscope

示范 shìfàn　set an example; demonstrate: 我先给大家～一下。I'll first show you how to do it. /～表演金属切削 put on a demonstration of metal-cutting technique /～飞行 demonstration flight /～农场 a demonstration farm; a pilot farm

示复 shìfù　(used in formal correspondence) give instructions in reply: 希即～。I am waiting for an early reply.

示功器 shìgōngqì　*mech.* indicator

示功图 shìgōngtú　*mech.* indicator card; indicator diagram

示寂 shìjì　(of a Buddhist monk) die; pass away

示警 shìjǐng　give a warning; warn: 鸣锣～ give a warning by beating a gong; beat an alarm on a gong

示例 shìlì　give typical examples; give a demonstration

示人 shìrén　show sth. to others; let others have a look

at sth.

示弱 shìruò　give the impression of weakness; take sth. lying down

示威 shìwēi　① demonstrate; hold a demonstration: ～群众 demonstrators ② put on a show of force; display one's strength

示威游行 shìwēi yóuxíng　demonstration; parade; march

示意 shìyì　signal; hint; motion: ～他出去 motion to him to go out /以目～ give a hint with the eyes; tip sb. the wink

示意图 shìyìtú　① sketch map: 边界东段～ a sketch map showing the eastern sector of the boundary /架设天线的～ illustrated instructions for installing antennae ② *mech.* schematic diagram; schematic drawing

示众 shìzhòng　publicly expose; put before the public: 游街～ parade sb. through the streets

示踪测定 shìzōng cèdìng　*phys.* tracer determination

示踪物 shìzōngwù　*phys.* tracer

示踪元素 shìzōng yuánsù　*phys.* tracer element

示踪原子 shìzōng yuánzǐ　*phys.* labelled atom; tagged atom; tracer

世（丗） shì　① lifetime; life: 一～ all one's life ② generation: 第七十～后裔 descendants of the 70th generation ③ from generation to generation; through generations: ～爵 hereditary rank or nobility ④ (used in terms of address among old family friends): ～伯（叔）uncle (friend of one's father) ⑤ age; era: 当今之～ at present; nowadays ⑥ the world: 公之于～ make known to the world; reveal to the public ⑦ *geol.* epoch: 古新世 Gǔxīnshì

世变 shìbiàn　changes in life or society; misfortunes in this world

世仇 shìchóu　① family feud ② ancient enemy

世传 shìchuán　be handed down through generations: ～秘方 a secret recipe handed down from generation to generation

世代 shìdài　① years; ages ② for generations; from generation to generation; generation after generation: 他家～务农。He comes from a long line of farmers.

世代交替 shìdài jiāotì　*biol.* alternation of generations

世代相传 shìdài xiāngchuán　pass on from generation to generation

世道 shìdào　the manners and morals of the time: 唉！别提那吃人的旧～了。Hm! Let's not talk about that man-eat-man society.

世道人心 shìdào-rénxīn　the ways of the world and public sentiment

世风 shìfēng　*formal* public morals: ～日下。Public morals are declining day by day. /～不古。Public morals are no longer what they used to be.

世故 shìgù　the ways of the world: 老于世故 lǎoyú shìgù

世故 shìgu　worldly-wise: 这人相当～。This chap is rather a smooth character.

世纪 shìjì　century

世纪末 shìjìmò　end of the century; *fin-de-siècle*

世家 shìjiā　① an old and well-known family; an aristocratic family: 音乐～ a family of musicians /～子弟 descendants of an aristocratic family ② *Hereditary Houses* (a section of the *Records of the Historian* 《史记》 giving detailed accounts of the feudal states): 《留侯～》"The Hereditary House of the Marquis of Liu"

世间 shìjiān　① in this world ② in society

世交 shìjiāo　① friendship spanning two or more generations ② old family friends: 王家跟李家是～。The Wangs and the Lis are old family friends.

世界 shìjiè　① world: 全～ the whole world /～大事 world events /～冠军 world champion /～纪录 world record ② *Buddhism* the universe: 大千世界 dàqiān

shìjiè ③ field; sphere; domain; realm: 内心～ a person's inner world / 科学～ the domain of sciences / 禽鸟～ the feathered world

世界博览会 Shìjiè Bólǎnhuì　World's Fair

世界大战 shìjiè dàzhàn　world war: 第一次～ the First World War (1914–1918); World War I / 第二次～ the Second World War (1939–1945); World War II

世界观 shìjièguān　world outlook

世界末日 shìjiè mòrì　*Christianity* Doomsday; Day of Last Judgment

世界人权宣言 Shìjiè Rénquán Xuānyán　Universal Declaration of Human Rights (Dec.10,1948)

世界时 shìjièshí　*astron.* universal time

世界语 Shìjièyǔ　Esperanto

世界主义 shìjièzhǔyì　cosmopolitanism

世局 shìjú　the world situation

世路 shìlù　the ways of the world

世论 shìlùn　the general opinion (of the time); public opinion

世面 shìmiàn　various aspects of society; society; world; life: 见过～ have seen the world; have experienced life

世情 shìqíng　worldly affairs; social trends: 不懂～ unsophisticated

世人 shìrén　common people

世上 shìshàng　in the world; on earth

世上无难事,只怕有心人 shìshàng wú nánshì, zhǐpà yǒuxīnrén　nothing in the world is difficult for one who sets his mind on it

世事 shìshì　affairs of human life

世事洞明皆学问,人情练达即文章 shìshì dòngmíng jiē xuéwen, rénqíng liàndá jǐ wénzhāng　a grasp of mundane affairs is genuine knowledge, and understanding of worldly wisdom is true learning

世俗 shìsú　① common customs: ～之见 common views ② secular; worldly

世态 shìtài　the ways of the world: ～人情 the ways of the world

世态炎凉 shìtài yánliáng　warmth or coldness is the way of the world—people are friendly or unfriendly, depending on whether one is successful or not

世途 shìtú　experiences in life: ～坎坷 a life full of frustrations

世外桃源 shìwài táoyuán　the Land of Peach Blossoms—a fictitious land of peace, away from the turmoil of the world; a haven of peace

世务 shìwù　current affairs; the trend of the times: 不达～ show no understanding of the times

世袭 shìxí　hereditary: ～财产 hereditary property; patrimony / ～制度 the hereditary system

世系 shìxì　pedigree; genealogy

世兄 shìxiōng　*old* a term of address for a student of one's father, the son of one's teacher, or the son of one's friend

世医 shìyī　a family of doctors of traditional Chinese medicine who have practised for generations; a long line of doctors

世谊 shìyì　*formal* friendship spanning generations

世子 shìzǐ　the eldest son of the emperor by his empress or of a feudal prince by his princess

世族 shìzú　an old and great family

仕　shì　① be an official; fill an office: 学而优则仕 xué ér yōu zé shì ② bodyguard, one of the pieces in Chinese chess

仕宦 shìhuàn　*formal* be an official; be in government service: ～之家 an official family / ～子弟 sons of an official family

仕进 shìjìn　*formal* pursue an official career: 不求～ give up all thought of an official career

仕路 shìlù　*formal* an official career

仕女 shìnǚ　① a maid· in an imperial palace; maid of honour ② *painting* traditional Chinese painting of beautiful women

仕途 shìtú　*formal* an official career: ～多蹇 an official career fraught with difficulties and danger

式　shì　① type; style: 雷锋～的人物 people of the Lei Feng type ② pattern; form: 程式 chéngshì ③ ceremony; ritual: 开幕式 kāimùshì ④ formula: 分子式 fēnzǐshì ⑤ *gram.* mood; mode: 叙述～ indicative mood

式微 shìwēi　*formal* (of a dynasty or a family) decline

式样 shìyàng　style; type; model: 各种～的服装 clothes in different styles / 不同～的房屋 houses of different designs / 各种～的车床 lathes of various models / ～美观 graceful-looking; stylish

式子 shìzi　① posture: 他的太极拳～摆得好。The postures he assumes when doing *taijiquan* exercises are correct and graceful. ② formula: 列出这道代数题的～。Write down the formula for this algebraic problem.

似　shì　see below ——see also sì

似的 shìde　*part.* (used after a noun, pronoun, or verb to indicate similarity): 像雪～那么白 as white as snow / 他仿佛睡着了～。He seems to be asleep.· / 这孩子乐得什么～。The child is as happy as a lark.

试　shì　① try; test: ～一～ have a try / ～穿 try on (a garment, shoes, etc.) / ～～绳子结实不结实 test the strength of a rope / ～产 trial production ② examination; test: 口试 kǒushì / 笔试 bǐshì

试巴 shìba　*inf.* have a try: 我来～～。Let me have a try.

试办 shìbàn　run an enterprise, etc. as an experiment; run a pilot scheme

试表 shìbiǎo　*inf.* take sb.'s temperature

试播 shìbō　trial broadcast or trial telecast

试场 shìchǎng　examination hall (*or* room)

试车 shìchē　test run (of a machine, car, etc.); trial run

试点 shìdiǎn　① make experiments; conduct tests at selected points; launch a pilot project: 进行以税代利的～ conduct experiments in substituting taxes for delivery of profits ② a place where an experiment is made; experimental unit

试电笔 shìdiànbǐ　*elec.* test pencil

试飞 shìfēi　test flight; trial flight: ～驾驶员 test pilot

试工 shìgōng　(of a worker or servant) be hired or engaged on a probational basis; be on probation: ～期间 during the probation or trial period / 顺利通过～ pass the probation with success / ～三个月 be on three-month probation

试管 shìguǎn　test tube

试管婴儿 shìguǎn yīng'ér　test-tube baby

试航 shìháng　① trial voyage or flight; shakedown cruise or flight; trial run ② shake down (a ship or an aeroplane)

试剂 shìjì　*chem.* reagent

试金石 shìjīnshí　touchstone (lit. and fig.)

试卷 shìjuàn　examination paper; test paper

试射 shìshè　*mil.* fire for adjustment; trial fire

试手 shìshǒu　① same as 试工 shìgōng ② have a try at sth: 我来试试手。Let me have a try at it.

试探 shìtàn　probe or explore (a question): ～宇宙的奥秘 probe the secrets of the universe

试探 shìtan　sound out; feel out: ～一下他对这个问题的看法 sound him out about the question

试探性 shìtànxìng　trial; exploratory; probing: ～攻击 probing attack / ～谈判 exploratory talks

试探性气球 shìtànxìng qìqiú　trial balloon

试题 shìtí　examination questions; test questions

试图 shìtú　attempt to (do sth.); try to (do sth.)

试问 shìwèn　we should like to ask; it may well be asked; may we ask

试想 shìxiǎng　(used in reasoning with sb.) just think: ～你这样干下去会有好结果吗? Just think. Will it do you any good if you go on like this?

试销 shìxiāo　① place goods on trial sale ② trial sale: ～专柜 trial sale counter

试行 shìxíng　try out: 先～，再推广 first try out, then popularize／由上级批准～ be ratified by the higher authorities for trial implementation

试选样品 shìxuǎn yàngpǐn　mech.　pilot model

试演 shìyǎn　① trial performance (of a play, etc.); preview; trial run ② give a trial performance or a preview (of a play, etc.); (of a play, etc.) have a trial run

试验 shìyàn　trial; experiment; test: 水力～ hydraulic test／进行反坦克武器～ try out antitank weapons

试验场 shìyànchǎng　proving ground; testing ground

试验农场 shìyàn nóngchǎng　experimental farm

试验田 shìyàntián　① agric.　experimental plot; experimental field ② a trial undertaking

试验性工厂 shìyànxìng gōngchǎng　pilot plant

试样[1] shìyàng　sample

试样[2] shìyàng　try on a partly finished garment

试剂 shìyào　same as 试剂 shìjì

试映 shìyìng　preview (of a film)

试用 shìyòng　① try out: 我想～一下。 I want to try it out. ② on probation: ～人员 person on probation; probationer／～期 probation period

试用本 shìyòngběn　trial edition (an edition put out to solicit comments)

试用品 shìyòngpǐn　trial products

试院 shìyuàn　examination hall (under the imperial examination system)

试运转 shìyùnzhuǎn　mech.　test run; running-in

试纸 shìzhǐ　chem.　test paper: 石蕊～ litmus test paper／万用～ universal test paper／姜黄～ turmeric test paper

试制 shìzhì　trial-produce; trial-manufacture: 一种新的播种机～成功了。 A new seeding machine has been successfully trial-produced.

试种 shìzhòng　plant experimentally: ～水稻 growing rice on a trial basis

势 (勢)

shì　① power; force; influence: 权势 quánshì ② momentum; tendency: 以排山倒海之～ with the momentum of an avalanche ③ the outward appearance of a natural object: 山～ the lie of a mountain ④ situation; state of affairs; circumstances: ～难从命。 Circumstances make it difficult for me to comply with your request. ⑤ sign; gesture: 手势 shǒushì ⑥ male genitals: 去势 qùshì

势必 shìbì　adv.　certainly will; be bound to: 饮酒过度，～影响健康。 Excessive drinking will undoubtedly affect one's health.

势不可当 shì bùkě dāng　irresistible: 革命的潮流汹涌澎湃，～。 The revolution is surging forward irresistibly.

势不两立 shì bù liǎng lì　be mutually exclusive; be extremely antagonistic; be irreconcilable

势成骑虎 shì chéng qí hǔ　like riding a tiger—a situation from which it is hard to extricate oneself ——see also 骑虎难下 qí hǔ nán xià

势家 shìjiā　old　an influential family

势均力敌 shìjūn-lìdí　match each other in strength: 双方～。 The two sides are evenly matched.／一场～的比赛 a close contest

势力 shìlì　force; power; influence: 壮大～ expand one's forces

势力范围 shìlì fànwéi　sphere of influence

势利 shìlì　snobbish: ～小人 snob

势利眼 shìlìyǎn　① snobbish attitude; snobbishness ② snob

势能 shìnéng　phys.　potential energy

势派 shìpai　dial.　① manner; style; air ② situation; circumstances

势如破竹 shì rú pò zhú　like splitting a bamboo; like a hot knife cutting through butter; with irresistible force: ～，所向披靡 smash all resistance and advance victoriously everywhere

势所必然 shì suǒ bìrán　inevitably; as a matter of course

势头 shìtóu　① impetus; momentum: 风的～越来越大。 It blew harder and harder. ② inf.　tendency; the look of things: 他见～不对, 转身就走。 Sensing that the odds were against him, he immediately turned back.

势焰 shìyàn　derog.　influence and power: ～万丈 aggressively powerful

势要 shìyào　formal　important and influential persons

势在必行 shì zài bì xíng　be imperative (under the circumstances): 此项改革～。 This reform must be enforced.

事

shì　① matter; affair; thing; business: 没你的～。 It's not your business.／这是怎么回～? What's this all about? ② trouble; accident: 出事 chūshì ③ job; work: 她找到～儿了。 She's got a job. ④ responsibility; involvement: 这件案子里还有他的～呢。 He was involved in the case too.／有我什么～, 干吗怪我? Why put the blame on me? It has nothing to do with me. ⑤ formal　wait upon; serve: ～父母 wait upon one's parents ⑥ be engaged in: 不～生产 lead an idle life

事半功倍 shìbàn-gōngbèi　get twice the result with half the effort

事倍功半 shìbèi-gōngbàn　get half the result with twice the effort

事必躬亲 shì bì gōngqīn　see (or attend) to everything oneself; take care of every single thing personally

事变 shìbiàn　① incident: 七七～ the July 7 Incident of 1937 ② emergency; exigency: 准备应付可能的突然～ be prepared against all possible emergencies ③ the course of events; events: 研究周围～的联系 look into the relations of events occurring around one

事不关己, 高高挂起 shì bù guān jǐ, gāogāo guàqǐ　let things drift if they do not affect one personally; stand aloof from things on the ground that they are no concern of one's

事不宜迟 shì bù yí chí　we must lose no time in doing it; we must attend to the matter immediately; this matter needs immediate attention

事出有因 shì chū yǒu yīn　there is good reason for it; it is by no means accidental

事到临头 shì dào líntóu　when things come to a head; when the situation becomes critical; at the last moment: 你如果没有思想准备, ～就会抓瞎。 If you don't anticipate what may happen, you'll find yourself at a loss when something crops up.

事端 shìduān　disturbance; incident: 挑起～ provoke incidents／制造～ create disturbances

事非经过不知难 shì fēi jīngguò bù zhī nán　you never know how hard a task is until you have done it yourself

事功 shìgōng　formal　achievement: 特殊～ remarkable achievements／急于～ be desirous of achievement

事故 shìgù　accident; mishap: 防止发生～ try to avert accidents／责任～ accident arising from sb.'s negligence

事过境迁 shìguò-jìngqiān　the affair is over and the situation has changed; the incident is over and the cir-

cumstances are different

事后 shìhòu　after the event; afterwards: 不要老是只作～的批评。Don't get into the habit of criticizing only after the event. / 仓库失火了，～我去看了现场。After the warehouse fire I went to make an on-the-spot investigation.

事后诸葛亮 shìhòu Zhūgé Liàng　be a Zhuge Liang only after something unpleasant has happened—be wise after the event

事机 shìjī　① affairs that should be kept secret ② situation

事迹 shìjì　deed; achievement: 英雄～ heroic deeds

事假 shìjià　leave of absence (to attend to private affairs); compassionate leave: 请两小时～ ask for two hours leave of absence

事件 shìjiàn　incident; event: 流血～ a bloody incident / 二十世纪最伟大的～ the greatest event in the 20th century

事理 shìlǐ　reason; logic: 明白～ be reasonable; be sensible

事例 shìlì　example; instance: 典型～ a typical case

事略 shìlüè　biographical sketch; short biographical account

事前 shìqián　before the event; in advance; beforehand: ～跟群众商量 consult the masses in advance / ～毫无准备 with no preparation at all / ～请示，事后报告 ask for instructions in advance and submit reports afterwards; ask for instructions beforehand and report back afterwards

事情 shìqing　affair; matter; thing; business: 急待解决的～ affairs to be settled right away / 大家的～大家管。Public business is everybody's business. / ～的真相 the truth of the matter; the facts of the case / ～也真巧 as luck would have it / ～是这样的。It happened like this.

事权 shìquán　duties and responsibilities

事实 shìshí　fact: 与～不符 not tally with the facts / ～恰恰相反。The facts are just the opposite. or The opposite is the case. / ～如此。This is how things are (or stand). / ～俱在，不容抵赖。The facts are all there and cannot be denied.

事实上 shìshíshang　in fact; in reality; as a matter of fact; actually: ～的承认 de facto recognition / ～的停火 de facto cease-fire / ～的分界线 de facto line

事实胜于雄辩 shìshí shèngyú xióngbiàn　facts are stronger than rhetoric; facts speak louder than words

事势 shìshì　state of affairs; situation: 想不到～竟会弄到这步田地。I never expected things to get into such a mess.

事事 shìshì　① everything: ～都要从人民的利益出发。In whatever we do, our primary concern should be the interests of the people. ② formal be engaged in some work or business: 无所事事 wú suǒ shìshì

事态 shìtài　state of affairs; situation: ～严重。The situation is serious. / ～在恶化。The situation is deteriorating. / ～的发展, 证明了我们的看法是完全正确的。The development of events entirely confirmed our view.

事体 shìtǐ　dial. matter; affair

事务 shìwù　① work; routine: ～繁忙 have a lot (of work) to do / ～性工作 routine work; daily routine ② general affairs: ～科 the general affairs section

事务所 shìwùsuǒ　office: 律师～ lawyer's office

事务员 shìwùyuán　office clerk

事务主义 shìwùzhǔyì　routinism: ～者 a person bogged down in routine matters

事物 shìwù　thing; object: ～的矛盾法则 the law of contradiction in things / ～都是一分为二的。Everything divides into two.

事先 shìxiān　in advance; beforehand; prior: ～做好准备 get everything ready beforehand / ～跟他们打个招呼。Notify them in advance. / ～磋商 prior (or preliminary) consultations / ～酝酿 prior deliberation; exchange of views in advance / ～策划的暗杀 a premeditated murder

事项 shìxiàng　item; matter: 注意～ matters needing attention; points for attention

事业 shìyè　① cause; undertaking; career: ～顺利 have a successful career / 革命～ revolutionary cause / 共产主义～ the cause of communism / 文化教育～ cultural and educational undertakings ② institution; facilities: 集体福利～ collective welfare facilities or services / 公用～ public utilities

事业单位 shìyè dānwèi　institution

事业费 shìyèfèi　operating expenses

事业家 shìyèjiā　entrepreneur

事业心 shìyèxīn　devotion to one's work; dedication

事宜 shìyí　(usu. used in official language) matters concerned; arrangements: 商谈有关建馆～ discuss matters relating to the establishment of the embassy / 讨论春耕～ discuss problems about the spring ploughing

事由 shìyóu　① the origin of an incident; particulars of a matter: 把～交代明白 give all the particulars about the incident ② (used in official language) main content ③ dial. job; work: 找～ hunt for a job

事与愿违 shì yǔ yuàn wéi　things turn out contrary to one's wishes

事在人为 shì zài rén wéi　it all depends on human effort; human effort is the decisive factor: 他们能够做到那样, 我们难道就做不到吗? ～嘛。If they could achieve so much, why can't we? Everything depends upon men's efforts.

事主 shìzhǔ　the victim of a crime

侍

　shì　wait upon; attend upon; serve: 服侍 fúshi

侍从 shìcóng　old attendants; retinue

侍从副官 shìcóng fùguān　aide-de-camp (A. D. C.); aide

侍儿 shì'ér　formal slave girl; servant-girl

侍奉 shìfèng　support and wait upon (one's elders): ～父母 support and wait upon one's parents

侍候 shìhòu　wait upon; look after; attend: ～病人 look after a patient / ～少爷 wait upon the young master

侍郎 shìláng　(in Ming-Qing times) Vice-President of one of the Six Boards (六部)

侍立 shìlì　be in attendance: ～两旁 stand on either side in attendance

侍弄 shìnòng　dial. tend with care (crops, domestic animals, etc.)

侍女 shìnǚ　maidservant; maid

侍卫 shìwèi　① guard ② imperial bodyguard

侍养 shìyǎng　support and wait upon (one's elders)

侍役 shìyì　attendants; servants

侍应生 shìyìngshēng　old a young attendant or odd-jobber (in banks, etc.)

侍者 shìzhě　attendant; servant; waiter

视

　shì　① look at: 注视 zhùshì ② regard; look upon: ～为莫大光荣 regard as a great honour / ～如仇敌 look upon sb. as one's enemy ③ inspect; watch: 巡视 xúnshì / 视察 shìchá

视差 shìchā　phys. parallax

视察 shìchá　① inspect: ～边防部队 inspect a frontier guard unit / 去外地～工作 be on an inspection tour ② watch; observe: ～地形 survey the terrain

视察团 shìchátuán　inspection team; inspectorate

视察员 shìcháyuán　inspector

视场 shìchǎng　field of vision (or view)

视唱 shìchàng　sightsinging

视唱练耳 shìchàng liàn'ěr　solfeggio

视地平 shìdìpíng *astron.* apparent horizon

视而不见 shì ér bù jiàn look but see not; turn a blind eye to; close (*or* shut) one's eyes to: 这是事实, 不能～。These are facts and you can't just ignore them.

视而不见, 听而不闻 shì ér bù jiàn, tīng ér bù wén look but see not; listen but hear not; turn a blind eye to and a deaf ear to; take no notice of; pretend not to see or hear

视轨道 shìguǐdào *astron.* apparent orbit

视角 shìjiǎo angle of view; visual angle

视界 shìjiè field of vision; visual field

视景 shìjǐng what comes into a driver's or a pilot's view as the vehicle or the craft proceeds

视觉 shìjué *physiol.* visual sense; vision; sense of sight

视觉象 shìjuéxiàng visual image

视觉印象 shìjué yìnxiàng eye impressions; visual impressions

视觉暂留 shìjué zànliú persistence of vision

视力 shìlì vision; sight: ～测验 eyesight test / ～好(差) have good (poor) eyesight

视力表 shìlìbiǎo visual chart

视亮度 shìliàngdù *astron.* apparent brightness

视频 shìpín *phys.* video frequency

视如敝屣 shì rú bìxǐ regard as worn-out shoes—cast aside as worthless

视如粪土 shì rú fèntǔ look upon as filth and dirt; consider as beneath contempt

视如寇仇 shì rú kòuchóu regard as an enemy

视若草芥 shì ruò cǎojiè regard as worthless

视若无睹 shì ruò wú dǔ take no notice of what one sees; shut one's eyes to; turn a blind eye to; ignore

视神经 shìshénjīng *physiol.* optic nerve

视事 shìshì *old* (of officials) attend to business after assuming office; assume office

视死如归 shì sǐ rú guī look upon death as going home; look death calmly in the face; face death unflinchingly

视听 shì-tīng seeing and hearing; what is seen and heard: 组织学生旅行参观, 以广～ arrange for touring trips and visits so as to broaden the students' views

视听教材 shì-tīng jiàocái audio-visual materials; audio-visuals

视听教具 shì-tīng jiàojù audio-visual aids

视同等闲 shì tóng děngxián regard sb. or sth. as unimportant; treat lightly or casually

视同儿戏 shì tóng érxì treat (a serious matter) as a trifle; trifle with

视同路人 shì tóng lùrén regard as a stranger; treat like a stranger

视图 shìtú *mech.* view: 前～ front view / 侧～ side view / 上～ top view

视网膜 shìwǎngmó *physiol.* retina

视网膜脱离 shìwǎngmó tuōlí detachment of retina

视网膜炎 shìwǎngmóyán retinitis

视为畏途 shì wéi wèitú regard as a dangerous road to take; be afraid to undertake

视线 shìxiàn line of vision; view; line of sight (in surveying): 请观众脱帽, 以免挡住别人的～。Spectators are requested to take off their hats so as not to block others' view.

视星等 shìxīngděng *astron.* apparent magnitude

视学 shìxué *old* educational inspector

视野 shìyě field of vision (*or* view): 广阔的～ a wide field of vision / 开拓～ broaden one's vision / 登上山顶, 一片广袤的平原进入～。When we reached the top of the mountain, a wide plain came into view.

视阈 shìyù *physiol.* visual threshold

视紫质 shìzǐzhì *physiol.* visual purple

饰 shì ① decorations; ornaments: 窗～ window decorations ② adorn; dress up; polish; cover up: 修饰 xiūshì / 文过饰非 wénguò-shìfēi ③ play the role of; act the part of; impersonate: 她在《白毛女》里～喜儿。She played Xi'er in *The White-haired Girl*.

饰词 shìcí excuse; pretext

饰物 shìwù ① articles for personal adornment; jewelry ② ornaments; decorations

饰演 shìyǎn play the role of; act the part of; play

室 shì ① room: 有一～一套的, 也有两～一套的。There are one-room flats as well as two-room flats. ② a room as an administrative or working unit: 资料～ reference room / 档案～ files room ③ the thirteenth of the twenty-eight constellations (二十八宿) into which the celestial sphere was divided in ancient Chinese astronomy (consisting of two stars in a straight line in Pegasus)

室内 shìnèi indoor; interior: ～运动 indoor sport / ～溜冰场 indoor skating rink / ～游泳池 indoor swimming pool / ～装饰 interior decoration

室内乐 shìnèiyuè *mus.* chamber music

室内乐队 shìnèi yuèduì *mus.* chamber orchestra

室女 shìnǚ *old* an unmarried girl; virgin

室女座 Shìnǚzuò *astron.* Virgo

室外 shìwài outdoor; outside: ～活动 outdoor activities

恃 shì ① rely on; depend on: ～势欺人 use one's power to bully people ② *formal* mother: 失恃 shīshì

恃才傲物 shì cái ào wù be inordinately proud of one's ability; be conceited and contemptuous

恃强凌弱 shì qiáng líng ruò use one's strength to bully the weak

拭 shì wipe away; wipe: ～泪 wipe away tears

拭除 shìchú wipe or brush sth. off: ～镜面上的灰尘 wipe the dust off the mirror; dust the mirror

拭目以待 shì mù yǐ dài wait and see; wait expectantly (for sth. to happen)

柿(柹) shì persimmon

柿饼 shìbǐng dried persimmon

柿蒂 shìdì *Chin. med.* the calyx and receptacle of a persimmon

柿霜 shìshuāng *Chin. med.* powder on the surface of a dried persimmon

柿子 shìzi persimmon

柿子椒 shìzijiāo sweet pepper; bell pepper

贳 shì *formal* ① hire out; let ② buy on credit ③ pardon

是¹ shì ① correct; right: 你说得～。What you said is right. / 应当早做准备才～。To make early preparations is the right thing to do. ② *formal* praise; justify: 是古非今 shìgǔ-fēijīn ③ (used in affirmative answers) yes; right: ～, 我们一定完成任务。Right, we will fulfil the task. / ～, 我就去。Yes, I'll go right away.

是² shì *formal* this; that: ～日天气晴朗。It was fine that day. / 由～可知 from this you can see / 如～ like this

是³ shì ① (used like "be" before nouns or pronouns to identify, describe or amplify the subject): 我～个医生。I am a doctor. / 中国～社会主义国家。China is a socialist country. / 《阿Q正传》的作者～鲁迅。The author of *The True Story of Ah Q* is Lu Xun. / 他真

心爱的～你。You are the girl he is truly in love with. / 这小孩～白皮肤，黄头发。That child is a blond. / 她还～一身中学生打扮。She still dresses simply, like a middle-school girl. / 院子里～冬天，屋子里～春天。It was winter outdoors, but spring indoors. / 火车从广州开出～早晨八点。The train leaves Kuangzhou at 8 a.m. ② (used after nouns denoting place or position to express existence): 前面～一片稻田。There is a stretch of rice fields ahead. / 他满身～汗。He is sweating all over. / 遍地～鲜花。The place is strewn with flowers. ③ (used with 的 at the end of the sentence, to indicate category, characteristic, etc.): 那儿的房屋～木头的。The houses there are built of wood. / 我～教书的。I am a teacher. / 马路边净～看热闹的。The street was crowded with people watching the excitement. / 这封电报～长春发来的。The telegram is from Changchun. / 被里被面全～新的。Both the facing and the underside of the quilt are new. ④ (used to emphasize a certain part of a sentence) ⓐ (used before the subject to stress it): ～谁告诉你的? Who told you? / 花瓶～我妹妹摔破的。It was my sister who broke the vase. ⓑ (used after a verb or adjective plus 的, to stress the predicate): 说的正～你。It's you we are talking about. / 麻烦的～他生病来不了。The trouble is he's taken ill and can't come at all. / 可惜的～把这么多时间全浪费了。It's a pity we've wasted so much of our time. ⓒ (used before the object, adverbial, etc. which is to be stressed): 我～专诚去看老王的。I made a special trip to see Lao Wang. / 他们看的～话剧，不～电影。They went to see a play, not a film. or What they saw was a play, not a film. / 我～昨天买的票。I bought the tickets yesterday. or It was yesterday that I bought the tickets. / 字写成这样，～因为毛笔不好。It was all because my brush was no good that I wrote the characters so poorly. / 好好的一次郊游搞成这样子，都～你! It was all your fault that the outing became such a flop. ⓓ (pronounced with stress; used to indicate certainty): 天气～冷。It is cold indeed. / 他的工作效率～高。He is really efficient. / 她～不知道。Really she doesn't know. / 他～去了。He did go. ⑤ be just right: 这场雨下的～时候。This rain has come at just the right time. / 工具放的不～地方。The tools are not put in the right place. ⑥ (used before nouns at the beginning of the sentence, followed by 都 or 就) every; all; any: ～什么种子，就开出什么花。Each kind of seed produces its own flowers. / ～什么样的老师，就教出什么样的学生。Like teacher, like student. / ～公众的事，大家都要关心。Whatever concerns the public concerns all of us. / ～重活，他都抢着干。When there's a tough job, he always rushes to do it. ⑦ (used between two identical words) ⓐ (used together with 就 or 总, to indicate actuality): 事实总～事实，谁也否认不了的。A fact is a fact, which no one can deny. / 不懂就～不懂，不要装懂。If you don't know, there you stand. Don't pretend to know what you don't. ⓑ (used in a clause of concession): 这东西旧～旧，可还能用。Yes, it's old, but it can still be used. / 诗～好诗，就是长了点。It is a good poem all right, but it's a bit too long. / 工作忙～忙，可是大家很愉快。We are busy to be sure, but every one of us is very happy. ⓒ (used in two parallel clauses to indicate mutual exclusiveness): 他～他，我～我，我们毫不相干。He is he, I am I; we have nothing to do with each other. / 敌～敌，友～友，必须分清敌我的界限。A friend is a friend, a foe is a foe; one must be clearly distinguished from the other. ⓓ (used in two or three parallel clauses to indicate thoroughness or excellence of performance): 他演得真好，表情～表情，身段～身段，做功～做功。He is a marvellous actor; his facial expressions, bodily movements and gesticulations are all the best that can be ex-

pected. ⑧ (used in yes-no questions): 你～不～明天去游泳? or 你～明天去游泳不～? Are you going swimming tomorrow? ⑨ (used in alternative questions): 你～累了还～病了? Are you tired or ill? / 你～坐火车呢，还～坐汽车? Are you going by train or by bus? / 今天该谁去，你去还～小王去? Whose turn is it to go today—yours or Xiao Wang's? / 这件事～真～假，谁也搞不清。Nobody knows whether it's true or not.

是的 shìde ① yes; right; that's it ② same as 似的 shìde

是凡 shìfán *dial.* every; any; all

是非 shìfēi ① right and wrong: ～问题 a matter of right and wrong / 明辨～ distinguish clearly between right and wrong ② quarrel; dispute: 惹起～ provoke a dispute; stir up trouble / 这儿～太多。There's too much gossip here.

是非曲直 shì-fēi qū-zhí rights and wrongs; truth and falsehood: 不问～ not bother to look into the rights and wrongs of a case / 根据事情本身的～进行裁断 decide the case on its merits

是非自有公论 shìfēi zì yǒu gōnglùn the public will judge the rights and wrongs of the case; public opinion is the best judge

是否 shìfǒu whether or not; whether; if: ～符合实际 whether or not it corresponds to reality / 他～能来，还不一定。It's not certain whether he can come or not.

是个儿 shìgèr *inf.* be a match: 你不是他的个儿。You are no match for him. / 跟我下棋，你～吗? Would you take me on at chess?

是古非今 shìgǔ-fēijīn praise the past and condemn the present

是可忍，孰不可忍 shì kě rěn, shú bùkě rěn if this can be tolerated, what cannot?

是味儿 shìwèir *inf.* ① (of food) have the right flavour; taste good: 这个汤不～。This soup doesn't have the right flavour. ② (of a person) feel good: 听了他那番话，我心里可真不～。I was really upset to hear those words of his.

是样儿 shìyàngr *inf.* look right or good: 这把椅子不～。This chair doesn't look quite right. / 衣服做得很～。This suit is of a very nice cut.

适¹（適）

shì ① fit; suitable; proper: ～于儿童阅读的书籍 books suitable for children ② just; right: ～因此故 just for this very reason / ～逢休假。It happened to be a holiday. ③ comfortable; well: 感到不～ not feel well

适²（適）

shì ① go; follow; pursue: 无所适从 wú suǒ shì cóng ② *formal* (of a girl) get married; marry: 适人 shìrén

适才 shìcái *old* just now

适当 shìdàng suitable; proper; appropriate: ～的工作 suitable work / ～的安排 proper arrangement / ～调整 appropriate readjustment / ～时机 an opportune moment; the right moment / 到～的时候 in due course

适得其反 shì dé qí fǎn run counter to one's desire; be just the opposite of what one wished: 多施肥能增产，但肥料过多会～。More fertilizer will raise the output, but too much will lead to just the opposite.

适度 shìdù appropriate measure; moderate degree: ～的体育活动有利于病人恢复健康。A moderate amount of physical exercise will help improve the patient's health. / 长短～ be the right length

适逢其会 shì féng qí huì happen to be present at the right moment (or on the occasion): 前次赴京，正值全国农业展览会开幕，我～，得以参加。The last time I was in Beijing, I chanced to witness the grand opening of the national agricultural exhibition of the year.

适航性 shìhángxìng airworthiness (of a plane); sea-

worthiness (of a ship)

适合 shìhé suit; fit: ～当地情况 be suited to local conditions / ～他的口味 suit his taste; be to his taste / 这类野生植物不～用作饲料。These wild plants are not fit for fodder. / 她～做教师。She's fit for teaching.

适婚 shìhūn of marriageable age: ～青年 young men and women of marriageable age

适间 shìjiān just now; a moment ago

适可而止 shìkě ér zhǐ stop before going too far; know when or where to stop; not overdo it: 初练长跑要～, 不能过量。A beginner at long-distance running must know when to stop and not overdo it.

适口 shìkǒu be agreeable to the taste; be palatable

适量 shìliàng an appropriate amount or quantity: 加一小匙盐, 糖～。Add a teaspoon of salt, and some sugar to taste.

适龄 shìlíng of the right age: ～儿童 children of school age / ～青年 young people old enough to join the army

适路 shìlù suit (or satisfy) the needs

适巧 shìqiǎo by chance; as chance would have it

适人 shìrén formal (of a girl) get married (to sb.)

适如 shìrú just as; just like: 事情的演变～你所想的那样。Things turned out just as you had expected.

适时 shìshí at the right moment; in good time; timely: ～的号召 a timely call / ～播种 begin sowing in good time / ～召开经验交流会 call timely meetings to exchange experience

适体 shìtǐ (of clothes) fit: 这件连衣裙你穿起来会很～的。This dress will fit you perfectly.

适销 shìxiāo salable: ～商品 salable goods

适销对路 shìxiāo duìlù salable and in good demand; marketable: 生产～、质量好的产品 produce popular products of good quality / 讲求产品～ ensure the ready marketability of products

适宜 shìyí suitable; fit; appropriate; favourable: 他～做卫生工作。He's suitable for public health work. / 游泳对老年人也是～的。Swimming is good for old people too. / 这种土壤～种花生。This kind of soil is good for growing peanuts. / 创造～的经济和社会环境 create a favourable economic and social environment

适意 shìyì agreeable; enjoyable; comfortable

适应 shìyìng suit; adapt to; adjust to; conform to: ～需要 meet the needs of / ～时代的要求 keep abreast of the times / ～环境 adapt oneself to circumstances / ～社会进步的新思想 new ideas which conform to social progress / 不～生产力的发展 be incompatible with the growth of the productive forces / 上层建筑要与经济基础相～。The superstructure should be suited to the economic base. / 人们的思想必须～已经变化了了的情况。People must adapt their thinking to the changed conditions.

适应性 shìyìngxìng biol. adaptability

适应症 shìyìngzhèng med. indication

适用 shìyòng be suitable; be applicable: 这种新的种植法对我们这个地区很～。The new method of cultivation is suitable for our area. / 普遍～的科技成果 scientific and technological achievements that are universally applicable / 这项原则并非～于一切情况。This rule does not apply in all cases.

适用性 shìyòngxìng applicability

适者生存 shìzhě shēngcún biol. survival of the fittest

适值 shìzhí formal just when; as it happens: 昨日来访, ～外出, 憾甚。Unfortunately you happened to be out when I called yesterday. / 上次赴京, ～全国农业展览会开幕。As it happened, the national agricultural exhibition opened the last time I was in Beijing.

适中 shìzhōng ① moderate: 雨量～ moderate rainfall / 大小～ moderate size ② well situated: 招待所地点～。The hostel is well situated.

逝 shì ① pass: 时光易～。Time passes quickly. ② die; pass away: 病～ die of illness

逝世 shìshì pass away; die

轼 shì arch. a horizontal bar in the front of a carriage used as an armrest

舐 shì formal lick

舐犊情深 shì dú qíng shēn the cow fondly licking her calf—parental love

莳(蒔) shì ① formal plant; cultivate: ～花 grow flowers ② dial. transplant: ～秧 transplant rice seedlings

铈 shì chem. cerium (Ce)

弑 shì formal murder (one's sovereign or parent): ～君 regicide / ～父 patricide

释¹(釋) shì ① explain; elucidate: 解释 jiěshì ② clear up; dispel: 释疑 shìyí ③ let go; be relieved of: 如释重负 rú shì zhòng fù ④ release; set free: ～俘 set prisoners free; release prisoners

释²(釋) Shì ① short for 释迦牟尼 Shìjiāmóuní ② Buddhism

释典 shìdiǎn Buddhist Scripture

释放 shìfàng ① release; set free: 要求～政治犯 demand the release of political prisoners ② phys. release: ～出能量 release energy

释怀 shìhuái (usu. used in the negative) dispel from one's bosom; dismiss from one's mind: 当年离别的情景使我久久不能～。I kept recalling the scene of our parting.

释迦牟尼 Shìjiāmóuní Sakyamuni, the founder of Buddhism (c. 565 B.C.–486 B.C.)

释教 Shìjiào Buddhism

释卷 shìjuàn put a book aside; leave off reading: 这本书妙趣横生, 令人不能～。This book is so interesting that you can't put it aside once you start reading it. ——see also 手不释卷 shǒu bù shìjuàn

释老 Shì-Lǎo Buddhism and Taoism

释然 shìrán formal feel relieved; feel at ease

释手 shìshǒu loosen one's grip; let go: 爱不释手 ài bù shìshǒu

释俗 shìsú explain in plain language

释文 shìwén annotations (often used in book titles): 《楚辞～》Annotations of "Chu Ci"

释疑 shìyí clear up (or remove) doubts; dispel suspicion

释义 shìyì explain the meaning (of a word, sentence, etc.)

释藏 Shìzàng the Buddhist Canon

谥(謚) shì ① a posthumous title (formerly bestowed on a ruler, a nobleman, or an eminent official; chosen as appropriate to the life and moral qualities of the deceased; e.g. the Wu 武"Mighty" of Han Wu Di 汉武帝): 诸葛亮～"忠武"。Zhuge Liang was given the posthumous title of "Loyally Martial." or Zhuge Liang was canonized as "Loyally Martial." ② call; name: ～之为保守主义 call it conservatism

筮 shì divination by means of the milfoil

嗜 shì have a liking for; be addicted to: ～酒 be addicted to drink

嗜好　shìhào　① hobby ② addiction; habit

嗜痂之癖　shì jiā zhī pǐ　(also 嗜痂成癖 shì jiā chéng pǐ) a depraved taste

嗜杀成性　shì shā chéng xìng　bloodthirsty; sanguinary: ～的法西斯匪徒 bloodthirsty fascists

嗜血　shìxuè　bloodthirsty; bloodsucking

嗜欲　shìyù　sensual desires

誓　shì　① swear; vow; pledge: ～报此仇 swear vengeance / ～将革命进行到底 vow to carry the revolution through to the end ② oath; vow: 发誓 fāshì

誓不罢休　shì bù bàxiū　(also 誓不甘休 shì bù gānxiū) swear not to stop; swear not to rest: 不达目的，～。We'll never stop until we reach our goal.

誓不两立　shì bù liǎng lì　swear not to coexist with sb.; resolve to destroy sb. or die in the attempt; be irreconcilable

誓词　shìcí　oath; pledge

誓师　shìshī　① a rally to pledge resolution before going to war ② take a mass pledge: ～大会 a meeting to pledge mass effort; an oath-taking rally

誓死　shìsǐ　pledge one's life; dare to die: ～保卫祖国 pledge to fight to the death in defending one's country; be ready to die in defence of one's country

誓死不二　shìsǐ bù èr　pledge to be true to death

誓言　shìyán　oath; pledge: 履行～ fulfil a pledge

誓愿　shìyuàn　vow

誓约　shìyuē　vow; pledge; solemn promise

噬　shì　bite: 吞噬 tūnshì

噬菌体　shìjùntǐ　biol. bacteriophage; phage

噬脐莫及　shì qí mò jí　(also 噬脐何及 shì qí hé jí) one cannot bite one's own navel—it is too late to repent

螫　shì　formal sting

螫针　shìzhēn　stinger (of insects, etc.); sting

shi

匙　shi　see 钥匙 yàoshi ——see also chí

殖　shi　see 骨殖 gǔshi ——see also zhí

shōu

收（收）　shōu　① receive; accept: 请～下作为纪念。Please accept this as a souvenir. / 学校今年又～了一批研究生。The college has enrolled another group of research students this year. / 这本词典共～词六万余条。The dictionary contains over 60,000 entries. ② put away; take in: ～工具 put the tools away / 洗的衣服～了没有? Have you brought in the washing? ③ collect: ～水电费 collect water and electricity bills / ～税 collect taxes / ～废品 collect scrap / ～money received; receipts; income: 税收 shuìshōu ⑤ harvest; gather in: ～庄稼 harvest (or gather in) crops / 一亩稻子～了八百斤。The rice yield was 800 jin per mu. ⑥ bring to an end; stop: 时间不早了，今天就～了吧。It's getting late. Let's call it a day. ⑦ restrain; control: 孩子玩得心都～不回来了。The boy can't get his mind off play.

收报机　shōubàojī　telegraphic or radiotelegraphic receiver

收编　shōubiān　incorporate into one's own forces

收兵　shōubīng　withdraw (or recall) troops; call off a battle: 不获全胜，决不～。We will not withdraw our forces till complete victory.

收藏　shōucáng　collect and store up: ～古画 collect old paintings / ～粮食 store up grain

收藏家　shōucángjiā　collector (of books, antiques, etc.)

收操　shōucāo　bring drill to an end

收操号　shōucāohào　a bugle call to dismiss; recall: 吹～ sound the recall

收场　shōuchǎng　① wind up; end up; stop: 他的话匣子一打开，就不容易～。Once he opens his trap, he just never stops. / 这件事不好～。It's hard to wind this matter up. / 咱们可不能就这样～。We can't wind up the matter in such a fashion. / 看他怎样～。Let's wait and see how he's going to end it all. ② end; ending; denouement: 圆满的～ a happy ending

收车　shōuchē　return the vehicle to the garage, terminal, etc. and knock off

收成　shōucheng　harvest; crop: 从来没有过的好～ a record harvest / ～不好 poor harvests; crop failures / 夺得秋季作物的好～ reap a good autumn harvest / 这次鱼汛中，带鱼的～好不好? Have you got a good catch of hairtail this season?

收存　shōucún　receive and keep: 这些重要文件要～好。These important documents must be kept in a safe place.

收到　shōudào　receive; get; achieve; obtain: ～一封信 receive a letter / ～良好效果 achieve good results

收发　shōufā　① receive and dispatch ② dispatcher

收发报　shōufābào　transmit and receive telegrams: 管～ be in charge of transmitting and receiving telegrams; be a telegraph operator

收发报机　shōufābàojī　transmitter-receiver; transceiver

收发室　shōufāshì　office for incoming and outgoing mail

收方　shōufāng　bookkeeping debit side; debit

收房　shōufáng　(in former times) take in a maidservant or a slave girl as a concubine

收费　shōufèi　collect fees; charge

收风　shōufēng　call prisoners in after letting them out for exercise

收服　shōufú　(also 收伏 shōufú) subdue; reduce to submission

收复　shōufù　recover; recapture: ～失地 recover lost territory / ～城市 recapture a city

收港　shōugǎng　(of ships) return to harbour

收割　shōugē　reap; harvest; gather in: ～小麦 gather in the wheat

收割机　shōugējī　harvester; reaper

收工　shōugōng　(of those who work in the fields or on construction sites) stop work for the day; knock off; pack up: 该～了。It's time to knock off. / 我们今天下午五点半～。We stop work at 5: 30 this afternoon.

收购　shōugòu　purchase; buy: ～农副产品 purchase farm produce and sideline products / ～价格 purchasing (or procurement) price

收购站　shōugòuzhàn　purchasing station (or centre)

收归　shōuguī　take back (rights, ownership, etc.): ～国有 nationalize

收回　shōuhuí　① take back; call in; regain; recall: ～发出的文件 recall the documents which have been issued / ～借出的书籍 call in books lent / ～主权 regain sovereignty / ～贷款 recall loans / ～投资 recoup capital outlay ② withdraw; countermand: ～建议 withdraw a proposal / 我～我的话。I take back what I said.

收回成命　shōuhuí chéngmìng　countermand (or retract) an order; revoke a command

收活　shōuhuó　① accept orders for repairs or processing ② dial. stop work for the day; knock off; pack up

收货人　shōuhuòrén　consignee

收获　shōuhuò　① gather (or bring) in the crops; har-

vest: 春天播种, 秋天～ sow in spring and reap in autumn ② results; gains: 一次很有～的访问 a most rewarding visit / 你们的艰苦劳动, 一定会有～。 Your hard work will be duly rewarded.

收获量 shōuhuòliàng harvest yield; yield; crop

收集 shōují collect; gather: ～民间验方 collect time-tested folk prescriptions / ～废铁 collect scrap iron

收监 shōujiān take into custody; put in prison

收件人 shōujiànrén addressee; consignee

收缴 shōujiǎo take over; capture: ～敌人的武器 take over the enemy's arms

收紧 shōujǐn tighten up

收据 shōujù receipt

收据簿 shōujùbù receipt book

收看 shōukàn watch television; look in

收口 shōukǒu ① (of a wound) close up; heal: 刀伤～了。 The sword wound has healed. ② (in knitting) cast off; bind off: 注意～别太紧。 Be careful not to cast off (or bind off) too tightly.

收款机 shōukuǎnjī popular name for 现金出纳机 xiànjīn chūnàjī

收款人 shōukuǎnrén payee

收揽 shōulǎn ① derog. draw over to one's side: ～民心 try to win the support of the people ② keep in one's grasp

收礼 shōulǐ accept gifts

收敛 shōuliǎn ① weaken or disappear: 她的笑容突然～了。 Her smile suddenly disappeared. ② restrain oneself: 碰了钉子以后, 他～些了。 He has pulled in his horns since that setback. / 他继续胡作非为, 毫无～。 Unrelentingly he pursued his course of evil. ③ math. convergence ④ med. astringent: ～剂 astringent (a drug)

收殓 shōuliàn lay a body in a coffin

收留 shōuliú take sb. in; have sb. in one's care

收拢 shōulǒng ① draw sth. in: 把网～ draw the net in ② derog. draw over to one's side: ～人心 try to win people's support by every artifice

收录 shōulù ① employ; recruit; take on: ～几个职员 recruit some office workers ② include: 这篇文章已～在他的选集里。 This essay is included in his selected works. ③ listen in and take down; take down; record: ～新闻广播 take down the news from the radio; make a recording of the news broadcast

收录机 shōulùjī (short for 收音录音两用机) radio-tape recorder; radio-cassette recorder

收罗 shōuluó collect; gather; enlist: ～人才 recruit qualified personnel / ～资料 collect data / ～社会渣滓 gather together the dregs of society / 这本小册子～了一些乌七八糟的东西。 This pamphlet is a jumble of all sorts of rubbish.

收买 shōumǎi ① purchase; buy in: ～旧书 buy used books ② buy over; bribe: 他们是想～你啊。 They are trying to buy you over.

收买人心 shōumǎi rénxīn buy popular support

收纳 shōunà receive; take in

收盘 shōupán closing quotation (on the exchange, etc.): ～汇率 closing rate / ～价格 closing price

收票员 shōupiàoyuán ticket collector

收起 shōuqǐ pack up; cut out; stop: ～你们那一套高调吧! Cut out your high-sounding talk! / ～你那套鬼把戏! None of your dirty tricks! / 你这些空话还是～为好。 You'd better stop this empty talk.

收讫 shōuqì ① payment received; paid ② (on a bill of lading, an invoice, etc.) all the above goods received; received in full

收清 shōuqīng received in full

收秋 shōuqiū gather in the autumn crops: 忙着～ be busy harvesting the autumn crops

收取 shōuqǔ receive; collect: ～手续费 collect service (or handling) charges

收容 shōuróng take in; accept; house: ～伤员 take in wounded soldiers / ～难民 house refugees

收容所 shōuróngsuǒ collecting post: 难民～ refugee camp

收入 shōurù ① income; revenue; receipts; earnings; proceeds: 集体(个人)～ collective (personal) income / 副业～ income from sideline occupations / 财政～ state revenue / 总～ gross income / 现金和粮食～ income in cash and grain / ～和支出 receipts and expenditures; revenue and expenditure / 人均～ average per capita income / ～相当可观 earn quite a handsome income ② take in; include: 修订版～许多新词语。 Many new words and phrases have been included in the revised edition.

收审 shōushěn detain for interrogation

收生 shōushēng midwifery

收生婆 shōushēngpó midwife

收市 shōushì (of markets or stores) close for the day

收拾 shōushí ① put in order; tidy; clear away: 把工具～一下。 Put the tools in order. / ～屋子 tidy up the room / ～床铺 make the bed / ～碗筷 clear away the bowls and chopsticks; clear the table ② get things ready; pack: ～药箱 get one's medical kit ready; pack one's medical kit / ～行李 pack one's luggage; pack up one's things / 咱们赶紧～～走吧。 Let's get our things together at once and be off. ③ repair; mend: ～鞋子 mend shoes ④ inf. settle with; punish: 早晚我们要～这个坏蛋。 We'll settle with the scoundrel one of these days.

收拾残局 shōushí cánjú clear up the mess; pick up the pieces

收受 shōushòu receive; accept; take: ～贿赂 take bribes

收束 shōushù ① bring together; collect: 把心思～一下 get into the frame of mind for work ② bring to a close: 写到这里, 我的信也该～了。 I think it is about time I wound up this letter. ③ pack (for a journey)

收缩 shōusuō ① contract; shrink: 金属遇冷就会～。 Metals contract as they become cool. / 这种布下水后要～。 This kind of cloth shrinks when it's washed. ② concentrate one's forces; draw back: 敌人～到几个据点里。 The enemy drew back into a few fortified points. ③ physiol. systole

收缩压 shōusuōyā systolic pressure

收摊儿 shōutānr pack up the stall—wind up the day's business or the work on hand

收条 shōutiáo receipt

收听 shōutīng listen in: ～元旦社论 listen in to the New Year's Day editorial / ～新闻广播 listen to the news broadcast / 你的收音机能～多少电台? How many stations can you get on your radio set?

收尾 shōuwěi ① bring to a conclusion; wind up: 你的文章可以用一句格言～。 Try to wind up your essay with a moral. / 我们正在做～工作。 We are winding up the job. ② ending (of an article, etc.): 这个剧本～太没劲。 The ending of the play is rather too tame.

收文 shōuwén incoming dispatches

收文簿 shōuwénbù register of incoming dispatches

收效 shōuxiào yield results; produce effects; bear fruit: ～显著 bring notable results / ～甚微 produce very little effect / 这些轻工业项目具有投资少、快的特点。 These light industry projects are characterized by small investments and quick returns.

收心 shōuxīn ① get into the frame of mind for work or study; concentrate on more serious things ② have a change of heart

收信人 shōuxìnrén the recipient of a letter; addressee

收押 shōuyā take into custody; detain

收养 shōuyǎng　take in and bring up; adopt: ～孤儿 adopt an orphan / 爹妈死后，周伯伯就把我～下来了。 After my parents died, Uncle Zhou took me in.

收益 shōuyì　income; profit; earnings; gains

收音 shōuyīn　① radio reception: 这里～情况良好。 Radio reception is good here. ② acoustics (of an auditorium, etc.)

收音电唱两用机 shōuyīn diànchàng liǎngyòngjī　radio-gramophone

收音机 shōuyīnjī　radio (set); wireless (set): 便携式～ portable radio / 落地式～ console set

收摘 shōuzhāi　pick (fruit, etc.): ～棉花 pick cotton

收账 shōuzhàng　① charge to an account ② collect debts

收针 shōuzhēn　(in knitting) decrease stitches; bind off; cast off

收支 shōu-zhī　revenue and expenditure; income and expenses: ～平衡。 Revenue and expenditure are balanced. / ～相抵 break even / 公布～帐目 publish a balance sheet

收支逆差 shōu-zhī nìchā　balance of payments deficit

收执 shōuzhí　① (of a certificate, etc.) be issued to the person concerned for safekeeping ② receipt (issued by a government agency)

shóu

熟 shóu　a variant pronunciation for 熟 shú used in colloquial speech

shǒu

手 shǒu　① hand: 双～捧着 hold in both hands / ～把～地教 take a person in hand and teach him how to do a job / ～织的毛衣 a hand-knitted woollen sweater ② have in one's hand; hold: 人手一册 rén shǒu yī cè ③ handy; convenient: 手册 shǒucè ④ personally: 手植 shǒuzhí ⑤ a person doing or good at a certain job: 拖拉机～ tractor driver / 机枪～ machinegunner ⑥ m. (for skill or dexterity): 他写一～好字。 He writes a fine hand. / 他真有两～。 He really knows his stuff.

手巴掌 shǒubāzhang　① palm (of the hand) ② dial. gloves

手版 shǒubǎn　a tablet held before the breast by officials when having an audience with the emperor

手板 shǒubǎn　① same as 手版 shǒubǎn ② dial. palm (of the hand)

手板儿 shǒubǎnr　ferule: 打～ punish a child with a ferule

手背 shǒubèi　the back of the hand

手本 shǒuběn　same as 手册 shǒucè

手笔 shǒubǐ　① a famous person's own handwriting or painting: 这一题词是鲁迅先生的～。 This inscription is in Lu Xun's own handwriting. ② literary skill: 大～ a well-known writer; master

手臂 shǒubì　① arm ② a reliable helper: 他是队长的得力～。 He's the team leader's right-hand man.

手边 shǒubiān　on hand; at hand: 我～没有现钱。 I don't have any cash on hand.

手表 shǒubiǎo　wrist watch

手不释卷 shǒu bù shìjuàn　always have a book in one's hand; be very studious; be a diligent reader

手不稳 shǒubùwěn　dial. have light fingers

手册 shǒucè　① handbook; manual: 教师～ teacher's manual ② record book; workbook: 劳动～ worker's book

手长 shǒucháng　pushing; grasping

手抄 shǒuchāo　① write by hand; handwrite ② handwritten

手抄本 shǒuchāoběn　handwritten copy

手车 shǒuchē　handcart; pushcart; barrow

手钏 shǒuchuàn　dial. bracelet

手锤 shǒuchuí　light hammer

手戳 shǒuchuō　inf. private seal; signet

手刺 shǒucì　handwritten visiting card (used among officials in former times)

手到病除 shǒu dào bìng chú　illness departs at a touch of the hand (said as a tribute to a doctor or a trouble-shooter)

手到擒来 shǒu dào qín lái　(also 手到擒拿 shǒu dào qín ná) just stretch the hand and bring it back—very easy: 要打赢他们还不是～？ Surely we can beat them hands down!

手倒立 shǒudàolì　sports handstand

手底下 shǒudǐxia　same as 手下 shǒuxià

手电筒 shǒudiàntǒng　electric torch; flashlight

手段 shǒuduàn　① means; medium; method: 达到目的的一种～ a means to an end / 高压～ high-handed measures / 强制～ coercive method; coercion / 利用合法的斗争～ utilize the legal form of struggle / 艺术～ artistic medium / 积累～ means of accumulation / 支付～ means of payment ② trick; artifice: 采用种种～ resort to all sorts of tricks; use every artifice ③ skill; finesse: 她应付那件事情很有～。 She managed that situation with great finesse.

手法 shǒufǎ　① skill; technique: 国画的传统～ traditional technique of Chinese painting / 艺术表现～ means of artistic expression ② trick; gimmick: 贼喊捉贼的拙劣～ the clumsy trick of thief crying "stop thief" / 一种反动的宣传～ a reactionary propaganda gimmick / 两面～ dual tactics / 惯用～ habitual (or customary) practice / 他的～并不高明。 Those tricks of his are none too clever.

手风琴 shǒufēngqín　accordion: 六角～ concertina

手扶拖拉机 shǒufú tuōlājī　walking tractor

手感 shǒugǎn　text. feel: ～柔软 have a soft feel / 我觉得这种料子的～好。 I like the feel of this cloth. / 这种布料的～仿佛毛料，又软又暖。 This cotton cloth has a soft, warm woolly feel.

手稿 shǒugǎo　original (or holograph) manuscript; manuscript

手工 shǒugōng　① handwork: 这件上衣的～做得很细。 This jacket is a fine piece of handwork. / ～费 payment for a piece of handwork ② by hand; manual: ～操作 done by hand; manual operations / ～织的布 hand-woven cloth / ～制纸 handmade paper ③ inf. charge for a piece of handwork: 你这件大衣～多少? How much did you pay for the tailoring of this overcoat?

手工工具 shǒugōng gōngjù　hand tools

手工业 shǒugōngyè　handicraft industry; handicraft: ～者 handicraftsman

手工业生产合作社 shǒugōngyè shēngchǎn hézuòshè handicraft producers' cooperative

手工艺 shǒugōngyì　handicraft art; handicraft

手工艺工人 shǒugōngyì gōngrén　craftsman; artisan

手工艺品 shǒugōngyìpǐn　articles of handicraft art; handicrafts

手鼓 shǒugǔ　a small drum similar to the tambourine (used by the Uygur and other nationalities)

手函 shǒuhán　a letter in one's own handwriting

手翰 shǒuhàn　formal a letter in one's own handwriting

手疾眼快 shǒují-yǎnkuài　quick of eye and deft of hand

手记 shǒují　① write down notes or records ② written

notes or records

手技 shǒujì ① handicraft; craftsmanship ② *acrobatics* juggling; jugglery

手迹 shǒujì sb.'s original handwriting or painting

手简 shǒujiǎn *formal* a letter in one's own handwriting

手脚 shǒujiǎo ① movement of hands or feet; motion: 〜利落 nimble; agile ② *dial.* underhand method; devious device; trick: 一定是有人从中弄了〜。Someone must have juggled things.

手脚不干净 shǒujiǎo bù gānjìng sticky-fingered; dishonest in money matters

手巾 shǒu·jīn ① towel ② *dial.* handkerchief

手巾架 shǒujīnjià towel rack

手紧 shǒujǐn ① closefisted; tightfisted ② be short of money; be hard up

手劲儿 shǒujìnr muscular strength of the hand

手锯 shǒujù handsaw

手卷 shǒujuàn hand scroll

手绢 shǒujuàn handkerchief

手铐 shǒukào handcuffs: 带上〜 be handcuffed

手快 shǒukuài deft of hand: 变戏法得〜。A juggler must have deft fingers.

手拉葫芦 shǒulā húlu *mech.* chain block

手拉手 shǒu lā shǒu hand in hand

手雷 shǒuléi *mil.* antitank grenade

手力千斤顶 shǒulì qiānjīndǐng *mech.* hand jack

手令 shǒulìng an order personally issued by sb. in command

手榴弹 shǒuliúdàn *mil.* hand grenade; grenade

手笼 shǒulǒng muff

手炉 shǒulú handwarmer

手轮 shǒulún *mech.* handwheel

手锣 shǒuluó same as 小锣 xiǎoluó

手慢 shǒumàn slow with one's hands; slow in movements; slow-moving

手忙脚乱 shǒumáng-jiǎoluàn in a rush; in a flurry: 我先去厨房通知一声，免得临时〜。I'm going to the kitchen to warn them so that they'll not have to rush about at the last moment. / 事情多，时间紧，搞得他〜。He's in a dreadful rush, with so much to do in so short a time.

手面 shǒumiàn *dial.* the extent of one's spending: 你〜太阔了，要节约一点才好。You spend too freely. You should be more thrifty.

手民 shǒumín *formal* typesetter

手民之误 shǒumín zhī wù *old* misprint; typographical error

手模 shǒumó fingerprint

手拿把掐 shǒuná-bǎqiā (also 手拿把攥 shǒuná-bǎzuàn) in the bag; a sure thing

手黏 shǒunián sticky-fingered; light-fingered; thievish

手帕 shǒupà same as 手绢 shǒujuàn

手蹼 shǒupǔ webbed gloves

手旗 shǒuqí *mil.* handflag; semaphore flag

手气 shǒuqì luck at gambling, card playing, etc.: 他今晚打牌的〜好得出奇。He's marvellously lucky at cards tonight.

手钳 shǒuqián hand vice; pliers

手枪 shǒuqiāng pistol

手枪慢加速比赛 shǒuqiāng mànjiāsù bǐsài *sports* centre-fire pistol

手枪速射 shǒuqiāng sùshè *sports* rapid-fire pistol

手枪套 shǒuqiāngtào holster

手巧 shǒuqiǎo skilful with one's hands; nimble-fingered; deft; dexterous: 那姑娘〜，裁剪、缝纫、刺绣、样样都来得。The girl is nimble-fingered and is good at garment-cutting, sewing and embroidery.

手勤 shǒuqín diligent; industrious; hardworking: 这徒弟〜脚快。This apprentice is keen and quick in his work.

手轻 shǒuqīng have gentle hands; not use too much force; handle gently: 那位护士的手很轻。That nurse has very gentle hands.

手球 shǒuqiú *sports* ① handball (a game) ② handball (the ball)

手刃 shǒurèn stab to death; kill with one's own hand

手软 shǒuruǎn be irresolute when firmness is needed; be softhearted: 对这种坏人可不能〜。We must not be soft on such scoundrels.

手刹车 shǒushāchē hand brake

手生 shǒushēng lack practice and skill; be out of practice

手势 shǒushì gesture; sign; signal: 打〜 make a gesture; gesticulate

手势语 shǒushìyǔ sign language

手书 shǒushū ① write in one's own hand ② personal letter: 顷接〜。I have just received your letter.

手术 shǒushù surgical operation; operation: 大（小）〜 major (minor) operation / 动〜 perform or undergo an operation / 高频电刀〜 high frequency electrotomy

手术刀 shǒushùdāo scalpel

手术刀包 shǒushùdāobāo surgical kit

手术室 shǒushùshì operating room; operating theatre

手术台 shǒushùtái operating table

手松 shǒusōng free with one's money; free-handed; open-handed

手套 shǒutào ① gloves; mittens ② baseball gloves; mitts

手提 shǒutí portable: 〜打字机 portable typewriter

手提包 shǒutíbāo handbag; bag

手提电话 shǒutí diànhuà another name for 移动电话 yídòng diànhuà

手提箱 shǒutíxiāng suitcase

手头 shǒutóu ① right beside one; on hand; at hand: 放在〜待用 place right beside one in case of need / 〜工作挺多 have a lot of work on hand; have one's hands full / 这本书我倒是有，可惜不在〜。I have a copy of the book, but unfortunately not with me. ② one's financial condition at the moment: 〜紧 be short of money; be hard up / 〜宽裕 be in easy circumstances; be quite well off at the moment

手推车 shǒutuīchē same as 手车 shǒuchē

手推婴儿车 shǒutuī yīng'érchē pushchair; light baby carriage

手腕 shǒuwàn ① trick; artifice: 耍〜 play tricks; use artifices / 他很有〜。He's quite crafty. ② skill; finesse; tactics: 外交〜 diplomatic skill (or finesse) / 政治〜 political tactics

手腕子 shǒuwànzi wrist

手纹 shǒuwén the lines of the palm

手无寸铁 shǒu wú cùntiě bare-handed; unarmed; defenceless

手无缚鸡之力 shǒu wú fù jī zhī lì lack the strength to truss a chicken—physically very weak

手舞足蹈 shǒuwǔ-zúdǎo dance for joy

手下 shǒuxià ① under the leadership (or guidance, direction) of; under: 他在我〜工作，就得听我的。He has to listen to me since he is working under me. ② at hand: 东西不在〜。I haven't got the thing with me. ③ at the hands of sb.: 我曾两次败在她〜。I have been defeated by her twice. ④ one's financial condition at the moment: 他每到月底，〜就紧了。He usually gets hard up by the end of the month.

手下败将 shǒuxià bàijiàng one's vanquished foe; one's defeated opponent

手下留情 shǒuxià liú qíng show mercy; be lenient; make allowances for (when dealing out punishment to sb.)

手下人 shǒuxiàrén ① one's subordinate ② servant

手相 shǒuxiàng　palmistry: 看～ practise palmistry ／～术士 palmist

手携手 shǒu xié shǒu　hand in hand

手写 shǒuxiě　① write by hand; handwrite; write in one's own hand ② handwritten; written in one's own hand

手写体 shǒuxiětǐ　handwritten form; script

手心 shǒuxīn　① the centre of the palm ② control: 这事儿全捏在他～里。 He's got the matter in the palm of his hand.

手续 shǒuxù　procedures; formalities: 办～ go through formalities ／行政～ administrative formalities ／法律～ legal formalities ／～不完备 have not completed the formalities

手续费 shǒuxùfèi　service charges; handling charges; commission

手癣 shǒuxuǎn　tinea manuum; fungal infection of the hand

手眼通天 shǒu-yǎn tōngtiān　exceptionally adept in trickery

手痒 shǒuyǎng　① one's fingers itch ② have an itch to do sth.

手摇泵 shǒuyáobèng　hand pump

手摇发电机 shǒuyáo fādiànjī　hand generator

手艺 shǒuyì　① craftsmanship; workmanship: ～高 be highly skilled ／那个裁缝的～很好。 That tailor has quite a bit of skill. ② handicraft; trade: 跟师傅学～ learn the trade from a master

手艺人 shǒuyìrén　craftsman

手淫 shǒuyín　masturbation; self-abuse: 犯～ masturbate

手印 shǒuyìn　① an impression of the hand ② thumb print; fingerprint: 按～ put one's thumb print on (a document, etc.)

手语 shǒuyǔ　sign language; dactylology

手谕 shǒuyù　old personally written orders or instructions

手泽 shǒuzé　formal handwriting or articles left by one's forefathers

手札 shǒuzhá　formal personal letter

手闸 shǒuzhá　hand brake

手章 shǒuzhāng　private seal; signet

手掌 shǒuzhǎng　palm (of the hand)

手掌心 shǒuzhǎngxīn　inf. ① the centre of the palm ② control: 我怎么也跳不出他的～。 No matter how hard I tried, I could never free myself from his control.

手杖 shǒuzhàng　walking stick; stick

手诏 shǒuzhào　an imperial edict written by the emperor himself

手折 shǒuzhé　old ① a record book in accordion form ② an account book in accordion form

手植 shǒuzhí　personally plant (a tree, etc.): 此树系周恩来～。 This tree was planted by Zhou Enlai.

手纸 shǒuzhǐ　toilet paper

手指 shǒuzhǐ　finger

手指甲 shǒuzhǐjiɑ　finger nail

手指头 shǒuzhǐtou　inf. finger

手指头肚儿 shǒuzhǐtoudùr　the inner side of the fingertip

手指字母 shǒuzhǐ zìmǔ　manual alphabet (used by deaf-mutes); deaf-and-dumb alphabet

手重 shǒuzhòng　use too much force: 她上药时～了些。 She pressed the wound a bit too hard when dressing it.

手镯 shǒuzhuó　bracelet

手足 shǒuzú　① movement ② brothers: ～之情 brotherly affection

手足无措 shǒu-zú wúcuò　all in a fluster; at a loss what to do

手钻 shǒuzuàn　hand drill

守

守 shǒu　① guard; defend: ～城 defend a city ／～球门 keep goal ／～住阵地 hold the position ② keep watch: ～了一夜 keep watch for the whole night ／～着伤员 watch over (or look after) the wounded ③ observe; abide by: ～纪律 observe discipline ／～规矩 behave well ／～信用 keep one's promise; be as good as one's word ／～着老一套 stick to the old practice ④ close to; near: ～着水的地方要多养鱼。 Where there is water nearby, make a special effort to breed fish.

守备 shǒubèi　perform garrison duty; be on garrison duty; garrison

守备部队 shǒubèi bùduì　garrison force; (holding) garrison

守财奴 shǒucáinú　miser

守场员 shǒuchǎngyuán　sports fielder (in baseball, softball or cricket)

守车 shǒuchē　(British) guard's van; (American) caboose

守成 shǒuchéng　formal maintain the achievements of one's predecessors

守敌 shǒudí　the enemy holding a fortress or a strategic point

守法 shǒufǎ　abide by (or observe) the law; be law-abiding

守法户 shǒufǎhù　law-abiding firm

守宫 shǒugōng　old name for 壁虎 bìhǔ

守寡 shǒuguǎ　remain a widow; live in widowhood

守恒 shǒuhéng　phys. conservation: 能量～ conservation of energy ／动量～ conservation of momentum

守恒定律 shǒuhéng dìnglǜ　phys. conservation law

守候 shǒuhòu　① wait for; expect: ～着前线的消息 wait for news from the front ② keep watch: ～在病人身旁 keep watch by the patient's bedside

守护 shǒuhù　guard; defend

守护神 shǒuhùshén　guardian spirit; tutelary spirit; patron saint

守活寡 shǒuhuóguǎ　be a grass widow

守家 shǒujiā　① look after the house; mind the house ② maintain what has been achieved or acquired by one's forefathers

守节 shǒujié　(of a woman in former times) remain unmarried after the death of her husband or her betrothed

守经达权 shǒujīng-dáquán　be mindful of principles but act according to circumstances; consider expediency as well as principle

守旧 shǒujiù　adhere to past practices; stick to old ways; be conservative

守旧派 shǒujiùpài　old-liners; conservatives

守军 shǒujūn　defending troops; defenders

守口如瓶 shǒu kǒu rú píng　keep one's mouth shut; breathe not a single word; be tight-mouthed; be tight-lipped

守垒员 shǒulěiyuán　sports baseman (in baseball or softball)

守灵 shǒulíng　stand as guards at the bier; keep vigil beside the coffin

守门 shǒumén　① be on duty at the door or gate: ～人 gatekeeper; doorkeeper ② sports keep goal

守门员 shǒuményuán　goalkeeper (in football, ice hockey, etc.)

守丧 shǒusāng　same as 守灵 shǒulíng

守身如玉 shǒushēn rú yù　keep oneself as pure as jade—preserve one's honour or integrity

守时 shǒushí　be on time; be punctual

守势 shǒushì　defensive: 采取～ be on the defensive ／迫使对方处于～ put one's opponent on the defensive

守岁 shǒusuì　stay up late or all night on New Year's Eve; see the Old Year out and the New Year in

守土 shǒutǔ　*formal* defend the territory of one's country: ～有责 be duty-bound to defend the territory of one's country

守望 shǒuwàng　keep watch

守望台 shǒuwàngtái　watchtower

守望相助 shǒuwàng xiāng zhù　(of neighbouring villages, etc.) keep watch and help defend each other; give mutual help and protection

守卫 shǒuwèi　guard; defend: 海防战士警惕地～着祖国的海疆。The coastguardsmen vigilantly guard our territorial waters.

守孝 shǒuxiào　observe a period of mourning for one's deceased parent

守信 shǒuxìn　keep one's word

守业 shǒuyè　maintain what has been achieved by one's forefathers or predecessors; safeguard one's heritage: 创业难,～更难。If it is difficult for a man to set up a business, it is even more so for his heirs to keep it up.

守夜 shǒuyè　keep watch at night; spend the night on watch

守约 shǒuyuē　① abide by an agreement ② keep an appointment

守则 shǒuzé　rules; regulations: 工作～ work regulations

守正不阿 shǒu zhèng bù ē　be strictly just and impartial

守职 shǒuzhí　stand fast at one's post; be faithful in the discharge of one's duties

守制 shǒuzhì　(in former times) observe the prescribed period of mourning (usu. 27 months) for one's deceased parent

守株待兔 shǒu zhū dài tù　stand by a stump waiting for more hares to come and dash themselves against it—trust to chance and strokes of luck

首[1]　shǒu　① head: 昂首 ángshǒu / 回首 huíshǒu ② first: ～批 the first batch ③ leader; head; chief: 元首 yuánshǒu ④ bring charges against sb.: 出首 chūshǒu

首[2]　shǒu　*m.* (for songs and poems): 一～歌 a song /《唐诗三百～》300 Tang Poems

首倡 shǒuchàng　be the first to advocate; initiate; start: ～改革 be the first to advocate reform

首车 shǒuchē　first bus (of a regular bus service)

首创 shǒuchuàng　originate; initiate; pioneer: ～一种新的汉字输入法 originate a new way of processing and inputting Chinese data into computers / ～精神 creative initiative; pioneering spirit

首次 shǒucì　for the first time; first: ～航行 maiden (or first) voyage / ～公演 first (or opening) performance; premiere

首当其冲 shǒu dāng qí chōng　be the first to be affected (by a disaster, etc.); bear the brunt

首都 shǒudū　capital (of a country)

首恶 shǒu'è　chief criminal; principal culprit

首发式 shǒufāshì　a ceremony celebrating the first publication of a book

首犯 shǒufàn　chief criminal; principal culprit

首府 shǒufǔ　① (in former times) head prefecture (the prefecture in which a provincial capital was located) ② the capital of an autonomous region or prefecture: 呼和浩特是内蒙古自治区的～。Huhhot is the capital of the Inner Mongolia Autonomous Region. ③ the capital of a dependency or colony

首富 shǒufù　(also 首户 shǒuhù) the wealthiest family in the locality

首告 shǒugào　report (an offender); inform against (an offender)

首功 shǒugōng　first-class merit

首航 shǒuháng　maiden voyage or flight

首级 shǒují　chopped-off head (in battle, etc.)

首季 shǒují　the first quarter (of a year)

首届 shǒujiè　the first occasion, term, session, etc.; ～全国农民运动会 the First All-China Agricultural Workers' Sports Meet / ～毕业生 the first class of graduates

首肯 shǒukěn　nod approval; nod assent; approve; consent

首领 shǒulǐng　① *formal* head and neck ② chieftain; leader; head

首难 shǒunàn　*formal* be the first to rise in revolt

首脑 shǒunǎo　head: 政府～ head of government / ～会议 conference of heads of state or government; summit conference / ～人物 leading figure

首屈一指 shǒu qū yī zhǐ　come first on the list; be second to none: 老王的棋艺在我们单位是～的。Lao Wang is the best chess player in our unit.

首任 shǒurèn　the first to be appointed to an office: ～驻中国大使 the first ambassador accredited to China

首日封 shǒurìfēng　first day cover (an envelope with a commemorative stamp and postmark affixed on the first day of issue of a set of commemorative stamps)

首善之区 shǒushàn zhī qū　the best of places (i.e. the capital of a country)

首饰 shǒushi　① (originally) head ornaments ② jewels; jewelry: 她戴很多～。She wears a lot of jewelry.

首饰店 shǒushidiàn　jewelry store

首饰盒 shǒushihé　jewel case

首鼠两端 shǒushǔ liǎng duān　be in two minds; shilly-shally

首途 shǒutú　*formal* set out on a journey; start a journey

首陀罗 Shǒutuóluó　Sudra

首尾 shǒu-wěi　① the head and the tail; the beginning and the end: ～不能相顾。The vanguard is cut off from the rear. ② from beginning to end: 我对这个问题的看法是～一贯的。I have always been consistent in my views on this subject.

首位 shǒuwèi　the first place: 放在～ put in the first place; place before everything else; give first priority to / 居于～ rank first

首乌 shǒuwū　*Chin. med.* the tuber of multiflower knotweed (*Polygonum multiform*)

首乌藤 shǒuwūténg　*Chin. med.* the vine of multiflower knotweed (*Polygonum multiform*)

首席 shǒuxí　① seat of honour: 坐～ be seated at the head of the table; be in the seat of honour ② chief: ～代表 chief representative or delegate / ～秘书 principal secretary / ～顾问 chief adviser

首先 shǒuxiān　*adv.* ① before all others; first: ～发言 speak first / ～到达工地 be the first to arrive at the construction site ② in the first place; first of all; above all: ～,我问你这个。First, let me ask you this.

首相 shǒuxiàng　prime minister

首演 shǒuyǎn　first (or opening) performance; premiere

首要 shǒuyào　of the first importance; first; chief: ～的事先办。First things first. / ～任务 the most important task / ～问题 a question of the first importance / 把这个问题放在～位置上 give first priority to this issue

首要分子 shǒuyào fènzǐ　*leg.* ringleader

首义 shǒuyì　*formal* be the first to rise in revolt

首映式 shǒuyìngshì　premiere (of a film)

首战告捷 shǒuzhàn gào jié　win in the very first battle or game

首长 shǒuzhǎng　leading cadre; senior officer: 团～ senior officers of the regiment / 我的老～ my old chief / 要～负责,亲自动手。The leading cadres should

take personal charge and pitch in.

首座 shǒuzuò ① seat of honour (at a banquet) ② abbot

shòu

寿 (壽、夀) shòu ① long life; old age: 福～ good fortune and long life ② life; age: 长寿 chángshòu ③ birthday: 祝寿 zhùshòu ④ *euph.* funerary: 寿木 shòumù ⑤ (Shòu) a surname

寿斑 shòubān senile plaque

寿比南山，福如东海 shòu bǐ nánshān, fú rú dōnghǎi may your age be as the southern mountain and your happiness as the eastern sea (said as birthday congratulations to an elderly person)

寿材 shòucái a coffin prepared before one's death; coffin

寿辰 shòuchén birthday (of an elderly person)

寿诞 shòudàn same as 寿辰 shòuchén

寿光鸡 shòuguāngjī shouguang chicken (a breed of chicken noted as both a layer and a broiler; originally developed in Shouguang county, Shandong Province)

寿酒 shòujiǔ birthday wine; birthday feast

寿考 shòukǎo *formal* long life; longevity: 富贵～ wealth, rank, and longevity

寿礼 shòulǐ birthday present (for an elderly person)

寿联 shòulián birthday couplets; birthday scrolls

寿面 shòumiàn birthday noodles; longevity noodles

寿命 shòumìng life span; life: 现代医学延长了人的～。 Modern medicine has increased man's life span. / 节省时间等于延长～。 To save time is to prolong life. / 机器～ a machine's life (or service life) / 中子～ neutron lifetime

寿木 shòumù (also 寿器 shòuqì) same as 寿材 shòucái

寿山石 shòushānshí shoushan stone (a translucent stone found at Shoushan, Fujian Province; prized as material for seals)

寿数 shòushu the allotted life span of an individual

寿堂 shòutáng ① *formal* mourning hall ② *formal* a grave prepared before one's death ③ longevity hall (for birthday celebrations)

寿桃 shòutáo ① peaches offered as a birthday present ② peach-shaped birthday cakes

寿险 shòuxiǎn life insurance

寿星 shòuxing ① the god of longevity ② an elderly person whose birthday is being celebrated

寿穴 shòuxué a grave prepared before one's death

寿筵 shòuyán birthday feast

寿衣 shòuyī graveclothes; shroud; cerements

寿幛 shòuzhàng birthday banner (with a congratulatory message)

寿终 shòuzhōng die of old age

寿终正寝 shòuzhōng-zhèngqǐn die in bed of old age; die a natural death

受 shòu ① receive; accept: ～教育 receive an education / 这种新产品很～欢迎。 The new product has been well received. ② suffer; be subjected to: ～损失 suffer losses / ～压迫 suffer oppression / ～监督 be subjected to supervision / ～法律制裁 be dealt with according to law ③ stand; endure; bear: 真够～的。 This is really hard to put up with. *or* It's really unbearable. ④ be pleasant: ～听 be pleasant to hear

受病 shòubìng catch (or contract) a disease; fall ill

受不了 shòubuliǎo cannot stand (or endure): 我冻得～。 I can't stand the cold. / 今天可真热得～。 It's unbearably hot today.

受不起 shòubuqǐ dare not accept; not deserve: 我可～你的重礼。 I don't deserve such expensive gifts from you.

受潮 shòucháo be affected with damp: 这屋子阴, 东西容易～。 The room gets no sun and things easily become damp.

受宠 shòuchǒng be in sb.'s favour

受宠若惊 shòuchǒng ruò jīng be overwhelmed by an unexpected favour; feel extremely flattered

受挫 shòucuò be foiled; be baffled; be thwarted; suffer a setback

受得了 shòudeliǎo can stand (or endure): 再苦再累我也～。 I can stand even greater hardships than this.

受敌 shòudí be attacked by the enemy: 四面～ be attacked on all sides

受罚 shòufá be punished

受粉 shòufěn *bot.* be pollinated

受害 shòuhài suffer injury; fall victim; be affected: ～的一方 the aggrieved (or injured) party / 这次霜冻, ～的庄稼不少。 A lot of crops were damaged by the frost.

受害不浅 shòuhài bù qiǎn suffer not a little; suffer a lot

受害者 shòuhàizhě victim; sufferer

受寒 shòuhán catch a chill; catch cold

受旱 shòuhàn suffer from drought; be drought-stricken

受话器 shòuhuàqì (telephone) receiver

受欢迎的人 shòu huānyíng de rén *diplomacy* persona grata

受贿 shòuhuì accept (or take) bribes

受惠 shòuhuì receive benefits

受惠国 shòuhuìguó *diplomacy* beneficiary country; beneficiary

受夹板气 shòu jiābǎnqì be blamed by both parties

受奖 shòujiǎng be rewarded: 立功者～。 Those who perform deeds of merit shall be rewarded.

受教 shòujiào receive instruction; learn from sb.; study under sb.

受戒 shòujiè *Buddhism* be initiated into monkhood or nunhood

受尽 shòujìn suffer enough from; suffer all kinds of; have one's fill of: ～旧社会的苦 have one's fill of sufferings in the old society; have experienced untold sufferings in the old days / ～帝国主义的压迫 have suffered enough from imperialist oppression / ～反动派的折磨 suffer all kinds of tortures at the hands of the reactionaries

受惊 shòujīng be frightened; be startled

受精 shòujīng be fertilized: 体内(外)～ internal (external) fertilization / 异体～ cross-fertilization / 自体～ self-fertilization

受精卵 shòujīngluǎn zygote: ～移植 zygote transplant

受窘 shòujiǒng be embarrassed; be in an awkward position

受看 shòukàn ① pleasant to look at; good-looking: 这块头巾挺～的。 This scarf looks quite nice. ② honourable; creditable: 孩子没出息, 做父母的脸上也不～。 If the boy proves to be no good, it will mean a loss of face for his parents.

受苦 shòukǔ suffer (hardships); have a rough time: 咱们俩都是受过苦的。 Both of us have suffered hardships. / 他受不得一点儿苦。 He can't stand the slightest hardship.

受苦受难 shòukǔ-shòunàn live in misery; have one's fill of sufferings

受累 shòulěi get involved on account of sb. else

受累 shòulèi be put to much trouble; be inconvenienced: 他为了我们大家, 可没少～。 He's been put to no little trouble for our sake. / 让您～了。 Sorry to have given you so much trouble.

受冷 shòulěng catch cold

受礼　shòulǐ　receive gifts

受理　shòulǐ　*leg.*　accept (a case)

受凉　shòuliáng　catch cold

受领　shòulǐng　accept (an assignment, etc.); appreciate (kind thoughts, etc.): ～任务 accept an assignment／你们的心意我～了, 东西可不能收下。I appreciate your kindness but must decline the gift.

受命　shòumìng　receive instructions or assignments

受难　shòunàn　suffer calamities or disasters; be in distress: 战争～者 war victim

受骗　shòupiàn　be deceived (*or* fooled, cheated, taken in)

受聘　shòupìn　① (of a girl) accept betrothal gifts ② accept an appointment (to a post): 他～为男排主教练。He was appointed head coach of the men's volleyball team.

受气　shòuqì　be bullied; suffer wrong

受气包　shòuqìbāo　a person whom anyone can vent his spite upon; one who always gets blamed (*or* takes the rap)

受穷　shòuqióng　suffer poverty; live in poverty: 她不愿～。She doesn't like being poor.

受屈　shòuqū　be wronged

受权　shòuquán　be authorized: 新华社～发表如下声明。Xinhua News Agency is authorized to issue the following statement.／～宣布 announce upon authorization／我～处理此事。I am empowered (*or* authorized) to deal with this matter.

受让人　shòuràngrén　*leg.*　assignee

受热　shòurè　① be heated: 物体～则膨胀。When matter is heated, it expands. ② be affected by the heat; have heatstroke (*or* sunstroke)

受辱　shòurǔ　be insulted; be disgraced; be humiliated

受伤　shòushāng　be injured; be wounded; sustain an injury: 头部受重伤 sustain a severe head injury

受赏　shòushǎng　be awarded

受审　shòushěn　stand trial; be tried; be on trial

受事　shòushì　*gram.*　a word denoting the receiver of an action (not necessarily an object, as in 饭准备好了 "Dinner is ready," where 饭, the subject, denotes the receiver of the action)

受暑　shòushǔ　suffer from heatstroke (*or* sunstroke)

受胎　shòutāi　become pregnant; be impregnated; conceive

受胎率　shòutāilǜ　*animal husbandry*　conception rate

受托　shòutuō　be commissioned; be entrusted (with a task): 受朋友之托买一块手表 be asked to buy a watch for a friend／～照看房子 be entrusted with the care of a house

受托国　shòutuōguó　*diplomacy*　mandatory power

受托人　shòutuōrén　*leg.*　trustee; fiduciary

受洗　shòuxǐ　*Christianity*　be baptized; receive baptism

受降　shòuxiáng　accept a surrender

受刑　shòuxíng　be tortured; be put to torture

受训　shòuxùn　receive (*or* undergo) training

受业　shòuyè　*formal*　① receive instruction ② (in letters to one's teacher) I , your pupil

受益　shòuyì　profit by; benefit from; be benefited: 这本书使我～不浅。This book has benefited me a great deal.／～面积达六万多亩。The area serviced exceeds 60,000 *mu.*

受益人　shòuyìrén　*leg.*　beneficiary

受用　shòuyòng　benefit from; profit by; enjoy: 终身～ benefit from sth. all one's life

受用不尽　shòuyòng bú jìn　benefit from sth. all one's life

受用　shòuyong　*dial.*　(usu. used in the negative) feel comfortable: 今天身体有点不～。I feel a bit under the weather today.

受援　shòuyuán　receive aid

受援国　shòuyuánguó　*diplomacy*　recipient country

受孕　shòuyùn　become pregnant; be impregnated; conceive

受灾　shòuzāi　be hit by a natural adversity (*or* calamity): ～地区 disaster area; stricken (*or* afflicted, affected) area

受之有愧　shòu zhī yǒu kuì　I don't deserve it; I am not worthy of it ——see also 却之不恭 què zhī bù gōng

受制　shòuzhì　① be controlled: ～于人 be under others' control ② endure hardships, tortures, rough conditions, etc.; suffer

受主　shòuzhǔ　*electron.*　acceptor

受阻　shòuzǔ　be obstructed; meet with obstruction: 撞车事故使交通～。A car crash held up the traffic.

受罪　shòuzuì　endure hardships, tortures, rough conditions, etc.; have a hard time: 大热天穿这么厚的衣服, 真～! It's really awful to be wearing such heavy clothes on a hot day like this.

狩

狩　shòu　*formal*　hunting (esp. in winter)

狩猎　shòuliè　hunting: ～专业队 professional hunting team

兽 (獸)

兽 (獸)　shòu　① beast; animal: 驯～ tame wild animals ② beastly; bestial: 兽行 shòuxíng

兽环　shòuhuán　animal-head knocker (on doors of old-type houses)

兽力车　shòulìchē　animal-drawn vehicle (*or* cart)

兽王　shòuwáng　the king of beasts—the lion

兽行　shòuxíng　brutal act; brutality

兽性　shòuxìng　brutish nature; barbarity

兽医　shòuyī　veterinary surgeon; veterinarian; vet

兽医学　shòuyīxué　veterinary science; veterinary medicine

兽医站　shòuyīzhàn　veterinary station

兽疫　shòuyì　epizootic disease; epizootic

兽疫学　shòuyìxué　epizootiology

兽欲　shòuyù　animal (*or* bestial) desire: 发泄～ gratify one's animal desires

授

授　shòu　① award; vest; confer; give: ～旗 present (sb. with) a flag／～以全权 vest sb. with full authority ② teach; instruct: 函授 hánshòu

授粉　shòufěn　*bot.*　pollination

授计　shòujì　confide a stratagem to sb.; tell sb. the plan of action

授奖　shòujiǎng　award (*or* give) a prize: ～仪式 prize-giving ceremony; medal-awarding ceremony

授精　shòujīng　insemination

授课　shòukè　give lessons; give instruction

授命[1]　shòumìng　*formal*　give (*or* lay down) one's life: 见危授命 jiàn wēi shòumìng

授命[2]　shòumìng　give orders: ～组阁 authorize sb. to form a cabinet

授权　shòuquán　empower; authorize: ～新华社发表声明 authorize Xinhua News Agency to make a statement

授权书　shòuquánshū　*leg.*　letter of authorization; letter of attorney

授时　shòushí　① *astron.*　time service ② (formerly of the government or the emperor) issue the official calendar

授时信号　shòushí xìnhào　time signal

授室　shòushì　*formal*　marry a woman; take a wife

授首　shòushǒu　*formal*　(of rebels, robbers, etc.) be beheaded

授受　shòu-shòu　grant and receive; give and accept: 男女～不亲。In giving and receiving, man and woman should not touch each other (according to Confucian rules of etiquette).

授衔 shòuxián　confer a title or a military rank

授勋 shòuxūn　confer orders or medals; award a decoration: ～仪式 medal-conferring ceremony

授业 shòuyè　*formal*　impart knowledge; give instruction

授艺 shòuyì　teach a trade or skill

授意 shòuyì　incite (*or* get) sb. to do sth.; inspire: 他这样干, 是谁～的? Who got him to do that? *or* Who put him up to it? / 我这封信是在老张～下写的。It was Lao Zhang who gave me the idea of writing the letter. *or* I drafted the letter at Lao Zhang's suggestion.

授予 shòuyǔ　confer; award: ～学位 award a degree / 被～"爱民模范连"的称号 be conferred the title "Model Company of Cherishing the People"

售

shòu　① sell: ～票 sell tickets / ～完 be sold out ② *formal*　make (one's plan, trick, etc.) work; carry out (intrigues): 其计不～。His plan didn't work.

售后服务 shòuhòu fúwù　after-sale service

售货 shòuhuò　sell goods

售货机 shòuhuòjī　vending machine

售货员 shòuhuòyuán　shop assistant; salesclerk: 女～ saleswoman; salesgirl; shopgirl

售价 shòujià　selling price; price

售卖 shòumài　sell

售票处 shòupiàochù　ticket office; booking office (at a railway station); box office (at a theatre, cinema, etc.)

售票口 shòupiàokǒu　wicket

售票员 shòupiàoyuán　ticket seller; (bus, tram, etc.) conductor; booking-office clerk; box-office clerk

绶

shòu　a silk ribbon attached to an official seal or a medal

绶带 shòudài　same as 绶 shòu

绶带鸟 shòudàiniǎo　paradise flycatcher

瘦

shòu　① thin; emaciated: 他长得很～。He is very thin. / 脸～ be thin in the face ② lean: ～肉 lean meat ③ tight: 这件上衣腰身～了点。The coat is a bit tight at the waist. ④ not fertile; poor: ～土薄田 poor soil and barren land

瘦长 shòucháng　long and thin; tall and thin; lanky: 他是～个儿。He's a tall, lean chap. *or* He's a spindle-legs.

瘦高挑儿 shòugāotiǎor　① a tall and slender figure ② a tall, slender person

瘦骨嶙峋 shòugǔ línxún　all skin and bones

瘦果 shòuguǒ　*bot.*　achene

瘦瘠 shòují　① thin and weak ② (of land) barren; sterile: ～的荒山 barren mountain wilds

瘦溜 shòuliu　*dial.*　slim: 身材～, 动作轻巧 slim and agile

瘦煤 shòuméi　lean coal; meagre coal

瘦俏 shòuqiào　slender; slim

瘦缺 shòuquē　(opp. 肥缺 féiquē) an unprofitable post

瘦弱 shòuruò　thin and weak; emaciated; frail

瘦小 shòuxiǎo　thin and small: 身材～ slight of figure (*or* stature)

瘦削 shòuxuē　very thin; gaunt; bony: ～的面孔 a haggard face

瘦子 shòuzi　a lean (*or* thin) person

shū

书 (書)

shū　① write: 振笔直～ take up the pen and write vigorously ② style of calligraphy; script: 楷书 kǎishū ③ book: 一本关于中国历史的新～ a new work on Chinese history ④ letter: 家书 jiāshū ⑤ document: 国书 guóshū / 证书 zhèngshū

书案 shū'àn　*formal*　writing desk

书包 shūbāo　satchel; schoolbag

书包带 shūbāodài　book strap (used by schoolchildren)

书报 shū-bào　books, newspapers, and periodicals

书背 shūbèi　the back of a book; spine; backbone

书本 shūběn　book: ～知识 book learning; book knowledge

书不尽言 shū bù jìn yán　I have much more to say than I can write in this letter (used at the end of a letter)

书茶馆儿 shūcháguǎnr　same as 书馆儿 shūguǎnr

书场 shūchǎng　a place of entertainment where *quyi* (曲艺) performances are given

书呈 shūchéng　*old* a letter submitted to one's superior

书痴 shūchī　*formal*　pedant; bookworm

书橱 shūchú　bookcase (often with glass doors)

书呆子 shūdāizi　pedant; bookworm

书丹 shūdān　write an epitaph (originally in red)

书挡 shūdǎng　bookend

书到用时方恨少 shū dào yòng shí fāng hèn shǎo　it is when you are using what you have learned from books that you wish you had read more books than you have

书店 shūdiàn　bookshop; bookstore; bookseller's

书牍 shūdú　*formal*　letters; correspondence

书蠹 shūdù　① bookworm; book louse ② pedant; bookworm

书法 shūfǎ　penmanship; calligraphy

书法家 shūfǎjiā　calligrapher; calligraphist

书坊 shūfāng　*old*　bookshop with printing works

书房 shūfáng　a study

书扉 shūfēi　title page

书稿 shūgǎo　manuscript

书格子 shūgézi　(also 书格子 shūgézi) bookshelf; a set of bookshelves

书贾 shūgǔ　*formal*　bookseller

书鼓 shūgǔ　a small drum played in *dagu* (大鼓) performances

书馆儿 shūguǎnr　*dial.* a teahouse featuring storytelling

书柜 shūguì　same as 书橱 shūchú

书函 shūhán　① slipcase ② letters; correspondence

书翰 shūhàn　*formal*　① calligraphy ② letters; correspondence

书后 shūhòu　postscript (by the author or sb. else)

书画 shū-huà　painting and calligraphy

书会 shūhuì　a gathering of calligraphers

书籍 shūjí　books; works; literature: 军事～ military literature

书脊 shūjǐ　spine (of a book); backbone

书记 shūji　① secretary: 党委～ secretary of the Party committee / 总～ general secretary ② clerk

书记处 shūjìchù　secretariat

书家 shūjiā　calligrapher; calligraphist

书架 shūjià　bookshelf; a set of bookshelves; bookcase

书简 shūjiǎn　(also 书柬 shūjiǎn) letters; correspondence

书经 Shūjīng　*The Book of History* ——see also 五经 Wǔ Jīng

书局 shūjú　publishing house; press; book company: 中华～ the Zhonghua Book Company

书卷 shūjuàn　*formal*　book

书卷气 shūjuànqì　bookishness; scholarliness

书刊 shū-kān　books and periodicals

书壳 shūké　slipcase

书口 shūkǒu　fore-edge (*or* foredge)

书库 shūkù　stack room

书吏 shūlì　*old*　government clerk

书林 shūlín　*formal*　a forest of books—a treasury of books: 《～漫步》*Browsing Among Books*

书录　shūlù　bibliography

书簏　shūlù　① a bamboo trunk for storing books ② *formal* a bookish person

书眉　shūméi　the top of a page; top margin

书迷　shūmí　① bibliomaniac ② storyteller's fan

书面　shūmiàn　written; in written form; in writing: ～材料 written material / ～通知 written notice / ～答复 written reply; answer in writing / ～声明 written statement

书面语　shūmiànyǔ　written language; literary language

书名　shūmíng　the title of a book; title

书名号　shūmínghào　punctuation marks used to enclose the title of a book or an article 《　》

书名页　shūmíngyè　title page

书目　shūmù　booklist; title catalogue: 参考～ a list of reference books; bibliography

书脑　shūnǎo　headband (of a hardcover book)

书皮　shūpí　① book cover: 塑料～ a plastic cover / 布面烫金～ a cloth gilt cover ② dust cover

书皮纸　shūpízhǐ　paper for covering books

书评　shūpíng　book review

书契　shūqì　*formal* characters; script

书签　shūqiān　① a title label pasted on the cover of a Chinese-style thread-bound book ② bookmark

书社　shūshè　① *old* literary club ② publishing house

书生　shūshēng　intellectual; scholar

书生气　shūshēngqì　bookishness; a bookish cast of mind: 不要～十足。 Don't be so bookish and unrealistic.

书生之见　shūshēng zhī jiàn　a bookish approach; a pedantic view

书市　shūshì　book fair

书手　shūshǒu　*old* scribe; copyist

书塾　shūshú　old-style private school

书肆　shūsì　*formal* bookshop; bookstore

书摊　shūtān　bookstall; bookstand

书坛　shūtán　① calligraphers' circle ② storytellers' circle

书套　shūtào　slipcase

书体　shūtǐ　style of calligraphy

书亭　shūtíng　book-kiosk; bookstall

书童　shūtóng　page boy

书屋　shūwū　*liter.* a study

书香　shūxiāng　(of a family) having literary or intellectual fame: ～人家 a literary (*or* intellectual) family; a family of scholars / 他家世代～。 He comes from a long line of scholars.

书香门第　shūxiāng méndì　a literary (*or* intellectual) family; a family of scholars

书写　shūxiě　write: ～标语 write slogans; letter posters

书写纸　shūxiězhǐ　writing paper

书心　shūxīn　type area (of a book page)

书信　shūxìn　letter; written message: 常有～往来 keep up a regular correspondence

书信电　shūxìndiàn　letter cable

书信体　shūxìntǐ　epistolary style: ～小说 epistolary novel

书页　shūyè　book page; printed page

书院　shūyuàn　(in former times) academy of classical learning: 白鹿洞～ the White Deer Hollow Academy (one of the leading academies in the Northern Song Dynasty)

书札　shūzhá　*formal* letters; correspondence

书斋　shūzhāi　a study

书展　shūzhǎn　book exhibition

书桌　shūzhuō　desk; writing desk

殳　shū　an ancient weapon made of bamboo

抒　shū　① express; give expression to; convey: 抒发 shūfā ② same as 纾 shū

抒发　shūfā　express; voice; give expression to: 这首诗～了战士的革命感情。 The poem expresses the revolutionary fervour of the army men. / 这一唱段～了一个开拓者的壮志豪情。 This aria conveys the determination and lofty ideals of a pioneer (*or* pathbreaker).

抒怀　shūhuái　pour out one's heart; unburden one's heart

抒情　shūqíng　express (*or* convey) one's emotion

抒情散文　shūqíng sǎnwén　lyric prose

抒情诗　shūqíngshī　lyric poetry; lyrics

抒写　shūxiě　express in writing; write of; describe: 这篇文章～了他在日内瓦工作时的一些感受。 The article describes how he felt while working in Geneva.

纾　shū　*formal* relax; relieve; remove: ～民困 relax the people's burden / ～难 give relief in time of distress

枢（樞）　shū　pivot; hub; centre

枢机　shūjī　① (in former times) a key government post or office ② *formal* a vital element

枢机主教　shūjī zhǔjiào　cardinal (of the Roman Catholic Church)

枢密院　shūmìyuàn　privy council

枢纽　shūniǔ　pivot; hub; axis; key position: ～作用 a pivotal role / 交通～ a hub of communications / 水利～工程 a key water control (*or* water conservancy) project

枢要　shūyào　*formal* the central administration

叔　shū　① father's younger brother; uncle ② (a form of address for a man about one's father's age) uncle: 刘大～ Uncle Liu ③ husband's younger brother: ～嫂 brother-in-law and sister-in-law ④ the third among brothers

叔伯　shūbai　relationship between cousins of the same grandfather or great-grandfather: ～兄弟 first or second cousins on the paternal side; cousins

叔父　shūfù　father's younger brother; uncle

叔公　shūgōng　① husband's father's younger brother ② *dial.* (paternal) granduncle (*or* great-uncle)

叔母　shūmǔ　wife of father's younger brother; aunt

叔婆　shūpó　① husband's father's younger brother's wife ② *dial.* (paternal) grandaunt (*or* great-aunt)

叔叔　shūshu　*inf.* ① father's younger brother; uncle ② (a child's form of address for any young man one generation its senior) uncle

叔子　shūzi　husband's younger brother; brother-in-law

叔祖　shūzǔ　(paternal) grandfather's younger brother; granduncle (*or* great-uncle)

叔祖母　shūzǔmǔ　wife of (paternal) grandfather's younger brother; grandaunt (*or* great-aunt)

姝　shū　*formal* ① pretty; lovely ② a pretty girl

殊　shū　① different: 无殊 wúshū ② outstanding; special; remarkable: 待以～礼 receive sb. with unusual ceremony ③ *formal* very much; extremely; really: ～觉歉然 feel most regretful / ～难相信 very difficult to believe; hardly credible ④ *formal* cut off; sever

殊不知　shūbùzhī　little imagine; hardly realize: 我以为他还在北京，～他已经走了。 I thought he had already left in Beijing. I never dreamt that he had already left. / 大家只知道西湖的风景好，～离杭州不远，富春江上的风光，才是天下的绝景呢! Most people only know that the scenery around the West Lake is very fine, but very few people

know that not far from Hangzhou, the countryside around the Fuchun River is the most magnificent in the world!

殊方 shūfāng *formal* ① different directions or tendencies: 好恶～ have different likes and dislikes ② strange lands; distant regions

殊功 shūgōng distinguished service; outstanding achievement

殊绩 shūjì same as 殊勋 shūxūn

殊荣 shūróng special honours

殊深轸念 shū shēn zhěnniàn express deep solicitude; feel deeply concerned

殊死 shūsǐ ① desperate; life-and-death: ～的搏斗 a life-and-death struggle / 作～战 fight to the death; fight a last-ditch battle; put up a desperate fight ② *arch.* the penalty of decapitation

殊途同归 shū tú tóng guī reach the same goal by different routes

殊效 shūxiào *formal* special effect: 有～ be especially effective

殊勋 shūxūn *formal* outstanding merit; distinguished service: 屡建～ rendered one distinguished service after another

殊异 shūyì ① different; divergent ② extraordinary; exceptional; unusual

殊遇 shūyù special treatment; special kindness

倏(倏)

shū *formal* suddenly; quickly: 羊城一别，～已半年。Six months have passed in a flash since we parted in the City of Rams (i.e. Guangzhou).

倏地 shūdì suddenly; quickly: 他～刹住了了车。He brought the car to a sudden stop.

倏尔 shū'ěr *formal* suddenly; quickly: ～不见 suddenly (*or* quickly) disappear

倏忽 shūhū suddenly; quickly: ～不见 suddenly (*or* quickly) disappear / 山地气候～变化。Mountain weather changes suddenly.

倏然 shūrán *formal* suddenly; abruptly: ～一阵暴雨。A rainstorm came on suddenly. / 一道流星，～而逝。A meteor shot across the sky and vanished.

淑

shū ① (of a woman) refined; pure; virtuous ② (of a woman) beautiful; lovely

淑德 shūdé female virtue

淑静 shūjìng (of a woman) refined and gentle

淑美 shūměi virtuous and beautiful; refined and beautiful

淑女 shūnǚ a fair maiden; a virtuous maiden; a noble lady

菽(尗)

shū beans

菽粟 shū-sù beans and grain—food ——see also 布帛菽粟 bù-bó-shū-sù

梳

shū ① comb: 木～ a wooden comb ② comb (one's hair, etc): ～头发 comb one's hair

梳篦 shū-bì thick- and fine-toothed combs

梳辫子 shū biànzi ① braid one's hair ② sort out matters, problems, etc: 先把问题梳梳辫子，再研究解决办法。First sort out and classify the problems, then try to find solutions to them.

梳理 shūlǐ ① *text.* carding ② comb out (one's hair); dress (one's hair): 她坐在镜前，～长发。She sat in front of the mirror, combing out her long hair.

梳棉 shūmián *text.* comb and parallel cotton fibers prior to spinning; card

梳棉机 shūmiánjī *text.* carding machine; card

梳头 shūtóu comb one's hair

梳洗 shūxǐ wash and dress

梳洗用具 shūxǐ yòngjù toilet articles

梳妆 shūzhuāng dress and make up

梳妆打扮 shūzhuāng-dǎbàn deck oneself out; dress smartly; be dressed up

梳妆台 shūzhuāngtái dressing table

梳子 shūzi comb: 一把～ a comb

舒

shū ① stretch; unfold; spread; smooth out ② *formal* easy; leisurely: 舒徐 shūxú ③ (Shū) a surname

舒畅 shūchàng happy; entirely free from worry: 心情～ have ease of mind; feel happy / 山上的空气使人感到～。Mountain air is very refreshing.

舒服 shūfu ① comfortable: 这把椅子又软又～。This chair is soft and comfortable. / 在这儿睡得还～吗? Were you comfortable sleeping here? / 舒舒服服地过日子 make a comfortable living; live in ease and comfort ② be well: 她今天不大～。She isn't well today. / 我浑身不～。I feel sore all over.

舒缓 shūhuǎn ① slow and unhurried; leisurely: 动作～ slow and unhurried in one's movements ② relaxed; mild: 语调～ in a mild tone ③ (of a slope) gentle; gradual: ～的斜坡 a gentle slope

舒筋活络 shūjīn-huóluò *Chin. med.* stimulate the circulation of the blood and cause the muscles and joints to relax

舒卷 shūjuǎn *formal* (of clouds or smoke) curl and uncurl; roll and unroll; roll back and forth: 白云～。White clouds massed and scattered.

舒快 shūkuài comfortable and relaxed; refreshed: 洗完蒸汽浴，我觉得浑身～。After the sauna bath I felt completely refreshed.

舒眉展眼 shūméi-zhǎnyǎn smiling eyes; a beaming face

舒气 shūqì ① get one's breath; catch one's breath: 到了半山腰，我们坐下来舒舒气。Halfway up the hill, we sat down to catch our breath. ② relax; have a breathing space: 险情排除了，大家才算舒了口气。We didn't get a breathing space until the crisis was over. ③ relieve one's feelings; let off steam: 他只知道发牢骚～。He's given to fussing and grumbling as a way of relieving his feelings.

舒散 shūsàn ① stretch and flex: ～一下筋骨 stretch oneself; flex one's limbs; relax one's muscles ② shake off one's fatigue or cares

舒适 shūshì comfortable; cosy; snug: ～的生活 a comfortable life / 房间不大，但很～。The rooms are not big but they're very cosy. / 孩子们都～地睡在小床上。All the children lay snug in their little beds.

舒适带 shūshìdài comfort zone (the range of temperature considered comfortable for most people, generally 20℃-24℃)

舒松 shūsōng relieved and relaxed

舒泰 shūtài free from worries; comfortable and at ease: 心里好～ feel completely relaxed / 问题解决了，我舒舒泰泰地睡了个好觉。With the problem solved, I got a good night's sleep.

舒坦 shūtan comfortable; at ease

舒心 shūxīn *dial.* comfortable; happy

舒徐 shūxú leisurely; unhurried: 溪水～地流淌着。The brook flows on sluggishly.

舒展 shū-zhǎn ① unfold; extend; smooth out: 荷叶～着，发出清香。The lotus leaves are unfolding, sending forth a delicate fragrance. / 问题解决了，老人家紧锁的眉头也～了。Once the problem was solved, the old man's knitted brows became smooth again. ② limber up; stretch: ～一下筋骨 limber up one's muscles and joints

舒张 shūzhāng *physiol.* diastole

舒张压 shūzhāngyā *med.* diastolic pressure

疏¹（疎）

shū ① dredge (a river, etc.): 疏浚 shūjùn ② thin; sparse; scattered: ～林 sparse woods / ～～的几根胡子 a sparse beard / 几点～星 a few scattered stars ③ (of family or social relations) distant; not familiar: 亲～ close and distant ④ neglect: ～于职守 negligent of one's duties / ～于防范 neglect to take precautions ⑤ scanty: 志大才疏 zhìdà-cáishū ⑥ disperse; scatter: 疏散 shūsàn

疏²

shū ① a memorial to the emperor ② sub-commentary: 注疏 zhùshū

疏不间亲 shū bú jiàn qīn casual acquaintances should not come between near relatives

疏财仗义 shū cái zhàngyì same as 仗义疏财 zhàngyì shū cái

疏淡 shūdàn ① sparse; thin: 白 云～ thin white clouds / ～的眉毛 thin eyebrows ② drift apart; become estranged: 由于志趣不同, 他俩的关系渐渐～了。Pursuing different interests, they gradually drifted apart.

疏导 shūdǎo ① dredge: ～淮河 dredge the Huai River ② remove obstructions: ～交通 relieve traffic congestion

疏放 shūfàng formal ① unrestrained ② (of style of writing) unconventional

疏港 shūgǎng clear out a harbour

疏果 shūguǒ agric. fruit thinning

疏忽 shūhu carelessness; negligence; oversight: ～大意就可能引起事故。Carelessness is liable to cause accidents. / 我一时～, 搞错了。I made the mistake through an oversight.

疏花 shūhuā agric. flower thinning

疏剪 shūjiǎn prune (trees, branches, etc.)

疏解 shūjiě ① mediate ② relieve (traffic congestion, etc.)

疏浚 shūjùn dredge: ～水道 dredge the waterways / ～港口 dredge a harbour

疏开 shūkāi mil. extend; disperse; deploy: ～队形 dispersed formation; extended order; open order (or formation)

疏狂 shūkuáng formal unrestrained; unbridled

疏阔 shūkuò formal ① inaccurate; rough ② (of relationship) distant ③ (of friends, etc.) long separated; far apart

疏懒 shūlǎn careless and lazy; indolent

疏朗 shūlǎng ① thinly scattered; sparse: 须 眉～ a sparse beard and thin eyebrows / 夜空中闪烁着疏疏朗朗的几点星光。A few scattered stars were twinkling in the night sky. ② cheerful; optimistic: 心胸渐渐～了 cheering up

疏理 shūlǐ formal put in order; sort out: ～古籍 reorganize ancient texts

疏漏 shūlòu careless omission; slip; oversight: 计划匆促拟成, 难免有～之处。The plan was drawn up in haste, so there are bound to be oversights and omissions.

疏略 shūlüè formal rough; sketchy

疏落 shūluò sparse; scattered: ～的村庄 scattered villages / 河边疏疏落落有几棵柳树。The river was sparsely lined with willow trees.

疏密 shūmì density; spacing: ～不匀 of uneven density / 花木栽得～有致。The flowers and trees are artistically spaced.

疏苗 shūmiáo seedling thinning

疏浅 shūqiǎn ① crude and superficial: 思虑～ immature and superficial thinking ② (of relationship) distant: 我和他关系～。He and I are not close friends.

疏散 shūsàn ① sparse; scattered; dispersed: ～的村落 scattered villages ② evacuate; disperse: 我们要做好地震预报工作, 以便及时～人口。We must do a good job of predicting earthquakes so that we can disperse the population in time.

疏神 shūshén relax one's attention; let one's attention wander

疏失 shūshī careless mistake; remissness

疏松 shūsōng ① loose: 土质～。The soil is porous. ② loosen: ～土壤 loosen the soil

疏通 shūtōng ① dredge: ～田间的排水沟 dredge the irrigation ditches in the fields ② mediate between two parties

疏挖 shūwā dredge: ～河道 dredge a river

疏懈 shūxiè careless; negligent

疏虞 shūyú formal carelessness; negligence; oversight

疏远 shūyuǎn drift apart; become estranged: 我们两个人越来越～了。We have become more and more estranged.

撽（攄）

shū formal ① express; set forth: ～所见 set forth one's views ② gallop

输¹

shū ① transport; convey: 油管把原油从油田直接～往港口。The pipeline carries crude oil direct from the oil field to the harbour. ② formal contribute money; donate: 输将 shūjiāng

输²

shū lose; be beaten; be defeated: ～了一局 lost one game in the set

输诚 shūchéng formal surrender

输出 shūchū ① send out: 血液从心脏～, 经血管分布全身。Blood is pumped by the heart through the blood vessels to all parts of the body. ② export: 资本～ export of capital / ～限额 export quota ③ elec. computer output: ～端数 fan-out / ～功率 output power / ～数据 data-out

输电 shūdiàn transmit electricity: 这个发电站已开始向山区～。The power station has begun to transmit electricity to the mountain area.

输电网 shūdiànwǎng power transmission network; grid system

输电线路 shūdiàn xiànlù transmission line

输家 shūjia loser (in a gambling game)

输将 shūjiāng formal contribute; donate: 慷慨～ make generous donations

输精管 shūjīngguǎn physiol. spermatic duct; seminal duct

输精管结扎术 shūjīngguǎn jiézāshù vasoligation

输精管炎 shūjīngguǎnyán deferentitis

输捐 shūjuān contribute; donate

输理 shūlǐ be in the wrong: 你输了理, 还有什么可辩的? You are in the wrong. Why argue?

输卵管 shūluǎnguǎn physiol. oviduct; Fallopian tube

输卵管结扎术 shūluǎnguǎn jiézāshù tubal ligation

输卵管炎 shūluǎnguǎnyán salpingitis

输纳 shūnà formal pay (taxes, etc.)

输尿管 shūniàoguǎn physiol. ureter

输尿管炎 shūniàoguǎnyán ureteritis

输钱 shūqián lose money (in gambling): 他输了十块钱。He lost ten dollars (in gambling).

输入 shūrù ① bring in; introduce: ～新思想 the influx of new ideas ② import: ～粮食 import grain / ～限额 import quota ③ elec. computer input: ～计算机三百万字 input 3,000,000 words / ～端数 fan-in / ～功率 input power / ～数据 data-in / ～员 data operator

输沙率 shūshālǜ water conservancy silt discharge

输送 shūsòng carry; transport; convey: 卡车把货物～到边疆地区。Commodities are transported to border areas by truck. / ～新鲜血液 infuse new blood / 大庆油田给其它油田～了大批工人、干部和技术人员。Daqing

has provided other oilfields with large numbers of workers, cadres and technical personnel.

输送带 shūsòngdài　conveyer belt

输送机 shūsòngjī　conveyer

输血 shūxuè　① blood transfusion ② give aid and support; bolster up; give sb. a shot in the arm: 这等于是给侵略者～打气。This is tantamount to giving the aggressor a shot in the arm.

输血者 shūxuèzhě　blood donor

输氧 shūyǎng　oxygen therapy

输液 shūyè　*med.* infusion

输赢 shū-yíng　① victory or defeat: 两个球队要较量一番，非见个～不可。The two teams are determined to fight it out. ② winnings and losses (in gambling): 他们常打麻将，而且～很大。They were always playing mahjong, and the winnings and losses were very high.

输油管 shūyóuguǎn　petroleum pipeline

觖

shū　see 氍觖 qúshū

蔬

shū　vegetables: 布衣蔬食 bùyī-shūshí

蔬菜 shūcài　vegetables; greens; greenstuff: ～栽培 vegetable growing; vegetable farming

蔬果 shūguǒ　vegetables and fruits

shú

秫

shū　*kaoliang*; sorghum

秫秸 shújiē　*kaoliang* stalk; sorghum stalk

秫米 shúmǐ　husked sorghum

秫秫 shúshú　*dial. kaoliang*; sorghum

孰

shú　*formal* ① who; which: ～胜～负? Who wins and who loses? / ～是～非? Which is right and which is wrong? ② what: 是可忍，孰不可忍 shì kě rěn, shú bùkě rěn

赎（贖）

shú　① redeem; ransom: 把东西～回来 redeem a pledge ② atone for (a crime)

赎当 shúdàng　redeem sth. pawned; take sth. out of pledge; redeem a pledge

赎价 shújià　ransom price; ransom

赎金 shújīn　ransom money; ransom

赎买 shúmǎi　redeem; buy out

赎买政策 shúmǎi zhèngcè　the policy of redemption (under which the government paid 5 percent annual interest to private shareholders of joint state-private enterprises for a period of ten years after the Socialist Transformation of 1955–1956)

赎身 shúshēn　(of slaves or prostitutes) redeem (*or* ransom) oneself; buy back one's freedom

赎刑 shúxíng　redeem sb. from punishment by paying a ransom

赎罪 shúzuì　atone for one's crime: 立功～ perform meritorious services to atone for one's crime

赎罪券 shúzuìquàn　indulgence (of the Roman Catholic Church in medieval times)

赎罪日 shúzuìrì　*Judaism* Yom Kippur; Day of Atonement

塾

shú　old-type private school; family school: 私塾 sīshú

塾师 shúshī　the tutor of an old-type private school; a private tutor

熟

shú　① ripe: 西红柿～了。The tomatoes are ripe. / 一年两～ two crops a year ② cooked; done: ～

肉 cooked meat / 饭～了。The rice is done. ③ processed: ～铜 wrought copper / ～皮子 tanned leather ④ familiar; well acquainted: 这个地方我很～。I'm familiar with this place. / 这口音听起来很～。The voice sounds familiar. / 这条路他最～。He knows this route best. ⑤ skilled; experienced; practised: 熟手 shúshǒu ⑥ deeply; thoroughly: 睡得很～ sleep soundly ——see also shóu

熟谙 shú'ān　*formal* be familiar with; be good at: ～水性 be an expert swimmer

熟菜 shúcài　cooked food; prepared food

熟道 shúdào　a familiar road (*or* route)

熟地[1] shúdì　cultivated land

熟地[2] shúdì　(also 熟地黄 shúdìhuáng) *Chin. med.* prepared rhizome of rehmannia (*Rehmannia glutinosa*)

熟番 shúfān　border tribes who were assimilated to Han Chinese

熟化 shúhuà　cultivate (land); till: ～地 cultivated land; tillable land

熟荒 shúhuāng　(also 熟荒地 shúhuāngdì) *agric.* once cultivated land; abandoned cultivated land

熟记 shújì　learn by heart; memorize; commit to memory

熟见 shújiàn　(of things) commonly seen: 人所～，不足为奇 a familiar sight—nothing to be surprised at

熟客 shúkè　frequent visitor

熟练 shúliàn　skilled; practised; proficient: ～工人 skilled worker / ～地操纵机器 skilfully operate the machine / 他枪法很～。He's a good shot.

熟料 shúliào　fired refractory material; grog; clinker

熟路 shúlù　a familiar road (*or* route); a beaten track

熟门熟路 shúmén-shúlù　a familiar road and a familiar door—things that one knows well

熟能生巧 shú néng shēng qiǎo　skill comes from practice; practice makes perfect

熟年 shúnián　a year of good harvests; bumper year

熟漆 shúqī　lacquer

熟人 shúrén　acquaintance; friend

熟稔 shúrěn　*formal* be familiar with; be conversant with

熟石膏 shúshígāo　plaster of Paris; plaster

熟石灰 shúshíhuī　slaked lime

熟食 shúshí　prepared food; cooked food

熟视无睹 shú shì wú dǔ　pay no attention to a familiar sight; turn a blind eye to; ignore: 对不良倾向决不能～。We must not turn a blind eye to unhealthy tendencies.

熟识 shúshi　be well acquainted with; know well: 我们交往不多，不太～。We haven't met often and don't know each other very well. / ～敌我双方各方面的情况 familiarize ourselves with all aspects of the enemy's situation and our own

熟手 shúshǒu　old hand; practised hand

熟睡 shúshuì　sleep soundly; be fast asleep

熟丝 shúsī　*text.* boiled-off silk

熟思 shúsī　ponder deeply; consider carefully; deliberate

熟铁 shútiě　wrought iron

熟土 shútǔ　*agric.* mellow soil

熟悉 shúxī　know sth. or sb. well; be familiar with; have an intimate knowledge of: 他们彼此很～。They know each other very well. / 用群众～的语言来写作 write in language familiar to the masses / 你到了那里，要先～当地的情况。When you get there, first of all familiarize yourself with the situation. / 他对各项生产数字很～。He has the various production figures at his fingertips. / 他对这工作不～。He is new to the task. / ～内情 know the ins and outs of the matter; know the inside story of; be in the know

熟习 shúxí　be skilful at; have the knack of; be prac-

tised in: ～业务 be practised (*or* well versed) in one's field of work / ～蔬菜的栽培法 have the knack of growing vegetables

熟橡胶 shúxiàngjiāo　vulcanized rubber
熟语 shúyǔ　idiom; idiomatic phrase
熟知 shúzhī　know very well; know intimately
熟字 shúzì　words already learned; familiar words

shǔ

黍 shǔ　broomcorn millet (*Panicum miliaceum*)
黍子 shǔzi　broomcorn millet (*Panicum miliaceum*)

属（屬） shǔ ① category: 金属 jīnshǔ ② *biol.* genus: 小麦和燕麦是同科的，但不同～。Wheat and oats are of the same family, but of different genera. ③ be under; be subordinate to: 这些厂～地方领导。These factories are run by the local authorities. / 所～单位和部门 subordinate units and departments ④ belong to: 我们两国同～第三世界。Both our countries belong to the Third World. / 西双版纳～亚热带气候。Xishuangbanna has a subtropical climate. / 胜利终～我们! The final victory is ours! ⑤ family members; dependants: 军属 jūnshǔ ⑥ be: 查明～实 prove to be true after investigation / 实～无理 be really unreasonable ⑦ be born in the year of (one of the 12 symbolic animals associated with a 12-year cycle): 她比我小一岁，是～牛的。She is one year younger than I am; she was born in the year of the ox. ——see also zhǔ

属地 shǔdì　possession; dependency
属国 shǔguó　vassal state; dependent state
属吏 shǔlì　*old* subordinate officials
属下 shǔxià　subordinates: 我是他的～。I'm one of his subordinates. *or* I work under him.
属相 shǔxiang　*inf.* popular name for 生肖 shēngxiào
属性 shǔxìng　attribute; property
属于 shǔyú　belong to; be part of: 西沙群岛～中国。The Xisha Islands belong to China. / 我们教师也～工人阶级。We schoolteachers also belong to the working class.
属员 shǔyuán　*old* staff member (of a government office)

暑 shǔ　heat; hot weather: 盛暑 shèngshǔ / 中暑 zhòngshǔ
暑假 shǔjià　summer vacation (*or* holidays)
暑期 shǔqī　summer vacation time: ～训练班 summer course / ～学校 summer school
暑气 shǔqì　summer heat; heat
暑热 shǔrè　hot summer weather
暑天 shǔtiān　hot summer days; dog days
暑瘟 shǔwēn　*Chin. med.* febrile diseases in summer, including encephalitis B, dysentry, malignant malaria, etc.

署¹ shǔ ① government office; office: 公署 gōngshǔ ② make arrangements for; arrange: 部署 bùshǔ ③ handle by proxy; act as deputy: 署理 shǔlǐ

署² shǔ　put one's signature to; sign: 请在信后～上你的名字。Please sign this letter.
署理 shǔlǐ　handle by proxy; act as deputy: ～部务 handle the ministry's affairs during the minister's absence
署名 shǔmíng　sign; put one's signature to: 全组同志都在信上署了名。The letter was jointly signed by all the comrades of the group. / 这条子没有～，不知是谁写的。

I don't know who wrote this note. It's unsigned.
署名人 shǔmíngrén　the undersigned
署名文章 shǔmíng wénzhāng　a signed article

数（數） shǔ ① count: 从一～到十 count from 1 to 10 / ～～看一行有多少棵苗。Count and see how many seedlings there are in a row. ② be reckoned as exceptionally (good, bad, etc.): 全班～他个儿最高。He is the tallest in the class. ③ enumerate; list: 历～其罪 enumerate the crimes sb. has committed ——see also shù; shuò

数不过来 shǔbuguòlái　too many to be counted; innumerable: 参观的人多得～。There were innumerable visitors.
数不清 shǔbuqīng　countless; innumerable: 天上有～的星星。There are countless stars in the sky.
数不胜数 shǔ bùshèng shǔ　innumerable; incalculable; countless
数不着 shǔbuzháo　(also 数不上 shǔbushàng) not count as outstanding, important, etc.: 论游泳技术，在我们厂里可～我。I don't count as a good swimmer in our factory.
数叨 shǔdao　*dial.* nag; scold
数得着 shǔdezháo　(also 数得上 shǔdeshàng) be reckoned as outstanding, important, etc.: 在我们村里，他是～的养猪能手。He is one of the outstanding pig-breeders of our village.
数典忘祖 shǔ diǎn wàng zǔ　give all the historical facts except those about one's own ancestors; forget one's own origins; be ignorant of the history of one's own country
数冬瓜道茄子 shǔdōnggua-dàoqiézi　same as 数葫芦道茄子 shǔhúlu-dàoqiézi
数伏 shǔfú　beginning of the three *fu* (三伏), the three hottest ten-day periods of the year; beginning of the hottest days of the year
数黑论黄 shǔhēi-lùnhuáng　(also 数黄道黑 shǔhuáng-dào-hēi) talk irresponsibly; gossip
数葫芦道茄子 shǔhúlu-dàoqiézi　rattle on; talk endlessly
数九 shǔjiǔ　beginning of the nine nine-day periods following the Winter Solstice; beginning of the coldest days of the year
数九寒天 shǔjiǔ hántiān　the coldest days of the year
数来宝 shǔláibǎo　rhythmic storytelling to clapper accompaniment
数落 shǔluo　*inf.* ① scold sb. by enumerating his wrongdoings; rebuke; reprove: 把他～一顿 give him a good scolding ② enumerate; cite one example after another
数米而炊 shǔ mǐ ér chuī　count the grains of rice before cooking them—fuss over small things; be miserly
数念 shǔniàn　① name one by one; enumerate ② read or recite sentence by sentence or line by line
数数儿 shǔshùr　count; reckon: 孩子们在学～。The children are learning how to count.
数说 shǔshuō　① enumerate ② scold; rebuke; reprove
数一数二 shǔyī-shǔ'èr　count as one of the very best; rank very high: 他在连里是～的射手。He is one of the very best marksmen in his company. / 他在当代山水画家中是～的。He ranks high among contemporary landscape painters.

蜀 Shǔ ① a state in the Zhou Dynasty, comprising the present-day Chengdu area in Sichuan Province ② short for 蜀汉 Shǔ Hàn ③ another name for 四川 Sìchuān
蜀汉 Shǔ Hàn　the Kingdom of Shu Han (221–263), one of the Three Kingdoms
蜀锦 shǔjǐn　Sichuan brocade

蜀葵　shǔkuí　hollyhock (*Althaea rosea*)

蜀犬吠日　Shǔ quǎn fèi rì　a dog of Shu, a misty region, barking at the sun—an ignorant person making a fuss about something that he alone finds strange

蜀黍　shǔshǔ　another name for 高粱 gāoliang

蜀绣　shǔxiù　Sichuan embroidery

鼠

　shǔ　mouse; rat

鼠辈　shǔbèi　mean creatures; scoundrels

鼠疮　shǔchuāng　*Chin. med.* scrofula

鼠窜　shǔcuàn　scamper off like a rat; scurry away like frightened rats

鼠胆　shǔdǎn　as timid as a mouse; chicken-hearted

鼠肚鸡肠　shǔdù-jīcháng　petty; narrow-minded

鼠害　shǔhài　a plague of rats; damage caused by rats

鼠耗　shǔhào　wastage of grain, etc. caused by rats

鼠夹　shǔjiā　mousetrap

鼠笼　shǔlóng　squirrel cage

鼠笼式电动机　shǔlóngshì diàndòngjī　squirrel-cage motor

鼠目寸光　shǔmù cùn guāng　a mouse can see only an inch; see only what is under one's nose; be short-sighted

鼠窃狗偷　shǔqiè-gǒutōu　filch like rats and snatch like dogs—play petty tricks on the sly

鼠曲草　shǔqūcǎo　(also 鼠麴草 shǔqūcǎo) affine cudweed (*Gnaphalium affine*)

鼠蹊　shǔxī　another name for 腹股沟 fùgǔgōu

鼠咬热　shǔyǎorè　rat-bite fever

鼠疫　shǔyì　the plague

薯（藷）

　shǔ　potato; yam: 白薯 báishǔ / 木薯 mùshǔ

薯莨　shǔliáng　dye yam (*Dioscorea cirrhosa*)

薯莨绸　shǔliángchóu　another name for 香云纱 xiāngyúnshā

薯芋类作物　shǔyùlèi zuòwù　tuber crops

薯蓣　shǔyù　Chinese yam (*Dioscorea batatas*)

曙

　shǔ　*formal* daybreak; dawn

曙光　shǔguāng　the first light of morning; dawn: 每天早晨，～初照，中山公园便有些上了年纪的人在那里打太极拳了。Every morning, in the first glimmer of dawn, some older people are seen practising *taijiquan* in Zhongshan Park. / 胜利的～ the dawn of victory

曙色　shǔsè　the light of early dawn: 从窗口透进了灰白的～。The pale light of early dawn slanted in through the window.

shù

术（術）

　shù　① art; skill; technique: 医术 yīshù / 美术 měishù ② method; tactics: 战术 zhànshù / 权术 quánshù ——see also zhú

术科　shùkē　technical courses offered in military or physical training (opp. 学科 xuékē③)

术士　shùshì　① a confucian scholar ② magician

术语　shùyǔ　technical terms; terminology: 军事～ military terms / 医学～ medical terminology

戍

　shù　defend; garrison: ～边 garrison the frontiers

戍楼　shùlóu　garrison watchtower

戍守　shùshǒu　defend; garrison: ～边疆 garrison the frontiers

戍卒　shùzú　garrison soldiers (at the frontiers)

束

　shù　① bind; tie: 腰～皮带 wear a belt round one's waist ② *m.* bundle; bunch; sheaf: 一～鲜花 a bunch of flowers / 一～稻草 a sheaf of straw ③ control; restrain: 拘束 jūshù ④ (Shù) a surname

束缚　shùfù　tie; bind up; fetter: ～手脚 bind sb. hand and foot; tie sb.'s hands; hamper the initiative of / ～生产力 fetter the productive forces / 冲破旧思想的～ smash the trammels of old ideas / 挣脱封建礼教的～ shake off the yoke of the feudal ethical code / 僵化思想～着一些人的头脑。An ossified way of thinking shackles some people's minds.

束射管　shùshèguǎn　*electron.* beam tube

束身　shùshēn　① control oneself; restrain oneself ② bind oneself: ～归罪 bind oneself with rope and surrender oneself to justice

束手　shùshǒu　have one's hands tied; be helpless

束手待毙　shùshǒu dài bì　fold one's hands and await destruction; helplessly wait for death; resign oneself to extinction

束手就擒　shùshǒu jiùqín　allow oneself to be seized without putting up a fight

束手束脚　shùshǒu-shùjiǎo　be over-cautious

束手无策　shùshǒu wú cè　be at a loss what to do; feel quite helpless; be at one's wit's end: 碰着类似这样的事，有时候连工程师们也～。Confronted with difficulties like this there were times when even the engineers were at a loss to know what to do.

束脩　shùxiū　*old* a private tutor's remuneration (*or* emolument)

束之高阁　shù zhī gāogé　tie sth. up and place it on the top shelf—lay aside and neglect; shelve; pigeonhole

束装　shùzhuāng　*formal* pack up (for a journey): ～就道 pack up and start off

述

　shù　state; relate; narrate: 略～其经过 relate briefly how it happened; give a brief account of the matter / 简～如下。A brief account is as follows.

述评　shùpíng　review; commentary: 每周时事～ weekly review of current affairs / 新华社记者～ commentary by a Xinhua correspondent

述说　shùshuō　state; recount; narrate

述职　shùzhí　report on one's work; report: 大使已回国～。The ambassador has gone back for consultations.

树（樹）

　shù　① tree: 苹果～ apple tree ② plant; cultivate: 十年树木，百年树人 shí nián shù mù, bǎi nián shù rén ③ set up; establish; uphold: ～正气 uphold (*or* foster) healthy tendencies / ～雄心 have lofty ambitions; aim high

树碑立传　shùbēi-lìzhuàn　erect a monument to sb. and write his biography—build up sb.'s public image: 这本所谓回忆录，实际上是为他自己～的。These so-called memoirs are, in fact, an attempt on his part to build up his own image.

树杈　shùchà　(also 树杈子 shùchàzi) crotch (of a tree)

树串儿　shùchuànr　*dial.* willow warbler (a bird)

树丛　shùcóng　grove; thicket

树大根深　shùdà-gēnshēn　a big tree with deep roots (said of an influential person or a huge organization)

树大招风　shù dà zhāofēng　a tall tree catches the wind—a person in a high position is liable to be attacked

树倒猢狲散　shù dǎo húsūn sàn　when the tree falls the monkeys scatter—when an influential person falls from power, his hangers-on disperse

树敌　shùdí　make an enemy of sb.; set others against oneself; antagonize: ～太多 make too many enemies; antagonize too many people

树墩　shùdūn　(also 树墩子 shùdūnzi) tree stump; stump

树蜂　shùfēng　wood wasp

树干　shùgàn　tree trunk; trunk

树高千丈,叶落归根　shù gāo qiānzhàng, yè luò guī gēn　a tree may grow a thousand *zhang* high, but its leaves fall back to the roots—a person residing away from home eventually returns to his native soil

树疙瘩　shùgēda　*dial.* tree stump; stump

树挂　shùguà　common name for 雾凇 wù·sōng

树冠　shùguān　crown (of a tree)

树海　shùhǎi　a sea of trees—an unbroken, limitless forest

树行子　shùhàngzi　rows of trees; woods

树胶　shùjiāo　gum (of a tree)

树懒　shùlǎn　*zool.* sloth

树立　shùlì　set up; establish: ～榜样 set an example /～标兵 set sb. up as a pacemaker /～远大理想 foster a lofty ideal /～正确的世界观 acquire a correct world outlook

树凉儿　shùliángr　(also 树阴凉儿 shùyīnliángr) the cool shade of a tree (as in summer)

树林　shùlín　(also 树林子 shùlínzi) woods; grove

树码　shùmǎ　(also 树码子 shùmǎzi) *dial.* scion (for grafting)

树苗　shùmiáo　sapling

树杪　shùmiǎo　*formal* the tip of a tree; treetop

树木　shùmù　trees generally

树皮　shùpí　bark

树皮画　shùpíhuà　bark picture

树鼩　shùqú　*zool.* tree shrew

树梢　shùshāo　the tip of a tree; treetop

树身　shùshēn　tree trunk; trunk

树薯　shùshǔ　another name for 木薯 mùshǔ

树趟子　shùtàngzi　rows of trees; woods

树蛙　shùwā　tree frog

树丫　shùyā　(also 树桠 shùyā) crotch (of a tree)

树阴　shùyīn　the shade of a tree

树欲静而风不止　shù yù jìng ér fēng bù zhǐ　the tree may crave calm, but the wind will not drop—things take their own course regardless of one's will

树栽子　shùzāizi　*inf.* sapling

树枝　shùzhī　branch; twig

树脂　shùzhī　resin

树脂酸　shùzhīsuān　resinic acid

树脂整理　shùzhī zhěnglǐ　*text.* resin finishing

树种　shùzhǒng　① kinds of trees: 阔叶～ broad-leaved trees / 针叶～ coniferous trees ② seeds of trees: 采集～ gather the seeds of trees

树桩　shùzhuāng　(also 树桩子 shùzhuāngzi) tree stump; stump

树籽　shùzǐ　seeds of trees

竖[1]（竖、豎）

shù　① vertical; upright; perpendicular: 画一条～线 draw a vertical line ② set upright; erect; stand: ～旗杆 erect a flagpole / 这杆子我～不起来。I can't get the pole to stand up. ③ vertical stroke (in Chinese characters): "王"字的写法是三横一～。The character 王 is composed of one vertical and three horizontal strokes.

竖[2]（竖、豎）

shù　*formal* a young servant

竖笛　shùdí　*mus.* recorder

竖井　shùjǐng　*min.* (vertical) shaft

竖立　shùlì　erect; set upright; stand: 门前～着一根旗杆。A flagpole stands outside the gate. / 宝塔～在山上。The pagoda stands at the top of the mountain.

竖起　shùqǐ　hold up; erect: ～大拇指 hold up one's thumb in approval; thumbs up /～一面大旗 hoist a huge banner /～耳朵听 prick up one's ears

竖琴　shùqín　*mus.* harp

竖蜻蜓　shù qīngtíng　*dial.* handstand

竖子　shùzǐ　*formal* ① boy; lad ② mean fellow; fellow

恕

shù　① consideration for others; forbearance ② forgive; pardon; excuse: ～罪 pardon an offence; forgive a sin ③ *pol.* excuse me; beg your pardon: 恕不奉陪 shù bù fèngpéi excuse me; beg your pardon

恕不奉陪　shù bù fèngpéi　excuse me (for not keeping you company)

恕难从命　shù nán cóngmìng　we regret that we cannot comply with your wishes

恕宥　shùyòu　*formal* forgive; pardon

庶[1]

shù　multitudinous; numerous: 富庶 fùshù

庶[2]

shù　of or by a concubine (as distinguished from the legal wife): ～出 be born of a concubine

庶[3]

shù　*conj. formal* so that; so as to: ～免误会 so as to avoid misunderstanding

庶乎　shùhū　*conj. formal* so that; so as to

庶几乎　shùjīhū　(also 庶几 shùjī) *conj. formal* so that; so as to

庶民　shùmín　*formal* the common people; the multitude

庶母　shùmǔ　concubine of one's father

庶人　shùrén　*formal* commoners; the common people: 夺去爵位, 废为～ be deprived of one's rank and reduced to the status of commoner

庶室　shùshì　concubine

庶务　shùwù　*old* ① general affairs; business matters ② a person in charge of business matters

庶子　shùzǐ　the son of a concubine

数（數）

shù　① number; figure: 代表人～ the number of delegates / 以万计 number tens of thousands ② *math.* number: 小数 xiǎoshù / 整数 zhěngshù ③ *gram.* number: 单数 dānshù / 复数 fùshù ④ several; a few: ～百人 several hundred people /～小时后 a few hours later ⑤ fate; destiny ——see also shǔ; shuò

数词　shùcí　*gram.* numeral

数额　shù'é　a fixed number; a definite amount: 超出～ exceed the number fixed / 不足规定～ fall short of the amount required

数据　shùjù　data: 科学～ scientific data

数据处理　shùjù chǔlǐ　data processing

数据存储系统　shùjù cúnchǔ xìtǒng　data-storage system

数据库　shùjùkù　data base; data bank

数控　shùkòng　numerical control (Nc): 总体～ total numerical control

数理化　shù-lǐ-huà　(short for 数学、物理、化学) mathematics, physics, and chemistry

数理逻辑　shùlǐ luójí　mathematical logic

数理统计学　shùlǐ tǒngjìxué　mathematical statistics

数量　shùliàng　quantity; amount: ～和质量并重 stress both quantity and quality /～上的差别 quantitative difference /～上的增减 increase or decrease in quantity / 在～上占优势 be superior in numbers; have numerical superiority

数量词　shùliàngcí　*gram.* numeral-classifier compound (e.g. 一次 "once," 两套 "two sets")

数列　shùliè　an ordered series of numbers

数码　shùmǎ　① numeral: 罗马～ Roman numerals ② number; amount

数目　shùmù　number; amount

数目字　shùmùzì　same as 数字 shùzì

数学　shùxué　mathematics: ～家 mathematician

数值　shùzhí　*math.* numerical value

数值天气预报 shùzhí tiānqì yùbào numerical weather forecast

数制 shùzhì a system of computation (based on the number 2, as the binary system 二进制, or on the number 10, as the decimal system 十进制)

数轴 shùzhóu *math.* number axis

数珠 shùzhū *Buddhism* beads

数字 shùzì ① numeral; figure; digit ② quantity; amount: 不要单纯追求〜。Don't just go after quantity.

数字计算机 shùzì jìsuànjī digital computer

数字控制 shùzì kòngzhì numerical control (Nc)

数字控制系统 shùzì kòngzhì xìtǒng numerical control system

腧（俞）
shù same as 腧穴 shùxué

腧穴 shùxué *Chin. med.* acupuncture points on the human body

漱
shù rinse (the mouth); gargle

漱口 shùkǒu rinse the mouth; gargle: 用盐水〜 gargle with salt water

漱口杯 shùkǒubēi a glass or mug for mouth-rinsing or teeth-cleaning; tooth glass

漱口剂 shùkǒujì gargle

墅
shù villa

澍
shù *formal* timely rain

shuā

刷¹
shuā ① a brush: 油漆〜 paintbrush ② clean with a brush; brush; scrub: 〜鞋 brush shoes / 〜地板 scrub the floor / 〜锅 clean (*or* scour) a pot ③ paint, daub, paste up, etc. with a brush: 用石灰浆〜墙 whitewash a wall / 〜标语 paste up posters ④ *inf.* eliminate; remove: 那个队直到半决赛才给〜下来。That team was not eliminated until the semifinals.

刷²（唰）
shuā *onom.* swish; rustle: 玉米叶子被风吹得〜〜 响。The corn leaves rustled in the wind.

——see also shuà

刷拉 shuālā *onom.* a swishing sound: 〜一声, 树上飞走一只鸟儿。Swish! A bird flew out of a tree.

刷洗 shuāxǐ scrub; scour: 〜地板 scrub the floor / 〜锅碗 scour the pots and pans

刷新 shuāxīn ① renovate; refurbish: 〜门面 repaint the front (of a shop, etc.); put up a new shopfront ② outdo; surpass: 〜纪录 break (*or* better) a record / 一再〜生产纪录 shatter the production records again and again

刷牙 shuāyá brush (*or* clean) one's teeth

刷子 shuāzi brush: 一把〜 a brush / 鞋〜 shoe brushes

shuǎ

耍
shuǎ ① *dial.* play: 叫孩子们到院子里去〜。Tell the children to go and play in the courtyard. / 这可不是〜的! It's no joke! ② play with; flourish: 〜刀 flourish a sword; give a performance of swordplay ③ play (tricks): 〜鬼把戏 play dirty tricks / 〜两面派 resort to double-dealing; be double-faced

耍把戏 shuǎ bǎxì ① give an acrobatic performance; perform juggling feats ② play tricks

耍把 shuǎbǎ *dial.* brandish

耍笔杆 shuǎ bǐgǎn wield a pen; be skilled in literary tricks: 他光会〜, 碰到实际问题就束手无策。He knows only how to wield a pen and is helpless in the face of practical problems.

耍逗 shuǎdòu play with; tease: 〜孩子 tease children

耍猴儿 shuǎhóur ① put on a monkey show ② make fun of sb.; tease; kid: 别以为我拿你〜, 我说的都是实话。Don't think I'm kidding you—I'm telling the truth.

耍花枪 shuǎ huāqiāng same as 耍花招 shuǎ huāzhāo

耍花腔 shuǎ huāqiāng cheat by glib talk; speak guilefully

耍花招 shuǎ huāzhāo ① display showy movements in *wushu* (武术), etc. ② play (*or* get up to) tricks: 别〜了! None of your tricks! / 你这是耍的什么花招? What are you up to? *or* What sort of game are you playing? / 他又在〜了。He is up to his tricks again.

耍滑 shuǎhuá (also 耍滑头 shuǎ huátóu) try to shirk work or responsibility; act in a slick way

耍奸 shuǎjiān same as 耍滑 shuǎhuá

耍赖 shuǎlài (also 耍赖皮 shuǎ làipí) act shamelessly; be perverse

耍流氓 shuǎ liúmáng behave like a hoodlum; take liberties with women; act indecently

耍闹 shuǎnào have horseplay: 上课铃响以前, 孩子们在教室里嘻嘻哈哈地〜着。Before the bell rang, the children were having horseplay in the classroom.

耍弄 shuǎnòng make fun of; make a fool of; deceive

耍排场 shuǎ páichang parade one's wealth; go in for ostentation and extravagance

耍盘子 shuǎ pánzi *acrob.* plate-spinning; disc-spinning

耍脾气 shuǎ píqi get into a huff; put on a show of bad temper

耍贫嘴 shuǎ pínzuǐ *dial.* be garrulous

耍钱 shuǎqián *dial.* gamble

耍人 shuǎrén make fun of others; poke fun at others; make a fool of sb.

耍手段 shuǎ shǒuduàn (also 耍手腕 shuǎ shǒuwàn) use artifices; play tricks

耍手艺 shuǎ shǒuyì make a living as a craftsman

耍死狗 shuǎ sǐgǒu *dial.* try to brazen it out

耍态度 shuǎ tàidu lose one's temper; get into a huff

耍坛子 shuǎ tánzi *acrob.* juggling with jars; jar balancing act

耍威风 shuǎ wēifēng make a show of authority; throw one's weight about; be overbearing

耍无赖 shuǎ wúlài act shamelessly; be perverse

耍笑 shuǎxiào ① joke; have fun ② make fun of; play a joke on: 他喜欢〜人。He delights in making fun of others.

耍心眼儿 shuǎ xīnyǎnr exercise one's wits for personal gain; be calculating; pull a smart trick

耍子 shuǎzi *old* have fun; have a good time

耍嘴皮子 shuǎ zuǐpízi ① talk glibly; be a slick talker ② mere empty talk; lip service

shuà

刷
shuà see below ——see also shuā

刷白 shuàbái *dial.* white; pale: 月亮把田野照得〜。The fields turned white under the moon. / 听到这个不幸的消息, 他的脸立刻变得〜。He turned pale when he heard the bad news.

shuāi

衰 shuāi decline; wane: 体力渐～ get weaker physically／风势渐～。The wind was dying down.／懒则～。Laziness leads to debility.

衰败 shuāibài decline; wane; be at a low ebb

衰惫 shuāibèi *formal* feeble and exhausted

衰敝 shuāibì decline; wane; be at a low ebb: 国力～。National strength is on the wane.／生产～。Production is at a low ebb.

衰变 shuāibiàn *phys.* decay: 核～ nuclear decay

衰草 shuāicǎo withering grass: ～败叶 withering grass and fallen leaves

衰减 shuāijiǎn ① weaken; fail; diminish: 我的记忆力日见～。My memory is failing fast. ② *elec.* attenuation: ～器 attenuator

衰竭 shuāijié *med.* exhaustion; prostration: 心力～ heart failure

衰老 shuāilǎo old and feeble; decrepit; senile: 一年不见, 他明显地～了。He's visibly aged and weakened since I saw him last a year ago.

衰落 shuāiluò decline; be on the wane; go downhill: 到了公元五世纪, 罗马帝国迅速～。The Roman Empire rapidly waned in power in the 5th century.

衰迈 shuāimài old and feeble; decrepit; senile

衰弱 shuāiruò ① weak; feeble: 久病之后身体～ be weak after a long illness／心脏～ have a weak heart ② weaken; diminish in strength: 攻势已经～。The offensive is losing momentum.

衰世 shuāishì an age of decline

衰替 shuāitì *formal* decline; be on the wane

衰颓 shuāituí weak and degenerate

衰退 shuāituì fail; decline: 视力～ one's eyesight is failing／记忆力～ be losing one's memory／经济～ economic recession／革命意志～的人, 要经过整风重新振作起来。Those whose revolutionary will has been waning should regain their ardour through rectification.

衰亡 shuāiwáng become feeble and die; decline and fall; wither away: 罗马帝国的～ the decline and fall of the Roman Empire

衰微 shuāiwēi *formal* (of a country, nation, etc.) decline; wane

衰萎 shuāiwěi wither; shrivel

衰谢 shuāixiè wither; fade

衰朽 shuāixiǔ *formal* feeble and decaying; decrepit: ～的王朝 a decadent dynasty／～残年 a decrepit old age

衰颜 shuāiyán an age-worn face

摔¹(蹤**)** shuāi fall; tumble; lose one's balance: 他～了好多次才学会骑自行车。He fell off many times before he learned to ride a bicycle.／他把腿～断了。He had a fall and broke his leg.

摔² shuāi ① hurtle down; plunge: 飞机一～下来了。The plane plunged to the ground. ② cause to fall and break; break: 我不小心把玻璃杯～了。I accidentally broke a glass. ③ cast; throw; fling: 把帽子往床上一～ throw one's cap onto the bed ④ same as 摔打 shuāidǎ①

摔打 shuāidǎ ① beat; knock: 把扫帚上的泥～～。Beat the dirt off the broom. ② rough it; temper oneself: 青年人应该到艰苦的环境中去～～。Young people should temper themselves in difficult circumstances. ／ 他从小就在渔船上, ～出一副结实的身子。He built up a robust constitution roughing it on the fishing boats ever since

he was small.

摔跟头 shuāi gēntou ① tumble; trip and fall ② trip up; come a cropper; make a blunder

摔交 shuāijiāo ① tumble; trip and fall: 他摔了一交, 把腿给摔折了。He had a fall and broke his leg. ② trip up; come a cropper; make a blunder ③ *sports* wrestling: ～运动员 wrestler

shuǎi

甩 shuǎi ① move backward and forward; swing: ～着胳膊 swinging one's arms／～鞭子 crack a whip／小女孩一跑, 辫子就来回一动。The girl's pigtails swing to and fro as she runs.／他袖子一～就走了。He flung up his hands in impatience and walked off. ② throw; fling; toss: ～手榴弹 throw hand grenades ③ leave sb. behind; throw off: 他加快速度, 一会儿就把别的运动员都～在后头了。Quickening his pace, he soon left all the other runners behind.／他的女朋友把他～了。His girlfriend gave him the brush-off.

甩车 shuǎichē uncouple railway coaches from the locomotive; uncouple

甩掉 shuǎidiào throw off; cast off; shake off; get rid of: ～包袱 cast off a burden; get a load off one's back／～尾巴 throw off a pursuer; throw off a tail

甩发 shuǎifà swaying hair—(in traditional opera) a long tuft of false hair inserted in the hole in the net which fits closely on the head (worn by actors representing persons in distress, who can sway the hair about to indicate distraction)

甩干 shuǎigān spin-dry (laundry in an automatic washing machine); tumble-dry

甩开膀子 shuǎikāi bǎngzi go all out; go full steam ahead: ～抓生产 go all out to increase production

甩脸子 shuǎi liǎnzi *dial.* pull a long face

甩卖 shuǎimài disposal of goods at reduced prices; markdown sale; reduction sale

甩手 shuǎishǒu ① swing one's arms ② refuse to do; wash one's hands of: 这事该你负责, 你可不能～不管。You can't wash your hands of this. It's your responsibility.

甩线 shuǎixiàn fishing line

甩子 shuǎizǐ *inf.* (of fish, insects, etc.) lay eggs: 青蛙正在～。The frogs are spawning.

甩子 shuǎizi fly whisk; whisk

shuài

帅¹(帥**)** shuài ① commander in chief: 统帅 tǒngshuài／挂帅 guàshuài ② commander in chief, the chief piece in Chinese chess ③ (Shuài) a surname

帅²(帥**)** shuài ① beautiful; graceful; smart: 他的字写得真～。He writes a beautiful hand.／他的双杠动作可～了! His movements on the parallel bars were very graceful. ② handsome; elegant: 这小伙子长得真～! What a handsome strapping young man!

帅旗 shuàiqí the flag of a commander in chief

帅气 shuàiqi same as 帅² shuài

帅印 shuàiyìn the seal of a commander in chief

率¹ shuài ① lead; command: ～师东征 lead troops on an eastern expedition／～众前往 go (to a place) at the head of many people／～所部向我投诚 come over to our side with his troops ② *formal* fol-

low; obey: 率由旧章 shuài yóu jiùzhāng

率²

shuài ① rash; hasty: 草率 cǎoshuài／轻率 qīng shuài ② frank; straightforward: 坦率 tǎn shuài／直率 zhíshuài ③ *formal* generally; usually: 大~如此。This is usually the case. ④ same as 帅² shuài
——see also lǜ

率常 shuàicháng *formal* usually; generally: ~如此。This is usually the case.

率尔 shuài'ěr *formal* rashly; hastily: 不可~应战。We should not rashly accept battle.

率尔操觚 shuài'ěr cāogū write at random

率领 shuàilǐng lead; head; command: ~代表团 lead (*or* head) a delegation／这支部队由他~。This unit is under his command./连长~全连战士冲锋。The company commander led his men in the charge.

率然 shuàirán hastily; rashly: ~回答 give a rash answer

率先 shuàixiān take the lead in doing sth.; be the first to do sth.

率意 shuàiyì *formal* as one pleases; at will: ~行事 act as one pleases

率由旧章 shuài yóu jiùzhāng act in accordance with set rules; follow the beaten track

率真 shuàizhēn forthright and sincere

率直 shuàizhí straightforward; unreserved; blunt

蟀

shuài see 蟋蟀 xīshuài

shuān

闩（檖）

shuān ① door bolt; latch: 上~ fasten with a bolt or latch ② fasten with a bolt or latch: 把门~上 bolt the door

拴

shuān tie; fasten: 把马~在树上 tie (*or* tether) a horse to a tree／~根绳子晒衣服 put up a clothes line／把船~住。Make the boat fast.

拴绑 shuānbǎng tie up; bind up

拴缚 shuānfù tie up; bind up

栓

shuān ① bolt; plug: 枪栓 qiāngshuān／消火栓 xiāohuǒshuān ② stopper; cork

栓剂 shuānjì *med.* suppository

栓皮 shuānpí cork (the outer bark of a kind of oak tree)

栓皮栎 shuānpílì oriental oak (*Quercus variabilis*)

栓塞 shuānsè *med.* embolism: 静脉~ venous embolism／肺（脑）~ pulmonary (cerebral) embolism

栓子 shuānzǐ *med.* embolus

shuàn

涮

shuàn ① rinse: 把衣服~一~。Rinse the clothes./把这瓶子~一下。Give this bottle a rinse. ② scald thin slices of meat in boiling water; instant-boil ③ *dial.* deceive; fool: 你别~我啦。Don't try to fool me.

涮锅子 shuànguōzi instant-boil slices of meat and vegetables in a chafing dish

涮羊肉 shuànyángròu ① instant-boil slices of mutton in a chafing dish ② instant-boiled mutton; Mongolian fire pot

shuāng

双（雙、隻）

shuāng ① two; twin; both; dual: ~目失明 blind in both eyes／~发动机飞机 a twin-engined plane／粮食、棉花~丰收 bumper harvests of both grain and cotton ② m. (for shoes, socks, chopsticks, etc.) pair: 一~鞋 a pair of shoes／一~袜子 a pair of socks ③ (opp. 单 "odd") even: 双数 shuāngshù／双号 shuānghào ④ double; twofold: ~份 double the amount; twice as much

双棒儿 shuāngbàngr *dial.* ① twins ② twin ice-lollies

双胞胎 shuāngbāotāi twins

双边 shuāngbiān bilateral: ~关系 bilateral relations／~会谈 bilateral talks／~贸易 bilateral trade; two-way trade／~条约 bilateral treaty／~最惠国条款 bilateral most-favoured-nation clause

双层 shuāngcéng double-deck; having two layers; of two thicknesses: ~桥 double-decker bridge／~床 double-deck bed; double-decker; bunk bed／~火车（公共汽车）double-decker／~玻璃窗 double window

双重 shuāngchóng double; dual; twofold: ~任务 a double (*or* dual) task／~标准 a double standard／~领导 dual leadership／~公民身份 dual citizenship／起~作用 serve a dual purpose／帝国主义和封建主义的~压迫 the twofold oppression of imperialism and feudalism

双重代表权 shuāngchóng dàibiǎoquán dual representation

双重国籍 shuāngchóng guójí dual (*or* double) nationality: ~人 dual nationals

双重间谍 shuāngchóng jiàndié double agent

双重人格 shuāngchóng réngé *derog.* dual personality

双唇音 shuāngchúnyīn *phonet.* bilabial consonant; bilabial (i.e. p, b, m in Chinese)

双打 shuāngdǎ *sports* doubles: 男子（女子）~ men's (women's) doubles／男女混合~ mixed doubles

双方 shuāngfāng both sides; the two parties: 缔约国~ both signatory states; the contracting parties／~各执一词。Each side persisted in its own views.／~同意 by mutual consent

双峰驼 shuāngfēngtuó two-humped camel; Bactrian camel

双幅 shuāngfú double width: 这块料子是单幅的还是~的? Is this material single or double width?

双杠 shuānggàng *sports* parallel bars

双宫丝 shuānggōngsī *text.* doupion silk

双挂号 shuāngguàhào double registered mail (which requires a receipt for the sender)

双关 shuāngguān having a double meaning: 一语双关 yī yǔ shuāngguān

双关语 shuāngguānyǔ pun

双管 shuāngguǎn double-barrelled: ~猎枪 double-barrelled shotgun

双管齐下 shuāng guǎn qí xià paint a picture with two brushes at the same time—work along both lines

双轨 shuāngguǐ double track: ~铁路 double-track railway

双号 shuānghào even numbers (of tickets, seats, etc.)

双簧 shuānghuáng (also 双锖 shuānghuáng) a two-man act, with one acting in pantomime and another hiding behind him doing all the speaking or singing: 唱~ give a two-man comic show; collaborate

双簧管 shuānghuángguǎn *mus.* oboe

双季稻 shuāngjìdào double cropping of rice; double-harvest rice

双交 shuāngjiāo *agric.* double cross

双款 shuāngkuǎn upper and lower inscriptions (for

paintings, calligraphy, etc.; i.e. both dedication and signature)

双料 shuāngliào of reinforced material; extra quality: ～脸盆 special quality basin; extra good quality basin

双轮 shuānglún ① *sports* double round: 五十米～射箭 50-metre double round archery event ② two-wheeled: ～马车 a two-wheeled cab or hansom / ～车 two-wheeler

双轮双铧犁 shuānglúnshuānghuálí two-wheeled double-shared plough

双面 shuāngmiàn two-sided; double-edged; double-faced; reversible: ～刀片 a double-edged razor blade

双面绣 shuāngmiànxiù double-faced embroidery

双面摇纱机 shuāngmiàn yáoshājī double reeling frame

双面印刷机 shuāngmiàn yìnshuājī perfecting press; perfector

双面织物 shuāngmiàn zhīwù reversible cloth; reversibles

双名 shuāngmíng two-character given name

双目显微镜 shuāngmù xiǎnwēijìng binocular microscope

双抢 shuāngqiǎng rush-harvesting and rush-planting

双亲 shuāngqīn (both) parents; father and mother

双球菌 shuāngqiújūn diplococcus

双曲面 shuāngqūmiàn *math.* hyperboloid: 单叶～ hyperboloid of one sheet / 双叶～ hyperboloid of two sheets

双曲线 shuāngqūxiàn *math.* hyperbola

双全 shuāngquán complete in both respects; possessing both: 父母～。 Both parents are alive.

双人床 shuāngrénchuáng double bed

双人房 shuāngrénfáng double-bedded room; twin-bedded room

双人舞 shuāngrénwǔ a dance for two performers; *pas de deux*

双日 shuāngrì even-numbered days (of the month)

双身子 shuāngshēnzi *inf.* a pregnant woman: 她不是发胖，是～。 She isn't really getting fat, she is with child (*or* she's in the family way).

双生 shuāngshēng twin: ～姐妹 twin sisters / ～兄弟 twin brothers / ～子 twins

双声 shuāngshēng *linguis.* alliterative compound (a compound consisting of two syllables with the same initial consonant; e.g. 踟蹰 chíchú, 回环 huíhuán)

双十二事变 Shuāng Shí'èr Shìbiàn the December 12 Incident (another name for 西安事变 Xī'ān Shìbiàn)

双手 shuāngshǒu both hands: 用我们的～建设社会主义新农村 build a new socialist countryside with our own hands / 我举～赞成。 I'm all for it.

双数 shuāngshù even numbers

双双 shuāngshuāng in pairs

双糖 shuāngtáng *chem.* disaccharide

双体船 shuāngtǐchuán catamaran

双筒望远镜 shuāngtǒng wàngyuǎnjìng binoculars; field glasses

双喜 shuāngxǐ double happiness

双喜临门 shuāngxǐ línmén a double blessing has descended upon the house

双下巴 shuāngxiàba double chin

双响 shuāngxiǎng double-bang firecracker (which goes off twice—once on the ground, and then again in the air)

双向 shuāngxiàng two-way: ～交通 two-way traffic / ～通信 two-way communication

双向飞碟射击 shuāngxiàng fēidié shèjī *sports* skeet shooting

双向开关 shuāngxiàng kāiguān two-way switch

双薪 shuāngxīn double pay: 工作量加倍的发给～ give double pay for double work

双星 Shuāngxīng ① *astron.* double star ② Altair and Vega (see also 牛郎织女 Niúláng Zhīnǚ)

双姓 shuāngxìng two-character surname (e.g. 欧阳 Ōuyáng, 司徒 Sītú)

双眼井 shuāngyǎnjǐng a twin-mouthed well

双眼皮 shuāngyǎnpí double-edged eyelid

双氧水 shuāngyǎngshuǐ *pharm.* hydrogen peroxide solution

双翼机 shuāngyìjī biplane

双音节词 shuāngyīnjiécí *phonet.* disyllabic word; disyllable

双鱼座 Shuāngyúzuò *astron.* Pisces

双元音 shuāngyuányīn *phonet.* diphthong

双月刊 shuāngyuèkān bimonthly (magazine)

双职工 shuāngzhígōng man and wife both at work; working couple

双周刊 shuāngzhōukān biweekly (magazine); fortnightly

双绉 shuāngzhòu *text.* crêpe de Chine

双子叶植物 shuāngzǐyè zhíwù *bot.* dicotyledon

双子座 Shuāngzǐzuò *astron.* Gemini

双座 shuāngzuò two-seater; double-seater: ～飞机 two-seater aircraft

泷（瀧）

shuāng used in ～水 (a place in Guangdong Province)——see also lóng

霜

shuāng ① frost (the white powdery substance) ② frostlike powder: 糖～ icing; frosting ③ white; hoar: ～鬓 grey (*or* hoary) temples

霜晨 shuāngchén a frosty morning

霜冻 shuāngdòng frost (the frozen condition)

霜害 shuānghài frost injury; frost: 受～的农作物 frosted crops

霜花 shuānghuā ① frostwork ② (soft) rime

霜降 Shuāngjiàng ① Frost's Descent—the 18th of the 24 solar terms ② the day marking the beginning of the 18th solar term (Oct. 23 or 24, when hoarfrost descends and is likely to bring the first film of ice)——see also 节气 jiéqì; 二十四节气 èrshí sì jiéqì

霜霉病 shuāngméibìng *agric.* downy mildew

霜期 shuāngqī frost season

霜天 shuāngtiān frosty sky—frosty weather

霜条 shuāngtiáo *dial.* ice-lolly; popsicle; ice-sucker; frozen sucker

霜叶 shuāngyè frosty leaves—autumn maple leaves: 停车坐爱枫林晚，～红于二月花。(杜牧) I stop my carriage to admire the maple grove at nightfall, Whose frosty leaves are redder than the flowers of early spring.

孀

shuāng widow

孀妇 shuāngfù *formal* widow

孀居 shuāngjū *formal* be a widow; live in widowhood

骦

shuāng see 骕骦 sùshuāng

鸘

shuāng see 鹔鸘 sùshuāng

shuǎng

爽¹

shuǎng ① bright; clear; crisp: 神清目～ uplifting to the mind and the eye ② frank; straightforward; openhearted: 豪爽 háoshuǎng ③ feel well: 身体不～ not feel well

爽²

shuǎng deviate: 毫厘不爽 háolí bù shuǎng

爽脆 shuǎngcuì ① (of sounds or voices) sharp and clear ② frank; straightforward ③ quick; brisk ④ (of

food) crisp and tasty

爽口 shuǎngkǒu　tasty and refreshing

爽快 shuǎngkuai　① refreshed; comfortable: 洗完澡身上～多了 feel much refreshed after a bath ② frank; straightforward; outright: 为人～ be frank and straightforward / 他～地说出了对我的看法。He told me frankly what he thought of me. ③ with alacrity; readily: ～地答应帮忙 readily agree to help / 办事～ work readily and briskly

爽朗 shuǎnglǎng　① bright and clear: 深秋的天空异常～。In late autumn the sky is crystal clear. ② hearty; candid; frank and open; straightforward: ～的笑声 hearty laughter / ～的性格 a frank and open personality

爽利 shuǎnglì　brisk and neat; efficient and able: 办事～ be brisk and neat in one's work

爽亮 shuǎngliàng　① loud and clear; resounding; sonorous ② cheerful; sanguine

爽目 shuǎngmù　pleasing to the eye

爽气 shuǎngqì　① formal cool and refreshing air ② dial. refreshed; comfortable ③ dial. frank; straightforward

爽然 shuǎngrán　formal at a loss; confused

爽然若失 shuǎngrán ruò shī　not know what to do; be at a loss

爽身粉 shuǎngshēnfěn　talcum powder

爽声 shuǎngshēng　(in) a loud and clear voice: ～笑了 laughed aloud

爽失 shuǎngshī　formal slip; fault; mistake; error

爽信 shuǎngxìn　formal fail to keep one's promise; break one's promise; go back on one's word

爽性 shuǎngxìng　may just as well: 没多少活了,～干完了再休息。There isn't much work left. We might as well finish it before we have a rest.

爽约 shuǎngyuē　formal fail to keep an appointment; break an appointment

爽直 shuǎngzhí　frank; straightforward; candid

shuí

谁 shuí, also shéi　① who: 他是～? Who is he? / 他在跟～说话? Who is he talking to? / 这是～的意见? Whose idea is this? ② (used in rhetorical questions) who: ～不说他好? Who wouldn't speak well of him? ③ someone; anyone: 有～能帮助我就好了! If only someone would help me! / 我没跟～说话。I didn't talk to anyone. / 你要找～吗? Are you looking for someone? ④ (used before 都 or 也) everyone; anyone: ～都喜欢他。Everybody likes him. / ～也不要。Nobody wants it. ⑤ (repeated in two phrases) whoever: ～先到,～先吃。Whoever arrives first will eat first. / 大家看～合适就选～。You may elect whoever you think is suitable. ⑥ (used both before and after a verb, indicating that one person does sth. to another): ～先到谁等着。Whoever arrives first should wait for the other. / 他们俩～也说不服。Neither of them could convince the other.

谁边 shuíbiān　where

谁个 shuígè　dial. who: ～敲门? Who is it (at the door)?

谁们 shuímen　dial. who (plural): ～来了? Who have come? / 你那屋里都是～? Who are they in your room?

谁人 shuírén　who: ～不知,哪个不晓? Everybody knows. / 这是～造的谣? Who started this rumour?

谁谁 shuíshuí　so-and-so

谁知 shuízhī　(also 谁知道 shuí zhīdào) who knows; who would have thought: 我只是开个玩笑,～她竟当真了。I

was only joking; who would have thought she would take it seriously.

谁知盘中餐,粒粒皆辛苦 shuízhī pánzhōng cān, lìlì jiē xīnkǔ (李绅) Who knows that every grain in the bowl Is the fruit of so much pain and toil?

shuǐ

水 shuǐ　① water: 请给我一杯～。Give me a glass of water, please. ② river: 汉～ the Han River ③ a general term for rivers, lakes, seas, etc.; water: ～陆运输 land and water transportation / ～平如镜。The surface of the water is as smooth as a mirror. ④ a liquid 汽水 qìshuǐ / 药水 yàoshuǐ ⑤ extra charges or incomes: 贴水 tiēshuǐ / 外水 wàishuǐ ⑥ m. washing (of a garment): 这件衬衫洗了三～了。This shirt has gone through three washings. ⑦ (Shuǐ) a surname

水坝 shuǐbà　dam

水半球 shuǐbànqiú　geog. water hemisphere

水饱儿 shuǐbǎor　dial. feel bloated after eating much liquid food: 喝了两大碗粥,落了个～。I gulped down two big bowls of porridge and felt terribly bloated.

水泵 shuǐbèng　water pump

水笔 shuǐbǐ　① a stiff-haired writing brush or water-colour paintbrush ② dial. fountain pen

水标 shuǐbiāo　water gauge

水表 shuǐbiǎo　water meter

水鳖 shuǐbiē　bot. frogbit (Hydrocharis morsus-ranae)

水鳖子 shuǐbiēzi　popular name for 蜣虫 hòuchóng

水滨 shuǐbīn　waterside; waterfront

水兵 shuǐbīng　seaman; sailor; bluejacket

水波 shuǐbō　wave; ripple: 清风徐来,～不兴。(苏轼) A cool wind blew gently, without starting a ripple.

水玻璃 shuǐbōli　chem. water glass

水彩 shuǐcǎi　watercolour

水彩画 shuǐcǎihuà　watercolour (painting)

水彩颜料 shuǐcǎi yánliào　watercolours

水仓 shuǐcāng　min. sump

水草 shuǐcǎo　① water and grass: ～丰美 (a place) with plenty of water and lush grass / 逐～而居 (of nomads) live where there is water and grass; rove about seeking water and grass ② waterweeds; water plants

水涔涔 shuǐcéncén　① (of eyes) bright and intelligent ② soaking wet

水虿 shuǐchài　zool. the nymph of the dragonfly, etc.

水产 shuǐchǎn　aquatic products: ～丰富 abound in aquatic products / ～资源 aquatic resources

水产品 shuǐchǎnpǐn　aquatic product

水产养殖 shuǐchǎn yǎngzhí　aquaculture

水产业 shuǐchǎnyè　aquatic products industry

水车 shuǐchē　① waterwheel (for raising water or driving machinery) ② watercart; water waggon

水丞 shuǐchéng　a small receptacle for holding water for use on an inkslab

水成岩 shuǐchéngyán　another name for 沉积岩 chénjīyán

水城 shuǐchéng　waterside town

水程 shuǐchéng　journey by boat; voyage: 一百公里的～ a 100-kilometre journey by boat

水池 shuǐchí　pond; pool; cistern

水池子 shuǐchízi　① same as 水池 shuǐchí ② sink

水尺 shuǐchǐ　water conservancy water gauge

水处理 shuǐchǔlǐ　chem. water treatment

水次 shuǐcì　formal waterside: 亭临～。The pavilion stands by the waterside.

水荡 shuǐdàng　① pond ② puddle

水到渠成 shuǐ dào qú chéng　when the water comes, a channel is formed—when conditions are ripe, success

is achieved

水道 shuǐdào ① water course ② waterway; water route: 这次去上海，我想打～走。This time I'll go to Shanghai by water. ③ lanes in a swimming pool

水稻 shuǐdào paddy (rice); rice

水稻插秧机 shuǐdào chāyāngjī rice (*or* paddy) transplanter

水稻土 shuǐdàotǔ rice (*or* paddy) soil

水滴石穿 shuǐ dī shí chuān dripping water wears through rock; little strokes fell great oaks

水底电缆 shuǐdǐ diànlǎn submarine cable; subaqueous cable

水地 shuǐdì ① irrigated land ② paddy field

水电 shuǐdiàn ① short for 水力发电 shuǐlì fādiàn ② water and electricity: ～供应 water and electricity supply

水电费 shuǐdiànfèi charges for water and electricity

水电站 shuǐdiànzhàn short for 水力发电站 shuǐlì fādiànzhàn

水貂 shuǐdiāo *zool.* mink

水痘 shuǐdòu *med.* varicella; chicken pox; water pox

水碓 shuǐduì water-powered trip-hammer (for husking rice)

水遁 shuǐdùn escape by water

水饭 shuǐfàn ① cooked rice reboiled in water or soup ② *old* porridge

水飞蓟 shuǐfēijì *bot.* milk thistle (*Silybum marianum*)

水肥 shuǐféi liquid manure

水粉 shuǐfěn ① *dial.* soaked noodles made from beans or sweet potatoes ② a cosmetic made from face powder and glycerine

水粉画 shuǐfěnhuà *painting* gouache

水分 shuǐfēn ① moisture content: 吸收～ absorb moisture ② exaggeration: 这个数字有～。This figure is inflated. / 这份报告有～。This report is somewhat exaggerated.

水浮莲 shuǐfúlián another name for 大藻 dàpiáo

水疙瘩 shuǐgēda salted (*or* pickled) rutabaga

水阁 shuǐgé waterside pavilion

水工 shuǐgōng short for 水利工程 shuǐlì gōngchéng

水工建筑物 shuǐgōng jiànzhùwù hydraulic structure

水沟 shuǐgōu ditch; drain; gutter

水垢 shuǐgòu scale; incrustation: 除去锅炉里的～ scour out a boiler

水鸪鸪 shuǐgūgū *inf.* popular name for 鹁鸪 bógū

水臌 shuǐgǔ *Chin. med.* ascites

水管 shuǐguǎn waterpipe

水柜 shuǐguì ① water tank ② *dial.* cistern; reservoir ③ *old* counter (in a shop)

水果 shuǐguǒ fruit

水果罐头 shuǐguǒ guàntou tinned (*or* canned) fruit

水果软糖 shuǐguǒ ruǎntáng fruit jelly

水果糖 shuǐguǒtáng fruit drops

水旱 shuǐ-hàn ① floods and droughts ② land and water: ～码头 a dock for land and water transport service

水合 shuǐhé *chem.* hydration

水合水 shuǐhéshuǐ hydrate water

水合物 shuǐhéwù hydrate

水红 shuǐhóng bright pink; cerise

水壶 shuǐhú ① kettle ② canteen ③ watering can

水葫芦 shuǐhúlu *bot.* water hyacinth

水花 shuǐhuā ① spray ② *dial.* chicken pox; water pox

水化 shuǐhuà another name for 水合 shuǐhé

水化物 shuǐhuàwù another name for 水合物 shuǐhéwù

水患 shuǐhuàn flood; inundation

水荒 shuǐhuāng water shortage

水火 shuǐ-huǒ ① fire and water—two things diametrically opposed to each other ② extreme misery: 拯救人民于～之中 save the people from untold miseries

水火不相容 shuǐ-huǒ bù xiāng róng be incompatible as fire and water

水火地 shuǐhuǒdì an area afflicted alternately with drought and waterlogging

水火无情 shuǐ-huǒ wúqíng *inf.* floods and fires have no mercy

水鸡 shuǐjī ① water bird ② frog ③ a drenched chicken; a drowned rat: 淋得～似的 be soaked through; be drenched and bedraggled

水碱 shuǐjiǎn scale; incrustation

水浆 shuǐ-jiāng plain water and liquid food: ～不进 not take a drop or a morsel

水浇地 shuǐjiāodì *agric.* irrigated land

水饺 shuǐjiǎo boiled dumplings

水脚 shuǐjiǎo *dial.* charges for water transport

水解 shuǐjiě *chem.* hydrolysis

水解产物 shuǐjiě chǎnwù hydrolysate

水解蛋白 shuǐjiě dànbái *pharm.* protein hydrolysate

水解质 shuǐjiězhì hydrolyte

水津津 shuǐjīnjīn moist with sweat or water

水晶 shuǐjīng crystal; rock crystal

水晶包 shuǐjīngbāo a steamed dumpling stuffed with diced pig fat and sugar

水晶玻璃 shuǐjīng bōli crystal (glass)

水晶宫 shuǐjīnggōng the Crystal Palace (of the Dragon King)

水晶棺 shuǐjīngguān crystal sarcophagus

水晶体 shuǐjīngtǐ *physiol.* crystalline lens

水井 shuǐjǐng well

水警 shuǐjǐng water police; coastal guard

水酒 shuǐjiǔ *hum.* watery wine (said by a host of his own wine)

水军 shuǐjūn waterborne troops (in former times)

水客 shuǐkè *old* ① boatman ② itinerant trader

水坑 shuǐkēng puddle; pool; water hole: 臭～ cesspool; cesspit

水库 shuǐkù reservoir

水牢 shuǐláo water dungeon

水老鸦 shuǐlǎoyā (also 水老鸹 shuǐlǎoguā) cormorant

水涝 shuǐlào waterlogging

水涝地 shuǐlàodì waterlogged land

水雷 shuǐléi *mil.* (submarine) mine: 敷设～ lay mines (in water) / ～密布的河道 a heavily mined river

水冷 shuǐlěng water-cooling: ～式发动机 water-cooled engine / ～系统 water-cooling system

水力 shuǐlì waterpower; hydraulic power

水力发电 shuǐlì fādiàn hydraulic power generation

水力发电站 shuǐlì fādiànzhàn hydroelectric (power) station; hydropower station

水力开采 shuǐlì kāicǎi *min.* hydraulic mining; hydraulicking

水力学 shuǐlìxué hydraulics

水力资源 shuǐlì zīyuán hydroelectric resources (*or* potential); waterpower resources

水利 shuǐlì ① water conservancy: ～设施 water conservancy facilities ② irrigation works; water conservancy project: 兴修～ build irrigation works

水利工程 shuǐlì gōngchéng irrigation works; water conservancy project (*or* works)

水利工程学 shuǐlì gōngchéngxué hydraulic engineering

水利灌溉网 shuǐlì guàngàiwǎng irrigation network

水利化 shuǐlìhuà bring all farmland under irrigation

水利枢纽 shuǐlì shūniǔ key water control project

水利资源 shuǐlì zīyuán water resources

水帘 shuǐlián cascade; waterfall

水疗 shuǐliáo hydropathy

水疗法 shuǐliáofǎ *med.* hydrotherapy

水淋淋 shuǐlínlín dripping wet

水灵 shuǐlíng *dial.* ① (of fruit, greens, etc.) fresh and

juicy ② (of appearance) bright and beautiful; radiant and vivacious: 两只～的大眼睛 a pair of bright, beautiful eyes

水流 shuǐliú ① rivers; streams; waters: 在我国一切矿藏、～都属于全民所有。 In China, all mineral resources and waters are the property of the whole people. ② current; flow: ～湍急(迟缓) rapid (sluggish) flow; rushing current

水流星 shuǐliúxīng *acrob.* spinning bowls of water; water meteors

水溜 shuǐliù eaves gutter

水龙 shuǐlóng (also 水龙带 shuǐlóngdài) fire hose; hose

水龙骨 shuǐlónggǔ *bot.* wall fern; golden locks

水龙卷 shuǐlóngjuǎn *meteorol.* waterspout

水龙头 shuǐlóngtóu (water) tap; faucet; bibcock: 开(关)～ turn on (off) the tap / 用后将～关紧。 Don't leave the tap running after use.

水漉漉 shuǐlùlù wet; damp

水陆 shuǐ-lù ① land and water: ～并进 proceed by both land and water; conduct a combined operation by army and navy ② delicacies from land and sea: ～俱陈 a feast with dainties of every kind

水陆交通线 shuǐlù jiāotōngxiàn land and water communication lines

水陆联运 shuǐlù liányùn water-land transshipment

水陆联运码头 shuǐlù liányùn mǎtou a dock for joint land and water transport service

水陆两用 shuǐlù liǎngyòng amphibious

水陆坦克 shuǐlù tǎnkè amphibious tank

水陆运输 shuǐlù yùnshū transportation by land and water

水路 shuǐlù waterway; water route: 由上海到武汉可以走～。 One can travel from Shanghai to Wuhan by water.

水铝矿 shuǐlǚkuàng gibbsite (a mineral)

水绿 shuǐlǜ light green

水轮 shuǐlún waterwheel

水轮泵 shuǐlúnbèng (water) turbine pump

水轮泵站 shuǐlúnbèngzhàn (water) turbine-pump station

水轮发电机 shuǐlún fādiànjī water turbogenerator

水轮机 shuǐlúnjī hydraulic (*or* water) turbine

水落管 shuǐluòguǎn same as 雨水管 yǔshuǐguǎn

水落石出 shuǐluòshíchū when the water subsides the rocks emerge—the whole thing comes to light: 把事情辩个～ argue a matter out / 我们一定要把这事弄个～。 We must get to the bottom of this matter.

水煤气 shuǐméiqì *chem.* water gas

水门 shuǐmén water valve

水门事件 Shuǐmén Shìjiàn the Watergate Affair (1972)

水门汀 shuǐméntīng *dial.* cement

水锰矿 shuǐměngkuàng manganite (a mineral)

水米无交 shuǐmǐ wú jiāo ① have no relations or contact with each other ② (of officials) be upright and accept no gifts from the people

水密 shuǐmì *mech.* watertight

水密桃 shuǐmìtáo honey peach

水面 shuǐmiàn ① the surface of the water ② the area of a body of water

水磨 shuǐmó polish with a waterstone ——see also shuǐmò

水磨功夫 shuǐmó gōngfu patient and precise work; painstaking work

水磨石 shuǐmóshí *archit.* terrazzo: ～地面 terrazzo floor

水墨画 shuǐmòhuà *painting* ink and wash; wash painting: 中国～ Chinese ink and wash

水磨 shuǐmò ① watermill ② grind grain, etc. fine while adding water: ～年糕 New Year cake made from finely ground rice flour ——see also shuǐmó

水母 shuǐmǔ *zool.* jellyfish; medusa

水能载舟, 亦能覆舟 shuǐ néng zài zhōu, yì néng fù zhōu while the waters can bear the boat, they can also sink it: 舟所以比人君, 水所以比黎庶, ～。(吴兢《贞观政要》) For if the emperor is a boat, then the people are the waters of the river. And while the waters can bear the boat, they can also sink it.

水泥 shuǐní cement

水泥标号 shuǐní biāohào strength of cement; cement grade

水泥厂 shuǐníchǎng cement plant

水泥船 shuǐníchuán concrete boat; plastered boat

水泥瓦 shuǐníwǎ cement tile

水碾 shuǐniǎn water-powered roller (for grinding grain)

水鸟 shuǐniǎo aquatic bird; water bird

水牛 shuǐniú (water) buffalo

水牛儿 shuǐniúr *dial.* snail

水暖 shuǐnuǎn ① hot water central heating system ② water supply and heating: ～设备 water supply and heating installations

水暖工 shuǐnuǎngōng plumber

水牌 shuǐpái a black or white board for writing temporary accounts or records on

水泡子 shuǐpāozi *dial.* small lake; pond

水泡 shuǐpào bubble

水疱 shuǐpào blister: 脚上打了～ get blisters on one's feet

水培法 shuǐpéifǎ water culture; hydroponics

水皮儿 shuǐpír *dial.* water surface

水瓢 shuǐpiáo (gourd) water ladle

水平 shuǐpíng ① horizontal; level: ～梯田 level terraced field; level terrace ② standard; level: 生活～ living standard / 文化～ standard of education; cultural level / 认识～ level of one's understanding / 赶超世界先进～ attain and surpass advanced world levels / 提高领导～ improve one's art of leadership

水平飞行 shuǐpíng fēixíng horizontal (*or* level) flight

水平轰炸 shuǐpíng hōngzhà *mil.* horizontal (*or* level) bombing

水平贸易 shuǐpíng màoyì *econ.* horizontal trade

水平面 shuǐpíngmiàn level surface; level

水平线 shuǐpíngxiàn level line; level

水平仪 shuǐpíngyí (also 水准器 shuǐzhǔnqì) level; spirit level

水萍 shuǐpíng same as 浮萍 fúpíng

水泼不进, 针插不进 shuǐ pō bù jìn, zhēn chā bù jìn same as 针插不进, 水泼不进 zhēn chā bù jìn, shuǐ pō bù jìn

水汽 shuǐqì water vapour; steam

水汽浓度 shuǐqì nóngdù *meteorol.* vapour concentration

水枪 shuǐqiāng *min.* giant; (hydraulic) monitor: 水采～ hydraulic giant

水橇 shuǐqiāo water ski: ～运动 water skiing

水禽 shuǐqín *zool.* waterfowl; water bird

水青冈 shuǐqīnggāng another name for 山毛榉 shānmáojǔ

水情 shuǐqíng *water conservancy* regimen

水球 shuǐqiú *sports* water polo

水曲柳 shuǐqūliǔ *bot.* Manchurian ash (*Fraxinus, mandshurica*)

水渠 shuǐqú ditch; canal

水圈 shuǐquān *geol.* hydrosphere

水溶液 shuǐróngyè *chem.* aqueous solution

水乳交融 shuǐ-rǔ jiāoróng as well blended as milk and water—in complete harmony: 干部和群众的关系亲密无间, ～。 The relationship between the cadres and the masses is one of perfect harmony. / 好的翻译可以使宾主谈得～。 A competent interpreter can help bring about a meeting of minds like milk mingling with water.

水杉 shuǐshān *bot.* metasequoia (*Metasequoia glyptostroboides*)

水上 shuǐshàng on, or above water: ～飞行 overwater flight

水上飞机 shuǐshàng fēijī seaplane; hydroplane

水上居民 shuǐshàng jūmín boat dwellers

水上运动 shuǐshàng yùndòng aquatic sports; water sports: ～会 aquatic sports meet

水筲 shuǐshāo a pail made of wood or bamboo strips; bucket

水蛇 shuǐshé *zool.* water snake

水蛇腰 shuǐshéyāo a very slender waist

水深火热 shuǐshēn-huǒrè deep water and scorching fire —an abyss of suffering; extreme misery: 旧社会劳动人民生活在～之中。The working people lived in an abyss of misery in the old society. *or* Life was hell on earth for the working people in the old society. / 反动政府发动的国内战争陷全国人民于～之中。The reactionary government plunged the whole nation into dire suffering by waging a civil war.

水生动物 shuǐshēng dòngwù aquatic animal

水生植物 shuǐshēng zhíwù water (*or* aquatic) plant; hydrophyte

水声学 shuǐshēngxué *phys.* marine acoustics

水师 shuǐshī waterborne forces (in former times)

水虱 shuǐshī *zool.* beach louse

水蚀 shuǐshí erosion by the action of running water

水势 shuǐshì the flow of water; the rise and fall of flood-water: 密切注意～ keep a close eye on the flow of the water / ～有所减退。The flood subsided (*or* abated) a little.

水手 shuǐshǒu seaman; sailor

水手长 shuǐshǒuzhǎng boatswain

水刷石 shuǐshuāshí *archit.* granitic plaster

水松 shuǐsōng *bot.* China cypress (*Glyptostrobus pensilis*)

水塔 shuǐtǎ water tower

水獭 shuǐtǎ *zool.* otter

水潭 shuǐtán puddle; pool

水塘 shuǐtáng pool; pond

水天一色 shuǐ-tiān yī sè the water and the sky blended in one colour (said of a vast body of water)

水田 shuǐtián paddy field; paddy

水田犁 shuǐtiánlí paddy plough

水田耙 shuǐtiánpá paddy harrow

水汀 shuǐtīng *dial.* steam heat

水桶 shuǐtǒng pail; bucket

水头 shuǐtóu ① *water conservancy* head ② flood peak; peak of flow

水土 shuǐtǔ ① water and soil: 植树可以保持～。Tree-planting helps to conserve water and prevent soil erosion. ② natural environment and climate: ～不服 unaccustomed to the climate of a new place; not acclimatized

水土保持 shuǐtǔ bǎochí water and soil conservation

水土流失 shuǐtǔ liúshī soil erosion

水汪汪 shuǐwāngwāng ① full of water; very wet: 刚下过大雨，地里～的。A heavy rain had fallen, and the fields were flooded. ② (of children's or young women's eyes) bright and intelligent

水网 shuǐwǎng a network of rivers, rivulets, lakes and ponds: ～地带 an area crisscrossed with rivers, rivulets, lakes and ponds

水位 shuǐwèi water level: 高 (低)～ high (low) water level / 地下～ water table; groundwater level

水位计 shuǐwèijì fluviograph

水文 shuǐwén hydrology: ～测验 hydrologic survey / ～工作者 hydrologist / ～资料 hydrological data

水文地理学 shuǐwén dìlǐxué hydrography

水文地质学 shuǐwén dìzhìxué hydrogeology

水文队 shuǐwénduì hydrological team

水文年鉴 shuǐwén niánjiàn Water Year Book

水文气象学 shuǐwén qìxiàngxué hydrometeorology

水文图 shuǐwéntú hydrological map

水文学 shuǐwénxué hydrology

水文预报 shuǐwén yùbào hydrologic forecast

水文站 shuǐwénzhàn hydrometric station; hydrologic station

水污染 shuǐwūrǎn water pollution; water contamination

水螅 shuǐxī *zool.* hydra

水系 shuǐxì river system; hydrographic net

水下 shuǐxià under water: ～导弹 submarine-based missile

水仙 shuǐxiān *bot.* narcissus (the plant and its flower)

水险 shuǐxiǎn marine insurance

水线 shuǐxiàn waterline

水乡 shuǐxiāng a region of rivers and lakes

水箱 shuǐxiāng water tank

水泻 shuǐxiè *med.* watery diarrhoea

水泄不通 shuǐ xiè bù tōng not even a drop of water could trickle through; be watertight: 挤得～ be packed with people / 围得～ be so closely besieged that not a drop of water could trickle through

水榭 shuǐxiè waterside pavilion

水星 Shuǐxīng *astron.* Mercury

水性 shuǐxìng ① ability in swimming: 这姑娘的～很好。This girl is a good swimmer. ② the depth, currents and other characteristics of a river, lake, etc. ③ (of a woman) of easy virtue

水性杨花 shuǐxìngyánghuā (of a woman) of easy virtue; wanton

水袖 shuǐxiù water sleeves (double white-silk sleeves attached to the cuffs of a costume, used in traditional Chinese opera)

水锈 shuǐxiù ① scale; incrustation ② watermark (in water vessels)

水选 shuǐxuǎn seed or ore selection by immersion

水靴 shuǐxuē water boots

水循环 shuǐxúnhuán hydrologic cycle; water cycle

水压 shuǐyā hydraulic (*or* water) pressure

水压机 shuǐyājī hydraulic press

水烟 shuǐyān shredded tobacco for water pipes: 抽～ smoke a water pipe

水烟袋 shuǐyāndài water pipe

水杨 shuǐyáng *bot.* bigcatkin willow

水杨酸 shuǐyángsuān *chem.* salicylic acid

水杨酸钠 shuǐyángsuānnà sodium salicylate

水舀子 shuǐyǎozi dipper; ladle; scoop (for water)

水翼船 shuǐyìchuán hydrofoil

水银 shuǐyín *chem.* mercury; quicksilver

水银灯 shuǐyíndēng mercury-vapour lamp

水银气压表 shuǐyín qìyābiǎo *meteorol.* mercury (*or* mercurial) barometer

水银温度计 shuǐyín wēndùjì *meteorol.* mercury (*or* mercurial) thermometer

水银柱 shuǐyínzhù mercury column

水印¹ shuǐyìn (also 水印木刻 shuǐyìn mùkè) watercolour block printing

水印² shuǐyìn watermark

水印³ shuǐyìn *dial.* shop seal (in former times)

水莹莹 shuǐyíngyíng (of eyes, etc.) radiant and crystal-clear; bright and clear

水有源，树有根 shuǐ yǒu yuán, shù yǒu gēn every river has its source and every tree its roots—everything has its origin

水域 shuǐyù waters; water area; a body of water: 内陆～ inland waters / 国际～ an international body of water; international waters

水源 shuǐyuán ① the source of a river; headwaters; waterhead: 黄河的～ the headwaters of the Yellow River ② source of water: 寻找～ seek new sources of water

水运 shuǐyùn water transport

水运码头 shuǐyùn mǎtou a port handling river or ocean cargo

水灾 shuǐzāi flood; inundation

水栽培 shuǐzāipéi hydroponics; water culture

水葬 shuǐzàng water burial

水蚤 shuǐzǎo water flea

水藻 shuǐzǎo algae

水泽 shuǐzé a region of rivers, lakes and marshes

水闸 shuǐzhá sluice; water gate

水战 shuǐzhàn a battle on water

水涨船高 shuǐ zhǎng chuán gāo when the river rises the boat goes up: 通货一膨胀, 物价就涨,～嘛。 Prices rise in proportion to inflation, like boats going up with the level of the water.

水针疗法 shuǐzhēn liáofǎ *Chin. med.* acupuncture therapy with medicinal injection

水蒸气 shuǐzhēngqì steam; water vapour

水至清则无鱼, 人至察则无徒 shuǐ zhì qīng zé wú yú, rén zhì chá zé wú tú water which is too clean has few fish; he who is too critical has few friends

水质 shuǐzhì water quality

水质保护 shuǐzhì bǎohù *environ. protec.* water quality protection

水蛭 shuǐzhì leech

水中捞月 shuǐzhōng lāo yuè fish for the moon—make impractical or vain efforts

水肿 shuǐzhǒng *med.* oedema; dropsy

水珠 shuǐzhū (also 水珠子 shuǐzhūzi) *inf.* a drop of water

水柱 shuǐzhù water column

水准 shuǐzhǔn level; standard: 高 (低) 于一般～ above (below) average

水准点 shuǐzhǔndiǎn bench mark

水准面 shuǐzhǔnmiàn level surface; level plane

水准仪 shuǐzhǔnyí surveyor's level

水渍险 shuǐzìxiǎn *econ.* with particular average (W. P. A.)

水族 Shuǐzú the Sui (Shui) nationality, or the Suis (Shuis), mainly inhabiting Guizhou Province

水族 shuǐzú aquatic animals

水族馆 shuǐzúguǎn aquarium

shuì

说 shuì try to persuade: 游说 yóushuì ——see also shuō; yuè

税 shuì tax; duty: 营业～ business tax / 进口 (出口)～ import (export) duty

税额 shuì'é the amount of tax to be paid

税负 shuìfù tax burden: 减轻～ ease the tax burden

税金 shuìjīn same as 税款 shuìkuǎn

税捐 shuìjuān taxes and levies

税款 shuìkuǎn tax payment; taxation

税率 shuìlǜ tax rate; rate of taxation; tariff rate

税目 shuìmù tax items; taxable items

税收 shuìshōu tax revenue

税收政策 shuìshōu zhèngcè tax policy

税务局 shuìwùjú tax bureau

税务员 shuìwùyuán tax collector

税则 shuìzé tax regulations

税制 shuìzhì tax system; taxation: 累进～ progressive taxation

税种 shuìzhǒng tax category

睡 shuì sleep: 他～了。 He's gone to bed. / 他～着了。 He's asleep. / 一～就～到大天亮 sleep like a log till broad daylight / 他～得早起得也早。 He goes to bed early and gets up early.

睡袋 shuìdài sleeping bag

睡觉 shuìjiào sleep: 该～了。 It's time to go to bed. / 睡午觉 take a nap after lunch / 睡懒觉 get up late; sleep in; sleep late / 马上上床, 好好地睡一觉。 Get straight into bed and have a good sleep.

睡裤 shuìkù pyjama trousers

睡莲 shuìlián *bot.* water lily

睡帽 shuìmào nightcap

睡梦 shuìmèng sleep; slumber: 一阵敲门声把他从～中惊醒了。 He was roused from sleep by a heavy pounding on the door.

睡眠 shuìmián sleep: ～不足 not have enough sleep

睡眠疗法 shuìmián liáofǎ *med.* physiological sleep therapy

睡魔 shuìmó extreme sleepiness

睡袍 shuìpáo nightgown; nightdress; nightie

睡乡 shuìxiāng dreamland: 进入～ fall asleep

睡醒 shuìxǐng wake up

睡眼惺忪 shuìyǎn xīngsōng eyes still heavy with sleep; eyes still fogged with sleep

睡衣 shuìyī nightclothes; pyjamas

睡椅 shuìyǐ reclining chair; deck chair

睡意 shuìyì sleepiness; drowsiness: 有几分～ feel somewhat sleepy; be drowsy

shǔn

吮 shǔn suck: ～奶 suck milk

吮吸 shǔnxī suck (usu. fig.): 剥削阶级贪婪地～劳动人民的血汗。 The exploiting classes greedily suck the blood of the labouring people.

吮痈舐痔 shǔnyōng-shìzhì lick sb.'s ulcers and piles —debase oneself in trying to please sb. important or powerful

shùn

顺 shùn ① *prep.* in the same direction as; with: ～流而下 go downstream / ～时针方向 clockwise ② *prep.* along: ～着这条道儿走。 Follow this road. / 水～着渠道流进地里。 Water runs along the channel to the fields. ③ arrange; put in order: 这篇文章还得～一～。 This essay needs polishing. / 把这些讲义一一～, 不要放得乱七八糟的。 Please put these teaching materials in order and don't leave them in a mess. ④ obey; yield to; act in submission to: 他不对嘛, 怎么能～着他呢? How can we do as he wishes when he's obviously wrong? ⑤ fall in with; suit; agree with: 顺意 shùnyì ⑥ at one's convenience; conveniently: 顺手 shùnshǒu ⑦ (used at the close of a letter) take the opportunity to: ～颂大安。 With best wishes for your health. / ～致最崇高的敬意。 I avail myself of this opportunity to renew to you the assurances of my highest consideration. ⑧ (of writings) smooth; readable; clear and well-written ⑨ in sequence: 顺延 shùnyán

顺坝 shùnbà *water conservancy* longitudinal dike

顺便 shùnbiàn *adv.* (do sth.) in addition to what one is already doing, without much extra effort: 你去图书馆

的时候，～把我这本书还了吧。When you go to the library, please return this book for me. / 我下班回家，常～到书店看看。I often look in at the bookstore on my way home from work. / 这一点现在～提一下，以后还会讲到。I mention this point now in passing and shall refer to it again.

顺差 shùnchā favourable balance; surplus: 贸易～ favourable balance of trade / 国际收支～ favourable balance of payments; balance of payments surplus

顺产 shùnchǎn *med.* natural labour

顺畅 shùnchàng smooth and easy; unhindered: 病人的呼吸渐渐～了。The patient is beginning to breathe more easily. / 保障城乡物资的～交流 ensure the smooth flow of goods and materials between urban and rural areas

顺磁 shùncí *phys.* paramagnetic: ～共振 paramagnetic resonance / ～性 paramagnetism

顺次 shùncì in order; in succession; in proper sequence: 按问题的轻重缓急～解决 dispose of the problems one by one in order of importance and urgency

顺从 shùncóng be obedient to; submit to; yield to

顺带 shùndài same as 顺便 shùnbiàn

顺当 shùndang *inf.* smooth; without a hitch; plain sailing: 不可能每一件事都那么～。Not everything could be that plain sailing.

顺导 shùndǎo guide or steer (a movement, etc.) along its proper course

顺道儿 shùndàor same as 顺路 shùnlù

顺丁橡胶 shùndīng xiàngjiāo *chem.* butadiene rubber

顺耳 shùn'ěr pleasing to the ear: 不要只爱听～的话。You shouldn't just listen to what pleases you.

顺访 shùnfǎng visit (a place, person, etc.) on the way: 总理在出访西欧归途中～了意大利。On the journey back from his official visits to Western Europe, the Premier visited Italy in transit.

顺风 shùnfēng ① have a favourable wind; have a tail wind: ～行船 sail with the wind ② favourable wind; tail wind

顺风吹火 shùnfēng chuī huǒ take advantage of favourable conditions

顺风耳 shùnfēng'ěr ① a person in traditional Chinese novels who can hear voices a long way off ② a well-informed person

顺风转舵 shùnfēng zhuǎn duò *derog.* trim one's sails; take one's cue from changing conditions

顺服 shùnfú obey; be obedient; be docile

顺竿儿爬 shùngānrpá take one's cue from sb. and say everything to please him

顺光 shùnguāng *photog.* frontlighting

顺和 shùnhe genial; gentle; affable

顺脚 shùnjiǎo ① (do sth.) on the way or without going out of one's way ② be a direct route: 这么走太绕远儿，不～。If you go that way, you'll be taking a roundabout and much longer route.

顺境 shùnjìng easy or favourable circumstances: 身处～ be in easy or favourable circumstances

顺口 shùnkǒu ① read smoothly: 稿子经过这样一改，念起来就～多了。After being touched up, the essay reads more smoothly. ② say offhandedly: 他也不想想就～答应了。He agreed without thinking. ③ *dial.* suit one's taste: 这鱼我吃着很～。I like the taste of this fish. / 不知我这些菜你吃来～不～? I wonder if my dishes are to your taste.

顺口搭音 shùnkǒu dā yīn echo what others say; chime in with others

顺口溜 shùnkǒuliū doggerel; jingle

顺理成章 shùn lǐ chéng zhāng (of a statement, argument, etc.) logical; well reasoned

顺利 shùnlì smooth; successful; without a hitch: 工作正在～进行。The work is going on smoothly. / 会议进行得很～。The meeting went off without a hitch. / 在～的情况下，要看到还会有困难。When circumstances are favourable, we must not forget that there will still be difficulties.

顺溜 shùnliu *dial.* ① orderly; tidy ② smooth; easy ③ obedient; agreeable

顺路 shùnlù ① on the way: 我昨天回家时～去看了看李大爷。I dropped in at Uncle Li's on my way home yesterday. ② be a direct route: 到王家庄这么走不～。This is not the most direct route to Wangjiazhuang Village.

顺民 shùnmín *derog.* docile citizens under a new regime or alien rulers

顺气 shùnqì *inf.* happy; free from worry

顺势 shùnshì ① take advantage of an opportunity (as provided by an opponent's reckless move): 他向旁边一闪，～把敌人摔倒了。He dodged the enemy's assault and threw him to the ground. ② conveniently; in passing

顺手 shùnshǒu ① smooth; without a hitch; without difficulty: 事情办得相当～。It was done without a hitch. / 开始试验有时不很～，也是很自然的。It is to be expected that an experiment will sometimes run into a snag at first. ② conveniently; without extra trouble: 出去时请～关上门。Would you close the door when you go out? ③ (do sth.) as a natural sequence or simultaneously: 我们扫完院子，～把房间也扫一扫好了。After sweeping the courtyard, we might as well clean the rooms. ④ handy; convenient and easy to use: 这把扳子使起来挺～。This spanner is very handy.

顺手牵羊 shùnshǒu qiān yáng lead off a goat in passing—pick up sth. on the sly; walk off with sth.

顺水 shùnshuǐ downstream; with the stream

顺水人情 shùnshuǐ rénqíng a favour done at little or no cost

顺水推舟 shùnshuǐ tuī zhōu push the boat along with the current—make use of an opportunity to gain one's end

顺遂 shùnsuì (of things) go well; go smoothly

顺藤摸瓜 shùn téng mō guā follow the vine to get the melon—track down sb. or sth. by following clues

顺心 shùnxīn be satisfactory: 诸事～。All is well. / 他父亲晚年过得挺～。His father spent the evening of his life in happiness.

顺行 shùnxíng *astron.* direct motion

顺序 shùnxù ① sequence; order: 文物按年代～展出。The cultural relics are displayed in chronological sequence. / 按字母～排列 in alphabetical order ② in proper order; in turn

顺延 shùnyán postpone: 运动会定于六月四日举行，遇雨～。The sports meet is scheduled for June 4th—subject to postponement in case of rain.

顺眼 shùnyǎn pleasing to the eye: 看着不～ be offensive to the eye; be an eyesore

顺应 shùnyìng comply with; conform to: ～历史发展的潮流 conform to the historical trend of the times; go with the tide of historical development

顺证 shùnzhèng *Chin. med.* a serious case which improves steadily

顺之者昌，逆之者亡 shùn zhī zhě chāng, nì zhī zhě wáng those who submit will prosper, those who resist shall perish

顺嘴 shùnzuǐ same as 顺口 shùnkǒu①②

舜 Shùn Shun, a legendary sage king in ancient China

瞬 shùn wink; twinkling

瞬时　shùnshí　instantaneous

瞬时速度　shùnshí sùdù　instantaneous velocity

瞬时性　shùnshíxìng　instantaneity

瞬时值　shùnshízhí　instantaneous value

瞬息　shùnxī　twinkling: ～间 in the twinkling of an eye

瞬息万变　shùnxī wàn biàn　undergoing a myriad changes in the twinkling of an eye; fast changing: 股票市场～。There are so many unpredictable fluctuations on the stock exchange.

shuō

说　shuō　① speak; talk; say: 他会～法语。He speaks French. / 请～慢一点儿。Please speak more slowly. / ～得多做得少 talk much but do little / 你～得很对。What you say is quite true. / 那未免～得太轻了。That's putting it too mildly. ② explain: 他～了又～, 我还是不懂。He explained and explained, but I still couldn't understand. / 我一～他就明白了。I told him how and he caught on at once. ③ theory; teachings; doctrine: 著书立说 zhùshū-lìshuō ④ scold: 他父亲～了他一顿。His father gave him a scolding (or talking-to). ⑤ act as matchmaker: 给他～个媳妇儿 find a wife for him ⑥ refer to; indicate: 你的话是～谁呢? Who did your remarks refer to? ——see also shuì; yuè

说白　shuōbái　spoken parts in an opera

说不得　shuōbude　① unspeakable; unmentionable ② scandalous ③ dial. have no say; have to comply

说不定　shuōbudìng　perhaps; maybe: ～她已经走了。Maybe she's already left. / ～要下雨。It looks as if it might rain.

说不过　shuōbuguò　cannot outspeak sb.; cannot match sb.'s eloquence

说不过去　shuōbuguòqù　cannot be justified or explained away: 条件这样好, 再不增产, 可～。With such favourable conditions, we'll have no excuse if we fail to increase output.

说不好　shuōbuhǎo　be unable to say for certain; not be certain; can't say: 我～她肯不肯来我们这儿工作。I can't say whether she would like to come and work here or not.

说不来　shuōbulái　① cannot get along (with sb.): 我跟他～。I don't see eye to eye with him. ② dial. not know how to put it

说不清　shuōbuqīng　be unable to explain clearly: 到底发生了什么事, 谁也～。Nobody can explain clearly what really happened.

说不上　shuōbushàng　① cannot say; cannot tell: 他也～问题在哪儿。He can't put his finger on what's wrong. / 我～他来不来。I can't say whether he is coming or not. ② not worth mentioning: 这些材料～有什么史料价值。These materials can't be said to have much value as historical records.

说不下去　shuōbuxiàqù　be unable to finish what one is saying

说部　shuōbù　old novels, anecdotes, etc.

说曹操曹操就到　shuō Cáo Cāo Cáo Cāo jiù dào　mention Cao Cao and there he is—talk of the devil (and he will appear)

说长道短　shuōcháng-dàoduǎn　gossip: 在她身上找不出一点让人家～的地方。There was not a single thing about her that one could find fault with.

说唱　shuōchàng　a genre of popular entertainment consisting mainly of talking and singing, e.g. comic dialogue, dagu (大鼓), etc.

说唱文学　shuōchàng wénxué　a genre of popular literature partly in verse and partly in prose, used as material for storytelling and ballad-singing

说穿　shuōchuān　tell what sth. really is; reveal; disclose: ～了, 无非是想推卸责任。To put it bluntly, this is shifting responsibility.

说辞　shuōcí　excuse; pretext

说大话　shuō dàhuà　brag; boast; talk big

说到底　shuōdàodǐ　in the final analysis; at bottom: 偏差和片面性的产生, ～, 是主观认识脱离客观实际。In the final analysis, wrong and one-sided thinking is caused by the separation of subjective thinking from objective reality.

说到钱, 便无缘　shuō dào qián, biàn wúyuán　to speak of a loan is to put an end to friendship

说到做到　shuōdào zuòdào　do what one says; match one's deeds to one's words; live up to one's word

说道　shuōdào　say (the words quoted): 少先队员～: "我们要向雷锋叔叔学习"。"We must learn from Uncle Lei Feng," said the Young Pioneer.

说道　shuōdao　dial. ① say; tell: 你把刚才听到的广播给大家～～。Tell us what you heard over the radio just now. ② talk over; discuss: 我跟他～～再作决定。I'll talk it over with him before I make a decision. ③ dial. what lies behind sth.; reason: 他为什么突然改变主意, 这里头肯定有～。There must be a reason for his sudden change of mind.

说得过去　shuōdeguòqù　be justifiable; be passable: 他的英语发音还～。His English pronunciation is passable.

说得来　shuōdelái　① can get along; be on good terms: 找一个跟他～的人去动员他。Get someone who is on good terms with him to try and persuade him. ② have a glib tongue

说定　shuōdìng　settle; agree on: 这件事基本上已经～了。The matter is as good as settled.

说东道西　shuōdōng-dàoxī　chatter away on a variety of things: 昨天晚上, 她俩挤在一个炕上, 亲亲热热地～。They had spent the previous night squeezed together on the kang, chatting intimately of everything under the sun.

说短论长　shuōduǎn-lùncháng　gossip

说法　shuōfǎ　expound Buddhist teachings

说法　shuōfa　① way of saying a thing; wording; formulation: 换一个～ say it in another way / 这个意思可以有两种～。This idea can be formulated in two different ways. ② statement; version; argument: 那种～是不对的。That's a false statement. / 关于那件事, 各人～不同。Different people have different versions of the incident. / 这种～是完全正确的。This argument is very sound. / 照他的～去做。Do as he says.

说服　shuōfú　persuade; convince; prevail on; talk sb. over: 要耐心～他。Talk to him patiently to bring him round. / 她的话很有～力。What she says is very convincing. / 努力宣传, ～群众 carry on energetic propaganda to convince the masses / 用～教育的方法 by the method of persuasion and education

说好　shuōhǎo　come to an agreement or understanding: 我已经跟他～了, 明天一块去看足球赛。I've arranged to go with him to tomorrow's football match.

说好说歹　shuōhǎo-shuōdǎi　use every possible argument to convince sb.

说合　shuōhe　① bring two (or more) parties together: ～亲事 make a match ② talk over; discuss ③ same as 说和 shuōhe

说和　shuōhe　mediate a settlement; compose a quarrel: 你去给他们～～。Try to patch things up between them, will you?

说黑道白　shuōhēi-dàobái　criticize irresponsibly or thoughtlessly

说话[1]　shuōhuà　① speak; talk; say: 他不爱～。He doesn't like to talk. / 感动得说不出话来 be too moved

to say anything / 还是让事实来～吧。Let the facts speak for themselves. / ～算数 honour one's word; mean what one says / 我们～是算数的。What we say counts. / ～不算话 go back on one's word / 现在人民有了～的权利。Now the people have got the right to speak. ② chat; talk: 我找他～儿去。I'd like to have a chat with him. / 我们正说着话,他进来了。We were talking when he came in. ③ gossip; talk: 你这样干,别人当然要～。Considering what you've done, it's natural that people should be talking.

说话² shuōhuà *dial.* ① in a jiffy; in a minute; right away: ～就得。It'll be ready in a jiffy. ② word; talk: 他这句～很有道理。What he said was quite right. ③ a kind of storytelling popular in Tang and Song times

说黄道黑 shuōhuáng-dàohēi same as 数黑论黄 shǔhēi-lùnhuáng

说谎 shuōhuǎng tell a lie; lie

说教 shuōjiào ① deliver a sermon; preach ② preachify

说开 shuōkāi ① explain clearly: 你还是把事情的原委跟他～了,免得他猜疑。You'd better explain clearly to him how all this came about, so as not to leave him in doubt. ② (of words or expressions) be in current use: 这个词儿已经～了,大家都懂得。This word is in current use, and everybody understands it.

说客 shuōkè ① a person often sent to win sb. over or enlist his support through persuasion ② a persuasive talker

说来 shuōlái come to speak of it: ～都是老朋友。Come to speak of it, we are all old friends.

说来话长 shuōlái huà cháng it's a long story

说来说去 shuōlái-shuōqù repeat over and over again

说理 shuōlǐ ① argue; reason things out: 咱们找他～去。Let's go and reason things out with him. / 批评应该是充分～的。Criticism should be entirely reasonable. / 进行～斗争 wage a struggle by argument and reasoning ② (usu. used in the negative) listen to reason; be reasonable: 你这个人～不～? Won't you listen to reason? or How could you be so unreasonable?

说漏嘴 shuōlòuzuǐ let slip a remark; make a slip of the tongue: 我一句话说漏了嘴,把事情捅出去了。I made a slip of the tongue and gave the show away.

说媒 shuōméi act as matchmaker

说明 shuōmíng ① explain; illustrate: ～机器的用法 explain how a machine works / 举例～ illustrate by examples / ～理由 give reasons / ～真相 give the facts / 代表团认为有必要～自己的立场。The delegation deems it necessary to state its position. ② show; prove: 事实充分～这种做法是正确的。The results show clearly that this procedure is correct. ③ explanation; directions; caption: 图片下边附有～。There is a caption under the picture.

说明书 shuōmíngshū (a booklet of) directions; (technical) manual; synopsis (of a play or film)

说明文 shuōmíngwén expository writing; exposition

说破 shuōpò lay bare; reveal

说破嘴 shuōpòzuǐ talk till one is hoarse; talk oneself hoarse: 你～他也不会听你的。He won't listen to you even if you talk yourself hoarse.

说千道万 shuōqiān-dàowàn keep on stating one's point

说亲 shuōqīn act as matchmaker

说情 shuōqíng plead for mercy for sb.; intercede for sb.

说三道四 shuōsān-dàosì make irresponsible remarks

说啥 shuōshá *inf.* no matter what one says: ～他也不会同意的。No matter what you say to him, he won't agree. / ～她也不让我走,非要留我吃饭。She wouldn't let me go no matter what I said, and pressed me to stay for supper.

说时迟,那时快 shuō shí chí, nàshí kuài in the twinkling of an eye; in an instant

说是 shuōshì be said to; be supposed to; they say: 他有了女朋友了,～个大美人。He's got a girlfriend, and she is supposed to be quite a beauty. / ～留学生,可不知道他在哪儿留的学。He is said to have studied abroad, but I don't know what country he studied in.

说书 shuōshū storytelling

说死 shuōsǐ fix definitely; make it definite: 咱们～了,六点钟见面。Let's make it definite—we'll meet at 6 o'clock. / 咱们先别～吧。Let's leave the question open for the present.

说头儿 shuōtour ① something to talk about: 问题已经解决了,没什么～了。Now that the problem is solved, nothing remains to be said. ② excuse: 你批评他,他总有～。Whenever you criticize him, he always has an excuse.

说妥 shuōtuǒ come to an agreement

说戏 shuōxì (of a film or play director) explain (to one or more actors) how a part or a scene is to be acted

说闲话 shuō xiánhuà ① gossip; grumble: 有意见当面提,别在背后～。If you have any complaints, make them openly. Don't grumble behind our backs. ② chat: 她常上我家说个闲话什么的。She often drops in to have a chat.

说项 shuōxiàng put in a good word for sb.; intercede for sb.

说笑 shuōxiào chatting and laughing: 这时满屋子的人又说又笑,兴高采烈。The room was then full of people chatting animatedly and laughing.

说一不二 shuō yī bù èr mean what one says; stand by one's word: 老班长是～的,他答应的事一定能办到。The old squad leader is a man of his word; he never makes a promise he cannot keep.

说着玩儿 shuōzhewánr be joking; not be serious in saying sth.

说嘴 shuōzuǐ ① brag; boast: 咱们谁也别～。Let's not have any boasting. ② *dial.* argue; quarrel: 好跟人～ like to quarrel with people

shuò

妁 shuò see 媒妁 méishuò

烁(爍) shuò bright; shining: 闪烁 shǎnshuò

烁亮 shuòliàng dazzling; brilliant; resplendent: 电灯把大街照得～。The street was ablaze with lights.

烁烁 shuòshuò glitter; sparkle

铄¹(鑠) shuò *formal* ① melt (metal, etc.) ② waste away; weaken

铄²(鑠) shuò same as 烁 shuò

铄石流金 shuòshí-liújīn (hot enough to) make rocks and metals melt—sweltering

朔¹ shuò ① new moon ② the first day of the lunar month

朔² shuò north: ～方 the North / ～风 north wind

朔日 shuòrì the first day of the lunar month

朔望 shuò-wàng the first and the fifteenth day of the lunar month; syzygy

朔望月 shuòwàngyuè *meteorol.* lunar month; lunation; synodic month

朔月 shuòyuè new moon

硕 shuò large: ～大 very large

硕大无朋 shuòdà wú péng of enormous size; huge;

gigantic: 整个地球可以想像为一块～的磁石。The earth may be thought of as a gigantic magnet.

硕果 shuòguǒ rich fruits; great achievements: ～累累 numerous significant achievements / 多年的辛劳结出了～。Years of painstaking work brought great successes.

硕果仅存 shuòguǒ jǐn cún the sole rare survival

硕士 shuòshì Master: ～学位 Master's degree

硕学 shuòxué *formal* ① learned; erudite ② a learned scholar; an erudite person

硕学通儒 shuòxué tōngrú a wise and learned scholar

硕壮 shuòzhuàng big and strong; robust; full-grown: 他身体～。He's of strong build. / ～的果实 rich, full-grown fruits

数(數) shuò frequently; repeatedly ——see also shǔ; shù

数见不鲜 shuò jiàn bù xiān be a common occurrence; be nothing new

数脉 shuòmài *Chin. med.* rapid pulse (of more than 90 beats per minute)

蒴 shuò capsule: 芝麻～ sesame capsule

蒴果 shuòguǒ *bot.* capsule

搠 shuò thrust; stab

槊 shuò a spear-like ancient weapon

SĪ

司 sī ① take charge of; attend to; manage: 各～其事。Each attends to his own duties. / 各种组织要各～其职。Let each of the various organizations perform its own functions. ② department (under a ministry): 外交部礼宾～ the Protocol Department of the Ministry of Foreign Affairs ③ (Sī) a surname

司泵员 sībèngyuán pump man; pumper

司晨 sīchén *formal* herald the break of day

司铎 sīduó another name for 神甫 shénfu

司舵 sīduò ① be at the helm; steer a boat ② helmsman; steersman

司法 sīfǎ administration of justice; judicature

司法部门 sīfǎ bùmén judicial department; judiciary

司法机关 sīfǎ jīguān judicial organ

司法鉴定 sīfǎ jiàndìng expert testimony (*or* evidence)

司法权 sīfǎquán judicial powers

司号 sīhào *mil.* ① sound a bugle ② bugler; trumpeter

司号员 sīhàoyuán *mil.* bugler; trumpeter

司阍 sīhūn *formal* gatekeeper; janitor

司机 sījī driver; chauffeur: 火车～ engine driver; locomotive engineer

司空 sīkōng ① Minister of Works in ancient China ② (Sīkōng) a two-character surname

司空见惯 sīkōng jiàn guàn a common sight; a common occurrence: 在旧中国，穷人饿死街头是～的事情。People dying of hunger on the streets was a common sight in old China.

司寇 Sīkòu a two-character surname

司令 sīlìng commander; commanding officer

司令部 sīlìngbù headquarters; command

司令台 sīlìngtái review stand

司令员 sīlìngyuán commander; commanding officer

司炉 sīlú stoker; fireman

司马 sīmǎ ① Minister of War in ancient China ② (Sīmǎ) a two-character surname

司马昭之心，路人皆知 Sīmǎ Zhāo zhī xīn, lùrén jiē zhī Sima Zhao's ill intent is known to all—the villain's design is obvious

司事 sīshì *old* office clerk

司书 sīshū *old* copyist; clerk

司徒 sītú ① Minister of Education in ancient China ② (Sītú) a two-character surname

司务 sīwù ① a petty official in charge of miscellaneous duties (in Ming and Qing times) ② craftsman; workman: 厨～ cook

司务长 sīwùzhǎng ① mess officer ② company quartermaster

司线员 sīxiànyuán *sports* linesman

司药 sīyào pharmacist; druggist; chemist

司仪 sīyí master of ceremonies

司帐 sīzhàng *old* accountant

司钻 sīzuàn (head) driller: 副～ assistant driller

丝(絲) sī ① silk ② a threadlike thing: 蜘蛛～ a thread spun by a spider; cobweb / 铜～ copper wire / 把土豆切成细～儿 cut the potatoes into fine shreds; shred the potatoes ③ *m.* a thread or shred of: 一～亮光 a thread of light / 这盘菜里一～儿肉也见不着。Not a single shred of meat can you find in this dish. ④ one ten-thousandth of certain units of measure: 丝米 sīmǐ ⑤ si, a unit of length, also a unit of weight, equal to 0.1 hao (毫) or 0.01 li (厘) or 0.001 fen (分) ⑥ a tiny bit; trace: 一～不差 not a bit of difference / 她脸上没有一～笑容。There isn't a trace of a smile on her face. / 一～风也没有。There isn't a breath of air.

丝虫 sīchóng filaria (a parasitic worm)

丝虫病 sīchóngbìng filariasis

丝绸 sīchóu silk cloth; silk

丝绸之路 sīchóu zhī lù *hist.* the Silk Road

丝带 sīdài silk ribbon; silk braid; silk sash

丝杠 sīgàng *mech.* guide screw; leading screw

丝杠车床 sīgàng chēchuáng leading screw lathe

丝糕 sīgāo steamed millet or corn cake

丝瓜 sīguā towel gourd; dishcloth gourd

丝瓜络 sīguāluò loofah; vegetable sponge

丝光 sīguāng the silky lustre of mercerized cotton fabrics

丝光机 sīguāngjī mercerizing range

丝光纱线 sīguāng shāxiàn mercerized yarn

丝毫 sīháo (usu. used in the negative) the slightest amount or degree; a bit; a particle; a shred; an iota: 我们～也不应当松懈自己的斗志。We must not, in the slightest degree, weaken our will to fight. / 拿不出～证据 cannot provide a shred of evidence / ～不差 not err by a hair's breadth; tally in every detail; be just right

丝极 sījí *electron.* filament

丝萝 sīluó *liter.* the bond of marriage: 永结～ seal an everlasting bond of marriage

丝米 sīmǐ one ten-thousandth of a metre; 0.01 centimetre; 0.1 millimetre

丝绵 sīmián silk floss; silk wadding

丝绒 sīróng velvet; velour

丝丝入扣 sī sī rù kòu (mostly of a writing or artistic performance) (done) with meticulous care and flawless artistry

丝丝拉拉 sīsilālā off and on; intermittently: 小雨～地下了几天。It has been drizzling off and on for days.

丝袜 sīwà silk stockings or socks

丝网 sīwǎng *print.* silk screen

丝网印刷 sīwǎng yìnshuā screen printing

丝网印刷机 sīwǎng yìnshuājī screen process press

丝弦 sīxián ① silk string (for a musical instrument) ② a Hebei provincial opera

丝线　sīxiàn　silk thread (for sewing, embroidery, etc.); silk yarn

丝织品　sīzhīpǐn　① silk fabrics ② silk knit goods

丝竹　sīzhú　① traditional stringed and woodwind instruments: ～乐 *ensemble* of such instruments ② music

丝状　sīzhuàng　filiform

丝锥　sīzhuī　*mech.* tap: 粗制～ taper tap ／ 中～ second tap ／ 精～ bottoming tap

私　sī　① personal; private: ～信 personal (*or* private) letter ② selfish: 无私 wúsī ③ secret; private: ～话 confidential talk ④ illicit; illegal: ～卖违禁品 illicit sale of contraband goods

私奔　sībēn　elope

私弊　sībì　corrupt practices

私藏　sīcáng　① a private collection ② keep or possess illegally: ～枪支 possess firearms illegally

私产　sīchǎn　private property

私娼　sīchāng　unlicensed (*or* unregistered) prostitute

私仇　sīchóu　personal enmity (*or* grudge): 报～ satisfy a personal grudge

私党　sīdǎng　a personal clique or faction

私德　sīdé　private morality (concerned with individual perfection); personal morals

私觌　sīdí　*formal* have a private audience with sb.; meet each other privately

私邸　sīdǐ　private residence (of a high-ranking official)

私底下　sīdǐxia　in private; in secret

私法　sīfǎ　*leg.* private law

私贩　sīfàn　smuggle; traffic in contraband goods

私房　sīfáng　a privately owned house or building; private residence

私房　sīfang　① private savings: ～钱 private savings of a family member ② confidential: 谈～话 exchange confidences

私访　sīfǎng　(of officials) go incognito among the people to make investigations

私愤　sīfèn　personal spite: 泄～ vent personal spite

私股　sīgǔ　private shares (in a joint state-private enterprise)

私馆　sīguǎn　old-style private school: 教过～ taught at an old-style private school ／ 读过两年～ had a couple of years' schooling at an old-style private school

私孩子　sīháizi　*inf.* a child born out of wedlock; illegitimate child

私货　sīhuò　smuggled goods; contraband goods

私家　sījiā　privately owned or engaged: ～车 private car ／ ～车道 drive; driveway ／ ～侦探 private detective; private investigator

私见　sījiàn　① personal prejudice ② personal opinion

私交　sījiāo　personal friendship

私窠子　sīkēzi　old another name for 私窝子 sīwōzi

私立　sīlì　privately run; private: ～学校 private school

私利　sīlì　private (*or* selfish) interests; personal gain: 图～ pursue private ends; seek personal gain ／ 不谋～ seek no personal gain

私了　sīliǎo　settle privately; settle out of court: 这事你看是～还是公了? Would you prefer to settle the matter in court or out of court?

私囊　sīnáng　private purse: 饱～ line one's pockets; feather one's nest

私念　sīniàn　selfish motives (*or* ideas)

私情　sīqíng　personal relationships: 不徇～ not swayed by personal considerations

私人　sīrén　① private; personal: ～访问 private visit ／ ～关系 personal relations; personal connections ② one's own man: 任用～ fill a post with one's own man; practise nepotism

私人代表　sīrén dàibiǎo　personal representative

私人经济　sīrén jīngjì　private sector of the economy

私人劳动　sīrén láodòng　*econ.* individual labour

私人秘书　sīrén mìshū　private secretary

私人企业　sīrén qǐyè　private enterprise

私商　sīshāng　① privately owned shop ② businessman; merchant; trader

私设公堂　sī shè gōngtáng　set up an illegal court; set up a kangaroo court

私生活　sīshēnghuó　private life: 别打听别人的～。Don't pry into the private life of others.

私生子　sīshēngzǐ　a child born out of wedlock; illegitimate child

私事　sīshì　private (*or* personal) affairs

私塾　sīshú　old-style private school

私逃　sītáo　abscond

私通　sītōng　① have secret communication with: ～敌人 have secret communication with the enemy ② have illicit intercourse; commit adultery

私图　sītú　one's personal scheme or attempt

私窝子　sīwōzi　old unlicensed (*or* unregistered) prostitute

私下　sīxià　(also 私下里 sīxiàli) in private; in secret: ～商议 discuss a matter in private

私相授受　sī xiāng shòu-shòu　privately give and privately accept; illegally pass things between individuals; make an illicit transfer: 拿公家的东西～ illicit transfer of public property

私心　sīxīn　selfish motives (*or* ideas); selfishness

私心杂念　sīxīn-zániàn　selfish ideas and personal considerations; selfish considerations

私刑　sīxíng　illegal punishment (meted out by a kangaroo court); lynching

私行　sīxíng　do sth. in a private capacity or on one's own initiative: ～释放 set sb. free without official sanction

私蓄　sīxù　personal or private savings

私营　sīyíng　privately owned; privately run (*or* operated); private: ～工商业 privately owned industrial and commercial enterprises ／ ～企业 private enterprise ／ ～经济 the private sector of the economy

私有　sīyǒu　privately owned; private: 绝不能把公家财产占为～。One should never make public property one's private possession.

私有财产　sīyǒu cáichǎn　private property

私有观念　sīyǒu guānniàn　private ownership mentality

私有化　sīyǒuhuà　privatization; denationalization

私有制　sīyǒuzhì　private ownership (of means of production)

私语　sīyǔ　① whisper: 窃窃私语 qièqiè sīyǔ ② confidence

私欲　sīyù　selfish desire

私运　sīyùn　smuggle: ～毒品 smuggle drugs

私章　sīzhāng　personal seal; signet

私自　sīzì　privately; secretly; without permission: 本阅览室参考书不得～携出。No reference books are to be taken out of the reading room without permission.

咝（嘶）　sī　*onom.* (the sound of flying shells and bullets) whistle: 子弹～～～地从头顶上飞过。Bullets whistled overhead.

思　sī　① think; consider; deliberate: 多～ think more ② think of; long for: ～亲 think of one's parents with affection ③ thought; thinking: 文思 wénsī ／ 哀思 āisī

思潮　sīcháo　① trend of thought; ideological trend: 无政府主义～ the anarchist trend of thought ／ 文艺～ trends of thought in art and literature ② thoughts: ～

起伏 disquieting thoughts surging in one's mind

思忖 sīcǔn *formal* ponder; consider

思凡 sīfán (of an immortal or of a monk or a nun) long for the world; yearn for the company of the opposite sex

思过 sīguò ponder over one's mistakes; make an introspection into one's faults

思旧 sījiù think fondly of past times or old acquaintances

思考 sīkǎo think deeply; ponder over; reflect on: ～问题 ponder a problem / 独立～ think things out for oneself; think independently

思恋 sīliàn think fondly of; long for: ～故土 think fondly of one's native land

思量 sīliang ① consider: 反复～ turn sth. over and over in one's mind ② *dial.* miss; be concerned about; keep thinking about: 大家好～你啊! How we all miss you!

思路 sīlù train of thought; thinking: 打断～ interrupt one's train of thought / 她的～很清楚。She thinks very clearly.

思虑 sīlǜ consider; contemplate; deliberate: 他～周到。He considers everything carefully.

思摸 sīmo *inf.* think; consider: 我～了好久，觉得这事你去办最好。I've thought about it for a long time, and decided that you are the right person for the job.

思谋 sīmóu *dial.* think; consider

思慕 sīmù think of sb. with respect; admire

思念 sīniàn think of; long for; miss: ～战友 long for one's comrades-in-arms

思如泉涌 sī rú quán yǒng ideas teeming in one's mind

思索 sīsuǒ think deeply; ponder: 用心～ do some hard thinking / 周密地～ consider carefully / 我一夜没睡着，反复～这个问题。I lay awake all night, turning the problem over and over in my mind.

思维 sīwéi ① thought; thinking: ～方式 mode of thinking ② think; consider: 再三～ think over and over again

思惟 sīwéi same as 思维 sīwéi

思贤若渴 sī xián ruò kě (of a ruler) thirst for (or long for) the assistance of wise men

思乡 sīxiāng be homesick

思想 sīxiǎng thought; thinking; idea; ideology: 军事～ military thinking / 无产阶级～ proletarian ideology / 搞通～ straighten out one's thinking / ～见面 have a frank exchange of ideas / ～交锋 a confrontation of ideas / ～自由 freedom of thought / 有～准备 be mentally prepared / ～内容好 have good ideological content / 解除～顾虑 free one's mind of misgivings / ～跟不上 lag behind in one's understanding

思想包袱 sīxiǎng bāofu sth. weighing on one's mind

思想动向 sīxiǎng dòngxiàng ideological trend

思想斗争 sīxiǎng dòuzhēng ideological struggle; mental struggle (or conflict)

思想方法 sīxiǎng fāngfǎ method (or mode, way) of thinking

思想改造 sīxiǎng gǎizào ideological remoulding

思想工作 sīxiǎng gōngzuò ideological work

思想家 sīxiǎngjiā thinker

思想检查 sīxiǎng jiǎnchá check on one's thinking; examine one's wrong ideas

思想教育 sīxiǎng jiàoyù ideological education

思想境界 sīxiǎng jìngjiè ideological level

思想觉悟 sīxiǎng juéwù political consciousness (or awareness)

思想体系 sīxiǎng tǐxì ideological system; ideology

思想问题 sīxiǎng wèntí a problem arising from erroneous thinking; ideological problem

思想性 sīxiǎngxìng ideological content (or level)

思想意识 sīxiǎng yìshí ideology

思想作风 sīxiǎng zuòfēng one's way of thinking, workstyle, and life-style

思绪 sīxù ① train of thought; thinking: ～纷乱 a confused state of mind; a confused train of thought ② feeling: ～不宁 feel perturbed

思议 sīyì conceive; think; imagine: 不可思议 bùkě sīyì

鸶(鷥) sī see 鹭鸶 lùsī

螄(螄) sī see 螺螄 luósī

斯 sī ① *formal* this: ～时 at this moment / ～人 this person / 余生于～，长于～。I was born and brought up here. ② *formal* then; thus ③ (Sī) a surname

斯堪的纳维亚半岛 Sīkāndìnàwéiyà Bàndǎo the Scandinavian Peninsula

斯拉夫人 Sīlāfūrén Slav

斯里兰卡 Sīlǐlánkǎ Sri Lanka

斯里兰卡人 Sīlǐlánkǎrén Sri Lankan

斯洛伐克 Sīluòfákè Slovakia

斯洛伐克人 Sīluòfákèrén Slovak; Slovakian

斯洛伐克语 Sīluòfákèyǔ Slovak (language)

斯瓦希里语 Sīwǎxīlǐyǔ Swahili (language)

斯威士兰 Sīwēishìlán Swaziland

斯威士兰人 Sīwēishìlánrén Swazi

斯文 sīwén *formal* ① culture ② men of letters; scholars; literati

斯文 sīwen refined; gentle: 他说话挺～的。He's a soft-spoken person.

斯文败类 sīwén bàilèi scum of the literati

斯文扫地 sīwén sǎodì scholarly dignity swept into the dust

斯须 sīxū *formal* a little while; a moment

锶 sī *chem.* strontium (Sr)

澌 sī *formal* floating ice; (ice) floe

厮¹(廝) sī *old* ① male servant: 小厮 xiǎosī ② fellow; guy: 那～ that guy

厮²(廝) sī with each other; together: 厮混 sīhùn

厮缠 sīchán pester: 孩子～住他爸妈要买个机器人。The boy kept pestering his parents for a toy robot.

厮打 sīdǎ wrestle; grapple; tussle

厮混 sīhùn fool around (or about) with sb.; play around (or about) with sb.: 他整天和一些不三不四的人～。He fools around all the time with some rather dubious fellows.

厮杀 sīshā fight at close quarters (with weapons)

澌 sī *formal* drain dry; drain completely

澌灭 sīmiè *formal* totally disappear

撕 sī tear; rip: 把信～开 rip open a letter / ～得粉碎 tear to shreds / 从日历上～下一页 tear a page from the calendar / ～下假面具 tear off the mask; unmask / 上衣～了。The jacket is torn.

撕毁 sīhuǐ tear up; tear to shreds: ～手稿 tear up the manuscript / ～协定 (条约) tear up an agreement (a treaty); tear an agreement (a treaty) to shreds

撕票 sīpiào (of kidnappers) kill the hostage

撕破 sīpò tear; rip: 这种料子容易～。This material tears easily. / 衬衫～了。The shirt is torn.

撕破脸 sīpòliǎn put aside all considerations of face; not spare sb.'s sensibilities

嘶¹ sī *formal* ① neigh: 人喊马～ men shouting and horses neighing ② hoarse: 声嘶力竭 shēngsī-lìjié

嘶² sī same as 咝 sī

嘶喊 sīhǎn shout; yell

嘶叫 sījiào ① shout; yell; scream: 她吓得尖声～起来。 She shrieked (*or* screamed) with terror. ② (of horses) neigh; whinny; (of donkeys) bray

嘶鸣 sīmíng (of horses, donkeys, etc.) neigh; whinny; bray: 战马～。 The war-horses neighed.

嘶哑 sīyǎ hoarse: 他讲话过多, 嗓子都～了。 He has talked himself hoarse.

sǐ

死 sǐ ① die; be dead: 这棵树～了。 This tree is dead. / 他因病～于北京。 He died of illness in Beijing. / 那条金鱼快～了。 The goldfish is dying. / 这次车祸～了五人。 The accident took five people's lives. / ～一般的寂静 a deathly stillness / 被打～ be beaten to death / 我差点没笑～。 I just about died laughing. ② to the death: 死战 sǐzhàn ③ *adv.* extremely; to death: 高兴～了 be extremely happy / 累～了 be tired to death; be dog-tired / 渴得要～ be parched with thirst; be dying for a drink / ～咸～咸 terribly salty / ～沉～沉 awfully heavy / ～顽固 diehard ④ implacable; deadly: 死对头 sǐduìtou ⑤ fixed; rigid; inflexible: ～规矩 a rigid rule / ～教条 lifeless dogma ⑥ impassable; closed: 把漏洞堵～ plug the holes; stop up loopholes / 窗户钉～了。 The window has been nailed fast. ⑦ (used before verbs in the negative) stubbornly; adamantly; unyieldingly: ～不认错 stubbornly refuse to admit one's mistake / ～不放手 cling (*or* hold on, hang on) to sth. like grim death / ～不改悔 be absolutely unrepentant; be incorrigible / ～不要脸 be dead to all feelings of shame; be utterly shameless

死板 sǐbǎn rigid; stiff; inflexible: 动作～ stiff movements / 表情～ an expressionless face / 办事～ work in a mechanical way / ～的公式 stereotyped formula

死别 sǐbié be parted by death; part forever

死不瞑目 sǐ bù míngmù not close one's eyes when one dies—die with a grievance or everlasting regret; die discontent

死产 sǐchǎn *med.* stillbirth

死沉 sǐchén silent as the grave; still as death: 战地一片～的气氛。 A deathlike silence reigned over the battlefield.

死沉沉 sǐchénchén ① heavy as lead; extremely heavy ② silent as the grave; still as death ③ glum; sullen; gloomy: 脸色～的 look glum; put on a sullen countenance

死党 sǐdǎng sworn followers; diehard followers

死当 sǐdàng an overdue and unredeemable pawn

死得其所 sǐ dé qí suǒ die a worthy death: 我们为人民而死, 就是～。 When we die for the people it is a worthy death.

死等 sǐděng wait indefinitely: 我们不能在这里～, 应该派人去打听一下, 看出了什么事。 We can't wait here indefinitely. We should send someone to find out what's happened.

死敌 sǐdí deadly enemy; mortal enemy; implacable foe

死地 sǐdì a fatal position; deathtrap

死读书 sǐ dúshū study mechanically; rely on book learning rather than practical experience; be bookish

死对头 sǐduìtou deadly enemy; irreconcilable opponent

死而后已 sǐ érhòu yǐ until one's dying day; to the end of one's days —— see also 鞠躬尽瘁, 死而后已 jūgōng jìn cuì, sǐ érhòu yǐ

死工夫 sǐgōngfu hard persevering work; sheer hard work: 你想通过考试, 不下～是不行的。 You won't pass the exam unless you put in some real hard work.

死光 sǐguāng death ray

死鬼 sǐguǐ (usu. used in cursing or jocularly) devil: 你这个～, 刚才跑到哪儿去了? You devil! Where have you been all this while?

死海 Sǐhǎi the Dead Sea

死耗 sǐhào news of sb.'s death

死胡同 sǐhútòng blind alley; dead end

死缓 sǐhuǎn *leg.* (short for 判处死刑、缓期二年执行) death sentence with a two-year reprieve and forced labour; stay of execution

死灰 sǐhuī cold ashes (of an extinguished fire); dead ashes; burnt-out cinders

死灰复燃 sǐhuī fù rán *derog.* dying cinders glowing again—resurgence; revival

死活 sǐhuó ① life or death; fate: 不顾人民～的政府早晚要被人民推翻。 A government which doesn't give a thought to the welfare of the people will sooner or later be overthrown. ② *adv. inf.* anyway; simply: 他～不让我走。 I wanted to go, but he simply wouldn't hear of it.

死火山 sǐhuǒshān extinct volcano

死记 sǐjì memorize mechanically; learn by rote; learn without comprehension

死记硬背 sǐjì-yìngbèi memorize mechanically; learn by rote; learn without comprehension

死忌 sǐjì death anniversary

死寂 sǐjì *formal* deathly stillness: 夜深了, 山谷里一片～。 As night wore on, a deathly silence filled the valley.

死角 sǐjiǎo ① *mil.* dead angle; dead space ② a spot as yet untouched by a trend, political movement, etc.

死节 sǐjié *formal* die for the sake of honour; die to preserve one's moral or political integrity

死结 sǐjié a fast knot

死劲儿 sǐjìnr *inf.* ① all one's strength; all one's might: 大家用～推, 才把车子推出泥坑。 Using all their strength, they pushed the cart out of the mud. ② with all one's strength (*or* might); with might and main; for all one's worth: ～跑 run for all one's worth / ～盯住他 watch him closely

死静 sǐjìng deathly silent; deathly still

死扣儿 sǐkòur *inf.* a fast knot

死拉活拽 sǐlā-huózhuài drag sb. along against his will; drag by force

死老虎 sǐlǎohǔ a dead tiger—a man who has lost his power and influence

死里逃生 sǐlǐ táoshēng escape by the skin of one's teeth; have a narrow escape; barely escape with one's life

死力 sǐlì ① all one's strength: 出～ exert one's utmost effort ② with all one's strength: ～抵抗 resist with might and main; fight tooth and nail

死路 sǐlù ① blind alley ② the road to ruin (*or* destruction)

死马当做活马医 sǐmǎ dàngzuò huómǎ yī doctor a dead horse as if it were still alive—make every possible effort; not give up for lost

死面 sǐmiàn unleavened dough

死命 sǐmìng ① doom; death: 制敌于～ send the enemy to his doom; have the enemy by the throat ② desperately: ～挣扎 struggle desperately

死难 sǐnàn die in an accident or a political incident (esp. for a revolutionary cause): ～烈士 martyr

死脑筋 sǐnǎojīn one-track mind

死皮赖脸 sǐpí-làiliǎn thick-skinned and hard to shake off; brazen and unreasonable

死棋 sǐqí ① a dead piece in a game of chess ② a hopeless case; a stupid move

死气沉沉 sǐqì chénchén lifeless; spiritless; stagnant

死气白赖 sǐqìbáilài *dial.* pestering people endlessly

死契 sǐqì an irrevocable title deed

死囚 sǐqiú a convict sentenced to death; a convict awaiting execution

死球 sǐqiú *sports* dead ball

死去活来 sǐqù-huólái half dead; only half alive; hovering between life and death: 被打得～ be beaten half dead; be beaten within an inch of one's life; be brutally beaten／哭得～ cry oneself half dead; cry one's heart (or eyes) out

死伤 sǐ-shāng the dead and the wounded; casualties

死神 sǐshén Death (personified)

死生有命, 富贵在天 sǐ-shēng yǒu mìng, fùguì zài tiān life and death are a matter of Destiny; wealth and honour depend on Heaven

死尸 sǐshī corpse; dead body

死守 sǐshǒu ① defend to the death; defend to the last; make a last-ditch defence: ～阵地 defend the position to the last ② obstinately cling to; rigidly adhere to

死水 sǐshuǐ stagnant water

死说活说 sǐshuō-huóshuō beg and beg; try every means to persuade: 我～也没说动她的心。In spite of all my persuasions, she remained unmoved.

死塌塌 sǐtātā wooden; expressionless

死胎 sǐtāi *med.* stillborn foetus; stillbirth

死土 sǐtǔ *agric.* dead soil

死亡 sǐwáng death; doom: 挣扎在～线上 struggle for existence on the verge of death／把病人从～边缘抢救过来 snatch the patient from the jaws of death／殖民主义正走向～。Colonialism is heading for its doom.

死亡率 sǐwánglǜ death rate; mortality

死无对证 sǐ wú duìzhèng be totally devoid of evidence (because of the death of the principal witness, etc.); the witness, if any, is dead; dead men tell no tales

死无葬身之地 sǐwú zàngshēn zhī dì die without a place for burial—come to a bad end

死心 sǐxīn drop the idea forever; have no more illusions about the matter: 你还是死了这条心吧。You'd better give up the idea altogether.

死心塌地 sǐxīntādì be dead set; be hell-bent: ～跟他走的只是一小撮。Only a handful of people were dead set on following him.／～的反革命分子 a die-hard counterrevolutionary／～的奴才 a dyed-in-the-wool lackey

死心眼儿 sǐxīnyǎnr ① stubborn; as obstinate as a mule ② a person with a one-track mind

死信[1] sǐxìn dead letter

死信[2] sǐxìn news of sb.'s death

死刑 sǐxíng *leg.* death penalty; death sentence; capital punishment

死讯 sǐxùn news of sb.'s death

死因 sǐyīn cause of death: 查明他的～ find out the cause of his death

死硬 sǐyìng ① stiff; inflexible ② very obstinate; die-hard

死硬派 sǐyìngpài diehards

死有余辜 sǐ yǒu yú gū (used when denouncing a person guilty of the most heinous of crimes) even death would be too good for him; even death would not expiate all his crimes

死于非命 sǐ yú fēimìng die an unnatural (or a violent) death: 他遭敌人杀害, ～。He died a violent death, murdered by an enemy.

死战 sǐzhàn ① a life-and-death struggle or battle ② fight to the death

死仗 sǐzhàng a tough (or hard-fought) battle

死者 sǐzhě the dead; the deceased; the departed

死症 sǐzhèng an incurable disease

死罪 sǐzuì capital offence (or crime)

sì

巳（巳） sì the sixth of the twelve Earthly Branches (地支)——see also 干支 gān-zhī

巳时 sìshí the period of the day from 9 a.m. to 11 a.m.

四[1] sì four

四[2] sì *mus.* a note of the scale in *gongchepu* (工尺谱), corresponding to 6 in numbered musical notation

四倍体 sìbèitǐ *biol.* tetraploid

四边 sìbiān (on) four sides: ～儿围着篱笆 with a fence running all round

四边形 sìbiānxíng quadrilateral

四不像 sìbùxiàng ① *zool.* David's deer; mi-lu ② nondescript; neither fish nor fowl

四部 sìbù the four bibliographic categories—the four traditional divisions of a Chinese library (i.e. 经史子集 jīng-shǐ-zǐ-jí)

四重唱 sìchóngchàng *mus.* (vocal) quartet

四重奏 sìchóngzòu *mus.* (instrumental) quartet: 弦乐～ string quartet

四出 sìchū go hither and thither; go from place to place; go around: ～寻求资助 go around seeking financial support

四处 sìchù all around; in all directions; everywhere: ～逃窜 flee in all directions／～奔走 go hither and thither／～寻找 search high and low; look into every hole and corner

四川 Sìchuān Sichuan (Province)

四川清音 Sìchuān qīngyīn Sichuan ballad-singing

四大 sìdà (in Buddhism) the four elements—earth, water, fire, and wind

四大皆空 sìdà jiē kōng *Buddhism* the sensuous world is illusory; all physical existence is vanity

四大金刚 Sì Dà Jīngāng the Four Diamond Kings (same as 四大天王 Sì Dà Tiānwáng)

四大名旦 sì dà míng dàn the four great *dan* actors (i.e. Mei Lanfang 梅兰芳, Cheng Yanqiu 程砚秋, Xun Huisheng 荀慧生, and Shang Xiaoyun 尚小云)

四大天王 Sì Dà Tiānwáng the Four Heavenly Kings or Four Lokapālas (fierce-looking heavenly guardians whose gigantic statues stand inside the entrance of Buddhist temples, two on each side)

四叠体 sìdiétǐ *physiol.* corpora quadrigemina

四方[1] sìfāng the four directions (north, south, east, west); all sides; all quarters: ～响应。Response came from every quarter.

四方[2] sìfāng square; cubic: 一个～的盒子 a square box／一块四四方方的木头 a wooden cube

四方步 sìfāngbù leisurely and measured steps

四分五裂 sìfēn-wǔliè fall apart; be rent by disunity; be all split up; disintegrate: 内部～。The ranks are all split up (or disintegrating).

四分音符 sìfēn yīnfú *mus.* crotchet; quarter note

四伏 sìfú lurk on every side: 危机四伏 wēijī sìfú

四个现代化 sìgè xiàndàihuà the Four Modernizations (i.e. of industry, agriculture, defence, and science and technology)

四顾 sìgù look around (or about): ～无人 look around and find no one in sight

四国 Sìguó Shikoku

四海 sìhǎi the four seas; the whole country; the whole world

四海升平 sìhǎi shēngpíng peace in the world

四海为家 sìhǎi wéi jiā make one's home wherever one is: 到处流浪，～ wander from place to place, making one's home wherever one happens to be

四海之内皆兄弟 sìhǎi zhī nèi jiē xiōngdì within the four seas all men are brothers

四害 sìhài the four pests (i.e. rats, bedbugs, flies and mosquitoes)

四合房 sìhéfáng same as 四合院儿 sìhéyuànr

四合院儿 sìhéyuànr siheyuanr, a compound with houses around a square courtyard; quadrangle

四呼 sìhū phonet. the four classes of syllables (set up according to the form of the final 韵母; i.e. 开口呼 kāikǒuhū, 齐齿呼 qíchǐhū, 合口呼 hékǒuhū, and 撮口呼 cuōkǒuhū)

四胡 sìhú mus. sihu, a four-stringed bowed instrument

四化 sìhuà short for 四个现代化 sìgè xiàndàihuà

四环素 sìhuánsù pharm. tetracycline

四级风 sìjífēng meteorol. force 4 wind; moderate breeze

四极管 sìjíguǎn radio tetrode

四季 sìjì the four seasons: 昆明～如春。In Kunming it's like spring all the year round.

四季豆 sìjìdòu another name for 菜豆 càidòu

四郊 sìjiāo suburbs; outskirts

四郊多垒 sìjiāo duō lěi enemy forces closing in from all sides

四角号码 sìjiǎo hàomǎ the four-corner system (a system of classifying Chinese characters which assigns numbers to ten different stroke types and thus makes it possible to derive a four-digit number from the stroke types found in the four corners of each character)

四脚八叉 sì jiǎo bā chā (lie) sprawling

四脚朝天 sì jiǎo cháo tiān (fall) on one's back

四脚蛇 sìjiǎoshé popular name for 蜥蜴 xīyì

四近 sìjìn neighbourhood; vicinity

四旧 sìjiù the "four olds" (i.e. old ideas, old culture, old customs and old habits, used during the Cultural Revolution 1966–1976)

四开 sìkāi print. quarto

四开本 sìkāiběn quarto

四库 sìkù same as 四部 sìbù: 《～全书》Complete Library in Four Divisions or Complete Collection in Four Treasuries

四类分子 sìlèifènzǐ ① the four kinds of elements (landlords, rich peasants, counterrevolutionaries and bad elements) ② a person belonging to one of the above categories

四邻 sìlín one's near neighbours

四邻八舍 sìlín-bāshè all the neighbours; the neighbours all around

四六风 sìliùfēng med. umbilical tetanus of newborn babies (frequently occurring on the 4th to 6th day after birth)

四六体 sìliùtǐ the four-six style (a style of parallel prose 骈体, characterized by a preponderance of pairs of four- and six-character sentences)

四六文 sìliùwén four-six prose (a type of parallel prose 骈文; so called because a four-six composition was made up of four-character and six-character couplets preceding or following each other, or of one four-character sentence following another six-character sentence or vice versa)

四面 sìmiàn (on) four sides; (on) all sides: ～包围敌人 completely encircle the enemy forces

四面八方 sìmiàn-bāfāng all directions; all quarters; all around; far and near: 治河大军从～向工地。Hosts of river control workers rushed to the site from all directions.

四面出击 sìmiàn chūjī hit out in all directions

四面楚歌 sìmiàn Chǔ gē be besieged on all sides; be utterly isolated; be in desperate straits; find oneself under fire from all quarters

四面受敌 sìmiàn shòu dí be exposed to enemy attacks on all sides

四拇指 sìmuzhǐ dial. the third finger; the ring finger

四旁 sìpáng ① back and front, left and right; all around ② the "four sides" (i.e. house side, village side, roadside and waterside): ～绿化 turning the "four sides" green (as part of an afforestation campaign)

四平八稳 sìpíng-bāwěn ① very steady; well balanced: 文章写得～。It's a well-balanced piece of writing. ② overcautious and lacking in initiative: 办事～ be on the safe side in doing things; play safe

四起 sìqǐ rise from all directions: 歌声～。Sounds of singing were heard from all around. / 掌声～。Applause broke out all around.

四清运动 Sìqīng Yùndòng the "Four Clean-ups" Movement (a nationwide movement to "clean things up in the fields of politics, economy, organization and ideology", 1963–1966)

四人帮 Sìrénbāng the Gang of Four

四散 sìsàn scatter (or disperse) in all directions

四舍五入 sìshě-wǔrù math. round up or down; round off

四声 sìshēng ① the four tones of classical Chinese pronunciation (i.e. 平声 píngshēng, 上声 shàngshēng, 去声 qùshēng, and 入声 rùshēng) ② the four tones of modern standard Chinese pronunciation (i.e. 阴平 yīnpíng "ˉ", 阳平 yángpíng "ˊ", 上声 shǎngshēng "ˇ", and 去声 qùshēng "ˋ")

四时 sìshí the four seasons: ～鲜果 fresh fruits of every season

四时八节 sìshí-bājié the four seasons and the eight periods—throughout the year (the eight periods here referring to the eight solar periods Beginning of Spring 立春, Beginning of Summer 立夏, Beginning of Autumn 立秋, Beginning of Winter 立冬, Spring Equinox 春分, Autumn Equinox 秋分, Summer Solstice 夏至, and Winter Solstice 冬至): ～好风光, 不亚瀛洲仙景象。(《西游记》) A splendid scene in all four seasons, As good as the immortal Isle Yingzhou.

四书 Sì Shū the Four Books, namely, The Great Learning 《大学》, The Doctrine of the Mean 《中庸》, The Analects of Confucius 《论语》, and The Mencius 《孟子》

四体 sìtǐ formal the four limbs (of man); arms and legs

四体不勤，五谷不分 sìtǐ bù qín, wǔgǔ bù fēn can neither toil with one's four limbs nor tell the five cereals apart

四体书 sìtǐshū the four scripts (i.e. the regular script 正, the cursive script 草, the official script 隶, and the seal character 篆)

四通八达 sìtōng-bādá extend in all directions: 公路～。Highways radiate in all directions. / 全省交通运输～。Transport and communication lines link up all parts of the province.

四外 sìwài all around (esp. in the open): ～无人。Not a soul was to be seen all around.

四围 sìwéi on all sides; all around: 这村子～都是菜地。All around the village are vegetable fields.

四维 sìwéi ① the four social bonds (see also 礼义廉耻

lǐ-yì-lián-chǐ) ② *formal* the four directions (i.e. north-east, southeast, northwest and southwest) ③ *Chin. med.* the four limbs ④ *phys.* four-dimensional

四维空间 sìwéi kōngjiān *phys.* space-time; space-time continuum

四下里 sìxiàli (also 四下 sìxià) all around: ～都是伏兵。 All around were troops lying in ambush. / ～一看，都是果树。 Looking around, one can see a vast stretch of fruit trees.

四仙桌 sìxiānzhuō four immortals table (a small square table seating four people)

四乡 sìxiāng the countryside around a town

四项基本原则 sìxiàng jīběn yuánzé the Four Cardinal Principles (i.e. keeping to the socialist road, and upholding the people's democratic dictatorship, leadership by the Communist Party, and Marxism-Leninism and Mao Zedong Thought)

四言诗 sìyánshī four-character verse (the earliest verse form in Chinese, popular before the Han Dynasty):《诗经》里的诗篇大都是～。 The poems in *The Book of Songs* are for the most part four-character poems (or in four-character lines).

四仰八叉 sì yǎng bā chà same as 四脚八叉 sì jiǎo bā chà

四野 sìyě the surrounding country; a vast expanse of open ground: ～茫茫，寂静无声。 All is quiet on the vast expanse of open ground.

四月 sìyuè ① April ② the fourth month of the lunar year; the fourth moon

四则 sìzé *math.* the four fundamental operations of arithmetic (i.e. addition, subtraction, multiplication and division)

四战之地 sì zhàn zhī dì a place open to attack from all directions

四诊 sìzhěn *Chin. med.* the four methods of diagnosis (i.e. observation 望, auscultation and olfaction 闻, interrogation 问, and pulse feeling and palpation 切)

四肢 sìzhī the four limbs; arms and legs

四至 sìzhì the four boundaries of a piece of land or a construction site

四周 sìzhōu all around; on all sides

四周围 sìzhōuwéi *inf.* all around; on all sides

四足动物 sìzú dòngwù quadruped; tetrapod

四座 sìzuò all the people present: 语惊～ words that startle all present

寺 sì temple: 少林～ the Shaolin Temple

寺院 sìyuàn temple; monastery

似 sì ① similar; like: 相似 xiāngsì ② seem; appear: ～属可行 seem to be feasible ③ (used in a comparative) than: 生活一年强～一年。 Life is getting better every year. ——see also shì

似曾相识 sì céng xiāngshí seem to have met before

似⋯非⋯ sì⋯fēi⋯ (each followed by the same word) look like but be not quite; smack of: 似懂非懂 have only a hazy notion; not quite understand / 她似笑非笑。 There's a faint smile on her face. / 这东西似绸非绸, 不知是什么料子。 This looks like silk but it isn't—I don't know what it is.

似乎 sìhū *adv.* as if; seemingly: 他的意思～另有所指。 It seems he was referring to something else. / ～明天要起风。 It looks as if it'll be windy tomorrow.

似是而非 sì shì ér fēi apparently right but actually wrong; specious; plausible: ～的说法 a specious argument

似水流年 sì shuǐ liúnián time passes swiftly like flowing water; youth slips away like flowing water

姒 sì *arch.* ① elder sister ② wife of husband's elder brother

祀 sì offer sacrifices to the gods or the spirits of the dead: ～孔 offer sacrifices to Confucius / ～祖 offer sacrifices to one's ancestors

伺 sì watch; await ——see also cì

伺服 sìfú *electron.* servo: ～传动 servo drive / ～放大器 servo amplifier / ～控制机构 servo-control mechanism

伺机 sìjī watch for one's chance: ～反扑 wait for an opportunity to stage a comeback / ～而动 wait for the opportune moment to go into action

伺隙 sìxì wait for a chance; watch for an opportunity: ～越狱 wait for an opportunity to break prison

饲 sì ① raise; rear ② forage; fodder; feed

饲槽 sìcáo feeding trough

饲草 sìcǎo forage grass

饲料 sìliào forage; fodder; feed: 猪～ pig feed / ～加工厂 feed-processing plant

饲料粉碎机 sìliào fěnsuìjī feed (or fodder) grinder

饲料作物 sìliào zuòwù forage (or fodder, feed) crop

饲喂 sìwèi feed or raise (animals)

饲养 sìyǎng raise; rear: ～家禽 raise (or rear) poultry / ～牲畜 raise livestock

饲养场 sìyǎngchǎng feed lot; dry lot; farm

饲养员 sìyǎngyuán stockman; poultry raiser; animal keeper

泗 sì *formal* nasal mucus

泗州戏 sìzhōuxì Sizhou opera (a form of regional drama popular in the Huai River area; named after its place of origin Sizhou or present-day Sixian, Anhui Province)

驷 sì *formal* ① a team of four horses ② horse

驷不及舌 sì bùjí shé a team of four horses cannot overtake the tongue—what is said cannot be unsaid

驷马 sìmǎ *formal* a team of four horses: 一言既出, 驷马难追 yī yán jì chū, sìmǎ nán zhuī

食 sì *formal* give food to; feed: 饮之～之, 教之诲之。（《诗经》） Let him have a drink, let him have some food, Give him a lesson, scold him. ——see also shí

俟（竢） sì *formal* wait: ～机进攻 wait for an opportunity to attack / 一～准备就绪, 即行公开展出。 The exhibition will be opened as soon as everything is in order. ——see also qí

俟河之清, 人寿几何 sì Hé zhī qīng, rénshòu jǐhé how long does a man live, that he can wait for the River to run clear? (said in despair of realizing one's hopes; the River referring to the Yellow River)

笥 sì *formal* bamboo-plaited basket or suitcase

耜 sì ① a spade-shaped farm tool used in ancient China ② sth. resembling a ploughshare, used in ancient China

嗣 sì ① succeed; inherit: ～位 succeed to the throne ② heir; descendant: 无～ heirless; without issue

嗣后 sìhòu *formal* hereafter; subsequently; afterwards; later on

肆¹

肆² sì wanton; unbridled: 放肆 fàngsì

sì four (used for the numeral 四 on cheques, etc. to avoid mistakes or alterations)

肆³

sì *formal* shop: 酒肆 jiǔsì

肆口大骂 sìkǒu dàmà let loose a torrent of abuse

肆力 sìlì *formal* devote all one's efforts to: ～农事 devote oneself to farming

肆虐 sìnüè indulge in wanton massacre or persecution; wreak havoc

肆扰 sìrǎo harass

肆无忌惮 sì wú jìdàn unbridled; unscrupulous; impertinent: ～地攻击 make unbridled attacks

肆意 sìyì wantonly; recklessly; wilfully: ～歪曲事实 wantonly distort the facts / ～践踏别国主权 wilfully trample upon other countries' sovereignty / ～侮辱 resort to wanton insults

sōng

忪

sōng see 惺忪 xīngsōng

松¹

sōng ① pine (tree) ② (Sōng) a surname

松² (鬆)

sōng ① loose; slack: 这里的土质很～。The soil here is very loose. / 你的鞋带～了。Your shoelace has come loose. / 绳子太～了。The rope is too slack. ② loosen; relax; slacken: ～一～螺丝 loosen the screw a little bit ③ not be hard up: 现在手头～些 be better off ④ light and flaky; soft: 这点心～脆可口。The pastry is light and crisp. / 这种木料～, 做家具不合适。The wood is too soft for making furniture. ⑤ untie; unfasten; release: 松绑 sōngbǎng ⑥ dried meat floss; dried minced meat: 猪肉～ dried minced pork

松绑 sōngbǎng ① untie a person: 给囚犯～ untie the prisoner ② relax restrictions

松弛 sōngchí ① limp; flabby; slack: 肌肉～ flaccid muscles ② lax: 纪律～ lax discipline

松貂 sōngdiāo pine marten

松动 sōngdong ① become less crowded ② not hard up: 银根较之上月有所～。Money is not so tight as it was last month. ③ become flexible; show flexibility; relax: 他的口气有点～。He has become a bit more flexible. / 两国关系有所～。Relations between the two countries have moved forward. / 他们在这个问题上的立场没有～。They show no flexibility in their position on this issue. / 表现了某些～姿态 have somewhat relaxed one's stance

松果腺 sōngguǒxiàn (also 松果体 sōngguǒtǐ) same as 脑上体 nǎoshàngtǐ

松虎 sōnghǔ *dial.* pine moth

松花 sōnghuā (also 松花蛋 sōnghuādàn) a kind of preserved egg

松花江 Sōnghuājiāng the Songhua (Sungari) River

松缓 sōnghuǎn relax; ease up; mitigate: 紧张的空气～了一些。The tense atmosphere has eased up a little.

松鸡 sōngjī capercaillie; grouse

松焦油 sōngjiāoyóu pine tar

松节油 sōngjiéyóu turpentine (oil)

松紧 sōngjǐn ① degree of tightness ② elasticity

松紧带 sōngjǐndài elastic cord; elastic

松劲 sōngjìn relax one's efforts; slacken (off): ～情绪 slack mood

松口 sōngkǒu ① relax one's bite and release what is held ② be less unyielding; soften; relent: 最后大夫～了, 同意她出院。Finally the doctor relented and allowed her to leave the hospital.

松快 sōngkuai ① be less crowded: 搬走一张桌子, 屋里～多了。With a desk moved out, there's much more space in the room. ② feel relieved: 吃了药以后身上～多了。I feel much better after taking the medicine. ③ relax: 干了一天活, ～～吧。After the day's work, let's relax a bit.

松毛虫 sōngmáochóng pine moth

松明 sōngmíng pine torch

松气 sōngqì relax one's efforts: 在节骨眼上决不能～。At this critical juncture we must not relax our efforts. / 现在我们可以松一口气了。Now we can have a breathing spell. *or* Now we can relax.

松球 sōngqiú pinecone

松仁 sōngrén pine nut kernel

松软 sōngruǎn soft; spongy; loose: ～的表土 spongy topsoil / ～的羊毛 fluffy wool / ～的面包 spongy bread

松散 sōngsǎn ① loose: 文章结构～。The article is loosely organized. / 掺点沙子使土质～一些。Add sand to make the soil more porous. ② inattentive

松散 sōngsan relax; take one's ease: 屋里太闷热, 出去～～吧。It's too hot and stuffy in here. Let's go out for a breath of air.

松手 sōngshǒu loosen one's grip; let go: 抓紧了, 别～! Hold it tight and don't let go.

松鼠 sōngshǔ squirrel

松树 sōngshù pine tree; pine

松松垮垮 sōngsongkuǎkuǎ ① not solid or firm; unsteady ② slack; sluggish

松塔 sōngtǎ ① *dial.* pinecone ② *Chin. med.* the cone of lacebark pine

松涛 sōngtāo the soughing of the wind in the pines

松土 sōngtǔ loosen the soil; scarify the soil

松土机 sōngtǔjī loosener; scarifier

松闲 sōng·xián not busy; slack: 秋收一完, 农活就～点了。After the autumn harvest comes the slack season.

松香 sōngxiāng rosin; colophony

松香油 sōngxiāngyóu retinol; rosin oil

松懈 sōngxiè ① lax; slack: 工作～ be slack in one's work / 管理～ loose management ② relax; slacken: ～斗志 relax one's will to fight

松心 sōngxīn feel relieved; have ease of mind; feel carefree and happy: 有了个帮忙的, 老太太～多了。The old lady feels much relieved now that she's got a help.

松蕈 sōngxùn pine mushroom

松鸦 sōngyā jaybird; jay

松烟 sōngyān pine soot

松烟墨 sōngyānmò Chinese ink or ink stick made from pine soot; pine-soot ink or ink stick

松针 sōngzhēn pine needle

松脂 sōngzhī rosin; pine resin

松子 sōngzǐ ① pine nut ② *dial.* pine nut kernel

松嘴 sōngzuǐ *inf.* ① relax one's bite and release what is held ② be less unyielding; soften; relent

凇

sōng see 雾凇 wùsōng

淞

Sōng a river in Jiangsu Province which flows into the Huangpu River of Shanghai

菘

sōng ancient name for Chinese cabbage

菘菜 sōngcài *dial.* Chinese cabbage

嵩 (崧)

sōng *formal* ① a high mountain ② high; lofty

嵩山 Sōngshān Mount Song (in Henan Province) ——see also 五岳 Wǔyuè

sóng

尿（屍） sóng ① seminal fluid; semen ② weak and incompetent: 这人真是个～包。He really is a good-for-nothing.

sǒng

怂（慫） sǒng *formal* alarmed and panicky; terrified

怂恿 sǒngyǒng instigate; incite; egg sb. on; abet

悚 sǒng *formal* terrified; horrified

悚然 sǒngrán terrified; horrified: 毛骨悚然 máogǔ sǒngrán

耸（聳） sǒng ① towering; lofty ② alarm; shock: 耸听 sǒngtīng

耸动 sǒngdòng ① raise (one's shoulders); shrug ② stir up; rouse: ～视听 create a sensation

耸肩 sǒngjiān shrug one's shoulders: 他耸了耸肩, 说他对此事一无所知, 也丝毫不感兴趣。He shrugged his shoulders, saying he didn't know and didn't care.

耸立 sǒnglì tower aloft: 人民英雄纪念碑～在天安门广场上。The Monument to the People's Heroes towers aloft on Tian'anmen Square.

耸人听闻 sǒng rén tīngwén deliberately exaggerate so as to create a sensation: ～的谣言 a sensational rumour / 这不是～, 而是铁的事实。This is not alarmist talk, but a hard fact.

耸入云霄 sǒng rù yúnxiāo tower to the skies: ～的高山 a high mountain towering to the skies

耸身 sǒngshēn jump; leap: ～跳过水沟 leap across the ditch

耸听 sǒngtīng deliberately exaggerate so as to create a sensation

耸峙 sǒngzhì (of mountains or cliffs) stand towering; tower aloft

竦 sǒng ① *formal* respectful ② same as 悚 sǒng ③ same as 耸 sǒng

sòng

讼 sòng ① bring a case to court ② dispute; argue

讼案 sòng'àn lawsuit

讼词 sòngcí legal cases: 包揽～ engage in pettifoggery

讼棍 sònggùn legal pettifogger; shyster

讼师 sòngshī legal pettifogger

讼事 sòngshì lawsuit; litigation

宋 Sòng ① a feudal state in the Zhou Dynasty (c. 11th century–256 B.C.), covering the present-day Shangqiu (商丘) area in Henan Province ② the Song Dynasty (420–479), one of the Southern Dynasties ③ the Song Dynasty (960–1279) ④ a surname

宋词 sòngcí *ci* poetry of the Song Dynasty

宋锦 sòngjǐn Song brocade (a brocade modelled on the Song-style silk fabric famed for its rich, colourful and elegant designs)

宋体字 sòngtǐzì Song typeface, a standard typeface first used in the Ming Dynasty (1368–1644) but popularly attributed to the Song Dynasty (960–1279)

送 sòng ① deliver; carry: ～信 deliver a letter / ～粪 carry manure to the fields / ～公粮 deliver public grain / ～医～药上门 deliver medical care right to the patient's home / 给我们～来好消息 bring us good news ② give as a present; give: 姐姐～我一本书。My sister gave me a book. ③ see sb. off or out; accompany; escort: ～她回家 see her home / 到车站～人 see sb. off at the station / 把客人～到门口 see a guest to the door; walk a guest to the gate / 我～你一段路。Let me walk with you part of the way. / ～孩子上学 take a child to school

送别 sòngbié same as 送行 sòngxíng

送殡 sòngbìn attend a funeral; take part in a funeral procession

送风机 sòngfēngjī *mech.* forced draught blower; blower

送话器 sònghuàqì microphone

送还 sònghuán give back; return

送货 sònghuò deliver goods: ～上门 deliver goods right to the doorstep of a customer; deliver to domicile

送交 sòngjiāo deliver to; hand over to: 请把这封信～中国日报社。Please take this letter to the General Office of the *China Daily*. / 把犯罪分子～人民法院审判 hand the criminal over to the people's court for trial

送旧迎新 sòngjiù-yíngxīn see out the old and welcome the new

送客 sòngkè see a visitor out

送礼 sònglǐ give sb. a present; present a gift to sb.: 请客～ give dinners or send gifts (in order to curry favour)

送命 sòngmìng lose one's life; get killed; go to one's doom

送气 sòngqì *phonet.* aspirated

送气音 sòngqìyīn aspirated sound; aspirate (e.g. Chinese p, t, k, c, ch, q)

送亲 sòngqīn (of the bride's kinsfolk) escort the bride to the groom's home or the wedding hall

送情 sòngqíng *dial.* make a gift of sth.

送人 sòngrén give away; present someone with: 他的画从不～。He never gives away his paintings.

送人情 sòng rénqíng ① do favours at no great cost to oneself ② *dial.* make a gift of sth.

送丧 sòngsāng attend a funeral; take part in a funeral procession

送上门 sòngshàngmén deliver to the doorstep (fig): ～的买卖你还不做? A business right at the door, and you refuse to do it?

送审 sòngshěn submit to a higher level for approval or revision

送死 sòngsǐ *inf.* court death

送往迎来 sòngwǎng-yínglái see off those who depart and welcome those who arrive; speed the parting guests and welcome the new arrivals: 负责～事宜 be in charge of arrangements for receiving and seeing off guests

送瘟神 sòng wēnshén send away the god of plague —get rid of sb. or sth. undesirable

送信儿 sòngxìnr *inf.* send word; go and tell: 我已经给他～, 让他马上来看你。I have sent him word to come and see you at once. / 你哥从东北回来了, 去给你妈送个信儿。Go and tell your mother that your brother has come back from the Northeast.

送行 sòngxíng ① see sb. off; wish sb. bon voyage ② give a send-off party

送葬 sòngzàng take part in a funeral procession

送灶 sòngzào (in former times) the ceremony of sending off the kitchen god on his annual trip to Heaven held on the 23rd day of the 12th lunar month

送终 sòngzhōng attend upon a dying parent or other senior member of one's family; bury a parent

诵

sòng ① read aloud; chant ② recite ③ state; recount; narrate

诵读 sòngdú read aloud; chant

诵习 sòngxí *formal* chant and study: ～经典 read and study the classics

颂

sòng ① praise; extol; eulogize; laud: 歌颂 gēsòng ② express good wishes (in letters): 敬～大安 wishing you good health ③ one of the three sections of *The Book of Songs* (《诗经》), consisting of songs in praise of imperial ancestors sung on sacrificial occasions ④ song; ode; paean; eulogy: 《延安～》 *Ode to Yan'an*

颂词 sòngcí ① complimentary address; panegyric; eulogy ② a speech delivered by an ambassador on presentation of his credentials

颂歌 sònggē song; ode

颂古非今 sònggǔ-fēijīn eulogize the past and condemn the present

颂扬 sòngyáng sing praises of; laud; extol; eulogize

颂谀 sòngyú flatter (with overpraise); praise to the skies; fawn upon

颂赞 sòngzàn sing praises of; laud; extol; eulogize

sōu

溲

sōu *formal* urinate

溲血 sōuxiě *Chin. med.* haematuria

搜¹ (蒐)

sōu look for: 搜集 sōují

搜²

sōu search: 什么也没～着。 Nothing was found in the search.

搜捕 sōubǔ track down and arrest

搜查 sōuchá search; ransack; rummage

搜查证 sōucházhèng search warrant

搜肠刮肚 sōucháng-guādù rack one's brains: ～地想办法 rack one's brains for a way out

搜刮 sōuguā (also 搜括 sōukuò) extort; plunder; expropriate; fleece: 贪官污吏～人民大量钱财。 The corrupt officials extorted large sums of money from the people (*or* fleeced the people).

搜集 sōují hunt high and low for; collect; gather: ～标本 collect specimens / ～情报 gather information; collect intelligence / ～证据 search for evidence / ～群众意见 solicit opinions from the masses

搜剿 sōujiǎo track down and exterminate: ～残匪 track down and exterminate the remnants of the bandits

搜罗 sōuluó hunt high and low for (persons or things); collect; gather; recruit: ～大量史料 collect a large amount of historical data / ～人才 recruit qualified persons; scout for talent

搜拿 sōuná track down and take into custody; hunt down and arrest

搜求 sōuqiú seek; search for; hunt for: ～古书 hunt high and low for ancient books

搜身 sōushēn search the person; make a body search; frisk

搜索 sōusuǒ search for; hunt for; scout around: ～失踪船只 search for missing boats / 在山上～空投特务 comb the hills for air-dropped agents / ～前进 advance and reconnoitre

搜索飞行 sōusuǒ fēixíng scouting flight

搜索枯肠 sōusuǒ kūcháng rack one's brains (for fresh ideas or apt expressions)

搜寻 sōuxún search for; look for; hunt for; seek: ～失踪人员 hunt high and low for the missing (persons)

搜腰包 sōu yāobāo search sb.'s pockets; search sb. for money and valuables

嗖

sōu *onom.* whiz: 汽车～的一声从他身边开过。 The car whizzed by him.

馊

sōu turn sour; become spoiled: 饭菜～了。 The food has spoiled. *or* The food smells a bit off.

馊点子 sōudiǎnzi a stupid suggestion; a lousy idea: 谁出的这个～? Who made this stupid suggestion?

馊主意 sōuzhǔyi a stupid suggestion; a lousy idea: 别出～! Stop making stupid suggestions!

飕¹

sōu *dial.* (of wind) make sth. dry or cool: 洗的衣服～干了。 The washing has dried in the wind.

飕²

sōu same as 嗖 sōu

飕飗 sōuliú *liter.* (of wind) soughing; rustling

锼

sōu *dial.* engrave (on wood); carve (wood)

锼弓子 sōugōngzi *dial.* fret saw; scroll saw

艘

sōu *m.* (for boats or ships): 两～油船 two tankers / 四～巡洋舰 four cruisers

螋

sōu see 蠼螋 qúsōu

sǒu

叟 (叜)

sǒu an old man: 邻～ the old man who lives next door

瞍

sǒu *formal* ① have eyes without pupils; be blind ② a blind person

嗾

sǒu ① a whistling sound made as a signal to a dog ② *formal* whistle to a dog

嗾使 sǒushǐ instigate; abet

薮 (藪)

sǒu *formal* ① a shallow lake overgrown with wild plants ② a gathering place of fish or beasts; den; haunt: 渊薮 yuānsǒu

薮泽 sǒuzé *formal* lakes and ponds

擞 (擻)

sǒu see 抖擞 dǒusǒu ——see also sòu

sòu

嗽

sòu cough: 干～ a dry cough

撽 (擻)

sòu *dial.* poke the ashes of a stove fire; rake: ～火 poke the ashes off; poke the fire up / 把炉子好好～一～ give the stove fire a good poking (*or* raking) ——see also sǒu

sū

苏¹(蘇) sū *bot.* perilla; beefsteak plant

苏²(蘇、甦) sū revive; come to: 死而复～ come back to life

苏³(蘇) Sū ① short for 苏州 Sūzhōu: ～杭 Suzhou and Hangzhou ② short for 江苏 Jiāngsū: ～南 southern Jiangsu / ～北地区 the northern areas of Jiangsu Province ③ a surname

苏⁴(蘇) sū ① short for 苏维埃 sūwéi'āi ② (Sū) short for 苏联 Sūlián

苏⁵(嚕) sū see 嚕苏 lūsū

苏白 sūbái ① Suzhou dialect ② spoken parts in Suzhou dialect in Kunqu opera

苏必利尔湖 Sūbìlì'ěrhú Lake Superior

苏菜 sūcài Jiangsu cuisine; Jiangsu-style dishes

苏打 sūdǎ *chem.* soda; soda ash; sodium carbonate: ～饼干 soda biscuit; soda cracker

苏丹 sūdān ① sultan ② (Sūdān) the Sudan

苏丹人 Sūdānrén Sudanese

苏剧 sūjù Jiangsu opera

苏里南 Sūlǐnán Surinam

苏里南人 Sūlǐnánrén Surinamese

苏联 Sūlián the Soviet Union (1917-1990)

苏门答腊 Sūméndálà Sumatra

苏门羚 sūménlíng *zool.* serow

苏区 sūqū Chinese Soviet Areas (established during the Second Revolutionary Civil War period, 1927-1937)

苏生 sūshēng come back to life; revive: 春回大地, 万木～。 Spring returns to the earth, reviving all plants and trees.

苏铁 sūtiě *bot.* sago cycas (Cycas revoluta)

苏维埃 sūwéi'āi soviet: 地方各级～ the local and regional soviets / 最高～ the Supreme Soviet

苏醒 sūxǐng revive; regain consciousness; come to; come round: 他昏迷了一个多小时才～过来。 He remained unconscious for more than an hour before he came to.

苏绣 sūxiù Suzhou embroidery

苏伊士运河 Sūyīshì Yùnhé the Suez Canal

苏州码子 Sūzhōu mǎzi Suzhou numerals (traditionally used by shopkeepers to mark prices)

苏子 sūzǐ perillaseed

酥 sū ① ancient name for 酥油 sūyóu ② crisp; short: ～糖 crunchy candy ③ shortbread: 杏仁～ almond shortbread ④ (of a person's limbs) limp; weak; soft

酥脆 sūcuì crisp: ～的饼干 crisp (*or* short) biscuit

酥麻 sūmá limp and numb: 两腿～ one's legs feeling weak and numb

酥软 sūruǎn (of the body) limp; languid

酥松 sūsōng (of soil, etc.) loose; porous; (of pastries, etc.) flaky; crisp: ～的土壤 porous soil / ～的薄脆饼干 flaky crackers

酥胸 sūxiōng soft and white breasts (of a woman)

酥油 sūyóu butter

酥油茶 sūyóuchá buttered tea

窣 sū see 窸窣 xīsū

稣 sū same as 苏² sū

sú

俗 sú ① custom; convention: 陈规旧～ old habits and customs ② popular; common: 玉蜀黍～称棒子。 Corn is commonly called *bangzi*. ③ vulgar: 俗气 súqi ④ secular; lay: 僧俗 sēng-sú

俗不可耐 sú bùkě nài unbearably vulgar

俗话 súhuà *inf.* common saying; proverb: ～说 as the saying goes

俗家 sújiā ① (used by a monk or nun) my parents' home ② layman: ～打扮 in a layman's attire

俗名 súmíng popular name; local name

俗气 súqi vulgar; in poor taste: 她穿得很～。 The clothes she wears are in poor taste.

俗人 súrén ① layman (as distinguished from 出家人 chūjiārén) ② a vulgar person; philistine

俗尚 súshàng prevailing customs

俗套 sútào conventional pattern; convention: 不落俗套 bù luò sútào

俗体字 sútǐzì nonstandard forms of characters (e.g. 菓 for 果 "fruit")

俗文学 súwénxué popular literature (as novels, ballads, etc.)

俗务 súwù everyday matters; routine business: ～缠身 be tied up with routine business

俗物 súwù a vulgar or uncouth person

俗语 súyǔ common saying; folk adage

俗字 súzì same as 俗体字 sútǐzì

sù

夙 sù *formal* ① early in the morning: 夙兴夜寐 sùxīng-yèmèi ② long-standing; old: ～志 long-cherished ambition

夙仇 sùchóu ① a long-time enemy ② long-standing enmity

夙敌 sùdí an old enemy

夙诺 sùnuò an old promise

夙日 sùrì generally; usually; ordinarily: ～过往甚密 usually have close contact with each other

夙世 sùshì a previous incarnation: ～因缘 a relationship predestined from a previous incarnation / ～冤家 predestined enemies

夙嫌 sùxián an old grudge

夙兴夜寐 sùxīng-yèmèi rise early and retire late—hard at work night and day

夙夜 sù-yè day and night: ～不寐 not sleep a wink day and night

夙夜匪懈 sù-yè fěi xiè work tirelessly day and night

夙愿 sùyuàn a long-cherished wish: ～得偿 a long-cherished wish fulfilled

诉 sù ① tell; relate; inform: 告诉 gàosu ② complain; accuse: ～委屈 pour out one's grievances ③ appeal to; resort to: 上诉 shàngsù

诉告 sùgào recount (one's grievances, sufferings, etc.); air (one's complaints)

诉苦 sùkǔ vent one's grievances; pour out one's woes

诉苦会 sùkǔhuì a meeting for pouring out grievances

诉说 sùshuō (also 诉述 sùshù) tell; relate; recount: ～苦难家史 relate the family's sufferings in the past / ～苦衷 recount one's worries and difficulties; tell one's troubles

诉讼 sùsòng *leg.* lawsuit; litigation: 法律～ judicial

proceedings / ～案件 lawsuit / 民刑～ civil and criminal lawsuits / 对某人提出～ take (*or* start) legal proceedings against sb. / 撤销～ withdraw an accusation; drop a lawsuit / 提出离婚～ take (*or* start) divorce proceedings

诉讼代理人 sùsòng dàilǐrén　agent *ad litem*; legal representative

诉讼当事人 sùsòng dāngshìrén　litigant

诉讼法 sùsòngfǎ　procedural law

诉讼豁免 sùsòng huòmiǎn　immunity from suit

诉讼权利 sùsòng quánlì　procedural rights

诉讼条例 sùsòng tiáolì　rules of procedure

诉冤 sùyuān　complain of injustice; air one's grievances

诉愿 sùyuàn　lodge a complaint against a lower government organization with a higher one

诉诸武力 sù zhū wǔlì　resort to force; appeal to arms

诉状 sùzhuàng　*leg. old* plaint; indictment: 向法院提出～ file a plaint at court

肃（肅）

sù　① respectful: 肃立 sùlì ② solemn: 严肃 yánsù ③ eliminate; clean up; mop up: 肃反 sùfǎn

肃反 sùfǎn　elimination of counterrevolutionaries

肃静 sùjìng　solemn silence: 全场～无声。A solemn silence reigned.

肃立 sùlì　stand as a mark of respect: 奏国歌时全场～。All stood as the band struck up the national anthem. *or* Everyone stood when the national anthem was played. / ～默哀 stand in silent mourning

肃穆 sùmù　① solemn and quiet; solemn and respectful: 纪念会气氛～。The commemoration meeting was permeated with a solemn atmosphere. ② respectful and congenial

肃清 sùqīng　eliminate; clean up; mop up: ～敌军残部 mop up the remnants of the enemy / ～流毒 liquidate a pernicious influence

肃然起敬 sùrán qǐ jìng　be filled with deep veneration: 使我～ call forth in me a feeling of profound respect

肃杀 sùshā　*formal* (of autumn or winter) stern; harsh: 秋气～。The breath of autumn is harsh and raw.

素

sù　① white; unbleached and undyed: ～幡 white streamers ② plain; simple; quiet: ～色 plain colour ③ vegetable: 三荤一～ three meat dishes and one vegetable dish ④ native: 素性 sùxìng ⑤ basic element; element: 色素 sèsù ⑥ usually; habitually; always: ～不往来 have never had anything to do with each other

素白 sùbái　plain and white: ～手绢 a plain white handkerchief

素不相识 sù bù xiāngshí　have never met; not be acquainted with each other

素材 sùcái　source material (of literature and art); material: 搜集小说～ gather material for a novel

素菜 sùcài　vegetable dish

素餐 sùcān　① a vegetarian meal ② be a vegetarian ③ *formal* not work for one's living; eat the bread of idleness

素常 sùcháng　usually; habitually; ordinarily: ～他到十二点钟才睡觉。Ordinarily he doesn't go to bed until twelve o'clock.

素淡 sùdàn　plain; quiet: 衣着～ be plainly (*or* quietly) dressed

素服 sùfú　plain white clothes (esp. as mourning apparel)

素裹 sùguǒ　*formal* dressed in white

素混凝土 sùhùnníngtǔ　plain concrete

素洁 sùjié　white and pure

素净 sùjing　plain and neat; quiet: 一套～的蓝衣服 a plain blue suit / 花色～ a pattern in quiet colours / 穿着～ be plainly and neatly dressed

素酒 sùjiǔ　① wine served with vegetarian food ② *dial.* a vegetarian feast

素来 sùlái　*adv.* always; usually: 他～是严格遵守纪律的。He always strictly observes discipline. / 他在公司里～威信很高。He has always enjoyed high prestige in the company.

素昧平生 sù mèi píngshēng　have never met before; have never made sb.'s acquaintance: 我同他～。I have never had the honour of making his acquaintance. *or* I know nothing about him. / 一个～的人 a complete stranger

素面 sùmiàn　vegetarian noodles

素描 sùmiáo　① sketch ② literary sketch

素朴 sùpǔ　simple and unadorned; plain and simple: 这些描绘草原人民生活的画面～动人。These pictures depict life on the grasslands with a charming simplicity.

素日 sùrì　*adv.* generally; usually: 他～不爱说话。He is usually very quiet.

素什锦 sùshíjǐn　assorted vegetables dish

素食 sùshí　① vegetarian food; vegetarian diet ② be a vegetarian: ～者 a vegetarian

素手 sùshǒu　soft white hands; fair and satiny hands

素数 sùshù　*math.* prime number

素席 sùxí　a vegetarian feast

素心 sùxīn　① one's real intention; one's true will: 与～相违 go against one's true will ② clean and honest; pure in heart: 他是个～人。He is a simple and honest one.

素馨 sùxīn　*bot.* jasmine

素性 sùxìng　one's natural instincts; one's true disposition or temperament

素雅 sùyǎ　simple but elegant; plain and in good taste: 衣着～ be tastefully dressed in a simple style / 房间布置～。The room is simply and tastefully furnished.

素养 sùyǎng　accomplishment; attainment: 艺术～ artistic accomplishment

素因子 sùyīnzǐ　*math.* prime factor

素油 sùyóu　vegetable oil

素愿 sùyuàn　a long-cherished desire, wish, or aspiration

素月 sùyuè　the silver moon

素志 sùzhì　a long-cherished ambition

素质 sùzhì　① character; quality: 提高部队的军政～ enhance the military and political quality of the troops ② *psychol.* diathesis

速¹

sù　① fast; rapid; quick; speedy: 收效甚～ produce quick results; have a speedy effect ② speed; velocity: 音速 yīngsù

速²

sù　*formal* invite: 不速之客 bù sù zhī kè

速成 sùchéng　attain a goal in a much shorter time than usual; gain a quick mastery of a course or subject: ～教学法 a quick method of teaching / ～识字法 a quick method of achieving literacy / 英文打字～ a speeded-up teaching programme of English typing

速成班 sùchéngbān　an accelerated course; a crash course

速冻 sùdòng　quick-freeze: ～饺子 quick-frozen dumplings / ～对虾 quick-frozen fresh prawns

速度 sùdù　① *phys.* speed; velocity: 匀～ uniform velocity / 轨道～ orbital velocity ② *mus. tempo* ③ speed; rate; pace; tempo: 加快～ increase the speed / 生产～ the tempo of production / 经济发展的～ the rate of economic development / 工业化的～ the pace of industrialization

速度滑冰 sùdù huábīng　*sports* speed skating

速度计 sùdùjì　speed indicator; speedometer

速记 sùjì　shorthand; stenography

速记员　sùjìyuán　stenographer
速决　sùjué　quick decision
速决战　sùjuézhàn　war (*or* battle) of quick decision
速率　sùlǜ　speed; rate: 冷却～ rate of cooling
速射　sùshè　*mil.* rapid fire
速射炮　sùshèpào　quick-firing gun; quick-firer
速调管　sùtiáoguǎn　*radio* klystron
速效　sùxiào　quick results
速效肥料　sùxiào féiliào　quick-acting fertilizer
速写　sùxiě　① sketch ② literary sketch
速战速决　sùzhàn-sùjué　fight a quick battle to force a quick decision

宿¹　sù　① lodge for the night; stay overnight: 夜～古刹 stay in an ancient temple for the night; make an overnight stay in an ancient temple ② (Sù) a surname

宿²　sù　*formal* ① long-standing; old: ～志 a long-cherished ambition ② veteran; old: 宿将 sùjiàng ——see also xiǔ; xiù

宿弊　sùbì　a long-standing abuse: ～一清。The long-standing abuses are all rooted out.
宿逋　sùbū　*formal* a long-standing debt
宿仇　sùchóu　long-standing enmity
宿处　sùchù　lodgings; accommodation: 我不知道她的～。I don't know where she's staying.
宿敌　sùdí　an old enemy
宿根　sùgēn　*bot.* ① perennial root ② biennial root
宿憾　sùhàn　(also 宿恨 sùhèn) long-harboured resentment; long-standing regret
宿疾　sùjí　chronic complaint; old trouble
宿将　sùjiàng　a veteran general
宿酒　sùjiǔ　hangover: ～未醒 still having a hangover
宿命论　sùmìnglùn　*philos.* fatalism: ～者 fatalist
宿诺　sùnuò　an old promise
宿儒　sùrú　a learned old scholar
宿舍　sùshè　hostel; living quarters; dormitory: 学生～ students' hostel (*or* dormitory)／职工～ living quarters for staff and workers
宿头　sùtóu　a lodging for the night; inn: 再不快走，就赶不上～了。We won't be able to find a lodging for the night unless we hurry up.
宿夜　sùyè　stay for the night; make an overnight stay
宿营　sùyíng　(of troops) take up quarters; camp: ～地 temporary quarters for soldiers; camping site
宿缘　sùyuán　a predestined relationship
宿怨　sùyuàn　old grudges; old scores
宿愿　sùyuàn　a long-cherished wish
宿债　sùzhài　a long-standing debt; an old debt
宿主　sùzhǔ　*biol.* host: 中间～ intermediate host／终～ final host
宿醉　sùzuì　hangover: ～未醒 still having a hangover

骕（驌）　sù　see below
骕骦　sùshuāng　(also 骕骦 sùshuāng) a fine breed of horse mentioned in ancient texts

粟　sù　① foxtail millet; millet (Setaria italica) ② (Sù) a surname
粟米　sùmǐ　*dial.* maize; Indian corn; corn
粟子　sùzi　*dial.* millet

谡　sù　*formal* stand up; rise
谡谡　sùsù　tall and straight

溯（泝、遡）　sù　① go against the stream: ～流而上 go upstream ② trace back; recall: 回溯 huísù
溯源　sùyuán　trace (back) to the source

塑　sù　model; mould: ～一尊佛像 mould a statue of Buddha
塑胶　sùjiāo　plastic cement: ～跑道 plastic cement race track
塑炼　sùliàn　plasticate
塑炼机　sùliànjī　plasticator
塑料　sùliào　plastics: 通用～ general-purpose plastics／工程～ engineering plastics／氟～ fluoroplastics
塑料薄膜　sùliào bómó　plastic film; plastic sheeting
塑料胶布带　sùliào jiāobùdài　*elec.* plastic adhesive tape
塑料热合机　sùliào rèhéjī　plastic welder
塑料贴面板　sùliào tiēmiànbǎn　plastic veneer
塑料印版　sùliào yìnbǎn　plastic (printing) plate
塑料炸弹　sùliào zhàdàn　plastic bomb
塑像　sùxiàng　statue
塑性　sùxìng　*phys.* plasticity
塑造　sùzào　① model; mould: ～一座石膏像 mould (*or* model) a plaster figure ② portray: ～一个女警察的英雄形象 portray a heroic policewoman

嗉（膆）　sù　see below
嗉子　sùzi　① (also 嗉囊 sùnáng) crop (of a bird): 鸡～ chicken crop ② *dial.* tin or porcelain wine flask

愫　sù　*formal* sincere feeling; sincerity: 情愫 qíngsù

鹔（鷫）　sù　see below
鹔鹴　sùshuāng　(also 鹔鹴 sùshuāng) a bird mentioned in ancient texts

僳　sù　see 傈僳族 Lìsùzú

蔌　sù　*formal* vegetables: 山肴野蔌 shānyáo-yěsù

觫　sù　see 觳觫 húsù

簌　sù　see below
簌簌　sùsù　① *onom.* rustle: 风吹树叶～响。The leaves are rustling in the wind. ② (of tears) streaming down

suān

狻　suān　see below
狻猊　suānní　a legendary beast of prey

酸¹　suān　① *chem.* acid ② sour; tart: ～梨 sour pear／～果 tart fruit／牛奶～了。The milk has turned sour. ③ sick at heart; grieved; distressed: 大娘鼻子一～，流下泪来。The old woman felt a twinge in her nose and she began to weep. ④ pedantic; impractical: ～秀才 an impractical old scholar; a priggish pedant

酸²（痠）　suān　tingle; ache: 腰～背痛 have a pain in the back; have a backache
酸鼻　suānbí　have a sting in the nose; feel like crying: 令人～ make one feel like crying
酸不唧　suānbujī　① slightly sour or tart; sourish; tartish: 这草莓～的，挺好吃。These strawberries have a slightly sour taste; they taste quite nice. ② tired and feeling weak; exhausted; worn-out: 浑身～的 worn-out and aching all over
酸不拉唧　suānbulājī　unpleasantly sour
酸不溜丢　suānbuliūdiū　*dial.* unpleasantly sour
酸菜　suāncài　pickled Chinese cabbage; Chinese sauer-

kraut

酸处理 suānchǔlǐ *petroleum* acid treatment; acidation

酸楚 suānchǔ grieved; distressed; miserable

酸度 suāndù *chem.* acidity

酸腐 suānfǔ ① (of smell) bad; rotten; putrid: 豆腐已～变质。 The beancurd has gone bad. ② pedantic; antediluvian

酸酐 suāngān *chem.* acid anhydride

酸解 suānjiě *chem.* acidolysis

酸苦 suānkǔ bitterness; misery; hardship: 历尽～ have experienced all kinds of hardships / 心头一阵～ feel a twinge at the heart

酸辣汤 suānlàtāng vinegar-pepper soup

酸懒 suānlǎn *dial.* listless and aching

酸溜溜 suānliūliū ① sour; pungent ② tingle; ache: 走了一天路，我的腿肚子～的。 My legs ached after I'd been walking all day. ③ sad; mournful ④ envious; green with envy ⑤ pedantic; priggish

酸马奶 suānmǎnǎi koumiss

酸梅 suānméi smoked plum; dark plum

酸梅汤 suānméitāng sweet-sour plum juice

酸牛奶 suānniúnǎi (also 酸奶 suānnǎi) yoghurt; sour milk

酸软 suānruǎn aching and limp: 四肢～ one's limbs all aching and limp

酸式盐 suānshìyán *chem.* acid salt

酸疼 suānténg (of muscles) ache

酸甜 suāntián sweet and sour

酸甜苦辣 suān-tián-kǔ-là sour, sweet, bitter, hot—joys and sorrows of life

酸痛 suāntòng ache: 浑身～ ache all over

酸味 suānwèi tart flavour; acidity

酸文假醋 suānwén-jiǎcù priggish; prudish

酸洗 suānxǐ *metall.* pickling; acid pickling

酸洗试验 suānxǐ shìyàn acid washing test

酸心 suānxīn ① be grieved; feel sad: 这出戏看了叫人～。 It was heartrending to see the play. ② suffer from heartburn

酸辛 suānxīn same as 辛酸 xīnsuān

酸性 suānxìng *chem.* acidity: ～染料 acid dye

酸性反应 suānxìng fǎnyìng acid reaction

酸性试验 suānxìng shìyàn acid test

酸性岩 suānxìngyán acidic rock: 花岗岩是一种～。 Granite is an acidic rock.

酸雨 suānyǔ acid rain

酸枣 suānzǎo wild jujube

酸值 suānzhí *chem.* acid value

suàn

蒜 suàn garlic: 一辫～ a braid of garlic / 一头～ a bulb of garlic

蒜瓣儿 suànbànr garlic clove

蒜黄 suànhuáng blanched garlic leaves

蒜苗 suànmiáo garlic bolt

蒜泥 suànní mashed garlic

蒜薹 suàntái the flower stalk of garlic (edible when tender)

蒜头 suàntóu the head (or bulb) of garlic

算（祘） suàn ① calculate; reckon; compute; figure: ～～旅行的费用 calculate the cost of a journey / 能写会～ good at writing and reckoning / 请你一～一～我该付多少钱? Please reckon up how much I must pay. / 他们～了一下，完成这项工程需要两年。 They figured it would take two years to finish the project. ② include; count: ～上你，一共十个人。 There'll be ten people, in-

cluding you. / 把我也～上。 Count me in. ③ plan; calculate: 失算 shīsuàn ④ guess; think; suppose: 我～他今天该动身了。 I suppose he'll have started (or be starting) today. ⑤ consider; regard as; count as: 他可以～一个车把势。 He can be counted as a carter. / 比起南方，北京的夏天不～热。 Compared to the south, summer in Beijing isn't really hot. / 解放前，我们这里的小麦亩产一百斤就～不错的了。 Before liberation, we were lucky if we got 100 *jin* of wheat per *mu*. ⑥ carry weight; count: 我一个人说的不～，还得大伙儿说。 It's not just what I say, but what we all say, that counts. / 你怎么刚说了又不～了? You just made a promise and now you've gone back on it! / 这点困难～不了什么。 A little difficulty like this is nothing to us. / 这家公司里的事由他说了～。 What he says goes in the firm. / 世界上的事不应该由一两个国家说了～。 One or two powers should not have the final say on world affairs. ⑦ at long last; in the end; finally: 现在～把情况弄清楚了。 At long last we have got things clear. *or* We've finally sized up the situation. / 问题～解决了。 The problem is finally solved. ⑧ (followed by 了 le) let it be; let it pass: ～了，别说了。 That's enough! Let it go at that. *or* Forget it. / 他不愿意去就～了吧，咱们反正去。 If he doesn't want to go, he doesn't need to. We'll go anyway.

算尺 suànchǐ slide rule

算得 suàndé regard as; count as: 你有这样一位贤内助，可～幸福的了。 You can well count yourself fortunate in having such a good wife.

算法 suànfǎ *math.* algorithm

算卦 suànguà tell sb.'s fortune or divine by using the Eight Trigrams (八卦) ——see also 八卦 bāguà

算计 suànji ① calculate; reckon: ～一下全部收入 count up all one's earnings / 让我～～，看够不够。 Let me figure it out and see if it will be enough. ② consider; plan: 我正～着要上北京去。 I am planning a trip to Beijing. ③ expect; figure: 我～他昨天回不来，果然没回来。 I thought he wouldn't come back yesterday, and he didn't. ④ scheme; plot: 暗中～别人 secretly scheme against others

算计儿 suànjir *dial.* plan: 你心里总得有个～。 You must have a plan in mind.

算旧帐 suàn jiùzhàng settle an old account; settle an old score: 我要同他算一笔旧帐。 I've got an old score to settle with him.

算命 suànmìng fortune-telling: 那瞎子自称会给人～。 The blind man claimed that he could tell people's fortunes.

算命先生 suànmìng xiānsheng fortune-teller

算盘 suàn·pán ① abacus ② calculation; plan; scheme: 他满口答应了这件事，是有他自己的～的。 In agreeing so readily, he had an axe to grind.

算盘子儿 suàn·pánzǐr beads of an abacus

算式 suànshì mathematical formula or equation

算是 suànshì at last: 这一下你～猜着了。 At last you've guessed right. / 我们的计划～实现了。 At last our plan has materialized.

算术 suànshù arithmetic: 做～ do sums

算术级数 suànshù jíshù arithmetic progression; arithmetic series

算术平均值 suànshù píngjūnzhí arithmetic mean

算数 suànshù count; hold; stand: 个别情况不～。 Isolated instances do not count. / 这条规定仍然～。 This rule still holds (or stands). / 我们说话是～的。 We mean what we say. / 我们在国际上说话是～的。 We always live up to our international commitments.

算题 suàntí arithmetic problem; mathematical exercise

算学 suànxué ① mathematics ② arithmetic

算帐 suànzhàng ① do (or work out) accounts; balance

the books; make out bills: 他每十天算一次帐。He does his accounts every ten days. / ～算得快 be quick at accounts ② square (or settle) accounts with sb.; get even with sb.: 以后再找这坏蛋～。We'll get even with the scoundrel later. or We'll make the scoundrel pay for this.

算子 suànzǐ *math.* operator: 微分～ differential operator

SUÍ

尿 suī urine: 这孩子又尿 (niào) 了一泡～。The child has pissed again! ——see also niào

尿脬 suī·pāo (also 尿泡 suī·pāo) *dial.* bladder

虽(雖) suī *conj. formal* though; although; even if: 问题～小，但很典型。The question is small but typical. / ～死犹荣 honoured though dead; have died a glorious death

虽然 suīrán *conj.* (often used correlatively with 但是 dànshì, 可是 kěshì, etc.) though; although: 他～在北京住了十来年了，可是家乡口音一点没改。Though he has lived in Beijing for ten years or so, he still speaks with a heavy accent.

虽说 suīshuō *conj. inf.* though; although: ～我已认识他很久了，但我并不了解他。I don't know him very well, though I've known him for a long time.

虽死犹生 suī sǐ yóu shēng live on in spirit

虽则 suīzé *conj.* though; although

荽 suī see 芫荽 yánsui

睢 suī see 暴戾恣睢 bàolì-zìsuī

濉 Suī a river which rises in the northeastern part of Anhui Province and empties into the Hongze Lake (洪泽湖) of Jiangsu Province

SUÍ

绥 suí *formal* ① peaceful ② pacify

绥靖 suíjìng pacify; appease

绥靖政策 suíjìng zhèngcè policy of appeasement

隋 Suí ① the Sui Dynasty (581-618) ② a surname

随(隨) suí ① follow; come or go along with: ～我来。Follow me. or Come along with me. ② comply with; adapt to: 只要你们做得对，我都～着。So long as what you do is right, I'll go along with you. ③ let (sb. do as he likes): 去不去～你。Whether you go or not is up to you. ④ along with (some other action): 随手 suíshǒu ⑤ *dial.* look like; resemble: 她长得～她母亲。She looks like her mother. or She takes after her mother.

随笔 suíbǐ ① informal essay ② jottings

随便[1] suíbiàn do as one pleases: 随你的便。Do as you please. / ～吃吧。Help yourself.

随便[2] suíbiàn ① casual; random; informal: ～闲谈 chat; chitchat / ～说了几句 make some casual remarks / 你怎么能这样～答应呢? How could you agree so casually? / 我只是～问问。I was just asking. ② careless; slipshod: 说话～ not be careful about the way one talks ③ wanton; wilful; arbitrary: ～撕毁协议 wantonly tear up an agreement ④ anyhow; any: ～什么时候来都行。

Come any time you like.

随波逐流 suíbō-zhúliú drift with the tide (or current); go with the stream

随常 suícháng ordinary; common; everyday: ～的衣服 everyday clothes

随处 suíchù *adv.* everywhere; anywhere: 这种树在这一带～可见。This kind of tree can be seen everywhere in these parts.

随从 suícóng ① accompany or follow (one's superior); attend ② (also 随从人员 suícóng rényuán) retinue; suite; *entourage*

随大溜 suídàliù drift (or swim) with the stream; follow (or conform to) the trend; do as others do

随带 suídài ① going along with: 书籍一包，～书信一封。Accompanying the parcel of books is a letter. ② have sth. taken along with one: ～行李两件 two pieces of luggage which a passenger takes along with him

随地 suídì anywhere; everywhere: 不要～乱扔东西。Don't litter.

随动件 suídòngjiàn *mech.* follower: 凸轮～ cam follower

随访 suífǎng (of doctors, etc.) follow up a case by regular visits to or correspondence with a patient

随份子 suí fènzi ① contribute one's share of a group gift ② present a gift of money for a wedding, funeral, etc.

随风倒 suífēngdǎo bend with the wind—be easily swayed (by whichever side has more power or influence)

随风转舵 suí fēng zhuǎn duò same as 顺风转舵 shùn fēng zhuǎn duò

随感 suígǎn random thoughts: 《旅欧～》*Random Thoughts on Travels in Europe*

随行就市 suí háng jiù shì (of prices) fluctuate in line with market conditions

随和 suíhe amiable; obliging: 脾气～ have an amiable disposition

随后 suíhòu *adv.* soon afterwards: 你先走，我～就去。You go first. I'll follow. or You go ahead. I'll be there right away.

随机 suíjī ① *statistics* random ② *math.* stochastic

随机变数 suíjī biànshù *statistics* random variable

随机抽样 suíjī chōuyàng *statistics* random sampling

随机存取存储器 suíjī cúnqǔcúnchǔqì *computer* random access memory (RAM)

随机过程 suíjī guòchéng *math.* stochastic process

随机应变 suíjī-yìngbiàn do as the changing circumstances demand; suit one's actions to changing conditions; act according to circumstances

随即 suíjí soon after that; immediately; presently: 他挂了电话～出门。He went out as soon as he hung up.

随军 suíjūn go along with an army: 派干部～南下 send cadres south with the army

随军记者 suíjūn jìzhě war correspondent

随军家属 suíjūn jiāshǔ camp family (i.e. an army officer's family allowed to settle at an army camp)

随口 suíkǒu speak thoughtlessly or casually; blurt out whatever comes into one's head: ～答应 say "yes" absent-mindedly; agree without thinking

随群 suíqún do as everybody else does; follow the crowd

随人俯仰 suí rén fǔ-yǎng be at sb.'s beck and call; follow sb. servilely

随身 suíshēn (carry) on one's person; (take) with one: 他～没有带钱。He had no money on him. / 我～可以带几公斤行李? How many kilograms of luggage can I take with me? / ～衣服 clothes for change taken along during a trip

随身行李 suíshēn xíngli accompanying luggage; carry-on

items

随声附和 suí shēng fùhè　echo what others say; chime in with others

随时 suíshí　*adv.*　① at any time; at all times: 你～都可以来。Come any time (*or* whenever) you like. *or* You are welcome at all times. / ～掌握工作进程 constantly have a grip on the progress of the work; always know clearly how the work is progressing / 有了问题～向我报告。Keep me informed of any problems that may arise. ② whenever necessary; as the occasion demands: ～纠正错误 correct mistakes as soon as they occur / ～表扬好人好事 commend good people for their good deeds when the occasion arises

随时随地 suíshí-suídì　*adv.*　at all times and all places: ～都要注意卫生。Pay attention to hygiene at all times and all places.

随侍 suíshì　*formal*　① attend (*or* wait) upon one's elders and betters ② personal attendant

随手 suíshǒu　conveniently (when doing sth.); without extra trouble: 出门时～关灯。Turn the light off as you go out. / ～关门。Shut the door after you.

随顺 suíshùn　be obedient to; comply with; yield to

随俗 suísú　comply with convention; follow the customs; do as everybody else does

随…随… suí…suí…　(each 随 followed by a verb, indicating that the latter action immediately follows the former): 随叫随到 be on call at any hour / 雪随下随化。The snow melted as it fell.

随同 suítóng　be in company with; be accompanying: ～代表团出国访问 accompany a delegation on a visit abroad

随喜 suíxǐ　① *Buddhism* join in charitable and pious deeds ② join in an enjoyable activity ③ *old* visit a temple

随乡入乡 suí xiāng rù xiāng　wherever you are, follow local customs; when in Rome do as the Romans do

随想曲 suíxiǎngqǔ　*mus.* caprice; capriccio

随心 suíxīn　① follow one's inclinations: 随心所欲 suí xīn suǒ yù ② find sth. satisfactory; be gratified

随心所欲 suí xīn suǒ yù　follow one's inclinations; have one's own way; do as one pleases

随行 suíxíng　① accompany or follow sb. on a trip ② retinue; suite; *entourage*

随行人员 suíxíng rényuán　*entourage*; suite; party: 总统及其～ the President and his *entourage*

随宜 suíyí　as one sees fit: 请～改动。Please make alterations as you see fit.

随意 suíyì　at will; as one pleases: ～抽查 random check / 请各位～! Make yourselves at home, everybody!

随意肌 suíyìjī　*physiol.*　voluntary muscle

随遇而安 suí yù ér ān　feel at home wherever one is; be able to adapt oneself to different circumstances

随遇平衡 suíyùpínghéng　*phys.*　indifferent equilibrium

随员 suíyuán　① suite; retinue; *entourage* ② *diplomacy* attaché

随员领事 suíyuán lǐngshì　*diplomacy*　attaché consul

随葬物 suízàngwù　(also 随葬品 suízàngpǐn) funerary objects; burial articles

随着 suízhe　*prep.*　along with; in the wake of; in pace with: ～时间的推移 as time goes on; with the lapse (*or* passage) of time / ～生产的稳步上升 alongside the steady growth of production / ～我国工业的蓬勃发展, 产业工人的队伍不断壮大。The ranks of industrial workers are steadily expanding along with the vigorous development of our country's industry. / ～经济建设的高潮的到来, 必将出现一个文化建设的高潮。An upsurge in economic construction is bound to be followed by an upsurge in the cultural field.

遂 suí　see 半身不遂 bànshēn bùsuí ——see also suì

髓 suǐ　① *physiol.* marrow: 脊髓 jǐsuǐ ② *bot.* pith

岁 (歲、崴、歲) suì　① year: ～末 the end of the year / 辞旧～, 迎新年 ring out the Old Year and ring in the New ② *m.* year (of age): 三～女孩儿 a three-year-old girl; a little girl three years old / 这匹马两～口。This horse is two years old. ③ *formal* the year's harvest: 歉岁 qiànsuì

岁差 suìchā　*astron.* precession of the equinoxes

岁出 suìchū　annual expenditure (in a state budget)

岁除 suìchú　*formal*　New Year's Eve

岁寒三友 suì hán sān yǒu　the three plant friends who thrive in cold weather—the pine, the bamboo, and the plum

岁寒知松柏 suì hán zhī sōng-bǎi　only when the year grows cold do we see the qualities of the pine and the cypress; adversity reveals virtue

岁杪 suìmiǎo　*formal*　the end of the year; year-end

岁暮 suìmù　*formal*　the close of the year: ～天寒。Cold weather sets in as the year draws to its close.

岁入 suìrù　annual income (in a state budget); revenue

岁时 suìshí　the four seasons

岁收 suìshōu　annual income (in a state budget); revenue

岁首 suìshǒu　*formal*　the beginning of the year; the first month of the lunar year

岁数 suìshu　*inf.*　age; years: 老大爷, 您多大～了? How old are you, Grandpa? / 我是上了～的人了。I'm getting on in years.

岁星 Suìxīng　the Year Star (old name for 木星 Mùxīng)

岁修 suìxiū　annual repairs

岁月 suìyuè　years: 艰苦斗争的～ years of arduous struggle / ～不居。Time and tide wait for no man.

岁朝 suìzhāo　*formal*　the first day of the lunar New Year

祟 suì　① an evil spirit; ghost ② haunt and plague

遂¹ suì　① satisfy; fulfil: 遂愿 suìyuàn ② succeed: 所谋不～ fail in an attempt

遂² suì　*formal*　then; thereupon: 病人服药后腹痛～止。The patient's stomachache stopped after he took the medicine.　——see also suí

遂心 suìxīn　after one's own heart; to one's liking: ～如意 be perfectly satisfied / 这几件事办得太不遂他的心了。He was far from being satisfied with the way the things were done.

遂意 suìyì　to one's liking

遂愿 suìyuàn　have one's wish fulfilled

碎 suì　① break to pieces; smash: 碗掉地下就～了。The bowl smashed on the floor. ② broken; fragmentary: ～玻璃 bits of broken glass / ～布 oddments of cloth ③ garrulous; gabby: 嘴太～ talk too much; be a regular chatterbox

碎步儿 suìbùr (also 碎步子 suìbùzi) quick short steps

碎尸万段 suì shī wàn duàn tear the body to thousands of pieces (said when swearing to destroy sb.)

碎石 suìshí *archit.* crushed stone; broken stone; macadam

碎石混凝土 suìshí hùnníngtǔ *archit.* crushed stone concrete

碎石机 suìshíjī stone crusher

碎石路 suìshílù broken stone road; macadam road; macadam: 铺~面 pave the road with macadam; macadamize the road

碎屑岩 suìxièyán clastic rock

碎音 suìyīn *mus.* acciaccatura

碎嘴子 suìzuǐzi *dial.* ① chatter; jabber; prate: 两句话能说完的事就别犯~了。Don't talk on and on (*or* jabber away) when you can say it in a few words. ② a garrulous person; chatterbox

隧
　　suì see below

隧道 suìdào tunnel

隧道管 suìdàoguǎn *electron.* tunneltron

隧道效应 suìdào xiàoyìng *electron.* tunnel effect

隧洞 suìdòng tunnel

燧
　　suì ① flint ② beacon fire (in ancient China)

燧人氏 Suìrénshì a legendary ruler of antiquity (the last of the Three August Ones 三皇, supposed to have discovered fire)

燧石 suìshí flint

燧石玻璃 suìshí bōli flint glass

邃
　　suì *formal* ① remote (in time or space): ~古 remote antiquity ② deep; profound

邃密 suìmì ① deep: 屋宇~。The houses were deep and spacious. ② profound: ~的理论 a comprehensive and profound theory

穗¹
　　suì the ear of grain; spike: 麦穗 màisuì

穗²（繐）
　　suì tassel; fringe: 黄~红罩的宫灯 red-shaded palace lanterns fringed with yellow tassels

穗³
　　Suì another name for 广州 Guǎngzhōu

穗选 suìxuǎn *agric.* ear selection (i.e. seed selection done ear by ear)

穗状花序 suìzhuàng huāxù *bot.* spike

穗子¹ suìzi the ear of grain; spike

穗子² suìzi tassel; fringe: 有~的旗 a banner fringed with tassels

sūn

孙（孫）
　　sūn ① son's son; grandson ② generations below that of the grandson: 玄孙 xuánsūn ③ relatives belonging to grandson's generation: 外孙 wàisūn / 侄孙 zhísūn ④ second growth of plants: ~竹 new shoots of bamboo from an old stump ⑤ (Sūn) a surname

孙女 sūn·nǚ son's daughter; granddaughter

孙女婿 sūnnǚxu granddaughter's husband; grandson-in-law

孙悟空跳不出如来佛的掌心 Sūn. Wùkōng tiàobuchū Rúláifóde zhǎngxīn like the Monkey King who cannot jump out of Buddha's palm—be unable to get out of sb.'s control

孙媳妇 sūnxífu grandson's wife; granddaughter-in-law

孙子兵法 Sūnzǐ Bīngfǎ *The Art of War* by Sunzi

孙子 sūnzi son's son; grandson

狲（猻）
　　sūn see 猢狲 húsūn

荪（蓀）
　　sūn a sweet-smelling grass mentioned in ancient texts

飧（飱）
　　sūn *formal* supper

sǔn

笋（筍）
　　sǔn bamboo shoot

笋鞭 sǔnbiān the subterranean stem of bamboo

笋干 sǔngān air-dried (cooked) bamboo shoots

笋瓜 sǔnguā winter squash

笋鸡 sǔnjī young chicken; broiler

笋尖 sǔnjiān tender tips of bamboo shoots

笋子¹ sǔnzi *dial.* bamboo shoot

笋子² sǔnzi same as 榫子 sǔnzi

损
　　sǔn ① decrease; lose: 增~ increase and decrease ② harm; damage: 有益无~ can only do good, not harm / 以~人开始，以害己告终 begin with injuring others and end up ruining oneself ③ *dial.* sarcastic; caustic; cutting: 他爱~人。He delights in making caustic remarks. / 说话别太~。Don't be so sarcastic. ④ *dial.* mean; shabby: 这法子真~。That's a mean trick.

损兵折将 sǔnbīng-zhéjiàng suffer heavy casualties

损德 sǔndé injure one's virtue (by misdeeds)

损公肥私 sǔngōng-féisī seek private gain at public expense; feather one's nest at public expense

损害 sǔnhài ① do harm to; damage; impair: ~庄稼 damage crops; be harmful to crops / ~健康 impair one's health / ~他人的名誉 impair (*or* damage) another's reputation; defame another's character / ~两国关系 impair bilateral relations / ~第三者的利益 jeopardize the interests of the third party; do sth. at the expense of the third party / 在光线不好的地方看书，容易~视力。Reading in poor light is bad for one's eyes. / 决不能~群众的利益。On no account should the interests of the masses be infringed upon. ② harm; injury; damage: 造成严重~ do great harm to; inflict serious damage on / 重大~ substantial damage

损耗 sǔnhào ① loss; wear and tear: 摩擦~ friction loss ② *com.* wastage; spoilage: 运输过程中造成的~ damage and spoilage incurred during transportation

损耗费 sǔnhàofèi cost of wear and tear

损耗率 sǔnhàolù *com.* proportion of goods damaged

损坏 sǔnhuài damage (objects): ~公物要赔。Pay for public property you damage. / 不要~树木。Do not damage the trees and bushes. / 在这次事故中两辆汽车都受到严重~。The accident did great damage to both cars.

损毁 sǔnhuǐ damage or destroy: 数万株树木遭~。Tens of thousands of trees were damaged or destroyed.

损人利己 sǔnrén-lìjǐ harm others to benefit oneself; benefit oneself at the expense of others

损伤 sǔnshāng ① harm; damage; injure: 不要~群众的积极性。Don't dampen the enthusiasm of the masses. ② loss: 敌军兵力~很大。The enemy forces suffered heavy losses.

损失 sǔnshī ① lose: ~坦克五辆 lost five tanks / ~了八百万元 lost 8 million *yuan* / ~殆尽 nearly lost everything ② loss; damage: 遭受重大~ suffer (*or* sustain) heavy losses / 生命和财产的~ loss in lives and property

损益 sǔnyì ① increase and decrease: 斟酌~ consider

making necessary adjustments ② profit and loss; gains and losses: ～相抵。The gains offset the losses.

损益计算书 sǔnyì jìsuànshū profit and loss statement

隼 sǔn falcon

榫 sǔn tenon

榫头 sǔntou tenon

榫眼 sǔnyǎn mortise

榫子 sǔnzi same as 榫头 sǔntou

suō

娑 suō see below

娑罗树 suōluóshù sal tree (*Shorea robusta*)

莎 suō see below——see also shā

莎草 suōcǎo nutgrass flatsedge (*Cyperus rotundus*)

唆 suō instigate; abet: 教唆 jiàosuō

唆弄 suō-nòng incite; instigate: ～是非 sow discord

唆使 suōshǐ instigate; abet: ～者 instigator; abettor

挲（挱） suō see 摩挲 mósuō——see also sa; sha

杪 suō see below

杪椤 suōluó *bot.* spinulose tree fern (*Cyathea spinulosa*)

梭 suō shuttle: 无～织机 shuttleless loom

梭镖 suōbiāo spear: ～队 spear corps

梭梭 suōsuō *bot.* sacsaoul (*Holoxylon ammodendron*)

梭巡 suōxún *formal* move around to watch and guard; patrol to and fro

梭鱼 suōyú (redeye) mullet

梭子¹ suōzi weaver's shuttle

梭子² suōzi ① cartridge clip ② *m.* a clip (of bullets): 打了一～子弹 fire a whole clip of ammunition

梭子蟹 suōzixiè swimming crab

梭子鱼 suōziyú barracuda

睃 suō look askance at

羧 suō *chem.* carboxyl

羧基 suōjī *chem.* carboxyl; carboxyl group

羧酸 suōsuān *chem.* carboxylic acid

嗍 suō suck

蓑（簔） suō alpine rush or palm-bark rain cape

蓑草 suōcǎo (also 蓑衣草 suōyīcǎo) *dial.* Chinese alpine rush (*Eulaliopsis binata*)

蓑衣 suōyī alpine rush or palm-bark rain cape

缩 suō ① contract; shrink: 热胀冷～ expand with heat and contract with cold / 这种布下水不～。This cloth won't shrink when it's washed. ② draw back; withdraw; recoil: 他把身子一～。He shrank back (in shame, horror, etc.). / 冷得～成一团 huddle oneself up with cold / 敌人一～回去了。The enemy has drawn back.

缩编 suōbiān (of troops, government organs, etc.) reduce the staff

缩脖子 suō bózi draw back one's neck—draw back; shrink back: 碰上困难就～ shrink from difficulty

缩尺 suōchǐ reduced scale; scale

缩尺图 suōchǐtú scale drawing

缩短 suōduǎn shorten; cut down; cut short: ～学制 shorten the period of schooling / ～距离 reduce the distance; narrow the gap / ～我们在经济技术上同发达国家之间的差距 narrow the economic and technological gaps between China and the developed countries / 把报告～一半 cut a report down to half its length / 把停留时间～一天 cut short one's stay by one day / 期限从五天～到三天。The time allowed has been reduced from 5 to 3 days.

缩短战线 suōduǎn zhànxiàn contract the front—narrow the scope of an activity: 缩短基建战线 slash unnecessary projects in capital construction; curtail capital construction

缩放仪 suōfàngyí pantograph

缩合 suōhé *chem.* condensation

缩合反应 suōhé fǎnyìng condensation reaction

缩合物 suōhéwù condensation compound

缩减 suōjiǎn reduce; cut: ～开支 reduce (*or* cut) spending / ～军费 cut back military expenditure / ～重叠的机构 trim overlapping organizations / ～行政人员，增加科技人员 retrench administrative staff and expand scientific and technological staff

缩聚 suōjù *chem.* condensation polymerization

缩聚物 suōjùwù condensation polymer

缩手 suōshǒu ① draw back one's hand ② shrink (from doing sth.)

缩手缩脚 suōshǒu-suōjiǎo ① shrink with cold ② be overcautious: 不要～，放开手脚干。Don't be overcautious. Go ahead boldly with your work.

缩水 suōshuǐ (of cloth through wetting) shrink: 毛织品泡在热水里就～。Wool shrinks when soaked in hot water. *or* Hot water shrinks wool.

缩水率 suōshuǐlǜ shrinkage: ～高达每10米15公分 a shrinkage of 15cm. in a length of 10m.

缩头虫 suōtóuchóng bamboo worm

缩头缩脑 suōtóu-suōnǎo ① be timid; be fainthearted ② shrink from responsibility

缩微 suōwēi microform

缩微技术 suōwēi jìshù microphotography

缩微胶卷 suōwēi jiāojuǎn microfilm

缩微胶片 suōwēi jiāopiàn microfiche; microcopy

缩微照片 suōwēi zhàopiàn microfilm; microphotograph

缩小 suōxiǎo ① reduce (in width, size, scope, etc.); lessen; narrow; shrink: ～范围 reduce the scope; narrow the range / 逐步～城乡差别 gradually reduce the distinction between town and country ② be reduced; shrink: 他的毛衣放到热水里一洗就～了。His sweater shrank when he washed it in hot water. / 他们的机构～了许多。Their organization has been greatly reduced in size.

缩写 suōxiě ① abbreviation ② abridge

缩写本 suōxiěběn abridged edition (*or* version)

缩写签字 suōxiě qiānzì initials

缩印 suōyìn reprint books in a reduced format

缩影 suōyǐng epitome; miniature

suǒ

所¹（処） suǒ ① place: 住所 zhùsuǒ / 休养所 xiūyǎngsuǒ ② office; bureau; institute: 指挥所 zhǐhuīsuǒ / 派出所 pàichūsuǒ ③ *m.* (for houses, schools, hospitals, etc.): 一～房子 a house / 两～学校 two schools / 这～医院 this hospital

所²（処） suǒ *part. formal* (used before a

verb to form a noun construction) what, that which, those whom, etc. ① noun or pronoun + 所 + verb ⓐ (used with 的 to modify a noun): 我～认识的人 the people I know / 大家～提的意见 the opinions various people put forward ⓑ (used with 的 as a noun): 他～说的未必确实. What he says is not necessarily true. / 我～知道的就这些。That's all I know. ⓒ (used as a noun without 的, esp. when the verb is monosyllabic): 尽我～能 do all I can / 据你～说 from what you say ② 所 + verb ⓐ (used with 的 to modify a noun): ～用的方法 the methods which are used / ～需的费用 the necessary expenses ⓑ (used with 的 as a noun): ～需的并不多。What is needed is not much. / ～考虑的正是这一点。That's just what we have under consideration. ⓒ (used as a noun without 的, esp. in set phrases in which the verb is monosyllabic): ～见～闻 what one has seen and heard / 各尽～能 from each according to his ability ③ 为 or 被 + noun or pronoun + 所 + verb (expressing a passive meaning): 为人～笑 be laughed at by other people / 被表面现象～迷惑 be misled by outward appearances ④ 所 + verb used as the object of 有 or 无 ⓐ (as the object of 有): 有～创造 create something or other / 有～准备 be prepared in some way or other ⓑ (as the object of 无, esp. in set phrases): 无～准备 need do nothing in preparation for it / 无～用心 not give serious thought to anything

所部 suǒbù　troops under one's command: 此炮兵师为李将军～. This artillery division is under General Li's command.

所长 suǒcháng　what one is good at; one's strong point; one's forte: 数学非我～. Maths is not my strong point. / 有～必有所短。Where you are strong on one thing, you are weak on another. ——see also suǒzhǎng

所答非所问 suǒ dá fēi suǒ wèn　not give a direct answer to a question; not answer to the point; give an irrelevant answer

所得 suǒdé　what one has gained or acquired; gains; earnings; income: 略有～ have gained something / ～大于所失。The gains offset the losses. or We have gained more than we have lost.

所得税 suǒdéshuì　income tax

所费不赀 suǒ fèi bùzī　incur a considerable or great expense: 工程浩大，～. The project is on such a gigantic scale that the cost is hard to calculate.

所罗门群岛 Suǒluómén Qúndǎo　Solomon Islands

所属 suǒshǔ　① what is subordinate to one or under one's command: 命令～部队立即反攻 order the units under one's command to counterattack at once / 外交部～单位 the organizations under the Foreign Ministry ② what one belongs to or is affiliated with: 向～派出所填报户口 apply to or register with the local police station for residence

所谓 suǒwèi　① what is called; what is known as: ～华北 what is called North China / ～四个现代化，是指工业、农业、国防和科学技术的现代化。By the "four modernizations" we mean modernization in industry, agriculture, national defence, and science and technology. ② so-called: 他的～"朋友"都背弃了他。All his so-called friends deserted him.

所向披靡 suǒ xiàng pīmǐ　(of troops) carry all before one; sweep away all obstacles; send the enemy fleeing helter-skelter

所向无敌 suǒ xiàng wúdí　be all-conquering; be ever-victorious; break all enemy resistance: 其声势之浩大，威力之猛烈，简直是～的。Its influence has been so great and its impact so powerful that it is invincible wherever it goes.

所向无前 suǒ xiàng wú qián　carry all before one; be irresistible

所学非所用 suǒ xué fēi suǒ yòng　be employed in a job not in one's line: 可惜他～。Pity he's employed in a job not in his line.

所以 ·suǒyǐ　① conj. ⓐ (used to introduce a clause of result, preceded by a clause of reason or cause with or without an introductory 因为 or 由于) as a result; so; therefore: 因为熊猫是珍稀动物，～要尽一切努力保护它。Pandas are a very rare animal; therefore we should do our best to protect them. / 由于临行匆忙，～来不及通知你了。I was in a hurry to leave, so I didn't let you know. / 天太冷，～我不去了。It's too cold, so I'm not going. ⓑ (used between the subject and the predicate of a clause of result, followed by a clause of reason or cause introduced by 是因为 or 是由于) the reason why: 我们～没有去，是因为我们得到通知太晚了。The reason why we didn't go was that we were notified too late. / 我～对他比较熟悉，是因为我和他在一起工作过两三年。The reason why I know him pretty well is that he and I have worked together for a couple of years. ⓒ (used in the pattern 是…所以… 的原因, preceded by a clause of reason or cause) that's why: 我和他在一起工作过两三年，这就是我～对他比较熟悉的原因。He and I have worked together for a couple of years. That's why I know him pretty well. ⓓ inf. that's just the reason; that's just the point: ～呀，要不我怎么会这么说呢? That's just the point; otherwise I wouldn't have said it. ② (used in certain set phrases as the object of the verb, to refer to sth. indefinite but understood): 不知所以 bù zhī suǒyǐ / 忘乎所以 wàng hū suǒyǐ

所以然 suǒyǐrán　the reason why; the whys and wherefores: 他说了半天还是没说出个～来。He talked a lot but made you none the wiser.

所有 suǒyǒu　① own; possess: 这些乐器属学校～。These musical instruments belong to the school. ② possessions: 尽其所有 jìn qí suǒyǒu ③ all: 把～的劲儿都使出来 exert all one's strength

所有格 suǒyǒugé　gram. the possessive case

所有权 suǒyǒuquán　proprietary rights; ownership; title

所有制 suǒyǒuzhì　system of ownership; ownership: 生产资料～ the system of ownership of the means of production

所在 suǒzài　① place; location: 那是个风景优美的～。It is a picturesque place (or a lovely scenic spot). ② where sb. or sth. is: 这是我们的力量～。That is where our strength lies. or Herein lies our strength. / ～单位 the organization one belongs to

所在地 suǒzàidì　location; seat; site

所在多有 suǒzài duō yǒu　be found almost everywhere

所长 suǒzhǎng　the head of an office, institute, etc.: 研究所～ the director of a research institute / 托儿所～ the head of a nursery ——see also suǒcháng

所致 suǒzhì　be caused by; be the result of: 这次事故是由于疏忽～。The accident was the result of (or was due to) negligence.

所作所为 suǒzuò-suǒwéi　one's behaviour or conduct: 看他平时的～，就可以想见他在这种场合的表现。Just look at his usual behaviour and you can imagine how he will behave on this occasion.

索¹　suǒ　① a large rope: 麻～ a hempen rope / 船～ a ship's rigging ② (Suǒ) a surname

索²　suǒ　① search: 遍～不得 search high and low for sth. in vain ② demand; ask; exact: ～债 demand payment of a debt

索³　suǒ　formal ① all alone; all by oneself: 离群索居 líqún suǒjū ② dull; insipid: 索然 suǒrán

索道 suǒdào　cableway; ropeway: 在河上架起～ throw

a cableway across the river／高架～ telpher

索价 suǒjià　ask (*or* demand) a price; charge: ～极高 demand an exorbitant price

索解 suǒjiě　seek an answer or explanation: ～人生的意义 ponder the meaning of life

索马里 Suǒmǎlǐ　Somalia

索马里人 Suǒmǎlǐrén　Somali

索马里语 Suǒmǎlǐyǔ　Somali (language)

索寞 suǒmò　(also 索莫, 索漠 suǒmò) *formal* ① downhearted; dejected; dispirited: 神情～ look dejected ② lonely; desolate: 岛上杂草丛生, 异常～。The island was overgrown with weeds and looked extremely desolate.

索赔 suǒpéi　claim damages; claim an indemnity

索桥 suǒqiáo　chain bridge; cable bridge

索取 suǒqǔ　ask for; demand; exact; extort: ～样品 ask for a sample／～巨额赔款 extort a huge indemnity

索然 suǒrán　dull; dry; insipid: 兴致～ uninterested; bored stiff

索然寡味 suǒrán guǎ wèi　(also 索然无味 suǒrán wú wèi) flat and insipid

索索 suǒsuǒ　① *onom.* a rustling sound: 微风吹动树叶～作响。The leaves rustled in the breeze. ② trembling: 他吓得脸色苍白, ～发抖。He turned ashen pale and trembled with fear.

索性 suǒxìng　*adv.* simply; just; might as well: 既然已经做了, ～就把它做完。Since you have started the job, you might as well finish it.／找了几个地方都没找着, ～不再找了。It was nowhere to be found, so we simply gave it up for lost.／～都捅出来。Why not just let the whole thing out?

索要 suǒyào　ask for; claim; demand

索引 suǒyǐn　index: 卡片～ card index／书名～ title index／作者～ author index／标题～ subject index

唢 suǒ　see below

唢呐 suǒnà　*suona* horn, a woodwind instrument

琐 suǒ　trivial; petty

琐事 suǒshì　trifles; trivial matters: 家庭～ household affairs

琐碎 suǒsuì　trifling; trivial: 摆脱这些～的事, 多抓些大问题。Don't get bogged down in these trivialities; try to grasp the essentials.

琐闻 suǒwén　bits of news; scraps of information

琐细 suǒxì　same as 琐碎 suǒsuì

琐屑 suǒxiè　*formal* trifling; trivial

锁 suǒ　① lock: 门上加了一把～。An extra lock has been fixed on the door. ② lock (up): ～门 lock a door／～在保险箱里 be locked up in a safe／双眉紧～ with knitted brows ③ lock and chains; chains: 枷锁 jiāsuǒ ④ lockstitch: ～眼 do a lockstitch on a buttonhole／～边 lockstitch a border

锁匙 suǒchí　*dial.* key

锁骨 suǒgǔ　*physiol.* clavicle; collarbone

锁国 suǒguó　see 闭关锁国 bìguān-suǒguó

锁簧 suǒhuáng　*mech.* locking spring

锁匠 suǒjiang　locksmith

锁紧 suǒjǐn　*mech.* locking: 自～ self-locking

锁链 suǒliàn　(also 锁链子 suǒliànzi) ① chain ② shackles; fetters; chains

锁阳 suǒyáng　*Chin. med.* Chinese cynomorium (*Cynomorium songaricum*)

锁钥 suǒyuè　① key (fig.): 解决问题的～ a key to the problem ② strategic gateway (to an important centre or a major city): 北门～ Key to the North Gate (the north gate of an old fort at the Badaling 八达岭 section of the Great Wall northwest of Beijing)

SUO

嗦 suo　see 哆嗦 duōsuo; 啰嗦 luōsuo

T

tā

它（牠） tā it: 这杯牛奶你喝了～。Drink up this glass of milk. / 有个东西在黑影里蹲着, 我也看不清～到底是猫还是狗。Some animal was crouching in the shadow. I couldn't make out whether it was a cat or a dog. / 这些画报我都看过了, 你把～拿去吧。I've finished with these pictorials. You can take them away.

它们 tāmen they or them (plural of 它): 猿、猴子、猩猩虽然是高等动物, 但～都不会制造工具。Apes, monkeys and orangutans are higher animals, but they can't make tools.

他 tā ① he or him: ～刚才给你送票来了。He came just now with a ticket for you. / 谁没有票, 问～要。Anyone without a ticket can ask him for one. / ～俩 the two of them / ～哥(老婆) his elder brother (wife) / ～家在农村。His home is in the countryside. / ～家是新搬来的。He and his family moved in here recently. ② (used for either sex when the sex of a person is unknown or unimportant): 从远处看不出～是男的还是女的。I can't tell if it's a man or a woman from a distance. / 每个孩子都讲了～学习雷锋的收获。Each child told what he or she had learnt from Lei Feng. ③ (used before a person's name for emphasis): 这事儿成与不成就看～老张了。The success or failure of this all depends on no one else but Lao Zhang. / 老王～也提前到了。Lao Wang also came a bit early. ④ (used as a meaningless mock object): 好好睡～一觉 have a good sleep / 咱们喝几杯去。Let's go and have a few drinks. / 你写～两三本书就出名了。If you can publish a couple of books, you'll become famous. ⑤ formal other; another; some other: 别无～求 have no other request / 留作～用 reserve for other uses / 调往～处 be transferred to another place / 此人早已～去。He has long since left.

他动 tādòng propelled by outside force

他动词 tādòngcí same as 及物动词 jíwù dòngcí

他加禄语 Tājiālùyǔ Tagalog (language)

他妈的 tāmāde offens. damn it; blast it; to hell with it: ～! 又下雨了! Damn it! It's raining again. / 我～才不干呢! I'll be damned if I will!

他们 tāmen ① they or them (referring to people): ～刚来, 你找～去。They've just come. You may go and see them now. / ～俩(仨) the two (three) of them / ～三位科学家都是国际知名的。The three scientists are well-known throughout the world. / ～的猫(意图) their cat (intentions) / ～家有一架钢琴。They have a piano in their home. ② (used before or after a noun or nouns for emphasis): ～弟兄都是钳工。The two brothers are fitters. / ～湖南人喜欢吃辣的。These Hunanese are fond of hot food. / 赵先生、钱先生～都下班走了。Both Mr. Zhao and Mr. Qian have left the office for the day. ③ (used after the name or title of a person to mean "and the others"): 队长～都在体育馆里练球。The captain and his team (or men) are in the gym practising.

他人 tārén another person; other people; others: 关心～比关心自己为重 be more concerned about others than oneself / 事必躬亲, 不假手～ attend to everything personally and never make sb. else do it

他日 tārì formal some other time or day; some day: ～再来看望。I'll call on you again some other time.

他杀 tāshā leg. homicide

他山攻错 tāshān gōng cuò there are other hills whose stones are good for working jade—other people's advice is of help

他乡 tāxiāng a place far away from home; an alien land

他乡遇故知 tāxiāng yù gùzhī meet an old friend in a distant land

他志 tāzhì formal other ambition; infidelity; disloyalty

她 tā she or her: ～好久没来这儿了。She hasn't been here for a long time. / 我明天找～去。I'm going to see her tomorrow.

她们 tāmen (used when the referent is feminine) they or them: ～都是女子排球队队员。All of them are members of the women's volleyball team.

铊 tā chem. thallium (Tl)

趿（靸） tā same as 趿拉 tāla

趿拉 tāla wear cloth shoes with the backs turned in; shuffle about with the backs of one's shoes trodden down: 别～着鞋走路。Don't walk around with the backs of your shoes turned in. or Don't use your shoes as slippers.

趿拉儿 tālar dial. slippers

趿拉板儿 tālabǎnr dial. wooden slippers; clogs

溻 tā dial. (of clothes, etc.) become soaked with sweat: 天太热, 我衣服都～了。It's too hot and my clothes become soaked with sweat.

塌 tā ① collapse; fall down; cave in: 墙～了。The wall collapsed. / 地震的时候～了几间房。Several houses collapsed during the earthquake. / 没什么好怕的, 天不会～下来。There's nothing to be afraid of. The sky won't fall down. ② sink; droop: 他病了好久, 两腮都～下去了。His cheeks were sunken after his long illness. / ～鼻梁 a flat nose / 花儿晒～秧了。The flowers drooped in the hot sun. ③ calm down; settle down: ～下心去 set one's mind at ease; settle down to (work, etc.)

塌方 tāfāng ① cave in; collapse: 大坝出现～。A section of the dam has caved in. ② landslide; landslip

塌架 tājià ① (of a building, etc.) collapse; topple down ② fall from power

塌落 tāluò cave in; collapse: 天花板～了, 打在他们身上。The ceiling caved in on them.

塌实 tāshi ① steady and sure; dependable: 工作～ be a steady worker; be steadfast in one's work ② free from anxiety; having peace of mind: 等事情办完, 我就

觉得～了。I'll be able to put my mind at rest when the matter is settled. / 睡得很～ enjoy a deep, quiet sleep; have a good, sound sleep / 经过检查, 发电机并没有毛病, 我们心里就～了。We felt relieved when the generator was checked and found in order.

塌台 tātái fall from power; collapse

塌陷 tāxiàn subside; sink; cave in: 这座房子的地基～了。The foundations of this building have subsided.

遢

tā see 邋遢 lāta

踏

tā see below ——see also tà

踏实 tāshi same as 塌实 tāshi

tǎ

溚

tǎ old name for 焦油 jiāoyóu

塔(墖)

tǎ ① Buddhist pagoda; pagoda ② tower: 水塔 shuǐtǎ ③ *chem.* column; tower: 氧化～ oxidizing column (or tower) / 蒸馏～ distillation column (or tower)

塔吊 tǎdiào tower crane

塔夫绸 tǎfūchóu taffeta

塔吉克斯坦 Tǎjíkèsītǎn Tadzhikistan

塔吉克斯坦人 Tǎjíkèsītǎnrén Tajik

塔吉克族 Tǎjíkèzú the Tajik nationality, or the Tajiks, inhabiting the Xinjiang Uygur Autonomous Region

塔楼 tǎlóu ① tower ② turret

塔轮 tǎlún *mech.* cone pulley; stepped pulley

塔式起重机 tǎshì qǐzhòngjī same as 塔吊 tǎdiào

塔塔尔族 Tǎtǎ'ěrzú the Tatar nationality, or the Tatars, inhabiting the Xinjiang Uygur Autonomous Region

塔台 tǎtái *aviation* control tower

塔钟 tǎzhōng tower clock; turret clock

獭

tǎ otter: 水獭 shuǐtǎ

鳎

tǎ *zool.* sole

tà

拓(搨)

tà make rubbings from inscriptions, pictures, etc. on stone tablets or bronze vessels ——see also tuò

拓本 tàběn a book of rubbings

拓片 tàpiàn rubbing (from a stone tablet or bronze vessel)

沓

tà *formal* crowded; repeated: 杂沓 zátà ——see also dá

沓乱 tàluàn numerous and disorderly: ～的脚步声 the clatter of footsteps

傝(儚)

tà see 佻傝 tiāotà

闼(闥)

tà *formal* door; small door; wicket gate: 排闼直入 pái tà zhí rù

迖(澾)

tà *formal* slippery; smooth

挞(撻)

tà *formal* flog; whip: 鞭挞 biāntà

挞伐 tàfá *formal* send armed forces to suppress; send a punitive expedition against

嗒

tà see below ——see also dā

嗒然 tàrán *formal* dejected; despondent; depressed

嗒然若丧 tàrán ruò sàng deeply despondent; mournful and dejected

嗒丧 tàsàng in low spirits; dejected; despondent: ～着脸 wear a sad look; put on a long face

逿

tà see 杂逿 zátà

榻

tà a long, narrow and low bed; couch: 竹～ bamboo couch / 藤～ rattan (or cane) couch

踏

tà ① step on; tread; stamp: 把火～灭 tread out a fire / ～平匪巢 smash the bandits' lair / ～上贵国的土地 set foot on the soil of your country / ～着先烈的血迹前进 march ahead along the path crimson with the blood of martyrs / 勘探队～遍了祖国的山山水水。The prospecting team has traversed the length and breadth of the land. ② go to the spot (to make an investigation or survey): 踏勘 tàkān ——see also tā

踏板 tàbǎn ① treadle; footboard; footrest: 缝纫机～ the treadle of a sewing machine ② footstool (usu. placed beside a bed) ③ *mus.* pedal (of a piano, etc.): 强音～ damper (or loud) pedal / 弱音～ soft pedal

踏步 tàbù ① mark time; march in place ② *dial.* a flight of steps; steps leading up to a house, etc.

踏歌 tàgē singing accompanied by stamping of feet, or rhythmic dancing

踏勘 tàkān ① make an on-the-spot survey (of a railway line, construction site, etc.) ② *old* (of an official) make a personal investigation on the spot

踏看 tàkàn go to the spot to make an investigation

踏破铁鞋无觅处, 得来全不费工夫 tàpò tiěxié wú mìchù, délái quán bù fèi gōngfu you can wear out iron shoes in fruitless searching, and yet by a lucky chance you may find the lost thing without even looking for it; fancy finding by sheer luck what one has searched for far and wide

踏青 tàqīng walk on the green grass—go for an outing in early spring

踏雪 tàxuě walk in the snow

踏月 tàyuè walk in the moonlight

蹋

tà see 糟蹋 zāota

tāi

苔

tāi see 舌苔 shétāi ——see also tái

胎[1]

tāi ① foetus; embryo: ～形 the form of the foetus / 有了～了 become (or be) pregnant / ～掉了 have a miscarriage ② birth: 头～ first baby; firstborn / 一～十五只小猪 fifteen piglets at a litter (or at one farrow) ③ padding; stuffing; wadding: 棉花胎 miánhuatāi ④ roughcast (in the making of china, *cloisonné*, etc.): 泥胎儿 nítāir

胎[2]

tāi tyre: 内胎 nèitāi / 外胎 wàitāi

胎动 tāidòng movement of the foetus which can be felt by the mother

胎动不安 tāidòng bù'ān *Chin. med.* a sign of approaching abortion characterized by movement of the foetus causing pain in the lower abdomen

胎毒 tāidú *Chin. med.* skin infections of newborn infants such as boils, blisters, eczema, etc. considered to be caused by febrile toxin transmitted from the mother

胎儿 tāi'ér ① (human) foetus ② foetus (of a domestic animal)

胎发 tāifà　foetal hair; lanugo

胎教 tāijiào　antenatal instruction (i.e. influencing the development of the foetus by maternal impressions)

胎里富 tāilǐfù　a person born with a silver spoon in his mouth

胎里坏 tāilǐhuài　a born villain

胎里素 tāilǐsù　a born vegetarian

胎毛 tāimáo　foetal hair; lanugo

胎膜 tāimó　foetal membrane

胎盘 tāipán　placenta

胎气 tāiqì　nausea, vomiting and oedema of legs during pregnancy; pregnancy complications

胎生 tāishēng　*zool.* viviparity

胎生动物 tāishēng dòngwù　viviparous animal; vivipara

胎位 tāiwèi　*med.* position of a foetus

胎衣 tāiyī　same as 胞衣 bāoyī

胎痣 tāizhì　birthmark: 她脸上有颗红色的～。She has a red birthmark on her face.

胎座 tāizuò　*bot.* placenta

tái

台¹（臺、枱） tái ① platform; stage; terrace: ～上坐着主席团。Seated on the rostrum was the presidium. ② anything shaped like a platform, etc.: 灶台 zàotái / 窗台 chuāngtái ③ stand; support: 灯台 dēngtái / 蜡台 làtái ④ *m.* (for certain machinery, apparatus, instruments, etc.): 一～打字机（计算机、拖拉机）a typewriter (computer, tractor) ⑤ *m.* (for a whole performance on the stage): 一～戏（话剧、歌舞）a performance (modern drama, song and dance performance) ⑥ special telephone service: 长途台 chángtútái / 查号台 cháhàotái ⑦ broadcasting station: 电视台 diànshìtái

台²（檯） tái　table; desk: 写字台 xiězìtái / 梳妆台 shūzhuāngtái

台³ tái　*honor. formal* your: ～启 for your information (used after the name of the addressee on an envelope) / ～鉴 for your inspection (used after the name in the salutation of a business letter)

台⁴（臺） Tái　short for Taiwan Province

台⁵（颱） tái　see 台风¹ táifēng

台本 táiběn　a playscript with stage directions

台布 táibù　tablecloth

台步 táibù　(in traditional opera) stage walk: 梅兰芳的～非常优美。Mei Lanfang's stage walk was very graceful.

台秤 táichèng ① platform scale; platform balance ② *dial.* counter scale

台词 táicí　actor's lines

台灯 táidēng　desk lamp; table lamp; reading lamp

台地 táidì ① *geol.* platform; tableland ② *mil.* mesa

台度 táidù　old name for 墙裙 qiángqún

台端 táiduān　*honor. formal* you (used in business letters)

台风¹ táifēng　typhoon: 强～ a violent typhoon / ～动向 typhoon movement / ～警戒线 typhoon detective line / ～路径 typhoon track / ～眼 typhoon eye

台风² táifēng　an actor's demeanour on the stage: ～稳健 a calm and steady stage demeanour

台甫 táifǔ　*honor. formal* your honoured style (used in asking sb.'s courtesy name): ～？ May I ask your honoured style?

台虎钳 táihǔqián　*mech.* bench vice

台阶 táijiē ① a flight of steps; steps leading up to a house, etc. ② chance to extricate oneself from an awkward position: 给他个～下吧。Give him an out. ③ *min.* bench: 上～ upper bench ——see also 下台阶 xià táijiē

台历 táilì　desk calendar

台面¹ táimiàn　*electron.* mesa: ～型晶体管 mesa transistor

台面² táimiàn　*dial.* ① on the table; aboveboard; in public ② winnings and losses (in gambling)

台钳 táiqián　*mech.* bench clamp

台球 táiqiú ① billiards ② billiard ball ③ *dial.* table tennis; ping-pong

台田 táitián　*agric.* raised fields; platform fields

台湾 Táiwān　Taiwan (Province)

台钟 táizhōng　*dial.* desk clock

台柱子 táizhùzi ① star or leading member (of a theatrical troupe) ② soul member (of an organization); mainstay; pillar

台子 táizi ① *inf.* platform; stage ② *dial.* table; desk ③ billiard table ④ table tennis table; ping-pong table

台钻 táizuàn　*mech.* bench drill

邰 Tái　a surname

抬（擡） tái ① lift; raise: ～胳膊 raise one's arm / 把桌子～起来 lift (up) the table ② (of two or more persons) carry: ～担架 carry a stretcher ③ same as 抬杠¹ táigàng

抬秤 táichèng　huge steelyard (usu. worked by three persons, with two lifting the steelyard on a shoulder pole and the third adjusting the weight)

抬杠¹ táigàng　*inf.* argue for the sake of arguing; bicker; wrangle: 他俩抬起杠来就没完。Those two can go on arguing for hours and hours.

抬杠² táigàng　*old* carry a coffin on stout poles

抬高 táigāo　raise; heighten; enhance: ～声誉 raise sb.'s reputation / ～物价 force up commodity prices / 打击别人，～自己 attack others so as to build oneself up

抬价 táijià　force up commodity prices

抬肩 táijian　(also 抬裉 táikèn) half the circumference of the sleeve where it joins the shoulder

抬轿子 tái jiàozi　carry sb. in a sedan chair—flatter (rich and influential people); sing the praises of; boost

抬举 táiju　praise or promote sb. to show favour; favour sb. ——see also 不识抬举 bù shí táiju

抬手 táishǒu ① raise one's hand ② be magnanimous; not be too hard on sb.; make an exception in sb.'s favour: 这事只要您抬手，就过去了。I'll get off if you will make an exception in my case.

抬头¹ táitóu ① raise one's head: ～一看 look up ② gain ground; look up; rise

抬头² táitóu ① begin a new line, as a mark of respect, when mentioning the addressee in letters, official correspondence, etc. ② *com.* (on receipts, bills, etc.) name of the buyer or payee, or space for filling in such a name

抬头纹 táitóuwén　wrinkles on one's forehead

苔 tái　*bot.* liverwort ——see also tāi

苔藓动物 táixiǎn dòngwù　bryozoan

苔藓植物 táixiǎn zhíwù　bryophyte

苔原 táiyuán　*geog.* tundra

骀 tái　*formal* an inferior horse; a broken-down nag: 驽骀 nútái

炱　tái　soot: 煤炱 méitái

鲐　tái　chub mackerel

薹[1]　tái　*bot.*　a kind of sedge

薹[2]　tái　the bolt of garlic, rape, etc.

tài

太　tài ① highest; greatest: 太空 tàikōng ② remotest: 太古 tàigǔ ③ more or most senior: ～老伯 granduncle; great-uncle／～老师 father of one's teacher or teacher of one's father ④ *adv.* excessively; too; over: 你车开得～快，不安全。You're driving too fast for safety.／那～过分了。That's going too far.／这座城市人口～多。The city is over-populated.／水～热，烫手。The water is scalding to the touch.／您～客气了。You are being too modest. *or* You are too kind.／你～夸奖了。You flatter me.／他～坚持己见了。He stubbornly adheres to his opinions.／你～相信这家伙了。You place too much trust in this fellow. ⑤ *adv.* ⓐ (used to express admiration or exclamation with 了 at the end of the sentence): 她的发音～好了。Her pronunciation is excellent.／长城～伟大了。The Great Wall is really great.／我～感激你了。I feel very much indebted to you.／哥儿俩长得～像了。The two brothers are very much alike.／又见到您，～高兴了。I'm extremely glad to see you again. ⓑ (used before another adverb 不 to emphasize negation): 这～不好了。It's very bad.／你～不虚心了。You're being immodest.／这个人～不讲道理。This man is so impervious to all reason.／这～不像话了! This is simply outrageous! *or* This is the height of absurdity! ⓒ (used after 不 to soften the tone of negation): 不～好 not very good／这车看起来不～漂亮，可就是快。The car isn't much to look at, but it's fast.／你这样做不～合适吧。That's not a very good way to go about it.／他不～愿意结交新朋友。He's hesitant about making new friends.

太白星　Tàibáixīng　Grand White (old name for 金星 Jīnxīng)

太仓一粟　tàicāng yī sù　a grain of millet in a granary—a drop in the ocean

太阿倒持　Tài'ē dào chí　hold the sword by the blade—surrender one's power to another at one's own peril

太公　tàigōng　*dial.*　great-grandfather

太公钓鱼，愿者上钩　Tàigōng diào yú, yuànzhě shàng gōu　like the fish rising to Jiang Taigong's hookless and baitless line—a willing victim letting himself be caught

太古　tàigǔ　remote antiquity

太古代　Tàigǔdài　*geol.*　the Archean (or Archaeozoic) Era

太古界　Tàigǔjiè　*geol.*　the Archean Erathem

太后　tàihòu　mother of an emperor; empress dowager; queen mother

太湖石　tàihúshí　*taihu* rocks (boulders found on the edge of the Tai Lake, highly prized by builders of rock gardens for their convolutions caused by weathering)

太极　tàijí　the Supreme Ultimate (the Absolute in ancient Chinese cosmology, presented as the primary source of all created things 万物)

太极拳　tàijíquán　*taijiquan*, a system of physical exercises that emphasizes balance, coordination, and effortlessness in movements, designed for attaining bodily or mental control and wellbeing and also as an art

of self-defence ——see also 打太极拳 dǎ tàijíquán

太极图　tàijítú　Diagram of the Supreme Ultimate (consisting of a wavy or double curved line bisecting a circle, one half of which is white and the other black; a symbol of Taoism and a motif in art)

太监　tàijiàn　(court) eunuch

太空　tàikōng　the firmament; outer space

太空梭　tàikōngsuō　another name for 航天飞机 hángtiān fēijī

太庙　tàimiào　the Imperial Ancestral Temple

太平　tàipíng　peaceful and tranquil; having good social order and without war

太平花　tàipínghuā　Beijing mockorange (*Philadelphus pekinensis*)

太平间　tàipíngjiān　mortuary

太平龙头　tàipíng lóngtóu　fire hydrant; fire plug

太平门　tàipíngmén　exit (of a building, etc.)

太平鸟　tàipíngniǎo　waxwing

太平盛世　tàipíng shèngshì　times of peace and prosperity; the piping times of peace

太平水缸　tàipíng shuǐgāng　a vat filled with water for use in case of fire

太平梯　tàipíngtī　fire escape

太平天国　Tàipíng Tiānguó　the Taiping Heavenly Kingdom (1851-1864), established by Hong Xiuquan 洪秀全 during the Taiping Revolution, the largest of peasant uprisings in China's history

太平无事　tàipíng wú shì　all is well

太平洋　Tàipíngyáng　the Pacific (Ocean)

太婆　tàipó　*dial.*　great-grandmother

太上皇　tàishànghuáng ① a title assumed by an emperor's father who abdicated in favour of his son ② overlord; supersovereign; backstage ruler

太上老君　Tàishàng Lǎojūn　Most Exalted Lord Lao (a Taoist deity, identified with Lao Zi 老子)

太甚　tàishèn　too far; to the extreme: 欺人太甚 qī rén tàishèn

太师椅　tàishīyǐ　an old-fashioned wooden armchair

太岁　tàisuì ① the Master of the Year (an ancient name for 木星 Mùxīng) ② the God of the Year (a god supposed to change his dwelling on earth every year and to allow no construction work where he happens to dwell and preside, the location of his new home being set by the almanac) ③ *derog.* a nickname for the most powerful man in a locality: 镇山～ the Lord of the Mountain (a brigand chief)／花花～ the King of Lechers

太岁头上动土　tàisuì tóushang dòng tǔ　break ground where Taisui (a god) presides—defy the mighty

太太　tàitai ① Mrs.; madame: 王～ Mrs. Wang; Madame Wang ② the mistress of a household; madam; lady ③ (usu. preceded by a personal pronoun) wife: 我～ my wife ④ *dial.* (paternal) great-grandmother or great-grandfather

太息　tàixī　*liter.*　heave a deep sigh

太虚　tàixū　*liter.*　the great void; the universe

太学　tàixué　the Imperial College (in feudal China)

太阳　tàiyáng ① the sun: ～光 the sun's rays; sunshine; sunlight ② the sun's rays; sunshine; sunlight: 晒～ bask in the sun／今天～很好。It's a lovely sunny day.

太阳常数　tàiyáng chángshù　solar constant

太阳灯　tàiyángdēng　*med.*　sunlamp; sunlight lamp

太阳地儿　tàiyángdìr　a place where there is sunshine; sunny spot

太阳电池　tàiyáng diànchí　solar cell

太阳风　tàiyángfēng　solar wind

太阳辐射　tàiyáng fúshè　*meteorol.*　solar radiation

太阳光谱　tàiyáng guāngpǔ　*phys.*　solar spectrum

太阳黑子　tàiyáng hēizǐ　sunspot

太阳活动周　tàiyáng huódòngzhōu　solar cycle

太阳镜　tàiyángjìng　sunglasses

太阳历　tàiyánglì　solar calendar

太阳炉　tàiyánglú　solar furnace

太阳帽　tàiyángmào　sun helmet; topee

太阳目视镜　tàiyáng mùshìjìng　helioscope

太阳能　tàiyángnéng　solar energy

太阳年　tàiyángnián　another name for 回归年 huíguīnián

太阳鸟　tàiyángniǎo　sunbird

太阳系　tàiyángxì　the solar system

太阳穴　tàiyángxué　the temples

太阳灶　tàiyángzào　solar energy stove; solar cooker

太爷　tàiyé　① (paternal) grandfather ② *dial.* (paternal) great-grandfather

太医　tàiyī　① an imperial physician ② *dial.* medical man; doctor

太阴　tàiyīn　① *dial.* the moon ② *astron.* lunar

太阴历　tàiyīnlì　lunar calendar

太阴年　tàiyīnnián　lunar year

太阴月　tàiyīnyuè　lunar month; lunation

太原　Tàiyuán　Taiyuan (capital of Shanxi Province)

太子　tàizǐ　crown prince

汰　tài　discard; eliminate: 淘汰 táotài

态 (態)　tài　① form; appearance; condition: 形态 xíngtài ② *phys.* state: 气态 qìtài ③ *gram.* voice: 语态 yǔtài

态度　tàidu　① manner; bearing; how one conducts oneself: ～大方 have an easy manner / ～和蔼 amiable; kindly / ～恶劣 behave badly / 你这是什么～? What sort of attitude is that? *or* Is this the way to behave? / 他今天～有些异常。He is not his usual self today. ② attitude; approach: 劳动～ attitude towards labour / 改变自己的～ change one's attitude; shift one's position / 把革命热情和科学～结合起来 combine revolutionary enthusiasm with a scientific approach / 他在改革问题上～坚决。He stands firm on the reform issue. / 在原则问题上要表明我们的～。We must state our position on matters of principle. / 这家饭馆的服务～很好。The service is good at this restaurant. ——see also 耍态度 shuǎ tàidu

态势　tàishì　state; situation; posture: 战略～ strategic situation / 军事～ military posture

肽　tài　*chem.* peptide

钛　tài　*chem.* titanium (Ti)

钛白　tàibái　(also 钛白粉 tàibáifěn) *chem.* titanium white; titanium dioxide

钛铁矿　tàitiěkuàng　ilmenite

泰　tài　① safe; peaceful: 康泰 kāngtài ② extreme; most: 泰西 Tàixī

泰斗　tàidǒu　Mount Tai and the North Star—an eminent scholar, musician, artist, etc.: 音乐界的～ the prince of musicians / 京剧～ the foremost actor of Beijing opera

泰阿倒持　Tài'ē dào chí　same as 太阿倒持 Tài'ē dào chí

泰国　Tàiguó　Thailand

泰国人　Tàiguórén　Thailander; Thai

泰然　tàirán　calm; composed; self-possessed

泰然处之　tàirán chǔ zhī　take sth. calmly; bear sth. with equanimity: ～, 行若无事 take sth. calmly as if nothing had happened

泰然自若　tàirán zìruò　behave with perfect composure; be self-possessed

泰山　Tàishān　① Mount Tai (in Shandong Province) (see also 五岳 Wǔyuè) ② a symbol of great weight or import: 有眼不识泰山 yǒu yǎn bù shí Tàishān ③ *old* wife's father; father-in-law

泰山北斗　Tàishān Běidǒu　Mount Tai and the North Star (a respectful epithet for a person of distinction)

泰山压顶　Tàishān yā dǐng　bear down on one with the weight of Mount Tai: ～不弯腰 not bend one's head even under the weight of Mount Tai; not give in to any pressure or difficulty

泰山压卵　Tàishān yā luǎn　like Mount Tai bearing down on an egg—with overwhelmingly superior force

泰西　Tàixī　*old* the West (chiefly Europe); the Occident: ～各国 the countries of Europe

泰语　Tàiyǔ　Thai (language)

酞　tài　*chem.* phthalein

tān

坍 (坍)　tān　collapse; fall; tumble: 土墙～了。The earthen wall collapsed.

坍方　tānfāng　same as 塌方 tāfāng

坍架　tānjià　same as 塌架 tājià

坍圮　tānpǐ　*formal* cave in; collapse

坍塌　tāntā　cave in; collapse

坍台　tāntái　*dial.* ① (of enterprises, etc.) collapse; fold ② fall into disgrace; lose face

坍陷　tānxiàn　same as 塌陷 tāxiàn

贪　tān　① embezzle; practise graft; be corrupt: 贪污 tānwū ② have an insatiable desire for: ～女色 be fond of women; be a womanizer / 他～吃, 这回把肚子吃坏了。He's a glutton; he ate himself sick this time. ③ covet; hanker after: ～安逸 seek ease and comfort / ～大求全 go in for grandiose projects

贪杯　tānbēi　be excessively fond of drinking; love a drop too much

贪鄙　tānbǐ　*formal* be insatiably avaricious

贪财　tāncái　be greedy for money; be a money-grubber

贪馋　tānchán　① greedy (for food); gluttonous ② insatiable; greedy: ～地读一本小说 read a novel greedily

贪得无厌　tān dé wú yàn　be insatiably avaricious

贪多嚼不烂　tānduō jiáo bù làn　bite off more than one can chew

贪多务得　tānduō wù dé　greedy and acquisitive

贪官污吏　tānguān-wūlì　corrupt officials; venal officials: 铲除～, 建立廉洁政府 throw out corrupt officials and establish clean government

贪贿无艺　tān huì wú yì　be infinitely greedy for gain; be inordinately rapacious

贪婪　tānlán　avaricious; greedy; rapacious: ～的目光 greedy eyes / ～地掠夺别国的资源 rapaciously plunder the resources of other countries / ～地追求知识 be greedy for knowledge

贪恋　tānliàn　be reluctant to part with; hate to leave; cling to: ～西湖景色 hate to leave the beautiful West Lake / ～舒适的生活 be reluctant to give up ease and comfort

贪墨　tānmò　*formal* embezzle; practise graft; be corrupt

贪便宜　tān piányi　eager to get things on the cheap; keen on gaining petty advantages

贪求　tānqiú　seek; hanker after; covet

贪色　tānsè　be fond of women; be a womanizer

贪生怕死　tānshēng-pàsǐ　cravenly cling to life instead of braving death; care for nothing but saving one's skin; be mortally afraid of death

贪天之功　tān tiān zhī gōng　arrogate to oneself the

merits of others; claim credit for other people's achievements

贪图 tāntú　seek; hanker after; covet: ～安逸 seek ease and comfort / ～小利 covet small advantages; hanker after petty gains / ～享受 seek a life of pleasure / ～金钱 be greedy for money; be a money-grubber / 他～凉快，着了凉。He wanted to cool off, but he ended up catching a chill.

贪玩 tānwán　be too fond of play

贪污 tānwū　embezzle; practise graft; be corrupt: ～5,000 元 embezzle 5,000 *yuan* / ～和浪费是极大的犯罪。Corruption and waste are very serious crimes. / ～分子 a person guilty of corruption; grafter; embezzler

贪污盗窃 tānwū dàoqiè　graft and embezzlement

贪污腐化 tānwū fǔhuà　corruption and degeneration; corruption

贪小失大 tān xiǎo shī dà　covet a little and lose a lot; seek small gains but incur big losses

贪心 tānxīn　① greed; avarice; rapacity ② greedy; avaricious; insatiable; voracious: ～不足 insatiably greedy

贪欲 tānyù　greed; avarice; rapacity

贪赃 tānzāng　take bribes; practise graft

贪赃枉法 tānzāng wǎngfǎ　take bribes and bend the law; pervert justice for a bribe

贪嘴 tānzuǐ　greedy (for food); gluttonous

滩 (灘) tān　① beach; sands: 海滩 hǎitān ② shoal: ～多水急 with many shoals and rapids

滩头堡 tāntóubǎo　*mil.* beachhead

滩羊 tānyáng　a kind of sheep known for its fine thick wool

摊 (攤) tān　① spread out: 把豆子～开晒一晒 spread the beans out to dry in the sun / 书～了一桌子。Books are strewn all over the desk. / 把事情～到桌面上来谈 put the problems on the table and thrash them out ② vendor's stand; booth; stall: 水果～儿 fruit stand; fruit stall / 报～ news-stand; news stall ③ *m.* (for paste or thick liquid): 一～稀泥 a mud puddle / 一～血 a pool of blood ④ fry batter in a thin layer: ～煎饼 make pancakes ⑤ take a share in: 每人～五毛钱。Each person will contribute 5 *mao.* ⑥ (of unpleasant things) befall; happen to: ～上这种事真倒霉! What luck to have this happen to me!

摊场 tāncháng　spread harvested grain on a threshing floor

摊贩 tānfàn　street pedlar

摊鸡蛋 tānjīdàn　omelette

摊开 tānkāi　spread out: ～双手 spread out one's hands / 把问题～来谈 discuss the questions with all cards on the table

摊牌 tānpái　lay one's cards on the table; show one's hand (*or* cards); have a showdown: 迫使对方～ force one's opponent to show his hand; force a showdown

摊派 tānpài　apportion (expenses, work, etc.)

摊晒机 tānshàijī　*agric.* tedder

摊市 tānshì　bazaar (of booths)

摊手 tānshǒu　loosen one's grip; let go

摊售 tānshòu　(of a vendor's stand) sell goods; set up a stall

摊子 tānzi　① vendor's stand; booth; stall: 菜～ vegetable stall (*or* stand) ② the structure of an organization; setup: ～铺得太大 do sth. on too large a scale

瘫 (癱) tān　be physically paralysed: 吓～了 be paralysed with fright / 他～了两年了。He's been paralysed for two years.

瘫痪 tānhuàn　① paralysis; palsy: ～病人 paralytic ②

(of transportation, etc.) be paralysed; break down; be at a standstill: 交通运输陷于～。Transportation was at a standstill.

瘫软 tānruǎn　(of arms, legs, etc.) become weak and limp: 被告一听到判决, 浑身都～了。On hearing the verdict, the defendant collapsed.

瘫子 tānzi　a person suffering from paralysis; paralytic

tán

坛¹ (壇) tán　① altar: 天坛 Tiāntán ② a raised plot of land for planting flowers, etc.: 花坛 huātán ③ platform; forum: 讲坛 jiǎngtán ④ circles; world: 文坛 wéntán

坛² (壜、罎、墰、罈) tán　earthen jar; jug: 一～醋 a jar of vinegar / 酒～ a wine jug

坛坛罐罐 tántánguànguàn　pots and pans—personal possessions: 不怕打烂～ not be afraid of having one's pots and pans smashed—not fear loss of possessions or destruction of property (in time of war)

坛子 tánzi　earthen jar; jug

昙 (曇) tán　cloudy; overcast

昙花 tánhuā　broad-leaved epiphyllum (*Epiphyllum oxypetalum*)

昙花一现 tánhuā yī xiàn　flower briefly as the broad-leaved epiphyllum; last briefly; be a flash in the pan: ～的人物 a transient figure; a person of ephemeral importance

谈 tán　① talk; chat; discuss: 他～了自己的看法。He offered his personal views. / 第一次见面他们就～得很投机。They had a most agreeable chat when they first met. / 他～到我国工业发展的前景。He talked about the prospects for industrial development in our country. / 我们好好～～。Let's have a good chat. / 我想同你们～～文学创作问题。I would like to discuss with you the question of creative writing. ② what is said or talked about: 奇谈 qítán ③ (Tán) a surname

谈柄 tánbǐng　butt of jokes

谈不到 tánbudào　(also 谈不上 tánbushàng) out of the question: 没有政治上的独立, 就～经济上的独立。Without political independence, you can't begin to talk about economic independence.

谈不来 tánbùlái　not get along well

谈得到 tándedào　(also 谈得上 tándeshàng) take into consideration: 有了组合音响才～买激光唱片。I can only consider buying a CD after I've bought a hi-fi set.

谈得来 tándelái　get along well

谈锋 tánfēng　volubility; eloquence: ～甚健 talk volubly; be a good talker; have the gift of the gab

谈何容易 tán hé róngyì　easier said than done; by no means easy

谈虎色变 tán hǔ sè biàn　turn pale at the mention of the tiger—turn pale at the mere mention of something terrifying

谈话 tánhuà　① talk; chat; discuss: 我已经跟他谈过话了。I've talked to him. / 他们正在屋里～。They're having a discussion inside. / 进行亲切友好的～ have a cordial and friendly conversation ② statement: 发表书面～ make a written statement

谈家常 tán jiācháng　talk about everyday matters; engage in small talk; chitchat

谈论 tánlùn　discuss; talk about: ～国事 discuss state affairs / 同学们纷纷～着今天发生的事。The students are all talking about what happened today.

谈判　tánpàn　negotiate; hold talks: 两国代表就边界问题～了几个星期。The representatives of the two countries negotiated the boundary question for several weeks. / 他们为签订和约进行了～。They held negotiations for the signing of a peace treaty. / 开始～ enter into (or open) negotiations with / 重开～ resume the talks / 举行～ hold talks (or negotiations) / 贸易～ trade negotiations (or talks) / 两次～都没有达成协议。Twice the negotiations ended without having reached any agreement. / ～中断了。The talks broke down. / ～桌 conference table

谈情说爱　tánqíng-shuō'ài　be courting; talk love

谈天　tántiān　(also 谈闲天 tánxiántiān) chat; make conversation

谈天说地　tántiān-shuōdì　talk of everything under the sun

谈吐　tántǔ　style of conversation: ～不俗 talk in good taste

谈笑　tánxiào　talk (or chat) and laugh

谈笑风生　tánxiào fēng shēng　talk and laugh cheerfully (or merrily)

谈笑自若　tánxiào zìruò　go on talking and laughing as if nothing had happened: 沉着镇静，～ go on talking and laughing without turning a hair / 临危不惧，～ talk and laugh imperturbably in face of danger

谈心　tánxīn　heart-to-heart talk: 在同学间开展～活动 encourage heart-to-heart talks among fellow students

谈兴　tánxìng　mood for conversation: ～正浓 be having an animated conversation

谈言微中　tán yán wēi zhòng　speak tactfully but to the point; make one's point through hints

谈助　tánzhù　formal (also 谈资 tánzī) topic of conversation: 足资～ serve as a good topic of conversation

佟
tán　(used esp. in a person's name) quiet; peaceful

弹 (彈)
tán　① shoot (as with a catapult, etc.); send forth: ～石子 shoot pebbles with a catapult ② fluff; tease: ～棉花 fluff (or tease) cotton (with a bow) ③ flick; flip: ～烟灰 flick the ash off a cigarette / 把帽子上的灰尘～掉 flick the dust off a hat ④ play (a stringed musical instrument); pluck: ～钢琴 play the piano / ～琵琶 pluck the pipa ⑤ spring; leap: 球从篮板上～回来。The ball rebounded from the backboard. / 从跳板上～起来 leap from the springboard ⑥ elastic: 弹性 tánxìng ⑦ accuse; impeach: 弹劾 tánhé ——see also dàn

弹拨　tánbō　play (a stringed musical instrument); pluck

弹拨乐器　tánbō yuèqì　plucked string (or stringed) instrument; plucked instrument

弹词　táncí　① storytelling (esp. in Suzhou dialect) to the accompaniment of stringed instruments ② script for this kind of storytelling

弹冠相庆　tán guān xiāng qìng　congratulate each other in anticipation of fat jobs (upon hearing of a mutual friend's appointment to a high post); congratulate each other on the prospect of getting good appointments

弹劾　tánhé　impeach (a public official)

弹花机　tánhuājī　cotton fluffer

弹簧　tánhuáng　spring: 回动～ return spring / 保险～ relief spring

弹簧秤　tánhuángchèng　spring balance

弹簧床　tánhuángchuáng　spring bed

弹簧钢　tánhuánggāng　spring steel

弹簧铰链　tánhuáng jiǎoliàn　spring hinge

弹簧门　tánhuángmén　swing door

弹簧圈　tánhuángquān　spring coil

弹簧锁　tánhuángsuǒ　spring lock

弹力　tánlì　elastic force; elasticity; resilience; spring: 失去～的橡皮圈 a perished rubber band

弹力尼龙　tánlì nílóng　stretch nylon; elastic nylon

弹力纱　tánlìshā　stretch yarn

弹力袜　tánlìwà　stretch socks

弹球　tánqiú　(play) marbles

弹射　tánshè　① mil. launch (as with a catapult); catapult; shoot off; eject ② formal pick faults and criticize; censure: ～利病 pick faults

弹射器　tánshèqì　ejector; catapult

弹射座舱　tánshè zuòcāng　ejection capsule

弹射座椅　tánshè zuòyǐ　ejection (or ejector) seat

弹跳　tántiào　bounce; spring: ～力好 have a lot of spring

弹跳板　tántiàobǎn　sports springboard

弹涂鱼　tántúyú　mudskipper

弹性　tánxìng　elasticity; resilience; spring: 又软又有～的地毯 soft and springy carpets / 这种毛～大，拉力强。This wool possesses high resilience and tensile strength. / 球的～符合标准。The balls reach the specifications for bounce.

弹性极限　tánxìng jíxiàn　elastic limit

弹性计　tánxìngjì　elastometer

弹性抗　tánxìngkàng　phys. elastic reactance

弹性塑料　tánxìng sùliào　elastoplast

弹性体　tánxìngtǐ　elastomer

弹压　tányā　suppress by force; quell

弹指　tánzhǐ　snap one's fingers—(of time) quickly pass: ～光阴 time zipping by / ～又过了三四年。So another three or four years quickly passed.

弹指之间　tánzhǐ zhījiān　during the snapping of the fingers—in a flash; in the twinkling of an eye; in an instant

弹奏　tánzòu　play (a stringed musical instrument); pluck

覃
tán　① formal deep: ～思 deep in thought ② (Tán) a surname ——see also Qín

替
tán　dial. (usu. used as part of a place name) pool; pond

痰
tán　phlegm; sputum

痰喘　tánchuǎn　Chin. med. asthma due to excessive phlegm

痰厥　tánjué　Chin. med. coma due to blocking of the respiratory system

痰气　tánqì　dial. ① mental disorder ② apoplexy

痰桶　tántǒng　inf. spittoon

痰盂　tányú　spittoon; cuspidor

谭
tán　① same as 谈 tán ② (Tán) a surname

潭
tán　① deep pool; pond: 水潭 shuǐtán ② dial. pit; depression

潭第　tándì　formal honor. your house

潭府　tánfǔ　formal ① a deep pool ② honor. your house

澹
tán　see below ——see also dàn

澹台　Tántái　a two-character surname

燂
tán　dial. heat sth. on a fire

檀
tán　① wingceltis (Pteroceltis tatarinowii): 青檀 qīngtán ② (Tán) a surname

檀板　tánbǎn　hardwood clappers

檀香　tánxiāng　bot. white sandalwood; sandalwood

檀香木　tánxiāngmù　sandalwood
檀香山　Tánxiāngshān　Honolulu
檀香扇　tánxiāngshàn　sandalwood fan
檀香油　tánxiāngyóu　sandalwood oil
檀香皂　tánxiāngzào　sandal soap

tǎn

忐　tǎn　see below
忐忑　tǎntè　perturbed; mentally disturbed
忐忑不安　tǎntè bù ān　uneasy; fidgety; restless

坦　tǎn　① level; smooth: 平坦 píngtǎn ② calm; composed: 坦然 tǎnrán ③ open; candid: 坦率 tǎnshuài
坦白　tǎnbái　① honest; frank; candid: 他很～, 没有私心。He's honest and selfless. / 对你说 to be frank with you; frankly speaking ② confess; make a confession; own up (to): 他～了自己的罪行。He confessed his crime. / 彻底～交代 make a clean breast of (one's crimes) / ～从宽, 抗拒从严 leniency to those who confess their crimes and severity to those who refuse to
坦诚　tǎnchéng　frank and sincere; frank and open: ～相见 deal with sb. in all sincerity; treat sb. open-heartedly
坦荡　tǎndàng　① (of a road, etc.) broad and level ② magnanimous; bighearted: 胸怀～ have largeness of mind; be open-hearted and aboveboard
坦缓　tǎnhuǎn　(of land) level; smooth
坦克　tǎnkè　(also 坦克车 tǎnkèchē) tank: ～乘员 tank crew / ～手 tankman
坦克兵　tǎnkèbīng　same as 装甲兵 zhuāngjiǎbīng
坦然　tǎnrán　calm; unperturbed; having no misgivings: ～无惧 calm and fearless / 他很～, 没有一点不安的样子。He's calm and completely at ease.
坦然自若　tǎnrán zìruò　calm and confident; completely at ease
坦桑尼亚　Tǎnsāngníyà　Tanzania
坦桑尼亚人　Tǎnsāngníyàrén　Tanzanian
坦率　tǎnshuài　candid; frank; straightforward: 他为人～。He's frank and open with people. / 双方～地交换了意见。The two sides had a frank exchange of views. / 她～地提出了自己的看法。She frankly expressed her views. / ～的答复 a straightforward answer
坦途　tǎntú　(fig) level road; highway: 攀登科学高峰, 既无捷径, 又无～。There are neither shortcuts nor easy paths to the heights of science.
坦挚　tǎnzhì　frank and sincere; frank and open

衵　tǎn　① leave (the upper part of the body) uncovered; be stripped to the waist or have one's shirt unbuttoned: 袒胸露臂 tǎnxiōng-lùbì ② give unprincipled protection to; shield; shelter: 偏袒 piāntǎn
袒护　tǎnhù　give unprincipled protection to; be partial to; shield: ～一方 be partial to one side / 公然～ openly shield / 你别～他。Don't make excuses for him. / 三个孩子一吵架, 妈妈总是～老三。Whenever the three kids fight, Mother always comes to protect her youngest darling.
袒露　tǎnlù　expose; uncover
袒胸露臂　tǎnxiōng-lùbì　(of a woman) exposing one's neck and shoulders; décolleté

钽　tǎn　chem. tantalum (Ta)

毯　tǎn　blanket; rug; carpet: 毛毯 máotǎn / 地毯 dìtǎn

毯子　tǎnzi　blanket

tàn

叹(嘆、歎)　tàn　① sigh: ～一声 heave a sigh ② exclaim in admiration; acclaim; praise: ～为奇迹 admire and praise sth. as a wonderful achievement
叹词　tàncí　gram. interjection; exclamation
叹服　tànfú　gasp in admiration: 令人～ compel (or command) admiration
叹观止矣　tàn guān zhǐ yǐ　same as 叹为观止 tàn wéi guān zhǐ
叹气　tànqì　sigh; heave a sigh: 叹了一口气 heave a sigh / 他～道:"这一次出门真倒霉!"He said with a sigh, "This trip has really had its share of bad luck!"
叹赏　tànshǎng　admire; express admiration for: ～不绝 express profuse admiration (for)
叹惋　tànwǎn　sigh with regret
叹为观止　tàn wéi guān zhǐ　acclaim (a work of art, etc.) as the acme of perfection
叹息　tànxī　formal heave a sigh
叹惜　tànxī　sigh with regret
叹羡　tànxiàn　formal sigh with admiration

炭(煭)　tàn　① charcoal ② dial. coal
炭棒　tànbàng　crayon
炭化　tànhuà　carbonize
炭画　tànhuà　charcoal drawing; charcoal
炭火　tànhuǒ　charcoal fire
炭精　tànjīng　① general name for charcoal products ② dial. general name for artificial charcoal and graphite
炭精棒　tànjīngbàng　carbon stick
炭精灯　tànjīngdēng　arc lamp; arc light
炭疽　tànjū　med. anthrax
炭疽病　tànjūbìng　agric. anthracnose
炭盆　tànpén　charcoal brazier
炭窑　tànyáo　charcoal kiln

探　tàn　① try to find out; explore; sound: ～情况 try to find out how the situation is / 他用竹竿～了～河水的深浅。He used a bamboo pole to sound the river. ② scout; spy; detective: 密探 mìtàn ③ visit; pay a call on: 探视 tànshì ④ stretch forward: 探身 tànshēn
探案　tàn'àn　detective story: 《福尔摩斯～》Tales of Sherlock Holmes
探宝　tànbǎo　① hunt for treasure ② prospect for mineral deposits: 深山～ prospect in the mountains / 海底～ explore the deep sea resources
探病　tànbìng　visit a sick person or a patient
探测　tàncè　survey; sound; probe: ～海底情况 survey the seabed / ～水深 take soundings / ～悬崖高度 gauge the height of a bluff
探测器　tàncèqì　sounder; probe; detector
探查　tànchá　look over; examine; scout: ～敌情 gather intelligence about the enemy
探察　tànchá　watch; look carefully at; observe: ～地形 survey the terrain
探访　tànfǎng　① seek by inquiry or search: ～民间秘方 seek out secret medicinal recipes from among the people ② pay a visit to; visit: ～亲友 visit one's relatives and friends
探风　tànfēng　make inquiries about sb. or sth.; fish for information
探戈　tàngē　tango (a transliteration)
探花　tànhuā　title conferred on the one who won third place in the highest imperial examination in the Ming and Qing Dynasties

探家　tànjiā　make a brief trip home: 你抽空探一回家。Find time to make a trip home.

探监　tànjiān　visit a prisoner (usu. a relative or a friend)

探井　tànjǐng　① *min.* prospect (*or* test) pit; exploring (*or* exploratory) shaft ② *petroleum* test well; exploratory well: 野猫～ wildcat

探究　tànjiū　make a thorough inquiry; probe into: ～原因 look into the causes

探勘　tànkān　same as 勘探 kāntàn

探看　tànkàn　① visit: ～病人 visit a sick person or a patient ② look about; watch: 四处～ look around

探空　tànkōng　*meteorol.* sounding: ～气球 sounding balloon

探口气　tàn kǒuqi　ascertain (*or* find out) sb.'s opinions or feelings; sound sb. out

探矿　tànkuàng　go prospecting; prospect

探雷　tànléi　detect (*or* locate) a mine: ～器 mine detector

探骊得珠　tàn lí dé zhū　(in writing) grasp the point of the theme; expound the essence of the theme

探路　tànlù　explore the way

探马　tànmǎ　*old* mounted scout

探明　tànmíng　① ascertain; verify: 已～的 煤 储 量 proven (*or* known) coal deposits / 新油田的含油层结构已 经～。The oil-bearing structure of the new oilfield has been verified. ② get a clear understanding of sth.; find out: ～来访者的用意 try to find out what the visitor has come for

探囊取物　tàn náng qǔ wù　(like) taking sth. out of one's pocket—as easy as winking; as easy as falling off a log

探亲　tànqīn　go home to visit one's family or go to visit one's relatives: 到故乡～访友 return to one's homeland to visit one's relatives and friends

探亲假　tànqīnjià　home leave

探求　tànqiú　seek; pursue; search after (*or* for): ～真理 seek truth

探丧　tànsāng　*dial.* visit the bereaved to offer one's condolences; pay a condolence call

探伤　tànshāng　*metall.* detect a flaw (*or* crack): ～仪 flaw detector

探身　tànshēn　lean forward: 他～去听她在说些什么。He leaned forward (*or* over) to hear what she was saying. / 行车时不要～窗外。Don't lean out of the window while the bus is in motion.

探视　tànshì　visit: ～病人 visit a patient

探视时间　tànshì shíjiān　visiting hours (in a hospital)

探索　tànsuǒ　explore; probe: ～宇宙的秘密 probe (*or* explore) the secrets of the universe / 星际～ interplanetary exploration / ～事物的本质 probe into the essence of things / ～真理 seek truth / 对一些具体政策问题, 我们应当继续考察和～。We must further investigate and study certain specific policies.

探讨　tàntǎo　inquire into; probe into: 从不同角度对问题进行～ approach a subject from different angles / 对针麻原理作进一步的～ delve further into the principles governing acupuncture anaesthesia / ～性的访问 an exploratory visit

探听　tàntīng　try to find out; make inquiries: ～下落 inquire about the whereabouts of sb. or sth. / ～消息 make inquiries about sb. or sth.; fish for information / ～人家的私事 pry into other people's private affairs / ～虚实 try to find out about an opponent, adversary, etc.; try to ascertain the strength of the enemy / ～敌人的动静 try to find out the movements of the enemy / 你去～～她对这件事有什么看法。Will you go and sound her out on this issue?

探头　tàntóu　pop one's head in; crane one's neck: 有人从门口探进头来。Somebody popped his head in at the door. / ～张望 crane one's neck and look around

探头探脑　tàntóu-tànnǎo　pop one's head in and look about: 他正乘着凉, 只见一个人～在那里张望。He was enjoying the cool breeze, when all at once he saw a man stealthily spying.

探望　tànwàng　① look about: 我在车站上四处～, 哪儿也找不到那位朋友。I looked all around the station but couldn't find my friend anywhere. / 她不时向窗外～。She looked out the window every now and then. ② call on sb. (usu. from afar); visit; see: 回国～亲友 return to one's home country to visit relatives and friends / 我路过重庆时, 顺便～了几个老朋友。When I passed through Chongqing, I used the opportunity to see a few of my old friends there.

探问　tànwèn　① make cautious inquiries about: 他们一再～此事。They inquired about the matter time and again. ② inquire after

探悉　tànxī　ascertain; learn; find out: 从有关方面～ learn from those concerned

探险　tànxiǎn　explore; make explorations; venture into the unknown: 到原始森林去～ explore a primeval forest

探险队　tànxiǎnduì　exploring (*or* exploration) party; expedition

探险家　tànxiǎnjiā　explorer

探信　tànxìn　*inf.* make inquiries about sb. or sth.; fish for information

探寻　tànxún　seek; pursue; search after (*or* for)

探询　tànxún　make cautious inquiries about

探鱼仪　tànyúyí　fish detector; fish-finder

探赜索隐　tànzé-suǒyǐn　delve into the abstruse; unravel mysteries

探照灯　tànzhàodēng　searchlight: ～的灯光 searchlight beam

探针　tànzhēn　*med.* probe

探知　tànzhī　get to know; find out; learn

探子[1]　tànzi　*old* scout

探子[2]　tànzi　a thin tube used to extract samples of food grains, etc.

碳

　　tàn　*chem.* carbon (C)

碳酐　tàngān　*chem.* carbonic anhydride

碳钢　tàngāng　same as 碳素钢 tànsùgāng

碳黑　tànhēi　*chem.* carbon black

碳化　tànhuà　carbonize

碳化钙　tànhuàgài　calcium carbide

碳化硅　tànhuàguī　carborundum; silicon carbide

碳化物　tànhuàwù　carbide

碳精　tànjīng　*elec.* pure carbon

碳精棒　tànjīngbàng　carbon stick (*or* rod)

碳精电极　tànjīng diànjí　carbon electrode; baked carbon

碳氢化合物　tànqīng huàhéwù　hydrocarbon

碳14断代法　tàn shísì duàndàifǎ　*archaeol.* C14 dating (another name for 放射性碳素断代法 fàngshèxìng tànsù duàndàifǎ)

碳刷　tànshuā　*elec.* carbon brush

碳水化合物　tànshuǐ huàhéwù　carbohydrate

碳丝　tànsī　*elec.* carbon filament

碳丝灯　tànsīdēng　carbon lamp

碳素钢　tànsùgāng　carbon steel

碳酸　tànsuān　carbonic acid

碳酸钙　tànsuāngài　calcium carbonate

碳酸钠　tànsuānnà　sodium carbonate; soda

碳酸气　tànsuānqì　carbon dioxide; chokedamp

碳酸氢钠　tànsuānqīngnà　sodium bicarbonate; baking soda

碳酸盐　tànsuānyán　carbonate

碳酰基　tànxiānjī　another name for 羰 tāng

tāng

汤（湯） tāng ① hot water; boiling water: 温汤浸种 wēntāng jìnzhǒng ② (usu. used as part of a place name) hot springs ③ water in which sth. has been boiled: 饺子～ jiaozi water / 姜～ ginger tea ④ soup; broth: 鸡～ chicken soup / 三菜一～ soup and three other courses / 喝点儿～吧。Have some soup. ⑤ a liquid preparation of medicinal herbs; decoction: 柴胡～ a decoction of Chinese thorowax root (with other ingredients) ⑥ (Tāng) a surname

汤包 tāngbāo steamed dumplings filled with minced meat and gravy

汤饼 tāngbǐng noodle soup: ～会 noodle soup feast held to celebrate the third day after a child's birth

汤池 tāngchí ① see 金城汤池 jīnchéng-tāngchí ② hot water bathing pool (in a public bath-house)

汤匙 tāngchí tablespoon; soupspoon

汤罐 tāngguàn a jug (fitted in an old-style kitchen range) used for heating up water

汤锅 tāngguō ① a butcher's cauldron in a slaughterhouse ② slaughterhouse

汤壶 tānghú metal or earthenware hot-water bottle

汤剂 tāngjì Chin. med. decoction (of herbal medicine)

汤加 Tāngjiā Tonga

汤加人 Tāngjiārén Tongan

汤料 tāngliào soup stock: 固体～ soup cubes / 浓缩～ concentrated soup

汤面 tāngmiàn noodles in soup

汤婆子 tāngpózi dial. metal or earthenware hot-water bottle

汤泉 tāngquán arch. hot spring

汤勺 tāngsháo soup ladle

汤头 tāngtóu Chin. med. a prescription for a medical decoction: ～歌诀 medical recipes in jingles; prescriptions in rhyme

汤团 tāngtuán dial. stuffed dumplings made of glutinous rice flour served in soup

汤碗 tāngwǎn soup bowl

汤药 tāngyào Chin. med. a decoction of medicinal ingredients

汤圆 tāngyuán (usu. stuffed) dumplings made of glutinous rice flour served in soup

锡（錫） tāng see below

锡锣 tāngluó a small brass gong

嗵 tāng onom. a loud ringing sound (of a gong, etc.); clang

趟 tāng same as 蹚 tāng ——see also 趟 tàng

羰 tāng chem. carbonyl (group)

羰基 tāngjī chem. carbonyl (group): ～键 carbonyl bond (or link)

镗 tāng same as 嗵 tāng ——see also táng

蹚¹（蹚） tāng wade; ford: ～水过河 wade (across) a stream / ～了一脚泥 get one's feet muddy through wading

蹚²（蹚） tāng turn the soil and dig up weeds (with a hoe, etc.)

táng

唐¹ táng ① exaggerative; boastful ② for nothing; in vain

唐² Táng ① the Tang Dynasty (618-907): ～诗 Tang poetry ② a surname

唐菖蒲 tángchāngpú gladiolus (Gladiolus gandavensis)

唐棣 tángdì same as 棠棣 tángdì

唐花 tánghuā hothouse flower

唐人街 Tángrénjiē Chinatown

唐三彩 tángsāncǎi archaeol. trio-coloured glazed pottery of the Tang Dynasty; Tang tricolour

唐宋八大家 Táng-Sòng bā dà jiā the eight prose masters of the Tang-Song period (i.e. Han Yu 韩愈, Liu Zongyuan 柳宗元, Ouyang Xiu 欧阳修, Su Xun 苏洵, Su Shi 苏轼, Su Zhe 苏辙, Zeng Gong 曾巩, and Wang Anshi 王安石)

唐突 tángtū formal ① rudely offend sb.; blaspheme; profane: ～古人 profane an ancient sage / 出言～ make a blunt remark / ～的行动 a presumptuous act / 恕我～。Excuse me if I'm being too blunt. ② pass oneself off as; pass sth. off as

堂 táng ① the main room of a house: 堂屋 tángwū ② a hall (or room) for a specific purpose: 课堂 kètáng / 食堂 shítáng ③ old court of law; a principal hall in a yamen: 过堂 guòtáng ④ relationship between cousins, etc. of the same paternal grandfather or great-grandfather: ～兄弟 (male) cousins on the paternal side; cousins ⑤ m. (for furniture, classes, and in old use for trials): 一～家具 a set (or suite) of furniture / 每天上四～课 have four classes every day / 过了两～ have been through two sessions (of a trial)

堂奥 táng'ào formal ① the innermost recess of a hall ② the interior of a country ③ profundity of thought or knowledge; profundities

堂而皇之 táng ér huáng zhī ① openly and legally ② do sth. in grand style

堂房 tángfáng relationship between cousins, etc. of the same paternal grandfather or great-grandfather: ～姐妹 (female) cousins on the paternal side; cousins

堂鼓 tánggǔ a barrel-shaped drum, high and narrow (used in traditional operas)

堂倌 tángguān old. waiter

堂花 tánghuā same as 唐花 tánghuā

堂皇 tánghuáng grand; stately; magnificent: 富丽堂皇 fùlì tánghuáng

堂会 tánghuì old home celebrations with hired performers

堂客 tángkè dial. ① women ② wife

堂上 tángshàng ① one's parents ② old (a term of address to magistrates or judges) Your Honour

堂堂 tángtáng ① dignified; impressive: 相貌～ dignified in appearance; impressive-looking ② (of a man) having high aspirations and boldness of vision ③ imposing; awe-inspiring; formidable

堂堂正正 tángtángzhèngzhèng ① impressive or dignified: 他身材高大结实，～的，不愧是个山东大汉。He was a credit to the big men of Shandong with his height and solidity. ② open and above-board

堂堂之阵 tángtáng zhī zhèn an imposing array of troops; awe-inspiring military strength

堂屋 tángwū ① central room (of a one-storey Chinese traditional house consisting of several rooms in a row) ② principal rooms (in a courtyard, usu. facing south)

堂子　tángzi　① an imperial sacrificial temple (in the Qing Dynasty) ② *dial.*　brothel

棠　táng　same as 棠梨 tánglǐ

棠棣　tángdì　*bot.*　① Chinese bush cherry ② a kind of white poplar

棠梨　tánglí　birchleaf pear (*Pyrus betulaefolia*)

溏　táng　half congealed; viscous

溏便　tángbiàn　*Chin. med.*　semiliquid (*or* unformed) stool

溏心　tángxīn　(of eggs) with a soft yolk: ～儿蛋 soft-boiled or soft-fried egg / ～儿松花 preserved egg with a jelly-like yolk

塘　táng　① dyke; embankment: 河塘 hétáng ② pool; pond: 鱼塘 yútáng ③ hot-water bathing pool: 澡塘 zǎotáng

塘肥　tángféi　pond sludge used as manure

塘鳢　tánglǐ　*zool.*　sleeper

塘泥　tángní　pond sludge; pond silt

塘堰　tángyàn　(also 塘坝 tángbà) a small reservoir (in a hilly area)

搪¹　táng　① ward off; keep out: ～风 keep out the wind / ～饥 allay one's hunger ② evade; do sth. perfunctorily: ～帐 put off a creditor / ～差事 perform a duty perfunctorily

搪²　táng　spread (clay, paint, etc.) over; daub: ～炉子 line a stove with clay

搪³　táng　same as 镗 táng

搪瓷　tángcí　enamel: ～茶缸 enamel mug / ～器皿 enamelware

搪瓷钢板　tángcí gāngbǎn　*archit.*　enamelled pressed steel

搪塞　tángsè　stall sb. off; do sth. perfunctorily: ～他几句 stall him off with a vague answer / ～差事 perform a duty perfunctorily / 他模棱两可地想把我的问话～过去。He tried to put me off by giving me an equivocal answer.

樘　táng　*archit.*　door or window frame

膛　táng　① thorax; chest: 这小鸡儿的～肥。The chick has a plump breast. ② an enclosed space inside sth.; chamber: 这炉子的～儿大。The stove has a large chamber.

膛线　tángxiàn　rifling

糖¹(醣)　táng　another name for 碳水化合物 tànshuǐ huàhéwù

糖²　táng　① sugar: 咖啡里少搁点儿～。Don't put too much sugar in the coffee. / 你喝茶搁～吗? Do you take sugar in your tea? ② sweets; candy; sweetmeats: 一袋～ a bag of sweets / 吃块～。Have a candy.

糖包　tángbāo　steamed bun stuffed with sugar

糖厂　tángchǎng　sugar refinery

糖醋　tángcù　sugar and vinegar; sweet and sour

糖醋排骨　tángcù páigǔ　sweet and sour spareribs

糖醋鱼　tángcùyú　fish in sweet and sour sauce

糖弍　tángdài　same as 弍 dài

糖弹　tángdàn　short for 糖衣炮弹 tángyī pàodàn

糖房　tángfáng　*old*　sugar refinery

糖苷　tángdài　another name for 弍 dài

糖膏　tánggāo　massecuite; fillmass

糖果　tángguǒ　sweets; candy; sweetmeats: ～店 sweet shop; candy store; confectionery / 这孩子～吃得太多。That child eats too much candy.

糖葫芦　tánghúlu　sugarcoated haws on a stick

糖化　tánghuà　*chem.*　saccharification: ～饲料 saccharified pig feed; fermented feed

糖姜　tángjiāng　sugared ginger; ginger in syrup

糖浆　tángjiāng　① medicinal syrup: 咳嗽～ cough syrup ② syrup (for making candy, etc.)

糖精　tángjīng　saccharin; gluside

糖类　tánglèi　*chem.*　carbohydrate

糖量计　tángliàngjì　*chem.*　saccharometer; saccharimeter

糖寮　tángliáo　*dial.*　sugar refinery (a workshop)

糖料作物　tángliào zuòwù　sugar crop

糖萝卜　tángluóbo　① *inf.*　beet ② *dial.*　preserved carrot

糖酶　tángméi　*chem.*　carbohydrase

糖蜜　tángmì　molasses; treacle

糖尿病　tángniàobìng　diabetes: ～患者 diabetic

糖人儿　tángrénr　sugar figurine

糖三角　tángsānjiǎo　steamed bun in triangular shape stuffed with sugar

糖食　tángshí　sweet food; sweets

糖霜　tángshuāng　icing; frosting

糖水　tángshuǐ　syrup: ～桔子(荔枝) tangerines (lichees) in syrup

糖蒜　tángsuàn　garlic in syrup; sweetened garlic

糖稀　tángxī　malt sugar; maltose

糖衣　tángyī　sugarcoating: 这种药片有～。These pills are sugarcoated.

糖衣炮弹　tángyī pàodàn　sugarcoated bullet

糖原　tángyuán　(also 糖元 tángyuán) *chem.*　glycogen

螗　táng　*arch.*　a smaller kind of cicada

镗　táng　*mech.*　boring——see also tāng

镗床　tángchuáng　*mech.*　boring machine; boring lathe; borer: 坐标～ jig boring machine

镗刀　tángdāo　*mech.*　boring cutter; boring tool

镗孔　tángkǒng　*mech.*　bore hole; boring

螳　táng　mantis

螳臂当车　tángbì dāng chē　a mantis trying to obstruct a chariot—overrate oneself and try to hold back an overwhelmingly superior force

螳螂　tángláng　mantis

螳螂捕蝉，黄雀在后　tángláng bǔ chán, huángquè zài hòu　the mantis stalks the cicada, unaware of the oriole behind—covet gains ahead, unaware of danger behind

糖　táng　(of complexion) red

tǎng

帑　tǎng　*formal*　state treasury: funds in the state treasury: 公～ public funds

帑藏　tǎngzàng　*formal*　state treasury

倘(儻)　tǎng　*conj. formal*　if; supposing; in case: ～有不测 in case of accidents; if anything untoward should happen

倘或　tǎnghuò　*conj. formal*　if; supposing; in case

倘来之物　tǎng lái zhī wù　an unexpected gain; windfall

倘然　tǎngrán　same as 倘若 tǎngruò

倘若　tǎngruò　*conj.*　if; supposing; in case: 你～有空，请到我家来谈谈。Please come to my place for a chat if you have time. / ～发现情况，立即报告。In case you find

anything unusual, report immediately.

倘使 tǎngshǐ　same as 倘若 tǎngruò

惝 tǎng　see 迷离惝恍 mílí-tǎnghuǎng

淌 tǎng　drip; shed; trickle: ～眼泪 shed tears / ～口水 let saliva dribble from the mouth; slaver; slobber / 伤口～血。Blood trickled from the wound. / 他脸上～着汗水。Sweat was dripping from his face. / 这桶漏水,～了一地。The pail leaked, so water ran all over the place.

傥(儻) tǎng　① same as 倘 tǎng ② see 倜傥 tìtǎng

耥 tǎng　weed and loosen the soil (in a paddy field)

耥耙 tǎngbà　paddy-field harrow

躺 tǎng　lie; recline: ～下歇歇 lie down and rest a while / 他正～床上呢。He's lying in bed. / 不要～在过去的成绩上睡大觉。Don't rest content with past achievements. *or* Don't rest on your laurels.

躺倒不干 tǎngdǎo bù gàn　stay in bed—refuse to shoulder responsibilities any longer

躺柜 tǎngguì　a long low box with a lid on top; chest

躺椅 tǎngyǐ　deck chair; sling chair

铴(鐋) tǎng　a kind of ancient weapon, resembling a fork

---

tàng

烫(燙) tàng　① scald; burn: 让开水～着了 be scalded by boiling water / ～了个泡 get a blister through being scalded (*or* burnt) ② heat up in hot water; warm: ～酒 heat wine (by putting the container in hot water) / ～澡 take a hot bath / ～脚 bathe one's feet in hot water ③ iron; press: ～衣服 iron (*or* press) clothes ④ very hot; scalding; boiling hot: 这汤真～! This soup is boiling hot! ⑤ perm; have one's hair permed: 她头发刚～过。She just got her hair permed.

烫发 tàngfà　give or have a permanent wave; perm: 她烫了头发显得精神了。Her new permanent makes her look perky.

烫金 tàngjīn　*print.*　gild; bronze: 布面～ cloth gilt

烫金机 tàngjīnjī　gilding press; bronzing machine

烫蜡 tànglà　polish with melted wax; wax (a floor, etc.)

烫面 tàngmiàn　dough made with boiling water: ～饺 steamed dumplings (made of dough prepared with boiling water)

烫伤 tàngshāng　*med.*　scald

烫手 tàngshǒu　① burn (*or* scald) the hand: 热得～ so hot that it burns (*or* scalds) one's hand; scalding to the touch / 钱不～。Money doesn't burn the hand—the more money, the better. ② troublesome; knotty: 这事有些～。This is a sticky business.

烫头 tàngtóu　same as 烫发 tàngfà

趟 tàng　① *m.* (for a round trip): 昆明我只去过一～。I have been to Kunming only once. / 这辆卡车昨天往工地跑了三～。Yesterday the truck made three trips to the construction site. / 这车运了两～煤。This truck has transported two loads of coal. / 这一～来, 是专给你们送好消息的。I've come to bring you a piece of good news. / 他左一～右一～地跑飞机场迎接朋友。He went to the airport again and again to meet his

friends. ② *m.* (for a single trip of a train): 刚开出一～列车。A train has just left. / 一下子到了好几～车, 站台上挤满了人。A number of trains arrived almost at the same time, and the platforms were crowded. / 我坐上了最后一～去天津的火车。I caught the last train to Tianjin. / 这～车是去广州的。This train goes to Guangzhou. *or* This is the Guangzhou train. ③ sth. that is going on: 跟不上～ lag behind ④ *m. dial.* (for a street or things arranged in a row): 一～街 a street / 两～桌子 two rows of tables / 几～大字 a few lines of big characters ——see also tāng

趟马 tàngmǎ　a set of stage motions symbolizing trotting and galloping (in traditional operas)

---

tāo

叨 tāo　① *formal pol.* be unworthy of the honour: ～在知己, 幸勿见怪。Having the honour, though I am unworthy of it, to be counted among your intimate friends, I hope that you will not take offence. (an apology in a classical-style letter) ② be favoured with; get the benefit of: 叨光 tāoguāng ——see also dāo; dáo

叨光 tāoguāng　*pol.* be much obliged to you: 有劳你们二位, 我只能～了。You two will have to do all the work. I'm much obliged to you.

叨教 tāojiào　*pol.*　thank you for your advice

叨扰 tāorǎo　*pol.*　thank you for your hospitality

涛(濤) tāo　great waves; billows: 波涛 bōtāo / 松涛 sōngtāo

绦(縧、縚、絛) tāo　silk ribbon; silk braid

绦虫 tāochóng　tapeworm; cestode: ～病 taeniasis; cestodiasis

绦子 tāozi　silk ribbon; silk braid

掏(搯) tāo　① draw out; pull out; fish out: 从口袋里～出笔记本 pull a notebook from one's pocket; take a notebook out of one's pocket / ～手枪 draw a pistol / ～炉灰 clear the ashes from a stove / ～鸟窝 take young birds or eggs out of a nest; go bird's-nesting / ～耳朵 pick one's ears / ～蛐蛐儿 catch crickets / 这顿饭是他～的钱。He footed the bill for the meal. ② dig (a hole, etc.); hollow out; scoop out: 在墙上～一个洞 make a hole in the wall ③ steal from sb.'s pocket: 他的皮夹子被～了。His wallet was stolen (by a pickpocket).

掏槽 tāocáo　*min.*　cutting

掏底 tāodǐ　try to find out the real intention or situation

掏坏 tāohuài　*dial.* be up to mischief; play a dirty trick

掏窟窿 tāo kūlong　*dial.* run (*or* get, fall) into debt

掏摸 tāomō　① draw out; pull out; fish out ② steal; pilfer; make off with

掏心 tāoxīn　from the bottom of one's heart: 说句～的话, 你真不该发那么大脾气。To be frank, you shouldn't have lost your temper like that.

掏腰包 tāo yāobāo　*inf.* ① pay out of one's own pocket; foot a bill: 这顿饭我～。This meal is on me. ② pick sb.'s pocket

滔 tāo　inundate; flood

滔滔 tāotāo　① torrential; surging: 白浪～ whitecaps surging ② keeping up a constant flow of words

滔滔不绝 tāotāo bù jué　pouring out words in a steady

flow: 口若悬河，～ talk on and on in a flow of eloquence / 他在房里走来走去，～地讲着城里发生的事情。Drifting around the room, he poured forth a steady stream of small talk about goings-on in the city.

滔天 tāotiān ① (of billows, etc.) dash to the skies: 波浪～ waves running high ② heinous; monstrous: ～罪行 monstrous crimes

滔天大罪 tāotiān dàzuì a monstrous crime; a heinous crime; a towering crime

韬 (韜、弢)

tāo *formal* ① sheath or bow case ② hide; conceal: 韬晦 tāohuì ③ the art of war: 韬略 tāolüè

韬光养晦 tāoguāng-yǎnghuì hide one's capacities and bide one's time

韬晦 tāohuì conceal one's true features or intentions; lie low

韬略 tāolüè military strategy

饕

tāo *formal* be greedy for money or food: 老饕 lǎotāo

饕餮 tāotiè ① *taotie*, a mythical ferocious animal ② a fierce and cruel person ③ voracious eater; glutton; gourmand

饕餮纹 tāotièwén *archaeol.* taotie design

táo

逃 (迯)

táo ① run away; escape; flee: 从监狱里～出去 escape from prison / ～出虎口 flee from the jaws of death ② evade; dodge; shirk; escape: 逃债 táozhài

逃奔 táobèn run away to (another place)

逃避 táobì escape; evade; shirk: ～现实 try to escape reality / ～斗争 evade struggle / ～责任 shirk responsibility / ～困难 avoid (or dodge) a difficulty

逃兵 táobīng army deserter; deserter

逃窜 táocuàn run away; flee in disorder: 敌军狼狈～。The enemy troops fled helter-skelter. / 这个罪犯已经～外地。The criminal has already fled to another part of the country.

逃遁 táodùn flee; escape; evade: 仓皇～ flee in panic / 警察跟踪追击，罪犯无处～。Being hotly pursued by the police, the criminal could find no refuge.

逃反 táofǎn *old* flee from war or banditry

逃犯 táofàn escaped criminal or convict

逃荒 táohuāng flee from famine; get away from a famine-stricken area

逃汇 táohuì evade foreign exchange

逃命 táomìng run (or flee, fly) for one's life

逃难 táonàn flee from a calamity (esp. a war); be a refugee: 抗日战争爆发后他家从无锡～到了上海。When the War of Resistance Against Japan broke out, his family fled from Wuxi to Shanghai.

逃匿 táonì escape and hide; go into hiding

逃跑 táopǎo run away; flee; take flight; take to one's heels

逃跑主义 táopǎozhǔyì flightism (the advocacy or practice of running away from the battlefield or from difficulties in revolutionary struggle)

逃散 táosàn become separated in flight

逃生 táoshēng flee (or run, fly) for one's life; escape with one's life

逃税 táoshuì evade (or dodge) a tax

逃脱 táotuō succeed in escaping; make good one's escape; get clear of: ～责任 succeed in evading responsibility / 不法分子～不了法律的制裁。The law-

breakers will never escape punishment according to law.

逃亡 táowáng become a fugitive; flee from home; go into exile: 1927年他～日本。In 1927 he went into exile in Japan. / ～地主 a runaway (or fugitive) landlord

逃席 táoxí take French leave during a feast (to avoid being pressed to drink)

逃学 táoxué play truant; cut class

逃逸 táoyì *formal* escape; run away; abscond

逃逸速度 táoyì sùdù *space* escape velocity

逃债 táozhài dodge (or avoid) a creditor

逃之夭夭 táo zhī yāoyāo decamp; make one's getaway; slip away; show a clean pair of heels (a humorous adaptation of the homophonous line 桃之夭夭 "Buxom is the peach tree" in *The Book of Songs* 《诗经》)

逃走 táozǒu run away; flee; take flight; take to one's heels

逃罪 táozuì escape responsibility for an offence (or crime); get away with it

咷

táo cry loudly; wail

桃

táo ① peach ② a peach-shaped thing: 棉桃 miántáo

桃符 táofú ① peachwood charms against evil, hung on the gate on lunar New Year's Eve in ancient times: 千门万户瞳瞳日, 总把新桃换旧符。(王安石) To every home the sun imparts its brighter rays, Old peachwood charms, renewed, 'gainst evil shall insure. ② Spring Festival couplets

桃脯 táofǔ preserved peach

桃红 táohóng pink

桃红柳绿 táohóng-liǔlǜ red peach flowers and green willows—a spring scene

桃花 táohuā peach blossom

桃花心木 táohuāxīnmù mahogany

桃花雪 táohuāxuě spring snow

桃花汛 táohuāxùn (also 桃汛 táoxùn) spring flood

桃花鱼 táohuāyú minnow

桃花运 táohuāyùn ① a man's luck in love affairs: 走～ be lucky in love affairs ② good luck

桃李 táolǐ peaches and plums—one's pupils or disciples: ～盈门 have many disciples

桃李不言, 下自成蹊 táo-lǐ bù yán, xià zì chéng xī the peach and the plum do not speak, yet a path is worn beneath them—a man of true worth attracts admiration

桃李满天下 táolǐ mǎn tiānxià have pupils everywhere (usu. said in praise of a teacher)

桃仁 táorén ① *Chin. med.* peach kernel ② walnut meat; shelled walnut

桃腮杏眼 táosāi-xìngyǎn peach-like cheeks and almond-shaped eyes—the beauty of a woman

桃色 táosè ① pink colour ② *euph.* illicit love and sex: ～新闻 reports of love affairs and sex scandals / ～案件 legal cases involving love and sex

桃树 táoshù peach (tree)

桃源 táoyuán see 世外桃源 shìwài táoyuán

桃子 táozi peach

陶[1]

táo ① pottery; earthenware: 彩陶 cǎitáo ② make pottery: 陶冶 táoyě ③ cultivate; mould; educate: 熏陶 xūntáo ④ (Táo) a surname

陶[2]

táo contented; happy: 乐陶陶 lètáotáo

陶瓷 táocí pottery and porcelain; ceramics: ～工 potter / ～业 ceramic industry; ceramics

陶瓷片 táocípiàn *archaeol.* potsherd

陶瓷学　táocíxué　ceramics
陶管　táoguǎn　*archit.* earthenware pipe
陶匠　táojiàng　potter
陶钧　táojūn　*formal* ① potter's wheel ② train (talents)
陶粒　táolì　*archit.* ceramsite: ～混凝土 ceramsite concrete
陶器　táoqì　pottery; earthenware
陶然　táorán　happy and carefree
陶陶　táotáo　happy; carefree
陶土　táotǔ　potter's clay; pottery clay; kaolin
陶文　táowén　*archaeol.* inscription on pottery
陶冶　táoyě　① make pottery and smelt metal ② exert a favourable influence (on a person's character, etc.); mould: ～性情 mould a person's temperament
陶俑　táoyǒng　*archaeol.* pottery figurine
陶铸　táozhù　*formal* ① mould; cast ② train (talents)
陶醉　táozuì　be intoxicated (with happiness, etc.); revel in: 她的歌声使我～。Her song made me feel intoxicated. / 我们不能～于已取得的成绩。We mustn't let success go to our heads.

桃　táo　see below
桃黍　táoshǔ　*dial.* sorghum

淘¹　táo　wash in a pan or basket: ～米 wash rice
淘²（掏）　táo　clean out; dredge: ～阴沟 clean out a drain (*or* sewer) / ～茅房 remove night soil from a latrine / ～井 dredge a well

淘³　táo　① tax (a person's energy): 淘神 táoshén ② *dial.* naughty; mischievous: 这孩子特～。The child is very naughty.
淘河　táohé　another name for 鹈鹕 tíhú
淘换　táohuan　try to get; search for: 这本书好不容易才给你～来的。I've just managed to get a copy of this book for you.
淘金　táojīn　wash (for gold); pan
淘箩　táoluó　a basket for washing rice in
淘气　táoqì　① naughty; mischievous: 这孩子很聪明，可就是有些～。The child is very bright, but a bit too mischievous. / ～鬼 a mischievous imp; a regular little mischief ② *dial.* get angry
淘神　táoshén　*inf.* be trying; be bothersome: 干那事才～呢。That job is a real pain in the neck. / 那孩子可～了。That kid really gets on my nerves (*or* is a terrible nuisance)!
淘汰　táotài　① eliminate through selection or competition: 他在第一轮比赛中就被～了。He was eliminated in the very first round. / 她～了两名种子选手。She's knocked two seeded players out of the running. ② die out; fall into disuse: 这种机器已经～了。This kind of machine is already obsolete.
淘汰赛　táotàisài　*sports* elimination series

萄　táo　grapes: 葡萄 pútao
萄酒　táojiǔ　same as 葡萄酒 pútaojiǔ
萄糖　táotáng　same as 葡萄糖 pútaotáng

嗃　táo　see 号嗃 háotáo

梼（檮）　táo　see below
梼昧　táomèi　*formal hum.* ignorant
梼杌　táowù　*arch.* ① a kind of legendary beast of prey ② a fierce person

tǎo

讨　tǎo　① send armed forces to suppress; send a punitive expedition against: 征讨 zhēngtǎo ② denounce; condemn: 声讨 shēngtǎo ③ demand; ask for; beg for: ～账 demand the payment of a debt; dun / 去跟老张～点墨汁。Go and ask Lao Zhang for some Chinese ink. ④ marry (a woman): ～老婆 take a wife; get married ⑤ incur; invite: ～了个没趣儿 court a rebuff; ask for a snub / 大熊猫温和驯良，～人喜欢。The gentleness and good nature of the giant panda makes them especially likable. ⑥ discuss; study: 商讨 shāngtǎo
讨保　tǎobǎo　get sb. to go bail for one: ～出狱 be released on bail; be bailed out
讨底　tǎodǐ　try to find out the real intention or situation: 向人讨个底 sound sb. out
讨伐　tǎofá　send armed forces to suppress; send a punitive expedition against
讨饭　tǎofàn　beg for food; be a beggar: 他爸爸以前讨过饭。His father used to be a beggar.
讨好　tǎohǎo　① ingratiate oneself with; fawn on; toady to; curry favour with: ～领导 curry favour with the leadership / 他想～经理。He tried to ingratiate himself with the manager. ② (usu. used in the negative) be rewarded with a fruitful result; have one's labour rewarded: 这个工作怎么干也讨不了好儿。No matter how hard you work on this job, it's always a thankless task. ——see also 费力不讨好 fèilì bù tǎohǎo
讨还　tǎohuán　get sth. back
讨还血债　tǎohuán xuèzhài　demand payment of a blood debt; make sb. pay for his bloody crimes: 向恶霸地主～ make the despotic landlord pay his blood debt
讨价　tǎojià　ask (*or* name) a price
讨价还价　tǎojià-huánjià　bargain; haggle
讨教　tǎojiào　ask for advice
讨究　tǎojiū　observe and study; investigate: 这个问题值得～。This problem merits serious attention.
讨脸　tǎoliǎn　ingratiate oneself with; fawn on; toady to; curry favour with
讨论　tǎolùn　discuss; talk over: 他们～了今后的计划。They discussed their plans for the future. / 这件事我们得～～。We must talk it over. / 关于这个问题我们进行了长时间的～。We held a long discussion about this problem. / 经过充分～，问题得到了解决。After much discussion, the matter was finally settled.
讨论会　tǎolùnhuì　discussion; symposium: 科学～ science symposium
讨便宜　tǎo piányi　seek undue advantage; try to gain sth. at the expense of others; look for a bargain
讨平　tǎopíng　send armed forces to suppress and put down (a rebellion): ～叛乱 put down a rebellion
讨乞　tǎoqǐ　beg alms; beg
讨巧　tǎoqiǎo　act artfully to get what one wants; get the best for oneself at the least expense; choose the easy way out
讨俏　tǎoqiào　try to be witty or humorous
讨亲　tǎoqīn　*dial.* take a wife; get married
讨情　tǎoqíng　*dial.* plead for sb.; beg sb. off: ～告饶 plead for leniency; beg for pardon
讨饶　tǎoráo　beg for mercy; ask for forgiveness
讨扰　tǎorǎo　*pol.* trespass on sb.'s hospitality
讨生活　tǎo shēnghuó　① seek a living ② drift along aimlessly
讨嫌　tǎoxián　disagreeable; annoying: 这孩子真讨人嫌。That child is a nuisance.

讨厌 tǎoyàn ① disagreeable; disgusting; repugnant: 〜的天气 abominable weather / 每天刮风, 真〜! It's been windy every day. What a nuisance! / 他老说这些不三不四的话, 〜! He's always talking twaddle. How repulsive! ② hard to handle; troublesome; nasty: 气管炎是很〜的病。Tracheitis is a nasty illness. ③ dislike; loathe; be disgusted with: 工人们很〜他那官僚架子。The workers detest his bureaucratic airs. / 他是个老油子, 谁都〜。He's a wily old bird. Everybody is disgusted by his behaviour.

讨债 tǎozhài demand the payment of a debt or loan

讨债鬼 tǎozhàiguǐ ① a child dying young ② a person difficult to deal with or shake off

tào

套 tào ① sheath; case; cover: 毛笔〜 cap of a writing brush / 沙发〜 slipcover for a sofa; sofa cover / 给电视机加上一个〜儿 put a cover on the TV set ② cover with; slip over; encase in: 〜上毛衣 slip on a pullover / 把枕套〜上 put the pillow in the pillowcase / 〜上罩衣 put on a dustcoat ③ that which covers (other garments, etc.): 套鞋 tàoxié ④ overlap; interlink: 生产上一个环节〜一个环节 a closely linked succession in the production chain ⑤ the bend of a river or curve in a mountain range: 河套 hétào ⑥ dial. cotton padding (or wadding); batting: 袄〜 the padded lining of a Chinese jacket ⑦ dial. pad a quilt or jacket with cotton or silk floss ⑧ traces; harness: 牲口〜 harness for a draught animal / 雇〜 hire a draught animal and a plough ⑨ harness (a draught animal); hitch up (a draught animal to a cart): 我去〜牲口。I'll go and harness the beast. ⑩ knot; loop; noose: 拴个〜儿 tie a knot; make a loop / 活〜儿 slipknot; running knot ⑪ put a ring, etc. round; tie: 〜上救生圈 put on a life buoy / 用绳子〜一只狼 catch a wolf with a lasso ⑫ model on (or after); copy: 〜公式 apply a formula / 这是从欧阳修的《秋声赋》〜下来的。This is modelled on Ouyang Xiu's "Autumn Fu". ⑬ convention; formula: 客套 kètào ⑭ coax a secret out of sb.; pump sb. about sth.: 拿话〜他 coax the secret out of him; trick him into telling the truth / 〜口供 trick the accused into confession ⑮ try to win (sb.'s friendship): 套交情 tào jiāoqing ⑯ m. (for books, furniture, rooms, methods, remarks, etc.) set; suit; suite: 一〜书 a set of books / 一〜唱片 a set of phonograph records / 一〜邮票 a set of stamps / 一〜西服 a suit (of Western-style clothes) / 一〜房间 a suite of rooms or a flat / 一〜规章制度 a set of rules and regulations / 一〜唱腔 a score of voices (in a Chinese opera) / 你这一〜把戏我们早就识破了。We have already seen through all these tricks of yours. / 他讲了一大〜客气话。He made a lot of polite remarks. / 种庄稼他很有一〜。He's proficient in growing crops. / 别来这一〜! Don't give me that stuff! / 我不听你那一〜。I won't listen to any more of your nonsense. / 嘴里一〜, 心里一〜, 这样不好。Saying one thing and meaning another, that's not a good way to be. ⑰ cut the thread (of a screw) with a die or tap

套版 tàobǎn ① print. register ② same as 套色版 tàoshǎibǎn

套包 tàobāo (also 套包子 tàobāozi) collar (for a horse)

套裁 tàocái make suitable arrangements on one piece of cloth so that two or more jackets, dresses, etc. can be cut out of it

套车 tàochē harness a draught animal to a cart: 我得〜去拉农药。I must get the cart ready to haul back the pesticide.

套房 tàofáng same as 套间 tàojiān

套服 tàofú suit (of clothes)

套耕 tàogēng till the land with two ploughs simultaneously, the second one along the line of the first so as to plough deeper

套购 tàogòu fraudulently purchase (state-controlled commodities); illegally buy up: 〜统购统销物资 illegally buy up goods for which there is a state monopoly of purchase and marketing

套管 tàoguǎn petroleum casing pipe; casing: 〜程序 casing programme

套话 tàohuà ① polite formula; conventionality ② stereotyped expressions

套换 tàohuàn buy or get (goods, etc.) by illegal means: 〜外汇 engage in arbitrage (of foreign exchange); arbitrage

套汇 tàohuì ① buy foreign exchange by illegal means ② engage in arbitrage (of foreign exchange); arbitrage

套间 tàojiān ① a small room opening off another; inner room ② apartment; flat

套交情 tào jiāoqing try to get in good with sb.

套近乎 tào jìnhu derog. try to be friendly with sb.; try to chum (or pal) up with sb.; cotton up to sb.: 他总想跟人家〜, 可就是没人理他这茬儿。He always tries to cotton up to others, but no one pays any attention to him.

套裤 tàokù trouser legs worn over one's trousers; leggings

套犁 tàolí same as 套耕 tàogēng

套路 tàolù a series of skills and tricks in wushu (武术)

套马 tàomǎ lasso a horse

套曲 tàoqǔ mus. divertimento: 〜形式 cyclical (or cycle) form

套色 tàoshǎi print. chromatography; colour process

套色版 tàoshǎibǎn process plate; colourplate

套色木刻 tàoshǎi mùkè coloured woodcut

套衫 tàoshān pullover

套绳 tàoshéng lasso; noose

套数 tàoshù ① a sequence of songs, dramatic (戏曲) or non-dramatic (散曲), with one rhyme and a common set of melodies ② a series of skills and tricks in wushu (武术), etc. ③ conventional (or stereotyped) remark; conventionality

套索 tàosuǒ lasso; noose

套套 tàotao dial. ways; tricks: 他的〜可多了。He is very resourceful.

套筒 tàotǒng mech. sleeve; muff: 〜扳手 box spanner (or wrench); socket wrench / 〜联轴节 muff coupling

套问 tàowèn find out by asking seemingly casual questions; tactfully sound sb. out

套鞋 tàoxié overshoes; rubbers; galoshes

套袖 tàoxiù oversleeve

套印 tàoyìn print. chromatography: 彩色〜 process printing / 〜本 chromatograph edition

套用 tàoyòng apply mechanically; use indiscriminately: 不能到处〜这个公式。This formula cannot be applied indiscriminately.

套语 tàoyǔ polite formula; conventionality

套种 tàozhòng (also 套作 tàozuò) interplant: 实行间作〜 adopt intercropping and interplanting / 小麦地里〜棉花 interplant cotton with wheat

套装 tàozhuāng same as 套服 tàofú

套子 tàozi ① sheath; case; cover: 照相机〜 camera case / 沙发〜 slipcover for a sofa; sofa cover / 唱片〜 (phonograph) record sleeve / 给雨伞做个〜 make a cloth cover for the umbrella ② conventional (or stereotyped) remark; conventionality: 俗〜 a conventional pattern ③ dial. cotton padding (or wadding);

batting: 棉花～ cotton padding ④ snare; trap

tè

忒 tè *formal* make a mistake; err: 差忒 chàtè ——see also tēi; tuī

忐 tè see 忐忑 tǎntè

特[1] tè ① special; particular; unusual; exceptional: 奇特 qítè ② *adv.* for a special purpose; specially: 他～为此事而来。He's come specially for this purpose. ③ *adv.* very; especially: 这个医生扎针～灵。That doctor is very good at giving acupuncture treatment. ④ secret agent; spy: 敌特 dítè

特[2] tè *conj. formal* but; only

特别 tèbié ① special; particular; out of the ordinary: ～开支 special expenses / ～的爱好 a special hobby / 这种花每当夜晚就散发出一种～的香味儿。As evening approaches, this flower gives off a distinctive fragrance. / 这楼的设计没有什么～的地方。The design of this building is nothing out of the ordinary. / 他的口音很～。He has a peculiar accent. / 他的脾气很～。He has a peculiar temperament. ② *adv.* especially; particularly: 工作～努力 be especially hardworking / 建设一支～能战斗的队伍 train a contingent of especially good fighters / 质量～好 be of extra fine quality / 今天～热。It's extremely hot today. / 老红军的报告～有教育意义。The veteran Red Army man's talk was particularly instructive. / 这里最需要医务人员，～是外科医生。We're very much in need of medical workers, especially surgeons. ③ *adv.* for a special purpose; specially: 这些花是我～为你摘的。I picked these flowers specially for you. / 他临走时～去向女主人道谢。He made a point of thanking his hostess before he left the party.

特别法 tèbiéfǎ *leg.* special law

特别会议 tèbié huìyì special meeting; special session

特别监护病房 tèbié jiānhù bìngfáng intensive care unit (ICU)

特别快车 tèbié kuàichē express train; express; special express

特别提款权 tèbié tíkuǎnquán special drawing rights (SDR)

特别条款 tèbié tiáokuǎn special clause

特别许可证 tèbié xǔkězhèng special license

特产 tèchǎn special local product; speciality; specialty: 东北～ specialities (or special local products) of the Northeast / 桐油是中国的～。Tung oil is a special product of China.

特长 tècháng what one is skilled in; strong point; speciality: 他有什么～? What is he skilled in? / 绘画不是他的～。Painting is not his strong point. / 发挥每个人的～ give scope to everyone's special skill

特出 tèchū outstanding; prominent; extraordinary: ～的成绩 outstanding achievements / ～的作用 a prominent role

特此 tècǐ *adv.* (used in a document or formal letter) hereby: 定于明天上午八点在礼堂开会，～通知。It is hereby announced that there will be a meeting in the auditorium at 8 tomorrow morning.

特大 tèdà especially (or exceptionally) big; the most: ～喜讯 excellent news; most welcome news / ～丰收 an exceptional bumper harvest / 百年未遇的～干旱 the worst drought in a century / ～自然灾害 extraordinarily serious natural calamities / ～洪水 a catastrophic flood / ～号服装 outsize garments; extra large size

特等 tèděng special grade (or class); top grade: ～舱 stateroom; *de luxe* cabin / ～劳模 special-class model worker / ～射手 crack shot; expert marksman

特地 tèdì *adv.* for a special purpose; specially: 我们是～来向您学习育秧的。We came specially to learn from you how to raise rice seedlings.

特点 tèdiǎn characteristic; distinguishing feature; peculiarity; trait: 生理～ physiological characteristics / 照顾妇女的～ pay attention to the special needs of women / 这个厂的产品具有工艺精湛，经久耐用的～。The products of this factory are noted for their fine workmanship and durability.

特定 tèdìng ① specially designated (or appointed): ～的人选 a person specially designated for a post ② specific; specified; given: 在～的条件下 under given (or specified) conditions / 这种钢有～的用途。This kind of steel is used for specific purposes.

特氟隆 tèfúlóng *chem.* teflon

特工 tègōng secret service: ～人员 special agent; secret service personnel

特惠待遇 tèhuì dàiyù preferential treatment

特惠关税 tèhuì guānshuì preferential tariff

特混舰队 tèhùn jiànduì (naval) task force

特级 tèjí special grade (or class); superfine: ～茉莉花茶 superfine jasmine tea / ～教师 teacher of a special classification / ～战斗英雄 special-class combat hero; combat hero special grade

特急 tèjí extra urgent: ～电 extra urgent telegram; flash message

特辑 tèjí ① special number (or issue) of a periodical ② a special collection of short films

特技 tèjì ① stunt; trick: ～跳伞 trick parachuting ② *film* special effects: ～镜头 trick shot / ～摄影 trick photography

特技飞行 tèjì fēixíng *mil.* stunt flying; aerobatics

特价 tèjià special offer; bargain price: ～出售 sell at a bargain price

特刊 tèkān special issue (or number); special: 国庆～ special National Day issue

特克斯群岛和凯科斯群岛 Tèkèsī Qúndǎo hé Kǎikēsī Qúndǎo Turks and Caicos Islands

特快 tèkuài short for 特别快车 tèbié kuàichē

特立独行 tèlì-dúxíng independent in mind and action

特立尼达和多巴哥 Tèlìnídá hé Duōbāgē Trinidad and Tobago

特例 tèlì a special case

特洛伊木马 Tèluòyī mùmǎ Trojan horse

特命全权大使 tèmìng quánquán dàshǐ ambassador extraordinary and plenipotentiary

特命全权公使 tèmìng quánquán gōngshǐ envoy extraordinary and minister plenipotentiary

特派 tèpài specially appoint: ～王先生为首席代表 specially appoint Mr. Wang the chief representative / ～记者 special correspondent; accredited journalist

特派员 tèpàiyuán special commissioner

特遣部队 tèqiǎn bùduì task force

特区 tèqū special zone

特屈儿 tèqū'ér *chem.* tetryl

特权 tèquán privilege; prerogative: ～地位 privileged position / 不把职权变～ not use one's power to seek privileges / ～阶层 privileged stratum / ～思想 the idea that prerogatives and privileges go with position; the "special privilege" mentality

特色 tèsè characteristic; distinguishing feature (or quality): 艺术～ artistic characteristics / 富有民族～的歌舞节目 songs and dances with distinctive national features / 象牙雕刻的传统～ the traditional features of ivory carving / 建设有中国～的社会主义 build socialism with Chinese characteristics

特设　tèshè　*ad hoc*: ～委员会 *ad hoc* committee
特赦　tèshè　① grant a special pardon ② grant a special amnesty: ～战犯 grant a special amnesty to war criminals
特赦令　tèshèlìng　a decree (*or* writ) of special pardon or amnesty
特使　tèshǐ　special envoy
特殊　tèshū　special; particular; peculiar; exceptional: ～情况 an exceptional case; special circumstances / 革命战争的～规律 the specific laws of revolutionary war / 这个病人的症状比较～。This patient has rather peculiar symptoms. / 她不希望别人给她～的照顾。She didn't want to be given any special attention.
特殊化　tèshūhuà　(esp. of leading cadres) become privileged: 不搞～ seek no personal privileges / 反对～ oppose privileges
特殊教育　tèshū jiàoyù　special education (for disabled or mentally retarded people)
特殊性　tèshūxìng　particularity; peculiarity; specific characteristics: 矛盾的～ the particularity of contradiction / 那个地区有它的～。That region has its specific characteristics.
特斯拉　tèsīlā　*phys.* tesla
特为　tèwèi　*adv.* for a special purpose; specially: 我～来请你们去帮忙。I've come specially to ask you for help.
特务　tèwù　special task (*or* duties): ～营 special task battalion
特务　tèwu　special (*or* secret) agent; spy: ～活动 espionage / ～机关 secret service; espionage agency / ～组织 secret service; spy organization
特效　tèxiào　specially good effect; special efficacy: ～药 specific drug; specific; effective cure / 这药治胃溃疡有～。This medicine is especially effective in curing gastric ulcers.
特写　tèxiě　① feature article or story; feature ② *film* close-up: ～镜头 close-up (shot)
特性　tèxìng　specific property (*or* characteristic): 坚硬是金刚钻的～。Hardness is a property of diamonds.
特许　tèxǔ　specially permit: ～证书 special permit; letters patent
特压　tèyā　*chem.* extreme pressure: ～添加剂 extreme pressure additive
特邀　tèyāo　specially invite: ～代表 a specially invited representative
特异　tèyì　① exceptionally good; excellent; superfine: 成绩～ an excellent record (*or* performance); extraordinary results ② peculiar; distinctive: ～的风格 distinctive style
特异功能　tèyì gōngnéng　extraordinary powers
特异体质　tèyì tǐzhì　(also 特异质 tèyìzhì) *med.* idiosyncrasy
特意　tèyì　same as 特地 tèdì
特有　tèyǒu　peculiar; characteristic: 表现出青年～的热情 display the characteristic enthusiasm of youth / 这是广东人～的一种说法。This is an expression peculiar to people from Guangdong.
特约　tèyuē　engage by special arrangement: 这一期我们～钱教授写了一篇书评。For this issue we have specially requested Professor Qian to write a book review. / ～稿 special contribution (to a publication) / ～记者 special correspondent / ～经售处 special sales agency / ～评论员 special commentator / ～维修店 special repair shop / ～演员 guest actor / ～撰稿人 special contributor
特征　tèzhēng　characteristic; feature; trait: 面部～ facial characteristics / 地理～ geographical features / 民族～ national traits / 社会主义经济的基本～ basic features of the socialist economy

特指　tèzhǐ　refer in particular to: 我们所说的"小老虎"是～我们的副班长王发奋。The "Little Tiger" we're talking about is our deputy squad leader Wang Fafen.
特制　tèzhì　specially made (for specific purpose or by special process)
特种　tèzhǒng　special type; particular kind: ～技术部队 special technical units / ～战争 special warfare
特种兵　tèzhǒngbīng　special technical troops
特种工艺　tèzhǒng gōngyì　special arts and crafts; special handicraft products (of a particular place)

铽　tè　*chem.* terbium (Tb)

慝　tè　*formal* evil; wickedness

te

忒　te (also de)　see 肋忒 lēde

tēi

忒　tēi　see below——see also tè; tuī
忒儿　tēir　*onom. dial.* the sound of flapping wings: 麻雀～一声飞了。With a flap of its wings the sparrow flew off.

tēng

熥　tēng　heat up by steaming: 馒头凉了，～一～吧。The steamed buns are cold, let's heat them up.

鼟　tēng　*onom.* the sound of a drumbeat: ～～的鼓声 the roll of drums

téng

疼　téng　① ache; have a pain; be sore: 胃～ have a stomachache / 嗓子～ have a sore throat / 腿～ have a pain in the leg / 浑身都～ be aching all over / 你那个牙还～吗?Does your tooth still hurt? ② love dearly; be fond of; dote on: 奶奶最～小孙子。Granny dotes on her little grandson. / 这孩子怪招人～的。This child is really lovable.
疼爱　téng'ài　love dearly; be fond of; dote on: 做父母的都～自己的孩子。All parents love their children. / 他就是特别～圆圆。He just dotes on Yuanyuan.
疼痛　téngtòng　pain; ache; soreness
疼惜　téngxī　love tenderly; have tender affection for

誊 (謄)　téng　transcribe (by hand); copy out: 她在～一封信。She's copying out a letter. / 这稿子太乱，要～一遍。This draft is too messy. It must be recopied. / 照底稿～一份 make a clean copy of the draft
誊录　ténglù　transcribe (by hand); copy out: ～文稿 copy out a manuscript
誊清　téngqīng　make a clean copy of: ～稿 a clean (*or* fair) copy
誊写　téngxiě　transcribe (by hand); copy out: 把这篇文章连同我的修改部分～出来。Copy out the article, including all the corrections I have made.
誊写版　téngxiěbǎn　*print.* stencil

誊写钢版 téngxiě gāngbǎn　steel plate for cutting stencils

誊写蜡纸 téngxiě làzhǐ　stencil paper

誊写油墨 téngxiě yóumò　stencil ink

誊印社 téngyìnshè　mimeograph service

腾

腾 téng ① gallop; jump; prance: ～身而过 jump over sth. ② rise; soar: 升腾 shēngténg ③ make room; clear out; vacate: ～出自己的房子给客人住 vacate one's own room to put up a visitor / 给新来的人～个地方 make room for a newcomer / ～出更多的人来参加麦收 release more people to help with the wheat harvest / ～出时间学英语 try and find time to learn English / 你～出手来帮我包馄饨好不好?Will you stop working for a moment and help me make *won ton*? ④ (used after certain verbs to show repeated actions): 翻腾 fānteng

腾达 téngdá *formal* ① rise; soar ② make rapid advances in one's career; rise to power and position

腾飞 téngfēi ① fly swiftly upward; soar ② make rapid advance; develop rapidly: 祖国在～。Our country is developing rapidly.

腾贵 téngguì　(of prices) shoot up; soar; skyrocket

腾空 téngkōng　soar; rise high into the air; rise to the sky: 五彩缤纷的礼花～而起。Colourful fireworks shot into the sky.

腾挪 téngnuó ① transfer (funds, etc.) to other use: 专款专用,不得任意～。Funds earmarked for specific purposes are not to be transferred at will. ② move sth. to make room: 把仓库里的东西～一下, 好装水泥。Move the things in the storehouse to make room for the cement.

腾闪 téngshǎn　avoid; elude; dodge: ～不及 too late to dodge

腾腾 téngténg　steaming; seething: 烟雾～ hazy with smoke; smoke-laden / 烈焰～ raging flames

腾跃 téngyuè ① prance; bounce ② *formal* (of prices) go up; rise

腾越 téngyuè　jump over: ～障碍 jump over obstacles

腾云驾雾 téngyún-jiàwù ① (of mythical beings) ride the clouds and mount the mist ② feel giddy (*or* dizzy)

滕

滕 Téng　a surname

藤(籐)

藤 téng ① cane; rattan: ～制品 rattan work / ～椅 cane chair; rattan chair / ～盔 rattan helmet ② vine: 西瓜～。watermelon vine

藤本植物 téngběn zhíwù　liana; vine

藤黄 ténghuáng *bot.* ① garcinia ② gamboge

藤萝 téngluó *bot.* Chinese wistaria (*Wisteria sinensis*)

藤牌 téngpái　cane (*or* rattan) shield; shield

藤球 téngqiú *sports* sepak takraw

藤条 téngtiáo　rattan

藤子 téngzi *inf.* ① cane; rattan ② vine

螣

螣 téng *zool.* stargazer

tǐ

体(體)

体 tǐ　see below——see also tī

体己 tǐjǐ ① intimate; confidential: ～人 a person one can confide in; bosom friend / ～话 things one says only to one's intimates; words spoken in confidence ② private (savings): ～钱 private savings of a family member

剔

剔 tī ① clean with a pointed instrument; pick: ～

指甲 clean the fingernails / ～骨头 pick a bone / ～牙 pick one's teeth ② pick out and throw away; reject: 把烂梨～出去 pick out the rotten pears ③ rising stroke (in Chinese characters)

剔除 tīchú　reject; get rid of: 继承文化遗产要吸取精华,～糟粕 absorb the essence and reject the dross in inheriting the cultural legacy / 1990年人均生活费为1,387元,～价格因素,比1980年增长68.1%。In 1990 the average per capita cost of living reached 1,387 *yuan*, an increase of 68.1% over 1980 after allowing for price rises.

剔红 tīhóng　carved lacquerware

剔庄货 tīzhuānghuò　goods (usu. general merchandise or clothing) sold at reduced prices; shopworn or substandard goods

梯

梯 tī ① ladder; steps; stairs: 楼梯 lóutī ② shaped like a staircase; terraced: 梯田 tītián

梯次队形 tīcì duìxíng *mil.* echelon formation

梯度 tīdù *phys.* gradient

梯队 tīduì ① *mil.* echelon formation; echelon ② a group of persons of one level or grade in an organization, kept for use if needed

梯恩梯 tī'ēntī *chem.* trinitrotoluene (TNT): ～当量 TNT equivalent

梯己 tījǐ　stair; step

梯己 tījǐ　same as 体己 tǐjǐ

梯田 tītián *agric.* terraced fields; terrace: 修～ build terraced fields; terrace mountain slopes

梯形 tīxíng ① *math.* trapezoid; trapezium ② ladder-shaped

梯形翼 tīxíngyì *aviation* trapezoidal wing; tapered airfoil

梯子 tīzi　ladder; stepladder

锑

锑 tī *chem.* antimony; stibium (Sb)

踢

踢 tī ① kick: 一脚把门～开 open the door with a kick; kick the door open / 把凳子～翻 kick over a stool / 小心这马～人! Be careful! This horse kicks. / ～开绊脚石 kick away a stumbling block ② play (football); kick: ～足球 play football / ～进一个球 kick (*or* score) a goal / 他～中锋。He plays centre forward.

踢踏 tīdā *onom.* the sound of footsteps

踢踏 tīda ① kick at random ② spend freely; squander

踢踏舞 tīdāwǔ　tap dance: 表演～ perform a tap dance

踢蹬 tīdeng ① kick at random: 这孩子坐在那儿还乱～。That child can't keep his legs still even when he's sitting down. / 那马赛完后还～着蹄儿。The horse was still pawing the ground after the race. ② spend freely; squander: 把家产～光 squander away one's family fortune ③ handle; deal with; dispose of: 他用了一个晚上才把这些琐碎事～完。It took him a whole evening to dispose of these trivial matters.

踢脚板 tījiǎobǎn *archit.* skirting board; skirtboard

踢皮球 tī píqiú ① kick a ball or play children's football ② kick sth. back and forth like a ball; pass the buck; shift responsibility onto each other

踢腾 tīteng　same as 踢蹬 tīdeng

鹏

鹏 tī　see 鹏鹏 pītī

擿

擿 tī *formal* expose; unmask; bring to light

tí

荑

荑 tí *formal* ① sprout; shoot: 柔荑 róutí ② barn-

yard grass ——see also yǐ

绨

绨　tí　a kind of thick silk ——see also tì

提

提　tí　① carry (in one's hand with the arm down): 手里～着个篮子 carry a basket in one's hand / 我去～壶水来。I'm going to fetch a kettle of water. ② lift; raise; promote: 这种自行车十分轻便, 一只手就能～起来。This bicycle is very light. You can lift it with one hand. / 从井里～水 draw water from a well / 把鞋～上。Pull your shoes on. / 把某人～到领导岗位上去 promote sb. to a position of leadership / 把问题～到原则高度来分析 analyse a problem from the high plane of principle ③ shift to an earlier time; move up a date: 把会议的日期往前～ move the date of the meeting up ④ put forward; bring up; raise: ～问题 ask a question / ～意见 make a criticism; make comments or suggestions / ～抗议 lodge a protest / ～条件 put forward conditions / ～要求 make demands / ～方案 suggest (or propose) plans / 把事情～到会上去讨论 take (or submit) the matter to the meeting for discussion / 把计划生育～到议事日程上来 put family planning on the agenda ⑤ draw (or take) out; extract: 银行里的这笔款子你～了没有?Have you drawn the money from the bank? / 我到车站～行李去。I'm going to collect my luggage at the station. ⑥ summon (a prisoner) for interrogation: ～犯人 fetch a prisoner for interrogation ⑦ mention; refer to; bring up: 他～了一下这个计划, 没有说明细节。He mentioned the plan, but gave no details. / 别再～那件事了。Don't bring that up again. / 论文有几处～到了《实践论》。The paper contains several references to On Practice. ⑧ dipper: 油提 yóutí ⑨ rising stroke (in Chinese characters) ——see also dī

提案　tí'àn　motion; proposal; draft resolution: ～国 sponsor country (of a resolution); sponsor / ～审查委员会 motions examination committee

提拔　tí·bá　promote: ～某人担任领导工作 promote sb. to a position of leadership

提包　tíbāo　handbag; shopping bag; bag; valise

提笔　tíbǐ　take up one's pen; start writing

提拨　tíbo　dial. remind; warn; call attention to

提倡　tíchàng　advocate; promote; encourage; recommend: ～晚婚和计划生育 advocate late marriage and family planning / ～说普通话 promote the use of putonghua / ～勤俭建国 spread the idea of building the country through diligence and thrift / ～奉献精神 encourage the spirit of self-devotion / 这种做法值得～。This method deserves recommendation.

提成　tíchéng　deduct a percentage (from a sum of money, etc.)

提出　tíchū　put forward; advance; pose; raise: ～建议 put forward a proposal; make a suggestion / ～一种新的理论 advance a new theory / ～程序问题 raise a point of order / ～警告 give (or serve) a warning / ～抗议 lodge a protest / 向自己～更高的要求 make still greater demands on oneself / ～入党申请 submit an application to join the Party; apply for Party membership / ～修改和补充意见 propose amendments and addenda / 新的形势向我们～了新的课题。The new situation has put new questions before us. / ～响亮的口号 raise a clarion call

提纯　tíchún　purify; refine: ～器 purifier

提纯复壮　tíchún fùzhuàng　agric. purification and rejuvenation

提词　tící　theat. prompt: 他忘了台词, 还得让人～。He forgot his lines and had to be prompted. / 我来～。I'll be the prompter.

提单　tídān　bill of lading (B / L): 直达～ direct bill of lading / 联运～ through bill of lading

提灯　tídēng　barn lantern; lantern

提调　tídiào　① supervise ② superviser: 舞台～ stage manager

提兜　tídōu　handbag; bag; valise

提督　tídū　a provincial commander in imperial China

提法　tífǎ　the way sth. is put; formulation; wording: 他们不同意你对这个问题的～。They take exception to the way you put the question. / 这是个新的～。This is a new formulation. / 这只是个～问题。This is just a matter of wording.

提干　tígàn　① make sb. a cadre ② promote a cadre to a higher position

提纲　tígāng　outline: 写发言～ make an outline for a speech

提纲挈领　tígāng-qièlǐng　take a net by the headrope or a coat by the collar——concentrate on the main points; bring out the essentials: 我来～地谈一谈。I'll just touch briefly on the essentials.

提高　tígāo　raise; heighten; enhance; increase; improve: ～水位 raise the water level / ～警惕 enhance (or heighten, sharpen) one's vigilance / ～认识 deepen one's understanding / ～勇气 pluck up one's courage / ～部队的战斗力 increase the combat effectiveness of the troops / ～单位面积产量 raise the per unit yield / ～产品质量 improve the quality of products / 人民生活水平逐年～。The living standards of the people rise year by year. / 也许我的方法不对头, 所以工作效率提不高。Maybe my method is incorrect, so I haven't been able to raise my working efficiency.

提供　tígōng　provide; supply; furnish; offer: 为轻工业～原料 supply light industry with raw materials / ～援助 give aid; provide assistance / ～贷款 offer a loan / ～新的证据 furnish fresh evidence / 历史给我们～了有益的经验教训。History affords us useful lessons. / 破案的线索他们～不出来。They weren't able to come up with clues that would solve the case.

提灌　tíguàn　irrigate by lifting water to a higher level with a water pump, etc.

提行　tíháng　begin a new line (in writing or printing)

提盒　tíhé　a tiered lunchbox with several round compartments one above the other and a handle

提花　tíhuā　jacquard weave: ～枕巾 a jacquard pillow cover / ～织机 jacquard loom

提婚　tíhūn　same as 提亲 tíqīn

提货　tíhuò　pick up goods; take delivery of goods: 到火车站～ pick up goods at the railway station / 请于三日内来车站～。Please take delivery of the goods at the station within three days.

提货单　tíhuòdān　same as 提单 tídān

提及　tíjí　speak of; talk about; refer to; mention: 这部小说文学史上从未～。The novel has received no mention in any history of literature.

提价　tíjià　raise the price

提交　tíjiāo　submit (a problem, etc.) to; refer to: 将决议草案～大会讨论 submit the draft resolution to the congress for discussion / 把问题～董事会 refer the matter to the board of directors

提款　tíkuǎn　draw money (from a bank)

提篮　tílán　hand-basket

提炼　tíliàn　extract and purify; abstract; refine: 从矿石中～金属 extract (or abstract) metal from ore / ～蔗糖 refine cane sugar / 将生活素材～加工 refine the literary raw material gathered from life

提梁　tíliáng　handle (of a basket, etc.); straps (of a handbag, etc.); loop handle

提梁卣　tíliángyǒu　archaeol. a ewer with a loop handle

提名　tímíng　nominate (for election): ～某人为代表 nominate sb. for representative

提起 tíqǐ ① mention; speak of: ～这个爱乐乐团没有一个不夸的。No one ever mentions the Philharmonic Orchestra without praising it. / 昨天他还～你来着。He spoke of you only yesterday. ② raise; arouse; brace up: ～精神 raise one's spirits; brace oneself up / ～人们的注意 call (or arouse) people's attention

提前 tíqián ① shift to an earlier date; move up (a date); advance: 总攻的时间～了。The time for the general offensive has been moved up. ② do sth. in advance or ahead of time: 下星期要是有演出，请～通知我们。If we are going to put on a performance next week, please notify us in advance. / ～两个月完成全年生产指标 meet the year's production target two months ahead of time / ～释放战犯 release war criminals before their sentences expire / ～召开大会 convene the congress before the due date

提前量 tíqiánliàng *mil.* lead

提挈 tíqiè *formal* ① lead; take with one; marshal: ～全军 marshal all one's (military) forces ② guide and support; give guidance and help to

提亲 tíqīn (also 提亲事 tí qīnshi) propose a marriage alliance

提琴 tíqín the violin family: 小提琴 xiǎotíqín

提请 tíqǐng submit sth. to: ～大会批准 submit to the congress for approval / ～大家注意 call everybody's attention to sth.

提取 tíqǔ ① draw; pick up; collect: ～银行存款 draw money from a bank; withdraw bank deposits / 到车站～行李 pick up (or collect) one's luggage at the railway station ② extract; abstract; recover: 从油页岩中～石油 extract oil from shale / 从废水中～有用物质 recover useful materials from waste water

提取器 tíqǔqì extractor

提取塔 tíqǔtǎ extraction column

提神 tíshén refresh oneself; give oneself a lift: 喝杯茶提提神 refresh oneself with a cup of tea

提审 tíshěn ① bring (a prisoner) before the court; bring (sb. in custody) to trial; fetch (a detainee) for interrogation ② review (a case tried by a lower court)

提升 tíshēng ① promote: ～他当排长 promote him to be platoon leader ② hoist; elevate: ～机 hoist; elevator

提示 tíshì point out; prompt: 请把学习重点向大家一下。Please brief us on the main points to be studied. / 如果她忘了台词，你就给她～一下。Prompt her if she forgets her lines.

提手 tíshǒu same as 提梁 tíliáng

提头儿 títóur start a conversation or discussion going: 一个人一～，大家就议论起来了。When the ball had started rolling in the discussion, everyone began to join in.

提味 tíwèi render palatable (by adding condiments); season: 搁点儿味精提提味。Add a little MSG to make it more flavourful.

提问 tíwèn (esp. of a teacher) put question to; quiz: 老师～以后，他答不上来。The teacher put the question to him, but he couldn't answer it.

提线木偶 tíxiàn mùǒu marionette

提箱 tíxiāng suitcase

提携 tíxié ① lead (a child) by the hand ② guide and support; give guidance and help to

提心 tíxīn worry; feel anxious

提心吊胆 tíxīn-diàodǎn have one's heart in one's mouth; be on tenterhooks: 他对考试结果感到～的。He was on tenterhooks about the result of the exam.

提醒 tíxǐng remind; warn; call attention to: 如果我忘了，请你～我一下。Please remind me in case I should forget. / ～他早点儿来。Remind him to come early. / ～司机在这一带要低速行驶。Warn the driver to drive slowly in this area.

提选 tíxuǎn select; choose: ～耐旱品种 select drought-resistant varieties

提讯 tíxùn bring (a prisoner) before the court; bring (sb. in custody) to trial; fetch (a detainee) for interrogation

提要 tíyào *précis*; summary; abstract; epitome; synopsis: 《哥达纲领批判》的～和注释 *précis* of and notes to *Critique of the Gotha Programme* / 论文～ abstract of the thesis / 本书内容～ capsule summary of the book

提要钩玄 tíyào-gōuxuán pick out the essentials and extract the essence (when reading a book)

提议 tíyì ① propose; suggest; move: 我～为两国人民的友谊干杯。I propose a toast to the friendship between the peoples of the two countries. / 我～现在休会。I move the meeting be adjourned. ② proposal; motion: 大会一致通过了他们的～。The meeting unanimously adopted their proposal. / 根据会议主席的～ on the motion of the chairman of the meeting

提掖 tíyè *formal* guide and support sb.

提早 tízǎo shift to an earlier time; be earlier than planned or expected: 汛期～了。The flood season is here earlier than expected. / ～出发 set out earlier than planned / ～通知一声 notify in advance

提制 tízhì obtain through refining; distil; extract: 香草香精是从一种热带兰～出来的。Vanilla is extracted from a tropical orchid.

啼 (嗁)

tí ① cry; weep aloud: 哭哭啼啼 kūkutítí ② (of certain birds and animals) crow; caw; screech: 鸡～。Cocks crow. / 月落乌～。The crows caw when the moon goes down.

啼号 tíháo cry loudly; wail

啼饥号寒 tíjī-háohán wail with hunger and cold; cry out from hunger and cold

啼哭 tíkū cry; wail

啼鸣 tímíng (of birds) crow; caw

啼笑皆非 tí-xiào jiē fēi not know whether to laugh or cry; find sth. both funny and annoying

缇

tí *formal* orange red

鹈

tí see below

鹈鹕 tíhú pelican

题

tí ① topic; subject; title; problem: 讨论～ topic for discussion / 这道～我没答对。I didn't give the correct answer to the problem. ② inscribe: ～诗一首 inscribe a poem (on a painting, fan, wall, etc.) / 某某～ (an inscription) by so-and-so

题跋 tíbá ① preface and postscript ② short comments, annotations, etc. on a scroll (of painting or calligraphy); colophon: 《东坡～》 *Dongpo's Postscripts and Colophons*

题壁 tíbì ① write on a wall: 苏轼《题西林壁》 "Written on the Wall at West Forest" by Su Shi ② inscriptions on a wall: 洞内有不少文人的～。There were many literary men's inscriptions on the walls of the cave temple.

题材 tícái subject matter; theme: ～范围 range of subjects / 这个剧本以土地革命为～。The theme of the play is the agrarian revolution. / 这是写小说的好～。This is good material for a novel.

题词 tící ① write a few words of encouragement, appreciation or commemoration ② inscription; dedication ③ foreword

题花 tíhuā title design

题解 tíjiě ① explanatory notes on the title or background of a book ② key to exercises or problems: 《平面几何～》 *Key to Exercises in Plane Geometry*

题名 tímíng ① inscribe one's name; autograph: 在照片

上～ autograph a photograph / ～留念 give one's autograph as a memento ② autograph ③ title (of an article, etc.)

题目 tímù ① title; subject; topic: 辩论的～ subject (or topic) for a debate / 这篇文章的～叫做《光明与真理》。The article is entitled "Light and Truth". ② exercise problems; examination questions

题签 tíqiān ① write the title of a book on a label to be stuck on the cover ② a label with the title of a book on it

题旨 tízhǐ ① the meaning of the title of an article ② the theme of a literary work

题字 tízì ① write a few words of commemoration (on an autograph album, etc.) ② inscription; autograph: 书上有作者亲笔～。The book is autographed by the author.

醍

tí see below

醍醐 tíhú arch. clarified butter; ghee (used by Buddhists as a metaphor for the perfect truth of Buddha)

醍醐灌顶 tíhú guàn dǐng ① be filled with wisdom; be enlightened ② suddenly feel refreshed

蹄 (蹏)

tí ① hoof: 马有四个～儿。A horse has four hoofs. ② trotter: 猪～ pig's trotters

蹄筋 tíjīn tendons of beef, mutton or pork: 红烧～ tendons stewed in soy sauce

蹄膀 típang dial. the upper part of a leg of pork

蹄子 tízi ① inf. hoof ② dial. upper part of a leg of pork

鳀 (鯷)

tí anchovy

tǐ

体 (體、躰)

tǐ ① body or part of the body: 肢体 zhītǐ ② substance or state of a substance: 固体 gùtǐ ③ style; form: 文体 wéntǐ ④ personally do or experience sth.; put oneself in another's position: 身体力行 shēntǐ-lìxíng ⑤ system: 政体 zhèngtǐ ⑥ style of calligraphy: 你写的什么～? What style of calligraphy do you do? ⑦ typeface: 注解你要排什么～? What typeface would you like the notes to be printed in? ⑧ gram. aspect (of a verb) ——see also tī

体壁 tǐbì zool. body wall

体裁 tǐcái types or forms of literature

体操 tǐcāo gymnastics: 自由体操 zìyóu tǐcāo

体操表演 tǐcāo biǎoyǎn gymnastic exhibition (or display)

体操服 tǐcāofú gym outfit (or clothes, suit)

体操器械 tǐcāo qìxiè gymnastic apparatus

体察 tǐchá experience and observe: 虚心～情况 ready to look into matters with an open mind; not be prejudiced in sizing up situations / ～下情 try to understand what is going on at the lower levels

体词 tǐcí gram. general term for nouns, pronouns, numerals and measure words; substantive

体大思精 tǐdà-sījīng (of a book) extensive in scope and brilliant in conception

体罚 tǐfá corporal (or physical) punishment

体格 tǐgé physique; build: ～强壮 of strong physique (or constitution); of powerful build

体格检查 tǐgé jiǎnchá physical examination; health checkup

体会 tǐhuì ① know (or learn) from experience; realize: 他深深～到这友情的温暖。He deeply felt the warmth of the friendship. / 不付出辛勤的劳动就无法～真正的幸

福。You won't know real happiness if you don't put in a lot of hard work. / 他在牧民中间生活多年,真能～他们的思想感情。Having lived among the herdsmen for years, he can have a true understanding of their thoughts and feelings. ② knowledge; understanding: 深有～ have an intimate knowledge of sth. / 谈谈我个人的～。I'll say a few words about my personal experience (or understanding). / 参加了这次科学讨论会,我有两点～。The symposium enlightened me on two points.

体积 tǐjī volume; bulk: ～大 bulky / 容器的～ the volume of a container

体积膨胀 tǐjī péngzhàng phys. volume expansion

体检 tǐjiǎn short for 体格检查 tǐgé jiǎnchá

体节 tǐjié zool. body segment

体力 tǐlì physical (or bodily) strength; physical power: 增强～ build up one's strength / 消耗～ be a drain on one's (physical) strength; consume (or sap) one's strength / 他～好,打满五局击败对手。He had good stamina and beat his opponent at the end of the fifth game. / 下半时队员们显得～不支。The players showed signs of tiredness during the second half.

体力劳动 tǐlì láodòng physical (or manual) labour: 参加～ take part in (or do) physical labour

体例 tǐlì stylistic rules and layout; style: 印刷～ style sheet; stylebook

体谅 tǐliàng show understanding and sympathy for; make allowances for: 充分～人家的困难 make full allowances for their difficulties / 她是很～人的。She is quite understanding.

体貌 tǐmào one's figure and features—general physical appearance

体面 tǐmian ① dignity; face: 他并不认为干这些事就会有失～。He did not consider it a loss of face (or beneath his dignity) to concern himself with these things. / 维持～ keep up appearances ② honourable; creditable: 不～的行为 disgraceful (or disreputable) conduct ③ good-looking: 长得～ be handsome / 你要出去的话得穿～一些。You're not going out unless you're decently dressed.

体能 tǐnéng (physical) stamina

体念 tǐniàn give sympathetic consideration to

体魄 tǐpò formal physique: 强壮的～ strong (or powerful) physique; vigorous health / 锻炼～ go in for physical training

体气 tǐqì formal literary style

体腔 tǐqiāng physiol. body cavity

体热 tǐrè body heat

体虱 tǐshī body louse

体式 tǐshì ① form of characters or letters: 汉语拼音字母有手写体和印刷体两种～。There are two forms of the Chinese phonetic alphabet, the cursive and the printed. ② formal form of literary works: 词和律诗～不同。Ci poems are different in form from lüshi poems.

体视 tǐshì phys. stereo: ～显微镜 stereomicroscope / ～望远镜 stereotelescope

体态 tǐtài posture; carriage: ～轻盈 have a graceful carriage

体坛 tǐtán the sports world; sports circles

体贴 tǐtiē show consideration for; give every care to: ～病人 show a patient every consideration / 他对妻子很～。He's very considerate of his wife. / 她能～人。She's considerate.

体贴入微 tǐtiē rù wēi look after with great care; care for with great solicitude; show every possible consideration; be extremely thoughtful

体统 tǐtǒng decorum; propriety; decency: 有失～ be disgraceful; be scandalous / 他这样无理取闹,成何～! He's being difficult on purpose and it's so unseemly! ——see also 不成体统 bù chéng tǐtǒng

体外受精 tǐwài shòujīng external fertilization

体外循环 tǐwài xúnhuán extracorporeal circulation

体味 tǐwèi appreciate; savour: 仔细～这首诗的含义 savour the meaning of the poem

体温 tǐwēn (body) temperature: 给孩子量～. Take the child's temperature. / 她的～在上升. Her temperature is going up. / ～过低 hypothermia

体温计 tǐwēnjì (clinical) thermometer

体无完肤 tǐ wú wán fū ① have cuts and bruises all over the body; be a mass of bruises: 被打得～ be beaten black and blue ② be thoroughly refuted or exposed; be scathingly criticized; be torn to pieces (or shreds): 这种谬论早已被批得～. This fallacy has long since been torn to shreds.

体惜 tǐxī understand and sympathize with

体系 tǐxì system; setup: 建成独立的、比较完整的工业～和国民经济～ complete an independent and fairly comprehensive industrial complex and economic system

体细胞 tǐxìbāo biol. somatic cell

体现 tǐxiàn embody; incarnate; reflect; give expression to: 《国际歌》～了巴黎公社的革命精神. The Internationale embodies the revolutionary spirit of the Paris Commune. / 这个提案～了发展中国家的利益和要求. This proposal reflects the interests and demands of the developing countries.

体形 tǐxíng bodily form; build

体型 tǐxíng ① type of build or figure ② somatotype

体恤 tǐxù understand and sympathize with; show solicitude for: ～烈士遗孤 show solicitude for the children of revolutionary martyrs

体癣 tǐxuǎn ringworm of the body

体循环 tǐxúnhuán physiol. systemic circulation; greater circulation

体验 tǐyàn learn through practice; learn through one's personal experience: ～生活 observe and learn from real life

体液 tǐyè body fluid; humour

体育 tǐyù ① physical culture; physical training: ～锻炼 physical training / 今天下午有一节～课. We'll have an hour of PE (physical education) this afternoon. ② sports: ～活动 sports activities / ～器械 sports apparatus

体育场 tǐyùchǎng ① sports field (or ground) ② stadium

体育道德 tǐyù dàodé sportsmanship

体育馆 tǐyùguǎn gymnasium; gym

体育疗法 tǐyù liáofǎ physical exercise therapy

体育用品 tǐyù yòngpǐn sports goods (or requisites)

体育运动 tǐyù yùndòng sports

体征 tǐzhēng med. sign

体制 tǐzhì system (of organization); structure: 国家～ state system / 管理～ managerial system / 经济和政治～ economic and political structures

体质 tǐzhì physique; constitution: 增强～ build up health / 他们的～都很好. They all have good physiques. / 各人的～不同, 对疾病的抵抗力也不同. People's constitutions differ; so does their resistance to disease.

体重 tǐzhòng (body) weight: ～增加 put on weight; gain weight / ～减轻 lose weight / 她～六十公斤. She weighs 60 kilograms.

屉（屜）

tì

tì ① a food steamer with several trays; steamer tray: ～帽 the lid (or cover) of a steamer / 一～馒头 a trayful of steamed buns / ～跟锅不合

适. The steamer tray doesn't fit into the pot. ② drawer: 三～桌 three-drawer desk

屉子 tìzi ① (one of) a set of removable trays (in furniture or a utensil) ② dial. drawer

剃

tì shave: ～胡子 have a shave; shave oneself

剃刀 tìdāo razor

剃刀鲸 tìdāojīng another name for 蓝鲸 lánjīng

剃度 tìdù Buddhism tonsure

剃光头 tì guāngtóu have one's head shaved—score no points (in games): 我们队给对方剃了个光头, 五比〇. Our team blanked the other, 5-0.

剃头 tìtóu ① have one's head shaved ② have one's hair cut; have a haircut

剃须膏 tìxūgāo shaving cream

剃枝虫 tìzhīchóng dial. armyworm

俶

tì same as 涕 tì

倜

tì see below

倜傥 tìtǎng same as 倜傥 tìtǎng

涕

tì ① tears: 痛哭流涕 tòngkū liútì ② mucus of the nose; snivel: 鼻涕 bítì

涕泪 tìlèi ① tears ② tears and snivel

涕零 tìlíng shed tears

涕泣 tìqì liter. weep

涕泗 tìsì liter. tears and snivel

涕泗交流 tìsì jiāo liú tears and snivel streaming down at the same time—crying piteously: 戎马关山北, 凭轩涕泗流.（杜甫）War rages in the northern mountain passes; Leaning on a balustrade I shed tears.

涕泗滂沱 tìsì pāngtuó be drenched with tears and snivel

悌

tì formal love and respect one's elder brother

绨

tì a silk and cotton fabric ——see also tí

倜

tì see below

倜然 tìrán formal ① aloof; detached ② drifting apart; estranged

倜傥 tìtǎng formal elegant; free and easy

惕

tì be cautious; be watchful: 警惕 jǐngtì

替[1]

tì ① take the place of; replace; substitute for: 今天老王没来, 谁～他? Lao Wang is absent today. Who'll take his place? / 你歇会儿, 我～你干. Have a rest. Let me take over. / 假日期间他～赵大夫值班. He'll be Dr. Zhao's substitute during the holidays. / 这里的工作谁也～不了谁. We cannot substitute for one another in our work here. / 三号上场, ～下五号. Player No.3 for No.5. / 他身体不好, 快去把他～下来. He's not well. Go and replace him at once. ② prep. for: ～别人买火车票 buy a train ticket for sb. / ～顾客着想 think about the interests of the customers / 大家都～你高兴. We all feel happy for your sake. / 别～我担心. Don't worry about me. / 你能～小王也画一张像吗? Will you also draw a portrait for Xiao Wang? / 他们都到机场～她送行. They all went to see her off at the airport.

替[2]

tì formal decline: 兴替 xīngtì

替班 tìbān take sb. else's place (in a work shift)

替补 tìbǔ substitute for: ～队员 substitute (player); reserve (player)

替代 tìdài substitute for; replace; supersede: 用石油～煤 replace coal with petroleum; substitute petroleum

for coal

替工 tìgōng ① work as a temporary substitute ② a temporary substitute (worker): 找一个～ find a substitute; get a replacement

替换 tìhuàn replace; substitute for; displace; take the place of: 教练决定让 3 号～ 8 号。The coach decided to replace player No. 8 with No. 3. / 我们去～值夜班的同志。We are going to relieve the comrades on night duty. / 带上一套～的衣服。Take a change of clothes with you.

替角儿 tìjuér understudy

替身 tìshēn ① substitute; replacement; stand-in ② scapegoat

替身演员 tìshēn yǎnyuán stunt man or stunt woman

替手 tìshǒu ① take the place of; replace; substitute for ② substitute; replacement

替死鬼 tìsǐguǐ inf. scapegoat; fall guy

替天行道 tì tiān xíngdào right wrongs in accordance with heaven's decree (a slogan often used by leaders of peasant uprisings)

替续器 tìxùqì another name for 继电器 jìdiànqì

替罪羊 tìzuìyáng scapegoat

嚏

tì formal sneeze

嚏喷 tìpen sneeze

tiān

天

tiān ① the sky; the heavens: 明朗的～ a clear sky / 太阳一出满～红。The sky is aglow with the rising sun. ② overhead: 天桥 tiānqiáo ③ day: 每～ every day / 开学第二～ on the second day of the new term / 忙了一～ have had a busy day; have done a good day's work / 夏天～长夜短。In summer the days are long and the nights short. / 二月份是几～? How many days are there in the month of February? ④ a period of time in a day: 五更～ around four in the morning / ～不早啦。It's getting late. ⑤ season: 冷～ the cold season; cold days ⑥ weather: 下雨～ wet (or rainy) weather / ～越来越冷了。It's getting colder and colder. / ～晴了, 咱们走吧。It's cleared up now. Let's go. ⑦ natural; inborn; innate: 天性 tiānxìng ⑧ nature: 人定胜天 rén dìng shèng tiān ⑨ God; Heaven: ～知道! God knows! / ～哪! Good Heavens!

天安门 Tiān'ānmén Tian An Men (the Gate of Heavenly Peace): ～广场 Tian'anmen Square / ～城楼 the rostrum of Tian An Men

天崩地坼 tiānbēng-dìchè (also 天崩地裂 tiānbēng-dìliè) heaven felling and earth rending—violent political or social upheavals

天边 tiānbiān horizon; the ends of the earth; remotest places: ～的渔帆 the sails of the fishing boats that appear on the horizon

天兵 tiānbīng troops from heaven—an invincible army

天禀 tiānbǐng formal natural gift; talent; natural endowments

天不怕, 地不怕 tiān bù pà, dì bù pà fear neither Heaven nor Earth; fear nothing on earth; nothing daunted

天才 tiāncái genius; talent; gift; endowment: 世界上不存在什么生而知之的～。There is no such thing as a genius born with knowledge. / 这孩子有音乐～。The child has musical talent (or a gift for music). / 爱因斯坦是个伟大的科学～。Einstein was a great scientific genius.

天才论 tiāncáilùn the theory of innate genius (according to which history is not made by the people but by heroes born with knowledge)

天蚕 tiāncán giant silkworm; wild silkworm

天蚕蛾 tiāncán'é giant silkworm moth

天差地远 tiānchā-dìyuǎn be poles apart; differ in thousands of ways

天长地久 tiāncháng-dìjiǔ enduring as the universe; everlasting and unchanging

天长日久 tiāncháng-rìjiǔ same as 日久天长 rìjiǔ-tiān-cháng

天车 tiānchē mech. overhead travelling crane; shop traveller

天秤座 Tiānchèngzuò astron. Libra

天窗 tiānchuāng archit. skylight ——see also 开天窗 kāi tiānchuāng

天赐 tiāncì be bestowed by heaven: ～我也! This is indeed a godsend!

天从人愿 tiān cóng rényuàn Heaven grants man's wish; by the grace of God

天大 tiāndà as large as the heavens; extremely big: ～的好事 an excellent thing (or event) / ～的面子 a mark of special favour / ～的笑话 a colossal absurdity

天道 tiāndào ① old the natural laws; heavenly laws ② dial. weather

天敌 tiāndí biol. natural enemy

天底 tiāndǐ astron. nadir

天底下 tiāndǐxia inf. in the world; on earth: ～哪有这种道理! Nobody on earth would reason that way. or How preposterous!

天地 tiāndì ① heaven and earth; world; universe: 炮声震动～。The earth shook with the roar of guns. ② field of activity; scope of operation: 开辟科学研究的新～ open up a new field for scientific research ——see also 拜天地 bài tiāndì

天地不容 tiān-dì bù róng a towering crime or a sinner that neither god nor men can forgive

天地良心 tiāndì liángxīn can say in all honesty; must point out in all fairness: ～, 我是尽力而为了。I can say in all honesty that I did it as best I could. / ～, 这绝不是他的过错。In all fairness it must be pointed out that this is none of his fault.

天地头 tiāndìtóu print. top and bottom margins of a page; upper and lower margins of a page

天帝 tiāndì the Lord of Heaven

天电 tiāndiàn elec. atmospherics; static: ～干扰 static disturbances

天顶 tiāndǐng astron. zenith

天鹅 tiān'é swan: 小～ cygnet / ～绒毛 swansdown

天鹅绒 tiān'éróng velvet

天鹅座 Tiān'ézuò astron. Cygnus

天蛾 tiān'é hawkmoth; sphinx

天翻地覆 tiānfān-dìfù heaven and earth turning upside down: ～的变化 earthshaking (or tremendous) changes / 游击队把这个城镇闹了个～。The guerrilla fighters turned the town upside down. / 虎踞龙盘今胜昔, ～慨而慷。(毛泽东) The City, a tiger crouching, a dragon curling, outshines its ancient glories; In heroic triumph heaven and earth have been overturned.

天方 Tiānfāng old name for the Arabian countries in the Middle East

天方夜谭 ① Tiānfāng Yètán The Arabian Nights ② (tiānfāng yètán) a cock-and-bull story; a most fantastic tale

天分 tiānfèn natural gift; talent; special endowments: ～高 gifted; talented

天府之国 tiānfǔ zhī guó (usu. referring to Sichuan Province) Nature's storehouse—a land of abundance; a land of plenty

天赋 tiānfù ① inborn; innate; endowed by nature ② natural gift; talent; endowments

天赋人权论 tiānfù rénquánlùn the theory of natural

rights

天干 tiāngān the ten Heavenly Stems, used as serial numbers and also in combination with the twelve Earthly Branches (地支) to designate years, months, days and hours

天罡 tiāngāng *arch.* ① the Big Dipper ② the handle of the Big Dipper

天罡星 Tiāngāngxīng *astron.* the Big Dipper

天高地厚 tiāngāo-dìhòu as high as the heavens and as deep as the earth—① (of kindness) profound; deep ② complexity of things ——see also 不知天高地厚 bù zhī tiāngāo-dìhòu

天高皇帝远 tiāngāo huángdì yuǎn heaven is high and the emperor far away—① justice is tardy ② one may do whatever one wishes without fear of interference

天高气爽 tiāngāo-qìshuǎng the sky is clear and the air is crisp—fine autumn weather

天各一方 tiān gè yī fāng (of relatives or friends) each in a different corner of the world: 妻离子散，～ a family torn asunder, each member in a different corner of the world

天公 tiāngōng the ruler of heaven; God

天公不作美 tiāngōng bù zuòměi Heaven is not cooperative; the weather isn't cooperating: 我们正想去郊游，～，下起雨来了。We were just thinking of going on an outing, but the gods were against us and it began to rain.

天公地道 tiāngōng-dìdào absolutely fair: 在我看来，她这样处理真是～。In my opinion, the way she disposed of the matter was perfectly fair and reasonable.

天宫 tiāngōng heavenly palace (in mythology)

天沟 tiāngōu *archit.* gutter

天光 tiānguāng ① daylight; time of the day: ～不早了。It's getting late. ② *dial.* morning

天癸 tiānguǐ *Chin. med.* menses; menstruation; period

天国 tiānguó ① *Christianity* the Kingdom of Heaven; paradise ② utopia

天寒地冻 tiānhán-dìdòng the weather is cold and the ground is frozen

天河 tiānhé common name for 银河 yínhé

天黑 tiānhēi ① deepening dusk; dusk ② dark

天候 tiānhòu *meteorol.* weather

天花 tiānhuā *med.* smallpox

天花板 tiānhuābǎn ceiling (of a room)

天花粉 tiānhuāfěn *Chin. med.* the root of Chinese trichosanthes (*Trichosanthes kirilowii*)

天花乱坠 tiānhuā luàn zhuì flowers cascading from the sky—an extravagantly colourful description: 吹得～ give an extravagant account of; make a wild boast about

天荒地老 tiānhuāng-dìlǎo same as 地老天荒 dìlǎo-tiānhuāng

天皇 tiānhuáng ① the Son of Heaven—the emperor ② the emperor of Japan; Mikado

天昏地暗 tiānhūn-dì'àn ① murky heavens over a dark earth; dark all round: 呼啸的西北风夹着黄沙，刮得～。A howling northwest wind swept by, carrying yellow dust that darkened the sky and obscured everything./～，日月无光。There was gloom above and darkness below, with the rays of the sun and the moon completely shut out. ② in a state of chaos and darkness: 当时军阀混战，真是～哪! In those years, with the warlords fighting among themselves, the country was plunged into chaos and darkness.

天火 tiānhuǒ fire caused by lightning or other natural phenomena

天机 tiānjī ① nature's mystery; something inexplicable ② God's design; secret: 泄漏～ give away a secret / 一

语道破～ lay bare the secret of sth. with one remark

天机不可泄漏 tiānjī bùkě xièlòu God's design must not be revealed to mortal ears; Heaven's secrets must not be divulged; don't say a word about it to a soul

天极 tiānjí *astron.* celestial pole

天际 tiānjì *liter.* horizon: 孤帆远影碧空尽，唯见长江～流。(李白) Lonely sail, distant shadow, Vanish in blue emptiness; All I see is the great river Flowing into the far horizon.

天津 Tiānjīn Tianjin (a seaport on the coast of the Bohai Sea)

天经地义 tiānjīng-dìyì (in line with) the principles of heaven and earth—right and proper; perfectly justified: 给国家纳税是～的事。It's only right and proper that we should pay taxes to the state.

天井 tiānjǐng ① small yard; courtyard ② skylight ③ *min.* raise: 通风～ air raise

天空 tiānkōng the sky; the heavens

天籁 tiānlài *liter.* sounds of nature (i.e. the sound of the wind or flowing waters, the call of the bird, etc.)

天蓝 tiānlán sky blue; azure

天狼星 Tiānlángxīng *astron.* Sirius

天朗气清 tiānlǎng-qìqīng the sky is clear and the air is fresh

天老儿 tiānlǎor (human) albino

天老爷 tiānlǎoye God; Heavens

天理 tiānlǐ ① heavenly principles—feudal ethics as propounded by the Song Confucianists ② (divine) justice: 是无～。That would be a gross injustice.

天理难容 tiānlǐ nán róng an intolerable injustice

天理昭彰 tiānlǐ zhāozhāng Heaven's laws are fully manifest

天良 tiānliáng conscience: ～发现 be stung by conscience; be conscience-stricken

天亮 tiānliàng daybreak; dawn: ～以前赶到 get there before daybreak

天灵盖 tiānlínggài top of the skull; crown (of the head)

天龙座 Tiānlóngzuò *astron.* Draco

天伦 tiānlún *formal* the natural bonds and ethical relationships between members of a family

天伦之乐 tiānlún zhī lè family happiness: 共叙～ enjoy family happiness together

天罗地网 tiānluó-dìwǎng nets above and snares below—tight encirclement: 布下～ spread a dragnet from which there is no escape; cast an escape-proof net

天麻 tiānmá *Chin. med.* the tuber of elevated gastrodia (*Gastrodia elata*)

天马行空 tiānmǎ xíng kōng a heavenly steed soaring across the skies—a powerful and unconstrained style (of writing, calligraphy, etc.)

天门冬 tiānméndōng *Chin. med.* lucid asparagus (*Asparagus cochinchinensis*)

天明 tiānmíng daybreak; dawn

天命 tiānmìng God's will; the mandate of heaven; destiny; fate

天幕 tiānmù ① the canopy of the heavens ② backdrop (of a stage)

天南地北 tiānnán-dìběi ① far apart: 他们哥儿俩～，见一次面不容易。The two brothers live so far apart they don't often get a chance to see each other. ② from different places or areas: 来自～ come from different parts of the country (*or* from all over the country)

天南海北 tiānnán-hǎiběi ① all over the country ② discursive; rambling: ～地谈起来 start chattering away about this and that; start a bull session; talk about everything under the sun

天年 tiānnián ① a natural span of life; one's allotted span: 尽其～ die a natural death; live one's full span ② *dial.* the year's harvest ③ *dial.* times; age; era

天牛 tiānniú *zool.* longicorn; long-horned beetle

天怒人怨 tiānnù-rényuàn the wrath of God and the anger of men; widespread indignation and discontent

天女 tiānnǚ (in Buddhist mythology) a female *deva*; a heavenly maiden:《~散花》*The Heavenly Maiden Scattering Flowers* (an operatic dance drama)

天疱疮 tiānpàochuāng pemphigus

天棚 tiānpéng ① *archit.* ceiling ② awning or canopy, usu. made of reed matting and bamboo poles

天平 tiānpíng balance; scales

天平动 tiānpíngdòng *astron.* libration

天气 tiānqì weather: ~要变。The weather is changing. / ~转晴。It's clearing up. / 初春~, 早晨还有些凉意。It's early spring now—still a bit chilly in the morning. / 不管~如何, 也要继续施工。Construction will go on no matter what the weather is like (*or* in all weathers).

天气图 tiānqìtú weather map; synoptic chart

天气形势预报 tiānqì xíngshì yùbào weather prognostics

天气学 tiānqìxué synoptic meteorology

天气预报 tiānqì yùbào weather forecast: 数值~ numerical weather forecast

天堑 tiānqiàn natural moat (usu. referring to the Changjiang River): 长江~ the natural moat of the Changjiang River

天桥 tiānqiáo overline bridge; platform bridge; overhead walkway

天琴座 Tiānqínzuò *astron.* Lyra

天青 tiānqīng reddish black

天穹 tiānqióng the vault of heaven

天球 tiānqiú *astron.* celestial sphere

天球赤道 tiānqiú chìdào *astron.* celestial equator

天球仪 tiānqiúyí celestial globe

天球子午圈 tiānqiú zǐwǔquān *astron.* celestial meridian

天球坐标 tiānqiú zuòbiāo *astron.* celestial coordinates

天趣 tiānqù natural charm (of writings, paintings, etc.): ~盎然 instinct with a natural charm

天然 tiānrán natural: ~财富 natural resources (*or* wealth) / ~景色 natural scenery / ~障碍物 natural barrier; topographical barrier / 中国无产阶级和广大的农民有一种~的联系。The Chinese proletariat has natural ties with the peasant masses.

天然堤 tiānrándī natural levee

天然港 tiānrángǎng natural harbour

天然更新 tiānrán gēngxīn *forestry* natural regeneration

天然免疫 tiānrán miǎnyì *med.* innate immunity; native immunity; natural immunity

天然牧地 tiānrán mùdì natural pasture

天然气 tiānránqì natural gas: 干~ dry gas; poor gas / 湿~ wet gas; rich gas

天然气回注 tiānránqì huízhù *petroleum* gas injection

天壤 tiānrǎng *formal* ① heaven and earth: ~间 between heaven and earth ② high heaven and deep sea; poles apart

天壤之别 tiānrǎng zhī bié as far apart as heaven and earth; worlds (*or* poles) apart; a world of difference

天人 tiānrén ① Heaven and man ② a man of great talent or a woman of matchless beauty

天日 tiānrì the sky and the sun—light ——see also 暗无天日 àn wú tiānrì; 重见天日 chóng jiàn tiānrì

天若有情天亦老 tiān ruò yǒu qíng tiān yì lǎo if Heaven has feelings, Heaven too will become aged: ~, 人间正道是沧桑。(毛泽东) Were Nature sentient, she too would pass from youth to age, But Man's world is mutable, seas become mulberry fields.

天色 tiānsè colour of the sky; time of the day as shown by the colour of the sky; weather: ~已晚。It's getting dark. / ~突变。The weather suddenly changed. /

看~要晴。It seems to be clearing up. / 看~怕要下雨。It looks like rain.

天上 tiānshàng the sky; the heavens

天神 tiānshén god; deity

天生 tiānshēng born; inborn; inherent; innate: 本事不是~的, 是锻炼出来的。Ability is not innate, but comes through practice. / 他~聋哑。He was born a deaf-mute.

天生桥 tiānshēngqiáo natural bridge

天师 Tiānshī Heavenly Teacher (the title of the head of the Taoist religion)

天时 tiānshí ① weather; climate: ~不正 abnormal weather / 庄稼活儿一定要趁~, 早了晚了都不好。Farming should be done in season, neither too early nor too late. ② timeliness; opportunity

天使 tiānshǐ angel

天授 tiānshòu bestowed by heaven

天书 tiānshū ① a book from heaven—abstruse or illegible writing: 对我来说, 这本书就跟~一样难懂。To me this book is as difficult as a book from heaven. *or* This book is all Greek to me. / 这封信字迹太潦草, 像~似的。This letter is as illegible as hieroglyphics. ② imperial edict (in ancient China)

天数 tiānshù predestination; fate

天塌地陷 tiāntā-dìxiàn ① same as 天崩地坼 tiānbēng-dìchè ② serious; grave; critical

天台乌药 tiāntái wūyào same as 乌药 wūyào

天坛 Tiāntán the Temple of Heaven (in Beijing)

天堂 tiāntáng paradise; heaven

天梯 tiāntī very tall ladder on high buildings and structures

天体 tiāntǐ *astron.* celestial body

天体光谱学 tiāntǐ guāngpǔxué astrospectroscopy

天体力学 tiāntǐ lìxué celestial mechanics

天体物理学 tiāntǐ wùlǐxué astrophysics

天体演化学 tiāntǐ yǎnhuàxué cosmogony

天体照相仪 tiāntǐ zhàoxiàngyí astrograph

天天 tiāntiān every day: ~锻炼身体 do physical training every day

天条 tiāntiáo ① Heaven's commandments ② prohibition decrees of the Taiping Heavenly Kingdom (太平天国, 1851-1864)

天庭 tiāntíng the middle of the forehead: ~饱满, 地角方圆 a full forehead and a strong square jaw (auspicious features according to physiognomy)

天头 tiāntóu the top (*or* upper) margin of a page

天外 tiānwài beyond the highest heavens—far, far away

天王 tiānwáng heavenly king—① an epithet for the emperor ② the title assumed by Hong Xiuquan (洪秀全), founder of the Taiping Heavenly Kingdom (太平天国, 1851-1864) ③ a name for certain deities (e.g. the Pagoda-bearing Heavenly King 托塔天王)

天王星 Tiānwángxīng *astron.* Uranus

天网恢恢, 疏而不漏 tiānwǎng huīhuī, shū ér bù lòu the net of Heaven has large meshes, but it lets nothing through; the mills of God grind slowly, but they grind exceeding small; justice has a long arm; the guilty can never escape Heaven's justice

天威 tiānwēi *formal* heavenly might

天文 tiānwén astronomy

天文单位 tiānwén dānwèi astronomical unit

天文导航 tiānwén dǎoháng astronavigation; celestial navigation

天文馆 tiānwénguǎn planetarium

天文年历 tiānwén niánlì astronomical yearbook; astronomical almanac

天文时 tiānwénshí astronomical time

天文数字 tiānwén shùzì astronomical figure; enormous figure

天文台　tiānwéntái　(astronomical) observatory

天文学　tiānwénxué　astronomy: 航海～ nautical astronomy / 恒星～ stellar astronomy / 空间～ space astronomy / 球面～ spherical astronomy / 射电～ radio astronomy / ～家 astronomer

天文仪　tiānwényí　astroscope

天文照相术　tiānwén zhàoxiàngshù　astrophotography

天文制导　tiānwén zhìdǎo　celestial guidance

天文钟　tiānwénzhōng　astronomical clock

天无二日,民无二王　tiān wú èr rì, mín wú èr wáng　there cannot be two kings for the people just as there cannot be two suns in the heavens

天无绝人之路　tiān wú jué rén zhī lù　Heaven never seals off all the exits—there is always a way out

天物　tiānwù　products of nature

天下　tiānxià　① land under heaven—the world or China ② rule; domination: 打～坐～ conquer and rule the country / 新中国是劳动人民的～。The working people are masters of New China.

天下大乱　tiānxià dà luàn　great disorder under heaven —a state of great confusion

天下大势　tiānxià dàshì　the momentum of history; historical trends: 话说～, 分久必合, 合久必分。(《三国演义》) They say the momentum of history was ever thus: the empire, long divided, must unite; long united, must divide.

天下大治　tiānxià dà zhì　great order throughout the land; a well ordered world

天下第一　tiānxià dìyī　the first under heaven—unequalled; peerless

天下奇闻　tiānxià qíwén　a most fantastic tale; a very strange story; the most absurd thing in the world

天下太平　tiānxià tàipíng　peace reigns under heaven; the world (or the country) is at peace

天下为公　tiānxià wéi gōng　the whole world as one community: 大道之行也,～。(《礼记》) When the Great Tao prevailed, the whole world was one community.

天下文章一大抄　tiānxià wénzhāng yī dà chāo　all writings under heaven are nothing but copyings

天下乌鸦一般黑　tiānxià wūyā yībān hēi　all crows under the sun are black—evil people are bad all over the world

天下无不散的宴席　tiānxià wú bù sàn de yànxí　there never was a feast but the guests had to depart—all good things must come to an end

天下无敌　tiānxià wú dí　invincible; ever-victorious; all-conquering

天下无难事,只怕有心人　tiānxià wú nánshì, zhǐpà yǒuxīnrén　nothing in the world is difficult for one who sets his mind on it: 谁也不是天生就会, 俗话说:"～"。Nobody's born capable. The old proverb's right: "Every difficulty on earth can be overcome if men but give their minds to it."

天下无双　tiānxià wú shuāng　unparalleled in the world; unique; without equal; matchless

天仙　tiānxiān　① goddess ② a beautiful young woman; a beauty

天仙子　tiānxiānzǐ　Chin. med. henbane seed (Hyoscyamus niger)

天险　tiānxiǎn　natural barrier: 此山向有～之称。This mountain has long been known as a natural barrier.

天线　tiānxiàn　aerial; antenna: 架设～ put up an aerial / 定向～ beam (or directional) antenna / 拉杆～ telescopic antenna

天香国色　tiānxiāng-guósè　same as 国色天香 guósè-tiānxiāng

天象　tiānxiàng　astronomical phenomena; celestial phenomena: 观测～ observe the heavenly bodies; astronomical observation

天象仪　tiānxiàngyí　planetarium

天晓得　tiānxiǎode　inf. God (or Heaven) knows: ～他在那儿待了多久。He stayed there God knows how long.

天蝎座　Tiānxiēzuò　astron. Scorpio; Scorpius

天心¹　tiānxīn　① right overhead: 太阳升到了～。The sun is shining right overhead. ② God's will; the will of Heaven ③ the intention of the emperor

天心²　tiānxīn　balance staff (of a balance wheel)

天行赤目　tiānxíngchìmù　Chin. med. red and swollen eyes; conjunctivitis

天性　tiānxìng　natural instincts; nature: ～忠厚 have a sincere and kindly nature / ～聪明 be intelligent by nature

天幸　tiānxìng　a providential escape; a close shave (or call)

天悬地隔　tiānxuán-dìgé　same as 天差地远 tiānchā-dìyuǎn

天旋地转　tiānxuán-dìzhuàn　(feel as if) the sky and earth were spinning round; dizzy: 昏沉沉, 只觉得～ feel faint and dizzy as if the earth were spinning round

天涯　tiānyá　the end of the world; the remotest corner of the earth

天涯海角　tiānyá-hǎijiǎo　the ends of the earth; the remotest corners of the earth: 我们必将追寻他们至～, 务使归案法办。We will hunt them down, even to the four corners of the earth, and will surely bring them to trial and punishment.

天阉　tiānyān　impotency

天衣无缝　tiānyī wú fèng　a seamless heavenly robe—flawless: 这篇文章, 论证严密,～。The article is close-knit and its argument flawless.

天意　tiānyì　God's will; the will of Heaven: 事在人为, 不存在什么～。There is no such thing as the will of Heaven. It is man that decides everything.

天鹰座　Tiānyīngzuò　astron. Aquila

天有不测风云　tiān yǒu bùcè fēngyún　a storm may arise from a clear sky—something unexpected may happen any time: ～, 人有旦夕祸福。Storms gather without warning and bad luck befalls men overnight. or In nature there are unexpected storms and in life unpredictable vicissitudes.

天宇　tiānyǔ　① the sky; the heavens ② liter. land under heaven—the world or China

天渊　tiānyuān　formal high heaven and deep sea; poles apart: 两人的诗作相去～。There is a world of difference between the two poets.

天渊之别　tiānyuān zhī bié　same as 天壤之别 tiānrǎng zhī bié

天灾　tiānzāi　natural disaster (or calamity): 遭受～ suffer natural disasters

天灾人祸　tiānzāi-rénhuò　natural and man-made calamities

天葬　tiānzàng　celestial burial (by which bodies are exposed to birds of prey)

天造地设　tiānzào-dìshè　created by nature; heavenly; ideal: 这里山水秀丽, 真是个～的游览区。This beautiful place is a heavenly tourist resort. / 我看他二人恰是一对～的夫妻。I think they will make a perfect match. / 莫扎特的作品好似～, 自然形成。Like a work of Nature, a work by Mozart seems inevitable as it stands.

天真　tiānzhēn　innocent; simple and unaffected; artless; naive: ～活泼的女孩子 an artless, vivacious girl / ～的幻想 a naive delusion / 你要相信这样的话, 那就太～了。If you believe that sort of talk you're really naive.

天真烂漫　tiānzhēn lànmàn　innocent and artless; simple and unaffected: ～的儿童 innocent and artless children

天之骄子　tiān zhī jiāozǐ　God's favoured one—an unusually lucky person

天知道　tiānzhīdao　God (or Heaven) knows

天职 tiānzhí bounden duty; vocation: 保卫国家是军人的～。Safeguarding the country is a soldier's bounden duty.

天轴 tiānzhóu ① *mech*. line shaft ② *astron*. celestial axis

天诛地灭 tiānzhū-dìmiè (used in cursing or taking vows) be destroyed by heaven and earth; stand condemned by God: 我要是说谎，～! May heaven strike me down if I lie!

天竹 tiānzhú same as 南天竹 nántiānzhú

天竺 Tiānzhú ancient name for 印度 Yìndù

天竺鲷 tiānzhúdiāo cardinal fish

天竺葵 tiānzhúkuí fish pelargonium (*Pelargonium hortorum*)

天竺鼠 tiānzhúshǔ guinea pig; cavy

天主 Tiānzhǔ *Catholicism* God

天主教 Tiānzhǔjiào Catholicism: ～会 the Roman Catholic Church / ～徒 Catholic

天主堂 tiānzhǔtáng a Catholic church

天姿国色 tiānzī-guósè reigning beauty; a woman of matchless beauty

天资 tiānzī natural gift; talent; natural endowments

天子 tiānzǐ the Son of Heaven—the emperor

天字第一号 tiān zì dìyī hào number one; A1

天足 tiānzú natural feet (opp. 小脚 bound feet)

天尊 tiānzūn celestial worthy (the title of some deities in the Taoist pantheon): 元始～ the Celestial Worthy of the Original Beginning (controlling time past)

天作孽，犹可违；自作孽，不可活 tiān zuòniè, yóu kě wéi; zì zuòniè, bù kě huó when Heaven sends down calamities, there is hope of weathering them; when man brings them upon himself, there is no hope of escape

天作之合 tiān zuò zhī hé a heaven-made match (used in congratulations on marriage)

添 tiān ① add; increase: ～煤 add (or put in more) coal; stoke / ～衣服 put on more clothes / ～一碗饭 have one more bowl of rice / ～了几根白头发 have grown a few more white hairs / 给你们～麻烦了。Sorry to have troubled you. / 锅炉里的水已经～满了。The boiler has already been filled with water. / 年纪大了容易～病。As one gets older, one is more liable to have health problems. ② *dial*. have a baby: 她最近～了个女孩儿。She recently had a daughter.

添办 tiānbàn add to one's possessions; acquire

添补 tiānbu replenish; get more: 需要～机器零件 need a fresh supply of machine parts

添丁 tiāndīng *old* have a baby (esp. a boy) born into the family

添加剂 tiānjiājì *chem*. additive

添设 tiānshè add; increase: ～早晚服务部 set up an additional department for after-hours service

添箱 tiānxiāng *old* ① give wedding presents to a bride ② wedding presents given to a bride

添枝加叶 tiānzhī-jiāyè (also 添油加醋 tiānyóu-jiācù) add colour and emphasis to (a narration); add highly coloured details to (a story); embellish (a story): 照我说的对他讲，可别～。Tell him exactly what I said and don't embroider it. / 接着，他就～，甚至公开扯谎。Then he started to embellish and even lie outright.

添置 tiānzhì add to one's possessions; acquire: ～家具 buy more furniture

添砖加瓦 tiānzhuān-jiāwǎ do what little one can to help: 为建设社会主义～ do one's bit to help build socialism

覘 tiān see below

覘鹿 tiānlù fallow deer

tián

田¹ tián ① field; farmland; cropland: 犁～ plough a field / 在～里劳动 work in the fields; work on the land ② an open area abounding in some natural product; field: 煤田 méitián ③ (Tián) a surname

田² tián *formal* go hunting: 田猎 tiánliè

田鳖 tiánbiē giant water bug; fish killer

田产 tiánchǎn (property in the form of) land; landed property; estate

田塍 tiánchéng *dial*. a low bank of earth between fields; ridge

田畴 tiánchóu *formal* farmland; cultivated land; fields

田地 tiándì ① field; farmland; cropland ② wretched situation; plight: 真没想到事情会发展到这步～。I never dreamt things would come to such a pass. / 你怎么落到这步～! How did you get into such a plight?

田凫 tiánfú *zool*. lapwing

田父 tiánfù *formal* an aged farmer

田赋 tiánfù feudal land tax

田埂 tiángěng a low bank of earth between fields; ridge

田鸡 tiánjī common name for 青蛙 qīngwā

田家 tiánjiā a farming family

田间 tiánjiān ① field; farm ② countryside

田间持水量 tiánjiān chíshuǐliàng *agric*. field capacity

田间管理 tiánjiān guǎnlǐ field management

田间劳动 tiánjiān láodòng field labour; farm work

田菁 tiánjīng *bot*. sesbania

田径 tiánjìng track and field; athletics

田径队 tiánjìngduì track and field team

田径赛 tiánjìngsài track and field meet: ～项目 track and field events

田径运动 tiánjìng yùndòng track and field sports; athletics: ～员 athlete

田坎 tiánkǎn same as 田埂 tiángěng

田猎 tiánliè *formal* go hunting

田鹨 tiánliù *zool*. paddy-field pipit

田螺 tiánluó river snail

田陌 tiánmò a path between fields

田亩 tiánmǔ general name for 田地 tiándì①

田七 tiánqī same as 三七 sānqī

田契 tiánqì title deed for farmland; land deed

田赛 tiánsài *sports* field events

田舍 tiánshè *formal* ① farm ② farmhouse ③ a farming family

田舍翁 tiánshèwēng *formal* an old countryman

田鼠 tiánshǔ vole: 普通～ field vole

田野 tiányě field; open country: 广阔的～ a vast field; a vast expanse of farmland / ～静悄悄的。It was very quiet in the fields.

田野工作 tiányě gōngzuò *old* fieldwork

田园 tiányuán fields and gardens; countryside: ～生活 idyllic life / ～风光 rural scenery / 贝多芬的《～交响曲》*Pastoral Symphony* by Beethoven

田园诗 tiányuánshī idyll; pastoral poetry: ～人 pastoral poet

田庄 tiánzhuāng country estate

田字草 tiánzìcǎo another name for 蘋 pín

恬 tián *formal* ① quiet; tranquil; calm: 恬适 tiánshì ② not care at all; remain unperturbed: 恬不知耻 tián bù zhī chǐ

恬不知耻 tián bù zhī chǐ not feel ashamed; have no sense of shame; be shameless

恬淡 tiándàn　indifferent to fame or gain

恬静 tiánjìng　quiet; peaceful; tranquil

恬美 tiánměi　quiet and happy

恬谧 tiánmì　*formal*　quiet; peaceful; tranquil

恬然 tiánrán　unperturbed; calm; nonchalant: 处之～ remain unruffled

恬适 tiánshì　*formal*　quiet and comfortable

畋 tián　*formal*　go hunting

钿 tián　*dial.*　① coin: 铜钿 tóngtián① ② money: 几～? How much is it? ③ fund; sum: 车～ (bus, train or taxi) fare ——see also diàn

菾 tián　see below

菾菜 tiáncài　same as 甜菜 tiáncài

甜 tián　① sweet; honeyed: 这西瓜好～哪! This watermelon is really sweet! / 她话说得很～。Her words were honeyed. ② (of sleep) sound: 睡得真～ have a sound (or sweet) sleep; sleep soundly

甜不唧 tiánbujī　having a sweet taste; slightly sweet

甜菜 tiáncài　① beet: 糖～ sugar beet / ～糖 beet sugar ② beetroot

甜点 tiándiǎn　sweet snacks; sweets

甜甘 tiángān　*inf.*　(of words) sweet; honeyed

甜瓜 tiánguā　muskmelon

甜津津 tiánjīnjīn　same as 甜丝丝 tiánsīsī

甜美 tiánměi　① sweet; luscious: 味道～ taste sweet; have a sweet taste / ～多汁的桃儿 luscious and juicy peaches ② pleasant; refreshing: ～的生活 a happy life / 睡了个～的午觉 have a refreshing nap after lunch

甜蜜 tiánmì　sweet; happy: ～的回忆 happy (or sweet) memories / 孩子们笑得多么～! How merrily the children laughed! / 他们俩的日子过得非常～。The couple led a very happy life together.

甜面酱 tiánmiànjiàng　(also 甜酱 tiánjiàng) a sweet sauce made of fermented flour

甜品 tiánpǐn　sweet snacks; sweets

甜软 tiánruǎn　(of voice) gentle and pleasant

甜润 tiánrùn　(of voice) sweet; melodious

甜食 tiánshí　sweet food; sweets: 他爱吃～。He has a sweet tooth. or He likes sweet things.

甜爽 tiánshuǎng　(of food) sweet and refreshing

甜水 tiánshuǐ　① fresh water: ～井 fresh water well ② sugar water—happiness; comfort: 这孩子是在～里长大的。The child's grown up in happy times.

甜睡 tiánshuì　sleep soundly; be fast asleep

甜丝丝 tiánsīsī　① pleasantly sweet: 这个菜～儿的。This dish is sweet and delicious. ② quite pleased; gratified; happy: 心里感到～的 feel quite pleased (or happy)

甜酸儿 tiánsuānr　(of food) sweet and sour

甜头 tiántou　① sweet taste; pleasant flavour ② good; benefit (as an inducement): 尝到～ become aware of the benefits of; come to know the good of

甜味 tiánwèi　sweet taste: 有点～ taste sweet; have a sweet taste

甜言蜜语 tiányán-mìyǔ　sweet words and honeyed phrases; fine-sounding words: 他们的～不过是引鱼上钩的诱饵罢了。Their honeyed words are nothing but bait to hook the fish.

甜滋滋 tiánzīzī　same as 甜丝丝 tiánsīsī

甜嘴蜜舌 tiánzuǐ-mìshé　speaking honeyed words; honey-mouthed

闐 tián　*formal*　be full of: 宾客～门。The house is full of guests.

填 tián　① fill; stuff: 往坑里～土 fill a pit with

earth / ～枕芯 stuff a pillow ② write; fill in: ～表 fill in a form / 别～错日期。Don't fill in the wrong date.

填报 tiánbào　fill in a form and submit it to the leadership: 每周～工程进度 make a weekly progress report on a project

填补 tiánbǔ　fill (a vacancy, gap, etc.): ～缺额 fill a vacancy / ～亏空 make up a deficit / ～科学技术领域的空白 fill in the gaps in the fields of science and technology / ～精神上的空虚 fill (or remedy) one's sense of spiritual barrenness

填充 tiánchōng　① fill up; stuff ② fill in the blanks (in a test paper)

填充塔 tiánchōngtǎ　*petroleum*　packed column (or tower)

填词 tiáncí　fill in the words to fit a given tune—compose a *ci* poem by choosing a tune and then writing words to it (e.g., a *ci* poem may be written to the tune "Spring Floods the Garden" 沁园春 and then be called by the name of that tune) ——see also 词 cí③

填堵 tiándǔ　stop up; block up

填发 tiánfā　fill in and issue a certificate, etc.

填方 tiánfāng　*archit.*　fill

填房 tiánfáng　① marry a widower ② a second wife a widower marries

填空 tiánkòng　① fill a vacant position; fill a vacancy ② fill in the blanks (in a test paper)

填窟窿 tián kūlong　fill up a hole—make up a deficit

填料 tiánliào　*mech.*　packing; stuffing; filling; filler: ～函 gland box; stuffing box

填密 tiánmì　*mech.*　packing: 液压～ hydraulic packing / ～函 packing box

填平 tiánpíng　fill and level up: ～弹坑 fill up bomb craters / 搬倒土山～山沟 flatten hills to fill up gullies / ～补齐 fill up the gaps

填塞 tiánsè　stop up; block up: ～洞隙 stop up a loophole

填写 tiánxiě　fill in; write: ～表格 fill in a form / ～入党志愿书 fill out an application form for Party membership / 这里～你的姓名和住址。Please fill in the blanks here with your name and address.

填鸭 tiányā　① force-feed a duck ② a force-fed duck

填鸭式教学法 tiányāshì jiàoxuéfǎ　cramming (or forced-feeding) method of teaching

tiǎn

忝 tiǎn　*formal hum.*　be unworthy of the honour: ～在相知之列 having the honour, though I'm unworthy of it, to be counted among your acquaintances

殄 tiǎn　extirpate; exterminate: 暴殄天物 bàotiǎntiǎnwù

殄灭 tiǎnmiè　*formal*　annihilate; wipe out

惵 tiǎn　*formal*　be ashamed

湕 tiǎn　*formal*　muddy; turbid

腆 tiǎn　① sumptuous; rich ② *dial.*　protrude; thrust out: ～着胸脯 stick out one's chest

靦 tiǎn　① *formal*　be ashamed: ～颜 shamefaced ② *inf.*　brazen: ～着脸 brazen it out

舔 tiǎn　lick; lap: ～～嘴唇 moisten one's lips with the tongue / 这孩子～了一下蛋卷冰淇淋。The child licked his ice cream cone.

tiàn

掭 tiàn ① (when preparing to write) dip a writing brush in ink and bring it to a fine point by twisting the tip gently on the inkstone, round in a circular movement ② *dial.* poke: ～灯心 raise the wick of a lamp

tiāo

佻 tiāo frivolous: 轻佻 qīngtiāo
佻薄 tiāobó *formal* frivolous; skittish; giddy
佻㒓 tiāotà *formal* given to philandering; frivolous

挑[1] tiāo ① choose; select; pick out: ～个好日子举行婚礼 choose a propitious day for the wedding / 最好的作种子 select the best for seeds / 把那筐西红柿～一～。Pick over that basket of tomatoes. / 她～出了一件特别喜欢的连衣裙。She picked out one dress that she particularly liked. ② nitpick; be hypercritical; be fastidious: ～毛病 find fault / 他讲的话你就别～错儿了。Stop picking holes in what he said.

挑[2] tiāo ① carry (or tote) on the shoulder with a pole; shoulder: ～着一担菜 carrying two baskets of vegetables on a shoulder pole / ～水点种 carry (or fetch) water for dibbling (seeds, young plants, etc.) / ～起领导生产的重担 shoulder the heavy load of leadership in production ② same as 挑子 tiāozi ③ *m.* (for a load carried on a shoulder pole): 一～水 two buckets of water carried on a shoulder pole ——see also tiǎo

挑刺儿 tiāocìr *dial.* find fault; pick holes; be captious: 他就爱～。He's always finding fault with people.
挑大梁 tiāo dàliáng ① be a leading actor or actress ② shoulder a heavy responsibility or a demanding task
挑肥拣瘦 tiāoféi-jiǎnshòu pick the fat or choose the lean—choose whatever is to one's personal advantage
挑夫 tiāofū *old* porter (carrying luggage on a shoulder pole)
挑拣 tiāojiǎn pick; pick and choose: 挑挑拣拣 be choosy / 苹果都是好的，用不着～。All the apples are good. There's no need to pick and choose.
挑脚 tiāojiǎo *old* carry luggage on a shoulder pole
挑礼 tiāolǐ quibble about etiquette; reproach sb. with a faux pas
挑毛拣刺 tiāomáo-jiǎncì find fault deliberately; pick holes; be captious
挑三拣四 tiāosān-jiǎnsì ① pick and choose; be choosy ② same as 挑剔 tiāoti
挑食 tiāoshí be very choosy about what one eats
挑剔 tiāoti nitpick; be hypercritical; be fastidious: 总的来说，这个计划是好的，我们不应过于～。On the whole it's a good plan and we shouldn't nitpick.
挑选 tiāoxuǎn choose; select; pick out: 百货商店有很多童装可供～。The department store has a large selection of children's clothes. / 这堆书我要过一遍，～我所需要的。I'll go through this pile of books and pick out those I want. / 指挥～了一位女高音担任领唱。The conductor selected a soprano to lead the chorus.
挑眼 tiāoyǎn *dial.* be fastidious (about etiquette, etc.)
挑字眼儿 tiāo zìyǎnr find fault with the choice of words; quibble: 我可是随便说的，你别～。I said it just off the cuff, so don't get hung up on my choice of words.

挑子 tiāozi carrying pole with its load; load carried on a shoulder pole

桃 tiāo *formal* ① be or become heir to: 承桃 chéngtiāo ② (of an ancestor's memorial tablet) be removed to the memorial temple for the remote ancestors: 不桃之祖 bù tiāo zhī zǔ

tiáo

条(條) tiáo ① twig: 这棵葡萄长出了许多新～。This grapevine has grown many new twigs. ② a long narrow piece; strip; slip: 把一块布撕成～ tear a piece of cloth into strips ③ a brief informal note: 经理不在，请你给他留个～吧。The manager is out. Will you leave a note for him please? ④ item; article: 这项条约的正文共八～。The main body of the treaty consists of eight articles. ⑤ order: 有条不紊 yǒutiáo-bùwěn ⑥ *m.* (for long or narrow or thin things): 一～床单 a bed sheet / 两～鱼 two fish / 三～船 three ships / 一～大街 an avenue / 一～肥皂 a bar of soap / 一～香烟 a carton of cigarettes / 一～裤子 a pair of trousers ⑦ *m.* (for certain nouns): 一～好汉 a brave-man / 两～新闻 two pieces (or items) of news / 四～建议 four proposals / 一～好嗓子 a good voice / 一～妙计 a brilliant scheme / 三～人命 three human lives
条案 tiáo'àn a long narrow table
条播 tiáobō *agric.* drilling
条播机 tiáobōjī seed drill; drill
条畅 tiáochàng *formal* (of writing) smooth and well-organized
条陈 tiáochén ① state item by item ② *old* itemized memorandum (to one's superior)
条凳 tiáodèng bench
条分缕析 tiáofēn-lǚxī make a careful and detailed analysis
条幅 tiáofú a vertically-hung scroll of painting or calligraphy; a wall scroll
条钢 tiáogāng bar iron
条贯 tiáoguàn *formal* proper arrangement or presentation; orderlyness; systematicness
条规 tiáoguī rules; regulations
条痕 tiáohén *min.* streak
条几 tiáojī same as 条案 tiáo'àn
条件 tiáojiàn ① condition; term; factor: 自然～ natural conditions / 贸易～ terms of trade / 利用有利的～ make use of the favourable factors / 在目前～下 given the present conditions; under present circumstances / 在对等的～下给予优惠待遇 give preferential treatment on a reciprocal basis / 为马克思主义政党的诞生准备～ prepare the ground for the founding of a Marxist party / 这个工厂生产～好。This factory has very good conditions for production. ② requirement; prerequisite; qualification: 提出～ list the prerequisites; put forward the requirements / 做这项工作需要具备什么～?What qualifications do you need for this job? / 当宇航员对身体～要求很严。The physical fitness requirements for being an astronaut are very stiff.
条件刺激 tiáojiàn cìjī *physiol.* conditioned stimulus
条件反射 tiáojiàn fǎnshè *physiol.* conditioned reflex
条款 tiáokuǎn clause (in a formal document); article; provision: 法律～ legal provision
条理 tiáolǐ proper arrangement or presentation; orderliness; method: 她工作很有～。She is a methodical worker. / 这篇文章～清楚。The article is well-organized.
条例 tiáolì regulations; rules; ordinances: 劳保～

labour insurance regulations / 组织～ organizational rules

条令 tiáolìng *mil.* regulations: 内务～ routine service regulations (for barracks)

条目 tiáomù ① clauses and subclauses (in a formal document) ② entry (in a dictionary)

条绒 tiáoróng same as 灯心绒 dēngxīnróng

条石 tiáoshí a rectangular slab of stone

条鳎 tiáotǎ *zool.* striped sole

条条框框 tiáotiáokuāngkuàng rules and regulations; regulations and restrictions; conventions and taboos: ～太多,办事效率不高。There are too many regulations and restrictions, and that makes it impossible to get things done quickly. / 思想上的～ the trammels of conventional (*or* outmoded) ideas

条文 tiáowén article (in laws and regulations); clause: ～范例 standard clause

条纹 tiáowén stripe; streak: 斑马身上有～。A zebra has stripes on its body.

条纹布 tiáowénbù striped cloth; stripe

条形码 tiáoxíngmǎ bar code; (U. S.) Universal Product Code (UPC)

条锈病 tiáoxiùbìng *agric.* stripe rust; yellow rust

条约 tiáoyuē treaty; pact

条子 tiáozi ① strip: 纸～ a narrow strip of paper; a slip of paper ② a brief informal note ③ *dial.* gold bar

苕 tiáo ancient name for 凌霄花 língxiāohuā ——see also sháo

迢 tiáo see below

迢迢 tiáotiáo far away; remote: ～牵牛星,皎皎河汉女。(《古诗十九首》) Far away twinkles the Herd-boy star; Brightly shines the Lady of the Silver River.

调[1] tiáo ① suit well; fit in perfectly: 失调 shītiáo ② mix; adjust: 牛奶里加点糖～一下。Mix some sugar into the milk. / ～工资 adjust wages (usu. upwards) / ～房子 change accommodations (usu. to improve conditions) ③ mediate: 调解 tiáojiě

调[2] tiáo ① provoke; tease; tantalize: 调笑 tiáoxiào ② incite; instigate; sow discord: 调唆 tiáo·suō ——see also diào

调处 tiáochǔ mediate; arbitrate: ～争端 arbitrate a dispute; act as mediator

调词架讼 tiáocí jiàsòng incite sb. to take legal proceedings against sb. else

调挡 tiáodǎng *mech.* gear shift

调幅 tiáofú *radio* amplitude modulation; AM: ～广播 AM broadcast

调羹 tiáogēng spoon

调和 tiáohé ① be in harmonious proportion: 雨水～。Rainfall is well distributed. / 这两种颜色配得很～。These two colours blend well. ② mediate; reconcile: 从中～ mediate; act as mediator ③ (usu. used in the negative) compromise; make concessions: 进行不～的斗争 wage uncompromising struggles / 两国的边界争端看来没有～的余地。There seems to be no room for compromise in the border dispute between the two countries.

调和漆 tiáohéqī ready-mixed paint

调护 tiáohù take care of a patient during convalescence; nurse: 病人需要特别～。The patient needs special care during his convalescence.

调级 tiáojí adjust a wage scale (usu. upwards)

调剂[1] tiáojì make up (*or* fill) a prescription

调剂[2] tiáojì adjust; regulate: ～劳动力 redistribute

labour power / 适当地看看电视,～～生活。Watching an appropriate amount of television will help to enliven one's life (*or* to break the monotony of life). / 这两家工厂有时候互相～原料。The two factories sometimes exchange raw materials.

调价 tiáojià readjust (*or* modify) prices

调浆 tiáojiāng *text.* size mixing

调焦 tiáojiāo *photog.* focusing: ～镜头 focusing lens / ～毛玻璃 focusing screen

调教 tiáojiào ① look after and guide (children) ② feed and train (domestic animals)

调节 tiáojié regulate; adjust: ～室温 regulate the room temperature / ～水流 regulate the flow of water / 对货币的流通不断进行～ constantly readjust the amount of money in circulation / 市场～ market regulation

调节器 tiáojiéqì regulator; conditioner: 空气调节器 kōngqì tiáojiéqì

调解 tiáojiě mediate; make peace: ～家庭纠纷 mediate in (*or* patch up) a family quarrel

调经 tiáojīng *Chin. med.* regulate the menstrual function

调侃 tiáokǎn ridicule; jeer at; deride

调理 tiáo·lǐ ① nurse one's health; recuperate: 吃点中药～一下身体 take some Chinese medicine to regain one's health / 精心～ nurse with great care; careful nursing ② take care of; look after: ～牲口 look after livestock ③ subject sb. to discipline ④ *dial.* make fun of; play tricks on; tease

调料 tiáoliào condiment; seasoning; flavouring

调弄 tiáonòng ① make fun of; tease ② arrange; adjust ③ instigate; stir up

调配 tiáopèi mix; blend: ～颜色 mix colours ——see also diàopèi

调皮 tiáopí ① naughty; mischievous: ～的孩子 a naughty child ② unruly; tricky: ～的牲口 skittish beasts / 科学是老老实实的学问,任何一点～都是不行的。Science means honest, solid knowledge; you can't just play around. ③ insincere; scheming

调皮捣蛋 tiáopí-dǎodàn mischievous; troublesome; making trouble

调频 tiáopín *radio* frequency modulation; FM: ～广播 FM broadcast

调情 tiáoqíng flirt

调人 tiáorén mediator

调三窝四 tiáosān-wōsì (also 调三斡四 tiáosān-wòsì) sow discord; foment dissension; incite one against the other

调色板 tiáosèbǎn palette

调色刀 tiáosèdāo palette knife; painting knife

调色碟 tiáosèdié colour mixing tray

调色 tiáoshǎi mix colours

调摄 tiáoshè *formal* take good care of oneself (as in poor health or after an illness); build up one's health by rest and by taking nourishing food; be nursed back to health

调试 tiáoshì *computer* debug

调速器 tiáosùqì *mech.* governor

调唆 tiáosuō incite; instigate

调停 tiáotíng mediate; intervene; act as an intermediary: 对争端进行～ mediate (*or* intervene in) a dispute

调味 tiáowèi flavour; season: 加点生姜调调味 flavour (*or* season) food with some ginger

调味品 tiáowèipǐn condiment; seasoning; flavouring

调戏 tiáo·xì take liberties with (a woman); assail (a woman) with obscenities

调弦 tiáoxián tune a stringed instrument

调相 tiáoxiàng *radio* phase modulation

调笑 tiáoxiào make fun of; poke fun at; tease

调协 tiáoxié coodinate; harmonize; bring into line

调谐 tiáoxié ① harmonious ② *radio* tune: 〜范围 tuning range / 〜旋钮 tuning knob

调谑 tiáoxuè same as 调笑 tiáoxiào

调压器 tiáoyāqì *elec.* voltage regulator

调养 tiáoyǎng take good care of oneself (as in poor health or after an illness); build up one's health by rest and by taking nourishing food; be nursed back to health

调音 tiáoyīn *mus.* tune

调匀 tiáoyún mix well: 和面时, 水跟面粉要〜。When you make dough, you must mix flour and water well. / 今年雨水〜, 丰收可望。Rainfall has been well distributed this year and a good harvest can be expected.

调整 tiáozhěng adjust; regulate; revise: 〜价格 readjust (*or* modify) prices / 〜供求关系 regulate (*or* readjust) supply and demand / 〜生产计划 revise production plans / 〜作息时间 adjust the work timetable / 〜人力 make adjustments in the use of manpower

调整杆 tiáozhěnggān *mech.* adjusting rod

调整工资 tiáozhěng gōngzī adjust wages (usu. upwards)

调整器 tiáozhěngqì *mech.* adjuster: 自动松紧〜 automatic slack adjuster

调治 tiáozhì recuperate under medical treatment

调制 tiáozhì *radio* modulation: 〜间隙 modulation gap

调资 tiáozī short for 调整工资 tiáozhěng gōngzī

调嘴学舌 tiáozuǐ-xuéshé tittle-tattle; tell tales; gossip

笤

tiáo see below

笤帚 tiáozhou whisk broom; small broom

齠

tiáo *formal* (of a child) shed baby (*or* milk) teeth; grow permanent teeth

齠龀 tiáochèn *formal* ① child ② childhood

齠年 tiáonián *formal* childhood

蜩

tiáo *arch.* cicada

髫

tiáo *arch.* a child's hanging hair

髫龄 tiáolíng *formal* childhood

髫年 tiáonián *formal* childhood

tiāo

挑

tiāo ① push sth. up with a pole or stick; raise: 把帘子〜起来 raise the curtain / 〜眉毛 raise one's eyebrows / 〜大姆指 hold up one's thumb (in approval) / 〜灯笼 hang a lantern (from a pole) ② poke; pick: 〜火 poke a fire / 〜刺 pick out a splinter / 〜破水泡 prick a blister with a needle / 把问题〜开来说吧。Let's put all the cards on the table. ③ stir up; instigate: 〜事 stir up trouble; sow discord / 这口舌是他〜起来的。It was he who stirred up the quarrel. ④ rising stroke (in Chinese characters) ——see also tiǎo

挑拨 tiǎobō instigate; incite; sow discord: 〜是非 foment discord / 〜民族关系 sow dissension among the various nationalities

挑拨离间 tiǎobō líjiàn sow discord; foment dissension; incite one against the other; drive a wedge between: 〜, 兴风作浪 foment dissension and stir up trouble / 竭尽〜之能事 stop at nothing to sow discord

挑灯 tiǎodēng ① raise the wick of an oil lamp ② hang a lantern from a pole: 〜夜战 fight by torchlight (in ancient times) or continue working by lamplight

挑动 tiǎodòng give rise to; lead to; touch off; arouse: 〜好奇心 arouse curiosity / 〜是非 give rise to

(*or* touch off) a dispute ② provoke; stir up; incite: 〜内战 provoke civil war / 〜群众斗群众 incite the masses to struggle against each other

挑逗 tiǎodòu provoke; tease; tantalize

挑费 tiāo·fèi *inf.* daily expenses; running expenses

挑花 tiāohuā cross-stitch work

挑明 tiǎomíng no longer keep it back; let it all out; bring it out into the open

挑弄 tiǎonòng ① instigate; incite; sow discord ② make fun of; play tricks on; tease; kid

挑起 tiǎoqǐ provoke; stir up; instigate: 〜边境冲突 provoke a border conflict (*or* clash)

挑三窝四 tiǎosān-wōsì same as 调三窝四 tiáosān-wōsì

挑唆 tiǎosuō incite; abet; instigate: 警惕有人在背后〜。Beware of people stirring up trouble behind the scenes.

挑头 tiǎotóu take the lead; be the first to do sth.: 〜提意见 be the first to make suggestions / 这是你挑的头儿吧? You started all this, didn't you?

挑衅 tiǎoxìn provoke: 进行武装〜 carry out armed provocation / 故意〜 deliberately provoke / 提出〜性的问题 raise provocative questions / 他向我〜。He was trying to provoke me.

挑战 tiǎozhàn ① throw down the gauntlet; challenge to battle: 〜的口吻 a provocative tone / 接受〜 take up the gauntlet; accept a challenge ② challenge to a contest: 他向我〜, 下一盘围棋。He challenged me to a game of *weiqi* (go chess)

挑战书 tiǎozhànshū a letter of challenge; challenge

朓

tiǎo *arch.* (of the moon) appear in the west at the end of a lunar month

窕

tiǎo see 窈窕 yǎotiǎo

斛

tiǎo *dial.* exchange; change; swop

tiào

眺

tiào look into the distance from a high place: 远眺 yuǎntiào

眺望 tiàowàng look into the distance from a high place

粜 (糶)

tiào sell (grain)

跳

tiào ① jump; leap; bounce: 高兴得〜起来 jump for (*or* with) joy / 〜下自行车 jump off a bicycle / 〜过一条沟 leap over a ditch / 他〜过了二米的高度。He cleared two metres in the high jump. / 球在篮框上〜了一下滚入篮内。With one bounce on the ring the ball rolled into the basketball net. ② move up and down; beat: 他激动得心直〜。His heart was throbbing with excitement. / 我眼皮老是〜。My eyelids keep twitching all the time. ③ skip (over); make omissions: 从第一页〜到第五页 jump from page 1 to page 5 / 〜过了三页 skip over three pages / 〜一针 drop a stitch (in knitting)

跳班 tiàobān (of pupils) skip a grade

跳板 tiàobǎn ① gangplank ② springboard; diving board

跳板跳水 tiàobǎn tiàoshuǐ *sports.* springboard diving

跳布札 tiào bùzhá devil's dance (performed by lamas) at religious festivals to exorcize evil spirits

跳槽 tiàocáo (also 跳槽子 tiàocáozi) jump the manger——① (of a horse, etc.) leave its own manger to eat at another ② throw up one job and take on another

跳虫 tiàochóng springtail; snowflea

跳弹 tiàodàn *mil.* ricochet: ～轰炸 ricochet bombing; skip bombing

跳荡 tiàodàng move up and down; throb; pulsate: 他的心兴奋地～着。His heart throbbed with excitement.／拉美舞曲～的节拍 the pulsating beat of Latin American dance music

跳到黄河洗不清 tiào dào Huánghé xǐbuqīng be unable to cleanse oneself even if one plunges into the Yellow River—find it hard to clear oneself (of a charge)

跳动 tiàodòng move up and down; beat; pulsate: 只要我的心脏还在～,我就要为人民工作。As long as my heart still beats, I will go on working for the people.

跳房子 tiào fángzi (also 跳间 tiàojiān) ① play hop-scotch ② hopscotch

跳高 tiàogāo high jump: ～运动员 high jumper

跳行 tiàoháng ① skip a line (in reading or transcribing) ② start a new paragraph ③ change one's profession (*or* occupation, trade)

跳级 tiàojí (of pupils) skip a grade

跳脚 tiàojiǎo stamp one's foot: 气得～ stamp with rage

跳井 tiàojǐng drown oneself in a well

跳栏 tiàolán hurdle race; the hurdles

跳雷 tiàoléi *mil.* bounding mine

跳梁小丑 tiàoliáng xiǎochǒu buffoon; clown; a contemptible scoundrel

跳马 tiàomǎ *sports* ① vaulting horse ② horse-vaulting

跳蝻 tiàonǎn same as 蝗蝻 huángnǎn

跳皮筋儿 tiào píjīnr (also 跳猴皮筋儿 tiào hóupíjīnr) rubber band skipping; skipping and dancing over a chain of rubber bands

跳棋 tiàoqí Chinese checkers; Chinese draughts

跳球 tiàoqiú *basketball* jump ball

跳伞 tiàosǎn ① parachute; bale (*or* bail) out ② *sports* parachute jumping: ～运动员 parachutist; parachuter

跳伞区 tiàosǎnqū parachute drop zone

跳伞塔 tiàosǎntǎ parachute tower

跳神 tiàoshén ① sorcerer's dance in a trance ② same as 跳布扎 tiào bùzhá

跳绳 tiàoshéng rope skipping; jump rope

跳虱 tiàoshī *dial.* flea

跳鼠 tiàoshǔ jerboa

跳水 tiàoshuǐ *sports* diving: ～表演 diving exhibition ／面对池反身～ reverse dive ／向前(后)～ front (back) dive／面对板向内～ inward dive

跳台 tiàotái diving tower; diving platform

跳台跳水 tiàotái tiàoshuǐ *sports* platform diving: 高(低)难度～ variety (plain) high diving

跳汰选 tiàotàixuǎn *min.* jigging: ～煤 coal jigging

跳舞 tiàowǔ ① dance (as a performance) ② dance (socially or in a ballroom)

跳箱 tiàoxiāng *sports* ① box horse; vaulting box ② jump over the box horse

跳鞋 tiàoxié a kind of leather shoes specially made for high jumping or long jumping

跳远 tiàoyuǎn long jump; broad jump

跳月 tiàoyuè moon dance (a festive dance performed in the moonlight by young people of the Miao and Yi nationalities)

跳跃 tiàoyuè jump; leap; bound: ～前进 bound forward ／人们欢呼着,～着。People were cheering and jumping.

跳跃着陆 tiàoyuè zhuólù *mil.* rebound landing

跳蚤 tiàozao flea

---

tiē

帖（贴） tiē ① submissive; obedient: 服帖 fútiē ② well-settled; well-placed: 妥帖 tuǒtiē ──see also tiě; tiè

帖服 tiēfú *formal* docile; obedient; submissive

贴[1] tiē ① paste; stick; glue: ～邮票 stick on a stamp ／～海报 put up a playbill ／～膏药 apply a (medicated) plaster to ／～上胶布 stick on a piece of adhesive tape ／请把这几张纸～在一块儿。Please paste these sheets of paper together. ② keep close to; nestle closely to: ～墙站着 be standing against the wall ／这孩子紧紧～在妈妈身边。The child was nestling closely to its mother. ③ subsidize; help (out) financially: 我每月～他十块钱。I help him out by giving him 10 *yuan* each month. ④ subsidies; allowance: 米～ food allowance ⑤ *m.* (for medicated plaster): 一～膏药 a piece of (medicated) plaster

贴[2] tiē same as 帖 tiē

贴边 tiēbiān hem (of a garment)

贴饼子 tiēbǐngzi ① bake corn or millet cakes on a pan ② corn or millet cakes so baked

贴补 tiē·bǔ ① subsidize (one's relatives or friends); help (out) financially: ～家用 help out with the family expenses ② use stored material or savings to cover daily needs or expenses: 还有存的料子～着用,现在先不买。Make do with the piece of cloth we've got on hand. You don't have to buy something new.

贴兜 tiēdōu patch pocket

贴花 tiēhuā *text.* appliqué

贴画 tiēhuà ① pinup picture (e.g. a New Year picture, a picture poster, etc.) ② matchbox picture

贴换 tiē·huàn *old* trade sth. in (for); trade in

贴己 tiējǐ ① intimate; close; confidential: ～朋友 a person one can confide in; bosom friend ／～话 things one says only to one's intimates; words spoken in confidence ／表现出十分～的样子 try to be very friendly (with sb.) ② *dial.* private savings: ～钱 private savings of a family member

贴金 tiējīn ① cover with gold leaf (*or* gold foil); gild ② touch up; prettify: 别尽往自己脸上～了。Don't put feathers in your own cap. *or* Don't go blowing your own trumpet.

贴金漆 tiējīnqī gold size

贴近 tiējìn press close to; nestle up against: 那孩子～他身边,轻声说了几句话。The child nestled up against him and murmured a few words.

贴邻 tiēlín close neighbour; next-door neighbour

贴面舞 tiēmiànwǔ cheek-to-cheek dancing

贴谱 tiēpǔ proper; appropriate; sound; relevant: 这个分析很～。This analysis is quite sound.

贴切 tiēqiè (of words) apt; suitable; appropriate; proper: 这个比喻很～。This metaphor is very appropriate. ／我找不到～的词儿来表达我的意思。I can't find suitable words to express what I mean. ／这样说不～。That's not the right word for it. ／措词～ aptly worded; well-put

贴身 tiēshēn ① next to the skin: ～衣服 underclothes; underclothing ② *old* constantly accompanying: ～丫鬟 a maidservant who constantly accompanies her mistress; personal maid

贴实 tiēshí ① sturdy; strong ② quiet; untroubled

贴水 tiēshuǐ *banking* ① pay an agio ② agio

贴题 tiētí relevant; pertinent; to the point: 着墨不多,但是十分～ brief but very much to the point ／你的话

不～。What you say is irrelevant (*or* beside the point).

贴体 tiētǐ　(of clothes) fit

贴息 tiēxī　*banking* ① pay interest in the form of a deduction when selling a bill of exchange, etc. ② interest so deducted; discount

贴现 tiēxiàn　discount (on a promissory note): ～率 discount rate

贴心 tiēxīn　intimate; close: ～朋友 a person one can confide in; bosom friend / ～话 words spoken in confidence / 群众的～人 a close friend of the masses

萜

tiē　*chem.* terpene

tiě

帖

tiě　① invitation: 请帖 qǐngtiě ② note; card: 字帖儿 zìtiěr ③ *m. dial.* (for herbal medicine): 一～药 a dose (*or* draught) of herbal medicine ——see also tiē; tiè

帖子 tiězi　① invitation ② note; card

铁(鐵、銕)

tiě　① *chem.* iron (Fe) ② arms; weapon: 手无寸铁 shǒu wú cùn tiě ③ hard or strong as iron: 铁拳 tiěquán ④ be resolved; be determined: 铁心 tiěxīn ⑤ indisputable; unalterable: ～的事实 hard fact; ironclad evidence / ～的纪律 iron discipline ⑥ (Tiě) a surname

铁案如山 tiě'àn rú shān　a case borne out by ironclad evidence; an ironclad case

铁板 tiěbǎn　iron plate; sheet iron

铁板钉钉 tiěbǎn dìng dīng　that clinches it; that's final; no two ways about it

铁板一块 tiěbǎn yī kuài　a monolithic bloc: 不要以为这帮人是～, 他们是可以分化的。Don't think this gang is monolithic—it can be split up.

铁笔 tiěbǐ　① a cutting tool used in carving seals, etc. ② stylus for cutting stencils; stencil pen

铁箅子 tiěbìzi　① grate (of a stove) ② gridiron; grill

铁壁铜墙 tiěbì-tóngqiáng　same as 铜墙铁壁 tóngqiáng-tiěbì

铁饼 tiěbǐng　① discus throw ② discus

铁驳 tiěbó　iron barge

铁蚕豆 tiěcándòu　roasted broad bean

铁杵磨成针 tiěchǔ móchéng zhēn　see 只要功夫深, 铁杵磨成针 zhǐyào gōngfu shēn, tiěchǔ móchéng zhēn

铁窗 tiěchuāng　① a window with iron grating ② prison bars; prison

铁窗风味 tiěchuāng fēngwèi　prison life; life behind bars

铁磁共振 tiěcí gòngzhèn　*phys.* ferromagnetic resonance

铁磁性 tiěcíxìng　ferromagnetism

铁搭 tiědā　*dial.* an iron rake with three to six teeth

铁打 tiědǎ　iron-forged—unshakable: ～的江山 unshakable state power

铁道 tiědào　railway; railroad

铁道兵 tiědàobīng　railway corps: 中国人民解放军～ the PLA railway engineering corps

铁道炮兵 tiědào pàobīng　railway artillery

铁定 tiědìng　ironclad; fixed; unalterable: ～的事实 hard fact; ironclad evidence / ～的局面 unalterable situation

铁饭碗 tiěfànwǎn　iron rice bowl—a secure job

铁杆儿 tiěgǎnr　① stubborn; inveterate; dyed-in-the-wool: ～汉奸 out-and-out traitor ② of guaranteed high yield; surefire: ～庄稼 guaranteed high-yielding crop

铁工 tiěgōng　① ironwork ② ironworker; blacksmith

铁公鸡 tiěgōngjī　iron cock (from which no feathers can be plucked)—a stingy person; miser

铁姑娘 tiěgūniang　iron girl—a girl who can do heavy physical labour

铁箍 tiěgū　iron hoop

铁骨铮铮 tiěgǔ zhēngzhēng　firm and unyielding

铁观音 tiěguānyīn　a variety of oolong (乌龙) tea

铁管 tiěguǎn　iron pipe; iron tube

铁轨 tiěguǐ　rail (s) (for trains, etc.); tracks

铁柜 tiěguì　strongbox; safe

铁汉 tiěhàn　man of iron (*or* steel); man of iron will; a strong determined person

铁合金 tiěhéjīn　ferroalloy

铁黑 tiěhēi　*chem.* ① iron oxide black ② iron black

铁红 tiěhóng　*chem.* iron oxide red

铁花 tiěhuā　*arts & crafts* ornamental work of iron; iron openwork

铁画 tiěhuà　*arts & crafts* iron picture

铁画银钩 tiěhuà-yíngōu　vigorous flourishes (*or* strokes) (in calligraphy); forceful strokes

铁环 tiěhuán　iron hoop: 滚～ trundle a hoop; play with a hoop

铁黄 tiěhuáng　*chem.* iron oxide yellow

铁活 tiěhuó　ironwork

铁蒺藜 tiějíli　*mil.* caltrop

铁甲 tiějiǎ　① mail; armour ② *mil.* armour for vessels, vehicles, etc.

铁甲车 tiějiǎchē　same as 装甲车 zhuāngjiǎchē

铁甲舰 tiějiǎjiàn　same as 装甲舰 zhuāngjiǎjiàn

铁将军把门 tiějiāngjūn bǎmén　General Iron guarding the door—the door is padlocked

铁匠 tiějiang　blacksmith; ironsmith

铁匠铺 tiějiangpù　smithy; blacksmith's shop

铁脚板 tiějiǎobǎn　iron soles—toughened feet

铁筋 tiějīn　same as 钢筋 gāngjīn

铁紧 tiějǐn　very tight: 门关得～。The door was shut tight. / 事情瞒得～。Secrecy was strictest.

铁军 tiějūn　iron army—invincible army

铁铠 tiěkǎi　same as 铁甲 tiějiǎ①

铁矿 tiěkuàng　① iron ore ② iron mine

铁矿石 tiěkuàngshí　iron ore

铁力木 tiělìmù　*bot.* ferreous mesua (*Mesua ferrea*)

铁链 tiěliàn　iron chain; shackles

铁路 tiělù　railway; railroad: ～运输 railway transportation; railway (*or* rail) transport; shipping by rail / ～电气化 railway electrification

铁路干线 tiělù gànxiàn　trunk railway

铁路公路两用桥 tiělù-gōnglù liǎngyòngqiáo　(railway and highway) combined bridge; road and rail bridge

铁路路基 tiělù lùjī　railway bed

铁路网 tiělùwǎng　railway network

铁路线 tiělùxiàn　railway line

铁路油槽车 tiělù yóucáochē　rail tank car; rail tanker

铁马[1] tiěmǎ　*liter.* iron-clad (*or* armoured) horses—strong mounted forces: 夜阑卧听风吹雨, ～冰河入梦来。(陆游) Night deepening, I lie and listen to winds buffeting the rain, And iron-clad horses over frozen rivers come charging into my dreams. ——see also 金戈铁马 jīngē-tiěmǎ

铁马[2] tiěmǎ　tinkling pieces of metal hanging from the eaves of pagodas, temples, etc.

铁门 tiěmén　① iron gate ② grille

铁闷子 tiěmènzi　boxcar

铁面无私 tiěmiàn wú sī　impartial and incorruptible; strictly impartial

铁鸟 tiěniǎo　iron bird—aircraft; aeroplane; plane

铁牛 tiěniú　iron ox—tractor

铁皮 tiěpí　iron sheet: 白～ tinplate; galvanized iron sheet / 黑～ black sheet (iron)

铁骑 tiěqí　*liter.* armoured horses—strong cavalry

铁器　tiěqì　ironware

铁器时代　Tiěqì Shídài　the Iron Age

铁锹　tiěqiāo　spade; shovel

铁青　tiěqīng　ashen; livid; ghastly pale: 气得脸色～ turn livid with rage

铁拳　tiěquán　iron fist—powerful striking force

铁人　tiěrén　iron man—a person of exceptional physical and moral strength

铁纱　tiěshā　wire gauze; wire cloth

铁砂　tiěshā　① iron sand ② shot (in a shotgun cartridge); pellets

铁杉　tiěshān　Chinese hemlock (Tsuga chinensis)

铁石心肠　tiěshí xīncháng　be ironhearted; have a heart of stone; be hardhearted; be heartless

铁树　tiěshù　① sago cycas (Cycas revoluta) ② common name for 苏铁 sūtiě

铁树开花　tiěshù kāi huā　the iron tree in blossom—sth. seldom seen or hardly possible: 千年的铁树开了花, 银针使得聋哑人说了话。Miraculously, like the thousand-year-old iron tree bursting into blossom, many deaf-mutes have regained their power of speech after acupuncture treatment.

铁水　tiěshuǐ　molten iron

铁丝　tiěsī　iron wire

铁丝网　tiěsīwǎng　① wire netting; wire meshes ② wire entanglement: 有刺～ barbed wire entanglement

铁素体　tiěsùtǐ　metall. ferrite

铁算盘　tiěsuàn·pán　iron abacus—① careful calculation and strict budgeting ② an astute businessman; a financial wizard

铁索　tiěsuǒ　iron chain; cable: ～吊车 cable car

铁索桥　tiěsuǒqiáo　chain bridge

铁塔　tiětǎ　① iron tower; iron pagoda ② elec. pylon; transmission tower

铁蹄　tiětí　iron heel—cruel oppression of the people

铁桶　tiětǒng　metal pail (or bucket); drum: 包围得～似的 be tightly encircled

铁腕　tiěwàn　① iron hand: ～人物 an ironhanded (or despotic, tyrannical) person; strong man or iron lady ② strong rule (over a country)

铁锨　tiěxiān　shovel; spade

铁线订书机　tiěxiàn dìngshūjī　wire stitcher; wire stitching machine

铁线蕨　tiěxiànjué　(also 铁线草 tiěxiàncǎo) bot. venus-hair fern (Adiantum capillarus-veneris)

铁线莲　tiěxiànlián　bot. cream clematis (Clematis florida)

铁屑　tiěxiè　① iron filings ② iron chippings and shavings

铁心[1]　tiěxīn　be unshakable in one's determination: ～务农 be a very determined farmer / 他扎根农村可是铁了心啦。He was unshakable in his determination to settle in the countryside.

铁心[2]　tiěxīn　elec. (iron) core

铁锈　tiěxiù　rust

铁盐　tiěyán　molysite

铁陨石　tiěyǔnshí　iron meteorite

铁则　tiězé　an iron rule; an inviolable rule

铁砧　tiězhēn　anvil

铁铮铮　tiězhēngzhēng　firm; staunch; steadfast

铁证　tiězhèng　ironclad proof; irrefutable evidence

铁证如山　tiězhèng rú shān　a mass of ironclad evidence; irrefutable, conclusive evidence

铁中铮铮　tiě zhōng zhēngzhēng　the finest of metals—an outstanding person

tiè

帖　tiè　a book containing models of handwriting or painting for learners to copy: 看着～写字 practise calligraphy after a model ——see also tiē; tiě

餮　tiè　formal　be greedy for food: 饕餮 tāotiè③

tīng

厅(廳、厛)　tīng　① hall (for holding meetings, concerts, receiving guests, etc.): 休息～ lounge (in a hotel, theatre, etc.); foyer / 这个(门)～很大。This (entrance) hall is very spacious. / 人民大会堂台湾～Taiwan Room in the Great Hall of the People ② a department in a big government organization, such as a ministry; office: 办公厅 bàngōngtīng ③ a government department at the provincial level: 湖南省教育～ the Education Department of Hunan Province

厅房　tīngfáng　dial. hall

厅事　tīngshì　same as 听事 tīngshì②

厅堂　tīngtáng　same as 厅 tīng①

汀　tīng　formal　low, level land along a river; spit of land

汀洲　tīngzhōu　islet in a river; sand bar

听[1](聽、聴)　tīng　① listen; hear: 请仔细～。Please listen carefully. / ～广播 listen to the radio / 打开收音机～～新闻 Let's turn on the radio and listen in to the news. / 我没～过这样好的音乐。I've never heard such beautiful music before. / 请～我说完。Please hear me out. / 这一句我没～清。I didn't quite catch that sentence. / ～, 好象有人敲门。Listen, it sounds like somebody's knocking on the door. / 你～着, 我在给你讲呢! Listen to me, will you? I'm talking to you. / 请～一下电话。Answer the phone, please. / 厂长要你～电话。The director wants to talk to you on the phone. / 到群众中走一走, ～～他们的意见。Go among the masses and hear what they have to say. / ～声音不像他。The voice didn't sound like him. / 他罗唆了半天, 我实在～不下去了。He'd rambled on for hours. I really couldn't stand it any longer. / 他的四川口音我～不出来。I can't detect his Sichuan accent. / 这些话～起来倒也有些道理。Those words sound quite reasonable after all. / 他的话～起来不诚恳。What he said seemed insincere. or His words rang hollow. ② heed; obey; listen to: ～我的没错儿。Do as I say and you won't go wrong. / 我劝他别去, 他不～。I advised him not to go, but he wouldn't listen. / 她要～了我的话, 哪儿会有今天。If she'd listened to me, things would be different today. / 对批评～不进去 turn a deaf ear to criticism / 老了, 胳膊腿儿不～使唤了。I'm getting old. My limbs won't do what I want them to. / 家里的事我都～她的。When it comes to household affairs, I listen to her. / 工地上一切都～他指挥。Everything on the construction site is under his command. ③ administer; manage: 听政 tīngzhèng

听[2](聽、聴)　tīng　allow; let: 听凭 tīngpíng

听[3](聽、聴)　tīng　m. dial. tin; can: 三～咖啡 three tins of coffee / 六～啤酒 six cans of beer

听便　tīngbiàn　do as one pleases: 去留～。You may go

or stay as you please.

听差 tīngchāi *old* manservant; office attendant

听从 tīngcóng obey; heed; comply with: ～指挥 obey orders / ～吩咐 be at sb.'s beck and call; do sb.'s bidding / ～劝告 accept sb.'s advice / ～召唤 answer sb.'s call

听断 tīngduàn *formal* try (a case)

听而不闻 tīng ér bù wén see 视而不见, 听而不闻 shì ér bù jiàn, tīng ér bù wén

听风是雨 tīng fēng shì yǔ hear the wind and mistake it for the rain—believe rumours

听骨 tīnggǔ *physiol.* ear bones

听喝 tīnghē do sb.'s bidding; be at sb.'s beck and call

听候 tīnghòu wait for (a decision, settlement, etc. from higher authorities): ～分配 wait for one's job assignment / ～上级指示 pending further instructions from the higher authorities

听话 tīnghuà heed what an elder or superior says; be obedient: 这孩子不～。 The child won't do as he is told. *or* The child doesn't behave himself. / ～, 做功课去。 Be a good boy (*or* girl). Go and do your homework.

听话儿 tīnghuàr wait for a reply: 你的要求我们正在研究, 过几天～。 We're considering your request and will give you a reply in a few days.

听话听音儿 tīng huà tīng yīnr when you hear people talk, listen to their tone

听会 tīnghuì be a visitor at a meeting

听见 tīng·jiàn hear: 我～有人敲门。 I heard a knock at the door. / 她说的什么你～了吗? Did you catch what she said? / 说话的声音小得几乎听不见 speak in a scarcely audible voice / 你小点儿声, 我听得见。 Lower your voice. I can hear you. / 我听了一会儿, 可什么也没～。 I listened for a while, but heard nothing. / 他耳背, 听不见。 He's hard of hearing. He can't hear you.

听讲 tīngjiǎng listen to a talk; attend a lecture: 一面～, 一面记笔记 take notes while listening to a lecture

听觉 tīngjué sense of hearing

听课 tīngkè ① visit (*or* sit in on) a class ② attend a lecture

听力 tīnglì ① hearing (ability): 经过针刺恢复了～ regain one's hearing after receiving acupuncture treatment ② aural comprehension (in language teaching)

听命 tīngmìng ① take orders from; be at sb.'s command: ～于人 be at sb.'s beck and call ② same as 听天由命 tīngtiān-yóumìng

听凭 tīngpíng allow; let (sb. do as he pleases): ～别人的摆布 be at the mercy of others / 去也罢, 不去也罢, ～你自己作主。 You decide whether or not to go. It's up to you.

听其言而观其行 tīng qí yán ér guān qí xíng listen to a person's words and watch his deeds; judge people by their deeds, not just by their words

听其自然 tīng qí zìrán let things take their own course; let matters slide

听墙根 tīng qiánggēn eavesdrop

听取 tīngqǔ listen to: 经常～群众的意见 constantly heed the opinions of the masses / ～工作报告 listen to a work report / ～汇报 hear reports (from below); debrief

听任 tīngrèn *formal* allow; let (sb. do as he pleases): 不能～黄色书刊充斥市场。 We cannot allow pornographic books to flood the market.

听神经 tīngshénjīng *physiol.* auditory (*or* acoustic) nerve

听事 tīngshì *formal* ① (of a monarch or regent) hold court; administer affairs of state ② hall (in a government office)

听说 tīngshuō ① be told; hear of: 她明天走。—我～了。

She's leaving tomorrow. — So I've been told. / 你～过李一这个人没有? Have you heard of a man called Li Yi? / 我听人说她到南方去了。 I hear she has gone to the South. / 这种事我们从来没～过。 We've never heard of such a thing. / 这只不过是～而已。 This is only hearsay. *or* It's nothing but hearsay. / 老王～病得很重。 I heard that Lao Wang was very ill. ② *dial.* heed what an elder or superior says; be obedient

听讼 tīngsòng *formal* try a case

听随 tīngsuí allow; let (sb. do as he pleases)

听天由命 tīngtiān-yóumìng submit to the will of Heaven; resign oneself to one's fate; trust to luck: 得了这种病只好～。 When you get this kind of disease, there's nothing you can do but put yourself in the hands of God.

听筒 tīngtǒng ① (telephone) receiver ② headphone; earphone ③ *med.* stethoscope

听头儿 tīngtour worth listening to: 这段唱腔有～。 This aria is a joy to listen to.

听闻 tīngwén *formal* ① listening ② what one hears: 以广～ in order to widen one's knowledge

听戏 tīngxì go to the opera (esp. Beijing opera)

听写 tīngxiě dictation: 教师让学生～。 The teacher gave the pupils (a piece of) dictation.

听信¹ tīngxìn wait for information: 今天开会就决定这件事儿, 你～吧。 The matter will be decided at today's meeting and we'll let you know the result.

听信² tīngxìn believe what one hears (usu. sth. incorrect or one-sided); believe: 不要～这种谣言。 Don't believe such rumours.

听诊 tīngzhěn *med.* auscultation

听诊器 tīngzhěnqì stethoscope

听政 tīngzhèng (of a monarch or regent) hold court; administer affairs of state

听之任之 tīngzhī-rènzhī let sth. (undesirable, evil, etc.) go unchecked; take a laissez-faire attitude; let sb. have his own way; let matters drift: 对于损害群众利益的事情, 我们不能～。 We cannot shut our eyes to things that harm the interests of the masses.

听众 tīngzhòng audience; listeners

听装 tīngzhuāng *dial.* tinned; canned: ～奶粉 tinned milk powder

听子 tīngzi *dial.* tin; can

烃 (烴) tīng *chem.* hydrocarbon: 开链～ open chain hydrocarbon / 闭链～ closed chain hydrocarbon

烃气 tīngqì *chem.* hydrocarbon gas

桯 tīng ① the shaft of an awl ② a small bedside table used in ancient China

桯子 tīngzi ① the shaft of an awl ② the floral axis of a vegetable

tíng

廷 tíng the court of a feudal ruler; the seat of a monarchical government: 清～ the Qing government

廷杖 tíngzhàng flogging with a big stick at court (a punishment in ancient China)

亭¹ tíng ① pavilion (in a park or beside a road for people to rest): 八角～ octagonal pavilion ② stall; kiosk: 书亭 shūtíng

亭² tíng *formal* well-balanced; in the middle; even: 亭午 tíngwǔ

亭亭 tíngtíng　*formal*　① erect; upright ② same as 婷婷 tíngtíng

亭亭如盖 tíngtíng rú gài　(of a tree) standing straight with a canopy of leaves

亭亭玉立 tíngtíng yù lì　① (of a woman) fair, slim and graceful ② (of a tree, etc.) tall and straight

亭午 tíngwǔ　*formal*　midday; noon

亭匀 tíngyún　same as 停匀 tíngyún

亭子 tíngzi　pavilion (in a park or beside a road for people to rest)

亭子间 tíngzijiān　*dial.*　a small, dark back room over a kitchen; garret

庭 tíng　① hall ② front courtyard; front yard ③ law court: 开庭 kāitíng

庭除 tíngchú　*formal*　courtyard: 黎明即起, 洒扫~。《朱子家训》Rise at dawn and sweep the courtyard.

庭训 tíngxùn　*formal*　paternal instructions and admonitions

庭园 tíngyuán　flower garden; grounds

庭院 tíngyuàn　courtyard

庭长 tíngzhǎng　*old*　the president of a law court; presiding judge

莛 tíng　the stem of a herb, etc.: 麦~儿 stalks of wheat

停[1] tíng　① stop; cease; halt; pause: ~下工作 stop work / 雨~了。The rain has stopped. / 演奏序曲之后, 乐队~下来又调了调音。After the overture, the orchestra stopped to tune up again. / 她~了一会儿, 又接着讲下去。She paused a moment before going on with the story. / 他不~地写着。He kept on writing. / 蟋蟀叫个不~。The crickets were chirruping ceaselessly. ② stop over; stay: 我在杭州~了五天。I stopped over at Hangzhou for five days. / 火车在这些小站都只~一分钟。The train stops only for one minute at these small stations. ③ (of cars) be parked; (of ships) lie at anchor; (of a dead body or coffin) be placed: 门口~着一辆奔驰牌轿车。Parked in front of the gate was a Benz sedan. / 汽车~在哪儿？Where can we park the car? / 船~在江心。The ship anchored in the middle of the river. / 轮船在港口已经~了三天了。The steamship has been lying at anchor in the harbour for three days. / 将灵柩~在中央大厅内 place the coffin in the central hall ④ ready; settled: 停妥 tíngtuǒ

停[2] tíng　*inf.*　part (of a total); portion: 十~儿有九~儿是好的。Nine out of ten are good.

停摆 tíngbǎi　(of a pendulum) come to a standstill; stop: 钟~了。The clock's stopped.

停办 tíngbàn　stop a business; close down: 这个学校已经~三年了。The school has been closed down for three years.

停闭 tíngbì　close a business; go out of business

停表 tíngbiǎo　stopwatch

停泊 tíngbó　anchor; berth: 这个码头可以~五十多艘轮船。The docks can berth over fifty vessels. / 你们的货船~在五号码头。Your cargo boat is berthed at No.5 wharf. / 港口里~着我国新造的一艘远洋巨轮。One of our new oceangoing ships is lying at anchor in the harbour.

停泊处 tíngbóchù　berth; anchorage; roads; roadstead

停产 tíngchǎn　stop production

停车 tíngchē　① stop; pull up: 下一站~十分钟。At the next station we'll have a ten-minute stop. ② park (a car): 此处不准~! No Parking! ③ (of a machine) stall; stop working: 机器~了, 得加点油。The machine's stalled. It needs oiling. / 三号车间~修理。No.3 Workshop has stopped working to undergo repairs.

停车场 tíngchēchǎng　car park; parking lot; parking area

停当 tíngdang　ready; settled: 一切准备~。Everything's ready. *or* All set.

停电 tíngdiàn　① cut off the power supply; have a power failure ② power cut; power failure; blackout

停顿 tíngdùn　① stop; halt; pause; be at a standstill: 交通陷于~。The traffic was at a standstill. / 水库工程~了好些年。The reservoir project has been suspended for quite a few years. ② pause (in speaking): 念到这里要~一下。When you've read up to here, you pause.

停放 tíngfàng　① park (a vehicle): 人行道上不准~自行车。Don't park bicycles on the pavement. ② place (a coffin)

停飞 tíngfēi　grounding of aircraft

停工 tínggōng　stop work; shut down: ~待料 work being held up for lack of material

停航 tíngháng　suspend air or shipping service: 班机因气候恶劣~。The regular flight is suspended on account of bad weather.

停火 tínghuǒ　cease fire: ~协议 cease-fire agreement

停机坪 tíngjīpíng　aircraft parking area; parking apron

停建 tíngjiàn　stop construction

停刊 tíngkān　stop publication (of a newspaper, magazine. etc.)

停靠 tíngkào　(of a train) stop; (of a ship) berth: 从上海开来的十四次列车~在二号站台。Train No.14 from Shanghai stops at Platform No. 2. / 六艘万吨货轮可以同时在这个码头~。Six 10,000-ton freighters can berth at this dock.

停靠港 tíngkàogǎng　port of call

停课 tíngkè　suspend classes: 那天学校~了。Classes were suspended that day.

停灵 tínglíng　keep a coffin in a temporary shelter before burial; rest the coffin temporarily

停留 tíngliú　stay for a time; stop; remain: 代表团在延安~了一周。The delegation stayed in Yan'an for a week. / 在武汉~过夜 make an overnight stop at Wuhan / 他在西安作短暂~。He had a brief stopover in Xi'an. / 人类对自然界的认识在不断发展, 永远不会~在一个水平上。Man's understanding of nature is developing all the time; it never remains at the same level.

停留时间 tíngliú shíjiān　*environ. protec.*　retention period

停食 tíngshí　*Chin. med.*　gastric disorder; indigestion

停水 tíngshuǐ　cut off the water supply; cut off the water: 明天上午八点至下午三点~。There will be no water tomorrow from 8 a.m. to 3 p.m.

停妥 tíngtuǒ　be well arranged; be in order: 事情已商议~。The matter has been discussed and satisfactorily arranged.

停息 tíngxī　stop; cease: 暴风雨~了。The storm has subsided.

停闲 tíngxián　(usu. used in the negative) stop; cease: 一连三天也没个~ work nonstop for three days running / 手脚一刻也不~ never let up with hands or feet

停歇 tíngxiē　① close a business; go out of business ② stop; cease: 从上午八点工作到下午两点一直没有~ work nonstop from 8 a.m. until 2 p.m. ③ stop for a rest; rest: 队伍在小树林里~。The troops rested in a grove.

停学 tíngxué　stop going to school; drop out of school

停业 tíngyè　① stop doing business: 修理内部, 暂时~。Closed temporarily for repairs. ② close a business; go out of business

停匀 tíngyún　*formal*　① (of the human figure) well-proportioned; well-balanced ② (of the rhythm of a melody) regular; balanced

停战 tíngzhàn　armistice; truce; cessation of hostilities:

～谈判 armistice talks (or negotiations) / ～协定 armistice; truce agreement

停职 tíngzhí suspend sb. from his duties: ～反省 be temporarily relieved of one's post for self-examination

停止 tíngzhǐ stop; cease; halt; suspend; call off: ～工作 stop working / ～营业 business suspended / ～前进! Halt! / ～敌对行动 cease hostilities / ～供水 cut off the water supply; cut off the water / ～广播 stop broadcasting; go off the air; close down / ～会籍 suspend sb.'s membership / 他的心脏～了跳动。His heart stopped beating. / 他们的争论还没有～。Their debate was still going on. / 病人的呼吸～了。The patient stopped breathing.

停滞 tíngzhì stagnate; be at a standstill; bog down: 那几年国民经济处于～状态。The national economy stagnated in those years. / 工厂生产～了。Production at the factory has come to a standstill.

停滞不前 tíngzhì bù qián stagnant; at a standstill: 他们的国民经济～。Their national economy is stagnant. / 会谈～。The negotiations have bogged down (or reached a stalemate). / 马克思主义一定要向前发展，要随着实践的发展而发展，不能～。(毛泽东) Marxism must necessarily advance; it must develop along with practice and cannot stand still.

停潴 tíngzhū (of water) stagnate: 污水～ stagnation of waste water

蜓 tíng see 蜻蜓 qīngtíng

婷 tíng see below
婷婷 tíngtíng graceful

霆 tíng thunderbolt: 雷霆 léitíng

tǐng

町 tǐng formal raised path between farm fields

侹 tǐng formal smooth and straight

挺[1] tǐng ① straight; erect; stiff: 直挺挺 zhítǐngtǐng ② stick out; straighten up (physically): ～胸 throw out one's chest; square one's shoulders / ～起腰杆 straighten one's back; straighten up / 他～着脖子，气呼呼的样子。His neck stiffened and he seemed to be in a huff. ③ endure; stand; hold out: 他肝疼得厉害，都～不住了。The pain in his liver was too sharp for him to endure. ④ outstanding; prominent; extraordinary: 英挺 yīngtǐng ⑤ adv. inf. very; rather; quite: ～好 very good / 今天～冷。It's rather (or pretty, quite) cold today. / 分量～轻的。It's rather light. / 这花～香。The flower has a very sweet smell. / 他讲得～生动的。His talk was quite lively. / 我～喜欢这部协奏曲。I quite like this concerto. / 他～能吃苦的。He can really bear hardships. / 你这样做～不好的。It's quite wrong of you to do such a thing.

挺[2] tǐng m. (for machine guns): 轻重机枪六十余～ over sixty heavy and light machine guns

挺拔 tǐngbá ① tall and straight: ～的白杨 tall, straight poplars ② forceful: 笔力～ forceful strokes in handwriting or drawing

挺杆 tǐnggǎn mech. tappet: 阀门～ valve tappet / ～间隙 tappet clearance

挺括 tǐng·guā dial. ① (of cloth, paper, etc.) stiff and smooth ② (of clothes) neat; trim; well pressed

挺进 tǐngjìn (of troops) boldly drive on; press onward; push forward: ～敌后 boldly drive into the areas behind the enemy lines

挺劲 tǐngjìng same as 挺拔 tǐngbá

挺举 tǐngjǔ weight lifting clean and jerk

挺俊 tǐngjùn tall and graceful

挺立 tǐnglì stand upright; stand firm: 几棵青松～在山坡上。Several pine trees stand erect on the hillside.

挺身 tǐngshēn straighten one's back: ～反抗 stand up and fight; stand up to (an enemy, reactionaries, etc.)

挺身而出 tǐngshēn ér chū step forward bravely; come out boldly: 他～，对这种谬论加以反驳。He stepped forward bravely and refuted the fallacy.

挺尸 tǐngshī offens. lie sleeping like a corpse

挺实 tǐngshí strong; sturdy

挺脱 tǐngtuō dial. ① strong; sturdy; tough: 这匹马真～。This is a very strong horse. ② (of clothes) neat; trim; well pressed

挺秀 tǐngxiù tall and graceful

挺直 tǐngzhí ① straighten (the body or a part of it): 走路腰板儿要～。Keep your back straight when you walk. ② straight; erect

梃 tǐng ① formal club; cudgel; bludgeon ② frame ③ dial. stem of a flower

梃子 tǐngzi frame

铤 tǐng formal (run) quickly

铤而走险 tǐng ér zǒu xiǎn take a risk in desperation; make a reckless move

艇 tǐng a light boat: 汽艇 qìtǐng

tōng

通 tōng ① open; through: 路～了。The road is now open. / 管子是～的。The pipe is not blocked. / 电话～了。The call has been put through. / 他思想～了。He's got his thinking straightened out. ② open up or clear out by poking or jabbing: 用铅丝～烟嘴儿 poke a piece of wire through a cigarette holder to clean it / ～炉子 poke the fire ③ lead to; go to: 这趟列车直～昆明。This train goes straight to Kunming. or This is a through train to Kunming. ④ connect; communicate: 两个房间是～着的。The two rooms are connected (or open into each other). / 互～情报 exchange information ⑤ notify; tell: 互～姓名 each telling his name to the other / ～消息 tell sb. the news; let sb. know / ～一个电话 give sb. a ring; call (or phone) sb. up ⑥ understand; know: 他～三种语言。He knows three languages. / 他念过哲学，但是根本没有念～。He's studied philosophy but has never been very good at it. ⑦ authority; expert: 日本～ an expert on Japan / 中国～ an old China hand; Sinologue ⑧ logical; coherent: 这个句子是～的，不必改了。This is a coherent sentence. It needs no correction. ⑨ general; common: 共通 gòngtōng ⑩ all; whole: ～观全局 take an overall view of the situation ⑪ m. formal (for letters, telegrams, etc.): 一～电报 a telegram / 手书两～ two personal letters ——see also tòng

通报 tōngbào ① circulate a notice: ～表扬 (批评) circulate a notice of commendation (criticism) ② circular: 关于情况的～ a circular on the situation ③ bulletin; journal: 《科学～》Science Bulletin / 《经济～》 Economic Journal ④ notify or report to (one's superior or master)

通便 tōngbiàn ease constipation

通便剂 tōngbiànjì med. laxative; cathartic

通禀 tōngbǐng report (to one's superior or master)

通病 tōngbìng common failing; common fault: 六朝诗人用典过多是一~。An excessive use of allusions was a common fault among Six Dynasties poets.

通才 tōngcái an all-round (or versatile) person; a universal genius

通草 tōngcǎo *Chin. med.* the stem pith of the rice-paper plant (*Tetrapanax papyriferus*)

通常 tōngcháng ① general; usual; normal: ~的方法 a usual way / ~情况下 under normal conditions ② *adv.* generally; usually; ordinarily; as a rule: 我~六点钟起床。I generally get up at six o'clock. / ~消息可靠人士 usually reliable sources / 我~在晚间不外出。I don't go out in the evening as a rule.

通畅 tōngchàng ① unobstructed; clear: 道路~。The road is clear. / 血液循环~ free circulation of the blood / 大便~ free movement (of the bowels) / 保持运输通畅 keep transportation going ② easy and smooth: 文字~ smooth writing

通车 tōngchē ① (of a railway or highway) be open to traffic ② have transport service: 从县城到每个乡都通了汽车。There's bus service from the county seat to every township. or Buses run from the county seat to every township.

通彻 tōngchè have a thorough knowledge of; thoroughly understand

通称 tōngchēng ① be generally called; be generally known as: 汞~水银。Mercury is generally known as quicksilver. ② a general (or common) term

通达 tōngdá understand things; be sensible or be reasonable: ~人情 be understanding and considerate / 见解~ hold sensible views; show good sense

通道 tōngdào thoroughfare; passageway; passage

通敌 tōngdí collude (or collaborate) with the enemy; have illicit relations with the enemy

通电¹ tōngdiàn set up an electric circuit; electrify; energize: ~的铁丝网 electrified (or live) wire entanglements

通电² tōngdiàn ① publish an open telegram (making known one's political views): ~全国 publish an open telegram to the nation ② circular (or open) telegram: 大会~ the circular telegram of the conference

通牒 tōngdié diplomatic note: 最后通牒 zuìhòu tōngdié

通都大邑 tōngdū-dàyì a large city; metropolis

通读¹ tōngdú read over (or through): ~《毛泽东选集》第五卷 read the fifth volume of the *Selected Works of Mao Zedong* from cover to cover

通读² tōngdú acquire a good knowledge of; have a good grasp of

通匪 tōngfěi collude (or collaborate) with bandit gangs

通分 tōngfēn *math.* reduction of fractions to a common denominator

通风 tōngfēng ① ventilate; aerate: 把窗子打开通通风。Open the windows to ventilate the room. or Open the windows to let in some fresh air. / ~降温 ventilation and cooling / ~装置 ventilation installation / ~管道 ventilating duct / 这屋里不~。This room is badly ventilated (or is stuffy). / 炉子不~。The stove doesn't draw well. ③ divulge information

通风报信 tōngfēng-bàoxìn furnish secret information; tip sb. off

通风机 tōngfēngjī ventilator; fanner

通风井 tōngfēngjǐng ventilation shaft; air shaft

通风口 tōngfēngkǒu air vent; vent

通告 tōnggào ① give public notice; announce ② public notice; announcement; circular

通共 tōnggòng *adv.* in all; altogether; all told: 我们~十八个人。There are eighteen of us altogether.

通古斯 Tōnggǔsī the Tunguses

通关节 tōng guānjié get round (laws, rules, etc.) by bribery

通过¹ tōngguò ① pass through; get past; traverse: 电流~导线。Electricity passes through the wires. / 路太窄，汽车通不过。The road is too narrow for cars to get by (or pass through). / 注意交通安全，一慢二看三~。Pay attention to traffic safety; slow down, look around and then go ahead. / 火车~大桥向南奔去。The train was crossing the bridge towards the south. / 游击队~了敌人的封锁线。The guerrillas managed to get through the enemy blockade. / 代表们~大厅进入会场。The delegates went through the lobby and into the assembly hall. or The delegates entered the assembly hall by way of the lobby. / 她~了入学考试。She's passed the entrance examination. / 我们要打开局面就必须~这一关。We must overcome this obstacle to open a new phase in our work. ② adopt; pass; carry: ~宪法 adopt a constitution / 以压倒多数~ be passed by an overwhelming majority / 这个提案已一致~。The motion was carried unanimously. / 我认为这议案未必通得过。I don't think the bill will get (or go) through. ③ ask the consent or approval of: 这个问题要~群众才能做出决定。No decision can be made on this matter until the masses have been consulted.

通过² tōngguò *prep.* by means of; by way of; by; through: ~什么方式我才能见到他？By what means can I meet him? / ~讨论取得一致 reach unanimity through discussion / 这位法国教授~译员同我进行了交谈。The French professor and I had a conversation through an interpreter. / ~老张介绍，我认识了她。I got to know her through Lao Zhang. / 植物~阳光照射，能把水和二氧化碳制成有机物质。Plants can turn water and carbon dioxide into organic substance by means of sunshine.

通航 tōngháng be open to navigation or air traffic: 北京与拉萨之间已~了。There is now air service between Beijing and Lhasa. / ~水域 navigable waters

通好 tōnghǎo *formal* (of nations) have friendly relations

通红 tōnghóng very red; red through and through: 孩子的脸冻得~。The child's face was bright red from the cold. / 她羞得满脸~。She blushed scarlet with shyness. / 高炉照得满天~。The sky was aglow with the fires of the blast furnaces.

通话 tōnghuà ① converse ② communicate by telephone

通话计时器 tōnghuà jìshíqì peg count meter

通婚 tōnghūn be (or become) related by marriage; intermarry

通货 tōnghuò *econ.* currency; current money

通货紧缩 tōnghuò jǐnsuō (of money) deflation

通货膨胀 tōnghuò péngzhàng (of money) inflation

通缉 tōngjī order the arrest of a criminal at large; list (sb.) as wanted; put (sb.) on the wanted list: 下~令 issue a wanted circular

通家 tōngjiā *formal* long and deep friendship between two families

通假 tōngjiǎ interchangeability of Chinese characters

通奸 tōngjiān commit adultery

通解 tōngjiě *formal* thoroughly understand; have a good knowledge of; be well versed in

通今博古 tōngjīn-bógǔ same as 博古通今 bógǔ-tōngjīn

通经 tōngjīng ① *Chin. med.* stimulate the menstrual flow (by emmenagogues or acupuncture) ② be well versed in Confucian classics

通栏 tōnglán the layout of a page of a book or a periodical without columns: ~标题 banner (or streamer) headline; banner

通览 tōnglǎn take an overall view of (a situation, etc.)

通礼 tōnglǐ established etiquette

通力 tōnglì put in a concerted effort: ～合作 make a concerted (or united) effort; give full cooperation to

通例 tōnglì ① general rule; usual practice: 星期天休息是学校的～。It is a general rule that schools close on Sundays. ② *formal* universal law

通连 tōnglián be connected; lead to: 浴室和卧室是～的。The bathroom is off the bedroom.

通联 tōnglián communications and liaison: ～工作 correspondence and liaison work

通亮 tōngliàng well-illuminated; brightly lit: 火光～。The flames lit up brightly. / 照明弹照得满天～。Star shells lit up the sky.

通量 tōngliàng *phys.* flux

通令 tōnglìng ① issue a circular (or general) order: ～各省 issue a general order to all provinces / ～嘉奖 issue an order of commendation ② circular (or general) order

通路 tōnglù ① thoroughfare; passageway; route: 将兵力集结于敌军必经的～两侧 concentrate forces on both sides of the route the enemy is sure to take ② way; channel

通论 tōnglùn ① a well-rounded argument ② (usu. used in book titles) a general survey:《地震学～》*General Seismology*

通脉 tōngmài *Chin. med.* ① promote blood circulation by invigorating vital energy ② promote lactation

通名 tōngmíng ① introduce oneself ② a general (or common) term

通明 tōngmíng well-illuminated; brightly lit: 灯火～ be ablaze with lights; be brightly lit

通年 tōngnián throughout the year; all the year round

通盘 tōngpán overall; all-round; comprehensive: ～计划 overall planning / ～估计 an all-round estimate / ～安排 a comprehensive arrangement / 把这个问题～研究一下 examine the question in its entirety

通票 tōngpiào through ticket

通铺 tōngpù same as 统铺 tǒngpù

通气 tōngqì ① ventilate; aerate: 粘土结构紧，不容易～。Clayey soils are dense and poorly aerated. ② be in touch (or communication) with each other; keep each other informed: 各单位要经常～。The various work units must keep in touch with each other. / 这件事你得跟他通个气。You should let him know of this matter.

通气孔 tōngqìkǒng air vent; vent

通窍 tōngqiào understand things; be sensible or reasonable: 道理讲得很明白，可他就是不～。The reason was explained to him clearly, but he couldn't see it.

通情 tōngqíng ① understanding and considerate; reasonable ② communicate the affection between a man and a woman

通情达理 tōngqíng-dálǐ showing good sense; understanding and reasonable; sensible: 群众是～的。The masses are reasonable. / ～地解决问题 solve a problem in a reasonable way

通衢 tōngqú *formal* thoroughfare

通权达变 tōngquán-dábiàn act as the occasion requires; adapt oneself to circumstances; follow a flexible course of action

通人 tōngrén *formal* a person of wide knowledge and sound scholarship

通融 tōng·róng ① stretch rules, get around regulations, etc., to accommodate sb.; make an exception in sb.'s favour: 这事可以～。We can make an exception in this case. ② accommodate sb. with a short-term loan: 我想跟你～二十块钱。I wonder if you can lend me 20 yuan.

通儒 tōngrú *old* an erudite scholar; a man of prodigious learning

通商 tōngshāng (of nations) have trade relations: 订立～条约 conclude a trade treaty; sign a treaty of commerce / ～口岸 trading port

通身 tōngshēn the whole body: ～是汗 sweat all over

通史 tōngshǐ comprehensive history; general history: 中国～ general history of China

通式 tōngshì *chem.* general formula

通事 tōngshì *old* interpreter

通书 tōngshū almanac

通顺 tōngshùn (of writing) clear and coherent; smooth: 文理～ coherent writing / 这个句子不～。This sentence doesn't read smoothly.

通俗 tōngsú popular; common: ～易懂 easy to understand / 拿一句～的话来讲 to use a common expression / 用～的语言说明深刻的道理 expound a profound truth in simple language

通俗读物 tōngsú dúwù books for popular consumption; popular literature

通俗化 tōngsúhuà popularize

通泰 tōngtài refreshed; relieved

通体 tōngtǐ the entire body or mass: 水晶～透明。Crystal is entirely transparent. / ～寒栗 shudder all over

通天 tōngtiān ① exceedingly high or great: ～的本事 exceptional ability; superhuman skill / 罪恶～ be guilty of monstrous crimes ② direct access to the highest authorities

通条 tōngtiáo ① (stove) poker ② cleaning rod (for a gun)

通通 tōngtōng *adv.* all; entirely; completely: 唱片～卖完了。The discs are all sold out. / ～拿去吧。Take away the lot. *or* Take them all. / ～到了吗? Is everybody here? *or* Are we (you) all here?

通同 tōngtóng collude; gang up: ～作弊 act fraudulently in collusion with sb.; gang up to cheat

通统 tōngtǒng same as 通通 tōngtōng

通透 tōngtòu penetrating; thorough

通途 tōngtú *formal* thoroughfare: 一桥飞架南北，天堑变～。(毛泽东) A bridge will fly to span the north and south, Turning a deep chasm into a thoroughfare.

通脱 tōngtuō *formal* not bother about trifles; be unconventional

通脱木 tōngtuōmù *bot.* rice-paper plant (*Tetrapanax papyriferus*)

通显 tōngxiǎn *formal* hold high office

通宵 tōngxiāo all night; the whole night; throughout the night: 干了个～ work all night / ～值班 on duty all night / ～服务部 a shop that is open all night; an all-night shop

通宵达旦 tōngxiāo-dádàn all night long; all through the night

通晓 tōngxiǎo thoroughly understand; be well versed in; be proficient in: ～几种文字 have a good command of several languages / ～中国历史 have a good knowledge of Chinese history; be well versed in Chinese history

通心粉 tōngxīnfěn macaroni

通信 tōngxìn communicate by letter; correspond: 他经常跟我们～。He often writes to us. / 我们好久没有～了。We haven't corresponded for a long time.

通信保密 tōngxìn bǎomì *mil.* communication (or traffic) security

通信兵 tōngxìnbīng ① signal corps (or unit, troops) ② signalman

通信处 tōngxìnchù mailing address

通信鸽 tōngxìngē homing pigeon; carrier pigeon

通信连 tōngxìnlián *mil.* signal company

通信联络 tōngxìn liánluò *mil.* signal communication;

communications and liaison

通信犬 tōngxìnquǎn messenger dog

通信枢纽 tōngxìn shūniǔ signal (*or* communication) centre

通信卫星 tōngxìn wèixīng communications satellite; telecommunication satellite

通信员 tōngxìnyuán messenger; orderly

通行 tōngxíng ① pass (*or* go) through: 自由～ can pass freely; have free passage / 道路泥泞, 卡车无法～。The road was too muddy for trucks. / 没有特别通行证, 一律不准～。Nobody is allowed through without a special pass. / 停止～ closed to traffic / 此巷不～ Blind Alley; Dead End; No Thoroughfare ② current; general: 这是全国～的办法。This is the current practice throughout the country. / 这项规定在一些地区仍然～。This regulation is still in force in some districts.

通行费 tōngxíngfèi toll

通行能力 tōngxíng nénglì traffic capacity

通行权 tōngxíngquán right of way

通行税 tōngxíngshuì transit duty

通行证 tōngxíngzhèng pass; permit; safe-conduct; laissez-passer: 边境～ border pass / 军事～ military pass / 临时～ provisional pass

通性 tōngxìng general character; generality

通宿 tōngxiǔ all night; the whole night; throughout the night

通学生 tōngxuéshēng *old* day student; nonresident student

通讯 tōngxùn ① communication: 无线电～ radio (*or* wireless) communication / 红外线～ infrared ray communication / 微波～ microwave communication / 激光～ laser communication / ～方法 means of communication / ～设备 communication apparatus (*or* equipment) ② news report; news dispatch; correspondence; newsletter: 新华社～ Xinhua dispatches / ～报导 news report; news dispatch; news story / ～文学 reportage

通讯录 tōngxùnlù address book

通讯社 tōngxùnshè news agency; news (*or* press) service: 新华～ Xinhua News Agency

通讯网 tōngxùnwǎng communication network

通讯线路 tōngxùn xiànlù communication line

通讯员 tōngxùnyuán reporter; (press) correspondent

通夜 tōngyè all night; the whole night; throughout the night: ～不眠 lie awake all night

通译 tōngyì *old* ① interpret ② interpreter

通用 tōngyòng ① in common use; current; general: ～语种 commonly used languages / 国际会议～的语言 languages used at international conferences / 全国～教材 national textbooks ② interchangeable: 这两个字可以～。These two words are interchangeable.

通用货币 tōngyòng huòbì current money

通用机械厂 tōngyòng jīxièchǎng universal machine works

通用月票 tōngyòng yuèpiào a monthly ticket for all urban and suburban lines

通邮 tōngyóu accessible by postal communication

通则 tōngzé general rule

通知 tōngzhī ① notify; inform; give notice: 请马上～他。Please notify him immediately. *or* Please let him know at once. / 请把我们的决定～他。Please inform him of our decision. / 将集合地点～大家。Notify everyone of the place of assembly. / 预先～ give advance notice ② notice; circular: 发出～ send out (*or* dispatch) a notice / 《中共中央～》 Circular of the CPC Central Committee

通知书 tōngzhīshū ① notice: 终止条约～ notice of termination of a treaty; notice of denunciation ② *com.* advice note

通直 tōngzhí perfectly straight; straight as a ramrod; bolt upright

tóng

仝
同

tóng same as 同 tóng

同 tóng ① same; alike; similar: ～年级 of the same grade ② be the same as: "鎚"～"锤"。鎚 is the same as 锤。③ *adv.* together; in common: 和工人～吃, ～住, ～劳动 eat, live and work together with the workers; live with the workers, eat the same food and join them in physical labour / 我们两国～属第三世界。Both our countries belong to the Third World. ④ *prep.* (used to indicate accompaniment, relationship, involvement, etc.) with: 我～你一起去。I'll go with you. / 这～你没有关系。This has nothing to do with you. / 这件事～他有牵连。He was implicated in the affair. ⑤ *prep.* (used to introduce the recipient of an action): 他上午来～我告别了。He came to say good-bye to me this morning. / 他～我商量下一步该怎么办。He consulted with me about what we should do next. ⑥ *prep.* (used to show comparison): 恶霸地主～豺狼一样凶恶。The despotic landlords were as ferocious as wolves. / ～去年相比, 产量增加了百分之二十。Output has increased by 20% over last year. / 湖面～明镜一样清澈。The limpid lake is like a mirror. ⑦ *dial.* for: 这封信我一直～你保存着。I've kept this letter for you all this time. / 别着急, 我～你想个办法。Don't worry. I'll find a way out for you. ⑧ *conj.* and: 老师～学生 teachers and students ——see also tòng

同班 tóngbān ① be in the same class: ～同学 classmate ② classmate

同伴 tóngbàn companion

同胞 tóngbāo ① born of the same parents: ～兄弟 (姐妹) full brothers (sisters) ② fellow countryman; compatriot: 台湾～ our compatriots in Taiwan

同辈 tóngbèi of the same generation

同病相怜 tóng bìng xiāng lián those who have the same illness sympathize with each other——fellow sufferers commiserate with each other

同步 tóngbù ① *phys.* synchronism: 载波～ carrier synchronization ② in step with; in pace with: ～增长 grow in step with; grow in pace with

同步电动机 tóngbù diàndòngjī *elec.* synchronous motor

同步回旋加速器 tóngbù huíxuán jiāsùqì *phys.* synchrocyclotron

同步加速器 tóngbù jiāsùqì *phys.* synchrotron

同步卫星 tóngbù wèixīng short for 地球同步卫星 dìqiú tóngbù wèixīng

同侪 tóngchái *formal* of the same generation

同仇敌忾 tóngchóu-díkài share a bitter hatred of the enemy; be bound by a common hatred for the enemy

同窗 tóngchuāng ① study in the same school ② schoolmate

同床异梦 tóngchuáng-yìmèng share the same bed but dream different dreams——be strange bedfellows

同党 tóngdǎng ① belong to the same political faction or party ② fellow member of a political faction or party

同道 tóngdào ① people cherishing the same ideals and following the same path; people having a common goal ② people of the same trade or occupation

同等 tóngděng of the same class, rank, or status; on an equal basis (*or* footing): ～重要 of equal importance / ～对待 put on an equal footing

同等学力 tóngděng xuélì　the same educational level: 具有～ have the same educational level (as graduates or a certain grade of students)

同调 tóngdiào　people having the same aspiration and interest; people engaged in the same pursuit

同恶相济 tóng è xiāng jì (*also* 同恶相求 tóng è xiāng qiú) the wicked help the wicked

同犯 tóngfàn　accomplice

同房[1] tóngfáng　*euph.* (of husband and wife) sleep together; have sexual intercourse

同房[2] tóngfáng　of the same branch of a family

同分异构体 tóngfēnyìgòutǐ　*chem.* isomer

同甘共苦 tónggān-gòngkǔ　share weal and woe (*or* comforts and hardships, joys and sorrows): ～的战友 comrades-in-arms sharing weal and woe; fellow fighters through thick and thin / 与人民群众～ share the comforts and hardships of the masses

同感 tónggǎn　the same feeling (*or* impression): 老张认为这部小说的人物写得很成功, 我也有～。Lao Zhang feels—and so do I—that the characters of this novel are very well drawn.

同庚 tónggēng　*formal* of the same age

同工同酬 tónggōng-tóngchóu　equal pay for equal work; equal remuneration for work of equal value: 男女应当～。Men and women should enjoy equal pay for equal work.

同工异曲 tónggōng-yìqǔ　same as 异曲同工 yìqǔ-tónggōng

同功酶 tónggōngméi　*biochem.* isoenzyme

同归 tóngguī　reach the same goal: 殊途同归 shū tú tóngguī

同归于尽 tóng guī yú jìn　perish together; end up in common ruin

同行 tóngháng　① of the same trade or occupation ② people of the same trade or occupation ——see also 同行 tóngxíng

同好 tónghào　people having similar interests or tastes: 公诸同好 gōng zhū tónghào

同呼吸, 共命运 tóng hūxī, gòng mìngyùn　share a common fate; throw in one's lot with sb.

同化 tónghuà　① assimilate (ethnic groups, etc.) ② *phonet.* assimilation

同化政策 tónghuà zhèngcè　the policy of national assimilation (as pursued by reactionary rulers)

同化作用 tónghuà zuòyòng　*biol.* assimilation

同伙 tónghuǒ　① work in partnership; collude (in doing evil) ② partner; confederate

同居 tóngjū　① live together: 父母死后, 他和叔父～。After his parents died, he lived with his uncle. ② cohabit

同类 tónglèi　of the same kind

同僚 tóngliáo　*old* colleague; fellow official

同龄 tónglíng　of the same age or about the same age: 他和我～。He is my contemporary. / 和新中国～ born in the same year as the New China

同龄人 tónglíngrén　contemporary

同流合污 tóngliú-héwū　wallow in the mire with sb.; associate with an evil person; go along with sb. in his evil deeds

同路 tónglù　go the same way: 咱俩～, 一块儿走吧。Come along with me. I'm going that way too.

同路人 tónglùrén　fellow traveller

同门 tóngmén　*formal* ① study under the same master ② fellow disciples

同盟 tóngméng　alliance; league: 结成～ form (*or* enter into) an alliance

同盟罢工 tóngméng bàgōng　joint strike

同盟国 tóngméngguó　① ally; allied nations ② the Central Powers (during World War Ⅰ) ③ the Allies (during World War Ⅱ)

同盟会 Tóngménghuì　short for 中国同盟会 Zhōngguó Tóngménghuì

同盟军 tóngméngjūn　allied forces; allies

同盟条约 tóngméng tiáoyuē　treaty of alliance

同名 tóngmíng　of the same title or name: 根据～小说摄制的电影 a film based on a novel of the same name / 他与我～。He is my namesake.

同谋 tóngmóu　① conspire (with sb.) ② confederate; accomplice

同谋犯 tóngmóufàn　*leg.* accessory: 事前～ accessory before the fact / 事后～ accessory after the fact

同年 tóngnián　① the same year: ～九月大桥竣工。The bridge was completed in September of the same year. ② *dial.* of the same age ③ candidates who passed the imperial examinations in the same year

同袍 tóngpáo　① same as 袍泽 páozé ② intimate friend; bosom friend

同期 tóngqī　① the corresponding period: 他们第一季度的钢产量超过了历史～的最高水平。Their steel output in the first quarter of the year was higher than their previous record for the period. ② the same term (in school, etc.): 我和他～毕业。I graduated the same time as he.

同前 tóngqián　ditto; idem

同衾共枕 tóngqīn-gòngzhěn　(of husband and wife) share the same quilt and pillow—sleep together

同情 tóngqíng　sympathize with; show sympathy for: 博得～ win sympathy / 我很～你。I heartily sympathize with you. *or* I have every sympathy for you.

同情罢工 tóngqíng bàgōng　sympathetic strike; strike in sympathy

同情心 tóngqíngxīn　sympathy; fellow feeling

同人 tóngrén　(also 同仁 tóngrén) colleagues

同上 tóngshàng　ditto; idem

同生死, 共患难 tóng shēngsǐ, gòng huànnàn　share weal and woe

同声 tóngshēng　in chorus; in unison: ～欢呼 cheer in unison / ～呼喊 shout in chorus (*or* in unison)

同声传译 tóngshēng chuányì　simultaneous interpretation: 有七种语言的～设备 be provided with facilities for simultaneous interpretation in seven languages

同声相应, 同气相求 tóng shēng xiāng yìng, tóng qì xiāng qiú　like attracts like

同时 tóngshí　① at the same time; simultaneously; meanwhile; in the meantime: ～发生 happen at the same time; coincide; concur / ～存在 exist simultaneously; exist side by side; coexist / 我们在加快工程进度的～, 必须注意质量。While speeding up the work on the project, we must pay attention to ensuring its quality. ② *conj.* moreover; besides; furthermore: 任务艰巨, ～时间又很紧迫。The task is arduous; besides, there's not much time. / 造林可以保持水土, ～也可以制止流沙。Afforestation conserves soil and water; it also checks drift sand.

同事 tóngshì　① work in the same place; work together: 我们～已经多年。We've worked together for years. / 我和他同过事。He and I have been colleagues before. ② colleague; fellow worker: 老～ an old colleague

同室操戈 tóng shì cāo gē　members of one family drawing swords on each other—fratricidal strife; internal strife; internecine feud

同素异形 tóngsù yìxíng　*chem.* allotropy: ～体 allotrope; allotropic substance

同岁 tóngsuì　① of the same age: 我们两人～。We two are the same age. ② same as 同年 tóngnián③

同榻 tóngtà　*formal* sleep in the same bed; share a bed

同位角 tóngwèijiǎo　*math.* corresponding angles

同位素 tóngwèisù *chem.* isotope: 放射性～ radioisotope / ～分离 isotope separation / ～扫描器 radioisotope scanner / ～探伤仪 isoscope

同位语 tóngwèiyǔ *gram.* appositive

同温层 tóngwēncéng old name for 平流层 píngliúcéng

同屋 tóngwū ① share a room ② roommate

同系物 tóngxìwù *chem.* homologue

同乡 tóngxiāng a person from the same village, town or province; a fellow villager, townsman or provincial

同乡会 tóngxiānghuì *old* an association of fellow provincials or townsmen

同心 tóngxīn ① concentric ② with one heart: ～干 work with one heart; fight as one man

同心度 tóngxīndù *mech.* concentricity

同心同德 tóngxīn-tóngdé be of one heart and one mind; be dedicated to the same cause: 广大军民～，坚决打败侵略者。The broad masses of people and armymen fought staunchly with one heart and one mind to defeat the aggressors.

同心协力 tóngxīn-xiélì work in full cooperation and with unity of purpose; work together with one heart; make concerted efforts

同心圆 tóngxīnyuán *math.* concentric circles

同行 tóngxíng travel together ——see also tónghǎng

同性 tóngxìng ① of the same sex ② of the same nature or character: ～的电互相排斥。Two like electric charges repel each other.

同性恋爱 tóngxìng liàn'ài (also 同性恋 tóngxìngliàn) homosexuality: 他搞～。He's homosexual.

同姓 tóngxìng of the same surname: 他与我～。He is my namesake.

同学 tóngxué ① be in the same school; be a schoolmate of sb.: 我和他同过三年学。I studied in the same school with him for three years. ② fellow student; schoolmate ③ a form of address used in speaking to a student

同砚 tóngyàn *old* fellow student; schoolmate

同样 tóngyàng same; equal; similar: ～的方法 the same method / ～情况下 under similar circumstances / ～地懂得 know equally well / 他说英语和法语～流利。He speaks English and French with equal fluency. / 对中国古代的文化，我们要吸收其中有益的东西，～，对外国的也应如此。We should assimilate whatever is beneficial in ancient Chinese culture, and deal with foreign culture likewise.

同业 tóngyè ① the same trade or business ② a person of the same trade or business

同业公会 tóngyè gōnghuì *old* trade council; trade association; guild

同一 tóngyī same; identical: 向～目标前进 advance towards the same goal / 抱～观点的人 those who hold identical views

同一律 tóngyīlǜ *log.* the law of identity

同一性 tóngyīxìng *philos.* identity

同义词 tóngyìcí synonym

同意 tóngyì agree; consent; approve: 我的意见你～吗？Do you agree with me? / 他～这项建议。He consented to the proposal. / 父母不～我的婚事。My parents don't approve of my marriage. / 征求对大使提名的～ request for agreement to the nomination of an ambassador / 表示～前一位发言人的意见 express agreement with the previous speaker

同音词 tóngyīncí homonym; homophone

同寅 tóngyín ① same as 同僚 tóngliáo ② *dial.* of the same age

同余 tóngyú *math.* congruence: ～数 congruent numbers

同源多倍体 tóngyuánduōbèitǐ *biol.* autopolyploid

同志 tóngzhì comrade: 李～ Comrade Li / ～们辛苦了。You comrades have been working hard. / 致以～的敬礼 with comradely greetings

同种 tóngzhǒng of the same race

同舟共济 tóng zhōu gòng jì cross a river in the same boat—pull together in times of trouble

同轴 tóngzhóu *elec.* coaxial: ～电缆 coaxial cable

同宗 tóngzōng of the same clan; have common ancestry: 同姓不～ of the same surname, but not the same clan

同族 tóngzú ① same as 同宗 tóngzōng ② same as 同种 tóngzhǒng

佟

佟 Tóng a surname

彤

彤 tóng *liter.* red

彤云 tóngyún *liter.* ① red clouds ② dark clouds: ～密布。Dark clouds were gathering. *or* The sky was overcast.

苘

苘 tóng see below

苘蒿 tónghāo *bot.* crowndaisy chrysanthemum

砼

砼 tóng concrete

桐

桐 tóng *bot.* ① paulownia ② Chinese parasol (tree); phoenix tree ③ tung oil tree; tung tree

桐油 tóngyóu tung oil

桐油树 tóngyóushù common name for 油桐 yóutóng

桐子 tóngzǐ seeds of a tung oil tree

铜

铜 tóng *chem.* copper (Cu)

铜氨液 tóng'ānyè cuprammonia

铜铵人造丝 tóng'ǎn rénzàosī *text.* cuprammonium (or copper) rayon

铜板 tóngbǎn *dial.* copper coin; copper

铜版 tóngbǎn *print.* copperplate

铜版画 tóngbǎnhuà copperplate etching (or engraving); copperplate

铜版印刷 tóngbǎn yìnshuā copperplate printing

铜版印刷机 tóngbǎn yìnshuājī copperplate press; etching press

铜版纸 tóngbǎnzhǐ art (printing) paper

铜币 tóngbì copper coin; copper

铜臭 tóngchòu the stink of money—profits-before-everything mentality: 满身～ stinking (or filthy) with money; filthy rich

铜鼓 tónggǔ bronze drum

铜管乐 tóngguǎnyuè music for or played by a brass band

铜管乐队 tóngguǎn yuèduì brass band

铜管乐器 tóngguǎn yuèqì brass-wind instrument; brass instrument; brass wind; brass

铜壶滴漏 tónghú dīlòu *archaeol.* copper clepsydra

铜活 tónghuó ① brass or copper fittings, accessories, etc. ② work in copper; coppersmithing

铜匠 tóngjiang coppersmith

铜筋铁骨 tóngjīn-tiěgǔ copper muscles and iron bones—strongly built; robust

铜镜 tóngjìng *archaeol.* bronze mirror

铜扣子 tóngkòuzi brass button

铜蓝 tónglán *min.* covellite; indigo copper

铜绿 tónglǜ *chem.* verdigris

铜模 tóngmú *print.* matrix; (copper) mould

铜模雕刻机 tóngmú diāokèjī matrix cutting machine

铜牌 tóngpái bronze medal; bronze

铜器 tóngqì bronze, brass or copper ware

铜器时代 Tóngqì Shídài the Bronze Age

铜钱 tóngqián copper cash

铜墙铁壁 tóngqiáng-tiěbì a bastion of iron—an impreg-

nable fortress

铜丝 tóngsī copper wire

铜钿 tóngtián *dial.* ① copper coin; copper ② money

铜像 tóngxiàng bronze statue

铜元 tóngyuán (also 铜圆 tóngyuán) copper coin; copper

铜子儿 tóngzǐr *inf.* copper coin; copper

童¹

tóng ① child: 顽童 wántóng ② virgin: 童男 tóngnán / 童女 tóngnǚ ③ bare; bald: 童山 tóngshān ④ (Tóng) a surname

童²(僮)

tóng *old* boy servant: 书童 shū-tóng

童骏 tóng'ái *formal* young and ignorant

童便 tóngbiàn *Chin. med.* boys' urine (the urine of boys under 12, used in cases of hemorrhage and extravasated blood)

童工 tónggōng ① child labour ② child labourer

童话 tónghuà children's stories; fairy tales

童婚 tónghūn child marriage

童伶 tónglíng boy actor (in traditional opera)

童蒙 tóngméng *formal* childish ignorance

童男 tóngnán virgin boy

童年 tóngnián childhood

童女 tóngnǚ maiden; virgin

童仆 tóngpú *formal* ① houseboys ② menservants; servants

童山 tóngshān bare hills: ～秃岭 bare hills and mountains

童山濯濯 tóngshān zhuózhuó bare and barren hills; hills denuded of vegetation

童生 tóngshēng (in Ming and Qing times) a scholar without a *xiucai* (秀才) degree

童声 tóngshēng child's voice: ～合唱 children's chorus

童叟 tóng-sǒu children and old men—the old and the young

童叟无欺 tóng-sǒu wú qī (a shop sign) neither old nor young cheated (i.e. honest with all customers)

童心 tóngxīn child's heart; childlike innocence

童心未泯 tóngxīn wèi mǐn (of a grown-up, esp. an aged person) still preserve traces of childishness or childlike innocence

童星 tóngxīng a child film (*or* movie) star

童颜鹤发 tóngyán-hèfà same as 鹤发童颜 hèfà-tóngyán

童养媳 tóngyǎngxí a girl taken into the family as a daughter-in-law-to-be; child daughter-in-law; child bride

童谣 tóngyáo children's folk rhymes

童贞 tóngzhēn virginity (esp. of a woman); chastity

童真 tóngzhēn child's simplicity or innocence

童稚 tóngzhì ① child ② child's naivety

童装 tóngzhuāng children's wear (*or* clothing)

童子 tóngzǐ boy; lad

童子鸡 tóngzǐjī *dial.* young chicken; broiler

童子军 tóngzǐjūn boy scouts

童子痨 tóngzǐláo *Chin. med.* ① pulmonary tuberculosis suffered by children ② general debility caused by chronic diseases

酮

tóng *chem.* ketone

酮化 tónghuà *chem.* ketonize

瞳

tóng pupil (of the eye)

瞳孔 tóngkǒng *physiol.* pupil: 放大～ have one's pupils dilated

瞳孔开大 tóngkǒng kāidà *med.* mydriasis

瞳孔缩小 tóngkǒng suōxiǎo *med.* myosis

瞳人 tóngrén (also 瞳仁 tóngrén) common name for 瞳

孔 tóngkǒng

tǒng

统¹

tǒng ① interconnected system: 传统 chuán-tǒng / 系统 xìtǒng ② gather into one; unite: 由老李～管 be under Lao Li's overall leadership ③ *adv.* all; together: 这些东西～归你用。You have all these things at your disposal.

统²

tǒng any tube-shaped part of an article of clothing, etc: 皮统子 pítǒngzi

统舱 tǒngcāng steerage (passenger accommodation): ～旅客 steerage passenger / 坐～ travel steerage

统称 tǒngchēng ① be called by a joint name: 武昌、汉口和汉阳常～为武汉。The cities of Wuchang, Hankou and Hanyang are often referred to as Wuhan. ② a general designation; a general term (*or* name)

统筹 tǒngchóu plan as a whole: ～全局 take the whole situation into account and plan accordingly / ～规划 overall planning

统筹兼顾 tǒngchóu-jiāngù unified planning with due consideration for all concerned; making overall plans and taking all factors into consideration: ～、全面安排的方针 the policy of overall consideration and all-round arrangement / 根据～的原则安排劳动就业 provide employment in accordance with the principle of overall consideration

统带 tǒngdài ① command ② a regiment commander (in the Qing Dynasty)

统共 tǒnggòng *adv.* altogether; in all: 我们小组～七个人。There are altogether seven people in our group.

统购统销 tǒnggòu tǒngxiāo state monopoly for purchase and marketing (of grain, cotton, etc.)

统计 tǒngjì ① statistics: ～资料 statistical data / 据不完全～ according to incomplete statistics (*or* figures) ② add up; count: ～出席人数 count up the number of people present (at a meeting, etc.) / 将图书分类整理并加以～ have the books classified, arranged in order and counted

统计地图 tǒngjì dìtú statistical map

统计力学 tǒngjì lìxué statistical mechanics

统计数字 tǒngjì shùzì statistical figures; statistics: 这些～很说明问题。These statistics throw a lot of light on the matter. *or* These statistics are very eloquent.

统计图表 tǒngjì túbiǎo statistical graph (*or* chart, table)

统计推断 tǒngjì tuīduàn *math.* statistical inference

统计学 tǒngjìxué statistics (a science): ～家 statistician

统计员 tǒngjìyuán statistician

统考 tǒngkǎo (short for 统一考试) a general examination with a common test paper for all students from different schools

统领 tǒnglǐng ① command; lead ② commander; leader

统铺 tǒngpù a wide bed for a number of people (as in barracks, hostels, etc.)

统摄 tǒngshè *formal* have under one's command; exercise control over; govern

统属 tǒngshǔ subordination: 彼此不相～。Neither is subordinate to the other.

统帅 tǒngshuài ① commander in chief; commander ② command

统帅部 tǒngshuàibù supreme command

统率 tǒngshuài command: 中国共产党中央委员会主席～全国武装力量。The Chairman of the Central Committee of the Communist Party of China commands the country's armed forces.

统统 tǒngtǒng *adv.* all; entirely; completely: 把杂草～除掉 get rid of all the weeds / ～讲出来 make a clean breast of it

统辖 tǒngxiá have under one's command; exercise control over; govern

统一 tǒngyī ① unify; unite; integrate: ～思想 seek unity of thinking; reach a common understanding / ～行动 seek unity of action; coordinate actions; act in unison / 把理论同实践～起来 integrate theory with practice / ～度量衡 standardize the system of weights and measures / 完成～祖国的神圣事业 accomplish the sacred task of unifying the country / 革命的政治内容和尽可能完美的艺术形式的～ the unity of revolutionary political content and the highest possible perfection of artistic form / 大家的意见逐渐～了。People gradually reached unanimity of opinion. *or* A consensus gradually emerged. / 我们的意见在有些方面不～。Our views differ in several ways. / 秦始皇于公元前二二一年～中国。The First Emperor of Qin unified China in 221 B.C. ② unified; unitary; centralized: ～(的)领导 unified leadership / ～(的)计划 unified planning / ～(的)分配 unified (*or* centralized) distribution; centralized placement (of college graduates, etc.) / ～的意见 consensus of opinion / ～的多民族的国家 a unitary multi-national state

统一体 tǒngyītǐ *philos.* entity; unity

统一性 tǒngyīxìng *philos.* unity

统一战线 tǒngyī zhànxiàn united front

统御 tǒngyù (also 统驭 tǒngyù) *formal* control; rule

统战 tǒngzhàn short for 统一战线 tǒngyī zhànxiàn

统治 tǒngzhì rule; dominate: 反动～ reactionary rule / 占～地位 occupy a dominant position / 国家是阶级的机关。The state is an organ of class domination. / ～者 ruler

统治阶级 tǒngzhìjiējí ruling class

统制 tǒngzhì control: 严格～军用物资 exercise strict control over military supplies / 经济～ economic control

捅（搧） tǒng ① poke; stab: 在硬纸盒上～个洞 poke a hole in the cardboard box / 把炉子～～ give the fire a poke / 用刺刀～ stab with a bayonet ② touch; push; nudge: 他用胳膊肘～了我一下。He gave me a nudge. ③ disclose; give away; let out: 谁把秘密给～出去了? Who gave away (*or* let out) the secret? / 他是个直性子, 把看到的事儿都～出来了。He's a straightforward man, and told everything he'd seen.

捅咕 tǒnggu ① touch; push; nudge ② instigate; incite

捅娄子 tǒng lóuzi get (oneself or others) into trouble through a blunder; make a blunder; make a mess of sth.

捅马蜂窝 tǒng mǎfēngwō stir up a hornet's nest; bring a hornets' nest about one's ears

桶 tǒng ① tub; pail; bucket; keg; barrel: 汽油～ petrol drum / 一～牛奶 a pail of milk / ～装啤酒 barrelled beer; draught beer ② barrel (of petroleum)

筒（筩） tǒng ① a section of thick bamboo: 竹筒 zhútǒng ② a thick tube-shaped object: 笔筒 bǐtǒng / 邮筒 yóutǒng ③ any tube-shaped part of an article of clothing, etc.: 袜筒 wàtǒng

筒管 tǒngguǎn *text.* bobbin

筒状花 tǒngzhuànghuā *bot.* tubular flower

筒子 tǒngzi tube or tube-shaped object: 枪～ barrel of a gun

tòng

同 tòng see 胡同儿 hútòngr ——see also tóng

恸（慟） tòng *formal* deep sorrow; grief: 大～ weep (*or* cry) bitterly; wail

恸哭 tòngkū wail; cry one's heart out

通 tòng *m.* ① a complete course or spell of activity in playing certain musical instruments: 擂鼓三～ beat the drum in three rolls / 唢呐已经吹过两～。The *suona* horn has blared in two rounds. ② (used after the numeral 一) an instance of doing sth. unpleasant: 胡说一～ talk as much nonsense as one likes / 闹了一～ kick up a row / 乱讲一～ make irresponsible remarks / 发一～牢骚 give out a torrent of grumbles / 挨一～骂 get a dressing down / 说了他一～ give him a talking-to / 借机大做了一～文章 seize upon the matter and make an issue of ——see also tōng

通红 tònghóng same as 通红 tōnghóng

痛 tòng ① ache; pain: 肚子～ have a stomachache / 嗓子～ have a sore throat / 觉得很～ feel a great deal of pain / ～不～? Does it hurt? ② sadness; sorrow: 悲痛 bēitòng ③ extremely; deeply; bitterly: 痛哭 tòngkū

痛痹 tòngbì same as 寒痹 hánbì

痛不欲生 tòng bù yù shēng be so grieved as to wish one were dead

痛陈 tòngchén state or present in strong terms: ～民间疾苦 give an accusing account of the people's sufferings

痛斥 tòngchì bitterly attack; scathingly denounce: ～谬论 sharply denounce a fallacy

痛楚 tòngchǔ pain; anguish; suffering

痛处 tòngchù sore spot; tender spot: 触及～ touch sb.'s sore spot; touch sb. on the raw

痛打 tòngdǎ give a good thrashing; beat soundly

痛悼 tòngdào mourn with deep grief

痛定思痛 tòng dìng sī tòng recall a painful experience; draw a lesson from a bitter experience

痛风 tòngfēng *med.* gout

痛改前非 tòng gǎi qiánfēi sincerely mend one's ways; thoroughly rectify one's errors

痛感 tònggǎn keenly feel: ～自己知识不足 keenly feel one's lack of knowledge

痛恨 tònghèn hate bitterly; utterly detest

痛悔 tònghuǐ bitterly repent; deeply regret; be filled with remorse

痛击 tòngjī deal a severe blow; deliver a telling blow

痛歼 tòngjiān wipe out; annihilate

痛经 tòngjīng *med.* dysmenorrhoea

痛觉 tòngjué *physiol.* sense of pain

痛哭 tòngkū cry (*or* weep) bitterly; wail: ～一场 have a good cry / ～失声 be choked with tears

痛哭流涕 tòngkū liútì weep bitter tears; cry one's heart out: 他～, 表示愿意改正错误。He wept bitter tears of remorse, saying he would mend his ways.

痛苦 tòngkǔ pain; suffering; agony: 我得离开老家, 感到很～。It pains me to have to leave my old home. / 关心病人的～ be concerned about the sufferings of the patient / 精神上的～ mental agony

痛快 tòngkuai ① very happy; delighted; joyful: 看见麦子堆成了山, 心里真～ be delighted at the sight of a mountain of wheat / 感到从来没有过的～ be filled with joy as never before / 图一时的～ seek momentary gra-

tification / 今天遇到了一件不～的事。I had an unpleasant experience today. ② to one's heart's content; to one's great satisfaction: 喝个～ drink one's fill / 玩个～ have a wonderful time / 这个澡洗得真～。I had a very refreshing bath. ③ simple and direct; forthright; straightforward: 说话很～ speak simply and directly; not mince matters / 她这人～，心里有什么就说什么。She is frank and says what's on her mind. / 他～地答应了。He readily agreed. / 你当时认为那不公平，为什么没有痛痛快快地说呢? If you thought that wasn't fair, why didn't you speak up?

痛快淋漓 tòngkuai línlí　impassioned and forceful

痛骂 tòngmà　severely scold; roundly curse

痛切 tòngqiè　with intense sorrow; most sorrowfully: ～反省 examine oneself with feelings of deep remorse

痛诉 tòngsù　give a bitter account

痛恶 tòngwù　bitterly detest; abhor: 他的两面派行为令人～。His double-dealing was disgusting.

痛惜 tòngxī　deeply regret; deplore: 我们都为失去一个好同志而感到～。We all deeply regretted the loss of such a good comrade.

痛心 tòngxīn　pained; distressed; grieved: 这样浪费粮食令人～。It is distressing to see food being wasted like this. / 他对自己的错误感到很～。He keenly regretted his mistake.

痛心疾首 tòngxīn-jíshǒu　with bitter hatred: 他～地说: "我上了这个坏家伙的当。" "I was duped by that villain!" he said, his voice filled with hate.

痛痒 tòngyǎng　① sufferings; difficulties: 关心群众的～ be concerned with the well-being of the masses ② (usu. used in the negative) importance; consequence: 无关痛痒 wúguān tòngyǎng

痛痒相关 tòngyǎng xiāng guān　share a common lot

痛饮 tòngyǐn　drink one's fill; drink to one's heart's content

痛饮黄龙 tòngyǐn Huánglóng　hold victory celebrations at a conquered enemy stronghold ——see also 直捣黄龙 zhídǎo Huánglóng

痛阈 tòngyù　*med.* threshold of pain

痛责 tòngzé　severely rebuke; castigate

衕

tòng　see. 衚衕 hútòng

tōu

偷[1]

tōu　① steal; pilfer; make off with : 有人把我的雨衣～走了。Someone has made off with my raincoat. ② stealthily; secretly; on the sly: 他没跟人说就～着跑了。He sneaked off without telling anyone. ③ find (time): 偷空 tōukòng

偷[2]（媮）

tōu　drift along: 偷安 tōu'ān

偷安 tōu'ān　seek temporary ease: 苟且偷安 gǒuqiě-tōu'ān

偷盗 tōudào　steal; pilfer

偷渡 tōudù　slip out of a blockade in a water area; run a blockade

偷惰 tōuduò　*formal* loaf on the job; be idle; be indolent

偷工减料 tōugōng-jiǎnliào　do shoddy work and use inferior material; scamp work and stint material; jerry-build

偷汉子 tōu hànzi　(also 偷汉 tōuhàn) (of a married woman) have illicit relations with a man; commit adultery

偷合苟容 tōu hé gǒu róng　toady to sb. for mere survival

偷换 tōuhuàn　substitute one thing for another surreptitiously: ～概念 play tricks with concepts

偷鸡不着蚀把米 tōu jī bùzháo shí bǎ mǐ　try to steal a chicken only to end up losing the rice; go for wool and come back shorn

偷鸡摸狗 tōujī-mōgǒu　① steal chickens and dogs—pilfer ② (of a man) always having affairs with women

偷奸取巧 tōujiān-qǔqiǎo　seize every chance to gain advantage by trickery; be opportunistic

偷看 tōukàn　steal a glance; peek; peep: 捂上眼睛，别～。Cover your eyes and don't peek. / 从门背后～某人 take a peep at sb. from behind the door

偷空 tōukòng　take time off (from work to do sth. else); snatch a moment

偷懒 tōulǎn　loaf on the job; be lazy

偷老婆 tōu lǎopo　(of a man) have an affair with sb.'s wife; commit adultery

偷垒 tōulěi　(in baseball and softball) steal a base; steal

偷梁换柱 tōuliáng-huànzhù　steal the beams and change the pillars—perpetrate a fraud

偷漏 tōulòu　tax evasion

偷期 tōuqī　*formal* (of lovers) make a rendezvous (*or* an assignation)

偷巧 tōuqiǎo　*dial.* resort to trickery to serve oneself

偷窃 tōuqiè　steal; pilfer

偷情 tōuqíng　carry on a clandestine love affair

偷人 tōurén　same as 偷汉子 tōu hànzi

偷生 tōushēng　drag out an ignoble existence

偷税 tōushuì　evade taxes

偷天换日 tōutiān-huànrì　steal the sky and put up a sham sun—perpetrate a gigantic fraud

偷听 tōutīng　eavesdrop: ～别人谈话 eavesdrop on a conversation

偷偷 tōutōu　stealthily; secretly; covertly; on the sly (*or* quiet): ～地溜走 sneak away / ～地瞧了一眼 steal a glance at / ～告诉他 tell him on the quiet / 这些孩子～地抽烟。The boys smoked on the sly.

偷偷摸摸 tōutōumōmō　furtively; surreptitiously; covertly

偷袭 tōuxí　sneak attack; sneak raid; surprise attack

偷暇 tōuxiá　snatch a moment of leisure

偷闲 tōuxián　①snatch a moment of leisure: 忙里偷闲 mánglǐ tōuxián ② *dial.* loaf on the job; be idle

偷香窃玉 tōuxiāng-qièyù　philander; womanize

偷眼 tōuyǎn　steal a glance; take a furtive glance: 他～看了一下母亲的神色。He stole a glance at his mother's face.

偷营 tōuyíng　make a surprise attack on an enemy camp; raid an enemy camp

偷越 tōuyuè　cross (a border, etc.) illegally or stealthily: ～封锁线 run a blockade; slip through a cordon

偷嘴 tōuzuǐ　take food on the sly

tóu

头（頭）

tóu　① head ② hair or hair style: 您理什么～? How shall I cut your hair? / 这～理得好。That's a good haircut. ③ top; end: 村西～ the west end of a village / 这条胡同儿走到～就是60号。No. 60 is at the end of the lane. ④ beginning or end: 你这故事讲到什么时候才是个～儿呀! When ever will you finish your story? ⑤ remnant; end: 蜡～儿 candle end / 铅笔～儿 pencil stub (*or* stump) ⑥ chief; head; leader: 头儿 tóur ⑦ side; aspect: 他们是一～儿的。They are on the same side. / 事情不能只顾一～。We mustn't pay attention to only one aspect of the matter. ⑧ first: 头等 tóuděng / 头号 tóuhào ⑨ leading: 头马 tóumǎ ⑩ (used

before a numeral) first: 〜一遍 the first time / 〜半场比赛 the first half of a game / 〜三天 the first three days / 〜两排位子 the two front rows of seats / 他跑了个百米〜一名。He came in first in the 100-metre dash. ⑪ *dial.* (used before 年 or 天) previous; last: 头年 tóunián / 头天 tóutiān ⑫before; prior to: 〜五点就得动身 have to start before (*or* by) five / 〜吃饭要洗手。Wash your hands before meals. / 〜鸡叫我就起来了。I got up before cockcrow. ⑬ (used between two numerals, indicating an approximate number) about: 三〜五百 three or five hundred; several hundred ⑭ *m.* ⓐ (for certain domestic animals): 三十〜牛 thirty head of cattle / 两〜骡子 two mules ⓑ (for garlic): 一〜蒜 a bulb of garlic ⓒ (after the numeral 一, for a marriage): 那一〜亲事怎么样了? What about the marriage? / 他许过我一〜亲事。He's promised me a wife (husband).

头(頭)

tou (noun suffix) ① (added to a noun, verb, or adjective): 木头 mùtou / 看头 kàntou / 甜头 tiántou ② (added to a word of locality): 上头 shàngtou / 下头 xiàtou / 前头 qiántou

头儿 tóur *inf.* head; chief; leader; boss: 她是我们组的〜。She is the head of our group. / 〜，有火柴没有? Have you got a match, boss?

头版 tóubǎn front page (of a newspaper): 〜新闻 front-page news

头半天 tóubàntiān forenoon; morning

头边 tóubian *dial.* in front; ahead: 他跑咱们〜去啦! He's shot ahead of us.

头彩 tóucǎi first prize in a lottery: 中〜 win first prize in a lottery

头寸 tóucùn *banking* ① money market; money supply: 〜紧(松)。Money is tight (easy). ② cash

头灯 tóudēng *min.* head lamp

头等 tóuděng first-class; first-rate: 〜重要任务 a task of primary importance / 〜舱 first-class cabin / 〜品 first-rate (*or* top-quality) goods

头等大事 tóuděng dàshì a matter of prime importance; a major event: 这两件事，是目前咱们的〜。Both are of paramount importance to us today.

头顶 tóudǐng the top (*or* crown) of the head

头发 tóufa hair (on the human head)

头发菜 tóufacài same as 发菜 fàcài

头发夹子 tóufajiāzi hairpin

头缝儿 tóufèngr parting (of combed hair): 她的〜偏一边儿。Her hair is arranged with a side parting.

头伏 tóufú the first *fu* (another name for 初伏 chūfú)

头盖 tóugài ① skull; cranium ② red cloth or gauze kerchief for a bride

头盖骨 tóugàigǔ *physiol.* cranium; skull

头功 tóugōng greatest service; highest merit: 立〜 render the greatest service; acquire the highest merit

头骨 tóugǔ *physiol.* skull; cranium

头号 tóuhào ① number one; size one: 〜字 size one type / 〜敌人 number one enemy; archenemy ② first-rate; top quality: 〜大米 top-grade rice

头花 tóuhuā *arts & crafts* headdress flower

头昏 tóuhūn dizzy; giddy: 我〜。I feel dizzy. *or* My head is swimming.

头昏脑胀 tóuhūn-nǎozhàng feel giddy (*or* dizzy); feel one's head swimming: 他又热又累，〜。He was hot and tired and his head was swimming. / 工作忙得〜 be overwhelmed with work

头昏眼花 tóuhūn-yǎnhuā feel giddy (*or* dizzy); feel one's head swimming: 我飞快地转着圈儿跳舞，都〜了。I was dancing round so fast that I felt quite giddy.

头髻 tóují hair worn in a bun or coil

头家 tóujiā organizer of a gambling party who take a percentage (*or* cut) of the winnings

头奖 tóujiǎng first prize (in a contest, etc.): 得〜 win first prize

头角 tóujiǎo brilliance (of a young person); talent

头角峥嵘 tóujiǎo zhēngróng (of a youth) brilliant; very promising; outstanding

头巾 tóujīn scarf; kerchief

头巾气 tóujīnqì pedantry; bookishness

头颈 tóujǐng *dial.* neck

头口 tóukǒu *dial.* draught animals; beasts of burden; livestock

头盔 tóukuī (steel) helmet

头佬 tóulǎo *dial.* foreman; overseer

头里 tóuli ① in front; ahead: 老张在〜。Lao Zhang is in front. / 您〜走，我马上就来。Please go ahead. I won't be a minute. / 她事事都走在〜。She takes the lead in everything. ② in advance; beforehand: 咱们把话说在〜。Let's make this clear in advance. ③ before; ago: 十年〜 ten years ago

头脸 tóuliǎn ① head and face ② face; features ③ reputation; prestige: 有〜的人 a prominent figure

头领 tóulǐng *old* chieftan; leader; head

头颅 tóulú head

头鲈鱼 tóulúyú silver-spotted grunt

头路¹ tóulù first class (goods, etc.); first-rate

头路² tóulù *dial.* ① parting (of combed hair) ② main threads (of a complicated affair)

头马 tóumǎ lead horse

头面人物 tóumiàn rénwù a prominent figure; a big shot; a bigwig

头面 tóumiàn *old* woman's head-ornaments

头名 tóumíng first place (in a contest, etc.)

头目 tóumù head of a gang; ringleader; chieftain: 小〜 head of a small group in a gang

头目人 tóumùrén *dial.* leader; head: 他是村里的〜。He is the head of this village.

头难 tóunán *dial.* the first step is difficult: 什么事情总是〜。Everything's hard in the beginning. *or* The first step is always difficult.

头脑 tóunǎo ① brains; mind: 她很有〜。She has plenty of brains. / 不用〜 not use one's head / 简单〜 simple-minded; seeing things too simply / 〜清醒 clearheaded; sober-minded / 有政治〜 be politically-minded / 有冷静的〜 have a cool head; be sober-minded / 把〜里的错误思想清除出去 rid one's mind of erroneous ideas ② main threads; clue: 摸不着〜 cannot make head or tail of sth. ③*inf.* chieftain; leader; head

头年 tóunián ① the first year ② *dial.* last year or the previous year

头帕 tóupà *dial.* scarf; kerchief

头牌 tóupái star actor or actress (in traditional opera)

头皮 tóupí ① scalp: 搔〜 scratch one's head ② dandruff; scurf: 他的上衣肩上白白的净是〜。The shoulders of his jacket were white with dandruff.

头破血流 tóu pò xuè liú one's head covered with bumps and bruises—be badly battered; be beaten; be crushed: 在事实面前碰得〜 bump one's head against a wall of hard facts

头秋 tóuqiū shortly before autumn harvest

头球 tóuqiú *football* header: 〜破门 head the ball into the goal

头人 tóurén *old* tribal chief; headman

头纱 tóushā gauze kerchief worn on a woman's head

头晌 tóushǎng *dial.* forenoon; morning

头上安头 tóu shàng ān tóu needless duplication; needless repetition

头上长疮，脚底流脓——坏透了 tóushàng zhǎng chuāng, jiǎodǐ liú nóng—huàitòule with boils on the head and feet running with pus—rotten from head to foot; rotten

to the core

头生　tóushēng　firstborn

头绳　tóushéng　① string for binding a plait, bun, etc. ② *dial.* knitting wool

头虱　tóushī　head louse

头式　tóushì　hair style; hairdo; coiffure

头饰　tóushì　head ornaments

头势　tóu·shì　*dial.* ① impetus; momentum ② *inf.* tendency; the look of things

头水　tóushuǐ　① (of goods) of the best quality; top-quality: ～货 first-rate (*or* top-quality) goods ② (of utensils) be used for the first time ③ be washed for the first time: 这件衣服刚洗了～就缩了好多。This coat shrank badly in the first wash.

头胎　tóutāi　firstborn

头套　tóutào　actor's headgear

头疼　tóuténg　(have a) headache

头疼脑热　tóuténg-nǎorè　a headache and a slight fever; a slight illness

头天　tóutiān　① the previous day ② the first day

头挑　tóutiāo　choicest: ～苹果 the choicest apples

头条新闻　tóutiáo xīnwén　front-page headline: 成为各报的～ hit (*or* make) front-page headlines in the press; be the top story of the paper

头童齿豁　tóutóng-chǐhuō　hair gone and teeth falling out—decrepit

头痛　tóutòng　(have a) headache: ～得厉害 have a bad headache / 这件事真让我～。This business is a headache for me.

头痛医头，脚痛医脚　tóutòng yī tóu, jiǎotòng yī jiǎo　treat the head when the head aches, treat the foot when the foot hurts—treat the symptoms but not the disease; take stopgap measures; apply palliative remedies

头头是道　tóutóu shì dào　clear and logical; systematic and orderly; closely reasoned and well argued; coherent and cogent: 他说得～。What he said was clear and logical. / 战争的学问，有些人可以在书本上讲得～，但打起仗来却不一定能取胜。Some people may appear impressive when discoursing on military science in books, but when it comes to actual fighting, they may not win a battle.

头头儿　tóutour　*inf.* head; chief; leader; boss

头陀　tóutuó　mendicant Buddhist monk

头晚　tóuwǎn　the previous night

头午　tóuwǔ　*dial.* about noon

头衔　tóuxián　title (a sign of rank, profession, etc.)

头像　tóuxiàng　head (portrait or sculpture)

头屑　tóuxiè　dandruff; scurf: 有的洗发香波能去～。Some shampoos help to get rid of scurf (*or* dandruff).

头囟儿　tóuxìnr　*dial.* the fontanel (of a baby's head)

头行人　tóu·xíngrén　*dial.* head; chief; leader

头胸部　tóuxiōngbù　*zool.* cephalothorax

头绪　tóuxù　main threads (of a complicated affair): ～太多 have too many things to attend to / 理出个～来 get things into shape / 事情渐渐有了～。Things are settling into shape.

头癣　tóuxuǎn　favus of the scalp

头雁　tóuyàn　the wild goose that leads the flock flying in formation

头羊　tóuyáng　bellwether

头由　tóuyóu　pretext

头油　tóuyóu　hair oil; pomade

头晕　tóuyūn　dizzy; giddy: ～目眩 have a dizzy spell; be afflicted with vertigo / 有点～ feel a bit dizzy (*or* giddy)

头针疗法　tóuzhēn liáofǎ　*Chin. med.* head-acupuncture therapy

头重脚轻　tóuzhòng-jiǎoqīng　top-heavy and unsteady

头状花序　tóuzhuàng huāxù　*bot.* capitulum; head

头子　tóuzi　*derog.* chieftain; chief; boss: 土匪～ bandit chief

头足动物　tóuzú dòngwù　cephalopod

投　tóu　① throw; fling; hurl: ～手榴弹 throw a hand grenade ② put in; drop: 把信～进邮筒 drop a letter into the pillar-box ③ throw oneself into (a river, well, etc. to commit suicide): 投河 tóuhé ④ project; cast: 树影～在窗户上。The tree cast its shadow on the window. / 把眼光～到来访者身上 cast one's eyes on the visitor ⑤ send; deliver: 投书 tóushū ⑥ go to; join: 投店 tóudiàn ⑦ fit in with; agree with; cater to: 意气相投 yìqì xiāngtóu ⑧ before; prior to: ～明 before daybreak / ～暮 towards dusk

投案　tóu'àn　give oneself up (*or* surrender oneself) to the police: ～自首 surrender oneself to the police or judicial department

投保　tóubǎo　insure; take out an insurance policy: 为这批货物～了十万元 insure the merchandise for 100,000 yuan / 他为自己的房子投了保。He took out an insurance policy on his house.

投保方　tóubǎofāng　policy-holder

投奔　tóubèn　go to (a friend or a place) for shelter: ～亲戚 seek refuge with relatives; go to one's relatives for help / ～解放区参加革命 go to the liberated areas to join in the revolution

投笔从戎　tóu bǐ cóng róng　cast aside the pen and join the army—renounce the pen for the sword; give up intellectual pursuits for a military career

投畀豺虎　tóu bì cháihǔ　throw them to the jackals and tigers; death to them

投鞭断流　tóu biān duàn liú　(of a vast and mighty army) could fling its whips into a river and stem its flow

投标　tóubiāo　submit a tender; enter a bid

投产　tóuchǎn　(of a factory) go into operation; put into production: 这个农具厂是去年～的。This farm implement factory went into operation last year.

投诚　tóuchéng　(of enemy troops, rebels, bandits, etc.) surrender; cross over: 向人民～ cross over to the side of the people

投弹　tóudàn　① drop a bomb ② throw a hand grenade

投弹高度　tóudàn gāodù　release altitude

投弹角　tóudànjiǎo　dropping angle

投弹器　tóudànqì　bomb rack control; bomb release mechanism

投弹手　tóudànshǒu　bombardier; grenadier

投敌　tóudí　go over to the enemy; defect to the enemy

投递　tóudì　deliver: ～信件 deliver letters / 无法～，退回原处。Undeliverable, returned to sender. / 无法～的信 dead letter

投递员　tóudìyuán　postman; letter (*or* mail) carrier; mailman

投店　tóudiàn　put up at an inn for the night

投放　tóufàng　① throw in; put in: ～鱼饵 throw in the bait / 在井里～毒药 put poison into a well ② put (money) into circulation; put (goods) on the market: 这个新产品已～市场。This new product has been put on market.

投分　tóufèn　*formal* be alike in temperament; be congenial

投稿　tóugǎo　submit a piece of writing for publication; contribute (to a newspaper or magazine): 欢迎～。Contributions are welcome. / 我给《中国日报》投了篇稿。I submitted an article to the *China Daily*.

投函　tóuhán　same as 投书 tóushū

投合　tóuhé　① agree; get along: 他们俩脾气很～。The two of them are quite congenial. ② cater to: ～顾客的口味 cater to the tastes of the customers

投河　tóuhé　drown oneself in a river

投壶 tóuhú pitch-pot game (formerly, a game played at a drinking party, in which the participants threw arrows into a pot)

投缳 tóuhuán *formal* hang oneself

投簧 tóuhuáng ① (of a key) fit into a locking spring ② (of a method) practical and effective

投机 tóujī ① congenial; agreeable: 谈得很～ talk very congenially; have a most agreeable chat ② speculate: 投机倒把 tóujī-dǎobǎ ③ seize a chance to seek private gain; be opportunistic: 投机取巧 tóujī qǔqiǎo

投机倒把 tóujī-dǎobǎ engage in speculation and profiteering: ～分子 speculator; profiteer

投机分子 tóujī fēnzǐ opportunist; political speculator

投机取巧 tóujī qǔqiǎo seize every chance to gain advantage by trickery; be opportunistic

投机商 tóujīshāng speculator; profiteer

投寄 tóujì send (a letter, etc.) by post; post

投井 tóujǐng drown oneself in a well

投井下石 tóu jǐng xià shí same as 落井下石 luò jǐng xià shí

投军 tóujūn *old* join the army

投考 tóukǎo sign up for an examination: ～大学 sign up for a college entrance examination

投靠 tóukào go and seek refuge with sb.: ～亲友 go and seek refuge with one's relatives and friends / ～反动派 throw in one's lot with the reactionaries

投篮 tóulán *basketball* shoot (a basket): 远（近）距离～ long (close-in) shot / 跳起～ jump up and shoot / ～不准 inaccurate shooting / ～不中 miss the basket / 钩手～ hook shot / 单手～ one-hand shot

投票 tóupiào vote; cast a vote: 我投了他一票。 I cast (*or* gave) my vote for him. / ～赞成 vote for; vote in favour of / ～反对 vote against / ～表决 decide (*or* vote) by ballot / 无记名～ secret ballot / 去投票处～ go to the polls

投票日 tóupiàorì polling day

投票箱 tóupiàoxiāng ballot box

投票站 tóupiàozhàn polling booth (*or* station); the polls

投其所好 tóu qí suǒ hào cater to sb.'s likes (*or* tastes)

投契 tóuqì *formal* see eye to eye; get along well; be congenial

投洽 tóuqià agree; get along: 谈得很～ talk very congenially; have a most agreeable chat

投枪 tóuqiāng javelin; (throwing) spear

投亲 tóuqīn go and live with relatives; seek refuge with relatives: ～靠友 go and seek refuge with one's relatives and friends

投入 tóurù ① throw into; put into: ～某人的怀抱 throw oneself into sb.'s arms / ～战斗 throw (oneself, troops, etc.) into the battle / ～生产 put into production; go into operation / ～全部劳动力 throw in the whole labour force / 他演这个角色很～。 He got into the character that he was playing. ② input

投射 tóushè ① throw (a projectile, etc.); cast ② project (a ray of light); cast: 金色的阳光～到平静的海面上。 The sun cast its golden rays on the calm sea. / 周围的人都对他～出惊异的眼光。 All those around him looked at him with amazement.

投身 tóushēn throw oneself into: ～到事业中去 throw oneself into a career / ～革命 join the revolutionary ranks; join in the revolution

投生 tóushēng ① be reincarnated in a new body; be reborn ② seek a livelihood outside one's home town

投师 tóushī seek instruction from a master: ～访友 learn from a master and call on friends to exchange knowledge or skills

投手 tóushǒu (in baseball and softball) pitcher: ～犯规 balk

投售 tóushòu sell on the market

投书 tóushū write or send a letter (to a newspaper, etc.)

投鼠忌器 tóu shǔ jì qì hesitate to pelt a rat for fear of smashing the dishes—hold back from taking action against an evil-doer for fear of involving or harming good people

投诉 tóusù ① appeal: ～法院 appeal to a court ② (of a customer) complain

投宿 tóusù seek temporary lodging; put up for the night: ～客栈 put up at an inn for the night

投胎 tóutāi reincarnation

投桃报李 tóu táo bào lǐ give a plum in return for a peach—return present for present; exchange gifts

投纬 tóuwěi *text.* picking: 每分钟～数 picks per minute

投闲置散 tóuxián-zhìsǎn (of a man of ability) stay idle; occupy an insignificant position

投降 tóuxiáng surrender; capitulate

投降派 tóuxiángpài capitulators; capitulationist clique

投降主义 tóuxiángzhǔyì capitulationism

投效 tóuxiào *formal* go and offer one's services

投药 tóuyào offer medicine (to take)

投医 tóuyī seek medical advice; go to a doctor

投影 tóuyǐng projection: 极～ polar projection / 墨卡托地图～ Mercator (map) projection

投影几何学 tóuyǐng jǐhéxué *math.* projective geometry

投影图 tóuyǐngtú *mech.* projection drawing

投邮 tóuyóu send (a letter, etc.) by post; post

投缘 tóuyuán find each other congenial; hit it off: 两人一见面就～。 The two of them hit it off as soon as they met. / 两人越谈越～。 As they talked, they warmed up to each other.

投掷 tóuzhì throw; hurl: ～标枪（铁饼、手榴弹） throw a javelin (discus, hand grenade)

投置 tóuzhì throw oneself into; join

投注 tóuzhù throw (energy, etc.) into: 把全副精力～到工作里 throw all one's energies into one's work

投资 tóuzī ① invest: ～工矿企业 invest in industrial and mining enterprises / ～五千万元 make an investment of 50,000,000 *yuan* ② money invested; investment: 国家～ state investment / 发挥～效果 realize returns on an investment / 收回本厂～ recoup the plant's capital outlay

投资场所 tóuzī chǎngsuǒ outlet for investment

投资基金 tóuzī jījīn investment funds

投资市场 tóuzī shìchǎng investment market

骰

骰 tóu see below

骰子 tóuzi *dial.* dice: 掷～ throw dice; play dice

tǒu

敨

敨 tǒu *dial.* ① open (sth. folded) ② shake off (dust, etc.)

tòu

透

透 tòu ① pass through; seep through; penetrate: 爱克斯光能～过肌体检查病变。 X-rays can pass through the human body and show inside pathological changes. / 血从绷带里～了出来。 Blood seeped out through the bandage. / 阳光～过窗户照进来。 Sunlight came in through the windows. / 这个手钻钻不～这种钢板。 This hand drill cannot penetrate the steel plate. /

这双鞋不～水。These shoes are waterproof. / ～过现象看本质 see through the appearance to get at the essence ② tell secretly; let out; reveal: ～消息 tell sb. news on the quiet / 只听他～了一句半句的,详细情况还不清楚。I only heard the fragmentary information he let out. Details are still unknown. / 这次谈判,一点情况也没～出来。Little was revealed about the talks. ③ fully; completely; thoroughly: 恨～ be full of hatred for sb.; bitterly hate / 天已经黑～了。It was completely dark. / 道理讲得很～ thoroughly explain one's reasons; drive the point home / 我笨～了,第一次测试都没通过。I was stupid enough to have failed the first test. / 有意思～了 be extremely interesting / 桃熟～了。The peaches are quite ripe. / 火～了 be in a terrible fury / 对问题了解得很～ have an intimate knowledge of the subject; know the subject inside out / 雨下～了。It was a real good soaker. / 我猜不～他在想什么。I can't make out what really is in his mind. / 这个谱子我记得熟～了。I have the music score off pat. / 她这样惹她母亲生气,真是不懂事～了。She's a very thoughtless girl to upset her mother like that. ④ appear; show: 他脸上～出幸福的微笑。A happy smile appeared on his face. / 她的一双大眼睛～着机灵。Her large eyes show intelligence. / 白里～红 white touched with red

透彻 tòuchè penetrating; thorough: 她把问题分析得很～。She made a penetrating analysis of the problem. / 有～的了解 have a thorough understanding / 这一番话说得非常～。Those words really drove the point home.

透翅蛾 tòuchì'é clearwing (moth)

透底 tòudǐ reveal the exact details

透顶 tòudǐng *derog.* thoroughly; downright; in the extreme; through and through: 反动～ downright reactionary; out-and-out reactionary / 腐败～ thoroughly corrupt; rotten to the core; decadent in the extreme / 这么明显的错误你都没看出来,真是糊涂～! How stupid of you to overlook such an obvious mistake!

透风 tòufēng ① let in air; ventilate: 打开窗户透透风 open the window and let in some air / 这门关不严,有点～。This door doesn't fit very tightly and the wind blows through. ② dry in the air; air ③ divulge a secret; leak: 这个人嘴很紧,一点风也不透。The man was closemouthed and didn't drop a hint.

透骨 tòugǔ ① (of cold air) chill one to the bone; be piercing: 冷得～ be chilled to the bone ② deep; profound; penetrating: 看得～ a keen observation; a penetrating analysis

透汗 tòuhàn a good sweat: 出一身～ break into a sweat; sweat all over / 出一身～感冒就会好。A good sweat will cure a cold.

透话 tòuhuà drop a hint; hint; suggest: 他～要买这所房子。He hinted that he would buy the house.

透镜 tòujìng *phys.* lens: 分光～ beam-splitting lens / 复合～ compound lens

透亮 tòuliàng ① bright; transparent: 这间房子又向阳,又～。This room is sunny and bright. ② perfectly clear: 经你这么一说,我心里就～了。Thanks to your explanation, it's clear to me now.

透亮儿 tòuliàngr allow light to pass through: 这个暗室有点～。This darkroom lets in light.

透漏 tòulòu divulge; leak; reveal: 消息～出去了。The news has leaked out.

透露 tòulù divulge; leak; disclose; reveal: ～风声 leak (*or* disclose) information / 真相～出来了。The truth has come to light (*or* has come out). / 她跟她娘～过这个意思。She said to her mother something to that effect.

透明 tòumíng transparent; diaphanous: ～度 transparency; diaphaneity / ～的纱巾 a diaphanous veil

透明计 tòumíngjì diaphanometer

透明漆 tòumíngqī celluloid paint; clear lacquer

透明体 tòumíngtǐ *phys.* transparent body

透明纸 tòumíngzhǐ cellophane paper; cellophane

透辟 tòupì penetrating; incisive; thorough: ～的分析 a penetrating analysis

透平机 tòupíngjī (also 透平 tòupíng) another name for 涡轮机 wōlúnjī

透气 tòuqì ① ventilate: 屋子太闷了,打开窗子透透气。The room is too stuffy. Open the windows and let some air in. ② breathe freely: 透不过气来 feel suffocated ③ leak (*or* disclose) information; drop a hint; tip off

透热疗法 tòurè liáofǎ diathermy

透热性 tòurèxìng *phys.* diathermancy; diathermaneity

透闪石 tòushǎnshí *geol.* tremolite

透射 tòushè ① (of light) pass through ② *phys.* transmission: 定向～ regular transmission / ～比 transmittance / ～率 transmissivity

透视 tòushì ① perspective ② *med.* fluoroscopy; roentgenoscopy ③ see through

透视图 tòushìtú perspective drawing

透熟 tòushú know well; be familiar with

透水层 tòushuǐcéng *geol.* pervious bed; permeable stratum

透心儿 tòuxīnr to the core; to the marrow: 这萝卜都糠透了心儿了。This radish has gone spongy to the core. / 冷风吹了我个～凉。The cold wind chilled me to the bone. / 我一听他变卦了,马上就觉得～凉。I felt bitterly disappointed when I heard that he had changed his mind.

透信 tòuxìn leak (*or* disclose) information; drop a hint; tip off: 如果有什么变化,你事先给我透个信儿。If there should be any changes, please let me know beforehand. / 老王～给我,说她要来。Lao Wang tipped me off about her arrival. / 咱俩的计划该跟你妈透个信儿了。I think we'll have to let your mother in on our plans.

透雨 tòuyǔ saturating (*or* soaking) rain; soaker

透支 tòuzhī ① *banking* overdraw; make an overdraft: ～的帐户 overdrawn account ② expenditure exceeds revenue; overspend ③ *old* draw one's salary in advance

tū

凸 tū protruding; raised: ～花银瓶 a silver vase with a raised floral design / ～面 convex

凸岸 tū'àn *geol.* convex bank

凸版 tūbǎn *print.* relief printing plate: ～轮转机 rotary letterpress machine / ～印刷 letterpress; relief (*or* typographic) printing

凸窗 tūchuāng bay window

凸轮 tūlún *mech.* cam: 推动～ actuating cam / 急升～ quick lift cam / ～轴 cam shaft

凸面镜 tūmiànjìng (also 凸镜 tūjìng) *phys.* convex mirror

凸透镜 tūtòujìng *phys.* convex lens

凸缘 tūyuán *mech.* flange: 环状～ collar flange / 接头～ joint flange / 管～ pipe flange

秃 tū ① bald; bare: 他的头开始～了。He's getting (*or* going) bald. / ～山 bare (*or* barren) hills / ～树 bare trees; defoliated trees ② blunt; without a point: 铅笔～了。The pencil is blunt. ③ incomplete; unsatisfactory: 这篇文章的结尾显得有点～。This article seems to end rather lamely.

秃笔 tūbǐ bald writing brush—poor writing ability; low

skill at composition: 我这支～不行，得找个笔杆子。I'm no good at writing; you'll have to find someone who is. /非我这支～所能形容 beyond the power of my poor pen

秃疮 tūchuāng *inf.* favus of the scalp

秃顶 tūdǐng ① bald ② bald head

秃发病 tūfàbìng alopecia

秃鹫 tūjiù cinereous vulture

秃头[1] tūtóu bareheaded; hatless

秃头[2] tūtóu ① bald head ② shaven head

秃子 tūzi ① baldhead; baldpate ② *dial.* favus of the scalp

突

突 tū ① dash forward; charge: ～入敌阵 charge into enemy positions ② *adv.* suddenly; abruptly; unexpectedly: 气温～降。The temperature suddenly dropped. ③ projecting; sticking out ④ *formal* chimney: 灶突 zàotū

突变 tūbiàn ① sudden change: 认识过程中的～ a sudden change in the process of cognition ② *philos.* leap ③ *biol.* mutation: 自发～ spontaneous mutation /～体 mutant

突出[1] tūchū break through: ～重围 break through a tight encirclement

突出[2] tūchū ① protruding; projecting; sticking out: 眼球～ bug-eyed /～的岩石 projecting rocks ② outstanding; prominent: ～的成就 outstanding achievements /这个例子～地说明了他的态度是错误的。This is a glaring example of his wrong attitude. /他的优点和缺点都很～。His virtues are as conspicuous as his defects. ③ give prominence to; stress; highlight: 他的发言没有～重点。In his speech he failed to stress the main points. /她老想～自己。She always tries to push herself forward. *or* She is very pushy.

突出部 tūchūbù *mil.* salient

突飞猛进 tūfēi-měngjìn advance by leaps and bounds; advance with seven-league strides; make giant strides: 我国社会主义建设事业～。Socialist construction is going ahead by leaps and bounds in our country. /生产力～的发展 the rapid development of the productive forces

突击 tūjī ① make a sudden and violent attack; assault ② make a concentrated effort to finish a job quickly; do a crash job: ～麦收 do a rush job of harvesting the wheat /～任务 rush job; shock work

突击点 tūjīdiǎn point of assault

突击队 tūjīduì shock brigade

突击手 tūjīshǒu shock worker

突击战术 tūjī zhànshù shock tactics

突厥 Tūjué Tujue (Turk), a nationality in ancient China

突尼斯 Tūnísī Tunisia

突尼斯人 Tūnísīrén Tunisian

突破 tūpò ① break through; make (*or* effect) a breakthrough: ～防线 break through a defence line /医学上的～ a medical breakthrough ② surmount; break; top: ～难关 break the back of a tough job /～定额 overfulfil a quota /我们村粮食亩产早已～五百公斤。Our village topped 500 kilos in its per *mu* grain yield long ago. ③ (in football, etc.) break through a defence

突破地区 tūpò dìqū *mil.* area of penetration (*or* breakthrough)

突破点 tūpòdiǎn *mil.* breakthrough point; point of penetration

突破口 tūpòkǒu *mil.* breach; gap

突起 tūqǐ ① break out; suddenly appear: 战事～。Hostilities broke out. ② rise high; tower: 奇峰～。Peaks tower magnificently.

突然 tūrán ① sudden; abrupt; unexpected: ～死亡 sudden (*or* unexpected) death /这场冰雹～极了。The hail

was totally unexpected. /他病得太～了。His illness was very sudden. /听到这消息我感到～。The news took me by surprise. /准备对付一切～事变 prepare for all eventualities (*or* contingencies) ② *adv.* suddenly; abruptly; unexpectedly: 灯～都灭了。Suddenly the lights went out. /～间，火车停住了，许多乘客从座位上摔了下来。The train came to an abrupt stop, making many passengers fall off their seats. /～哭起来 burst into tears

突然袭击 tūrán xíjī surprise attack; sudden onslaught

突如其来 tū rú qí lái arise suddenly; come all of a sudden; appear out of nowhere

突突 tūtū *onom.* 她的心～地跳。Her heart went pit-a-pat. /汽艇～地驶入港口。The motorboat chugged its way into the harbour.

突围 tūwéi break out of an encirclement

突兀 tūwù ① lofty; towering: ～的山石 towering crags /怪峰～。A grotesque peak thrusts itself towards the sky. ② sudden; abrupt; unexpected: 事情来得这么～，使他简直不知所措。It all happened so suddenly he didn't know what to do.

突袭 tūxí surprise attack

葵

葵 tū see 菩葵 gūtū

tú

图（圖）

图 tú ① picture; drawing; chart; map: 制图 zhìtú /草图 cǎotú ② scheme; plan; attempt: 另作他～ find another way out; work out a different scheme ③ pursue; seek: ～私利 pursue private ends /～一时痛快 seek momentary satisfaction /不～名，不～利，～的是共产主义 strive for neither fame nor gain, but for communism /～一时之苟安，贻百年之大患。One moment's false security can bring a century of calamities. ④ intention; intent

图案 tú'àn pattern; design: 几何～ geometrical pattern

图案操 tú'àncāo callisthenic performance forming patterns

图板 túbǎn drawing board

图版 túbǎn plate (for printing photos, maps, illustrations, etc.)

图报 túbào seek ways to return sb.'s kindness

图表 túbiǎo chart; diagram; graph

图财害命 túcái-hàimìng same as 谋财害命 móucái-hàimìng

图存 túcún strive for survival

图钉 túdīng drawing pin; thumbtack

图画 túhuà drawing; picture; painting

图画文字 túhuà wénzì *linguis.* picture writing; pictography

图画纸 túhuàzhǐ drawing paper

图籍 tújí *formal* maps and census records of the border regions

图记 tújì seal; stamp

图鉴 tújiàn (usu. used in book titles) illustrated (*or* pictorial) handbook: 《中草药～》 *Pictorial Handbook of Chinese Medicinal Herbs*

图解 tújiě ① diagram; graph; figure: 用～说明 explain through diagrams ② *math.* graphic solution: ～法 graphic method

图景 tújǐng view; prospect: 展现出一幅壮丽的～ open up a magnificent prospect

图卷 tújuàn picture scroll

图例 túlì legend (of a map, etc.); key

图赖 túlài ① repudiate a debt ② falsely incriminate: ～好人 incriminate innocent people

图谋 túmóu　plot; scheme; conspire

图谋不轨 túmóu bùguǐ　plot sth. unlawful; engage in conspiratorial activities

图片 túpiàn　picture; photograph: ～展览 photo (or picture) exhibition／～说明 caption

图谱 túpǔ　a collection of illustrative plates; atlas:《古玉～》An Illustrated Catalogue of Ancient Jades

图穷匕首见 tú qióng bǐshǒu xiàn (also 图穷匕见 tú qióng-bǐxiàn)　when the map was unrolled, the dagger was revealed—hidden intentions are revealed in the end (from the story of Jing Ke 荆轲, who tried to assassinate Qin Shi Huang 秦始皇 and had his dagger hidden in a rolled-up map)

图书 túshū　books: ～资料 books and reference materials／～目录 catalogue of books; library catalogue

图书 túshu　seal; stamp

图书馆 túshūguǎn　library: ～馆长 librarian (in charge of a library)／～管理员 librarian (a library worker)

图书馆学 túshūguǎnxué　library science

图腾 túténg　totem

图瓦卢 Túwǎlú　Tuvalu

图文并茂 tú-wén bìng mào　(of a book, magazine, etc.) both pictures and texts are excellent

图文传真 túwén chuánzhēn　fax

图像 túxiàng　picture; image

图像识别 túxiàng shíbié　electron. pattern recognition

图形 túxíng　① graph; figure ② short for 几何图形 jǐhé túxíng

图样 túyàng　pattern; design; draft; drawing: 机器～ a draft for a machine

图章 túzhāng　seal; stamp

图纸 túzhǐ　blueprint; drawing: 建筑物的～ drawing of a building

涂¹（塗）

　tú　① spread on; apply; smear: ～漆 apply a coat of paint; paint／～点软膏 apply some ointment／给机器部件～油 smear machine parts with grease／木桩子上～了沥青。The wooden stakes are coated with pitch. ② scribble; scrawl: 别在墙上乱～。Don't scribble (or scrawl) on the wall. ③ blot out; cross out: ～掉几个字 cross out a few words

涂²（涂）

　Tú　a surname

涂层 túcéng　coat; coating: 减磨～ friction coat／反雷达～ antiradar coating

涂改 túgǎi　alter: ～无效 invalid if altered

涂画 túhuà　scribble; scrawl; daub

涂料 túliào　coating; paint: 防腐～ anticorrosive paint／耐火～ refractory coating

涂抹 túmǒ　① daub; smear; paint ② scribble; scrawl: 信笔～ doodle

涂片 túpiàn　med. smear: 血～ blood smear

涂饰 túshì　① cover with paint, lacquer, colour wash, etc. ② daub (plaster, etc.) on a wall; whitewash

涂刷 túshuā　apply paint, etc. with a brush

涂炭 tútàn　formal mud and ashes—utter misery; great affliction; misery and suffering ——see also 生灵涂炭 shēnglíng tútàn

涂写 túxiě　scribble; scrawl; doodle: 墙上净～着名字。The wall was scribbled over with names.／禁止～! No scribbling!／老师在讲话，他却在纸上乱涂乱写。He made doodles on paper while the teacher was talking.

涂鸦 túyā　hum. poor handwriting; scrawl; chicken tracks

涂乙 túyǐ　formal prune (an essay, etc.); delete and change

涂泽 túzé　formal gloss over; whitewash

涂脂抹粉 túzhī-mǒfěn　apply powder and paint—prettify; whitewash: 为自己～ try to whitewash oneself

荼

　tú　arch. ① a bitter edible plant ② the white flower of reeds, etc.

荼毒 túdú　formal afflict with great suffering; torment

荼毒生灵 túdú shēnglíng　plunge the people into the depths of suffering

荼蘼 túmí　bot. roseleaf raspberry (Rubus rosaefolius var. Coronarius)

途

　tú　way; road; route: ～中 on the way; en route

途程 túchéng　(fig.) road; way; course: 人类进化的～ the evolution of the human species

途次 túcì　formal stopover; travellers' lodging

途经 tújīng　by way of; via: ～武汉前往广州 go to Guangzhou by way of Wuhan

途径 tújìng　way; channel: 寻找消除分歧的～ seek ways to eliminate differences／探索和平解决的～ explore avenues to a peaceful settlement／外交～ diplomatic channels

徒¹

　tú　① on foot: 徒涉 túshè ② empty; bare: 徒手 túshǒu ③ adv. merely; only: ～具形式 be a mere formality／不～无益，反而有害 not only useless, but harmful ④ adv. in vain; for nothing; to no avail: ～自惊扰 frighten oneself for no apparent reason; become needlessly alarmed

徒²

　tú　① apprentice; pupil: 学徒 xuétú ② follower; believer: 信徒 xìntú ③ derog. people of the same faction: 党徒 dǎngtú ④ derog. person; fellow: 歹徒 dǎitú／暴徒 bàotú ⑤ (prison) sentence; imprisonment: 徒刑 túxíng

徒步 túbù　on foot: ～旅行 travel on foot

徒弟 túdi　apprentice; disciple

徒费唇舌 tú fèi chúnshé　waste one's breath: 我的主意已定，你别～了。I've made up my mind, you're wasting your breath.

徒歌 túgē　formal singing without accompaniment

徒工 túgōng　apprentice

徒唤奈何 tú huàn nàihé　utter unavailing cries of despair

徒劳 túláo　make a futile effort; work fruitlessly: 去跟他争辩是～的。It would be futile to argue with him.

徒劳往返 túláo wǎng-fǎn　make a futile journey; hurry back and forth for nothing

徒劳无功 túláo wú gōng　(also 徒劳无益 túláo wú yì) make a futile effort; work to no avail

徒乱人意 tú luàn rényì　(of a statement, argument, etc.) can only confuse people's minds

徒然 túrán　① in vain; for nothing; to no avail: ～耗费精力 waste one's energy (or effort) ② merely; only: 如果那么办，～有利于敌人。To do that will only be to the advantage of the enemy.

徒涉 túshè　formal wade through; ford

徒手 túshǒu　bare-handed; unarmed

徒手操 túshǒucāo　free-standing exercises

徒孙 túsūn　disciple's disciple

徒托空言 tú tuō kōngyán　make empty promises; pay lip service to

徒刑 túxíng　leg. imprisonment; (prison) sentence: 判三年～ sentence sb. to three years' imprisonment

徒有虚名 tú yǒu xūmíng　have a false (or unearned, undeserved) reputation

徒长 túzhǎng　agric. excessive growth (of branches and leaves); spindling

徒子徒孙 túzǐ-túsūn　① disciples and followers ② hangers-on and their spawn

屠

　tú　① slaughter (animals for food) ② mas-

sacre; slaughter: 屠杀 túshā ③ (Tú) a surname

屠场 túchǎng　slaughterhouse

屠城 túchéng　massacre the inhabitants of a captured city

屠刀 túdāo　butcher's knife

屠夫 túfū　① *old* butcher ② a ruthless ruler

屠户 túhù　*old* butcher or butcher's

屠龙之技 tú lóng zhī jì　the art of butchering dragons —an art of a high order but of little value

屠戮 túlù　*formal* massacre; butcher; slaughter

屠门大嚼 túmén dà jué　same as 过屠门而大嚼 guò túmén ér dà jué

屠杀 túshā　massacre; butcher; slaughter: 军阀～罢工工人。The warlords butchered the strikers.

屠苏 túsū　an ancient wine: 爆竹声中一岁除，春风送暖入～。(王安石) Amid the din of crackers goes the parting year, The winds of spring bring warmth to help the wine mature.

屠宰 túzǎi　butcher; slaughter: ～牲畜 slaughter animals; butcher fat stock

屠宰场 túzǎichǎng　slaughterhouse

屠宰率 túzǎilǜ　dressing percentage

屠宰税 túzǎishuì　tax on slaughtering animals

菟 tú　see 於菟 wūtú——see also tù

圖 túshūguǎn　popular written form for 图书馆 túshūguǎn

酴 tú　see below

酴醾 túmí　① *arch.* a double-fermented wine ② same as 荼蘼 túmí

---

tǔ

土 tǔ　① soil; earth: 一把～ a handful of soil／～坷拉 a lump of earth; clod／用～把种子盖上 cover seeds with earth／～台 an earthen platform／他鞋上都是～。There's dust all over his shoes. ② land; ground: 国土 guótǔ／领土 lǐngtǔ ③ local; native: 他穿着那件大褂显着～得很。He looks very rustic in his gown.／他说的是很～的北京话。He speaks with a broad Beijing accent. ④ homemade; indigenous: ～办法 indigenous methods／～杂肥 farmyard manure ⑤ unrefined; unenlightened: 土里土气 tǔlǐtǔqì ⑥ (crude) opium: 烟土 yāntǔ

土坝 tǔbà　earth-filled dam; earth dam

土邦 tǔbāng　a local independent region under British colonial rule

土包子 tǔbāozi　clodhopper; (country) bumpkin

土豹 tǔbào　buzzard

土崩瓦解 tǔbēng-wǎjiě　disintegrate; crumble; fall apart; collapse: 陷于不可挽救的～的状态 be hopelessly disintegrated／他们的反动统治机构终于～，归于消灭。The whole structure of their reactionary regime finally crumbled and perished.

土鳖 tǔbiē　ground beetle

土拨鼠 tǔbōshǔ　marmot

土布 tǔbù　handwoven (*or* handloomed) cloth; homespun cloth

土蚕 tǔcán　*dial.* ① the larva of a noctuid ② grub

土产 tǔchǎn　① produced in a locality ② local (*or* native) product

土地 tǔdì　① land; soil: 肥沃的～ fertile land; good soil ② territory: 我国～辽阔，资源丰富。Our country has a vast territory and abundant resources.

土地报酬递减律 tǔdì bàochóu dìjiǎnlǜ　the law of dimin-

---

ishing returns

土地法 tǔdìfǎ　land law; agrarian law

土地分红 tǔdì fēnhóng　dividend on land shares

土地改革 tǔdì gǎigé　land reform; agrarian reform

土地革命战争 Tǔdì Gémìng Zhànzhēng　the Agrarian Revolutionary War (1927–1937)

土地集中 tǔdì jízhōng　concentration of landholdings

土地税 tǔdìshuì　land tax

土地证 tǔdìzhèng　land certificate; land deed

土地制度 tǔdì zhìdù　land system

土地 tǔdi　(also 土地爷 tǔdiyé, 土地老 tǔdilǎo) local god of the land; village god

土地庙 tǔdimiào　(also 土地堂 tǔditáng) a tiny temple housing the village god

土电影 tǔdiànyǐng　*dial.* slide show

土豆 tǔdòu　*inf.* potato

土耳其 Tǔ'ěrqí　Turkey

土耳其人 Tǔ'ěrqírén　Turk

土耳其语 Tǔ'ěrqíyǔ　Turkish (language)

土耳其浴 tǔ'ěrqíyù　Turkish bath

土法 tǔfǎ　indigenous method; local method: ～上马 get on the job with local methods

土方¹ tǔfāng　① cubic metre of earth ② earthwork: ～工程 earthwork

土方² tǔfāng　*Chin. med.* folk recipe

土房 tǔfáng　an abode house

土匪 tǔfěi　bandit; brigand

土粉子 tǔfěnzi　*dial.* chalk (used to whitewash walls)

土风 tǔfēng　① folk song ② local custom

土风舞 tǔfēngwǔ　old name for 民间舞蹈 mínjiān wǔdǎo

土改 tǔgǎi　short for 土地改革 tǔdì gǎigé

土岗 tǔgǎng　(also 土岗子 tǔgǎngzi) (earthen) mound

土狗子 tǔgǒuzi　*dial.* mole cricket

土棍 tǔgùn　a local rascal; a local bully; ruffian

土豪 tǔháo　local tyrant

土豪劣绅 tǔháo lièshēn　local tyrants (*or* bullies) and evil gentry

土话 tǔhuà　local, colloquial expressions; local dialect

土皇帝 tǔhuángdì　local despot; local tyrant

土黄 tǔhuáng　colour of loess; yellowish brown

土货 tǔhuò　local product; native produce

土墼 tǔjī　*dial.* sun-dried mud brick; adobe

土家族 Tǔjiāzú　the Tujia (Tuchia) nationality, or the Tujias (Tuchias), distributed over Hunan and Hubei Provinces

土芥 tǔjiè　*formal* a trifling thing; trifle

土炕 tǔkàng　heatable adobe sleeping platform; adobe kang

土库曼斯坦 Tǔkùmànsītǎn　Turkmenistan

土库曼斯坦人 Tǔkùmànsītǎnrén　Turkman

土牢 tǔláo　dungeon

土老儿 tǔlǎor　*old* clodhopper; (country) bumpkin

土老财 tǔlǎocái　countrified moneybags

土老冒儿 tǔlǎomàor　(also 土冒儿 tǔmàor) *inf.* clodhopper; (country) bumpkin

土礼 tǔlǐ　local product presented as a gift

土沥青 tǔlìqīng　natural asphalt; natural bitumen ——see also 沥青 lìqīng

土里土气 tǔlǐtǔqì　rustic; uncouth; countrified

土路 tǔlù　dirt road

土霉素 tǔméisù　*pharm.* terramycin; oxytetracycline

土名 tǔmíng　popular name

土木 tǔmù　building; construction

土木工程 tǔmù gōngchéng　civil engineering: ～师 civil engineer

土偶 tǔ'ǒu　clay idol

土坯 tǔpī　sun-dried mud brick; adobe

土气 tǔ·qì　① rustic style ② rustic; uncouth; countrified

土丘 tǔqiū　mound; hillock

土壤 tǔrǎng　soil: 多腐植质的～ humus-rich soil / 战争的～ soil for war / ～改良 soil improvement; soil amelioration / ～结构 soil structure / ～湿度 soil moisture / ～通气性 soil aeration / ～渗透性 soil permeability / ～质地 soil texture

土壤学 tǔrǎngxué　soil science; pedology: ～家 pedologist

土人 tǔrén　natives; aborigines

土生土长 tǔshēng-tǔzhǎng　locally born and bred; born and brought up in the locality

土石方 tǔshífāng　cubic metre of earth and stone

土司 tǔsī　① system of appointing national minority hereditary headmen in the Yuan, Ming and Qing Dynasties ② such a headman

土俗 tǔsú　① local custom ② vulgar; coarse

土特产 tǔtèchǎn　collective name for 土产 tǔchǎn and 特产 tèchǎn

土头土脑 tǔtóu-tǔnǎo　rustic; uncouth; countrified

土豚 tǔtún　zool.　earth pig

土围子 tǔwéizi　fortified village

土卫 tǔwèi　astron.　satellite of Saturn; Saturnian satellite

土温 tǔwēn　agric.　soil temperature

土物 tǔwù　local (or native) product

土星 Tǔxīng　Saturn: ～光环 Saturn's rings

土腥气 tǔxīngqì　(also 土腥味儿 tǔ·xīngwèir) the smell of soil

土燕 tǔyàn　common name for 燕鸻 yànhéng

土洋并举 tǔ-yáng bìngjǔ　use both indigenous and foreign methods; use both traditional and modern methods; use both simple and sophisticated methods

土洋结合 tǔ-yáng jiéhé　combine indigenous and foreign methods; combine traditional and modern methods; combine simple and sophisticated methods

土仪 tǔyí　formal　local product presented as a gift

土音 tǔyīn　local accent

土语 tǔyǔ　local, colloquial expressions; local dialect

土葬 tǔzàng　burial (of the dead) in the ground

土造 tǔzào　make sth. with local methods: ～手榴弹 grenades of local make

土政策 tǔzhèngcè　local policy (regulations of a locality or a government department designed to further its own interests and more often than not running counter to the state policy)

土纸 tǔzhǐ　handmade paper

土质 tǔzhì　the quality and composition of the soil: ～肥沃 the fertility of the soil

土冢 tǔzhǒng　grave mound

土著 tǔzhù　original inhabitants; aboriginals; aborigines

土专家 tǔzhuānjiā　self-taught expert; local expert

土族 Tǔzú　the Tu nationality, or the Tus, mainly inhabiting Qinghai Province

吐 tǔ　① spit: ～核儿 spit out the pips, stone or pits / 蚕～丝。Silkworms spin silk. / 机枪～着火舌。The machine gun was spitting fire. ② say; tell; pour out: ～实 tell the truth / ～怨气 vent one's grievances ——see also tù

吐蕃 Tǔfān　Tibetan regime in ancient China

吐刚茹柔 tǔgāng-rúróu　bully the weak and fear the strong

吐根 tǔgēn　bot.　ipecac (Cephaelis ipecacuanha)

吐根素 tǔgēnsù　(also 吐根碱 tǔgēnjiǎn) pharm.　emetine

吐故纳新 tǔgù-nàxīn　exhale the old and inhale the new; get rid of the stale and take in the fresh

吐话 tǔhuà　give the go-ahead; give one's OK: 你一～，我们就开始干。We'll start as soon as we get the go-ahead from you.

吐口 tǔkǒu　① tell truth ② put forward a claim; make a demand

吐苦水 tǔ kǔshuǐ　pour out one's grievances (or bitterness): 翻身农奴吐出了千年的苦水。The emancipated serfs poured out the accumulated bitterness of hundreds of years.

吐露 tǔlù　reveal; tell

吐露真情 tǔlù zhēnqíng　unbosom oneself; come out with the truth

吐气[1] tǔqì　feel elated after unburdening oneself of resentment; feel elated and exultant: 扬眉吐气 yángméi-tǔqì

吐气[2] tǔqì　same as 送气 sòngqì

吐弃 tǔqì　spurn; cast aside; reject

吐舌头 tǔ shétou　put (or stick) out one's tongue

吐绶鸡 tǔshòujī　turkey

吐属 tǔshǔ　formal　style of conversation

吐诉 tǔsù　come out with what's on one's mind; pour out (one's heart, etc.)

吐穗 tǔsuì　agric.　earing (up); heading (of cereal plants)

吐痰 tǔtán　spit; expectorate: 不准随地～! No Spitting!

吐絮 tǔxù　agric.　opening of bolls; boll opening

吐字 tǔzì　(of an actor in traditional opera) enunciate: ～清楚 enunciate clearly

钍 tǔ　chem.　thorium (Th)

tù

吐 tù　① vomit; throw up: 病人不断地～。The patient was vomiting repeatedly. / 恶心要～ feel sick; feel like vomiting (or throwing up) ② give up unwillingly; disgorge: 吐赃 tùzāng ——see also tǔ

吐酒石 tùjiǔshí　pharm.　tartar emetic

吐沫 tùmo　saliva; spittle; spit

吐血 tùxiě　spitting blood; haematemesis

吐泻 tù-xiè　vomiting and diarrhoea

吐赃 tùzāng　disgorge ill-gotten gains

兔（兎） tù　hare; rabbit

兔唇 tùchún　med.　harelip

兔毫 tùháo　a writing brush made of rabbit's hair

兔起鹘落 tùqǐ-húluò　the falcon swoops down as the hare starts out—① rapid action ② a rapid, flowing style (of a writer, calligrapher, or painter)

兔死狗烹 tù sǐ gǒu pēng　kill the hounds for food once the hares are bagged—eliminate trusted aids when they have outlived their usefulness

兔死狐悲 tù sǐ hú bēi　(usu. used in) ～, 物伤其类 the fox mourns the death of the hare—like feels for like

兔狲 tùsūn　zool.　steppe cat

兔脱 tùtuō　formal　run away like a hare; escape; flee

兔儿爷 tùryé　a clay figurine with the head of a rabbit (children's toy at the Mid-Autumn Festival)

兔崽子 tùzǎizi　offens.　brat; bastard

兔子 tùzi　hare; rabbit

兔子不吃窝边草 tùzi bù chī wōbiān cǎo　a rabbit doesn't eat the grass near its own hole (for its own protection)—a villain doesn't harm his nextdoor neighbours

兔子尾巴长不了 tùzi wěiba chángbùliǎo　derog.　the tail of a rabbit can't be long—won't last long

塊 tù　the ramp of a bridge: 桥塊 qiáotù

菟 tù　see below ——see also tú

菟丝子　tùsīzǐ　(also 菟丝 tùsī) *Chin. med.*　the seed of Chinese dodder (*Cuscuta chinensis*)

tuān

湍　tuān　*formal* ① (of a current) rapid; torrential ② rapids; rushing waters: 急湍 jítuān

湍急　tuānjí　(of a current) rapid; torrential: 水流～。The current is swift.

湍流　tuānliú　① *formal* swift current; rushing waters; torrent; rapids ② *phys.* turbulent flow; turbulence

tuán

团¹(團)　tuán　① round; circular: 团扇 tuánshàn ② roll sth. into a ball; roll: ～纸团儿 roll paper into a ball / ～药丸 roll pills ③ unite; conglomerate: 团结 tuánjié ④ group; society; organization: 剧团 jùtuán / 乐团 yuètuán ⑤ *mil.* regiment ⑥ (short for 中国共产主义青年团) the Communist Youth League of China; the League: ～籍 League membership ⑦ sth. shaped like a ball: 把面揉成一个～ knead dough into a ball / 缩成一～ curl up into a ball ⑧ *m.* (for sth. in the shape of a ball): 一～毛线 a ball of wool / 一～面 a lump of dough

团²(糰)　tuán　dumpling: 汤团 tāngtuán

团拜　tuánbài　gather together to exchange greetings (as on New Year's Day)

团粉　tuánfěn　cooking starch

团伙　tuánhuǒ　gang; band; clique: 流氓～ a gang of hooligans (*or* hoodlums)

团结　tuánjié　unite; rally: ～一致 unite as one / ～对敌 unite to oppose the enemy; close ranks to fight the enemy / ～一切可以～的力量 unite with all the forces that can be united / ～在党中央的周围 rally around the Party's Central Committee / 发扬～战斗的精神 carry forward the spirit of solidarity and militancy / ～就是力量。Unity is strength. / ～、紧张、严肃、活泼。Be united, alert, earnest and lively.

团聚　tuánjù　① reunite: 被旧社会拆散的亲骨肉, 解放不久就～了。Separated in the old society, the family was reunited soon after liberation. / 全家～ family reunion ② unite and gather

团课　tuánkè　League class; League lecture

团矿　tuánkuàng　*metall.* nodulizing; briquetting

团粒　tuánlì　*agric.* granule: ～结构 granular structure

团圞　tuánluán　(also 团栾 tuánluán) *liter.* ① (of the moon) round: 一轮～的明月 a bright full moon ② reunion

团年　tuánnián　family reunion during the Spring Festival

团弄　tuánnong　*dial.* ① roll sth. into a ball with the palms ② manipulate; swindle; control

团脐　tuánqí　① broad and rounded abdomen of a female crab ② female crab

团扇　tuánshàn　a round fan

团体　tuántǐ　organization; group; team

团体操　tuántǐcāo　group callisthenics

团体冠军　tuántǐ guànjūn　team title

团体票　tuántǐpiào　group ticket

团体赛　tuántǐsài　team competition

团团　tuántuán　round and round; all round: ～围住 surround completely; encircle

团团簇簇　tuántuáncùcù　swarm; flock; cluster: 人们～地

跑去看足球比赛。People flocked to the football match. / 花渐渐开得～的了。Flowers were blooming in clusters.

团团转　tuántuánzhuàn　round and round (used esp. in) 忙得～ be up to one's ears in work; run round in circles / 急得～ pace up and down in a state of agitation

团鱼　tuányú　soft-shelled turtle

团员　tuányuán　① member: 代表团～ a member of a delegation ② a member of the Communist Youth League of China; League member

团圆　tuányuán　① reunion (of family members): 全家～ family reunion / ～饭 family reunion dinner ② round: 这男孩儿～脸。The boy has a round face.

团圆节　Tuányuánjié　Family Reunion Festival (another name for 中秋节 Zhōngqiūjié)

团藻　tuánzǎo　*bot.* volvox

团长　tuánzhǎng　① *mil.* regimental commander ② head (*or* chief, chairman) of a delegation, troupe, etc.

团子　tuánzi　dumpling: 糯米～ dumpling made of glutinous rice / 菜～ cornmeal dumpling with vegetable stuffing / 饭～ rice ball

团坐　tuánzuò　(of a group of people) sit in a circle: 围炉～ sit around a fire

抟(摶)　tuán　① *liter.* spiral; circle; wheel ② same as 团¹ tuán②

tuǎn

疃(畽)　tuǎn　village (used in place names): 王～ Wang Village (in Hebei Province)

tuī

忒　tuī　*dial.* too; very: ～小 too small / 路～滑。The road is very slippery. ——see also tè; tēi

推　tuī　① push; shove: ～车 push a cart / ～了他一下 give him a push / 把门～开 push (*or* shove) the door open / 把竹排～进河里 shove (*or* push) the bamboo raft into the river / 把子弹～上膛 ram a cartridge into the rifle chamber ② turn a mill or grindstone; grind: ～点白面 grind some wheat into flour ③ cut; pare: 用刨子～光 make smooth with a plane; plane ④ push forward; promote; advance: 把运动～向高潮 push the movement to a climax ⑤ infer; deduce: 类推 lèituī ⑥ push away; shirk; shift: 不要把重担子～给人家。Don't shift burdensome tasks onto others. ⑦ put off; postpone: 这项工作得抓紧, 不能老是往后～。We have to get on with this job, we can't put it off day after day. / 往后～几天 postpone for a few days ⑧ elect; choose: ～他担任小组长 elect him group leader; choose him to be group leader ⑨ hold in esteem; praise highly: 推许 tuīxǔ

推扳　tuībān　(also 推班 tuībān) *dial.* no good; poor: 质量忒～ poor quality / 耳朵～ be a bit hard of hearing

推刨　tuībào　*dial.* plane (a carpenter's tool)

推本溯源　tuīběn-sùyuán　trace the origin; ascertain the cause

推波助澜　tuībō-zhùlán　make a stormy sea stormier; add fuel to the flames: 煽风点火, ～, 极尽挑拨离间之能事 fan the flames, add fuel to the fire and do one's utmost to incite one against the other

推测　tuīcè　infer; conjecture; guess: 根据～ by inference / 不过是～而已 mere guesswork; nothing but conjecture / 猿人化石可以帮助我们～猿人的生活情况。The fossil

remains of ape-men can help us infer how they lived.

推陈出新 tuī chén chū xīn weed through the old to bring forth the new ——see also 百花齐放, 推陈出新 bǎihuā qífàng, tuī chén chū xīn

推诚相见 tuīchéng xiāngjiàn deal with sb. in good faith; treat sb. with sincerity

推迟 tuīchí put off; postpone; defer: ～作出决定 defer making a decision / 这个会议～几天开。The meeting will be postponed for a few days.

推斥 tuīchì *phys.* repulsion: ～力 repulsive force

推崇 tuīchóng hold in esteem; praise highly: ～备至 have the greatest esteem for

推出 tuīchū introduce; put out; present: ～新产品 put out a new product / ～两部新双语词典 put out two new bilingual dictionaries / ～一部新影片 present a new film

推辞 tuīcí decline (an appointment, invitation, etc.)

推戴 tuīdài *formal* support sb. assuming leadership

推挡 tuīdǎng *table tennis* half volley with push

推宕 tuīdàng delay; procrastinate

推导 tuīdǎo derivation (in math, physics, etc.)

推倒 tuīdǎo ① push over; overturn: 把他～在地 shove him to the ground ② repudiate; cancel; reverse: 这个计划不切实际，要～重来。The plan is not practical and has to be replaced with a new one. / 一切诬蔑不实之词, 应予～。All slanders and libels should be repudiated.

推定 tuīdìng ① elect; choose ② infer; deduce

推动 tuīdòng push forward; promote; give impetus to: ～工作 push the work forward; expedite the work / ～社会向前发展 propel the society forward / ～力 motive (or driving) force

推断 tuīduàn infer; deduce: 经过周密的调查和分析才能作出正确的～。Correct inferences can be drawn only from careful investigation and analysis.

推度 tuīduó infer; conjecture; guess

推而广之 tuī ér guǎng zhī likewise; in the same way

推翻 tuīfān ① overthrow; overturn; topple: ～帝国主义、封建主义和官僚资本主义的统治 overthrow the rule of imperialism, feudalism and bureaucrat-capitalism ② repudiate; cancel; reverse: ～协议 repudiate an agreement / ～原定计划 cancel the original plan

推服 tuīfú praise and admire

推杆 tuīgǎn *mech.* push rod

推毂 tuīgǔ *formal* ① help sb. to achieve his aim ② recommend (sb. for a post)

推故 tuīgù give (or find) a pretext; make an excuse: 他～不去开会。He excused himself from the meeting.

推广 tuīguǎng popularize; spread; extend: ～普通话 popularize the common spoken Chinese / ～先进经验 spread advanced experience

推及 tuījí spread to; reach by analogy

推己及人 tuī jǐ jí rén put oneself in the place of another; treat other people as you would like to be treated; be considerate

推挤 tuījǐ ① push and shove: 人们～着上了公共汽车。There was a lot of pushing and shoving to get on the bus. ② *formal* push out; squeeze out; elbow out

推见 tuījiàn imagine; reckon: 从这些事情, 可以～其为人。From these instances you can gather what kind of person he is.

推荐 tuījiàn recommend: ～她去当拖拉机手 recommend her for training as a tractor driver / 向青年～优秀的文学作品 recommend outstanding literary works to the youth

推奖 tuījiǎng praise; commend

推襟送抱 tuījīn-sòngbào deal with sb. in good faith; treat sb. with sincerity

推进 tuījìn ① push on; carry forward; advance; give

impetus to: 把两国之间的友好关系～到一个新阶段 carry the friendly relations between the two countries to a new stage / 这项发明对纺织工业的发展起了新的～作用。This invention gave a fresh impetus to the development of the textile industry. ② *mil.* move forward; push; drive: 战线再次向前～。The battlefront has again moved forward. / 我团～到距离敌人只有几公里的地方。Our regiment drove to within a few kilometres of the enemy.

推进剂 tuījìnjì propellant

推进力 tuījìnlì propulsive force; driving power

推进器 tuījìnqì propeller

推究 tuījiū examine; study: ～事理 study the whys and wherefores of things

推举 tuījǔ ① elect; choose: 大家～他到大会发言。They chose him to speak on their behalf at the meeting. ② *weight lifting* clean and press; press: ～一百三十七公斤 press 137 kilograms

推拒 tuījù refuse; decline

推理 tuīlǐ *log.* inference; reasoning: 用～方法 by inference / 类比～ reasoning from analogy

推力 tuīlì thrust: 螺旋桨～ propeller thrust / 喷气发动机～ jet thrust

推论 tuīlùn inference; deduction; corollary

推磨 tuīmò turn a millstone

推拿 tuīná *Chin. med.* massage

推迁 tuīqiān *formal* ① (of time) elapse; pass: 日月～。Time goes by. or Time flies. ② play for time; stall (for time)

推敲 tuīqiāo weigh; deliberate: ～词句 weigh one's words; seek the right word / 这个提法是经过反复～的。This formulation was worked out after repeated deliberation. / 他写的东西经得起～。His writings can stand close scrutiny.

推求 tuīqiú inquire into; ascertain: ～地面沉降的原因 inquire into the causes of surface subsidence

推却 tuīquè refuse; decline: 他要请我吃饭, 我～了。I declined his invitation to dinner.

推让 tuīràng decline (a position, favour, etc. out of modesty)

推人犯规 tuīrén fànguī pushing (in basketball, etc.)

推三阻四 tuīsān-zǔsì decline with all sorts of excuses; give the runaround

推事 tuīshì *old* judge (in a court)

推说 tuīshuō ① *dial.* offer as an excuse (for not doing sth.); plead ② infer; deduce

推算 tuīsuàn calculate; reckon: 日食发生的时间可以～出来。The time when a solar eclipse will occur can be calculated.

推索 tuīsuǒ inquire into; ascertain

推涛作浪 tuītāo-zuòlàng stir up (or make) trouble; create disturbances

推头 tuītóu *inf.* ① cut sb.'s hair (with clippers) ② have a haircut

推土机 tuītǔjī bulldozer

推推搡搡 tuīīsǎngsǎng push and shove: 大家慢慢走, 别～的。Take it easy, don't push and shove.

推托 tuītuō offer as an excuse (for not doing sth.); plead: 她～嗓子疼, 不肯唱。Pleading a sore throat, she refused to sing.

推脱 tuītuō evade; shirk: ～责任 evade (or shirk) responsibility

推挽[1] tuīwǎn *formal* recommend (sb. for a post)

推挽[2] tuīwǎn *elec.* push-pull: ～电路 push-pull circuit

推委 tuīwěi (also 推诿 tuīwěi) shift responsibility onto others

推问 tuīwèn investigate; cross-examine

推详 tuīxiáng study or consider carefully; examine closely

推想　tuīxiǎng　imagine; guess; reckon: 按现在的速度, 可以～两年内我们县就能实现农业机械化了。At this speed, we expect our county's farming to be mechanized within two years.

推销　tuīxiāo　promote sales; market; peddle: ～商品 promote the sale of goods / ～员 salesman

推卸　tuīxiè　shirk (responsibility): ～责任, 委过于人 shirk responsibility and shift the blame onto others

推谢　tuīxiè　find an excuse to decline (an appointment, invitation, etc.)

推心置腹　tuīxīn-zhìfù　repose full confidence in sb.; confide in sb.: ～地交换意见 have a confidential (or heart-to-heart) exchange of views

推行　tuīxíng　carry out; pursue; practise: ～新的政策 pursue a new policy / ～学分制 introduce a credit system

推许　tuīxǔ　praise; commend; approve

推选　tuīxuǎn　elect; choose

推延　tuīyán　put off; postpone: 把讨论～到明天 put off the discussion till tomorrow

推演　tuīyǎn　deduce

推移　tuīyí　① (of time) elapse; pass: 随着时间的～ with the lapse (or passage) of time; as time goes on (or by) ② (of a situation, etc.) develop; evolve

推移质　tuīyízhì　*water conservancy*　bed load

推知　tuīzhī　know by inference; deduce

推重　tuīzhòng　have a high regard for; hold in esteem: 《本草纲目》问世之后, 深受人们的～。The *Compendium of Materia Medica* has been held in high esteem since it was first published.

推子　tuīzi　hair-clippers; clippers

推尊　tuīzūn　have a high regard for; hold in esteem

tuí

颓

颓　tuí　① ruined; dilapidated: 颓垣断壁 tuíyuán-duànbì ② declining; decadent: 衰颓 shuāituí ③ dejected; dispirited: 颓丧 tuísàng

颓败　tuíbài　*formal*　declining; decadent

颓放　tuífàng　*formal*　abandoned and dissolute

颓废　tuífèi　dispirited; decadent: ～情绪 decadent sentiments / ～派 the decadent school; the decadents

颓风　tuífēng　depraved customs; corrupt morals

颓坏　tuíhuài　ruined; dilapidated

颓靡　tuímǐ　downcast; dejected; crestfallen

颓圮　tuípǐ　*formal*　collapse; topple down

颓然　tuírán　*formal*　dejected; disappointed

颓丧　tuísàng　dejected; dispirited; listless: 敌军士气～。The enemy is demoralized.

颓势　tuíshì　declining tendency: 挽回～ retrieve oneself from an inferior position; turn the tide in one's favour

颓唐　tuítáng　dejected; dispirited

颓萎　tuíwěi　downcast; dejected; crestfallen

颓朽　tuíxiǔ　rotten; decayed

颓阳　tuíyáng　*formal*　the setting sun

颓垣断壁　tuíyuán-duànbì　same as 断垣残壁 duànyuán-cánbì

颓运　tuíyùn　*formal*　adversity; misfortune

tuǐ

腿

腿　tuǐ　① leg: 他～长。He has long legs. ② a leg-like support: 桌子(椅子)～ legs of a table (chair) ③ ham: 火腿 huǒtuǐ

腿肚子　tuǐdùzi　*inf.*　calf (of the leg)

腿脚　tuǐjiǎo　legs and feet—ability to walk: ～不灵便 have difficulty walking / 这位老奶奶的～还很利落。This old lady still moves briskly.

腿快　tuǐkuài　quick-footed; swift-footed

腿懒　tuǐlǎn　disinclined to move about; lazy about paying visits

腿勤　tuǐqín　be tireless in running around; love to run around

腿腕子　tuǐwànzi　ankle

腿子　tuǐzi　① *inf.*　hired thug; lackey; henchman ② *dial.*　leg

tuì

退

退　tuì　① move back; retreat: 他往后～了几步。He stepped back a few paces. *or* He backed up several steps. / 敌人已经～了。The enemy has retreated. / ～一步说 even if that is so; even so ② cause to move back; withdraw; remove: 把子弹～出来 remove a cartridge from the breech of a gun; unload a gun ③ withdraw from; quit: 退党 tuìdǎng ④ decline; recede; ebb: 潮水～了。The tide has receded. *or* The tide is on the ebb. ⑤ fade: 退色 tuìshǎi ⑥ return; give back; refund: 把这份礼～掉。Return this gift. / 空瓶不～。Empty bottles are not refundable. / cancel; break off: ～掉订货 cancel an order (for merchandise)

退避　tuìbì　withdraw and keep off; keep out of the way

退避三舍　tuìbì sān shè　retreat ninety *li*—give way to avoid a conflict

退兵　tuìbīng　① retreat; withdrawal: 传令～ order a retreat ② force the enemy to retreat: ～之计 a plan for repulsing the enemy

退步[1]　tuìbù　lag (or fall) behind; retrogress: 这孩子功课～了。The boy's not doing so well in his studies as he used to. / 他思想上～了。He has slipped back ideologically.

退步[2]　tuìbù　room for manoeuvre; leeway: 留个～ leave some room for manoeuvre; leave some leeway

退场　tuìchǎng　① (of athletes) withdraw from the arena (as after the opening ceremony); march off the arena ② (of an audience) leave the theatre (as when a play ends)

退潮　tuìcháo　ebb tide; ebb

退出　tuìchū　withdraw from; secede; quit: ～战斗 withdraw from action; break contact / ～会场 walk out of a meeting / ～组织 withdraw (or resign) from an organization / ～比赛 withdraw from a competition; scratch / ～历史舞台 step down from the stage of history

退磁　tuìcí　demagnetize

退党　tuìdǎng　withdraw from (or resign, quit) a political party

退敌　tuìdí　repulse (or repel) the enemy

退佃　tuìdiàn　(of a landlord) cancel a tenancy

退股　tuìgǔ　withdraw shares (from a joint-stock company)

退化　tuìhuà　① *biol.*　degeneration ② degenerate; deteriorate; retrograde

退还　tuìhuán　return: ～公物 return public property / ～抗议照会 reject a protest note

退换　tuìhuàn　exchange (or replace) a purchase: 产品不合规格, 保证～。Replacement is guaranteed if the products are not up to standard. *or* We undertake to replace any product not up to specifications. / 货物出门, 概不～。Goods sold are not returnable.

退回　tuìhuí　① return; send (or give) back: ～押金 return a deposit / 无法投递, ～原处。Undeliverable, returned to sender. / 原稿已经～。The manuscript has

been sent back. ② go (or turn) back: 道路不通，我们只得～。Finding the road impassable, we had to turn back.

退婚 tuìhūn　break off an engagement

退火 tuìhuǒ　*metall.*　annealing

退伙[1] tuìhuǒ　*old*　withdraw from a secret society or underworld gang

退伙[2] tuìhuǒ　cancel an arrangement to eat at a mess; withdraw from a mess

退货 tuìhuò　return goods (or merchandise): ～退钱 return merchandise for a refund

退居 tuìjū　① retire from a prominent position and take (a less important one): ～二线 withdraw to the second line of duty—retire from active life and take up a nominal post (usu. in a consultant capacity) / ～幕后 withdraw to a position behind the scenes ② be reduced to (a lower rank): 该厂产品已～第二位。The products of that factory have dropped to second place now.

退路 tuìlù　① route of retreat: 切断敌军～ cut off the enemy's retreat ② room for manoeuvre; leeway: 留个～ leave some leeway

退落 tuìluò　① (of water levels) fall after a rise ② decline; be on the wane; go downhill

退赔 tuìpéi　return what one has unlawfully taken or pay compensation for it

退票 tuìpiào　① return a ticket; get a refund for a ticket ② a returned (or unused) ticket: 等～ look for a returned (or unused) ticket

退坡 tuìpō　fall off; backslide: ～思想 falling off of revolutionary will or zeal

退钱 tuìqián　refund: 音乐会取消，买票的人都退了钱。When the concert was cancelled, the people who had bought tickets had their money refunded. / 这鞋如果不合适，商店管～。If the shoes do not wear well, the shop will refund your money.

退亲 tuìqīn　same as 退婚 tuìhūn

退却 tuìquè　① *mil.*　retreat; withdraw: 战略～ strategic retreat ② hang back; shrink back; flinch

退让 tuìràng　make a concession; yield; give in: 稍微～一点 give in a little / 决不～一步 never yield an inch / 在原则问题上从不～ never make concessions on matters of principle

退热 tuìrè　same as 退烧 tuìshāo

退色 tuìshǎi　fade: 这种布～吗？Will this cloth fade? or Is this cloth colourfast?

退烧 tuìshāo　① bring down (or allay) a fever ② (of a person's temperature) come down: 他已经～了。His fever is gone. or His temperature has come down.

退烧药 tuìshāoyào　antipyretic

退守 tuìshǒu　withdraw and stand on the defensive

退税 tuìshuì　*econ.*　drawback

退缩 tuìsuō　shrink back; flinch; cower: 在困难面前从不～ never flinch from difficulty

退庭 tuìtíng　withdraw from the court

退团 tuìtuán　withdraw from a youth league; give up league membership

退位 tuìwèi　give up the throne; abdicate

退伍 tuìwǔ　retire or be discharged from active military service; be demobilized; leave the army: ～军人 demobilized soldier; ex-serviceman; veteran

退席 tuìxí　① leave a banquet or a meeting ② walk out: ～以示抗议 walk out in protest

退闲 tuìxián　*formal*　go into retirement

退省 tuìxǐng　*formal*　introspection; self-questioning; self-examination

退休 tuìxiū　retire

退休工人 tuìxiū gōng·rén　retired worker

退休金 tuìxiūjīn　retirement pay; pension

退休年龄 tuìxiū niánlíng　retirement age

退学 tuìxué　leave school; discontinue one's schooling: 因病～ leave school owing to bad health / 勒令～ order to quit school

退押 tuìyā　① return a deposit ② (of a landlord) return deposits to tenants in the land reform

退役 tuìyì　retire or be released from military service (on completing the term of reserve) / ～军官 retired officer / ～军人 ex-serviceman

退隐 tuìyǐn　*old*　(of an official) retire from public life; go into retirement

退赃 tuìzāng　give up (or surrender, disgorge) ill-gotten gains

退职 tuìzhí　resign or be discharged from office; quit working

退走 tuìzǒu　retreat; withdraw

煺（煺、䍚）

tuì　scald (a pig, chicken, etc.) in order to remove hairs or feathers: ～毛 remove the hairs or feathers (of a pig, chicken, etc.)

蜕

tuì　① slough off; exuviate; moult ② exuviae: 蛇蜕 shétuì

蜕变 tuìbiàn　① change qualitatively; transform; transmute ② *phys.*　decay: 感生～ induced decay / 自发～ spontaneous decay

蜕化 tuìhuà　① slough off; exuviate ② degenerate

蜕化变质 tuìhuà-biànzhì　become morally degenerate: ～分子 degenerate element; degenerate

蜕皮 tuìpí　*zool.*　cast off (or shed) a skin; exuviate

褪

tuì　① take off (clothes); shed (feathers): ～去冬衣 leave off winter clothes / 小鸭～了黄毛。The ducklings have shed their yellow down. ② (of colour) fade: 褪色 tuìshǎi ——see also tùn

褪色 tuìshǎi　same as 退色 tuìshǎi

tūn

吞

tūn　① swallow; gulp down: 把药丸～下去 swallow the pills / 一口～掉 gobble up in one go; devour in one gulp ② take possession of; annex: 独吞 dútūn

吞并 tūnbìng　annex; gobble (or swallow) up

吞吃 tūnchī　① swallow; gulp down ② embezzle; misappropriate

吞金 tūnjīn　swallow gold (to commit suicide)

吞灭 tūnmiè　conquer and annex (a country)

吞没 tūnmò　① embezzle; misappropriate: ～巨款 misappropriate a huge sum ② swallow up; engulf: 小船被波浪～了。The little boat was engulfed in the waves.

吞声 tūnshēng　*formal*　gulp down one's sobs; dare not cry out

吞食 tūnshí　swallow; devour: 大鱼～小鱼。Big fish eat small fish. / 我刚好看见一条蛇在～青蛙。I came upon a snake devouring a frog.

吞蚀 tūnshí　① embezzle; misappropriate ② corrode; erode

吞噬 tūnshì　swallow; gobble up; engulf: 白血球～细菌。White corpuscles engulf bacteria. / 洪水～了整个村庄。The flood waters engulfed the whole village.

吞噬细胞 tūnshì xìbāo　*physiol.*　phagocyte

吞噬作用 tūnshì zuòyòng　*physiol.*　phagocytosis

吞吐 tūntǔ　swallow and spit—take in and send out in large quantities: 这个港口一年可～三千万吨货物。This port can handle up to 30,000,000 tons of cargo a year.

吞吐量 tūntǔliàng　handling capacity (of a harbour); the

volume of freight handled

吞吞吐吐 tūntūntǔtǔ hesitate in speech; hem and haw; mutter and mumble: 有话说清楚, 不要～。You've got to speak up clearly. No humming and hawing.

吞咽 tūnyàn swallow; gulp down: 他嗓子疼得厉害,～有困难。His throat was so painful that he could hardly swallow. / 他话到嘴边, 却又～下去了。He was on the point of saying something when he checked himself.

吞云吐雾 tūnyún-tǔwù swallow clouds and blow out fog—smoke (opium or cigarette)

吞占 tūnzhàn ① embezzle; misappropriate ② invade and occupy; seize

暾 tūn *liter.* newly-risen sun: 朝～ the early morning sun

tún

屯 tún ① collect; store up: ～粮 store up grain ② station (troops); quarter (troops): 驻屯 zhùtún ③ village (often used in village names): 皇姑～ Huanggu Village (in Liaoning Province)

屯兵 túnbīng station troops

屯积 túnjī same as 囤积 túnjī

屯集 túnjí assemble; collect

屯聚 túnjù (of troops, etc.) concentrate; assemble

屯垦 túnkěn station troops to open up wasteland

屯落 túnluò village; hamlet

屯田 túntián have garrison troops or peasants open up wasteland and grow food grain (a policy pursued by feudal rulers since the Han Dynasty)

屯扎 túnzhā station (troops); quarter (troops)

屯驻 túnzhù same as 驻屯 zhùtún

屯子 túnzi *dial.* village; hamlet

囤 tún store up; hoard: ～货 store goods ——see also dùn

囤积 túnjī hoard for speculation; corner (the market): ～小麦 corner the wheat market

囤积居奇 túnjī jūqí hoarding and cornering; hoarding and profiteering: 禁止高抬粮价和～ ban the forcing up of grain prices and hoarding and cornering

囤聚 túnjù store up (goods)

饨 tún see 馄饨 húntun

豚(独) tún ① suckling pig ② pig

豚儿 tún'ér *hum.* my son

豚鼠 túnshǔ guinea pig; cavy

鲀 tún another name for 河豚 hétún

臀 tún buttocks

臀部 túnbù buttocks: 在～打一针 give or have an injection in the buttock

臀尖 túnjiān pork rump

臀鳍 túnqí *zool.* anal fin

臀疣 túnyóu *zool.* monkey's ischial callosities; monkey's seat pads

tǔn

氽 tǔn *dial.* ① float; drift ② deep-fry: 油～花生米 fried peanuts

tùn

褪 tùn ① slip out of sth.: ～下一只袖子 slip one's arm out of one's sleeve ② *dial.* hide sth. in one's sleeve: ～着手 hide one's hands in sleeves ——see also tuì

褪去 tùnqù take off (clothes, etc.)

褪套儿 tùntàor ① break loose; free oneself; get oneself free: 狗褪了套儿跑了。The dog broke loose and ran away. ② shake off responsibility

tuō

托[1] tuō ① hold in the palm; support with the hand or palm: ～着盘子 hold a tray on one's palm / 两手一～腮 cup one's chin in one's hands ② sth. serving as a support: 花托 huātuō ③ serve as a foil (*or* contrast); set off: 衬托 chèntuō

托[2] **(託)** tuō ① ask; entrust: ～人买书 ask sb. to buy books for one / ～人照看孩子 leave a child in sb.'s care / 这事就～给她吧。Let's leave the matter to her. / 我想～你给他捎点东西。I'd like you to take something to him. ② plead; give as a pretext: 托病 tuōbìng ③ rely upon; owe to: 托庇 tuōbì

托[3] tuō *phys.* torr (a unit of pressure)

托儿 tuōr *inf.* a partner of a street pedlar or shopkeeper who pretends to be a customer and lures people into buying; salesperson's decoy

托庇 tuōbì rely upon one's elder or an influential person for protection

托病 tuōbìng plead illness

托词 tuōcí (also 托辞 tuōcí) ① find a pretext; make an excuse: ～谢绝 decline on some pretext ② pretext; excuse; subterfuge: 他说有事, 不过是～。He said he was busy, but that was just an excuse.

托大 tuōdà ① give oneself airs; be self-important; be conceited and arrogant ② *old* careless; negligent

托地 tuōdì *adv.* suddenly; abruptly; unexpectedly

托儿所 tuō'érsuǒ nursery; child-care centre; crèche

托福[1] tuōfú ① *pol.* (usu. responding to greetings) thanks to you: 托您的福, 我身体好多了。I'm much better now, thank you. ② rely upon; owe to: 托共产党的福, 我们才能过上今天的好日子。We owe our happy life to the Communist Party.

托福[2] tuōfú transliteration of TOEFL—see below

托福考试 tuōfú kǎoshì Test of English as a Foreign Language (TOEFL)

托付 tuōfù entrust; commit sth. to sb.'s care: 我们把这任务～给他了。We have entrusted him with the task.

托孤 tuōgū (of a dying emperor) entrust his young son to the care of a minister

托故 tuōgù give (*or* find) a pretext; make an excuse: ～早退 leave early under some pretext

托管 tuōguǎn (also 托管制 tuōguǎnzhì) trusteeship

托管国 tuōguǎnguó trustee state; trustee

托管理事会 tuōguǎn lǐshìhuì Trusteeship Council

托管领土 tuōguǎn lǐngtǔ trustee territory

托管区 tuōguǎnqū trust area

托管制度 tuōguǎn zhìdù trusteeship system; trusteeship

托灰板 tuōhuībǎn *archit.* hawk

托疾 tuōjí *formal* plead illness

托架 tuōjià *mech.* bracket: 发动机～ engine bracket /

～臂 bracket arm

托克劳群岛 Tuōkèláo Qúndǎo the Tokelau Islands

托拉斯 tuōlāsī *econ.* trust

托里拆利真空 tuōlǐchāilì zhēnkōng *phys.* Torricellian vacuum

托洛茨基主义 Tuōluòcíjīzhǔyì Trotskyism

托门子 tuō ménzi solicit help from potential backers; gain one's end through pull

托梦 tuōmèng (of the ghost of one's kith and kin) appear in one's dream and make a request

托名 tuōmíng do sth. in sb. else's name

托墨 tuōmò (of *Xuan* paper 宣纸) support ink well

托派 Tuōpài ① Trotskyite; Trotskyist ② *humor.* college students who are set on passing TOEFL (托福考试); TOEFL buffs; TOEFL maniacs

托盘 tuōpán (serving) tray

托人情 tuō rénqíng (also 托情 tuōqíng) ask an influential person to help arrange sth.; gain one's end through pull; seek the good offices of sb.

托身 tuōshēn ① find a place to live in ② seek a living

托生 tuōshēng reincarnation; transmigration

托叶 tuōyè *bot.* stipule

托幼 tuōyòu short for 托儿所 tuō'érsuǒ and 幼儿园 yòu'éryuán

托运 tuōyùn consign for shipment; check: 你的行李～了吗? Have you checked your baggage? / 你的行李都拿下来了吗? 有～的没有? Have you got all your baggage off? Is there any checked through? / 你有几件～的行李? How many pieces of consigned baggage have you got?

托运人 tuōyùnrén consignor

托嘱 tuōzhǔ entrust

托子 tuōzi base; support: 花瓶～ vase support (or holder)

托足 tuōzú *formal* have a foothold somewhere

饦

tuō see 馎饦 bótuō

拖

tuō ① pull; drag; haul: 火车头～着十二个车皮。The locomotive was pulling (or drawing) twelve carriages. / 拖轮～着几条小船。The tugboat was towing some small boats. / 把箱子从床底下～出来 drag (or haul) a trunk out from under the bed / ～着根竹竿 trail a bamboo pole along / ～地板 mop the floor / ～住敌人 pin down the enemy / 把身体～垮 wear oneself down ② delay; drag on; procrastinate: 再一就太晚了。Don't delay any more, or it'll be too late. / 这件工作～得太久了。This work has been dragging on far too long.

拖把 tuōbǎ (also 拖布 tuōbù) mop

拖驳 tuōbó barge (towed by a tugboat or motorboat)

拖车 tuōchē trailer

拖船 tuōchuán ① tugboat; tug; towboat ② *dial.* a wooden boat (towed by a tugboat)

拖带 tuōdài traction; pulling; towing

拖宕 tuōdàng *formal* delay; put off; procrastinate

拖儿带女 tuō'ér-dàinǚ be burdened with children

拖粪 tuōfèn *dial.* mop

拖后腿 tuō hòutuǐ (also 拖腿 tuōtuǐ) hinder (or impede) sb.; hold sb. back; be a drag on sb.: 孩子要到西藏去工作,你可别～。The kid wants to go and work in Xizang; you shouldn't try to hold him back. / 一个车间完不成任务,就要拖全厂的后腿。One workshop failing to fulfil its quota will be a drag on the whole factory.

拖家带口 tuōjiā-dàikǒu (also 拖家带眷 tuōjiā-dàijuàn) be burdened with a family

拖拉 tuōlā dilatory; slow; sluggish: 办事拖拖拉拉的 be dilatory in doing things / ～作风 dilatory style of work / 她工作从不～。She never puts off her work.

拖拉机 tuōlājī tractor: ～厂 tractor plant / ～手 tractor driver / ～站 tractor station

拖累 tuōlěi ① encumber; be a burden on: 受家务～ be tied down by household chores / 子女过多是个～。Too many children are a burden. ② implicate; involve

拖轮 tuōlún tugboat; tug; towboat

拖泥带水 tuōní-dàishuǐ messy; sloppy; slovenly: 这篇文章写得～。This article is sloppily written. / 办事要利落,不要～。Do things deftly, not sloppily. / 签订这个协定我们得准备应付许多～的事情。In signing this agreement, we must be prepared to deal with many messy matters.

拖欠 tuōqiàn be behind in payment; be in arrears; default: ～税款 be in arrears with tax payment

拖三拉四 tuōsān-lāsì (also 拖三阻四 tuōsān-zǔsì) put off one's work with all sorts of excuses; give the runaround

拖沓 tuōtà dilatory; sluggish; laggard

拖堂 tuōtáng (of a teacher) not dismiss class when time is up: 下课铃打了,老师还在滔滔不绝地～。The teacher was still holding forth after the bell had rung.

拖网 tuōwǎng trawlnet; trawl; dragnet: ～渔船 trawler

拖尾巴 tuō wěiba ① same as 拖后腿 tuō hòutuǐ ② leave a project, etc. unfinished; leave loose ends: 问题要彻底解决,不要拖个尾巴。The problem must be solved once for all, without leaving any loose ends.

拖鞋 tuōxié slippers

拖延 tuōyán delay; put off; procrastinate: 期限快到了,不能再～了。The deadline is drawing near; we can't delay any more. / ～时间 play for time; stall (for time)

拖延战术 tuōyán zhànshù dilatory (or delaying, stalling) tactics

拖曳 tuōyè pull; tow; draw

拖油瓶 tuōyóupíng ① (of a widow) remarry and take her children to her second husband's home ② such children

拖债 tuōzhài be behind in paying one's debt; be in arrears with one's debt: 不～ pay one's debt in time / 他拖的债还没有还清。He hasn't cleared up (or paid off) his debt yet.

脱

tuō ① (of hair, skin) shed; come off: 他脸晒～皮了。His face is peeling because of sunburn. / 头发～光了 lose all one's hair; become bald ② take off; cast off: ～鞋(衣服) take off one's shoes (clothes) ③ escape from; get out of: 逃脱 táotuō ④ miss out (words): 这一行里～了三个字。Three characters are missing in this line. ⑤ *formal* neglect; slight: 轻脱 qīngtuō ⑥ *formal* if; in case: ～有不测 if anything untoward should happen

脱靶 tuōbǎ miss the target in shooting practice

脱班 tuōbān ① be late for work ② (of a bus, train, etc.) be behind schedule

脱产 tuōchǎn be released from production or one's regular work to take on other duties: ～学习一年 be released from work for one year's study / 不～的理论队伍 a contingent of theoretical workers not withdrawn from production

脱出 tuōchū deviate from; shake off; break away from: ～常轨 break away from normal practice; break precedent / ～被动局面 regain the initiative

脱党 tuōdǎng quit (*or* leave) a political party (esp. the Chinese Communist Party); give up party membership

脱档 tuōdàng (of goods) be out of supply (*or* stock)

脱发 tuōfà *med.* loss of the hair; alopecia

脱肛 tuōgāng *med.* prolapse of the anus

脱稿 tuōgǎo (of a manuscript) be completed: 这本书已～,即可付印。The book is completed and is ready for printing.

脱钩 tuōgōu break off relations; cut ties

脱轨　tuōguǐ　be derailed: 火车～了。The train was derailed.

脱滑　tuōhuá　try to shirk work or responsibility; act in a slick way

脱货　tuōhuò　be in short supply; be out of stock

脱缰之马　tuō jiāng zhī mǎ　a runaway horse—uncontrollable; running wild: 通货膨胀如～ runaway inflation / 物价飞腾,有如～。Prices were running wild.

脱胶　tuōjiāo　① (of parts joined with gum or glue) come unglued; come unstuck: 这件橡皮雨衣～了。The rubber of this raincoat has disintegrated. ② *chem.* degum: 生丝～ degumming of silk

脱节　tuōjié　come apart; be disjointed; be out of line with: 管子焊得不好,容易～。Faultily welded piping is apt to come apart. / 理论与实践不能～。Theory must not be divorced from practice.

脱臼　tuōjiù　same as 脱位 tuōwèi

脱壳机　tuōkéjī　huller; sheller

脱空　tuōkōng　① come to nothing; fail; fall through: 希望～ fail to attain one's hope ② *dial.* tell a lie; lie; resort to deception: ～汉 liar

脱口而出　tuō kǒu ér chū　say sth. unwittingly; blurt out

脱蜡　tuōlà　*petroleum* dewaxing

脱懒　tuōlǎn　loaf on the job; shy away from work; be lazy

脱离　tuōlí　separate oneself from; break away from; be divorced from: ～群众 cut oneself off from the masses; be divorced from the masses / ～革命队伍 drop out of the revolutionary ranks / ～实际 lose contact with reality; be divorced from reality / 使双方武装力量～接触 disengage (or separate) the armed forces of the two sides / ～关系 break off relations; cut ties / 病人～危险了。The patient is out of danger.

脱离速度　tuōlí sùdù　*space* second cosmic velocity ——see also 宇宙速度 yǔzhòu sùdù

脱粒　tuōlì　*agric.* ① threshing ② shelling

脱粒机　tuōlìjī　① thresher ② sheller

脱磷　tuōlín　*chem.* dephosphorization

脱硫　tuōliú　*chem.* desulphurization; sweetening: ～原油 sweet crude

脱漏　tuōlòu　be left out; be omitted; be missing: 这里～了一行。A line is missing here. / ～一针 drop a stitch (in knitting)

脱略　tuōlüè　*formal* ① unrestrained ② treat sb. without proper respect; slight

脱落　tuōluò　drop; fall off (or away); come off: 毛发～ lose (one's) hair / 门的把手～了。The door handle has come off. / 墙上油漆已经～了。The paint on the wall has peeled off. / 蕾铃～ shedding of young bolls

脱盲　tuōmáng　become literate

脱毛　tuōmáo　lose hair or feathers; moult; shed: 那只骆驼刚脱了毛。That camel has just shed.

脱帽　tuōmào　take off (or raise) one's hat (in respect): ～致敬 take off one's hat in salutation / ～默哀 bare one's head and mourn in silence

脱模　tuōmú　*metall.* drawing of patterns

脱泡　tuōpào　*text.* deaeration: ～桶 deaerator

脱坯　tuōpī　mould adobe blocks

脱贫　tuōpín　shake off poverty; lift oneself out of poverty: ～致富 shake off poverty and build up a fortune

脱期　tuōqī　(of a periodical) fail to come out on time

脱氢　tuōqīng　*chem.* dehydrogenation

脱色　tuōsè　① decolour; decolourize: ～剂 decolourant; decolourizer ② fade

脱涩　tuōsè　take away the puckery taste (from persimmons); depuckerise

脱身　tuōshēn　get away; get free; extricate oneself: 我事情太多,脱不开身。I have so much to do that I just can't get away. / 他跳上一辆汽车脱了身。He jumped into a car and made his escape.

脱手　tuōshǒu　① slip out of the hand: 他用力一扔,石块～飞了出去。With a powerful fling he sent the stone flying. ② get off one's hands; dispose of; sell: 这些货不好～。These goods are difficult to dispose of.

脱水　tuōshuǐ　① *med.* deprivation (or loss) of body fluids; dehydration: 严重～ serious dehydration ② *chem.* dehydration; dewatering

脱水机　tuōshuǐjī　hydroextractor; whizzer

脱水蔬菜　tuōshuǐ shūcài　dehydrated vegetables

脱俗　tuōsú　free from vulgarity; refined

脱粟　tuōsù　*formal* brown rice; unpolished rice

脱榫　tuōsǔn　be out of joint

脱胎　tuōtāi　① emerge from the womb of; be born out of: 社会主义社会是从资本主义社会～而来的。Socialist society emerges from the womb of capitalist society. / 这部小说～于民间传说。This novel has been developed out of a folk story. ② a process of making bodiless lacquerware: ～漆器 bodiless lacquerware

脱胎换骨　tuōtāi-huàngǔ　be reborn; cast off one's old self; thoroughly remould oneself: 得到～的改造 cast off one's old self and take on a new self; make a change in one's very nature

脱逃　tuōtáo　run away; escape; flee

脱兔　tuōtù　a fleeing hare—fast speed: 动如～ as quick as a fleeing hare

脱位　tuōwèi　*med.* dislocation

脱误　tuōwù　omissions and errors (in a book, etc.)

脱险　tuōxiǎn　escape (or be out of) danger: 经过抢救,孩子～了。The child was out of danger after the emergency treatment.

脱销　tuōxiāo　out of stock; sold out: 这本书～了。The book is out of stock. or The book is sold out.

脱孝　tuōxiào　take off one's mourning—the mourning period is over

脱卸　tuōxiè　shirk (responsibility)

脱盐　tuōyán　desalination

脱氧　tuōyǎng　*chem.* deoxidation; deoxidization: ～剂 deoxidizer; deoxidant

脱氧核糖　tuōyǎng hétáng　*biochem.* deoxyribose

脱氧核糖核酸　tuōyǎng hétáng hésuān　*biochem.* deoxyribonucleic acid (DNA)

脱衣舞　tuōyīwǔ　striptease

脱易　tuōyì　rash; hasty; indiscreet

脱颖而出　tuō yǐng ér chū　the point of an awl sticking out through a bag—talent revealing itself

脱羽　tuōyǔ　(of birds) moult

脱证　tuōzhèng　*Chin. med.* exhaustion of vital energy at the critical stage of an illness

脱脂　tuōzhī　de-fat; degrease

脱脂剂　tuōzhījì　*leather* degreasing agent

脱脂棉　tuōzhīmián　absorbent cotton

脱脂奶粉　tuōzhī nǎifěn　de-fatted milk powder; nonfat dried milk

脱脂乳　tuōzhīrǔ　skimmed milk

脱脂纱布　tuōzhī shābù　absorbent gauze

tuó

驮　tuó　carry (or bear) on the back: 这头驴子能～三袋粮食。This donkey can carry three sacks of grain. ——see also duò

驮畜　tuóchù　pack animal

驮轿　tuójiào　litter carried by a horse or mule

驮筐　tuókuāng　pannier

驮马　tuómǎ　pack horse

陀　tuó　see below

陀螺　tuóluó　top (a toy): 抽～ whip a top

陀螺仪　tuóluóyí　*aviation* gyroscope; gyro

驼　tuó　① camel: 骆驼 luòtuo ② hunchbacked; humpbacked: 老爷爷的背～了。The grandpa's back has become bent.

驼背　tuóbèi　① hunchback; humpback ② hunchbacked; humpbacked

驼峰　tuófēng　① hump (of a camel) ② *transportation* hump: ～调车场 hump yard / ～调车法 hump switching

驼铃　tuólíng　camel bells

驼鹿　tuólù　elk; moose

驼绒　tuóróng　① camel's hair ② camel hair cloth

驼色　tuósè　the colour of camel's hair; light tan

驼子　tuózi　*inf.* hunchback; humpback

沱　tuó　① see 滂沱 pāngtuó ② *dial.* a small bay in a river (often used in place names)

沱茶　tuóchá　a bowl-shaped compressed mass of tea leaves

坨　tuó　① (of cooked wheaten food) stick together: 面条～了。These noodles are sticking together. ② same as 坨子 tuózi

坨子　tuózi　① lump: 泥～ a lump of mud; clod ② heap: 盐～ salt mound

柁　tuó　*archit.* girder

砣¹（铊）　tuó　the sliding weight of a steel-yard

砣²　tuó　① stone roller ② cut or polish jade with an emery wheel

砣子　tuózi　an emery wheel for cutting or polishing jade

鸵　tuó　ostrich

鸵鸟　tuóniǎo　ostrich

鸵鸟政策　tuóniǎo zhèngcè　ostrich policy; ostrichism

跎　tuó　see 蹉跎 cuōtuó

酡　tuó　*liter.* (of one's face) be flushed with drink

酡颜　tuóyán　*liter.* flushed face (from drinking)

橐¹（橐）　tuó　*formal* a kind of bag

橐²（橐）　tuó　*onom.*: ～～的脚步声 the tread of footsteps

橐驼　tuótuó　*formal* camel

鼧　tuó　see below

鼧鼥　tuóbá　an ancient name for marmot

鼍（鼉）　tuó　(also 鼍龙 tuólóng) *zool.* Chinese alligator

tuǒ

妥　tuǒ　① appropriate; proper: 请～ 为 保 存。Please look after it carefully. / 以上意见～否, 请指示。Please indicate whether you consider the above views sound or not. ② (usu. used after a verb) ready; settled; finished: 款已备～。The money is ready. / 事已办～。The matter has been settled.

妥便　tuǒbiàn　proper and convenient

妥当　tuǒdang　appropriate; proper: 办得很～ well handled; quite well done

妥靠　tuǒkào　reliable; dependable

妥善　tuǒshàn　appropriate; proper; well arranged: ～安排 make appropriate arrangements / 问题比较复杂, 需要～ 处理。The problem is rather complicated and needs careful and skilful handling. / 互阅全权证书, 认为～ examine each other's full powers and find them in good and due form

妥实　tuǒshí　appropriate; proper; well-done

妥帖　tuǒtiē　appropriate; fitting; proper: 看来这段译文不十分～。That doesn't seem to be an apt translation. / 办事～ manage things properly; handle matters well

妥协　tuǒxié　come to terms; compromise: 达成～ reach a compromise / ～性 a tendency towards compromise (*or* accommodation)

庹　tuǒ　*m.* arm spread; span

椭（橢）　tuǒ　see below

椭率　tuǒlǜ　*math.* ellipticity

椭面　tuǒmiàn　*math.* ellipsoid

椭圆　tuǒyuán　*math.* ellipse

椭圆截面　tuǒyuánjiémiàn　oval cross section

椭圆星云　tuǒyuán xīngyún　*astron.* elliptical nebula

椭圆柱面　tuǒyuánzhùmiàn　elliptic cylinder

椭圆锥面　tuǒyuánzhuīmiàn　elliptic cone

tuò

拓　tuò　open up; develop: 拓宽 tuòkuān ——see also tà

拓地　tuòdì　*formal* extend (*or* expand) territory

拓荒　tuòhuāng　open up virgin soil; reclaim wasteland: ～者 pioneer; pathbreaker; trailblazer

拓宽　tuòkuān　widen

拓落　tuòluò　*formal* ① be frustrated; be disappointed ② broad; extensive; vast

拓扑学　tuòpūxué　*math.* topology

拓展　tuòzhǎn　expand; spread; extend; develop

拓殖　tuòzhí　plant a colony; colonize

柝（欜）　tuò　*formal* watchman's clapper (*or* knocker)

唾　tuò　① saliva; spittle ② spit ③ spit (to show one's contempt)

唾骂　tuòmà　spit on and curse; revile: 为世人所～ be the opprobrium of the community

唾面自干　tuò miàn zì gān　let the spit on one's face dry of itself—meekly submit to humiliation; turn the other cheek

唾沫　tuòmo　saliva; spittle

唾沫星子　tuòmoxīngzi　a spray of saliva

唾弃　tuòqì　cast aside; spurn: 逆历史潮流而动的人终将被人民所～。Those who go against the trend of history will be cast aside by the people.

唾手可得　tuò shǒu kě dé　extremely easy to obtain

唾涎　tuòxián　saliva; spittle

唾液　tuòyè　saliva; spittle

唾液腺　tuòyèxiàn　(also 唾腺 tuòxiàn) salivary gland

唾余　tuòyú　idle talk; casual remarks: 拾人～ repeat other people's casual remarks

箨(**蘀**)　tuò　*formal*　fallen bark or leaves

魄　tuò　see 落拓（魄）luòtuò ——see also bó; pò

箨(**籜**)　tuò　*formal*　sheaths of bamboo shoots

W

wā

洼（窪） wā ① hollow; low-lying: 这地太～, 不适于种棉花。 This is low-lying land and not suitable for cotton. ② low-lying area; depression: 水～儿 a waterlogged depression

洼地 wādì　depression; low-lying land

洼下 wāxià　low-lying

洼陷 wāxiàn　(of ground) be sunken; be low-lying

洼子 wāzi　depression: 水～ a waterlogged depression

挖 wā　dig; excavate: ～井 dig (or sink) a well / ～隧道 excavate a tunnel / ～塘泥 scoop up sludge from a pond / ～煤 mine coal / ～防空洞 dig an air-raid shelter

挖补 wābǔ　mend by replacing a damaged part

挖槽机 wācáojī　mech. groover

挖兜 wādōu　inset pocket

挖耳 wā'ěr　dial. ① pick one's ears (to get rid of the wax) ② earpick

挖方 wāfāng　archit. ① excavation (of earth or stone) ② cubage of excavation

挖根 wāgēn　dig sth. up by the roots; uproot: 从思想上～ analyse one's ideological roots (when examining one's mistakes)

挖沟机 wāgōujī　ditcher; trencher; trench digger

挖角 wājué　lure a star actor or actress away from a theatrical company by the prospect of higher pay

挖掘 wājué　excavate; unearth: ～古物 excavate ancient relics / ～地下宝藏 unearth buried treasure

挖掘机 wājuéjī　(also 挖土机 wātǔjī) excavator; navvy: 迈步式～ walking excavator / 履带式～ caterpillar excavator / 索斗～ dragline excavator

挖空心思 wākōng xīnsi　derog. rack one's brains: ～为自己辩护 rack one's brains trying to justify oneself

挖苦 wāku　speak sarcastically or ironically: 那话是～我的。 That was a dig at me.

挖苦话 wākuhuà　ironical remarks; verbal thrusts

挖泥船 wāníchuán　dredger; dredge

挖潜 wāqián　(short for 挖掘潜力) tap the latent power (or potentialities)

挖墙脚 wā qiángjiǎo　inf. sap the wall; undermine the foundation; cut the ground from under sb.'s feet: 你把我们最好的教师都弄走了，你这是在挖我们系的墙脚。 You've taken away our best teachers, so you're undermining the foundation of the department.

挖肉补疮 wāròu bǔchuāng　same as 剜肉补疮 wānròubǔchuāng

挖树机 wāshùjī　tree mover

哇 wā　onom. the sound of crying or vomiting: ～的一声哭了起来 burst out crying ——see also wa

哇啦 wālā　(also 哇喇 wālā) onom. hullabaloo; uproar; din: 老师叫学生别那么～～的。 The teacher told the pupils to stop making such a hullabaloo.

哇哇 wāwā　onom. the crying of a child, the cawing of a crow, etc.

娲（媧） wā　see 女娲 Nǚwā

蛙（鼃） wā　frog

蛙人 wārén　frogman

蛙式打夯机 wāshì dǎhāngjī　frog rammer

蛙泳 wāyǒng　sports breaststroke: ～蹬腿 frog kick

wá

娃 wá　① baby; child ② dial. newborn animal: 鸡～ chick / 猪～ piglet

娃娃 wáwa　baby; child: 胖～ a chubby child

娃娃床 wáwachuáng　crib; cot

娃娃亲 wáwaqīn　the betrothal of a little boy and a little girl arranged by parents of both sides

娃娃生 wáwashēng　a subdivision of the xiaosheng (小生) role in traditional opera, representing loud-voiced boys

娃娃鱼 wáwayú　giant salamander

娃崽 wázǎi　dial. child; kid

娃子¹ wázi　dial. ① baby; child ② newborn animal: 猪～ piglet

娃子² wázi　old slave (among the minority nationalities in the Liangshan Mountains)

wǎ

瓦¹ wǎ　① tile: 无棱～ plain tile ② made of baked clay: 瓦器 wǎqì

瓦² wǎ　elec. short for 瓦特 wǎtè
——see also wà

瓦当 wǎdāng　archaeol. eaves tile

瓦房 wǎfáng　tile-roofed house

瓦釜雷鸣 wǎfǔ léimíng　an earthen crock sounding like thunder—an unworthy man in a high position

瓦工 wǎgōng　① bricklaying, tiling or plastering ② bricklayer; tiler; plasterer

瓦棺 wǎguān　earthen coffin (used in ancient times)

瓦罐 wǎguàn　earthen jar

瓦灰 wǎhuī　dark grey

瓦匠 wǎjiang　bricklayer; tiler; plasterer

瓦解 wǎjiě　disintegrate; collapse; crumble: ～敌军 disintegrate the enemy forces / 经过三个月战斗，敌军全线～。 After three months' fighting the whole enemy front crumbled. / ～士气 sap morale

瓦解冰消 wǎjiě-bīngxiāo　same as 冰消瓦解 bīngxiāowǎjiě

瓦块 wǎkuài　(also 瓦片 wǎpiàn) fragments of tiles; broken tiles

瓦蓝 wǎlán　azure; sky blue: ～的天空 a bright blue sky

瓦楞　wǎléng　① rows of tiles on a roof ② corrugated

瓦楞铁皮　wǎléngtiěpí　corrugated sheet iron

瓦楞纸　wǎléngzhǐ　corrugated paper

瓦楞子　wǎléngzi　(also 瓦垄子 wǎlǒngzi) zool. blood clam

瓦利思群岛和富图纳群岛　Wǎlìsī Qúndǎo hé Fùtúnà Qúndǎo　Wallis and Futuna

瓦砾　wǎlì　rubble; debris: 成了一片～ be reduced to rubble

瓦亮　wǎliàng　very bright: 锅擦得锃光～的。The pot was polished shining bright.

瓦垄　wǎlǒng　same as 瓦楞 wǎléng①

瓦努阿图　Wǎnǔ'ātú　Vanuatu

瓦圈　wǎquān　rim (of a bicycle wheel, cart wheel, etc.)

瓦全　wǎquán　see 宁为玉碎，不为瓦全 nìng wéi yù suì, bù wéi wǎ quán

瓦舍　wǎshè　① tile-roofed house ② pleasure quarters in cities in Song and Yuan times

瓦时　wǎshí　elec. watt-hour

瓦斯　wǎsī　gas: ～爆炸 gas explosion / ～筒 gas cylinder / ～弹 gas bomb; gas shell

瓦松　wǎsōng　bot. Orostachys fimbriatus

瓦特　wǎtè　elec. watt: ～计 wattmeter

瓦砚　wǎyàn　tile inkslab

瓦窑　wǎyáo　tile kiln

佤　Wǎ　see below

佤族　Wǎzú　the Va (Wa) nationality, or the Vas (Was), inhabiting Yunnan Province

wà

瓦　wà　cover (a roof) with tiles; tile ——see also wǎ

瓦刀　wàdāo　(bricklayer's) cleaver

袜（襪、韤）　wà　socks; stockings; hose

袜带　wàdài　suspenders; garters

袜底儿　wàdǐr　sole of a sock

袜套　wàtào　ankle socks; socks

袜筒　wàtǒng　the leg of a stocking

袜子　wàzi　socks; stockings; hose

膃　wà　see below

膃肭　wànà　formal obese

膃肭脐　wànàqí　Chin. med. the penis and testes of an ursine seal

膃肭兽　wànàshòu　zool. fur seal; ursine seal

wa

哇　wa　part. (used in place of 啊 a after a word ending in u or ao): 你怎么还不走～? Why haven't you gone yet, eh? / 你好～? Well, how are you? ——see also wā

wāi

歪　wāi　① askew; crooked; inclined; slanting: ～戴帽子 have one's hat on crooked / 这堵墙有点～。This wall is a little out of the perpendicular. / 小女孩儿～着头聚精会神地听故事。The little girl listened attentively to the story with her head tilted to one side. ② de-

vious; underhand; crooked: ～点子 evil ideas; devil's advice ③ recline to take a rest ④ dial. domineering; bossy: 他在乡下～得很。He is a local bully.

歪缠　wāichán　plague sb. with unreasonable demands

歪词儿　wāicír　worthless talk; defamatory talk

歪打正着　wāidǎ-zhèngzháo　hit the mark by a fluke; score a lucky hit

歪道　wāidào　① evil ways; depraved life; vice: 走～ lead a depraved life; abandon oneself to evil ways ② evil ideas; devil's advice

歪风　wāifēng　evil wind; unhealthy trend: 打击～，发扬正气 combat evil trends and foster a spirit of uprightness

歪风邪气　wāifēng-xiéqì　evil winds and noxious influences; unhealthy trends and evil practices: 有力地打击～ hit hard at evil trends

歪话　wāihuà　lie; falsehood

歪理　wāilǐ　false reasoning

歪路　wāilù　crooked ways; underhand ways; dishonest practices

歪门邪道　wāimén-xiédào　same as 邪门歪道 xiémén-wāidào

歪扭　wāiniǔ　twisted; awry: 他的嘴有些～。His mouth was a little twisted.

歪七扭八　wāiqī-niǔbā　crooked; askew; shapeless and twisted: ～地写几个字 scrawl a few words

歪曲　wāiqū　① distort; misrepresent; twist: ～事实 distort the facts / 事实不容～。The facts brook no distortion. / ～作者原意 misrepresent the author's meaning / ～别人的话 twist people's words ② crooked; askew; aslant

歪诗　wāishī　inelegant verses; doggerel

歪歪倒倒　wāiwāidǎodǎo　① rickety; shaky: 这椅子～。This chair is rather rickety. / 那醉汉～地走着。The drunk man reeled along. ② uneven; irregular; untidy: 他那～写的也算是字? Does he call that scribble handwriting?

歪歪扭扭　wāiwāiniǔniǔ　crooked; askew; shapeless and twisted: 字写得～ write a poor hand; scrawl; scribble

歪斜　wāixié　crooked; askew; aslant

㖞（喎）　wāi　(of the mouth) awry

㖞僻不遂　wāipì bùsuí　Chin. med. facial paralysis and hemiplegia after apoplexy

哇　wāi　interj. hey: ～，你去哪儿? Hey, where are you going?

wǎi

崴[1]　wǎi　rugged (mountain path)

崴[2]（踓）　wǎi　sprain; twist: 把脚～了 sprain one's ankle

崴泥　wǎiní　fail; fall through: 事先没准备，怕会～。The plan may fall through unless preparations are made well beforehand. / 这下子他可崴了泥了。He's got into a fix.

崴子　wǎizi　dial. (usu. used as part of a place name) river bend and mountain recess

揻　wǎi　dial. ladle out; spoon up (or out); scoop up: ～水 ladle out water

wài

外[1]　wài　① outer; outward; outside: 窗～ outside the window ② other: 外埠 wàibù ③ foreign; external: 外国 wàiguó ④ (relatives) of one's mother, sisters or daughters: 外孙 wàisūn ⑤ not of the same organization, class, etc.; not closely related: 见外 jiànwài ⑥ besides; in addition; beyond: 预算～的开支 extra-budgetary expenditure / 计划～的项目 projects not included in the plan ⑦ unofficial: 外传 wàizhuàn

外[2]　wài　a role for old men in traditional opera

外办　wàibàn　short for 外事办公室 wàishì bàngōngshì

外邦　wàibāng　*formal* foreign country

外币　wàibì　foreign currency: ～汇票 foreign currency bill / ～申报单 foreign currencies declaration / ～折合率 foreign currency conversion rate

外边　wàibian　① outside; out: 到～散步 go out for a walk / 咱们上～去谈, 好不好? Let's go outside to talk, shall we? ② a place other than where one lives or works: 她儿子在～工作。Her son works somewhere away from home. ③ exterior; outside: 行李卷儿～再裹一层塑料布。Wrap a plastic sheet round the bedroll.

外表　wàibiǎo　outward appearance; exterior; surface: ～美观 have a fine exterior; look nice / 事物的～ the outward appearance of things / 从～看人 judge people by appearances

外宾　wàibīn　foreign guest (*or* visitor)

外部　wàibù　① outside; external: 事物的～联系 external relations of things / ～世界 the external world ② exterior; surface

外埠　wàibù　towns or cities other than where one is

外财　wàicái　extra income

外层空间　wàicéng kōngjiān　outer space: ～导弹 outer-space missile

外层焰　wàicéngyàn　*chem.*　outer flame

外差　wàichā　*elec.*　heterodyne: 超～ superheterodyne

外场　wàicháng　sociable: 她是个～人儿, 人头儿挺广。She's a good mixer and has a large circle of acquaintances.

外场　wàichǎng　outfield (in baseball and softball): ～手 outfielder

外钞　wàichāo　foreign bank note

外出　wàichū　go out: 他有事～, 我没见到他。He had gone out on business so I didn't see him.

外出血　wàichūxuè　*med.*　external haemorrhage

外带[1]　wàidài　outer cover (of a tyre); tyre: ～和里带都扎穿了。The tyre and the inner tube are both punctured.

外带[2]　wàidài　as well; besides; into the bargain: 这个厂生产农业机械, ～修理农具。This factory, which produces agricultural machinery, repairs farm tools as a sideline.

外待　wàidài　treat sb. as a stranger or an outsider

外道儿　wàidàor　*inf.*　stranger; outsider

外道　wàidao　*inf.*　over-polite: 我们都是老同学, 你还～什么? We are all old classmates so why stand on ceremony?

外敌　wàidí　foreign enemy

外地　wàidì　parts of the country other than where one is: 代表团将在首都访问三天, 然后再到～游览。The delegation will pay a three-day visit to the capital before leaving for other parts of the country.

外电　wàidiàn　dispatches from foreign news agencies: 据～报导 according to reports from foreign news agencies

外调　wàidiào　① transfer (materials or personnel) to other localities: ～物资 materials allocated for transfer to other places ② go out to another work unit to make investigations

外毒素　wàidúsù　*med.*　exotoxin

外耳　wài'ěr　external ear

外耳道　wài'ěrdào　external auditory meatus

外耳炎　wài'ěryán　otitis externa

外翻足　wàifānzú　*med.*　talipes valgus

外藩　wàifān　vassal state

外分泌　wàifēnmì　*physiol.*　exocrine; external secretion: ～腺 exocrine gland

外敷　wàifū　*med.*　apply (ointment, etc.)

外敷药　wàifūyào　medicine for external application

外感　wàigǎn　*Chin. med.*　diseases caused by external factors: ～风寒 be affected by the cold; have a cold

外港　wàigǎng　outport

外公　wàigōng　*dial.*　(maternal) grandfather

外功　wàigōng　exercises to benefit the muscles and bones

外观　wàiguān　outward appearance; exterior: 这座大楼～很美。This is a fine-looking building.

外国　wàiguó　foreign country: ～朋友 foreign friends / ～干涉 foreign intervention (*or* interference) / 到～学习 go abroad to study

外国管辖权　wàiguó guǎnxiáquán　foreign jurisdiction

外国货　wàiguóhuò　(also 外货 wàihuò) foreign goods; imported goods

外国军事基地　wàiguó jūnshì jīdì　foreign military base

外国人　wàiguórén　foreigner; alien: ～居留证 residence permit for foreigners

外国语　wàiguóyǔ　foreign language

外国驻华机构　wàiguó zhùhuá jīgòu　foreign institutions in China

外国驻华使领馆　wàiguó zhùhuá shǐ-lǐngguǎn　foreign diplomatic and consular missions in China

外国租界　wàiguó zūjiè　foreign settlement; foreign concession

外果皮　wàiguǒpí　*bot.*　exocarp

外行　wàiháng　① layman; nonprofessional ② lay; unprofessional: 种庄稼他可不～。He's no amateur in farming. / 我对股票很～。I'm quite ignorant about stocks. / ～话 lay language; a mere dabbler's opinion

外号　wàihào　nickname

外话　wàihuà　*dial.*　unduly polite words that a friend is not expected to say

外踝　wàihuái　external malleolus; malleolus lateralis

外患　wàihuàn　foreign aggression

外汇　wàihuì　foreign exchange: ～储备 foreign exchange reserve / ～官价 official exchange rate / ～管理 (foreign) exchange control / ～行情 exchange quotations / ～交易 foreign exchange transaction / ～牌价 foreign exchange rate / ～平价 par of exchange; exchange parity / ～收入 foreign exchange earnings (*or* income) / ～收入留成 retention of a share of the foreign currency earned

外汇兑换券　wàihuìduìhuànquàn　(also 外汇券 wàihuìquàn) foreign exchange certificate (FEC)

外汇率　wàihuìlǜ　exchange rate

外汇平准基金　wàihuì píngzhǔn jījīn　exchange stabilization fund

外活　wàihuó　*dial.*　① orders taken by factories or craftsmen ② work taken in by housewives

外祸　wàihuò　foreign aggression

外籍　wàijí　foreign nationality: ～工作人员 foreign personnel

外寄生物　wàijìshēngwù　ectoparasite

外加　wàijiā　more; additional; extra: 给你们十份报纸, ～三本小册子。Here you are—ten copies of the newspa-

per, plus three pamphlets.

外加电压 wàijiā diànyā applied voltage

外家 wàijiā ① maternal grandparents' home ② mistress; concubine; kept woman ③ house for a mistress or concubine

外间 wàijiān ① outer room ② *formal* the external world; outside circles

外交 wàijiāo diplomacy; foreign affairs: 通过～途径解决 be settled through diplomatic channels

外交部 wàijiāobù ministry of foreign affairs; foreign ministry

外交部长 wàijiāobùzhǎng minister of (*or* for) foreign affairs; foreign minister

外交程序 wàijiāo chéngxù diplomatic procedure

外交辞令 wàijiāo cílìng diplomatic language (*or* parlance)

外交大臣 wàijiāo dàchén Foreign Secretary (in Britain)

外交代表 wàijiāo dàibiǎo diplomatic agent (*or* representative): ～机构 diplomatic mission

外交法 wàijiāofǎ diplomatic law

外交关系 wàijiāo guānxi diplomatic relations: 建立大使级的～ establish diplomatic relations at ambassadorial level / 断绝～ sever (*or* break off) diplomatic relations / 恢复～ resume diplomatic relations / 中止～ suspend diplomatic relations / ～升格 upgrade diplomatic relations / ～降格 downgrade diplomatic relations

外交官 wàijiāoguān diplomat

外交惯例 wàijiāo guànlì diplomatic practice; diplomatic usage; customary diplomatic practice

外交护照 wàijiāo hùzhào diplomatic passport

外交豁免权 wàijiāo huòmiǎnquán diplomatic immunity

外交机关 wàijiāo jīguān diplomatic establishments

外交家 wàijiāojiā diplomat

外交界 wàijiāojiè diplomatic circles

外交礼节 wàijiāo lǐjié diplomatic protocol (*or* etiquette)

外交签证 wàijiāo qiānzhèng diplomatic visa

外交使节 wàijiāo shǐjié diplomatic envoy

外交使团 wàijiāo shǐtuán diplomatic mission

外交特权 wàijiāo tèquán diplomatic prerogative (*or* privilege)

外交团 wàijiāotuán diplomatic corps: ～团长 dean (*or* doyen) of the diplomatic corps

外交文书 wàijiāo wénshū diplomatic papers

外交衔 wàijiāoxián diplomatic rank

外交信使 wàijiāo xìnshǐ diplomatic courier

外交邮袋 wàijiāo yóudài diplomatic pouch; diplomatic bag

外交邮件 wàijiāo yóujiàn diplomatic mail

外交政策 wàijiāo zhèngcè foreign policy

外交制裁 wàijiāo zhìcái diplomatic sanction

外角 wàijiǎo *math.* exterior angle

外教 wàijiào (short for 外籍教员) foreign teacher

外接圆 wàijiēyuán *math.* circumscribed circle; circumcircle

外界 wàijiè ① the external (*or* outside) world: 对～的认识 knowledge of the external world ② outside: 向～征求意见 solicit comments and suggestions from people outside one's organization / 顶住～的种种压力 withstand all kinds of outside pressure

外借 wàijiè lend out: 工具书恕不～。Reference books are not for lending. / 电话不～。This telephone is not for public use.

外景 wàijǐng outdoor scene; a scene shot on location; exterior: 拍摄～ film the exterior; shoot a scene on location

外径 wàijìng *mech.* external diameter; outside (*or* outer) diameter

外径千分尺 wàijìng qiānfēnchǐ outside micrometer

外舅 wàijiù *formal* wife's father; father-in-law

外卡钳 wàikǎqián *mech.* outside callipers

外科 wàikē *med.* surgical department: ～病房 surgical ward / ～手术 surgical operation; surgery / ～医生 surgeon

外科学 wàikēxué surgery

外壳 wàiké outer covering (*or* casing); shell; case: 热水瓶～ the outer casing of a thermos flask / 电池～ battery case

外客 wàikè a visitor or guest who is an outsider

外寇 wàikòu invading army; aggressor troops

外快 wàikuài extra income: 捞～ make extra money

外来 wàilái outside; external; foreign: ～干涉 outside interference; foreign (*or* external) intervention / ～干部 cadres not native to the locality

外来户 wàiláihù a household from another place; nonnative

外来语 wàiláiyǔ word of foreign origin; foreign word; loanword

外力 wàilì ① outside force ② *phys.* external force

外流 wàiliú outflow; drain: 美元～ dollar outflow / 黄金～ gold bullion outflow

外路 wàilù from outside; not local: ～货 imported goods / ～人 stranger; outsider

外露 wàilù reveal; show: 他感情从不～。He never reveals his true feelings.

外贸 wàimào short for 对外贸易 duìwài màoyì

外贸部 wàimàobù ministry of foreign trade

外貌 wàimào appearance; exterior; looks: 不要以～取人。Don't judge people by their appearance.

外面 wàimiàn outward appearance; exterior; surface

外面 wàimian outside; out: 把椅子搬到～去 take the chair out / 今天我们要在～吃饭。We'll eat (*or* dine) out today.

外面儿光 wàimiànrguāng deceptively smooth appearance; outward show: 做事要考虑实际效果, 不能追求～。In handling matters, we must pay attention to actual results and not try to be flashy.

外胚层 wàipēicéng *biol.* ectoblast; ectoderm; epiblast

外婆 wàipó *dial.* (maternal) grandmother

外戚 wàiqī relatives of a king or emperor on the side of his mother or wife

外企 wàiqǐ short for 外资企业 wàizī qǐyè

外强中干 wàiqiáng-zhōnggān outwardly strong but inwardly weak; strong in appearance but weak in reality

外侨 wàiqiáo (short for 外国侨民) foreign national; alien

外切形 wàiqiēxíng *math.* circumscribed figure

外勤 wàiqín ① work done outside the office or in the field (as surveying, prospecting, news gathering, etc.): 跑～ do fieldwork; run errands ② field personnel

外倾 wàiqīng *psychol.* extroversion

外圈 wàiquān *sports* outer lane; outside lane

外燃机 wàiránjī external-combustion engine

外人 wàirén ① stranger; outsider: 别客气, 我又不是～。Don't stand on ceremony. I'm no stranger. / 不足为～道 not to be mentioned to outsiders / 你说吧, 这里没～。Speak up. You're among friends. ② foreigner; alien

外柔内刚 wàiróu-nèigāng soft outside but hard inside—outwardly yielding but inwardly firm

外伤 wàishāng an injury or wound; trauma: ～性休克 traumatic shock

外伤学 wàishāngxué traumatology

外商 wàishāng (short for 外国商人) foreign businessman; foreign merchant

外肾 wàishèn *Chin. med.* testis; testicle

外生殖器 wàishēngzhíqì external genital organs

外省 wàishěng provinces other than where one is; other provinces

外甥 wàisheng ① sister's son; nephew ② *dial.* daugh-

ter's son; grandson

外甥打灯笼,照舅（旧） wàisheng dǎ dēnglong, zhàojiù the nephew carrying a lantern to give light to his uncle—the same as before (a pun on 照舅 zhàojiù and 照旧 zhàojiù)

外甥女 wàishengnǚ ① sister's daughter; niece ② *dial.* daughter's daughter; granddaughter

外史 wàishǐ unofficial history; informal history: 《儒林～》 *Unofficial* (or *Informal*) *History of the Literati* or *The Scholars*

外事 wàishì foreign affairs; external affairs: ～往来 dealings with foreign nationals or organizations / ～服务单位 service units for foreigners / ～活动 external public functions

外事办公室 wàishì bàngōngshì office of foreign affairs; foreign affairs office: 地方～ office in charge of local foreign affairs

外事局 wàishìjú bureau of foreign affairs, foreign affairs bureau

外事口 wàishìkǒu *inf.* (lit. "foreign affairs mouth") a collective name for all government organs that have to do with foreign affairs

外事组 wàishìzǔ ① foreign affairs section ② a section dealing with foreign personnel and foreign visitors

外室 wàishì ① mistress; concubine; kept woman ② house for a mistress or concubine

外手 wàishǒu (when driving a vehicle or operating a machine) the right-hand side

外首 wàishǒu *dial.* outside; out

外水 wàishuǐ extra income

外孙 wàisūn daughter's son; grandson

外孙女 wàisūn·nǚ daughter's daughter; granddaughter

外孙子 wàisūnzi *inf.* daughter's son; grandson

外胎 wàitāi outer cover (of a tyre); tyre

外逃 wàitáo ① flee to some other place ② flee the country: ～出境 run out of the country / ～分子 deserter; escapee

外套 wàitào ① overcoat ② loose coat; outer garment

外听道 wàitīngdào *physiol.* external auditory meatus

外头 wàitou outside; out: 汽车在～。 The car is outside. / 这事儿～全知道了。 Even those on the outside know about it. / 夏天我常在～睡。 In summer I often sleep outdoors.

外围 wàiwéi periphery: 首都～ the periphery of the capital

外围防线 wàiwéi fángxiàn outer defence line

外围组织 wàiwéi zǔzhī peripheral organization

外文 wàiwén foreign language

外屋 wàiwū outer room

外侮 wàiwǔ foreign aggression; external aggression: 抵御～ resist foreign aggression

外务 wàiwù ① matters outside one's job ② foreign affairs; external affairs

外务大臣 wàiwù dàchén minister of (or for) foreign affairs; foreign minister

外务省 wàiwùshěng the Ministry of Foreign Affairs (as in Japan)

外骛 wàiwù *formal* get involved in things which are not one's business: 心无～。 His heart is in his work.

外县 wàixiàn counties other than where one is; other counties

外线 wàixiàn ① *mil.* exterior lines: ～作战 fight on exterior lines; exterior-line operations ② outside (telephone) connections

外乡 wàixiāng another part of the country; some other place: ～口音 a nonlocal accent / 他是～人。 He is not from these parts.

外向 wàixiàng *psychol.* extroversion

外向型经济 wàixiàngxíng jīngjì export-oriented econ-

omy

外相 wàixiàng foreign minister

外销 wàixiāo for sale abroad or in another part of the country: ～产品 products for export; articles for sale in other areas

外心 wàixīn ① unfaithful intentions (of husband or wife) ② *math.* circumcentre

外形 wàixíng appearance; external form; contour

外姓 wàixìng (people) not of the same surname

外延 wàiyán *log.* extension

外焰 wàiyàn *chem.* outer flame

外洋 wàiyáng *old* outer ocean—foreign countries

外衣 wàiyī ① coat; jacket; outer clothing; outer garment ② semblance; appearance; garb

外因 wàiyīn *philos.* external cause

外阴 wàiyīn *physiol.* vulva

外阴炎 wàiyīnyán vulvitis

外用 wàiyòng *pharm.* external use; external application: ～药水 lotion / 只能～ for external use only

外语 wàiyǔ foreign language

外域 wàiyù *formal* foreign lands

外遇 wàiyù extramarital relations: 她怀疑她丈夫有～。 She suspected her husband of carrying on with some other woman.

外圆内方 wàiyuán-nèifāng round outside but spuare inside—outwardly gentle but inwardly stern

外援 wàiyuán foreign aid; outside help; external assistance

外在 wàizài external; extrinsic: ～因素 external factor

外在性 wàizàixìng externalism

外债 wàizhài external debt; foreign debt

外长 wàizhǎng short for 外交部长 wàijiāobùzhǎng

外罩 wàizhào outer garment; dustcoat; overall

外痔 wàizhì external piles (or haemorrhoids)

外传 wàizhuàn unofficial life history; unauthorized biography: 《杨太真～》 "The Unofficial Life History of Yang Taizhen" (i.e. Yang Guifei or Lady Yang 杨贵妃, Taizhen being her Taoist name)

外资 wàizī foreign capital: 引进～ absorb foreign capital / ～流入 foreign capital inflow

外资企业 wàizī qǐyè foreign enterprise (i.e. a company, enterprise or other economic organization registered within Chinese territory with foreign capital that is operating independently or engaged in cooperative production or cooperative management with a Chinese enterprise)

外子 wàizǐ *old* my husband

外族 wàizú ① people not of the same clan ② foreigner; alien ③ other nationalities

外祖父 wàizǔfù (maternal) grandfather

外祖母 wàizǔmǔ (maternal) grandmother

wān

弯（彎） wān ① curved; tortuous; crooked: ～～的月牙儿 a crescent moon / 累累的果实把树枝都压～了。 Clusters of fruit weighed the branches down. ② bend; flex: ～着腰插秧 bend over to transplant rice ③ turn; curve; bend: 这胡同有个～儿。 There's a curve in the lane.

弯度 wāndù curvature

弯弓 wāngōng *formal* draw a bow; bend a bow

弯路 wānlù ① crooked road; tortuous path ② roundabout way; detour: 少走～ avoid detours / 由于缺少经验, 我们工作走了～。 Owing to lack of experience we took a roundabout course in our work.

弯扭 wānniǔ crooked; twisted; winding: 一条～的小路

a winding path / 字写得弯弯扭扭 write a poor hand; scrawl; scribble

弯曲 wānqū winding; meandering; zigzag; crooked; curved: 一条～的山间小道 a winding mountain path / 一根～的木棍 a crooked stick / 小河弯弯曲曲地向东流去。The brook meanders eastwards.

弯头 wāntóu *mech.* elbow; bend: 回转～ return bend / 接合～ joint elbow

弯子 wānzi (also 弯儿 wānr) bend; turn; curve ——see also 绕弯子 rào wānzi; 转弯子 zhuǎn wānzi

剜 wān cut out; gouge out; scoop out: 把苹果烂的地方～掉。Scoop out the rotten part of the apple. / 凶残的奴隶主～掉了奴隶的双眼。The brutal slave owner gouged out the slave's eyes.

剜肉补疮 wānròu bǔchuāng (also 剜肉医疮 wānròu yīchuāng) cut out a piece of flesh to cure a boil—resort to a remedy worse than the ailment; resort to a stop-gap measure detrimental to long-term interests

湾（灣） wān ① a bend in a stream: 河～ river bend ② gulf; bay: 渤海～ Bohai Bay / 波斯～ the Persian Gulf ③ cast anchor; moor: 把船～在那边。Moor the boat over there.

湾泊 wānbó anchor; berth

蜿 wān see below

蜿蜒 wānyán ① (of snakes, etc.) wriggle ② wind; zigzag; meander: 小溪～流过田野。The stream winds through the fields. / 小路～而上。The path zigzagged upwards.

豌 wān see below

豌豆 wāndòu pea

豌豆黄 wāndòuhuáng pea-flour cake

豌豆象 wāndòuxiàng *zool.* pea weevil

wán

丸 wán ① ball; pellet: 泥丸 níwán ② pill; bolus: 每服两～ take two pills each time

丸剂 wánjì pill

丸药 wányào pill (or bolus) of Chinese medicine

丸子 wánzi ① a round mass of food; ball: 肉～ meatball ② pill; bolus

纨 wán *formal* fine silk fabrics

纨绔 wánkù (also 纨袴 wánkù) *formal* silk clothes—a rich family

纨绔子弟 wánkù zǐdì profligate son of rich parents; fop; dandy; playboy

纨扇 wánshàn round silk fan

完 wán ① intact; whole: 完好 wánhǎo ② run out; use up: 我们的煤快烧～了。We're running out of coal. / 听～别人的话 hear sb. out / 信纸用～了。The writing pad is used up. ③ finish; complete; be over; be through: 我马上就～。I'll be through soon. / 会开～了。The meeting is over. / 下期续～ to be concluded in the next issue ④ pay: 完税 wánshuì

完备 wánbèi complete; perfect: 一套～的工具 a complete set of tools / 指出不～之处 point out the imperfections / 设施～ be equipped with all sorts of facilities / 这本当代文集还是很不～的。This collection of contemporary prose is by no means a complete one.

完毕 wánbì finish; complete; end: 第一期工程已经～。The first phase of the project has been completed. / 一

切准备～。Everything is ready.

完璧归赵 wánbì guī Zhào return the jade intact to the State of Zhao—return sth. to its owner in perfect condition

完成 wánchéng accomplish; complete; fulfil; bring to success (or fruition): ～任务 complete one's mission; accomplish a task; discharge one's duty / ～国家计划 fulfil the state plan / ～生产指标 hit the production target; fulfil the production quota / ～作业 finish one's homework / 他的论文～了。He has finished off his thesis.

完蛋 wándàn *inf.* be done for; be finished: 要是银行不借钱,我们就～了。If the bank refuses to lend us the money, we're finished.

完稿 wángǎo finish a piece of writing; complete the manuscript

完工 wángōng complete a project, etc.; finish doing sth.; get through: 这座桥一个月就～了。It took only one month to complete the bridge.

完好 wánhǎo intact; whole; in good condition: ～无缺 intact; undamaged / 货物已到,～无损。The goods have arrived in good condition. / 鞋子修理后～如新。When the shoes were repaired, they looked as good as new.

完婚 wánhūn *formal* (of a man) get married; marry

完结 wánjié end; be over; finish: 事情并没有～。This is not the end of the matter.

完具 wánjù *formal* complete; perfect

完聚 wánjù *formal* reunite

完竣 wánjùn (of a project, etc.) be completed

完粮 wánliáng pay the grain tax

完了 wánliǎo come to an end; be over

完满 wánmǎn satisfactory; successful: 找个～的解决办法 seek a satisfactory solution / 会议～结束。The meeting came to a satisfactory close.

完美 wánměi perfect; consummate: ～的演奏 give a perfect performance

完美无缺 wánměi wú quē (also 完美无疵 wánměi wú cī) perfect; flawless: 舒伯特的《未完成交响曲》看来不完整,却是～的。Schubert's *Unfinished Symphony* is perfect in its incomplete state.

完密 wánmì careful; meticulous; deliberate

完全 wánquán ① complete; whole: 他话没说～。He didn't give a full picture. ② *adv.* completely; fully; wholly; entirely; absolutely: ～错了 be completely wrong / ～不同 be totally different; have nothing in common / ～相反 be the exact opposite / ～正确 perfectly right; absolutely correct / ～有资格 fully qualified; fully eligible / ～彻底为人民服务 serve the people heart and soul / 他～同意我们的意见。He fully agrees with us. / 她～不考虑个人得失。She gave no thought whatsoever to personal gain or loss.

完全变态 wánquán biàntài *biol.* complete metamorphosis

完全燃烧 wánquán ránshāo complete combustion

完全小学 wánquán xiǎoxué primary school with the full six grades

完全叶 wánquányè *bot.* complete leaf

完人 wánrén perfect man: 人无～。No man is perfect.

完善 wánshàn ① perfect; consummate: 设备～ very well equipped / 新生事物难免有不够～的地方。Imperfections are almost unavoidable in newborn things. / 我们厂的规章制度日趋～。The rules and regulations of our factory are being perfected. ② make perfect; improve: ～生产责任制 perfect the responsibility system of production / ～教育制度 improve the educational system

完事 wánshì finish; get through; come to an end: 你～了没有? Have you finished (the job)? / 他们校对到深夜才～。They didn't finish their proofreading until late

at night.

完税　wánshuì　pay taxes

完小　wánxiǎo　short for 完全小学 wánquán xiǎoxué

完整　wánzhěng　complete; integrated; intact: ～的工业体系 an integrated (*or* all-round, comprehensive) industrial system / 维护领土～ safeguard territorial integrity / 许多珍贵的历史文物～地保存下来了。Many precious historical relics have been preserved intact. / 没有经济上的独立，一个国家的独立是不～的。Without economic independence, no country can achieve complete independence.

玩¹(頑)　wán　① play; have fun; amuse oneself: ～儿牌 play cards / 咱们～儿盘棋好吗? Shall we have a game of chess? / 孩子们都喜欢～儿。Children all love to play. / 我们在青岛～了几天。We spent a few days enjoying ourselves in Qingdao. / 他是说着～儿的。He only said it for fun. *or* He was only joking. ② employ; resort to: ～儿邪的 employ underhand means; not play fair / ～手段 resort to crafty manoeuvres; play tricks

玩²(翫)　wán　① trifle with; treat lightly: 玩世不恭 wán shì bù gōng ② enjoy; appreciate: ～月 enjoy a beautiful moonlight / ～儿邮票 make a hobby of collecting stamps ③ object for appreciation: 古玩 gǔwán

玩儿不转　wánrbuzhuàn　*inf.*　can't handle; can't manage: 要他领导这班人，根本～。He's not up to the task of leading such a group.

玩法　wánfǎ　trifle with the law

玩忽　wánhū　neglect; trifle with: ～职守 neglect (*or* dereliction) of duty; be remiss in one's duty

玩话　wánhuà　joking remarks; joke: 他说的准是～吧? I'm sure his remarks were meant jokingly?

玩儿坏　wánrhuài　*dial.*　be up to mischief; play a dirty trick

玩火　wánhuǒ　play with fire

玩火自焚　wánhuǒ zìfén　he who plays with fire will get burnt; whoever plays with fire will perish by fire

玩具　wánjù　toy; plaything: ～汽车 toy car / ～汽枪 popgun / ～店 toyshop

玩儿命　wánrmìng　*inf.*　① gamble (*or* play) with one's life; risk one's life needlessly: 在大街上撒把骑车简直是～。To ride a bicycle in the street without holding the handlebars is simply to play with one's own life. ② exerting the utmost strength; for all one is worth; with all one's might: ～地干 work like hell / 他们正在～地赶时间。They're doing their damnedest to meet the deadline.

玩弄　wánnòng　① dally with: ～女性 philander; dally with women ② play with; juggle with: ～词句 juggle with words; go in for rhetoric ③ resort to; employ: ～种种阴谋诡计 resort to all sorts of schemes and intrigues / ～新花招 employ some new tricks / ～两面派手法 engage in double-dealing

玩偶　wán'ǒu　doll; toy figurine

玩儿票　wánrpiào　play a role in Beijing opera as an amateur

玩儿去　wánrqù　*inf.*　get away; clear off

玩赏　wánshǎng　enjoy; take pleasure (*or* delight) in: ～风景 enjoy (*or* admire) the scenery

玩世不恭　wán shì bù gōng　thumb one's nose at the world; be cynical

玩耍　wánshuǎ　play; have fun; amuse oneself

玩儿完　wánrwán　*inf.*　① be done for; be finished: 一场大火他的买卖全～了。After the fire, his business was done for. ② dead

玩味　wánwèi　ponder; ruminate: 他的话很值得～。His

words are worth pondering.

玩物　wánwù　plaything; toy

玩物丧志　wán wù sàng zhì　riding a hobby saps one's will to make progress; pursuit of petty pleasures thwarts high aims

玩狎　wánxiá　*formal*　trifle with; dally with

玩笑　wánxiào　① joke with; play a prank on: 他这是～，你别认真。He's only joking; don't take him seriously. ② joke; jest; prank ——see also 开玩笑 kāi wánxiào

玩意儿　wányìr　(*also* 玩艺儿 wányìr) *inf.*　① toy; plaything ② acrobatics, cross talks, ballad singing, magic, etc. ③ thing: 新鲜～ newfangled gadget / 他手里拿的是什么～? What's that thing in his hand? / 他是什么～! What kind of louse is he! / 我早知道他不是个好～。I know all along that he was no good.

顽¹　wán　① stupid; dense; insensate: 冥顽 míngwán ② stubborn; obstinate: 顽敌 wándí ③ naughty; mischievous

顽²　wán　same as 玩¹ wán

顽磁　wáncí　*phys.*　magnetic retentivity

顽敌　wándí　stubborn enemy; inveterate

顽钝　wándùn　*formal*　① dull and obtuse; stupid; thickheaded ② lacking moral courage ③ blunt

顽梗　wángěng　obstinate; perverse

顽固　wángù　① obstinate; stubborn; headstrong: ～地坚持错误立场 stubbornly cling to one's wrong position ② bitterly opposed to change; die-hard

顽固不化　wángù bù huà　incorrigibly obstinate

顽固分子　wángù fènzǐ　diehard; die-hard element

顽固派　wángùpài　the diehards

顽疾　wánjí　chronic and stubborn disease; persistent ailment

顽抗　wánkàng　stubbornly resist: 敌人再～就消灭它。If the enemy continue to resist stubbornly, wipe them out.

顽廉懦立　wánlián nuòlì　make a dishonest man become honest and a weak man become resolute (said of the influence of a man of integrity)

顽劣　wánliè　stubborn and stupid; stubborn and obstreperous

顽民　wánmín　*old*　unruly people

顽皮　wánpí　naughty; mischievous

顽强　wánqiáng　indomitable; staunch; tenacious: ～的精神 indomitable spirit / 同疾病进行～的斗争 carry on a tenacious struggle against illness

顽躯　wánqū　*formal hum.*　my person; my health

顽石　wánshí　hard rock; insensate stone

顽石点头　wánshí diǎntóu　the insensate stones nodding in agreement (said of persuasive powers)

顽童　wántóng　naughty boy; urchin

顽癣　wánxuǎn　*Chin. med.*　stubborn dermatitis (e.g. neurodermatitis)

顽症　wánzhèng　chronic and stubborn disease; persistent ailment

烷　wán　*chem.*　alkane

烷化　wánhuà　*chem.*　alkanisation; alkylation: ～汽油 alkylation gasoline

烷基　wánjī　*chem.*　alkyl: ～胺 alkylamine

wǎn

宛¹　wǎn　winding; tortuous

宛²　wǎn　*formal*　as if: 音容宛在 yīnróng wǎn zài

宛然 wǎnrán　as if: 这里山清水秀，～江南风景。The scenery here has great charm, reminding one of the land south of the Changjiang River.

宛如 wǎnrú　(also 宛似 wǎnsì, 宛若 wǎnruò) just like: 欢腾的人群～大海的波涛。The jubilant crowds are just like the surging waves of the sea.

宛延 wǎnyán　*formal*　wind; zigzag; meander

宛转 wǎnzhuǎn　① same as 辗转 zhǎnzhuǎn ② same as 婉转 wǎnzhuǎn

莞 wǎn　see below

莞尔 wǎn·ěr　*formal*　smile: 不觉～ cannot help smiling

挽[1] wǎn　① draw; pull: ～弓 draw a bow / 手～着手 arm in arm ② roll up: ～起袖子 roll up one's sleeves

挽[2]（輓） wǎn　① pull; draw: ～车 pull (or draw) a cart or carriage ② lament sb.'s death

挽[3] wǎn　same as 绾 wǎn

挽词 wǎncí　(also 挽辞 wǎncí) memorial speech

挽歌 wǎngē　dirge; elegy

挽回 wǎnhuí　retrieve; redeem: ～败局 retrieve a defeat / ～面子 save face / ～劣势 retrieve oneself from an inferior position; improve one's position / ～损失 retrieve a loss / ～影响 redeem (or retrieve) one's reputation / 他们觉得情况一定很严重，不能～了。They thought that the situation must be desperate, past saving.

挽救 wǎnjiù　save; remedy; rescue: ～病人的生命 save the patient's life / 想出一个有效的～办法 think out an effective remedy / 不顾党对他的教育和～ disregard the Party's efforts to educate and redeem him / ～失足青少年 make great efforts to reform juvenile delinquents

挽联 wǎnlián　elegiac couplet

挽留 wǎnliú　urge (or persuade) sb. to stay: 再三～ repeatedly urge sb. to stay; press sb. to stay

挽马 wǎnmǎ　draught horse

挽诗 wǎnshī　elegy

惋 wǎn　*formal*　sigh

惋伤 wǎnshāng　heave a sigh of grief

惋叹 wǎntàn　sigh mournfully; lament

惋惜 wǎnxī　feel sorry for sb. or about sth.; regret: 他才华未展，英年早逝，十分令人～。It is much to be regretted that he died so young, his potential unfulfilled. / 我把旧书全卖了，一直感到～。I've always regretted selling all my old books.

菀 wǎn　see 紫菀 zǐwǎn

晚 wǎn　① evening; night: ～风 evening breeze ② far on in time; late: ～唐 the late Tang Dynasty / 睡得～ go to bed late / ～做总比不做好。Better late than never. / 现在去还不～。It's still not too late to go. ③ younger; junior: 晚辈 wǎnbèi

晚安 wǎn·ān　*pol.*　good night

晚班 wǎnbān　night shift: 上～ be on the night shift

晚半天儿 wǎnbàntiānr　*inf.*　in the late afternoon; towards dusk; dusk

晚半晌儿 wǎnbanshǎngr　*dial.*　dusk

晚报 wǎnbào　evening paper

晚辈 wǎnbèi　the younger generation; one's juniors

晚餐 wǎncān　supper; dinner

晚场 wǎnchǎng　evening show; evening performance

晚车 wǎnchē　night train

晚春 wǎnchūn　late spring; late in the spring

晚稻 wǎndào　late rice

晚点 wǎndiǎn　(of a train, ship, etc.) late; behind schedule: 火车～了。The train is late. / 火车～十五分钟。The train is 15 minutes overdue.

晚饭 wǎnfàn　supper; dinner

晚会 wǎnhuì　an evening of entertainment; soirée; social evening; evening party: 除夕～ New Year's Eve entertainment

晚婚 wǎnhūn　marry late; late marriage: 提倡～ encourage late marriage

晚间 wǎnjiān　(in the) evening; (at) night: ～新闻 evening news

晚节 wǎnjié　integrity in one's later years: 保持革命～ maintain (or uphold) one's revolutionary integrity in one's later years

晚近 wǎnjìn　in recent years; during the past few years

晚景 wǎnjǐng　① evening scene ② one's circumstances in old age: ～凄凉 lead a miserable and dreary life in old age

晚礼服 wǎnlǐfú　evening dress; evening clothes

晚年 wǎnnián　old age; one's later (or remaining) years: 过着幸福的～ spend one's remaining years in happiness

晚娘 wǎnniáng　*dial.*　stepmother

晚期 wǎnqī　late period: ～作品 sb.'s later works; the works of sb.'s later period / 十九世纪～ the late 19th century; the latter part of the 19th century / 他的病已到～。His illness has reached an advanced stage. / ～癌症 terminal cancer

晚秋 wǎnqiū　① late autumn; late in the autumn ② late-autumn crops

晚秋作物 wǎnqiū zuòwù　late-autumn crops

晚晌 wǎn·shǎng　*dial.*　(in the) evening; (at) night

晚上 wǎnshang　(in the) evening; (at) night: ～好。Good evening.

晚生 wǎnshēng　*old hum.*　I (used when speaking to an elder or a senior)

晚世 wǎnshì　*formal*　modern times

晚熟 wǎnshú　*agric.*　late-maturing: ～品种 late variety

晚霜 wǎnshuāng　late frost

晚岁 wǎnsuì　*formal*　old age; one's later (or remaining) years

晚田 wǎntián　*dial.*　late-autumn crops

晚霞 wǎnxiá　sunset glow; sunset clouds

晚香玉 wǎnxiāngyù　*bot.*　tuberose

晚学 wǎnxué　① *formal hum.*　I (used when speaking to an elder or a senior) ② attend school or seek knowledge in old age ③ *dial.*　afternoon classes

晚宴 wǎnyàn　dinner party

晚育 wǎnyù　late childbirth: 晚婚～应予鼓励。Late marriage and late childbirth should be encouraged.

脘 wǎn　see 胃脘 wèiwǎn

婉 wǎn　① mild and indirect; tactful: 婉商 wǎnshāng ② *formal*　gentle; gracious: 婉顺 wǎnshùn ③ *formal*　beautiful; graceful; elegant: 婉丽 wǎnlì

婉词 wǎncí　gentle words; euphemism

婉辞[1] wǎncí　same as 婉词

婉辞[2] wǎncí　graciously decline; politely refuse

婉和 wǎnhé　mild and roundabout; tactful: ～的语气 a mild tone

婉丽 wǎnlì　*formal*　beautiful; lovely

婉曼 wǎnmàn　*formal*　soft and graceful

婉媚 wǎnmèi　*formal*　gentle and charming

婉妙 wǎnmiào　(of voice) sweet; soft

婉商 wǎnshāng　consult with sb. tactfully or politely

婉顺 wǎnshùn　*formal*　(of a woman) meek; docile

婉谢 wǎnxiè　graciously decline; politely refuse

婉言 wǎnyán gentle words; tactful expressions: ～相劝 gently persuade; plead tactfully

婉言谢绝 wǎnyán xièjué graciously decline; politely refuse

婉约 wǎnyuē *formal* ① graceful and restrained: ～风流，异西施之被教。(徐陵《玉台新咏序》) Graceful and seductive, different from Xi Shi, who had to be taught. ② subtle and concise (said of a style of the *ci* 词, regarded as the orthodox style, suitable for the portrayal of picturesque scenery and feminine beauty and for the expression of delicate feelings and tender thoughts)

婉转 wǎnzhuǎn ① mild and indirect; tactful: 措词～ put it tactfully / 他那话虽然说得～, 意见却很尖锐。His remark, for all its mildness, is nevertheless a sharp criticism. ② sweet and agreeable: 歌喉～ a sweet voice; sweet singing

缩

wǎn coil up: 把头发～起来 coil one's hair / ～个扣儿 tie a knot

皖

Wǎn another name for 安徽 Ānhuī

碗（盌、椀）

wǎn ① bowl: 摆～筷 put out bowls and chopsticks for a meal; set (*or* lay) the table ② bowl-like thing

碗柜 wǎnguì kitchen cupboard

碗盏 wǎnzhǎn crockery; chinaware

wàn

万（萬）

wàn ① ten thousand ② a very great number; myriad: ～事～物 myriads of things; all nature / ～里长空 vast clear skies ③ *adv.* (used in the negative) absolutely: 你～不可去。You absolutely may not go. / 此事～不可泄漏出去。Be sure not to let it out. ④ (Wàn) a surname ——see also mò

万儿八千 wànr bāqiān *inf.* ten thousand or a bit less

万般 wànbān ① all the different kinds ② utterly; extremely

万般皆下品, 惟有读书高 wànbān jiē xiàpǐn, wéiyǒu dúshū gāo the worth of other pursuits is small, the study of books excels them all (a parodical reversed version runs: 万般皆上品, 惟有读书糟 all other callings now rank first, the study of books is last and worst)

万般无奈 wànbān wúnài have no alternative (but to): 她～, 只好自寻短见。She took her own life: there was no alternative. *or* As a last resort she took her own life.

万变不离其宗 wàn biàn bù lí qí zōng change ten thousand times without leaving the original aim or stand; change time and again, yet stay much the same

万不得已 wànbùdéyǐ out of absolute necessity; as a last resort: 他知道这只是～的办法。He knew it was a last resort. / 不到～, 他不亲自出马。He never appeared personally unless it was absolutely essential. / 倘不是～, 我是不和他来往的。I would have nothing to do with him if I could help it.

万次闪光灯 wàncì shǎnguāngdēng *photog.* multitime flash lamp

万代 wàndài same as 万世 wànshì

万端 wànduān multifarious: 变化～ multifarious changes; kaleidoscopic changes

万恶 wàn'è extremely vicious; absolutely vicious: ～的旧社会 the vicious (*or* evil) old society / ～的殖民主义制度 the diabolical system of colonialism / ～之源 the root of all evil

万方 wànfāng ① all places ② extremely; incomparably: 仪态万方 yítài wànfāng

万分 wànfēn *adv.* very much; extremely: ～感谢 thank you very much indeed / ～抱歉 be extremely sorry / ～高兴 be very happy; be highly pleased

万夫莫当 wànfū mò dāng more than a match for ten thousand men (said of a brave warrior)

万福 wànfú *old* a woman's bow; curtsy: 道～ make (*or* drop) a curtsy; curtsy

万古 wàngǔ through the ages; eternally; forever

万古长存 wàngǔ chángcún last forever; be everlasting

万古长青 wàngǔ chángqīng remain fresh forever; be everlasting: 祝两国人民的友谊～! May the friendship between our two peoples last forever!

万古流芳 wàngǔ liúfāng leave a good name that will live forever; achieve immortal fame

万古千秋 wàngǔ-qiānqiū through unnumbered ages; for eons

万贯 wànguàn ten thousand strings of cash—great wealth: 他有～家财。He is extremely wealthy. *or* He is a millionaire.

万国 wànguó *old* all nations

万户侯 wànhùhóu a marquis with a fief of 10,000 families—a high noble; a high official

万花筒 wànhuātǒng kaleidoscope

万汇 wànhuì *formal* all things on earth

万机 wànjī a myriad of state affairs: 日理万机 rì lǐ wànjī

万家灯火 wànjiā dēnghuǒ a myriad twinkling lights (of a city): 飞机降落时, 但见～, 一片灿烂。As the plane was landing, a myriad lights greeted the eye.

万箭穿心 wànjiàn chuān xīn (as if) ten thousand arrows have pierced the heart—in extreme grief

万劫不复 wànjié bù fù lost forever; beyond redemption: 陷于～之地 be doomed forever

万金油 wànjīnyóu ① a balm for treating headaches, scalds and other minor ailments ② Jack of all trades and master of none

万钧 wànjūn ten thousand *jun*—very heavy; very powerful: 雷霆万钧 léitíng wànjūn

万籁俱寂 wànlài jù jì all is quiet and still; silence reigns supreme: 当夜～, 月色初上。The night was very still and the moon had just risen.

万类 wànlèi all creation; all living things: 鹰击长空, 鱼翔浅底, ～霜天竞自由。(毛泽东) Eagles cleave the air, Fish glide in the limpid deep; Under freezing skies a million creatures contend in freedom.

万里长城 Wànlǐ Chángchéng the Great Wall

万里长征 wànlǐ chángzhēng a long march of ten thousand *li*: 夺取全国胜利, 这只是～走完了第一步。(毛泽东) To win countrywide victory is only the first step in a long march of ten thousand *li*.

万流景仰 wànliú jǐngyǎng command the respect and admiration of all

万隆 Wànlóng Bandung: ～会议 the Bandung Conference (1955)

万马奔腾 wànmǎ bēnténg ten thousand horses galloping ahead—all going full steam ahead

万马齐喑 wànmǎ qí yīn ten thousand horses standing mute—a lifeless atmosphere: 九州生气恃风雷, ～究可哀。(龚自珍) Only in wind and thunder can the country show its vitality; Alas, the ten thousand horses all muted!

万民伞 wànmínsǎn umbrella of ten thousand people (formerly an umbrella presented to a popular official when he left his district as a token of respect and gratitude; made of red silk or satin and inscribed with the names of the donors in gilt characters)

万难 wànnán ① extremely difficult; utterly impossible: ～照办 impossible to do as requested / ～同意 can by

no means agree ② all sorts of difficulties: 排除万难 páichú wàn nán

万能 wànnéng ① omnipotent; all-powerful ② universal; all-purpose: ～材料试验机 universal testing machine／～工具机 all-purpose machine／～虎钳 universal vice／～胶 all-purpose adhesive／～润滑脂 multipurpose grease／～工作台 universal table／～拖拉机 multipurpose tractor

万年 wànnián ten thousand years; all ages; eternity: 遗臭万年 yí chòu wànnián

万年历 wànniánlì perpetual calendar

万年青 wànniánqīng bot. ① evergreen ② Japanese rohdea (Rohdea japonica)

万念俱灰 wànniàn jù huī abandon oneself to despair; be in the slough of despond

万千 wànqiān multifarious; myriad: 变化～ eternally changing; changing all the time／思绪～ myriads of thoughts welling up in one's mind

万全 wànquán perfectly sound; surefire

万全之计 wànquán zhī jì a completely safe plan; a surefire plan

万人坑 wànrénkēng a pit of ten thousand corpses—a mass grave

万人空巷 wànrén kōng xiàng the whole town turns out (to celebrate or to welcome sb.)

万世 wànshì all ages; generation after generation

万世师表 wànshì shībiǎo the Model Teacher of a Myriad Ages (an honorific title for Confucius 孔子)

万事 wànshì all things; everything: 人生～ everything in life

万事大吉 wànshì dàjí everything is just fine; everything goes off without a hitch; everything's O.K.: 以为这次胜利了便～的思想是危险的。It is dangerous to think that after this one victory everything will go off without a hitch.

万事亨通 wànshì hēngtōng everything goes well

万事俱备, 只欠东风 wànshì jù bèi, zhǐ qiàn dōngfēng everything is ready, all we need is an east wind—all is ready except what is crucial

万事起头难 wànshì qǐtóu nán (also 万事开头难 wànshì kāitóu nán) everything's hard in the beginning; the first step is always difficult

万事通 wànshìtōng know-all

万寿无疆 wànshòu wújiāng (may you enjoy) boundless longevity

万水千山 wànshuǐ-qiānshān ten thousand torrents and a thousand crags—the trials of a long and arduous journey: 红军不怕远征难,～只等闲。(毛泽东) The Red Army fears not the trials of the Long March, Scorning ten thousand torrents, a thousand crags.

万死 wànsǐ die ten thousand deaths

万死不辞 wànsǐ bù cí willing to risk any danger (to fulfil a task)

万岁 wànsuì ① long live: 全世界人民大团结～! Long live the great unity of the people of the world! ② the emperor; Your Majesty; His Majesty

万万 wànwàn ① adv. (used in the negative) absolutely: 我～没有想到。This idea never occurred to me.／那是～不行的。That's absolutely out of the question. or That won't do at all.／对此～不可大意。You must under no circumstances take this lightly. ② hundred million

万无一失 wàn wú yī shī no danger of anything going wrong; no risk at all; perfectly safe

万物 wànwù the ten thousand things of creation; all things of creation all things on the earth: 夫天地者,～之逆旅。(李白) Heaven and earth are an inn for the ten thousand things of creation.

万向 wànxiàng mech. universal: ～阀 universal valve／～

联轴节 universal coupling

万象 wànxiàng every phenomenon on earth; all manifestations of nature

万象更新 wànxiàng gēngxīn all things take on a new aspect; everything looks new and fresh: 春回大地,～。Spring comes to the earth again and all looks fresh and gay.

万幸 wànxìng very lucky (or fortunate); by sheer luck: 他差点儿没淹死, 真是～。What luck he escaped being drowned!

万姓 wànxìng ten thousand names—the people; the masses

万言书 wànyánshū a 10,000-word (i.e. long) memorial

万一 wànyī ① conj. just in case; if by any chance: ～有人找我, 就请他留个条。If by any chance somebody comes to see me, ask him to leave a message. ② adv. what if: ～这传闻是事实呢? What if the rumour is true? ③ contingency; eventuality: 防备～ be ready for all eventualities; be prepared for the worst ④ one ten thousandth; a very small percentage: 笔墨不能形容其～。It simply beggars description.

万应灵丹 wànyìng língdān cure-all; panacea

万用电表 wànyòng diànbiǎo elec. avometer; multimeter

万有引力 wànyǒuyǐnlì phys. (universal) gravitation; gravitational attraction

万有引力定律 wànyǒuyǐnlì dìnglù the law of universal gravitation

万丈 wànzhàng lofty or bottomless: 怒火～ a towering rage; a fit of violent anger

万丈高楼平地起 wànzhàng gāolóu píngdì qǐ the loftiest towers are built up from the ground; great oaks from little acorns grow

万丈深渊 wànzhàng shēnyuān a bottomless chasm; abyss

万众 wànzhòng millions of people; the multitude: 喜讯传来,～欢腾。Millions of people rejoiced at the happy news.

万众一心 wànzhòng yīxīn millions of people all of one mind: 我们～建设社会主义现代化强国。We are building a modern, powerful socialist country with one heart and one mind.

万状 wànzhuàng in the extreme; extremely: 危险～ extremely dangerous

万紫千红 wànzǐ-qiānhóng a riot (or blaze) of colour: 百花盛开,～。Flowers of all sorts are blooming in a riot of colour.

萬 wàn ten thousand (used for the numeral 万 wàn on cheques, etc. to avoid mistakes or alterations)

腕 wàn wrist

腕儿 wànr same as 大腕 dàwàn

腕力 wànlì wrist strength

腕子 wànzi wrist: 手～ wrist

腕足动物 wànzú dòngwù brachiopod

蔓 wàn a tendrilled vine: 这棵黄瓜爬～了。This cucumber plant is climbing. ——see also mán; màn

wāng

汪[1] wāng ① formal (of a body of water) deep and vast ② (of liquid) collect; accumulate: 汤里～着油。There are blobs of fat in the soup. ③ dial. pond; pool ④ m. (for liquid): 一～雨水 a puddle of rainwater ⑤ (Wāng) a surname

汪²

汪　wāng　*onom.*　bark; bowwow

汪汪　wāngwāng　① tears welling up; tearful: 泪汪汪 lèiwāngwāng ② *onom.* bark; yap; bowwow: 狗～地叫。 A dog is barking. ③ *formal* (of a body of water) vast; boundless

汪洋　wāngyáng　(of a body of water) vast; boundless: 一片～ a vast expanse of water

汪洋大海　wāngyáng dàhǎi　a vast (*or* boundless) ocean: 陷敌于人民战争的～之中 engulf the enemy in the boundless ocean of people's war

汪子　wāngzi　*inf.*　pond; pool

wǎng

亡（亾）

wáng　① flee; run away: 出亡 chūwáng ② lose; be gone: 亡失 wángshī ③ die; perish: 阵亡 zhènwáng ④ deceased: ～妻 deceased wife / ～友 deceased friend ⑤ conquer; subjugate: 亡国 wángguó

亡故　wánggù　die; pass away; decease

亡国　wángguó　① subjugate a nation; let a state perish ② a conquered nation: ～之民 the people of a conquered nation

亡国灭种　wángguó-mièzhǒng　national doom and racial extinction

亡国奴　wángguónú　a slave without a country; a conquered people

亡魂　wánghún　soul of the newly deceased; ghost

亡魂丧胆　wánghún-sàngdǎn　be scared out of one's wits; be half dead with fright

亡灵　wánglíng　soul of a deceased person; ghost; spectre

亡命　wángmìng　① flee; seek refuge; go into exile ② desperate

亡命之徒　wángmìng zhī tú　desperado

亡失　wángshī　be lost; be missing

亡羊补牢　wáng yáng bǔ láo　mend the fold after the sheep is lost: ～，犹未为晚。 It is not too late to mend the fold even after the sheep is lost.

亡佚　wángyì　*formal*　be lost; be missing

王

wáng　① king; monarch: 国王 guówáng ② duke; prince: 亲王 qīnwáng ③ *formal* grand; great: ～父 grandfather ④ best or strongest of its kind: 拳王 quánwáng ⑤ (Wáng) a surname ——see also wàng

王八　wángba　① tortoise ② *offens.* cuckold

王八蛋　wángbadàn　(also 王八羔子 wángbagāozi) *offens.*　bastard; son of a bitch

王不留行　wángbùliúxíng　*Chin. med.*　the seed of cowherb (*Vaccaria segetalis*)

王朝　wángcháo　① imperial court; royal court ② dynasty: 封建～ feudal dynasties

王储　wángchǔ　crown prince

王道　wángdào　kingly way; benevolent government

王法　wángfǎ　the law of the land; the law

王府　wángfǔ　palace of a prince

王公　wánggōng　princes and dukes; the nobility: ～大臣 princes, dukes and ministers / ～贵族 the nobility

王宫　wánggōng　(imperial) palace

王顾左右而言他　wáng gù zuǒ-yòu ér yán tā　the king looked right and left, and spoke of other things (an allusion to King Xuan of Qi 齐宣王, who was embarrassed when Mencius 孟子 asked him a question about his government)—trying to evade a question by changing the subject

王官　wángguān　officials of feudal dynasties

王冠　wángguān　imperial crown; royal crown

王国　wángguó　① kingdom ② realm; domain: 自由王国 zìyóu wángguó

王侯　wánghóu　princes and marquises; the nobility

王后　wánghòu　queen consort; queen

王浆　wángjiāng　royal jelly

王母娘娘　Wángmǔ niángniang　the Lady Queen Mother (popular name for 西王母 Xīwángmǔ)

王牌　wángpái　trump card

王牌军　wángpáijūn　*elite* troops; crack units

王权　wángquán　monarchical power

王室　wángshì　① royal family: ～成员 a member of the royal family ② imperial court; royal court

王水　wángshuǐ　*chem.*　*aqua regia*

王孙　wángsūn　prince's descendants; offspring of the nobility

王孙公子　wángsūn gōngzǐ　same as 公子王孙 gōngzǐ wángsūn

王位　wángwèi　throne: 继承～ succeed to the throne

王子　wángzǐ　king's son; prince

王族　wángzú　persons of royal lineage; imperial kinsmen

wǎng

网（網）

wǎng　① net: 一张～ a net / 捉蝴蝶的～ a butterfly-net ② network: 铁路网 tiělùwǎng ③ catch with a net; net: ～鱼 net a fish ④ cover or enclose as with a net: 眼里～着红丝 have bloodshot eyes

网点　wǎngdiǎn　a network of commercial establishments

网兜　wǎngdōu　string bag

网纲　wǎnggāng　head rope (of a fishnet)

网获量　wǎnghuòliàng　*fishery* haul

网巾　wǎngjīn　hairnet

网开三面　wǎng kāi sān miàn　leave three sides of the net open—give the wrongdoer a way out; be lenient

网开一面　wǎng kāi yī miàn　leave one side of the net open—give the wrongdoer a way out; be lenient

网篮　wǎnglán　a basket with netting on top

网漏吞舟　wǎng lòu tūn zhōu　the meshes of the net are so large that a whale could slip through—the laws are too lax

网罗　wǎngluó　① a net for catching fish or birds; trap ② enlist the services of: ～人材 enlist able men / ～一小撮不法分子 scrape together a handful of lawbreakers

网络　wǎngluò　① network: 开放式、～型的经济区 an open and interconnected economic zone ② *elec.* network: 有源～ active network / 无源～ passive network

网屏　wǎngpíng　(also 网版 wǎngbǎn) *print.*　screen

网球　wǎngqiú　① tennis: ～场 tennis court / ～拍 tennis racket / 软式～ soft tennis ② tennis ball

网坛　wǎngtán　tennis circles

网眼　wǎngyǎn　(also 网目 wǎngmù) mesh

网状脉　wǎngzhuàngmài　*bot.* netted (*or* reticulated) veins: ～叶 net-veined (*or* reticulate) leaf

网子　wǎngzi　① net ② hairnet

枉

wǎng　① crooked: 矫枉过正 jiǎo wǎng guò zhèng ② twist; pervert: 枉法 wǎngfǎ ③ treat unjustly; wrong: ～杀无辜 kill an innocent person ④ in vain; to no avail: ～活了半辈子 have wasted half a lifetime

枉尺直寻　wǎngchǐ-zhíxún　bend the foot in order to straighten the yard—lose a little in order to gain a great deal

枉道　wǎngdào　① make a detour; go by a roundabout route ② *formal* curry favour by crooked means

枉断　wǎngduàn　settle a case by perverting the law

枉法 wǎngfǎ　pervert (or bend) the law: 贪脏枉法 tān-zāng wǎngfǎ

枉费 wǎngfèi　waste; try in vain; be of no avail: ～工夫 waste time and energy

枉费唇舌 wǎngfèi chúnshé　waste one's breath

枉费心机 wǎngfèi xīnjī　hatch plots in vain; scheme to no avail: 他想在我们中间挑拨离间，结果是～。He tried in vain to sow dissension among us.

枉顾 wǎnggù　(also 枉临 wǎnglín) formal pol. I am honoured by your visit

枉己正人 wǎngjǐ-zhèngrén　be crooked yet try to set others straight

枉驾 wǎngjià　formal pol. ① I am honoured by your visit ② would you be kind enough to see sb.

枉然 wǎngrán　futile; in vain; to no purpose: 既然他不讲理, 跟他争辩也是～。It's no use arguing with him when he refuses to listen to reason.

枉死 wǎngsǐ　die uncleared of a false charge; die a victim of injustice: ～鬼 wronged souls

枉自 wǎngzì　futile; in vain; to no purpose: ～讨论了那么多次, 问题还是没解决。We have discussed the problem several times but to no purpose.

罔[1] wǎng　formal deceive: 欺罔 qīwǎng

罔[2] wǎng　formal no; not: 置若罔闻 zhì ruò wǎng wén

往 wǎng　① go: 何～? Where are you going? ② prep. in the direction of; towards; to: ～东走去 go in an eastward direction; go eastwards / 劲～一处使 all directing their efforts towards the same goal / 从上海飞～香港 fly from Shanghai to Hong Kong / ～左拐 turn to the left / 汽艇～湖州开去了。The motorboat is heading for Huzhou. / ～前看 look forward ③ past; previous: 往事 wǎngshì

往常 wǎngcháng　habitually in the past; as one used to do formerly: 他～不这样。He was not like that before. / 我们～都是天黑了才收工。We used to go on working until it got dark. / 他比～回来得晚。He came back later than usual.

往初 wǎngchū　formal in ancient times

往返 wǎngfǎn　go there and back; journey to and fro: ～于成都、重庆之间 travel to and fro between Chengdu and Chongqing / ～要多少时间? How long does it take to go there and back? / ～运费 freight out and home

往返票 wǎngfǎnpiào　return ticket; round-trip ticket

往复 wǎngfù　① move back and forth; reciprocate: ～泵 reciprocating pump / ～式发动机 reciprocating engine / ～运动 reciprocating motion; alternating motion ② contact; dealings; intercourse

往古 wǎnggǔ　formal in ancient times: ～来今 from ancient times to the present; from time immemorial

往后 wǎnghòu　from now on; later on; in the future: ～我们要更加倍努力。From now on we'll redouble our efforts. / ～的日子会更好。As time goes on we'll live an even better life. / ～我一定要仔细点。I'll be more careful from now on.

往还 wǎnghuán　contact; dealings; intercourse: 经常有书信～ write to each other regularly; keep in contact by correspondence

往迹 wǎngjì　past events; a thing of the past

往来 wǎnglái　① come and go ② contact; dealings; intercourse: 贸易～ trade contacts; commercial intercourse / 友好～ exchange of friendly visits; friendly intercourse / 他们俩～密切。The two of them are in close contact. or They see a lot of each other.

往来帐 wǎngláizhàng　current (or open, running) account

往年 wǎngnián　(in) former years: ～人们不怎么外出旅游。In former years people did not travel so much.

往前 wǎngqián　before; formerly; in the past: ～的事不要再提了。Don't bring up those things of the past again.

往日 wǎngrì　(in) former days; (in) bygone days: ～这个地区全是些低矮的小房子。In the past, all houses in this area were small and low.

往时 wǎngshí　in the past; formerly; previously: 他和～大不一样了。He is very different from what he used to be.

往事 wǎngshì　past events; the past: 回忆～ recollections of the past / ～已成空, 还如一梦中。(李煜) Past events have turned to emptiness, become like things in a dream.

往事如烟 wǎngshì rú yān　past events have vanished like smoke

往往 wǎngwǎng　adv. often; frequently; more often than not: 这里春天～刮大风。It often blows hard here in spring. / 有些人～只看到当前的、局部的、个人的利益。Some people are prone to see only immediate, partial and personal interests. / 有雾的时候班机～取消。During foggy weather the flights are cancelled more often than not.

往昔 wǎngxī　in the past; in former times

惘 wǎng　feel frustrated; feel disappointed: 怅惘 chàngwǎng

惘然 wǎngrán　frustrated; disappointed

惘然若失 wǎngrán ruò shī　feel lost

辋 wǎng　rim (of a wheel)

蜩 wǎng　see below

蜩蛴 wǎngliǎng　same as 魍魉 wǎngliǎng

魍 wǎng　see below

魍魉 wǎngliǎng　demons and monsters: 魑魅魍魉 chīmèi-wǎngliǎng

wàng

王 wàng　arch. govern; rule: ～天下 rule over the empire ——see also wáng

妄 wàng　① absurd; preposterous: 狂妄 kuáng-wàng ② presumptuous; rash: ～作主张 make a presumptuous decision / ～加评论 make improper comments

妄称 wàngchēng　declare falsely or presumptuously

妄动 wàngdòng　rash (or reckless, ill-considered) action: 轻举妄动 qīngjǔ-wàngdòng

妄断 wàngduàn　draw a rash conclusion; jump to a conclusion

妄口巴舌 wàngkǒu-bāshé　old talk nonsense

妄念 wàngniàn　wild fancy; improper thought

妄求 wàngqiú　inappropriate request; presumptuous demand

妄取 wàngqǔ　take sth. without authorization or permission

妄人 wàngrén　formal an ignorant and presumptuous person

妄说 wàngshuō　talk irresponsibly; talk nonsense

妄图 wàngtú　try in vain; vainly attempt: ～打破一个缺口 vainly attempt to make a breach / ～掩盖事实真相 try in vain to cover up the truth; vainly attempt to conceal the facts

妄为 wàngwéi　act recklessly or wildly: 胆大妄为 dǎndà wàngwéi

妄下雌黄 wàng xià cíhuáng ① make irresponsible comments ② make wrong corrections

妄想 wàngxiǎng ① vainly hope to do sth.: ～挽回败局 in a vain attempt to retrieve the defeat ② vain hope (*or* attempt); wishful thinking ③ *med.* delusion

妄想狂 wàngxiǎngkuáng *med.* paranoia: 医生说他是～。The doctor says that he is paranoiac.

妄言 wàngyán ① talk tactlessly; speak carelessly; make irresponsible remarks ② wild talk; rant

妄言妄听 wàngyán wàngtīng loose talk not to be taken seriously

妄语 wàngyǔ ① tell lies; talk nonsense ② wild talk; rant

妄自菲薄 wàng zì fěibó belittle oneself; be unduly humble: 不可骄傲自满，也不可～。Be neither conceited nor excessively humble.

妄自尊大 wàng zì zūndà have too high an opinion of oneself; be overweening; be self-important

忘 wàng ① forget: 他把这事全～了。He forgot all about it. *or* He clean forgot about the whole thing. / 别～了给我打电话。Don't forget to phone me. / 我～了拿笔记本。I've left my notebook behind. / 我永远也～不了离家的那一天。I'll always remember the day I left home. ② overlook; neglect: 不要只看到事物的一面而～了另一面。Don't look at only one aspect of the thing and neglect the other.

忘本 wàngběn forget one's past suffering; forget where one's happiness comes from: 我们过上了幸福的生活，可不能～。We must not forget our old sufferings, now that we are living happy lives.

忘掉 wàngdiào forget; let slip from one's mind: 我当时忙于工作，把这件事给～了。I was so busy working it simply slipped my mind. / 咱们把这件不愉快的事～吧。Let's forget the unpleasantness.

忘恩负义 wàng'ēn-fùyì devoid of gratitude; ungrateful

忘乎所以 wàng hū suǒyǐ (also 忘其所以 wàng qí suǒyǐ) forget oneself: 心血来潮，～ be carried away by a sudden impulse; lose one's head in a moment of excitement / 不要因为胜利而～。Don't get swollen-headed because of victory.

忘怀 wànghuái forget; dismiss from one's mind: 当时情景我久久不能～。For a long time afterwards I could not get the scene out of my mind. / ～得失 not worried about personal gains or losses

忘机 wàngjī *formal* with a mind free of schemes; at peace with the world

忘记 wàngjì ① forget: 我永远不会～我们初次见面的那一天。I'll never forget the day we first met. / 他紧张地工作，～了去吃晚饭。He was working so hard that he forgot to go for supper. ② overlook; neglect: 不能～自己的责任。One mustn't neglect one's duties.

忘旧 wàngjiù forget old friends (after making new friends)

忘年交 wàngniánjiāo ① friendship between generations ② good friends despite great difference in age

忘情 wàngqíng ① (usu. used in the negative) be unruffled by emotion; be unmoved; be indifferent: 不能～ be still emotionally attached ② let oneself go: ～地歌唱 let oneself go and sing lustily

忘却 wàngquè forget: 一件～了的往事 a forgotten event in one's past

忘我 wàngwǒ oblivious of oneself; selfless: ～地工作 work selflessly; work untiringly / ～的精神 spirit of selflessness

忘形 wàngxíng be beside oneself (with glee, etc.); have one's head turned: 得意忘形 déyì wàngxíng

忘性 wàngxing forgetfulness: ～大 be forgetful; have a poor memory

旺 wàng prosperous; flourishing; vigorous: 人畜两～。Both men and livestock are flourishing. / 屋中炉火烧得正～。There was a roaring fire in the room.

旺炽 wàngchì flaming; blazing: 火焰～。The fire was blazing.

旺季 wàngjì peak period; busy season: 西红柿～ tomato season

旺健 wàngjiàn strong and healthy; vigorous; exuberant

旺年 wàngnián *dial.* on-year (for fruit trees)

旺盛 wàngshèng vigorous; exuberant: 他精力～。He is vigorous. / 士气～ have high morale / ～的生命力 exuberant vitality / 麦子长势～。Wheat is growing luxuriantly.

旺销 wàngxiāo be in great demand; sell well

旺月 wàngyuè busy month (in business)

望¹ wàng ① gaze into the distance; look over: 登山远～ climb a mountain and gaze far afield / 放眼～去 look ahead as far as the eye can reach / ～了他一眼 shoot a glance at him ② call on; visit: 拜望 bàiwàng / 看望 kànwàng ③ hope; expect: ～速归。Hoping you'll return as soon as possible. / ～回信。Awaiting your reply. ④ reputation; prestige: 一乡之～ a respected man in a township ⑤ resentment; enmity: 怨望 yuànwàng ⑥ *prep.* to; towards: ～我点点头 nod to me / ～他笑了笑 smile at him

望² wàng ① full moon ② the 15th day of a lunar month

望板 wàngbǎn *archit.* roof boarding

望尘莫及 wàng chén mò jí so far behind that one can only see the dust of the rider ahead—too far behind to catch up; too inferior to bear comparison

望穿秋水 wàngchuān qiūshuǐ keep gazing anxiously till one's eyes are strained; await with great anxiety

望断 wàngduàn *formal* watch sth. in the distance until it vanishes: 天高云淡，～南飞雁。(毛泽东) The sky is high, the clouds are pale, We watch the wild geese vanish southward.

望而却步 wàng ér quèbù shrink back at the sight of (sth. dangerous or difficult); flinch; hang back: 这座桥看来很不稳，行人都～。The bridge looked so unsafe that the travellers all hung back in fear.

望而生畏 wàng ér shēng wèi be terrified (*or* awed) by the sight of sb. or sth.: 这位老教授态度严肃，令人～。The old professor seemed stern and forbidding.

望风 wàngfēng be on the lookout (while conducting secret activities); keep watch

望风捕影 wàngfēng-bǔyǐng same as 捕风捉影 bǔfēng-zhuōyǐng

望风而逃 wàng fēng ér táo flee at the mere sight of the oncoming force: 敌军～。The enemy fled pell-mell (*or* helter-skelter) before our army.

望风披靡 wàng fēng pīmǐ scatter at the mere sight of the oncoming force

望江南 wàngjiāngnán *bot.* coffee senna (*Cassia occidentalis*)

望楼 wànglóu watchtower; lookout tower

望梅止渴 wàng méi zhǐkě quench one's thirst by thinking of plums—console oneself with false hopes; feed on fancies

望门寡 wàngménguǎ ① (of a woman) remain unmarried all her life after the death of her betrothed ② such a woman

望门投止 wàng mén tóu zhǐ (of a fugitive or refugee) ask for shelter at any house one happens upon

望日　wàngrì　the 15th day of a lunar month

望天田　wàngtiāntián　fields on hill tops which depend on rains for water

望头　wàngtou　*dial.* sth. hoped for and likely to happen; good prospects: 近来事情有了～，我也不那么愁了。Things have been looking up lately and most of my worries have disappeared.

望文生义　wàng wén shēng yì　misinterpret words through taking them too literally

望闻问切　wàng-wén-wèn-qiè　see 四诊 sìzhěn

望乡台　wàngxiāngtái　① *old* a terrace from which one can see one's home in the distance ② a terrace in hell from which the dead can see their homes

望眼欲穿　wàng yǎn yù chuān　keep gazing anxiously till one's eyes are strained; have long been looking forward with eager expectancy

望洋兴叹　wàng yáng xīngtàn　lament one's littleness before the vast ocean—bemoan one's inadequacy in the face of a great task

望远镜　wàngyuǎnjìng　telescope: 色球～ chromospheric telescope / 射电～ radio telescope / 双筒～ binoculars; field glasses / 天文～ astronomical telescope / 剧场用小～ opera glasses / 反射～ reflecting telescope; reflector / 折射～ refracting telescope; refractor / 折反射～ catodioptric telescope / ～瞄准器 telescopic sight

望月　wàngyuè　full moon

望诊　wàngzhěn　*Chin. med.* observation of the patient's complexion, tongue, expression, behaviour, etc., one of the four methods of diagnosis ——see also 四诊 sìzhěn

望子成龙　wàng zǐ chéng lóng　long to see one's son become a dragon (i.e. win success in the world); long to see one's son succeed in life

望子　wàngzi　shop sign in the form of a streamer

望族　wàngzú　*formal* distinguished family; prominent family

wēi

危　wēi　① danger; peril: 居安思危 jū ān sī wēi ② endanger; imperil: 危害 wēihài ③ dying: 病危 bìngwēi ④ *formal* high; precipitous: ～崖 a precipitous cliff ⑤ *formal* proper: 危坐 wēizuò ⑥ the twelfth of the twenty-eight constellations (二十八宿) into which the celestial sphere was divided in ancient Chinese astronomy (consisting of three stars in the shape of an obtuse-angled triangle, one in Aquarius and two in Pegasus) ⑦ (Wēi) a surname

危殆　wēidài　*formal* in great danger; in jeopardy; in a critical condition: 病势～ be dangerously ill; be critically ill

危地马拉　Wēidìmǎlā　Guatemala

危地马拉人　Wēidìmǎlārén　Guatemalan

危笃　wēidǔ　*formal* critically ill; on the point of death

危房　wēifáng　buildings that are ready to collapse; unsafe buildings

危害　wēihài　harm; endanger; jeopardize: ～国家主权和领土完整 endanger the sovereignty and territorial integrity of the state / ～国际和平及安全 endanger international peace and security / ～健康 be detrimental to health / ～农作物 harm the crops / ～治安 jeopardize public security / ～公共利益 harm the public interest / ～社会秩序罪 offense against social order

危害性　wēihàixìng　harmfulness; perniciousness

危机　wēijī　crisis: 财政～ a financial crisis / ～重重 bogged down in crises; crisis-ridden

危机四伏　wēijī sì fú　danger lurks on every side

危及　wēijí　endanger: 酒后开车～他人生命。Drunk drivers endanger the lives of others.

危急　wēijí　critical; in imminent danger; in a desperate situation: ～关头 critical juncture (or time, moment) / 情况十分～。The situation is desperate. / 伤势～。The wound may be fatal.

危急存亡　wēijí-cúnwáng　danger and crisis: ～之秋 a most critical moment (for a nation)

危境　wēijìng　a desperate situation

危局　wēijú　a dangerous (or critical, desperate) situation

危惧　wēijù　worry and fear; be apprehensive

危楼　wēilóu　a high building; a high tower

危难　wēinàn　danger and disaster; calamity: 处于～之中 be in dire peril

危迫　wēipò　critical; in imminent danger; in a desperate situation

危浅　wēiqiǎn　*formal* critically ill; at one's last gasp: 人命危浅, 朝不虑夕 rénmìng wēiqiǎn, zhāo bù lǜ xī

危如累卵　wēi rú lěi luǎn　as precarious as a pile of eggs; in an extremely precarious situation: 故曹小国也。而迫于晋、楚之间。其君之危犹累卵也。《韩非子》Cao was a small state hemmed in between Jin and Chu, and the safety of its ruler was as precarious as a pile of eggs.

危途　wēitú　a dangerous road

危亡　wēiwáng　in peril; at stake: 民族～的时刻 when the nation's existence is in peril; when the fate of the nation hangs in the balance

危险　wēixiǎn　dangerous; perilous: 冒生命～ at the risk of one's life / 脱离～ out of danger / 有电, ～! Danger! Electricity! / ～地带 danger zone / ～人物 a dangerous person; a danger / ～信号 danger signal / ～工作津贴 danger money

危险品　wēixiǎnpǐn　dangerous articles; dangerous goods: 严禁携带～上车。It is strictly forbidden to take dangerous articles aboard.

危险性　wēixiǎnxìng　dangerous nature; danger

危象　wēixiàng　*med.* crisis; critical state

危言　wēiyán　① *formal* speak bluntly; state outright ② exaggerate; overstate

危言耸听　wēiyán sǒngtīng　(aslo 危辞耸听 wēicí sǒngtīng) say frightening things just to cause alarm; exaggerate just to scare people: 这不是～, 而是历史多次证明了的真理。This is not alarmist talk; it is a truth repeatedly borne out by history.

危在旦夕　wēi zài dànxī　in imminent danger; on the verge of death or destruction: 生命～。Death is expected at any moment. / 该城～。The city may fall at any moment.

危重　wēizhòng　critically ill

危坐　wēizuò　*formal* sit bolt upright; sit properly: 正襟危坐 zhèngjīn-wēizuò

委　wēi　see below ——see also wěi

委蛇　wēiyí　① same as 逶迤 wēiyí ② see 虚与委蛇 xū yǔ wēiyí

威　wēi　① impressive strength; might; power: ～震四方 known far and wide for one's military prowess ② by force: 威逼 wēibī

威逼　wēibī　threaten by force; coerce; intimidate

威逼利诱　wēibī-lìyòu　(also 威胁利诱 wēixié-lìyòu) alternate intimidation and bribery; combine threats with inducements; use both coercion and cajolery

威风　wēifēng　① power and prestige; might: 农民一起来就把地主的～打下去了。As soon as the peasants were aroused, they smashed the power and prestige of the landlord class. / 灭敌人的～ puncture (or deflate) the enemy's arrogance / 游击队在敌占区大显～。The

guerrillas impressively demonstrated their courage and power in the enemy-occupied area. ② imposing; impressive; awe-inspiring: 瞧! 这些女民兵多么～! Look at the militant bearing of these militia women! ——see also 抖威风 dǒu wēifēng

威风凛凛 wēifēng lǐnlǐn have an awesome bearing; have a commanding presence: 此人相貌堂堂，～。The man had an impressive bearing and a commanding presence.

威风扫地 wēifēng sǎodì with every shred of one's prestige swept away—completely discredited

威吓 wēihè intimidate; threaten; bully: 证人受到～未能作证。The witness was kept from testifying by intimidation.

威克岛 Wēikèdǎo Wake Island

威棱 wēiléng *formal* power and influence; prestige

威力 wēilì power; might: 人民战争～无穷。The might of people's war knows no bounds. *or* People's war is an invincible force.

威灵仙 wēilíngxiān *Chin. med.* the root of Chinese clematis (*Clematis chinensis*)

威猛 wēiměng brave and fierce

威名 wēimíng fame based on great strength or military exploits; mighty name; mighty reputation: 人民子弟兵,～天下扬。The fame of the people's soldiers has spread far and wide.

威尼斯 Wēinísī Venice

威迫 wēipò same as 威逼 wēibī

威权 wēiquán authority; power

威容 wēiróng awe-inspiring bearing

威慑 wēishè terrorize with military force; deter: ～力量 deterrent force; deterrent / ～均势 balance of deterrence / ～政策 deterrent policy

威士忌 wēishìjì whisky

威势 wēishì power and influence

威望 wēiwàng prestige: 崇高的～ high prestige

威武 wēiwǔ ① might; force; power ② powerful; mighty: ～雄壮 full of power and grandeur

威武不屈 wēiwǔ bù qū not to be subdued by force; unyielding in the face of force: 富贵不能淫, 贫贱不能移, 威武不能屈, 此之谓大丈夫。《孟子》He whom riches and honours cannot corrupt nor poverty and obscurity divert, whom neither threats nor violence itself can bend—he it is that I call a great man.

威胁 wēixié threaten; menace; imperil: ～邻国的安全 threaten (*or* menace) the security of a neighbouring country / ～世界和平 imperil world peace / 受到战争～ be menaced by war / 以武力相～ resort to threat of force / 洪水～着这座城市。Flood waters are threatening the town.

威信 wēixìn prestige; popular trust: 他在群众中有很高的～。He has high prestige among the masses. / 有～的人 men of prestige; prestigious people

威信扫地 wēixìn sǎodì with every shred of prestige swept away—completely discredited: 丧失人心, ～ forfeit popular support and prestige / 使此人～ sweep every bit of his prestige into the dust; discredit him completely

威严 wēiyán ① dignified; stately; majestic; awe-inspiring: 将军的举止～。The general had a dignified manner. ② prestige; dignity: 保持～ keep up one's prestige

威仪 wēiyí impressive and dignified manner

逶

　　wēi see below

逶迤 wēiyí winding; meandering: ～的山路 a winding mountain path / 这条铁路～在群山之中。The railway winds its way through the mountains.

偎

　　wēi snuggle up to; lean close to: 看电影时她～着他。She snuggled up to him in the darkened cinema.

偎抱 wēibào hug; cuddle: 小女孩～着她的洋娃娃。The little girl cuddled her doll.

偎红倚翠 wēihóng-yǐcuì embrace red and caress green—dally with prostitutes

偎贴 wēitiē snuggle up to; lean close to: 她～在妈妈身上睡着了。She snuggled up to her mother and went to sleep.

偎依 wēiyī (also 偎倚 wēiyǐ) snuggle up to; lean close to: 孩子～在母亲的怀里。The child snuggled up in its mother's arms.

隈

　　wēi *formal* ① river bend ② mountain recess

葳

　　wēi see below

葳蕤 wēiruí *liter.* luxuriant (foliage)

煨

　　wēi ① cook over a slow fire; stew; simmer: ～牛肉 stewed beef ② roast (sweet potatoes, etc.) in fresh cinders

微

　　wēi ① minute; tiny; slight: 相差甚～。The difference is slight (*or* negligible). / ～云 thin clouds / ～雨 drizzle / 我跟他～说了一下。I just mentioned it to him. ② profound; abstruse: 精微 jīngwēi ③ decline: 衰微 shuāiwēi ④ one millionth part of; micro-: 微米 wēimǐ

微安 wēi'ān *elec.* microampere: ～计 microammeter

微巴 wēibā microbar

微波 wēibō ① ripples ② *electron.* microwave: ～半导体 microwave semiconductor / ～管 microwave tube / ～理疗机 microwave therapeutic apparatus / ～区 microwave region / ～遥感 microwave remote sensing / ～遥感器 microwave remote sensor

微波炉 wēibōlú microwave oven

微薄 wēibó meagre; scanty: 收入～ have a meagre income / 尽我们～的力量。We'll exert what little strength we have. *or* We'll do what little we can.

微不足道 wēi bùzú dào too trivial or insignificant to mention; insignificant; inconsiderable; negligible: ～的人物 an insignificant figure; a nobody / ～的损失 a trivial loss / ～的贡献 an insignificant contribution / 要付的钱～。The sum of money involved is trifling.

微处理机 wēichǔlǐjī microprocessor

微词 wēicí (also 微辞 wēicí) *formal* veiled criticism; complaints: 观众对裁判的执法多有～。The spectators muttered their disapproval of the judge's performance.

微雕 wēidiāo miniature sculpture

微法拉 wēifǎlā *elec.* microfarad

微分 wēifēn *math.* differential: 二项式～ binomial differential / ～法 differentiation / ～分析 differential analysis

微分学 wēifēnxué differential calculus

微风 wēifēng ① *meteorol.* gentle breeze ② breeze

微伏 wēifú *elec.* microvolt (μV)

微服 wēifú (of officials) in disguise; in incognito: ～私访 travel incognito

微观 wēiguān microcosmic

微观经济学 wēiguān jīngjìxué microeconomics

微观世界 wēiguān shìjiè microcosmos; microcosm

微观物理学 wēiguān wùlǐxué microphysics

微观现象 wēiguān xiànxiàng *phys.* microphenomenon

微乎其微 wēi hū qí wēi very little; next to nothing: 我一个人的力量是～的。On my own I can do very little. / 双方达成协议的可能性是～的。There is hardly any possibility of the two parties reaching agreement.

微火 wēihuǒ slow fire; gentle heat

微积分学 wēijīfēnxué *math.* infinitesimal calculus; cal

culus

微贱　wēijiàn　humble; lowly: 出身～ be of humble origin; be from a humble background

微刻　wēikè　miniature carving

微粒　wēilì　① particle ② *phys.* corpuscle

微粒体　wēilìtǐ　*bot.* microsome

微量　wēiliàng　trace; micro-: ～分析 microanalysis

微量化学　wēiliàng huàxué　microchemistry

微量天平　wēiliàng tiānpíng　microbalance

微量元素　wēiliàng yuánsù　trace element

微脉　wēimài　*Chin. med.* scarcely perceptible pulse

微茫　wēimáng　*formal* blurred; hazy

微米　wēimǐ　micron (μ)

微妙　wēimiào　delicate; subtle: 关系～ subtle relations / 谈判进入～阶段。The negotiations have entered a delicate stage.

微末　wēimò　trifling; insignificant: ～的贡献 an insignificant contribution / ～的成就 an achievement of minor importance

微气象计　wēiqìxiàngjì　micrometeorograph

微热　wēirè　*med.* low-grade fever

微弱　wēiruò　faint; feeble; weak: 呼吸～ faint breath / 光线～ faint light; glimmer / 脉搏～ feeble pulse / ～的声音 a thin voice / ～的多数 a slender majority

微生物　wēishēngwù　microorganism; microbe: ～农药 microbial pesticide

微生物学　wēishēngwùxué　microbiology

微调　wēitiáo　*electron.* fine tuning; trimming: ～电容器 trimmer (condenser); padder

微微　wēiwēi　① *adv.* slightly; faintly: ～一笑 smile faintly ② micromicro-: pico-: ～法拉 micromicrofarad; picofarad / ～秒 picosecond

微熹　wēixī　*formal* (of morning sunlight) dim; pale

微细　wēixì　very small; tiny: ～的血管 very small blood vessels

微小　wēixiǎo　small; little: 极其～ infinitely small; infinitesimal / ～的希望 slender hopes / ～的进步 meagre progress

微笑　wēixiào　smile

微笑服务　wēixiào fúwù　service with a smile

微行　wēixíng　travel incognito

微型　wēixíng　miniature; mini-: ～化 microminiaturization / ～汽车 minicar; mini / ～照相机 miniature camera; minicam / ～计算机 microcomputer

微血管　wēixuèguǎn　(blood) capillary

微言大义　wēiyán-dàyì　sublime words with profound meaning

微恙　wēiyàng　slight illness; indisposition

微音器　wēiyīnqì　microphone

微震　wēizhèn　① slight shock ② *geol. phys.* microseism

薇　wēi　see 蔷薇 qiángwēi

巍　wēi　towering; lofty

巍峨　wēi'é　towering; lofty: ～的群山 lofty mountains

巍然　wēirán　towering; lofty; majestic; imposing: 大桥～横跨在江上。The bridge stands majestic astride the river.

巍然屹立　wēirán yìlì　stand lofty and firm; stand rock-firm: 人民英雄纪念碑～在天安门广场中央。The Monument to the People's Heroes stands majestic in the middle of Tian'anmen Square.

巍巍　wēiwēi　towering; lofty: ～井岗山 the towering Jinggang Mountains

wéi

为[1] (为、爲)　wéi　① do; act: 敢作敢～ be decisive and bold in action; act with daring ② act as; serve as: 选她～人民代表 elect her a people's deputy / 以此～凭。This will serve as a proof. / 有诗～证。A poem testifies to that. ③ become: 变沙漠～良田 turn the desert into arable land ④ be; mean: 一公里～二华里。One kilometer is equivalent to two *li*.

为[2] (为、爲)　wéi　*prep.* (used with 所 in a passive sentence): ～人民所爱戴 be loved and respected by the people / 不～表面现象所迷惑 not be confused by superficial phenomena

为[3] (为、爲)　wéi　*part. formal* (used in a rhetorical question with 何) 何以家～? What need have I of a home? (usu. said during a national crisis)

为[4] (为、爲)　wéi　① (used after an adjective to form an adverb): 大～高兴 very happy / 广～流传 widely spread ② (used after an adverb for emphasis): 极～重要 extremely important
——see also wèi

为非作歹　wéifēi-zuòdǎi　do evil; commit crimes; perpetrate outrages: 欺压百姓，～ ride roughshod over the people and commit all sorts of crimes

为富不仁　wéi fù bù rén　be rich and cruel; be one of the heartless rich

为害　wéihài　cause harm; cause damage: 蚜虫～蔬菜。Aphids are destructive to vegetables.

为患　wéihuàn　bring trouble: 洪水～ suffer from floods

为力　wéilì　put forth one's strength; exert oneself: 这件事他是不能～的。He can do nothing about it.

为难　wéinán　① feel embarrassed; feel awkward: ～的事 an awkward matter / 使人～ embarrass sb.; put sb. in an awkward situation ② make things difficult for: 故意～ deliberately make things difficult for sb.

为期　wéiqī　(to be completed) by a definite date: 以两周～ not to exceed two weeks / 举办～一个月的摄影展览 hold a photo exhibition lasting a month / 会议～三天。The meeting is scheduled to last three days.

为期不远　wéi qī bù yuǎn　the day is not far off

为人　wéirén　behave; conduct oneself: ～正直 be upright

为人处世　wéirén-chǔshì　the way one conducts oneself in society; one's attitude towards life

为人师表　wéi rén shībiǎo　be worthy of the name of teacher; be a paragon of virtue and learning

为生　wéishēng　make a living: 以狩猎～ make a living as a hunter

为时过早　wéi shí guò zǎo　premature; too early; too soon: 现在下结论～。It's still too early to reach a conclusion.

为首　wéishǒu　with sb. as the leader; headed (*or* led) by: 以某某～的代表团 a delegation headed (*or* led) by so-and-so

为数　wéishù　amount to; number: ～不少 come up to a large number; amount to quite a lot / ～不多 have only a small number

为所欲为　wéi suǒ yù wéi　act wilfully; do whatever one likes; have one's own way

为伍　wéiwǔ　associate with: 与坏分子～ associate with bad elements

为限　wéixiàn　be within the limit of; not exceed: 费用以一百元～。The expenses shall not exceed 100 *yuan*.

为止 wéizhǐ up to; till: 迄今～ up to now; so far / 到去年年底～ up to the end of last year / 一直等到他回来～ wait till he returns / 今天的讨论到此～。That's all for today's discussion.

为重 wéizhòng attach most importance to: 以大局为～ put the general interest first / 以人民的利益～ value the interests of the people above everything else

为主 wéizhǔ give first place to; give priority to: 以自力更生～，外援为辅 rely mainly on one's own efforts while making external assistance subsidiary / 精神鼓励和物质鼓励相结合、而以精神鼓励～的方针 the policy of combining moral encouragement with material reward, with stress on the former

韦（韋）
wéi ① *formal* leather ② short for 韦伯 wéibó ③ (Wéi) a surname

韦编三绝 wéibiān sān jué be diligent in one's studies

韦伯 wéibó *phys.* weber (Wb)

圩
wéi dyke; embankment: 筑～ build dykes ——see also xū

圩田 wéitián ① low-lying paddy fields surrounded with dykes ② polder

圩垸 wéiyuàn protective embankments in lakeside areas

圩子 wéizi ① protective embankments surrounding low-lying fields ② same as 围子 wéizi①

违（違）
wéi ① disobey; violate: 违法 wéifǎ ② be separated: 久违 jiǔwéi

违碍 wéi'ài taboo; prohibition

违拗 wéi'ào defy (one's superiors or elders); disobey

违背 wéibèi violate; go against; run counter to: ～原则 violate a principle / ～人民的意志 go against the will of the people / ～马克思主义 run counter to Marxism / 自己的诺言 go back on one's word / ～历史事实 be contrary to the historical facts

违法 wéifǎ break the law; be illegal: ～行为 illegal activities; unlawful practice / ～失职 transgression of the law and neglect of duty

违法乱纪 wéifǎ-luànjì violate law and discipline; break the law and violate discipline

违反 wéifǎn violate; run counter to; transgress; infringe: ～政策 run counter to the policy / ～纪律 violate discipline / ～交通规则 violate traffic regulations / ～刑法 commit a criminal offence / ～事实 fly in the face of facts / ～历史潮流 run counter to the trend of history / ～决议的精神 be contrary to the spirit of the resolution / ～社会发展规律 go against the laws of social development

违犯 wéifàn violate; infringe; act contrary to: ～纪律 violation of discipline; breach of discipline

违和 wéihé *euph.* indisposed: 贵体～。You are indisposed.

违禁 wéijìn violate a ban: ～品 contraband (goods)

违抗 wéikàng disobey; defy: ～命令 disobey orders; act in defiance of orders / ～上级 defy the higher leading body; defy one's superiors; be insubordinate

违例 wéilì *sports* breach of rules; violation

违令 wéilìng disobey orders

违逆 wéinì violate; go against; run counter to

违忤 wéiwǔ *formal* violate; go against; run counter to; disobey

违误 wéiwù (used in official documents) disobey orders and cause delay: 迅速办理，不得～。This is to be acted upon without delay.

违宪 wéixiàn violate the constitution; be unconstitutional: ～行为 an unconstitutional act

违心 wéixīn against one's will; contrary to one's convictions: 做～事 act against one's conscience

违心之论 wéixīn zhī lùn words uttered against one's conscience; insincere talk

违约 wéiyuē ① break a contract; violate a treaty ② break one's promise; break off an engagement

违章 wéizhāng break rules and regulations: ～行驶 drive against traffic regulations / ～冒险作业 work in a risky way in violation of the rules

围（圍）
wéi ① enclose; surround: 用篱笆把菜园子～上 enclose the vegetable patch with a fence / 团团～住 completely surround; encircle; besiege / ～着他问长问短 gather round him, asking all sorts of questions ② all round; around: 周围 zhōuwéi ③ m. arm span: 树大十～ a tree trunk ten arm spans around

围脖儿 wéibór *dial.* muffler; scarf

围捕 wéibǔ surround and seize; round up

围场 wéichǎng imperial hunting park

围城 wéichéng ① encircle (*or* besiege) a city ② besieged city

围城打援 wéichéng dǎyuán lay siege to a city to annihilate the enemy relief force; besiege the enemy in order to strike at his reinforcements

围簇 wéicù gather round; cluster round: 孩子们～在老人身边。The children gathered round the old man.

围攻 wéigōng ① besiege; lay siege to: 停止～ abandon a siege ② jointly speak or write against sb.; jointly attack sb.: 遭到～ come under attack from all sides; be caught in a cross fire

围观 wéiguān (of a crowd of people) watch; look on: 一群人在那里～。A crowd of people were looking on. / ～的人群 a crowd of onlookers

围湖造田 wéihú zàotián (build dykes to) reclaim land from a lake; reclaim lake bottom land and plant it to crops

围护 wéihù go along with sb. to guard him

围击 wéijī besiege; lay siege to

围歼 wéijiān surround and annihilate

围剿 wéijiǎo encircle and suppress

围巾 wéijīn muffler; scarf

围聚 wéijù crowd around; gather round

围垦 wéikěn (build dykes to) reclaim land from marshes; enclose tideland for cultivation

围困 wéikùn besiege; hem in; pin down: 把敌人～在少数据点中 pin down the enemy in a few strongholds

围猎 wéiliè round up and hunt

围拢 wéilǒng crowd around; gather round

围炉 wéilú sit around a fire: ～夜话 spend the evening chatting around a fire / ～烤火 sit round a fire to get warm

围屏 wéipíng (folding) screen

围棋 wéiqí *weiqi*, a game played with black and white pieces on a board of 361 crosses; go

围墙 wéiqiáng enclosure; enclosing wall

围裙 wéi·qún apron

围绕 wéirào ① encircle; go round: 月亮～着地球旋转。The moon revolves round the earth. ② centre on: ～中心任务安排其他工作 arrange other work around the central task

围网 wéiwǎng *fishery* purse seine; purse net: ～渔船 purse seiner; purse boat

围魏救赵 wéi Wèi jiù Zhào besiege Wei to rescue Zhao——relieve the besieged by besieging the base of the besiegers

围岩 wéiyán country rock; surrounding rock

围堰 wéiyàn cofferdam; coffer

围桌 wéizhuō a piece of embroidered cloth or silk covering the front side of a table (used on festive occasions or on the stage)

围子 wéizi ① defensive wall or stockade surrounding a village: 土～ fortified village ② curtain ③ protective embankments surrounding low-lying fields

围嘴儿 wéizuǐr　bib

围坐 wéizuò　sit around sb. or sth.

闱（闈） wéi ① a side gate of an imperial palace: 宫闱 gōngwéi ② imperial examination hall (in feudal China) 秋闱 qiūwéi

闱墨 wéimò　selections from papers of successful candidates at imperial examinations

帏（幃） wéi　same as 帷 wéi

桅 wéi　mast: 船～ mast

桅灯 wéidēng ① mast head light; range light ② barn lantern

桅顶 wéidǐng　masthead

桅杆 wéigān　mast

桅樯 wéiqiáng　mast

惟¹ wéi adv. ① only; alone: ～你是问。 You'll be held personally responsible. ② formal but: 母已痊愈，～体力尚未恢复。 Mother's well now, but she hasn't fully recovered her strength yet.

惟² wéi part. formal (used before a year, month or day): ～二月既望 on the 16th of the second lunar month

惟³ wéi　thinking; thought: 思惟 sīwéi

惟独 wéidú adv. only; alone: 人家都回家了，～她还在工作。 She kept on working when all the others had gone home. / 他心里总是装着别人，～没有他自己。 His thoughts always turn to other people; hardly ever does he think of himself.

惟恐 wéikǒng　for fear that; lest: ～落后 for fear that one should lag behind / 我几次提醒他，～他忘了。 I reminded him several times lest he should forget.

惟恐天下不乱 wéikǒng tiānxià bù luàn　crave nothing short of nationwide chaos; desire to see the world plunged into chaos; desire to stir up trouble

惟利是图 wéi lì shì tú　be bent solely on profit; be intent on nothing but profit; put profit first: ～的思想 profit-before-everything mentality

惟妙惟肖 wéimiào-wéixiào　same as 维妙维肖 wéimiào-wéixiào

惟命是听 wéi mìng shì tīng　(also 惟命是从 wéi mìng shì cóng) be at sb.'s bidding; be obedient to sb.

惟其 wéiqí conj. formal precisely because: ～知者甚少，故必须多加宣传。 It's precisely because very few people know about it that we must publicise it.

惟我独尊 wéi wǒ dú zūn　overweening; extremely conceited

惟一 wéiyī　only; sole: ～可行的办法 the only feasible way / ～合法的政府 the sole legitimate government / ～出路 the only way out / ～继承人 the sole heir

惟有 wéiyǒu conj. only; alone: ～充分发动群众，才能取得胜利。 Only when the masses are fully mobilized can victory be won. / 大家都愿意去，～他不愿意。 Everybody is willing to go except him.

唯 wéi adv. only; alone——see also wěi

唯成分论 wéichéngfènlùn　the theory of the unique importance of class origin

唯恐 wéikǒng　same as 惟恐 wéikǒng

唯理论 wéilǐlùn philos. rationalism

唯利是图 wéi lì shì tú　same as 惟利是图 wéi lì shì tú

唯美主义 wéiměizhǔyì　aestheticism

唯名论 wéimínglùn philos. nominalism

唯命是听 wéi mìng shì tīng　same as 惟命是听 wéi mìng shì tīng

唯能说 wéinéngshuō phys. energetics

唯我独尊 wéi wǒ dú zūn　same as 惟我独尊 wéi wǒ dú zūn

唯我主义 wéiwǒzhǔyì philos. solipsism

唯武器论 wéiwǔqìlùn　the theory that weapons alone decide the outcome of war

唯物辩证法 wéiwù biànzhèngfǎ philos. materialist dialectics

唯物论 wéiwùlùn philos. materialism

唯物史观 wéiwùshǐguān　same as 历史唯物主义 lìshǐ-wéiwùzhǔyì

唯物主义 wéiwùzhǔyì philos. materialism

唯心论 wéixīnlùn philos. idealism

唯心史观 wéixīnshǐguān　same as 历史唯心主义 lìshǐ-wéixīnzhǔyì

唯心主义 wéixīnzhǔyì philos. idealism

唯一 wéiyī　same as 惟一 wéiyī

维¹ wéi ① tie up; hold together: 维系 wéixì ② maintain; safeguard; preserve: 维护 wéihù

维² wéi　same as 惟³ wéi

维³ wéi math. dimension: 三维空间 sānwéi kōngjiān

维持 wéichí　keep; maintain; preserve: ～秩序 keep order; maintain order / ～现状 maintain the status quo; let things go on as they are / ～生活 support oneself or one's family

维持和平部队 wéichí hépíng bùduì　peace-keeping force

维持会 wéichíhuì　peace preservation association (a local puppet organization during the War of Resistance Against Japan, 1937-1945)

维持原判 wéichí yuánpàn leg. affirm the original judgment

维多利亚湖 Wéiduōlìyàhú　Lake Victoria

维尔京群岛 Wéi'ěrjīng Qúndǎo　the Virgin Islands

维管束 wéiguǎnshù bot. vascular bundle

维护 wéihù　safeguard; defend; uphold: ～团结 uphold unity / ～人民的利益 safeguard the people's interests / ～国家主权 defend state sovereignty / ～民族尊严 vindicate (or defend) national honour / ～国际和平与安全 maintain international peace and security

维纶 wéilún text. polyvinyl alcohol fibre

维棉布 wéimiánbù　vinylon and cotton blend

维妙维肖 wéimiào-wéixiào　remarkably true to life; absolutely lifelike: 这幅画把儿童天真活泼的神态画得～。 This picture catches the innocent vivacity of children.

维尼纶 wéinílún　(also 维尼龙 wéinílóng) vinylon

维生素 wéishēngsù　vitamin: ～E vitamin E / 丁种～ vitamin D / ～缺乏症 vitamin-deficiency; avitaminosis / ～过多症 hypervitaminosis

维数 wéishù math. dimension; dimensionality: ～论 dimension theory

维他命 wéitāmìng　old name for 维生素 wéishēngsù

维吾尔族 Wéiwú'ěrzú　the Uygur (Uighur) nationality, or the Uygurs (Uighurs), inhabiting the Xinjiang Uygur Autonomous Region

维系 wéixì　hold together; maintain: ～人心 maintain popular morale

维新 wéixīn　reform; modernization: 百日～ the Hundred Days' Reform (1898) / 日本明治～ the Meiji Reformation of Japan (1868)

维修 wéixiū　keep in (good) repair; service; maintain: ～房屋 maintain houses and buildings / ～汽车 service

a car / 设备～ maintenance (*or* upkeep) of equipment / ～得很好 be in good repair / ～费 maintenance cost; upkeep / ～工 maintenance worker / ～车 maintenance vehicle

维族 Wéizú short for 维吾尔族 Wéiwú'ěrzú

帷 wéi bed-curtain

帷幕 wéimù (also 帷幔 wéimàn) heavy curtain

帷幄 wéiwò *formal* army tent: 运筹帷幄 yùnchóu wéiwò

帷帐 wéizhàng bed-curtain

帷子 wéizi curtain: 床～ bed-curtain

嵬 wéi *formal* lofty; towering: 崔嵬 cuīwéi[②]

wěi

伪（偽、僞） wěi ① false; fake; bogus: 作伪 zuòwěi ② puppet; collaborationist: ～政权 puppet regime

伪币 wěibì ① counterfeit money; counterfeit (*or* forged) bank note; spurious coin ② money issued by a puppet government

伪钞 wěichāo counterfeit (*or* forged) bank note

伪顶 wěidǐng *min.* false roof

伪军 wěijūn puppet army or soldier

伪君子 wěijūnzǐ hypocrite

伪科学 wěikēxué pseudoscience

伪善 wěishàn hypocritical: ～的言词 hypocritical words / ～者 hypocrite

伪书 wěishū ancient books found to have been incorrectly dated, forged, or attributed to a wrong author; ancient books of dubious authenticity

伪托 wěituō forge ancient literary or art works, or pass off modern works as ancient ones

伪造 wěizào forge; falsify; fabricate; counterfeit: ～签名 forge a signature / ～证件 forge a certificate / ～帐目 falsify accounts / ～历史 fabricate history; falsify history / ～货币 counterfeit money; forge money / ～的文件 spurious (*or* fake, forged) document; pseudograph

伪造品 wěizàopǐn counterfeit; forgery

伪造罪 wěizàozuì forgery

伪证 wěizhèng perjury; false evidence (*or* testimony): 那证人有意作～。 The witness intentionally gave false testimony.

伪撰 wěizhuàn write an essay under sb. else's name (esp. that of a writer of the past)

伪装 wěizhuāng ① pretend; feign: ～进步 pretend to be progressive / ～中立 feign neutrality ② disguise; guise; mask: 他～成传教士。 He disguised himself as a missionary. / 假的就是假的，～应当剥去。 Sham is sham, and the mask must be stripped off. ③ *mil.* camouflage: 高射炮已经用树枝～起来。 The antiaircraft guns have been camouflaged with boughs of trees. / ～工事 camouflage works / ～猎潜舰 Q-boat / ～网 camouflage net; garnished net

伪足 wěizú *zool.* pseudopodium

伟（偉） wěi big; great: 魁伟 kuíwěi

伟岸 wěi'àn *formal* tall and sturdy; stalwart; husky; strapping: 身材～ tall and sturdy; of great height and powerful build

伟大 wěidà great; mighty: 我们～的祖国 our great country / ～的事业 a great undertaking / ～的胜利 a signal victory

伟观 wěiguān a grand (*or* magnificent) sight: 钱塘江潮是我国自然～之一。 The Qiantang Bore is one of the magnificent sights of Nature in our country.

伟绩 wěijì great feats; great exploits; brilliant achievements

伟晶岩 wěijīngyán *geol.* pegmatite

伟举 wěijǔ a great undertaking; a magnificent feat

伟力 wěilì mighty force

伟人 wěirén a great man; a great personage: 当代的～ a great man of our time

伟业 wěiyè *formal* great cause; exploit

苇（葦） wěi reed

苇箔 wěibó reed matting

苇丛 wěicóng a clump of reeds

苇荡 wěidàng reed marsh

苇塘 wěitáng reed pond

苇席 wěixí reed mat

苇子 wěizi reed

纬（緯） wěi ① weft; woof ② *geog.* latitude: 北纬 běiwěi

纬编 wěibiān *text.* weft knitting: ～针织物 weft-knitted fabric

纬度 wěidù *geog.* latitude: 高（低）～ high (low) latitudes

纬密 wěimì *text.* weft density

纬纱 wěishā *text.* ① weft (yarn); woof; filling ② pick

纬线 wěixiàn ① *geog.* parallel ② *text.* weft

尾 wěi ① tail ② the sixth of the twenty-eight constellations (二十八宿) into which the celestial sphere was divided in ancient Chinese astronomy (consisting of nine stars in the shape of a hook in Scorpio) ③ tail-like part: 机尾 jīwěi ④ end: 排尾 páiwěi ⑤ remaining part; remnant: 扫尾 sǎowěi ⑥ *m.* (for fish): 两～鱼 two fish ——see also yǐ

尾巴 wěiba ① tail: 猴子～ monkey's tail / 夹起～逃跑 run away with one's tail between one's legs / 夹着～做人 behave oneself tuck one's tail between one's legs; pull one's head in ② tail-like part: 飞机～ the tail of a plane / 彗星～ the tail of a comet ③ servile adherent; appendage: 你为什么老做别人的～，难道自己一点主见也没有？ Why are you always tailing behind others? Don't you have any ideas of your own? ④ remaining part: 留尾巴 liú wěiba ⑤ a person shadowing sb.: 甩掉～ throw off one's tail ——see also 翘尾巴 qiào wěiba; 拖尾巴 tuō wěiba

尾巴主义 wěibazhǔyì tailism

尾大不掉 wěi dà bù diào ① leadership rendered ineffectual by recalcitrant subordinates ② (of an organization) too cumbersome to be effective

尾灯 wěidēng tail light; tail lamp

尾骨 wěigǔ *physiol.* coccyx

尾矿 wěikuàng *min.* tailings

尾轮 wěilún tail-wheel (of an aircraft)

尾闾[1] wěilǘ lower reaches (of a river)

尾闾[2] wěilǘ *Chin. med.* sacrum

尾期 wěiqī last stage; last phase; final phase

尾鳍 wěiqí tail fin; caudal fin

尾气 wěiqì tail gas

尾欠 wěiqiàn ① owe a small balance ② balance due

尾声 wěishēng ① *mus.* coda ② epilogue: 序幕和～ prologue and epilogue ③ end: 会谈已接近～。 The talks are drawing to an end.

尾数 wěishù odd amount in addition to the round number (usu. of a credit balance)

尾水 wěishuǐ *water conservancy* tail water

尾随 wěisuí tail behind; tag along after; follow at sb.'s heels: 孩子们～着巡回演出队走了好远。 The kids followed the mobile cultural troupe for quite a distance.

尾须　wěixū　*zool.*　cercus

尾翼　wěiyì　tail surface (of an aircraft); empennage

尾音　wěiyīn　last or end syllable

尾蚴　wěiyòu　*zool.*　cercaria

尾追　wěizhuī　in hot pursuit; hot on the trail of

尾子　wěizi　*dial.*　odd amount in addition to the round number (usu. of a credit balance): 伙 食～ mess savings

尾座　wěizuò　*mech.*　tailstock

炜(煒)　wěi　*formal*　bright

玮(瑋)　wěi　*formal*　① a kind of jade ② valuable; precious: ～宝 rare treasure

委[1]　wěi　① entrust; appoint: 委托 wěituō ② throw away; cast aside: 委弃 wěiqì ③ shift: 委过于人 wěi guò yú rén

委[2]　wěi　indirect; roundabout: 委婉 wěiwǎn

委[3]　wěi　*formal*　① gather; accumulate; build up: 委积 wěijī ② end: 原委 yuánwěi

委[4]　wěi　listless; dejected: 委靡 wěimǐ

委[5]　wěi　*formal*　actually; certainly: ～系实情。This is the true story.

委[6]　wěi　① (short for 委员) committee member: 常委 chángwěi ② (short for 委员会) committee; commission; council: 党委 dǎngwěi ——see also wèi

委顿　wěidùn　tired; exhausted; weary

委过于人　wěi guò yú rén　put the blame on sb. else; shift the blame on to sb. else

委积　wěijī　*formal*　gather; accumulate; pile up; build up

委决不下　wěi jué bù xià　hesitate to make a decision; be undecided

委令　wěilìng　appointment

委靡　wěimǐ　listless; dispirited; dejected: 精神～ listless; dispirited and inert

委靡不振　wěimǐ bù zhèn　dejected and apathetic; dispirited; in low spirits

委内瑞拉　Wěinèiruìlā　Venezuela

委内瑞拉人　Wěinèiruìlārén　Venezuelan

委派　wěipài　appoint; delegate; designate

委弃　wěiqì　abandon; forsake; cast aside

委曲　wěiqū　① (of roads, rivers, etc.) winding; tortuous ② *formal* ins and outs; all the details

委曲求全　wěiqū qiú quán　make concessions to achieve one's aim; compromise for the sake of the general interest

委屈　wěiqu　① feel wronged; nurse a grievance: 诉～ pour out one's grievances (*or* troubles) ② put sb. to great inconvenience: 你只好～一点。You'll have to put up with it. / 对不起，～你了。Sorry to have made you go through all this. *or* Sorry to have put you to such inconvenience.

委任　wěirèn　appoint: ～某人为首席顾问 appoint sb. chief adviser

委任书　wěirènshū　certificate of appointment

委任统治　wěirèn tǒngzhì　mandate: ～地 mandated territory

委任状　wěirènzhuàng　certificate of appointment

委身　wěishēn　submit to; give oneself to: ～事人 submit oneself to the service of sb.

委实　wěishí　*adv.*　really; indeed: 我～不知道。I really

don't know. / ～不容易 by no means easy

委琐　wěisuǒ　① *formal*　petty; trifling ② of wretched appearance

委托　wěituō　entrust; trust: ～他负责这项工作 entrust him with responsibility for the work / 行长～我主持今天的会议。The president asked me to chair the meeting on his behalf. / 这事就～你了。I leave this matter in your hands. / 代表们带着人民的～，聚集一堂，共商国家大事。Mandated by the people, the delegates assembled to discuss state affairs.

委托人　wěituōrén　*leg.*　trustor

委托商店　wěituō shāngdiàn　commission shop; commission house

委托书　wěituōshū　trust deed; a power of attorney

委婉　wěiwǎn　(also 委宛 wěiwǎn) mild and roundabout; tactful: ～的语气 a mild tone / 他批评得很～。He made his criticism very tactfully.

委婉语　wěiwǎnyǔ　euphemism

委员　wěiyuán　committee member

委员会　wěiyuánhuì　committee; commission; council

委罪　wěizuì　put the blame on sb. else

娓　wěi　see below

娓娓　wěiwěi　(talk) tirelessly: ～不倦 talk tirelessly

娓娓动听　wěiwěi dòngtīng　speak most interestingly

娓娓而谈　wěiwěi ér tán　talk in a kindly and informal fashion

诿　wěi　same as 委[1] wěi ③

诿过于人　wěi guò yú rén　same as 委过于人 wěi guò yú rén

萎　wěi　wither; wilt; fade

萎顿　wěidùn　same as 委顿 wěidùn

萎靡　wěimǐ　same as 委靡 wěimǐ

萎蔫　wěiniān　*bot.*　wilting

萎缩　wěisuō　① wither; shrivel ② listless; dispirited; dejected ③ (of a market, economy, etc.) shrink; sag ④ *med.* atrophy: 肝～ hepatatrophy; atrophy of the liver / 肌肉～ muscular atrophy; amyotrophy

萎陷疗法　wěixiàn liáofǎ　*med.*　collapse therapy

萎谢　wěixiè　wither; fade

唯　wěi　*formal*　yea ——see also wéi

唯唯诺诺　wěiwěinuònuò　be a yes-man; be subservient

陒　Wěi　a surname ——see also Kuí

猥　wěi　① numerous; multifarious: ～杂 miscellaneous ② base; obscene; salacious; indecent

猥鄙　wěibǐ　*formal*　base; mean; despicable

猥辞　wěicí　(also 猥词 wěicí) obscene (*or* dirty, foul) language; obscenities

猥獕　wěicuī　*old*　ugly looking; vulgar and unrefined

猥贱　wěijiàn　lowly; humble

猥劣　wěiliè　*formal*　abject; base; mean

猥陋　wěilòu　*formal*　base; mean; despicable

猥琐　wěisuǒ　of wretched appearance

猥屑　wěixiè　*formal*　base; mean; comtemptible; despicable

猥亵　wěixiè　① obscene; salacious ② act indecently towards (a woman)

骩　wěi　*formal*　twist; bend: ～法 pervert the law

痿　wěi　see below

痿症　wěizhèng　*Chin. med.*　flaccid paralysis; motor impairment as shown by weakness and numbness of the limbs, etc.

鳚（鳚）

zhī dà bùwěi　wěi　see 冒天下之大不鳚 mào tiānxià

鲔

wěi　① (mentioned in ancient texts) sturgeon ② yaito tuna

wèi

卫（衛、衞）

wèi　① defend; guard; protect: 保家～国 protect our homes and defend our country ② (Wèi) a surname

卫兵　wèibīng　guard; bodyguard

卫道　wèidào　defend traditional moral principles

卫道士　wèidàoshì　derog.　apologist

卫队　wèiduì　squad of bodyguards; armed escort: ～长 captain of the guard

卫顾　wèigù　protect; guard; look after

卫护　wèihù　protect; guard

卫矛　wèimáo　bot.　winged euonymus (Euonymus alatus)

卫冕　wèimiǎn　defend one's championship; defend one's title

卫气营血辨证　wèiqì-yíngxuè biànzhèng　Chin. med. analysing, differentiating and judging the development of a (usually febrile) disease by studying the four conditions of the human body: superficial resistance, nutrition, vital function and blood

卫生　wèishēng　hygiene; health; sanitation: 讲～ pay attention to hygiene / 个人～ personal hygiene / 工业～ industrial hygiene / 劳动～ labour hygiene / 喝生水，不～。Drinking unboiled water is bad for the health. / ～知识 hygienic knowledge

卫生带　wèishēngdài　sanitary belt; sanitary napkin

卫生队　wèishēngduì　medical unit; medical team

卫生防疫站　wèishēng fángyìzhàn　sanitation and anti-epidemic station

卫生间　wèishēngjiān　toilet (room)

卫生巾　wèishēngjīn　feminine napkin

卫生裤　wèishēngkù　dial.　sweat pants

卫生棉　wèishēngmián　cotton wool

卫生球　wèishēngqiú　(also 卫生丸 wèishēngwán) camphor ball; mothball

卫生设备　wèishēng shèbèi　sanitary equipment

卫生室　wèishēngshì　clinic

卫生学　wèishēngxué　hygiene; hygienics

卫生衣　wèishēngyī　dial.　sweat shirt

卫生员　wèishēngyuán　health worker; medical orderly; medic

卫生院　wèishēngyuàn　① formerly a commune hospital ② a small hospital

卫生纸　wèishēngzhǐ　toilet paper

卫士　wèishì　bodyguard

卫戍　wèishù　garrison: 北京～区 the Beijing Garrison Command / ～部队 garrison force

卫星　wèixīng　① satellite; moon: 木星有几个～? How many moons has the planet Jupiter? ② artificial satellite; man-made satellite: 低轨～ low altitude satellite / 高轨～ high altitude satellite / 军用～ military satellite / 气象～ weather satellite; meteorological satellite / 通讯～ telecommunications satellite

卫星城　wèixīngchéng　satellite town

卫星国　wèixīngguó　satellite state; satellite country

卫星天线　wèixīng tiānxiàn　satellite antenna

为（為、爲）

wèi　① prep.　in the interest of; for: ～什么人的问题，是一个根本的问题，原则的问题。The question of "for whom?" is fundamental; it is a question of principle. / ～大多数人谋利益 work in the interests of the vast majority of people ② prep. because of: ～我们的友谊干杯! A toast to our friendship! / ～胜利而欢呼 hail a victory ③ prep. for the purpose of; for the sake of: ～方便起见 for the sake of convenience / 不～名，不～利 seek no personal fame or gain / 让我们～实现这一宏伟目标而共同努力。Let us strive together to attain this splendid goal. ④ prep. to; towards: 他～我送来一份请帖。He's sent an invitation to me. / 且～诸君言之。Now I'll inform you about it. ⑤ formal　stand for; support ——see also wéi

为此　wèicǐ　to this end; for this reason (or purpose); in this connection: ～而作出种种努力 make every effort to that end / ～, 大会作出一项重要决定。The conference made a very important decision in this connection. / 我们都～感到欢欣鼓舞。We all feel delighted and encouraged by this. / ～, 我们不能投票。For this reason we must abstain from voting.

为国捐躯　wèi guó juānqū　lay down one's life for one's country

为何　wèihé　why; for what reason

为虎傅翼　wèi hǔ fù yì　(also 为虎添翼 wèi hǔ tiān yì) give wings to a tiger—aid an evildoer

为虎作伥　wèi hǔ zuò chāng　play the jackal to the tiger—help a villain do evil

为了　wèile　prep.　for; for the sake of; in order to: ～健康戒烟 give up smoking for the sake of health / 他们现在学英语是～以后学工。They are learning English in order that they can study engineering. / ～准确起见, 他再次核查数字。To make sure, he checked all the figures over again.

为民除害　wèi mín chú hài　rid the people of an evil; rid the people of a scourge

为民请命　wèi mín qǐngmìng　plead in the name of the people; plead for the people: 打着～的幌子 pose as a spokesperson of the people

为人作嫁　wèi rén zuò jià　sewing sb. else's trousseau—doing work for others with no benefit to oneself

为什么　wèishénme　why; why (or how) is it that: 你～没来? Why didn't you come? / ～犹豫不决呢? Why hesitate? / 我不知道～, 心里直害怕。I don't know why, but I'm afraid. / 我还没做完呢。——～没做完? I haven't finished yet. —Why not?

为我之物　wèi wǒ zhī wù　philos.　thing-for-us

为渊驱鱼, 为丛驱雀　wèi yuān qū yú, wèi cóng qū què drive the fish into deep waters and the sparrows into the thickets—drive friends over to the side of the enemy

未1

wèi　adv.　① have not; did not: 意犹～尽 have not given full expression to one's views / 走访～遇。I called but you were out. / 尚～恢复健康 not yet recovered (from illness); not yet restored to health ② not: ～知可否 not know whether sth. can be done

未2

wèi　the eighth of the twelve Earthly Branches (地支) ——see also 干支 gān-zhī

未爆弹　wèibàodàn　mil.　dud

未必　wèibì　adv.　may not; not necessarily: 他～知道。He doesn't necessarily know. / 事情～会如此。Things may not necessarily turn out that way.

未便　wèibiàn　not be in a position to; find it hard to: ～擅自处理 cannot do it without authorization / ～立即答复 find it difficult to give an immediate reply

未卜先知　wèi bǔ xiān zhī　know without consulting the oracle—have foreknowledge

未曾　wèicéng　adv.　have not; did not: ～听说过 never heard of it / 历史上～有过的奇迹 a miracle unprec-

edented in history

未尝 wèicháng *adv.* ①have not; did not: 她一夜～合眼。She didn't get a wink of sleep the whole night. ②(used before a negative word, in making a guarded assertion): 这～不是好主意。That might not be a bad idea. / 那样也～不可。That should be all right. / ～没有可取之处 not without its merits

未成年 wèichéngnián not yet of age; under age

未成年人 wèichéngniánrén *leg.* minor

未达一间 wèi dá yī jiàn there is not much difference; pretty much the same

未定 wèidìng uncertain; undecided; undefined: 行期～。The date of departure is not yet fixed.

未定稿 wèidìnggǎo (also 未定草 wèidìngcǎo) manuscript not yet finalized; draft

未定界 wèidìngjiè undefined boundary; undemarcated boundary

未定之天 wèidìng zhī tiān an unknown factor; uncertainty

未敢苟同 wèi gǎn gǒutóng *formal* beg to differ; cannot agree: 你的意见,我～。I beg to differ. *or* I'm sorry but I don't agree.

未婚 wèihūn unmarried; single

未婚夫 wèihūnfū *fiancé*

未婚妻 wèihūnqī *fiancée*

未及 wèijí ① there's not enough time (to do sth.); it's too late (to do sth.): 他匆促起程,～向朋友告别。He set out in such a haste that he didn't have time to say good-bye to his friends. ② not touch upon; leave unmentioned: 他只谈到了奏鸣曲的结构,而～于它的起源。He only talked about the structure of the sonata without mentioning its origin.

未几 wèijǐ ① soon; before long: 他上周来此,～即悄然离去。He came here last week, and soon afterwards left quietly. ② not many; very few

未竟 wèijìng unfulfilled; unaccomplished: ～之志 an unfulfilled ambition / ～之业 an unaccomplished task

未决 wèijué unsettled; outstanding: 胜负～。The outcome (of the battle or contest) is not yet decided.

未决犯 wèijuéfàn prisoner awaiting trial; culprit

未可 wèikě cannot: 前途～限量 have a brilliant future

未可厚非 wèi kě hòu fēi not be altogether unjustifiable; give little cause for criticism

未可乐观 wèi kě lèguān give no cause for optimism; nothing to be optimistic about

未来 wèilái ① coming; approaching; next; future: ～的一年 the coming year; next year / 在～的岁月中 in the years to come / ～二十四小时内将有暴雨。There will be a rainstorm within 24 hours. ② future; tomorrow: 美好的～ a glorious future / ～是属于人民的。Tomorrow belongs to the people.

未来派 wèiláipài futurism

未来学 wèiláixué futurology

未老先衰 wèi lǎo xiān shuāi frail and failing before one's time

未了 wèiliǎo unfinished; outstanding: ～事宜 unsettled matters; unfinished business / ～的手续 formalities still to be complied with / ～的债务 outstanding debts / ～的心愿 an unfulfilled wish

未免 wèimiǎn ① *adv.* rather; a bit too; truly: 这～太过份。This is really going too far. / 他的话～太多。He's rather talkative. / 你这样作～操之过急。You were a bit too impetuous in doing that. ② *formal* unavoidable

未能 wèinéng fail to; cannot: ～实现 fail to materialize / 阴谋～得逞 be frustrated in one's plot / 他们～取得预期的结果。They have failed to achieve the expected result. / ～忘怀 cannot get sth. out of one's mind; still remember

未能免俗 wèinéng miǎn sú be unable to rise above the

convention; cannot but follow conventional practice

未然 wèirán see 防患未然 fánghuàn wèirán

未识别飞行物 wèishíbié fēixíngwù same as 不明飞行物 bùmíng fēixíngwù

未时 wèishí the period of the day from 1 p.m. to 3 p.m.

未始 wèishǐ same as 未尝 wèicháng②

未遂 wèisuì not accomplished; abortive: 政变～。The coup d'état aborted. / 自杀～ an attempted suicide

未遂犯 wèisuìfàn one who attempts to commit a crime

未遂罪 wèisuìzuì attempted crime; attempt

未完 wèiwán unfinished: ～待续 to be continued

未亡人 wèiwángrén the bereaved one (a form of self-address formerly used by a widow)

未详 wèixiáng unknown: 本书作者～。The author of the book is unknown. / 病因～。What brought on the illness is not clear.

未央 wèiyāng *formal* not ended: 夜未央 yèwèiyāng

未雨绸缪 wèi yǔ chóumóu repair the house before it rains; provide for a rainy day; take precautions

未知量 wèizhīliàng *math.* unknown quantity

未知数 wèizhīshù ① *math.* unknown number ② unknown; uncertain: 这事能不能办成还是个～。It's still uncertain whether this can be arranged.

位

wèi ① place; location: 座位 zuòwèi ② position: 名位 míngwèi ③ throne: 即位 jíwèi ④ *math.* place; figure; digit: 个～ unit's place / 十～ ten's place / 小数～ decimal place / 计算到小数点后五～ calculate to five decimal places / 四～数 four-figure number; four-digit number ⑤ *m. pol.* (for people): 各～代表! Fellow Delegates! / 今天我们家要来几～朋友。We have some friends coming to see us today.

位次 wèicì ① precedence; seating arrangement: ～卡 place card ② rank

位能 wèinéng *phys.* potential energy

位势米 wèishìmǐ *meteorol.* geopotential metre

位望 wèiwàng (social) position and prestige

位移 wèiyí *phys.* displacement

位于 wèiyú *formal* be located; be situated; lie: ～亚洲东部 be situated in the eastern part of Asia

位置 wèizhi ① seat; place: 请按指定的～坐。Will everybody please take his proper seat. / 地理～ geographical position / 在地图上找出西安的～ locate Xi'an on a map / 这个路口建个超级市场～很好。This corner would make a good location for a supermarket. ② place; position: 《红楼梦》在中国文学史上占有重要～。*A Dream of the Red Mansions* occupies an important place in the history of Chinese literature.

位子 wèizi seat; place

味

wèi ① taste; flavour: ～儿甜 taste sweet / 这糖有巧克力～儿。The candy has a chocolate flavour. ② smell; odour: 香～儿 a sweet smell; fragrance; perfume; aroma / 臭～儿 an offensive (*or* foul) smell; stench; stink ③ interest; delight: 趣味 qùwèi ④ distinguish the flavour of: 细～其言 ponder his words ⑤ *m.* (for ingredients of a Chinese medicine prescription): 这个方子共有七～药。The prescription specifies seven medicinal herbs. *or* Seven medicinal herbs are prescribed.

味道 wèidao taste; flavour: 这个菜～很好。This dish is delicious. / 感冒的时候吃东西没有～。When you have a cold, your food has very little flavour. / 你们年轻人没尝过当童工是什么～。You young people don't know what it was like to slave away as a child labourer. / 心里有一股说不出的～ have an indescribable feeling / 他的话里有点讽刺的～。There's a touch of irony in his remarks.

味精 wèijīng monosodium glutamate; gourmet powder; MSG

味觉　wèijué　sense of taste

味蕾　wèilěi　*physiol.*　taste bud

味美思　wèiměisī　vermouth

味素　wèisù　same as 味精 wèijīng

味同嚼蜡　wèi tóng jiáo là　like chewing wax——insipid: 世人见了功名，便舍着性命去求他，及至到手之后，～。《儒林外史》Men will risk their lives in search of success and fame; yet once they have them, the taste is no better than chewed tallow.

畏

wèi　① fear: 不～强敌 stand in no fear of a formidable enemy ② respect: 后生可畏 hòushēng kě wèi

畏避　wèibì　avoid sth. out of fear; recoil from; flinch from

畏怖　wèibù　*formal*　fear; dread

畏服　wèifú　submit from fear; yield from awe

畏光　wèiguāng　*med.*　photophobia

畏忌　wèijì　have scruples; fear; dread

畏惧　wèijù　fear; dread: 他和这位强手比赛并不感到～。He played fearlessly against his strong opponent.

畏难　wèinán　be afraid of difficulty: ～情绪 fear of difficulty

畏怯　wèiqiè　cowardly; timid; chickenhearted

畏首畏尾　wèishǒu-wèiwěi　be full of misgivings; be overcautious

畏缩　wèisuō　recoil; shrink; flinch: 在困难面前从不～ never shrink (*or* flinch) from difficulty

畏缩不前　wèisuō bù qián　(also 畏葸不前 wèixǐ bù qián) recoil in fear; hesitate to press forward; hang back

畏途　wèitú　*formal*　a dangerous road——a perilous undertaking: 视为畏途 shì wéi wèitú

畏葸　wèixǐ　*formal*　timid; afraid

畏友　wèiyǒu　an esteemed friend

畏罪　wèizuì　dread punishment for one's crime: ～潜逃 abscond to avoid punishment / ～自杀 commit suicide to escape punishment

胃

wèi　① stomach ② the seventeenth of the twenty-eight constellations (二十八宿) into which the celestial sphere was divided in ancient Chinese astronomy (consisting of three stars in Musca Borealis)

胃癌　wèi'ái　cancer of the stomach; gastric carcinoma

胃病　wèibìng　stomach trouble; gastric disease; gastropathy

胃肠炎　wèichángyán　gastroenteritis

胃出血　wèichūxuè　gastric bleeding; gastric hemorrhage; gastrorrhagia

胃穿孔　wèichuānkǒng　gastric perforation; stomach perforation

胃蛋白酶　wèidànbáiméi　*physiol.*　pepsin

胃痉挛　wèijìngluán　gastrospasm

胃镜　wèijìng　gastroscope: ～检查 gastrocopy; stomachoscopy

胃口　wèi·kǒu　① appetite: ～好 have a good appetite / 没有～ have no appetite ② liking: 对～ to one's liking ——see also 倒胃口 dǎo wèi·kǒu

胃溃疡　wèikuìyáng　gastric ulcer

胃扩张　wèikuòzhāng　dilatation of the stomach; gastrectasis

胃切除术　wèiqiēchúshù　gastrectomy

胃酸　wèisuān　hydrochloric acid in gastric juice: ～过多 hyperchlorhydria; hyperacidity / ～过少 hypochlorhydria; hypoacidity

胃痛　wèitòng　stomachache; gastralgia

胃脘　wèiwǎn　*Chin. med.*　gastral cavity

胃萎缩　wèiwěisuō　lipogastry

胃下垂　wèixiàchuí　ptosis of the stomach; gastroptosis

胃腺　wèixiàn　*physiol.*　gastric gland

胃炎　wèiyán　gastritis

胃液　wèiyè　*physiol.*　gastric juice

谓

wèi　① say: 或～ someone says ② call; name: 此之～形式主义。This is what is called formalism. ③ meaning; sense: 无谓 wúwèi

谓词　wèicí　*log.*　predicate: ～演算 predicate calculus

谓语　wèiyǔ　*gram.*　predicate

尉

wèi　① see 尉官 wèiguān ② (Wèi) a surname ——see also yù

尉官　wèiguān　a military officer above the rank of warrant officer and below that of major; a junior officer

遗

wèi　*formal*　offer as a gift; make a present of sth.: ～之千金 present sb. with a generous gift of money ——see also yí

喂¹

wèi　① *interj.*　hello; hey: ～，请接三一三号分机。Hello, extension 313, please! / ～，你的围巾快掉了。Hey, your scarf is slipping off.

喂²（餵、餧）

wèi　feed: ～猪 feed pigs / 给病人～饭 feed a patient

喂料　wèiliào　feed (draught animals)

喂奶　wèinǎi　breast-feed; suckle; nurse

喂养　wèiyǎng　feed; raise; keep: ～家禽 keep fowls

渭

Wèi　(also 渭河 Wèihé) a river rising in Gansu and flowing east into southern Shaanxi where it empties into the Huanghe River

猬（蝟）

wèi　*zool.*　hedgehog

猬集　wèijí　*formal*　(of matters) as numerous as the spines of a hedgehog: 诸事～ have too many things to attend to; have too many irons in the fire

蔚

wèi　*formal*　① luxuriant; grand ② colourful: 云蒸霞蔚 yúnzhēng-xiáwèi

蔚蓝　wèilán　azure; sky blue: ～的天空 a bright blue sky / ～的海洋 the blue sea

蔚然成风　wèirán chéng fēng　become common practice; become the order of the day: 学习外语～。Studying foreign languages is the order of the day.

蔚为大观　wèi wéi dàguān　present a splendid sight; afford a magnificent view: 展出的美术作品，～。There's a splendid array of works of art on display.

慰

wèi　① console; comfort: 慰勉 wèimiǎn ② be relieved: 知你平安到达，甚～。I am greatly relieved to learn that you have arrived safely.

慰抚　wèifǔ　comfort; console; soothe

慰藉　wèijiè　*formal*　comfort; console

慰劳　wèiláo　bring gifts to, or send one's best wishes to, in recognition of services rendered

慰留　wèiliú　urge sb. to stay on

慰勉　wèimiǎn　comfort and encourage

慰情胜无　wèi qíng shèng wú　a little comfort is better than none

慰问　wèiwèn　express sympathy and solicitude for; extend one's regards to; convey greetings to; salute: 对灾区人民表示～ express sympathy and solicitude for the people of disaster areas / 同志们辛苦了，我们特来～你们。Comrades, you've been working hard. We've come to salute you. / 请向他们转达我们亲切的～。Please convey to them our sincere solicitude. / ～袋 gift bag / ～团 a group sent to convey greetings and appreciation / ～信 a letter expressing one's appreciation or sympathy / ～演出 a special performance as an ex-

pression of gratitude or appreciation

慰唁 wèiyàn　condole with sb.

魏

Wèi ① one of the Warring States into which China was divided during the Eastern Zhou period (770-256 B.C.), occupying what is now northern Henan, eastern Shaanxi, southwestern Shanxi, and southern Hebei ② one of the Three Kingdoms into which China was divided during the period 220-280, occupying the present-day provinces in the Yellow River valley and what is now northern Hubei, Anhui, and Jiangsu and central Liaoning ③ one of the Northern Dynasties (北朝), better known as the Northern Wei (北魏) ④ a surname

魏碑 Wèibēi　① tablet inscriptions of the Northern Dynasties (386-581) ② model calligraphy represented by the aforesaid inscriptions

魏阙 wèiquè　① gate of the imperial palace where imperial edicts were issued ② imperial court

鳂

wèi　*zool.*　blenny

wēn

温

wēn ① warm; lukewarm: ～水 lukewarm water ② temperature: 体温 tǐwēn ③ warm up: 把酒～一下 warm up the wine ④ review; revise: ～课 review (or revise) one's lessons ⑤ same as 瘟 wēn ⑥ (Wēn) a surname

温饱 wēnbǎo　dress warmly and eat one's fill; have adequate food and clothing: 终年劳累, 不得～ toil all the year round without enough to eat and wear / 提高人民生活, 从～达到小康水平 raise the living standards of the people from simply having enough food and clothing to leading a relatively comfortable life

温标 wēnbiāo　*phys.*　thermometric scale: 华氏～ Fahrenheit's thermometric scale / 摄氏～ Celsius' thermometric scale / 开氏～ Kelvin's thermometric scale

温差 wēnchā　difference in temperature; range of temperature: 这里白天和夜晚的～很大。The temperature here varies greatly between day and night.

温差电 wēnchādiàn　*phys.*　thermoelectricity: ～检波器 thermodetector / ～偶 thermoelectric couple; thermocouple

温床 wēnchuáng　① *agric.* hotbed ② (fig.) breeding ground; hotbed: 官僚主义是贿赂和腐败的～。Bureaucracy is a hotbed of bribery and corruption.

温存 wēncún　① attentive (usu. to a person of the opposite sex) ② gentle; kind

温带 wēndài　temperate zone

温度 wēndù　temperature: 室内(外)～ indoor (outdoor) temperature

温度表 wēndùbiǎo　thermometer: 摄氏～ centigrade (or Celsius) thermometer / 华氏～ Fahrenheit thermometer

温度计 wēndùjì　thermograph

温故知新 wēngù-zhīxīn　① gain new knowledge by reviewing old ② understand the present by reviewing the past

温和 wēnhé　① temperate; mild; moderate: 气候～ a temperate climate ② gentle; mild: 性情～ a gentle disposition / 语气～ a mild tone ——see also wēnhuo

温和派 wēnhépài　moderates

温厚 wēnhòu　gentle and kind; good-natured

温乎乎 wēnhūhū　warm; lukewarm: 我不爱喝～的汤。I hate lukewarm soup.

温乎 wēnhu　warm; lukewarm: 烙饼还有点儿～。The pancake is still warm.

温和 wēnhuo　warm; lukewarm: 汤还～呢。The soup is still warm. ——see also wēnhé

温居 wēnjū　housewarming

温觉 wēnjué　*physiol.*　sense of heat

温良 wēnliáng　gentle and kindhearted

温良恭俭让 wēn-liáng-gōng-jiǎn-ràng　temperate, kind, courteous, restrained and magnanimous

温暖 wēnnuǎn　warm: 天气～ warm weather / 对同志像春天般的～ be as mild as spring towards one's comrades / 他的一席话～了我的心。What he said warmed my heart.

温情 wēnqíng　① tender feeling ② too softhearted: 你对他太～了。You're too lenient with him.

温情脉脉 wēnqíng mòmò　full of tenderness

温情主义 wēnqíngzhǔyì　excessive tenderheartedness; undue leniency

温泉 wēnquán　hot spring

温柔 wēnróu　(usu. of a woman) gentle and soft

温柔敦厚 wēnróu-dūnhòu　gentle and kind

温柔乡 wēnróuxiāng　the land of warmth and tenderness—a place where a man can find solace in feminine charms

温润 wēnrùn　① gentle; kindly: ～的面容 a kindly face ② mild (or temperate) and moist: 气候～ a temperate and moist climate

温湿计 wēnshījì　hygrothermograph; thermohygrograph

温室 wēnshì　hothouse; greenhouse; glasshouse; conservatory: ～育苗 nurse young plants in hothouses

温室效应 wēnshì xiàoyìng　greenhouse effect

温淑 wēnshū　*formal*　(of a woman) gentle and kind

温顺 wēnshùn　docile; meek: 像小羊一般～ as meek as a lamb

温汤 wēntāng　① lukewarm water ② *formal* hot spring

温汤浸种 wēntāng jìnzhǒng　*agric.*　hot water treatment of seeds

温暾 wēn·tūn　(also 温吞 wēn·tūn)　*dial.*　① lukewarm; tepid: ～水 lukewarm water ② (of language) not to the point; irrelevant

温文尔雅 wēnwén-ěryǎ　refined and cultivated

温习 wēnxí　review; revise: ～功课 review one's lessons

温馨 wēnxīn　soft and sweet; warm: ～的春夜 a soft spring evening / ～的情谊 warm friendship

温煦 wēnxù　warm

温血动物 wēnxuè dòngwù　warm-blooded animal

温驯 wēnxún　(of animals) docile; meek; tame

温雅 wēnyǎ　gentle and refined: ～的少年 a gentle and elegant young man

榅

wēn　see below

榅桲 wēnpo　*bot.*　quince (*Cydonia oblonga*)

瘟

wēn ① *Chin. med.* acute communicable diseases ② (of traditional opera) dull and insipid

瘟病 wēnbìng　*Chin. med.*　seasonal febrile diseases

瘟神 wēnshén　god of plague

瘟疫 wēnyì　pestilence

瘟疹 wēnzhěn　infectious diseases characterized by rashes (such as scarlet fever, typhus, etc.)

鰛

wēn　*zool.*　sardine

鰛鲸 wēnjīng　*zool.*　sei whale; rorqual

wén

文

wén ① character; script; writing: 甲骨文 jiǎgǔwén ② language: 英文 yīngwén ③ literary composition;

writing: 文如其人 wén rú qí rén ④ literary language: 这句话太～了，不好懂。 This sentence is too bookish to be readily intelligible. ⑤ culture: 文物 wénwù ⑥ formal ritual: 虚文 xūwén ⑦ civilian; civil: 文职 wénzhí ⑧ gentle; refined: 文雅 wényǎ ⑨ certain natural phenomena: 天文 tiānwén / 水文 shuǐwén ⑩ cover up; paint over: 文过饰非 wénguò-shìfēi ⑪ tattoo: 文身 wénshēn ⑫ m. (for copper cash): 一～钱 a cash / 一～不值 not worth a farthing ⑬ (Wén) a surname

文案 wén'àn old ① official documents and correspondence ② secretary; clerk

文本 wénběn text; version: 本合同两种～同等有效。Both texts of the contract are equally valid. / 如对本协定在解释上遇有分歧，应以中文～为准。In case there is any divergence of interpretation of this agreement, the Chinese text shall prevail.

文笔 wénbǐ style of writing: ～流利 write in an easy and fluent style

文不对题 wén bù duì tí irrelevant; beside the point (or mark); wide of the mark

文不加点 wén bù jiā diǎn never make the slightest change in one's writing; have a facile pen: 时邯郸淳年方十三岁，～，一挥而就。《三国演义》At that time Handan Chun was only thirteen, but the composition of the inscription was so perfect that neither jot nor tittle could be added, and yet it had come impromptu from his pen.

文才 wéncái literary talent; aptitude for writing

文采 wéncǎi ① rich and bright colours ② literary grace; literary talent: 这个人很有～。This is a man of unusual literary talent.

文昌鱼 wénchāngyú lancelet

文场[1] wénchǎng (also 文场面 wénchǎngmiàn) civil division (one of the two divisions of the orchestra in traditional opera, consisting of stringed and wind instruments)——see also 武场 wǔchǎng

文场[2] wénchǎng ① examination hall (for the imperial civil service examinations) ② same as 文坛 wéntán

文抄公 wénchāogōng plagiarist

文丑 wénchǒu (in traditional opera) a comedian in civil plays (文戏)

文辞 wéncí (also 文词 wéncí) diction; language: ～优美 exquisite diction; elegant language

文从字顺 wéncóng-zìshùn readable and fluent

文旦 wéndàn dial. pomelo

文典 wéndiǎn formal ① classics ② models of style

文电 wéndiàn message; cable: 来往～ received and delivered messages (or cables)

文斗 wéndòu verbal struggle; nonviolent struggle

文牍 wéndú ① official documents and correspondence ② old secretary; clerk

文牍主义 wéndúzhǔyì red tape

文法 wénfǎ ① rules of composition and rhetoric ② old name for 语法 yǔfǎ

文房 wénfáng formal study (a room)

文房四宝 wénfáng sìbǎo the four treasures of the study (writing brush, inkstick, inkslab and paper)

文风 wénfēng style of writing: ～朴实 a simple style of writing

文风不动 wénfēng bù dòng absolutely still

文稿 wéngǎo manuscript; draft

文告 wéngào proclamation; statement; message

文革 Wéngé short for 无产阶级文化大革命 Wúchǎnjiējí Wénhuà Dàgémìng

文蛤 wéngé zool. clam

文工团 wéngōngtuán song and dance ensemble; art troupe; cultural troupe

文官 wénguān civil official

文冠果 wénguānguǒ bot. shiny-leaved yellowhorn (Xanthoceras sorbifolia)

文过饰非 wénguò-shìfēi conceal faults and gloss over wrongs; gloss over one's faults; cover up (or explain away) one's errors

文翰 wénhàn formal ① essay; article ② official documents and correspondence

文豪 wénháo literary giant; great writer; eminent writer

文虎 wénhǔ literary riddles

文化 wénhuà ① civilization; culture: 中国～ Chinese civilization (or culture) / ～合作 cultural cooperation / ～交流 cultural exchange / ～侵略 cultural aggression; cultural penetration / ～渗透 cultural infiltration / ～遗产 cultural heritage / ～遗址 a site of ancient cultural remains; remains of an ancient culture ② education; culture; schooling; literacy: 学～ acquire an elementary education; learn to read and write / ～课 literacy class; general knowledge course / ～事业 cultural establishments; cultural undertakings / ～水平 cultural level; educational level

文化参赞 wénhuà cānzàn cultural counsellor; cultural attaché

文化程度 wénhuà chéngdù cultural level; cultural standard: 她的～比我高。She's had more education than I. or She's better educated than I.

文化大革命 Wénhuà Dàgémìng short for 无产阶级文化大革命 Wúchǎnjiējí Wénhuà Dàgémìng

文化宫 wénhuàgōng palace of culture; cultural palace

文化馆 wénhuàguǎn (also 文化站 wénhuàzhàn) cultural centre

文化机关 wénhuà jīguān cultural institution

文化界 wénhuàjiè cultural circles

文化人 wénhuàrén cultural worker; intellectual

文化水儿 wénhuàshuǐr inf. cultural level; education level

文化用品 wénhuà yòngpǐn stationery

文化专员 wénhuà zhuānyuán cultural attaché

文化专制主义 wénhuàzhuānzhìzhǔyì cultural tyranny

文火 wénhuǒ slow fire; gentle heat: ～焖四十分钟 simmer gently for forty minutes

文集 wénjí collected works

文籍 wénjí books

文件 wénjiàn documents; papers; instruments: ～编号 the reference or serial number of a document / ～袋 documents pouch; dispatch case / ～柜 filing cabinet

文教 wénjiào (short for 文化教育) culture and education: ～事业 cultural and educational work; culture and education

文教界 wénjiàojiè cultural and educational circles

文静 wénjìng gentle and quiet

文具 wénjù writing materials; stationery: ～店 stationer's; stationery shop

文据 wénjù written pledge

文科 wénkē liberal arts: ～学校 liberal arts school / ～院校 colleges of arts

文库 wénkù (usu. used in book titles) a series of books issued in a single format by a publisher; library: 《万有～》 Everyman's Library

文侩 wénkuài literary scavenger

文莱 Wénlái Brunei

文理 wénlǐ unity and coherence in writing: ～不通 illogical and ungrammatical; ungrammatical and incoherent / ～通顺 have unity and coherence; make smooth reading

文林 wénlín formal a galaxy of literary talent; literary men as a class

文盲 wénmáng an illiterate person; illiterate: 据计算，该国百分之十的人是～。Ten per cent of the country is reckoned to be illiterate.

文面　wénmiàn　*formal*　tattoo the face

文庙　wénmiào　Confucian temple

文名　wénmíng　literary fame

文明　wénmíng　① civilization; culture: ～古国 a country with an ancient civilization ② civilized: ～国家 an civilized country / ～经商 do business with civility / ～礼貌 decorum; courtesy; manners / 这人一点都不～。He is not at all civil. / 说话～点! Keep a civil tongue in your head! *or* Please watch your language a little.

文明棍　wénmínggùn　*old*　walking stick; stick

文明戏　wénmíngxì　*old*　early form of spoken drama（话剧）

文墨　wénmò　writing: 粗通～ barely know the rudiments of writing

文墨人　wénmòrén　collective name for painters, calligraphers, writers, teachers, etc.

文鸟　wénniǎo　*zool.*　mannikin

文痞　wénpǐ　literary prostitute

文凭　wénpíng　diploma

文气　wénqì　vigour of style

文气　wénqi　*dial.*　gentle and quiet

文契　wénqì　contracts concerning the buying and selling of real estate, etc.

文情并茂　wén qíng bìng mào　(of writing) elegant in style and rich in sentiment

文人　wénrén　man of letters; scholar; *literati*

文人画　wénrénhuà　*literati* painting (the ideal of the Chinese scholar-painter who was more interested in individual expression and learning than in outward representation and immediate visual appeal)

文人无行　wénrén wúxíng　men of letters are nowhere in point of moral conduct (i.e. are frivolous, pleasure-loving persons)

文人相轻　wénrén xiāng qīng　scholars tend to scorn each other

文人学士　wénrén-xuéshì　scholars; men of letters

文如其人　wén rú qí rén　the writing mirrors the writer; the style is the man

文弱　wénruò　gentle and frail-looking: ～书生 a frail scholar

文山会海　wénshān-huìhǎi　a mountain of papers and a sea of meetings—the intricate routine that a leading cadre gets bogged down in

文身　wénshēn　*formal*　tattoo

文史　wénshǐ　literature and history: ～资料 historical accounts of past events

文史馆　Wénshǐguǎn　Research Institute of Culture and History

文饰　wénshì　① polish (a piece of writing) ② gloss over (one's mistakes); cover up

文书　wénshū　① document; official dispatch ② copy clerk

文殊　Wénshū　Manjusri (the Bodhisattva 菩萨 personifying supreme wisdom, depicted seated on a lion or on a lotus; the patron deity of Mt. Wutai 五台山 in Shanxi Province)

文思　wénsī　the thread of ideas in writing; the train of thought in writing: ～敏捷 have a ready pen

文坛　wéntán　the literary world (*or* arena, circles); the world of letters

文韬武略　wéntāo-wǔlüè　civil and military skills

文体[1]　wéntǐ　type of writing; literary form; style

文体[2]　wéntǐ　(short for 文娱体育) recreation and sports: ～活动 recreational and sports activities

文恬武嬉　wéntián-wǔxī　(of a corrupt regime) the officials are indolent and the officers frivolous

文武　wén-wǔ　civil and military: ～官员 civil and military officials

文武双全　wén-wǔ shuāngquán　be well versed in both polite letters and martial arts; adept with both pen and sword

文物　wénwù　cultural relic; historical relic

文物保护　wénwù bǎohù　preservation of cultural relics; protection of historical relics: 重点～单位 major historical and cultural sites under state protection

文戏　wénxì　(in traditional opera) civil plays (opp. 武戏 wǔxì; concerned with domestic joy or sorrow, filial piety, marital fidelity, and the effect of ghosts and spirits on the lives of ordinary people)

文献　wénxiàn　document; literature: 历史～ historical documents / 马列主义～ Marxist-Leninist literature

文献记录片　wénxiàn jìlùpiàn　documentary film

文选　wénxuǎn　(usu. used in book titles) selected works; literary selections: 《列宁～》 *Selections from Lenin*

文选烂, 秀才半　Wén Xuǎn làn, xiùcai bàn　the *Wen Xuan* (a general anthology of prose and verse made by Xiao Tong 萧统) thoroughly done, half a licentiate won

文学　wénxué　literature: ～家 writer; man of letters; *literati* / ～流派 schools of literature / ～批评 literary criticism / ～作品 literary works

文学士　wénxuéshì　bachelor of arts (B. A.)

文学语言　wénxué yǔyán　① standard speech ② literary language

文雅　wényǎ　elegant; refined; cultured; polished: 举止～ refined in manner

文言　wényán　classical Chinese

文言文　wényánwén　writings in classical Chinese; classical style of writing

文以载道　wén yǐ zài dào　the function of literature is to convey the *Tao* (a moralist view of literature, advanced by Confucian writers of the past, notably Han Yu 韩愈, who by the *Tao* meant of course only Confucian philosophical and moral principles)

文艺　wényì　literature and art: ～创作 literary and artistic creation / ～队伍 ranks of writers and artists / ～工作 work in the literary and artistic fields / ～工作者 literary and art workers; writers and artists / ～理论 theory of literature and art / ～路线 line in literature and art / ～思潮 trend of thought in literature and art / ～团体 literature and art organization; theatre company; theatre troupe / ～作品 literary and artistic works / ～座谈会 forum on literature and art

文艺复兴　Wényìfùxīng　the Renaissance

文艺会演　wényì huìyǎn　theatrical festival

文艺节目　wényì jiémù　programme of entertainment; theatrical items; theatrical performance

文艺界　wényìjiè　literary and art circles; the world of literature and art

文艺批评　wényì pīpíng　literary or art criticism: ～家 literary or art critic

文艺语言　wényì yǔyán　same as 文学语言 wénxué yǔyán[2]

文友　wényǒu　literary friend

文娱　wényú　(short for 文化娱乐) cultural recreation; entertainment: ～活动 recreational activities

文苑　wényuàn　① the literary world (*or* arena, circles); the world of letters ② literary and art circles; the world of literature and art

文约　wényuē　contract; deed

文责　wénzé　the responsibility an author should assume for his own writings; author's responsibility

文责自负　wénzé zì fù　the author takes sole responsibility for his views

文摘　wénzhāi　abstract; digest

文章　wénzhāng　① essay; article ② literary works; writings ③ hidden meaning; implied meaning: 话里有～。There is an insinuation in that remark. *or* That's

an insinuating remark. / 其中大有～. There is a lot behind all this. ——see also 做文章 zuò wénzhāng

文职 wénzhí civilian post: ～人员 nonmilitary personnel

文治 wénzhì *formal* civil administration

文治武功 wénzhì-wǔgōng cultural and military achievements

文质彬彬 wénzhì bīnbīn gentle; urbane; suave: 他举止大方,～, 和霭可亲. He is composed, urbane, and affable.

文绉绉 wénzhōuzhōu genteel: 说话～的 speak in a genteel manner; be soft-spoken

文竹 wénzhú *bot.* asparagus fern (*Asparagus plumosus*)

文字 wénzì ① characters; script; writing ② written language: ～宣传 written propaganda / 有～可考的历史 recorded history ③ writing (as regards form or style): ～清通 lucid writing

文字处理机 wénzì chǔlǐjī word processor

文字方程 wénzì fāngchéng *math.* literal equation

文字改革 wénzì gǎigé reform of a writing system (as in China)

文字交 wénzìjiāo pen friends; literary friends

文字学 wénzìxué philology

文字游戏 wénzì yóuxì play with words; juggle with terms

文字狱 wénzìyù *hist.* imprisonment or execution of an author for writing sth. considered offensive by the imperial court; literary inquisition

文宗 wénzōng *formal* an outstanding literary figure: 一代～ the most outstanding literary figure of the time

纹 wén lines; veins; grain: 皱纹 zhòuwén

纹理 wénlǐ veins; grain: 有～的大理石 veined marble / 这木头的～很好看. This wood has a beautiful grain.

纹路儿 wénlur lines; grain

纹缕儿 wénlǚr same as 纹路儿 wénlur

纹饰 wénshì decorative pattern (on utensils); figure

纹丝不动 wénsī bù dòng absolutely still: 没有一点风, 柳条儿～. There wasn't a breath of wind and the willow twigs were perfectly still.

纹银 wényín *old* fine silver

炆 wén *dial.* cook food on a slow fire; simmer

闻 wén ① hear: 耳闻 ěrwén ② news; story: 要闻 yàowén ③ well-known; famous: 闻人 wénrén ④ reputation: 秽闻 huìwén ⑤ smell: 你～～这是什么味儿? Smell this and see what it is. / 我～到煳味儿了. I can smell something burning. ⑥ (Wén) a surname

闻达 wéndá *formal* illustrious and influential; eminent: 不求～ seek neither fame nor position

闻风而动 wén fēng ér dòng act without delay upon hearing the news; immediately respond to a call; go into action without delay

闻风丧胆 wén fēng sàng dǎn become terror-stricken (*or* panic-stricken, terrified) at the news: 我军向前推进, 敌人～. The enemy trembled with fear on hearing of our advance.

闻过则喜 wén guò zé xǐ be glad to have one's errors pointed out

闻鸡起舞 wén jī qǐ wǔ rise at cock's crow—diligent and self-disciplined

闻见 wénjiàn what one sees and hears; knowledge; information

闻见 wénjian ① notice by smell; smell: 我～了花香. I smell the fragrance of a flower. ② hear

闻名 wénmíng ① well-known; famous; renowned: ～全国 well-known throughout the country / 世界～ world-famous; world-renowned ② be familiar with sb.'s name; know sb. by repute

闻名不如见面 wénmíng bùrú jiànmiàn knowing a person by repute is not as good as meeting him face to face

闻人 wénrén well-known figure; famous man; celebrity

闻所未闻 wén suǒ wèi wén hear what one has never heard before; unheard-of: 他们给我讲了很多～的事情. They told me a lot of things I had never heard before.

闻悉 wénxī *formal* hear; learn; be informed: ～贵体欠安, 希早日康复. I've heard you are slightly indisposed these days. I wish you a speedy recovery.

闻讯 wénxùn hear the news: 消防队～赶到. On hearing the alarm the fire brigade rushed to the scene.

闻一知十 wén yī zhī shí learn one thing and know ten things—very intelligent

闻诊 wénzhěn *Chin. med.* auscultation and smelling, one of the four methods of diagnosis ——see also 四诊 sìzhěn

蚊 wén mosquito: 按蚊 ànwén

蚊虫 wénchóng *dial.* mosquito

蚊香 wénxiāng mosquito-repellent incense

蚊帐 wénzhàng mosquito net: ～纱 mosquito netting

蚊子 wénzi mosquito

雯 wén *formal* cloud tints

wěn

刎 wěn cut one's throat: 自刎 zìwěn

刎颈之交 wěn jǐng zhī jiāo friends that are ready to die for each other: 两人相与为～. The two men were such devoted friends that they would have died for each other.

拉 wěn *formal* wipe: ～泪 wipe one's tears

吻(脗) wěn ① lips: 接吻 jiēwěn ② kiss: ～别 kiss sb. good-bye ③ an animal's mouth

吻合 wěnhé ① be identical; coincide; tally: 意见～ have identical views / 他讲的情况和我听到的～. His account tallies with what I heard. ② *med.* connect by anastomosis

吻合术 wěnhéshù *med.* anastomosis

吻兽 wěnshòu same as 鸱尾 chīwěi

紊 wěn disorderly; confused: 有条不紊 yǒutiáobùwěn

紊流 wěnliú *phys.* turbulence; turbulent flow

紊乱 wěnluàn disorder; chaos; confusion: 秩序～ in a state of chaos / 新陈代谢功能～ metabolic disorder

稳(穩) wěn ① steady; firm: 把桌子放～ make the table steady / 坐～ sit tight / 她做事很～. She is steady and reliable in doing things. ② sure; certain: 这场比赛他～赢. He is certain to win the game.

稳便 wěnbiàn ① safe and convenient: ～的办法 a safe and convenient method ② *old* do as you wish; suit your own convenience

稳步 wěnbù with steady steps; steadily: ～前进 advance steadily; make steady progress / 生产～上升. Production is going up steadily.

稳操左券 wěn cāo zuǒquàn (also 稳操胜券 wěn cāo shèngquàn) be certain (*or* confident) of success

稳产 wěnchǎn stable yields: ～高产田 land (*or* fields) with high, stable yields

稳当 wěndang ① reliable; secure; safe: ～的办法 a reliable method ② steady; stable: 这张桌子不～. The

table isn't steady. / 把梯子扶～。Hold the ladder steady.

稳定 wěndìng ① stable; steady: 物价～。Prices remain stable. / 情绪～ be in a calm, unruffled mood / ～的多数 a stable majority / 不～的国际金融市场 a shaky international monetary market / 保持该地区的～和繁荣 maintain the stability and prosperity of the area ② stabilize; steady: ～物价 stabilize commodity prices / ～情绪 set sb.'s mind at rest; reassure sb.

稳定剂 wěndìngjì *chem.* stabilizer

稳定平衡 wěndìng pínghéng *phys.* stable equilibrium

稳定装置 wěndìng zhuāngzhì stabilization plant; stabilizer

稳固 wěngù ① firm; stable: ～的基础 a firm (or solid) foundation ② stabilize: ～政权 stabilize a government

稳健 wěnjiàn firm; steady: 迈着～的步子 walk with firm steps / 办事～ go about things steadily / 他这个人很～。He's a steady person.

稳健派 wěnjiànpài moderates

稳练 wěnliàn steady and proficient

稳流 wěnliú *phys.* steady flow

稳拿 wěnná be certain to win, achieve, etc.: 他～第一名。He is certain to win first place.

稳婆 wěnpó *old* midwife

稳如泰山 wěn rú Tàishān as stable as Mount Tai

稳妥 wěntuǒ (also 稳帖 wěntiē) safe; reliable: ～的计划 a safe plan / 我看这样办更～。I think it's safer to do it this way.

稳扎稳打 wěnzhā-wěndǎ ① go ahead steadily and strike sure blows (in war) ② go about things steadily and surely: 事情要一步一步地,～地去进行。The business should be conducted step by step, slowly and surely.

稳重 wěnzhòng steady; staid; sedate: 她既～又热情。She's both steady and warmhearted. / 他年纪不大,说话做事都很～。Young as he is, he is steady in what he says and what he does. / 他年纪大了,～多了。He became more sedate as he grew older.

稳住阵脚 wěnzhù zhènjiǎo maintain (or secure) one's position; hold one's ground

稳准狠 wěn-zhǔn-hěn sure, accurate and relentless: ～地打击 strike surely, accurately and relentlessly at sb.

稳坐钓鱼船 wěn zuò diàoyúchuán see 任凭风浪起,稳坐钓鱼船 rènpíng fēnglàng qǐ, wěn zuò diàoyúchuán

wèn

问 wèn ① ask; inquire: ～路 ask the way / 不懂就～。Ask when you don't know. / 我～他为什么要那样做。I asked him why he did it. / 他在食堂～了一下开饭的时间。He inquired about the meal times at the canteen. ② ask after; inquire after: 他信里～起你。He asks after you in his letter. ③ interrogate; examine: 审问 shěnwèn ④ hold responsible: 出了事唯你是～。You'll be held responsible if anything goes wrong. ⑤ ask (sb.) for sth: 我去～他借那本书。I'll ask him to lend me the book.

问安 wèn'ān pay one's respects (usu. to elders); wish sb. good health

问案 wèn'àn try (or hear) a case

问卜 wènbǔ divine by the Eight Trigrams

问长问短 wèncháng-wènduǎn make detailed inquiries; inquire with concern about sb.'s well-being; ask about this and that: 她见医生走出手术室,急忙上前～。When she saw the surgeon coming out of the operating room, she stepped forward and asked many solicitous questions.

问答 wèn-dá questions and answers: ～练习 question-and-answer drills

问道于盲 wèn dào yú máng ask a blind man the way—seek advice from one who can offer none

问鼎 wèndǐng ① inquire about the tripods—aspire after the throne; have monarchic ambitions (a reference to the Nine Tripods 九鼎, bronze tripods used only by the ruler in grand ceremonial observances of the state and regarded as emblems of royal authority) ② compete for a championship; try to carry off the first prize

问寒问暖 wènhán-wènnuǎn inquire with concern about sb.'s well-being; be solicitous for sb.'s welfare

问好 wènhǎo send one's regards to; say hello to: 请代我向你父亲～。Please give my regards to your father. or Remember me to your father. / 他向您～。He wished to be remembered to you.

问号 wènhào ① question mark; interrogation mark (or point) (?) ② unknown factor; unsolved problem: 致癌的真正原因还是个～。The exact cause of cancer is still unknown. / 他究竟有多大能力,还得打上一个～。There is still some doubt as to his ability.

问候 wènhòu send one's respects (or regards) to; extend greetings to: 致以亲切的～ extend cordial greetings

问话 wènhuà ask about; inquire: 老师要找你～。The teacher wants to ask you some questions.

问津 wènjīn *formal* (usu. used in the negative) make inquiries (as about prices or the situation): 不敢问津 bùgǎn wènjīn / 无人问津 wú rén wènjīn

问荆 wènjīng *bot.* meadow pine (*Equisetum arvense*)

问柳寻花 wènliǔ-xúnhuā same as 寻花问柳 xúnhuā-wènliǔ

问难 wènnàn raise difficult questions for discussion: 质疑问难 zhìyí-wènnàn

问世 wènshì be published; come out: 这本词典于1978年～。This dictionary was first published in 1978. / 本书作者的一部新小说即将～。A new novel by the same author will soon come out.

问事 wènshì ① inquire; ask ② run affairs; be in charge: 找他没有用,他现在已经不～了。It's no use asking him. He is no longer in charge now.

问事处 wènshìchù inquiry office; information desk

问题 wèntí ① question; problem; issue: 我提个～行吗? May I ask a question? / 他的能力没～。There's no question about his ability. / 关键～ a key problem / 家庭～ a family problem / 研究新～ study new problems / 这如何防止还是个～。How to prevent it is a problem. / 这个星期给我稿子行吗?—没～。Can you give me your article by the end of the week? —No problem. / ～儿童 a problem child / 这是个用法～。This is a matter of usage. / ～是我们去还是不去。The thing is shall we go or not. / 那不是～之所在。That's just not the issue. ② trouble; mishap: 那台车床出～了。Something has gone wrong with that lathe. / 一路上没出～。The trip went off without mishap.

问题单 wèntídān questionnaire

问心无愧 wèn xīn wú kuì feel no qualms upon self-examination; have a clear conscience: 你只要～,就不必感到不安。You have nothing to worry about as long as you have a clear conscience. / 我～。I have done nothing to be ashamed of!

问心有愧 wèn xīn yǒu kuì feel a twinge of conscience; have a guilty conscience

问讯 wènxùn inquire; ask

问讯处 wènxùnchù inquiry office; information desk

问斩 wènzhǎn *old* behead; decapitate

问诊 wènzhěn *Chin. med.* interrogation, one of the four methods of diagnosis——see also 四诊 sìzhěn

问住 wènzhù stump sb. with a question: 我一句话就把

他～了。I stumped him with a question. / 这下子你把我～了。You've got me there.

问罪 wènzuì　denounce; condemn

汶
Wèn　(also 汶水 Wènshuǐ) a river in Shangdong Province

搵
wèn　*formal*　press or rub with fingers

璺(纹)
wèn　crack (on glassware or earthenware): 碗上有一道～。The bowl has a crack.

wēng

翁
wēng　① old man: 渔翁 yúwēng ② father ③ father-in-law: 翁姑 wēnggū ④ (Wēng) a surname

翁姑 wēnggū　a woman's parents-in-law
翁婿 wēngxù　father-in-law and son-in-law
翁仲 wēngzhòng　stone statue placed in front of a tomb

嗡
wēng　*onom.*　drone; buzz; hum: 蜜蜂～～地飞。Bees are buzzing all around.

鶲
wēng　*zool.*　flycatcher

wěng

蓊
wěng　see below
蓊郁 wěngyù　*formal*　lush; luxuriant

wèng

瓮(甕、罋)
wèng　urn; earthen jar: 水～ water jar / 菜～ a jar for pickling vegetables

瓮城 wèngchéng　the *enceinte* of a city gate; a barbican entrance to a city
瓮声瓮气 wèngshēng-wèngqì　in a low, muffled voice
瓮中之鳖 wèng zhōng zhī biē　like a turtle in a jar—bottled up; trapped
瓮中捉鳖 wèng zhōng zhuō biē　catch a turtle in a jar—go after an easy prey

蕹
wèng　see below
蕹菜 wèngcài　water spinach

鼼
wèng　see below
鼼鼻儿 wèngbír　① speak with a nasal twang due to a stuffy nose ② a person who speaks with a nasal twang

wō

挝(撾)
wō　see 老挝 Lǎowō

涡(渦)
wō　whirlpool; eddy: 水～ eddies of water

涡虫 wōchóng　*zool.*　turbellarian worm; turbellarian
涡流 wōliú　① the circular movement of a fluid; whirling fluid; eddy ② *phys.*　eddy current; vortex flow
涡轮 wōlún　turbine: ～壳 turbine casing / ～叶片 turbine blade / ～轴 turboshaft

涡轮发电机 wōlún fādiànjī　turbogenerator
涡轮机 wōlúnjī　turbine
涡轮螺旋桨发动机 wōlún luóxuánjiǎng fādòngjī　turboprop (engine)
涡轮喷气发动机 wōlún pēnqì fādòngjī　turbojet (engine)
涡旋 wōxuán　*meteorol.*　vortex: 大气～ atmospheric vortex

倭
Wō　(old name for 日本) Japan

倭瓜 wōguā　*dial.*　pumpkin; cushaw
倭寇 Wōkòu　*hist.*　Japanese pirates (operating in Chinese coastal waters from the fourteenth to the sixteenth century)

莴(萵)
wō　see below

莴苣 wō·jù　lettuce
莴笋 wōsǔn　asparagus lettuce

窝(窩)
wō　① nest: 燕子在我家房檐下做了个～。The swallows built a nest under the roof of our house. ② lair; den: 土匪～ bandits' lair; bandits' nest ③ a hollow part of the human body; pit: 心口～ the pit of the stomach ④ *dial.*　place: 挪窝儿 nuówōr ⑤ harbour; shelter: 窝赃 wōzāng ⑥ hold in; check: 窝火 wōhuǒ ⑦ bend: 把铁丝～个圆圈 bend the wire into a circle / 别把画片～了。Be careful not to bend (or crease) the picture. ⑧ *m.*　(for animals) litter; brood: 一～十只小猪 ten piglets at a litter / 一～小鸡 a brood of chickens

窝瘪 wōbiě　hollow; sunken; depressed: 他脸色苍白, 两腮～。His face was pale and his cheeks were sunken.
窝憋 wōbie　*dial.*　① feel frustrated: 事情没办好, 心里老觉得～得慌。I feel frustrated about having botched the job. ② shut oneself indoors; stay at home ③ narrow and small; poky: 我这间卧室太～。This bedroom is too poky for me.
窝脖儿 wōbór　(also 窝脖子 wōbózi) *dial.*　meet with a rebuff; strike a snag; be crossed
窝藏 wōcáng　harbour; shelter: ～罪犯 give shelter to (or harbour) a criminal / ～赃物 conceal booty
窝匪 wōfěi　give shelter to (or harbour) a bandit
窝工 wōgōng　enforced idleness due to poor organization of work; holdup in the work through poor organization
窝火 wōhuǒ　be filled with anger: 窝了一肚子火 be filled with pent-up anger; be simmering with rage; be forced to bottle up one's anger
窝家 wōjiā　same as 窝主 wōzhǔ
窝眍眼 wōkōuyǎn　*dial.*　sunken eyes
窝儿里反 wōrlǐfǎn　*inf.*　internal strife; family quarrel
窝儿里横 wōrlǐhèng　*dial.*　a terror at home (but a coward outside)
窝囊 wōnang　① feel vexed; be annoyed: 受～气 be subjected to petty annoyances / 这事办得真～。That's really botched it up. ② good-for-nothing; hopelessly stupid
窝囊废 wōnangfèi　*dial.*　good-for-nothing; worthless wretch
窝棚 wōpeng　shack; shed; shanty
窝气 wōqì　choke with resentment; feel injured and resentful: 窝了一肚子气 have pent-up grievances
窝缩 wōsuō　roll up; huddle up; curl up
窝窝头 wōwotóu　(also 窝头 wōtóu) steamed bread of corn, sorghum, etc.
窝赃 wōzāng　harbour stolen goods; conceal booty
窝主 wōzhǔ　a person who harbours criminals, loot or contraband goods

喔
wō　*onom.*　cock's crow: ～～～! Cock-a-

doodle-doo! ——see also ō

蜗（蝸）　wō　snail

蜗杆　wōgǎn　*mech.*　worm: ～轴 worm shaft
蜗居　wōjū　*formal*　humble abode
蜗轮　wōlún　*mech.*　worm gear; worm wheel
蜗牛　wōniú　snail
蜗行牛步　wōxíng-niúbù　at a snail's pace
蜗旋　wōxuán　spiral; helix: 阶梯绕着中间的石柱～而上。 The stairs spiralled round the central pillar.

踒　wō　sprain (one's ankle or wrist); strain

wǒ

我　wǒ　① I or me ② we or us: ～方 our side; we / ～军 our army ③ (used coordinately with 你 in parallel structures) one; anyone: 大家你帮～，～帮你，很快就把活儿干完了。 With each one giving the other a hand, they soon got the job done. ④ self: 自我 zìwǒ／忘我 wàngwǒ

我辈　wǒbèi　*formal*　we or us
我见　wǒjiàn　my opinion: 以我之见 in my opinion
我们　wǒmen　we or us
我行我素　wǒ xíng wǒ sù　persist in one's old ways (no matter what others say); stick to one's old way of doing things

wò

沃　wò　① fertile; rich: 肥沃 féiwò ② irrigate: ～田 irrigate farmland

沃壤　wòrǎng　(also 沃土 wòtǔ) fertile soil; rich soil
沃野千里　wòyě qiānlǐ　a thousand *li* of fertile fields; a vast expanse of fertile land

肟　wò　*chem.*　oxime

卧（臥）　wò　① lie: 仰卧 yǎngwò ② (of animals or birds) crouch; sit ③ for sleeping in: 卧室 wòshì ④ *dial.*　poach (eggs): ～个鸡子儿 poach an egg

卧病　wòbìng　be confined to bed; be laid up
卧车　wòchē　① sleeping car; sleeping carriage; sleeper ② automobile; car; limousine; sedan
卧床　wòchuáng　① (of the old or the sick) lie in bed; be confined to bed: 活动期肺结核患者需要严格～休息。 Patients with active tuberculosis require strict rest in bed.／～不起 take to one's bed and never rise again ② *dial.*　bed
卧倒　wòdǎo　drop to the ground; take a prone (*or* lying-down) position: ～! (word of command) Lie down! *or* Hit the ground!
卧底　wòdǐ　*dial.*　be a planted agent
卧房　wòfáng　bedroom
卧佛　wòfó　reclining Buddha (a huge statue of a recumbent Buddha)
卧轨　wòguǐ　lay oneself on the railway tracks (either to commit suicide or as a form of protest)
卧果儿　wòguǒr　*dial.*　① poach an egg ② poached egg
卧具　wòjù　bedding (provided on a train or ship)
卧龙　wòlóng　sleeping dragon—a talent in obscurity
卧铺　wòpù　sleeping berth; sleeper
卧射　wòshè　*mil.*　prone fire
卧式　wòshì　*mech.*　horizontal: ～镗床 horizontal bor-

ing machine / ～发动机 horizontal engine
卧室　wòshì　bedroom
卧榻　wòtà　*formal*　bed
卧榻之侧，岂容他人鼾睡　wòtà zhī cè, qǐ róng tārén hānshuì　how can one tolerate people snoring at one's bedside?—how can one tolerate others encroaching on one's preserve?
卧薪尝胆　wò xīn cháng dǎn　sleep on brushwood and taste gall—undergo self-imposed hardships (to strengthen one's resolve to wipe out a national humiliation or to accomplish some ambition)
卧姿　wòzī　*sports*　prone position

渥　wò　*formal*　① wet; moisten ② strong; rich: 优渥 yōuwò

握　wò　hold; grasp: ～笔 hold a writing brush or pen

握别　wòbié　shake hands at parting; part: ～以来, 已逾三月。 It is more than three months since we parted.
握管　wòguǎn　*formal*　hold a writing brush or pen —write
握力　wòlì　the power of gripping; grip
握力器　wòlìqì　*sports*　spring-grip dumb-bells
握拳　wòquán　make a fist; clench one's fist
握手　wòshǒu　shake hands; clasp hands
握手言欢　wòshǒu yán huān　hold hands and chat cheerfully (esp. in making up a quarrel)

硪　wò　a flat stone or iron rammer with ropes attached at the sides

幄　wò　*formal*　tent

斡　wò　*formal*　revolve; spin; rotate

斡旋　wòxuán　① mediate: 由于他从中～, 双方的争端得到了解决。 Through his mediation the dispute between the two parties was settled. ② *leg.*　good offices

龌　wò　see below

龌龊　wòchuò　① dirty; filthy ② base; unprincipled: 卑鄙～ sordid; foul ③ *formal*　narrow-minded

wū

乌¹（烏）　wū　① crow ② black; dark: 乌云 wūyún ③ (Wū) a surname

乌²（烏）　wū　*formal*　(used in rhetorical questions): ～足道哉? What's there worth mentioning about it? ——see also wù

乌鲳　wūchāng　*zool.*　black pomfret
乌尔都语　Wū'ěrdūyǔ　Urdu
乌饭树　wūfànshù　oriental blueberry (*Vaccinium bracteatum*)
乌飞兔走　wūfēi-tùzǒu　the crow flies and the rabbit runs—time flies (the crow and the rabbit stand for the sun and the moon respectively)
乌干达　Wūgāndá　Uganda
乌干达人　Wūgāndárén　Ugandan
乌龟　wūguī　① tortoise ② cuckold
乌龟壳　wūguīké　① tortoiseshell ② *inf.*　enemy's pillbox or tank
乌合之众　wūhé zhī zhòng　a disorderly band; a motley crowd; rabble; mob
乌黑　wūhēi　pitch-black; jet-black

乌红　wūhóng　deep red

乌呼　wūhū　same as 呜呼 wūhū

乌金　wūjīn　black gold—coal

乌桕　wūjiù　*bot.* Chinese tallow tree

乌克兰　Wūkèlán　Ukraine

乌拉　wūlā　(also 乌喇 wūlā) ① *wula*, corvée labour formerly imposed on Xizang serfs ② *wula* labourer ——see also wùlā

乌拉尔　Wūlā'ěr　Ural

乌拉尔山　Wūlā'ěrshān　the Ural Mountains; the Urals

乌拉圭　Wūlāguī　Uruguay

乌拉圭人　Wūlāguīrén　Uruguayan

乌兰牧骑　wūlánmùqí　a Nei Monggol cultural troupe mounted on horseback

乌蓝　wūlán　dark blue

乌鳢　wūlǐ　*zool.* snakehead; snakeheaded fish

乌亮　wūliàng　glossy black; jet-black: ～ 的头发 dark, glossy hair; raven locks

乌溜溜　wūliūliū　(of eyes) dark and liquid: 一双～的眼睛 sparkling, black eyes

乌龙茶　wūlóngchá　oolong (tea)

乌鲁木齐　Wūlǔmùqí　Ürümqi (capital of the Xinjiang Uygur Autonomous Region)

乌梅　wūméi　smoked plum; dark plum

乌木　wūmù　*bot.* ebony

乌娘　wūniáng　*dial.* newly-hatched silkworm

乌七八糟　wūqībāzāo　① in a horrible mess; in great disorder ② obscene; dirty; filthy: 那本小说里全是些～的东西。That novel is filled with filth.

乌漆墨黑　wūqī-mòhēi　pitch-dark; pitch-black

乌青　wūqīng　blue (as with cold)

乌纱帽　wūshāmào　① black gauze cap (worn by feudal officials) ② official post: 丢～ be dismissed from office

乌苏里江　Wūsūlǐjiāng　the Wusuli River

乌头　wūtóu　*Chin. med.* the rhizome of Chinese monkshood (*Aconitum carmichaeli*)

乌涂　wūtu　① (of drinking water) lukewarm; tepid ② not clear-cut

乌托邦　wūtuōbāng　Utopia

乌鸦　wūyā　crow

乌烟瘴气　wūyān-zhàngqì　a foul (*or* pestilential) atmosphere: 搞得～ create a foul atmosphere; foul things up / 旧中国的官场～, 腐败得很。In old China officialdom was simply foul and rotten.

乌药　wūyào　*Chin. med.* the root of three-nerved spicebush (*Lindera strychnifolia*)

乌油油　wūyōuyōu　shiny black: ～ 的头发 black and glossy hair

乌有　wūyǒu　*formal* nothing; naught: ～乡 Utopia

乌鱼　wūyú　another name for 乌鳢 wūlǐ

乌云　wūyún　black clouds; dark clouds: ～遮天。Black clouds blotted out the sky. *or* The sky was covered with dark clouds.

乌枣　wūzǎo　smoked jujube; black jujube

乌贼　wūzéi　*zool.* cuttlefish; inkfish

乌鲗　wūzéi　another name for 乌贼 wūzéi

乌孜别克族　Wūzībiékèzú　the Ozbek (Uzbek) nationality, or the Ozbeks (Uzbeks), inhabiting the Xinjiang Uygur Autonomous Region

乌兹别克斯坦　Wūzībiékèsītǎn　Uzbekistan

污（汙、洿）

wū ① dirt; filth: 血污 xuèwū ② dirty; filthy; foul: 污泥 wūní ③ corrupt: 贪官污吏 tānguān-wūlì ④ defile; smear: 玷污 diànwū

污点　wūdiǎn　stain; spot; blemish; smirch

污毒　wūdú　dirty and noxious

污垢　wūgòu　dirt; filth

污秽　wūhuì　*formal* filthy; foul

污迹　wūjì　(also 污痕 wūhén) stain; smear; smudge

污蔑　wūmiè　① same as 诬蔑 wūmiè ② defile; sully; tarnish

污泥　wūní　mud; mire; sludge

污泥浊水　wūní-zhuóshuǐ　filth and mire: 荡涤旧社会遗留下来的～ clean up the filth left by the old society

污七八糟　wūqībāzāo　same as 乌七八糟 wūqībāzāo

污染　wūrǎn　pollute; contaminate: 这条河已为该厂的废水所～。The river has been polluted by the waste water from that factory. / ～地带 contaminated zone

污染报警系统　wūrǎn bàojǐng xìtǒng　pollution warning system

污染计数管　wūrǎn jìshùguǎn　contamination counter

污染气象学　wūrǎn qìxiàngxué　air pollution meteorology; pollution meteorology

污染物　wūrǎnwù　pollutant; contaminant

污染源　wūrǎnyuán　pollution source

污染指示生物　wūrǎn zhǐshì shēngwù　pollution indicating organism

污辱　wūrǔ　① humiliate; insult ② defile; sully; tarnish

污水　wūshuǐ　foul (*or* polluted, waste) water; sewage; slops: 生活～ domestic sewage / ～ 管 sewage pipe; sewer (pipe) / ～管道 sewage conduit; sewer line

污水处理　wūshuǐ chǔlǐ　sewage disposal; sewage treatment: ～厂 sewage treatment plant

污水灌溉　wūshuǐ guàngài　sewage irrigation

污水净化　wūshuǐ jìnghuà　sewage purification

污浊　wūzhuó　(of air, water, etc.) dirty; muddy; foul; filthy

圬（杇）

wū *formal* ① trowel used for plastering ② plaster

圬工　wūgōng　*old* bricklaying; tiling or plastering

邬（鄔）

Wū　a surname

巫

wū ① shaman; witch; wizard ② (Wū) a surname

巫婆　wūpó　witch; sorceress

巫神　wūshén　wizard; sorcerer

巫师　wūshī　wizard; sorcerer

巫术　wūshù　witchcraft; sorcery

巫医　wūyī　witch doctor

呜（嗚）

wū *onom.* toot; hoot; zoom: 轮船上的汽笛～～叫。The ship's whistle kept hooting. / 汽车～的一声飞驰而过。The car zoomed past.

呜呼　wūhū　① *arch.* alas; alack: ～! 盛衰之理, 虽曰天命, 岂非人事哉?（欧阳修）Alas for the law of prosperity and decline! Although regarded as Heaven's decree, is it not truly the handiwork of men? ② die: 一命呜呼 yī mìng wūhū

呜呼哀哉　wūhū-āizāi　① (formerly usu. used in funeral orations) alas: ～, 尚飨!（韩愈《祭十二郎文》）Alas! I am woebegone! I beg you to partake of this sacrifice. ② dead and gone; all is lost: 挨到晚上, 痰响了一阵, 喘息一回, ～, 断气身亡。(《儒林外史》) In the evening the death-rattle sounded in his throat, and with a last gasp for breath he gave up the ghost.

呜曠　wūnang　mumbling (due to a stuffy nose)

呜咽　wūyè　sob; whimper

诬

wū　accuse falsely: 诬告 wūgào

诬告　wūgào　(also 诬控 wūkòng) lodge a false accusation against; bring a false charge against; trump up a charge against: ～案件 frame-up; trumped-up case

诬害　wūhài　injure by spreading false reports about; calumniate; malign

诬赖　wūlài　falsely incriminate: ～好人 incriminate innocent people

诬蔑　wūmiè　slander; vilify; calumniate; smear: 〜不实之词 slander and libel

诬枉　wūwǎng　slander; calumniate

诬陷　wūxiàn　frame a case against; frame sb.

诬栽　wūzāi　calumniate and frame; fabricate a charge against sb.

屋 wū ① house: 一座小〜 a small house ② room: 〜里坐。Come in and sit down please.

屋顶　wūdǐng　roof; housetop

屋顶花园　wūdǐng huāyuán　roof garden

屋脊　wūjǐ　ridge (of a roof): 帕米尔高原有世界〜之称。The Pamirs are known as the roof of the world.

屋架　wūjià　roof truss

屋里人　wūlirén　(also 屋里的 wūlide) dial. wife

屋面　wūmiàn　roofing: 瓦〜 tile roofing / 〜板 roof boarding

屋上架屋　wū shàng jià wū　build one house on top of another—needless duplication

屋头　wūtou　dial. ① home ② room

屋檐　wūyán　eaves

屋宇　wūyǔ　formal house

屋子　wūzi　room: 三间〜 three rooms

钨(鎢) wū chem. tungsten; wolfram (W)

钨钢　wūgāng　wolfram steel; tungsten steel

钨砂　wūshā　tungsten ore

钨丝　wūsī　tungsten filament: 〜灯 tungsten lamp

恶(惡) wū formal ① same as 乌² wū ② interj. (expressing surprise) oh: 〜! 是何言也! Oh! What a thing to say! ——see also ě; è; wù

唔 wū see 咿唔 yīwū

wú

无(無) wú ① nothing; nil: 从无到有 cóng wú dào yǒu ② not have; there is not; without: 〜一定计划 without a definite plan ③ adv. not: 〜碍大局 not affect the situation as a whole ④ regardless of; no matter whether, what, etc.: 事〜大小, 都有人负责。Everything, big and small, is properly taken care of. ⑤ same as 毋 wú ——see also mó

无伴奏合唱　wúbànzòu héchàng　a cappella

无被选权　wúbèixuǎnquán　ineligible

无比　wúbǐ　incomparable; unparalleled; matchless: 〜的优越性 incomparable (or unparalleled) superiority / 〜的毅力 tremendous determination / 〜英勇 unrivalled in bravery / 〜愤怒 furiously indignant

无边无际　wúbiān-wújì　boundless; limitless; vast: 〜的大海 a boundless ocean / 〜的沙漠 a vast expanse of desert

无柄叶　wúbǐngyè　bot. sessile leaf

无病呻吟　wú bìng shēnyín　① moan and groan without being ill; make a fuss about an imaginary illness ② adopt a sentimental pose (in writing or speech)

无补　wúbǔ　of no help; of no avail: 空谈〜于实际。Mere words won't help matters.

无补于事　wúbǔ yú shì　of no avail: 这样恐怕〜。That would be of no avail. / 这样做不但〜, 反而会把事情弄糟。This won't do any good; on the contrary, it will make things even worse.

无不　wúbù　all without exception; invariably: 同志们对这种英勇行为〜表示钦佩。All the comrades, without exception, expressed great admiration for this heroic act. / 大家〜为之感动。None were unmoved.

无产阶级　wúchǎnjiējí　the proletariat: 〜化 acquire proletarian qualities

无产阶级文化大革命　Wúchǎnjiējí Wénhuà Dàgémìng　the Great Proletarian Cultural Revolution (1966-1977); the Great Cultural Revolution

无产阶级专政　wúchǎnjiējí zhuānzhèng　dictatorship of the proletariat; proletarian dictatorship: 巩固和加强〜 consolidate and strengthen the dictatorship of the proletariat

无产者　wúchǎnzhě　proletarian

无肠公子　wúcháng gōngzǐ　the bowelless master—a literary name for crab

无常¹　wúcháng　variable; changeable: 反复无常 fǎnfù wúcháng / 变化无常 biànhuà wúcháng

无常²　wúcháng　① a demon regarded as the messenger of death ② euph. die: 一旦〜万事休。When death comes, everything is ended.

无偿　wúcháng　free; gratis; gratuitous: 〜援助 aid given gratis (or gratuitously) / 提供〜经济援助 render economic assistance gratis; give free economic aid

无成　wúchéng　accomplish nothing: 毕生〜 a life of utter failure

无耻　wúchǐ　shameless; brazen; impudent: 〜谰言 shameless slander / 人不可以〜, 〜之耻, 〜矣。《孟子》 A man must not be without shame, for the shame of being without shame is shamelessness indeed.

无耻之徒　wúchǐ zhī tú　a person who has lost all sense of shame; a shameless person

无耻之尤　wúchǐ zhī yóu　brazen in the extreme; the height of shamelessness

无酬劳动　wúchóu láodòng　econ. unpaid labour

无出其右　wú chū qí yòu　second to none; matchless; unequalled

无从　wúcóng　adv. have no way (of doing sth.); not be in a position (to do sth.): 我们不了解情况, 〜答复这类问题。As we do not know the facts, we are in no position to answer such questions. / 心中千言万语, 一时〜说起 have a thousand things to say but not know where to begin / 〜下手 not know where to start; not know how to set about a job

无党派　wúdǎngpài　without party affiliation; nonparty: 〜人士 a public figure without party affiliation; nonparty personage / 〜民主人士 a nonparty democratic personage

无道　wúdào　not follow the Way; be without principles: 天下〜。The Way does not prevail under Heaven (or in the empire). or Bad government prevails. / 〜昏君 an unprincipled, dim-witted ruler / 往者秦为〜, 残贼天下。《史记》 In former times the Qin emperor ruled with utter disregard for principles, plundering and enslaving the empire.

无敌　wúdí　unmatched; invincible; unconquerable

无敌于天下　wúdí yú tiānxià　unmatched anywhere in the world; invincible

无底洞　wúdǐdòng　a bottomless pit (fig.)

无地自容　wú dì zì róng　can find no place to hide oneself for shame; feel too ashamed to show one's face; look for a hole to crawl into

无的放矢　wú dì fàng shǐ　shoot an arrow without a target; shoot at random: 批评要有针对性, 不要〜。Criticism should have an aim; it shouldn't be undirected.

无调性　wúdiàoxìng　mus. atonality

无冬无夏　wúdōng-wúxià　be it winter or summer—throughout the year; all the year round

无动于衷　wú dòng yú zhōng　aloof and indifferent; unmoved; untouched; unconcerned: 对这种情况, 我们不能〜。We cannot remain indifferent in such a situation. / 他对我的忠告〜。He turned a deaf ear to my advice.

无独有偶 wúdú-yǒu'ǒu it is not unique, but has its counterpart

无毒不丈夫 wú dú bù zhàngfu every real man has his venom; all great men are ruthless ——see also 恨小非君子, 无毒不丈夫 hèn xiǎo fēi jūnzǐ, wú dú bù zhàngfu

无毒蛇 wúdúshé nonpoisonous snake

无度 wúdù immoderate; excessive: 饮食～ excessive (or immoderate) eating and drinking／挥霍～ squander wantonly

无端 wúduān for no reason: ～侮辱 a gratuitous insult／～气恼 become angry over nothing／～生事 create a disturbance for no reason; wilfully make trouble

无恶不作 wú è bù zuò stop at nothing in doing evil; stop at no evil; commit all manner of crimes: 杀人放火, ～ commit murder, arson and every crime imaginable

无法 wúfǎ unable; incapable: ～应付 unable to cope with; at the end of one's resources／～形容 beyond description／～解脱的困境 an inextricable dilemma／局势～控制 The situation was out of control.

无法无天 wúfǎ-wútiān defy laws human and divine; become absolutely lawless; run wild: ～的人 a lawless, ungovernable creature

无方 wúfāng not in the proper way; in the wrong way; not knowing how: 经营～ mismanagement

无妨 wúfāng adv. there's no harm; may (or might) as well: 你～试一试。There's no harm in having a try.／我们～同他取得联系。We might get in touch with him.

无纺织物 wúfǎng zhīwù text. adhesive-bonded fabric

无非 wúfēi adv. nothing but; no more than; simply; only: 我想说的～是那么几句话。What I want to say is no·more than (or nothing but) this.／～是好坏两种可能。There are only two possibilities, a good one and a bad one.

无风 wúfēng meteorol. calm

无风不起浪 wú fēng bù qǐ làng there are no waves without wind; there's no smoke without fire

无风带 wúfēngdài meteorol. calm belt; calm zone

无峰骆驼 wúfēngluòtuo llama

无缝钢管 wúfèng gāngguǎn seamless steel tube (or pipe): ～厂 seamless (steel) tubing mill

无干 wúgān have nothing to do with: 这事与你～。It has nothing to do with you. or It's none of your business.／这全是我的过错, 跟别人～。It was entirely my fault; nobody else had anything to do with it.

无告 wúgào with nowhere to turn to: 孤苦～ forlorn and helpless

无功受禄 wú gōng shòu lù get a reward without deserving it

无辜 wúgū ① not guilty; innocent ② an innocent person

无故 wúgù without cause or reason: 不得～缺席。Nobody may be absent without reason.

无怪 wúguài (also 无怪乎 wúguàihu) adv. no wonder; not to be wondered at: 门是锁着的, ～你打不开。The door was locked. No wonder you couldn't open it.

无关 wúguān have nothing to do with: 此事与他～。It has nothing to do with him.

无关大局 wúguān dàjú not affecting (or having no bearing on) the general situation; insignificant; of little account: 那也～。That does not matter very much.

无关宏旨 wúguān hóngzhǐ insignificant; minor; immaterial

无关紧要 wúguān jǐnyào of no importance; immaterial

无关痛痒 wúguān tòngyǎng of no consequence; immaterial: ～的自我批评 irrelevant or superficial self-criticism／～的话 comment without any bite; irrelevant or pointless remarks／～的文章 innocuous articles

无官一身轻 wú guān yīshēn qīng happy is the man who

is relieved of his official duties

无规 wúguī phys. random: ～介质 random media／～取向 random orientation

无轨电车 wúguǐ diànchē trackless trolley; trolleybus

无国籍 wúguójí absent nationality; stateless: ～者 a stateless person／～状态 statelessness

无害 wúhài harmless: 这种农药对农作物～。This pesticide is harmless to crops.

无害通过 wúhài tōngguò leg. innocent passage; inoffensive passage

无何 wúhé formal ① soon; before long ② nothing else

无核 wúhé nuclear-free; nonnuclear

无核化 wúhéhuà denuclearize

无核区 wúhéqū nuclear-free zone

无核武器国家 wúhéwǔqì guójiā (also 无核国家 wúhé guójiā) nonnuclear country

无核武器区 wúhéwǔqìqū nuclear-weapon-free zone

无恒 wúhéng lack perseverance

无后 wúhòu without male offspring; without issue

无后坐力炮 wúhòuzuòlìpào recoilless gun

无花果 wúhuāguǒ bot. fig

无华 wúhuá simple and unadorned: 文章质朴～ written in a simple style

无话不谈 wú huà bù tán keep no secrets from each other; be in each other's confidence

无机 wújī chem. inorganic: ～界 the inorganic world

无机肥料 wújī féiliào inorganic fertilizer; mineral fertilizer

无机化合物 wújī huàhéwù inorganic compound

无机化学 wújī huàxué inorganic chemistry

无机酸 wújīsuān inorganic acid

无机物 wújīwù inorganic substance; inorganic matter

无机盐 wújīyán inorganic salts

无稽 wújī unfounded; fantastic; absurd

无稽之谈 wújī zhī tán an unfounded statement; fantastic talk; sheer nonsense: 我们坚决地斥责那些～。We categorically repudiate these absurd views.

无及 wújí it's too late (to do sth.); there's not enough time (to do sth.): 后悔～ too late to repent

无级 wújí mech. stepless: ～调速 stepless speed regulation／～变速装置 stepless speed change device

无疾而终 wú jí ér zhōng (of an old person) pass peacefully away

无几 wújǐ very few; very little; hardly any: 所剩～。There's very little left.／两人的年岁相差～。The two are almost the same age.

无脊椎动物 wújǐzhuī dòngwù invertebrate

无计可施 wú jì kě shī have exhausted one's whole bag of tricks; at one's wits' end; at the end of one's resources

无记名投票 wújìmíng tóupiào secret ballot

无际 wújì boundless; limitless; vast: 一望无际 yī wàng wújì

无济于事 wú jì yú shì not help matters; of no help; of no avail; to no effect: 在他病中医生们用了许多办法, 但都～。Many remedies were employed by the physicians in his sickness, but all were of no avail.

无家可归 wú jiā kě guī wander about with no home to go to; be homeless

无价之宝 wú jià zhī bǎo a priceless treasure; an invaluable asset

无坚不摧 wú jiān bù cuī overrun all fortifications; carry all before one; be all-conquering

无间 wújiàn formal ① not keeping anything from each other; very close to each other: 亲密无间 qīnmì wújiàn ② continuously; without interruption: 坚持户外锻炼, 寒暑～ keep on doing outdoor exercise all the year round

无疆 wújiāng boundless; limitless: 万寿无疆 wànshòu wújiāng

无尽无休 wújìn-wúxiū incessant; endless: 这个讨论好像～似的。The discussion seemed endless.

无精打采 wújīng-dǎcǎi listless; in low spirits; out of sorts; lackadaisical: 许多人碰到下雨天就～。Many people feel listless on rainy days. / 他不时长吁短叹,～的。He kept sighing and looked very downcast.

无拘无束 wújū-wúshù unrestrained; unconstrained; free and easy: 在～的气氛中 in an unconstrained atmosphere / 大家～地发表意见。Everyone expressed his views freely.

无菌 wújūn *med.* asepsis

无菌操作法 wújūn cāozuòfǎ *med.* aseptic manipulation

无可比拟 wúkě bǐnǐ incomparable; unparalleled; matchless; beyond compare: 有史以来～的大变化 a tremendous change unparalleled in history

无可不可 wúkě-bùkě ① do what one likes; do as one pleases ② extremely (happy); highly (pleased): 老大娘搬进了新房子,喜欢得～。When the old woman moved into the new house, she was as pleased as pleased could be.

无可非议 wúkě fēiyì irreproachable; blameless; beyond (*or* above) reproach; above criticism: 他的行为～。His conduct is irreproachable (*or* beyond reproach).

无可奉告 wúkě fènggào no comment

无可厚非 wúkě hòu fēi not be altogether unjustifiable; give little cause for criticism

无可讳言 wúkě huìyán there is no hiding (*or* denying) the fact: 这些都是～的事实。All these are undeniable (*or* indisputable) facts.

无可救药 wúkě jiùyào same as 不可救药 bùkě jiùyào

无可奈何 wúkě nàihé have no way out; be utterly helpless; have no alternative: 他虽然每日抱怨,也～了。Grumble as he might, he had to put up with it. / 我们～,只得应允。We had no choice but to give in. / 他说完了,～地叹了口气。Having said this, he sighed as much as to say there was nothing he could do about it. / ～的供状 a confession of helplessness / ～花落去,似曾相识燕归来。(晏殊) Flowers fall, do what one may; Swallows return, no strangers they.

无可挽回 wúkě wǎnhuí irretrievable; irredeemable; irrevocable: ～的损失 an irretrievable loss / 那是最后决定,～。The decision is final and irrevocable.

无可无不可 wúkě-wúbùkě not care one way or the other: 我去也行,不去也行,～。I don't care whether I go or not. / 对原则问题不应采取～的态度。One should not take an indifferent (*or* nonchalant) attitude towards questions of principle.

无可争辩 wúkě zhēngbiàn indisputable; irrefutable: ～的事实 an indisputable (*or* irrefutable) fact / 这件事情是非分明,～。The rights and wrongs of the case are perfectly clear and admit of no dispute.

无可置疑 wúkě zhìyí indubitable; unquestionable: 证据充分,～。The evidence is strong and admits of no doubt.

无孔不入 wú kǒng bù rù get in by every opening; seize every opportunity: 他是～,有空就钻。He slips into every opening. / 广泛的～的宣传 widespread, all-pervasive propaganda

无愧 wúkuì feel no qualms; have a clear conscience: ～于共产党员的称号 be worthy of the name of a communist

无赖 wúlài ① rascally; scoundrelly; blackguardly: 要～ act shamelessly ② rascal

无理 wúlǐ unreasonable; unjustifiable: ～要求 unreasonable demands / ～阻挠 unjustifiable obstruction / ～指责 unwarranted accusations; groundless charges

无理方程 wúlǐ fāngchéng *math.* irrational equation; radical equation

无理取闹 wúlǐ qǔnào wilfully make trouble; be deliberately provocative: 他简直是～。He's being difficult on purpose.

无理式 wúlǐshì *math.* irrational expression

无理数 wúlǐshù *math.* irrational number

无力 wúlì ① lack strength; feel weak: 四肢～ feel weak in one's limbs ② unable; incapable; powerless: 一个人是～完成这项任务的。One person alone can't accomplish this task. *or* No one can do this job single-handed.

无梁殿 wúliángdiàn beamless hall

无两 wúliǎng unparalled; unrivalled; matchless

无量 wúliàng measureless; immeasurable; boundless: 前途无量 qiántú wúliàng

无聊 wúliáo ① bored: 整天呆在家里,他感到～透了。He felt very much bored to stay at home all day long. ② senseless; silly; stupid: 不要讲这种～的话。Don't make such silly remarks.

无聊赖 wú liáolài *formal* dejected; dispirited ——see also 百无聊赖 bǎi wú liáolài

无虑[1] wúlù *formal* approximately; about: ～一千五百人 about 1,500 people

无虑[2] wúlù worry about nothing; be free from care

无论 wúlùn *conj.* no matter what, how, etc.; regardless of: ～是谁都不能违反劳动纪律。Nobody is supposed to break labour discipline, no matter who he is. / ～发生什么情况,你都要保持冷静。Keep calm, whatever happens.

无论如何 wúlùn rúhé in any case; at any rate; whatever happens; at all events: 你～得来一趟。You've got to come, whatever happens. / 我们～得把丢失的文件找到。At all costs, we have to find the missing document. / ～,现在已经来不及了。Anyhow, it's too late now. / 我们～不能急躁。On no account must we be impetuous. / 我～不能再吃了。I can't possibly eat any more.

无米之炊 wú mǐ zhī chuī cook a meal without rice; make bricks without straw ——see also 巧妇难为无米之炊 qiǎo fù nán wéi wú mǐ zhī chuī

无冕帝王 wú miǎn dìwáng a crownless king—reporter

无名 wúmíng ① nameless; unknown ② indefinable; indescribable: ～的恐惧 an indefinable feeling of terror

无名高地 wúmíng gāodì *mil.* an unnamed hill

无名氏 wúmíngshì an anonymous person: 这本小说系～所作。This novel was written by an anonymous author.

无名帖 wúmíngtiě poison-pen letter

无名小卒 wúmíng xiǎozú a nobody; nonentity

无名英雄 wúmíng yīngxióng ① unknown hero; unsung hero ② unknown soldier: ～纪念碑 monument to the unknown fallen soldiers

无名指 wúmíngzhǐ the third finger; ring finger

无名肿毒 wúmíng zhǒngdú *Chin. med.* nameless sores or boils

无明火 wúmínghuǒ (also 无名火 wúmínghuǒ) flames of anger: ～起 get angry; fly into a rage

无奈 wúnài ① cannot help but; have no alternative; have no choice: 他出于～,只得表示同意。He had no choice but to agree. ② *conj.* but; however: 他本想来的,～临时有会,来不了。He had meant to come, but was prevented by an unexpected meeting.

无奈何 wúnàihé ① can do nothing about it: 他整天游手好闲,他母亲也无奈他何。He just fools around all day long, and his mother can do nothing about it. ② same as 无可奈何 wú kě nàihé

无能 wúnéng incompetent; incapable: 教练～,该队屡遭败绩。The coach was incompetent and the team suffered repeated defeats.

无能为力 wú néng wéi lì powerless; helpless; incapable of action: 人类对于自然界不是～的。Man is not powerless before nature. / 我对她不幸的遭遇非常同情, 可惜～。I sympathize with her in her misfortune, but I'm afraid I can do nothing to help. / 这事我～。That's beyond my power.

无宁 wúnìng same as 毋宁 wúnìng

无偏无党 wúpiān-wúdǎng unbiased; impartial

无期徒刑 wúqī túxíng life imprisonment: 判处～ be sentenced to imprisonment for life; be given a life sentence

无奇不有 wú qí bù yǒu there is no lack of strange things

无其数 wúqíshù inf. innumerable; countless

无牵无挂 wúqiān-wúguà have no cares; be free from care

无前 wúqián ① unmatched; invincible; unconquerable: 所向无前 suǒ xiàng wú qián ② unprecedented: 成绩～ an unprecedented success / 诗人兴会更～。(毛泽东) And the poet is inspired as never before.

无巧不成书 wú qiǎo bù chéng shū without coincidences there would be no stories: 真是～, 我的顶头上司就是被我在街上撞倒的那个人。What a coincidence: My immediate superior was the man I had knocked down on the street.

无巧不巧 wú qiǎo bù qiǎo by coincidence; as it happens; as luck would have it: 我正要找他, 他自己来了, 真是～。What a coincidence! He came just as I was looking for him.

无情 wúqíng merciless; ruthless; heartless: ～的打击 a merciless blow / ～的事实 harsh reality; hard facts / 历史的辩证法是～的。The dialectics of history is inexorable.

无穷 wúqióng infinite; endless; boundless; inexhaustible: ～的烦恼和忧虑 endless troubles and worries

无穷大 wúqióngdà math. infinitely great; infinity

无穷无尽 wúqióng-wújìn inexhaustible; endless: 人民群众的创造力是～的。The creative power of the masses is inexhaustible.

无穷小 wúqióngxiǎo math. infinitely small; infinitesimal

无趣 wúqù same as 没趣 méiqù

无权 wúquán have no right: ～干预 have no right to interfere / ～享受豁免 not be entitled to immunities

无权追索 wúquán zhuīsuǒ leg. without recourse

无拳无勇 wúquán-wúyǒng lacking both in strength and in courage

无缺 wúquē intact; whole

无人 wúrén ① unmanned: ～火箭 unmanned rocket / ～驾驶飞机 unmanned plane; pilotless plane; robot plane ② depopulated: ～区 a depopulated zone ③ self-service: ～售书处 self-service bookstall

无人地带 wúrén dìdài mil. no man's land

无人问津 wú rén wènjīn nobody troubles to ask; nobody is interested: 这种蹩脚货现在～。This shoddy commodity is now a drug on the market.

无任 wúrèn formal extremely; immensely: ～感激 be deeply grateful

无任所大使 wúrènsuǒ dàshǐ ambassador-at-large; roving ambassador

无日 wúrì adv. ① all the time; not a single day: ～不在想念你。Not a single day passed without my thinking of you. ② soon; before long

无如 wúrú same as 无奈 wúnài②

无伤大雅 wú shāng dàyǎ not matter much; not affect things as a whole: 他以文才著称, 虽然脾气有些古怪, 但～。His claim to fame rests on his literary talents. His eccentric behaviour is considered immaterial.

无上 wúshàng supreme; paramount; highest: ～权力 supreme power / ～光荣 the highest honour

无神论 wúshénlùn atheism: ～者 atheist

无生代 Wúshēngdài geol. the Azoic Era

无生物 wúshēngwù inanimate object; nonliving matter

无声 wúshēng noiseless; silent: ～打字机 noiseless typewriter

无声片 wúshēngpiàn silent film

无声手枪 wúshēng shǒuqiāng pistol with a silencer

无声无臭 wúshēng-wúxiù unknown; obscure: 不甘心～地过一辈子 hate to live out one's life unknown

无师自通 wú shī zì tōng learn sth. wihout a teacher; be self-taught

无时无刻 wúshí-wúkè all the time; incessantly: 我们～不在想念你。You are constantly in our thoughts. / 登山队员～不在和风雪搏斗。The mountaineers had to fight the blizzard the whole time.

无事不登三宝殿 wú shì bù dēng sānbǎodiàn one never goes to the temple for no reason; I wouldn't come to you if I hadn't something to ask of you

无事忙 wúshìmáng busy oneself over nothing; make much ado about nothing

无事生非 wú shì shēng fēi make trouble out of nothing; be deliberately provocative

无视 wúshì ignore; disregard; defy: ～别国主权 disregard the sovereignty of other countries / ～人民的意志 defy the will of the people / ～我方的警告 in defiance of our warning

无殊 wúshū formal not different from; tantamount to

无熟料水泥 wúshúliào shuǐní archit. clinker-free cement

无数 wúshù ① innumerable; countless: 天上有～的星星。There are innumerable (or countless) stars in the sky. / ～的事实 innumerable facts ② not know for certain; be uncertain: 这计划是否可行, 我心中～。I'm not too sure whether the plan will work.

无双 wúshuāng unparalleled; unrivalled; matchless: 举世无双 jùshì wúshuāng

无霜期 wúshuāngqī frost-free period

无水 wúshuǐ chem. anhydrous: ～溶剂 anhydrous solvent / ～酸 anhydrous acid

无丝分裂 wúsīfēnliè bot. amitosis

无私 wúsī selfless; disinterested; unselfish: 给予～的援助 give (or render) disinterested assistance / ～才能无畏 Only the selfless can be fearless.

无算 wúsuàn formal innumerable; countless: 这位医生活人～。The doctor has saved countless lives.

无损 wúsǔn ① cannot harm; be harmless; will not lessen: 有益～ can only do good, not harm / 狂犬吠日, ～于太阳的光辉。A cur barking at the sun cannot detract from its glory. ② intact; whole; in good condition: 那包易碎物品寄到时完好～。The fragile parcel arrived intact.

无梭织机 wúsuō zhījī text. shuttleless loom

无所不包 wú suǒ bù bāo all-embracing; all-inclusive; all-encompassing

无所不能 wú suǒ bù néng ① omnipotent ② versatile: 琴棋书画, ～ be equally adept in music, chess, calligraphy, and painting

无所不为 wú suǒ bù wéi do all manner of evil; stop at nothing: 匪徒烧杀掳掠, ～。Stopping at nothing, the bandits massacred, burned and looted.

无所用其极 wú suǒ bù yòng qí jí resort to every conceivable means; stop at nothing; go to any extreme; go to any length(s): 这个家伙造谣诽谤, 挑拨离间, ～。That scoundrel went all the way in rumour-mongering, mudslinging and sowing dissension. / 他们到处杀戮人民, 奸淫妇女, 焚毁村庄, 掠夺财物, ～。Wherever they went, they massacred and raped, burned and looted, and stopped at nothing.

无所不在 wú suǒ bù zài omnipresent; ubiquitous

无所不知 wú suǒ bù zhī omniscient

无所不至 wú suǒ bù zhì ① penetrate everywhere: 细菌活动的范围很广，～。 Bacteria are active practically everywhere. ② spare no pains (usu. to do evil); be capable of anything; stop at nothing: 威胁利诱，～ use intimidation, bribery and every other means

无所措手足 wú suǒ cuò shǒuzú have nowhere to put hand or foot—be at a loss to know how to conduct oneself: 规章制度如果常常改动，会使人们～。 If rules and regulations are changed too often, people will be at a loss to know how to conduct themselves.

无所事事 wú suǒ shì shì be occupied with nothing; have nothing to do; idle away one's time: 他们本来可以工作却～。 They were idling about when they might have been working. / 一个人老是～就会懒散成性。 Too much idleness makes one indolent.

无所适从 wú suǒ shì cóng not know what to do; not know whom to turn to: 领导意见分歧，群众～。 The leaders are divided, and the rank and file don't know whom to turn to.

无所畏惧 wú suǒ wèijù fearless; dauntless; undaunted: 彻底的唯物主义者是～的。 Thoroughgoing materialists are fearless.

无所谓 wúsuǒwèi ① cannot be called; not deserve the name of: 这是随便说的，～什么批评。 It was a passing remark; I didn't mean it as a criticism. ② be indifferent; not matter: 采取～的态度 adopt an indifferent attitude / 你替他着急，他自己却好象～似的。 You are worried about him, but he himself doesn't seem to care. / 他去不去～。 It makes no difference whether he goes or not.

无所用心 wú suǒ yòngxīn not give serious thought to anything——see also 饱食终日，无所用心 bǎoshí zhōngrì, wú suǒ yòngxīn

无所作为 wú suǒ zuòwéi attempt nothing and accomplish nothing; be in a state of inertia

无题 wútí no title (used as a title for writings for which the author cannot find, or chooses not to give, a title): ～诗 a poem without a title; titleless poem

无条件 wútiáojiàn unconditional; without preconditions: 建议～地立即举行谈判 propose that negotiations be held at once without preconditions / ～地、全心全意地到群众中去 go among the masses unreservedly and wholeheartedly

无条件反射 wútiáojiào fǎnshè physiol. unconditional reflex

无条件投降 wútiáojiàn tóuxiáng unconditional surrender

无头公案 wútóu gōng'àn (also 无头案 wútóu'àn) an intricate case without a clue; an unsolved mystery

无土栽培 wútǔ zāipéi soilless culture

无往不利 wú wǎng bù lì go smoothly everywhere; be ever successful: 依靠党，依靠群众，工作就～。 Rely on the Party and the masses and you will succeed wherever you go.

无往不胜 wú wǎng bù shèng ever-victorious; invincible

无妄之灾 wú wàng zhī zāi an unexpected calamity; an undeserved ill turn

无望 wúwàng hopeless: 局势已经～。 The situation is hopeless. / 康复～。 There is no hope of recovery.

无微不至 wú wēi bù zhì meticulously; in every possible way: 他对青年的关怀～。 He takes the greatest care of the youth. / 服务人员对我们照顾得～。 The attendants showed us every consideration.

无为 wúwéi (lit. "do nothing") inaction; nonaction (a basic concept in Taoism, understood as no unnatural action rather than complete passivity): ～而无不为。 Do nothing and everything is done. / ～而治 govern by noninterference (i. e. by keeping to a minimum governmental organization and regulation)

无味 wúwèi ① tasteless; unpalatable ② dull; insipid; uninteresting: 语言～ insipid language; colourless language

无畏 wúwèi fearless; dauntless

无谓 wúwèi meaningless; pointless; senseless: ～的争吵 a pointless quarrel / ～的牺牲 a meaningless (or senseless) sacrifice / ～的话 senseless talk; twaddle

无物 wúwù empty; devoid of substance: 言之无物 yán zhī wúwù / 空洞无物 kōngdòng wúwù

无误 wúwù no mistake; errorless: 核查～ checked and found correct

无息 wúxī interest-free: ～存款 interest-free deposit / ～贷款 interest-free loan / ～信贷 interest-free credit

无隙可乘 wú xì kě chéng no crack to get in by; no loophole to exploit; no weakness to take advantage of; no chink in one's armour: 他们时刻保持警惕，敌人～。 They were always on the alert so that no opening was left for the enemy to exploit.

无暇 wúxiá have no time; be too busy: ～顾及 have no time to attend to / ～他顾 be too busy to attend to other things

无瑕 wúxiá flawless: 完美～ perfect; flawless

无限 wúxiàn infinite; limitless; boundless; immeasurable: ～光明的未来 a future of incomparable brightness / ～忠诚 boundless loyalty; absolute loyalty; absolute devotion / 人民群众有～的创造力。 The masses have unlimited creative power. / 批评要实事求是，不要～上纲。 Criticism should be fair and not exaggerated.

无限大 wúxiàndà same as 无穷大 wúqióngdà

无限公司 wúxiàn gōngsī unlimited company

无限花序 wúxiàn huāxù bot. indefinite inflorescence

无限期 wúxiànqī indefinite duration: ～罢工 a strike of indefinite duration / ～搁置动议 shelve a motion sine die / ～休会 adjourn indefinitely; adjourn sine die

无限小 wúxiànxiǎo same as 无穷小 wúqióngxiǎo

无限制 wúxiànzhì unrestricted; unbridled; unlimited

无线电 wúxiàndiàn radio

无线电报 wúxiàn diànbào wireless telegram; radiotelegram

无线电测向器 wúxiàndiàn cèxiàngqì radio direction finder; radio goniometer

无线电传真 wúxiàndiàn chuánzhēn radiofacsimile

无线电导航 wúxiàndiàn dǎoháng radio navigation: ～设备 radio navigation aid

无线电发射机 wúxiàndiàn fāshèjī radio transmitter

无线电干扰 wúxiàndiàn gānrǎo radio jamming

无线电跟踪 wúxiàndiàn gēnzōng radio tracking

无线电话 wúxiàn diànhuà radiotelephone; radiophone

无线电收发两用机 wúxiàndiàn shōu-fā liǎngyòngjī transceiver

无线电收音机 wúxiàndiàn shōuyīnjī radio receiver

无线电探空仪 wúxiàndiàn tànkōngyí radiosonde

无线电天文学 wúxiàndiàn tiānwénxué radio astronomy

无线电通信 wúxiàndiàn tōngxìn radio communication; wireless communication

无线电遥测 wúxiàndiàn yáocè radio telemetry

无线电遥控 wúxiàndiàn yáokòng wireless remote control

无效 wúxiào of (or to) no avail; invalid; null and void: 医治～ fail to respond to medical treatment / 宣布合同～ declare a contract invalid (or null and void); invalidate (or nullify) a contract / 宣布选举～ nullify an election / 逾期～ invalid after the specified date

无效分蘖 wúxiào fēnniè agric. ineffective tillering

无效劳动 wúxiào láodòng fruitless labour; labour lost

无懈可击 wú xiè kě jī with no chink in one's armour;

unassailable; invulnerable: 这篇文章论证周密, ～。The article is closely reasoned and the arguments are unassailable.

无心 wúxīn ① not be in the mood for: 他工作还没做完, ～去看电影。He was in no mood to go to the film, as he hadn't finished his work. ② not intentionally; unwittingly; inadvertently: 他说这话是～的, 你可别见怪。Don't take offence. He didn't say it intentionally.

无行 wúxíng *formal* be a man of loose conduct: 文人无行 wénrén wúxíng

无形 wúxíng invisible; intangible: ～的枷锁 invisible shackles / ～的战线 invisible fronts / ～贸易 invisible trade / ～进(出)口 invisible import (export) / ～资产 intangible asset / ～利益 intangible benefit / ～损耗 nonphysical wear

无形中 wúxíngzhōng imperceptibly; virtually: 这～成了风气。This has imperceptibly become a common practice. / 他～成了我的助手。He's virtually become my assistant.

无性生殖 wúxìng shēngzhí *biol.* asexual reproduction

无性世代 wúxìng shìdài *biol.* asexual generation

无性杂交 wúxìng zájiāo *biol.* asexual (or vegetative) hybridization

无休止 wúxiūzhǐ ceaseless; endless: ～地争论 argue on and on

无须 wúxū (also 无须乎 wúxū·hū) *adv.* need not; not have to: ～顾虑 need not worry / ～细说。It's unnecessary to go into details. / ～着急。There's no need to get excited.

无需 wúxū (also 无需乎 wúxū·hū) same as 无须 wúxū

无涯 wúyá boundless; limitless: 一望～ stretching beyond the horizon; boundless

无烟火药 wúyān huǒyào smokeless powder; ballistite

无烟煤 wúyānméi anthracite

无言以对 wú yán yǐ duì have nothing to say in reply

无颜见江东父老 wú yán jiàn jiāngdōng fùlǎo cannot bear to see again the elders east of the river—be ashamed to go back to one's people after a defeat or failure

无恙 wúyàng *formal* in good health; well; safe: 安然无恙 ānrán wúyàng / 别来无恙 bié lái wúyàng

无业 wúyè ① be out of work; be unemployed ② have no property

无业游民 wúyè yóumín vagrant

无依无靠 wúyī-wúkào have no one to depend on (or to turn to); be helpless: ～的孤儿 a helpless orphan

无遗 wúyí nothing left: 破坏～ be totally destroyed

无疑 wúyí beyond doubt; undoubtedly: 这种行为～是错误的。Such conduct is undoubtedly wrong. / 他～是对的。He is right, beyond doubt. / 确凿～ well established and irrefutable

无已 wúyǐ *formal* ① endlessly; incessantly: 赞叹～ praise again and again; be profuse in praise ② have no alternative but to; have to

无以复加 wú yǐ fù jiā in the extreme: 荒谬到了～的地步 be absurd in the extreme

无以为生 wú yǐ wéi shēng have no means of livelihood; have no means of support

无艺 wúyì *formal* ① have no standards or regulations (to go by) ② unlimited: 贪贿无艺 tān huì wú yì

无异 wúyì not different from; tantamount to; as good as: 这件复制品几乎与原作～。The reproduction is almost as good as the original. / 他撤回声明～于表示歉意。The withdrawal of his statement is tantamount to an apology.

无益 wúyì unprofitable; useless; no good: 读这种无聊的东西非但～, 而且有害。Reading that trash is not only unprofitable but harmful.

无意 wúyì ① have no intention (of doing sth.); not be inclined to: ～参加 have no intention of joining / ～于此 not interested in that; not keen on it ② inadvertently; unwittingly; accidentally: 他们在挖井时, ～中发现了一些古代文物。While digging a well they accidentally unearthed some ancient relics.

无意识 wúyìshí unconscious: ～的动作 an unconscious act (or movement)

无翼鸟 wúyìniǎo kiwi

无垠 wúyín *formal* boundless; vast: 一望～的草原 a boundless prairie

无影灯 wúyǐngdēng *med.* shadowless lamp

无影无踪 wúyǐng-wúzōng without a trace: 那小偷早跑得～了。The thief had disappeared without a trace.

无庸 wúyōng need not

无庸讳言 wúyōng huìyán no need for reticence

无庸赘述 wúyōng zhuìshù there is no need to go into details; it is pointless to belabour the obvious

无用 wúyòng useless; of no use

无用能 wúyòngnéng *mech.* unavailable energy

无忧无虑 wúyōu-wúlù free from care; free from all anxieties; carefree

无由 wúyóu *formal* not be in a position (to do sth.); have no way (of doing sth.)

无余 wúyú nothing left: 一览无余 yīlǎn wúyú

无与伦比 wú yǔ lúnbǐ incomparable; unparalleled; peerless; unique; without equal: 他在地质学方面的贡献是～的。His contribution in the field of geology was unparalleled.

无原则 wúyuánzé unprincipled: ～纠纷 an unprincipled dispute

无援 wúyuán have no support; be cut off from help

无缘 wúyuán ① have not the chance or luck (to do sth.): 久闻大名, 但恨～拜识。I have long been aware of your exalted name, and I regret never getting a chance to make your acquaintance. / 我和酒～。I never touch the bottle. ② have no way (of doing sth.); not be in a position (to do sth.)

无缘无故 wúyuán-wúgù without cause or reason; without rhyme or reason; for no reason at all: 世上决没有～的爱, 也没有～的恨。There is absolutely no such thing in the world as love or hate without cause or reason.

无源 wúyuán *radio* passive: ～天线 passive antenna

无源之水, 无本之木 wú yuán zhī shuǐ, wú běn zhī mù water without a source, a tree without roots: 理论脱离实际, 就成了～。Theory divorced from practice would be like water without a source, or a tree without roots.

无韵诗 wúyùnshī blank verse

无照 wúzhào without a licence: ～营业 do business without a licence

无政府主义 wúzhèngfǔzhǔyì anarchism

无知 wúzhī ignorant: ～妄说 ignorant nonsense / 出于～ out of ignorance

无止境 wúzhǐjìng have no limits; know no end: 科学的发展是～的。The development of science has no limits.

无中生有 wú zhōng shēng yǒu purely fictitious; fabricated: 纯粹是～, 当面造谣。Nothing but rumours fabricated out of thin air and brazen lies.

无重力 wúzhònglì *space* agravic: ～状态 null-gravity state

无着 wúzhuó ① nowhere: 寻找～ nowhere to be found; whereabouts unknown ② unassured: 生活～ have one's livelihood unassured / 经费～ no funds available

无足轻重 wú zú qīng-zhòng of little importance (or consequence); insignificant: ～的人物 a nobody; a nonentity / 他们看不起我们, 认为～。They looked down upon us as of little importance. / 此事～。It's a matter

of no consequence.

无阻　wúzǔ　without hindrance; unimpeded: 拿着这张通行证就可以通行～。This pass will let you through.

无罪　wúzuì　innocent; not guilty: ～释放　set a person free with a verdict of "not guilty"

无坐力炮　wúzuòlìpào　same as 无后坐力炮 wúhòuzuòlìpào

毋　wú　*adv. formal*　no; not: ～令逃逸。You must not let him escape.

毋宁　wúnìng　*adv.*　rather...(than); (not so much...) as: 与其固守，～出击。Better to strike out than to entrench oneself in defence. / 这与其说是奇迹，～说是历史发展的必然。It is the necessary outcome of historical development rather than a miracle.

毋庸　wúyōng　same as 无庸 wúyōng

吾　wú　*formal*　I or me; we or us: ～国　my or our country

吾辈　wúbèi　*formal*　we or us

吾侪　wúchái　*formal*　we or us

吾人　wúrén　*formal*　we or us

芜(蕪)　wú　*formal*　① overgrown with weeds: 荒芜 huāngwú ② grassland: 平芜 píngwú ③ mixed and disorderly; miscellaneous: 芜词 wúcí

芜鄙　wúbǐ　(of writing) confused and disorderly

芜词　wúcí　superfluous words

芜秽　wúhuì　overgrown with weeds and brambles

芜菁　wújīng　*bot.*　turnip

芜劣　wúliè　(of writing) confused and disorderly

芜杂　wúzá　(of writing) mixed and disorderly; jumbled

吴(吳)　Wú　① one of the Warring States into which China was divided during the Eastern Zhou period (770-256 B.C.), comprising parts of modern Jiangsu and Zhejiang ② one of the Three Kingdoms into which China was divided during the period 220-265, occupying the middle and lower Yangtze valley ③ a name for an area comprising southern Jiangsu and northern Zhejiang ④ a surname

吴牛喘月　Wú niú chuǎn yuè　the water buffalo (which dreads the heat of summer) panting at the sight of the moon (mistaking it for the sun)—fear of a thing due to mistaking it for sth. else

吴语　wúyǔ　the Wu dialect (a variety of Chinese spoken in southeastern Jiangsu and most of Zhejiang, major cities in which the Wu dialect is spoken including Shanghai, Suzhou, Ningbo and Wenzhou)

梧　wú　see below

梧桐　wútóng　Chinese parasol (tree); phoenix tree (a beautiful Chinese tree which figures prominently in literature and whose euphonious Chinese name is often left untranslated): ～树，三更雨，不道离情正苦。(温庭筠) Wutong trees, third watch rain, care not for separation's sorrow's utter bitterness.

鹀　wú　*zool.*　bunting

蜈　wú　see below

蜈蚣　wúgong　centipede

蜈蚣草　wúgongcǎo　ciliate desert-grass (*Eremochloa ciliaris*)

鼯　wú　see below

鼯鼠　wúshǔ　flying squirrel

wǔ

五[1]　wǔ　five: ～公斤　five kilos / ～个班　five classes / ～班　the fifth class; class 5 / ～路公共汽车　No. 5 bus

五[2]　wǔ　*mus.*　a note of the scale in *gongchepu* (工尺谱), corresponding to 6 in numbered musical notation

五保户　wǔbǎohù　a household enjoying the five guarantees (childless and infirm old persons who are guaranteed food, clothing, medical care, housing and burial expenses)

五倍子　wǔbèizǐ　*Chin. med.*　Chinese gall; gallnut

五倍子虫　wǔbèizǐchóng　gall makers

五边形　wǔbiānxíng　pentagon

五步蛇　wǔbùshé　long-noded pit viper

五彩　wǔcǎi　① the five colours (blue, yellow, red, white and black) ② multicoloured

五彩缤纷　wǔcǎi bīnfēn　colourful; blazing with colour: ～的礼花腾空而起。Colourful fireworks shot into the sky.

五重唱　wǔchóngchàng　*mus.*　(vocal) quintet

五重奏　wǔchóngzòu　*mus.*　(instrumental) quintet

五大三粗　wǔdà-sāncū　big and tall; tall and stalwart; strapping

五代　Wǔ Dài　the Five Dynasties (907–960), namely, the Later Liang Dynasty (后梁，907–923)，the Later Tang Dynasty (后唐，923–936)，the Later Jin Dynasty (后晋，936–946)，the Later Han Dynasty (后汉，947–950)，and the Later Zhou Dynasty (后周，951–960)

五帝　Wǔdì　the Five Lords ——see also 三皇五帝 Sānhuáng-Wǔdì

五斗柜　wǔdǒuguì　(also 五屉橱 wǔtìchú) chest of drawers

五毒　wǔdú　① the five poisonous creatures (scorpion, viper, centipede, house lizard and toad) ② the "five evils" (see also 五反运动 Wǔfǎn Yùndòng)

五短三粗　wǔduǎn-sāncū　short and sturdy; stumpy

五短身材　wǔduǎn shēncái　(of a man) squat

五反运动　Wǔfǎn Yùndòng　the movement, begun in 1952, against the "five evils" (bribery, tax evasion, theft of state property, cheating on government contracts and stealing of economic information, as practised by owners of private industrial and commercial enterprises)

五方　wǔfāng　the five directions (i.e. the four cardinal points and the centre)

五方杂处　wǔfāng záchǔ　(of a big city) be inhabited by people from all parts; have a mixed (or cosmopolitan) population

五分制　wǔfēnzhì　the five-grade marking system

五更　wǔgēng　① the five watches (or periods) of the night ② the fifth watch of the night; just before dawn: 起～，睡半夜　retire at midnight and rise before dawn

五古　wǔgǔ　(short for 五言古体诗) pentasyllabic (or five-syllable) ancient-style poetry ——see also 古体诗 gǔtǐshī

五谷　wǔgǔ　① the five cereals (rice, two kinds of millet, wheat and beans) ② food crops

五谷不分　wǔgǔ bù fēn　see 四体不勤，五谷不分 sìtǐ bù qín, wǔgǔ bù fēn

五谷丰登　wǔgǔ fēngdēng　an abundant harvest of all food crops; a bumper grain harvest: 天下太平，～，万民乐业。(《水浒》) The crops were abundant, and there

was general peace and prosperity.

五官 wǔguān ① *Chin. med.* the five sense organs (ears, eyes, lips, nose and tongue) ② facial features

五官端正 wǔguān duānzhèng have regular features

五光十色 wǔguāng-shísè ① multicoloured; bright with many colours ② of great variety; of all kinds; multifarious

五行八作 wǔháng-bāzuò five professions and eight workshops—all trades and professions

五合板 wǔhébǎn five-ply board; plywood

五湖四海 wǔhú-sìhǎi all corners of the land: 来自～ hail from all corners of the country

五花八门 wǔhuā-bāmén multifarious; of a wide (*or* rich) variety

五花大绑 wǔhuā dàbǎng tie a person's hands behind his back with a rope that is looped round his neck

五花肉 wǔhuāròu streaky pork

五级风 wǔjífēng *meteorol.* force 5 wind; fresh breeze

五极管 wǔjíguǎn *electron.* pentode

五加 wǔjiā *bot.* slender acanthopanax (*Acanthopanax gracilistylus*)

五加皮 wǔjiāpí ① *Chin. med.* bark of the slender acanthopanax ② a medicinal wine made by soaking the bark of the slender acanthopanax in liquor

五角大楼 Wǔjiǎo Dàlóu the Pentagon

五角星 wǔjiǎoxīng five-pointed star

五金 wǔjīn ① the five metals (gold, silver, copper, iron and tin) ② metals; hardware: ～厂 hardware factory / ～店 hardware store / ～商 dealer in hardware; ironmonger

五经 wǔjīng the Five Classics, namely, *The Book of Songs* (《诗经》), *The Book of History* (《书经》), *The Book of Changes* (《易经》), *The Book of Rites* (《礼记》), and *The Spring and Autumn Annals* (《春秋》)

五绝 wǔjué (short for 五言绝句) pentasyllabic (*or* five-syllable) quatrain ——see also 绝句 juéjù

五劳 wǔláo *Chin. med.* exhaustion or lesion of the five internal organs (heart, liver, spleen, lungs and kidneys)

五劳七伤 wǔláo qīshāng *Chin. med.* general debility

五里雾 wǔlǐwù thick fog—bewilderment ——see also 如堕五里雾中 rú duò wǔlǐwù zhōng

五敛子 wǔliǎnzǐ *bot.* carambola (*Averrhoa carambola*) ② the fruit of carambola; star fruit

五粮液 wǔliángyè a famous spirit distilled from five kinds of grain

五岭 wǔlǐng the Five Ridges (across the borders between Hunan and Jiangxi on the one hand and Guangdong and Guangxi on the other)

五律 wǔlǜ (short for 五言律诗) pentasyllabic (*or* five-syllable) regulated verse ——see also 律诗 lǜshī

五氯硝基苯 wǔlǜxiāojīběn pentachloronitrobenzene; PCNB

五伦 wǔlún the five human relationships (i.e. between ruler and subject 君臣, father and son 父子, husband and wife 夫妇, brothers 兄弟, and friends 朋友)

五马分尸 wǔ mǎ fēn shī dismemberment by five horses—dividing up; sharing out

五内 wǔnèi *formal* viscera

五内如焚 wǔnèi rú fén one's heart rent with grief; one's heart torn by anxiety

五年计划 wǔnián jìhuà Five-Year Plan

五七干校 Wǔ Qī gànxiào May 7 cadre school (named after Mao Zedong's May 7 Directive of 1966)

五日京兆 wǔ rì jīngzhào (of an official) not expecting to remain long in office; holding office only for a brief period

五卅运动 Wǔ Sà Yùndòng the May 30th Movement (1925)

五色 wǔsè same as 五彩 wǔcǎi

五色斑斓 wǔsè bānlán a riot of colour

五声音阶 wǔshēng yīnjiē *mus.* five-tone scale; pentatonic scale

五十步笑百步 wǔshí bù xiào bǎi bù one who retreats fifty paces mocks one who retreats a hundred—the pot calls the kettle black

五四青年节 Wǔ Sì Qīngniánjié Youth Day (May 4)

五四运动 Wǔ Sì Yùndòng the May 4th Movement of 1919 (an anti-imperialist, anti-feudal, political and cultural movement influenced by the October Revolution and led by intellectuals having the rudiments of Communist ideology)

五体投地 wǔ tǐ tóu dì prostrate oneself before sb.: 佩服得～ prostrate oneself before sb. in admiration; admire sb. from the bottom of one's heart; worship sb.

五味 wǔwèi ① the five flavours (sweet, sour, bitter, pungent and salty) ② all sorts of flavours

五味子 wǔwèizǐ *Chin. med.* the fruit of Chinese magnoliavine (*Schisandra chinensis*)

五线谱 wǔxiànpǔ *mus.* staff; stave

五香 wǔxiāng ① the five spices (prickly ash, star aniseed, cinnamon, clove and fennel) ② spices

五香豆 wǔxiāngdòu spiced beans

五项全能运动 wǔ xiàng quánnéng yùndòng *sports* pentathlon

五小工业 wǔxiǎo gōngyè the five small industrial enterprises (producing iron and steel, coal, chemical fertilizer, cement and machinery)

五星红旗 Wǔxīng Hóngqí the Five-Starred Red Flag (the national flag of the People's Republic of China)

五星级 wǔxīngjí five-star: ～旅馆 a five-star hotel

五星上将 wǔxīng shàngjiāng five-star general (referring to the U. S. General of the Army, Fleet Admiral and General of the Air Force)

五刑 wǔxíng the five chief forms of punishment in ancient China (tattooing the face 墨, cutting off the nose 劓, cutting of the feet 剕, castration 宫 and decapitation 大辟)

五行 wǔxíng the five elements (metal, wood, water, fire and earth; held by the ancients to compose the physical universe and later used in traditional Chinese medicine to explain various physiological and pathological phenomena)

五言诗 wǔyánshī a poem with five characters to a line ——see also 古体诗 gǔtǐshī; 绝句 juéjù; 律诗 lǜshī

五颜六色 wǔyán-liùsè of various (*or* all) colours; multicoloured; colourful: ～的云霞 clouds of many colours / 一叠～的纸 a heap of papers of various colours

五一 Wǔ Yī short for 五一国际劳动节 Wǔ Yī Guójì Láodòngjié

五一国际劳动节 Wǔ Yī Guójì Láodòngjié May 1, International Labour Day; May Day

五音 wǔyīn *mus.* the five notes of the ancient Chinese five-tone scale

五月 wǔyuè ① May ② the fifth month of the lunar year; the fifth moon

五月节 Wǔyuèjié the Dragon Boat Festival (the 5th day of the 5th lunar month)

五岳 Wǔ Yuè the Five Sacred Mountains (i.e. 东岳泰山 Tàishān, the Eastern Mountain in Shandong Province; 南岳衡山 Héngshān, the Southern Mountain in Hunan Province; 西岳华山 Huàshān, the Western Mountain in Shaanxi Province; 北岳恒山 Héngshān, the Northern Mountain in Shanxi Province; and 中岳嵩山 Sōngshān, the Central Mountain in Henan Province)

五脏 wǔzàng *Chin. med.* the five internal organs (heart, liver, spleen, lungs and kidneys)

五脏六腑 wǔzàng-liùfǔ the internal organs of the body;

the viscera

五指 wǔzhǐ the five fingers (thumb, index finger, middle finger, third finger and little finger)

五中 wǔzhōng *formal* the five internal organs (heart, liver, spleen, lungs and kidneys): 铭感～ thank sb. from the bottom of one's heart; be deeply grateful

五洲 wǔzhōu the five continents; the whole world

五子棋 wǔzǐqí gobang

午 wǔ ① noon; midday ② the seventh of the twelve Earthly Branches (地支) (see also 干支 gān-zhī)

午餐 wǔcān midday meal; lunch

午餐肉 wǔcānròu (pork) luncheon meat

午饭 wǔfàn midday meal; lunch

午后 wǔhòu afternoon

午间 wǔjiān noon; midday

午觉 wǔjiào afternoon nap; noontime snooze

午前 wǔqián forenoon; before noon; morning

午时 wǔshí (also 午刻 wǔkè) the period of the day from 11 a.m. to 1 p.m.

午睡 wǔshuì ① afternoon nap; noontime snooze ② take (*or* have) a nap after lunch

午休 wǔxiū noon break; midday rest; noontime rest; lunch hour

午宴 wǔyàn luncheon

午夜 wǔyè midnight

仵 wǔ *old* coroner

仵作 wǔzuò *old* coroner

伍 wǔ ① five (used for the numeral 五 on cheques, banknotes, etc. to avoid mistakes or alterations) ② the basic five-man unit of the army in ancient China; army: 入伍 rùwǔ ③ company: 羞与为伍 xiū yǔ wéiwǔ ④ (Wǔ) a surname

妩(嫵、娬) wǔ see below

妩媚 wǔmèi (of a woman) lovely; charming: 唐小姐～端正的圆脸，有两个浅酒窝。On Miss Tang's charming, well-proportioned round face were two shallow dimples.

迕 wǔ *formal* ① meet ② violate; go against; run counter to

忤(悟) wǔ ① disobedient ② uncongenial: 与人无～ bear no ill will against anybody

忤逆 wǔnì disobedient (to parents)

武 wǔ ① military: 黩武 dúwǔ / 尚武 shàngwǔ ② connected with boxing skill, swordplay, etc.: 武术 wǔshù ③ valiant; fierce: 威武 wēiwǔ ④ (Wǔ) a surname

武备 wǔbèi *formal* defence preparations, specifically the condition of the armed forces and armaments

武昌鱼 wǔchāngyú *zool.* blunt-snout bream (*Megalobrama amblycephala*)

武场 wǔchǎng (also 武场面 wǔchǎngmiàn) military division (one of the two divisions of the orchestra in traditional opera, consisting of percussion instruments like drums, gongs, cymbals, etc.) ——see also 文场 wénchǎng

武丑 wǔchǒu (in traditional opera) a comedian in military plays (武戏)

武打 wǔdǎ acrobatic fighting in Chinese opera or dance

武旦 wǔdàn one of the main divisions of the *dan* or female role in traditional opera (representing a military maiden, a princess of martial character, or a woman bandit; combining the most charming feminine virtues with those of masculine character)

武斗 wǔdòu resort to violence (in a debate, dispute, etc.)

武断 wǔduàn arbitrary; subjective assertion: 这样说太～了。This is a subjective assertion.

武夫 wǔfū ① a man of great physical prowess ② soldier; military man

武工 wǔgōng (in traditional opera) the basic physical training which enables an actor to perform acrobatic feats and stage fighting and conditions his body generally; acrobatic skills

武工队 wǔgōngduì (short for 武装工作队) armed working team (operating under the leadership of the Chinese Communist Party in enemy-occupied areas during the War of Resistance Against Japan, 1937–1945)

武功 wǔgōng ① *formal* military accomplishments (*or* achievements) ② same as 武工 wǔgōng

武官 wǔguān ① military officer ② *diplomacy* military attaché

武官处 wǔguānchù *diplomacy* military attaché's office

武汉 Wǔhàn Wuhan (capital of Hubei Province; collective name for Wuchang 武昌, Hankou 汉口, and Hanyang 汉阳, three closely linked municipalities)

武行 wǔháng (in traditional opera) specialists in acrobatics (actors who take minor parts in military combats)

武火 wǔhuǒ high heat (in cooking)

武将 wǔjiàng military officer; general

武警 wǔjǐng short for 武装警察 wǔzhuāng jǐngchá

武剧 wǔjù same as 武戏 wǔxì

武力 wǔlì ① force ② military force; armed might; armed strength; force of arms: ～镇压 armed suppression

武林 wǔlín (also 武坛 wǔtán) martial arts circles

武庙 wǔmiào temple to the God of War (i.e. dedicated to Guan Yu 关羽)

武器 wǔqì weapon; arms: 放下～ lay down one's arms / 拿起～ take up arms / ～交易 arms deal; arms trade

武器禁运 wǔqì jìnyùn arms embargo

武器库 wǔqìkù (also 武库 wǔkù) arsenal; armoury

武器装备 wǔqì zhuāngbèi weaponry

武生 wǔshēng one of the main divisions of the *sheng* or male role in traditional opera (portraying military heroes, high-ranking generals, and heroic outlaws; the *wusheng* actor being majestic in bearing and skilled in acrobatics, swift movement, and agile play with weapons)

武师 wǔshī a man versed in martial arts; martial arts master

武士 wǔshì ① palace guards in ancient times ② man of prowess; warrior; knight

武士道 wǔshìdào *bushido*

武士俑 wǔshìyǒng warrior figure

武术 wǔshù *wushu*, martial arts such as shadowboxing, swordplay, etc., formerly cultivated for self-defence, now a form of physical culture

武松 Wǔ Sōng one of the Mount Liang heroes (梁山好汉) in *Water Margin* (《水浒传》), a tiger-killer and a champion of the oppressed, noted for his prowess and feats of strength

武戏 wǔxì (in traditional opera) military plays (opp. 文戏 wénxì; heroic in nature; full of loyal generals, glorious emperors, and wise government officials, all of whom struggle against traitorous opposing forces)

武侠 wǔxiá a person adept in martial arts and given to chivalrous conduct (in olden times)

武侠小说 wǔxiá xiǎoshuō swordsman fiction; knight-

errant fiction

武艺 wǔyì　skill in *wushu* ——see also 武术 wǔshù

武职 wǔzhí　military post

武装 wǔzhuāng ① arms; military equipment; battle outfit: 全副～ fully armed; in full battle gear / ～人员 armed personnel ② armed forces: ～夺取政权 seizure of power by armed force ③ equip (*or* supply) with arms; arm: ～到牙齿 be armed to the teeth / 用马列主义、毛泽东思想～头脑 arm one's mind with Marxism-Leninism-Mao Zedong Thought

武装部队 wǔzhuāng bùduì　armed forces

武装冲突 wǔzhuāng chōngtū　armed clash

武装带 wǔzhuāngdài　Sam Browne belt

武装斗争 wǔzhuāng dòuzhēng　armed struggle

武装干涉 wǔzhuāng gānshè　armed intervention

武装警察 wǔzhuāng jǐngchá　armed police

武装力量 wǔzhuāng lìliàng　armed power; armed forces

武装起义 wǔzhuāng qǐyì　armed uprising (*or* insurrection)

武装泅渡 wǔzhuāng qiúdù　swim with one's weapons; swim in battle gear

侮 wǔ　insult; bully: 欺侮 qīwǔ

侮骂 wǔmà　abuse; call sb. names; hurl insults

侮慢 wǔmàn　slight; treat disrespectfully

侮蔑 wǔmiè　despise; look down on

侮辱 wǔrǔ　insult; humiliate; subject sb. to indignities

捂（搗） wǔ　seal; cover; muffle: ～鼻子 cover one's nose with one's hand / ～着耳朵 stop one's ears

捂盖子 wǔ gàizi　keep the lid on—try to cover up the truth (about a crime, etc.)

捂捂盖盖 wǔwǔgǎigài　*dial.* try to cover up; hedge and dodge: 有了错误不能～。You shouldn't try to cover up your mistakes.

悟 wǔ　see 抵悟 dǐwǔ

鹉 wǔ　see 鹦鹉 yīngwǔ

舞 wǔ ① dance: 集体舞 jítǐwǔ ② move about as in a dance: 手舞足蹈 shǒuwǔ-zúdǎo ③ dance with sth. in one's hands: 舞剑 wǔjiàn ④ flourish; wield; brandish: 挥舞 huīwǔ

舞伴 wǔbàn　dancing partner

舞弊 wǔbì　fraudulent practices; malpractices; irregularities; embezzlement: 我们在清查帐目时发现了他的～行为。We discovered his irregularities while checking the accounts.

舞步 wǔbù　step (in dancing)

舞场 wǔchǎng　dance hall; ballroom

舞池 wǔchí　dance floor

舞蹈 wǔdǎo　dance: ～动作 dance movement / ～家 dancer / ～设计 choreography

舞蹈病 wǔdǎobìng　*med.* chorea

舞动 wǔdòng　wave; brandish

舞会 wǔhuì　dance; ball: 举行～ hold a dance

舞剑 wǔjiàn　perform a sword-dance

舞剧 wǔjù　dance drama; ballet

舞客 wǔkè　dance hall customer

舞迷 wǔmí　dance fiend

舞弄 wǔnòng　wave; wield; brandish: ～刀枪 brandish swords and spears

舞女 wǔnǚ　dancing girl; dance-hostess; taxi dancer

舞曲 wǔqǔ　dance music; dance

舞台 wǔtái　stage; arena: ～布景 (stage) scenery; décor / ～灯光 stage lights; lighting / ～工作人员 stagehand / ～监督 stage director / ～设计 stage design / ～效果 stage effect / ～艺术 stagecraft / 政治～ poli-

tical arena (*or* scene, stage) / 在国际～上 in the international arena

舞台记录片 wǔtái jìlùpiàn　stage documentary

舞厅 wǔtīng　dance hall; ballroom

舞文弄法 wǔwén-nòngfǎ　pervert the law by playing with legal phraseology

舞文弄墨 wǔwén-nòngmò　engage in phrase-mongering

舞艺 wǔyì　(also 舞技 wǔjì) dancing skill

舞姿 wǔzī　a dancer's posture and movements

wù

兀 wù　*formal* ① rising to a height; towering ② bald

兀傲 wù'ào　*formal* supercilious; arrogant; haughty

兀鹫 wùjiù　griffon vulture

兀立 wùlì　stand upright

兀臬 wùniè　same as 杌陧 wùniè

兀突 wùtū　sudden; abrupt; unexpected: 事情来的那么～，我们毫无准备。It happened so suddenly that we were caught unprepared.

兀自 wùzì　still

乌（烏） wù　see below ——see also wū

乌拉 wùlā　leather boots lined with *wula* sedge ——see also wūlā

乌拉草 wùlācǎo　*bot.* *wula* sedge

勿 wù　*adv.* (used in prohibitions, admonitions, etc.) do not; never: 请～入内 No Admittance / 请～吸烟 No Smoking

勿忘草 wùwàngcǎo　forget-me-not (*Myosotis sylvatica*)

勿谓言之不预 wù wèi yán zhī bù yù　do not say that you have not been forewarned; do not blame us for not having forewarned you

勿以善小而不为，勿以恶小而为之 wù yǐ shàn xiǎo ér bù wéi, wù yǐ è xiǎo ér wéi zhī　don't fail to do good even if it's small; don't engage in evil even if it's small

戊 wù　the fifth of the ten Heavenly Stems (天干) ——see also 干支 gān-zhī

戊戌变法 Wùxū Biànfǎ　the Reform Movement of 1898 (whose leading spirits, Kang Youwei, Liang Qichao and Tan Sitong, represented the interests of the liberal bourgeoisie and the enlightened landlords)

务（務） wù ① affair; business: 公务 gōngwù ② be engaged in; devote one's efforts to: 务农 wùnóng ③ *adv.* must; be sure to: ～使大家明了这一点。Be sure to make this point clear to everyone. / ～请光临指导。You are cordially invited to come and give guidance. ④ (used as part of a place name): 曹家～ Caojiawu (in Hebei)

务本 wùběn　attend to the basic or the fundamental

务必 wùbì　*adv.* must; be sure to: 你～在本周内去看望他一次。Be sure to go and see him before the week is out. / 这信请你～带到。Please deliver this letter without fail. / 此事～认真考虑。We must think about this seriously.

务农 wùnóng　be engaged in agriculture; be a farmer

务期 wùqī　must; be sure to: ～按时归来。Be sure to come back on time.

务求 wùqiú　must; be sure to: 此事～妥善解决。We must find a satisfactory solution to the problem.

务实 wùshí　deal with concrete matters relating to work; be pragmatic: ～的政府 a pragmatically-inclined government / ～的政治家 a pragmatic politician

务使 wùshǐ make sure; ensure: ～老年人得到适当照顾 ensure that old people are properly cared for / ～同志们保持艰苦奋斗的作风。The comrades must be helped to preserve the style of plain living and hard struggle.

务须 wùxū same as 务必 wùbì

务虚 wùxū discuss principles or ideological guidelines

务正 wùzhèng (usu. used in the negative) do honest work ——see also 不务正业 bù wù zhèngyè

荮 wù *chem.* fluorene

杌 wù a square stool

杌凳 wùdèng same as 杌子 wùzi

杌陧 wùniè *formal* ① (of a situation, etc.) unsettled; unstable ② uneasy; disturbed; restless

杌子 wùzi a square stool

坞（隖、隖） wù ① a depressed place: 船坞 chuánwù ② *formal* a fortified building; castle

物 wù ① thing; matter: 公物 gōngwù ② the outside world as distinct from oneself; other people: 待人接物 dàirén-jiēwù ③ content; substance: 言之无物 yán zhī wú wù

物产 wùchǎn products; produce

物腐虫生 wùfǔ-chóngshēng worms breed in decaying matter: 物必先腐也，而后虫生之；人必先疑也，而后谗入之。(苏轼) Something must be rotten before worms multiply, and a man must first have some suspicion before slander takes effect.

物阜民丰 wùfù-mínfēng products abound and the people live in plenty

物故 wùgù *formal* pass away; die

物归原主 wù guī yuánzhǔ return sth. to its rightful owner

物候学 wùhòuxué phenology

物化 wùhuà *formal* pass away; die

物换星移 wùhuàn-xīngyí things change and the stars move—change of the seasons: 闲云潭影日悠悠，～几度秋。(王勃) Calm clouds, reflected in pools, go on and on each day, But things change, stars move—how many autumns gone by?

物极必反 wù jí bì fǎn things turn into their opposites when they reach the extreme

物价 wùjià (commodity) prices: ～稳定。Prices remain stable. / ～波动 price fluctuation / ～飞涨。Prices skyrocketed. / ～冻结 price freeze / ～管理 price control

物价补贴 wùjià bǔtiē subsidies paid out to compensate for price rises

物价政策 wùjià zhèngcè pricing policy

物价指数 wùjià zhǐshù price index

物件 wùjiàn thing; article

物尽其用 wù jìn qí yòng make the best use of everything; let all things serve their proper purpose

物镜 wùjìng *phys.* objective (lens)

物理 wùlǐ ① innate laws of things ② physics

物理变化 wùlǐ biànhuà physical change

物理化学 wùlǐ huàxué physical chemistry

物理疗法 wùlǐ liáofǎ physical therapy; physiotherapy

物理性质 wùlǐ xìngzhì physical property

物理学 wùlǐxué physics: ～家 physicist

物理诊断 wùlǐ zhěnduàn physical diagnosis

物力 wùlì material resources; *matériel*: 节约人力～ use manpower and material resources sparingly / 我军人力～的来源 our army's sources of manpower and *matériel*

物美价廉 wùměi-jiàlián same as 价廉物美 jiàlián-wùměi

物品 wùpǐn article; goods: 零星～ sundries; odds and ends / 随身携带的～ things carried on one's person

物色 wùsè look for; seek out; choose: ～这方面的人才 look for qualified persons in this field

物伤其类 wù shāng qí lèi like feels for like ——see also 兔死狐悲 tù sǐ hú bēi

物事 wùshì ① *formal* matter; affair; thing; business ② *dial.* tangible thing; visible thing

物体 wùtǐ body; substance; object: 运动～ a body in motion / 透明～ a transparent substance (or object)

物外 wùwài beyond the region of objective existence; transcendental: 超然物外 chāorán wùwài

物望 wùwàng *formal* popular confidence; popular trust

物象¹ wùxiàng image

物象² wùxiàng visible phenomena

物以类聚，人以群分 wù yǐ lèi jù, rén yǐ qún fēn things of a kind come together, people of a mind fall into the same group; like attracts like; birds of a feather flock together

物以稀为贵 wù yǐ xī wéi guì when a thing is scarce, it is precious

物议 wùyì *formal* criticism from the public: 免遭～ so as to avoid public censure; so as not to incur criticism by the masses

物欲 wùyù material desires

物证 wùzhèng material evidence

物质 wùzhì ① matter; substance: ～形体有三种：气体、液体、固体。All matter has one of three forms: gas, liquid, or solid. / 所有的宗教都说～以外还有灵魂。All religions teach the existence of spirit as well as matter. ② material: ～财富 material wealth / ～储备 reserve supply; stockpile / ～力量 material strength; material force / ～利益 material benefits; material gains / ～条件 material conditions or prerequisites / ～享受 material comforts / ～资料 material goods

物质不灭定律 wùzhì bùmiè dìnglǜ the law of conservation of matter

物质刺激 wùzhì cìjī material incentive

物质鼓励 wùzhì gǔlì material reward; material incentive

物质基础 wùzhì jīchǔ material base

物质生活 wùzhì shēnghuó material life

物质世界 wùzhì shìjiè the material (or physical) world

物质文明 wùzhì wénmíng material civilization: 在建设～的同时，进行精神文明的建设。In building a civilization, we have to pay attention to its moral as well as its material aspect.

物质性 wùzhìxìng *philos.* materiality

物质运动 wùzhì yùndòng the motion of matter

物种 wùzhǒng *biol.* species

物主 wùzhǔ owner (esp. of lost or stolen property)

物资 wùzī goods and materials: ～调度 distribution of materials / ～管理 handling of goods and materials / ～交流 interflow of commodities

误（悮） wù ① mistake; error: ～把友谊当爱情 mistake friendship for love ② miss: ～了火车 miss a train ③ hinder; impede: 生产学习两不～。Neither production nor study is to suffer. ④ by mistake; by accident: 误伤 wùshāng

误差 wùchā error: ～极微的精密零件 precision parts with very close tolerances / ～不超过千分之三毫米 with a tolerance of less than three-thousandths of a millimetre / 平均～ mean error; average error / 仪器～ instrumental error / 概然～ probable error

误差函数 wùchā hánshù error function

误差率 wùchālǜ error rate

误场 wùchǎng (of an actor) fail to turn up for the show

误点 wùdiǎn late; overdue; behind schedule: 飞机～了。

The plane is overdue (*or* late). / 火车～十分钟。The train was ten minutes late (*or* behind schedule).

误工 wùgōng ① delay one's work ② loss of working time

误国 wùguó endanger the realm: 严嵩父子欺君～。Yan Song and his son deceived their sovereign and endangered the realm.

误会 wùhuì ① misunderstand; mistake; misconstrue: 你～了我的意思。You've mistaken my meaning. / 你一定是搞～了。You must have misunderstood. *or* You must be mistaken. ② misunderstanding: 小小的～ a minor misunderstanding

误解 wùjiě ① misread; misunderstand: 你～了我的话。You misunderstood what I said. ② misunderstanding: 产生～ produce misunderstanding / 消除～ clear up a misunderstanding / 你亲自去和他谈谈，以免引起～。Go and talk to him yourself so that there will be no misunderstanding.

误期 wùqī exceed the time limit; be behind schedule: 这项工程～了。The project is behind schedule.

误人子弟 wù rén zǐdì (of a teacher) harm the younger generation; lead young people astray

误入歧途 wù rù qítú go astray

误杀 wùshā *leg.* manslaughter

误伤 wùshāng ① accidentally injure ② accidental injury

误事 wùshì ① cause delay in work or business; hold things up ② bungle matters

误诊 wùzhěn make a wrong diagnosis: ～病例 missed case

悟 wù realize; awaken: ～出其中的道理 realize why it should be so

悟彻 wùchè understand thoroughly; realize completely

悟道 wùdào awake to the truth; attain enlightenment: ～之言 enlightened views

悟解 wùjiě understand; comprehend; grasp

悟性 wùxìng power of understanding; comprehension

恶(惡) wù loathe; dislike; hate: 好恶 hàowù / 可恶 kěwù ——see also ě; è; wū

恶寒 wùhán *Chin. med.* aversion to cold

晤 wù meet; interview; see: 会晤 huìwù

晤面 wùmiàn (also 晤见 wùjiàn) meet; see

晤谈 wùtán meet and talk; have a talk; interview

焐 wù warm up: 把被褥～热 warm up the bedding / 用热水袋～一～手 warm one's hands with a hot-water bottle

痦(疿) wù see below

痦子 wùzi *med.* naevus; mole

靰 wù see below

靰鞡 wùla same as 乌拉 wùla

骛 wù *formal* ① move about freely and quickly; sweep through the length and breadth ② go after; seek for: 好高骛远 hàogāo-wùyuǎn

雾(霧) wù ① fog: 中午时分～就散了。Around midday, the fog lifted. ② fine spray: 喷雾器 pēnwùqì

雾霭 wù'ǎi *formal* fog; mist; vapour

雾标 wùbiāo fog buoy

雾沉沉 wùchénchén misty; foggy: 天气～的，我不得不开得很慢。It was very foggy. I had to drive very slowly.

雾滴 wùdī *environ. protec.* droplet

雾虹 wùhóng fogbow

雾化 wùhuà atomize

雾化器 wùhuàqì atomizer

雾里看花 wù lǐ kàn huā look at flowers in a fog——a blurred vision

雾茫茫 wùmángmáng misty; foggy: 山上～的，只看见一个模糊的轮廓。The mountains were covered in thick mist and only a faint outline could be seen.

雾气 wùqì fog; mist; vapour

雾凇 wùsōng *meteorol.* (soft) rime: ～雾 rime fog

雾腾腾 wùtēngtēng misty; foggy: 水面上～的。There's cloud of mist over the water.

寤 wù *formal* ① awake ② same as 悟 wù

鹜 wù *formal* duck: 趋之若鹜 qū zhī ruò wù

X

xī

夕 xī ① sunset: 夕阳 xīyáng / 朝发夕至 zhāofā-xīzhì ② evening; night: 风雨之～ a stormy night

夕晖 xīhuī evening twilight

夕烟 xīyān evening mist

夕阳 xīyáng the evening sun; the setting sun: ～反照 evening (or sunset) glow / ～西下。The evening sun is sinking in the west. or The sun is setting in the west. / ～无限好，只是近黄昏。(李商隐) The setting sun has boundless beauty; Only the yellow dusk is so near.

夕照 xīzhào the glow of the setting sun; evening glow: 满目青山～明。On all sides, verdant sunset-bathed hills greet the eye.

兮 xī *part. liter.* (representing a meaningless sound, somewhat like 啊, used in an old song form between the two divisions of each line presumably to carry the singing voice through parts of the melody for which there are no corresponding words): 风萧萧～易水寒，壮士一去～不复还。(荆轲) The wind is wailing, cold the River Yi, And a hero sets forth, never to return.

汐 xī tide during the night; nighttide

西 xī ① west: ～屋 west room / ～海岸 the west coast / 太原以～ to the west of Taiyuan / 往～去 head west ② (Xī) Occidental; Western: 西服 xīfú / 西药 xīyào

西安 Xī'ān Xi'an (capital of Shaanxi Province)

西安事变 Xī'ān Shìbiàn the Xi'an Incident (which occurred in Xi'an on December 12, 1936, when Generals Zhang Xueliang 张学良 and Yang Hucheng 杨虎城 took Chiang Kai-shek hostage and demanded that he cease the civil war and unite with the Communist Party in a national war against Japanese aggression)

西班牙 Xībānyá Spain

西班牙人 Xībānyárén a Spaniard; the Spanish

西班牙语 Xībānyáyǔ Spanish (language)

西半球 xībànqiú the Western Hemisphere

西北 xīběi ① northwest ② (Xīběi) northwest China; the Northwest (including Shaanxi, Gansu, Qinghai, Ningxia, and Xinjiang)

西北风 xīběifēng northwest wind; northwesterly wind

西边 xībian same as 西面 xīmian

西宾 xībīn same as 西席 xīxí

西伯利亚 Xībólìyà Siberia

西餐 xīcān Western-style food

西餐馆 xīcānguǎn a restaurant which serves Western food

西点 xīdiǎn Western-style pastry

西法 xīfǎ Western method: ～洗染 Western method of laundering and dyeing

西番莲 xīfānlián ① passionflower ② dahlia

西方 xīfāng ① the west ② (Xīfāng) the West; the

Occident: ～国家 the Western countries ③ same as 西天 xītiān②

西非 Xī Fēi West Africa

西风 xīfēng ① west wind; westerly wind ② autumn wind ③ decaying influences (fig.)

西风带 xīfēngdài westerlies

西凤酒 xīfèngjiǔ a famous hard liquor distilled in Fengxiang County (凤翔县), Shaanxi Province

西服 xīfú Western-style clothes; suit

西服料 xīfúliào suiting

西府海棠 xīfǔ hǎitáng *bot.* midget crabapple

西宫 xīgōng ① western palace—palace quarters for imperial concubines ② imperial concubines: ～娘娘 imperial concubine of the highest rank

西瓜 xīguā watermelon

西瓜子 xīguāzǐ watermelon seed

西汉 Xī Hàn the Western Han Dynasty (206 B.C.-A.D. 24)

西河大鼓 xīhé dàgǔ a variety of *dagu* popular in Hebei and Henan Provinces

西红柿 xīhóngshì same as 番茄 fānqié

西湖 Xīhú the West Lake, name of various lakes in a number of places in China, the most famous of all being in Hangzhou

西葫芦 xīhúlu *bot.* pumpkin; summer squash

西化 xīhuà be westernized: 向西方学习不等于全盘～。To learn from the West does not mean to be completely westernized.

西画 xīhuà short for 西洋画 xīyánghuà

西晋 Xī Jìn the Western Jin Dynasty (265-316)

西经 xījīng west longitude: ～一百六十五度 longitude 165°W.

西口 xīkǒu gates in the western sections of the Great Wall: 出～ go north of the Great Wall through one of the gates in the western sections

西历 xīlì *old* the Gregorian calendar

西门 Xīmén a two-character surname

西米 xīmǐ *bot.* sago

西面 xīmian west: 电影院～ (to the) west of the cinema / 剧场在商店的～。The theatre is to the west of the store. / ～的窗子 a window facing west

西南 xīnán ① southwest ② (Xīnán) southwest China; the Southwest (including Sichuan, Yunnan, Guizhou, and Tibet)

西南风 xīnánfēng southwest wind; southwesterly wind

西宁 Xīníng Xining (capital of Qinghai Province)

西欧 Xī Ōu Western Europe

西皮 xīpí *xipi*, one of the two chief types of music in traditional Chinese operas ——see also 皮黄 píhuáng

西撒哈拉 Xīsāhālā Western Sahara

西萨摩亚 Xīsàmóyà Western Samoa

西沙群岛 Xīshā Qúndǎo the Xisha Islands

西晒 xīshài (of a room) have a western exposure (hot on summer afternoons)

西施 Xīshī ① the name of a famous beauty in the late Spring and Autumn Period ② a beautiful woman; a beauty: 情人眼里出西施 qíngrén yǎnli chū Xīshī

西式 xīshì Western style: ～点心 Western-style pastry

西天　xītiān　① Western Heaven (ancient Chinese Buddhists' name for India): 孙悟空保护唐僧往～取经。Sun Wukong accompanied the Tang monk to acquire scriptures in the Western Heaven. ② *Buddhism* Western Paradise ——see also 上西天 shàng xītiān

西王母　Xīwángmǔ　the Queen Mother of the West (a mythological figure, usu. described as a beautiful immortal, who dwells at Jasper Lake 瑶池 in the Kunlun Mountains and in whose huge palace grow the magic peach trees which bear the fruits of immortality 蟠桃 once every three thousand years)

西魏　Xī Wèi　the Western Wei Dynasty (535–556), one of the Northern Dynasties ——see also 北朝 Běi Cháo

西西　xīxī　cc; c.c. (a transliteration; old name for 毫升 háo shēng)

西席　xīxí　*old honor.* a private tutor or secretary

西夏　Xī Xià　the Western Xia regime (1038–1227)

西学　xīxué　Western learning (a late Qing Dynasty term for Western natural and social sciences)

西亚　Xī Yà　(also 西南亚 Xīnán Yà) Southwest Asia

西洋　Xīyáng　the West; the Western world: ～文学 Western literature

西洋画　xīyánghuà　Western painting

西洋景　xīyángjǐng　(also 西洋镜 xīyángjìng) ① peep show ② hanky-panky; trickery: 拆穿～ expose sb.'s tricks; strip off the camouflage

西洋人　xīyángrén　Westerner

西洋参　xīyángshēn　American ginseng (*Panax quinquefolium*)

西洋史　xīyángshǐ　history of the Western world (*or* Western countries)

西药　xīyào　Western medicine

西医　xīyī　① Western medicine (as distinguished from traditional Chinese medicine) ② a doctor trained in Western medicine

西印度群岛　Xīyìndù Qúndǎo　the West Indies

西语　xīyǔ　① Western languages: ～系 the Department of Western Languages ② (Xīyǔ) short for 西班牙语 Xībānyáyǔ

西域　Xīyù　the Western Regions (a Han Dynasty term for the area west of Yumenguan 玉门关, including what is now Xinjiang 新疆 and parts of Central Asia)

西元　xīyuán　old name for 公元 gōngyuán

西乐　xīyuè　Western music

西岳　Xī Yuè　the Western Mountain (another name for 华山 Mount Hua in Shaanxi Province) ——see also 五岳 Wǔ Yuè

西崽　xīzǎi　*old derog.* a man or boy working at odd jobs in a foreign firm, restaurant, etc.

西藏　Xīzàng　Tibet

西藏自治区　Xīzàng Zìzhìqū　the Tibet Autonomous Region

西周　Xī Zhōu　the Western Zhou Dynasty (c. 11th century–771 B.C.)

西装　xīzhuāng　Western-style clothes; suit

西子　Xīzǐ　another name for 西施 Xīshī

吸　xī　① inhale; breathe in; draw: ～进新鲜空气 inhale fresh air / 深深～一口气 draw a deep breath ② suck (liquids): ～奶 suck milk; nurse / 蚊子～人血。Mosquitoes suck human blood. ③ absorb; suck up: 用粉笔把墨水～干 blot ink with a piece of chalk / 海绵～水。A sponge absorbs water. ④ attract; draw to oneself: 磁石～铁。A magnet attracts iron.

吸尘器　xīchénqì　dust catcher; dust collector: 真空～ vacuum cleaner

吸虫　xīchóng　fluke: 肺～ lung fluke / 肝～ liver fluke

吸顶灯　xīdǐngdēng　lamp with its shade affixed to the ceiling

吸毒　xīdú　take addictive drugs; be addicted to a narcotic

吸毒者　xīdúzhě　drug addict; narcotic addict

吸附　xīfù　*chem.* adsorb: ～作用 adsorption / 活性炭～毒气和液体中的杂质。Active carbon adsorbs poisonous gases and impurities in liquids.

吸附剂　xīfùjì　adsorbent

吸附器　xīfùqì　adsorber

吸附水　xīfùshuǐ　adsorbed water

吸管　xīguǎn　straw

吸力　xīlì　suction; attraction: 相互～ mutual attraction

吸力计　xīlìjì　suction gauge

吸墨纸　xīmòzhǐ　blotting paper

吸奶器　xīnǎiqì　breast pump

吸泥泵　xīníbèng　dredge pump

吸盘　xīpán　sucking disc (of certain animals); sucker

吸取　xīqǔ　absorb; draw; assimilate: ～水分 absorb water / ～精华 absorb the quintessence / ～教训 draw a lesson / 从书本里可以～到大量的科学知识。Much scientific knowledge can be acquired through reading. / 这项设计～了老工人的先进经验。The design incorporates the experience of veteran workers.

吸热　xīrè　absorption of heat

吸热反应　xīrè fǎnyìng　*chem.* endothermic reaction

吸声　xīshēng　sound-absorbing; acoustic: ～材料 sound-absorbing material / ～瓷砖 acoustic tiles

吸湿　xīshī　moisture-absorbing

吸湿剂　xīshījì　hygroscopic agent; moisture absorbent

吸湿性　xīshīxìng　hygroscopicity; moisture absorbency

吸食　xīshí　suck; take in (liquid foods, narcotic drugs, etc.)

吸收　xīshōu　① absorb; suck up; assimilate; imbibe; draw: ～养分 assimilate nutriment / ～水分 suck up moisture / ～知识 absorb (*or* imbibe) knowledge / ～古代文化遗产 assimilate ancient cultural heritage / 叶子～阳光。Leaves take in sunlight. ② recruit; enrol; admit: ～入党 admit into the Party / 要～更多的同志参加这项工作。We should recruit more comrades for the work. *or* We should draw more comrades into the work. / 我们决定～他为正式会员。We have decided to admit him to full membership.

吸收光谱　xīshōu guāngpǔ　*phys.* absorption spectrum

吸收剂　xīshōujì　absorbent

吸收率　xīshōulù　absorptivity

吸收塔　xīshōutǎ　*chem.* absorption tower

吸收作用　xīshōu zuòyòng　absorption

吸吮　xīshǔn　suck; absorb: 婴儿在～母亲的奶汁。The baby is nursing at his mother's breast. / ～穷人的血汗 suck the blood of the poor

吸铁石　xītiěshí　magnet; lodestone

吸血鬼　xīxuèguǐ　bloodsucker; vampire

吸烟　xīyān　smoke: 他一天吸一包烟。He smokes a pack of cigarettes a day. / 严禁～。No smoking.

吸烟室　xīyānshì　smoking room

吸引　xīyǐn　attract; draw; fascinate: ～注意力 attract attention / 把敌人火力～过来 draw enemy fire on oneself / 被工地热火朝天的场面～住了 be fascinated by the hustle and bustle of the construction site / 这部电影对观众很有～力。This film has a strong appeal to the audience.

吸引器　xīyǐnqì　*med.* aspirator

希¹　xī　① hope: 敬～读者指正。It is hoped that the readers will kindly point out our errors. / ～准时到会。Please get to the meeting on time.

希²　xī　same as 稀 xī①

希伯来语　Xībóláiyǔ　Hebrew (language)

希罕　xīhan　① rare; scarce; uncommon: 骆驼在南方

是～的东西。Camels are a rare sight in the south. ② value as a rarity; cherish: 你不～, 我还～呢。You may not cherish it, but I do. / 谁～你的臭钱? Who cares about your lousy money? ③ a rare thing; rarity: 看～儿 enjoy the rare sight of sth. / 这么大的人参可是个～儿。Such a big ginseng root is certainly a rarity.

希冀 xījì　*formal*　hope for; wish for; aspire after

希腊 Xīlà　Greece

希腊人 Xīlàrén　Greek

希腊语 Xīlàyǔ　Greek (language)

希腊正教 Xīlà Zhèngjiào　the Greek Orthodox Church

希腊字母 Xīlà zìmǔ　the Greek alphabet

希奇 xīqí　rare; strange; curious: 十月下雪在这儿不是什么～的事。Snow in October is nothing strange in this place.

希求 xīqiú　① hope for; wish for ② what one hopes or wishes for

希少 xīshǎo　same as 稀少 xīshǎo

希世 xīshì　rare on earth

希世之珍 xīshì zhī zhēn　a rare treasure: 故宫博物院收藏着许多～。Many rare treasures are housed in the Palace Museum.

希图 xītú　harbour the intention of; intend to; attempt to: ～蒙混过关 try to wangle; try to get by under false pretences / ～牟取暴利 go after quick profits

希望 xīwàng　① hope; wish; expect: 他～长大了当医生。He hopes to become a doctor when he grows up. / ～你明天能来。Hope you'll be here tomorrow. / 那时候我们是多么～能把河水引到这儿来啊! How we wished then that the water over there could be diverted to our area! ② hope; wish; expectation: 把～变成现实 turn hopes into reality / 大有成功的～ promise high hopes of success; stand a very good chance of success / 他康复的～不大。There is little hope of his recovery. / 这就是同志们对你的～。This is what the comrades expect of you. / ～寄托在你们青年人身上。Our hope is placed on you young people. / 我们的国家是大有～的。Our country is full of promise. ③ a person or thing on which hope is placed: 青少年是我们的未来, 是我们的～。The youngsters are our future, our hope.

希有 xīyǒu　same as 稀有 xīyǒu

希珍 xīzhēn　rare and precious: 海獭是一种～的哺乳动物。The sea otter is a rare and precious mammal.

夌

xī　see 窀夌 zhūnxī

昔

xī　former times; the past: 今胜于～。The present is superior to the past.

昔年 xīnián　*formal*　(in) former years

昔日 xīrì　(in) former days (*or* times): ～荒坡, 今日良田。The once barren hillsides are now good farmland.

昔者 xīzhě　*formal*　① (in) the past; (in) former times ② yesterday

析

xī　① divide; separate: 析居 xījū / 分崩离析 fēn-bēng-líxī ② analyse; dissect; resolve: 析义 xīyì / 剖析 pōuxī

析出 xīchū　① find (results) on analysis ② *chem.* separate out

析㸑 xīcuàn　*formal*　(of family members) cook and eat separately

析居 xījū　(of family members) live separately

析像管 xīxiàngguǎn　*electron.*　image dissector

析疑 xīyí　*formal*　resolve a doubt; clear up a doubtful point

析义 xīyì　analyse the meaning (of a word, etc.)

矽

xī　*chem.*　silicon (Si)

矽肺 xīfèi　*med.*　silicosis (a disease)

矽钢 xīgāng　silicon steel

郗

Xī　a surname

悕

xī　see below

悕惶 xīhuáng　*formal*　vexed; troubled

悕悕 xīxī　*formal*　vexed; troubled

茜

xī　used in women's names——see also qiàn

唏

xī　*formal*　sigh

唏里呼噜 xīlihūlū　same as 稀里呼噜 xīlihūlū

唏里哗啦 xīlihuālā　same as 稀里哗啦 xīlihuālā

唏嘘 xīxū　same as 歔欷 xīxū

奚

xī　① *formal*　why; how ② (Xī) a surname

奚落 xīluò　scoff at; taunt; gibe at: 他就爱～人。He's always gibing at (*or* making gibes about) others. / 我被他～了一顿。I was scoffed at by him.

奚幸 xīxìng　same as 傒倖 xīxìng

牺(犧)

xī　*formal*　a beast of a uniform colour for sacrifice; sacrifice: ～牛 sacrificial ox

牺牲 xīshēng　① a beast slaughtered for sacrifice; sacrifice ② sacrifice oneself; die a martyr's death; lay down one's life: 英勇～ die a heroic death / 他为了救别人～了自己的宝贵生命。He sacrificed (*or* gave) his life to rescue another. ③ sacrifice; give up; do sth. at the expense of: ～个人利益 sacrifice one's personal interests / ～质量而去追求数量是错误的。It is wrong to sacrifice quality to quantity. / 老张～休息时间为村里赶修脱粒机。Lao Zhang gave up his spare time to repair the village thresher.

牺牲品 xīshēngpǐn　victim; prey

牺尊 xīzūn　an ancient wine vessel (often in the shape of an ox)

息

xī　① breath: 战斗到最后一～ fight to one's last breath ② news: 信息 xìnxī ③ cease; stop: 风止雨～。The wind subsided and the rain stopped. / 生命不～, 战斗不止 fight as long as one breathes; go on fighting till one breathes one's last ④ rest: 歇息 xiēxi / 作息 zuòxī ⑤ grow; multiply: 蕃息 fánxī ⑥ interest: 年息 niánxī / 无息 wúxī ⑦ *formal*　one's children: 子息 zǐxī

息兵 xībīng　cease fire

息肩 xījiān　*formal*　rest one's shoulders——free oneself from certain responsibilities

息交绝游 xījiāo-juéyóu　shut oneself in and cut oneself off from social life

息率 xīlù　a fixed rate of interest; interest rate

息男 xīnán　a son of one's own

息怒 xīnù　cease to be angry; calm one's anger

息女 xīnǚ　a daughter of one's own

息票 xīpiào　interest coupon

息钱 xīqián　interest (money)

息肉 xīròu　*med.*　polyp; polypus

息事宁人 xīshì-níngrén　① patch up a quarrel ② give way to avoid trouble; gloss things over to stay on good terms: 我们的人恐怕他们捣乱, 为了～, 便放他们进去了。We were afraid they'd disturb the audience with the racket they were making, so we let them in, just to keep them quiet.

息讼 xīsòng　drop a lawsuit

息息相关 xīxī xiāngguān　(also 息息相通 xīxī xiāngtōng) be closely linked; be closely bound up

息影 xīyǐng　(also 息景 xīyǐng) *formal*　retire into private life: ～银坛 retire from the screen

息战 xīzhàn　cease fire; stop fighting

浙 xī *formal* wash rice

浙沥 xīlì *onom.* the sound of a light rain, a breeze, falling leaves, etc.: 雨声～。The rain went pitter-pattering.

浙飒 xīsà *onom.* the sound of a light wind, rain, etc.: 风吹得杨树叶浙浙飒飒直响。The wind set the poplar leaves a-rustling.

惜 xī ① cherish; value highly; use sparingly; care for tenderly: ～寸阴 value every bit of time; make good use of every moment ② spare; grudge; stint: 吝惜 lìnxī ③ have pity on; feel sorry for: 怜惜 wǎnxī

惜别 xībié be reluctant to part; hate to see sb. go: 依依～ be reluctant to part / 老师们怀着～的心情，送走了毕业同学。The teachers reluctantly parted with the graduates.

惜老怜贫 xīlǎo-liánpín have compassion for the old and the poor

惜力 xīlì be sparing of one's energy; not do one's best: 小张干活从不～。Xiao Zhang never spares himself in his work.

惜墨如金 xī mò rú jīn (of a painter, calligrapher, or writer) use ink as if it were gold—work with scrupulous care: 那些了不得的作家，谨严入骨，～，要把一生的作品，只删存一个或者三四个字。(鲁迅) Some important writers are so strict with themselves, so sparing of ink, that they like to pare down the work of a lifetime to three or four words.

惜售 xīshòu be loath to sell

惜指失掌 xīzhǐ-shīzhǎng stint a finger and lose a hand—try to save a little only to lose a lot; spoil the ship for a ha'p'orth of tar

烯 xī see below

烯烃 xītīng *chem.* alkene

硒 xī *chem.* selenium (Se)

晞 xī *liter.* ① dry: 晨露未～ the morning dew has not yet dried—early in the morning ② the first light of day; daybreak: 东方未～ the east is not yet red—before daybreak

欷 xī see below

欷歔 xīxū *formal* sob or sigh: 相对～ stare at each other, sobbing

悉[1] xī all; entire: 悉心 xīxīn / 悉数 xīshù

悉[2] xī know; learn; be informed of: 熟悉 shúxī / 获悉 huòxī

悉力 xīlì go all out; spare no effort: 定～相助。I will do all I can to help you.

悉数 xīshǔ *formal* enumerate in full detail: 不可～ too many to enumerate

悉数 xīshù *formal* all; every single one: ～奉还 return all that has been borrowed or taken away

悉心 xīxīn devote all one's attention; take the utmost care: ～研究 devote oneself to the study of sth. / ～照料病人 take the utmost care of the patient

晰(晳) xī clear; distinct: 明晰 míngxī / 清晰 qīngxī

傒 xī see below

傒倖 xīxìng *old* be vexed; be worried

翕 xī *formal* ① amiable and compliant ② furl;

fold; shut: ～张 furl and unfurl; close and open

翕动 xīdòng *formal* (of lips, nostrils, etc.) open and close; quiver: 他的嘴唇～着，可已经说不出话来。He kept moving his lips but could not utter a word. / 受了伤的小鸟～了几下翅膀就死了。With a few flaps of its wings, the wounded bird died.

翕然 xīrán *formal* (of opinions, actions, etc.) be in unison; be in harmony: 舆论～。Public opinion is unanimous.

稀 xī ① rare; scarce; uncommon: 物以稀为贵 wù yǐ xī wéi guì / 稀少 xīshǎo ② sparse; scattered: 月明星～。The moon is bright and the stars are few. / 他的头发长得特别～。He has very thin hair. / 这块地的麦苗太～。The wheat seedlings in this field are too sparse. ③ watery; thin: 粥太～了。This gruel is too thin. / 我想喝点儿～的。I'd like to have some liquid food.

稀薄 xībó thin; rare: 山顶空气～。The air at the top of the mountain is thin.

稀饭 xīfàn rice or millet gruel; porridge

稀罕 xīhan same as 希罕 xīhan

稀客 xīkè a rare visitor

稀拉 xīlā ① sparse; scanty; thinly scattered: 几根～的枯草 a few withered grass scattered here and there ② *dial.* slovenly; sloppy; slack: 作风～ lax

稀烂 xīlàn ① completely mashed; pulpy: 肉煮得～。The meat was cooked to a pulp. ② (also 稀巴烂 xībā-làn) smashed to pieces (or smithereens); broken to bits: 鸡蛋掉在地上，摔了个～。The egg fell on the ground and smashed. / 敌人碉堡被打得～。The enemy blockhouse was smashed to smithereens.

稀朗 xīlǎng (of lights or stars) sparse or scattered but bright

稀里呼噜 xīlihūlū *onom. inf.* the sound of snoring, guzzling porridge, etc.: 他端起那大碗粥，～地喝起来。He took up that big bowl of porridge and started guzzling it down at once.

稀里糊涂 xīlihútú ① not knowing what one is about; muddleheaded: 这道算题他讲了两遍，我还是～的。He explained the problem twice, but I was none the wiser. ② careless; casual; perfunctory: 这个提案没经过认真讨论，就～地通过了。The motion was carried perfunctorily, without any adequate discussion.

稀里哗啦 xīlihuālā *inf.* ① *onom.* the sound of rain or of sth. falling down: 雨～下了起来。The rain came down in sheets (or came pouring down). / 院墙～倒了下来。The courtyard walls fell with a crash. ② badly battered; broken to pieces; utterly shattered: 大厅里的摆设给打了个～。All the furnishings in the hall were shattered into splinters. / 这一回咱们定要把他们打个～。This time we'll beat them hollow.

稀料 xīliào solvent or diluent

稀溜溜 xīliūliū (of porridge, soup, etc.) very thin

稀落 xīluò ① become sparse; be thinning: 她的头发～了。Her hair is thinning out. / 枪声～了。The gunfire dwindled off. ② sparse; scattered; thin: 小河边只有几株～的柳树。There are only a few scattered willow trees by the stream.

稀奇 xīqí same as 希奇 xīqí

稀缺 xīquē in short supply; scarce; in pressing demand: ～商品 goods in short supply

稀少 xīshǎo few; rare; scarce: 人口～ be sparsely populated / 街上行人～。There were few people in the street.

稀释 xīshì dilute: 应该把柠檬汁～一下。You are supposed to dilute the lemon juice with water.

稀释测定 xīshì cèdìng *chem.* dilution metering

稀释剂 xīshìjì *chem.* diluent; thinner

稀疏 xīshū (of objects, sounds, etc.) few and scattered;

few and far between; thin; sparse: 〜的晨星 a few scattered morning stars ／ 〜的头发 thin hair; sparse hair ／ 〜的枪声 scattered shots; sporadic firing ／ 林木〜。The woods are sparse.

稀松 xīsōng ① sloppy; lax: 这活儿干得〜。This is sloppy work. ／ 他们干起活儿来，哪个也不〜。When they set to work, not one of them is lax. ② unimportant; trivial: 别把这些〜的事放在心上。Don't take such trivial matters to heart. ③ loose; porous: 这土够〜的。This soil is loose enough.

稀汤寡水 xītāng-guǎshuǐ (of porridge, soup, etc.) watery; thin and tasteless

稀土金属 xītǔ jīnshǔ *chem.* rare-earth metal

稀土元素 xītǔ yuánsù *chem.* rare-earth element

稀稀拉拉 xīxilālā (also 稀稀落落 xīxiluòluò) ① sparse; thinly scattered: 这块地的庄稼怎么长得这么〜的? How is it that the crops on this plot are so sparse? ／ 天上只有〜的几颗晨星。There were only a few scattered stars in the morning sky. ／ 看这场球赛的〜，没有几个人。The ball game was poorly attended. ② slack; remiss: 昨天的大会开得〜，真没劲。Yesterday's meeting was a dull affair.

稀有 xīyǒu rare; unusual: 十月下雪在这儿并不是〜的事。Snow in October is not unusual around here.

稀有金属 xīyǒu jīnshǔ *chem.* rare metal

稀有元素 xīyǒu yuánsù *chem.* rare element

稀糟 xīzāo *dial.* very bad: 你把事情弄了个〜。You have made a mess of things.

稀珍 xīzhēn same as 希珍 xīzhēn

腊 xī *arch.* dried meat ——see also là

犀 xī *zool.* rhinoceros

犀角 xījiǎo rhinoceros horn

犀利 xīlì sharp; incisive; trenchant: 〜的目光 sharp eyes ／ 谈锋〜 be incisive in conversation ／ 文笔〜 have or wield a trenchant pen

犀鸟 xīniǎo hornbill

犀牛 xīniú common name for 犀 xī

溪 xī a small stream; brook; rivulet

溪涧 xījiàn mountain stream

溪流 xīliú brook; rivulet

锡¹ xī *chem.* tin; stannum (Sn)

锡² xī *formal* grant; bestow

锡伯族 Xībózú the Xibe (Sibo) nationality, or the Xibes (Sibos), distributed over the Xinjiang Uygur Autonomous Region and Liaoning Province

锡箔 xībó tinfoil paper (formerly used as funeral offerings)

锡匠 xījiang tinsmith

锡金 Xījīn Sikkim

锡剧 xījù Wuxi opera, a local opera popular in southern Jiangsu and Shanghai

锡矿 xīkuàng tin ore

锡镴 xīla *dial.* ① tin solder; soldering tin ② tin

锡兰肉桂 xīlán ròuguì Ceylon cinnamon (*Cinnamomum zeylanicum*)

锡石 xīshí *min.* cassiterite; tinstone

锡杖 xīzhàng Buddhist abbot's staff

锡纸 xīzhǐ tinfoil; silver paper

裼 xī *formal* unbutton or divest one's upper garment

皙 xī *formal* fair-skinned; light-complexioned: 白皙 báixī

傒 xī *arch.* ① wait ② same as 蹊 xī

熄 xī ① extinguish; put out: 〜灯 put out the light ② (of a fire, light, etc.) go out; die out: 火〜了。The fire has gone out.

熄灯号 xīdēnghào lights-out; taps

熄风 xīfēng *Chin. med.* relieve dizziness, high fever, infantile convulsions, epilepsy, etc.

熄火 xīhuǒ ① (of fuel, a stove, etc.) stop burning; die out ② (of an engine, etc.) stop working; go dead ③ stop (fuel) from burning; stop (an engine, etc.)

熄灭 xīmiè (of a fire, light, etc.) go out; die out: 篝火〜。The campfire died out. ／ 把灯〜 put out the light

豨 xī *arch.* pig; hog

豨莶 xīxiān *bot.* common St. Paulswort (*Siegesbeckia orientalis*)

熙 xī ① bright; sunny ② prosperous ③ gay; merry

熙和 xīhé ① *formal* congenial and happy ② pleasantly warm; genial: 〜的南风 a genial wind from the south

熙来攘往 xīlái-rǎngwǎng same as 熙熙攘攘 xīxī-rǎngrǎng

熙熙攘攘 xīxīrǎngrǎng bustling with activity; with people bustling about: 马路上〜的尽是人。The pavement was packed with jostling crowds. ／ 集市上人们〜，好不热闹。The country fair was busy with people coming and going all the time.

蜥 xī see below

蜥蜴 xīyì lizard

僖 xī *formal* happy

嘻 xī ① *interj. formal* (used when exclaiming in admiration, wonder, etc.): 〜，技至此乎! How wonderful! What superb skill! ② *onom.* the sound of merry laughter: 〜〜地笑 giggle

嘻和 xīhe *inf.* ① affable looks and soft words: 你去递个〜儿，他就会答应的。Be pleasant to him and he will agree. ② please sb. with affable looks and soft words

嘻闹 xīnào same as 嬉闹 xīnào

嘻皮笑脸 xīpí-xiàoliǎn same as 嬉皮笑脸 xīpí-xiàoliǎn

嘻嘻哈哈 xīxihāhā laughing and joking; laughing merrily; mirthful

嘻笑 xīxiào same as 嬉笑 xīxiào

膝 xī knee: 双〜跪下 kneel on both knees ／ 左 (右) 〜 the left (right) knee

膝盖 xīgài common name for 膝 xī

膝盖骨 xīgàigǔ another name for 髌骨 bìngǔ

膝关节 xīguānjié knee joint

膝腱 xījiàn patellar tendon

膝腱反射 xījiàn fǎnshè *physiol.* patellar reflex; knee jerk

膝上型文字处理机 xīshàngxíng wénzìchǔlǐjī lap-top word processor; lap-top

膝下 xīxià *old* ① at one's knees (used in saying whether one has children or not): 〜无子 have no son ／ 〜一儿一女 have a son and a daughter ② (used in the salutations of letters to one's parents or grandparents): 父亲大人〜 Dear Father

膝行 xīxíng *formal* move forward on one's knees (in submission, supplication, etc.); grovel; crawl

膝痒搔背 xī yǎng sāo bèi not scratch at the itch; not scratch where it itches—fail to handle a matter prop-

erly; miss the point; miss fire

嬉 xī *formal* play; sport

嬉和 xīhe same as 嬉和 xīhe

嬉闹 xīnào laugh and frolic: 姑娘们～了好一阵。The girls laughed and frolicked for a long time.

嬉皮士 xīpíshì hippie; hippy

嬉皮笑脸 xīpí-xiàoliǎn grinning cheekily; smiling and grimacing

嬉耍 xīshuǎ play; sport; frolic: 孩子们光着脚在河边～。The kids were playing barefoot by the riverside.

嬉戏 xīxì *formal* play; sport: 湖面上鸭群在～。Ducks are sporting on the lake.

嬉笑 xīxiào be laughing and playing: 孩子们的～声 the happy laughter of children at play

嬉笑怒骂 xīxiào-nùmà laughing merrily or cursing angrily: ～，皆成文章。Anything, from a merry laugh to an angry curse, can make good writing.

嬉游曲 xīyóuqū *mus.* divertimento

嗋 xī *arch.* ① same as 吸 xī ② contract; draw back

嗋动 xīdòng same as 翕动 xīdòng

窸 xī see below

窸窣 xīsū *onom.* a succession of slight, soft sounds, as of leaves, silks, papers, etc.; rustle

熹 xī *liter.* dawn; brightness

熹微 xīwēi *liter.* (of morning sunlight) dim; pale

榽 xī see 木犀(木榽) mùxi

螅 xī see 水螅 shuǐxī

歙 xī *formal* inhale

蹊 xī *formal* footpath ——see also qī

蹊径 xījìng *formal* path; way

螅 xī see below

螅蟀 xīshuài cricket (an insect)

螅蟀草 xīshuàicǎo *bot.* yard grass

谿 xī *formal* ① same as 溪 xī ② see 勃谿 bóxī

谿谷 xīgǔ *formal* valley

谿壑 xīhè *formal* gorge; gully; ravine (often fig.): ～之心 insatiable desire or greed

谿卡 xīkǎ a plantation belonging to an official, a slave-owner, or a temple in Tibet before the democratic reform

谿刻 xīkè *formal* scathing; mean

羲 Xī see 伏羲 Fú Xī

醯 xī *formal* vinegar

巇 xī see 险巇 xiǎnxī

曦 xī *formal* sunlight (usu. of early morning): 晨曦 chénxī

曦光 xīguāng morning sunlight

騱 xī see below

騱鼠 xīshǔ another name for 小家鼠 xiǎojiāshǔ

习 (習) xí ① practise; exercise; review: 自习 zìxí / 复习 fùxí ② get accustomed to; be used to; become familiar with: ～闻 often hear / 不～水性 be not good at swimming ③ habit; custom; usual practice: 积习 jīxí / 陋习 lòuxí ④ (Xí) a surname

习兵 xíbīng *formal* ① undergo military training ② be versed in military affairs

习非成是 xí fēi chéng shì get used to what is wrong and regard it as right

习惯 xíguàn ① be accustomed to; be used to; be inured to: 他～早起。He is used to getting up early. / 我已经～了北方的气候。I've become accustomed to the northern climate. / 这样潮湿的天气我实在不～。I just can't get used to this damp weather. ② habit; custom; usual practice: 从小培养劳动～ cultivate from childhood the habit of working with one's own hands / 别养成抽烟的～。Don't get into the habit of smoking. / 破除旧～，树立新风尚 break down outmoded customs and establish new ones / ～势力 force of habit

习惯成自然 xíguàn chéng zìrán once you form a habit, it comes natural to you; habit becomes second nature

习惯法 xíguànfǎ common law; customary law

习好 xíhào an inveterate habit

习见 xíjiàn commonly seen (thing or sight): ～的现象 a common sight

习气 xíqì a bad habit; bad practice: 官僚～ habitual practice of bureaucracy; bad bureaucratic habits / 流氓～ hooliganism

习染 xírǎn *formal* ① contract (a bad habit); fall into a bad habit of ② a bad habit

习尚 xíshàng common practice; custom

习俗 xísú custom; convention

习题 xítí exercises (in school work)

习习 xíxí (of a wind) blow gently: 微风～。A gentle breeze is blowing.

习性 xíxìng habits and characteristics: 熊猫的～ the habits and characteristics of the giant panda

习焉不察 xí yān bù chá too accustomed to sth. to call it in question

习以为常 xí yǐ wéi cháng be used (or accustomed, inured) to sth.: 渐渐地人们对这种现象也～了。Gradually people got used to it.

习艺 xíyì learn a trade, skill, handicraft, etc.

习用 xíyòng habitually use

习用语 xíyòngyǔ (also 习语 xíyǔ) idiom

习与性成 xí yǔ xìng chéng habit becomes second nature

习字 xízì practise penmanship; do exercises in calligraphy

习字帖 xízìtiè copybook; calligraphy model

习作 xízuò ① do exercises in composition ② an exercise in composition, drawing, etc.

席¹ (蓆) xí mat: 一领～ a mat

席² xí ① seat; place: 入席 rùxí / 退席 tuìxí ② seat (in a legislative assembly): 该党在议会选举中失去了十五～。That party lost 15 seats in the parliamentary election. ③ feast; banquet; dinner: 宴席 yànxí ④ *m.*: 一～酒 a banquet / 一～话 a talk (with sb.); a conversation ⑤ (Xí) a surname

席不暇暖 xí bù xiá nuǎn not sit long enough to warm the seat; be in a tearing hurry; be constantly on the go

席次 xícì the order of seats; seating arrangement; one's

place among the seats arranged: 按指定～入座 take one's assigned seat; sit down in one's place

席地 xídì have a mat on the ground; (sit or lie) on the ground: ～而坐 sit on the ground

席间 xíjiān at or during the feast: ～宾主频频举杯。 Again and again the host and guests raised their glasses during the feast.

席卷 xíjuǎn ① roll up like a mat; carry everything with one; take away everything: ～而去 make off with everything that one can lay hands on ② sweep across; engulf: 暴风雨～大草原。 A blizzard swept across the prairie. / 一九二九年一场空前的经济危机～了整个资本主义世界。 In 1929, an economic crisis of unprecedented dimensions engulfed the entire capitalist world.

席梦思 xímèngsī Simmons (a transliteration); innerspring mattress

席面 xímiàn the dishes served at a feast

席棚 xípéng mat shed; mat hoarding

席位 xíwèi seat (at a conference, in a legislative assembly, etc.)

席子 xízi *dial.* mat

袭¹（襲） xí make a surprise attack on; raid: 花气～人。 The fragrance of flowers assails one's nose.

袭²（襲） xí ① follow the pattern of; carry on as before: 因袭 yīnxí / 抄袭 chāoxí ② *m. formal* a suit or set (of clothes): 一～棉衣 a set of cotton-padded clothes (consisting of trousers and a coat)

袭夺 xíduó take by surprise

袭封 xífēng inherit a feudal title (of nobility)

袭击 xíjī ① make a surprise attack on; attack by surprise: ～敌军阵地 make a surprise attack on the enemy positions / 沿海一带受到台风的～。 The coastal areas were hit by a typhoon. ② a surprise attack; raid: 敌人向我们发动了一次突然～。 The enemy launched a surprise attack on us.

袭爵 xíjué same as 袭封 xífēng

袭取¹ xíqǔ take by surprise

袭取² xíqǔ take over (something that has long been used in the past): 后人～这个故事, 写成了戏。 Later people adapted this story for the stage.

袭扰 xírǎo *mil.* harass; attack repeatedly: ～敌军 harass the enemy troops

袭用 xíyòng take over (something that has long been used in the past): ～古方 take over an age-old recipe / ～老谱 follow old practice

袭占 xízhàn take (a place) by surprise

媳 xí daughter-in-law

媳妇 xífù ① son's wife; daughter-in-law ② the wife of a relative of the younger generation: 侄媳妇 zhíxífu / 孙媳妇 sūnxífu

媳妇儿 xífur *dial.* ① wife: 你～ your wife ② a young married woman: 这小～长得甚好标致! How pretty this young woman is!

隰 xí low marshy land; swamp

檄 xí ① (a literary genre) a war proclamation setting forth the purpose of the expedition and enumerating the crimes of the enemy: 骆宾王《为徐敬业讨武曌～》 Luo Binwang's "Xi (War Proclamation) for Xu Jingye's Expedition Against Wu Zhao" (i.e. Wu Zetian 武则天) ② *formal* send such a war proclamation to sb., or denounce sb. in it: 陈琳之～豫州, 壮有骨鲠, …钟会～蜀, 征验甚明, 桓公～胡, 观衅尤切。(刘勰《文心雕龙》) Chen Lin's *xi* (war proclamation) against Cao

Cao（曹操）is marked with strength and courage;… Zhong Hui, in his *xi* to the generals in Shu, cited his evidence convincingly, and the *xi* of Huan Wen（桓温）against the barbarians is even more telling in recounting their ruthlessness.

檄书 xíshū war proclamation

檄文 xíwén war proclamation

xǐ

洗 xǐ ① wash; bathe: ～衣服 wash clothes / ～伤口 bathe a wound; apply wash to a wound / 袜子没～干净。 The socks have not been washed clean. / 用肥皂～～手 wash one's hands with soap ② baptize: 受洗 shòuxǐ ③ redress; right: ～冤 right a wrong; redress a grievance ④ kill and loot; sack: ～城 massacre the inhabitants of a captured city ⑤ *photog.* develop; process: ～胶卷 develop an exposed film / ～相片 process a photo / 照片～出来了。 The photos have been processed. ⑥ clear (a recording, etc.); erase: 那段讲话的录音已经～了。 The recording of the talk has been erased. ⑦ shuffle (cards, etc.): 这牌没～开。 The cards weren't shuffled properly. ⑧ a small vessel containing water for washing writing brushes: 笔洗 bǐxǐ ——see also Xiǎn

洗不掉 xǐbudiào can't be washed off; can't wash out: 衣服上的这块墨迹～。 I can't get rid of this ink stain on my coat. *or* This ink stain didn't wash out.

洗尘 xǐchén give a dinner of welcome (to a visitor from afar)

洗涤 xǐdí wash; cleanse

洗涤槽 xǐdícáo washing tank; sink

洗涤剂 xǐdíjì detergent

洗涤器 xǐdíqì washing appliance; washer; scrubber

洗涤塔 xǐdítǎ *chem.* washing tower

洗耳恭听 xǐ ěr gōng tīng listen with respectful attention

洗发剂 xǐfàjì shampoo

洗剂 xǐjì lotion; wash

洗碱 xǐjiǎn same as 洗盐 xǐyán

洗劫 xǐjié loot; sack: 屋子里的东西被匪徒们～一空。 The bandits made off with everything in the house.

洗井 xǐjǐng *petroleum* flushing

洗礼 xǐlǐ ① baptism ② a severe test: 炮火的～ a baptism of fire / 受过战斗的～ have gone through the test of battle

洗脸盆 xǐliǎnpén washbasin; washbowl

洗练 xǐliàn (also 洗炼 xǐliàn) succinct; clear: 文笔～。 The language is very succinct. / 剧情处理得很～。 The plot is well-knit.

洗煤 xǐméi coal washing

洗煤厂 xǐméichǎng coal washery; coal cleaning plant

洗面膏 xǐmiàngāo (facial) cleansing cream

洗牌 xǐpái shuffle cards; make the pack: 该你～了。 Your turn to make (the pack).

洗片 xǐpiàn *photog.* develop a film or process a photo

洗片机 xǐpiànjī developing machine

洗染店 xǐrǎndiàn cleaners and dyers; laundering and dyeing shop

洗三 xǐsān give a baby a bath on the third day after its birth (an old Chinese custom)

洗手不干 xǐshǒu bù gàn ① (of a thief, etc.) stop doing wrong and reform oneself ② wash one's hands of sth.

洗手间 xǐshǒujiān toilet; lavatory; washroom; rest room

洗刷 xǐshuā ① wash and brush; scrub: ～地板 scrub the floor ② wash off; clear oneself of (opprobrium,

stigma, guilt, etc.): ～耻辱 clear oneself of opprobrium

洗涮 xǐshuàn　rinse: 把蔬菜放在自来水龙头下～干净。 Give the vegetables a good rinse with running water.

洗头 xǐtóu　wash one's hair; shampoo one's hair; have a shampoo

洗碗机 xǐwǎnjī　dishwasher

洗胃 xǐwèi　*med.* gastric lavage

洗洗涮涮 xǐxǐshuànshuàn　laundering, washing of utensils and other household cleaning jobs

洗心革面 xǐxīn-gémiàn　turn over a new leaf; thoroughly reform oneself

洗选 xǐxuǎn　*min.* ore dressing (by washing)

洗雪 xǐxuě　wipe out (a disgrace); redress (a wrong): ～国耻 wipe out a national disgrace

洗盐 xǐyán　desalinization of soil by flooding or leaching

洗眼杯 xǐyǎnbēi　eyecup

洗眼剂 xǐyǎnjì　*pharm.* eyewash

洗衣板 xǐyībǎn　washboard

洗衣店 xǐyīdiàn　laundry

洗衣粉 xǐyīfěn　laundry detergent (powder); washing powder

洗衣机 xǐyījī　washing machine

洗衣刷 xǐyīshuā　wash brush

洗印 xǐyìn　*photog.* develop and print (photos); process

洗印机 xǐyìnjī　(film) processor

洗澡 xǐzǎo　have (*or* take) a bath; bathe: 我刚洗完澡。 I've just had a bath.

洗澡间 xǐzǎojiān　bathroom

洗澡盆 xǐzǎopén　bathtub

洗濯 xǐzhuó　*formal* wash; cleanse

玺（璽） xǐ　imperial or royal seal: 玉玺 yùxǐ

徙 xǐ　move from one place to another: 迁徙 qiānxǐ

徙居 xǐjū　move house: ～内地 move up-country

徙倚 xǐyǐ　*formal* ① pace up and down ② hesitate; waver

铣 xǐ　mill (metals) ——see also xiǎn

铣床 xǐchuáng　*mech.* milling machine; miller

铣刀 xǐdāo　*mech.* milling cutter

铣工 xǐgōng　① milling (work) ② miller; milling machine operator

喜 xǐ　① happy; delighted; pleased: 心中暗～ secretly feel pleased / ～不自胜 be delighted beyond measure; be beside oneself with joy / 笑在脸上，～在心里 with a smile on one's face and joy in one's heart / ～获丰收 reap a bumper harvest / 华北地区～降瑞雪。 There was a welcome fall of seasonable snow in north China. ② a happy event (esp. wedding); an occasion for celebration: 喜事 xǐshì / 报喜 bàoxǐ ③ *inf.* pregnancy: 有喜 yǒuxǐ ④ be fond of; like; have an inclination for: ～读书 be fond of reading / 猴子性～攀缘。 Monkeys have a natural inclination for climbing.

喜爱 xǐ'ài　like; love; be fond of; be keen on: ～户外活动 be keen on outdoor activities / 我们最～这首歌曲。 We like this song best. / 这花真惹人～。 This flower is really attractive.

喜报 xǐbào　a bulletin of glad tidings: 大红～ a report of happy tidings written on crimson paper / 立功～ a bulletin announcing meritorious service

喜病 xǐbìng　morning sickness

喜冲冲 xǐchōngchōng　look exhilarated; be in a joyful mood

喜出望外 xǐ chū wàng wài　be overjoyed (at an unexpected gain, good news, etc.); be pleasantly surprised:

听说我们队得了冠军，大家～。 We were overjoyed to hear that our team had won the championship.

喜从天降 xǐ cóng tiān jiàng　a heaven-sent fortune; a heavenly blessing—an unexpected piece of good fortune; a gift from the gods

喜蛋 xǐdàn　same as 红蛋 hóngdàn

喜房 xǐfáng　*dial.* ① bridal chamber ② a private room temporarily given over to the delivery of a baby

喜封 xǐfēng　*old* gift envelope (enclosed with money, given on a happy occasion)

喜光植物 xǐguāngzhíwù　same as 阳性植物 yángxìng zhíwù

喜果 xǐguǒ　① wedding fruits (assorted nuts and dried fruits served to guests on the occasion of a wedding) ② *dial.* same as 喜糖 xǐtáng ③ *dial.* same as 红蛋 hóngdàn

喜好 xǐhào　like; love; be fond of; be keen on: 她从小就～音乐。 She's been a music lover since childhood.

喜欢 xǐhuan　① like; love; be fond of; be keen on: ～看电视 like watching TV / 我～热闹。 I like company. / 这孩子真讨人～。 This is a lovable child. / 她最不～吹吹拍拍。 She loathes boasting and flattery. ② happy; elated; filled with joy: 听到胜利的消息好不～ become elated at the news of victory / 快把这好消息告诉奶奶，让她老人家～～。 Tell Grandma the good news quick. She'll be delighted to hear it.

喜酒 xǐjiǔ　drinks offered to guests at a wedding; wedding feast: 什么时候喝你们的～啊? When's your wedding? *or* When do I wish you joy? / 吃～ attend a wedding feast or any other kind of wedding celebration

喜剧 xǐjù　comedy

喜剧演员 xǐjù yǎnyuán　comedian

喜联 xǐlián　wedding couplets; wedding scrolls

喜马拉雅山 Xǐmǎlāyǎshān　the Himalayas

喜眉笑眼 xǐméi-xiàoyǎn　be all smiles; be smiling all over

喜娘 xǐniáng　a woman employed to attend to the bride's wants on her wedding day

喜怒哀乐 xǐ-nù-āi-lè　happiness, anger, grief and joy—the gamut of human feeling

喜怒无常 xǐ-nù wúcháng　be subject to changing moods: 他这个人～。 He is a man of moods.

喜期 xǐqī　the happy occasion—wedding day: ～已近，得加紧准备。 You must speed up your preparations, as it will soon be your wedding day.

喜气 xǐqì　a cheerful atmosphere or countenance: 满脸～ a face beaming with joy

喜气洋洋 xǐqìyángyáng　full of joy; jubilant: 农民们～庆丰收。 The farmers are jubilantly celebrating their bumper harvest.

喜钱 xǐqián　*old* tips given on a happy occasion (e.g. a wedding, birthday celebration, etc.)

喜庆 xǐqìng　① joyous; jubilant: 在这～的日子里 on this day of jubilation; on this happy occasion ② a happy event or occasion

喜鹊 xǐque　*zool.* magpie

喜人 xǐrén　give pleasure and satisfaction; be gratifying or satisfactory: 取得～的成果 achieve satisfactory results / 形势～。 The situation is gratifying. / 好一派～的丰收景象! What a fine sight this good harvest is! / 麦苗长势～。 The wheat is coming on beautifully.

喜色 xǐsè　a happy expression; a joyful look: 面有～ wear a happy expression

喜上眉梢 xǐ shàng méishāo　be radiant with joy; look very happy

喜事 xǐshì　① a happy event; a joyous occasion: 瞧你这么高兴，有什么～? You look so happy. What's the good news? ② marriage; wedding: 什么时候办～? When will the marriage (*or* wedding) take place?

喜堂　xǐtáng　wedding hall

喜糖　xǐtáng　wedding sweets (*or* candies): 吃～ have wedding sweets—attend a wedding celebration

喜帖　xǐtiě　*old* wedding invitation card

喜闻乐见　xǐwén-lèjiàn　love to see and hear: 人民大众～的作品 literary and artistic works loved by the people

喜相　xǐxiang　*dial.* kindly; affable; amiable: 这姑娘不算好看,可是总那么～。The girl is not exactly pretty, but she always has a kindly smile for you.

喜笑颜开　xǐxiào-yánkāi　a face wreathed in smiles; a face lit up with pleasure: 看着院子里堆成山的粮食,全家人都～。Looking at the grain piled high in the courtyard, the whole family were wreathed in smiles.

喜新厌旧　xǐxīn-yànjiù　love the new and loathe the old—be fickle in one's affections: 唉,你们男人家,我是晓得的,都有～的毛病。Ai! You men, I know you all have the same fault—off with the old love and on with the new.

喜形于色　xǐ xíng yú sè　a face lit up with pleasure; visibly pleased; beaming with happiness: 男女老少,个个～。Men and women, old and young, all beamed with happiness.

喜讯　xǐxùn　happy news; good news; glad tidings

喜洋洋　xǐyángyáng　beaming with joy; radiant

喜雨　xǐyǔ　a seasonable rain; a welcome fall of rain: 普降～ have a widespread seasonable rainfall; have a seasonable fall of rain over a wide area

喜悦　xǐyuè　happy; joyous: 怀着万分～的心情 with a feeling of immeasurable joy / 内心充满了～ be filled with joy

喜幛　xǐzhàng　wedding banner (with congratulatory message)

喜滋滋　xǐzīzī　feeling greatly pleased; filled with joy: 听到这好消息,她心里～的。When she heard the good news, she was immensely pleased.

蒽　xǐ　*formal*　fear; dread; be afraid: 畏蒽 wèixǐ

葸　xǐ　*arch.*　a five-fold increase

屣　xǐ　*formal*　shoe: 敝屣 bìxǐ

禧（釐）　xǐ　auspiciousness; happiness; jubilation: 恭贺新禧 gōnghè xīnxǐ

鱚　xǐ　sand borer (a fish)

xì

戏（戲、戱）　xì　① play; sport: 鸳鸯～水 mandarin ducks sporting in water / 二龙～珠 two dragons playing with a pearl ② make fun of; joke: 戏言 xìyán ③ drama; play; show: 古装～ a drama in ancient costume / 这场～演得很精彩。It was a wonderful performance.

戏班　xìbān　(also 戏班子 xìbānzi) *old* theatrical troupe

戏本　xìběn　(also 戏本子 xìběnzi) *old* opera script

戏出儿　xìchūr　a representation of a theatrical scene (in the form of a poster or a set of figurines)

戏词　xìcí　actor's part or lines

戏单　xìdān　(theatrical) programme

戏德　xìdé　actors' ethics (i.e. one's attitude towards playacting and fellow actors)

戏法　xìfǎ　conjuring; juggling; tricks; magic: ～人人会变,各有巧妙不同。Many are the magicians, but each has his own tricks.

戏份儿　xìfènr　*old* bonus (for performers after a show)

戏馆子　xìguǎnzi　*old* theatre

戏剧　xìjù　drama; play; theatre: 现代～ modern drama; the modern theatre / ～评论 dramatic criticism

戏剧家　xìjùjiā　playwright; dramatist

戏剧界　xìjùjiè　theatrical circles

戏剧性　xìjùxìng　dramatic: 一起富有～的事件 a dramatic event / 政治局势发生了～变化。Spectacular changes in the political situation are taking place.

戏路　xìlù　(also 戏路子 xìlùzi) the range of character types that an actor can portray: ～宽（窄）can portray a wide (narrow) range of character types

戏码　xìmǎ　*old* (theatrical) programme

戏迷　xìmí　theatre fan

戏目　xìmù　(theatrical) programme

戏弄　xìnòng　make fun of; play tricks on; tease; kid: 你别老～人。Don't you go playing tricks on others.

戏票　xìpiào　theatre ticket

戏评　xìpíng　a review of a play

戏曲　xìqǔ　① traditional opera: 地方～ local operas ② singing parts in *chuanqi* 传奇 and *zaju* 杂剧

戏曲片　xìqǔpiàn　a screen adaptation of a traditional or local opera

戏耍　xìshuǎ　tease; play tricks on

戏台　xìtái　*inf.* stage

戏文　xìwén　actor's part or lines

戏匣子　xìxiázi　*dial.* ① gramophone ② radioset

戏箱　xìxiāng　costume trunk

戏笑　xìxiào　① a merry laugh: 一阵～ a burst of merry laughter ② ridicule; jeer at; laugh at

戏谑　xìxuè　banter; crack jokes

戏言　xìyán　joking remarks; pleasantries

戏衣　xìyī　stage costume

戏园子　xìyuánzi　*old* opera house; theatre

戏院　xìyuàn　theatre

戏照　xìzhào　a photo of a person in stage costume

戏装　xìzhuāng　theatrical or stage costume

戏子　xìzi　*old derog.* opera singer; actor: 女～ actress

系¹　xì　① system; series: 太阳～ tàiyángxì / 语系 yǔxì ② department (in a college); faculty: 哲学～ the department of philosophy ③ *geol.* system: 奥陶～ the Ordovician system

系²（係、繫）　xì　(used with abstractions) relate to; bear on: 名誉所～ have a direct bearing on one's reputation / 成败～于此举 stand or fall by this

系³（繫）　xì　① tie; fasten; bind: ～马 tether a horse to a hitching post / 从窖里～几筐土豆上来 hoist up some potatoes from the cellar with the corded basket ② take into custody; put in prison: ～狱 be put in prison ③ feel anxious; be concerned: 系念 xìniàn

系⁴（係）　xì　*formal* be: 其母～山东人。His mother is a native of Shandong. / 纯～试验性质 be purely experimental / 确～实情 be nothing but the truth

——see also jì

系绊　xìbàn　trammels; yoke

系词　xìcí　① *log.* copula ② *linguis.* copulative verb; linking verb

系风捕影　xìfēng-bǔyǐng　same as 捕风捉影 bǔfēng-zhuōyǐng

系缚　xìfù　*formal* tie; bind up; fetter

系累　xìlěi　tie down; burden

系恋　xìliàn　be reluctant to leave; can't bear to part (from sb. or with sth.)

系列　xìliè　series; set: 一～的问题 a series of problems /

一～政策 a whole set of policies / 运载～ vehicle series / 这类产品将发展22个～, 171个新品种。We intend to turn out 171 new varieties of those products in 22 lines.

系列化 xìlièhuà serialize; come out in serial form

系列片 xìlièpiàn serial

系念 xìniàn *formal* be anxious about; worry about; feel concerned about

系谱 xìpǔ *biol.* family; genealogy

系谱树 xìpǔshù *biol.* family tree

系数 xìshù *math.* coefficient: 光学～ optical coefficient

系统 xìtǒng ① system: 灌溉系统 guàngài xìtǒng / 财贸系统 cáimào xìtǒng ② systematic: 作～的研究 make a systematic study / ～地说明 explain in a systematic way / 有～地进行经济体制改革 reform the economic structure systematically

系统分析 xìtǒng fēnxi systems analysis

系统工程 xìtǒng gōngchéng systems engineering

系统化 xìtǒnghuà systematize; systemize

系统性 xìtǒngxìng systematic nature; systematicness; system

厸（屭） xì see 赑屭 bìxì

细

细 xì ① thin; slender: ～铁丝 thin wire / 她们纺的线又～又匀。The thread they spin is thin and smooth. ② in small particles; fine: ～沙 fine sand / 玉米面磨得很～。The corn flour has been ground very fine. ③ thin and soft: ～嗓子 a thready voice ④ fine; exquisite; delicate: ～瓷 fine porcelain (*or* china) / 这几件玉雕做得真～! What exquisite (*or* delicate) jade carvings these are! / 粗粮～作 make delicacies out of coarse food grain ⑤ careful; meticulous; detailed: ～看 examine carefully; scrutinize / ～问 make detailed inquiries; ask about details / 工作做得～ be meticulous in one's work ⑥ minute; trifling: 事无巨～ all matters, big and small / 分工很～ have an elaborate division of labour

细胞 xìbāo cell

细胞壁 xìbāobì cell wall

细胞分裂 xìbāo fēnliè cell division

细胞核 xìbāohé cell nucleus

细胞膜 xìbāomó cell membrane

细胞学 xìbāoxué cytology

细胞质 xìbāozhì cytoplasm

细别 xìbié ① a fine distinction ② make (*or* draw) fine distinctions between

细布 xìbù muslin

细部 xìbù detail (of a drawing)

细长 xìcháng long and thin; tall and slender: ～身材 a tall and slender figure

细齿 xìchǐ *mech.* serration: ～拉刀 serration broach / ～螺母 serrated nut

细大不捐 xì-dà bù juān reject nothing, big or small

细点 xìdiǎn choice refreshments; dainty pastries; delicatesse

细发 xìfa *dial.* fine; smooth: 她的皮肤真～。Her skin is really smooth and soft.

细纺 xìfǎng *text* finespun

细高挑儿 xìgāotiǎor *dial.* ① a tall and slender figure ② a tall, slender person

细工 xìgōng fine workmanship

细故 xìgù trivial matter; trifle: 因～而勃豀终日 bicker over trifles all day

细活 xìhuó a job requiring fine workmanship or meticulous care; skilled work

细火 xìhuǒ slow fire; gentle heat: 用～烤十五分钟 bake over a slow fire for 15 minutes

细嚼慢咽 xìjiáo-mànyàn chew carefully and swallow slowly; chew one's food well before swallowing it

细节 xìjié details; particulars: 讨论计划的～ discuss the details of a plan; go into the particulars of a plan / 通过～描写来表现人物性格 portray a character through the description of detail

细菌 xìjūn germ; bacterium

细菌肥料 xìjūn féiliào bacterial fertilizer

细菌农药 xìjūn nóngyào bacterial pesticide

细菌武器 xìjūn wǔqì bacteriological weapon

细菌性痢疾 xìjūnxìng lìji bacillary dysentery

细菌学 xìjūnxué bacteriology

细菌学家 xìjūnxuéjiā bacteriologist

细菌战 xìjūnzhàn bacteriological warfare

细粮 xìliáng fine food grain (usu. referring to wheat flour and rice)

细脉 xìmài *Chin. med.* thready pulse

细毛 xìmáo fine, soft fur

细毛羊 xìmáoyáng fine-wool sheep

细密 xìmì ① fine and closely woven; close: 质地～ of close texture / 针脚～ in fine close stitches / ～的纹理 a close grain ② meticulous; detailed: ～的分析 a detailed analysis / 现代企业分工～。Modern enterprises have a fine division of labour.

细木工 xìmùgōng ① joinery ② joiner; cabinetmaker

细目 xìmù ① detailed catalogue ② specific item; detail

细嫩 xìnèn delicate; tender: ～的皮肤 delicate skin / 肉质～ tender meat

细腻 xìnì ① fine and smooth ② exquisite; minute: ～的描写 a minute description / ～的表演 an exquisite performance

细皮白肉 xìpí-báiròu (also 细皮嫩肉 xìpí-nènròu) delicate skin and fair complexion: 一身～ be delicate-skinned and fair-complexioned

细巧 xìqiǎo exquisite; dainty; delicate: ～的图案 an exquisite design

细情 xìqíng details: 我不了解～, 所以不好说。I can't say for sure because I don't know the details. / 其中～, 一言难尽。It would take a whole book to give all the details.

细绒线 xìróngxiàn fingering yarn

细柔 xìróu fine and soft; gentle and slender; fine-textured: ～的声音 a fine, gentle voice / ～的皮革 soft and smooth leather / ～的柳枝迎风摇曳。The slender willow branches were swaying gently in the breeze.

细软 xìruǎn jewelry, expensive clothing and other valuables: 席卷～, 逃之夭夭 make off with all the valuables one can lay hands on

细润 xìrùn fine and glossy: 瓷质～。The porcelain is fine and glossy.

细弱 xìruò thin and delicate; slim and fragile: ～的身子 of slim and delicate build / 声音～ a feeble voice

细纱 xìshā *text.* spun yarn

细纱机 xìshājī spinning frame

细声细气 xìshēng-xìqì in a soft voice; soft-spoken: 他举止文雅, 说话～的。He is gentle and soft-spoken.

细石器 xìshíqì *archaeol.* microlith

细石器文化 xìshíqì wénhuà *archaeol.* microlithic culture

细水长流 xìshuǐ cháng liú ① economize to avoid running short ② go about sth. little by little without a letup

细说 xìshuō (also 细谈 xìtán) recount or describe in detail; tell at length: ～分明 give a clear and detailed account / 这是后话, 暂不～。We shan't go into detail about it right now; we'll take it up later.

细碎 xìsuì in small, broken bits: ～的布片 scraps of cloth / ～的脚步声 the sound of light and hurried foot-

steps

细挑 xìtiāo (also 细条 xìtiáo) tall and slender: 〜个儿 a tall, slender figure

细微 xìwēi slight; fine; subtle: 〜的声响 a slight sound / 〜的动作 a scarcely perceptible movement / 〜的变化 slight (or subtle) changes / 〜差别 a fine distinction; a subtle difference

细纹木 xìwénmù fine-grained wood

细细儿 xìxìr ① very thin; very fine: 他把那些木棍儿都削〜的。He pared each of the sticks down to a thin strip. ② very careful: 你〜想想，当时在场的都有哪些人？Now think very carefully who were present at the time.

细小 xìxiǎo very small; tiny; fine; trivial: 〜的零件 small parts (of a machine) / 〜的雨点 tiny raindrops / 〜的事情 trivial matters

细心 xìxīn careful; attentive: 〜观察 carefully observe / 〜护理伤员 nurse the wounded with care / 她做什么事都很〜。She's meticulous in whatever she does. / 他是个人。He's a careful man.

细辛 xìxīn Chin. med. the root of Chinese wild ginger (Asarum sieboldi)

细腰 xìyāo slender waist (esp. of a woman)

细雨 xìyǔ drizzle; fine rain

细语 xìyǔ speak softly; whisper: 低声〜 speak in a soft low voice

细则 xìzé detailed rules and regulations:《中华人民共和国商标法实施〜》Rules for the Implementation of the Trademark Law of the People's Republic of China

细帐 xìzhàng itemized account

细针密缕 xìzhēn-mìlǚ in fine, close stitches—(work) in a meticulous way

细支纱 xìzhīshā text. fine-count yarn

细枝末节 xìzhī-mòjié minor details; nonessentials

细致 xìzhì careful; meticulous; painstaking: 做〜的思想工作 do painstaking ideological work / 她想得很〜。She thought it out in detail. / 这活做得很〜。This is a careful piece of work.

细作 xìzuò old spy; secret agent

阅（闃）
xì formal quarrel; strife: 兄弟阋墙 xiōngdì xì qiáng

舄
xì ① formal shoe ② same as 潟 xì

隙
xì ① crack; chink; crevice: 墙〜 a crack in the wall / 云〜 a rift in the clouds ② gap; interval: 农〜 interval between busy seasons in farming ③ loophole; opportunity: 乘隙 chéngxì ④ discord; rift: 嫌隙 xiánxì

隙地 xìdì unoccupied place; open space

隙罅 xìxià crack; slit; fissure

潟
xì formal salinized soil

潟卤 xìlǔ formal saline-alkali soil

xiā

呷
xiā dial. sip: 〜一口茶 take a sip of tea

虾（蝦）
xiā shrimp: 〜群 a shoal of shrimps

虾兵蟹将 xiābīng-xièjiàng shrimp soldiers and crab generals—ineffective troops; hopeless soldiers

虾干 xiāgān dried shrimps

虾蛄 xiāgū mantis shrimp

虾酱 xiājiàng salted shrimp paste

虾米 xiāmi ① dried, shelled shrimps ② dial. small shrimps

虾皮 xiāpí (also 虾米皮 xiāmipí) dried, unshelled small shrimps

虾仁 xiārén shelled fresh shrimps; shrimp meat

虾油 xiāyóu shrimp sauce

虾子 xiāzǐ shrimp roe (or eggs): 〜酱油 shrimp-roe soy sauce / 〜豆腐 bean curd stewed with shrimp roe

瞎
xiā ① blind: 〜了一只眼 be blind in one eye / 我真〜了眼，把他当做好人了。I was so blind as to take him for a gentleman. ② adv. groundlessly; foolishly; to no purpose: 〜讲 speak groundlessly / 〜花钱 spend money foolishly / 〜干 go it blind / 〜猜 make a wild guess / 〜费劲儿 make a vain effort ③ dial. (of thread, etc.) become tangled: 我的头发〜得梳也梳不开了。My hair's so tangled that it can't be combed out. ④ (of a bullet, grenade, shell, or bomb) fail to explode; be a dud: 炮炮不〜。None of the shells failed to go off (or was a dud). or Every one of the shells went off beautifully.

瞎掰 xiābāi inf. ① talk nonsense ② do stupid things

瞎扯 xiāchě ① talk groundlessly or irresponsibly; talk nonsense: 他尽〜，别信他的。He's just talking nonsense. Don't believe him. ② talk at random about anything under the sun; waffle; natter: 她没说什么正经事，〜了一通就走了。She didn't talk about anything serious. She just chattered away for a while and left.

瞎吹 xiāchuī boast in the most fantastic of terms

瞎话 xiāhuà untruth; lie: 说〜 tell a lie; tell a fib

瞎聊 xiāliáo chat at random about anything under the sun; chat idly: 没事也不能整天地〜啊。Even if you are free, you still shouldn't waste your time chatting the whole day away.

瞎忙 xiāmáng (also 瞎忙活 xiāmánghuo) make a fuss about nothing: 〜了几天，什么也没搞成。For days we made ourselves busy but got nothing done. / 这些日子你干什么呢？—〜。What have you been doing for the last few days?—Nothing much.

瞎蒙 xiāmēng inf. make a wild guess: 他并不知道答案，全是〜上的。He didn't really know the answers. He just made a lucky guess.

瞎奶 xiānǎi ① breasts with sunken nipples ② dry breasts

瞎闹 xiānào (also 瞎胡闹 xiāhúnào) ① act senselessly; mess about ② fool around; be mischievous: 赶快做作业，别〜。Hurry up and get your homework done; don't fool around.

瞎炮 xiāpào ignited dynamite or a fired artillery shell that fails to explode; dud

瞎说 xiāshuō talk groundlessly or irresponsibly; talk nonsense

瞎说八道 xiāshuōbādào same as 胡说八道 húshuōbādào

瞎指挥 xiāzhǐhuī issue confused orders; give arbitrary and impracticable directions; mess things up by giving wrong orders

瞎诌 xiāzhōu dial. make up wild stories; tell cock-and-bull stories

瞎抓 xiāzhuā do things without a plan; go about sth. in a haphazard way: 事先把要带的东西都准备好，免得临时〜。Get everything ready beforehand so that you won't be in a rush when it's time to leave.

瞎字儿不识 xiā zìr bù shí inf. cannot read a single word; be completely illiterate: 他从小没上过学，到现在〜。He's never had any schooling, and even now can't read a single word.

瞎子 xiāzi a blind person

瞎子点灯白费蜡 xiāzi diǎn dēng báifèi là a blind person lighting a candle—a sheer waste

瞎子摸象 xiāzi mō xiàng the blind men sizing up the elephant—take a part for the whole

瞎子摸鱼 xiāzi mō yú a blind person groping for fish—act blindly: 敌人真是～，他要去的地方鬼都没有一个! The enemy are like blind men trying to catch fish with their bare hands. They're rushing to a place that's inhabited by neither man nor ghost!

鰕　xiā same as 虾 xiā

---

xiá

匣　xiá a small box (*or* case); casket: 木～ a wooden box (*or* case) / 买两～点心 buy two boxes of pastries

匣子 xiázi a small box (*or* case); casket: 梳头～ a casket for hairdressing articles

狎　xiá be improperly familiar with; be too close with (usu. a woman)

狎妓 xiájì visit prostitutes; go whoring

狎客 xiákè a frequenter of brothels

狎昵 xiánì be improperly familiar with

侠（俠）　xiá ① a person adept in martial arts and given to chivalrous conduct (in olden times) ② having a strong sense of justice and ready to help the weak; chivalrous

侠骨 xiágǔ *formal* chivalry: ～义胆 chivalry and loyalty

侠客 xiákè (also 侠士 xiáshì) a person adept in martial arts and given to chivalrous conduct (in olden times)

侠义 xiáyì having a strong sense of justice and ready to help the weak; chivalrous: ～心肠 a generous and gallant heart / ～行为 a chivalrous act / ～之士 a chivalrous man

峡（峽）　xiá (usu. used as part of a place name) gorge: 三门～ the Sanmen Gorge / 长江三～ the Three Gorges on the Yangtze

峡谷 xiágǔ gorge; canyon

峡湾 xiáwān *geog.* fiord

狭（狹）　xiá narrow: 坡陡路～. The slope is steep and the path narrow.

狭隘 xiá'ài ① narrow: ～的山道 a narrow mountain path ② (of mind, views, etc.) narrow and limited; parochial: ～的看法 a narrow view / 心胸～ be narrow-minded

狭隘民族主义 xiá'àimínzúzhǔyì narrow nationalism

狭长 xiácháng long and narrow: ～的山谷 a long and narrow valley

狭路相逢 xiálù xiāng féng (of adversaries) meet face to face on a narrow path—come into unavoidable confrontation

狭小 xiáxiǎo narrow and small; narrow: ～的阁楼 a poky attic / 气量～ be intolerant; be narrow-minded / 走出～的圈子 step out of one's narrow circle

狭斜 xiáxié (also 狭邪 xiáxié) *formal* narrow (streets) and crooked (lanes)—brothels: 作～游 visit brothels; go whoring

狭心症 xiáxīnzhèng another name for 心绞痛 xīnjiǎotòng

狭义 xiáyì narrow sense

狭窄 xiázhǎi ① narrow; cramped: ～的走廊 a narrow corridor / ～的胡同 a narrow lane (*or* alley) ② (of mind, experience, etc.) narrow and limited; narrow: 心地～ be narrow-minded / 见识～ be limited in knowledge and narrow in experience ③ *med.* stricture

柙　xiá ① a cage for wild beasts ② prisoner's cage (in former times)

遐　xiá *formal* ① far; distant ② lasting; long: ～龄 advanced age

遐迩 xiá'ěr *formal* far and near

遐迩闻名 xiá'ěr wénmíng be known far and wide; enjoy widespread renown

遐思 xiásī same as 遐想 xiáxiǎng

遐想 xiáxiǎng reverie; daydreaming: 满天的繁星会引起人们无边无际的～。A star-studded sky induces fantastic reveries.

瑕　xiá ① flaw in a piece of jade ② flaw; defect; shortcoming

瑕不掩瑜 xiá bù yǎn yú one flaw cannot mar the jade—small defects cannot obscure great virtues

瑕疵 xiácī flaw; blemish

瑕玷 xiádiàn *formal* blemish; stain; defect

瑕瑜互见 xiá-yú hù jiàn have defects as well as merits; have both strong and weak points

暇　xiá free time; leisure: 有～望即来信。Hope you'll write to me when you have time.

辖¹（鎋、舝）　xiá linchpin

辖²　xiá have jurisdiction over; administer; govern: 省～市 a municipality (*or* city) under the jurisdiction of the provincial government / 下～四个兵团 have four army corps under its command

辖区 xiáqū area under one's jurisdiction

辖制 xiázhì *formal* control

霞　xiá rosy clouds; morning or evening glow: 晚霞 wǎnxiá

霞光 xiáguāng rays of morning or evening sunlight: ～万道 a myriad of sun rays / 彩云万朵，～四射。Rays of sunlight shine through multihued clouds.

霞帔 xiápèi an embroidered tasselled cape worn as part of ceremonial dress by noblewomen in former times

霞石 xiáshí *min.* nepheline

黠　xiá *formal* crafty; cunning: 狡黠 jiǎoxiá

黠慧 xiáhuì *formal* cunning; artful

黠吏 xiálì *formal* a vicious and crafty official

---

xià

下¹　xià ① (used alone, esp. in contrast to 上) below: 上有父母，～有儿女 have parents above and children below—have a large family to take care of / 上至市长，～至一般市民 from the mayor down to the ordinary townspeople ② (used after a preposition) down; downward: 往～看 look down at sth. / 他将帽沿向～拉了拉。He pulled his hat down a little. ③ (used after a noun) under: 树～ under a tree / 山～ at the foot of a hill / 零～五度 five degrees below zero / 在月光～散步 take a walk in the moonlight ④ (used before a noun) lower (in position, rank, or quality): 分为上、中、～三等 divided into three grades: the upper, the middle and the lower / 那本书在书架的最～一层。The book is on the bottom shelf. ⑤ next (in time or order); latter; second: ～次 next time / ～礼拜 next week / ～个世纪 next century / ～两批 the next two batches / ～一

班车 the next bus or train ⑥ the second or the last of three: ～集 Volume Two or Three; Vol. II or III / 这部词典有上、中、～三册。 This dictionary is in three volumes, first, second, and third. / ～半学期 the second (*or* latter) half of the term ⑦ (used before a verb) downward; down: 防止圆木～滑 prevent the logs from rolling down ⑧ (indicating scope, state, condition, etc.): 在党的领导～ under the leadership of the Party / 在这种情况～ in (*or* under) such circumstances / 在同志们的帮助～ with the help of one's comrades ⑨ (used in certain time expressions): 时下 shíxià / 年下 niánxià ⑩ (used after numerals to indicate aspect or direction): 四下 sìxià / 两下里 liǎngxiàli

下² xià ① come or go down from; descend: ～山 descend the mountain; come or go down a mountain / ～楼 descend the stairs; go or come downstairs / ～床 get out of bed / 顺流而～ sail or go downstream ② get off (a conveyance); alight: ～车 get off a car or bus / ～电梯 get off an elevator / ～飞机 get off a plane; alight from a plane ③ (of rain, snow, etc.) come down; fall: ～雨 rain / ～雪 snow / ～雹子了。 It's hailing. / ～雾了。 There's a fog. / ～霜了。 There is frost. / 雪～得很大。 The snow is falling heavily. *or* It's snowing hard. ④ issue (an order, etc.); deliver; send out (an invitation, etc.): ～命令 issue (*or* give) orders / ～请帖 send an invitation / 我们早～过通知了。 We have already sent out notices. ⑤ go to (a place thought of as lower or below): ～地狱 go down to hell / ～馆子 go and eat in a restaurant / 厂长～车间了。 The factory director has gone to the workshop. / 师长～连队去了。 The division commander has gone to the company. ⑥ leave (the stage, field, etc.); exit: 这场戏你从右边的旁门～。 In this scene you are to exit from the right-hand door. / 换人，四号～，三号上。 Substitution, No. 3 for No. 4. ⑦ put in (ingredients of food, fertilizer, poison, capital, etc.); cast: ～作料 put in the condiments; add the ingredients / ～肥料 apply fertilizer / ～面条 put noodles in a pot of boiling water to cook; cook noodles in boiling water / ～网捞鱼 cast a net to catch fish ⑧ play (a board game); make a move (in a board game): ～围棋 play *go* / 该你～了。 Your turn to make a move. ⑨ take down or off; dismantle; unload: ～了俘房的枪 disarm the captured soldier / 把纱窗～下来 take the screen window off / 船上的货还没～完。 The cargo hasn't all been unloaded yet. ⑩ give (a definition, conclusion, etc.): ～定义 give a definition; define / ～决心 make a resolution; determine / ～结论 draw a conclusion ⑪ apply; use: ～力气 put forth strength; make an effort; exert oneself / ～刀 get a knife into sth. ⑫ (of animals) give birth to; drop (a litter); lay (eggs): ～了一窝小猪 give birth to (*or* drop) a litter of piglets ⑬ capture (a city); take: 连～数城 take several cities in succession ⑭ give in: 相持不下 xiāngchí bù xià ⑮ get off (work); get out of (class): ～夜班 come off night duty / 课早～了。 The class has long been dismissed. ⑯ (used in the negative) be less than: 参加大会的不～三千人。 No less than 3,000 people attended the conference.

下³ xià ① m. ⓐ (for verbs of action) stroke; time(s): 钟敲了三～。 The clock struck three times. / 推了我一～ gave me a push / 打了孩子儿～ gave the child two or three slaps / 摇了几～旗子 waved the flag a few times / 敲三～门 give three knocks on the door ⓑ *dial.* (for the capacity of a container): 瓶子里装了半～墨水。 The bottle is half full of ink. / 这么大碗面条，他足足吃了三～。 He guzzled down three big bowlfuls of noodles. ② (used after 两 or 几) what one is good at or capable of: 想不到他还有几～。 I never expected

him to be so capable. / 我就会这么两～。 That's all I can do.

下 ·xià (used as a complement to a verb) ① down: 坐～ sit down / 躺～ lie down / 传～一道命令 send down an order / 走～楼 go downstairs / 跑～山 run down a hill / 她激动得流～了眼泪。 She was moved to tears. ② (indicating the capacity for holding or containing): 坐得～ can seat / 坐不～ cannot seat / 这房间能坐～五十人。 The room can hold (*or* seat) fifty people. / 这么多菜我吃不～。 I can't eat all this food. ③ (indicating the finalizing of an action): 记～地址 write down an address / 打～基础 lay a foundation / 攻～难关 break down a barrier / 准备～必需的材料 get all the necessary materials ready

下巴 xiàba ① the lower jaw ② chin

下巴颏儿 xiàbakēr *inf.* chin

下摆 xiàbǎi the lower hem of a gown, jacket or shirt

下拜 xiàbài make obeisance; kneel down to pay respect; *kowtow*

下班 xiàbān get off work; knock off: 每天下午六点～。 We knock off at six p. m. every weekday.

下板儿 xiàbǎnr *dial.* take down the shutters—start the business of the day

下半辈子 xiàbànbèizi the latter half of one's life; the rest of one's life

下半场 xiàbànchǎng second half (of a game, concert, etc.): ～，客队踢进了一个球。 The visiting team scored one goal in the second half of the game.

下半旗 xià bànqí fly a flag at half-mast

下半晌 xiàbànshǎng *inf.* afternoon: ～我见她来着。 I saw her this afternoon.

下半身 xiàbànshēn the lower part of the body; below the waist

下半天 xiàbàntiān afternoon: 天气预报说～有雨。 The weather forecast predicts rain in the afternoon.

下半夜 xiàbànyè the time after midnight; the latter half of the night

下辈 xiàbèi ① future generations; offspring ② the younger generation of a family

下辈子 xiàbèizi the next life

下本钱 xià běnqián (also 下本儿 xiàběnr) put in time, money and effort; make an investment: 要舍得～培养人才。 Don't begrudge time, money and effort in training qualified personnel.

下笔 xiàbǐ put pen to paper; begin to write or paint: 不知如何～ be at a loss as to how to begin writing or painting / 想好了再～。 Think it out before you put pen to paper.

下笔成章 xiàbǐ chéng zhāng produce a piece of writing as soon as the pen is put to paper (said of a good and fast writer)

下笔千言，离题万里 xiàbǐ qiānyán, lítí wànlǐ a thousand words flow from the pen, but ten thousand *li* away from the theme—write fast and at length but not to the point; long-winded and irrelevant

下边 xiàbian same as 下面 xiàmian

下不来 xiàbulái ① cannot come down: 她的体温～。 Her temperature won't come down. ② cannot be accomplished; won't do: 这道墙没有五千块砖～。 You can't build that wall with less than 5,000 bricks. ③ feel embarrassed: 几句话说得他脸上～。 He was visibly embarrassed at the remarks.

下不来台 xiàbuláitái (also 下不了台 xiàbuliǎotái) be unable to get out of an embarrassing situation; be unable to back down with good grace; be on the spot; feel embarrassed: 给他一个～ put him on the spot / 你的话说得太重，弄得他～了。 Your remarks were much too harsh for him to swallow with good grace.

下不为例　xià bù wéi lì　not to be taken as a precedent; not to be repeated: 就这一回，～。Just this once.

下部　xiàbù　① the lower part ② the lower part of the body

下操　xiàcāo　① have drills: 我们上午～，下午听课。We have drills in the morning and lectures in the afternoon. ② finish drilling: 他刚～回来。He's just back from drill.

下策　xiàcè　a bad plan; an unwise decision; the worst thing to do; a stupid move: 为何出此～? Why do you resort to such an unwise move?

下层　xiàcéng　① lower levels: 深入～ go to lower-level units; go down to the grass-roots level ② lower strata: ～社会 the lower strata of society

下场　xiàchǎng　① go off stage; exit ② leave the playing field or court (in a game)

下场　xiàchang　an end that a person comes to, usu. bad; fate: 遭到可耻～ come to a disgraceful end; meet with an ignominious fate / 搞阴谋诡计的人绝不会有好～。Those who plot and conspire will certainly come to no good end.

下场门　xiàchǎngmén　exit (of a stage)

下场头　xiàchǎngtou　dial.　same as 下场 xiàchang

下车伊始　xià chē yī shǐ　the moment one alights from the official carriage—the moment one takes up a post; immediately on arrival at a new post

下沉　xiàchén　sink; subside; submerge: 敌舰起火～。The enemy warship caught fire and sank. / 潜水艇逐渐～。The submarine gradually submerged. / 地基～。The foundations have subsided.

下乘　xiàchéng　① Buddhism same as 小乘 xiǎochéng ② low order; inferior quality: ～之作 a literary or artistic work of low order or inferior quality

下厨房　xià chúfáng　go to the kitchen (i.e. to cook or to prepare a meal): 今天他要亲自～招待你们。Today he'll treat you to a meal he cooks himself.

下处　xiàchu　one's temporary lodging during a trip: 找到～了没有? Have you found a lodging yet?

下穿交叉　xiàchuānjiāochā　transportation underpass; undercrossing

下船　xiàchuán　① go ashore; disembark ② dial.　get down into a junk; go aboard

下垂　xiàchuí　① hang down; droop: 她软弱无力，双手～。Her hands hung limply. ② med.　prolapse: 子宫～ prolapse of the uterus; metroptosis

下存　xiàcún　(of a sum) remain after deduction: 这笔款子提了两万元，～八万元。Twenty thousand yuan has been drawn from the account and there is still eighty thousand yuan left.

下达　xiàdá　make known (or transmit) to lower levels: ～作战命令 issue orders of operation / 任务已经～。The task has been assigned.

下蛋　xiàdàn　lay eggs: 咱们的鸭子～了。Our ducks are laying. / 那只母鸡下了一百多个蛋了。That hen has laid over a hundred eggs.

下等　xiàděng　of low grade or caste; inferior

下等人　xiàděngrén　old　a person belonging to one of the lower social strata

下地　xiàdì　① go to the fields: ～劳动 go to work in the fields ② leave a sickbed: 他病好多了，现在能～了。He is getting much better now and can get up and move about a bit.

下第　xiàdì　① fail at imperial examinations ② formal low-grade; inferior

下店　xiàdiàn　put up at an inn

下跌　xiàdiē　(of water level, prices, etc.) fall; drop: 黄河水位逐渐～。The water level of the Yellow River is gradually falling. / 导致物价急剧～ cause a sharp drop in prices

下碇　xiàdìng　cast anchor: 船在九江～。The ship anchored at Jiujiang.

下毒　xiàdú　put in poison

下毒手　xià dúshǒu　resort to cruel treachery; strike a vicious blow; lay murderous hands on sb.: 背后～ stab sb. in the back / 对他～ lay murderous hands on him; do him in

下颚　xià'è　① maxilla (of certain arthropods) ② the lower jaw or mandible (of vertebrates)

下法　xiàfǎ　Chin. med.　laxative (or purgative) remedy

下凡　xiàfán　(of gods or immortals) descend to the world

下饭[1]　xiàfàn　① go with rice: 你这两个菜都不喜欢，拿什么～呀? If you don't like either of the two dishes, what are you going to have with your rice? ② go well with rice: 这个菜下酒不～。This dish goes well with wine, but not with rice.

下饭[2]　xiàfàn　dial.　any food served at table other than staple food

下房　xiàfáng　servant quarters; servant's room

下放　xiàfàng　① transfer to a lower level: 权力～ transfer (or delegate) power to lower levels / 企业～ put an enterprise under a lower administrative level ② transfer (cadres, etc.) to work at the grass-roots level or to do manual labour in the countryside or in a factory: ～农村 be transferred to work in the countryside

下放干部　xiàfàng gànbù　a cadre transferred to a lower level to work in the countryside or in a factory

下风　xiàfēng　① leeward: 工业区一般都设在城市的～。Industrial districts are generally situated to the leeward of the cities. ② disadvantageous position: 占～ be at a disadvantage / 暂时处于～ be temporarily at a disadvantage

下疳　xiàgān　med.　chancre (either hard or soft chancre)

下岗　xiàgǎng　come or go off sentry duty

下工　xiàgōng　come or go off work; stop work; knock off: 今天～下得早。We knocked off early today.

下工夫　xià gōngfu　(also 下功夫 xià gōngfu) put in time and energy; concentrate one's efforts: 在技术革新上狠～ devote a lot of time and energy to technical innovation / 你要学好一门外语就要舍得～。If you want to master a foreign language, you must put in a lot of effort. / 改造世界观要在理论联系实际上～。In remoulding one's world outlook, one must concentrate one's efforts on integrating theory with practice.

下官　xiàguān　old　I (used by an official before his superior)

下跪　xiàguì　kneel down; go down on one's knees

下锅　xiàguō　put food in the pot or pan (ready to be cooked): 肉已～。The pork is already in the pot. / 无米～ destitute of rice; starving

下海　xiàhǎi　① go to sea: ～去游泳 go swimming in the sea ② (of fishermen) go fishing on the sea; put out to sea: ～捕鱼 go fishing on the sea / 初次～，难免晕船 You can't help being seasick on your first trip at sea. ③ (of non-professionals in traditional opera) turn professional ④ inf.　engage in trade

下颌　xiàhé　physiol.　the lower jaw

下颌骨　xiàhégǔ　lower jawbone

下怀　xiàhuái　one's heart's desire: 正中下怀 zhèng zhòng xiàhuái

下回　xiàhuí　next time

下级　xiàjí　① lower level: ～服从上级。The lower level is subordinate to the higher level. / ～干部 a subordinate (or junior) cadre / ～机关 a lower-level government office / ～军官 a low-ranking (or junior) officer / ～组织 a subordinate organization ② subordinate: 帮助～解决工作中的问题 help one's subordinates to

solve the problems they encounter in their work

下家 xiàjiā (in mahjong, card games, or in wine games) the player whose turn comes next

下嫁 xiàjià (of a girl of high birth) marry a man of lower social status

下贱 xiàjiàn ① of humble origin; low in social status ② low; mean; degrading: 有些人把劳动看作～的事情。Some people look upon labour as something degrading. /～女人 a cheap woman

下江 xiàjiāng the lower reaches of the Changjiang (Yangtze) River: ～人 a native of one of the provinces on the lower reaches of the Changjiang (Yangtze) River

下降 xiàjiàng descend; go or come down; drop; fall; decline: 飞机开始～。The plane began to descend. /气温显著～。There was a marked drop in the temperature. /药品价格平均～百分之三十七。The prices of medicines dropped 37% on an average. /生产成本逐年～。Production costs come down every year. /出生率～ a decline in the birth rate

下焦 xiàjiāo *Chin. med.* the part of the body cavity below the umbilicus, housing the bladder, kidneys and bowels

下脚[1] xiàjiǎo get a foothold; plant one's foot: 没有～的地方 be unable to gain a footing (or foothold); have nowhere to plant one's foot

下脚[2] xiàjiǎo leftover bits and pieces: ～棉 cotton waste

下脚货 xiàjiǎohuò unsalable leftover goods of inferior quality

下脚料 xiàjiǎoliào leftover bits and pieces (of industrial material, etc.); scrap

下届 xiàjiè the next session of a regular meeting; next (graduating class, etc.): ～会议 the next session of the conference /～毕业生 students graduating next year

下界[1] xiàjiè the world of mortals; the world of man

下界[2] xiàjiè same as 下凡 xiàfán

下劲 xiàjìn exert oneself; go all out: 他学习很～。He works really hard. /要想成功就得下死劲干。You have to go all out if you want to be a success.

下井落石 xià jǐng luò shí (also 下井投石 xià jǐng tóu shí) same as 落井下石 luò jǐng xià shí

下酒 xiàjiǔ ① go with wine: 买点花生米～ buy some peanuts to go with the wine ② go well with wine: 这菜不～。This dish doesn't go very well with wine.

下酒菜 xiàjiǔcài a dish that goes with alcoholic drinks

下颏儿 xiàkēr *dial.* chin

下课 xiàkè get out of class; finish class: ～后再去。Go there after class. /现在～。The class is dismissed. *or* The class is over.

下筷 xiàkuài apply one's chopsticks to the food—start eating

下款 xiàkuǎn ① the name of the donor (as inscribed on a painting or a calligraphic scroll presented as a gift) ② the signature at the end of a letter

下来 xià·lái ① come down: 梯子不牢，快～! Come down at once! The ladder isn't steady. /你自个儿下得来下不来? Can you get down by yourself? ② come down to a place regarded as being lower or below: 昨天省里～两位领导干部。Two leading cadres came down from the provincial capital yesterday. /新任务～了。A new task has fallen on us. /司令部～一道命令。An order has come down from headquarters. ③ (of farm crops) be harvested: 麦子已经～了。The wheat has been harvested. ④ (of a period of time) be over; come to an end: 一年～，他的技术大有提高。After one year's work, his skills have improved a lot.

下来 xià·lái (used as a complement to a verb) ① (indicating motion toward a lower or nearer position)

down (here): 把树上的苹果都摘～。Pick all the apples off the trees. /溪水从山上流～。The stream flows down from the mountain. /扔条绳子～。Throw down a rope. ② (used after a verb of duration) up to the present; till the end (or finish): 古代流传～的寓言 fables handed down from ancient times /所有上夜校的人都坚持～了。All those who joined the evening classes persisted to the end. ③ (used after a verb, expressing completion or finality of an action): 风突然停了～。The wind dropped all of a sudden. /剩～的就这么些了。This is all that's left. /方案今天定得～定不～? Can the plan be finalized today? /四堂课连上～，老师的嗓子都哑了。Four classes in a row made the teacher's voice hoarse. ④ (used after an adjective, indicating increasing degree): 他的声音慢慢低了～。His voice trailed off. /天色渐渐黑～。It was getting darker and darker. /会场刚刚安静～。The audience has just quieted down.

下里巴人 xiàlǐ Bārén Songs of the Rustic Poor (folk songs of the state of Chu)—popular literature or art

下里 xiàlǐ *inf.* (used after numerals): 三～都同意了。The three sides have all agreed.

下联 xiàlián the second (or latter) line of a couplet

下僚 xiàliáo *formal* officials of lower status; subordinates

下列 xiàliè listed below; following: 应注意～几点。Attention should be paid to the following points. /～人员明日上午到校医院体检。All those listed below please come to the school hospital for a checkup tomorrow morning.

下令 xiàlìng give orders; order: 团长～紧急集合。The regiment commander ordered (or gave orders for) an emergency muster.

下流 xiàliú ① lower reaches (of a river): 黄河～ the lower reaches of the Huanghe River ② low-down; mean; obscene; dirty: ～的谩骂 scurrilous attacks; coarse invectives /～的勾当 a base act; a dirty deal /～的玩笑 dirty (or obscene) jests; coarse jokes /～话 obscene (or dirty, foul) language; obscenities

下落 xiàluò ① whereabouts: 打听某人的～ inquire about sb.'s whereabouts /有一件古物现在～不明。The whereabouts of one of the antiques is unknown. /失踪者至今还没有～。We still have no idea of the whereabouts of those missing persons. ② drop; fall: 气球～的地点 the place where the balloon has fallen

下马 xiàmǎ ① get down (or dismount) from a horse ② (of a project, plan, etc.) be discontinued; be given up: 这项工程不能～。This project should not be abandoned. /建钢厂的计划～了。The plan to set up a steel mill here has been abandoned.

下马看花 xiàmǎ kàn huā (also 下马观花 xiàmǎ guānhuā) get off one's horse to look at the flowers—go deep into the realities of life and make thorough investigations

下马威 xiàmǎwēi severity shown by an official on assuming office; the severity of a newly-appointed official: 给他个～ deal him a head-on blow at the first encounter

下面 xiàmian ① below; under; underneath: 大桥～ under the bridge /图表～的说明 the caption below the chart /褥子～铺着一领席。There is a mat underneath the mattress. ② the next in order; following: ～该谁了? Who's next? /～一个 the next one /必须记住～几点。The following points should be borne in mind. /～请老李谈谈。Now we'll ask Lao Li to say something. /这个问题我～还要谈到。I'll come back to this point later on. ③ lower level; subordinate: 细心倾听～的意见 listen carefully to the views of one's subordinates /了解～的情况 find out about how things are at the lower

levels

下奶　xiànǎi　stimulate or increase the secretion of milk (of nursing mothers)

下女　xiànǚ　*old*　a girl of low status; servant girl

下品　xiàpǐn　of the lowest grade or quality

下聘　xiàpìn　(of the bridegroom-to-be's family) send betrothal gifts and money over to the bride

下坡路　xiàpōlù　① a downhill path; a downhill journey ② decline: 走～ go downhill; be on the decline

下铺　xiàpù　lower berth; bottom berth

下棋　xiàqí　play chess; have a game of chess

下欠　xiàqiàn　① still owe (after paying part of one's debt): ～八百元 with 800 *yuan* still owing ② a sum still owing: 全数还清，并无～。 The debt has been fully paid up. Nothing owing.

下情　xiàqíng　① conditions at the lower levels; feelings or wishes of the masses or one's subordinates: 不了解～ not know what is going on at the lower levels / ～上达 make the situation below known to those above ② *old hum.* the situation I am in; my feelings or wishes: 还望体念～。 Hope you will give sympathetic consideration to my situation.

下去　xià·qù　① go down; descend: ～看看是谁在敲门。 Go downstairs and see who's knocking at the door. / 到站了，快～。 Here we are, let's get off at once. / ～一百米左右就到井底了。 Go down 100 metres or so and you'll reach the bottom of the well. ② go down to a place regarded as lower or below; step down (from the stage, platform, etc.): 你应该～了解一下情况。 You should go down there to size up the situation. / 连长受了重伤～了。 The company commander was seriously wounded and had to leave the battlefront. ③ lessen; be reduced; go down: 手上的泡全～了。 All the blisters on my hand have gone down. / 他的气还没～吗? Hasn't he calmed down yet? / 我不饿，中午吃的还没～呢。 I am not hungry at all. I haven't finished digesting my lunch yet.

下去　xià·qù　(used as a complement to a verb) ① (indicating motion toward a lower or farther position) down (there): 跳～ jump down / 从窗口扔～ throw sth. down through the window / 洪水退～了。 The flood has receded. / 把犯人带～ take the prisoner away / 把敌人的火力压～ silence the enemy's fire ② go on (doing sth.); continue: 坚持～ stick it out / 她激动得说不～。 She was so overcome with emotion that she couldn't go on. / 希望两国人民世世代代友好～。 We hope the people of the two countries will remain friendly from generation to generation. ③ (used after an adjective, indicating increasing degree) develop; grow: 看来天气还会冷～。 It seems it will get even colder. / 她一天天地瘦～。 She's getting thinner every day. / 情况还可能坏～。 The situation may grow even worse.

下人　xiàrén　*old*　(domestic) servant

下山　xiàshān　① go down a hill or mountain ② (of the sun) set; sink below the horizon: 太阳已经～。 The sun has sunk in the west.

下身　xiàshēn　① the lower part of the body ② private parts; genitals ③ trousers

下神　xiàshén　(of a witch, sorceress, etc.) act as if possessed by a god or spirit

下生　xiàshēng　be born

下剩　xiàshèng　*inf.*　be left: ～的种子不多了。 There aren't many seeds left. / 刨去开支，～三十元。 After subtracting expenses, there is 30 *yuan* left.

下士　xiàshì　(U. S. & Brit. Army, Brit. Air Force, U. S. & Brit. Marine Corps) corporal; (U. S. Navy) petty officer third class; (Brit. Navy) petty officer second class

下世[1]　xiàshì　next life

下世[2]　xiàshì　①　*formal*　leave this world—die ②

dial.　be born

下手[1]　xiàshǒu　① (also 下首 xiàshǒu) right-hand side or seat; seat of lower priority: 坐在主宾的～ sit on the right hand of the guest of honour ② same as 下家 xiàjiā

下手[2]　xiàshǒu　put one's hand to; start doing sth.; set about; set to: 不知从何～ not know where to start; not know how to set about a job / 我完全不了解情况，无从～。 I'm entirely in the dark about this matter, so I have no idea how to handle it. / 敌人就要对我们～了。 The enemy is going to strike out at us. / 让我宰鸡，我怎么也下不了手。 I can never bring myself to kill a chicken.

下手[3]　xiàshǒu　*inf.*　assistant; helper: 打～ act as assistant

下书　xiàshū　*formal*　deliver a letter

下属　xiàshǔ　subordinate: 他像使唤用人一样对待他的～。 He treated his subordinates like servants. / 这个厂是我们公司的～单位。 That's one of the subsidiary factories of our company.

下水[1]　xiàshuǐ　① enter the water; be launched: 又一艘新船～了。 Another new ship was launched. / 新船～典礼 the launching ceremony of a new ship ② soak in water to shrink cloth or fabrics before use ③ take to evil-doing; fall into evil ways: 拖人～ involve sb. in evildoing; drag sb. into the mire

下水[2]　xiàshuǐ　going downstream; downriver: ～船 a downriver boat

下水　xiàshui　tripe or chitterlings: 猪～ pig's tripe and chitterlings

下水道　xiàshuǐdào　sewer

下榻　xiàtà　*formal*　stay (at a place during a trip): ～于新侨饭店 stay at the Xinqiao Hotel

下台　xiàtái　① step down from the stage or platform ② fall out of power; leave office: 被赶～ be driven out of office; be thrown out / 总统快～。 The President will soon leave office. ③ (usu. used in the negative) get out of a predicament or an embarrassing situation: 没法～ be unable to back down with good grace / 叫他下不了台 put him on the spot

下台阶　xià táijiē　get out of a predicament or an embarrassing situation: 自己想法～ try to find oneself a way out of a predicament / 趁势～ take an opportunity to back down with good grace

下堂　xiàtáng　① (of women in the old society) be abandoned or divorced by one's husband: 糟糠之妻不～。 A wife who has shared her husband's hard lot must never be cast aside. ② *dial.*　finish class; get out of class

下体　xiàtǐ　*formal*　① the lower part of the body ② private parts; genitals

下帖　xiàtiě　*formal*　send an invitation card

下同　xiàtóng　(used in annotation) similarly hereinafter; the same below

下头　xiàtou　same as 下面 xiàmian①③

下晚儿　xiàwǎnr　*inf.*　near dusk: 他～就回来。 He'll be back towards evening.

下文　xiàwén　① what follows in the passage, paragraph, article, etc.: ～再作阐述 be explained in the ensuing chapters or paragraphs ② later development; outcome; sequel: 申请书交上去两个星期了，还没有～。 The application was handed in a couple of weeks ago, but so far there's been no reply. / 事情并没有就此结束，还有～哩。 The matter didn't end there; there was a sequel to it.

下午　xiàwǔ　afternoon: ～有场电影。 There's a movie this afternoon. / ～见! See you in the afternoon!

下弦　xiàxián　*astron.*　last (*or* third) quarter (of the moon)

下弦月　xiàxiányuè　the moon at the last (*or* third) quarter

下限　xiàxiàn　the latest or minimum permissible; lower limit; prescribed minimum; floor level; floor: 溶液比重不能低于～。The specific gravity of the solution should be kept above the prescribed minimum. / 申请书要求在两周内交齐,～为月底。All applications must be handed in within the next two weeks, by the end of the month at the latest.

下陷　xiàxiàn　be sunken; be hollow; form a depression: 眼眶～ with sunken eyes / 双颊～ with sunken cheeks / 一下雨,地面～的地方就成了水坑。Rain formed puddles in the depressions on the ground.

下乡　xiàxiāng　go to the countryside: ～务农 go in for farming in the countryside

下乡知识青年　xiàxiāng zhīshiqīngnián　educated urban youth working in the countryside

下泻　xiàxiè　① (of water) flow down: 激流～不畅。The torrents were impeded in their downflow. ② (of prices, etc.) drop sharply: 年初以来,美元对日元的汇价一路～。Since the beginning of the year, there have been sharp drops in the dollar-yen conversion rate. ③ have loose bowels (see also 上吐下泻 shàngtǔ-xiàxiè)

下行　xiàxíng　① (of trains) going from the capital to any other part of the country; down: ～列车 down train / 在中国,～列车编号用奇数。In China, the down trains are given odd numbers. ② (of boats) going downstream; downriver: ～船 a downstream boat ③ (of documents) being issued to the lower levels: ～公文 documents issued to the lower levels

下旋　xiàxuán　*sports* underspin; backspin: 他擅长打～球。He's good at cutting underspins.

下学　xiàxué　finish classes and leave school (for the day): ～后早点回家! Come home right after school!

下旬　xiàxún　the last ten-day period of a month

下咽　xiàyàn　swallow (food or other things): 难以～ find it hard to swallow

下药　xiàyào　① prescribe medicine: 李大夫～比较重。Dr. Li usually prescribes heavy doses. ② put in poison

下野　xiàyě　(of a ruler) retire from the political arena; be forced to relinquish power

下议院　xiàyìyuàn　① lower house; lower chamber ② the House of Commons (the lower house of the British Parliament)

下意识　xiàyìshí　subconsciousness: 有一种～的恐惧 have a subconscious fear / 我～地感到要出事。Subconsciously I felt something untoward was going to happen.

下游　xiàyóu　① lower reaches (of a river): 长江～ the lower reaches of the Changjiang (Yangtze) River ② backward position: 甘居～ be resigned to being backward

下狱　xiàyù　throw into prison; imprison

下葬　xiàzàng　be interred; be buried

下诏　xiàzhào　issue an imperial edict: ～大赦天下。An imperial edict was given for an amnesty.

下肢　xiàzhī　lower limbs; legs

下中农　xiàzhōngnóng　lower-middle peasant

下种　xiàzhǒng　sow (seeds): 麦子该～了。It's time to sow wheat.

下注　xiàzhù　lay down a stake (in gambling): 他在那匹马身上下了大注。He staked a lot of money on that horse.

下箸　xiàzhù　apply one's chopsticks to the food—start eating

下装　xiàzhuāng　remove theatrical makeup and costume

下坠　xiàzhuì　*med.* straining (at stool); tenesmus

下子　xiàzi　(used after 两 or 几) what one is good at or capable of: 他打起篮球来还有两～。He's no mean basketball player.

下钻　xiàzuàn　*petroleum* run the drilling tool into a well: ～速度 drilling speed

下作　xiàzuo　① low-down; mean; obscene; dirty: 那个老家伙太～。That man is a mean old bird. ② *dial.* greedy (for food); gluttonous ③ *dial.* assistant; helper: 打～ act as assistant

吓 (嚇)

吓　xià　frighten; scare; intimidate: 别～着孩子。Be careful not to frighten the child. / ～坏了 be terribly frightened; be overcome with fear / ～破了胆 be scared out of one's wits / 把我～一跳 give me a start (*or* scare) / 这种困难～不倒我们。Difficulties like this don't scare us. ——see also hè

吓唬　xiàhu　*inf.* frighten; scare; intimidate: 别～她,她胆儿小。Don't frighten her; she's rather timid. / 他净～人。He's always trying to intimidate people.

吓人　xiàrén　be frightening: 山洞又黑又深,进去可真～。It was really frightening to get into that deep and pitch-dark cave.

夏¹
夏²

夏¹　xià　summer

夏²　Xià　① the Xia Dynasty (c. 21st–c. 16th century B.C.) ② an ancient name for China: 华夏 Huáxià ③ a surname

夏播　xiàbō　summer sowing

夏布　xiàbù　grass linen; grass cloth

夏锄　xiàchú　summer hoeing and weeding

夏管　xiàguǎn　field management in summer

夏侯　Xiàhóu　a two-character surname

夏候鸟　xiàhòuniǎo　summer resident (e.g. barn swallows, cuckoos, etc. in China)

夏季　xiàjì　summer (season)

夏枯草　xiàkūcǎo　*Chin. med.* selfheal (*Prunella vulgaris*)

夏历　xiàlì　the traditional Chinese calendar; the lunar calendar

夏粮　xiàliáng　summer grain crops

夏令　xiàlìng　① summertime: ～时装 summer fashions / ～商品 commodities for summer use ② summer weather: 春行～ have summerlike weather in spring; see exceptionally warm days in spring

夏令时　xiàlìngshí　summer time; daylight-saving time

夏令营　xiàlìngyíng　summer camp

夏炉冬扇　xiàlú-dōngshàn　stoves in summer and fans in winter—things that do not meet the needs of the time

夏眠　xiàmián　aestivation (of certain animals)

夏时制　xiàshízhì　the practice of adopting daylight-saving time in summer

夏收　xiàshōu　summer harvest: ～季节快到了。It's about time for the summer harvest. / ～作物 summer crops

夏熟　xiàshú　ripen in summer: ～作物 summer crops

夏天　xiàtiān　summer: 这里的～特别热。It's very hot here in summer.

夏娃　Xiàwá　Eve (the first woman according to the Bible)

夏衣　xiàyī　summer clothing; summer wear

夏耘　xiàyún　*formal* summer hoeing and weeding

夏至　Xiàzhì　① the Summer Solstice—the 10th of the 24 solar terms ② the day marking the beginning of the 10th solar term (June 21 or 22, the longest day of the year) ——see also 节气 jiéqì; 二十四节气 èrshí sì jiéqì

夏至点 xiàzhìdiǎn the Summer Solstice (the northernmost point in the ecliptic reached by the sun about June 21 or 22)

夏至线 xiàzhìxiàn another name for 北回归线 běihuíguīxiàn

夏种 xiàzhòng summer sowing

夏装 xiàzhuāng summer clothing; summer wear

唬 xià same as 吓 xià ——see also hǔ

厦（廈） xià see below ——see also shà

厦门 Xiàmén Xiamen (Amoy), a city in Fujian Province

罅 xià formal crack; rift; chink: 石～ a crack in a rock / 云～ a rift in the clouds

罅缝 xiàfèng same as 罅隙 xiàxì

罅漏 xiàlòu formal omission; shortcoming; deficiency: ～之处, 有待订补. Shortcomings will be remedied in future editions.

罅隙 xiàxì formal crack; rift; chink: 了无～ crackless

xiān

仙（僊） xiān celestial being; immortal: 成仙 chéngxiān / 仙人 xiānrén

仙丹 xiāndān elixir of life

仙风道骨 xiānfēng-dàogǔ the demeanour of a transcendent being

仙姑 xiāngū ① female immortal (or celestial) ② sorceress

仙鹤 xiānhè ① another name for 丹顶鹤 dāndǐnghè ② white crane (kept by immortals in Chinese mythology)

仙鹤草 xiānhècǎo Chin. med. hairyvein agrimony (Agrimonia pilosa)

仙后座 Xiānhòuzuò astron. Cassiopeia

仙境 xiānjìng fairyland; wonderland; paradise

仙客来 xiānkèlái bot. cyclamen

仙女 xiānnǚ female celestial; fairy maiden

仙女座 Xiānnǚzuò astron. Andromeda

仙人 xiānrén celestial being; immortal

仙人果 xiānrénguǒ bot. prickly-pear cactus; prickly pear

仙人球 xiānrénqiú bot. ball cactus

仙人掌 xiānrénzhǎng bot. cactus

仙山琼阁 xiānshān qiónggé a jewelled palace on the mountain of the immortals

仙逝 xiānshì euph. pass away

仙桃 xiāntáo peach of immortality in Chinese mythology

仙王座 Xiānwángzuò astron. Cepheus

仙游 xiānyóu euph. travel to fairyland—die

仙姿 xiānzī fairy-like beauty

仙子 xiānzǐ ① female celestial ② celestial being; immortal

先 xiān ① adv. earlier; before sb. else; before doing sth. else; first; in advance: 他比我～到. He arrived earlier than I did. / 我～说两句. Let me say a few words first. / 你～拟个提纲再写. Make an outline before you start writing. / 你不必～付款. You don't have to pay in advance. / 没有什么～于经验的知识. There is no knowledge prior to experience. ② adv. (used with a negative word "不", "别", etc.) for the time being; for the moment: 你～别走, 我有话跟你说. Don't leave yet, I want to have a word with you. / 这个问题～不谈吧. Let's put aside this problem for the time being. ③ adv. inf. earlier on; before; at first: 你～怎么不告诉我呢？

Why didn't you tell me before? / 他～说不去, 后来却又改变了主意. At first he refused to go, but later on he changed his mind. ④ elder generation; ancestor: 祖先 zǔxiān ⑤ deceased; late: 先父 xiānfù

先辈 xiānbèi elder generation; ancestors: 继承革命～的事业 carry on the cause of the older generation of revolutionaries

先妣 xiānbǐ formal my late mother

先鞭 xiānbiān formal do sth. before sb. else

先慈 xiāncí formal my late mother

先导 xiāndǎo guide; forerunner; precursor: 错误常常是正确的～. Error is often the precursor of what is correct.

先帝 xiāndì the previous emperor; the late emperor

先睹为快 xiān dǔ wéi kuài consider it a pleasure to be among the first to read (a poem, article, etc.) or see (a play, ballet, etc.)

先端 xiānduān tip (of a leaf, flower, fruit, etc.)

先发制人 xiān fā zhì rén gain the initiative by striking the first blow; forestall the enemy: 采取～的手段 take preemptive measures

先锋 xiānfēng vanguard; van: 打～ fight in the van; be a pioneer / ～模范作用 exemplary vanguard role / 八路军是抗日救国的～. The Eighth Route Army was the vanguard in the fight against Japanese aggression.

先锋队 xiānfēngduì vanguard: 共产党是工人阶级的～. The Communist Party is the vanguard of the working class.

先夫 xiānfū my late husband

先父 xiānfù my late father

先公后私 xiān gōng hòu sī public interest comes before private or personal interests

先河 xiānhé the beginning of sth.: 开……之～ be a forerunner of …

先后 xiān-hòu ① being early or late; priority; order: 革命不分～. Whether one makes revolution early or late, one is equally welcome. / 这些事都该办, 可也得有个～. All these matters should be tackled, but they should be taken up in order of priority. ② adv. successively; one after another: 代表团～在北京、上海等地参观访问. The delegation first went to Beijing and afterwards to Shanghai and other places. / 代表们～入了座. One after another the deputies took their seats. / 他～三次访美. He visited America three times.

先见之明 xiān jiàn zhī míng prophetic vision; foresight: 缺乏～ lack foresight

先进 xiānjìn advanced: ～单位 advanced unit / ～分子 advanced element / ～个人 advanced individual / ～经验 advanced experience / ～事迹 meritorious (or exemplary) deeds / 赶超世界～水平 surpass the world's most advanced level

先进工作者 xiānjìn gōngzuòzhě advanced worker

先进集体 xiānjìn jítǐ advanced group (or collective)

先决 xiānjué prerequisite: ～条件 prerequisite; precondition / 社会安定是社会发展的～条件. Social order and stability is a prerequisite to social development.

先觉 xiānjué a person with foresight (in social and political affairs); advanced thinker

先君 xiānjūn formal my late father

先考 xiānkǎo formal my late father

先来后到 xiānlái-hòudào in the order of arrival; first come, first served: 请按～的次序排队. Please line up in order of arrival.

先礼后兵 xiān lǐ hòu bīng take strong measures only after courteous ones fail; try peaceful means before resorting to force

先例 xiānlì precedent: 开～ set (or create) a precedent / 有～可援 have a precedent to go by

先烈 xiānliè martyr: 革命～ revolutionary martyr

先令 xiānlìng ① shilling (a monetary unit of Britain until 1971) ② shilling (a monetary unit of Uganda, Kenya, Somalia and Tanzania) ③ schilling (a monetary unit of Austria)

先民 xiānmín *formal* ① ancients: ～时代 ancient times ② ancient worthies

先母 xiānmǔ my late mother

先期 xiānqī earlier than the date scheduled; earlier on; in advance: 代表团的部分团员已～到达。Some members of the delegation had arrived at an earlier date.

先前 xiānqián before; previously: 这孩子比～高多了。The child is much taller than before. / ～咱们村压根儿就没诊疗所。Previously there was no clinic in our village at all.

先遣 xiānqiǎn sent in advance: ～部队 advance troops (*or* force) / ～队 advance party

先秦 Xiān Qín the pre-Qin days (i.e. before 221 B.C. when the First Emperor of Qin united China; usually referring to the Spring and Autumn Period and the Period of the Warring States)

先驱 xiānqū pioneer; forerunner; harbinger: 聂耳、冼星海是中国革命音乐的～。Nie Er and Xian Xinghai were pioneers of China's revolutionary music.

先人 xiānrén ① ancestor; forefather ② my late father

先人后己 xiān rén hòu jǐ put others before oneself; put other people's interest ahead of one's own

先容 xiānróng *formal* speak for sb. beforehand

先入为主 xiān rù wéi zhǔ first impressions are strongest; prejudices die hard

先入之见 xiān rù zhī jiàn preconception; preconceived idea; prejudice

先声 xiānshēng first signs; herald; harbinger: 一七八九年的法国革命是十九世纪各国资产阶级革命的～。The French Revolution of 1789 heralded other bourgeois revolutions in the 19th century.

先声夺人 xiān shēng duó rén demoralize one's opponent by a show of strength; overawe people by displaying one's strength: 湖南队～，一上场就连中三球。The Hunan team got the better of their opponents by scoring three baskets in a row at the beginning.

先生 xiānsheng ① teacher: 要做人民的～，先做人民的学生。To be a teacher of the people, one must first be their pupil. ② Mister (Mr.); gentleman; sir: 总统～ Mr. President / 女士们，～们! Ladies and Gentlemen! ③ husband: 她～出差去了。Her husband is away on business. / 我～不在家。My husband is out. ④ *dial.* doctor ⑤ *old* (usu. used in) 帐房～ bookkeeper / 算命～ fortune-teller

先世 xiānshì forefathers; ancestors

先是 xiān·shì *adv.* before this; originally

先手 xiānshǒu offensive position (in chess): ～棋 an offensive move

先天 xiāntiān ① congenital; inborn: ～畸形 congenital malformation ② *philos.* a priori; innate: 人的知识不是～就有的，而是从社会实践中来的。Man's knowledge is not innate but comes from social practice.

先天不足 xiāntiān bùzú congenital deficiency; inborn weakness: 这孩子体弱多病，医生说他～。The child is always ailing. The doctor says he's congenitally deficient. / ～，后天失调 born weak and ill cared for after birth

先天下之忧而忧，后天下之乐而乐 xiān tiānxià zhī yōu ér yōu, hòu tiānxià zhī lè ér lè be the first to become concerned with the world's troubles and the last to rejoice in its happiness; be concerned before anyone else and enjoy oneself only after everyone else finds enjoyment

先天性疾病 xiāntiānxìng jíbìng congenital disorders

先天性免疫 xiāntiānxìng miǎnyì congenital immunity

先天性缺陷 xiāntiānxìng quēxiàn birth defects

先天性心脏病 xiāntiānxìng xīnzàngbìng *med.* congenital heart disease

先头 xiāntóu ① ahead; in front; in advance: ～部队 an advance party of soldiers; vanguard / 走在最～ walk ahead of all other people ② *adv.* before; formerly; in the past: 你～没说过这事。You didn't mention this before. / 她～已来过两次。She's been here twice already. / 一切结论产生于调查情况的末尾，而不是在它的～。Conclusions invariably come after investigation, and not before.

先王 xiānwáng former sovereigns: 法～ follow the example of former rulers

先下手为强 xiān xiàshǒu wéi qiáng he who strikes first gains the advantage; to take the initiative is to gain the upper hand: ～，后下手遭殃。He who strikes first prevails, he who strikes late fails.

先贤 xiānxián *old* sages of the past

先小人后君子 xiān xiǎorén hòu jūnzǐ let's allow impoliteness to precede courtesy (said when discussing the terms of a deal)

先行 xiānxíng ① go ahead of the rest; start off before the others: 兵马未动，粮草先行 bīngmǎ wèi dòng, liángcǎo xiānxíng ② beforehand; in advance: ～通知 notify in advance / 新产品将在本市～试销。The new products will first be put on trial sale in this city.

先行官 xiānxíngguān commander of an advance unit or vanguard: 铁路运输是国民经济的～。Railway transportation is the vanguard of the national economy.

先行者 xiānxíngzhě forerunner: 纪念伟大的革命～孙中山先生! Let us pay tribute to our great revolutionary forerunner, Dr. Sun Yat-sen!

先兄 xiānxiōng my late elder brother

先严 xiānyán *formal* my late father

先验 xiānyàn *philos.* a priori: ～知识 a priori knowledge

先验方法 xiānyàn fāngfǎ transcendental method

先验论 xiānyànlùn *philos.* apriorism

先意承志 xiān yì chéng zhì anticipate and attend to the wishes of another to please him

先斩后奏 xiān zhǎn hòu zòu execute sb. first and report to the emperor afterwards—act first and report afterwards

先兆 xiānzhào omen; portent; sign; indication: 地震的～ indications of an impending earthquake / 不祥的～ ill omen

先兆流产 xiānzhào liúchǎn *med.* early signs of miscarriage; threatened miscarriage

先兆子痫 xiānzhào zǐxián *med.* pre-eclampsia

先哲 xiānzhé a great thinker of the past; sage

先知 xiānzhī ① a person of foresight ② *religion* prophet

先知先觉 xiānzhī-xiānjué ① a person of foresight ② having foresight

先祖 xiānzǔ ① my late grandfather ② my forefathers

纤(纖) xiān fine; minute: 纤尘 xiānchén ——see also qiàn

纤尘 xiānchén fine dust

纤尘不染 xiānchén bù rǎn ① without a speck of dust: 室内窗明几净，～。The room is bright and spotlessly clean. ② untainted with evil thoughts or bad habits

纤度 xiāndù *text.* fibre number; size

纤毫 xiānháo the least bit; the minutest detail: 无～差别 without the slightest difference / 人物形象在这些牙雕艺术品里刻得～毕见。These ivory figures are so minutely and elaborately carved that the finest details can be distinguished.

纤毫不爽 xiānháo bù shuǎng be extremely accurate; be free from the slightest error

纤介 xiānjiè (also 纤芥 xiānjiè) *formal* minute; tiny; very small: 无～之失 without the slightest flaw or mishap

纤毛 xiānmáo *biol.* cilium: ～运动 ciliary movement

纤毛虫 xiānmáochóng *zool.* ciliate; infusorian

纤巧 xiānqiǎo dainty; delicate: 这些精美的绣品都出自她那～的双手。 All these elegant embroideries are creations of her dainty and dexterous hands.

纤柔 xiānróu soft and slender; delicate and soft: ～的双手 delicate, soft hands

纤弱 xiānruò slim and fragile; delicate: ～的身影 a slim and frail figure

纤手 xiānshǒu dainty (or delicate) hands (of a woman)

纤维 xiānwéi fibre; staple: 天然(合成、人造)～ natural (synthetic, man-made) fibre / ～长度 fibre length; staple

纤维板 xiānwéibǎn fibreboard

纤维蛋白 xiānwéi dànbái *biochem.* fibrin

纤维蛋白原 xiānwéi dànbáiyuán *biochem.* fibrinogen

纤维光学 xiānwéi guāngxué *phys.* fibre optics

纤维集束 xiānwéi jíshù *chem. fibre* collection of filaments

纤维瘤 xiānwéiliú *med.* fibroma

纤维束 xiānwéishù *chem. fibre* tow

纤维素 xiānwéisù *chem.* cellulose

纤维素分解菌 xiānwéisù fēnjiějūn cellulose-decomposing bacterium; cellvibrio

纤维植物 xiānwéi zhíwù fibre plant

纤悉 xiānxī *formal* extremely detailed

纤悉无遗 xiānxī wúyí with not a single detail left out

纤细 xiānxì very thin; slender; fine; tenuous: ～的头发 fine hair / ～的游丝 tenuous gossamer

纤纤 xiānxiān *formal* long and slender: 十指～ long and slender fingers

纤小 xiānxiǎo fine; tenuous

纤腰 xiānyāo slender waist (of a woman)

纤指 xiānzhǐ delicate fingers (of a woman)

氙 xiān *chem.* xenon (Xe)

氙灯 xiāndēng xenon lamp

祆 Xiān see below

祆教 Xiānjiào another name for 拜火教 Bàihuǒjiào

籼(秈) xiān see below

籼稻 xiāndào long-grained nonglutinous rice; *indica* rice

籼米 xiānmǐ polished long-grained nonglutinous rice; polished *indica* rice

苬(蘞) xiān see 稀苬 xīxiān

掀 xiān lift (a cover, etc.): ～门帘 lift the door curtain / ～掉盖子 take the lid off / 把对手～翻在地 throw the opponent off his balance / 把被子～起来 pull the quilt off / 别一会儿～一次锅盖, 热气都跑了。 Don't keep lifting the pot's lid, or you'll let all the steam out.

掀动 xiāndòng ① launch (a war) ② lift; start; set in motion: 春风～了她的衣襟。 The spring breeze lifted the edge of her blouse. / 壶里的蒸汽把壶盖都～了。 The steam in the kettle is jiggling the lid.

掀风鼓浪 xiānfēng-gǔlàng raise a storm—stir up trouble

掀开 xiānkāi open; lift; draw: ～窗帘 draw the curtains open / ～锅盖 lift the lid off the pot / 在两国关系史上～了新的一页 open a new chapter in the annals of relations between the two countries

掀起 xiānqǐ ① lift; raise: 一阵狂风～了她的大衣衣角。 A sudden gust lifted the corners of her overcoat. ② surge; cause to surge: 大海～了巨浪。 Big waves surged on the sea. ③ set off (a movement, etc.); start: ～社会主义劳动竞赛的新高潮 set off (or start) a new upsurge of socialist labour emulation / 就这个问题～了一场激烈的辩论。 This question set off a fierce debate.

掀天揭地 xiāntiān-jiēdì shaking heaven and earth—bringing about great changes; achieving wonders; exerting a profound and far-reaching influence

锨(枚、杴) xiān shovel

跹(躚) xiān see 翩跹 piānxiān

酰 xiān *chem.* acyl

鲜 xiān ① fresh: ～奶 fresh milk / ～蘑 fresh mushrooms / ～鱼 fresh fish ② bright-coloured; bright: 这块布颜色太～。 The colour of this cloth is too bright. ③ (of salty dishes or soup) delicious; tasty: 这汤味道很～。 The soup tastes delicious. ④ delicacy: 尝尝～ have a taste of a delicacy of the season ⑤ seafood; aquatic foods: 海鲜 hǎixiān ——see also xiǎn

鲜卑 Xiānbēi Xianbei (Sienpi), an ancient nationality in China

鲜果 xiānguǒ fresh fruit

鲜红 xiānhóng bright red; scarlet: ～的旗帜 a bright red flag

鲜花 xiānhuā fresh flowers; flowers

鲜货 xiānhuò fresh fruit, vegetables, or seafood, etc.

鲜亮 xiānliang *dial.* (of colour) shining bright

鲜灵 xiān·líng *dial.* ① fresh: 你看这鱼多～呀! See how fresh the fish is! ② shining bright: 石榴花红得那么～可爱。 The pomegranate blossoms, ablaze with a fiery red, are really eye-catching.

鲜美 xiānměi ① (of cooked food, fruit, etc.) delicious; tasty ② *formal* (of flowers, grass, etc.) fresh and pleasing: 芳草～。 There were scented grasses, fresh and pleasing to the eye.

鲜明 xiānmíng ① (of colour) bright: 色彩～ in bright colours; bright-coloured ② clear-cut; distinct; distinctive: ～的对照 a striking (or sharp) contrast / ～的节奏 strongly accented rhythms / 主题～ have a distinct theme / 富有～的地方特色 be characterized by a distinctive local style or flavour / 我们必须坚持真理, 而真理必须旗帜～。 We must firmly uphold the truth, and truth requires a clear-cut stand.

鲜嫩 xiānnèn fresh and tender: ～的藕 fresh and tender lotus roots

鲜皮 xiānpí fresh hide; greenhide

鲜血 xiānxuè (red) blood: 她的手沾满了～。 Her hands are covered with blood. / ～凝成的战斗友谊 militant friendship cemented (or sealed) with blood

鲜艳 xiānyàn (also 鲜妍 xiānyán) bright-coloured; gaily-coloured: 颜色～ in gay colours / 穿着～的民族服装 wearing bright national costume

鲜艳夺目 xiānyàn duómù dazzlingly beautiful; resplendent: 那～的浆果, 在绿叶的衬托下, 显得格外娇妍。 The contrast of the bright, eye-catching red of the berries against the green of the leaves looked particularly charming. / 她穿戴仍然～。 She is dressed and bejewelled as brightly and dazzlingly as ever.

鲜衣怒马 xiānyī-nùmǎ be dressed in fine clothes and ride on well-groomed horses—lead a luxurious life

鲜于 Xiānyú a two-character surname

暹 xiān see below

暹罗 Xiānluó Siam, former name for Thailand 泰国

xián

闲（閒）

xián ① not busy; idle; unoccupied: 我这两天～着没事。I've had nothing to do for the last couple of days. / 妈妈老是这么忙，没～过一天。Mother is always so busy; she's never been free for a single day. ② not in use; unoccupied; lying idle: 别让机器～着! Don't let the machine stand idle. / 没有一辆车～着。There's not a single free vehicle. or All the vehicles are in use. ③ spare or free time; leisure: 今天她不得～。She has no time to spare today. ④ having nothing to do with business: 闲谈 xiántán

闲步 xiánbù take a stroll: ～海滨 take a stroll along the seashore

闲不住 xiánbuzhù refuse to stay idle; always keep oneself busy

闲扯 xiánchě chat; engage in chitchat: 你别在这儿扯了，快回家去吧。Don't hang around here and gab. Get yourself home, quick.

闲荡 xiándàng saunter; stroll; loaf: 他把大好时光都给～掉了。He spent all his precious time loafing around.

闲房 xiánfáng a vacant room; an unoccupied room

闲工夫 xiángōngfu spare time; leisure

闲官 xiánguān an official with a sinecure

闲逛 xiánguàng saunter; stroll: 星期天在街上～的人比平时多。On Sundays there are more people strolling along the streets than on weekdays.

闲花野草 xiánhuā-yěcǎo same as 野草闲花 yěcǎo-xiánhuā

闲话 xiánhuà ① digression: ～少说，书归正传。Enough of this digression; let's return to our story. or However, to continue the story. ② complaint; gossip: 别让人说咱们的～。We mustn't give anyone cause for complaint. / 她可不爱说人～。She's not fond of gossip. ③ formal talk casually about; chat about: ～当年 chat about bygone days

闲静 xiánjìng ① serene; tranquil: 旷野～。It was quiet and serene in the wilderness. ② (of manners or bearing) calm and relaxed

闲居 xiánjū stay at home idle; lead a quiet life

闲磕牙 xiánkēyá dial. have an idle chat

闲空 xiánkòng free time; spare time; leisure

闲聊 xiánliáo chat: 她俩正在院子里～呢。They are in the courtyard chatting.

闲磨牙 xiánmóyá have an idle chat

闲盘儿 xiánpánr ① a matter that does not concern one; other people's business: 我没工夫管这些～。I've no time for these things. They are none of my business. ② rigmarole; meaningless talk; idle chatter: 我正忙着呢，没法听你这些～。I'm too busy right now to listen to your idle chatter.

闲篇 xiánpiān dial. rigmarole; meaningless talk; idle chatter: 扯～儿 talk idly; chatter

闲气 xiánqì anger about trifles: 我可没工夫生这份儿～。I'm too busy to lose my temper over such a little thing. or I've no time to get angry about such a trivial matter.

闲钱 xiánqián inf. spare cash

闲情逸致 xiánqíng-yìzhì (be in) a leisurely and carefree mood; (have) the leisure and (be in the) mood for enjoyment: 大家都在紧张地工作着，谁还有～去跳舞呢! Everybody is busy working and is in no mood for going to a dance.

闲人 xiánrén ① an unoccupied person; idler: 现在正是农忙季节，村里一个～也没有。It's the busy season for farmers and nobody in the village is idle. ② persons not concerned: ～免进。No admittance except on business. or Admittance to staff only. or Employees only.

闲散 xiánsǎn ① free and at leisure; at loose ends ② unused; idle: ～资金 idle capital / ～土地 scattered plots of unutilized land

闲时 xiánshí leisure; free time

闲事 xiánshì ① a matter that does not concern one; other people's business: 爱管～ like to poke one's nose into other people's business / 别管～! Mind your own business. or None of your business. ② an unimportant matter

闲是闲非 xiánshì-xiánfēi idle gossip: 别人爱说个～的，随他们说去。Some people like to engage in idle gossip. Don't pay any attention to them.

闲适 xiánshì leisurely and comfortable: ～的心情 a leisurely and placid mood

闲书 xiánshū light reading

闲谈 xiántán chat; engage in chitchat

闲庭 xiántíng a quiet and peaceful courtyard: 不管风吹浪打，胜似～信步。(毛泽东) Let the wind blow and waves beat, Better far than idly strolling in a courtyard.

闲暇 xiánxiá leisure

闲心 xiánxīn leisurely mood: 没有～管这种事 be too busy to think about such matters; not be in the mood to bother about such matters

闲雅 xiányǎ same as 娴雅 xiányǎ

闲言碎语 xiányán-suìyǔ ① idle chatter; irrelevancies ② gossip; backbiting; groundless rumour; slander

闲云野鹤 xiányún-yěhè (like) drifting clouds and wild storks—free and unrestrained

闲杂 xiánzá without fixed duties: ～人员 people without fixed duties; miscellaneous personnel

闲在 xiánzài dial. leisurely; with nothing to do: 今天你怎么这么～，能出来溜达溜达? How come you have so much time today to loiter around?

闲章 xiánzhāng a seal as an object of artistic value (not used for practical purposes, usu. inscribed with a motto or a line of poetry)

闲职 xiánzhí an extremely light and easy job; sinecure

闲置 xiánzhì leave unused; let sth. lie idle; set aside: ～的机器 idle machines / ～资金 idle funds

闲坐 xiánzuò sit back for a chat or enjoy one's leisure

贤（賢）

xián ① virtuous and able; worthy: 贤明 xiánmíng ② a worthy person; an able and virtuous person: 让～ relinquish one's post in favour of sb. better qualified ③ pol. (used in addressing people of the same or of a younger generation): 贤弟 xiándì / 贤侄 xiánzhí

贤才 xiáncái a man of superior capacity

贤达 xiándá a prominent and worthy personage: 社会～ the worthies

贤德 xiándé ① virtue and kindheartedness ② virtuous: ～夫人 a virtuous and kindhearted lady

贤弟 xiándì a term of respect for one's younger brother or sb. younger than oneself

贤惠 xiánhuì (also 贤慧 xiánhuì) (of a woman) virtuous; genial and prudent; kindhearted and understanding: 他有一位十分～的夫人。He has a genial and devoted wife.

贤劳 xiánláo formal industrious; hardworking (usu. used in commending sb. for his good work)

贤良 xiánliáng ① (of a man) able and virtuous ② able and virtuous men

贤路 xiánlù formal openings for the able and the worthy: 广开～ do everything possible for able and worthy men to rise in the world

贤妹　xiánmèi　a term of respect for one's younger sister or sb. younger than oneself

贤明　xiánmíng　wise and able; sagacious

贤内助　xiánnèizhù　① pol. (said of another person's wife) a good wife: 大家都羡慕你有一位～。Everybody envies you for having such a good wife. ② humor. my better half; my good wife: 这是我的～。This is my better half.

贤能　xiánnéng　a virtuous and talented person

贤妻　xiánqī　old (a term of respect) my good (or worthy) wife

贤妻良母　xiánqī-liángmǔ　a good wife and loving mother

贤契　xiánqì　formal pol. (an old term for one's junior, esp. one's pupil or a son of one's friend) my worthy pupil, nephew, etc.

贤人　xiánrén　a person of virtue (or merit); a person of outstanding worth

贤淑　xiánshū　formal (of a woman) virtuous, kind and genial

贤哲　xiánzhé　a good and wise man

贤侄　xiánzhí　pol. a term for one's nephew or for a son of one's friend

弦¹　xián　① bowstring; string ② dial. spring (of a watch, etc.) ③ math. chord ④ math. hypotenuse

弦²（絃）　xián　the string of a musical instrument

弦脉　xiánmài　Chin. med. taut pulse

弦外之音　xián wài zhī yīn　overtones; implication: 我懂得他的～: 这事儿总工程师也有责任。I'm quite aware of the overtones of what he was saying: the chief engineer should also be held responsible.

弦线　xiánxiàn　the string of a musical instrument

弦月　xiányuè　crescent or half moon

弦乐队　xiányuèduì　string orchestra (or band); string ensemble

弦乐器　xiányuèqì　stringed instrument

弦柱　xiánzhù　the post or neck to which the strings of a musical instrument are attached

弦子　xiánzi　a popular name for 三弦 sānxián

涎　xián　saliva: 流～ slobber; slaver; drool

涎皮赖脸　xiánpí-làiliǎn　brazen; cheeky; shameless and loathsome

涎水　xiánshuǐ　dial. saliva

涎着脸　xiánzheliǎn　be brazenfaced; be cheeky

咸¹　xián　adv. formal all: ～受其益。All benefited from it. / 老少～宜 suitable for old and young alike

咸²（鹹）　xián　salted; salty: ～鱼 salt fish / ～蛋 salted egg / 菜太～了。The dish is too salty.

咸不唧儿　xiánbùjīr　(also 咸不滋儿 xiánbuzīr) dial. saltish

咸菜　xiáncài　salted vegetables; pickles

咸淡　xiándàn　degree of saltiness: 这汤的～正合适。This soup tastes just right, neither too salty nor too flat.

咸津津　xiánjīnjīn　with a nice saltish taste: 这瓜子～的, 吃着怪有味儿。These melon seeds have a nice saltish flavour which is quite tasty.

咸肉　xiánròu　salted meat; bacon

咸水　xiánshuǐ　salt water

咸水湖　xiánshuǐhú　saltwater lake

咸水鱼　xiánshuǐyú　saltwater fish

咸丝丝　xiánsīsī　slightly saline or salty; saltish: 海边的空气～的, 沁人心脾。The seaside air is a bit saline, very pleasant and refreshing.

咸盐　xiányán　dial. table salt; salt

挦（撏）　xián　pull out (hair); pluck: ～鸡毛 pluck chicken feathers; pluck a chicken

娴（嫻）　xián　formal ① refined: 娴静 xiánjìng ② adept; skilled: 娴熟 xiánshú

娴静　xiánjìng　gentle and refined

娴熟　xiánshú　adept; skilled: 弓马～ adept in archery and horsemanship / ～的技巧 consummate skill / 她在平衡木上动作～。She showed great skill in her exercises on the balance beam.

娴习　xiánxí　be skilful at; be adept in; be expert at: 她～竖琴。She is expert at playing the harp.

娴雅　xiányǎ　(of a woman) refined; elegant: 举止～ poised and elegant

娴于辞令　xián yú cílìng　be skilled in the use of words; be gifted with a silver tongue

舷　xián　the side of a ship or aircraft: 左舷 zuǒxián / 右舷 yòuxián

舷边　xiánbiān　gunwale; gunnel

舷窗　xiánchuāng　porthole

舷梯　xiántī　① gangway ladder; accommodation ladder ② (boarding) ramp

衔¹（啣）　xián　① hold in the mouth: ～着烟斗 have a pipe between one's teeth / 燕子～泥筑窠。Swallows carry bits of earth in their bills to build nests. ② harbour; bear: 衔恨 xiánhèn ③ formal receive (orders, etc.): 衔命 xiánmìng ④ link up; join: 衔接 xiánjiē

衔²　xián　rank; title: 大使～常驻代表 permanent representative with the rank of ambassador

衔恨　xiánhèn　harbour resentment; bear a grudge: ～终生 nurse a deep grudge to the end of one's days

衔环结草　xiánhuán-jiécǎo　same as 结草衔环 jiécǎo-xiánhuán

衔接　xiánjiē　link up; join: 大桥把两条公路～起来。The bridge links up the two highways. / 使计划互相～ make the plans dovetail

衔枚　xiánméi　formal (formerly of soldiers on the march) have a wooden gag in their mouths to ensure silence: 赴敌之兵, ～疾走。Soldiers were advancing against the enemy, running swiftly with the gag between their teeth.

衔命　xiánmìng　formal carry out an order

衔铁　xiántiě　elec. armature

衔头　xiántóu　title (of a person by right of office, attainment, etc.)

衔尾　xiánwěi　formal close behind: ～相随 one close behind another

衔冤　xiányuān　nurse a bitter sense of wrong; have a simmering sense of injustice

鹇（鷳）　xián　see 白鹇 báixián

痫（癇）　xián　Chin. med. epilepsy

嫌　xián　① suspicion: 避嫌 bìxián ② ill will; resentment; enmity; grudge: 前嫌 qiánxián ③ dislike; mind; complain of: ～麻烦 not want to take the trouble; think it troublesome / ～脏 think sth. too dirty / ～孩子吵 think the children too noisy / 大家都～他脾气太急。Everybody disliked him because of his hot temper. / 你不～我们在这里抽烟吧? You don't mind us smoking here, do you? / 这文章内容不错, 只是文字略～啰唆。

The article is good in content, only it's a bit wordy.

嫌烦 xiánfán find sth. annoying or trying: 老人很难待候, 但她从没嫌过烦。 The old man was very hard to please, but she never grew impatient waiting on him.

嫌气细菌 xiánqìxìjūn anaerobic bacteria; anaerobes

嫌弃 xiánqì dislike and avoid; cold-shoulder: 不要～犯过错误的同志。 Don't cold-shoulder comrades who have made mistakes.

嫌恶 xiánwù detest; loathe: 我们办公室里没有一个人不～他的。 There's no one in our office who doesn't detest him.

嫌隙 xiánxì feeling of animosity; enmity; ill will; grudge

嫌疑 xiányí suspicion: 有间谍～ be suspected of being a spy

嫌疑犯 xiányífàn suspect

嫌疑分子 xiányí fènzǐ *leg.* suspect

嫌怨 xiányuàn grudge; resentment; enmity

嫌憎 xiánzēng be disgusted with; dislike intensely

xiǎn

冼 Xiǎn a surname

洗 Xiǎn a surname ——see also xǐ

险 (險) xiǎn ① a place difficult of access; a narrow pass; defile: 凭～据守 be entrenched at a strategical vantage point / 无～可守 have no tenable defence position; be strategically indefensible ② dangerous; perilous: 山又高又陡, 而且雪深没膝, 爬上去好～呀。 The mountain was high and steep, and the snow knee-deep. It was really dangerous to climb. / 湍流急而～。 The rapids are swift and perilous. ③ sinister; vicious; venomous: 阴险 yīnxiǎn ④ by a hair's breadth; by inches; nearly: ～遭不幸 come within an ace of death / 好～哪! That was a near thing!

险隘 xiǎn'ài a strategic pass; defile

险地 xiǎndì ① a strategical vantage point ② a perilous situation; dangerous circumstances

险恶 xiǎn'è ① dangerous; perilous; ominous: 处境～ be in a perilous position / 病情～ be dangerously ill ② sinister; vicious; malicious; treacherous: ～的用心 sinister (*or* vicious) intentions; evil motives

险峰 xiǎnfēng a perilous peak

险工 xiǎngōng a dangerous section (of a dyke or embankment)

险固 xiǎngù *formal* strategically secure; unassailable; strong in defence

险境 xiǎnjìng dangerous situation: 脱离～ be out of danger

险峻 xiǎnjùn dangerously steep; precipitous: 山峰～。 The mountains are precipitous.

险情 xiǎnqíng dangerous state or situation: 河水不断上涨, 大堤出现～。 The river keeps rising and the dam is threatened.

险球 xiǎnqiú (mostly football) a near miss (goal): 守门员身手不凡, 接连救起了几个～。 He's a very good goalkeeper and made several spectacular saves.

险区 xiǎnqū danger zone

险胜 xiǎnshèng win by a narrow margin: 以二十一比十九～ win the game by the close score of 21-19

险滩 xiǎntān dangerous shoal; rapids

险巇 xiǎnxī *formal* (of roads, paths, etc.) dangerous and difficult: 世路～。 Life is full of difficulties and dangers.

险象环生 xiǎnxiàng huán shēng dangers lurking on all sides; beset (*or* surrounded) by perils

险些 xiǎnxiē *adv.* narrowly (escape from sth. untoward); just barely; nearly: ～掉到水里 nearly fall into the water / 马往旁边一闪, ～把我摔下来。 The horse suddenly shied and I was nearly thrown off.

险要 xiǎnyào strategically located and difficult of access

险语 xiǎnyǔ startling remarks: 他好作～。 He has a way of coming out with startling remarks.

险韵 xiǎnyùn a difficult rhyme

险遭不测 xiǎn zāo bùcè have a near (*or* narrow) escape

险诈 xiǎnzhà sinister and crafty

险症 xiǎnzhèng dangerous illness

险阻 xiǎnzǔ (of roads) dangerous and difficult: 崎岖～的山路 a dangerous and difficult mountain path

显 (顯) xiǎn ① be apparent; be obvious; be noticeable: 药的效果还不～。 The effect of the medicine is not yet noticeable. ② show; display; manifest: ～本领 display one's skill / 深色衣服不～脏。 Dark clothes do not show the dirt. ③ illustrious and influential: 显达 xiǎndá

显摆 xiǎnbai (also 显白 xiǎnbai) *dial.* show off; brag about; flaunt

显鼻子显眼儿 xiǎnbízi-xiǎnyǎnr *inf.* be too conspicuous (*or* too exposed): 钱包放在上衣兜儿里太～, 你可要小心点儿。 Your wallet in your jacket pocket will attract too much attention. You'd better be careful.

显妣 xiǎnbǐ *formal* my late mother

显出 xiǎnchū show; reveal: 脸上～不耐烦的神色 with impatience written on one's face / 东方刚刚～鱼肚白。 Day was just breaking.

显达 xiǎndá illustrious and influential

显得 xiǎnde look; seem; appear: 他～有点紧张。 He seems a bit nervous. / 屋子这么一布置, ～宽敞多了。 Arranged the way it is, the room looks much more spacious.

显而易见 xiǎn ér yì jiàn obviously; evidently; clearly

显贵 xiǎnguì ① occupying a distinguished position; of high position ② high officials (in former times)

显赫 xiǎnhè illustrious; celebrated: ～的战功 illustrious war exploits / 声势～ have a powerful influence / ～的名声 great renown / ～一时的殖民帝国 the once mighty colonial empire

显花植物 xiǎnhuāzhíwù *bot.* phanerogam

显宦 xiǎnhuàn high officials (in former times)

显豁 xiǎnhuò obvious and clear: 他作了一篇内容～的报告。 He gave a lucid talk.

显见 xiǎnjiàn be obvious; be self-evident; be apparent: ～的理由 an obvious (*or* apparent) reason

显考 xiǎnkǎo *formal* my late father

显灵 xiǎnlíng (of a ghost or spirit) make its presence or power felt

显露 xiǎnlù become visible; appear; manifest itself: 他脸上～出亲切的笑容。 A genial smile appeared on his face. / 随着乌云的消散, 月亮逐渐～出来了。 As the dark clouds dispersed, the moon gradually came into view. / 通过这次技术革新, 他的才智～出来了。 His ability manifested itself through this technical innovation.

显明 xiǎnmíng obvious; manifest; distinct; marked: ～的道理 an obvious truth / ～的对照 a sharp contrast / ～的特点 a distinct (*or* marked) characteristic

显目 xiǎnmù conspicuous

显能 xiǎnnéng show off one's talent or competence: 你在行家面前显什么能? What have you to show off before those experts?

显然 xiǎnrán *adv.* obviously; evidently; clearly: 这～是另一码事。 That's obviously quite another matter. / 很～, 这么大的工程靠几个人的力量是完不成的。 It is

quite evident that a project of such magnitude cannot be accomplished through the effort of just a few persons. / 孩子们的体质～提高了。The physical condition of the children has obviously improved.

显色染料 xiǎnsèrǎnliào *chem.* developing dye

显身手 xiǎn shēnshǒu display one's talent or skill

显圣 xiǎnshèng (of the ghost of a saintly person) make its presence or power felt

显示 xiǎnshì ① show; display; demonstrate; manifest: ～力量 make a show of force; display one's strength / 这些文物～出中国古代劳动人民的高度智慧。These cultural relics demonstrate the great intelligence of the labouring people of ancient China. / 我们在战胜自然灾害中～了巨大威力。We have manifested our tremendous strength in conquering the natural calamities. ② *petroleum* show; indication: 石油(天然气)～ oil (gas) shows / 地面～ surface indications

显微胶片 xiǎnwēijiāopiàn microfilm; microfiche; bibliofilm

显微镜 xiǎnwēijìng microscope

显微术 xiǎnwēishù microscopy

显微外科 xiǎnwēiwàikē microsurgery

显微阅读机 xiǎnwēiyuèdújī microfilm viewer (*or* reader)

显微照片 xiǎnwēizhàopiàn micrograph

显微照相术 xiǎnwēizhàoxiàngshù microphotography; photomicrography

显现 xiǎnxiàn manifest (*or* reveal) oneself; appear; show: 雾气逐渐消失,重叠的山峦一层一层地～出来。As the mist lifted, the mountains revealed themselves one behind the other.

显像管 xiǎnxiàngguǎn *electron.* kinescope

显效 xiǎnxiào ① produce effects: 这种药～快。This medicine produces quick results. ② tangible results

显形 xiǎnxíng show one's (true) colours; betray oneself

显性 xiǎnxìng *biol.* dominance: ～性状 dominant character

显眼 xiǎnyǎn conspicuous; showy: 把布告贴在～的地方 put up the notice in a conspicuous place / 穿得太～ be loudly (*or* showily) dressed

显扬 xiǎnyáng *formal* ① commend; extol; glorify: ～先祖 glorify one's ancestors ② eminent; of undisputed fame

显要 xiǎnyào ① powerful and influential: ～人物 an influential figure ② an influential figure; an important personage; VIP

显耀 xiǎnyào ① show off: ～自己的身份 show off one's status ② be of high repute: ～一时 be highly renowned for a time

显影 xiǎnyǐng *photog.* develop

显影机 xiǎnyǐngjī developing machine

显影剂 xiǎnyǐngjì developer

显影盘 xiǎnyǐngpán developing dish

显影纸 xiǎnyǐngzhǐ developing-out paper

显著 xiǎnzhù notable; marked; striking; remarkable; outstanding: 收效～ yield notable results / 有～的进步 make marked progress / 取得～的成就 achieve remarkable success / ～的特征 outstanding characteristics / 各报均以～地位刊载了这条消息。This news was prominently featured in all the papers.

显字管 xiǎnzìguǎn *electron.* charactron

蚬

xiǎn a species of small clam living in fresh water (*Corbicula leana*)

铣

xiǎn see below ——see also xǐ

铣铁 xiǎntiě cast iron

筅(箲)

xiǎn see below

筅帚 xiǎnzhǒu *dial.* a brush (usu. made of bamboo) for cleaning pots and pans

跣

xiǎn *formal* barefoot: ～足 with bare feet; barefoot; barefooted

鲜(尠、尟)

xiǎn little; rare: ～见 rarely seen; seldom met with ——see also xiān

藓

xiǎn *bot.* moss

燹

xiǎn *formal* wild fires

xiàn

见(見)

xiàn show; appear; become visible: 图穷匕首见 tú qióng bǐshǒu xiàn ——see also jiàn

苋

xiàn amaranth (a herbaceous plant)

苋菜 xiàncài three-coloured amaranth (*Amaranthus tricolor*)

县(縣)

xiàn county

县城 xiànchéng county seat; county town

县份 xiànfèn (not used with specific place names) county: 我们那儿是个小～。Ours is a small county.

县官 xiànguān same as 县令 xiànlìng

县令 xiànlìng *old* county magistrate

县太爷 xiàntàiyé a colloquial term for 县令 xiànlìng

县委 xiànwěi county Party committee

县长 xiànzhǎng the head of a county; county magistrate

县志 xiànzhì general records of a county; county annals

县治 xiànzhì *old* the seat of a county government; county seat

现

xiàn ① present; current; existing: ～阶段 the present stage / ～况 the existing (*or* present) situation / ～派张同志前往你处接洽。We are now sending Comrade Zhang along to get in touch with you. ② (do sth.) in time of need; extempore: ～打的烧饼 sesame cakes just out of the oven / 这点技术也是工作中～学的。What skill I have has been picked up on the job. / 他在晚会上～编了一首诗。He improvised a poem at the evening party. ③ (of money, etc.) on hand: 现钱 xiànqián / 现货 xiànhuò ④ cash; ready money: 付现 fùxiàn ⑤ show; appear; become visible: 她脸上～出一丝笑容。A faint smile appeared on (*or* crept over) her face. / ～原形 show one's true colours

现报 xiànbào same as 现世报 xiànshìbào

现场 xiànchǎng ① scene (of an incident): 作案～ the scene of a crime / 保护～ keep the scene (of a crime or accident) intact ② site; spot: 工作～ worksite / 试验～ testing ground / ～表演 on-the-spot (*or* live) demonstration / ～采访 spot coverage / ～会议 on-the-spot meeting / ～勘验 inspection of the scene of a crime or accident / ～指导 on-the-spot guidance

现成 xiànchéng ready-made: 买～衣服 buy ready-made clothes; buy clothes off the peg / 吃～的 eat whatever is ready or prepared by others

现成饭 xiànchéngfàn food ready for the table; unearned gain

现成话 xiànchénghuà an onlooker's unsolicited comments; a kibitzer's comments: 说～ kibitz

现存 xiàncún extant; in stock: ～的手稿 extant manuscripts／～物资 goods and materials in stock

现代 xiàndài ① modern times; the contemporary age ② modern; contemporary: ～交通工具 modern means of communication／～作家 modern (or contemporary) writers／～题材 contemporary themes

现代化 xiàndàihuà modernize: ～企业 modernized enterprise／～设备 sophisticated equipment／实现四个～ achieve the four modernizations (of agriculture, industry, national defence, and science and technology)

现代派 xiàndàipài modernist school

现代史 xiàndàishǐ contemporary history

现代舞 xiàndàiwǔ modern dance

现代戏 xiàndàixì drama with a contemporary theme

现代艺术 xiàndài yìshù modern art

现地作业 xiàndì zuòyè mil. terrain exercise

现而今 xiàn'érjīn dial. now; at present

现货 xiànhuò merchandise on hand; spots: ～价格 spot price／～交易 spot transaction; over-the-counter trading／～市场 spot market

现浇 xiànjiāo archit. cast-in-place; cast-in-situ: ～混凝土 cast-in-place (or cast-in-situ) concrete

现今 xiànjīn nowadays; these days

现金 xiànjīn ① ready money; cash: ～付款 cash payment; payment in cash／～交易 cash transaction／～支出 out-of-pocket expenses ② cash reserve in a bank

现金出纳机 xiànjīn chūnàjī cash register

现金帐 xiànjīnzhàng cash account; cash book

现局 xiànjú current situation

现款 xiànkuǎn ready money; cash

现蕾 xiànlěi ① budding (of flowers) ② squaring (of cotton plants): ～期 squaring period (or stage)

现钱 xiànqián inf. ready money; cash

现任 xiànrèn ① at present hold the office of: 她～工会主席。At present she holds the position of chairman of the labour union. ② currently in office; incumbent: ～邮局局长过去是邮递员。The present postmaster used to be a postman.

现身说法 xiàn shēn shuō fǎ advise sb. or explain sth. by citing one's own experience

现时 xiànshí now; at present

现实 xiànshí ① reality; actuality: 脱离～ be divorced from reality; be unrealistic／面对～ face the facts／理想变成了～。A dream has come true. ② real; actual: ～生活 real (or actual) life／～意义 practical or immediate significance／采取～的态度 adopt a realistic attitude／这是一个比较～的办法。This is a more realistic way of doing things.

现实主义 xiànshízhǔyì realism: ～文学 realistic literature／～者 realist

现世[1] xiànshì this life

现世[2] xiànshì lose face; be disgraced; bring shame on oneself: 活～ really disgraceful (or shameful)

现世报 xiànshìbào retribution in this life

现势 xiànshì the trend of the times

现下 xiànxià inf. now; at present

现…现… xiàn…xiàn… (used with two verbs, expressing the idea of doing sth. extempore for a certain need): 现吃现做 cook for immediate consumption／现编现唱 make up a song as one sings／现学现教 learn while one teaches／现用现买 buy for immediate use

现象 xiànxiàng appearance (of things); phenomenon: 社会～ social phenomenon／向不良～作斗争 combat unhealthy phenomena／看事情不要只看～，要看本质。We should not judge things simply by their appearance; we must grasp their essence.

现行 xiànxíng ① currently in effect; in force; in operation: ～法令 decrees in effect／～规章制度 rules and regulations in force／～政策 present policies ② (of a criminal) active

现行犯 xiànxíngfàn leg. active criminal (a criminal caught in, or immediately before or after the act)

现形 xiànxíng reveal one's true features; betray oneself

现眼 xiànyǎn dial. make a spectacle (or fool) of oneself; lose face: 丢人现眼 diūrén-xiànyǎn

现洋 xiànyáng (also 现大洋 xiàndàyáng) silver dollar

现役 xiànyì ① active service; active duty: 服～ be on active service ② on active service; on active duty; active: ～兵员 personnel on active service／～军队 active military unit／～军官 officer on the active list／～年限 term of active service

现役军人 xiànyì jūnrén a member of the armed forces in active service; serviceman

现有 xiànyǒu now available; existing: ～材料 materials now available (or on hand); available information

现在 xiànzài now; at present; today: 我～不跟你争论。I will not argue with you now.／～的年轻人可讲究穿着了。Young people of today are particular about their clothing.

现状 xiànzhuàng present (or current) situation; status quo; existing state of affairs: 研究这个国家的历史和～ study the history and present condition of this country／改变(维持)～ change (maintain) the status quo

限

限 xiàn ① limit; bounds: 以年底为～ set the end of the year as the deadline ② set a limit; limit; restrict: ～你一个月完成。You are allowed one month to finish the job.／每人～购四张票。Each customer is limited to four tickets.／人数不～。There is no restriction (or limit) on the number of people.／不要～得太死，要有点灵活性。Don't make rigid restrictions; allow a certain latitude.

限定 xiàndìng prescribe (or set) a limit to; limit; restrict: ～时间完成 prescribe a time limit for fulfilment／参加这次座谈会的人数～为四十人。Participation in the forum will be limited to 40.／讨论的范围没有～。The subject matter of the discussion is not limited.

限度 xiàndù limit; limitation: 超过～ go beyond (or exceed) the limit／最大(最小)～ the maximum (minimum) limit／最高(最低)～ the highest (lowest) limit／最大～地发挥人的主观能动性 bring people's subjective initiative into full play／把非生产性的开支减少到最低～ reduce nonproductive expenditures to a minimum／我们的忍耐是有～的。There is a limit to our patience.

限额 xiàn'é norm; quota: ～以上(以下)的工业企业 above-norm (below-norm) industrial enterprises

限幅器 xiànfúqì radio limiter: 接收机～ receiver limiter

限价[1] xiànjià fix the official price

限价[2] xiànjià the (officially) fixed price: 最高～ the ceiling price／最低～ the floor price

限界 xiànjiè boundary limit

限量 xiànliàng limit the quantity of; set bounds to: 前途不可～ have boundless prospects

限令 xiànlìng order sb. to do sth. within a certain time: ～某人于四十八小时内离境 order sb. to leave the country within 48 hours; give sb. 48 hours' notice to leave the country

限期 xiànqī ① prescribe (or set) a time limit: ～报到 report for duty by the prescribed time／～撤退 withdraw within a stated time／这项工程～完成。This project must be completed within the specified time. ② time limit; deadline: ～已满。The time limit has been reached.／给他三天～ give him three days (to do sth.)

限位 xiànwèi mech. spacing

限于 xiànyú be confined to; be limited to: 学习雷锋的群众运动不～部队和青年。The mass movement to

learn from Lei Feng is not confined to the army and young people. / ～篇幅，来电不能一一登载。 As space is limited, it is impossible to publish all the messages we have received. / ～个人的思想水平 due to one's limited ideological level / 本文讨论的范围，～一些原则问题。 The subject matter of this article is limited to a few questions of principle.

限止 xiànzhǐ place (or impose) restrictions on; restrict; keep within limits

限制 xiànzhì ① place (or impose) restrictions on; restrict; limit; confine: ～数量 limit to a number or amount / ～发言时间 restrict (or limit) the time allowed for a speaker / ～在必要的范围内 confine sth. within necessary limits / 文章的字数不加～。 There is no restriction on the length of the article. ② restriction; limit; confinement: 年龄～ age limit / 受健康状况的～ be handicapped by one's poor health / 有一定的～ have specified restrictions

限制器 xiànzhìqì elec. limiter

限制性 xiànzhìxìng restricted; restrictive: ～会议 restricted meeting

限制性内切酶 xiànzhìxìng nèiqiēméi biochem. restriction enzyme

线(綫)

xiàn ① thread; string; wire: 一根～ piece of thread / ～团 a ball of string; a reel of thread / 铜～ copper wire / ～衣～裤 cotton knitwear ② math. line: 直线 zhíxiàn ③ sth. shaped like a line, thread, etc.: 光线 guāngxiàn ④ route; line: 供应～ supply route (or line) / 铁道～ railway line / 沪宁～ the Shanghai-Nanjing Railway (Line) ⑤ demarcation line; boundary: 边界～ boundary line / 海岸～ coastline ⑥ (political) line ⑦ brink; verge: 在死亡～上 on the verge of death / 在饥饿～上 on the brink of starvation ⑧ clue; thread: 案子的～儿断了。 The clue could not be followed up. ⑨ m. (used with numeral 一 before abstract things, indicating very little): 一～希望 a ray (or gleam) of hope

线材 xiàncái metall. wire rod

线虫 xiànchóng nematode

线虫病 xiànchóngbìng nematodiasis

线春 xiànchūn a silk fabric with a geometric design (for spring wear)

线电压 xiàndiànyā elec. line voltage

线段 xiànduàn math. line segment

线桄子 xiànguàngzi a reel or spool for winding thread

线规 xiànguī mech. wire gauge

线画 xiànhuà line drawing

线间 xiànjiān mus. space

线脚 xiànjiǎo dial. stitch: ～很密 sewn with close stitches

线路 xiànlù ① elec. circuit; line: 电话～ telephone line / ～工人 wireman; lineman ② communication line; route: 公共汽车～ bus line / 航空～ air route

线路图 xiànlùtú elec. circuit diagram

线麻 xiànmá same as 大麻 dàmá①

线描 xiànmiáo line drawing

线呢 xiànní cotton suiting

线膨胀 xiànpéngzhàng phys. linear expansion

线坯子 xiànpīzi coarse cotton thread

线圈 xiànquān elec. coil: 初级（次级）～ primary (secondary) coil

线人 xiànrén old an inner connection; spy; informer

线绳 xiànshéng cotton rope

线速度 xiànsùdù phys. linear velocity

线索 xiànsuǒ clue; thread: 破案的～ clues for solving a case / 故事的～ threads of a story / 为深入研究提供～ provide leads for further study / 关于他的下落，没有找到任何～。 No clues have been found as to his whereabouts.

线毯 xiàntǎn a blanket woven of thick cotton yarn; cotton (thread) blanket

线条 xiàntiáo arts line; contour; figure: 粗犷、雄浑的～ bold and vigorous lines / 这幅画的～非常柔和。 The lines of this painting are very soft. / 这个陶俑～非常优美。 The lines of this pottery figurine are very graceful. / 那个少女～很美。 The girl has a beautiful figure.

线头 xiàntóu ① the end of a thread: ～上打个结 secure the end of the thread with a knot ② an odd piece of thread; a bit of thread

线香 xiànxiāng a slender stick of incense

线形动物 xiànxíng dòngwù roundworm

线形叶 xiànxíngyè bot. linear leaf

线性 xiànxìng math. linear: ～方程 linear equation / ～规划 linear programming / ～函数 linear function

线衣 xiànyī cotton knitwear

线闸 xiànzhá cable brake (of a bicycle); caliper brake

线轴儿 xiànzhóur ① a reel for thread; bobbin ② a reel (or spool) of thread

线装 xiànzhuāng traditional thread binding (of Chinese books): ～本 thread-bound edition / ～书 thread-bound Chinese book

宪(憲)

xiàn ① statute ② constitution: 制～ draw up a constitution

宪兵 xiànbīng military police; military policeman; gendarme: ～队 gendarmerie; military police corps

宪法 xiànfǎ constitution; charter: ～草案 draft constitution / 中华人民共和国～ the Constitution of the People's Republic of China

宪章 xiànzhāng ① formal follow the example of; model oneself on; learn from ② formal institutions, decrees and regulations ③ charter: 联合国～ the United Nations Charter

宪政 xiànzhèng constitutional government; constitutionalism

陷

xiàn ① pitfall; trap: 陷阱 xiànjǐn ② get stuck or bogged down: ～进泥里 get stuck in the mud / ～在日常事务堆里 get bogged down in everyday routine / 在错误的泥坑里越～越深 sink deeper and deeper into the quagmire of error ③ sink; cave in: 深～的两颊 sunken cheeks / 他病了几天，眼睛都～进去了。 After being ill for a few days, his eyes became sunken. ④ frame (up): ～人于罪 frame sb. (up); incriminate sb. ⑤ (of a town, etc.) be captured; fall: 城～之日 the day the city fell ⑥ defect; deficiency: 缺陷 quēxiàn

陷害 xiànhài frame (up); make a false charge against: ～好人 frame up an innocent person / 政治～ political frame-up

陷阱 xiànjǐng pitfall; pit; trap; snare: 布设～ lay a trap

陷坑 xiànkēng pitfall; pit

陷落 xiànluò ① subside; sink in; cave in: 许多盆地都是因地壳～而形成的。 Many basins were formed by the subsidence of the earth's crust. ② sink (or fall) into; land oneself in: ～重围 find oneself tightly encircled / ～困境 land oneself in a predicament; be put in a tight spot; be cornered ③ (of territory) fall into enemy hands: 南京于1937年十二月～。 Nanjing fell into enemy hands in December 1937.

陷落地震 xiànluò dìzhèn depression earthquake

陷入 xiànrù ① sink (or fall) into; land oneself in; be caught in; get bogged down in: ～被动地位 fall into a passive position / ～重围 find oneself tightly encircled / ～困境 land oneself in a predicament; be put in a tight spot; be cornered / ～无休止的争论 be bogged down in endless debates / ～唯心论和形而上学 degenerate into idealism and metaphysics ② be lost in; be immersed

in; be deep in: ～沉思 be lost in thought; be deep in meditation

陷入僵局 xiànrù jiāngjú　come to a deadlock; reach an impasse: 谈判～。The negotiations came to a deadlock. *or* The negotiations reached an impasse.

陷身 xiànshēn　fall into; land in: ～虎口 fall into the tiger's mouth—fall into a very dangerous position

陷身图圄 xiànshēn língyǔ　be thrown into prison; be taken prisoner; be behind prison bars: 军长力竭负伤,～。The commander, wounded and exhausted in the fighting, was taken prisoner.

陷型模 xiànxíngmú　*mech.* swage

陷于 xiànyú　fall into (an unfavourable position): 双方谈判～僵局。The talks between the two sides were in a deadlock. / ～孤立 find oneself isolated

陷阵 xiànzhèn　break through enemy lines: 冲锋陷阵 chōngfēng xiànzhèn

馅

xiàn　filling; stuffing: 饺子～儿 stuffing for dumplings

馅儿饼 xiànrbǐng　meat pie

羡（羨）

xiàn　admire; envy: 称羡 chēngxiàn

羡慕 xiànmù　admire; envy: 她很～我有这样一个好丈夫。She envies me my good husband.

线

xiàn　same as 线 xiàn

献（獻）

xiàn　① offer; present; dedicate; donate: ～哈达 present a *hada* (a Tibetan ceremonial silk scarf) / ～血 donate blood / 敬～花圈 lay a wreath / 把青春～给祖国 dedicate one's youth to the motherland / 为革命～出生命 give one's life for the cause of the revolution ② show; put on; display: 献殷勤 xiàn yīnqín / 献技 xiànjì

献宝 xiànbǎo　① present a treasure ② offer a valuable piece of advice or one's valuable experience ③ show off what one treasures

献策 xiàncè　offer advice; make suggestions

献丑 xiànchǒu　*hum.* (speaking of one's own performance) show oneself up; show one's incompetence (*or* inadequacy): 一定要我唱, 就只好～了。Since you insist, i'll make a fool of myself and sing.

献词 xiàncí　congratulatory message: 新年～ New Year message

献花 xiànhuā　present flowers or bouquets

献计 xiànjì　offer advice; make suggestions: 在技术革新中人人～献策。Everyone suggested ways and means for technical innovation.

献技 xiànjì　show one's skill (in a performance)

献礼 xiànlǐ　present a gift: 以优异成绩向国庆～ greet National Day with new and outstanding successes

献媚 xiànmèi　try to ingratiate oneself with; make up to

献旗 xiànqí　present a banner

献身 xiànshēn　devote (*or* dedicate) oneself to; give one's life for: ～教育事业 devote oneself to the cause of education / 愿为共产主义事业～ be ready to give one's life for the cause of communism

献艺 xiànyì　(of actors, singers, etc.) show one's skill; give a performance: 登台～ go up on the stage and give a performance

献殷勤 xiàn yīnqín　do everything to please; pay attentions to; pay one's addresses to: 他不断地向姑娘～, 倒把姑娘惹恼了。His constant attentions annoyed the girl.

腺

xiàn　gland: 汗 (泪、唾液) ～ sweat (lachrymal, salivary) gland

腺瘤 xiànliú　*med.* adenoma

霰

xiàn　*meteorol.* graupel ——see also sǎn

xiāng

乡（鄉）

xiāng　① country; countryside; village; rural area: 城乡 chéngxiāng ② native place; home village or town: 丝绸之～ the home of silk ③ township (a rural administrative unit under the county)

乡巴佬儿 xiāngbālǎor　*derog.* (country) bumpkin

乡愁 xiāngchóu　homesickness: ～满肠 be overcome with homesickness

乡村 xiāngcūn　village; countryside; rural area: 那是一个边远的～。That is a remote village. / ～的空气比城市新鲜。The air is cleaner and fresher in the country than in the cities. / ～风格 rustic style / ～生活 country life

乡党 xiāngdǎng　*formal* ① village communities ② fellow villagers or townsmen

乡规民约 xiāngguī-mínyuē　local rules and regulations valid for the whole village

乡宦 xiānghuàn　a retired official living in the country (in former times)

乡间 xiāngjiān　in the village; in the country: ～小贩 village pedlar / ～别墅 country villa

乡井 xiāngjǐng　*formal* native place; home village or town

乡里 xiānglǐ　① home village or town ② fellow villagers or townsmen: 都是～乡亲的, 有什么不好开口的。As we are all fellow townsmen, there's nothing you can't bring up before us.

乡邻 xiānglín　fellow villagers; neighbours (in the same village): 那个村里～之间关系一向很好。The people of that village have always been on very good terms with each other.

乡民 xiāngmín　villagers; country people

乡僻 xiāngpì　far from town; out-of-the-way

乡气 xiāng-qì　rustic; countrified; uncouth: 她的穿着有点～。She looks rather rustic in the way she dresses.

乡亲 xiāngqīn　① a person from the same village or town; fellow villager or townsman ② local people; villagers; folks: 给～们办个示范性的养鸡场 set up an exemplary poultry farm for the villagers ③ a term of direct address for local people or villagers: ～们, 八路军回来啦! Folks, the Eighth Route Army is back with us again!

乡曲 xiāngqū　*formal* remote countryside; an out-of-the-way village: 久居～ have lived in a remote village for a long time

乡人 xiāngrén　① village people ② fellow villagers; people from the same village

乡绅 xiāngshēn　country gentleman; squire

乡试 xiāngshì　provincial examination (under the Ming-Qing civil service examination system, the examination for the selection of *juren* 举人 out of *xiucai* 秀才, held triennially in the various provincial capitals)

乡思 xiāngsī　homesickness; nostalgia

乡俗 xiāngsú　local customs; village customs: 按照～, 他得叩三个头。According to local customs, he had to *kowtow* three times.

乡谈 xiāngtán　local dialect: 二人打起～, 十分投机。Lapsing into their local dialect, the two of them began to talk most amicably.

乡土 xiāngtǔ　native soil; one's native land; local: ～风味 local flavour / 富于～气息 be imbued with local colour / ～教材 teaching material reflecting local conditions and suited to local needs

乡土观念 xiāngtǔ guānniàn　provincialism

乡土志 xiāngtǔzhì　local records or annals

乡下 xiāngxia　*inf.* countryside; village: 他刚从～来。He's just come from the countryside. / ～来人了。Someone is here from the village.

乡下人 xiāngxiarén　country folk; country cousin; rustic: 我好像～头回进城,见啥都觉得新鲜。I felt like a country bumpkin coming to town for the first time. Everything which met my eyes was a novelty.

乡贤 xiāngxián　country worthy

乡谊 xiāngyì　*formal* friendship between people from the same native place

乡音 xiāngyīn　accent of one's native place; local accent: 她说话～挺重的。She speaks with a strong local accent.

乡邮 xiāngyóu　rural postal service

乡邮员 xiāngyóuyuán　rural postman

乡愿 xiāngyuàn　*formal* hypocrite

乡约 xiāngyuē　local rules and regulations valid for all the inhabitants of a township: 村有村规,乡有～。Every village and township have their own rules and regulations.

乡镇 xiāngzhèn　① villages and towns ② small towns in general

乡镇企业 xiāngzhèn qǐyè　village and township enterprises

乡梓 xiāngzǐ　*formal* one's native place

芎(蔴)

xiāng　① a fragrant herb mentioned in ancient texts ② same as 香 xiāng

芎剧 xiāngjù　a local opera popular in Taiwan and southern Fujian

相¹

xiāng　*adv.* ① each other; one another; mutually: ～见 meet (each other) / ～聚 get together / ～视而笑 look and smile at each other / 不～符合 not tally with each other / 理论要与实际～联系。Theory must be integrated with practice. / 这里的山水和我老家的～仿佛。The scenery here looks much the same as that in my home town. ② (indicating an action performed by one person toward another): 实不～瞒 to tell you the truth / 他既然不愿意去,就不要～强。Since he doesn't want to go, don't force him to. / 连日承友好～邀,遍游京都名胜古迹。For days, friends invited me out to visit the historical sites and scenic spots in the capital. ③ (Xiāng) a surname

相²

xiāng　see for oneself (whether sb. or sth. is to one's liking): ～女婿 take a look at one's prospective son-in-law ——see also xiàng

相爱 xiāng'ài　be in love with each other

相安无事 xiāng'ān wú shì　live in peace with each other

相帮 xiāngbāng　*dial.* help; aid; assist

相比 xiāngbǐ　compare: 二者不能～。There's no comparison between the two (of them). / 跟先进单位～,我们还有很大差距。We still have a long way to go to catch up with the advanced units. *or* We are far behind the advanced units. / ～之下,他的作文比你写得好。By comparison, his composition is better than yours.

相差 xiāngchà　differ: 两者～无几。There's hardly any difference between the two. / 我们的工作跟大家的要求～还很远。Our work still falls far short of the expected standard.

相称 xiāngchèn　match; suit: 这两种颜色配在一起很～。The two colours match very well. / 这头巾跟你的年龄不～。This kerchief doesn't suit a person of your age. / 你这种工作作风与党员的称号很不～。Your work style

is not worthy of a Party member. ——see also xiāngchēng

相称 xiāngchēng　call each other; address each other (as ...): 以姐弟～ address each other as brother and sister ——see also xiāngchèn

相承 xiāngchéng　pass on from one to another: 世代～ pass on from generation to generation

相持 xiāngchí　be locked in a stalemate: 双方已～很久。The two sides have been locked in a stalemate for a long time. / 战争处于～阶段。The war was at a stalemate.

相持不下 xiāngchí bù xià　each sticks to his own stand; be locked in a stalemate: 双方～。Neither side was ready to yield.

相处 xiāngchǔ　get along (with one another): 不好～ difficult to get along with / ～得很好 get on well with each other / 我们～时间不长,但已经结下了深厚的友谊。We've not been together long, but we've become close friends.

相传 xiāngchuán　① tradition has it that...; according to legend: ～这里是当年孔明祭风处。According to legend, this is where Kong Ming supplicated the wind. ② hand down or pass on from one to another: 世代相传 shìdài xiāngchuán

相待 xiāngdài　treat: 以诚～ treat another with all sincerity / 拿他当朋友～ treat him as a friend

相当 xiāngdāng　① match; balance; correspond to; be about equal to; be commensurate with: 得失～。The gains balance the losses. / 他们俩年龄～。They are well-matched in age. *or* They're about the same age. / 两队实力～。The two teams are about equal in strength. / ～于省一级的自治区 autonomous regions analogous to provinces / 水坝高达七十八米,～于二十层的大楼。The dam rises to a height of 78 metres, or the height of a 20-storey building. ② suitable; fit; appropriate: 他一时想不出～的字眼来。At the time he couldn't think of a suitable word for it. / 这个工作还没有找到～的人。We haven't found a fit person for the job yet. ③ *adv.* quite; fairly; considerably: ～好 fairly good / 演出～成功。The performance was quite a success. / 社会主义社会是一个～长的历史阶段。Socialist society covers a historical period of considerable length.

相得 xiāngdé　*formal* get along well: 相处多年,甚为～ have lived and worked together for years and got along well

相得益彰 xiāng dé yì zhāng　each shining more brilliantly in the other's company; bring out the best in each other; complement each other

相等 xiāngděng　be equal: 数量～ be equal in amount (*or* quantity, number); be numerically equal / 这两间房子的面积～。The two rooms have the same amount of floor space.

相抵 xiāngdǐ　offset; balance; counterbalance: 收支～ one's accounts balance / 收支～,我还有一百五十元盈余。My accounts show a favourable balance of 150 *yuan*.

相对 xiāngduì　① opposite to each other; face to face: ～而坐 sit opposite (*or* facing) each other; sit face to face / 两山遥遥～。The two hills stand opposite each other at a distance. / 美是与丑～的。Beauty is the opposite of ugliness. ② relative: 平衡是～的,不平衡是绝对的。Balance is relative, imbalance is absolute. ③ relatively; comparatively: ～稳定 relatively stable / ～地说 comparatively speaking

相对高度 xiāngduì gāodù　relative altitude (*or* height)

相对论 xiāngduìlùn　*phys.* the theory of relativity; relativity: 广(狭)义～ the general (special) theory of relativity

相对论性 xiāngduìlùnxìng *phys.* relativistic: ～量子理论 relativistic quantum theory / ～物理学 relativistic physics

相对湿度 xiāngduì shīdù relative humidity

相对速度 xiāngduì sùdù *phys.* relative velocity

相对误差 xiāngduì wùchā *math.* relative error

相对性 xiāngduìxìng relativity

相对运动 xiāngduì yùndòng *phys.* relative motion

相对真理 xiāngduì zhēnlǐ *philos.* relative truth

相对值 xiāngduìzhí relative value

相对主义 xiāngduìzhǔyì *philos.* relativism

相烦 xiāngfán *formal* trouble (*or* bother) you: 有事～。May I trouble you for something?

相反 xiāngfǎn ① contrary; opposite: 我的意思跟你正～。My opinion is contrary to yours (*or* is just the opposite of yours). / 结果与我们的愿望恰好～。The result turned out contrary to our expectations. / 他们朝着～的方向开走了。They drove off in opposite directions. / 他跟他弟弟对政治持～的观点。He and his brother had contrary points of view on politics. ② *adv.* on the contrary: 他一点儿也不吝啬，～，没有比他更大方的了。He is not stingy; on the contrary, no one could be more generous. / 他们根本不是好朋友，～，是死对头。Far from being best friends, they are bitter enemies.

相反相成 xiāngfǎn-xiāngchéng things that oppose each other also complement each other; be both opposite and complementary to each other; oppose each other and yet also complement each other: 战争中勇敢牺牲和保存自己并不矛盾，他们是～的。Heroic sacrifice in war does not contradict self-preservation. They are both opposite and complementary to each other.

相仿 xiāngfǎng be similar; resemble each other; be more or less the same: 内容～ be similar in content / 年纪～ be about the same age

相逢 xiāngféng meet (by chance); come across: 想不到我和儿时好友竟在异国他乡～。I never thought I would meet my childhood companion in a foreign land.

相符 xiāngfú conform to; tally (*or* agree) with; correspond to (*or* with): 报告与事实～。The report tallies with the facts. / 名实～。The name corresponds to the reality.

相辅而行 xiāng fǔ ér xíng be complementary to each other; proceed in coordination; go together

相辅相成 xiāngfǔ-xiāngchéng supplement and complement each other: 行政命令同用说服教育的方法去解决人民内部的矛盾，是～的两个方面。Administrative regulations and the method of persuasion and education complement each other in resolving contradictions among the people.

相干 xiānggān ① (used in the negative or in a rhetorical question) have sth. to do with; be concerned with: 这件事与她有什么～? What has this to do with her? / 这事与你不～。This has nothing to do with you. ② *phys.* coherent: ～散射 coherent scattering

相干性 xiānggānxìng *phys.* coherence; coherency

相告 xiānggào inform (*or* tell) you: 有要事～。I have something important to tell you. / 实话～ to tell you the truth

相隔 xiānggé be separated by; be apart; be at a distance of: ～万里 be thousands of *li* apart; be a long way away from each other / ～多年 after an interval of many years / ～千山万水 be separated by numerous rivers and mountains / 从我上次来到现在～不过两三个月，情况已经发生了很大的变化。It's only two or three months since my last visit here, but the situation has greatly changed.

相顾 xiānggù look at each other: 在座的人～无言。All those present just looked at each other and kept si-lent. / ～一笑 smile at each other knowingly

相关 xiāngguān be mutually related; be interrelated: 体育事业和人民健康密切～。Physical culture has a direct bearing on the people's health. / 与此～的事物 things correlated with this

相好 xiānghǎo ① be on intimate terms ② an intimate friend ③ have an affair with ④ lover or mistress

相互 xiānghù ① mutual; reciprocal: 增进～了解 promote mutual understanding / 援助是～的。Aid is usually mutual. / ～关系 mutual relation; interrelation / ～作用 interaction; interplay ② *adv.* mutually; reciprocally; each other: ～影响 influence each other; interact / ～支持 support each other

相会 xiānghuì meet: 我期待着在西安再一次和你～。I'm looking forward to meeting you again in Xi'an.

相继 xiāngjì in succession; one after another: 代表们～发言。The delegates spoke one after another.

相煎太急 xiāng jiān tài jí (of brothers) bitter against each other; no love lost between them ——see also 煮豆燃其 zhǔdòu ránqí

相见恨晚 xiāngjiàn hèn wǎn regret not having met earlier: 两人谈得情投意合，～。The two found so much in common that they regretted not having met earlier.

相间 xiāngjiàn alternate with: 黑白～ black alternating with white; in black and white check

相交 xiāngjiāo ① intersect: 圆的直径必～于圆心。Any two diameters of a circle intersect each other. ② make friends with: ～有年 have been friends for years

相较 xiāngjiào compare: 双方实力～，我方略优于对方。Compared with our opponent, we are a cut above them in strength.

相接 xiāngjiē (of one or more trains, buses, etc.) connect (with): 这个航班在广州同飞往桂林的航班～。This flight connects with a flight for Guilin at Guangzhou.

相近 xiāngjìn ① close; near: 地点～的两个学校 two neighbouring schools / 比分～。The score was very close. ② similar; about the same: 两人性格～。The two of them are similar in character.

相敬如宾 xiāng jìng rú bīn (of husband and wife) treat each other with the respect due to a guest

相救 xiāngjiù come to sb.'s rescue; save sb. from danger: 拼死～ risk one's life to help save sb.

相距 xiāngjù be separated by (a distance of ...); be ... apart; be ... away from: 两地～不到二公里。The two places are less than two kilometres apart. / 这两个桥墩之间～二十米。The distance between the two piers of the bridge is 20 metres.

相连 xiānglián be linked together; be joined: 两地有铁路～。The two places are linked by rail. / 两国山水～。The two countries are joined by common mountains and rivers. / 虽然他们俩分驻两地，但是他们的心是～的。Though the two of them are stationed in two different places, their hearts are linked together.

相骂 xiāngmà abuse each other; exchange hot words

相骂无好言，相打无好拳 xiāngmà wú hǎo yán, xiāngdǎ wú hǎo quán there are no quarrels with nice words nor fights with weak blows

相能 xiāngnéng *formal* (usu. used in the negative) be on good terms: 两人素不～。The two have never been on good terms. *or* The two are always at loggerheads.

相陪 xiāngpéi keep company with; be a companion to: 他孤身一人，无人～。He is all alone without a companion.

相配 xiāngpèi be well-matched; be a good match: 小两口儿很～。The young couple are a perfect match. / 她的打扮和她的年龄很不～。Her clothes and her make-up do not fit her age.

相扑 xiāngpū *sports* sumo (wrestling)

相契 xiāngqì *formal* be in accord; be on friendly

terms

相切 xiāngqiē *math.* have a common tangent at a point; be tangent: 这两个弧 (圆) ~。These two curves (circles) are tangent.

相亲 xiāngqīn size up a prospective mate in an arranged meeting

相亲相爱 xiāngqīn-xiāng'ài be friendly or on intimate terms: 同学们~，关系十分融洽。The students are very friendly and get on very well together.

相去无几 xiāng qù wújǐ there is not much difference; pretty much the same

相劝 xiāngquàn try to persuade sb.; offer advice to sb.: 好意~ offer well-meaning advice / 尽管我好言~，她依然执意不从。Though I tried hard to persuade her to do it, she flatly refused.

相扰 xiāngrǎo ① interfere with or disturb each other: 如果我们再有一个房间就可以各不~了。If we had an extra room, we wouldn't disturb each other. ② *pol.* disturb you; trouble you: 对不起，~了! Sorry to have disturbed you. / 无事不敢~。If it weren't something important, I wouldn't bother you with it.

相忍为国 xiāng rěn wéi guó show forbearance for the sake of the nation

相濡以沫 xiāng rú yǐ mò (of stranded fish) moisten each other with spit—give one's meagre resources to help another in time of need

相若 xiāngruò *formal* be about the same; be similar; be alike

相商 xiāngshāng ① consult each other ② consult you: 有要事~。I have something important to consult you about.

相生相克 xiāngshēng-xiāngkè mutual promotion and restraint between the five elements (a concept held by the ancients to explain natural phenomena and later used in traditional Chinese medicine, etc.) ——see also 五行 wǔxíng

相识 xiāngshí ① be acquainted with each other: 此人似曾~。It seems I've met him before. ② an acquaintance: 老~ an old acquaintance

相率 xiāngshuài one after another: 宾客~离座。The guests rose one after another.

相思 xiāngsī pine with love; yearn for sb.'s love; languish with lovesickness

相思病 xiāngsībìng lovesickness: 害~ be lovesick

相思鸟 xiāngsīniǎo red-billed leiothrix

相思子 xiāngsīzǐ ① jequirity (the plant) ② jequirity bean; love pea ③ ormosia seed

相似 xiāngsì resemble; be similar; be alike: 兄弟俩面貌~。The two brothers look alike. / 历史往往有惊人的~之处。Astonishing parallels can often be found in history.

相似形 xiāngsìxíng *math.* similar figures

相提并论 xiāngtí-bìnglùn (usu. used in the negative) mention in the same breath; place on a par: 两者不能~。The two cannot be mentioned in the same breath. / 怎么能拿我这个初出茅庐的和巴金这样的大作家~呢? How can you mention a fledgling like me in the same breath with a great writer like Ba Jin?

相通 xiāngtōng communicate with each other; be interlinked: 这是两间~的屋子。These are two communicating rooms. / 这两个院子有门~。The two courtyards open onto (*or* into) each other. / 我们的心是~的。Our hearts beat in harmony.

相同 xiāngtóng identical; the same; alike: 我们在这个问题上观点~。We have identical (*or* the same) views on this question. / 两者毫无~之处。The two have nothing in common. / 不同性质的矛盾不能用~的方法去处理。Contradictions different in nature must not be treated alike (*or* in the same way).

相投 xiāngtóu be congenial; agree with each other: 兴趣~ have similar tastes and interests; find each other congenial

相托 xiāngtuō entrust sb. with sth.; commit to sb.'s care; ask sb. to do sth.: 以国事~ entrust sb. with state affairs / 我有要事~。I have something important to entrust you with (*or* to ask you to do).

相违 xiāngwéi disagree; be opposed to each other: 双方意见~。The two sides could not find any common ground. / 这种做法与我们的本意~。This way of doing things runs counter to our original ideas.

相闻 xiāngwén be able to hear each other; be within hearing distance of each other: 鸡犬之声~ the crowing of their cocks and the barking of their dogs are within hearing of each other (said of country people living not far from each other)

相向 xiāngxiàng ① in opposite directions: ~而行 go in opposite directions ② face to face; facing each other: ~无言 look each other in the face without saying a word

相像 xiāngxiàng resemble; be similar; be alike: 这两种花很~。These two flowers are very much alike.

相偕 xiāngxié accompany each other (in doing sth.); keep each other company: 两人出入~，形影不离。The two are always together, inseparable like shadows. / ~出游 go on an outing together

相信 xiāngxìn believe in; be convinced of; trust; have faith in: 我~你的话。I believe what you say. / ~我吧。Trust me. / ~群众 have faith in the masses / ~真理 believe in truth / ~自己的事业是正义的 be convinced of the justice of one's cause

相形见绌 xiāng xíng jiàn chù prove inferior by comparison; pale by comparison; be outshone: 鬼见愁，名字听来令人生畏; 但是，比起我们爬过的一些高山来，未免~了。The Devil's Frown, despite its forbidding name, pales beside some of the mountains we have climbed.

相形之下 xiāng xíng zhī xià by contrast; by comparison

相沿成习 xiāng yán chéng xí become common practice through long usage

相依 xiāngyī depend on each other; be interdependent: 唇齿相依 chún-chǐ xiāngyī

相依为命 xiāngyī wéi mìng depend on each other for survival: 从此，母女俩~。Since then the mother and the daughter had been dependent on each other for survival.

相宜 xiāngyí suitable; fitting; appropriate: 在那个场合你说这样的话是不~的。What you said on that occasion was not appropriate. / 秋分种麦最~。The Autumnal Equinox is the best time for wheat-sowing.

相应 xiāngyīng (used in official language between organizations of the same level) ought to; should: ~函达。We should inform you of this by letter. ——see also xiāngyìng; xiāngying

相迎 xiāngyíng welcome sb.: 笑脸~ give sb. a cheerful welcome

相应 xiāngyìng corresponding; relevant; fitting; appropriate: 随着工业的发展，对环境保护也采取了~的措施。With the development of industry, appropriate measures have been taken to protect the environment. / 大会一致谴责这种侵略行为，并通过了~的决议。The conference unanimously condemned this act of aggression and passed relevant resolutions. ——see also xiāngyīng; xiāngying

相应 xiāngying *dial.* inexpensive ——see also xiāngyīng; xiāngyìng

相映 xiāngyìng reflect each other; set each other off; form a contrast: 山光水色，上下~。The hills and the waters form a beautiful contrast.

相映成趣 xiāngyìng chéng qù set each other off and

form a pleasing contrast; contrast pleasingly with each other: 湖光塔影，～。 The lake's shimmer and the pagoda's reflection make a pleasing scene.

相与 xiāngyǔ ① get along with sb.; deal with sb.: 此人极难～。 That person is extremely difficult to get along with (*or* deal with). ② *adv.* with each other; together: ～大笑 have a good laugh together ③ *old* an intimate friend

相遇 xiāngyù meet: 我二人在美术馆偶然～。 We ran across each other in the art gallery.

相约 xiāngyuē agree (on meeting place, date, etc.); reach agreement; make an appointment

相赠 xiāngzèng present to sb.; give as a present: 她以亲笔签名的著作～。 She gave me an autographed copy of her book.

相知 xiāngzhī ① be well acquainted with each other; know each other well: ～有素 have known each other long ② a bosom friend; a great friend

相知恨晚 xiāngzhī hèn wǎn regret that one has not got to know sb. sooner

相中 xiāngzhòng take a fancy to; settle on: 这些姑娘当中他好像～了一个。 He seems to have taken a fancy to one of these girls. / 这些姑娘我一个也相不中。 I'm interested in none of these girls.

相助 xiāngzhù come to sb.'s help; aid: 一人有难, 众人～。 When one man is in difficulty, all come to his help (*or* aid).

相撞 xiāngzhuàng collide: 两机～, 同时坠毁。 Both planes crashed within seconds of a midair collision. / 两车～。 The two vehicles had a head-on crash.

相左 xiāngzuǒ *formal* ① fail to meet each other ② conflict with each other; fail to agree; be at odds with: 意见～ hold different views; be at variance

香

xiāng ① fragrant; sweet-smelling; aromatic; scented: 稻～千里 the fragrance of ripening rice spreading a thousand *li* / 茉莉花好～! What a sweet scent the jasmine flowers give off! ② savoury; appetizing: 这饭真～。 This rice is really appetizing. / 炒什么菜啊? 好～呀! Mmm! What's cooking? It smells delicious. ③ with relish; with good appetite: 吃得很～ eat with relish; enjoy the food / 昨晚没睡好, 吃饭不～。 I have no appetite because I didn't sleep well last night. ④ (of sleep) sound: 她睡得正～呢。 She's sound asleep. ⑤ popular; welcome: 这种摩托车在农村可～了。 This type of motorcycle is most popular in the countryside. ⑥ perfume or spice: 麝香 shèxiāng / 檀香 tánxiāng ⑦ incense; joss stick: 盘香 pánxiāng / 蚊香 wénxiāng

香案 xiāng'àn a long altar on which incense burners are placed; incense burner table

香槟酒 xiāngbīnjiǔ champagne

香波 xiāngbō shampoo

香饽饽 xiāngbōbo *dial.* a person who is liked best; favourite

香菜 xiāngcài common name for 芫荽 yánsui

香草 xiāngcǎo vanilla: ～冰淇淋 vanilla ice cream

香草醛 xiāngcǎoquán *chem.* vanillic aldehyde; vanillin; vanilla

香肠 xiāngcháng sausage

香臭 xiāng-chòu good and foul smells—good and bad: 不知～ not know whether a thing is good or bad / ～不分 unable to tell good from bad

香椿 xiāngchūn ① Chinese toon (*Toona sinensis*; the tree) ② the tender, edible leaves and stems of Chinese toon (used as a vegetable)

香袋 xiāngdài sachet

香榧 xiāngfēi Chinese torreya (*Torreya grandis*)

香榧子 xiāngfěizi Chinese torreya nut

香粉 xiāngfěn cosmetic powder

香馥馥 xiāngfùfù strongly scented; richly fragrant

香附子 xiāngfùzǐ *Chin. med.* the rhizome of nutgrass flatsedge (*Cyperus rotundus*)

香干 xiānggān smoked bean curd

香港 Xiānggǎng ① Hong Kong (*or* Hongkong) Island ② the entire Hong Kong area (including Hong Kong Island, Kowloon 九龙 and the New Territories 新界)

香港脚 xiānggǎngjiǎo *dial.* Hong Kong foot; athlete's foot

香港特别行政区 Xiānggǎng Tèbié Xíngzhèngqū the Hong Kong Special Administrative Region (HKSAR)

香菇 xiānggū (also 香菰 xiānggū) *Xianggu* mushroom

香瓜 xiāngguā muskmelon

香闺 xiāngguī *old* lady's bedchamber

香花 xiānghuā fragrant flowers—views, opinions, writings, artistic works, etc. useful to the people

香灰 xiānghuī incense ash

香会 xiānghuì a group of Buddhists going together on a pilgrimage; a company of Buddhist pilgrims

香火[1] xiānghuǒ ① joss sticks and candles burning at a temple: ～甚盛 (of a temple) have many worshippers; attract a large number of pilgrims ② temple attendant ③ ancestral sacrifices: 继～ continue the family line

香火[2] xiānghuǒ burning joss sticks, incense coil, etc.: 用～点爆竹 light a firecracker with a burning joss stick

香蕉 xiāngjiāo banana

香蕉苹果 xiāngjiāo píngguǒ a species of apple with a bananalike odor

香蕉水 xiāngjiāoshuǐ *chem.* banana oil (used as a paint solvent)

香精 xiāngjīng essence: 食用～ flavouring essence / 合成～ compound essence / ～油 essential oil

香客 xiāngkè a worshipper at a Buddhist temple; a Buddhist pilgrim

香兰素 xiānglánsù another name for 香草醛 xiāngcǎoquán

香料 xiāngliào ① perfume ② spice

香料厂 xiāngliàochǎng perfumery

香炉 xiānglú incense burner

香茅 xiāngmáo *bot.* lemongrass

香茅醛 xiāngmáoquán *chem.* citronellal

香茅油 xiāngmáoyóu citronella oil

香囊 xiāngnáng sachet

香喷喷 xiāngpēnpēn ① sweet-smelling ② savoury; appetizing: 一碗～的炖肉 a bowl of savoury (pork) stew

香片 xiāngpiàn scented tea

香蒲 xiāngpú *bot.* cattail

香气 xiāngqì a sweet smell; fragrance; aroma: 门一开, 一阵～扑鼻而来。 The door opened and a sweet smell reached (*or* assailed) my nostrils.

香钱 xiāngqián incense money—gifts to a temple and its monks

香石竹 xiāngshízhú *bot.* carnation

香水 xiāngshuǐ perfume; scent

香酥鸡 xiāngsūjī crisp fried chicken (a Chinese dish)

香梭鱼 xiāngsuōyú *zool.* red barracuda

香甜 xiāngtián ① fragrant and sweet: 味道～ taste and smell sweet / ～的瓜果 sweet melons and fruits ② (of sleep) sound: 小伙子们劳动了一天, 晚上睡得格外～。 The boys slept soundly after a day's work.

香豌豆 xiāngwāndòu sweet pea (an ornamental climbing plant, with butterfly-shaped flowers)

香蕈 xiāngxùn another name for 香菇 xiānggū

香烟[1] xiāngyān ① incense smoke: ～缭绕 smoke coiling up from burning incense ② ancestral sacrifices: 断了～ die without issue

香烟[2] xiāngyān cigarette: ～盒 cigarette case / ～头 cigarette butt (*or* end)

香艳 xiāngyàn amorous; erotic: 〜小说 an amorous novel

香胰子 xiāngyízi dial. perfumed (or scented) soap; toilet soap

香油 xiāngyóu sesame oil

香鼬 xiāngyòu zool. alpine weasel

香鱼 xiāngyú zool. sweetfish; ayu

香橼 xiāngyuán bot. citron

香云纱 xiāngyúnshā text. gambiered Guangdong gauze

香皂 xiāngzào perfumed (or scented) soap; toilet soap

香泽 xiāngzé formal ① perfumed hair cream or oil ② fragrance (esp. of a lady)

香獐子 xiāngzhāngzi popular name for 麝 shè

香脂 xiāngzhī ① face cream ② balm; balsam

香烛 xiāngzhú joss sticks and candles (burned when offering sacrifices to gods or ancestors)

香资 xiāngzī same as 香钱 xiāngqián

香子兰 xiāngzǐlán bot. vanilla: 〜豆 vanilla bean / 〜精 vanilla extract; vanilla

厢(廂) xiāng ① wing (usu. of a one-storeyed house); wing-room: 一正两〜 a central room with two wing-rooms ② railway carriage or compartment; (theatre) box: 车厢 chēxiāng / 包厢 bāoxiāng ③ the vicinity outside of a city gate: 城厢 chéngxiāng ④ old side: 这〜 this side; here /那〜 that side; there

厢房 xiāngfáng wing (usu. of a one-storeyed house); wing-room: 东〜 the east wing

湘 Xiāng ① short for 湘江 (a river in Hunan Province) ② another name for 湖南 Húnán

湘妃竹 xiāngfēizhú bamboo of the Ladies of the Xiang (another name for 斑竹 bānzhú; from the legend that the two sister-queens of the sage King Shun 舜, called "Ladies of the Xiang," wept so copiously after Shun died that the tears they shed speckled the bamboos, thus giving rise to the spotted variety of the plant)

湘剧 xiāngjù Hunan opera

湘帘 xiānglián a curtain made of bamboo of the Xiang; mottled-bamboo curtain

湘莲 xiānglián Hunan lotus seeds

湘绣 xiāngxiù Hunan embroidery

湘竹 xiāngzhú bamboo of the Xiang (another name for 湘妃竹 xiāngfēizhú)

莦 xiāng see 青莦 qīngxiāng

箱 xiāng ① chest; box; case; trunk: 大木〜 wooden trunk; chest / 纸〜 cardboard box; carton / 货〜 packing box /书〜 a box for books ② anything in the shape of a box: 风箱 fēngxiāng

箱底 xiāngdǐ ① the bottom of a chest: 旧衣服都压〜了。The old clothes are stowed away at the bottom of the chest. ② valuables stowed away at the bottom of the chest; one's store of valuables: 她家〜厚。Her family has accumulated a large store of valuables.

箱笼 xiānglǒng (a traveller's) boxes and baskets; luggage; baggage

箱型照相机 xiāngxíng zhàoxiàngjī box camera

箱子 xiāngzi chest, box, case, trunk, etc.

襄 xiāng formal assist; help: 共〜义举 let everybody help to promote this worthy undertaking

襄礼 xiānglǐ ① assist in officiating a ceremony at a wedding, funeral, etc. (in former times) ② assistant master of ceremonies

襄理 xiānglǐ assistant manager second to 协理 xiélǐ (in a bank, business enterprise, etc. in former times)

襄赞 xiāngzàn formal support and assist in: 〜军务 assist in military affairs

襄助 xiāngzhù formal assist

骧 xiāng formal ① (of horses) gallop ② rear (one's head)

镶 xiāng ① inlay; set; mount: 金〜玉嵌 inlaid with gold and jade / 〜宝石 set gems; mount precious stones /〜满口假牙 have a full set of false teeth put in one's mouth / 给窗子〜玻璃 glaze a window ② rim; edge; border: 给裙子〜花边 edge a skirt with lace / 给镜子〜上个框儿 mount (or set) the mirror in a frame

镶板 xiāngbǎn archit. panelling

镶边 xiāngbiān edge; border; rim: 她衣领上镶着一道红边。The collar of her jacket is edged with red. / 他的眼镜是镶金边的。His glasses have gold rims.

镶嵌 xiāngqiàn ① inlay; set; mount: 〜银丝漆器 silver-inlaid lacquerware / 〜细工 inlaid work; marquetry ② mosaic; tessellate: 〜玻璃 mosaic glass / 〜图案 mosaic; tessellation

镶嵌画 xiāngqiànhuà a picture or design made of mosaic; mosaic

镶牙 xiāngyá put in a false tooth; insert an artificial tooth

xiáng

详 xiáng ① detailed; minute: 〜谈 speak in detail (or at length); go into details /〜述自己的论点 elaborate one's thesis ② details; particulars: 〜见附录。For details, see the appendix. ③ know clearly: 作者生卒年月不〜。The author's dates are unknown.

详尽 xiángjìn detailed and complete; exhaustive; thorough: 〜的记载 a detailed record / 〜的调查 a thorough investigation /对问题进行〜的研究 make an exhaustive study of a subject

详略 xiáng-lüè details and omissions: 〜得宜 necessary details and appropriate omissions / 这本书的注释〜不很一致。The book is not quite consistent in its annotations, some detailed, and some very sketchy.

详密 xiángmì elaborate; meticulous: 〜的计划 a meticulous plan

详明 xiángmíng full and clear: 〜的注解 full and clear annotations

详情 xiángqíng detailed information; details; particulars: 我不了解这件事的〜。I don't know the details of the matter. /〜后报。Details to follow. /〜请问办事处。Please apply to the office for particulars.

详实 xiángshí full and accurate: 〜的材料 full and accurate data (or material)

详图 xiángtú detail drawing: 发动机〜 engine detail

详悉 xiángxī ① know the details of: 来信收到, 情况〜。I've received your letter and got a good knowledge of the situation. ② detailed and complete

详细 xiángxì detailed; minute: 〜的报导 a detailed news report / 〜了解情况 acquire detailed knowledge of the situation /〜占有材料 collect all the available material; have all the relevant data at one's fingertips /〜地描述 give a minute description /请说〜点。Please explain in greater detail.

详注 xiángzhù ① annotate fully ② detailed annotations

庠 xiáng a government-run local school in ancient China

庠生 xiángshēng student of an ancient local school

庠序 xiángxù same as 庠 xiáng

降

xiáng ① surrender; capitulate: 宁死不～ rather die than surrender ② subdue; vanquish; tame: ～妖伏魔 vanquish demons and monsters——see also jiàng

降表 xiángbiǎo *formal* petition of surrender

降敌 xiángdí surrender to the enemy

降伏 xiángfú subdue; vanquish; tame: ～野马 break in a wild horse / 谁～得了那野小子? Who could tame that unruly boy?

降服 xiángfú yield; surrender and acknowledge allegiance

降将 xiángjiàng a general who has surrendered (*or* come over from the enemy camp)

降龙伏虎 xiánglóng-fúhǔ subdue the dragon and tame the tiger—overcome powerful adversaries

降旗 xiángqí flag of surrender; white flag

降顺 xiángshùn *formal* yield and pledge allegiance to

祥

xiáng auspicious; propitious; lucky: 吉祥 jíxiáng

祥和 xiánghé ① happy and auspicious ② kind; benign

祥瑞 xiángruì auspicious sign; propitious omen

祥云 xiángyún auspicious clouds

祥兆 xiángzhào good omen

翔

xiáng circle in the air: 翱翔 áoxiáng

翔实 xiángshí full and accurate: ～的材料 full and accurate data / 她的叙述～可信。The account she gave was full and accurate and reliable.

xiǎng

曏（曏）

xiǎng *formal* in the past; before

享

xiǎng enjoy: 享受 xiǎngshòu

享福 xiǎngfú enjoy a happy life; live in ease and comfort: 我指望着老来能享点儿清福。I'm looking forward to a peaceful, quiet and easy life in my old age.

享乐 xiǎnglè lead a life of pleasure; indulge in creature comforts: ～思想 preoccupation with pleasure-seeking

享乐主义 xiǎnglèzhǔyì hedonism; pleasure-seeking

享年 xiǎngnián (of a deceased, generally old person) die at the age of; live to the age of: 他～七十四岁。He died at the age of 74.

享受 xiǎngshòu ① enjoy: ～公费医疗 enjoy public health services ② enjoyment; treat: 贪图～ seek ease and comfort / 看这样的好戏是一种艺术～。A good play like this is an artistic treat.

享用 xiǎngyòng enjoy the use of; enjoy

享有 xiǎngyǒu enjoy (rights, prestige, etc.): ～崇高的威望 enjoy high prestige; be held in esteem / 在我国, 妇女～同男子平等的权利。Women in our country enjoy equal rights with men.

享誉 xiǎngyù enjoy good fame: ～海内外 enjoy great prestige both at home and abroad

响（響）

xiǎng ① sound; noise: 一声炮～ the report of a cannon / 两～的爆竹 double-bang firecrackers ② make a sound; sound; resound; ring: 锣～了。The gong sounded. / 电话铃～了。The telephone rang. / 全场～起暴风雨般的掌声。A stormy applause broke out in the hall. *or* The hall resounded with stormy applause. / 炮声～彻山谷。The roar of guns reverberated in the valley. / 扩音器不～了。The loudspeaker's stopped working. ③ make sth. emit a sound; sound: 敲起鼓, ～起锣 sound the drum and the gong ④ noisy;

loud: 收音机开得太～了。The radio's too loud (*or* noisy).

响儿 xiǎngr *dial.* noise; sound: 小心! 别弄出～来。Be careful. Don't make any noise. / 听不见～。Not a sound was heard.

响板 xiǎngbǎn *mus.* castanets

响鼻 xiǎngbí snort (of a horse, mule, etc.): 打～儿 snort

响鞭 xiǎngbiān ① the crack of a whip: 抽一～ crack a whip ② *dial.* a string of small firecrackers

响彻云霄 xiǎngchè yúnxiāo resound (*or* reverberate) across the heavens: 一曲～的凯歌 a song of triumph that resounds across the heavens / 锣鼓声～。The beating of gongs and drums resounded to the skies. / 歌声～。The strains echoed to the sky.

响当当 xiǎngdāngdāng ① (of the sound made by a bell, a gong, etc.) loud and resounding ② (of a person) of resounding fame; outstanding; worthy: 一个～的劳动英雄 a labour hero worthy of his name

响动 xiǎngdòng the sound of sth. astir: 夜很静, 一点～也没有。The night was quiet, and there was no sound of anything astir. / 有什么～就叫醒我。Wake me up if there's anything astir.

响度 xiǎngdù *phys.* degree of loudness; volume

响遏行云 xiǎng è xíngyún (of singing) be so sonorous it stops the passing clouds: 至今耳边还留下他那～、充溢着激情的歌声。Even now, his sonorous singing is still resounding in my ears, full of fire and passion.

响箭 xiǎngjiàn a whistling arrow (used as a signal)

响雷 xiǎnglèi ① be thundering: ～了, 暴风雨快来了。It's thundering. There's a storm coming on. ② a crash of thunder; thunderclap

响亮 xiǎngliàng loud and clear; resounding; resonant; sonorous: ～的回答 a loud and clear reply; an unequivocal reply / ～的声音 a resounding voice / 一记～的耳光 a heavy slap in the face; a smart box on the ear

响铃 xiǎnglíng jingle bell; cascabel: 小马的脖子上挂着一串～。Round the neck of the pony is tied a string of jingle bells.

响马 xiǎngmǎ *old* bandit; mounted highwayman (who shot whistling arrows as a signal for attack)

响器 xiǎngqì *mus.* Chinese percussion instruments

响晴 xiǎngqíng cloudless: 白鸽在～的天空中飞翔。White doves are circling in the cloudless sky.

响声 xiǎngshēng sound; noise: 沙沙的～ rustling sound

响尾蛇 xiǎngwěishé rattlesnake

响杨 xiǎngyáng another name for 毛白杨 máobáiyáng

响音 xiǎngyīn *phonet.* ① resonant (i.e. vowel, semi-vowel, or sonorant; e.g. a, e, ou, j, w, m, n, ng, r, l) ② sonorant (e.g. m, n, ng, r, l)

响应 xiǎngyìng respond; answer: ～党的号召 respond to (*or* answer) the Party's call / 他们一提出倡议, 我们就全力～。As soon as they put forward the proposal, we responded with full support.

饷

xiǎng ① *formal* entertain (with food and drink): ～客 entertain a visitor with food and wine ② pay (for soldiers, policemen, etc.): 月～ monthly pay

饷银 xiǎngyín *old* army pay

飨（饗）

xiǎng *formal* provide dinner for; entertain: ～客 entertain a guest / 以～读者 offer to the readers

想

xiǎng ① think; ponder: ～问题 think over a problem / ～办法 think of a way; try to find a solution (*or* a way out) / 让我～一～。Let me think it over. *or* Let me see. / 你～得真周到。You have really thought of

everything. / 你～清楚了没有? Have you thought it out (*or* through)? / 我在～下一步该怎么走。I'm thinking about what my next move should be. / 我们也要～～困难。We must also anticipate difficulties. ② think back; try to remember; recall; recollect: ～往事 recall the past events / 你好好～～钥匙搁哪儿了。Think carefully, and see if you can remember where you put the key. ③ suppose; reckon; consider; think: 我～他今天不会来。I don't think he'll be coming today. / 你～他能买到票吗? Do you think he can get the tickets? / 我～不至于吧。I don't believe things could go so far as that. / 我～我该走了。I'm afraid I must be going now. ④ want to; would like to; feel like (doing sth.): 你～看足球赛吗? Do you want to see (*or* feel like seeing) a football match? / 他很～上大学。He wants very much to go to college. / 我也～试试。I'd also like to have a try. / 她不～跟我们去。She doesn't feel like coming with us. ⑤ remember with longing; miss: 你走了以后, 我们都很～你。After you left, we all missed you. / 王大娘～女儿都～病了。Auntie Wang misses her daughter so much that she's taken ill.

想儿 xiǎngr *dial.* hope; something to look forward to: 车票买到了, 去青岛玩儿的事有～了。The train tickets are booked, so we can look forward to a holiday in Qingdao.

想必 xiǎngbì *adv.* presumably; most probably (*or* likely): 这事～你知道。You most probably know this. / 他没有答复, ～没有收到我的信。No word from him yet; presumably he hasn't received my letter.

想不到 xiǎngbudào never expect; be unexpected: 这真是～的事! This is something quite unexpected! / 真～家乡变化这么大。I never expected my village would have changed so much. / 真～会在这儿见到你。Fancy seeing you here!

想不开 xiǎngbukāi take things too hard; take a matter to heart: 别为这些小事～。Don't take such small things to heart. / 她遭人遗弃, 一时～就自杀了。She was deserted by her lover, and in despair she took her own life.

想出 xiǎng·chū (object obligatory) think out; think up: 她～一条妙计。She thought out a brilliant scheme. / 想不出什么办法 can't think up any solution to it / 想了半天, 我也没～个好主意。I've tried hard, but still can't come up with any good ideas.

想出来 xiǎng·chū·lái think out; think up: 这主意是谁～的? Whose idea was this? / 办法我是～了, 就是不知道行不行。I've thought out (*or* up) a plan, but I'm not sure whether it will work.

想当然 xiǎngdāngrán assume sth. as a matter of course; take sth. for granted: 我们不能凭～办事。We must not act on assumptions.

想到 xiǎngdào think of; call to mind: 忽然～一件重要的事情 suddenly think of something important / 经常～人民的利益 always have the interests of the people at heart / 在这紧要关头, 工人们首先～的是抢救国家财产。At this critical moment, the workers' first thought was to save state property. ② expect sth. to happen; expect that sth. will happen: 他～这次考试可能通不过。He expects possible failure in this examination. / 我们没～你会来。We didn't expect you (to come).

想得到 xiǎngdedào (usu. used in rhetorical questions) think; imagine; expect: 谁～会出事故? Who would have thought there'd be an accident?

想得开 xiǎngdekāi not take to heart; take philosophically; try to look on the bright side of things: 这老太太最～了。This old lady always looks at the bright side of things.

想法 xiǎngfǎ think of a way; do what one can; try: ～给大伙儿弄点水喝喝。Try and get some drinking water for everyone.

想法 xiǎngfa idea; opinion; what one has in mind: 这个～不错。This is a good idea. / 按我的～ in my opinion; to my mind / 把你的～给大家说说。Tell us what you have in mind.

想方设法 xiǎngfāng-shèfǎ do everything possible; try every means; try by hook or by crook: ～去打听消息 try every means to find out what's happening

想家 xiǎngjiā be homesick: 我非常～。I'm terribly homesick.

想见 xiǎngjiàn infer; gather: 从这些事情上, 你可以～他的为人。From these instances you can gather what kind of person he is.

想开 xiǎngkāi accept a situation; not take to heart: ～点儿, 别生气了。Calm down, don't take it to heart.

想来 xiǎnglái it may be assumed that; presumably: 他的话～不是没有根据的。I suppose what he says is not groundless. / ～你都知道了。Presumably you know all about it.

想来想去 xiǎngláixiǎngqù turn over and over in one's mind: 我～, 还是认为自己没有错。I've thought it over and over, and still think I'm right.

想念 xiǎngniàn remember with longing; long to see again; miss: 我们都很～你。We all miss you very much. / 侨胞～祖国。Overseas Chinese cherish the memory of their home land.

想起 xiǎngqǐ remember; recollect; recall; think of; call to mind: 你想得起他的原话吗? Can you recall his exact words? / 这人很面熟, 可就是想不起他的名字。He looks familiar to me, but I just can't think of his name. / 我忽然～忘了锁门了。It suddenly occurred to me that I had left the door unlocked.

想起来 xiǎng·qǐ·lái remember; recollect; recall; think of; call to mind: 我～了, 她当时在场。Now I remember, she was present at the time. / 隔了这么久, 谁还想得起来呀! No one can still remember after such a long time. / 我怎么也想不起来在哪儿见过他。I just can't recollect where I met him before. / 他一看到这件纪念品, 就想起他以前的女朋友来。The sight of the souvenir always reminds him of his former girlfriend.

想入非非 xiǎngrùfēifēi indulge in fantasy; allow one's fancy to run wild

想通 xiǎngtōng straighten out one's thinking; become convinced; come round: 我～了。I've come round to the idea now. / 只要～了, 他就会积极地去干。Once he's straightened out his thinking, he'll go all out on the job. / 你要是一时想不通, 还可以再想想。Think the matter over again if you're still not convinced. / 我想不通他为什么说出那样的话来。I can't figure out why he said that.

想头 xiǎngtou *inf.* ① idea: 老李有个～。Lao Li's got an idea. ② hope: 没什么～了。There's no hope now.

想望 xiǎngwàng ① desire; long for; yearn for: 他从小就～着当一名工程师。He's longed to be an engineer ever since he was a child. / ～家里来信 yearn for letters from home ② *formal* admire; look up to: ～其风采 admire his elegant bearing

想像 xiǎngxiàng ① imagination: 完美无缺的人只存在于人们的～之中。A flawless person exists only in imagination. ② imagine; fancy; visualize: 难以～ hard to imagine (*or* visualize) / ～不到的困难 unimaginable difficulties

想像力 xiǎngxiànglì the power (*or* faculty) of imagination; imagination: 激发人们的～ fire people's imagination / 充分发挥～ give full play to one's imagination / 具有丰富的～ be endowed with great power of imagination / 我这个人缺乏～。I'm not an imaginative sort of person.

想着 xiǎngzhe keep in mind; not forget: 这事你～点儿。

Please keep this in mind. / 到了那儿～给我们写信。Don't forget to write to us after you get there. / 你～把东西带走。Don't forget to take this with you.

鲞（鮝）

xiǎng　dried fish (with all insides taken out and the body flattened): 鳗～ dried eel

xiāng

向¹（嚮）

xiàng　① direction: 风向 fēngxiàng / 志向 zhìxiàng　② face; turn towards: 那间屋子～东。That room faces east. / 葵花～太阳。Sunflowers turn towards the sun.　③ *formal* shortly before; towards: ～明 towards dawn

向²

xiàng　① take sb.'s part; side with; be partial to: ～理不～人 stand by what is right, not by a particular person; side with whoever is right / 穷人～穷人。The poor people side with each other.　② *prep.* to; towards; in the direction of: ～上看 look upward / ～后撤 withdraw / 河水～东流去。The river flows east. / 这条小路通～果园。This path leads to the orchard. / ～上级汇报工作 report to one's superior on one's work / ～人民宣传 carry on propaganda among the people / ～自然开战 wage a battle against nature / ～纵深发展 develop in depth / ～雷锋同志学习。Learn from Comrade Lei Feng. / 从胜利走～胜利! March from victory to victory!　③ (Xiàng) a surname

向³

xiàng　*adv.* all along; always: ～无此例。There's no precedent for this. / 他对此～有研究。He has always been doing research in this field.

向背 xiàng-bèi　support or oppose: 人心向背 rénxīn xiàng-bèi

向壁虚构 xiàng bì xūgòu　(also 向壁虚造 xiàng bì xūzào) make up out of one's head; fabricate

向导 xiàngdǎo　① show sb. the way; lead sb. somewhere; act as a guide　② a guide; an escort: 探险队急需一位～。The exploring party needs a guide urgently. / 我来给你们做～, 怎么样? How about taking me as a guide?

向光性 xiàngguāngxìng　*bot.* phototropism

向后 xiànghòu　towards the back; backward: ～看 look back / ～转! (word of command) About face! *or* About turn! / ～转走! (word of command) To the rear, march!

向火 xiànghuǒ　*dial.* warm oneself in front of a fire

向来 xiànglái　always; all along: ～如此。It has always been so. / 我～不抽烟。I have never smoked. / 他做事～认真。He's always been conscientious in his work.

向例 xiànglì　usual practice: 打破～ break with the usual practice / 我们这里～起得早。Here, as a rule, we get up early.

向量 xiàngliàng　*math.* vector: ～分析 vector analysis

向慕 xiàngmù　admire: 他是我十分～的一位作曲家。He's one of the composers I admire tremendously.

向前 xiàngqián　forward; onward; ahead: 奋勇～ forge ahead / 科学的～发展 the forward march of science / ～看! (word of command) Eyes front! *or* Ready, front!

向前看 xiàngqiánkàn　look to the future; look forward: 采取～的态度 adopt a forward-looking attitude

向日 xiàngrì　*formal* in former days; formerly

向日葵 xiàngrìkuí　sunflower

向日性 xiàngrìxìng　*bot.* heliotropism

向善 xiàngshàn　be inclined to goodness or charity

向上 xiàngshàng　① upward; up: 卡车沿着盘山公路～爬去。The trucks climbed the twisting mountain road.　②

advance; make one's way up or forward: 好好学习, 天天～。Study well and make progress every day.

向上爬 xiàngshàngpá　① climb (up)　② seek personal advancement; be a social climber; be a careerist: 有～的思想 have the mentality of a careerist (*or* social climber) / 一心～ set one's mind on personal advancement

向使 xiàngshǐ　*formal* if

向水性 xiàngshuǐxìng　*biol.* hydrotropism

向晚 xiàngwǎn　towards evening; about dusk

向往 xiàngwǎng　yearn for; look forward to: ～着北京 yearn for Beijing / ～幸福的新生活 look forward to a happy new life / 我终于登上了～已久的长城。At long last, I climbed to the top of the Great Wall, which I had long been looking forward to seeing.

向下 xiàngxià　downward; down: 滑雪运动员飞快地～滑去。The skiers sped down the slope. / 他把帽沿～拉了拉。He pulled the visor of his cap down a little. / 领导干部要善于～作调查。Leading cadres should be good at investigating conditions at the lower levels.

向晓 xiàngxiǎo　towards dawn; about daybreak: ～雨止。The rain stopped shortly before daybreak.

向斜 xiàngxié　*geol.* syncline

向斜谷 xiàngxiégǔ　*geog.* synclinal valley

向心力 xiàngxīnlì　*phys.* centripetal force

向性 xiàngxìng　*biol.* tropism

向学 xiàngxué　be determined to study or pursue one's studies

向阳 xiàngyáng　be exposed to the sun; have a sunny exposure: 这间屋～。The room has a southern exposure.

向阳花 xiàngyánghuā　*liter.* sunflower

向右 xiàngyòu　towards the right: ～转! (word of command) Right face! *or* Right turn! / ～转走! (word of command) By the right flank, march!

向隅 xiàngyú　*formal* stand in a corner—be disappointed for lack of opportunity; feel left out

向隅而泣 xiàngyú ér qì　weep all alone in a corner; be left to grieve in the cold

向着 xiàngzhe　① turn towards; face: ～光明的未来前进 advance towards a bright future　② *inf.* take sb.'s part; side with; be partial to: 她说话在理, 我就～她。I take her part because she's right. / 老奶奶～小孙女儿。Grandma favours her little granddaughter.

向左 xiàngzuǒ　towards the left: ～转! (word of command) Left face! *or* Left turn! / ～转走! (word of command) By the left flank, march!

巷

xiàng　lane; alley ——see also hàng

巷口 xiàngkǒu　entrance to a lane

巷陌 xiàngmò　*formal* streets and lanes

巷尾 xiàngwěi　end of a lane

巷议 xiàngyì　street gossip

巷战 xiàngzhàn　street fighting

项¹

xiàng　① nape (of the neck)　② (Xiàng) a surname

项²

xiàng　① *m.* (for itemized things): 两～声明 two statements / 八～原则 eight principles / 一～一～地进行解释 explain item by item / 第五条第二款第三～ article 5, clause 2, item 3 / 还有一～工作要做。There is another job to do.　③ sum (of money): 进项 jìnxiàng / 欠项 qiànxiàng　④ *math.* term

项背 xiàngbèi　a person's back: 不可望其～ cannot hold a candle to sb.

项背相望 xiàngbèi xiāng wàng　walk one after another in close succession

项链 xiàngliàn　(also 项练 xiàngliàn) necklace

项目 xiàngmù item: 出口～ goods for export; export items / 基本建设～ capital construction project / 援助～ aid project / 训练～ training courses / 田径～ track and field events

项圈 xiàngquān neckband (a band of gold or silver, worn around the neck as an ornament); necklet

项庄舞剑, 意在沛公 Xiàng Zhuāng wǔ jiàn, yì zài Pèigōng Xiang Zhuang performed the sword dance as a cover for his attempt on Liu Bang's life—act with a hidden motive

相¹
xiàng ① looks; appearance: 一副可怜～ a pitiful appearance; a sorry figure ② bearing; posture: 站没站～、坐没坐～ not know how to stand or sit properly / 这孩子睡～不好。 The child sleeps sprawled all over the bed. ③ look at and appraise: ～马 look at a horse to judge its worth ④ photograph: 照相 zhàoxiàng ⑤ geol. facies: 海～ marine facies / 浅海～ neritic facies / 煤～ coaly facies ⑥ phys. phase: 三～变压器 three-phase transformer / 调～ phase modulation ⑦ (Xiàng) a surname

相²
xiàng ① formal assist: ～夫教子 assist one's husband and teach one's children ② chief minister: 周瑜十三岁拜～。 Zhou Yu was given the post of chief minister when he was only 13 years of age. ③ minister (as in Japan) ④ elephant, one of the pieces in Chinese chess (象棋) ⑤ old a person who helps the host receive guests: 傧相 bīnxiàng
——see also xiàng

相册 xiàngcè photo album

相公 xiànggōng ① honor. a term of address used by a wife to her husband (in feudal China) ② a term of address for young men of rich or cultured families (in feudal China)

相国 xiàngguó the chief minister of state; premier (in feudal China)

相机¹ xiàngjī camera

相机² xiàngjī ① watch for an opportunity: ～而动 wait for an opportunity to act; bide one's time ② do as one sees fit

相机行事 xiàngjī xíngshì act as the occasion demands; do as one sees fit

相控阵雷达 xiàngkòngzhèn léidá mil. phased-array radar

相貌 xiàngmào facial features; looks; appearance: ～端正 have regular features / ～堂堂 be elegant in appearance / 那小伙子好～! That young man is really handsome.

相面 xiàngmiàn tell sb.'s fortune by reading his face; practise physiognomy

相片儿 xiàngpiānr inf. photo (of a person); snapshot

相片 xiàngpiàn photo (of a person); snapshot

相声 xiàngsheng comic dialogue; cross talk: 说～ perform a comic dialogue

相士 xiàngshì fortune-teller

相手术 xiàngshǒushù palmistry

相术 xiàngshù fortune-telling by ·studying facial features; physiognomy

相态 xiàngtài phase: 水蒸气、水和冰是同一物质的三个～。 Steam, water and ice constitute the three phases of one and the same matter.

相体裁衣 xiàng tǐ cáiyī same as 量体裁衣 liáng tǐ cáiyī

相印 xiàngyìn the chief minister's seal—chief minister's office or power

相纸 xiàngzhǐ (photographic) printing paper; photographic paper

象¹
xiàng ① elephant ② elephant, one of the pieces in Chinese chess (象棋)

象²
xiàng ① appearance; shape; image: 景象 jǐngxiàng / 印象 yìnxiàng / 抽象 chōuxiàng ② imitate: 象声 xiàngshēng / 象形 xiàngxíng

象鼻 xiàngbí trunk; proboscis

象鼻虫 xiàngbíchóng weevil; snout beetle

象脚鼓 xiàngjiǎogǔ mus. a drum on a pedestal, shaped like an elephant's leg, used by several minority nationalities in Yunnan

象皮病 xiàngpíbìng med. elephantiasis

象皮鱼 xiàngpíyú another name for 马面鲀 mǎmiàntún

象棋 xiàngqí Chinese chess

象声 xiàngshēng linguis. onomatopoeia

象声词 xiàngshēngcí onomatope

象限 xiàngxiàn math. quadrant

象限仪 xiàngxiànyí astron. quadrant

象形 xiàngxíng pictographic characters or pictographs (e.g. 日 sun and 月 moon)—one of the six categories of Chinese characters (六书)

象形文字 xiàngxíng wénzì pictograph; hieroglyph

象形字 xiàngxíngzì pictographic character

象牙 xiàngyá elephant's tusk; ivory: ～雕刻 ivory carving (or sculpture) /～制品 ivories

象牙海岸 Xiàngyá Hǎi'àn the Ivory Coast

象牙之塔 xiàngyá zhī tǎ ivory tower (fig.)

象牙质 xiàngyázhì ① (made of) ivory: ～刀把 the ivory handle of a knife ② dentine (of teeth)

象征 xiàngzhēng ① symbolize; signify; stand for: 鸽子～和平。 The dove symbolizes peace. / 斧头镰刀～工人农民。 The hammer and sickle symbolize (or stand for) the workers and peasants. ② symbol; emblem; token: 友谊的～ emblem (or symbol) of friendship

象征性 xiàngzhēngxìng symbolic; emblematic; token: 韶山—北京～长跑 a symbolic "Shaoshan—Beijing" long-distance run

像
xiàng ① be like; resemble; take after: 姐妹俩长得很～。 The two sisters are very much alike. / 这孩子～他父亲。 The child takes after its father. / ～猛虎下山一样向敌人扑去 charge at the enemy like tigers dashing down a mountain / ～雷锋一样全心全意为人民服务 serve the people wholeheartedly as Lei Feng did ② look as if; seem: ～要下雨了。 It looks like rain. / ～是有人在敲门。 It sounds like somebody's knocking on the door. ③ such as; like: ～黄继光这样的英雄人物, 将永远活在人民的心里。 Heroes such as Huang Jiguang will always live in the hearts of the people. ④ likeness (of sb.); portrait; picture: 画像 huàxiàng / 铜像 tóngxiàng ⑤ phys. image: 虚～ virtual image / 实～ real image

像差 xiàngchā phys. aberration

像个人样儿 xiàng ge rényàngr inf. like a decent person: 他有了正式工作, 也结了婚, 现在活得～了。 Now that he is married and has a regular job, he's beginning to live like a decent person.

像话 xiànghuà (usu. used in the negative or in rhetorical questions) reasonable; proper; right: 大家都忙, 就我在家休息, ～吗? How can I take it easy at home when everybody else is so busy? / 你发这么大脾气～吗? Aren't you ashamed to fly into such a rage? / 真不～! That's really the limit. or It's simply outrageous.

像回事儿 xiànghuíshìr inf. just like the real thing: 瞧这些孩子, 演得还真挺～的。 Look at those kids. They act just like professionals.

像模像样 xiàngmó-xiàngyàng up to the mark; presentable; decent

像散 xiàngsàn phys. astigmatism

像散镜 xiàngsànjìng phys. astigmatoscope

像散透镜 xiàngsàn tòujìng ,astigmatic lens

像煞有介事 xiàng shà yǒu jiè shì make a show of being in earnest; pretend to be serious (about doing sth.)

像生 xiàngshēng a lifelike imitation: 〜花果 imitation flowers and fruit

像样 xiàngyàng (also 像样子 xiàngyàngzi) up to the mark; presentable; decent; sound: 他的针线活还挺〜的。His needlework is quite presentable. / 这屋里连张〜的桌子也没有。There isn't even a decent table in this room. / 他提不出〜的理由来解释他的行动。He couldn't give any sound reason for his action.

像赞 xiàngzàn inscriptions on a portrait

像章 xiàngzhāng badge (or button) with sb.'s likeness on it

橡

橡 xiàng ① oak ② rubber tree

橡浆 xiàngjiāng rubber latex

橡胶 xiàngjiāo rubber: 天然〜 natural rubber / 合成〜 synthetic rubber / 海棉〜 foam rubber / 〜厂 rubber plant / 〜轮胎 rubber tyre / 〜种植园 rubber plantation

橡胶草 xiàngjiāocǎo bot. Russian dandelion; koksaghyz

橡胶树 xiàngjiāoshù another name for 印度橡胶树 Yìndù xiàngjiāoshù

橡皮 xiàngpí ① (vulcanized) rubber: 〜胶水 rubber cement / 〜手套 rubber (operating) gloves ② eraser; rubber

橡皮版 xiàngpíbǎn print. rubber plate

橡皮船 xiàngpíchuán rubber boat

橡皮膏 xiàngpígāo med. adhesive plaster

橡皮筋 xiàngpíjīn rubber band

橡皮泥 xiàngpíní plasticine

橡皮圈 xiàngpíquān ① inflatable life preserver (for swimming learners) ② rubber ring or band (for binding or tying things together)

橡皮树 xiàngpíshù another name for 印度橡胶树 Yìndù xiàngjiāoshù

橡皮艇 xiàngpítǐng pneumatic boat; rubber dinghy

橡皮图章 xiàngpí túzhāng rubber stamp: 盖〜 rubber-stamp

橡皮线 xiàngpíxiàn elec. rubber-sheathed wire

橡实 xiàngshí (also 橡子 xiàngzǐ) acorn

橡实管 xiàngshíguǎn electron. acorn tube

xiāo

肖

肖 Xiāo a surname (a popular written form for 萧 Xiāo) ——see also xiào

肖氏回跳硬度 Xiāoshì huítiào yìngdù phys. Shore hardness

枭(梟)

枭 xiāo ① owl ② brave; valiant: 〜将 a brave general ③ smuggler: 盐〜 salt smuggler (in former times) / 毒〜 drugpusher

枭首示众 xiāoshǒu shìzhòng cut off a person's head and hang it up as a warning to all

枭雄 xiāoxióng a fierce and ambitious person; a formidable man

枵

枵 xiāo formal empty; hollow

枵腹从公 xiāo fù cóng gōng attend to one's duties on an empty stomach

削

削 xiāo ① pare (or peel) with a knife: 〜苹果 pare (or peel) an apple / 〜铅笔 sharpen a pencil / 把木棍再〜细点儿。Whittle the stick down a bit more. ② sports chop; cut: 这个球〜得好漂亮! What a beautiful chop! ——see also xuē

削尖脑袋往里钻 xiāojiān nǎodai wàng lǐ zuān try hard to worm one's way in

削球 xiāoqiú chop; cut: 他削得一手好球。He's especially good at chopping.

哓(嘵)

哓 xiāo see below

哓哓 xiāoxiāo shouting and arguing noisily

哓哓不休 xiāoxiāo bù xiū argue (or talk) endlessly

骁(驍)

骁 xiāo valiant; brave; spirited

骁将 xiāojiàng formal a valiant general

骁骑 xiāoqí formal a well-trained cavalry; a dashing cavalryman

骁勇 xiāoyǒng formal brave; valiant: 〜善战 brave and battlewise

消

消 xiāo ① disappear; vanish: 火灭了,烟还没〜尽。The fire had gone out, but the smoke had not cleared yet. / 红肿已〜。The swelling has gone down. / 他的气〜了。He has cooled down. ② cause to disappear; eliminate; dispel; remove: 〜肿 cause a swelling to go down / 〜烟除尘 eliminate smoke and dust / 〜痰 reduce phlegm ③ pass (time) in a leisurely way; while away (time): 消夏 xiāoxià ④ dial. (used after 不, 只, 何, etc.) need; take (time, etc.): 来回只〜一个星期。It takes only a week to get there and back. / 只〜几句话就可以说清楚。A few words will be enough to make it clear.

消沉 xiāochén downhearted; low-spirited; dejected; depressed: 意志〜 demoralized; despondent / 她近来有些〜。She's rather depressed these days.

消愁 xiāochóu dispel or allay worries: 借酒〜 try to drown one's worries in wine

消愁解闷 xiāochóu-jiěmèn divert oneself from boredom; dispel depression or melancholy

消除 xiāochú eliminate; dispel; remove; clear up: 〜分歧 eliminate (or iron out) differences / 〜顾虑 dispel misgivings / 〜隐患 remove a hidden danger / 〜误会 clear up a misunderstanding / 轻音乐能帮助你〜疲劳。Light music will help you to relax.

消导 xiāodǎo Chin. med. a treatment for relieving indigestion and constipation

消毒 xiāodú ① disinfect; sterilize: 用酒精〜 sterilize in (or with) alcohol / 用漂白粉〜 disinfect with bleaching powder / 经过高压〜 have been sterilized under pressure / 〜器械 sterilizer ② disinfected; sterilized; pasteurized: 〜棉花 sterilized cotton / 〜牛奶 sterilized (or pasteurized) milk

消毒剂 xiāodújì disinfectant

消防 xiāofáng ① fire fighting: 〜设备 fire-fighting equipment / 〜水龙 fire hose / 〜演习 fire drill / 加强力量 improve fire-fighting capabilities ② fire prevention and control: 普及基本的〜知识 spread among the people an elementary knowledge of fire prevention and control / 建筑物的设计和施工一定要遵守〜规程。Rules of fire prevention and control must be observed in the designing and construction of buildings.

消防车 xiāofángchē fire engine

消防队 xiāofángduì fire brigade; fire department: 〜员 fireman; fire fighter

消防艇 xiāofángtǐng fireboat

消防站 xiāofángzhàn fire station

消费 xiāofèi consume: 城市建设〜大量物资。Urban construction consumes large stocks of material resources.

消费城市 xiāofèi chéngshì consumer-city

消费合作社 xiāofèi hézuòshè consumer cooperative

消费基金 xiāofèi jījīn funds for consumption

消费结构 xiāofèi jiégòu consumption patterns

消费品 xiāofèipǐn　consumer goods

消费水平 xiāofèi shuǐpíng　level of consumption

消费税 xiāofèishuì　consumption tax

消费者 xiāofèizhě　consumer: 保护~权益 consumerism

消费资料 xiāofèi zīliào　means of subsistence; consumer goods

消光剂 xiāoguāngjì　*chem. fibre* dulling agent

消耗[1] xiāohào　consume; use up; deplete; expend: ~精力 consume one's energy / ~大量武器弹药 expend large amounts of arms and ammunition / ~敌人的有生力量 wear down the enemy's effective strength / 战争~大量的人力物力. War is a drain on manpower and material resources. /减少能源的~. Try to reduce the consumption of energy.

消耗[2] xiāohào　*old* message; news

消耗热 xiāohàorè　*med.* hectic fever

消耗战 xiāohàozhàn　war of attrition

消化 xiāohuà　① digest (food): 这种药片有助于~脂肪. These tablets will help to digest fats. / 奶酪不好~. Cheese doesn't digest easily. / 我~很好. I have good digestion. / ~功能紊乱 disorders of digestion ② think over and absorb; digest (knowledge): 帮助学生~所学的东西 help the students digest what they have learnt / 引进和~新的技术 import and assimilate new technology from abroad

消化不良 xiāohuà bùliáng　① indigestion: 我有点儿~. I'm suffering from indigestion. ② *med.* dyspepsia

消化道 xiāohuàdào　alimentary canal; digestive tract

消化酶 xiāohuàméi　digestive enzyme; digestive ferment

消化器官 xiāohuà qìguān　digestive organ

消化系统 xiāohuà xìtǒng　digestive system

消化性溃疡 xiāohuàxìng kuìyáng　peptic ulcer

消化液 xiāohuàyè　digestive juice

消魂 xiāohún　same as 销魂 xiāohún

消火栓 xiāohuǒshuān　fire hydrant

消极 xiāojí　① negative: ~因素 negative factor / ~言论 negative statement / ~现象 undesirable phenomenon / ~影响 negative (*or* harmful) influence ② passive; inactive: ~抵抗(防御) passive resistance (defence) / 态度~ take a passive attitude; remain inactive / 情绪~ be dispirited / ~怠工 be slack in work

消减 xiāojiǎn　diminish; decrease: ~痛楚 relieve pain / 他年纪大了,但学习热情并未~. Though he was getting on in years, his enthusiasm for learning never diminished.

消解 xiāojiě　clear up; dispel; remove: 疑窦~. The mystery was cleared up. / 前嫌~,和好如初. With all past ill will dispelled, good relations were restored.

消渴 xiāokě　*Chin. med.* any disease with symptoms of frequent drinking and urination (e.g. diabetes mellitus 糖尿病, diabetes insipidus 尿崩症, etc.)

消弭 xiāomǐ　*formal* put an end to (an evil); prevent: ~祸患 put an end to a disaster / ~战祸 stop or prevent a war / ~水患 eliminate the menace of floods; prevent floods

消灭 xiāomiè　① perish; die out; pass away: 许多古生物早已~了. Many prehistoric forms of life have long since died out. / 自行~ perish (*or* die out) of itself / 一切事物都有一个发生、发展和~的过程. All things go through the process of coming into being, developing and passing away. ② eliminate; abolish; exterminate; wipe out: ~差错 eliminate errors / ~病虫害 wipe out insect pests and plant diseases / ~敌人一个师 wipe out an enemy division / ~种族歧视 put an end to racial discrimination

消泯 xiāomǐn　① die out ② exterminate

消磨 xiāomó　① wear down; fritter away: ~志气 sap one's will / ~精力 fritter away one's energy / 接二连三的不幸遭遇并没有把她的意志~掉. Repeated misfor-

tunes did not get her down. ② while away; idle away: ~时间 kill time; pass the time / ~岁月 while away the time

消气 xiāoqì　cool down; be mollified: 我向她赔个不是, 她也就消了气. Her anger melted as soon as I said sorry.

消遣 xiāoqiǎn　① divert oneself; while away the time: 在火车上打扑克~ beguile the train journey by playing cards ② diversion; pastime: 下棋是我喜爱的一种~. Playing chess is one of my favourite pastimes.

消融 xiāoróng　(also 消溶 xiāoróng) (of ice or snow) melt; thaw: 冰雪~ melting of ice and snow / 待到冰雪~时 wait till the thaw sets in

消散 xiāosàn　(of smoke, fog, odor, heat, etc.) scatter and disappear; dissipate: 晨雾~了. The morning mist has lifted. / 他脸上的愁容~了. The worried expression has disappeared from his face. / 睡了一觉, 疲劳完全~了. After a good sleep, my fatigue was all gone.

消色差 xiāosèchā　*phys.* achromatism

消色差透镜 xiāosèchā tòujìng　*phys.* achromatic lens; achromat

消声 xiāoshēng　diminish or eliminate noises

消声器 xiāoshēngqì　muffler

消声室 xiāoshēngshì　anechoic chamber (of a recording room, TV studio, etc.)

消失 xiāoshī　disappear; vanish; dissolve; die (*or* fade) away: ~在浓雾中 disappear in the dense fog / ~在人群中 be lost in a crowd / 痛楚~了. The pain subsided.

消食 xiāoshí　help digestion: 山楂糕开胃~, 老少皆宜. Haw jelly is good for both the old and the young because it whets one's appetite and helps digestion.

消逝 xiāoshì　die (*or* fade) away; vanish; elapse: 火车的隆隆声慢慢~了. The rumbling of the train gradually died away. / 一抹残霞渐渐在天边~. A few stray rosy clouds were disappearing from the horizon. / 岁月~, 人生易老. Time slips by, and a man ages all too soon. / 随着时间的~ with the lapse of time

消释 xiāoshì　dispel (misunderstanding, misgivings, enmity, pain, etc.); clear up; dissipate: ~疑虑 dispel misgivings / ~前嫌 dispel past grudges / 误会~了. The misunderstanding has been cleared up (*or* ironed out).

消受 xiāoshòu　① (usu. used in the negative) enjoy (having sth.): 无福~ not have the luck to enjoy; be unable to enjoy ② endure, bear, or stand (hardship, ill treatment, etc.)

消瘦 xiāoshòu　emaciated; thinning down: 身体一天天~下去 be getting thinner every day / 显得有点~ look a bit emaciated

消暑 xiāoshǔ　① spend a summer holiday ② relieve summer heat

消损 xiāosǔn　① reduce bit by bit; decrease: 他的锐气~了. His dashing spirit has diminished. ② fritter away: 坐食嘉谷, ~白日 sit idle enjoying the choicest of foods and fritter away the best time of the day

消停 xiāoting　*dial.* ① tranquil; quiet: 孩子们都上学去了, 家里可~了. Now that the children have gone to school, we'll have some peace and quiet at last. / 大伙儿~点, ~点! Quiet, everybody! Quiet, please! ② cease; stop: 枪炮到后半夜才~下来. The bursts of gunfire didn't stop until after midnight.

消退 xiāotuì　decrease; disappear: 暑热~了. The summer heat is ending. / 他的笑容渐渐~了. His smile gradually disappeared.

消亡 xiāowáng　wither away; die out: 到了共产主义, 国家就自行~了. With the coming of communism the state will wither away. / 这些旧习惯在逐渐~. These old customs are dying out.

消息 xiāoxi　① news; information: 本地~ local news / 头版~ a front-page story / 据新华社~ according to a

Xinhua dispatch ② tidings; news: 你弟弟最近有～了吗? Have you had any news of your brother? / 他至今毫无～。We haven't had any news of him yet.

消息儿 xiāoxir *dial.* contraption; floor trap: 一脚踩在～上, 人就会掉下去。Once you step on the floor trap you'll fall in.

消息灵通人士 xiāoxí língtōng rénshì　well-informed sources

消夏 xiāoxià　spend a summer holiday: 到北戴河去～ spend the summer at Beidaihe / ～音乐会 summer concert

消闲 xiāoxián　fill one's spare time; while away the time: 为了～, 他学会了打麻将。He's learned to play mahjong as a way to spend his spare time.

消歇 xiāoxiē　*formal* cease; disappear: 风雨～。The wind and rain died down.

消炎 xiāoyán　*med.* diminish (*or* counteract, reduce) inflammation; dephlogisticate

消炎剂 xiāoyánjì　antiphlogistic

消炎片 xiāoyánpiàn　antiphlogistic tablets

消夜 xiāoyè　*dial.* ① food (*or* refreshments) taken late at night; midnight snack ② have a midnight snack

消灾 xiāozāi　rid calamities: 祈求神灵～降福 pray to the gods to ward off calamities and send down blessings

消长 xiāo-zhǎng　decrease and increase; growth and decline; wax and wane: 双方力量的～ the growth and decline of the relative strength of the two sides

消肿 xiāozhǒng　① cause a swelling to go down: 抹这种药膏可以～。This ointment will reduce the swelling. / 很快就会～的。The swelling will soon go down. ② *med.* detumescence

宵
xiāo　night: 今～ tonight

宵遁 xiāodùn　*formal* escape by night: 狡寇～。The cunning enemy escaped under cover of night.

宵旰 xiāogàn　short for 宵衣旰食 xiāoyī-gànshí

宵禁 xiāojìn　curfew: 实行～ impose a curfew / 解除～ lift a curfew

宵小 xiāoxiǎo　*formal* thieves or robbers who act under cover of night; bad people in general: ～之徒 the bad sort

宵夜 xiāoyè　same as 消夜 xiāoyè①

宵衣旰食 xiāoyī-gànshí　dress and get up before dawn and not eat until dark—be busy all day with affairs of state

逍
xiāo　see below

逍遥 xiāoyáo　free and unfettered

逍遥法外 xiāoyáo fǎ wài　go scot-free; be (*or* remain) at large

逍遥自在 xiāoyáo zìzài　free and unfettered; leisurely and carefree

绡
xiāo　*formal* ① raw silk ② raw silk fabric

虓
xiāo　*formal* (of tigers) roar: ～虎 a roaring tiger

鸮
xiāo　*zool.* owl

鸮卣 xiāoyǒu　*archaeol.* an owl-shaped bronze wine jar

萧(蕭)
xiāo　① desolate; dreary: 萧瑟 xiāosè ② (Xiāo) a surname

萧规曹随 Xiāo guī Cáo suí　Cao Can (曹参), a Han Dynasty chief minister, followed the rules set by Xiao He (萧何), his predecessor—follow established rules

萧墙 xiāoqiáng　*formal* the screen wall facing the gate of a Chinese house: ～之内 behind the screen wall; within one's home

萧墙之祸 xiāoqiáng zhī huò　trouble behind the screen wall—trouble at home; trouble from within; internal strife ——see also 祸起萧墙 huò qǐ xiāoqiáng

萧然 xiāorán　*formal* ① desolate: 四壁～ four bare walls with nothing inside ② empty: 囊橐～。The purse is empty. *or* One is poverty-stricken.

萧洒 xiāosǎ　same as 潇洒 xiāosǎ

萧瑟 xiāosè　(also 萧飒 xiāosà) ① rustling in the air; soughing: 秋风～。The autumn wind is soughing. ② bleak; desolate

萧森 xiāosēn　*formal* dreary and desolate

萧疏 xiāoshū　*formal* ① desolate ② (of trees, leaves, a person's hair, etc.) sparse; thinly scattered: 枝叶～。The tree's leaves are few and sparse. / ～鬓已斑。His (My, etc.) scant hair is already frosted.

萧索 xiāosuǒ　① bleak and dreary; dull and desolate: ～的晚秋气象 a bleak late autumn scene ② (of a person's mood) melancholy; depressed

萧条 xiāotiáo　① desolate; bleak: 一片～的景象 a desolate scene on all sides ② *econ.* depression: 市面～。The market is dull. / 生意～。Business is bad (*or* slack). / 经济～ economic depression; slump

萧萧 xiāoxiāo　*onom. formal* ① the sound of a horse neighing or whinnying: 车辚辚, 马～。Chariots rumble and roll; horses whinny and neigh. ② the sound of a whistling wind, pattering rain, etc.: 风～, 雨～。The wind soughs and sighs; the rain goes pitter-pattering.

硝
xiāo　① nitre; saltpetre ② taw (animal skin): ～皮 taw an animal skin into leather

硝化 xiāohuà　*chem.* nitrify: ～棉 nitrocotton

硝化甘油 xiāohuà gānyóu　nitroglycerine

硝基 xiāojī　*chem.* nitro-: ～苯 nitrobenzene / ～烷 nitroalkane / ～化合物 nitro compound

硝镪水 xiāoqiāngshuǐ　popular name for 硝酸 xiāosuān

硝石 xiāoshí　nitre; saltpetre: 智利～ Chile nitre (*or* saltpetre); sodium nitre

硝酸 xiāosuān　*chem.* nitric acid

硝酸铵 xiāosuān'ǎn　ammonium nitrate

硝酸甘油片 xiāosuāngānyóupiàn　*pharm.* nitroglycerine tablets

硝酸钾 xiāosuānjiǎ　potassium nitrate

硝酸钠 xiāosuānnà　sodium nitrate

硝酸纤维素 xiāosuān xiānwéisù　nitrocellulose; cellulose nitrate

硝酸盐 xiāosuānyán　nitrate (e.g. 硝酸钾 xiāosuānjiǎ, etc.)

硝烟 xiāoyān　smoke of gunpowder: ～滚滚 billows of powder smoke / 战场上空～弥漫。Gun smoke filled the air over the battlefield.

硝盐 xiāoyán　salt made from earth containing a comparatively high percentage of sodium chloride

销¹
xiāo　① melt (metal) ② cancel; annul: 这笔帐已经～了。This item has been written off (the account). *or* The score is settled. ③ sell; market: 这种产品～得出去吗? Are these products marketable? / 一天～不少货 sell quite a lot of goods a day ④ expend; spend: 开销 kāixiāo

销²
xiāo　① bolt; pin: 门～ door bolt ② fasten with a bolt; bolt: 把窗户～上! Bolt the window, please!

销案 xiāo'àn　close a case; bring a case to a close

销差 xiāochāi　report the accomplishment of a task or termination of a mission (*or* assignment): 你先去～, 销完差可以休息几天。You'll have to report your return from the assignment before you can have a few days

off.

销钉 xiāodīng same as 销子 xiāozi

销户口 xiāo hùkǒu cancel one's residence registration: 我销完户口就离开了北京。I left Beijing after I had my name cancelled from the residence register.

销毁 xiāohuǐ destroy by melting, burning, etc.: ～罪证 destroy incriminating evidence / ～核武器 have the nuclear weapons destroyed

销魂 xiāohún be overwhelmed with sorrow or joy; feel transported

销假 xiāojià report back after leave of absence

销金 xiāojīn ① melt gold ② gold-sprinkled (paper, curtain, shawl, etc.); adorned with gold: ～纸 gold-sprinkled paper / ～帐 a curtain embroidered with gold thread

销金窟 xiāojīnkū money-squandering den (e.g. a brothel, gambling house, etc.)

销量 xiāoliàng the quantity (of goods) sold; sales made: 本月～猛增。This month has seen a sharp increase in sales.

销路 xiāolù sale; market: ～很好 have a good sale; find a good market; sell well / 没有～ find no sale (or market)

销声匿迹 xiāoshēng-nìjì keep silent and lie low; disappear from the scene: 这位大明星近来～, 不知去向。The renowned film star has of late disappeared from the scene and is nowhere to be found.

销蚀 xiāoshí corrode: ～作用 corrosion

销蚀剂 xiāoshíjì corrodent

销售 xiāoshòu sell; market: ～价格 selling price / ～量 sales volume / ～费用 selling expenses / ～净额 net sales / ～总额 gross (or aggregate) sales / ～收入 income from sales / ～利润 profit on sales / ～税金 sales tax; tax on sales / ～与推销 marketing and merchandizing

销铄 xiāoshuò formal ① smelt (metals) ② remove; eliminate: 国仇未～。The national grievances have not yet been removed. ③ thin and frail after a long illness: 肌肤～, 不似人形。He is all skin and bones and hardly looks human.

销行 xiāoxíng sell; be on sale: ～各地 be on sale everywhere / ～百万册 have sold a million copies / 本地土产开始～国外。We have commenced the sale of local products abroad.

销赃 xiāozāng dispose of stolen goods: 一定有人帮助窃贼～。Somebody must have helped the thief sell the stolen goods.

销帐 xiāozhàng cancel or remove from an account; write off

销子 xiāozi pin; peg; dowel; bolt

蛸 xiāo see 螵蛸 piāoxiāo

翛 xiāo formal free and unrestrained; unconstrained

潇(瀟) xiāo ① formal (of water) deep and clear ② (Xiāo) Xiao River, a tributary of the Xiang River (湘江 or 湘水)

潇洒 xiāosǎ (of a person's appearance, demeanour, carriage, etc.) natural and unrestrained: 举止～ carry oneself with ease and natural poise / 神情～ look natural and unaffected / 书法～ write a free and easy hand

潇湘 Xiāoxiāng ① poetic name for 湘江 (the Xiang River in Hunan Province) ② poetic name for 湖南 Húnán

潇潇 xiāoxiāo ① (of wind and rain) driving; whistling and pattering: 风雨～ a driving wind and a heavy rain ② drizzling; drizzly: ～细雨 a fine, gentle drizzle

箫(簫) xiāo xiao, a vertical bamboo flute

霄 xiāo ① clouds: 云霄 yúnxiāo ② sky; heaven: 九霄云外 jiǔxiāo yúnwài

霄汉 xiāohàn liter. the sky; the firmament

霄壤 xiāo-rǎng heaven and earth

霄壤之别 xiāo-rǎng zhī bié as far apart (or as different) as heaven and earth; a world of difference

魈 xiāo see 山魈 shānxiāo

嚣(嚻) xiāo clamour; hubbub; din: 叫嚣 jiàoxiāo

嚣张 xiāozhāng rampant; arrogant; aggressive: ～一时 run rampant (or wild) for a time / 他也太～了。He's really too aggressive.

xiáo

淆 xiáo confuse; mix: 混淆 hùnxiáo

淆惑 xiáohuò formal confuse; bewilder

淆乱 xiáoluàn ① mixed and disorderly ② confuse; befuddle: ～视听 befuddle the minds of the public

淆杂 xiáozá mixed

xiǎo

小 xiǎo ① small; little; petty; minor: ～屋 a small room or house / ～河 a small river / ～姑娘 a little girl / ～国 a small country / ～事 a small matter / ～问题 a minor question / ～手术 a minor operation / 那个数量很～。That's a very small amount. / 你的声音太～。Your voice is too soft. / 风～些了。The wind has dropped a little. / 鞋～了点儿。These shoes are a bit too tight. ② young: 他还～呢。He's still young. / 你也不～了。You're not young any more. / 她比我～。She is younger than I am. ③ of short duration: ～坐片刻 sit for a while ④ the last in order of seniority: ～儿子 the youngest son / 他是我的～弟弟。He is my youngest brother. ⑤ (used before names of animals to indicate the young): ～鸡 chick / ～鸭 duckling / ～狗 pup; puppy / ～猫 kitten; kitty / ～牛 calf; heifer / ～羊 lamb; kid / ～马 pony; foal; colt / ～猪 piggy; piglet; shoat / ～鹿 deerlet; fawn / ～老虎 tiger cub ⑥ little ones; children: 一家大～ the whole family, old and young / 上有老, 下有～ have the old above and the young below—have parents and children to care for ⑦ concubine: 讨个～ take a concubine ⑧ hum. my; our: ～女 my daughter / ～店 my store ⑧ (used before family name, given name, etc.): ～张 Xiao Zhang / ～强 Xiao Qiang / ～三儿 Xiao Sanr (childhood name for one's third child)

小儿 xiǎor inf. ① (used after 从, 自, 打) early childhood: 这孩子从小(自, 打)～就伶俐。He has been a bright kid since his early childhood. ② a baby boy: 胖～ a chubby baby boy ——see also xiǎo'ér

小白菜 xiǎobáicài a variety of Chinese cabbage; pakchoi

小白脸儿 xiǎobáiliǎnr derog. a young fair face—a handsome, effeminate young man

小百货 xiǎobǎihuò small articles of daily use

小摆设 xiǎobǎishè little curios, handicrafts, statuettes, etc. placed on shelves and desks for decoration; bric-a-bracs; ornamental knick-knacks

小班 xiǎobān the bottom class in a kindergarten (for

children from 2 or 3 to 4 years of age)

小半 xiǎobàn less than half; the lesser (*or* smaller) half

小报 xiǎobào small-sized newspaper; tabloid

小报告 xiǎobàogào a little report—a secret report to the higher authority on the shortcomings or wrongdoings of sb.: 打～ tell on sb.

小辈 xiǎobèi junior members of a family or of families more or less related

小本经营 xiǎoběn jīngyíng do business with little capital—go in for sth. in a small way

小扁豆 xiǎobiǎndòu lentil

小便 xiǎobiàn ① urinate; pass (*or* make) water; empty one's bladder ② urine ③ penis

小便池 xiǎobiànchí urinal

小辫儿 xiǎobiànr short braid; pigtail: 她梳着两条～。She wears her hair in two pigtails.

小辫子 xiǎobiànzi a mistake or shortcoming that may be exploited by others; vulnerable point; handle: 有～给人抓 have vulnerable points that others may capitalize on／抓住～不放 get a handle on sb. to make things hard for him

小标题 xiǎobiāotí subheading; subhead

小病大养 xiǎobìng dà yǎng take an unduly long rest for a slight illness

小不忍则乱大谋 xiǎo bù rěn zé luàn dàmóu lack of forbearance in small matters upsets great plans

小步舞 xiǎobùwǔ minuet (the dance)

小步舞曲 xiǎobùwǔqǔ minuet (the music)

小不点儿 xiǎobudiǎnr *dial.* ① very small; tiny ② a tiny tot

小菜 xiǎocài ① pickled vegetables; pickles ② *dial.* meat, fish and vegetable dishes; common dishes

小菜儿 xiǎocàir *inf.* something extremely easy to do or manage

小册子 xiǎocèzi booklet; pamphlet

小差 xiǎochāi see 开小差 kāi xiǎochāi

小产 xiǎochǎn have a miscarriage

小肠 xiǎocháng *physiol.* small intestine

小肠串气 xiǎocháng chuànqì popular name for 疝气 shànqì

小抄儿 xiǎochāor *inf.* a slip of paper with facts, figures, or answers to questions, used for cheating in examinations

小朝廷 xiǎocháotíng little court—① a court in exile or forced into the border regions ② the court of a vassal state or a weak neighbouring state

小潮 xiǎocháo neap tide

小车 xiǎochē ① wheelbarrow; handbarrow; handcart; pushcart ② car; sedan

小乘 xiǎochéng Little Vehicle (a school of Buddhism); Hinayana

小吃 xiǎochī ① snacks; refreshments ② cold dishes (of western food)

小吃部 xiǎochībù snack counter

小吃店 xiǎochīdiàn snack bar

小丑[1] xiǎochǒu clown; buffoon: 扮演～角色 play the buffoon

小丑[2] xiǎochǒu a contemptible wretch; a vile character

小丑跳梁 xiǎochǒu tiàoliáng a contemptible wretch making trouble

小除夕 xiǎochúxī same as 小年夜 xiǎoniányè①

小春 xiǎochūn *dial.* ① the tenth lunar month; late autumn ② (also 小春作物 xiǎochūn zuòwù) crops sown in late autumn

小词 xiǎocí minor term (in a syllogism)

小葱 xiǎocōng shallot; spring onion

小聪明 xiǎocōngmíng *derog.* cleverness in trivial matters; petty trick: 要～ play petty tricks／有点儿～ be

clever in some small ways／靠～过日子 live by one's wits

小旦 xiǎodàn the role of a young woman in traditional opera

小刀 xiǎodāo pocket knife

小刀会起义 Xiǎodāohuì Qǐyì Small-Sword Society Uprising (an uprising led in 1853 by the Small-Sword Society, a secret society, against the foreign imperialists in Shanghai and Xiamen)

小道 xiǎodào minor arts (used by Confucianists to refer to agriculture, medicine, divination and other professions unworthy of the 君子 jūnzǐ)

小道儿 xiǎodàor a small lane; path

小道理 xiǎodàoli minor principle

小道儿消息 xiǎodàor xiāoxi side-street news; grapevine news; hearsay: 那是他听来的～。That's something he heard on the grapevine.

小的 xiǎode ① little ones; children: 家里老的～都等着我回去忙饭吃呢。My parents and children are all waiting for me to come home and cook the meal. ② old I (used by commoners when speaking to officials, or servants to masters)

小弟 xiǎodì ① youngest brother ② old hum. your younger brother (a form of self-address used among male friends)

小调 xiǎodiào ① ditty; tune ② *mus.* minor: A～协奏曲 concerto in A minor

小动作 xiǎodòngzuò ① mean and petty action; little trick or manoeuvre: 搞～ get up to little tricks ② fidgety movements (made by schoolchildren in class): 李刚，坐好听课，别做～了! Li Gang, stop fidgeting! Sit still and pay attention!

小豆 xiǎodòu another name for 赤小豆 chìxiǎodòu

小豆蔻 xiǎodòukòu cardamom; cardamon

小肚鸡肠 xiǎodù-jīcháng petty; narrow-minded

小肚子 xiǎodùzi popular name for 小腹 xiǎofù

小队 xiǎoduì the lowest-level unit of a group organized for a particular purpose; team; squad: 少先队～长 a squad leader of the Young Pioneers

小额 xiǎo'é small amount: ～储蓄 small savings deposit

小恩小惠 xiǎo'ēn-xiǎohuì little or small favours; economic sops or bait

小儿 xiǎo'ér ① children ② *hum.* my son ——see also xiǎor

小儿科 xiǎo'érkē (department of) paediatrics: ～医生 paediatrician

小儿麻痹症 xiǎo'ér mábìzhèng infantile paralysis; poliomyelitis; polio

小二 xiǎo'èr (also 小二哥 xiǎo'èrgē) old a young waiter in a wineshop or an inn

小贩 xiǎofàn pedlar; vendor; hawker

小费 xiǎofèi tip; gratuity

小分队 xiǎofēnduì a small detachment; a group sent out for a special task: 民兵～ a militia detachment／文艺～ an itinerant art troupe

小斧 xiǎofǔ hatchet: 单刃～ half hatchet

小腹 xiǎofù underbelly; lower abdomen

小钢炮 xiǎogāngpào *inf.* a small steel cannon—a bold, outspoken person ready to give sharp criticisms, comments, etc.

小个子 xiǎogèzi a short person; a small fellow

小工 xiǎogōng unskilled labourer

小恭 xiǎogōng *formal* urinate; pass (*or* make) water; empty one's bladder

小姑 xiǎogū *inf.* ① (also 小姑子 xiǎogūzi) husband's younger sister; sister-in-law ② one's youngest paternal aunt

小鼓 xiǎogǔ *mus.* side drum; snare drum

小褂　xiǎoguà　Chinese-style shirt (worn next to the skin)

小馆儿　xiǎoguǎnr　a small restaurant; cafeteria

小广播　xiǎoguǎngbō　spreading of hearsay information; grapevine; bush telegraph

小鬼　xiǎoguǐ　① little devil; a demon servant in Hell ② child; imp (a term of endearment used in addressing a child)

小孩儿　xiǎoháir　(also 小孩子 xiǎoháizi) inf. child

小寒　Xiǎohán　① Lesser Cold—the 23rd of the 24 solar terms ② the day marking the beginning of the 23rd solar term (Jan. 5, 6, or 7) ——see also 节气 jiéqì; 二十四节气 èrshí sì jiéqì

小号¹　xiǎohào　① (also 小号儿 xiǎohàor) small size (of clothes, etc.): ～鞋 small-size shoes / 这种风衣型号齐全, 从～到特大号都有。 Wind jackets of this style come in all sizes, from small to extra large. / 我要小一号的。 I want one size smaller. ② hum. my (or our) store

小号²　xiǎohào　trumpet

小黑麦　xiǎohēimài　triticale

小胡桃　xiǎohútáo　dial. ① hickory ② hickory nut

小户　xiǎohù　① (also 小户人家 xiǎohù rénjiā) a poor, humble family; a family of limited means and without powerful connections ② a small family

小花脸　xiǎohuāliǎn　small flowery face (another name for 丑³ chǒu, cf. 大花脸 dàhuāliǎn)

小鬟　xiǎohuán　old a little slave girl

小黄鱼　xiǎohuángyú　little yellow croaker

小汇报　xiǎohuìbào　same as 小报告 xiǎobàogào

小惠　xiǎohuì　a small favour (usu. as economic bait)

小伙子　xiǎohuǒzi　inf. a young man; lad; a young fellow (or chap); youngster

小鸡儿　xiǎojīr　(also 小鸡子 xiǎojīzi) humor. little cock (said of a little boy's penis)

小集团　xiǎojítuán　clique; faction

小蓟　xiǎojì　Chin. med. field thistle (Cephalanoplos segetum)

小家碧玉　xiǎojiā bìyù　a pretty girl of humble birth

小家伙　xiǎojiāhuo　(also 小傢伙 xiǎojiāhuo) kid: 我那～调皮得很。 My kid is very naughty.

小家鼠　xiǎojiāshǔ　house mouse (Mus musculus)

小家庭　xiǎojiātíng　a small family: 建立～ get married and set up one's own home

小家子气　xiǎojiāziqì　(also 小家子相 xiǎojiāzixiàng) small-minded; petty: 不要太～了! Don't be so petty! / 她的～很重。 Her small-town manners are unmistakable.

小建　xiǎojiàn　a lunar month of 29 days

小将　xiǎojiàng　① a young general ② a young militant; a young pathbreaker

小脚　xiǎojiǎo　bound feet (of women in the old days)

小轿车　xiǎojiàochē　sedan; car

小节　xiǎojié　① a small matter; trifle: 生活～ matters concerning personal life ② mus. bar; measure: ～线 bar line; bar

小结　xiǎojié　① a brief sum-up; a preliminary or interim summary: 期末～ an end-of-term summary ② summarize briefly: ～一下前阶段的工作 summarize briefly the work done in the previous stage

小解　xiǎojiě　urinate; pass (or make) water; empty one's bladder

小姐　xiǎojie　① a young (unmarried) lady ② Miss: 张～ Miss Zhang

小襟　xiǎojīn　the small inner piece on the right side of a Chinese garment which buttons on the right

小尽　xiǎojìn　same as 小建 xiǎojiàn

小径　xiǎojìng　① a narrow path ② (of timber) small in diameter

小舅子　xiǎojiùzi　inf. wife's younger brother; brother-in-law

小开　xiǎokāi　dial. (an old term of address for a rich man's son) young master

小楷　xiǎokǎi　① the regular script in small characters (in Chinese calligraphy) ② lowercase letter (in printing)

小看　xiǎokàn　inf. look down upon; underestimate; belittle: 你不该这么～人。 You really shouldn't look down on people like this. / 你可别～了这件事。 Don't underestimate the importance of this matter.

小康　xiǎokāng　a relatively comfortable life: 家道～。 The family was comfortably off.

小康之家　xiǎokāng zhī jiā　a family with a modest competence; a comfortably-off family

小考　xiǎokǎo　minor examination (i.e. quiz, test, mid-term examination, etc.)

小可　xiǎokě　old your servant—I

小客车　xiǎokèchē　minibus

小口径　xiǎokǒujìng　small-bore; small-calibre: ～步枪 small-bore rifle

小老婆　xiǎolǎopo　concubine

小老树　xiǎolǎoshù　a stunted tree

小老头儿　xiǎolǎotóur　inf. a prematurely old man

小礼拜　xiǎolǐbài　alternate Sunday which is a working day

小礼拜堂　xiǎolǐbàitáng　chapel

小两口　xiǎoliǎngkǒu　inf. a young (married) couple: 那～儿真是天生的一对儿。 That young couple were meant for each other.

小量　xiǎoliàng　a small amount or quantity

小令　xiǎolìng　① a short metre for ci (词) poems that contains relatively few syllables (say 62 or fewer) ② a single sanqu (散曲 sǎnqǔ) song (i.e. not in a sequence, corresponding to one aria in the drama; cf. 散套 sǎntào)

小绺　xiǎoliǔ　dial. pickpocket

小炉匠　xiǎolújiàng　tinker

小路　xiǎolù　path; trail

小萝卜　xiǎoluóbo　radish

小萝卜头儿　xiǎoluóbotóur　dial. ① child; tot ② a mere nobody

小骂大帮忙　xiǎomà dàbāngmáng　condemn on minor issues but support on major ones

小买卖　xiǎomǎimai　small business: 做～ do small business

小麦　xiǎomài　wheat

小麦赤霉病　xiǎomài chìméibìng　wheat scab

小麦吸浆虫　xiǎomài xījiāngchóng　wheat midge

小麦线虫　xiǎomài xiànchóng　nematode of wheat (Anguina tritici)

小麦线虫病　xiǎomài xiànchóngbìng　nematode disease of wheat

小麦腥黑穗病　xiǎomài xīnghēisuìbìng　bunt of wheat

小卖　xiǎomài　snacks: 应时～ seasonal snacks

小卖部　xiǎomàibù　① a small shop attached to a school, factory, theatre, etc. (selling cigarettes, confectionery, cold drinks, etc.) ② buffet; snack counter

小满　Xiǎomǎn　① Lesser Fullness of Grain—the 8th of the 24 solar terms ② the day marking the beginning of the 8th solar term (May 20, 21, or 22, when the winter wheat, sown the previous autumn, is filling out its ears) ——see also 节气 jiéqì; 二十四节气 èrshí sì jiéqì

小猫熊　xiǎomāoxióng　lesser panda

小毛　xiǎomáo　short-haired pelt (as that of the grey squirrel, snow weasel, etc.)

小毛头　xiǎomáotóu　dial. baby

小门小户　xiǎomén-xiǎohù　poor humble families; families of limited means and without powerful connections

小米 xiǎomǐ millet: ～粥 millet gruel / ～面 millet flour

小名 xiǎomíng pet name for a child; childhood name: 他～叫毛毛。His childhood name is Maomao.

小命儿 xiǎomìngr *inf.* life: 他差一点儿送了～。He barely escaped with his life.

小拇哥 xiǎomugē *dial.* little finger

小拇指 xiǎomuzhǐ *inf.* little finger

小脑 xiǎonǎo *physiol.* cerebellum

小年 xiǎonián ① a lunar year in which the last month has 29 days ② a festival on the 23rd or 24th of the 12th month of the lunar year when sacrifices are made to the kitchen god ③ an off year (for fruit trees, bamboos, etc.)

小年轻 xiǎoniánqīng young people; boys and girls (about 20 years of age)

小年夜 xiǎoniányè ① the night before the lunar New Year's Eve ② the 23rd or 24th of the 12th month of the lunar year

小娘 xiǎoniáng *old* ① father's concubine ② prostitute

小娘儿们 xiǎoniángrmen *derog.* a young woman

小娘子 xiǎoniángzǐ *old* ① a young married woman ② young lady (used in direct address)

小鸟依人 xiǎoniǎo yī rén an endearing little bird (said of a lovely young girl)

小妞儿 xiǎoniūr *inf.* a young girl

小牛肉 xiǎoniúròu veal

小农 xiǎonóng small farmer

小农经济 xiǎonóng jīngjì small-scale peasant economy; small-scale farming by individual owners

小女 xiǎonǚ *hum.* my daughter

小跑 xiǎopǎo *inf.* trot; jog: 他是一溜～着来的。He came jogging all the way here.

小朋友 xiǎopéngyǒu ① children: 幼儿园的～ children of the kindergarten / 一群～ a bunch of children ② (a term of address used by an adult to a child) little friend; little boy or girl

小便宜 xiǎopiányi small gain; petty advantage: 贪～ go after petty advantages / 占～ gain petty advantages

小票儿 xiǎopiàor bank notes of small denominations

小品 xiǎopǐn a short, simple literary or artistic creation; essay; sketch: 历史～ a short historical essay / 广播～ a short piece for broadcasting / 电视～ a TV sketch

小品文 xiǎopǐnwén familiar essay; essay

小评论 xiǎopínglùn a short comment

小铺儿 xiǎopùr a small store

小瀑布 xiǎopùbù cascade

小气候 xiǎoqìhòu microclimate

小憩 xiǎoqì *formal* take a short rest: 公园里辟有茶座, 供游人～。There are teahouses in the park where visitors can sit and relax.

小气 xiǎoqi ① stingy; niggardly; mean ② *dial.* narrow-minded; petty

小前提 xiǎoqiántí *log.* minor premise (in a syllogism)

小钱 xiǎoqián ① copper coin; copper ② a small amount of money ③ a small amount of money given as a bribe

小瞧 xiǎoqiáo *inf.* look down upon; underestimate: 别～人, 你能干的我也能干! Now don't underestimate me. What you can do I can do too!

小巧玲珑 xiǎoqiǎo línglóng small and exquisite

小青年 xiǎoqīngnián young people; boys and girls (about 20 years of age)

小青瓦 xiǎoqīngwǎ small black tile (a name for the old-style curved roof-tile)

小秋收 xiǎoqiūshōu the lesser autumn harvest (i.e. the gathering of wild herbs or fruits before or after the autumn harvest)

小球藻 xiǎoqiúzǎo chlorella

小曲儿 xiǎoqǔr ditty; popular tune

小觑 xiǎoqù despise; look down upon; underestimate

小圈子 xiǎoquānzi ① a small social circle; a narrow area of activity: 走出家庭的～ come out of the narrow family circle ② a small circle (*or* set) of people; a small clique: 搞～ form a small clique

小犬 xiǎoquǎn *hum.* my son

小犬座 Xiǎoquǎnzuò *astron.* Canis Minor

小人 xiǎorén ① a small man: 君子求诸己,～求诸人。《论语》The demands that a gentleman makes are upon himself; those that a small man makes are upon others. ② *old hum.* I (used by a man of low social position when speaking to his betters) ③ a base person; a vile character; villain

小人儿 xiǎorénr *dial.* (an endearing term for a young person) baby

小人得志 xiǎorén dézhì a small man intoxicated by success; a small man having greatness thrust upon him; villains holding sway

小人儿书 xiǎorénrshū *inf.* children's picture-story book

小人物 xiǎorénwù an unimportant person; a nobody; cipher; nonentity

小日子 xiǎorìzi the easy life of a small family (esp. of a young couple): 他们的～过得挺舒坦。They lead a happy and snug life.

小嗓儿 xiǎosǎngr falsetto (used in traditional opera)

小商品 xiǎoshāngpǐn small commodities

小商品经济 xiǎoshāngpǐn jīngjì small commodity economy

小晌午 xiǎoshǎngwu *dial.* late morning; the time just before noon

小舌 xiǎoshé *physiol.* uvula

小婶儿 xiǎoshěnr (also 小婶子 xiǎoshěnzi) *dial.* wife of husband's younger brother

小生 xiǎoshēng ① one of the main divisions of the *sheng* or male role in traditional opera (representing young students, scholars, or warriors; the *xiaosheng* actor never wears a beard and speaks and sings in a mixture of high falsetto and tenor) ② *old* (used by a young student or scholar to refer to himself): ～姓张, 名琪, 字君瑞, 本贯西洛人也。(王实甫《西厢记》) My name is Zhang Qi, my style Junrui. I am a native of Xiluo.

小生产 xiǎoshēngchǎn small (*or* small-scale) production

小生产者 xiǎoshēngchǎnzhě small producer

小狮座 Xiǎoshīzuò *astron.* Leo Minor

小时 xiǎoshí hour

小时候 xiǎoshíhou *inf.* in one's childhood; when one was young: 这是他～的照片。These are his childhood photos. / ～, 我们常在一块儿玩儿。We used to play together when we were young.

小市民 xiǎoshìmín a town-dweller of the lower middle class; urban petty bourgeois; plebeian; philistine: ～习气 plebeian ways and habits

小视 xiǎoshì *formal* slight; look down upon: 这件事对今后的工作关系重大, 不可～。This is not to be slighted, for it has an important bearing on our future work.

小事 xiǎoshì trifle; petty thing; minor matter: 大事做不来,～又不做 disdain minor assignments while being unequal to major ones / ～一桩, 不必挂在心上。It's a trifling matter. *or* It's nothing. Forget it.

小试锋芒 xiǎo shì fēngmáng display only a small part of one's talent or capability

小手工业者 xiǎoshǒugōngyèzhě small handicraftsman

小手小脚 xiǎoshǒu-xiǎojiǎo ① stingy; mean ② lacking boldness; timid; niggling

小书 xiǎoshū ① children's picture-story book ② children's primer (in the old days) ③ *dial.* a term referring to 弹词 táncí

小叔子 xiǎoshūzi *inf.* husband's younger brother; brother-in-law

小暑 Xiǎoshǔ ① Lesser Heat—the 11th of the 24 solar terms ② the day marking the beginning of the 11th solar term (July 6, 7, or 8) ——see also 节气 jiéqi; 二十四节气 èrshí sì jiéqì

小数 xiǎoshù *math.* decimal

小数点 xiǎoshùdiǎn *math.* decimal point

小水 xiǎoshuǐ *Chin. med.* urine

小睡 xiǎoshuì nap: 〜片刻 take a short nap

小说 xiǎoshuō novel; fiction

小说家 xiǎoshuōjiā novelist; writer of fiction

小厮 xiǎosī *old* ① a young male servant; page boy; page ② boy; a young lad

小苏打 xiǎosūdá *chem.* sodium bicarbonate

小算盘 xiǎosuànpan small abacus—selfish calculations: 〜打得精 be very calculating; be very shrewd in looking after one's own interests

小提琴 xiǎotíqín violin

小提琴手 xiǎotíqínshǒu violinist: 首席〜 concertmaster

小题大作 xiǎo tí dà zuò make a fuss over a trifle; make a mountain out of a molehill

小天地 xiǎotiāndì one's own little world: 不要把自己关在办公室一里。Don't confine yourself within the four walls of an office.

小艇 xiǎotǐng a small boat; dinghy; skiff (rowed or sailed by one person)

小偷 xiǎotōu petty (*or* sneak) thief; pilferer

小偷小摸 xiǎotōu-xiǎomō pilfering

小土地出租者 xiǎotǔdìchūzūzhě a lessor of small plots of land

小团体主义 xiǎotuántǐzhǔyì cliquism; small-group mentality

小腿 xiǎotuǐ shank; lower leg

小玩艺儿 xiǎowányìr ① ornamental knick-knacks; bric-a-bracs ② insignificant skills

小我 xiǎowǒ the individual; the self: 牺牲〜 sacrifice self

小巫见大巫 xiǎowū jiàn dàwū a minor magician in the presence of a great one—feel dwarfed; pale into insignificance by comparison: 我过去所受的那些委屈和刺激，比起他来，也只是〜，算不得什么。What little pain and adversity I've experienced so far is simply nothing compared to what he's gone through.

小五金 xiǎowǔjīn metal fittings (e.g. nails, wires, hinges, bolts, locks, etc.); hardware

小媳妇 xiǎoxífu ① a married young woman ② one who always gets blamed (*or* takes the rap)

小先生 xiǎoxiānsheng little teacher—a student playing the role of a teacher to his classmates

小小不言 xiǎoxiǎo bù yán too trivial to talk about: 〜的事儿，不必计较。The matter is too small to be worth niggling over.

小鞋 xiǎoxié tight shoes—difficulties created, or unfair treatment given, by one's boss or superior when he cannot punish openly ——see also 穿小鞋 chuān xiǎoxié

小写 xiǎoxiě ① the ordinary form of a Chinese numeral (e.g. 一，二，三，as against 壹，贰，叁) ② a small letter; minuscule

小心 xiǎoxīn take care; be careful; be cautious: 〜火烛! Guard against fire! / 〜轻放! Handle with care! / 过马路要〜。Be careful when crossing the street. / 〜油漆! Mind the wet paint! / 路滑，〜摔倒。The road is slippery. Be careful not to slip and fall. ——see also 赔小心 péi xiǎoxīn

小心谨慎 xiǎoxīn-jǐnshèn careful; cautious; discreet; prudent

小心眼儿 xiǎoxīnyǎnr narrow-minded; petty: 你也太〜了，为这点儿事还生气。You are a bit too touchy to get angry about such a small thing.

小心翼翼 xiǎoxīn yìyì with the greatest of care; very cautiously: 她〜地把门打开，生怕把孩子惊醒。She opened the door gently so as not to wake the baby. / 他〜地接过鱼缸，放在桌上。He took the goldfish bowl gingerly and put it on the table.

小星 xiǎoxīng *euph.* little star—a concubine (usu. with reference to another man's concubine)

小行星 xiǎoxíngxīng *astron.* minor planet

小型 xiǎoxíng small-size; small-scale; miniature: 〜马 pony / 〜鸮 owlet / 〜企业 small enterprise / 〜运动会 a small-scale athletic meet / 〜拖拉机 baby (*or* small) tractor / 〜照相机 miniature camera / 〜摄像机 minicam

小性儿 xiǎoxìngr (also 小性子 xiǎoxìngzi) *dial.* childish temper; peevishness: 她动不动就闹〜，让她闹去，甭理她。She's always fretful and peevish like this, so just leave her alone.

小熊猫 xiǎoxióngmāo popular name for 小猫熊 xiǎomāoxióng

小熊座 Xiǎoxióngzuò *astron.* Ursa Minor

小婿 xiǎoxù *hum.* ① my son-in-law (used when speaking of him to sb. else) ② your son-in-law—I (used when speaking to one's parent-in-law)

小学 xiǎoxué ① primary (*or* elementary) school ② philological studies

小学生 xiǎoxuéshēng primary school pupil; schoolchild; schoolboy or schoolgirl: 甘当群众的〜 be willing to be a pupil of the masses

小学生 xiǎo xuésheng ① a student younger in age (than others of his class) ② *dial.* a little boy

小雪 Xiǎoxuě ① Lesser Snow—the 20th of the 24 solar terms ② the day marking the beginning of the 20th solar term (Nov. 22 or 23) ——see also 节气 jiéqi; 二十四节气 èrshí sì jiéqì

小循环 xiǎoxúnhuán *physiol.* pulmonary circulation

小阳春 xiǎoyángchūn the little spring (a period of mild, warm weather occurring in some parts of China in the 10th lunar month): 十月〜。The 10th (lunar) month brings us the little spring.

小样 xiǎoyàng *print.* galley proof (of a separate news item or an article in a newspaper)

小业主 xiǎoyèzhǔ small (*or* petty) proprietor

小叶 xiǎoyè *bot.* leaflet (one of the separate blades of a compound leaf)

小夜曲 xiǎoyèqǔ *mus.* serenade

小衣 xiǎoyī *dial.* underpants; drawers

小衣裳 xiǎoyīshang ① underclothes (worn next to the skin) ② children's clothing

小姨 xiǎoyí mother's youngest sister—aunt

小姨子 xiǎoyízi (also 小姨儿 xiǎoyír) *inf.* wife's younger sister; sister-in-law

小意思 xiǎoyìsi ① *pol.* a small token of one's regard: 这是我的一点儿〜，送给你做个纪念。This is a token of my esteem—just a little keepsake for you. ② a mere trifle; nothing important: 这种事〜，一两个小时就可以完。This job is nothing to me. I can finish it in a couple of hours.

小音阶 xiǎoyīnjiē *mus.* minor scale

小引 xiǎoyǐn a brief or short introductory note (to a poem, essay, etc.); foreword

小影 xiǎoyǐng a snapshot of oneself: 秋日登长城，留〜数帧。One autumn day I climbed to the top of the Great Wall and had a few snapshots taken.

小雨 xiǎoyǔ light rain; drizzle

小月 xiǎoyuè lesser month—a solar month of 30 days or a lunar month of 29 days

小月 xiǎo·yuè (also 小月子 xiǎoyuèzi) miscarriage; abortion

小灶 xiǎozào small mess—a mess hall where higher-grade food is prepared and served to a restricted group of diners

小帐 xiǎozhàng inf. tip; gratuity

小照 xiǎozhào a small-sized photograph of oneself

小侄 xiǎozhí hum. ① my nephew (used when speaking to others) ② your nephew—I (used when speaking to people of one's father's generation)

小指 xiǎozhǐ little finger or toe

小住 xiǎozhù formal stay for a few days: 假期我将赴京～数日。I will spend a few days in Beijing during the vacation.

小注 xiǎozhù notes in smaller print (incorporated in the text)

小传 xiǎozhuàn a brief biography; biographical sketch; profile

小篆 xiǎozhuàn the lesser seal character (a simplified form of 大篆 dàzhuàn, adopted c. 213 B.C. during the Qin Dynasty for the purpose of standardizing the script)

小酌 xiǎozhuó formal drinks with snacks: 餐馆设有雅座，供顾客随意～。There are special tables serving drinks with snacks in this restaurant.

小资产阶级 xiǎozīchǎnjiējí petty bourgeoisie

小子 xiǎozǐ formal ① the younger male generation ② old a term of address used by seniors to juniors ③ old I (a term referring to oneself, used by juniors to elders or to betters)

小子 xiǎozi inf. ① boy: 一个胖～ a chubby little boy / 他有两个孩子，一个闺女，一个～。He has two children, one girl and one boy. ② derog. bloke; fellow; guy: 这～真不是东西。That guy is really despicable.

小字 xiǎozì ① handwritten small characters ② childhood name

小字辈 xiǎozìbèi juniors; younger members; persons of lower status

小卒 xiǎozú foot soldier

小组 xiǎozǔ a small group: 领导～ the leading group / ～讨论 group discussion / ～委员会 subcommittee

晓（曉）

xiǎo ① dawn; daybreak: 拂晓 fúxiǎo ② know: 谁人不知，哪个不～? Everybody knows. ③ let sb. know; tell: 晓谕 xiǎoyù

晓畅 xiǎochàng ① be familiar with; have a deep understanding of: ～军事 be versed in military affairs / ～音律 have a deep understanding of music ② (of a piece of writing) smooth and explicit: 文笔～ write in a smooth and clear style

晓得 xiǎode know: 天～! God knows! / 明天你要提早十分钟来啊! ——～! You must get here ten minutes earlier tomorrow.—I know.

晓市 xiǎoshì morning market

晓示 xiǎoshì tell explicitly; notify

晓事 xiǎoshì sensible; intelligent: 这人好不～! How thoughtless he is!

晓行夜宿 xiǎoxíng-yèsù (of a person on a long journey) start at dawn and stop at dusk: 他～，风尘仆仆，一路来到陕西。Travelling by day and resting by night, he came to the Province of Shaanxi, travel-worn and weary.

晓以大义 xiǎo yǐ dàyì instil in sb.'s mind the righteousness of a cause

晓以利害 xiǎo yǐ lì·hài (also 晓以利弊 xiǎo yǐ lì-bì) warn sb. of the possible consequences; impress on sb. the gains and losses involved

晓谕 xiǎoyù formal (of higher authorities to sub-ordinates) give explicit instructions (or directions)

筱（篠）

xiǎo ① formal little slender bamboo ② a substitute for 小, often used in a person's name

xiào

孝

xiào ① filial: 孝子 xiàozǐ ② filial piety; filial obedience: 尽孝 jìnxiào ③ the conventional mourning rites for a deceased elder member of one's family: 守孝 shǒuxiào ④ mourning apparel: 穿孝 chuānxiào

孝道 xiàodào filial duty: 尽～ fulfil one's filial duty to one's parents

孝道 xiàodao inf. be a good son or daughter: 他的儿子、儿媳都很～。He has a good son and daughter-in-law.

孝服 xiàofú ① mourning apparel ② a conventional period of mourning (for a deceased elder member of one's family): ～已满。The mourning period is over.

孝敬 xiàojìng ① show filial respect to (one's elders) ② give presents to (one's elders or superiors) to show one's respect; pay a tribute of respect to: 他带了些南边的土产来～他奶奶。He brought his grandmother some local produce from the south as a gift.

孝幔 xiàomàn the curtain or screen before a bier

孝男 xiàonán old bereaved son (a term used in an obituary or on a tombstone)

孝女 xiàonǚ ① old bereaved daughter (a term used in an obituary or on a tombstone) ② a filial daughter; a dutiful daughter

孝顺 xiàoshùn show filial obedience: 她对父母十分～。She is extremely filial towards her parents.

孝悌 xiàotì show filial piety to one's parents and love and respect to one's elder brothers

孝心 xiàoxīn filial sentiments; filial devotion

孝行 xiàoxíng filial behaviour

孝衣 xiàoyī mourning apparel

孝子 xiàozǐ ① a filial son; a dutiful son ② son in mourning

孝子贤孙 xiàozǐ-xiánsūn worthy progeny; a fine son: 地主阶级的～ worthy progeny of the landlord class

肖

xiào resemble; be like: 维妙维肖 wéimiào-wéixiào ——see also Xiāo

肖像 xiàoxiàng portrait; portraiture

肖像画 xiàoxiànghuà portrait-painting

哮

xiào ① heavy breathing; wheeze: 哮喘 xiàochuǎn ② roar; howl: 咆哮 páoxiào

哮喘 xiàochuǎn med. asthma

效¹

xiào effect: 见效 jiànxiào

效²（傚）

xiào imitate; follow the example of: 上行下效 shàngxíng-xiàxiào

效³（効）

xiào devote (one's energy or life) to; render (a service): 效死 xiàosǐ / 报效 bàoxiào

效法 xiàofǎ follow the example of; model oneself on; learn from: 他治学严谨，值得～。His meticulous scholarship is worthy of emulation. or We have much to learn from his meticulous scholarship.

效仿 xiàofǎng imitate; follow the example of

效果 xiàoguǒ ① effect; result: ～不大 not be very effective; produce little effect / 试验治虫药的～ test the effectiveness of the insecticide / 取得良好的～ achieve

good results / 动机与～有时会发生矛盾。Motives sometimes conflict with results. ② *theat.* sound and lighting effects

效劳 xiàoláo work in the service of; work for: 为祖国～ work for the benefit of one's country / 乐于为您～. I'm only too glad to offer you my services.

效力 xiàolì ① render a service to; serve: 为国～ serve one's country ② effect: 这药很有～. The medicine is efficacious. / 两种文本具有同等～. Both texts (in two different languages) are equally authentic. / 你的话对他没有发生什么～. Your advice (or words) had no effect on him whatever.

效力射 xiàolìshè *mil.* fire for effect

效率 xiàolù efficiency: ～高 efficient / ～低 inefficient / 这项革新使工作～提高五倍. The innovation raised (or increased) efficiency fivefold.

效命 xiàomìng go all out to serve sb. regardless of the consequences: ～疆场 ready to lay down one's life on the battlefield

效能 xiàonéng efficacy; usefulness: 充分发挥水、肥的～ make the best possible use of irrigation and fertilizer

效颦 xiàopín imitate unintelligently and awkwardly; be an awkward, incompetent imitator; mimic ——see also 东施效颦 Dōngshī xiàopín

效死 xiàosǐ be ready to give (or relinquish) one's life for a cause; devote one's life to: 愿～沙场 be willing to give one's life on the battlefield

效验 xiàoyàn intended effect; desired result: 没有～ prove ineffective; fall flat / 这种方法具有明显的～. This method produces tangible results.

效益 xiàoyì beneficial result; benefit: 灌溉～ irrigation benefit / 经济～ economic returns (or results, benefits) / 社会～ social effect / 投资～ investment results / 充分发挥水库的～ try to reap the fullest benefits that the reservoir can provide / ～指标 targets set for better results

效应 xiàoyìng (physical or chemical) effect: 热～ fuel factor; heat effect; thermal results / 光电～ photoelectric effect; electro-optic effect / 陀螺～ gyroscopic effect / 微观～ microeffect

效用 xiàoyòng effectiveness; usefulness: 发挥明显的～ show obvious effectiveness

效尤 xiàoyóu knowingly follow the example of a wrongdoer: 以儆效尤 yǐ jǐng xiàoyóu

效忠 xiàozhōng pledge loyalty to; devote oneself heart and soul to: ～于祖国 pledge one's loyalty to one's country; devote oneself heart and soul to one's motherland / ～宣誓 oath of allegiance / ～信 letter pledging allegiance; letter of fealty

校[1] xiào school: 全～同学 all students of the school / ～办工厂 school-run workshop; campus workshop

校[2] xiào field officer; field grade officer ——see also jiào

校车 xiàochē school bus

校董 xiàodǒng members of the Board of Directors of a school, college, etc.: ～会 the School (College, etc.) Board of Directors

校风 xiàofēng school spirit: 这所学校以具有良好的～闻名. The school boasts of excellent school spirit. / 重振～ revive the school spirit

校服 xiàofú school uniform

校官 xiàoguān *mil.* field officer; field grade officer

校规 xiàoguī school regulations

校花 xiàohuā campus belle

校徽 xiàohuī school badge

校刊 xiàokān school publication; college journal

校历 xiàolì school calendar

校庆 xiàoqìng the anniversary of the founding of a school or college

校舍 xiàoshè schoolhouse; school building

校外 xiàowài outside school; outside the school campus: 住～ not live on the school campus

校外辅导员 xiàowài fǔdǎoyuán guest counsellor for schoolchildren's activities

校外活动 xiàowài huódòng after-school activities: ～站 after-school activities club (or centre) / ～辅导员 after-school activities counsellor

校务 xiàowù administrative affairs of a school or college

校训 xiàoxùn school motto

校医 xiàoyī school doctor

校友 xiàoyǒu alumnus or alumna: ～会 alumni association

校园 xiàoyuán campus; school grounds

校长 xiàozhǎng ① headmaster (of a middle or primary school); principal ② president (of a university, college, etc.); chancellor

校址 xiàozhǐ the location of a school or college; school or college address

笑 xiào ① smile; laugh: 哈哈大～ laugh heartily; roar with laughter / 真～死人 be terribly funny / 小伙子被批准入伍，～得合不拢嘴. The young man grinned from ear to ear when his application to join the army was approved. ② ridicule; laugh at: 他刚学，别～他. He's just started learning. Don't laugh at him.

笑柄 xiàobǐng laughingstock; butt; joke: 他这句话已成为～. That remark of his has become a standing joke.

笑不可仰 xiào bù kě yǎng double up with laughter

笑掉大牙 xiào diào dàyá laugh one's head off: 叫人～ ridiculous enough to make people laugh their heads off

笑哈哈 xiàohāhā laughingly; with a laugh

笑呵呵 xiàohēhē be smiling happily; be all smiles: 她一天到晚总是～的. She's always all smiles.

笑话 xiàohua ① joke; jest: 说～ crack a joke ② laugh at; ridicule: ～人 laugh at sb. / 咱们一定要赢，别让人～咱们. We must win the game, and not give others any chance to laugh at us. ——see also 闹笑话 nào xiàohua; 看笑话 kàn xiàohua

笑话百出 xiàohua bǎi chū make many stupid mistakes; make oneself utterly ridiculous

笑剧 xiàojù same as 闹剧 nàojù

笑里藏刀 xiào lǐ cáng dāo hide a dagger behind a smile—with murderous intent behind one's smiles: 世界上多少人被他们的甜言蜜语所蒙蔽，而不知道他们～的可怕. Quite a number of people have been fooled by their honeyed words, failing to see the murderous intent behind their smiles.

笑脸 xiàoliǎn smiling face: ～相迎 greet with a genial smile ——see also 赔笑脸 péi xiàoliǎn

笑料 xiàoliào something funny or laughable; laughingstock; joke

笑骂 xiàomà ① deride and upbraid; taunt: ～由他～，好官我自为之. Let them laugh who will—I am a good official (defiant, self-revealing words put into the mouth of a dishonest official). ② scold in jest (or jokingly)

笑貌 xiàomào smiling face; smiling expression: 音容～，宛然俱在. The voice, the smiles, the facial expression of the deceased are still there (or can still be felt), as alive as ever.

笑眯眯 xiàomīmī smiling; with a genial smile on one's face: 他老是～的. He's always smiling.

笑面虎　xiàomiànhǔ　a smiling tiger—an outwardly kind but inwardly cruel person

笑纳　xiàonà　*pol.*　kindly accept (this small gift of mine): 送上薄酬, 还望～。Hope you will kindly accept this little remuneration we are sending you.

笑诺　xiàonuò　say "yes" with a smile; cheerfully promise; gladly agree

笑破肚皮　xiào pò dùpí　split one's sides with laughter

笑气　xiàoqì　*chem.*　laughing gas; nitrous oxide

笑容　xiàoróng　smiling expression; smile: 慈祥的～ a kindly smile /～满面 be all smiles; have a broad smile on one's face / 她脸上露出一丝～。A faint smile crept over her face.

笑容可掬　xiàoróng kě jū　be radiant with smiles

笑谈　xiàotán　① laughingstock; object of ridicule: 传为～ become a standing joke ② a funny remark; joke; jest

笑窝　xiàowō　(also 笑涡 xiàowō) dimple

笑嘻嘻　xiàoxīxī　grinning; smiling broadly

笑颜　xiàoyán　smiling face: ～常开 be always beaming with joy

笑靥　xiàoyè　*formal*　① dimple ② smiling face

笑吟吟　xiàoyínyín　smiling winsomely; with a winsome smile on one's face

笑影　xiàoyǐng　the image of a smiling face: 她的～重又浮上我的脑海。Again, her smiling face came back to my mind.

笑语　xiàoyǔ　cheerful chatting interspersed with hearty laughter

笑逐颜开　xiào zhú yán kāi　beam with smiles; one's face wreathed in smiles: 张太太不由得～。Mrs. Zhang couldn't restrain a smile of joy.

啸（嘯、歗）

xiào　① (of humans) make a whistling sound: 长啸 chángxiào ② (of certain birds and animals) give a long, loud cry: 虎～ tigers roaring (*or* growling) / 鸟～ birds screeching ③ (of the wind, the sea, etc.) howl; roar: 风～ the wind howling / 海水的～声 the roaring of the sea ④ (of bullets, airplanes, etc.) whistle; whizz: 枪弹的～声 the whistling of bullets / 飞机尖～着飞过顶空。A plane whizzed overhead.

啸傲　xiào'ào　*liter.*　whistle arrogantly, free of worries and social conventions (usu. referring to a hermit): ～山泉 lead a hermit's life in the woods and by the brooks

啸聚　xiàojù　*formal*　holler to each other and band together (*or* gang up)

啸聚山林　xiàojù shānlín　holler to each other, form a band and take to the greenwood: 竟岁～, 亦有何乐? There is no pleasure in leading a lawless life all the year round.

啸鸣　xiàomíng　① whistle; whizz; screech; howl: 烈风～ A strong wind was howling. ② a loud, shrill and long sound: 汽笛的～把人们从睡梦中惊醒。The wails of the siren woke the people out of their dreams.

xiē

些

xiē　*m.*　① some; a few: 作了～改进 have made some improvements / 买～东西 do some shopping / 前～日子 a few days ago; sometime ago ② (used after adjectives) a little more; a little: 这个稍大～。This is a little bigger. / 我好～了。I'm a little better. / 请大声～! Louder, please! / 留神～! Be careful! / 他的烧退了～。His fever has come down a little.

些个　xiēge　*inf.*　some; a few: 这～人都来干吗? What are all these people doing here? / 他是弟弟, 你就该让他～。He is your younger brother, so you should humour him a little. / 我要不了那么～。I can't take that many.

些微　xiēwēi　slightly; a little; a bit: ～有点儿疼 hurt slightly; be a bit painful / 这颜色～深了一点。The colour is a trifle too dark. / 一阵秋风吹来, 感到～的凉意。The autumn wind sprang up, and there was a slight chill in the air.

些须　xiēxū　*old*　a little; trifling: ～小事, 何足挂齿? It's a trifling matter, not worth mentioning.

些许　xiēxǔ　a little; a few: ～礼物 some small presents

揳

xiē　*dial.*　drive (a wedge, nail, etc.): 在墙上～个钉子 drive (*or* knock) a nail into the wall

楔

xiē　① wedge ② peg ③ same as 揳 xiē

楔规　xiēguī　*mech.*　wedge gauge

楔形文字　xiēxíng wénzì　cuneiform characters (as of ancient Babylonia, Assyria, Persia, and some other areas of the Near East); sphenogram

楔子　xiēzi　① wedge ② peg ③ prologue or interlude in Yuan Dynasty drama ④ prologue in some modern novels

歇

xiē　① have a rest: ～一会儿 have a short rest / 累得我都～不过来了。I'm completely done in. ② stop (work, etc.); knock off: 咱们～会儿, 喝杯茶。Let's knock off for a cup of tea. / 我已经～了一个礼拜没上班了。I've been off from work for a week. ③ *dial.*　go to bed: 你～了吗? Are you in bed? ④ *dial.*　a little while: 过了一～ after a while / 等一～ wait for a while

歇班　xiēbān　be off duty; have time off: 今天小王～。Xiao Wang is off duty today.

歇顶　xiēdǐng　get a bit thin on top; be balding: 他年龄并不老, 可是已经～了。He is not old but is already balding.

歇乏　xiēfá　have a rest in order to relieve one's fatigue: 歇不过乏来 cannot recover from one's fatigue; be completely done in

歇伏　xiēfú　stop work during the hottest days of the year

歇工　xiēgōng　stop work; knock off: 今天我们早早就～了。We stopped work early today.

歇后语　xiēhòuyǔ　a two-part allegorical saying, of which the first part, always stated, is descriptive, while the second part, sometimes unstated, carries the message, e.g. 泥菩萨过河—自身难保 like a clay idol fording a river—hardly able to save oneself (let alone anyone else)

歇肩　xiējiān　take the load off one's shoulder (*or* put down one's shoulder pole) for a rest

歇脚　xiējiǎo　rest the feet—stop on the way for a rest: 咱们到那边荫凉地歇歇脚吧。Let's stop for a rest in the shade over there.

歇凉　xiēliáng　*dial.*　enjoy the cool in some shade; relax in a cool place

歇气　xiēqì　have a short break: 歇口气儿 stop for a breather; take (*or* have) a breather / 他一连干了一天一夜没～。He worked the whole day and night without a break.

歇晌　xiēshǎng　take a midday nap or rest

歇手　xiēshǒu　stop doing sth.

歇斯底里　xiēsīdǐlǐ　① *med.*　hysteria ② unnaturally excited or emotional; hysterical: ～大发作 go into hysterics; become hysterical / 她～地大哭起来。She broke into hysterical sobs.

歇宿　xiēsù　put up (somewhere) for the night; make an overnight stop: 晚上在旅店～ put up at a hotel for the night

歇腿　xiētuǐ　same as 歇脚 xiējiǎo

歇息　xiēxi　① have a rest ② put up for the night; go to bed: 今晚就在我这儿～吧。Stay here for the night.

歇夏　xiēxià　same as 歇伏 xiēfú

歇闲　xiēxián　*dial.* stop to rest: 他一天到晚不～。He works from morning till night, without ever stopping to rest.

歇心　xiēxīn　in a relaxed mood; free from worries

歇业　xiēyè　close a business; go out of business

歇枝　xiēzhī　(of fruit trees) bear less or no fruit after a big crop the previous year

蝎(蠍)　xiē　scorpion

蝎虎　xiēhǔ　(also 蝎虎子 xiēhǔzi) gecko; house lizard

蝎子　xiēzi　scorpion

xié

叶　xié　be in harmony; be in accord ——see also yè

叶韵　xiéyùn　rhyme

协(協)　xié　① joint; common: ～办 do sth. jointly ② assist: 协理 xiélǐ

协定　xiédìng　① agreement; accord: 文化合作～ agreement on cultural cooperation ② reach an agreement on sth.; conclude a convention: 我们应该～一个共同的纲领。We should reach an agreement on a common programme.

协定边界　xiédìng biānjiè　conventional boundary

协定关税　xiédìng guānshuì　conventional tariff

协和　xiéhé　coordinate; harmonize

协和音　xiéhéyīn　consonance: 不～ dissonance

协会　xiéhuì　association; society: 中国人民对外友好～ the Chinese People's Association for Friendship with Foreign Countries

协理　xiélǐ　① assist in the management (of an enterprise, etc.) ② assistant manager (in a bank, business enterprise, etc.)

协理员　xiélǐyuán　common name for 政治协理员 zhèngzhì xiélǐyuán

协力　xiélì　unite efforts; join in a common effort: ～进攻 launch a joint assault

协商　xiéshāng　consult; talk things over: ～一致的原则 the principle of reaching unanimity through consultation; principle of consensus / 需要和有关部门～。It's necessary to consult with the departments concerned. / 有问题可以～解决。The problems can be solved through consultation.

协商会议　xiéshāng huìyì　consultative conference

协商委员会　xiéshāng wěiyuánhuì　consultative committee or commission

协调　xiétiáo　① coordinate; concert; harmonize; bring into line: 一定要使我们的行动～起来。We must coordinate our activities. / 国民经济各部门的发展必须互相～。Development of the different branches of the national economy should be well coordinated. ② in a concerted way; balanced; harmonious; in tune: 建立～的关系 establish harmonious relations (between parts) / ～ (work) in concert and harmony / 比例关系逐渐趋于～。The ratio is becoming more balanced. / 他的意见好像和大家的不太～。His opinions don't seem to be in tune with those of the others. / 体操运动员的动作～优美。The gymnast's movements are harmonious and graceful.

协调委员会　xiétiáo wěiyuánhuì　coordination committee

协同　xiétóng　work in coordination with; cooperate with: ～作战 fight in coordination / ～动作 coordinated action / 民兵～解放军守卫海岛。The militia cooperate with the PLA

men in guarding the island. / 此事请～办理。Your cooperation is requested in handling this matter.

协议　xiéyì　① agree on: 一致～的文件 a document unanimously agreed upon / 双方～提高收购价格。The two sides agreed to raise the purchasing price. / ～声明 agreed announcement / ～联合声明 agreed joint statement ② agreement: 达成～ reach an agreement / 口头～ verbal agreement / ～条款 terms of agreement

协约国　Xiéyuēguó　the *Entente* countries (during World War I)

协约国际法　xiéyuē guójìfǎ　conventional international law

协助　xiézhù　assist; help; give assistance; provide help: 副总理～总理工作。The Vice-Premiers assist the Premier in his work.

协奏曲　xiézòuqǔ　*mus.* concerto: 钢琴 (小提琴) ～ piano (violin) concerto

协作　xiézuò　cooperate; coordinate; combine (in efforts): 发扬共产主义的～精神 bring into play the communist spirit of cooperation / 实行几个行业间的大～ organize extensive cooperation (*or* coordination) between different trades / ～项目 joint-operated project / 双方～得很好。The two sides cooperated harmoniously. / 这是几个厂～的产物。This is a product of the combined efforts of several factories.

邪　xié　① evil; heretical; weird; irregular: 咱们按原则办事，决不搞～的歪的。We'll stick to principles and never engage in irregularities. ② *Chin. med.* unhealthy environmental influences that cause disease: 寒～ disease caused by catching cold ③ disaster (caused by supernatural beings): 中邪 zhòngxié

邪不胜正　xié bù shèng zhèng　(also 邪不敌正 xié bù dí zhèng) the evil will not triumph over the virtuous

邪财　xiécái　*dial.* ill-gotten gains

邪道　xiédào　evil ways; a depraved life; vice: 走～ lead a depraved life; abandon oneself to evil ways

邪恶　xié'è　evil; wicked; vicious: ～的念头 wicked thoughts

邪乎　xiéhu　*inf.* ① extraordinary; abnormal; terrible: 天旱得～。This drought is abnormal. / 疼得～。The pain is terrible. ② fantastic; incredible: 他说得～。His story sounds incredible.

邪路　xiélù　evil ways; vice: 走上～ take to evil ways / 把某人引向～ lead sb. astray

邪门儿　xiéménr　*dial.* strange; odd; abnormal: 这天气真～，这时候还下雪。What strange weather—snowing at this time of the year! / 真～，钥匙刚才还在这儿呢! That's strange! The key was here just a minute ago. ② crooked ways; underhand means; dishonest practices (*or* methods)

邪门歪道　xiémén-wāidào　crooked ways; underhand means; dishonest practices (*or* methods)

邪魔　xiémó　evil spirit; demon

邪魔外道　xiémó-wàidào　① *Buddhism* evil demons and heretics ② unorthodox ways; crooked ways and means

邪念　xiéniàn　an evil thought; a wicked idea: 他起了～。A wicked idea came into his head.

邪气　xiéqì　a perverse trend; an evil influence: 使正气上升，～下降 encourage healthy trends and check unhealthy ones

邪术　xiéshù　black magic; sorcery; witchcraft

邪说　xiéshuō　heresy; heretical ideas; fallacy

邪心　xiéxīn　same as 邪念 xiéniàn

邪行　xiéxíng　evil deed; wicked conduct

邪行　xiéxing　*dial.* strange; unusual: 你瞧这事儿有多～! Just look how strange the whole thing is! / 天气冷得～。The weather is unusually cold. / 他们俩好得～。Those two are unusually close.

胁(脅、脇)　xié　① the side of the human body from the armpit to the waist ② coerce; force: 裹胁 guǒxié / 威胁 wēixié

胁变 xiébiàn *phys.* strain: 局部～ local strain / 过度～ overstrain / ～硬化 strain hardening / ～张量 strain tensor

胁持 xiéchí same as 挟持 xiéchí

胁从 xiécóng be an accomplice under duress: ～者 reluctant (*or* unwilling) follower; accomplice under duress

胁肩谄笑 xiéjiān chǎnxiào cringe and smile obsequiously; bow and scrape

胁迫 xiépò coerce; force: 被～参与犯罪 be coerced into participating in a crime

胁强 xiéqiáng *phys.* stress: 外施～ applied stress / 张～ tensile stress

挟(挾) xié ① hold sth. under the arm: 挟泰山以超北海 xié Tàishān yǐ chāo běihǎi ② coerce; force sb. to submit to one's will: 要挟 yāoxié ③ harbour (resentment, etc.): 挟仇 xiéchóu

挟持 xiéchí ① (usu. of bad people) seize sb. on both sides by the arms ② hold sb. under duress

挟仇 xiéchóu harbour a grudge

挟恨 xiéhèn harbour intense hatred

挟泰山以超北海 xié Tàishān yǐ chāo běihǎi jumping over the northern sea with Mount Tai under one's arm—an impossibility

挟天子以令诸侯 xié tiānzǐ yǐ lìng zhūhóu have the emperor in one's power and order the nobles about in his name; control the emperor and command the nobles

挟嫌 xiéxián *formal* harbour resentment; bear a grudge: ～报复 bear resentment against sb. and retaliate

挟怨 xiéyuàn harbour a grudge

挟制 xiézhì take advantage of sb.'s weakness to enforce obedience; force sb. to do one's bidding

谐 xié ① in harmony; in accord: 和谐 héxié / 谐调 xiétiáo ② *formal* come to an agreement; settle: 事～之后，即可动身。We shall set out immediately once the matter is settled. ③ humorous: 诙谐 huīxié

谐和 xiéhé harmonious; concordant

谐趣 xiéqù ① wit and humour: ～横生 full of wit and humour ② harmonious interests or charms: ～园 the Garden of Harmonious Interests (a small exquisite garden in the Summer Palace 颐和园)

谐声 xiéshēng same as 形声 xíngshēng

谐戏 xiéxì *formal* crack a pleasant joke; exchange pleasantries

谐谑 xiéxuè banter: 语带～ speak somewhat jokingly

谐谑曲 xiéxuèqǔ *mus.* scherzo

谐音 xiéyīn ① euphony ② *mus.* partials ③ homophony

谐振 xiézhèn *phys.* resonance: 空腔～ cavity resonance

谐振腔 xiézhènqiāng *phys.* resonant cavity

偕 xié together with; in the company of

偕老 xiélǎo (used in blessing newly-weds) live together to a ripe old age

偕同 xiétóng in the company of; accompanied by; along with

偕行 xiéxíng ① travel (*or* go) together: 携手～ go together hand in hand ② coexist

斜 xié oblique; slanting; inclined; tilted: 这根线～了。The line is slanting. / 柱子有点～。The pillar is a little tilted. / ～躺在沙发上 recline on a sofa / 把桌子～过来 turn the table sideways / ～着眼看人 cast sidelong glances at sb.; look sideways at sb.

斜边 xiébiān ① *math.* hypotenuse ② *mech.* bevel edge

斜长石 xiéchángshí plagioclase (a mineral)

斜度 xiédù degree of inclination; gradient

斜度标 xiédùbiāo gradient sign

斜对面 xiéduìmiàn (also 斜对过 xiéduìguò) opposite slightly to the right or left: 车站在学校的～。The station is almost opposite the school.

斜风细雨 xiéfēng-xìyǔ gentle wind and light rain

斜高 xiégāo *math.* slant height

斜晖 xiéhuī *formal* the slanting rays of the setting sun; the last evening rays

斜角 xiéjiǎo ① *math.* oblique angle ② *mech.* bevel angle

斜角规 xiéjiǎoguī *mech.* bevel square

斜井 xiéjǐng ① *min.* inclined shaft; slope ② *petroleum* inclined well; slant hole

斜楞 xiéleng *inf.* slanting: ～着眼儿 look askance; glance sideways

斜楞眼 xiélengyǎn *inf.* squint; walleye

斜路 xiélù wrong path: 走到～上去 go astray / 正路不走走～ turn from the right road and take the wrong one —give up an honest life for a dishonest one

斜率 xiélù *math.* slope

斜面 xiémiàn ① *math.* inclined plane ② *mech.* oblique plane; bevel (face)

斜睨 xiénì cast a sidelong glance at: 她～了我一眼。She cast a sidelong glance at me.

斜坡 xiépō slope

斜射 xiéshè ① cast oblique rays (*or* beams) on: ～的光线 oblique light (*or* beams) / ～的阳光穿过树丛, 洒落在大道上。The rays of the setting sun slanted through the trees onto the road. ② *mil.* oblique fire

斜视 xiéshì ① *med.* strabismus ② look sideways; cast a sidelong glance: 目不斜视 mù bù xiéshì

斜视图 xiéshìtú *mech.* oblique drawing

斜体字 xiétǐzì *print.* italics

斜纹 xiéwén *text.* twill (weave)

斜纹布 xiéwénbù *text.* twill; drill

斜线 xiéxiàn *math.* oblique line

斜线号 xiéxiànhào slant (/)

斜眼 xiéyǎn ① *med.* strabismus ② walleye or cross-eye; squint ③ a walleyed or cross-eyed person

斜阳 xiéyáng the setting sun

斜照 xiézhào ① cast oblique rays (*or* beams) on ② the setting sun

斜轴线 xiézhóuxiàn *math.* oblique axis

颉 xié *formal* (of birds) fly upwards

颉颃 xiéháng *formal* ① (of birds) fly up and down ② be equally matched; rival each other

携(攜、擕) xié ① carry; take along: ～眷 bring one's wife and children along / ～款潜逃 abscond with funds / ～械投诚 come over from the enemy's side bringing weapons ② take (*or* hold) sb. by the hand: 携手 xiéshǒu

携带 xiédài carry; take along: ～方便 be easy to carry about / 随身～的物品 things carried on one's person / 旅客每人可～行李二十公斤。Each passenger can take up to twenty kilograms of luggage.

携贰 xié'èr *formal* be halfhearted; be disloyal

携手 xiéshǒu join hands: ～并进 go forward hand in hand / 让我们携起手来, 共同前进。Let us join hands and advance together.

鞋 xié shoes

鞋拔子 xiébázi shoehorn

鞋帮 xiébāng upper (of a shoe)

鞋带 xiédài shoelace; shoestring

鞋底 xiédǐ sole (of a shoe)

鞋垫 xiédiàn shoe-pad; insole

鞋粉 xiéfěn shoe powder

鞋跟 xiégēn heel (of a shoe)

鞋匠 xiéjiàng shoemaker; cobbler

鞋扣 xiékòu　shoe buckle
鞋里 xiélǐ　shoe lining
鞋面 xiémiàn　instep; vamp
鞋刷 xiéshuā　shoe brush
鞋楦 xiéxuàn　a last for shaping a shoe; shoe tree
鞋样 xiéyàng　shoe pattern; outline of a shoe's upper and sole
鞋油 xiéyóu　shoe polish (or cream)

擷 xié　formal pick; pluck: 采擷 cǎixié

xiě

写(寫) xiě　① write: ～封信 write a letter / ～得一手好字 have good handwriting; write a good hand / 这支笔不好～。This pen doesn't write well. / ～副对联 write a couplet / 我喜欢～钢笔字，不喜欢～毛笔字。I like to write with a pen and not with a writing-brush. ② compose; write (as an author, reporter, etc.): ～小说 write a novel / ～诗 compose a poem / ～日记 make an entry in one's diary; keep a diary / ～科学论文 write a scientific paper; write a thesis on a scientific subject / 文章～成了吗? Have you finished writing the article? ③ describe; depict: ～景 describe the scenery / ～人物的心理活动 depict the characters' mental activities / 这个人物叫他～活了。His portrayal of the character is vivid and true to life. ④ paint; draw: 写生 xiěshēng ——see also xiè
写本 xiěběn　a handwritten copy
写法 xiěfǎ　① style of writing; literary style: 文体不同，～也不同。Different types of writing call for different styles of writing. ② style of handwriting; penmanship
写稿 xiěgǎo　write for (or contribute to) a magazine, etc.: 你给我们的晚报写篇稿好吗? Will you write an article for our evening paper? / 他经常为儿童刊物～。He is a regular contributor to children's magazines.
写生 xiěshēng　arts sketch from life; do a still life painting; paint or sketch from nature: 人物～ portrait from life
写生画 xiěshēnghuà　sketch
写实 xiěshí　write or paint realistically
写实主义 xiěshízhǔyì　old name for 现实主义 xiànshízhǔyì
写意 xiěyì　arts freehand brushwork in traditional Chinese painting (characterized by vivid expression and bold outline) ——see also xièyì
写照 xiězhào　① portray (a person or character): 传神～ give a vivid and lifelike portrayal ② portrayal; picture: 真实的～ a portrayal true to life / 百花盛开春满园是今日文坛的～。The world of letters can be portrayed today as a garden with a hundred flowers in bloom.
写真 xiězhēn　① portray a person; draw a portrait ② portrait ③ a true-to-life depiction; a faithful representation
写字间 xiězìjiān　dial. office
写字楼 xiězìlóu　office building
写字台 xiězìtái　writing desk; desk; bureau
写作 xiězuò　writing: 从事～ take up writing as one's career / ～技巧 writing technique
写作班子 xiězuò bānzi　writing group

血 xiě　inf. blood: 一滴～ a drop of blood / 一摊～ a pool of blood / ～的教训 a lesson paid for (or written) in blood / 流了一点～，不要紧。There was just a little bleeding. Nothing serious. ——see also xuè
血肠 xiěcháng　blood sausage
血道子 xiědàozi　welt; wale
血糊糊 xiěhūhū　bloodstained; bloody: ～的伤口 a bloody wound / 地上～的一片。There was a pool of blood on

the ground.
血块 xiěkuài　blood clot; clot
血淋淋 xiělínlín　① dripping with blood; bloody; gory ② grim; bitter; cruel: ～的现实 a grim reality / ～的教训 a bitter lesson
血丝 xiěsī　a trace of blood: 他咯出的痰带有～。There are detectable traces of blood in his sputum. / 由于睡眠不足，他两眼布满～。His eyes are bloodshot because of lack of sleep.
血晕 xiěyùn　contusion; bruise ——see also xuèyùn

xiè

写(寫) xiè　see below ——see also xiě
写意 xièyì　dial. comfortable; enjoyable ——see also xiěyì

泻(瀉) xiè　① flow swiftly; rush down; pour out: 一泻千里 yī xiè qiānlǐ ② have loose bowels; have diarrhoea
泻肚 xièdù　have loose bowels; have diarrhoea
泻湖 xièhú　geog. lagoon
泻盐 xièyán　Epsom salts; salts
泻药 xièyào　laxative; cathartic; purgative

泄(洩) xiè　① let out (a fluid or gas); discharge; release: 排泄 páixiè / 泄洪 xièhóng ② let out (a secret); leak (news, secrets, etc.): 泄底 xièdǐ ③ give vent to; vent: 泄愤 xièfèn
泄底 xièdǐ　reveal or expose what is at the bottom of sth.
泄愤 xièfèn　(also 泄恨 xièhèn) give vent to one's pent-up anger: 泄私愤，图报复 try to revenge a personal grudge
泄洪 xièhóng　water conservancy release floodwater: 开闸～ open a sluice to release floodwater
泄洪道 xièhóngdào　flood-relief channel; floodway
泄洪隧道 xièhóng suìdào　flood-discharge tunnel
泄劲 xièjìn　lose heart; feel discouraged; be disheartened; slacken one's efforts: 他近来有点～。He has been a bit disheartened lately. / 继续努力，不要～! Keep at it, don't slacken your efforts!
泄漏 xièlòu　① (of a fluid or gas) leak; escape ② (of a secret, etc.) leak; let out; divulge; give away: ～秘密 let out (or divulge, give away) a secret / 消息已～出去了。The news has leaked out.
泄露 xièlù　let out; reveal: 敌人无意中～了行动计划。The enemy unwittingly revealed their plan of action. / ～国家机密 divulge a state secret
泄密 xièmì　divulge a secret; betray confidential matters: ～事件 (a case of) leakage of a state or Party secret
泄气 xièqì　① lose heart; feel discouraged; be disheartened: 困难面前不～ keep one's end up in the face of difficulties / 我不该说那些～话。I shouldn't have made those discouraging (or pessimistic) remarks. ② disappointing; frustrating; pathetic: 这么矮他都跳不过去，真～! He can't even jump that high. How pathetic! / 我队一比五输了，真～! Our team was beaten one to five. What a disappointment!
泄水 xièshuǐ　water conservancy sluicing: ～工程 outlet work
泄水道 xièshuǐdào　sluiceway
泄水孔 xièshuǐkǒng　outlet
泄水闸 xièshuǐzhá　sluice gate; sluice
泄泻 xièxiè　Chin. med. have loose bowels; have diarrhoea
泄殖腔 xièzhíqiāng　zool. cloacal chamber; cloaca

绁(紲、緤) xiè　formal ① ropes; reins: 缧

继 léixiè ② tie; bind; fasten

卸 xiè ① unload; discharge; lay down: ～担子 lay down a burden / ～牲口 unhitch a draught animal ② remove; strip: ～零件 remove parts from a machine; strip a machine / 把门～下来 lift a door off its hinges ③ get rid of; shirk: 卸责 xièzé

卸车 xièchē unload (goods, etc.) from a vehicle; unload a truck, car, etc.

卸货 xièhuò unload (or discharge) a cargo; unload: 从船上～ unload a ship; land goods from a ship / 这些船明天～。 The ships will unload (the cargoes) tomorrow.

卸货港 xièhuògǎng transportation port of discharge; unloading port

卸肩 xièjiān lay down one's burden; shirk one's responsibility

卸磨杀驴 xiè mò shā lǘ kill the donkey the moment it leaves the millstone—get rid of sb. as soon as he has done his job

卸任 xièrèn be relieved of one's office

卸责 xièzé shirk responsibility and shift the blame onto others

卸妆 xièzhuāng (of a female) remove ornaments and formal dress

卸装 xièzhuāng (of an actor or actress) remove stage makeup and costume

屑 xiè ① bits; scraps; crumbs: 纸～ scraps of paper / 煤～ (coal) slack / 金属～ metal filings / 面包～ crumbs (of bread) ② trifling: 琐屑 suǒxiè ③ (usu. used in the negative) consider sth. to be worth doing: 不屑 bùxiè

屑屑 xièxiè trifling; trivial: ～小事 a trifling matter

屑意 xièyì mind; take offence: 毫不～ not mind a bit

械 xiè ① tool; instrument: 机械 jīxiè ② weapon: 持～抢劫 (commit) armed robbery ③ formal fetters, shackles, etc.

械斗 xièdòu a fight with weapons between groups of people

谢 xiè ① thank: ～了又～ thank again and again / 多～。 Thanks a lot. / 不用～。 Don't mention it. ② formal make an apology; excuse oneself: ～过 apologize for having done sth. wrong / ～病 excuse oneself on grounds of illness ③ decline: 谢绝 xièjué ④ (of flowers, leaves) wither: 凋谢 diāoxiè ⑤ (Xiè) a surname

谢忱 xièchén gratitude; thankfulness: 承蒙协助, 谨致～。 Allow us to express our thanks for your kindly help.

谢词 xiècí a thank-you speech

谢顶 xièdǐng get a bit thin on top; be balding

谢恩 xiè'ēn (usually of a minister to an emperor) express gratitude for a favour

谢绝 xièjué politely refuse; decline: ～参观。 Not open to visitors.

谢客 xièkè ① decline to receive visitors; not be seeing any visitors: 闭门～ not at home to visitors ② thank a guest for his visit

谢礼 xièlǐ a gift in token of gratitude; a return present

谢媒 xièméi (of newly-weds) express thanks to the matchmaker

谢幕 xièmù answer (or respond to) a curtain call

谢却 xièquè politely refuse; decline

谢世 xièshì formal pass away; die

谢天谢地 xiètiān-xièdì thank goodness; thank heaven: ～, 你总算回来了! Thank goodness, you're back at last!

谢帖 xiètiě a note of thanks; a thank-you note

谢孝 xièxiào after the period of mourning for a parent, visit and thank those friends and relatives who have offered condolences

谢谢 xièxie thank: ～! Thanks! or Thank you! / ～你的好意。 Thank you for your kindness. / 请替我～他。 Please give my thanks to him.

谢仪 xièyí same as 谢礼 xièlǐ

谢意 xièyì gratitude; thankfulness: 预致～ thank you in anticipation / 谨致薄礼, 聊表～。 Please accept this gift and my gratitude.

谢罪 xièzuì apologize for an offence; offer one's apology for a fault

亵(褻) xiè ① treat with irreverence; be disrespectful: 亵渎 xièdú ② obscene; indecent: ～语 obscene utterances; obscenities

亵渎 xièdú blaspheme; profane; pollute: ～神明 a blasphemy against gods

亵慢 xièmàn formal show disrespect

亵玩 xièwán dally with (women)

亵衣 xièyī formal underwear; underclothes

解¹ xiè ① inf. understand; see: ～不开这个道理 can't see the point

解² xiè old acrobatics: 卖～的 a street performer of acrobatics

解³ Xiè a surname
——see also jiě; jiè

解数 xièshù ① postures in martial arts ② skill; art; competence: 使出浑身解数 shǐchū húnshēn xièshù

榭 xiè a pavilion or house on a terrace: 水榭 shuǐxiè

懈 xiè slack; lax: 松懈 sōngxiè

懈怠 xièdài slack; sluggish: 学习上不可～。 Don't slack off in your studies.

懈劲 xièjìn relax one's exertions; lose one's drive; slack off

懈气 xièqì relax one's exertions; lose one's drive; slack off

澥 xiè ① (of paste, glue, etc.) become thin; thin down: 剩粥～了。 The leftover porridge has lost its glueyness. ② dial. add water to make a paste, etc. thinner: 糨糊太稠, 加点热水～一～。 The paste is too thick. Add some hot water to make it thinner.

廨 xiè arch. government office

邂 xiè see below

邂逅 xièhòu formal meet (a relative, friend, etc.) unexpectedly; run into sb.; meet by chance

邂逅相遇 xièhòu xiāngyù meet unexpectedly; meet by chance

獬 xiè see below

獬豸 xièzhì a fabulous animal reputed to be able to distinguish between good and evil

薤 xiè ① Chinese onion (Allium chinense) ② the bulb of the plant

燮(爕) xiè formal mediate; harmonize: ～理 harmonize; adjust; coordinate

蟹(蠏) xiè crab

蟹粉 xièfěn dial. crab meat

蟹黄 xièhuáng the reddish-yellow crab meat (made up of the ovary and digestive glands)

蟹獴 xièméng zool. crab-eating mongoose

蟹钳　xièqián　the crab's claws
蟹青　xièqīng　greenish-grey (colour)

漤　xiè　see 沆漤 hàngxiè

蹀　xiè　see 蹀蹀 diéxiè

xīn

心　xīn　① the heart ② heart; mind; feeling; intention: 羞耻之～ sense of shame / 伤人的～ wound (or hurt) sb.'s feelings / 你的～是好的, 但是事情办得不好。 You meant well but you didn't handle the job well. / 他人在这儿，～不在。 He himself is here, but his thoughts are elsewhere. ③ centre; core: 白菜～ the heart of a Chinese cabbage / 江～ the middle of a river; halfway across the river ④ the fifth of the twenty-eight constellations (二十八宿) into which the celestial sphere was divided in ancient Chinese astronomy (consisting of three stars in Scorpio)

心爱　xīn'ài　loved; treasured; dear to one's heart: ～的人 one's beloved; loved one / ～的东西 treasured (or prized) possession

心安理得　xīn'ān-lǐdé　feel at ease and justified; have an easy conscience; with mind at rest and conscience clear: 你能～地把全部责任都推到他一人身上吗? Can you shift the blame onto him alone and yet have a clear conscience?

心瓣膜　xīnbànmó　physiol. heart valve
心包　xīnbāo　physiol. pericardium
心包炎　xīnbāoyán　pericarditis
心病　xīnbìng　① worry; anxiety: 这事老悬着, 一直是他的～。 Not having this matter settled has always worried him. ② sore point; secret trouble

心病难医　xīnbìng nán yī　mental worries cannot be cured by medicine

心搏　xīnbó　physiol. heartbeat

心不在焉　xīn bù zài yān　absent-minded; inattentive; preoccupied (with sth. else): ～地听着 listen absent-mindedly / 她拿起一本小说，～地看着。 She took up a novel to read, but could not concentrate.

心材　xīncái　heartwood
心裁　xīncái　idea; conception; mental plan: 独出心裁 dú chū xīncái

心肠　xīncháng　① heart; intention: ～软 have a soft heart; be softhearted / 好～ kindhearted / 他真是个热～! He's a really warmhearted person! ② dial. state of mind; mood: 没～去看电影 be in no mood to see a movie

心潮　xīncháo　a tidal surge of emotion; surging thoughts and emotions: 她～翻滚, 无法入睡。 Her mind being in a tumult, she could not go to sleep.

心潮澎湃　xīncháo péngpài　feel an upsurge of emotion

心驰神往　xīnchí-shénwǎng　one's thoughts fly to (a place or person); have a deep longing for

心传　xīnchuán　① Buddhism mind-to-mind instruction from master to disciple (without the aid of scriptures) ② a doctrine or theory passed on from generation to generation

心慈面软　xīncí-miànruǎn　kindhearted and obliging: 他是个～的人, 肯定会答应你的要求。 He is a kindhearted and obliging person and will certainly grant your request.

心慈手软　xīncí-shǒuruǎn　softhearted: 对怙恶不悛的犯罪分子不能～。 We should not be softhearted towards hardened criminals.

心粗　xīncū　be careless or thoughtless by nature
心粗气浮　xīncū-qìfú　hotheaded; thoughtless and impetuous

心胆俱裂　xīn-dǎn jù liè　be frightened out of one's wits; be terror-stricken: 吓得敌人～ strike terror into the enemy's hearts

心得　xīndé　what one has learned from work, study, etc.: 谈谈学习～ talk about what one has gained from study

心底　xīndǐ　the bottom of one's heart: 从～里 from the bottom of one's heart; from one's heart of hearts; from one's heart / 我从～里佩服他。 I worship (or admire) him from the bottom of my heart. / 这是她出自～的话。 The words were spoken from her heart.

心地　xīndì　a person's mind, character, moral nature, etc.: ～坦白 candid; open / ～单纯 simpleminded / ～善良 good-natured; kindhearted / ～光明 always open and aboveboard

心电描记器　xīndiàn miáojìqì　med. electrocardiograph
心电图　xīndiàntú　med. electrocardiogram
心动　xīndòng　① heartbeat ② same as 动心 dòngxīn
心动过速　xīndòng guòsù　med. tachycardia: 阵发性～ paroxysmal tachycardia
心动徐缓　xīndòng xúhuǎn　med. bradycardia
心动周期　xīndòng zhōuqī　physiol. cardiac cycle
心毒　xīndú　wicked; vicious; malignant: ～如蛇蝎 as vicious as a viper
心耳　xīn'ěr　physiol. auricle (of the heart); auricular appendage

心烦　xīnfán　be vexed; be perturbed: 这事真叫人～。 This is really a bother. or This is really upsetting.

心烦意乱　xīnfán-yìluàn　be terribly upset; be perturbed: ～, 不知所从。 His mind was in such a turmoil that he did not know which way to turn. / 就是那些家事也够叫人～。 The problems of housekeeping alone would be enough to drive one to distraction.

心房　xīnfáng　physiol. atrium (of the heart)
心房纤颤　xīnfáng xiānchàn　med. atrial fibrillation

心扉　xīnfēi　the door of one's heart: 我愿意敞开自己的～, 向你倾诉一切。 I wish to open my heart and tell you everything.

心浮　xīnfú　flighty and impatient; unstable
心浮气躁　xīnfú-qìzào　flighty and impetuous
心服　xīnfú　be genuinely convinced; acknowledge (one's defeat, mistake, etc.) sincerely

心服口服　xīnfú-kǒufú　be sincerely convinced: 我觉得他说的有理, 听得～。 All this made such good sense that I was won round completely. / 在这一帮人中, 大伙就对老王～。 In the whole group the most respected man was Lao Wang.

心腹　xīnfù　① trusted subordinate; reliable agent ② confidential: 说～话 tell sb. sth. in strict confidence; confide in sb.; exchange confidences / ～事 a secret in the depth of one's heart

心腹之患　xīnfù zhī huàn　disease in one's vital organs — danger from within; serious hidden trouble or danger

心甘　xīngān　same as 甘心 gānxīn

心甘情愿　xīngān-qíngyuàn　be most willing to; be perfectly happy to: 为了革命, 就是牺牲生命也～。 If need be, I will willingly give my life for the revolution. / ～当人民的勤务员 be a willing servant of the people

心肝　xīngān　① conscience: 没～ heartless ② (a term of endearment mostly used with one's small children) darling; dear; sweetheart; honey

心高气傲　xīngāo-qì'ào　(also 心高气盛 xīngāo-qìshèng) ambitious and proud

心广体胖　xīnguǎng-tǐpán　carefree and contented; fit and happy

心寒　xīnhán　dial. be bitterly disappointed: 令人～ chill the heart; be bitterly disappointing

心狠　xīnhěn　cruel; merciless
心狠手辣　xīnhěn-shǒulà　cruel and ruthless; wicked and merciless

心花怒放 xīnhuā nùfàng burst with joy; be wild with joy; be elated

心怀[1] xīnhuái ① intention; purpose ② state of mind; mood

心怀[2] xīnhuái harbour; entertain; cherish: ～不满 feel discontented; nurse a grievance

心怀鬼胎 xīnhuái guǐtāi have evil intentions; have sinister motives

心怀叵测 xīnhuái pǒcè harbour unfathomable evil designs; have sinister intentions: 这个人～, 对他的一举一动, 都要严加提防。That man has sinister designs. You must guard against his every move.

心慌 xīnhuāng ① be flustered; be nervous; get alarmed: 我考试的时候～。I was nervous while I was taking the exam. ② *dial.* (of the heart) palpitate

心慌意乱 xīnhuāng-yìluàn be alarmed and confused; be nervous and flustered

心灰意懒 xīnhuī-yìlǎn be disheartened; be downhearted; be dispirited: 他连输三场, ～。Three defeats in a row dispirited him.

心活 xīnhuó be indecisive and changeable: 耳软～ be easily swayed by others' words

心火 xīnhuǒ ① *Chin. med.* internal heat, symptoms of which include mental uneasiness, thirst, rapid pulse, etc. ② hidden anger or annoyance; pent-up fury or worries

心机 xīnjī thinking; scheming: 她年龄不大, 但很有～。Young as she is, she has a mind of her own.

心肌 xīnjī *physiol.* cardiac muscle; myocardium

心肌梗塞 xīnjī gěngsè (also 心肌梗死 xīnjī gěngsǐ) *med.* myocardial infarction

心肌炎 xīnjīyán myocarditis

心急 xīnjí impatient; short-tempered

心急火燎 xīnjí-huǒliǎo burning with impatience; in a nervous state

心急如焚 xīnjí rú fén (also 心急如火 xīnjí rú huǒ) burning with impatience: 他的全身滚热, ～。He was boiling hot all over, his mind tense with a great sense of urgency.

心计 xīnjì calculation; scheming; planning: 工于～ adept at scheming; very calculating / 这个年轻人做事很有～。This young chap does things intelligently.

心迹 xīnjì the true state of one's mind; true motives or feelings: 表明～ lay bare one's true feelings

心悸 xīnjì ① *med.* palpitation ② *formal* be scared: 令人～ terrifying; frightening

心尖 xīnjiān ① *physiol.* the apex of the heart; apex cordis ② the heart considered as the centre of the emotions ③ *dial.* darling; dear

心坚石穿 xīn jiān shí chuān the strength of will can pierce a stone—determination can overcome all difficulties (from the legend of a Taoist who persisted at drilling a hole in a huge millstone with wooden drills and succeeded after 47 years of hard work)

心焦 xīnjiāo anxious; worried: 真叫人～! This is really worrying! / 我们等得好～! How anxiously we waited!

心绞痛 xīnjiǎotòng *med.* angina pectoris

心劲 xīnjìn ① thought; idea: 我们大伙儿是一个～, 要尽快把事情办成。We have only one thought: to get the job done as quickly as possible. ② brains

心旌 xīnjīng *formal* a fluttering heart—nervous excitement; flurry

心惊胆战 xīnjīng-dǎnzhàn tremble with terror; shake with fright; quake with fear

心惊肉跳 xīnjīng-ròutiào be jumpy; have the jitters

心净 xīnjìng one's mind is pure: ～孤明独照, 心存万境皆清。《西游记》When the mind is pure, it shines forth as a solitary lamp, and when the mind is secure, the entire phenomenal world becomes clarified.

心境 xīnjìng state (*or* frame) of mind; mental state; mood: ～不好 be in a bad mood / ～非常愉快 be in a very happy mood

心静 xīnjìng calm: ～自然凉。So long as one keeps calm, one doesn't feel the heat too much.

心坎 xīnkǎn ① the pit of the stomach: 他把手放在～上。He laid his hand on his heart. ② the bottom of one's heart: 我从～里感谢您。I thank you from the bottom of my heart. / 字字句句都说到我～上。Each word struck a chord in my heart. / 我把您的话牢记在～上。Your words are engraved on my heart (*or* mind).

心口 xīnkǒu the pit of the stomach

心口如一 xīn-kǒu rú yī say what one thinks; speak from the heart; be frank and forthright

心宽体胖 xīnkuān-tǐpán see 心广体胖 xīnguǎng-tǐpán

心旷神怡 xīnkuàng-shényí relaxed and joyful; carefree and happy: 登斯楼也, 则有～, 宠辱皆忘, 把酒临风, 其喜洋洋者矣。(范仲淹) Men coming up to this pavilion may feel complete freedom of heart and ease of spirit, forgetting every worldly gain or setback to hold their wine-cups in the breeze in absolute elation, delighted with life.

心劳计绌 xīnláo-jìchù rack one's brains in vain; be at one's wit's end

心劳日拙 xīn láo rì zhuō fare worse and worse for all one's scheming

心理 xīnlǐ mentality; psychology: 这位保育员很懂得孩子们的～。That kindergarten teacher understands the children's psychology very well. / 不要养成依赖别人的～。Don't get into the habit of depending on others. / 这是一般人的～。This is how ordinary people feel about it. / 他老说有心脏病, 其实是～作用。He's always complaining of heart trouble; but it's only his imagination. / ～因素 psychological factor

心理病态 xīnlǐ bìngtài morbid state of mind

心理测验学 xīnlǐcèyànxué psychometry

心理分析 xīnlǐfēnxi psychoanalysis

心理疗法 xīnlǐliáofǎ psychotherapy

心理学 xīnlǐxué psychology: ～家 psychologist

心理战 xīnlǐzhàn psychological warfare

心理治疗 xīnlǐzhìliáo psychotherapy

心力 xīn-lì mental and physical efforts: 费尽～ make strenuous efforts

心力交瘁 xīn-lì jiāo cuì be mentally and physically exhausted

心力衰竭 xīnlìshuāijié *med.* heart failure

心里 xīnli in the heart; at heart; in (the) mind: ～发闷 feel constriction in the area of the heart / ～不痛快 feel bad about sth. / 记在～ keep (*or* bear) in mind / ～有事 have sth. on one's mind / ～装着亿万人民 have at heart the wellbeing of hundreds of millions / 他将永远活在我们～。He will live forever in our hearts.

心里话 xīnlihuà one's innermost thoughts and feelings: 说出自己的～ give voice to one's innermost feelings / 我看他没有说～。I don't think he has come out with what's on his mind. / 说～, 我真不想去。To be honest, I just don't want to go.

心里美 xīnliměi a kind of sweet turnip with green peel and purple-red flesh

心连心 xīn lián xīn heart linked to heart: 我国各族人民～。The hearts of the people of all our nationalities are linked to each other. / 解放军和我们～。The PLA men's hearts and ours beat as one.

心灵[1] xīnlíng clever; intelligent; quick-witted: ～手巧 clever and deft

心灵[2] xīnlíng heart; soul; spirit: ～深处 deep in one's heart / 在她幼小的～里 in her childish heart

心领 xīnlǐng *pol.* (expressing a polite refusal): 雅意～。I appreciate your kindness but must decline the offer.

心领神会 xīnlǐng-shénhuì understand tacitly; readily take a hint: 这个奴才对主子的意图～。The lackey immediately understood what his master wanted.

心路 xīnlù ① wit; intelligence ② motive; intention ③ tolerance

心律 xīnlǜ *med.* rhythm of the heartbeat

心律不齐 xīnlǜ bù qí *med.* arrhythmia

心率 xīnlǜ heart rate

心乱如麻 xīn luàn rú má have one's mind all in a tangle; be utterly confused and disconcerted; be terribly upset

心满意足 xīnmǎn-yìzú be perfectly content (*or* satisfied)

心明眼亮 xīnmíng-yǎnliàng see and think clearly; be sharp-eyed and clear-headed

心目 xīnmù ① mood; frame of mind: 以娱～ to amuse oneself ② memory: 动人情景犹在～。The moving scene remains (*or* is still) fresh in my memory. ③ mind; mental view: 在某些人的～中 in some people's eyes / 在我的～中, 他是个好同志。In my view (*or* To my mind), he is a good comrade.

心皮 xīnpí *bot.* carpel

心平气和 xīnpíng-qìhé even-tempered and good-humoured; calm: ～地交换意见 exchange views calmly / 有话～地讲。Let's try to talk things over without getting excited.

心魄 xīnpò soul: 动人～ soul-stirring

心气 xīnqì ① motive; intention ② aspiration: ～高 have high aspirations ③ mood; frame of mind: ～不顺 in a bad mood ④ tolerance: ～窄 narrow-minded

心窍 xīnqiào capacity for clear thinking: 权迷～ be obsessed by a lust for power / 他的话打开了我的～, 知道该怎么办了。What he said cleared up my thinking and then I knew what to do next.

心切 xīnqiè eager; impatient; anxious: 求胜～ be anxious to gain victory / 求官～ seek office eagerly / 回国～ be anxious to return to one's country

心情 xīnqíng frame (*or* state) of mind; mood: ～愉快 be in a cheerful frame (*or* state) of mind; be in a good (*or* happy) mood; have a light heart / ～沉重 with a heavy heart / ～舒畅 have ease of mind / ～激动 be excited; be thrilled / ～不一样, 感受也不同。People in different frames of mind feel differently about things.

心曲 xīnqǔ ① innermost being; mind: 乱我～ disturb my peace of mind ② sth. weighing on one's mind: 倾诉～ pour out one's secret concern (*or* pent-up feelings); lay one's heart bare

心如刀割 xīn rú dāo gē feel as if a knife were piercing one's heart: 她听到这不幸的消息～。The sad news stabbed her to the heart.

心如死灰 xīn rú sǐhuī one's heart is like dead ashes—hopelessly apathetic

心如铁石 xīn rú tiěshí have a heart of iron; be stony-hearted; be hard-hearted

心软 xīnruǎn be softhearted; be tenderhearted

心上 xīnshang in the heart: 这等小事你千万别搁在～。Please don't take such trifles to heart.

心上人 xīnshangrén person of one's heart; one's beloved

心神 xīnshén mind; state of mind: ～不安 feel uneasy (*or* restless); be disturbed

心神不定 xīnshén bù dìng have no peace of mind; feel restless; be distracted

心声 xīnshēng heartfelt wishes; aspirations; thinking: 表达人民的～ voice the aspirations of the people

心事 xīnshì sth. weighing on one's mind; a load on one's mind; worry: 了结一桩～ take a load off one's mind / 她好像有什么～似的。She seems to have something on her mind.

心事重重 xīnshì chóngchóng be laden with anxiety; be weighed down with care: 他好像～。He gave the impression of a man whose heart was heavy.

心室 xīnshì *physiol.* ventricle

心室纤颤 xīnshì xiānchàn *med.* ventricular fibrillation

心手相应 xīn-shǒu xiāngyìng the hand responding perfectly to the mind—amazingly skilful

心输出量 xīnshūchūliàng *physiol.* cardiac output

心术 xīnshù ① intention; design: ～不正 harbour evil intentions (*or* designs) ② calculation; scheming; planning: 他是个有～的人。He is a calculating person.

心数 xīnshù calculation; scheming; planning

心顺 xīnshùn be in a good mood: 趁他～的时候去跟他说。Go and tell him while he is in a good mood.

心死 xīnsǐ one's will dies within one—see the futility of one's attempt

心思 xīnsi ① thought; idea: 坏～ a wicked idea / 他在想～。He is pondering over something. / 我猜不透他的～。I can't read his mind. *or* I can't figure out what's on his mind. ② thinking: 用～ do a lot of thinking; think hard / 白费～ bother one's head for nothing ③ state of mind; mood: 没有～去看戏 not be in the mood to see a play

心酸 xīnsuān be grieved; feel sad: 她的遭遇听了令人～。Hers is a heart-rending story.

心算 xīnsuàn mental arithmetic; doing sums in one's head

心髓 xīnsuǐ the depths of one's heart

心碎 xīnsuì be heartbroken: 听到她的小妹妹的死讯, 她的心都碎了。She was heartbroken at the news of her little sister's death.

心疼 xīnténg ① love dearly: 这样惯孩子不是～他。Pampering a child like this is not loving him. ② feel sorry; be distressed: 这么浪费, 叫人看了～。It makes one's heart ache to see such waste.

心田 xīntián ① heart ② intention

心跳 xīntiào palpitation: 我有些～。My heart is beating a bit too fast. / 他吓得心直跳。His heart jumped with fright.

心痛 xīntòng same as 痛心 tòngxīn

心头 xīntóu mind; heart: 记在～ bear (*or* keep) in mind / ～恨 rankling hatred / ～火起 burn with anger / 抑制不住～的喜悦 be unable to conceal one's delight

心头肉 xīntóuròu a dearly loved person or a treasured possession: 孩子是她的～。Her children are closest to her heart.

心土 xīntǔ *agric.* subsoil

心往一处想, 劲往一处使 xīn wǎng yīchù xiǎng, jìn wǎng yīchù shǐ think with one mind and work with one heart

心窝儿 xīnwōr *inf.* ① the pit of the heart or stomach: 他一拳打在我～里, 痛得我半天直不起腰来。I doubled up with pain when he struck me in the pit of my stomach. ② deep down in one's heart: 他第一次把掏～的话都和她说了。For the first time he told her all his innermost thoughts and feelings.

心无二用 xīn wú èr yòng one cannot keep one's mind on two things at the same time; one should concentrate on one thing at a time

心细 xīnxì careful; scrupulous: 胆大～ bold but cautious

心弦 xīnxián heartstrings: 动人心弦 dòng rén xīnxián

心想 xīnxiǎng think to oneself; think: 我～他早晚总会来的。I thought he would turn up sooner or later.

心向往之 xīn xiàngwǎng zhī yearning for sb. or sth.

心心念念 xīnxīnniànniàn longingly; yearningly: 他～地想当个飞行员。He is set on becoming a pilot.

心心相印 xīn-xīn xiāng yìn have mutual affinity; be kindred spirits

心性 xīnxìng disposition; temperament

心胸 xīnxiōng ① breadth of mind: ～开阔 broad-minded; unprejudiced / ～狭窄 narrow-minded; intolerant ② aspiration; ambition: 他有～, 有气魄。He is a man of vision with high ambitions.

心秀 xīnxiù be intelligent without looking so

心虚 xīnxū ① afraid of being found out; with a guilty conscience ② lacking in self-confidence; diffident: 对于这种生

疏的工作, 我感到～。I don't know much about the job, and I'm diffident about my ability to do it properly.

心许 xīnxǔ ① tacitly consent to; acquiesce in ② appreciate; think highly of

心绪 xīnxù state of mind: ～烦乱 emotionally upset; in an emotional turmoil

心绪不宁 xīnxù bù níng in a disturbed state of mind; in a flutter

心血 xīnxuè painstaking care (or effort): 费尽～ expend all one's energies / 多年～的结晶 the fruit of many years' painstaking labour

心血管监护病房 xīnxuèguǎn jiānhù bìngfáng cardiovascular care unit

心血管系统 xīnxuèguǎn xìtǒng physiol. cardiovascular system: ～疾病和功能障碍 cardiovascular system diseases and disorders

心血管造影 xīnxuèguǎn zàoyǐng angiocardiography

心血来潮 xīnxuè lái cháo be prompted by a sudden impulse; be seized by a whim: ～, 忘乎所以 forget oneself in an impulsive moment; be carried away by one's whims and act recklessly

心眼儿 xīnyǎnr ① heart; mind: 一个～为集体 devote oneself heart and soul to the collective; work for the collective wholeheartedly / 打～里热爱新社会 love the new society with all one's heart / 看到孩子们这么幸福, 大家从～里感到高兴。It warms the cockles of the heart to see the children so happy. ② intention; a person's mind: ～好 good-natured; kindhearted / 没安好～ have bad intentions; be up to no good ③ intelligence; cleverness: 他有～, 什么事都想得周到。He is alert and thoughtful. / 长点～, 别上人家的当。Smarten up and don't be taken in. ④ unfounded doubts; unnecessary misgivings: ～太多 full of unnecessary misgivings; oversensitive ⑤ tolerance: ～小 oversensitive; petty ——see also 斗心眼儿 dòu xīnyǎnr

心痒 xīnyǎng have an itch for: 一见那清凉的水, 个个都～, 巴不得马上跳下去。When they saw the clear cool water, they all had an itch to dive in at once.

心仪 xīnyí formal admire; respect: ～已久 have long had a high regard for sb.

心疑 xīnyí become or be suspicious

心意 xīnyì ① regard; kindly feelings: 这点礼物是我们大家的一点～。This little gift is a token of our regard. ② intention; purpose: 你们不了解他的～。You don't understand his intention.

心音 xīnyīn physiol. heart sounds; cardiac sounds: 第一 (第二)～ the first (second) heart sound

心硬 xīnyìng hard-hearted; stony-hearted; callous; unfeeling

心有灵犀一点通 xīn yǒu língxī yī diǎn tōng hearts which beat in unison are linked

心有余而力不足 xīn yǒuyú ér lì bùzú one's ability falls short of one's wishes; the spirit is willing, but the flesh is weak

心有余悸 xīn yǒu yújì one's heart still fluttering with fear; have a lingering fear

心余力绌 xīnyú-lìchù same as 心有余而力不足 xīn yǒuyú ér lì bùzú

心猿意马 xīnyuán-yìmǎ a heart like a capering monkey and a mind like a galloping horse—restless; perturbed

心愿 xīnyuàn cherished desire; aspiration; wish; dream: 这就了却了我的一桩～。This serves to fulfil a cherished desire of mine.

心悦诚服 xīnyuè chéngfú be completely convinced; feel a heartfelt admiration: 她爸爸的一番话说得她～。She was completely convinced by her father's arguments. / 他对你们的批评～。He fully accepted your criticism.

心杂音 xīnzáyīn med. heart murmur

心脏 xīnzàng ① the heart: ～搏动 heartbeat ② the central or most vital part of anything: 首都是一个国家的～。The capital is the heart of a country.

心脏病 xīnzàngbìng heart disease

心脏导管 xīnzàng dǎoguǎn cardiac catheter

心脏地带 xīnzàng dìdài heartland

心脏起搏器 xīnzàng qǐbóqì (cardiac) pacemaker

心脏移植 xīnzàng yízhí heart transplant

心窄 xīnzhǎi narrow-minded

心照 xīnzhào understand without being told: 彼此～ have a tacit understanding with sb.

心照不宣 xīnzhào bù xuān have a tacit understanding

心折 xīnzhé be filled with admiration

心之官则思 xīn zhī guān zé sī the office of the mind is to think

心直口快 xīnzhí-kǒukuài frank and outspoken; straightforward and plain-spoken: 他喜欢这个小伙子, ～, 有啥说啥。He has always liked this straightforward, outspoken youngster.

心志 xīnzhì will; resolution

心中 xīnzhōng in the heart; in the mind: 牢记～ keep firmly in mind

心中无数 xīnzhōng wú shù have no idea of how things stand; not know for certain: 这计划是否可行, 我～。I'm not too sure whether this plan will work.

心中有数 xīnzhōng yǒu shù know the score; have a pretty good idea of how things stand; know fairly well; know what's what: 对计划执行情况～ have a pretty clear idea of how the plan is being carried out / 进行调查研究, 做到～。Make investigations to find out how things stand. / 摸了这样的底, 就～了。With this stock-taking we know where we are.

心轴 xīnzhóu mech. mandrel: 花键～ splined mandrel

心拙口笨 xīnzhuō-kǒubèn dull-witted and slow-tongued

心子 xīnzi ① centre (of sth.); heart; core ② dial. the heart of a pig, sheep, etc. as food

心醉 xīnzuì be charmed; be enchanted; be fascinated

心醉魂迷 xīnzuì-húnmí the heart is intoxicated and the soul possessed—be overcome with admiration

芯 xīn rush pith: 灯～ lampwick; wick ——see also xìn

辛[1] xīn ① hot (in taste, flavour, etc.); pungent ② hard; laborious: 艰辛 jiānxīn ③ suffering: 辛酸 xīnsuān ④ (Xīn) a surname

辛[2] xīn the eighth of the ten Heavenly Stems (天干) ——see also 干支 gān-zhī

辛迪加 xīndíjiā econ. syndicate

辛亥革命 Xīnhài Gémìng the Revolution of 1911 (the Chinese bourgeois democratic revolution led by Dr. Sun Yat-sen which overthrew the Qing Dynasty)

辛苦 xīnkǔ ① hard; strenuous; toilsome; laborious: 犁地这活儿很～。Ploughing is hard work. ② pol. work hard; go to great trouble; go through hardships: 这事恐怕还得～您一趟。I'm afraid you'll have to take the trouble of going there to see about it. / 同志们～了。You comrades have been working hard. / 路上～了。You must have had a tiring journey. or You must be very tired after the journey.

辛辣 xīnlà pungent; hot; bitter: ～的味道 a sharp (or pungent) flavour / ～的讽刺 bitter irony; biting sarcasm

辛劳 xīnláo work hard; toil: 日夜～ toil day and night / 不辞～ spare no pains

辛勤 xīnqín industrious; hardworking: ～劳动 work hard; labour assiduously

辛酸 xīnsuān sad; bitter; miserable: ～泪 hot and bitter tears / ～的往事 sad (or poignant) memories / 饱尝旧社会的～ taste to the full the bitterness of life in the old society

辛烷值 xīnwánzhí chem. octane number (or value)

辛辛苦苦 xīnxīnkǔkǔ take a lot of trouble; take great pains; work laboriously: 她～地攒了几个钱。She saved up some money with great difficulty. / ～地一年干到头 toil all the

year round / 〜的官僚主义 a painstaking but bureaucratic style of work

辛夷 xīnyí *Chin. med.* the flower bud of lily magnolia (*Magnolia liliflora*)

忻 xīn ① same as 欣 xīn ② (Xīn) a surname

欣(訢) xīn glad; happy; joyful: 〜逢佳节 on the happy occasion of the festival

欣快 xīnkuài glad; joyful: 火车驶进他的家乡车站时, 他心里觉得非常〜。His heart swelled with joy as the train pulled into the station of his home town.

欣慕 xīnmù admire: 她的杰出表演使我〜不已。Her excellent performance filled me with admiration.

欣然 xīnrán *formal* joyfully; with pleasure: 〜接受 accept with pleasure / 〜同意 gladly consent; readily agree

欣赏 xīnshǎng appreciate; enjoy; admire: 音乐〜 music appreciation / 〜风景 enjoy (*or* admire) the scenery / 我很〜这个花园的格局。I admire the layout of this garden. *or* I like the way the garden is laid out.

欣慰 xīnwèi be gratified: 我们对实验的成功感到〜。We were gratified at the success of the experiment. / 获悉你身体康复, 至感〜。I am relieved to learn that you have recovered from your illness.

欣悉 xīnxī *formal* be glad (*or* happy) to learn

欣喜 xīnxǐ glad; joyful; happy: 听说王涛即将学成归国, 〜万分。We are extremely glad to learn that Wang Tao will soon complete his studies abroad and return home.

欣喜若狂 xīnxǐ ruò kuáng be wild with joy; go into raptures

欣羡 xīnxiàn *formal* admire

欣欣 xīnxīn ① joyful; glad; happy: 〜然有喜色 wear a joyful expression ② thriving; flourishing

欣欣向荣 xīnxīn xiàng róng thriving; flourishing; prosperous: 一派〜的景象 a picture of prosperity / 我国国民经济〜。Our national economy is thriving.

欣幸 xīnxìng be glad and thankful

锌 xīn *chem.* zinc (Zn)

锌白 xīnbái *chem.* zinc white

锌版 xīnbǎn *print.* zinc plate; zincograph

锌版印刷术 xīnbǎn yìnshuāshù zincography

锌钡白 xīnbèibái *chem.* lithopone

锌粉 xīnfěn *chem.* zinc powder

歆 xīn *formal* admire

歆慕 xīnmù (also 歆羡 xīnxiàn) *formal* admire

新 xīn ① new; fresh; up-to-date: 〜技术 new (*or* up-to-date) technique / 〜品种 a new variety / 最〜消息 the latest news / 〜社会 the new society ② brand new; unused: 〜笔 a new pen / 〜衣服 new clothes ③ newly; freshly; recently: 〜建的工厂 a newly built factory / 〜漆的门 a freshly painted door / 他是〜来的。He's a new arrival. / 这本书是我〜买的。This is the book I've just bought. ④ recently married or just being married: 〜女婿 a man newly married to one's daughter; daughter's bridegroom / 〜媳妇 a woman newly married to one's son; son's bride ⑤ (Xīn) short for 新疆维吾尔自治区 Xīnjiāng Wéiwúěr Zìzhìqū ⑥ (Xīn) the Xin Dynasty (8-23 A.D., between the Western Han and the Eastern Han)

新兵 xīnbīng recruit; (Brit. Navy) ordinary seaman; (Brit. Air Force) aircraftsman

新兵报到站 xīnbīng bàodàozhàn reception centre (*or* station); recruiting depot

新茶 xīnchá newly picked and processed tea leaves

新潮 xīncháo new trend; new fashion: 〜服装 new fashions

新陈代谢 xīn-chén dàixiè ① *biol.* metabolism: 生物都有〜, 有生长、繁殖和死亡。All living matter undergoes a process of metabolism: it grows, reproduces and perishes.

② the new superseding the old: 〜是宇宙间普遍的永远不可抵抗的规律。The supersession of the old by the new is a general, eternal and inviolable law of the universe.

新仇旧恨 xīnchóu-jiùhèn new hatred piled on old; old scores and new

新春 xīnchūn the 10 to 20 days following lunar New Year's Day

新词 xīncí new word; new expression: 〜、新义、新用法 new words, new meanings and new usages

新村 xīncūn new residential quarter; new housing development (*or* estate): 工人〜 new housing estate for workers

新大陆 Xīn Dàlù the New World—the Americas

新法 xīnfǎ ① new law ② new method

新房 xīnfáng bridal chamber

新妇 xīnfù bride

新寡 xīnguǎ ① have recently been widowed ② a woman who has recently been widowed

新官上任三把火 xīnguān shàngrèn sān bǎ huǒ a new official applies strict measures; a new broom sweeps clean

新贵 xīnguì a newly appointed high official

新赫布里底 Xīn Hèbùlǐdǐ New Hebrides

新欢 xīnhuān new sweetheart (esp. a woman): 另结〜 be taken up with another woman

新婚 xīnhūn newly-married: 〜夫妇 a newly-married couple; newlyweds / 〜旅行 go on a honeymoon trip

新婚燕尔 xīnhūn yàn'ěr same as 宴尔新婚 yàn'ěr xīnhūn

新纪录 xīnjìlù a new record: 创造〜 set a new record

新纪元 xīnjìyuán a new era; a new epoch: 开创〜 usher in a new epoch; open a new era

新霁 xīnjì clear up after a rain or snow: 雪后〜。It had stopped snowing and was clearing up.

新加坡 Xīnjiāpō Singapore

新嫁娘 xīnjiàniáng bride

新疆 Xīnjiāng Xinjiang

新疆维吾尔自治区 Xīnjiāng Wéiwúěr Zìzhìqū the Xinjiang Uygur (Uighur) Autonomous Region

新交 xīnjiāo a new acquaintance; a new friend: 他与老王是〜。He and Lao Wang have become acquainted only recently. / 〜与故知 old and new friends

新教 Xīnjiào Protestantism

新教徒 Xīnjiàotú Protestant

新近 xīnjìn recently; lately; in recent times

新旧约全书 Xīn-Jiùyuē Quánshū *Christianity* the Old and New Testaments

新居 xīnjū new home; new residence

新喀里多尼亚 Xīn Kālǐduōníyà New Caledonia

新来乍到 xīnlái-zhàdào newly arrived: 我〜, 请多帮助。I'm a newcomer here and would be glad to have your help.

新郎 xīnláng bridegroom

新郎官 xīnlángguān *inf.* bridegroom

新历 xīnlì the new calendar—the Gregorian calender

新绿 xīnlǜ (of spring vegetation) fresh green: 春天来了, 大地一片〜。Spring is come and the earth is a fresh green.

新马 Xīn-Mǎ Singapore and Malaysia

新霉素 xīnméisù *pharm.* neomycin

新民主主义 xīnmínzhǔzhǔyì new democracy

新民主主义革命 xīnmínzhǔzhǔyì gémìng new-democratic revolution

新名词 xīnmíngcí ① new term; new expression ② vogue word; newfangled phrase: 满口〜 mouthing newfangled phrases

新年 xīnnián New Year: 〜好! Happy New Year! / 〜献词 New Year message

新娘 xīnniáng (also 新娘子 xīnniángzi) bride

新女性 xīnnǚxìng *old* new woman (a term used in the earlier years of the 20th century for a woman with progressive ideas)

新篇章 xīnpiānzhāng new page: 两国关系史上的〜 a new page in the history of relations between the two countries

新瓶装旧酒　xīnpíng zhuāng jiùjiǔ　old wine in a new bottle——the same old stuff with a new label

新奇　xīnqí　strange; novel; new: ～的想法 a novel idea／他初到矿山时，处处觉得～。When he first got to the mine, everything struck him as new.

新巧　xīnqiǎo　new and ingenious: ～的手工艺品 curious and exquisite handicrafts

新秋　xīnqiū　early autumn

新区　xīnqū　① newly developed area; newly added district ② newly liberated area (during the Third Revolutionary Civil War, 1945—1949)

新人　xīnrén　① people of a new type: 一代～在茁壮成长。A new generation is reaching maturity. ② new personality; new talent: 科学界涌现出了一批～。A new batch of gifted people has emerged in the world of science. ③ bride and bridegroom ④ bride ⑤ Neoanthropus; *Homo sapiens*

新人新事　xīnrén-xīnshì　new people and new things: ～不断涌现。New people and new things are constantly coming to the fore.

新任　xīnrèn　① newly appointed: ～部长 the newly appointed minister ② new post: 赶赴～ go to take up a new post

新生[1]　xīnshēng　① newborn; newly born: ～婴儿 newborn (baby) ② new life; rebirth; regeneration: 一九四九年一月三十一日北京解放了，这个古城从此获得了～。With its liberation on January 31, 1949, the centuries-old city of Beijing was reborn.／解放后这种古老的民间艺术获得了～。Liberation gave this age-old folk art a new life.

新生[2]　xīnshēng　a new student or pupil

新生代　Xīnshēngdài　*geol.* the Cenozoic Era

新生界　Xīnshēngjiè　*geol.* the Cenozoic Erathem

新生力量　xīnshēng lìliàng　newly emerging force; new rising force; new force

新生事物　xīnshēng shìwù　newly emerging things; new things

新诗　xīnshī　(opp. 旧诗 jiùshī) new verse (free verse written in the vernacular)

新石器时代　Xīnshíqì Shídài　the Neolithic Age; the New Stone Age

新式　xīnshì　new type; latest type; new style: ～农具 new types of farm implements; improved farm implements／～武器 modern weapons

新手　xīnshǒu　a new hand; a raw recruit

新书　xīnshū　① new book ② new title

新斯的明　xīnsīdímíng　*pharm.* neostigmine

新四军　Xīnsìjūn　the New Fourth Army (led by the Chinese Communist Party during the War of Resistance Against Japan)

新文化运动　Xīnwénhuàyùndòng　the New Culture Movement (around the time of the May 4th Movement in 1919)

新文学　xīnwénxué　new-vernacular literature (promoted by the May 4th Movement in 1919)

新闻　xīnwén　news: 头版～ front-page news (or story)／简明～ news in brief／电视～ TV news／～简报 news summary／～图片橱窗 newsphoto display case

新闻处　xīnwénchù　office of information; information service

新闻稿　xīnwéngǎo　press (or news) release

新闻工作者　xīnwén gōngzuòzhě　journalist

新闻公报　xīnwén gōngbào　press *communiqué*

新闻广播　xīnwén guǎngbō　newscast

新闻记者　xīnwén jìzhě　newsman; newspaperman; reporter; journalist

新闻检查　xīnwén jiǎnchá　press censorship

新闻界　xīnwénjiè　press circles; the press

新闻联播　xīnwén liánbō　news hookup

新闻片　xīnwénpiàn　newsreel; news film

新闻司　xīnwénsī　department of information (of the Foreign Ministry)

新闻通讯　xīnwén tōngxùn　newsletter

新闻业　xīnwényè　journalism

新闻纸　xīnwénzhǐ　① *old* newspaper ② newsprint

新西兰　Xīnxīlán　New Zealand

新西兰人　Xīnxīlánrén　New Zealander

新媳妇儿　xīnxífur　*inf.* bride

新禧　xīnxǐ　good fortune for the new year: 恭贺～ Happy New Year

新鲜　xīnxiān　① fresh: ～空气 fresh air／～牛奶 fresh milk／～的水果 fresh fruit／鱼有点不～了。The fish is slightly off.／尝个～ have a taste of what is just in season ② new; novel; strange: ～经验 new (or fresh) experience／这话真～。That's a strange thing to say.

新兴　xīnxīng　new and developing; rising; burgeoning: ～工业城市 a developing industrial city／～的独立国家 newly independent countries／～势力 the rising forces; the forces in the ascendant

新星　xīnxīng　① *astron.* nova ② new star: 羽毛球～ a new badminton star

新型　xīnxíng　new type; new pattern: ～厨房用具 modern cooking equipment; modern kitchenware

新秀　xīnxiù　new star: 影坛～ a new film (or movie) star

新学　xīnxué　new learning ——see also 西学 xīxué

新医　xīnyī　① new Chinese medicine (Chinese medicine integrated with Western medicine) ② Western medicine

新义　xīnyì　new meaning

新异　xīnyì　strange; novel; newfangled

新意　xīnyì　new meaning; new conception

新颖　xīnyǐng　new and original; novel: 题材～ original in choice of subject (or theme)／式样～ in a novel style

新雨　xīnyǔ　① rain in early spring; newly fallen rain ② *formal* new friends: 旧知～ friends, old and new

新约　Xīnyuē　*Christianity* the New Testament

新月　xīnyuè　① crescent (moon) ② *astron.* new moon (invisible to men)

新月形沙丘　xīnyuèxíng shāqiū　*geog.* barchan

新张　xīnzhāng　(of a new shop) begin doing business

新正　xīnzhēng　the first month of the lunar year

新政　xīnzhèng　new political measures; new policies

新殖民主义　xīnzhímínzhǔyì　neocolonialism

新殖民主义者　xīnzhímínzhǔyìzhě　neocolonialist

新址　xīnzhǐ　the new address of an establishment

新制　xīnzhì　new system

新妆　xīnzhuāng　① the new look of a woman after make-up ② (women's) new fashion

新装　xīnzhuāng　new clothes: 她正在试～。She's trying on a new dress.／山村换～。The mountain village takes on a new look.

薪

薪　xīn　① firewood; faggot; fuel: 采木为～ gather wood for fuel ② salary: 加～ increase (or raise) the salary

薪传　xīnchuán　*formal* the torch of learning passes on from teacher to student ——see also 薪尽火传 xīnjìn-huǒchuán

薪俸　xīnfèng　salary; pay

薪给　xīnjǐ　pay (in any form); salary

薪金　xīnjīn　pay in money; salary

薪尽火传　xīnjìn-huǒchuán　as one piece of fuel is consumed, the flame passes on to another——the torch of learning is passed on from teacher to student

薪水　xīnshui　salary; pay; wages

薪炭林　xīntànlín　*forestry* fuel forest

薪饷　xīnxiǎng　pay for soldiers, policemen, etc.

薪资　xīnzī　wages; pay

馨

馨　xīn　*formal* strong and pervasive fragrance: 如兰之～ a strong and pervasive fragrance like the orchid's

馨香　xīnxiāng　*formal* ① fragrance: 桂花盛开，～四溢。The osmanthus is in full bloom, filling the air with its fragrance. ② the sweet smell of burning incense

馨香祷祝 xīnxiāng dǎozhù burn incense and pray to the gods—earnestly pray for sth.; sincerely wish

鑫
xīn (usu. used in names of persons or shops) prosperous; making a good profit

xìn

囟(顖)
xìn short for 囟门 xìnmén

囟门 xìnmén fontanel (of a baby's head)

芯(信)
xìn core ——see also xīn

芯子 xìnzi ① fuse (as in a firecracker); wick (as in a candle) ② the forked tongue of a snake

信
xìn ① true; real: 信史 xìnshǐ ② confidence; trust; faith: 守信 shǒuxìn / 失信 shīxìn ③ believe: ～不一由你。Believe it or not. / 别一他的话。Don't believe him. / 我不一他能赢。I don't believe he can win. ④ profess faith in; believe in: ～佛 profess Buddhism ⑤ at will; at random; without plan: 信步 xìnbù ⑥ sign; evidence: 信号 xìnhào / 印信 yìnxìn ⑦ letter; mail: 写封～ write a letter ⑧ message; word; information: 还没有～儿呢。No news yet. / 你到了那儿就给我来个～儿。Please send me word of your arrival. ⑨ fuse: 信管 xìnguǎn ⑩ same as 芯 xìn ⑪ (Xìn) a surname

信笔 xìnbǐ write at random; write without premeditation: 我一写了几个字就寄出了。I dashed off a few words and posted the note. / 他一写来，尽是文章。With just a flourish of his pen, he produces an article.

信标灯 xìnbiāodēng beacon light

信步 xìnbù take a leisurely walk; stroll; walk aimlessly

信不过 xìnbuguò distrust; have no trust in: 你是～我，所以不肯对我讲真话。You are not telling me the truth because you don't trust me.

信差 xìnchāi old ① courier ② postman

信从 xìncóng trust and follow the advice of: 国王只～他的宠臣。The king only trusted and listened to his favourite ministers.

信贷 xìndài credit: 长期～ long-term credit / ～额度 line of credit / ～资金 credit funds; funds for extending credit

信得过 xìndeguò ① trust: 你要是～我，就交给我去办。If you trust me, let me do it for you. ② trustworthy; dependable

信而有征 xìn ér yǒu zhēng borne out by evidence

信访 xìn-fǎng (short for 人民来信来访) letters and calls (i.e. letters of complaint from the people and the calls they make to lodge complaints)

信风 xìnfēng meteorol. trade winds; trades

信风带 xìnfēngdài trade-wind zone

信封 xìnfēng envelope

信奉 xìnfèng believe in: ～上帝 believe in God / ～伊斯兰教 be a Moslem

信服 xìnfú completely accept; be convinced: 令人～的论据 convincing argument; argument that carries conviction

信鸽 xìngē carrier pigeon; homing pigeon; homer

信管 xìnguǎn fuse: 炸药～ fuse in a blasting charge / 触发～ contact fuse / 延期～ delay-action fuse / 近炸～ proximity fuse

信函 xìnhán letters

信号 xìnhào signal: 灯光～ light signal / 识别～ identification signal

信号兵 xìnhàobīng signalman

信号刺激 xìnhào cìjī psychol. signal stimulus

信号弹 xìnhàodàn signal flare: 放～ send up a signal flare

信号灯 xìnhàodēng signal lamp; semaphore

信号旗 xìnhàoqí signal flag; semaphore

信号枪 xìnhàoqiāng mil. flare pistol; signal pistol

信汇 xìnhuì mail transfer (M/T)

信笺 xìnjiān letter paper; notepaper

信件 xìnjiàn letters, papers, printed matter, etc. (sent either by post or by messenger)

信教 xìnjiào profess a religion; be religious

信据 xìnjù reliable evidence; authentic evidence; absolute proof

信口 xìnkǒu speak thoughtlessly or casually: ～说出 blurt out / ～回答 answer casually

信口雌黄 xìnkǒu cíhuáng make irresponsible remarks; wag one's tongue too freely: 一个～的无赖 a shameless liar and scoundrel

信口开河 xìnkǒu kāihé (also 信口开合 xìnkǒu kāihé) talk irresponsibly; wag one's tongue too freely; talk at random

信赖 xìnlài trust; count on; have faith in: 她是群众～的好干部。She's a good cadre trusted by the masses.

信马由缰 xìnmǎ-yóujiāng ① ride a horse without holding the reins ② stroll about aimlessly; act or do as one pleases

信念 xìnniàn faith; belief; conviction: 坚定的～ a firm conviction / 我的～决不会动摇。Nothing can shake my belief.

信女 xìnnǚ female Buddhist devotee: 善男信女 shànnán-xìnnǚ

信皮儿 xìnpír inf. envelope

信然 xìnrán formal true; really so; indeed

信瓤儿 xìnrángr dial. the letter in an envelope

信任 xìnrèn trust; have confidence in: 得到人民的～ enjoy the trust (or confidence) of the people

信任投票 xìnrèn tóupiào vote of confidence

信赏必罚 xìnshǎng-bìfá due rewards and punishments will be meted out without fail

信石 xìnshí arsenic in a natural state

信实 xìnshí trustworthy; honest; reliable: 他为人～。He is honest and reliable.

信史 xìnshǐ true (or authentic) history; faithful historical account

信使 xìnshǐ courier; messenger: 外交～ diplomatic messenger / ～证明书 courier's credentials

信士 xìnshì ① male Buddhist devotee ② formal a man of his (my, your) word; a man of honour

信誓旦旦 xìnshì dàndàn pledge in all sincerity; vow solemnly

信手 xìnshǒu do sth. spontaneously or without much thought or effort: 他一进门就～把大衣扔在沙发上。He threw his overcoat on the sofa as he entered. / 她抱起琵琶，～弹来，竟十分动听。She took up the pipa and began to play, effortlessly and melodiously. / ～写来的文章很少是好文章。Ready writing is seldom good writing.

信手拈来 xìnshǒu niānlái have the words at hand; have materials, etc. at one's fingertips

信守 xìnshǒu abide by; stand by: ～协议 abide by (or stand by) an agreement / ～诺言 keep a promise; be as good as one's word

信守不渝 xìnshǒu bù yú be unswervingly true (to one's promise, etc.)

信水 xìnshuǐ formal menstruation

信宿 xìnsù formal a stay of two nights; two nights' time

信天翁 xìntiānwēng zool. albatross

信天游 xìntiānyóu rambles in the sky—the name of a number of tunes used for the folk songs of northern Shaanxi

信条 xìntiáo article of creed (or faith); creed; precept; tenet

信筒 xìntǒng pillar-box; mailbox

信徒 xìntú believer; disciple; follower; adherent; devotee: 佛教～ Buddhist

信托 xìntuō trust; entrust

信托公司 xìntuō gōngsī trust company

信托基金 xìntuō jījīn trust fund

信托商店 xìntuō shāngdiàn commercial shop (or house,

agent)

信托投资公司 xìntuō tóuzī gōngsī trust and investment corporation: 中国国际～ China International Trust and Investment Corporation (CITIC)

信望 xìnwàng prestige

信物 xìnwù authenticating object; token; keepsake

信息 xìnxī ① information; news; message: ～传递 information transmission / ～中心 information centre ② math. information

信息编码 xìnxī biānmǎ computer information encoding

信息存储器 xìnxī cúnchǔqì computer information storing device

信息论 xìnxīlùn math. information theory

信息体 xìnxītǐ biochem. informosome

信息学 xìnxīxué information science; informatics

信息载体 xìnxī zàitǐ information carrier

信息子 xìnxīzǐ biochem. informofer

信箱 xìnxiāng ① letter box; mailbox ② post-office box (P.O.B.)

信心 xìnxīn confidence; faith: 满怀～ full of confidence / 有～提前完成任务 be confident of fulfilling a task ahead of schedule / 我对这药～不大。 I haven't much faith in this medicine.

信仰 xìnyǎng faith; belief; conviction: 政治～ political conviction / 宗教～ religious belief / ～自由 freedom of belief / ～危机 credibility crisis

信仰主义 xìnyǎngzhǔyì philos. fideism

信以为真 xìn yǐwéi zhēn accept sth. as true: 因为他说得有凭有据，大家～。 Since his statement seemed well founded, all the others immediately accepted it.

信义 xìnyì good faith; faith: 有～ act in good faith / 无～ be perfidious

信用 xìnyòng ① trustworthiness; credit: 他～好，完全可以信任。 His credit is good. You can trust him. / 讲～ keep one's word / 失去～ lose one's credit ② credit: ～贷款 unsecured loan; loan on credit

信用合作社 xìnyòng hézuòshè credit cooperative

信用卡 xìnyòngkǎ credit card

信用证 xìnyòngzhèng letter of credit (L/C)

信誉 xìnyù prestige; credit; reputation: 享有很高的国际～ enjoy high international prestige

信札 xìnzhá letters

信纸 xìnzhǐ letter paper; writing paper

衅（釁）

xìn quarrel; dispute: 寻衅 xúnxìn

衅端 xìnduān formal a cause for a quarrel or dispute

衅起萧墙 xìn qǐ xiāoqiáng same as 祸起萧墙 huò qǐ xiāoqiáng

xīng

兴（興）

xīng ① prosper; rise; prevail; become popular: 我们这儿不～这一套。 We don't go in for that sort of thing here. / 现在又～超短裙了。 Miniskirts are coming into fashion again. ② start; begin: 兴工 xīnggōng / 兴建 xīngjiàn ③ encourage; promote: 大～调查研究之风 energetically encourage the practice of investigation and study ④ formal get up; rise: 晨～ get up in the morning ⑤ dial. (often used in the negative) permit; allow: 不～胡说! None of your nonsense! ⑥ dial. maybe; perhaps: 明天他也～来, 也～不来。 He may or may not come tomorrow. ⑦ (Xīng) a surname

兴办 xīngbàn initiate; set up: ～新型企业 initiate enterprises of a new type

兴兵 xīngbīng start military operations; send an army: ～讨伐 send a punitive expedition against

兴废 xīng-fèi formal rise and fall

兴奋 xīngfèn ① be excited: 他～过度, 睡不着觉。 He was too excited to fall asleep. ② physiol. excitation

兴奋剂 xīngfènjì excitant; stimulant; dope

兴奋剂检测中心 xīngfènjì jiǎncè zhōngxīn doping control centre

兴奋性 xīngfènxìng excitability

兴风作浪 xīngfēng-zuòlàng stir up trouble; make trouble; fan the flames of disorder

兴革 xīng-gé formal initiation (of the new) and abolition (of the old); reforms

兴工 xīnggōng start construction: 破土～ break ground and start construction

兴建 xīngjiàn build; construct: 正在～一座大坝。 A dam is now under construction. / 又～了一个钢铁联合企业。 Another iron and steel complex has been built.

兴利除弊 xīnglì-chúbì promote what is beneficial and abolish what is harmful

兴隆 xīnglóng prosperous; thriving; flourishing; brisk: 生意～。 Business is brisk.

兴起 xīngqǐ ① rise; spring up; be on the upgrade: 激光是六十年代初期～的一门新科学。 Laser is a new branch of science which rose in the early 1960s. / 一个社会主义建设的新高潮正在～。 A new upsurge in socialist construction is in the making. ② formal rise in excitement; be aroused

兴盛 xīngshèng prosper; flourish; thrive; be in the ascendant: 国家～。 The nation is prosperous. / 事业～。 Business is thriving.

兴师 xīngshī formal send an army; dispatch troops

兴师动众 xīngshī-dòngzhòng move troops and stir up people—draw in many people (to do sth.): 这点小事, 用不着～。 It's only a small matter; you needn't make a fuss about it and draw in a lot of people.

兴师问罪 xīngshī-wènzuì send a punitive expedition

兴时 xīngshí fashionable; in vogue; popular: 这种款式现在不那么～了。 This style is no more in vogue.

兴衰 xīng-shuāi rise and decline; rise and fall

兴叹 xīngtàn formal heave a sigh; lament; bemoan: 望洋兴叹 wàng yáng xīngtàn

兴替 xīng-tì formal the rise of a power and its supersession by another; rise and fall: 朝代的～ the rise and fall of a dynasty

兴亡 xīng-wáng rise and fall (of a nation)

兴旺 xīngwàng prosper; flourish; thrive: 他们的企业越办越～。 Their enterprise is growing more and more prosperous. / 青年人朝气蓬勃, 正在～时期。 Young people, full of vitality, are in the heyday of life. / 我们的队伍必定会～起来。 Our ranks will surely swell. / 我国的科学技术一定会～发达起来。 China's science and technology will certainly grow and flourish

兴修 xīngxiū start construction (on a large project); start building (on an extensive scale): ～水利 undertake new water conservancy projects / ～居民楼 construct apartment buildings on a large scale / ～铁路 start railway construction

兴许 xīngxǔ dial. perhaps; maybe

兴学 xīngxué (of private individuals or groups of people) set up schools: 捐资～ make donations for the setting up of schools

兴妖作怪 xīngyāo-zuòguài conjure up demons to make trouble—stir up trouble

星

xīng ① star: 月明～稀。 The moon is bright and the stars are sparse. ② heavenly body: 彗星 huìxīng / 卫星 wèixīng ③ bit; particle: 火星儿 huǒxīngr ④ small marks on the arm of a steelyard indicating jin and its fractions ⑤ the twenty-fifth of the twenty-eight constellations (二十八宿) into which the celestial sphere was divided in ancient Chinese astronomy (consi-

sting of seven stars in Hydra)

星表 xīngbiǎo *astron.* star catalogue

星辰 xīngchén stars and constellations; the stars: 日月～ the sun, the moon and the stars

星虫 xīngchóng sipunculid worm

星等 xīngděng *astron.* magnitude

星斗 xīngdǒu stars: 满天～ a star-studded sky

星光 xīngguāng starlight: 在～下漫步 go for a walk under the starlight／一个～闪烁的夜晚 one starlit night

星汉 xīnghàn *liter.* the Milky Way; Galaxy

星号 xīnghào asterisk (*)

星河 xīnghé the Milky Way; Galaxy

星火¹ xīnghuǒ spark

星火² xīnghuǒ shooting star; meteor: 急如星火 jí rú xīnghuǒ

星火燎原 xīnghuǒ liáoyuán a single spark can start a prairie fire

星际 xīngjì interplanetary; interstellar

星际航行 xīngjì hángxíng interplanetary flight (*or* travel); interstellar flight (*or* travel); space flight (*or* travel)

星际物质 xīngjì wùzhì interstellar medium

星空 xīngkōng a starry sky; a star-studded sky; a starlit sky

星离雨散 xīnglí-yǔsàn (also 星离云散 xīnglí-yúnsàn) (of family members, friends, etc.) separate; be scattered far and wide

星罗棋布 xīngluó-qíbù scattered all over like stars in the sky or men on a chessboard; spread all over the place: 全国中小型水利工程～。Small and medium-sized irrigation works spread all over the country.

星命 xīngmìng astrology

星期 xīngqī ① week: 三个～ three weeks ② (used before 日, 一, 二, 三, 四, 五, 六, 几) day of the week: 今天～几? What day (of the week) is it today? ③ short for 星期日 xīngqīrì

星期二 xīngqī'èr Tuesday (Tues.)

星期六 xīngqīliù Saturday (Sat.)

星期日 xīngqīrì (also 星期天 xīngqītiān) Sunday (Sun.)

星期三 xīngqīsān Wednesday (Wed.)

星期四 xīngqīsì Thursday (Thur. or Thurs.)

星期五 xīngqīwǔ Friday (Fri.)

星期一 xīngqīyī Monday (Mon.)

星球 xīngqiú celestial body; heavenly body

星散 xīngsàn *formal* (of family members, friends, etc.) be scattered about like the stars; be scattered far and wide

星鲨 xīngshā *zool.* gummy shark

星速 xīngsù as fast as a shooting star; at lightning speed: 队伍接到号令便～南下。As soon as they received orders, the army marched south without a moment of delay.

星体 xīngtǐ *astron.* celestial body; heavenly body

星条旗 xīngtiáoqí Stars and Stripes; the Star-Spangled Banner (the national flag of U. S. A.)

星图 xīngtú *astron.* star chart; star map; star atlas

星团 xīngtuán *astron.* star cluster

星系 xīngxì *astron.* galaxy: 总～ metagalaxy／～团 cluster of galaxies

星系天文学 xīngxì tiānwénxué extragalactic astronomy

星系晕 xīngxìyùn *astron.* galactic halo

星相 xīngxiàng horoscope

星象 xīngxiàng configurations of the stars (formerly studied for their supposed influence on human affairs)

星协 xīngxié stellar association

星星 xīngxīng a tiny spot; speck: 天空晴朗, 一～云彩也没有。The sky is clear and bright without a speck of cloud.

星星 xīngxing *inf.* star

星星点点 xīngxīngdiǎndiǎn tiny spots; bits and pieces: 对于科学的最新成就我只是～知道一些。I have only a scrappy knowledge of the latest scientific achievements.

星星之火, 可以燎原 xīngxīng zhī huǒ, kěyǐ liáoyuán a single spark can start a prairie fire

星宿 xīngxiù constellation

星夜 xīngyè a starlit (*or* starry) night: ～启程 set out by starlight; set out in great haste

星移斗转 xīngyí-dǒuzhuàn change in the positions of the stars—change of the seasons; passage of time

星云 xīngyún *astron.* nebula: 旋涡～ spiral nebula／银河～ galactic nebula／蟹状～ Crab Nebula／网状～ network nebula／～团 nebulous cluster

星占 xīngzhān divine by astrology; cast a horoscope

星占术 xīngzhānshù astrology

星震 xīngzhèn *astron.* starquake

星子 xīngzi ① (also 星儿 xīngr) tiny particles: 唾沫～ sputtered drops of saliva; sputter／他一着急, 说起话来就唾沫～四溅。He sputters terribly when excited. ② *astron.* planetesimal

星座 xīngzuò *astron.* constellation

惺

xīng see below

惺忪 xīngsōng (also 惺松 xīngsōng) ① (of eyes) not yet fully open on waking up: 睡眼～ eyes still heavy with sleep; sleepy eyes ② *formal* awake; conscious; clearheaded: 不～ not awake; still unconscious

惺惺 xīngxīng ① clearheaded; awake ② wise; intelligent ③ an intelligent person; a wise man

惺惺惜惺惺 xīngxīng xī xīngxīng the wise appreciate one another: ～, 好汉识好汉。Intelligent people like intelligence in others, and so good folk recognize the good in others.

惺惺作态 xīngxīng zuòtài be affected; simulate (friendship, innocence, etc.)

猩

xīng *zool.* orangutan

猩红 xīnghóng scarlet; bloodred: ～的石榴花 the fiery red pomegranate flowers

猩红热 xīnghóngrè scarlet fever; scarlatina

猩猩 xīngxing *zool.* orangutan——see also 大猩猩 dàxīngxing; 黑猩猩 hēixīngxing

猩猩草 xīngxingcǎo *bot.* painted euphorbia (*Euphorbia heterophylla*)

腥

xīng ① raw meat or fish: 荤腥 hūnxīng ② having the smell of fish, seafood, etc.

腥臭 xīngchòu stinking smell as of rotten fish; stench

腥风血雨 xīngfēng-xuèyǔ a foul wind and a rain of blood—reign of terror

腥黑穗病 xīnghēisuìbìng bunt (a smut disease of wheat); stinking smut

腥气 xīngqi ① the smell of fish, seafood, etc.: 一股子～ a fishy smell ② stinking; fishy: 好～! How stinky!

腥臊 xīngsāo stench

腥膻 xīngshān the smell of fish, mutton, etc.

腥味儿 xīngwèir the foul smell of fish; a fishy smell

xíng

刑

xíng ① punishment (inflicted for a crime); penalty; sentence: 判刑 pànxíng ② torture; corporal punishment: 用刑 yòngxíng

刑部 Xíngbù the Board of Punishments——see also 六部 Liùbù

刑场 xíngchǎng execution ground

刑典 xíngdiǎn penal code; criminal law

刑罚 xíngfá *leg.* penalty (for a criminal offence); punishment

刑法 xíngfǎ *leg.* penal code; criminal law

刑法 xíngfa corporal punishment; torture: 动了～ administer corporal punishment / 受了～ suffer corporal punishment

刑房 xíngfáng ①(in former times) department of criminal prosecution in a *yamen* ② torture chamber: 私设～ set up an illegal torture chamber

刑警 xíngjǐng short for 刑事警察 xíngshì jǐngchá

刑具 xíngjù instruments of torture; implements of punishment

刑律 xínglǜ *leg.* criminal law: 触犯～ violate the criminal law

刑满释放 xíngmǎn shìfàng *leg.* be released upon completion of a sentence (or one's term)

刑名 xíngmíng ① *arch.* law (esp. criminal law) ② names of punishments (e.g. death sentence, imprisonment, etc.)

刑名师爷 xíngmíng shīye (in the Qing Dynasty) a *yamen* secretary handling criminal cases

刑期 xíngqī term of imprisonment; prison term: ～已满 have completed a term of imprisonment; have served one's sentence / ～七年 a sentence of seven years in prison; a 7-year prison sentence

刑事 xíngshì *leg.* criminal; penal: ～案件 criminal case / ～处分 criminal sanction / ～管辖权 criminal jurisdiction

刑事法庭 xíngshì fǎtíng criminal court

刑事犯 xíngshìfàn criminal offender; criminal

刑事犯罪 xíngshì fànzuì criminal offence; criminal act

刑事警察 xíngshì jǐngchá criminal police

刑事诉讼 xíngshì sùsòng criminal procedure; criminal suit

刑事诉讼法 xíngshì sùsòngfǎ code of criminal procedure; criminal procedure law

刑事责任 xíngshì zérèn criminal responsibility

刑事侦查 xíngshì zhēnchá criminal investigation

刑庭 xíngtíng short for 刑事法庭 xíngshì fǎtíng

刑讯 xíngxùn inquisition by torture: ～逼供 extort a confession by torture; subject a criminal suspect to the third degree

刑杖 xíngzhàng a club, rod, or bunch of sticks for torture

邢
邢 Xíng a surname

行
行 xíng ① *formal* go; walk; travel: 日～三千步 walk three thousand steps a day (for exercise) / 日～百里 cover a hundred *li* a day / 儿～千里母担忧。When children travel far from home, mothers never stop worrying. / 非洲之～ a trip to Africa ② temporary; makeshift: 行营 xíngyíng / 行灶 xíngzào ③ be current; circulate: 发行 fāxíng / 行销 xíngxiāo ④ do; perform; carry out: 简便易～ simple and easy to do ⑤ (used before a disyllabic verb, indicating the performance of some action): 即～通知 notify sb. at once / 另～安排 make separate arrangements ⑥ behaviour; conduct: 品行 pǐnxíng / 言行 yánxíng ⑦ be all right; will do: 咱们走着去，～不～? Will it be all right if we go on foot? / 没有铅丝，用绳子也～。If there is no wire, a cord will do. / 在快车道上骑车可不～。Cycling along the motorway is not allowed. / 你替我到邮局跑一趟，～吗? ——～! Would you run over to the post office for me? — O.K.! (or All right!) ⑧ capable; competent: 老王，你真～! Lao Wang, you are really terrific (or something great)! / 你看他干这工作～吗? Do you think he is up to it? / 不要认为只有自己才～。Don't think you're the only cap-

able one. ⑨ *formal* soon: 别来～复四年。It is four years since we parted. ——see also háng

行百里者半九十 xíngbǎilǐzhě bàn jiǔshí ninety *li* is only half of a hundred-*li* journey—the going is toughest towards the end of a journey; one must sustain one's effort when a task is nearing completion

行板 xíngbǎn *mus.* andante

行波 xíngbō *radio* travelling wave

行波管 xíngbōguǎn travelling wave tube

行不通 xíngbutōng won't do (or work); will get nowhere: 这个计划～。This plan won't work. / 这样的作法是绝对～的。This course of action will get us absolutely nowhere.

行藏 xíngcáng *formal* conduct ——see also 用舍行藏 yòngshě xíngcáng

行车 xíngchē drive a vehicle: 千万注意～安全。Ensure safety in driving. / ～时刻表 a train or bus time-table / ～里程 distance travelled by a vehicle; mileage / ～速率 driving speed / ～执照 driver's (or driving) license

行成于思 xíng chéng yú sī a deed is accomplished through taking thought; success depends on forethought: ～毁于随。(韩愈) The way of life is attained through deliberate thought but ruined by casual negligence.

行程 xíngchéng ① route or distance of travel: ～一万多公里 travel over 10,000 kilometres ② *mech.* stroke; throw; travel: 活塞～ piston travel / 滑枕～ ram stroke / 偏心轮～ throw of eccentric

行船 xíngchuán sail a boat; navigate: 大运河有几段仍可以～。The Grand Canal is still navigable in certain sections.

行刺 xíngcì assassinate

行道 xíngdào *old* preach one's doctrine; propagate one's belief

行道树 xíngdàoshù trees that line a street

行得通 xíngdetōng will do (or work); be practicable: 这个主意～。This idea will work.

行动 xíngdòng ① move (or get) about: ～不便 have difficulty getting about / ～缓慢 move slowly; be slow-moving ② act; take action: ～起来 go into action / 按计划～。Proceed according to plan. ③ action; operation: 军事～ military operations / ～纲领 programme of action

行都 xíngdū a provisional capital

行方便 xíng fāngbian make things convenient for sb.; be accommodating

行房 xíngfáng (of a married couple) have sexual intercourse; make love

行宫 xínggōng imperial palace for short stays away from the capital; temporary dwelling place of an emperor when away from the capital

行贾 xínggǔ *formal* ① itinerant trader; travelling merchant ② travel about to do business

行好 xínghǎo act charitably; be merciful; be charitable; do a good turn: 您行行好，就饶了我这一回吧! Please have a heart and let me off this time!

行贿 xínghuì bribe; offer a bribe; resort to bribery

行迹 xíngjì tracks (of a person); traces: ～无定 wander about; lead a vagrant life; have no fixed whereabouts

行奸 xíngjiān commit adultery

行检 xíngjiǎn *formal* conduct; behaviour: 不修～ be loose in conduct; be a person of loose conduct

行将 xíngjiāng *formal* be about to; be just going to; be on the verge of: ～就道 be about to set out on a journey / ～灭亡的反动势力 reactionary forces on the verge of extinction / ～完工。The project will soon be completed.

行将就木 xíngjiāng jiùmù be getting closer and closer to the coffin—be fast approaching death; have one foot

in the grave

行脚　xíngjiǎo　(of a monk) travel far and wide

行脚僧　xíngjiǎosēng　itinerant monk

行劫　xíngjié　commit robbery; rob

行进　xíngjìn　(usu. of troops) march forward; advance

行经[1]　xíngjīng　*physiol.*　menstruate; be in the period

行经[2]　xíngjīng　go (or pass) by: 火车～沈阳的时候, 已是半夜了。 It was midnight when the train passed through Shenyang.

行径　xíngjìng　*derog.*　act; action; move: 侵略～ act of aggression / 野蛮～ barbarous act / 一切扩张主义的～是注定要失败的。 All expansionist moves are doomed to failure.

行酒　xíngjiǔ　*formal*　serve a round of liquor to the guests

行军　xíngjūn　(of troops) march: ～警戒 protection while on the move; security on the march

行军床　xíngjūnchuáng　camp bed; camp cot; a light-weight folding bed

行军锅　xíngjūnguō　field cauldron

行军壶　xíngjūnhú　canteen

行军灶　xíngjūnzào　field kitchen

行乐　xínglè　*formal*　indulge in pleasures; seek amusement; make merry

行礼　xínglǐ　① salute ② *dial.*　present gifts

行李　xíngli　luggage; baggage: 超重～ excess luggage / 手提～ hand-luggage

行李车　xínglichē　① luggage van; baggage car ② luggage cart

行李寄存处　xíngli jìcúnchù　left-luggage office; checkroom

行李架　xínglijià　luggage rack; baggage rack

行李卷儿　xínglijuǎnr　bedroll; bedding roll; bedding pack

行李票　xínglipiào　luggage (or baggage) check

行猎　xíngliè　*formal*　go hunting

行令　xínglìng　play drinking games

行旅　xínglǚ　traveller; wayfarer: ～称便 travellers find it convenient

行囊　xíngnáng　*formal*　travelling bag

行骗　xíngpiàn　practise fraud; swindle; cheat: 用伪钞～ cheat with counterfeit bank notes

行期　xíngqī　date of departure: ～已近。 The date of departure is drawing near。/ 推迟～ postpone one's trip

行乞　xíngqǐ　beg one's bread; beg alms; beg

行腔　xíngqiāng　(in traditional opera) an actor's rendering of an operatic tune

行窃　xíngqiè　steal; thieve: 在～时被抓住 be caught in the act of stealing

行箧　xíngqiè　*formal*　travelling box

行人　xíngrén　pedestrian; foot traveller: ～走便道。 Pedestrians, keep to the sidewalk (or footpath)! / 公路上～稀少。 There were very few pedestrians on the highway.

行人情　xíng rénqíng　do what is required of social etiquette (as offering congratulations, expressing condolences, sending gifts on certain occasions)

行若无事　xíng ruò wú shì　behave as if nothing had happened

行色　xíngsè　circumstances or style of departure: 以壮～ (give a grand send-off, etc.) to enable sb. to depart in style

行色匆匆　xíngsè cōngcōng　be in a hurry to set out

行善　xíngshàn　do good; do kind deeds; practise philanthropy: ～人 philanthropist; a charitable person

行商　xíngshāng　itinerant trader; travelling merchant; pedlar

行赏　xíngshǎng　give awards; dispense rewards or honours

行尸走肉　xíngshī-zǒuròu　a walking corpse—one who vegetates; an utterly worthless person

行时　xíngshí　① (of a thing) be in vogue; be all the rage ② (of a person) be in the ascendant

行使　xíngshǐ　exercise; perform: ～检察权 exercise procuratorial authority / ～职权 exercise one's functions and powers / ～主权 exercise sovereignty

行驶　xíngshǐ　(of a vehicle, ship, etc.) go; ply; travel: 列车向南～。 The train is going south。/ 长江下游可以～万吨轮。 The lower reaches of the Changjiang River are navigable by 10,000-ton steamers。/ 汽车正以每小时八十公里的速度～着。 The car was doing eighty kilometres an hour.

行事　xíngshì　① act; handle matters: 按计划～ act according to plan ② behaviour; conduct: 言谈～ speech and conduct

行书　xíngshū　running hand (in Chinese calligraphy)

行署　xíngshǔ　short for 行政公署 xíngzhèng gōngshǔ

行述　xíngshù　a brief biography of a deceased person (usu. accompanying an obituary notice)

行水　xíngshuǐ　*formal*　① flowing water ② (of boats) travel on water ③ prevent floods by water control ④ inspect rivers for purposes of flood control

行同狗彘　xíng tóng gǒu-zhì　behave like dogs and pigs

行头　xíngtou　① actor's costumes and paraphernalia ② *humor.*　dress; clothing; apparel; outfit: 她的～可多了。 She has a large wardrobe。/ 新娘的～ a bride's outfit (or apparel)

行为　xíngwéi　action; behaviour; conduct: 正义的～ righteous action / 不法的～ an illegal act / ～不端 dishonourable behaviour; bad conduct

行为主义　xíngwéizhǔyì　*psychol.*　behaviourism

行文　xíngwén　① style or manner of writing: 这篇作文～流畅。 This composition reads smoothly。② (of a government office) send an official communication to other organizations: 即将～各部委。 An official communication will soon be sent to all the ministries and commissions.

行销　xíngxiāo　be on sale; sell: ～全国 be on sale throughout the country

行星　xíngxīng　planet

行星际　xíngxīngjì　interplanetary: ～航行 interplanetary flight (or travel)

行刑　xíngxíng　carry out a death sentence; execute

行刑队　xíngxíngduì　executioners; firing squad

行凶　xíngxiōng　commit physical assault or murder; do violence

行医　xíngyī　practise medicine (usu. on one's own)

行吟　xíngyín　hum, chant or sing while taking a stroll

行营　xíngyíng　field headquarters

行辕　xíngyuán　field headquarters

行远自迩　xíng yuǎn zì ěr　no matter how distant your goal, you must start from where you are—in doing anything we must proceed step by step, from near to far

行云流水　xíngyún-liúshuǐ　(of style of writing) like floating clouds and flowing water—natural and spontaneous: 苏轼认为作文应如水, "行于所当行, 止于所不可不止。" Su Shi believed that writing should resemble floating clouds and flowing water, "going whither it wants to go and stopping whenever it is right to stop."

行在　xíngzài　*old*　temporary lodging for an emperor on tour

行灶　xíngzào　makeshift cooking stove

行者　xíngzhě　① *formal*　passerby ② a Buddhist monk prior to his tonsure

行政　xíngzhèng　administration: 管～ be in charge of administrative affairs / ～部门 administrative department; executive branch; administration / ～单位

administrative unit / ～委员会 administrative council

行政处分 xíngzhèng chǔfèn administrative sanction; disciplinary sanction

行政村 xíngzhèngcūn administrative village (a grassroots administrative unit in some old liberated areas during the War of Resistance Against Japan and the early days of liberation)

行政公署 xíngzhèng gōngshǔ administrative office (within a province)

行政管理 xíngzhèng guǎnlǐ administration

行政命令 xíngzhèng mìnglìng administrative decree (or order)

行政区 xíngzhèngqū administrative area

行政人员 xíngzhèng rényuán administrative personnel (or staff)

行政长官 xíngzhèng zhǎngguān chief executive

行之有效 xíng zhī yǒuxiào effective (in practice); effectual: ～的办法 effective measures

行止 xíngzhǐ *formal* ① whereabouts: ～不明 whereabouts unknown / ～无定 there's no telling where sb. is ② behaviour; conduct: ～有亏 His conduct has some shortcomings.

行舟 xíngzhōu sail a boat; navigate

行装 xíngzhuāng outfit for a journey; luggage: 整理～ pack (for a journey)

行状 xíngzhuàng same as 行述 xíngshù

行踪 xíngzōng whereabouts; track: ～不定 be of uncertain whereabouts / 特务企图隐匿～。The spy tried to cover his tracks.

行走 xíngzǒu walk: 起重机下，禁止～或停留。Walking or standing under the crane is prohibited. / 他在崎岖的山路上艰难地～着。He was trudging laboriously on the rugged mountain path.

形

xíng ① form; shape: 鸡心～的胸针 a heart-shaped brooch ② body; entity: 形影不离 xíng-yǐng bù lí ③ appear; look: 喜形于色 xǐ xíng yú sè ④ compare; contrast: 相形之下 xiāng xíng zhī xià

形变 xíngbiàn *phys.* deformation: 弹性～ elastic deformation

形成 xíngchéng take shape; form: 石灰岩经地下水长时期的侵蚀，～岩洞。Caves are formed by the erosion of limestone by groundwater over many thousands of years. / 一种切实可行的经济体制正在～。A viable economy is shaping up. / 近代自然科学是从有了实验科学之后才～的。Modern natural science came into being only after the emergence of experimental science. / 这个艺术团已经～了独特的风格。This performing arts troupe has evolved a style of its own. / ～鲜明的对比 form a sharp contrast / ～风气 become a common practice

形成层 xíngchéngcéng *bot.* cambium

形单影只 xíngdān-yǐngzhǐ a solitary form, a single shadow—extremely lonely; solitary

形而上学 xíng'érshàngxué *philos.* metaphysics

形格势禁 xínggé-shìjìn be hampered by circumstances; be in an unfavourable situation

形骸 xínghái *formal* the human skeleton; the human body

形迹 xíngjì ① a person's movements and expression: 不露～ betray nothing in one's expression and movements ② formality: 不拘～ without formality; not standing on ceremony

形迹可疑 xíngjì kěyí of suspicious appearance; suspicious-looking: 你进大楼时看到什么～的人没有? Did you notice anyone suspicious-looking when you came into the building?

形旁 xíngpáng (also 形符 xíngfú) *linguis.* the pictographic element of a pictophonetic character which indicates a general category of meaning (e.g., the pictophonetic characters 草 "grass," 花 "flower," and 芳 "fragrant" share the pictographic element 艹 "grass")——see also 形声 xíngshēng

形容 xíngróng ① *formal* appearance; countenance: ～枯槁 look haggard ② describe: 难以～ difficult to describe; beyond description

形容词 xíngróngcí *gram.* adjective

形容憔悴 xíngróng qiáocuì wan-looking; thin and pallid

形声 xíngshēng pictophonetic characters, with one element indicating meaning and the other sound, e.g. 江 "river"—one of the six categories of Chinese characters (六书)

形胜 xíngshèng *formal* with favourable geographical conditions: ～之地 advantageous terrain

形式 xíngshì form; shape: 艺术～ art form / 组织～ organizational makeup / 以公开信～提出建议 put suggestions in the form of an open letter / 那次选举只不过是个～。The elections were conducted only as a matter of form. / ～地看问题 consider a question in a mechanical way

形式逻辑 xíngshì luójí *log.* formal logic

形式上 xíngshìshang in form; formal: ～的一致 formal unity / ～的独立 nominal independence / 在～保持外交关系 maintain formal diplomatic relations

形式主义 xíngshìzhǔyì formalism

形势 xíngshì ① terrain; topographical features: ～险要 strategically important terrain ② situation; circumstances: ～越来越好。The situation is getting better and better. / ～逼人。The situation is pressing. or The situation demands immediate action. / ～发展的必然结果 the inevitable result of developing circumstances

形似 xíngsì likeness in form or appearance; formal likeness (or resemblance): 绘画不仅要求～，而且要求神似。Painters aim at a likeness not only in appearance, but also in spirit. / 士大夫游戏翰墨，妙在意足，不求～。(吴太素) In scholar-officials' playing with brush and ink, excellence consists in meaning's being there, not in the attempt to capture formal likeness.

形态 xíngtài ① form; shape; pattern: 社会经济～ social-economic formation; the economic formation of society ② *gram.* morphology

形态学 xíngtàixué ① *biol.* morphology ② *gram.* morphology

形体 xíngtǐ ① shape (of a person's body); physique; body ② form and structure: 汉字的～ the form of Chinese characters

形同虚设 xíng tóng xūshè perform practically no function: 这个机构～。This organization is nothing but an empty shell.

形相 xíngxiàng outward appearance; exterior; looks

形象 xíngxiàng ① image; form; figure: 图画教学通过～发展儿童认识事物的能力。The use of pictures in classroom teaching helps children to understand things through images. ② literary or artistic image; imagery: 塑造英雄～ create images of heroes and heroines / 这个电视剧～地表现了拓荒者们坚韧不拔的精神。The teleplay vividly depicts the dauntless spirit of the trailblazers.

形象思维 xíngxiàng sīwéi thinking in (terms of) images: 诗是运用～的。Poetry conveys ideas by means of images.

形销骨立 xíngxiāo-gǔlì be all (or mere) skin and bones; be worn to a shadow of one's former self; be just a skeleton

形形色色 xíngxíngsèsè of every hue; of all shades; of all forms; of every description: ～的时髦衣裙 fashionable dresses and skirts of every colour and design / ～的反动派 reactionaries of every hue / ～的错误思想

erroneous ideas of every description

形影不离 xíng-yǐng bù lí　be inseparable as body and shadow; be always together

形影相吊 xíng-yǐng xiāng diào　body and shadow comforting each other——extremely lonely; sad and solitary ——see also 茕茕孑立, 形影相吊 qióngqióng jié lì, xíng-yǐng xiāng diào

形影相随 xíng-yǐng xiāng suí　be as close as body and shadow; be always together

形于辞色 xíngyú císè　show in one's words and expression: 他欣喜之情，～。 There was joy in his words and on his face.

形制 xíngzhì　structure; design: ～古朴 a design of primitive simplicity

形诸笔墨 xíng zhū bǐmò　commit to writing

形状 xíngzhuàng　form; appearance; shape: 凤梨和苹果～不同。 A pineapple is different in shape from an apple.

形"左"实右 xíng "zuǒ" shí yòu　"Left" in form but Right in essence

饧(餳)

xíng ① *formal* treacle; molasses; syrup ② (of dough, sweets, etc.) get soft; get sticky: 让和好的面～一～。 Let the dough stand and soften a bit. / 奶糖～了。 These toffees have got soft and sticky. ③ (of eyes) drowsy; sleepy: 她的眼睛发～, 眼看就要睡着了。 Her eyelids drooped. She looked as if she was falling asleep.

型

xíng ① mould: 砂型 shāxíng ② model; type; pattern: 人类血液分为 O～、A～、B～和 AB～四种血型。 Human blood is classified into four blood types (*or* blood groups), namely, type O, type A, type B and type AB.

型板 xíngbǎn　*mech.*　template; templet

型锻 xíngduàn　*mech.*　swaged forging; swaging

型钢 xínggāng　*metall.*　section steel; shape

型钢轧机 xínggāng zhájī　shape rolling mill

型号 xínghào　model; type: 他的车子是什么牌子、什么～的? What make and model is his car?

型砂 xíngshā　moulding sand

型心 xíngxīn　*metall.*　core: 干砂～ baked core / 粘土～ loam core

硎

xíng　*formal*　① whetstone ② grind; polish

xǐng

省

xǐng ① examine oneself critically: 吾日三～吾身。《论语》 I daily examine myself on three points. ② visit (esp. one's parents or elders): 省亲 xǐngqīn ③ become conscious; be aware: 不省人事 bù xǐng rénshì ——see also shěng

省察 xǐngchá　examine oneself critically; examine one's thoughts and conduct

省墓 xǐngmù　*formal*　visit one's parents' or elders' graves

省亲 xǐngqīn　pay a visit to one's parents or elders (living at another place)

省视 xǐngshì　① call upon; pay a visit to ② examine carefully; inspect

省悟 xǐngwù　same as 醒悟 xǐngwù

醒

xǐng ① regain consciousness; sober up; come to: 酒醉未～ be drunk and not sobered up yet / 他昏迷了三天, 刚刚～过来。 He was unconscious for three days and has just come to. ② wake up; be awake: 今天早晨我～得早。 I woke up early this morning. / ～一～! Wake up! / 半夜里一声怪响把我吵～了。 In the middle of the night, a strange noise woke me up. / 他还～着呢。 He is still awake. ③ be clear in mind: 清醒 qīngxǐng ④ be striking; catch one's attention: 醒目 xǐngmù

醒盹儿 xǐngdǔnr　*dial.*　wake up from a nap; shake off drowsiness

醒豁 xǐnghuò　clear; explicit: 道理说得～。 The argument is clearly presented.

醒酒 xǐngjiǔ　dispel the effects of alcohol; sober up: 浓茶可以用来～。 Strong tea can help to dispel the effects of alcohol. / 吃个梨醒醒酒。 Have a pear to sober yourself up.

醒木 xǐngmù　story-teller's gavel

醒目 xǐngmù　(of written words or pictures) catch the eye; attract attention; be striking to the eye: ～的标语 eye-catching slogans / ～的标题 bold headlines

醒脾 xǐngpí　① be amusing; be entertaining ② (often used with the preposition 拿) tease; make fun of: 你这是拿我～! You're making fun of me.

醒世 xǐngshì　rouse the public; awaken the world: ～之言 words to rouse the public / 冯梦龙《～恒言》 Feng Menglong's *Lasting Words to Awaken the World* (a collection of stories)

醒睡 xǐngshuì　keep alert while in bed; sleep very lightly: 你得～着点儿, 有什么动静就起来。 You must keep alert in bed and be ready to get up at the slightest sound.

醒悟 xǐngwù　come to realize (*or* see) the truth, one's error, etc.; wake up to reality

醒眼 xǐngyǎn　*dial.*　(of written words or pictures) catch the eye; attract attention; be striking to the eye

擤(搇)

xǐng　blow (one's nose): ～鼻涕 blow one's nose

xìng

兴(興)

xìng　mood or desire to do sth.; interest; excitement: 助兴 zhùxìng / 雅兴 yǎxìng ——see also xīng

兴冲冲 xìngchōngchōng　(do sth.) with joy and expedition; excitedly: 他～地跑进来, 告诉我这个好消息。 He rushed into the room excitedly and told me the good news.

兴高采烈 xìnggāo-cǎiliè　in high spirits; excited; jubilant: 人们～地参加祝捷大会。 People were jubilant at the victory celebration. / 孩子们听说去动物园都～。 The children were all excited when they heard they were going to the zoo.

兴会 xìnghuì　a sudden flash of inspiration; brain wave: 这首诗是乘一时的～写成的。 This poem was improvised on the spur of the moment. / 万方乐奏有于阗, 诗人～更无前。(毛泽东) Here is music from all our peoples, from Yutian too, And the poet is inspired as never before.

兴趣 xìngqù　interest: 对文学产生了～ become interested in literature / 怀着极大的～观看农民画家的作品 look at the paintings by peasant artists with great interest / 我对下棋不感～。 I'm not interested in chess.

兴头 xìngtóu　enthusiasm; keen interest: 我们厂的工人对体育活动～可大了。 The workers of our factory are very keen on sport.

兴头儿上 xìngtóurshàng　at the height of one's enthusiasm: 小青年们跳舞正在～, 忘记了休息。 The young people were dancing in such high spirits that they forgot to go to bed.

兴味 xìngwèi interest: 青少年们～盎然地阅读各种新出版的小说。Teen-agers read the newly-published novels with keen interest.

兴味索然 xìngwèi suǒrán have lost all interest in sth.; be bored stiff: 大凡一件事的性质由"消遣的"而变为"义务的"，便觉得～。Any pastime which is converted into an obligation loses its taste.

兴致 xìngzhì interest; mood to enjoy: 他对集邮的～很浓。He's very much interested in collecting stamps.

兴致勃勃 xìngzhì bóbó full of zest; in high spirits

杏
xìng apricot

杏脯 xìngfǔ sun-dried sweetened apricot; preserved sweetened apricot

杏红 xìnghóng yellowish pink; apricot pink

杏核儿 xìnghúr inf. apricot stone

杏黄 xìnghuáng pinkish yellow; apricot (colour)

杏仁 xìngrén apricot kernel; almond

性
xìng ① nature: 天命之谓～。What is God-given is called nature. ② character; disposition: 本性 běnxìng / 性急 xìngjí ③ property; quality: 弹性 tánxìng / 药性 yàoxìng ④ a suffix designating a specified quality, property, scope, etc.: 科学～ the state or quality of being scientific / 综合～ comprehensive / 先天～ congenital ⑤ sex: ～的要求 sexual desire ⑥ gram. gender: 阳性 yángxìng / 阴性 yīnxìng

性爱 xìng'ài love between the sexes; sexual love; love

性别 xìngbié sexual distinction; sex

性别歧视 xìngbié qíshì sexism; sexual discrimination; discrimination against women

性病 xìngbìng venereal disease; V. D.

性感 xìnggǎn sex appeal; sexiness: 那个女演员很～。That actress has a lot of sex appeal (or is awfully sexy).

性格 xìnggé nature; disposition; temperament: ～开朗 have a bright and cheerful disposition

性激素 xìngjīsù physiol. sex hormone

性急 xìngjí impatient; short-tempered

性交 xìngjiāo ① sexual intercourse ② make love; have sex

性教育 xìngjiàoyù sex education

性灵 xìnglíng ① formal personality; temperament; character: 陶冶～ mould a person's temperament, personality, etc. ② intelligent; bright; brilliant: 我还不曾遇到过这样～的学生。I've never had any student as brilliant as he is.

性命 xìngmìng life (of a man or animal): 差一点儿把～丢了 nearly lose one's life; narrowly escape death

性命交关 xìngmìng jiāoguān (also 性命攸关 xìngmìng yōuguān) (a matter) of life and death; of vital importance

性能 xìngnéng function (of a machine, etc.); performance; property: ～试验 performance test / 反应堆～ reactor behaviour / 阻冻～ antifreezing property / 这种电脑～良好。This kind of computer performs satisfactorily.

性气 xìngqì temper; temperament; character: ～不好 bad-tempered

性器官 xìngqìguān physiol. sexual organs; genitals

性情 xìngqíng disposition; temperament; temper: ～温柔 have a gentle disposition / ～暴躁 have an irascible temperament; be short-tempered

性骚扰 xìngsāorǎo sexual harassment

性卫生 xìngwèishēng sex hygiene

性腺 xìngxiàn physiol. sexual (or sex) gland

性行为 xìngxíngwéi sexual behaviour; sex act

性学 xìngxué sexology

性欲 xìngyù sexual desire (or urge): ～冲动 sexual impulse; sexual excitement

性知识 xìngzhīshi sex knowledge

性质 xìngzhì quality; nature; character: 硫酸的化学～ the chemical properties of sulphuric acid / 弄清问题的～ ascertain the nature of the problem / 中国革命的～ the character of the Chinese revolution

性状 xìngzhuàng shape and properties; properties; character: 土壤的理化～ the physicochemical properties of soil / 显性～ dominant character / ～分歧 character divergence

性子 xìngzi ① temper: 使～ get into a temper / 这匹马的～很野。This is a vicious horse. ② strength; potency: 这药～平和。This is a mild drug. / 这酒的～很烈。This liquor is very strong.

幸[1]
xìng ① fortunate; lucky: 荣幸 róngxìng / 不幸 bùxìng ② rejoice: 庆幸 qìngxìng ③ formal (I) hope; (I) trust: ～勿推却。I hope that you will not refuse. or Pray do not refuse. ④ fortunately; luckily: ～未成灾。Fortunately it didn't cause a disaster. / 该工程在雨季来临前～告完成。Happily the project was completed before the rainy season set in. ⑤ (of a monarch) tour one's dominions: 巡幸 xúnxìng

幸[2] (倖)
xìng formal (imperial) favour: 得～ get imperial favours

幸臣 xìngchén derog. a favourite at the court; court favourite; favourite courtier

幸而 xìng'ér adv. luckily; fortunately: ～是你。Luckily it was you and not anyone else.

幸福 xìngfú ① happiness; well-being: 人生的～ happiness of life / 为人民谋～ work for the well-being of the people / 祝你～。I wish you happiness. ② happy: ～的回忆 happy memories / 老人在敬老院里过着～的晚年。In the Home of Respect for the Aged, the old people are leading a happy life in their remaining years.

幸好 xìnghǎo same as 幸亏 xìngkuī

幸会 xìnghuì pol. (a rather formal greeting) very pleased to meet you: 久仰, 久仰!～,～! I am most honoured to meet you after hearing so much about you!

幸亏 xìngkuī adv. fortunately; luckily: 我～走得早, 才没叫雨淋了。Luckily I left early and wasn't caught in the rain. / ～你提醒我, 不然我就忘了。I'm happy you reminded me; otherwise I would have forgotten all about it.

幸免 xìngmiǎn escape by sheer luck; have a narrow escape: ～于难 escape death by sheer luck; escape death by a hair's breadth / 侵略者在村里大肆屠杀, 连小孩也难～。The invaders massacred the villagers, not even sparing little children.

幸甚 xìngshèn formal be very lucky; be blessed indeed: 如是则国家～, 民族～。If so, blessed indeed are the country and the people.

幸事 xìngshì a piece of good fortune; a stroke of luck; blessing

幸喜 xìngxǐ same as 幸亏 xìngkuī

幸运 xìngyùn ① good fortune; good luck ② fortunate; lucky

幸运儿 xìngyùn'ér fortune's favourite; lucky fellow: 她是个～。She was born under a lucky star (or with a silver spoon in her mouth).

幸灾乐祸 xìngzāi-lèhuò take pleasure in (or gloat over) other people's misfortune

姓
xìng surname; family (or clan) name: 他～王。He is surnamed Wang. or His surname is Wang. / 您贵姓?——敝～陈。May I know your surname?——(My surname is) Chen.

姓名　xìngmíng　surname and personal name; full name

姓甚名谁　xìngshènmíngshéi　what one's full name is: 你不问问他～，就让他把东西拿走，太荒唐了! It's ridiculous that you should let him take the thing away without as much as asking for his name.

姓氏　xìngshì　surname: 以～笔划为序 arranged in the order of the number of strokes in the surnames

荇(莕)　xìng　see below

荇菜　xìngcài　floating heart (*Nymphoides peltatum*)

悻　xìng　see below

悻然　xìngrán　enraged

悻悻　xìngxìng　angry; resentful: ～而去 go away angry; leave in a huff

xiōng

凶[1]　xiōng　① inauspicious; ominous: 凶兆 xiōngzhào / 吉凶未卜 jí-xiōng wèi bǔ ② bad for crops; unproductive; threatened with famine: 凶年 xiōngnián

凶[2](兇)　xiōng　① fierce; ferocious: 这个人样子真～. This chap looks really fierce. ② terrible; fearful: 病势很～ be terribly ill / 闹得太～了! What a terrific row! / 这场雨来势很～. The rain came down with a vengeance. ③ act of violence; murder: 行凶 xíngxiōng

凶暴　xiōngbào　fierce and brutal

凶残　xiōngcán　① fierce and cruel; savage and cruel: ～成性 be cruel by nature ② *formal* a fierce and cruel person

凶多吉少　xiōngduō-jíshǎo　bode ill rather than well; be fraught with grim possibilities

凶恶　xiōng'è　(of temper, appearance or behaviour) fierce; ferocious; fiendish

凶犯　xiōngfàn　one who has committed homicide or mayhem; murderer

凶服　xiōngfú　*formal* mourning apparel

凶悍　xiōnghàn　fierce and tough

凶耗　xiōnghào　news of sb.'s death; death notice

凶狠　xiōnghěn　① fierce and malicious ② powerful; vigorous: 拼抢～ scramble furiously for a ball / 射门～ make powerful shots at the goal

凶横　xiōnghèng　fierce and arrogant; rude and ferocious

凶狂　xiōngkuáng　fierce; savage; ferocious

凶猛　xiōngměng　violent; ferocious: 山洪来势～. The mountain torrents rushed down with a devastating force. / 虎豹都是～的野兽 Both tigers and leopards are ferocious beasts.

凶年　xiōngnián　a year of crop failure or famine; a famine year; a bad year

凶虐　xiōngnüè　brutal; tyrannical

凶殴　xiōng'ōu　strike vicious blows (at sb.)

凶气　xiōngqì　fierce manner; ferocious expression: 满脸～ with murder written on one's face

凶器　xiōngqì　a tool or weapon for criminal purposes; a lethal weapon

凶杀　xiōngshā　homicide; murder: 这是一起～案. This is a case of murder.

凶神　xiōngshén　demon; fiend

凶神恶煞　xiōngshén-èshà　devils; fiends

凶事　xiōngshì　① unlucky incidents—deaths, burials, etc. ② violence that involves casualties—killings, hostilities, etc.

凶手　xiōngshǒu　murderer; assassin; assailant (who has caused injury to sb.)

凶死　xiōngsǐ　die by violence; meet a violent end; get killed or kill oneself

凶岁　xiōngsuì　*formal* a year of crop failure or famine; a famine year; a bad year

凶徒　xiōngtú　ruffian; cut-throat

凶险　xiōngxiǎn　① dangerous; perilous; critical: 病情～ dangerously ill; critically ill; in a critical condition / 情势～ / in a very dangerous situation ② ruthless and treacherous

凶相　xiōngxiàng　ferocious features; fierce look; fiendish look: 一脸的～ look fiendish

凶相毕露　xiōngxiàng bìlù　look thoroughly ferocious; unleash all one's ferocity

凶信　xiōngxìn　news of sb.'s death

凶焰　xiōngyàn　ferocity; aggressive arrogance: ～万丈 swell with aggressive arrogance

凶宅　xiōngzhái　a haunted house; an unlucky abode

凶兆　xiōngzhào　ill omen; boding of evil

兄　xiōng　① elder brother: 胞～ elder brother of the same parents ② elder male relative of the same generation: 姻～ elder brother-in-law ③ a courteous form of address between male friends: 王～，久违了! Hi, Wang! Haven't seen you for ages!

兄弟　xiōngdì　① brothers: ～二人都还没结婚. Neither of the two brothers is married. / 我们～三人都是新闻工作者. We three brothers are all journalists. / 阶级～ class brothers ② fraternal; brotherly: ～情谊 fraternal affection / ～般的团结 fraternal solidarity; brotherly unity / ～单位 fraternal units (i.e. units having common purposes, interests, etc.)

兄弟　xiōngdi　*inf.* ① younger brother ② a familiar form of address for a man younger than oneself: 大～, 这件事就托你了. And so, brother, I'll leave the matter in your hands. ③ *hum.* (used by a man, usu. in a public speech) I

兄弟阋墙　xiōngdì xìqiáng　quarrel between brothers; internal dispute

兄弟阋于墙，外御其侮　xiōngdì xì yú qiáng, wài yù qí wǔ　brothers quarrelling at home join forces against attacks from without; internal disunity dissolves at the threat of external invasion

兄嫂　xiōng-sǎo　one's elder brother and his wife

兄长　xiōngzhǎng　① a respectful form of address for an elder brother ② a respectful form of address for a male friend

芎　xiōng　see below

芎䓖　xiōngqióng　same as 川芎 chuānxiōng

匈　xiōng　*arch.* breast

匈奴　Xiōngnú　Xiongnu, or the Huns, an ancient nationality in China

匈牙利　Xiōngyálì　Hungary

匈牙利人　Xiōngyálìrén　Hungarian

匈牙利语　Xiōngyálìyǔ　Hungarian (language)

讻(訩、哅)　xiōng　see below

讻讻　xiōngxiōng　same as 汹汹 xiōngxiōng

汹(洶)　xiōng　see below

汹汹　xiōngxiōng　*formal* ① the sound of turbulent waves: 波涛～ roaring waves ② violent; truculent: 来势～ bear down menacingly ③ tumultuous; agitated: 议论～ tumultuous debate; heated discussion / 群情～. Public feeling ran high. *or* Public opinion was deeply stirred.

汹涌　xiōngyǒng　surging; turbulent; tempestuous: 波涛～ turbulent waves / ～的洪水威胁着堤坝的安全.

The surging floodwaters threatened the dykes and dams. / 革命洪流～向前。Th raging tide of revolution surges forward.

汹涌澎湃 xiōngyǒng péngpài surging; turbulent; tempestuous: ～的历史潮流 a tempestuous historical trend / 人们像一股潮水似的～地直涌到大厅门口。People surged towards the entrance to the hall like a raging torrent.

胸（胷）

xiōng ① thorax; chest; breast; bosom: 孩子把脸贴在母亲的～前。The child buried its face in its mother's bosom. ② mind; heart: 心胸 xīnxiōng / 胸襟 xiōngjīn

胸靶 xiōngbǎ chest silhouette (used as a target in shooting practice)

胸部 xiōngbù thorax; chest: ～手术 thoracic operation

胸次 xiōngcì formal heart; mind; frame of mind: ～舒畅 have ease of mind; feel happy; be in a happy frame of mind

胸骨 xiōnggǔ physiol. sternum; breastbone

胸怀[1] xiōnghuái mind; heart: ～坦白 openhearted; frank / ～狭窄 narrow-minded; small-minded / ～宽广 broad-minded / 暖人～的同志情谊 heartwarming comradeship / 共产主义者的伟大～ a communist's breadth of vision

胸怀[2] xiōnghuái keep in the mind; cherish: ～大志 cherish high ideals; have lofty aspirations

胸甲 xiōngjiǎ cuirass; breastplate

胸襟 xiōngjīn mind; breadth of mind: ～开阔 broad-minded; large-minded / ～狭窄 narrow-minded; small-minded

胸口 xiōngkǒu the pit of the stomach; chest: 我～疼得厉害。I have severe pains in my chest.

胸膜 xiōngmó physiol. pleura

胸膜炎 xiōngmóyán med. pleurisy

胸脯 xiōngpú chest; breast: 挺起～ throw out one's chest / 拍～保证 strike one's chest as a gesture of guarantee or reassurance / 鸡～ chicken breast

胸鳍 xiōngqí pectoral fin

胸腔 xiōngqiāng thoracic cavity; chest cavity

胸墙 xiōngqiáng mil. breastwork; parapet

胸膛 xiōngtáng chest: 挺起～ throw out one's chest

胸围 xiōngwéi chest measurement; bust: 量～ measure one's bust / 他～90厘米。He measures 90 cm. round the chest.

胸无城府 xiōng wú chéngfǔ artless; simple and candid

胸无点墨 xiōng wú diǎn mò unlearned; unlettered

胸无宿物 xiōng wú sùwù frank; candid; guileless

胸像 xiōngxiàng (sculptured) bust

胸臆 xiōngyì what is deep in one's heart; thoughts or feelings deep in one's heart: 直抒～ pour out one's heart

胸有成竹 xiōng yǒu chéngzhú have a well-thought-out plan, stratagem, etc.: 明年的生产计划, 厂长已～。The factory director has a well-thought-out plan for next year's production.

胸章 xiōngzhāng badge

胸罩 xiōngzhào brassiere; bra

胸针 xiōngzhēn brooch

胸中无数 xiōngzhōng wú shù same as 心中无数 xīnzhōng wú shù

胸中有数 xiōngzhōng yǒu shù same as 心中有数 xīnzhōng yǒu shù

胸椎 xiōngzhuī physiol. thoracic vertebra

xióng

雄

xióng ① male; (of plants) staminate: ～猫 male cat; tomcat / ～狮 (male) lion / ～冬青 staminate (or male) holly ② grand; imposing: 雄伟 xióngwěi ③ powerful; mighty: 雄兵 xióngbīng ④ a person or state having great power and influence: 战国七～ the seven powerful states of the Warring States Period (475-221 B.C.)

雄辩 xióngbiàn convincing argument; eloquent speech: 事实胜于雄辩 shìshí shèngyú xióngbiàn ② convincing; eloquent: ～地证明 prove incontrovertibly; be eloquent proof of / 最～的莫过于事实。Nothing is more convincing than facts.

雄兵 xióngbīng a powerful army: ～百万 a million bold warriors

雄才大略 xióngcái-dàlüè (a man of) great talent and bold vision; (a statesman or general of) rare gifts and bold strategy: 此人名虽儒生, 实有～。He is reputed to be a scholar, but really he is a bold and capable man.

雄飞 xióngfēi push ahead vigorously; strive for higher aims

雄风 xióngfēng ① a strong wind ② an awe-inspiring bearing; a stately appearance

雄蜂 xióngfēng drone; male bee

雄关 xióngguān an impregnable pass

雄豪 xióngháo ① hero ② grand and heroic; full of power and grandeur

雄厚 xiónghòu (of strength, resources, etc.) ample; rich; solid; abundant: ～的人力物力 rich human and material resources / 资金～ abundant funds / 国力～ have solid national strength

雄花 xiónghuā bot. male flower; staminate flower

雄黄 xiónghuáng min. realgar; red orpiment

雄黄酒 xiónghuángjiǔ realgar wine (traditionally drunk during the Dragon Boat Festival 端午节 to ward off poisonous creatures)

雄浑 xiónghún vigorous and firm; forceful: ～的诗篇 powerful poetry / 笔力～ vigour of strokes in calligraphy or drawing / ～高亢的乐曲 resounding music

雄鸡 xióngjī cock; rooster: ～报晓。The cock heralds the dawn. / 一唱～天下白。(毛泽东) Now the cock has crowed and all under heaven is bright.

雄激素 xióngjīsù physiol. androgen

雄健 xióngjiàn robust; vigorous; powerful: 迈着～的步伐 in vigorous strides

雄杰 xióngjié ① of exceptional ability; of great talent: ～之士 a man of great talent ② a man of great talent: 一代～ the greatest talent of the time

雄精 xióngjīng Chin. med. realgar; red orpiment

雄劲 xióngjìng vigorous and powerful: 笔势～ forceful strokes (in calligraphy)

雄赳赳 xióngjiūjiū valiant; gallant

雄赳赳，气昂昂 xióngjiūjiū, qì'áng'áng valiant and spirited; full of mettle

雄峻 xióngjùn (of mountains) high, steep and imposing

雄蕊 xióngruǐ bot. stamen

雄师 xióngshī a powerful army; a mighty army

雄图 xióngtú a great ambition; a grandiose plan: ～大业 a grandiose and noble enterprise; a great cause

雄威 xióngwēi full of power and grandeur; strong and imposing; awe-inspiring

雄伟 xióngwěi grand; imposing: ～壮丽 grand; magnificent; sublime / ～的天安门 the magnificent Tian An Men

雄文 xióngwén profound and powerful writing; great works

雄心 xióngxīn great ambitions; lofty aspirations: 树～, 立壮志, 向科学技术现代化进军。Foster lofty ideals, set high goals and march forward for the modernization of science and technology.

雄心勃勃 xióngxīn bóbó very ambitious

雄心壮志 xióngxīn-zhuàngzhì lofty aspirations and high ideals: 树立～ set high aims and have lofty aspirations; set one's sights high

雄性 xióngxìng male

雄性不育 xióngxìng bùyù biol. male sterility: ～系 male-sterile line; A-line / ～保持系 maintain line; B-line / ～恢复系 restorer line; R-line

雄蚁 xióngyǐ male ant; aner

雄主 xióngzhǔ a ruler of great talent and bold vision

雄壮 xióngzhuàng full of power and grandeur; magnificent; majestic: ～的军乐 majestic martial music

雄姿 xióngzī majestic appearance; heroic posture: 喷气式战斗机编队飞行的～ the imposing sight of jet fighters flying in formation / 南京长江大桥的～ a magnificent view of the Changjiang Bridge at Nanjing

雄姿英发 xióngzī yīngfā majestic and spirited; dashing and debonair

熊¹ xióng ① bear: 玩具～ teddy bear / 幼～ bear cub ② (Xióng) a surname

熊² xióng dial. rebuke; upbraid; scold: 挨了一顿～ got a scolding

熊白 xióngbái the fatty portion of a bear's back (a rare delicacy)

熊包 xióngbāo (also 熊蛋包 xióngdànbāo) dial. a good-for-nothing; coward

熊蹯 xióngfán formal bear's paw (a rare delicacy)

熊蜂 xióngfēng bumblebee

熊猴 xiónghóu zool. Assamese macaque

熊猫 xióngmāo panda (popular name for 猫熊)

熊罴 xióngpí fierce fighters; valiant warriors

熊瞎子 xióngxiāzi dial. bear

熊心豹胆 xióngxīn-bàodǎn bear's heart and leopard's gall—fearlessness; courage; guts

熊熊 xióngxióng flaming; ablaze; raging: 手持～燃烧的火炬 bear a blazing torch in hand / ～的烈火 raging flames

熊掌 xióngzhǎng bear's paw (a rare delicacy)

xiòng

诇 xiòng formal reconnoitre; scout; pry; spy

xiū

休¹ xiū ① stop; cease: 争论不～ argue ceaselessly ② rest: ～大礼拜 have every other Sunday off ③ (in former times) cast off one's wife and send her home: ～妻 put one's wife away ④ adv. don't: ～要胡言乱语! Don't talk nonsense! / 闲话～提 No more of this digression.

休² xiū formal good fortune: 休咎 xiū-jiù

休兵 xiūbīng formal stop fighting; have a cease-fire

休怪 xiūguài don't blame: 我们之间的问题解决不了，～我到法院去起诉。Don't blame me for going to court since we can't settle it between us.

休会 xiūhuì adjourn: 无限期～ adjourn indefinitely (or sine die) / 会议～一周。The meeting was adjourned for a week. / ～期间 between sessions; when the meeting stands adjourned / 会议主席宣布～十分钟。The chairman of the meeting announced a ten-minute recess.

休假 xiūjià (of workers, students, etc.) have (or take, go on) a holiday or vacation; (of soldiers, personnel working abroad, etc.) be on leave or furlough: ～一周 have a week's holiday / 回国～ go home on furlough

休咎 xiū-jiù formal good and bad fortune; weal and woe

休刊 xiūkān suspend publication (of a newspaper or journal)

休克 xiūkè med. shock: 电～ electric shock / 病人～了。The patient is suffering from shock.

休眠 xiūmián biol. dormancy

休眠火山 xiūmián huǒshān dormant volcano

休眠期 xiūmiánqī biol. rest period

休眠芽 xiūmiányá bot. resting (or dormant) bud

休戚 xiū-qī weal and woe; joys and sorrows

休戚相关 xiū-qī xiāngguān share joys and sorrows; be bound together by common interests: ～, 患难与共 be bound by a common cause and go through thick and thin together

休戚与共 xiū-qī yǔ gòng share weal and woe; stand together through thick and thin: ～, 生死相依 share weal and woe, and stick together in life and death

休弃 xiūqì (of a husband in feudal China) cast off one's wife and send her home; put one's wife away

休憩 xiūqì have (or take) a rest; rest

休书 xiūshū a bill of divorcement

休息 xiūxi have (or take) a rest; rest: ～一会儿 rest for a while; have a rest / 幕间～ intermission; interval / 课间～ break (between classes) / ～一天 have (or take) a day off / 百货公司元旦不～。The department store is open as usual on New Year's Day.

休息室 xiūxishì lounge; lobby; vestibule; foyer

休闲 xiūxián agri. lie fallow: ～地 fallow (land)

休想 xiūxiǎng don't imagine that it's possible: 你～逃脱。Don't imagine you can get away.

休学 xiūxué suspend one's schooling without losing one's status as a student

休养 xiūyǎng recuperate; convalesce: 逐步扩充劳动者休息和～的物质条件 gradually expand material facilities for the working people to rest and recuperate / 他到北戴河～去了。He has gone to Beidaihe for recuperation.

休养生息 xiūyǎng shēngxī (of a nation) recuperate and multiply; rest and build up strength; rehabilitate: 大战之后, 各国都需要时间～。After a great war, every country needs time to recuperate and multiply its population.

休养所 xiūyǎngsuǒ sanatorium; rest home

休业 xiūyè ① suspend business; be closed down: 今天～。Closed today. ② (of a short-term course, etc.) come to an end; wind up

休战 xiūzhàn truce; cease-fire; armistice: ～状态 (state of) cease-fire

休整 xiūzhěng rest and reorganization (of troops, etc.)

休止 xiūzhǐ stop; cease: 这座火山已进入～状态。The volcano is inactive.

休止符 xiūzhǐfú mus. rest

咻 xiū formal make a din

咻咻 xiūxiū onom. ① the sound of heavy breathing: ～的鼻息 noisy breathing / ～地喘气 pant noisily ② the sound made by certain birds and animals: 小鸭～地叫着。The ducklings are cheeping.

修¹ xiū ① embellish; decorate: 装修 zhuāngxiū ② repair; mend; overhaul: ～收音机 repair a radio / ～鞋 mend shoes ③ write; compile: ～史 write history / ～县志 compile the historical and other records of a county ④ study; cultivate: 自修 zìxiū ⑤ build; construct: ～铁路 build a railway / ～水库 construct a reservoir / ～渠 dig irrigation ditches ⑥ trim; prune: ～指

甲 trim (*or* manicure) fingernails / 〜铅笔 sharpen a pencil ⑦ (short for 修正主义) revisionism ⑧ (Xiū) a surname

修²

　　xiū *formal* long; tall and slender: 茂林〜竹 dense forests and tall bamboos

修补 xiūbǔ ① mend; patch up; repair; revamp: 〜渔网 mend fishing nets / 〜衣服 patch clothes / 〜篱笆 mend a fence ② *med.* repair

修长 xiūcháng tall and thin; slender: 〜身材 a slender figure

修饬 xiūchì *formal* repair and maintain

修船厂 xiūchuánchǎng shipyard; dockyard

修辞 xiūcí rhetoric

修辞格 xiūcígé *linguis.* figures of speech

修辞学 xiūcíxué *linguis.* rhetoric

修道 xiūdào cultivate oneself according to a religious doctrine

修道院 xiūdàoyuàn monastery or convent

修订 xiūdìng revise: 〜条约 revise a treaty / 〜教学计划 revise a teaching plan / 〜课本 revise textbooks

修订本 xiūdìngběn revised edition

修短 xiū-duǎn *formal* length: 身材适中，〜合度 of medium height, neither too tall nor too short

修复 xiūfù ① repair; restore; renovate: 这段铁路已〜通车。This section of the railway has been repaired and reopened to traffic. / 〜有历史意义的建筑物 renovate historic buildings ② *med.* repair (of destroyed cells or tissues)

修改 xiūgǎi revise; modify; amend; alter: 〜计划 revise a plan / 〜宪法 amend (*or* revise) a constitution / 对宣言草案提出建设性的〜意见 submit constructive amendments to the draft declaration / 小修小改 minor alterations

修盖 xiūgài build (houses)

修函 xiūhán *formal* write a letter

修好 xiūhǎo ① *formal* foster cordial relations between states ② *dial.* do good works

修剪 xiūjiǎn prune; trim; clip: 〜果枝 prune fruit trees / 〜指甲 trim one's fingernails

修建 xiūjiàn build; construct; erect: 〜机场 build an airport / 〜纪念碑 erect a monument / 〜桥梁 construct a bridge / 〜铁路 build (*or* construct) a railway

修脚 xiūjiǎo pedicure

修脚师 xiūjiǎoshī pedicurist

修旧利废 xiūjiù-lìfèi repair and utilize old or discarded things

修浚 xiūjùn dredge: 〜河道 dredge a river

修理 xiūlǐ ① repair; mend; overhaul; fix: 〜机器 repair (*or* fix) a machine / 正在〜 be under repair / 当场〜，立等可取。Repairs done while you wait. ② prune; trim

修理厂 xiūlǐchǎng fix-it shop; repair shop

修理行业 xiūlǐ hángyè repairing trades

修炼 xiūliàn (of Taoists) practise austerities; practise asceticism

修面 xiūmiàn *dial.* shave; have a shave

修面膏 xiūmiàngāo shaving cream

修面刷 xiūmiànshuā shaving brush

修明 xiūmíng *formal* (of a government) honest and enlightened

修女 xiūnǚ nun (of the Roman Catholic and Greek Orthodox churches); sister: 当〜 become a nun; enter a convent

修配 xiūpèi make repairs and supply replacements: 〜车间 repair and spare parts workshop

修葺 xiūqì repair; renovate: 〜一新 take on a new look after renovation; be completely renovated

修桥补路 xiūqiáo-bǔlù build or repair bridges and mend roads—do philanthropic acts; finance philan-

thropic projects

修润 xiūrùn polish (a piece of writing): 对此文略加〜 touch up this article

修缮 xiūshàn repair; renovate: 〜房屋 repair houses

修身 xiūshēn cultivate one's moral character

修士 xiūshì monk (of the Roman Catholic and Greek Orthodox churches); brother; friar

修饰 xiūshì ① decorate; adorn; embellish: 〜公园，准备迎接五一。The parks are decorated for the May Day celebrations. ② make up and dress up ③ polish (a piece of writing): 请你把这篇稿子〜一下。Please polish this piece of writing. ④ *linguis.* qualify; modify: 定语的作用是〜或限制名词的。An attribute is a word or phrase used to modify or limit the meaning of a noun.

修饰剂 xiūshìjì dressing agent

修饰语 xiūshìyǔ *linguis.* modifier

修书 xiūshū *old* ① compile a book ② write a letter

修仙 xiūxiān train and cultivate oneself to attain immortality

修心养性 xiūxīn-yǎngxìng cultivate oneself through meditation

修行 xiū·xíng practise Buddhism or Taoism: 出家〜 become a Buddhist or Taoist monk or nun

修修补补 xiūxiūbǔbǔ patch up; tinker

修养 xiūyǎng ① accomplishment; training; mastery: 马列主义〜 one's understanding of Marxism-Leninism / 有艺术〜 be artistically accomplished / 在文学上很有〜 be widely read in literature ② accomplishment in self-cultivation; self-possession: 他无论做什么事总是非常稳重，不急躁，的确很有〜。He is always steady and reliable in whatever he does. He is really self-possessed.

修业 xiūyè study at school: 〜年限 length of schooling / 〜期满 one's term of schooling completed

修业证书 xiūyè zhèngshū certificate for the completion of a course of study; certificate showing courses attended

修造 xiūzào build as well as repair: 〜轮船 build or repair ships

修整 xiūzhěng ① repair and maintain: 〜农具 repair and maintain farm implements ② prune; trim: 〜果树 prune fruit trees

修正 xiūzhèng ① revise; amend; correct: 坚持真理，〜错误 uphold the truth and correct one's mistakes / 〜草案 a revised draft / 〜后的决议草案 the draft resolution as amended / 对建议提出〜意见 put forward amendments to the proposal / 不到之处，请予以〜。I stand to be corrected. ② mutilate (Marxism-Leninism); revise

修正案 xiūzhèng'àn amendment

修正角 xiūzhèngjiǎo *aviation* correction angle

修正主义 xiūzhèngzhǔyì revisionism: 〜思潮 revisionist trend / 〜者 revisionist / 〜分子 revisionist element; revisionist

修枝 xiūzhī prune

修枝剪 xiūzhījiǎn pruning scissors; pruning shears

修治 xiūzhì repair and renovate; dredge (a river): 〜河道 the dredging and realignment of a river

修竹 xiūzhú tall bamboos

修筑 xiūzhù build; construct; put up: 〜桥梁 build bridges / 〜工事 construct defences; build fortifications (*or* defence works) / 〜堤坝 put up dykes

修纂 xiūzuǎn *formal* compile

脩¹

　　xiū *old* dried meat as gift to a teacher in lieu of tuition: 脩金 xiūjīn / 束脩 shùxiū

脩²

　　xiū same as 修 xiū

脩金 xiūjīn *old* tuition fees

羞[1] xiū ① shy; bashful: ～红了脸 blush ② make sb. feel ashamed or embarrassed ③ shame; disgrace: 遮羞 zhēxiū ④ feel ashamed: 羞与为伍 xiū yǔ wéiwǔ

羞[2] xiū same as 馐 xiū

羞惭 xiūcán be ashamed: 满面～ be shamefaced

羞耻 xiūchǐ sense of shame; shame: ～之心 sense of shame / 不知～ lose all sense of shame

羞答答 xiūdādā (also 羞羞答答 xiūxiudādā) coy; shy; bashful

羞愤 xiūfèn ashamed and resentful

羞口 xiūkǒu find it difficult to bring the matter up

羞愧 xiūkuì ashamed; abashed: ～难言 be ashamed beyond words / ～地低着头 hang one's head for shame

羞明 xiūmíng med. photophobia

羞赧 xiūnǎn formal blush

羞恼 xiū-nǎo be angry and ashamed

羞怯 xiūqiè shy; timid; sheepish: ～得说不出话来 be too shy to utter a word

羞人 xiūrén feel embarrassed or ashamed: 羞死人了 simply die of shame; feel terribly embarrassed

羞人答答 xiūréndādā feel shy or awkward

羞辱 xiūrǔ ① shame; dishonour; humiliation ② humiliate; put sb. to shame

羞涩 xiūsè shy; bashful; embarrassed

羞恶 xiūwù formal be ashamed of and disgusted with one's own or other people's faults: ～之心, 人皆有之。 Everyone has a sense of shame.

羞与为伍 xiū yǔ wéiwǔ feel ashamed to associate with sb.; think it beneath one to associate with sb.

鸺 xiū see below

鸺鹠 xiūliú owl

馐 xiū formal delicacy; dainty: 珍馐 zhēnxiū

貅 xiū see 貔貅 píxiū

髹(髤) xiū formal coat sth. with lacquer

xiǔ

朽 xiū ① rotten; decayed: 枯木～株 withered trees and rotten stumps ② senile: 老朽 lǎoxiū

朽败 xiǔbài decayed; rotten

朽坏 xiǔhuài decayed; rotten

朽迈 xiǔmài formal old and weak; senile; decrepit

朽木 xiǔmù ① rotten wood or tree ② a hopeless case; a good-for-nothing

朽木粪土 xiǔmù-fèntǔ rotten wood and worthless soil—a worthless person; useless stuff: 朽木不可雕也, 粪土之墙不可圬也。《论语》 Rotten wood cannot be carved, nor a wall of dried dung be trowelled.

宿 xiǔ m. (used for counting nights): 住一～ stay for one night / 谈了半～ chat till midnight ——see also sù; xiù

xiù

秀[1] xiù (of grain crops, etc.) put forth flowers or ears: ～穗 put forth ears

秀[2] xiù ① elegant; beautiful: 秀丽 xiùlì / 清秀 qīng-

xiù ② excellent: 优秀 yōuxiù

秀拔 xiùbá beautiful and forceful: 书法～ a fine and forceful calligraphic style / 文辞～ elegant and forceful language

秀才 xiùcai ① xiucai, one who passed the imperial examination at the county level (in the Ming and Qing Dynasties) ② scholar; skilful writer: 他是我们班里的～。 He is the scholar in our class.

秀才不出门, 能知天下事 xiùcai bù chūmén, néng zhī tiān-xià shì without stepping outside his gate the scholar knows all the wide world's affairs

秀才人情纸半张 xiùcai rénqíng zhǐ bànzhāng a scholar's gift can be a half sheet of paper (i.e. needn't be expensive)

秀而不实 xiù ér bù shí flowering but bearing no fruit —fine in appearance but empty in substance

秀丽 xiùlì beautiful; handsome; pretty: 这个小姑娘长得很～。 This little girl is very pretty. / ～的桂林山水 the beautiful mountains and waters of Guilin

秀美 xiùměi graceful; elegant: 书法～ beautiful handwriting

秀媚 xiùmèi pretty and charming; lovely

秀气 xiùqi ① delicate; elegant; fine: 眉眼生得～ have beautiful eyes / 她的字写得很～。 She writes a beautiful hand. ② (of manners) refined; urbane ③ (of articles of use) delicate and well-made; exquisite: 这表可真～。 The watch is really exquisite.

秀色可餐 xiùsè kě cān be a feast to the eye (usu. said of a very attractive woman, sometimes of beautiful scenery)

秀外慧中 xiùwài-huìzhōng (also 秀外惠中 xiùwài-huìzhōng) beautiful and intelligent

秀雅 xiùyǎ tasteful and refined; graceful; elegant: 服饰～ tastefully dressed and adorned

秀异 xiùyì outstanding; excellent

岫 xiù formal ① cave; cavern ② mountain peak; mountain: 窗中列远～。(谢朓) The distant peaks stand framed in my window.

袖 xiù ① sleeve: 长 (短)～ long (short) sleeves / ～长 the length of the sleeves ② tuck inside the sleeve: 他～着手, 踱来踱去。 He paced the floor, his hands tucked deep in his sleeves. / ～刃 hide a dagger in one's sleeve

袖标 xiùbiāo armband or badge worn on the sleeve for identification

袖管 xiùguǎn dial. sleeve

袖箭 xiùjiàn a dart hidden in the sleeve (for throwing by a spring device)

袖口 xiùkǒu cuff (of a sleeve): 衬衫～ wristband

袖扣 xiùkòu cuff links

袖手旁观 xiùshǒu pángguān look on (or stand by) with folded arms; look on unconcerned: 看到损害国家财产的现象, 不能～。 We must not stand by with folded arms when people damage state property.

袖套 xiùtào oversleeve

袖筒 xiùtǒng sleeve

袖头 xiùtóu dial. cuff (of a sleeve)

袖章 xiùzhāng armband; sleeve badge

袖珍 xiùzhēn pocket-size; pocket: ～式半导体收音机 pocket-size transistor radio / ～计算器 pocket calculator / ～字典 pocket dictionary / ～照相机 vest-pocket camera / ～潜艇 midget submarine

袖珍本 xiùzhēnběn pocket edition

袖子 xiùzi sleeve: 卷起～ roll (or turn) up one's sleeves / 一把抓住他的～ seize him by the sleeve

绣(繡) xiù ① embroider: 她在围裙上～了一

只小白兔。She embroidered a little white rabbit on the apron. / 那孩子的衣服上～着名字。On the child's clothes is embroidered his name. ② embroidery: 苏绣 sūxiù

绣墩 xiùdūn a ceramic stool with an embroidered cover

绣房 xiùfáng old a young lady's bedchamber

绣阁 xiùgé same as 绣房 xiùfáng

绣工 xiùgōng ① embroidery worker ② embroidery; embroidery work

绣花 xiùhuā embroider; do embroidery: ～被面 embroidered quilt cover

绣花丝线 xiùhuā sīxiàn floss silk; embroidery silk

绣花鞋 xiùhuāxié embroidered shoes

绣花针 xiùhuāzhēn embroidery needle

绣花枕头 xiùhuā zhěntou a pillow with an embroidered case—an outwardly attractive but worthless person

绣画 xiùhuà arts & crafts embroidered picture

绣货 xiùhuò embroideries; embroidered works

绣球 xiùqiú a ball made of rolled coloured silk

绣球花 xiùqiúhuā bot. big-leaf hydrangea (hydrangea macrophylla)

绣像 xiùxiàng ① tapestry portrait; embroidered portrait ② exquisitely drawn portrait

绣鞋 xiùxié embroidered shoes

绣眼鸟 xiùyǎnniǎo zool. silvereye; white-eye

臭 xiù ① odour; smell: 纯空气是无色无～的。Pure air is colourless and odourless. ② same as 嗅 xiù ——see also chòu

臭味相投 xiùwèi xiāngtóu have the same tastes, interests, etc.; be kindred spirits ——see also 臭味相投 chòuwèi xiāngtóu

臭腺 xiùxiàn zool. scent gland (a gland which secretes an odoriferous substance)

宿 xiù astron. an ancient term for constellation ——see also sù; xiǔ

锈(鏽) xiù ① rust ② become rusty: 门上的锁～住了。The lock on the door is rusty and won't open.

锈病 xiùbìng agric. rust: 小麦秆～ wheat stem rust

锈菌 xiùjūn rust fungus: 小麦秆～ wheat stem rust fungus

锈蚀 xiùshí corroded by rust; spoilt by rust

溴 xiù chem. bromine (Br)

溴化物 xiùhuàwù chem. bromide

溴水 xiùshuǐ chem. bromine water

溴酸 xiùsuān chem. bromic acid

嗅 xiù smell; scent; sniff: 警犬～来～去, 终于找到了踪迹。The police dog scented about till he found the trail. / 我们对任何东西都要用鼻子～一～, 鉴别其好坏。We should take a sniff at everything and distinguish the good from the bad.

嗅觉 xiùjué (sense of) smell; scent: ～很灵 have a keen sense of smell / 政治～灵敏 be politically sharp

嗅神经 xiùshénjīng physiol. olfactory nerve

xū

圩(墟) xū country fair: 赶～ go to a fair ——see also wéi

圩场 xūcháng dial. country fair; market

戌 xū the eleventh of the twelve Earthly Branches (地支) ——see also 干支 gān-zhī

戌时 xūshí the period of the day from 7 p. m. to 9 p. m.

吁 xū formal ① sigh: 长吁短叹 chángxū-duǎntàn ② interj. (expressing surprise or amazement) why; oh ——see also yū; yù

吁吁 xūxū onom.: 气喘～ pant; puff hard

盱 xū formal look up with eyes wide open

盱衡 xūhéng formal ① stare ② survey; take stock of: ～大局 take stock of the general situation

胥[1] xū ① formal petty official ② (Xū) a surname

胥[2] xū formal all; each and every: 万事～备。Everything is ready.

胥吏 xūlì formal petty official

须[1] xū must; have to: 我们～作出很大努力。We'll have to make a great effort.

须[2] xū formal wait; await: ～我片刻。Wait a moment for me.

须[3] **(鬚)** xū ① beard; mustache: 留～ grow a beard ② zool. palpus; feeler: 触须 chùxū ③ bot. tassel: 花须 huāxū

须发 xū-fà beard and hair: ～皆白 white hair and beard

须根 xūgēn bot. fibrous root

须鲸 xūjīng baleen whale; toothless whale

须眉 xū-méi formal beard and eyebrows—a man

须生 xūshēng another name for 老生 lǎoshēng

须要 xūyào must; have to: 做这项工作～细心。This work needs to be done carefully. / 这问题～好好研究和处理。This problem must be carefully studied and tackled.

须臾 xūyú formal moment; instant: ～之间, 雨过天晴。In an instant the rain stopped and the sky cleared up. / ～不可离 cannot do without even for a moment / 哀我生之～, 羡长江之无穷。(苏轼) I repine at the shortness of life, and envy the Great River its eternal course.

须知 xūzhī ① one should know that; it must be understood (or borne in mind) that: ～胜利来之不易。It must be borne in mind that the victory is hard-won. ② points for attention; notice: 游览～ tourist guide; information for tourists / 旅客～ notice to travellers, passengers, etc.

须子 xūzi ① zool. palpus; feeler: 虾～ feelers of a shrimp ② bot. tassel: 玉米～ tassels of maize

虚 xū ① emptiness; void: 乘虚 chéngxū / 太虚 tàixū ② empty; void; unoccupied: ～位 leave a seat vacant ③ diffident; timid; shy: 胆～ timid; milk-livered / 心里有点～ feel rather diffident ④ in vain: 箭不～发。Not a single arrow missed its target. ⑤ false; nominal: 虚名 xūmíng / 虚构 xūgòu ⑥ humble; modest: 谦虚 qiānxū ⑦ weak; in poor health: 身体很～be very weak physically ⑧ abstract; theory; guiding principles: 以～带实。Let correct ideology guide practical work. ⑨ phys. virtual: ～阴极 virtual cathode ⑩ the eleventh of the twenty-eight constellations (二十八宿) into which the celestial sphere was divided in ancient Chinese astronomy (consisting of two stars in a straight line, one in

Aquarius and the other in Equuleus)

虚报 xūbào　make a false report; report untruthfully: ～帐目 cook accounts; falsify accounts / ～冒领 make a fraudulent application and claim

虚词 xūcí　*gram.* function word; form word

虚诞 xūdàn　absurd; preposterous; fantastic

虚度 xūdù　spend time in vain; waste: 我们不能让青春～。We must not let our youth slip idly by.

虚度光阴 xūdù guāngyīn　fritter away one's time

虚度年华 xūdù niánhuá　idle away one's time; waste one's life

虚浮 xūfú　impractical; superficial: ～的计划 an impractical plan / 作风～ have a superficial style of work

虚根 xūgēn　*math.* imaginary root

虚构 xūgòu　fabricate; make up: ～的情节 a made-up story; a trumped-up story / ～的人物 a fictitious character / 纯属～ an out-and-out fabrication; a sheer fabrication

虚汗 xūhàn　abnormal sweating due to general debility

虚华 xūhuá　ostentation; empty show

虚话 xūhuà　① empty talk; empty words ② lie; falsehood; unfounded statement

虚怀若谷 xūhuái ruò gǔ　have a mind as open as a valley—be extremely modest; be open-minded

虚幻 xūhuàn　unreal; illusory: ～的情景 a mere illusion

虚晃一枪 xū huǎng yī qiāng　feint a thrust with one's spear; make a feint

虚己以听 xū jǐ yǐ tīng　listen to advice with an open mind; listen to criticisms attentively

虚假 xūjiǎ　false; sham: ～证明 false testimony / ～现象 false appearance / ～的安全感 a false sense of security / ～的可能性 spurious possibility / ～的友谊 hypocritical friendship / 我感到他对人有点～。I don't think he is quite honest with people. / 做学问要老老实实，不能有半点～。Academic work must be honest, without any sophistry.

虚价 xūjià　*econ.* nominal price

虚骄 xūjiāo　false pride

虚焦点 xūjiāodiǎn　*phys.* virtual focus

虚惊 xūjīng　false alarm: 受了一场～ be the victim of a false alarm

虚空 xūkōng　hollow; void

虚夸 xūkuā　exaggerative; bombastic; boastful

虚痨 xūláo　*Chin. med.* consumptive disease; consumption

虚礼 xūlǐ　mere formalities; conventional courtesies

虚脉 xūmài　*Chin. med.* feeble pulse

虚名 xūmíng　false reputation; undeserved reputation: 徒有～，并无实学 have a false reputation and no real learning

虚拟 xūnǐ　① invented; fictitious: 这个故事是～的。This is a fictitious story. ② suppositional

虚拟语气 xūnǐ yǔqì　*gram.* the subjunctive mood

虚胖 xūpàng　puffiness

虚飘飘 xūpiāopiāo　shaky; unsteady: 他喝了几杯，感到两腿～的。After a few drinks, he felt quite wobbly.

虚情假意 xūqíng-jiǎyì　a false display of affection; a hypocritical show of friendship

虚荣 xūróng　vanity: 不慕～ not affected by vanity; not vain / 爱慕～ be vain

虚荣心 xūróngxīn　vanity

虚弱 xūruò　① in poor health; weak; debilitated: 病后身体很～ suffer from general debility after an illness; be very weak after an illness / 爷爷近来的身体越发～了。Grandfather has been getting feebler lately. ② weak; feeble: 兵力～ weak in military strength / ～的本质 inherent (*or* intrinsic) weakness / 一切反动派在本质上都是～的。All reactionaries are in essence feeble.

虚设 xūshè　nominal; existing in name only: 形同虚设

xíng tóng xūshè

虚声 xūshēng　① false reputation; undeserved reputation ② an empty show of strength

虚声恫吓 xūshēng dònghè　bluff and bluster

虚实 xū-shí　① false or true—the actual situation (as of the opposing side): 探听～ try to find out about an opponent, etc.; try to ascertain the strength (of the enemy) ② theoretical and practical: ～并举 do both ideological and practical work

虚数 xūshù　① unreliable figure ② *math.* imaginary number

虚岁 xūsuì　nominal age (reckoned by the traditional method, i.e. considering a person one year old at birth and adding a year each lunar new year)

虚套子 xūtàozi　mere formalities; conventionalities

虚土 xūtǔ　*dial.* loosened soil

虚脱 xūtuō　*med.* collapse; prostration

虚妄 xūwàng　unfounded; fabricated; invented: ～的故事 a fabricated story

虚伪 xūwěi　sham; false; hypocritical: 这个人很～。That chap is a hypocrite. / 他为人实在，没有一点～。He is perfectly candid and never two-faced. / 知识的问题是一个科学问题，来不得半点～和骄傲。Knowledge is a matter of science, and no dishonesty or conceit whatsoever is permissible.

虚位以待 xū wèi yǐ dài　(also 虚席以待 xū xí yǐ dài) leave a seat vacant (*or* save a seat) for sb.: 这次宴会你一定要来，我们将～。You must come to the dinner party. We'll have a seat especially for you. / 宁可～，也不要让不称职的人滥竽充数。We'd rather leave the place vacant than have someone incompetent fill the position.

虚温 xūwēn　*meteorol.* virtual temperature

虚文 xūwén　① rules and regulations that have become a dead letter; dead letter ② empty forms: ～浮礼 mere formalities; conventionalities

虚无 xūwú　nihility; nothingness

虚无缥缈 xūwú-piāomiǎo　purely imaginary; entirely unreal; visionary; illusory: 忽闻海上有仙山，山在～间。(白居易) And then he heard accounts of an enchanted isle at sea, A part of the intangible and incorporeal world.

虚无主义 xūwúzhǔyì　nihilism: ～者 nihilist

虚线 xūxiàn　① dotted line or line of dashes ② *math.* imaginary line

虚像 xūxiàng　*phys.* virtual image

虚心 xūxīn　open-minded; modest: ～学习 learn modestly; learn with an open mind / ～体察情况 look into matters with an open mind / ～听取别人的意见 listen to people's criticisms with an open mind / ～使人进步，骄傲使人落后。Modesty helps one to go forward, whereas conceit makes one lag behind.

虚虚实实 xūxūshíshí　the true mingled with the false; a mixture of truth and falsehood: 以～的战术使敌人疲于奔命 tire out the enemy by feints and ambushes

虚言 xūyán　*formal* ① empty talk; empty words ② lie; falsehood; unfounded statement

虚言妄语 xūyán-wàngyǔ　lies and falsehoods; unfounded remarks

虚掩 xūyǎn　(of a door or window) be left unlocked or unlatched

虚应故事 xū yìng gùshì　do sth. perfunctorily as a mere matter of form or routine: 国家承平日久，近来的地方官办事，件件都是～。(《儒林外史》) The country has been at peace for so long that local government has become a mere empty show.

虚有其表 xū yǒu qí biǎo　look impressive but lack real worth; appear better than it is

虚与委蛇 xū yǔ wēiyí　deal with sb. courteously but

without sincerity; pretend politeness and compliance

虚张声势 xū zhāng shēngshì make an empty show of strength; bluff and bluster; be swashbuckling

虚症 xūzhèng *Chin. med.* chronic diseases marked by deficiency of vital energy and lowering of body resistance

虚掷 xūzhì waste (time, money, effort, etc.): ～光阴 waste one's time on useless things; fritter away one's time

虚字 xūzì (also 虚字眼儿 xūzìyǎnr) empty word; function word; form word

需 xū ① need; want; require: 所～物品 goods in great need / ～款甚巨 require a big sum of money ② necessaries; needs: 军需 jūnxū

需求 xūqiú requirement; demand: 满足消费者的～ supply consumer demand; meet the consumers' demands / 人们对商品的～越来越高。There is an ever-growing demand for commodities.

需索 xūsuǒ exact; extort: ～无厌 make rapacious extortions

需要 xūyào ① need; want; require; demand: 这本书我非常～。I need this book badly. / 他～一本汉英词典。He is in need of a Chinese-English dictionary. / 到党和人民最～的地方去 go wherever the Party and the people need us most / 这所房子～修理。The house wants repairing. / 这种情况～立即采取措施。This situation requires (*or* demands) immediate action. / 坏习惯一旦养成,～很长的时间才能根除。A bad habit once contracted takes a very long time to uproot (*or* root up). ② needs: 从群众的～出发 make the needs of the masses our starting point / 保证人民吃穿的基本～ ensure the people their basic needs in food and clothing / 适应形势发展的～ adapt oneself to the needs of the developing conditions

嘘 xū ① breathe out slowly: ～气 exhale slowly ② utter a sigh: 仰天而～ staring up at the sky and sighing deeply ③ (of cooking fire, steam, etc.) come into contact with sth.; scald; burn: 揭笼屉时小心热气～着手。Don't scald your hands when you open the steamer. / 把馒头在火上一～一～。Put the steamed bread over the fire for a while. ④ *interj. dial.* sh; hush: ～!轻一点儿,孩子们刚睡下。Hush! The kids have just gone to bed. ⑤ *dial.* hiss; boo: 把他～下台去 hiss (*or* boo) him off the platform ——see also shī

嘘寒问暖 xūhán-wènnuǎn inquire after sb.'s well-being; be solicitous about sb.'s health

嘘唏 xūxī *formal* sob

墟 xū ① ruins: 废墟 fèixū ② same as 圩 xū

歔 xū see below

歔欷 xūxī *formal* sob: 暗自～ sob in secret / ～不已 sob on and on

魆 xū see 黑魆魆 hēixūxū

徐 xú

徐 xú ① *formal* slowly; gently: 清风～来。A refreshing breeze was blowing gently. ② (Xú) a surname

徐步 xúbù *formal* walk slowly (*or* leisurely); stroll

徐娘半老,风韵犹存 Xúniáng bàn lǎo, fēngyùn yóu cún Xuniang in middle age, attractive all the same—an attractive middle-aged woman (originally said of Xuniang, or Lady Xu, a concubine of Emperor Yuan of

the Liang Dynasty 梁元帝, who carried on amorous affairs even when getting old)

徐图 xútú *formal* plan deliberately to achieve sth.: ～扩展 plan deliberately for expansion

徐徐 xúxú *formal* slowly; gently: 鲜艳的五星红旗～升起。The bright Five-Star Red Flag slowly went up the pole.

许 xǔ

许[1] xǔ ① praise: ～为佳作 praise sth. as an excellent piece of work ② promise: 他～过我一张票。He promised me a ticket. ③ allow; permit: 每组只～去一个人。Only one person is allowed from each group. ④ maybe; perhaps: 他今天没来,～是生病了。He didn't come today; perhaps he's ill. ⑤ (of a girl) be betrothed to: 姑娘～了人了。The girl is engaged (to be married).

许[2] xǔ (indicating a rough estimate): 年四十～ about forty years old

许[3] xǔ *formal* place: 何～人? Where does he come from?

许[4] Xǔ a surname

许多 xǔduō many; much; a great deal of; a lot of: ～人 many people / 积累了～经验 have accumulated much experience / 我们有～工作要做。We have a lot of work to do. / 他讲的内容,～是我不知道的。Much of what he said was new to me. / 她好像一下子老了～。She seems to have aged a lot. / 现在也顾不得这～了,送病人去医院要紧。We have no time to consider anything else. We have to rush the patient to hospital without delay.

许国 xǔguó *formal* dedicate oneself to one's country: 以身～ pledge to give one's life for one's country

许婚 xǔhūn (of a girl herself or her parents on her behalf) accept a proposal of marriage

许久 xǔjiǔ for a long time; for ages: 大家商量了～。We talked things over for a long time. / 我们～没有通信了。We have not corresponded for ages.

许可 xǔkě permit; allow: 凡是条件～的地方 wherever conditions permit / 得到领导的～ get permission from the leadership

许可证 xǔkězhèng license; permit: 出口～ an export license

许诺 xǔnuò make a promise; promise: 他～过帮我解决困难。He promised that he would help me out.

许配 xǔpèi (of a girl) be betrothed to sb. (in an arranged match): 她才满十岁就～人了。She was betrothed to her husband when she was only ten.

许身 xǔshēn dedicate oneself to: ～报国 dedicate oneself to one's country

许愿 xǔyuàn ① make a vow to a god: 烧香～ burn incense and make vows ② promise sb. a reward: 我给孩子许了愿,要是他这次考好了带他去海边玩。I promised the child to take him to the seaside if he did well in the exam.

许字 xǔzì *formal* (of a girl) be betrothed to sb.

诩 xǔ *formal* brag; boast: 自诩 zìxǔ

栩 xǔ see below

栩栩 xǔxǔ vivid; lively: ～欲活 lifelike; to the life

栩栩如生 xǔxǔ rú shēng lifelike; to the life: 他画的奔马,～,极其神似。The galloping horses he paints are extremely lifelike. / 唐代的《纨扇仕女图》～地描绘出宫

女们倦绣无聊的情态。The Tang painting "Ladies with Silken Fans" is a vivid portrayal of the languid ennui of court ladies.

醑 xǔ ① *formal* fine wine ② *pharm.* spirit; essence: 樟脑～ camphor spirit (*or* essence)

醑剂 xǔjì *pharm.* spirit; essence

xù

旭 xù *formal* brilliance of the rising sun

旭日 xùrì the rising sun

旭日东升 xùrì dōng shēng the sun rising in the eastern sky—a display of youthful vigour and vitality

序[1] xù ① order; sequence: 顺序 shùnxù / 程序 chéngxù ② arrange in order: 序齿 xùchǐ ③ introductory; initial: 序幕 xùmù ④ preface: 能否请您为这本书写一篇～? Would you write a preface to this book?

序[2] xù a type of local school in ancient times

序跋 xùbá preface and postscript

序齿 xùchǐ *formal* in order of seniority: ～坐下 sit down in order of seniority

序次 xùcì ① order; sequence ② *formal* arrange in order

序列 xùliè alignment; array: 战斗～ battle array; battle order

序论 xùlùn introduction

序目 xùmù preface and table of contents

序幕 xùmù ① prologue (to a play) ② prologue (to a major event, etc.); prelude: 五四运动是我国新民主主义革命的～。The May 4th Movement was the prelude to China's new-democratic revolution.

序曲 xùqǔ ① *mus.* overture ② prelude (to an event, action, etc.)

序时帐 xùshízhàng *accounting* journal

序数 xùshù ordinal number; ordinal

序文 xùwén preface; foreword

序言 xùyán preface; foreword

序战 xùzhàn *mil.* initial battle

洫 xù *formal* ditch: 沟～ ditches running between plots of farmland (for irrigation or drainage)

恤（卹、賉） xù ① pity; sympathize: 体恤 tǐxù ② give relief; compensate: 抚恤 fǔxù

恤金 xùjīn pension for a person disabled while on duty; pension for the dependants of a person who died while on duty

叙（敘、敍） xù ① talk; chat: ～家常 chitchat ② narrate; recount; relate ③ assess; appraise: 叙功 xùgōng ④ introductory; initial: 叙文 xùwén / 叙言 xùyán

叙别 xùbié have a farewell talk

叙次 xùcì *formal* same as 序次 xùcì

叙功 xùgōng *formal* assess sb.'s services: ～授奖 assess sb.'s services and give him a reward

叙旧 xùjiù talk about the old days

叙利亚 Xùlìyà Syria

叙利亚人 Xùlìyàrén Syrian

叙事 xùshì narrate (in writing); recount

叙事歌剧 xùshìgējù ballad opera

叙事剧 xùshìjù epic theatre

叙事曲 xùshìqǔ *mus.* ballade

叙事诗 xùshìshī narrative poem; ballade

叙事文 xùshìwén narrative; narrative prose

叙述 xùshù narrate (in speech or writing); recount; relate

叙说 xùshuō tell; narrate (in speech)

叙谈 xùtán chat; chitchat

叙文 xùwén same as 序文 xùwén

叙言 xùyán same as 序言 xùyán

叙用 xùyòng appoint (an official); employ (as a government official)

畜 xù raise (domestic animals) ——see also chù

畜产 xùchǎn livestock (*or* animal) products

畜牧 xùmù raise (*or* rear) livestock or poultry: 从事～ go in for animal husbandry

畜牧场 xùmùchǎng animal farm; livestock (*or* stock) farm

畜牧业 xùmùyè animal husbandry; livestock husbandry; livestock farming

畜养 xùyǎng raise (domestic animals)

酗 xù see below

酗酒 xùjiǔ indulge in excessive drinking: ～滋事 get drunk and create a disturbance

绪 xù ① the beginning of a matter: 绪论 xùlùn / 头绪 tóuxù ② thread ends; remnants: ～余 surplus; remnants ③ mental or emotional state: 心绪 xīnxù ④ task; cause; undertaking: 续未竟之～ carry on an unfinished task; take up where another has left off

绪论 xùlùn introduction

绪言 xùyán introduction

续（續） xù ① continuous; successive: 连续 liánxù ② continue; extend; join: ～会 extended session; follow-up meeting / 这条绳子太短，再～上一截儿吧。This piece of string is too short. Join another piece onto it. ③ add; supply more: 蒸锅要烧干了，赶快～水。The steamer (on the fire) is nearly dry. Put some more water in it, quick. / 炉子该～煤了。The fire needs more coal.

续编 xùbiān continuation (of a book); sequel

续貂 xùdiāo see 狗尾续貂 gǒuwěi xùdiāo

续订 xùdìng renew one's subscription (to a newspaper or magazine)

续断 xùduàn *Chin. med.* teasel root

续航 xùháng (of an airplane or ship) continue (*or* pursue) a journey without refuelling

续航力 xùhánglì endurance; flying range (of an airplane); cruising radius (of a ship)

续集 xùjí continuation (of a book); sequel

续假 xùjià extend one's leave of absence; extend leave: ～一星期 have one's leave extended for another week

续借 xùjiè renew (a library book)

续命汤 xùmìngtāng a decoction to stimulate a dying person; lifesaver

续娶 xùqǔ remarry after the death of one's wife

续弦 xùxián ① remarry after the death of one's wife ② a second wife (after the death of one's first wife)

续约 xùyuē ① renew a treaty or contract ② a renewed treaty or contract; a supplementary contract

勖（勗） xù *formal* encourage

勖勉 xùmiǎn *formal* encourage; prompt

絮[1] xù ① (cotton) wadding ② old name for coarse silk floss ③ sth. resembling cotton: 芦～ (reed) catkin ④ wad with cotton: ～被子 wad a quilt with cotton / ～棉衣 line (*or* wad) one's clothes with cotton

絮[2]

絮 xù　long-winded; garrulous

絮叨 xùdao　be long-winded; be garrulous; be wordy: 他老是～个没完, 所以大家都烦他。Everybody is fed up with his endless chatter.

絮烦 xùfan　tired; bored: 她老说她穷, 人们都听～了。She was always harping on her poverty, and people were bored stiff.

絮聒 xùguō　① same as 絮叨 xùdao ② trouble sb.

絮棉 xùmián　cotton for wadding

絮窝 xùwō　(of birds or animals) do up a nest or lair

絮絮 xùxù　garrulous; loquacious; chattering endlessly

絮语 xùyǔ　① prattle on ② endless chatter

婿（壻）

xù　① son-in-law ② husband: 妹～ younger sister's husband

蓄

xù　① store up; save up: 储蓄 chǔxù / 蓄水 xùshuǐ ② grow: ～须 grow a beard / ～发 wear one's hair long ③ entertain (ideas); harbour: 蓄意 xùyì

蓄藏 xùcáng　save and preserve; lay in; lay up; store

蓄电池 xùdiànchí　storage battery; accumulator

蓄电池车 xùdiànchíchē　accumulator vehicle

蓄洪 xùhóng　store floodwater: ～防旱 store floodwater for use against a drought / ～工程 flood storage project

蓄积 xùjī　store up; save up: ～粮食 store up grain / 水库可以～雨水。Reservoirs can store up rainwater.

蓄谋 xùmóu　premeditate: ～已久 long premeditated / ～迫害 harbour a design of persecuting sb.

蓄念 xùniàn　harbour an idea (or a thought, an intention): ～已久 have long entertained the idea

蓄水 xùshuǐ　retain (or store) water: 在山坡上建池～ dig ponds on the slopes to store water / 这个水库能蓄多少水? How much water can this reservoir hold? / 这水库能～两千万立方米。This reservoir has a storage capacity of 20 million cubic metres. / ～工程 (water) storage project

蓄水池 xùshuǐchí　cistern; reservoir

蓄养 xùyǎng　build up; accumulate: ～力量 build up (or accumulate) strength

蓄意 xùyì　premeditated; deliberate: ～挑衅 premeditated provocation / ～进行破坏 deliberately sabotage / ～干涉别国内政 be bent on interfering in other countries' internal affairs

蓄志 xùzhì　harbour an ambition

煦

xù　formal warm; balmy: 和煦 héxù

xu

蓿

xu　see 苜蓿 mùxu

xuān

轩[1]

xuān　formal high; lofty

轩[2]

xuān　① (formerly often used in names of studies, restaurants or teahouses) a small room or veranda with windows ② a high-fronted, curtained carriage used in ancient times ③ formal window or door

轩昂 xuān'áng　dignified; imposing

轩敞 xuānchǎng　spacious and bright

轩豁 xuānhuò　① (of a room or hall) light and spa-cious: 客厅十分～。The drawing room is light and spacious. ② (of disposition or temperament) sanguine; cheerful: 性格～ of a sanguine disposition; always cheerful

轩然大波 xuānrán dàbō　a great disturbance; a mighty uproar: 没料到芝麻大的事儿竟会引起这样一场～。Who could have thought that a trivial matter would cause such a stir (or cause so much agitation)?

轩辕 Xuānyuán　another name for 黄帝 Huángdì

轩轾 xuān-zhì　formal high and low chariots—high or low; good or bad: 不分轩轾 bù fēn xuān-zhì

宣

xuān　① declare; proclaim; announce: ～赦 proclaim a general amnesty ② lead off (liquids); drain: 宣泄 xuānxiè ③ (Xuān) a surname

宣笔 xuānbǐ　Xuan writing-brush, a high-quality writing-brush made in Xuancheng 宣城 in Anhui Province

宣布 xuānbù　declare; proclaim; announce: ～独立 declare (or proclaim) independence / ～会议开始 declare a meeting open; call a meeting to order / ～无效 declare sth. invalid (or null and void) / ～戒严 declare (or proclaim) martial law / ～进入紧急状态 proclaim a state of emergency / ～一件事 make an announcement / 当众～ announce in public

宣称 xuānchēng　assert; declare; profess: 被告～自己是无辜的。The accused declared that he was innocent. or The accused pleaded not guilty.

宣传 xuānchuán　conduct propaganda; propagate; dis-seminate; give publicity to: ～共产主义思想 disseminate communist ideas / ～党的方针政策 publicize the Party's general and specific policies / ～群众 spread propaganda among the masses / 广为～ give wide publicity to / 做～要看对象。In doing propaganda we must consider our audience.

宣传队 xuānchuánduì　propaganda team: 文艺～ per-forming arts propaganda team

宣传工具 xuānchuán gōngjù　instrument (or means) of propaganda or publicity

宣传工作者 xuānchuán gōngzuòzhě　propagandist

宣传画 xuānchuánhuà　picture poster

宣传机构 xuānchuán jīgòu　propaganda organ

宣传机器 xuānchuán jīqì　propaganda machine

宣传品 xuānchuánpǐn　propaganda (or publicity) mate-rial

宣传网 xuānchuánwǎng　propaganda network

宣传员 xuānchuányuán　propagandist

宣读 xuāndú　read out (in public): ～中央文件 read out a Central Committee document

宣告 xuāngào　declare; proclaim: ～成立 proclaim the founding of (a state, organization, etc.) / ～无效 de-clare sth. null and void / ～破产 declare bankruptcy; go bankrupt

宣讲 xuānjiǎng　① explain and publicise (a policy, de-cree, etc.) ② preach (a religious doctrine)

宣教 xuānjiào　propaganda and education

宣明 xuānmíng　declare; make clear: ～立场 declare one's stand

宣判 xuānpàn　leg. pronounce judgment: ～有罪 pro-nounce sb. guilty / ～无罪 pronounce sb. not guilty; ac-quit sb. of a crime or charge

宣示 xuānshì　declare openly; make publicly known

宣誓 xuānshì　take (or swear) an oath; make a vow; make a pledge: 庄严～ make a solemn vow / 入党～ take the oath on being admitted to the Party / ～就职 take an oath of office; be sworn in; be sworn into office

宣腿 xuāntuǐ　Xuanwei ham (after Xuanwei 宣威, a town in Yunnan Province where it is made)

宣泄 xuānxiè　① lead off (liquids); drain: ～洪水 drain

off floodwaters ② get sth. off one's chest; unbosom oneself: ～心中的积郁 give vent to one's pent-up feelings

宣叙调 xuānxùdiào *mus.* recitative

宣言 xuānyán declaration; manifesto: 《共产党～》 *Manifesto of the Communist Party* / 开罗～ Cairo Declaration / 和平与裁军～ Declaration on Peace and Disarmament

宣扬 xuānyáng publicise; propagate; advocate; advertise: ～好人好事 give publicity to good people and their good deeds / ～自己的成绩 advertise one's own success

宣战 xuānzhàn declare war

宣战书 xuānzhànshū a declaration of war

宣召 xuānzhào (of a king or an emperor) summon to court; summon to an audience

宣旨 xuānzhǐ proclaim an imperial edict

宣纸 xuānzhǐ *Xuan* paper, a high quality paper made in Xuancheng (宣城) in Anhui Province, esp. good for traditional Chinese painting and calligraphy

萱 (蕿) xuān see below

萱草 xuāncǎo day lily

萱堂 xuāntáng *formal honor.* your mother

喧 (誼) xuān noisy: 结庐在人境, 而无车马～。(陶潜) I built my house where others dwell, And yet there is no clamour of carriages and horses.

喧宾夺主 xuān bīn duó zhǔ a presumptuous guest usurps the role of the host; the secondary supersedes the primary

喧哗 xuānhuá ① confused noise; hubbub; uproar: 笑语～ uproarious talk and laughter / 门外一阵～。There was a hubbub outside the door. ② make an uproar; make a racket: 请勿～。Please keep quiet (a sign in a public place).

喧闹 xuānnào noise and excitement; bustle; racket

喧嚷 xuānrǎng make an uproar; make a racket: 人声～ a hubbub of voices; loud confused voices / 千万别把事情～出去呀! For heaven's sake, don't spread it around!

喧扰 xuānrǎo stir up a disturbance; make a commotion

喧腾 xuānténg noise and excitement; hubbub: 广场上一片～。A hubbub filled the square.

喧天 xuāntiān fill the air with noises; be terribly noisy: 锣鼓喧天 luógǔ xuāntiān

喧阗 xuāntián *formal* fill the air with noises; be terribly noisy: 鼓乐～。Drums and gongs made a terrible racket.

喧嚣 xuānxiāo ① noisy: ～的车马声 the noise of dense traffic ② make a clamour; make a hullabaloo; raise a din: ～鼓噪 make a clamour; stir up a commotion / 诸如此类的论调～一时。This sort of talk created quite a stir.

揎 xuān ① pull up the sleeves and bare the arms: ～拳捋袖 pull up the sleeves and raise the fists —get ready to fight ② *dial.* push: ～开房门 push a door open

暄[1] xuān *formal* warm and sunny: 负～ bask in the sunshine

暄[2] xuān *dial.* fluffy; soft: 馒头很～。The steamed bread is very fluffy. / 沙土地～, 不好走。It's hard to walk on the soft sand.

暄和 xuānhuo (also 暄乎 xuānhu) fluffy; soft: 晒过的被子多～。How fluffy the quilts are after sunning!

暄暖 xuānnuǎn *formal* warm: 三月天气, 阳光～。It

was March, and the sun shone bright and warm.

暄腾 xuānteng *dial.* soft and springy; fluffy; spongy: 这屉馒头蒸得好～! How nice and soft this steamed bread is!

煊 xuān same as 暄[1] xuān

煊赫 xuānhè of great renown and influence

儇 xuān *formal* ① frivolous ② cunning; artful

儇薄 xuānbó *formal* frivolous

xuán

玄 xuán ① black; dark: 玄青 xuánqīng ② profound; abstruse: 玄理 xuánlǐ ③ *inf.* unreliable; incredible: 这话太～了。That's a pretty tall story.

玄狐 xuánhú another name for 银狐 yínhú

玄乎 xuánhu *inf.* fantastic; incredible: 说得那么～, 有谁相信! Who'd believe such a fantastic story!

玄机 xuánjī *Taoism* arcane truth

玄理 xuánlǐ abstruse theory

玄妙 xuánmiào mysterious; abstruse

玄明粉 xuánmíngfěn *Chin. med.* compound of glauber-salt and liquorice

玄青 xuánqīng deep black

玄参 xuánshēn ① figwort ② *Chin. med.* the root of figwort

玄孙 xuánsūn great-great-grandson; grandson of one's grandson

玄武 xuánwǔ the Black Warrior—① an epithet for the tortoise ② a collective name for the northern group (Nos. 8-14) of the twenty-eight constellations (二十八宿) ③ the guardian spirit of the north in Taoism

玄武湖 Xuánwǔhú Xuanwu Lake, a scenic spot in Nanjing (南京)

玄武岩 xuánwǔyán *geol.* basalt

玄想 xuánxiǎng fancy; imagination

玄虚 xuánxū deceitful trick; mystery: 故弄玄虚 gù nòng xuánxū

玄学 xuánxué ① dark learning—a mystical school that developed in the 3rd and 4th centuries, characterized by metaphysical speculations seeking to adapt Taoist theories to a Confucian milieu ② another name for 形而上学 xíng'érshàngxué

玄远 xuányuǎn *formal* (of doctrines, principles, etc.) abstruse; profound

玄之又玄 xuán zhī yòu xuán the mystery of mysteries—extremely mysterious and abstruse

旋 xuán ① revolve; circle; spin: 盘旋 pánxuán / 旋绕 xuánrào ② return; come back: 凯旋 kǎixuán ③ part of the scalp where the hair is whorled ④ *formal* soon: 旋即 xuánjí ——see also xuàn

旋耕 xuángēng rotary tillage

旋耕机 xuángēngjī rotary cultivator; rotocultivator

旋管 xuánguǎn *chem.* coil; coiled pipe; coiler

旋光性 xuánguāngxìng *phys.* optical rotation

旋回 xuánhuí ① *geol.* cycle: 造山～ orogenic cycle / 构造～ tectonic cycle ② turn round; circle round

旋即 xuánjí *formal* soon: 入场券～售完。All the tickets were soon sold out.

旋里 xuánlǐ *formal* return to one's home town; return home

旋律 xuánlǜ *mus.* melody

旋毛虫 xuánmáochóng trichina

旋木雀 xuánmùquè tree creeper

旋钮 xuánniǔ knob

旋桥　xuánqiáo　swing bridge

旋绕　xuánrào　curl up; wind around: 炊烟～。Smoke is curling up from the kitchen chimneys. / 他们的歌声在山谷中～。Their songs reverberated throughout the valley.

旋塞　xuánsāi · mech.　cock: 放水～ drain cock / 三通～ three-way cock

旋涡　xuánwō　whirlpool; vortex; eddy

旋涡星云　xuánwō xīngyún　astron.　spiral nebula

旋舞　xuánwǔ　dance in a circle; whirl: 彩蝶在花丛中～。Butterflies fluttered about among the flowers.

旋翼机　xuányìjī　rotary-wing aircraft; rotorcraft

旋踵　xuánzhǒng　formal　in the brief time it takes to turn round on one's heel—in an instant: ～即逝 vanish before one has time to turn round; disappear in the twinkling of an eye

旋转　xuánzhuǎn　revolve; gyrate; rotate; spin: 陀螺在～。The top is spinning. / 地球绕地轴～，同时也围绕太阳。The earth revolves round the sun on its own axis. / 顺时针方向～ clockwise rotation / 逆时针方向～ counterclockwise rotation / ～球 a spinning ball

旋转乾坤　xuánzhuǎn qiánkūn　effect a drastic change in nature or the established order of a country; be earth-shaking

旋转钻井　xuánzhuǎn zuànjǐng　petroleum　rotary drilling

悬¹（懸）　xuán ① hang; suspend: ～在空中 suspend in midair ② lift; raise: 悬腕 xuánwàn ③ outstanding; unresolved: 这事儿不能老～着，得抓紧解决。We can't leave the matter unresolved any longer. Let's have it settled without delay. / 这笔帐～了好久了。This account has remained unsettled for a long time. ④ feel anxious; be solicitous: 悬念 xuánniàn ⑤ imagine: 悬拟 xuánnǐ ⑥ far apart: 悬隔 xuángé

悬²（懸）　xuán dial.　dangerous: 在快车道上骑自行车，可真～。Cycling in the fast traffic lane is really dangerous.

悬案　xuán'àn ① an unsettled law case ② an outstanding issue; an unsettled question

悬臂　xuánbì　mech.　cantilever

悬臂梁　xuánbìliáng　cantilever (beam)

悬臂起重机　xuánbì qǐzhòngjī　cantilever crane

悬臂桥　xuánbìqiáo　cantilever bridge

悬肠挂肚　xuáncháng-guàdù　same as 牵肠挂肚 qiāncháng-guàdù

悬揣　xuánchuǎi　speculate; conjecture

悬灯结彩　xuándēng-jiécǎi　hang up lanterns and festoons; adorn with lanterns and coloured streamers

悬而未决　xuán ér wèi jué　outstanding; unresolved: ～的 an outstanding question

悬浮　xuánfú　suspension: ～染色 suspension dyeing

悬浮固体　xuánfú gùtǐ　environ. protect.　suspended solid

悬浮体　xuánfútǐ　suspended substance; suspension

悬隔　xuángé　be separated by a great distance; be far apart: 两地～。The two places are far apart. / ～千里 be a thousand li apart; be a great distance apart

悬钩子　xuángōuzi　raspberry

悬谷　xuángǔ　geog.　hanging valley

悬挂　xuánguà ① hang; suspend; fly (a flag): ～国旗 fly the national flag of China / 圣诞树上上下下～着亮晶晶的花彩。Glistening trimmings were hung over the Xmas tree. / 半空中～着两个彩色大汽球。Two big coloured balloons were suspended in midair. ② suspension (of a motor vehicle)

悬挂犁　xuánguàlí　mounted plough

悬挂式滑翔　xuánguàshì huáxiáng　sports　hang gliding: ～运动员 hang glider

悬挂式滑翔机　xuánguàshì huáxiángjī　hang glider

悬河　xuánhé ① hanging river—a river (or a section of it) high above the surrounding countryside ② formal cataract; waterfall ③ a copious, rapid flow of words: 口若悬河 kǒu ruò xuánhé

悬河泻水　xuánhé xiè shuǐ　a hanging river in flood—a flood of eloquence

悬壶　xuánhú　formal　practise medicine (on one's own)

悬乎　xuánhu　dial.　dangerous; unsafe: 真～! 她差点让汽车给撞了。Whew, that was dangerous! She nearly got run over by the car. / 这件事让他去办，有点～。It's not safe to leave the matter in his hands.

悬胶　xuánjiāo　chem.　suspensoid: ～态 suspensoid state

悬空　xuánkōng　hang in the air—be unsettled; be impractical: 这件事不能老～着，要抓紧解决。Let's deal with the matter now; it's hung in the air too long.

悬梁　xuánliáng　hang oneself from a beam: ～自尽 commit suicide by hanging oneself from a beam; hang oneself

悬梁刺股　xuánliáng-cìgǔ　tie one's hair to a beam to keep from nodding off, or prod oneself awake with an awl in the thigh—study assiduously

悬料　xuánliào　metall.　hanging

悬铃木　xuánlíngmù　plane tree

悬拟　xuánnǐ　fabricate; make up

悬念　xuánniàn ① formal be concerned about (sb. who is elsewhere) ② suspense (felt as a story, play, etc. builds to a climax): 一篇充满～的侦探小说 a suspenseful detective story / 这部片子使观众自始至终处于～之中。The audience were kept in suspense until the very end of the film.

悬赏　xuánshǎng　offer (or post) a reward: ～缉拿逃犯 offer a reward for the capture of a runaway criminal; set a price on a runaway criminal's head

悬首示众　xuánshǒu shìzhòng　display sb.'s chopped-off head at a public place as a warning to all

悬饰　xuánshì　pendant

悬殊　xuánshū　a great disparity; a wide gap: 力量～ a great disparity in strength / 众寡～ a great disparity in numbers / 贫富～ a wide gap between the rich and the poor

悬索结构　xuánsuǒ jiégòu　archit.　suspended-cable structure

悬索桥　xuánsuǒqiáo　suspension bridge

悬梯　xuántī　hanging ladder

悬停　xuántíng ·　(of helicopters, etc.) hover

悬腕　xuánwàn　suspend the wrist (i.e. hold both wrist and elbow above the table when writing large characters, thus allowing the brush to operate over a greater ambit)

悬望　xuánwàng　wait or expect anxiously ·

悬想　xuánxiǎng　imagine; fancy

悬心　xuánxīn　be on tenterhooks

悬心吊胆　xuánxīn-diàodǎn　have one's heart in one's mouth; be on tenterhooks

悬崖　xuányá　overhanging (or steep) cliff; precipice

悬崖勒马　xuányá lè mǎ　rein in at the brink of the precipice—wake up to danger at the last moment

悬崖峭壁　xuányá-qiàobì　(also 悬崖绝壁 xuányá-juébì) sheer precipices and overhanging rocks; (perilous) cliffs and precipices

悬雍垂　xuányōngchuí　physiol.　uvula

悬肘　xuánzhǒu　same as 悬腕 xuánwàn

漩　xuán　whirlpool; eddy

漩涡　xuánwō　same as 旋涡 xuánwō

璇(璿)　xuán *formal* fine jade

璇玑 xuánjī a circumpolar constellation template (a serrated jade template used in ancient China to determine the positions of the celestial pole and certain circumpolar stars and the direction of the summer and winter solstices)

xuǎn

选(選)　xuǎn ① select; choose; pick: ～个好日子 choose an auspicious day. / ～一种你喜欢的样式 select a style that takes your fancy ② elect: ～学生会主席 elect a chairman of the student union / 我们～她当代表。We elected her (as) our representative. *or* We elected her to represent us. ③ the person or thing selected: 人选 rénxuǎn ④ selections; anthology: 诗～ selected poems / 民歌～ selections of folk songs / 散文～ an anthology of prose

选拔 xuǎnbá select; choose: ～运动员 select athletes / ～人才 select talented people

选拔赛 xuǎnbásài (selective) trial

选拔委员会 xuǎnbá wěiyuánhuì selection board

选本 xuǎnběn anthology; selected works

选编 xuǎnbiān ① select and compile: ～一本清代诗集 make a collection of selected Qing poems ② (usu. used in book titles) a collection of selected materials: 《现代诗歌～》*Selected Modern Poems*

选材 xuǎncái ① select a suitable person ② select suitable materials

选场 xuǎnchǎng selected scenes (from an opera, etc.)

选调 xuǎndiào recruit: ～各地优秀运动员集中训练 recruit top-notch athletes from all over the country for intensified training

选定 xuǎndìng decide on; fix: ～日期 fix the date

选读 xuǎndú ① pick out (pieces or passages) to read; read excerpts ② selected readings: 文学～ selected readings in literature

选购 xuǎngòu pick out and buy; choose from a variety of goods: 她为小女儿～了一件漂亮衣服。She chose a pretty dress for her little daughter. / 那家商店有多种旅游鞋可供～。That shop has got a large choice of sneakers. / 新到各种花布, 欢迎～。A new variety of cotton prints awaits your choice.

选集 xuǎnjí selected works (or writings); selections; anthology: 《毛泽东～》*Selected Works of Mao Zedong* / 《现代戏剧～》*An Anthology of Modern Drama*

选辑 xuǎnjí ① select and compile ② selected works (or writings)

选举 xuǎnjǔ elect: ～会议主席 elect a chairperson / 民主～产生的代表 democratically elected representatives / ～已于昨天举行。The election took place yesterday. / 无记名投票～ elect by secret ballot / ～程序 electoral procedure (or proceedings) / ～单位 electoral unit / ～结果 election results (or returns)

选举法 xuǎnjǔfǎ electoral law

选举权 xuǎnjǔquán the right to vote; franchise: 有～和被选举权 have the right to vote and to stand for election

选举人 xuǎnjǔrén voter

选矿 xuǎnkuàng ore dressing; mineral separation; beneficiation: ～厂 ore dressing plant; concentration plant

选录 xuǎnlù collect (writings): 这本集子～当代知名学者的十篇文章。This collection consists of ten articles by famous contemporary writers.

选民 xuǎnmín voter; elector: ～登记 registration of voters / ～名册 voting register / 全体 ～ the constituency; the electorate

选民榜 xuǎnmínbǎng list of eligible voters

选民证 xuǎnmínzhèng elector's certificate; voter registration card

选派 xuǎnpài select; detail: ～五名民兵守仓库 detail five militiamen to guard the warehouse / ～代表参加会议 depute sb. to attend a conference; select sb. as representative to a conference

选票 xuǎnpiào vote; ballot

选区 xuǎnqū electoral (or election) district; electoral ward; constituency

选曲 xuǎnqǔ selected songs or tunes: 《茶花女》～ selected tunes from *La Traviata*

选取 xuǎnqǔ select; choose

选任 xuǎnrèn select (a suitable person) for a post

选手 xuǎnshǒu an athlete selected for a sports meet; (selected) contestant; player: 参加体操比赛的～有几百名。There were hundreds of contestants in the gymnastics competition.

选送 xuǎnsòng select and recommend sb. (for a position or for admission to a school, etc.)

选题 xuǎntí ① select a title, subject or topic (for writing or research) ② the title, subject or topic selected

选贤举能 xuǎnxián-jǔnéng (also 选贤任能 xuǎnxián-rènnéng) select the worthy and promote the capable

选修 xuǎnxiū take as an elective course: 我们班大部分同学～欧洲史。Most of the students of our class take European history as an elective course.

选修课 xuǎnxiūkè elective course

选样 xuǎnyàng sampling; sample

选用 xuǎnyòng select for employment or for use

选育 xuǎnyù ① *agric.* seed selection: ～良种小麦 develop improved varieties of wheat by selection ② *animal husbandry* breeding

选择 xuǎnzé select; choose; opt: ～日期 choose a date / ～职业 choose an occupation / ～发型 choose a hair style / 没有～的余地 have no choice at all / 有～地应用新的科技成果 make selective use of new scientific and technological achievements

选择场地 xuǎnzé chǎngdì *sports* choice of ends

选择题 xuǎnzétí multiple-choice question; multiple-choice test

选择问句 xuǎnzé wènjù *gram.* alternative question

选种 xuǎnzhǒng seed selection

选中 xuǎnzhòng pick on; decide on; settle on: 她最后～了黄白条儿的那种料子。Finally she decided on the white and yellow striped material.

选准 xuǎnzhǔn make the right choice: ～时机 choose the right moment

炟　xuǎn *formal* ① ablaze ② bright

炟赫 xuǎnhè of great renown and influence

炟赫一时 xuǎnhè yīshí have renown and influence for a time

癣　xuǎn tinea; ringworm

癣疥之疾 xuǎnjiè zhī jǐ only a skin complaint—some slight ailment: 张鲁犯界, 乃～; 刘备入川, 乃心腹之大患。(《三国演义》) A Zhang Lu invasion would be but a skin disease. Liu Bei's entry into this country would be a mortal malady.

xuàn

泫　xuàn *formal* drip; trickle: 花上露犹～。The flowers are still dripping with dew.

泫然 xuànrán *formal* (usu. of tears) falling; trickling:

～泪下 tears rolling down one's cheeks; tears trickling from one's eyes

券 xuàn see 拱券 gǒngxuàn ——see also quàn
券门 xuànmén arched door or gate; arch

炫[1] xuàn *formal* dazzle: 光彩～目 blindingly bright; with dazzling brightness

炫[2]（衒） xuàn *formal* show off; display: 自～其能 show off one's ability
炫惑 xuànhuò *formal* dazzle and delude
炫弄 xuànnòng show off; display; parade: ～技巧 show off one's skill
炫示 xuànshì show off; display; parade: ～自己的知识 parade one's knowledge
炫耀 xuànyào make a display of; show off; flaunt: ～力量 flaunt one's strength / ～武力 make a show of force / ～自己的学问 parade one's learning

绚 xuàn gorgeous: 绚丽 xuànlì
绚烂 xuànlàn splendid; gorgeous: ～的朝霞 gorgeous morning clouds / ～的杜鹃花 splendid azaleas
绚丽 xuànlì gorgeous; magnificent: ～的景色 magnificent scenery / ～的鲜花 gorgeous flowers / 文采～ literary brilliance
绚丽多彩 xuànlì duōcǎi bright and colourful; gorgeous

眩 xuàn *formal* ① dizzy; giddy: 头晕目～ feel dizzy ② dazzled; bewildered: ～于名利 dazzled by the prospect of fame and wealth; obsessed with a desire for fame and wealth
眩目 xuànmù dazzle the eyes
眩晕 xuànyùn ① dizziness: 一阵～ a fit of dizziness ② *med.* vertigo

旋[1] xuàn whirl

旋[2]（鏇） xuàn ① cut or shape on a lathe, or pare with a knife: ～根车轴 shape a piece of steel into an axle on a lathe / 给孩子～一个苹果吃。Peel an apple for the child. ② same as 旋子 xuànzi

旋[3] xuàn *adv.* at the time; at the last moment: ～用～买 buy for immediate use / 客人到了～做就来不及了。It'll be too late to start preparing dinner after your guests have arrived.
——see also xuán
旋床 xuànchuáng *mech.* (turning) lathe
旋风 xuànfēng whirlwind
旋工 xuàngōng turner
旋子 xuànzi ① copper plate (for making sheets of bean-starch jelly) ② hot water container for warming wine

渲 xuàn same as 渲染 xuànrǎn①
渲染 xuànrǎn ① (in Chinese painting) add washes of ink or colour to a drawing ② play up; exaggerate; pile it on: ～战争恐怖 play up the horrors of war / 一件小事情，用不着这么～。No need to exaggerate a trifling matter like that. / 轻快的舞蹈给这场戏～了欢乐气氛。The lively dance heightened the joyous atmosphere of the scene.

楦（楥） xuàn ① shoe last or hat block ② shape with a last or block: ～鞋 last a shoe / ～帽子 block a hat ③ *dial.* fill up with padding
楦子 xuànzi (also 楦头 xuàntóu) shoe last or hat block

---

xuē

削 xuē (mainly as part of a compound word; otherwise pronounced xiāo) pare; whittle; cut: 剥削 bōxuē / 削减 xuējiǎn ——see also xiāo
削壁 xuēbì precipice; cliff
削发 xuēfà cut off the hair (as a sign of renouncing the worldly life and entering the monkhood or nunhood); take the tonsure
削籍 xuējí *formal* remove the name (of an erring official) from the rolls; remove from office
削价 xuējià cut the price; lower the price: ～处理 disposal of goods at reduced prices; a clearance sale
削肩 xuējiān sloping shoulders; drooping shoulders
削减 xuējiǎn cut (down); reduce; slash; whittle down: ～非生产性开支 cut down nonproductive expenditures; cut back on nonproductive spending / ～军费 cut down military expenditures
削平 xuēpíng *formal* quell; suppress; subdue
削弱 xuēruò weaken; cripple: 人民的武装只能加强，不能～。The people's armed forces must be strengthened, not weakened. / ～敌人的力量 cripple (or weaken) the enemy
削铁如泥 xuē tiě rú ní cut through iron as if it were mud (said of an exceptionally sharp sword)
削正 xuēzhèng *formal pol.* (please) make corrections
削职 xuēzhí remove from office
削足适履 xuē zú shì lǚ cut the feet to fit the shoes

靴（鞾） xuē boots: 雨靴 yǔxuē / 靴子 xuēzi
靴筒 xuētǒng (also 靴统 xuētǒng) the leg of a boot; bootleg
靴勒 xuēyào same as 靴筒 xuētǒng
靴子 xuēzi boots

薛 Xuē a surname

---

xué

穴 xué ① cave; den; hole: 蚁～ ant hole / 匪～ bandits' den ② coffin pit ③ *Chin. med.* acupuncture point; acupoint
穴播 xuébō dibble seeding; dibbling
穴道 xuédào same as 穴位 xuéwèi
穴居人 xuéjūrén cave dweller; troglodyte
穴居野处 xuéjū-yěchǔ dwell in caves in the wilds (as primitive man did)
穴位 xuéwèi *Chin. med.* acupuncture point; acupoint: ～注射疗法 therapy of point injection

学（學、斈） xué ① study; learn: ～文化 acquire an elementary education; learn to read and write / ～外语 learn (or study) a foreign language / ～游泳 learn swimming / ～先进 emulate the advanced / 跟人～绘画 take lessons in painting / 把新技术～到手 master a new skill ② imitate; mimic: 这孩子～他爸爸走路的样子。The boy imitates his father's way of walking. / ～鸡叫 mimic the crowing of a cock ③ learning; knowledge: 博学 bóxué ④ subject of study; branch of learning: 数学 shùxué / 文学 wénxué ⑤ school; college: 大学 dàxué / 上学 shàngxué
学报 xuébào learned journal; journal: 《清华～》 *Qing Hua University Journal* / 《中国考古～》 *Chinese Journal of Archaeology*

学步　xuébù　learn to walk: 刚会～的孩子 a toddler

学步邯郸　xuébù Hándān　same as 邯郸学步 Hándān xuébù

学部　xuébù　① the Board of Education in the Qing Dynasty ② departments of the Chinese Academy of Sciences (中国科学院)

学潮　xuécháo　student unrest; campus upheaval

学而不思则罔, 思而不学则殆　xué ér bù sī zé wǎng, sī ér bù xué zé dài　learning without thought is labour lost, thought without learning is perilous

学而不厌　xué ér bù yàn　have an insatiable desire to learn; be insatiable in learning

学而优则仕　xué ér yōu zé shì　when a student finds that he can more than cope with his studies, then he takes office

学阀　xuéfá　scholar-lord; scholar-tyrant

学非所用　xué fēi suǒ yòng　what one is doing has nothing to do with one's training

学费　xuéfèi　① tuition fee; tuition: 交～pay tuition ② a price for what one has learned to one's cost

学分　xuéfēn　educ.　credit: ～制 the credit system

学风　xuéfēng　① academic atmosphere; academic discipline: 那个学院以优良～著称。That college is noted for its academic atmosphere and discipline. / ～不正 lack of academic discipline ② style of study: 发扬理论联系实际的好～ carry forward the good style of study of integrating theory with practice

学府　xuéfǔ　seat of learning; institution of higher learning

学富五车　xué fù wǔ chē　have read five cartloads of books—be very learned

学贯古今　xué guàn gǔ-jīn　be well versed in both ancient and modern learning

学棍　xuégùn　educator-despot

学海　xuéhǎi　① like streams flowing ceaselessly until they reach the sea—persevering in one's studies until one reaches the goal ② sea of learning—a learned scholar

学好　xuéhǎo　learn from good examples; emulate good

学坏　xuéhuài　① follow bad examples ② (used with 了) be corrupted by bad examples

学会[1]　xuéhuì　① learn; master: 你的功课～了吗? Have you learned your lessons? / 她～了游泳。She's learned to swim. / ～多种外国语 master quite a number of foreign languages

学会[2]　xuéhuì　learned society; society; institute: 中国人民外交～ the Chinese People's Institute of Foreign Affairs / 物理～ the Physics Society

学级　xuéjí　old　classes and grades in school

学籍　xuéjí　one's status as a student; one's name on the school roll: 保留～ retain one's status as a student / 取消～ be struck off the school roll

学监　xuéjiān　old　proctor

学界　xuéjiè　educational circles

学究　xuéjiū　pedant: ～气 pedantry

学科　xuékē　① a branch of learning; discipline ② a school subject; a course of study ③ theoretical courses offered in military or physical training (opp. 术科 shùkē)

学理　xuélǐ　scientific principle or theory

学力　xuélì　educational level; scholastic or academic attainments

学历　xuélì　record of formal schooling; academic credentials

学联　xuélián　① (short for 学生联合会) students' federation ② (short for 中华全国学生联合会) All-China Students' Federation

学龄　xuélíng　school age: ～儿童 children of school age; school-age children / ～前儿童 preschool children; preschoolers

学名　xuémíng　① scientific name (e.g. Latin name for plants, etc.) ② formal name used at school (as distinguished from infant name or pet name at home)

学年　xuénián　school (or academic) year: ～考试 year-end examination

学派　xuépài　school of thought; school

学期　xuéqī　school term; term; semester

学前教育　xuéqiánjiàoyù　preschool education; infant school education

学前期　xuéqiánqī　preschool years

学然后知不足　xué ránhòu zhī bùzú　the more you learn, the less you feel you know

学人　xuérén　scholar; a learned man; a man of learning

学舌　xuéshé　① mechanically repeat other people's words; parrot; ape ② inf.　wag one's tongue spreading hearsay

学生　xuésheng　① student; pupil: 医科～ a medical student / ～时代 school days / ～腔 schoolboy or schoolgirl talk; classroom tone of a schoolboy or schoolgirl ② disciple; follower ③ dial.　boy; lad

学生会　xuéshenghuì　student union; student association

学生运动　xuésheng yùndòng　student movement

学生证　xuéshengzhèng　student's identity card

学生装　xuéshengzhuāng　(in former times) student dress—a jacket with three pockets without flaps and a narrow, stand-up collar, with western-style trousers to match

学时　xuéshí　class hour; period: 小学一～四十五分钟。In primary schools, a class hour has 45 minutes (or a period is 45 minutes long).

学识　xuéshí　learning; knowledge; scholarly attainments: ～渊博 have great learning; be learned / ～浅薄 have little learning

学士　xuéshì　① scholar ② a holder of the bachelor's degree; bachelor

学塾　xuéshú　an old-style private school

学术　xuéshù　systematic learning; science: ～领域 sphere of learning / 国际～交流活动 international academic exchanges / ～报告 learned report; academic report / ～地位 academic position or standing / ～论文 research paper; scientific paper; thesis / ～讨论会 academic discussion; scientific conference; symposium / ～团体 learned society / ～研究 academic research / ～性刊物 learned journal

学术界　xuéshùjiè　academic circles

学说　xuéshuō　theory; doctrine: 马克思主义的～ the theory of Marxism / 达尔文的进化论～ Darwin's theory of evolution

学堂　xuétáng　old　school

学田　xuétián　(in former times) community land the income from which was used to support a school

学徒　xuétú　① apprentice; trainee ② serve an apprenticeship: 在机床厂～ be an apprentice in a machine tool plant / ～期满 have served out one's apprenticeship / ～期未满 not out of one's apprenticeship / 他跟一位木匠师傅学了三年徒。He has served an apprenticeship of three years with (or to) a master carpenter.

学徒工　xuétúgōng　apprentice

学位　xuéwèi　academic degree; degree: 硕士～ master's degree / 博士～ doctor's degree; doctorate / 名誉～ an honorary degree

学问　xuéwen　① systematic learning; a branch of knowledge: 生物工程是一门新兴的～。Bioengineering is an emergent branch of learning. / 语言学是一门研究语言的～。Linguistics is a science concerned with the study of language or languages. ② learning; knowledge; scholarship: ～高深的人 a man of great learning; an erudite scholar / 别看种菜好像没啥, 其实大有～。

Growing vegetables looks easy, but actually it takes a lot of learning.

学无常师 xué wú cháng shī a learner has no need of a constant teacher

学无止境 xué wú zhǐjìng knowledge is infinite; there is no limit to knowledge

学习 xuéxí study; learn; emulate: ～文化 acquire an elementary education; learn to read and write /～先进经验 learn from others' advanced experiences /～的过程是丰富知识的过程。The process of study is a process of enriching one's knowledge. /～别人的长处，克服自己的弱点。Emulate others' strong points and overcome one's own weaknesses. / 以王铁人为～的榜样 model oneself on lron Man Wang; follow the example of lron Man Wang /～成绩 academic record; school record /～年限 period of schooling

学衔 xuéxián academic rank (or title)

学校 xuéxiào school; educational institution: 师范～ teachers school; normal school / 专业～ specialized school; vocational school / 高等～ institution of higher learning

学行 xuéxíng scholarship and moral conduct

学行车 xuéxíngchē walker (for a baby learning to walk)

学兄 xuéxiōng same as 学长 xuézhǎng

学养 xuéyǎng formal scholarship and self-cultivation

学业 xuéyè one's studies; school work

学以致用 xué yǐ zhì yòng study for the sake of application; study sth. in order to apply it

学艺 xuéyì ① learn a craft or trade ② knowledge and skills

学友 xuéyǒu schoolmates; fellow students

学员 xuéyuán student (usu. of a college or a training course)

学院 xuéyuàn college; academy; institute: 师范～ teachers training college / 建筑工程～ institute of civil engineering / 美术～ school of art

学运 xuéyùn short for 学生运动 xuésheng yùndòng

学长 xuézhǎng formal a term of respect for one's schoolmate

学者 xuézhě scholar; a learned man; a man of learning

学制 xuézhì ① educational (or school) system: ～改革 reform in the school system ② length of schooling: 缩短～ shorten the period of schooling

学子 xuézǐ formal student

茓　xué store grain in a matting silo

茓子 xuézi a matting silo

踅　xué walk to and fro; turn back halfway: 他在大门口一来一去。He was hanging about the gate.

踅摸 xuémo same as 寻摸 xúnmo

踅子 xuézi same as 茓子 xuézi

嚛　xué dial. laugh: 发～ make one laugh; excite laughter ——see also jué

嚛头 xuétóu dial. ① words or act meant to amuse or to excite laughter: 这个丑角～真多。That clown is full of amusing tricks. / 卖弄～ play to the gallery ② tricks meant to deceive: 不要摆～! Don't try any tricks! or None of your tricks! ③ funny; amusing; comical: 实在～ really funny

xuě

雪[1]　xuě ① snow: 一场大～ a heavy fall of snow ② resembling snow; snowy: 雪白 xuěbái / 雪亮 xuěliàng

雪[2]　xuě wipe away (or off, out); clean: 雪耻 xuěchǐ / 昭雪 zhāoxuě

雪白 xuěbái snow-white; snowy white

雪板 xuěbǎn skis

雪豹 xuěbào zool. snow leopard; ounce (Panthera uncia)

雪暴 xuěbào snowstorm; blizzard

雪崩 xuěbēng snowslide; avalanche

雪崩效应 xuěbēng xiàoyìng phys. avalanche effect

雪车 xuěchē sled; sledge; sleigh

雪耻 xuěchǐ avenge an insult; wipe out a disgrace or humiliation

雪堆 xuěduī snowbank; snow drift

雪纺绸 xuěfǎngchóu text. chiffon

雪糕 xuěgāo dial. ice cream

雪恨 xuěhèn wreak vengeance; avenge

雪花 xuěhuā snowflake

雪花膏 xuěhuāgāo vanishing cream

雪花莲 xuěhuālián bot. snowdrop

雪花石膏 xuěhuāshígāo alabaster

雪鸡 xuějī zool. snow cock

雪茄 xuějiā cigar

雪窖冰天 xuějiào-bīngtiān a land of ice and snow

雪晶 xuějīng meteorol. snow crystal

雪里红 xuělǐhóng (also 雪里蕻 xuělǐhóng) potherb mustard (Brassica cernua, a vegetable quite palatable when pickled)

雪里送炭 xuě lǐ sòng tàn same as 雪中送炭 xuě zhōng sòng tàn

雪莲 xuělián (also 雪莲花 xuěliánhuā) snow lotus (Saussurea involucrata)

雪亮 xuěliàng bright as snow; shiny: 把自行车擦得～ polish the bike till it has a good shine / 灯光～ dazzling lamplight / 人民群众的眼睛是～的。The people's eyes are discerning.

雪柳 xuěliǔ bot. fontanesia (Fontanesia fortunei)

雪盲 xuěmáng snow blindness

雪泥鸿爪 xuění hóngzhǎo marks left by goose claws in the snow—traces of past events

雪片 xuěpiàn snowflake (usu. fig.): 贺电如～飞来。Messages of congratulation poured in. / 读者来信～似地飞向报社。The newspaper office was swamped by a flood of readers' letters.

雪橇 xuěqiāo sled; sledge; sleigh

雪青 xuěqīng lilac (colour)

雪球 xuěqiú snowball ——see also 滚雪球 gǔn xuěqiú

雪雀 xuěquè zool. snow finch

雪人[1] xuěrén snowman: 堆～ make a snowman

雪人[2] Xuěrén the Abominable Snowman (a hairy man-like creature reported to live in the snows of the Himalayas)

雪山 xuěshān a snow-capped mountain; a snowy mountain

雪上加霜 xuě shàng jiā shuāng snow plus frost—one disaster after another

雪上汽车 xuěshàngqìchē snowmobile

雪上汽车运动 xuěshàngqìchēyùndòng sports snowmobiling

雪糁 xuěshēn (also 雪糁子 xuěshēnzi) dial. snow pellets; graupel

雪松 xuěsōng bot. cedar

雪条 xuětiáo dial. ice-lolly; frozen sucker; popsicle

雪线 xuěxiàn geog. snow line

雪冤 xuěyuān clear sb. of a false charge; redress a wrong

雪原 xuěyuán snowfield

雪杖 xuězhàng ski pole; ski stick

雪中送炭 xuě zhōng sòng tàn send charcoal in snowy

weather—provide timely help

鳕

鳕　xuě　cod

鳕鱼　xuěyú　cod

xuè

血　xuè　① blood: ～从伤口流出来了。Blood was flowing from the wound ② related by blood: 血亲 xuè-qīn ③ energetic and high-spirited: 血性 xuèxìng ④ menses —see also xiě

血癌　xuè'ái　a popular name for 白血病 báixuèbìng

血案　xuè'àn　a murder case; a bloody incident

血本　xuèběn　principal; original capital

血崩症　xuèbēngzhèng　*med.* metrorrhagia

血沉　xuèchén　*med.* erythrocyte sedimentation rate (ESR)

血仇　xuèchóu　blood feud

血防　xuèfáng　(short for 血吸虫病防治) the prevention and cure of schistosomiasis (*or* snail fever)

血粉　xuèfěn　blood meal

血管　xuèguǎn　blood vessel

血管瘤　xuèguǎnliú　*med.* haemangioma; angioma

血管硬化　xuèguǎn yìnghuà　*med.* vascular sclerosis

血管造影　xuèguǎn zàoyǐng　*med.* angiography

血海　xuèhǎi　a sea of blood; bloodbath

血海深仇　xuèhǎi shēnchóu　a huge debt of blood; intense and deep-seated hatred: 我们誓死要报这～! We swear to collect this blood debt!

血汗　xuèhàn　blood and sweat; sweat and toil: ～钱 money earned by hard toil／～工厂 sweatshop／资本家吮吸工人的～。Capitalists fatten themselves on the workers' sweat and toil.／粮食是农民用～换来的。The grain is reaped through the hard labour of the peasants.

血红　xuèhóng　blood red

血红蛋白　xuèhóngdànbái　*biochem.* haemoglobin

血花　xuèhuā　spattered drops of blood

血迹　xuèjì　bloodstain: ～斑斑 bloodstained／踏着烈士的～前进 march along the path crimson with the martyrs' blood

血痂　xuèjiā　scab

血浆　xuèjiāng　*physiol.* (blood) plasma

血竭　xuèjié　*Chin. med.* dragon's blood (*Daemonorops draco*)

血口喷人　xuèkǒu pēn rén　make unfounded and malicious attacks upon sb.; venomously slander: 你～, 纯粹是造谣! You're slinging mud at me—that's a pack of lies!

血库　xuèkù　*med.* blood bank

血亏　xuèkuī　*Chin. med.* anaemia

血泪　xuèlèi　tears of blood: ～帐 debts of blood and tears／旧社会劳苦大众家家都有一部～史。In the old society all working people had a family history written in blood and tears.

血泪斑斑　xuèlèi bānbān　full of blood and tears: ～的家史 a family history of blood and tears

血淋淋　xuèlīnlīn　dripping with blood; bloody

血流成河　xuè liú chéng hé　blood flowing like a river—bloodbath

血流飘杵　xuè liú piāo chǔ　shields floating upon a river of blood—a bloody battle

血流如注　xuè liú rú zhù　blood streaming down

血路　xuèlù　a bloody path; an escape route: 杀出一条～ open up a bloody path; cut an escape route

血脉　xuèmài　① *Chin. med.* blood vessels; blood circulation ② blood relationship; blood lineage: ～相通

be related by blood

血尿　xuèniào　*med.* haematuria; blood in the urine

血浓于水　xuè nóng yú shuǐ　blood is thicker than water

血泊　xuèpō　a pool of blood: 倒在～中 lie in a pool of blood

血气　xuèqì　① animal spirits; sap; vigour: 血气方刚 xuèqì fāng gāng ② courage and uprightness: 有～的青年 a courageous and upright youth

血气方刚　xuèqì fāng gāng　full of animal spirits; full of sap; full of vigour and vitality

血亲　xuèqīn　blood relations

血亲婚配　xuèqīn hūnpèi　incest

血清　xuèqīng　*physiol.* (blood) serum

血清病　xuèqīngbìng　*med.* serum sickness; serum disease

血球　xuèqiú　*physiol.* blood cell; blood corpuscle

血染沙场　xuè rǎn shāchǎng　stain the battlefield with blood—die in battle

血肉　xuèròu　flesh and blood; the human body

血肉横飞　xuèròu héngfēi　blood and flesh flying in every direction: "砰", 一颗手榴弹, 把那一伙鬼子兵打得～。Then with a loud explosion a hand-grenade immediately blew the whole group of enemy soldiers into a disorderly pile of dead bodies.

血肉模糊　xuèròu móhu　be badly mangled

血肉相连　xuèròu xiānglián　as close as flesh and blood: 台湾同胞和我们～。Our compatriots in Taiwan are as close to us as flesh and blood.／和人民群众～ maintain flesh-and-blood ties with the masses of the people

血肉之躯　xuèròu zhī qū　the human body; flesh and blood

血色　xuèsè　redness of the face; colour: 她脸上几乎没有～。She has very little colour.／她脸上逐渐恢复了～。Little by little a healthy complexion came back to her face.

血色素　xuèsèsù　*physiol.* haemochrome

血书　xuèshū　a letter (expressing one's determination, last wish, etc.) written in one's own blood

血栓　xuèshuān　*med.* thrombus

血栓形成　xuèshuānxíngchéng　*med.* thrombosis

血水　xuèshuǐ　watery blood (esp. as flowing out from a part of the body)

血糖　xuètáng　*physiol.* blood sugar

血统　xuètǒng　blood relationship; blood lineage; extraction: 中国～的外国人 foreign nationals of Chinese descent／德国～的美国人 Americans of German extraction

血统工人　xuètǒng gōngrén　(industrial) worker of working-class parentage

血污　xuèwū　bloodstain

血吸虫　xuèxīchóng　blood fluke; schistosome

血吸虫病　xuèxīchóngbìng　*med.* schistosomiasis; snail fever

血洗　xuèxǐ　flood (a place) with blood—massacre the inhabitants of (a city, etc.)

血细胞计数　xuèxìbāo jìshù　*med.* blood count

血像　xuèxiàng　*med.* blood picture; hemogram

血小板　xuèxiǎobǎn　*physiol.* (blood) platelet

血小板病　xuèxiǎobǎnbìng　*med.* thrombocytopathy

血腥　xuèxīng　reeking of blood; bloody; sanguinary: ～的白色恐怖 bloody white terror／～味 smell of blood／～统治 sanguinary (*or* bloodstained) rule／反动统治者～地镇压人民。The reactionary rulers carried out a bloody suppression of the people.

血型　xuèxíng　*physiol.* blood group; blood type: ～分类 blood grouping; blood typing

血性　xuèxìng　courage and uprightness: ～汉子 a courageous and upright man

血胸　xuèxiōng　*med.* haemothorax

血虚 xuèxū *Chin. med.* deficiency of blood and its ensuing pathological changes

血循环 xuèxúnhuán *physiol.* blood circulation

血压 xuèyā blood pressure: 高～ high blood pressure; hypertension / 低～ low blood pressure; hypotension

血压计 xuèyājì sphygmomanometer

血样 xuèyàng blood sample; blood specimen

血液 xuèyè ① (human) blood: 新鲜～ fresh blood ② lifeblood; lifeline: 石油是工业的～。Petroleum is the lifeblood of industry.

血液病 xuèyèbìng *med.* blood diseases

血液透析 xuèyètòuxī *med.* haemodialysis

血液透析器 xuèyètòuxīqì haemodialyser

血衣 xuèyī a bloodstained garment; clothes covered with gore

血印 xuèyìn bloodstain

血友病 xuèyǒubìng *med.* haemophilia

血雨腥风 xuèyǔ-xīngfēng wind and rain reeking of blood—a reign of terror; a bloodbath on a battlefield

血郁 xuèyù *Chin. med.* blood stasis

血缘 xuèyuán ties of blood; consanguinity; blood relationship

血缘婚 xuèyuánhūn consanguineous marriage

血缘家庭 xuèyuán jiātíng connsanguine family

血晕 xuèyùn *Chin. med* coma after childbirth due to excessive loss of blood

血债 xuèzhài a debt of blood

血债累累 xuèzhài lěilěi have a mountain of blood debts

血债要用血来还 xuèzhài yào yòng xuè lái huán debts of blood must be paid in blood; blood will have blood

血战 xuèzhàn ① a bloody (*or* sanguinary) battle: 一场～ a bloody battle ② fight a very fierce battle

血战到底 xuèzhàn dào dǐ fight to the last drop of one's blood; fight to the bitter end: 为保卫祖国而～ fight to the finish in defence of one's country / 我们中华民族有同自己的敌人～的气概。We Chinese have the spirit to fight the enemy to the last drop of our blood.

血肿 xuèzhǒng *med.* haematoma

血渍 xuèzì bloodstain: ～斑斑 full of bloodstains; bloodstained

谑 xuè *formal* crack a joke; banter; tease: 戏谑 xìxuè

谑而不虐 xuè ér bù nüè tease without hurting or embarrassing; banter

xūn

勋(勳) xūn merit; meritorious service; achievement: 功勋 gōngxūn

勋臣 xūnchén an official with meritorious records

勋绩 xūnjì meritorious service; outstanding contribution

勋爵 xūnjué ① a feudal title of nobility conferred for meritorious service ② Lord (in Great Britain)

勋劳 xūnláo meritorious service: 卓著～ noted for meritorious service

勋业 xūnyè *formal* meritorious service and great achievement

勋章 xūnzhāng medal; decoration

埙(塤) xūn an ancient egg-shaped, holed wind instrument

熏¹(燻) xūn ① expose to smoke or fumes; fumigate: 烟把厨房的墙壁～黑了。The kitchen walls were blackened by cooking fumes. / 我被烟～得直流眼泪。The smoke brought tears to my eyes. / ～蚊子 smoke out mosquitoes / 用醋～房间 fumigate a room with vinegar vapour / 臭气～天 stink to heaven ② treat (meat, fish, etc.) with smoke; smoke: 熏鱼 xūnyú

熏² xūn ① make fragrant with incense, etc.: 用茉莉花～茶叶 scent tea with jasmine ② warm; mild: 熏风 xūnfēng
——see also xùn

熏风 xūnfēng *formal* a warm southeasterly or southerly breeze

熏干 xūngān smoke-dried beancurd

熏鸡 xūnjī smoked chicken

熏笼 xūnlóng a frame placed over a brazier for drying things or over a censer for scenting clothes

熏炉 xūnlú censer

熏沐 xūnmù have a bath and burn incense (preparatory to exercises of devotion)

熏染 xūnrǎn exert a gradual, corrupting influence on: 受坏思想的～ be gradually influenced by evil ideas

熏肉 xūnròu smoked meat

熏陶 xūntáo exert a gradual, uplifting influence on; nurture; edify: 起～作用 exert an edifying influence on / 在集体主义精神的～下，孩子们互相关心，互相帮助。Nurtured in the spirit of collectivism, the children care for each other and help each other.

熏衣草 xūnyīcǎo lavender (*Lavandula angustifolia*)

熏鱼 xūnyú smoked fish

熏蒸 xūnzhēng ① sultry; sweltering; stifling; suffocating: 暑气～ sweltering summer weather; stifling summer heat ② *Chin. med.* fuming or steaming—treating diseases with fumes as in moxibustion or with steam generated by boiling medicinal herbs ③ fumigate

熏蒸剂 xūnzhēngjì fumigant

熏制 xūnzhì cure (meat, etc.) by smoking; smoke

窨 xūn same as 熏² xūn, limited to use in ～茶叶 (scent tea with jasmine, etc.) ——see also yìn

薰¹ xūn *formal* ① a kind of sweet grass ② fragrance (of flowers, etc.)

薰² xūn same as 熏² xūn

薰莸不同器 xūn-yóu bù tóng qì (*also* 薰莸异器 xūn-yóu yì qì) fragrant herbs and stinking weeds must be kept in separate vessels—good people must stay away from bad

曛 xūn *formal* ① the dim glow of the setting sun ② dusk; nightfall

醺 xūn drunk: 微～ tipsy

xún

旬 xún ① a period of ten days: 按～计算 calculate in ten-day periods ② a period of ten years in a person's age (applied only to old persons): 八～老母 80-year-old mother

旬刊 xúnkān a publication appearing once every ten days

旬日 xúnrì ten days

寻¹(尋) xún an ancient measure of length, equal to eight *chi* (尺)

寻²(尋) xún look for; search; seek: ～人

look for sb. missing / ～物 look for sth. lost

寻常 xúncháng ordinary; usual; common: 不～ unusual; out of the ordinary / ～人家 an ordinary family / 男人干一部分家务活在今天是很～的事情了。It's quite common these days for men to do part of the housework. / 发明这种东西，确实不是～事。An invention like this is really something out of the ordinary (*or* something exceptional).

寻的 xúndì *mil.* target-seeking; homing: ～导弹 homing missile

寻短见 xún duǎnjiàn commit suicide; take one's own life

寻访 xúnfǎng look for (sb. whose whereabouts is unknown); try to locate; make inquiries about

寻根究底 xúngēn-jiūdǐ get to the bottom (*or* root) of things; inquire deeply into: 她最爱～，寻求事物的隐藏的、内在的缘由。She liked to get to the root of a matter and find out its hidden and internal causes.

寻呼 xúnhū page; bleep

寻呼机 xúnhūjī pager; bleeper; beeper

寻花问柳 xúnhuā-wènliǔ sport with flowers and willows——① enjoy a beautiful spring scene ② dally with prostitutes; visit houses of ill repute

寻欢作乐 xúnhuān-zuòlè seek pleasure and make merry

寻机 xúnjī *formal* look for an opportunity: ～突围 seek an opportunity to break out of an encirclement

寻开心 xún kāixīn *dial.* make fun of; poke fun at; joke: 别太认真了，她不过是在～罢了。Don't take it too seriously. She is only joking.

寻觅 xúnmì seek; look for: 这幅古画我们已～多年了。We have been looking for this old painting for years.

寻摸 xúnmo *inf.* look around for: 你在这儿～什么呢? What are you looking around here for? / 我到商场～～，看有什么可买的没有。I'll look around the department store and see if I can pick up something.

寻求 xúnqiú seek; explore; go in quest of: ～知识 seek knowledge / ～真理 seek truth / ～打开僵局的途径 explore possible paths for ending the stalemate / 通过改革～出路 seek (*or* find) a way out through reform

寻声 xúnshēng follow the sound (to find sb. or sth.): 我们～向东望去，只见一片瀑布从半山腰里倾泻而下。Following the noise, we looked towards the east and saw a waterfall tumbling down from halfway up the mountain. / 我在远处听着像是你的说话声，所以就～而来了。I heard a voice like yours at some distance from here, and have followed it and found you here.

寻事生非 xúnshì-shēngfēi seek a quarrel; stir up or make trouble

寻死 xúnsǐ ① try to commit suicide; attempt suicide ② commit suicide

寻死觅活 xúnsǐ-mìhuó attempt suicide (usu. as a threat)

寻思 xúnsi think to oneself; think: 你～～这事该怎么办。Think over what to do about it. / 我～她最适合做这个工作。I thought (*or* thought to myself) she was best suited for this job.

寻味 xúnwèi chew sth. over; ruminate; think over

寻问 xúnwèn inquire about: 不断有人来～这件事。People kept coming to inquire about that affair.

寻衅 xúnxìn pick a quarrel; provoke: ～滋事 pick quarrels and stir up trouble

寻幽访胜 xúnyōu-fǎngshèng travel around visiting quiet and secluded scenic spots

寻章摘句 xúnzhāng-zhāijù cull phrases and cite passages; write in *clichés*: 历观史籍, 采其大旨, 不效书生～而已。(《三国演义》) He reads the histories and annals, for the sake of the general lessons to be learned therefrom. He is no dryasdust pedant seeking remarkable passages and culling model sentences.

寻找 xúnzhǎo seek; look for: ～失物 look for lost articles / ～真理 seek truth

巡 (廵) xún ① patrol; make one's rounds: 巡逻 xúnluó ② *m.* a round of drinks: 酒过三～。The wine has gone round three times.

巡边员 xúnbiānyuán *sports* linesman

巡捕 xúnbǔ police or policeman (in former foreign concessions)

巡捕房 xúnbǔfáng police station (in former foreign concessions)

巡查 xúnchá go on a tour of inspection; make one's rounds

巡风 xúnfēng keep watch

巡抚 xúnfǔ ① (in the Ming Dynasty) an imperial inspector ② (in the Qing Dynasty) the governor of a province

巡更 xúngēng ① (in former times) go the rounds as a night watchman ② go on night patrol

巡官 xúnguān old police inspector

巡航 xúnháng cruise: ～半径 cruising radius / ～速度 cruising speed

巡航导弹 xúnháng dǎodàn cruise missile

巡回 xúnhuí go the rounds; tour; make a circuit of: 剧团正在全国各地～演出。The theatrical troupe is touring the country. / 教师到放牧点上进行～教学。The teachers make a circuit of the herding centres to give lessons.

巡回大使 xúnhuí dàshǐ roving ambassador

巡回放映队 xúnhuí fàngyìngduì mobile film projection unit

巡回剧团 xúnhuí jùtuán touring theatrical troupe; touring company

巡回医疗队 xúnhuí yīliáoduì mobile medical team

巡警 xúnjǐng old policeman

巡礼 xúnlǐ ① visit a sacred land; go on a pilgrimage ② tour; sight-seeing

巡逻 xúnluó go on patrol; patrol: 执行～任务 be on patrol duty; be on one's beat

巡逻队 xúnluóduì patrol party; patrol

巡逻护卫舰 xúnluó hùwèijiàn patrol escort

巡逻哨 xúnluóshào roving sentry; patrol

巡逻艇 xúnluótǐng patrol boat

巡逻线 xúnluóxiàn patrol route

巡哨 xúnshào (of security men) go on patrol

巡视 xúnshì ① make (*or* be on) an inspection tour; tour: ～各地 make an inspection tour of various places ② cast one's eyes around

巡行 xúnxíng go the rounds; tour; make a circuit of

巡幸 xúnxìng *formal* (of an emperor) go on an inspection tour: ～江南 go on an imperial tour of the Southland

巡洋舰 xúnyángjiàn cruiser

巡夜 xúnyè go on night patrol; keep night watch

巡弋 xúnyì (of a warship) cruise

巡游 xúnyóu ① stroll about; ramble ② go the rounds

巡诊 xúnzhěn (of a doctor) make one's rounds; go on one's rounds

询 xún ask; inquire

询问 xúnwèn ask about; inquire about: ～我们的学习情况 ask us about our studies / ～病状 inquire about sb.'s illness / 他关切地～着家乡的一切。With great concern he asked about everything of his home town.

洵 xún *formal* truly; indeed: ～属可贵 truly valuable

峋 xún see 嶙峋 línxún

荨（蕁、藡） xún see below ——see also qián

荨麻疹 xúnmázhěn *med.* nettle rash; urticaria

浔（潯） xún ① *formal* waterside: 江～ riverside ② (Xún) another name for 九江 Jiujiang (a city in Jiangxi Province)

串（嘽） xún, also yīngxún old form for 英寻 yīngxún

荀 Xún a surname

循 xún follow; abide by: ～此前进 proceed along this line / ～例 follow the usual practice; follow a precedent

循分 xúnfèn *formal* be dutiful

循规蹈矩 xúnguī-dǎojǔ observe rules, obey orders, etc. docilely; conform to convention; toe the line: 学生们都很～。 All the students conscientiously obeyed the rules of the school.

循环 xúnhuán circulate; cycle: ～不息 move in endless cycles / 四季的～ the cycle of the seasons

循环论证 xúnhuán lùnzhèng *log.* argue in a circle

循环赛 xúnhuánsài *sports* round robin

循环往复 xúnhuán-wǎngfù move in cycles: ～，以至无穷 repeat itself in endless cycles

循环系统 xúnhuánxìtǒng *physiol.* the circulatory system

循环小数 xúnhuán xiǎoshù *math.* recurring decimal

循环信用证 xúnhuán xìnyòngzhèng revolving letter of credit

循吏 xúnlì *formal* an upright official; an honest official

循良 xúnliáng *formal* be law-abiding

循名责实 xún míng zé shí see that the reality matches the name: ～，这就是今天的工作。 Our present task is to create the reality that will fit the name.

循序 xúnxù in proper order or sequence

循序渐进 xúnxù jiàn jìn follow in order and advance step by step; proceed in an orderly way and step by step: ～地进行教学。 Instruction is given step by step.

循循善诱 xúnxún shàn yòu be good at giving systematic guidance; teach with skill and patience

鲟（鱘、鱏） xún sturgeon

xùn

讯 xùn ① interrogate; question: 审讯 shěnxùn ② information; news; message; dispatch: 据新华社～ according to a Xinhua dispatch

讯号 xùnhào radio signal; signal

讯实 xùnshí prove to be true after interrogation

讯问 xùnwèn ① ask about; inquire about: 向医生～病人的病情 ask a doctor about the condition of a patient / ～事情的原委 inquire about all the details of a matter ② interrogate; question: ～被告人 interrogate the defendant / ～案件 hear (or try) a case

训 xùn ① instruct; admonish; give sb. a lecture: 他没做作业，老师～了他一顿。 His teacher gave him a lecture for not doing his homework. / 他专爱～人。 He's always lecturing people. ② instructions; teachings: 家训 jiāxùn ③ standard; model; example: 不足为训 bù zú wéi xùn ④ critical explanation or interpretation of a

text: 训诂 xùngǔ

训斥 xùnchì reprimand; rebuke; dress down: 他数学不及格，受到爸爸的～。 He failed his maths examination and got a dressing-down from his father.

训词 xùncí admonition; instructions

训导 xùndǎo instruct and guide

训导长 xùndǎozhǎng (formerly in college) the dean of students

训迪 xùndí *formal* instruct and enlighten

训诂 xùngǔ exegetical studies (esp. of ancient texts); exegesis

训诂学 xùngǔxué exegetics

训话 xùnhuà give an admonitory talk to subordinates

训诲 xùnhuì *formal* instruct; teach

训诫 xùnjiè (also 训戒 xùnjiè) ① admonish; advise ② rebuke; reprimand ③ *leg.* admonishing

训练 xùnliàn train; drill: ～部队 train troops / 经他～的射击运动员一个个都成了优秀射手。 The shooters he trained have all become crack shots. / 这些警犬都受过很好的～。 All these police dogs are well trained.

训练班 xùnliànbān training class; training course: 园艺～ a training course in horticulture / 短期～ a short course of training / 为外国人开设的暑期汉语口语～ a summer course in spoken Chinese for foreigners

训练有素 xùnliàn yǒusù have received a regular and thorough training; be well-trained: ～的运动员 a well-trained athlete

训令 xùnlìng written instructions from superiors

训勉 xùnmiǎn exhort and encourage

训示 xùnshì instructions or orders (to subordinates or younger members of one's family)

训诱 xùnyòu *formal* teach and guide

训育 xùnyù (formerly in school) moral education

驯 xùn ① tame and docile: 这匹马很～。 This horse is very tame. ② tame; domesticate: 善于～虎 good at taming tigers / ～马 break in a horse

驯服 xùnfú ① docile; tame; tractable: 猫是很～的。 Cats are very docile. ② tame; break; domesticate: 这匹野马终于被～了。 The wild horse was finally broken in. / ～洪水 bring a flood under control

驯化 xùnhuà domesticate; tame: 鹿群经过～，可以放牧。 Deer can be tamed and trained to go out to pasture.

驯良 xùnliáng tractable; docile; tame and gentle

驯鹿 xùnlù *zool.* reindeer

驯善 xùnshàn tractable; docile; tame and gentle: ～的羔羊 a tame and gentle lamb

驯顺 xùnshùn tame and docile

驯养 xùnyǎng raise and train (animals); domesticate

汛 xùn seasonal flood; high water: 伏～ midsummer floods

汛期 xùnqī flood (or high-water) season

汛情 xùnqíng flood situation: ～严重。 The flood (situation) is serious.

迅 xùn fast; swift: ～跑 run swiftly

迅即 xùnjí immediately; at once: 此事望～处理。 It is hoped that immediate action will be taken on this matter.

迅急 xùnjí very fast; rapidly; at high speed

迅疾 xùnjí swift; rapid

迅捷 xùnjié fast; agile; quick

迅雷不及掩耳 xùnléi bùjí yǎn ěr a sudden peal of thunder leaves no time to cover the ears—as sudden as a flash of lightning: 以～之势袭击敌人 fall on the enemy with the suddenness of a thunderbolt / 给他个～的突然袭击 hit him like a thunderbolt so fast he won't have

time to cover his ears

迅猛 xùnměng swift and violent: 水势～异常。The flood roared on, swift and violent.

迅速 xùnsù rapid; swift; speedy; prompt: 动作～ swift in action; quick-moving / 工农业的～发展 rapid development of industry and agriculture / ～取得成效 produce speedy results / ～作出决定 come to a prompt decision / ～召开现场会 lose no time in calling an on-the-spot meeting

逊(遜)

xùn ① abdicate ② modest: 谦逊 qiānxùn / 出言不逊 chūyán bù xùn ③ *formal* inferior: 稍～一筹 be slightly inferior

逊尼派 Xùnnípài *Islam* Sunnite

逊色 xùnsè be inferior: 毫无～ be by no means inferior / 其他玉雕跟这件相比大为～。Other jade carvings pale beside this.

逊位 xùnwèi abdicate

徇(狥)

xùn ① *formal* give in to; submit to; comply with ② same as 殉 xùn②

徇情 xùnqíng *formal* act wrongly out of personal considerations; practise favouritism

徇情枉法 xùnqíng-wǎngfǎ bend the law to help one's friends or relatives

徇私 xùnsī same as 徇情 xùnqíng

徇私舞弊 xùnsī-wǔbì do wrong to serve one's friends or relatives

殉

xùn ① be buried alive with the dead ② sacrifice one's life for

殉道 xùndào die for a cause

殉道者 xùndàozhě martyr

殉国 xùnguó die (*or* give one's life) for one's country

殉教 xùnjiào die for a religious cause

殉节 xùnjié ① die out of loyalty to one's country or to a dynasty or regime ② (of a woman) die in defence of one's virtue ③ (of a widow) commit suicide rather than remarry

殉难 xùnnàn die for a just cause or for one's country

殉情 xùnqíng die for love

殉死 xùnsǐ ① be buried alive with the dead ② commit suicide at the death of sb.

殉葬 xùnzàng be buried alive with the dead: ～的奴隶 slaves buried alive with their deceased masters

殉葬品 xùnzàngpǐn funerary object; sacrificial object

殉职 xùnzhí die at one's post; die in the course of performing one's duty; die in line of duty

巽

xùn the sign ☴, symbolizing the wind in the Eight Diagrams (八卦)

熏

xùn *dial.* be poisoned or suffocated by coal gas: 他被煤气～死了。He died from suffocation by coal gas. / 小心别让煤气～着。Guard against coal gas poisoning. ——see also xūn

蕈

xùn *bot.* gill fungus

噀(潠)

xùn *formal* spurt (*or* spout) from the mouth

Y

yā

丫 yā bifurcation; fork

丫巴儿 yābar *dial.* bifurcation; fork: 树～ fork (of a tree); crotch

丫杈 yāchà same as 桠杈 yāchà

丫鬟 yāhuan slave girl; servant girl

丫头 yātou ① *dial.* girl ② slave girl

压（壓） yā ① press; push down; hold down; weigh down: ～扁 press flat; flatten / ～碎 crush to pieces / ～死 crush to death / ～坏 damage by pressure / 用石头～住地图的四角 put a stone on each corner of the map to hold it down / 果子把树枝～弯了。 The fruit weighed the branches down. / 这盒子压了～。 This box won't stand much weight. / 中国人民推翻了～在头上的三座大山。 The Chinese people overthrew the three big mountains (imperialism, feudalism and bureaucrat capitalism) that had lain like a dead weight on their backs. ② keep under control; control; keep under; quell: 喝点热水把咳嗽～一～ drink some hot water to ease a cough / ～低嗓门 lower one's voice; speak under one's breath / 强～住心头怒火 try hard to control one's anger; hold back one's rage / 我们的重机枪～住了敌人的火力。 Our heavy machine guns stilled the enemy's fire. ③ bring pressure to bear on; suppress; daunt; intimidate: 不受捧，不怕～ withstand both flattery and pressure / 别拿大帽子～人。 Don't you try to intimidate people by pinning labels on them. / 再大的自然灾害也～不垮我们。 Even a greater natural calamity cannot daunt us. / 资本家妄图～工人复工。 The capitalists vainly tried to force the workers to end the strike. ④ approach; be getting near: 太阳～山了。 The setting sun was touching the hilltop. ⑤ pigeonhole; shelve: 这份公文～了不少时间。 This document was pigeonholed for quite some time. / 这事儿先～几天再说。 Shelve this matter for a few days. ⑥ risk (money); stake ⑦ pressure: 血压 xuèyā ——see also yà

压宝 yābǎo a gambling game, played with dice under a bowl; stake

压不住 yābuzhù cannot keep under control: ～心头怒火 cannot control one's anger (*or* hold back one's rage) / 这个班除了他谁也～。 No one can keep this class under control except him.

压仓物 yācāngwù *navigation* ballast

压场 yāchǎng ① have a meeting, an audience, etc. well under one's control: 压不住场 cannot hold the audience's attention ② same as 压台 yātái

压车 yāchē same as 押车 yāchē

压秤 yāchèng be relatively heavy per unit volume: 干稻草不～。 Dry straw doesn't weigh much. / 这些劈柴太湿，～。 This firewood is too wet and weighs much more than usual.

压床 yāchuáng *mech.* press (machine): 手扳～ arbor press

压倒 yādǎo overwhelm; overpower; prevail over: ～一切的任务 an overriding task / 以～多数通过一项决议 pass a resolution by an overwhelming majority / 困难压不倒我们。 No difficulty can overwhelm us. / 我们已经～了敌人。 We have prevailed over our enemies. / 任何敌人也不能～我们。 No enemy can crush us. / ～性的胜利 an overwhelming victory; a landslide victory

压得住 yādezhù can keep under control: ～火 can control (*or* hold down) one's anger; can control oneself / 他有魄力，～手下的人。 He is forceful enough to control his men.

压低 yādī lower; drop: ～声音说话 speak in a lowered voice / ～物价 keep the prices down

压电 yādiàn (also 压电现象 yādiàn xiànxiàng) *phys.* piezoelectricity

压电晶体 yādiàn jīngtǐ *phys.* piezocrystal; piezoelectric crystal

压电拾音器 yādiàn shíyīnqì piezoelectric pickup

压电效应 yādiàn xiàoyìng piezoelectric effect

压顶 yādǐng bear down on one; weigh heavily on one: 乌云～。 Dark clouds hung overhead.

压锻 yāduàn *metall.* press forging

压队 yāduì bring up the rear

压服 yāfú force (*or* compel) sb. to submit: 解决思想问题只能靠说服，不能～。 Ideological problems can be solved only through persuasion, not by coercion. / ～手段 coercive measure

压盖 yāgài *mech.* gland

压盖填料 yāgài tiánliào gland packing

压花玻璃 yāhuābōli pattern glass

压挤 yājǐ *mech.* extrude: 塑料从微孔～出来形成纤维。 Plastic material is extruded through very small holes to form fibres.

压挤成形 yājǐ chéngxíng *mech.* extrusion moulding

压价 yājià force prices down; demand a lower price: ～出售 undersell / ～百分之二十五 force the price down by 25 per cent

压惊 yājīng help sb. get over a shock (by entertaining him, etc.)

压井 yājǐng *petroleum* kill the well

压境 yājìng (of enemy troops) press on to the border: 大军～。 A large enemy force is bearing down upon the border.

压卷 yājuàn (also 压卷之作 yājuàn zhī zuò) a piece of writing that surpasses all the others

压力 yālì ① *phys.* pressure: 大气～ atmospheric (*or* barometric) pressure ② overwhelming force; pressure: 外界～ outside pressure / 对某人施加～ bring pressure to bear on sb. / 在舆论的～下 under the pressure of public opinion

压力锅 yālìguō pressure cooker: 用～蒸煮 pressure-cook

压力机 yālìjī another name for 冲床 chōngchuáng

压力计 yālìjì pressure gauge; manometer

压裂 yāliè *petroleum* fracture: 水力～ hydraulic fracturing

压裂车 yālièchē fracturing unit truck

压路机 yālùjī　road roller; roller

压迫 yāpò　① oppress; repress: 地主～农民。The landlords oppressed the peasants. / ～其他民族的民族不可能是自由的。No nation can be free if it oppresses other nations. / ～者 oppressor / ～阶级 oppressor class ② constrict: 肿瘤～神经, 引起疼痛。The tumour constricts the nerves and causes pain. / 病人胸部有～感。The patient feels a constriction in the chest.

压气 yāqì　calm sb.'s anger: 说几句好话给他压压气。Say a few agreeable words to calm him down.

压强 yāqiáng　*phys.* intensity of pressure; pressure

压强计 yāqiángjì　pressure gauge

压青 yāqīng　*agric.* green manuring; green dressing

压热效应 yārè xiàoyìng　*phys.* piezocaloric effect

压舌板 yāshébǎn　*med.* tongue depressor

压岁钱 yāsuìqián　money given to children as a lunar New Year gift

压缩 yāsuō　① compress: 空气是可以～的气体。Air is a compressible gas. ② condense; reduce; cut down: ～开支 cut down (or reduce) expenses; retrench / 这篇文章可以～一下。The article can be cut down. / 你能把这故事～到不超过五千字吗? Can you condense the story into not more than 5,000 words?

压缩饼干 yāsuō bǐnggān　hardtack; ship biscuit (or bread); pilot biscuit (or bread)

压缩机 yāsuōjī　compressor: 空气～ air compressor

压缩空气 yāsuō kōngqì　compressed air

压台 yātái　present a theatrical performance as the last item on a programme

压台戏 yātáixì　the last item on a theatrical programme

压条 yātiáo　*agric.* layering

压痛 yātòng　*med.* tenderness: 伤口好了, 可是胳臂还有～。The cut has healed, but my arm is still tender.

压头 yātóu　*water conservancy* pressure head: 有效～ effective head

压蔓 yāwàn　keep down the vines of a creeping plant by covering them with earth at regular intervals (for protection against animals or the wind and for facilitating the growth of adventitious roots)

压线 yāxiàn　*sports* line ball

压延 yāyán　*mech.* mangle

压抑 yāyì　constrain; inhibit; depress; hold back: ～群众的积极性 inhibit the initiative of the masses / 心情～ feel constrained (or oppressed) / 这部影片气氛比较～。The film is rather depressing. / 胸口感到～ feel tight in the chest

压韵 yāyùn　rhyme: 这两句不～。These two lines don't rhyme.

压载舱 yāzàicāng　*navigation* ballast tank

压榨 yāzhà　① extract (juice, etc.) by pressure; press; squeeze: ～甘蔗 press sugarcane ② oppress and exploit; extort (or exact) money from; squeeze; bleed: 垄断资本家加紧对劳动人民的～。The monopoly capitalists are intensifying their exploitation of the working people.

压榨机 yāzhàjī　squeezer; mangle

压寨夫人 yāzhài fūren　mistress of the fort (a sobriquet for the wife of a brigand chief)

压阵 yāzhèn　① same as 压队 yāduì ② keep a situation well under one's control

压枝 yāzhī　same as 压条 yātiáo

压纸型机 yāzhǐxíngjī　*print.* stereotype press

压制[1] yāzhì　① suppress; stifle; inhibit: ～民主 suppress democracy / ～批评 suppress (or muzzle) criticism / ～不同意见 clamp down on (or stifle) differing opinions / ～群众的首创精神 inhibit the initiative of the masses / 采取～手段 adopt repressive measures / ～不住自己的愤怒 cannot suppress one's anger ② *mil.* neutralize (enemy fire by massive bombardment, etc.): ～射击 neutralizing (or neutralization) fire

压制[2] yāzhì　*mech.* pressing: ～砖坯 make unfired bricks by pressing / ～玻璃 pressed glass / ～茶 pressed tea

压制板 yāzhìbǎn　pressboard

压轴子 yāzhòuzi　① the last item but one on a theatrical programme ② present a theatrical performance as the last but one item on a programme: 明儿晚上拿《空城计》来～。Let's have *The Empty City Ruse* as the second major item for tomorrow evening's performance.

压铸 yāzhù　*metall.* (short for 压力铸造) die-casting

呀

yā　① *interj.* (expressing surprise) ah; oh: ～, 下雪了! Oh, it's snowing! ② *onom.* creak: 门～的一声开了。The door opened with a creak. ——see also yɑ

押[1]

yā　① give as security; mortgage; pawn; pledge: 以手表作～ leave one's watch as security ② detain; take into custody: 拘押 jūyā ③ escort: ～行李 escort luggage / 把小偷～到派出所去 escort the thief to the police station / ～下去! Take him away. ④ same as 压 yā, limited to use in 押宝 yābǎo, 押队 yāduì, 押韵 yāyùn, etc.

押[2]

yā　signature or mark in lieu of signature: 画押 huàyā

押宝 yābǎo　same as 压宝 yābǎo

押车 yāchē　escort goods on a train, truck, etc.

押当 yādàng　① pawn sth. ② a small pawnshop

押队 yāduì　same as 压队 yāduì

押解 yājiè　send (a criminal or captive) under escort; escort: ～出境 deport under escort

押金 yājīn　cash pledge; deposit

押款 yākuǎn　*com.* ① borrow money on security; raise a mortgage ② mortgage loan; loan on security; secured loan

押送 yāsòng　① send (a prisoner or captive) under escort; escort ② escort (goods) in transportation

押头 yātou　*dial.* security; pledge; collateral

押尾 yāwěi　sign or mark in lieu of signature at the end of a document

押运 yāyùn　escort (goods) in transportation

押韵 yāyùn　same as 压韵 yāyùn

押帐 yāzhàng　leave (or offer) sth. as security for a loan

押租 yāzū　rent deposit

哑（啞）

yā　same as 呀 yā ——see also yǎ

哑哑 yāyā　*onom.* ① the cries of a crow ② the sound of a baby learning to speak; babble

垭（埡）

yā　*dial.* (usu. used as part of a place name) a strip of land between hills: 马头～ Matou Ya (in Hubei Province)

鸦（鴉）

yā　crow (a bird)

鸦胆子 yādǎnzi　*bot.* Java brucea (*Brucea javanica*)

鸦片 yāpiàn　opium

鸦片战争 Yāpiàn Zhànzhēng　the Opium Wars (1840-1842)

鸦雀 yāquè　crow tit (a bird)

鸦雀无声 yā-què wú shēng　not a crow or sparrow is heard—silence reigns; all is quiet; no birds sing

桠（椏、枒）

yā　fork (of a tree)

桠杈 yāchà　① fork (of a tree); crotch ② crotched; forked

桠枫　yāfēng　same as 三角枫 sānjiǎofēng

鸭　yā　duck: 母～ duck / 公～ drake / 小～ duckling

鸭步鹅行　yābù-éxíng　same as 鸭行鹅步 yāxíng-ébù

鸭蛋　yādàn　① duck's egg ② inf. zero (as a score or mark); nought; goose egg

鸭蛋脸　yādànliǎn　oval face

鸭蛋青　yādànqīng　pale blue

鸭蛋圆　yādànyuán　dial. oval

鸭黄　yāhuáng　dial. duckling

鸭儿梨　yārlí　a fine species of pear grown in Hebei Province

鸭绒　yāróng　duck's down; eiderdown; down: ～被 eiderdown quilt; down quilt / ～背心 down waistcoat; down vest

鸭舌帽　yāshémào　peaked cap

鸭行鹅步　yāxíng-ébù　walk in a slow, rocking manner; waddle

鸭掌　yāzhǎng　duck's web (a delicacy)

鸭胗儿　yāzhēnr　duck's gizzard (a delicacy)

鸭跖草　yāzhícǎo　bot. dayflower (Commelina communis)

鸭子儿　yāzǐr　inf. duck's egg

鸭子　yāzi　inf. duck

鸭嘴笔　yāzuǐbǐ　drawing pen; ruling pen

鸭嘴兽　yāzuǐshòu　platypus; duckbill; duckmole

雅　yā　same as 鸭 yā——see also yǎ

雅皮士　yāpíshì　yuppie; yuppy (a transliteration)

雅片　yāpiàn　same as 鸦片 yāpiàn

yá

牙[1]　yá　① tooth: 这颗～疼。This tooth hurts. / 孩子长～了。The baby is teething. ② tooth-like thing: 轮～ cog ③ ivory: ～筷 ivory chopsticks / ～章 ivory seal

牙[2]　yá　old middleman; broker: 牙行 yáháng

牙白　yábái　creamy white; ivory-coloured

牙白口清　yábái-kǒuqīng　speak articulately

牙本质　yáběnzhì　physiol. dentine

牙碜　yáchen　① (of food) gritty ② (of language) coarse; jarring

牙齿　yáchǐ　tooth

牙床[1]　yáchuáng　physiol. gum

牙床[2]　yáchuáng　a richly carved ivory-inlaid bed

牙雕　yádiāo　ivory carving

牙粉　yáfěn　tooth powder

牙缝　yáfèng　space between the teeth: 剔～ pick one's teeth

牙疳　yágān　same as 走马疳 zǒumǎgān

牙缸　yágāng　a mug for mouth-rinsing or tooth-cleaning; tooth mug

牙膏　yágāo　toothpaste

牙根　yágēn　gum: 咬定～不说 clench one's teeth and refuse to say anything

牙垢　yágòu　tartar; dental calculus

牙骨质　yágǔzhì　physiol. cementum; cement

牙关　yáguān　mandibular joint: ～紧闭 lockjaw

牙冠　yáguān　physiol crown (of a tooth)

牙行　yáháng　old ① middleman; broker ② broker house; brokerage

牙花　yáhuā　(also 牙花子 yáhuāzi) dial. ① tartar; dental calculus ② gum

牙慧　yáhuì　see 拾人牙慧 shí rén yáhuì

牙祭　yájì　an unusually good meal (with plenty of meat): 打牙祭 dǎ yájì

牙具　yájù　tooth-cleaners (e.g. toothbrush, toothpaste, etc.)

牙科　yákē　(department of) dentistry: ～诊疗所 dental clinic

牙科学　yákēxué　dentistry

牙科医生　yákē yīshēng　dentist; dental surgeon

牙口　yákou　① the age of a draught animal as shown by the number of its teeth: 看一看～ look at a draught animal's teeth to determine its age ② the condition of an old person's teeth: 您这么大年纪,～可不错呀! You've certainly got good teeth for your age.

牙侩　yákuài　formal middleman; broker

牙轮　yálún　common name for 齿轮 chǐlún

牙买加　Yámǎijiā　Jamaica

牙买加人　Yámǎijiārén　Jamaican

牙牌　yápái　dominoes (made of ivory, bone, etc.)

牙鲆　yápíng　zool. lefteye flounder (Paralichthys)

牙婆　yápó　old a woman trafficking in young girls

牙签　yáqiān　toothpick

牙色　yásè　ivory-coloured; creamy white

牙商　yáshāng　old middleman; broker

牙石　yáshí　same as 牙垢 yágòu

牙刷　yáshuā　toothbrush

牙髓　yásuǐ　physiol. dental pulp

牙髓炎　yásuǐyán　pulpitis

牙痛　yátòng　toothache

牙线　yáxiàn　dental floss

牙牙　yáyá　onom. the sound of baby talk; babble

牙牙学语　yáyá xué yǔ　babble one's first sounds; learn to speak

牙医　yáyī　short for 牙科医生 yákē yīshēng

牙龈　yáyín　physiol. gum; gingiva

牙龈炎　yáyínyán　gingivitis

牙釉质　yáyòuzhì　physiol. enamel

牙獐　yázhāng　another name for 獐子 zhāngzi

牙质　yázhì　① made of ivory: ～的刀把 an ivory knife handle ② same as 牙本质 yáběnzhì

牙周病　yázhōubìng　periodontosis

牙周炎　yázhōuyán　periodontitis

牙子[1]　yázi　inf. serrated edge

牙子[2]　yázi　old middleman; broker

伢　yā　dial. child; kid

伢崽　yázǎi　dial. child; kid

伢子　yázi　dial. child; kid

芽　yá　bud; sprout; shoot

芽孢　yábāo　biol. gemma (of a fungus)

芽变　yábiàn　bot. bud mutation

芽茶　yáchá　young tea leaves; bud-tea

芽豆　yádòu　sprouted broad bean

芽接　yájiē　bud grafting; budding

芽眼　yáyǎn　eye (the bud of a potato)

蚜　yá　aphid; aphis; plant louse

蚜虫　yáchóng　aphid; aphis; plant louse: 苹果～ apple aphid / 烟～ tobacco aphid

涯　yá　① water margin ② margin; limit: 吾生也有～,而知也无～。(庄子) Our life has a limit but knowledge has none.

崖(厓、崕)　yá　① precipice; cliff ② limit; bound; boundary: 崖略 yálüè

崖壁　yábì　precipice; cliff

崖略　yálüè　formal outline; general idea

睚　yá　*formal*　the corner of the eye

睚眦　yázì　*formal*　① an angry stare ② a small grievance: ～之怨 a trifling (*or* trivial) grievance

睚眦必报　yázì bì bào　seek revenge just for an angry look: 一饭之德必偿，睚眦之怨必报《史记》 make a point of repaying the kindness of a single meal and taking revenge for one angry look

衙　yá　*yamen*

衙门　yámen　*yamen*, government office in feudal China: ～八字开，有理无钱莫进来。The *yamen* gate is open wide; with right but no money, don't go inside.

衙内　yánèi　*old* (a title for the son of a high official) master: 高～ Master Gao

衙署　yáshǔ　same as 衙门 yámen

衙役　yáyi　*yamen* runner

yǎ

哑（啞）　yǎ　① mute; dumb: 他又聋又～。He's deaf and dumb. ② hoarse; husky: ～嗓子 a husky (*or* hoarse) voice / 嗓子喊～了 shout oneself hoarse ③ (of a shell, bomb, etc.) fail to explode: ～弹 dud ——see also yā

哑巴　yǎba　① a dumb person; mute ② be dumb; keep mum: 你今儿个怎么～啦? Why are you so silent today? *or* Have you lost your tongue?

哑巴吃黄连，有苦说不出　yǎba chī huánglián, yǒu kǔ shuōbuchū　a dumb person tasting bitter herbs—be unable to express one's discomfort; be forced to suffer in silence

哑巴亏　yǎbakuī　a grievance that one has to keep to oneself: 吃～ be unable to speak out about one's grievances; be forced to keep one's grievances to oneself

哑场　yǎchǎng　an awkward silence at a meeting

哑号儿　yǎhàor　*dial.* a secret signal (*or* sign)

哑火　yǎhuǒ　① (of a shell, bomb, etc.) fail to explode ② remain dumb; keep mum

哑剧　yǎjù　dumb show; pantomime: ～演员 pantomimist

哑口无言　yǎkǒu wúyán　be left without an argument; be reduced to silence; be rendered speechless: 他论辩有力，把对方说得～。His forceful arguments silenced his opponent. / 他没料到她这样严厉的反问，一时～。He had not expected his question to be countered so sternly and for the moment he could think of nothing to say.

哑铃　yǎlíng　*sports* dumbbell

哑谜　yǎmí　a puzzling remark; enigma; riddle: 别给我们打～啦! Don't keep us guessing.

哑炮　yǎpào　same as 瞎炮 xiāpào

哑然[1]　yǎrán　*formal* soundless; silent: ～无声。Silence reigns.

哑然[2]　yǎrán　*formal* the sound of laughing: ～失笑 be unable to stifle a laugh; can't help laughing

哑语　yǎyǔ　same as 手语 shǒuyǔ

哑子　yǎzi　*dial.* a dumb person; mute

雅[1]　yǎ　① *formal* standard; proper; correct: 雅正 yǎzhèng ② refined; elegant: 你这房间的布置～得很。Your room is furnished in excellent taste. ③ one of the three sections of *The Book of Songs*《诗经》, consisting of festal songs sung at court during banquets and entertainment of guests ④ *honor.* your: 雅意 yǎyì

雅[2]　yǎ　*formal* ① acquaintance; friendship: 无一日之～ not have the pleasure of knowing sb. ② usually; often: 妇赵女也，～善鼓瑟。(杨恽) My wife is from Zhao and so plays the zither very well. ③ extremely; very much: ～以为美 really consider it beautiful ——see also yā

雅淡　yǎdàn　simple and tasteful; quietly elegant: ～梳妆 be simply but tastefully dressed

雅尔塔　Yǎěrtǎ　Yalta

雅观　yǎguān　(usu. used in the negative) refined (in manner, etc.); in good taste: 很不～ most unseemly; rather unsightly

雅号　yǎhào　① *honor.* your elegant name ② *humor.* nickname: 我倒不晓得他还有这么一个～呢。I never knew he had such a nickname.

雅教　yǎjiào　*honor.* your esteemed opinion; your excellent advice

雅洁　yǎjié　elegant and immaculate

雅量　yǎliàng　① magnanimity; generosity ② great capacity for liquor

雅鲁藏布江　Yǎlǔzàngbùjiāng　the Yarlung Zangbo (Yalu Tsangpo) River

雅趣　yǎqù　refined (*or* cultivated) tastes

雅人　yǎrén　a person of refined tastes

雅人深致　yǎrén shēn zhì　a man of refinement with a profound mind

雅士　yǎshì　a refined scholar: 文人～ men of letters and refined scholars

雅俗共赏　yǎ-sú gòng shǎng　(of a work of art or literature) appeal to all; suit both refined and popular tastes

雅玩　yǎwán　① refined enjoyment ② *pol.* (said when presenting sb. with an object of artistic value) for your refined enjoyment

雅兴　yǎxìng　an aesthetic mood: ～不浅 be really in an aesthetic mood; have a really keen interest in sth. / 无此～ not be in such a poetic mood; be in no mood for such things

雅驯　yǎxùn　*formal* (of diction or language) refined; elegant

雅意　yǎyì　① kindly thoughts ② *honor.* your kindness; your kind offer

雅乐　yǎyuè　(in ancient times) ceremonial music; court music

雅正　yǎzhèng　① *formal* standard; correct ② *formal* upright; righteous ③ *pol.* (said when presenting sb. with a specimen of one's calligraphy, a copy of one's book, etc.) would you kindly point out my inadequacies

雅致　yǎzhì　refined; tasteful: 陈设～ tastefully furnished

雅座　yǎzuò　private room (in a restaurant, etc.)

yà

轧[1]　yà　① roll; run over: 把路面～平 roll a road surface / 被车～伤 get run over and injured by a car / ～碎 crush to pieces / ～棉花 gin cotton ② oust; squeeze out; push out: 倾轧 qīngyà

轧[2]　yà　*onom.* the sound of a machine running: 缝纫机～～～～地响着。The sewing machine was clicking away. ——see also gá; zhá

轧板机　yàbǎnjī　*metall.* mangle

轧场　yàcháng　① thresh grain on a threshing ground with a stone roller ② level a threshing floor with a stone roller

轧道机 yàdàojī *dial.* road roller; roller

轧光 yàguāng *text.* calendering

轧光机 yàguāngjī *text.* calender

轧花 yàhuā *text.* cotton ginning: ～厂 cotton ginning mill

轧花机 yàhuājī cotton gin

亚[1]（亞） yà inferior; second: 不～于人 second to none; not inferior to anyone

亚[2]（亞） Yà short for 亚洲 Yàzhōu

亚当 Yàdāng Adam (the first man according to the Bible)

亚得里亚海 Yàdélǐyàhǎi the Adriatic (Sea)

亚非会议 Yà-Fēi Huìyì the Asian-African Conference

亚砜 yàfēng *chem.* sulphoxide

亚急性 yàjíxìng *med.* subacute: ～病 subacute disease

亚军 yàjūn second place (in a sports contest); runner-up: 他在百米赛跑中得了～。He came second in the 100-metre dash. *or* He was runner-up in the 100-metre dash. / 上海队获～。The Shanghai team won second place.

亚硫酸 yàliúsuān *chem.* sulphurous acid

亚麻 yàmá *bot.* flax (*linum usitatissimum*)

亚麻布 yàmábù linen (cloth)

亚麻精纺机 yàmá jīngfǎngjī *text.* flax spinning frame

亚麻籽 yàmázǐ linseed; flaxseed

亚麻籽油 yàmázǐyóu linseed oil

亚马孙河 Yàmǎsūnhé the Amazon (River)

亚美尼亚 Yàměiníyà Armenia

亚美尼亚人 Yàměiníyàrén Armenian

亚美尼亚语 Yàměiníyàyǔ Armenian (language)

亚平宁山脉 Yàpíngníng Shānmài the Apennines

亚热带 yàrèdài subtropical zone; subtropics; semitropics

亚赛 yàsài (*also* 亚似 yàsì) can be compared to; may be likened to; be just like

亚圣 yàshèng the lesser sage—Mencius (opp. 至圣 zhìshèng)

亚速尔群岛 Yàsù'ěr Qúndǎo the Azores

亚铁 yàtiě *chem.* ferrous: 氯化～ ferrous chloride

亚细亚 Yàxìyà Asia

亚硝酸 yàxiāosuān *chem.* nitrous acid

亚音速 yàyīnsù *phys.* subsonic speed: ～飞机 subsonic aircraft

亚油酸 yàyóusuān *chem.* linoleic acid

亚运会 Yàyùnhuì (short for 亚洲运动会) the Asian Games: 第十一届～ the 11th Asian Games

亚种 yàzhǒng *biol.* subspecies

亚洲 Yàzhōu Asia

亚洲开发银行 Yàzhōu Kāifā Yínháng the Asian Development Bank (ADB): ～理事 governor of the Asian Development Bank; ADB governor / ～理事会 the board of governors of the Asian Development Bank

压（壓） yà see below ——see also yā

压板 yàbǎn seesaw; teeterboard; teeter-totter

压根儿 yàgēnr *inf.* (usu. used in the negative) from the start; in the first place; altogether: ～就不知道 have had no idea from the start; not know anything about it / 他全忘了，好像～就没有这回事。He's clean forgotten about it, as if it had never happened. / 我不是新搬来的，我是～就住在这儿的。I'm no newcomer. I've been living here all along.

讶 yà *formal* be surprised; be astonished; wonder: 惊讶 jīngyà

讶然 yàrán *formal* be surprised; be astonished: ～失色 turn pale with fright

讶异 yàyì be surprised; be amazed; be astonished: 大家听了他的话，都十分～。We were all amazed at what he said.

迓 yà *formal* welcome; meet: 迎迓 yíngyà

研 yà press and smooth (leather, cloth, paper, etc.); calender; mangle

研光 yàguāng *mech.* calendering; mangling

研光机 yàguāngjī *mech.* calender; mangle

娅（婭） yà see 姻娅 yīnyà

挜（掗） yà *dial.* force sb. to take or buy sth.

氩（氬） yà *chem.* argon (Ar)

揠 yà *formal* pull up; tug upward

揠苗助长 yà miáo zhù zhǎng try to help shoots grow by pulling them up—spoil things by excessive enthusiasm

ya

呀 ya *part.* (used in place of 啊 when the preceding word ends in sound a, e, i, o, or ü): 她是谁～? Who is she? / 快来～! Come here, quick! ——see also yā

yān

咽 yān *physiol.* pharynx ——see also yàn; yè

咽鼓管 yāngǔguǎn *physiol.* Eustachian tube

咽喉 yānhóu ① *physiol.* pharynx and larynx; throat ② strategic (*or* vital) passage; key junction (*or* link): 直布罗陀海峡是地中海通向大西洋的～。The Straits of Gibraltar are the strategic passage between the Mediterranean and the Atlantic.

咽喉炎 yānhóuyán sore throat

咽喉要地 yānhóu yàodì strategic (*or* vital) passage; key junction (*or* link)

咽头 yāntóu another name for 咽 yān

咽峡炎 yānxiáyán angina

咽炎 yānyán pharyngitis

恹（懕、厭） yān see below

恹恹 yānyān *formal* weak and weary through illness; run-down: ～欲睡 feel weak and sleepy

烟[1]（煙） yān ① smoke ② mist; vapour: 云烟 yúnyān / 烟雾 yānwù ③ (of eyes) be irritated by smoke: 谁在这里生火啊! 都～得睁不开眼了。Who's lighting the stove here? I can't even open my eyes for the smoke. ④ cigarette or pipe tobacco: 抽支～ have a cigarette; have a smoke / 一袋～的功夫 time enough to smoke a pipeful of tobacco ⑤ opium: 烟土 yāntǔ / 禁烟 jìnyān

烟[2]（煙、菸） yān the tobacco plant: 烟叶 yānyè / 烤烟 kǎoyān

烟霭 yān'ǎi *formal* mist and clouds

烟波 yānbō mist-covered waters

烟波浩渺 yānbō hàomiǎo a vast expanse of misty, roll-

ing waters: 远望洞庭，～。 Far in the distance lies the Dongting Lake, a vast expanse of misty, rolling waters.

烟草　yāncǎo　the tobacco plant; tobacco: ～种植园 tobacco plantation

烟尘　yānchén　① smoke and dust ② *old* battle; war: 扫荡～ quell a rebellion

烟囱　yāncōng　chimney; funnel; stovepipe

烟村　yāncūn　a village shrouded in mist

烟袋　yāndài　a long-stemmed pipe or a water pipe

烟袋杆儿　yāndàigǎnr　the stem of a pipe

烟袋锅　yāndàiguō　(also 烟袋锅子 yāndàiguōzi) ① the bowl of a long-stemmed pipe; pipe bowl ② a long-stemmed pipe

烟袋荷包　yāndài hébāo　tobacco pouch

烟袋嘴儿　yāndàizuǐr　the mouth-piece of a long-stemmed pipe

烟道　yāndào　flue: ～尘 flue dust / ～气 flue gas

烟灯　yāndēng　a small lamp used for roasting prepared opium

烟蒂　yāndì　cigarette end (*or* stub, butt, stump)

烟斗　yāndǒu　(tobacco) pipe

烟斗架　yāndǒujià　pipe rack

烟斗丝　yāndǒusī　pipe tobacco

烟缸　yāngāng　same as 烟灰缸 yānhuīgāng

烟膏　yāngāo　prepared opium paste

烟馆儿　yānguǎnr　opium den

烟鬼　yānguǐ　① opium addict ② a heavy smoker

烟锅　yānguō　pipe bowl

烟海　yānhǎi　*formal* a sea of fog or mist—vast and voluminous: 浩如烟海 hào rú yānhǎi

烟盒　yānhé　cigarette case

烟花　yānhuā　① *formal* a lovely spring scene ② *old* prostitution: ～女 prostitute / ～巷 a red-light district ③ fireworks

烟花炮竹　yānhuā pàozhú　fireworks

烟灰　yānhuī　tobacco or cigarette ash

烟灰缸　yānhuīgāng　ashtray

烟火　yānhuǒ　① smoke and fire: 动～ light a fire and cook / 严禁～! Smoking or lighting fires strictly forbidden. ② cooked food: 不食人间～ do not eat cooked food; live the life of an immortal

烟火　yānhuo　fireworks: 放～ let off fireworks; put on a display of fireworks

烟火食　yānhuǒshí　cooked food

烟火探测器　yānhuǒ tàncèqì　smoke detector

烟碱　yānjiǎn　*chem.* nicotine: ～中毒 nicotinism

烟晶　yānjīng　*geol.* smoky quartz; smoky topaz

烟具　yānjù　smoking paraphernalia; smoking set

烟卷儿　yānjuǎnr　*inf.* cigarette

烟煤　yānméi　bituminous coal; soft coal

烟幕　yānmù　smoke screen

烟幕弹　yānmùdàn　① smoke shell; smoke bomb ② smoke screen

烟农　yānnóng　tobacco grower

烟泡儿　yānpàor　a small ball of roasted opium

烟屁股　yānpìgu　*inf.* cigarette end (*or* stub, butt, stump)

烟枪　yānqiāng　opium pipe

烟圈　yānquān　smoke ring: 他躺在沙发上，口含烟斗，欣赏着自己吐出来的～。 With a pipe in his mouth, he lounged on the sofa, admiring the smoke rings he was blowing.

烟色　yānsè　dark brown

烟丝　yānsī　cut tobacco; pipe tobacco

烟酸　yānsuān　*chem.* nicotinic acid; niacin

烟酸缺乏症　yānsuānquēfázhèng　*med.* pellagra

烟筒　yāntong　chimney; funnel; stovepipe

烟头　yāntóu　cigarette end (*or* stub, butt, stump)

烟突　yāntū　*formal* chimney; funnel; stovepipe

烟土　yāntǔ　crude opium

烟雾　yānwù　① smoke, mist, or vapour; a mixture of smoke and vapour: 厨房里～腾腾。 The kitchen is filled with steam and smoke. ② smog: ～笼罩着那座城市。 The city was shrouded in a thick smog.

烟雾弥漫　yānwù mímàn　be full of smoke; be enveloped in mist

烟霞　yānxiá　mists and clouds

烟霞癖　yānxiápǐ　① *formal* a deep love for mists and clouds (i.e. the beauty of nature) ② *humor.* addiction to opium smoking; the opium habit

烟消云散　yānxiāo-yúnsàn　vanish like smoke and disperse like clouds—completely vanish: 她方才那一阵兴奋又～了。 Her high spirits of a moment ago suddenly passed away like a breath of wind. / 他紧张的心情，被我这一番笑谈，一下子冲得～了。 At my friendly jesting, his tension melted away.

烟叶　yānyè　tobacco leaf; leaf tobacco

烟瘾　yānyǐn　a craving for opium; a craving for tobacco: 他～可大了。 He's a heavy smoker. *or* He smokes like a chimney. / 他～发了。 He's dying for a smoke.

烟油子　yānyóuzi　tobacco tar; cigarette tar

烟雨　yānyǔ　misty rain: 南朝四百八十寺，多少楼台～中。 (杜牧) Of four hundred and eighty monasteries of the Southern Dynasties, How many towers and terraces loom in the misty rain?

烟云　yānyún　smoke, mists and clouds

烟柱　yānzhù　a column of smoke

烟子　yānzi　soot

烟嘴儿　yānzuǐr　cigarette holder

殷
yān　*formal* blackish red; dark red ——see also yīn

殷红　yānhóng　blackish red; dark red: ～的血迹 blackish red bloodstains / ～的鸡冠花 the dark red cockscombs

胭（臙）
yān　see below

胭脂　yānzhi　rouge

胭脂红　yānzhihóng　① carmine ② famille rose

淹¹（湮）
yān　flood; submerge; inundate: 暴雨过后，整个村子的地都被水～了。 The heavy rains flooded all the fields of the village. / 修好河堤，庄稼就不怕～了。 When the river dyke is completed, the crops will be safe against floods.

淹²
yān　① (of sweat, etc.) irritate the skin: 我胳肢窝被汗～得难受。 My armpits are tingling from sweat. ② *formal* wide: 淹博 yānbó ③ *formal* delay: 淹留 yānliú

淹博　yānbó　*formal* wide; broad: 学识～ have a wide (*or* broad) knowledge; be well-read; be learned

淹贯　yānguàn　*formal* have a thorough understanding of: ～群书 be well-read; be learned

淹灌　yānguàn　*agric.* basin irrigation

淹蹇　yānjiǎn　① *formal* be frustrated: 宦途～。 An official career is full of frustrations. ② delay; hold up: 他老不回来，不知道什么事情～住了。 He isn't back yet. I wonder what's holding him up.

淹浸　yānjìn　flood; inundate: 洪水～了数千亩农田。 Floodwaters inundated thousands of *mu* of farmland.

淹浸　yānjin　*dial.* ruin; spoil

淹留　yānliú　*formal* stay for a long period

淹埋　yānmái　(of mud, sand, etc.) flow or blow over and cover completely: 一段铁路被淤泥～了。 A section of the railway was buried in mud.

淹没　yānmò　submerge; flood; inundate; drown: 河里涨水，小桥都～了。 The river flooded and submerged the

small bridge. / 被～的田地 inundated fields / 企图阻挡历史潮流的人终将被历史潮流所～。Those who try to hold back the tide of history will eventually be drowned by it. / 他的讲话被欢呼声～了。His speech was drowned out by cheers.

淹死　yānsǐ　be drowned

阉　yān　① castrate or spay: ～鸡 capon / ～牛 bullock; steer / ～羊 wether / ～猪 barrow; hog ② *formal* eunuch: 阉党 yāndǎng

阉党　yāndǎng　the eunuchs as a clique

阉割　yāngē　① castrate or spay ② deprive a theory, etc. of its essence; emasculate

阉宦　yānhuàn　eunuch

阉人　yānrén　① a castrated person ② eunuch

阉寺　yānsì　*formal* eunuch

阏　yān　see below

阏氏　yānzhī　the consort of a Xiongnu (匈奴) chief

焉　yān　*formal* ① (used to refer to an important element placed at the beginning of the sentence) to, on, in, from, by, or than it: 寡人之于国也, 尽心～耳矣。(《孟子》) As for my attitude towards the state, I do indeed devote my whole attention to it. ② (used in rhetorical questions) to or in what place; in what respect; for what; how: ～能不去? How could I possibly not go? / 未知生, ～知死? If you know nothing about life, what can you know about death? ③ (preceded by an expression of condition) not unless; then and only then: 必知乱之所自起, ～能治之。You have to know how the trouble arose before you can deal with it. ④ *part.*: 幸勿哂～。Please don't laugh at me. / 天何言哉? 四时行～, 百物生～。(《论语》) What does Heaven ever say? Yet there are the four seasons going round and the hundred things coming into being.

湮　yān　*formal* ① fall into oblivion; bury in oblivion: 湮没 yānmò ② clog up; stop

湮灭　yānmiè　bury in oblivion; annihilate

湮没　yānmò　① fall into oblivion; be neglected; be forgotten: 在封建社会, 劳动人民有许多发明创造都被～了。In feudal society many of the inventions of the working people were neglected. ② *phys.* annihilation: ～光子 annihilation photon

湮没无闻　yānmò wúwén　sink into oblivion; fall into obscurity

腌(醃)　yān　preserve in salt, sugar, etc.; pickle; salt: 剩下的肉可以～一下以后吃。The rest of the meat can be salted down for later use. / ～菜 pickled vegetables; pickles / ～鱼 salted fish / ～肉 salted meat; bacon ② marinate: 肉片要用黄酒、醋、酱油～过再炸。Marinate the sliced pork in rice wine, vinegar and soy sauce before frying it. ——see also ā

腌制　yānzhì　make by pickling or salting: ～火腿 make ham / ～酱菜 make pickles

腌渍　yānzì　preserve in brine, vinegar, etc.; pickle: ～的黄瓜很爽口。Pickled cucumbers are crisp and refreshing. / 跑了一天的路, 汗～得身上好难受。After walking for a whole day, I was all sticky with sweat.

鄢　Yān　a surname

嫣　yān　*formal* handsome; beautiful

嫣红　yānhóng　bright red

嫣然　yānrán　*formal* beautiful; sweet: ～一笑 give a charming (*or* winsome) smile

燕　Yān　① one of the Warring States into which China was divided during the Eastern Zhou period (770–256 B.C.), comprising parts of modern Hebei and Liaoning ② old name for 河北 Héběi ③ a surname ——see also yàn

燕京　Yānjīng　old name for 北京 Běijīng

yán

延　yán　① prolong; extend; protract: 蔓延 mànyán ② postpone; delay: 顺延 shùnyán ③ *formal* engage (a teacher, adviser, etc.); send for: ～医 send for a doctor

延挨　yán'ái　delay; stall: ～时日 play for time; stall (for time)

延安　Yán'ān　Yan'an

延安精神　Yán'ān jīngshén　the Yan'an Spirit—the spirit of self-reliance and hard struggle developed by the people of Yan'an and the Shaanxi-Gansu-Ningxia Border Region during 1936–1948

延长　yáncháng　lengthen; prolong; extend: 输油管～了二百公里。The oil pipeline has been extended another 200 kilometres. / 会议～了三天。The conference was prolonged for three more days. / ～合同期限 extend the contract period

延长号　yánchánghào　*mus.* pause

延长线　yánchángxiàn　extension (*or* extended) line

延迟　yánchí　delay; defer; postpone: 展览会开幕的日期～了。The opening of the exhibition has been postponed.

延宕　yándàng　procrastinate; delay; keep putting off

延发　yánfā　*mil.* delayed action

延发引信　yánfā yǐnxìn　delayed-action fuse; delay fuse

延搁　yángē　delay; procrastinate: 这事已经～多天。This matter has been delayed for quite a few days.

延胡索　yánhúsuǒ　① *bot.* yanhusuo (*Corydalis remota* or *Corydalis ambigua*) ② *Chin. med.* tuber of yanhusuo

延缓　yánhuǎn　delay; postpone; put off: ～工作进度 retard the progress of work / 这个手术可以～几天再做。The operation can be put off for a few days.

延会　yánhuì　postpone a meeting or conference

延见　yánjiàn　*formal* grant an interview with; give an audience to

延接　yánjiē　*formal* receive (a guest): ～来宾 receive visitors

延颈企踵　yánjǐng-qǐzhǒng　(also 延颈举踵 yánjǐng-jǔzhǒng) crane one's neck and stand on tiptoe—eagerly look forward to; anxiously expect

延揽　yánlǎn　*formal* enlist the services of: ～人才 enlist the services of able people

延袤　yánmào　*formal* stretch; extend: 长城自西至东～万余里。From west to east the Great Wall stretched for over ten thousand li.

延年益寿　yánnián-yìshòu　(of tonics, etc.) prolong life; promise longevity

延聘　yánpìn　*formal* engage; invite (sb. to do sth. in a particular capacity): ～某人为法律顾问 engage sb. as one's legal adviser

延期　yánqī　postpone; defer; put off: ～付款 defer payment / 比赛因雨～。The game was put off on account of rain. / 要求～十年偿还债务 demand a ten-year moratorium / 办理签证～手续 have one's visa extended; extend a visa / ～审理 postponement of the hearing

延期偿付权　yánqīchángfùquán　*leg.* moratorium

延期炸弹　yánqī zhàdàn　delayed-action bomb

延企　yánqǐ　*formal* crane one's neck and stand on tip-

toe—eagerly look forward to; anxiously expect: 对您的来访, 我们正～以待。 We are eagerly looking forward to your visit.

延请　yánqǐng　invite (sb. to do a particular job); engage

延烧　yánshāo　(of a fire) spread: 这场森林大火～五百平方公里。 The forest fire spread over an area of five hundred square kilometres.

延伸　yánshēn　extend; stretch; elongate: 铁路一直～到海边。 The railway line stretches right to the coast.

延伸火力　yánshēn huǒlì　*mil.* creeping fire; lift fire

延伸率　yánshēnlǜ　*metall.* percentage elongation

延绳钓　yánshéngdiào　longline fishing; long-lining

延时摄影　yánshíshèyǐng　time-lapse photography

延寿　yánshòu　lengthen (*or* prolong) one's life

延髓　yánsuǐ　*physiol.* medulla oblongata

延误　yánwù　incur loss through delay: ～时机 miss an opportunity because of a delay / ～时日 lose time

延性　yánxìng　*phys.* ductility

延续　yánxù　continue; go on; last: 不能让这种状况～下去。 This state of affairs must not be allowed to continue. / 旱象～了半年之久。 The drought lasted for as long as six months.

延续性　yánxùxìng　continuity

延音　yányīn　*mus.* tenuto

延誉　yányù　*formal* spread sb.'s fame

延展　yánzhǎn　extend; stretch: 公路一直～到海滩上。 The highway extends as far as the beach.

言

言　yán　① speech; word: 言语 yányǔ / 有言在先 yǒu yán zài xiān ② say; talk; speak: ～明 state explicitly; clearly stipulate ③ character; word: 全书近二十万～。 It is a book of nearly 200,000 words. ④ (Yán) a surname

言必信, 行必果　yán bì xìn, xíng bì guǒ　insist on keeping one's word and seeing one's actions through to the end; always stand by one's word, and undertake nothing that one does not bring to achievement

言必有中　yán bì yǒu zhòng　when one speaks, one speaks to the point; whenever one says something one hits the mark: 夫人不言, ～。(《论语》) That man is no talker; but when he does say anything, he invariably hits the mark.

言不及义　yán bù jí yì　never say anything serious; talk frivolously: 群居终日, ～, 好行小慧, 难矣哉。(《论语》) To be together all day long and never talk about fundamentals but take pleasure only in showing one's cleverness—indeed it's a hopeless case!

言不尽意　yán bù jìn yì　I should like to say more (but I must bring my letter to a close)

言不由衷　yán bù yóuzhōng　speak insincerely; speak with one's tongue in one's cheek

言差语错　yánchā-yǔcuò　mistakes or slips in speaking: 偶尔有个～, 谁也不会责怪。 Nobody would blame you for an occasional slip of the tongue.

言出法随　yán chū fǎ suí　upon promulgation this law shall be strictly enforced

言传　yánchuán　explain in words: 只可意会, 不可言传 zhǐkě yìhuì, bùkě yánchuán

言传身教　yánchuán-shēnjiào　teach by personal example as well as verbal instruction; teach by precept and example

言辞　yáncí　(also 言词 yáncí) one's words; what one says: ～恳切 be sincere in what one says / ～不逊 make impertinent remarks; speak insolently

言次　yáncì　*formal* in the course of the conversation: ～有退隐之意。 As he talked, he hinted at his intention of going into retirement.

言道　yándào　*old* say: 他～他和林先生只有一面之交。 He said he was only casually acquainted with Mr. Lin.

言定　yándìng　decide; agree: 他们～过了春节就动手。 They decided to start work immediately after the Spring Festival.

言多语失　yán duō yǔshī　(also 言多必失 yán duō bì shī) he who talks too much is prone to error

言而无信　yán ér wú xìn　fail to keep faith; go back on one's word

言而有信　yán ér yǒu xìn　be true to one's word; be as good as one's word

言归于好　yán guī yú hǎo　make it up (with sb.); become reconciled

言归正传　yán guī zhèngzhuàn　to come back to our story; to return to the subject

言过其实　yán guò qí shí　exaggerate; overstate

言和　yánhé　make peace; become reconciled; bury the hatchet: 握手～ shake hands and make it up

言次　yánhuān　chat cheerfully: 杯酒～ chat cheerfully over a cup of wine

言简意赅　yánjiǎn-yìgāi　concise and comprehensive; compendious

言讲　yánjiǎng　say: 听人～, 他得的是癌症。 They say he's got cancer.

言教　yánjiào　teach by word of mouth; give verbal directions: ～不如身教。 Example is better than precept.

言近旨远　yánjìn-zhǐyuǎn　simple words but deep meaning; simple in language but profound in meaning

言路　yánlù　channels through which criticisms and suggestions may be communicated to the leadership: 堵塞～ stifle criticisms and suggestions

言论　yánlùn　opinion on public affairs; expression of one's political views; speech: 我们的一切～和行动都应符合人民的利益。 Everything we say and do must be in the interests of the people. / 我们看一个人, 不仅要听他的～, 还要看他的行动。 We must judge a person not only by his words, but also by his deeds. / ～自由 freedom of speech

言情小说　yánqíng xiǎoshuō　a romantic or sentimental novel

言人人殊　yán rén rén shū　different people, different versions; each person tells a different story

言三语四　yánsān-yǔsì　make irresponsible remarks

言声儿　yánshēngr　utter a sound or a word: 他不言一声儿。 He didn't say a word.

言说　yánshuō　put into words; say: 一种难以～的心情 an indescribable mood

言谈　yántán　the way one speaks or what he says: ～举止 speech and deportment / ～之间可以看出他很懂行。 It's clear from the way he talks that he knows the subject well.

言听计从　yántīng-jìcóng　listen to sb.'s words and follow his counsels; always follow sb.'s advice; act upon whatever sb. says; have implicit faith in sb.

言外之意　yán wài zhī yì　what is actually meant; the real meaning; implication: 他摆了一大堆困难, ～是需要补助。 He gave a long account of his troubles, with the implication that he needed financial aid. / 体会其～ read between the lines

言为心声　yán wéi xīnshēng　words are the voice of the mind; speech is the picture of the mind; what the heart thinks the tongue speaks: 人的心理真是奇妙, ～一点不假。 A person's psychology is a subtle thing. How true it is that "words are echoes of the heart."

言行　yán-xíng　words and deeds; statements and actions

言行不一　yán-xíng bù yī　the deeds do not match the words; one's actions do not square with one's promises

言行录　yánxínglù　records of the words and deeds (of a

famous person)

言行一致 yán-xíng yīzhì the deeds match (*or* square with) the words; one's actions are in keeping with one's promises; one's deeds are consistent with one's words; be as good as one's word

言犹在耳 yán yóu zài ěr the words still ring (*or* reverberate) in one's ears

言有尽而意无穷 yán yǒu jìn ér yì wúqióng the words come to an end, but the meaning is inexhaustible: 如空中之音，相中之色，水中之月，镜中之像，～。(严羽《沧浪诗话》) Like an echo in the void, and colour in a form, the moon reflected in water, and an image in a mirror, the words come to an end, but the meaning is inexhaustible.

言语 yányǔ spoken language; speech: ～和文字 spoken and written language / ～粗鲁 speak rudely

言语 yányu *dial.* speak; talk; answer: 他这个人不爱～。He is a man of few words. / 人家问你这事儿，怎么不～? Why didn't you say something when people asked you about it? / 你走的时候～一声儿。Let me know when you leave.

言责 yánzé ① a subject's responsibility of offering advice to the ruler ② responsibility for what one says

言者无心，听者有意 yánzhě wúxīn, tīngzhě yǒuyì a casual remark sounds significant to a suspicious listener; a careless word may reveal much to an attentive listener

言者无罪，闻者足戒 yánzhě wú zuì, wénzhě zú jiè blame not the speaker but be warned by his words; blame not the critic, heed what he says

言者谆谆，听者藐藐 yánzhě zhūnzhūn, tīngzhě miǎomiǎo the speaker is earnest but the hearer is casual; the words are earnest but they fall on deaf ears

言之成理 yán zhī chéng lǐ speak in a rational and convincing way; sound reasonable: 人家～，他无法驳斥。He didn't see how he could turn down the suggestion which sounded plausible enough.

言之无物 yán zhī wú wù (of speech or writing) be devoid of substance; be mere verbiage; be empty talk: 最不应该、最要反对的是～的文章。Articles devoid of substance are the least justifiable and the most objectionable.

言之有据 yán zhī yǒu jù speak on good grounds (*or* on good authority)

言之凿凿 yán zhī záozáo say sth. with certainty

言重 yánzhòng overstate; exaggerate

严（嚴）

yán ① tight: 把窗户关～了。Shut the window tight. / 他的嘴很～。He is tight-mouthed. ② strict; severe; stern; rigorous: 纪律要～。Be strict in discipline. / 高标准，～要求 high standards and strict demands / ～加批驳 sternly refute / ～是爱，松是害。Strictness helps, indulgence spoils. ③ *formal* father: 家严 jiāyán ④ (Yán) a surname

严办 yánbàn deal with severely; punish with severity

严惩 yánchéng punish severely: ～入侵之敌 deal the invaders a crushing blow

严惩不贷 yánchéng bù dài punish without leniency; punish with severity: 违者～。Those who disobey will be severely punished.

严饬 yánchì *formal* ① give strict orders: ～部下 give strict orders to one's subordinates ② careful and precise: 治家～ be careful and meticulous in managing one's household

严词 yáncí strong terms; stern words: ～谴责 denounce in strong terms; sternly condemn / ～拒绝 give a stern rebuff; sternly refuse

严冬 yándōng a severe winter; a hard winter

严防 yánfáng be strictly on guard against; take strict

precautions against: ～敌人破坏 take strict precautions against sabotage by the enemy

严父 yánfù stern father; father

严父慈母 yánfù-címǔ stern father and compassionate mother (the conventional conception of parenthood, according to which the father is to be stern while the mother should temper the father's severity with compassion)

严格 yángé ① strict; rigorous; rigid; stringent: 队长对我们要求很～。Our team leader is very strict with us. / ～履行协定条款 strictly implement the terms of the agreement / ～训练，～要求 go in for rigorous training and set strict demands; train hard and strictly / 作出～的规定 set rigid (*or* stringent) rules / ～按规定办事 act in strict accordance with the rules / ～说来 strictly speaking ② rigorously enforce: ～规章制度 rigorously enforce rules and regulations

严固 yángù (of defences) strong: 防守～。The defences are strong.

严寒 yánhán severe cold; bitter cold

严紧 yánjǐn tight; close: 窗户糊得挺～。The windows are tightly sealed. / 那个山口防守～。The mountain pass was closely guarded.

严谨 yánjǐn ① rigorous; strict; careful and precise: ～的科学态度 a rigorous scientific approach / 办事～ be meticulous and precise in one's work ② compact; well-knit: 文章结构～。The essay is well-knit.

严禁 yánjìn strictly forbid (*or* prohibit): ～体罚 strictly forbid corporal punishment / ～吸烟。Smoking is strictly prohibited.

严峻 yánjùn stern; severe; rigorous; grim: 神色～ look stern / ～的考验 a severe test; a rigorous test / ～的态度 a stern (*or* an uncompromising) attitude / 局势十分～。The situation is pregnant with grim possibilities.

严酷 yánkù ① harsh; bitter; grim: ～的现实 harsh reality / ～的教训 a bitter lesson / ～的斗争 a grim struggle ② cruel; ruthless: ～的剥削 cruel exploitation

严冷 yánlěng ① cold and stern: 板着～的面孔 put on a cold, stern expression ② bitter cold: ～的天气 bitter cold weather

严厉 yánlì stern; severe: 态度～ be stern in manner / 声音很～ speak in a very stern voice / ～的批评 severe criticism / ～的措施 severe (*or* stringent) measures / ～声讨 sternly (*or* strongly) denounce

严令 yánlìng give strict orders: ～缉拿归案 give strict orders to bring the criminal to justice

严密 yánmì tight; close: ～封锁 impose a tight blockade / ～监视 put under close surveillance; keep close watch over / ～防范 take strict precautions against / ～注视国际局势的发展 closely follow the development of world events / 组织～ be well-organized / 安全措施很～。Security was tight. / 这篇小说的结构十分～。The novel has a well-knit plot.

严明 yánmíng ① strict and impartial: 赏罚～ be strict and impartial in meting out rewards and punishments; give rewards and punishments impartially / 纪律～ observe strict discipline; be highly disciplined ② strictly enforce (discipline): ～军纪 enforce and maintain strict military discipline

严命 yánmìng *formal* ① give strict orders ② father's orders: 奉～返里 return home by order of one's father

严声 yánshēng (speak) in a stern voice: ～喝问 snap out one's questions

严声厉色 yánshēng-lìsè stern in voice and countenance

严师 yánshī a strict teacher

严师诤友 yánshī-zhèngyǒu a strict teacher and a friend who will give unpalatable advice

严实 yánshi *dial.* ① tight; close: 门关得挺～。The door is shut tight. / 她的嘴～着呢! She has tight lips. /

她那嘴可不～。She has a loose tongue. ② (hide) safely: 游击队把粮食藏～了才转移。The guerrillas carefully hid their food grain before they moved on.

严守 yánshǒu　① observe strictly: ～纪律 observe strict discipline / ～合同 abide by a contract faithfully ② guard closely: ～国家机密 strictly guard state secrets

严霜 yánshuāng　a severe (*or* heavy) frost: 一场～，把白菜秧儿都给冻坏了。A severe frost killed the cabbage sprouts.

严丝合缝 yánsī héfèng　fit together perfectly; join tightly; dovetail

严肃 yánsù　① serious; solemn; earnest: ～认真 serious and conscientious / ～的气氛 a solemn atmosphere / ～的态度 a serious attitude / 他是个很～的人。He is a serious (*or* serious-minded) man. / ～地指出 point out in all earnestness ② strictly enforce: ～党纪 enforce Party discipline / ～法制 maintain the legal system

严细 yánxì　careful and precise; meticulous: ～的工作作风 a meticulous work style

严刑 yánxíng　cruel torture: ～逼供 extort a confession by cruel torture

严刑峻法 yánxíng-jùnfǎ　harsh laws and severe punishments; draconian laws

严刑拷打 yánxíng kǎodǎ　subject sb. to severe torture; cruelly beat up

严以律己，宽以待人 yán yǐ lǜ jǐ, kuān yǐ dài rén (*also* 严于责己，宽以待人 yán yú zé jǐ, kuān yǐ dài rén) be strict with oneself and lenient towards others

严阵以待 yán zhèn yǐ dài　be in full battle array; stand in combat readiness

严整 yánzhěng　(usu. of troops) be in neat formation: 军容～。The troops are in gallant array.

严正 yánzhèng　solemn and just; serious and principled; stern: ～立场 solemn and just stand / 发表～声明 issue a solemn statement; solemnly declare / ～警告 serve a stern warning / 提出～抗议 lodge a stern protest

严重 yánzhòng　serious; grave; critical: ～后果 serious (*or* grave) consequences / ～关头 critical juncture / 病情～ be seriously ill / 事态～。The situation is grave. / 感到～不安 feel grave concern; feel deeply disturbed / 充分认识到问题的～性 be fully aware of the gravity of the question

芫 yán　see below——see also yuán
芫荽 yánsui　*bot.* coriander

妍（姸） yán　*formal* beautiful: 百花争～。A hundred flowers contend in beauty.

妍媸 yán-chī　*formal* beautiful and ugly: 不辨～ be unable to distinguish the beautiful from the ugly

沿（沿） yán　① *prep.* along: ～街栽着一排排法国梧桐。Along the streets grow lines of plane trees. / ～着海岸航行 sail along the coast / ～着公路一直去 go straight ahead along the highway / ～着党指引的方向前进 advance along the course charted by the Party ② follow (a tradition, pattern, etc.): 世代相～ be handed down from generation to generation ③ trim (with tape, ribbon, etc.): ～鞋口 trim the top of a shoe ④ edge; border: 缸～儿 the brim of a jar / 沟～儿 the edge of a ditch / 河～ riverside

沿岸 yán'àn　along the bank or coast; littoral or riparian: 长江～ along (the banks of) the Changjiang River / 地中海～国家 the littoral countries of the Mediterranean / 尼日尔河～国家 riparian states along the Niger

沿边儿 yánbiānr　trim (with tape, ribbon, etc.): 用白缎带在衣领上沿一道边儿 trim the collar of a garment with white ribbon

沿革 yángé　the course of change and development; evolution: 社会风俗的～ the evolution of social customs

沿海 yánhǎi　along the coast; coastal; littoral: ～城市 coastal cities / ～岛屿 offshore islands / ～地区 coastal areas; coastland / ～国家 coastal states (*or* countries); littoral states (*or* countries) / ～航船 coaster / ～航行 coastal navigation; cabotage / ～贸易 coasting trade; cabotage / ～渔业 inshore fishing / ～自然资源 the natural resources of coastal waters

沿洄 yán-huí　*formal* go upstream and downstream

沿江 yánjiāng　along the river (esp. the Changjiang); riparian; riverine

沿阶草 yánjiēcǎo　*bot.* dwarf lilyturf

沿例 yánlì　follow the usual practice; follow the established precedents

沿路 yánlù　along the road; on the way: ～林木成行，郁郁葱葱。Along the road stand rows of green and luxuriant trees.

沿门托钵 yán mén tuō bō　beg alms from door to door; go begging from place to place

沿条儿 yántiáor　trimming tape or ribbon

沿途 yántú　on the way; throughout a journey: 参观团～受到热情的接待。The visiting group was warmly received throughout its journey. / 这艘客轮～停靠五个码头。This liner calls at five ports on her voyage.

沿袭 yánxí　carry on as before; follow: ～陈规 follow convention / ～成说 adopt an accepted theory

沿线 yánxiàn　along the line (i.e. a railway, highway, air or shipping line): 铁路～的村镇 villages and towns along the railway line

沿用 yányòng　continue to use (an old method, etc.): ～原来的名称 continue to use the old name

炎 yán　① scorching; burning hot: 炎夏 yánxià ② inflammation: 发炎 fāyán / 阑尾炎 lánwěiyán

炎帝 Yán Dì　Yan Di, also known as Shen Nong (神农), a legendary ruler——see also 炎黄 Yán-Huáng; 炎黄子孙 Yán-Huáng zǐsūn

炎旱 yánhàn　hot and dry: ～的夏季 a hot and dry summer; a scorching, droughty summer

炎黄 Yán-Huáng　Yan Di and Huang Di (*or* the Yellow Emperor), two legendary rulers of remote antiquity

炎黄子孙 Yán-Huáng zǐsūn　descendants of Yan Di and Huang Di—the Chinese people

炎凉 yán-liáng　see 世态炎凉 shìtài yán-liáng

炎热 yánrè　(of weather) scorching; blazing; burning hot: 冒着～ braving the sweltering heat / ～的暑天 the sweltering summer days

炎日 yánrì　the burning (*or* scorching) sun

炎暑 yánshǔ　hot summer; sweltering summer days; dog days

炎天 yántiān　① hot weather; summer ② *formal* the South

炎威 yánwēi　fierce heat

炎夏 yánxià　a torrid (*or* scorching) summer

炎炎 yányán　scorching; sweltering; blazing: 赤日～ the scorching sun

炎阳 yányáng　the scorching sun

炎症 yánzhèng　inflammation

岩（巖、嵒） yán　① rock: 岩石 yánshí ② cliff; crag: 七星～ the Seven-Star Cliff (in Guilin)

岩岸 yán'àn　rocky coast
岩壁 yánbì　crag; cliff
岩层 yáncéng　rock stratum; rock formation
岩洞 yándòng　grotto
岩鸽 yángē　rock dove; rock pigeon
岩壑 yánhè　a rocky mountain valley

岩画　yánhuà　rock painting

岩浆　yánjiāng　*geol.*　magma: ～分异作用 magmatic differentiation / ～作用 magmatism

岩浆岩　yánjiāngyán　magmatic rock

岩羚羊　yánlíngyáng　*zool.*　chamois (*Rupicapra rupicapra Linnaeus*)

岩溶　yánróng　*geol.*　karst

岩溶地貌　yánróng dìmào　karst features; karst topography

岩石　yánshí　rock

岩石力学　yánshílìxué　rock mechanics

岩石圈　yánshíquān　lithosphere

岩石学　yánshíxué　petrology

岩相　yánxiàng　*geol.*　lithofacies: ～图 lithofacies map

岩心　yánxīn　*geol.*　(drill) core: ～回收 core recovery / ～样品 core sample

岩心筒　yánxīntǒng　core barrel

岩性学　yánxìngxué　*geol.*　lithology

岩穴　yánxué　cavern; cave: ～之士 a hermit

岩崖　yányá　cliff

岩盐　yányán　rock salt; halite

岩羊　yányáng　*zool.*　blue sheep; bharal (*Pseudois nayaur Hodgson*)

岩样　yányàng　① *geol.*　rock specimen ② *min.*　core sample

研(硏)

yán　① grind; pestle: ～成粉末 grind into fine powder; pulverize by grinding / ～墨 rub an ink stick on an inkslab (to prepare ink for brush writing) ② study: 研读 yándú

研钵　yánbō　mortar (a vessel)

研杵　yánchǔ　pestle; grinder; pulverizer

研读　yándú　study carefully: ～电影剧本 make a careful study of the scenario

研究　yánjiū　① study; research: ～自然规律 study the laws of nature / 科学～ scientific research / 癌症病源～ researches into the causes of cancer ② consider; discuss; deliberate: 这些问题正在～。These matters are under review (*or* consideration).

研究工作者　yánjiū gōngzuòzhě　research worker

研究生　yánjiūshēng　postgraduate (student); graduate student

研究生院　yánjiūshēngyuàn　graduate school

研究室　yánjiūshì　research room

研究所　yánjiūsuǒ　research institute

研究员　yánjiūyuán　research fellow

研究院　yánjiūyuàn　① research institute ② graduate school

研磨　yánmó　① grind; pestle ② abrade; polish: ～粉 abrasive powder / ～料 abrasive / ～器 abrader

研讨　yántǎo　deliberate; study and discuss

研讨会　yántǎohuì　symposium; seminar

研习　yánxí　study; research

研修　yánxiū　do research work

研修生　yánxiūshēng　researcher

研制　yánzhì　① develop (drugs, weapons, etc.): ～新式武器 develop new weapons ② *Chin. med.*　prepare medicinal powder by pestling

盐(鹽)

yán　① table salt; salt: 加点儿～ add a little salt ② *chem.*　salt (a product formed by the neutralization of an acid by a base): 酸式～ acid salt / 碱式～ basic salt

盐巴　yánbā　*dial.*　table salt; salt

盐层　yáncéng　salt deposit; salt bed

盐场　yánchǎng　saltern; saltworks

盐池　yánchí　salt pond

盐分　yánfèn　salt content

盐肤木　yánfūmù　*bot.*　Chinese sumac

盐肤木根皮　yánfūmùgēnpí　*Chin. med.*　the root bark of Chinese sumac

盐罐　yánguàn　saltcellar; saltshaker

盐湖　yánhú　salt lake

盐花　yánhuā　a little salt; a pinch of salt: 汤里搁点儿～儿。Put just a little salt in the soup.

盐碱地　yánjiǎndì　saline or alkaline land

盐碱化　yánjiǎnhuà　salinization or alkalinization (of soil); salinization of alkaline soil; alkalinization of saline soil

盐碱土　yánjiǎntǔ　saline or alkaline soil; salinized alkaline soil; alkalinized saline soil; saline-alkaline soil

盐井　yánjǐng　salt well; brine pit

盐矿　yánkuàng　salt mine

盐卤　yánlǔ　bittern

盐瓶　yánpíng　saltcellar; saltshaker

盐汽水　yánqìshuǐ　salt soda water

盐泉　yánquán　brine (*or* salt) spring

盐霜　yánshuāng　salt efflorescence

盐水　yánshuǐ　salt solution; brine

盐水输液　yánshuǐ shūyè　*med.*　saline infusion

盐水选种　yánshuǐ xuǎnzhǒng　seed sorting by salt water

盐酸　yánsuān　*chem.*　hydrochloric acid

盐滩　yántān　① a beach for making sea salt ② another name for 盐沼 yánzhǎo

盐田　yántián　salt pan; salina

盐土　yántǔ　solonchak; saline soil

盐析　yánxī　*chem.*　saltout: ～效应 salting-out effect

盐业　yányè　salt industry

盐液　yányè　saline solution

盐液比重计　yányè bǐzhòngjì　(also 盐重计 yánzhòngjì) salinometer; salimeter

盐沼　yánzhǎo　salt marsh

盐渍土　yánzìtǔ　salinized soil

阎¹

yán　*formal*　the entrance to a lane

阎²(閻)

Yán　a surname

阎罗　Yánluó　*Buddhism*　Yama, King of Hell

阎王　Yánwang　① Yama, King of Hell: 活～ a living King of Hell; a devil incarnate / 见～ die ② an extremely cruel and violent person

阎王殿　yánwangdiàn　the Palace of the King of Hell

阎王帐　yánwangzhàng　(also 阎王债 yánwangzhài) *inf.*　a usurious loan; shark's loan

筵

yán　① *formal*　formerly, a bamboo mat spread on the floor for people to sit ② feast; banquet: 喜～ a wedding feast

筵席　yánxí　① seats arranged at a banquet ② feast; banquet

蜒

yán　see 蜿蜒 wānyán; 蜒蚰 yányóu; 蚰蜒 yóuyán

蜒蚰　yányóu　*dial.*　slug

颜

yán　① face; countenance: 容颜 róngyán ② prestige; face: 无～见人 not have the face to appear in public ③ colour: 颜料 yánliào ④ (Yán) a surname

颜厚　yánhòu　thick-skinned; brazen-faced; shameless

颜料　yánliào　pigment; colouring: 天然～ natural pigments / 人造～ artificial pigments

颜面　yánmiàn　① face: ～神经 facial nerve ② prestige; face: 顾全～ save face / ～扫地 lose face altogether; be thoroughly discredited

颜色　yánsè　① colour: 你最喜欢什么～? What colour do you like most? ② countenance; facial expression: 给他一点～看看 make it hot for him; teach him a lesson

颜色　yánshǎi　*inf.*　pigment or dyestuff

颜体　Yántǐ　the Yan style (a calligraphic style created by Yan Zhenqing 颜真卿 of the Tang Dynasty)

檐（簷）

　yán　① eaves: ～下 under the eaves ② ledge; brim: 帽檐 màoyán

檐沟　yángōu　*archit.*　eaves gutter

檐子　yánzi　*inf.*　eaves

yǎn

奄

　yǎn　*formal*　① cover; include ② all of a sudden; suddenly

奄忽　yǎnhū　*formal*　suddenly; all of a sudden; all at once

奄奄　yǎnyǎn　breathing feebly: 气息奄奄 qìxī yǎnyǎn

奄奄一息　yǎnyǎn yī xī　at one's last gasp; on the verge of death: 他被打得～。 He was flogged till there was barely any breath left in his body.

俨（儼）

　yǎn　*formal*　majestic; solemn; dignified

俨然　yǎnrán　*formal*　① solemn; dignified: 望之～ look dignified ② neatly arranged: 屋舍～ houses set out in neat order ③ just like: 这孩子说起话来～是个大人。 This child speaks just like a grown-up. / ～以恩人自居 assume the airs of a benefactor

俨如　yǎnrú　just like: ～白昼 as bright as day

衍¹

　yǎn　*formal*　① spread out; develop; amplify: 衍变 yǎnbiàn ② redundant; superfluous: 衍文 yǎnwén

衍²

　yǎn　*formal*　① low-lying flatland: 广～沃野 a broad expanse of fertile flatland ② marsh; swamp; bog

衍变　yǎnbiàn　develop; evolve

衍射　yǎnshè　*phys.*　diffraction: ～角 diffraction angle / ～线 diffracted ray

衍生　yǎnshēng　*chem.*　derive

衍生物　yǎnshēngwù　*chem.*　derivative: 醋酸是酒精的一种～。 Acetic acid is a derivative of alcohol. / 纤维素～ cellulose derivatives

衍文　yǎnwén　redundancy due to misprinting or miscopying

掩（揜）

　yǎn　① cover; hide: ～口而笑 hide one's smile / ～鼻而过 pass by (sth. nauseating) holding one's nose ② shut; close: ～卷 close a book / 虚～着门 with the door left unlocked or unlatched ③ *dial.* get squeezed (*or* pinched) while shutting a door, lid, etc.: 小心门～了手。 Don't get your fingers caught in the door. ④ attack by surprise: ～袭 launch a surprise attack

掩蔽　yǎnbì　screen; shelter; cover: 高射炮上有树枝～着。 The antiaircraft guns were camouflaged with tree branches. / 堤埂很高，正好做我们的～。 The embankment was high enough to provide cover for us.

掩蔽阵地　yǎnbì zhèndì　*mil.*　covered position

掩藏　yǎncáng　hide; conceal

掩耳盗铃　yǎn ěr dào líng　plug one's ears while stealing a bell—deceive oneself; bury one's head in the sand

掩盖　yǎngài　① cover; overspread: 大雪～着田野。 The fields were covered with snow. ② conceal; cover up: 一个倾向～着另一个倾向。 One tendency conceals another. / 谎言～不了事实。 Lies cannot cover up (*or* conceal) the facts. / ～不住内心的喜悦 be unable to conceal one's joy

掩护　yǎnhù　screen; shield; cover: ～进攻 screen an advance / 用身体～战友 shield one's comrade-in-arms with one's body / 游击队～村里的群众转移。 The guerrillas covered the villagers' evacuation. / 他这样做，实际上是给他上司打～。 In so doing, he was actually trying to shield his boss. / 他以修鞋为～从事党的秘密活动。 He did underground work for the Party under the guise of a cobbler.

掩护部队　yǎnhù bùduì　*mil.*　covering force

掩护火力　yǎnhù huǒlì　*mil.*　covering fire

掩埋　yǎnmái　bury: ～尸首 bury a corpse / 那些露营的人每天都把垃圾～起来。 The campers buried their garbage every day.

掩泣　yǎnqì　cover one's face with one's hands and start weeping

掩人耳目　yǎn rén ěr-mù　deceive the public; hoodwink people

掩杀　yǎnshā　*formal*　make a surprise attack; pounce on (the enemy)

掩饰　yǎnshì　cover up (faults, mistakes, etc.); gloss over; conceal: ～错误 gloss over (*or* cover up) one's mistakes / ～真实的意图 conceal one's true intentions / ～不住内心的恐慌 be unable to hide (*or* conceal) one's fears / 毫不～自己的感情 make no secret of one's feelings

掩体　yǎntǐ　*mil.*　blindage; bunker: 炮兵～ emplacement

掩星　yǎnxīng　*astron.*　occultation: 月～ lunar occultation

掩眼法　yǎnyǎnfǎ　cover-up; camouflage

掩映　yǎnyìng　(of things screening part of each other from view) show off (each other); set off (one another): 红楼翠竹交相～。 The red buildings and green bamboos set each other off. / 竹木扶疏，交相～。 Bamboos and shady trees set each other off to advantage.

眼

　yǎn　① eye: 左(右)～ left (right) eye / 我眯～了。 Something has got into my eye. ② look; glance: 瞪了他一～ give him a hard look / 瞥了他一～ shoot a glance at him / 一～就认出是她 recognize her at first glance ③ a small hole; aperture: 拿锥子扎个～儿 pierce with an awl / 打个～ bore a hole ④ key point: 节骨～儿 critical juncture ⑤ (*weiqi*) trap ⑥ an unaccented beat in traditional Chinese music: 一板三～ one accented and three unaccented beats in a bar ⑦ *m.*: 两～井 two wells

眼巴巴　yǎnbābā　① (expecting) eagerly; anxiously: 大家～地盼着他回来。 We were eagerly looking forward to his return. ② helplessly (watching sth. unpleasant happen): 他～地看着老鹰把小鸡抓走了。 He helplessly looked on when the hawk snatched the chick away.

眼白　yǎnbái　*dial.*　the white of the eye

眼波　yǎnbō　*formal*　glances (of a young lady)

眼不见，心不烦　yǎn bù jiàn, xīn bù fán　what the eye doesn't see the heart doesn't grieve for: 几时我闭了眼，断了这口气，任凭你们两个冤家闹上天去，我"～"。(《红楼梦》) Once I've closed my eyes and breathed my last, you can quarrel and storm as much as you like. What the eye doesn't see the heart doesn't grieve for.

眼岔　yǎnchà　mistake one for another: 刚才看见的不是他，是我～了。 He's not the person I saw just now. I mistook someone else for him.

眼馋　yǎnchán　cast covetous eyes at sth.; eye sth. covetously

眼眵　yǎnchī　gum (in the eyes)

眼虫藻　yǎnchóngzǎo　(also 眼虫 yǎnchóng) euglena (a green flagellate protozoan having a reddish eyespot)

眼瞅着　yǎnchōuzhe　*dial.*　① see sth. happen: 我～一根大梁掉下来把他砸死了。 I saw with my own eyes a

girder fall and crush him to death. ② soon; in no time: 他～要红起来了。He'll be a celebrity in no time.

眼底 yǎndǐ ① eyeground; the fundus of the eye (*fundus oculi*) ② in one's eyes; in sight: 登楼一望，全城景色尽收～。The top of the building commands a panoramic view of the city.

眼底检查 yǎndǐ jiǎnchá *med.* funduscopy

眼底镜 yǎndǐjìng *med.* funduscope

眼底下 yǎndǐxia ① right before one's eyes: 他的眼睛近视得利害，放到～才看得清。He is so nearsighted that he can only see clearly things placed right before his eyes. / 侦察兵就在敌人～活动。The scouts were operating under the enemy's very eyes (*or* nose). ② at the moment: 先处理～的事。Let's settle the business on hand first.

眼点 yǎndiǎn eyespot (of a protozoan); stigma

眼福 yǎnfú the good fortune of seeing sth. rare or beautiful: ～不浅 be lucky enough to see sth. / 一饱～ feast one's eyes on sth.

眼干症 yǎngānzhèng *med.* xerophthalmia

眼高手低 yǎngāo-shǒudī have high standards but little ability; be fastidious but incompetent

眼膏 yǎngāo eye ointment

眼格 yǎngé *dial.* field of vision (*or* view); outlook

眼观六路，耳听八方 yǎn guān liùlù, ěr tīng bāfāng have sharp eyes and keen ears; be observant and alert

眼光 yǎnguāng ① eye: 大家的～都集中到他身上。Everyone turned their eyes on him. / 她的～锐利，什么事情都瞒不过她。You can hide nothing from her sharp eyes. ② sight; foresight; insight; vision: ～远大 farsighted / ～短浅 shortsighted / 政治～ political foresight / 历史～ historical perspective / 有～的政治家 a farsighted statesman / 他开始用新的～来观察周围事物。He began to view everything around him in a different light. / 不能用老～来看新事物。One mustn't judge new things by old standards.

眼黑 yǎnhēi *dial.* pupil (of the eye)

眼红 yǎnhóng ① covet; be envious; be jealous ② eyes burning with fury; be furious: 仇人相见，分外眼红 chóurén xiāngjiàn, fènwài yǎnhóng

眼花 yǎnhuā have dim eyesight; have blurred vision: 耳不聋眼不花 (of an old person) be neither hard of hearing nor dim-sighted

眼花缭乱 yǎnhuā liáoluàn be dazzled: 使人～的杂技表演 a dazzling display of acrobatics

眼犄角儿 yǎnjījiǎor *dial.* the corner of the eye; canthus

眼疾手快 yǎnjí-shǒukuài quick of eye and deft of hand

眼尖 yǎnjiān be sharp-eyed; have sharp eyes; have keen sight

眼睑 yǎnjiǎn *physiol.* eyelid

眼见 yǎnjiàn soon; in no time: ～就要立冬了，可娃娃的棉衣还没做好。It will be winter here very soon, and I haven't got the baby's warm clothes ready yet.

眼见得 yǎnjiànde *dial.* (of sth. unpleasant) be evident: 病人～不行了。It's clear that the patient won't pull through.

眼角 yǎnjiǎo the common name for 眦 zì

眼睫毛 yǎnjiémáo *inf.* eyelash

眼界 yǎnjiè field of vision (*or* view); outlook: ～不广 have a narrow outlook / 扩大～ widen one's field of vision; broaden one's horizon / 形而上学限制了他的～。Metaphysics limited his outlook. / 这次访华，大开～。The China trip was a real eye-opener to me.

眼镜 yǎnjìng eyeglasses; glasses; spectacles: 一付～ a pair of spectacles / 戴～ wear glasses / 摘下～ take off one's glasses

眼镜猴 yǎnjìnghóu tarsier (*Tarsius spectrum*; a small arboreal, nocturnal mammal having a long tail and large goggle eyes)

眼镜框 yǎnjìngkuàng rims (of spectacles); spectacles frame

眼镜蛇 yǎnjìngshé cobra (*Naja naja*)

眼睛 yǎnjing eye: 她那双～十分动人。Her eyes are very beautiful. / 群众的～是雪亮的。The masses are sharp-sighted. *or* The masses have sharp eyes.

眼看 yǎnkàn ① soon; in a moment: 暴风雨～就要来了。The storm will start any moment. / ～天就要亮了。It'll be daylight soon. ② watch helplessly; look on passively: 咱们哪能～着他走邪道不管呢? How can we sit idly by and watch him go astray?

眼科 yǎnkē (department of) ophthalmology

眼科学 yǎnkēxué ophthalmology

眼科医生 yǎnkē yīshēng oculist; ophthalmologist; eye-doctor

眼快 yǎnkuài be sharp-eyed (*or* sharp-sighted); have sharp eyes; have keen sight

眼眶 yǎnkuàng ① eye socket; eyehole; orbit: 他～里含着热泪。His eyes were filled with tears. ② rim of the eye: 揉揉～ rub one's eyes

眼泪 yǎnlèi tears: 流～ shed tears / 强咽下～ choke down (*or* back) one's tears / 为这件事她没少掉～。It cost her many tears. / 她的～说来就来。She breaks out into tears at a moment's notice.

眼泪汪汪 yǎnlèi wāngwāng eyes brimming with tears; in tears

眼离 yǎnlí *dial.* have hallucinations; see things: 牲口一～就惊了。The animal shied the moment it began to see things.

眼力 yǎnlì ① eyesight; vision: ～好（差）have good (poor) eyesight ② judgment; discrimination: 老支书看人很有～。The old Party branch secretary is good at sizing people up.

眼里 yǎnlǐ in one's eyes; in one's view: 她说话时～闪着泪花。Tears glistened in her eyes as she spoke. / 在他的～，我还是个孩子。In his eyes, I'm still a child. / 看在～，记在心里 bear in mind what one sees; see and heed / ～有活 see where there's work to be done; know where one can be of use / ～没有群众 care nothing for the masses / 这点困难她根本不放在～。She thinks nothing of a difficulty like that. / 中国人～的美国 the United States through Chinese eyes

眼帘 yǎnlián *liter.* eyes: 一片丰收的景色映入～。A lively scene of farmers bringing in bumper crops greeted the eye.

眼眉 yǎnméi *dial.* eyebrow

眼明手快 yǎnmíng-shǒukuài quick of eye and deft of hand; sharp-eyed and deft-handed

眼明心亮 yǎnmíng-xīnliàng same as 心明眼亮 xīnmíng-yǎnliàng

眼目 yǎnmù ① eyes: 强烈的灯光炫人～。Strong lights dazzle the eyes. ② one who spies for sb. else

眼内压 yǎnnèiyā same as 眼压 yǎnyā

眼泡 yǎnpāo upper eyelid: 肉～儿 heavy eyelids / 她～儿都哭肿了。Her eyes were swollen from crying.

眼皮 yǎnpí (also 眼皮子 yǎnpízi) eyelid: 我～直跳。My eyes kept twitching. / 困得我上下～直打架。I was so sleepy I couldn't keep my eyes open.

眼皮底下 yǎnpídǐ·xià (also 眼皮子底下 yǎnpízidǐ·xià) same as 眼底下 yǎndǐxia

眼皮子高 yǎnpízi gāo fastidious; hard to please

眼皮子浅 yǎnpízi qiǎn short-sighted; shallow

眼前 yǎnqián ① before one's eyes: ～是一片碧绿的稻田。Before our eyes was a stretch of green paddy fields. ② at the moment; at present; now: ～利益服从长远利益 subordinate immediate interests to long-term interests / 不能只顾～，不管将来。One must not think only of the present and neglect the future. / 胜利就

在～。Victory is at hand.

眼前欢　yǎnqiánhuān　pleasure of the moment

眼前亏　yǎnqiánkuī　trouble right before the eyes: 好汉不吃眼前亏 hǎohàn bùchī yǎnqiánkuī

眼球　yǎnqiú　eyeball

眼圈　yǎnquān　① eye socket; orbit: ～红了 be on the verge of tears ② rim of the eye

眼热　yǎnrè　cast covetous eyes at sth.; eye sth. covetously: 她见了那些珠宝怪～的。She eyed those jewels covetously.

眼色　yǎnsè　a hint given with the eyes; a meaningful glance; wink: 使～ tip sb. the wink; wink at sb. / 她给我递了个～。She cast me a meaningful glance. / 看某人的～行事 take one's cue from sb.

眼神　yǎnshén　① expression in one's eyes: 从他的～里，我能猜测到他的心事 I can guess what's on his mind from the expression in his eyes. ② dial. eyesight: ～不好 have poor eyesight / 我的～不济了。My eyesight is failing.

眼生　yǎnshēng　look unfamiliar: 来客很～。I haven't seen the visitor before. / 几年没来这儿，连从前很熟悉的地方都～了。I have been away for only a few years, but even those places I knew quite well look unfamiliar to me now.

眼时　yǎnshí　dial. at the moment; at present; nowadays

眼屎　yǎnshǐ　dial. gum (in the eyes)

眼熟　yǎnshú　look familiar: 这人看着很～。That person looks familiar.

眼跳　yǎntiào　twitching of the eyelid

眼窝　yǎnwō　eye socket; eyehole; orbit

眼下　yǎnxià　at the moment; at present; now: ～正是秋收大忙季节。We're right in the middle of the autumn harvest rush. / 这种八角帽～不时兴了。These octagonal caps are now out of fashion.

眼弦赤烂　yǎnxián chìlàn　Chin. med. blepharitis

眼线[1]　yǎnxiàn　informer; stool-pigeon

眼线[2]　yǎnxiàn　eye-liner

眼压　yǎnyā　intraocular pressure

眼药　yǎnyào　medicament for the eyes; eye ointment or eyedrops

眼药水　yǎnyàoshuǐ　eyedrops

眼晕　yǎnyùn　dizziness (owing to defective vision)

眼影　yǎnyǐng　eye-shadow

眼罩儿　yǎnzhàor　① eyeshade ② blinkers (for a horse, donkey, etc.)

眼睁睁　yǎnzhēngzhēng　looking on helplessly or unfeelingly: 咱不能～地看着庄稼被水淹了。We can't just sit here and watch the crops being flooded.

眼中钉　yǎnzhōngdīng　a thorn in one's flesh (or side)

眼中钉，肉中刺　yǎnzhōngdīng, ròuzhōngcì　a thorn in one's flesh (or side): 快叫个人牙子来，多少卖几两银子，拔去肉中刺，眼中钉。(《红楼梦》) Fetch a broker at once. We'll sell her for whatever she'll fetch and rid ourselves of this pest, this thorn in the flesh.

眼珠子　yǎnzhūzi　inf. ① (also 眼珠儿 yǎnzhūr) eyeball ② the apple of sb.'s eye

眼拙　yǎnzhuō　pol. my bad eyes; my bad memory: 恕我～，咱们在哪儿见过面? Excuse me for my bad memory, but have we met before?

偃　yǎn　formal ① fall on one's back: ～卧 lie supine; lie on one's back ② lay down ③ desist; cease: 偃武修文 yǎnwǔ-xiūwén

偃旗息鼓　yǎnqí-xīgǔ　lower the banners and muffle the drums—cease all activities: 于是传令，教众军～，只作无人把守之状。(《三国演义》) Then he issued orders to furl all the banners and to silence all the drums as if the city was empty of defenders.

偃武修文　yǎnwǔ-xiūwén　desist from war and encourage the arts of peace; desist from military activities and encourage culture and education

罨　yǎn　formal ① net for catching birds or fish ② cover: 热罨 rèyǎn

演　yǎn　① develop; evolve: 演变 yǎnbiàn ② deduce; elaborate: 演绎 yǎnyì ③ drill; practise: 演算 yǎnsuàn ④ perform; play; act; put on: 她在《洪湖赤卫队》里～韩英。She plays the part of Han Ying in the opera Red Guards of Honghu Lake. / ～电影 show a film / ～五场 give (or put on) five performances

演变　yǎnbiàn　develop; evolve: 从猿到人的～过程 evolution from ape to man

演播　yǎnbō　telecast (a play, performance, etc.)

演唱　yǎnchàng　sing (in a performance)

演出　yǎnchū　perform; show; put on a show: 为工人～ perform (or put on a performance) for the workers / 登台～ appear on the stage / 首次～ first performance or show; première (of a play, film, etc.); début (of an actor or actress) / ～结束后，领导同志登台祝贺～成功。After the final curtain, the leading comrades went up onto the stage to congratulate the actors and actresses on their fine performances. / ～节目 items on the programme; programme

演出本　yǎnchūběn　acting version; playscript; script

演出单位　yǎnchū dānwèi　producer

演化　yǎnhuà　evolution: 生物的～ the evolution of living things

演技　yǎnjì　acting; stage performance: 她的～好极了。Her acting is excellent.

演讲　yǎnjiǎng　give a lecture; make a speech; lecture: ～比赛 oratorical contest

演进　yǎnjìn　gradual progress; evolution

演剧　yǎnjù　act in a play

演练　yǎnliàn　drill: ～场 drill ground / 地面～ aviation ground drill

演示　yǎnshì　demonstrate: 工人们为我们～了他们自己的发明创造。The workers gave us a demonstration of their own inventions.

演说　yǎnshuō　① deliver a speech; make an address ② speech

演说术　yǎnshuōshù　oratory

演算　yǎnsuàn　perform mathematical calculations

演替　yǎntì　biol. succession: 植物～ succession of plants

演武　yǎnwǔ　practise traditional martial arts

演习　yǎnxí　manoeuvre; exercise; drill; practice: 军事～ military manoeuvre; war exercise / 民兵～ militia drill / 实弹～ live ammunition manoeuvres / 消防～ fire drill

演戏　yǎnxì　① put on a play; act in a play ② playact; pretend: 别再～了。Stop playacting.

演义　yǎnyì　historical novel; historical romance: 《三国～》The Romance of the Three Kingdoms

演艺　yǎnyì　performing arts

演绎　yǎnyì　deduce

演绎法　yǎnyìfǎ　the deductive method; deduction

演员　yǎnyuán　actor or actress; performer: 挑选～ choose the cast / ～表 the cast

演奏　yǎnzòu　give an instrumental performance; play a musical instrument (in a performance): ～琵琶 play the pipa / ～能手 virtuoso

演奏家　yǎnzòujiā　an accomplished performer (of a musical instrument): 著名的小提琴～ a celebrated violinist; a violin virtuoso

魇（魘）　yǎn　① have a nightmare ② dial. talk in one's sleep

黡（黶） yǎn *formal* black mole

鼹（鼴） yǎn mole (a small burrowing insectivorous mammal)

鼹鼠 yǎnshǔ common name for 鼹 yǎn

yàn

厌（厭） yàn ① be disgusted with; detest: 厌弃 yànqì ② be fed up with; be bored with; be tired of: 看～了 have seen more than enough of sth. / 吃～了 be sick of eating sth. ③ be satisfied: 贪得无厌 tān dé wú yàn

厌烦 yànfán be sick of; be fed up with: 他非常～他现在做的工作。He is thoroughly fed up with his job. / 这支小夜曲我听多少遍也不觉得～。I never tire of listening to this serenade.

厌倦 yànjuàn be weary of; be tired of: 整天坐办公室，我早就～了。I've long been tired of sitting in an office all day.

厌弃 yànqì detest and reject; detest; loathe

厌气 yànqi *dial.* ① be sick of; be fed up with ② lonely; lonesome

厌食症 yànshízhèng *med.* (esp. in young women) anorexia; anorexia nervosa

厌世 yànshì be world-weary; be pessimistic

厌恶 yànwù detest; abhor; abominate; be disgusted with: 大家都～他。Everybody is disgusted with him. / 他的所作所为，实在令人～。His behaviour is simply disgusting.

厌恶疗法 yànwù liáofǎ *psychol.* aversion therapy

厌氧微生物 yànyǎng wēishēngwù anaerobe

厌战 yànzhàn be weary of war; be war-weary: ～情绪 war-weariness

砚 yàn inkstone; inkslab: 笔～ writing brush and inkslab

砚池 yànchí inkstone; inkslab

砚弟 yàndì *old* junior fellow student

砚台 yàntái inkstone; inkslab

砚兄 yànxiōng *old* senior fellow student

砚友 yànyǒu *old* fellow student; classmate

咽（嚥） yàn swallow: ～一口水 take a swallow of water / 吃东西要多嚼一嚼再～。Chew your food well before you swallow it. / 我嗓子疼得～不下东西。My throat is so sore that I can hardly swallow. / 他话到嘴边又～了回去。He was on the point of saying something when he checked himself. / 她恐怕～不下这口气。I don't think she can stomach (*or* swallow, take) an insult like that. ——see also yān; yè

咽气 yànqì breathe one's last; die: 爸爸刚～，几个子女就争开了遗产。No sooner had the father died than the sons and daughters started to quarrel over the inheritance.

彦 yàn *formal* a man of virtue and ability

宴 yàn ① entertain at a banquet; fête: ～客 entertain guests at a banquet; give a banquet ② feast; banquet: 盛～ a grand banquet; a magnificent feast / 婚～ wedding (*or* marriage) feast ③ ease and comfort: ～安 yàn'ān

宴安 yàn'ān live in ease and comfort

宴安鸩毒 yàn'ān zhèndú seeking pleasure is like drinking poisoned wine; voluptuous comfort is poison

宴尔 yàn'ěr recently happily married: ～之乐 happiness of newly-weds

宴尔新婚 yàn'ěr xīnhūn same as 新婚燕尔 xīnhūn yàn'ěr

宴会 yànhuì banquet; feast; dinner party: 举行～ give a banquet / 主持～ host a dinner party

宴会厅 yànhuìtīng banquet hall: 国宴在人民大会堂～举行。State banquets are given in the banquet hall of the Great Hall of the People.

宴乐 yànlè ① live in ease and comfort; enjoy an easy life ② wine and dine ——see also yànyuè

宴请 yànqǐng entertain (to dinner); fête: ～贵宾 entertain the distinguished guests

宴席 yànxí banquet; feast

宴饮 yànyǐn feast and carouse; wine and dine

宴乐 yànyuè music played at court feasts in ancient times ——see also yànlè

晏 yàn ① late: ～起 get up late ② ease and comfort ③ (Yàn) a surname

晏驾 yànjià (of an emperor) die; pass away

艳（艷、豔） yàn ① gorgeous; colourful; gaudy: 这布的花色太～了。The cloth is too gaudy. ② amorous: ～诗 love poem in a flowery style ③ *formal* admire; envy: 艳羡 yànxiàn

艳福 yànfú a man's good fortune in love affairs: ～不浅 have a lot of good fortune in love affairs; have a beautiful wife or girl friend

艳歌 yàngē love song

艳红 yànhóng bright red; scarlet: ～的太阳从海上冉冉升起。A bright red sun slowly rose from the sea.

艳丽 yànlì bright-coloured and beautiful; gorgeous: ～夺目 of dazzling beauty / 词藻～ flowery diction / 打扮得非常～ be gorgeously dressed

艳绿 yànlǜ bright green: 柳树在蒙蒙的雨丝中更显得～。In the fine drizzle the willows take on a brighter green.

艳情 yànqíng erotic: ～小说 erotic fiction

艳如桃李，冷若冰霜 yàn rú táolǐ, lěng ruò bīngshuāng (of a woman) as beautiful as peach and plum blossoms, but as cold as frost and ice

艳诗 yànshī erotic poetry

艳史 yànshǐ erotic adventures; amorous adventures: 《隋炀帝～》*Merry Adventures of Emperor Yang of the Sui Dynasty*

艳羡 yànxiàn *formal* admire immensely

艳阳天 yànyángtiān bright spring day; bright sunny skies

艳冶 yànyě *formal* pretty and coquettish

艳装 yànzhuāng (also 艳妆 yànzhuāng) gaudy attire

唁 yàn extend condolences: 吊唁 diàoyàn

唁电 yàndiàn telegram (*or* cable) of condolence; message of condolence

唁函 yànhán letter (*or* message) of condolence

验（驗、騐） yàn ① examine; check; test: ～货 check goods / ～小便 have a urine test / ～护照 examine (*or* check) a passport ② prove effective; produce the expected result: 屡试屡～ prove successful in every test ③ intended effect; desired result: 效验 xiàoyàn

验潮器 yàncháoqì *meteorol.* tide gauge

验电器 yàndiànqì electroscope

验方 yànfāng *Chin. med.* proved recipe

验关 yànguān customs examination

验光 yànguāng optometry

验核 yànhé examine; check

验看 yànkàn examine; inspect: ～护照 examine a pass

port

验明正身 yànmíng zhèngshēn verify the identity of a convict prior to execution

验讫 yànqì checked; examined

验枪 yànqiāng *mil.* inspect arms

验墒 yànshāng check the moisture of the soil

验尸 yànshī *leg.* postmortem; autopsy

验尸官 yànshīguān coroner

验收 yànshōu check and accept; check before acceptance; check upon delivery: 逐项～ check item by item before acceptance / 工程已由国家～. The completed project has been checked and accepted by the government. / ～单 receipt (issued after examination and acceptance of goods) / ～试验 acceptance test

验算 yànsuàn *math.* checking computations: ～公式 check formula

验血 yànxiě blood test

验证 yànzhèng verify: ～理论 verify a theory

谚 yàn proverb; saying; adage; saw: 谚语 yànyǔ / 古谚 gǔyàn

谚语 yànyǔ proverb; saying; adage; saw

焰(燄) yàn flame; blaze: 烈～ blazing (or raging) flames

焰火 yànhuǒ fireworks

雁(鴈) yàn wild goose; goose

雁过拔毛 yàn guò bá máo pluck feathers from each goose as it passes by—squeeze whenever possible

雁行 yànháng geese flying in a line—brothers

雁来红 yànláihóng *bot.* tricolour amaranth (*Amaranthus tricolor*)

雁序 yànxù *formal* geese flying in a line—brothers

雁阵 yànzhèn the flying formation of geese

堰 yàn weir

堰塞湖 yànsèhú *geog.* barrier lake

滟(灔) yàn see 潋滟 liànyàn

酽(釅) yàn (of tea, etc.) thick; strong: 茶太～. The tea's too strong.

餍(饜) yàn *formal* ① have enough (food); be satiated ② satisfy

餍足 yànzú *formal* satisfy (esp. selfish desires)

谳(讞) yàn *formal* decide a law case

燕¹(鷰) yàn swallow (a bird)

燕²(讌、醼) yàn ① entertain at a banquet; fête ② banquet; feast

燕³(讌) yàn ease and comfort
——see also Yān

燕菜 yàncài delicacies made from bird's nests

燕巢幕上 yàn cháo mù shàng a swallow nesting on a canopy—in a precarious position

燕尔 yàn'ěr same as 宴尔 yàn'ěr

燕尔新婚 yàn'ěr xīnhūn same as 新婚燕尔 xīnhūn yàn'ěr

燕颔虎颈 yànhàn-hǔjǐng a majestic and awe-inspiring appearance

燕好 yànhǎo *formal* (of husband and wife) be very fond of each other; be happily married: 百年～ remain a devoted couple to the end of their lives

燕鸻 yànhéng *zool.* pratincole; swallow plover

燕乐 yànlè live in ease and comfort; enjoy an easy life

——see also yànyuè

燕麦 yànmài oats

燕鸥 yàn'ōu *zool.* tern

燕雀 yànquè *zool.* brambling; bramble finch (*Fringilla montifringilla*)

燕雀安知鸿鹄之志 yàn-què ān zhī hónghú zhī zhì how could a sparrow understand the ambitions of a swan?—the lofty aims of the great are beyond the understanding of the lowly

燕雀处堂 yàn-què chǔ táng swallows nesting in a hall that is about to be on fire—unaware of one's danger

燕隼 yànsǔn *zool.* hobby

燕尾服 yànwěifú swallowtail; swallow-tailed coat; tailcoat; tails

燕窝 yànwō edible bird's nest

燕鱼 yànyú *zool.* Spanish mackerel

燕乐 yànyuè music played at court feasts in ancient times ——see also yànlè

燕子 yànzi swallow

赝(贗) yàn *formal* counterfeit; spurious; fake: 赝品 yànpǐn

赝本 yànběn spurious edition or copy

赝币 yànbì *formal* counterfeit coin

赝晶体 yànjīngtǐ *phys.* pseudocrystal

赝品 yànpǐn art forgery

yāng

央¹ yāng entreat; beg: 我～你一件事。May I ask a favour of you?

央² yāng centre: 中央 zhōngyāng

央³ yāng *formal* end; finish: 夜未～. The night is not yet spent.

央告 yānggao beg; plead; implore: 苦苦～ beg piteously

央求 yāngqiú beg; plead; implore: ～宽恕 beg for mercy / 不管我怎么～, 她就是不答应。No matter how earnestly I pleaded with her, she wouldn't agree.

央托 yāngtuō entreat sb. to do sth.

泱 yāng see below

泱泱 yāngyāng *formal* ① (of waters) vast ② grand; great; magnificent; glorious: ～大国 a great and proud country

殃 yāng ① calamity; disaster; misfortune: 遭殃 zāoyāng ② bring disaster to: 祸国殃民 huòguó-yāngmín

殃及 yāngjí bring disaster to: 这场暴风雪～上万牧民。The snowstorm was a disaster to thousands of herdsmen.

殃及池鱼 yāngjí chí yú see 城门失火, 殃及池鱼 chéngmén shīhuǒ, yāngjí chí yú

秧 yāng ① seedling; sprout: 黄瓜～儿 cucumber sprout ② rice seedling: 插秧 chāyāng ③ vine: 白薯～ sweet potato vine ④ young; fry: 鱼～ young fish; fry / 猪～ piglet

秧歌 yāngge yangge (dance), a popular rural folk dance: 扭～ do the yangge

秧歌剧 yānggejù yangge opera

秧鸡 yāngjī *zool.* rail

秧龄 yānglíng the length of time rice seedlings grow in seedling beds until they are transplanted

秧苗 yāngmiáo rice shoot; rice seedling

秧田　yāngtián　rice seedling bed
秧子　yāngzi　same as 秧 yāng①③④

莺　yāng　see 鸳莺 yuānyāng

yāng

羊　yáng　① sheep: 放～ put sheep out to pasture; graze sheep / ～叫 baa; bleat ② (Yáng) a surname
羊肠线　yángchángxiàn　*med.* catgut suture
羊肠小道　yángcháng xiǎodào　a narrow winding trail; a meandering footpath: 这条崎岖的～非常难走。This bumpy, meandering byway is difficult to negotiate.
羊齿　yángchǐ　*bot.* bracken; fern
羊痘　yángdòu　*animal husbandry* sheep pox
羊肚儿手巾　yángdǔr shǒujin　*dial.* towel
羊肚蕈　yángdǔxùn　*bot.* morel
羊羔　yánggāo　① lamb ② the name of a wine
羊羹　yánggēng　a sweet gelatinized red-bean cake
羊工　yánggōng　hired herdsman
羊倌　yángguān　shepherd
羊毫　yángháo　writing brush made of goat's hair
羊角锤　yángjiǎochuí　claw hammer
羊角风　yángjiǎofēng　common name for 癫痫 diānxián
羊脚碾　yángjiǎoniǎn　*archit.* sheepfoot roller
羊圈　yángjuàn　sheepfold; sheep pen
羊毛　yángmáo　sheep's wool; wool; fleece
羊毛出在羊身上　yángmáo chū zài yáng shēnshang　after all, the wool still comes from the sheep's back—in the long run, whatever you're given, you pay for
羊毛衫　yángmáoshān　woollen sweater; cardigan
羊毛袜　yángmáowà　woollen socks or stockings
羊毛脂　yángmáozhī　lanolin; wool fat
羊茅　yángmáo　fescue grass; fescue
羊膜　yángmó　*physiol.* amnion
羊排　yángpái　mutton chop; lamb chop
羊皮　yángpí　sheepskin: 一双～靴子 a pair of sheepskin boots / 披着～的狼 a wolf in sheep's clothing
羊皮纸　yángpízhǐ　parchment
羊群里头出骆驼　yángqún lǐtou chū luòtuo　stand out like a camel in a flock of sheep
羊绒　yángróng　cashmere
羊绒衫　yángróngshān　cashmere sweater
羊肉　yángròu　mutton
羊肉串　yángròuchuàn　mutton cubes roasted on a skewer; shish kebab (*or* kabob); shashlik
羊水　yángshuǐ　*physiol.* amniotic fluid: ～过多 hydramnios
羊桃　yángtáo　① another name for 五敛子 wǔliǎnzǐ ② another name for 猕猴桃 míhóutáo
羊驼　yángtuó　alpaca (*Lama alpacos*)
羊驼毛　yángtuómáo　alpaca fibre
羊痫风　yángxiánfēng　common name for 癫痫 diānxián
羊踯躅　yángzhízhú　*bot.* Chinese azalea
羊质虎皮　yángzhì-hǔpí　a sheep in a tiger's skin—outwardly strong, inwardly weak

阳(陽)　yáng　① (in Chinese thought) *yang*, the masculine or positive principle in nature (opp. 阴 yīn) ② the sun: 阳光 yángguāng ③ south of a hill or north of a river: 衡～ Hengyang (a city situated on the south side of Hengshan Mountain) / 洛～ Luoyang (a city situated on the north side of the Luohe River) ④ in relief: 阳文 yángwén ⑤ open; overt: 阳沟 yánggōu / 阳奉阴违 yángfēng-yīnwéi ⑥ belonging to this world; concerned with living beings: 阳间 yángjiān ⑦ *phys.* positive: 阳离子 yánglízǐ ⑧ male genitals

阳春　yángchūn　spring (season)
阳春白雪　yángchūn báixuě　Spring Snow (melodies of the *élite* in the State of Chu)—highbrow art and literature: 现在是"～"和下里巴人统一的问题,是提高和普及统一的问题。(毛泽东) The question now is to bring about a unity between "Spring Snow" and the "Song of the Rustic Poor", between higher standards and popularization.
阳春面　yángchūnmiàn　noodles in a simple sauce
阳地植物　yángdì zhíwù　sun plant
阳电　yángdiàn　positive electricity
阳电子　yángdiànzǐ　same as 正电子 zhèngdiànzǐ
阳奉阴违　yángfēng-yīnwéi　overtly agree but covertly oppose; comply in public but oppose in private; feign compliance: ～,口是心非,当面说得好听,背后又在捣鬼,这就是两面派行为的表现。(毛泽东) To comply in public but oppose in private, to say yes and mean no, to say nice things to a person's face but play tricks behind his back—these are all forms of double-dealing.
阳刚　yánggāng　manly; virile: ～之气 manliness; virility
阳沟　yánggōu　open drain; ditch
阳关道　yángguāndào　(also 阳关大道 yángguāndàdào) a broad highway; a broad road; thoroughfare: 你走你的～,我过我的独木桥。You take the open road, I'll cross the log bridge—you go your way, I'll go mine.
阳光　yángguāng　sunlight; sunshine: ～充足 full of sunlight; with plenty of sunshine (*or* sun); sunny / ～普照大地。Sunlight floods the earth. *or* The sun illuminates every corner of the land.
阳极　yángjí　*phys.* positive pole; positive electrode; anode: ～板 positive plate / ～栅 anode grid / ～射线 positive ray
阳间　yángjiān　this world
阳狂　yángkuáng　same as 佯狂 yángkuáng
阳离子　yánglízǐ　positive ion; cation
阳历　yánglì　① solar calendar ② the Gregorian calendar
阳平　yángpíng　rising tone (the second of the four tones in modern standard Chinese pronunciation)
阳畦　yángqí　*agric.* seed bed with windbreaks; cold bed
阳起石　yángqǐshí　actinolite (a mineral)
阳伞　yángsǎn　parasol; sunshade
阳世　yángshì　this world
阳台　yángtái　balcony or veranda
阳痿　yángwěi　*med.* impotence
阳文　yángwén　characters or designs cut in relief; relief
阳性　yángxìng　① *med.* positive: ～反应 positive reaction ② *linguis.* masculine gender
阳性植物　yángxìng zhíwù　sun plant
阳虚　yángxū　*Chin. med.* deficiency of *yang*; lack of vital energy

扬(揚、敭)　yáng　① raise: ～手 raise one's hand (and beckon) / ～起灰尘 raise (*or* kick up) a dust / ～鞭催马 flourish the whip to urge on the horse; whip one's horse on ② throw up and scatter; winnow: ～谷去糠 winnow the chaff from the grain ③ spread; make known: 宣扬 xuānyáng
扬长避短　yángcháng-bìduǎn　show one's strong points and hide one's weaknesses; maximize favourable factors and minimize unfavourable ones
扬长补短　yángcháng-bǔduǎn　bring out one's strengths to make up for one's weaknesses
扬长而去　yángcháng ér qù　stalk off; swagger off
扬场　yángcháng　*agric.* winnowing
扬场机　yángchángjī　winnowing machine; winnower
扬程　yángchéng　*water conservancy* lift: 高～ high lift / 高～水泵 high-lift pump / 高～抽水站 high-lift pump-

ing station

扬帆 yángfān *formal* hoist the sails; set sail

扬幡招魂 yángfān zhāohún fly a funeral banner to summon the soul—try to revive what is obsolete

扬花 yánghuā *agric.* (of cereal crops) be flowering

扬眉吐气 yángméi-tǔqì feel proud and elated

扬名 yángmíng make a name for oneself; become famous: ～天下 become world-famous; become known throughout the country

扬旗 yángqí *railway* semaphore

扬弃 yángqì ① develop what is useful or healthy and discard what is not ② *philos.* sublate

扬琴 yángqín dulcimer

扬清激浊 yángqīng-jīzhuó same as 激浊扬清 jīzhuó-yángqīng

扬声 yángshēng ① raise one's voice ② make public; disclose ③ *formal* make a name for oneself; become famous

扬声器 yángshēngqì loudspeaker: 高频～ tweeter / 低频～ woofer

扬水 yángshuǐ pump up water

扬水泵 yángshuǐbèng lift pump

扬水站 yángshuǐzhàn pumping station

扬汤止沸 yáng tāng zhǐ fèi try to stop water from boiling by skimming it off and pouring it back—apply a palliative

扬言 yángyán threaten (that one is going to take action): ～要进行报复 threaten to retaliate

扬扬 yángyáng triumphantly; complacently: 意气～ in buoyant spirits; elated (over success)

扬扬得意 yángyáng déyì be immensely proud with success; look triumphant: 她～举起手来招呼新到的客人。She raised her hand with a self-satisfied gesture to greet some newly-arrived guests.

扬扬自得 yángyáng zìdé be very pleased with oneself; be complacent

扬州 Yángzhōu Yangzhou (in Jiangsu Province)

扬子鳄 yángzǐ'è *zool.* Chinese alligator

杨（楊） yáng ① poplar ② (Yáng) a surname

杨柳 yángliǔ ① poplar and willow ② willow

杨梅 yángméi *bot.* red bayberry (*Myrica rubra*)

杨梅疮 yángméichuāng *dial.* syphilis

杨树 yángshù poplar

杨桃 yángtáo see 羊桃 yángtáo

杨枝鱼 yángzhīyú pipefish

炀（煬） yáng *formal* ① smelt (metals) ② in flames; blazing

飏（颺） yáng be blown about by the wind; fly

佯 yáng pretend; feign; sham: ～作不知 feign ignorance; pretend not to know / ～死 feign death; play dead

佯称 yángchēng same as 佯言 yángyán

佯动 yángdòng *mil.* make a feint

佯攻 yánggōng *mil.* feign (*or* simulate) attack; make a feint

佯狂 yángkuáng *formal* feign madness; pretend to be mad

佯言 yángyán *formal* allege falsely; tell lies; lie; pretend: ～不知情 pretend ignorance

佯装 yángzhuāng *formal* pretend; feign: ～惊诧 pretend to be surprised

疡（瘍） yáng *med.* sore: 溃疡 kuìyáng

洋 yáng ① vast; multitudinous: 洋溢 yángyì ② ocean: 四大～ the four oceans ③ foreign: ～房 Western-style house ④ modern: ～办法 modern methods ⑤ silver dollar or coin: 罚～一百元 impose a fine of one hundred silver dollars

洋八股 yángbāgǔ foreign stereotyped writing; foreign stereotypes

洋白菜 yángbáicài cabbage

洋布 yángbù *old* (as distinguished from 土布 hand-loomed cloth) machine-woven cloth; calico

洋财 yángcái an unexpected big fortune; windfall money: 发洋财 fā yángcái

洋菜 yángcài common name for 琼脂 qióngzhī

洋场 yángchǎng metropolis infested with foreign adventurers (usu. referring to preliberation Shanghai): ～恶少 rich young bully in a metropolis (in old China)

洋车 yángchē *inf.* rickshaw: 拉～ pull a rickshaw / 拉～的 rickshawman

洋瓷 yángcí *inf.* enamel: ～器皿 enamelware

洋葱 yángcōng onion

洋地黄 yángdìhuáng *bot.* digitalis (a Chinese medicine)

洋粉 yángfěn common name for 琼脂 qióngzhī

洋服 yángfú Western-style clothes

洋橄榄 yánggǎnlǎn common name for 油橄榄 yóugǎnlǎn

洋镐 yánggǎo common name for 鹤嘴镐 hèzuǐgǎo

洋鬼子 yángguǐzi foreign devil (a term used in preliberation China for foreign invaders): 假～ imitation foreign devil—comprador, etc.

洋行 yángháng foreign firm (in preliberation China)

洋红 yánghóng carmine; crimson pigment

洋槐 yánghuái another name for 刺槐 cìhuái

洋灰 yánghuī popular name for 水泥 shuǐní

洋火 yánghuǒ *inf.* matches

洋货 yánghuò foreign goods; imported goods

洋姜 yángjiāng *inf.* Jerusalem artichoke

洋金花 yángjīnhuā *bot.* datura flower (*Datura metel*)

洋泾浜 yángjīngbāng pidgin English; pidgin

洋里洋气 yánglǐyángqi in an ostentatious Western style: 打扮得～ be dressed in an ostentatious Western style

洋流 yángliú *geol.* ocean current

洋码子 yángmǎzi *dial.* Arabic numerals

洋奴 yángnú slave of a foreign master; flunkey of imperialism; worshipper of everything foreign: ～买办 lackeys and compradors in the service of foreign bosses / ～思想 slavish mentality towards all things foreign / ～哲学 slavish comprador philosophy; blind worship of everything foreign

洋盆 yángpén same as 海盆 hǎipén

洋气 yángqì ① foreign flavour; Western style ② in an ostentatious Western style: 穿着～ be dressed in an ostentatious Western style; be stylishly dressed

洋钱 yángqián *inf.* silver dollar

洋琴 yángqín another name for 扬琴 yángqín

洋人 yángrén foreigner (usu. a Westerner)

洋伞 yángsǎn *old* Western-style umbrella

洋嗓子 yángsǎngzi a voice trained in the Western style of singing

洋纱 yángshā *old* ① machine-spun cotton yarn ② plain cloth; calico; muslin

洋柿子 yángshìzi *dial.* tomato

洋钿 yángtián *dial.* silver dollar

洋铁 yángtiě *old* galvanized iron or tinned iron

洋铁皮 yángtiěpí *old* tinplate

洋娃娃 yángwáwa (Western-style) doll

洋为中用 yáng wéi Zhōng yòng make foreign things

serve China: 利用外国工业技术来提高我们的劳动生产力就是～的一个例子。When we use foreign industrial know-how to raise our labour productivity, we are making foreign things serve the needs of China.

洋务 yángwù *old* foreign affairs

洋务运动 Yángwù Yùndòng Westernization Movement (to introduce techniques of capitalist production, initiated by comprador bureaucrats in the latter half of the 19th century in order to preserve the feudal rule of the Qing government)

洋相 yángxiàng see 出洋相 chū yángxiàng

洋绣球 yángxiùqiú another name for 天竺葵 tiānzhúkuí

洋洋 yángyáng ① numerous; copious: ～万言 run to ten thousand words—be very lengthy ② same as 扬扬 yángyáng

洋洋大观 yángyáng dàguān spectacular; grandiose; imposing

洋洋得意 yángyáng déyì same as 扬扬得意 yángyáng déyì

洋洋洒洒 yángyángsǎsǎ voluminous; of great length: ～一大篇 a magnificent piece of writing

洋洋自得 yángyáng zìdé same as 扬扬自得 yángyáng zìdé

洋溢 yángyì be permeated with; brim with: 宴会上～着团结友好的热烈气氛。The banquet was permeated with a warm atmosphere of unity and friendship.

洋油 yángyóu *dial.* imported oil; kerosene: 中国人民依靠～的日子已经一去不复返了。The days when the Chinese people had to rely on imported oil are gone forever.

洋芋 yángyù *dial.* potato

洋装[1] yángzhuāng Western-style clothes

洋装[2] yángzhuāng Western-style binding: ～书 a book in a Western-style binding

徉 yáng see 徜徉 chángyáng

烊 yáng *dial.* melt; go soft: 天太热，这糖都～了。The sweets have gone soft in this hot weather. ——see also yàng

yǎng

仰 yǎng ① face upward: ～着睡 sleep on one's back / ～头 raise one's head; raise one's eyes ② admire; respect; look up to: 瞻仰 zhānyǎng ③ rely on: 仰仗 yǎngzhàng ④ *old* (used in official documents, transmitting orders or requests): ～即遵照。We hope that you will act accordingly at once. / ～请允准。We beg for your kind permission.

仰八叉 yǎngbāchā *inf.* (fall) on one's back: 摔了个～ fall flat on one's back

仰尘 yǎngchén *formal* ceiling

仰承 yǎngchéng ① *formal* rely on ② *pol.* in compliance with your wishes

仰毒 yǎngdú *formal* take poison: ～自尽 commit suicide by taking poison

仰给 yǎngjǐ rely on sb. for support: ～于人 rely on others for support

仰角 yǎngjiǎo *math.* angle of elevation

仰壳 yǎngké *dial.* (fall) on one's back: 摔了个大～ fall flat on one's back

仰赖 yǎnglài rely on: 我们～您的资助。We rely on you for financial support.

仰面 yǎngmiàn face upward: ～朝天 lie on one's back / ～倒下 fall on one's back

仰慕 yǎngmù admire; look up to: 久已～盛名。I have

long been aware of your high fame. *or* I feel honoured to meet you.

仰攀 yǎngpān *formal* ① climb up; clamber up ② associate with people above one's social position

仰人鼻息 yǎng rén bíxī be dependent on the whims of others; be slavishly dependent

仰韶文化 Yǎngsháo wénhuà the Yangshao culture (a Neolithic culture characterized by a fine painted pottery; named after Yangshao, Henan Province, where remains were first found in 1921)

仰食 yǎngshí *formal* depend on another for food (*or* for one's living)

仰视 yǎngshì look up: ～天空 look up at the sky / 俯伏在地，不敢～ lie prostrate on the ground, not daring to look up

仰首 yǎngshǒu *formal* raise one's head: ～望明月 raise one's head and gaze at the moon

仰首伸眉 yǎngshǒu-shēnméi hold one's head high, feeling proud and elated

仰天 yǎngtiān look up to heaven: ～长叹 look up to heaven and heave a deep sigh / ～大笑 laugh sardonically

仰望 yǎngwàng ① look up at: ～星空 look up at the starlit sky / ～天安门城楼 look up at the gate tower of Tian An Men ② *formal* respectfully seek guidance or help from; look up to

仰卧 yǎngwò lie on one's back; lie supine

仰卧起坐 yǎngwòqǐzuò *sports* sit-up: 一气儿做四十个～ do forty sit-ups at a stretch

仰屋兴叹 yǎng wū xīngtàn look up at the ceiling and sigh—be at the end of one's resources

仰屋著书 yǎng wū zhùshū look up at the ceiling as one writes—take great pains with one's writings

仰药 yǎngyào *formal* take poison

仰泳 yǎngyǒng *sports* backstroke

仰仗 yǎngzhàng rely on; look to sb. for backing (*or* support): 我们～你啦! We rely on you.

养 (養)

yǎng ① support; provide for: ～家 support a family / 我从小没了父母，是姑姑把我～大的。I lost my parents when I was a child, and was brought up by my aunt. ② raise; keep; grow: ～鸭 raise ducks / ～鸟 keep pet birds / ～花 grow flowers ③ give birth to: 她～了个儿子。She gave birth to a boy. ④ foster; adoptive: ～父 (母) foster father (mother) / ～子 (女) adopted son (daughter) ⑤ form; acquire; cultivate: ～成良好的习惯 cultivate good habits ⑥ rest; convalesce; recuperate one's health; heal: ～身体 recuperate / 你这回病得不轻，应该好好～～。You've been seriously ill and should take a good rest. ⑦ let (one's hair) grow ⑧ maintain; keep in good repair: 养路 yǎnglù

养兵 yǎngbīng maintain an army

养兵千日，用兵一时 yǎngbīng qiānrì, yòngbīng yīshí maintain an army for a thousand days to use it for an hour

养病 yǎngbìng take rest and nourishment to regain one's health; recuperate: 他在家～呢。He's recuperating at home.

养蚕 yǎngcán engage in sericulture

养蚕业 yǎngcányè sericulture

养地 yǎngdì increase soil fertility (by fertilization, crop rotation, etc.)

养儿防老，积谷防荒 yǎng ér fáng lǎo, jī gǔ fáng huāng just as one stores up grain against lean years, one rears children against old age

养分 yǎngfèn nutrient: 土壤～ soil nutrient

养蜂 yǎngfēng raise or keep bees; engage in apiculture (*or* beekeeping)

养蜂场 yǎngfēngchǎng　apiary; bee farm

养蜂业 yǎngfēngyè　apiculture; beekeeping

养汉 yǎnghàn　(of a woman) have a lover

养虎遗患 yǎng hǔ yí huàn　to rear a tiger is to court calamity—appeasement brings disaster

养护 yǎnghù　① maintain; conserve: 道路～ road maintenance / 生物资源～ conservation of living resources ② curing: 混凝土～ concrete curing

养活 yǎnghuo　inf.　① support; feed: ～一家子 support (or feed) a family / 农民的血汗～了地主老财。The landlords lived off the sweat and blood of the peasants. ② raise (animals): 他家～了上百头猪。His family raises nearly a hundred pigs. ③ give birth to: ～孩子 have a baby

养鸡场 yǎngjīchǎng　chicken run; chicken farm

养家活口 yǎngjiā-huókǒu　support one's family

养精蓄锐 yǎngjīng-xùruì　conserve strength and store up energy

养疴 yǎngkē　formal　recuperate from an illness

养老 yǎnglǎo　① provide for the aged (usu. one's parents) ② live out one's life in retirement

养老金 yǎnglǎojīn　old-age pension

养老送终 yǎnglǎo-sòngzhōng　look after one's parents in their old age and give them a proper burial after they die

养老院 yǎnglǎoyuàn　old people's home; rest home

养廉 yǎnglián　formal　(of government officials) nourish honesty—refrain from squeeze and graft: 俭以～ nourish honesty by living a frugal life

养料 yǎngliào　nutriment; nourishment: 树根从土壤中吸取水分和～。The roots of trees draw water and nourishment from the soil. / 作家应该从现实生活中吸取创作的～。Writers should try to draw nourishment for their creative work from real life.

养路 yǎnglù　maintain a road or railway: ～道班 road maintenance crew

养路费 yǎnglùfèi　road toll

养马场 yǎngmǎchǎng　(horse) ranch

养气 yǎngqì　formal　① foster the spirit of nobility (by moral cultivation or through a moral life, as advocated by Confucianists) ② conserve one's vital powers (by avoiding conflict with the unchangeable laws of nature, as practised by Taoists)

养伤 yǎngshāng　nurse one's injuries or wounds

养神 yǎngshén　rest to attain mental tranquility; repose: 闭目～ sit in repose with one's eyes closed

养生 yǎngshēng　care for life; conserve one's vital powers; preserve one's health; keep in good health

养生之道 yǎngshēng zhī dào　how to care for life (or conserve one's vital powers); how to maintain good health

养兔场 yǎngtùchǎng　rabbit warren

养息 yǎngxī　rest and take nourishing food to build up one's health; recuperate

养媳妇 yǎngxífù　dial.　same as 童养媳 tóngyǎngxí

养性 yǎngxìng　nourish one's nature: 修真～ cultivate one's native sensibility and nourish one's inborn nature

养痈成患 yǎng yōng chéng huàn　(also 养痈遗患 yǎng yōng yí huàn) a boil neglected becomes the bane of one's life—leaving evil unchecked spells ruin

养鱼 yǎngyú　breed fish; engage in pisciculture

养鱼池 yǎngyúchí　fishpond

养育 yǎngyù　bring up; rear: ～子女 bring up children

养殖 yǎngzhí　breed (aquatics): ～海带 cultivate kelp / 淡水～ freshwater aquiculture / 海水～ seawater aquiculture

养殖珍珠 yǎngzhí zhēnzhū　cultured pearl

养猪场 yǎngzhūchǎng　pig farm; piggery

养尊处优 yǎngzūn-chǔyōu　enjoy high position and live in comfort; live in clover

氧　yǎng　chem.　oxygen (O)

氧合作用 yǎnghé zuòyòng　physiol.　oxygenation

氧化 yǎnghuà　chem.　oxidize; oxidate: ～作用 oxidation

氧化还原酶 yǎnghuàhuányuánméi　chem.　oxido-reducing enzyme; oxidoreductase

氧化剂 yǎnghuàjì　oxidizer; oxidant

氧化数 yǎnghuàshù　oxidation number; oxidation state

氧化态 yǎnghuàtài　oxidation state; oxidation number

氧化铁 yǎnghuàtiě　ferric oxide

氧化物 yǎnghuàwù　oxide

氧化焰 yǎnghuàyàn　another name for 外焰 wàiyàn

氧化抑制剂 yǎnghuà yìzhìjì　oxidation retarder (or inhibitor)

氧气 yǎngqì　oxygen: ～炼钢 oxygen steelmaking

氧气顶吹转炉 yǎngqì dǐngchuī zhuànlú　oxygen top-blown convertor

氧气面具 yǎngqì miànjù　oxygen mask

氧气瓶 yǎngqìpíng　oxygen cylinder

氧气枪 yǎngqìqiāng　metall.　oxygen lance

氧气帐 yǎngqìzhàng　med.　oxygen tent

氧乙炔吹管 yǎngyǐquē chuīguǎn　mech.　oxyacetylene blowpipe

痒（癢）　yǎng　itch; tickle: 浑身发～ itch all over / 搔到～处 scratch where it itches—hit the nail on the head / 怕～ ticklish

痒痒 yǎngyang　inf.　itch; tickle: 蚊子咬得腿上直～。The mosquito bites on my legs itch terribly.

yàng

快　yàng　see below

怏怏 yàngyàng　disgruntled; sullen: ～不乐 unhappy about sth.; morose

恙　yàng　formal　ailment; illness: 无恙 wúyàng

恙虫 yàngchóng　zool.　tsutsugamushi mite

恙虫热 yàngchóngrè　tsutsugamushi disease; scrub typhus

样（樣）　yàng　① appearance; shape: 这两支笔～儿差不多, 色儿却不一样。These two pens are alike except that they're different colours. / 几年没见, 他还是那个～儿。It's years since I last saw him, but he still looks the same. ② sample; model; pattern: 鞋样 xiéyàng / 样品 yàngpǐn ③ m.　kind; type: 三～儿点心 three kinds of pastries / 商店虽小, 各～货物俱全。Small as it is, the shop stocks all kinds of wares.

样板 yàngbǎn　① sample plate ② templet ③ model; prototype; example

样板戏 yàngbǎnxì　(a term used during the Cultural Revolution) model opera: 京剧～ model Peking opera

样本 yàngběn　① sample book ② print.　sample; specimen: 字体～ type specimen book

样稿 yànggǎo　sample manuscript

样机 yàngjī　the prototype of a machine

样片 yàngpiàn　the sample copy of a film

样品 yàngpǐn　sample (product); specimen

样式 yàngshì　pattern; type; style; form: 各种～的羊毛衫 woollen sweaters in all styles

样样 yàngyàng　every kind; each and every; all: 地里的活她～都会。She knows how to do every kind of farm work. / 这孩子德、智、体～都好。The child is developing

in every way, morally, intellectually and physically.

样张 yàngzhāng *print.* specimen page

样子 yàngzi ① appearance; shape: 这件大衣的～很好看。This coat is well cut. / 这活做得不像～。This job has been done too crudely. ② manner; air: 看他那高兴的～。How happy he looks! / 装出一副公正的～ assume a righteous posture (*or* manner, air) ③ sample; model; pattern: 衣服～ clothes pattern / 给我个～照着做。Give me a model to follow. / 做出～来 set an example ④ *inf.* tendency; likelihood: 天像是要下雨的～。It looks like rain. / 看～这星期他来不了。It seems (*or* looks as if) he won't be able to come this week. ——see also 摆样子 bǎi yàngzi

烊 yàng see 打烊 dǎyàng ——see also yáng

漾 yàng ① ripple: 荡漾 dàngyàng ② brim over; overflow: 碗里的汤快～出来了。The soup in the bowl is brimming over. / 她脸上～出了笑容。Her face broadened into a smile. ③ *dial.* lakelet; pool; pond

漾奶 yàngnǎi (of a baby) throw up milk

yāo

幺（么） yāo ① one (used for the numeral 一 orally) ② *dial.* youngest (among brothers and sisters): ～妹 youngest sister

幺麽 yāomó *formal* petty; insignificant; paltry: ～小丑 a despicable wretch

夭¹（殀） yāo die young

夭² yāo *formal* tender and luxuriant

夭殇 yāoshāng *formal* die young

夭桃秾李 yāotáo-nónglǐ georgeous in beauty as the bloom of peach or plum (said of a beautiful young lady, esp. in congratulations on marriage)

夭亡 yāowáng die young

夭折 yāozhé ① die young ② come to a premature end: 谈判中途～。The negotiations came to a premature end.

吆（吆） yāo see below

吆喊 yāohǎn cry out; call: 他～了几声，也没人回答。He called several times, but no one answered.

吆喝 yāohe ① cry out; call; shout: 走的时候～一声。Give us a shout when it's time to leave. ② cry one's wares: 她头一次上街卖菜，不好意思～。The first time she went out selling vegetables, she was too shy to cry out for customers. ③ loudly urge on (an animal): 牲口不听～。The animal wouldn't obey its driver.

吆唤 yāohuan cry out; call: 你～几个小伙子来帮忙。Call some of the boys over here to help.

约 yāo *inf.* weigh in a balance (*or* on a scale): 给我～一公斤猪肉。Weigh me out one kilo of pork. / ～～多重。See how much it weighs. ——see also yuē

约克夏猪 yāokèxiàzhū Yorkshire (hog)

妖 yāo ① goblin; demon; evil spirit: 妖魔 yāomó ② evil and fraudulent: 妖术 yāoshù ③ seductive: 妖里妖气 yāoliyāoqì

妖道 yāodào Taoist sorcerer or witch

妖氛 yāofēn demonic aura; evil portent; evil influence

妖风 yāofēng evil wind; noxious trend

妖怪 yāoguài monster; bogy; goblin; demon

妖精 yāojing ① evil spirit; demon ② seductress; siren

妖里妖气 yāoliyāoqì seductive; sexy: 打扮得～的 be seductively dressed

妖媚 yāomèi seductively charming; bewitching; sexy

妖魔 yāomó evil spirit; demon

妖魔鬼怪 yāomó-guǐguài demons and ghosts; monsters of every description; all forces of evil

妖孽 yāoniè *formal* ① person or event associated with evil or misfortune ② evildoer

妖娆 yāoráo *formal* enchanting; fascinating; bewitching

妖人 yāorén sorcerer; enchanter

妖声妖气 yāoshēng-yāoqì (also 妖声怪气 yāoshēng-guàiqì) speak in an affected voice and manner

妖术 yāoshù sorcery; witchcraft; black art

妖妄 yāowàng fantastic; absurd: ～之说 fallacy

妖物 yāowù evil spirit; monster

妖言 yāoyán heresy; fallacy

妖言惑众 yāoyán huòzhòng spread fallacies to deceive people

妖艳 yāoyàn seductive; bewitching

妖冶 yāoyě seductive; bewitching

要 yāo ① demand; ask: 要求 yāoqiú ② force; coerce: 要挟 yāoxié ③ same as 邀 yāo ——see also yào

要功 yāogōng same as 邀功 yāogōng

要击 yāojī same as 邀击 yāojī

要买人心 yāomǎi rénxīn same as 邀买人心 yāomǎi rénxīn

要求 yāoqiú ① ask; demand; require; claim: ～增加工资 demand a raise in pay / ～发言 ask to be heard; ask for the floor / ～入党 ask to join the Party; apply for admission to the Party / 严格～自己 set strict demands on oneself; be strict with oneself / ～赔偿 claim compensation / 这项工作～精神高度集中。This job calls for intense concentration. / 对他不要～过高。Don't ask too much of him. ② requirement; demand; claim: 达到质量～ fulfil quality requirements / 提出领土～ make territorial claims / 满足他的～ satisfy (*or* meet) his demands

要挟 yāoxié coerce; put pressure on; threaten: 对小国进行～ use coercion against small nations / ～对方 put pressure on the other party

腰 yāo ① waist; the small of the back: 齐～深 waist-deep; up to the waist / 弯～ bend down; stoop / ～酸腿疼 aching back and legs / 扭了～ sprain one's back muscles ② waist (of a garment): 裤～ waist of trousers ③ pocket: 我～里还有些钱。I've still got some money in my pocket. ④ middle: 半山～ halfway up the mountain

腰板儿 yāobǎnr ① back: 直起～ straighten one's back ② physique; build: 他八十多了，～还挺硬朗。He's well over eighty, but he's still quite strong.

腰包 yāobāo purse; pocket: 肥了投机商的～ line the pockets of the profiteers / 把钱装进自己的～ pocket the money ——see also 掏腰包 tāo yāobāo

腰部 yāobù waist; the small of the back

腰缠万贯 yāochán wànguàn be loaded; be very rich

腰带 yāodài belt; girdle

腰肥 yāoféi waistline; waist measurement: ～64厘米 measure 64 cm. round the waist

腰杆子 yāogǎnzi (also 腰杆儿 yāogǎnr) ① back: 挺起～ straighten one's back—be confident and unafraid ② backing; support: ～硬 have strong backing

腰鼓 yāogǔ ① waist drum ② waist drum dance

腰果 yāoguǒ cashew nut; cashew

腰果树 yāoguǒshù *bot.* cashew (tree)

腰花 yāohuā scalloped pork or lamb kidneys: 炒～

stir-fried kidneys

腰肌劳损 yāojī láosǔn strain of lumbar muscles; psoatic strain

腰身 yāoshēn waistline; waist; waist measurement; girth: 她的～很细。She has a slender waist. / 这条裤子～太大。These trousers are too big in the waist.

腰酸背痛 yāosuān-bèitòng have a sore waist and an aching back—be aching all over

腰痛 yāotòng lumbago

腰围 yāowéi ① waistline; waist measurement: 你的～粗了。Your waistline is getting bigger. ② girdle

腰眼 yāoyǎn either side of the small of the back

腰斩 yāozhǎn ① cutting sb. in two at the waist (a capital punishment in ancient China) ② cut sth. in half

腰肢 yāozhī waist: ～纤细 have a slim waist

腰椎 yāozhuī physiol. lumbar vertebra

腰椎穿刺 yāozhuī chuāncì med. lumbar puncture

腰子 yāozi inf. kidney

邀 yāo ① invite; ask: ～几个朋友来打桥牌 invite (or ask) some friends over for a game of bridge ② solicit; seek: ～准 seek approval; ask permission ③ intercept: 邀击 yāojī

邀宠 yāochǒng try to win sb.'s favour; curry favour with sb.

邀功 yāogōng formal take credit for someone else's achievements: ～请赏 take credit and seek rewards for someone else's achievements

邀击 yāojī intercept (the enemy); waylay

邀集 yāojí invite to meet together; call together: 今天～大家来开个座谈会。You have been invited here today to hold a forum.

邀买人心 yāomǎi rénxīn buy popular support; court popularity

邀请 yāoqǐng invite: ～代表团来中国访问 invite a delegation to visit China / 应中国政府的～ at the invitation of the Chinese Government / 发出～ send (or extend) an invitation / 愉快地接受～ accept an invitation with pleasure

邀请国 yāoqǐngguó host country

邀请赛 yāoqǐngsài sports invitational tournament: 足球～ invitational soccer tournament

邀请信 yāoqǐngxìn letter of invitation

邀赏 yāoshǎng ask to be rewarded for service rendered

yáo

尧（堯） Yáo Yao, a legendary sage king in ancient China

尧舜 Yáo-Shùn Yao and Shun, legendary sage kings in ancient China—ancient sages

尧天舜日 Yáotiān-Shùnrì the days of Yao and Shun —the golden age of Chinese history (according to the Confucianists)

肴（餚） yáo meat and fish dishes: 酒～ wine and dainties

肴肉 yáoròu a kind of cured pork

肴馔 yáozhuàn formal sumptuous courses at a meal

姚 Yáo a surname

姚黄魏紫 yáohuáng-wèizǐ Yao Yellow and Wei Purple —rare varieties of peonies (originally varieties developed by a Yao and a Wei family of the Song Dynasty)

珧 yáo see 江珧 jiāngyáo

窑（窯、窰） yáo ① kiln: 石灰～ limekiln ② (coal) pit: 小煤～ small coal pit ③ cave dwelling ④ dial. brothel

窑变 yáobiàn kiln transmutation—the technique of making iridescent chinaware by the irregular application of glaze: ～花瓶 a flambé vase

窑洞 yáodòng cave dwelling

窑灰钾肥 yáohuījiǎféi flue ash potash

窑姐儿 yáojiěr dial. prostitute

窑子 yáozi dial. brothel

谣 yáo ① ballad; rhyme: 民谣 mínyáo ② rumour: 造谣 zàoyáo

谣传 yáochuán ① rumour; hearsay ② it is rumoured that; rumour has it that

谣俗 yáosú formal customs and habits; folkways

谣言 yáoyán rumour; unfounded report; groundless allegation: 散布～ spread (or circulate) rumours / 戳穿～ give the lie to a rumour / ～攻势 rumourmongering campaign

谣谚 yáoyàn folk songs and proverbs

谣诼 yáozhuó formal slander; calumny

猺 yáo see 青猺 qīngyáo

遥 yáo formal distant; remote; far: 千里之～ at a distance of a thousand li; a thousand li away

遥测 yáocè telemetering: 空间～ space telemetry

遥测计 yáocèjì telemeter

遥测术 yáocèshù telemetry

遥测温度计 yáocè wēndùjì telethermometer

遥感 yáogǎn electron. remote sensing: 红外～ infrared remote sensing

遥控 yáokòng remote control; telecontrol: ～飞机 remote control aircraft; telecontrolled airplane / ～开关 teleswitch / ～无人驾驶飞机 drone (aircraft) / 计算机～操作 remote computer operation / ～测量 telemetric measurement

遥控力学 yáokòng lìxué telemechanics

遥望 yáowàng look into the distance

遥相呼应 yáo xiāng hūyìng echo each other at a distance; coordinate with each other from afar

遥想 yáoxiǎng recall; recollect; reminisce: ～当年 reminisce about the good old days

遥遥 yáoyáo far away; a long way off: ～相对 stand far apart facing each other

遥遥领先 yáoyáo lǐngxiān be far ahead; hold a safe lead

遥遥无期 yáoyáo wú qī not (realizable, etc.) within the foreseeable future: 工程竣工～。Completion of the project is nowhere in sight.

遥夜 yáoyè formal a long night: ～深思 sit up all night, thinking

遥远 yáoyuǎn distant; remote; faraway: ～的将来 the distant (or remote) future / ～的山村 a remote mountain village / ～的边疆 remote frontiers / 路途～ a long journey; a long way to go

遥瞻 yáozhān formal view from a great distance

遥指 yáozhǐ point in the direction of

摇 yáo shake; wave; rock; turn: ～铃 ring a bell / ～扇子 wave a fan / ～辘轳 turn a windlass / ～橹 scull; sweep / 小狗～着尾巴跑了。The little dog ran off wagging its tail.

摇摆 yáobǎi sway; swing; rock; vacillate: 柳枝迎风～。The branches of the willow trees swayed in the

breeze. / 船身～。The ship rocked. / 左右～ vacillate now to the left, now to the right

摇摆舞 yáobǎiwǔ ① swing ② rock and roll; rock

摇摆乐 yáobǎiyuè swing; swing music

摇臂 yáobì *mech.* rocker (*or* rock, rocking) arm: ～轴 rocker shaft / ～钻床 radial drilling machine

摇船 yáochuán row a boat

摇床 yáochuáng *min.* table: 选矿～ cleaning table / 粗选～ roughing table

摇唇鼓舌 yáochún-gǔshé flap one's lips and beat one's tongue; wag one's tongue; engage in loose talk (to stir up trouble)

摇荡 yáodàng rock; sway

摇动 yáodòng ① wave; shake: 欢迎的群众～着花束。The welcoming crowd waved their bouquets. ② sway; rock: 大树在狂风中～。The big tree rocked in the strong wind.

摇鹅毛扇 yáo émáoshàn wave a goose-feather fan —mastermind (a plot, etc.)

摇滚乐 yáogǔnyuè rock and roll; rock (music)

摇撼 yáohàn give a violent shake to; shake to the root or foundation; rock

摇晃 yáohuang rock; sway; shake: 地震时大楼都～了。The tall buildings shook during the earthquake. / 这椅子有点～。The chair is a bit rickety (*or* shaky). / 他病了很久，走起路来摇摇晃晃的。He walked with faltering steps after a long illness.

摇奖 yáojiǎng lottery

摇篮 yáolán cradle: 她把孩子放在～里，把他摇睡着了。She rocked the bady to sleep in the cradle. / 延安是中国革命的～。Yan'an was the cradle of the Chinese revolution. / 黄河是我国文化的～。The Yellow River was the cradle of Chinese civilization.

摇篮曲 yáolánqǔ *mus.* cradle-song; lullaby; berceuse

摇耧 yáolóu rock a drill barrow in sowing; sow with a drill barrow

摇蜜 yáomì extract honey

摇蜜机 yáomìjī honey extractor

摇旗呐喊 yáo qí nàhǎn wave flags and shout battle cries—bang the drum for sb.: 团练使黄安带领人马上船，～，杀奔金沙滩来。《水浒》Huang An, the drill master, embarked his soldiers and horses on the boats, and with much shouting and fluttering of flags they set out for the Golden Sand Bund.

摇钱树 yáoqiánshù a legendary tree that sheds coins when shaken—a ready source of money

摇纱机 yáoshājī *text.* reeling frame

摇身一变 yáo shēn yī biàn *derog.* give oneself a shake and change into another form—suddenly change one's identity: 解放初期，这个特务～，钻进了革命队伍。At the time of liberation this special agent changed his identity and sneaked into the revolutionary ranks.

摇手 yáoshǒu shake one's hand in admonition or disapproval

摇头 yáotóu shake one's head: 每逢提起这件事，他总是苦笑着摇摇头。Each time this was mentioned, he would give a bitter smile and shake his head.

摇头摆尾 yáotóu-bǎiwěi shake the head and wag the tail—assume an air of complacency or levity

摇头晃脑 yáotóu-huàngnǎo wag one's head—look pleased with oneself; assume an air of self-approbation or self-satisfaction

摇尾乞怜 yáo wěi qǐ lián wag the tail ingratiatingly —fawn obsequiously

摇蚊 yáowén midge; chironomid (a small gnatlike insect)

摇摇欲坠 yáoyáo yù zhuì tottering; crumbling; on the verge of collapse: 保守党政府～。The Conservative Government was tottering. / ～的反动政权 a crumbling

reactionary regime

摇曳 yáoyè flicker; sway: ～的灯光 flickering light / 垂柳在微风中轻轻～。The willow branches swayed gently in the breeze.

摇椅 yáoyǐ rocking chair

徭（傜）

yáo see below

徭役 yáoyì corvée

徭役地租 yáoyì dìzū another name for 劳役地租 láoyì dìzū

瑶

yáo *formal* precious jade; jasper: ～琴 a lute with jasper mountings

瑶池 Yáochí Jasper Lake (the dwelling-place of the Queen Mother of the West 西王母)——see also 西王母 Xīwángmǔ

瑶族 Yáozú the Yao nationality, or the Yaos, distributed over the Guangxi Zhuang Autonomous Region and Hunan, Yunnan, Guangdong and Guizhou Provinces

鳐

yáo skate (a fish)

yǎo

杳

yǎo *formal* distant and out of sight: ～无踪迹 disappear without a trace; vanish

杳渺 yǎomiǎo (also 杳眇 yǎomiǎo) *formal* distant and indistinct

杳冥 yǎomíng same as 窈冥 yǎomíng

杳然 yǎorán *formal* quiet; still

杳如黄鹤 yǎo rú huánghè leave like the yellow crane—leave never to return; be gone for ever (from Cui Hao's 崔颢 lines 黄鹤一去不复返，白云千载空悠悠 "The yellow crane, once it has gone, will never come again, But white clouds of a thousand years go aimlessly on and on.")

杳无音信 yǎo wú yīnxìn there has been no news whatsoever about sb.; never been heard of since: 他走后～。We have not heard from him since he left. *or* No word has come from him since he left.

咬（齩、鲛）

yǎo ① bite; snap at: ～不动 too tough to bite (*or* chew) / ～一口 take a bite / 被蛇～了 be bitten by a snake / 被疯狗～死 be bitten to death by a mad dog / 我吃饭吃得太快，～着舌头了。I ate too fast and bit my tongue. ② grip; bite: 这个旧螺母～不住扣儿了。This old nut won't bite (*or* grip). / 双方比分一直得很紧。The score was very close throughout the match. ③ (of a dog) bark: 鸡叫狗～ cocks crow and dogs bark ④ incriminate another person (usu. innocent) when blamed or interrogated: 别～好人。Don't implicate the innocent. ⑤ *dial.* corrode (metals); irritate (the skin): 我最怕漆～。I'm allergic to paint. *or* My skin is allergic to paint. / 这把刀埋在地里让土～了。The knife had been buried in the ground and was corroded. ⑥ pronounce; articulate: 这个字他～不准。He can't pronounce this word correctly. ⑦ be nitpicking (about the use of words): 咬字眼儿 yǎozìyǎnr

咬耳朵 yǎo ěrduo *inf.* whisper in sb.'s ear; whisper

咬合 yǎohé (of gear wheels, etc.) interlock; engage; mesh: 这两个齿轮相～。These two gear wheels engage (*or* mesh).

咬紧牙关 yǎojǐn yáguān grit (*or* clench) one's teeth; endure with dogged will: 他～忍受。He gritted his teeth and resolved to hold out.

咬啮 yǎoniè gnaw: 恐惧和焦虑正～着她的心。Fear and

anxiety were gnawing at her heart.

咬群 yǎoqún *inf.* ① (of a domestic animal) be prone to fight within the herd ② (of a person) be apt to pick a quarrel within a group

咬舌儿 yǎoshér (also 咬舌子 yǎo shézi) ① lisp ② lisper

咬文嚼字 yǎowén-jiáozì pay excessive attention to wording

咬牙 yǎoyá ① grit (or set, clench, gnash) one's teeth: 恨得直～ gnash one's teeth in hatred / 痛得直～ grit one's teeth in pain / 咬咬牙干下去 go at it with set (or clenched) teeth ② grind one's teeth (in sleep)

咬牙切齿 yǎoyá-qièchǐ gnash one's teeth: ～地咒骂 curse between one's teeth / 所有的人都气得握紧拳头，～。They were all so enraged that they clenched their fists and ground their teeth.

咬住 yǎozhù ① bite into; grip with one's teeth: 用嘴～绳子 grip the rope with one's teeth ② grip; take firm hold of; refuse to let go of: 别老～我那句话不放。Don't keep nagging me about that remark of mine. / 追击部队紧紧～敌人。The pursuing troops were close on the heels of the enemy. / 他掉转机头，～了敌机。He swung his fighter around and got on the tail of the enemy plane.

咬字儿 yǎozìr pronounce; articulate: 她～清楚。Her articulation is clear.

咬字眼儿 yǎozìyǎnr be nitpicking on words

咬嘴 yǎozuǐ be difficult to articulate; be awkward-sounding

窈

yǎo see below

窈冥 yǎomíng *formal* ① dim; dusky ② deep; profound; abstruse

窈窕 yǎotiǎo *liter.* ① (of a woman) gentle and graceful: ～淑女，君子好逑。(《诗经》) Lovely is the good lady, Fit bride for our lord. ② (of a palace, landscape, etc.) secluded

窅

yǎo *formal* far and deep; remote and obscure

窅然 yǎorán *formal* far and deep; remote and obscure: 桃花流水～去，别有天地非人间。(李白) Peach blossoms and flowing waters go without a trace; There is another heaven and earth beyond the world of man.

舀

yǎo ladle out; spoon up (or out); scoop up: ～汤 ladle out soup

舀子 yǎozi dipper; ladle; scoop

yào

疟(瘧)

yào see below——see also nüè

疟子 yàozi *inf.* malaria

药(藥)

yào ① medicine; drug; remedy: 你吃过～了吗? Have you taken your medicine yet? / 这种～得有大夫处方才能买。This drug is sold only on a doctor's prescription. / 一种治高血压的新～ a new remedy for high blood pressure / 进口～ imported drugs ② certain chemicals: 杀虫～ insecticide; pesticide ③ *formal* cure with medicine: 不可救药 bùkě jiùyào ④ kill with poison: 把老鼠～死 kill rats with rat poison

药补 yàobǔ build up one's health by taking tonic: ～不如食补。Nourishing food is better than tonic.

药材 yàocái medicinal materials; crude drugs

药草 yàocǎo medicinal herbs

药叉 yàochā same as 夜叉 yèchā

药厂 yàochǎng pharmaceutical factory

药单 yàodān (medical) prescription

药典 yàodiǎn pharmacopoeia

药店 yàodiàn drugstore; chemist's shop; pharmacy

药饵 yào'ěr same as 药物 yàowù

药方 yàofāng prescription: 开～ write out a prescription

药房 yàofáng ① drugstore; chemist's shop; pharmacy ② hospital pharmacy; dispensary

药费 yàofèi expenses for medicine; charges for medicine

药粉 yàofěn (medicinal) powder

药膏 yàogāo ointment; salve

药罐子 yàoguànzi ① a pot for decocting herbal medicine ② a chronic invalid

药衡 yàohéng apothecaries' measure or weight

药剂 yàojì medicament; drug

药剂师 yàojìshī pharmacist; pharmaceutist; druggist

药剂学 yàojìxué pharmaceutics; pharmacy

药箭 yàojiàn a poisoned arrow

药劲儿 yàojìnr efficacy of a drug (or medicine)

药酒 yàojiǔ medicinal liquor

药理 yàolǐ ① pharmacodynamics ② pharmacology

药理学 yàolǐxué pharmacology

药力 yàolì efficacy of a drug (or medicine): ～发作。The drug is taking effect. / ～达不到。The medicine was not potent enough to produce the desired effect.

药麻 yàomá *med.* drug anaesthesia

药棉 yàomián absorbent cotton

药面儿 yàomiànr (medicinal) powder

药捻儿 yàoniǎnr ① fuse (for igniting an explosive charge) ② same as 药捻子 yàoniǎnzi

药捻子 yàoniǎnzi a slender roll of medicated paper or gauze (to be inserted into wounds, boils, etc.)

药农 yàonóng a peasant who cultivates or collects medicinal herbs; medicinal herb grower or collector; herbalist

药片 yàopiàn (medicinal) tablet

药品 yàopǐn medicines and chemical reagents

药瓶 yàopíng medicine bottle

药铺 yàopù herbal medicine shop

药签 yàoqiān swab

药球 yàoqiú another name for 实心球 shíxīnqiú

药膳 yàoshàn medicated food; food cooked with medicinal herbs: ～餐厅 a restaurant serving medicated food (or medicinal dishes)

药石 yàoshí medicines and stone needles for acupuncture—remedies: ～罔效。All medical treatment has failed.

药石之言 yàoshí zhī yán (also 药言 yàoyán) unpalatable but salutary advice

药水 yàoshuǐ ① liquid medicine; medicinal liquid ② lotion

药丸 yàowán (also 药丸子 yàowánzi) pill: 大～ bolus

药味 yàowèi ① herbal medicines in a prescription ② flavour of a drug

药物 yàowù pharmaceuticals; materia medica; medicines; drugs: ～生产 production of pharmaceuticals

药物过敏 yàowù guòmǐn drug allergy

药物化学 yàowù huàxué pharmaceutical chemistry

药物学 yàowùxué materia medica; pharmacognosy

药物牙膏 yàowù yágāo medicated toothpaste

药物中毒 yàowù zhòngdú drug poisoning

药箱 yàoxiāng medical kit; medicine-chest: 急救～ first-aid kit

药效 yàoxiào efficacy of a drug (or medicine)

药性 yàoxìng property of a medicine: 这种药～平和。This medicine is quite mild.

药性气 yàoxìngqi the flavour of medicinal decoctions

药学 yàoxué pharmacy

药引子 yàoyǐnzi *Chin. med.* an ingredient added to enhance the efficacy of a dose of medicine; a medical supplement

药用炭 yàoyòngtàn medical charcoal

药浴 yàoyù *animal husbandry* dipping: 羊～ sheep dipping / ～池 dipping vat

药皂 yàozào medicated soap

药渣 yàozhā dregs of a decoction

药疹 yàozhěn *med.* drug rash; drug eruption

要¹ yào ① important; essential: ～事 an important matter (*or* affair) / 上述规定希严格执行为～。It is imperative that the above rules be strictly observed. ② main points; essentials: 择～记录 note down the essential points

要² yào ① want; ask for; wish; desire: 他～一架手风琴。He wants an accordion. / 这双鞋我还～呢。I want to keep these shoes. / 中国～和平, 不～战争。China wants peace, not war. / 谁没有票, 问她～。Anyone without a ticket can ask her for one. / 我～了两个菜。I ordered two dishes. ② ask (*or* want) sb. to do sth.: 老大爷～我替他写封信。The old man asked me to write a letter for him. / 班长～我们五点以前归队。The squad leader told us to get back before five o'clock. / 不是你～我来的吗? Wasn't it you who asked me to come? ③ want to; wish to: 这位先生～见总经理。This gentleman wishes to see the general manager. / 我还有几句话～说。I'd like to say a few more words. / 他～学游泳。He wants to learn swimming. ④ must; should; it is necessary (*or* imperative, essential): ～相信群众。We must have faith in the masses. / 借东西～还。One should return what one borrows. / 我～不～留下来? Shall I stay? / 这个问题～仔细考虑。This question calls for careful consideration. / 早点儿睡吧, 明天还～起早呢! Let's go to bed now. We'll have to get up early tomorrow morning. ⑤ shall; will; be going to: ～下雨了。It's going to rain. / 天～黑了, 快走吧! It's getting dark. Let's hurry up! / 他快～回来了。He will soon be back. / 会议～到月底才能结束。The conference will not end till the end of the month. ⑥ need; take: 这项任务～十天才能完成。It will take ten days to get the work done. / 这活儿～不了这么多人。You don't need so many people for this job. ⑦ *adv.* (used in comparisons to indicate an estimate): 你们～比我们辛苦得多。You must have had a much tougher time than we did. / 树阴底下比屋子里～凉快些。It is cooler under the tree than in the room.

要³ yào *conj.* ① if; suppose; in case: 明天～下雨, 我们就不去了。If it rains tomorrow, we won't go. / 他～来不了呢? Suppose he can't come? / 我～赶不回来, 你替我说一声。In case I can't get back in time, please apologize for me. / 这有什么可怕的, ～我就不怕。What is there to be afraid of? I wouldn't be afraid if I were you. ② (usu. used with 就 or 就是) or; either... or...: ～就去跳舞, ～就去听音乐, 别处我不去。Let's go either to the dance or to the concert. I won't go anywhere else.
——see also yāo

要隘 yào'ài strategic pass

要不 yàobù (also 要不然 yàoburán) *conj.* otherwise; or else; or: 我得马上走, ～就赶不上火车了。I have to leave at once or I'll miss the train. / 你可以坐船去, ～坐火车也行。You may go there by boat—or by train.

要不得 yàobude be no good; be intolerable: 这种自私行为～。Such selfish acts are not to be tolerated.

要不是 yàobushì if it were not for; but for: ～他们勇敢地抢救国家财产, 那损失可就大了。If it weren't for their courage in rescuing the state property, the loss would have been enormous. / ～下雨, 我们早就出门了。We would have gone out long ago but for the rain.

要冲 yàochōng communications centre (*or* hub): 军事～ strategic point / 兰州是西北交通的～。Lanzhou is the communications hub of the Northwest.

要道 yàodào thoroughfare: 交通～ important line of communications; vital communications line

要得 yàodé *dial.* good; fine; desirable: 这个办法～! That's a good idea!

要地 yàodì important place; strategic point: 徐州是历史上的军事～。Xuzhou has been well known in history as a hotly contested strategic point.

要点 yàodiǎn ① main points; essentials; gist: 抓住～ grasp the main points / 讲话的～ the gist of a speech ② key strongpoint: 战略～ strategic point

要端 yàoduān same as 要点 yàodiǎn①

要犯 yàofàn an important criminal

要饭 yàofàn beg (for food or money): ～的 beggar

要害 yàohài ① vital part; crucial point: ～部位 vital part / ～部门 key department / 回避～问题 evade the crucial question (*or* issue) / 击中～ hit home / 抓住～ scratch where it itches ② strategic point: 地处～ be located at a strategic point

要好 yàohǎo ① be on good terms; be close friends: 她们俩从小就很～。The two of them have been close friends since childhood. ② be eager to improve oneself; try hard to make progress: 这孩子很～。The kid is eager to make progress.

要谎 yàohuǎng (of a seller) ask an exorbitant price

要价 yàojià ask a price; charge: ～过高 demand an exorbitant price; ask too much / 对方在谈判中～越来越高。The other party demanded more and more in the negotiations.

要价还价 yàojià-huánjià bargain; haggle

要件 yàojiàn ① an important document ② an important condition

要津 yàojīn ① *formal* key place ② key post: 位居～ hold a key post

要紧 yàojǐn ① important; essential: 随便做什么工作, 最～的是实事求是。In whatever we do, the most important thing is to be realistic and down-to-earth. / 我有点儿的事儿跟他商量。I have something urgent to discuss with him. ② be critical; be serious; matter: 没什么～的, 你明天去也可以。You can go tomorrow. It doesn't matter. / 他只受了点儿轻伤, 没什么～的。He was only slightly injured—nothing serious. ③ *dial.* be in a hurry to; be anxious to: ～去上班 be in a hurry to go to work

要诀 yàojué important tricks of the trade; knack

要脸 yàoliǎn be keen on face-saving; care much about one's reputation

要领 yàolǐng ① main points; gist: 不得要领 bù dé yàolǐng ② essentials (of an exercise in military or athletic training): 掌握～ grasp the essentials

要略 yàolüè outline; summary

要么 yàome (also 要末 yàome) *conj.* or; either...or...: 赶快给他发个电报, ～挂个长途也行。Send him a telegram at once, or call him long-distance. / ～她来, ～我去, 我们总得碰个头。Either she comes here or I go there; in any case we've got to see each other.

要面子 yào miànzi be keen on face-saving; be anxious to keep up appearances

要命 yàomìng ① drive sb. to his death; kill: 这样短的期限, 要了我的命, 也完成不了定额。I cannot fulfil the quota in such a short time even if I kill myself. ② confoundedly; extremely; awfully; terribly: 热得～ awfully hot / 渴得～ terribly thirsty ③ a nuisance: 真～, 车胎又

没气了。What an awful nuisance. The tyre's flat again. / 这姑娘可真～, 火车都快开了, 她还没影儿呢。That girl is quite impossible. The train starts in a minute and there's still no sign of her.

要强 yàoqiáng　be eager to excel; be anxious to outdo others

要人 yàorén　very important person (V.I.P.); important personage

要塞 yàosài　fort; fortress; fortification

要事 yàoshì　an important matter: 她说有～相商。She says she has something important to consult you about.

要是 yàoshi　*conj. inf.*　if; suppose; in case: ～下雨怎么办?What if it rains? *or* Suppose it rains? / ～有人问的话, 就说我去看病了。If anyone asks for me, just say I've gone out to see a doctor. / ～别人, 我才不管呢。If it had been somebody else, I wouldn't have bothered myself.

要死 yàosǐ　extremely; awfully; terribly: 怕蛇怕得～ be terribly afraid of snakes

要素 yàosù　essential factor; key element

要图 yàotú　an important plan (*or* programme)

要闻 yàowén　important news; front-page story: ～版 the front page of a newspaper

要言不烦 yào yán bù fán　terse; succinct; pithy

要员 yàoyuán　important official

要帐 yàozhàng　demand payment of a debt; press for repayment of a loan; dun

要职 yàozhí　an important post: 身居～ hold an important post

要旨 yàozhǐ　main idea; gist

要子 yàozi　① a straw cord for bundling up rice or wheat stalks ② a baling strap or hoop

钥(鑰)
yào　see below ——see also yuè

钥匙 yàoshi　key

鞠
yào　the leg of a boot: 这双靴子的～儿矮了点儿。The legs of these boots are a bit too short. / 高～靴子 boots; wellington boots / 矮～雨鞋 galoshes

鹞
yào　sparrow hawk (another name for 雀鹰 quèyīng)

鹞鹰 yàoyīng　common name for 雀鹰 quèyīng

鹞子 yàozi　① common name for 雀鹰 quèyīng ② *dial.* kite

曜
yào　*formal*　① sunlight ② shine; illuminate ③ luminary (i.e. the sun, the moon, or the stars; used in old names of the days of the week): 日～日 Sunday / 月～日 Monday / 火～日 Tuesday / 水～日 Wednesday / 木～日 Thursday / 金～日 Friday / 土～日 Saturday

耀
yào　① shine; illuminate; dazzle: 照耀 zhàoyào ② boast of; laud: 夸耀 kuāyào ③ honour; credit: 荣耀 róngyào

耀斑 yàobān　*astron.*　solar flare

耀武扬威 yàowǔ-yángwēi　make a show of one's strength; swagger around; throw one's weight around: 表面上～, 骨子里贪生怕死! All bluff and bluster; in their bones they're afraid to die!

耀眼 yàoyǎn　dazzling: 车灯～。The headlights are dazzling. / ～的红旗 bright red flags

yē

耶
yē　see below ——see also yé

耶和华 Yēhéhuá　*Christianity*　Jehovah (an Old Testa-

ment name for God)

耶路撒冷 Yēlùsālěng　Jerusalem

耶稣 Yēsū　(also 耶稣基督 Yēsū Jīdū) Jesus; Jesus Christ

耶稣会 Yēsūhuì　the Society of Jesus; the Jesuits

耶稣教 Yēsūjiào　Protestantism

倻
yē　see 伽倻琴 jiāyēqín

掖
yē　tuck in; thrust in between: 把被角～好 tuck in the corner of the quilt / 把衬衫条到裤子里边 tuck one's shirt in / 把纸条从门缝里～进去 slip a note under the door / 腰里～着枪 with a pistol in one's belt ——see also yè

椰
yē　*bot.*　coconut palm; coconut tree; coco

椰雕 yēdiāo　*arts & crafts*　coconut shell carving

椰干 yēgān　desiccated coconut; copra

椰壳 yēké　coconut husk

椰壳纤维 yēké xiānwéi　coir fibre; coir

椰仁 yērén　coconut kernel; coconut meat

椰仁干 yēréngān　desiccated coconut; copra

椰蓉 yēróng　fine coconut mash (used as a filling for cakes): ～月饼 coconut moon cake (with such a filling)

椰丝 yēsī　shredded coconut meat (used as a topping for cakes)

椰油 yēyóu　coconut oil; coconut butter

椰枣 yēzǎo　*bot.*　date palm; date

椰子 yēzi　① coconut palm; coconut tree; coco ② coconut (the fruit): ～肉 coconut kernel; coconut meat / ～糖 coconut candy / ～汁 coconut milk

噎
yē　① choke: 慢点吃, 留神别～着。Eat slowly. Be careful not to choke. ② *dial.*　render sb. speechless by saying sth. blunt or rude; choke off: 他一句话就把她给～回去了。She was just going to say something when that one remark of his choked her off.

噎嗝 yēgé　*Chin. med.*　cancer of the esophagus

yé

爷(爺)
yé　① *dial.* father: ～娘 father and mother ② *dial.* grandfather ③ (a respectful form of address for an elderly man) uncle: 李～ Uncle Li / 四～ Fourth Uncle ④ *old* (a form of address for an official or rich man) sir; master; lord: 少爷 shàoye / 县太爷 xiàntàiyé ⑤ (a worshipper's form of address for a god): 土地～ God of the Land / 阎王～ Yama, King of Hell

爷儿 yér　*inf.*　(often followed by 俩, 几个, etc.) a senior male member of a family together with one or more junior members: ～俩并肩战斗。Father and son fought side by side. / ～几个在树荫下乘凉。The grandpa and his grandchildren were enjoying the cool under the tree.

爷们 yémen　*dial.*　① man or menfolk ② husband

爷们儿 yémenr　*dial.*　a collective term for men of two or more generations

爷儿们 yérmen　*inf.*　a collective term for men of two or more generations

爷爷 yéye　*inf.*　① (paternal) grandfather ② grandpa (a respectful form of address for any old man)

耶
yé　*formal part.*　(used at the end of a question): 是～非～? Is it or isn't it? *or* Yes or no? ——see also yē

揶
yé　see below

揶揄 yéyú　*formal*　ridicule; deride: 她的微笑中带有一丝

～。There was a trace of derision in her smile.

也¹

yě *part.* formal ① (used at the end of a sentence, indicating an explanation or a judgment): 陈胜者, 阳城人～。Chen Sheng was a native of Yangcheng. / 是不为～, 非不能～。This is a case of choosing not to, not of being unable to. / 不可不慎～。You must be very careful. / 何其毒～! How pernicious! ② (used at the end of a question or counterquestion): 何～? How is that? *or* Why so? / 是可忍也, 孰不可忍～? If this can be tolerated, what cannot? ③ (used in the middle of a sentence, marking off a sentence element about which there is to be a statement): 大道之行～, 天下为公。(《礼记》) When the Great Tao prevailed, the whole world was one community.

也²

yě *adv.* ① also; too; as well; either: 我妹妹～是售货员。My sister is a shop assistant too. / 你不去, 我～不去。If you're not going, I'm not going either. / 中国是一个社会主义国家, ～是一个发展中国家。China is a socialist country, and a developing country as well. / 水库可以灌溉, ～可以养鱼。Reservoirs can be used for irrigation, and also for fish breeding. ② (used for emphasis, often before a negative expression): 他病得一点～不想吃。He is so ill that he doesn't feel like eating anything. / 他忙得连饭～顾不上吃。He is so busy that he can't even stop for a meal. / 她一天假～没请过。She has never asked for leave, not even for a day. / 他什么～不知道。He knows nothing about it. ③ (used correlatively with 虽然, 即使, etc.) still; yet: 我虽然没见过, ～听人说过。I've heard about it, though I have never seen it. / 我即使干不了重活, ～可以干点轻活嘛。If I can't do heavy work, I can still do some light work. / 你不说我～知道。You don't have to tell me. I know already. / 我怎么想～想不起来。I simply couldn't recall it however hard I tried. ④ (used in a hesitant or guarded statement): ～只好这样了。We'll have to leave it at that. / 这袋土豆～就一百公斤。This sack of potatoes weighs a hundred kilos at most. / 他的英语～还可以。His English is passable.

也罢¹ yěbà *part.* (used to express forbearance, resignation, etc.) well; all right: 这次不去～, 下次可一定要让我去。All right, I won't go this time but next time you must let me go. / ～, 你一定要走, 我就不留你了。All right, I won't keep you any longer since you insist on going.

也罢² yěbà *part.* (reduplicated) whether...or...; no matter whether: 刮风～, 下雪～, 他都坚持跑步。He keeps up his jogging whether it's blowing or snowing. / 你去～, 不去～, 反正是一样。It makes no difference whether you go or not.

也好 yěhǎo *part.* ① it may not be a bad idea; may as well: 说明一下～。Better give an explanation. / 让他们自己干一干～, 实践出真知嘛。We might as well let them do it themselves, since real knowledge comes from practice. ② (reduplicated) whether...or...; no matter whether: 学习～, 劳动～, 他都很积极。He is enthusiastic about both study and physical labour.

也门 Yěmén Yemen

也门人 Yěménrén Yemeni; Yemenite

也许 yěxǔ *adv.* perhaps; probably; maybe: 他～病了。Perhaps he's ill. / 我～来, ～不来。I may or may not come. / ～我不该告诉他的。Perhaps I shouldn't have told him.

也…也… yě…yě… ① both...and...; either...or...: 也有好的, 也有坏的。There are both good ones and bad ones. / 操场上也有打球的, 也有跑步的。Some of the people on the sports ground are playing ball games, some are running. / 他也不抽烟, 也不喝酒。He neither smokes nor

drinks. ② no matter (whether, who, etc.): 天好我们也干, 天不好我们也干。We never stop working, rain or shine. / 你去也得去, 不去也得去。You've got to go, whether you want to or not. / 他左想也不是, 右想也不是。He just couldn't make up his mind either way.

冶¹

yě smelt (metal): 冶金 yějīn

冶²

yě *formal* seductively dressed or made up: 妖冶 yāoyě

冶荡 yědàng lewd; lascivious

冶金 yějīn metallurgy: ～工业 metallurgical industry

冶金学 yějīnxué metallurgy

冶炼 yěliàn smelt: ～操作 smelting operation / ～厂 smeltery / ～炉 smelting furnace / ～时间 duration of heat

冶容 yěróng ① be seductively made up ② seductive looks

冶笑 yěxiào a seductive smile

冶艳 yěyàn *formal* seductive and bewitching

冶游 yěyóu frequent brothels; go whoring

冶铸 yězhù smelting and founding

野 (埜)

yě ① open country; the open: 田野 tiányě / 野火 yěhuǒ ② limit; boundary: 视野 shìyě ③ not in power; out of office: 在野 zàiyě ④ (of plants or animals) wild; uncultivated; undomesticated; untamed: ～花 wild flowers / ～狗 homeless dogs ⑤ rude; rough: 说话太～ use coarse language; speak rudely / 动作太～ rough play ⑥ unrestrained; abandoned; unruly: 放了几天假, 这孩子的心都玩～了。After the fun he's had during the holidays, the boy can't concentrate on his school work.

野菜 yěcài edible wild herbs

野餐 yěcān picnic

野蚕 yěcán wild silkworm: ～丝 wild silk

野草 yěcǎo weeds: ～丛生 be overgrown (*or* choked) with weeds

野草闲花 yěcǎo-xiánhuā ① weeds and wild flowers ② mistress; prostitute

野传 yěchuán *baseball & softball* wild throw: ～球 passed ball

野炊 yěchuī cook in the open air

野地 yědì wild country; wilderness

野调无腔 yě diào wú qiāng coarse (*or* uncouth) in speech and manner

野鸽 yěgē another name for 原鸽 yuángē

野葛 yěgě another name for 钩吻 gōuwěn

野果 yěguǒ wild fruit

野汉子 yěhànzi a woman's lover

野合 yěhé *formal* have illicit sexual relations; commit adultery

野鹤闲云 yěhè-xiányún same as 闲云野鹤 xiányún-yěhè

野狐禅 yěhúchán *Buddhism* heresy

野火 yěhuǒ prairie fire; bush fire

野火烧不尽, 春风吹又生 yěhuǒ shāo bù jìn, chūnfēng chuī yòu shēng even a prairie fire cannot destroy the grass; it grows again when the spring breeze blows (said of what cannot be suppressed, from Bai Juyi's lines 白居易诗: 离离原上草, 一岁一枯荣。～。Grasses grow tall and flourish then wither and die only to rise again; A wild fire may burn them, yet with the spring winds they will grow back again.)

野鸡 yějī ① common name for 雉 zhì ② streetwalker; unlicensed prostitute

野鸡大学 yějī dàxué diploma mill

野景 yějǐng wild scenery

野菊花 yějúhuā mother chrysanthemum

野驴 yělǘ Asiatic wild ass; kiang

野麻 yěmá ① wild flax; wild hemp ② popular name for 罗布麻 luóbùmá

野马 yěmǎ ① wild horse; untamed horse ② Przhevalski's horse (*Equus przewalskii*)

野蛮 yěmán ① uncivilized; savage ② barbarous; cruel; brutal: ～的种族主义 barbarous racism / ～的屠杀 brutal massacre / ～行为 barbarous act; savage behaviour / 遭受～的虐待 be subjected to barbarous (*or* brutal) treatment

野猫 yěmāo ① wildcat ② a stray cat ③ *dial.* hare

野牛 yěniú wild ox (*Bos gaurus*)

野炮 yěpào field gun; field artillery

野蔷薇 yěqiángwēi *bot.* multiflora rose

野禽 yěqín wild fowl

野趣 yěqù rustic charm: 园子虽然荒凉，却富有～。The garden, in its neglected and forlorn state, has a rustic charm of its own.

野人 yěrén ① an uncouth person; rustic ② savage; barbarian

野生 yěshēng wild; undomesticated; uncultivated; feral: ～植物 wild plant

野生动物 yěshēngdòngwù wildlife: 保护～ conserve wildlife

野食儿 yěshír ① animals' food picked up in the wilds ② ill-gotten (*or* illicit) gains

野史 yěshǐ unofficial history

野兽 yěshòu wild beast; wild animal

野兔 yětù hare

野外 yěwài open country; field: 在～工作 do fieldwork / ～生活 outdoor life / ～演习 field exercise / ～作业 fieldwork; field operation

野豌豆 yěwāndòu *bot.* vetch (*Vicia sativa*)

野味 yěwèi game (as food)

野心 yěxīn wild ambition; careerism: 侵略～ aggressive ambitions / ～不死 cling to one's ambitious designs

野心勃勃 yěxīn bóbó be overweeningly ambitious; be obsessed with ambition

野心家 yěxīnjiā careerist

野心狼 yěxīnláng a vicious wolf—a person of evil ambitions

野性 yěxìng wild nature; unruliness: ～难驯 untamable

野营 yěyíng camp; bivouac: 出外～ go camping / ～训练 camp and field training

野战 yězhàn *mil.* field operations: ～仓库 field depot / ～工事 fieldwork

野战军 yězhànjūn field army

野战炮 yězhànpào fieldpiece; field gun

野战医院 yězhàn yīyuàn field hospital

野猪 yězhū wild boar (*Sus scrofa*)

yè

业¹（業） yè ① line of business; trade; industry: 工业 gōngyè / 矿业 kuàngyè ② occupation; profession; employment; job: 我家世代以农为～。I come from a long line of farmers. ③ course of study: 结业 jiéyè ④ cause; enterprise: 创业 chuàngyè ⑤ estate; property: 家业 jiāyè ⑥ *Buddhism* karma ⑦ engage in: ～农 engage in farming

业²（業） yè *adv.* already: ～已核实 have already been verified

业报 yèbào *Buddhism* retribution for sins

业海 yèhǎi *Buddhism* sea of retribution

业绩 yèjī outstanding achievement: 光辉～ glorious achievements / 医学界的最新～ the latest achievements in medical science

业经 yèjīng already: ～批准 have been approved

业精于勤 yè jīng yú qín mastery of work comes from diligent application; a subject is mastered through diligent study: ～，荒于嬉。(韩愈) The scholar becomes proficient in learning through diligence but suffers from indolence.

业师 yèshī one's (former) teacher

业务 yèwù vocational work; professional work; business: 钻研～ diligently study one's profession / 恢复正常～ resume normal business / 办理信托投资～ handle trust and investment business / ～范围 scope of business / ～能力 professional ability (*or* proficiency) / ～水平 professional skill; vocational level / ～协定 business agreement / ～学习 vocational study / ～知识 professional knowledge

业余 yèyú ① sparetime; after-hours: 他利用～时间给同志们修收音机。He repaired radios for his comrades during his spare time. / ～爱好 hobby / ～理论学习 theoretical study after workhours ② nonprofessional; amateur: ～文艺工作者 amateur literary and art workers / ～剧团 an amateur theatrical troupe

业余教育 yèyú jiàoyù sparetime education

业余学校 yèyú xuéxiào sparetime school

业障 yèzhàng ① *Buddhism* retribution in this life for the sins of a previous existence ② *offens.* (said to one's children) medium of retribution

业种 yèzhǒng same as 孽种 nièzhǒng

业主 yèzhǔ owner (of an enterprise or estate); proprietor

叶¹（葉） yè ① leaf; foliage: 红花绿～ red flowers and green leaves ② leaf-like thing: 一～扁舟 a small boat ③ same as 页 yè ④ (Yè) a surname

叶²（葉） yè part of a historical period: 清朝末～ the closing period of the Qing Dynasty / 十九世纪中～ (in) the middle of the 19th century

叶斑病 yèbānbìng *agric.* leaf spot

叶柄 yèbǐng *bot.* petiole; leafstalk

叶蝉 yèchán leafhopper (an insect)

叶蜂 yèfēng sawfly (an insect)

叶公好龙 Yègōng hào lóng Lord Ye's love of dragons —professed love of what one really fears

叶红素 yèhóngsù another name for 胡萝卜素 húluóbosù

叶猴 yèhóu leaf monkey

叶黄素 yèhuángsù *biochem.* xanthophyll; lutein

叶蜡石 yèlàshí pyrophyllite (a mineral)

叶绿素 yèlǜsù *biochem.* chlorophyll

叶绿体 yèlǜtǐ *biochem.* chloroplast

叶轮 yèlún *mech.* impeller; vane wheel: ～泵 vane pump

叶落归根 yè luò guī gēn the falling leaves settle on the roots—a person residing elsewhere finally returns to his ancestral home

叶脉 yèmài *bot.* leaf vein

叶片 yèpiàn ① leaf blade ② *mech.* vane: ～式压缩机 vane compressor

叶鞘 yèqiào *bot.* leaf sheath

叶肉 yèròu *bot.* mesophyll

叶酸 yèsuān *med.* folic acid; folacin

叶锈病 yèxiùbìng *agric.* leaf rust

叶序 yèxù *bot.* phyllotaxy; leaf arrangement

叶芽 yèyá *bot.* leaf bud

叶子 yèzi leaf

叶子烟 yèziyān dried tobacco leaves

页（頁、葉、箂） yè page or leaf: 这本书掉了一～。A leaf is missing from the book. / 一本三百～的书 a book of three hundred pages / 打开新的

一～ open up a new chapter

页边 yèbiān margin

页理 yèlǐ the laminated structure of shale

页码 yèmǎ page number

页心 yèxīn *print.* type page

页岩 yèyán *geol.* shale

页岩油 yèyányóu shale oil

曳 (拽、抴) yè drag; haul; tug; tow

曳白 yèbái *formal* hand in a blank paper in an imperial examination

曳扯 yèche *dial.* take great pains to bring up (a child)

曳光弹 yèguāngdàn *mil.* tracer bullet or shell; tracer

曳力 yèlì *phys.* drag force

曳绳钓 yèshéngdiào *fishery* trolling

曳引 yèyǐn tow; tug: 拖轮～着三艘驳船，溯运河而上。The tugboat was towing three barges up the canal.

夜 (亱) yè night; evening: 冬天昼短～长。In winter the days are short and the nights long. / 三天三～讲不完。It would take days to tell it all.

夜班 yèbān night shift: 值～ be on night shift

夜半 yèbàn midnight: 姑苏城外寒山寺，～钟声到客船。(张 继) Outside Gusu City, Cold Mountain Temple —late at night the sound of its bell reaches a traveller's boat.

夜不闭户 yè bù bì hù doors are not bolted at night —law and order prevail ——see also 道不拾遗 dào bù shí yí

夜餐 yècān midnight snack

夜叉 yèchā ① *Buddhism* yaksha (a malevolent spirit) ② a hideous, ferocious person

夜长梦多 yècháng-mèngduō a long night is fraught with dreams—a long delay means trouble

夜场 yèchǎng evening show; evening performance

夜车 yèchē night train ——see also 开夜车 kāi yèchē

夜出动物 yèchū dòngwù nocturnal animal

夜大学 yèdàxué evening university

夜饭 yèfàn *dial.* supper; dinner

夜分 yèfēn *formal* midnight

夜儿个 yèrge *dial.* yesterday

夜工 yègōng night work; night job: 打～ work at night; do a night job

夜光杯 yèguāngbēi a cup of phosphorescent jade: 葡萄美酒～，欲饮琵琶马上催。(王翰) Fine wine of the grape, cup of phosphorescent jade, Ready to drink, the *pipa* plays wildly on horseback.

夜光表 yèguāngbiǎo luminous watch

夜光虫 yèguāngchóng noctiluca

夜光螺 yèguāngluó green snail

夜航 yèháng night flight or navigation

夜合 yèhé ① silk tree ② *dial.* the tuber of multiflower knotweed (Polygonum multiflorum)

夜壶 yèhú chamber pot

夜间 yèjiān at night: ～行军 march by night; night march / ～施工 carry on construction work at night / ～演习 night exercise / ～战斗机 night fighter

夜交藤 yèjiāoténg *Chin. med.* the vine of multiflower knotweed (Polygonum multiflorum)

夜禁 yèjìn curfew

夜景 yèjǐng night scene (or view): 一幅壮丽的长江大桥～ the magnificent view of the Changjiang bridge at night

夜课 yèkè evening class

夜空 yèkōng the night sky: 一道道探照灯光划破～。Searchlight beams pierced the night sky.

夜来 yèlái *formal* ① yesterday ② in the night: ～风雨声，花落知多少。(孟浩然) Last night, the sound of

wind and rain—Flowers have fallen, I wonder how many.

夜来香 yèláixiāng *bot.* cordate telosma

夜阑 yèlán *formal* late at night

夜阑人静 yèlán-rénjìng (also 夜深人静 yèshēn-rénjìng) in the dead of night; in the still (or quiet) of the night

夜郎自大 Yèláng zìdà ludicrous conceit of the King of Yelang—parochial arrogance

夜礼服 yèlǐfú same as 晚礼服 wǎnlǐfú

夜里 yèlǐ at night

夜盲 yèmáng *med.* nyctalopia; night blindness

夜猫子 yèmāozi *dial.* ① owl ② a person who goes to bed late; night owl

夜明珠 yèmíngzhū night-luminescent pearl

夜幕 yèmù curtain (or veil) of night; gathering darkness: ～笼罩着大地。The land is enveloped in a curtain of darkness. / ～降临。Night has fallen.

夜尿症 yèniàozhèng enuresis; bed-wetting

夜勤 yèqín night duty

夜曲 yèqǔ *mus.* nocturne

夜入私宅罪 yèrùsīzháizuì *leg.* burglary

夜色 yèsè the dim light of night: 趁着～ by starlight or moonlight / ～苍茫 in gathering dusk

夜生活 yèshēnghuó night life

夜市 yèshì night market

夜视仪 yèshìyí *mil.* night vision device (or instrument)

夜啼 yètí morbid night crying of babies

夜晚 yèwǎn night

夜望镜 yèwàngjìng *mil.* snooperscope

夜未央 yèwèiyāng *liter.* the night is yet young; the night is not yet spent

夜袭 yèxí night attack (or raid)

夜宵 yèxiāo (also 夜消 yèxiāo) food (or refreshments) taken late at night; midnight snack

夜校 yèxiào (also 夜学 yèxué) night (or evening) school

夜行 yèxíng ① go out walking in the night; travel by night ② night flight or navigation

夜行军 yèxíngjūn night march

夜夜 yèyè every night

夜以继日 yè yǐ jì rì day and night; round the clock: 工程正在～地进行。Work on the project is going on day and night.

夜莺 yèyīng nightingale

夜鹰 yèyīng nightjar; goatsucker

夜游神 yèyóushén the legendary god on patrol at night—a person who is up and about at night; night owl

夜战 yèzhàn ① *mil.* night fighting ② night work: 打两个～ put in two nights' work

夜总会 yèzǒnghuì nightclub; cabaret

夜作 yèzuò night work; night job: 打～ work at night; do a night job

咽 yè see 哽咽 gěngyè; 呜咽 wūyè ——see also yān; yàn

烨 (燁、爗) yè *formal* ① firelight or sunlight ② (of light) bright

晔 (曄) yè *formal* (of light) bright

液 yè liquid; fluid; juice: 体液 tǐyè / 溶液 róngyè

液果 yèguǒ juicy fruit; pulpy fruit (as berries, drupes, etc.)

液化 yèhuà liquefaction

液化器 yèhuàqì liquefier

液化石油气 yèhuà shíyóuqì liquefied petroleum gas

(LPG)

液化天然气 yèhuà tiānránqì　liquefied natural gas (LNG)

液晶 yèjīng　liquid crystal

液冷 yèlěng　liquid cooling (*or* cooled): ～式内燃机 liquid cooled engine

液力 yèlì　*mech.* hydraulic: ～变速箱 hydraulic transmission box / ～传动 hydraulic power / ～制动器 hydraulic brake

液泡 yèpào　*physiol.* vacuole

液态 yètài　liquid state: ～空气 liquid air

液体 yètǐ　liquid

液体比重计 yètǐ bǐzhòngjì　hydrometer

液体燃料 yètǐ ránliào　liquid fuel: ～火箭发动机 liquid-fuel rocket engine

液压 yèyā　hydraulic pressure: ～传动 hydraulic transmission (*or* drive) / ～联轴节 hydraulic coupling

液压泵 yèyābèng　hydraulic pump

液压表 yèyābiǎo　hydraulic pressure gauge

液压机 yèyājī　hydraulic press

掖 yè　① support sb. by the arm ② help; assist; promote: 奖掖 jiǎngyè ——see also yē

谒 yè　*formal* call on (a superior or an elder person); pay one's respects to: ～陵 pay homage at sb.'s mausoleum

谒见 yèjiàn　call on (a superior or a senior in the clan hierarchy); have an audience with

腋 yè　① *physiol.* axilla; armpit ② *bot.* axil

腋臭 yèchòu　underarm odour

腋毛 yèmáo　armpit hair

腋窝 yèwō　armpit

腋芽 yèyá　same as 侧芽 cèyá

靥(靨) yè　dimple: 酒靥 jiǔyè

yī

一[1]　yī　① one: ～匹马 a horse / ～瓶牛奶 one bottle of milk / ～万～ eleven thousand / 三千～百 three thousand one hundred / ～营～连 the First Company of the First Battalion / 棉纺～厂 No. 1 Cotton Mill ② single; alone; only one: ～枪就打中了目标 hit the target with a single shot / 你～个人行吗?Can you manage all by yourself? ③ same: 意见不～。Opinions differ. / ～根藤上的苦瓜 bitter gourds from the same vine—people with a similar bitter past / 军民～家。The army and the people are of one family. / 这姑娘跟她妈妈～个模样。The girl is the image of her mother. / 这不是～码事。They are not the same thing. ④ whole; all; throughout: ～冬 the whole winter; all winter; throughout the winter / 他～脸的土。His face was covered with dust. / ～屋子的人都欢腾起来。Everybody in the room was overjoyed. ⑤ each; per; every time: 四个小组,～组五人 four groups with five people in each / ～小时六十公里 at 60 kilometres per hour / 大家～提起那艰苦创业的日子,总有说不完的话。Every time we talk about the hard pioneering days, we have so much to say that we can't get it all out. ⑥ also; otherwise: 汞溴红～名红汞。Merbromin is also known as mercurochrome. ⑦ concentrated; wholehearted: 专心～意 single-minded; concentrated ⑧ (used to indicate that the action occurs just once or lasts for a short time) ⓐ (used in the middle of a reduplicated verb): 笑～笑 give a smile / 歇～歇 have a rest / 等～等 wait a bit / 出去走～走 go out for a stroll / 让我闻～闻。Let me smell it. ⓑ (used between

a verb and a verbal measure): 瞧～眼 take a look / 咳～声 give a cough / 咬～口 take a bite / 打他～巴掌 give him a slap ⑨ (used before a verb or a verbal measure to indicate an action to be followed by a result): ～跳跳了过去 get over in one jump / 他～脚把球踢进了球门。He kicked the ball into the goal. *or* He kicked a goal. / 经他这么～说,大家又都有信心了。His words restored our confidence. / 医生～检查,果然是肺炎。The doctor's check-up confirmed that it was pneumonia. ⑩ (used before a verb or an adjective, indicating the suddenness or thoroughness of an action or a change in the situation): 那马猛然～惊,直立起来。All of a sudden the horse shied and reared in fright. / 这部电影值得～看。This movie is well worth seeing. / 喜讯传来,大家精神为之～振。Everyone's spirits were instantly buoyed up by the good news. ⑪ *part. formal* (used before certain words for emphasis): 事态之严重～至于此! To think that things should have come to such a pass! / 吏呼～何怒,妇啼～何苦。(杜甫) The officer's shouting, how angry it was; The woman's cry, how mournful and bitter!

一[2]　yī　*mus.* a note of the scale in *gongchepu* (工尺谱), corresponding to 7 in numbered musical notation

一把手 yībǎshǒu　① a party to an undertaking; a member; a hand: 我们准备搭伙干,你也算上～吧。We're going to pool our efforts. Shall we count you in? ② a good hand: 她干农活可真是～。She is really good at farm work. ③ same as 第一把手 dìyībǎshǒu

一把死拿 yībǎsǐná　*dial.* inflexible; stubborn

一把钥匙开一把锁 yī bǎ yàoshi kāi yī bǎ suǒ　open different locks with different keys—use different methods to solve different problems: 不能拿一个药方去医治百病,～就是这意思。We cannot use one prescription to cure all diseases. This is what we mean by using the right key to open the lock.

一把抓 yībǎzhuā　① take everything into one's own hands ② try to tackle all problems at once regardless of their relative importance

一百一 yībǎiyī　perfect; faultless; ideal: 他是～的正人君子。He is a perfect gentleman. / 她护理病人那份精心可是～呀! She nurses the patients with the best of care.

一败如水 yī bài rú shuǐ　sustain a crushing defeat

一败涂地 yī bài tú dì　fail completely; suffer a crushing defeat; be routed: 我们有准备,决不会～。We just can't possibly fail completely, after all the preparations we've made. / 他在西药business信用～。He had become completely discredited in the Western drug business.

一班人 yībānrén　members of a squad—a small body of people working together: 党委～ the members of the Party committee

一般 yībān　① same as; just like: 他们俩～高。The two of them are the same height. / 火车飞～地驰去。The train flashed past like lightning. ② general; ordinary; common: ～号召和个别指导相结合 combine general calls (for action) with specific guidance / 从～到具体 from generalities to particulars / ～工作人员 ordinary personnel; an ordinary member of the staff / ～的做法 common practice / ～说来 generally speaking / ～等价物 universal equivalent / ～规律 universal law; general rule / ～性辩论 general debate / 我～早上六点起床。I usually get up at 6 in the morning. / 他只是～地说了说,没有详谈。He just spoke in general terms and didn't elaborate. / 这部小说写得～。This novel is only mediocre. *or* There's nothing striking about this novel.

一般化 yībānhuà　vague generalization: 防止领导～ avoid giving only vague, general directions

一般见识 yībān jiànshi　(lower oneself to) the same

level as sb.: 别跟他～。You don't want to bother yourself arguing with the likes of him. / 太太不必和她小孩子～，等我们说她。She's just a child with no sense, madam. Let her be! We'll give her a good talking-to presently. / 由他便了，你也和他～。Let him alone, that is all. Do you want to behave like him?

一斑 yībān one spot (on a leopard); one of a number of similar things ——see also 管中窥豹，可见一斑 guǎn zhōng kuī bào, kě jiàn yībān

一板一眼 yìbǎn-yìyǎn following a prescribed (or set) pattern in speech or action; scrupulous and methodical: 他办事总是那么～的。He is always very methodical in his work.

一板正经 yì bǎn zhèngjīng same as 一本正经 yì běn zhèngjīng

一半 yíbàn one half; half; in part: ～以上 more than half / 歉收～由于干旱，～由于虫灾。The crop failure was due in part to drought and in part to insect pests. / 把菜籽平分一下，给他们～儿，咱们留～儿。Let's share the vegetable seeds with them, share and share alike.

一…半… yī…bàn… (used with synonymous words, forming a phrase implying not much or many or not a long time): 这活儿一时半会儿完不了。This job can't be finished in a short while. / 我只听到一句半句的。What I heard was very fragmentary. / 我去个一年半载就回来。I'll be back within a year.

一半天 yíbàntiān in a day or two: 过～就给你送回去。I'll return it to you in a day or two. / 他～回不来。He won't be able to get back for a couple of days.

一包在内 yī bāo zài nèi all included: 车钱、店钱、饭钱、～，花了二百块钱。I spent 200 yuan, fares, hotel, meals all included.

一报还一报 yī bào huán yī bào retribution paid out in kind

一辈子 yíbèizi inf. all one's life; throughout one's life; as long as one lives; a lifetime: ～也忘不了。I won't forget as long as I live. / 这工作我准备干它～。I'm taking this as a lifelong job. / ～不干，～不会。If you never do a thing yourself, you'll never know how to do it. / 一个人做点好事并不难，难的是一～做好事。It is not hard for one to do a bit of good. What is hard is to do good all one's life.

一本万利 yī běn wàn lì a small investment brings a ten thousand-fold profit; make big profits with a small capital

一本正经 yī běn zhèngjīng in all seriousness; in dead earnest: 装得～的样子 assume a mock-serious manner; be sanctimonious / 他蓦地站起来，～地讲了起来。Suddenly he stood up and began his speech in a serious tone.

一鼻孔出气 yī bíkǒng chūqì derog. breathe through the same nostrils—sing the same tune

一笔勾销 yìbǐ gōuxiāo write off at one stroke; cancel: 我们的旧帐可以～。It's time we wrote off all our old scores. / 不是早就～了吗?But wasn't the whole of the debt cancelled at one stroke? / 他所有的抱负、志向、希望、前程，全被～了。All his ambitions, aims, hope and future had been blasted at one fell swoop.

一笔抹杀 yìbǐ mǒshā blot out at one stroke; condemn out of hand; totally negate: 这些成绩是不能～的。These achievements cannot be gainsaid. / 我们对资产阶级民主不能～，说他们的宪法在历史上没有地位。(毛泽东) We should not write off bourgeois democracy with one stroke of the pen and deny bourgeois constitutions a place in history.

一碧 yíbì formal an expanse of blue or green: 到处都是树木，～无际。There were trees everywhere, forming a boundless expanse of green. / 辽阔的草原～如洗。The grasslands were an unbroken stretch of fresh green.

一壁 yíbì old at the same time; simultaneously: 那人～招架，～夺门而出。The man forced his way out as he warded off the blows.

一壁厢 yíbìxiāng old side: 在～观望 look on from the sidelines; watch from the wings

一臂之力 yī bì zhī lì a helping hand: 助我～ lend me a hand / 设有困难，当助～。You can count on me to help out in case of difficulty.

一边 yìbiān ① one side; side: 这块木料只有～光滑。Only one side of this piece of wood is smooth. / 大楼的～是花园，另～是网球场。On one side of the building there is a garden, on the other side a tennis court. / 她站在～看着我们玩桥牌。She stood on one side watching us play bridge. / 站在人民群众～ side with the masses of the people / 两方面争论，总有～儿理屈。In a dispute between two parties there is always one which is in the wrong. ② either side: 在他身旁，～儿站着一个保镖。A bodyguard stood at either of his sides. ③ adv. at the same time; simultaneously: 他悠闲地往前走，～唱着歌儿。He sang as he strolled leisurely along. / ～喝茶，～聊天 chat over a cup of tea

一边倒 yìbiāndǎo ① lean to one side; side with sb. without reservation ② predominate; enjoy overwhelming superiority

一表人材 yī biǎo réncái a man of striking appearance

一并 yìbìng adv. along with all the others; in the lump: 连同类似情况～考虑 to be considered together with all similar cases / 读者提出的几个疑问，现在～答复如下。What follows is an answer to all the questions raised by the readers.

一病不起 yī bìng bù qǐ take to one's bed and never leave it again; fall ill and die

一波三折 yī bō sān zhé full of twists and turns or ups and downs

一波未平，一波又起 yī bō wèi píng, yī bō yòu qǐ hardly has one wave subsided when another rises—one trouble follows another

一…不… yī…bù… ① (used with two verbs to indicate the unalterability of a situation): 一去不返 gone never to return / 一定不易 unalterable ② (used with a noun and a verb) not a single; not the slightest: 一字不漏 without missing a single word / 一笔不苟 be scrupulous about every stroke (in writing or painting)

一不怕苦，二不怕死 yī bù pà kǔ, èr bù pà sǐ fear neither hardship nor death

一不做，二不休 yī bù zuò, èr bù xiū carry it through, whatever the consequences; in for a penny, in for a pound: 到这地步，～，我是打算拼一拼了! Now that we've gone as far as this, we must either go the whole hog or else drop it altogether. I'm in favour of putting up a fight, myself.

一步登天 yī bù dēng tiān reach the sky in a single bound—attain the highest level in one step; have a meteoric rise

一步一个脚印儿 yī bù yīge jiǎoyìnr every step leaves its print—work steadily and make solid progress

一差二错 yīchā-èrcuò a possible mistake or mishap: 万一有个～ just in case there is a slip somewhere; just in case of accidents / 他要是有个～，怎么办? What if something happens to him?

一刹 yíchà in an instant; in a split second; in the twinkling of an eye: ～间，布景换了。In a twinkling the scene changed. / ～时，黄沙滚滚，天昏地暗。In an instant, yellow dust came flying and churning, obscuring heaven and earth.

一刹那 yíchànà see 刹那 chànà

一划 yíchàn dial. without exception: 这些大楼～都是新盖的。The buildings are all newly built.

一长两短　yīchǎng-liǎngduǎn　same as 三长两短 sān-cháng-liǎngduǎn

一场春梦　yī chǎng chūnmèng　a spring dream — a fleeting illusion

一场空　yīchǎngkōng　all in vain; futile —— see also 竹篮子打水一场空 zhúlánzi dǎshuǐ yīchǎngkōng

一场秋雨一场寒　yī chǎng qiūyǔ yī chǎng hán　a spell of autumn rain, and a spell of cold

一唱百和　yīchàng-bǎihè　(also 一倡百和 yīchàng-bǎihè) when one starts singing, the others join in — meet with general approval

一唱一和　yīchàng-yīhè　sing a duet; sing the same tune; echo each other

一朝天子一朝臣　yī cháo tiānzǐ yī cháo chén　every new sovereign brings his own courtiers — a new chief brings in new aides

一尘不染　yī chén bù rǎn　not soiled by a speck of dust; spotless: 仪器上～。The apparatus is spotlessly clean. / 身居闹市，～ remain uncontaminated amidst the temptations of a big city

一成不变　yī chéng bùbiàn　immutable and frozen; invariable; unalterable: ～的东西是没有的。Nothing is immutable (or unchangeable). / 没有～的规则。There is no hard-and-fast rule.

一程子　yīchéngzi　dial. a number of days: 我母亲来住了～，昨天刚走。My mother was here with us a number of days. She left only yesterday.

一筹莫展　yī chóu mò zhǎn　can find no way out; be at one's wits' end; be at the end of one's tether

一触即发　yī chù jí fā　may break out at any moment; be on the verge of breaking out: 武装冲突有～之势。Armed conflict may break out at any moment. / 形势～。It's an explosive situation.

一触即溃　yī chù jí kuì　collapse at the first encounter: 敌军士气涣散，～。The enemy were demoralized and collapsed at the first encounter.

一传十，十传百　yī chuán shí, shí chuán bǎi　(of news) spread from one to ten, and from ten to a hundred — pass quickly from mouth to mouth; get around quickly

一锤定音　yī chuí dìng yīn　set the tune with one beat of the gong — give the final word

一锤子买卖　yī chuízi mǎimai　"once-for-all" deal — the one and only business deal to be made with sb. (from which the greatest possible advantage is to be derived)

一词多义　yīcíduōyì　polysemy

一次　yīcì　once: 我只跟他见过～面。I've met him only once. / 机器～试运成功。The machine worked successfully on its first test run. / ～或分期缴纳 to be paid in a lump sum or in installments

一次方程　yīcì fāngchéng　math. linear equation

一次函数　yīcì hánshù　math. linear function

一次能源　yīcì néngyuán　primary energy

一次性　yīcìxìng　① once only (without a second time): ～补助 a lump-sum grant ② disposable: ～筷子 disposable chopsticks / ～注射器 disposable syringes / ～尿布 disposable nappies

一蹴而就　yī cù ér jiù　reach the goal in one step; accomplish one's aim in one move: 在中国这样一个幅员广大的国家里，要实现现代化，不可能～。Modernization of a vast country like China cannot be done at one go.

一寸光阴一寸金　yī cùn guāngyīn yī cùn jīn　time is gold; time is precious

一搭　yīdā　dial. ① at the same place: 他俩在～上的小学。The two of them went to the same primary school. ② together: 他们常在～打乒乓球。They often play table tennis together.

一搭两用儿　yīdāliǎngyòngr　one thing serving two purposes: 带件大衣比较方便，白天穿，晚上当被子盖，～。It's convenient to take an overcoat with you. You can wear it during the day and use it as a quilt at night — having one thing serving two purposes.

一打一拉　yīdǎ-yīlā　strike and stroke alternately; alternate hard and soft tactics; use the carrot and the stick

一大早　yīdàzǎo　inf. early in the morning: 他～就走了。He left early in the morning.

一代　yīdài　① a dynasty ② an era; the present age: ～英豪 outstanding figures of our time ③ all one's life; a lifetime; a generation: 我们的祖先在这块土地上，～～地辛勤劳动，创造出灿烂的文化。Generation after generation, our forefathers worked hard and created a splendid culture on this land of ours.

一带　yīdài　the area around a particular place: 京津唐～ the Beijing-Tianjin-Tangshan area / 江南～雨量充足。The area south of the Yangtze River enjoys plentiful rainfall. / 他是这～出名的猎手。He is one of the most famous hunters around here. / 他在那～打过游击。He once fought in that area as a guerrilla.

一旦　yīdàn　① in a single day; in a very short time ② once; in case; now that: 理论～为群众所掌握，就会产生巨大的物质力量。Once grasped by the masses, theory will generate a tremendous material force. / 他们多年相处，～分别，不免依依不舍。After being together for years, they can't bear to part from each other.

一担儿挑　yīdànrtiāo　dial. husbands of sisters; brothers-in-law

一刀两断　yī dāo liǎng duàn　sever at one stroke — make a clean break

一刀切　yīdāoqiē　cut it even at one stroke — make everything rigidly uniform; impose uniformity in all cases; prescribe a single solution for diverse problems

一道　yīdào　adv. together; side by side; alongside: 我们～走吧。Let's go together. / 干部应当和工人～参加生产劳动。Cadres should take part in productive labour alongside the workers. / 学校、家长和社会～担负起教育下一代的责任。School, parents and society share the responsibility of educating the younger generation.

一得之功　yī dé zhī gōng　just an occasional, minor success: 不要沾沾自喜于～。Don't feel self-satisfied over just a minor success.

一得之愚　yī dé zhī yú　pol. my humble opinion: ～，仅供参考。This is my humble opinion, for what it's worth.

一等　yīděng　first-class; first-rate; top-grade; top-notch: ～品 first-rate (or top-quality) product / ～奖 first prize / ～舱 first class

一等兵　yīděngbīng　(U.S. Army) private first class; (Brit. Army) lance corporal; (U.S. Navy) seaman first class; (Brit. Navy) leading seaman; (U. S. Air Force) airman first class; (Brit. Air Force) senior aircraftsman; (U.S. Marine Corps) private first class; (Brit. Marine Corps) marine first class

一等功　yīděnggōng　Merit Citation, First Class

一等秘书　yīděng mìshū　diplomacy First Secretary

一点儿　yīdiǎnr　① a bit; a little: 有～累 feel a bit tired / 这事我知道～。I know a little (or something) about it. / 请往右边移～。Please move a little to the right. / 还有～希望。There is still a gleam of hope. ② (used after 这么 or 那么, or with a negative expression) the least bit: ～也不累 not feel the least bit tired / ～都不知道 have not the faintest idea / ～用处也没有 utterly useless / 桌上没有～灰尘。There isn't a speck of dust on the desk. / 这事我就知道那么～。That's all I know about it. / 壶里就剩下这么～水了。This is all the water that's left in the kettle.

一点论　yīdiǎnlùn　the doctrine that everything has only

one aspect; the doctrine affirming only one aspect

一点一滴 yīdiǎn-yīdī every little bit: ～地积累资料 collect material bit by bit / 我知道的东西是～地学来的, 不是一下子就学来的。What I know I learn bit by bit, not all at once.

一丁点儿 yīdīngdiǎnr *dial.* a wee bit

一定 yīdìng ① fixed; specified; definite; regular: 工人们每个月都有～的生产指标。The workers have fixed monthly production quotas. / 按照～的规格进行生产 work according to specifications / 勘探队员成天在野外作业, 没有～的住处。The prospectors are always out in the field and never settle down in a fixed place. / 她一忙起来, 吃饭睡觉都没有～的时间了。When she gets really busy, she doesn't keep regular hours for eating or sleeping. ② *adv.* certainly; surely; necessarily: 我们的目的～要达到。我们的目的～能够达到。Our goal must be attained. Our goal can unquestionably be attained. / ～要搞好同志间的团结。It is imperative to achieve unity among comrades. / 六点以前我～回家。I shall certainly be home by six o'clock. / 告诉他～不让说出去。Tell him that under no circumstances is he to let it out. / 他～是被什么要紧事拖住了。He must have been held up by some urgent business. / 星期天～来啊! Be sure to come on Sunday. / 我们不～能找到她。I doubt whether we can find her. / 可以口头汇报, 不～要写成书面材料。An oral report will do; it isn't necessary to put it in writing. ③ given; particular; certain: 在～意义上 in a certain sense / 在～程度上 to a certain degree / 在～条件下 under given conditions ④ proper; fair; due: 具有～规模的工厂 a fair-sized factory / 作出了～的贡献 have made some contributions / 达到～水平 reach a fairly high level / 给以～的重视 attach due importance to

一定之规 yīdìng zhī guī ① a fixed pattern; a set rule ② one's own way

一动 yīdòng easily; frequently; at every turn: 他～就生气。He takes offence easily.

一动不如一静 yī dòng bùrú yī jìng to stay put is better than to move (said when questioning the necessity of a move)

一肚子 yīdùzi a stomachful of; full of: ～委屈 be full of grievances / 憋了一肚子的气 be full of pent-up anger / 他这人～坏水儿。He's full of evil ideas.

一度 yīdù ① once: 一年～ once a year; yearly; annually ② *adv.* on one occasion; for a time: 他因病～休学。He stopped going to school for a time on account of illness.

一端 yīduān one aspect (*or* side) of the matter: 此其～。This is one aspect of the matter. / 各执～ each sticking to his own argument

一堆儿 yīduīr together: 我们小时候常～玩。We often played together in our childhood days. / 快毕业了, 我们在～的时间不多了。Before long we'll graduate and separate.

一多半 yīduōbàn the greater part: 一张双人床占了房间的～。A double bed took up the greater part of the room.

一…而… yī…ér… (used with two verbs to indicate that one action follows another as an immediate result): 一怒而去 go away in a temper; leave in anger / 一饮而尽 empty the glass at one gulp / 一掠而过 skim over

一而再, 再而三 yī ér zài, zài ér sān again and again; time and again; repeatedly

一二 yī-èr one or two; just a few; just a little: 邀请～知己 invite a few close friends

一二报数 yī'èr bàoshù *mil.* By twos, number!

一·九运动 Yī'èr Jiǔ Yùndòng the December 9th Movement (a demonstration staged on December 9,

1935 by Beijing students under the leadership of the Chinese Communist Party, calling for resistance to Japanese aggression and national salvation)

一发 yīfā *adv.* ① all the more; even more: 如果处理不当, 就～不可收拾了。If not handled properly, the situation will become even more hopeless. ② together; along with all the others: 你把你的信留在这儿, 等明天和我的信～寄出。Leave your letter with me, and I'll post it together with mine tomorrow.

一发千钧 yī fà qiān jūn a hundredweight hanging by a hair—in imminent peril: 在这～的时刻 at this critical moment

一帆风顺 yī fān fēng shùn plain sailing; smooth sailing

一反常态 yī fǎn chángtài depart from one's normal behaviour; act out of character

一方面 yīfāngmiàn ① one side: 这只是事情的～。This is only one side of the matter. ② on the one hand..., on the other hand...; for one thing..., for another...: 他们～很想去医院看望班长, ～又怕影响他休息。On the one hand, they wanted very much to visit their squad leader in hospital; on the other hand, they didn't want to disturb his rest. / 这场球打输了, ～是由于对方实力较强, 另～也是因为我们没有配合好。We lost the game because, for one thing, our opponents were quite strong and, for another, our teamwork was poor.

一分钱一分货 yīfēn qián yīfēn huò the higher the price, the better the quality; what price, what goods

一分为二 yī fēn wéi èr one divides into two—everything has its good and bad sides; there are two sides to everything

一风吹 yīfēngchuī scatter to the winds—dismiss all charges, etc.; cancel the whole thing

一佛出世, 二佛涅槃 yī fó chūshì, èr fó nièpán (usu. used in) 被打得～ be beaten half dead; be beaten within an inch of one's life

一夫当关, 万夫莫开 yī fū dāng guān, wàn fū mò kāi if one man guards the pass, ten thousand cannot get through

一夫多妻制 yīfūduōqīzhì polygyny; polygamy

一夫一妻制 yīfūyīqīzhì monogyny; monogamy

一概 yīgài *adv.* one and all; without exception; totally; categorically: ～拒绝 reject without exception / ～排斥 totally exclude / 这些事情我～不知。I know nothing whatever about these matters.

一概而论 yīgài ér lùn (usu. used in the negative) treat (different matters) as the same: 不能～ not to be lumped together / 同样是儿童, 各有各的个性; ～就不对了。Every child's an individual and is different from the rest. You can't just treat them all alike.

一干 yīgān all those involved: ～人犯 the criminals and all those involved in the case

一干二净 yīgān-èrjìng thoroughly; completely: 把菜吃个～ eat up all the food / 忘得～ clean (*or* completely) forget / 把自己洗刷得～ try to absolve oneself from all blame

一竿子到底 yī gānzi dào dǐ (also 一竿子插到底 yī gānzi chā dào dǐ) carry (a task or directive) right down to the grass-roots level; carry sth. through to the end

一个巴掌拍不响 yīge bāzhang pāibuxiǎng one hand alone can't clap—it takes two to make a quarrel: 有一个让着点, 也吵不起来。～。If only one of them were more easy-going, this would never have started. It takes two to make a quarrel.

一个和尚挑水吃, 两个和尚抬水吃, 三个和尚没水吃 yīge héshang tiāo shuǐ chī, liǎngge héshang tái shuǐ chī, sānge héshang méi shuǐ chī one monk will shoulder two buckets of water, two monks will share the load, but add a third and no one will want to fetch water

一个劲儿 yīgejìnr continuously; persistently: 雨～地下。

It kept on raining. / 她～地要求到边疆去。She persistently asked for permission to go to work in a frontier region.

一个萝卜一个坑 yīge luóbo yīge kēng one radish, one hole—① each has his own task, and nobody is dispensable: 我们是～，腾不出人手来。We're so busy that no one can be spared for any other work. ② steady and reliable: 他是～的人，不会有什么闪失。He is steady and reliable, so nothing'll go wrong.

一个心眼儿 yīge xīnyǎnr ① have one's heart set on sth.; devotedly; stubbornly: ～跟党走 devotedly follow the Party ② be of one mind: 我们大家都是～。We are all of one mind.

一共 yīgòng adv. altogether; in all; all told: ～二十个。There are twenty in all (or all told). / ～多少人？How many are there altogether?

一股劲儿 yīgǔjìnr without a break; at one go; at a stretch: ～地干 do sth. without a break

一股脑儿 yīgǔnǎor (also 一古脑儿 yīgǔnǎor) dial. completely; lock, stock and barrel; root and branch: 好! ～告诉你罢! All right, I'll tell you everything. / 她兴奋得很，把要讲的话～都倒出来了。She got so excited that she poured out all she had to say at once.

一鼓作气 yī gǔ zuò qì press on to the finish without letup; get sth. done in one sustained effort: 他们～爬上山顶。They pressed on without letup until they got to the top of the hill.

一官半职 yīguān-bànzhí some official post or other: 将来熬的环哥大了，得个～，那时你要做多大功德，还怕不能么?《红楼梦》Just hold out till Master Huan grows up and gets an official post. Then you can do all the good works you want.

一贯 yīguàn consistent; persistent; all along: ～政策 consistent policy / ～为群众做好事 have persistently (or all along) been doing good for the people / 我们～主张国家不分大小，一律平等。We've always held that all nations, big or small, are equal.

一贯道 Yīguàndào a reactionary secret society which, under the cover of religious activities, served the Japanese invaders and Kuomintang reactionaries

一棍子打死 yī gùnzi dǎsǐ knock sb. down at one stroke; finish off with one blow; completely negate: 对待犯错误的同志，要批评帮助，不能～。Instead of bludgeoning our erring comrades, we should help them with criticism.

一锅粥 yīguōzhōu a pot of porridge—a complete mess; all in a muddle: 乱成～ in a mess; in utter confusion

一锅煮 yīguōzhǔ cook all things in one pot—treat different persons or things alike (or indiscriminately)

一国两制 yīguó-liǎngzhì one country, two systems

一国三公 yīguó-sāngōng a state with three rulers—a divided leadership

一哄而起 yī hōng ér qǐ (of a group of people) be roused to precipitate action; rush headlong into mass action

一哄而散 yī hōng ér sàn break up (or disperse) in a hubbub: 听说今晚的戏不演了，人们～。When word came that there wasn't going to be any show that evening, the crowd broke up in a hubbub.

一呼百诺 yīhū-bǎinuò have hundreds at one's beck and call

一呼百应 yīhū-bǎiyìng hundreds respond to a single call

一忽儿 yīhūr dial. same as 一会儿 yīhuìr

一环扣一环 yī huán kòu yī huán one ring linked with another—a closely linked succession

一晃 yīhuǎng flash: 窗外有个人影，～就不见了。A figure flashed past the window. ——see also yīhuàng

一晃 yīhuàng (of time) pass in a flash: ～几年又过去

了。Several years passed in a flash. ——see also yīhuǎng

一挥而就 yī huī ér jiù a flourish of the pen and it's done: 提笔～ finish (a piece of writing or a painting) at one go

一回生，二回熟 yī huí shēng, èr huí shú strangers at the first meeting, friends at the second; ill at ease the first time, at home the second; difficult the first time, easy the second

一回事 yīhuíshì ① one and the same (thing): 他们所说的是～。They were talking about the same thing. ② one thing: 主观愿望是～，实际情况又是～。Subjective wishes are one thing, objective reality is another.

一会儿 yīhuìr ① a little while: 咱们歇～。Let's rest for a while. ② in a moment; presently: 我～就来。I'll be coming in a moment. or I won't be a minute. / ～地上就积起了一层雪。Soon the ground was covered with a layer of snow. ③ now...now...; one moment...the next...: 天气～晴～阴。The weather is now clear, now cloudy. / 他～这么说，～那么说。He says one thing one moment and another thing the next.

一级风 yījífēng meteorol. force 1 wind; light air

一级战备 yījí zhànbèi first-degree combat readiness

一级准尉 yījí zhǔnwèi (Brit. Army, Navy, Air Force & Marine Corps) warrant officer (Class I); (U.S. Army & Air Force) chief warrant officer; (U.S. Navy & Marine Corps) commissioned warrant officer

一己 yījǐ oneself: ～之私 one's own selfish interests

一技之长 yī jì zhī cháng proficiency in a particular line (or field); professional skill; speciality

一家之言 yī jiā zhī yán a distinctive doctrine or theory; an original system of thought

一家子 yījiāzi ① a family: 那～是新搬来的。That family has just moved in. / 我们不是～。We are not of the same family. ② the whole family: ～都高兴极了。The whole family was overjoyed.

一见倾心 yī jiàn qīngxīn fall in love at first sight

一见如故 yī jiàn rúgù feel like old friends at the first meeting; hit it off well right from the start: 我和你～，这是人生最难得的事。You and I are like old friends from the start, and that doesn't happen to many men.

一见钟情 yī jiàn zhōngqíng fall in love at first sight

一箭双雕 yījiàn-shuāngdiāo hit two hawks with one arrow; kill two birds with one stone

一箭之仇 yī jiàn zhī chóu the wrong of an arrow shot—a loss or defeat to be retrieved: 他们去年赢了我们，这回我们以二比一击败他们，报了～。Last year they defeated us, but now we have got even with them by beating them 2:1.

一箭之地 yī jiàn zhī dì as far as the arrow flies—a short distance: 他家离火车站不过～。He lives only a short distance from the railway station.

一将功成万骨枯 yī jiàng gōng chéng wàn gǔ kū a single general's reputation is made out of ten thousand corpses; what millions died that Caesar might be great: 凭君莫话封侯事，～。(曹松) I charge thee, sir, not to talk of high honours; A single general achieves fame on the rotting bones of ten thousand.

一经 yījīng adv. as soon as; once: 错误～发现，就应立即纠正。Mistakes should be corrected as soon as detected.

一径 yījìng straight; directly; straightaway: 他一下车，～走进大厅，没和别人打招呼。As soon as he got out of the car, he went straight into the hall without greeting anyone.

一…就… yī…jiù… no sooner...than...; the moment...; as soon as; once: 这情况她一看就明白了。She took in the situation at a glance. / 他一接到通知就动身了。He started off as soon as he got the message. / 他一吃就

吐。He throws up everything he eats. / 我一教他就会了。He caught on as soon as I told him how. / 一干完就睡觉去吧。Once you're finished, go to bed.

一举 yìjǔ one action; one stroke; one fell swoop: 成败在此一～。Success or failure hinges on this one action. / ～粉碎政变阴谋 smash the coup plot at one blow / ～歼灭来犯之敌 wipe out the invaders in one fell swoop / ～成名 become famous overnight; achieve instant fame

一举两得 yìjǔ-liǎngdé gain two ends at once; kill two birds with one stone

一举手之劳 yī jǔshǒu zhī láo the effort of lifting the hand—a slight effort

一举一动 yìjǔ-yídòng every act and every move; every action: 我们新来乍到，得注意自己的～。We're newcomers here and must be careful what we do.

一句话 yíjùhuà in a word; in short

一决雌雄 yī jué cí-xióng same as 决一雌雄 jué yī cí-xióng

一蹶不振 yī jué bù zhèn collapse after a single setback; be unable to recover after a setback

一看二帮 yī kàn èr bāng observe and help: 对犯错误的同志要～。With comrades who have made mistakes, we should not only see how they behave but give them help.

一刻千金 yíkè qiānjīn one moment is worth a thousand pieces of gold—time is gold

一客不烦二主 yī kè bùfán èr zhǔ one guest should not bother two hosts (said when asking an additional favour of sb.)

一孔之见 yī kǒng zhī jiàn a peephole view; a narrow view; a very limited outlook: 有一种人，抱着一技之长和一，再也没有进步。There are some people who, contented with a single skill or a peephole view, never make any progress.

一口 yìkǒu ① a mouthful; a bite: 吸～气 draw a breath / 咬～ take a bite ② a manner of speech: 他讲～流利英语。He speaks fluent English. / 她～美国音。She speaks with an American accent. / 他是～的广东话。He speaks Guangdong dialect. ③ with certainty; readily; flatly: ～断定 arbitrarily assert; allege / ～答应 readily agree; readily promise / ～回绝 flatly refuse

一口吃不成个胖子 yī kǒu chībuchéng ge pàngzi you can't get fat on one mouthful—you must keep at it

一口气 yìkǒuqì ① one breath: 只要我还有一～，就要为党和人民工作。As long as there's a breath left in me, I'll work for the Party and the people. ② in one breath; without a break; at one go; at a stretch: ～干完 finish the work at one go / ～跑了五千米 run 5,000 metres at a stretch

一口咬定 yīkǒu yǎodìng state categorically; assert positively; insist emphatically: 他～当时他不在现场。He stated categorically that he was not at the scene of the crime.

一口钟 yīkǒuzhōng dial. mantle; cape; cloak

一块儿 yīkuàir ① at the same place: 在～工作 work at the same place / 两个人说不到～。The two of them can never see eye to eye. ② together: 我们～走吧。Let's go together. / 这两个问题最好～研究。It would be best to consider the two questions together. / 老见他们俩在～。The two of them are always seen together.

一块石头落地 yī kuài shítou luòdì the mind is at last set at rest: 听到她平安无事的消息，大家心里才～。Not until they heard that she was safe and sound were their minds set at rest.

一来二去 yìlái-èrqù in the course of frequent contact; in the course of time: 他们常在地里一块儿干活，～地也就熟了。They often worked together in the fields, and in time they got to know each other quite well.

一览 yìlǎn general survey; bird's-eye view: 《北京名胜古迹～》 *A Guide to the Historical Relics and Scenic Spots of Beijing*

一览表 yìlǎnbiǎo table; schedule: 火车行车时刻～ railway timetable

一览无余 yī lǎn wú yú take in everything at a glance

一揽子 yìlǎnzi wholesale; package: ～计划 package plan / ～交易 package deal

一浪接一浪 yī làng jiē yī làng wave upon wave

一劳永逸 yī láo yǒng yì by one supreme effort gain lasting repose—settle a matter once and for all: ～的解决办法 a solution that holds good for all time; a permanent solution / 咱们这次好好儿修一下，就～了。Let's fix it for good this time. / 自买计算机，才是～的办法呢。To buy a computer of our own is the only way to get rid of such trouble once and for all.

一力 yīlì do one's best; do all one can: ～成全 do one's best to help (sb. to achieve his aim)

一例 yīlì same; alike: ～看待 treat in the same way

一连 yìlián adv. in a row; in succession; running: ～三年获得丰收 reap good harvests for three years in a row / ～下了三天雨。It rained for three days running.

一连串 yìliánchuàn a succession of; a series of; a string of; a chain of: ～的事件 a succession of events / ～问题 a series of questions

一连气儿 yìliánqìr dial. in a row; in succession; running: 她～唱了四五个歌。She sang four or five songs in a row.

一了百了 yī liǎo bǎi liǎo all troubles end when the main trouble ends: 一去世，他的苦恼就～了。With his death all his woes ended.

一鳞半爪 yīlín-bànzhǎo odd bits; fragments: ～的情况 odd bits (or scraps) of information / ～的知识 fragmentary knowledge

一零儿 yīlíngr a fraction: 我知道的这一点儿，连他的～也比不上啊。What little I know isn't even a fraction of what he knows.

一流 yīliú ① a kind; the same kind: 他属于抽象派～人物。He belongs to the abstractionist school. or He is an abstractionist. ② first-class; first-rate; top-notch: ～作家 a first-class writer / ～作品 a first-rate work

一溜儿 yīliùr dial. ① a row: ～平房 a row of one-storey houses ② neighbourhood; vicinity: 他就住在那～。He lives somewhere around there. ③ a short period of activity: 他～小跑来到村边。He came running all the way to the village.

一溜歪斜 yīliùwāixié dial. (walk, etc.) unsteadily in a zigzag: 他挑着一挑儿水，～地从河边走上来。He wobbled up the slope from the river, carrying two buckets of water on a shoulder pole.

一溜烟 yīliùyān like a streak of smoke—very quickly: 小汽车～开走了。The car sped off. / 他～就没影儿了。He disappeared in an instant (or a flash).

一溜风 yīliùfēng like a gust of wind—very quickly

一路 yílù ① all the way; throughout the journey: ～上说说笑笑 chat cheerfully all the way / ～多保重。Take care of yourself on the journey. / 客队～领先。The visiting team led from the beginning. ② of the same kind: 一路货色 yílù huòsè ③ go the same way; take the same route: 咱们是～吗？Are we going the same way? ④ single file: ～纵队 single column / 成～纵队齐步走 march (in) single file

一路货色 yílù huòsè (also 一路货 yílùhuò) the same sort of stuff; one of a kind; birds of a feather

一路平安 yílù píng'ān (also 一路顺风 yílù shùnfēng) have a pleasant journey; have a good trip; *bon voyage*

一律 yílù ① same; alike; uniform: ～对待 treat in the same way (or equally) / 不宜强求～。No rigid uniformity should be sought. ② all; without exception: 国家不分大小，应该～平等。All countries, big or small, should be equal (or on an equal footing). / 值勤人员～佩戴臂

章。All personnel on duty are to wear an armband.

一落千丈　yī luò qiānzhàng　drop a thousand *zhang* in one fall—suffer a drastic decline: 社会风气～。Morals and manners have declined to an enormous extent.

一抹平　yīmāpíng　① the same; equal: 要按质定价，不能～。The prices should be different, fixed according to quality. ② level; smooth: 路修得～。The road is very smooth.

一麻黑　yīmāhēi　(also 一抹黑 yīmāhēi) pitch-dark: 山洞里～，什么也看不见。It was pitch-dark in the cave; you couldn't see a thing. / 人生地不熟，两眼～ all alone and helpless in a strange place

一马当先　yī mǎ dāngxiān　gallop at the head—take the lead; be in the forefront: 我们队长干什么活儿都是～。Our team leader takes the lead in whatever work we do.

一马平川　yī mǎ píngchuān　a wide expanse of flat land; a wide stretch of flat country

一脉相承　yī mài xiāngchéng　(also 一脉相传 yī mài xiāngchuán) come down in one continuous line; can be traced to the same origin; in direct line of descent (*or* succession): 汉儒与孔孟～。The Han Confucianists were direct successors of Confucius and Mencius.

一毛不拔　yī máo bù bá　unwilling to give up even a hair—very stingy

一门心思　yī mén xīnsi　heart and soul; wholeheartedly: ～搞设计 throw oneself wholeheartedly into designing

一秘　yīmì　short for 一等秘书 yīděng mìshū

一面　yīmiàn　① one side: 这座房子朝南的～有两个窗户。The house has two windows on the south side. ② one aspect: 这里的条件既有有利的～，也有不利的～。The situation here has both favourable and unfavourable aspects. / 这只是问题的～。This is only one aspect of the question. ③ at the same time; simultaneously: ～教，～学 learn while teaching / 他～说着，～朝门口走去。So saying, he made for the door. ④ *formal* have met once before: 未尝～ have never met before

一面儿官司　yīmiànr guānsi　a one-sided lawsuit (a lawsuit in which one party has a great advantage over the other)

一面儿理　yīmiànrlǐ　one party's account or version; a lopsided (*or* one sided) argument

一面之词　yīmiàn zhī cí　the statement of only one of the parties: 这个案子其说不一，你不要听人家～。There are different versions of this case. You mustn't listen to only one side of the story.

一面之交　yī miàn zhī jiāo　(also 一面之雅 yī miàn zhī yǎ) have met only once; be casually acquainted

一面之缘　yī miàn zhī yuán　having met once (as ordained by fate): 有～ have met once / 有些人他不认识，或者只不过～，他也亲热地招呼。He extended his greetings—cordial greetings—even to those people whom he did not know at all or whom he had only met once before.

一鸣惊人　yī míng jīngrén　(of an obscure person) amaze the world with a single brilliant feat; set the world on fire

一瞑不视　yī míng bù shì　close one's eyes never to open them again—die

一命归天　yī mìng guītiān　(also 一命归阴 yī mìng guīyīn) quit this world; pass away; die

一命呜呼　yī mìng wūhū　die; kick the bucket; give up the ghost

一模活脱　yī mú huótuō　*dial.* cast in the same mould—exactly alike; as like as two peas

一模一样　yīmú-yīyàng　exactly alike; as like as two peas: 她长得跟她母亲～。She's the image of her mother.

一木难支　yī mù nán zhī　same as 独木难支 dú mù nán zhī

zhī

一目了然　yī mù liǎorán　be clear at a glance: 那门却是开着的，里面有几支枪、几把刀，～。The gate was open, and you could see at a glance the number of guns and bayonets.

一目十行　yī mù shí háng　take in ten lines at a glance—read rapidly

一男半女　yīnán-bànnǚ　a son or a daughter; a child or two (usu. used in the case of people who have no children)

一年半载　yīnián-bànzǎi　in a year or so; in about a year: 这座桥～可望竣工。Completion of this bridge is expected in a year or so.

一年到头　yī nián dào tóu　throughout the year; all the year round

一年生　yīniánshēng　*bot.* annual: ～植物 annual plant; annual

一年四季　yīnián-sìjì　throughout (the four seasons of) the year; all the year round

一年之计在于春　yī nián zhī jì zàiyú chūn　the whole year's work depends on a good start in spring

一念之差　yī niàn zhī chā　a wrong decision made in a moment of weakness; a momentary slip with serious consequences

一诺千金　yī nuò qiānjīn　a promise worth a thousand pieces of gold—a promise that can be counted on

一拍即合　yī pāi jí hé　*derog.* fit in readily; chime in easily

一盘散沙　yī pán sǎnshā　a sheet of loose sand—a state of disunity (formerly said of a country)

一旁　yīpáng　one side: 院子的～栽了一些小树。There was a growth of bushes on one side of the courtyard. / 他接过去，随手放在～。He took it, and put it aside. / 我们玩牌的时候，他站在～看着。He stood by watching while we played cards.

一偏　yīpiān　one-sided: ～之见 a one-sided view

一瞥　yīpiē　① a quick glance: 就在这～之间，我看出了她非常激动。In a quick glance I noticed her agitation. ② a glimpse; a brief survey: 《长城～》A Glimpse of the Great Wall

一贫如洗　yī pín rú xǐ　penniless; utterly destitute

一品　yīpǐn　the highest official rank in imperial China: ～官 highest-ranking official / 当朝～ highest court official

一品红　yīpǐnhóng　*bot.* poinsettia (*Euphorbia pulcherrima*)

一平二调　yīpíng-èrdiào　equalitarianism and indiscriminate transfer of resources

一瓶子不响，半瓶子晃荡　yī píngzi bù xiǎng, bàn píngzi huàngdang　the half-filled bottle sloshes, the full bottle makes no sound—the dabbler in knowledge chatters away, the wise man stays silent

一抔黄土　yī póu huángtǔ　a handful of yellow earth—sth. utterly insignificant

一暴十寒　yīpù-shíhán　(also 一曝十寒 yīpù-shíhán) have one day's sun and then ten days' cold—work by fits and starts

一妻多夫制　yīqīduōfūzhì　polyandry; polygamy

一齐　yīqí　*adv.* at the same time; simultaneously; in unison: ～努力 make a concerted effort / 观众～鼓起掌来。The audience started clapping in unison. / 人和行李～到了。The luggage arrived at the same time as the passengers.

一起　yīqǐ　① in the same place: 住在～ live in the same place / 我们俩在～工作了四年。We two worked at the same place for four years. ② *adv.* together; in company: 奶奶和孙女儿～进城。Grandma went downtown with her granddaughter. / 我不跟他～走。I won't go along with him. / 让我们团结在～，战斗在～，胜利在～。

Let us stand together, fight together and win together. ③ *dial.* altogether; in all: 这几件东西〜多少钱? How much is that altogether? ④ *dial.* a batch of people: 那〜人刚走, 这〜人又到了。This batch of people arrived as soon as the other batch left.

一气 yīqì ① at one go; without a break; at a stretch: 〜儿游了三千米 swim three thousand metres at a stretch ② of the same gang; hand in glove: 通同〜 act in collusion ③ a spell; a fit: 瞎闹〜 raise hell; kick up a row / 胡吹〜 tell tall stories

一气呵成 yīqì hē chéng ① (of an essay) form a coherent whole; make smooth reading ② get sth. done at one go; carry sth. through without stopping

一气之下 yī qì zhī xià in a fury; in a fit of anger: 他〜不辞而别。Greatly angered, he left without saying goodbye。

一钱不值 yī qián bù zhí not worth a penny; utterly worthless; mere trash

一腔 yīqiāng be full of (zeal, grievances, etc.): 〜热情 be full of zeal / 〜冤仇 be full of grievances

一窍不通 yī qiào bù tōng know nothing about (a subject); lack the slightest knowledge of; be utterly ignorant of: 我对原子核物理学〜。I'm out of my depth when it comes to nuclear physics.

一切 yīqiè ① all; every: 抓住〜机会 seize every opportunity / 〜行动听指挥。Obey orders in all your actions. / 调动〜积极因素 bring every positive factor into play ② everything; all: 把〜献给祖国 give one's all to one's country / 〜为了前线的胜利! Everything for victory at the front! / 这里〜都好, 请放心。Don't worry. Everything here is O.K. / 〜向钱看 put money above all else

一清二白 yīqīng-èrbái perfectly clean; blameless; unimpeachable

一清二楚 yīqīng-èrchǔ perfectly clear: 他把什么事都交代得〜。He made everything perfectly clear. / 他把情况打听得〜。He has found out all about it.

一清早 yīqīngzǎo early in the morning

一穷二白 yīqióng-èrbái poor and blank: 改变我国"〜"的面貌 lift our country from the state of "poverty and blankness"

一丘之貉 yī qiū zhī hé jackals from the same lair; birds of a feather

一去不复返 yī qù bù fù fǎn gone never to return; gone for ever: 人民所厌恶的国家分裂和混乱的局面, 已经〜了。The days of national disunity and chaos which the people detested are gone, never to return.

一犬吠影, 百犬吠声 yī quǎn fèiyǐng, bǎi quǎn fèishēng when one dog barks at a shadow a hundred others join in—blindly follow others

一人得道, 鸡犬升天 yī rén dédào, jī-quǎn shēngtiān when a man attains the Tao, even his pets ascend to heaven—when a man gets to the top, all his friends and relations get there with him

一任 yīrèn *formal* allow: 岂能〜他胡作非为? How can we let him run amuck?

一仍旧贯 yī réng jiù guàn stick to the old practice; follow the old routine

一日不见, 如隔三秋 yīrì bùjiàn, rú gé sānqiū one day apart seems like three years—miss sb. very much

一日千里 yīrì qiānlǐ a thousand *li* a day—at a tremendous pace; with giant strides: 当前电子工业的发展〜。At present the electronics industry is developing at a tremendous pace.

一日三秋 yīrì sānqiū same as 一日不见, 如隔三秋 yīrì bùjiàn, rú gé sānqiū

一日为师, 终身为父 yīrì wéi shī, zhōngshēn wéi fù a teacher for a day is a father for a lifetime

一日之长 yīrì zhī cháng a slight superiority: 争〜 strive for a slight superiority

一日之雅 yīrì zhī yǎ (usu. used in) 无〜 not have the pleasure of knowing sb.

一如 yīrú just like; the same as: 〜所见 just like what we've seen / 〜所闻 the same as what we've heard

一如既往 yīrú jìwǎng just as in the past; as before; as always: 我们将〜坚决支持你们的正义斗争。We will, as always, firmly support your just struggle.

一若 yīruò same as 一如 yīrú

一若以往 yīruò yǐwǎng same as 一如既往 yīrú jìwǎng

一扫而光 yī sǎo ér guāng (also 一扫而空 yī sǎo ér kōng) make a clean sweep of; clear off; finish off; get rid of sth. lock, stock and barrel: 孩子们一来就把水果〜。The children came and finished off all the fruit. / 节日的气氛把他的沉郁的心情〜。The festive atmosphere swept his melancholy thoughts clean away.

一色 yīsè ① of the same colour: 秋水共长天〜。(王勃) Autumnal waters merge with the limitless sky. ② of the same type; uniform: 〜的瓦房 tiled houses of a uniform style

一霎 yīshà in an instant; in a moment: 〜间 in a flash / 〜时 in a flash

一闪念 yīshǎnniàn a fleeting thought

一晌 yīshǎng ① a short time; a little while: 他坐了〜就走了。He sat for a while and went away. ② same as 一向 yīxiàng ③ a period of time: 前〜雨水太多了。There was too much rain recently.

一上来 yīshànglái at first; at the beginning: 〜就劲头十足 be full of zest (*or* enthusiasm) from the very beginning

一勺烩 yīsháohuì same as 一锅煮 yīguōzhǔ

一身 yīshēn ① the whole body; all over the body: 〜是泥 be covered all over with mud / 〜是汗 be sweating all over ② a suit: 〜新衣服 a new suit of clothes ③ a single person: 独自〜 solitary; all alone

一身两役 yī shēn liǎng yì hold two jobs at the same time; serve in a dual capacity

一身是胆 yī shēn shì dǎn one's whole body is all pluck —know no fear; be absolutely fearless: 据说赵子龙〜。It is said of Zhao Zilong that his whole body was all pluck.

一神论 yīshénlùn (also 一神教 yīshénjiào) monotheism

一生 yīshēng all one's life; throughout one's life: 鲁迅的〜是战斗的〜, 革命的〜。Lu Xun's was a fighting life, a revolutionary life.

一生一世 yīshēng-yīshì all one's life; throughout one's life

一声不响 yī shēng bù xiǎng not say a word; not utter a sound

一失足成千古恨 yī shīzú chéng qiāngǔ hèn one false step brings everlasting grief; a single slip may cause lasting sorrow; a moment's error can bring a lifelong regret

一时 yīshí ① a period of time: 此〜彼〜。Times have changed. ② for a short while; temporary; momentary: 〜的多数 a temporary majority / 为〜的表面现象所迷惑 be misled by transient phenomena; be taken in by appearances / 不凭〜的热情 not rely on a moment's enthusiasm / 〜想不起来 can't recall offhand (*or* for the moment) / 看一个人不要光看他的〜一事。Don't judge a person by a single act or a short period of his life. ③ (used in pairs) now..., now..., one moment..., the next: 他的病〜好, 〜坏。He'd be better for a while and then have a relapse.

一时半刻 yīshí-bànkè (also 一时半会儿 yīshí-bànhuìr) a short time; a little while: 他〜还回不来。He won't be back for a little while yet.

一时三刻 yīshí-sānkè a short time; a little while: 要这么多钱, 〜叫我上哪儿去找哇? Where can I find so much money in so short a time?

一时一刻 yīshí-yīkè　every moment: ～也不要脱离群众。Never for a single moment cut yourself off from the masses. / 我～也不能忘记这个教训。I shall never forget this lesson.

一世 yīshì　① all one's life; a lifetime: 他～没出过远门。All his life he's never been away from home. ② an age: 固一之雄也，而今安在哉?(苏轼) Truly he was the hero of his age, but where is he now?

一式 yīshì　the same form: ～两份 in duplicate / ～三份 in triplicate

一事 yīshì　dial. be related (organizationally or professionally); belong to the same organization: 你们都是～吗?Are you all together? / 这两家公司实际是～。The two firms are actually one and the same outfit.

一事无成 yī shì wú chéng　accomplish nothing; get nowhere: 知识分子如果不和工农民众相结合，则将～。The intellectuals will accomplish nothing if they fail to integrate themselves with the workers and peasants.

一视同仁 yī shì tóng rén　treat equally without discrimination

一手 yīshǒu　① proficiency; skill: 露～ show off one's skill / 业务上有～ be proficient in one's own line; know one's stuff / 他有～好手艺。He's a real craftsman. or He's a master of his craft. / 这个篮球队在防守上很有～。This basketball team has a very strong defence. ② trick; move: 他这～可真毒辣! What a vicious trick he played! ③ single-handed; all by oneself; all alone: 这场争端是他们～挑起的。The dispute was all started by them. / 小王是他叔叔～拉扯大的。Xiao Wang was brought up all along by his uncle.

一手包办 yīshǒu bāobàn　keep everything in one's own hands; take everything on oneself

一手遮天 yīshǒu zhē tiān　shut out the heavens with one hand—hide the truth from the masses; hoodwink the public: 他想～，颠倒是非，这只能是徒劳的。He was merely wasting his time trying to hoodwink the people of the whole world and confound right with wrong.

一顺儿 yīshùnr　in the same direction or order: 村里新盖的房子，～都是朝南的。The newly built houses in the village all face south.

一瞬 yīshùn　an instant; a flash; the twinkling of an eye: ～即逝 vanish in a flash / 二百年时间在中国文明史上只不过是～间。Two hundred years is but a fleeting moment in the history of Chinese civilization.

一丝不苟 yī sī bù gǒu　not be the least bit negligent; be scrupulous about every detail; be conscientious and meticulous: 她把眼睛睁得大大的，～地接着线头。She strained to keep her eyes wide open and continued mending the broken threads with conscientious thoroughness.

一丝不挂 yī sī bù guà　not have a stitch on; be stark naked

一丝一毫 yīsī-yīháo　a tiny bit; an iota; a trace: 没有～的差别 without the least difference / 这是死命令! 不能改变～! This is an order and it must be obeyed down to the last detail.

一似 yīsì　formal just like; the same as

一塌刮子 yītāguāzi　dial. ① all; entirely; completely ② in all; altogether

一塌糊涂 yītāhútú　in a complete mess; in an awful (or terrible) state: 他把事情弄得～。He has made a mess of the job. / 屋子乱得～。The room was a complete mess. / 为了一件小事争得～ make a fearful row over a mere trifle

一潭死水 yītán sǐshuǐ　a pool of stagnant water—a stagnant or lifeless condition

一体 yītǐ　① an organic (or integral) whole: 融成～ merge into an organic whole ② all people concerned; to a man: 上述各项望～遵照。It is expected that the above stipulations will be observed by all.

一体化 yītǐhuà　integration: 经济～ economic integration / ～区域合作 integrated regional cooperation

一天 yītiān　① a day: ～二十四小时都有人值班。There are people on duty round the clock. ② one day (in the past): ～，老李谈起他参加红军的经过。One day, Lao Li talked about how he had joined the Red Army. ③ dial. the whole day; all (the) day; from morning till night: 忙碌了～ have been busy all day

一天到晚 yī tiān dào wǎn　from morning till night; from dawn to dusk; all day long: ～就是忙，不是工作，就是开会，还要学习。I'm busy day and night, not only with work, but also with meetings or classes. / ～光抄着手休息，那还不把人憋出病来了! If I had to sit around with folded hands all day I'd go mad.

一条道儿跑到黑 yītiáodàor pǎo dào hēi　follow one road until it's dark—cling obstinately to one course

一条龙 yītiáolóng　① one continuous line: 十几辆卡车排成～，向前开动。A dozen trucks moved ahead one after another in a long line. ② a connected sequence; a coordinated process: 实行产、运、销～ make production, transportation and marketing a coordinated process

一条心 yītiáoxīn　be of one mind; be at one: 跟党～ be at one with the Party / 众人～，黄土变成金。If we're all of one heart and one mind, we can change clay into gold.

一通百通 yī tōng bǎi tōng　master one and you'll master a hundred; grasp this and you'll grasp everything

一同 yītóng　adv. together; at the same time and place: ～出发 set out together

一统 yītǒng　unify (a country): 大～ a unified domain

一统天下 yītǒng tiānxià　the whole empire under one ruler

一头 yītóu　① adv. at the same time; simultaneously: 他～走，～说。He talked as he walked. ② adv. all of a sudden; all at once: 我刚进门，～碰见了他。I bumped into him the moment I came in. ③ adv. directly; headlong: ～扎进水里 plunge headlong into the water / 他打开车门，～钻了进去。He opened the door and dived into the car. ④ a head: 他比我高～。He is a head taller than I am. / 白马领先～获胜。The white horse won by a head. ⑤ one end: 扁担的～挑着篮子，另～挂着水罐。A basket was being carried at one end of the shoulder pole, and a water pitcher at the other. ⑥ dial. in a group; together: 咱们玩桥牌，我们俩～，你们俩～。Let's play bridge, we two against you two. / 他们是～来的。They came together.

一头儿沉 yītóurchén　dial. ① heavy-at-one-end, a desk with a cupboard or drawers at one end ② be partial (in mediation)

一吐为快 yī tǔ wéi kuài　cannot rest until one has one's say

一团和气 yī tuán héqì　keep on good terms with everyone (at the expense of principle); keep on the right side of everyone

一团漆黑 yī tuán qīhēi　same as 漆黑一团 qīhēi yī tuán

一团糟 yītuánzāo　a complete mess; a chaotic state: 他的事情～。His affairs are in a mess.

一退六二五 yī tuì liù èr wǔ　(also 一推六二五 yī tuī liù èr wǔ) evade or deny all responsibility

一碗水端平 yīwǎnshuǐ duānpíng　hold a bowl of water level—be impartial: 处理争执要～，不能有偏向。When settling a dispute, one must be fair to both sides.

一网打尽 yī wǎng dǎjìn　catch the whole lot in a dragnet; round up the whole gang at one fell swoop

一往情深 yīwǎng qíngshēn　be deeply attached; be passionately devoted; be head over heels in love

一往无前 yīwǎng wúqián　press forward with an in-

domitable will: 这个军队具有～的精神。This army has an indomitable spirit.

一望无际 yī wàng wújì stretch as far as the eye can see; stretch to the horizon: ～的大草原 a boundless stretch of grassland /～的大海 a vast expanse of ocean stretching to the horizon /沙地种着～的碧绿的西瓜。The sand flats were planted as far as the eye could see with jade-green watermelons.

一位论派 Yīwèilùnpài *Christianity* Unitarianism

一味 · yīwèi *adv.* blindly: ～蛮干 persist in acting blindly /～地固执己见 stubbornly stick to one's opinions /～迁就 make endless concessions; make one concession after another

一文不名 yī wén bù míng not have a penny to one's name; be penniless: 她一天只吃了两个小烧饼，身上已经～。She had only two small cakes for the whole day and had not a penny with her.

一文不值 yī wén bùzhí not worth a farthing; utterly worthless; mere trash

一问三不知 yī wèn sān bù zhī say "I don't know" to every question—not know a thing; be entirely ignorant: 她是拿定了主意"不干己事不张口，一问摇头三不知"。She's made up her mind not to open her mouth about matters that don't concern her, but to shake her head in answer to all questions. /一谈到什么党呀派呀，他就～。When the conversation turned to politics he assumed complete ignorance.

一窝蜂 yīwōfēng like a swarm of bees: 孩子们～似地拥上来。The children came swarming round.

一无可取 yī wú kěqǔ have nothing to recommend one; be worthless: 这家饭馆儿除了价钱便宜之外，～。This restaurant has nothing to recommend it except that it's cheap.

一无是处 yī wú shìchù without a single redeeming feature; devoid of any merit; having no saving grace: 把他说得～ make him out to be without a saving grace

一无所长 yī wú suǒ cháng have no special skill

一无所有 yī wú suǒyǒu not own a thing in the world; not have a thing to one's name: 我除了行李被褥之外，～。Apart from clothes and bedding I have nothing. /他们所到的集镇、村庄，都是～，一无可吃的了。Every market town and village they came to was quite empty and afforded nothing to eat.

一无所知 yī wú suǒ zhī know nothing about; not have the least inkling of; be absolutely ignorant of: 真奇怪，他们至今对那样重要的事还～。It's really surprising that they should still be in the dark about such important events.

一五一十 yīwǔ-yīshí (narrate) systematically and in full detail: 他把事情～地都给同志们讲了。He told his comrades the whole story exactly as it had happened. /你去找她，～对她实说。Go and tell her all about it from beginning to end.

一物降一物 yī wù xiáng yī wù one thing conquers another; everything has its superior

一误再误 yī wù zài wù ① make one error after another; keep on making mistakes ② make things worse by repeated delays: 你这病要抓紧治，可不能～了。You should go and see a doctor at once. You mustn't put it off any more.

一息尚存 yī xī shàng cún so long as one still has a breath left; till one's last gasp: 我只要～，就要努力为祖国工作。I'll work hard for my country as long as I live.

一席话 yīxíhuà what one says during a conversation: 他的～打动了我的心。What he said touched my heart. /听君一席话，胜读十年书。I profit more from one consultation with you than from ten years of reading.

一系列 yīxìliè a series of: ～问题 a whole series of questions /～的事件 a whole train of events /～措施 a series of measures

一下[1] yīxià (also 一下子 yīxiàzi) one time; once: 亲～孩子的脸 give the baby a kiss on the cheek /拍～他的肩膀 give him a pat on the shoulder /～打死两个苍蝇 kill two flies with one swat /让我想～。Let me think a bit. *or* Let me see. /打听～再说。Better make some inquiries first. /老鹰～就把小鸡叼走了。The hawk snatched away the chick at one swoop.

一下[2] yīxià (also 一下子 yīxiàzi) in a short while; all at once; all of a sudden: 灯～又亮了。After a little while the lights went on again. /请等～。Wait a minute, please. /这天气，～冷，～热。Look at this weather. It's cold one moment and hot the next. /～阴了下来。It became overcast all of a sudden. /不能希望人们把旧观念～都清除掉。One cannot expect people to get rid of their old ideas overnight.

一线 yīxiàn a ray of; a gleam of: ～希望 a gleam of hope /～光明 a ray (or gleam) of light /～生机 a slim chance of survival; a gleam of hope

一相情愿 yī xiāng qíngyuàn (also 一厢情愿 yī xiāng qíngyuàn) one-sided wish; one's own wishful thinking

一向 yīxiàng ① earlier on; lately: 前～雨水多。There was quite a lot of rain earlier on. /这～进步不小吧? You must have made a lot of progress lately. ② *adv.* consistently; all along: 我国～支持世界各国人民的正义斗争。China has consistently supported the just struggles of the peoples of the world. /她对工作～认真负责。She's always been conscientious in her work.

一小儿 yīxiǎor since childhood: 他～就爱画画儿。He has loved to paint ever since childhood.

一小撮 yīxiǎocuō a handful: ～战争贩子 a handful of warmongers

一笑置之 yī xiào zhì zhī dismiss with a laugh (or smile); laugh off

一些 yīxiē *m.* a number of; certain; some; a few; a little: 有～国家 some (or a number of) countries /作～适当的调整 make certain appropriate readjustments /有～事情我还不明白。There are a few things that still puzzle me. /只剩这～了，够吗? There's only this much left. Is it enough? /我想说的就这～。That's all I wanted to say.

一泻千里 yī xiè qiānlǐ ① (of a river) rush down a thousand *li*—flow powerfully: 牡丹江水，汹涌澎湃，犹如万马奔腾，～。The raging Peony River raced down its long course like ten thousand stampeding horses. ② (of a writer's style) bold and flowing

一蟹不如一蟹 yī xiè bùrú yī xiè each crab is smaller than the one before—each one is worse than the last

一心 yīxīn ① wholeheartedly; heart and soul: ～为人民 serve the people heart and soul /～为四化 devote oneself wholeheartedly to the Four Modernizations /她～想着厂里的工作。She always has the work of her factory at heart. /他～想上大学。He is set on going to college. ② of one mind; at one: 全国～。The country is of one mind.

一心一德 yīxīn-yīdé be of one heart and one mind; be dedicated to the same cause

一心一意 yīxīn-yīyì heart and soul; wholeheartedly: 他～进行科学实验。He wholeheartedly engaged in scientific experiments. /他～要叫儿子去上学。He was set on sending his son to school.

一新 yīxīn become something entirely new: 房屋已修缮～。The house has been renovated. /房间已粉刷～。The room has been whitewashed and become bright and tidy again.

一星半点 yīxīng-bàndiǎn a tiny bit; a very small amount: 这可是细活，不能有～差错。This is a high precision job. There mustn't be the slightest slip.

一行 yīxíng a group travelling together; party: 代表

团～十五人于昨日下午抵京。The fifteen-person delegation arrived in Beijing yesterday afternoon. / 副总理及其～ the Vice-Premier and his party / 总统及其～ the President and accompanying officials

一宿 yīxiǔ *inf.* one night: ～没睡好 not sleep well the whole night; not sleep a wink the whole night

一言不发 yī yán bù fā not say (*or* utter) a word; keep one's mouth shut: 他在会上～。He sat through the meeting without saying a word.

一言抄百总 yī yán chāo bǎi zǒng to make a long story short; in a word; in short; in brief

一言既出，驷马难追 yī yán jì chū, sìmǎ nán zhuī a word once spoken cannot be taken back even by a team of four horses—what is said cannot be unsaid

一言难尽 yī yán nán jìn it's hard to explain in a few words; it's a long story: 说来话长，其中底细，～。It would take too long to tell you that in full. / 这些年你都上哪儿啦?——一～哪! Where have you been all these years?—That's a long story.

一言堂 yīyántáng a conference hall where one person has all the say—what I say goes; one person alone has the say; one person lays down the law: 要搞"群言堂"，不搞"～"。Let all have a say, not just one.

一言为定 yī yán wéi dìng that's settled then: 一点不错，就这样办，～。Absolutely right. That's the way to do it. So it's settled. / 你两人～，各无翻悔。Now that you have both agreed to this, you must neither of you go back on your word.

一言以蔽之 yī yán yǐ bì zhī to sum up in a word: 《诗》三百，一言以蔽之，曰:"思无邪。"(《论语》) The *Songs* are three hundred in number. They can be summed up in one phrase: Let there be no evil in your thoughts.

一氧化碳 yīyǎnghuàtàn carbon monoxide: ～中毒 carbon monoxide poisoning

一氧化物 yīyǎnghuàwù *chem.* monoxide

一样 yīyàng the same; alike; as...as...: 我买的伞和你的～。The umbrella I've bought is the same as yours. / 这两根针～粗。The two needles are of the same thickness. / 哥儿俩相貌～，脾气也～。The two brothers are alike in appearance and temperament. / 他跟他哥哥跑得～快。He runs as fast as his brother. / 我们的意见很不～。Our opinions differ radically. / 谁去都～。It won't make any difference who goes. / 李大娘把我们当做自己的亲生儿女～。Grandma Li treats us as her own children.

一叶障目，不见泰山 yī yè zhàng mù, bù jiàn Tàishān a leaf before the eye shuts out Mount Tai—have one's view of the important overshadowed by the trivial

一叶知秋 yī yè zhī qiū the falling of one leaf heralds the autumn; it is a straw in the wind; a small sign can indicate a great trend

一夜夫妻百夜恩 yī yè fūqī bǎi yè ēn husband and wife for one night, love lingers on for a hundred nights

一一 yīyī one by one; one after another: ～检查 examine one by one / 没时间～介绍 have no time to go into details or cover everything / ～告别 say goodbye to everyone; bid farewell to all, one after another

一…一… yī…yī… ① (used with two nouns) ⓐ all; the whole of: 一生一世 one's whole life; all one's life ⓑ each; every; single: 一言一行 every word and deed / 不拿群众一针一线 not take a single needle or piece of thread from the masses ② (used with two verbs similar in meaning, to indicate two successive actions): 一瘸一拐 limping along / 一蹦一跳 skipping and hopping ③ (used with two verbs contrasting in meaning, to indicate the coordination or alternation of the two actions): 一问一答 one asking and the other answering ④ (used with two words opposite in meaning, to indicate opposition or contrast): 一东一西 one east, one west; poles apart / 一长一短 one short, one long

一衣带水 yīyīdàishuǐ a narrow strip of water: ～的邻邦 close neighbours separated by only a strip of water

一意孤行 yī yì gū xíng cling obstinately to one's course; act wilfully; insist on having one's own way

一应 yīyīng all; everything: ～工具均已备齐。All the tools are ready.

一应俱全 yīyīng jù quán everything needed is there: 日用百货～。All varieties of goods for daily use are available.

一拥而上 yī yōng ér shàng rush up in a crowd: 战士们跟在这勇敢的人后面，～，一下就冲上山峰。Infected with his courage, the soldiers surged after him and at once charged up the heights.

一隅 yīyú a corner: ～之地 a very small area / ～之见 a very narrow (*or* limited) view

一隅三反 yīyú sān fǎn same as 举一反三 jǔ yī fǎn sān

一语道破 yī yǔ dàopò lay bare the truth with one remark; hit the nail on the head: ～其中奥秘 lay bare the secret of sth. with one remark

一语破的 yī yǔ pò dì hit the mark with a single comment

一语双关 yī yǔ shuāngguān a single phrase with a double meaning

一元方程 yīyuán fāngchéng equation with one unknown

一元化 yīyuánhuà centralized; unified: 实行～的领导 exercise unified (*or* centralized) leadership

一元论 yīyuánlùn *philos.* monism

一元酸 yīyuánsuān *chem.* monoacid; monoatomic acid

一院制 yīyuànzhì unicameral (*or* one chamber) legislature

一月 yīyuè January

一再 yīzài time and again; again and again; repeatedly: ～宣称 declare time and again / ～表示感谢 express one's gratitude again and again

一…再… yī…zài… (used with two identical verbs) repeatedly: 一错再错 keep on making mistakes / 一让再让 make one concession after another / 一拖再拖 postpone again and again

一早 yīzǎo *inf.* early in the morning: 我明天～就告诉他。I'll let him know first thing tomorrow morning. / 苏先生今天～就来过了。Mr. Su was here early this morning.

一张一弛 yīzhāng-yīchí tension alternating with relaxation

一长制 yīzhǎngzhì system of one-man leadership

一着不慎，满盘皆输 yī zhāo bù shèn, mǎn pán jiē shū one careless move and the whole game is lost

一朝 yīzhāo ① in one day: ～覆亡 collapse (*or* be toppled) in one short day ② once: ～失足，悔恨终生。A moment's error can bring a lifelong regret.

一朝被蛇咬，十年怕井绳 yīzhāo bèi shé yǎo, shínián pà jǐngshéng once bitten by a snake, one shies at coiled rope for ten years; he that hath been bitten by a serpent is afraid of a rope; once bitten, twice shy

一朝一夕 yīzhāo-yīxī in one morning or evening; overnight; in one day: 非～之功 not the work of a single day / 不是～所能完成的 cannot be accomplished overnight

一针见血 yī zhēn jiàn xiě pierce to the truth with one pertinent remark; hit the nail on the head: 他～地指出，那个男孩误入歧途，责任在家长与教师。He hit the nail on the head when he said that the boy's going astray was the fault of his parents and teachers. / 他把我们的毛病讲得～。He put his finger on our weak spot.

一枕黄粱 yī zhěn huángliáng Golden Millet Dream—a brief dream or delusion of grandeur

一阵 yīzhèn (also 一阵子 yīzhènzi) ① a burst; a fit; a

peal: ～掌声 a burst of applause / ～咳嗽 a fit (or spasm) of coughing / 一阵阵笑声 peals of laughter / ～狂风 a violent gust of wind; a blast (of wind) / ～枪声 a burst of gunfire / 脸上红～、白～ one's face turning now red, now pale ② a period of time; a spell: 这～尽下雨。We've had a spell of rainy weather recently. / 她病了好一～了。She has been ill for quite a long time.

一之谓甚 yī zhī wèi shèn　even once is too much: ～，其可再乎! Even once is too much, how can it be permitted again?

一知半解 yīzhī-bànjiě　have a smattering of knowledge; have scanty (or half-baked) knowledge: 我对于国际事务只是～。I have only a scanty knowledge of world affairs.

一直 yīzhí　adv. ① straight: ～走 go straight ahead; keep straight on / ～往西走 go straight towards the west / 从窗口～望出去 look straight ahead out of the window ② continuously; all along; always; all the way: 雪～下了两天两夜。It snowed for two days and nights on end. / 我们～配合得很好。We have cooperated very well all along. / 我～在等你。I've been waiting for you all the time. / 她～把我送到车站。She went with me all the way to the station. / 从年初起～到现在 from the beginning of the year right up to now; ever since the beginning of the year

一纸空文 yī zhǐ kōngwén　a mere scrap of paper: 协定如不执行，只是～。An agreement, if not implemented, is a mere scrap of paper.

一致 yīzhì　showing no difference; identical; unanimous; consistent: 观点～ hold identical views; be of the same view / 步调～ march in step; act in unison / 官兵～ unity between officers and men / ～行动 concerted action / 双方～认为 both sides agree (that...) / 通过大家的～努力 thanks to the concerted efforts of all / 取得完全～的意见 reach unanimity; reach a consensus / 提案～通过了。The resolution was adopted (or carried) unanimously. / 举国上下，～努力。The whole nation is working together with one mind. / 体例前后不～。The style is inconsistent.

一掷千金 yī zhì qiānjīn　stake a thousand pieces of gold on one throw—throw away money like dirt; spend money like water

一柱擎天 yī zhù qíngtiān　one pillar supporting the sky—shouldering the heavy responsibility of high office

一专多能 yī zhuān duō néng　expert in one thing and good at many

一准 yīzhǔn　inf. adv.　sure; surely; certainly: 他～来吗？Is he sure to come? / 今年的收成～比去年强。This year's harvest will surely top last year's.

一字儿 yīzìr　in a row; in a line: 靶场上～站着十名射手。Ten marksmen stood in a row on the range.

一字褒贬 yī zì bāo-biǎn　one word clearly expressing praise or censure—a strict, deliberate choice of words

一字长蛇阵 yīzì chángshézhèn　single-line battle array: 摆开～ draw up in single-line formation; string out in a long line

一字千金 yī zì qiānjīn　each word worth a thousand pieces of gold—a highly finished literary product

一字师 yīzìshī　one's single-correction teacher

一字一板 yīzì-yībǎn　(speak) calmly and clearly: 他慢吞吞地从座位上站起来，开始～地讲话。He rose slowly from his chair and began to speak in a deliberate way.

一总 yīzǒng　① altogether; all told; in all: ～二十个人。There are twenty people altogether. / 我们～花了三十块钱。We spent thirty yuan in all. ② all: 那～是你的错儿。It was all your fault.

衣　yī　① clothing; clothes; garment: 衣服 yīfu / 内衣 nèiyī ② coating; covering: 糖衣 tángyī / 炮衣 pàoyī

③ Chin. med. afterbirth: 胞衣 bāoyī ——see also yì

衣胞 yībāo　Chin. med.　(human) afterbirth

衣钵 yībō　a Buddhist monk's mantle and alms bowl which he hands down to his favourite disciple; legacy: 继承～ inherit the mantle of sb.

衣不蔽体 yī bù bì tǐ　be dressed in rags; have nothing but rags on one's back: 过着～、食不果腹的生活 have rags on one's back and little in one's belly

衣橱 yīchú　wardrobe

衣兜 yīdōu　pocket

衣蛾 yī'é　casemaking clothes moth

衣分 yīfēn　agric.　ginning outturn; gin turnout

衣服 yīfu　clothing; clothes: 外边冷，多穿些～。It's cold outside. Put on more clothes.

衣钩 yīgōu　clothes hook

衣冠 yīguān　hat and clothes; dress: ～不整 be sloppily dressed

衣冠楚楚 yīguān chǔchǔ　be immaculately dressed

衣冠禽兽 yīguān qínshòu　a beast in human clothing; brute

衣冠冢 yīguānzhǒng　a tomb containing personal effects of the deceased, whose remains are either missing or buried elsewhere

衣柜 yīguì　wardrobe

衣架 yījià　① coat hanger; clothes-rack ② clothes tree; clothes stand

衣架饭囊 yījià-fànnáng　a clothes-horse and a food bag—a useless person; a good-for-nothing

衣襟 yījīn　the one or two pieces making up the front of a Chinese jacket

衣锦还乡 yī jǐn huánxiāng　(also 衣锦荣归 yī jǐn róngguī) go back to one's old home in silken robes (i.e. after acquiring wealth and honour)

衣料 yīliào　material for clothing; dress material: 这种～适合做工作服。This material is suitable for making overalls.

衣领 yīlǐng　collar

衣履 yīlǚ　clothes and shoes; clothes: ～不整 not properly dressed

衣帽架 yīmàojià　clothes tree; clothes stand

衣帽间 yīmàojiān　cloakroom

衣衾 yīqīn　burial clothes: ～棺椁 burial clothes and coffin

衣衫 yīshān　clothes: ～不整 not properly dressed

衣衫褴褛 yīshān lánlǚ　shabbily dressed; out at elbows; in rags

衣裳 yīshang　inf.　clothing; clothes

衣食住行 yī-shí-zhù-xíng　food, clothing, shelter and transportation—basic necessities of life

衣食足而知荣辱 yī-shí zú ér zhī róng-rǔ　when food and clothing are enough, men have a sense of honour and shame

衣饰 yīshì　dress and personal adornment; dress: ～华丽 be gorgeously dressed

衣物 yīwù　clothing and other articles of daily use

衣箱 yīxiāng　trunk; suitcase

衣鱼 yīyú　silverfish; fish moth; bookworm

衣装 yīzhuāng　① dress; attire ② clothes and luggage: 整治～ pack (for a journey)

衣着 yīzhuó　clothing, headgear and footwear: ～整洁 be neatly dressed

伊[1]　yī　① part. formal (used before a word or an expression): ～谁之力? To whom should the credit go? / 其效～何?What was the result of it all? ② (Yī) a surname

伊[2]　yī　formal　he or she

伊甸园 yīdiànyuán　Christianity　the Garden of Eden;

paradise

伊克度 yīkèdù *pharm.* ichthyol; ichthammol

伊拉克 Yīlākè Iraq

伊拉克人 Yīlākèrén Iraqi

伊朗 Yīlǎng Iran

伊朗人 Yīlǎngrén Iranian

伊人 yīrén *formal* that person (referring esp. to a woman)

伊始 yīshǐ beginning: 就职～ upon assuming office

伊斯兰教 Yīsīlánjiào Islam; Islamism: ～国家 Islamic country

伊斯兰教历 Yīsīlánjiàolì the Moslem Calendar

伊斯兰教徒 Yīsīlánjiàotú Moslem

伊蚊 yīwén yellow-fever mosquito

伊于胡底 yī yú hú dǐ where will it all end: 长此以往, 不知～。If things go on like this, I wonder where it will all end (or what will happen).

医 (醫、毉) yī ① doctor (of medicine): 边远农村缺～少药。Remote rural areas are short of doctors and medicine. ② medical science; medical service; medicine: 她是学～的。She studies medicine. / ～用温度计 clinical thermometer / 送～送药到山寨 take medicine and medical service to mountain villages ③ cure; treat: 给牧民～病 give medical treatment to herdsmen / 把他的病～好 cure him of his illness

医道 yīdào art of healing; medical knowledge; physician's skill: ～高明 be a highly skilled doctor

医德 yīdé medical ethics: ～高尚 be an ethical doctor

医护 yīhù doctors and nurses

医经 yījīng *Chin. med.* ancient Chinese medical classics

医科 yīkē medical courses in general; medicine: ～大学 medical university

医理 yīlǐ principles of medical science; medical knowledge: 精通～ have a profound knowledge of medicine

医疗 yīliáo medical treatment: ～卫生工作 medical and health work / ～机构 medical establishment (or institution) / ～器械 medical apparatus and instruments / ～事故 unskilful and faulty medical or surgical treatment; malpractice

医疗队 yīliáoduì medical team

医疗辐射学 yīliáo fúshèxué atomic (or radiological) medicine

医疗体育 yīliáo tǐyù medico-athletics

医疗站 yīliáozhàn medical station; health centre

医生 yīshēng doctor; medical man: 内科～ physician / 外科～ surgeon / 实习～ intern / 主治～ doctor in charge / 住院～ resident doctor

医师 yīshī (qualified) doctor

医士 yīshì practitioner with secondary medical school education

医书 yīshū medical book

医术 yīshù medical skill; art of healing: ～高超 have superb medical skill

医务 yīwù medical matters: ～工作者 medical worker / ～人员 medical personnel (or staff, workers); public health worker

医务所 yīwùsuǒ clinic

医学 yīxué medical science; medicine: ～文献 medical literature / ～遗产 medical heritage

医学科学院 yīxué kēxuéyuàn academy of medical sciences

医药 yīyào medicine: ～常识 general medical knowledge / ～费 medical expenses (or costs)

医院 yīyuàn hospital: 儿童～ children's hospital / 综合性～ general hospital

医治 yīzhì cure; treat; heal: ～无效 fail to respond to any medical treatment / ～战争创伤 heal war wounds

医嘱 yīzhǔ doctor's advice (or orders): 用量: 遵～ dosage: as directed by the physician

医助 yīzhù assistant doctor (in the army)

依 yī ① depend on: 依靠 yīkào ② comply with; listen to; yield to: 不能因为孩子小, 就什么都～着他。You shouldn't comply with every wish of his just because he is a child. / ～着你该怎么办? What do you suggest I should do? / 我怎么劝, 他还是不～。No matter what I said, he just wouldn't listen. / 你要是把这些资料弄丢了, 我可不～你。If you lose these data, I'll never forgive you. ③ according to; in the light of; judging by: ～我看 in my view; as I see it / ～当时情况来说 in the light of the situation at the time; as matters then stood / ～着我的性子, 非揍他一顿不行。If I had had my way, I would have given him a sound beating.

依傍 yībàng ① depend on; rely on: 互相～ rely on each other / 无可～ without anyone to rely on ② imitate; model oneself on: ～前人 model oneself on one's predecessors

依此类推 yī cǐ lèituī the rest may be inferred; and so on and so forth

依次 yīcì in proper order; successively: 他们～入座。They take their seats in proper order. / ～递补 fill vacancies in order of precedence / ～说明下列问题 illustrate the following points in their given order

依从 yīcóng comply with; yield to: 她坚持要单独去, 我只好～她了。Since she insisted on going alone, I had to comply.

依存 yīcún depend on sb. or sth. for existence: 相互～ be interdependent

依法 yīfǎ according to law; in conformity with legal provisions; in accordance with the law: ～惩办 punish according to law; deal with in accordance with the law; bring to justice / ～办案 handle cases in conformity with legal provisions

依附 yīfù depend on; attach oneself to; become an appendage to: ～权贵 attach oneself to bigwigs / 有些小国往往～大国。Some small countries tend to attach themselves to big powers.

依归 yīguī ① what one turns to for guidance or support: 以人民的意志为～ take the will of the people as a guide ② same as 皈依 guīyī

依旧 yījiù as before; still: 书房的陈设～未变。The study is furnished as it was before. / 他～是那个老样子。He still looks his old self. / 山河～。The landscape remains unchanged.

依据 yījù ① according to; in the light of; on the basis of; judging by: ～上述意见 in accordance with the above views / ～马列主义的理论 on the basis of Marxist-Leninist theory ② basis; foundation: 有～的 well-founded / 毫无～ utterly baseless (or groundless) / 提供科学～ provide scientific basis for sth. / 这些遗址是我们研究殷代文化的重要～。These sites form an important basis for our study of the culture of the Yin Dynasty. / 当时我们没有什么蓝图可以作～。We didn't have any blueprints to go by at that time.

依靠 yīkào ① rely on; depend on: ～自己的力量 depend on one's own strength / 垄断资本家～战争发财。The monopolists look to war for profits. or Monopoly capital battens on war. ② something to fall back on; support; backing: 寻找～ seek support / 生活有～ have one's livelihood assured

依赖 yīlài rely on; be dependent on: ～别人 be dependent on others / 这个国家的石油完全～进口。This country relies on imports for all its oil supplies. / 工业和农业是互相～, 互相支援的。Industry and agriculture depend on and support each other. / ～思想 the de-

pendent mentality / ～性 dependence

依恋 yīliàn　be reluctant to leave; feel regret at parting from

依凭 yīpíng　rely on; depend on

依然 yīrán　still; as before: ～有效 still hold good; remain valid / 风景～。The landscape is just the same as before.

依然故我 yīrán gù wǒ　I'm still my same old self; I'm just the same as before

依然如故 yīrán rúgù　remain as before; remain the same

依山傍水 yīshān-bàngshuǐ　at the foot of a hill and beside a stream

依实 yīshí　① comply with; yield to: 老太太见他说得有理, 就～了。The old lady thought what he said was reasonable and so complied. ② according to the facts; as things really are: 要～说, 不要说谎。Tell the truth, don't tell lies.

依恃 yīshì　same as 依仗 yīzhàng

依顺 yīshùn　be obedient

依随 yīsuí　agree to; yield to; comply with: 孩子说什么她都～。She agrees to whatever her child says.

依托 yītuō　① rely on; depend on ② support; prop; backing: 经济特区的建设没有国内其他地区作～是不行的。The construction of special economic zones would have been impossible without the backing of the rest of the country.

依偎 yīwēi　snuggle up to; lean close to

依违 yī-wéi　formal equivocal; undecided: ～两可 be equivocal; be ambiguous / ～不决 be undecided; shilly-shally

依稀 yīxī　vaguely; dimly: ～记得 vaguely remember / ～可见 faintly (or dimly) visible

依循 yīxún　follow; abide by

依样画葫芦 yī yàng huà húlu　draw a gourd according to the model—copy mechanically

依依 yīyī　① liter. luxuriant: 杨柳～。The willows are fresh and green (or are spreading their shade). ② reluctant to part: 在此～惜别的时刻 at this moment when we reluctantly bid farewell to each other

依依不舍 yīyī bù shě　be reluctant to part; cannot bear to part: 出了门, 他又回过头去看了看, 心上～的, 不忍离开他的母校。Once out of the gate he looked back, reluctant to leave his old school.

依允 yīyǔn　assent; consent: 点头～ nod assent

依仗 yīzhàng　count on; rely on: ～权势 rely on one's power and position; count on one's powerful connections

依照 yīzhào　according to; in accordance with; in the light of: ～他的指示 in accordance with his instructions / ～情况而定 decide as circumstances require / ～法律规定的条件 under conditions prescribed by law

咿（吚） yī　see below

咿唔 yīwú　onom. the sound of reading aloud

咿呀 yīyā　① onom. squeak; creak: ～的桨声 the squeak of oars in oarlocks / 咿咿呀呀的提琴声 squeaky notes of a violin ② prattle; babble

铱 yī　chem. iridium (Ir)

铱金笔 yījīnbǐ　iridium-point pen

猗 yī　formal ① part. (used like 啊 a): 河水清且涟～。The clear river ripples on. ② interj. (expressing approval): ～欤盛哉! Magnificent! or Superb!

揖 yī　make a bow with hands clasped

揖别 yībié　formal make a bow and say good-bye

揖让 yīràng　formal (of host and guest) bow and

make way for each other

壹（弌） yī　one (used as the numeral 一 on cheques, banknotes, etc. to avoid mistakes or alterations)

漪 yī　formal ripples: 清～ clear ripples

噫 yī　interj. arch. (expressing grief or regret) alas: ～, 艳冶之貌, 则代有之矣; 洁朗之操, 则人鲜闻乎。(皇甫枚) Alas! Every age has its captivating women, but one rarely hears of one who is truly pure and upright.

繄嘻 yīxī　same as 噫 yī

繄 yī　formal ① only; alone ② be tantamount to

黟 Yī　(also 黟县 Yīxiàn) Yi County; Yixian (in Anhui Province)

yí

匜 yí　archaeol. a gourd-shaped ladle (used for washing one's hands and face)

仪¹（儀） yí　① appearance; bearing: 仪表¹ yíbiǎo / 威仪 wēiyí ② ceremony; rite: 司仪 sīyí ③ present; gift: 贺～ present for wedding, birthday, etc.

仪²（儀） yí　apparatus; instrument: 仪器 yíqì / 地震仪 dìzhènyí

仪表¹ yíbiǎo　appearance; bearing: ～大方 poised and graceful

仪表² yíbiǎo　meter: ～板 instrument panel; dashboard / ～厂 instrument and meter plant

仪表堂堂 yíbiǎo tángtáng　dignified in appearance; impressive-looking

仪节 yíjié　etiquette; protocol

仪器 yíqì　instrument; apparatus: 精密～ precision instrument / 自记～ recording instrument / ～厂 instrument plant / ～制造工业 instrument-making industry

仪容 yíróng　looks; appearance: ～俊秀, 举止大方 pretty and poised

仪式 yíshì　ceremony; rite; function: 协定签字～ a ceremony for signing an agreement / 宗教～ religious rites / 奠基～ foundation stone laying ceremony / 举行了庄严而隆重的～。A solemn and grand ceremony was held.

仪态 yítài　formal bearing; deportment

仪态万方 yítài wànfāng　(of a beauty) appear in all her glory

仪仗 yízhàng　① insignia carried before the emperor ② flags, weapons, etc. carried by a guard of honour

仪仗队 yízhàngduì　guard of honour; honour guard: 陆海空三军～ a guard of honour of the three services / 检阅～ review the guard of honour

圯 yí　formal bridge: ～上 on the bridge

夷¹ yí　formal ① smooth; safe: 化险为夷 huàxiǎn wéi yí ② raze: ～为平地 level to the ground; raze ③ exterminate; wipe out: ～族 extermination of an entire family (a punishment in ancient times)

夷² yí　① (Yí) the name for ancient tribes in the east ② old foreign country; foreigner

沂 Yí (also 沂河 Yíhé) the Yihe River (a river rising in Shandong and flowing through northern Jiangsu into the Yellow Sea)

诒 yí same as 贻 yí

宜 yí ① suitable; appropriate; fitting: 老幼咸～ suitable (or good) for both young and old ② (usu. used in the negative) should; ought to: 对孩子不～要求过高。You shouldn't ask too much of a child. / 讲演～短不～长。A short speech is preferable to a long one.

宜人 yírén pleasant; delightful: 气候～ pleasant (or delightful) weather / 景物～ attractive (or charming) scenery

宜兴壶 yíxīnghú Yixing teapot (a famous earthen teapot made in Yixing, a town in Jiangsu Province)

宜于 yíyú be suitable for: 这种土壤～种西瓜。This kind of soil is good for growing watermelons.

怡 yí formal happy; joyful; cheerful: 心旷神怡 xīnkuàng-shényí

怡和 yíhé formal affable; genial

怡乐 yílè cheerful; happy

怡情悦性 yíqíng-yuèxìng cheer the heart and compose the mind

怡然 yírán happy and contented

怡然自得 yírán zìdé be happy and pleased with oneself; feel a glow of happiness: 听着风动树梢, 听着小鸟欢噪, 他～, 觉得很不愿离开这种景致。Listening to the breeze in the branches and the merry chirping of birds, he was filled with content and felt reluctant to tear himself away from such a scene. / 热带小鱼在绿茵茵的水藻中～地游来游去。Small tropical fish were swimming placidly to and fro in the green water-weed.

怡神 yíshén formal soothe the spirit

怡神养性 yíshén-yǎngxìng soothe one's spirit and nourish one's nature

怡悦 yíyuè happy; joyous

迤(迱) yí see 逶迤 wēiyí ——see also yǐ

饴 yí maltose; malt sugar

饴糖 yítáng maltose; malt sugar

迻 yí same as 移 yí

迻录 yílù formal copy out; transcribe

迻译 yíyì formal translate

贻 yí formal ① make a gift of sth.; present ② bequeath; leave behind; hand down

贻贝 yíbèi zool. mussel

贻臭万年 yí chòu wànnián same as 遗臭万年 yí chòu wànnián

贻害 yíhài leave a legacy of trouble

贻害无穷 yíhài wúqióng entail untold troubles; involve endless trouble

贻患 yíhuàn leave a legacy of trouble

贻人口实 yí rén kǒushí provide one's critics with a handle; give occasion for talk

贻误 yíwù affect adversely; bungle: ～工作 affect the work adversely / ～战机 bungle the chance of winning a battle; forfeit a chance for combat / ～青年 mislead young people

贻笑大方 yíxiào dàfāng make a laughingstock of oneself before experts; incur the ridicule of experts

贻训 yíxùn teachings of the deceased

薞 yí formal clear the fields of weeds; weed

——see also tí

咦 yí interj. (expressing surprise) well; why: ～, 你怎么又来了? Why, you're here again! / ～, 这是怎么回事? Hey, what's all this about?

姨 yí ① mother's sister; maternal aunt; aunt ② wife's sister; sister-in-law: 小姨子 xiǎoyízi

姨儿 yír inf. mother's sister; maternal aunt; aunt: 三～ mother's third sister

姨表 yíbiǎo the relationship between the children of sisters (or maternal cousins); cousinship: ～兄弟 male maternal cousins / ～姐妹 female maternal cousins

姨夫 yífu (also 姨父 yífu) the husband of mother's sister (or one's maternal aunt); uncle

姨姐 yíjiě elder sister of one's wife; sister-in-law

姨姥姥 yílǎolao sister of one's maternal grandmother; great-aunt

姨妈 yímā inf. (married) maternal aunt; aunt

姨妹 yímèi younger sister of one's wife; sister-in-law

姨母 yímǔ (married) maternal aunt; aunt

姨奶奶 yínǎinai ① sister of one's paternal grandmother; great-aunt ② inf. concubine

姨娘 yíniáng ① old a term of address for father's concubine ② dial. (married) maternal aunt; aunt

姨婆 yípó same as 姨姥姥 yílǎolao

姨太太 yítàitai inf. concubine

姨丈 yízhàng the husband of mother's sister (or one's maternal aunt); uncle

胰 yí physiol. pancreas

胰蛋白酶 yídànbáiméi biochem. trypsin

胰岛 yídǎo physiol. pancreas islet

胰岛素 yídǎosù med. insulin: 完全人工合成结晶牛～ total synthetic crystalline bovine insulin

胰淀粉酶 yídiànfěnméi biochem. amylopsin

胰酶 yíméi med. pancreatin

胰腺 yíxiàn physiol. pancreas

胰腺炎 yíxiànyán pancreatitis

胰液 yíyè physiol. pancreatic juice

胰皂 yízào dial. soap

胰脂酶 yízhīméi biochem. pancreatic lipase; steapsin

胰子 yízi ① inf. pancreas (of pigs, sheep, etc.) ② dial. soap

痍 yí formal wound; trauma: 疮痍 chuāngyí

移 yí ① move; remove; shift: 把桌子～到那边去 move the table over there / ～沙造田 create farmland by removing sand drifts ② change; alter: 献身革命志不～ dedicate oneself to the revolution with unshakable will

移调 yídiào mus. transposition: ～乐器 transposing instrument

移动 yídòng move; shift: 冷气团正向南～。A cold air mass is moving southward. / 把靶位向左～两米。Shift the target two metres to the left.

移动电话 yídòng diànhuà cellular telephone; mobile phone

移防 yífáng be shifted elsewhere for garrison duty

移风易俗 yífēng-yìsú change prevailing habits and customs; transform social traditions; reform the ways and manners of the people

移晷 yíguǐ formal the sun's shadow moves—time passes: 伏案攻读, ～忘倦。I sat at the table reading, and hours passed without fatigue.

移行 yíháng (in English usage) divide a word with a hyphen at the end of a line

移花接木 yíhuā-jiēmù graft one twig on another—

stealthily substitute one thing for another

移交 yíjiāo ① turn over; transfer; deliver into sb.'s custody: 那批仪器已经～给研究所了。Those instruments have been turned over to the research institute. ② hand over one's job to a successor: 他临走前把工作～给我了。Before he left he handed over his job to me.

移解 yíjiè transfer (a prisoner) from one place to another under escort

移居 yíjū move one's residence; migrate: ～国外 emigrate to a foreign country / ～我国 immigrate into our country / 从外地～北京的人很多。Many people have moved to Beijing from other parts of the country.

移苗 yímiáo transplant seedlings

移民 yímín ① migrate; emigrate or immigrate ② emigrant or immigrant

移民点 yímíndiǎn settlement

移民法 yímínfǎ immigration laws

移山倒海 yíshān-dǎohǎi move mountains and drain seas—exercise magic powers; transform nature: 用～之力 make superhuman efforts

移时 yíshí *formal* after a short while

移天易日 yítiān-yìrì (also 移天换日 yítiān-huànrì) move the sky and change the sun—perpetrate a gigantic fraud

移徙 yíxǐ move; migrate: 牧民随牲畜～。Herdsmen move about with their herds.

移项 yíxiàng *math.* transposition

移译 yíyì same as 迻译 yíyì

移易 yíyì *formal* change; alter; transform

移用 yíyòng divert (materials, funds, etc.) from one use to another

移玉 yíyù *formal pol.* may I request your company at (some place)

移栽 yízāi transplant

移植 yízhí ① transplant: ～秧苗 transplant seedlings / 近年来京剧从各种地方戏曲～了不少优秀的剧目。In recent years many good local operas have been adapted as Beijing operas. ② *med.* transplanting; grafting

移樽就教 yízūn jiùjiào take one's wine cup and go to sb.'s table to ask his advice—go to sb. for advice

蛇
yí see 委蛇 wēiyí ——see also shé

遗
yí ① lose: 遗失 yíshī ② something lost: 路不拾遗 lù bù shíyí ③ omit: 遗忘 yíwàng / 补遗 bǔyí ④ leave behind; keep back; not give: 遗憾 yíhàn ⑤ leave behind at one's death; bequeath; hand down: 遗骨 yígǔ / 遗作 yízuò ⑥ involuntary discharge of urine, etc.: 梦遗 mèngyí ——see also wèi

遗笔 yíbǐ writings left behind by the deceased

遗产 yíchǎn legacy; inheritance; heritage: 留下(继承)～ bequeath (inherit) a legacy / 历史～ a legacy of history / 文化～ cultural heritage

遗产承受人 yíchǎn chéngshòurén legatee

遗产税 yíchǎnshuì inheritance tax; succession duty

遗臭万年 yíchòu wànnián leave a name that will stink to eternity; go down in history as a byword for infamy

遗传 yíchuán *biol.* heredity; inheritance: 这种病会～。The disease is hereditary. / ～特征 hereditary feature; heredity

遗传病 yíchuánbìng hereditary disease

遗传工程 yíchuán gōngchéng *biol.* genetic engineering

遗传基因 yíchuán jīyīn genetic genes

遗传密码 yíchuán mìmǎ genetic code

遗传信息 yíchuán xìnxī hereditary (*or* genetic) information

遗传学 yíchuánxué genetics

遗传学家 yíchuánxuéjiā geneticist

遗传因子 yíchuán yīnzǐ genetic factor

遗存 yícún ① be left over; be handed down: 这些石刻～至今已千余年。These stone inscriptions have been in existence for over a thousand years. ② remnants; remains: 恐龙的化石～ the fossil remains of a dinosaur

遗大投艰 yídà-tóujiān entrust sb. with a heavy task

遗毒 yídú evil legacy; harmful tradition; pernicious influence

遗范 yífàn the example set by the deceased: ～犹存 a shining example to posterity

遗风 yífēng customs which have been handed down: 太白～ the ways of Taibai the Drinking Immortal (a common sign in wineshops)

遗腹子 yífùzǐ a posthumous child

遗稿 yígǎo a manuscript left unpublished by the author at his death; a posthumous manuscript

遗孤 yígū orphan

遗骨 yígǔ remains (of the dead): 烈士～ the remains of the martyrs / 猿人～化石 the fossil remains of an apeman

遗骸 yíhái remains (of the dead): 烈士～ the remains of the martyrs

遗害 yíhài leave a legacy of trouble: ～后人 bring calamity upon posterity

遗憾 yíhàn regret; pity: 对此表示～ express regret over the matter / 一点不感到～ have no regrets / 十分～地指出 point out with great (*or* deep) regret / 非常～,我不能接受你的邀请。I am very sorry I will not be able to accept your invitation. / 今晚的音乐会你不能来,实在～。It's really a pity that you can't come to the concert this evening.

遗痕 yíhén marks; traces; vestiges

遗恨 yíhèn eternal regret

遗患 yíhuàn leave a legacy of trouble: 养虎遗患 yǎnghǔ yíhuàn / 养痈遗患 yǎng yōng yíhuàn

遗祸 yíhuò leave a legacy of trouble

遗迹 yíjì historical remains; traces; vestiges: 古代村落的～ the remains of ancient villages / 原始人的～ the traces of primitive man / 封建～ the vestiges of feudalism

遗教 yíjiào teachings of the deceased

遗精 yíjīng *med.* (seminal) emission

遗老 yílǎo ① a surviving adherent of a former dynasty; an old fogy; an old diehard ② *formal* old people who have witnessed big social changes

遗老遗少 yílǎo-yíshào old fogies and young diehards; diehards old and young

遗留 yíliú leave over; hand down: ～的痕迹 surviving traces / 历史上～下来的边界问题 boundary questions left over by history / 帝国主义统治～下来的问题 a legacy of imperialist rule / 草案中仍然～几个问题。There are still a few points to clear up in the draft.

遗漏 yílòu omit; leave out: 重要～ an important omission / 名单上有～。There are some names missing from the list. / 她把你的话全记下来了,没有一点～。She took down everything you said without leaving out anything.

遗民 yímín ① adherents of a former dynasty ② survivors of a great upheaval

遗命 yímìng last will; final charge

遗墨 yímò letters, manuscripts, scrolls of painting or calligraphy, etc. left behind by the deceased

遗尿 yíniào *med.* enuresis; bed-wetting

遗篇 yípiān writings left behind by the deceased

遗弃 yíqì ① abandon; forsake; desert; walk out on: ～妻儿 forsake one's wife and children ② leave behind; cast away; abandon: 敌军～大批辎重。The enemy abandoned (*or* left behind) large quantities of supplies.

遗缺 yíquē vacancy (caused by sb.'s death, resignation, transfer, etc.); a vacated post

遗容 yíróng ① the looks of the deceased: ～安详, 就像在熟睡中。The deceased looked serene and peaceful, as if in a deep sleep. / 瞻仰～ pay one's respects to the remains of sb. ② a portrait of the deceased

遗少 yíshào a young man with the mentality of an old fogy; a young diehard

遗失 yíshī lose: 他的借书证～了。He has lost his library card. / ～声明 lost property notice / ～招领 lost and found

遗矢 yíshǐ formal empty one's bowels; defecate

遗世独立 yíshì dúlì leave the world of men; be freed from this world: 浩浩乎如冯虚御风, 而不知其所止; 飘飘乎如～, 羽化而登仙。(苏轼) Now we seemed to be borne aloft by the wind, not knowing where to stop; now we seemed to float away and, freed from this world, to take wing and become immortal.

遗事 yíshì ① incidents of past ages ② deeds of those now dead

遗书 yíshū ① (usu. used in book titles) surviving works; posthumous works; collected writings published after the author's death: 《船山～》Collected Writings of Wang Chuanshan ② a letter or note left by one immediately before death or suicide ③ formal lost books

遗属 yíshǔ members of the deceased's family; family dependants of the deceased: 烈士～ family dependants of the martyr

遗孀 yíshuāng widow; relict

遗俗 yísú same as 遗风 yífēng

遗体 yítǐ remains (of the dead): 向～告别 pay one's last respects to the remains

遗蜕 yítuì formal remains (esp. of a Taoist priest)

遗忘 yíwàng forget: 他学过的知识, 很多都已经～了。He's forgotten much of what he learned. / 童年的生活, 至今尚未～。I still remember how I spent my childhood. / 一个早已～了的名字 a name long forgotten

遗忘症 yíwàngzhèng amnesia

遗闻 yíwén tradition; lore

遗物 yíwù ① things left behind by the deceased ② relic: 这把石斧是旧石器时代的～。This stone axe is a relic of the Old Stone Age.

遗像 yíxiàng a portrait of the deceased

遗训 yíxùn teachings of the deceased

遗言 yíyán words of the deceased; (a person's) last words

遗业 yíyè work left unfinished by one's predecessor or ancestor: 继承先人～ carry on where one's ancestor left off

遗愿 yíyuàn unfulfilled wish of the deceased; last wish; behest: 为实现革命先烈的～而努力奋斗 strive to carry out the behests of the revolutionary martyrs

遗赠 yízèng bequeath: ～物 legacy; bequest

遗诏 yízhào testamentary edict

遗照 yízhào a photograph of the deceased

遗址 yízhǐ site (where sth. was): 古城～ the site of an ancient city / 平型关战役～ the site of the Battle of Pingxingguan (Sept. 1937) / 半坡～ (新石器时代仰韶文化～, 在西安东郊半坡村) the Banpo Village site (a neolithic site of the Yangshao culture, at Banpo Village on the eastern outskirts of Xi'an)

遗志 yízhì unfulfilled wish; behest; work bequeathed by the deceased: 继承先烈～ carry out the behest of the martyrs; continue the work left by the martyrs

遗珠 yízhū a lost pearl—unrecognized talent

遗嘱 yízhǔ testament; will; dying words: 立～ make (or draw up) a will / 未立～ intestate; will-less / ～检验 probate / ～执行人 executor

遗著 yízhù posthumous work (of an author)

遗族 yízú the family of the deceased

遗作 yízuò posthumous work (of art or literature)

颐[1] yí formal chin or cheek: 支颐 zhīyí

颐[2] yí formal nourish; take good care of one's health: 颐养 yíyǎng

颐和园 Yíhéyuán the Summer Palace (in Beijing)

颐养 yíyǎng formal keep fit; take good care of oneself: ～天年 take good care of oneself so as to fulfil one's allotted life span

颐指气使 yízhǐ-qìshǐ order people about by gestures; be insufferably arrogant

疑 yí ① doubt; disbelieve; suspect: 深信不～ unquestioningly believe; not have the slightest doubt ② doubtful; uncertain: 疑点 yídiǎn / 疑义 yíyì

疑案 yí'àn a doubtful (or disputed) case; an open question; mystery

疑兵 yíbīng troops deployed to mislead the enemy; deceptive deployment (of soldiers)

疑病 yíbìng med. hypochondriasis

疑猜 yícāi harbour suspicions; be suspicious; have misgivings

疑点 yídiǎn a doubtful (or questionable) point; an uncertain (or unclear) point: 这个案件还有几个～。There are still a few questionable points in the case. / 听了他的解释, 我仍有不少～。After hearing his explanations, I was still not quite clear about a number of points.

疑窦 yídòu formal cause for suspicion; suspicion: 顿生～ suddenly feel suspicious / 启人～ arouse (or awaken, raise) sb.'s suspicion

疑惑 yíhuò feel uncertain; not be convinced: ～不解 feel puzzled; have doubts

疑惧 yíjù apprehensions; misgivings

疑虑 yílǜ misgivings; doubts: 消除心中的～ clear one's mind of doubt; free sb. from doubts and misgivings / 这件事在我们心中引起许多～。It raised many doubts in our minds. / ～重重 be laden with misgivings

疑难 yínán difficult; knotty: ～问题 a knotty problem / ～病症 difficult and complicated cases (of illness)

疑念 yíniàn suspicions; doubts

疑神疑鬼 yíshén-yíguǐ be terribly suspicious; be even afraid of one's own shadow

疑似 yísì doubtful: ～之间 doubtful / ～之词 ambiguous words

疑团 yítuán doubts and suspicions: 满腹～ be full of doubts and suspicions / ～顿释。The suspicions were cleared up at once.

疑问 yíwèn query; question; doubt: 毫无～ doubtless; without a doubt; without question / 有人对他是否胜任这项工作提出～。Some people question his ability to do the job.

疑问句 yíwènjù gram. interrogative sentence

疑心 yíxīn suspicion: 起～ become suspicious / 一看村里整个儿变了样, 我真～自己走错了路。Finding the village completely changed, I really began to wonder whether I had come to the right place.

疑心病 yíxīnbìng a suspicious frame of mind: 犯～ be oversuspicious (or paranoiac)

疑心生暗鬼 yíxīn shēng ànguǐ suspicions create fantastic fears

疑义 yíyì doubt; doubtful point: 毫无～ no doubt / 对这一点难道还有～吗?Can there be any doubt about it?

疑云 yíyún misgivings or suspicions clouding one's mind: ～消散。The misgivings were dispelled.

疑阵 yízhèn deceptive battle array to mislead the enemy; stratagem

嶷 yí (used as part of a place name): 九～ Mount

Jiuyi (in Hunan Province)

彝[1]（彝）　yí　*archaeol.* wine vessel: ～器 sacrificial vessel

彝[2]（彝）　Yí　the Yi nationality

彝族　Yízú　the Yi nationality, or the Yis, distributed over Yunnan, Sichuan, and Guizhou Provinces, and the Guangxi Zhuang Autonomous Region

yǐ

乙[1]　yǐ　① the second of the ten Heavenly Stems （天干）(see also 干支 gān-zhī) ② second: ～等 second class; Class B ③ (used for an unspecified person or thing): 某甲与某～ Mr. A and Mr. B / 甲方和～方 the first party and the second party / 甲队和～队 team A and team B

乙[2]　yǐ　*mus.* a note of the scale in *gongchepu* （工尺谱）, corresponding to 7 in numbered musical notation

乙[3]　yǐ　use a mark like 乙 to show where something is to be added

乙胺　yǐ'àn　*chem.* ethylamine; aminoethane
乙苯　yǐběn　*chem.* ethylbenzene; phenylethane
乙醇　yǐchún　*chem.* ethyl alcohol; ethanol; alcohol
乙肝　yǐgān　short for 乙型肝炎 yǐxíng gānyán
乙醚　yǐmí　*chem.* ether
乙脑　yǐnǎo　short for 流行性乙型脑炎 liúxíngxìng yǐxíng nǎoyán
乙醛　yǐquán　*chem.* acetaldehyde; ethanal
乙炔　yǐquē　*chem.* acetylene; ethyne: ～焊 acetylene welding
乙酸　yǐsuān　another name for 醋酸 cùsuān
乙烷　yǐwán　*chem.* ethane
乙烯　yǐxī　*chem.* ethylene
乙烯基　yǐxījī　*chem.* vinyl
乙酰　yǐxiān　*chem.* acetyl
乙酰胆碱　yǐxiāndǎnjiǎn　*biochem.* acetylcholine
乙酰基　yǐxiānjī　*chem.* the acetyl group
乙酰水杨酸　yǐxiānshuǐyángsuān　① *chem.* acetylsalicylic acid ② *pharm.* aspirin
乙酰唑胺　yǐxiānzuò'àn　*pharm.* acetazolamide; diamox
乙型超声波　yǐxíng chāoshēngbō　B-mode ultrasound (popularly called B超)
乙型肝炎　yǐxíng gānyán　*med.* hepatitis B
乙夜　yǐyè　the second watch (the second of the five two-hour periods into which the night was formerly divided, corresponding to around 10 p.m.)
乙种粒子　yǐzhǒng lìzǐ　*phys.* beta particle
乙种射线　yǐzhǒng shèxiàn　*phys.* beta ray

已　yǐ　① stop; cease; end: 争论不～ argue endlessly; be bogged down in endless argument ② *adv.* already: 问题～解决。The problem has already been solved. / 雨季～过。The rainy season is over. / 为时～晚。It's too late. / ～成定局 be a foregone conclusion ③ *formal* thereafter; afterwards: 已而 yǐ'ér ④ *formal* too: 已甚 yǐshèn

已而　yǐ'ér　*formal* ① then; afterwards: 突然雷电大作，～大雨倾盆。Suddenly it thundered and lightened, and then rain fell in torrents. ② that's all; simply that; no more
已故　yǐgù　deceased; late: ～地质学家李四光 the late geologist Li Siguang

已极　yǐjí　to the utmost; in the extreme: 狂妄～ extremely arrogant
已经　yǐjīng　*adv.* already: 天～黑了。It's already dark. / 这样～不错了。It's good enough as it is. / 这点前面～说过了。This has been dealt with above. / ～两点了。It's already two o'clock. / 我们～十年不见了。It's ten years since we last saw each other.
已决犯　yǐjuéfàn　*leg.* convicted prisoner; convict
已然　yǐrán　be already so; have already become a fact: 与其补救于～，不如防患于未然。To forestall is better than to amend. *or* Prevention is better than cure.
已甚　yǐshèn　*formal* excessively: 病之～ be seriously ill
已往　yǐwǎng　before; previously; in the past
已知数　yǐzhīshù　*math.* known number

以[1]　yǐ　① *prep.* with; by means of: ～诚相待 treat sb. with all sincerity / ～我之长，攻敌之短 utilize our strong points to attack the enemy's weak points / 赠～鲜花 present sb. with a bouquet / 喻之～理 reason with sb.; try to make sb. see reason ② *prep.* according to: ～时启闭 open and close according to schedule / ～此类推 on the analogy of this / ～到达先后为序 in order of arrival ③ *prep.* because of: 不～失败自馁，不～成功自满 not lose heart because of failure nor feel conceited because of success / 何～知之? How do you know? ④ *conj.* in order to; so as to: ～示区别 so as to distinguish this from other cases / ～应急需 in order to answer an urgent need ⑤ *prep. formal* at (a certain time); on (a fixed date): 余～三月一日返。I returned on March the first. ⑥ *conj. formal* and; as well as: 淅沥～潇飒 raindrops pattering and wind rustling / 城高～厚。The city wall is high and thick.

以[2]　yǐ　(used before certain localizers to form compound localizers): 以前 yǐqián / 以内 yǐnèi / 以上 yǐshàng
以暴易暴　yǐ bào yì bào　replace one tyranny by another
以备不虞　yǐ bèi bùyú　be prepared for any contingency
以便　yǐbiàn　*conj.* so that; in order to; so as to; with the aim of; for the purpose of: 集中兵力包围敌人，～聚而歼之 encircle the enemy with a concentrated force with the aim of annihilating him / 今晚作好准备，～明天一早动身 make preparations today for an early start tomorrow
以不变应万变　yǐ bùbiàn yìng wàn biàn　meet all changes by remaining unchanged—cope with a constantly changing situation by sticking to a fixed principle or policy
以词害意　yǐ cí hài yì　let the words interfere with the sense
以此为戒　yǐ cǐ wéi jiè　take this as a lesson; take warning from this
以次　yǐcì　① in proper order: 主人～给来宾斟酒。The host filled the guests' glasses in turn. ② the following: ～各章 the following chapters
以德报怨　yǐ dé bào yuàn　return good for evil; repay evil with good; requite ingratitude with kindness
以点带面　yǐ diǎn dài miàn　fan out from point to area; use the experience of selected units to promote work in the entire area
以毒攻毒　yǐ dú gōng dú　fight poison with poison; use poison as an antidote for poison
以讹传讹　yǐ é chuán é　incorrectly relay an erroneous message (so that it becomes increasingly distorted); spread an error or a falsehood: 我是亲眼看见的，让我去对他们说说，免得～。I am an eyewitness. Let me go and tell them so that they will not be wrongly informed.

以耳代目 yǐ ěr dài mù　rely upon hearsay instead of seeing for oneself

以防万一 yǐ fáng wànyī　be prepared for all contingencies; be ready for any eventuality: 也许不会下雨, 不过还是带把伞, ～. It may not rain, but you'd better take an umbrella just in case.

以丰补歉 yǐ fēng bǔ qiàn　store up in fat years to make up for lean ones; have high-yield areas help low-yield areas

以工代赈 yǐ gōng dài zhèn　provide work as a form of relief; give relief by providing labour

以攻为守 yǐ gōng wéi shǒu　use attack as a means of defence; attack in order to defend

以古非今 yǐ gǔ fēi jīn　disparage the present by extolling the past

以寡敌众 yǐ guǎ dí zhòng　pit few against many; fight against heavy odds

以观后效 yǐ guān hòu xiào　(lighten a punishment and) see how the offender behaves

以广招徕 yǐ guǎng zhāolái　so as to attract more customers; with a view to promoting sales

以后 yǐhòu　after; afterwards; later; hereafter: 全国解放～ after (or following) the liberation of the whole country / 从今(那)～ from now (then) on / 至于～怎么样, 我就不知道了。 I don't know what happened later on. / 会议今天开始, 大概一星期～结束。 The conference begins today and will probably close in a week's time. / 别着急, ～你会有机会去的。 Don't worry. You'll have a chance to go.

以及 yǐjí　*conj.*　as well as; along with; and: 党和国家领导人～各有关方面负责人 Party and government leaders as well as responsible cadres of departments concerned / 拖拉机、收割机、～各种小农具 tractors, harvesters and small farm implements of all kinds as well

以己度人 yǐ jǐ duó rén　judge others by oneself; measure others' corn with one's own bushel

以假乱真 yǐ jiǎ luàn zhēn　mix the false with the true; mix the spurious with the genuine

以解倒悬 yǐ jiě dàoxuán　so as to relieve sb.'s distress

以近 yǐjìn　*transportation*　up to: 济南～的火车票 train tickets up to Jinan

以儆效尤 yǐ jǐng xiàoyóu　to warn others against following a bad example; as a warning to others

以来 yǐlái　*part.*　since: 建国～ since the founding of the People's Republic / 长期～ for a long time past / 三年～ in the past three years / 自古～ ever since the ancient times

以泪洗面 yǐ lèi xǐ miàn　have a tearful face; wear a woebegone look

以蠡测海 yǐ lí cè hǎi　measure the sea with an oyster shell—make an appraisal in the light of limited knowledge

以礼相待 yǐ lǐ xiāngdài　treat sb. with due respect

以理服人 yǐ lǐ fú rén　convince by reasoning

以力服人 yǐ lì fú rén　force people to submit; dominate others by force

以邻为壑 yǐ lín wéi hè　use one's neighbour's field as a drain—shift one's troubles onto others

以卵投石 yǐ luǎn tóu shí　(also 以卵击石 yǐ luǎn jī shí) throw an egg against a rock—court defeat by fighting against overwhelming odds

以貌取人 yǐ mào qǔ rén　judge people solely by their appearance

以免 yǐmiǎn　*conj.*　in order to avoid; so as not to; lest: 仔细检查～出错 check carefully to avoid mistakes / 自行车要放在存车处, ～影响交通。 Bicycles should be left at parking lots so as not to block the traffic.

以沫相濡 yǐ mò xiāng rú　same as 相濡以沫 xiāng rú yǐ mò

以内 yǐnèi　within; less than: 本年度～ within this year / 营房～ within the barracks / 五十人～ less than fifty people

以偏概全 yǐ piān gài quán　take a part for the whole

以期 yǐqī　in the hope of: 这个问题必须反复讲, ～引起各方面的重视。 This question must be brought up time and again in the hope of attracting universal attention.

以其昏昏, 使人昭昭 yǐ qí hūnhūn, shǐ rén zhāozhāo　try to enlighten others while in darkness oneself: ～, 是不行的。 Those in darkness are in no position to enlighten others.

以其人之道, 还治其人之身 yǐ qírén zhī dào, huán zhì qírén zhī shēn　deal with a man as he deals with you; pay sb. back in his own coin

以前 yǐqián　before; formerly; previously: 解放～ before liberation / 十年～ ten years ago / 我～的同事 a former colleague of mine / ～各版 all the preceding (or previous) editions / 我～没看过这个戏 I've never seen this opera before. / ～他当过理发员。 He used to be a barber.

以强凌弱 yǐ qiáng líng ruò　oppress the weak by sheer strength

以求 yǐqiú　in the hope of; in an attempt to: ～一逞 in the hope of realizing one's ambition; in a bid for success / ～全胜 in an attempt to achieve complete victory

以屈求伸 yǐ qū qiú shēn　bend in order to straighten up—retreat in order to advance; make concessions to gain advantages

以权谋私 yǐ quán móu sī　seek personal gain by abusing one's position and authority; abuse power for personal gain

以色列 Yǐsèliè　Israel

以色列人 Yǐsèlièrén　Israeli; Israelite

以色列议会 Yǐsèliè yìhuì　Knesset

以上 yǐshàng　① more than; over; above: 五十人～ over (or more than) fifty people / 县和县～的人民代表大会 people's congresses at county level and above / 十岁～的孩子 children of ten and over / 半山～石级更陡。 From halfway up the mountain, the stone steps become even steeper. ② the above; the foregoing; the above-mentioned: ～各位同志会后请留下。 The above-mentioned comrades will please remain after the meeting. / ～是我的几点建议。 Those are a few of my suggestions. / 我完全同意～几位代表的发言。 I fully agree with the delegates who have already spoken.

以身试法 yǐ shēn shì fǎ　defy the law

以身相许 yǐ shēn xiāng xǔ　(of a girl) pledge to marry sb.

以身殉职 yǐ shēn xùnzhí　die at one's post: 他不幸～。 He died at his post, to our great sorrow.

以身作则 yǐ shēn zuò zé　set a good example with one's own conduct; set an example

以售其奸 yǐ shòu qí jiān　in order to carry out an evil plot; to achieve a treacherous purpose: 利用别人的无知～ take advantage of other people's ignorance to achieve one's treacherous purposes

以税代利 yǐ shuì dài lì　(of a state enterprise) replace profit delivery to the state by taxation; substitute taxation for profit delivery to the state

以太 yǐtài　*phys.*　ether

以汤沃雪 yǐ tāng wò xuě　melting snow with hot water—easily done

以汤止沸 yǐ tāng zhǐ fèi　trying to stop water from boiling by adding boiling water to it—an ineffective measure

以退为进 yǐ tuì wéi jìn　retreat in order to advance; make concessions in order to gain advantages

以外 yǐwài　beyond; outside; other than: 长城～ beyond

the Great Wall / 营房～ outside the barracks / 一百公里～ a hundred kilometres away from here / 汉族～的各兄弟民族代表 delegates of fraternal nationalities other than the Han nationality / 雾太大，五米～就看不见了。There was such a heavy fog that one could not see further than five metres. / 除了这间～，所有的屋子都打扫了。All the rooms have been cleaned except this one. / 除此～，还有一件事要麻烦你。There's another thing I have to trouble you about.

以往 yǐwǎng before; formerly; in the past: 今年的收成比～哪年都好。This year's harvest is better than any previous year's. / 这里～是一片荒野。This place used to be a vast expanse of wasteland.

以为 yǐwéi think; believe; consider: 我还～是她呢。I thought it was her. / 他～那样做比较好。He considers it better to do it that way. / 我们不要～自己不了解的东西，广大群众也不了解。We must not assume that things we ourselves cannot understand are not understood by the masses.

以…为… yǐ…wéi… take…as…; regard…as…: 以事实为根据，以法律为准绳 take the facts as a basis and the law as a criterion / 以大局为重 regard the interests of the whole as of prime importance / 以我为主 take ourselves (or our side, our way, etc.) as the dominant factor; keep the initiative in our own hands / 以姓氏笔划为序 in the order of the number of strokes in the surnames

以文会友 yǐ wén huì yǒu make friends through literary activities

以下 yǐxià ① below; under: 零度～ below zero; sub-zero / 三岁～儿童 children under three / 俘获敌师长～三千人。3,000 of the enemy, from their divisional commander down, were taken prisoner. / 我左腿膝盖～都麻木了。My left leg has gone numb from the knee down. / 宜昌～，江面逐渐变宽。Below Yichang the river gradually widens. ② the following; hereafter: ～是代表名单。The following is a list of the delegates. / ～就来谈谈具体办法。Now I'm coming to the concrete measures. / 外国公司、企业和其他经济组织或个人（～简称外国合营者）foreign companies, enterprises, and other economic organizations or individuals (hereafter referred to as "foreign joint venturers")

以销定产 yǐ xiāo dìng chǎn plan production according to sales

以小人之心，度君子之腹 yǐ xiǎorén zhī xīn, duó jūnzǐ zhī fù gauge the heart of a gentleman with one's own mean measure

以眼还眼，以牙还牙 yǐ yǎn huán yǎn, yǐ yá huán yá an eye for an eye and a tooth for a tooth

以一当十 yǐ yī dāng shí pit one against ten: 我们的战略是"～"，我们的战术是"以十当一"，这是我们制胜敌人的根本法则之一。(毛泽东) Our strategy is "pit one against ten" and our tactics are "pit ten against one"—this is one of our fundamental principles for gaining mastery over the enemy.

以逸待劳 yǐ yì dài láo wait at one's ease for an exhausted enemy

以远 yǐyuǎn transportation beyond: 只售济南～的车票。Only tickets for Jinan and beyond are available.

以远权 yǐyuǎnquán transportation the right to extend a flying route; the right to fly beyond designated points

以怨报德 yǐ yuàn bào dé return evil for good; repay good with evil; requite kindness with ingratitude; bite the hand that feeds one

以正视听 yǐ zhèng shì-tīng in order to ensure a correct understanding of the facts

以直报怨 yǐ zhí bào yuàn meet resentment with upright dealing

以至 yǐzhì ① conj. down to; up to: 团长、师长～军长

都到这个连队来帮助总结经验。Commanders of the regiment, the division and even the army came to this company to help sum up its experience. ② (also 以至于 yǐzhìyú) to such an extent as to…; so…that…: 他工作非常专心，～连饭都忘了吃了。He was so absorbed in his work that he even forgot his meals. / 形势发展得这样快，～很多人都感到惊奇。Things have been developing so fast that many people are amazed.

以致 yǐzhì conj. (usu. referring to bad results) so that; with the result that; consequently; as a result: 小王平时训练不刻苦，～射击考核没有及格。Xiao Wang didn't practise hard, so he failed the marksmanship test. / 有些人不认真学习，～思想落后于形势。Some people don't study hard, with the result that their thinking lags behind events.

以资 yǐzī as a means of: ～证明 in testimony thereof; this is to certify that / ～弥补 to make up the deficit; to make up a shortage / ～鼓励 as an encouragement / ～比较 for the sake of comparison

以子之矛，攻子之盾 yǐ zǐ zhī máo, gōng zǐ zhī dùn set a person's own spear against his own shield—refute sb. with his own argument

钇 yǐ chem. yttrium (Y)

矣 yǐ part. formal ① (used at the end of a sentence like 了 le): 悔之晚～。It's too late for regrets. ② (used in exclamatory sentences): 毒～哉! Diabolical! or How ruthless!

尾 yǐ ① hairs on a horse's tail ② spikelets on a cricket's tail ——see also wěi

苡 yǐ same as 薏苡 yìyǐ

苡米 yǐmǐ another name for 薏米 yìmǐ

苡仁 yǐrén another name for 薏米 yìmǐ

迤（迆） yǐ go (or extend) towards: 天安门～西是中山公园。To the west of Tian An Men is Zhongshan Park. ——see also yí

迤逦 yǐlǐ winding; tortuous; meandering: 队伍沿着山道～而行。The troops marched along the winding mountain path.

蚁（蟻、螘） yǐ ant: 雄蚁 xióngyǐ / 雌蚁 cíyǐ

蚁蚕 yǐcán same as 蚕蚁 cányǐ

蚁巢 yǐcháo ant nest

蚁封 yǐfēng ant hill

蚁后 yǐhòu queen (of an ant colony); gyne

蚁䴕 yǐliè wryneck (a bird)

蚁丘 yǐqiū ant hill

蚁醛 yǐquán another name for 甲醛 jiǎquán

蚁酸 yǐsuān another name for 甲酸 jiǎsuān

酏 yǐ see below

酏剂 yǐjì pharm. elixir

倚 yǐ ① lean on or against; rest on or against: ～栏远眺 lean on the parapet and gaze into the distance ② rely on; count on: ～势欺人 take advantage of one's position to bully people ③ formal biased; partial: 不偏不倚 bùpiān-bùyǐ

倚官仗势 yǐguān-zhàngshì rely on one's power and position; count on one's powerful connections

倚靠 yǐkào ① lean on or against; rest on or against ② same as 依靠 yīkào

倚赖 yǐlài same as 依赖 yīlài

倚老卖老 yǐ lǎo mài lǎo take advantage of one's seniority or old age (to ignore manners, regulations, etc.);

flaunt one's seniority

倚马可待 yǐ mǎ kě dài　can write at the side of a horse—can write very fast ——see also 倚马千言 yǐ mǎ qiānyán

倚马千言 yǐ mǎ qiānyán　dash off a thousand words at the side of a horse—write with great facility (a reference to Yuan Hu 袁虎 in the Jin Dynasty, who once dashed off a document using the side of his horse for a table)

倚音 yǐyīn　*mus.* appoggiatura

倚仗 yǐzhàng　rely on; count on: 〜权势 rely on one's power and position; count on one's powerful connections

倚重 yǐzhòng　rely heavily on sb.'s service

椅 yǐ　chair
椅背 yǐbèi　the back of a chair
椅披 yǐpī　a colourful silk chair cover
椅套 yǐtào　a slipcover for a chair
椅子 yǐzi　chair
椅子顶 yǐzidǐng　*acrob.* balancing on a pyramid of chairs

旖 yǐ　see below
旖旎 yǐnǐ　*liter.* charming; enchanting: 〜风光 an enchanting scene / 解舞腰肢娇又软，千般袅娜，万般〜，似垂柳晚风前。(王实甫《西厢记》) Her dancing waist, how soft and supple! A thousand graces and ten thousand charms she has, Like a drooping willow before the evening breeze.

yì

义 yì　*formal* bring under control; put in order: 〜安 at peace

弋 yì　*formal* shoot a retrievable arrow
弋获 yìhuò　*formal* ① shoot (birds) ② catch (criminals, etc.); capture
弋取 yìqǔ　*formal* catch; seize
弋阳腔 yìyángqiāng　(also 弋腔 yìqiāng) an opera style of the Ming Dynasty, which originated in Yiyang, Jiangxi Province, and spread to many other places, and which was noteworthy for its use of a chorus as well as of soloists

义¹(義) yì　① justice; righteousness: 见〜不为，无勇也。(《论语》) To see what is right and not do it is cowardice. ② righteous; equitable; just: 〜行 a righteous deed ③ human ties; relationship: 情义 qíngyì ④ adopted or adoptive: 〜子(女) adopted son (daughter) / 〜父(母) adoptive father (mother) ⑤ artificial; false: 〜发 false hair

义²(義) yì　meaning; significance: 字〜 the meaning of a word
义兵 yìbīng　a righteous army: 举〜 raise an army to fight a just war
义不容辞 yì bùróng cí　be duty-bound; have an unshirkable duty
义仓 yìcāng　(in former times) a public granary for storing relief grain
义齿 yìchǐ　false tooth; artificial tooth
义地 yìdì　(in former times) a free burial ground for the destitute
义方 yìfāng　*formal* the right way of conduct
义愤 yìfèn　righteous indignation; moral indignation: 激

于〜 be stirred by righteous indignation / 革命〜 revolutionary indignation
义愤填膺 yìfèn tián yīng　be filled with indignation
义和团运动 Yìhétuán Yùndòng　the Yihetuan Movement (an anti-imperialist armed struggle waged by north China peasants and handicraftsmen in 1900)
义举 yìjǔ　a magnanimous act undertaken for the public good; an undertaking in public interests
义捐 yìjuān　donations for public welfare: 〜门诊 free consultations
义理 yìlǐ　① reason and good sense ② argumentation (of a speech or essay)
义烈 yìliè　*formal* staunch and upright
义卖 yìmài　a sale of goods for charity or other worthy causes; (charity) bazaar
义旗 yìqí　the banner of an army fighting a just war; banner of righteousness: 举〜 raise the banner of righteousness; rise against injustice
义气 yìqi　code of brotherhood; personal loyalty: 讲〜 be loyal (to one's friends) / 〜深重 have a strong sense of obligation
义犬 yìquǎn　a faithful dog
义师 yìshī　an army fighting a just war; a righteous army: 兴〜 raise an army to fight for a just cause
义士 yìshì　a high-minded or chivalrous person; a person who upholds justice; a righteous man
义疏 yìshū　commentaries on classics: 《尔雅〜》 *Exegesis of the Literary Expositor*
义塾 yìshú　same as 义学 yìxué
义无反顾 yì wú fǎngù　honour permits no turning back; be duty-bound not to turn back
义务 yìwù　① duty; obligation: 子女对父母有赡养的〜。 Children have the duty to support their parents. / 公民的基本权利与〜 the fundamental rights and duties of citizens / 条约规定的〜 treaty obligations / 履行所承担的〜 carry out commitments ② volunteer; voluntary: 我是来尽〜的。 I've come to do voluntary service.
义务兵 yìwùbīng　compulsory serviceman
义务兵役制 yìwù bīngyìzhì　compulsory military service; conscription
义务教育 yìwù jiàoyù　compulsory education
义务劳动 yìwù láodòng　voluntary labour; volunteer labour
义项 yìxiàng　senses of a dictionary entry
义形于色 yì xíng yú sè　with righteous indignation written on one's face
义学 yìxué　(in former times) a private or community-run school charging no tuition; free school
义演 yìyǎn　benefit performance
义勇 yìyǒng　righteous and courageous
义勇军 yìyǒngjūn　army of volunteers; volunteers
义勇军进行曲 Yìyǒngjūn Jìnxíngqǔ　*March of the Volunteers* (the national anthem of the People's Republic of China)
义园 yìyuán　same as 义地 yìdì
义蕴 yìyùn　same as 意蕴 yìyùn
义战 yìzhàn　a just war: 《春秋》无〜。(《孟子》) *The Spring and Autumn Annals* acknowledges no just wars.
义诊 yìzhěn　(of a doctor) treat patients free
义正词严 yìzhèng-cíyán　speak out sternly from a sense of justice; speak with the force of justice
义肢 yìzhī　*med.* artificial limb
义冢 yìzhǒng　(in former times) a burial ground for the remains of unidentified persons

亿(億) yì　a hundred million
亿万 yìwàn　hundreds of millions; millions upon millions: 〜人民 hundreds of millions of people; the people in their hundreds of millions / 〜富翁 billionaire;

multimillionaire

亿万斯年 yìwàn sī nián (for) billions of years; (for) aeons; time without end; eternity

忆(憶)
yì recall; recollect; remember: 回忆 huíyì

忆苦 yìkǔ recall one's suffering in the old society: ～饭 a poor meal specially prepared to recall past suffering (of the working people) / ～会 a meeting to recall past suffering

忆苦思甜 yìkǔ-sītián recall the sorrows of the past and savour the joys of the present; tell of one's sufferings in the old society and one's happiness in the new; contrast past misery with present happiness

忆念 yìniàn cherish the memory of; think of: ～战友 think of one's old comrades-in-arms

忆昔抚今 yìxī-fǔjīn recall the past and compare it with the present; reflect on the past in the light of the present

忆想 yìxiǎng recall; recollect; call to mind: ～往事 recollect the past

艺(藝)
yì ① skill: 学艺 xuéyì ② art: 文艺 wényì

艺高人胆大 yì gāo rén dǎn dà boldness of execution stems from superb skill

艺妓 yìjì geisha (in Japan)

艺林 yìlín the world of art; art circles

艺龄 yìlíng length of sb.'s stage career: 他有三十多年～。 He's been on the stage for over thirty years.

艺名 yìmíng stage name (of an actor or actress)

艺能 yìnéng mastery of a skill or technique; technical ability; skill

艺人 yìrén ① actor or entertainer (in local drama, storytelling, acrobatics, etc.) ② artisan; handicraftsman

艺术 yìshù ① art: ～标准 artistic criterion / ～风格 artistic style / ～技巧 artistry; craftsmanship / ～形式 artistic form; forms of art / ～造诣 artistic attainments / 为～而～ art for art's sake ② skill; art; craft: 领导～ art of leadership ③ conforming to good taste: 这个房间布置得很～。 The room is tastefully furnished.

艺术家 yìshùjiā artist

艺术界 yìshùjiè art circles

艺术品 yìshùpǐn work of art

艺术体操 yìshù tǐcāo sports rhythmic gymnastics

艺术团 yìshùtuán art ensemble; art troupe

艺术性 yìshùxìng artistic quality; artistry

艺术指导 yìshù zhǐdǎo art director

艺坛 yìtán art circles: ～新秀 a new star in art circles

艺徒 yìtú dial. apprentice

艺文 yìwén ① books ② art and literature

艺文志 yìwénzhì descriptive accounts of books in dynastic histories

艺苑 yìyuàn the realm of art and literature; art and literary circles: ～奇葩 exquisite works of art

刈
yì mow; cut down: ～草 mow grass

刈草机 yìcǎojī mowing machine; mower

刈除 yìchú cut off; root out; eradicate: ～杂草 weeding

艾
yì ① same as 乂 yì ② punish: 惩艾 chéngyì ——see also ài

议(議)
yì ① opinion; view: 异议 yìyì / 提议 tíyì ② discuss; exchange views on; talk over: 我们对各种方案都～了～。 We exchanged views on each of the different proposals.

议案 yì'àn proposal; motion

议程 yìchéng agenda: 列入～ place on the agenda; include in the agenda / 会议有三项～。 There are three items on the agenda of the meeting.

议定 yìdìng decide through consultation; agree on

议定书 yìdìngshū protocol: 贸易～ trade protocol / 附加～ additional protocol / 任择～ optional protocol / 最后～ final protocol (or act)

议而不决 yì ér bù jué discuss sth. without reaching a decision; have a fruitless discussion

议购 yìgòu buy at negotiated prices

议和 yìhé negotiate peace; carry on peace negotiations

议会 yìhuì parliament; congress; legislative assembly: 召开(解散)～ convene (dissolve) parliament / ～党团 parliamentary groups / ～斗争 parliamentary struggle / ～法 parliamentary law / ～领袖 parliamentary leader (or chief); floor leader

议会制 yìhuìzhì parliamentarism

议会走廊 yìhuì zǒuláng lobby

议价 yìjià ① negotiate a price ② negotiated price

议决 yìjué resolve after deliberation; pass a resolution

议论 yìlùn comment; talk; discuss: 大发～ speak at great length / ～不休 carry on endless discussions / 大家都在～这件事。 Everybody is talking about the matter.

议论纷纷 yìlùn fēnfēn all sorts of comments; widespread comment: 人们对这件事～。 This is a subject of widespread comment.

议论文 yìlùnwén argumentation

议事 yìshì discuss official business: ～规则 rules of procedure; rules of debate / ～日程 agenda; order of the day

议题 yìtí item on the agenda; subject under discussion; topic for discussion

议席 yìxí seat in a legislative assembly

议销 yìxiāo sell at negotiated prices

议员 yìyuán member of a legislative assembly; assemblyman; (in Great Britain) Member of Parliament (MP); (in U. S.) Congressman or Congresswoman

议院 yìyuàn legislative assembly; parliament; congress

议长 yìzhǎng speaker (of a legislative body); president: 众议院～ Speaker of the (U. S.) House of Representatives

议政 yìzhèng discuss affairs of government

亦
yì adv. formal also; too: 反之～然 and the reverse is also true; and vice versa / ～工～农 be both worker and peasant

亦步亦趋 yìbù-yìqū ape sb. at every step; imitate sb.'s every move; blindly follow suit

亦即 yìjí that is; i.e.; namely; viz.

亦且 yìqiě formal moreover

亦庄亦谐 yìzhuāng-yìxié serious and comical at the same time; seriocomic

屹
yì formal towering like a mountain peak

屹立 yìlì stand towering like a giant; stand erect: 人民英雄纪念碑～在天安门广场上。 The Monument to the People's Heroes stands like a giant on Tiananmen Square.

屹然 yìrán towering; majestic: ～不动 stand firm and erect

衣
yì formal wear; clothe: ～布衣 wear cotton clothes / 解衣～人 doff one's own garments to clothe sb. else ——see also yī

异(異)
yì ① different: ～姓 a different surname ② strange; unusual; extraordinary: ～兆 a strange omen / 奇才～能 extraordinary talents and

abilities ③ surprise: 深以为～ be greatly surprised ④ other; another: 异日 yìrì ⑤ separate: 离异 líyì

异邦 yìbāng a foreign country: 漂泊～ lead a wandering life in a foreign country

异步 yìbù *phys.* asynchronous: ～发电机 asynchronous generator／～计算机 asynchronous computer

异才 yìcái exceptional talents

异彩 yìcǎi extraordinary (*or* radiant) splendour: 戏剧舞台大放～。New forms of traditional opera are blossoming in radiant splendour.

异常 yìcháng ① unusual; abnormal: ～现象 abnormal phenomena／神色～ not be one's usual self ② *adv.* extremely; exceedingly; particularly: ～危险 extremely dangerous／～丰富 exceedingly rich／～需要 particularly necessary

异词 yìcí dissenting words

异地 yìdì a place far away from home; a strange land

异读 yìdú variant pronunciation

异端 yìduān heterodoxy; heresy

异端邪说 yìduān-xiéshuō heresies; heretical beliefs; unorthodox opinions

异构化 yìgòuhuà *chem.* isomerization

异国 yìguó a foreign country (*or* land): ～情调 an exotic atmosphere

异乎寻常 yì hū xúncháng unusual; extraordinary: ～地冷 extraordinarily cold／～地热心 unusually enthusiastic／在最近的一个多月里，她～地快乐。For the past month *or* more she had been unusually happy.

异花传粉 yìhuā chuánfěn *bot.* cross pollination

异花受精 yìhuā shòujīng *bot.* allogamy; cross fertilization

异化 yìhuà ① *philos.* alienation ② *linguis.* dissimilation

异化作用 yìhuà zuòyòng *biol.* dissimilation

异己 yìjǐ dissident; alien: 排除～ discriminate against those who hold different views; get rid of dissidents

异教 yìjiào paganism; heathenism

异教徒 yìjiàotú pagan; heathen

异军突起 yìjūn tūqǐ a new force suddenly coming to the fore

异口同声 yìkǒu-tóngshēng with one voice; in unison: 大家～地称赞她献身教育事业的精神。Everybody spoke in praise of her devotion to the cause of education.／"没问题。"战士们～地回答。"We can do it," the men replied with one voice.／"好。"大家～说。"Agreed," was the unanimous reply.

异类 yìlèi ① *old* foreign peoples ② a different class or species (of plants or animals)

异曲同工 yìqǔ-tónggōng different tunes sung with equal skill—different approaches but equally satisfactory results

异人 yìrén ① *old* an extraordinary person (referring to a supernatural being or an immortal) ② another person

异日 yìrì *formal* ① some other day ② (in) former days

异兽 yìshòu strange animals; rare animals: 珍禽异兽 zhēnqín-yìshòu

异说 yìshuō ① dissenting views; different views ② absurd remarks

异体受精 yìtǐ shòujīng ① *zool.* cross-fertilization ② *bot.* allogamy; cross-fertilization

异体字 yìtǐzì a variant form of a Chinese character

异同 yì-tóng ① similarities and differences ② *formal* objection; dissent

异途同归 yì tú tóng guī same as 殊途同归 shū tú tóng guī

异外 yìwài unusual; exceptional: ～舒畅 feel unusually happy

异味 yìwèi ① a rare delicacy ② a peculiar smell

异物 yìwù ① foreign matter; a foreign body: 食管～ a foreign body in the esophagus ② *formal* a dead person; ghost: 化为～ give up the ghost; die ③ a rare object

异乡 yìxiāng a foreign land; a strange land

异香 yìxiāng an unusually sweet smell; a rare perfume: ～扑鼻。Strong whiffs of rare perfume assailed the nostrils.

异想天开 yì xiǎng tiān kāi indulge in the wildest fantasy; have a most fantastic idea: 休要～。Don't let your imagination run away with you.

异心 yìxīn infidelity; disloyalty

异形钢材 yìxíng gāngcái special-shaped steel

异形管 yìxíngguǎn *mech.* special pipe

异性 yìxìng ① the opposite sex ② different in nature: ～的电互相吸引。Unlike electric charges attract each other.

异烟肼 yìyānjīng *med.* isoniazid; rimifon

异言 yìyán *formal* dissenting words: 并无～ raise no objection

异样 yìyàng ① difference: 多年没见了，看不出他有什么～。We haven't seen each other for many years, but he doesn't look any different. ② unusual; peculiar: ～服装 peculiar dress／人们都用～的眼光打量他。Everyone sized him up with curious eyes.

异议 yìyì objection; dissent: 提出～ raise an objection; take exception to; challenge／独持～ be the only one to dissent／如果没有～, 提案就算通过了。If there are no objections, we shall consider the resolution adopted.

异域 yìyù ① a foreign country ② an alien land; a strange land

异源多倍体 yìyuánduōbèitǐ *biol.* allopolyploid

异重流 yìzhòngliú density current

异族 yìzú a different race or nation: ～通婚 mixed marriages

译（譯）

yì translate; interpret: ～成英语 translate into English／～成电码 coding／～成密码 enciphering

译本 yìběn translated version (of a book); translation: 《石头记》的英～ an English translation of *The Story of the Stone*

译笔 yìbǐ the quality or style of a translation: ～流畅。The translation reads smoothly.

译电 yìdiàn ① encode or encipher a telegram ② decode or decipher a telegram

译电员 yìdiànyuán decoder; code clerk; cryptographer

译电组 yìdiànzǔ code and cipher section

译稿 yìgǎo the manuscript of a translation

译介 yìjiè translate and write an introduction to (a book)

译码 yìmǎ decode; decipher

译码器 yìmǎqì decoder; decipherer

译名 yìmíng a translated term or name

译述 yìshù translate (*or* render) freely

译文 yìwén translated text; translation: 正式～ an official translation／非正式～ an unofficial translation／把～跟原文核对一下 check the translation against the original

译意风 yìyìfēng simultaneous interpretation installation

译音 yìyīn transliteration

译员 yìyuán interpreter

译者 yìzhě translator

译制 yìzhì dub (a film, etc.)

译制片 yìzhìpiàn a dubbed film

译注 yìzhù translate and annotate: ～古籍 translate and annotate ancient books

译著 yìzhù translations

译作 yìzuò translations

抑[1] yì press down; restrain; repress; curb: ～价 keep down the prices

抑[2] yì *conj. formal* ① or: 人歟,～鬼歟? Is it a human being or is it a ghost? ② but: 非惟天时,～亦人谋也。It's not only a matter of Heaven-sent occasions but also a matter of human endeavour.

抑遏 yì'è curb; repress; restrain: 不可～的悲痛 irrepressible sorrow

抑或 yìhuò *conj.* or: 不知他们是赞成,～是反对。I wonder if they are for or against this.

抑菌作用 yìjūnzuòyòng *med.* bacteriostasis

抑强扶弱 yìqiáng-fúruò curb the strong and help the weak; uphold the weak against the strong

抑且 yìqiě *conj. formal* also; moreover; furthermore

抑压 yìyā same as 压抑 yāyì

抑扬 yìyáng (of sound) rise and fall; modulate

抑扬顿挫 yì-yáng-dùn-cuò cadence; modulation in tone: 那～的音乐节奏,听来非常悦耳。The rhythm and cadence of the music delighted the ear.

抑郁 yìyù depressed; despondent; gloomy: ～不平 feel disgruntled

抑郁症 yìyùzhèng *med.* depression

抑止 yìzhǐ hold in check; hold back: 眼泪～不住直往下流 can't hold back one's tears

抑制 yìzhì ① restrain; control; check: ～自己的愤怒 restrain one's anger / ～自己的感情 control one's emotion / 利用辐射～洋葱发芽 check the sprouting of onions by radiation ② *physiol.* inhibition

抑制剂 yìzhìjì *chem.* inhibitor

抑制神经 yìzhì shénjīng *physiol.* inhibitory nerve

呓（囈、讛） yì talk in one's sleep

呓语 yìyǔ ① talk in one's sleep ② crazy talk; ravings: 狂人～ ravings of a madman

邑 yì ① town; city ② county

佚 yì same as 逸 yì

佚失 yìshī scatter and disappear; be lost: 那部古书久已～。That ancient work has long been lost.

佚游 yìyóu *formal* roam freely about

役 yì ① labour; service: 劳役 láoyì ② military service: 现役 xiànyì / 兵役 bīngyì ③ use as a servant: ～万物 make all things serve man ④ servant: 仆役 púyì ⑤ battle; campaign: 平型关之～ the Battle of Pingxingguan (Sept. 1937)

役畜 yìchù draught animal; beast of burden

役龄 yìlíng enlistment age

役使 yìshǐ work (an animal); use: 地主把长工当牛马一样～。The landlord made the farmhands toil like beasts of burden.

怿（懌） yì *formal* pleased; happy

诣 yì *formal* ① go to (a place); call on (sb. one respects): ～烈士墓参谒 go to the graves of revolutionary martyrs to pay one's respects ② (academic or technical) attainments: 造诣 zàoyì

易[1] yì ① easy: 不～解决 not easy to solve / 得来不～ not easily won; hard-earned / ～学 easy to learn / ～患感冒 catch cold easily; be susceptible to colds / 涝地区 areas liable to waterlogging ② amiable: 平易 píngyì ③ *formal* despise

易[2] yì ① change: ～地疗养 go to another place for recuperation / 数～寒暑。Several years have passed. ② exchange: 以～物 barter / ～地而处 change places with another person ③ (Yì) a surname

易爆物 yìbàowù explosive substance

易感者 yìgǎnzhě *med.* susceptible person; susceptible

易货贸易 yìhuòmàoyì barter

易货协定 yìhuòxiédìng an agreement on the exchange of commodities

易经 Yìjīng *The Book of Changes* ——see also 五经 wǔjīng

易拉罐 yìlāguàn pop-top; pull-top; flip-top

易洛魁人 Yīluòkuírén Iroquois

易燃物 yìránwù combustibles; inflammables

易熔点 yìróngdiǎn *phys.* eutectic point

易熔合金 yìróng héjīn *metall.* fusible alloy

易如反掌 yì rú fǎnzhǎng as easy as turning one's hand over; as easy as falling off a log

易手 yìshǒu change hands

易于 yìyú be easy to: 这件事～处理。This is easy to manage.

易辙 yìzhé *formal* change one's course; strike out on a new path

易帜 yìzhì *formal* change one's banner—change one's principles or allegiance

驿（驛） yì same as 驿站 yìzhàn, now used mainly as part of a place name: 龙泉～ Longquanyi (in Sichuan Province)

驿丞 yìchéng posthouse official

驿道 yìdào (also 驿路 yìlù) post road

驿馆 yìguǎn (also 驿舍 yìshè) posthouse

驿吏 yìlì posthouse officer

驿马 yìmǎ post horse

驿使 yìshǐ courier; post

驿站 yìzhàn (in former times) post station; courier station

驿卒 yìzú posthouse runner

绎（繹） yì *formal* ① unravel silk; sort out: 抽绎 chōuyì ② continuous; unceasing: 络绎不绝 luòyì bù jué

狋 yì see 林狋 línyì

奕 yì *formal* grand; great

奕奕 yìyì ① grand; great: ～梁山。(《诗经》) How great is Mount Liang! ② radiating power and vitality: 神采奕奕 shéncǎi yìyì

弈 yì *formal* ① *weiqi*, a game played with black and white pieces on a board of 361 crosses; *go* ② play chess: 对弈 duìyì

弈林 yìlín chess-playing circles: ～高手 a master chess player

疫 yì epidemic disease; pestilence: 鼠疫 shǔyì / 防疫 fángyì

疫病 yìbìng epidemic disease

疫疠 yìlì plague; pestilence

疫苗 yìmiáo vaccine

疫情 yìqíng information about and appraisal of an epidemic; epidemic situation: 报告～ report epidemic diseases

疫区 yìqū an epidemic-stricken area

轶 yì same as 逸③④

轶材 yìcái *formal* talents above the average

轶伦 yìlún *formal* tower above one's generation; surpass one's contemporaries

轶事 yìshì anecdote

益[1] yì ① benefit; profit; advantage: 受益 shòuyì / 利益 lìyì ② beneficial: 益虫 yìchóng

益[2] yì ① increase: 延年益寿 yánnián-yìshòu ② *adv.* all the more; increasingly: 〜觉困难 find sth. increasingly difficult

益虫 yìchóng beneficial insect

益处 yìchu benefit; profit; good

益发 yìfā (also 益加 yìjiā) *adv.* all the more; even more

益母草 yìmǔcǎo *bot.* motherwort (*Leonurus heterophyllus*)

益鸟 yìniǎo beneficial bird

益友 yìyǒu friend and mentor

谊 yì friendship: 〜同手足 be as close as brothers

挹 yì *formal* ① ladle out; scoop up: 〜酒浆 ladle out wine ② pull

挹彼注兹 yìbǐ-zhùzī draw from one to make good the deficits of another

挹取 yìqǔ *formal* ladle out; scoop up

挹注 yìzhù short for 挹彼注兹 yìbǐ-zhùzī

悒 yì *formal* sad; worried: 〜〜不乐 feel depressed; mope

悒闷 yìmèn *formal* depressed; dejected; in low spirits

悒郁 yìyù *formal* depressed; despondent; gloomy

悒郁寡欢 yìyù guǎhuān same as 郁郁寡欢 yùyù guǎhuān

逸 yì ① ease; leisure: 有劳有〜 alternate work with rest ② escape; flee: 逃逸 táoyì ③ be lost: 〜书 ancient works no longer extant ④ excel: 超逸 chāoyì

逸乐 yìlè comfort and pleasure

逸民 yìmín hermit; recluse

逸趣 yìqù refined interests or tastes

逸群 yìqún be head and shoulders above others; excel all others

逸史 yìshǐ unofficial history

逸事 yìshì anecdote

逸闻 yìwén anecdote

逸豫 yìyù *formal* idleness and pleasure: 〜亡身。 Idleness and pleasure lead to ruin.

逸致 yìzhì a carefree mood: 闲情逸致 xiánqíng-yìzhì

翌 yì *formal* immediately following in time; next: 〜日 next day / 〜年 next year

翊 yì *formal* assist (a ruler): 〜戴 assist and support (a ruler)

勚 yì ① *arch.* toil; hard work ② (of an edge, point, etc.) become worn; become dull or blunt: 螺丝扣〜了。 The threads of the screw are worn.

溢 yì ① overflow; spill: 河水四〜。 The river overflowed. ② excessive: 〜誉 excessive praise

溢出 yìchū spill over; overflow

溢洪道 yìhóngdào *water conservancy* spillway

溢流 yìliú overflow; brim over

溢流坝 yìliúbà *water conservancy* overfall dam; spillway dam

溢美 yìměi *formal* excessive praise; fulsome praise; undeserved praise

溢目 yìmù *formal* more than the eye can take in: 珍宝〜。 There are too many treasures for the eye to take in.

溢于言表 yì yú yán-biǎo (of feelings) show clearly in one's words and manner: 愤激之情,〜。 Indignation showed clearly in his words and manner.

意[1] yì ① meaning; idea; thought: 同意 tóngyì / 来意 láiyì ② wish; desire; intention: 好意 hǎoyì / 中意 zhōngyì ③ anticipate; expect: 不意 bùyì ④ suggestion; hint; trace: 颇有秋〜 make one feel that autumn has set in

意[2] Yì short for 意大利 Yìdàlì

意表 yìbiǎo what one expects; expectation: 出人意表 chū rén yìbiǎo

意大利 Yìdàlì Italy

意大利人 Yìdàlìrén Italian

意大利肉饼 yìdàlì ròubǐng pizza

意大利语 Yìdàlìyǔ Italian (language)

意会 yìhuì perceive by intuition; sense: 只可意会,不可言传 zhǐkě yìhuì, bùkě yánchuán

意见 yì·jiàn ① idea; view; opinion; suggestion: 交换〜 exchange ideas (*or* views); compare notes / 倾听群众的〜 listen carefully to the views (*or* opinions) of the masses / 提出修改〜 make suggestions for revision / 〜一致 have identical views; be of one mind / 〜分歧 have a difference (*or* divergence) of opinion; disagree ② objection; differing opinion; complaint: 我对这种办法很有〜。 I strongly object to this method. *or* I take vigorous exception to this approach. / 大家对你〜很大。 People have a lot of complaints about you. / 有〜要拿到桌面上来。 Those who differ should air their views openly.

意见簿 yìjiànbù visitors' book, customers' book, etc.

意见箱 yìjiànxiāng suggestion box

意匠 yìjiàng artistic conception (of a poem, painting, etc.); artistic design: 别具〜 show originality in artistic conception

意境 yìjìng the mood of a literary work or a work of art

意料 yìliào anticipate; expect: 这是〜中的事。 That's to be expected.

意马心猿 yìmǎ-xīnyuán same as 心猿意马 xīnyuán-yìmǎ

意念 yìniàn idea; thought: 这时每人脑子里都只有一个〜:"胜利!" At that moment victory was the one idea that occupied everyone's mind. *or* Then, everybody had only one thought in mind: victory.

意气 yìqì ① will and spirit: 〜高昂 high-spirited ② temperament: 意气相投 yìqì xiāngtóu ③ personal feelings (*or* prejudice): 〜之争 a dispute caused by personal feelings

意气风发 yìqì fēngfā high-spirited and vigorous; daring and energetic

意气相投 yìqì xiāngtóu be alike in temperament; be congenial

意气用事 yìqì yòng shì be swayed by personal feelings

意趣 yìqù interest and charm (of a literary work or a work of art); flavour; mood: 余家董源雾景横披全幅, 山骨隐显, 林梢出没,〜高古。(米芾) In the landscape of a cloudy scene by Dong Yuan in my collection, when one unrolls the whole scroll, the structure of the mountains is hidden and revealed, the branches of trees emerge and disappear, and the mood is lofty and antique.

意识 yìshí ① consciousness; awareness: 法律〜 law awareness / 宗教〜 religious consciousness / 增强全民的人口〜 increase the nation's awareness of the population problem / 增强全民族的环境〜 enhance the

whole nation's awareness of the need to protect the environment ② (usu. used with 到) be conscious (*or* aware) of; awake to; realize: 他～到自己的责任了。He is conscious of his responsibilities. / 她充分～到将会遇到的困难。She is fully aware of the difficulties awaiting her. / 这一点我当时还没～到。I didn't realize this at the time.

意识流 yìshíliú　*psychol.*　stream of consciousness: ～小说 a stream-of-consciousness novel

意识形态 yìshí xíngtài　*philos.*　ideology: 社会～ social ideology / ～方面普遍存在的问题 problems prevalent in the realm of ideology

意识域 yìshíyù　*psychol.*　sphere of consciousness

意思 yìsi　① meaning; idea: 这个字的～是什么? What is the meaning of this word? / 我不明白你的～。I don't understand what you mean. / 你这是什么～? What do you mean by that? / 文章的中心～ the central idea of an article　② opinion; wish; desire: 我的～是走着去。In my opinion, (*or* I think) we should walk. / 你是不是有～跟她见见面? Do you wish to meet her? ③ a token of affection, appreciation, gratitude, etc.: 这不过是我的一点儿～, 请收下吧。Please accept this little gift as a token of my appreciation. ④ suggestion; hint; trace: 天有点要下雨的～。It looks like rain. ⑤ interest; fun: 他觉得年画展览很有～。He found the exhibition of New Year pictures very interesting. / 打桥牌很有～。Bridge is a lot of fun. / 他这个人没～。He's dull. / 学校闹派系, 真没有～。All this factionalism in the school is so silly. ⑥ (reduplicated) as a mere token: 她要走了, 咱们送她一条丝巾～～。She's leaving. Let's give her a silk kerchief as a token of our friendship.

意态 yìtài　mien; demeanor; bearing: ～自若 appear calm and at ease / ～潇洒 be natural and unrestrained

意图 yìtú　intention; intent: 领会上级～ understand the intentions of the higher organization / 他的～很明显。His intention is obvious. / 如果方法不好, ～再好, 也往往无济于事。Ineffective means often defeat the best intentions.

意外 yìwài　① unexpected; unforeseen: ～损失 unexpected loss / ～利润 windfall profit / 感到～ be surprised; be taken by surprise / 你太出乎我的～了! You astound me! ② accident; mishap: 以免发生～ so as to avoid accidents

意味 yìwèi　① meaning; significance; implication: 我揣摩不透他那番话的～所在。I can't figure out the implications of what he said. ② interest; overtone; flavour: 这首诗～无穷。This is a poem of unlimited interest. / 带有文学～的新闻报道 a news report with a literary flavour

意味深长 yìwèi shēncháng　having deep meaning; pregnant with meaning; of profound significance: ～的一笑 a meaningful smile / 他的话～。What he says is significant.

意味着 yìwèizhe　signify; mean; imply: 这一数字～生产提高了两倍。This figure means a twofold increase in production.

意下 yìxià　① in the mind; in the heart: 别人的闲话, 她全不放在～。She didn't take the idle gossip to heart at all. ② opinion; idea; view: 老兄～如何? What do you think of it? *or* What's your opinion?

意想 yìxiǎng　imagine; expect: ～不到的效果 unexpected results / 这种事谁～得到! Who would have expected such a thing?

意向 yìxiàng　intention; purpose: 敌军～不明。The enemy's intentions are not clear.

意向书 yìxiàngshū　letter of intent: 签订～ sign a letter of intent

意象 yìxiàng　images; imagery

意兴 yìxìng　interest; enthusiasm: ～索然 have lost all interest in sth.; be no longer interested in sth. / ～勃勃 be highly enthusiastic

意绪 yìxù　state of mind; mood: ～低沉 low-spirited; depressed

意义 yìyì　meaning; sense; significance: 在某种～上 in a sense / ～略有不同 a slight difference of meaning / 具有重大历史～的事件 an event of historic significance / 一部富有教育～的影片 a very instructive film / 这是一项有～的工作。This is an important job. / 这样做没有～。There's no point in doing that. / 这个词有三个～。This word has three distinct meanings.

意译 yìyì　free translation

意意思思 yìyìsīsī　hesitate in speech

意欲 yìyù　intend to; want to: 他～独自前去。He intends to go all by himself.

意愿 yìyuàn　wish; desire; aspiration: 表达人民的～ express the wishes of the people / 这并不是我们的～。This is not what we'd like to see.

意蕴 yìyùn　meaning; implication; connotation

意在笔先 yì zài bǐ xiān　have an idea in the mind before starting writing or painting

意在言外 yì zài yán wài　the meaning is implied: 古人为诗, 贵于～。The poets of old made a point of implying their meaning rather than making it explicit.

意旨 yìzhǐ　intention; wish; will: 秉承某人的～ in compliance with sb.'s wish

意志 yìzhì　will; willpower; determination: 钢铁～ iron will; iron determination / ～薄弱 weak-willed / ～坚强 strong-willed / ～消沉 demoralized; despondent / 锻炼～ temper one's willpower / 不以人的～为转移 independent of man's will

意中人 yìzhōngrén　the person one is in love with; the person of one's heart; the beloved one

意中事 yìzhōngshì　sth. that is to be expected

裔 yì　*formal*　① descendants; posterity: 后裔 hòuyì / 华裔 huáyì　② a distant land; a remote region: 四～ the borderlands; the frontiers　③ (Yì) a surname

裔孙 yìsūn　*formal*　remote descendants

肄 yì　study: 肄业 yìyè

肄业 yìyè　study in school or at college: 他曾在大学～二年。He was in college for two years.

缢 yì　*formal*　die or be put to death by hanging: 自缢 zìyì

蝎 yì　see 蜥蜴 xīyì

瘗 (瘞) yì　*formal*　bury

蓺 yì　*formal*　plant; grow: ～菊 grow chrysanthemums

熠 yì　*formal*　bright; brilliant

熠熠 yìyì　*formal*　sparkling; glittering

镒 yì　an ancient unit of weight equal to 20 or 24 *taels* of silver

毅 yì　firm; resolute; staunch: 刚毅 gāngyì

毅力 yìlì　willpower; will; stamina; tenacity: 惊人的～ amazing willpower / 百折不回的～ indomitable will / 以无比的～跟疾病作斗争 battle against illness with matchless stamina / 完成这项工作需要坚强的～。It'll require great willpower to accomplish the task.

毅然 yìrán　resolutely; firmly; determinedly

毅然决然 yìrán-juérán　resolutely; determinedly: 她～地离开了家, 跟自己的恋人一起生活。Resolutely she left

home to embark on a new life with the man she loved.

薏 yì　see below

薏米 yìmǐ　(also 薏仁米 yìrénmǐ) the seed of Job's tears

薏苡 yìyǐ　*bot.* Job's tears

劓 yì　cutting off the nose (a punishment in ancient China)

臆(肊) yì　① the chest: 胸臆 xiōngyì ② subjectively: 臆测 yìcè

臆测 yìcè　conjecture; surmise; guess

臆断 yìduàn　form a subjective judgment; assume

臆度 yìduó　*formal* conjecture; surmise; guess

臆见 yìjiàn　a subjective view

臆说 yìshuō　assumption; supposition

臆造 yìzào　fabricate (a story, reason, etc.); concoct

翼 yì　① the wings of a bird, an insect, etc. ② the wings of an aeroplane ③ flank (of an army, etc.); wing (of a building): 从左右两～夹攻敌人 attack the enemy on both flanks / 主楼的两～ the two wings of the main building ④ the twenty-seventh of the twenty-eight constellations (二十八宿) into which the celestial sphere was divided in ancient Chinese astronomy (consisting of twenty-two stars in Crater and Hydra) ⑤ *formal* assist (a ruler): ～助 render assistance (to a ruler)

翼蔽 yìbì　*formal* shield; protect; screen

翼侧 yìcè　*mil.* flank: ～攻击 flank attack / ～迂回 outflank

翼翅 yìchì　wing

翼护 yìhù　shield sb. with one's own body: 她在敌机扫射下～过伤员。 She once shielded a wounded soldier with her own body when enemy planes were strafing our troops.

翼手动物 yìshǒudòngwù　*zool.* chiropter (e.g. the bat)

翼手目 yìshǒumù　*zool.* Chiroptera

翼型 yìxíng　*aviation* wing section; aerofoil

翼翼 yìyì　*formal* ① reverent and cautious: 小心翼翼 xiǎoxīn yìyì ② in neat formation; in orderly array ③ thriving; abundant

翼指龙 yìzhǐlóng　pterodactyl (an extinct reptile)

翼状胬肉 yìzhuàngnǔròu　*med.* pterygium

翳 yì　① *formal* screen; conceal ② *Chin. med.* slight corneal opacity; nebula

翳翳 yìyì　*formal* ① dim; obscure; hazy ② veiled; vague

癔 yì　see below

癔病 yìbìng　*med.* hysteria: ～患者 hysteriac

镱 yì　*chem.* ytterbium (Yb)

懿 yì　*formal* (esp. of women) virtuous; exemplary: ～行 exemplary conduct

懿德 yìdé　*formal* admirable virtue; moral excellence

懿亲 yìqīn　*formal* closest relative

懿旨 yìzhǐ　the empress's decree

yīn

因 yīn　① *formal* follow; carry on: 因袭 yīnxí ② *formal* rely on; accord with: ～病下药 suit the medicine to the illness / ～其自然 let things take their natural course ③ cause; reason: 必有他～ there must be some other reason ④ *prep.* because of; as a result of: ～病请假 ask for sick leave / ～公牺牲 die while on duty; die at one's post / 会议～故延期。 The meeting has been postponed for some reason. ⑤ *conj.* because: 他～有其他事情未能出席。 He was absent because he had other things to attend to.

因变数 yīnbiànshù　another name for 函数 hánshù

因材施教 yīn cái shī jiào　teach students according to their aptitude; suit the instruction to the student's level

因此 yīncǐ　*conj.* so; therefore; for this reason; consequently: 这个干部办事公道，～同志们都拥护他。 He is a fair-minded cadre, so all the comrades support him. / 她的话引得大家都笑了，室内的空气～轻松了很多。 What she said set everyone laughing, and consequently the party livened up a lot. / 雪融化时吸收热量，气温～下降。 Melting snow absorbs heat, and so makes the temperature drop.

因次 yīncì　*phys.* dimension: ～分析 dimensional analysis

因地制宜 yīn dì zhì yí　take measures suited to local conditions; suit measures to local conditions: ～地进行密植 carry out close planting in line with local conditions / 实行这种～、及时指导的方法，就可以保证我们的工作少犯一些错误。 This method of suiting our measures to local conditions and of giving timely guidance ensures that fewer mistakes will be made in our work.

因而 yīn'ér　*conj.* thus; as a result; therefore: 新机器的运转速度要快一倍，～会大大降低成本。 The new machines will work twice as fast, thus greatly reducing costs.

因果 yīnguǒ　① cause and effect: ～关系 causality / ～性 causality / ～倒置 confuse cause and effect ② *Buddhism* karma; preordained fate

因果报应 yīnguǒ bàoyìng　*Buddhism* retribution; karma

因果律 yīnguǒlù　the law of cause and effect; the law of causality (or causation)

因祸得福 yīn huò dé fú　derive gain from misfortune; profit by misfortune

因陋就简 yīn lòu jiù jiǎn　make do with whatever is available; do things simply and thriftily: 实验室设备是不够理想，但我们只好～。 Our laboratory equipment isn't perfect, but we must make do.

因明 yīnmíng　a system of Hindu logic

因人成事 yīn rén chéng shì　depend on others for success in one's work

因人而异 yīn rén ér yì　vary with each individual: 疗效～。 The effect of the treatment varies with the individual.

因人设事 yīn rén shè shì　create a job to accommodate a person

因人制宜 yīn rén zhì yí　do what is suited to each individual; take measures suited to each person

因仍 yīnréng　*formal* carry on as before; follow: ～旧习 follow the old customs

因时制宜 yīn shí zhì yí　do what is suited to the occasion; take measures suited to the time

因式 yīnshì　*math.* factor (which is an algebraic expression): a＋b 和 a－b 都是 a²－b² 的～。 a＋b and a－b are both factors of a^2-b^2. / ～分解 factorization (into algebraic expressions)

因势利导 yīn shì lì dǎo　guide a matter along its course of development; adroitly guide action according to circumstances: ～，夺取胜利 make the best use of the situation and guide the struggle to victory

因数 yīnshù　*math.* factor (which is a whole number): 2、3、4 和 6 都是 12 的～。 2, 3, 4 and 6 are all factors of 12. / ～分解 factorization (into whole numbers)

因素 yīnsù factor; element: 积极～ positive factors / 人的～ the human factor / 生产力的基本～是生产资料和劳动力。The basic factors in the productive forces are the means of production and manpower.

因素论 yīnsùlùn *philos.* theory of factors

因头 yīntóu *dial.* ① excuse; pretext: 这出戏我实在不想看，就借个～出去了。I really didn't like the play, so I found an excuse and left. ② cause; reason; origin: 看来事体总有点～，不会无中生有。There must be some reason or other for things being the way they are. There can't be something coming out of nothing.

因为 yīn·wèi ① *conj.* because: ～天冷，奶奶今天没有出门。Grandma didn't go out today because it was cold. / 我～事情太多，所以直到今天才来看你。I didn't come and see you till today because I was terribly busy. / ～治疗及时，他的伤好得很快。His wound healed quickly because of timely treatment. ② *prep.* because of; on account of; owing to: ～天气的关系，飞机不能按时起飞。Because of bad weather, the plane didn't take off on time. / 这花儿～缺水死了。The flowers died for lack of water.

因袭 yīnxí follow (old customs, methods, rules, etc.); copy: ～陈规 follow outmoded rules / ～前人 follow in the footsteps of one's predecessors

因小失大 yīn xiǎo shī dà try to save a little only to lose a lot; penny wise and pound foolish; spoil the ship for a ha'p'orth of tar

因循 yīnxún ① follow (old customs, etc.); continue in the same old rut: ～旧习 follow the old customs ② procrastinate: ～坐误 sit back and allow the situation to deteriorate; procrastinate until it is too late

因循守旧 yīnxún shǒujiù stick to old ways; follow the beaten track

因噎废食 yīn yē fèi shí give up eating for fear of choking—refrain from doing what one should for fear of running a risk

因由 yīnyóu *inf.* reason; cause; origin

因缘 yīnyuán ① *Buddhism* principal and subsidiary causes; cause ② predestined relationship

因之 yīnzhī *conj.* therefore; for this reason; consequently

因子 yīnzǐ ① another name for 因数 yīnshù ② another name for 因式 yīnshì

阴（陰、隂）

yīn ① (in Chinese thought) *yin*, the feminine or negative principle in nature (opp. 阳 *yang*) ② the moon: 阴历 yīnlì ③ overcast: 天～了。The sky is overcast. / 多云转～ cloudy to overcast ④ shade: 树阴 shùyīn ⑤ north of a hill or south of a river: 华～ Huayin (a county situated on the north side of Huashan Mountain) / 江～ Jiangyin (a county situated on the south side of the Changjiang River) ⑥ the back side: 碑～ the back of a stone tablet ⑦ in intaglio: 阴文 yīnwén ⑧ hidden; secret: 阴沟 yīngōu ⑨ sinister: 这个人真～。This chap's very sinister. ⑩ of the nether world; of ghosts: 阴宅 yīnzhái / 阴间 yīnjiān ⑪ *phys.* negative: 阴极 yīnjí ⑫ private parts (esp. of the female) ⑬ (Yīn) a surname

阴暗 yīn'àn dark; gloomy: 地下室里～而潮湿。It's dark and damp in the basement. / 天色～。The sky is dark. / ～的角落 a dark corner / ～的脸色 a glum face / ～的心理 mentality marked by antipathy and gloom

阴暗面 yīn'ànmiàn the dark (or seamy) side of things

阴部 yīnbù *physiol.* private parts; genitals; pudenda

阴曹 yīncáo (also 阴曹地府 yīncáo dìfǔ) the nether world; the Hades

阴沉 yīnchén cloudy; overcast; gloomy; sombre: 天色～。The sky is cloudy (or grey). / 脸色～ have a sombre countenance; look glum

阴沉木 yīnchénmù hard wood which has long been buried in earth

阴唇 yīnchún *physiol.* labia (of the vulva)

阴错阳差 yīncuò-yángchā (also 阴差阳错 yīnchā-yángcuò) a mistake or error due to a strange combination of circumstances

阴丹士林 yīndānshìlín ① indanthrone (a deep blue dye) ② a cotton cloth dyed with indanthrone

阴道 yīndào *physiol.* vagina

阴道炎 yīndàoyán vaginitis

阴德 yīndé good deeds done in secret; hidden acts of merit: 积～ accumulate hidden merit

阴地 yīndì a shaded place; shade

阴地植物 yīndì zhíwù shade plant

阴电 yīndiàn negative electricity

阴毒 yīndú insidious; sinister and ruthless

阴风 yīnfēng ① a cold wind ② an ill (or evil) wind

阴干 yīngān be placed in the shade to dry; dry in the shade

阴功 yīngōng same as 阴德 yīndé

阴沟 yīngōu sewer; covered drain

阴河 yīnhé underground river

阴黑 yīnhēi dark and gloomy; murky; sombre: 天色～。The sky was dark and gloomy. / 脸色～ have a sombre countenance; look glum

阴户 yīnhù *physiol.* vaginal orifice

阴晦 yīnhuì dark; gloomy

阴魂 yīnhún ghost; spirit; apparition

阴魂不散 yīnhún bù sàn the ghost lingers on—the evil influence remains

阴极 yīnjí *phys.* negative pole; negative electrode; cathode: 冷～ cold cathode / ～激励 cathode drive

阴极射线 yīnjí shèxiàn *phys.* cathode ray: ～管 cathode-ray tube

阴间 yīnjiān the nether world; the Hades

阴茎 yīnjīng *physiol.* penis: ～勃起 penile erection

阴冷 yīnlěng ① (of weather) gloomy and cold; raw ② (of a person's look) sombre; glum

阴离子 yīnlízǐ another name for 负离子 fùlízǐ

阴历 yīnlì lunar calendar: ～正月 the first month of the lunar year

阴凉 yīnliáng ① shady and cool: 此药宜置于～处。The medicine should be kept in a cool, dark place. ② a cool place; shade: 找个～儿歇歇。Let's have a rest in the shade.

阴灵 yīnlíng same as 阴魂 yīnhún

阴霾 yīnmái haze

阴毛 yīnmáo *physiol.* pubes

阴门 yīnmén same as 阴户 yīnhù

阴面 yīnmiàn the shady side; the back side

阴谋 yīnmóu ① conspire; plot; scheme: ～破坏 plot sabotage / ～复辟 plot to restore the old order / ～篡权 scheme to usurp power / ～推翻政府 conspire to overthrow the government ② conspiracy; plot; scheme: ～诡计 schemes and intrigues / ～手段 conspiratorial means / 政变～ a coup plot / 外交～ a diplomatic intrigue

阴谋集团 yīnmóu jítuán a conspiratorial clique (or group)

阴谋家 yīnmóujiā schemer; intriguer; conspirator

阴囊 yīnnáng *physiol.* scrotum

阴平 yīnpíng high and level tone (the first of the four tones in modern standard Chinese pronunciation)

阴燃 yīnrán glow

阴森 yīnsēn gloomy; gruesome; ghastly: ～的树林 a deep, dark forest / ～可怕 ghastly and bloodcurdling

阴山 Yīnshān the Yinshan Mountains

阴山背后 yīnshān bèihòu a remote and desolate place

阴生植物 yīnshēng zhíwù same as 阴地植物 yīndì zhíwù

阴虱 yīnshī *zool.* crab louse

阴湿 yīnshī dark and damp

阴事 yīnshì *formal* secret matters

阴司 yīnsī same as 阴间 yīnjiān

阴私 yīnsī shameful secret

阴天 yīntiān an overcast sky; a cloudy day

阴文 yīnwén characters or designs cut in intaglio; intaglio

阴险 yīnxiǎn sinister; insidious; treacherous: ～毒辣 sinister and ruthless / ～的计谋 a sinister design (*or* scheme) / ～的敌人 an insidious enemy (*or* foe)

阴笑 yīnxiào a sinister smile: 他脸上露出一丝～。A sinister smile crept over his face.

阴性 yīnxìng ① *med.* negative: ～反应 negative reaction ② *linguis.* feminine gender

阴虚 yīnxū *Chin. med.* deficiency of *yin* (insufficiency of body fluid), with irritability, thirst, constipation, etc. as symptoms

阴阳 yīnyáng ① (in Chinese thought) *yin* and *yang*, the two opposing principles in nature, the former feminine and negative, the latter masculine and positive ② ancient Chinese astronomy (esp. the study of the movements of the celestial bodies) ③ occult arts (e.g. astrology, geomancy, etc.) ④ same as 阴阳生 yīnyángshēng

阴阳怪气 yīnyángguàiqì ① (of a person's manner of speaking) mystifying; enigmatic; deliberately ambiguous ② eccentric; queer; cynical: 他这个人～的。He's a queer chap. / 他来往的人都是有些～的。The people he has to do with are all a rather peculiar lot.

阴阳家 yīnyángjiā ① geomancer ② (Yīnyángjiā) the Yin-Yang School or School of Naturalists (in the Warring States Period, 475–221 B.C.)

阴阳历 yīnyánglì lunisolar calendar

阴阳人 yīnyángrén a bisexual person; hermaphrodite

阴阳生 yīnyángshēng *yin-yang* adept (e.g. astrologer, diviner, geomancer, etc.)

阴阳水 yīnyángshuǐ *Chin. med. yin-yang* water (a mixture of hot and cold water, or of river and well water, used for washing down or preparing medicine)

阴阳先生 yīnyáng xiānsheng geomancer (usu. employed as a funeral adviser)

阴一套,阳一套 yīn yī tào, yáng yī tào act one way in public and another in private; be engaged in double-dealing

阴翳 yīnyì *formal* ① be shaded or hidden by foliage: 柳树～的河边 river banks shaded by willows ② with luxuriant foliage: 桃李～ peach and plum trees covered with luxuriant foliage

阴影 yīnyǐng shadow: 树木的～ shadows of trees / 肺部有～ have a shadow on one's lungs

阴雨 yīnyǔ overcast and rainy: ～连绵 cloudy and drizzly for days on end; an unbroken spell of wet weather

阴郁 yīnyù gloomy; dismal; depressed: 天色～。The weather is gloomy. / 心情～ feel gloomy (*or* depressed)

阴云 yīnyún dark clouds: ～密布。The sky is overcast. *or* The sky is covered with dark clouds. / 笼罩着两国关系的～会迅速消散。The dark clouds hanging over the relations between the two countries will soon vanish.

阴宅 yīnzhái grave; tomb

阴着儿 yīnzhāor *dial.* a treacherous act

阴鸷 yīnzhì *formal* sinister and ruthless

阴骘 yīnzhì good deeds done in secret

音 yīn ① sound: 噪音 zàoyīn / 口音 kǒuyīn ② musical sound; note: 这个～得延长一点儿。The note must be held longer. ③ news; tidings: 佳音 jiāyīn ④ syllable: 一字一～。Each character stands for a syllable.

音儿 yīnr *dial.* ① voice: 他急得连说话的～都变了。He was so excited that even his voice changed. ② implication: 听话听音儿 tīng huà tīng yīnr

音爆 yīnbào *aviation* sonic boom

音标 yīnbiāo *phonet.* phonetic symbol; phonetic transcription

音波 yīnbō *phys.* sound wave

音叉 yīnchā tuning fork

音长 yīncháng the duration of a sound

音尘 yīnchén *formal* news; message; information

音程 yīnchéng *mus.* interval

音调 yīndiào tone: ～铿锵 a ringing tone

音读 yīndú pronunciation (of a character)

音符 yīnfú *mus.* note

音高 yīngāo *linguis. mus.* pitch

音耗 yīnhào news; message; information

音阶 yīnjiē *mus.* scale

音节 yīnjié *phonet.* syllable

音节表 yīnjiébiǎo syllabary

音节文字 yīnjié wénzì syllabic language

音量 yīnliàng volume (of sound): ～控制 volume control

音律 yīnlǜ *mus.* temperament

音名 yīnmíng *mus.* musical alphabet

音频 yīnpín *phys.* audio frequency

音频调制 yīnpín tiáozhì *radio* voice modulation

音品 yīnpǐn another name for 音色 yīnsè

音强 yīnqiáng intensity of sound

音容 yīnróng *formal* voice and face (of sb. as recalled after his death): 室内陈设依然, 而～已杳。Everything in the room was as it had always been, except that the voice and face of the one I love were no longer there.

音容宛在 yīnróng wǎn zài the same voice and face seem still there (said as one thinks fondly of a dead person; usu. inscribed on a funeral banner)

音色 yīnsè tone colour; timbre

音诗 yīnshī *mus.* tone poem

音势 yīnshì another name for 音强 yīnqiáng

音素 yīnsù old name for 音位 yīnwèi

音素文字 yīnsù wénzì old name for 音位文字 yīnwèi wénzì

音速 yīnsù *phys.* velocity (*or* speed) of sound

音位 yīnwèi *phonet.* phoneme

音位文字 yīnwèi wénzì *linguis.* phonemic language

音位学 yīnwèixué *phonet.* phonemics

音问 yīnwèn news; tidings

音响 yīnxiǎng ① sound; acoustics: ～水雷 sonic (*or* sound, acoustic) mine / ～效果 sound effects; acoustics ② short for 组合音响 zǔhé yīnxiǎng

音像 yīnxiàng audiovisual: ～出版社 audiovisual publishing house

音信 yīnxìn (also 音讯 yīnxùn) mail; message; news: 互通～ communicate with each other; be in correspondence with each other / 他走后就一直没有～。We have not heard from him since he left.

音型 yīnxíng *mus.* figure

音义 yīnyì ① pronunciation and meaning ② (formerly used in book titles) explanations of pronunciation and meaning: 《毛诗～》*Pronunciation and Meaning for the Book of Songs*

音译 yīnyì transliteration

音域 yīnyù *mus.* range; compass; register

音乐 yīnyuè music: 你喜欢什么～? What kind of music do you like? / 学～ study music / ～形象 musical image

音乐电视 yīnyuè diànshì music TV (MTV)

音乐会 yīnyuèhuì concert

音乐家 yīnyuèjiā musician

音乐片 yīnyuèpiàn　musical film
音乐厅 yīnyuètīng　concert hall
音乐学 yīnyuèxué　musicology
音乐学院 yīnyuè xuéyuàn　conservatory (of music)
音韵 yīnyùn　① harmonious sounds; rhyme and rhythm ② the initial, final and tone of a Chinese character
音韵学 yīnyùnxué　*linguis.* phonology: ～家 phonologist
音障 yīnzhàng　*phys.* sound (*or* sonic) barrier
音值 yīnzhí　*linguis.* value
音质 yīnzhì　① tone quality ② acoustic fidelity
音缀 yīnzhuì　another name for 音节 yīnjié
音准 yīnzhǔn　*mus.* accuracy in pitch

茵（裀）
yīn　mattress: 绿草如～ a carpet of green grass
茵陈 yīnchén　*bot.* capillary artemisia (*Artemisia capillaris*)
茵褥 yīnrù　*formal* mattress
茵茵 yīnyīn　(of grass, etc.) lush; luxuriant: 芳草～ fragrant grass growing lush and long／一片～嫩绿的麦苗 a stretch of lush, tender wheat seedlings

洇（湮）
yīn　(of ink) spread and sink in: 这种纸写字容易～。Ink blots on this paper.
洇色 yīnsè　diffusion or running of colouring matter; bleeding

姻（婣）
yīn　① marriage: 婚姻 hūnyīn ② relation by marriage: ～兄弟 brothers-in-law
姻伯 yīnbó　brother or sister's father-in-law
姻亲 yīnqīn　relation by marriage: ～关系 relationship by marriage; affinity
姻娅 yīnyà　(also 姻亚 yīnyà) *formal* relatives by marriage; in-laws
姻缘 yīnyuán　the happy fate which brings lovers together: 美满～ a happy marriage; conjugal felicity

絪
yīn　see below
絪缊 yīnyūn　same as 氤氲 yīnyūn

氤
yīn　see below
氤氲 yīnyūn　① (in ancient Chinese thought) the generative forces of heaven and earth ② *liter.* (of smoke or mist) dense; thick; enshrouding: 云烟～ enshrouding mists／灵山多秀色, 空水共～。(张九龄《湖口望庐山瀑布泉》) The mountains in beauty dressed stand awed by that magical sight Of the wedding of Heaven and Earth in a waterfall's headlong flight.

殷¹
yīn　*formal* ① abundant; rich: 殷实 yīnshí ② eager; ardent: 期望甚～ cherish high hopes ③ hospitable: 招待甚～ offer cordial hospitality

殷²
Yīn　① the Yin Dynasty (c. 14th–11th century B.C.; a name for the latter part of the Shang 商 Dynasty) ② a surname
——see also yān
殷富 yīnfù　wealthy; well-off
殷钢 yīngāng　*metall.* invar
殷鉴 yīnjiàn　*formal* setback which serves as a warning to others: 可资～ may serve as a warning (*or* lesson)
殷鉴不远 Yīnjiàn bù yuǎn　a lesson for Yin lies not far behind—one need not look far back for a warning; the lessons of history are close at hand
殷切 yīnqiè　ardent; eager: ～的期望 ardent expectations
殷勤 yīnqín　eagerly attentive; solicitous: 受到～接待 be

accorded solicitous hospitality ——see also 献殷勤 xiàn yīnqín
殷实 yīnshí　well-off; substantial: ～人家 well-off families／～的商号 a substantial firm／家道～ be a man of substance
殷墟 Yīnxū　*archaeol.* the Yin ruins
殷殷 yīnyīn　ardent; sincere: ～期望 entertain ardent hopes／～嘱咐 enjoin sincerely
殷忧 yīnyōu　great worry; deep anxiety

铟
yīn　*chem.* indium (In)

堙
yīn　*formal* ① mound ② block up

喑（瘖）
yīn　*formal* mute; dumb
喑哑 yīnyǎ　mute; dumb: 一排子弹射去, 敌人的机枪～了。At our first volley the enemy machine gun was silenced.

yín

吟（唫）
yín　① chant; recite: ～诗 recite or compose poetry／两句三年得, 一～双泪垂。(贾岛) Two lines of poetry in three years! Each time I sing, two streams of tears. ② song (as a type of classical poetry): 《秦妇～》 *Song of a Qin Lady* ③ the cry of certain animals or insects: 猿～ monkeys squealing／蝉～ cicadas stridulating
吟唱 yínchàng　sing; chant: ～毛泽东诗词 chant Mao Zedong's poems
吟哦 yín'é　recite (poetry) with a cadence; chant
吟风弄月 yínfēng-nòngyuè　(also 吟风咏月 yínfēng-yǒngyuè) sing of the moon and the wind—write sentimental verse: 明末的小品虽然比较的颓放, 却并非全是～。Though the essays of the late Ming Dynasty are rather decadent, they are not entirely devoted to the wind and the moon.
吟诵 yínsòng　chant; recite: ～唐诗 recite a Tang poem
吟味 yínwèi　recite with relish; recite with appreciation: 反复～ recite again and again in appreciation
吟咏 yínyǒng　recite (poetry) with a cadence; chant

垠
yín　*formal* boundary; limit: 无垠 wúyín

狺
yín　see below
狺狺 yínyín　*formal* yap; yelp: ～狂吠 bark frenziedly

淫¹
yín　① excessive: 淫雨 yínyǔ ② wanton: 乐而不淫 lè ér bù yín

淫²（婬）
yín　① licentious; lewd; lascivious: 万恶～为首。Lewdness is the worst of all vices. ② obscene; pornographic: ～书 pornographic books (*or* publications)／～画 obscene pictures
淫奔 yínbēn　(esp. of a woman) elope
淫辞 yíncí　(also 淫词 yíncí) ① *formal* extravagant speech ② obscene language; lewd expressions
淫荡 yíndàng　loose in morals; lascivious; licentious; lewd
淫风 yínfēng　wanton customs; lascivious practices
淫妇 yínfù　a wanton woman; adulteress
淫棍 yíngùn　libertine; womanizer; wolf
淫秽 yínhuì　obscene; salacious; bawdy: ～书刊 pornographic literature
淫乐 yínlè　indulge in sensual pleasures; gratify carnal desires ——see also yīnyuè
淫乱 yínluàn　(sexually) promiscuous; licentious

淫靡　yínmǐ　① obscene; decadent: ～的歌曲 obscene or decadent songs ② extravagant: 风气～。Extravagance has become a common practice.

淫威　yínwēi　abuse of power; despotic power

淫猥　yínwěi　obscene

淫亵　yínxiè　① obscene; salacious ② act indecently towards (a woman)

淫刑　yínxíng　formal　① mete out excessive punishments ② excessive punishments

淫羊霍　yínyánghuò　bot.　longspur epimedium (Epimedium macranthum)

淫雨　yínyǔ　excessive rains: ～成灾。Excessive rains caused a flood.

淫乐　yínyuè　formal　decadent music; obscene music ——see also yínlè

寅 yín　the third of the twelve Earthly Branches (地支)——see also 干支 gān-zhī

寅吃卯粮　yín chī mǎo liáng　(also 寅支卯粮 yín zhī mǎo liáng) eat next year's food; anticipate one's income

寅时　yínshí　the period of the day from 3 a. m. to 5 a. m.

银 yín　① chem. silver (Ag): 纯～ pure silver ② relating to currency or money: 银行 yínháng ③ silver-coloured: ～色 silvery／红地～字 silver characters on a red background

银白　yínbái　silvery white

银白杨　yínbáiyáng　white poplar (Populus alba)

银杯　yínbēi　silver cup

银本位　yínběnwèi　econ.　silver standard

银币　yínbì　silver coin

银鲳　yínchāng　another name for 鲳鱼 chāngyú

银川　Yínchuān　Yinchuan (capital of the Ningxia Hui Autonomous Region)

银锭　yíndìng　silver ingot

银耳　yín'ěr　tremella (Tremella fuciformis)

银发　yínfà　silver (or silvery) hair: 满头～ silver-haired

银根　yíngēn　econ.　money market; money: ～紧。Money is tight. or The money market is tight.／～松。Money is easy. or The money market is easy.

银汉　yínhàn　liter.　the Milky Way

银汉鱼　yínhànyú　zool.　silverside

银行　yínháng　bank: ～储备金 bank reserve／储备～ reserve bank／储蓄～ savings bank／外汇指定～ authorized bank for dealing in foreign exchange／～存款 bank deposit／～存折 bankbook; passbook／～汇款 bank remittance／～汇票 bank draft／～帐户 bank account／～贴现 bank discount／～贴现率 bank discount rate; bank rate／～信贷 bank credit

银行家　yínhángjiā　banker

银毫　yínháo　(also 银毫子 yínháozi) same as 毫 háo①

银号　yínhào　banking house

银河　yínhé　astron.　the Milky Way

银河系　yínhéxì　astron.　the Milky Way system; the Galaxy

银河星团　yínhé xīngtuán　astron.　galactic cluster

银狐　yínhú　silver fox

银灰　yínhuī　silver grey

银婚　yínhūn　silver wedding

银匠　yínjiàng　silversmith

银角子　yínjiǎozi　dial.　silver coin of small denominations

银两　yínliǎng　silver (used as currency)

银亮　yínliàng　bright as silver

银楼　yínlóu　silverware shop; jeweller's shop

银幕　yínmù　(motion-picture) screen; projection screen

银鸥　yín'ōu　zool.　herring gull (Larus argentatus vegae)

银牌　yínpái　silver medal

银票　yínpiào　(in former times) silver draft (a form of paper money)

银器　yínqì　silverware

银钱　yínqián　money

银鼠　yínshǔ　zool.　snow weasel

银条　yíntiáo　silver bar

银屑病　yínxièbìng　med.　psoriasis

银杏　yínxìng　bot.　ginkgo; gingko

银燕　yínyàn　silver swallow——aeroplane

银洋　yínyáng　silver dollar

银样镴枪头　yín yàng làqiāngtóu　a pewter spearhead that shines like silver——an impressive-looking but useless person

银鱼　yínyú　whitebait; salangid

银圆　yínyuán　(also 银元 yínyuán) silver dollar

银质奖　yínzhìjiǎng　silver medal

银朱　yínzhū　vermilion: ～涂料 vermilion paint

银子　yínzi　silver; money

龈 yín　gum

蒙 yín　formal　① hold sb. in respectful awe ② deep: 蒙夜 yínyè

蒙夜　yínyè　formal　in the depth of the night; at the dead of night

蒙缘　yínyuán　formal　make use of one's connections to climb up; try to advance one's career by currying favour with important people

霪 yín　formal　excessive rains

霪雨　yínyǔ　same as 淫雨 yínyǔ

yǐn

尹 yǐn　① an ancient official title: 府尹 fǔyǐn ② (Yǐn) a surname

引 yǐn　① draw; stretch: ～弓 draw a bow ② lead; guide: ～滦入津 divert the water of the Luan River to Tianjin ③ leave: ～避 keep (or stay, steer) clear of; make way for ④ stretch out: 引颈 yǐnjǐng ⑤ induce; attract: 劈柴太湿, 火～不着。The firewood is too wet to kindle. ⑥ cause; make: 他这一句话～得大家笑起来。His remark set everybody laughing. ⑦ quote; cite: ～某人的话 quote sb.／～自《中国日报》quoted from China Daily／～书为证 cite a book as proof ⑧ a traditional unit of length equal to 10 zhang 市丈 and equivalent to 33⅓ metres

引爆　yǐnbào　ignite; detonate: ～装置 igniter

引柴　yǐnchái　(also 引火柴 yǐnhuǒchái) kindling

引产　yǐnchǎn　med.　induce labour

引出　yǐnchū　draw forth; lead to: ～正确的结论 draw correct conclusions／在一定的条件下, 坏的东西可以～好的结果, 好的东西也可以～坏的结果。In given conditions, a bad thing can lead to good results and a good thing to bad results.

引导　yǐndǎo　guide; lead: 主人～贵宾们参观了车间。The hosts showed the distinguished guests around the workshops.／伟大的党～我们走向胜利。Our great Party guides us to victory.

引得　yǐndé　index (a transliteration)

引动　yǐndòng　cause; arouse; stir up (feelings)

引逗　yǐndòu　① tantalize; tease ② lure; entice

引渡　yǐndù　leg.　extradite

引而不发　yǐn ér bù fā　(of a teacher of archery) draw the bow but not release the arrow——show people what

to do without doing it for them

引发 yǐnfā initiate; touch off; spark off; trigger off: 〜炸药的导火线 a fuse that ignites an explosive / 那个事件〜了一场暴乱。 The incident touched off (or sparked off) a riot.

引发剂 yǐnfājì *chem.* initiator

引港 yǐngǎng ① pilot a ship (into or out of a harbour) ② pilot (of a ship)

引吭高歌 yǐn háng gāogē sing joyfully in a loud voice; sing heartily

引航 yǐnháng same as 引水 yǐnshuǐ①

引航员 yǐnhángyuán another name for 引水员 yǐnshuǐ-yuán

引号 yǐnhào quotation marks (" "): 双〜 double quotation marks (" ") / 单〜 single quotation marks (' ')

引河 yǐnhé ① irrigation channel ② diversion canal

引火 yǐnhuǒ light a fire: 连〜的木头片儿也找不到 can't even find a piece of wood for kindling

引火烧身 yǐn huǒ shāo shēn draw fire against oneself—make self-criticism to invite criticism from others; criticize oneself so as to get criticism from others

引火线 yǐnhuǒxiàn fuse

引疾 yǐnjí *formal* resign on grounds of ill health

引见 yǐnjiàn present (a person) to another; introduce: 他把我〜给市长。 He presented me to the mayor.

引荐 yǐnjiàn recommend (a person)

引酵 yǐnjiào *dial.* leavening dough

引进 yǐnjìn ① recommend (a person) ② introduce from elsewhere: 〜新的小麦品种 introduce new varieties of wheat / 〜技术装备 import technology and equipment

引经据典 yǐnjīng-jùdiǎn quote the classics; quote authoritative works

引颈 yǐnjǐng crane one's neck: 〜四望 crane one's neck to look around / 〜企待 eagerly look forward to

引咎 yǐnjiù *formal* hold oneself responsible for a serious mistake; take the blame: 〜辞职 take the blame and resign

引狼入室 yǐn láng rù shì invite a wolf into the house—open the door to an enemy

引理 yǐnlǐ *math.* lemma

引力 yǐnlì *phys.* gravitation; gravitational force; attraction: 核〜 nuclear attraction / 〜场 gravitational field

引领 yǐnlǐng *formal* crane one's neck to look into the distance—eagerly look forward to sth.

引领而望 yǐnlǐng ér wàng crane one's neck to see; eagerly look forward to

引流 yǐnliú *med.* drainage: 十二指肠〜 duodenal drainage

引流管 yǐnliúguǎn *med.* drainage tube

引路 yǐnlù lead the way

引起 yǐnqǐ give rise to; lead to; set off; touch off; cause; arouse: 〜严重后果 lead to grave consequences / 〜连锁反应 set off a chain reaction / 〜公愤 arouse (or touch off) public indignation / 〜强烈的反响 cause strong repercussions / 〜怀疑 arouse suspicion / 〜注意 bring to sb.'s attention / 〜一场热烈的讨论 evoke a heated discussion / 由此而〜的一切后果 all consequences arising therefrom / 事故是由于粗心大意而〜的。 The accident was caused by carelessness.

引桥 yǐnqiáo *transportation* bridge approach

引擎 yǐnqíng engine: 〜盖 bonnet; hood

引燃管 yǐnránguǎn ignitron

引人入胜 yǐn rén rù shèng (of scenery, literary works, etc.) fascinating; enchanting; bewitching: 山路盘旋而上, 风景优美, 〜。 As the mountain path spirals up, the

beauty of the scene fills one with enchantment. / 把报纸办得〜 make the newspaper interesting and absorbing

引人注目 yǐn rén zhùmù noticeable; conspicuous; spectacular: 〜的横幅标语 an eye-catching slogan on a banner / 〜的特点 conspicuous features / 〜的变化 spectacular changes

引入 yǐnrù lead into; draw into; introduce from elsewhere: 〜圈套 lure into a trap; ensnare / 〜新品种 introduce new varieties

引入歧途 yǐnrù qítú lead sb. onto a wrong path; lead sb. astray

引申 yǐnshēn extend (the meaning of a word, etc.): "兵"字的本义是武器, 〜为"战士"。 Originally 兵 meant "weapon" and has by extension come to mean "soldier".

引申义 yǐnshēnyì extended meaning

引首 yǐnshǒu raise one's head; crane one's neck

引述 yǐnshù quote sb.'s words; quote from sb.'s speech

引水 yǐnshuǐ ① pilot a ship (through difficult waters, or into or out of a harbour) ② draw or channel water: 〜灌田 channel water into the fields / 〜上山 draw water up a hill

引水工程 yǐnshuǐ gōngchéng diversion works

引水员 yǐnshuǐyuán pilot (of a ship)

引头 yǐntóu take the lead: 只要你来引个头, 这件事就好办了。 This can be easily arranged if you will take the lead.

引退 yǐntuì retire from office; resign

引文 yǐnwén (also 引语 yǐnyǔ) quoted passage; quotation

引线 yǐnxiàn ① fuse ② go-between ③ *dial.* sewing needle

引信 yǐnxìn detonator; fuse: 触发〜 contact fuse / 延期〜 delay fuse

引言 yǐnyán foreword; introduction

引以为耻 yǐn yǐ wéi chǐ regard it as a disgrace; consider it shameful

引以为憾 yǐn yǐ wéi hàn deem it regrettable

引以为鉴 yǐn yǐ wéi jiàn take warning from it

引以为戒 yǐn yǐ wéi jiè (also 引为鉴戒 yǐn wéi jiànjiè) draw a lesson (from a mistake, etc.); take warning: 过去我们就是鉴于他们的经验教训, 少走了一些弯路, 现在当然更要〜。 It was by drawing lessons from their experience that we were able to avoid certain detours in the past, and there is all the more reason for us to do so now.

引以为荣 yǐn yǐ wéi róng regard it as an honour; take it as an honour

引用 yǐnyòng ① quote; cite: 他在文章中〜了鲁迅的话。 In his article he quoted Lu Xun. ② recommend; appoint

引诱 yǐnyòu lure; entice; seduce: 〜敌人进入伏击圈 lure the enemy into a trap / 企图用金钱和美女来〜意志薄弱的人 try to lure the weak-willed with money and women / 〜少女离家出走 entice a girl away from home / 物质〜 material enticements

引玉之砖 yǐn yù zhī zhuān a brick cast to attract jade——see also 抛砖引玉 pāozhuān-yǐnyù

引证 yǐnzhèng quote or cite as proof or evidence

引种 yǐnzhǒng introduce a fine variety

引种 yǐnzhòng plant an introduced variety

引子 yǐnzi ① *theat.* an actor's opening words (either spoken or sung) ② *mus.* introductory music ③ introductory remarks; introduction: 这一段话是下文的〜。 This paragraph is an introduction to what follows. / 我简单说几句做个〜, 希望大家多发表意见。 I'll just say a few words to start the ball rolling. ④ *Chin. med.* an added ingredient (to enhance the efficacy of

medicines)

饮 yǐn ① drink: ～茶 drink tea / ～酒 drink wine or liquor / 一～而尽 drink it down in one gulp ② drinks: 冷饮 lěngyǐn ③ keep in the heart; nurse: 饮恨 yǐnhèn ④ *Chin. med.* a decoction of Chinese medicine to be taken cold ——see also yìn

饮弹 yǐndàn *formal* be hit by a bullet: ～身亡 be killed by a bullet

饮恨 yǐnhèn *formal* nurse a grievance: ～而终 die with a grievance in one's heart

饮恨吞声 yǐnhèn-tūnshēng swallow one's resentment and choke back one's sobs; endure insults and injuries

饮料 yǐnliào beverage; drink (esp. a soft drink)

饮片 yǐnpiàn *Chin. med.* prepared herbal medicine in small pieces ready for decoction

饮泣 yǐnqì *formal* weep in silence: ～吞声 swallow one's tears; weep silent tears

饮食 yǐnshí food and drink; diet: 给病人规定～ put a patient on a diet / ～卫生 dietetic hygiene / ～习惯 dietary habits / ～有度 temperance in eating and drinking / ～无味 have no appetite

饮食店 yǐnshídiàn eating house; café; snack bar

饮食疗法 yǐnshí liáofǎ *med.* dietotherapy

饮食男女 yǐnshí-nánnǚ food, drink and sex—man's prime wants

饮食业 yǐnshíyè the catering trade

饮水 yǐnshuǐ drinking water; potable water

饮水不忘掘井人 yǐn shuǐ bùwàng juéjǐngrén when you drink the water, think of those who dug the well ——see also 饮水思源 yǐn shuǐ sī yuán

饮水器 yǐnshuǐqì drinking bowl; drinker

饮水思源 yǐn shuǐ sī yuán when drinking water, think of its source—bear in mind where one's happiness comes from

饮用水 yǐnyòngshuǐ drinking water; potable water

饮鸩止渴 yǐn zhèn zhǐ kě drink poison to quench thirst—seek quick relief regardless of the consequences

饮子 yǐnzi same as 饮 yǐn④

蚓 yǐn see 蚯蚓 qiūyǐn

隐（隱） yǐn ① hidden from view; concealed: 隐蔽 yǐnbì ② latent; dormant; lurking: 隐患 yǐnhuàn

隐蔽 yǐnbì conceal; take cover: 公开的和～的活动 overt and covert activities / 游击队～在高粱地里。The guerrillas took cover in the sorghum fields. / ～! Take cover! / ～运动 *mil.* concealed movement / ～阵地 covered position

隐藏 yǐncáng hide; conceal; remain under cover: 她把负伤的战士～在地窖里。She hid the wounded soldier in the cellar.

隐恶扬善 yǐn'è-yángshàn cover up sb.'s faults and publicize his merits; hide sb.'s evil deeds and praise his good ones

隐伏 yǐnfú lie concealed (*or* hidden); lie low: 小猫～在草丛里。The cat lay hidden in the grass. / 平静中～着危险。Danger lurked where all was quiet.

隐睾症 yǐngāozhèng *med.* cryptorchidism

隐含 yǐnhán imply

隐函数 yǐnhánshù *math.* implicit function

隐花植物 yǐnhuā zhíwù *bot.* cryptogam

隐患 yǐnhuàn hidden trouble; hidden danger; snake in the grass: 消除～ remove a hidden peril

隐讳 yǐnhuì avoid mentioning; cover up: 不要～自己的缺点。One should not gloss over one's shortcomings.

隐晦 yǐnhuì obscure; veiled: 文字写得很～ be couched in ambiguous terms / 这首诗写得十分～, 不容易懂。The poem is too obscure to understand.

隐晦曲折 yǐnhuì qūzhé (of a statement) veiled and roundabout

隐疾 yǐnjí unmentionable disease (e.g. V. D.)

隐居 yǐnjū live in seclusion; withdraw from society and live in solitude; be a hermit

隐君子 yǐnjūnzǐ *humor.* retired scholar—drug addict; opium addict (a pun on 隐 yǐn "retired" and 瘾 yǐn "addicted")

隐瞒 yǐnmán conceal; hide; hold back; cover up: ～错误 conceal one's mistakes / ～事实 withhold the truth; hide (*or* hold back) the facts

隐秘 yǐnmì ① conceal; hide: ～不说 not disclose a secret / 地道的出口开在～的地方。The exit of the tunnel is concealed. ② secret: 刺探～ pry into sb.'s secrets

隐没 yǐnmò (also 隐灭 yǐnmiè) hide and disappear: 东方露白, 繁星～。The east paled and the stars disappeared.

隐匿 yǐnnì *formal* conceal; hide; go into hiding; lie low: ～罪证 conceal criminal evidence

隐情 yǐnqíng facts or circumstances one wishes to hide; secrets

隐然 yǐnrán dim; faint: ～可见 dimly visible / ～可闻 faintly audible

隐忍 yǐnrěn bear patiently; forbear: ～不言 forbear from speaking

隐射 yǐnshè insinuate; hint; throw out innuendoes

隐身草 yǐnshēncǎo a person or thing acting as cover

隐士 yǐnshì recluse; hermit

隐事 yǐnshì secrets

隐私 yǐnsī one's secrets; private matters one wants to hide

隐私权 yǐnsīquán rights of privacy; privacy: 侵犯～ violate sb.'s privacy

隐慝 yǐntè *formal* hidden evil thoughts; concealed wickedness

隐痛 yǐntòng secret anguish

隐头花序 yǐntóu huāxù *bot.* hypanthodium

隐退 yǐntuì go and live in seclusion; retire from political life

隐显墨水 yǐnxiǎn mòshuǐ invisible ink

隐现 yǐnxiàn be now visible, now invisible; be dimly visible: 水天相接, 岛屿～。The water merges with the sky; the islands are dimly visible.

隐形轰炸机 yǐnxíng hōngzhàjī stealth bomber

隐形眼镜 yǐnxíng yǎnjìng contact lens

隐性 yǐnxìng *biol.* recessiveness: ～性状 recessive character

隐姓埋名 yǐnxìng-máimíng conceal one's identity; keep one's identity hidden; live incognito

隐血 yǐnxuè *med.* occult blood

隐逸 yǐnyì *formal* ① live in seclusion; withdraw from society and live in solitude; be a hermit ② hermit; recluse

隐隐 yǐnyǐn indistinct; faint: ～的雷声 a distant roll of thunder / ～可见 faintly visible / 感到～作痛 feel a dull pain

隐隐绰绰 yǐnyǐnchuòchuò indistinct; faint: 远处～有个人影在移动。A figure loomed in the distance.

隐忧 yǐnyōu secret worry

隐语 yǐnyǔ enigmatic language; insinuating language; riddle

隐喻 yǐnyù metaphor

隐约 yǐnyuē indistinct; faint: ～可以听到远处传来的歌声。We could faintly hear singing in the distance. / 晨雾中一座座井架～可见。Derricks could be seen dimly in the morning mist.

隐约其词 yǐnyuē qí cí use ambiguous language; speak in equivocal terms

隐衷　yǐnzhōng　feelings or troubles one wishes to keep to oneself

瘾（癮）　yǐn　① addiction; habitual craving: 他喝酒的～真大。He's too fond of the cup. ② strong interest (in a sport or pastime): 有球～ have a passion for ball games / 他看武侠小说都有～了。He's crazy about swordsman fiction.

瘾头　yǐntóu　addiction; strong interest: 你们游泳的～儿可真不小。You people are certainly keen on swimming.

yìn

印　yìn　① seal; stamp; chop: 盖～ affix a seal; stamp a seal ② mark; trace; print: 脚印 jiǎoyìn ③ print; engrave: ～书 print books / 这照片～得不清楚。This photo is not well printed. / 深深～在脑子里 be engraved on one's mind ④ tally; conform: 印证 yìnzhèng ⑤ (Yìn) a surname

印把子　yìnbàzi　the handle of an official seal—an official seal; the seal of authority: ～掌握在人民手里。The people hold the seal of authority (or wield political power).

印版　yìnbǎn　printing plate

印本　yìnběn　printed copy

印鼻　yìnbí　the knob (or handle) of a seal

印次　yìncì　print. impression

印第安人　Yìndì'ānrén　American Indian; Red Indian; Indian

印地语　Yìndìyǔ　Hindi

印度　Yìndù　India

印度教　Yìndùjiào　Hinduism

印度尼西亚　Yìndùníxīyà　Indonesia

印度尼西亚人　Yìndùníxīyàrén　Indonesian

印度尼西亚语　Yìndùníxīyàyǔ　Indonesian (language)

印度人　Yìndùrén　Indian

印度橡胶树　Yìndù xiàngjiāoshù　India rubber plant; India rubber tree (Ficus elastica)

印度洋　Yìndùyáng　the Indian Ocean

印度支那　Yìndù-Zhīnà　Indo-China: ～半岛 the Indo-Chinese Peninsula; Indo-China

印发　yìnfā　print and distribute: ～传单 print and distribute leaflets

印盒　yìnhé　seal box

印痕　yìnhén　mark; trace

印花[1]　yìnhuā　text. printing: ～丝绸 printed silk / ～布 print / ～厂 printworks / ～机 printing machine / ～棉布 cotton print / ～平布 calico

印花[2]　yìnhuā　short for 印花税票 yìnhuāshuìpiào

印花税　yìnhuāshuì　stamp duty; stamp tax

印花税票　yìnhuāshuìpiào　revenue stamp; fiscal stamp

印记　yìnjì　① the seal or stamp of a government organization in old China ② the impression of a seal; trace; mark: 鲜红的～ the red impression of a seal / 鲜明的时代～ a marked imprint of the times ③ impress deeply on one's mind

印迹　yìnjì　trace; mark; vestige

印加人　Yìnjiārén　Inca

印鉴　yìnjiàn　a specimen seal impression for checking when marking payments

印泥　yìnní　red ink paste used for seals; Chinese vermilion seal paste

印纽　yìnniǔ　the knob (or handle) of a seal

印欧语系　Yìn-Ōu yǔxì　the Indo-European languages; Indo-European

印谱　yìnpǔ　a collection of impressions of seals by fa-

mous seal-engravers; a book of ancient seals

印染　yìnrǎn　printing and dyeing (of textiles): ～厂 printing and dyeing mill

印色　yìnsè　red ink paste used for seals; Chinese vermilion seal paste

印绶　yìnshòu　old an official seal and the ribbon attached to it; an official seal

印数　yìnshù　print. the number of copies of a book printed at one impression; impression: ～八万册 an impression of 80,000 copies

印刷　yìnshuā　printing: 这本书正在～中。The book is in the press. / 第一次～ first impression (or printing) / 立体～ stereoscopic printing; three-dimensional printing / 三色版～ three-colour halftone

印刷厂　yìnshuāchǎng　printing house; press

印刷错误　yìnshuā cuòwù　misprint; typographic error

印刷电路　yìnshuā diànlù　printed circuit

印刷工人　yìnshuā gōngrén　printing worker; printer

印刷合金　yìnshuā héjīn　type metal

印刷机　yìnshuājī　printing machine; press: 滚筒～ cylinder press / 轮转～ rotary press / 双面～ perfecting press; perfector

印刷品　yìnshuāpǐn　printed matter

印刷术　yìnshuāshù　art of printing; printing

印刷体　yìnshuātǐ　block letter; print hand: 请用～把姓名写清楚。Please print your name clearly.

印刷纸　yìnshuāzhǐ　printing paper

印台　yìntái　ink pad; stamp pad

印堂　yìntáng　the space between the eyebrows

印纹陶文化　yìnwéntáo wénhuà　archaeol. Stamped Pottery Culture

印玺　yìnxǐ　imperial seal

印相纸　yìnxiàngzhǐ　photographic paper

印象　yìnxiàng　impression: 我对他～很好。I have a good impression of him. / 这个城市给外宾们留下了深刻的～。The city left a deep impression on foreign visitors.

印象派　yìnxiàngpài　impressionist school; impressionist

印象主义　yìnxiàngzhǔyì　impressionism

印信　yìnxìn　official seal

印行　yìnxíng　print and distribute; publish

印油　yìnyóu　stamp-pad ink

印张　yìnzhāng　print. printed sheet (equal to a half sheet of printing paper)

印章　yìnzhāng　seal; signet; stamp

印章学　yìnzhāngxué　sigillography; sphragistics

印证　yìnzhèng　confirm; corroborate; verify: 有待～ yet to be confirmed

印子　yìnzi　① mark; trace; print: 脚～ footprint ② same as 印子钱 yìnziqián

印子钱　yìnziqián　usury: 放～ practise usury / 借～ borrow from a usurer

饮　yìn　give (animals) water to drink; water: ～马 water a horse ——see also yǐn

饮场　yìnchǎng　(in former times) the practice of opera singers having a drink of water onstage before starting on a long aria

茚　yìn　chem. indene

荫[1]（蔭）　yìn　inf. sunless; damp and chilly: 朝北的屋子太～。The rooms with a northern exposure are too damp and chilly.

荫[2]（蔭、廕）　yìn　① formal shelter; protect ② a hereditary rank or privilege granted sb. as a recognition of the services of his ancestors

荫庇　yìnbì　shelter; protect; bless

荫蔽 yìnbì ① be shaded or hidden by foliage: 野战医院～在树林中。The field hospital lies hidden among the trees. ② cover; conceal: ～集结 concentrate under cover /～的斗争 a covert struggle

荫凉 yìnliáng shady and cool: 大树下～得很。It's very shady and cool under the tree.

荫生 yìnshēng (in Ming and Qing times) a student admitted to the Imperial College (国子监) in recognition of the distinguished services of his deceased father or his ancestors

荫翳 yìnyì same as 阴翳 yīnyì

胤 yìn formal offspring; posterity

鲥 yìn remora; shark sucker

窨 yìn basement ——see also xūn

窨井 yìnjǐng inspection shaft; inspection well

yīng

应[1]（應） yīng ① answer; respond: 喊他他不～。I called him, but he didn't answer. ② agree (to do sth.); promise; accept: 这事是我一～下来的, 由我负责吧。I'm the one who took on the job, so let me take care of it. ③ (Yīng) a surname

应[2]（應） yīng should; ought to: ～享受的权利 a right one is entitled to /～尽的义务 one's bounden duty /～予考虑 merit consideration /发现错误～立即纠正。When a mistake is discovered, it should be corrected at once. ——see also yìng

应当 yīngdāng should; ought to: 咱们是同志, ～互相帮助。As comrades we ought to help each other. /～不成问题。There should be no problem.

应得 yīngdé (well) deserved; due: ～的一份 a due share /～的惩罚 a deserved punishment

应分 yīngfèn part of one's job: 帮助顾客选购商品是我们售货员～的事。It's part of our job as shop assistants to help customers choose what they want to buy.

应付帐款 yīngfùzhàngkuǎn bookkeeping account payable

应该 yīnggāi should; ought to: 你～冷静些。You should cool down. /事情就～这样。This is as it should be. /你这样说话可不～。You shouldn't talk like this. /你～知道。You ought to know. /哪谢, 这是我们～做的。Don't mention it, we've only done our duty.

应届毕业生 yīngjiè bìyèshēng graduating students or pupils; this year's graduates

应名儿 yīngmíngr ① hold a title but have no real power or responsibility: 我当主席只是应个名儿。I'm the chairman in name only. ② only in name; nominally: 他们～是近亲, 实际上不大来往。Nominally they're close relatives, but they don't see much of each other.

应声 yīngshēng inf. answer; respond: 我敲了一阵门, 里边没有人～儿。I knocked and knocked, but no one answered. ——see also yìngshēng

应收帐款 yīngshōu zhàngkuǎn bookkeeping account receivable

应许 yīngxǔ ① agree; promise: 他～明天来谈。He agreed to come and talk it over with us tomorrow. ② permit; allow: 谁～他把写字台搬走的? Who gave him permission to take the desk away?

应有 yīngyǒu due; proper; deserved: 发挥它～的作用 play its proper role / 做出～的贡献 make a due contribution / 遭到～的回击 receive a deserved rebuff

应有尽有 yīngyǒu-jìnyǒu have everything that one could wish for: 这家商店日用品～。This general store has just about everything you could wish for.

应允 yīngyǔn assent; consent: 点头～ nod assent; nod approval

英[1] yīng ① liter. flower; petal: 落英 luòyīng ② hero; outstanding person: 群英会 qúnyīnghuì ③ (Yīng) a surname

英[2] Yīng short for 英国 Yīngguó

英镑 yīngbàng pound sterling: ～结存 sterling balance

英镑区 yīngbàngqū the sterling area

英才 yīngcái a person of outstanding ability; a person of superior talents

英尺 yīngchǐ foot (a measure)

英寸 yīngcùn inch

英断 yīngduàn a wise (or brilliant) decision

英吨 yīngdūn long ton; gross ton

英发 yīngfā formal (of talent, etc.) brilliant; transcendent

英国 Yīngguó Britain; England: ～护照 British passport /～文学 English literature /～国民 British national /～公民 British subject

英国管 yīngguóguǎn mus. English horn

英国人 Yīngguórén the British; Englishman or Englishwoman

英豪 yīngháo heroes; outstanding figures

英华 yīnghuá the best or most outstanding persons or things; cream; quintessence

英魂 yīnghún spirit of the brave departed; spirit of a martyr

英吉利海峡 Yīngjílì Hǎixiá the English Channel

英杰 yīngjié heroes; outstanding figures

英俊 yīngjùn ① eminently talented; brilliant: ～有为 brilliant and promising ② handsome and spirited; smart: 一个～的小伙子 a handsome young chap

英里 yīnglǐ mile

英联邦 Yīngliánbāng the British Commonwealth (of Nations)

英两 yīngliǎng old name for 盎司 àngsī

英烈 yīngliè ① heroic; valiant: ～女子 a heroic woman ② heroic martyr ③ formal brilliant achievement

英灵 yīnglíng ① spirit of the brave departed; spirit of a martyr ② formal a person of outstanding ability

英名 yīngmíng heroic name; illustrious name

英明 yīngmíng wise; brilliant: ～领袖 wise leader /～的论断 brilliant thesis /～远见 wisdom and foresight; sagacity (or acumen) and farsightedness

英亩 yīngmǔ acre

英年 yīngnián youthful years; youth

英气 yīngqì heroic spirit: ～勃勃 full of heroic spirit

英石 yīngshí a limestone from Yingde County (英德县) in Guangdong Province (used for building rockeries)

英特耐雄纳尔 Yīngtènàixióngnà'ěr Internationale (a transliteration)

英挺 yīngtǐng dashing: 一位～的青年军官 a dashing young officer

英伟 yīngwěi tall and handsome; strapping

英文 Yīngwén English (language)

英武 yīngwǔ of soldierly (or martial) bearing

英仙座 Yīngxiānzuò astron. Perseus

英雄 yīngxióng ① hero: 女～ heroine /～本色 the true quality of a hero / 传奇式的～ a legendary hero / 人民～ the people's heroes ② heroic: ～气概 heroic spirit; mettle /～业绩 heroic exploits /～行为 heroic deeds

英雄气短 yīngxióng qì duǎn brief is the spirit of a hero ——see also 儿女情长 ér-nǚ qíng cháng

英雄所见略同 yīngxióng suǒjiàn lüètóng great minds

think alike

英雄无用武之地 yīngxióng wú yòngwǔ zhī dì　a hero with no place to display his prowess—have no scope for the exercise of one's abilities

英秀 yīngxiù ① handsome and spirited: 眉目～ have handsome features ② a person of outstanding ability

英寻 yīngxún　fathom (= 6 feet)

英勇 yīngyǒng　heroic; valiant; brave; gallant: ～奋斗 fight heroically / ～善战 brave and skilful in battle / ～就义 die a heroic death (on the enemy's execution ground) / ～不屈 show unyielding heroism

英语 Yīngyǔ　English (language): 英国～ British English / 美国～ American English / 纯正～ pure English / 标准～ standard English; king's (or queen's) English / 当代～ contemporary (or present-day) English / 现代～ modern English / ～国家 English-speaking countries / ～水平测验 English Proficiency Test (EPT)

英制 yīngzhì　the English system

英姿 yīngzī　heroic bearing

英姿焕发 yīngzī huànfā　dashing and spirited

英姿飒爽 yīngzī sàshuǎng　valiant and heroic in bearing; bold and brave

莺（鶯、鸎） yīng　warbler; oriole

莺歌燕舞 yīnggē-yànwǔ　orioles sing and swallows dart —the joy of spring; a scene of prosperity

莺声燕语 yīngshēng-yànyǔ　like an oriole trilling or a swallow twittering (said of a woman speaking in a sweet, delicate voice)

婴[1] yīng　baby; infant

婴[2] yīng　arch. run against; surround: ～疾 fall ill

婴儿 yīng'ér　baby; infant

婴儿车 yīng'érchē　pram; baby carriage; stroller; pushchair

婴儿死亡率 yīng'ér sǐwánglǜ　infant mortality

婴孩 yīnghái　baby; infant

罂（甖） yīng　formal a small-mouthed jar

罂粟 yīngsù (also 罂子粟 yīngzisù) bot. opium poppy (Papaver somniferum): ～花 poppy flower

罂子桐 yīngzitóng　another name for 油桐 yóutóng

嘤 yīng　onom. formal trill; chirp

嘤鸣 yīngmíng ① (of birds) trill; chirp ② formal friend seeking friend

嘤其鸣矣，求其友声 yīng qí míng yǐ, qiú qí yǒu shēng　a bird sings to call forth a mate's response

嘤泣 yīngqì　sob

嘤嘤 yīngyīng　onom. the sound of chirping, whispering, or sobbing: 鸟鸣～ birds chirping / ～啜泣 sobbing

缨 yīng ① tassel: 红缨枪 hóngyīngqiāng ② sth. shaped like a tassel: 萝卜～儿 radish leaves ③ ribbon

缨帽 yīngmào　red-tasselled official hat (worn by Qing Dynasty officials)

缨子 yīngzi ① ornamental tassels ② sth. shaped like a tassel: 萝卜～ radish leaves

撄 yīng　arch. ① run against; oppose: ～其锋 blunt the thrust (of an attacking force) / ～怒 incur sb.'s displeasure ② disturb; stir up

樱 yīng ① cherry ② oriental cherry

樱唇 yīngchún　cherry lips (the red lips of a pretty woman)

樱花 yīnghuā　oriental cherry: 日本～ Japanese flower-

ing cherry

樱桃 yīngtáo　cherry

璎 yīng　jade-like gem

璎珞 yīngluò　pearl and jade necklace

鹦 yīng　see below

鹦哥 yīng·gē　common name for 鹦鹉 yīngwǔ

鹦哥绿 yīng·gēlǜ　parrot green

鹦鹉 yīngwǔ　parrot: 长尾～ parakeet / 虎皮～ budgerigar

鹦鹉螺 yīngwǔluó　nautilus

鹦鹉热 yīngwǔrè　med. psittacosis; parrot fever

鹦鹉学舌 yīngwǔ xuéshé　repeat another person's words like a parrot; parrot

鹦嘴鱼 yīngzuǐyú　parrot fish

膺[1] yīng　formal breast: 义愤填膺 yìfèn tián yīng

膺[2] yīng　formal ① bear; receive: ～此重任 hold this post of great responsibility ② strike; smite: 膺惩 yīngchéng

膺惩 yīngchéng　formal send armed forces to suppress; send a punitive expedition against

膺赏 yīngshǎng　formal receive an award

膺选 yīngxuǎn　formal be elected

鹰 yīng　hawk; eagle

鹰鼻鹞眼 yīngbí-yàoyǎn　hawk-nosed and vulture-eyed—sinister and fierce-looking

鹰钩鼻子 yīnggōubízi　aquiline nose

鹰犬 yīngquǎn　falcons and hounds—lackeys; hired thugs

鹰隼 yīngsǔn　formal hawks and falcons—brutal or fierce people

鹰洋 yīngyáng　Mexican silver dollar

鹰爪毛儿 yīngzhǎomáor　a kind of curly sheep's wool

呎 yīngchǐ, also chǐ　old form for 英尺 yīngchǐ

吋 yīngcùn, also cùn　old form for 英寸 yīngcùn

哩 yīnglǐ, also lǐ　old form for 英里 yīnglǐ

唡（啢） yīngliǎng, also liǎng　old form for 盎司 àngsī

嗼 yīngmǔ, also mǔ　old form for 英亩 yīngmǔ

哶 yīngxún, also xún　old form for 英寻 yīngxún

yíng

迎 yíng ① go to meet; greet; welcome; receive: 到门口去～客 go to meet a visitor at the gate / ～上前去同客人握手 step forward to greet the guest and shake hands with him / 喜～新春 joyously see in the lunar New Year ② move towards; meet face to face: ～着困难上 meet difficulties head-on

迎宾 yíngbīn　receive visitors: ～曲 a tune of welcome

迎春 yíngchūn (also 迎春花 yíngchūnhuā) winter jasmine (Jasminum nudiflorum)

迎风 yíngfēng ① facing (or against) the wind: ～的一面 the windward side / ～飞翔 fly against the wind / 坐在这里正～, 特别凉爽。 It's nice and cool to sit here against the wind. ② down the wind; with the wind: 彩旗～招展。 Coloured flags fluttered in the breeze.

迎合 yínghé　cater to; pander to: ～对方心理 go along with the other side / ～低级趣味 pander to low tastes / ～上司意图 cater to the wishes of one's superiors

迎候 yínghòu　await the arrival of: 在宾馆门口～一个贵宾 await the arrival of the distinguished guest at the entrance of the guest house

迎击 yíngjī　meet (an approaching enemy) head-on

迎接 yíngjiē　meet; welcome; greet: 到机场～一个朋友 meet a friend at the airport / ～新的挑战 meet a new challenge / ～新的一年 usher in (or greet) the New Year / 工人们决心以新的成绩来～五一节。The workers are determined to greet May Day with new achievements.

迎面 yíngmiàn　head-on; in one's face: ～走上去同他们打招呼 step forward to greet them / 微风～吹来 a breeze blowing in one's face

迎亲 yíngqīn　(of the bridegroom) send a party to meet the bride at the bride's home and escort her to the bridegroom's home for the wedding

迎娶 yíngqǔ　(of a man) get married

迎刃而解 yíng rèn ér jiě　(bamboo) splits as it meets the edge of the knife—(of a problem) be readily solved: 抓住了这个主要矛盾，一切问题就～了。Once this principal contradiction is grasped, all problems can be readily solved.

迎头 yíngtóu　head-on; directly

迎头赶上 yíngtóu gǎnshàng　try hard to catch up

迎头痛击 yíngtóu tòngjī　deal a head-on blow:《兵法》云:"敌人喘息未定，即予以～。" The Art of War says, "Launch a frontal assult before the enemy has a chance to catch his breath."

迎新 yíngxīn　① see the New Year in: 送旧迎新 sòngjiù-yíngxīn ② welcome new arrivals: ～晚会 an evening party to welcome newcomers

迎迓 yíngyà　formal meet; welcome

迎战 yíngzhàn　meet (an approaching enemy) head-on

茔（塋） yíng　formal grave: 祖～ ancestral graves / ～地 graveyard; cemetery

盈 yíng　① be full of; be filled with: 丰盈 fēngyíng ② have a surplus of: 盈余 yíngyú

盈亏 yíng-kuī　① profit and loss: ～包干 (of enterprises) be responsible for their own profits or losses ② the waxing and waning of the moon: 月有～。The moon waxes and wanes.

盈利 yínglì　same as 赢利 yínglì

盈千累万 yíngqiān-lěiwàn　thousands and tens of thousands; thousands upon thousands

盈盈 yíngyíng　① clear; lucid: 荷叶上露珠～。The lotus leaves glistened with dewdrops. ② delicate; dainty: ～顾盼 look about daintily (or gracefully) ③ brimming over: 喜气～ brimming over with joy ④ graceful; lissom: ～起舞 dancing gracefully

盈余 yíngyú　surplus; profit: ～两千元 have a surplus of 2,000 yuan / 略有～ with a small favourable balance

荧（熒） yíng　formal ① glimmering; shimmering; twinkling: 一灯～然。A light is glimmering. ② dazzled; perplexed: 荧惑 yínghuò

荧光 yíngguāng　phys. fluorescence; fluorescent light

荧光灯 yíngguāngdēng　fluorescent lamp; daylight lamp

荧光粉 yíngguāngfěn　fluorescent powder

荧光镜 yíngguāngjìng　fluoroscope

荧光屏 yíngguāngpíng　fluorescent screen

荧惑 yínghuò　① formal bewilder; confuse: ～人心 confuse people's minds ② the Sparkling Deluder (old name for 火星[1] Huǒxīng)

荧屏 yíngpíng　① same as 荧光屏 yíngguāngpíng ② television: 这个连续剧下周即可在～上和观众见面。The serial will be on television next week.

荧荧 yíngyíng　(of stars, lights, etc.) twinkling; glimmering: 明星～ stars twinkling / 一灯～。A light is glimmering.

莹（瑩） yíng　formal ① jade-like stone ② lustrous and transparent

莹白 yíngbái　shining and white

莹澈 yíngchè　lustrous and transparent; sparkling and crystal: ～的露珠 sparkling dewdrops

莹洁 yíngjié　shining and clean

莹莹 yíngyíng　sparkling; glistening: 泪水～ eyes glistening with tears

营[1]（營） yíng　① seek: 营利 yínglì ② operate; run: 营业 yíngyè / 国营 guóyíng

营[2]（營） yíng　① camp; barracks: 安营 ānyíng ② battalion: ～部 battalion headquarters / ～教导员 battalion political instructor

营巢 yíngcháo　(of birds) build a nest

营地 yíngdì　campsite; camping ground

营房 yíngfáng　barracks

营工 yínggōng　old work as a hired labourer: ～度日 earn a living as a hired labourer

营混子 yínghùnzi　old army riffraff; army ruffian

营火 yínghuǒ　campfire

营火会 yínghuǒhuì　campfire party; campfire

营建 yíngjiàn　construct; build

营救 yíngjiù　succour; rescue: 设法～被捕的同志 try to rescue the arrested comrades

营垒 yínglěi　① barracks and the enclosing walls ② camp: 革命～ revolutionary camp

营利 yínglì　seek profits

营林 yínglín　afforest

营盘 yíngpán　old military camp; barracks

营求 yíngqiú　① seek: ～私利 seek personal gain ② look for

营舍 yíngshè　barracks

营生 yíngshēng　earn a living; make a living: 靠修鞋～ earn a living as a cobbler

营生 yíngsheng　dial. job: 找个～ look for a job

营私 yíngsī　seek private gain; feather one's nest

营私舞弊 yíngsī-wǔbì　engage in fraud for selfish ends; practise graft

营养 yíngyǎng　nutrition; nourishment: 富于～ nourishing; nutritious / ～状况 nutritional status / ～不良 malnutrition; undernourishment

营养体 yíngyǎngtǐ　nutritive cube

营养级 yíngyǎngjí　trophic level

营养价值 yíngyǎng jiàzhí　nutritive (or nutritional) value: ～很高的食品 foods of high nutritive value

营养链 yíngyǎngliàn　another name for 食物链 shíwùliàn

营养品 yíngyǎngpǐn　nutriment

营养师 yíngyǎngshī　dietitian; dietician; nutritionist

营养霜 yíngyǎngshuāng　nourishing cream

营养素 yíngyǎngsù　nutrient

营养学 yíngyǎngxué　nutriology

营业 yíngyè　do business: 商店上午九时开始～。The shops open at nine in the morning. / 暂停～ business temporarily suspended / 照常～ business as usual / ～收入 business income (or earnings, receipts) / ～支出 operating expenses / ～项目 business items / ～执照 business license

营业额 yíngyè'é　turnover; volume of business

营业时间 yíngyè shíjiān　business hours; banking hours (of a bank)

营业税 yíngyèshuì　business tax; transactions tax; turn-

over tax; sales tax

营业员 yíngyèyuán shop employees (including buyers, travelling salespersons and shop assistants)

营营 yíngyíng *formal* running hither and thither: 毕生～，追求名利 running hither and thither all one's life in quest of fame and wealth

营运 yíngyùn operation (of vehicles, ships, airliners, etc.): 这条新船即将投入～。 This new ship will soon go into operation.

营葬 yíngzàng manage a funeral

营造 yíngzào construct; build: ～防风林 plant wind-break forests

营造尺 yíngzàochǐ the standard foot adopted by the Board of Works (工部) during the Qing Dynasty (equal to 0.32 metre)

营寨 yíngzhài *old* military camp; barracks

营长 yíngzhǎng battalion commander

营帐 yíngzhàng tent

萤(螢) yíng firefly; glowworm; lightning bug

萤火虫 yínghuǒchóng firefly; glowworm; lightning bug

萤石 yíngshí fluorite; fluorspar

萦(縈) yíng *formal* entangle; encompass: 琐事～身 be preoccupied with trivialities; get bogged down in petty matters

萦怀 yínghuái occupy one's mind

萦回 yínghuí hover; linger: ～脑际 linger in one's mind

萦念 yíngniàn think of; long for: 回到日夜～的祖国 return to one's sorely missed homeland

萦绕 yíngrào hover; linger

滢(瀅) yíng *formal* crystal-clear

楹 yíng principal columns (or pillars) of a hall

楹联 yínglián couplet written on scrolls and hung on the pillars of a hall

潆(瀠) yíng see below

潆洄 yínghuí swirl

蝇(蠅) yíng fly; housefly

蝇虎 yínghǔ a kind of spider that feeds on flies (*Menemerus*)

蝇拍 yíngpāi flyswatter; flyflap

蝇甩儿 yíngshuǎir *dial.* horsetail whisk

蝇头 yíngtóu fly's head—very small; tiny: ～小楷 small characters of the size of a fly's head; very small handwritten characters

蝇头小利 yíngtóu xiǎolì (also 蝇头微利 yíngtóu wēilì) a fly's head of profit; a pittance of profit; a petty profit

蝇营狗苟 yíngyíng-gǒugǒu shamelessly seek personal gain

蝇子 yíngzi *inf.* fly; housefly

嬴 Yíng a surname

赢 yíng ① win; beat: 这场比赛谁～了? Who won the game? / 我象棋下不～他。 I can't beat him at Chinese chess. ② gain (profit)

赢得 yíngdé win; gain: ～独立 win (or attain) independence / ～长时间的掌声 draw prolonged applause / ～群众的赞扬 win praise from the masses / ～大多数的支持 obtain (or win, gain) the support of the great majority / 使中国在国际上～了信誉和朋友 earn China prestige and friendship in the world

赢利 yínglì profit; gain: ～五百万元 net a profit of five million *yuan*

赢余 yíngyú same as 盈余 yíngyú

瀛 yíng *formal* sea; ocean

瀛海 yínghǎi *formal* sea; ocean

瀛寰 yínghuán *formal* the world

瀛洲 Yíngzhōu a fabled abode of immortals

yǐng

郢 Yǐng capital of the ancient State of Chu (楚)

颖 yǐng *formal* ① glume; grain husk ② tip (as of a writing brush); point ③ clever: 聪颖 cōngyǐng

颖果 yǐngguǒ *bot.* caryopsis

颖慧 yǐnghuì *formal* (of a teen-ager) clever; bright; intelligent

颖悟 yǐngwù *formal* (of a teen-ager) clever; bright

影 yǐng ① shadow: 树～ the shadow of a tree ② reflection; image: 湖光塔～ a lake with the reflection of a pagoda in it ③ trace; sign; vague impression: 至今也没见他的～儿。 I haven't seen any sign of him yet. / 他长得什么样，我早就忘得没～儿了。 I've clean forgotten what he looked like. ④ photograph; picture: 合影 héyǐng ⑤ film; movie: 影评 yǐngpíng ⑥ *dial.* hide; conceal: 一只野兔～在草丛里。 There was a hare hiding in the grass. ⑦ copy; trace: ～宋本 a facsimile edition of a Song book

影壁 yǐngbì ① screen wall (facing the gate inside or outside a traditional Chinese courtyard) ② a wall with carved murals

影抄 yǐngchāo make an exact copy of a rare book: ～本 a facsimile edition

影调剧 yǐngdiàojù a newly developed local opera popular in the Tangshan area of Hebei Province

影格儿 yǐnggér copy-slip for tracing over

影集 yǐngjí photograph (or picture, photo) album

影剧界 yǐngjùjiè film and drama circles

影剧院 yǐngjùyuàn theatre

影迷 yǐngmí film (or movie) fan

影片儿 yǐngpiānr *inf.* film; movie

影片 yǐngpiàn film; movie: 故事～ feature film

影评 yǐngpíng film review

影射 yǐngshè allude to; hint obliquely at; insinuate: ～攻击 attack by innuendo

影视 yǐng-shì (short for 电影电视) film and television: 在文化艺术、广播～等方面都取得了新成绩。 Progress was registered in the fields of culture, art, broadcasting, film, television and so forth. / ～新星 a new film and TV star

影视界 yǐng-shìjiè film and TV circles

影坛 yǐngtán film (or movie) circles

影条 yǐngtiáo *text.* shadow stripes: ～巴里纱 shadow-stripe voile

影戏 yǐngxì ① leather-silhouette show; shadow play ② *dial.* film; movie

影响 yǐngxiǎng ① influence; effect: 月亮对潮汐的～ the influence of the moon on the tides / 榜样对青年人的～ the influence of example on the young / 产生巨大～ exert a tremendous influence; produce a great impact / 消除天灾的～ fight off the effects of natural calamities / 这样做～不好。 This would create a bad impression. / 这篇文章很有～。 This article is making a strong impact. ② affect; influence: 吸烟～健康。 Smoking affects health. / 用自己的榜样去～孩子 try to influence children by personal example／～质量 impair the quality／～威信 lower (or undermine) one's prestige／～工程进度 hold up the project／～群众的积极性 chill (or

dampen) the enthusiasm of the masses / ～工作 interfere with one's work / 别～他复习功课。Don't disturb him while he is reviewing his lessons. / 灯光不好会～演出效果。Poor lighting will spoil the stage effect. ③ hearsay; gossip: ～之谈 speaking from hearsay

影像 yǐngxiàng ① image ② *old* portrait

影写 yǐngxiě ① make a tracing of; trace ② same as 影抄 yǐngchāo

影写版 yǐngxiěbǎn photogravure

影星 yǐngxīng film star; movie star

影业 yǐngyè the film industry; the motion picture industry; the cinema: 他毕生从事～。He worked in the cinema all his life.

影印 yǐngyìn photomechanical printing; photo-offset process: ～珍本书籍 photolithograph rare books / ～版 process plate / ～本 photo-offset copy; facsimile / ～件 photocopy / ～照相机 process camera / ～制版 photomechanical process

影影绰绰 yǐngyǐngchuòchuò vague; dim; indistinct: 远处～地有一些小山。A few hills loomed in the distance.

影院 yǐngyuàn (usu. used as part of the name of a cinema) cinema; movie (house)

影展 yǐngzhǎn ① photo exhibition ② film exhibition

影子 yǐngzi ① shadow ② reflection ③ trace; sign; vague impression: 找了他半天, 连个～也没见。I looked for him a long time but never even caught a glimpse of him. / 事情已经过了好多年, 我脑子里连点～都没有了。It happened so long ago that I haven't the vaguest recollection of it. / 谈判进行了很久, 但问题的解决还没有～呢。The talks have been going on for a long time, but there is no sign of a solution as yet.

影子内阁 yǐngzi nèigé shadow cabinet

影踪 yǐngzōng same as 踪影 zōngyǐng

瘿

瘿 yǐng ① *Chin. med.* goitre ② *bot.* gall

瘿虫 yǐngchóng gall insect

yìng

应(應)

yìng ① answer; respond; echo: 山鸣谷～。The valleys echo the sounds of the mountains. ② comply with; grant: 以～急需 in order to fill an urgent need / 为～广大读者需要 to meet the needs of the broad reading public / ～中国政府的邀请 at the invitation of the Chinese government ③ suit; respond to: 应景 yìngjǐng ④ deal with; cope with: 从容～敌 meet the enemy calmly ——see also yīng

应变[1] yìngbiàn meet an emergency (*or* contingency): ～措施 emergency measure

应变[2] yìngbiàn *phys.* strain: ～硬化 strain hardening

应变规 yìngbiànguī strain gauge

应变计 yìngbiànjì strainometer

应差 yìngchāi accept an assignment

应承 yìngchéng agree (to do sth.); promise; consent: 这件事他一口～下来了。He agreed to do it without hesitation.

应酬 yìngchou ① have social intercourse with; treat with courtesy: 不善～ socially inept / ～几句 exchange a few polite words / ～信件 courtesy letter ② a social engagement (e.g. dinner party, luncheon party, etc.): 今天晚上有个～。I've been invited to dinner this evening.

应从 yìngcóng assent to; comply with: 他点头～了大家的要求。He nodded assent to our demands.

应答 yìngdá reply; answer

应答如流 yìngdá rú liú (also 应对如流 yìngduì rú liú) reply readily and fluently

应电流 yìngdiànliú induced current

应对 yìngduì reply; answer: 善于～ be good at repartee

应付 yìngfu ① deal with; cope with; handle: ～复杂局面 deal with complicated situations / 准备～可能的突然事变 be prepared against possible emergencies / 定单过多, 难于～。We cannot cope with such a flood of orders. ② do sth. perfunctorily; do sth. after a fashion: ～事儿 go through the motions / 采取～的态度 take a perfunctory attitude ③ make do: 我这双凉鞋今年夏天还可以～过去。I'll make do with these sandals for this summer.

应付裕如 yìngfu yù rú (also 应付自如 yìngfu zìrú) handle the situation with ease; be equal to the occasion; be master of the situation

应机 yìngjī take an opportunity when it offers (*or* presents itself): ～立断 make a quick decision when an opportunity presents itself

应急 yìngjí meet an urgent need; meet an emergency (*or* contingency): ～措施 emergency measure / ～计划 contingency plan; crash programme

应接不暇 yìngjiē bù xiá have more (visitors or business) than one can attend to: 顾客很多, 售货员～。There were so many customers that the shop assistants couldn't attend to them all. / 提出的问题太多, 我真有点～了。I could hardly cope with such a volley of questions fired at me.

应景 yìngjǐng ① do sth. for the occasion: 他本来不大会喝酒, 可是在宴会上也不得不应个景儿。He hardly ever drinks, but at banquets he doesn't mind drinking just a little for the occasion. / 端午吃粽子是～儿。It is customary to eat *zongzi* during the Dragon Boat Festival. / ～诗 occasional verses

应举 yìngjǔ sit for the imperial examinations (esp. for the provincial examination 乡试)

应考 yìngkǎo take (*or* sit for) an entrance examination: ～的人很多。Many sat for the examination.

应力 yìnglì *phys.* stress

应卯 yìngmǎo answer the roll call at *maoshi* (卯时, i.e. 5a.m.–7a.m.)—put in a routine appearance

应门 yìngmén *formal* answer the door

应募 yìngmù respond to a call for recruits; enlist; join up

应诺 yìngnuò agree (to do sth.); promise; undertake

应聘 yìngpìn accept an offer of employment: 她～到宁波大学执教。She accepted a teaching post at Ningbo University.

应声 yìngshēng happen right at the sound of sth.: 鸟枪一响, 野鸭～而落。The wild duck fell at the report of the shotgun. / 警官扣动扳机, 逃犯～而倒。The police officer pulled the trigger, and the fugitive fell at the bang. ——see also yīngshēng

应声虫 yìngshēngchóng yesman; echo

应时 yìngshí ① seasonable; in season: ～货品 seasonable goods / ～瓜果 fruits of the season / 西红柿正～。Tomatoes are in season. ② at once; immediately: 敌人一推门, 地雷～就炸了。No sooner had the enemy soldier pushed the door open than the mine exploded.

应市 yìngshì go on the market; be offered for sale: 新产品即将～。The new product will soon be put on the market.

应试 yìngshì same as 应考 yìngkǎo

应选 yìngxuǎn be a candidate for election; be an election candidate; run for election

应验 yìngyàn come true; be confirmed; be fulfilled: 他的话～了。What he said has come true.

应邀 yìngyāo at sb.'s invitation; on invitation: ～出席大会的有在京的外国友人。Among those invited to attend the meeting were some of the foreign friends in Beijing. / ～派代表团参加庆祝活动 send a delegation to attend the celebrations at sb.'s invitation

应用 yìngyòng ① apply; use: 把理论～于实践 apply theory to practice / 防御和进攻的交替～ the alternate use of defence and attack / 这种方法～得相当普遍。This is a most widely used method. ② applied: ～化学 applied chemistry / ～数学 applied mathematics

应用科学 yìngyòng kēxué applied science

应用文 yìngyòngwén practical writing (as in official documents, notices, receipts, etc.)

应援 yìngyuán respond to a call for help; come to sb.'s aid

应运而生 yìngyùn ér shēng arise at the historic moment; emerge as the times demand

应战 yìngzhàn ① meet an enemy attack: 沉着～ meet the attack calmly ② accept (or take up) a challenge

应战书 yìngzhànshū a letter accepting a challenge

应招 yìngzhāo respond to a call for recruits or candidates

应召 yìngzhào formal respond to a call or summons

应召女郎 yìngzhào nǚláng call girl

应诏 yìngzhào do sth. in response to an imperial decree

应诊 yìngzhěn (of a doctor) see patients

应征 yìngzhēng ① be recruited: ～入伍 be recruited into the army ② respond to a call for contributions (to a publication): ～的稿件 contributions to a periodical, etc. at the editor's public invitation

映

映 yìng reflect; mirror; shine: 朝霞～在湖面上。The glory of the dawn is mirrored on the lake. / 他的脸被炉火～得通红。His cheeks shone red before the glowing oven.

映衬 yìngchèn ① set off: 红墙碧瓦,互相～。The red walls and green tiles set each other off beautifully. ② antithesis

映带 yìngdài liter. enhance each other's beauty; set off each other: 湖光山色,～左右。The lake and the hills side by side—each a foil for the other. / 又有清流激湍,～左右。(王羲之) Here are also clear streams and gurgling rapids, catching one's eye from the right and left.

映山红 yìngshānhóng bot. azalea

映射 yìngshè shine upon; cast light upon: 阳光～在江面上。The sun shines upon the river.

映托 yìngtuō set off; serve as a foil to

映照 yìngzhào shine upon; cast light upon

硬

硬 yìng ① hard; stiff; tough: ～铅笔 a hard pencil / ～领 a stiff collar / ～刷子 a stiff brush / 这根铁丝太～,弯不动。The iron wire is too strong to bend. ② strong; firm; tough; obstinate: 心肠～ hardhearted / 话说得～ express oneself in strong terms / ～不承认错误 obstinately refuse to admit one's error / ～的不行来软的。When hard tactics failed, soft methods were used. ③ manage to do sth. with difficulty: ～充好汉 act the hero / ～压住心头怒火 choke down one's anger / ～搬别人的经验 copy other people's experience mechanically ④ good (quality); able (person): 货色～ goods of high quality / 牌子～ a trademark of high standing; a prestigious trademark

硬邦邦 yìngbāngbāng very hard; very stiff: 这个馒头～的,像块石头。This steamed bun is as hard as rock.

硬棒 yìngbang dial. strong; hale and hearty; sturdy: 老人的身体还挺～。The old man is still hale and hearty.

硬绷绷 yìngbēngbēng same as 硬邦邦 yìngbāngbāng

硬币 yìngbì ① coin; specie: 一个五分的～ a five-fen piece (or coin) / 用～支付 payment in specie ② hard currency

硬撑 yìngchēng hold out or keep on in spite of difficul-

---

ties: 有病不要～。Don't force yourself to work when you are ill.

硬顶 yìngdǐng ① resist stubbornly: 你对上级的指示不能这样～。You cannot disobey orders from above like this. ② contradict rudely: 你对长辈怎么老这样～? Why are you always contradicting your elders so rudely?

硬度 yìngdù phys. hardness: 维氏～ Vickers hardness

硬度计 yìngdùjì sclerometer

硬腭 yìng'è physiol. hard palate

硬弓 yìnggōng a strong bow

硬功夫 yìnggōngfu great proficiency; masterly skill: 练就一身～ acquire masterly skill through intensive training

硬骨头 yìnggǔtou hard bone—a dauntless, unyielding person: ～六连 the Hard-Boned Sixth Company

硬骨鱼 yìnggǔyú bony fish

硬汉 yìnghàn (also 硬汉子 yìnghànzi) a dauntless, unyielding man; a man of iron

硬化 yìnghuà ① harden: 生橡胶遇冷容易～。Raw rubber is apt to harden when subjected to low temperatures. / 经久～ age hardening ② med. sclerosis: 血管～ vascular sclerosis ③ become rigid or inflexible in attitudes, opinions, etc.; ossify

硬话 yìnghuà tough words; strong terms

硬货 yìnghuò ① coin; specie ② hard currency

硬货币 yìnghuòbì hard currency

硬件 yìngjiàn computer hardware

硬结 yìngjié ① indurate; harden ② med. scleroma

硬撅撅 yìngjuējuē dial. very stiff; very rigid: 衬衫浆得～的,穿着不舒服。The starched shirt is stiff and uncomfortable to wear.

硬朗 yìnglang inf. hale and hearty: 他七十多了,身子骨还挺～。He's over seventy but still going strong.

硬煤 yìngméi dial. hard coal; anthracite

硬锰矿 yìngměngkuàng psilomelane

硬面 yìngmiàn stiff dough

硬模 yìngmú mech. die: ～铸造 diecasting

硬木 yìngmù hardwood: ～家具 hardwood furniture

硬磐 yìngpán geol. hardpan

硬碰硬 yìng pèng yìng ① confront the tough with toughness; meet force with force ② (of a job) demanding solid, painstaking work or real skill: 改山造田可是～的事。To transform hills into fields is an extremely tough job.

硬皮病 yìngpíbìng scleroderma; scleriasis

硬拼 yìngpīn fight recklessly

硬气 yìngqi dial. ① strong-willed; firm; staunch; unyielding ② have no qualms; have an easy conscience: 她觉得自己挣的钱用着～。She had no qualms about spending money she'd earned herself.

硬砂岩 yìngshāyán geol. greywacke

硬设备 yìngshèbèi another name for 硬件 yìngjiàn

硬石膏 yìngshígāo anhydrite

硬是 yìngshì ① actually (accomplish sth. extremely difficult): 民工们～打通了这座大山,修成了隧道。The peasant labourers literally (or actually) hewed a tunnel through that rocky mountain. ② just; simply: 医生嘱咐他卧床休息,可他～不听。The doctor advised him to stay in bed, but he just wouldn't listen.

硬实 yìngshi dial. strong; sturdy; robust: 别看他年过八十,身子骨儿还挺～。Though over eighty, he's still going strong. / 这东西挺牢固,挺～。This is quite solid and strong.

硬手 yìngshǒu a skilled (or good) hand

硬水 yìngshuǐ hard water

硬说 yìngshuō stubbornly insist; obstinately assert; allege: 他～他做得对。He obstinately asserted that he had done the right thing. / 她～她不累。She insisted that she wasn't tired.

硬挺 yìngtǐng　endure with all one's will; hold out with all one's might: 你牙疼别～, 快去治治吧。Don't just try to put up with your toothache. Go and see the dentist. / 那小伙子受了伤, 还～着把活干完。In spite of his injuries, the young man stuck it out. / 这场官司叫他～了过来。He barely survived the lawsuit.

硬通货 yìngtōnghuò　hard currency

硬卧 yìngwò　short for 硬席卧铺 yìngxí wòpù

硬席 yìngxí　hard seats or berths (on a train)

硬席卧铺 yìngxí wòpù　sleeping carriage with hard berths; hard sleeper

硬橡胶 yìngxiàngjiāo　hard rubber; ebonite; vulcanite

硬性 yìngxìng　rigid; stiff; inflexible: 至于具体做法, 不作～规定。As for the details of the procedure, we won't lay down any hard and fast (or rigid) rules.

硬玉 yìngyù　jadeite

硬仗 yìngzhàng　a tough (or hard-fought) battle; a formidable task: 打～ fight a hard battle / 一支能打～的石油钻井队 a drilling crew equal to the most formidable tasks

硬着头皮 yìngzhe tóupí　toughen one's scalp—brace oneself; force oneself to do sth. against one's will: ～顶住 brace oneself and bear it; hold out tenaciously / 我～把这碗苦药喝了下去。I forced myself to gulp down the bowl of bitter medicine. / ～, 装出不在乎的样子 brazen it out and pretend that one does not care

硬脂 yìngzhī　chem. tristearin; stearin

硬脂酸 yìngzhīsuān　chem. stearic acid

硬脂酸盐 yìngzhīsuānyán　chem. stearate

硬脂油 yìngzhīyóu　chem. stearine oil

硬纸板 yìngzhǐbǎn　hardboard; cardboard

硬指标 yìngzhǐbiāo　a mandatory quota; an inflexible standard

硬质合金 yìngzhì héjīn　metall. hard alloy; hard metal: ～刀具 hard alloy cutter; hard metal tool

硬质塑料 yìngzhì sùliào　chem. rigid plastics: 半～ semirigid plastics

媵 yìng　formal ① accompany a bride to her new home ② a maid accompanying a bride to her new home ③ concubine

yō

哟 yō　interj. ① (expressing slight surprise): ～, 你踩我的脚了。Oh! You've stepped on my foot. ② see 啊哟 āyō; 哎哟 āiyō ——see also yo

唷 yō　see 哼唷 hēngyō; 喔唷 ōyō

yo

哟 yo　part. ① (used at the end of an imperative sentence): 用力拉～! Heave ho! ② (used as a syllable filler in a song): 呼儿嗨～! Hu-er-hei-yo! ——see also yō

yōng

佣(傭) yōng　① hire (a labourer): 雇佣 gùyōng ② servant: 女～ woman servant; maid ——see also yòng

佣妇 yōngfù　woman servant; maid

佣工 yōnggōng　hired labourer; servant

佣人 yōngrén　(domestic) servant

拥(擁) yōng　① hold in one's arms; embrace; hug: 把孩子紧紧～在怀里 hug the child tightly ② gather around; wrap around: 一群青年～着一位老教师走出来。An old teacher came out, surrounded by a group of young people. / 病人～被而坐。The patient sat wrapped in a quilt. ③ crowd; throng; swarm: 大门一开, 人群一窝蜂似的往里～。The crowd swarmed in as soon as the gate opened. / 欢乐的人群～向天安门。Jubilant crowds surged towards Tian An Men. ④ support: 军爱民, 民～军。The army cherishes the people and the people support the army. ⑤ have; possess: ～兵十万 have an army of 100,000 / ～书万卷 possess a large collection of books

拥抱 yōngbào　embrace; hug; hold in one's arms: 两国选手热烈～, 互致问候。The players of the two countries warmly embraced and greeted each other.

拥脖 yōngbó　dial. collar for a horse

拥簇 yōngcù　cluster round

拥戴 yōngdài　support (sb. as leader): 受到全国人民的～ enjoy the support of the whole nation

拥护 yōnghù　support; uphold; endorse: ～中国共产党的领导 support the leadership of the Chinese Communist Party / 我们～这个决定。We endorse this decision.

拥挤 yōngjǐ　① be crowded; be packed: 上下班时间, 公共汽车特别～。The buses are especially crowded during the rush hours. ② push and squeeze: 不要～! Don't push!

拥进 yōngjìn　crowd into; swarm into

拥军优属 yōngjūn-yōushǔ　(of civilians) support the army and give preferential treatment to families of revolutionary armymen and martyrs

拥塞 yōngsè　jam; congest: 街道～ streets jammed with traffic / 来往货船经常～河道。The river is often congested with the traffic of freighters.

拥有 yōngyǒu　possess; have; own: ～核武器 possess nuclear weapons / ～丰富的矿藏 have rich mineral resources; abound in mineral resources / ～广大的人力资源 command vast reserves of manpower / 一个～十万人口的新城市 a new town of 100,000 people

拥政爱民 yōngzhèng-àimín　(of the army) support the government and cherish the people

痈(癰) yōng　med. carbuncle

痈疽 yōngjū　ulcer

邕 Yōng　① (also 邕江 Yōngjiāng) a river in Guangxi ② another name for 南宁 Nánníng

邕剧 yōngjù　a local opera popular in the Cantonese-speaking districts of Guangxi

庸[1] yōng　① commonplace; mediocre: ～言～行 commonplace words and deeds ② inferior; second-rate: 平庸 píngyōng

庸[2] yōng　formal ① (usu. used in the negative) need: 无～细述。This needn't be related in detail. or There is no need to go into details. ② (used in rhetorical questions) how; in what way: ～可弃乎? How could this possibly be relinquished?

庸才 yōngcái　formal a mediocre person; a person of mediocre ability; mediocrity

庸常 yōngcháng　commonplace; mediocre: ～之才 mediocre ability or a person of mediocre ability

庸夫 yōngfū　a mediocre person

庸劣 yōngliè　inferior; low-grade

庸碌 yōnglù　mediocre and unambitious: ～无能 mediocre and incompetent

庸人 yōngrén　a mediocre person

庸人自扰 yōngrén zì rǎo　worry about imaginary troubles; alarm oneself needlessly

庸俗 yōngsú　vulgar; philistine; low: 相互吹捧的～作风 the vulgar ways of logrolling / 趣味～ have vulgar (or unrefined) tastes / ～化 vulgarize; debase

庸医 yōngyī　quack; charlatan

庸中佼佼 yōng zhōng jiǎojiǎo　a giant among dwarfs

雍　yōng　① formal harmony ② (Yōng) a surname

雍和 yōnghé　harmony

雍容 yōngróng　natural, graceful and poised: 态度～ have a dignified bearing

雍容大雅 yōngróng dàyǎ　display poise and refinement

雍容华贵 yōngróng huáguì　(of a woman) elegant and poised; stately

慵　yōng　formal weary; lethargic; languid

慵惰 yōngduò　formal lazy; indolent

慵倦 yōngjuàn　(also 慵困 yōngkùn) tired and sleepy

慵懒 yōnglǎn　formal sluggish; indolent; lethargic

堳(隃)　yōng　formal city wall; high wall

壅　yōng　① stop up; obstruct: 壅塞 yōngsè ② heap soil or fertilizer over and around the roots (of plants and trees): ～土 hilling / ～肥 heap fertilizer around the roots

壅蔽 yōngbì　formal hide from view; cover; conceal

壅塞 yōngsè　be clogged up; be jammed; be congested: 水道～。The waterway is blocked up.

臃　yōng　formal swelling

臃肿 yōngzhǒng　① too fat to move: 穿得太～ be cumbersomely dressed; be encumbered by too much clothing ② overstaffed: ～的机构 overstaffed organizations

鳙　yōng　variegated carp; bighead (Aristichthys nobilis)

鳙鱼 yōngyú　variegated carp; bighead (Aristichthys nobilis)

饔　yōng　formal ① cooked food ② breakfast

饔飧 yōng-sūn　formal breakfast and supper

饔飧不继 yōng-sūn bù jì　not know where the next meal will come from

yóng

喁　yóng　formal a fish sticking its mouth out of the water

喁喁 yóngyóng　formal ① everyone looking up to sb. ② whisper: ～私语 talk in whispers / ～情话 whisper tender words to each other

yǒng

永　yǒng　adv. perpetually; forever; always: ～放光芒 shine forever / ～葆青春 always keep one's spirit young; keep alive the fervour of youth / ～不变心 remain loyal till one's dying day

永别 yǒngbié　part never to meet again; part forever; be parted by death

永垂不朽 yǒng chuí bùxiǔ　sb.'s memory will live forever; be immortal: 人民英雄～! Eternal glory to the people's heroes! or Immortal are the people's heroes! / ～的杰作 a masterpiece that will live forever

永磁 yǒngcí　phys. permanent magnetism

永磁发电机 yǒngcí fādiànjī　magneto

永磁体 yǒngcítǐ　permanent magnet

永冻层 yǒngdòngcéng　geol. permafrost horizon

永恒 yǒnghéng　eternal; perpetual: ～的友谊 eternal friendship / ～的真理 eternal truth

永恒运动 yǒnghéng yùndòng　phys. perpetual motion

永久 yǒngjiǔ　permanent; perpetual; everlasting; forever; for good (and all): ～会员 permanent member / ～和平 perpetual (or everlasting) peace / ～主权 permanent sovereignty / ～中立 permanent neutrality / ～性居民身份证 permanent identity card

永久磁铁 yǒngjiǔ cítiě　permanent magnet

永久冻土 yǒngjiǔ dòngtǔ　permafrost

永久雪线 yǒngjiǔ xuěxiàn　firn line

永诀 yǒngjué　formal part forever; be separated by death: 蓉城一别, 竟成～。When we parted at chengdu, I little thought that we were never to meet again in this world.

永眠 yǒngmián　euph. die; be dead

永年 yǒngnián　① the whole year; throughout the year; all the year round ② long life; longevity

永生 yǒngshēng　① eternal life ② (usu. used in mourning for the dead) be immortal; live forever: ～的战士 immortal fighter / 为争取民族解放斗争而牺牲的烈士们～! Those who died for national liberation shall live forever in our memory.

永生永世 yǒngshēng-yǒngshì　for ever and ever

永世 yǒngshì　forever: ～难忘 will never forget it for the rest of one's life / ～长存 live forever; be everlasting; be immortal

永逝 yǒngshì　pass away; be gone forever

永夜 yǒngyè　formal a long night

永远 yǒngyuǎn　adv. always; forever; ever: ～记住我的劝告。Always remember my advice. / 我不想～住在这儿。I don't plan to live here forever. / 中国现在不做超级大国, 将来也～不做超级大国。China is not a superpower, nor will she ever become one. / 我～不再去了。I'll never go there again.

永志不忘 yǒng zhì bù wàng　will forever bear in mind; will always cherish the memory of sb. or sth.

甬　Yǒng　① (also 甬江 Yǒngjiāng) a river in Zhejiang Province ② another name for 宁波 Ningbo (a city in Zhejiang Province)

甬道 yǒngdào　① (also 甬路 yǒnglù) a paved path leading to a main hall or a tomb ② corridor

甬剧 yǒngjù　a local opera popular in the Ningbo area of Zhejiang Province

泳　yǒng　swim: 仰泳 yǎngyǒng / 潜泳 qiányǒng

泳道 yǒngdào　lane (in a swimming race): 他游的是第四～。He swam in the fourth lane.

咏(詠)　yǒng　① chant; intone: ～诗 chant poems ② express or narrate in poetic form: 《～梅》 Ode to the Plum Blossom

咏唱 yǒngchàng　chant; sing

咏怀 yǒnghuái　singing from one's heart (a literary subgenre): ～诗 poems of one's heart (in which the poet reveals his innermost feelings)

咏史 yǒngshǐ　singing of history (a literary subgenre): ～诗 poems on history (in which the poet mentions

some historical event to point a moral or as an excuse for comment on contemporary political affairs)

咏叹 yǒngtàn　intone; chant; sing

咏叹调 yǒngtàndiào　*mus.* aria

咏赞 yǒngzàn　sing the praises of; praise

俑 yǒng　wooden or earthen human figure buried with the dead in ancient times; tomb figure; figurine: 陶～ pottery figurine / 武士～ warrior figure

勇 yǒng　brave; valiant; courageous: 越战越～ one's courage mounts as the battle progresses

勇敢 yǒnggǎn　brave; courageous: 勤劳～ 的人民 a brave and industrious people / ～善战 courageous and skilful in battle

勇冠三军 yǒng guàn sānjūn　the bravest of the brave in the whole army; distinguish oneself by peerless valour

勇悍 yǒnghàn　brave and fierce

勇健 yǒngjiàn　brave and strong

勇决 yǒngjué　*formal* brave and resolute

勇猛 yǒngměng　bold and powerful; full of valour and vigour: ～前进 march boldly forward

勇气 yǒngqì　courage; nerve: 鼓起～ pluck up (*or* muster up) one's courage / 见她满脸的不高兴，我没有～再问下去。 She looked so displeased that I didn't have the nerve to ask her further questions.

勇士 yǒngshì　a brave and strong man; warrior

勇往直前 yǒng wǎng zhí qián　march forward courageously; advance bravely

勇武 yǒngwǔ　valiant: ～过人 surpass others in valour; be surpassingly valorous

勇毅 yǒngyì　brave and steadfast

勇于 yǒngyú　be brave in; be bold in; have the courage to: ～负责 be brave in shouldering responsibilities / 承认错误 have the courage to admit one's mistakes / ～创新 be bold in making innovations

涌 yǒng　① gush; pour; surge: 石油喷～而出。 Oil gushed out. / 风啸浪～。 The wind howls; the waves surge. / 一排排巨浪向石滩～来。 Huge waves surged over the rocks. / 大家都向外～。 The crowd was pouring out. ② rise; spring; well; emerge: 海上～出一轮红日。 A red sun rose above the sea. / 多少往事～上心头。 Memories of the past welled up in my mind.

涌潮 yǒngcháo　tidal bore

涌进 yǒngjìn　pour into: 人们从四面八方～广场。 Crowds of people poured into the square from all directions.

涌浪 yǒnglàng　turbulent waves

涌流 yǒngliú　flow rapidly; pour

涌现 yǒngxiàn　emerge in large numbers; spring up; come to the fore: 新人新事不断～。 New people and new things are constantly emerging.

涌溢 yǒngyì　gush out: 清泉～ crystal spring water gushing out

恿（慂） yǒng　see 怂恿 sǒngyǒng

湧 yǒng　same as 涌 yǒng

蛹 yǒng　pupa: 蝶～ chrysalis

踊（踴） yǒng　leap up; jump up

踊跃 yǒngyuè　① leap; jump: ～欢呼 leap and cheer ② vying with one another; eagerly; enthusiastically: ～响应号召 respond to a call enthusiastically / ～参军 vie with one another to join the army / 会上发言～。 People took the floor one after another. / 今晚的晚会大家肯定会～参加的。 I'm sure everybody will be eager to come to this evening's party.

鲬 yǒng　flathead; sand gurnard

yòng

用 yòng　① use; employ; apply: ～双手 use both hands / 你会不会～计算机? Do you know how to operate a computer? / 把你的剪子借我～～，好吗? May I use your scissors? / 酒精常～作溶剂。 Alcohol is often used as a solvent. / 你应该把主要精力～在学习上。 You should devote your chief energies to your studies. ② *prep.* with: ～手掰 break with one's hands / ～剪子剪 cut with scissors / ～火烤 bake over the fire / ～水煮 boil in water / ～针刺麻醉做外科手术 employ acupuncture anaesthesia in surgery / ～严格的科学态度从事研究工作 do research with a strictly scientific attitude / ～五十八秒钟跑完全程 run the course in 58 seconds ③ expenses; outlay: 家用 jiāyòng / 零用 língyòng ④ usefulness; use: 有～ useful / 没～ useless; worthless / 有点～ be of some use ⑤ (usu. used in the negative) need: 不～开灯。 There's no need to turn on the light. / 不～担心。 Don't worry. ⑥ *pol.* eat; drink: 请～茶。 Won't you have some tea, please. ⑦ *formal* (usu. used in letter-writing) hence; therefore: ～特函达。 Hence this letter.

用兵 yòngbīng　use military forces; resort to arms: 不得已而～ have no alternative but to resort to arms / 善于～ be well versed in the art of war

用兵如神 yòngbīng rú shén　direct military operations with miraculous skill; be a superb military commander

用不了 yòngbuliǎo　① have more than is needed: 把～ 的钱存在银行里 put the spare money in the bank ② less than: ～三天，他们就可以把地全部耕完。 They will finish ploughing the fields in less than three days. / 这种鞋～二十块钱就能买到。 You can get a pair of these shoes at less than 20 *yuan*.

用不着 yòngbuzháo　① not need; have no use for: 天不冷，～穿大衣。 It isn't very cold today. You don't need an overcoat. / 把～的书放回书架 Put back the books you are not using on the shelves. / 活儿不多，～这么些人。 There aren't enough jobs for so many people. ② there is no need to; it is not worthwhile to: ～为这些小事争论不休。 There's no need to keep arguing about such triflings.

用材林 yòngcáilín　commercial forest; timber forest

用场 yòngchǎng　use: 有～ be useful / 没有～ be useless / 派大～ be turned to good account / 派新～ be put to new uses

用出来 yòngchulai　① use; exert: 他把吃奶的劲儿都～了。 He exerted his utmost strength. ② become easier to handle with use; be broken in: 这台缝纫机刚买来的时候不好用，现在已经～了。 The sewing machine was rather hard to handle when it was bought, but now it has been broken in.

用处 yòngchu　use; good: 水库的～很多。 A reservoir has many uses. / 这两件东西，各有各的～。 Each of the two things has its own use. / 抱怨有什么～? What's the use (*or* good) of complaining? / 不要扔掉，将来会有～。 Don't throw it away; it may come in handy.

用得了 yòngdeliǎo　need that much or many: 你要这么多钱，～吗? Do you need all that money?

用得着 yòngdezháo　① find sth. useful; need: 这个材料没准儿会～，别扔掉。 This material may come in useful one day, so don't throw it away. / 别看这台机器旧，我们目前正～。 Although the machine is old, it serves our purpose at present. / 这里可能～古代希腊的一段寓言。

Here it might be useful to quote an ancient Greek fable. / 没多少活儿了, 还～那么多人吗? There isn't much work left. Do we still need so many people? ② there is need to; it is necessary to; it is worthwhile to: ～派车去接他们吗? Is it necessary to send a car for them? / ～你亲自去吗? Is there any need for you to go in person?

用度 yòngdù　expenditure; expense; outlay: 他家人口多, ～大。 He has a big family and many expenses.

用法 yòngfǎ　use; usage: ～说明 directions (for use) / 《英语～词典》 A Dictionary of English Usage

用非所长 yòng fēi suǒ cháng　what one is doing is not one's strong point

用非所学 yòng fēi suǒ xué　what one is doing has nothing to do with one's training

用费 yòngfèi　expense; cost

用工 yònggōng　recruit and use (workers): ～制度 the system of recruitment / 企业有权自行决定～办法。 An enterprise has the power to decide how to recruit and use its work force.

用工夫 yòng gōngfu　study or work hard; spend time and energy

用功 yònggōng　hardworking; diligent; studious: ～读书 be studious; study diligently; be diligent in one's studies / 学生都很～。 All the students are very diligent. / 他还在图书馆里～呢。 He's still working hard in the library.

用惯 yòngguàn　be accustomed to the use of: 欧美人用不惯筷子。 Westerners are not used to eating with chopsticks.

用户 yònghù　consumer; user: 征求～意见 ask for consumers' opinions / 电话～ telephone subscriber

用户电报 yònghù diànbào　telex

用劲 yòngjìn　exert oneself (physically); put forth one's strength: 大家一齐～, 把大石头搬开了。 We all heaved together and removed the boulder.

用具 yòngjù　utensil; apparatus; appliance: 炊事～ kitchen (or cooking) utensils / 消防～ fire-fighting apparatus / 救生～ lifesaving equipment / 狩猎～ hunting gear

用开 yòngkāi　be widely used; become popular: 煤气灶这些年～了。 In the past few years the gas oven has become widely used. / 新换的街道名称不知用得开用不开。 I wonder if those new street names will ever become popular.

用力 yònglì　exert oneself (physically); put forth one's strength: ～把门推了一下 give the door a hard push / ～喊叫 shout at the top of one's voice / ～过度 overexert oneself

用品 yòngpǐn　articles for use: 生活～ articles for daily use; daily necessities / 办公～ things for office use; stationery

用人 yòngrén　① choose a person for a job; make use of personnel: 善于～ know how to choose the right person for the right job; know how to make proper use of personnel; know how to employ people to the best advantage / ～不当 not choose the right person for the job / ～制度 the system of personnel placement / ～单位 employing unit ② need hands: 现在正是～的时候。 Now's the time when we are in need of personnel.

用人 yòngren　servant: 女～ woman servant; maid

用上 yòngshang　be made use of; be put to use: 这些资料今天还都～了。 All these data proved useful today. / 他主意倒不少, 就是用不上。 He is full of ideas; none of them will work out, though. / 把这几件工具都带上, 一会儿干起活儿来都用得上。 Take along all these tools. You'll find them handy when you are working.

用舍行藏 yòng shě xíng cáng　(also 用行舍藏 yòngxíngshěcáng) go forward when employed and stay out of sight when set aside

用事 yòngshì　① act: 意气用事 yìqì yòngshì ② formal be in power: 奸臣～ treacherous officials in power ③ formal make literary allusions

用途 yòngtú　use: 橡胶的～很广。 Rubber has many uses. / 一套设备, 多种～ one set of equipment serving many purposes

用武 yòngwǔ　use force; display one's abilities or talents: 大有～之地。 There's ample scope for one's abilities

用项 yòngxiàng　items of expenditure; expenditures

用心[1] yòngxīn　diligently; attentively; with concentrated attention: ～学习 concentrate on one's studies; study diligently / ～听讲 listen attentively to a lecture / ～思索 think hard

用心[2] yòngxīn　motive; intention: ～险恶 have vicious intentions; harbour sinister motives / ～何其毒也! How vicious his intentions are!

用心良苦 yòngxīn liángkǔ　have really given much thought to the matter; have expended much care and thought on sth.

用刑 yòngxíng　put sb. to torture; torture

用以 yòngyǐ　in order to; so as to: 略举数例, ～说明这一原理。 Here are a few examples to illustrate this principle.

用意 yòngyì　intention; purpose: ～很好 with good intentions / 你这是什么～? Just what are you up to? or What's your game? / 我说这话的～, 只是想劝告他一下。 I said all that just to give him some advice.

用印 yòngyìn　affix an official seal (to a document); seal (a document)

用语 yòngyǔ　① choice of words; wording: ～不当 inappropriate choice of words; incorrect wording ② phraseology; term: 商业～ commercial phraseology / 外交～ diplomatic terms

佣

佣　yòng　commission ——see also yōng

佣金 yòngjīn　commission; brokerage; middleman's fee

佣钱 yòngqian　same as 佣金 yòngjīn

yōu

优[1]（優）

yōu　excellent: 择优 zéyōu

优[2]（優）

yōu　actor or actress: 名优 míngyōu

优待 yōudài　① give preferential (or favoured, special) treatment: ～军属 give favoured treatment to servicemen's families / ～外宾 give special consideration to foreign guests / 学生半价～票 special half-price tickets for students ② preferential (or favoured, special) treatment: 我们受到了特别的～。 We were accorded preferential treatment.

优待券 yōudàiquàn　complimentary ticket

优等 yōuděng　high-class; first-rate; excellent: ～品 high-class (or first-rate) product / ～生 top student

优点 yōudiǎn　merit; strong (or good) point; advantage; virtue: ～和缺点 merits and demerits; virtues and defects; strong and weak points / 这个办法有很多～。 This method has many advantages. / 每个人都有自己的～。 Each person has his own strong points.

优抚 yōufǔ　(short for 优待和抚恤) give special care to disabled servicemen, and to family members of revolutionary martyrs and servicemen: 烈属～金 allowance to the family members of revolutionary martyrs

优厚 yōuhòu　munificent; liberal; favourable: 待遇～ excellent pay and conditions; liberal wages and benefits

优弧 yōuhú　math.　major arc

优化 yōuhuà optimize: ～经济结构 optimize the economic structure / ～产业结构 optimize the industrial structure

优化组合 yōuhuà zǔhé optimization grouping or regrouping

优惠 yōuhuì preferential; favourable: ～贷款 loan on favourable terms / ～价格 preferential price / ～的贸易安排 preferential trade arrangement

优惠待遇 yōuhuì dàiyù preferential treatment; favoured treatment

优惠关税协定 yōuhuì guānshuì xiédìng preferential tariff agreement

优惠国 yōuhuìguó favoured nation

优惠权 yōuhuìquán preferential rights

优惠条件 yōuhuì tiáojiàn favourable terms; concessional terms: 按～提供的经济援助 economic aid given on favourable terms

优惠条款 yōuhuì tiáokuǎn preferential clause

优礼 yōulǐ treat with great courtesy: ～教师 treat teachers with great courtesy / 对远方来客～有加 give an exceptionally warm reception to visitors from afar

优良 yōuliáng fine; good: 成绩～ get good marks; make a good showing / 艰苦朴素的～作风 the fine style of hard work and plain living / 推广水稻～品种 popularize fine (or good) varieties of rice

优劣 yōu-liè good and bad; superior and inferior: 不分～ make no distinction between the good and the bad

优伶 yōulíng old actor or actress

优美 yōuměi graceful; fine; exquisite: 风景～ fine scenery / 姿态～ graceful postures / ～的舞蹈动作 graceful dance movements / ～的民间艺术 exquisite folk arts / ～的语言 beautiful language

优孟衣冠 yōu Mèng yīguān the actor Meng in costume—act on the stage; imitate others

优俳 yōupái arch. farce

优人 yōurén same as 优伶 yōulíng

优容 yōuróng formal treat with leniency

优柔 yōuróu ① formal leisurely; unhurried ② formal gentle; amiable ③ weak in character; hesitant

优柔寡断 yōuróu guǎduàn irresolute and hesitant; indecisive: 他是个～的人。He's indecisive.

优生学 yōushēngxué biol. eugenics

优生优育 yōushēng-yōuyù bear and rear better children

优胜 yōushèng winning; superior: ～红旗 championship red banner / ～奖 winning prize / ～者 winner; champion

优胜劣败 yōushèng-lièbài survival of the fittest

优势 yōushì superiority; preponderance; dominant position: 军事～ military superiority / ～兵力 superior force / 占～ occupy a dominant position; gain the upper hand / 我军的力量占压倒～。Our forces are overwhelmingly superior to those of the enemy. / 充分发挥自己的～ give full play to one's own advantages

优渥 yōuwò formal liberal; munificent; favourable

优先 yōuxiān have priority; take precedence: ～发展基础工业 give priority to the development of the basic industries / 必须～考虑的一个问题 a question which claims precedence over all others; a first (or top) priority

优先股 yōuxiāngǔ preference shares; preferred shares

优先权 yōuxiānquán priority; preference

优闲 yōuxián carefree; leisurely

优秀 yōuxiù outstanding; excellent; splendid; fine: ～作品 (literary or artistic) works of excellence / ～电影 highly rated films / ～人才 talented persons / ～生 excellent students / ～的共产党员 an exemplary Communist / 中华民族的～儿女 worthy sons and daughters of the Chinese nation / 今天打靶，他得了个～。He got

an "excellent" in today's target practice. / 成绩～ get excellent results or marks

优选法 yōuxuǎnfǎ optimum seeking method; optimization

优雅 yōuyǎ graceful; elegant; in good taste: 客厅布置得十分～。The drawing room was furnished with elegance and taste. / 她弹的竖琴～动听。She played the harp beautifully.

优异 yōuyì excellent; outstanding; exceedingly good: 考试成绩～ do exceedingly well in an examination / 他们在修建新铁路的工作中作出了～的成绩。They have performed brilliant exploits in building the new railway.

优游 yōuyóu formal leisurely and carefree: ～自在 leisurely and carefree / ～岁月 pass one's days in carefree leisure

优裕 yōuyù affluent; abundant: 生活～ be well-off; be well-to-do; live in affluence

优遇 yōuyù give special treatment: 格外～ accord exceptionally good treatment

优越 yōuyuè superior; advantageous: 处于～的地位 be in an advantageous position / ～条件 favourable conditions / 她总觉得自己比别人～。She always considers herself superior to others.

优越感 yōuyuègǎn sense of superiority; superiority complex

优越性 yōuyuèxìng superiority; advantage

优哉游哉 yōuzāi-yōuzāi leisurely and carefree; leisurely and unhurried

优质 yōuzhì high (or top) quality; high grade: ～高产 high quality and high yield / ～名牌产品 high-quality famous-brand products / ～混凝土 quality concrete / 提供～服务 provide good service / ～奖 high-quality award

忧（憂）

yōu ① worry about; be worried: 忧国忧民 yōuguó-yōumín ② sorrow; anxiety; concern; care: 无忧无虑 wúyōu-wúlǜ

忧愁 yōuchóu worried; troubled; depressed: 面容～ look worried

忧烦 yōufán worried; vexed

忧愤 yōufèn worried and indignant

忧国忧民 yōuguó-yōumín be concerned about one's country and one's people

忧患 yōuhuàn suffering; misery; hardship: 饱经～ have gone through a good deal

忧患余生 yōuhuàn yúshēng a person who has known adversity and sorrow

忧惶 yōuhuáng worried and apprehensive

忧煎 yōujiān be extremely worried

忧惧 yōujù worried and apprehensive

忧劳 yōuláo care-laden and overworked: ～成疾 fall ill from care and overwork

忧虑 yōulǜ ① be worried; be anxious; be concerned: 为孩子的前途～ worry about one's son's future / ～不安 be worried and restless / 深感～ feel extremely anxious; be very worried ② worry; anxiety: 无穷的～ endless worries / 他的～不是没有根据的。His anxiety is not uncalled-for.

忧闷 yōumèn depressed; feeling low; weighed down with cares

忧戚 yōuqī formal distressed; weighed down with sorrow; laden with grief

忧容 yōuróng a worried look: 面带～ look worried

忧伤 yōushāng distressed; weighed down with sorrow; laden with grief

忧思 yōusī ① be worried; be anxious ② troubled thoughts

忧心 yōuxīn formal a troubled heart

忧心忡忡　yōuxīn chōngchōng　heavyhearted; care-laden; weighed down with anxieties

忧心如焚　yōuxīn rú fén　burning with anxiety; extremely worried

忧悒　yōuyì　*formal*　anxious and restless

忧郁　yōuyù　melancholy; heavyhearted; dejected

忧郁症　yōuyùzhèng　*med.*　melancholia

攸　yōu　*formal* (used like the particle 所 in certain phrases): 名誉～关 affect one's reputation

呦　yōu　*interj.* (expressing surprise): ～! 你怎么也来了? Hey! Fancy seeing you here.

呦呦　yōuyōu　*formal*　the cry of a deer

幽[1]　yōu　① deep and remote; secluded; dim: ～林 a secluded wood ② secret; hidden: 幽怨 yōuyuàn / 幽会 yōuhuì ③ quiet; tranquil; serene: 幽深 yōushēn ④ imprison: 幽囚 yōuqiú ⑤ of the nether world: 幽魂 yōuhún

幽[2]　yōu　an ancient administrative district, comprising parts of modern Hebei and Liaoning

幽暗　yōu'àn　dim; dark; gloomy: ～的角落 a dark corner / ～的山谷 a deep and gloomy valley

幽闭　yōubì　*formal*　① put under house arrest ② confine oneself indoors

幽愤　yōufèn　hidden resentment

幽谷　yōugǔ　a deep and secluded valley

幽光　yōuguāng　dim light

幽篁　yōuhuáng　*liter.*　a secluded and restful bamboo grove: 独坐～里, 弹琴复长啸。(王维) Beneath the bamboo grove, alone, I seize my lute and sit and croon.

幽会　yōuhuì　a secret meeting of lovers; a lovers' rendezvous; tryst

幽魂　yōuhún　ghost; spectre; spirit

幽寂　yōujì　secluded and lonely

幽禁　yōujìn　put under house arrest; imprison

幽径　yōujìng　a quiet and secluded path

幽静　yōujìng　quiet and secluded; peaceful: 这里环境很～。It's rather peaceful and secluded around here.

幽居　yōujū　① live in seclusion ② a place of seclusion; retreat

幽兰　yōulán　*liter.*　orchid

幽蓝　yōulán　dull blue

幽灵　yōulíng　ghost; spectre; spirit

幽美　yōuměi　secluded and beautiful: ～的庭院 a secluded and beautiful courtyard

幽门　yōumén　*physiol.*　pylorus

幽门梗阻　yōumén gěngzǔ　*med.*　pyloric stenosis

幽眇　yōumiǎo　*formal*　profound and subtle

幽明　yōu-míng　*formal*　the nether world and this world: ～永隔。The dead and the living are separated forever.

幽冥　yōumíng　① dark; gloomy; sombre ② the nether world

幽默　yōumò　humour: 马克·吐温以～著称。Mark Twain was famous for his humour. / 他很～。He's full of humour. *or* He is very humorous. / ～感 a sense of humour / ～大师 humorist

幽默曲　yōumòqǔ　*mus.*　humoresque

幽期　yōuqī　a secret meeting of lovers; a lover's rendezvous; tryst

幽情　yōuqíng　exquisite feelings: 发思古之～ muse over things of the remote past

幽囚　yōuqiú　imprison; put in jail; keep in captivity

幽趣　yōuqù　the delightful serenity of seclusion

幽人　yōurén　*formal*　recluse; hermit

幽深　yōushēn　(of forests, palaces, etc.) deep and serene; deep and quiet: ～的峡谷 a deep gorge

幽思　yōusī　① ponder; muse; meditate ② deep contemplation; melancholy brooding

幽邃　yōusuì　*formal*　deep and quiet

幽婉　yōuwǎn　(also 幽宛 yōuwǎn) subtle and delicate; exquisite: ～的诗篇 exquisite poems

幽微　yōuwēi　(of sound, smell, etc.) faint; weak

幽闲[1]　yōuxián　(also 幽娴 yōuxián) (of a woman) gentle and serene

幽闲[2]　yōuxián　same as 悠闲 yōuxián

幽香　yōuxiāng　a delicate (*or* faint) fragrance: 兰花～四溢。The orchids give out a delicate fragrance. / 野芳发而～, 佳木秀而繁阴。(欧阳修) As wild flowers bloom, a quiet fragrance is emitted; as beautiful trees thrive, the shade becomes dense.

幽雅　yōuyǎ　(of a place) quiet and tastefully laid out

幽燕　Yōu-Yān　an ancient region comprising parts of modern Hebei and Liaoning: 大雨落～, 白浪滔天。(毛泽东) A rainstorm sweeps down on this northern land, White breakers leap to the sky.

幽咽　yōuyè　*formal*　① whimpering: ～的哭泣 low sobs; whimpers ② murmuring: 泉水～ a murmuring spring

幽忧　yōuyōu　*formal*　distressed; weighed down with sorrow; laden with grief

幽幽　yōuyōu　① (of light or sound) faint: ～啜泣 sob quietly / ～的路灯 dim street lamps ② *formal* looming in the distance

幽怨　yōuyuàn　hidden bitterness (of a young woman thwarted in love)

悠[1]　yōu　① long-drawn-out; remote in time or space: 悠久 yōujiǔ ② leisurely: 悠闲 yōuxián

悠[2]　yōu　*inf.*　swing: 他抓住绳子～了过去。He held on to the rope and swung across.

悠长　yōucháng　long; long-drawn-out: ～的岁月 long years / ～的汽笛声 the drawn-out sound of a siren

悠荡　yōudàng　swing (to and fro); sway (back and forth)

悠忽　yōuhū　*formal*　lazy and idle

悠缓　yōuhuǎn　leisurely and unhurried

悠久　yōujiǔ　long; long-standing; age-old: 历史～ have a long history / ～的文化 a civilization (*or* culture) of long standing / ～的传统 an age-old tradition

悠邈　yōumiǎo　*formal*　remote (in space or time): 年代～ of the remote past

悠谬　yōumiù　(also 悠缪 yōumiù) *formal*　fantastic; absurd; incredible

悠然　yōurán　carefree and leisurely: ～神往 one's thoughts turn to things distant / 采菊东篱下, ～见南山。(陶潜) Plucking chrysanthemums under the eastern hedge, I see the southern hills in the light of Eternity.

悠然自得　yōurán zìdé　be carefree and content

悠闲　yōuxián　leisurely and carefree: ～自在 leisurely and carefree

悠扬　yōuyáng　(of music, etc.) rising and falling; melodious; mellifluous: ～的歌声 melodious singing / ～的小提琴声 mellifluous notes flowing from the violin

悠悠　yōuyōu　① long; long-drawn-out; remote: ～长夜。The night seemed to drag. / ～山川。Oh, this vast, everlasting land! ② leisurely; unhurried: ～自得 carefree and content ③ *formal* absurd; preposterous: ～之谈 a preposterous statement

悠悠荡荡　yōuyōudàngdàng　floating about; swinging to and fro

悠悠忽忽　yōuyōuhūhū　① loitering languidly; lounging around ② be in a trance

悠游　yōuyóu　① move about unhurriedly: 有几艘小艇在湖面上～。There were a few yachts sailing leisurely on

the lake. ② leisurely and carefree: ～自在 leisurely and carefree

悠远 yōuyuǎn ① a long time ago; long ago; distant: ～的往事 events of the distant past ② far off (*or* away); remote; distant: 山川～ mountains and rivers far, far away

悠着 yōuzhe (also 悠停着 yōutíngzhe) *dial.* take things easy: ～点劲，别太猛了。Take it easy (*or* Easy)! Don't go at it so hard.

yóu

尤¹（尢） yóu ① outstanding: 择～ pick out the best / 拔其～ select and promote those of outstanding ability ② *adv.* particularly; especially: 这一点～为重要。This is even more important. / 此地盛产水果，～以梨桃著称。The place abounds with fruit, especially pears and peaches. ③ (Yóu) a surname

尤²（尢） yóu ① fault; mistake: 效尤 xiàoyóu ② have a grudge against; blame: 怨天尤人 yuàntiān-yóurén

尤其 yóuqí *adv.* especially; particularly: 大家干得都很猛，～是小王。Everyone was working energetically, especially Xiao Wang. / 讲话的第一部分～重要。The first part of the speech is particularly important. / 多喝酒对身体不好，～影响心脏。Heavy drinking is harmful to health, especially to the heart. / 我喜欢音乐，～喜欢古典音乐。I love music, especially classical music.

尤甚 yóushèn more so; especially so: 夏季多雨，七月下旬～。We have abundant rains in summer, especially in the last ten days of July.

尤物 yóuwù *formal* ① a rare thing ② an extraordinary person; a woman of great beauty: 大凡天之所命也，不妖其身，必妖于人。(元稹) It is a general rule that those women endowed by Heaven with great beauty invariably either destroy themselves or destroy someone else.

尤异 yóuyì *formal* excellent; outstanding

由 yóu ① cause; reason: 因由 yīnyóu / 理由 lǐyóu ② pass through; go by way of: 必由之路 bì yóu zhī lù ③ be up to sb.; rest with sb.: 事不～己。Things are beyond one's control. *or* Things are getting out of hand. / ～着性子 do as one pleases / ～她去吧。Let her do as she pleases. / 花色很多，～你挑选。There's a great variety of designs and colours for you to choose from. ④ *prep.* by; through; via: ～边门出去。Exit by the side door. / ～此入内。This way in. *or* Entrance. / ～水路而来 come by the water route ⑤ *prep.* (done) by sb.: 这个钱该～我付。This money should be paid by me. / 这件事～他处理。Leave it to him. / 会议～老李主持。Lao Li will preside over the meeting. / 须～大会通过 be subject to acceptance by a general meeting ⑥ *prep.* because of; due to: ～粗心大意造成的错误 mistakes due to carelessness ⑦ *prep.* by means of: 水～氢与氧化合而成。Water is composed of hydrogen and oxygen. / 代表～民主协商选举产生。The representatives were elected after democratic consultation. / 句子是～词组成的。A sentence is made up of words. ⑧ *prep.* from: ～银川出发 set off from Yinchuan / ～点到面 spread over a whole area from one point / ～下而上 from bottom to top; from the lower level upward; from below / ～汉语译成英语 translate from Chinese into English / ～早上六点一直到晚上十点 from 6 a.m. up to 10 p.m. ⑨ (Yóu) a surname

由表及里 yóu biǎo jí lǐ from the outside to the inside; from the surface to the centre: 指挥员将得来的各种材料加以由此及彼、～的思索。The commander pondered on the information gathered about the situation, proceeding from one thing to another and from the outside to the inside.

由不得 yóubude ① not be up to sb. to decide; be beyond the control of: 这件事～我。It's not up to me. / 事到如今就～你了。You have no choice in the matter at this late hour. ② cannot help: ～笑了起来 can't help laughing

由此 yóucǐ from this; therefrom; hence; thus: ～前进 go forward from here / ～看来 judging from this; in view of this / ～产生的一切后果 all consequences arising therefrom / ～弄出许多错误 make many mistakes as a consequence / ～引起了他们两人之间的误会 hence the misunderstanding between the two of them

由此及彼 yóu cǐ jí bǐ from one to the other

由此可见 yóu cǐ kě jiàn thus it can be seen; this shows; that proves: ～，多数人是赞成这个计划的。Thus it can be seen that the majority are in favour of the plan.

由打 yóudǎ *dial.* ① since; from: ～今年五月份起，工厂的产量就逐月上升。Since May the factory's output has been rising month after month. / ～家乡来的客人 a guest from one's hometown ② via; by way of; through: 河水～这儿往北，再向东入海。The river flows north from here, then turns east and empties into the sea.

由俭入奢易，由奢入俭难 yóu jiǎn rù shē yì, yóu shē rù jiǎn nán it is easy to go from frugality to extravagance, but difficult to go from extravagance to frugality

由简及繁 yóu jiǎn jí fán from the simple to the complex

由近及远 yóu jìn jí yuǎn from the near to the distant

由来 yóulái ① origin; source: 分歧的～ the origin of differences ② up to now; so far: 由来已久 yóulái yǐjiǔ

由来已久 yóulái yǐ jiǔ long-standing; time-honoured: 争论～。The dispute is of long standing. / 这种风俗～。This is a time-honoured custom. / 这个问题～。This is a long-standing issue.

由浅入深 yóu qiǎn rù shēn from the easy to the difficult; from the elementary to the profound

由头 yóutou pretext: 找～ find a pretext

由性 yóuxìng do as one likes; act wilfully: 别让她～儿乱说。Don't let her talk as she pleases without any restraint.

由于 yóuyú ① *prep.* owing to; thanks to; as a result of; due to; in virtue of: ～健康关系 on health grounds / ～各种原因 for various reasons / ～同志们的共同努力，工作进行得很顺利。Owing to the concerted efforts of the comrades, work is going on smoothly. ② *conj.* because; since: ～各人的观点不同，我们没有能够取得一致意见。Since our points of view differ, we can't reach an agreement.

由衷 yóuzhōng from the bottom of one's heart; sincere; heartfelt: 表示～的感激 extend one's heartfelt thanks / 对于你的进步，我感到～的高兴。I heartily rejoice at the progress you've made.

由衷之言 yóuzhōng zhī yán words from the bottom of one's heart; sincere words

由子 yóuzi *dial.* pretext

邮（郵） yóu ① post; mail: 信～了吗? Has the letter been posted (*or* mailed)? / 我上月给家里～去二百元。I remitted home 200 *yuan* by post last month. ② postal; mail: 邮路 yóulù / 邮局 yóujú

邮包 yóubāo postal parcel; parcel: ～保险 parcel post insurance

邮差 yóuchāi *old* postman

邮车 yóuchē postal (*or* mail) car

邮传 yóuchuán *formal* ① send by post (*or* mail) ② postal (*or* mail) delivery

邮船 yóuchuán ocean liner; liner; packet ship

邮戳　yóuchuō　postmark

邮袋　yóudài　mailbag; postbag; (mail) pouch

邮递　yóudì　① send by post (*or* mail) ② postal (*or* mail) delivery

邮递员　yóudìyuán　postman; mailman

邮电　yóudiàn　post and telecommunications: ～业务 postal and telecommunication service

邮电部　yóudiànbù　Ministry of Post and Telecommunications

邮电局　yóudiànjú　post and telecommunications office

邮费　yóufèi　*inf.* postage: ～免收 post-free

邮购　yóugòu　mail-order: ～部 mail-order department

邮花　yóuhuā　*dial.* postage stamp; stamp

邮汇　yóuhuì　remit by post

邮寄　yóujì　send by post; post: ～书籍 send books by post

邮件　yóujiàn　postal matter; post; mail: 挂号～ registered post / 航空～ air mail / 小包～ a postal packet / 早班～几点到? When does the morning post come in? / 末班～几点走? When does the last post go out? / 今天的～量特别大。There's an unusually heavy post (*or* mail) today.

邮局　yóujú　post office

邮路　yóulù　postal (*or* mail) route: ～遍布全国。A postal network now covers the whole country.

邮轮　yóulún　same as 邮船 yóuchuán

邮票　yóupiào　postage stamp; stamp: 一套纪念～ a set of commemorative stamps / 特种～ special stamps

邮亭　yóutíng　postal kiosk

邮筒　yóutǒng　pillar-box; postbox; mailbox

邮箱　yóuxiāng　postbox; mailbox

邮展　yóuzhǎn　philatelic exhibition

邮政　yóuzhèng　postal service

邮政包裹　yóuzhèng bāoguǒ　postal parcel

邮政编码　yóuzhèng biānmǎ　(British) postcode; (American) zip code; zip

邮政储蓄　yóuzhèng chǔxù　postal savings deposit

邮政代办所　yóuzhèng dàibànsuǒ　postal agency

邮政汇票　yóuzhèng huìpiào　postal money order; postal order

邮政局　yóuzhèngjú　post office: ～局长 postmaster

邮政网　yóuzhèngwǎng　postal network

邮政信箱　yóuzhèng xìnxiāng　post-office box (P.O.B.): 5130号～ P.O.Box 5130

邮资　yóuzī　postage: 国内～ postage paid for inland mail / 国外～ postage paid for overseas mail / ～已付 postage paid; postpaid

犹(猶)　yóu　*formal* ① just as; like: 虽死犹生 suī sǐ yóu shēng ② still: ～未定夺 still undecided; not decided yet / ～有可为 can still do something about it

犹大　Yóudà　Judas

犹然　yóurán　*adv.* still; just as before: 虽然时隔多年, 那事他～记得很清楚。After so many years, he still remembers it clearly.

犹如　yóurú　just as; like; as if: 灯火辉煌, ～白昼。The place was lit up as bright as day.

犹太复国主义　Yóutài fùguózhǔyì　Zionism

犹太教　Yóutàijiào　Judaism: ～教士 rabbi / ～教徒 Judaist; Jew / ～堂 synagogue

犹太人　Yóutàirén　Jew

犹疑　yóuyí　hesitate

犹豫　yóuyù　hesitate; be irresolute: ～不定 hesitate; remain undecided / 毫不～ without the least hesitation / 犹犹豫豫 shilly-shally / 他～了一下才回答。He hesitated for a minute before he answered.

犹豫不决　yóuyù bù jué　hesitate; remain undecided; be irresolute

犹之乎　yóuzhīhū　*formal* just as: 人离不开土地, ～鱼离不开水。Man cannot leave the soil just as fish cannot leave the water.

犹子　yóuzǐ　*formal* brother's son; nephew

犹自　yóuzì　still: 现在想起那件事, ～叫人心惊肉跳。Even to this day, I still shudder at the very thought of it.

油　yóu　① oil; fat; grease; petroleum: 摊鸡蛋要多放点～。You have to put in more oil when making an omelet. / 汽车该加～了。The car's engine is in need of oil. ② apply tung oil, varnish, or paint: ～门窗 paint the doors and windows ③ oily; greasy; stained or smeared with oil or grease: 这炖肉太～了。The stewed pork is too greasy. / 你的上衣～了。Your coat has got oil stains on it. ④ oily; glib: 这家伙嘴～得很。That fellow has a very glib tongue. / 这个人～极了。That chap is much too slippery (*or* tricky). / 他打麻将打得可～了。He is an old hand at mahjong.

油泵　yóubèng　*mech.* oil pump

油饼¹　yóubǐng　oilcake (as animal feed or fertilizer)

油饼²　yóubǐng　deep-fried dough cake

油驳　yóubó　oil barge

油布　yóubù　oilcloth; oilskin; tarpaulin

油彩　yóucǎi　greasepaint: 演员们用～化装。Actors and actresses make themselves up with greasepaint.

油菜　yóucài　① rape (*Brassica napus*): ～籽 rapeseed ② Chinese cabbage (*Brassica chinensis*)

油藏　yóucáng　oil deposit; oil pool: 地层～ stratigraphic oil pool / 构造～ structural oil pool / 岩性～ lithogical oil pool

油层　yóucéng　oil reservoir; oil layer; oil horizon: ～压力 reservoir pressure / ～动态 reservoir behaviour (*or* performance)

油茶¹　youcha, yóuchá　tea-oil tree; oil-tea camellia (*Camellia oleifera*)

油茶²　yóuchá　youcha, a gruel of sweetened, fried flour

油茶面儿　yóuchámiànr　flour fried in beef fat with sugar and sesame (for making youcha 油茶)

油船　yóuchuán　oil tanker; tanker; oil carrier

油淬火　yóucuìhuǒ　*mech.* oil hardening; oil quenching

油灯　yóudēng　oil lamp

油底子　yóudǐzi　*inf.* oil dregs

油坊　yóufáng　oil mill

油封　yóufēng　*mech.* oil seal

油橄榄　yóugǎnlǎn　(also 油榄 yóulǎn) olive (*Olea europaea*)

油膏　yóugāo　ointment

油垢　yóugòu　greasy filth; greasy dirt

油瓜　yóuguā　*bot.* large-fruited hodgsonia (*Hodgsonia macrocarpa*)

油管　yóuguǎn　① oil pipe: 铺设～ lay oil pipes ② oil tube: 未下～的井 untubed well / ～深度 tubing depth

油罐　yóuguàn　oil tank; storage tank: ～汽车 oil car (*or* truck)

油光　yóuguāng　glossy; shiny; varnished: 把车子擦得～锃亮 put a good shine on the car

油光水滑　yóuguāng-shuǐhuá　smooth and shining; sleek: 她的头发～的。Her hair is sleek and healthy.

油耗　yóuhào　oil consumption: 降低汽车的～ reduce the oil consumption of motor vehicles

油黑　yóuhēi　glossy black: 她的两条辫子～发亮。She wears two glossy black braids.

油乎乎　yóuhūhū　oily; greasy: 工作服～的。The overalls are smeared with oil.

油壶　yóuhú　oilcan; oiler

油葫芦　yóuhulú　*zool.* a kind of field cricket (*Gryllus testaceus*)

油花儿　yóuhuār　drops of oil on the surface of soup;

blobs of fat

油滑　yóuhuá　slippery; foxy

油画　yóuhuà　oil painting: 画～ paint in oils

油画色　yóuhuàsè　(also 油画颜料 yóuhuà yánliào) oil colours; oils

油灰　yóuhuī　*archit.* putty

油鸡　yóujī　a fine breed of chicken with thick brownish feathers

油迹　yóujī　oil stains; grease spots: ～斑斑 covered with grease spots

油煎火燎　yóujiān-huǒliǎo　in a state of great agitation; in a stew

油匠　yóujiàng　same as 油漆工 yóuqīgōng

油脚　yóujiǎo　same as 油底子 yóudǐzi

油井　yóujǐng　oil well: 钻一口～ drill (*or* bore) a well

油锯　yóujù　chain saw: ～手 chain-saw operator

油枯　yóukū　another name for 油饼[1] yóubǐng

油库　yóukù　oil depot; tank farm: 转运～ oil terminal

油矿　yóukuàng　① oil deposit ② oilfield

油亮　yóuliàng　(often reduplicated) glossy; shiny: 刚下过雨，花草树木的叶子都是～～的。The rain had just stopped, and the leaves of plants and trees all took on a beautiful sheen.

油料　yóuliào　oil-bearing seed; oilseed

油料作物　yóuliào zuòwù　oil-bearing crops; oil crops

油绿　yóulù　glossy dark green

油轮　yóulún　oil tanker; tanker; oil carrier

油码头　yóumǎtou　oil jetty; oil wharf; tanker (loading) terminal

油麦　yóumài　same as 莜麦 yóumài

油毛毡　yóumáozhān　same as 油毡 yóuzhān

油门　yóumén　① throttle ② *inf.* accelerator: 踩～ step on the accelerator

油焖　yóumèn　braise: ～茄子 braised eggplant slices / ～笋 braised bamboo shoots

油苗　yóumiáo　*petroleum* oil seepage

油墨　yóumò　printing ink: 快干～ quicksetting ink

油母页岩　yóumǔyèyán　same as 油页岩 yóuyèyán

油泥　yóuní　greasy filth: 这表需要擦～。The watch needs cleaning and oiling.

油腻　yóunì　① greasy; fatty; oily: 不爱吃～的东西 not care for greasy (*or* fatty, oily) food ② greasy food; fatty food; oily food

油盘　yóupán　food tray

油皮　yóupí　*dial.* ① outermost layer of skin; epidermis: 只是擦破了点～儿。It's only a scratch. ② skin of soya-bean milk

油漆　yóuqī　① paint: 一层～ a coat of paint / ～未干! Wet paint! *or* Fresh paint! ② cover with paint; paint: 把大门～一下 have the gate painted

油漆工　yóuqīgōng　painter

油气　yóuqì　short for 油田伴生气 yóutián bànshēngqì

油气比　yóuqìbǐ　*petroleum* oil-gas ratio

油气界面　yóuqì jièmiàn　*petroleum* the interface of oil and gas; oil-gas interface

油枪　yóuqiāng　*mech.* oil gun

油腔滑调　yóuqiāng-huádiào　glib: 说起话来～ speak glibly; have a glib tongue

油泉　yóuquán　oil spring

油裙　yóuqún　kitchen apron; apron

油然　yóurán　① spontaneously; involuntarily ② (of clouds) gathering: ～作云 clouds beginning to gather

油然而生　yóurán ér shēng　(of a feeling) rise of itself; be produced of itself: 敬慕之心，～。Admiration wells up in one's heart.

油溶性染料　yóuróngxìng rǎnliào　oil-soluble dyes

油鞣　yóuróu　oil tanning

油色　yóusè　oil colours; oils

油砂　yóushā　oil sand: 稠～ heavy oil sand / ～层 pay

sand

油石　yóushí　oilstone (for sharpening cutting tools)

油饰　yóushì　cover or decorate with paint; paint; varnish: ～一新 freshly painted or varnished

油柿　yóushì　wild kaki persimmon (*Diospyros kaki* var. *silvestris*)

油刷　yóushuā　cover with paint or varnish; paint: ～门面 paint the shop front

油水　yóushui　① grease: 这个菜～太大。This dish is too greasy. ② pickings; profit: ～不大 not very profitable / 捞到一点～ pick up a few crumbs; make a profit

油松　yóusōng　Chinese pine (*Pinus tabulaeformis*)

油酥　yóusū　short; crisp; flaky: ～点心 short pastry

油酸　yóusuān　*chem.* oleic acid

油提　yóutí　oil-dipper

油田　yóutián　oilfield: ～开发 oilfield development (*or* exploitation) / 多层～ multi-pay oilfield

油田伴生气　yóutián bànshēngqì　*petroleum* associated gas

油田气　yóutiánqì　short for 油田伴生气 yóutián bànshēngqì

油条　yóutiáo　deep-fried twisted dough sticks

油桐　yóutóng　tung oil tree; tung tree (*Aleurites fordii*)

油桶　yóutǒng　oil drum

油头粉面　yóutóu-fěnmiàn　sleek-haired and creamy-faced—heavily made-up; dressy or foppish

油头滑脑　yóutóu-huánǎo　slick; smooth; oily: 一个～的家伙 a shifty-looking fellow

油汪汪　yóuwāngwāng　① dripping with oil; full of grease ② glossy; shiny

油位　yóuwèi　*mech.* oil level

油位表　yóuwèibiǎo　oil (level) gauge

油污　yóuwū　greasy dirt: 一个满身～的老工人 an old worker covered all over with greasy dirt

油箱　yóuxiāng　fuel tank

油香　yóuxiang　a salted cake fried in sesame oil (a Moslem food)

油鞋　yóuxié　oiled shoes (for wet weather)

油星　yóuxīng　(also 油星子 yóuxīngzi) same as 油花儿 yóuhuār

油性　yóuxìng　oiliness; greasiness

油靴　yóuxuē　oiled boots (for wet weather)

油压　yóuyā　oil pressure

油压泵　yóuyābèng　oil pressure pump

油压表　yóuyābiǎo　oil pressure gauge

油压传动　yóuyā chuándòng　hydraulic transmission

油压机　yóuyājī　hydraulic press; oil press

油压千斤顶　yóuyā qiānjīndǐng　hydraulic jack; oil jack

油烟　yóuyān　(also 油烟子 yóuyānzi) lampblack; soot

油椰子　yóuyēzi　another name for 油棕 yóuzōng

油页岩　yóuyèyán　oil-shale

油衣　yóuyī　*dial.* oilskins

油印　yóuyìn　mimeograph: ～一百份 mimeograph a hundred copies

油印机　yóuyìnjī　mimeograph

油印蜡纸　yóuyìn làzhǐ　stencil; stencil paper

油油　yóuyóu　*formal* ① glossy; shiny ② flowing smoothly and incessantly ③ luxuriant and dense

油浴　yóuyù　*chem.* oil bath

油渣　yóuzhā　① dregs of fat ② *petroleum* oil residue

油渣果　yóuzhāguǒ　another name for 油瓜 yóuguā

油炸　yóuzhá　deep-fry: ～土豆片 (potato) chips; French fries

油炸鬼　yóuzháguǐ　deep-fried dough strips or rings

油毡　yóuzhān　asphalt felt

油脂　yóuzhī　oil; fat: 植物～ vegetable fat or oil / 动物～ animal fat or oil; tallow; grease

油脂麻花　yóuzhīmáhuā　*dial.* smeared or spotted with grease; grease-stained

油纸　yóuzhǐ　oilpaper

油子　yóuzi　① black sticky substance: 烟袋～ tar inside a tobacco pipe ② *dial.* a foxy old hand

油棕　yóuzōng　*bot.* oil palm (*Elaeis guineensis*)

油嘴　yóuzuǐ　① glib ② a glib talker ③ spray nozzle; spray head

油嘴滑舌　yóuzuǐ-huáshé　glib-tongued: 一个～的家伙 a glib talker

疣(肬)　yóu　*med.* wart

疣赘　yóuzhuì　① wart ② anything superfluous or useless

柚　yóu　see below ——see also yòu

柚木　yóumù　teak; teakwood (*Tectona grandis*)

莜　yóu　see below

莜麦　yóumài　*bot.* naked oats

莸(蕕)　yóu　① *bot.* common bluebeard (*Caryopteris incana*) ② a stinking grass mentioned in ancient texts (used to refer to an evil man): 薰莸不同器 xūn-yóu bù tóng qì

铀　yóu　*chem.* uranium (U)

铀后元素　yóuhòuyuánsù　*chem.* transuranium element; transuranium

蚰　yóu　see 蚰蜒 yóuyan; 蜒蚰 yányóu

蚰蜒　yóuyan　common house centipede

蚰蜒草　yóuyancǎo　common name for 蓍 shī

遊　yóu　same as 游②③④

游　yóu　① swim: 这条河太宽，我～不过去。I can't swim across the river; it's too wide. ② rove around; saunter; stroll; travel; tour: ～遍北京的山山水水 visit all the scenic spots in Beijing ③ moving about; roving; floating: 游资 yóuzī / 游民 yóumín ④ *formal* associate with: 交游 jiāoyóu ⑤ part of a river; reach: 上游 shàngyóu ⑥ (Yóu) a surname

游伴　yóubàn　travel companion

游标　yóubiāo　*mech.* vernier; vernier scale: ～卡尺 vernier calliper / ～千分尺 vernier micrometer

游程　yóuchéng　① distance of swimming ② route of travel ③ itinerary

游船　yóuchuán　pleasure-boat

游春　yóuchūn　go on a spring outing

游词　yóucí　(also 游辞 yóucí) *formal* ① unfounded remarks; a groundless statement ② joke; jest

游荡　yóudàng　loaf about; loiter; wander

游动　yóudòng　① move about; go from place to place: 白云在天空中徐徐～。White clouds are slowly floating in the sky. ② mobile; moving; roving: ～探照灯 mobile floodlight

游动哨　yóudòngshào　a roving sentry; patrol

游斗　yóudòu　parade sb. through the streets and denounce him publicly

游方　yóufāng　① roam all around the world: ～僧 an itinerant monk ② a form of institutionalized courtship among Miao（苗族）young people, involving antiphonal singing, engaging each other in conversation, or exchanging mementos

游舫　yóufǎng　pleasure-boat

游逛　yóuguàng　go sight-seeing; stroll about

游宦　yóuhuàn　*formal* serve as an official away from home

游魂　yóuhún　a wandering ghost

游击　yóujī　guerrilla warfare ——see also 打游击 dǎ yóujī

游击队　yóujīduì　guerrilla forces; a guerrilla detachment: ～员 guerrilla; partisan

游击区　yóujīqū　guerrilla area

游击战　yóujīzhàn　guerrilla war; guerrilla warfare

游记　yóujì　travel notes; travels: 《徐霞客～》 *Travels of Xu Xiake*

游街　yóujiē　parade sb. through the streets: ～示众 parade sb. through the streets to expose him before the public

游客　yóukè　visitor (to a park, etc.); tourist; excursionist; sightseer

游览　yóulǎn　go sight-seeing; tour; visit: ～西湖 go sight-seeing on the West Lake / ～长城 visit the Great Wall

游览车　yóulǎnchē　tourist coach

游览地　yóulǎndì　place for sight-seeing; excursion centre

游览区　yóulǎnqū　tourist area

游览图　yóulǎntú　tourist map

游廊　yóuláng　covered corridor (linking two or more buildings); veranda

游乐　yóulè　make merry; amuse oneself: ～场所 places of recreation

游乐园　yóulèyuán　amusement park; pleasure ground (*or* garden)

游离　yóulí　① dissociate; drift away: ～分子 one who quits the collective ② *chem.* free: ～酸 free acid / ～状态 free state

游离电子　yóulí diànzǐ　*phys.* free electron

游离基　yóulíjī　*chem.* free radical

游历　yóulì　travel for pleasure; travel; tour: ～过很多地方 have travelled extensively

游猎　yóuliè　go on a hunting trip

游民　yóumín　vagrant; vagabond

游民无产者　yóumín wúchǎnzhě　*lumpen*-proletariat

游目骋怀　yóumù-chěnghuái　look as far as one's eyes can see and give free rein to one's thoughts and feelings

游牧　yóumù　move about in search of pasture; rove around as a nomad: ～部落 nomadic tribe / ～生活 nomadic life; nomadism

游气　yóuqì　① faint breath: 病人只剩一丝～。The patient was at his last breath. ② *formal* floating clouds

游憩　yóuqì　stroll about or have a rest; play and relax

游禽　yóuqín　*zool.* natatorial bird

游人　yóurén　visitor (to a park, etc.); sightseer; tourist: 每年深秋，北京香山红叶烂漫，～如织。The Fragrant Hills in Beijing, ablaze with red maple leaves in late autumn, attract throngs of visitors.

游刃有余　yóu rèn yǒu yú　handle a cleaver with skill —do a job with skill and ease; be more than equal to a task

游散　yóusàn　take a stroll

游山玩水　yóushān-wánshuǐ　travel from one beauty spot to another; visit various scenic spots

游赏　yóushǎng　enjoy the sights: 缓步～ stroll about enjoying the sights

游手好闲　yóushǒu-hàoxián　idle about; loaf: ～，不务正业 idle about and do no decent work / 别～的，干点正经活儿。Stop fooling around, do some serious work.

游耍　yóushuǎ　play; amuse oneself; have fun

游水　yóushuǐ　swim

游说　yóushuì　go about selling an idea; go about drumming up support for an idea; go canvassing

游丝　yóusī　① gossamer ② *mech.* hairspring

游艇　yóutǐng　yacht; pleasure-boat

游玩　yóuwán　① amuse oneself; play: 孩子们经常去海滨～。The children often go to the beach to play. ②

go sight-seeing; stroll about

游息　yóuxī　① stroll about or have a rest; play and relax: 公园是人们～的地方。A park is a place for amusement and relaxation. ② (of fish, birds, etc.) move about and rest: 这里水草茂盛, 最适合水鸟～。There is plenty of water and grass here—a natural habitat for water birds.

游嬉　yóuxī　play; sport; frolic

游戏　yóuxì　① recreation; game: 做～ play games ② play: 孩子们在公园里～。The children are playing in the park.

游戏机　yóuxìjī　(short for 电子游戏机) video game player; TV game player

游侠　yóuxiá　(in former times) roving brave; knight-errant

游仙诗　yóuxiānshī　poem of mystical excursion (a type of poem, popular during the Wei and Jin Dynasties, in which the poet, discontent with conventional society and desirous of escaping from it, portrays the mystical journey of a Taoist master into the realm of the immortals)

游乡　yóuxiāng　① parade sb. around the villages ② go from village to village soliciting custom

游行　yóuxíng　parade; march; demonstration: 节日～ gala parade / 抗议～ protest march / 饥饿～ hunger march / 举行～示威 hold a demonstration / ～队伍 contingents of paraders or marchers; procession

游兴　yóuxìng　interest in going on an excursion or sight-seeing

游学　yóuxué　old study away from home or abroad: 他早年～日本。He went to study in Japan in his early years.

游医　yóuyī　an itinerant (or travelling) doctor

游移　yóuyí　(of attitude, policy, etc.) waver; vacillate; wobble: ～不定 keep on vacillating / ～于两者之间 waver between the two / 一点～的余地也没有了。There is no wavering.

游弋　yóuyì　cruise: 在海上～ cruise on the sea

游艺　yóuyì　entertainment; recreation: ～节目 programme of musical and other performances / ～室 recreation room

游艺会　yóuyìhuì　an entertainment gathering (for watching performances and playing games)

游泳　yóuyǒng　swim: 去～ go for a swim; go swimming / 参加～比赛 take part in a swimming contest / 在～中学习～ learn to swim by swimming

游泳池　yóuyǒngchí　swimming pool

游泳馆　yóuyǒngguǎn　natatorium

游泳裤　yóuyǒngkù　bathing (or swimming) trunks

游泳帽　yóuyǒngmào　bathing (or swimming) cap

游泳衣　yóuyǒngyī　swimsuit; swimming suit (or costume); bathing suit (or costume)

游勇　yóuyǒng　see 散兵游勇 sǎnbīng-yóuyǒng

游园　yóuyuán　① visit a garden or park: 陪外宾～ accompany a foreign guest on a visit to a park ② mass celebrations in parks: 党和国家领导人和群众一道参加五一节～联欢。Party and state leaders joined the masses in the parks for the May Day celebrations.

游园会　yóuyuánhuì　garden gathering; garden carnival; garden party

游资　yóuzī　idle fund; idle money; floating capital

游子　yóuzǐ　formal a man travelling or residing in a place far away from home: 慈母手中线, ～身上衣。(孟郊) The thread from a fond mother's hand Is now in the jacket of her absent son.

游子　yóuzi　same as 圝子 yóuzi

游踪　yóuzōng　the whereabouts of a traveller: ～无定 travel from place to place without a fixed plan or route

鱿　yóu　squid

鱿鱼　yóuyú　common name for 枪乌贼 qiāngwūzéi —see also 炒鱿鱼 chǎoyóuyú

鲉　yóu　scorpionfish

猷　yóu　formal plan; scheme: 鸿～ a great plan

蝣　yóu　see 蜉蝣 fúyóu

蝤　yóu　see below

蝤蛑　yóumóu　another name for 梭子蟹 suōzixiè

圝　yóu　see below

圝子　yóuzi　a bird used to lure other birds into a trap; decoy

yǒu

友　yǒu　① friend: 好～ a good (or great) friend / 敌～不分 not distinguish between friend and foe ② friendly: 友爱 yǒu'ài / 友邦 yǒubāng

友爱　yǒu'ài　friendly affection; fraternal love: 团结～ fraternal unity / 阶级～ class brotherhood

友邦　yǒubāng　friendly nation (or country)

友好　yǒuhǎo　① close friend; friend: 生前～ friends of the deceased ② friendly; amicable: ～访问 friendly visit / 会谈在～的气氛中进行。The talks proceeded in a friendly atmosphere. / 发表热情～的讲话 make a warm and friendly speech / ～往来 friendly contacts (or exchanges) / ～代表团 goodwill mission / ～人士 friendly personage; friend / ～使者 envoy of friendship / ～条约 treaty of friendship / ～协会 friendship association

友好城市　yǒuhǎo chéngshì　cities of friendship; twin cities; sister cities

友好邀请赛　yǒuhǎo yāoqǐngsài　friendship invitational tournament

友军　yǒujūn　friendly forces

友邻　yǒulín　friendly neighbours; good neighbours

友朋　yǒupéng　formal friends

友情　yǒuqíng　friendly sentiments; friendship

友人　yǒurén　friend: 国际～ foreign friend

友善　yǒushàn　formal friendly; amicable

友谊　yǒuyì　friendship: 深厚的～ profound friendship / 建立～ build (or forge) ties of friendship

友谊赛　yǒuyìsài　friendly match

友谊商店　yǒuyì shāngdiàn　friendship store (a large retail store established in the major cities specifically to cater to foreign visitors)

有　yǒu　① have; possess: 我～一个弟弟。I have a younger brother. / 我～充分时间搞科研。I have plenty of time to do scientific research. / 她～热情, ～朝气。She is full of vigour and enthusiasm. / ～百利而无一弊 have every advantage and no drawback ② there is; exist: 屋里～人吗? Is there anyone in the room? / 这座位～人吗? Is this seat taken? / 树上～两只小鸟。There are two birds in the tree. / 还～许多工作要做。Much still remains to be done. / 你的话很～道理。There is a lot of sense in what you say. ③ (used in making an estimate or a comparison): 水～三米多深。The water is more than 3 metres deep. / 这条鱼～四公斤重。This fish weighs about four kilos. / 他～你这么高。He is as tall as you. / 他～十岁了吧? He is about ten, I guess. / 我不知道鱼还～那么贵。I didn't know fish was that expensive. / 问题～那么严重吗? Is the problem that

serious? ④ (used to indicate sth. appearing or occurring): ～一问题就去解决 deal with a problem as soon as it crops up / 他～病了。He is ill. / 他～过肺病。He has had TB before. / 北京～了很大变化。Beijing has changed a lot. / 形势～了新发展。There are new developments in the situation. / 在同志们的帮助下，他～了很大进步。With the help of his comrades, he has made great progress. ⑤ (used to express the idea of having plenty of): ～经验 be experienced / ～本事 be capable / ～了年纪 be getting on in years / 他很～学问。He is quite a scholar. ⑥ (used with the meaning of "certain" or "some"): ～一天我在街上碰见他了。One day I ran into him in the street. / ～些事还需要商量。Certain things are still open to discussion. / ～人说可以，～人说不可以。Some say yes, some say no. / 这里～时候也能热到三十九度。The temperature here sometimes goes up to thirty-nine degrees centigrade. / 这个措施～地方适用，～地方不适用。This measure is suited to some localities, but not to others. ⑦ (used after certain monosyllabic verbs, the combination functioning as a single word): 瓶上刻～花纹。On the vase is carved an ornamental design. / 墙上题～诗句。On the wall are inscribed lines of poetry. / 这家伙怀～不可告人的目的。That fellow has an underhand scheme. / 这种水果含～多种维生素。This fruit contains vitamins. ⑧ (used before certain verbs in polite formulas): 有劳 yǒuláo / 有请 yǒuqǐng ⑨ prefix formal (used before the names of certain dynasties): ～夏 the Xia Dynasty / ～宋一代 the Song period / 诗至～唐为极盛。During the Tang period poetry attained the acme of its development. ——see also yòu

有碍 yǒu'ài be a hindrance to; get in the way of; obstruct: ～交通 hinder traffic

有碍观瞻 yǒu'ài guānzhān be unsightly; offend the eye; be an eyesore

有案可稽 yǒu àn kě jī (also 有案可查 yǒu àn kě chá) be a matter of record; be on record; be documented: 中国始终坚持和平共处五项原则，这是～的。The record shows that China has consistently adhered to the Five Principles of Peaceful Coexistence.

有板有眼 yǒubǎn-yǒuyǎn rhythmical; measured; orderly: 他说话～。Whatever he says is well presented.

有备无患 yǒubèi-wúhuàn where there is precaution, there is no danger; preparedness averts peril: 有备才能无患，无备必定吃亏。If one is prepared, one will be safe; if not, one will suffer. or Preparedness ensures security; unpreparedness invites disaster.

有鼻子有眼儿 yǒubízi-yǒuyǎnr with every detail described: 她说得～，就像真有那么一回事。She described the whole thing in such vivid detail that it sounded quite real.

有产阶级 yǒuchǎnjiējí propertied class

有偿 yǒuchǎng with compensation; compensated; paid: ～技术转让 compensated transfer of technology / ～服务 paid services

有成 yǒuchéng formal achieve success: 双方意见已渐接近，谈判可望～。Since the two sides are beginning to see eye to eye, we are hopeful that the talks will be a success.

有酬劳动 yǒuchóu láodòng econ. paid labour

有错必纠 yǒu cuò bì jiū every wrong will be righted

有待 yǒudài remain (to be done); await: ～解决 remain to be solved / ～证明 have yet to be proved / ～研究 await research / ～上级作出最后决定 await final decision by the higher level / ～进一步讨论 pending further discussion

有袋类 yǒudàilèi zool. marsupial

有道 yǒudào have attained the Way; be accomplished in the Way; adhere to principles of truth and right: 天

下～。The Way prevails under Heaven (or in the empire). or Good government prevails. / ～之士 a man who has attained the Way (or is accomplished in the Way) / ～明君 a wise, enlightened ruler

有得 yǒudé have learned sth.; have gained some knowledge: 学习～ have profited from one's studies

有的 yǒude some: ～这样说，～那样说。Some say one thing, some say another. / 这些衣服，～好看，～不太好看。Some of these clothes look nice, some don't.

有的是 yǒudeshì have plenty of; there's no lack of: 她～时间。She has all the time in the world. / 这种草药山上～。There are plenty of these herbs in the hills. / 有关这个题目的文献～。There is no lack of literature on this subject.

有底 yǒudǐ know how things stand and feel confident of handling them; be fully prepared for what is coming: 他心里～，一点不慌。He was not at all nervous, for he knew what to expect.

有的放矢 yǒu dì fàng shǐ shoot the arrow at the target—have an object in view

有点儿 yǒudiǎnr ① some; a little: 水壶里还～水。There's still some water in the kettle. / 干这事得要～勇气。It requires some courage to do this. / 现在看来还～希望。It looks a bit hopeful now. ② adv. somewhat; rather; a bit: ～反感 feel a bit resentful; have a touch of resentment / ～不好意思 be somewhat embarrassed / 好像～不高兴 seem a bit out of sorts / ～不大舒服 feel a little under the weather

有法可依，有章可循 yǒu fǎ kě yī, yǒu zhāng kě xún there are laws and regulations to go by

有方 yǒufāng with the proper method; in the right way: 领导～ exercise able leadership / 计划周详，指挥～ carefully planned and well directed

有份儿 yǒufènr have a share; have taken a part in: 这件事我～，要承担责任我也～。I have a share in the business and must bear my share of responsibility. / 分红利她也该～。She should also have a share of the profits.

有福同享，有祸同当 yǒu fú tóng xiǎng, yǒu huò tóng dāng share joys and sorrows; share weal and woe; stick together through thick and thin

有感 yǒugǎn thoughts on sth. (usu. used in the title of a literary sketch): 《重访延安～》 "Thoughts on Revisiting Yan'an"

有功 yǒugōng have rendered great service; have performed meritorious service: ～部队 troops with a fine record of service; meritorious army unit

有关 yǒuguān ① have something to do with; have a bearing on; relate to; concern: 这件事与他～。He has something to do with the matter. / 这些问题都跟哲学～。All these questions relate to philosophy. / ～全局 have a bearing on the situation as a whole ② related; concerned; relevant; pertinent: ～部门 the department concerned / ～当局 the authorities concerned; the proper authorities / ～方面 the parties concerned / ～组织 related organizations / ～规定 pertinent regulations / 阅读～的文件 read the relevant documents / 保证～国家的合法权利 safeguard the legitimate rights of such countries as may be affected

有光 yǒuguāng ① glazed: ～纸 glazed paper ② text. bright: ～人造丝 bright rayon

有轨电车 yǒuguǐ diànchē tramcar; streetcar

有鬼 yǒuguǐ there's something fishy: 这里面～。There's something fishy about it. or One smells a rat here. / 他心里～。He's got a guilty conscience.

有过之无不及 yǒu guò zhī wú bùjí go even farther than; outdo

有害 yǒuhài harmful; pernicious; detrimental: 对健康～ harmful (or detrimental) to one's health / ～的影响

pernicious effects / 我们不做任何～于我们两国友好关系的事。We will do nothing detrimental (*or* harmful) to the friendly relations between our two countries.

有行无市 yǒuháng-wúshì (of a market) have only quotations but no actual trading

有核国家 yǒuhéguójiā　nuclear power; nuclear

有恒 yǒuhéng　persevering

有会子 yǒuhuìzi　*inf.* quite a long while; quite some time: 他出去了一～啦! He's been out for quite a while.

有机 yǒujī　① *chem.* organic: ～酸 organic acid / ～盐 organic salt ② organic: ～的整体 an organic whole / ～的组成部分 an organic part; a component part

有机玻璃 yǒujī bōli　polymethyl methacrylate; plexiglass; perspex

有机肥料 yǒujī féiliào　organic fertilizer; manure

有机耕作 yǒujī gēngzuò　organic farming; organic gardening

有机合成 yǒujī héchéng　organic synthesis

有机化合物 yǒujī huàhéwù　organic compound

有机化学 yǒujī huàxué　organic chemistry

有机可乘 yǒu jī kě chéng　there's an opportunity to take advantage of; there's a loophole that can be used

有机染料 yǒujī rǎnliào　organic dyestuff

有机体 yǒujītǐ　organism

有机物 yǒujīwù　same as 有机化合物 yǒujī huàhéwù

有机物质 yǒujī wùzhì　organic matter (*or* substance)

有奇 yǒujī　*formal* (used after round numbers) odd: 一百～ just over a hundred

有计划 yǒu jìhuà　in a planned way; according to plan: ～地发展国民经济 develop the national economy in a planned way

有加利 yǒujiālì　eucalyptus (a transliteration, now replaced by 桉 ān)

有加无已 yǒujiā-wúyǐ　same as 有增无已 yǒuzēng-wúyǐ

有价证券 yǒujiàzhèngquàn　negotiable securities; securities

有奖储蓄 yǒujiǎng chǔxù　lottery-attached deposit

有教无类 yǒu jiào wú lèi　in education there should be no class distinctions (a saying of Confucius, who undertook to make his students into gentlemen and accepted them from the lowest as well as the highest social strata)

有旧 yǒujiù　*formal* have been friends in the past

有救 yǒujiù　can be saved (*or* cured, remedied): 好了, 这病～了! Thank goodness, we've found a cure for the disease.

有孔虫 yǒukǒngchóng　foraminifer

有口皆碑 yǒu kǒu jiē bēi　win universal praise; be universally acclaimed

有口难分 yǒu kǒu nán fēn　(also 有口难辩 yǒu kǒu nán biàn) find it hard to defend or vindicate oneself

有口难言 yǒu kǒu nán yán　cannot bring oneself to mention sth.; find it hard or embarrassing to bring up a matter

有口无心 yǒukǒu-wúxīn　be sharp-tongued but not malicious: 他是～, 你别见怪。He didn't really mean what he said, so don't take it to heart.

有愧 yǒukuì　feel qualms about sth.; have a guilty conscience

有来有往 yǒulái-yǒuwǎng　give-and-take; reciprocal

有赖 yǒulài　depend on; rest on: 要实现这项革新～于大家共同努力。The success of the innovation depends on our concerted efforts.

有劳 yǒuláo　*pol.* may I trouble you; sorry to bother you: ～您代我买本书。May I trouble you to buy a book for me? / 这件事～您了。Sorry to have bothered you with this matter. / ～远迎 I deeply appreciate your kindness in coming so far to meet me.

有了 yǒule　*inf.* ① (said when hitting upon an idea)

I've got it ② *euph.* be pregnant: 我～。I'm going to have a baby.

有理 yǒulǐ　① reasonable; justified; in the right: 你讲的～。What you say is quite reasonable. ② *math.* rational

有理分式 yǒulǐ fēnshì　*math.* rational fraction

有理函数 yǒulǐ hánshù　*math.* rational function

有理式 yǒulǐshì　*math.* rational formula

有理数 yǒulǐshù　*math.* rational number

有理无情 yǒulǐ-wúqíng　① stick to the principle and disregard personal feelings ② for no apparent reason; without rhyme or reason

有理走遍天下, 无理寸步难行 yǒulǐ zǒubiàn tiānxià, wúlǐ cùn bù nán xíng　with justice on your side, you can go anywhere; without it, you can't take a step

有力 yǒulì　strong; powerful; forceful; energetic; vigorous: 进行～的斗争 conduct a vigorous struggle; wage an energetic struggle / 给以～的支援 give strong (*or* effective) support / 提供～的证据 provide strong evidence; furnish convincing proof / 作出～的回答 give a forceful answer / ～地打击了歪风邪气 hit hard at evil trends / ～无处使 have no outlet for one's surplus energy

有利 yǒulì　advantageous; beneficial; favourable: ～于国计民生 be beneficial to the national economy and the people's livelihood / 向～于人民的方向发展 develop in a direction favourable to the people / ～于改进领导作风 help improve the style of leadership / ～于世界和平 be in the interest of world peace / 形势对我们～。The situation is to our advantage. / ～地形 favourable terrain / ～时机 opportune time / ～条件 favourable conditions or terms

有利可图 yǒu lì kě tú　have good prospects of profit; stand to gain; be profitable

有利无弊 yǒulì-wúbì　have every advantage and not a single disadvantage; be advantageous in every respect

有利有弊 yǒulì-yǒubì　there are both advantages and disadvantages

有例在先 yǒu lì zài xiān　there is a precedent for that

有脸 yǒuliǎn　① have prestige; command respect: 你～, 这事得由你出面去调停。You have prestige, and so are in a position to arbitrate. ② have the face: 我骂过他, 现在叫我怎么～去求他? I once insulted him. How could I have the face to ask a favour of him? / 看你有什么脸见人。I'd just like to see if you can face anyone.

有两下子 yǒuliǎngxiàzi　*inf.* have real skill; know one's stuff: 他干活又快又好, 真～。He works fast and well; he obviously knows his stuff.

有零 yǒulíng　(used after round numbers) odd: 三十～ thirty odd / 一千～ just over a thousand

有令不行, 有禁不止 yǒu lìng bù xíng, yǒu jìn bù zhǐ　orders are not carried out, and prohibitions are not heeded

有门儿 yǒuménr　*inf.* ① find the beginning of a solution; be hopeful (of success): 听他的口气, 这事看来～了。Judging by the way he spoke, he might get the matter off the ground now. ② get the hang: 这活儿他干了几次, 现在有点门儿了。After several trials, he began to get the hang of the work.

有名 yǒumíng　well-known; famous; celebrated: ～的跳水运动员 a famous diver / ～的科学家 a celebrated scientist

有名无实 yǒumíng-wúshí　in name but not in reality; merely nominal; titular: 校长和院长都是～的。The president and the deans are only nominal heads. / 那个委员会～。That committee exists only in name.

有名有姓 yǒumíng-yǒuxìng　identifiable by both given name and surname—of established identity

有目共睹 yǒu mù gòng dǔ　(also 有目共见 yǒu mù gòng

jiàn) be obvious to anyone who has eyes; be perfectly obvious: 他成就之大～。 The greatness of his achievements is obvious. / 滥伐森林造成水土流失, 对农作物危害之大～。 It is perfectly obvious that deforestation, which causes soil erosion, has done great damage to the crops.

有目共赏 yǒu mù gòng shǎng have a universal appeal; appeal to all alike

有奶便是娘 yǒu nǎi biàn shì niáng whoever suckles me is my mother; submit to whoever feeds one; lick the hand of anyone who throws a few crumbs

有你的 yǒunǐde *inf.* ① you really are something; good for you ② you'll get your deserts; you'll suffer for this

有年 yǒunián *formal* for years

有盼儿 yǒupànr *dial.* become hopeful

有朋自远方来, 不亦乐乎 yǒu péng zì yuǎnfāng lái, bù yì lè hū is it not a joy to have friends come from afar?

有凭有据 yǒupíng-yǒujù fully substantiated; well-documented: 因为他说得～, 大家信以为真。 Since his statement seemed well founded, we all accepted it.

有谱儿 yǒupǔr have sth. to go by; have confidence: 做事儿～ do things with confidence; know what one is doing

有期徒刑 yǒuqī túxíng *leg.* fixed-term imprisonment: 判～七年 be sentenced to seven years' imprisonment

有其父, 必有其子 yǒu qí fù, bì yǒu qí zǐ like father, like son

有气 yǒuqì be or get angry; take offence: 我越想越～。 The more I thought of it, the angrier I became.

有气儿 yǒuqìr be breathing: 他还～, 快叫救护车。 He's still breathing. Call an ambulance, quick.

有气无力 yǒuqì-wúlì feeble; weak; faint; listless: 说话～ speak in a faint (*or* feeble) voice / 老人拄着拐棍儿, ～地走开了。 The old man walked feebly away, supporting himself with a cane. / 天气闷热使人觉得身上～。 A hot, sticky day makes a person listless. / 他只～地鼓了几下掌。 He gave just a few half-hearted claps. / 墙洞里搁着一盏小油灯, 黄色的火苗～地跳动着。 A small oil lamp flickered weakly in a niche in the wall.

有钱 yǒuqián rich; wealthy: 他很～。 He has a lot of money. *or* He's very rich. / ～人 the rich; the wealthy

有钱能使鬼推磨 yǒuqián néng shǐ guǐ tuīmò with money you can make the devil turn the millstone; money makes the mare go

有情 yǒuqíng be in love: 你～, 我有意。 You are all heart, and my heart is for you.

有情人 yǒuqíngrén lovers

有情人终成眷属 yǒuqíngrén zhōng chéng juànshǔ lovers will be married; Jack shall have Jill, all shall be well

有顷 yǒuqǐng *formal* after a little while; not long after; soon after

有请 yǒuqǐng *pol.* ask the visitor in

有求必应 yǒu qiú bì yìng respond to every plea; grant whatever is requested

有求于 yǒuqiúyú have to look to sb. for help; have a favour to ask of sb.: ～人 have to look to others for help / 他们以为我们～他们, 所以要价越来越高。 Thinking we are asking favours of them, they are demanding more and more in return.

有去无还 yǒuqù-wúhuán gone never to return; gone forever

有趣 yǒuqù interesting; fascinating; amusing: ～的故事 an interesting story / ～的游戏 a fascinating game; an amusing game

有染 yǒurǎn *formal* have illicit sexual relations

有扰 yǒurǎo *pol.* thanks for your hospitality

有人家儿 yǒurénjiār (of a girl) be engaged

有日子 yǒu rìzi ① for quite a few days; for days: 咱们～没见面了。 We haven't seen each other for quite a few days. ② have fixed a date: 你们结婚～了没有? Have you fixed the date for the wedding?

有如 yǒurú just like; as if; as though

有色 yǒusè coloured: 戴着～眼镜看事情 look at things through coloured spectacles—take a distorted view

有色金属 yǒusè jīnshǔ nonferrous metal

有色人种 yǒusè rénzhǒng coloured race (*or* people)

有身 yǒushēn (also 有娠 yǒushēn) *formal* be pregnant

有身子 yǒushēnzi *inf.* be pregnant; be in the family way

有神论 yǒushénlùn theism: ～者 theist

有生 yǒushēng (also 有生以来 yǒushēng yǐlái) ever since one's birth: ～第一次 the first time in one's life (*or* in all one's born days)

有生力量 yǒushēng lìliàng effective strength; effectives: 歼灭敌人～ wipe out the enemy's effective strength; annihilate the enemy effectives

有生之年 yǒushēng zhī nián one's remaining years: 我今年八十岁了, 希望能在～看到祖国统一的实现。 I'm eighty now. I hope I shall live to see the reunification of our country.

有声片 yǒushēngpiàn sound film; talkie

有声有色 yǒushēng-yǒusè full of sound and colour—vivid and dramatic: 故事讲得～ tell a story dramatically / 他把他看到的情形～地描述了一番。 He gave a vivid and spirited description of what he had seen.

有识之士 yǒu shí zhī shì a person with breadth of vision; a man of insight

有时 yǒushí sometimes; at times; now and then: 他～也写几句诗。 Sometimes he writes a few lines of poetry. / 那里的天气, ～冷, ～热。 The weather there is now cold, now hot.

有史以来 yǒu shǐ yǐlái since the beginning (*or* dawn) of history; throughout history: ～最大的陨石雨 the biggest meteorite shower in history / ～最大的骗局 the biggest fraud ever

有始无终 yǒushǐ-wúzhōng start sth. but not carry it through

有始有终 yǒushǐ-yǒuzhōng carry sth. through to the end: 她做事总是～。 Once she starts a job, she goes through with it.

有事 yǒushì ① have a job; be employed; be occupied; be busy: 她现在～了, 待遇还不错。 She's got a job now, and is pretty well paid, too. / 对不起, 我这会儿～。 Sorry, I'm busy now. ② have sth. happen; meet with an accident; get into trouble: 你放心, 我看不会～的。 Don't worry, I don't think there'll be any trouble. / 做好准备, 一旦～, 马上出动。 Get prepared so that you can set off immediately if something happens. ③ (used with 心里) have sth. on one's mind; be anxious; worry: 看他这几天愁眉苦脸的, 心里一定～。 Just look at the worried look he's been wearing all these days. There must be something weighing on his mind.

有恃无恐 yǒushì-wúkǒng when one has something to fall back upon one has nothing to fear; feel secure in the knowledge that one has strong backing

有数[1] yǒushù know exactly how things stand; have a definite idea of what one's doing: 这样一摸底, 大家心里就～了。 With this stocktaking, we know where we are. / 你放心, 怎么做我心里～。 Don't worry. I know what I'm doing.

有数[2] yǒushù not many; only a few: 只剩下～的几天了, 得加把劲儿。 There are only a few days left. We must get a move on.

有说有笑 yǒushuō-yǒuxiào talk and laugh: 两人～。 The two of them talked and laughed together.

有司 yǒusī *formal* officials

有丝分裂 yǒusī fēnliè *biol.* mitosis

有素 yǒusù ① be always or usually as specified: 训练有素 xùnliàn yǒusù ② *formal* have known sb. for a long time; have long been friends with sb.: 余与张生～。I have known Student Zhang for a long time.

有所 yǒusuǒ to some extent; somewhat: 两国关系～改善。The relations between the two countries have improved to some extent. / 物价～降低。Prices have gone down a little. / 我对这一决议,～保留。I have my reservations about this resolution. / 人类总得不断地总结经验,～发现,～发明,～创造,～前进。Man has constantly to sum up his experience and go on discovering, inventing, creating and advancing.

有所不为而后可以有为 yǒu suǒ bù wéi érhòu kěyǐ yǒuwéi you must leave some things undone if you want to get others done; refrain from doing some things in order to be able to do other things

有蹄动物 yǒutí dòngwù ungulate

有天没日 yǒutiān-méirì (also 有天无日 yǒutiān-wúrì) ① wanton; unbridled; outrageous: 他那些～的话简直听不得。Those outrageous remarks of his were simply intolerable to the ear. ② complete darkness—total absence of justice

有条不紊 yǒutiáo-bùwěn in an orderly way; methodically; systematically: 他做事～。He's a methodical worker. / ～地进行生产 carry on production in a systematic fashion

有条有理 yǒutiáo-yǒulǐ methodical; systematic; orderly

有头无尾 yǒutóu-wúwěi have a beginning but no end; start sth. but not finish it; leave sth. unfinished; give up sth. halfway

有头有脸 yǒutóu-yǒuliǎn have prestige; command respect: 他在村里是个～的,说话很有分量。He is a prestigious figure in his village and what he says carries a lot of weight.

有头有尾 yǒutóu-yǒuwěi have a beginning and an end; do sth. from beginning to end; start sth. and finish it: 他太激动了,没法把自己的事～地讲给大家听。He was too excited to tell them his story from beginning to end.

有望 yǒuwàng hopeful: 丰收～。There's hope of a bumper harvest.

有为 yǒuwéi promising: ～的青年 a promising young person / 年轻～ young and promising

有味儿 yǒuwèir ① (of food) be tasty; be delicious: 这个酸辣汤真～。This vinegar-pepper soup is so delicious. ② (of food) smell bad; be off: 这个鱼～了,不能吃了。This fish has gone off—we can't eat it. ③ be interesting; be meaningful: 这首诗越读越～。The more you read this poem, the more meaningful you find it.

有闻必录 yǒu wén bì lù record whatever one hears

有喜 yǒuxǐ *inf.* be pregnant; be expecting; be in the family way

有戏 yǒuxì hopeful: 这事还～。There is still hope.

有隙 yǒuxì ① *formal* bear a grudge: 二人～。They harbour a grudge against each other. ② there is a loophole: 有隙可乘 yǒuxì kě chéng

有隙可乘 yǒuxì kě chéng there is a crack to squeeze through—there is a loophole to exploit

有闲 yǒuxián have leisure: ～阶级 the leisured classes; the idle rich

有限 yǒuxiàn limited; finite: 为数～ limited in number; not many / 文化水平～ have had little schooling / 对情况了解～ have a limited knowledge of the situation / 人的生命是～的,但为人民服务是无限的。There is a limit to one's life, but no limit to serving the people.

有限公司 yǒuxiàn gōngsī limited company; limited-liability company

有限花序 yǒuxiàn huāxù *bot.* definite inflorescence

有限级数 yǒuxiàn jíshù *math.* finite progression; finite series

有线 yǒuxiàn wired: ～通讯 wire communication

有线传真 yǒuxiàn chuánzhēn wirephoto

有线电报 yǒuxiàn diànbào wire telegraph

有线电话 yǒuxiàn diànhuà wire (or wired) telephone

有线电视 yǒuxiàn diànshì cable television

有线广播 yǒuxiàn guǎngbō wire (or wired) broadcasting; rediffusion on wire: ～网 wire-broadcasting network; wired broadcast network / ～站 wired broadcast station; rediffusion station

有效 yǒuxiào efficacious; effective; valid: 采取～步骤 take effective steps / 这药治哮喘病很～。This is an efficacious (or effective) drug for asthma. / 这张车票三日内～。This train ticket is good (or valid) for three days. / 这个指示仍然～。The directive still holds good.

有效分蘖 yǒuxiào fēnniè *agric.* effective tillering

有效功率 yǒuxiào gōnglǜ *elec.* effective power; useful power

有效荷载 yǒuxiào hèzài useful load

有效库容 yǒuxiào kùróng *water conservancy* effective storage

有效票 yǒuxiàopiào valid ballot paper

有效期 yǒuxiàoqī term (or period) of validity; time of efficacy: 延长合同的～ prolong the contract's period of validity / 本条约～为三十年。The present treaty shall be valid for 30 years. / 这个胶卷已过了～。This film has passed its expiry date.

有效数字 yǒuxiào shùzì significant digits

有些 yǒuxiē ① some: ～人在看书,～人在谈天。Some people were reading, some were talking. / ～旧机器还能用。Some of the old machines are still serviceable. ② *adv.* somewhat; rather: ～不满意 be somewhat dissatisfied / ～失望 be rather disappointed / 他心里～着急。He is rather worried.

有心 yǒuxīn ① have a mind to; set one's mind on: 我～去看看他,又怕打扰他。I'd like to go and see him, but I don't want to disturb him. ② intentionally; purposely: 他是～说给你听的。What he said was intended for you.

有心人 yǒuxīnrén a person who sets his mind on doing sth. useful; a person with high aspirations and determination; an observant and conscientious person

有形 yǒuxíng tangible; visible; physical

有形贸易 yǒuxíng màoyì visible trade

有形损耗 yǒuxíng sǔnhào material loss

有形资产 yǒuxíng zīchǎn tangible assets; tangibles

有性 yǒuxìng *biol.* sexual: ～孢子 sexual spore

有性生殖 yǒuxìng shēngzhí sexual reproduction; zogamy

有性世代 yǒuxìng shìdài sexual generation

有性杂交 yǒuxìng zájiāo sexual hybridization

有幸 yǒuxìng be lucky to; have the good fortune to: 我们～再次相会。We are happy to meet again.

有血有肉 yǒuxuè-yǒuròu lifelike; true to life; vivid: 这个人物写得～。The portrayal of the character is lifelike. / 这篇报道～。This news report is full of vivid details.

有言在先 yǒu yán zài xiān make clear beforehand; forewarn: 不是～,过时不候吗? Wasn't it clearly understood that we wouldn't wait for anyone who was late?

有眼不识泰山 yǒu yǎn bù shí Tàishān have eyes but not see Mount Tai; entertain an angel unawares: 小人"～"! 一时冒渎兄长,望乞恕罪!(《水浒》) I failed to recognize your eminence and I hope that you will forgive me for that blunder.

有眼无珠 yǒuyǎn-wúzhū have eyes but see not; possess no true discernment

有要没紧 yǒuyào-méijǐn unimportant; insignificant; immaterial: 谁管那些～的闲事! Who would like to poke

his nose into those trivial matters?

有一搭没一搭 yǒuyīdā-méiyīdā ① trying to engage sb. in small talk; conversing for the sake of conversing ② not essential; not indispensable

有一得一 yǒu yī dé yī no more, no less; just that much

有一分热，发一分光 yǒu yī fēn rè, fā yī fēn guāng give as much light as the fuel can produce—do one's best, however little it may be

有益 yǒuyì profitable; beneficial; useful: ～的格言 good popular maxims / 作出～的贡献 make valuable contributions / ～于健康 good for one's health / 做一个～于人民的人 be a person who is of value to the people / 会谈对双方都～。The talks were beneficial to both sides.

有意 yǒuyì ① have a mind to; be inclined (or disposed) to: ～帮忙 be disposed to help ② intentionally; deliberately; purposely: ～歪曲 deliberately distort / ～刁难 make things difficult for sb. on purpose / 这书是他～留给我们看的。He has left this book here especially for us to read.

有意识 yǒu yìshi consciously: ～地克服自己的缺点 make conscious efforts to overcome one's weaknesses

有意思 yǒu yìsi ① significant; meaningful: 他说的话很～。What he said was significant. ② interesting; enjoyable: 今天的晚会很～。The performance this evening was most enjoyable.

有意无意 yǒuyì-wúyì wittingly or unwittingly; consciously or unconsciously; by accident or design

有影没影 yǒuyǐng-méiyǐng groundless; unfounded: 那些～的话很快传开了。Such idle gossip spread quickly.

有勇无谋 yǒuyǒng-wúmóu have valour but lack strategy; be brave but not resourceful; be foolhardy

有余 yǒuyú ① have a surplus; have enough and to spare: 粮食自给～ have grain enough and to spare ② odd: 二十～ twenty odd

有缘 yǒuyuán be predetermined by fate; be predestined; have a bond; have an affinity: 我们真～, 又碰见了。It's fate for us, we meet again. / 你两个结为夫妻, 是前世～。Your union was predestined from a previous incarnation. / 余平生与梅～, 既画之, 又赋之。All my life I have had an affinity with plum blossoms. Having painted them, I also versify them.

有缘千里能相会，无缘对面不相逢 yǒuyuán qiānlǐ néng xiānghuì, wúyuán duìmiàn bù xiāngféng if there is a bond between them, the two will meet across a thousand li; without a bond, they will not meet though face to face

有源 yǒuyuán elec. active: ～电路 active circuit / ～器件 active device; active parts

有则改之，无则加勉 yǒu zé gǎi zhī, wú zé jiā miǎn correct mistakes if you have made any and guard against them if you have not

有增无已 yǒuzēng-wúyǐ ever-increasing; increasingly

有朝一日 yǒuzhāo-yīrì should the day come when...; if by chance...

有着 yǒuzhe possess; have: 计算机的发明～伟大的意义。The invention of the computer was an event of great significance.

有枝添叶 yǒuzhī-tiānyè same as 添枝加叶 tiānzhī-jiāyè

有职无权 yǒuzhí-wúquán hold a post but have no real power or authority; be a figurehead

有职有权 yǒuzhí-yǒuquán hold both the post and the power; have the authority that goes with one's post; exercise the power that goes with one's post

有志者事竟成 yǒuzhìzhě shì jìng chéng (also 有志竟成 yǒuzhì jìng chéng) where there's a will there's a way

有志之士 yǒuzhì zhī shì a person of noble aspirations; a person with lofty ideals

有种 yǒuzhǒng inf. have guts; be plucky; be gritty: ～

的站出来! Let anyone who has guts step forward!

有助于 yǒuzhùyú contribute to; be conducive to; conduce to: 这次访问～增进我们两国人民的相互了解。This visit has contributed to a better understanding between the peoples of our two countries. / 体育锻炼～增强体质。Exercise is conducive to good health.

有滋有味儿 yǒuzī-yǒuwèir ① tasty; delicious ② with relish; avidly: 他吃得～。He ate with relish.

有嘴无心 yǒuzuǐ-wúxīn same as 有口无心 yǒukǒu-wúxīn

有罪 yǒuzuì be guilty of a crime; be guilty

卣 yǒu an ancient small-mouthed wine vessel

酉 yǒu the tenth of the twelve Earthly Branches (地支)——see also 干支 gān-zhī

酉时 yǒushí the period of the day from 5 p.m. to 7 p.m.

莠 yǒu ① bot. green bristlegrass ② formal bad; vicious; undesirable: 良莠不齐 liáng-yǒu bù qí

铕 yǒu chem. europium (Eu)

牖 yǒu formal window

黝 yǒu see below

黝黑 yǒuhēi dark; swarthy: 胳膊晒得～ with sunburnt arms

yòu

又 yòu adv. ① (used for an actual action) again: 他～来了。Here he comes again. / 我～到那儿去了。I went there again. / 他说了～说。He said it over and over again. ② also; in addition: 他要买肉～要买鱼。He wants to buy meat and also fish. / 这个很好, ～便宜。This is very good, and inexpensive too. / 天很黑, ～下着雨, 路更难走了。On top of it being dark it was raining, which made the going even tougher. ③ (used between a whole number and a fraction) and: 一～二分之一 one and a half ④ (used, sometimes in pairs, to indicate contrary actions or ideas): 他答应了来～不来。He promised to come but didn't. / 刚才太冷, 现在～太热了。Just a moment ago it was too cold, now it's too hot. / 我想去, ～怕没时间。I'd like to go, but I'm not sure if I can find the time. / 她～想去, ～想不去, 拿不定主意。She couldn't make up her mind whether to go or not. ⑤ (used in a negative statement or a rhetorical question for emphasis): 我～没说你不对, 你何必生气呢? I didn't say you were wrong; why should you be so angry? / 这活儿～不重, 我一个人顶得下来。That's not a hard job. I'm sure I can manage it alone. / 这样做～有什么好处呢? What good is there in doing that? ⑥ (reduplicated, with verbs or adjectives) both ... and ...; not only ... but also ...: 坐飞机～快～舒服。The plane is both quick and comfortable. / 这儿的东西～便宜～好。Things here are not only inexpensive but also good. / ～哭～闹 make a tearful scene

又打又拉 yòudǎ-yòulā strike and stroke alternately; use both the carrot and the stick

又红又专 yòuhóng-yòuzhuān both red and expert; both socialist-minded and professionally proficient; both politically conscious and professionally competent

又及 yòují postscript (PS)

又惊又喜 yòujīng-yòuxǐ be both startled and delighted; be pleasantly surprised

又名 yòumíng also called; alias; also known as: 沈雁

冰～茅盾 Shen Yanbing, also known as Mao Dun

又想当婊子，又想立牌坊 yòu xiǎng dāng biǎozi, yòu xiǎng lì páifang lead the life of a whore and want a monument put up to one's chastity

又要马儿好，又要马儿不吃草 yòu yào mǎ'ér hǎo, yòu yào mǎ'ér bù chī cǎo expect the horse to run fast but not let it graze; eat one's cake and have it

右 yòu ① the right side; the right: 向～拐 turn right / 靠～走 keep to the right ② west: 山～ areas west of the Taihang Mountains, specifically Shanxi Province ③ the right side as the side of precedence: 无出其右 wú chū qí yòu ④ the Right: 思想太～ too far to the Right in thinking ⑤ *formal* favour; give emphasis to: ～文 give emphasis to civil affairs

右边锋 yòubiānfēng *football* outside right; right wing

右边 yòubian the right (*or* right-hand) side; the right

右侧 yòucè same as 右边 yòubian

右舵 yòuduò right standard rudder; right rudder

右锋 yòufēng *basketball* right forward

右后卫 yòuhòuwèi *football* right back

右面 yòumiàn the right (*or* right-hand) side; the right

右内锋 yòunèifēng *football* inside right

右派 yòupài the Right; the right wing; Rightist: 国民党～ the right wing of the Kuomintang; the Kuomintang right-wingers

右前轮 yòuqiánlún off-front wheel (of a car)

右前卫 yòuqiánwèi *football* right halfback; right half

右倾 yòuqīng Right deviation: ～保守 Right-deviationist conservatism / ～思想 Right-deviationist thinking

右倾机会主义 yòuqīngjīhuìzhǔyì Right opportunism

右手 yòushǒu ① the right hand ② same as 右首 yòushǒu

右手定则 yòushǒu dìngzé *elect.* the right-hand rule

右首 yòushǒu the right-hand side; the right: 他～坐着一位老大娘。An old woman was seated on his right.

右袒 yòutǎn *formal* take sides with; be partial to

右舷 yòuxián starboard (of a ship)

右旋 yòuxuán *chem.* dextrorotation: ～物质 dextrorotatory substance

右旋糖 yòuxuántáng *chem.* dextrose; glucose; grape sugar

右翼 yòuyì ① *mil.* right wing; right flank ② the right wing; the Right: ～分子 Rightist; Right-winger

幼 yòu ① young; under age: ～畜 young animal; young stock ② children; the young: 扶老携幼 fúlǎo-xiéyòu

幼虫 yòuchóng larva

幼雏 yòuchú young bird; baby bird; nestling

幼儿 yòu'ér child; infant

幼儿教育 yòu'ér jiàoyù preschool education

幼儿园 yòu'éryuán kindergarten; nursery school; infant school

幼功 yòugōng skills (of actors, acrobats, etc.) acquired during childhood

幼教 yòujiào short for 幼儿教育 yòu'ér jiàoyù

幼龄林 yòulínglín *forestry* young growth

幼苗 yòumiáo seedling

幼嫩 yòunèn ① tender; delicate: ～的秧苗 tender rice seedlings / 婴儿的皮肤 a baby's delicate skin ② immature; naive: 他太～，根本不懂人情世故。He is too naive and knows nothing at all of the ways of the world.

幼年 yòunián childhood; infancy

幼女 yòunǚ a young girl

幼弱 yòuruò young and delicate

幼时 yòushí childhood; infancy

幼体 yòutǐ *biol.* the young; larva

幼童 yòutóng child

幼小 yòuxiǎo young and small; immature: ～的心灵 a childish heart

幼芽 yòuyá young shoot; bud

幼稚 yòuzhì ① young ② childish; puerile; naive: ～可笑 ridiculously childish / ～的想法 naive ideas

幼稚病 yòuzhìbìng ① *psychol.* infantilism ② infantile disorder: 《共产主义运动中的"左派"～》 "Left-Wing" Communism, an Infantile Disorder

幼稚园 yòuzhìyuán old name for 幼儿园 yòu'éryuán

幼株 yòuzhū young plant; seedling

幼子 yòuzǐ the youngest son

有 yòu *formal* (used between a round number and its remainder) and: 三十～八年 thirty-eight years ——see also yǒu

佑（祐） yòu help; protect; bless

佑护 yòuhù protect; bless

佑助 yòuzhù help; aid; assist

侑 yòu *formal* press (sb. to eat or drink); urge: ～食 press sb. to eat / ～觞 urge a guest to drink

宥 yòu *formal* excuse; pardon; forgive: 尚希～见。Please accept my apologies.

柚 yòu *bot.* shaddock; pomelo (*Citrus grandis*) ——see also yóu

柚子 yòuzi common name for 柚 yòu

囿 yòu *formal* ① animal farm; enclosure; park: 鹿～ deer farm; deer park ② limited; hampered: ～于习俗 be constrained by custom / ～于见闻 be handicapped by lack of knowledge and experience

囿于成见 yòu yú chéngjiàn be blinded by prejudice

诱 yòu ① guide; lead; induce: 诱导 yòudǎo ② lure; seduce; entice: ～良为娼 induce innocent girls into prostitution

诱逼 yòubī (also 诱迫 yòupò) cajole and coerce

诱变 yòubiàn *biol.* mutagenesis; mutagenicity

诱变因子 yòubiànyīnzǐ (also 诱变剂 yòubiànjì) *biol.* mutagen; mutagenic agent

诱捕 yòubǔ trap (animals)

诱虫灯 yòuchóngdēng (also 诱蛾灯 yòu'édēng) moth-killing lamp

诱导 yòudǎo ① guide; lead; induce: 这些问题可以～大家去思考。These are thought-provoking questions. ② *phys.* induce: ～作用 induction

诱导反应 yòudǎo fǎnyìng *chem.* induced reaction

诱敌深入 yòu dí shēnrù lure the enemy in deep

诱饵 yòu'ěr bait: 用金钱作～ use money as bait

诱发 yòufā bring out (sth. potential or latent); induce; cause to happen: 把麻疹～出来 bring out the rash of measles (by administering medicine)

诱供 yòugòng trap a person into a confession; induce a person to make a confession: 既不～也不逼供。Neither trickery nor coercion is used to secure confessions.

诱拐 yòuguǎi abduct; carry off (a woman) by fraud; kidnap (a child)

诱惑 yòuhuò ① entice; tempt; seduce; lure: 用黄色书刊～青少年 tempt the young with pornographic books and periodicals ② attract; allure: 窗外是一片～人的景色。The window commands a charming view.

诱奸 yòujiān entice into unlawful sexual intercourse; seduce

诱骗 yòupiàn inveigle; cajole; trap; trick: ～某人投赞成

票 cajole sb. into voting in one's favour / 被～成婚 be tricked into a marriage

诱人 yòurén alluring; fascinating; captivating; enchanting: ～的景色 captivating scenery

诱杀 yòushā trap and kill; lure to destruction: 用灯光～棉铃虫 lure bollworms to their death with lamps

诱使 yòushǐ trick into; inveigle into; lure into: ～她上当受骗 lure her into a trap / ～犯罪 entrapment

诱降 yòuxiáng lure into surrender

诱胁 yòuxié cajole and coerce

诱掖 yòuyè formal guide and encourage; lead and help: ～青年 guide and encourage young people

诱因 yòuyīn cause (esp. of an illness): 他这场病的～是着了凉。 His illness was brought on by a chill.

诱致 yòuzhì lead to; cause: ～堕落 lead to one's degeneration

蚴 yòu the larva of a tapeworm or the cercaria of a schistosome: 毛蚴 máoyòu / 尾蚴 wěiyòu

釉 yòu glaze: 青～瓷器 blue glazed porcelain / ～里红 underglaze red

釉工 yòugōng glazer

釉面砖 yòumiànzhuān glazed tile

釉陶 yòutáo glazed pottery

釉质 yòuzhì physiol. enamel

釉子 yòuzi glaze

鼬 yòu zool. weasel

鼬獾 yòuhuān zool. ferret badger

yū

迂 yū ① circuitous; winding; roundabout: ～道访问 make a detour to call on sb. ② clinging to outworn rules and ideas; pedantic: 这人有点～。 He's a bit of a pedant.

迂夫子 yūfūzǐ pedant

迂腐 yūfǔ stubbornly clinging to outworn rules and ideas; pedantic: ～的见解 pedantic ideas

迂缓 yūhuǎn slow in movement; dilatory

迂回 yūhuí ① circuitous; tortuous; roundabout: 历史的发展是曲折的，～的。 History moves in zigzags and by roundabout ways. / ～前进 advance by a roundabout route ② outflank: 向敌人左侧～ outflank the enemy on the left

迂回曲折 yūhuí qūzhé full of twists and turns; circuitous; tortuous

迂回战术 yūhuí zhànshù outflanking tactics

迂见 yūjiàn pedantic ideas

迂阔 yūkuò high-sounding and impracticable: ～之论 impractical views

迂论 yūlùn impractical views

迂气 yū·qì stubborn adherence to outworn rules and ideas; pedantry

迂曲 yūqū tortuous; circuitous: ～的山路 a tortuous mountain path

迂儒 yūrú a pedantic scholar; pedant

迂拙 yūzhuō impractical and stupid

吁 yū onom. a call to an animal to stop; whoa ——see also xū; yù

纡 yū winding; tortuous

纡徐 yūxú formal unhurried; leisurely

纡尊降贵 yūzūn-jiàngguì condescend

淤 yū ① become silted up; be choked with silt: 水渠里～了很多泥沙。 The channel is almost choked with silt. ② silt: 引～肥田 fertilize the soil with silt / 河～ sludge from a riverbed ③ same as 瘀 yū

淤地 yūdì alluvial plain

淤地坝 yūdìbà water conservancy silt arrester

淤淀 yūdiàn silt up: 河身～。 The river is silted up.

淤灌 yūguàn agric. warping

淤积 yūjī silt up; deposit: 洪水过后，地里～了一层泥浆。 When the flood subsided, it left a layer of mud in the fields.

淤泥 yūní silt; sludge; ooze

淤塞 yūsè silt up; be choked with silt: 航道～。 The waterway is silted up.

淤血 yūxuè med. extravasated blood

淤滞 yūzhì ① (of the flow of a river, etc.) be retarded by silt; silt up ② med. stasis (of blood or other bodily fluids): 静脉～ venous stasis / 尿～ urinary stasis

瘀 yū Chin. med. stasis of blood: 活血化～ reduce stasis and improve blood circulation

瘀斑 yūbān med. ecchymosis

瘀点 yūdiǎn med. petechiae

瘀血 yūxuè Chin. med. stasis of blood

yú

于¹**(於)** yú prep. ① (indicating time or place) in; on; at: 生～上海 be born in Shanghai / 就学～北京大学 study at Beijing University / 驰名～全世界 be famous all over the world; be of world renown / 第一次世界大战爆发～一九一四年。 The First World War broke out in 1914. / 来信～十五日收到。 Your letter was received on the 15th. / 此项工程将～三年内完成。 This engineering project is to be completed within three years. ② (indicating direction): 求助～人 ask people for help / 热衷～集邮 be keen on stamp collecting ③ (indicating giving or yielding to sb.): 腐朽的势力让位～新生的势力。 Decaying forces give way to new rising forces. ④ with regard to; concerning; to: 有利～提高产量 be conducive to higher yields / 这样～你自己不利。 It won't do you any good. / 操之过急～事无补。 It would be of no avail to act with undue haste. ⑤ (indicating beginning or origin) from: 黄河发源～青海。 The Yellow River rises in Qinghai Province. / 他毕业～上海圣约翰大学。 He graduated from St. John's University of Shanghai. / 认识来源～实践。 Knowledge comes from practice. ⑥ (indicating comparison): 不少～五千人 no less than 5000 people / 友谊贵～黄金。 Friendship is more precious than gold. / 金星略小～地球。 Venus is a little smaller than the earth. ⑦ (indicating the doer of an action) by: 主队败～客队。 The home team was defeated by the visiting team. / 见笑～人 be laughed at (by others)

于² Yú a surname

于飞 yúfēi formal flying side by side—conjugal happiness (from 凤凰～ in The Book of Songs《诗经》: The phoenixes are in flight.)

于归 yúguī formal go home—(of a girl) get married (from 之子～, 宜其室家 in The Book of Songs《诗经》: Our lady going home Brings good to family and house.)

于今 yújīn ① up to the present; since: 延安一别，～十年。 It is ten years since we parted in Yan'an. ② nowadays; today; now: 这城市建设得真快，～已看不出它原来

的面貌了。The city has been built up really fast; it's changed beyond recognition.

于是 yúshì (also 于是乎 yúshìhū) *conj.* so; then; thereupon; hence

于心不忍 yú xīn bù rěn not have the heart to; can't bear to

于心有愧 yú xīn yǒu kuì have a guilty conscience; have something on one's conscience; feel ashamed

与(與)
yú same as 欤 yú —— see also yǔ; yù

予
yú *formal* I; me —— see also yǔ

予取予求 yúqǔ-yúqiú take from me whatever you please—make unlimited demands

余¹
yú ① *formal* I; me ② (Yú) a surname

余²(餘)
yú ① surplus; spare; remaining: ～钱 spare money (or cash) / 收支相抵, 尚～五十元。After paying all the expenses, there is a balance of fifty *yuan*. ② more than; odd; over: 五十～年 fifty odd years / 二百～公斤 over 200 kilos ③ beyond; after: 工作之～ after working hours; after work

余波 yúbō the swell after a storm—repercussions: 这场纠纷～未平。The trouble hasn't ended; there are still repercussions.

余存 yúcún balance; remainder: 取出一百元, ～五十元。The balance is 50 *yuan* after the withdrawal of 100. / 核对销售数量和～数量 check the amount of sales and stock

余党 yúdǎng remnants of an overthrown clique (or gang); remaining confederates

余地 yúdì leeway; margin; room; latitude: 还有改进的～。There is still room for improvement. / 订计划要留有～。When drawing up a plan, one should leave some margin.

余毒 yúdú residual poison; pernicious vestige; pernicious influence: 肃清封建思想的～ eliminate the pernicious influence of feudalist ideas

余额 yú'é ① vacancies yet to be filled ② remaining sum; balance

余风 yúfēng lingering remnants of past customs

余割 yúgē *math.* cosecant

余暇 yúguǐ *formal* spare time

余函数 yúhánshù *math.* complementary function

余痕 yúhén trace; vestige

余晖 yúhuī (also 余辉 yúhuī) sunset glow; evening glow: 落日～ the last rays of the setting sun; afterglow

余悸 yújì lingering fear: 犹有～ still have a lingering fear

余角 yújiǎo *math.* complementary angle

余烬 yújìn ashes; embers: 劫后余烬 jié hòu yújìn

余可类推 yú kě lèituī the rest may be inferred by analogy

余款 yúkuǎn spare money (or cash)

余力 yúlì surplus energy or strength: 不遗余力 bù yí yúlì

余利 yúlì profit

余沥 yúlì *formal* heeltap—a small share of benefit

余粮 yúliáng surplus grain: 把～卖给国家 sell surplus grain to the state / ～户 household with grain to spare

余留 yúliú be left; remain: 家里一场大火, 什么都没有了。The house was burned down and nothing was left.

余年 yúnián one's remaining years

余孽 yúniè remaining evil element; leftover evil; surviving supporter of an evil cause: 封建～ dregs of feudalism

余怒未息 yúnù wèi xī (also 余怒未消 yúnù wèi xiāo) be still angry; be still fuming

余切 yúqiē *math.* cotangent

余缺 yú-quē surplus and deficiency: 互通有无, 调剂～ each making up the other's deficiency from his own surplus

余热 yúrè ① surplus energy: 利用～取暖 use surplus energy for heating purposes ② old people's capacity for work: 发挥～ do what one can in one's old age

余生 yúshēng ① the remainder of one's life; one's remaining years ② survival (after a disaster): 虎口余生 hǔkǒu yúshēng

余剩 yúshèng same as 剩余 shèngyú

余矢 yúshǐ *math.* coversed sine (covers)

余数 yúshù *math.* remainder (after division)

余头 yútóu *inf.* remainder

余唾 yútuò same as 唾余 tuòyú

余外 yúwài *dial.* besides; apart from this

余威 yúwēi remaining prestige or influence

余味 yúwèi agreeable aftertaste; pleasant impression: ～无穷 leave a lasting and pleasant impression or aftertaste

余隙 yúxì *mech.* clearance: 切屑～ chip clearance

余暇 yúxiá spare time; leisure time; leisure

余下 yúxià remaining: ～的钱 the remaining sum / ～的同志 the rest of the comrades; the other comrades

余闲 yúxián same as 余暇 yúxiá

余弦 yúxián *math.* cosine: ～定律 the cosine law

余兴 yúxìng ① lingering interest; a wish to prolong a pleasant diversion ② entertainment after a meeting or a dinner party

余蓄 yúxù bank balance

余因子 yúyīnzǐ *math.* complementary divisor

余音 yúyīn lingering sound (of music or singing): ～缭绕。The music lingered in the air.

余音绕梁 yúyīn ràoliáng the music lingering around the beams; the music lingering in the air long after the performance

余荫 yúyìn *formal* the blessings of one's ancestors

余勇可贾 yúyǒng kě gǔ with plenty of fight left in one; with strength yet to spare

余裕 yúyù enough and to spare; ample: ～的时间 time to spare

余震 yúzhèn *geol.* aftershock

好
yú see 婕好 jiéyú

欤(歟)
yú *part. formal* (expressing doubt, surprise, etc.): 嗟～! Alas! / 可不慎～! How could one fail to exercise caution?

盂
yú a broad-mouthed receptacle for holding liquid; jar: 痰盂 tányú

盂兰盆会 yúlánpénhuì the Buddhist name of the Ghost Festival (on the 15th of the seventh lunar month)

臾
yú see 须臾 xūyú

鱼(魚)
yú ① fish: 两条～ two fish ② (Yú) a surname

鱼白¹ yúbái fish sperm; milt

鱼白² yúbái the whitish colour of a fish's belly—grey dawn: 东方一线～, 黎明已经到来。A streak of light in the east heralded the dawn.

鱼鳔 yúbiào air bladder (of fish); swim bladder

鱼叉 yúchā fish spear; fishgig; fish fork

鱼池 yúchí fish pond

鱼翅 yúchì shark's fin (a delicacy)

鱼虫 yúchóng water flea (used as fish feed)

鱼唇 yúchún shark's lip (as food)

鱼刺 yúcì fishbone: 剔掉～ bone a fish

鱼大水小　yúdà-shuǐxiǎo　a big fish in shallow water—a ponderous apparatus without sufficient resources for maintenance

鱼道　yúdào　fishway; fish ladder

鱼肚　yúdǔ　fish maw (as food)

鱼肚白　yúdùbái　the whitish colour of a fish's belly—grey dawn: 东方已露出～。The sky is turning bright in the east. or Day is breaking.

鱼饵　yú'ěr　(fish) bait

鱼粉　yúfěn　fish meal

鱼肝油　yúgānyóu　cod-liver oil

鱼竿　yúgān　fishing rod

鱼缸　yúgāng　fish bowl; fish tank

鱼钩　yúgōu　fishhook

鱼狗　yúgǒu　zool. kingfisher

鱼鼓　yúgǔ　same as 渔鼓 yúgǔ

鱼贯　yúguàn　one following the other; in single file: ～人场 enter in single file; file in

鱼贯而入　yúguàn ér rù　enter in single file; file in

鱼花　yúhuā　(fish) fry

鱼胶　yújiāo　① fish glue; isinglass ② dial. air bladder; swim bladder

鱼具　yújù　fishing tackle (or gear)

鱼口　yúkǒu　(also 鱼口疔 yúkǒudīng) Chin. med. lymphogranuloma inguinale; climatic (or tropical) bubo

鱼雷　yúléi　torpedo: ～发射管 torpedo tube

鱼雷艇　yúléitǐng　(also 鱼雷快艇 yúléi kuàitǐng) torpedo boat

鱼类学　yúlèixué　ichthyology

鱼鳞　yúlín　fish scale; scale: 刮去～ scale a fish

鱼鳞病　yúlínbìng　(also 鱼鳞癣 yúlínxuǎn) ichthyosis; fishskin disease

鱼鳞坑　yúlínkēng　pits arranged like fish scales, dug on mountain slopes for holding water or planting trees; fish-scale pits

鱼龙　yúlóng　archaeol. ichthyosaur

鱼龙混杂　yú-lóng hùnzá　dragons and fishes jumbled together—good and bad people mixed up

鱼篓　yúlǒu　bamboo fish hamper

鱼露　yúlù　fish sauce

鱼卵　yúluǎn　(fish) roe

鱼米之乡　yú-mǐ zhī xiāng　a land of fish and rice—a well-watered place where fish and rice are abundant

鱼苗　yúmiáo　(fish) fry

鱼目混珠　yúmù hùn zhū　pass off fish eyes as pearls—pass off sth. sham as genuine

鱼片　yúpiàn　sliced fish meat

鱼漂　yúpiāo　cork on a fishing line; float

鱼鳍　yúqí　fin

鱼群　yúqún　a shoal of fish

鱼肉　yúròu　① the flesh of fish ② (yú-ròu) fish and meat: 人为刀俎，我为鱼肉 rén wéi dāo-zǔ, wǒ wéi yú-ròu ③ cut up like fish and meat—cruelly oppress: 反动官吏～百姓。The reactionary officials savagely oppressed the people.

鱼生　yúshēng　finely sliced raw fish

鱼生粥　yúshēngzhōu　rice gruel with finely sliced fish

鱼石脂　yúshízhī　pharm. ichthammol; ichthyol

鱼水　yú-shuǐ　fish and water: 军民关系亲如～。The army and the people are as inseparable as fish and water.

鱼水情　yúshuǐqíng　relationship between fish and water—close relationship

鱼水情深　yú-shuǐ qíng shēn　be close as fish and water

鱼死网破　yúsǐ-wǎngpò　either the fish dies or the net gets torn—a life-and-death struggle

鱼松　yúsōng　(also 鱼肉松 yúròusōng) dried fish floss

鱼塘　yútáng　fish pond

鱼藤　yúténg　bot. trifoliate jewelvine (Derris trifoliata)

鱼藤精　yúténgjīng　agric. derris extract

鱼藤酮　yúténgtóng　agric. rotenone

鱼梯　yútī　fishway; fish ladder

鱼丸子　yúwánzi　fish ball

鱼网　yúwǎng　fishnet; fishing net

鱼尾号　yúwěihào　boldface square brackets (【　】)

鱼尾纹　yúwěiwén　crow's feet: 她的眼角已有几道明显的～。At the corners of her eyes the crow's feet are quite noticeable.

鱼鲜　yúxiān　seafood

鱼香肉丝　yúxiāng ròusī　fish-flavoured shredded pork

鱼腥草　yúxīngcǎo　bot. cordate houttuynia (Houttuynia cordata)

鱼汛　yúxùn　fishing season

鱼雁　yú-yàn　liter. fish and wild geese—letters (from the legends of fish and wild geese as bearers of letters): 频通～ often write to each other / ～鲜通 hardly ever write to each other

鱼秧子　yúyāngzi　fingerling

鱼鹰　yúyīng　① a large hawk that feeds on fish; fish hawk ② a diving bird leashed by fishermen to catch fish; cormorant

鱼油　yúyóu　fish oil

鱼游釜中　yú yóu fǔ zhōng　like fish swimming in a cooking pot—in imminent peril

鱼圆　yúyuán　dial. fish ball

鱼跃　yúyuè　fish dive: ～救球 diving save; diving retrieve

鱼闸　yúzhá　fish lock

鱼种　yúzhǒng　fingerling

鱼子　yúzǐ　(fish) roe

鱼子酱　yúzǐjiàng　caviare

俞

俞　Yú　a surname

俞允　yúyǔn　formal accede to (a request); consent; approve

竽

竽　yú　an ancient wind instrument: 滥竽充数 lànyú chōngshù

舁

舁　yú　dial. (of two or more persons) carry

谀

谀　yú　formal flatter 阿谀 ēyú

谀辞　yúcí　(also 谀词 yúcí) flattering words; flattery

娱

娱　yú　① give pleasure to; amuse: 聊以自～ just to amuse oneself ② joy; pleasure; amusement: 耳目之～ pleasures of the senses

娱老　yúlǎo　spend one's remaining years in happiness

娱乐　yúlè　amusement; entertainment; recreation: 象棋是他爱好的～。Chess is his favourite recreation. / ～场所 public place of entertainment / ～活动 recreational activities; recreation / ～室 recreation room

嵎

嵎　yú　see 犰嵎 qiúyú

隅

隅　yú　① corner; nook: 城～ the corner of a city wall ② an outlying place; border: 海隅 hǎiyú

萸

萸　yú　see 茱萸 zhūyú

渔（漁）

渔　yú　① fishing; fishery: 渔业 yúyè ② take sth. one is not entitled to: 渔利 yúlì

渔霸　yúbà　a local despot who monopolizes the fishing market

渔叉　yúchā　fish spear; fishgig; fish fork

渔产　yúchǎn　aquatic products

渔场　yúchǎng　fishing ground; fishery

渔船 yúchuán fishing boat

渔村 yúcūn fishing village

渔夫 yúfū *old* fisherman

渔父 yúfù *formal* an old fisherman

渔妇 yúfù fisherwoman

渔港 yúgǎng fishing port (*or* harbour)

渔歌 yúgē fisherman's song

渔钩 yúgōu fishhook

渔鼓 yúgǔ ① a percussion instrument made of bamboo, used to accompany the chanting of folk tales ② same as 渔鼓道情 yúgǔ dàoqíng

渔鼓道情 yúgǔ dàoqíng chanting of folk tales to the accompaniment of a bamboo percussion instrument

渔火 yúhuǒ lights on fishing boats: 月落乌啼霜满天, 江枫～对愁眠。(张继) Moonset, rooks caw, frost fills the sky, Maples and fishing lights, and sorrow before my bed.

渔获量 yúhuòliàng a catch (of fish)

渔家 yújiā fisherman's family: ～姑娘 a fisherman's daughter

渔具 yújù fishing tackle (*or* gear)

渔捞 yúlāo fishery

渔利 yúlì ① reap unfair gains; profit at others' expense: 从中渔利 cóngzhōng yúlì ② easy gains; spoils: 坐收渔利 zuò shōu yúlì

渔猎 yú-liè fishing and hunting

渔轮 yúlún fishing vessel

渔民 yúmín fisherman; fisherfolk

渔区 yúqū fishing zone

渔人 yúrén fisherman; fisherfolk

渔人之利 yúrén zhī lì the fisherman's gains—profit reaped by a third party ——see also 鹬蚌相争, 渔人得利 yù bàng xiāng zhēng, yúrén dé lì; 坐收渔利 zuò shōu yúlì

渔色 yúsè *formal* love woman's beauty; be fond of women: ～之徒 lecher; libertine

渔网 yúwǎng fishnet; fishing net

渔翁 yúwēng an old fisherman

渔线 yúxiàn fishing line; fishline

渔汛 yúxùn fishing season

渔业 yúyè fishery: ～区 fishing zone / ～协定 fisheries agreement / ～资源 fishery resources

渔舟 yúzhōu *formal* fishing boat

渝¹ yú (of one's attitude or feeling) change: 忠贞不渝 zhōngzhēn bù yú

渝² Yú another name for 重庆 Chóngqìng (a city in Sichuan Province)

腴 yú ① fat; plump: 丰腴 fēngyú ② fertile: 膏腴 gāoyú

愉 yú pleased; happy; joyful; cheerful: 面有不～之色 wear an annoyed expression; look displeased

愉快 yúkuài happy; joyful; cheerful: ～的微笑 a happy smile / ～的事 something pleasant; a joyful event / 心情～ be in a cheerful frame of mind / 祝你在中国逗留期间过得～。I hope you'll have a pleasant stay in China.

愉乐 yúlè happy; joyful; cheerful: 家庭融和～ have a happy and harmonious family

愉悦 yúyuè joyful; cheerful; delighted

逾¹(踰) yú exceed; go beyond: ～额 exceed the allowed amount / 情～骨肉 dearer than one's own flesh and blood / 这位老人已年～七十。The old man is over seventy.

逾² yú *formal* even more: 痛乃～甚。Then the pain became even more acute.

逾常 yúcháng out of the ordinary; unusual: 欣喜～ be overjoyed

逾分 yúfèn excessive; undue: ～的要求 excessive demands

逾恒 yúhéng *formal* out of the common; unusual: 勤奋～ be exceedingly diligent

逾期 yúqī exceed the time limit; be overdue: ～一星期 be a week overdue / 在图书馆借书～不还要罚款。You must pay a fine for overdue library books.

逾限 yúxiàn exceed the time limit; be overdue

逾越 yúyuè exceed; go beyond: ～权限 overstep one's authority / ～界限 go beyond the limit; go out of bounds / ～常规 depart from the usual practice

揄 yú *formal* ① draw ② raise

揄扬 yúyáng *formal* ① praise ② publicize; advocate

畲 yú *formal* fields in the third year of cultivation ——see also shē

愚 yú ① foolish; stupid: 愚笨 yúbèn ② make a fool of; fool: 为人所～ be fooled (*or* duped) by sb. ③ *hum.* I: ～以为不然。I beg to differ. / ～兄 your unworthy elder brother—I

愚骏 yú'ài *formal* ignorant and stupid; idiotic

愚笨 yúbèn foolish; stupid; clumsy

愚不可及 yú bùkě jí couldn't be more foolish; be hopelessly stupid; the height of folly: 知其不可为而为之, ～也。To know it's no use, but keep on doing it—there can be no greater folly than this.

愚蠢 yúchǔn stupid; foolish; silly: ～无知 foolish and ignorant

愚钝 yúdùn slow-witted; stupid

愚公移山 Yúgōng yí shān like the Foolish Old Man who removed the mountains—with dogged perseverance: ～, 改造中国。Transform China in the spirit of the Foolish Old Man who removed the mountains.

愚见 yújiàn (also 愚意 yúyì) *hum.* my humble opinion

愚陋 yúlòu stupid and ignorant

愚鲁 yúlǔ dull-witted; stupid

愚昧 yúmèi ignorant; benighted: ～落后 ignorant and backward

愚昧无知 yúmèi wúzhī benighted; unenlightened; ignorant

愚氓 yúméng fool

愚蒙 yúméng *formal* ignorant; benighted

愚民 yúmín ① ignorant people ② try to keep the people in ignorance; try to prevent the people from knowing the truth

愚民政策 yúmín zhèngcè policy of keeping the people in ignorance; obscurantist policy; obscurantism

愚弄 yúnòng deceive; hoodwink; make a fool of; dupe

愚懦 yúnuò stupid and timid

愚人 yúrén fool; simpleton

愚人节 Yúrénjié All Fools' Day (April 1); April Fool's (*or* Fools') Day

愚顽 yúwán ignorant and stubborn

愚妄 yúwàng ignorant but self-important; stupid but conceited

愚者千虑, 必有一得 yúzhě qiān lù, bì yǒu yī dé the greatest fool, in a thousand schemes, must hit once on the truth; even a fool occasionally hits on a good idea

愚忠 yúzhōng blind devotion (to a master, ruler, etc.)

愚拙 yúzhuō stupid and clumsy

瑜 yú ① fine jade; gem ② lustre of gems—

virtues; good points: 瑕不掩瑜 xiá bù yǎn yú

瑜珈　yújiā　(also 瑜伽 yújiā) yoga

榆

榆　yú　elm

榆荚　yújiá　elm seeds

榆钱儿　yúqiánr　inf. elm seeds

榆树　yúshù　elm tree; elm

榆叶梅　yúyèméi　flowering plum

觎

觎　yú　see 觊觎 jìyú

虞¹

虞　yú　formal ① supposition; prediction: 以备不虞 yǐ bèi bùyú ② anxiety; worry: 兴修水利，水旱无～ build irrigation works so as to have no worries about drought or flood / 无冻馁之～ be secure against hunger and cold ③ deceive; cheat; fool: 尔虞我诈 ěryú-wǒzhà

虞²

虞　Yú　① the name of a legendary dynasty founded by Shun (舜) ② the name of a state in the Zhou (周) Dynasty ③ a surname

虞美人　yúměirén　bot. corn poppy

舆¹

舆　yú　formal ① carriage; chariot: 舍～登舟 change from a carriage to a boat ② the part of a carriage for passengers or goods ③ sedan chair: 彩～ a decorated sedan chair

舆²

舆　yú　area; territory: 舆地 yúdì

舆³

舆　yú　public; popular: 舆论 yúlùn

舆地　yúdì　formal land; territory

舆论　yúlùn　public opinion: 作～准备 prepare public opinion / 大造～ whip up opinion / 国际～ world opinion

舆论工具　yúlùn gōngjù　mass media; the media

舆论界　yúlùnjiè　the media; press circles

舆情　yúqíng　public sentiment; popular feelings: 洞察～ know public sentiment well

舆图　yútú　formal map

窬（踰）

窬（踰）　yú　formal climb over a wall: 穿窬 chuānyú

蝓

蝓　yú　see 蛞蝓 kuòyú

yǔ

与¹（與）

与　yǔ　① give; offer; grant: ～人方便 give help to others; make things easy for others / 信件已交～本人。 The letter has been given to the person concerned. ② get along with; be on good terms with: 此人易～。 He is easy to get along with. or He is not difficult to approach. / ～国 friendly country; allied state ③ help; support: 与人为善 yǔ rén wéi shàn

与²（與）

与　yǔ　① prep. (used to indicate involvement, relationship, etc.) with: 他～此事有关。 He has something to do with the matter. ② (used to introduce the recipient of an action): ～困难作斗争 strive to overcome difficulties / ～人民为敌 be hostile to the people; set oneself against the people ③ conj. and: 工业～农业 industry and agriculture / 《战争～和平》War and Peace

——see also yú; yù

与夺　yǔ-duó　same as 予夺 yǔ-duó

与虎谋皮　yǔ hǔ móu pí　ask a tiger for its skin—expect sb. (usu. an evil person) to act against his own interests

与君一夕话，胜读十年书　yǔ jūn yī xī huà, shèng dú shí nián shū　I have learnt much more from this evening's talk with you than I could have learnt from ten years of study

与其　yǔqí　conj. (used correlatively with 不如 or 毋宁) rather than; better than: ～你去，不如我去。 Rather than having you go, it'd be better if I went. / 你～坐车，不如坐船。 It's better for you to go by boat than by train. / ～说是粗心大意，不如说是不负责任。 It's not so much carelessness as irresponsibility.

与人方便，自己方便　yǔ rén fāngbiàn, zìjǐ fāngbiàn　he who helps others helps himself

与人为善　yǔ rén wéi shàn　well-intentioned; well-meaning: ～的批评 well-meaning criticism

与日俱增　yǔ rì jù zēng　grow with each passing day; be steadily on the increase: 学习英语的人～。 The number of people learning English is on the increase.

与世长辞　yǔ shì chángcí　depart from the world for ever; pass away

与世浮沉　yǔ shì fúchén　drift with the current of the times; swim with the tide

与世无争　yǔ shì wú zhēng　stand aloof from worldly strife; hold oneself aloof from the world

与众不同　yǔ zhòng bù tóng　out of the ordinary; different from the common run

予

予　yǔ　give; grant; bestow: 免～处分 exempt sb. from punishment ——see also yú

予夺　yǔ-duó　formal ① (the power) to give and take away: 生杀予夺 shēng-shā yǔ-duó ② commend and depreciate

予人口实　yǔ rén kǒushí　give people a handle

予以　yǔyǐ　give; grant: ～表扬 commend sb. / ～照顾 give preferential treatment

宇

宇　yǔ　① eaves ② house: 庙宇 miàoyǔ ③ space; universe; world: ～内 in the world

宇称　yǔchēng　phys. parity: ～不守恒 parity nonconservation / ～守恒 parity conservation

宇航　yǔháng　short for 宇宙航行 yǔzhòu hángxíng

宇航员　yǔhángyuán　short for 宇宙航行员 yǔzhòu hángxíngyuán

宇宙　yǔzhòu　universe; cosmos

宇宙尘　yǔzhòuchén　cosmic dust

宇宙飞船　yǔzhòu fēichuán　spaceship; spacecraft

宇宙飞行　yǔzhòu fēixíng　space flight; space travel

宇宙飞行员　yǔzhòu fēixíngyuán　astronaut; spaceman; cosmonaut

宇宙服　yǔzhòufú　spacesuit

宇宙观　yǔzhòuguān　world view; world outlook

宇宙航行　yǔzhòu hángxíng　space flight; space travel

宇宙航行学　yǔzhòuhángxíngxué　astronautics; cosmonautics

宇宙航行员　yǔzhòu hángxíngyuán　astronaut; spaceman; cosmonaut

宇宙火箭　yǔzhòu huǒjiàn　space rocket

宇宙空间　yǔzhòu kōngjiān　cosmic space; outer space

宇宙射线　yǔzhòu shèxiàn　(also 宇宙线 yǔzhòuxiàn) cosmic rays; cosmic radiation

宇宙速度　yǔzhòu sùdù　cosmic velocity (or speed): 第一～ first cosmic velocity; circular (or orbital) velocity / 第二～ second cosmic velocity; earth escape velocity / 第三～ third cosmic velocity; solar escape velocity

宇宙学　yǔzhòuxué　(also 宇宙论 yǔzhòulùn) cosmology

宇宙站　yǔzhòuzhàn　space station

屿（嶼）

屿（嶼）　yǔ　small island; islet: 岛屿 dǎoyǔ

羽[1]　yǔ　feather; plume

羽[2]　yǔ　*mus.* a note of the ancient Chinese five-tone scale, corresponding to 6 in numbered musical notation

羽翅　yǔchì　wing

羽缎　yǔduàn　(also 羽毛缎 yǔmáoduàn) sateen

羽冠　yǔguān　crest (of a bird)

羽化[1]　yǔhuà　① sprout wings—become an immortal: ～而登仙 rise as an immortal on newly sprouted wings ② *euph.* (used by Taoists) pass away; die

羽化[2]　yǔhuà　*zool.* eclosion

羽林　yǔlín　another name for 禁军 jìnjūn

羽毛　yǔmáo　feather; plume: 美丽的～ beautiful plumage

羽毛丰满　yǔmáo fēngmǎn　become full-fledged; mature

羽毛画　yǔmáohuà　feather patchwork; feather picture

羽毛球　yǔmáoqiú　① badminton ② shuttlecock

羽毛扇　yǔmáoshàn　feather fan: 摇～的 the man with a feather fan—the mastermind behind a plot

羽毛未丰　yǔmáo wèi fēng　unfledged; young and immature

羽人　yǔrén　① immortal (in Chinese mythology) ② Taoist priest

羽绒　yǔróng　fine soft feathers; eiderdown; down: ～背心 down vest／～服 down jacket

羽纱　yǔshā　camlet

羽扇　yǔshàn　feather fan: ～纶巾 feather fan and silk kerchief (traditional accoutrement for a scholar-official at ease, esp. as used by 诸葛亮 Zhuge Liang)

羽士　yǔshì　(also 羽客 yǔkè) Taoist priest

羽书　yǔshū　(also 羽檄 yǔxí) feather despatch (a military despatch with a feather attached to show its urgency, used in ancient times)

羽坛　yǔtán　badminton circles; the badminton world

羽衣　yǔyī　① *formal* garment or robe made of feathers ② robe worn by a Taoist priest ③ Taoist priest

羽翼　yǔyì　① wing ② assistant

羽族　yǔzú　birds

伛（傴）　yǔ　*formal* bow (to show respect)

伛偻　yǔlǚ　*formal* ① hunchbacked; humpbacked ② bow (to show respect)

雨　yǔ　rain: 天气预报说明天有～。It will rain tomorrow according to the weather forecast.／～下得很大。It's raining hard. ——see also yù

雨暴　yǔbào　*meteorol.* rainstorm

雨布　yǔbù　waterproof cloth; waterproof

雨层云　yǔcéngyún　*meteorol.* nimbostratus

雨滴　yǔdī　raindrop

雨点　yǔdiǎn　raindrop

雨刮　yǔguā　windscreen (*or* windshield) wiper (of a car)

雨过地皮湿　yǔ guò dìpí shī　do sth. as a mere formality; go through the motions; do sth. perfunctorily or superficially

雨过天晴　yǔ guò tiān qíng　(also 雨过天青 yǔ guò tiān qīng) the sun shines again after the rain—after gloom comes brightness

雨后春笋　yǔ hòu chūnsǔn　(spring up like) bamboo shoots after a spring rain: 专业户像～一样蓬勃发展起来。Specialized households sprang up like mushrooms.

雨后送伞　yǔ hòu sòng sǎn　give sb. an umbrella after the rain has stopped—offer help when it's too late; offer help when it's no longer needed

雨花石　yǔhuāshí　*yuhua* pebbles (colourful fine-grained pebbles found in the Yuhuatai 雨花台 area at Nanjing)

雨季　yǔjì　rainy season

雨具　yǔjù　rain gear (i.e. umbrella, raincoat, etc.)

雨涝　yǔlào　waterlogging caused by excessive rain

雨帘　yǔlián　(also 雨帘子 yǔliánzi) same as 雨幕 yǔmù

雨量　yǔliàng　rainfall: ～强度 rainfall density／～站 precipitation station; rainfall station

雨量计　yǔliàngjì　rain gauge; udometer

雨露　yǔlù　① rain and dew ② favour; grace; bounty

雨帽　yǔmào　① rain cap ② hood

雨幕　yǔmù　a curtain of rain—a thick rain

雨棚　yǔpéng　*archit.* canopy

雨前　yǔqián　a kind of green tea, picked before Grain Rain (about mid-April)

雨情　yǔqíng　rainfall (in a given area)

雨区　yǔqū　rain area; rain field

雨伞　yǔsǎn　umbrella

雨师　Yǔshī　Rain God

雨势　yǔshì　the force of rain: ～渐弱。The rain gradually died down.

雨水[1]　yǔshuǐ　rainwater; rainfall; rain: ～足 adequate rainfall／～调和。The rainfall is just right.

雨水[2]　Yǔshuǐ　① Rain Water—the 2nd of the 24 solar terms ② the day marking the beginning of the 2nd solar term (Feb. 18, 19, or 20, after which there should be no more snow, but rain showers may be expected) ——see also 节气 jiéqi; 二十四节气 èrshí sì jiéqi

雨水管　yǔshuǐguǎn　another name for 水落管 shuǐluòguǎn

雨丝　yǔsī　a very light rain

雨蛙　yǔwā　*zool.* tree toad

雨雾　yǔwù　misty rain

雨鞋　yǔxié　galoshes; rubbers

雨靴　yǔxuē　rubber boots; rain boots

雨烟　yǔyān　misty rain

雨燕　yǔyàn　*zool.* swift

雨衣　yǔyī　raincoat; waterproof

雨意　yǔyì　signs of approaching rain: 颇有～。It looks like rain.

雨云　yǔyún　*meteorol.* nimbus

雨珠　yǔzhū　raindrop

语　yǔ　① language; tongue; words: 汉语 Hànyǔ ② speak; say: 低语 dīyǔ ③ set phrase; proverb; saying: ～云，"将欲取之，必先与之。" As the saying goes, "Give in order to take." ④ nonlinguistic means of communicating ideas; sign; signal: 旗语 qíyǔ／手语 shǒuyǔ ——see also yù

语病　yǔbìng　faulty wording or formulation (causing ambiguity)

语词　yǔcí　words and phrases

语调　yǔdiào　*phonet.* intonation

语法　yǔfǎ　grammar

语锋　yǔfēng　thread of discourse; topic of conversation

语感　yǔgǎn　an instinctive feel for the language

语汇　yǔhuì　vocabulary: 汉语的～是极其丰富的。Chinese has a very rich vocabulary.

语惊四座　yǔ jīng sìzuò　the words startle all present

语句　yǔjù　sentence

语录　yǔlù　recorded utterance; quotation: 毛主席～ quotations from Chairman Mao

语妙天下　yǔ miào tiānxià　speak with inimitable wit

语气　yǔqì　① tone; manner of speaking: ～友好 a friendly tone／用婉转的～说 speak in a tactful manner／听他的～，这事大概有点不妙。From the way he spoke about the matter, I gathered something had gone wrong. ② *gram.* mood: 祈使～ imperative mood

语塞　yǔsè　be unable to utter a word (due to excitement, anger, etc.): 悲愤之下，一时～ be speechless with

grief and indignation

语失 yǔshī make an indiscreet remark: 言多语失 yán duō yǔshī

语素 yǔsù *linguis.* morpheme

语态 yǔtài *gram.* voice: 主动·(被动)～ active (passive) voice

语体 yǔtǐ type of writing; style: 口语～ colloquialism / 科学～ scientific style of writing

语体文 yǔtǐwén prose written in the vernacular

语文 yǔwén ① Chinese (as a subject of study or a means of communication): 他的～程度怎么样? How good is his Chinese? ② (short for 语言和文学) language and literature

语无伦次 yǔ wú lúncì speak incoherently

语系 yǔxì *linguis.* family of languages; language family

语序 yǔxù *gram.* word order

语焉不详 yǔ yān bù xiáng ① not speak in detail; not elaborate ② (of a statement) be rather too brief or sketchy

语言 yǔyán language: ～隔阂 language barrier /～与文字 spoken and written language /～规范化 standardization of speech /～科学 linguistic science

语言学 yǔyánxué linguistics; philology: 比较～ comparative linguistics / 普通～ general linguistics / 应用～ applied linguistics /～家 linguist; philologist

语义 yǔyì semantic meaning

语义学 yǔyìxué semantics

语意 yǔyì meaning of one's words: ～深长。The words are full of meaning.

语音 yǔyīn ① speech sounds ② pronunciation: 她的～好。She has good pronunciation. /～课 phonetics class

语音学 yǔyīnxué phonetics: ～家 phonetician

语源学 yǔyuánxué etymology

语种 yǔzhǒng languages

语重心长 yǔzhòng-xīncháng sincere words and earnest wishes: ～的劝告 earnest advice

语助词 yǔzhùcí (also 语气助词 yǔqì zhùcí) *gram.* an auxiliary word that indicates mood ——see also 助词 zhùcí

语族 yǔzú branch: 印欧语系日耳曼～ the Germanic branch of the Indo-European language family

禹 Yǔ ① the reputed founder of the Xia Dynasty (c. 21st–16th century B.C.) ② a surname

圄 yǔ see 囹圄 língyǔ

圉 yǔ *formal* horse stable

庾 yǔ *formal* an enclosure for storing grain

瘐 yǔ see below

瘐死 yǔsǐ (also 瘐毙 yǔbì) *formal* (of a prisoner) die of disease

龉 yǔ see 龃龉 jǔyǔ

窳 yǔ *formal* corrupt; bad: 窳败 yǔbài

窳败 yǔbài *formal* corrupt; rot

窳惰 yǔduò *formal* lazy and dissipated

窳劣 yǔliè *formal* of inferior quality

yù

与(與) yù take part in; participate in: 参与 cānyù ——see also yú; yǔ

与会 yùhuì participate in a conference: ～国 countries attending a conference; participating countries /～者 conferee; participant

与闻 yùwén have a participant's knowledge of; be let into (a secret, etc.): ～其事 have a participant's knowledge of a matter; be in the know / 不能让这样的人～国家机密。We mustn't allow such a person access to confidential matters of the state.

玉 yù ① jade ② *formal* (of a person, esp. a woman) pure; fair; handsome; beautiful: 玉颜 yùyán ③ *honor.* your: 玉照 yùzhào

玉版宣 yùbǎnxuān strong white *Xuan* paper

玉版纸 yùbǎnzhǐ a fine-quality writing paper

玉帛 yùbó *formal* jade objects and silk fabrics, used as state gifts in ancient China

玉不琢, 不成器 yù bù zhuó, bù chéng qì jade cannot be made into anything without being cut and polished—one cannot become useful without being educated

玉成 yùchéng *pol.* kindly help secure the success of sth.

玉成其事 yùchéng qí shì kindly help make a success of it: 深望～。It is earnestly hoped that you will help accomplish the matter.

玉带 yùdài jade belt (worn by high-ranking officials in ancient China)

玉雕 yùdiāo jade carving; jade sculpture: ～工人 jade carver

玉钩 yùgōu ① jade hook ② *liter.* the crescent moon; the new moon

玉皇大帝 Yùhuáng Dàdì (also 玉帝 Yùdì) the Jade Emperor (the Supreme Deity of Taoism)

玉茭 yùjiāo (also 玉茭子 yùjiāozi) *dial.* maize; corn: ～面 maize flour; cornmeal

玉洁 yùjié pure as jade: ～的月亮 the jade-pure moon

玉洁冰清 yùjié-bīngqīng pure as jade and chaste as ice; pure and noble

玉筋鱼 yùjīnyú sand lance

玉兰 yùlán *bot.* yulan magnolia (*Magnolia denudata*)

玉兰片 yùlánpiàn dried slices of tender bamboo shoots

玉立 yùlì ① slim and graceful ② *formal* steadfast to principles

玉麦 yùmài *dial.* maize; Indian corn; corn

玉米 yùmǐ ① maize; Indian corn; corn ② ear of maize (*or* corn)

玉米楂 yùmǐchá (also 玉米楂子 yùmǐcházi) hulled, coarsely ground corn (*or* maize); hominy

玉米大斑病 yùmǐ dàbānbìng *agric.* leaf blight of corn

玉米黑粉病 yùmǐ hēifěnbìng *agric.* corn smut

玉米花儿 yùmǐhuār popcorn

玉米粒儿 yùmǐlìr kernel of corn; grain of corn

玉米面 yùmǐmiàn maize flour; cornmeal

玉米螟 yùmǐmíng corn borer

玉米脱粒机 yùmǐ tuōlìjī maize sheller

玉米芯 yùmǐxīn corncob; cob

玉米粥 yùmǐzhōu maize gruel

玉面狸 yùmiànlí another name for 果子狸 guǒzilí

玉女 yùnǚ the Jade Maiden ——see also 金童玉女 jīntóng-yùnǚ

玉盘 yùpán ① jade plate ② *liter.* a bright full moon

玉器 yùqì jade article; jade object; jadeware: ～工厂 jade workshop

玉人 yùrén ① *arch.* jade worker ② jade figure ③ *liter.* a handsome man or (esp.) a beautiful woman: 拂墙花影动, 疑是～来。(元稹《莺莺传》) Sweeping the wall the flower shadows move: I imagine it is my lover who comes.

玉容 yùróng *liter.* beautiful face (usu. of a woman); good looks

玉润　yùrùn　smooth as jade

玉搔头　yùsāotóu　jade hairpin

玉色　yùsè　jade green; light bluish green

玉石　yùshí　*inf.* jade: 这座人像是～的。This statue is carved in jade.

玉石俱焚　yù-shí jù fén　jade and stone burned together—destruction of good and bad alike

玉手　yùshǒu　*liter.* jade hands—slender white hands (of a pretty woman)

玉蜀黍　yùshǔshǔ　another name for 玉米 yùmǐ

玉树　yùshù　same as 桉 ān

玉碎　yùsuì　be like a broken piece of jade—die in glory——see also 宁为玉碎, 不为瓦全 nìng wéi yù suì, bù wéi wǎ quán

玉体　yùtǐ　① *honor.* your person; your health ② *liter.* jadelike frame—the naked body of a beautiful woman: 佳人洗处冰肌滑, 涤荡尘烦～新。(《西游记》) The beauties wash their smooth, ice-white skins, All dirt removed, their jadelike frames renewed.

玉兔　yùtù　*liter.* the Jade Hare—the moon: ～东升。The moon was rising in the east.

玉玺　yùxǐ　imperial jade seal

玉言　yùyán　*honor.* your words

玉颜　yùyán　fair complexion

玉液　yùyè　*liter.* jadelike wine; good wine

玉音　yùyīn　*honor.* your letter (used mostly in letters)

玉宇　yùyǔ　① residence of the immortals ② the universe

玉簪　yùzān　① jade hairpin ② *bot.* fragrant plantain lily (*Hosta plantaginea*)

玉札　yùzhá　another name for 地榆 dìyú

玉照　yùzhào　*honor.* your photograph

驭

yù　drive (a carriage)

驭手　yùshǒu　soldier in charge of pack animals; driver of a military pack train: 炮车～ gun-carriage driver

芋

yù　*bot.* ① taro ② tuber crops: 洋芋 yángyù / 山芋 shānyù

芋艿　yùnǎi　*bot.* taro

芋头　yùtou　*bot.* ① taro ② *dial.* sweet potato

吁 (籲)

yù　appeal; plead: 呼吁 hūyù ——see also xū; yù

吁请　yùqǐng　implore; plead; petition

吁求　yùqiú　implore; plead; petition

聿

yù　*formal* then; and then

雨

yù　*formal* (of rain, snow, etc.) fall: ～雪 be snowing ——see also yǔ

妪 (嫗)

yù　*formal* old woman: 老妪 lǎoyù

育

yù　① give birth to: 生儿～女 give birth to children; have children ② rear; raise; bring up: ～花 cultivate flowers / ～蚕 raise silkworms / ～婴 feed and take care of babies ③ educate: 德育 déyù ——see also yō

育才　yùcái　cultivate (*or* educate) people of ability

育成品种　yùchéng pǐnzhǒng　*agric.* improved variety

育雏　yùchú　raise young fowl

育雏器　yùchúqì　brooder

育儿袋　yù'érdài　*zool.* brood pouch; marsupium

育肥　yùféi　same as 肥育 féiyù

育林　yùlín　afforest: ～区 an afforested area

育龄　yùlíng　childbearing age: ～夫妇 couples of childbearing age / ～妇女 women of childbearing age

育苗　yùmiáo　*agric.* grow (*or* raise) seedlings: ～区 nursery garden

育性　yùxìng　*agric.* fertility

育秧　yùyāng　raise rice seedlings

育养　yùyǎng　① bring up; rear ② breed (aquatics); cultivate

育婴堂　yùyīngtáng　foundling hospital

育种　yùzhǒng　*agric.* breeding: 杂交～ crossbreeding / 作物～ crop breeding / ～家 breeder

郁[1]

yù　① strongly fragrant: 馥郁 fùyù ② (Yù) a surname

郁[2] (鬱)

yù　① luxuriant; lush ② gloomy; depressed: 忧郁 yōuyù

郁闭　yùbì　*forestry* closing: 林冠～ canopy closure / ～度 canopy density

郁葱　yùcōng　① verdant; luxuriantly green ② strong; rich

郁愤　yùfèn　worried and indignant: 满腔～ extremely worried and indignant; burning with anxiety

郁馥　yùfù　strong fragrance; heavy fragrance

郁积　yùjī　pent up: ～的愤怒 pent-up fury / 仇恨～在心头 hatred smouldering in one's bosom

郁结　yùjié　pent up: ～在心头的烦闷 worries pent up inside one

郁金　yùjīn　*Chin. med.* the root-tuber of aromatic turmeric (*Curcuma aromatica*)

郁金香　yùjīnxiāng　*bot.* tulip (*Tulipa gesneriana*)

郁烈　yùliè　strongly fragrant; full of fragrance

郁闷　yùmèn　gloomy; depressed: ～之感 a feeling of oppression

郁怒　yùnù　disgruntled; sulky

郁然　yùrán　① sad; worried; depressed ② *formal* luxuriant; lush

郁热　yùrè　hot and suffocating; sultry; muggy

郁血　yùxuè　*med.* stagnation of the blood; venous stasis

郁抑　yùyì　depressed; despondent; gloomy

郁悒　yùyì　*formal* depressed; dejected; melancholy

郁郁[1]　yùyù　*formal* ① elegant; refined: 文采～ displaying literary elegance ② strongly fragrant

郁郁[2]　yùyù　*formal* ① lush; luxuriant: 青青河畔草, ～园中柳。(《古诗十九首》) Green, green the riverside grass, Dense, dense the garden willows.

郁郁不乐　yùyù bù lè　depressed; melancholy; gloomy

郁郁葱葱　yùyùcōngcōng　(also 郁郁苍苍 yùyùcāngcāng) lush and green: 苍松翠柏～。Green and luxuriant are the pines and cypresses.

郁郁寡欢　yùyù guǎ huān　depressed; melancholy; joyless

郁蒸　yùzhēng　*formal* hot and suffocating; sultry; muggy

语

yù　*formal* tell; inform: 不以～人 not to be divulged ——see also yǔ

昱

yù　*formal* ① sunlight; sunshine ② shine; illuminate

狱 (獄)

yù　① prison; jail: ～中的生活 life in prison ② lawsuit; case: 冤狱 yuānyù

狱警　yùjǐng　prison guard; jailer

狱吏　yùlì　*old* warder; prison officer; jailer

狱室　yùshì　prison; jail

狱卒　yùzú　*old* prison guard; turnkey

浴

yù　bath; bathe: 淋浴 línyù / 日光浴 rìguāngyù

浴场　yùchǎng　outdoor bathing place: 海滨～ bathing beach

浴池　yùchí　① common bathing pool (in a public bathhouse) ② public bathhouse; public baths

浴缸　yùgāng　*dial.* bathtub

浴巾　yùjīn　bath towel

浴盆　yùpén　*dial.* bathtub

浴室　yùshì　bathroom or shower room

浴血　yùxuè　bathed in blood; bloody: ～奋战 fight a bloody battle

浴衣　yùyī　bathrobe

彧　yù　*formal* have literary talent

钰　yù　*formal* treasure

峪　yù　(usu. used as part of a place name) valley; ravine: 嘉～关 Jiayuguan (a mountain pass in Gansu Province, at the westernmost end of the Great Wall)

预¹　yù　in advance; beforehand: 预支 yùzhī

预²　yù　same as 与 yù

预报　yùbào　forecast: 天气～ weather forecast / 商情～ commercial prediction

预备　yùbèi　prepare; get ready: ～功课 prepare lessons / 你们～好了吗? Are you all ready? / 各就各位，～，跑! Ready! Set! Go! *or* On your mark! Get set! Go!

预备党员　yùbèi dǎngyuán　probationary Party member

预备队　yùbèiduì　reserve force; reserves

预备会议　yùbèi huìyì　preparatory meeting or conference

预备金　yùbèijīn　reserve fund

预备军　yùbèijūn　reserve army

预备期　yùbèiqī　probationary period

预备役　yùbèiyì　*mil.* reserve duty (*or* service)

预卜　yùbǔ　augur; foretell: ～吉凶 try to predict good or bad fortune / 结果如何尚难～。 The result is hard to foretell.

预测　yùcè　calculate; forecast: ～日蚀 calculate an eclipse of the sun / ～台风 detect a typhoon / 市场～ market forecasting

预产期　yùchǎnqī　expected date of childbirth

预处理　yùchǔlǐ　pretreatment

预订　yùdìng　subscribe; book; place an order: ～杂志 subscribe to a magazine / ～火车票 book a train ticket / ～旅馆 make hotel reservations / 您～(房间、餐桌)了吗? Have you a reservation, sir? / ～一本书 place an order for a book / 座位已经～一空。 All seats are booked.

预定　yùdìng　fix in advance; predetermine; schedule: 在～时间 at the fixed time / 在～地点着陆 make a landing in a predetermined area / 这项工程～在明年完成。 The project is scheduled for completion next year. / 会议将按～的计划进行。 The meeting will take place as planned.

预断　yùduàn　prejudge

预防　yùfáng　prevent; take precautions against; guard against: 贯彻以～为主的医疗方针 carry out the policy of putting prevention first in medical work / 采取～措施 take preventive measures / ～火灾 take precautions against fire

预防接种　yùfáng jiēzhòng　preventive (*or* prophylactic) inoculation

预防性拘留　yùfángxìng jūliú　*leg.* preventive detention

预防医学　yùfáng yīxué　preventive medicine

预付　yùfù　pay in advance: ～费用 advanced charges / ～货款 cash before delivery / ～款项 advance payment

预感　yùgǎn　① premonition; presentiment: 不祥的～ an ominous presentiment ② have a premonition

预告　yùgào　① announce in advance; herald ② advance notice: 新书～ notice on forthcoming books; books in preparation

预购　yùgòu　place an order or purchase in advance: ～合同 forward purchasing contract

预后　yùhòu　*med.* prognosis: ～良好 favourable prognosis

预计　yùjì　calculate in advance; estimate: 大楼～十个月可以完工。 It is estimated that the building will be completed in ten months. / ～产量 estimated output / ～数据 predicted data; scheduled data

预计到达时间　yùjì dàodá shíjiān　*navigation* estimated time of arrival (E.T.A.)

预见　yùjiàn　① foresee; predict: ～不到的困难 unforeseen difficulties / 这是可以～到的。 This can be predicted. ② foresight; prevision: 英明的～ brilliant foresight / ～性 foresight; farsightedness

预警　yùjǐng　early warning: ～系统 early warning system / ～雷达 early warning radar / ～飞机 early warning plane

预科　yùkē　preparatory course (in a college)

预料　yùliào　expect; predict; anticipate: 和我们的～相反 contrary to our expectations / 今年的收成比人们～的要好得多。 This year's harvest was much better than expected (*or* anticipated).

预谋　yùmóu　premeditate; plan beforehand: ～杀人 premeditated murder; murder with malice prepense

预期　yùqī　expect; anticipate: 达到～的效果 achieve the desired (*or* hoped-for) results / 结果和～的相反。 The results are contrary to expectations.

预热　yùrè　*mech.* preheat

预赛　yùsài　*sports* preliminary contest; preliminary heats; preliminary; trial match

预审　yùshěn　preliminary (*or* first) hearing

预示　yùshì　betoken; indicate; presage; forebode: 灿烂的晚霞～明天又是好天气。 The splendid evening glow in the sky means another fine day tomorrow.

预收　yùshōu　collect money in advance: ～定金 collect a deposit

预算　yùsuàn　budget: ～经费 budgetary resources / ～赤字 budget deficit / ～结余 budget surplus / ～年度 budget year / ～收入 budgetary receipts / ～项目 budget items / ～外资金 extra-budgetary funds / ～内拨款 budgetary appropriations

预闻　yùwén　same as 与闻 yùwén

预习　yùxí　(of students) prepare lessons before class

预先　yùxiān　in advance; beforehand: ～通知 notify in advance / ～声明 state explicitly beforehand / ～警告 forewarn / ～感谢 thank sb. in anticipation

预想　yùxiǎng　anticipate; expect: 得到～的结果 obtain the anticipated results

预行　yùxíng　① carry out ahead of schedule ② trial run

预选　yùxuǎn　preliminary election; primary election

预言　yùyán　① prophesy; predict; foretell: 马克思～社会主义必定要取代资本主义。 Marx foretold that socialism would inevitably replace capitalism. ② prophecy; prediction: 他的～得到了证实。 Things turned out as he predicted.

预言家　yùyánjiā　prophet

预演　yùyǎn　preview (of a performance or motion picture)

预应力　yùyìnglì　*phys.* prestressing force: ～构件 prestressed component / ～混凝土 prestressed concrete

预约　yùyuē　make an appointment: 门诊～挂号 have an appointment with a doctor / ～会见某人 meet sb. by appointment

预展　yùzhǎn　preview (of an exhibition)

预兆　yùzhào　omen; presage; sign; harbinger: 吉祥的～ an auspicious omen / 胜利的～ a harbinger of victory / 下雨的～ a sign of coming rain / 某些动物烦躁不安可能是地震临震前的～。 Agitated activity by certain

animals may be a sign of an impending earthquake.

预支 yùzhī ① pay in advance: 这本书我们要给作者～五百元稿费。 We'll give the author an advance of 500 *yuan* on this book. / 给我～了一个月的工资。 I was given an advance of a month's pay. ② get payment in advance: ～一百块钱 get an advance of 100 *yuan* / 我能～工资吗? Can I have an advance on my salary?

预知 yùzhī know beforehand

预制 yùzhì prefabricate: ～装配式房屋 prefabricated house; prefab

预制构件 yùzhì gòujiàn *archit.* prefabricated components

预祝 yùzhù congratulate beforehand; wish: ～你取得成功。 I wish you success.

欲[1]（慾） yù desire; longing; wish: 食欲 shíyù

欲[2] yù ① wish; want; desire: 从心所～ follow what the heart desires / ～言又止 make as if to speak, and then stop ② about to; just going to; on the point of: 摇摇欲坠 yáoyáo yù zhuì

欲罢不能 yù bà bùnéng unable to stop even though one wants to; try to stop but cannot; cannot refrain from going on: 敌人于是就陷入了～、而又不能不罢的被动地位。 The enemy were thus reduced to a passive position in which they found it hard to give up the battle and yet had to give it up.

欲盖弥彰 yù gài mí zhāng the more one tries to hide, the more one is exposed; try to cover up a misdeed, only to make it more conspicuous; protest too much

欲壑难填 yùhè nán tián greed is a valley that can never be filled; avarice knows no bounds

欲火 yùhuǒ the fire of lust; lewd desire: ～中烧 burning with lewd desire

欲加之罪，何患无词 yù jiā zhī zuì, hé huàn wú cí if you are out to condemn sb., you can always trump up a charge

欲念 yùniàn desire; wish; lust

欲擒故纵 yù qín gù zòng leave sb. at large the better to apprehend him; allow sb. more latitude first to keep a tighter rein on him afterwards

欲求 yùqiú desire; wish; lust

欲取姑与 yù qǔ gū yǔ give in order to take; make concessions for the sake of future gains

欲速则不达 yù sù zé bù dá haste brings no success; more haste, less speed

欲望 yùwàng desire; wish; lust

域 yù land within certain boundaries; territory; region: 领域 lǐngyù

域外 yùwài outside the country

域中 yùzhōng inside the country

谕 yù *formal* (of superiors or elders) instruct; tell: 面谕 miànyù

谕告 yùgào *formal* (of superiors or elders) give explicit instructions (*or* directions); tell

谕令 yùlìng *formal* order

谕示 yùshì *formal* (of seniors or elders) instruct

谕旨 yùzhǐ imperial edict

尉 yù see below ——see also wèi

尉迟 Yùchí a two-character surname

阈 yù *formal* threshold; doorsill

寓（庽） yù ① reside; live: 暂～友人处 be staying with a friend ② residence; abode: 公寓 gōngyù ③ imply; contain: 这个故事～有深意。 This story con-

tains a profound lesson. *or* The moral of the story is profound.

寓处 yùchù residence; abode; dwelling place

寓邸 yùdǐ the residence of a high official

寓公 yùgōng ① formerly, a government official residing away from home (usu. in a big city) ② bureaucrats or rich people in exile

寓居 yùjū make one's home in (a place other than one's native place): 他晚年～上海。 He made Shanghai his home in his old age.

寓目 yùmù *formal* look over: 室内展览品我已大致～。 I've looked over all the exhibits in the room.

寓舍 yùshè residence; abode; dwelling place

寓所 yùsuǒ residence; abode; dwelling place

寓言 yùyán fable; allegory; parable

寓意 yùyì implied meaning; moral; message; import: ～深刻 be pregnant with meaning

寓于 yùyú be contained in; reside in: 矛盾的普遍性即～矛盾的特殊性之中。 It is precisely in the particularity of contradiction that the universality of contradiction resides. / 寓教育于娱乐之中 combine education with recreation

寓斋 yùzhāi *formal* residence; abode; dwelling place

裕 yù ① abundant; plentiful: 富裕 fùyù ② *formal* make (a country or people) rich: 富国～民 make one's country and people rich

裕固族 Yùgùzú the Yugur (Yuku) nationality, or the Yugurs (Yukus), inhabiting Gansu Province

裕如 yùrú effortlessly; with ease: 应付～ handle the situation with ease; be equal to the occasion

遇 yù ① meet: 我在路上没～着他。 I didn't see him on the way. / ～雨 be caught in a rain ② treat; receive: 待遇 dàiyù ③ chance; opportunity: 机遇 jīyù

遇便 yùbiàn when it's convenient; at sb.'s convenience

遇刺 yùcì be attacked by an assassin: ～身死 be assassinated

遇到 yùdào run into; encounter; come across: 在路上～一个老同学 run into an old schoolmate on the way / ～意外的问题 come across unforeseen problems / ～埋伏 run into an ambush

遇害 yùhài be murdered

遇合 yùhé ① meet; come across; run into ② meet and get on well together

遇见 yùjiàn meet; come across: ～一位朋友 meet a friend

遇救 yùjiù be rescued; be saved

遇难 yùnàn ① die (*or* be killed) in an accident: 他在一次飞机失事中～。 He was killed in an air crash. ② be murdered

遇事 yùshì when anything crops (*or* comes) up: ～不慌 be unruffled whatever happens / ～和群众商量 consult with the masses when problems arise

遇事生风 yù shì shēng fēng sow discord whenever possible

遇险 yùxiǎn meet with a mishap; be in danger; be in distress: ～船只 ship in distress

遇险信号 yùxiǎn xìnhào (also 遇难信号 yùnàn xìnhào) distress signal; GMDSS

遇缘 yùyuán as luck would have it; by chance; by a lucky coincidence: 我正想找你，不料想你来了，可谓～。 It is strange that I was looking for you when you came, but coincidences do happen.

喻 yù ① explain; make clear; inform: ～之以理 reason with sb.; try to make sb. see reason ② understand; know: 家喻户晓 jiāyù-hùxiǎo ③ analogy: 比喻 bǐyù ④ (Yù) a surname

御[1]
yù ① drive (a carriage): 〜者 carriage driver ② manage; control: 〜众 rule or control the masses / 〜夫(妻) control one's husband (wife) ③ of an emperor; imperial: 御宝 yùbǎo

御[2](禦)
yù resist; keep out; ward off: 防御 fángyù

御宝 yùbǎo imperial seal

御笔 yùbǐ imperial brush—handwriting or painting of the emperor

御赐 yùcì bestowed by the emperor

御道 yùdào a road for the imperial carriage

御敌 yùdí resist the enemy

御夫座 Yùfūzuò astron. Auriga

御寒 yùhán keep out the cold

御花园 yùhuāyuán imperial garden

御极 yùjí formal ascend the throne

御驾 yùjià imperial carriage: 〜亲征。The emperor personally led the expedition.

御览 yùlǎn ① for the emperor's inspection ② books for the emperor's inspection:《太平〜》Taiping Reign-Period Imperial Encyclopaedia

御林军 yùlínjūn ① imperial guards ② derog. elite troops or crack units

御路 yùlù a road for the imperial carriage

御膳 yùshàn the food of the imperial household

御膳房 yùshànfáng imperial kitchen

御手 yùshǒu same as 驭手 yùshǒu

御侮 yùwǔ resist foreign aggression

御医 yùyī imperial physician; court physician

御用 yùyòng ① for the use of an emperor ② serve as a tool; be in the pay of: 资产阶级的〜政党 a political party in the pay of the bourgeoisie / 〜报刊 hired (or controlled, paid) press / 〜文人 hired scribbler; hack writer

御苑 yùyuàn imperial garden or park

御制 yùzhì made by the emperor or by imperial order

鹆
yù see 鸲鹆 qúyù

誉(譽)
yù ① reputation; fame: 名誉 míngyù ② praise; eulogize: 〜不绝口 praise profusely; be full of praise

誉满全球 yù mǎn quánqiú of world renown; famed the world over

蒉
yù see 薯蒉 shǔyù

煜
yù formal illuminate; shine

愈[1](瘉、癒)
yù heal; recover; become well: 痊愈 quányù

愈[2]
yù formal be better; excel: 彼〜于此。That one is better than this one.

愈[3]
yù adv. 愈…愈… the more ... the more ...: 〜多〜好 the more the better / 山路〜走〜陡。The mountain path becomes steeper and steeper as you go up. / 真理〜辩〜明。Truth becomes clearer through debate. / 人民武装力量〜战〜强。The people's armed forces grow stronger and stronger through fighting.

愈合 yùhé (of a wound) heal: 伤口很快〜了。The wound healed quickly.

愈加 yùjiā adv. all the more; even more; further: 变得〜模糊 become even more indistinct / 过了中秋，天气〜凉快了。After the Mid-Autumn Festival, it became increasingly cool.

愈演愈烈 yù yǎn yù liè grow in intensity; become increasingly intense

蝛(魊)
yù see 鬼蝛 guǐyù

毓
yù formal (used esp. in a person's name) give birth; nurture

熨
yù see below ——see also yùn

熨贴 yùtiē ① (of wording) apt; suitable; appropriate ② (of the mind) calm; tranquil ③ dial. (of a matter) be settled

豫[1]
yù formal ① pleased; delighted: 悦豫 yuèyù ② comfort: 逸豫 yìyù

豫[2]
yù same as 预[1] yù

豫[3]
Yù another name for 河南 Hénán

豫剧 yùjù Henan opera

鹬
yù sandpiper; snipe

鹬蚌相争，渔人得利 yù bàng xiāng zhēng, yúrén dé lì when the snipe and the clam grapple, it's the fisherman who stands to benefit—it's the third party that benefits from the tussle

鹬鸵 yùtuó another name for 无翼鸟 wúyìniǎo

燠
yù formal warm: 寒〜 cold and heat

燠热 yùrè formal extremely hot; sultry

鬻
yù formal sell; vend: 〜文为生 make a living with one's pen / 〜画 sell one's paintings / 自〜 sell oneself

yuān

鸢
yuān zool. kite

鸢尾 yuānwěi bot. iris

冤(寃)
yuān ① wrong; injustice: 含冤 hányuān ② feeling of bitterness; hatred; enmity: 结冤 jiéyuān ③ dial. kid; fool; pull sb.'s leg: 我不〜你。I'm not kidding. ④ bad luck; loss; disadvantage: 白跑一趟，真〜! What bad luck, nothing came of my trip.

冤案 yuān'àn a case in which a person is unjustly charged or sentenced; an unjust case

冤仇 yuānchóu rancour; enmity

冤大头 yuāndàtóu a person who spends money wastefully and foolishly; squanderer; wastrel

冤愤 yuānfèn resentment; rancour

冤魂 yuānhún the ghost of one who was wrongly put to death or was murdered

冤家 yuān·jiā ① enemy; foe ② old (usu. used in dramas or folk songs) one's destined love; sweetheart; lover

冤家对头 yuānjiā-duìtou opponent and foe

冤家路窄 yuānjiā lù zhǎi enemies are bound to meet on a narrow road—one can't avoid one's enemy (much as one wants to)

冤家宜解不宜结 yuānjiā yí jiě bùyí jié better make friends than make enemies

冤结 yuānjié gross injustice; unrighted wrong

冤苦 yuānkǔ ① wrong; injustice: 饱尝〜 suffer a great wrong; be wrongly wronged ② wrong sb.; do sb. an injustice: 我〜了她。I wronged her.

冤孽 yuānniè evil, misfortune, or trouble regarded as

retribution for bad deeds done in a previous existence

冤气 yuānqì resentment; rancour: 一肚子～ be resentful

冤钱 yuānqián (usu. used in) 花～ waste money; not get one's money's worth

冤情 yuānqíng facts of an injustice

冤屈 yuānqū ① treat unjustly; wrong ② wrongful treatment; injustice: 受～ be wronged; suffer an injustice

冤桶 yuāntǒng *inf.* fool

冤头 yuāntou *dial.* enemy; foe: 老百姓的直接～ the mortal and immediate enemies of the people

冤枉 yuānwang ① treat unjustly; wrong: 我是～的。I was wrongly accused. *or* I am innocent. / ～好人 wrong an innocent person ② not worthwhile; not repaying the effort: 在这件小事上, 花那么多时间, 真～。It wasn't worthwhile to spend so much time on such a trifle. / 花～钱 waste money; not get one's money's worth

冤枉路 yuānwanglù a longer way; a roundabout way: 走～ take a roundabout way; go the long way round

冤枉气 yuānwangqì unjust treatment; mistreatment

冤诬 yuānwū wrong sb.; frame sb.

冤抑 yuānyì unrighted wrong; unredressed injustice

冤有头, 债有主 yuān yǒu tóu, zhài yǒu zhǔ every injustice has its perpetrator, every debt has its debtor

冤狱 yuānyù an unjust charge or verdict; a miscarriage of justice; frame-up: 平反～ reverse an unjust verdict

冤冤相报 yuān yuān xiāng bào injury for injury

鸳 yuān see below

鸳鸯 yuānyang ① mandarin duck ② an affectionate couple

鸳鸯座 yuānyangzuò love seat

渊 (淵) yuān ① a deep pool ② deep: ～泉 a deep spring

渊博 yuānbó broad and profound; erudite: 学识渊博 xuéshí yuānbó

渊海 yuān-hǎi abyss and ocean—deep and vast; profound and extensive

渊默 yuānmò *formal* profound (*or* deep) silence

渊深 yuānshēn profound; deep; erudite

渊薮 yuānsǒu a gathering place of fish or beasts; den; haunt: 盗贼的～ a den (*or* haunt) of bandits and thieves / 罪恶的～ a hotbed (*or* breeding ground) of crime; a sink of iniquity

渊源 yuānyuán origin; source: 历史～ historical origins / 江藩《宋学～记》Jiang Fan's *An Account of the Sources of Song Confucianism*

yuán

元[1] yuán ① first; primary: 元月 yuányuè ② chief; principal: 元首 yuánshǒu / 元凶 yuánxiōng ③ basic; fundamental: 元素 yuánsù ④ unit; component: 单元 dānyuán / 一元化 yīyuánhuà

元[2] yuán same as 圆 yuán⑤⑥

元[3] Yuán ① the Yuan Dynasty (1271–1368) ② a surname

元宝 yuánbǎo a shoe-shaped gold or silver ingot used as money in feudal China

元宝铁 yuánbǎotiě *mech.* V-block

元旦 Yuándàn New Year's Day

元恶 yuán'è chief criminal; principal culprit (*or* offender)

元古代 Yuángǔdài *geol.* the Proterozoic Era

元古界 Yuángǔjiè *geol.* the Proterozoic Erathem

元件 yuánjiàn element; component; cell: 传输～ transfer element / 电光～ electrooptic cell / 电路～ circuit component / 敏感～ sensor

元老 yuánlǎo senior statesman; founding member (of a political organization, etc.)

元麦 yuánmài another name for 青稞 qīngkē

元煤 yuánméi same as 原煤 yuánméi

元谋猿人 Yuánmóu yuánrén (also 元谋人 Yuánmóurén) Yuanmou Man, whose fossil remains, about 1,700,000 years old, were found in Yuanmou, Yunnan Province, in 1965

元年 yuánnián the first year of an era or of the reign of an emperor

元配 yuánpèi first wife

元气 yuánqì vitality; vigour: ～旺盛 full of vitality / 大伤～ undermine one's constitution; sap one's vitality / 恢复～ regain one's strength (*or* health, vigour)

元器件 yuánqìjiàn components and parts (of an apparatus, etc.)

元青 yuánqīng black: ～布 black cloth

元曲 yuánqǔ ① Yuan songs (a collective name for 杂剧 zájù② and 散曲 sǎnqǔ) ② Yuan drama (another name for 杂剧 zájù②): 臧晋叔《～选》Zang Jinshu's *Selections from the Yuan Drama*

元日 yuánrì the first day of the first lunar month; the lunar New Year's Day

元戎 yuánróng *formal* supreme commander

元首 yuánshǒu head of state

元书纸 yuánshūzhǐ a kind of writing paper (produced in Zhejiang Province)

元帅 yuánshuài ① marshal; (Brit. Army) Field Marshal; (Brit. Air Force) Marshal of the Royal Air Force; (Brit. Navy) Admiral of the Fleet ② supreme commander (in ancient times)

元素 yuánsù ① element ② *math. chem.* element: 稀有～ rare element / ～分析 ultimate analysis

元素周期表 yuánsùzhōuqībiǎo periodic table of elements

元宵 yuánxiāo ① the night of the 15th of the 1st lunar month ② sweet dumplings made of glutinous rice flour (for the Lantern Festival)

元宵节 yuánxiāojié the Lantern Festival (the 15th of the 1st lunar month)

元凶 yuánxiōng prime culprit; arch-criminal

元勋 yuánxūn a man of great merit; founding father: 革命～ a veteran revolutionary of great distinction / 开国～ founders of a state

元夜 yuányè *formal* the night of the 15th of the 1st lunar month

元音 yuányīn *phonet.* vowel

元鱼 yuányú same as 鼋鱼 yuányú

元元 yuányuán *formal* the common people

元元本本 yuányuánběnběn same as 原原本本 yuányuánběnběn

元月 yuányuè ① January ② the first month of the lunar year; the first moon

沅 Yuán (also 沅江) a river flowing from Guizhou Province through Hunan into Dongting Lake

芫 yuán see below ——see also yán

芫花 yuánhuā lilac daphne

园 (園) yuán ① an area of land for growing plants: 葡萄～ vineyard; grapery / 苹果～ apple orchard ② a place for public recreation: 动物园 dòngwùyuán / 公园 gōngyuán

园地 yuándì ① garden plot ② field; scope: 扩大文学创

作的～ broaden the scope of literary creation / 为科学家开辟广阔的～ open up vast fields of activity for scientists

园丁 yuándīng ① gardener ② school teacher

园林 yuánlín gardens; park

园陵 yuánlíng tombs surrounded by a park; cemetery

园圃 yuánpǔ garden; ground used for growing vegetables, flowers or fruit

园容 yuánróng the appearance of a park, garden, etc.

园田 yuántián vegetable garden: 耕作～化 garden-style cultivation of farmland; intensive cultivation

园艺 yuányì horticulture; gardening: ～家 horticulturist

园艺学 yuányìxué horticulture; gardening

园囿 yuányòu *formal* ① garden ② zoological garden; zoo

园子 yuánzi orchard or garden: 菜～ vegetable garden; vegetable farm

员 yuán ① a person engaged in some field of activity: 指挥员 zhǐhuīyuán / 售货员 shòuhuòyuán ② member: 集体的一～ a member of the collective ③ *m.* (for generals): 一～大将 an able general

员额 yuán'é specified number of personnel

员工 yuángōng staff; personnel: 师生～ teachers, students, administrative personnel and workers

员司 yuánsī *old* junior clerks or functionaries in government offices

员外 yuánwài ① (also 员外郎 yuánwàiláng) an ancient official title ② *old* landlord; squire

垣 yuán *formal* ① wall: 城垣 chéngyuán ② city: 省垣 shěngyuán

爰 yuán *formal* ① whence; from what place ② hence; thereupon; consequently: ～书其事以告。Therefore I have written an account of what happened for your information.

原[1] yuán ① primary; original; former: ～计划 original plan / ～单位 the organization (*or* unit) one formerly belonged to / ～有规定 already existing provisions ② unprocessed; raw: ～矿石 raw ore ③ (Yuán) a surname

原[2] yuán excuse; pardon: 情有可原 qíng yǒu kě yuán

原[3] yuán open country; plain; level: 平原 píngyuán / 草原 cǎoyuán

原班人马 yuánbān rénmǎ the old cast; the former staff

原版 yuánbǎn original edition (of a book, etc.)

原本[1] yuánběn ① original manuscript; master copy ② the original (from which a translation is made)

原本[2] yuánběn *adv.* originally; formerly: 他～住在山东。Originally he lived in Shandong Province.

原材料 yuáncáiliào raw and processed materials: ～消耗下降 a drop in consumption of raw and other materials / ～工业 raw and semifinished materials industries

原肠 yuáncháng *zool.* primitive gut; archenteron

原虫 yuánchóng *zool.* protozoon

原初 yuánchū *adv.* originally; formerly; at first: 我～不同意, 可很快就改变了主意。At first I didn't agree, but I soon changed my mind. / 她～不像现在这样爱说话。She wasn't so talkative as she is now.

原动力 yuándònglì motive power (*or* force); motivity

原防 yuánfáng place where troops were originally stationed; original station or position (of a unit): 撤回～ withdraw troops to their original positions

原封 yuánfēng with the seal unbroken; intact: ～退回 return to the sender a parcel or letter unopened

原封不动 yuánfēng bù dòng be left intact; remain untouched

原稿 yuángǎo original manuscript; master copy

原稿纸 yuángǎozhǐ same as 稿纸 gǎozhǐ

原告 yuángào *leg.* (in civil cases) plaintiff; (in criminal cases) prosecutor

原鸽 yuángē wild pigeon; dove

原故 yuángù same as 缘故 yuángù

原鸡 yuánjī ① jungle fowl ② jungle cock or hen

原级 yuánjí *gram.* positive degree

原籍 yuánjí ancestral home: 他～广东。His ancestral home is in Guangdong Province.

原价 yuánjià original price

原件 yuánjiàn ① original manuscript (of a document); master copy ② the original (from which a replica is made)

原旧 yuánjiù *dial.* ① former; original ② still; as before

原来 yuánlái ① original; former: ～的计划 the original plan / 他还是住在～的地方。He still lives in the same place. ② *adv.* originally; formerly; at first: 他家～是福建人。Originally his family came from Fujian. / 他～在一家工厂干活。He formerly worked in a factory. / 我～抽烟, 现在不抽了。I used to smoke, but not now. ③ *adv.* as a matter of fact; as it turns out; actually: 这～是个骗局。It turned out to be a fraud. / ～是你呀! So it's you. / 你～是这样的朋友! So that's the kind of friend you are!

原来如此 yuánlái rúcǐ so that's how it is; so that's what's happened; I see

原理 yuánlǐ principle; tenet: 根本的～ a cardinal principle / 数学的基本～ fundamentals of mathematics / 马克思列宁主义的基本～ the fundamental tenets of Marxism-Leninism

原粮 yuánliáng unprocessed food grains

原谅 yuánliàng excuse; forgive; pardon: 我来晚了, 请～。Please excuse me for being late. / 不能～的错误 an unpardonable mistake

原料 yuánliào raw material

原貌 yuánmào original appearance (of things): 保存～ keep sth. as it is

原煤 yuánméi raw coal

原棉 yuánmián raw cotton: ～等级 grades of raw cotton

原木 yuánmù log

原配 yuánpèi same as 元配 yuánpèi

原人 yuánrén same as 猿人 yuánrén

原任 yuánrèn ① formerly held the post of ② predecessor

原色 yuánsè *phys.* primary colours

原审 yuánshěn *leg.* first trial

原生动物 yuánshēng dòngwù protozoon: ～学 protozoology

原生矿物 yuánshēng kuàngwù primary mineral

原生林 yuánshēnglín (also 原始林 yuánshǐlín) primeval forest; virgin forest

原生生物 yuánshēng shēngwù protist

原生植物 yuánshēng zhíwù protophyte

原生质 yuánshēngzhì *physiol.* protoplasm

原始 yuánshǐ ① original; firsthand: ～记录 original record / ～资料 firsthand information (*or* data); source material ② primeval; primitive: ～人 primitive man / ～森林 primeval forest; virgin forest / ～细胞 primordial cell

原始公社 yuánshǐ gōngshè primitive commune

原始积累 yuánshǐ jīlěi primitive accumulation: 资本～ primitive accumulation of capital

原始群 yuánshǐqún primitive horde

原始社会　yuánshǐ shèhuì　primitive society

原诉　yuánsù　*leg.*　plaintiff's or prosecutor's accusation

原索动物　yuánsuǒ dòngwù　protochordate; prochordate

原糖　yuántáng　raw sugar

原田　*dial.*　farmland on a plateau

原委　yuánwěi　how a thing happened from beginning to end; the whole story; all the details: 我来跟你说明事情的～。I'll tell you the whole story. / 不明～，妄加评论 make presumptuous comments out of ignorance

原文　yuánwén.　① the original (from which a translation is made): 我没看过这本书的～。I have not read the book in the original. ② original text: 引用～要加引号。Put quoted passages in quotation marks. / 如此 *sic* / 把抄件跟～核对一下 check the copy against the original

原物　yuánwù　the original thing: ～归还 return the thing borrowed or taken

原先　yuánxiān　① original; former: 照～的计划做 act according to the original plan ② *adv.* originally; formerly; at first: 我～挺喜欢他的，现在不了。I liked him originally but I don't now. / 他～是个海员，现在已经成了一位作家。He used to be a sailor, but now he's become a writer. / 我～以为他不会同意，没想到他居然答应了。I thought that he would not agree, but to my surprise he said "Yes".

原线圈　yuánxiànquān　*elec.*　primary coil

原形　yuánxíng　original shape; the true shape under the disguise: 现～ show one's true colours; betray oneself

原形毕露　yuánxíng bì lù　be revealed for what one is; show one's true colours

原型　yuánxíng　model; prototype

原盐　yuányán　crude salt

原样　yuányàng　① the same old way: 照～每月一号付房租。As usual, rent is paid on the first day of each month. ② original state; previous condition: 几年没见，你还是～，一点不见老。It's years since I last saw you, but you still look the same as before and haven't aged at all.

原野　yuányě　open country; champaign

原义　yuányì　original (*or* primary) meaning (of a word or phrase)

原意　yuányì　meaning; original intention: 曲解～ distort the meaning / 这不是我们的～。This was not our original intention. *or* This is not what we meant.

原因　yuányīn　cause; reason: ～和结果 cause and effect / 成功的～ reasons for the success / 产生这种现象有两方面的～。Two things account for the occurrence.

原由　yuányóu　cause; reason

原油　yuányóu　crude oil; crude: 含硫～ sour crude / 低硫～ sweet crude / 多蜡～ waxy crude / 无蜡～ wax-free crude / ～分馏塔 crude fractionating tower / ～裂化设备 crude cracker

原宥　yuányòu　pardon; forgive

原原本本　yuányuánběnběn　from beginning to end: 我把这件事～讲给他们听了。I told them the whole story exactly as it had happened. / 把上级的指示～地向群众传达 make known to the masses the directives of the higher authorities exactly as they are

原韵　yuányùn　the rhyme sequence of one person's poem which is used in another person's poem written in reply: 步～ use the rhyme sequence of a poem (when replying to it)

原则　yuánzé　principle: ～问题 a question (*or* matter) of principle / ～分歧 differences in principle / 具有高度的～性 be highly principled; have a strong sense of principle / 坚持马克思列宁主义的～立场 adhere to the principled stand of Marxism-Leninism / 我们～上同意这个计划。We agree to the plan in principle. / 我的～是绝不走穴。I never moonlight on principle. / 把～作交

易 barter away principles; trade in principles

原职　yuánzhí　former post

原址　yuánzhǐ　former address

原主　yuánzhǔ　original owner (*or* proprietor)

原注　yuánzhù　original annotation

原著　yuánzhù　original work; original: 我不懂俄文，没有读过高尔基的～。As I don't know Russian, I've never read Gorky in the original.

原状　yuánzhuàng　original state; previous condition; *status quo ante*: 恢复～ restore the *status quo ante*; restore to the former state

原子　yuánzǐ　atom: 标记～ labelled atom / ～动力船 atomic-powered ship / ～辐射 atomic radiation / ～结构 atomic structure / ～时代 atomic age

原子笔　yuánzǐbǐ　old name for 圆珠笔 yuánzhūbǐ

原子尘　yuánzǐchén　fallout

原子弹　yuánzǐdàn　(also 原子炸弹 yuánzǐ zhàdàn) atom bomb; atomic bomb; A-bomb

原子反应堆　yuánzǐ fǎnyìngduī　atomic reactor; atomic pile

原子核　yuánzǐhé　atomic nucleus

原子价　yuánzǐjià　valence; atomicity

原子键　yuánzǐjiàn　atomic bond

原子量　yuánzǐliàng　atomic weight

原子论　yuánzǐlùn　atomic theory; atomism

原子能　yuánzǐnéng　atomic energy

原子炮　yuánzǐpào　atomic gun

原子团　yuánzǐtuán　atomic group

原子武器　yuánzǐ wǔqì　atomic weapon

原子物理学　yuánzǐ wùlǐxué　atomic physics

原子序数　yuánzǐ xùshù　(also 原子序 yuánzǐxù) atomic number

原子战争　yuánzǐ zhànzhēng　atomic war (*or* warfare)

原子钟　yuánzǐzhōng　atomic clock

原罪　yuánzuì　*Christianity*　original sin

原作　yuánzuò　original work; original: 译文保持了～的风格。The translation reproduces the style of the original.

袁

袁　Yuán　a surname

袁头　yuántóu　(also 袁大头 yuándàtóu) silver coins minted in the early years of the Republic of China with the head of Yuan Shikai on the obverse side

圆

圆　yuán　① round; circular; spherical: ～孔 a round hole / ～锉 round file / 月～了。The moon is full. ② *math.* circle ③ tactful; satisfactory: 他这话说得不～。What he said was not very tactful. ④ make plausible; justify: 圆谎 yuánhuǎng ⑤ *yuan*, the monetary unit of China, equal to 10 *jiao* or 100 *fen* ⑥ a coin of fixed value and weight: 银圆 yínyuán

圆白菜　yuánbáicài　common name for 结球甘蓝 jiéqiú gānlán

圆材　yuáncái　roundwood; log

圆场　yuánchǎng　mediate; help to effect a compromise: 打～ mediate a dispute; smooth things over

圆成　yuánchéng　help sb. to attain his aim

圆唇元音　yuánchúnyuányīn　*phonet.*　round vowel

圆到　yuándào　full; thorough; comprehensive: 他的话说得很～。He expressed his ideas quite fully.

圆雕　yuándiāo　sculpture

圆顶　yuándǐng　dome: 小～ cupola

圆嘟嘟　yuándūdū　(also 圆敦敦 yuándūndūn) full and plump; chubby: ～的脸庞 plump (*or* chubby) cheeks

圆房　yuánfáng　(in former times of a foster daughter-in-law and her husband) consummate the union on reaching adulthood

圆钢　yuángāng　steel strip

圆工　yuángōng　(also 圆功 yuángōng) achieve the de-

sired results; complete a project, etc.

圆骨碌 yuángūlu　good and round; rounded

圆鼓鼓 yuángǔgǔ　rounded and bulging: 挺着～的肚子 with a rounded, bulging belly

圆规 yuánguī　compasses: 一个～ a pair of compasses / 制图～ drawing compasses / 长杆～ beam compasses

圆滚滚 yuángǔngǔn　good and round; rounded: ～的石子儿 rounded pebbles / ～的乳房 rounded breasts / ～的脸蛋儿 a chubby face / ～的小肥猪 a podgy pigling

圆号 yuánhào　*mus.* French horn; horn

圆和 yuánhe　① mediate (a dispute); help to effect a compromise ② flexible; accommodating ③ mellow and full: 她的嗓音～洪亮。Her sweet and mellow voice carries well.

圆乎乎 yuánhūhū　roundish: ～的脸颊 plump (*or* chubby) cheeks / 两眼睁得～的 be round-eyed; with one's eyes opened wide

圆乎 yuánhu　roundish: 他中等个儿，～脸。He is of medium height and has a roundish face.

圆滑 yuánhuá　smooth and evasive; slick and sly: 他这个人太～。He's a sly customer.

圆滑线 yuánhuáxiàn　*mus.* slur

圆谎 yuánhuǎng　patch up a lie

圆浑 yuánhún　*formal* ① (of voice) round and mellow: 这段唱腔流畅而～。This aria is soft and melodious. ② (of writing) natural and spontaneous

圆活 yuán·huó　① flexible; smooth: 说话～ speak in a tactful way / 办事～ be flexible in handling a matter ② mellow and full: 声音～ a sweet, mellow voice

圆寂 yuánjì　(of Buddhist monks or nuns) pass away; die

圆锯 yuánjù　*mech.* circular saw

圆括号 yuánkuòhào　parentheses; curves (( ))

圆溜溜 yuánliūliū　good and round; rounded: ～的眼睛 round eyes

圆笼 yuánlóng　a big round tierred lunchbox with several compartments one above the other and a handle

圆颅方趾 yuánlú-fāngzhǐ　round skull and square feet —human being

圆满 yuánmǎn　satisfactory: ～成功 complete success / ～的答案 a satisfactory answer / 问题～地解决了。The problem has been solved satisfactorily. / 邀请赛在友好团结的气氛中～结束。The invitational tournament was rounded off in an atmosphere of friendship and solidarity.

圆梦 yuánmèng　same as 占梦 zhānmèng

圆明园 Yuánmíngyuán　Yuanming Yuan (the Round Bright Garden or the Garden of Perfect Brightness, the old Summer Palace a few miles to the northwest of Beijing, destroyed by British and French troops in 1860)

圆盘 yuánpán　disc

圆盘耙 yuánpánbà　disc harrow

圆盘犁 yuánpánlí　disc plough

圆圈 yuánquān　circle; ring

圆全 yuánquán　*dial.* full; thorough; comprehensive: 他办事处得～。He's thorough in doing things.

圆润 yuánrùn　mellow and full: ～的嗓音 a sweet, mellow voice / 他的书法～有力。He writes a round, vigorous hand.

圆鲹 yuánshēn　*zool.* round scad

圆实 yuánshi　round and filled out; plump; chubby: ～而红润的脸膛儿 rosy plump cheeks

圆熟 yuánshú　skilful; proficient; dexterous

圆说 yuánshuō　speak in defence of; argue in favour of; defend

圆台 yuántái　short for 圆锥台 yuánzhuītái

圆通 yuántōng　flexible; accommodating: 他为人～。He's a very flexible person.

圆舞曲 yuánwǔqǔ　waltz

圆心 yuánxīn　the centre of a circle

圆心角 yuánxīnjiǎo　*math.* central angle

圆形 yuánxíng　round; circular

圆形动物 yuánxíng dòngwù　another name for 线形动物 xiànxíng dòngwù

圆形建筑 yuánxíng jiànzhù　thoios; rotunda

圆形剧场 yuánxíng jùchǎng　amphitheatre

圆凿方枘 yuánzáo-fāngruì　like a square tenon for a round mortise—at variance with each other

圆周 yuánzhōu　circumference

圆周角 yuánzhōujiǎo　*math.* angle in a circular segment

圆周接缝 yuánzhōu jiēfèng　*mech.* circumferential seam

圆周率 yuánzhōulǜ　ratio of the circumference of a circle to its diameter (π)

圆周运动 yuánzhōu yùndòng　*phys.* circular motion

圆珠笔 yuánzhūbǐ　ball-point pen; ball-pen

圆柱 yuánzhù　*math.* cylinder

圆柱根 yuánzhùgēn　*math.* cylindrical root

圆柱体 yuánzhùtǐ　cylinder

圆锥 yuánzhuī　circular cone; taper

圆锥根 yuánzhuīgēn　*bot.* conical root

圆锥花序 yuánzhuī huāxù　*bot.* panicle

圆锥曲线 yuánzhuī qūxiàn　*math.* conic section

圆锥台 yuánzhuītái　*math.* frustum of a cone

圆桌 yuánzhuō　round table

圆桌会议 yuánzhuō huìyì　round-table conference

圆桌面 yuánzhuōmiàn　a detachable round tabletop (which can be put on a square table)

圆子 yuánzi　① dumpling (made of glutinous rice flour) ② *dial.* (meat, fish, etc.) ball

溒 yuán　see 潺溒 chányuán

媛 yuán　see 婵媛 chányuán ——see also yuàn

援 yuán　① pull by hand; hold: 援笔 yuánbǐ ② quote; cite: 援例 yuánlì ③ help; aid; rescue: 求援 qiúyuán

援笔 yuánbǐ　take up a pen: ～疾书 take up a pen and write quickly / ～立就 take up a pen and dash (*or* write) off sth.

援兵 yuánbīng　relief troops; reinforcements

援救 yuánjiù　rescue; save; deliver from danger

援军 yuánjūn　relief troops; reinforcements

援款 yuánkuǎn　aid fund

援例 yuánlì　quote (*or* cite) a precedent: 有例可援。There's a precedent to quote.

援手 yuánshǒu　*formal* aid; save; rescue

援外 yuánwài　foreign aid: ～物资 materials in aid of a foreign country

援引 yuányǐn　① quote; cite: ～例证 cite an example / ～法律条文 invoke a legal provision ② recommend or appoint one's friends or favourites

援用 yuányòng　quote; cite; invoke: ～成例 cite a precedent / ～条约 invoke a treaty

援助 yuánzhù　help; support; aid: 给他们一切可能的～ give them every possible help / 不附带条件的～ aid with no strings attached / 技术～ technical assistance / 国际～ international support

鼋(黿) yuán　soft-shelled turtle

鼋鱼 yuányú　*inf.* soft-shelled turtle

源 yuán　① source (of a river); fountainhead: 水源

shuǐyuán ② **source; cause**: 货源 huòyuán

源流 yuánliú　source and course (of a river, etc.); origin and development: 词韵～ metrical origins of the *ci*

源泉 yuánquán　source; fountainhead; well-spring: 生活是文艺创作的～。Life is the source of literary and artistic creation.

源头 yuántóu　fountainhead; source: 民歌是文学的一个～。Folk songs are one of the sources of literature.

源源 yuányuán　in a steady stream; continuously: 大庆石油通过这条输油管～不断地流往北京。Through this pipeline, crude oil flows from Daqing to Beijing in a steady stream.

源源本本 yuányuánběnběn　same as 原原本本 yuányuánběnběn

源源不绝 yuányuán bù jué　in an endless stream; continuously: 运往市场的蔬菜～。There is a steady flow of vegetables to the market.

源源而来 yuányuán ér lái　come in a steady (*or* continuous) stream

源远流长 yuányuǎn-liúcháng　a distant source and a long stream—of long standing and well established: 我们两国人民的友谊～。The friendship between our two peoples goes back to ancient times.

猿（猨）

yuán　ape: 从～到人 from ape to man

猿猴 yuánhóu　apes and monkeys

猿人 yuánrén　ape-man ——see also 北京猿人 Běijīng yuánrén

缘

yuán　① reason: ～何到此? What's your reason for coming here? ② edge; fringe; brink: 外～ outer fringe (*or* edge) / 这个城市处于沙漠南～。This city is located on the southern fringe of the desert. ③ along: ～溪而行 walk along the stream ④ predestined relationship: 姻缘 yīnyuán /《铁弓～》*Marriage Through a Steel Bow* (a Beijing opera)

缘簿 yuánbù　records of contributions kept at Buddhist or Taoist temples

缘法 yuán·fǎ　same as 缘分 yuánfèn

缘分 yuánfèn　lot or luck by which people are brought together: 咱俩又在一起了,真是有～。So we're together again. It must be fate. / 烟、酒跟我没有～。Smoking and drinking don't appeal to me.

缘故 yuángù　reason; cause: 他这样生气,不知什么～。I wonder what reason he had for getting so angry. / 那个孩子身体虚弱,是因为营养不良的～。Malnutrition was the cause of the child's weakness. / 西红柿在这土里长不好,其中必有～。There must be some reason why tomatoes will not flourish in this soil.

缘木求鱼 yuán mù qiú yú　climb a tree to catch fish—a fruitless approach

缘起 yuánqǐ　① genesis; origin: 文章～ the origins of literary forms ② an account of the founding of an institution or the beginning of a project:《中国科学院～》*The Chinese Academy of Sciences: Its Origins and Founders* (an assumed book title)

缘悭一面 yuán qiān yīmiàn　it was never my good fortune to meet him

缘由 yuányóu　cause; reason

辕

yuán　① shafts of a cart or carriage ② the outer gate of a government office in ancient times ③ a government office in ancient times: 行辕 xíngyuán

辕马 yuánmǎ　horse in the shafts; shaft-horse

辕门 yuánmén　the outer gate of a government office in ancient times

辕子 yuánzi　*inf.* shafts of a cart or carriage: 车～ shafts of a cart

羱

yuán　*zool.* ibex

羱羊 yuányáng　*zool.* ibex

螈

yuán　see 蝾螈 róngyuán

橼

yuán　see 枸橼 jǔyuán; 香橼 xiāngyuán

yuǎn

远（遠）

yuǎn　① far away (in time or space); distant; remote: 别走～了。Don't go far. / 离这儿多～? How far is it from here? / 我家离学校不～。It's not far from my home to school. / 到山顶上挺～的。It's a long way to the top of the mountain. / ～在公元十一世纪,中国已使用火药。Gunpowder was used in China as far back as the 11th century. / 谁能看得这样～? Who could have seen so far ahead? ② distant (in relationship): 远亲 yuǎnqīn ③ *adv.* by far; far and away: 这个问题～比那个重要。This problem is far more important than that. / 城里这家饭店～比别家好。This is by far the best hotel in town. / ～不及 far inferior to / ～～超过 far exceed ④ keep away from; keep at a distance: 他这个人很危险,你最好～着他一点儿。He is quite dangerous; you'd better keep away from him. / 亲贤臣,～小人,此先汉所以兴隆也;亲小人,～贤臣,此后汉所以倾颓也。(诸葛亮) Attracting worthy men and repelling mean men—this achieved the glory of the Former Han; attracting mean men and repelling worthy men—this ruined the Later Han.

远程 yuǎnchéng　long-range; long-distance: ～导弹 long-range missile / ～火箭 long-range rocket / ～航行 long (sea) voyage

远处 yuǎnchù　a distant point or place: 我看见一个人从～走来。I saw a man coming towards me from a long way off. / 那座楼从～看还不错。At a distance the building seems attractive.

远大 yuǎndà　long-range; broad; ambitious: 眼光～ be farsighted; have a broad vision / 前途～ (of a person) have a bright future / ～的计划 a long-range plan; an ambitious plan / ～的理想 lofty ideals

远道 yuǎndào　a long way: ～而来 come a long way; come from afar

远地点 yuǎndìdiǎn　*astron.* apogee

远东 Yuǎndōng　the Far East

远渡 yuǎndù　travel across a vast expanse of water: ～重洋 travel all the way from across the oceans; travel across the oceans

远方 yuǎnfāng　a distant place: ～的来客 a guest from afar

远房 yuǎnfáng　distantly related: ～亲戚 a distant relative; remote kinsfolk

远隔重洋 yuǎn gé chóngyáng　be separated by vast oceans

远古 yuǎngǔ　remote antiquity: 在～时代 in remote antiquity / 从～流传下来的故事 a legend from ancient times

远海 yuǎnhǎi　distant sea waters

远航 yuǎnháng　take a long (sea) voyage; sail to a distant place

远话 yuǎnhuà　a stranger's words: 一家人怎么说起～来了? How come you, one of the family, are speaking like a stranger? / 近人不说～。Friends don't speak like strangers.

远见 yuǎnjiàn　foresight; vision: 有～ have breadth of vision; be farsighted

远见卓识 yuǎnjiàn zhuōshí　foresight and sagacity: 只有

具备～，才能不失前进的方向。Only farsightedness can prevent us from losing our bearings in the march forward. ／～的决策 a farsighted policy decision

远交近攻 yuǎnjiāo-jìngōng befriend distant states while attacking those nearby

远郊 yuǎnjiāo the outer suburbs; the remoter outskirts of a city

远近 yuǎnjìn ① far and near: ～闻名 be known far and wide; be widely known ② distance: 不论～我都去。I'll go no matter how far it is. ／这两条路～差不多。The distance is about the same by either road.

远景 yuǎnjǐng ① distant view; long-range perspective; prospect: ～规划 a long-range plan ／共产主义的壮丽～ the splendid prospects of communism ② film long shot

远距离操纵 yuǎnjùlí cāozòng remote control; telecontrol

远客 yuǎnkè a guest from afar

远路 yuǎnlù ① a long way: 走～ go a long way; take a long journey ② same as 冤枉路 yuānwanglù

远虑 yuǎnlǜ foresight; long view

远门 yuǎnmén far away from home: 出～ travel far away from home; go on a long journey

远谋 yuǎnmóu a long-term plan

远年 yuǎnnián many years ago; of long standing: ～陈酒 aged wine

远僻 yuǎnpì remote; out-of-the-way

远期 yuǎnqī at a specified future date; forward: ～汇价 forward rate ／～外汇 forward exchange

远亲 yuǎnqīn distant relative (or relation); remote kinsfolk

远亲不如近邻 yuǎnqīn bùrú jìnlín a relative far off is less help than a neighbour close by; neighbours are dearer than distant relatives

远人 yuǎnrén ① people living in faraway places ② stranger; a mere acquaintance

远日点 yuǎnrìdiǎn astron. aphelion

远涉 yuǎnshè make a long, arduous journey (esp. across the sea): ～重洋 travel all the way from across the oceans; travel across the oceans

远射程炮 yuǎnshèchéngpào long-range gun

远摄镜头 yuǎnshè jìngtóu ① film long shot ② telephoto lens

远识 yuǎnshí foresight; vision

远视 yuǎnshì med. long sight; farsightedness; hyperopia; hypermetropia: ～眼镜 spectacles for long sight; spectacles for the farsighted

远水不解近渴 yuǎnshuǐ bù jiě jìnkě distant water can't quench present thirst—the aid is too slow in coming to be of any help

远水救不了近火 yuǎnshuǐ jiùbuliǎo jìnhuǒ distant water won't put out a fire close at hand—a slow remedy cannot meet an urgency

远台 yuǎntái table tennis far from the table: ～防守 long defence; far-from-table defence ／～削球 off-table chop

远天 yuǎntiān the distant sky

远眺 yuǎntiào look far into the distance (from a high place): 亭在山脊，～颇畅。The pavilion was situated on a knoll and commanded an open view of the distance.

远图 yuǎntú a long-term plan

远销 yuǎnxiāo sell goods to distant places: ～海外 find a good sale overseas; find a market abroad

远行 yuǎnxíng go on a long journey

远扬 yuǎnyáng (of fame, reputation, etc.) spread far and wide: 声威～。His mighty fame spread far and wide.

远飏 yuǎnyáng formal flee to a faraway place: 凶犯闻风～。The murderer fled away at the first sign of

danger.

远洋 yuǎnyáng ① ocean ② of the open sea beyond the littoral zone; oceanic: ～航行 oceangoing voyage ／～货轮 oceangoing freighter ／～客轮（班轮）ocean liner ／～渔业 deep-sea (or pelagic) fishing ／～救助拖轮 oceangoing salvage tug

远因 yuǎnyīn remote cause

远缘杂交 yuǎnyuán zájiāo agric. distant hybridization

远月点 yuǎnyuèdiǎn astron. apocynthion

远在天边，近在眼前 yuǎn zài tiānbiān, jìn zài yǎnqián seemingly far away, actually close at hand (said playfully to call attention to sb. or sth. right in front of sb.'s eyes)

远征 yuǎnzhēng expedition: ～军 expeditionary army (or force)

远支 yuǎnzhī a remote branch of a clan

远志[1] yuǎnzhì great and far-reaching ambition; high aspiration

远志[2] yuǎnzhì Chin. med. the root of the narrow-leaved polygala (polygala tenuifolia)

远走高飞 yuǎnzǒu-gāofēi fly far and high; be off to distant parts; flee to faraway places

远足 yuǎnzú pleasure trip on foot; hike; walking tour

远祖 yuǎnzǔ remote ancestor

yuàn

苑 yuàn ① formal enclosed ground for growing trees, keeping animals, etc.; gardens: 御苑 yùyuàn ② formal centre (of art and literature, etc.): 文苑 wényuàn ③ (Yuàn) a surname

苑囿 yuànyòu animal farm (or park)

怨 yuàn ① resentment; enmity: 面有～色 wear a resentful (or discontented) look ／《清宫～》The Malice of Empire (a play) ② blame; complain: 这件事～我。I am to blame for this.

怨不得 yuànbude ① cannot blame: 这件事～老李，都怪我。Lao Li is not to blame for this. It's all my fault. ② no wonder; so that's why: 班车坏了，～他们迟到了。The bus broke down. No wonder they were late.

怨仇 yuànchóu hatred; enmity

怨敌 yuàndí foe; enemy

怨毒 yuàndú formal enmity; hatred

怨怼 yuànduì formal resentment; enmity

怨愤 yuànfèn discontented and indignant

怨府 yuànfǔ formal object of general indignation

怨怪 yuànguài blame: 他～我多嘴。He blamed me for not keeping my mouth shut when I should.

怨恨 yuànhèn ① have a grudge against sb.; hate ② resentment; grudge; enmity

怨悔 yuànhuǐ repent remorsefully

怨嗟 yuànjiē formal sigh in resentment

怨苦 yuànkǔ bitter resentment

怨詈 yuànlì formal rail fretfully

怨懑 yuànmèn discontented and indignant; resentful

怨怒 yuànnù resentful

怨女 yuànnǚ liter. a grumbling maid; a girl pining for a husband: 当是时也，内无～，外无旷夫。《孟子》At that time, there were neither girls pining for a husband nor men without a wife.

怨偶 yuàn'ǒu formal an unhappy couple

怨气 yuànqì grievance; complaint; resentment: 出～ air one's grievances; vent one's resentment ／一肚子～ be full of complaints (or grievances)

怨声载道 yuànshēng zài dào cries of discontent rise all round; complaints (or voices of discontent) are heard

everywhere

怨天尤人 yuàntiān-yóurén blame god and man—blame everyone and everything but oneself: 唉声叹气，～ groaning and sighing and cursing fate

怨望 yuànwàng *formal* resentment; grudge; enmity

怨言 yuànyán complaint; grumble: 他工作负担很重，但从未发过一句～。He was overworked but never uttered a word of complaint. / 人们对物价上涨颇有～。There were a lot of complaints about the rising prices.

怨艾 yuànyì *formal* resentment; grudge

怨尤 yuànyóu resentment; grudge; enmity

院 yuàn ① courtyard; yard; compound: ～里种了几棵枣树。There are some jujube trees in the courtyard. ② a designation for certain government offices and public places: 法院 fǎyuàn / 科学院 kēxuéyuàn ③ college; academy; institute

院本 yuànběn ① professional script—a name for a type of drama known to have flourished in North China in the Jin-Yuan 金元 period (the dramatic script being used by professionals including both courtesans and regular actors) ② a general term used in the Ming-Qing period for 杂剧 zájù② and 传奇 chuánqí②

院落 yuànluò courtyard; yard; compound

院墙 yuànqiáng the walls that surround a house

院士 yuànshì academician

院套 yuàntào *dial.* courtyard; yard; compound

院体画 yuàntǐhuà imperial-court decorative painting

院校 yuànxiào educational institutions; universities and colleges

院子 yuànzi courtyard; yard; compound: 我们家有个～，孩子们可以在那里玩儿。Our house has a yard for the children to play in. / ～里练不出千里马，温室里长不出万年松。A fiery steed is not trained in a courtyard, nor does a pine grow sturdy in a greenhouse.

坑 yuàn *dial.* protective embankments (built around houses or fields in riverside and lakeside areas in Hunan and Hubei): ～田 fields with protective embankments

坑子 yuànzi protective embankments (built around houses or fields in riverside and lakeside areas in Hunan and Hubei)

媛 yuàn *formal* a beautiful woman ——see also yuán

掾 yuàn *formal* minor official; subordinate

愿[1] yuàn *formal* honest and cautious: 谨～ cautious in conduct

愿[2]（願） yuàn ① hope; wish; desire: 平生之～ one's lifelong wish ② be willing; be ready: 我～为共产主义奋斗终生。I will devote my entire life to the cause of communism. ③ vow (made before Buddha or a god): 还愿 huányuàn

愿望 yuànwàng desire; wish; aspiration: 从团结的～出发 start from the desire for unity / 全世界人民的共同～ the common aspirations of the world's people / 她出国进修的～终于实现了。Her wish to go abroad for advanced studies has at last come true.

愿心 yuànxīn a vow made to a god or Buddha

愿意 yuàn·yì ① be willing; be ready: 她～尽力帮忙。She's willing to help in any way she can. / 我～听听你的意见。I'm ready to listen to your idea. ② wish; like; want: 他们～你留在这里。They want you to remain here.

yuē

曰 yuē *formal* ① say: 子～：“温故而知新，可以为师矣。”《论语》The Master says, "A man is worthy of being a teacher who gets to know what is new by keeping fresh in his mind what he is already familiar with." ② call; name: 无以名之，故名之～… call it sth. for lack of a better name

约 yuē ① make an appointment; arrange: 我想跟王经理～个时间谈谈。I'd like to make an appointment with Mr. Wang, the manager. / 我们～好下星期一碰头。We agreed to meet next Monday. ② ask or invite in advance: 请～他来。Please ask him to come. / 我已～了王同志。I've invited Comrade Wang. ③ pact; agreement; appointment: 立约 lìyuē ④ restrict; restrain: 约束 yuēshù ⑤ economical; frugal: 节约 jiéyuē ⑥ simple; brief: ～言之 in brief; in a word ⑦ *adv.* about; around; approximately: ～五十人 about fifty people ⑧ *math.* reduction of a fraction: 十分之五可以～成二分之一。Five over ten can be reduced to one over two.——see also yāo

约旦 Yuēdàn Jordan

约旦人 Yuēdànrén Jordanian

约定 yuēdìng agree on; appoint; arrange: ～会晤地点 agree on a meeting place / 在～的时间 at the appointed time

约定俗成 yuēdìng súchéng established (*or* sanctioned) by popular usage; accepted through common practice

约法 yuēfǎ provisional constitution

约法三章 yuē fǎ sān zhāng agree on a three-point law—make a few simple rules to be observed by all concerned

约分 yuēfēn *math.* reduction of a fraction

约翰斯岛 Yuēhànsīdǎo Johnston Island

约合 yuēhé invite to meet together; call together

约会 yuē·huì ① arrange a meeting; make an appointment: 大伙儿～好在这儿碰头。We've arranged to meet here. / 他们～过我，我没去。They invited me, but I didn't go. ② appointment; engagement; date: 订个～ make an appointment / 我今天晚上有个～。I have an engagement this evening.

约集 yuējí invite to meet together; call together

约计 yuējì count roughly; come roughly to

约见 yuējiàn make an appointment to meet (esp. a foreign diplomatic official); ask for (*or* request) an appointment with

约据 yuējù general name for 合同 hétong, 契约 qìyuē, etc.

约略 yuēlüè ① rough; approximate: ～的估计 a rough (*or* approximate) estimate ② *adv.* roughly; approximately; about: 这件事我～知道一些。I know something about the matter.

约莫 yuēmo (also 约摸 yuēmo) about; roughly: 现在～有十点钟。It is about ten now. / 我们等了～有一个小时的光景。We waited for an hour or so. / 离这儿～有三公里路。It's about three km. from here.

约期 yuēqī ① fix a date; appoint a time: ～会谈 fix a date to hold talks ② appointment or engagement; the appointed time: 误了～ fail to keep the appointment ③ the term or duration of an agreement: ～已满。The contract has expired.

约请 yuēqǐng invite; ask

约束 yuēshù keep within bounds; restrain; bind: 用纪律～自己 keep oneself within the bounds of discipline

约束力 yuēshùlì binding force: 本联合声明及其附件具有

同等～。This Joint Declaration and its Annexes shall be equally binding.

约数 yuēshù ① approximate number ② *math.* divisor

约谈 yuētán arrange talks

约同 yuētóng *formal* ask sb. to join one

约言 yuēyán promise; word; pledge: 遵守～ keep one's promise (*or* word) / 违背～ break one's promise; go back on one's word / 实行～ redeem one's pledge

约制 yuēzhì keep within bounds; restrain; bind

燺

yuē *formal* yardstick; measure; scale: 矩燺 jǔyuē

yuě

哕（噦）

yuě ① *onom.* the sound of vomiting ② *inf.* vomit; throw up: 她刚吃完药，又都～出来了。She threw up all the medicine she had just taken.

yuè

月

yuè ① the moon ② month: 这孩子才两个～。The baby is only two months old. ③ monthly: 我的～收入为300元。My monthly income is 300 *yuan*. / ～产量 monthly output ④ full-moon-shaped; round: 月饼 yuèbing

月白 yuèbái bluish white; very pale blue

月白风清 yuèbái-fēngqīng a bright moon and a gentle breeze—a beautiful night

月半 yuèbàn the 15th day of a month (esp. of a lunar month)

月报 yuèbào ① monthly magazine; monthly: 《小说～》*Short Story Monthly* ② monthly report

月饼 yuèbing moon cake (esp. for the Mid-Autumn Festival)

月长石 yuèchángshí *min.* moonstone

月尘 yuèchén *astron.* lunar dust

月城 yuèchéng *formal* the *enceinte* of a city gate; a barbican entrance to a city

月初 yuèchū the beginning of the month

月底 yuèdǐ the end of the month

月洞门 yuèdòngmén moon gate

月度 yuèdù monthly: ～计划 a monthly plan

月房 yuèfáng *dial.* a lying-in woman's bedroom

月份 yuèfèn month: 上～ last month / 八～的产量比七～提高了百分之五。In August output was 5% higher than in July.

月份牌 yuèfènpái *inf.* calendar

月俸 yuèfèng monthly pay

月工 yuègōng a labourer hired by the month

月宫 yuègōng the Lunar Palace (a legendary palace on the moon; also another name for the moon)

月光 yuèguāng ① moonlight; moonbeam ② *dial.* the moon

月光花 yuèguānghuā large moonflower (*Calonction aculeatum*)

月规钱 yuèguīqián *old* monthly allowances given to apprentices

月桂树 yuèguìshù laurel; bay tree; bay

月海 yuèhǎi lunar maria

月黑天 yuèhēitiān (also 月黑夜 yuèhēiyè) a moonless night

月黑头 yuèhēitóu *dial.* a moonless night

月华 yuèhuá ① moonlight: ～如水 watery moonbeams; a flood of translucent moonlight ② *meteorol.* lunar corona

月季 yuèjì Chinese rose

月家疾 yuèjiājí *dial.* puerperal fever

月建 yuèjiàn month

月经 yuèjīng menses; menstruation; period: ～不调 menoxenia; abnormal menstruation / ～过多 menorrhagia; excessive menstruation / ～周期 menstrual cycle

月经带 yuèjīngdài sanitary belt (*or* napkin)

月刊 yuèkān monthly magazine; monthly

月窠 yuèkē (also 月窝 yuèwō) *dial.* a baby's first month of life: 出～ a month old / ～儿 a baby less than a month old

月蓝 yuèlán pale blue

月老 yuèlǎo same as 月下老人 yuèxià lǎorén

月历 yuèlì monthly calendar

月利 yuèlì monthly interest: ～率 monthly interest rate

月亮 yuèliang the moon

月亮地儿 yuèliangdìr a place where there is moonlight; moonlit spot

月亮门 yuèliangmén moon gate

月令 yuèlìng a lunar month as characterized by climatic and agricultural conditions

月轮 yuèlún full moon

月门 yuèmén moon gate

月杪 yuèmiǎo *formal* the end of the month

月末 yuèmò the end of the month

月票 yuèpiào monthly ticket

月婆子 yuèpózi *dial.* lying-in woman

月钱 yuèqian monthly allowances

月琴 yuèqín a four-stringed plucked instrument with a full-moon-shaped sound box

月球 yuèqiú the moon: ～背面 the far side of the moon / ～轨道 lunar orbit

月球探测 yuèqiútàncè moon exploration

月球学 yuèqiúxué selenology

月入 yuèrù monthly income: ～甚微 have a meagre monthly income

月色 yuèsè moonlight: 西湖～ the moon over the West Lake / 雨洗东坡～清。(苏轼) Rain has washed Eastern Slope, the moon shines clear.

月石 yuèshí *Chin. med* borax

月食 yuèshí (also 月蚀 yuèshí) *astron.* lunar eclipse: 月全食 total lunar eclipse / 月偏食 partial lunar eclipse

月事 yuèshì *formal* menses; menstruation; period

月台 yuètái railway platform

月台票 yuètáipiào platform ticket

月头儿 yuètóur *inf.* ① the beginning of the month ② time for monthly payment: 到～了，该付房租了。It's time to pay the month's rent.

月尾 yuèwěi the end of the month

月夕 yuèxī *formal* ① moonlit (*or* moonlight) night ② the end of the month

月息 yuèxī monthly interest

月下老人 yuèxià lǎorén (also 月下老儿 yuèxiàlǎor) ① the Old Man of the Moon (the god of marriage, who has on record in a book the marriage fates of those on earth and attaches betrothed couples with a red cord which will bind them for life) ② matchmaker

月相 yuèxiàng *astron.* phases of the moon (the four chief ones being 朔 new moon, 上弦 first quarter, 望 full moon, and 下弦 last quarter)

月薪 yuèxīn monthly pay

月信 yuèxìn menses; menstruation; period

月牙 yuèyá (also 月芽 yuèyá) *inf.* crescent moon

月岩 yuèyán moon rock

月夜 yuèyè moonlit (*or* moonlight) night

月红 yuèhóng another name for 月季 yuèjì

月晕 yuèyùn lunar halo

月晕而风, 础润而雨 yuè yùn ér fēng, chǔ rùn ér yǔ a

halo round the moon means wind; a damp plinth means rain—premonitory signs of future events

月震 yuèzhèn moonquake

月氏 Yuèzhī a nomadic people living in the Western Regions (西域) during the Han Dynasty, identified as the Indo-Scyths of Western sources

月中 yuèzhōng the middle of the month

月终 yuèzhōng the end of the month

月子 yuèzi ① month of confinement after giving birth to a child: 她还没出～。She's still in confinement. ② time of childbirth; confinement: 她的～是二月初。She's expecting her baby at the beginning of February.

月子病 yuèzibìng puerperal fever

乐(樂)
yuè ① music: 奏乐 zòuyuè ② (Yuè) a surname ——see also lè

乐池 yuèchí orchestra pit; orchestra

乐段 yuèduàn *mus.* period

乐队 yuèduì orchestra; band

乐队指挥 yuèduì zhǐhuī conductor; bandmaster

乐府 yuèfǔ ① Music Bureau (a government office created during the reign of Emperor Wu of the Han Dynasty to collect folk songs and their music for ceremonial occasions at court) ② such folk songs or their imitations by literary men (many *yuefu* songs are in a regular five-syllable line)

乐歌 yuègē ① music and songs ② a song with accompaniment

乐工 yuègōng same as 乐师 yuèshī

乐户 yuèhù (in former times) ① female musicians under government control ② brothel

乐句 yuèjù *mus.* phrase

乐理 yuèlǐ *mus.* music theory

乐律 yuèlǜ *mus.* temperament

乐迷 yuèmí music lover

乐谱 yuèpǔ music score; music

乐谱架 yuèpǔjià music stand

乐器 yuèqì musical instrument; instrument

乐曲 yuèqǔ musical composition; composition; music

乐师 yuèshī musician (who performs on a musical instrument)

乐坛 yuètán the musical world; music circles

乐团 yuètuán ① philharmonic society ② philharmonic orchestra

乐舞 yuèwǔ a dance with accompaniment

乐音 yuèyīn musical sound; tone

乐章 yuèzhāng *mus.* movement

刖(跀)
yuè cutting off the feet (a form of punishment in ancient China)

岳[1](嶽)
yuè high mountain: 五岳 Wǔyuè

岳[2]
yuè ① wife's parents: 岳父 yuèfù ② (Yuè) a surname

岳父 yuèfù (also 岳丈 yuèzhàng) wife's father; father-in-law

岳家 yuèjiā wife's parents' home

岳母 yuèmǔ wife's mother; mother-in-law

钥
yuè key: 锁钥 suǒyuè ——see also yào

说
yuè same as 悦 yuè ——see also shuì; shuō

栎(櫟)
yuè used in 栎阳 (a place in Shaanxi Province) ——see also lì

悦
yuè ① happy; pleased; delighted: 大～ feel very pleased / ～色 a pleased look (or expression) ②

please; delight: 悦耳 yuè'ěr

悦耳 yuè'ěr pleasing to the ear; sweet-sounding: ～的音乐 sweet (or melodious) music / 歌声～。The singing is pleasant.

悦服 yuèfú heartily admire

悦目 yuèmù pleasing to the eye; good-looking

悦豫 yuèyù *formal* pleased; delighted

阅
yuè ① read; go over: ～报 read newspapers ② review; inspect: 阅兵 yuèbīng ③ experience; pass through: 试行已～三月。Three months have passed since we started to try this out.

阅兵 yuèbīng review troops: ～场 parade ground / ～典礼 dress parade / ～式 military review; parade

阅操 yuècāo review soldiers at drill

阅读 yuèdú read: ～杂志 read magazines

阅卷 yuèjuàn go over examination papers

阅览 yuèlǎn read

阅览室 yuèlǎnshì reading room

阅历 yuèlì ① see, hear or do for oneself: ～过很多事 have seen much of the world ② experience: ～浅 having little experience; inexperienced

阅世 yuèshì *formal* see the world: ～渐深 gain more and more experience of life

钺(戉)
yuè a battle-axe used in ancient China

跃(躍)
yuè leap; jump: ～上马背 leap onto a horse / 一～而起 get up with a jump; jump up all of a sudden / ～居世界首位 leap to first place in the world

跃动 yuèdòng move up and down; quiver

跃进 yuèjìn make (or take) a leap; leap forward: 电子工业出现了～的局面。The electronics industry is developing by leaps and bounds. / 他们县小麦亩产由二百公斤～到五百公斤。Their county's output of wheat has jumped from 200 kilos to 500 kilos per *mu*.

跃马 yuèmǎ spur the horse on

跃迁 yuèqiān *phys.* transition: 自发～ spontaneous transition / 俘获～ capture transition / ～概率 transition probability

跃然 yuèrán appear vividly

跃然纸上 yuèrán zhǐshàng show forth in one's writing: 义愤之情～。Righteous indignation shows forth in his writing.

跃跃欲试 yuèyuè yù shì be eager to have a try; itch to have a go

越[1]
yuè ① get over; jump over: ～墙而逃 escape by climbing over the wall ② exceed; overstep: ～出范围 overstep the bounds; exceed the limits / ～出政策界限 go beyond the bounds of policy ③ (of one's voice or emotion) be at a high pitch: 清越 qīngyuè

越[2]
Yuè ① one of the Warring States into which China was divided during the Eastern Zhou period (770–256 B.C.), comprising parts of modern Zhejiang and Jiangsu ② a name for eastern Zhejiang ③ a surname

越次 yuècì *formal* not in proper sequence or order

越冬 yuèdōng live through (or survive) the winter

越冬作物 yuèdōng zuòwù winter crop; overwintering crop

越发 yuèfā *adv.* ① all the more; even more: 两年不见，这姑娘～长得标致了。I haven't seen the girl for two years, and she's grown prettier than ever. / 他～沉不住气了。He got all the more excited. / 她一听这话，～不高兴了。She became even more displeased at this. ② (used correlatively with a preceding 越 or 越是) (the

more...) the more...: 越是性急，～容易出差错。The more impatient you are, the more mistakes you'll make.

越分 yuèfèn　overstepping the bounds of propriety; assuming; presumptuous

越瓜 yuèguā　same as 菜瓜 càiguā

越轨 yuèguǐ　exceed the bounds; transgress: ～行为 impermissible behaviour; transgression

越过 yuèguò　cross; surmount; negotiate: ～戈壁沙漠 cross the Gobi Desert / ～障碍 surmount obstacles / ～激流险滩 negotiate turbulent rivers and treacherous shoals

越级 yuèjí　① bypass the immediate leadership: ～提出申诉 bypass the immediate leadership and present one's appeals and complaints to higher levels ② (of personnel promotion) skip a grade or rank: ～提升 promote sb. more than one grade at a time

越加 yuèjiā　adv.　all the more; even more

越界 yuèjiè　overstep the boundary; cross the border

越境 yuèjìng　cross the boundary illegally; sneak in or out of a country

越橘 yuèjú　bot.　cowberry

越剧 yuèjù　Shaoxing opera

越来越… yuèláiyuè…　more and more: 越来越好 get better and better / 发挥越来越大的作用 play an increasingly important role / 天气越来越热了。It's getting warmer and warmer. / 越来越深入人心 go deeper and deeper into the hearts of the people; become more and more popular

越礼 yuèlǐ　improper; indecorous

越理 yuèlǐ　unreasonable

越南 Yuènán　Viet Nam

越南人 Yuènánrén　Vietnamese

越南语 Yuènányǔ　Vietnamese (language)

越权 yuèquán　exceed (or overstep) one's power or authority; ultra vires

越位 yuèwèi　sports　offside: 裁判判进球无效，因为有个球员处在～位置。The referee disallowed the goal because one of the players was offside.

越席 yuèxí　leave one's seat at the table

越野 yuèyě　cross-country: ～汽车 cross-country (motor) vehicle

越野赛跑 yuèyě sàipǎo　cross-country race

越铀元素 yuèyóu yuánsù　chem.　transuranic element

越狱 yuèyù　escape from prison; break prison: 组织～ organize a jailbreak

越狱犯 yuèyùfàn　prison breaker

越…越… yuè…yuè…　the more...the more...: 越多越好 the more the better / 越战越强 grow stronger with the fighting / 风越刮越大。The wind was blowing harder and harder. / 脑子越用越灵。The more you use your brains, the keener they'll become. / 犯了错误则要求改正，改正得越迅速，越彻底，越好。Once a mistake is made, we should correct it, and the more quickly and thoroughly the better.

越俎代庖 yuè zǔ dài páo　exceed one's functions and meddle in other people's affairs; take sb. else's job into one's own hands

粤 Yuè　① another name for 广东 Guǎngdōng ② (used in) 两～ the two Yues (i.e. Guangdong and Guangxi)

粤菜 yuècài　Guangdong style of cooking; Guangdong food; Guangdong cuisine

粤剧 yuèjù　Guangdong opera

龠[1] yuè　a unit of measure used in ancient China (equal to 0.5 合 gě)

龠[2]（籥） yuè　an ancient musical instrument, similar to the dizi (笛子)

瀹 yuè　formal　① boil (tea) ② dredge (a river)

yūn

晕 yūn　① same as 晕 yùn[1], limited to use in 头晕 tóuyūn, 头晕晕脑 yūntóu-yūnnǎo, 晕头转向 yūntóu zhuànxiàng, etc. ② swoon; faint: ～了过去 lose consciousness; faint; swoon ——see also yùn

晕倒 yūndǎo　fall in a faint; pass out

晕糊 yūnhu　(also 晕乎 yūnhu) dizzy; giddy: 他才喝了一杯白兰地就～了。One glass of brandy and he felt dizzy.

晕厥 yūnjué　med.　syncope; faint

晕头晕脑 yūntóu-yūnnǎo　① dizzy; giddy ② muddleheaded

晕头转向 yūntóu zhuànxiàng　confused and disoriented: 把敌人打得～ hit the enemy so hard that he's thrown into confusion / 这道算题真难，把我搞得～。This mathematical problem is really difficult; it's got me confused. / 这几天简直把人忙得～的。I've been as busy as hell these last few days. I'm getting quite dizzy.

晕眩 yūnxuàn　same as 眩晕 xuànyùn

晕晕忽忽 yūnyunhūhū　① dizzy; giddy ② muddleheaded

缊 yūn　see 纲缊 yīnyūn ——see also yùn

氲 yūn　see 氤氲 yīnyūn

yún

云[1] yún　① formal　say: 《诗》～:"战战兢兢，如临深渊，如履薄冰。"(《论语》) The Songs says: "In fear and trembling, As if approaching a deep abyss, As if walking on thin ice." ② part. arch.: 岁～暮矣。The year is drawing to its end.

云[2]（雲） yún　cloud

云[3]（雲） Yún　① short for 云南 Yúnnán ② a surname

云霭 yún'ǎi　thin, floating clouds

云豹 yúnbào　clouded leopard

云表 yúnbiǎo　formal　high above the clouds

云鬓 yúnbìn　liter.　cloudlike hair (the beautiful hair of a woman): 当窗理～，对镜贴花黄。(《木兰诗》) Facing the window, I arrange my cloudlike hair; Looking into the mirror, I adorn myself with a yellow patch.

云彩 yúncai　inf.　cloud

云层 yúncéng　cloud layer: 在～上面飞行 fly above the clouds

云顶 yúndǐng　meteorol.　cloud top

云豆 yúndòu　same as 芸豆 yúndòu

云端 yúnduān　high in the clouds: 飞机从～飞来。A plane was coming down from behind the clouds.

云朵 yúnduǒ　flaky clouds

云尔 yún'ěr　part. formal　(used to mark off the end of a statement, emphasizing its finality): 十月三日之夕于怀仁堂观西南各民族文工团、新疆文工团、吉林省延边文工团、内蒙文工团联合演出歌舞晚会，毛主席命填是阕，用纪大团结之盛况～! (柳亚子) On October 3 [1950], I attended a soirée in Huai Ren Tang. Performances were given by ensembles from the various nationalities

in the Southwest, Xinjiang, Yanbian in Jilin Province, and Inner Mongolia. At Chairman Mao's request, I composed the following poem to celebrate the great unity of the nationalities.

云贵高原 Yún-Guì Gāoyuán　the Yunnan-Guizhou Plateau

云海 yúnhǎi　a sea of clouds

云汉 yúnhàn　*liter.*　the Milky Way

云鬟 yúnhuán　bun (of hair)

云集 yúnjí　come together in crowds; gather; converge: 各地代表～首都。Representatives from all over the country gathered in the capital.

云际 yúnjì　*formal*　high in the clouds

云锦 yúnjǐn　cloud-pattern brocade (a kind of high quality brocade)

云谲波诡 yúnjué-bōguǐ　bewilderingly changeable

云开见日 yún kāi jiàn rì　same as 开云见日 kāi yún jiàn rì

云量 yúnliàng　*meteorol.*　cloudiness

云锣 yúnluó　chiming gongs (a percussion instrument consisting of ten gong-shaped pieces of brass of the same diameter but varying thickness hung in a wooden frame; only nine of the gongs are struck, hence another name 九音锣 jiǔyīnluó); Chinese gong chimes

云幂 yúnmì　*meteorol.*　ceiling: ～高度 ceiling height / ～气球 ceiling balloon

云母 yúnmǔ　mica: ～板岩 mica-slate / ～电容器 mica condenser / ～片 mica sheet; sheet mica / ～片岩 mica schist; micacite

云南 Yúnnán　Yunnan (Province)

云泥之别 yún-ní zhī bié　as far apart as clouds and mud—worlds (*or* poles) apart; a world of difference

云霓 yúnní　rain clouds

云片糕 yúnpiàngāo　a kind of ricecake in thin strips

云起龙骧 yúnqǐ-lóngxiāng　dragons rise as clouds gather—great men come to the fore when opportunity offers

云气 yúnqì　thin, floating clouds

云雀 yúnquè　skylark

云扰 yúnrǎo　*formal*　disturbed and confused like the clouds: 四方～。Turmoil prevails on all sides.

云散 yúnsàn　disperse like the clouds: 旧友～。Old friends dispersed like the clouds. ——see also 烟消云散 yānxiāo-yúnsàn

云山雾罩 yún shān wù zhào　① be enveloped in mist; misty ② rambling; discursive: 他们在～地闲聊。They were chatting aimlessly. ③ dazed; confused; muddled: 这人～的, 刚说过的事就忘了。He's all in a muddle and doesn't even remember what he's just said.

云杉 yúnshān　*bot.*　dragon spruce (*Picea asperata*)

云室 yúnshì　*phys.*　cloud chamber: 威耳孙～ Wilson (cloud) chamber

云涛 yúntāo　billowy clouds: ～滚滚 clouds surging

云梯 yúntī　scaling ladder

云天 yúntiān　the skies: 高耸～ rising to the skies / 高峰直插～ peaks towering into the clouds

云头 yúntóu　*dial.*　cloud cluster; clouds

云头儿 yúntóur　cloud pattern

云图 yúntú　*meteorol.*　cloud atlas; cloud chart; cloud picture

云团 yúntuán　*meteorol.*　cloud cluster

云腿 yúntuǐ　Yunnan ham

云屯 yúntún　*formal*　come together in crowds; gather; converge

云雾 yúnwù　(usu. fig.) cloud and mist; mist: 拨开～见青天 scatter the clouds and see the blue sky

云雾天 yúnwùtiān　soupy weather

云霞 yúnxiá　rosy clouds

云消雾散 yúnxiāo-wùsàn　the clouds melt and the mists disperse—vanish into thin air

云霄 yúnxiāo　the skies: 响彻云霄 xiǎngchè yúnxiāo

云崖 yúnyá　mountain peaks towering into the clouds; steep cliffs: 金沙水拍～暖, 大渡桥横铁索寒。(毛泽东) Warm the steep cliffs lapped by the waters of Golden Sand, Cold the iron chains spanning the Dadu River.

云烟 yúnyān　cloud and mist; mist

云涌 yúnyǒng　like surging clouds—in large numbers; in force: 民工从四面八方～而来。Volunteer workers arrived in force from different parts of the country. / 才思～ in a moment of literary effusion

云游 yúnyóu　(of a Buddhist monk or a Taoist priest) wander about; roam about: 吴教授从此舍俗出家,～天下。(《警世通言》) From then on, Schoolmaster Wu renounced the world to follow the Way, and he drifted all around the country.

云雨 yúnyǔ　*liter.*　the sport of cloud and rain—sexual intercourse

云云 yúnyún　*formal*　(used at the end of a direct or indirect quotation, implying that some words of the same purport are left unquoted): 他来信说读了不少新书, 颇有心得～。He wrote to say that he had read several new books and profited greatly from them.

云遮雾障 yúnzhē-wùzhàng　enveloped in mist; blurred; indistinct; hazy

云蒸霞蔚 yúnzhēng-xiāwèi　(also 云兴霞蔚 yúnxīng-xiāwèi) (of scenery) magnificent

匀 yún　① even: 颜色涂得不～。The colour is not evenly spread. / 麦苗出得很～。The wheat sprouts are growing very evenly. ② even up; divide evenly: 这两份多少不均, 再～一～吧。These two shares are not equal. Please even them up. ③ spare: 我们种子比较多, 可以～给你们一些。We've got more seeds than we need. We can spare you some.

匀称 yúnchen　well-proportioned; well-balanced; symmetrical: 身材～ of proportional build / 字写得～ write a neat hand

匀兑 yúnduì　spare; share: 给某人～一间屋子 spare sb. a room

匀和 yúnhuo　(also 匀乎 yúnhu) *inf.*　even; neat; uniform

匀净 yúnjing　uniform; even; neat: 这块布染得很～。This cloth is evenly dyed.

匀脸 yúnliǎn　rub powder and paint evenly on one's face

匀溜 yúnliu　*inf.*　of the right size, thickness, consistency, etc.

匀染 yúnrǎn　*text.*　level dyeing: ～剂 levelling agent

匀实 yúnshi　*inf.*　even; neat; uniform

匀速运动 yúnsù yùndòng　*phys.*　uniform motion

匀调 yúntiao　even; well-proportioned: 气息～ even breathing / 眉眼～ have regular features

匀停 yúnting　*dial.*　the right amount: 吃东西要～。We should eat just enough, neither too much nor too little.

匀妥 yúntuǒ　even; equitable: 分配～ be evenly (*or* equitably) distributed

匀细 yúnxì　even and fine; even and light: ～洁白的牙齿 even and fine white teeth / ～的鼾声 even and light snoring

匀圆 yúnyuán　nicely rounded: ～饱满的樱桃 full and round cherries; plump cherries

匀整 yún·zhěng　neat and well spaced; even and orderly: 他的字写得很～。His handwriting is very neat.

芸[1]　yún　*bot.*　rue

芸[2] **(蕓)**　yún　see 芸薹 yúntái

芸豆 yúndòu　kidney bean

芸薹　yúntái　*bot.* rape

芸香　yúnxiāng　*bot.* rue

芸芸　yúnyún　numerous; multitudinous

芸芸众生　yúnyún zhòngshēng　all living things; all mortal beings

纭　yún　see below

纭纭　yúnyún　numerous and disorderly; diverse and confused

耘　yún　weed: 春耕夏～ spring ploughing and summer weeding

耘锄　yúnchú　hoe (a farm tool)

耘田　yúntián　weed the fields

筼　yún　*formal* ① skin of bamboo ② bamboo

yǔn

允[1]　yǔn　permit; allow; consent: 不～ refuse to consent

允[2]　yǔn　fair; just: 公允 gōngyǔn

允承　yǔnchéng　agree or promise to do sth.; undertake: ～一项任务 undertake a task

允从　yǔncóng　consent to; assent to

允当　yǔndàng　proper; suitable

允诺　yǔnnuò　promise; consent; undertake: 欣然～ readily consent / 实行自己所作的～ fulfil one's promise (*or* commitment)

允许　yǔnxǔ　permit; allow: 不～任何破坏纪律的现象存在 permit no breach of discipline / 这是我国内政, 不～任何外来干涉。This is our internal affair which brooks no outside interference. / 请～我代表全厂职工向你们致谢。Allow me to thank you on behalf of our factory.

允许误差　yǔnxǔ wùchā　*mech.* allowable (*or* permissible) error

允许载荷　yǔnxǔ zàihè　allowable load

允准　yǔnzhǔn　approve; permit; allow

陨　yǔn　fall from the sky or outer space

陨落　yǔnluò　(of a meteorite, etc.) fall from the sky or outer space

陨灭　yǔnmiè　① fall from outer space and burn up ② *formal* meet one's death; perish

陨石　yǔnshí　*astron.* aerolite; stony meteorite: ～雨 meteorite shower

陨铁　yǔntiě　*astron.* meteoric iron; iron meteorite; siderite

陨星　yǔnxīng　*astron.* meteorite: 石～ aerolite; stony meteorite / 铁～ siderite; iron meteorite / 石铁～ siderolite; stony iron meteorite / ～学 meteoritics

陨越　yǔnyuè　*formal* fall into error; fail to fulfil one's duties: 幸免～ be lucky to escape committing an error

殒　yǔn　perish; die

殒灭　yǔnmiè　*formal* meet one's death; perish

殒命　yǔnmìng　*formal* meet one's death; perish

殒殁　yǔnmò　*formal* pass away; die

殒身　yǔnshēn　*formal* meet one's death; perish

殒阵　yǔnzhèn　be killed in action; fall in battle

yùn

孕　yùn　① pregnant: 孕妇 yùnfù ② pregnancy:

有～在身 be pregnant; be in the family way

孕畜　yùnchù　pregnant domestic animal

孕妇　yùnfù　pregnant woman

孕期　yùnqī　*med.* pregnancy; gestation

孕穗　yùnsuì　*agric.* booting: ～期 boot stage

孕吐　yùntù　vomiting during pregnancy; morning sickness

孕育　yùnyù　(fig.) give birth to; be pregnant with; breed: 黄河流域～了中国古代文明。The Huanghe valley gave birth to ancient Chinese civilization. / 局势中～着危险。The situation is pregnant with grim possibilities.

运[1]（運）　yùn　① motion; movement: 运行 yùnxíng ② carry; transport; ship: ～货 transport (*or* ship) goods ③ use; wield; utilize: 运笔 yùnbǐ / 运思 yùnsī

运[2]（運）　yùn　fortune; luck; fate: 幸运 xìngyùn

运笔　yùnbǐ　wield the pen (in writing or painting): 他时而搁笔沉思, 时而～如飞。Now he was lost in thought, his pen laid down; now he was wielding the pen with rapid, vigorous strokes. / 书法之道在于～。Calligraphy is the way of the brush.

运程　yùnchéng　*transportation* haul

运筹　yùnchóu　draw up plans; devise strategies

运筹帷幄　yùnchóu wéiwò　plan strategies within a command tent: ～之中, 决胜千里之外 sit within a command tent and devise strategies that will assure victory a thousand *li* away

运筹学　yùnchóuxué　operational research; operations research

运道　yùndao　*dial.* fortune; luck

运动　yùndòng　① motion; movement: ～的物质 matter in motion / ～的形式 form of motion / 行星的～ the movement of a planet / ～是物质的存在方式。Motion is the mode of existence of matter. / 乘敌～之际, 打击敌人。Attack the enemy while he is on the move. ② sports; athletics; exercise: 室外～ outdoor sports / 游泳是我喜爱的～。Swimming is my favourite sport. / 散步也是一种～。Walking is also a form of exercise. ③ (political) movement; campaign; drive: 竞选～ election campaign / 技术革新～ a drive for technological innovation

运动　yùndong　arrange things through pull

运动场　yùndòngchǎng　sports (*or* athletic) ground; playground; stadium

运动服装　yùndòng fúzhuāng　sportswear

运动会　yùndònghuì　sports meet; athletic meeting; games: 世界大学生～ World University Games; Universiade / 全国～ national games

运动健将　yùndòng jiànjiàng　master of sports; sportsmaster

运动衫　yùndòngshān　sports shirt

运动神经　yùndòng shénjīng　same as 传出神经 chuánchū shénjīng

运动学　yùndòngxué　*phys.* kinematics

运动医学　yùndòng yīxué　sports medicine

运动员　yùndòngyuán　sportsman or sportswoman; athlete; player: 参加比赛的～ contestant; competitor

运动战　yùndòngzhàn　mobile war (*or* warfare)

运动知觉　yùndòng zhījué　*psychol.* consciousness of motion

运费　yùnfèi　transportation expenses; freight; carriage: 到付～ freight payable at destination / ～表 freight list / ～单 freight note / ～吨 freight ton / ～率 freight rate / ～免付 carriage free / ～条款 freight clause / ～已付 freight (*or* carriage) paid / ～预付 freight prepaid; advanced freight

运河　yùnhé　canal: ～税 canal dues

运脚　yùnjiǎo　*dial.*　transport charge; freight; carriage

运斤成风　yùn jīn chéng fēng　whirl the hatchet with a noise like the wind—an uncanny feat (from a story in *Zhuang Zi*《庄子》about a carpenter who, at the request of a plasterer, whirled his hatchet with a noise like the wind and sliced off a speck of mud on the tip of the plasterer's nose no thicker than a fly's wing, removing every bit of mud without injury to the nose)

运煤船　yùnméichuán　coal carrier; collier

运气　yùnqì　(the art of) directing one's strength, through concentration, to a part of the body

运气　yùnqì　fortune; luck: 他～好, 提升了。He had the good fortune to be promoted. / 唉,～老是不好。Just my luck! / 这回可来了～了。This time my luck's in.

运球　yùnqiú　*basketball hockey*　dribble

运输　yùnshū　transport; carriage; conveyance: 陆上 (水路)～ land (water) transport; transport by land (water) / 地面 (空中)～ surface (air) transport /～部队 transportation troops /～船 cargo ship; transport ship /～队 transport corps (*or* team) /～方式 modes of transport /～工具 means of transport; conveyance /～公司 transport company /～里程 transport mileage /～量 freight volume /～能力 transport capacity; carrying capacity /～网 transport network /～业 transport service; carrying trade; transportation

运输机　yùnshūjī　① *aviation* transport plane; air-freighter ② *min.* conveyor

运输舰　yùnshūjiàn　transport ship; naval transport

运数　yùnshù　*formal*　destiny; fate

运思　yùnsī　exercise one's mind (in writing)

运送　yùnsòng　transport; ship; convey: ～物资 ship (*or* transport) goods and materials

运算　yùnsuàn　*math.*　operation: 四则～ the four fundamental operations of arithmetic / 每秒钟～二百万次 capable of 2,000,000 calculations per second /～分析 operational analysis /～微积分 operational calculus /～误差 arithmetic error

运算器　yùnsuànqì　*computer*　arithmetic unit

运腕　yùnwàn　(in practising calligraphy) exercise control over the brush with wrist and elbow

运销　yùnxiāo　(commodity) transportation and sale

运行　yùnxíng　① move; be in motion: 在轨道上～ move in orbit / 地球绕太阳～。The earth revolves round the sun. / 列车～时, 请勿打开车门。Don't open the door while the train is in motion. ② operate; function: 推动经济～ keep the economy functioning

运营　yùnyíng　(of buses, ships, etc.) run; ply

运用　yùnyòng　use; wield; apply: ～你自己的判断力 use your own judgment / 成功地～外国先进经验 make good use of the advanced experience of foreign countries /～国家机器 wield the state machinery / 灵活～ apply in a flexible way / 她把课堂上学到的东西～在这项实验里。She applied what she had learned in class to the experiment.

运用之妙, 存乎一心　yùnyòng zhī miào, cún hū yī xīn　ingenuity in varying tactics depends on mother wit

运用自如　yùnyòng zìrú　handle very skilfully; have a perfect command of

运载　yùnzài　deliver; carry

运载工具　yùnzài gōngjù　means of delivery: 战略～ strategic vehicles

运载火箭　yùnzài huǒjiàn　carrier rocket; launch vehicle

运载技术　yùnzài jìshù　delivery technology

运转　yùnzhuàn　① revolve; turn round: 行星绕着太阳～。The planets revolve round the sun. ② work; operate: 机器～正常。The machine is running well. /～不灵 not work well; be out of order

运祚　yùnzuò　*formal*　fate (esp. of a dynasty); fortunes: 汉明帝时始有佛法, 明帝在位才十八年耳。其后乱亡相

继,～不长。(韩愈) It was in the reign of Emperor Ming of the Han Dynasty that Buddhism was first introduced into China, and yet this emperor was on the throne for only eighteen years. Subsequently, disorder followed upon disorder, and rulers did not reign for long.

郓

郓　Yùn　① (also 郓城 Yùnchéng) a county in Shandong Province ② a surname

恽

恽　Yùn　a surname

晕

晕　yūn　① dizzy; giddy; faint: 他一坐汽车就～。He feels dizzy (*or* sick) whenever he travels by car. ② *meteorol.* halo: 日晕 rìyùn / 月晕 yuèyùn ——see also yùn

晕场　yùnchǎng　have stage fright; feel nervous and dizzy at an examination

晕车　yùnchē　carsickness: 好～ be liable to carsickness

晕池　yùnchí　(also 晕堂 yùntáng) have a fainting spell in a bathhouse

晕船　yùnchuán　suffer from seasickness

晕高儿　yùngāor　*dial.*　feel giddy when on a height

晕机　yùnjī　suffer from airsickness

晕针　yùnzhēn　*Chin. med.*　have a fainting spell during acupuncture treatment

酝 (醞)

酝　yùn　*formal*　① ferment (wine) ② wine

酝酿　yùnniàng　① (fig.) brew; ferment: 这场大辩论～已久。This great debate has been brewing for a long time. ② have a preliminary informal discussion; deliberate on: ～候选人名单 consider and talk over the list of candidates / 大家先～一下。Let's have an exchange of views first. / 经过反复～协商, 选举了出席大会的代表。Delegates to the congress were elected after repeated deliberations and consultations.

愠

愠　yùn　*formal*　angry; irritated: 愠色 yùnsè

愠恼　yùnnǎo　angry; indignant; furious

愠怒　yùnnù　be inwardly angry

愠容　yùnróng　*formal*　angry look; irritated look

愠色　yùnsè　*formal*　angry look; irritated look: 面有～ look irritated

缊

缊　yùn　*arch.*　① coarse hemp ② old silk floss: ～袍 a gown padded with old silk floss ——see also yūn

韵 (韻)

韵　yùn　① musical (*or* agreeable) sound: 琴～悠扬。Sweet music was being played on the lute. ② rhyme: 押韵 yāyùn / 韵文 yùnwén ③ charm: 风韵 fēngyùn

韵白　yùnbái　① spoken parts in Beijing opera where the traditional pronunciation of certain words is slightly different from that in current Beijing dialect ② rhyming spoken parts in traditional opera

韵调　yùndiào　musical tone

韵腹　yùnfù　*phonet.*　the head vowel of a final ——see also 韵母 yùnmǔ

韵脚　yùnjiǎo　the rhyming word that ends a line of verse; rhyme

韵律　yùnlǜ　① metre (in verse) ② rules of rhyming; rhyme scheme

韵律学　yùnlǜxué　prosody

韵母　yùnmǔ　*phonet.*　the final of a syllable (i.e. the syllable minus the initial 声母 shēngmǔ, e.g. -iang in 娘 niáng), (The longest form of a final consists of a medial 韵头 or 介音, a head vowel 韵腹, and an ending 韵尾. Thus, in the final -iang of 娘 niáng, -i- is the medial, -a-, the

head vowel, and -ng the ending. There may be no medial or ending, but there must be at least a head vowel.)

韵目 yùnmù　rhyme classes (in traditional rhyming dictionaries)

韵事 yùnshì　① literary or artistic pursuits, often with pretence to good taste and refinement ② romantic affair

韵书 yùnshū　(traditional) rhyming dictionary

韵头 yùntóu　another name for 介音 jièyīn ——see also 韵母 yùnmǔ

韵尾 yùnwěi　*phonet.* the ending of a final ——see also 韵母 yùnmǔ

韵味 yùnwèi　lingering charm; lasting appeal: 她的唱腔很有～。Her singing has a special pleasing quality about it. / 这首诗～很浓。This poem is charged with meaning and feeling.

韵文 yùnwén　literary composition in rhyme; verse

韵语 yùnyǔ　rhymes

韵致 yùnzhì　charm; beauty: 水仙另有一种淡雅的～。The narcissus has a quiet charm of its own.

熨

　　yùn　iron; press: ～衣服 iron (*or* press) clothes ——see also yù

熨斗 yùndǒu　flatiron; iron: 电～ electric iron

熨衣板 yùnyībǎn　ironing board

蕴

　　yùn　*formal* accumulate; hold in store; contain

蕴藏 yùncáng　hold in store; contain: 我国地下～着丰富的矿物资源。Our country is rich in mineral resources. / 这部百科全书～着丰富的信息。This encyclopedia is a vast storehouse of information. / 群众中～了极大的社会主义的积极性。The masses have a vast reservoir of enthusiasm for socialism. / ～量 reserves; deposits

蕴涵 yùnhán　① (also 蕴含 yùnhán) *formal*　contain: 这个故事虽然很短，但却～着深刻的哲理。The story, short as it is, contains a profound philosophy. ② *log.*　implication

蕴结 yùnjié　pent up

蕴藉 yùnjiè　*formal*　temperate and refined; cultured and restrained: ～的微笑 a bland smile

蕴蓄 yùnxù　lie hidden and undeveloped; be latent

Z

zā

扎(紥、紮) zā tie; bind: ～小辫儿 tie up one's plaits; plait one's hair; wear one's hair in plaits / ～一根红头绳 tie one's plait with a piece of red yarn / 腰里～一条皮带 tie a leather belt around one's waist ——see also zhā; zhá

扎把子 zābǎzi *dial.* ① tie up; bundle up ② unite; pull together

扎彩 zācǎi hang up festoons

匝(帀) zā *formal* ① circle; circumference: 绕树三～ circle a tree three times ② surround; encircle; revolve around ③ dense; full: 匝地 zādì

匝道 zādào *formal* ring road

匝地 zādì *formal* all over the ground; everywhere: 柳荫～。The willow trees cast their shadows all around.

匝月 zāyuè *formal* a full month

咂 zā ① sip; suck: ～一口酒 take a sip of wine ② make clicks (of admiration, praise, etc.) ③ taste (*or* savour) carefully

咂嘴 zāzuǐ make clicks (of admiration, praise, surprise, etc.)

拶 zā *formal* force; compel; coerce ——see also zǎn

zá

杂(杂、雜、襍) zá ① miscellaneous; sundry; mixed: ～事儿 miscellaneous affairs / ～而不乱 mixed but not confused / 到会的人很～。A mixed bag of people attended the meeting. ② mix; mingle: 这片苹果树中～有几棵梨树。There are a few pear trees scattered among these apple trees.

杂拌儿 zábànr ① assorted preserved fruits; mixed sweetmeats ② mixture; miscellany; medley; hotchpotch

杂草 zácǎo weeds; rank grass: ～丛生 be overgrown with weeds

杂处 záchǔ (of people from different places) live together

杂凑 zácòu knock together: 由流氓、土匪等～成的一支反动武装 a reactionary force knocked together of hooligans, bandits, and the like

杂肥 záféi miscellaneous fertilizers (e. g. urban refuse)

杂费 záfèi ① incidental (*or* miscellaneous) expenses; incidentals ② sundry fees (*or* charges); extras

杂感 zágǎn ① random (*or* stray) thoughts ② a type of literature recording such thoughts

杂环 záhuán *chem.* heterocycle; heterocyclic ring: ～化合物 heterocyclic compound

杂烩 záhuì ① a stew of various ingredients; mixed stew; hotchpotch ② mixture; miscellany; medley; hotchpotch

杂活儿 záhuór odd jobs: 他在这家餐厅干～挣点钱。He earns some money by doing odd jobs at the restaurant.

杂货 záhuò sundry goods; groceries: 日用～ various household supplies

杂货店 záhuòdiàn (also 杂货铺 záhuòpù) grocery; sundry store; general store

杂和菜 záhuocài mixed stew (of leftovers)

杂和面儿 záhuomiànr maize flour mixed with a little soya bean flour

杂记 zájì ① jottings; notes ② miscellanies (as a type of literature): 《西京～》*Miscellany of the Western Capital*

杂技 zájì acrobatics

杂技团 zájìtuán acrobatic troupe

杂技演员 zájì yǎnyuán acrobat

杂家 zájiā the Eclectics, a school of thought flourishing at the end of the Warring States Period and the beginning of the Han Dynasty

杂交 zájiāo *biol.* hybridize; cross: 苹果与梨～ cross the apple with the pear / 通过～改良水稻品种 improve paddy varieties through hybridization

杂交后代 zájiāo hòudài *biol.* filial generation

杂交水稻 zájiāo shuǐdào hybrid rice

杂交玉米 zájiāo yùmǐ hybrid (*or* crossbred) maize

杂交育种 zájiāo yùzhǒng crossbreeding

杂居 zájū (of people of two or more nationalities) live together: 少数民族～地区 an area inhabited by several minority nationalities

杂剧 zájù ① (in the Song Dynasty) a variety play consisting of a prelude, the main play in one or two scenes, and a musical epilogue (none of the Song variety plays is extant) ② (in the Yuan Dynasty) a poetic drama consisting of four acts or song sequences 折, occasionally including a "wedge" 楔子 in the form of a prologue (placed before the first act) or an interlude (placed between acts), all the sung parts in the four acts being assigned to the protagonist, whether male or female (e.g. Guan Hanqing's 关汉卿 *Injustice Suffered by Dou E*《窦娥冤》and Ma Zhiyuan's 马致远 *Autumn in the Palace of Han*《汉宫秋》)

杂粮 záliáng food grains other than wheat and rice

杂乱 záluàn mixed and disorderly; in a jumble; in a muddle: 抽屉里的东西很～。The things in the drawer were all in a jumble.

杂乱无章 záluàn wú zhāng disorderly and unsystematic; confused and disorderly; chaotic: 无意义的、～的议论 pointless, random talk / 这篇报告～，文理不通。This report is just a jumble of words, lacking logic and coherence.

杂乱信号 záluàn xìnhào hash (in radio, radar or TV reception)

杂面 zámiàn ① flour made from various kinds of beans ② noodles made from such flour

杂念 zániàn distracting thoughts: 排除～ banish dis-

tracting thoughts from one's mind

杂牌 zápái a less known and inferior brand: ～货 goods of an inferior brand

杂牌军 zápáijūn miscellaneous troops; troops of miscellaneous brands

杂品 zápǐn (also 杂件 zájiàn) sundry goods; groceries

杂七杂八 záqīzábā mixed; assorted; miscellaneous: 刀子、勺子之类～的东西 a motley assortment of knives and ladles and so on

杂糅 záróu mix; mingle; blend: 古今～ a blending of the ancient and the modern

杂散 zásǎn phys. stray: ～磁场 stray magnetic field / ～辐射 stray radiation

杂色 zásè ① variegated; parti-coloured; motley ② an inferior brand

杂食动物 záshí dòngwù omnivorous animal

杂史 záshǐ miscellaneous histories (i.e. private records or records of particular events)

杂耍 záshuǎ variety show; vaudeville

杂税 záshuì miscellaneous levies

杂说 záshuō ① different versions (of sth.): 对这个事件～不一。 There have been different versions of this incident. ② formal fragmentary writing

杂碎 zásui chopped cooked entrails of sheep or oxen

杂沓 zátà numerous and disorderly: ～的脚步声 the clatter of footsteps

杂文 záwén essay

杂务 záwù odd jobs; sundry duties

杂役 záyì old odd-job man

杂音 záyīn ① noise ② elec. static ③ med. murmur: 心脏～ heart murmur

杂院儿 záyuànr a compound occupied by many households

杂志 zázhì ① magazine: 订一份～ subscribe to a magazine ② (often used in book titles) miscellaneous notes; notes: 王念孙《读书～》 Wang Niansun's *Miscellaneous Reading Notes*

杂志架 zázhìjià magazine rack

杂质 zázhì ① impurity: ～含量 impurity content / ～限度 limit of impurities ② chem. foreign matter (or substance)

杂种 zázhǒng ① biol. hybrid; crossbreed: ～猪 crossbred pig / ～狗 mongrel dog ② offens. bastard; son of a bitch

杂种不育性 zázhǒng bùyùxìng biol. hybrid sterility

杂种优势 zázhǒng yōushì biol. hybrid vigour; heterosis

砸 zá ① pound; tamp: 把地基～实 tamp the foundations solid / ～了脚 have one's foot squashed ② break; smash: 碗～了。 The bowl is broken. / ～核桃 crack walnuts / ～碎锁链 smash the shackles / 把门～开 smash (or ram) the door open ③ dial. fail; fall through; be bungled: 考～了 failed the test / 事儿办～了。 The job was bungled. / 戏演～了。 The performance was a fiasco.

砸饭碗 zá fànwǎn smash sb.'s rice bowl—make sb. lose his job; dismiss sb. from his job: 这可砸了我的饭碗了。 Now I've lost my job.

砸锅 záguō dial. fail; fall through; be bungled

砸锅卖铁 zá guō mài tiě give away all one has

zǎ

咋（喒） zǎ dial. how; why: 情况～样? How are things? / 你看该～办? What do you think we should do? / 你～不去? Why don't you go? ——see

also zhā; zhà

咋个 zǎge dial. how; why: 你～没去上学? Why didn't you go to school?

za

臜 za see 腌臜 āza

zāi

灾（災） zāi ① calamity; disaster: 一场大～ a great calamity / 去年有～。 There was a natural calamity last year. ② personal misfortune; adversity: 没病没～ good health and good luck; with one's health all right and luck not bad

灾变说 zāibiànshuō geol. catastrophism

灾害 zāihài calamity; disaster

灾患 zāihuàn calamity; disaster: 屡经～ suffer calamity after calamity

灾荒 zāihuāng famine due to crop failures: 去年他老家闹了～。 Famine hit his home district last year.

灾祸 zāihuò disaster; calamity; catastrophe: ～临头。 A great disaster is befalling (or imminent).

灾民 zāimín victims of a natural calamity

灾难 zāinàn suffering; calamity; disaster; catastrophe: ～性的后果 disastrous consequences / 避免一场大～ avert a catastrophe / 给殖民地人民带来巨大的～ bring great suffering to the colonial people

灾难深重 zāinàn shēnzhòng disaster-ridden: 经过一百多年的反帝反封建斗争，～的中华民族终于站起来了。 After more than a hundred years of anti-imperialist, anti-feudal struggle, the calamity-ridden Chinese nation at last stood up.

灾年 zāinián famine (or lean) year

灾情 zāiqíng the condition of a disaster: ～严重。 The losses caused by the disaster were serious. / 这场雨减轻了～。 The rain reduced the effects of the drought.

灾区 zāiqū disaster area: 地震～ earthquake-stricken area / 旱～ drought-stricken area / 水～ flooded area / 重～ severely afflicted area

灾星 zāixīng the star of calamity—sb. or sth. that brings disaster

灾殃 zāiyāng suffering; calamity; disaster

甾 zāi chem. steroid

哉 zāi part. formal ① (used in exclamations): 诚～斯言! How true that is! ② (used with an interrogative word in asking a question or making a retort): 胡为乎来～? Why has it come? / 何～? Why? or Wherefore? / 有何难～? What's so difficult about it?

栽[1] zāi ① plant; grow: ～树 plant trees / ～花 grow flowers ② stick in; insert; plant: ～电线杆子 erect a wire pole ③ force sth. on sb.; impose: ～上罪名 frame sb.; fabricate a charge against sb. ④ young plant; seedling

栽[2] zāi tumble; fall: ～倒 fall down

栽插 zāichā plant; transplant: ～水稻 transplant rice seedlings

栽跟头 zāi gēntou ① tumble; fall ② come to grief; come a cropper: 他非常自负, 到头来忘乎所以, 栽了跟

头。He was very proud of himself until he overreached himself and came a cropper.

栽交 zāijiāo　same as 栽跟头 zāi gēntou

栽培 zāipéi　① cultivate; grow: 先进的～技术 advanced cultivation techniques / 棉花～ the culture of cotton / ～野生植物 domesticate wild plants ② foster; train; educate: 我们今天的成就离不开老师对我们的～. We owe our success to the education and training our teachers gave us. ③ help advance sb.'s career; patronize

栽培品种 zāipéi pǐnzhǒng　cultivar

栽培植物 zāipéi zhíwù　cultivated plant

栽绒 zāiróng　*text.* synthetic tuft

栽诬 zāiwū　frame sb.; frame a case against sb.

栽秧 zāiyāng　transplant seedlings (as of tomatoes or eggplants)

栽赃 zāizāng　① plant stolen or banned goods on sb. ② frame sb.; fabricate a charge against sb.

栽植 zāizhí　plant; transplant: 在山坡上～了树苗。The hillside was planted with saplings.

栽种 zāizhòng　plant; grow

栽子 zāizi　young plant; seedling: 柳树～ willow slips / 桃树～ peach seedlings

zǎi

仔 zǎi　*dial.* ① son ② young animal; whelp
——see also zī; zǐ

宰[1] zǎi　① govern; rule: 主宰 zhǔzǎi ② (in ancient times) warden; prefect

宰[2] zǎi　① slaughter; butcher: ～猪 butcher pigs ② *inf.* overcharge; soak; fleece: 那家饭馆特～人。They really fleeced us at that restaurant.

宰割 zǎigē　invade, oppress and exploit

宰杀 zǎishā　slaughter; butcher

宰牲节 Zǎishēngjié　another name for 古尔邦节 Gǔ'ěrbāngjié

宰相 zǎixiàng　prime minister (in feudal China); chancellor

宰相肚里能撑船 zǎixiàng dùli néng chēng chuán　a prime minister's heart is big enough to pole a boat in—a great person is large-hearted or magnanimous

宰制 zǎizhì　rule; dominate

载[1] zǎi　year: 一年半载 yīnián-bànzǎi

载[2] zǎi　put down in writing; record: ～入记录 record in the minutes; place on record / 据报～ according to press reports / 条约中～明 be clearly stated in the treaty
——see also zài

载入史册 zǎirù shǐcè　be written into the annals of history; go down in history

崽(仔) zǎi　*dial.* ① son ② young animal; whelp

崽子 zǎizi　*offens.* whelp; bastard: 狗崽子 gǒuzǎizi

zài

再 zài　*adv.* ① (for an action yet to take place or contemplated) again; once more; further: 我叫他别～来, 可他又来了。I told him not to come again, but here he is again. / 有工夫, 请～来玩。Please come again whenever you are free. / 要是～下雨, 那还得改日子。If it rains again, the date will have to be changed again. / 我还得～去几次。I have to go there a few more times. / 我不能～喝了。I can't drink any more. / 我～也不去了。I won't go there any more. / ～创新纪录 try to set another new record / 青春不～。One's youth never returns. / 良机难～。Opportunity knocks but once. ② (used before adjectives) more; -er: 还有～大点儿的吗? Have you got a bigger one? / 声音～大一点。Still louder, please. / ～冷的天我也不怕。I can stand colder weather than this. / ～好不过了。It couldn't be any better. ③ (used to indicate the continuing of a situation in conditional or suppositional clauses): ～过几年, 这个村子就要整个变样了。A few more years and there will be a complete change in the village. / ～不走我们就赶不上火车了。We'll miss the train if we delay any longer. ④ (for a delayed action, preceded by an expression of time or condition) then; only then: 先到张家, ～到李家。First go to the Zhangs', and then to the Lis'. / 你做完了功课～出去。Finish your homework before you go out. / 雨住了～走吧。Let's leave when the rain stops. / 这件事等明年～说。This business can keep till next year. ⑤ in addition; on top of that: 到会的有教职员工, ～就是学生代表。Present at the meeting were teachers, administrative personnel, and workers, and also representatives of the students. ⑥ ～…也 (followed by a negative expression) no matter how…still (not): 你～劝他也没有用。No matter how hard you try, you can never persuade him. / 他～卖力也升不了职。No matter how hard he works, he'll never get promoted.

再版 zàibǎn　① second edition ② *old* reprint; second impression

再不 zàibu　*inf.* or else; or: 派老王去, ～小李也行。Send Lao Wang, or else Xiao Li.

再不然 zàiburán　or else; otherwise: 书肯定在这儿, ～就是你把它弄丢了。The book must be here, or else you've lost it.

再出口 zàichūkǒu　*com.* reexport

再次 zàicì　once more; a second time; once again: ～感谢你们的帮助。Thank you once again for your help. / 防止类似事件～发生 prevent the occurrence of similar incidents

再度 zàidù　once more; a second time; once again: ～访问贵国 visit your country a second time / ～当选 be reelected

再分配 zàifēnpèi　*econ.* redistribution

再会 zàihuì　goodbye; see you again

再婚 zàihūn　remarry; marry again

再加 zàijiā　in addition; besides; on top of that: 下着大雨, ～道儿不熟, 所以他迟到了。What with the heavy rain and his not knowing the way, he was late.

再嫁 zàijià　(of a woman) remarry

再见 zàijiàn　goodbye; see you again

再教育 zàijiàoyù　reeducation: 接受～ receive reeducation; be reeducated

再醮 zàijiào　*old* (of a widow) remarry

再接再厉 zàijiē-zàilì　make persistent efforts; continue to exert oneself: 他们百折不挠, ～, 终于达到了目的。The goal has been finally attained through their dauntless and persistent efforts.

再进口 zàijìnkǒu　*com.* reimport

再来一个 zài lái yīgè　encore

再起 zàiqǐ　recurrence; resurgence; revival: 防止边境冲突～ prevent the recurrence of border clashes

再三 zàisān　*adv.* over and over again; time and again; again and again; repeatedly: ～再四 over and over again / ～考虑 consider over and over again / ～

嘱咐 bid or tell again and again

再审 zàishěn ① review ② *leg.* retrial

再生 zàishēng ① be a second so-and-so (a well-known figure already dead): 他手艺真巧，简直是鲁班～。His carpentry is really exquisite. He's another Lu Ban. ② *biol.* regeneration ③ reprocess; regenerate: ～稻 ratooning rice /～纤维素 regenerated cellulose /～橡胶 reclaimed (*or* regenerated) rubber

再生产 zàishēngchǎn *econ.* reproduction

再生父母 zàishēng fùmǔ one's second parent (said with gratitude of a person who has saved or spared one's life)

再生检波器 zàishēng jiǎnbōqì *radio* regenerative detector

再衰三竭 zài shuāi sān jié be nearing exhaustion; be weakened and demoralized

再说 zàishuō ① put off until some time later: 这事先搁两天～。Let's put the matter aside for a couple of days. / 等他打定了主意～。Wait until he's made up his mind. ② *conj.* what's more; besides: 现在去找他太晚了，～我路也不熟。It's too late to go and see him now; besides, I don't quite know the way.

再贴现 zàitiēxiàn *econ.* rediscount

再投资 zàitóuzī *econ.* reinvest; plough back

再现 zàixiàn (of a past event) reappear; be reproduced: ～在眼前 reappear before one's eyes / 使红军过雪山的场面在银幕上～ reproduce on the screen scenes of the Red Army crossing snowcapped mountains

再造 zàizào give sb. a new lease of life: 恩同再造 ēn tóng zàizào

再则 zàizé *conj. formal* moreover; furthermore; besides

再者 zàizhě *conj. formal* moreover; furthermore; besides

在 zài ① exist; be alive: 问题还～，并没有解决。The problem still exists. It's not solved yet. / 他父亲还～，母亲早就不～了。His father is still alive, but his mother passed away long ago. / 刘胡兰已经死了，但是她的精神永～。Liu Hulan is dead, but her spirit lives on. / 人～人情～。Friendship lasts as long as the man is there. ② be at, in or on (a place): 我父母～农村。My parents are in the countryside. / 你的钢笔～桌子上呢。Your pen is on the table. / 他～家，不～这儿。He's at home, not here. / 你去那儿找他，他准～。Go and see him; he must be there. ③ depend on; rest with: 学习好，主要～自己努力。Getting good results in one's studies depends mainly on one's own efforts. / 去不去～你自己。It's up to you whether you go or not. / 收不收他～学校领导。Whether to admit him or not rests with the school authorities. ④ lie in; consist in: 我们的希望～青年一代。Our hopes lie in the younger generation. / 这首诗妙～含蓄而不明言。The appeal of this poem lies in suggestion rather than direct statement. / 学习贵～坚持。In study the important thing is to keep at it. / 她美就美～那双眼睛。Her charm lies in that pair of eyes. / 工作人员不～多，而～有效率。A staff need not be large; it must be efficient. ⑤ join or belong to an organization; be a member of an organization: ～组织 belong to a certain organization ⑥ be on the job or at the post: 在职 zàizhí ⑦ *prep.* at, in, or on (a place or time): 他～工厂工作。He works in a factory. / 事情发生～去年。It happened last year. /～会上发言 speak at a meeting / 运动会安排～四月份。The sports meet has been arranged for some time in April. / 阳光照射～水面上。The sunlight fell on the water. / 狗～地上打滚儿。The dog rolled on the ground. /～我看来 in my opinion; as I see it /～理论上 in theory; theoretically /～和平共处五项原则的基础上 on the basis of the Five Prin-

ciples of Peaceful Coexistence /～这种情况下 under these circumstances /～国际事务中 in international affairs /～党中央的领导下 under the leadership of the Party Central Committee /～党内 within (*or* inside) the Party /～全国范围内 throughout the country /～此期间 during this period /～革命的重要关头 at important junctures of the revolution /～这方面 in this respect ⑧ *adv.* (used to indicate action in progress): 他～看电视。He's watching TV. / 他～干什么？—他还～睡觉呢。What's he doing?—He's still sleeping. / 她～游泳。She is swimming.

在案 zài'àn be on record: 记录～ be put on record; be a matter of record / 声明～ have a statement placed on record

在帮 zàibāng (formerly) be a member of the Qing Gang (青帮 Qīng Bāng) or the Hong Gang (洪帮 Hóng Bāng)

在编 zàibiān (of personnel) be on the permanent staff; be on the regular payroll: ～人员 personnel on the permanent staff; personnel on the regular payroll

在场 zàichǎng be on the scene; be on the spot; be present: 当时我没～。I wasn't there at the time.

在朝 zàicháo hold office at court

在朝党 zàicháodǎng a party in power; ruling party

在党 zàidǎng *inf.* be a member of a political party (esp. the Chinese Communist Party)

在行 zàiháng be expert at sth.; know a job, trade, etc. well: 这方面我不～。I'm no expert at that. / 他打草鞋很～。He's good at weaving straw sandals. / 她对计算机很～。She knows a lot about computers.

在乎 zàihu ① depend on; rest with: 干不干～你自己。It's up to you whether you do it or not. / 诗之所以为诗，～意境，不～辞藻。It is the mood and atmosphere evoked, not poetic diction, that makes poetry what it is. ② lie in; consist in: 背景的作用～衬托。The function of a background is to set off. ③ (usu. used in the negative) care about; mind; take to heart: 只要能学会，不～少睡点觉。As long as I can learn it, I don't mind if I have to cut down on my sleep. / 不～他怎么说，要看他怎么做。Never mind what he says, let's see what he does. / 他爱怎么想就怎么想，我才不～呢。I don't care what he thinks. / 难道你还～这几个钱? Surely you won't grudge such a small sum. / 人家会说你，你～不～? Don't you care what people will say?

在即 zàijí near at hand; shortly; soon: 完工～ will soon be completed; be nearing completion / 毕业～ will soon be graduating / 成功～。Success is in sight.

在家 zàijiā ① be at home; be in: 你爸～吗? Is your father in? / 我们让她～好好休息。We told her to stay home and have a good rest. ② have not renounced the family and become a monk or nun: ～人 layman

在家千日好，出外时时难 zài jiā qiān rì hǎo, chū wài shí shí nán at home you may be a thousand days in comfort, away from home you are in constant trouble

在教 zàijiào *inf.* ① believe in a religion ② believe in Islam; be a Muslim

在劫难逃 zài jié nán táo if you're doomed, you're doomed; there's no escape

在理 zàilǐ reasonable; sensible; right: 这话说得～。That's a perfectly reasonable statement. / 她说得～，我当然听她的。She's right, so of course I'll do what she says.

在内 zàinèi included: 邮费～ postage included / 连我～，小组有七个人。There are seven people in the group, including me.

在旗 zàiqí ① be a bannerman ② be a Manchu ——see also 八旗 bāqí

在世 zàishì be living: 他～的时候 in his lifetime / 他妈要是还～，看到这样的好光景，该有多高兴啊! If his

mother were alive, how happy she would be to see such good times.

在所不辞 zài suǒ bù cí　will not refuse under any circumstances; will not hesitate to: 为革命赴汤蹈火～。I wouldn't hesitate to go through fire and water for the revolution.

在所不惜 zài suǒ bù xī　will not grudge; will never balk at: 为了共产主义事业, 即使牺牲生命也～。To advance the cause of communism, we will balk at no sacrifice, even that of our lives.

在所难免 zài suǒ nánmiǎn　can hardly be avoided; be unavoidable: 工作没有经验, 出点差错～。Slips are unavoidable when you are new to your work. / 本词典虽非草率之作, 但错误仍～。This dictionary, despite the care exercised in compiling it, cannot in the nature of things be free from error.

在逃 zàitáo　*leg.*　has escaped; be at large

在逃犯 zàitáofàn　*leg.*　escaped criminal; criminal at large; fugitive

在天之灵 zài tiān zhī líng　sb.'s soul in heaven (said when thinking fondly of a dead person)

在外 zàiwài　excluded: 住招待所每天得花五十元, 伙食还～。The hostel charges 50 *yuan* per day, food not included. / 这是饭钱, 服务费～。That is the price of the meal exclusive of service charge.

在望 zàiwàng　① be visible; be in sight; be in view: 山头隐隐～。The mountain top was dimly visible. ② will soon materialize; be in sight; be in the offing: 胜利～。Victory is in sight. / 小麦丰收～。The wheatfields promise a good harvest.

在位 zàiwèi　① be on the throne; reign: 万历皇帝十岁登基, ～四十八年。Emperor Wanli acceded to the throne at the age of ten and occupied it for 48 years (1573–1620). ② be at one's post

在握 zàiwò　be in one's hands; be within one's grasp; be under one's control: 大权～ with power in one's hands / 胜利～。Victory is within grasp.

在昔 zàixī　*formal*　in former times; in the past; formerly

在下 zàixià　*hum.*　I: ～看来 in my humble opinion

在先 zàixiān　(also 在前 zàiqián) formerly; in the past; before

在心 zàixīn　feel concerned; mind; be attentive: 别看他大大咧咧的, 什么事他都很～。He appears unconcerned, but nothing escapes his attention. / 这事儿请您在点儿心。Please keep an eye on the matter.

在学 zàixué　be at school

在押 zàiyā　*leg.*　be under detention; be in custody; be in prison

在押犯 zàiyāfàn　*leg.*　criminal in custody; prisoner

在野 zàiyě　not be in office; be out of office

在野党 zàiyědǎng　a party not in office

在意 zàiyì　(usu. used in the negative) take notice of; care about; mind; take to heart: 他只顾看信, 别人对他说的话, 他都没～。He was poring over the letter and didn't take any notice of what people were saying to him. / 这些小事他是不会～的。He won't take such trifles to heart.

在于 zàiyú　① depend on; rest with; be determined by: 有收无收～水, 多收少收～肥。Water determines whether or not we have a harvest, and fertilizer determines whether the harvest is big or small. / 最后怎么决定～你。The final decision rests with you. ② lie in; consist in: 我们的力量～人民群众。Our strength lies in the mass of the people. / 战争的目的～消灭战争。The aim of war is to eliminate war. / 这项工程的问题不～进度, 而～质量。The question of this project is one not of speed but of quality.

在在 zàizài　*formal*　everywhere; in all aspects: ～皆是 can be seen everywhere

在职 zàizhí　be on the job; be at one's post: ～训练 in-service training; on-the-job training / ～期间 during one's tenure of office

在职干部 zàizhí gànbù　cadres at their posts; cadres at work

在职研究生 zàizhí yánjiūshēng　cadres admitted to a postgraduate programme

在职总统 zàizhí zǒngtǒng　incumbent president

在座 zàizuò　be present (at a meeting, banquet, etc.): ～的还有几位归国华侨。Among those present were a few returned overseas Chinese. / 有客人～, 她没好意思说。She was too embarrassed to bring it up in front of the guest. / 请～的同志们多提意见。We hope you comrades here will not hesitate to give your opinions and criticisms.

载¹　zǎi　① carry; hold; be loaded with: 宇宙飞船正把他们～向月球。The spaceship was carrying them to the moon. ② all over the road; everywhere along the way: 风雪～途。Whirling snow swept over the road.

载²　zǎi　*formal*　and; as well as; at the same time: ～笑～言 talking and laughing
——see also zǎi

载波 zàibō　carrier wave; carrier: 三路～ three-channel carrier / ～电报 carrier telegraphy / ～电话机 carrier telephone / ～电流 carrier current / ～抑制 carrier suppression

载歌载舞 zàigē-zàiwǔ　festively singing and dancing: 人们～热烈欢迎贵宾。Singing and dancing, people gave the distinguished guests a warm welcome.

载荷 zàihè　load

载货 zàihuò　carry cargo (*or* freight): ～吨位 cargo tonnage / ～甲板 cargo deck / ～容积 cargo carrying capacity

载客 zàikè　carry passengers

载流子 zàiliúzǐ　*elec.*　carrier; charge carrier

载频 zàipín　*radio*　carrier frequency: ～放大器 carrier amplifier / ～振荡器 carrier oscillator

载人飞行器 zàirén fēixíngqì　manned vehicle

载体 zàitǐ　*chem.*　carrier: 催化剂～ catalyst carrier

载运 zàiyùn　convey by vehicles, ships, etc.; transport; carry: 本市公共汽车每天～乘客十万左右。The city buses carry about 100,000 passengers a day.

载重 zàizhòng　load; carrying capacity: 这辆卡车～多少? What's the carrying capacity of this truck?

载重表尺 zàizhòng biǎochǐ　deadweight scale

载重吨位 zàizhòng dūnwèi　deadweight tonnage

载重量 zàizhòngliàng　loading capacity; deadweight capacity (of a ship, etc.)

载重汽车 zàizhòng qìchē　lorry; truck

载重线 zàizhòngxiàn　load line; load waterline: ～标志 load line mark; freeboard mark; Plimsoll mark

zān

糌　zān　see below

糌粑 zānba　*zanba*, roasted *qingke* barley (青稞) flour, a staple food of the Zang nationality

簪　zān　① hairpin: 碧玉～ emerald hairpin ② wear in one's hair: ～花 wear flowers in one's hair

簪缨 zānyīng　*formal*　high-ranking official: 诗礼～之家 a cultured family of official status

簪子 zānzi　hair clasp

zǎn

咱（喒、偺）　zán　① we or us (including both the speaker and the person or persons spoken to): ～班的人呢? Where are our classmates? ② *dial.* I or me: ～不会说英语。 I don't speak English.

咱们　zánmen　① we or us (including both the speaker and the person or persons spoken to): ～军民是一家。 We, the army and the people, are all one family. / ～商量一下。 Let's talk it over. / ～三个的 the three of us ② *dial.* I or me: ～是个大老粗, 说话只会直来直去。 As I'm an uneducated person, I can only put this bluntly. ③ *dial.* you: ～别哭, 妈出去一会儿就回来。 Don't cry, Mom will be back in a little while. / 同志, ～这儿有牙膏吗? (to a shop assistant) Comrade, do you have toothpaste?

zǎn

拶（桚）　zǎn　press or squeeze hard ——see also zā

拶指　zǎnzhǐ　squeezing a person's fingers between sticks (a torture in old China)

拶子　zǎnzi　sticks for squeezing a person's fingers (as a torture in old China)

攒（儹）　zǎn　accumulate; hoard; save: ～钱 save (or scrape) up money / 他把～的钱都买了书。 He spent all his savings on books. ——see also cuán

趱　zǎn　① *old* hurry (or rush) through: 紧～了一程 rush through one part of the journey ② urge; hasten: ～马向前 urge on a horse

zàn

暂　zàn　① of short duration: 短暂 duǎnzàn ② *adv.* temporarily; for the time being; for the moment: ～别 temporary separation / ～不答复 put off replying / ～代 act for sb. / ～住 stay temporarily (at a place) / 工作～告一段落。 The work has been brought to a temporary close.

暂定　zàndìng　arranged for the time being; tentative; provisional: ～议程 tentative agenda / ～办法 provisional measures; tentative measures / 学习期限～两年。 The term of study is tentatively fixed at two years.

暂缓　zànhuǎn　postpone; put off; defer: ～成行 postpone one's trip / ～作出决定 put off (or defer) making a decision

暂记帐　zànjìzhàng　suspense account

暂且　zànqiě　*adv.* for the time being; for the moment: 讨论～告一段落吧。 Let's stop the discussion for the time being. / 这是后话, ～不提。 But I'm anticipating.

暂缺　zànquē　① (of a post) be left vacant for the time being ② (of a commodity) be out of stock at the moment

暂时　zànshí　① temporary; transient: ～的需要 temporary needs / ～现象 transient phenomenon / 比赛的胜负是～的, 而友谊是长久的。 The results of contests are transient, but friendship is lasting. / ～利益服从长远利益 subordinate temporary interests to long-range (or long-term) ones ② *adv.* temporarily; for the time

being; for the moment: 这事～就这样定了吧。 Let's make it a tentative decision. / 他～来不了。 He can't come right away. / ～停刊 (of a periodical, etc.) temporarily suspend publication / 我～住在家里。 I'm staying at home for the time being.

暂停　zàntíng　① suspend: ～付款 suspend payment / 修理内部, ～营业 business suspended for internal repairs / 会议～, 明天继续举行。 The meeting is adjourned till tomorrow. ② *sports* time-out: 要求～ ask for time-out

暂星　zànxīng　same as 新星[1] xīnxīng

暂行　zànxíng　provisional; temporary; interim: ～条例 provisional (or interim) regulations / ～规定 interim (or temporary) provisions / 安理会～议事规则 Provisional Rules of Procedure of the Security Council

錾

錾　zàn　① engrave on gold or silver; carve; chisel: ～字 engrave characters / ～花 carve flowers or patterns ② engraving tool; chisel

錾刀　zàndāo　(engraver's) burin; graver

錾子　zànzi　chisel (for cutting stone)

赞[1]（賛）　zàn　support; favour; assist: 赞助 zànzhù

赞[2]（賛、讚）　zàn　① praise; commend: 盛赞 shèngzàn ② eulogy: 像～ an inscription eulogizing the subject of a portrait /《天安门～》 Ode to Tian An Men

赞比亚　Zànbǐyà　Zambia

赞比亚人　Zànbǐyàrén　Zambian

赞不绝口　zàn bù jué kǒu　be profuse in praise; be full of praise

赞成　zànchéng　① approve of; favour; agree with; endorse: 咱们明天去郊游, 你～吗? How about going on an outing tomorrow? / 我完全～。 I'm all for it. / 他最不～你这样搞。 He doesn't like the way you do it at all. / 六票～, 三票反对 six votes for and three against / ～意见 assenting views / ～的请举手。 Those in favour please raise their hands. ② *formal* help sb. accomplish sth.

赞成票　zànchéngpiào　affirmative vote

赞词　zàncí　(also 赞辞 zàncí) words of praise; praise

赞歌　zàngē　song of praise; paean: 一曲民族团结的～ a paean of national solidarity

赞礼　zànlǐ　*old* ① act as master of ceremonies ② master of ceremonies

赞美　zànměi　praise; eulogize: 他的大公无私受到人们的～。 He was praised for his selflessness.

赞美诗　zànměishī　(also 赞美歌 zànměigē) *Christianity* hymn; psalm

赞佩　zànpèi　(also 赞服 zànfú) esteem; admire: 我对他的勇气深为～。 I have great admiration for his courage.

赞赏　zànshǎng　appreciate; admire: 对这一友好行动表示～ express appreciation for this friendly act / 他们非常～这些精美的工艺品。 They greatly admired the exquisite handicrafts.

赞颂　zànsòng　extol; eulogize; sing the praises of

赞叹　zàntàn　gasp in (or with) admiration; highly praise: 演员们的高超演技令人～。 People gasped with admiration at the superb skill of the performers.

赞同　zàntóng　approve of; agree with; endorse: 这一主张得到普遍的～。 This proposition met with general approval (or acceptance). / 我们～这项决议。 We subscribe to the resolution. / 全厂一致～这项改革。 The whole factory unanimously agreed to this reform. / 我完全～你的意见。 I fully endorse your opinions.

赞许　zànxǔ　speak favourably of; praise; commend: 得到很多人的～ win the approval of many / 值得～ de-

serve commendation; be commendable; be worthy of praise

赞扬 zànyáng　speak highly of; praise; commend: 这种一心为公的精神值得～. This spirit of selflessness deserves commendation. / 热烈～两国人民之间的友谊 pay warm tribute to the friendship between the two peoples / 他们的良好体育作风博得广泛的～. Their fine sportsmanship won widespread acclaim. / ～声中找差距 see out one's shortcomings amidst a shower of praise

赞仰 zànyǎng　esteem; admire

赞语 zànyǔ　words of praise; praise

赞誉 zànyù　praise; acclaim; commend: 这个厂的产品质量赢得了用户的～. The factory has been commended by the consumers for the high quality of its products.

赞助 zànzhù　support; assistance: 这个展览会得到当地华侨的～. The exhibition had the help and support of the overseas Chinese there. / 这次音乐会得到了多家公司的～. The concert was under the auspices of various companies.

zāng

赃（贓、贜） zāng　① stolen goods; booty; spoils: 分赃 fēnzāng ② bribes: 贪赃 tānzāng

赃官 zāngguān　a corrupt official

赃款 zāngkuǎn　money stolen, embezzled or received in bribes; illicit money

赃物 zāngwù　① stolen goods; booty; spoils ② bribes

脏（髒） zāng　dirty; filthy: ～衣服 dirty (or soiled) clothes; dirty linen / ～水 filthy water; slops; sewage / 别把桌布弄～了. Don't dirty the tablecloth. ——see also zàng

脏病 zāngbìng　popular name for 性病 xìngbìng

脏话 zānghuà　obscene (or dirty, foul) language; obscenities: 他用～骂人. He shouted obscenities at someone.

脏乱 zāngluàn　(of a place) dirty and messy

脏钱 zāngqián　inf. ill-gotten money

脏土 zāngtǔ　rubbish; garbage

脏字 zāngzì　obscene word; swearword; dirty word: 说话别带～. Don't swear.

臧 zāng　① formal good; right ② (Zāng) a surname

臧否 zāngpǐ　formal pass judgment (on people): ～人物 pass judgment on people

zǎng

驵 zǎng　formal fine horse; steed

驵侩 zǎngkuài　formal ① horse broker ② broker

zàng

脏（臟） zàng　internal organs of the body, usu. referring to the heart, liver, spleen, lungs and kidneys; viscera: 心脏 xīnzàng ——see also zāng

脏腑 zàngfǔ　Chin. med. internal organs including the heart, liver, spleen, lungs, kidneys, stomach, gall, intestines and bladder; viscera

脏器 zàngqì　internal organs of the body; viscera

脏象 zàngxiàng　Chin. med. state of internal organs (visceral manifestations indicating physiological function as well as pathological changes of the internal organs)

脏躁症 zàngzàozhèng　another name for 癔病 yìbìng

葬 zàng　bury; inter: 他～在西山. He was buried in the Western Hills.

葬礼 zànglǐ　funeral (or burial) rites; funeral

葬埋 zàngmái　entomb; bury; inter

葬身 zàngshēn　be buried: ～大海 lose one's life in the sea; be drowned / ～在人民战争的汪洋大海之中 get drowned in the vast ocean of people's war

葬身鱼腹 zàngshēn yúfù　become food for the fishes; be swept to a watery grave; be drowned

葬送 zàngsòng　ruin; spell an end to: 封建婚姻制度～了她一生的幸福. The feudal marriage system condemned her an unhappy married life. / 右倾机会主义路线～了一九二四——一九二七年的大革命. The Right opportunist line was the ruin of the Great Revolution of 1924-1927.

藏[1] zàng　① storing place; depository: 宝藏 bǎozàng ② Buddhist or Taoist scriptures: 道藏 dàozàng

藏[2] Zàng　① short for 西藏 Xīzàng ② the Zang nationality ——see also cáng

藏羚獭 zànghàntǎ　Himalayan marmot

藏红花 zànghónghuā　① bot. saffron crocus (Crocus sativus) ② Chin. med. saffron

藏剧 zàngjù　(also 藏戏 zàngxì) Zang opera

藏蓝 zànglán　purplish blue

藏历 zànglì　lunar calendar used by the Zang nationality

藏青 zàngqīng　dark blue

藏青果 zàngqīngguǒ　another name for 诃子 hēzǐ

藏香 zàngxiāng　a kind of joss stick produced in Xizang

藏族 Zàngzú　the Zang (Tibetan) nationality, or the Zangs (Tibetans), distributed over the Xizang Autonomous Region, and Qinghai, Sichuan, Gansu and Yunnan Provinces

奘 zàng　① formal (usu. used in a person's name, as in 玄奘, a famous monk of the Tang Dynasty) strong; robust ② dial. rude; stiff in manner ——see also zhuǎng

zāo

遭[1] zāo　meet with (disaster, misfortune, etc.); suffer: 几～挫折 suffer repeated setbacks / 惨～杀害 be murdered in cold blood; be brutally killed / ～人白眼 be treated with disdain / 你是～他骗了. You have been taken in by him.

遭[2] zāo　m. ① round: 用绳子绕两～ wind the string around twice ② time; turn: 在这么多人面前讲话, 我还是头一～. This is the first time I have ever spoken to such a big audience. / 一～生, 两～熟. Strangers at first meeting become familiar at the next.

遭到 zāodào　suffer; meet with; encounter: ～失败 suffer (or meet with) defeat / ～拒绝 meet with refusal; be turned down / ～困难 encounter (or run up against) difficulties / ～攻击 come under attacks; be attacked by / 这个工厂在地震中～严重破坏. This factory was

seriously damaged during the earthquake.

遭逢 zāoféng　meet with; come across; encounter: ～盛世 live in prosperous times / ～不幸 suffer misfortune

遭际 zāojì　*formal*　① circumstances; lot ② meet with; encounter; run up against: ～艰危 be confronted with difficulties and dangers

遭劫 zāojié　meet with catastrophe

遭难 zāonàn　meet with misfortune; suffer disaster

遭受 zāoshòu　suffer; be subjected to; sustain: ～剥削 suffer exploitation / ～压迫 suffer (*or* be subjected to) oppression / ～损失 sustain losses / ～水灾 be hit by floods

遭殃 zāoyāng　suffer disaster; suffer

遭遇 zāoyù　① meet with; encounter; run up against: ～不幸 meet with misfortune; have hard luck / 先头部队与敌人～了。The advance unit encountered (*or* ran into) the enemy. ② (bitter) experience; (hard) lot: 咱们有着共同的历史～。We have shared the same historical experiences. *or* We have had a common lot. / 他后来的～我就不知道了。I don't know what became of him later.

遭遇战 zāoyùzhàn　meeting engagement; encounter (action); contact battle

遭灾 zāozāi　be hit by a natural calamity

遭罪 zāozuì　(also 遭孽 zāoniè) endure hardships, tortures, rough conditions, etc.; have a hard time

糟 zāo　① distillers' grains; grains ② be pickled with grains or in wine: ～鱼 fish pickled with grains or in wine; pickled fish ③ rotten; poor: 这案板～了。The chopping board is rotten. / 他身体很～。He is in very poor health. ④ in a wretched (*or* terrible) state; in a mess: 把事情搞～了 make a mess of sth. / ～了, 饭糊啦! Damn it! The rice is burning!

糟改 zāogǎi　*dial.*　satirize; tease; make fun of

糟糕 zāogāo　*inf.*　how terrible; what bad luck; too bad: ～, 我把钥匙锁在屋里了。Oh, no, I've locked the key in the room! / 真～, 误了火车啦。What bad luck! We've missed the train. / 更～的是, 他把介绍信丢了。To make things worse, he lost the letter of introduction.

糟害 zāo·hài　*dial.*　(of birds or beasts) damage; make havoc of: 野兔～庄稼。Hares damage crops.

糟行 zāoháng　(also 糟坊 zāofáng) distiller

糟践 zāojian　① waste; ruin; spoil: 别～粮食。Don't waste grain. ② insult; trample on; ravage ③ violate (a woman); rape

糟糠 zāokāng　distillers' grains, husks, chaff, etc.—foodstuffs for the poor: 原宪不厌～, 匿于穷巷。(《史记》) Yuan Xian (one of Confucius' disciples) could not get even enough chaff and husks to satisfy his hunger, and lived hidden away in a wretched lane.

糟糠之妻 zāokāng zhī qī　the wife of one's "chaff and husks" days—a wife who has shared her husband's hard lot

糟糠之妻不下堂 zāokāng zhī qī bù xià táng　the wife of one's "chaff and husks" days shall never go down from the hall; a wife who has shared her husband's hard lot must never be cast aside

糟粕 zāopò　waste matter; dross; dregs

糟蹋 zāo·tà　(also 糟踏 zāo·tà) ① waste; ruin; spoil: ～粮食 waste grain / 剪裁时要小心, 别把料子～了。Cut the material carefully, don't spoil it. ② insult; trample on; ravage: 侵略军把这个村子～得不成样子。The invading troops left the village in a terrible state. / 说话可不要这样～人。You shouldn't talk about anyone like that. ③ violate (a woman); rape

糟心 zāoxīn　vexed; annoyed; dejected: 事情搞得这样, 真～。I'm really vexed (*or* It's a damned nuisance)

things have turned out this way.

zǎo

凿¹ (鑿) záo　① chisel ② cut a hole; chisel or dig: ～一个窟窿 bore a hole / ～山劈岭 tunnel through mountains and cut across ridges / ～冰 make a hole in the ice / 把船～沉 scuttle the ship

凿² (鑿) záo　① mortise: 圆凿方枘 yuánzáo-fāngruì ② *formal*　certain; authentic; irrefutable: 确凿 quèzáo

凿井 záojǐng　① dig (*or* sink, bore) a well ② *min.* shaft sinking; pit sinking: 冻结法～ freeze sinking

凿空 záokōng　*formal*　forced; farfetched: ～之论 a farfetched argument

凿密 záomì　*mech.*　caulking

凿枘 záoruì　*formal*　① mortise and tenon—compatible ② short for 圆凿方枘 yuánzáo-fāngruì

凿死理儿 záo sǐlǐr　*dial.*　obstinate; stubborn; dogged

凿岩 záoyán　*min.*　(rock) drilling: ～机 rock drill

凿凿 záozáo　*formal*　true; certain; verified: 言之～ say sth. with certainty / ～有据 supported by irrefutable evidence

凿子 záozi　chisel

zǎo

早 zǎo　① (early) morning: 从～到晚 from morning till night ② *adv.*　long ago; as early as; for a long time: 他～走了。He went away a long time ago. / 我～知道了。I knew that long ago. *or* That's no news to me. / 我～就想来看你了。I've been wanting to see you for a long time. / ～在二十世纪初 as early as the beginning of the twentieth century ③ early; in advance; beforehand: 你～点儿来。Come early. / 爷爷睡得～。Grandfather goes to bed early. / ～作准备 get prepared in advance; make timely preparations / 他来得比我～。He came earlier than I. / 火车～到了十分钟。The train was ten minutes early. / ～两天我还看见他的。I saw him a couple of days ago. / ～知如此, 我就不回去了。If I'd know this beforehand I would not have gone back. / 电影离开演还～哩。It's still quite a while before the film starts. ④ good morning

早安 zǎo'ān　good morning

早班 zǎobān　morning shift: 上～ be on the morning shift

早半天儿 zǎobàntiānr　(also 早半晌儿 zǎobànshǎngr) *inf.*　forenoon; morning

早餐 zǎocān　breakfast

早操 zǎocāo　morning (setting-up) exercises

早茶 zǎochá　morning tea

早产 zǎochǎn　*med.*　premature delivery

早场 zǎochǎng　morning show (at a cinema, theatre, etc.)

早车 zǎochē　morning train or coach

早晨 zǎochén　(early) morning

早春 zǎochūn　early spring; early in spring

早稻 zǎodào　early (season) rice

早点 zǎodiǎn　(light) breakfast

早饭 zǎofàn　breakfast

早花 zǎohuā　*agric.*　early blossoming

早慧 zǎohuì　*formal*　(of a child) precocious

早婚 zǎohūn　marry too early: ～妨碍工作和学习。Marrying too early hinders one's work and study.

早年 zǎonián　one's early years: 他～参加辛亥革命。He took part in the Revolution of 1911 in his early years.

早期 zǎoqī　early stage; early phase; early days; initial stage: ～作品 sb.'s early works; the works of sb.'s earlier period / ～食道癌 early stage carcinoma of the esophagus

早期白话 zǎoqī báihuà　early vernacular (the vernacular style of written Chinese used before the May 4th Movement of 1919)

早起 zǎoqǐ　*dial.*　(early) morning

早秋 zǎoqiū　early autumn; early in autumn

早日 zǎorì　at an early date; early; soon: 请～答复。Your early reply is requested. *or* Please reply at your earliest convenience. / 祝你～恢复健康。I hope you'll get well soon. *or* I wish you a speedy recovery. / ～完工 complete the project as soon as possible

早上 zǎoshang　(early) morning: ～好。Good morning.

早市 zǎoshì　① morning market ② morning business: 本店～供应豆浆。We sell soya-bean milk in the morning.

早熟 zǎoshú　① *physiol.*　precocity: ～的孩子 a precocious child ② early-maturing; early-ripe: ～品种 early-maturing variety; early variety / ～作物 early-maturing crop; early crop

早衰 zǎoshuāi　*med.*　premature senility (*or* decrepitude); early ageing

早霜 zǎoshuāng　early frost

早岁 zǎosuì　one's early years

早退 zǎotuì　leave earlier than one should; leave early

早晚 zǎowǎn　① morning and evening: ～各服一丸 take one pill in the morning and one in the evening ② *adv.*　sooner or later: 他～得去。He'll have to go there sooner or later. / 他～要栽跟头。One of these days he will come a cropper. ③ time: 他一清早就走了，这～多半已经到家了。He left early in the morning and should be home by now. ④ *dial.*　some time in the future; some day: 你～上城里来，到我们这里坐坐。Drop in on us when you come to town.

早晚服务部 zǎowǎn fúwùbù　before-and-after-hours shop; department for after-hours service

早先 zǎoxiān　*adv.*　previously; before; in the past: 他～是中国驻悉尼总领事。He was previously Chinese consul general in Sydney. / 我～没见过他。I haven't seen him before. / 这儿～是臭水塘，现在成了工人新村了。There used to be a stagnant pond here; now there are workers' flats.

早泄 zǎoxiè　*med.*　premature ejaculation

早已 zǎoyǐ　*adv.*　long ago; for a long time: 他～打定主意了。He made up his mind long ago. / 你要的东西，我～给你买来了。I've already bought all the things you want.

早育 zǎoyù　early childbirth

早早儿 zǎozǎor　*adv.*　as early as possible; well in advance: 要来，明天～来。If you want to come, come early tomorrow. / 既然要办, 就～办。Since we've decided to do it, let's do it as soon as possible.

枣(棗) zǎo　jujube; (Chinese) date; *tsao*

枣红 zǎohóng　purplish red; claret

枣泥 zǎoní　jujube paste

枣树 zǎoshù　jujube tree

枣椰 zǎoyē　date palm

枣子 zǎozi　*dial.*　Chinese date

蚤 zǎo　flea: 跳蚤 tiàozao

澡 zǎo　bath: 洗澡 xǐzǎo

澡盆 zǎopén　bathtub

澡堂 zǎotáng　(also 澡堂子 zǎotángzi) public baths; bathhouse

澡塘 zǎotáng　① common bathing pool (in a bathhouse) ② same as 澡堂 zǎotáng

藻 zǎo　① algae ② aquatic plants ③ literary embellishment: 辞藻 cízǎo

藻井 zǎojǐng　*archit.*　sunk panel; caisson ceiling

藻类学 zǎolèixué　algology: ～家 algologist

藻类植物 zǎolèi zhíwù　algae

藻丽 zǎolì　*formal*　(of language) flowery; ornate

藻煤 zǎoméi　boghead coal

藻饰 zǎoshì　*formal*　embellishments in writing

zào

灶(竈) zào　① kitchen range; cooking stove ② kitchen; mess; canteen: 学生～ students' dining room (*or* canteen)

灶火 zàohuo　*dial.*　① kitchen range; cooking stove ② kitchen

灶间 zàojiān　kitchen

灶具 zàojù　*dial.*　cooking utensils

灶君 Zàojūn　same as 灶神 Zàoshén

灶马 zàomǎ　*zool.*　a kind of house cricket found in a kitchen (*Diestrammena unicolor*)

灶披间 zàopījiān　*dial.*　kitchen

灶神 Zàoshén　kitchen god

灶台 zàotái　the top of a kitchen range

灶膛 zàotáng　chamber of a kitchen range

灶糖 zàotáng　malt sugar; maltose (formerly used as a sacrificial offering to the kitchen god)

灶头 zàotou　*dial.*　kitchen range; cooking stove

灶突 zàotū　*formal*　chimney (of a kitchen stove)

灶王爷 Zào-wángyé　same as 灶神 Zàoshén

灶屋 zàowū　(also 灶房 zàofáng) *dial.*　kitchen

皂(皁) zào　① black: ～鞋 black shoes ② *yamen* runner: 皂隶 zàolì ③ soap: 香皂 xiāngzào

皂白 zào-bái　black and white—right and wrong: ～不分 make no distinction between right and wrong

皂化 zàohuà　*chem.*　saponification: ～剂 saponifier

皂荚 zàojiá　(also 皂角 zàojiǎo) *bot.*　Chinese honey locust

皂隶 zàolì　*yamen* runner

皂片 zàopiàn　soap flakes

皂素 zàosù　(also 皂苷 zàogān) saponin

皂洗机 zàoxǐjī　*text.*　soaper: 平幅～ open soaper

唣(唕) zào　see 啰唣 luózào

造¹ zào　① make; build; create: ～一台铣床 make (*or* manufacture) a milling machine / ～房子 build a house / ～舆论 create (*or* prepare) public opinion / ～预算 make (*or* draw up) a budget / ～表 draw up a form or list / ～册 compile a register ② invent; cook up; concoct: ～假帐 cook accounts

造² zào　① *leg.*　one of the two parties in a legal agreement or a lawsuit: 两～ both parties (in a lawsuit) ② *dial.*　crop: 早～ early crops / 一年三～ three crops a year

造³ zào　① *formal*　go to; arrive at: 造府 zàofǔ ② achievements; attainments: 造诣 zàoyì ③ train; educate: 深造 shēnzào

造币厂 zàobìchǎng　mint (a place where money is made)

造成 zàochéng create; cause; give rise to; bring about: ～生动活泼的政治局面 create a lively political situation / ～革命声势 build up revolutionary momentum / ～既成事实 bring about a *fait accompli* / ～巨大损失 cause enormous losses / ～假象 put up a facade; create a false impression / ～一种尊重知识,尊重人才的空气 create the atmosphere of respecting both knowledge and intellectuals

造船 zàochuán shipbuilding

造船厂 zàochuánchǎng shipyard; dockyard

造船工业 zàochuán gōngyè shipbuilding industry

造次 zàocì *formal* ① hurried; hasty: ～之间 in one's hurry; in a moment of haste ② rash; impetuous: ～行事 act rashly

造端 zàoduān *formal* begin; originate

造反 zàofǎn rise in rebellion; rebel; revolt

造饭 zàofàn *old* do the cooking; prepare a meal

造访 zàofǎng *formal* pay a visit (*or* call); call on: 登门～ call at sb.'s house; pay sb. a visit

造福 zàofú bring benefit to; benefit: ～于人类 bring benefit to mankind / 为后代～ benefit future generations

造府 zàofǔ *formal pol.* call at your house: 能否～请教? May I call at your house and ask for your advice?

造化 zàohuà *formal* the Creator; Nature; Creation: ～赋形,支体必双;神理为用,事不孤立。(刘勰《文心雕龙》) Nature, creating living beings, endows them with limbs in pairs. The Divine Reason operates in such a way that nothing stands alone. / ～锺神秀,阴阳割昏晓。(杜甫) Here Creation concentrated unearthly glory, Dark north slope, the sunlit south divide dusk and dawn. / 夺天地～之功 rob Heaven and Earth of their creative powers

造化 zàohua good luck; good fortune: 有～ be born under a lucky star; be lucky / 好～! What luck! / 真是天大的～! What a stroke of good fortune! / 你的～不小。I envy your good fortune.

造价 zàojià cost (of building or manufacture): 这种桥～比较低。It costs less to build this kind of bridge.

造就 zàojiù ① bring up; train: ～一代新人 bring up a new generation / ～良好的社会风气 foster high standard of social conduct / 伟大的革命斗争会～伟大的人物。A great revolutionary struggle creates great figures. ② achievements; attainments (usu. of young people)

造句 zàojù make a sentence: ～练习 a sentence-making exercise

造块 zàokuài *metall.* agglomeration

造林 zàolín afforestation: ～面积 afforestation (*or* afforested) area

造林学 zàolínxué silviculture

造陆运动 zàolù yùndòng *geog.* epeirogenic (*or* epeirogenetic) movement; epeirogeny; epeirogenesis

造孽 zàonie *Buddhism* do evil; commit a sin

造山带 zàoshāndài *geog.* orogenic zone

造山运动 zàoshān yùndòng *geog.* orogenic movement; orogeny; orogenesis

造物 zàowù the divine force that created the universe; Nature

造物主 zàowùzhǔ *Christianity* God; the Creator

造像 zàoxiàng statue

造型 zàoxíng ① modelling; mould-making: 这些古代工艺品～优美。These ancient art objects are beautifully shaped. ② model; mould ③ *mech.* moulding: 干砂～ dry sand moulding / 潮砂～ green sand moulding / 开砂～ open sand moulding

造型板 zàoxíngbǎn *mech.* mould board

造型艺术 zàoxíng yìshù plastic arts

造谣 zàoyáo cook up a story and spread it around; start a rumour

造谣惑众 zàoyáo huòzhòng fabricate rumours to mislead people

造谣生事 zàoyáo shēngshì start a rumour to create trouble; stir up trouble by rumour-mongering

造谣诬蔑 zàoyáo wūmiè rumour-mongering and mud-slinging; calumny and slander

造谣中伤 zàoyáo zhòngshāng spread slanderous rumours

造诣 zàoyì (academic or artistic) attainments: 他是一位～很高的学者。He is a scholar of great attainments. / 她是一位很有～的歌唱家。She's an accomplished singer.

造影 zàoyǐng *med.* radiography: 支气管～ bronchography

造渣 zàozhā *metall.* slag making; slag formation

造纸 zàozhǐ papermaking

造纸厂 zàozhǐchǎng paper mill

造纸机 zàozhǐjī paper machine

造作 zàozuò make; manufacture

造作 zàozuo affected; artificial

簉 zào *formal* secondary; subsidiary

簉室 zàoshì *formal* concubine

噪¹ zào (of birds, insects, etc.) chirp: 蝉～ the chirping of cicadas / 群鸦乱～。Crows were cawing.

噪²(譟) zào a confusion of voices: 鼓噪 gǔzào

噪聒 zàoguō *dial.* noisy; clamorous

噪鹃 zàojuān Chinese koel

噪鹛 zàoméi *zool.* laughing thrush

噪音 zàoyīn (also 噪声 zàoshēng) noise: 机器的～ the noise of machinery / 这些飞机～很大。Those planes make an awful noise. / 低～马达 low-noise motor

噪音污染 zàoyīn wūrǎn noise pollution

噪音抑制 zàoyīn yìzhì *radio* noise suppression

噪杂 zàozá noisy: 街上的～声使我不能入睡。The noise on the street kept me awake. / 人声～ a hubbub of voices

燥 zào dry

燥热 zàorè hot and dry

躁 zào rash; impetuous; restless: 性子～ quick-tempered; hot-tempered

躁动 zàodòng move restlessly

躁急 zàojí restless; uneasy

躁狂 zàokuáng *med.* mania: ～者 maniac

zé

则¹ zé ① standard; norm; criterion: 准则 zhǔnzé ② rule; regulation: 法则 fǎzé / 细则 xìzé ③ *formal* imitate; follow: ～先烈之言行 follow the example of the martyrs in word and deed ④ *m.* (for news, writing, etc.) piece; item: 新闻一～ an item of news / 寓言四～ four fables

则² zé *formal* ① *conj.* ⓐ (used to indicate cause, condition, etc.): 物体热～胀,冷～缩。Objects expand when heated and contract when cooled. / 不战～已,战～必胜。Fight no battle unless victory is sure. / 少～几年,多～几十年 several years at least and several decades at most; between several years and several decades ⓑ (used to indicate concession, con-

trast, etc.): 好～好，只是太贵。It's good but too expensive. / 今～不然。However, things are quite different today. ② (used to list reasons, preceded by 一，二，三，or 一，再，三): 这篇课文不合适，一～太长，二～太难。This text is unsuitable. For one thing it's too long, for another it's too difficult. ③ *formal* be: 此～余之过也。This is my fault.

则甚 zéshèn *old* what for: 问他～? Why ask him? / 只管担搁人～! What's the idea, just wasting people's time like this!

则声 zéshēng make a sound; utter a word: 不～ keep silent

责 zé ① duty; responsibility: 爱护公物，人人有～。It is everybody's duty to take good care of public property. ② demand; require: ～明于垢鉴 look for brilliance in a tarnished mirror—expect the impossible ③ question closely; call sb. to account: 责问 zéwèn ④ reproach; blame; reprove: 痛责 tòngzé ⑤ punish: 笞责 chīzé

责备 zébèi reproach; blame; reprove; take sb. to task: ～的眼光 a look of reproach / 受到良心的～ feel a prick of conscience / 她～丈夫对母亲粗暴无礼。She took her husband to task for his rudeness to her mother.

责成 zéchéng instruct (sb. to fulfil a task); charge (sb. with a task); enjoin (sb. to do sth.): ～小组委员会提出报告 instruct the subcommittee to submit a report

责打 zédǎ punish by beating

责罚 zéfá punish

责怪 zéguài blame: 这事不应该～他。He should not be blamed for this.

责令 zéling order; instruct; charge: ～主管部门采取有力措施 instruct the department in charge to take effective measures / 这个饭馆因卫生差而被～停业。The restaurant has been ordered to stop business for being unhygienic.

责骂 zémà scold; rebuke; dress down: 老师～他不该考试作弊。The teacher rebuked him for cheating in the exam.

责难 zénàn censure; blame: 受到各方面的～ incur censure from various quarters

责任 zérèn ① duty; responsibility: ～重大 have a grave responsibility / 先进的有～帮助后进的。The advanced are duty-bound to help those lagging behind. / 我不过是尽了自己的～罢了。I've done no more than my duty. / 负起～来。Shoulder your responsibility. ② responsibility for a fault or wrong; blame: 对由此而产生的严重后果承担全部～ bear full responsibility for the serious consequences arising therefrom / 追究～ ascertain where the responsibility lies / 你不应该把～推到别人身上。You shouldn't shift the blame onto others. / 这事如果搞不好，你要负～。If anything goes wrong, you'll have to answer for it.

责任编辑 zérèn biānjí executive editor

责任感 zérèngǎn (also 责任心 zérènxīn) sense of responsibility (*or* duty)

责任事故 zérèn shìgù accident due to negligence; accident involving criminal or civil liability

责任制 zérènzhì system of job responsibility

责问 zéwèn call (*or* bring) sb. to account: 小组长～他为何不来开会。The group leader called him to account for his absence from the meeting.

责无旁贷 zé wú páng dài there is no shirking the responsibility; be duty-bound

责有攸归 zé yǒu yōu guī responsibility must rest somewhere: 如因循坐误，则～。The responsibility will fall on those who procrastinate and allow the situation to deteriorate.

泽（澤） zé ① pool; pond: 湖泽 húzé ② damp; moist: 润泽 rùnzé ③ lustre (of metals, pearls, etc.): 光泽 guāngzé ④ *formal* favour; beneficence

泽国 zéguó *formal* ① a land that abounds in rivers and lakes ② inundated area: 全区尽成～。The whole area became submerged.

泽兰 zélán *bot.* Japanese Eupatorium (*Eupatorium japonicum*)

泽润 zérùn same as 润泽 rùnzé

泽泻 zéxiè ① *bot.* oriental water plantain (*Alisma plantago-aquatica* var. *orientale*) ② *Chin. med.* the rhizome of such a plant

择（擇） zé select; choose; pick: ～友 choose friends / 二者任～其一 choose either of the two / ～日起程 fix a departure date ——see also zhái

择伐 zéfá *forestry* selective cutting (*or* felling)

择吉 zéjí select (*or* choose) an auspicious day (for a marriage, funeral, etc.): ～开张 select an auspicious day for opening a business

择交 zéjiāo choose friends: 慎重～ choose friends with care

择偶 zé'ǒu choose a spouse

择期 zéqī select a day or time : ～完婚 select a day for the marriage ceremony

择取 zéqǔ select; choose

择善而从 zé shàn ér cóng choose and follow what is good

择优 zéyōu select the superior ones: ～录取 employ or enroll on the basis of competitive selection

择捉 Zézhuō Etorofu

啧 zé ① *formal* same as 赜 zé ② click of the tongue

啧有烦言 zé yǒu fán yán there are a lot of complaints

啧啧 zézé ① clicking the tongue; chattering ② *liter.* chirping: 雀声～。Sparrows were chirping.

啧啧称羡 zézé chēngxiàn (also 啧啧称赞 zézé chēngzàn) click the tongue in admiration

帻 zé man's headdress used in ancient China

箦 zé *formal* bed mat made of woven strips of bamboo

赜 zé *formal* subtle; abstruse: 探赜索隐 tànzésuǒyǐn

zè

仄¹ zè ① narrow: 逼仄 bīzè ② feel sorry

仄² zè same as 仄声 zèshēng

仄声 zèshēng *phonet.* oblique tones, i.e., the falling-rising tone (上声), the falling tone (去声) and the entering tone (入声), as distinct from the level tone (平声) in classical Chinese pronunciation

昃 zè *formal* the sun past the meridian; afternoon

zéi

贼¹ zéi ① thief ② traitor; enemy: 工贼 gōngzéi ③

crooked; wicked; evil; furtive: 贼心 zéixīn ④ crafty; sly; cunning; deceitful: 老鼠真～。Rats are really cunning. ⑤ *formal* injure; harm; murder: 戕贼 qiāngzéi

贼² zéi *dial.* (usu. used to show disapproval) extremely; disagreeably: ～冷 terribly cold / ～亮 disagreeably glossy or dazzling

贼船 zéichuán pirate ship: 上～ board the pirate ship —join a reactionary faction or a criminal gang

贼骨头 zéigǔtou *dial.* thief

贼喊捉贼 zéi hǎn zhuō zéi a thief crying "Stop thief"

贼眉鼠眼 zéiméi-shǔyǎn shifty-eyed; thievish-looking

贼去关门 zéi qù guānmén (also 贼走关门 zéi zǒu guānmén) lock the door after the thief has gone; lock the stable door after the horse is stolen

贼人 zéirén *old* thief

贼死 zéisǐ *dial.* extremely; utterly: 这么重的活儿把她累得个～。The hard work completely exhausted her.

贼头贼脑 zéitóu-zéinǎo behaving stealthily like a thief; stealthy; furtive

贼窝 zéiwō thieves' den

贼心 zéixīn wicked heart; evil designs; evil intentions

贼心不死 zéixīn bù sǐ refuse to give up one's evil designs

贼星 zéixīng popular name for 流星 liúxīng

贼眼 zéiyǎn shifty eyes; furtive glance

贼赃 zéizāng stolen goods; booty; spoils

鲗 zéi see 乌鲗 wūzéi

zěn

怎 zěn *inf.* why; how: 这样的好收成，我们～能不高兴呢? How can we help rejoicing over such a good harvest? / 你～不早说呀? Why didn't you say so earlier?

怎的 zěndi (also 怎地 zěndi) *dial.* what; why; how: 他就是不去，我能～? He just won't go, so what can I do about it? / 你～还没做完? Why haven't you finished yet?

怎么 zěnme ① how; what; why: 你是～来的? How did you come here? / 这个字～写? How do you write this character? / ～办? What's to be done? / 这是～回事? What's all this about? / ～你不告诉他? Why don't you tell him? / 你～不去? Why aren't you going? / 我～没听说过这事儿? How come I never heard of it? / 你～啦? What's the matter with you? or Why, is anything the matter? / 你～搞的! See what you've done! ② in a certain way; in any way; no matter how: 不知道一来我就滑倒了。Somehow I slipped and fell. / 他把～来～去都告诉了大家。He told us everything, from beginning to end. / 你～说，我就～做。I'll do just as you say. or I'll do whatever you say. / 该～办就～办 do what must be done / 这本词典～贵我也要买。I'll buy the dictionary no matter how expensive it is. / 健康的重要性，～强调也不过分。The importance of good health cannot be emphasized too strongly (or cannot be overemphasized). ③ (used in the negative as an understatement) (not) very; (not) much; (not) quite; (not) too: 那个不～贵。That's not very expensive. / 他不～说话。He doesn't talk much. / 今天我不～舒服。I'm not quite well today. / 这个地方我不～熟。I'm not too familiar with the place. / 这首歌我还没～学会。I haven't quite learnt the song yet. ④ (used by itself at the beginning of a sentence to show surprise) what: ～, 他还没来吗? What? Isn't he here yet? / ～, 连你也不知道! What? Even you don't know it!

怎么得了 zěnme déliǎo where will it all end; what a terrible thing it would be; this is one hell of a mess

怎么样 zěnmeyàng ① how; what: 你觉得～? How are you feeling? / 演出的情况～? How was the performance? / 后来这孩子～了? What became of the child? / 你能把他～? What can you do to him? ② what's it like; how are things; what do you think: ～, 忙吗? How are things, busy? Have a cigarette. / 四个菜，一个汤，～? Four dishes and one soup—what do you think? / 骑车去～? How (or What) about going by bike? ③ in a certain way; in any way; no matter how: 人家～做，你也～做。Do as everybody does. / 我～做都不对。No matter how I did it, I did it wrong. ④ (used in the negative as a mild understatement) (not) up to much: 这个电影不～。The film isn't up to much. / 她唱歌不～。She's not much of a singer. / 他一时不小心，我们也不好把他～。We couldn't be too hard on him—he was just being careless.

怎么着 zěnmezhe ① what to do; what: 我一点儿也不知道～好。I'm at a loss to know what to do. / 看完戏我就回家，你打算～? I'm going straight home after the play. What about you? / 下午干什么?是小组讨论还是～? What's on this afternoon, group discussion or what? ② no matter what; whatever: ～也得把试验进行下去。The experiment must be carried on whatever happens. / ～都行。It'll be all right whatever it is. / 你不能想～就～。You can't just do what (or as) you please. ③ (used by itself at the beginning of the sentence to show surprise) what: ～, 你不去了? What? You're not going? / ～, 他敢打人! What? He dares hit people!

怎奈 zěnnài *old* but; however

怎生 zěnshēng *arch.* how: 守着窗儿，独自～得黑! (李清照) I stay at the window, All alone; Oh, how dark it gets!

怎样 zěnyàng ① how; what: 你现在感觉～? How are you feeling now? / 这件事你～解释? How do you explain it? / 奏鸣曲是～一种乐曲形式呢? What musical form is the sonata? ② in a certain way; in any way; no matter how: 想想从前～, 再看看现在～ think of the past and look at the present / 他说那地方的风景～～好，引得大家都想去。He described the scenic beauties in such a way that everybody wanted to go there for a visit. / 人家～做，你也～做。Do as everybody does.

zèn

谮 zèn *formal* falsely charge; slander; calumniate: ～言 slander; calumny

zēng

曾 zēng ① relationship between great-grandchildren and great-grandparents ② (Zēng) a surname —see also céng

曾母暗沙 Zēngmǔ Ànshā Zengmu Reef

曾孙 zēngsūn great-grandson

曾孙女 zēngsūn·nǚ great-granddaughter

曾祖 zēngzǔ (paternal) great-grandfather

曾祖母 zēngzǔmǔ (paternal) great-grandmother

憎 zēng hate; detest; abhor: 憎恶 zēngwù

憎称 zēngchēng derogatory name for sb. one hates or loathes

憎恨 zēnghèn hate; detest

憎恶 zēngwù abhor; loathe; abominate: 有些人～现代

艺术。Some people loathe modern art.

增

增 zēng　increase; gain; add: 产量猛～。Output increased sharply. / ～拨资金 allocate more funds / ～兵 throw in more troops; augment one's forces; reinforce

增白剂 zēngbáijì　*chem.* brightening agent; brightener

增白霜 zēngbáishuāng　fair complexion cream

增补 zēngbǔ　augment; supplement: 人员略有～。The staff has been slightly augmented. / 该书内容有所～。The book has been supplemented with new material.

增补本 zēngbǔběn　an enlarged edition

增产 zēngchǎn　increase production: ～节约 increase production and practise economy / ～不增人 increase production without increasing the work force

增充剂 zēngchōngjì　*chem.* extender

增订 zēngdìng　revise and enlarge (a book)

增订本 zēngdìngběn　a revised and enlarged edition

增多 zēngduō　grow in number or quantity; increase: 来华参观访问的外国朋友日益～。More and more foreign friends come to visit China.

增高 zēnggāo　① get higher; rise; increase: 正在建筑的电视发射台日见～。The TV tower under construction is getting higher each day. ② make higher; heighten; raise; increase: ～温室的温度 raise the temperature of a hothouse

增光 zēngguāng　add lustre to; do credit to; add to the prestige of: 为国～ do credit to one's country

增辉 zēnghuī　add lustre to; do credit to

增加 zēngjiā　increase; raise; add: ～积累 increase accumulation / ～收入 increase income / ～工资 get a raise in pay / ～困难 add to the difficulties; multiply the difficulties / ～复种面积 extend the area of double or triple cropping; enlarge the multiple-cropping area / ～体重 put on weight / ～抵抗力 build up one's resistance to disease / 产量比去年～一倍。Output is double that of last year. / 报名人数由三千～到五千。The number of applicants has gone up from 3,000 to 5,000.

增减 zēngjiǎn　increase and decrease; fluctuate

增进 zēngjìn　enhance; promote; further: ～各国人民的相互了解和友谊 promote (or further) mutual understanding and friendship between the peoples of all countries / ～健康 improve one's health / ～食欲 whet one's appetite

增刊 zēngkān　supplement (to a newspaper or periodical); supplementary issue

增量 zēngliàng　*math.* increment

增强 zēngqiáng　strengthen; heighten; enhance: ～战斗力 strengthen fighting capacity; increase combat effectiveness / ～信心 heighten one's confidence / ～斗志 raise (or heighten, boost) one's morale / ～党性 enhance Party spirit / ～防御力量 strengthen defence / 发展体育运动，～人民体质。Promote physical culture and build up the people's health. / 夜间风力将～到六级。The wind will rise to force 6 at night.

增强塑料 zēngqiáng sùliào　reinforced plastics

增色 zēngsè　add colour to; add beauty to: 这幅画给这间屋子～不少。The picture adds beauty to the room.

增删 zēng-shān　additions and deletions

增设 zēngshè　establish an additional or new (organization, unit, course, etc.): ～一个新机构 set up a new organization / ～新课程 establish a new course; offer a new course

增生 zēngshēng　*med.* hyperplasia; proliferation; multiplication

增塑剂 zēngsùjì　*chem.* plasticizer; plastifier

增添 zēngtiān　add; increase: ～设备 get additional equipment / ～力量和信心 gain strength and confidence / 新出土的文物为研究古代史～了资料。The new archaeological finds provide fresh material for the

study of ancient history. / 为社会主义大厦～一砖一瓦 add a brick and a tile to the edifice of socialism; do one's bit towards building socialism / 对不起，给你～了麻烦。Sorry to have put you to so much trouble.

增效剂 zēngxiàojì　*chem.* synergist

增益 zēngyì　① increase; raise; add ② *elec.* gain: 高～ high gain / 分贝～ decibel gain / ～控制 gain control

增音机 zēngyīnjī　repeater (used in telegraphy)

增援 zēngyuán　*mil.* reinforce: ～部队 reinforcements; reinforcing units

增长 zēngzhǎng　increase; rise; grow: 平均～百分之四十 register an average increase of 40% / 有计划地控制人口的～ control population growth in a planned way / 持续～ sustained growth / ～才干 enhance (or develop) one's abilities / ～知识 broaden (or enrich) one's knowledge / 产量比解放前～了七倍半。Output is 8.5 times what it was before liberation. / 人口已无～。The population has reached zero growth.

增长率 zēngzhǎnglǜ　rate of increase; growth rate

增值 zēngzhí　*econ.* ① rise (or increase) in value; appreciation; increment ② value added

增值税 zēngzhíshuì　*econ.* value added tax (V.A.T.)

增殖 zēngzhí　① *med.* hyperplasia; proliferation; multiplication: 细胞～ proliferation of cells ② breed; reproduce; multiply; propagate: ～耕牛 breed farm cattles

增殖率 zēngzhílǜ　*animal husbandry* rate of increase

缯

缯 zēng　an ancient term for silk fabrics ——see also zèng

罾

罾 zēng　a square-shaped fishing net with poles as supports

zèng

综

综 zèng　*text.* heddle; heald: ～框 heald frame ——see also zōng

锃

锃 zèng　*dial.* (of utensils, etc.) polished

锃光瓦亮 zèngguāngwǎliàng　*dial.* shiny

锃亮 zèngliàng　*dial.* shiny

缯

缯 zèng　*dial.* bind; fasten ——see also zēng

甑

甑 zèng　① an ancient earthen utensil for steaming rice ② rice steamer ③ a utensil for distilling water, etc.: 曲颈甑 qūjǐngzèng

甑子 zèngzi　rice steamer

赠

赠 zèng　give as a present; present as a gift: 此砚乃老友所～。This inkstone is a present from an old friend of mine.

赠别 zèngbié　present a friend with gifts, poems, etc. at parting

赠答 zèngdá　present each other with gifts, poems, etc.

赠礼 zènglǐ　① present sb. with a gift ② gift; present

赠书 zèngshū　① present sb. with a book ② same as 赠阅 zèngyuè ③ complimentary copy

赠品 zèngpǐn　(complimentary) gift; giveaway

赠送 zèngsòng　give as a present; present as a gift: 向演员～花篮 present a basket of flowers to the performers

赠送仪式 zèngsòng yíshì　presentation ceremony

赠言 zèngyán　words of advice or encouragement given to a friend at parting

赠予 zèngyǔ　(also 赠与 zèngyǔ) present to; donate to:

将五千册图书～这所大学 present (*or* donate) 5,000 copies of books to this university

赠予国 zèngyǔguó　donor country

赠阅 zèngyuè　(of a book, periodical, etc.) given free by the publisher

赠阅本 zèngyuèběn　complimentary copy

zhā

扎¹　zhā　① prick; run or stick (a needle, etc.) into: 手指上～了一根刺 prick one's finger on a thorn; have a splinter in one's finger / ～一刀 stab with a knife ② *dial.* plunge into; get into: ～到人群里 dash into the crowd / 扑通一声, 他～进水里去了。He dived into the water with a splash. / 一头～进书堆里 bury oneself in books

扎²（紥、紮）　zhā　be stationed; be quartered: 扎营 zhāyíng ——see also zā; zhá

扎堆儿 zhāduīr　*dial.* get together: ～聊天 get together to gossip

扎耳朵 zhā ěrduo　*inf.* grate (*or* jar) on the ear; be ear-piercing: 用小刀儿划玻璃的声音～。A knife scraping against glass makes a grating sound. / 这些尖刻的话听起来真～。Such sharp words jar on the ear.

扎耳朵眼儿 zhā ěrduoyǎnr　pierce the earlobe (in order to wear earrings)

扎根 zhāgēn　take root: 水和阳光充足, 树苗很快就会～。Saplings take root quickly with plenty of water and sunlight. / ～于群众之中 take root among the masses

扎工 zhāgōng　a mutual aid system devised for poor peasants in northwest China before the setting up of farm cooperatives

扎花 zhāhuā　*dial.* embroider

扎猛子 zhā měngzi　*dial.* swim with the head kept submerged in water; dive

扎煞 zhāsha　same as 挓挲 zhāsha

扎实 zhāshí　① sturdy; strong ② solid; sound; down-to-earth: 工作很～ do a solid job / 扎扎实实地开展技术革新的群众运动 develop the mass movement for technical innovation in a down-to-earth manner / 这门基础课她学得很～。She has a good grasp of this basic course.

扎手 zhāshǒu　① prick the hand: 树上有刺, 留神～。The tree is thorny. Mind you don't prick your hands. ② difficult to handle; thorny: 这事真～。This is really a hard nut to crack.

扎眼 zhāyǎn　① dazzling; offending to the eye; loud; garish: 这块布的颜色太～。This cloth is too dazzling. / 她穿得很～。She's loudly dressed. ② offensively conspicuous

扎伊尔 Zhāyī'ěr　Zaïre

扎伊尔人 Zhāyī'ěrrén　Zaïrian

扎营 zhāyíng　pitch a camp; camp

扎寨 zhāzhài　pitch a camp; camp

扎针 zhāzhēn　*Chin. med.* give or have an acupuncture treatment: 上医务室～ go to the clinic for acupuncture treatment

吒　zhā　used in names of mythical beings (e.g. 金吒, 木吒)

咋　zhā　see below ——see also zǎ; zhà

咋呼 zhāhu　(also 咋唬) *dial.* ① shout blusteringly; show off; make a fuss: 甭听他瞎～。Don't take any notice of him—he's just showing off. / 他有点小事儿就爱～。He's rather fussy about small things.

挓　zhā　see below

挓挲 zhāsha　*dial.* ① (of hands, branches, etc.) spread; stretch out: 他～着两只手, 不知道干什么好。He spread out his arms, not knowing what to do. ② (of hair, etc.) stand on end

查（查）　zhā　① same as 楂 zhā ② (Zhā) a surname ——see also chá

咥　zhā　see 啁咥 zhāozhā

渣　zhā　① dregs; sediment; residue: 豆腐～ soya-bean residue (after making bean curd) / 猪油～儿 cracklings ② broken bits: 饼干～儿 biscuit crumbs

渣油 zhāyóu　*petroleum* residual oil; residuum: ～路 residual-oil road

渣滓 zhā·zǐ　dregs; sediment; residue: 溶液的～ dregs of a solution / 社会～ dregs of society

渣子 zhāzi　*inf.* ① dregs; sediment; residue ② broken bits: 点心～ cake crumbs

喳　zhā　① aye (formerly used by servants to indicate polite attentiveness) ② *onom.* chirp; chatter: 喜鹊～～地叫。Magpies were chattering. ——see also chá

揸（摣、䥯）　zhā　*dial.* ① pick up sth. with the fingers ② spread one's fingers

楂（樝）　zhā　see 山楂 shānzhā ——see also chá

劄　zhā　① prick; run or stick (a needle, etc.) into ② be stationed; be quartered ——see also zhá

zhá

扎　zhá　see below ——see also zā; zhā

扎挣 zházheng　*dial.* move with difficulty (because of physical weakness)

札　zhá　① thin pieces of wood used for writing on in ancient China ② *formal* letter: 适奉大～。I have just received your esteemed letter.

札记 zhájì　reading notes

轧　zhá　roll (steel) ——see also gá; yà

轧钢 zhágāng　steel rolling: ～机 rolling mill

轧钢厂 zhágāngchǎng　steel rolling mill: 大型～ heavy rolling mill

轧辊 zhágǔn　*metall.* roll; roller: ～调整装置 roll adjusting device

轧机 zhájī　*metall.* rolling mill: 二辊式～ two-high mill / 可逆式～ reversing mill / 连续式～ continuous mill

轧制 zházhì　*metall.* rolling: ～钢 rolled steel / ～公差 rolling tolerance

闸（牐）　zhá　① floodgate; sluice gate ② dam up a stream, river, etc.: ～住河水防洪 dam up a river to control flooding ③ brake ④ *inf.* switch: 扳～ operate a switch; switch on or off

闸盒 zháhé　fuse box

闸流管 zháliúguǎn　*electron.* thyratron

闸门 zhámén　① sluice gate ② (ship) lock gate ③ *mech.* throttle valve

闸瓦 zháwǎ　*mech.* brake shoe

炸(煠) zhá ① fry in deep fat or oil; deep-fry: 把花生～一～ deep-fry the peanuts / ～豆腐 deep-fried bean curd / ～糕 fried cake ② *dial.* scald (as a way of cooking) ——see also zhà

炸酱 zhájiàng fried bean sauce (usu. with minced meat)

炸酱面 zhájiàngmiàn noodles served with fried bean sauce

炸土豆条 zhátǔdòutiáo chips; French fries

铡 zhá ① hand hay cutter; fodder chopper ② cut up with a hay cutter: ～猪草 chop fodder for pigs

铡草机 zhácǎojī hay cutter; chaffcutter

铡刀 zhádāo hand hay (*or* straw) cutter; fodder chopper

喋 zhá see 唼喋 shàzhá ——see also dié

劄 zhá a kind of official document used in former times ——see also zhà

劄记 zhájì reading notes

劄子 zházi a kind of official document (in former times)

zhǎ

拃(搾) zhǎ ① measure by handspans; span ② *m.* span: 这块布有三～宽。This cloth is three spans wide.

眨 zhǎ blink; wink: 眼睛一～ blink (one's eyes) / 他向我～了～眼。He winked at me.

眨巴 zhǎba *dial.* blink: 这孩子的眼睛直～, 想是困了。The child is blinking his eyes. He must be sleepy.

眨眼 zhǎyǎn very short time; wink; twinkle: 一～的工夫 in the twinkling of an eye

砟 zhǎ tiny fragments of stone, coal, etc.: 炉灰～儿 cinder

砟子 zhǎzi tiny fragments of stone, coal, etc.

鲝 zhǎ *formal* salted fish

鲝肉 zhǎròu *dial.* pork steamed with ground glutinous rice

zhà

乍 zhà *adv.* ① first; for the first time: ～一听 at first hearing / ～看起来 at first glance / 天～晴。The rain has just stopped. ② suddenly; abruptly: 天气～冷～热。The temperature changes abruptly. ③ spread; extend: ～翅 spread wings

乍得 Zhàdé Chad

乍得人 Zhàdérén Chadian

乍猛的 zhàměngde *dial.* suddenly; unexpectedly: 他～提出这问题, 我不知怎么回答。He sprang the question on me and I didn't know what to say.

乍暖还寒 zhà nuǎn huán hán after suddenly getting warmer, it's turned cold again: ～时候, 最难将息。(李清照) In a season that is barely warm but still cool It is hard to nourish oneself and rest.

乍然 zhàrán *adv.* suddenly; unexpectedly; abruptly: ～相逢 suddenly find oneself face to face with sb.

诈 zhà ① cheat; swindle: ～人钱财 swindle people out of their money; get money by fraud ② pretend; feign: ～死 feign (*or* fake) death; play dead / ～败 feign defeat ③ bluff sb. into giving information: 他是拿话～我。He was trying to draw me out.

诈唬 zhàhu bluff; bluster

诈骗 zhàpiàn defraud; swindle

诈骗犯 zhàpiànfàn swindler

诈取 zhàqǔ obtain sth. by cheating; swindle sb. out of sth.; defraud

诈尸 zhàshī ① a corpse come to life (from the superstitious belief that the bodies of the dead, before they are placed in coffins, are liable to rise suddenly from the bed and dash out of the house in pursuit of sb.) ② *dial. offens.* as if being chased by a corpse come to life (said of sb. running or screaming like mad)

诈降 zhàxiáng pretend to surrender; feign surrender

诈语 zhà·yǔ lie; falsehood; fabrication

咋 zhà *formal* bite ——see also zǎ; zhā

咋舌 zhàshé *formal* be left speechless or breathless (with wonder or fear): 杂技演员的惊险动作使观众为之～。The acrobat's feat took the audience's breath away.

咤(吒) zhà see 叱咤 chìzhà

炸 zhà ① explode; burst: 暖瓶～了。The thermos flask has burst. ② blow up; blast; bomb: ～桥 blow up a bridge / ～毁 blow up; blast to pieces; demolish / 把障碍物～掉 blast away the barriers / ～平 bomb flat / ～沉 bomb and sink / 把敌人的工事～开一个口子 blow a hole in the enemy fortifications ③ *inf.* fly into a rage; flare up: 肺都气～了 flare up; explode with rage ④ *dial.* scamper; flee in terror: 炸窝 zhàwō ——see also zhá

炸弹 zhàdàn bomb: ～坑 bombcrater; crater

炸胶 zhàjiāo *chem.* blasting gelatine

炸雷 zhàléi *dial.* a clap of thunder

炸窝 zhàwō *dial.* scamper; flee in terror: 鸡炸了窝了。The chickens have all fled from their coop. / 饭店着火, 旅客炸了窝。The guests stampeded out of the burning hotel.

炸药 zhàyào explosive (charges); dynamite

炸药包 zhàyàobāo pack (*or* satchel) of dynamite; explosive package; satchel charges

柞 zhà used in 柞水 (a place in Shaanxi Province) ——see also zuò

奓 zhà *dial.* open out: ～着头发 with hair dishevelled (*or* in disarray)

奓着胆子 zhàzhedǎnzi *dial.* pluck up one's courage

栅(柵) zhà railings; paling; bars: 木～ paling; palisade / 铁～ iron railings; metal rails; iron bars / 炉～ grate ——see also shān

栅栏 zhàlan ① railings; paling; bars ② *mil.* boom: ～网 boom nets

痄 zhà see below

痄腮 zhàsai common name for 流行性腮腺炎 liúxíngxìng sāixiànyán

蚱 zhà see below

蚱蜢 zhàměng grasshopper

榨¹(搾) zhà press; extract: ～甘蔗 press

sugar cane／～干血汗 wring every ounce of sweat and blood out of sb.

榨² zhà　a press for extracting juice, oil, etc.
榨菜 zhàcài ① mustard tuber (*Brassica juncea* var. *tsatsai*) ② hot pickled mustard tuber
榨寮 zhàliáo *dial.* sugar refinery
榨取 zhàqǔ squeeze; extort: ～果汁 squeeze juice out of oranges, etc.／～钱财 extort money from sb.
榨油 zhàyóu extract oil: ～机 oil press

zhāi

斋¹ (齋) zhāi ① same as 斋戒 zhāijiè ② vegetarian diet adopted for religious reasons: 吃斋 chīzhāi ③ give alms (to a monk)

斋² (齋) zhāi room or building: 学生宿舍第三～ Student Hostel No. 3
斋饭 zhāifàn food given to Buddhist monks as alms
斋公 zhāigōng ① acolyte ② vegetarian
斋果 zhāiguǒ *dial.* offerings
斋戒 zhāijiè abstain from meat, wine, etc. (when offering sacrifices to gods or ancestors); fast
斋期 zhāiqī fast days; fast
斋堂 zhāitáng dining hall in a Buddhist temple
斋月 zhāiyuè *Islam* Ramadan; the month of fast

摘 zhāi ① pick; pluck; take off: ～棉花(苹果) pick cotton (apples)／～花 pluck flowers／把眼镜～下来 take off one's glasses／把灯泡～下来 remove the bulb／～白菜帮子 strip a cabbage of its outer leaves ② select; make extracts from: 摘译 zhāiyì ③ borrow money when in urgent need: ～几个钱救急 borrow some money to meet an urgent need
摘编 zhāibiān ① select and edit; make extracts ② extracts
摘抄 zhāichāo ① take passages; make extracts; extract; excerpt ② extracts; excerpts: 雷锋日记～ pages (*or* excerpts) from Lei Feng's diary
摘除 zhāichú *med.* excise: ～腹部肿瘤 excise an abdominal tumour
摘登 zhāidēng publish excerpts (*or* extracts) of sth.: 今天报纸～了他的发言。Today's paper carried excerpts of his speech.
摘记 zhāijì ① take notes: 报告很长，我只～了要点。The report was rather long. I just jotted down the main points. ② extracts; excerpts
摘借 zhāijiè borrow money when in urgent need
摘录 zhāilù ① take passages; make extracts; extract; excerpt ② extracts; excerpts: 文件～ extracts from a document
摘帽子 zhāi màozi ① take off one's hat or cap ② cast off (*or* remove) a label: 摘掉落后帽子 cast off (*or* remove) the label of "backwardness"; catch up with the others
摘棉铃机 zhāimiánlíngjī *agric.* cotton stripper
摘要 zhāiyào ① make a summary: ～发表 publish excerpts (*or* extracts) of sth. ② summary; abstract; *précis*: 社论～ the summary of an editorial
摘译 zhāiyì ① translate selected passages ② translations of selected passages
摘引 zhāiyǐn quote
摘由 zhāiyóu key extracts (of a document); *résumé*

侧 zhāi *dial.* tilt; slant ——see also cè
侧楞 zhāileng *dial.* incline; slant: ～着身子睡 sleep on one's side

侧歪 zhāiwai *dial.* slant: 帽子～在一边儿 have one's hat on crooked

zhái

宅 zhái residence; house: 赵～ the Zhaos' residence
宅第 zháidì a large house; mansion
宅基 zháijī the foundations of a house; the site of a house
宅门 zháimén ① gate of an old-style big house ② family living in such a house
宅院 zháiyuàn a house with a courtyard; house
宅子 zháizi *inf.* residence; house

择 (擇) zhái same as 择 zé, limited to use in the following entry words ——see also zé
择不开 zháibukāi ① unable to disentangle (*or* undo): 线乱成了一团, 怎么也～了。The thread is all in a tangle. I simply can't undo it. ② cannot get away from: 一点儿工夫也～ not have a moment to spare
择菜 zháicài trim vegetables for cooking
择铺 zháipù (also 择床 zháichuáng) *dial.* be unable to sleep well in a new place
择席 zháixí be unable to sleep well in a new place: 我从来不～。I never have trouble sleeping in a strange place.

翟 Zhái a surname

zhǎi

窄 zhǎi ① narrow: ～道 narrow path ② petty; narrow: 心眼儿～ petty; oversensitive ③ hard up; badly off: 父亲死后, 家里的日子过得挺～。We were very hard up after my father died.
窄轨铁路 zhǎiguǐ tiělù narrow-gauge railway
窄小 zhǎixiǎo narrow and small: 房屋～ a small house

觯 zhǎi *dial.* blemishes; scars

zhài

债 zhài debt: 一笔十万元的～ a debt of 100,000 *yuan*／他的～还清了。He was out of debt.
债户 zhàihù debtor
债款 zhàikuǎn loan
债利 zhàilì interest on loans
债权 zhàiquán *leg.* creditor's rights
债权国 zhàiquánguó creditor nation
债权人 zhàiquánrén creditor
债券 zhàiquàn bond; debenture: ～持有者 bondholder
债台高筑 zhàitái gāo zhù be heavily in debt; be up to one's ears in debt; be debt-ridden
债务 zhàiwù debt; liabilities
债务国 zhàiwùguó debtor nation
债务人 zhàiwùrén debtor
债主 zhàizhǔ creditor

砦 zhài see 鹿砦 lùzhài; 桩砦 zhuāngzhài

寨 zhài ① stockade ② stockaded village ③ *old*

camp: 营寨 yíngzhài ④ mountain stronghold

寨主 zhàizhǔ (in former times) brigand chief

寨子 zhàizi stockaded village

攃 zhài dial. sew sth. on: ～花边 trim (a dress) with lace

zhān

占 zhān practise divination ——see also zhàn

占卜 zhānbǔ practise divination; divine

占卦 zhānguà divine by means of the Eight Diagrams (八卦)

占课 zhānkè divine by tossing coins

占梦 zhānmèng prognostication by dreams; oneiromancy

占星 zhānxīng divine by astrology; cast a horoscope: ～术 astrology

沾¹(霑) zhān ① moisten; wet; soak: 泪～襟 tears wet the front of one's jacket ② be stained with: ～水 get wet / ～上了泥 be stained with mud / 双手～满人民鲜血的刽子手 a butcher stained with the blood of the people

沾² zhān ① touch: 他跑得真快, 脚不～地似的。He ran so fast that his feet seemed hardly to touch the ground. / 一～枕头就着 fall asleep as soon as one's head hits the pillow / 烟酒不～ touch neither tobacco nor alcohol / ～上了association with sb. or sth.: ～点便宜 get a bargain ③ dial. all right; O.K.

沾包 zhānbāo dial. get involved (in trouble); be tied up with

沾边 zhānbiān ① touch on (or upon) only lightly: 检讨多少遍, 思想不～ make self-criticism again and again but never touch on one's real thinking / 他讲的那些话跟他的真实思想根本不～。What he said wasn't at all what he was really thinking. / 这事他也沾了点边儿。He was involved in the affair to a certain extent. ② be close to what it should be; be relevant: 他唱得不怎么样, 就是这几句还沾点边。He didn't sing well and those were the only lines that sounded anything like the way they should. / 你讲的一点也不～。What you say is completely irrelevant.

沾溉 zhāngài formal bestow bounties on; benefit: ～后人 benefit future generations

沾光 zhānguāng benefit from association with sb. or sth.: 我们工厂每周放电影, 附近小孩儿都～。Kids in the neighbourhood enjoy the chance of seeing our factory's weekly film.

沾花惹草 zhānhuā-rěcǎo same as 拈花惹草 niānhuā-rěcǎo

沾亲带故 zhānqīn-dàigù be related somehow or other; have ties of kinship or friendship

沾染 zhānrǎn be infected with; be contaminated by; be tainted with: 伤口～了细菌。The wound was infected with germs. / ～市侩作风 be contaminated by philistine ways / ～坏习气 be tainted with bad habits / ～官僚主义的灰尘 be tainted with the dust of bureaucracy

沾染区 zhānrǎnqū contaminated area

沾手 zhānshǒu ① touch with one's hand: 雪花一～就化。Snowflakes melt as they fall on one's hand. ② have a hand in: 看来这事他沾了手。It seems that he has a hand in the matter. / 这活儿她一～就会了。She got the hang of the job the moment she started it.

沾污 zhānwū ① make dirty; dirty; soil ② contaminate

沾沾自喜 zhānzhān zì xǐ feel complacent; be pleased

with oneself: 不要～于一得之功。Don't be complacent over an occasional success. or Don't feel self-satisfied over a minor success.

毡(氊、氈) zhān felt: ～帽 felt hat

毡房 zhānfáng yurt

毡条 zhāntiáo dial. felt rug

毡子 zhānzi felt; felt rug; felt blanket

旃¹ zhān same as 毡 zhān

旃² zhān part. formal (a fusion of 之 and 焉): 勉～! Do it as best you can.

旃檀 zhāntán sandalwood (used in ancient texts)

粘 zhān glue; stick; paste: 把两块木片～在一起 glue the two chips of wood together / 把信封～上 seal (up) an envelope / 这糖不～牙。This candy doesn't stick to your teeth. ——see also nián

粘连 zhānlián med. adhesion: 瘢痕性～ cicatricial adhesion

粘贴 zhāntiē paste; stick: 在墙上～标语 paste slogans on the wall

詹 Zhān a surname

谵 zhān formal rave; be delirious: 谵语 zhānyǔ

谵妄 zhānwàng med. delirium

谵语 zhānyǔ formal delirious speech; wild talk; ravings

瞻 zhān look up or forward: 观瞻 guānzhān

瞻顾 zhāngù formal look ahead and behind

瞻念 zhānniàn look to; think of: ～前途 think of the future

瞻前顾后 zhānqián-gùhòu peer ahead and look behind — ① think over carefully ② be over-cautious and indecisive

瞻望 zhānwàng look forward; look far ahead: ～未来 look to the future

瞻仰 zhānyǎng (also 瞻拜 zhānbài) look at with reverence: ～毛主席遗容 pay one's respects to the remains of Chairman Mao / ～烈士陵园 pay a visit to the martyrs' mausoleum

瞻谒 zhānyè formal call on (a superior or an elder person); have an audience with

zhǎn

斩 zhǎn slay: chop; cut: ～敌将 slay (or cut down) an enemy general / 言降者～! Whosoever mentions surrender dies! / ～断侵略者的魔爪 chop off the claws of the invaders

斩草除根 zhǎncǎo-chúgēn cut the weeds and dig up the roots—stamp out the source of trouble

斩钉截铁 zhǎndīng-jiétiě resolute and decisive; categorical: ～地拒绝 give a round rebuff / 他说得～。He spoke with curt finality.

斩假石 zhǎnjiǎshí archit. artificial stone; imitation stone

斩尽杀绝 zhǎnjìn-shājué kill all; wipe out; exterminate

斩决 zhǎnjué execute by decapitation

斩齐 zhǎnqí same as 崭齐 zhǎnqí

斩首 zhǎnshǒu behead; decapitate

斩新 zhǎnxīn same as 崭新 zhǎnxīn

展 zhǎn ① open up; spread out; unfold; unfurl:

风～红旗。The red flags are fluttering in the wind. / 舒眉～眼 beam with joy ② put to good use; give free play to: ～技 give full play to one's skill / 一～才华 display one's talents / 立大志，～宏图 cherish high aspirations and carry out a great plan ③ postpone; extend; prolong: 展期 zhǎnqī ④ exhibition: 画展 huàzhǎn ⑤ (Zhǎn) a surname

展播 zhǎnbō a special TV programme: 迎春文艺节目～ a Spring Festival art and literature TV programme

展翅 zhǎnchì spread the wings; get ready for flight: ～高飞 soar to great heights

展出 zhǎnchū put on display; be on show (or view); exhibit: 展览会上～了各种各样的机床。A good variety of machine tools are on display at the exhibition.

展读 zhǎndú open and read; read: ～家信 read a letter from home

展缓 zhǎnhuǎn postpone; extend; prolong: 行期一再～。The date for departure was postponed again and again. / 限期不得～。The time limit is not to be extended.

展卷 zhǎnjuàn open a book; read

展开 zhǎnkāi ① spread out; unfold; open up: 把地图～ unfold the map / 把队伍～ deploy the forces ② launch; unfold; develop; carry out: ～社会主义劳动竞赛 launch a socialist emulation drive / ～攻势 unfold an offensive / ～思想斗争 wage an ideological struggle / 热烈的讨论 set off an animated discussion / 运动会的各项比赛已全面～。The sports meet is now in full swing.

展览 zhǎnlǎn put on display; exhibit; show: 工业～ industrial exhibition / 菊花～ chrysanthemum show / 故宫博物院里有瓷器～。There is an exhibit of porcelain in the Palace Museum. / 部分新出土的文物正在国外～。Some of the ancient relics recently unearthed are on display abroad.

展览馆 zhǎnlǎnguǎn exhibition centre (or hall)

展览会 zhǎnlǎnhuì exhibition

展览室 zhǎnlǎnshì exhibition room; showroom

展眉 zhǎnméi formal lift the brows—look delighted; beam with joy

展品 zhǎnpǐn (also 展览品 zhǎnlǎnpǐn) exhibit; item on display: 请勿抚摸～。Please do not touch the exhibits.

展评 zhǎnpíng display and appraise: 这家百货商店正在举办家电商品～会。The department store is holding an appraisal exhibition of home electrical appliances.

展期 zhǎnqī ① extend a time limit; postpone: 会议～举行。The meeting has been postponed. / 交易会～两天结束。The fair will be extended for another two days. ② duration of an exhibition; exhibition period

展示 zhǎnshì open up before one's eyes; reveal; show; lay bare: ～人物的内心世界 reveal a character's inner world / 这场辩论～了问题的实质。The debate laid bare the essence of the issue.

展示会 zhǎnshìhuì exhibition; show

展望 zhǎnwàng ① look into the distance: 登上山顶向四周～ climb to the top of the mountain and get a view of the surrounding country ② look into the future; look ahead: ～未来 look forward to the future / 前程，信心百倍。Looking ahead, we are filled with boundless confidence. ③ forecast; prospect: 二十一世纪～ prospects for the 21st century; the 21st century in prospect

展现 zhǎnxiàn unfold before one's eyes; emerge; develop: 到了工地，一派繁忙的景象～在我们眼前。As we reached the construction site, a scene of bustling activity presented itself before our eyes.

展限 zhǎnxiàn extend a time limit

展销 zhǎnxiāo display and sell (goods)

展销会 zhǎnxiāohuì commodities fair

展性 zhǎnxìng phys. malleability

展转 zhǎnzhuǎn same as 辗转 zhǎnzhuǎn

盏（盞） zhǎn ① a small cup: 酒～ a small wine cup ② m. (for lamps): 一～电灯 an electric lamp

崭 zhǎn ① formal towering (over) ② dial. fine; swell: 滋味真～! How delicious!

崭露头角 zhǎn lù tóujiǎo (of a young person) begin to show one's brilliant talents; display remarkable ability or talent

崭齐 zhǎnqí perfectly uniform; perfectly even: ～的一行树 a row of trees in perfect alignment

崭然 zhǎnrán formal towering; outstanding

崭新 zhǎnxīn brand-new; completely new: 穿一身～的制服 wear a brand-new tunic suit / ～的阶段 a completely new stage / ～的面貌 a completely new look / 文艺界呈现出一派～的气象。An entirely new atmosphere prevails in artistic and literary circles.

搌 zhǎn wipe or dab (with a soft dry object) to sop up liquid: 纸上落了一滴墨水，快拿吸墨纸～一～吧。A drop of ink has fallen on the paper; blot it up quickly.

搌布 zhǎnbu dishcloth; dish towel

辗 zhǎn see below

辗转 zhǎnzhuǎn ① pass through many hands or places: 他从上海～到达陕北。He left Shanghai and reached northern Shaanxi after passing through many different places. ② toss about (in bed): ～不能成眠 toss and turn (in bed); unable to go to sleep

辗转反侧 zhǎnzhuǎn fǎncè toss about (in bed); toss and turn

辗转流传 zhǎnzhuǎn liúchuán pass through many hands; spread from place to place

辗转相除法 zhǎnzhuǎnxiāngchúfǎ math. division algorithm

黵 zhǎn dial. make dirty; dirty; soil: 深色布禁(jīn)～。Dark cloth doesn't show the dirt.

zhàn

占（佔） zhàn ① occupy; seize; take: ～用不少时间 take up much time ② constitute; hold; make up; account for: ～多（少）数 constitute the majority (minority) / ～统治地位 hold (or occupy) a dominant position / ～世界第一位 rank first in the world / ～总产值的百分之四十 make up (or account for, amount to) 40 per cent of the total output value / 海洋几乎～地球表面四分之三。The sea covers nearly three-fourths of the earth's surface. ——see also zhān

占地 zhàndì (of a garden, farm, etc.) cover an area of: 故宫～72公顷。The Imperial Palace covers an area of 72 hectares.

占据 zhànjù occupy; hold: ～重要的战略地位 occupy a position of strategic importance

占理 zhànlǐ reasonable; sensible; right: 她的话～，我们按她说的办。She's right. We'll do what she says.

占领 zhànlǐng capture; occupy; seize: ～要塞 capture a fort / ～市场 dominate the market / 第二次世界大战中德国～法国达四年之久。During World War Ⅱ German occupation of France lasted four years.

占领军 zhànlǐngjūn occupation army

占领区 zhànlǐngqū occupied area

占便宜 zhàn piányi ① gain extra advantage by unfair means; profit at other people's expense: 别老想占我的～。Don't always try to take advantage of me. ② advantageous; favourable: 你个子高，打篮球～。A tall fellow like you has an advantage in playing basketball.

占上风 zhàn shàngfēng get the upper hand; win an advantage; prevail: 我队下半场占了上风。Our team gained the upper hand in the second half of the game.

占先 zhànxiān get ahead of: 上个月劳动竞赛，第一组～了。The first team led all the others in last month's emulation drive.

占线 zhànxiàn the line (of a telephone) is busy (or engaged)

占线通道 zhànxiàn tōngdào elec. active channel

占小便宜 zhàn xiǎopiányi gain petty advantages; secure small advantages at other people's expense; make small gains at other people's expense

占用 zhànyòng occupy and use: 不能随便～耕地。It is illegal to occupy cultivated land and put it to other uses without authorization. / 政治学习～了一部分工作时间。Political study sessions take up part of the working hours.

占有 zhànyǒu ① own; possess; have: ～生产资料 own the means of production / ～第一手资料 have firsthand data ② occupy; hold: 商业在国民经济中～重要地位。Commerce occupies an important place in the national economy.

占着茅坑不拉屎 zhànzhe máokēng bù lāshǐ sit on the (toilet) seat but not shit—hold on to a post without doing any work and not let anyone else take over; be a dog in the manger

战¹(戰)
zhàn ① war; warfare; battle; fight: 淝水之～ the battle of the Fei Shui (A.D. 383) ② fight: ～而胜之 fight and defeat the enemy / 为保卫祖国而～ fight to defend one's motherland / 《～马超》Combat with Ma Chao (a Beijing opera) / 《～上海》The Battle for Shanghai (a film) ③ (Zhàn) a surname

战²(戰)
zhàn shiver; tremble; shudder: 寒战 hánzhàn

战败 zhànbài ① be defeated; be vanquished; suffer a defeat; lose (a battle or war): 敌军～了。The enemy troops were defeated. ② defeat; vanquish; beat

战败国 zhànbàiguó vanquished (or defeated) nation

战报 zhànbào war communiqué; battlefield report

战备 zhànbèi war preparedness; combat readiness: 加强～ step up combat readiness / ～观念强 be prepared against war / ～工作 preparations against war / ～行军 tactical march; tactical movement

战备等级 zhànbèi děngjí degree of combat readiness

战备粮 zhànbèiliáng grain stockpiled in case of war

战备状态 zhànbèi zhuàngtài combat readiness

战表 zhànbiǎo written challenge to war; letter of challenge

战场 zhànchǎng battlefield; battleground; battlefront: 开辟新～ open another front / 西北～ the Northwest theatre / 奔赴～ go to the front

战车 zhànchē war chariot

战船 zhànchuán man-of-war; naval vessel; warship

战刀 zhàndāo sabre

战地 zhàndì battlefield; battleground; combat zone: ～指挥部 field headquarters

战地记者 zhàndì jìzhě war correspondent

战抖 zhàndǒu tremble; shiver; shudder

战斗 zhàndòu ① fight; battle; combat; action: 英勇～ put up a heroic fight / 进行了数十次～ have fought scores of battles / 作好～准备 get ready for action; be combat ready / 投入～ go into battle / 在～中牺牲 be killed in action / 每一次胜利都是经过激烈～赢得的。Each victory was won through fierce struggle. / ～部队 combat forces / ～部署 tactical disposition / ～队形 battle formation / ～命令 combat orders / ～任务 combat mission; fighting task / ～序列 order of battle; battle array / ～意志 will to fight ② militant; fighting: ～的友谊 militant friendship / ～的诗篇 militant poem / ～岗位 fighting post / ～性 militancy / 致以～的敬礼 with militant greetings / 满怀～豪情 be filled with militant pride / 充分发挥支部的～堡垒作用 give full play to the role of the Party branch as a fighting bastion

战斗轰炸机 zhàndòu hōngzhàjī fighter-bomber

战斗机 zhàndòujī old name for 歼击机 jiānjījī

战斗力 zhàndòulì combat effectiveness (or strength, capability); fighting capacity: ～强(弱) high (low) combat effectiveness / 有～ combat-worthy / 党组织的～ the fighting power (or capacity) of a Party organization

战斗英雄 zhàndòu yīngxióng combat hero

战斗员 zhàndòuyuán fighter

战端 zhànduān the beginning of a war: 重启～。War broke out again.

战犯 zhànfàn war criminal

战费 zhànfèi war expenses

战俘 zhànfú prisoner of war (P.O.W.): ～营 prisoner-of-war camp / ～收容所 prisoner-of-war collecting post

战歌 zhàngē battle song; fighting song

战功 zhàngōng meritorious military service; outstanding military exploit; battle achievement: 立～ distinguish oneself in action

战鼓 zhàngǔ war drum; battle drum

战国 Zhànguó the Warring States (475–221 B.C.)

战果 zhànguǒ results of battle; combat success; victory: 取得辉煌～ achieve splendid results on the battlefield / 扩大～ exploit the victory (or success)

战壕 zhànháo trench; entrenchment

战后 zhànhòu postwar: ～时期 postwar period

战火 zhànhuǒ flames of war: 海湾燃起了～。Flames of war rose over the gulf.

战火纷飞 zhànhuǒ fēnfēi flames of war raging everywhere: 在那～的岁月里 in those war-ridden years

战祸 zhànhuò disaster of war

战机 zhànjī opportunity for combat: 抓住～消灭敌人有生力量 seize the opportunity for wiping out enemy effectives / 丧失～ miss the opportunity to win a battle

战绩 zhànjì military successes (or exploits, feats); combat gains

战舰 zhànjiàn warship

战将 zhànjiàng warrior

战局 zhànjú war situation: ～大有好转。The war situation has improved a lot.

战具 zhànjù weapon; arms

战况 zhànkuàng situation on the battlefield; progress of a battle

战利品 zhànlìpǐn spoils of war; captured equipment; war trophies (or booty)

战例 zhànlì a specific example of a battle (in military science): 有名的～ a famous battle / 赤壁之战（公元208年）是一个以少胜多的～。The battle of the Red Cliffs (A. D. 208) is an instance of the few defeating the many.

战栗 zhànlì tremble; shiver; shudder: 吓得全身～ tremble all over with fear

战列舰 zhànlièjiàn (also 战斗舰 zhàndòujiàn) battleship

战列巡洋舰 zhànliè xúnyángjiàn battle cruiser

战乱 zhànluàn chaos caused by war; war

战略 zhànlüè strategy: 保持实力，作～上的撤退 maintain military strength through strategic retreats / 全球～ global strategy / ～部署 strategic plan (or deployment, disposition) / ～储备 strategic reserves (or

stockpiles) /～反攻 strategic counteroffensive /～核武器 strategic nuclear weapons /～决战 decisive strategic engagement; strategically decisive battle /～思想 strategic thinking /～物资 strategic materials /～要地 strategic area (*or* place); important strategic point

战略家 zhànlüèjiā strategist

战略学 zhànlüèxué science of strategy

战马 zhànmǎ battle steed; war-horse

战幕 zhànmù war curtain: (used esp. in) 拉 (揭) 开～ lift the war curtain—start a war or a match

战袍 zhànpáo (in former times) war robe; soldier's garb

战前 zhànqián prewar: ～时期 prewar period /～动员 mobilization before a battle

战勤 zhànqín civilian war service

战区 zhànqū war zone; theatre of operations

战胜 zhànshèng defeat; triumph over; vanquish; overcome: ～敌人 defeat (*or* vanquish) the enemy /～困难 overcome (*or* surmount) difficulties /～自然灾害 conquer natural disasters / 甲队～乙队。Team A beat Team B.

战胜国 zhànshèngguó victorious nation

战时 zhànshí wartime: ～编制 wartime establishment; war footing /～内阁 wartime cabinet

战史 zhànshǐ military history; war history

战士 zhànshì ① soldier; man: 人民解放军～ a PLA soldier (*or* man) / 新～ a new recruit ② champion; warrior; fighter: 国际主义～ champion of internationalism / 杰出的共产主义～ an outstanding fighter for communism

战事 zhànshì war; hostilities: ～结束 conclusion of the war; termination of hostilities / 大军渡江前暂无～。There was a lull in the fighting before the army crossed the Yangtze.

战书 zhànshū written challenge to war; letter of challenge: 下～ deliver a letter of challenge

战术 zhànshù (military) tactics: ～核武器 tactical nuclear weapons /～训练 tactical training /～演习 tactical manoeuvre /～指挥员 commander of a tactical operation

战术学 zhànshùxué science of tactics

战死 zhànsǐ die (*or* be killed) in battle

战天斗地 zhàntiān-dòudì fight against heaven and earth; combat nature; brave the elements

战无不胜 zhàn wú bù shèng invincible; ever-victorious; all-conquering —— see also 攻无不克 gōng wú bù kè

战线 zhànxiàn battle line; battlefront; front: 长达五百公里的～ a front of 500 kilometres / 思想～ the ideological front / 在各条～上 on every front of endeavour; on all fronts / 基本建设规模过大、～过长。Capital construction was overextended and too large in scale.

战役 zhànyì campaign; battle: 淮海～ the Huai-Hai Campaign /～性的进攻 offensive campaign /～指挥员 commander of a campaign

战役学 zhànyìxué science of campaigns

战鹰 zhànyīng fighting eagle (an affectionate term for a fighter plane)

战友 zhànyǒu comrade-in-arms; battle companion: ～的情谊 comradeship-in-arms / 老～ one's old comrade-in-arms

战云 zhànyún war cloud: ～密布 gathering war clouds

战战兢兢 zhànzhànjīngjīng trembling with fear; with fear and trepidation; gingerly: 敌军怕遭埋伏，～地向前移动。Fearing an ambush, the enemy troops advanced cautiously.

战争 zhànzhēng war; warfare: 挑起～ provoke a war /～的双方 the two sides in a war; both belligerents / 从～中学习～。Learn warfare through fighting in war. /

～是政治的继续。War is the continuation of politics. /～冒险 war venture; war gamble /～升级 war escalation /～温床 hotbed of war /～政策 policy of war; bellicose policy

战争边缘政策 zhànzhēngbiānyuánzhèngcè brink of war policy; brinkmanship

战争贩子 zhànzhēng fànzi warmonger

战争机器 zhànzhēng jīqì war machine; war apparatus

战争狂 zhànzhēngkuáng war mania; war hysteria: ～人 war maniac

战争状态 zhànzhēng zhuàngtài state of war

栈（棧）

zhàn ① warehouse: 货栈 huòzhàn ② inn: 客栈 kèzhàn ③ shed; pen: 羊～ sheep pen ④ see 栈道 zhàndào

栈道 zhàndào a plank roadway built along perpendicular rock-faces by means of wooden brackets fixed into the cliff

栈房 zhànfáng ① warehouse; storehouse ② *dial.* inn

栈桥 zhànqiáo landing stage (in a port); loading bridge (at a railway station)

站¹

zhàn stand; be on one's feet; take a stand: ～起来 stand up; rise to one's feet / 往后～～! Stand back! / 别拿椅子了，就～着看吧。Don't bother to get chairs. Let's just stand and watch. / 我都～了一天了。I've been on my feet all day. /～在党的立场上 uphold the stand of the Party

站²

zhàn ① stop; halt: 这车中途不～。This bus makes no stops along the way. / 东京是总统此次亚洲之行的第二～。Tokyo is the President's second stop on his Asia trip. ② station; stop: 长途汽车～ bus station / 我下一～下车。I get off at the next stop. ③ station or centre for rendering certain services: 供应～ supply centre

站得高，看得远 zhàndegāo, kàndeyuǎn stand high and see far; have vision; be far-sighted

站队 zhànduì line up; fall in; stand in line: 我们站好了队准备出发。We lined up and got ready to start.

站岗 zhàngǎng stand (*or* mount) guard; be on sentry duty; stand sentry: 今天晚上我～。I'm on sentry duty tonight. / 站好最后一班岗 (of one who is about to leave his job) continue working hard till the last minute

站柜台 zhàn guìtái serve as a shop assistant; serve behind the counter: 商业局干部经常到商店～。Cadres of the Commerce Bureau often go to shops to serve behind the counter.

站立 zhànlì stand; be on one's feet: 他腿疼，不能～。His leg was so painful that he could hardly stand.

站笼 zhànlóng pillory cage (used in former times)

站票 zhànpiào ticket for standing room; standing ticket: ～观众 standee / 本处只售～。Standing room only.

站哨 zhànshào *dial.* stand (*or* mount) guard; be on sentry duty; stand sentry

站台 zhàntái platform (in a railway station)

站台票 zhàntáipiào platform ticket

站稳 zhànwěn ① come to a stop: 等车～了再下。Don't get out until the car stops. ② stand firm; take a firm stand: ～脚跟 get a firm foothold; stand firm /～无产阶级立场 take a firm proletarian stand

站长 zhànzhǎng head of a station, centre, etc.: 火车站～ stationmaster

站住 zhàn·zhù ① stop; halt: 他听到有人叫他～。He heard someone calling to him to stop. /～，要不就开枪了! Halt, or I fire! / 谁? ～! Who's that? Don't move! ② stand firmly on one's feet; keep one's feet: 风刮得人都站不住了。The wind was so strong that one could

hardly keep one's feet. ③ stand (*or* hold) one's ground; consolidate one's position ④ hold water; be tenable: 他的说法站不住。His opinion doesn't hold water.

站住脚 zhàn·zhùjiǎo ① stop; halt: 他跑得太快, 一下子站不住脚。He was running too fast to stop suddenly. ② stand (*or* hold) one's ground; consolidate one's position: 我们向敌人猛烈攻击, 打得他们站不住脚。We attacked the enemy so fiercely that they couldn't hold their ground. / 游击队不依靠群众就站不住脚。The guerrillas would be unable to hold their ground if they failed to rely on the masses. ③ stay put: 忙得站不住脚 be so busy one can't stand still ④ hold water; be tenable: 这些论点没有一个是站得住脚的。None of these arguments are tenable.

绽 zhàn split; burst: 衣裳～线了。The seam has split (*or* burst).

绽放 zhànfàng (of flowers) burst forth; burst into bloom

绽裂 zhànliè split open; burst open: 棉桃～, 露出雪白的棉花。The cotton bolls burst open, revealing masses of snow-white fibres.

湛 zhàn ① profound; deep: 精湛 jīngzhàn ② crystal clear ③ (Zhàn) a surname

湛蓝 zhànlán (of the sky, the sea, a lake, etc.) azure blue; azure: ～的天空 azure skies

湛清 zhànqīng limpid; clear: ～的溪水 a limpid stream

湛深 zhànshēn same as 深湛 shēnzhàn

颤 zhàn tremble; shiver; shudder: 打颤 dǎzhàn ——see also chàn

颤栗 zhànlì same as 战栗 zhànlì

蘸 zhàn dip in (ink, sauce, etc.): ～墨水 dip in ink / 大葱～酱 scallions dipped in thick sauce

蘸火 zhànhuǒ *inf.* quench

蘸水钢笔 zhànshuǐ gāngbǐ pen (with a nib fixed into a penholder)

zhāng

张(張) zhāng ① open; spread; stretch: ～开手 open one's hand / ～翅膀 spread the wings / ～网 spread a net / ～开双臂 stretch out both arms / ～弓 draw a bow / ～帆 make sail; hoist sail ② set out; display: 大～筵席 lay on a feast ③ magnify; exaggerate: 夸张 kuāzhāng ④ look: 张望 zhāngwàng ⑤ opening of a new shop: 开张 kāizhāng ⑥ *m.*: 一～桌子 a table / 两～床 two beds / 一～纸 a piece (*or* sheet) of paper / 一～弓 a bow / 你这～嘴啊! What a tongue you've got! ⑦ the twenty-sixth of the twenty-eight constellations (二十八宿) into which the celestial sphere was divided in ancient Chinese astronomy (consisting of five stars in the shape of a drawn bow in Hydra) ⑧ (Zhāng) a surname

张榜 zhāngbǎng put up a notice; post a notice

张本 zhāngběn ① an anticipatory action ② a hint foreshadowing later developments in a story; an anticipatory remark

张弛 zhāngchí tension and relaxation; tightness and looseness ——see also 一张一弛 yīzhāng-yīchí

张大 zhāngdà *formal* magnify; exaggerate; publicize widely: ～其词 exaggerate; overstate / ～其事 publicize widely; play up

张灯结彩 zhāngdēng-jiécǎi be decorated with lanterns and coloured streamers; be decked with lanterns and bunting; be decked out and hung with lanterns; be gay with lanterns and decorations

张挂 zhāngguà hang up (a picture, curtain, etc.)

张冠李戴 Zhāng guān Lǐ dài put Zhang's hat on Li's head—attribute sth. to the wrong person or confuse one thing with another

张皇 zhānghuáng *formal* alarmed; scared; flurried; flustered

张皇失措 zhānghuáng-shīcuò be in a flurry of alarm; lose one's head; get into a panic: 一个很棘手的问题摆在他面前, 他～了。Here was a thorny question requiring an answer from him. He was too flurried to think properly. / 他讲话的时候, 神色有点～。He looked rather flustered when he spoke.

张家长, 李家短 Zhāng jiā cháng, Lǐ jiā duǎn the virtues of the Zhangs and the defects of the Lis—gossip

张口 zhāngkǒu ① same as 张嘴 zhāngzuǐ ② *dial.* yawn

张口结舌 zhāngkǒu-jiéshé be agape and tongue-tied; be at a loss for words: 他被问得～, 半天说不出话来。He was stumped by the questions and remained tongue-tied for a long time.

张狂 zhāngkuáng flippant and impudent; insolent

张力 zhānglì *phys.* ① tension ② pulling force

张力计 zhānglìjì tensiometer

张量 zhāngliàng *math.* tensor

张罗 zhāngluo ① take care of; get busy about: 场院的活让王大爷～。Uncle Wang will take care of the work on the threshing floor. / 要带的东西早点儿收拾好, 不要临时～。Get your things ready in good time to avoid a last-minute rush. / 他还没有对象, 您给～～。He hasn't got a girl to marry yet. Can't you do something about it? ② raise (funds); get together (money, etc.): ～一笔钱 raise a sum of money ③ greet and entertain (guests); attend to (customers, etc.): 她正忙着～客人。She's busy looking after the guests. / 我们坐一会儿就走, 您别～。We'll only stay for a few minutes. Please don't bother (about serving tea, etc.). / 顾客很多, 一个售货员～不过来。There were too many customers for one shop assistant to attend to.

张目 zhāngmù ① open one's eyes wide: ～注视 watch wide-eyed ② (usu. used in) 为某人～ boost sb.'s arrogance; build up another

张三李四 Zhāng Sān Lǐ Sì Zhang, Li or anybody—any Tom, Dick or Harry

张贴 zhāngtiē put up (a notice, poster, etc.): ～海报 put up posters / ～通告 post a notice / 禁止～。Post no bills.

张望 zhāngwàng ① peep (through a crack, etc.) ② look around: 探头～ crane one's neck and look around

张牙舞爪 zhāngyá-wǔzhǎo bare fangs and brandish claws—make threatening gestures; engage in sabre rattling

张扬 zhāngyáng make widely known; make public; publicize: 四处～ publicize everywhere; spread (a story) all over the place / 这事还没定下来, 先别～出去。The final decision hasn't been made yet, so don't spread this around.

张应力 zhāngyìnglì *phys.* tensile stress

张嘴 zhāngzuǐ ① open one's mouth (to say sth.): 他正要～, 一个年轻妇女抢先说了。He was on the point of saying something when a young woman started to speak. ② ask for a loan or a favour: 我想找他帮忙, 又不好意思～。I would have liked him to give me a hand, but found it embarrassing to ask.

章[1] zhāng ① chapter; section: 全书共二十～。The book has twenty chapters. ② order: 杂乱无章 zá-

luàn wú zhāng ③ rules; regulations; constitution: 规章 guīzhāng ④ item; clause: 约法三章 yuē fǎ sān zhāng ⑤ (Zhāng) a surname

章² zhāng ① seal; stamp: 刻个～ engrave a seal ② badge; medal: 领章 lǐngzhāng

章草 zhāngcǎo a type of the cursive script (草书), bearing some of the characteristics of the official script (隶书) (reputedly developed by Shi You 史游 of the Han Dynasty, so called from its use in *Zouzhang* 奏章 "memorials")

章程 zhāngchéng rules; regulations; constitution: 会员～ membership regulations

章程 zhāngcheng *dial.* solution; way: 我心里还没个准～. I'm not sure yet what's the best way.

章动 zhāngdòng *astron.* nutation: 黄经～ nutation in longitude / 倾角～ nutation in obliquity

章法 zhāngfǎ ① presentation of ideas in a piece of writing; art of composition: 文章结构严谨, 很有～. The article is well organized and the ideas are skilfully presented. ② orderly ways; methodicalness: 他办事很有～. He is quite methodical in his work. / 碰到这样意外的事, 他乱了～. He was thrown off balance by such an unexpected turn of events.

章回体 zhānghuítǐ a type of traditional Chinese novel with each chapter headed by a couplet giving the gist of its content

章回小说 zhānghuí xiǎoshuō same as 章回体 zhānghuítǐ

章节 zhāngjié chapters and sections

章句 zhāngjù ① chapters, sections, sentences and phrases in ancient texts ② syntactic and semantic analysis of ancient texts: ～之学 the philological study of ancient texts

章鱼 zhāngyú octopus

章则 zhāngzé rules and regulations

章子 zhāngzi *dial.* seal; stamp

章奏 zhāngzòu same as 奏章 zòuzhāng

彰 zhāng ① clear; evident; conspicuous: 昭彰 zhāozhāng ② make known; display: 表彰 biǎozhāng

彰明较著 zhāngmíng jiàozhù very obvious; conspicuous; easily seen

彰善瘅恶 zhāngshàn-dàn'è praise good and denounce evil; uphold virtue and condemn vice

彰彰 zhāngzhāng clear; evident; conspicuous: ～若是 as clear (or obvious) as that / ～在人耳目 be clear for all to see

嫜 zhāng *formal* husband's father; father-in-law: 姑嫜 gūzhāng

獐（麞） zhāng river deer

獐头鼠目 zhāngtóu-shǔmù with the head of a buck and the eyes of a rat—repulsively ugly and sly-looking

獐子 zhāngzi river deer

璋 zhāng a jade tablet

樟 zhāng camphor tree

樟蚕 zhāngcán a kind of wild silkworm (*Eriogyna pyretorum*)

樟木 zhāngmù camphorwood

樟脑 zhāngnǎo camphor

樟脑丸 zhāngnǎowán camphor ball; moth-ball

樟脑油 zhāngnǎoyóu camphor oil

樟树 zhāngshù camphor tree

蟑 zhāng see below

蟑螂 zhāngláng cockroach; roach

zhǎng

长¹**（長）** zhǎng ① older; elder; senior: 比他年～ older than him / 他比我～一辈. He belongs to my father's generation. / 他比我～两岁. He is senior to me by two years. *or* He is two years my senior. ② eldest; oldest: ～兄 eldest brother / ～女 eldest daughter ③ chief; head: 科长 kēzhǎng / 首长 shǒuzhǎng

长²**（長）** zhǎng ① grow; develop: 青年时期是～身体的时期. Youth is the time of physical growth. / 庄稼～得很旺. The crops are growing very well. ② come into being; begin to grow; form: ～疮 have a boil / ～癌 get cancer / ～锈 get rusty / 孩子～牙了. The baby is teething. ③ 叶子～了. The leaves are coming out. / 桃树～虫了. The peach tree is wormy. ③ acquire; enhance; increase: ～见识 increase one's knowledge; gain experience / ～工资 get an increase in salary; get a pay rise (or pay raise) / 此风不可～. Such a tendency is not to be encouraged. / ～自己的志气, 灭敌人的威风 boost our morale and dampen the enemy's spirit ——see also cháng

长辈 zhǎngbèi elder member of a family; elder; senior

长膘 zhǎngbiāo (of a domestic animal) get fat; put on flesh; flesh out

长大 zhǎngdà grow up; be brought up: 我～了当医生. I'm going to be a doctor when I grow up. / 在红旗下～ be brought up (or grow up) under the red flag

长房 zhǎngfáng the eldest branch of a family (i.e. that of the eldest son)

长个儿 zhǎnggèr grow taller

长官 zhǎngguān *old* senior officer or official; commanding officer

长机 zhǎngjī *mil.* lead aircraft; leader

长进 zhǎngjìn progress: 在学习上很有～ make good progress in one's studies

长老 zhǎnglǎo ① *formal* elder ② (a respectful term of address for an old monk) elder

长老会 Zhǎnglǎohuì *Christianity* the Presbyterian Church

长毛 zhǎngmáo *dial.* become mildewed; be covered with mildew: 馒头放久了就会～. Steamed bread will go mouldy if kept long. ——see also 长毛 chángmáo

长年 zhǎngnián *dial.* owner of a ship ——see also chángnián

长亲 zhǎngqīn senior relatives

长肉 zhǎngròu put on flesh; fill out: 这孩子光长个儿, 不～. The child keeps growing taller but doesn't fill out.

长上 zhǎngshàng ① elder member of a family; elder; senior ② superior; boss

长势 zhǎngshì the way a crop is growing: 作物～良好. The crops are doing well. / 棉花～喜人. The cotton is coming along fine.

长孙 zhǎngsūn ① eldest son's eldest son ② eldest grandson ③ (Zhǎngsūn) a two-character surname

长相 zhǎngxiàng *inf.* looks; features; appearance: ～好 be good-looking / 看她们的～好像是姐儿俩. They look like sisters.

长者 zhǎngzhě ① elder; senior ② venerable elder

长子 zhǎngzǐ eldest son

长子继承权 zhǎngzǐ jìchéngquán (right of) primogeniture; birthright

涨 (漲)
zhǎng (of water, prices, etc.) rise; go up: 潮～了。The tide is rising. *or* The tide is in. / 火车票又～了。Train fares are rising again. ——see also zhàng

涨潮 zhǎngcháo rising tide; flood tide: 正在～。The tide is at the flood.

涨风 zhǎngfēng upward trend of prices: 股市掀起了～。There was an upswing of prices on the stock market.

涨价 zhǎngjià rise in price

涨落 zhǎng-luò (of water, prices, etc.) rise and fall; fluctuate: 潮水的～ ebb and flow of the tide / 价格的～ fluctuations of prices

涨水 zhǎngshuǐ (of a river) rise

掌
zhǎng ① palm: 击掌 jīzhǎng ② strike with the palm of the hand; slap: 掌嘴 zhǎngzuǐ ③ hold in one's hand; be in charge of; control; wield: 掌权 zhǎngquán ④ the bottom of certain animals' feet; pad; sole: 鸭掌 yāzhǎng shoe sole or heel: 鞋子打前后～ have a shoe soled and heeled ⑥ horseshoe: 这匹马该钉～了。It's time for the horse to be shod. ⑦ *dial.* mend (a shoe sole): ～鞋 have a shoe sole mended ⑧ *dial.* put in (salt, oil, etc.): ～点酱油 put in some soy sauce ⑨ *dial.* (used in the same way as 把² bǎ): ～门关上。Close the door.

掌案儿的 zhǎng'ànrde *old* butcher

掌班 zhǎngbān *old* the manager of a theatrical troupe or a brothel

掌鞭 zhǎngbiān (also 掌鞭的 zhǎngbiānde) *dial.* cart driver; carter

掌灯 zhǎngdēng ① hold a lamp in one's hand ② light an oil lamp

掌舵 zhǎngduò ① be at the helm; operate the rudder; take the tiller; steer a boat ② helmsman; steersman

掌骨 zhǎnggǔ *physiol.* metacarpal bone

掌故 zhǎnggù anecdotes: 文坛～ literary anecdotes / 他熟悉这座城市的～。He knows a lot of historical anecdotes about this city.

掌管 zhǎngguǎn be in charge of; administer: ～财政 administer finances / 一个部门 be in charge of a department / 各项事务都有专人。Everything is taken care of by specially assigned people.

掌柜 zhǎngguì (also 掌柜的 zhǎngguìde) ① shopkeeper; manager (of a shop) ② *dial.* husband

掌权 zhǎngquán be in power; wield power; exercise control

掌上明珠 zhǎngshàng míngzhū a pearl in the palm—a beloved daughter: 女儿是他的～。His daughter was the apple of his eye.

掌勺儿 zhǎngsháor (also 掌锅 zhǎngguō, 掌灶 zhǎngzào) be the *chef*: ～的 *chef*

掌声 zhǎngshēng clapping; applause: 经久不息的～ prolonged applause

掌声雷动 zhǎngshēng léidòng thunderous applause: 全场～。The audience burst into thunderous applause.

掌事 zhǎngshì *dial.* be in charge of; administer

掌握 zhǎngwò ① grasp; master; know well: ～马列主义 grasp Marxism-Leninism / ～党的政策 have a good grasp of the Party's policies / ～新情况 keep abreast of new developments / ～第一手材料 possess firsthand material / ～工作进程 keep informed on how the work is progressing / ～一门外国语 have a good command of a foreign language / ～现代生产技能和科学知识 master modern techniques of production and scientific knowledge ② have in hand; take into one's hands; control: ～办公室的钥匙 keep the key to the office / ～局势 have the situation well in hand; have the situation under control / ～主动权 have the initiative in

one's hands / ～自己的命运 take one's destiny into one's own hands; be master of one's own destiny / ～国家的经济命脉 control the economic lifelines of the country / ～会议 preside over a meeting / ～分寸 exercise sound judgment; act or speak properly

掌心 zhǎngxīn ① the centre (*or* hollow) of the palm ② control; influence: 他好像跳不出她的～。He cannot seem to be able to break free from her control.

掌印 zhǎngyìn keep the seal—be in power

掌子¹ zhǎngzi (also 掌子面 zhǎngzimiàn) *min.* face; work area

掌子² zhǎngzi horseshoe

掌嘴 zhǎngzuǐ slap sb.'s face; box sb.'s ears

礃
zhǎng see below

礃子 zhǎngzi same as 掌子¹ zhǎngzi

zhàng

丈¹
zhàng ① *zhang*, a unit of length (= 3⅓ metres) ② measure (land): 春耕前要把地～完。We must finish measuring the land before spring ploughing.

丈²
zhàng ① senior; elder: 老丈 lǎozhàng ② husband (used in certain kinship terms): 姑丈 gūzhàng / 姐丈 jiězhàng

丈二和尚,摸不着头脑 zhàng èr héshang, mōbuzháo tóunǎo you can't touch the head of the ten-foot monk —you can't make head or tail of it; be very much in the dark

丈夫 zhàngfū man: ～气概 manliness

丈夫 zhàngfu husband

丈量 zhàngliáng measure (land): ～土地 measure land; take the dimensions of a field

丈母 zhàngmu (also 丈母娘 zhàngmuniáng) wife's mother; mother-in-law

丈人 zhàngrén *arch.* old gentleman

丈人 zhàngren wife's father; father-in-law

仗¹
zhàng ① *formal* weaponry; weapons: 仪仗 yízhàng ② hold (a weapon): ～剑 hold a sword ③ rely on; depend on: 这事我一人干不了, 全～大家帮忙。I can't manage it on my own. I must rely on all of you for help.

仗²
zhàng battle; war: 那是这场战争中的最后一～。That was the last battle of the war. / 打好春耕这一～ make a success of this spring ploughing.

仗势欺人 zhàng shì qī rén take advantage of one's own or sb. else's power to bully people; bully people on the strength of one's powerful connections or position; abuse one's power and bully people

仗恃 zhàngshì rely on (an advantage)

仗腰 zhàngyāo *inf.* support; back up; bolster up

仗义 zhàngyì ① *formal* uphold justice ② be loyal (to one's friends)

仗义疏财 zhàng yì shū cái be generous in aiding needy people

仗义执言 zhàng yì zhí yán speak out from a sense of justice

杖
zhàng ① cane; stick: 扶～而行 walk with a cane ② rod or staff used for a specific purpose: 擀面杖 gǎnmiànzhàng ③ flogging with a stick (a punishment in ancient China)

杖子 zhàngzi (usu. used as part of a place name)

hedge: 大～ Dazhangzi (in Hebei Province)

帐¹(帳)

zhàng　curtain; canopy: 营帐 yíng-zhàng / 蚊帐 wénzhàng

帐²(帳、賬)

zhàng　① account: ～算出来没有? Have you figured out the account? / 从～上看我们超支了。 The accounts show we have spent more than we received. ② account book: 一本～ an account book ③ debt; bill: ～都还清了。 All of the debt was paid off. / ～付了没有? Have you paid the bill?

帐簿 zhàngbù　(also 帐本 zhàngběn) account book

帐册 zhàngcè　account book

帐单 zhàngdān　bill; check: 侍者拿来了～。 The waiter came with the bill.

帐房 zhàngfáng　*old* ① accountant's office ② accountant

帐钩 zhànggōu　bed-curtain or mosquito net hook

帐号 zhànghào　number of a bank account

帐户 zhànghù　account: 非贸易～ noncommercial account / 在银行开立(结束)～ open (close) an account with a bank

帐款 zhàngkuǎn　funds on account; credit

帐面 zhàngmiàn　as shown in an account book: ～价值 book value / ～利润 book profit / ～损失 book loss / ～盈余 book surplus / ～余额 book balance / ～债务 book debt

帐目 zhàngmù　items of an account; accounts: 清理～ square accounts / 定期公布～ publish the accounts regularly / 公开 accounts open to public inspection / ～不清。 The accounts (or books) are not in order.

帐幕 zhàngmù　tent

帐篷 zhàngpeng　tent: 搭(拆)～ pitch (strike) a tent

帐主子 zhàngzhǔzi　*dial.* creditor

帐子 zhàngzi　① bed-curtain ② mosquito net

胀(脹)

zhàng　① expand; distend: 热～冷缩 expand with heat and contract with cold ② swell; be bloated: 我吃多了, 肚子有点～。 I've overeaten and feel bloated.

胀闸 zhàngzhá　hub brake

涨(漲)

zhàng　① swell after absorbing water, etc.: 豆子泡～了。 The beans swelled up after being soaked. ② (of the head) be swelled by a rush of blood: 气得～红了脸 redden (or flush) with anger ③ be more, larger, etc. than expected: 上个月他钱花～了。 Last month he couldn't make ends meet. / 把布一量, ～出了半尺。 When the cloth was measured, it was found to be half a *chi* longer than expected. ——see also zhǎng

障

zhàng　① hinder; obstruct: 障碍 zhàng'ài ② barrier; block: 路障 lùzhàng

障碍 zhàng'ài　① hinder; obstruct: ～物 obstacle; barrier; entanglement ② obstacle; obstruction; barrier; impediment: 扫清～ clear away obstacles / 制造～ erect barriers; create obstacles / 两国正在进行的谈判遇到了～。 The current talks between the two countries have run into obstacles. / 语言交流上的～ language barrier / 经济发展的主要～ a major impediment to economic growth

障碍船 zhàng'àichuán　*mil.* blockship

障碍赛跑 zhàng'ài sàipǎo　steeplechase; obstacle race

障蔽 zhàngbì　block; obstruct; shut out: ～视线 obstruct one's view

障眼法 zhàngyǎnfǎ　cover-up; camouflage: 玩弄～ throw dust into people's eyes

障翳 zhàngyì　*formal* hide from view; cover; screen

障子 zhàngzi　a barrier made of reeds, sorghum stalks

or closely planted shrubs; hedge

幛

zhàng　a large, oblong sheet of silk with an appropriate message attached, presented at a wedding, birthday or funeral: 喜幛 xǐzhàng

幛子 zhàngzi　same as 幛 zhàng

嶂

zhàng　a screen-like mountain peak

瘴

zhàng　miasma

瘴疠 zhànglì　communicable subtropical diseases, such as pernicious malaria, etc.

瘴气 zhàngqì　miasma

zhāo

钊

zhāo　(obsolete except in given names) encourage; exhort

招¹

zhāo　① beckon: 他把手一～, 要我跟上。 He beckoned me to follow. ② recruit; enlist; enrol: 学校下学期～二百人。 The school will enrol 200 pupils next term. ③ attract; incur; court: ～苍蝇 attract flies / ～灾 court disaster; invite calamity / ～人嫌 incur odium / ～人喜欢的孩子 a charming (or lovable) child ④ provoke; tease: 这孩子爱哭, 别～他。 He's a crybaby. Don't tease him. ⑤ *dial.* infect; be contagious: 这病～人。 This disease is catching.

招²

zhāo　confess; own up: 犯人已经～了。 The prisoner has confessed. / 他死也不肯～。 Nothing could make him own up.

招³

zhāo　same as 着¹ zhāo

招安 zhāo'ān　(of feudal rulers) offer amnesty and enlistment to rebels: 受～ (of former rebels) accept amnesty and serve the ruler

招标 zhāobiāo　invite tenders (or bids, public bidding)

招兵 zhāobīng　recruit soldiers; raise troops

招兵买马 zhāobīng-mǎimǎ　recruit men and buy horses ——raise or enlarge an army; recruit followers

招财进宝 zhāocái-jìnbǎo　let riches and treasures come into the house

招待 zhāodài　receive (guests); entertain; serve (customers): 设宴～外宾 give a dinner for (or in honour of) foreign guests / ～客人 entertain guests / 谢谢你们的热情～。 Thank you for your kind hospitality. / ～费 entertainment allowance or expenses

招待会 zhāodàihuì　reception: 冷餐～ buffet reception / 举行～ give (or hold) a reception

招待券 zhāodàiquàn　complimentary ticket

招待所 zhāodàisuǒ　guest house; hostel

招风 zhāofēng　catch the wind——attract too much attention and invite trouble

招风耳 zhāofēng'ěr　protruding ears; flappy ears

招蜂引蝶 zhāofēng-yǐndié　attract bees and butterflies ——(of a woman) flirtatious

招抚 zhāofǔ　same as 招安 zhāo'ān

招柑 zhāogān　a kind of orange

招工 zhāogōng　advertise for workers; recruit workers

招供 zhāogòng　make a confession of one's crime; confess

招股 zhāogǔ　raise capital by floating shares

招呼 zhāohu　① call: 那边有人～你。 Someone over there is calling you. ② hail; greet; say hello to: 热情地打～ greet warmly ③ notify; tell: ～他赶快来开会。 Tell him to come to the meeting at once. / 你要是不去, 事

先打个～。Let me know beforehand if you won't be going. ④ take care of: ～老人 take care of old people ⑤ *dial.* mind; take care: 路上有冰,～滑倒了。The road is icy. Mind you don't slip.

招唤 zhāohuàn summon; call: 把孩子～过来。Call the boy over here.

招魂 zhāohún call back the spirit of the dead

招集 zhāojí call together; convene

招架 zhāojià ward off blows; hold one's own: ～不住 be unable to hold one's own; unable to withstand / 只有～之功, 没有还手之力 can only parry sb.'s blows without being able to hit back

招考 zhāokǎo give public notice of entrance examination; admit (students, applicants, etc.) by examination

招徕 zhāolái solicit (customers or business); canvass: ～顾客 solicit customers / 以广～ so as to have more customers

招揽 zhāolǎn solicit (customers or business); canvass: ～主顾 solicit customers / ～生意 canvass; seek business orders; drum up trade

招领 zhāolǐng announce the finding of lost property: 失物～ (a notice) Found / 拾物～处 Lost and Found

招募 zhāomù recruit; enlist

招纳 zhāonà *formal* recruit: ～贤士 recruit men of worth

招女婿 zhāo nǚxu take a man into the family as a son-in-law

招牌 zhāopai shop sign; signboard: 据说这～是一位名书法家写的。This signboard is said to have been written by a famous calligrapher. / 打着人道主义的～ under the signboard of humanitarianism

招盘 zhāopán put a business up for sale

招聘 zhāopìn same as 征聘 zhēngpìn

招亲 zhāoqīn ① same as 招女婿 zhāo nǚxu ② marry into and live with one's bride's family

招权纳贿 zhāoquán-nàhuì seize power and accept bribes

招惹 zhāore ① provoke; incur; court: ～麻烦 bring trouble ② *dial.* (usu. used in the negative) tease; provoke: 这人～不得。You'd better not provoke that fellow.

招惹是非 zhāore shìfēi bring trouble on oneself

招认 zhāorèn confess one's crime; plead guilty

招商 zhāoshāng invite outside investment

招生 zhāoshēng enrol new students; recruit students: ～制度 enrolment system; admissions system / ～简章 school admission brochure

招式 zhāoshì movements in martial arts or traditional opera

招事 zhāoshì bring trouble on oneself; invite trouble

招收 zhāoshōu recruit; take in: ～工人 recruit workers / ～大学生 enrol new students in universities and colleges

招手 zhāoshǒu beckon; wave: 他～要我进去。He beckoned me in. / ～致意 wave one's greetings; wave back in acknowledgement / 胜利在向我们～。Victory beckons.

招数 zhāoshù same as 着数 zhāoshù

招贴 zhāotiē poster; placard; bill

招贴画 zhāotiēhuà pictorial poster (or placard)

招贤 zhāoxián ① (of a ruler) summon men of worth to serve their country ② call the able to service

招降 zhāoxiáng summon sb. to surrender

招降纳叛 zhāoxiáng-nàpàn recruit deserters and traitors

招笑儿 zhāoxiàor *dial.* laughable; funny

招眼 zhāoyǎn eye-catching: 你这身儿打扮太～。Your clothes are rather too loud.

招摇 zhāoyáo act ostentatiously

招摇过市 zhāoyáo guò shì swagger through the streets —blatantly seek publicity

招摇撞骗 zhāoyáo-zhuàngpiàn swindle and bluff; bluff one's way around: 他冒充记者, 到处～。He passed himself off as a reporter to go about cheating people.

招引 zhāoyǐn attract; induce: 灯光～蛾子。Lights attract moths.

招怨 zhāoyuàn incur hatred

招灾惹祸 zhāozāi-rěhuò court disaster; invite trouble: 这孩子老给大人～。This child is always making trouble for his parents. / 他性情暴躁, 准会～。His fiery temper will get him into trouble.

招展 zhāozhǎn flutter; wave: 工地上红旗～。Red flags fluttered over the construction site.

招致 zhāozhì ① recruit (followers); scout about for (talents, etc.) ② incur; bring about; lead to: ～意外的损失 incur unexpected losses / ～失败 cause defeat / ～无穷后患 lead to endless trouble

招赘 zhāozhuì same as 招女婿 zhāo nǚxu

招子 zhāozi ① poster; placard; bill ② shop sign ③ trick; device; move

招租 zhāozū (house) for rent: 此屋～。Room to let.

昭 zhāo clear; obvious: 昭著 zhāozhù

昭布 zhāobù make known to the public

昭告 zhāogào declare to the public

昭然 zhāorán clear; obvious

昭然若揭 zhāorán ruò jiē abundantly clear; all too clear

昭示 zhāoshì make clear to all; declare publicly: ～全国 declare to the whole nation

昭苏 zhāosū *formal* come to life; wake up: 大地回春, 万物～。Spring comes round, quickening all creation.

昭雪 zhāoxuě exonerate; rehabilitate: 冤案得到了～。The wrong has been righted. *or* The person wronged has been rehabilitated.

昭彰 zhāozhāng clear; manifest; evident: 罪恶昭彰 zuì'è zhāozhāng

昭著 zhāozhù clear; evident; obvious: 成绩～ have achieved signal successes

着¹ **(招)** zhāo ① a move in chess: 妙～儿 a clever move / 走错一～ make a false move; take a wrong step ② trick; device; move: 这一～厉害。That's a shrewd move. / 他没～儿了。He's at the end of his tether. / 你这一～可真高。That was really a brilliant stroke (*or* move, idea) of yours.

着² zhāo *dial.* ① put in; add: ～点儿盐 put some salt in it ② all right; O.K.: ～, 咱们就这么办。O.K., that's what we'll do then.
——see also zháo; zhe; zhuó

着数 zhāoshù (also 着法 zhāofǎ) ① a move in chess ② a movement in *wushu* (武术) ③ trick; device

啁 zhāo see below ——see also zhōu

啁哳 zhāozhā *formal* twitter

朝 zhāo ① early morning; morning: 一朝一夕 yīzhāo-yīxī ② day: 今朝 jīnzhāo ——see also cháo

朝不保夕 zhāo bù bǎo xī not know at dawn what may happen by dusk; be in a precarious state

朝不谋夕 zhāo bù móu xī (also 朝不虑夕 zhāo bù lǜ xī) be unable to plan one's day; be in a precarious state

朝发夕至 zhāo fā xī zhì start at dawn and arrive at dusk—a day's journey

朝晖 zhāohuī morning sunlight: 祖国大地尽～。This vast land of ours is glowing in the morning sun.

朝令夕改 zhāo lìng xī gǎi issue an order at dawn and

rescind it at dusk; make unpredictable changes in policy

朝露 zhāolù *liter.* morning dew—ephemeral; transitory: 浩浩阴阳移，年命如～。(《古诗十九首》) In infinite succession light and darkness shift, And years vanish like the morning dew.

朝暮 zhāomù ① morning and evening ② from morning to night; from dawn to dusk; all day long: ～相处 be together from morning to night; be closely associated

朝气 zhāoqì youthful spirit; vigour; vitality: 革命～ revolutionary vigour / 富有～ be full of vigour

朝气蓬勃 zhāoqì péngbó full of youthful spirit; full of vigour and vitality; imbued with vitality: ～的青年 spirited young people / ～的先锋队组织 a vigorous vanguard organization

朝乾夕惕 zhāoqián-xītì work hard and conscientiously from morning till night

朝秦暮楚 zhāo Qín mù Chǔ serve (the State of) Qin in the morning and (the State of) Chu in the evening—be quick to switch sides; be fickle; be inconstant

朝日 zhāorì the morning sun

朝三暮四 zhāosān-mùsì blow hot and cold; chop and change

朝思暮想 zhāosī-mùxiǎng yearn day and night: 我～，连做梦也见到她。I think about her from dawn to dusk; I see her even in my dreams.

朝夕 zhāoxī ① morning and evening; from morning to night; day and night; daily: ～相处 be together from morning to night; be closely associated ② a very short time: 只争朝夕 zhǐ zhēng zhāoxī

朝霞 zhāoxiá rosy clouds of dawn; rosy dawn

朝阳 zhāoyáng the rising sun; the morning sun ——see also cháoyáng

zhāo

着 zhāo ① touch; come in contact with: 孩子太小，坐在那把椅子上脚不能～地。The child is so small that his feet can't touch the floor when he sits in that chair. / 我手上的烫伤一～水就疼。The burns on my hand hurt when they get in contact with water. ② be affected by (cold, etc.); be troubled with; suffer: 着凉 zháoliáng ③ be ignited; be lit: 火～了。The fire is lit. / 炉子～得很旺。The stove is going strong. / 天黑了，路灯都～了。It's dark, and the street lights are all on. / 汽油一点就～。Gasoline is highly inflammable. ④ *dial.* fall asleep: 他困得很，一上床就～了。He was so tired that he fell asleep the moment he got into bed. ⑤ (used as a complement to another verb) hitting the mark; succeeding in: 这回你可说～了。This time you really hit the nail on the head. / 灯点～了。The lamp is lit. / 他整夜翻来复去睡不～。He tossed about all night, unable to get to sleep. / 猫逮～一只老鼠。The cat caught a rat. / 票我买～了。I've bought my ticket. / 今天真把你累～了。You really must be worn out today. / 我们到处找他都找不～。We looked everywhere for him, but couldn't find him. ——see also zhāo; zhe; zhuó

着风 zháofēng be chilled by the wind: 我两个肩膀酸疼，想是夜里起来解手着了风。My shoulders ache. I must have been chilled by the wind when I got up to relieve myself during the night.

着慌 zháohuāng get nervous; get alarmed; become flustered (*or* jittery); be thrown into a panic: 这下子他可～了。At that point he panicked.

着火 zháohuǒ catch fire; be on fire: ～啦! Fire! / 房子～了。The house is on fire. / 木头容易～。Wood catches fire easily. / 上星期有家工厂着了一场大火。There was a very bad fire in a factory last week.

着火点 zháohuǒdiǎn same as 燃点 rándiǎn

着急 zháojí get worried; get excited; feel anxious: 别～, 安心养病。Just take care of yourself and don't worry. / 冷静点，别～。Keep calm. Don't get excited. / 你着什么急呢? 不会有什么问题的。What are you worrying about? Everything will be all right.

着凉 zháoliáng catch cold; catch a chill: 外面有点冷，当心～。It's chilly outside; be careful not to catch cold.

着忙 zháománg be in a hurry; be in a rush: 别～, 还来得及。Don't be in such a hurry; there's still time.

着迷 zháomí be fascinated; be captivated: 观众越看越～。The audience watched the performance with growing fascination. / 孩子们听故事都听得着了迷。The children were spellbound by the story. / 他对音乐着了迷。He's crazy about music.

着魔 zháomó be bewitched; be possessed: 他着了魔似的站在那里不动。He stood still like a man possessed. / 他这几天练乒乓球像着了魔似的。He's been practising ping-pong like crazy these few days.

着恼 zháonǎo get angry; be annoyed: 你别～, 咱们可以好好商量。Don't get excited. We can talk it over calmly. / 最近他心情不好，动不动就～。He has been in a bad mood lately and is very irritable.

着三不着两 zháo sān bù zháo liǎng erratic; ill-considered; thoughtless: 说话～ speak thoughtlessly

zhǎo

爪 zhǎo claw; talon ——see also zhuǎ

爪哇 Zhǎowā Java

爪牙 zhǎoyá talons and fangs—lackeys; underlings: 帝国主义的～ a lackey of imperialism

找[1] zhǎo ① look for; try to find; seek: 他到处在～你。He's been looking for you all over the place. / ～矿 look for mineral deposits / ～到油田 discover an oil field / ～出地震的规律 discover the laws of earthquakes / ～工作 look (*or* hunt) for a job / ～机会 look for (*or* seek) an opportunity / ～出路 seek a way out / 从世界观上～原因 seek the cause (of an error) in a person's world outlook / ～答案 try to find the answer ② want to see; call on; approach; ask for: 有人～你。Someone wants to see you. / 有人来～过我吗? Did anyone ask for me? / 明天再来～你。I'll call on you again tomorrow. / 干吗不去～老杨帮忙? Why not go and ask Lao Yang for help? / ～我有什么事? What can I do for you? *or* What do you want to see me about? / 出了问题可得～你。If anything goes wrong, we'll hold you responsible.

找[2] zhǎo give change: 这张唱片三十元，我给了你五十元，～我二十元。This disc costs 30 *yuan* and I gave you 50 *yuan*, so I want 20 *yuan* change. / 她～我二十元。She gave me 20 *yuan* change (*or* in change). / 甭～了。(to a taxi driver, etc.) Keep the change.

找病 zhǎobìng bring vexation on oneself

找补 zhǎobu make up a deficiency: 请点一下，不够再～。Count it, please. We'll make it up if there's any shortage. / 这儿没焊好，再～两下。The welding is faulty here. Let's touch it up.

找不开 zhǎobukāi have no small change for (money of a higher denomination): 对不起，你这张十元票子我～。Sorry, I have no small change for your 10-*yuan* note.

找不自在 zhǎobuzìzài *inf.* ask for trouble; borrow

trouble; bring trouble upon oneself: 你去劝他是～。 You are borrowing trouble if you try to persuade him.

找茬儿 zhǎocházr　find fault; pick holes; pick a quarrel: 我觉得我干得满不错了，可他老～。 I think my work is quite satisfactory, but he's always finding fault. / 他在～吵架。 He's trying to find some excuse and start a quarrel.

找对象 zhǎo duìxiàng　look for a partner in marriage

找缝子 zhǎofèngzi　(also 找岔子 zhǎochàzi; 找刺儿 zhǎocìr) find fault; pick holes; nitpick

找麻烦 zhǎo máfan　① look for trouble; ask for trouble ② cause sb. trouble: 对不起，给你们～了。 I'm sorry to have caused you so much trouble.

找平 zhǎopíng　make level; level up or down: 右手边儿还差两层砖，～了再下班。 The right side needs two more layers of bricks. Let's lay them before knocking off for the day.

找婆家 zhǎo pójia　look for a husband: 她今年二十八了，还没～。 She is twenty-eight this year, and still unmarried.

找齐 zhǎoqí　① make uniform; even up: 打埂得～。 The tops of ridges should be made even. ② make up a deficiency: 先付一部分，差多少交货时～。 We'll pay you part of the sum now. The balance will be paid on delivery of the goods.

找钱 zhǎoqián　give change: 售货员找了我钱。 The shop assistant gave (or handed) me my change. / 这是找给你的钱。 Here's your change.

找事 zhǎoshì　① look (or hunt) for a job ② pick a quarrel

找死 zhǎosǐ　court death: 你～啊! (as said by a driver to another driver or a pedestrian trying to cut him off) What are you up to? Do you want to kill yourself?

找头 zhǎotou　change (from money paid): 这是给你的～。 Here is your change.

找寻 zhǎoxún　look for; seek

找寻 zhǎoxun　*dial.*　find fault with; pick on: 他爱～人。 He likes to pick on someone or other.

找辙 zhǎozhé　*inf.*　find an excuse (or pretext)

沼 zhǎo　natural pond: 池沼 chízhǎo

沼气 zhǎoqì　marsh gas; firedamp; methane; sewage gas; sludge gas: ～池 methane-generating pit; methane tank

沼泽 zhǎozé　marsh; swamp; bog: ～地 marshland; swamp / ～土 bog soil

zhào

召¹ zhào　call together; convene; summon: 号召 hàozhào

召² zhào　(usu. used as part of a place name) temple; monastery

召唤 zhàohuàn　call (usu. fig.): 大草原在～着我们。 The grasslands are calling us. / 共产党员听从党的～。 A communist heeds the Party's call.

召回 zhàohuí　recall: ～大使 recall an ambassador / ～国书 letter of recall

召祸 zhàohuò　*formal*　court disaster

召集 zhàojí　call together; convene: 把干部～在一起 call the cadres together / ～会议 call (or convene) a conference

召集人 zhàojírén　convener

召见 zhàojiàn　① call in (a subordinate) ② *diplomacy* summon (an envoy) to an interview

召开 zhàokāi　convene; convoke: 庆祝全国人民代表大会的～ celebrate the convening (or opening) of the National People's Congress / ～一次国际会议 convene an international conference

召之即来 zhào zhī jí lái　come as soon as called; be on call: ～，来之能战，战之能胜。 Be ready to assemble at the first call and be capable of fighting and winning.

兆¹ zhào　① sign; omen; portent: 不祥之兆 bùxiáng zhī zhào ② portend; foretell: 瑞雪兆丰年 ruìxuě zhào fēngnián

兆² zhào　① million; mega- ② (in ancient times) a million millions; billion

兆赫 zhàohè　*electron.*　megahertz (MHz); megacycle per second

兆头 zhàotou　(also 兆候 zhàohòu) sign; omen; portent: 好(坏)～ a good (bad) omen / 早晨有雾是晴天的～。 Mist in the morning is a sign of good weather.

兆周 zhàozhōu　*radio*　megacycle

诏 zhào　*formal*　① instruct ② imperial edict

诏令 zhàolìng　imperial edict

诏书 zhàoshū　imperial edict

炤 zhào　same as 照 zhào

赵(趙) Zhào　① one of the Warring States into which China was divided during the Eastern Zhou period (770-256 B.C.), occupying what is now northern and central Shanxi and western and southern Hebei ② (in classical prose and poetry) a name for what is now southern Hebei: 家本秦也，能为秦声；妇—女也，雅善鼓瑟。(西汉文《杨恽报孙会宗书》) My own family came originally from Qin and so I can make music in the Qin style, while my wife is from Zhao and consequently plays the zither very well. ③ a surname

赵公元帅 Zhàogōng yuánshuài　Marshal Zhao, or Zhao Gongming, God of Wealth in Chinese folklore

笊 zhào　see below

笊篱 zhàoli　a bamboo, wicker or wire strainer

棹(櫂、桌) zhào　*dial.*　① oar ② row (a boat)

照 zhào　① shine; illuminate; light up: 金色的太阳～在天安门城楼上。 The golden sun shines upon the gate tower of Tian An Men. / 车灯把大路～得通亮。 The headlights lit up the road. / 拿手电～路 light the way with a torch ② reflect; mirror: ～镜子 look in the mirror / 湖面～出了她的倒影。 Her image was reflected in the lake. ③ take a picture (or photograph); photograph; film; shoot: 这镜头可不容易～。 This scene is by no means easy to shoot. / 这张照片里我没～好。 I don't come out well in this photo. ④ photograph; picture: 小照 xiǎozhào ⑤ license; permit: 禁止无～行车。 It is forbidden to drive without a license. ⑥ take care of; look after: 照看 zhàokàn ⑦ notify: 知照 zhīzhào ⑧ contrast: 对照 duìzhào ⑨ understand: 心照不宣 xīnzhào bù xuān ⑩ *prep.*　in the direction of; towards: 这个方向走。 Go in this direction. / 拿起茶碗～脸就打 pick up a teacup and throw it in sb.'s face ⑪ *prep.*　according to; in accordance with: ～他们的说法 according to what they say / ～规章办事 act in accordance with the regulations / ～我看，线路有毛病。 It seems to me there's something wrong with the circuit.

照搬 zhàobān　indiscriminately imitate; copy: 全盘～人家的经验 copy indiscriminately the experience of others

照办 zhàobàn　act accordingly; act in accordance with; act upon; comply with; follow: 你说得对，我们就照你的办。If what you propose is right, we will act upon it. / 你们提出的要求我们尽量～。We'll try our best to comply with your request.

照本宣科 zhào běn xuān kē　read item by item from the text; repeat what the book says

照壁 zhàobì　(also 照墙 zhàoqiáng) a screen wall facing the gate of a house

照常 zhàocháng　as usual: ～营业 business as usual / 遇雨比赛～进行。The match will be played as scheduled in the event of rain.

照抄 zhàochāo　① copy word for word: 这个材料请你一份。Please make a copy of this material. ② same as 照搬 zhàobān

照登 zhàodēng　publish sth. as it is (i.e. without alterations)

照度 zhàodù　phys. intensity of illumination; illuminance

照发 zhàofā　① issue as before: 女工产假期间工资～。Women workers are entitled to maternity leave with full pay. or Women workers receive full pay during maternity leave. ② approved for distribution (used for notices or circulars submitted for approval)

照拂 zhàofú　formal　look after; care for; attend to: 请惠予～。Please be so kind as to take good care of him.

照顾 zhàogu　① give consideration to; show consideration for; make allowance(s) for: ～到两国的友好关系 out of consideration for the friendship of the two countries / ～全局 take the whole into account; consider the situation as a whole / ～多数 make allowance for the majority; think in terms of the majority / ～实际需要 consider actual needs / ～他的困难 take his difficulties into account / 给予适当～ give appropriate preferential treatment / 青年团的工作要～青年的特点。The Youth League in its work must take the characteristics of youth into consideration. ② look after; care for; attend to: ～伤员 look after the wounded / 烈军属受到政府的特别～。Families of martyrs and servicemen receive special care from the government. ③ (of a customer) patronize

照管 zhàoguǎn　look after; tend; be in charge of: ～孩子 look after a child; mind a child / ～机器 tend a machine / ～仓库 be in charge of a storehouse

照葫芦画瓢 zhào húlu huà piáo　draw a dipper with a gourd as a model—copy; imitate

照护 zhàohù　look after (patients, the wounded, etc.)

照会 zhàohuì　① present (or deliver, address) a note to (a government) ② note: 提出～ present (or deliver, address) a note / 交换～ exchange notes / 普通～ note verbale / 正式～ personal note; formal note; official note

照价 zhàojià　according to the set (or arranged) price: ～付款 pay according to the arranged price / 如有损坏，～赔偿 pay the full price for anything damaged

照旧 zhàojiù　as before; as usual; as of old: 程序～。The procedure remains unchanged. / 参观改期，入场券～有效。Visit postponed. Tickets remain valid.

照看 zhàokàn　look after; attend to; keep an eye on: 她在幼儿园～孩子。She looks after children in the kindergarten. / ～病人 attend to a patient / 劳驾帮我～一下行李。Will you please keep an eye on my luggage.

照理 zhàolǐ　according to reason; in the ordinary course of events; normally: ～他现在该来了。He ought to be here by now.

照例 zhàolì　as a rule; as usual; usually: 我们～是在星期一下午开全组会。As a rule, we have our group meeting on Monday afternoon. / 那天早上，他～起得很早。That morning he got up very early, as usual.

照料 zhàoliào　take care of; attend to: ～烈士子女 care for the children of revolutionary martyrs / 她把小女儿托给一位老大娘～。She left her baby daughter in the care of an old woman. / 你放心走吧，这里的事有我们～。Don't you worry. We'll take care of everything while you're away.

照临 zhàolín　shine on; illuminate; light up: 曙光～大地。The early sun bathes the land in light.

照猫画虎 zhào māo huà hǔ　draw a tiger with a cat as a model—copy sth. without catching its spirit

照面儿 zhàomiànr　① (usu. used in the negative) put in an appearance; show up; turn up: 他始终不～。He never showed up. / 互不～ avoid each other ② encounter; come across: 打个～ come face to face with sb.; run into sb.

照明 zhàomíng　illumination; lighting: 舞台～ stage illumination / ～电路 lighting circuit / ～装置 lighting installation

照明弹 zhàomíngdàn　flare; star shell

照明炮弹 zhàomíng pàodàn　illuminating shell

照片儿 zhàopiānr　inf.　photo

照片子 zhào piānzi　take an X-ray; X-ray: 医生要给我的胸部～。The doctor will take an X-ray of my chest. / 我的胳膊得照个片子。I must have my arm X-rayed.

照片 zhàopiàn　photograph; picture: 彩色～ colour photograph / 加印～ print off copies from a negative; make copies of a print

照射 zhàoshè　shine; illuminate; light up; irradiate: 用紫外线～ irradiate with ultraviolet rays

照实 zhàoshí　according to the facts: 情况怎样，你～说好了。Tell us the truth about the situation.

照说 zhàoshuō　ordinarily; as a rule: ～这时候该热了。As a rule, it should be warm by now. / ～我们早就应当通知你的。We ought to have told you much earlier.

照相 zhàoxiàng　(also 照像 zhàoxiàng) take a picture (or photograph); photograph: 我想照张相。I want to have a picture taken. / 我们星期天～去。Let's go and take photographs this Sunday. / 宾主在一起照了相。Guests and host were photographed together. / 缩微～ microphotograph

照相版 zhàoxiàngbǎn　process plate

照相簿 zhàoxiàngbù　photo album

照相弹 zhàoxiàngdàn　mil.　photo-flash bomb; flash bomb

照相复制 zhàoxiàng fùzhì　photocopy

照相馆 zhàoxiàngguǎn　photo studio

照相机 zhàoxiàngjī　camera: 反射式～ reflex camera / 立体～ stereoscopic (or stereo) camera / 全景～ panoramic camera / 傻瓜～ foolproof camera / 小型～ miniature camera; minicamera; minicam / 折叠式～ folding camera / 制版～ process camera

照相排字 zhàoxiàng páizì　filmsetting; phototype setting

照相枪 zhàoxiàngqiāng　mil.　gun camera

照相纸 zhàoxiàngzhǐ　photographic paper

照相制版 zhàoxiàng zhìbǎn　photomechanical process

照相制图 zhàoxiàng zhìtú　photomap

照样 zhàoyàng　① after a pattern or model: 照着样儿画 draw after a model / 照这个样儿做 do it this way ② in the same old way; as before; as usual: ～办理 go about it in the same old way / 没有他，我们～可以做。We can do it without him, as we have before.

照妖镜 zhàoyāojìng　monster-revealing mirror; demon-detector

照耀 zhàoyào　shine; illuminate: 灿烂的阳光～着祖国大地。A bright sun is shining over our country.

照应 zhàoyìng　coordinate; correlate: 文章要前后～。A composition must be well organized.

照应 zhàoying　look after; take care of: 火车上乘务员对旅客～很好。The attendants on the train took good

care of the passengers.

照章 zhàozhāng in accordance with rules or regulations: ～罚款。A fine will be imposed in accordance with the regulations.

照直 zhàozhí ① (go) straight on: ～走就到学校了。Go straight ahead and you'll find the school. ② straightforward; direct: 有话就～说。Say directly what you have to say.

照准 zhàozhǔn ① (used in official documents) request granted ② aim at: ～靶子射击 aim at the target and fire

照准仪 zhàozhǔnyí *mech.* alidade

罩 zhào ① cover; overspread; wrap: 工人们下班时都细心地把仪器～好。The workers carefully covered all the instruments before they went off work. / 山坡上～着一层薄雾。The mountain slope was wrapped in a thin mist. / 棉袄外面～着一件蓝布褂儿 wear a blue dustcoat over one's cotton-padded jacket ② cover; shade; hood; casing: 玻璃～ glass cover / 发动机～ (engine) hood / 保险～ protecting casing ③ a bamboo fish trap ④ a bamboo chicken coop

罩袍 zhàopáo dust-robe; dust-gown; overall

罩棚 zhàopéng an awning over a gateway or a courtyard

罩衫 zhàoshān *dial.* overall; dustcoat

罩袖 zhàoxiù *dial.* oversleeve; sleevelet

罩衣 zhàoyī (also 罩褂儿 zhàoguàr) dustcoat; overall

罩子 zhàozi cover; shade; hood; casing

肇(肇) zhào *formal* ① start; commence; initiate: 肇始 zhàoshǐ ② cause (trouble, etc.): 肇事 zhàoshì

肇端 zhàoduān *formal* beginning

肇祸 zhàohuò cause trouble; cause an accident

肇始 zhàoshǐ *formal* start; commence; initiate

肇事 zhàoshì cause trouble; create a disturbance: ～者 a person who has created a disturbance; troublemaker

zhē

折 zhē *inf.* ① roll over; turn over: 折跟头 zhē gēntou ② pour back and forth between two containers: 开水太烫，拿两个杯子～一～就凉了。The water's boiling hot. Pour it from one cup to another to cool it. ——see also shé; zhé

折跟头 zhē gēntou turn a somersault

折腾 zhēteng *inf.* ① turn from side to side; toss about: 他～了好几个钟头才睡着。He tossed about in bed for hours before he got to sleep. ② do sth. over and over again: 徒工把旧机器拆了又安，安了又拆，～了好多回。The young apprentice again and again took the old machine apart and then put it together. ③ cause physical or mental suffering; get sb. down: 牙疼真～人。A toothache can get you down. ④ spend freely; squander: 没多久他就把那份家产～光了。It didn't take him long to squander away his family fortune.

蜇 zhē ① (of bees, wasps, etc.) sting: 马蜂～人。Wasps sting people. ② smart; sting: 碘酒擦在伤口上～得慌。Iodine smarts when it is put on a cut. / 切洋葱～眼睛。When you slice an onion it makes your eyes sting. ——see also zhé

蜇针 zhēzhēn *zool.* sting; stinger

遮 zhē ① hide from view; cover; screen: 月亮给云彩～住了。The moon was hidden by clouds. / 拿塑料布把脱粒机～起来 spread a plastic sheet over the thresher / 乌鸦的翅膀～不住太阳的光辉。A crow's wings can never shut out the sunlight. / ～不住内心的喜悦 cannot conceal one's delight ② block; obstruct; impede: ～道 block the way ③ keep out: ～风挡雨 keep out wind and rain

遮蔽 zhēbì ① hide from view; cover; screen ② obstruct; block: ～视线 obstruct the view ③ *mil.* defilade: ～物 defilade / ～阵地 defiladed position

遮藏 zhēcáng hide; conceal; cover up

遮丑 zhēchǒu gloss over one's blemishes; hide one's shame; cover up one's defect

遮挡 zhēdǎng ① shelter from; keep out: ～寒风 keep out the cold wind / 用帘子把窗户～起来 cover the window with a curtain ② a shelter; a cover

遮断 zhēduàn *mil.* interdict: ～射击 interdiction fire

遮盖 zhēgài ① cover; overspread: 山路全给大雪～住了。The mountain paths were all covered by snow. ② hide; conceal; cover up: 错误总是～不住的。Mistakes can never be hidden.

遮光罩 zhēguāngzhào *photog.* lens hood

遮拦 zhēlán block; obstruct; impede

遮瞒 zhēmán conceal; hide; hold back

遮没 zhēmò hide from view; cover; screen: 山被浓雾～了。The hills were covered in thick mist.

遮天蔽日 zhētiān-bìrì blot out the sky and the sun (said of a dense forest)

遮天盖地 zhētiān-gàidì blot out the sky and cover up the earth (said of a snowstorm or sandstorm or of an invading army)

遮羞 zhēxiū hush up a scandal; cover up one's embarrassment

遮羞布 zhēxiūbù fig leaf

遮掩 zhēyǎn ① cover; overspread; envelop: 远山被云雾～着。The distant hills were enveloped in clouds and mist. ② cover up; hide; conceal: 大胆承认错误，不要遮遮掩掩。Admit your mistakes courageously. Don't try to cover them up.

遮眼法 zhēyǎnfǎ cover-up; camouflage

遮阳 zhēyáng sunshade

遮阳板 zhēyángbǎn *archit.* sunshading board

遮阴 zhēyīn (also 遮荫 zhēyīn) shelter from heat or light; shade: ～的树 a shade tree

zhé

折[1] zhé ① break; snap: ～断一根树枝 break off a branch / ～断腿 fracture (or break) one's leg ② suffer the loss of; lose: 损兵折将 sǔnbīng-zhéjiàng ③ bend; twist: 曲折 qūzhé ④ turn back; change direction: 边界由此～向西南。From here the boundary turns southwestward. ⑤ be convinced; be filled with admiration: 心～ be deeply convinced; be filled with heartfelt admiration ⑥ convert into; amount to: 把市斤～成公斤 convert (or change) jin into kilograms / 这笔外币～成人民币是多少? How much does this sum of foreign money amount to in Renminbi? ⑦ discount; rebate: 打八～ give 20% discount; charge 80% of the original price ⑧ an act of 杂剧 zájù[2] ⑨ turning stroke (in Chinese characters)

折[2]**(摺)** zhé ① fold: 把信～好 fold the letter / 把纸对～起来 fold the sheet of paper in two ② booklet in accordion form with a slipcase, used for keeping accounts, etc.; folder: 存折 cúnzhé ——see also shé; zhē

折板结构 zhébǎn jiégòu *archit.* folded plate structure

折半 zhébàn　reduce (a price) by half; give 50% discount: 按原价～出售 sell at 50% discount; sell at half price

折变 zhébiàn　*dial.* sell off (one's property)

折布机 zhébùjī　*text.* folding machine

折尺 zhéchǐ　folding rule

折冲 zhéchōng　*formal* repulse or subdue the enemy: ～御侮 repel foreign aggression

折冲樽俎 zhéchōng zūnzǔ　① outmanoeuvre the enemy over glasses of wine; win by superior diplomacy ② engage in diplomatic negotiations

折叠 zhédié　fold: 把报纸～好 fold up the newspaper

折叠床 zhédiéchuáng　folding bed

折叠剪 zhédiéjiǎn　folding scissors

折叠椅 zhédiéyǐ　folding chair

折叠翼飞机 zhédiéyì fēijī　folding-wing aircraft

折兑 zhéduì　exchange (gold or silver) for money; convert

折返 zhéfǎn　turn back (halfway)

折服 zhéfú　① subdue; bring into submission; convince: 艰难困苦～不了为正义事业而奋斗的人。No hardship can subdue people fighting for a just cause. / 强词夺理不能～人。You cannot convince people by sophistry. ② be convinced; be filled with admiration: 令人～ compel admiration

折福 zhéfú　*old* have one's good fortune compromised by having or getting more than one deserves: 王老三欲待回礼，陈青就坐上一把按住道：“你老人家不须多礼。却不怕折了那小厮一世之福？”(《醒世恒言·陈多寿生死夫妻》) Wang Laosan was about to return the civility when Chen Qing pressed the old man down firmly in his chair, saying, "You mustn't be so formal with him. To treat him like this will only compromise his fortune!"

折干 zhégān　give money as a gift

折光 zhéguāng　(of water, glass, etc.) refract light

折光度 zhéguāngdù　*phys.* dioptre

折桂 zhéguì　pluck the cassia—① pass the imperial examinations ② carry off the first prize; win a championship

折合 zhéhé　convert into; amount to: 把美元～成瑞士法郎 convert dollars into Swiss francs / 一英镑～成人民币是多少? How much is a pound in terms of Renminbi? or How many Renminbi *yuan* to the pound? / 水泥每包五十公斤，～一百market斤。Each bag of cement weighs 50 kilogrammes, that is, 100 *jin*.

折回 zhéhuí　turn back (halfway): 他刚走出不远又～来了。He hadn't gone very far when he turned back.

折戟沉沙 zhé jǐ chén shā　broken halberds embedded in sand—reminder of a fierce battle or a beaten army

折价 zhéjià　convert into money; evaluate in terms of money: ～退赔 pay compensation at the market price

折旧 zhéjiù　*econ.* depreciation (in value of property): ～费 depreciation charge / ～基金 depreciation fund / ～率 rate of depreciation

折扣 zhé·kòu　discount; rebate: 这价钱已经打了～了。This is the discounted price. / 执行上级指示不打～ carry out instructions to the letter

折门 zhémén　*archit.* folding door; accordion door

折磨 zhémó　cause physical or mental suffering; torment: 受疾病的～ suffer severely from a lingering illness / 在狱中受尽～ be subjected to various torments in prison

折辱 zhérǔ　*formal* humiliate

折杀 zhéshā (also 折煞 zhéshā)　*old* overwhelm sb. with special favour: 慌得婆子没理会处，连声应道：“是，是，莫要～老身! 大官人请起。老身有话讲。”(《今古奇观·蒋兴哥重会珍珠衫》) The old woman was too startled to know what to do, and she said again and again, "All

right, all right! You're overwhelming me with all this. Now, please get up. There is something I have to say."

折扇 zhéshàn　folding fan

折射 zhéshè　*phys.* refraction: ～本领 refractivity; refringence / ～波 refracted wave / ～计 refractometer / ～角 angle of refraction; refraction angle / ～率 index of refraction; refracting power / ～望远镜 refracting telescope / ～线 refracted ray

折实 zhéshí　① reckon the actual amount after a discount ② adjust payment in accordance with the price index of certain commodities

折寿 zhéshòu　have one's allotted portion of life reduced by having or getting more than one deserves

折受 zhéshou　*dial.* be overwhelmed by attentions, favours, etc.

折算 zhésuàn　convert: 把人民币～成法郎 convert Renminbi into francs / ～率 conversion rate

折头 zhétou　*dial.* discount; rebate

折线 zhéxiàn　*math.* broken line

折腰 zhéyāo　*liter.* bend one's back—bow in obeisance; cringe: 陶渊明不能为五斗米～。Tao Yuanming found it impossible to bend his back (*or* to cringe) for five pecks of rice (which was the regulation salary of a magistrate). / 江山如此多娇，引无数英雄竞～。(毛泽东) This land so rich in beauty Has made countless heroes bow in homage.

折页 zhéyè　*print.* folding: ～机 folding machine

折帐 zhézhàng　pay a debt in kind

折纸 zhézhǐ　paper folding

折中 zhézhōng　(also 折衷 zhézhōng) compromise: ～方案 a compromise proposal

折衷主义 zhézhōngzhǔyì　eclecticism

折子 zhézi　booklet in accordion form with a slipcase, used for keeping accounts, etc.

折子钱 zhéziqián　*dial.* usury

折子戏 zhézixì　highlights from operas

哲(喆) zhé　① wise; sagacious: 哲人 zhérén ② wise man; sage: 先哲 xiānzhé

哲理 zhélǐ　philosophic theory; philosophy: 这首诗富有～性。This poem is philosophical.

哲人 zhérén　*formal* sage; philosopher

哲学 zhéxué　philosophy: ～家 philosopher

辄(輒) zhé　*formal* ① always; often: 所言～听 always heed sb.'s advice ② then: 饮少～醉 get drunk after a few sips

蛰(蟄) zhé　*formal* hibernate

蛰伏 zhéfú　① *zool.* dormancy; hibernation ② same as 蛰居 zhéjū

蛰居 zhéjū　*formal* live in seclusion: ～书斋 cloister oneself in one's study

蜇 zhé　see 海蜇 hǎizhé ——see also zhē

谪(謫) zhé　*formal* ① relegate a high official to a minor post in an outlying district (as a form of punishment in feudal times); banish; exile: 贬谪 biǎnzhé ② (of immortals) be banished from Heaven ③ censure; blame: 众口交～ be censured by everybody

谪居 zhéjū　(of officials in former times) live in banishment: 苏东坡曾～黄州。At one time Su Dongpo lived at Huangzhou in banishment.

谪迁 zhéqiān　*formal* (of court officials in former times) be banished to a minor post in an outlying district

谪戍 zhéshù　(of officials in former times) be banished to a frontier post

谪仙 zhéxiān banished immortal—a wayward genius: 李～ Li the Banished Immortal (a fancy name for Li Bai 李白) (it was believed that immortals who had misbehaved in Heaven were as a punishment banished to live on earth for a fixed period, where they figured as wayward and extraordinary human beings)

磔[1] zhé dismemberment of the body (as a form of punishment in ancient China)

磔[2] zhé *formal* right-falling stroke (in Chinese characters)

辙 zhé ① the track of a wheel; rut ② direction of traffic: 戗～儿行驶 drive in the wrong direction (against traffic regulations) ③ rhyme (of a song, poetic drama, etc.): 合辙 hézhé ④ *dial.* (usu. used after 有 or 没) way; idea: 没辙 méizhé

辙叉 zhéchā *railway* frog

辙口 zhékǒu rhyme (of a song, poetic drama, etc.)

辙乱旗靡 zhéluàn-qímǐ crisscross chariot tracks and drooping banners (said of an army in headlong flight)

zhě

者[1]**(者)** zhě *part.* ① (used after a verb or adjective, or a verb or adjective phrase to indicate a class of persons or things) one or those who; the thing or things which; -er: 译～ translator / 出版～ publisher / 符合标准～ those which are up to standard / 老～ old man / 大～ the big one / 前(后)～ the former (latter) / 贫(富)～ the poor (rich) ② (used after a noun phrase ending with 工作 "work" or 主义 "ism" to indicate the person or persons doing the stated work or holding the stated doctrine) -er; -ist: 医务工作～ medical worker / 马克思主义～ Marxist ③ *formal* (used with the numbers 二、三、数, etc.): 二～ these two things / 三～ these three things / 两～缺一不可。 Neither is dispensable. ④ *formal* (used after a word, phrase, or clause to mark a pause, as in giving definitions): 仁～, 人也; 义～, 宜也。(《中庸》) Benevolence is acting like a human being; righteousness is doing what is right. ⑤ *old* (used at the end of a command): 路上小心在意～! Take care on the way.

者[2]**(者)** zhě *old* this: ～边 this side; here / ～番 on this occasion; this time

锗 zhě *chem.* germanium (Ge)

赭 zhě reddish brown; burnt ochre

赭石 zhěshí ochre (a mineral)

褶(襵) zhě pleat; crease: 把衬衫上的～儿熨平 iron the wrinkles out of the shirt

褶皱 zhězhòu ① *geol.* fold: ～作用 folding / ～山 folded mountain ② wrinkle (in the skin)

褶子 zhězi ① pleat: 她的裙子有～。 Her skirt has pleats. ② crease; fold; wrinkle: 用熨斗把～熨平。 Iron out the wrinkles. ③ wrinkle (on the face)

zhè

这(這) zhè ① this: ～地方 this place / ～一回 this time / ～究竟是怎么回事? What's all this

about? / ～都是我们厂的新产品。 These are new products from our plant. / ～才是好孩子! That's a good boy (girl)! *or* That's a dear! / ～消息我知道了。 I've heard that news already. *or* Yes, so I've heard. / ～就对了。 Now, you're on the right track. *or* Now, that's better. ② now: 他～才知道锻炼身体的好处。 Only now does he see the good of taking exercise. / 我～就走。 I'm leaving right now. ——see also zhèi

这儿 zhèr *inf.* ① here ② (used after 打, 从 or 由 only) now; then: 打～起我就要天天学英语了。 From now on I'm going to study English every day. / 从～以后我再也没见着他。 Since then I haven't seen him again.

这般 zhèbān such; so; like this: ～仔细 so careful / ～大小 this size; this big

这边 zhèbiān this side; here: 到～来。 Come over here. / 正义在我们～。 Justice is on our side. / 踏遍青山人未老, 风景～独好。(毛泽东) Crossing these blue hills adds nothing to one's years, The landscape here is beyond compare.

这程子 zhèchéngzi *dial.* these days; recently: 你～到哪儿去了? Where have you been these last few days?

这次 zhècì this time; present; current: ～会议 the present session / ～运动 the current movement (*or* campaign) / ～我们提前三天完成了任务。 This time we fulfilled our task three days ahead of schedule.

这等 zhèděng like this; so; such: 天下哪有～事? How can there be such a thing? / 何必～费心? Why take so much trouble?

这番 zhèfān this; these: 感谢你～好意。 I appreciate your kindness.

这个 zhège ① this one; this: ～孩子真乖。 This child is a little dear. / ～比那个沉。 This one is heavier than that one. / 他为了～忙了好几天。 He's been busy with this for quite a few days. ② *inf.* (used before a verb or adjective to give force to it) so; such: 看见大象吹口琴, 孩子们～乐啊! When they saw the elephant blowing the mouth organ, the children roared with laughter. ③ (repeated to show hesitation): 他叫～～我想不起来了。 His name is…ah…I cannot remember.

这号人 zhèhàorén *dial.* people of this sort: 像他～, 还是少跟他来往好。 You'd better have less to do with people of his sort.

这会儿 zhèhuìr (also 这会子 zhèhuìzi) *inf.* now; at the moment; at present: 你～又上哪儿去呀? Where are you going now? / ～电话占线。 The line's busy at the moment. / 去年～我还在深圳呢。 I was in Shenzhen at this time last year.

这里 zhèlǐ here: 我们～一年种两季稻子。 We grow two crops of rice a year here.

这么 zhème (also 这末 zhème) so; such; this way; like this: 他就是～个人。 That's just like him. / 那个句子应该～译。 The sentence should be translated this way. / 大家都～说。 So they say. / 往～挪一挪。 Move over this way a little bit. / 有～回事。 Yes, that's true.

这么点儿 zhèmediǎnr such a little bit: ～水, 怕不够喝。 I'm afraid so little water won't be enough to drink. / ～路一会儿就走到了。 It is so close, we can walk there in a short time.

这么些 zhèmexiē so much; so many: ～活儿, 得有个人帮帮你吧? Surely you need some help with so much work? / ～人, 坐得开吗? Is there seating for that many people?

这么样 zhèmeyàng so; such; like this; this way: 那蛇差不多有～长。 The snake was about so long. / 他老～说话吗? Does he often talk like this? / 要是～, 事情会闹大的。 That would blow up the affair.

这么着 zhèmezhe like this; so: ～才能瞄得准。 You should take aim like this. / ～好。 It's better this way. /

要是～, 那我就去吧。In that case, I'll go.

这山望着那山高 zhè shān wàngzhe nà shān gāo　it's always the other mountain that looks higher; always think the grass is greener on the other side of the hill; never be happy where one is

这些 zhè·xiē (also 这些个 zhèxiēge) these: ～日子我们特别忙。We've been particularly busy these days.

这样 zhèyàng　so; such; like this; this way: 别走～快。Don't walk so fast. / 有～的事? How could such a thing happen? / ～的文学作品很受群众欢迎。Literary works of this kind are well received by the masses. / 他怎么病成～了? How did he get so ill? / 如果你们觉得可以～办, 就～办。If you people feel this is the right thing to do, then do it. / 一会儿～, 一会儿那样 now one way, now another / 情况就是～。That's how it is.

这样那样 zhèyàng-nàyàng　this or that; of one kind or another; in one way or another: 由于～的原因 for this or that reason / 存在～的分歧 have differences of one kind or another / ～的问题 one question or another; various problems; all sorts of problems

这咱 zhèzan　dial.　now; at the moment; at present: ～我该走了。I must be going now.

这早晚儿 zhèzǎowǎnr　so late: ～还去干什么! It's too late to go.

柘 zhè　bot.　three-bristle cudrania (Cudrania tricuspidata)

浙(淛) Zhè　short for 浙江 Zhèjiāng

浙江 Zhèjiāng　Zhejiang (Province)

蔗 zhè　sugarcane

蔗螟 zhèmíng　sugarcane borer

蔗农 zhènóng　sugarcane grower

蔗糖 zhètáng ① chem.　sucrose: ～酶 sucrase / ～蜜 cane molasses ② cane sugar

蔗渣 zhèzhā　bagasse

嗻 zhè　aye (formerly used by servants to indicate attentiveness)

鹧 zhè　see below

鹧鸪 zhègū　zool.　Chinese francolin; partridge

鹧鸪菜 zhègūcài　zhegucai (Caloglossa leprieurii)

zhe

着(著) zhe　part. ① (added to a verb or adjective to indicate a continued action or state, often with the particle 呢 at the end of the sentence): 大门敞～。The gate is wide open. / 他穿～一身新衣服。He is wearing new clothes. / 雪正下～呢。It's snowing. / 别站～, 坐下吧。Don't just stand there; sit down. / 他们正谈～话呢, 请你在外头等几分钟吧。They are having a talk just now. Will you please wait outside for a few minutes. / 夜深了, 屋里的灯却还亮～。It was late at night, but the lights in the room were still on. ② (in sentences beginning with a place word, added to the verb to indicate a resultant state, the verb plus 着 having the force of "there is"): 桌儿上放～好些东西。There are a lot of things lying on the table. / 墙上挂～一幅山水画。On the wall hangs a landscape painting. / 水渠两旁栽～高高的白杨树。On either side of the ditch were planted tall white poplars. ③ (verb plus 着 placed before another verb, indicating an accompanying action or state) ⓐ (verb plus 着 serving as an adverbial modifier): 他爱吃～饭看报。He likes to read

the newspaper while eating. / 路不远, 咱们走～去吧。It's quite near, let's go there on foot. / 他老低～头走路。He always walks with his head bent down. / 探险队冒～大雪上山。The expedition climbed the mountain in spite of the heavy snow. / 孩子们急～要出去玩儿。The children are in a hurry to go outside and play. / 他正忙～准备考试。He is busy preparing for the examination just now. ⓑ (verb plus 着 repeated, indicating that while one action is in progress the occurrence of another is expected): 她想～想～笑了起来。She thought and thought and then burst out laughing. / 我们走～走～天色已经暗了下来。As we walked along, it began to grow dark. ④ (in imperative sentences, used after verbs or adjectives for emphasis, often with 点儿 added): 等～! Wait! / 慢～! Hold it! / 你听～。You just listen. / 快～点儿。Be quick. / 这事儿你记～点儿。Be sure to remember this. / 过马路看着～点儿。Mind how you cross the street. ——see also zhāo; zháo; zhuó

着呢 zhene (also 着哩 zheli)　inf.　(used as an intensive at the end of a sentence, after adjectives or verbs that admit of differences of degree) very (much); quite; awfully: 他阔～。He is awfully rich. / 天儿冷～。It's dreadfully cold. / 那条路难走～。The going is very hard over that road. / 我想你～。I miss you terribly. / 街上热闹～。The streets are full of noise and excitement. / 他会说～。He's a very good talker.

zhèi

这(這) zhèi　a variant pronunciation for 这 zhè, used in colloquial speech before a classifier or a numerial-classifier compound: ～本词典 this dictionary / ～三架飞机 these three planes

zhēn

贞¹ zhēn ① loyal; faithful: 坚贞 jiānzhēn ② (of women) chastity or virginity: 贞女 zhēnnǚ

贞² zhēn　divination (in ancient times)

贞操 zhēncāo ① chastity or virginity ② loyalty; moral integrity

贞节 zhēnjié ① loyalty; constancy ② chastity or virginity (i.e. remaining chaste and faithful to one's husband or betrothed, even after his death, as demanded by the feudal moral code)

贞洁 zhēnjié　chaste and undefiled

贞烈 zhēnliè　ready to die to preserve one's chastity

贞女 zhēnnǚ　a chaste girl; virgin

贞淑 zhēnshū　formal　chaste and gentle

针(鍼) zhēn ① needle: 缝纫～ sewing needle ② stitch: 在袜子上缝两～ sew (or put) a couple of stitches in a sock / 织漏一～ drop a stitch / 伤口缝了四～。The wound was closed with four stitches. ③ anything like a needle: 松针 sōngzhēn / 时针 shízhēn ④ injection; shot: 打针 dǎzhēn ⑤ acupuncture: 针灸 zhēnjiǔ

针鼻儿 zhēnbír　the eye of a needle

针砭 zhēnbiān ① an ancient form of acupuncture ② point out sb.'s errors and offer salutary advice

针布 zhēnbù　text.　card clothing

针插不进, 水泼不进 zhēn chā bù jìn, shuǐ pō bù jìn　impenetrable and watertight (said of an exclusive group, etc.)

针刺疗法　zhēncì liáofǎ　acupuncture treatment

针刺麻醉　zhēncì mázuì　acupuncture anaesthesia: ～心脏手术 heart surgery with acupuncture anaesthesia

针对　zhēnduì　① be directed against; be aimed at; counter: 这个条约～任何第三国。The treaty is not directed against any third country. / 这个讲话～性很强。There was no mistaking what the talk was aimed at. / ～这种倾向，我们需要加强自然科学的基础理论的研究。To counter this tendency, we must strengthen research in the basic theories of natural science. ② in the light of; in accordance with; in connection with: ～儿童的特点进行教育 educate children in accordance with their special characteristics / ～这种情况 in view of this situation

针锋相对　zhēnfēng xiāng duì　give tit for tat; be diametrically opposed to: 进行～的斗争 wage a tit-for-tat (or blow-for-blow) struggle against

针箍　zhēngū　dial.　thimble

针剂　zhēnjì　pharm.　injection

针尖　zhēnjiān　the point of a needle; pinpoint

针尖大的窟窿，斗大的风　zhēnjiān dà de kūlong, dǒu dà de fēng　a big wind can blow through a small hole; a little leak can sink a great ship

针尖对麦芒　zhēnjiān duì màimáng　a pin against an awl; diamond cut diamond: 这妯娌俩可真是针尖对住麦芒了。These two sisters-in-law are like diamond cutting diamond.

针脚　zhēnjiao　stitch: 把～缝得密一些。Make your stitches closer together. / 她缭贴边～又细又匀。She sewed the hem with small, neat stitches. / ～太大了。The stitches are too long. / 顺着线头找～ pick up clues

针灸　zhēnjiǔ　acupuncture and moxibustion: ～铜人 a bronze figure marked with acupuncture points

针麻　zhēnmá　short for 针刺麻醉 zhēncì mázuì

针梳机　zhēnshūjī　text.　gill box

针头　zhēntóu　med.　syringe needle

针头线脑　zhēntóu-xiànnǎo　inf.　odds and ends needed for sewing; needle and thread; sewing kit

针尾鸭　zhēnwěiyā　zool.　pintail

针线　zhēnxian　needlework: ～活儿 needlework; stitching; sewing / ～学 learn how to do needlework

针线包　zhēnxianbāo　sewing kit

针眼　zhēnyǎn　① the eye of a needle ② pinprick

针眼　zhēnyan　med.　sty

针鼹　zhēnyǎn　zool.　echidna; spiny anteater

针叶树　zhēnyèshù　coniferous tree; conifer

针织　zhēnzhī　knitting: ～外衣 knitted (or knit) coat / ～机 knitting machine

针织厂　zhēnzhīchǎng　knitting mill; knit goods mill

针织品　zhēnzhīpǐn　knit goods; knitwear; hosiery

针黹　zhēnzhǐ　formal　needlework

侦

侦　zhēn　detect; scout; investigate: 侦探 zhēntàn

侦查　zhēnchá　leg.　investigate (a crime)

侦察　zhēnchá　reconnoitre; scout: 敌后～ reconnoitre the enemy rear / 进行～活动 conduct reconnaissance / ～敌情 gather intelligence about the enemy / ～飞行 reconnaissance flight

侦察兵　zhēnchábīng　scout

侦察部队　zhēnchá bùduì　reconnaissance troops (or unit); scouting force

侦察机　zhēnchájī　reconnaissance plane; scout

侦察卫星　zhēnchá wèixīng　reconnaissance (or spy) satellite

侦察员　zhēncháyuán　scout

侦缉　zhēnjī　track down and arrest

侦破　zhēnpò　investigate and uncover; detect; solve: ～案件 solve a case; crack a criminal case

侦探　zhēntàn　① do detective work ② detective; spy

侦探小说　zhēntàn xiǎoshuō　detective story; detective fiction; crime novel: ～作家 writer of detective fiction; crime-writer

侦听　zhēntīng　intercept (enemy radio communications); monitor: ～器 detectaphone / ～台 intercept station

珍 (珎)

珍 (珎)　zhēn　① treasure: 珍宝 zhēnbǎo ② precious; valuable; rare: 珍品 zhēnpǐn ③ value highly; treasure: 珍惜 zhēnxī

珍爱　zhēn'ài　treasure; love dearly; be very fond of: 他非常～老战士送给自己的针线包。He treasures the sewing kit the old soldier gave him.

珍宝　zhēnbǎo　jewellery; treasure: ～馆 Treasures Hall (in the Palace Museum)

珍本　zhēnběn　rare edition; rare book

珍藏　zhēncáng　collect (rare books, art treasures, etc.)

珍贵　zhēnguì　valuable; precious: ～药材 valuable ingredients of traditional Chinese medicine / ～的历史文物 precious historical relics / ～的纪念品 precious mementos

珍品　zhēnpǐn　treasure: 艺术～ art treasure

珍奇　zhēnqí　rare: ～的动物 rare animals

珍禽异兽　zhēnqín-yìshòu　rare birds and animals

珍赏　zhēnshǎng　treasure and delight in (curios, etc.); highly value and appreciate

珍摄　zhēnshè　formal　(used in letters) take good care of yourself: 至盼善自～。I hope you'll take good care of yourself.

珍视　zhēnshì　value; prize; cherish; treasure: 教育青年人～今天的美好生活 teach young people to prize the happy life they lead today / ～我们两国人民之间的友谊 treasure the friendship between the peoples of our two countries

珍玩　zhēnwán　rare curios

珍味　zhēnwèi　rare delicacies; dainties

珍闻　zhēnwén　news titbits; fillers: 世界～ world briefs (or miscellany)

珍惜　zhēnxī　treasure; value; cherish: ～革命的成果 treasure the fruits of the revolution / ～时间 value one's time / ～劳动人民创造出来的财富 cherish the wealth created by the labouring people. / ～人才 value people of ability

珍稀　zhēnxī　rare and precious: ～动物 rare animals

珍馐　zhēnxiū　(also 珍羞 zhēnxiū)　formal　delicacies; dainties

珍异　zhēnyì　same as 珍奇 zhēnqí

珍重　zhēnzhòng　① highly value; treasure; set great store by: 我～你对我的信任。I highly value the trust you place in me. ② take good care of yourself: 两人紧紧握手，互道～。They clasped hands, each asking the other to take good care of himself.

珍珠　zhēnzhū　pearl

珍珠贝　zhēnzhūbèi　pearl shell; pearl oyster

珍珠港　Zhēnzhūgǎng　Pearl Harbour

珍珠鸡　zhēnzhūjī　guinea fowl

珍珠梅　zhēnzhūméi　bot.　false spiraea

珍珠米　zhēnzhūmǐ　dial.　maize; (Indian) corn

珍珠岩　zhēnzhūyán　pearlite

胗

胗　zhēn　gizzard: 鸡～儿 chicken's gizzard

胗肝儿　zhēngānr　gizzard and liver (esp. chicken's or duck's)

帧

帧　zhēn　m.　(for a picture, etc.): 一～油画 an oil painting

帧频　zhēnpín　TV　frame frequency; picture frequency

祯

祯　zhēn　formal　auspicious; propitious

桢 zhēn ① hardwood ② terminal posts used in building a wall in ancient times

桢干 zhēngàn *formal* core member; backbone (element)

真 zhēn ① true; real; genuine: ～丝 real silk / 这幅宋人的画是～的。This is a genuine Song painting. / 我～的要走了。It's true I'm leaving. ② *adv.* really; truly; indeed: 我～不知道。I really don't know. / 他～信了。He actually believed it. / 时间过得～快。How time flies! / 演出～精采。The performance was just splendid. / 这家伙～能说。That fellow is a very glib talker. / 给你添了不少麻烦，～过意不去。I'm very sorry to have put you to so much trouble. / 你～不害臊。You've got some nerve! / 你通过了考试，～行! You've passed the exams—good for you! / ～有你的! You're a smart fellow, you are! ③ clear; unmistakable: 你看得～么? Can you see clearly? / 字音咬得～ pronounce words distinctly ④ short for 真书 zhēnshū

真北 zhēnběi true north

真才实学 zhēncái-shíxué real ability and learning; genuine talent: 有～的人 a person of real ability and learning / 有～的科技人员 well-trained scientific and technical personnel / 我决不计较学位，我只讲～。I won't quibble about a degree. I'm only concerned with true talent and learning.

真诚 zhēnchéng sincere; genuine; true: ～的愿望 a sincere wish (or desire) / ～的友谊 true friendship / ～悔过 sincerely (or genuinely) repent / ～合作 sincerely cooperate / ～地执行协议 implement the agreement in good faith

真传 zhēnchuán be handed down in a direct line from the master

真刀真枪 zhēndāo-zhēnqiāng real swords and spears—the real thing: ～地干起来 start a shooting war; start in real earnest

真地平 zhēndìpíng *astron.* true horizon

真谛 zhēndì true essence; true meaning: 人生的～ the true meaning of life

真鲷 zhēndiāo genuine porgy; red porgy

真分数 zhēnfēnshù *math.* proper fraction

真格的 zhēngéde *dial.* real; true: 你别再装着玩儿啦，说～吧。Stop joking and tell me the truth. / ～，你到底去不去? Seriously, are you going or not? / 动～ start a shooting war or do sth. in real earnest

真个 zhēngè *dial.* really; truly; indeed: ～了不起 really wonderful

真果 zhēnguǒ *bot.* true fruit

真话 zhēnhuà the truth: 你要说～。You must tell the truth.

真迹 zhēnjì authentic work (of painting or calligraphy): 这一幅画是宋人的～。This is an authentic Song painting.

真金不怕火炼 zhēnjīn bù pà huǒ liàn true gold fears no fire—a person of integrity can stand severest tests

真菌 zhēnjūn fungus

真空 zhēnkōng *phys.* vacuum: 未尽～ partial vacuum / ～泵 vacuum pump / ～处理 vacuum treatment / ～弹道 vacuum trajectory; vacuum flight path / ～电弧炉 vacuum arc furnace / ～镀膜 vacuum coating / ～过滤 vacuum filtration / ～技术 vacuum technique / ～吸尘器 vacuum cleaner / ～压铸 vacuum die casting

真空地带 zhēnkōng dìdài *mil.* no-man's-land

真空管 zhēnkōngguǎn same as 电子管 diànzǐguǎn

真理 zhēnlǐ truth: 马克思列宁主义的普遍～ the universal truth of Marxism-Leninism / 坚持～，修正错误 uphold the truth and correct mistakes

真面目 zhēnmiànmù true features; true colours: 认清其～ see sb. in his true colours; know sb. for what he is / 露出～ reveal one's true colours; betray oneself

真名实姓 zhēnmíng-shíxìng real name

真命 zhēnmìng ordained by Heaven: ～之主 an ordained ruler / ～天子 an ordained Son of Heaven

真皮 zhēnpí ① *physiol.* derma ② genuine leather

真凭实据 zhēnpíng-shíjù genuine evidence; hard evidence; conclusive proof

真漆 zhēnqī lacquer

真枪实弹 zhēnqiāng-shídàn real guns and bullets; live ammunition: 进行～的演习 conduct exercises (or manoeuvres) with live ammunition

真切 zhēnqiè vivid; clear; distinct: 这篇通讯写得～感人。The report is vividly written and very moving. / 看得～ see clearly

真情 zhēnqíng ① the real (or true) situation; the facts; the actual state of affairs; truth ② true feelings; real sentiments: ～的流露 a revelation of one's true feelings

真确 zhēnquè ① true; real; authentic: ～的消息 authentic (or reliable) news ② clear; distinct

真人 zhēnrén true man (i.e. a man who has attained enlightenment or immortality; used esp. in official Taoist titles): 太乙～ True Man of the Grand Unity / 玉鼎～ True Man of the Jade Tripod

真人真事 zhēnrén-zhēnshì real people and real events; actual persons and events: 这个电影说的是～。The film is a story of real people and real events. *or* The film is based on a true story.

真溶液 zhēnróngyè another name for 分子溶液 fēnzǐ róngyè

真善美 zhēn-shàn-měi the true, the good and the beautiful

真实 zhēnshí true; real; authentic: ～的感情 true feelings; real sentiments / ～情况 the real (or true) situation; how things actually stand / ～记录 authentic records / ～感 sense of reality / ～性 truthfulness; authenticity / ～的故事 a true story

真释 zhēnshì a correct explanation or interpretation

真是 zhēnshi (also 真是的 zhēnshide) (used to express displeasure or annoyance): 他把一支新笔丢了，～。It's too bad he's lost his new pen. / ～，做这种笨事。Well, really! What a stupid thing to do. / 下点雨就不让我们去，～。Just because of a bit of rain we're not allowed to go. The idea! / 你也～，连灯也不关，就走了。Look at this! You didn't even turn off the light when you left.

真书 zhēnshū (in Chinese calligraphy) regular script

真率 zhēnshuài sincere; unaffected; straightforward

真髓 zhēnsuǐ essence

真相 zhēnxiàng (also 真象 zhēnxiàng) the real (or true) situation; the real (or actual) facts; the actual state of affairs; truth: 掩盖～ cover up the facts / 弄清事情的～ clarify the truth of the matter / 给人以假象，而将～荫蔽着 conceal one's true features and give a false impression / 这就是事情的～。This is the actual state of affairs. *or* This is how things actually stand.

真相大白 zhēnxiàng dàbái the whole truth has come out; the whole affair is now out in the open

真心 zhēnxīn wholehearted; heartfelt; sincere: ～拥护 give wholehearted support to / ～话 sincere words / 说～话 speak from the bottom of one's heart / ～悔改 sincerely repent and earnestly reform oneself / ～爱某人 love sb. devotedly / 我知道你是～对我好。I know your affections for me are genuine.

真心实意 zhēnxīn-shíyì genuinely and sincerely; truly and whole-heartedly: ～地为人民谋福利 sincerely and whole-heartedly work for the well-being of the people / ～地把国家的事情办好 sincerely and honestly set the affairs of state to rights / 我们是～找你帮忙。We are asking you to do us this favour in dead earnest.

真性 zhēnxìng *med.* genuine: ～痴呆 genuine dementia / ～血友病 hemophilia vera

真赃实犯 zhēnzāng-shífàn irrefutable proof of guilt; material evidence of a crime

真真假假 zhēnzhēnjiǎjiǎ the true mingled with the false; a mixture of truth and falsehood

真正 zhēnzhèng genuine; true; real: ～的吉林人参 genuine Jilin ginseng / ～的朋友 a true friend / ～的革命者 a true (*or* genuine) revolutionary / ～领会文件的精神实质 have a real grasp of the essence of the document / ～的马列主义政党 genuine Marxist-Leninist parties / ～负起责任来 shoulder the responsibilities in earnest / ～有力量的是人民。 It's the people who are really powerful.

真知 zhēnzhī genuine (*or* real) knowledge

真知灼见 zhēnzhī-zhuójiàn real knowledge and deep insight; penetrating judgment

真值表 zhēnzhíbiǎo *phys.* truth table

真挚 zhēnzhì sincere; cordial: ～的友谊 sincere friendship

真珠 zhēnzhū same as 珍珠 zhēnzhū

真珠层 zhēnzhūcéng *zool.* pearly (*or* nacreous) layer

真主 Zhēnzhǔ *Islam* Allah

砧(碪) zhēn hammering block; anvil: 锻～ smith anvil

砧板 zhēnbǎn chopping block

砧骨 zhēngǔ *physiol.* incus; anvil

砧木 zhēnmù *agric.* stock

砧子 zhēnzi *inf.* hammering block; anvil

斟 zhēn pour (tea or wine): 给她～一杯酒。 Pour her a glass of wine.

斟酌 zhēnzhuó consider; deliberate: 再三～ consider carefully again and again / ～词句 weigh one's words / ～办理 act at one's discretion; act as one sees fit / ～情况作适当调整 make appropriate adjustments according to circumstances

甄 zhēn ① *formal* discriminate; distinguish; examine: 甄选 zhēnxuǎn ② (Zhēn) a surname

甄拔 zhēnbá select: ～人才 select people of talent

甄别 zhēnbié ① examine and distinguish; screen; discriminate ② reexamine a case

甄录 zhēnlù employ by an examination

甄审 zhēnshěn examine; screen

甄选 zhēnxuǎn select

蓁 zhēn see below

蓁蓁 zhēnzhēn *formal* ① luxuriant ② overgrown with brambles

榛 zhēn *bot.* hazel

榛鸡 zhēnjī hazel grouse

榛莽 zhēnmǎng *formal* luxuriant vegetation

榛实 zhēnshí hazelnut

榛子 zhēnzi ① hazel ② hazelnut

箴 zhēn *formal* ① admonish; exhort ② a type of didactic literary composition

箴言 zhēnyán *formal* admonition; exhortation; maxim

臻 zhēn *formal* ① attain (a high level): 交通日～便利。 Transportation and communications are becoming easier day by day. / 方法日～完善。 The methods are being perfected. ② reach; arrive: 百福并～。 May every blessing descend upon you!

鱵 zhēn *zool.* halfbeak

诊 zhěn examine (a patient): 出诊 chūzhěn

诊病 zhěnbìng diagnose a disease

诊察 zhěnchá examine (a patient)

诊断 zhěnduàn diagnose: 物理～ physical diagnosis / 医生～这病是胸膜炎。 The doctor diagnosed the illness (*or* case) as pleurisy.

诊断书 zhěnduànshū medical certificate

诊金 zhěnjīn consultation fee; hospital fee

诊例 zhěnlì hospital case: 临床～ a clinical case

诊疗 zhěnliáo make a diagnosis and give treatment: ～器械 medical instruments

诊脉 zhěnmài feel the pulse

诊视 zhěnshì examine (a patient)

诊室 zhěnshì (also 诊疗室 zhěnliáoshì) consulting room

诊所 zhěnsuǒ (also 诊疗所 zhěnliáosuǒ) clinic; dispensary: 王医生开了一个私人～。 Dr. Wang runs a private clinic.

诊治 zhěnzhì make a diagnosis and give treatment

枕 zhěn ① pillow ② rest the head on: ～着胳臂睡觉 sleep with one's head resting on one's arm ③ *mech.* block: 转～ swivel block

枕戈待旦 zhěn gē dài dàn lie with one's head pillowed on a spear, waiting for day to break—be ready for battle; maintain combat readiness

枕骨 zhěngǔ *physiol.* occipital bone

枕藉 zhěnjiè *formal* lying about; lying close together: 战场上尸体～。 The battlefield was strewn with corpses.

枕巾 zhěnjīn a towel used to cover a pillow

枕木 zhěnmù *railway* sleeper; tie

枕套 zhěntào (also 枕头套 zhěntoutào) pillowcase; pillowslip

枕头 zhěntou pillow

枕头箱 zhěntouxiāng pillow casket (a small box for valuables)

枕席 zhěnxí ① a mat used to cover a pillow; pillow mat ② bed

枕心 zhěnxīn (also 枕头心儿 zhěntouxīnr) pillow (without the pillowcase)

轸¹ zhěn *formal* ① the cross board at the rear of an ancient carriage ② carriage ③ the last of the twenty-eight constellations (二十八宿) into which the celestial sphere was divided in ancient Chinese astronomy (consisting of four stars in Corvus)

轸² zhěn *formal* sorrowful; distressed: ～悼 mourn with deep grief

轸念 zhěnniàn *formal* sorrowfully cherish the memory of sb.; think anxiously about: 殊深～ express great solicitude for sb.

疹 zhěn rash: 麻疹 mázhěn

疹子 zhěnzi *inf.* measles

畛 zhěn *formal* raised paths between fields

畛域 zhěnyù *formal* boundary: 不分畛域 bù fēn zhěnyù

缜(稹) zhěn see below

缜密 zhěnmì careful; meticulous; deliberate: ～的计划 a deliberate (*or* carefully thought-out) plan / ～的分析 a careful (*or* minute) analysis / ～的研究 a meticulous

study

zhèn

阵[1]　zhèn　① battle array (or formation): 长蛇阵 chángshézhèn ② position; front: 上阵 shàngzhèn

阵[2]　zhèn　① a period of time: 病了一～儿 be ill for some time / 那～儿 in those days; then / 这～儿 these days; recently ② m. short period; spell: 一～雨 a spatter of rain / 一～风 a gust (or blast) of wind / 一～寒潮 a cold spell / 一～咳嗽 a fit (or spasm) of coughing / 一～热烈的掌声 a burst of warm applause

阵地　zhèndì　position; front: 进入～ get into position / 人在～在 fight to the death in defence of one's position; hold one's position at all costs / ～攻击 (防御) positional attack (defence) / 前沿～ forward position / 思想～ ideological front

阵地战　zhèndìzhàn　positional warfare

阵法　zhènfǎ　tactical deployment of troops

阵风　zhènfēng　a gust of wind

阵脚　zhènjiǎo　① front line: 压住～ keep the troops in battle array; hold the line ② position; situation; circumstances: 乱了～ be thrown into confusion

阵容　zhènróng　① battle array (or formation) ② lineup: ～强大 have a strong lineup / 演员～整齐 a well-balanced cast

阵势　zhènshì　① battle array (or formation); a disposition of combat forces: 摆开～ deploy the ranks in battle array / 敌人的～全给打乱了。The enemy formations were completely broken up. ② situation; condition; circumstances

阵痛　zhèntòng　med. labour pains; throes (of childbirth)

阵头雨　zhèntóuyǔ　dial. thunder shower

阵图　zhèntú　a system of battle formations: 八～ the Eightfold Maze (Zhuge Liang's 诸葛亮 deployment of rock formations)

阵亡　zhènwáng　be killed in action; fall in battle

阵线　zhènxiàn　front; ranks; alignment: 革命～ an alignment of revolutionary forces / 民族统一～ national united front

阵型　zhènxíng　formation: 在这场足球比赛中，我队始终保持了4-3-3～。Our team played in 4-3-3 formation throughout the match.

阵雪　zhènxuě　snow shower

阵营　zhènyíng　a group of people who pursue a common interest; camp: 革命～ a revolutionary camp

阵雨　zhènyǔ　shower

阵仗　zhènzhang　① war; battle; combat: 咱见过大～，打过硬仗。I have seen action in a big war. ② dial. situation; occasion; spectacle

阵子　zhènzi　same as 阵[2] zhèn

圳(甽)　zhèn　dial. a ditch between fields

鸩[1]　zhèn　a legendary bird with poisonous feathers

鸩[2](酖)　zhèn　formal ① poisoned wine: 饮鸩止渴 yǐn zhèn zhǐ kě ② kill sb. with poisoned wine

鸩毒　zhèndú　formal poisoned wine: 宴安鸩毒 yàn'ān zhèndú

鸩酒　zhènjiǔ　poisoned wine

振　zhèn　① shake; flap: ～翅 flap the wings; flutter / ～笔直书 wield the pen furiously ② rise with force and spirit; brace up: 精神为之一～ feel one's spirits buoyed up / 我军士气大～。The morale of our troops was greatly boosted.

振拔　zhènbá　formal extricate oneself from a predicament and brace oneself up to action

振臂　zhènbì　raise one's arm: ～高呼 raise one's arm and shout (slogans, etc.)

振臂一呼　zhènbì yī hū　raise one's arm and cry for action—issue a call for action; sound the trumpet call of action

振荡　zhèndàng　① phys. vibration ② elec. oscillation: 本机～ local oscillation / 寄生～ parasitic oscillation / ～电路 oscillating circuit / ～管 oscillator valve / ～器 oscillator

振捣器　zhèndǎoqì　archit. vibrator

振动　zhèndòng　phys. vibration: 简谐～ simple harmonic vibration / 等时～ isochronous vibration / ～计 vibrometer / ～频率 vibration frequency

振奋　zhènfèn　① rouse oneself; rise with force and spirit; be inspired with enthusiasm: 人人～, 个个当先 everyone full of vigour, each one forging ahead ② inspire; stimulate: ～士气 boost (or raise) the morale (of the troops) / ～革命精神 inspire revolutionary enthusiasm; enhance revolutionary vigour; encourage a revolutionary spirit / 令人～的消息 heartening news

振奋人心　zhènfèn rénxīn　inspire people; fill people with enthusiasm: ～的事迹 inspiring deeds

振幅　zhènfú　phys. amplitude (of vibration): 脉冲～ pulse amplitude / 畸变～ amplitude distortion

振聋发聩　zhènlóng-fākuì　rouse the deaf, enlighten the benighted: 先生这番议论，真可谓之～。Your arguments, sir, would make a deaf man hear and a blind man see.

振刷　zhènshuā　formal bestir (or exert) oneself; display vigour

振兴　zhènxīng　develop vigorously; promote: ～中华 rejuvenate China / ～教育事业 vitalize education / ～工业 vigorously develop industry / 开创一个新的经济～时期 start a new period of vigorous economic growth

振振有词　zhènzhèn yǒu cí　speak plausibly and volubly (in self-justification)

振作　zhènzuò　bestir (or exert) oneself; display vigour: ～精神 bestir oneself; brace (or cheer) up / ～起来! Brace up! or Pull yourself together!

朕[1]　zhèn　I, the sovereign; we (used by a royal person in proclamations instead of I)

朕[2]　zhèn　formal sign; omen

朕兆　zhènzhào　formal sign; omen; portent: 有～可寻。There are signs for us to read.

赈　zhèn　relieve; aid: 赈灾 zhènzāi

赈济　zhènjì　relieve; aid: ～灾民 relieve the people in stricken areas; aid the victims of natural calamities

赈款　zhènkuǎn　relief fund

赈灾　zhènzāi　relieve the people in stricken areas

震　zhèn　① shake; shock; vibrate; quake: 他捶了一下桌子，杯子被～得跳起来。He gave the table a thump which shook the cups. ② greatly excited; deeply astonished; shocked: ～骇 shocked; stunned; astounded ③ one of the Eight Trigrams (八卦)

震波　zhènbō　geol. seismic wave; earthquake wave: ～图 seismogram

震颤　zhènchàn　tremble; quiver

震颤性麻痹　zhènchànxìng mábì　paralysis agitans

震旦纪　Zhèndànjì　geol. the Sinian Period

震荡　zhèndàng　shake; shock; vibrate; quake: 1976年唐山大地震的时候北京都感到～。Tremors were felt in

Beijing when a great earthquake rocked Tangshan in 1976.

震动 zhèndòng shake; shock; vibrate; quake: 春雷～山谷。Spring thunder shook the valley. / 火车～了一下，开走了。The train pulled out with a jerk. / 十月革命～了全世界。The October Revolution shook the world. / ～全国 reverberate through the whole country / 引起了广泛的～ produce wide repercussions / 这番话对他的思想～很大。The talk made a great impact on him.

震耳欲聋 zhèn ěr yù lóng deafening: ～的鞭炮声 the deafening noise of firecrackers

震古烁今 zhèngǔ-shuòjīn (also 震古铄今 zhèngǔ-shuòjīn) surpassing the ancients and amazing contemporaries

震骇 zhènhài shock; appal; astonish

震撼 zhènhàn shake; shock; vibrate: ～天地的英雄气概 earthshaking heroism

震撼人心 zhènhàn rénxīn stirring; thrilling

震级 zhènjí magnitude (of an earthquake)

震惊 zhènjīng shock; amaze; astonish: 南京大屠杀～中外。The Nanjing Massacre shocked the country and the whole world. / 听到他去世的消息我感到～。I was stunned by the news of his death.

震怒 zhènnù be enraged; be furious

震慑 zhènshè awe; frighten

震悚 zhènsǒng formal tremble with fear; be terrified; be frightened

震天动地 zhèntiān-dòngdì (also 震天撼地 zhèntiān-hàndì) shake heaven and earth: 示威群众的怒吼～。The angry shouts of the demonstrators rent the air.

震音 zhènyīn mus. tremolo

震源 zhènyuán focus (of an earthquake)

震中 zhènzhōng epicentre: ～区 epicentral area

镇[1] zhèn ① press down; keep down; ease: 镇纸 zhènzhǐ / 镇痛 zhèntòng ② calm; tranquil; at ease: 镇定 zhèndìng ③ guard; garrison: 坐镇 zuòzhèn ④ garrison post: 重镇 zhòngzhèn ⑤ town ⑥ a comparatively large trading centre ⑦ cool with cold water or ice: 把西瓜放在冷水里——～ put the watermelon in cold water for a while to chill it

镇[2] zhèn old ① often; frequently: 十年～相随。For ten years we were often together. ② a whole period: 镇日 zhènrì

镇尺 zhènchǐ paperweight (in the shape of a ruler)

镇定 zhèndìng calm; cool; composed; unruffled: 神色～ be calm and collected; show composure and presence of mind / 保持～ keep cool; remain calm; keep one's head

镇反 Zhènfǎn short for 镇压反革命运动 Zhènyā Fǎngémìng Yùndòng

镇服 zhènfú force sb. into submission

镇静 zhènjìng calm; cool; composed; unruffled: 遇到紧急情况要～。Keep calm in an emergency. / 努力～下来 compose oneself with an effort

镇静钢 zhènjìnggāng metall. killed steel

镇静剂 zhènjìngjì sedative; tranquillizer

镇流管 zhènliúguǎn elec. ballast tube

镇流器 zhènliúqì elec. ballast

镇日 zhènrì old the whole day; all day; all day long

镇慑 zhènshè cow sb. into submission

镇守 zhènshǒu guard (a strategically important place); garrison

镇痛 zhèntòng ① ease pain; relieve pain ② med. analgesia: 针刺～ acupuncture analgesia / ～效果 analgesic effect

镇痛剂 zhèntòngjì anodyne; analgesic; pain-killer

镇星 Zhènxīng the Quelling Star (old name for 土星 Tǔxīng)

镇压 zhènyā ① suppress; repress; put down: ～叛乱 put down a rebellion ② inf. execute (a counterrevolutionary): 那个杀人犯已经依法～了。The murderer was executed according to law. ③ agric. rolling; compacting; tamping

镇压反革命运动 Zhènyā Fǎngémìng Yùndòng the Movement to Suppress Counterrevolutionaries (1950-1952)

镇压器 zhènyāqì agric. (land) roller

镇长 zhènzhǎng town head

镇纸 zhènzhǐ paperweight

镇住 zhènzhù bring or keep sb. under control; reduce sb. to submission: 她镇得住孩子。She is good at controlling children. / 她第一次在音乐厅登台演出就把听众～了。Her debut took the concert hall by storm.

镇子 zhènzi dial. small town; market town

zhēng

丁 zhēng see below ——see also dīng

丁丁 zhēngzhēng onom. liter. the sound of chopping wood, plucking the strings of a musical instrument, etc.: 伐木～。Clang, clang goes the woodman's axe.

正 zhēng the first month of the lunar year; the first moon: 新正 xīnzhēng ——see also zhèng

正旦 zhēngdàn formal the lunar New Year's Day ——see also zhèngdàn

正月 zhēngyuè the first month of the lunar year; the first moon: ～初一 the lunar New Year's Day

争[1] (**爭**) zhēng ① contend; vie; strive: ～领导权 contend for leadership / 不～一日之短长 not strive for only temporary superiority / 不～一城一地的得失 not contend for a city or a piece of ground (in mobile warfare) / ～挑重担 rush to carry the heaviest load; vie with each other for the hardest job / ～着发言 try to have the floor before others / 春～日，夏～时。In spring every day counts, in summer every hour. ② argue; dispute: 你们在～什么? What are you arguing about? ③ dial. short of; wanting: 总数还～多少? How many more are needed to make up the total?

争[2] (**爭**) zhēng old how; why: ～知 how does one know

争霸 zhēngbà contend (or struggle) for hegemony; scramble (or strive) for supremacy: ～世界 contend for world domination (or hegemony)

争辩 zhēngbiàn argue; debate; contend: 无休止的～ an endless debate / 真理不怕～。Truth does not fear contention.

争长论短 zhēngcháng-lùnduǎn squabble; argue

争吵 zhēngchǎo quarrel; wrangle; squabble: 无谓的～ a pointless quarrel / 激烈的～ fierce (or bitter) wrangling / ～不休 bicker (or squabble) endlessly

争持 zhēngchí refuse to give in; stick to one's guns

争宠 zhēngchǒng strive for sb's favour

争斗 zhēngdòu ① fight ② struggle; contend

争端 zhēngduān controversial issue; dispute; conflict: 国际～ an international dispute / 边界～ a border dispute / 引起～ give rise (or lead) to a dispute / 挑起～ provoke a dispute / 解决～ settle a dispute / 当事国～ parties to a dispute (between nations) / 调解两国～ act as mediator in a conflict between two countries

争夺 zhēngduó fight (or contend, scramble) for; enter into rivalry with sb. over sth.; vie with sb. for sth.: ～制高点 fight (or contend) for possession of a commanding height / ～市场 scramble for markets / ～势力范围

scramble for spheres of influence / ～核优势 vie for nuclear superiority / ～冠军 compete for a championship

争分夺秒 zhēngfēn-duómiǎo　race (*or* work) against time; make every minute and second count

争风吃醋 zhēngfēng-chīcù　fight for the affections of a man *or* woman

争锋 zhēngfēng　fight for mastery; strive for a decisive victory

争光 zhēngguāng　win honour (*or* glory) for: 为祖国～ win honour for our homeland; bring credit to (*or* be a credit to) our country

争衡 zhēnghéng　scramble for supremacy; strive for mastery; be in rivalry with

争斤论两 zhēngjīn-lùnliǎng　haggle over every ounce; be calculating

争竞 zhēngjing　*dial.*　haggle over; fuss about

争脸 zhēngliǎn　(also 争面子 zhēngmiànzi) try to win credit or honour

争论 zhēnglùn　controversy; dispute; debate; contention: 不同意见的～ controversies over differing opinions / 激烈的～ a heated dispute / ～不休 an endless debate / ～的双方 the two contending sides / ～之点 the point at issue / 科学上不同学派的自由～ free contention among different schools in science

争名夺利 zhēngmíng-duólì　strive (*or* scramble) for fame and gain: ～，唯利是图 scramble for fame and fortune and be interested only in personal gain

争鸣 zhēngmíng　contend: 百家争鸣 bǎijiā zhēngmíng

争奈 zhēngnài　*old*　nevertheless; unfortunately

争奇斗艳 zhēngqí-dòuyàn　(of flowers, etc.) vie with each other for glamour

争气 zhēngqì　try to make a good showing; try to win credit for; try to bring credit to: 为中国工人～ bring credit to the Chinese workers / 有人说妇女干不了这种工作，我们要争这口气。Some people say women can't do this job, but we'll show them.

争抢 zhēngqiǎng　fight for; scramble for

争取 zhēngqǔ　strive for; fight for; win over: ～民族解放 strive for national liberation / ～群众 win over the masses / ～选票 canvass for votes / ～入党 strive to qualify for Party membership / ～时间 race (*or* work) against time / ～主动 try to gain the initiative; contend for the initiative / 要～一切可以～的人，团结一切可以团结的人。We must win over all people who can be won over, unite with all people who can be united. / 你能给我们杂志写点什么吗?—我～吧。Can you write something for the magazine?—Well, I'll try.

争权夺利 zhēngquán-duólì　scramble for power and profit; struggle for power

争胜 zhēngshèng　compete for first place

争讼 zhēngsòng　contest a lawsuit

争先 zhēngxiān　try to be the first to do sth.: 大家～发言。Everyone tried to get the floor.

争先恐后 zhēngxiān-kǒnghòu　strive to be the first and fear to lag behind; vie with each other in doing sth.: ～地报名参军 vie with each other in signing up for military service / 大家～地抢好坐位。There was a scramble for the best seats.

争雄 zhēngxióng　contend for supremacy

争议 zhēngyì　dispute; controversy: 有～的地区 a disputed area / 有～的条款 a contentious clause / 一本有～的书 a controversial book / 一个有～的历史人物 a controversial historical figure

争战 zhēngzhàn　fight; war: 连年～ long years of war

争执 zhēngzhí　disagree; dispute; stick to one's position (*or* guns)

争执不下 zhēngzhí bù xià　each stands (*or* holds) his ground; each sticks to his own stand; each sticks to his guns

怔 zhēng　seized with terror; terrified; panic-stricken——see also zhèng

怔忡 zhēngchōng　*Chin. med.*　palpitation

怔营 zhēngyíng　*formal*　in a state of alarm (*or* trepidation)

怔忪 zhēngzhōng　*formal*　alarmed and panicky; terrified; panic-stricken; seized with terror

征[1]　zhēng　① go on a journey: 征途 zhēngtú ② go on an expedition (*or* a campaign): 出征 chūzhēng

征[2]（徵）　zhēng　① levy (troops); call up; draft: 征兵 zhēngbīng ② levy (taxes); collect; impose: 征粮 zhēngliáng ③ ask for; solicit: 征稿 zhēnggǎo

征[3]（徵）　zhēng　① evidence; proof: 有实物可～。There is solid evidence. / 无～之言 an unfounded assertion ② sign; portent: 特征 tèzhēng

征兵 zhēngbīng　conscription; draft; call-up: ～年龄 conscription age; age for enlistment / ～站 drafting centre

征兵法 zhēngbīngfǎ　conscription (*or* draft) law

征兵制 zhēngbīngzhì　universal military service; conscription system

征尘 zhēngchén　*liter.*　dust which settles on one during a journey: 衣上～杂酒痕，远游无处不销魂。(陆游) On my clothes the dust of travel mingled with wine stains; A distant journey—no place that doesn't jar the soul!

征程 zhēngchéng　journey

征调 zhēngdiào　requisition; call up: ～物资和人员 requisition supplies and draft personnel

征伐 zhēngfá　go on a punitive expedition

征帆 zhēngfān　*formal*　a ship on a long voyage

征服 zhēngfú　conquer; subjugate: 诺曼人在十一世纪～了英格兰。The Normans conquered England in the 11th century. / ～自然 conquer nature / ～黄河 tame the Huanghe River / 她的歌声～了北京听众。Her singing took Beijing by storm.

征稿 zhēnggǎo　solicit contributions (to a journal, etc.)

征购 zhēnggòu　requisition by purchase: 粮食～ grain purchases by the state / ～任务 state purchase quotas

征候 zhēnghòu　sign: 病人已有好转的～。The patient shows signs of a turn for the better.

征集 zhēngjí　① collect: ～签名 collect signatures (for an appeal) / ～军粮 collect grain for the army / ～物资 the acquisition of supplies ② draft; call up; recruit: ～新兵 recruitment / 战时～ wartime draft / ～补充兵员 call up new recruits to replenish the ranks / 定期～和退役 periodic call-up and demobilization

征粮 zhēngliáng　impose grain levies; collect grain taxes

征马 zhēngmǎ　battle steed; war horse

征募 zhēngmù　enlist; recruit

征聘 zhēngpìn　① give public notice of vacancies to be filled; invite applications for jobs; advertise for (a secretary, teacher, etc.): ～技术工人 advertise for skilled workers ② want ad; wanted (for a job): ～会计一名 Wanted: An Accountant

征求 zhēngqiú　solicit; seek; ask for: ～意见 solicit (*or* seek) opinions; ask for criticisms / 广泛～群众意见 consult the broad masses; solicit opinions from the general public / ～学生对教学的意见 gather students' opinions on teaching / ～订户 solicit (*or* canvass for) subscriptions / ～意见本 an edition for soliciting comments; trial edition

征人 zhēngrén　*formal*　① a traveller on a long jour-

ney ② a soldier sent on an expedition

征实 zhēngshí　levies in kind; grain levies (or tax)

征收 zhēngshōu　levy; collect; impose: ～赋税 levy (or collect) taxes / ～进口税 impose import duties / ～烟草税 put a tax on tobacco

征税 zhēngshuì　levy (or collect) taxes; taxation: ～货物 dutiable goods

征讨 zhēngtǎo　go on a punitive expedition

征途 zhēngtú　the road to be travelled; journey: 艰险的～ a perilous journey / 踏上～ start on a journey; set out / 踏上革命的～ embark on the road of revolution

征文 zhēngwén　solicit articles or essays: ～启事 a notice soliciting contributions for a special issue, etc.

征象 zhēngxiàng　sign; symptom

征询 zhēngxún　seek the opinion of; consult

征引 zhēngyǐn　quote; cite

征用 zhēngyòng　take over for use; commandeer; requisition: ～房屋 requisition buildings / 国家可以对城乡土地实行～。 The state may take over for use urban and rural land.

征战 zhēngzhàn　go on an expedition (or a campaign): 醉卧沙场君莫笑, 古来～几人回?(王翰) I lie drunk in this desert, sir, don't you laugh at me!—Since ancient days men have marched into battle, and how many have returned?

征召 zhēngzhào　① call up; enlist; draft; conscript: ～入伍 enlist in the army ② formal appoint to an official position

征兆 zhēngzhào　sign; omen; portent; indication: 地震的～ indications of an impending earthquake

挣
zhēng　see below——see also zhèng

挣扎 zhēngzhá　struggle: ～着坐起来 struggle to a sitting position / ～在死亡线上 struggle for existence on the brink of death; struggle for a bare subsistence

峥
zhēng　see below

峥嵘 zhēngróng　① lofty and steep; towering: 山势～ mountains towering high / 楼阁～ tall, towering buildings ② outstanding; extraordinary: 头角峥嵘 tóujiǎo zhēngróng

峥嵘岁月 zhēngróng suìyuè　memorable years (of one's life): 携来百侣曾游。忆往昔～稠。(毛泽东) I was here with a throng of companions, Vivid yet those crowded months and years.

狰
zhēng　see below

狰狞 zhēngníng　ferocious; savage; hideous

狰狞面目 zhēngníng miànmù　same as 面目狰狞 miànmù zhēngníng

症(癥)
zhēng　see below——see also zhèng

症瘕积聚 zhēngjiǎ jījù　Chin. med. a lump in the abdomen causing distension and pain

症结 zhēngjié　crux; crucial reason: 这就是问题的～所在。Therein lies the crux of the problem.

钲
zhēng　a bell-shaped percussion instrument, used in ancient times by troops on march

睁
zhēng　open (the eyes): ～开眼睛。Open your eyes.

睁眼瞎子 zhēngyǎn xiāzi　a blind person with eyes wide open—an illiterate

睁一只眼, 闭一只眼 zhēng yìzhī yǎn, bì yìzhī yǎn　turn a blind eye to sth.; wink at sth.

睁着眼睛说瞎话 zhēngzhe yǎnjing shuō xiāhuà　tell a bare-faced (or out-and-out) lie

铮
zhēng　see below

铮铞 zhēngcōng　onom. clank; clang

铮铮 zhēngzhēng　① onom. clank; clang ② see 铁铮铮 tiězhēngzhēng

筝
zhēng　① zheng, a 21- or 25-stringed plucked instrument in some ways similar to the zither ② see 风筝 fēngzheng

蒸
zhēng　① evaporate: 蒸气 zhēngqì ② steam: ～饭 steam rice / 菜凉了, ～一～。The food is cold. Let's warm it up in the steamer.

蒸饼 zhēngbǐng　steamed cake

蒸发 zhēngfā　evaporate: 沸水～很快。Boiling water evaporates rapidly.

蒸发计 zhēngfājì　evaporimeter

蒸锅 zhēngguō　a pot for steaming food; steamer

蒸饺 zhēngjiǎo　steamed dumpling (with meat and vegetable stuffing)

蒸馏 zhēngliú　distillation: 拔顶～ topping distillation / 常压～ atmospheric distillation / 真空～ vacuum distillation / ～器 distiller; retort / ～塔 distilling tower (or column)

蒸馏水 zhēngliúshuǐ　distilled water

蒸笼 zhēnglóng　food steamer (usu. made of bamboo)

蒸馍 zhēngmo　dial. steamed bun

蒸呢 zhēngní　text. decatizing; decating

蒸气 zhēngqì　vapour

蒸汽 zhēngqì　steam: ～发生器 steam generator / ～供暖 steam heating / ～锅炉 steam boiler / ～机车 steam locomotive / ～绞车 steam winch

蒸汽锤 zhēngqìchuí　same as 汽锤 qìchuí

蒸汽机 zhēngqìjī　steam engine

蒸汽浴 zhēngqìyù　steam bath

蒸球 zhēngqiú　paper making rotary spherical digester

蒸食 zhēngshi　steamed wheaten foods

蒸腾 zhēngténg　(of steam) rising: 热气～ steaming

蒸腾作用 zhēngténg zuòyòng　bot. transpiration

蒸蒸日上 zhēngzhēng rì shàng　becoming more prosperous every day; flourishing; thriving: 一派～、欣欣向荣的景象 a scene of prosperity / 随着机械化的发展, 农业生产～。With the development of mechanization, agriculture is flourishing. / 教育事业～。Education is spreading by leaps and bounds.

zhěng

拯
zhěng　save; rescue; deliver: ～民于水火之中 deliver the people from an abyss of misery

拯救 zhěngjiù　save; rescue; deliver: 改善环境, ～珍稀野生动物 improve the environment to save rare wild animals

整
zhěng　① whole; complete; full; entire: ～砖 a whole (or an unbroken) brick / ～夜 the whole night; all night long / 敌人～团一团地投降。Whole regiments of the enemy surrendered. / 一～页 a full page / 十二点～ twelve o'clock sharp / 恰好～一年。It's a year to the day. ② in good order; neat; tidy: 仪容不～ untidy in one's appearance / 衣冠不～ slovenly in one's dress; not properly dressed / ～然有序 be in good order ③ put in order; rectify: ～一下领带 adjust one's tie ④ repair; mend; renovate: ～旧如新 repair sth. old and make it as good as new ⑤ make sb. suffer; punish; fix: 挨整 áizhěng ⑥ dial. do; make; work: 这东西我看见

人～过，并不难。I once saw someone do it. It's not very difficult. / 绳子给～断了。The rope was broken.

整儿 zhěngr *dial.* round number; round figure: 把钱凑个～存起来。Let's make it a round sum and put it in the bank.

整备 zhěngbèi reorganize and outfit (troops)

整编 zhěngbiān reorganize (troops)

整补 zhěngbǔ reorganize and bring (an armed force) up to full strength

整饬 zhěngchì ① put in order; strengthen: ～纪律 strengthen discipline ② in good order; neat; tidy: 服装～ neatly dressed

整除 zhěngchú *math.* be divided with no remainder; divide exactly

整党 zhěngdǎng consolidate the Party organization: ～建党 Party consolidation and Party building

整地 zhěngdì soil preparation (i.e. preparation of land for sowing or planting by ploughing, harrowing, levelling, etc.)

整点 zhěngdiǎn *math.* integral point

整队 zhěngduì dress the ranks; get (or bring) the ranks into orderly alignment; line up: ～出发 get the ranks in good order and set out; set out in orderly formation / ～入场 file into the arena, auditorium, etc.

整顿 zhěngdùn rectify; consolidate; reorganize: ～财务 straighten out financial affairs / ～文风 rectify the style of writing / ～纪律 strengthen discipline / ～组织 overhaul and consolidate an organization / ～领导班子 consolidate or reorganize a leading body / ～规章制度 reestablish rules and regulations / ～城市治安 improve public order in the cities / ～好各方面的工作 straighten things out in every field of work / 我们的足球队要好好～一下。Our football team needs a good shake-up.

整风 zhěngfēng rectification of incorrect styles of work or thinking: ～就是全党通过批评和自我批评来学习马克思主义。Rectification means the whole Party studying Marxism through criticism and self-criticism.

整风运动 zhěngfēng yùndòng rectification movement

整改 zhěnggǎi rectify and reform

整个 zhěnggè whole; entire: ～上午 the whole morning / ～会场响起热烈的掌声。The whole hall resounded with applause. / ～国民经济 the whole national economy / ～社会 the whole of society / ～国际形势 the entire international situation / 在～社会主义阶段 throughout the stage of socialism / 他把这件事～儿给忘了。He clean forgot about that. / ～说来 (taken) as a whole; on the whole; by and large

整合 zhěnghé *geol.* conformity

整洁 zhěngjié clean and tidy; neat; trim: 房间收拾得很～。The room is kept clean and tidy (or spick-and-span). / 衣着～ neatly dressed

整经 zhěngjīng *text.* warping: 分段～ sectional warping / ～机 warping machine

整军经武 zhěngjūn jīngwǔ build up a country's military strength

整理 zhěnglǐ put in order; straighten out; arrange; sort out: ～房间 put a room in order; tidy a room / ～桌上的东西 straighten out the things on the table / ～书架上的书 rearrange the books on the shelves / ～资料 sort out the data / ～中国医药学 systematize Chinese medicine and pharmacology / 搜集～民歌 collect and collate folk songs / ～财政 regulate finances / ～行装 pack one's things for a journey; pack (for a journey) / ～文化遗产 sift our cultural heritage / ～化石 dress fossils

整料 zhěngliào material all in one piece for a given job

整流 zhěngliú *elec.* rectification: ～管 rectifier tube / ～子 commutator

整流器 zhěngliúqì *elec.* rectifier: 硅～ silicon rectifier /

硅可控～ silicon-controlled rectifier; thyristor

整齐 zhěngqí ① in good order; neat; tidy: 保持队伍～ keep the ranks in good order / 字写得清楚～ clear and neat handwriting / 服装～ neatly dressed / 被子叠得整整齐齐的。The quilts were rolled up tidily. ② even; regular: 出苗～ an even emergence of seedlings / ～的牙齿 regular teeth / 一排排～的工人住宅 well-laid-out blocks of workers' quarters / 迈着～的步伐 march in step / 这个篮球队阵容～。This basketball team has a well-balanced lineup.

整齐划一 zhěngqí huàyī uniform

整人 zhěngrén make sb. suffer; fix sb.

整容 zhěngróng ① tidy oneself up (i.e. have a haircut, a shave, etc.) ② face-lifting

整饰 zhěngshì renovate and decorate: 校舍～一新。The school buildings have been renovated.

整数 zhěngshù ① *math.* integer; whole number ② round number; round figure

整肃 zhěngsù *formal* ① strict; rigid: 军容～ soldiers drawn up in strict order ② rectify; consolidate: ～纪律 strengthen discipline; enforce discipline

整套 zhěngtào a complete (or whole) set of: ～设备 a complete set of equipment / 这就是他们的～观点。This is the sum total of their views. / 对这个问题他有一～看法。He has a lot of views of his own on this matter.

整体 zhěngtǐ whole; entirety: 从～上看形势 view the situation as a whole / ～的一个组成部分 an integral part of the whole / 为了～的利益牺牲局部的利益 give up individual or local interests for the sake of the whole / 以党和人民的～利益为出发点 starting out from the overall interests of the Party and the people / ～方案 an overall plan

整体吊装 zhěngtǐ diàozhuāng *archit.* integral hoisting

整体观念 zhěngtǐ guānniàn ① the concept of viewing the situation as a whole ② *Chin. med.* an organic conception of the human body, viewing its various parts as forming an organic whole

整天 zhěngtiān the whole day; all day; all day long: 干了三～ work for three whole days / 他拆洗被褥忙了一～。He's been busy all day (or the whole day) unstitching and washing his bedding.

整形 zhěngxíng *med.* plastic: ～手术 plastic operation / ～外科 plastic surgery; plastics

整修 zhěngxiū rebuild; renovate; recondition: ～水利工程 rebuild water conservancy projects / ～梯田 reinforce terraced fields / ～房子 renovate a house

整训 zhěngxùn train and consolidate (troops, etc.)

整整 zhěngzhěng whole; full: ～半小时 a whole half hour / ～两天 two whole days / ～一小时 a full (or good) hour / ～六公里 a good six kilometres / ～五十年 fully fifty years / ～一个月 a solid month / ～三百万元 a good three million *yuan*

整枝 zhěngzhī *agric.* training; pruning: 棉花～ pruning of cotton plants / 葡萄～ training of vines

整治 zhěngzhì ① renovate; repair; dredge (a river, etc.): ～房屋 renovate a house / ～机器 repair a machine / ～航道 dredge waterways / ～河道 the realignment of a river / 进行环境的综合～ carry out comprehensive ecological improvement ② punish; fix: 这坏蛋得～一下。That scoundrel needs to be punished. ③ do; work at: ～饭菜 prepare food / ～庄稼 field management

整装 zhěngzhuāng get one's things ready (for a journey, etc.): ～待命 be ready for orders

整装待发 zhěngzhuāng dài fā get ready for a journey or a march; be ready to start out

zhèng

正 zhèng ① straight; upright: ～前方 straight ahead / ～东(南、西、北) due east (south, west, north) / 把柱子扶～ set the post upright / 这幅画挂得不～。 This picture is not straight. ② situated in the middle; main: 正门 zhèngmén / 正厅 zhèngtīng ③ punctually; sharp: 九点～ at nine o'clock sharp ④ obverse; right: 布的这一面是～的吗? Is this the right side of the cloth? / 这件茄克～穿反穿都可以。 You can wear this jacket inside out. ⑤ honest; upright: 他作风不～. His behaviour is not proper. ⑥ correct; right: 路子走得～ follow a correct path ⑦ (of colour, flavour, etc.) pure; right: ～黄 pure yellow / 味儿不～ not the right flavour ⑧ regular; standard: 正楷 zhèngkǎi ⑨ (opp. 副 "secondary, vice-") principal; chief: ～副主任 director and deputy director / ～驾驶员 first pilot (opp. 副驾驶员"copilot") ⑩ (of figures, designs, etc.) regular: ～八边形 regular octagon / ～多面体 regular polyhedron ⑪ math. positive ⑫ phys. positive; plus: ～晶体 positive crystal / ～离子 positive ion; cation ⑬ rectify; straighten; set right: 把帽子～一～ put one's cap straight / 把领带～一～ straighten one's tie ⑭ make right; correct: 正误 zhèngwù / 正音 zhèngyīn ⑮ adv. just; right; precisely; exactly: ～如上文所述 just as mentioned above / 大小～合适 just the right size / 我～要谈这个问题。 I'm just coming to that point. / 这～是我想要的。 This is exactly what I want. / 那人～是张先生。 It was none other than Mr. Zhang. / 到剧场～赶上开演。 I got to the theatre just as the performance was starting. / ～是这些人创造了如此伟大的奇迹。 They are the very people who worked such wonders. ⑯ adv. just (doing sth.); just now: 他～吃着饭呢。 He's eating just now. / ～下着雨呢。 It's raining. ——see also zhēng

正儿八经 zhèngrbājīng dial. serious; earnest

正本 zhèngběn ① original (of a document): 将～送存档案库 deposit the original in the archives ② reserved copy (of a library book)

正本清源 zhèngběn-qīngyuán radically reform; thoroughly overhaul: 采取～的措施 take measures for thorough-going reform

正比 zhèngbǐ ① direct ratio ② short for 正比例 zhèngbǐlì

正比例 zhèngbǐlì math. direct proportion

正步 zhèngbù mil. parade step; goose step: ～走! (word of command) Parade step, march!

正餐 zhèngcān ① a regular meal served in a restaurant ② dinner

正册 zhèngcè regular register (used in the Qing Dynasty for listing honest people)

正茬 zhèngchá the main crop (in crop rotation)

正长石 zhèngchángshí orthoclase

正长岩 zhèngchángyán syenite

正常 zhèngcháng normal; regular: ～体温 normal body temperature / 在～情况下 under normal conditions / 发动机运转～。 The engine is functioning normally. / 恢复～ return to normal / ～的党内民主生活 normal practice of democracy in the Party / 两国关系～化 normalization of the relations between the two countries / 过～的生活 lead a normal life / 他的行为极不～。 His behaviour is far from normal. / ～心搏 regular heartbeats / 你大便～吗? Are your bowel movements regular? / 她月经不太～。 Her periods are not very regular.

正大 zhèngdà upright; honest; aboveboard: ～的理由 justifiable reasons

正大光明 zhèngdà guāngmíng open and aboveboard; just and honourable: ～的做法 a square and honest way of doing things / ～的立场 an open and aboveboard stand

正旦 zhèngdàn old name for 青衣 qīngyī ——see also zhēngdàn

正当 zhèngdāng just when; just the time for: ～春耕之时 just the time for spring ploughing / ～人手少的时候, 他们来了。 They came to help just when we were short of hands.

正当年 zhèngdāngnián in the prime of life; in one's prime

正当时 zhèngdāngshí the right season or time: 秋分种麦～。 The Autumnal Equinox is the right time for sowing wheat.

正当中 zhèngdāngzhōng same as 正中 zhèngzhōng

正当 zhèngdàng ① proper; appropriate; legitimate: ～收入 legitimate income / 通过～途径 in proper ways; by appropriate means; through proper channels / 他们的要求是完全～的。 Their demand is entirely justified. / 国家保护华侨和侨眷的～的权利和利益。 The state protects the just rights and interests of overseas Chinese and their relatives. ② (of behaviour, etc.) correct; proper: ～的行为 correct behaviour

正当防卫 zhèngdàng fángwèi legitimate defence; justified defence

正道 zhèngdào ① the right way (or course); the correct path: 走～ follow the correct path ② the correct principle; the correct way

正点 zhèngdiǎn (of ships, trains, etc.) on schedule; on time; punctually: ～运行 running on schedule / 火车～到达。 The train arrived on time (or punctually).

正电 zhèngdiàn positive electricity

正电荷 zhèngdiànhè positive charge

正电子 zhèngdiànzǐ positive electron; positron

正殿 zhèngdiàn main hall (in a palace or temple)

正定霉素 zhèngdìngméisù pharm. daunomycin

正多边形 zhèngduōbiānxíng (also 正多角形 zhèngduōjiǎoxíng) math. regular polygon

正法 zhèngfǎ execute (a criminal)

正反 zhèng-fǎn positive and negative: 总结～两方面的经验 sum up both positive and negative experience / ～两方面的看法 the pros and cons

正方 zhèngfāng square: ～盒子 a square box

正方体 zhèngfāngtǐ same as 立方体 lìfāngtǐ

正方形 zhèngfāngxíng square

正房 zhèngfáng ① principal rooms (in a courtyard, usu. facing south) ② legal wife (as contrasted with concubine)

正负电子对撞机 zhèngfù diànzǐ duìzhuàngjī electron-positron collider

正告 zhènggào earnestly admonish; warn sternly; warn in all seriousness

正割 zhènggē math. secant

正宫 zhènggōng ① empress's palace ② empress

正骨 zhènggǔ Chin. med. bonesetting

正规 zhèngguī regular; standard: ～部队 regular troops; regulars / ～化 regularize; standardize; be put on a regular basis / ～学校 regular school / ～教育 regular education

正规军 zhèngguījūn regular army

正规战 zhèngguīzhàn regular warfare

正轨 zhèngguǐ the right (or correct) path: 纳入～ lead onto the correct path; put on the right track

正果 zhèngguǒ Buddhism the right fruit—the proper consequence of a regulated life in this world: 因为修行, 得了～ have attained the right fruit by self-cultivation

正好 zhènghǎo ① just in time; just right; just enough: 你来得～。 You've come just in time. / 这双鞋我穿～。

This pair of shoes fits me nicely. /这笔钱～买台抽水机。This is just enough money for a pump. /天气不冷不热,～出去玩玩。It's neither too hot nor too cold —just the right weather for an outing. /这一证明我们的作法是对的。That only goes to prove that our approach is correct. ② happen to; chance to; as it happens: 小王～从那儿路过。Xiao Wang happened (or chanced) to be passing by. /我身边～有五块钱。As it happens, I have five *yuan* with me.

正号 zhènghào *math.* positive sign; plus sign

正话 zhènghuà ① serious words: 他那个人就是玩笑话多,～少。He often speaks in jest, and seldom says anything serious. ② what one really means: 她正在气头上,那话怕是～反说吧! She said that in a fit of anger, and it must surely have been the very opposite of what she really meant.

正火 zhènghuǒ *metall.* normalizing

正极 zhèngjí *elec.* positive electrode; positive pole; anode: ～板 positive plate

正教 Zhèngjiào the Orthodox Church

正襟危坐 zhèngjīn-wēizuò straighten one's clothes and sit properly

正经 zhèngjīng old name for 十三经 Shísān Jīng

正经 zhèngjing ① decent; respectable; honest: ～人 a decent person ② serious: 钱必须用在～地方。Money must be put to right uses. /～事儿 serious affairs /谈～事 talk business /说～的,你得注意点身体。Seriously now, you ought to take more care of your health. ③ standard: ～货 standard goods ④ *dial.* really; truly; indeed: 这黄瓜长得还～不错呢! The cucumbers are really doing fine.

正经八百 zhèngjingbābǎi (also 正经八摆 zhèngjingbābǎi) *dial.* serious; earnest: 这是～的事。This is a serious matter. *or* This is no joke.

正剧 zhèngjù serious drama

正角 zhèngjué same as 主角 zhǔjué

正楷 zhèngkǎi (in Chinese calligraphy) regular script

正课 zhèngkè required courses (in college)

正理 zhènglǐ correct principle; valid reason (or argument); the right thing to do

正梁 zhèngliáng *archit.* ridge purlin

正六面体 zhèngliùmiàntǐ *math.* regular hexahedron

正路 zhènglù the right way (or course); the correct path: 这才是～。That's the correct thing to do.

正论 zhènglùn a just opinion

正门 zhèngmén front door (or gate); main entrance

正面 zhèngmiàn ① front; frontage; facade: 房屋的～ the front (or facade) of a house /～进攻 frontal attack /～冲突 head-on confrontation (or clash) ② the obverse side; the right side: 牛皮纸的～ the right side of kraft paper /硬币的～ the obverse side of a coin /皮革的～ the grain side of leather /～和反面 the obverse and the reverse sides of a thing; both sides ③ positive: ～教育 educate by positive measures or examples; positive education /～阐明自己的观点 state one's views in a positive way /～和反面的历史经验 positive and negative historical lessons ④ directly; openly: 有问题请～提出来。Please ask your question directly.

正面人物 zhèngmiàn rénwù positive character

正面图 zhèngmiàntú same as 主视图 zhǔshìtú

正派 zhèngpài upright; honest; decent: ～人 a decent person /他为人～。He's honest and upright.

正片 zhèngpiàn ① *photog.* positive ② *film* copy ③ *film* feature (film)

正品 zhèngpǐn certified products (or goods); quality products (or goods)

正气 zhèngqì ① healthy atmosphere (or tendency): 发扬～ encourage healthy trends; encourage standing up for what is right /～上升。A healthy atmosphere pre-

vails. ② *Chin. med.* vital energy

正桥 zhèngqiáo the main structure of a bridge

正巧 zhèngqiǎo ① happen to; chance to; as it happens: 他们～带有仪器。They happened (or chanced) to have their instruments with them. /～两位民兵到那儿巡逻,及时发现了火情。As it happened, two militiamen were there on patrol and spotted the fire as soon as it started. ② just in time; in the nick of time; just at the right time: 你来得～,我们马上就要出发了。You've come just in time. We're leaving immediately.

正切 zhèngqiē *math.* tangent

正确 zhèngquè correct; right; proper: ～的答案 a correct answer /～的立场 a correct stand /你这样做是～的。What you are doing is right. /～处理国家、集体、个人三者之间的关系 maintain a proper balance in the relationship between the state, the collective and the individual /～对待自己 adopt a correct attitude towards oneself /～估计客观形势 accurately appraise the objective situation /～的批评 well-founded criticism /～性 correctness; soundness; validity

正人君子 zhèngrén-jūnzǐ a man of honour; a man of integrity; gentleman: 打扮成～ masquerade as a gentleman

正三角形 zhèngsānjiǎoxíng equilateral triangle

正色[1] zhèngsè *formal* pure colours

正色[2] zhèngsè adopt a stern countenance: ～拒绝 sternly refuse

正身 zhèngshēn in person; not by proxy

正史 zhèngshǐ history books written in biographical style ——see also 纪传体 jìzhuàntǐ

正式 zhèngshì formal; official; regular: ～列入记录 be officially placed on record /代表团的～成员 a regular (or full) member of the delegation /大会于八月二十四日～开幕。The conference formally opened on August 24. /～党员 full member of the Party; full Party member /～访问 official (or formal) visit /～会谈 formal talks /～记录 official records /～声明 official statement /～文本 official text

正视 zhèngshì face squarely; face up to; look squarely at: ～困难 face difficulties squarely; face up to difficulties /～现实 look reality in the face /～缺点 acknowledge one's shortcomings /不～事实 shut one's eyes to facts

正视图 zhèngshìtú same as 主视图 zhǔshìtú

正事 zhèngshì one's proper business: 现在咱们谈～。Now let's talk business.

正室 zhèngshì ① legal wife (as contrasted with concubine) ② *formal* the wife's eldest son

正手 zhèngshǒu *sports* forehand: ～抽球 forehand drive

正书 zhèngshū same as 正楷 zhèngkǎi

正数 zhèngshù *math.* positive number

正税 zhèngshuì regular tax

正态分布 zhèngtài fēnbù *statistics* normal distribution

正题 zhèngtí ① subject (or topic) of a talk or essay: 转入～ come to the subject /离开～ wander (or digress) from the subject /不离～ stick to one's text ② *philos.* thesis

正体 zhèngtǐ ① standardized form of Chinese characters ② same as 正楷 zhèngkǎi ③ block letter

正厅 zhèngtīng ① main hall (in the middle) ② stalls (in a theatre)

正统 zhèngtǒng ① legitimism ② orthodox: ～观念 orthodox ideas /～派 orthodox party or school

正投影 zhèngtóuyǐng orthographic projection

正文 zhèngwén main body (of a book, etc.); text: 书的～ the text of a book /词典～ the main body of a dictionary; the dictionary proper

正屋 zhèngwū principal rooms (in a courtyard, usu.

facing south)

正午 zhèngwǔ　high noon

正误 zhèngwù　correct (typographical) errors

正误表 zhèngwùbiǎo　errata; corrigenda

正弦 zhèngxián　*math.* sine

正弦波 zhèngxiánbō　*phys.* sine wave

正凶 zhèngxiōng　*leg.* principal murderer

正言厉色 zhèngyán-lìsè　in a serious tone and with a solemn look

正盐 zhèngyán　*chem.* normal salt

正颜厉色 zhèngyán-lìsè　serious and severe; with a stern look

正眼 zhèngyǎn　look straight: 他和我说话时不敢～看着我。He did not dare look me straight in the face when he spoke.

正业 zhèngyè　regular occupation; proper duties: 不务正业 bù wù zhèngyè

正义[1] zhèngyì　① justice: 主持～ uphold justice / 为～而战 fight for justice / ～之师 an army dedicated to a just cause ② just; righteous: ～立场 a just stand / ～的事业 a just cause / ～的战争 a just war

正义[2] zhèngyì　(formerly often used in book titles) orthodox or rectified interpretation (of ancient texts): 孙诒让《周礼～》Sun Yirang's *Rectified Interpretation of the "Rites of Zhou"*

正义感 zhèngyìgǎn　a sense of what is right; a sense of justice (*or* righteousness)

正音 zhèngyīn　① correct one's pronunciation ② standard pronunciation

正音法 zhèngyīnfǎ　*phonet.* orthoepy

正应力 zhèngyìnglì　*phys.* direct stress

正用 zhèngyòng　proper use: 省了这笔钱作～多好。Wouldn't it be better to save this money for more proper uses?

正院儿 zhèngyuànr　main courtyard

正在 zhèngzài　*adv.* in process of; in course of: 他们～聊天。They're having a chat. / 许多问题～讨论。Many questions are under discussion. / ～修建一条新铁路。A new railway is under construction. / ～进行磋商。Consultations are under way.

正直 zhèngzhí　honest; upright; fair-minded: ～的人 an honest person; a person of integrity

正职 zhèngzhí　the position of the chief of an office, department, etc.

正治 zhèngzhì　*Chin. med.* normal treatment, i.e. administering medicines of a cold nature to treat a febrile disease

正中 zhèngzhōng　right in the middle (*or* centre): 把茶具放在桌子～。Put the tea-things right in the middle (*or* centre) of the table.

正中下怀 zhèngzhòng xiàhuái　be just what one hopes for; fit in exactly with one's wishes

正传 zhèngzhuàn　main story (of a novel, etc.); subject under discussion ——see also 言归正传 yán guī zhèngzhuàn

正字 zhèngzì　① correct a wrongly written character or a misspelt word ② same as 正楷 zhèngkǎi ③ standardized form of Chinese characters

正字法 zhèngzìfǎ　orthography

正宗 zhèngzōng　① orthodox school ② genuine: ～川菜 genuine Sichuan cooking

正座 zhèngzuò　central seats that directly face the stage; stalls

证(證)

zhèng　① prove; demonstrate: ～几何定理 demonstrate (*or* prove) a geometric theorem ② evidence; proof; testimony: 以此为～ take this as an evidence ③ certificate; card: 工作证 gōngzuòzhèng

证词 zhèngcí　testimony

证婚人 zhènghūnrén　chief witness at a wedding ceremony

证件 zhèngjiàn　credentials; papers; certificate: 请出示～。Please show your credentials (*or* papers).

证据 zhèngjù　evidence; proof; testimony: 搜集～ collect evidence / 提出～ offer testimony / 大量～ an abundance of evidence / 直接～ direct evidence / ～确凿的叛徒 a proven renegade

证明 zhèngmíng　① prove; testify; bear out: 充分～ fully prove / 雄辩地～ give (*or* be) eloquent proof of / 无数事实已～了这一点。Countless facts have proved this point. / 事实～我是对的。The facts bear me out. ② certificate; identification; testimonial: 医生～ medical certificate / ～文件 certificate; testimonial; papers

证明书 zhèngmíngshū　certificate; testimonial: 质量～ certificate of quality / 产地～ certificate of origin / 健康～ health certificate

证券 zhèngquàn　negotiable securities

证券交易所 zhèngquàn jiāoyìsuǒ　stock exchange; stock market

证人 zhèngren　witness: ～席 witness-box; witness stand

证实 zhèngshí　confirm; verify; bear out: 有待～ remain to be confirmed / ～一个科学上的假设 verify (*or* bear out) a scientific hypothesis / 经过研究，他的理论得到了～。Research bore out his theory.

证书 zhèngshū　certificate; credentials: ～审查委员会 credentials committee

证物 zhèngwù　*leg.* exhibit (produced in court as evidence)

证言 zhèngyán　testimony

证验 zhèngyàn　① verify ② real results; efficacy

证章 zhèngzhāng　badge

怔

zhèng　*dial.* stare blankly; be in a daze: 那消息使她～住了。She was stunned by the news. ——see also zhēng

怔神儿 zhèngshénr　*dial.* stare blankly; be in a daze

怔怔 zhèngzhèng　*dial.* stare blankly; be in a daze; be in a trance: ～地站着 stand there as if in a trance; stand there staring blankly

诤

zhèng　*formal* criticize sb.'s faults frankly; admonish; expostulate: 诤友 zhèngyǒu

诤谏 zhèngjiàn　*formal* criticize sb.'s faults frankly

诤言 zhèngyán　*formal* forthright admonition

诤友 zhèngyǒu　*formal* a friend who will give forthright admonition

郑(鄭)

Zhèng　① one of the Warring states into which China was divided during the Eastern Zhou period (770–256 B.C.), occupying parts of modern Henan Province ② a surname

郑重 zhèngzhòng　serious; solemn; earnest: 态度～ be serious in one's attitude / ～表示 earnestly declare; solemnly state / ～声明 solemnly declare

郑重其事 zhèngzhòng qí shì　seriously; in earnest

郑州 Zhèngzhōu　Zhengzhou (capital of Henan Province)

政

zhèng　① politics; political affairs: 政治 zhèngzhì ② certain administrative aspects of government: 邮政 yóuzhèng ③ affairs of a family or an organization: 家政 jiāzhèng

政变 zhèngbiàn　coup d'état; coup: 发动～ stage a coup d'état / 粉碎～阴谋 smash a coup plot / 军事～ military coup d'état / 宫廷～ palace coup d'état / 不流血的～ bloodless coup d'état / 未遂～ abortive coup d'état

政柄 zhèngbǐng　*formal* political (*or* state) power;

regime

政策 zhèngcè policy: ～教育 education in policy / 提高～水平 enhance the understanding of policy / 划清～界限 draw clear lines of demarcation in applying a policy

政潮 zhèngcháo political unrest

政党 zhèngdǎng political party

政敌 zhèngdí political opponent

政法 zhèngfǎ politics and law

政法机构 zhèngfǎ jīgòu procuratorial, judicial and public security organizations

政法学院 zhèngfǎ xuéyuàn institute of political science and law

政府 zhèngfǔ government: ～部门 government departments / ～官员 government official / ～机构 government apparatus / ～机关 government bodies (or organizations) / ～人士 government circles / ～首脑 head of government

政纲 zhènggāng (short for 政治纲领) political programme; platform

政工 zhènggōng (short for 政治工作) political work: ～组 political work section (or office)

政躬 zhènggōng *formal pol.* your health: ～违和。 You are indisposed.

政纪 zhèngjì government discipline

政绩 zhèngjì achievements in one's official career

政见 zhèngjiàn political view: 持不同～ hold different political views / 持不同～者 dissident

政教分离 zhèng-jiào fēnlí separation of religion from politics; separation of the church from the state

政界 zhèngjiè political circles; government circles: 进入～ enter politics / 退出～ withdraw from political life

政局 zhèngjú political situation; political scene: ～稳定。 The political situation is stable.

政客 zhèngkè *derog.* politician

政令 zhènglìng government decree (or order)

政论 zhènglùn political comment: ～家 political commentator; political writer / ～文 political essay

政派 zhèngpài (short for 政治派别) political grouping (or faction)

政情 zhèngqíng political situation

政权 zhèngquán political (or state) power; regime: 革命～ a revolutionary regime / 革命的根本问题是～问题。 The fundamental question of revolution is political power.

政权机关 zhèngquán jīguān organs of state (or political) power

政审 zhèngshěn (short for 政治审查) examine sb.'s political behaviour or record

政声 zhèngshēng *old* an official's reputation for his administration

政事 zhèngshì government affairs

政体 zhèngtǐ system (or form) of government

政委 zhèngwěi short for 政治委员 zhèngzhì wěiyuán

政务 zhèngwù government affairs; government administration

政务院 zhèngwùyuàn the Government Administration Council (of the Central People's Government of the People's Republic of China, replaced in 1954 by the State Council)

政协 zhèngxié short for 政治协商会议 zhèngzhì xiéshāng huìyì

政治 zhèngzhì politics; political affairs: ～历史清白(清楚) have a clean (clear) political record / ～上可靠 politically reliable / ～表现 political behaviour or record / ～待遇 political treatment / ～挂帅 put politics in command / ～基础 political basis / ～交易 political deal (or transaction) / ～觉悟 political consciousness (or awareness, understanding) / ～空气 political atmos-

phere / ～立场 political stand / ～路线 political line / ～骗子 political swindler / ～生命 political life / ～态度 political attitude / ～舞台 political arena (or stage, scene) / ～信仰 political conviction (or belief) / ～性 political nature / ～嗅觉 political sense of smell; political acumen (or sensitiveness)

政治庇护 zhèngzhì bìhù political asylum

政治避难 zhèngzhì bìnàn political refuge; political asylum: 要求～ seek (or ask for) political asylum

政治部 zhèngzhìbù political department

政治犯 zhèngzhìfàn political offender; political prisoner

政治家 zhèngzhìjiā statesman: ～风度 statesmanship

政治教导员 zhèngzhì jiàodǎoyuán political instructor (of a PLA battalion)

政治经济学 zhèngzhìjīngjìxué political economy

政治局 zhèngzhìjú the Political Bureau: ～常务委员 member of the Standing Committee of the Political Bureau / ～委员 member of the Political Bureau

政治面目 zhèngzhì miànmù political affiliation or background: ～不清 of dubious political background

政治权利 zhèngzhì quánlì political rights

政治委员 zhèngzhì wěiyuán political commissar (of a PLA regiment and above); commissar

政治协理员 zhèngzhì xiélǐyuán political assistant (of a PLA regiment and above)

政治协商会议 zhèngzhì xiéshāng huìyì political consultative conference

政治学 zhèngzhìxué political science; government

政治指导员 zhèngzhì zhǐdǎoyuán political instructor (of a PLA company)

挣[1] zhèng struggle to get free; try to throw off: ～脱枷锁 throw off the shackles / 他把捆绑的绳子～开了。 He wrenched himself free from his bonds.

挣[2] zhèng earn; make: ～饭吃 earn a living / 一个月～二百五十块 earn (or make) 250 *yuan* a month / 工资的～ wage earner / 她～得挺多的。 She earns a high salary.
——see also zhēng

挣揣 zhèngchuài *formal* struggle; strive hard

挣命 zhèngmìng struggle to save one's life

挣钱 zhèngqián earn (or make) money: ～餬口 earn a living / 他挣的钱不够养家的。 His earnings are not sufficient to support his family. / 她的两个儿子都～了。 Her sons are both earning now.

阐 zhèng struggle; contend

症(證) zhèng disease; illness: 急症 jízhèng
——see also zhēng

症候群 zhènghòuqún another name for 综合病征 zōnghé bìngzhēng

症候 zhènghou ① disease ② symptom

症状 zhèngzhuàng symptom: 前驱～ premonitory (or signal) symptoms / 早期～ early (or incipient) symptoms

铮 zhèng *dial.* (of utensils, etc.) polished: 她把银匙擦得～亮。 She polished the silver spoons till they shone. ——see also zhēng

zhī

之[1] zhī *formal* go; leave for: 由京～渝 leave Beijing for Chongqing / 君将何～? Where are you bound for?

之² zhī *formal* ① (used in place of an objective noun or pronoun): 影片情节十分悲惨,观众无不为～感动。The film was so sad that none were unmoved. / 将如～何? What is to be done? ② (used in certain set phrases without definite designation): 我们三个人我最年长,李次～,张又次～。Of the three of us, I am the eldest, Li is younger, and Zhang is the youngest. / 手之舞～,足之蹈～ dance with joy ③ this or that: ～子于归。The maiden goes to her future home.

之³ zhī *part. formal* ① (used between an attribute and the word it modifies): 钟鼓～声 the sound of drums and bells / 原因～一 one of the reasons / 宝中～宝 the treasure of treasures / 一水～隔 be separated only by a river / 以我～长,攻敌～短 utilize our strong points to attack the enemy at his weak points / 三分～一 one-third / 百分～八十 eighty per cent / 急群众～急 be eager to meet the needs of the masses / 五千年～久 as long as five thousand years / 得意～极 be very much pleased with oneself / 感激～至 be deeply grateful / 抱歉～至 be awfully sorry / 不胜荣幸～至 feel greatly honoured / 非常～正确 absolutely right / 非常～需要 highly necessary / 我～所以讨厌他是因为他的嘴太贫。The reason why I dislike him is that he is too garrulous. / 弦乐器是指琵琶、二胡、小提琴～类。Stringed instruments refer to *pipa, erhu,* violin, etc. ② (used between the subject and the predicate in a S-P structure so as to make it nominalized): 如因势利导,则如水～就下,极为自然。If we guide the matter along its course of development, it will proceed as naturally as water flows downwards.

之后 zhīhòu later; after; afterwards: 三天～ after three days; three days later / 这次大会～ following this conference / 从那～她没来过。She hasn't been here since then. / 他又给我写了两封信。Afterwards he wrote to me twice.

之乎者也 zhī-hū-zhě-yě particles of literary Chinese —pedantic terms; literary jargon; archaisms: 他这信写得文绉绉的,没把～用错。His letter was couched in an elegant style without incorrectly using any of the various particles of literary Chinese. / 老学究满口～,教人半懂不懂。The old pedant used so many archaisms that half of what he said was unintelligible.

之前 zhīqián before; prior to; ago: 在她动身～ before (*or* prior to) her departure / 这药在睡觉～吃。Take the medicine before bedtime. / 两星期～他还在这儿。He was here until two weeks ago.

之死靡他 zhī sǐ mǐ tā ① till death no other—(of a widow) swear never to remarry ② be unwaveringly steadfast

之无 zhīwú the characters 之 and 无 —the simplest and most common characters: 略识～ know only a few simple characters / 不识～ be illiterate

之字路 zhīzìlù zigzag course; S curve in a road

支¹ zhī ① prop up; put up: ～帐篷 put up a tent / 用两张凳子把木板～起来 prop up the board with two stools / 两手～着头 rest one's head in both hands ② protrude; raise: ～着耳朵听 prick up one's ears / 他那两只虎牙朝两边～着。His two upper canine teeth protrude. ③ support; sustain; bear: 孩子疼得～不住了。The child couldn't bear the pain. ④ send away; put sb. off: 把他们～开 put them off with excuses; send them away upon some pretext / 这事甭～别人了,你自个儿去吧。Don't send anyone else; better go yourself. ⑤ pay or draw (money): ～拨 pay a sum of money or transfer a sum of money in payment / 上银行～款 go to the bank to draw money ⑥ (Zhī) a surname

支² zhī ① branch; offshoot: ～店 branch store / 邮政～局 branch post office ② *m.* ⓐ (for long, thin, inflexible objects): 一～钢笔 a pen / 一～箭 an arrow / 一～香烟 a cigarette ⓑ (for troops, fleets, etc.): 两～队伍 two contingents of troops / 一～舰队 a fleet ⓒ (for songs or musical compositions): 一～曲子 a tune / 一～新歌 a new song ⓓ (for the illuminating power of electric lights) watt: 一个四十～光的灯泡 a 40-watt bulb ⓔ (for the size or quality of yarn) count: 六十～纱 60-count yarn / 细(中)～棉纱 fine (medium) count yarn

支³ zhī short for 地支 dìzhī (see also 干支 gānzhī)

支边 zhībiān support the border areas

支部 zhībù branch (esp. of the Chinese Communist Party or the Chinese Communist Youth League): 党(团)～ Party (League) branch / ～大会 general membership meeting of the branch / ～书记 branch secretary / ～委员 member of the branch committee

支撑 zhīchēng ① prop up; sustain; support: 坑道顶儿用柱子～着。The pillars sustain the roof of the pit. / 病人～着坐了起来。The patient propped himself up into a sitting position. / 一家人的生活得由他～。He has to support his whole family. ② *archit.* strut; brace

支撑点 zhīchēngdiǎn *mil.* strong point; centre of resistance

支承 zhīchéng *mech.* support; bear: ～点 bearing point / ～力 supporting force / ～圈 backup ring; support ring

支持 zhīchí ① sustain; hold out; bear: 他冻得～不住了。He was so cold he couldn't hold out any longer. ② support; back; stand by: 在国际上得到越来越广泛的～ enjoy wider and wider international support / ～被压迫人民的斗争 support the struggle of the oppressed peoples / 给予坚决的～ give strong backing to / 全世界各国人民的正义斗争,都是互相～的。The just struggles of the people of all countries support each other. / 我完全～这个建议。I am all for this proposal.

支出 zhīchū ① pay (money); expend; disburse ② expenses; expenditure; outlay; disbursement 收入与～相抵。The income balances the expenditure.

支绌 zhīchù (of funds) not enough; insufficient: 由于经费～ due to insufficient funds

支单 zhīdān a certificate for drawing money; voucher

支点 zhīdiǎn *phys.* fulcrum

支队 zhīduì detachment: 游击～ a guerrilla detachment

支墩坝 zhīdūnbà *water conservancy* buttress dam

支付 zhīfù pay (money); defray: ～水电费 pay for electricity and water / ～手段 means of payment / ～协定 payments agreement

支行 zhīháng subbranch (of a bank)

支唤 zhīhuàn *dial.* order about

支架 zhījià support; stand; trestle: 自行车～ prop stand of a bicycle

支解 zhījiě dismemberment: ～一个国家 dismember a country

支棱 zhīleng *dial.* hold up; stick up: ～着耳朵听 prick up one's ears

支离 zhīlí ① fragmented; broken; disorganized ② (of writing) trivial and jumbled; incoherent

支离破碎 zhīlí-pòsuì torn to pieces; broken up; fragmented

支链反应 zhīliàn fǎnyìng same as 链式反应 liànshì fǎnyìng

支流 zhīliú ① tributary; affluent: 珠江的一条～ a tributary of the Zhujiang River ② minor aspects; nonessentials: 看问题时,不要把～当作主流。In considering a problem, one mustn't mistake the nonessentials for the

essentials.

支路 zhīlù branch road; byroad; side road

支脉 zhīmài offshoot (of a mountain range); branch range: 天山的～ a branch range of the Tianshan Mountains / 伏牛山是秦岭的～。The Funiu Mountains are an offshoot of the Qinling Mountain Range.

支那 Zhīnà China (a transliteration, used in translations of Buddhist scriptures, and by the Japanese until recently)

支派 zhīpài branch; sect; offshoot

支派 zhī·pài order; send; dispatch

支配 zhīpèi ① arrange; allocate; budget: 合理～劳动力 make a proper allocation of the labour force / 善于～自己的时间 be good at budgeting one's time ② control; dominate; govern: 受人～ be controlled by others / 受自然规律的～ be subject to the laws of nature / 思想～行动。People's actions are governed by their ideology.

支票 zhīpiào cheque; check: 开～ write a cheque / 划线～ crossed cheque / 空白～ blank cheque / 空头～ rubber cheque / 来人～ bearer cheque / 保付～ certified cheque / 旅行～ traveller's cheque / 转账～ cheque for transfer / 付讫～ paid cheque / 未兑现～ outstanding cheque / ～簿 chequebook / ～票根 stub of a cheque; counterfoil / ～挂失 report the loss of a cheque

支气管 zhīqìguǎn bronchus

支气管扩张 zhīqìguǎn kuòzhāng bronchiectasis

支气管性气喘 zhīqìguǎnxìng qìchuǎn bronchial asthma

支气管炎 zhīqìguǎnyán bronchitis

支前 zhīqián support the front

支渠 zhīqú branch (irrigation) canal

支取 zhīqǔ draw (money): ～存款 draw one's deposit (from a bank)

支使 zhīshi ① order about: 他老～人，我都烦了。I'm tired of him ordering me about all the time. ② send away; put sb. off

支书 zhīshū (short for 支部书记) secretary of a Party or League branch; branch secretary

支枢 zhīshū mech. pivot

支数 zhīshù text. number (of yarn); count: 纱线～ yarn number; yarn size

支吾 zhīwu prevaricate; equivocate; hum and haw: 他显然不知道该怎么回答我的问题，站在那里支支吾吾的。He obviously didn't know the answer to my question—he just stood there humming and hawing.

支吾其词 zhīwu qí cí speak evasively; hum and haw

支线 zhīxiàn branch line; feeder (line): 铁路～ feeder railway / 公路～ feeder highway

支颐 zhīyí formal cheek in palm

支应 zhīyìng ① cope with; deal with ② wait on; attend to: ～门户 attend to the door

支援 zhīyuán support; assist; help: 各行各业都要大力～农业。All trades and professions must do their best to support agriculture. / ～灾区 give aid (or send relief) to disaster areas

支援部队 zhīyuán bùduì support unit; supporting troops

支柱 zhīzhù pillar; prop; mainstay: 矿用～ pit prop / 国家的～ pillar of the state

支柱根 zhīzhùgēn bot. prop root

支子 zhīzi ① stand; support: 自行车～ kickstand of a bicycle / 火～ trivet ② gridiron (as a cooking utensil)

支嘴儿 zhīzuǐr (also 支着儿 zhīzhāor) dial. give advice; suggest ideas; make suggestions

氏 zhī see 阏氏 yānzhī; 月氏 Yuèzhī ——see also shì

汁 zhī juice: 西瓜红瓤多～。Watermelons have juicy red flesh.

汁水 zhīshui dial. juice: 这种果子～很多。This fruit is juicy.

汁液 zhīyè juice

只(隻) zhī ① single; one only: 只言片语 zhīyán-piànyǔ ② m. (for boats, birds, some animals, some containers, and one of certain paired things): 一～船 a boat / 两～喜鹊 two magpies / 一～老虎 a tiger / 三～箱子 three suitcases / 两～手 two hands / 一～眼睛 an eye ——see also zhǐ

只身 zhīshēn alone; by oneself: ～前往 go there alone / ～在外 be away from home all by oneself

只言片语 zhīyán-piànyǔ a word or two; a few isolated words and phrases: 只听见～ catch (or overhear) only a word or two / 未留下～ leave behind not even a single word

只字不提 zhī zì bù tí not say a single word about sth.; not so much as mention sth.

卮(巵) zhī ancient wine vessel

芝 zhī see below

芝加哥 Zhījiāgē Chicago

芝兰 zhīlán irises and orchids (symbolic of noble character, true friendship, or beautiful surroundings) ——see also 如入芝兰之室 rú rù zhīlán zhī shì

芝麻 zhīma ① sesame ② sesame seed

芝麻官 zhīmaguān humor. sesame official—petty official

芝麻酱 zhīmajiàng sesame paste

芝麻开花节节高 zhīma kāihuā jiéjié gāo sesame stalks putting forth flowers notch by notch, higher and higher—(of living standards, etc.) rising steadily

芝麻油 zhīmayóu sesame-seed oil; sesame oil

吱 zhī onom. a creaking sound: 门～地一声开了。The door creaked open. ——see also zī

枝 zhī ① branch; twig: 柳～ willow branches ② m. (for flowers with stems intact): 一～梅花 a spray of plum blossoms ③ m. (for long, thin, inflexible objects): 一～步枪 a rifle / 三～钢笔 three pens / 一～蜡烛 a candle

枝杈 zhīchà branch; twig

枝辞 zhīcí (also 枝词 zhīcí) formal ① superfluous words ② florid language

枝接 zhījiē agric. scion grafting

枝节 zhījié ① branches and knots—minor matters: ～问题 a minor problem; a side issue / 不要过多地注意那些枝枝节节。Don't pay too much attention to the minor issues. ② complication; unexpected difficulty: 横生枝节 héngshēng zhījié

枝解 zhījiě same as 支解 zhījiě

枝柯 zhīkē formal branch; twig

枝蔓 zhīmàn branches and tendrils—complicated and confused: 文字～，不得要领。The writing is confused and the main points are not clear.

枝条 zhītiáo branch; twig

枝头 zhītóu on a branch: ～小鸟 little birds on a branch

枝梧 zhīwú (also 枝语 zhīwǔ) formal prevaricate; equivocate; hum and haw

枝桠 zhīyā (also 枝丫 zhīyā) branch; twig

枝叶 zhīyè ① branches and leaves: 那棵大樟树～茂盛。That big camphor tree is a mass of branches and leaves. ② nonessentials; minor details

枝子 zhīzi branch; twig

知 zhī ① know; realize; be aware of: 这话不～是

谁说的。 We don't know who said this. ② inform; notify; tell: 通知 tōngzhī ③ knowledge: 求知 qiúzhī ④ administer; be in charge of: 知县 zhīxiàn

知彼知己,百战不殆 zhī bǐ zhī jǐ, bǎi zhàn bù dài know the enemy and know yourself, and you can fight a hundred battles without defeat

知宾 zhībīn *dial.* a person in charge of reception at ceremonies

知耻 zhīchǐ have a sense of shame

知耻近乎勇 zhīchǐ jìnhū yǒng to know the things of shame is to be near to fortitude

知单 zhīdān a notice of invitation with a list of the names of those invited (who are supposed to write against their names a 知 "notified" to indicate a promise of attendance or a 谢 "thanks" to indicate declination)

知道 zhīdao know; realize; be aware of: 我不~这事儿。 I know nothing about it. / 你的意思我~。 I know what you mean. *or* I see your point. / 他们~问题的严重性。 They realize how serious the problem is. / 我们~在前进的路上还会有困难。 We are aware that on our way forward there will still be difficulties;

知底 zhīdǐ know the inside story; be in the know

知法犯法 zhī fǎ fàn fǎ knowingly violate the law; deliberately break the law

知府 zhīfǔ (in former times) prefect

知根知底 zhīgēn zhīdǐ know sb.'s background; know sb. thoroughly

知更鸟 zhīgēngniǎo robin; redbreast

知过必改 zhī guò bì gǎi always correct an error when one becomes aware of it

知会 zhīhui *inf.* tell (orally): 你先去~他一声, 让他早点儿准备。 Go and tell him so that he can get ready in time.

知己 zhījǐ ① intimate; understanding: ~的朋友 bosom (*or* intimate) friend / 和他很~ be on intimate terms with him / ~话 intimate words; heart-to-heart talk ② bosom (*or* intimate) friend

知交 zhījiāo bosom (*or* intimate) friend: 他和我父亲是~。 He is an intimate friend of my father's.

知觉 zhījué ① consciousness: 失去~ lose consciousness; pass out / 恢复~ recover consciousness; come to ② *psychol.* perception

知觉常性 zhījué chángxìng *psychol.* perceptual constancies

知客 zhīkè ① *old* person in charge of reception at ceremonies ② (also 知客僧 zhīkèsēng) monk in charge of monastery reception

知了 zhīliǎo cicada

知名 zhīmíng well-known; noted; celebrated; famous: ~人士 a well-known figure; celebrity / 海内~ well-known throughout the country

知名度 zhīmíngdù popularity: 他的~很高。 He enjoys great popularity.

知命 zhīmìng *formal* ① understand the Decree of Heaven ② (used esp. in) ~之年 the age of fifty (from Confucius' saying 五十而知天命 "At fifty I understood the Decree of Heaven" / 年逾~ be over fifty

知母 zhīmǔ ① *bot.* wind-weed (*Anemarrhena asphodeloides*) ② *Chin. med.* rhizome of wind-weed

知难而进 zhī nán ér jìn press forward despite difficulties; advance in the face of difficulties

知难而退 zhī nán ér tuì beat a retreat in the face of difficulties; shrink back from difficulties

知其不可而为之 zhī qí bùkě ér wéi zhī know it's no use, but keep on doing it; do what one knows is impossible

知其然,不知其所以然 zhī qí rán, bù zhī qí suǒyǐrán know that sth. is so but not why it is so; know the hows but not the whys

知其一,不知其二 zhī qí yī, bù zhī qí èr know only one aspect of a thing; have a one-sided view: 总之,事物都有两点而不是一点。说只有一点, 叫~。 In short, there are two aspects to everything, not just one. To say there is only one is to be aware of one aspect and be ignorant of the other.

知青 zhīqīng short for 知识青年 zhīshi qīngnián

知情[1] zhīqíng know the facts of a case or the details of an incident; be in the know: ~不报 fail to report what one knows of a case / ~人 person in the know; insider

知情[2] zhīqíng feel grateful to sb.; appreciate the kindness: 你们的好意, 我很~。 I'm very grateful to you for your kindness.

知情达理 zhīqíng-dálǐ reasonable; sensible

知趣 zhīqù know how to behave in a delicate situation; be sensible; be tactful: 你还是~一些, 快走吧。 You'd better be sensible and quit. / 这人多嘴, 好不~。 The man is talkative and indiscreet.

知人善任 zhī rén shàn rèn know one's subordinates well enough to assign them suitable jobs; know how to judge and use people

知人之明 zhī rén zhī míng ability to appreciate a person's character and capability; a keen insight into a person's character: 有~ know how to judge people; be a good judge of people

知人知面不知心 zhī rén zhī miàn bù zhī xīn you may know a person's face but not his heart; one may know a person for a long time without understanding his true nature: 画虎画皮难画骨, ~。 Painting a tiger's skin is easy, but not so the bones. A man's face one can know, but not his heart.

知事 zhīshì *old* (in former times) county magistrate

知识 zhīshi knowledge; intellect: ~渊博 have a wide range of knowledge; be erudite; be learned / 技术~ technical know-how / 书本~ book learning / 获得生产斗争~ acquire a knowledge of the struggle for production / 跟这种没有~的人议论严肃音乐本来就没有意思。 There's no point discussing serious music with such ignorant people.

知识产权 zhīshi chǎnquán intellectual property rights

知识分子 zhīshifēnzǐ intellectual; the intelligentsia: 对~的政策 policy towards intellectuals / ~出身 with an intellectual background

知识界 zhīshijiè intellectual circles; the intelligentsia

知识就是力量 zhīshi jiù shì lìliàng knowledge is power

知识青年 zhīshi qīngnián school leavers; school graduates

知疼着热 zhīténg-zháorè (also 知冷知热 zhīlěng-zhīrè) love sb. (esp. one's husband or wife) tenderly: 他需要一个~的人。 He needs the loving care of a woman.

知无不言,言无不尽 zhī wú bù yán, yán wú bù jìn say all you know and say it without reserve

知悉 zhīxī know; learn; be informed of: 业已~ have already learned of the matter / 无从~ have no way of finding out about it

知县 zhīxiàn (in former times) county magistrate

知晓 zhīxiǎo know; be aware of; understand

知心 zhīxīn intimate; understanding: ~朋友 intimate (*or* bosom) friend / ~话 intimate words; heart-to-heart talk

知行 zhī-xíng *philos.* knowing and doing: ~统一观 the theory of the unity of knowing and doing

知行合一 zhī-xíng hé yī the unity of knowledge and practice (asserted by Wang Yangming 王阳明 of the Ming Dynasty, who believed that knowledge motivates action and that practice implies the execution of knowledge)

知音 zhīyīn a friend keenly appreciative of one's talents; an understanding friend: ~其难哉。 It is indeed

difficult to find an understanding friend. / 不惜歌者苦，但伤～稀。(《古诗十九首》) She does not regret that she is left so sad, But minds that so few can understand her song.

知遇 zhīyù　have found a patron or superior appreciative of one's ability: ～之恩 a debt of gratitude for sb.'s recognition and appreciation

知照 zhīzhào　inform; notify; tell: 你去～他一声，说我已经回来了。Please go and tell him I've come back.

知之为知之，不知为不知，是知也 zhī zhī wéi zhī zhī, bù zhī wéi bù zhī, shì zhī yě　to say you know when you know, and to say you do not when you do not, that is knowledge

知子莫若父 zhī zǐ mòruò fù　no one knows a son better than his father

知足 zhīzú　be content with one's lot

知足常乐 zhīzú chánglè　contentment brings happiness

肢

zhī　limb: 四肢 sìzhī

肢解 zhījiě　same as 支解 zhījiě

肢势 zhīshì　standing (or erect) posture (of domestic animals)

肢体 zhītǐ　① limbs ② limbs and trunk

织（織）

zhī　① weave: ～席 weave (or make) a mat ② knit: ～毛衣 knit a sweater

织补 zhībǔ　darning; invisible mending

织布 zhībù　weaving cotton cloth; weaving: ～工 weaver

织布鸟 zhībùniǎo　weaverbird

织机 zhījī　loom: 多梭箱～ multiple box loom

织锦 zhījǐn　① brocade ② picture-weaving in silk: 风景～ landscape woven in silk

织锦厂 zhījǐnchǎng　brocade mill

织锦缎 zhījǐnduàn　tapestry satin

织女 zhīnǚ　① old weaving-girl; weaving-maid; girl weaver ② (Zhīnǚ) the Weaving-girl (see also 牛郎织女 Niúláng Zhīnǚ)

织女星 Zhīnǚxīng　the Weaving-girl star—Vega

织品 zhīpǐn　textile; fabric

织袜机 zhīwàjī　hosiery machine

织物 zhīwù　fabric: 机织～ woven fabric / ～经纬密度 thread count / ～耐磨试验 wear testing

织造 zhīzào　weaving

织造厂 zhīzàochǎng　weaving mill

织针 zhīzhēn　knitting needle

织轴 zhīzhóu　text.　beam (of a loom)

祗

zhī　formal　venerate; respect

胝

zhī　see 胼胝 piánzhī

栀（梔）

zhī　see below

栀子 zhīzi　bot.　Cape jasmine

脂

zhī　① fat; grease; tallow: 含～羊毛 wool in the grease ② rouge: 脂粉 zhīfěn

脂肪 zhīfáng　fat: 动物～ animal fat / 植物～ vegetable fat

脂肪肝 zhīfánggān　med.　fatty liver

脂肪酶 zhīfángméi　biochem.　lipase

脂肪酸 zhīfángsuān　(also 脂酸 zhīsuān) fatty acid

脂肪组织 zhīfáng zǔzhī　physiol.　adipose tissue

脂粉 zhīfěn　rouge and powder; cosmetics: 薄施～ apply a light make-up

脂粉气 zhīfěnqì　womanlike ways; femininity: 温庭筠的词带有～。Wen Tingyun's ci poems are effeminate verse, redolent with the fragrance of women.

脂膏 zhīgāo　① fat; grease ② fruits of the people's labour; wealth of the people (see 民脂民膏 mínzhī-

míngāo)

脂瘤 zhīliú　med.　lipoma

脂麻 zhīma　same as 芝麻 zhīma

脂眼鲱 zhīyǎnfēi　zool.　Pacific round herring

脂油 zhīyóu　dial.　leaf fat; leaf lard

蜘

zhī　see below

蜘蛛 zhīzhū　spider: ～丝 the thread of a spider web; cobweb / ～网 spider (or spider's) web; cobweb

蜘蛛抱蛋 zhīzhūbàodàn　bot.　(common) aspidistra (*Aspidistra elatior*)

zhí

执（執）

zhí　① hold; grasp: 手～红旗 hold (or carry) a red banner ② take charge of; direct; manage: 执教 zhíjiào ③ stick to (one's views, etc.); persist: 各执一词 gè zhí yī cí ④ carry out; observe: 执礼 zhílǐ ⑤ formal　catch; capture: 战败被～ be captured after being defeated in battle ⑥ written acknowledgement: 回执 huízhí

执傲 zhí'ào　obstinate and arrogant

执笔 zhíbǐ　write; do the actual writing: 这封信是集体讨论，由老王～的。The letter was discussed by us all, but Lao Wang did the actual writing.

执鞭 zhíbiān　formal　hold the teacher's pointer—be a teacher

执法 zhífǎ　enforce (or execute) the law: 有法必依，～必严，违法必究。When there is a law, it must be obeyed, its enforcement must be strict, and lawbreakers must be prosecuted.

执法如山 zhífǎ rú shān　enforce the law strictly

执绋 zhífú　take part in a funeral procession

执管 zhíguǎn　be in charge of

执教 zhíjiào　be a teacher; teach: 他在北京师范学院～多年。He taught at Beijing Teachers College for many years.

执礼 zhílǐ　formal　observe the rules of etiquette: ～甚恭 be punctilious in observing the rules of etiquette / 执弟子礼 treat sb. with the deference expected of a pupil

执迷不悟 zhí mí bù wù　obstinately stick to a wrong course; be perverse; refuse to come to one's senses

执泥 zhíní　obstinate; stubborn

执牛耳 zhí niú'ěr　(of an ancient prince presiding over a ceremony marking the conclusion of an alliance) hold the plate on which lie the ears of a sacrificial bull—be the acknowledged leader; occupy a leading position

执拗 zhíniù　stubborn; pigheaded; wilful

执勤 zhíqín　be on duty

执行 zhíxíng　carry out; execute; implement: ～任务 carry out a task; perform a mission / ～命令 execute an order / ～纪律 enforce discipline / ～独立自主的外交政策 pursue (or implement, follow) an independent foreign policy

执行机构 zhíxíng jīgòu　executive body

执行机关 zhíxíng jīguān　executive organ

执行秘书 zhíxíng mìshū　executive secretary

执行委员会 zhíxíng wěiyuánhuì　executive committee

执行员 zhíxíngyuán　leg.　marshal (responsible for executing all civil case decisions and criminal case decisions concerning questions of property)

执行主席 zhíxíng zhǔxí　executive (or presiding) chairman

执刑 zhíxíng　carry out the execution

执意 zhíyì　insist on; be determined to; be bent on: 他～要走。He insisted on leaving. / 她～不收彩礼。She

firmly refused to accept betrothal presents from her *fiancé's* family.

执友 zhíyǒu *formal* intimate friend; bosom friend

执掌 zhízhǎng wield; be in control of: ～兵权 wield military power

执照 zhízhào license; permit: 驾驶～ driver's license

执政 zhízhèng be in power; be in office; be at the helm of the state

执政党 zhízhèngdǎng the party in power (*or* in office); the ruling (*or* governing) party

执中 zhízhōng *formal* fair and unbiased; impartial

执著 zhízhuó persistent; persevering: ～地追求艺术上的完美 strive perseveringly for artistic perfection

直

zhí ① straight: 街道又宽又～。The streets are wide and straight. / 把铁丝拉～ straighten a piece of wire ② straighten: ～起腰来 straighten one's back; stand up straight ③ vertical; perpendicular: ～行的文字 characters written from top to bottom / 这屋子～里有六米, 横里有三米。The room is 6 metres in length and 3 in width. ④ just; upright: 正直 zhèngzhí ⑤ frank; straightforward: ～认不讳 admit frankly; own up readily / 我就～说了。I'll speak very frankly. ⑥ stiff; numb: 天太冷, 手指都冻～。It was so cold that my fingers were frozen stiff. ⑦ vertical stroke (in Chinese characters) ⑧ *adv.* directly; straight: 一～走 go straight ahead / ～奔火车站 head direct for the railway station / ～通港口 lead directly to the harbour / ～飞北京 fly nonstop to Beijing ⑨ *adv.* continuously: 新井～往外喷油。Oil gushed continuously from the new well. / 他冻得～哆嗦。He was so cold that he kept shivering. / 这个故事逗得她～乐。The story tickled her fancy. ⑩ *adv.* just; simply: 待他～如兄弟 treat him just like a brother / 疼得～像针扎一样 feel a piercing pain

直笔 zhíbǐ a straight pen—unprejudiced writings: ～不讳 give a plain uncoloured account

直笔谠论 zhíbǐ-dǎnglùn unprejudiced writings and outspoken criticisms (usu. said of a newspaper); the mirror of truth

直播 zhíbō ① *agric.* direct seeding ② live radio or TV transmission

直布罗陀 Zhíbùluótuó Gibraltar

直布罗陀海峡 Zhíbùluótuó Hǎixiá the Strait(s) of Gibraltar

直肠 zhícháng *physiol.* rectum

直肠癌 zhícháng'ái carcinoma of the rectum

直肠镜 zhíchángjìng *med.* proctoscope

直肠炎 zhíchángyán proctitis; rectitis

直肠直肚 zhícháng-zhídù *inf.* straightforward; frank

直肠子 zhíchángzi *inf.* ① straightforward; downright; forthright ② a straightforward person

直陈 zhíchén speak frankly; state outright

直尺 zhíchǐ straightedge

直齿轮 zhíchǐlún *mech.* straight gear

直翅目昆虫 zhíchìmù kūnchóng orthopteran

直刺 zhícì ① straight thrust (in fencing) ② *Chin. med.* perpendicular inserting (in acupuncture)

直达 zhídá through; nonstop: ～福州的火车 a through train to Fuzhou / ～车 through train or through bus / ～车票 through ticket / ～路线 through route

直打直 zhídǎzhí *inf.* straightforward; blunt; point-blank: ～地说 put it bluntly

直待 zhídài wait until (a certain time or period)

直捣 zhídǎo drive straight on to: ～匪巢 drive straight on to the bandits' den

直捣黄龙 zhídǎo Huánglóng drive straight on to Huanglong (i.e. the enemy stronghold; Huanglong, or Huanglongfu, being an administrative centre of the Nuzhen Tartars 女真, in what is now Jilin Province, which the

Song general Yue Fei 岳飞 vowed to take)

直到 zhídào ① until: 我们～昨晚才接到通知。We didn't get the notice until last night. ② up to: ～现在我们还没有接到正式通知。We've received no official information about it up to now.

直道而行 zhídào ér xíng follow the straight path—act with rectitude

直裰 zhíduō a loose robe worn by a Buddhist monk or a Taoist priest

直根 zhígēn *bot.* taproot

直贡呢 zhígòngní *text.* venetian

直勾勾 zhígōugōu (stare) fixedly: 他～地望着我。He stared fixedly at me.

直观 zhíguān directly perceived through the senses; audio-visual: ～教具 aids to object teaching; audio-visual aids / ～教学 object teaching / ～教学课 object lesson

直话 zhíhuà straightforward talk: ～直说 speak frankly

直角 zhíjiǎo *math.* right angle

直角尺 zhíjiǎochǐ square

直角三角形 zhíjiǎo sānjiǎoxíng right (*or* right-angled) triangle

直接 zhíjiē direct; immediate: ～原因 immediate cause; direct cause / ～会晤 meet sb. in person / 由公司～经营 be run directly by the company / ～交涉 negotiate directly with sb.; talk things over face to face with sb.

直接宾语 zhíjiē bīnyǔ *gram.* direct object

直接经验 zhíjiē jīngyàn *philos.* direct experience

直接起飞 zhíjiē qǐfēi rolling (*or* follow-through) takeoff; rolling start

直接染料 zhíjiē rǎnliào direct dyes

直接税 zhíjiēshuì direct tax

直接推理 zhíjiē tuīlǐ immediate reasoning

直接选举 zhíjiē xuǎnjǔ direct election

直接着陆 zhíjiē zhuólù straight-in landing

直截 zhíjié (also 直捷 zhíjié) straightforward; blunt; point-blank

直截了当 zhíjié-liǎodàng straightforward; blunt; point-blank: ～的回答 a point-blank (*or* direct) answer / ～地说吧。Let's put it bluntly. *or* Come straight to the point. / ～地拒绝对方的无理要求 flatly reject the other side's unreasonable demands

直径 zhíjìng diameter: 大～ major diameter / 小～ minor diameter

直觉 zhíjué *psychol.* intuition

直觉主义 zhíjuézhǔyì *psychol.* intuitionism

直来直去 zhílái-zhíqù frank and outspoken; blunt: 他是个～的人, 说话有口无心。He's a blunt man, often speaking sharply but meaning no harm.

直立茎 zhílìjīng *bot.* erect stern

直溜溜 zhíliūliū perfectly straight: ～的大马路 a straight, broad avenue

直溜 zhíliu perfectly straight: 你看这棵小树, 长得多～儿。Look at this small tree—standing so erect.

直流电 zhíliúdiàn direct current (D.C.)

直眉瞪眼 zhíméi-dèngyǎn ① stare in anger; fume ② stare blankly; be in a daze; be stupefied: 他～地站在那里, 也不说话。He stood there staring blankly, saying nothing.

直射距离 zhíshè jùlí *mil.* battle-sight range; point-blank range

直升飞机 zhíshēng fēijī helicopter; copter: ～机场 heliport / ～母舰 helicopter carrier / ～运载 helilift

直抒己见 zhí shū jǐ jiàn state one's views frankly; be plainspoken

直属 zhíshǔ directly under; directly subordinate (*or* affiliated) to: 国务院～机关 departments directly under the State Council

直率 zhíshuài frank; candid; straightforward: 你～地告

诉我吧。Now tell me frankly. / 她说话很～。She is very straightforward in what she says.

直爽 zhíshuǎng frank; candid; straightforward; forthright: 性格～ forthright in character

直挺挺 zhítǐngtǐng straight; stiff; bolt upright: ～地站着 stand ramrod straight / ～地坐着 sit bolt upright

直筒子 zhítǒngzi a straightforward person

直系亲属 zhíxì qīnshǔ directly-related members of one's family—parents, spouse and children

直辖 zhíxiá directly under the jurisdiction of: 文化部～机构 organizations directly under the Ministry of Culture

直辖市 zhíxiáshì municipality directly under the Central Government

直线 zhíxiàn ① straight line: 两点之间以～为最短。A straight line is the shortest distance between 2 points. / ～距离二十里 twenty li as the crow flies / ～飞行 rectilinear (or straight) flight / ～爬高 rectilinear (or straight) climb ② steep; sharp (rise or fall): 捕鱼量～上升。The total catch of fish has shot up. / 废品率～下降。The rate of rejects fell sharply.

直线加速器 zhíxiàn jiāsùqì phys. linear accelerator

直线运动 zhíxiàn yùndòng phys. rectilinear motion

直心眼儿 zhíxīnyǎnr inf. open; frank; straightforward

直性 zhíxìng straightforward; downright; forthright

直性子 zhíxìngzi ① straightforward; downright; forthright ② a straightforward person: 他是个～，有什么说什么。He's a straightforward chap, always ready to say what's on his mind.

直言 zhíyán speak bluntly; state outright: 恕我～。Excuse me for speaking bluntly.

直言不讳 zhíyán bùhuì speak without reservation; not mince words; call a spade a spade: 他～地指出我们工作中的缺点。He pointed out the shortcomings in our work without mincing words.

直言贾祸 zhíyán gǔ huò straight talk brings trouble

直译 zhíyì word-for-word translation; literal translation

直音 zhíyīn phonet. traditional method of indicating the pronunciation of a Chinese character by citing another character with the same pronunciation

直展云 zhízhǎnyún meteorol. cloud with vertical development

直至 zhízhì ① until: 继续战斗，～胜利。Keep on fighting till victory is assured. ② up to: ～此时 up to this moment

侄（姪）

zhí brother's son; nephew

侄妇 zhífù formal wife of brother's son; nephew's wife

侄女 zhínǚ brother's daughter; niece

侄女婿 zhínǚxu husband of brother's daughter; niece's husband

侄孙 zhísūn brother's grandson; grandnephew

侄孙女 zhísūnnǚ brother's granddaughter; grandniece

侄媳妇 zhíxífu wife of brother's son; nephew's wife

侄子 zhízi (also 侄儿 zhír) brother's son; nephew

值

zhí ① value: 币值 bìzhí ② be worth: 这～多少钱? How much (or What) is this worth? / 这只戒指～五百元。This ring is worth 500 yuan. ③ happen to: 你上次来访，正～我外出。I happened to be out when you called. / ～此贵国三十周年国庆之际 on the occasion of the 30th anniversary of your National Day ④ be on duty; take one's turn at sth.: 轮值 lúnzhí ⑤ math. value

值班 zhíbān be on duty: ～员 person on duty / 今天谁～? Who's on duty today? / 他值夜班。He's on night duty. or He's on the night shift.

值不当 zhíbudàng dial. not be worthwhile

值乘 zhíchéng (of crewmen) be on duty

值当 zhídàng dial. be worthwhile; be to one's advantage

值得 zhíde be worth; merit; deserve: ～买 be worth buying / ～赞许 deserve commendation; be praiseworthy / ～怀疑 be open to doubt / ～仔细考虑 warrant careful consideration / 历史的经验～注意。Historical experience merits attention. / 李贺的诗很～一读。Li He's poems are well worth reading. / 这个展览会很～一看。The exhibition is well worth a visit. / 不～一提 not be worth mentioning / 这辆旧车不～修了。This old bike isn't worth repairing.

值分布理论 zhífēnbù lǐlùn math. value distribution theory

值价 zhíjià dial. costly; valuable

值钱 zhíqián costly; valuable: 这张画～。This is a valuable painting. / 这些邮票不～。These stamps are worthless.

值勤 zhíqín (of armymen, policemen, etc.) be on duty; be on point duty: 晚上有民兵～巡逻。There are night patrols by the militia. / ～交通警 policeman on point duty / ～人员 personnel on duty

值日 zhírì be on duty for the day; be one's turn to be on duty: 今天谁～打扫教室? Whose turn is it to clean the classroom today? / ～表 duty roster; rota / ～生 student on duty

值星 zhíxīng (of army officers) be on duty for the week: 本周是王连长～。Company commander Wang is the officer of the week.

值夜 zhíyè be on night duty; be on the night shift

值遇 zhíyù formal meet with; come across; encounter

职（職）

zhí ① duty; job: 尽职 jìnzhí ② post; office: 就职 jiùzhí / 在职 zàizhí ③ manage; direct: 职掌 zhízhǎng① ④ old (used in official reports to superiors) I ⑤ formal because of: ～是之故 for this particular reason

职别 zhíbié official rank

职称 zhíchēng the title of a technical or professional post (such as engineer, professor, lecturer, academician, etc.): 学术～和技术～ academic and technical titles

职分 zhífèn ① duty ② official post; position

职工 zhígōng ① staff and workers; workers and staff members ② old workers; labour: ～运动 labour movement; trade union movement

职官 zhíguān officials

职能 zhínéng function: 货币的～ the functions of money / ～机构 functional institution

职权 zhíquán powers or authority of office: 行使～ exercise one's functions and powers / 超越～ overstep one's authority; exceed one's powers

职权范围 zhíquán fànwéi limits (or scope) of one's functions and powers; terms of reference: 在自己的～内 within one's functions and powers / 委员会的～ terms of reference for a commission

职事 zhíshì ① post; duties; job ② old occupation; profession; vocation

职守 zhíshǒu post; duty: 忠于～ be faithful in the discharge of one's duties; be devoted to one's duty

职司 zhísī formal ① post; duties; job ② be in charge of; administer: ～财政 administer finances

职位 zhíwèi position; post

职务 zhíwù post; duties; job: 履行～ do (or perform) one's duties / ～工资 wages related to specific work posts / 我们～不同，但都是为人民服务。Our jobs may be different but we all serve the people.

职衔 zhíxián post and rank

职业 zhíyè occupation; profession; vocation: 从事各种～的人 people of all occupations / 这里填上你的姓名、～等等。Put down your name, occupation, etc. here. / 他的～是医生。He is a doctor by profession. / 我们的～有保障。Our jobs are secure.

职业病 zhíyèbìng occupational disease

职业团体 zhíyè tuántǐ professional organization

职业外交官 zhíyè wàijiāoguān career diplomat

职业学校 zhíyè xuéxiào vocational school

职业运动员 zhíyè yùndòngyuán professional athlete; professional

职员 zhíyuán office worker; staff member; functionary

职责 zhízé duty; obligation; responsibility: 应尽的～ bounden duty / 神圣～ sacred duty / 分清～ define the duties incumbent on each person or post

职掌 zhízhǎng formal ① be in charge of: ～财务 be in charge of financial affairs ② duty; charge

职志 zhízhì formal lifework; mission: 以教育为～ take education as one's lifework

填 zhí formal clay

植 zhí ① plant; grow: 植树 zhíshù / 移植 yízhí ② set up; establish: 植党营私 zhídǎng yíngsī

植保 zhíbǎo short for 植物保护 zhíwù bǎohù

植被 zhíbèi bot. vegetation

植党营私 zhídǎng yíngsī set up a clique for one's own selfish interests

植苗 zhímiáo plant seedlings

植皮 zhípí med. skin grafting

植绒 zhíróng text. flocking

植树 zhíshù tree planting: ～造林 afforestation

植树节 Zhíshùjié National Treeplanting Day (March 12)

植物 zhíwù plant; flora

植物保护 zhíwù bǎohù plant (or crop) protection: ～机械 equipment for plant protection / ～员 plant protector

植物病害 zhíwù bìnghài plant disease

植物检疫 zhíwù jiǎnyì plant quarantine

植物胶 zhíwù jiāo vegetable gum or glue

植物界 zhíwùjiè plant kingdom; vegetable kingdom

植物净化 zhíwù jìnghuà environ. protec. plant purification

植物区系 zhíwù qūxì flora

植物群落 zhíwù qúnluò plant community

植物人 zhíwùrén vegetable (a human being)

植物生长调节剂 zhíwù shēngzhǎng tiáojiéjì agric. plant growth regulator

植物纤维 zhíwù xiānwéi plant fibre

植物性神经 zhíwùxìng shénjīng physiol. autonomic nerve

植物学 zhíwùxué botany: ～家 botanist

植物油 zhíwùyóu vegetable oil

植物育种 zhíwù yùzhǒng plant breeding

植物园 zhíwùyuán botanical garden

植物志 zhíwùzhì flora

植株 zhízhū agric. plant

絷（縶） zhí formal ① tie up; fasten ② take into custody ③ horse reins

殖 zhí breed; multiply: 生殖 shēngzhí ——see also shi

殖民 zhímín establish a colony; colonize: 非～化 decolonize; decolonization / ～国家 colonialist power / ～扩张 colonial expansion / ～战争 colonialist war

殖民地 zhímíndì colony: 沦为～ be reduced to a colony / ～国家 colonial country / ～人民 people under colonial rule; colonial people

殖民主义 zhímínzhǔyì colonialism: ～祸害 the scourge of colonialism / 新～ new colonialism; neocolonialism / ～者 colonialist

跖 zhí same as 蹠 zhí

摭 zhí formal pick up

摭拾 zhíshí formal pick; gather; collect: ～群言 collect views from various sources

躑（躅） zhí see below

躑躅 zhízhú formal walk to and fro; loiter around: ～街头 tramp the streets

蹠 zhí ① physiol. metatarsus ② formal sole of the foot ③ formal tread

蹠骨 zhígǔ physiol. metatarsal bones

zhǐ

止 zhǐ ① stop: ～痒 stop or relieve itching / 不达目的不～ refuse to give up without attaining one's aim ② to; till: 从本月十号起到十六号～ from the 10th to the 16th of this month ③ only: ～此一家。This is the only shop.

止步 zhǐbù halt; stop; go no further: ～不前 halt; stand still / 如果就此～，就会前功尽弃。If we stop where we are, all our previous efforts will be wasted. / 游人～ no visitors; out of bounds

止动机构 zhǐdòng jīgòu mech. stop motion (mechanism)

止付 zhǐfù banking stop payment: ～通知书 stop-payment notice

止境 zhǐjìng end; limit: 科学的发展是没有～的。There is no limit to the development of science.

止咳 zhǐké relieve a cough

止咳糖浆 zhǐké tángjiāng cough syrup

止渴 zhǐkě quench one's thirst

止水 zhǐshuǐ stagnant water

止宿 zhǐsù stay; put up; get accommodation

止痛 zhǐtòng relieve pain; stop pain

止痛药 zhǐtòngyào anodyne; analgesic; pain-killer

止息 zhǐxī cease; stop

止泻药 zhǐxièyào antidiarrheal

止血 zhǐxuè stop bleeding; stanch bleeding

止血带 zhǐxuèdài tourniquet

止血器 zhǐxuèqì haemostat

止血药 zhǐxuèyào haemostatic

只（祇、衹） zhǐ adv. only; just; merely: ～剩一个了。There is only one left. / 我～想问一个问题。I have just one question. / 这～是个时间问题。It is merely a question of time. / 我们这车～能带三个人。We can only take three people in our car. / 屋子里～老王一个人。Old Wang was alone in the house. / ～那块地就打了八百斤小麦。That plot alone yielded 800 jin of wheat. ——see also zhī

只不过 zhǐbuguò adv. only; just; merely: 这～是一种猜测。It's just (or nothing but) a guess. / 别害怕，他～是吓唬你。Don't be afraid. He was only trying to frighten you. / ～拼错几个字罢了，有什么可大惊小怪的? It's only some spelling mistakes. What's there to be surprised at? / 我～拧了拧门把手，可它却掉了。The door knob came off when I gave it a mere turn.

只此一家，别无分店 zhǐ cǐ yī jiā, bié wú fēndiàn the only shop of this name—no branches anywhere (a shop sign warning of sham goods)

只得 zhǐdé *adv.* have no alternative but to; be obliged to; have to: 他们～把会议延期。 They had no alternative but to put the meeting off. / 没有桥，我们～涉水过去。 As there was no bridge, we were obliged to wade across. / 别人都走不开，～我自己去了。 Since all the others were tied up, I had to go myself. / 我知道着急没用，～冷静一点。 I knew that it was useless to worry about it, so I forced myself to keep calm.

只顾 zhǐgù ① be only concerned with; just think of: 你别～自己。 Don't just think of yourself. ② *adv.* (do sth.) single-mindedly; just (do sth.): 他～赚钱。 He's just trying to make money.

只管 zhǐguǎn *adv.* ① by all means: 有意见～提出来。 Don't hesitate to put forward your suggestions if you have any. / 你～干下去。 Go ahead by all means. ② simply; just: 我的话你～相信，不会有错。 You must believe me simply on my word. / 他不会使桨，小船～在湖中打转。 He couldn't use the oars, so the boat just turned round and round on the lake.

只好 zhǐhǎo *adv.* have to; be forced to: ～作罢 be forced to give up / 银行不给我们贷款，我们～另想办法。 As the bank refused to grant us a loan, we could not but seek other means. / 末班车过去了，我们～走回家。 As the last bus had gone, we had to walk home. / 十点钟他还不来，～我一个人先去了。 By ten o'clock he still hadn't turned up, so I had to go by myself.

只可意会，不可言传 zhǐkě yìhuì, bùkě yánchuán can be sensed, but not explained in words; can be apprehended but not expressed

只是 zhǐshì ① *adv.* only; just; merely: 我今天进城，～去看看朋友，没有什么要紧的事儿。 Today I'm going to town just to see friends, not on business. / 我说这个，开个玩笑罢了。 I said it merely as a joke. / 大家问他是什么事，他～一笑，不回答。 When people asked him what had happened, he simply laughed without replying. / 随便你怎么问，他～不吭声。 No matter how you question him, he just kept silent. ② *conj.* except that; only; but: 这架电视机不错，～小了点。 This TV set is quite good, only it's a bit too small. / 你那篇文章写得很好，～太长。 Your essay is good except that it is too long. / 他各方面都很好，～身体差些。 He's good in every respect except in health. / 他想去，～去不了。 He wants to go , only he can't.

只听楼梯响，不见人下来 zhǐ tīng lóutī xiǎng, bù jiàn rén xiàlai the stairs creak but no one comes down—much talk but no action

只消 zhǐxiāo *dial.* all one has to do is; you only need to: ～来个电话，货物马上送到。 Just give us a ring and the goods will be delivered without delay.

只许官放火，不许百姓点灯 zhǐ xǔ zhōuguān fànghuǒ, bù xǔ bǎixìng diǎndēng the magistrates are free to burn down houses, while the common people are forbidden even to light lamps; one may steal a horse while another may not look over the hedge

只要 zhǐyào *conj.* (usu. used correlatively with 就 or 便) if only; as long as; provided: ～你有钱就办得到。 You could do it if only you had the money. / ～你在这儿，我就放心了。 As long as you're here, I'll have nothing to worry about. / ～虚心，就会进步。 Provided you are modest, you'll surely make progress.

只要功夫深，铁杵磨成针 zhǐyào gōngfu shēn, tiěchǔ móchéng zhēn if you work at it hard enough, you can grind an iron rod into a needle—perseverance spells success

只有 zhǐyǒu ① *conj.* only; alone: ～依靠群众，才能做好工作。 Only by relying on the masses can you do your work well. / 他知道这事的内情。 He alone knows the inside story. / ～在紧急情况下，才能动用这笔款项。 We can draw on the fund only in an emergency. / 要上山，～这么一条路。 This is the only path up the mountain. ② *adv.* have to; be forced to: 如果下大雨，比赛～延期。 If it rains hard we have to put off the match. / 你～采取这个办法了。 This is the only way open to you.

只争朝夕 zhǐ zhēng zhāoxī seize the day, seize the hour; seize every minute; race against time

只重衣衫不重人 zhǐ zhòng yīshān bù zhòng rén only value the clothes and not the man himself; judge people by their clothes, not their qualities

旨¹
zhǐ *formal* tasty; delicious: 甘旨 gānzhǐ

旨² (恉)
zhǐ purport; purpose; aim: ～在唤起民众 for the purpose of arousing the masses / ～在加快工程进度的措施 measures aimed at speeding up the project

旨³
zhǐ decree: 圣旨 shèngzhǐ

旨酒 zhǐjiǔ *formal* excellent wine

旨趣 zhǐqù *formal* purport; objective

旨要 zhǐyào same as 指要 zhǐyào

旨意 zhǐyì decree; order: 你这样做是奉谁的～? On whose orders did you do this?

址 (阯)
zhǐ location; site: 地址 dìzhǐ

芷
zhǐ see 白芷 báizhǐ

纸 (帋)
zhǐ ① paper: 一张～ a piece (or sheet) of paper ② *m.* (for letters, documents, etc.): 一～公文 a document / 单据三～ three bills

纸板 zhǐbǎn paperboard; cardboard: ～盒 (箱) cardboard case or box; carton

纸版 zhǐbǎn *print.* paper mould; paper matrix

纸包不住火 zhǐ bāobuzhù huǒ you can't wrap fire in paper—there is no concealing the truth; truth will out

纸币 zhǐbì paper money; paper currency; note: 不兑现～ fiat money

纸锭 zhǐdìng paper ingots (burned as offerings to the dead)

纸贵洛阳 zhǐ guì Luòyáng same as 洛阳纸贵 Luòyáng zhǐ guì

纸花 zhǐhuā paper flower

纸浆 zhǐjiāng paper pulp; pulp: ～板 pulp board / ～厂 pulp mill / ～筛滤器 pulp strainer / ～原材 pulpwood / ～制造机 macerator

纸巾 zhǐjīn paper towel; towel

纸老虎 zhǐlǎohǔ paper tiger: 一切反动派都是～。 All reactionaries are paper tigers.

纸马 zhǐmǎ ① paper painted with pictures of idols and burned at the altar ② *dial.* human figures, carriages, horses, etc. made of paper and burned as offerings to the dead

纸煤儿 zhǐméir (also 纸媒儿 zhǐméir) paper rolled into a thin stick used to light a pipe, etc.

纸捻 zhǐniǎn spill of rolled paper used to light a pipe, etc.; (paper) spill

纸牌 zhǐpái playing cards

纸钱 zhǐqián paper made to resemble money and burned as an offering to the dead

纸上谈兵 zhǐshàng tán bīng fight only on paper; be an armchair strategist; engage in idle theorizing

纸绳 zhǐshéng paper string

纸头 zhǐtóu *dial.* paper

纸型 zhǐxíng *print.* paper mould; paper matrix: ～干燥机 scorcher

纸烟 zhǐyān cigarette

纸鹞 zhǐyào *dial.* kite

纸叶子　zhǐyèzi　*dial.*　playing cards
纸鱼　zhǐyú　silverfish; fish moth
纸鸢　zhǐyuān　kite
纸张　zhǐzhāng　paper
纸醉金迷　zhǐzuì-jīnmí　(a life of) luxury and dissipation

抵　zhǐ　*formal*　knock one's fist against the palm

抵掌　zhǐzhǎng　*formal*　knock one's fist against the palm (to show happiness): ～而谈 have a happy and intimate chat

祉　zhǐ　*formal*　happiness; blessedness: 福祉 fúzhǐ

指　zhǐ　① finger: 拇指 mǔzhǐ ② fingerbreadth; digit: 两～宽的纸条 a strip of paper two fingerbreadths wide／下了四～雨. We had about three inches of rain. ③ point at; point to: 时针～向十二点. The hour hand points to twelve.／他朝那个门～了。He pointed his finger at that door. ④ indicate; point out; refer to: 党中央给我们～航向. The Party's Central Committee charts our course.／～出正确方向 point out the correct way／～出缺点 point out sb.'s shortcomings／他的话不是～你说的。His remarks were not directed at you.／文学史上谈到李、杜，～的是李白和杜甫. In histories of Chinese literature, Li and Du refer to Li Bai and Du Fu. ⑤ depend on; count on: 一家子都～着我。My wife and children depend on me.／他们就～着你帮忙呢. They're counting on your help. ⑥ (of hair) stand: 发指 fàzhǐ

指北针　zhǐběizhēn　compass
指标　zhǐbiāo　target; quota; norm; index: 完成国家计划规定的～ attain the targets (*or* fulfil the norms) set in the state plan／招工～ recruitment quota
指不定　zhǐbudìng　*dial.*　perhaps; maybe: 你甭等他了，他～来不来呢. Don't wait for him; maybe he isn't coming.
指不胜屈　zhǐ bù shèng qū　too many to be counted on the fingers; a great many
指斥　zhǐchì　reprove; reprimand; denounce
指导　zhǐdǎo　guide; direct: ～我们思想的理论基础是马克思列宁主义. The theoretical basis guiding our thinking is Marxism-Leninism.／～战争的规律 laws for directing war／老农～青年干农活. The old peasants instructed (*or* directed) the youths in farm work.／教师正在～学生做实验. The teacher was supervising his students in doing the experiment.／～思想 guiding ideology
指导性计划　zhǐdǎoxìng jìhuà　guidance planning
指导员　zhǐdǎoyuán　① common name for 政治指导员 zhèngzhì zhǐdǎoyuán ② instructor
指点　zhǐdiǎn　① give directions (*or* pointers, advice); show how (to do sth.): 教练耐心地～他们. The coach patiently instructs them.／请给我们～～. Please show us how to do it.／经他一～，我就全明白了. A few pointers from him made it all clear to me. ② gossip about sb.'s faults
指定　zhǐdìng　appoint; assign: ～谈判代表 appoint representatives to the negotiations／在～地点见面 meet at the designated place／～一位副秘书长主持这项工作 assign an Under-Secretary-General to direct the work／～他为大会发言人. He was named as the spokesman of the Conference.
指东话西　zhǐdōng-huàxī　point to the east and talk west—make pointless comments; be irrelevant
指法　zhǐfǎ　*mus.*　fingering
指腹为婚　zhǐ fù wéi hūn　an antenatal (*or* prenatal) betrothal
指骨　zhǐgǔ　*physiol.*　phalanx
指顾　zhǐgù　*formal*　in an instant; in no time
指归　zhǐguī　*formal*　aim; intention

指画　zhǐhuà　① point at; point to ② finger drawing
指环　zhǐhuán　(finger) ring
指挥　zhǐhuī　① command; direct; conduct: ～一个连 command a company; be in command of a company／～交通 direct traffic／～乐队 conduct an orchestra／我们的原则是党～枪，而决不容许枪～党. Our principle is that the Party commands the gun, and the gun must never be allowed to command the Party. ② commander; director ③ *mus.*　conductor
指挥棒　zhǐhuībàng　*mus.*　baton: 指挥举起了～. The conductor raised his baton.
指挥部　zhǐhuībù　command post; headquarters: 防空～ air defence command／会战～ campaign headquarters
指挥舱　zhǐhuīcāng　*space*　command module
指挥车　zhǐhuīchē　command car
指挥刀　zhǐhuīdāo　officer's sword
指挥官　zhǐhuīguān　commanding officer; commander
指挥若定　zhǐhuī ruò dìng　direct (work, etc.) with perfect ease; give competent leadership
指挥所　zhǐhuīsuǒ　command post
指挥塔台　zhǐhuī tǎtái　*aviation*　control tower
指挥系统　zhǐhuī xìtǒng　command system
指挥员　zhǐhuīyuán　commander
指鸡骂狗　zhǐ jī mà gǒu　point at the chicken and abuse the dog—point at one but abuse another; make oblique accusations
指甲　zhǐjia　nail: 手～ fingernail／脚～ toenail
指甲锉刀　zhǐjia cuòdāo　nail file
指甲刀　zhǐjiadāo　nail clippers
指甲盖儿　zhǐjiagàir　nail
指甲花　zhǐjiahuā　popular name for 凤仙花 fèngxiānhuā
指甲心儿　zhǐjiaxīnr　nail
指甲油　zhǐjiayóu　nail polish
指教　zhǐjiào　*pol.*　give advice or comments: 请多多～. Kindly give us your advice.／望不吝～. I hope you won't spare your comments.
指靠　zhǐkào　depend on (for one's livelihood); look to (for help); count on: 这件事我们就～你了. We'll count on you for this.
指控　zhǐkòng　accuse; charge: 有人～他纳贿. He's been accused of taking bribes.
指令　zhǐlìng　① instruct; order; direct ② instructions; order; directive: ～指标 mandatory target ③ *computer* instruction
指令性计划　zhǐlìngxìng jìhuà　mandatory planning
指鹿为马　zhǐ lù wéi mǎ　call a stag a horse—deliberately misrepresent
指路明灯　zhǐlù míngdēng　(fig.) beacon light; beacon
指路牌　zhǐlùpái　signpost; fingerpost; guidepost
指名　zhǐmíng　mention by name; name: ～攻击 assail sb. by name／领导上～要小赵参加会议. The leadership named Xiao Zhao as the one to attend the meeting.
指名道姓　zhǐmíng-dàoxìng　mention sb.'s name; name names: 这些人是谁，大家都清楚，但是我不愿～. Their names are well known, but I forbear to mention them.
指明　zhǐmíng　show clearly; demonstrate; point out: ～两者之间的差别 show clearly the difference between the two／～出路 point the way out
指模　zhǐmó　(also 指摹 zhǐmó) finger print or thumb print (used mostly by illiterates as a signature on official or legal papers)
指南　zhǐnán　guide; guidebook: 《消费者～》A Consumer's Guide
指南车　zhǐnánchē　an ancient Chinese vehicle with a wooden figure always pointing to the south
指南针　zhǐnánzhēn　compass: 十二世纪初我国航海已普遍使用～. By the early twelfth century the compass was already in general use among Chinese navigators.

指派 zhǐpài　appoint; name; designate: 〜她当车间主任 appoint her (to be) workshop director／〜代表出席会议 name delegates to the conference／双方各〜一名大使级的首席代表。Each side shall designate a senior representative, who shall be of ambassadorial rank.

指日可待 zhǐ rì kě dài　can be expected soon; be just round the corner: 胜利〜。Victory is just round the corner.

指桑骂槐 zhǐ sāng mà huái　point at the mulberry and abuse the locust—point at one but abuse another; make oblique accusations

指使 zhǐshǐ　instigate; incite; put sb. up to sth.: 〜少数坏人闹事 incite a handful of bad elements to make trouble／受别人〜 act on sb.'s instigation／揭露幕后〜者 expose the person behind the scenes; unmask the hidden instigator／这件事幕后有人〜。There must have been an instigator behind the scenes.

指示 zhǐshì　① indicate; point out: 〜前进的方向 indicate the direction of advance ② instruct: 〜部队立即出发 instruct the troops to set out at once ③ directive; instructions: 下达〜 give instructions／奉上级〜 upon boss instructions

指示板 zhǐshìbǎn　indicator board

指示代词 zhǐshì dàicí　gram. demonstrative pronoun

指示灯 zhǐshìdēng　pilot lamp (or light); indicator lamp

指示功率 zhǐshì gōnglǜ　mech. indicated power

指示剂 zhǐshìjì　chem. indicator

指示器 zhǐshìqì　indicator: 刻度盘〜 dial indicator／液面〜 level indicator

指示植物 zhǐshì zhíwù　indicator plant

指事 zhǐshì　linguis. self-explanatory characters, e.g. 上 (above) and 下 (below)—one of the six categories of Chinese characters (六书)

指手画脚 zhǐshǒu-huàjiǎo (also 指手划脚 zhǐshǒu-huàjiǎo)　① make gestures; gesticulate: 〜地高谈阔论 talk volubly with animated gestures ② make indiscreet remarks or criticisms

指数 zhǐshù　index number; index: 〜化 indexation／综合〜 composite index／生活费〜 cost of living index

指数函数 zhǐshù hánshù　math. exponential function

指数律 zhǐshùlǜ　math. index law

指天画地 zhǐtiān-huàdì　gesticulate excitedly; speak without restraint

指头 zhǐtou　① finger ② toe

指头肚儿 zhǐtoudùr　dial. face of the fingertip

指望 zhǐwàng　① look to; count on: 〜有一天能实现这个计划 look forward to the day when this plan will be put in practice／〜他长大了好好为人民服务。We hope that he'll grow up to serve the people heart and soul.／别〜他能帮你的忙。You can't count on him for help. ② prospect; hope: 解放了，我们才有了〜。It was liberation which brought us hope.／他这病还有〜吗? Is there still hope of his recovery?

指纹 zhǐwén　① loops and whorls on a finger ② fingerprint

指纹学 zhǐwénxué　dactylography

指向 zhǐxiàng　directional: 〜天线 directional antenna／〜植物 compass plant

指要 zhǐyào　formal main idea; gist

指引 zhǐyǐn　point (the way); guide; show: 猎人〜他通过了林区。The huntsman showed him the way to pass through the forest.

指印 zhǐyìn　fingerprint; finger mark: 按〜 make a fingerprint

指责 zhǐzé　censure; criticize; find fault with: 横加〜 make unwarranted charges／受到舆论的〜 be subjected to the censure of public opinion／大家〜他玩忽职守。He was criticized for neglect of duty.／用事实回击他们的〜 answer their attacks with facts／我们怎能〜这种实事求是的态度呢? How can we find fault with this realistic approach?

指摘 zhǐzhāi　censure; criticize; find fault with

指战员 zhǐzhànyuán　(collective name for 指挥员 and 战斗员) officers and men (of the PLA)

指针 zhǐzhēn　① indicator; pointer; needle ② guiding principle; guide: 作为今后工作的〜 as a guide for future work ③ Chin. med. pressing with a finger (on an acupuncture point); finger-pressing

指正 zhǐzhèng　① point out mistakes so that they can be corrected ② pol. make a comment or criticism: 请惠予〜。Please oblige me with your valuable comments. or Be kind enough to give me your opinion.

指重表 zhǐzhòngbiǎo　petroleum weight indicator

枳
zhǐ　bot. trifoliate orange

枳机草 zhǐjīcǎo　another name for 芨芨草 jījīcǎo

枳壳 zhǐqiào　Chin. med. dried fruit of citron or trifoliate orange

枳实 zhǐshí　Chin. med. dried immature fruit of citron or trifoliate orange

咫
zhǐ　an ancient measure of length, equal to 8 cun (寸)

咫尺 zhǐchǐ　formal very close: 〜之间 close at hand

咫尺天涯 zhǐchǐ-tiānyá (also 咫尺千里 zhǐchǐ-qiānlǐ)　so near and yet so far—see little of each other though living close together

趾
zhǐ　① toe ② foot

趾高气扬 zhǐgāo-qìyáng　strut about and give oneself airs; be swollen with arrogance: 〜, 目中无人 give oneself airs and look down one's nose at everybody／工作无成绩, 可以使人悲观丧气; 工作有成绩, 又可以使人〜。Lack of achievement in work may breed pessimism and depression, while achievement may breed pride and arrogance.

趾骨 zhǐgǔ　metatarsal bones

趾甲 zhǐjiǎ　toenail

黹
zhǐ　formal needlework; embroidery: 针黹 zhēnzhǐ

酯
, zhǐ　chem. ester

酯化 zhǐhuà　chem. esterify

酯酶 zhǐméi　biochem. esterase

徵
zhǐ　mus. a note of the ancient Chinese five-tone scale, corresponding to 5 in numbered musical notation

zhì

至
zhì　① formal arrive; reach: 〜京之次日 the day following my arrival at Beijing／有风飒然而〜。A gust of wind blew in. ② prep. to; until: 从左〜右 from left to right／从早〜晚 from morning till night／〜上月底为止 up to the end of last month ③ adv. formal extremely; most: 是为〜盼。That is our sincerest hope.／〜嘱。See that you act accordingly.

至宝 zhìbǎo　most valuable treasure: 如获至宝 rú huò zhìbǎo

至不济 zhìbùjì　adv. inf. at (the) least: 他们当中有的会三、四种外语, 〜也会一种外语。They can all speak at least one foreign language; some can speak even three or four.

至诚 zhìchéng　complete sincerity: 出于〜 in all

sincerity; from the bottom of one's heart /～待人 treat people with absolute sincerity

至诚 zhìchéng sincere; straightforward: ～的朋友 a sincere friend

至迟 zhìchí at (the) latest: 这条铁路～五月通车。This railway will be opened to traffic in May at the latest.

至此 zhìcǐ up to this point; at this stage: 文章～为止。The article ends at this point. /～, 事情才逐渐清楚了。The matter is only now becoming clear. / 事已～, 后悔也没有用了。There is no room for regret when matters have reached this stage. or Now it's done, regrets are no use.

至当 zhìdàng formal most suitable; most appropriate

至多 zhìduō adv. at (the) most: 这张画～两个星期就能画好。It'll take two weeks at most to finish the painting. / 他～不过四十岁。He's at most in his forties. / 他不会来开会的, 只送一个书面发言来。He isn't coming to the meeting. A written statement from him is all that we can hope for.

至高无上 zhìgāo-wúshàng most lofty; paramount; supreme: ～的事业 most lofty undertaking /～的权力 supreme power (or authority) / 在封建国家中, 皇帝有～的权力。The emperor reigned supreme in the feudal state.

至关紧要 zhì guān jǐnyào the most important; of the utmost importance

至好 zhìhǎo most intimate friend; best friend

至极 zhìjí to the utmost point; extremely: 他愤怒～。His anger reached the boiling point. or He was extremely angry. / 他真是可恨～。He is unbearably hateful.

至交 zhìjiāo most intimate friend; best friend

至今 zhìjīn up to now; to this day; so far: ～没有人提出过反对意见。Up to now no one has raised any objections. / 我～未得到他的答复。So far I've had no reply from him.

至理名言 zhìlǐ-míngyán famous dictum; maxim; axiom

至品 zhìpǐn highest grade; best quality

至亲 zhìqīn very close relative; close kin: 骨肉～ close kin; one's own flesh and blood

至亲好友 zhìqīn-hǎoyǒu close relatives and good friends: ～, 概不赊欠 (a common sign in shops in former times) no credit given—not even to kith and kin

至情 zhìqíng true feelings; real sentiments

至日 zhìrì the Summer Solstice (10th solar term) or the Winter Solstice (22nd solar term)

至若 zhìruò prep. formal as for; as to

至上 zhìshàng supreme; the highest: 艺术～ put art above everything else

至少 zhìshǎo adv. at (the) least: ～有一万人参加了大会。At least ten thousand people attended the rally. / 他并不了解我, ～是了解得不全面。He doesn't understand me, or at any rate not fully. /～可以说, 这样处理不妥。This is not the proper way to handle the matter, to say the least. / 他～五十岁了。He's at least fifty. / 你虽然没有见过他, 但一听说过他的名字吧? You haven't met him, but you must surely have heard of him.

至圣 zhìshèng the greatest sage—Confucius

至圣先师 zhìshèng xiānshī the greatest sage and teacher—Confucius

至死 zhìsǐ unto death; till death: ～不屈 not yield even unto death

至死不变 zhìsǐ bù biàn will not change even unto death; stick to one's course until the end of one's days

至死不悟 zhìsǐ bù wù remain benighted to the end of one's days; be incorrigibly stubborn

至言 zhìyán pertinent remarks; profound words

至友 zhìyǒu most intimate friend; best friend

至于 zhìyú ① prep. as for; as to: ～其他问题, 以后再

说。As for other matters, we'll take them up later. / 我愿意读一读他写的书, ～出版吗, 那是另外一回事。I'm willing to read his book, but as to publishing it, that's a different matter. ② go so far as to: 你要是早请大夫看, 何～病成这样? If you had seen the doctor earlier, you wouldn't be so seriously ill.

至尊 zhìzūn the most revered and respected—the emperor

忮 zhì formal jealousy

识（識） zhì formal ① remember; commit to memory: 博闻强识 bówén-qiángzhì ② mark; sign: 款识 kuǎnzhì ——see also shí

志[1] zhì will; aspiration; ideal: ～坚如钢 have an iron will; have a will of steel

志[2] zhì dial. weigh; measure: 拿碗～～ measure sth. with a bowl

志[3]**（誌）** zhì ① keep in mind: 永志不忘 yǒng zhì bù wàng ② records; annals: 《三国～》History of the Three Kingdoms / 《昌黎方言～》A Survey of the Changli Dialect ③ mark; sign: 标志 biāozhì

志哀 zhì'āi indicate mourning: 下半旗～ fly a flag at half-mast as a sign of mourning

志大才疏 zhìdà-cáishū have great ambition but little talent; have high aspirations but little ability

志悼 zhìdào condole

志得意满 zhìdé-yìmǎn enormously proud of one's success; smug; complacent

志怪 zhìguài record or write about weird, uncanny or supernatural things: ～小说 tales of mystery and the supernatural

志留纪 Zhìliújì geol. the Silurian Period

志留系 Zhìliúxì geol. Silurian

志气 zhìqi aspiration; ambition: 中国人民有～。The Chinese people have high aspirations.

志趣 zhìqù aspiration and interest; inclination; bent: 她的～主要是在语言和文学方面。Her main interests are language and literature.

志士 zhìshì person of ideals and integrity: 爱国～ a noble-minded patriot

志士仁人 zhìshì-rénrén people with high ideals

志书 zhìshū district annals; local histories

志同道合 zhìtóng-dàohé cherish the same ideals and follow the same path; have a common goal: 两人～, 谈得投机, 只恨相见之晚。Having the same interests, they had a most agreeable chat. They only regretted that they had not met sooner.

志喜 zhìxǐ offer congratulations (as on sb.'s wedding day)

志向 zhìxiàng aspiration; ideal; ambition: 青年人应有远大的～。Young people should have lofty aspirations.

志行 zhìxíng one's aspirations and conduct

志学 zhìxué formal ① set one's mind on study ② (used esp. in) ～之年 the age of fifteen (from Confucius' saying 吾十有五而志于学 "At fifteen I set my heart on learning")

志愿 zhìyuàn ① aspiration; wish; ideal ② do sth. of one's own free will; volunteer

志愿兵 zhìyuànbīng volunteer (soldier)

志愿军 zhìyuànjūn people who volunteer to fight in another country; volunteers

志愿书 zhìyuànshū application form: 入党～ application for Party membership

志在必得 zhì zài bì dé be determined to win: 我队参加这次锦标赛, ～。We are determined to come in first in

the championships.

志子 zhìzi *dial.* a measure (implement)

豸 zhì *formal* insect without feet or legs (mentioned in ancient books): 虫豸 chóngzhì

治 zhì ① rule; govern; administer; manage: 统治 tǒngzhì ② order; peace: 治世 zhìshì ③ *old* seat of a local government: 县治 xiànzhì ④ treat (a disease); cure: 他的病不久就～好了。He was soon cured of his illness. /～好战争创伤 heal the wounds of war ⑤ control; harness (a river): ～淮 harness the Huai River ⑥ wipe out (injurious insects): 治蝗 zhìhuáng ⑦ punish: 他老是违反监规，非好好～～他不可。He always violates the prison regulations and should be given a good punishment. ⑧ study; research: 专～宋史 specialize in the history of the Song Dynasty

治安 zhì'ān public order; public security: 维持～ maintain public order / 该市～情况良好（不好）。Public order is good (poor) in that city. /～保卫委员会 public security committee

治本 zhìběn effect a permanent cure; get at the root (of a problem, etc.); take radical measures: 河流的～工程 project for the permanent control of a river

治标 zhìbiāo merely alleviate the symptoms of an illness; bring about a temporary solution (of a problem, etc.); take stopgap measures

治病救人 zhìbìng-jiùrén cure the sickness to save the patient: 要以"～"的态度帮助犯错误的同志。To help comrades who have made mistakes, we should adopt the approach of "curing the sickness to save the patient".

治产 zhìchǎn manage property

治国 zhìguó administer (*or* run) a country; manage state affairs

治国安民 zhìguó-ānmín run the country well and give the people peace and security

治蝗 zhìhuáng eliminate locusts

治绩 zhìjì the achievements of a regime or a government

治家 zhìjiā manage a household

治碱 zhìjiǎn combat alkalinity

治理 zhìlǐ ① administer; govern: ～国家 administer a country; run a state ② harness; bring under control; put in order: ～河流 harness a river; bring a river under control

治疗 zhìliáo treat; cure: 住院～ be hospitalized /～效果 therapeutic effect / 她还在医院～。She is still under treatment in hospital. / 预防胜于～。Prevention is better than cure.

治疗学 zhìliáoxué therapeutics

治丧 zhìsāng make funeral arrangements: ～委员会 funeral committee

治沙 zhìshā control sand

治山治水 zhìshān-zhìshuǐ transform mountains and tame rivers

治世 zhìshì times of peace and prosperity

治水 zhìshuǐ regulate rivers and watercourses; prevent floods by water control

治丝益棻 zhì sī yì fén try to sort silk threads only to tangle them further—try to help but only hinder; make matters worse; make confusion worse confounded

治所 zhìsuǒ *old* seat of local government

治外法权 zhìwài fǎquán extraterritoriality; exterritoriality; extrality

治学 zhìxué *formal* pursue one's studies; do scholarly research: 他以～严谨著称。He is noted for his meticulous scholarship. / 实事求是才是～的正确态度。To seek truth from facts is the correct approach in academic pursuits.

治愈率 zhìyùlǜ *med.* cure rate

治装 zhìzhuāng *formal* purchase things necessary (esp. clothes) for a long journey

治罪 zhìzuì punish sb. (for a crime)

帜（幟） zhì *formal* flag; banner: 旗帜 qízhì

炙 zhì ① broil; roast ② *formal* roast meat

炙手可热 zhì shǒu kě rè if you stretch out your hand you feel the heat (said of the imperative manner of a person with power)

帙 zhì *formal* ① cloth slip-case for a book ② *m.* (for books with a cloth slip-case)

郅 zhì *formal* most; extreme

质¹（質） zhì ① nature; character: 实质 shízhì ② quality: 按～分等 grade according to quality /～的飞跃 a qualitative leap /～优价廉 high quality and low price ③ matter; substance: 木～纤维 wood fibre / 铁～的器具 ironware ④ simple; plain: ～言之 to put it bluntly

质²（質） zhì question: 质疑 zhìyí

质³（質） zhì *formal* ① pawn: 以衣物～钱 put one's clothes, etc. in pawn ② pledge: 以此为～ with this as a pledge

质变 zhìbiàn *philos.* qualitative change: 部分～ partial qualitative change

质地 zhìdì ① quality of a material; texture; grain: ～细密 of close texture; fine-grained ② character; disposition

质点 zhìdiǎn *phys.* particle

质对 zhìduì confrontation (in court)

质检 zhìjiǎn quality testing

质粒 zhìlì *biol.* plasmid

质量 zhìliàng ① quality: ～好 of high quality /～不高 of low quality; inferior / 提高～ improve the quality /～检查制度 rules for testing quality /～指标 quality index ② *phys.* mass: 相对论～ relativistic mass

质量比 zhìliàngbǐ *phys.* mass ratio

质量守恒 zhìliàng shǒuhéng *phys.* conservation of mass

质量数 zhìliàngshù *phys.* mass number; nuclear number; nucleon number

质量作用定律 zhìliàng zuòyòng dìnglǜ *phys.* law of mass action

质料 zhìliào material: 这套衣服的～很好。This suit is made of very good material.

质难 zhìnàn blame; censure; reproach

质能关系式 zhì-néng guānxìshì *phys.* mass-energy relation

质朴 zhìpǔ simple and unadorned; unaffected; plain: 文字～ written in a simple style / 为人忠厚～ be simple and honest; be unsophisticated

质谱 zhìpǔ *phys.* mass spectra: ～分析 mass spectrographic analysis

质谱仪 zhìpǔyí mass spectrometer; mass spectrograph

质数 zhìshù *math.* prime number

质素 zhìsù ① quality ② factor; element ③ simple; plain

质问 zhìwèn question; interrogate; call to account: 提出～ bring sb. to account

质心 zhìxīn *phys.* centre of mass

质询 zhìxún address inquiries to; ask for an explanation: 人民代表大会代表有权向国家机关提出～。

Deputies to the People's Congresses have the right to address inquiries to state organs.

质言 zhìyán *formal* truthful words: ～之 to put it in plain words; frankly speaking

质疑 zhìyí call in question; query: 对他的说法提出～ query (*or* question) the validity of his statement

质疑问难 zhìyí-wènnàn raise doubts and difficult questions for discussion

质因数 zhìyīnshù *math.* prime (number) factor

质直 zhìzhí upright; straightforward: 为人～ be simple and upright / 文辞～简洁 written in a pithy style

质子[1] zhìzǐ (in feudal times) a prince sent to a neighbouring state to be held as hostage

质子[2] zhìzǐ proton: ～轰击 proton bombardment / ～加速器 proton accelerator

制[1]（製）　zhì make; manufacture: 中国～ made in China

制[2]　zhì ① work out; formulate: 制定 zhìdìng ② restrict; control: 限制 xiànzhì ③ system: 所有制 suǒyǒuzhì

制版 zhìbǎn *print.* plate making: 平版～ lithographic plate making

制备 zhìbèi *chem.* prepare: 氧的～ preparation of oxygen

制币 zhìbì standard national currency: ～厂 mint

制表 zhìbiǎo ① draw up a form or list ② *statistics* tabulation

制裁 zhìcái sanction; punish: 实行～ apply sanctions (against); impose sanctions (upon) / 受到法律～ be punished according to law / 予以～ mete out punishment to sb. or apply sanctions against sb.

制成品 zhìchéngpǐn finished products; manufactured goods; manufactures

制导 zhìdǎo control and guide (a missile, etc.): ～系统 guidance system / ～炸弹 guided bomb

制订 zhìdìng work (*or* map) out; formulate: ～《汉语拼音方案》work out *The Scheme for the Chinese Phonetic Alphabet*

制定 zhìdìng lay down; draw up; formulate; draft: ～操作规程 lay down operating rules / ～宪法 draw up a constitution / ～政策 formulate a policy / ～计划 work out a plan / ～法律 make laws / ～法令 enact decrees

制动 zhìdòng apply the brake; brake

制动火箭 zhìdòng huǒjiàn retro-rocket

制动距离 zhìdòng jùlí *transportation* braking (*or* stopping) distance

制动器 zhìdòngqì brake

制动闸 zhìdòngzhá damper brake

制度 zhìdù system; institution: 教育～ system of education / 奴隶～ the institution of slavery

制伏 zhìfú subdue; check; bring under control: ～敌人 subdue the enemy / ～风沙 check wind and sand / 这条河给～了。The river was brought under control.

制服 zhìfú ① uniform ② same as 制伏 zhìfú

制服呢 zhìfúní uniform suiting (*or* coating)

制高点 zhìgāodiǎn *mil.* commanding elevation (*or* point, ground, height)

制革 zhìgé process hides; tan: ～工人 tanner / ～厂 tannery

制海权 zhìhǎiquán *mil.* mastery of the seas; command of the sea

制剂 zhìjì *pharm.* preparation: 标准～ standard preparation

制件 zhìjiàn same as 作件 zuòjiàn

制空权 zhìkōngquán *mil.* control of the air; air domination

制冷 zhìlěng refrigeration: ～循环 refrigeration cycle /

～剂 refrigerant

制粒机 zhìlìjī granulator

制霉菌素 zhìméijūnsù nystatin

制片 zhìpiàn produce (a film): ～厂 a film studio / ～人 producer

制品 zhìpǐn products; goods: 奶～ dairy products / 黄麻～ jute goods / 竹～ articles made of bamboo; bamboo articles

制钱 zhìqián standard copper coins made by the imperial mint during the Ming and Qing Dynasties

制胜 zhìshèng get the upper hand of; subdue: ～敌人 subdue the enemy

制糖 zhìtáng refine sugar: ～厂 sugar refinery

制图 zhìtú charting; map-making; drafting: ～仪器 drawing (*or* drafting) instrument / ～员 cartographer; draftsman

制图学 zhìtúxué cartography

制宪 zhìxiàn draw up a constitution

制销 zhìxiāo *mech.* cotter

制药 zhìyào pharmacy: ～厂 pharmaceutical factory

制药学 zhìyàoxué pharmaceutics

制艺 zhìyì old name for 八股 bāgǔ[1]

制音器 zhìyīnqì *mus.* damper

制约 zhìyuē restrict; condition: 受历史条件的～ be restricted by historical conditions / 人民法院和人民检察院互相～，保证准确执行法律。The people's courts and the people's procuratorates restrain each other in order to guarantee the accurate enforcement of the law.

制造 zhìzào ① make; manufacture: 中国～的飞机 China-made aircraft / 这设备是我们自己～的。The equipment is of our own manufacture. ② engineer; create; fabricate: ～纠纷 create trouble; sow dissension / ～紧张局势 create tension / ～分裂 foment splits / ～谣言 fabricate rumours (*or* lies) / ～假象 put up a false front / ～重重障碍 raise one obstacle after another / ～烟幕 spread a smoke screen / ～内乱 stir up internal strife / ～舆论 mould public opinion

制造商 zhìzàoshāng manufacturer

制造业 zhìzàoyè manufacturing industry

制止 zhìzhǐ check; curb; prevent; stop: ～流沙 curb shifting sand / ～通货膨胀 check (*or* halt) inflation / ～派别活动 put an end to factional activities / 我做了一个手势，～他再说下去。I made a gesture to stop him from saying any more.

制作 zhìzuò make; manufacture: ～家具 make furniture / 精心～的银器 elaborately wrought silverware

栉（櫛）　zhì *formal* ① comb ② comb (one's hair): ～发 comb one's hair

栉比 zhìbǐ *formal* placed closely side by side (like the teeth of a comb)

栉风沐雨 zhìfēng-mùyǔ be combed by the wind and washed by the rain—travel or work in the open despite wind and rain

栉沐 zhìmù *formal* wash and dress

峙　zhì *formal* stand erect; tower: 对峙 duìzhì

峙立 zhìlì stand towering

陟　zhì *formal* ① ascend (a height); climb; scale ② promote

桎　zhì *formal* fetters

桎梏 zhìgù *formal* (fig.) fetters and handcuffs; shackles: 打碎精神上的～ smash spiritual shackles

轾　zhì see 轩轾 xuān-zhì

致[1]　zhì　① send; extend; deliver: 〜电 send a telegram／〜欢迎词 deliver a welcoming speech; make an address of welcome ② devote (one's efforts, etc.): 致力 zhìlì ③ incur; cause: 致病 zhìbìng ④ cause; result in: 致使 zhìshǐ

致[2]　zhì　manner or style that engages attention or arouses interest: 故事曲折有〜。The story with its many twists and turns is very intriguing.

致[3]（緻）　zhì　fine; delicate: 细致 xìzhì

致哀　zhì'āi　pay one's respects to the dead: 向革命烈士〜 pay one's respects to revolutionary martyrs

致癌　zhì'ái　cause (or produce) cancer; be carcinogenic: 〜物质 carcinogen; carcinogenic substance／吸烟能致肺癌。Cigarette smoking can cause lung cancer.／有些化学药品是〜的。Some chemicals are carcinogenic.

致病　zhìbìng　cause a disease: 〜菌 pathogenic bacteria; germs

致残　zhìcán　cause disability or become disabled

致辞　zhìcí　(also 致词 zhìcí) make (or deliver) a speech: 请来宾向大会〜 call upon a guest to address the conference／新年〜 New Year message

致富　zhìfù　become rich; make a fortune: 养鸡〜 make a fortune by raising chickens／劳动〜 become rich through sweat and toil

致函　zhìhán　write (a letter) to

致贺　zhìhè　extend one's congratulations

致敬　zhìjìng　salute; pay one's respects to; pay tribute to: 鸣礼炮二十一响 fire a 21-gun salute／向劳动模范〜! Salute the model workers!

致敬电　zhìjìngdiàn　a message of greeting

致力　zhìlì　devote oneself to; work for: 〜于中医学的研究 devote (or dedicate) oneself to the study of traditional Chinese medical science

致密　zhìmì　fine and close; compact: 〜的观察 careful (or close) observation／结构〜 fine and close in texture

致密结构　zhìmì jiégòu　geol. compact texture

致命　zhìmìng　causing death; fatal; mortal; deadly: 〜的打击 a deadly blow／〜伤 a mortal (or vital) wound／〜的弱点 fatal weakness

致使　zhìshǐ　cause; result in: 由于地址字迹不清,〜信件无法投递。It is impossible to deliver this letter because the address is illegible.

致仕　zhìshì　formal　resign from an official post

致死　zhìsǐ　cause death or die: 因伤〜 die of a severe wound (or injury)／〜原因 cause of death／〜剂量 lethal dose

致死性毒气　zhìsǐxìng dúqì　lethal gas

致谢　zhìxiè　express one's thanks (or gratitude); extend thanks to: 谨此〜。We hereby express our thanks.

致意　zhìyì　give one's regards (or best wishes); present one's compliments; send one's greetings: 请向边防战士们〜。Please give our best wishes to the frontier guards.／点头(挥手)〜 nod (wave) a greeting／向欢呼群众挥手〜 wave to the cheering crowd in acknowledgement

致知　zhìzhī　pursue knowledge; attain (or acquire) knowledge ——see also 格物致知 géwù-zhìzhī

秩[1]　zhì　formal　order: 〜然不紊 orderly; shipshape

秩[2]　zhì　formal　decade: 七〜寿辰 the seventieth birthday

秩[3]　zhì　official rank in feudal times

秩序　zhìxù　order; sequence: 工作〜 sequence of work／守〜 observe order／维持社会〜 maintain public order／紧张而有〜的工作 intense but orderly work

挚（摯）　zhì　formal　sincere; earnest: 真挚 zhēnzhì

挚爱　zhì'ài　true love: 深情〜 deep love

挚诚　zhìchéng　sincere; earnest

挚切　zhìqiè　sincere; earnest; cordial

挚情　zhìqíng　deep emotion; deep feeling

挚友　zhìyǒu　intimate friend; bosom friend

贽（贄）　zhì　formal　gift presented to a senior at one's first visit as a mark of esteem

贽见　zhìjiàn　formal　bring gifts along and present oneself to a senior

贽敬　zhìjìng　formal　ceremonial gifts presented to one's teacher at the first meeting

掷（擲）　zhì　throw; cast: 〜手榴弹 throw a grenade

掷标枪　zhì biāoqiāng　javelin throw

掷弹兵　zhìdànbīng　grenadier

掷弹筒　zhìdàntǒng　grenade discharger; grenade launcher

掷还　zhìhuán　pol.　please return (to the writer, etc.): 前请审阅之件, 请早日〜为荷。Please return at your earliest convenience the manuscript (or draft, material) submitted to you for approval.

掷界外球　zhì jièwàiqiú　throw-in (in football)

掷铁饼　zhì tiěbǐng　discus throw

窒　zhì　formal　stop up; obstruct: 窒塞 zhìsè

窒碍　zhì'ài　formal　have obstacles; be obstructed

窒闷　zhìmèn　close; stuffy

窒塞　zhìsè　stop up; block

窒息　zhìxī　stifle; suffocate: 〜而死 be stifled to death／浓烟几乎使他〜。The dense smoke almost suffocated him.

窒息弹　zhìxīdàn　stifling bomb

窒息性毒气　zhìxīxìng dúqì　asphyxiating (or choking) gas

鸷（鷙）　zhì　formal　ferocious; violent

鸷悍　zhìhàn　fierce and tough; ferocious

鸷鸟　zhìniǎo　birds of prey

痔　zhì　haemorrhoids; piles

痔疮　zhìchuāng　haemorrhoids; piles

痔漏　zhìlòu　med.　anal fistula

滞（滯）　zhì　stagnant; sluggish: 停滞 tíngzhì

滞碍　zhì'ài　block (up); obstruct

滞背　zhìbèi　unfashionable and unsalable: 〜货 a drug on the market

滞呆　zhìdāi　dull: 两眼〜 with a dull look in one's eyes; with lacklustre eyes

滞钝　zhìdùn　slow (in thought or action); obtuse: 脑筋〜 slow-witted

滞洪　zhìhóng　water conservancy　flood detention: 〜区 detention basin; retarding basin

滞缓　zhìhuǎn　slow; tardy; sluggish: 行动〜 act slowly／生产增长〜 a sluggish growth of production

滞留　zhìliú　be detained; be held up

滞纳金　zhìnàjīn　fine for delaying payment; fine for paying late; overdue fine

滞泥　zhìnì　be a sticker for (form, etc.); rigidly adhere to (formalities, etc.) ② slow (in speech or action)

滞涩 zhìsè ① slow; dull: 举止～ slow in movements / 目光～ look dull ② (of writing) unsmooth; obscure

滞塞 zhìsè block; obstruct; clog: 航运～。The river traffic is held up. / 他的思路～了。His train of thought is interrupted.

滞销 zhìxiāo unsalable; unmarketable: 消费品出现积压～现象。There has appeared the problem of overstocking and sluggish sales of consumer goods. / ～货 unsalable (or slow-selling) goods; a drug on the market

滞育 zhìyù zool. diapause

滞运 zhìyùn (of freight transport) be held up

痣 zhì nevus; mole: 他脸上有一颗～。He has a mole on his face.

蛭 zhì leech: 水蛭 shuǐzhì

蛭石 zhìshí vermiculite (a mineral)

骘 zhì see 评骘 píngzhì

智 zhì wisdom; resourcefulness; wit: 智谋 zhìmóu / 明智 míngzhì

智齿 zhìchǐ (also 智牙 zhìyá) wisdom tooth

智多星 zhìduōxīng wizard—resourceful person; mastermind (originally a nickname for Wu Yong, the resourceful strategist of the peasant army in the Water Margin《水浒传》)

智慧 zhìhuì wisdom; intelligence: 吸取群众的～ draw on the wisdom of the masses / 勤劳、～的人民 the industrious and ingenious people / 这些壮丽的古代建筑显示了劳动人民的高度～。These magnificent ancient buildings demonstrate the great intelligence of the labouring people.

智力 zhìlì intelligence; intellect: ～测验 intelligence test / ～开发 tap (or develop) intellectual resources / ～投资 investment in brainpower / ～竞赛 quiz game

智利 Zhìlì Chile

智利人 Zhìlìrén Chilean

智利硝石 Zhìlì xiāoshí another name for 硝酸钠 xiāosuānnà

智略 zhìlüè wisdom and resourcefulness

智谋 zhìmóu resourcefulness: 靠勇敢也靠～ rely on both courage and resourcefulness / 人多～高。More people mean more ideas.

智囊 zhìnáng brain truster: ～人物 brain truster; think tanker

智囊团 zhìnángtuán brain trust; think tank

智能 zhìnéng intellectual power; intellectual ability

智巧 zhìqiǎo brains and tact

智穷才尽 zhìqióng-cáijìn at the end of one's resources; at one's wits' end

智取 zhìqǔ take (a fort, town, etc.) by strategy: 只可～, 不可强攻。The only way to take the enemy position is by strategy, not by forceful attack.

智商 zhìshāng intelligence quotient (IQ): ～高（低）have a high (low) IQ

智术 zhìshù trickery; stratagem

智勇双全 zhì-yǒng shuāng quán both intelligent and courageous; both brave and resourceful: ～的将军 a brave and sagacious general

智育 zhìyù intellectual education; intellectual development: 使学生在德育、～、体育几方面都得到发展 enable the students to develop morally, intellectually and physically

智圆行方 zhìyuán-xíngfāng resourceful and upright; flexible and principled

智者千虑, 必有一失 zhìzhě qiān lǜ, bì yǒu yī shī the wisest man, in a thousand schemes, must make at least one mistake; even the wise are not free from error

智珠在握 zhì zhū zǎi wò be endowed with high native intelligence

彘 zhì formal pig; swine

锧（鑕） zhì formal ① chopping block ② (ancient) executioner's block: 斧锧 fǔzhì

置 zhì ① place; put: 安～于案头 be placed on one's desk ② set up; establish; install: ～酒款待 give a feast to entertain sb. ③ buy: ～一身衣服 buy a suit or have one made to order / ～一些家具 buy some furniture

置办 zhìbàn buy (durables); purchase: ～家具 buy furniture / ～图书仪器 procure books and instruments

置备 zhìbèi purchase (equipment, furniture, etc.)

置辩 zhìbiàn formal (usu. used in the negative) argue (in self-defence): 不屑～ disdain to argue

置产 zhìchǎn buy property (esp. an estate)

置放 zhìfàng put; lay up

置换 zhìhuàn chem. displacement; replacement

置喙 zhìhuì formal (usu. used in the negative) interfere; intervene: 不容置喙 bùróng zhìhuì

置买 zhìmǎi purchase; buy

置评 zhìpíng (usu. used in the negative) comment on; discuss: 不予～ give no comment

置若罔闻 zhì ruò wǎng wén turn a deaf ear to; pay no heed to: 我多次劝告, 他都～。I cautioned him many times but he paid no heed.

置身 zhìshēn place oneself; stay: ～于群众之中 place oneself in the midst of the masses / ～异域 find oneself in the midst of a foreign people

置身事外 zhìshēn shì wài stay aloof from the affair; keep out of the business; refuse to be drawn into the matter

置信 zhìxìn (usu. used in the negative) believe: 不可～ not to be believed; unbelievable

置疑 zhìyí (used in the negative) doubt: 不容置疑 bùróng zhìyí

置之不顾 zhì zhī bù gù leave out of account; ignore; disregard

置之不理 zhì zhī bù lǐ ignore; brush aside; pay no attention to: 对于这种挑衅, 我们不能～。We cannot ignore such provocations.

置之度外 zhì zhī dù wài give no thought to; have no regard for: 他为了抢救落水儿童, 把个人安危～。He went to the rescue of a drowning child regardless of his personal safety. / 把生死～ face death with equanimity

置之脑后 zhì zhī nǎo hòu banish from one's mind; ignore and forget

置之死地而后快 zhì zhī sǐdì érhòu kuài will be content with nothing less than sb.'s destruction

置之死地而后生 zhì zhī sǐdì érhòu shēng confront a person with the danger of death and he will fight to live: 兵法不曰"陷之死地而后生, 置之亡地而后存"?《史记》Does it not say in The Art of War: "Drive them into a fatal position and they will come out alive; place them in a hopeless spot and they will survive"?

雉[1] zhì pheasant

雉[2] zhì a parapet section of a city wall, 30 chi high and 10 chi long

雉堞 zhìdié crenelation

雉鸠 zhìjiū turtledove

稚（穉） zhì young; childish: 幼稚 yòuzhì

稚虫　zhìchóng　*zool.*　naiad

稚嫩　zhìnèn　① young and tender: ～的童音 child's piping voice／～的脸蛋儿 a delicate face／～的心灵 an innocent heart ② immature: 他的早期作品比较～。His early works are relatively immature.

稚气　zhìqì　childishness: 一脸～ innocent-looking

稚弱　zhìruò　childish and tender: ～的心灵 a tender heart

稚子　zhìzǐ　(innocent) child

觯（觶）　zhì　an ancient drinking vessel

踬（躓）　zhì　*formal* ① trip; stumble: 颠踬 diānzhì ② suffer a setback: 屡试屡～ fail at each trial

寘（寊）　zhì　*formal* ① encounter obstacles ② fall down

zhōng

中　zhōng　① centre; middle: 上、～、下 upper, middle, lower／冀～ central Hebei ② (Zhōng) China: 中文 Zhōngwén ③ in; among; amidst: 记在心～ keep in mind／跳入水～ jump into the water ④ middle; mid: 月中 yuèzhōng ⑤ medium; intermediate: 中号 zhōnghào ⑥ mean; halfway between two extremes: 适中 shìzhōng ⑦ intermediary: 作中 zuòzhōng ⑧ in the process of: 在修建～ being built; under construction／历史在斗争～发展, 世界在动荡～前进。History develops in struggle and the world advances amidst turbulence. ⑨ fit for; good for: 中看 zhōngkàn ⑩ *dial.* all right; O. K.: ～不～? Is it all right? ／这办法～! This way works! ——see also zhòng

中班　zhōngbān　① middle shift; swing shift: 上～ be on the middle shift; work the swing shift ② the middle class in a kindergarten

中板　zhōngbǎn　① *metall.* medium plate ② *mus.* moderato

中饱　zhōngbǎo　batten on money entrusted to one's care; line one's pockets with public funds or other people's money; embezzle

中保　zhōng-bǎo　middleman and guarantor

中表　zhōngbiǎo　first cousin, child of father's sister or mother's sister or brother

中波　zhōngbō　medium wave

中不溜儿　zhōngbùliūr　(also 中溜儿 zhōngliūr) *inf.* fair to middling; middling: 他不高不矮, 个子～的。He's neither tall nor short, but of middling height.

中部　zhōngbù　central section; middle part: 根据地～ the central section of the base area／在高原～ in the middle part of the plateau

中材　zhōngcái　person of average ability or ordinary talent; mediocre

中餐　zhōngcān　Chinese meal; Chinese food

中草药　zhōngcǎoyào　Chinese herbal medicine

中策　zhōngcè　the second best plan

中层　zhōngcéng　middle-level: ～干部 middle-level (or middle-ranking) cadres

中产阶级　zhōngchǎnjiējí　middle class; middle bourgeoisie

中常　zhōngcháng　middling; average: ～年景 average harvest／这孩子学习成绩～。The child's work at school is about average.

中场　zhōngchǎng　*football* midfield

中程　zhōngchéng　intermediate range; medium range: ～导弹 intermediate-range missile; medium-range missile／～轰炸机 medium bomber

中垂线　zhōngchuíxiàn　*math.* perpendicular bisector

中辍　zhōngchuò　stop (doing sth.) halfway; give up halfway

中词　zhōngcí　*log.* middle term

中道　zhōngdào　① halfway; midway: ～而废 give up halfway ② *formal* the golden mean (of the Confucian school)

中稻　zhōngdào　semilate rice; middle-season rice

中等　zhōngděng　① medium; moderate; middling: ～个儿 of medium height／～城市 medium-sized city ② secondary: ～职业学校 secondary vocational school

中等技术学校　zhōngděng jìshù xuéxiào　secondary technical school

中等教育　zhōngděng jiàoyù　secondary school education: 中等师范教育 secondary normal education

中等师范学校　zhōngděng shīfàn xuéxiào　secondary normal school

中等专科学校　zhōngděng zhuānkē xuéxiào　secondary specialized school; polytechnic school

中点　zhōngdiǎn　*math.* midpoint

中东　Zhōngdōng　the Middle East

中短波　zhōngduǎnbō　intermediate wave; medium-short wave

中断　zhōngduàn　suspend; break off; discontinue: ～谈判 break off the negotiations (*or* talks)／两国关系～了好多年。Relations between the two countries were suspended for many years. ／交通～了几小时。Traffic was held up for a few hours. ／地震后铁路运输～了。After the earthquake, railway service discontinued.

中队　zhōngduì　① *mil.* military unit corresponding to a company; squadron: 歼击机～ fighter squadron ② a unit composed of several groups: 交通～ a detachment of traffic police

中耳　zhōng'ěr　auris media; middle ear

中耳炎　zhōng'ěryán　otitis media

中饭　zhōngfàn　midday meal; lunch

中幡　zhōngfān　*acrobatics* flagpole-waving

中非　Zhōngfēi　Central Africa

中分　zhōngfēn　① divide sth. equally into two halves ② part hair in the middle

中锋　zhōngfēng　*sports* centre forward (as in football); centre

中缝　zhōngfèng　① the column on the folding line of a newspaper, usu. reserved for advertisements or notices ② the line sewn down the back of a jacket

中伏　zhōngfú　① the middle or second *fu*—the second hottest period of the year (10 or 20 days) ② the first day of the middle or second *fu* (falling in late July) ——see also 三伏 sānfú

中服　zhōngfú　same as 中装 zhōngzhuāng

中耕　zhōnggēng　*agric.* intertill: ～机 cultivator／～作物 intertilled crop

中共　Zhōng Gòng　short for 中国共产党 Zhōngguó Gòngchǎndǎng

中共中央　Zhōng Gòng Zhōngyāng　(short for 中国共产党中央委员会) the Central Committee of the Communist Party of China: ～军事委员会 the Military Commission of the Central Committee of the Chinese Communist Party／～全会 Plenary Session of the Central Committee of the CPC／～政治局 the Political Bureau of the Central Committee of the Chinese Communist Party

中古　zhōnggǔ　① the middle ancient times (in Chinese history, from the 3rd to the 9th century) ② medieval times; Middle Ages: ～史 medieval history

中国　Zhōngguó　China: ～大陆 China's mainland

中国工农红军　Zhōngguó Gōng-Nóng Hóngjūn　the Chinese Workers' and Peasants' Red Army (1928–1937); the Red Army

中国工农民主政府 Zhōngguó Gōng-Nóng Mínzhǔ Zhèngfǔ the Chinese Workers' and Peasants' Democratic Government (of the revolutionary base areas during the Second Revolutionary Civil War, 1927–1937)

中国共产党 Zhōngguó Gòngchǎndǎng the Communist Party of China (CPC); the Chinese Communist Party

中国共产主义青年团 Zhōngguó Gòngchǎnzhǔyì Qīngniántuán the Communist Youth League of China

中国话 zhōngguóhuà the Chinese language; Chinese

中国画 zhōngguóhuà traditional Chinese painting

中国科学院 Zhōngguó Kēxuéyuàn the Chinese Academy of Sciences; Academia Sinica

中国人 Zhōngguórén Chinese

中国人民解放军 Zhōngguó Rénmín Jiěfàngjūn the Chinese People's Liberation Army

中国人民政治协商会议 Zhōngguó Rénmín Zhèngzhì Xiéshāng Huìyì the Chinese People's Political Consultative Conference (CPPCC)

中国人民志愿军 Zhōngguó Rénmín Zhìyuànjūn the Chinese People's Volunteers

中国社会科学院 Zhōngguó Shèhuì Kēxuéyuàn the Chinese Academy of Social Sciences

中国同盟会 Zhōngguó Tóngménghuì the United League of China (1905–1912, the predecessor of the Kuomintang 国民党)

中国猿人 Zhōngguó yuánrén same as 北京人 Běijīngrén

中国字 zhōngguózì Chinese characters; the Chinese written language

中果皮 zhōngguǒpí *bot.* mesocarp

中号 zhōnghào medium size

中和 zhōnghé *chem. elec.* neutralization: ～剂 neutralizer

中华 Zhōnghuá ① the Chinese nation ② China

中华民族 Zhōnghuá Mínzú the Chinese nation

中华人民共和国 Zhōnghuá Rénmín Gònghéguó the People's Republic of China: ～国务院 the State Council of the People's Republic of China

中级 zhōngjí middle rank; intermediate: ～人民法院 intermediate people's court

中技 zhōngjì short for 中等技术学校 zhōngděng jìshù xuéxiào

中继 zhōngjì *elec.* relay

中继器 zhōngjìqì *electron.* repeater

中继线 zhōngjìxiàn trunk line

中继站 zhōngjìzhàn relay station

中间 zhōngjiān ① among; between: 生活在人民群众～ live among the masses of the people / 坐在他们两人～ sit between the two of them / 她是我们三人～最年轻的。She is the youngest of us three. ② centre; middle: ～突破 make a breakthrough at the centre (or in the middle) / ～剥削 middleman's exploitation / ～道路 middle road / ～地带 intermediate zone / ～分子 middle (or intermediate) element / ～路线 middle-of-the-road line; middle road / ～状态 intermediate state / 从我家到工厂,～要换车。I have to change buses on the way from home to the factory.

中间阶层 zhōngjiān jiēcéng intermediate strata

中间力量 zhōngjiān lìliàng middle-of-the-road forces; intermediate forces

中间派 zhōngjiānpài middle-of-the-roaders; middle elements; intermediate sections (or forces)

中间人 zhōngjiānrén middleman; go-between; mediator; intermediary

中间体 zhōngjiāntǐ *chem.* intermediate

中间线 zhōngjiānxiàn *mech.* medium line

中坚 zhōngjiān nucleus; hard core; backbone: ～分子 backbone elements / 干部的～力量 nucleus (or hard core) of cadres / 社会～ pillar of society; the salt of the earth / 贫农是农民协会的～。The poor peasants were the backbone of the peasant associations.

中将 zhōngjiàng (U. S. & Brit. Army, U. S. Air Force, U. S. & Brit. Marine Corps) lieutenant general; (U. S. & Brit. Navy) vice admiral; (Brit. Air Force) air marshal

中焦 zhōngjiāo *Chin. med.* the part of the body cavity between the diaphragm and the umbilicus housing the spleen, stomach, ect.

中觉 zhōngjiào afternoon nap; noontime snooze

中介 zhōngjiè intermediary; medium

中介子 zhōngjièzǐ *phys.* neutretto

中景 zhōngjǐng *film* medium shot

中距离 zhōngjùlí *sports* middle distance: ～赛跑 middle-distance race

中看 zhōngkàn be pleasant to the eye

中看不中吃 zhōngkàn bù zhōngchī look nice but taste nasty; be pleasing to the eye but not to the taste

中馈 zhōngkuì *formal* ① housewife's duties such as cooking: 主～ take up duties as a housewife; be a housewife ② wife: ～犹虚 have not yet taken a wife; be unmarried

中栏 zhōnglán *sports* intermediate hurdles

中立 zhōnglì neutrality: 守～ observe neutrality / 保持～ remain neutral / 永久～ permanent neutrality / ～地带 neutral zone / ～法 law of neutrality; neutrality law / ～政策 policy of neutrality

中立国 zhōnglìguó neutral state

中立主义 zhōnglìzhǔyì neutralism

中量级 zhōngliàngjí *sports* middleweight

中林 zhōnglín *forestry* middle forest

中流 zhōngliú midstream

中流砥柱 zhōngliú dǐzhù a firm rock in midstream; mainstay: 共产党领导的武装和民众是抗日战争的～。The armed forces and the people led by the Communist Party were the mainstay in the War of Resistance Against Japan.

中路 zhōnglù ① mediocre in quality: ～货 mediocre goods ② halfway; midway

中路梆子 zhōnglùbāngzi same as 晋剧 jìnjù

中略 zhōnglüè part omitted (used as an ellipsis mark within brackets in a quoted passage)

中落 zhōngluò (of family fortunes) decline; ebb

中美洲 Zhōng Měizhōu Central America

中拇指 zhōngmuzhǐ middle finger

中脑 zhōngnǎo mesencephalon; midbrain

中年 zhōngnián middle age: ～人 a middle-aged person / 我虽然还算年轻, 但心情已近～了。I may still be young, but I feel middle-aged.

中农 zhōngnóng middle peasant

中跑 zhōngpǎo middle-distance race

中胚层 zhōngpēicéng mesoderm; mesoblast

中篇小说 zhōngpiān xiǎoshuō medium-length novel; novelette

中频 zhōngpín *radio* intermediate frequency

中期 zhōngqī middle period: 二十世纪～ mid 20th century / ～选举 mid-term election / 棉花～管理 the mid-period management of cotton

中气候 zhōngqìhòu mesoclimate

中秋节 Zhōngqiūjié the Mid-autumn Festival (15th day of the 8th lunar month)

中人 zhōngrén ① middleman; go-between; mediator; intermediary ② one of ordinary stature, appearance, ability, etc.; an average man

中沙群岛 Zhōngshā Qúndǎo the Zhongsha Islands

中山狼 zhōngshānláng the Zhongshan wolf in the fable —one who repays good with evil ——see also 东郭先生 Dōngguō Xiānsheng

中山陵 Zhōngshānlíng the Sun Yat-sen Mausoleum (in Nanjing)

中山装 zhōngshānzhuāng Chinese tunic suit: 穿着一身

灰色～ in gray tunic and trousers

中生代 Zhōngshēngdài *geol.* the Mesozoic Era; the Mesozoic

中生界 Zhōngshēngjiè *geol.* the Mesozoic Erathem

中师 zhōngshī short for 中等师范学校 zhōngděng shīfàn xuéxiào

中石器时代 zhōngshíqì shídài Mesolithic Period; Middle Stone Age

中士 zhōngshì (U. S. & Brit. Army, Brit. Air Force, U. S. & Brit. Marine Corps) sergeant; (U. S. Navy) petty officer second class; (Brit. Navy) petty officer first class; (U. S. Air Force) staff sergeant

中世纪 zhōngshìjì Middle Ages

中式 zhōngshì Chinese style: ～服装 Chinese-style clothing——see also zhòngshì

中式盐 zhōngshìyán (also 中性盐 zhōngxìngyán) *chem.* neutral salt

中枢 zhōngshū centre: 领导～ leading centre / 电讯～ telecommunications centre / 神经～ nerve centre

中枢神经 zhōngshū shénjīng central nervous system

中水期 zhōngshuǐqī same as 平水期 píngshuǐqī

中碳钢 zhōngtàngāng *metall.* medium carbon steel

中堂 zhōngtáng ① same as 堂屋 tángwū ② central scroll of painting or calligraphy (hung in the middle of the wall of the main room)

中堂 zhōngtáng a form of address for a Grand Secretary in the Ming and Qing Dynasties

中提琴 zhōngtíqín viola

中天 zhōngtiān ① in the sky: 日丽～。The sun was shining bright in the sky. ② *astron.* culmination; meridian passage (*or* transit)

中听 zhōngtīng pleasant to the ear; agreeable to the hearer: 他觉得这句话～。He found these remarks very agreeable.

中统 zhōngtǒng (short for 中央执行委员会调查统计局) the Bureau of Investigation and Statistics of the Central Executive Committee (one of the Kuomintang's huge secret service agencies)

中途 zhōngtú halfway; midway: ～停留 stop halfway; stop over / ～下汽车 get off the car midway / 这趟公共汽车～不停。This is a nonstop bus. / 他原是学建筑的, ～改行搞地质了。At first he studied architecture, but later he switched to geology. / 开会不要～退场。Don't leave before the meeting is over. *or* Don't leave when the meeting is in progress.

中途岛 Zhōngtúdǎo Midway Island

中土 Zhōngtǔ ① same as 中原 Zhōngyuán ② *formal* China

中外 Zhōng-wài China and foreign countries: ～合营企业 a Chinese-foreign joint venture

中外比 zhōngwàibǐ another name for 黄金分割 huángjīn fēngē

中微子 zhōngwēizǐ *phys.* neutrino

中纬度 zhōngwěidù middle latitudes

中卫 zhōngwèi *football* centre halfback

中位数 zhōngwèishù *statistics* median

中尉 zhōngwèi (U. S. Army, Air Force & Marine Corps) first lieutenant; (Brit. Army & Marine Corps) lieutenant; (U. S. Navy) lieutenant junior grade; (Brit. Navy) sublieutenant; senior commissioned branch officer; (Brit. Air Force) flying officer

中文 Zhōngwén the Chinese language; Chinese: ～书刊 books and magazines in Chinese

中午 zhōngwǔ noon; midday

中西 Zhōng-Xī Chinese and Western: ～医结合 combine traditional Chinese and Western medicine / ～结合医 a doctor well versed in traditional Chinese and Western medicine

中夏 Zhōngxià ancient name for China

中线 zhōngxiàn ① *sports* centre line (in basketball and volleyball); halfway line (in football) ② *math.* central line

中宵 zhōngxiāo midnight

中校 zhōngxiào (U. S. & Brit. Army, U. S. Air Force, U. S. & Brit. Marine Corps) lieutenant colonel; (U. S. & Brit. Navy) commander; (Brit. Air Force) wing commander

中心 zhōngxīn centre; heart; core; hub: 在广场～ at the centre of the square / 抓住问题的～ get to the heart of the matter / 陆路交通的～ hub of overland communications / ～城市 key city / ～工作 central task / ～环节 key link; central link / ～问题 central issue; crucial question

中心规 zhōngxīnguī *mech.* centre gauge

中心角 zhōngxīnjiǎo same as 圆心角 yuánxīnjiǎo

中心思想 zhōngxīn sīxiǎng central idea; gist

中心线 zhōngxīnxiàn *mech.* centre line

中心项 zhōngxīnxiàng *philos.* central term

中新世 Zhōngxīnshì *geol.* the Miocene Epoch

中兴 zhōngxīng resurgence (of a nation); restoration (of a dynasty): 光武～ the restoration of Emperor Guangwu (of the Eastern Han Dynasty)

中星仪 zhōngxīngyí *astron.* meridian instrument; transit instrument

中型 zhōngxíng medium-sized; middle-sized: ～词典 a medium-sized dictionary

中性 zhōngxìng ① *chem.* neutral: ～反应 neutral reaction / ～树脂 neutral resin / ～土 neutral soil ② *gram.* neuter: ～名词 neuter noun

中休 zhōngxiū a break (between work, activities, etc.); a pause for rest

中学[1] zhōngxué middle school: 初(高)级～ junior (senior) middle school

中学[2] zhōngxué Chinese learning (a late Qing Dynasty term for Chinese traditional learning): ～为体, 西学为用 Chinese learning as the fundamental structure, Western learning for practical use

中学生 zhōngxuéshēng middle school student

中旬 zhōngxún the middle ten days of a month: 四月～ the middle ten days of April

中央 zhōngyāng ① centre; middle: 湖的～有一座亭子。At the centre of the lake, there is a pavilion. ② central authorities (of a state, party, etc.): 团～ the Central Committee of the League / 发挥～和地方两个积极性。Both central and local initiative should be brought into play. / ～和地方企业并举 simultaneous development of national and local enterprises / ～各部门 departments under the Party's Central Committee and the State Council / ～工作会议 the Central Working Conference / ～机构 central organs (*or* institutions) / ～领导同志 leading comrades of the central authorities / ～直属机关 departments under the Party Central Committee / ～军事委员会 the Central Military Commission / ～纪律检查委员会 the Central Commission for Discipline Inspection / ～顾问委员会 the Central Advisory Commission

中央候补委员 zhōngyāng hòubǔ wěiyuán alternate member of the Central Committee (of the Chinese Communist Party)

中央集权 zhōngyāng jíquán centralization (of authority): ～的国家 centralized state power / ～的封建君主制 centralized feudal monarchy

中央情报局 Zhōngyāng Qíngbàojú the (U. S.) Central Intelligence Agency (CIA)

中央全会 zhōngyāng quánhuì plenary session of the Central Committee

中央条约组织 Zhōngyāng Tiáoyuē Zǔzhī the Central Treaty Organization (CENTO)

中央委员 zhōngyāng wěiyuán member of the Central Committee (of the Chinese Communist Party)

中央银行 zhōngyāng yínháng central bank

中药 zhōngyào traditional Chinese medicine

中药铺 zhōngyàopù shop (or store) of traditional Chinese medicines; Chinese pharmacy

中药学 zhōngyàoxué traditional Chinese pharmacology

中叶 zhōngyè middle period: 十九世纪～ the mid-1800s; the middle of the 19th century

中衣 zhōngyī underpants; pants

中医 zhōngyī ① traditional Chinese medical science ② doctor of traditional Chinese medicine; practitioner of Chinese medicine

中医学 zhōngyīxué traditional Chinese medicine

中医学院 zhōngyī xuéyuàn college of traditional Chinese medicine

中医研究院 zhōngyī yánjiūyuàn academy of traditional Chinese medicine

中音号 zhōngyīnhào *mus.* althorn; alto horn

中庸 zhōngyōng ① the golden mean (of the Confucian school) ② *formal* of ordinary talent; common; mediocre ③ (Zhōngyōng) *The Doctrine of the Mean* (see also 四书 sìshū)

中庸之道 zhōngyōng zhī dào the doctrine of the mean: 采取～ opt for the golden mean

中用 zhōngyòng (usu. used in the negative) of use; useful: 不中用 bùzhōngyòng

中游 zhōngyóu ① middle reaches (of a river) ② the state of being middling

中雨 zhōngyǔ moderate rain

中元节 Zhōngyuánjié the Festival of the Dead Spirits (15th day of the seventh lunar month when sacrifices are offered to the dead)

中原 Zhōngyuán Central Plains (comprising the middle and lower reaches of the Huanghe River)

中岳 Zhōng Yuè the Central Mountain (another name for 嵩山 "Mount Song" in Henan Province) ——see also 五岳 Wǔ Yuè

中云 zhōngyún *meteorol.* medium cloud

中允 zhōngyǔn *formal* just; fair; impartial: 貌似～ seemingly impartial

中灶 zhōngzào mess for medium-ranking cadres

中正 zhōngzhèng *formal* just; fair; unbiased

中支 zhōngzhī *text.* medium-counts: ～纱 medium-count yarn

中止 zhōngzhǐ discontinue; suspend; break off: ～发行 discontinue publishing / ～谈判 suspend (or break off) negotiations / ～外交关系 suspend diplomatic relations / ～射击 lift fire

中指 zhōngzhǐ middle finger

中州 Zhōngzhōu Central Region (old name for Henan Province, so called from its central location in the country)

中州韵 zhōngzhōuyùn Zhongzhou intonations (used on finals 韵母 by actors in traditional opera)

中注管 zhōngzhùguǎn *metall.* running-gate

中专 zhōngzhuān short for 中等专科学校 zhōngděng zhuānkē xuéxiào

中转 zhōngzhuǎn change trains: ～环节 intermediate link / ～签字 sign a transfer (for a railway passenger)

中转港 zhōngzhuǎngǎng entrepot

中转站 zhōngzhuǎnzhàn transfer station

中装 zhōngzhuāng traditional Chinese clothing

中子 zhōngzǐ neutron: ～物理学 neutronics / ～源 neutron source / ～反应堆 neutron reactor

中子弹 zhōngzǐdàn neutron bomb

中子态 zhōngzǐtài neutron state

中子星 zhōngzǐxīng *astron.* neutron star

忪（忪） zhōng see 怔忪 zhēngzhōng ——see also sōng

忠 zhōng loyal; devoted; honest: 效忠 xiàozhōng

忠臣 zhōngchén official loyal to his sovereign

忠忱 zhōngchén loyal; faithful; staunch

忠诚 zhōngchéng loyal; faithful; staunch: ～的朋友 loyal friend / 对革命无限～ be boundlessly loyal to the revolution / ～党的教育事业。Be devoted to the Party's educational task. / 我们对人民必须～老实。We must be honest and faithful to the people.

忠告 zhōnggào ① sincerely advise; admonish ② sincere advice; advice

忠鲠 zhōnggěng loyal and outspoken; honest and upright

忠骨 zhōnggǔ loyal bones—remains of a martyr

忠厚 zhōnghòu honest and tolerant; sincere and kindly: 他为人～老实。He is kindly and simple-hearted.

忠君爱国 zhōngjūn-àiguó be loyal to the sovereign and devoted to the country

忠良 zhōngliáng ① faithful and upright; honest and staunch ② a faithful and upright person

忠烈 zhōngliè ① loyal till death ② martyr

忠实 zhōngshí loyal; true; faithful: ～执行协议条款 faithfully implement (or observe) the provisions of an agreement / ～于原文 true (or faithful) to the original / ～的信徒 a faithful disciple / ～的走狗 a faithful running dog; faithful lackey / ～的朋友 a faithful (or true, devoted) friend / ～的报道 a truthful news report / ～地反映情况 give a faithful account of what happened / 她丈夫对她不～。Her husband was unfaithful to her.

忠恕 zhōngshù loyal and considerate: 夫子之道, ～而已矣。《论语》 Our Master's Way is simply this: Loyalty, consideration.

忠顺 zhōngshùn loyal and obedient; obedient: ～的奴仆 a willing servant

忠孝 zhōngxiào loyalty and filial piety: ～不能两全。Loyalty and filial piety do not always complement each other.

忠心 zhōngxīn loyalty; devotion: 表～ express one's loyalty

忠心耿耿 zhōngxīn gěnggěng loyal and devoted; most faithful and true: ～为革命 be dedicated heart and soul to the revolution; work most faithfully for the revolution / 对党对人民～ be faithful to the Party and the people

忠信 zhōngxìn faithful and honest; loyal and trustworthy

忠言 zhōngyán sincere advice; earnest advice

忠言逆耳 zhōngyán nì ěr faithful words offend the ear; good advice jars on the ear: ～利于行。Honest advice, though unpleasant to the ear, benefits conduct. ——see also 良药苦口 liángyào kǔ kǒu

忠义 zhōngyì loyal and righteous

忠勇 zhōngyǒng loyal and brave; faithful and courageous: ～战士 loyal and gallant fighters / ～之心 loyalty and courage

忠于 zhōngyú true to; loyal to; faithful to; devoted to: ～祖国,～人民 be loyal to one's country and people / ～职守 be faithful in the discharge of one's duties; be devoted to one's duty

忠贞 zhōngzhēn loyal and steadfast: ～不屈 staunch and indomitable

忠贞不渝 zhōngzhēn bù yú unswervingly loyal

忠直 zhōngzhí loyal and upright

终 zhōng ① end; finish: 年终 niánzhōng ② die: ～其天年 live one's full span ③ *adv.* eventually; after

all; in the end: ～非良策。It's not a good plan after all./共产主义～将实现。Communism will ultimately be realized. ④ whole; entire; all: ～其一生 all his life

终场 zhōngchǎng ① end of a performance or game: ～前一分钟，主队又攻进一球。The host team scored another goal just before the final whistle. ② *old* final session in an examination

终底于成 zhōng dǐ yú chéng succeed in the end

终点 zhōngdiǎn ① terminal point; destination: 旅行的～ destination of a journey ② *sports* finish: ～线 finishing line; finishing tape

终点站 zhōngdiǎnzhàn terminus; terminal

终端 zhōngduān terminal: ～电缆 terminal cable

终端局 zhōngduānjú terminal station (in postal service)

终伏 zhōngfú same as 末伏 mòfú

终古 zhōnggǔ *formal* forever

终归 zhōngguī eventually; in the end; after all: 他可能迟到，来～会来的。He will probably be late but he'll come eventually. / 耍两面派～不会有好下场。Double-dealers will come to no good end. / 他～还是个新手。After all he is still a new hand. / 孩子～是孩子。Children will be children.

终极 zhōngjí ultimate: ～目标 ultimate aim

终结 zhōngjié end; final stage: 审判长在宣布辩论～后，被告人有最后陈述的权利。After the chief judge has announced the closing of debate, the defendant has the right to make a final statement.

终究 zhōngjiū *adv.* eventually; in the end; after all: 一个人的力量～有限。The strength of the individual is limited after all. / 你～会明白的。In the end you'll understand.

终久 zhōngjiǔ same as 终究 zhōngjiū

终局 zhōngjú end; outcome: 战争的～ the outcome of a war

终老 zhōnglǎo spend one's remaining years till death: ～故乡 spend one's remaining years in one's hometown

终了 zhōngliǎo end (of a period): 学期～ the end of the (school) term

终南捷径 Zhōngnán jiéjìng a short cut to high office; the high road to fame or success

终年 zhōngnián ① (all) the year round; throughout the year: ～积雪的高山 mountains perennially covered with snow ② the age at which one dies: 他～七十八岁。He died at the age of seventy-eight.

终篇 zhōngpiān *formal* finish writing, or finish reading a piece of writing

终曲 zhōngqǔ *mus.* finale

终日 zhōngrì all day long; all day

终身 zhōngshēn lifelong; all one's life: ～事业 one's lifework / 剥夺政治权利～ be deprived of political rights for life / ～职务 life tenure

终身伴侣 zhōngshēn bànlǚ lifelong companion—one's husband or wife

终身大事 zhōngshēn dàshì a great event in one's life (usu. referring to marriage): ～，一生至死，非同儿戏。《红楼梦》》Marriage is a serious business, not a joking matter; it's for life.

终审 zhōngshěn *leg.* last instance; final judgment: ～判决 final judgement / ～法院 court of last instance / ～权 power of final adjudication

终生 zhōngshēng all one's life: 为共产主义奋斗～ struggle for communism all one's life / ～难忘的教训 a lesson for life

终霜 zhōngshuāng *meteorol.* latest frost

终岁 zhōngsuì the whole year; throughout the year

终天 zhōngtiān ① all day long; all day: ～不停地写 write the whole day without stopping ② *formal* all

one's life

终天之恨 zhōngtiān zhī hèn lifelong regret; eternal regret

终席 zhōngxí (of a dinner party or meeting) end; come to a close: 没有等到～，他推说头疼，起身回家了。Pleading a headache, he left for home before the dinner party ended.

终宵 zhōngxiāo (also 终夜 zhōngyè) all night; the whole night; throughout the night

终于 zhōngyú *adv.* at (long) last; in the end; finally: 她～到了，晚了将近半小时。At long last she arrived, about half an hour late. / 中国登山队～胜利地登上了珠峰。The Chinese mountaineering expedition finally succeeded in scaling Mount Qomolangma. / 尽管多方医治，～还是把他受伤的腿锯了。All the treatments were to no avail and in the end they had to amputate his wounded leg.

终朝 zhōngzhāo *formal* ① all morning; the whole morning ② all day long; all day

终止 zhōngzhǐ ① stop; end: 要求～这种不正常状态 demand an end to this abnormal state of affairs / ～日期 closing date ② termination; annulment; abrogation: ～条约通知书 notice of termination of a treaty; notice of denunciation ③ *mus.* cadence

盅

盅 zhōng handleless cup: 酒盅 jiǔzhōng

盅子 zhōngzi *inf.* handleless cup

钟¹（鐘）

zhōng ① bell: 这口铜～是明永乐初年铸造的。The bronze bell was made in the early years of Yongle of the Ming Dynasty. ② clock: ～停了。The clock has stopped. ③ time as measured in hours and minutes: 六点～ six o'clock / 十分～ ten minutes

钟²（鍾）

zhōng ① concentrate (one's affections, etc.): 钟情 zhōngqíng ② (Zhōng) a surname

钟³（鍾）

zhōng same as 盅 zhōng

钟爱 zhōng'ài dote on (a child); cherish

钟摆 zhōngbǎi pendulum (of a clock)

钟表 zhōngbiǎo clocks and watches; timepiece: ～店 watchmaker's shop / ～油 watchmaker's oil

钟点 zhōngdiǎn *inf.* ① a time for sth. to be done or to happen: 到～儿了，我们快走吧! It's time; let's be off. ② hour: 我等了他一个～了。I've been waiting for him for an hour.

钟鼎文 zhōngdǐngwén same as 金文 jīnwén

钟馗 Zhōngkuí a deity supposed to be a chaser of demons (whose pictures used to be pasted as charms at the entrance to houses to ward off evil influences)

钟灵毓秀 zhōnglíng-yùxiù (of a place) pregnant with beauty and productive of talent

钟楼 zhōnglóu ① bell tower; belfry ② clock tower

钟鸣鼎食 zhōngmíng-dǐngshí partake of rich food in *ding* vessels to the accompaniment of music—affluency; extravagance: ～之家 a stately house (or mansion)

钟鸣漏尽 zhōngmíng-lòujìn the morning bell is striking and the night is waning—be in one's declining years

钟琴 zhōngqín *mus.* carillon

钟情 zhōngqíng be deeply in love

钟乳石 zhōngrǔshí *geol.* stalactite

钟头 zhōngtóu *inf.* hour: 这出戏演了三个半～。The play lasted for three and half hours.

衷

衷 zhōng ① inner feelings; heart: 由衷 yóuzhōng ② same as 中 zhōng

衷肠 zhōngcháng *formal* words right from one's heart: 畅叙～ pour out one's heart

衷情 zhōngqíng *formal* heartfelt emotion; inner feelings: 久别重逢，互诉～。Meeting again after a long separation, they opened their hearts to each other.

衷曲 zhōngqū *formal* heartfelt emotion; inner feelings: 倾吐～ pour out one's heart

衷心 zhōngxīn heartfelt; wholehearted; cordial: 表示～的感激（感谢）express one's heartfelt gratitude (thanks) / ～拥护 give wholehearted support / 表示～的祝贺 extend cordial greetings / ～感谢你的帮助。I thank you for your help from the bottom of my heart.

螽 zhōng　see below

螽斯 zhōngsī *zool.* katydid; long-horned grasshopper

zhǒng

肿（腫） zhǒng swelling; swollen: 我的腿～了。My legs are swollen. / ～消了一点。The swelling has gone down a little.

肿骨鹿 zhǒnggǔlù *palaeontology* thick-jawed deer

肿瘤 zhǒngliú tumour: 良（恶）性～ benign (malignant) tumour / ～医院 tumour hospital

肿胀 zhǒngzhàng ① swelling ② *Chin. med.* oedema and abdominal distension

种（種） zhǒng ① *biol.* species: 本地～ endemic species / 外地～ exotic species / 老虎是猫科的一～。The tiger belongs to the cat family. ② race: 黄种 Huángzhǒng / 白种 Báizhǒng ③ seed; strain; breed: 麦～ wheat seeds / 这水稻是什么～? What variety is this rice? ④ guts; grit: 有种 yǒuzhǒng ⑤ *m.* kind; sort; type: 各～仪器 all kinds of instruments / 这一～论调 this sort of argument / 四十～钢材 forty types of rolled steel / 一～现象 a phenomenon / 他有一～以前从未有过的感觉。He had a kind of feeling that he'd never had before. ——see also zhòng

种畜 zhǒngchù breeding stock; stud stock

种肥 zhǒngféi seed manure

种间杂交 zhǒngjiān zájiāo *agric.* interspecific hybridization (or cross)

种类 zhǒnglèi kind; type; variety: 不同～的刀具 cutters of different kinds / ～繁多 a great variety

种马 zhǒngmǎ stud: ～场 stud farm; stud

种内杂交 zhǒngnèi zájiāo *agric.* intraspecific hybridization (or cross)

种牛 zhǒngniú bull kept for covering

种仁 zhǒngrén kernel

种姓 zhǒngxìng caste (of India): ～制度 caste system

种种 zhǒngzhǒng all sorts (or kinds) of; a variety of: 设置了～障碍 put up all sorts of obstacles / 由于～原因 for a variety of reasons / 用～手段 by hook or by crook; resort to every means (or trick)

种子 zhǒng·zǐ ① seed: ～处理 seed treatment / ～清选机 seed cleaner / ～田 seed-breeding field / ～植物 seed plant ② *sports* seeded player; seed: 被列为～ be seeded / ～选手 seeded player; seed

种子队 zhǒng·zǐduì *sports* seeded team

种子地 zhǒngzǐdì same as 留种地 liúzhǒngdì

种族 zhǒngzú race: ～平等 racial equality / 不分～和信仰 irrespective of race or creed / ～问题实质上是阶级问题。The racial question is in essence a class question.

种族隔离 zhǒngzú gélí racial segregation; apartheid

种族灭绝 zhǒngzú mièjué genocide

种族歧视 zhǒngzú qíshì racial discrimination

种族主义 zhǒngzúzhǔyì racism; racialism: ～者 racist

冢（塚） zhǒng tomb; grave: 古～ an ancient tomb

踵 zhǒng *formal* ① heel: 接踵 jiēzhǒng ② call in person: ～门道谢 call in person to express one's thanks ③ follow close behind: 踵至 zhǒngzhì

踵事增华 zhǒng shì zēng huá carry on a predecessor's task and make a greater success of it; take over and carry forward

踵武 zhǒngwǔ *formal* follow in sb.'s footsteps; imitate; follow suit

踵至 zhǒngzhì *formal* arrive upon the heels of another; arrive immediately after sb.

zhòng

中 zhòng ① hit; fit exactly: 射～靶心 hit the bull's eye / 你说～了。You've hit it. *or* That's right. / 打三枪～两枪，第三枪没有～。Two shot hit the target out of three. The third shot missed the target. ② be hit by; fall into; be affected by; suffer: ～煤气 be gassed / 他腿上～了一枪。He got shot in the leg. ——see also zhōng

中标 zhòngbiāo get (or win) the bid or tender

中彩 zhòngcǎi win a prize in a lottery

中弹 zhòngdàn be hit by a bullet; get shot

中的 zhòngdì hit the mark; hit the nail on the head: 批驳有力，语语～。The refutation is forceful and every word hits home.

中毒 zhòngdú ① be poisoned (usu. accidentally) ② poisoning; toxicosis: 食物～ food poisoning

中风 zhòngfēng suffer from a stroke of apoplexy: 死于～ die of apoplexy

中计 zhòngjì play into sb.'s hands; fall into a trap; be taken in

中奖 zhòngjiǎng draw a prizewinning ticket (or win a prize) in a lottery; get the winning number in a bond

中举 zhòngjǔ pass the imperial examinations at the provincial level

中肯 zhòngkěn ① apropos; pertinent; to the point: ～的评语 pertinent remarks / 回答简短而～。The reply was brief and to the point. / 他的发言很～。He spoke very much to the point. *or* His speech hit the nail on the head. / 作出～的分析 make a sound analysis ② *phys.* critical: ～质量 critical mass

中魔 zhòngmó be possessed (by evil spirits): 他像中了魔似地手舞足蹈。He danced and waved like a man possessed.

中签 zhòngqiān be the lucky number (in drawing lots, etc.)

中伤 zhòngshāng slander; malign; vilify: ～好人 malign an innocent person

中式 zhòngshì pass the imperial examinations ——see also zhōngshì

中试 zhòngshì pass a test, etc.

中暑 zhòngshǔ ① suffer heatstroke (or sunstroke); be affected by the heat ② heatstroke; sunstroke

中邪 zhòngxié same as 中魔 zhòngmó

中选 zhòngxuǎn be chosen; be selected

中意 zhòngyì be to one's liking; take (or catch) the fancy of: 这些暖瓶，我一个都不～。None of these thermosflasks is to my liking. / 她花了一千元买了一件很～的西服连衣裙。She paid 1,000 *yuan* for a coat dress that had taken her fancy. / 这衣服不中我的意。This dress is not to my taste.

众（眾） zhòng ① many; numerous: 众多

zhòngduō ② crowd; multitude: 大众 dàzhòng / 观众 guānzhòng

众多 zhòngduō multitudinous; numerous: 我国人口～，地大物博。Our country has a large population, vast territory and abundant resources.

众寡悬殊 zhòng-guǎ xuánshū a great disparity in numerical strength

众口难调 zhòng kǒu nán tiáo it is difficult to cater for all tastes

众口铄金 zhòng kǒu shuò jīn public clamour can confound right and wrong

众口一词 zhòng kǒu yī cí with one voice; unanimously

众目睽睽 zhòng mù kuíkuí with everybody watching: ～之下 under the watchful eye of everyone; under the public gaze

众目昭彰 zhòng mù zhāozhāng seen clearly by everyone; clear to all

众怒 zhòngnù public wrath

众怒难犯 zhòngnù nán fàn one cannot afford to incur public wrath; it is dangerous to incur the anger of the masses

众叛亲离 zhòngpàn-qīnlí with the masses rising in rebellion and one's friends deserting; be opposed by the masses and deserted by one's followers; be utterly isolated

众擎易举 zhòng qíng yì jǔ with many people it's easy to lift a load—many hands make light work

众人 zhòngrén everybody

众人拾柴火焰高 zhòngrén shí chái huǒyàn gāo when everybody adds fuel the flames rise high—the more people, the more strength

众生 zhòngshēng all living creatures

众矢之的 zhòng shǐ zhī dì a target of public criticism (or censure)

众庶 zhòngshù formal common people

众数 zhòngshù statistics mode

众说纷纭 zhòng shuō fēnyún opinions vary; opinions are widely divided: ～，莫衷一是。As opinions vary, no unanimous conclusion can be drawn.

众所周知 zhòng suǒ zhōu zhī as everyone knows; as is known to all; it is common knowledge that: ～，中国一贯主张和平解决国际争端。As is well known, China has always stood for a peaceful settlement of international disputes. / 为了～的原因 for reasons known to all

众望 zhòngwàng people's expectations; popular confidence

众望所归 zhòngwàng suǒ guī enjoy popular confidence; command popular support

众星拱月 zhòng xīng gǒng yuè a myriad of stars surrounding the moon—a host of lesser lights around the leading one

众议员 zhòngyìyuán representative (in Congress); member of the House of Representatives; Congressman or Congresswoman

众议院 zhòngyìyuàn House of Representatives (in United States, Australia, Japan, etc.); Chamber of Deputies (in Italy, Mexico, Chile, etc.)

众志成城 zhòng zhì chéng chéng unity of will is an impregnable stronghold; unity is strength

仲 zhòng ① the second month of a season: 仲秋 zhòngqiū ② the second among brothers: ～兄 the second eldest brother ③ middle; intermediate: 仲裁 zhòngcái ④ (Zhòng) a surname

仲裁 zhòngcái arbitrate: 对争端进行～ arbitrate a dispute / ～法庭 arbitration tribunal; court of arbitration / ～人 arbitrator / ～书 (arbitration) award / ～协定 arbitration agreement

仲春 zhòngchūn second month of spring; the middle of spring

仲冬 zhòngdōng second month of winter; midwinter

仲家 Zhòngjiā old name for 布依族 Bùyīzú

仲秋 zhòngqiū second month of autumn; midautumn

仲夏 zhòngxià second month of summer; midsummer

种（種） zhòng grow; plant; cultivate: ～水稻 grow rice / ～庄稼 grow (or plant) crops / ～玉米的那六亩地 the six mu of land sown to maize / ～一块试验田 cultivate an experimental plot / 过去这里的水田多数只～一季，现在全部～两季。Most paddy fields here used to yield only one crop a year, but now they all yield two crops. ——see also zhǒng

种地 zhòngdì till (or cultivate) land; go in for farming

种痘 zhòngdòu (also 种牛痘 zhòng niúdòu) vaccinate sb. against smallpox: 这孩子～了吗? Has the baby been vaccinated?

种瓜得瓜，种豆得豆 zhòng guā dé guā, zhòng dòu dé dòu plant melons and you get melons, sow beans and you get beans—as you sow, so will you reap

种花 zhònghuā ① cultivate (or grow) flowers ② dial. vaccinate sb. against smallpox ③ dial. grow cotton

种田 zhòngtián till (or cultivate) land; go in for farming

种因 zhòngyīn do things that will entail grave consequences

种植 zhòngzhí plant; grow: 油菜～面积 rape-growing areas; areas sown to rape

种植园 zhòngzhíyuán plantation: ～主 plantation owner; planter

重 zhòng ① weight: 这条鱼有三斤～。This fish weighs three jin. / 你多～? What's your weight? ② heavy; weighty; important: 铁比木头～。Iron is weightier than wood. / 眉毛很～ have thick eyebrows / 工作很～ have a heavy work load / 以友谊为～ set store by friendship / 话说得太～了。That's putting it too strongly. / 为人民利益而死，就比泰山还～。To die for the people is weightier than Mount Tai. ③ considerable in amount or value: 重金 zhòngjīn ④ deep; heavy; serious: 情意～ deep affection / 私心很～ extremely selfish / 山东口音很～ have a marked (or heavy) Shandong accent / 病势很～ be seriously ill ⑤ lay stress on; attach importance to: ～调查研究 lay stress on investigation and study ⑥ discreet: 慎重 shènzhòng ——see also chóng

重办 zhòngbàn severely punish (a criminal)

重兵 zhòngbīng a large number of troops; massive forces: 派驻～ station massive forces / 有～把守 be heavily guarded

重柄 zhòngbǐng formal great political power

重病 zhòngbìng a serious illness: 得～ contract a serious illness; be seriously ill

重臣 zhòngchén formal minister (of a monarchy) holding an important post or shouldering heavy responsibilities; important official

重惩 zhòngchéng severely punish: ～不贷 punish with severity; punish without leniency

重酬 zhòngchóu ① generously reward ② a high (or handsome) reward

重创 zhòngchuāng inflict heavy losses (or casualties) on; maul (heavily)

重大 zhòngdà great; weighty; major; significant: 具有～的现实意义 be of great immediate significance / 取得～进展 make significant progress (or headway) / ～的原则分歧 a major difference of principle / ～成就 significant (or tremendous) achievements / ～胜利 a signal victory / ～问题 vital problem; major issue / ～损失 heavy losses / 他有作案的～嫌疑。There is a strong

suspicion that he committed the crime.

重担 zhòngdàn heavy burden; difficult task: 敢 挑～ dare to shoulder heavy burdens (or responsibilities) / 把～子留给自己 take the difficult tasks for oneself

重地 zhòngdì important place (usu. not open to the public): 施工～，闲人免进。Construction Site. No Admittance. / 军事～ a place of military importance

重典 zhòngdiǎn formal ① severe punishment; heavy sentence ② important ancient books and records

重点 zhòngdiǎn ① phys. weight ② focal point; stress; emphasis: 突出～ make the focal (or key) points stand out (as in one's speech) / ～工程 major (or priority) project / ～单位和企业 key units and enterprises / ～建设 construction of key project / ～进攻 attacks against key sectors / 工作～ focal point of the work / 今天～讨论技术革新问题。Our discussion today will centre on technical innovation. or We'll focus our discussion today on technical innovation.

重点学校 zhòngdiǎn xuéxiào key school, institute, or university

重读 zhòngdú phonet. stress: ～音节 stressed syllable / 非～音节 unstressed syllable

重犯 zhòngfàn major criminal

重负 zhòngfù heavy burden; heavy load

重工业 zhònggōngyè heavy industry

重过磷酸钙 zhòngguòlínsuāngài double superphosphate

重荷 zhònghè heavy burden; heavy responsibilities: 肩负～ shoulder heavy responsibilities

重轰炸机 zhònghōngzhàjī heavy bomber

重话 zhònghuà hard words; harsh words: 他俩结婚以来连句～都没有过。Hardly a harsh word has passed between them ever since their marriage.

重活 zhònghuó heavy work

重机关枪 zhòngjīguānqiāng heavy machine gun

重寄 zhòngjì heavy responsibilities of government

重价 zhòngjià high price: ～收购古物 offer high prices for antiques

重剑 zhòngjiàn sports épée: ～运动员 épée fencer; épéeist

重奖 zhòngjiǎng give ample rewards to: 对有特殊贡献的，要给以～。Those who have made outstanding contribution should be amply rewarded.

重金 zhòngjīn a huge sum (of money): ～购买 pay a high price for

重金属 zhòngjīnshǔ chem. heavy metal

重晶石 zhòngjīngshí barite; heavy spar (a mineral)

重力 zhònglì gravity; gravitational force: ～坝 gravity dam / ～场 gravitational field / ～秤 gravity balance / ～加速度 acceleration of gravity / ～水 gravitational water; free water / ～选矿 gravity separation (or concentration) / ～仪 gravity meter; gravimeter / ～异常 gravity anomaly

重利 zhònglì ① high interest ② huge profit

重量 zhòngliàng weight: ～单 weight list (or memo) / ～证明书 weight certificate; surveyor's report on weight

重量级 zhòngliàngjí sports heavyweight

重名 zhòngmíng great reputation

重男轻女 zhòngnán-qīngnǚ regard men as superior to women

重炮 zhòngpào heavy artillery; heavy artillery piece; heavy gun

重器 zhòngqì formal ① treasure ② a great mind

重切削 zhòngqiēxiāo mech. heavy cut

重氢 zhòngqīng chem. heavy hydrogen; deuterium

重任 zhòngrèn important task; heavy responsibility: 身负～ be charged with important tasks

重伤 zhòngshāng a severe injury: 受～ sustain (or receive) severe injuries; be severely injured

重商主义 zhòngshāngzhǔyì mercantilism

重赏 zhòngshǎng a high (or handsome) reward

重赏之下，必有勇夫 zhòngshǎng zhī xià, bì yǒu yǒngfū when a high reward is offered, brave fellows are bound to come forward

重身子 zhòngshēnzi ① be pregnant ② a pregnant woman

重视 zhòngshì attach importance to; pay attention to; think highly of; take sth. seriously; value: ～对妇女干部的培养 devote much attention to the training of women cadres / ～发展农业 attach great importance to agriculture / ～这件事 take the matter seriously / ～群众的意见 set great store by the opinions of the masses / ～基础理论的研究工作 pay great attention to basic theoretical research

重水 zhòngshuǐ chem. heavy water

重税 zhòngshuì heavy (or oppressive) taxation

重听 zhòngtīng hard of hearing: 他有点～，你说话得大点声儿。You have to raise your voice for he is hard of hearing.

重头戏 zhòngtóuxì traditional opera involving much singing and action

重托 zhòngtuō great trust: 不辜负人民对我们的～ justify the great trust placed in us by the people

重望 zhòngwàng ① good reputation ② high hopes; great expectations

重武器 zhòngwǔqì heavy weapons

重孝 zhòngxiào in deep mourning (usu. after the death of one's parent)

重心 zhòngxīn ① phys. centre of gravity ② heart; core; focus: 问题的～ the heart of a matter

重刑 zhòngxíng severe punishment; heavy sentence

重型 zhòngxíng heavy-duty; heavy: ～机床 heavy-duty machine tool / ～卡车 heavy-duty truck; heavy truck

重压 zhòngyā heavy (or strong) pressure: 树枝经不起雪的～，终于折断了。Weighed down by snow, the twig broke off in the end. / 承受着精神的～ be under heavy mental pressure

重要 zhòngyào important; significant; major: ～人物 important figure; prominent personage; VIP / ～关头 critical juncture / ～任务 vital task; important mission / ～原则 cardinal principle / ～政策 major policy / ～因素 key factor / ～性 importance; significance / 这文件很～。This document is very important.

重音 zhòngyīn ① phonet. stress; accent: 句子～ sentence stress / 单词～ word stress / ～符号 stress mark; accent ② mus. accent

重用 zhòngyòng put sb. in an important position: ～有真才实学的人 put people of real ability and learning in important positions / 一直受到～ have always been employed at high levels

重油 zhòngyóu heavy oil

重于泰山，轻于鸿毛 zhòngyú Tàishān, qīngyú hóngmáo (of one's death) weightier than Mount Tai or lighter than a feather: 人固有一死，或重于泰山，或轻于鸿毛。(司马迁) Though death befalls all men alike, it may be weightier than Mount Tai or lighter than a feather. or Death befalls all men alike, but the loss of some is heavier than Mount Tai, of others lighter than a feather.

重元素 zhòngyuánsù chem. heavy element

重载 zhòngzài (of a vehicle) be heavily loaded

重枣 zhòngzǎo reddish brown (like dried dates)

重责 zhòngzé ① heavy responsibility; important task ② severely reprimand or punish: ～四十大板 punish with 40 strokes of the rod

重镇 zhòngzhèn place of strategic importance: 军事～ a strategic post

重浊 zhòngzhuó ① (of voice) low and deep ②

overcast; lowering: 天色暗淡～。The sky was overcast. / 烟雾迷漫, 空气十分～。The air was heavy with smoke.

重子 zhòngzǐ *phys.* baryon

重罪 zhòngzuì serious crime; felony

zhōu

州 zhōu ① an administrative division in former times ② (autonomous) prefecture

舟 zhōu *formal* boat: 小～ a small (*or* light) boat

舟车 zhōuchē *formal* ① vessel and vehicle ② journey: ～劳顿 fatigued by a long journey; travel-worn

舟楫 zhōují *formal* vessels: 江河湖泽给我们以～和灌溉之利。Rivers and lakes provide us with water transport and irrigation.

舟子 zhōuzǐ *formal* boatman

诌 (謅) zhōu fabricate (tales, etc.); make up: 胡诌 húzhōu

周¹ (週) zhōu ① circumference; periphery; circuit: 运动员绕场一～。The athletes made a circuit of the arena. / 地球绕太阳一～是一年。It makes a year when the earth finishes a circuit around the sun. ② make a circuit; move in a circular course: 周而复始 zhōu ér fù shǐ ③ all; whole; all over; all around: 周身 zhōushēn ④ thoughtful; attentive: 周到 zhōudào ⑤ week: 上～ last week ⑥ short for 周波 zhōubō

周² (賙) zhōu help out (the needy); relieve: 周济 zhōují

周³ Zhōu ① the Zhou Dynasty (c.11th century-256 B.C.) ② a surname

周报 zhōubào a weekly newspaper or periodical; weekly: 《北京～》 *Beijing Review*

周备 zhōubèi be fully or satisfactorily (prepared); be carefully (worked out)

周边 zhōubiān *mech.* periphery

周遍 zhōubiàn all round; all over

周布 zhōubù extend (*or* spread) all over: 血管～全身。Blood vessels extend all over the body.

周波 zhōubō *elec.* cycle

周长 zhōucháng girth; circumference; perimeter: ～五米的烟筒 a funnel five metres in girth / 水库的～ the perimeter of a reservoir / 湖的～十二公里。The lake is 12 kilometres in circumference.

周到 zhōudào attentive and satisfactory; thoughtful; considerate: 服务～ offer good service / 想得很～ be very thoughtful (*or* considerate) / 安排得很～ be satisfactorily arranged; be carefully worked out / 照顾得很～ take good care of sb.; look after sb. well

周而复始 zhōu ér fù shǐ go round and begin again; go round and round; move in cycles: 四季更迭, ～。The seasons of the year make a cycle. When one cycle is completed, another begins.

周回 zhōuhuí *formal* ① circumference: 故城～九里余。The ancient city has a circumference of 9 *li.* ② surround; encircle: 四山～ be surrounded by hills

周忌 zhōují first anniversary of sb.'s death

周济 zhōují help out (the needy); relieve

周刊 zhōukān a weekly publication (e. g. a magazine, a supplement to a newspaper, etc.); weekly

周流 zhōuliú circulate: 血液～全身。Blood circulates through the body.

周率 zhōulǜ *phys.* frequency

周密 zhōumì careful; thorough: ～思考 think over carefully / 进行～的调查 carry out a thorough investigation / ～的分析 a detailed analysis / ～的计划 a well-conceived plan

周末 zhōumò weekend: 我们在北戴河度过了一个愉快的～。We spent a lovely weekend in Beidaihe.

周年 zhōunián anniversary: 建厂十五～ the 15th anniversary of the founding of the factory / 一百～ centenary / 二十五～纪念 silver jubilee / 五十～纪念 golden jubilee

周期 zhōuqī period; cycle

周期表 zhōuqībiǎo *chem.* periodic table

周期律 zhōuqīlǜ *chem.* periodic law

周期性 zhōuqīxìng periodicity; cyclicity: ～循环 periodic return / ～经济危机 periodic (*or* cyclical) economic crises / ～疟疾发作 periodic attacks of malaria / ～通货膨胀 cyclical inflation

周全 zhōuquán ① thorough; comprehensive: 计划要尽量订得～些。We should make the plan as comprehensive as we can. ② help sb. attain his aim

周身 zhōushēn the whole body; all over the body: ～疼痛 ache all over

周岁 zhōusuì one full year of life: 今天孩子满～。Today is the child's first birthday. / 他三十二～。He is thirty-two years old.

周围 zhōuwéi around; round; about: 关心～的群众 have concern for the people around one / 团结在党的～ rally round the Party / 环顾～ look about; look around / ～环境 surroundings; environment / ～温度 environment (*or* ambient) temperature

周围神经 zhōuwéi shénjīng *physiol.* peripheral nerves: ～系统 peripheral nervous system

周详 zhōuxiáng comprehensive; complete; careful: 考虑～ give careful consideration to

周恤 zhōuxù *formal* show pity on and give charity to; sympathise and help

周旋 zhōuxuán ① circle round; spiral ② mix with other people; socialize: ～于达官贵人之间 move in high society ③ deal with; contend with: 游击队长期在山区和侵略者～。For a long time, the guerrillas fought the invaders in hilly country.

周延 zhōuyán *log.* distribution

周游 zhōuyóu travel round; journey round: ～世界 travel round the world / ～各国 travel to many countries; travel far and wide

周缘 zhōuyuán outer edge (as of a wheel); rim

周遭 zhōuzāo the surrounding area: ～静悄悄的, 没有一个人。It was very quiet all around with nobody in sight. / 山围故国～在, 潮打空城寂寞回。(刘禹锡) Hills surround the ancient kingdom; they never change. The tide beats against the empty city, and silently, silently returns.

周章 zhōuzhāng *formal* ① be scared: ～失措 be flurried out of one's wits ② trouble; effort: 煞费～ take great pains; spare no effort

周折 zhōuzhé twists and turns; setbacks: 这事恐怕要费一番～。I'm afraid this business will cause us a good deal of bother. / 几经～, 才告成功。Only after many setbacks was success achieved.

周正 zhōuzhèng *dial.* straight; regular: 把帽子戴～。Put your hat on straight. / 她模样儿长得很～。She has regular features.

周知 zhōuzhī everybody knows or make known to all: 特此通告～。It is hereby announced that....

周至 zhōuzhì *formal* thoughtful; considerate: 丁宁～ give thoughtful advice

周转 zhōuzhuǎn ① *econ.* turnover: 加速资本～ speed up capital turnover / ～率 turnover rate / ～资金 working

fund; revolving fund; circulating fund / 〜天数 turnover period ② have enough to meet the need: 义务劳动的学生很多, 土筐〜不开。We have many students here to do volunteer labour, but there aren't enough carrying baskets to go round.

洲 zhōu ① continent ② islet in a river; sand bar

洲际 zhōujì intercontinental: 〜弹道导弹 intercontinental ballistic missile / 〜导弹 intercontinental missile

啁 zhōu see below ——see also zhāo

啁啾 zhōujiū onom. formal (of birds) twitter; chirp; warble

捣（撖） zhōu dial. hold one end or side of a heavy object and lift it

粥 zhōu gruel (made of rice, millet, etc.); porridge; congee: 小米〜 millet gruel

粥少僧多 zhōu shǎo sēng duō little gruel and many monks—not enough to go round

zhóu

妯 zhóu see below

妯娌 zhóuli wives of brothers; sisters-in-law

轴 zhóu ① axle; shaft: 这〜儿磨坏了。The axle is worn. ② axis: 椭圆的长（短）〜 the major (minor) axis of an ellipse ③ spool; rod: 画轴 huàzhóu ④ m.: 一〜线 a spool of thread / 一〜山水画 a scroll painting of scenery ——see also zhòu

轴衬 zhóuchèn same as 轴瓦 zhóuwǎ

轴承 zhóuchéng mech. bearing: 〜衬 bearing bush / 〜钢 bearing steel

轴对称 zhóuduìchèn math. axial symmetry

轴距 zhóujù wheelbase (of a vehicle)

轴流泵 zhóuliúbèng axial-flow pump; axial pump

轴套 zhóutào mech. axle sleeve

轴瓦 zhóuwǎ mech. axle bush

轴线 zhóuxiàn ① mech. axis: 垂直〜 normal axis ② spool thread; spool cotton

轴向 zhóuxiàng mech. axial: 〜剖面 axial section / 〜运动 axial motion

轴心 zhóuxīn ① mech. axle centre ② axis

轴心国 Zhóuxīnguó Axis powers (i. e. Germany, Italy and Japan during World War Ⅱ); the Axis

轴子 zhóuzi ① roller (for a scroll of calligraphy or painting) ② (tuning) peg (or pin)

zhǒu

肘 zhǒu elbow

肘接 zhǒujiē mech. toggle (or elbow) joint

肘节 zhǒujié mech. toggle: 制动〜 brake toggle

肘窝 zhǒuwō crook of the arm

肘腋 zhǒuyè formal elbow and armpit—close at hand ——see also 变生肘腋 biàn shēng zhǒuyè

肘子 zhǒuzi ① upper part of a leg of pork ② elbow

帚（箒） zhǒu broom: 笤帚 tiáozhou

zhòu

纣 Zhòu name of the last ruler of the Shang Dynasty (c. 16th–11th century B. C.), reputedly a tyrant

纣棍 zhòugùn crupper of a saddle

宙 zhòu time (conceived as past, present and future): 宇宙 yǔzhòu

怞（懤） zhòu dial. obstinate; stubborn

绉（縐） zhòu crape; crepe: 派力斯〜 palace crepe

绉布 zhòubù cotton crepe; crepe

绉纱 zhòushā crape

咒（呪） zhòu ① incantation: 念〜 chant incantations ② curse; damn: 你别〜我噢。Don't you curse me.

咒骂 zhòumà curse; swear; abuse; revile

咒语 zhòuyǔ incantation

胄[1] zhòu descendants of feudal rulers or aristocrats: 贵胄 guìzhòu

胄[2] zhòu helmet: 甲胄 jiǎzhòu

苃 zhòu dial. ① wrap with straw ② m. a bundle (of bowls, plates, ect. wrapped together with a straw rope)

昼（晝） zhòu daytime; daylight; day: 〜伏夜出 hide by day and come out at night

昼出动物 zhòuchū dòngwù diurnal animal

昼夜 zhòu-yè day and night; round the clock: 〜看守 keep watch round the clock / 〜警戒 be on a round-the-clock alert / 他们英勇地战斗了七〜。They battled heroically for seven days and nights.

轴 zhòu see 压轴子 yāzhòuzi; 大轴子 dàzhòuzi ——see also zhóu

皱（皺） zhòu wrinkle; crease; crumple: 我的上衣在箱子里搁久了, 〜得不像样子。My jacket has been in the suitcase so long that it's full of creases (or it's all creased). / 这种料子爱〜。This material crumples easily. / 注意别把地图弄〜了。Mind you don't crumple the map.

皱襞 zhòubì formal pleat; crease; wrinkle

皱痕 zhòuhén fine wrinkle

皱眉头 zhòu méitóu knit (or contract) one's brows; frown: 他看见有人吐痰, 皱了皱眉头。He frowned with displeasure when he saw someone spit.

皱胃 zhòuwèi zool. abomasum

皱纹 zhòuwén wrinkles; creases; lines: 他是满脸〜。His face is full of wrinkles. or He has many lines on his face. / 许多人过了四十, 眼睛周围就有了〜。After forty, many people get wrinkles round their eyes. / 长年的焦虑使他的额头起了〜。Years of worry had creased his brow. / 眼角的〜 crow's-feet

皱纹法兰绒 zhòuwén fǎlánróng crepe flannel

皱纹革 zhòuwéngé shrink leather

皱纹纸 zhòuwénzhǐ crepe paper

皱褶 zhòuzhě fold; crease; wrinkle

皱皱巴巴 zhòuzhoubābā (also 皱巴巴 zhòubābā) wrinkled; crumpled: 皱巴巴的瘦脸 a thin wrinkly face / 〜的

手绢儿 a crumpled handkerchief／脸上～的 a face full of wrinkles; having many lines on one's face／他那身衣服总是～的 His suit is always full of creases.

酎

酎 zhòu *formal* double-fermented wine
酎金 zhòujīn contributions of nobles to the emperor for sacrificial purposes in ancient times

骤

骤 zhòu ① (of a horse) trot: 驰骤 chízhòu ② sudden; abrupt: 一阵～雨 a passing heavy shower／天气～变。There was a sudden change of weather.／狂风～起。A sudden gale struck.／雨疏风～。The rain was light, the wind fierce.
骤然 zhòurán *adv.* suddenly; abruptly: ～离去 leave abruptly／～响起雷鸣般的掌声。Stormy applause broke forth suddenly.／～一惊 be startled; be stupefied

籀

籀 zhòu *formal* ① read aloud; recite ② see 籀文 zhòuwén
籀文 zhòuwén a style of calligraphy, current in the Zhou Dynasty (c. 11th century–256 B.C.)

zhou

碡

碡 zhou see 碌碡 liùzhou

zhū

朱¹

朱 zhū ① vermilion; bright red ② (Zhū) a surname

朱²(硃)

朱²(硃) zhū cinnabar
朱笔 zhūbǐ writing brush dipped in red ink (formerly used in marking students' papers or writing comments on official documents)
朱唇皓齿 zhūchún-hàochǐ red lips and shining teeth—very pretty or handsome
朱顶雀 zhūdǐngquè redpoll (linnet)
朱古力 zhūgǔlì same as 巧克力 qiǎokèlì
朱红 zhūhóng vermilion; bright red
朱槿 zhūjǐn Chinese Hibiscus (*Hibiscus rosa-sinensis*)
朱鹭 zhūlù (crested) ibis
朱轮华毂 zhūlún-huágǔ ornate carriage with wheels painted red (used by nobles in ancient times)
朱门 zhūmén vermilion gates—red-lacquered doors of wealthy homes
朱门酒肉臭，路有冻死骨 zhūmén jiǔròu chòu, lù yǒu dòngsǐgǔ behind the red doors meat and wine go to waste while out on the road lie the bones of the frozen
朱墨¹ zhūmò red and black: ～套印 printed in red and black／～本 an edition of ancient books printed in red and black
朱墨² zhūmò ink made of cinnabar
朱鸟 zhūniǎo same as 朱雀² zhūquè
朱批 zhūpī comments or remarks written in red with a brush
朱漆 zhūqī red paint; red lacquer: ～大门 vermilion gates／～木箱 red-lacquered chest
朱雀¹ zhūquè rosefinch
朱雀² zhūquè the Scarlet Bird—① a collective name for the southern group (Nos. 22-28) of the twenty-eight constellations (二十八宿) ② the guardian spirit of the south in Taoism
朱砂 zhūshā cinnabar
朱文 zhūwén characters on a seal carved in relief

朱颜 zhūyán ① beautiful face (of a woman) ② youthful colour

诛

诛 zhū *formal* ① put (a criminal) to death: 伏诛 fúzhū ② punish: 卖国贼人人得而～之。Everybody has the right to punish traitors.
诛锄异己 zhūchú yìjǐ wipe out (*or* liquidate) dissenters
诛戮 zhūlù *formal* kill; put to death
诛求 zhūqiú *formal* make exorbitant demands; extort; exact: ～无厌 demand greedily; be insatiably avaricious
诛求无已 zhūqiú wúyǐ make endless exorbitant demands
诛心之论 zhūxīn zhī lùn penetrating criticism; exposure of sb.'s ulterior motives

侏

侏 zhū *formal* ① short and small ② dwarf
侏罗纪 Zhūluójì *geol.* Jurassic Period
侏罗系 Zhūluóxì *geol.* Jurassic system
侏儒 zhūrú dwarf; midget; pygmy

茱

茱 zhū see below
茱萸 zhūyú see 山茱萸 shānzhūyú; 食茱萸 shízhūyú

珠

珠 zhū ① pearl: 明珠 míngzhū ② bead: 算盘～ beads on an abacus
珠蚌 zhūbàng pearl oyster
珠宝 zhūbǎo pearls and jewels; jewelry: ～店 a jeweller's (shop)／～商 jeweller
珠茶 zhūchá a kind of green tea (the tea leaves looking like beads)
珠翠 zhūcuì pearls and jade; ornaments made with pearls and jade
珠光宝气 zhūguāng-bǎoqì resplendent with jewels; bedecked with jewels
珠光体 zhūguāngtǐ *metall.* pearlite
珠花 zhūhuā pearl head-ornaments
珠还合浦 zhū huán Hépǔ same as 合浦还珠 Hépǔ huán zhū
珠玑 zhūjī *formal* ① pearl; gem ② exquisite or excellent wording of a writing: 字字珠玑 zì zì zhūjī
珠江 Zhūjiāng the Zhujiang River; the Pearl River
珠兰 zhūlán common name for 金粟兰 jīnsùlán
珠帘 zhūlián pearl-decorated screen or curtain; bead curtain
珠联璧合 zhūlián-bìhé strings of pearls and girdles of jade—a perfect pair; a happy combination
珠落玉盘 zhū luò yùpán pearls falling on a plate of jade—the sweet notes of the *pipa* lute: 大弦嘈嘈如急雨，小弦切切如私语；嘈嘈切切错杂弹，大珠小珠落玉盘。(白居易) The high notes wail like pelting rain, The low notes whisper like soft confidences; Wailing and whispering interweave Like pearls large and small cascading on a plate of jade.
珠母 zhūmǔ pearl oyster
珠母贝 zhūmǔbèi pearl shell
珠穆朗玛峰 Zhūmùlǎngmǎfēng Mount Qomolangma (known to the West as Mount Everest)
珠算 zhūsuàn reckoning by the abacus; calculation with an abacus
珠围翠绕 zhūwéi-cuìrào ① (of a woman) be gorgeously dressed and richly ornamented ② be surrounded by attending maids
珠圆玉润 zhūyuán-yùrùn round as pearls and smooth as jade—excellent singing or polished writing
珠子 zhūzi ① pearl ② bead

株

株 zhū ① trunk of a tree; stem of a plant ② individual plant; plant: 幼株 yòuzhū ③ *m.*: 两～梨树 two

pear trees

株距 zhūjù *agric.* spacing in the rows

株连 zhūlián involve (others) in a criminal case; implicate

株守 zhūshǒu hold on stubbornly to (a silly idea, etc.) ——see also 守株待兔 shǒu zhū dài tù

株选 zhūxuǎn select good strains in the field for seed

诸[1]

zhū ① all; various: 编辑部～同志 all the comrades of the editorial department / 自然科学～部门 the various branches of natural science ② (Zhū) a surname

诸[2]

zhū *formal* a fusing of 之于 or of 之乎: 付～ (＝之于) 实施 put into effect / 数易其稿, 而后公～(＝之于) 社会。It went through several drafts before it was published. / 不识有～(＝之乎)?一有之。I wonder if this is true?—It is.

诸多 zhūduō *formal* (used for abstract things) a good deal; a lot of: ～不便 quite a lot of trouble; rather inconvenient

诸葛 Zhūgé a two-character surname

诸葛亮 Zhūgé Liàng ① Zhuge Liang, a statesman and strategist in the period of the Three Kingdoms (220–265), who became a symbol of resourcefulness and wisdom in Chinese folklore ② a person of great wisdom and resourcefulness; mastermind

诸葛亮会 zhūgéliànghuì a meeting of Zhuge Liangs—a meeting to pool the wisdom of the collective

诸公 zhūgōng *pol.* (used in addressing a group of men) gentlemen

诸宫调 zhūgōngdiào a kind of ballad, popular in the Song, Jin and Yuan Dynasties

诸侯 zhūhóu dukes or princes under an emperor

诸君 zhūjūn *pol.* (used in addressing a group of people) ladies and gentlemen; you

诸亲好友 zhūqīn-hǎoyǒu friends and relatives

诸如 zhūrú such as: 他当总经理, 职务繁多, ～主持会议, 制定计划、预算, 洽谈贷款, 等等。His duties as general manager are complex and many, such as presiding over meetings, making plans and budgets, and negotiating loans.

诸如此类 zhūrú cǐ lèi things of that sort; and suchlike; and what not: ～, 不胜枚举。Such instances are too numerous to mention. / ～的科学发明, 都大大提高了劳动生产率。Scientific inventions such as these have raised labour productivity by a big margin.

诸色 zhūsè *formal* various; all kinds: ～人等 all kinds of people

诸事 zhūshì everything; every matter: 祝 您～ 顺遂。Hope everything goes well with you! *or* Wishing you every success!

诸位 zhūwèi *pol.* (used in addressing a group of people) ladies and gentlemen; you: ～有什么意见, 欢迎提出来。You are welcome to put forward your views. / ～早。Good morning, everybody. / ～女士, ～先生! Ladies and Gentlemen!

诸子百家 zhūzǐ bǎijiā the various schools of thought and their exponents during the period from pre-Qin times to the early years of the Han Dynasty

猪(豬)

zhū pig; hog; swine: 小～ pigling; piglet / 母～ sow / 公～ boar

猪八戒倒打一耙 Zhūbājiè dào dǎ yī pá Pigsy striking backwards with his rake—make a counterattack or countercharge

猪草 zhūcǎo greenfeed for pigs

猪场 zhūchǎng pig farm; piggery

猪丹毒 zhūdāndú swine erysipelas; diamond-skin disease

猪肚 zhūdǔ pork tripe

猪肝 zhūgān pork liver: ～色 liver-coloured; purplish red

猪倌 zhūguān swineherd

猪獾 zhūhuān sand badger

猪圈 zhūjuàn pigsty; pigpen; hogpen

猪苓 zhūlíng *Chin. med.* umbellate pore fungus (*Polyporus umbellata*)

猪笼草 zhūlóngcǎo *bot.* common nepenthes (*Nepenthes mirabilis*)

猪猡 zhūluó *dial.* pig; swine

猪苗 zhūmiáo piglet; pigling

猪囊虫病 zhūnángchóngbìng pork measles

猪排 zhūpái pork chop

猪皮 zhūpí pigskin; hogskin

猪婆龙 zhūpólóng common name for 鼍 tuó

猪气喘病 zhūqìchuǎnbìng swine enzootic pneumonia

猪肉 zhūròu pork

猪舍 zhūshè pig (*or* hog) house

猪食 zhūshí pig feed; pigwash; swill: ～缸 (pig) trough

猪蹄 zhūtí pig's trotters

猪头 zhūtóu pig's head: ～肉 pieces of meat cut from a pig's head served as a cold dish to go with drinks

猪腿 zhūtuǐ leg of pork; ham

猪瘟 zhūwēn swine fever; hog cholera

猪窝 zhūwō pigsty: 他的房间脏得像～。His room is as dirty as a pigsty.

猪血 zhūxiě coagulated pig's blood used as a food

猪腰子 zhūyāozi pork kidney

猪油 zhūyóu lard

猪油果 zhūyóuguǒ another name for 油瓜 yóuguā

猪鬃 zhūzōng (hog) bristles

猪鬃草 zhūzōngcǎo same as 铁线蕨 tiěxiànjué

铢

zhū an ancient unit of weight, equal to 1/24 *liang* (两)

铢积寸累 zhūjī-cùnlěi accumulate little by little; build up bit by bit

铢两悉称 zhū-liǎng xī chèn carry the same weight; be exactly equal

蛛

zhū spider: 蜘蛛 zhīzhū

蛛丝马迹 zhūsī-mǎjì the thread of a spider and the trail of a horse—clues; traces: 此案有～可寻。There are clues for solving the case.

蛛网 zhūwǎng spider web; cobweb

蛛形动物 zhūxíng dòngwù arachnid

蛛蛛 zhūzhu common name for 蜘蛛 zhīzhū

潴(瀦)

zhū *formal* ① (of water) collect; accumulate; store ② puddle; pool

潴留 zhūliú *med.* retention: 尿潴留 niàozhūliú

zhú

术

zhú see 白术 báizhú; 苍术 cāngzhú ——see also shù

竹

zhú bamboo: ～篓 bamboo crate (*or* basket) / ～林 bamboo forest; groves of bamboo

竹板 zhúbǎn bamboo clappers

竹板书 zhúbǎnshū story recited to the rhythm of bamboo clappers

竹算子 zhúbìzi bamboo grid (to be put in a pot for steaming food)

竹编 zhúbiān bamboo woven articles

竹帛　zhúbó　bamboo slips and silk (used for writing on during ancient times); ancient books

竹布　zhúbù　a light blue or white cotton cloth for making summer clothes

竹蛏　zhúchēng　*zool.* razor clam; razor shell

竹筹　zhúchóu　bamboo chip

竹雕　zhúdiāo　bamboo carving

竹筏　zhúfá　bamboo raft

竹竿　zhúgān　bamboo pole; bamboo

竹黄　zhúhuáng　(also 竹簧 zhúhuáng) handicraft articles made from bamboo with its green covering removed

竹黄菌　zhúhuángjūn　*Chin. med.* bamboo parasitic fungus

竹鸡　zhújī　bamboo partridge

竹荚鱼　zhújiāyú　saurel; horse mackerel

竹简　zhújiǎn　bamboo slip (used for writing on during ancient times)

竹节　zhújié　bamboo joint

竹节虫　zhújiéchóng　stick insect; walkingstick

竹节钢筋　zhújié gāngjīn　corrugated bar

竹刻　zhúkè　bamboo carving; bamboo engraving

竹篮子打水一场空　zhúlánzi dǎshuǐ yīchǎngkōng　draw water with a bamboo basket—achieve nothing; all in vain: 到头来只落得～。In the end all the efforts proved as futile as drawing water with a bamboo basket.

竹篱茅舍　zhúlí-máoshè　thatched cottage with bamboo fence—simple dwelling of a hermit

竹笠　zhúlì　bamboo hat (with a conical crown and broad brim)

竹帘　zhúlián　bamboo screen or curtain

竹帘画　zhúliánhuà　painting on a bamboo curtain

竹笼　zhúlóng　bamboo cage

竹马　zhúmǎ　① a bamboo stick used as a toy horse (see also 青梅竹马 qīngméi-zhúmǎ) ② a bamboo horse used in a folk dance

竹马之交　zhúmǎ zhī jiāo　friends from childhood days

竹篾　zhúmiè　thin bamboo strips used for weaving

竹幕　zhúmù　bamboo curtain

竹排　zhúpái　bamboo raft

竹器　zhúqì　articles made of bamboo

竹扦　zhúqiān　bamboo spike

竹鼠　zhúshǔ　bamboo rat

竹荪　zhúsūn　a kind of edible fungus found in bamboo groves in Sichuan and Guizhou Provinces

竹笋　zhúsǔn　bamboo shoots

竹筒　zhútǒng　a thick bamboo tube

竹筒倒豆子　zhútǒng dào dòuzi　pour beans out of a bamboo tube—withhold nothing: 你就来个～，都说了吧。Out with it—don't hold anything back.

竹头木屑　zhútóu-mùxiè　bamboo ends and wood shavings—things not of much value but of some use: ～皆有用。Bamboo ends and wood shavings all have their uses.

竹席　zhúxí　bamboo mat

竹叶青[1]　zhúyèqīng　green bamboo snake

竹叶青[2]　zhúyèqīng　bamboo-leaf-green liqueur, a pale green *Fen* (汾) liquor or a light yellow *Shaoxing* (绍兴) wine

竹椅　zhúyǐ　bamboo chair

竹芋　zhúyù　*bot.* arrowroot

竹枝词　zhúzhīcí　① ancient folk songs with love as their main theme ② occasional poems in the classical style devoted to local topics

竹纸　zhúzhǐ　paper made from young bamboo

竹子　zhúzi　bamboo

竺

zhú　a surname

烛(燭)

zhú　① candle: 喜～ wedding candles

② *formal* illuminate; light up: 火光～天。Leaping flames lit up the sky. ③ (common name for 瓦特) watt: 二十五～灯泡 a 25-watt bulb

烛光　zhúguāng　*phys.* candlepower; candle

烛花　zhúhuā　snuff: 剪～ trim off the snuff (of a candle); snuff

烛泪　zhúlèi　gutterings of a candle

烛台　zhútái　candlestick

烛心　zhúxīn　(also 烛芯 zhúxīn) candlewick

烛照　zhúzhào　*formal* illuminate; light up: 阳光～万物。The sun illuminates all things on earth.

逐

zhú　① pursue; chase: 追逐 zhuīzhú ② drive out; expel: ～出门外 drive out of the door ③ *prep.* one by one: ～项 item by item／～月 month by month

逐北　zhúběi　*formal* pursue the defeated enemy

逐步　zhúbù　*adv.* step by step; progressively: ～加以解决 settle sth. step by step／～降低生产成本 progressively reduce the production cost／战争正在～升级。The war was escalating.

逐臭之夫　zhú chòu zhī fū　① an eccentric person; eccentric ② a person of depraved tastes—striving after fame and gain

逐处　zhúchù　everywhere; in all respects

逐个　zhúgè　one by one: 我们得～研究这些问题。We must look into these matters one by one.

逐渐　zhújiàn　*adv.* gradually; by degrees: 他对情况～熟悉起来了。He's gradually getting better acquainted with the situation.／天～暗下来了。It's getting darker and darker.

逐客令　zhúkèlìng　order for guests to leave: 下～ show sb. the door

逐鹿　zhúlù　*formal* chase the deer—fight for the throne; bid for state power (from: 秦失其鹿，天下共逐之。《史记》Qin had lost the stag—the imperial power—and all the world was chasing after it.): 群雄～ feudal lords vying for the throne; powerful politicians fighting for supremacy

逐鹿中原　zhúlù Zhōngyuán　chase the deer on the Central Plains—try to seize control of the empire

逐年　zhúnián　year by year; year after year: 产量～增加。Production has been increasing year after year.

逐日　zhúrì　day by day; every day: 病情～好转。The patient's condition is improving day by day.

逐水　zhúshuǐ　*Chin. med.* relieve oedema or abdominal distension through diuresis or purgation

逐条　zhútiáo　item by item; point by point: ～加以说明 explain point by point

逐一　zhúyī　one by one: 对这些规定～加以说明 explain all these provisions one by one

逐字　zhúzì　word for word; verbatim: ～记录 verbatim record

逐字逐句　zhúzì-zhújù　word by word and sentence by sentence; word for word: ～地宣读文件 read the document word by word and sentence by sentence／～的翻译 a word-for-word (or literal) translation

舳

zhú　stern (of a ship)

舳舻　zhúlú　*formal* a convoy of ships, stem touching stern: ～千里，旌旗蔽空。(苏轼) His fleet from stem to stern covered a thousand *li*, His pennons and banners filled the sky.

筑

Zhú　another name for 贵阳 Guìyáng ——see also zhù

瘃

zhú　*formal* chilblain

蠋

zhú　larva of a butterfly or moth

躅（躅） zhú *formal* footprint; footmark

zhǔ

主 zhǔ ① host: 宾主 bīnzhǔ ② owner; master: ～仆 master and servant / 企业～ proprietor of an enterprise ③ person or party concerned: 买主 mǎizhǔ / 事主 shìzhǔ ④ God; Lord ⑤ Allah ⑥ main; primary: ～航道 main (*or* principal) channel ⑦ manage; direct; be in charge of: 主管 zhǔguǎn ⑧ indicate; signify: 早霞～雨，晚霞～晴。Rosy morning clouds indicate rain, and a rosy sunset means fine weather. ⑨ hold a definite view about sth.; advocate: 我一时心里没～。For a moment I just didn't know what to do.

主儿 zhǔr *dial.* ① master; employer ② person of a specified type: 他是个爱管闲事的～。He is the busybody type. / 碰上你这么个～，简直没法儿。Just my luck to come across a person like you. ③ a husband or fiancé: 她快三十了，也该找～了。She is about thirty and it's time she looked for a husband.

主办 zhǔbàn direct; sponsor: 展览会将由农业部～。The exhibition will be sponsored by (*or* held under the auspices of) the Ministry of Agriculture.

主笔 zhǔbǐ *old* ① editor in chief ② chief commentator

主编 zhǔbiān ① chief editor (*or* compiler); editor in chief ② supervise the publication of (a newspaper, magazine, etc.); edit

主宾 zhǔbīn guest of honour: ～在女主人右上方。The guest of honour is seated on the right side of the hostess. / ～席 head table (for guests of honour); seat for the guest of honour

主持 zhǔchí ① take charge (*or* care) of; manage; direct: ～日常事务 take care of routine matters / ～俱乐部的工作 be in charge of the club ② preside over; chair: ～讨论 chair a discussion / ～今晚的宴会 host this evening's banquet / 会议由校长～。The chancellor presided over the meeting. ③ uphold; stand for: ～正义 uphold justice

主厨 zhǔchú ① be the *chef* ② *chef*

主词 zhǔcí *log.* subject term; subject

主次 zhǔcì primary and secondary: 我们干工作要分清～。In our work we must differentiate what is primary from what is secondary.

主从 zhǔcóng principal and subordinate: ～关系 the relationship between the principal and the subordinate

主单位 zhǔdānwèi basic unit (as a standard of measurement)

主刀 zhǔdāo *med.* operator

主导 zhǔdǎo leading; dominant; guiding: 工业是国民经济的～。Industry is the leading factor in the national economy. / 起～作用 play a leading role / 占～地位 occupy the leading position; hold sway / ～思想 dominant ideas; guiding ideology / ～力量 the leading force; the main force

主导风 zhǔdǎofēng *archit.* prevailing wind

主导主题 zhǔdǎo zhǔtí *mus.* *leitmotiv*

主调 zhǔdiào ① *mus.* top melody of a homophonic piece ② keynote (of a speech, etc.)

主调音乐 zhǔdiào yīnyuè homophony

主动 zhǔdòng ① take the initiative; do sth. of one's own accord: 争取～ try to gain the initiative; contend for the initiative / ～帮助人 help others of one's own accord / 我们应～派人去支援。We ought to send people to help on our own initiative. ② *mech.* driving: ～齿轮 driving gear / ～轴 driving shaft; driving spindle

主动脉 zhǔdòngmài aorta

主动脉弓 zhǔdòngmàigōng arch of aorta

主动脉炎 zhǔdòngmàiyán aortitis

主动语态 zhǔdòng yǔtài *gram.* active voice

主队 zhǔduì *sports* home team; host team

主发动机 zhǔfādòngjī *space* sustainer

主伐 zhǔfá *forestry* final felling (*or* cutting)

主犯 zhǔfàn *leg.* prime culprit; principal criminal (*or* offender); principal: ～和从犯 principal and accessories in a crime

主峰 zhǔfēng the highest peak in a mountain range

主妇 zhǔfù housewife; hostess

主干 zhǔgàn ① *bot.* trunk ② main force; mainstay

主稿 zhǔgǎo be responsible for the first draft; be the chief writer (of a joint work)

主格 zhǔgé *gram.* the nominative case

主根 zhǔgēn *bot.* main root; taproot

主公 zhǔgōng same as 主上 zhǔshàng

主攻 zhǔgōng *mil.* main attack: ～部队 main attack force / ～方面 main phase of attack / ～方向 main direction of attack

主攻手 zhǔgōngshǒu *sports* ace spiker

主顾 zhǔgù customer; client

主观 zhǔguān subjective: ～努力 subjective efforts / ～愿望 subjective desire; wishful thinking / ～臆断 subjective and groundless conclusion / ～地对待问题 a subjective approach to problems / 在改造客观世界的同时改造～世界 transform one's subjective world while transforming the objective world

主观能动性 zhǔguān néngdòngxìng *philos.* subjective initiative; conscious activity

主观唯心主义 zhǔguānwéixīnzhǔyì subjective idealism

主观主义 zhǔguānzhǔyì subjectivism

主管 zhǔguǎn ① be responsible for; be in charge of: 谁～这项工作？Who is in charge of this job? / ～外事的副市长 vice-mayor in charge of external relations / ～部门 department responsible for the work / ～机关 competent authorities; responsible institution ② person in charge: 他是这项工程的～。He is the person in charge of the project.

主和 zhǔhé advocate peace; be for a peaceful settlement: ～派 peace party

主婚 zhǔhūn (usu. of the parents of the bride and the bridegroom) preside over a wedding ceremony

主机 zhǔjī ① *mech.* main engine; main processor ② *mil.* lead plane; leader

主祭 zhǔjì officiate at funeral or sacrificial rites

主家 zhǔjiā ① master's house ② manage household affairs

主见 zhǔjiàn ideas or thoughts of one's own; one's own judgment; definite view: 没有～ have no definite views of one's own / 她这人很有～。She knows her own mind.

主讲 zhǔjiǎng be the speaker; give a lecture

主将 zhǔjiàng chief commander; commanding general

主焦点 zhǔjiāodiǎn *phys.* prime (*or* principal) focus

主焦煤 zhǔjiāoméi same as 焦煤 jiāoméi

主教 zhǔjiào bishop

主井 zhǔjǐng *min.* main shaft

主句 zhǔjù *gram.* main (*or* principal) clause

主角 zhǔjué leading role; lead; protagonist: 在该片中演～ play the lead in the film

主考 zhǔkǎo ① be in charge of an examination ② chief examiner (in a school, etc.)

主考官 zhǔkǎoguān official in charge of an imperial examination; chief examiner

主客 zhǔkè ① host and guest ② guest of honour

主课 zhǔkè main subject; major course

主力 zhǔlì main force; main strength of an army: ～兵

团 main formations / ～队员 top players of a team

主力舰 zhǔlìjiàn capital ship

主力军 zhǔlìjūn main (or principal) force

主梁 zhǔliáng *archit.* girder

主粮 zhǔliáng staple food grain

主流 zhǔliú ① trunk stream; mainstream: 河的～ the mainstream of a river / 历史的～ the mainstream of history ② essential or main aspect; main trend: ～和支流 principal and secondary aspects / 该地区的改革～是好的。The general direction of reform in that area is correct.

主麻 zhǔmǎ *Islam* Djumah (Friday)

主谋 zhǔmóu ① head a conspiracy; be the chief plotter ② *leg.* chief instigator

主脑 zhǔnǎo ① control centre; centre of operation ② leader; chief

主权 zhǔquán sovereign rights; sovereignty: 领土～ territorial sovereignty / ～国家 a sovereign state / ～平等 sovereign equality / ～完整 full sovereignty

主人 zhǔrén ① master: 在我国社会主义制度下,人民是国家的～。Under our socialist system, the people are the masters of the country. ② host: 女～ hostess ③ owner: 房子的～ owner of the house

主人公 zhǔréngōng leading character in a novel, etc.; hero or heroine; protagonist

主人翁 zhǔrénwēng ① master: 新社会的～ masters of the new society / 有一种～感 have a sense of being the master of one's own affairs ② same as 主人公 zhǔréngōng

主任 zhǔrèn director; head; chairman: 总政治部～ Director of the General Political Department / 居民委员会～ head of the neighbourhood committee / 国家计划委员会～ Minister in charge of the State Planning Commission / 人大外事委员会～ Chairman of the Foreign Affairs Committee of the NPC / 教研室～ chief of teaching and research section / 内(外)科～ head of the medical (surgical) department

主日 zhǔrì Lord's Day; Sunday: ～学 Sunday school

主上 zhǔshàng (used in addressing a ruler) Your Majesty; my lord

主食 zhǔshí staple food; principal food

主使 zhǔshǐ instigate; incite; abet

主事 zhǔshì be in charge; take charge: 主其事 be in charge of the business; manage the affairs / 主不了事 have no say; have no power of decision

主视图 zhǔshìtú front view; elevation

主帅 zhǔshuài same as 主将 zhǔjiàng

主题 zhǔtí theme; subject; motif; *leitmotiv*: 诗的～ the subject of a poem / 作品的～思想 the theme of a literary work / 第一乐章第一～ the first subject (or theme) of the first movement

主题歌 zhǔtígē theme song

主体 zhǔtǐ ① main body; main part; principal part: 以贫农为～的农会 peasant associations with the poor peasants as their main body / 建筑群的～ the main part of a building complex / 一支以青年为～的突击队 a shock force composed mainly of young people / ～工程 principal part of a project ② *philos.* subject: ～和客体 subject and object; the perceiver and the world

主位 zhǔwèi ① status of a sovereign ② seat of the host (at table)

主谓词组 zhǔwèicízǔ *gram.* subject-predicate word group

主谓句 zhǔwèijù *gram.* subject-predicate sentence

主文 zhǔwén *leg.* main body of a court verdict

主席 zhǔxí ① chairman (of a meeting): 当～ be in the chair; preside over a meeting ② chairman or president (of an organization or a state)

主席台 zhǔxítái rostrum; platform: 登上～ go up to the rostrum / 在～上发表讲话 speak from the rostrum

主席团 zhǔxítuán presidium; bureau: ～成员 bureau members; members of a presidium

主线 zhǔxiàn thread (of a novel, etc.)

主心骨 zhǔxīngǔ ① backbone; mainstay; pillar: 他是我们队里的～。He is the mainstay of our team. ② a definite view; one's own judgment: 他这个人没有～。He has no judgment of his own.

主星 zhǔxīng *astron.* primary (component)

主星序 zhǔxīngxù *astron.* main sequence

主刑 zhǔxíng *leg.* principal penalty

主凶 zhǔxiōng prime (or chief) culprit (in a murder case); principal

主修 zhǔxiū ① specialize (in a subject); major: 她～原子物理。She majors in atomic physics. / ～科目 major subjects ② be responsible for the repair or overhaul (of a machine): 王师傅～这台磨床。Master Worker Wang is responsible for the overhaul of this grinder.

主旋律 zhǔxuánlǜ main melody; top melody; theme

主演 zhǔyǎn act the leading role (in a play or film); star: 她～过许多影片。She has starred in many films.

主要 zhǔyào main; chief; principal; major: ～理由 main reasons / ～对手 chief opponent / ～矛盾 principal contradiction / ～目的 major objective / ～因素 primary factor / ～农作物 staple crops / 会议～讨论了两个问题。The conference dealt mainly with two questions.

主义 zhǔyì doctrine; -ism: 唯物主义 wéiwùzhǔyì / 资本主义 zīběnzhǔyì

主意 zhǔyi ① idea; plan: 好～! That's a good idea. / 人多～多。More people mean a greater ferment of ideas. / 领导者的责任主要是出～、用干部两件事。Leadership involves two main responsibilities: to work out ideas and to make good use of cadres. ② decision; definite view: 打定～ make a decision; make up one's mind / 改变～ change one's view (or mind) / 拿不定～ be in two minds (about sth.) / 我一时没了～。I was quite at a loss, then. or For a moment I just didn't know what to do.

主因 zhǔyīn main reason; major cause

主音 zhǔyīn *mus.* keynote; tonic

主语 zhǔyǔ *gram.* subject

主宰 zhǔzǎi dominate; dictate; decide: ～自己的命运 decide one's own destiny; be master of one's own fate / 大国～世界的时代已经一去不复返了。Gone forever are the days when big powers could dominate the world. / 思想是人们行动的～。A man's action is determined by his thought.

主战 zhǔzhàn advocate war: ～派 war party

主张 zhǔzhāng ① advocate; stand for; maintain; hold: ～自力更生 advocate self-reliance / ～改革 favour reforms / 我们～文艺为工农兵服务。We maintain that literature and art should serve the workers, peasants and soldiers. / 我们～用和平的方式解决国际争端。We advocate a peaceful settlement of international disputes. ② view; position; stand; proposition: 这是我们一贯的～。That has been our consistent stand. / 听起来两种～都有理由。Both propositions sound reasonable.

主旨 zhǔzhǐ purport; substance; gist: 文章的～ the gist of the article

主治 zhǔzhì *med.* indications: ～食欲不振、失眠、神经衰弱、贫血等症 Indications: anorexia, insomnia, neurasthenia, anaemia, etc.

主治医生 zhǔzhì yīshēng physician-in-charge; doctor in charge of a case

主轴 zhǔzhóu *mech.* main shaft; spindle: ～箱 spindle box

主子 zhǔzi master; boss: ～和奴才 the boss and his flunkey; master and servant

拄 zhǔ lean on (a stick, etc.): ～着拐棍走 walk with a stick

渚 zhǔ *formal* small piece of land surrounded by water; islet: 江～ islet in a river

属(屬) zhǔ *formal* ① join; combine: ～文 compose a piece of prose writing / 前后相～ (of two parts) join together ② fix (one's mind) on; centre (one's attention, etc.) upon: 属望 zhǔwàng ——see also shǔ

属草 zhǔcǎo *formal* draft (or draw up) a document

属望 zhǔwàng *formal* centre one's hope on; look forward to; expect

属意 zhǔyì fix one's mind on sb. (as one's choice, favourite, etc.)

属垣有耳 zhǔ yuán yǒu ěr walls have ears; beware of eavesdroppers

煮 zhǔ boil; cook: ～鸡蛋 boil eggs or boiled eggs / ～饭 cook rice

煮豆燃萁 zhǔdòu ránqí burn beanstalks to cook beans—fratricidal strife (from Cao Zhi's 曹植 "Seven-pace Song"《七步诗》): 煮豆燃豆萁, 豆在釜中泣。本是同根生, 相煎何太急! Beans in flame that beanstalks feed Out from the pan cry, "Sprung from the same stalk, what need Each the other fry?")

煮鹤焚琴 zhǔhè-fénqín same as 焚琴煮鹤 fénqín-zhǔhè

煮呢 zhǔní *text.* potting

嘱(囑) zhǔ enjoin; advise; urge: 叮嘱 dīngzhǔ

嘱咐 zhǔfu (also 嘱告 zhǔgào) enjoin; tell; exhort: 再三～ exhort again and again; din sth. into sb. / ～他保守秘密 enjoin him to secrecy / 临终～ deathbed injunction / 大夫～他好好休息。The doctor told him to take a good rest.

嘱托 zhǔtuō entrust: 她～我办这件事。She entrusted me with the task.

瞩(矚) zhǔ gaze; look steadily: 瞩目 zhǔmù

瞩目 zhǔmù *formal* fix one's eyes upon; focus one's attention upon: 为世界所～ attract worldwide attention

瞩望 zhǔwàng *formal* ① look forward to: ～已久 have been eagerly looking forward to it for a long time ② gaze at; look long and steadily upon

zhù

伫(佇、竚) zhù *formal* stand for a long while

伫候 zhùhòu *formal* stand waiting: ～佳音 look forward to hearing good news from you

伫立 zhùlì *formal* stand still for a long while

苎(苧) zhù see below

苎麻 zhùmá ramie

助 zhù help; assist; aid: ～消化 aid digestion / ～一臂之力 lend sb. a helping hand

助爆药 zhùbàoyào *mil.* booster charge; booster

助产 zhùchǎn practise midwifery

助产士 zhùchǎnshì midwife

助词 zhùcí *gram.* auxiliary word, an unstressed form word which performs the grammatical functions of structure (as 的, 地, 得, 所), of tense (as 了, 着, 过) or of mood (as 呢, 吗, 吧, 啊); particle

助动词 zhùdòngcí *gram.* auxiliary verb

助攻 zhùgōng *mil.* holding (or secondary) attack: ～部队 holding element

助剂 zhùjì *text.* auxiliary

助教 zhùjiào assistant (of a college faculty)

助桀为虐 zhù Jié wéi nüè aid King Jie in his tyrannical rule—aid and abet the evil-doer

助理 zhùlǐ assistant: ～秘书长 assistant secretary-general

助力 zhùlì a helping hand; help; assistance: 在困难中, 他曾给过我很大的～。He gave me a lot of help when I was in difficulty.

助跑 zhùpǎo *sports* run-up; approach

助燃 zhùrán *chem.* combustion-supporting: ～气体 combustion-supporting gas

助人为乐 zhù rén wéi lè find it a pleasure to help others; take pleasure in helping people

助熔剂 zhùróngjì flux

助色团 zhùsètuán *chem.* auxochrome

助手 zhùshǒu assistant; helper; aide

助听器 zhùtīngqì audiophone; hearing aid; deaf-aid

助推级 zhùtuījí *space* booster

助威 zhùwēi (also 助阵 zhùzhèn) boost the morale of; cheer (for): 给我们的篮球队～ cheer for our basketball team

助兴 zhùxìng liven things up; add to the fun: 给大伙儿唱支歌助助兴。Sing us a song to liven things up.

助学 zhùxué give financial aid to students

助学金 zhùxuéjīn stipend; grant-in-aid: 领～的学生 a grant-aided student

助益 zhùyì benefit; help: 毫无～ be of no help at all

助战 zhùzhàn ① assist in fighting ② bolster sb.'s morale

助长 zhùzhǎng *derog.* encourage; abet; foster; foment: ～侵略者的野心 whet the ambitions of the aggressors / ～歪风邪气 encourage the evil trends / 恭维他只会～他的骄气。Flattery will make him more arrogant.

助纣为虐 zhù Zhòu wéi nüè aid King Zhou in his tyrannical rule—aid and abet the evil-doer

住 zhù ① live; reside; stay: 我～这间屋。I live in this room. / 他～在北京。He lives in Beijing. / 对面没人～。Nobody lives in the room opposite mine. / 我们～上了新房。We've moved into a new house. / ～城外 live in the suburbs / ～旅馆 stay at a hotel ② stop; cease: 雨～了。The rain has stopped. / 等风～了再走。Don't go until the wind drops. ③ (used after a verb) firmly; to a stop: 拿～了, 别撒手。Hold tight. Don't let go. / 悠扬的小提琴声把我吸引～了。The beautiful notes of a violin held me spellbound. / 这一下你可把我问～了。You've got me there. / 她挡～了我的去路。She blocked my way. / 听到这个消息我一下子楞～了。I was struck dumb at the news. / 扣～一封信 stop (or withhold) a letter / 支持不～ cannot withstand; cannot hold out

住持 zhùchí (Buddhist or Taoist) abbot

住处 zhùchù residence; dwelling (place); lodging; quarters: 找到～没有? Have you found accommodation? / 我不知道他的～。I don't know where he lives.

住地 zhùdì dwelling (place); lodging

住读 zhùdú (of a student) board at school

住房 zhùfáng housing; lodgings: ～问题 the housing problem; accommodation

住户 zhùhù household; resident: 院内有三家～。There are three households in the compound. / 这儿有姓马的～吗? Is there anyone named Ma living here?

住家 zhùjiā ① (of one's family) live; reside in: 他在郊区～。He lives with his family in the suburbs. ② household; resident

住居 zhùjū live; reside; inhabit: 少数民族～的地区 a region inhabited by minority nationalities

住口 zhùkǒu shut up; stop talking: 你给我～! Hold your tongue!

住声 zhùshēng stop talking, laughing, or crying: 他们有说有笑, 老半天没有～。They talked and laughed for a long time without stop. / 这孩子就没住过声儿。The child never stopped talking.

住手 zhùshǒu stay one's hand; stop: 他不做完不肯～。He won't stop until he finishes the job. / 老师看见孩子们在打架, 大声叫道: "～!" "Break it up!" shouted the teacher when he saw the boys were fighting.

住宿 zhùsù stay; put up; get accommodation: 他今晚在旅店～。He will put up at an inn for the night. / 给客人安排～ find lodgings (or arrange accommodation) for the visitors / 大学生大部分在校～。Most college students are boarders.

住所 zhùsuǒ dwelling place; residence; domicile: 固定～ permanent dwelling place; domicile

住闲 zhùxián stay at home idle; be unemployed

住校 zhùxiào (of a student) board at school

住院 zhùyuàn be in hospital; be hospitalized: 他断了腿, 住了一个月的院。He broke a leg and was hospitalized for a month. / ～期间 during one's hospitalization; while in hospital / ～费 hospitalization expenses

住院病人 zhùyuàn bìngrén inpatient

住院部 zhùyuànbù inpatient department

住院处 zhùyuànchù admission office (in a hospital)

住院医生 zhùyuàn yīshēng resident (physician)

住宅 zhùzhái residence; dwelling: ～区 residential quarters (or district) / ～建设 housing construction

住址 zhùzhǐ address

住嘴 zhùzuǐ stop talking: 老太太扯起东邻西舍的闲事, 总是不～。The old woman would keep on and on gossiping about her neighbours. / ～, 不许你胡说! Stop talking nonsense!

注[1] zhù ① pour; fill: 大雨如注 dàyǔ rú zhù ② concentrate; fix: 注视 zhùshì ③ stakes (in gambling): 下注 xiàzhù ④ m. (for deals or sums of money): 一～交易 a deal / 一～钱 a sum of money

注[2] (註) zhù ① annotate; explain with notes: 批注 pīzhù ② notes: 正文用大字, ～用小字。The text is to be in big type, the notes in small type. ③ record; register

注册 zhùcè register: ～处 registration office; registrar's office / ～商标 registered trademark / ～资本 registered capital / ～证书 registration certificate

注带 zhùdài text. casting

注定 zhùdìng be doomed; be destined: ～要失败 be doomed to failure / 命中～ decreed by fate; predestined

注脚 zhùjiǎo footnote

注解 zhùjiě ① annotate; explain with notes ② (explanatory) note; annotation

注明 zhùmíng give clear indication of: ～出处 give sources (of quotations, etc.) / 该表未～日期。That form is undated. / 本词典词类用下列方式～。Parts of speech are labelled in the following way in this dictionary.

注目 zhùmù gaze at; fix one's eyes on: 这个小县城成了全国～的地方。The small town became the country's centre of attention.

注目礼 zhùmùlǐ salute with eyes

注入 zhùrù ① pour into; empty into: 长江～东海。The Changjiang River empties into the East China Sea. / ～式教学法 the spoon-feeding way of teaching; cramming ② petroleum injection: ～井 injection well

注射 zhùshè med. inject: 肌肉 (皮下, 静脉)～ intra-muscular (hypodermic, intravenous) injection / 往静脉里～葡萄糖 inject glucose into the veins / 给病人～青霉素 give the patient an injection of penicillin / ～器 injector; syringe / ～针头 syringe needle

注视 zhùshì look attentively at; gaze at: 久久～着陌生人的脸 look fixedly at the stranger's face for a long time / 他爱慕地～着这位女演员。He gazed admiringly at the actress. / 密切～会议的进展 closely follow the progress of the conference / 雷达兵目不转睛地～着荧光屏。The radarman's eyes were glued to the screen. / 千万只眼睛～着她跳入水中时的压水花动作。Thousands of people were watching when she plunged into the water with a rip.

注释 zhùshì explanatory note; annotation: ～读物 annotated readings

注疏 zhùshū commentary and subcommentary: 《十三经～》 Commentary and Subcommentary to the Thirteen Classics

注水 zhùshuǐ petroleum water flooding: 边缘～ edge-water flooding / ～动态 flood performance

注塑 zhùsù mould plastics

注文 zhùwén explanatory notes; notes

注销 zhùxiāo cancel; write off: 把借条～ cancel a written acknowledgment of a loan; cancel an I.O.U. / 账已～。The account has been written off. / ～登记 nullify the registration

注意 zhùyì pay attention to; take note (or notice) of: ～工作方法 pay attention to methods of work / 必须～团结一切可以团结的人。Care must be taken to unite with all those that can be united with. / 我没～他什么时候走的。I didn't notice when he left. / ～, 马上就要点炮啦! Look out! We're ready to blast. / ～别摔倒。Mind you don't fall. / ～事项 matters needing attention; points for attention

注意广度 zhùyì guǎngdù psychol. attention span; range of attention

注意力 zhùyìlì attention: 他～不容易集中。His attention wanders.

注音 zhùyīn phonetic notation: 课文有～吗?Is the text marked with phonetic symbols?

注音字母 zhùyīn zìmǔ (also 注音符号 zhùyīn fúhào) the national phonetic alphabet (in use before the publication of the Scheme for the Chinese Phonetic Alphabet)

注油 zhùyóu ① oiling; greasing ② fuel-injection

注油枪 zhùyóuqiāng grease gun; oil gun

注重 zhùzhòng lay stress on; pay attention to; attach importance to: ～基本功的训练 lay stress on basic training / ～经济效益 lay stress on economic results / ～穿着 pay attention to dress; be particular about dress / 这个学校～爱国主义教育。The school attaches importance to education in patriotism.

杼 zhù ① text. reed ② shuttle

贮 (貯) zhù store; save; lay aside: ～粮备荒 store grain against a lean year

贮备 zhùbèi store up; have in reserve; lay aside

贮藏 zhùcáng store up; lay in: ～苹果 store apples / ～过冬的大白菜 lay in cabbages for the winter / 这一带地下～着丰富的矿产。This place is rich in mineral deposits.

贮存 zhùcún store; keep in storage: ～期 storage time

贮点红 zhùdiǎnhóng same as 朱顶雀 zhūdǐngquè

贮积 zhùjī store up; lay in; stockpile

贮木场 zhùmùchǎng timber depot; timber yard; lumber yard

贮蓄 zhùxù ① store up; lay in; conserve: ～土壤养分 conservation of soil nutrient ② storage or saving

贮运 zhùyùn storage and transportation

驻 zhù ① halt; stay: 敌～我扰。When the enemy halts, we harass him. ② be stationed: 一连～在黄村。The First Company is stationed at Huangcun Village. / 我国～英大使 our ambassador to Britain / 中国～埃及大使馆 Chinese Embassy in Egypt / ～京记者 resident correspondent in Beijing / ～外机构 institutions stationed abroad

驻跸 zhùbì formal (of a monarch on a tour) stay temporarily; stop over; put up

驻波 zhùbō phys. standing wave

驻地 zhùdì ① place where troops, etc. are stationed: 边防军～ frontier guard station / 地质勘探队的～ encampment of a geological prospecting team ② seat (of a local administrative organ)

驻防 zhùfáng be on garrison duty; garrison: ～福州 garrison Fuzhou / ～部队 garrison (troops)

驻节公使 zhùjié gōngshǐ minister resident

驻军 zhùjūn ① station troops ② garrison troops; garrison

驻守 zhùshǒu garrison; defend: ～山海关 garrison the Shanhaiguan Pass

驻屯 zhùtún (of troops) be stationed; be quartered

驻颜 zhùyán formal preserve youthful looks: ～有术 possess the secret of preserving youthful looks

驻在国 zhùzàiguó state to which a diplomatic envoy is accredited

驻扎 zhùzhá (of troops) be stationed; be quartered: ～重兵 station a huge force

驻足 zhùzú halt; stop; go no further: ～而观 stop to watch

炷 zhù formal ① wick (of an oil lamp) ② burn: ～香 burn a joss stick ③ m.: 一～香 a burning joss stick

祝 zhù ① express good wishes; wish: ～你健康。I wish you the best of health. / ～你旅途愉快。Have a pleasant journey. or Bon voyage! / ～我们两国人民的友谊万古长青! May the friendship between our two peoples be everlasting! ② (Zhù) a surname

祝词 zhùcí ① congratulatory speech (at a ceremony, etc.); congratulations ② prayers at sacrificial rites in ancient times

祝祷 zhùdǎo (also 祝告 zhùgào) pray; say one's prayers

祝福 zhùfú ① blessing; benediction: 为你～。Blessings on you. ② new year's sacrifice (an old custom in certain parts of Zhejiang Province)

祝贺 zhùhè congratulate: ～演出成功 congratulate the artists on their successful performance / 向你～! Congratulations! / ～你生了一个女儿。Congratulations! You have a daughter. / ～两国建交 acclaim the establishment of diplomatic relations between the two countries / 致以兄弟般的～ extend fraternal greetings

祝捷 zhùjié celebrate a victory: ～大会 victory celebration (meeting)

祝酒 zhùjiǔ drink a toast; toast: 向来宾们～ toast the guests / 致～辞 propose a toast / 答谢～ respond (or reply) to a toast

祝融 Zhùróng God of fire

祝寿 zhùshòu congratulate (an elderly person) on his or her birthday

祝颂 zhùsòng express good wishes

祝愿 zhùyuàn wish: 致以良好的～ with best wishes / ～贵国日益繁荣昌盛。We wish your country ever growing prosperity.

柱 zhù ① post; upright; pillar; column: 立一根～

儿 erect a post ② sth. shaped like a column: 水柱 shuǐzhù ③ math. cylinder

柱础 zhùchǔ stone base of a column; plinth

柱顶 zhùdǐng archit. capital

柱廊 zhùláng archit. colonnade

柱面 zhùmiàn math. cylinder: 椭圆～ elliptic cylinder

柱身 zhùshēn archit. shaft

柱石 zhùshí (fig.) pillar; mainstay: 中国人民解放军是无产阶级专政的～。The Chinese People's Liberation Army is the pillar of the dictatorship of the proletariat.

柱头 zhùtóu ① bot. stigma ② archit. column cap; column head ③ dial. post; pillar

柱状剖面 zhùzhuàng pōumiàn geol. columnar section; geologic column

柱子 zhùzi post; pillar

柱座 zhùzuò column base; plinth

疰 zhù see below

疰夏 zhùxià ① Chin. med. a summer disease, usu. contracted by children with symptoms of fever, loss of appetite, lassitude, etc. ② dial. loss of appetite and weight in summer

著 zhù ① marked; outstanding: 卓著 zhuózhù ② show; prove: 颇～成效 prove rather effective ③ write: ～书 write books ④ book; work: 新～ sb.'s latest work

著称 zhùchēng celebrated; famous: 以风景优美～ be celebrated for its scenic beauty / 杭州以西湖～于世。Hangzhou is world-famous for its West Lake.

著录 zhùlù put down in writing; record

著名 zhùmíng famous; celebrated; well-known: ～论断 a celebrated (or well-known) thesis / 李时珍是明代～的药物学家。Li Shizhen was a famous pharmacologist of the Ming Dynasty.

著书立说 zhùshū-lìshuō write books to expound a theory; write scholarly works

著述 zhùshù ① write; compile: 从事～ be engaged in writing or compiling scholarly works ② book; work: 主要～ major works

著述等身 zhùshù děng shēn one's writings piled up to one's own height—be a prolific writer

著者 zhùzhě author; writer

著作 zhùzuò ① work; book; writings: 古代医学～ ancient books on medicine; ancient medical literature ② write: 他一生～甚多。He wrote many books during his lifetime. or He was a prolific author.

著作权 zhùzuòquán copyright (of the author)

蛀 zhù ① moth or any other insect that eats books, clothes, wood, etc.: 蛀虫 zhùchóng ② (of moths, etc.) eat; bore through: 这件呢大衣给虫子～了。This woollen coat is moth-eaten.

蛀齿 zhùchǐ decayed tooth; dental caries

蛀虫 zhùchóng insect that eats books, clothes or wood; moth; borer

蛀心虫 zhùxīnchóng same as 钻心虫 zuānxīnchóng

筑(築) zhù build; construct: ～路 construct a road / ～堤 build a dyke ——see also Zhú

筑埂机 zhùgěngjī agric. ridger

筑室道谋 zhù shì dào móu ask every passerby how to build one's house—have no idea or plan of one's own (and accomplish nothing)

铸(鑄) zhù casting; founding: ～钟 cast a bell / ～钱 coin (or mint) money / 这口钟是铜～的。This bell is cast with bronze.

铸币 zhùbì coin; specie

铸币权 zhùbìquán mintage

铸成大错 zhùchéng dàcuò make a gross error (or stupendous mistake)

铸错 zhùcuò commit blunders; make grave mistakes

铸锭 zhùdìng ingot casting

铸钢 zhùgāng cast steel

铸工 zhùgōng ① foundry work: ～车间 foundry (shop) / ～鼓风机 foundry fan ② foundry worker; founder

铸件 zhùjiàn cast; casting: 干砂～ dry sand casting / 压～ die casting / 冷硬～ chill (or chilled) casting

铸模 zhùmú mould for casting; matrix

铸石 zhùshí cast stone; molten-rock casting; stone casting

铸铁 zhùtiě ① iron casting ② cast iron

铸型 zhùxíng casting mould

铸造 zhùzào casting; founding: 无砂～ sandless casting / 蜡模～ investment casting; lost wax casting / ～车间 foundry; casting shop

铸字 zhùzì typefounding; typecasting: ～工场 typefoundry / ～工人 typefounder / ～机 typecasting machine

翥 zhù formal (of birds) fly; soar

箸(筯) zhù dial. chopsticks

zhuā

抓 zhuā ① grab; seize; clutch: ～一把糖 take a handful of sweets / ～机会 seize an opportunity / 他～起帽子就往外走。 He grabbed (or snatched up) his cap and made for the door. ② scratch: ～痒痒 scratch an itch / 猫把孩子的手～了。 The cat scratched the child's hand. ③ arrest; catch: ～小偷 catch a thief ④ stress; pay special attention to: ～重点 stress the essentials / ～思想问题 pay special attention to ideological problems / ～苗头 watch out for the first signs ⑤ take charge of; be responsible for: 他是～工会工作的。 He is in charge of trade union work.

抓辫子 zhuā biànzi same as 揪辫子 jiū biànzi

抓膘 zhuābiāo fatten (pigs, cattle, etc.)

抓捕 zhuābǔ arrest; catch: ～逃犯 arrest an escaped prisoner

抓不起来 zhuābuqǐlái ① cannot get hold of or lift sth. ② cannot manage sth. (because of inability, etc.)

抓茬儿 zhuāchár dial. find fault; pick holes; pick a quarrel

抓差 zhuāchāi draft sb. for a particular task; press sb. into service

抓大头 zhuā dàtóu draw lots to decide who is to play the host

抓点 zhuādiǎn concentrate on work at selected units: ～带面 draw experience from selected units to promote overall work

抓丁 zhuādīng pressgang able-bodied men

抓斗 zhuādǒu grab bucket; grab: 双瓣式～ two-jaw grab

抓赌 zhuādǔ (of police) break up a gambling party and arrest the participants

抓耳挠腮 zhuā'ěr-náosāi tweak one's ears and scratch one's cheeks (as a sign of anxiety or delight)

抓夫 zhuāfū same as 拉夫 lāfū

抓哏 zhuāgén (of a comedian, etc.) throw in impromptu lines

抓工夫 zhuā gōngfu make good use of one's time; find time (to do sth.)

抓好 zhuāhǎo do a good job of; make great efforts to: 你得把工作～。 You must do a good job of it.

抓获 zhuāhuò catch (a criminal, etc.); capture; seize

抓髻 zhuāji same as 髻髻 zhuāji

抓尖儿卖快 zhuājiānr-màikuài go out of one's way to curry favour

抓紧 zhuājǐn firmly grasp; pay close attention to: ～学习 attend to one's studies in earnest; study hard / ～时机 seize or grasp the opportunity / ～时间 make the best use of one's time / 抓而不紧,等于不抓。 Not to grasp firmly is not to grasp at all. / 必须把农业～。 We must pay close attention to agriculture. / 要按时完成,我们得～一些。 We must work harder if we want to meet the deadline. / 经理对公司的财务抓得很紧。 The manager kept a firm hand on the finances of the company.

抓阄儿 zhuājiūr draw lots

抓举 zhuājǔ sports snatch

抓空子 zhuā kòngzi find time (to do sth.)

抓两头,带中间 zhuā liǎngtóu, dài zhōngjiān grasp the two ends to bring along the middle—sustain the advanced and help the backward so as to encourage the vast majority to move along

抓挠 zhuānao dial. ① scratch: ～几下就不痒了。 Scratch and it won't itch any more. ② mess about: 好孩子,别～东西! Don't mess things about, my child. ③ come to blows; fight: 他们俩又～起来了。 The two of them have got into a fight again. ④ prepare sth. hastily: 一下子来了这么多人吃饭,炊事员怕～不过来吧! With so many people here all of a sudden for a meal, I wonder how the cook can hustle them up something to eat. ⑤ sb. or sth. that one can rely on: 最好派个负责人来,咱好有个～。 We should have someone sent here to take responsibility, so that we can turn to him with our problems. ⑥ solution to a difficulty: 事前要慎重考虑,免得发生问题时没～。 Think it over well beforehand so as to be prepared for all eventualities.

抓拍 zhuāpāi ④ take a candid photograph (or picture) ② a candid photograph (or picture); candid

抓破 zhuāpò injure or damage by scratching or clawing

抓破脸 zhuāpòliǎn inf. scratch each other's face—quarrel openly

抓权 zhuāquán grab power

抓人 zhuārén arrest sb.; take sb. into custody: 抓了好些人。 A number of arrests were made.

抓瞎 zhuāxiā inf. find oneself at a loss; be in a rush and muddle; be thrown off balance: 早点儿做好准备,免得临时～。 Arrange everything in advance so that you won't be in a rush at the last moment.

抓岩机 zhuāyánjī grab loader; grab

抓药 zhuāyào ① make up (or fill) a prescription of Chinese herbal medicine ② have a prescription of Chinese herbal medicine made up (or filled)

抓早儿 zhuāzǎor as early as possible; before it is too late: 你～上街买东西去呀! You'd better hurry up and go shopping.

抓周 zhuāzhōu the grabbing test on the occasion of a baby's first birthday (in which various articles—e.g. a book, a writing brush, an inkstone, workman's tools, playthings and eatables, cosmetics and many an unexpected gadget—are assembled and spread out before the baby and the one particular article he picks up is supposed to give a general idea of his future character and pattern of life, his career and behaviour, his habits and hobbies)

抓住 zhuāzhù ① catch (or seize) hold of; grip: ～她的胳膊 catch hold of her arm / ～一点小事做文章 seize on a trifle and make an issue of it; make a fuss about something trivial / ～机遇 grasp the opportunity / ～要害 scratch where it itches ② catch; capture: ～个小偷

catch a thief ③ grip sb.'s attention: 这出戏一开场就～了观众。The play gripped the attention of the audience from the moment the curtain rose.

抓壮丁 zhuā zhuàngdīng　pressgang able-bodied men

抓总儿 zhuāzǒngr　*inf.* assume overall responsibility (in carrying out a project, etc.)

挝（撾）
zhuā　① knock at; beat: ～鼓 beat a drum ② same as 抓 zhuā ——see also wō

髽
zhuā　see below

髽髻 zhuāji　(also 髽鬏 zhuājiu) hair worn in two buns

zhuǎ

爪
zhuǎ　claw; talon ——see also zhǎo

爪儿 zhuǎr　*inf.* ① paw of a small animal ② foot of a utensil: 三～锅 a pan standing on three feet

爪尖儿 zhuǎjiānr　pig's trotters; pettitoes

爪子 zhuǎzi　*inf.* claw; paw; talon: 猫～ a cat's paws / 鹰～ an eagle's talons

zhuāi

拽
zhuāi　*dial.* fling; throw; hurl: 把皮球～出去 fling the ball out ——see also zhuài

zhuǎi

跩
zhuǎi　*dial.* waddle: 鸭子走起路来一～一～的。Ducks waddle.

zhuài

拽（撷）
zhuài　pull; drag; haul: 一把～住不放 catch hold of sb. or sth. and not let go ——see also zhuāi

zhuān

专（專、耑）
zhuān　① for a particular person, occasion, purpose, etc.; focussed on one thing; special: 心不～ not concentrate (on any one thing) / ～项贷款 special-purpose loans / 奎宁～治疟疾。Quinine is a specific for malaria. / 他～找重活干。He made a point of picking the heaviest jobs for himself. ② monopolize: 专制 zhuānzhì

专案 zhuān'àn　special case for investigation; case: 这件事应成立～。This should be made a special case for investigation. / ～材料 material connected with a case; dossier / ～人员 those engaged in the examination of a case / ～组 special group for the examination of a case

专差 zhuānchāi　① special mission (*or* errand): 他～去北京。He went to Beijing on a special mission. ② person sent on a special mission

专长 zhuāncháng　speciality; special skill or knowledge: 学有～ have specialized knowledge of a subject; be expert in a special field of study / 制图是她的～。Cartography is her speciality.

专场 zhuānchǎng　special performance; show intended for a limited audience: 相声～ a performance of comic dialogues / 学生～ a special show for students

专车 zhuānchē　a special train or car

专诚 zhuānchéng　for a particular purpose; specially: ～拜访 pay a special visit to sb.

专程 zhuānchéng　special trip: ～赴广州迎接贵宾 make a special trip to Guangzhou to welcome the honoured guests

专宠 zhuānchǒng　monopolize the favour (of a ruler)

专电 zhuāndiàn　special dispatch (sent by a reporter to a newspaper)

专断 zhuānduàn　make an arbitrary decision; act arbitrarily

专攻 zhuāngōng　specialize in; do special research on: 他～空间技术。He specializes in space technology.

专号 zhuānhào　special issue (of a periodical): 小说～ a fiction issue

专横 zhuānhèng　imperious; peremptory; domineering: ～跋扈 imperious and despotic; arrogant and domineering

专机 zhuānjī　① special plane ② private plane

专家 zhuānjiā　expert; specialist: 水稻～ expert in rice-growing / 眼科～ ophthalmologist; eye specialist

专刊 zhuānkān　① special issue or column ② monograph

专科 zhuānkē　① special field of study; specialized subject; specialty ② same as 专科学校 zhuānkē xuéxiào

专科学校 zhuānkē xuéxiào　college for professional training; training school

专科医生 zhuānkē yīshēng　(medical) specialist

专款 zhuānkuǎn　special fund: ～专用 earmark a fund for its specified purpose only

专栏 zhuānlán　special column: 书评～ book review column; book reviews / 评论～ opinion column; opion

专栏作家 zhuānlán zuòjiā　columnist

专力 zhuānlì　concentrate one's efforts or energy (to do sth.)

专利 zhuānlì　patent: ～品 patent; patented article

专利法 zhuānlìfǎ　patent law

专利权 zhuānlìquán　patent right; patent

专列 zhuānliè　(short for 专门列车) a special train

专卖 zhuānmài　exclusive possession of the trade in some commodity; monopoly

专美 zhuānměi　*formal* have an exclusive claim to fame; be the sole possessor of an honour: 青年演员钻研表演艺术, 不让上代艺人～于前。Challenging their predecessors' exclusive claim to fame, young actors are striving to perfect their skills.

专门 zhuānmén　special; specialized: ～研究化学 specialize in chemistry / ～为儿童写的故事 stories specially written for children / 今后你就～搞会计工作好了。From now on you'll concentrate on accounting alone. / ～机构 special agency; special organ / ～人材 people with professional skill; specialized personnel / ～术语 technical terms; nomenclature / ～知识 specialized knowledge; expertise; technical know-how

专门家 zhuānménjiā　expert; specialist

专门人民法院 zhuānmén rénmín fǎyuàn　special people's court

专名 zhuānmíng　proper name

专名号 zhuānmínghào　a line under or beside a word to show that it is a proper noun (e.g. 西安, 诸葛亮)

专区 zhuānqū　prefecture; subprovincial administrative region

专权 zhuānquán　arrogate all powers to oneself; monopolize power

专人 zhuānrén　person specially assigned for a task or job: 这项工作一定要有～负责。Someone must be put

in charge of the work. / 这个文件是～送来的。The document was brought by a special messenger.

专任 zhuānrèn　full-time; regular: ～教员 full-time teacher

专擅 zhuānshàn　*formal* usurp authority; act without authorization from one's superior

专神 zhuānshén　concentrate one's attention; be absorbed: ～贯注 concentrate one's attention on; be absorbed in; be preoccupied with

专史 zhuānshǐ　history of a particular subject (e.g. history of literature)

专使 zhùānshǐ　special envoy

专属 zhuānshǔ　exclusive: ～经济区 exclusive economic zone / ～渔区 exclusive fishing zone / ～主权 exclusive sovereignty

专署 zhuānshǔ　short for 专员公署 zhuānyuán gōngshǔ

专题 zhuāntí　special subject; special topic: ～报告 report (*or* lecture) on a special topic / ～调查 investigation of a special subject / ～讨论 seminar / ～研究 monographic study / ～著作 monograph; treatise

专线 zhuānxiàn　① special railway line ② special telephone line; line for special use

专心 zhuānxīn　concentrate one's attention; be absorbed: 学习必须～。Study requires undivided attention.

专心致志 zhuānxīn-zhìzhì　wholly absorbed; with single-hearted devotion

专修 zhuānxiū　specialize in: ～数学 specialize in mathematics

专修科 zhuānxiūkē　special (training) course

专业 zhuānyè　① special field of study; specialized subject; speciality; discipline: 该大学有十二个系，四十一个～。The university has 12 departments with 41 specialities. ② specialized trade or profession; special line: ～生产会议 a conference on specialized trades / ～队伍 professional contingent / ～人员 personnel in a specific field / ～知识 professional knowledge / 提供～服务 offer professional service / 中国银行是中国的外汇～银行。The Bank of China is the specialized foreign exchange bank of the People's Republic of China.

专业户 zhuānyèhù　a rural family that goes in for a special kind of production; specialized household: 粮食～ a household specializing in grain growing

专业化 zhuānyèhuà　specialize: 广泛实行～协作 carry out extensive coordination among specialized departments

专业课 zhuānyèkè　specialized course

专业学校 zhuānyè xuéxiào　vocational school; specialized school

专一 zhuānyī　single-minded; concentrated: 心思～ with concentrated attention / 爱情～ be constant in love

专意 zhuānyì　for a special purpose; specially

专用 zhuānyòng　for a special purpose: ～车床 special-purpose lathe / ～电话 telephone for special use

专有 zhuānyǒu　related to a particular person or thing: ～名词 technical term; nomenclature

专员 zhuānyuán　① assistant director; (administrative) commissioner: 礼宾司～ an assistant director of the Protocol Department / 商务～ commercial attaché ② prefectural commissioner ③ person specially assigned for a job

专员公署 zhuānyuán gōngshǔ　prefectural commissioner's office

专责 zhuānzé　specific responsibility: 分工明确，各有～。The division of labour is clear-cut, each one being charged with specific responsibilities.

专政 zhuānzhèng　dictatorship: ～对象 object (*or* target) of dictatorship / ～工具 instrument of dictatorship

专政机关 zhuānzhèng jīguān　organ of dictatorship

专职 zhuānzhí　① sole duty; specific duty ② full-time: 他是工会的～干部。He is a full-time cadre of the trade union.

专制 zhuānzhì　① autocracy ② autocratic; despotic: ～帝王 autocratic monarch; despotic emperor / ～君主 autocrat

专制政府 zhuānzhì zhèngfǔ　autocratic government

专制政体 zhuānzhì zhèngtǐ　autocracy

专挚 zhuānzhì　sincere; genuine; true

专注 zhuānzhù　concentrate one's attention on; be absorbed in; devote one's mind to: 心神～ wholly absorbed; with single-hearted devotion

专著 zhuānzhù　monograph; treatise; a book on a special subject: 这是一本有关计算机的～。This is a book about computers.

砖（磚、甎、塼）

zhuān　① brick: ～房 brick house / ～墙 brick wall ② sth. shaped like a brick: 茶砖 cházhuān / 煤砖 méizhuān

砖茶 zhuānchá　brick tea

砖厂 zhuānchǎng　brickfield; brickyard

砖红壤 zhuānhóngrǎng　laterite

砖红壤性土 zhuānhóngrǎngxìngtǔ　lateritic soil

砖坯 zhuānpī　unfired brick

砖头 zhuāntóu　fragment of a brick

砖头 zhuāntou　*dial.* brick

砖窑 zhuānyáo　brickkiln

颛

zhuān　*formal* ① ignorant; benighted ② same as 专 zhuān

颛蒙 zhuānméng　*formal* ignorant; benighted

颛顼 zhuānxū　a legendary ruler in ancient times

zhuǎn

转（轉）

zhuǎn　① turn; shift; change: 把全党工作重点～到经济建设上来 shift the focus of the work of the Party to economic construction / ～败为胜 turn defeat into victory / ～弱为强 transform (*or* grow) from weak to strong / 晴～多云 change from fine to cloudy; clear to cloudy / 她～过头来和我说话。She spoke to me over her shoulder. ② pass on; transfer: 这封信请你～给他。Please pass the letter on to him. / 把她的邮件～寄到她的新地址 forward her mail to her new address / 把钱从活期存款～为定期存款 transfer the money from a current to a fixed deposit account ——see also zhuàn

转氨基酶 zhuǎn'ānjīméi　(also 转氨酶 zhuǎn'ānméi) glutamic-pyruvic transaminase (GPT)

转背 zhuǎnbèi　*dial.* turn round; face about: 他一声不吭，～就走了。He turned and walked away without saying a word.

转变 zhuǎnbiàn　change; transform: ～立场 change one's stand; shift one's ground / 世界观的～ change in one's world outlook / 蒸汽机使热～为能。A steam engine transforms heat into energy. / 经过多次批评他仍无～。He remains unrepentant after repeated criticism. / 经过尖锐的思想斗争，他～了。Intense mental struggle has brought about a change in him.

转播 zhuǎnbō　relay (a radio or TV broadcast): ～台 relay station

转侧 zhuǎncè　*formal* ① change one's position ② toss about (in bed): 他在床上～许久，方才入睡。He tossed about for a long time before he fell asleep.

转产 zhuǎnchǎn　(of a factory) switch to the manufacture of another line of products; change the line of

production

转车 zhuǎnchē change trains or buses; transfer to another train or bus

转船 zhuǎnchuán change to another ship; transship

转达 zhuǎndá pass on; convey; communicate: 请向他～我的问候。Please give him my regards. / 我一定把你的话～给他。You can be assured I'll pass on your message to him.

转道 zhuǎndào make a detour; go by way of

转递 zhuǎndì pass on; transmit: 这信就由我～给他吧。I'll pass on this letter to him.

转调[1] zhuǎndiào *mus.* modulation: 从F调转到降B调 a modulation from F to B-flat / 乐曲在这里～了。At this point the music modulates.

转调[2] zhuǎndiào (of a government employee, etc.) be transferred to another post

转动 zhuǎndòng turn; move; turn round: ～手腕子 flex one's wrist / ～门把手 turn the door knob / 水龙头转不动。The tap's stuck. ——see also zhuàndòng

转发 zhuǎnfā transmit: 此件～全国。This document is to be transmitted throughout the country.

转法 zhuǎnfǎ *mil.* facing

转告 zhuǎngào pass on (word); communicate; transmit: 他把这消息～了他的姐姐。He passed on the news to his sister.

转关系 zhuǎnguānxi transfer the registration of Party membership, etc. from one unit to another

转化 zhuǎnhuà change; transform: 向反面～ transform oneself into one's opposite; change into the reverse / 将先进技术～为生产力 turn advanced technology into productive force

转圜 zhuǎnhuán ① save (a situation) ② mediate

转换 zhuǎnhuàn change; transform: ～方向 change direction / ～话题 change the subject of conversation; switch the conversation to another subject

转换开关 zhuǎnhuàn kāiguān change-over switch

转机 zhuǎnjī a favourable turn; a turn for the better: 他的病有了～。The patient has taken a turn for the better. or His condition is improving. / 战局出现～。The war situation was improving.

转嫁 zhuǎnjià ① (of women) marry again; remarry ② shift; transfer: 把责任～给他人 shift off one's responsibility; put the blame on someone else / 向别国～金融危机 shift a financial crisis on to other countries

转交 zhuǎnjiāo pass on; transmit: 请把这个包裹～给王同志。Please pass this parcel on to Comrade Wang. / 来信请由中国大使馆～。Address my mail care of (or c/o) the Chinese Embassy.

转角 zhuǎnjiǎo street corner; corner

转剧 zhuǎnjù aggravate; intensify; exacerbate: 战斗～。The fighting has intensified. / 病势～。The patient's condition was worsening.

转科 zhuǎnkē (of a patient) transfer from one department to another

转口 zhuǎnkǒu transit: ～货物 transit goods / ～贸易 *entrepôt* trade

转脸[1] zhuǎnliǎn turn one's face: 对手踢了我一脚，裁判却转过脸去，装作没看见。When my opponent kicked me, the referee looked the other way.

转脸[2] zhuǎnliǎn in no time; in the twinkling of an eye: 他刚才还在这儿，怎么～就不见了? He was here just now. How come he disappeared in a wink?

转捩点 zhuǎnlièdiǎn same as 转折点 zhuǎnzhédiǎn

转录 zhuǎnlù make a copy of a pre-recorded cassette tape or videotape; copy; dub

转卖 zhuǎnmài resell

转年 zhuǎnnián ① the coming year; next year ② *dial.* the following year (in past time)

转念 zhuǎnniàn reconsider and give up an idea; think

better of: 他刚想开口，但一～，又不说了。He was just going to speak when he thought better of it.

转蓬 zhuǎnpéng wander about like stray leaves in the wind—wandering; adrift; homeless; forsaken

转让 zhuǎnràng transfer the ownership of; make over: 技术～ technology transfer / 此票不得～ This ticket is not transferable. / 你不要，可以～给别人。You may give it to somebody else if you don't want it.

转让人 zhuǎnràngrén *leg.* assignor

转入 zhuǎnrù change over to; shift to; switch to: ～敌后 go into the enemy's rear / ～地下 go underground / ～正常 return to normal / ～下一个项目 move on to the next item / 由进攻～防御 switch (or shift) from the offensive to the defensive

转身 zhuǎnshēn (of a person) turn round; face about: 信还没有看完，他就～向屋里跑去。He turned and made for his room before he finished reading the letter.

转生 zhuǎnshēng *Buddhism* reincarnation; transmigration

转世 zhuǎnshì same as 转生 zhuǎnshēng

转手 zhuǎnshǒu ① pass on: 你就直接交给他，不必要我～了。Give it directly to him; there is no need to do it through me. ② sell what one has bought

转述 zhuǎnshù report; relate sth. as told by another: 我只是～他的话。I am merely reporting what he said.

转瞬 zhuǎnshùn in the twinkling of an eye; in an instant; in a flash: ～间他就到了。He arrived in the twinkling of an eye.

转送 zhuǎnsòng ① pass on; transmit on ② make a present of what one has been given

转体 zhuǎntǐ *sports* turn; twist: ～跳 turning leap / ～跳水 twist dive

转头 zhuǎntóu ① (of a person) turn round; face about ② (of a car, etc.) make a U-turn ③ repent

转托 zhuǎntuō ask someone else to do what is asked of one: 你让我办的事，我已～老张了。I've asked Lao Zhang to take care of the matter you spoke to me about.

转弯 zhuǎnwān turn a corner; make a turn: 邮局一～儿就是。The post office is just round (or right around) the corner. / 来一个一百八十度的大～ make a 180-degree turn; do an about-face / 他是个直性子，说话从来不会～儿。He's straightforward; he never minces his words. / 右～走! (word of command) Right wheel! (to a rank) Right turn march! or Column right march! (to a column) / 给他们一个～的余地 give them some leeway

转弯抹角 zhuǎnwān-mòjiǎo ① full of twists and turns: 我们～地走了好一会才找到那个地方。We had to take a tortuous route before we got to the place. / 这条路～的，可难走了。This road is full of twists and turns, which makes the going hard. ② beat about the bush; speak in a roundabout way: 有什么意见就痛快说，别这么～的。Say what you have to say and don't beat about the bush.

转弯子 zhuǎn wānzi ① beat about the bush; speak in a roundabout way ② change one's position or get one's thinking straightened out

转危为安 zhuǎn wēi wéi ān take a turn for the better and be out of danger; pull through

转文 zhuǎnwén lard one's speech with literary allusions

转徙 zhuǎnxǐ migrate from place to place; wander about

转系 zhuǎnxì (of a college student) transfer from one department to another: 从物理系转经济系 change (or switch) one's major from physics to economics

转向 zhuǎnxiàng ① change direction: ～装置 steering gear ② change one's political stand ——see also zhuànxiàng

转向架 zhuǎnxiàngjià　bogie (fitted under a railway carriage)

转学 zhuǎnxué　(of a student) transfer from one school to another

转眼 zhuǎnyǎn　in the twinkling of an eye; in an instant; in a flash: 这孩子一～就不见了。The child disappeared in the twinkling of an eye. / 一间, 一个月就过去了。A month passed before we knew it.

转业 zhuǎnyè　(of an armyman) be transferred to civilian work: ～军人 armyman transferred to civilian work / ～费 decommission pay; military severance pay

转移 zhuǎnyí　① shift; transfer; divert: ～兵力 shift forces; transfer troops / ～视线 divert sb.'s attention / ～目标 distract people's attention from sth. or sb. / ～斗争大方向 divert (or deflect) the general orientation of the struggle / 游击队～了。The guerrillas have moved away. ② change; transform: ～社会风气 change prevalent social customs / 阶级斗争是客观存在, 不依人的意志为～的。Class struggle is an objective reality independent of man's will. ③ med. metastasis: 癌～ the metastasis of a carcinoma / ～性癌 metastatic carcinoma

转义 zhuǎnyì　transferred meaning (a collective name for extended meaning and metaphorical meaning)

转引 zhuǎnyǐn　quote from a secondary source: ～自《政府工作报告》 quoted in the *Report on the Work of the Government*

转院 zhuǎnyuàn　(of a patient) transfer from one hospital to another

转运[1] zhuǎnyùn　have a change of luck; luck turns in one's favour

转运[2] zhuǎnyùn　transport; transfer; transship: ～公司 transport company; forwarding agency / ～站 transfer post

转韵 zhuǎnyùn　change rhyme (in a classic poem)

转载 zhuǎnzǎi　reprint sth. that has been published elsewhere; reprint: 各报都～了这篇报道。The report was reprinted in all the newspapers.

转赠 zhuǎnzèng　make a present of what one has been given

转战 zhuǎnzhàn　fight in one place after another: ～大江南北 fight successively in different parts north and south of the Changjiang River

转帐 zhuǎnzhàng　transfer accounts: 一万元钱已转到你的帐上。The 10,000 *yuan* has been transferred into your account. / 凭单 transfer document / 通过银行～结算 make settlement by means of transfer between bank accounts

转折 zhuǎnzhé　① a turn in the course of events: 世界历史上的急剧～ an abrupt turn in world history / 戏剧性的～ a dramatic turn ② transition (of an essay)

转折点 zhuǎnzhédiǎn　turning point: 我国经济建设的～ a turning point in the economic development of China

转辙器 zhuǎnzhéqì　*railway* switch

转正 zhuǎnzhèng　① (of a probationary member of the Communist Party of China) become a full member after completion of the probationary period ② (of a temporary worker) become a regular worker

转注 zhuǎnzhù　*linguis.* mutually explanatory or synonymous characters, e. g. 老 (old age) and 考 (long life, aged)—one of the six categories of Chinese characters (六书)

转租 zhuǎnzū　sublet; sublease

zhuàn

传(傳)

zhuàn　① commentaries on classics: 《左～》 *The Zuo Commentary* (on *The Spring and Autumn Annals*) ② biography: 名人～ biographies of famous people / 《贝多芬～》 *The Life of Beethoven* ③ story or novel (usu. used in titles): 《白蛇～》 *The Story of the White Snake* / 《水浒～》 *Water Margin* or *The Outlaws of the Marsh* / 《新儿女英雄～》 *Daughters and Sons*

传记 zhuànjì　biography

传略 zhuànlüè　brief biography; biographical sketch

传赞 zhuànzàn　historian's comments at the end of biographies in dynastic histories

转(轉)

zhuàn　① turn; revolve; rotate: 砂轮～得很快。The grinding wheel turns very quickly. / 地球绕着太阳～。The earth revolves round the sun. / 你在这儿～来～去干什么? What are you hanging around here for? ② m. revolution: 每分钟二千～ 2,000 revolutions per minute; 2,000 r.p.m. ——see also zhuǎn

转笔刀 zhuànbǐdāo　pencil sharpener

转碟 zhuàndié　*acrob.* plate-spinning

转动 zhuàndòng　turn; revolve; rotate: ～辘轳把儿 turn the crank of a windlass / 这个电厂的涡轮全是用核动力～的。All the turbines of this power plant are driven by nuclear energy. / 经过修理, 机器又～起来了。The machine started working again after being put right. ——see also zhuǎndòng

转筋 zhuànjīn　*Chin. med.* ① have a cramp (esp. in the leg); have a twisted muscle ② convulsion; spasm

转炉 zhuànlú　*metall.* converter: ～钢 converter steel / ～炼钢法 converting process

转轮手枪 zhuànlún shǒuqiāng　revolver

转门 zhuànmén　revolving door

转磨 zhuànmò　(also 转磨磨儿 zhuànmòmor) *dial.* go round and round a millstone—be at a loss what to do

转盘 zhuànpán　① turntable (as of a record player) ② *sports* giant stride ③ *acrob.* disc-spinning ④ *petroleum* rotary table: ～速度 rotary speed

转数 zhuànshù　*mech.* revolution: 每分钟～ revolutions per minute (r. p. m.) / 额定～ rated revolution

转速 zhuànsù　rotational speed

转速比 zhuànsùbǐ　same as 传动比 chuándòngbǐ

转速计 zhuànsùjì　tachometer

转台 zhuàntái　revolving stage

转向 zhuànxiàng　lose one's bearings; get lost: 房子真大, 我在里面直转了向。It was such a huge house that I got lost in it. ——see also zhuǎnxiàng

转椅 zhuànyǐ　swivel chair; revolving chair

转悠 zhuànyou　(also 转游 zhuànyou) *inf.* ① turn; move from side to side: 他眼珠一～就想出个主意。He rolled his eyes and hit upon an idea. ② stroll; saunter; take a leisurely walk: 星期天我上街～了一下。I strolled around the streets on Sunday.

转轴 zhuànzhóu　axle

转转 zhuànzhuan　take a short walk; go for a stroll: 他要我陪他一块到厂里～。He asked me to show him round the plant.

转子 zhuànzǐ　rotor: ～发动机 Wankel engine; Wankel

啭(囀)

zhuàn　*formal* (of birds) twitter; sing

赚

zhuàn　① make a profit; gain: 这家商行做出口生意～得可多了。The firm made large profits from exports. ② *inf.* profit ③ *dial.* earn (money) ——see also zuàn

赚钱 zhuànqián　make money; make a profit: ～生意 a profitable business; a paying proposition (*or* concern)

赚头 zhuàntou　*inf.* profit

饌 zhuàn *formal* food: 盛饌 shèngzhuàn

撰 zhuàn write; compose: 为报纸～稿 write articles for a newspaper

撰述 zhuànshù ① write; compile ② book; work

撰文 zhuànwén write an article

撰写 zhuànxiě write (usu. short articles): ～评论文章 write a commentary

撰著 zhuànzhù write; compose

篆 zhuàn ① seal character (a style of Chinese calligraphy) ② inscribe in such style: ～额 inscribe seal characters at the top of a tablet ③ seal

篆刻 zhuànkè seal cutting

篆书 zhuànshū seal character (a style of Chinese calligraphy, often used on seals)

篆字 zhuànzì same as 篆书 zhuànshū

zhuāng

妆(妆、粧) zhuāng ① apply makeup; make up: 梳妆 shūzhuāng ② woman's personal adornments ③ trousseau; dowry

妆扮 zhuāngbàn dress up; attire; deck out

妆点 zhuāngdiǎn decorate; dress up; deck out

妆奁 zhuānglián trousseau; dowry

妆饰 zhuāngshì ① adorn; dress up; deck out ② makeup

妆梳 zhuāngshū make up and dress up

妆台 zhuāngtái dressing table

妆新 zhuāngxīn *dial.* a complete outfit for newlyweds (including clothes and bedding)

庄¹(莊) zhuāng ① village: 王家～ Wangjiazhuang Village ② manor: 庄园 zhuāngyuán ③ a place of business: 钱庄 qiánzhuāng ④ banker (in a gambling game): 是谁的～? Who's the banker? ⑤ (Zhuāng) a surname

庄²(莊) zhuāng serious; grave; sedate: 端庄 duānzhuāng

庄户 zhuānghù peasant household: ～人 peasant / ～人家 peasant family

庄家 zhuāngjia banker (in a gambling game)

庄稼 zhuāngjia crops: 种～ grow (or plant) crops / 晚～ late crops

庄稼地 zhuāngjiadì *inf.* cropland; fields

庄稼汉 zhuāngjiahàn *inf.* farmer; peasant

庄稼活儿 zhuāngjiahuór *inf.* farm work

庄稼人 zhuāngjiarén *inf.* peasant; farmer

庄静 zhuāngjìng (usu. of a woman) dignified and reticent; demure

庄肃 zhuāngsù serious; solemn; earnest

庄田 zhuāngtián ① fields let out to tenant farmers by imperial families, etc. ② field; farmland; cropland

庄严 zhuāngyán solemn; dignified; stately: ～隆重的场面 a solemn, grand occasion / ～地声明 solemnly declare / 态度～ dignified in manner / 追悼会会场～肃穆。 The mourning hall was filled with a solemn silence. / ～国徽 the sacred national emblem

庄园 zhuāngyuán manor

庄院 zhuāngyuàn a big house in a village

庄重 zhuāngzhòng serious; grave; solemn; sedate: 法官神情分外～。 The judge looked grave. / 他讲话语调～。 He spoke in a solemn tone. / 一位～的中年妇女 a sedate, middle-aged woman

庄子 zhuāngzi *inf.* village; hamlet: 他是我们～里的人。 He's one of our fellow villagers.

桩(椿) zhuāng ① stake; pile: 木～ wood stake / 桥～ bridge stake ② *m.*: 一～大事 an important matter / 一～买卖 a business transaction

桩砦 zhuāngzhài *mil.* post obstacles

桩子 zhuāngzi stake; pile

装¹(裝) zhuāng ① dress up; attire; deck; play the part (*or* role) of; act: 她～老大娘真像。 She acted an old woman and really looked the part. ② outfit; clothing: 滑雪～ skiing suits ③ stage makeup and costume: 卸装 xièzhuāng ④ pretend; feign; make believe: 她不是真哭,是～的。 She wasn't really crying; she was only pretending. / ～出一副可怜相 assume a pitiable look / 不要不懂～懂。 Don't pretend to know what you don't know.

装²(裝) zhuāng ① load; pack; hold: ～车 load a truck (*or* cart) / ～箱 pack a box; put sth. in a crate; crate / ～烟袋 fill one's pipe / 这书包～不下这么多东西。 This satchel won't hold so many things. ② install; fit; assemble: 给门～上锁 fit a lock on the door / ～个无线电 assemble a radio set / 我们村家家户户都～上了电灯。 Electric lights have been installed in every house in our village.

装扮 zhuāngbàn ① dress up; attire; deck out ② disguise; masquerade: ～成朋友的敌人是最危险的。 The most dangerous enemy is one who disguises himself as a friend.

装备 zhuāngbèi ① equip; fit out: ～新式武器 be equipped with modern weapons ② equipment; outfit: 军事～ military equipment / 配置全套国产～ be fitted out with complete sets of Chinese-made equipment / 登山运动员的～ a mountaineer's outfit / 实验室配置了全新～。 The laboratory has been newly fitted out.

装裱 zhuāngbiǎo mount (a picture, etc.)

装病 zhuāngbìng pretend sickness; feign illness; malinger: 他是～。 His illness is feigned.

装舱 zhuāngcāng stow the hold (with cargo)

装船 zhuāngchuán shipment: 分批～ partial shipment

装点 zhuāngdiǎn decorate; dress; deck: 大厅里～着花彩。 The hall was decorated with festoons.

装订 zhuāngdìng binding; bookbinding: 布面～ clothbound / 皮面～ bound in leather / 硬面～ hardbound / ～车间 bookbindery; bindery / ～工人 bookbinder / ～机 bookbinding machine; binding machinery

装疯卖傻 zhuāngfēng-màishǎ feign madness and act like an idiot

装裹 zhuāngguo ① dress a corpse; wrap (a corpse) in a shroud ② shroud; burial suit

装糊涂 zhuāng hútu pretend not to know; feign ignorance; play the fool

装潢 zhuānghuáng (also 装璜 zhuānghuáng) ① mount (a picture, etc.); decorate; dress ② decoration; mounting; packaging: ～讲究的茅台酒 tastefully packaged bottles of *maotai*

装潢门面 zhuānghuáng ménmiàn do window dressing; put up a facade; keep up appearances

装幌子 zhuāng huǎngzi put up a front; maintain an outward show; keep up appearances

装货 zhuānghuò load (cargo)

装货单 zhuānghuòdān shipping order

装货港 zhuānghuògǎng port of shipment; port of loading

装机容量 zhuāngjī róngliàng *elec.* installed capacity

装甲 zhuāngjiǎ ① plate armour ② armoured: ～列车 armoured train

装甲兵 zhuāngjiǎbīng armoured force (or troops)

装甲车 zhuāngjiǎchē armoured car; armoured vehicle

装甲舰 zhuāngjiǎjiàn ironclad (a warship)

装甲师 zhuāngjiǎshī armoured division

装甲输送车 zhuāngjiǎ shūsòngchē armoured carrier

装假 zhuāngjiǎ pretend; feign; make believe

装殓 zhuāngliàn dress and lay a corpse in a coffin

装料 zhuāngliào ① feed (a machine) ② *metall.* loading; charging

装聋作哑 zhuānglóng-zuòyǎ pretend to be deaf and dumb; feign ignorance

装门面 zhuāng ménmian put up a front; maintain an outward show; keep up appearances

装模作样 zhuāngmú-zuòyàng be affected; attitudinize; put on an act; behave in an affected way

装配 zhuāngpèi assemble; fit together: ～机器 assemble a machine / ～车间 assembly shop; fitting shop / ～工 assembler; fitter / ～件 assembly parts

装配线 zhuāngpèixiàn assembly line

装腔 zhuāngqiāng behave affectedly; be artificial

装腔作势 zhuāngqiāng-zuòshì be affected or pretentious; strike a pose; put on airs: 他的那副派头完全是～，假得很。His mannerisms are affected and full of pretense.

装傻 zhuāngshǎ act dumb; pretend not to know; pretend to be naive or stupid

装傻充愣 zhuāngshǎ-chōnglèng *dial.* pretend to be naive or stupid; feign ignorance

装设 zhuāngshè install; fix; fit: ～电灯 install electric lights / ～发动机 install an engine

装神弄鬼 zhuāngshén-nòngguǐ purposely make a mystery of simple things; be deliberately mystifying

装饰 zhuāngshì decorate; adorn; ornament; deck: 彩旗和鲜花把公园～得十分绚丽。The park was gaily decorated with bunting and flowers. / ～图案 decorative pattern

装饰布 zhuāngshìbù upholstery fabrics

装饰品 zhuāngshìpǐn ornament

装饰音 zhuāngshìyīn *mus.* grace note; grace; ornament

装束 zhuāngshù ① dress; attire: 看他的～，可能是藏族。Judging from his dress, he's probably a Tibetan. ② *formal* pack up (for a journey)

装睡 zhuāngshuì pretend sleep; sham sleep

装死 zhuāngsǐ feign death; sham dead

装蒜 zhuāngsuàn *inf.* pretend not to know; feign ignorance: 你比谁都明白，别～了! Don't pretend; you know better than anybody else.

装孙子 zhuāng sūnzi *dial.* ① pretend to be helpless and miserable ② pretend not to know; feign ignorance

装填 zhuāngtián *mil.* load; ram

装相 zhuāngxiàng pretend; put on an act: 你明明不会为什么还硬～儿? Why pretend to know when obviously you don't?

装卸 zhuāngxiè ① load and unload: ～货物 load and unload a truck, ship, etc.; load and unload goods / 文明（野蛮）～ careful (careless) loading and unloading ② assemble and disassemble: 他会～自行车。He can take a bicycle apart and put it back again.

装卸工 zhuāngxiègōng loader; stevedore

装卸时间 zhuāngxiè shíjiān *water transport* lay day

装修 zhuāngxiū fit up (a house, etc.): ～门面 fit up the front of a shop

装佯 zhuāngyáng *dial.* practise fraud; be affected or pretentious; put on airs

装样子 zhuāng yàngzi put on an act; do sth. for appearance sake: 这个选手看来沉着自信，其实是在～。The player appeared calm and confident but it was just an act.

装药 zhuāngyào *mil.* powder charge; filling

装运 zhuāngyùn load and transport; ship: ～货物 ship cargo

装载 zhuāngzài loading: ～量 loading capacity

装帧 zhuāngzhēn binding and layout (of a book, magazine, etc.): 一本～精美的书 a beautifully designed and bound book

装置 zhuāngzhì ① install; fit: 仪器已经～好了。The instrument has been installed. ② installation; unit; device; plant: 雷达～ radar installation / 自停～ automatic stop arrangement / 磨煤～ coal-pulverizing plant / 配电～ power distribution unit / 减震～ damping device / 防护～ protective equipment

装作 zhuāngzuò pretend to be; disguise as: ～睡着了 pretend to be asleep / ～放羊的 be disguised as a shepherd / ～生气的样子 pretend to be angry; sham anger

zhuǎng

奘 zhuǎng *dial.* big and thick; stout, robust: 这棵树很～。The tree is very big and thick. / 那小伙子可真～。That young man is really strapping. ——see also zàng

zhuàng

壮¹(壮) zhuàng ① strong; robust: 他身体很～。He is sturdy. *or* He has a strong physique. ② magnificent; grand: 雄壮 xióngzhuàng ③ strengthen; make better: ～声势 to lend impetus and strength; to make it appear more vigorous and impressive / 以～观瞻 (deck out a place) to make it more sightly

壮²(壮) Zhuàng the Zhuang nationality ——see also 壮族 Zhuàngzú

壮大 zhuàngdà ① grow in strength; expand; strengthen: 第三世界的～ the growing strength of the Third World / ～集体经济 strengthen the collective economy / ～革命力量 expand the revolutionary forces / 科技工作人员的队伍不断～。The ranks of the scientists and technological workers are growing steadily. ② thick and strong; bulky: 手脚～ have thick and strong arms and legs

壮胆 zhuàngdǎn build up sb.'s courage; boost sb.'s courage: 你跟我一块儿去吧，起码可以壮壮我的胆。Do come with me. You can at the very least build up my courage.

壮丁 zhuàngdīng *old* able-bodied man (subject to conscription)

壮工 zhuànggōng unskilled labourer

壮观 zhuàngguān grand (or magnificent) sight: 节日的广场到处红旗飘扬，显得格外～。With red flags fluttering everywhere in celebration of the festival, the square looked most magnificent.

壮健 zhuàngjiàn healthy and strong; robust

壮锦 zhuàngjǐn Zhuang brocade

壮举 zhuàngjǔ magnificent feat; heroic undertaking: 史无前例的～ an unparalleled feat

壮阔 zhuàngkuò vast; grand; magnificent; grandiose: 规模～ grand in scale

壮劳力 zhuàngláolì ① strong labour power ② an able-bodied adult (esp. for farming)

壮丽 zhuànglì majestic; magnificent; glorious: ～的景色 magnificent scenery; majestic view / 一篇～的史诗 a

magnificent (*or* glorious) epic / 一曲～的凯歌 a stirring song of victory / 山河～ a land of glories

壮烈 zhuàngliè heroic; brave: ～牺牲 heroically give one's life; die a hero's death

壮美 zhuàngměi majestic; magnificent

壮苗 zhuàngmiáo strong sprout

壮年 zhuàngnián the more robust years of a person's life (between thirty and fifty); prime of life

壮士 zhuàngshì brave man; heroic man; hero; warrior

壮实 zhuàngshi sturdy; robust: 一个～的小伙子 a sturdy young chap

壮硕 zhuàngshuò thick and strong; robust: ～的身躯 a strong body

壮图 zhuàngtú great plan; grand prospect

壮伟 zhuàngwěi grand; lofty; magnificent: ～的山峰 lofty mountain peak

壮心 zhuàngxīn high aspirations; lofty (*or* noble) ideal

壮行 zhuàngxíng (give a grand send-off, etc.) to enable sb. to depart in style

壮志 zhuàngzhì great aspiration; lofty ideal

壮志凌云 zhuàngzhì língyún with soaring (*or* high) aspirations

壮志未酬 zhuàngzhì wèi chóu with one's lofty aspirations unrealized

壮族 Zhuàngzú the Zhuang (Chuang) nationality, or the Zhuangs (Chuangs), distributed over the Guangxi Zhuang Autonomous Region, and Yunnan and Guangdong Provinces

状 (狀)

zhuàng ① form; shape: 其～不一 of different forms ② state; condition: 现状 xiànzhuàng ③ describe: ～景～事易, 自～其情难。(王夫之) Bodying forth scenes and situations is easy; bodying forth one's own feelings is a matter of difficulty. ④ account; record: 功状 gōngzhuàng ⑤ written complaint; plaint: 告状 gàozhuàng ⑥ certificate: 奖状 jiǎngzhuàng

状词 zhuàngcí written complaint; plaint; indictment

状况 zhuàngkuàng condition; state; state of affairs: 健康～ physical condition; state of health; health / 改善这种～ remedy this state of affairs / 经济～ (a person's) financial situation; (a country's) economic situation

状貌 zhuàngmào appearance; form

状态 zhuàngtài state; condition; state of affairs: 固体～ solid state / 心理～ state of mind; psychology / 无组织～ disorganized state of affairs

状态图 zhuàngtàitú *metall.* state diagram

状语 zhuàngyǔ *gram.* adverbial modifier; adverbial

状元红 zhuàngyuánhóng a high quality Shaoxing wine

状元 zhuàngyuan ① Number One Scholar, title conferred on the one who came first in the highest imperial examination ② the very best (in any field): 养鸡"～" a champion chicken-raiser

状纸 zhuàngzhǐ *old* official form for filing a lawsuit

状子 zhuàngzi *inf.* written complaint; plaint; indictment

僮

Zhuàng old form for 壮² Zhuàng

撞

zhuàng ① bump against; run into; strike; collide: ～墙 bump against a wall / ～钟 toll (*or* strike) a bell / 一辆卡车～坏了我们的汽车。A lorry ran into our car and damaged it. / 被卡车～倒了 be knocked down by a truck / 两船在雾中相～。Two ships collided in the fog. ② meet by chance; bump into; run into: 我不想见他, 偏～上他了。I tried to avoid him, but it was just my luck to bump into him. ③ rush; dash; barge: 横冲直撞 héngchōng-zhízhuàng ④ take one's chance: ～运气 try one's luck; take a chance

撞车 zhuàngchē ① collision of vehicles ② clash of

opinions or interests ③ *inf.* (of two meetings, etc.) clash: 这两个会～了。The two meetings clash.

撞击 zhuàngjī ram; dash against; strike: 波浪～着岩石。The breakers dashed on the rocks.

撞见 zhuàngjiàn meet or discover by chance; run across; catch sb. in the act

撞骗 zhuàngpiàn look about for a chance to swindle; swindle

撞锁 zhuàngsuǒ ① spring lock ② *inf.* find that sb. is not home: 我昨儿晚上去你家串门, 没想到～了。I went to your place last night and found the door locked.

撞针 zhuàngzhēn firing pin (in a firearm)

幢

zhuàng *m. dial.*: 一～三层楼房 a three-storeyed building ——see also chuáng

戆

zhuàng *formal* blunt; simple ——see also gàng

戆直 zhuàngzhí *formal* blunt and tactless; simple and honest

zhuī

追

zhuī ① chase (*or* run) after; pursue: ～上他 catch up with him / 把比分～到十比十一 close the margin to 10-11; catch up and bring the score to 10-11 ② court (a woman); woo ③ trace; look into; get to the bottom of: 他们决心一定要把这事的根底～出来。They were determined to get to the bottom of the matter. / ～穷根 trace the root cause of one's poverty ④ seek; go after: 追名逐利 zhuīmíng-zhúlì ⑤ recall; reminisce: 追念 zhuīniàn ⑥ retroactively; posthumously: ～授一级战斗英雄称号 be posthumously awarded the title of Combat Hero Class 1

追奔逐北 zhuībēn-zhúběi (also 追亡逐北 zhuīwáng-zhúběi) give chase to a routed enemy

追本溯源 zhuīběn-sùyuán (also 追本穷源 zhuīběn-qióngyuán) trace to its source; get to the root of the matter

追逼 zhuībī ① pursue closely (a fleeing enemy) ② press for (repayment); extort (a confession)

追兵 zhuībīng pursuing troops

追补 zhuībǔ ① same as 追加 zhuījiā ② make up; remedy; make good: 不可～的损失 an irretrievable loss

追捕 zhuībǔ pursue and capture: ～逃犯 pursue and capture an escaped prisoner

追查 zhuīchá investigate; trace; find out: ～事故原因 investigate the causes of an accident / ～谣言 trace a rumour to its source

追悼 zhuīdào mourn over a person's death

追悼会 zhuīdàohuì memorial meeting

追肥 zhuīféi top application; topdressing

追风逐电 zhuīfēng-zhúdiàn chase after wind and lightning—(of a train, etc.) run swiftly

追赶 zhuīgǎn quicken one's pace to catch up; run after; pursue: 他已走远, 你～不上了。You won't be able to catch him now—he's too far away. / ～世界先进水平 measure up to advanced world levels

追根 zhuīgēn get to the root (*or* bottom) of sth.: 这件事一定得～究底。We must get to the root of the matter.

追怀 zhuīhuái call to mind; recall; reminisce: ～往事 reminisce about the old days

追回 zhuīhuí (also 追还 zhuīhuán) recover: ～赃物 recover stolen goods

追悔 zhuīhuǐ repent; regret: ～莫及 too late to repent

追击 zhuījī pursue and attack; follow up: ～敌人 pursue

and attack the enemy / 战略～ strategic pursuit / ～部队 pursuit troops / ～战 warfare of pursuit and attack

追缉 zhuījī　pursue and capture (an escaped criminal)

追记 zhuījì　① accounts of events given afterwards or from memory (usu. used in titles):《世界杯足球赛～》"World Cup Soccer Tournament in Retrospect" ② cite (*or* award) posthumously: ～特等功 be posthumously awarded a Special-Class Merit citation

追加 zhuījiā　add to (the original amount): ～支出 make an additional expenditure / ～预算 supplement a budget; make a supplementary budget / ～税 additional tax

追歼 zhuījiān　pursue and wipe out: ～残敌 pursue and wipe out the remnants of the enemy forces

追剿 zhuījiǎo　pursue and wipe out: ～队 pursuit detachment

追缴 zhuījiǎo　① demand payment (of tax arrears, etc.): ～税款 demand tax arrears ② recover: 犯罪分子非法所得的一切财物，应当予以～。All articles of property illegally obtained by the criminal element shall be recovered.

追究 zhuījiū　look into; find out; investigate: ～事故的责任 investigate and affix the responsibility for an accident; find out who is to blame for an accident / 凡是伪造证据的，必须受法律～。Anyone who falsifies evidence must be investigated under the law.

追名逐利 zhuīmíng-zhúlì　seek (*or* be after) fame and wealth

追念 zhuīniàn　think back; recall; reminisce: ～往事 recall early days; reminisce about the past

追蹑 zhuīniè　*formal* follow the trail of; track; trace

追求 zhuīqiú　① seek; pursue: ～真理 seek truth; be in pursuit of truth / ～名誉地位 be after fame and position / 单纯～数量 concentrate on quantity alone; lay stress on quantity at the expense of quality / 盲目～高指标 blindly chase high targets / 片面～产值 go exclusively after output value / ～利润 seek profits ② court (a woman); woo

追认 zhuīrèn　① subsequently confirm or endorse; recognize retroactively: ～一项法令 subsequently endorse a decree ② admit or confer posthumously: ～为共产党员 be posthumously admitted as a member of the Communist Party

追述 zhuīshù　tell about the past; relate; recount

追思 zhuīsī　recall; reminisce

追诉 zhuīsù　*leg.* prosecute

追溯 zhuīsù　trace back to; date from: 这个传说可以～到遥远的过去。The legend goes (*or* can be traced) back to remote antiquity. / 我们两国人民之间的友谊可以～到第五世纪。The friendship between our two peoples dates from the 5th century.

追随 zhuīsuí　follow: ～不舍 follow sb. closely / ～错误路线 follow an erroneous line / ～者 follower; adherent; following

追索 zhuīsuǒ　① seek; pursue; explore ② demand; exact; extort: ～一笔旧帐 demand payment of an old debt

追讨 zhuītǎo　demand payment of an old debt

追问 zhuīwèn　(also 追询 zhuīxún) question closely; make a detailed inquiry; examine minutely: ～事实真相 make detailed inquiries about the facts / 我们～他渔船失踪的原因。We questioned him trying to find out how the fishing boat got lost.

追想 zhuīxiǎng　recall; reminisce

追叙 zhuīxù　① tell about the past; relate; recount ② narration of earlier episodes; flashback

追寻 zhuīxún　pursue; search; track down

追忆 zhuīyì　recollect; recall; look back: ～往事，历历在目。As I look back, scenes of the past leap before my eyes. / 年代太久，难以～。It happened ages ago and I can't call it to mind.

追赃 zhuīzāng　order the return of stolen money or goods; recover stolen money or goods; make sb. disgorge the spoils

追赠 zhuīzèng　confer posthumously (a title)

追逐 zhuīzhú　① pursue; chase ② seek; quest: ～高额利润 seek exorbitant profits

追踪 zhuīzōng　follow the trail of; track; trace

骓 zhuī　*formal* a piebald horse

椎 zhuī　vertebra: 脊椎 jǐzhuī ——see also chuí

椎骨 zhuīgǔ　vertebra

椎间盘 zhuījiānpán　*physiol.* intervertebral disc

椎间盘突出症 zhuījiānpán tūchūzhèng　protrusion of the intervertebral disc

锥 zhuī　① awl ② anything shaped like an awl ③ bore; drill: ～孔 make a hole with an awl ④ *math.* cone

锥处囊中 zhuī chǔ náng zhōng　an awl in a bag—talent will reveal itself despite temporary obscurity

锥刀之末 zhuīdāo zhī mò　petty profits; small gains

锥度 zhuīdù　① coning; taper: ～规 taper gauge ② taper ratio

锥栗 zhuīlì　*bot.* chinquapin

锥面 zhuīmiàn　① *math.* conical surface ② *min.* pyramidal face

锥形 zhuīxíng　conical contour; cone; taper; pyramid

锥指 zhuīzhǐ　*formal* have a meagre knowledge of sth.; have a limited view of sth.

锥子 zhuīzi　awl

zhuì

坠（墜） zhuì　① fall; drop: ～马 fall off a horse / 飞机～入海中。The plane crashed into the sea. ② weigh down: 苹果把树枝～得弯弯的。The branches were bending down with the weight of the apples. *or* The apples weighed the branches down. ③ weight; a hanging object: 扇坠 shànzhuì

坠地 zhuìdì　*formal* (of a child) be born: 呱呱坠地 gūgū zhuìdì

坠毁 zhuìhuǐ　(of a plane, etc.) fall and break; crash: 飞机在山中～。The plane crashed in the mountains.

坠楼 zhuìlóu　① fall off a building ② commit suicide by jumping off a building

坠落 zhuìluò　fall; drop

坠琴 zhuìqín　(also 坠胡 zhuìhú) *zhuiqin,* a kind of bowed instrument

坠胎 zhuìtāi　same as 堕胎 duòtāi

坠子[1] zhuìzi　*dial.* ① weight; plummet; pendant ② ear pendant

坠子[2] zhuìzi　① same as 坠琴 zhuìqín ② ballad singing to the accompaniment of the *zhuiqin* (坠琴), popular in Henan Province

缀 zhuì　① sew; stitch: 你的袖子扯破了，我给你～上两针。Your sleeve's torn. I'll put in a few stitches for you. ② put words together correctly; compose: ～字成文 put words together to produce a piece of writing ③ embellish; decorate: 天上～满了星星。The sky was studded with twinkling stars.

缀合 zhuìhé　put together; make up; compose

缀辑 zhuìjí　compile; edit: ～成书 compile a book out of various materials

缀文　zhuìwén　compose an essay; write a composition

惴　zhuì　*formal* anxious and fearful

惴栗　zhuìlì　*formal* tremble with fear; shudder

惴惴不安　zhuìzhuì bùān　*formal* be anxious and fearful; be alarmed; be on tenterhooks

缒　zhuì　let down (with a rope): ～城而出 let oneself or sb. down a city wall by a rope

赘　zhuì　① superfluous; redundant: 赘言 zhuìyán ② (of a man) go to live in the household of one's in-laws on getting married; (of the bride's parents) gain a son-in-law in such a manner ③ *dial.* be burdensome; be cumbersome: 孩子多了真～人。It's really burdensome to have many children.

赘词　zhuìcí　superfluous words; redundancy

赘瘤　zhuìliú　anything superfluous or useless

赘述　zhuìshù　give more than is needed; say more than is needed: 不必一一～。It is unnecessary to go into details.

赘婿　zhuìxù　a son-in-law who lives in the home of his wife's parents

赘言　zhuìyán　① give unnecessary details; say more than is needed: 不再～。No more need be said. / 不待～。It would be pointless to dwell on the matter any more. ② superfluous words; redundancy

赘疣　zhuìyóu　① wart ② anything superfluous or useless

赘余　zhuìyú　unnecessary; superfluous; uncalled-for

zhūn

肫[1]　zhūn　*formal* sincere; genuine

肫[2]　zhūn　gizzard (of a fowl): 鸭～ duck gizzard

窀　zhūn　see below

窀穸　zhūnxī　*formal* grave; tomb

谆　zhūn　earnest; sincere: ～嘱 give earnest exhortations

谆谆　zhūnzhūn　earnest and tireless: ～教导 earnestly and tirelessly instruct / ～告诫 repeatedly admonish; tirelessly exhort

zhǔn

准[1]　zhǔn　allow; grant; permit: ～假两周 grant sb. two weeks' leave / 你要求调动工作，～了没有？ Has your request for a transfer been granted?

准[2]（準）　zhǔn　① in accordance with; follow: ～前例处理 to be settled by following precedent ② standard; norm; criterion: 以此为～ take this as the standard (*or* criterion) ③ accurate; exact: 投篮不～ inaccurate shooting (in basketball) / 这表走得～。The watch keeps good time. ④ *adv.* definitely; certainly: 我明天～去。I'll certainly be there tomorrow. / 他不～能来。He'll not possibly come. ⑤ quasi-: para-; ～军事组织 paramilitary organization / ～单色光 quasi-monochromatic light

准儿　zhǔnr　certain; sure: 心里有～ feel sure; know what one is doing / 成不成没～。The chances of success are uncertain. / 这种天气可没～。You can never

be certain about this kind of weather.

准保　zhǔnbǎo　*adv.* certainly; for sure: 你现在给他打电话，他～会来。He will certainly come if you ring him up now. / 我检查了两遍，～没错儿。I've checked twice. You can be sure there's no mistake.

准备　zhǔnbèi　① prepare; get ready: 为会议～文件 prepare documents for a meeting / 作最坏的～ prepare for the worst / 随时～歼灭入侵之敌 be prepared at all times to wipe out any invader / 你～好了吗？ Are you ready? / 可能还会有更大的洪水到来，我们必须有所～。Worse floods are likely, so we must get prepared. / ～阶段 preparatory stage ② intend; plan: 今年暑假我～回老家看看。I intend to visit my native place this summer vacation. / 我们～下星期一开始试验。We plan to start the experiment next Monday.

准备活动　zhǔnbèi huódòng　*sports* warming-up exercise; limbering-up exercise

准得　zhǔndéi　*adv.* certainly; for sure: 你看这黑云，今天～下雨。Look at those dark clouds! It's sure to rain today.

准定　zhǔndìng　*adv.* certainly; for sure: 明天我～来。I'll certainly come tomorrow.

准稿子　zhǔngǎozi　certain; sure: 什么时间盖好新宿舍，还没有～呢。Nobody can tell when the new dormitory will be completed.

准话　zhǔnhuà　definite message or answer: 什么时候定好日子，我再给您个～。I'll give you a definite answer when we've fixed the date.

准将　zhǔnjiàng　(U. S. Army, Air Force & Marine Corps) brigadier general; (Brit. Army & Marine Corps) brigadier; (U. S. & Brit. Navy) commodore; (Brit. Air Force) air commodore

准平原　zhǔnpíngyuán　paraplain

准谱儿　zhǔnpǔr　*inf.* certain; sure: 他们明天来不来没个～。It's not sure whether they'll come or not tomorrow.

准情　zhǔnqíng　agree to do sb. a favour

准确　zhǔnquè　accurate; exact; precise: 计算～ calculate accurately / ～有力的扣杀 accurate and powerful smashes / 他的英语发音～。His English pronunciation is accurate. / ～地说明 explain in precise terms / ～度 degree of accuracy; accuracy / ～性 accuracy

准绳　zhǔnshéng　criterion; yardstick: 以事实为根据，以法律为～ take facts as the basis and the law as the criterion

准时　zhǔnshí　punctual; on time; on schedule: ～起飞 take off at the scheduled time / 请～出席。Please be punctual. *or* You are requested to come on time.

准头　zhǔntou　*inf.* accuracy (in speech, marksmanship, etc.): 枪法挺有～ shoot well; be a good shot / 他说话没有～。You can't depend on what he says.

准尉　zhǔnwèi　warrant officer——see also 一级准尉 yījí zhǔnwèi; 二级准尉 èrjí zhǔnwèi

准信　zhǔnxìn　definite message or answer: 你什么时候来，先给我个～。Please let me know in advance exactly when you are coming.

准星　zhǔnxīng　front sight (of a gun)

准行　zhǔnxíng　*inf.* there won't be any problem: 这事你去跟他说～。If you go and talk to him there won't be any problem about his agreeing.

准许　zhǔnxǔ　permit; allow

准予　zhǔnyǔ　grant; approve; permit: ～入境 allow sb. to enter the country / ～休假 grant a leave

准则　zhǔnzé　norm; standard; criterion: 行为～ code of conduct / 外交～ diplomatic norms / 国际法的起码～ elementary requirements of international law / 热力学～ thermodynamic criterion

准直　zhǔnzhí　*phys.* collimation: ～透镜 collimating lens / ～仪 collimator

zhuō

拙 zhuō ① clumsy; awkward; dull: 手～ be all thumbs / ～于言词 be inarticulate; be clumsy in expressing oneself ② *hum.* my: 拙荆 zhuōjīng

拙笨 zhuōbèn clumsy; dull; unskilful: 口齿～ clumsy of speech; inarticulate

拙笔 zhuōbǐ *hum.* my (poor) writing or painting

拙稿 zhuōgǎo *hum.* my (poor) writing; my (poor) work

拙见 zhuōjiàn *hum.* my (humble) opinion

拙荆 zhuōjīng *old hum.* my wife

拙劣 zhuōliè clumsy; inferior: ～表演 a clumsy performance; a bad show / ～手法 inferior tactics; clumsy trick / 文笔～ bad (*or* poor) writing

拙朴 zhuōpǔ simple and unadorned

拙涩 zhuōsè clumsy and obscure: 译文～ clumsy and obscure translation

拙直 zhuōzhí straightforward and good-natured; simple and frank

拙著 zhuōzhù *hum.* my (poor) writing; my (poor) work

拙嘴笨腮 zhuōzuǐ-bènsāi (also 拙嘴笨舌 zhuōzuǐ-bènshé) clumsy-tongued; inarticulate

拙作 zhuōzuò *hum.* my (poor) writing, painting, etc.; my (poor) work

倬 zhuō *formal* notable; striking

捉 zhuō ① clutch; hold; grasp: ～笔 hold a pen / ～住不放 seize hold of sb. or sth. and not let go ② catch; capture: ～贼! Stop thief. / 小猫～到一只老鼠。 The little cat caught a rat.

捉刀 zhuōdāo write (an article, etc.) for sb. else; ghostwrite

捉刀人 zhuōdāorén ghostwriter

捉奸 zhuōjiān catch adulterers in the act

捉襟见肘 zhuōjīn-jiànzhǒu when one pulls together one's lapels, one's elbows poke through the sleeves—have too many difficulties (esp. financial) to cope with

捉迷藏 zhuōmícáng ① hide-and-seek; blindman's buff ② be tricky and evasive; play hide-and-seek: 你就直说吧，不要跟我～了。 Get straight to the point. Don't beat about the bush.

捉摸 zhuōmō (usu. used in the negative) fathom; ascertain: ～不定 difficult to ascertain; unpredictable; elusive

捉拿 zhuōná arrest; catch: ～逃犯 arrest an escaped prisoner / ～归案 arrest and bring a criminal to justice

捉弄 zhuōnòng tease; make fun of; play tricks on

桌 zhuō ① table; desk: 把它搁～上。 Put it on the table. ② *m.*: 三～客人 three tables of guests (at a dinner party) / 一～菜 a table of dishes

桌布 zhuōbù tablecloth

桌灯 zhuōdēng desk lamp

桌面 zhuōmiàn top of a table; tabletop

桌面儿上 zhuōmiànrshang on the table; aboveboard; in public: ～的话 polite and unimpeachable remarks / 把问题摆到～来 place problems on the table; bring problems out into the open

桌椅板凳 zhuō yǐ bǎndèng tables, chairs and benches —household furniture generally

桌子 zhuōzi table; desk

涿 Zhuō used in 涿县 and 涿鹿 (counties in Hebei Province)

zhuó

灼 zhuó ① burn; scorch: 灼伤 zhuóshāng ② bright; luminous: 灼亮 zhuóliàng

灼急 zhuójí anxious; worried

灼见 zhuójiàn profound view; penetrating view: 真知灼见 zhēnzhī-zhuójiàn

灼亮 zhuóliàng bright; shining: ～的灯光 bright lamplight

灼然 zhuórán quite obvious; fairly clear: ～可见 perfectly obvious; abduntly clear / ～无疑 indisputable; irrefutable; unquestionable

灼热 zhuórè scorching hot

灼伤 zhuóshāng (of fire, acid, etc.) burn

灼灼 zhuózhuó *formal* shining; brilliant: 目光～ with keen, sparkling eyes

卓 zhuó ① tall and erect: ～立 stand upright ② eminent; outstanding: 卓见 zhuójiàn ③ (Zhuó) a surname

卓尔不群 zhuó'ěr bù qún stand head and shoulders above all others; be preeminent

卓见 zhuójiàn excellent opinion; brilliant idea

卓绝 zhuójué unsurpassed; extreme; of the highest degree: 英勇～ extremely brave

卓荦 zhuóluò (also 卓跞 zhuóluò) *formal* unique; superb; extraordinary

卓然 zhuórán outstanding; splendid; remarkable: 成绩～ achieve outstanding results

卓识 zhuóshí judicious judgment; sagacity

卓午 zhuówǔ *formal* high noon

卓异 zhuóyì out of the ordinary; outstanding; unique; preeminent

卓有成效 zhuó yǒu chéngxiào fruitful; highly effective: 进行了～的努力 have made fruitful efforts / 几年来绿化荒山已～。 In the past few years good results have been attained in afforesting the barren hills. / 农村的改革～。 The reform in the rural areas has proved highly successful.

卓越 zhuóyuè outstanding; brilliant; remarkable: ～的成就 remarkable achievements / ～的科学家 a brilliant scientist / 作出～的贡献 make outstanding contributions

卓著 zhuózhù distinguished; outstanding; eminent: 该省农业机械化的工作成效～。 That province has achieved outstanding results in farm mechanization.

茁 zhuó thriving

茁实 zhuóshi *dial.* healthy and strong; sturdy

茁长 zhuózhǎng grow up strong and sturdy

茁壮 zhuózhuàng healthy and strong; sturdy: 小麦长得很～。 The wheat has grown sturdy.

茁壮成长 zhuózhuàng chéngzhǎng grow up strong and sturdy

浊(濁) zhuó ① turbid; muddy: ～水 turbid water / ～流 muddy stream ② deep and thick: ～声～气 in a deep, raucous voice ③ chaotic; confused; corrupted: 浊世 zhuóshì

浊点 zhuódiǎn *chem.* cloud point

浊世 zhuóshì ① *formal* the corrupted world; chaotic times ② *Buddhism* the mortal world

浊物 zhuówù *offens.* absurd creature; insensitive

creature; ignoramus

浊音 zhuóyīn *phonet.* voiced sound

斫 zhuó hack (with an axe or sword)

泏 zhuó pour; drench: 浑身都～湿了 be drenched from head to foot

酌 zhuó ① pour out (wine); drink: 独～ drink alone ② a meal with wine: 便酌 biànzhuó ③ consider; think over; use one's discretion: 请～加修改。Make any alterations as you may think fit.

酌办 zhuóbàn act according to one's judgment; act at one's discretion; do as one thinks fit

酌定 zhuódìng make a decision as one thinks fit; decide according to one's judgment: ～对策 work out (or develop) countermeasures / 以上几点意见是否可行,请～。Please weigh the above points and see if they are practicable.

酌量 zhuó-liáng consider; deliberate; use one's judgment: 这事儿你～着办吧。You can handle the matter as you think fit.

酌情 zhuóqíng take into consideration the circumstances; exercise discretion in the light of the circumstances; use one's discretion: ～处理 settle a matter as one sees fit; act at one's discretion

酌予 zhuóyǔ give sth. as one thinks fit: ～补助 give some financial assistance

诼 zhuó *formal* calumny; slander

着¹(著) zhuó ① wear (clothes): 吃～不尽 have as much food and clothing as one wants ② touch; come into contact with: 附着 fùzhuó ③ apply; use: 着墨 zhuómò ④ whereabouts: 无着 wúzhuó

着²(著) zhuó ① send: 请～人前来领取。Please send someone here for it. ② (used in official documents, expressing peremptory tone): 以上规定,～即施行。The above regulations are to be enforced immediately.
——see also zhāo; zháo; zhe

着笔 zhuóbǐ put (or set) pen to paper; begin to write or paint: 不知如何～ not know how to begin the writing or the painting

着花 zhuóhuā *formal* blossom; bear flowers

着力 zhuólì put forth effort; exert oneself: ～描写 concentrate one's efforts on depicting sb. or sth.; take great pains to describe / 无从～ fail to see where to direct one's efforts / 再着一把力 make one more effort; redouble one's efforts

着陆 zhuólù land; touch down: 飞机就要～了。The plane is about to land. or The plane is going to touch down. / ～场 landing field; landing ground / ～接地 touchdown

着陆舱 zhuólùcāng *space* landing module

着落 zhuóluò ① whereabouts: 遗失的行李已经有～了。The missing luggage has been found. ② assured source: 这笔经费还没有～。We still don't know where to get the funds from. ③ fall to sb.; rest with sb.: 这件事情得～在你身上了。It falls to you to handle the matter. ④ *old* settle: ～停当 all set; settled

着墨 zhuómò apply ink to paper—write or paint: ～不多 sketchily described or painted

着棋 zhuóqí *dial.* play chess

着色 zhuósè put colour on; colour: ～法 colouring / ～剂 colouring agent; colouring material

着实 zhuóshí ① really; indeed: 这台播种机～不错。This seeder is very good indeed. / 为了改装这台机器,他们～

花了些功夫。They really put in a good deal of time refitting the machine. / 这孩子～讨人喜欢。The child is really very cute. ② severely: ～说了他一顿 give him a good talking-to; lecture him severely

着手 zhuóshǒu put one's hand to; set about: ～一项工作 set about a job / ～编制计划 start drawing up plans / 从调查研究～ start with investigation and study

着手成春 zhuóshǒu chéng chūn same as 妙手回春 miàoshǒu huí chūn

着先鞭 zhuó xiānbiān take precedence; take the lead; get ahead of

着想 zhuóxiǎng consider (the interests of sb. or sth.): 为人民的利益～ think about the interests of the people / 他是为你～才劝你不要去的。It was for your good that he advised you not to go.

着眼 zhuóyǎn have sth. in mind; see (or view) from the angle of: ～于人民 have the people in mind / ～于未来 have one's eyes on the future / 这些措施都～于建立一支庞大的科技队伍。All these measures are aimed at building a huge contingent of scientists and technicians.

着眼点 zhuóyǎndiǎn starting point; focus of attention; object in mind

着意 zhuóyì act with care and effort; take pains: ～经营 manage with diligent care

着重 zhuózhòng stress; emphasize: ～指出 emphatically point out / ～说明问题的重要性 stress the importance of the matter / 这里我想～地讲一个问题。Here I would like to go into one question in particular.

着重号 zhuózhònghào mark of emphasis (as in 正是他本人)

着装 zhuózhuāng ① put on; wear ② clothing, headgear and footwear

啄 zhuó peck: 小鸡正在～米呢。The chicks are pecking at the rice.

啄花鸟 zhuóhuāniǎo flowerpecker

啄木鸟 zhuómùniǎo woodpecker

琢 zhuó chisel; carve: 翡翠～成的小茶壶 a small carved jadeite teapot ——see also zuó

琢磨 zhuómó ① carve and polish (jade) ② improve (literary works); polish; refine ——see also zuómó

斵 zhuó *formal* chop; hack

斵轮老手 zhuó lún lǎoshǒu expert wheelwright; old hand

斵丧 zhuósāng *formal* debauched; dissipated

濯 zhuó *formal* wash: ～足 wash one's feet

濯濯 zhuózhuó *formal* (of mountains) bare; bald: 童山濯濯 tóngshān zhuózhuó

擢 zhuó *formal* ① pull out; extract ② raise (in rank); promote

擢发难数 zhuó fà nán shǔ (of crimes) be as countless as the hairs on a head; be too numerous to count

擢升 zhuóshēng *formal* promote; advance (to a higher position or rank)

擢用 zhuóyòng *formal* promote to a post

镯(鋜) zhuó bracelet: 玉～ jade bracelet

镯子 zhuózi bracelet: 金～ gold bracelet

zī

仔 zī see below ——see also zǎi; zǐ

仔肩 zījiān *formal* official burdens or responsibilities

吱
zī *onom.* ① (of mice) squeak ② (of small birds) chirp; peep ——see also zhī

吱声 zīshēng *dial.* utter sth.; make a sound: 我们问他几遍，他都没～。We asked him several times, but couldn't get a peep out of him.

孜
zī see below

孜孜 zīzī diligent; industrious; hardworking: ～以求 diligently strive after; assiduously seek

孜孜不倦 zīzī bù juàn diligently; assiduously; indefatigably

咨（諮）
zī consult; take counsel: 咨询 zīxún

咨访 zīfǎng *formal* seek the opinion of; consult

咨嗟 zījiē *formal* ① heave a sigh; sigh ② gasp in admiration; highly praise

咨文 zīwén ① *old* official communication (between government offices of equal rank) ② report delivered by the head of a government on affairs of state; message: 总统～ presidential message; president's message

咨询 zīxún seek advice from; hold counsel with; consult: 进行～服务 provide consulting service / 技术～ technical consultation / ～机关 advisory body / ～委员会 consultative (or advisory) committee

姿
zī ① looks; appearance: 姿色 zīsè ② gesture; carriage; posture: 舞姿 wǔzī

姿媚 zīmèi *formal* lovely; charming

姿容 zīróng looks; appearance: ～秀美 good-looking; pretty

姿色 zīsè good looks (of a woman): 略有几分～ be rather good-looking

姿势 zīshì posture; gesture: 直立的～ an erect posture / ～优美 have a graceful carriage

姿首 zīshǒu *formal* good looks

姿态 zītài ① posture; carriage: 各种不同～的泥塑 clay figures in various postures ② attitude; pose: 以一个普通劳动者的～出现 (of a senior cadre) appear among the masses as an ordinary worker / 装出一副反帝的～ adopt a pose of fighting against imperialism / 作出强硬的～ take a strong posture

兹（茲）
zī *formal* ① this: ～事体大。This is indeed a serious matter. ② now; at present: ～将新到书籍开列如下。Below is a list of books recently received. ③ year: 今～ this year

资¹
zī ① money; expenses: 投资 tóuzī / 合资 hézī ② subsidize; support: 资助 zīzhù ③ provide; supply: 可～对比 provide a contrast ④ (Zī) a surname

资²
zī ① endowment; natural ability: 天资 tiānzī ② qualifications; record of service: 年资 niánzī

资本 zīběn ① capital: ～的周转 turnover of capital / ～输出 export of capital / ～投入 capital input ② what is capitalized on; sth. used to one's own advantage: 你怎么能把集体取得的成绩看作个人的～? How could you capitalize on what the group has achieved?

资本帝国主义 zīběndìguózhǔyì capitalist-imperialism

资本货物 zīběn huòwù capital goods

资本家 zīběnjiā capitalist

资本市场 zīběn shìchǎng capital market

资本主义 zīběnzhǔyì capitalism: ～道路 the capitalist road / ～复辟 the restoration of capitalism / ～经济成份 capitalist sector of the economy / ～倾向 tendencies towards capitalism / ～社会 capitalist society / ～生产方式 capitalist mode of production / ～制度 capitalist

system / ～自发势力 spontaneous capitalist forces

资本主义总危机 zīběnzhǔyì zǒngwēijī general crisis of capitalism

资材 zīcái goods, materials and equipments

资财 zīcái capital and goods; assets: 清点～ make an inventory of the assets (of a factory, etc.)

资产 zīchǎn ① property ② capital fund; capital ③ *econ.* assets: 固定（流动）～ fixed (liquid) assets / 无形～ intangible assets / ～冻结 freezing of assets

资产负债表 zīchǎn fùzhàibiǎo *econ.* statement of assets and liabilities; balance sheet

资产阶级 zīchǎnjiējí the capitalist class; the bourgeoisie: ～分子 bourgeois element / ～个人主义 bourgeois individualism / ～化 become bourgeoisified / ～民主 bourgeois democracy / ～权利 bourgeois right / ～世界观 bourgeois world outlook / ～思想 bourgeois ideas; bourgeois ideology / ～专政 the dictatorship of the bourgeoisie

资产阶级革命 zīchǎnjiējí gémìng bourgeois revolution

资产阶级民主革命 zīchǎnjiējí mínzhǔ gémìng bourgeois-democratic revolution

资产阶级自由化 zīchǎnjiējí zìyóuhuà bourgeois liberalization

资敌 zīdí aid the enemy; support the enemy

资方 zīfāng those representing capital; capital: ～人员 capitalists and their representatives / ～代理人 agent of the owner of a private enterprise; agent of a capitalist

资费 zīfèi expenses

资斧 zīfǔ *formal* travelling expenses

资格 zī-gé ① qualifications: 具备必要的～ have the requisite qualifications; be qualified / 取消比赛～ be disqualified from the contest / 取消预备党员～ annul the status of sb. as a probationary Party member / 你们有什么～向别的国家发号施令? What right have you to dictate to other countries? ② seniority: 他因～老而当选主席。He was elected chairman by virtue of his seniority.

资格审查委员会 zīgé shěnchá wěiyuánhuì credentials committee

资格证书 zīgé zhèngshū credentials

资金 zījīn fund: 建设～ funds for construction / 发展工业的～ funds for developing industry / ～短缺 shortage of funds / ～外流 capital outflow

资力 zīlì financial strength: ～雄厚 have a large capital; be financially powerful

资历 zīlì qualifications and record of service: 他的外交工作～很深。He has a long record of diplomatic service.

资料 zīliào ① means: 生产资料 shēngchǎn zīliào ② data; material: 参考～ reference material / 搜集～ gather material; collect data / ～处理 data processing / ～室 reference room

资遣 zīqiǎn dismiss sb. with severance pay

资送 zīsòng send sb. away with money provided: ～回籍 give sb. money and send him home / ～出国留学 finance sb.'s education abroad

资望 zīwàng seniority and prestige

资信可靠 zīxìn kěkào creditworthy

资性 zīxìng natural endowments; intelligence

资用 zīyòng *phys.* available: ～功 available work / ～假说 working hypothesis

资源 zīyuán natural resources; resources: ～丰富 abound (or be rich) in natural resources / 开发～ tap (or exploit) natural resources / 水产～ aquatic resources / 野生动物～ wild animal resources / 中国的妇女是一种伟大的人力～。Women form a great reserve of labour power in China.

资质 zīzhì natural endowments; intelligence: ～庸下 be

a person of mediocre intelligence

资助 zīzhù　aid financially; subsidize

赀 zī　① count; calculate (usu. used in) 不赀 bùzī ② money; expenses

缁 zī　formal　black

缁黄 zīhuáng　Buddhist monks and Taoist priests

滋[1] zī　① grow; multiply: 繁滋 fánzī ② more: 为害～甚 cause greater havoc than ever

滋[2] zī　dial.　spurt; burst: 水管裂缝了，直往外～水。Water is spurting from the crack in the pipe. / 电线～火。Sparks are spurting out from the electric wire.

滋补 zībǔ　nourishing; nutritious: ～食品 nourishing food; nourishment / ～气血药 tonics for building up vital energy and nourishing the blood / 人参是～身体的名药。Ginseng is well known for its tonic effect.

滋蔓 zīmàn　formal　grow and spread; grow vigorously: 湖中水藻～。Algae grow and spread quickly in the lake.

滋毛儿 zīmáor　same as 髭毛儿 zīmáor

滋扰 zīrǎo　cause trouble; create a disturbance

滋润 zīrùn　① moist: ～的土地 moist soil / 皮肤～ smooth skin ② moisten: 雨露～禾苗壮。Moistened by rain and dew, young crops grow strong. ③ dial. comfortable: 你这小日子过得可够～的啊。Your life is quite comfortable.

滋生 zīshēng　① multiply; breed; propagate: 防止蚊蝇～ prevent the breeding of flies and mosquitoes ② cause; create; provoke: ～事端 cause trouble; create a disturbance

滋事 zīshì　create (or stir up) trouble

滋味 zīwèi　taste; flavour: 这个菜很有～。This dish tastes good. / 尝尝艰苦生活的～ have a taste of hard life / 唱得有滋有味 sing with great gusto / 心里不是～ feel bad; be disturbed

滋芽 zīyá　dial.　sprout; germinate

滋养 zīyǎng　① nourish: ～身体 be nourishing ② nutriment; nourishment: 丰富的～ rich nutriment

滋养品 zīyǎngpǐn　nourishing food; nutriment; nourishment

滋阴 zīyīn　Chin. med.　method of treating yin deficiency by reinforcing body fluid and nourishing the blood

滋育 zīyù　grow; multiply; breed: 太阳～着万物生长。The sun gives life to all things on earth.

滋长 zīzhǎng　grow; develop: 防止～骄傲自满情绪 guard against arrogance and conceit / ～和平麻痹思想 engender a false sense of security

滋殖 zīzhí　grow; breed; propagate

嗞 zī　same as 吱 zī

嗞啦 zīlā　(also 嗞喇 zīlā)　onom.　sputtering sound

孳 zī　multiply; propagate

孳乳 zīrǔ　formal　① (of mammals) breed; multiply ② derive

孳生 zīshēng　multiply; breed; propagate: ～蚊蝇 breed flies and mosquitoes

孳孳 zīzī　same as 孜孜 zīzī

辎 zī　an ancient covered wagon

辎重 zīzhòng　impedimenta; supplies and gear of an army; baggage

趑（趦） zī　see below

趑趄 zījū　formal　① walk with difficulty; plough one's way ② hesitate to advance

趑趄不前 zījū bù qián　hesitate to advance

锱 zī　an ancient unit of weight, equal to one fourth of a liang (两)

锱铢必较 zī-zhū bì jiào　haggle over every penny; dispute over every detail

觜 zī　the twentieth of the twenty-eight constellations (二十八宿) into which the celestial sphere was divided in ancient Chinese astronomy (consisting of three stars in Orion)

龇（呲） zī　inf.　bare; show: ～着牙 bare one's teeth

龇牙咧嘴 zīyá-liězuǐ　① show one's teeth; look fierce ② contort one's face (in agony); grimace (with pain)

鲻 zī　mullet

髭 zī　moustache

髭毛儿 zīmáor　dial.　① lose one's temper; get angry ② create a disturbance; make trouble

髭须 zīxū　beard, moustache or whiskers

鼒 zī　small tripod

zǐ

子[1] zǐ　① son; child: 父与～ father and son / 他俩生有一～二女。The couple have a son and two daughters. ② person: 男子 nánzǐ / 女子 nǚzǐ ③ ancient title of respect for a learned or virtuous man: 荀～ Master Xun (313?–238 B.C.) / 先秦诸～ the pre-Qin philosophers ④ formal　you: 以子之矛，攻子之盾 yǐ zǐ zhī máo, gōng zǐ zhī dùn ⑤ same as 子书 zǐshū ⑥ seed: 结～儿 bear seed; go to seed / 这西瓜没～儿。This melon is seedless. ⑦ egg: 鱼子 yúzǐ / 鸡子儿 jīzǐr ⑧ young; tender; small: 子鸡 zǐjī ⑨ sth. small and hard: 棋～ qízǐ / 石头子儿 shí·tóuzǐr ⑩ copper coin; copper: 一个～儿不值 not worth a copper / 一个～儿也没有 penniless ⑪ m.　(used for sth. long and thin): 一～儿挂面 a bundle of fine dried noodles / 一～儿毛线 a hank of knitting wool

子[2] zǐ　the first of the twelve Earthly Branches (地支)

(see also 干支 gān-zhī)

子[3] zǐ　viscount: 子爵 zǐjué

子 zi　① (noun suffix): 帽子 màozi / 旗子 qízi / 胖子 pàngzi / 推子 tuīzi / 乱子 luànzi ② (added to certain measure words): 这档～事 this matter; this business / 我一下～想不起他的名字。I just can't recall his name at the moment. / 来了一伙～人。A group of people came.

子部 zǐbù　same as 子书 zǐshū

子城 zǐchéng　a small city within a larger one

子丑寅卯 zǐ-chǒu-yín-mǎo　the first four of the twelve Earthly Branches (地支)—in an orderly way; systematically: 你倒～讲得像模像样的。You've described the whole thing in such vivid detail that it sounds quite real. / 他支吾了半天，也没有说出个～来。He hummed and hawed for quite a while, failing to come out with a coherent story.

子畜 zǐchù　young animal; newborn animal

子代 zǐdài　biol.　filial generation: 第一～ the first filial

generation

子弹 zǐdàn　bullet; cartridge: 步枪～ rifle bullet / 汽枪～ air-gun pellet / 练习～ dummy cartridge / ～带 cartridge belt; bandoleer / ～箱 cartridge box

子堤 zǐdī　same as 子埝 zǐniàn

子弟 zǐdì　sons and younger brothers; juniors; children: 职工～ children of the workers and staff (of a factory, etc.)

子弟兵 zǐdìbīng　army made up of the sons of the people; our own army: 解放军是人民的～。The PLA is the people's own army.

子弟书 zǐdìshū　(in the Qing Dynasty) songs sung by groups of singers to the accompaniment of a drum (a popular form of entertainment originated by Manchu boys)

子房 zǐfáng　*bot.* ovary

子妇 zǐfù　① son and daughter-in-law ② one's son's wife; daughter-in-law

子公司 zǐgōngsī　subsidiary company; subsidiary

子宫 zǐgōng　uterus; womb

子宫颈 zǐgōngjǐng　cervix (of womb)

子宫颈炎 zǐgōngjǐngyán　cervicitis

子宫帽 zǐgōngmào　cervical cap

子宫切除术 zǐgōng qiēchúshù　uterectomy

子宫脱垂 zǐgōng tuōchuí　metroptosis; prolapse of uterus

子宫外孕 zǐgōngwàiyùn　ectopic (*or* extrauterine) pregnancy

子规 zǐguī　*zool.* cuckoo

子鸡 zǐjī　chick

子姜 zǐjiāng　tender ginger

子金 zǐjīn　interest (paid for the use of money)

子爵 zǐjué　viscount

子爵夫人 zǐjué fūrén　viscountess

子口 zǐkǒu　rim of the mouth of a bottle, etc. to fit the cap

子粒 zǐlì　seed; grain; kernel; bean: ～饱满 full grains

子棉 zǐmián　unginned cotton

子母弹 zǐmǔdàn　another name for 榴霰弹 liúxiàndàn

子母机 zǐmǔjī　*mil.* composite aircraft

子母扣儿 zǐmǔkòur　snap fastener; popper

子目 zǐmù　specific item; subtitle

子囊 zǐnáng　*bot.* ascus

子埝 zǐniàn　(also 子堤 zǐdī) an embankment added on top of a dyke when a flood is imminent

子女 zǐnǚ　sons and daughters; children; offspring

子时 zǐshí　the period of the day from 11 p. m. to 1 a. m.

子实 zǐshí　seed; grain; kernel; bean

子书 zǐshū　philosophical works—one of the four traditional divisions of a Chinese library ——see also 经史子集 jīng-shǐ-zǐ-jí

子嗣 zǐsì　son; male offspring

子孙 zǐsūn　children and grandchildren; descendants

子孙后代 zǐsūn hòudài　descendants; posterity; coming generations

子孙满堂 zǐsūn mǎntáng　(of a person) be blessed with many children

子午莲 zǐwǔlián　same as 睡莲 shuìlián

子午卯酉 zǐ-wǔ-mǎo-yǒu　from midnight to noon and from sunrise to sunset— ① from beginning to end; from start to finish: 问个～ get to the bottom of things ② reason; argument: 他吭哧了半天, 也没有说出个～。He hummed and hawed for quite a while, failing to come out with any convincing argument. ③ result; achievement: 没混出个～ have accomplished nothing; have got nowhere

子午线 zǐwǔxiàn　(also 子午圈 zǐwǔquān) meridian (line) ——see also 本初子午线 běnchū zǐwǔxiàn

子午仪 zǐwǔyí　meridian instrument

子息 zǐxī　① son; male offspring ② *formal* interest (paid for the use of money)

子细 zǐxì　same as 仔细 zǐxì

子弦 zǐxián　fine silk strings used for the outer strings of *sanxian* (三弦), *pipa* (琵琶), and *erhu* (二胡)

子痫 zǐxián　*med.* eclampsia

子虚 zǐxū　*formal* fictitious; unreal: 事属～。It is sheer fiction.

子虚乌有 zǐxū-wūyǒu　without foundation in fact; nonexistent; unreal; imaginary

子婿 zǐxù　*formal* son-in-law

子药 zǐyào　a collective name for 子弹 zǐdàn and 火药 huǒyào

子叶 zǐyè　*bot.* cotyledon

子夜 zǐyè　midnight

子音 zǐyīn　*phonet.* consonant

子侄 zǐzhí　sons and nephews generally

子猪 zǐzhū　pigling

仔

zǐ　(of domestic animals or fowls) young: 仔鸡 zǐjī ——see also zǎi; zī

仔畜 zǐchù　newborn animal; young animal

仔鸡 zǐjī　chick

仔密 zǐmì　(of knitwear) close-knitted; (of textiles) close-woven

仔细 zǐxì　① careful; attentive: ～分析 analyse carefully / ～地研究文件 pore over a document / 上课～听讲 listen attentively in class / 她做事很～。She's very careful in everything she does. ② be careful; look out: 路很滑, ～点儿。Watch your step! The road is very slippery. ③ *dial.* frugal; economical: 日子过得～ be frugal of one's expenses

仔猪 zǐzhū　piglet; pigling

姊

zǐ　elder sister; sister

姊妹 zǐmèi　elder and younger sisters; sisters

姊妹城 zǐmèichéng　sister city

姊妹船 zǐmèichuán　sister ship

姊妹花 zǐmèihuā　the two sisters

姊妹篇 zǐmèipiān　companion volume (*or* piece)

笫

zǐ　*formal* mat woven of fine bamboo strips: 床笫 chuángzǐ

籽

zǐ　seed: 棉籽 miánzǐ

籽棉 zǐmián　same as 子棉 zǐmián

梓

zǐ　① *bot.* Chinese catalpa (*Catalpa ovata*) ② cut blocks for printing: 付梓 fùzǐ

梓里 zǐlǐ　*formal* native place; home town

紫

zǐ　purple; violet

紫菜 zǐcài　*bot.* laver (*Porphyra spp.*)

紫草 zǐcǎo　Asian puccoon; Chinese gromwell (*Lithospermum erythrorhizon*)

紫草茸 zǐcǎoróng　*Chin. med.* shellac; lac

紫癜 zǐdiàn　*med.* purpura

紫貂 zǐdiāo　sable (*Martes zibellina*)

紫丁香 zǐdīngxiāng　(early) lilac (*Syringa oblata*)

紫毫 zǐháo　a writing brush made of rabbit's hair (which is dark purple)

紫绀 zǐgàn　*med.* cyanosis

紫河车 zǐhéchē　*Chin. med.* dried human placenta

紫红 zǐhóng　purplish red

紫花 zǐhuā　pale reddish brown: ～布 nankeen (a kind of coarse cloth)

紫花地丁 zǐhuādìdīng　*bot.* Chinese violet (*Viola philippica; V. philippica ssp. munda*)

紫花苜蓿　zǐhuāmùxu　alfalfa (*Medicago sativa*)

紫胶　zǐjiāo　shellac; lac

紫胶虫　zǐjiāochóng　lac insect (*Laccifer lacca*)

紫金牛　zǐjīnniú　*bot.*　Japanese ardisia (*Ardisia japonica*)

紫堇　zǐjǐn　*bot.*.　corydalis (*Corydalis edulis*)

紫禁城　Zǐjìnchéng　the Forbidden City (in Beijing)

紫荆　zǐjīng　*bot.*　Chinese redbud (*Cercis chinensis*)

紫羚羊　zǐlíngyáng　bongo

紫罗兰　zǐluólán　violet; common stock (*Matthiola incana*)

紫茉莉　zǐmòli　four-o'clock (*Mirabilis jalapa*)

紫萍　zǐpíng　duckweed (*Spirodela polyrrhiza*)

紫杉　zǐshān　*bot.*　(Japanese) yew (*Taxus cuspidata*)

紫石英　zǐshíyīng　amethyst

紫苏　zǐsū　*bot.*　purple perilla (*Perilla frutescens* var. *crispa*)

紫穗槐　zǐsuìhuái　*bot.*　false indigo (*Amorpha fruticosa*)

紫檀　zǐtán　*bot.*　red sandalwood; padauk (*Pterocarpus indicus*)

紫藤　zǐténg　*bot.*　Chinese wistaria (*Wistaria sinensis*)

紫铜　zǐtóng　red copper

紫外线　zǐwàixiàn　ultraviolet ray: ～灯 ultraviolet lamp

紫菀　zǐwǎn　*bot.*　aster (*Aster tataricus*)

紫葳　zǐwēi　another name for 凌霄花 língxiāohuā

紫薇　zǐwēi　*bot.*　crape myrtle (*Lagerstroemia indica*)

紫药水　zǐyàoshuǐ　common name for 龙胆紫 lóngdǎnzǐ

紫云英　zǐyúnyīng　*bot.*　Chinese milk vetch (*Astragalus sinicus*)

紫竹　zǐzhú　black bamboo (*Phyllostachys nigra*)

滓　zǐ　dregs; lees; sediment: 渣滓 zhāzǐ

訾　zǐ　*formal*　slander; calumniate

訾议　zǐyì　*formal*　discuss the failings of others; criticize; impeach: 无可～ above criticism; unimpeachable

zì

字　zì　① word; character: ～形 the form of a written character / ～义 meaning of a word / 你这个～写得不对。You wrote this character wrong. ② pronunciation (of a word or character): 说话～～清楚 pronounce every word clearly; have clear articulation ③ form of a written or printed character; style of handwriting; printing type: 篆～ seal character / 黑体～ boldface type / 柳～ style of calligraphy of Liu Gongquan (柳公权, 778-865) / 他写得一手好～。He writes a good hand. *or* He has good handwriting. ④ scripts; writings: 专藏～、不藏画 only collect scripts (*or* writings), not paintings ⑤ receipt; written pledge: 收到款子, 写个～儿给他。Write him a receipt when you get the money from him. ⑥ a style (*or* name) taken at the age of twenty, by which a man is sometimes called: 诸葛亮～孔明。Zhuge Liang styled himself Kongming. ⑦ *formal* (of a girl) be betrothed: 待字闺中 dàizì guīzhōng

字典　zìdiǎn　character dictionary (which defines only single characters, though including compounds as illustrative examples; e.g. the *Xinhua Zidian* 《新华字典》, the *Kangxi Zidian* 《康熙字典》)

字典纸　zìdiǎnzhǐ　India paper

字调　zìdiào　*phonet.*　tones of Chinese characters ——see also 四声 sìshēng

字幅　zìfú　horizontal or vertical scroll of calligraphy

字号　zìhao　① the name of a shop ② *dial.*　reputation

字盒　zìhé　*print.*　(type) mould

字画　zìhuà　calligraphy and painting

字汇　zìhuì　glossary; wordbook; lexicon

字迹　zìjì　handwriting; writing: ～工整 neat writing / ～模糊 illegible handwriting

字句　zìjù　words and expressions; writing: ～通顺 coherent and smooth writing

字据　zìjù　written pledge (e.g. receipt, IOU, contract, etc.)

字里行间　zìlǐ-hángjiān　between the lines: 他的信～流露出畏难情绪。His letter reveals, between the lines, that he's afraid of some difficulty.

字码儿　zìmǎr　*inf.*　numeral

字谜　zìmí　a riddle about a character or word

字面　zìmiàn　literal: ～上的意思 literal meaning / 从～上看 take (a word or expression) literally

字模　zìmú　*print.*　(type) matrix: 冲压～ punched matrix / ～雕刻机 matrix cutting machine

字母　zìmǔ　① letters of an alphabet; letter: 汉语拼音～ the Chinese phonetic alphabet / 英语～ the English alphabet / 大写～ a capital letter / 按～顺序排列 be arranged in alphabetical order; be arranged alphabetically ② (in phonology) a character representing an initial consonant (声母), as 明 míng for the initial m

字母表　zìmǔbiǎo　alphabet

字幕　zìmù　captions (of motion pictures, etc.); subtitles: 中文～ Chinese subtitles (*or* captions)

字盘　zìpán　*print.*　case: 大写～ upper case / 小写～ lower case

字书　zìshū　wordbook; lexicon; dictionary

字体　zìtǐ　① form of a written or printed character; script; typeface ② style of calligraphy ——see also 体 tǐ ⑨

字条儿　zìtiáor 、brief note; note: 他给我留了个～, 是关于这次演出的。He left me a note about the performance.

字帖儿　zìtiěr　a brief note

字帖　zìtiè　copybook (for calligraphy)

字眼　zìyǎn　wording; diction: 玩弄～ play with words / 我实在找不出适当的～来形容我的心情。I really can't find appropriate words to describe my feelings. ——see also 抠字眼儿 kōu zìyǎnr; 挑字眼儿 tiāo zìyǎnr

字样　zìyàng　① model of written characters ② printed or written words (which succinctly inform, instruct, warn, etc.): 封面上有"初稿"～。On the cover are the words "First Draft".

字斟句酌　zìzhēn-jùzhuó　choose one's words with care; weigh every word

字纸　zìzhǐ　wastepaper with characters written or printed on it

字纸篓　zìzhǐlǒu　wastepaper basket

字字珠玑　zì zì zhūjī　each word a gem (said in praise of sb.'s writing)

自¹　zì　① self; oneself; one's own: ～打耳光 slap one's own face; contradict oneself / ～顾～ each for himself ② *adv.*　certainly; of course; naturally: ～当努力 will certainly do one's best / 两人久别重逢, ～有许多话说。It was quite natural that they should have a lot to say to each other after such a long separation. / 现在多用功, 将来～有好处。It will certainly do you good if you study hard now. / 这电影部分情节～属有趣, 但终非佳片。Of course parts of it are funny but it's not really a good film.

自²　zì　*prep.*　from; since: ～即日起生效 become effective (as) from this date; with effect from (w.e.f.) / ～数十元至几千元不等 ranging from tens to thousands of *yuan* / ～远而近 from far to near / ～左而右 from left to right / 本次列车～北京开往南京。This train goes from Beijing to Nanjing. / 他～小在这儿长大。He was brought up here.

自爱 zì'ài regard for oneself; self-respect

自傲 zì'ào ① arrogant; conceited ② be proud of sth.; take pride in sth.

自拔 zìbá free oneself (from pain or evildoing); extricate oneself: 不能自拔 bùnéng zìbá

自白 zìbái make clear one's meaning or position; vindicate oneself

自白书 zìbáishū a written confession

自报公议 zì bào gōng yì self-assessment and public discussion

自暴自弃 zìbào-zìqì give oneself up as hopeless; have no urge to make progress; be resigned to one's backwardness

自卑 zìbēi feel oneself inferior; be self-abased: 不自满, 也不~ be neither self-satisfied nor self-abased

自卑感 zìbēigǎn inferiority complex; a sense of inferiority

自备 zìbèi provide for oneself: 在本食堂用饭请~碗筷。Will those who have their meals here please bring their own bowls and chopsticks.

自变数 zìbiànshù (also 自变量 zìbiànliàng) math. independent variable

自便 zìbiàn at one's convenience; as one pleases: 听其~。Let him do as he pleases. / 请~。Please do as you like.

自不待言 zì bù dài yán be self-evident; that goes without saying; that is taken for granted

自不量力 zì bù liànglì overestimate one's strength or oneself; not know one's own limitations

自裁 zìcái formal commit suicide; take one's own life

自惭 zìcán feel ashamed

自惭形秽 zìcán xínghuì feel unworthy (of others' company); have a sense of inferiority or inadequacy

自差 zìchā elec. autodyne: ~收音机 autodyne (radio receiver)

自嘲 zìcháo laugh at oneself

自沉 zìchén formal drown oneself

自称 zìchēng call oneself; claim to be; profess: ~内行 call oneself an expert; claim to be an old hand / 他~是孔子的后裔。He claims to be a descendant of Confucius. / ~不知情 profess ignorance

自成一家 zì chéng yī jiā (in calligraphy, painting, sculpture, etc.) have a style of one's own; have a unique or original style

自乘 zìchéng math. involution; squaring: 七~得四十九。The square of 7 is 49. or 7 squared is 49.

自持 zìchí ① control oneself; restrain oneself; exercise self-restraint ② reserved; self-possessed

自筹 zìchóu collect or raise (funds, etc.) independently: ~资金 raise funds independently or funds raised independently

自出机杼 zì chū jīzhù (of literary compositions) be original in conception

自出心裁 zì chū xīncái think up an idea of one's own; make a new departure

自吹自擂 zìchuī-zìléi blow one's own trumpet; crack oneself up

自从 zìcóng prep. from; since: ~去年秋天到现在 from last autumn till now; since last fall / 我~参加了体育锻炼, 身体好多了。I've been feeling much better since I started taking exercise.

自打 zìdǎ dial. from; since

自大 zìdà self-important; arrogant

自大狂 zìdàkuáng megalomania

自得 zìdé contented; self-satisfied: 安闲~ free and contented

自得其乐 zì dé qí lè derive pleasure from sth.; find enjoyment in sth.: 有人认为编纂词典枯燥无味, 他却~。Some people think that dictionary making is dull work, but he derives much pleasure from it.

自动 zìdòng ① voluntarily; of one's own accord: ~参加 participate voluntarily / ~帮忙 make a spontaneous offer of help / ~交待 make a voluntary confession; confess of one's own accord / 一切反动派都不会~退出历史舞台。No reactionary force will ever step down from the stage of history of its own accord. ② automatic: ~延长 (of a lease, etc.) be automatically extended / ~换梭织机 automatic shuttle-changing loom / ~绢网印花机 automatic screen printing machine / ~音量控制 automatic volume control / ~增益控制 automatic gain control / ~装配线 automatic assembly line / ~装填炮 autoloading gun

自动步枪 zìdòng bùqiāng automatic rifle

自动词 zìdòngcí same as 不及物动词 bùjíwù dòngcí

自动电话 zìdòng diànhuà automatic telephone

自动扶梯 zìdòng fútī escalator

自动化 zìdònghuà automate: 工艺过程~ process automation / 铁路编组站~ automation of a railway marshalling yard

自动控制 zìdòng kòngzhì automatic control

自动免疫 zìdòng miǎnyì med. active immunity

自动铅笔 zìdòng qiānbǐ propelling pencil

自动饲喂器 zìdòng sìwèiqì self-feeder

自动线 zìdòngxiàn transfer machine

自动饮水器 zìdòng yǐnshuǐqì automatic drinking bowl

自渎 zìdú formal self-abuse; masturbation

自发 zìfā spontaneous: ~的斗争 spontaneous struggle / ~罢工 wildcat strike / ~势力 spontaneous trend (or forces) / 小资产阶级的无政府主义~倾向 the spontaneous petty-bourgeois tendency towards anarchism / ~性 spontaneity

自反 zìfǎn ask oneself; examine oneself

自肥 zìféi fatten oneself; enrich oneself by misappropriating funds or material; feather one's nest

自费 zìfèi at one's own expense: ~旅行 travel at one's own expense

自焚 zìfén burn oneself to death

自分 zìfèn formal evaluate oneself; estimate oneself: ~不足以当此任 consider oneself not up to the task

自封 zìfēng ① proclaim (or style) oneself: ~为诗人 proclaim oneself a poet; profess to be a poet ② confine oneself; isolate oneself: 故步自封 gù bù zìfēng

自奉 zìfèng formal satisfy one's own needs or desires: ~甚俭 allow oneself few comforts or pleasures; practise self-denial / ~甚约 live economically; lead a frugal life

自负[1] zìfù be responsible for one's own action, etc.: 文责自负 wénzé zìfù

自负[2] zìfù think highly of oneself; be conceited: 这个人很~。This person is rather conceited.

自负盈亏 zìfù yíng-kuī (of an enterprise) assume sole responsibility for its profits or losses

自甘堕落 zì gān duòluò wallow in degeneration; abandon oneself to vice

自感应 zìgǎnyìng phys. self-induction

自高自大 zìgāo-zìdà self-important; conceited; arrogant

自告奋勇 zì gào fènyǒng offer to undertake (a difficult or dangerous task); volunteer (to do sth. difficult): ~参加突击队 volunteer to join the shock team

自割 zìgē zool. autotomy

自各儿 zìgěr (also 自个儿 zìgěr) dial. oneself; by oneself: 我很忙, 你~去, 好吗? I'm busy. Would you go there by yourself?

自耕农 zìgēngnóng owner-peasant; land-holding peasant

自供 zìgòng confess

自供状 zìgòngzhuàng confession

自古 zìgǔ since ancient times; from time immemorial:

～以来, 治乱无常。(《三国演义》) From ancient times periods of order and disorder have alternated quite unpredictably.

自顾不暇 zì gù bù xiá be unable even to fend for oneself (much less look after others); be busy enough with one's own affairs

自汗 zìhàn *Chin. med.* spontaneous perspiration (*or* sweating)

自豪 zìháo have a proper sense of pride or dignity; be proud of sth.: 我们为社会主义祖国的伟大成就而～。We are proud of the great achievements of our socialist country. / ～感 sense of pride

自好 zìhào regard for oneself; self-respect: 洁身自好 jié shēn zìhào

自花不稔性 zìhuā bùrěnxìng *bot.* self-sterility

自花传粉 zìhuā chuánfěn *bot.* self-pollination

自画像 zìhuàxiàng self-portrait

自毁 zìhuǐ *mil.* self-destruction: 导弹～ missile self-destruction

自己 zìjǐ ① referring to the person mentioned earlier in the sentence: 我觉得～错了。I felt that I was in the wrong. ② oneself: 生～的气 be angry with oneself / ～动手 use one's own hands / 打击别人, 抬高～ sling mud at others so as to boost oneself / 你～看看去! Go and see for yourself! / 瓶子不会～倒下来, 准是有人碰了它。The bottle couldn't have fallen down of itself. Someone must have knocked it over. ③ closely related; own: ～弟兄 one's own brothers / ～家里 one's own family

自己人 zìjǐrén people on one's own side; one of us: 他是～。He's one of us. / 都是～, 你别客气了。You're among friends, so make yourself at home.

自给 zìjǐ self-sufficient; self-supporting: 粮食～有余 be more than self-sufficient in grain / ～经济 self-supporting (*or* self-contained) economy / ～率 degree of self-sufficiency

自给自足 zìjǐ-zìzú self-sufficiency; autarky

自家 zìjiā *dial.* one or oneself: ～的小船 one's own boat

自家人 zìjiārén *dial.* people on one's own side; one of us

自荐 zìjiàn recommend oneself (for a job); offer one's services

自矜 zìjīn *formal* sing one's own praises; crack oneself up

自尽 zìjìn commit suicide; take one's own life

自经 zìjīng *formal* hang oneself

自刭 zìjǐng *formal* commit suicide by cutting one's throat; cut one's throat

自净 zìjìng *environ. protec.* self-purification

自疚 zìjiù feel compunction; have qualms of conscience

自咎 zìjiù blame oneself; rebuke oneself

自救 zìjiù save oneself; provide for and help oneself: 团结～ get united for one's own salvation / 生产～ provide for and help oneself by engaging in production

自居 zìjū consider oneself to be; pose as: 以功臣～ pose as one who has rendered great service; give oneself the airs of a hero / 以老资格～ pride oneself on one's seniority / 以专家～ claim to be an expert; be a self-styled expert

自决 zìjué self-determination: ～权 right to self-determination

自觉 zìjué ① (usu. used in the negative) be conscious; aware of: 这种病初起时, 患者每不～。Those suffering from the disease are often unaware of it in the early stages. ② on one's own initiative; conscious: 这孩子做作业挺～。The girl does her homework on her own initiative. / ～的共产主义战士 a politically conscious

fighter for communism / 这些人太不～了, 听音乐会呢还在讲话。These people are really awful. They are still talking while the concert is going on. / ～遵守纪律 conscientiously observe discipline / ～性 (level of political) consciousness

自觉症状 zìjué zhèngzhuàng subjective symptoms

自觉自愿 zìjué-zìyuàn voluntarily; willingly; of one's own free will

自绝 zìjué alienate oneself: ～于人民 alienate oneself from the people

自掘坟墓 zì jué fénmù dig one's own grave; work for one's own destruction

自控 zìkòng short for 自动控制 zìdòng kòngzhì

自苦 zìkǔ ① ask for trouble; bring trouble upon oneself ② be hard on oneself; mortify oneself

自夸 zìkuā sing one's own praises; crack oneself up

自郐以下 zì Kuài yǐ xià and the rest is not worth mentioning

自宽 zìkuān comfort oneself; console oneself

自况 zìkuàng compare oneself to; consider oneself to be

自愧不如 zì kuì bùrú (also 自愧弗如 zì kuì fúrú) feel ashamed of one's inferiority

自拉自唱 zìlā-zìchàng ① accompany one's own singing ② hold forth all alone in defence of one's own views or proposals; second one's own motion

自来 zìlái from the beginning; in the first place; originally

自来红 zìláihóng born red—born into a revolutionary family; born revolutionary: 没有～, 只有改造红。No one is born red; one becomes red only through ideological remoulding. *or* No one is born with a proletarian world outlook; one acquires it only through ideological remoulding.

自来火 zìláihuǒ *dial.* ① matches ② cigarette-lighter; lighter

自来水 zìláishuǐ running water; tap water

自来水笔 zìláishuǐbǐ fountain pen

自来水厂 zìláishuǐchǎng waterworks

自理 zìlǐ take care of or provide for oneself: 伙食～ make one's own eating arrangements / 旅费～ pay one's own travelling expenses

自力 zìlì do sth. through one's own efforts; rely on oneself

自力更生 zìlì gēngshēng regeneration (*or* reconstruction) through one's own efforts; self-reliance: ～重建家园 rebuild one's homeland through self-reliance (*or* one's own efforts)

自力霉素 zìlìméisù *pharm.* mitomycin C

自立 zìlì stand on one's own feet; support oneself; earn one's own living: 我的孩子们现在都能～了。My children are now self-supporting.

自量 zìliàng estimate one's own ability or strength: 不知～ overrate one's abilities

自料[1] zìliào expect; anticipate

自料[2] zìliào materials supplied by customers: ～加工 process materials supplied by customers; accept customers' materials for processing

自流 zìliú ① (of water, etc.) flow automatically; flow by itself ② (of a thing) take its natural course; (of a person) do as one pleases: 听其～ let things drift along; let people act freely without leadership

自流灌溉 zìliú guàngài gravity irrigation

自流井 zìliújǐng artesian well

自留 zìliú reserve sth. for one's own use: ～资金 funds an enterprise is entitled to retain

自留畜 zìliúchù livestock for personal needs; privately owned livestock

自留地 zìliúdì plot of land for personal needs; family

plot; private plot

自卖自夸 zì mài zì kuā praise the goods one sells; indulge in self-glorification; blow one's own trumpet ——see also 老王卖瓜, 自卖自夸 Lǎo Wáng mài guā, zì mài zì kuā

自满 zìmǎn complacent; self-satisfied: ～情绪 complacency; self-satisfaction / 要认真学习一点东西, 必须从不～开始。 We cannot really learn anything until we rid ourselves of complacency.

自明 zìmíng self-evident; self-explanatory; obvious: 其理～。 The principle involved is obvious. / 含义～, 无须多说。 This point is self-evident and needs no elaboration.

自鸣得意 zì míng déyì show self-satisfaction; be very pleased with oneself; preen oneself

自鸣清高 zì míng qīnggāo profess to be above politics and worldly considerations

自鸣钟 zìmíngzhōng striking clock; chime clock

自命 zìmìng consider oneself; regard oneself as: ～为历史学家 consider oneself a historian; profess to be a historian

自命不凡 zìmìng bù fán consider oneself no ordinary being; have an unduly high opinion of oneself; think no end of oneself

自馁 zìněi lose confidence; be discouraged

自捻纱 zìniǎnshā *text.* self-twisted yarn

自拍机 zìpāijī *photog.* self-timer

自喷井 zìpēnjǐng *petroleum* flowing well; gusher well

自喷期 zìpēnqī *petroleum* flush stage; flowing life

自欺欺人 zì qī qī rén deceive oneself as well as others: 完全是～之谈 a gross deception

自弃 zìqì give oneself up as hopeless; have no urge to make progress

自谦 zìqiān be modest: ～之词 self-deprecating remarks made as a gesture of politeness

自遣 zìqiǎn divert oneself from melancholy, etc.; cheer oneself up: 无以～ have no way to cheer oneself up (*or* amuse oneself); have nothing to divert oneself with

自谴 zìqiǎn blame oneself; reprove oneself

自戕 zìqiāng *formal* commit suicide; take one's own life

自强不息 zìqiáng bù xī constantly strive to become stronger; make unremitting (*or* unceasing) efforts to improve oneself

自轻自贱 zìqīng-zìjiàn demean oneself; belittle oneself; lack self-confidence and self-respect

自取灭亡 zì qǔ mièwáng court (*or* invite) destruction; take the road to one's doom

自取其咎 zì qǔ qí jiù bring blame on oneself; have only oneself to blame: 你这是～。 You asked for it.

自然 zìrán ① natural world; nature: 改造～ transform nature / 与～作斗争 struggle with nature; battle the elements / ～条件 natural conditions ② natural: 拍照时表情要～些。 Try to look natural for your photograph. / 像他这样年龄的孩子对女孩儿产生兴趣是很～的。 It's quite natural for a boy of his age to be interested in girls. ③ *adv.* naturally; in the ordinary course of events: ～归于消灭 die out naturally / 这病不用吃药, 休息一两天～会好的。 No medicine is necessary for this illness. With a couple of days of rest you'll be all right. / 你先别问, 到时候～明白。 Don't ask now. You'll understand in due course. ④ *adv.* of course; naturally: 你第一次登台～要感到紧张。 Naturally, you were keyed up when you went on the stage for the first time. / 只要努力, ～会取得好成绩。 If you work hard, you're bound to get good results.

自然 zìran at ease; natural; free from affectation: 态度非常～ be quite at ease / 她虽是初次演出, 但是演得很～。 Her acting was very natural although it was the first time she appeared on the stage. / 他不～地笑了一笑。 He forced a smile.

自然保护区 zìrán bǎohùqū nature reserve; nature preservation zone

自然辩证法 zìrán biànzhèngfǎ dialectics of nature

自然博物馆 zìrán bówùguǎn museum of natural history

自然村 zìráncūn natural village

自然地理 zìrán dìlǐ physical geography

自然而然 zìrán'érrán naturally; automatically; spontaneously; of oneself: 这孩子发育快, ～也就吃得多。 The boy is growing fast, so naturally he eats a lot of food. / 男女平等不是～就会到来的。 Equality of the sexes does not come of itself.

自然规律 zìrán guīlù natural law; law of nature

自然环境 zìrán huánjìng natural environment

自然界 zìránjiè natural world; nature

自然金属 zìrán jīnshǔ native metal

自然经济 zìrán jīngjì natural economy

自然科学 zìrán kēxué natural science

自然类群 zìrán lèiqún *biol.* natural group

自然力 zìránlì natural forces

自然免疫 zìrán miǎnyì same as 天然免疫 tiānrán miǎnyì

自然区域 zìrán qūyù natural regions

自然人 zìránrén *leg.* natural person

自然神论 zìránshénlùn deism: ～者 deist

自然数 zìránshù *math.* natural number

自然死亡 zìrán sǐwáng natural death

自然铜 zìrántóng native copper

自然现象 zìrán xiànxiàng natural phenomena

自然形态 zìrán xíngtài natural form

自然选择 zìrán xuǎnzé natural selection

自然灾害 zìrán zāihài natural calamity (*or* disaster)

自然增长率 zìrán zēngzhǎnglù natural growth: 人口～ the natural population growth

自然主义 zìránzhǔyì naturalism

自然资源 zìrán zīyuán natural resources (*or* wealth)

自燃 zìrán *chem.* spontaneous combustion (*or* ignition)

自认 zìrèn accept as unavoidable; resign oneself to: ～晦气 be resigned to one's bad luck; accept bad luck without complaint; grin and bear it

自如 zìrú *formal* freely; smoothly; with facility: 操纵～ operate with facility / 旋转～ rotate or revolve freely

自若 zìruò *formal* self-possessed; composed; calm and at ease: 神志～ appear calm and at ease; appear composed

自杀 zìshā commit suicide; take one's own life

自伤 zìshāng ① feel sorrow for oneself; be sick at heart; grieve: 余～幼年丧母。 I am grieved over the fact that I lost my mother when I was a child. ② *leg.* self-inflicted injury; self-injury

自上而下 zì shàng ér xià from above to below; from top to bottom: 军队中～的统一指挥 unified command from above in the army

自身 zìshēn self; oneself: ～思想革命化 revolutionization of one's thinking / ～的物质利益 one's own material benefits

自身难保 zìshēn nán bǎo be unable even to protect or fend for oneself ——see also 泥菩萨过河 nípúsà guò hé

自生自灭 zìshēng-zìmiè (of a thing) emerge of itself and perish of itself; run its course

自食其果 zì shí qí guǒ eat one's own bitter fruit—reap what one has sown

自食其力 zì shí qí lì support oneself by one's own labour; earn one's own living: ～的劳动者 working people living by their own labour

自食其言 zì shí qí yán go back on one's word; break one's promise; break faith with sb.

自始至终 zǐ shǐ zhǐ zhōng　from beginning to end; from start to finish: 大会～充满着团结战斗的气氛。The conference was held from beginning to end in a pervading atmosphere of solidarity and militancy.

自视 zìshì　consider (*or* think, imagine) oneself: ～甚高 think highly of oneself; be self-important

自恃 zìshì　① over confident and conceited ② *formal* be self-assured for having sth. or sb. to rely on; count on; capitalize on: ～有功 capitalize on one's achievements / ～有靠山 count on sb.'s backing

自是[1] zìshì　naturally; of course: 久别重逢，～高兴。It was of course a delight for them to meet again after such a long separation.

自是[2] zìshì　consider oneself (always) in the right; regard oneself as infallible; be opinionated: 他平日很～和倔强。He is always very opinionated and stubborn.

自首 zìshǒu　① (of a criminal) voluntarily surrender oneself; confess one's crime; give oneself up ② make a political recantation; surrender to the enemy: ～变节 recant and turn traitor

自首书 zìshǒushū　confession

自赎 zìshú　redeem oneself; atone for one's crime: 立功～ perform meritorious services to atone for one's crime

自述 zìshù　an account in one's own words

自说自话 zìshuōzìhuà　*dial.* ① act on one's own; decide for oneself ② talk to oneself; think aloud; soliloquize

自私 zìsī　selfish; self-centred: 他比较～。He's rather selfish.

自私自利 zìsī-zìlì　selfish: 毫无～之心的精神 the spirit of absolute selflessness / ～是可鄙的。Selfishness is contemptible. / 出于～的动机 act from selfish motives

自讼 zìsòng　*formal* blame oneself; reprove oneself

自诉 zìsù　*leg.* private prosecution; action initiated by an injured party without the participation of the public prosecutor: ～人 private party who prosecutes a case by himself; party who initiates a private prosecution

自讨苦吃 zì tǎo kǔ chī　ask for trouble; bring trouble upon oneself

自讨没趣 zì tǎo méiqù　ask for a snub; court a rebuff

自体不育性 zìtǐ bùyùxìng　*zool.* self-sterility

自投罗网 zì tóu luówǎng　cast oneself into the net; walk right into the trap; bite the hook; leap at the bait

自外 zìwài　stand by as an outsider; regard oneself as an outsider

自卫 zìwèi　defend oneself; self-defence: ～能力 the capacity to defend oneself / ～行动 an act in self-defence / ～原则 principle of self-defence / ～战争 war of self-defence

自卫反击 zìwèi fǎnjī　fight (*or* strike) back in self-defence: ～战 counterattack in self-defence

自卫军 zìwèijūn　self-defence corps

自为阶级 zìwéijiējí　class-for-itself

自慰 zìwèi　console oneself

自刎 zìwěn　commit suicide by cutting one's throat; cut one's throat

自问 zìwèn　① ask oneself; examine oneself: 反躬自问 fǎngōng zìwèn ② reach a conclusion after weighing a matter: 我～是花过不少力气的。I flatter myself that I have spared no pains. / 我～没有什么对不起他的地方。I don't remember ever doing him wrong.

自我 zìwǒ　(used before disyllabic verbs) self; oneself: ～介绍 introduce oneself / ～辩解 self-justification / ～安慰 self-consolation

自我暗示 zìwǒ ànshì　*psychol.* self-suggestion

自我暴露 zìwǒ bàolù　self-betrayal; self-exposure

自我标榜 zìwǒ biāobǎng　blow one's own trumpet; sing one's own praises

自我表现 zìwǒ biǎoxiàn　self-expression

自我吹嘘 zìwǒ chuīxū　self-glorification

自我催眠 zìwǒ cuīmián　autohypnosis

自我改造 zìwǒ gǎizào　self-remoulding

自我观察 zìwǒ guānchá　*psychol.* self-observation

自我检查 zìwǒ jiǎnchá　self-examination; introspection

自我教育 zìwǒ jiàoyù　self-education

自我解嘲 zìwǒ jiěcháo　find excuses to console oneself

自我批评 zìwǒ pīpíng　self-criticism

自我陶醉 zìwǒ táozuì　be intoxicated with self-satisfaction

自我完善 zìwǒ wánshàn　self-improvement: 社会主义制度的～和发展 self-improvement and development of the socialist system

自我牺牲 zìwǒ xīshēng　self-sacrifice

自我欣赏 zìwǒ xīnshǎng　self-appreciation; self-admiration: 对着镜子～ look in a mirror in self-admiration

自我作古 zì wǒ zuò gǔ　be the founder or originator of sth.

自习 zìxí　(of students) study by oneself in scheduled time or free time: ～时间 time for individual study

自下而上 zì xià ér shàng　from below: ～的监督 supervision from below

自相残杀 zì xiāng cánshā　(of persons within a group, party, etc.) kill each other; cause one another's death: ～的战争 a fratricidal war

自相惊扰 zì xiāng jīngrǎo　alarm one's own group, etc.; create a disturbance within one's ranks; raise false alarms

自相矛盾 zì xiāng máodùn　contradict oneself; be self-contradictory: 他的话～。What he says is self-contradictory. / 你这不是～吗？Aren't you contradicting yourself?

自销 zìxiāo　(of a factory, etc.) sell goods through one's own channels

自小 zìxiǎo　since childhood

自卸卡车 zìxiè kǎchē　dump truck; tip truck

自新 zìxīn　turn over a new leaf; make a fresh start: 走上～的道路 turn over a new leaf

自信 zìxìn　self-confident; confident: 有～心 have self-confidence; be confident (*or* sure) of oneself / 缺乏～ lack confidence in oneself / 她～自己能赢。She is confident that she will win. / 我～能够完成这项任务。I'm sure I can fulfil the task.

自行 zìxíng　① by oneself: ～解决 settle (a problem) by oneself / ～安排 arrange by oneself / ～设计 make designs of one's own ② of oneself; of one's own accord; voluntarily: ～到来 come of itself / 敌人是不会～消灭的。The enemy will not perish of himself. ③ *astron.* proper motion

自行车 zìxíngchē　bicycle; bike: 骑～ ride a bicycle / 骑～进城 go down town by bike

自行车架 zìxíngchējià　① bicycle frame ② bicycle stand (*or* rack)

自行车棚 zìxíngchēpéng　bicycle shed

自行车赛 zìxíngchēsài　cycle racing; cycling

自行火炮 zìxíng huǒpào　*mil.* self-propelled gun

自行其是 zì xíng qí shì　go one's own way; act wilfully

自省 zìxǐng　examine oneself; examine one's ability, conduct, etc.

自修 zìxiū　① (of students) study by oneself; have self-study ② study on one's own; study independently: ～法语 teach oneself French

自许 zìxǔ　① take pride in; pride oneself on ② call oneself; claim to be

自诩 zìxǔ　*formal* praise oneself; crack oneself up; brag

自序 zìxù　(also 自叙 zìxù) ① author's preface; preface

② autobiographic note; brief account of oneself

自选 zìxuǎn *sports* free; optional: ～手枪五十米赛 free pistol 50 m.

自选动作 zìxuǎn dòngzuò *sports* optional exercise

自选市场 zìxuǎn shìchǎng (also 自选商场 zìxuǎn shāng-chǎng) supermarket

自炫 zìxuàn *formal* sing one's own praises; flaunt; crack oneself up

自学 zìxué study on one's own; study independently; teach oneself: 培养～能力 cultivate (*or* foster) one's ability to study independently / ～成才 be self-taught

自学课本 zìxué kèběn teach-yourself books

自寻烦恼 zì xún fánnǎo worry oneself needlessly; bring vexation on oneself

自寻死路 zì xún sǐlù bring about one's own destruction

自言自语 zìyánzìyǔ talk to oneself; think aloud; solilo-quize

自养生物 zìyǎng shēngwù *biol.* autotroph

自养植物 zìyǎng zhíwù *bot.* autophyte; autotrophic plant

自贻伊戚 zì yí yī qī bring trouble on oneself

自以为得计 zì yǐwéi déjì be pleased with one's own scheming; think oneself smart

自以为非 zì yǐwéi fēi consider oneself in the wrong; recognize one's own fallibility

自以为是 zì yǐwéi shì consider oneself (always) in the right; regard oneself as infallible; be self-opinionated

自缢 zìyì *formal* hang oneself: ～而死 hanging oneself

自用 zìyòng ① *formal* obstinately holding to one's own views; self-opinionated; self-willed: 愚 而好～ ignorant and self-willed ② for private use; personal: ～物品 personal effects; personal belongings

自由 zìyóu ① freedom; liberty: 公民～权 civil liberties / 中国公民有言论、通信、出版、集会、结社、游行、示威、罢工的～。 Citizens of China enjoy freedom of speech, cor-respondence, the press, assembly, association, proces-sion, demonstration and the freedom to strike. ② *philos.* freedom: ～和必然 freedom and necessity ③ free; unrestrained: ～讨论 have a free exchange of views / ～选择 be free to choose; have a free choice / ～行动 act on one's own / ～发表意见 express one's views unreservedly

自由电子 zìyóu diànzǐ free electron

自由兑换 zìyóu duìhuàn *econ.* convertibility: 可以～的货币 convertible currency / 不能～的货币 inconvertible currency

自由泛滥 zìyóu fànlàn (of erroneous ideas, etc.) spread unchecked; run wild

自由放任 zìyóu fàngrèn let people do what they like; let things go their own way; follow one's own inclina-tions

自由放任主义 zìyóufàngrènzhǔyì *laissez-faire*

自由港 zìyóugǎng free port

自由化 zìyóuhuà liberalize

自由汇率 zìyóu huìlǜ free exchange rate

自由价格 zìyóu jiàgé free price

自由竞争 zìyóu jìngzhēng free competition

自由联想 zìyóu liánxiǎng *psychol.* free (*or* uncontrol-led) association

自由恋爱 zìyóu liàn'ài freedom to arrange one's own marriage; free courtship: 我们俩是～结合的。 We arranged our own marriage.

自由贸易 zìyóu màoyì free trade

自由民 zìyóumín *hist.* freeman

自由能 zìyóunéng *phys.* free energy

自由散漫 zìyóu-sǎnmàn slack; lax in discipline: ～现象 slackness (in discipline) / ～性 individualistic aversion to discipline

自由诗 zìyóushī free verse; unorthodox verse; *vers libre*

自由市场 zìyóu shìchǎng free (*or* open) market

自由体操 zìyóu tǐcāo free exercise; floor exercise; free callisthenics

自由王国 zìyóu wángguó *philos.* realm of freedom: 人类的历史，就是一个不断地从必然王国向～发展的历史。 The history of mankind is one of continuous develop-ment from the realm of necessity to the realm of freedom.

自由意志 zìyóu yìzhì free will

自由泳 zìyóuyǒng freestyle (swimming); crawl

自由职业 zìyóu zhíyè profession: ～者 professional

自由主义 zìyóuzhǔyì liberalism: ～的倾向 liberal tend-encies / ～者 liberal

自由资本主义 zìyóuzīběnzhǔyì non-monopoly capital-ism; *laissez-faire* capitalism

自由资产阶级 zìyóu zīchǎnjiējí non-monopoly bourgeoi-sie; liberal bourgeoisie

自由自在 zìyóu-zìzài leisurely and carefree; free and unrestrained: ～地畅所欲言 speak one's mind freely / 无事牵萦，～ lead a free and easy life without worries / 野生动物～地生活在这个自然保护区里。 Wild animals roam unmolested in this nature reserve.

自由组合规律 zìyóu zǔhé guīlǜ *biol.* law of independ-ent assortment

自幼 zìyòu since childhood

自娱 zìyú please oneself; amuse oneself: 作诗～ com-pose poems to please oneself

自育 zìyù *zool.* self-fertile

自圆其说 zì yuán qí shuō make one's statement valid; justify oneself: 这样解释能～吗? Is this a plausible ex-planation? / 不能～ cannot offer a tenable argument; cannot justify oneself

自怨自艾 zìyuàn-zìyì be full of remorse; repent

自愿 zìyuàn voluntary; of one's own accord; of one's own free will: 出于～ on a voluntary basis; of one's free will / ～参加山区建设 volunteer to work in a mountainous area / ～互利的原则 the principles of voluntary participation and mutual benefit / 按照群众的需要和～ in accordance with the needs and wishes of the masses

自在 zìzài free; unrestrained: 日子过得挺～ lead a free and easy life / 始知锁向金笼听，不及林间～啼。(欧阳修) Now I know in a cage of gold she never sang so sweet As when she roams freely in the woods.

自在 zìzai comfortable; at ease: 主人太客气了，反而使他们有些不～。 The host's assiduous attentions made them feel rather ill at ease. / 身体有点不～ feel a little out of sorts; not be quite oneself

自在阶级 zìzàijiējí *philos.* class-in-itself

自在之物 zìzài zhī wù *philos.* thing-in-itself

自责 zìzé blame oneself; reprove oneself

自找 zìzhǎo suffer from one's own actions; ask for it: 这是你～的嘛! You asked for it. / ～麻烦 be looking for trouble

自知之明 zìzhī zhī míng knowledge of oneself: 无～ lack of self-knowledge / 人贵有～。 It is important to know one's own limitations. *or* Self-knowledge is wisdom.

自治 zìzhì autonomy; self-government: ～的权限 auton-omous jurisdiction / ～条例 regulations on the exercise of autonomy

自治机关 zìzhì jīguān organ of self-government

自治领 zìzhìlǐng self-governing dominion; dominion

自治区 zìzhìqū autonomous region

自治权 zìzhìquán autonomy

自治县 zìzhìxiàn autonomous county

自治州 zìzhìzhōu autonomous prefecture

自制[1] zìzhì made by oneself: 这台铣床是我们厂～的。 This milling machine was made in our own plant.

自制[2] zìzhì self-control; self-restraint: 失去～ lose self-

control

自重[1] zìzhòng　conduct oneself with dignity; be self-possessed: 请～。Please behave yourself.

自重[2] zìzhòng　dead weight: 车皮～ the dead weight of a wagon

自主 zìzhǔ　act on one's own; decide for oneself; keep the initiative in one's own hands: 男女婚姻～。Men and women shall marry the partners of their choice. / ～经营 be independent in management

自主权 zìzhǔquán　power to make one's own decisions: 扩大企业的～ enlarge the decision-making power of local enterprises

自主神经 zìzhǔ shénjīng　same as 植物性神经 zhíwùxìng shénjīng

自专 zìzhuān　formal act on one's own; make arbitrary decisions and take peremptory action

自传 zìzhuàn　autobiography

自转 zìzhuàn　astron. rotation: 地球的～ the rotation of the earth / ～轴 axis of rotation

自走式 zìzǒushì　self-propelled: ～联合收割机 self-propelled combine harvester

自足 zìzú　self-satisfied; complacent; smug

自尊 zìzūn　self-respect; self-esteem; proper pride: 伤了他的～心 injure his self-esteem; wound his pride / ～感 sense of self-respect

自作自受 zìzuō-zìshòu　suffer from one's own actions; stew in one's own juice: 这是你～。As you make your bed, so you must lie on it. / 他这是～, 没人可怜他。Nobody feels sorry for him; he's got what he deserves.

自作聪明 zì zuò cōngmíng　think oneself clever (in making suggestions, etc.); try to be smart (by acting on one's own, etc.)

自作多情 zì zuò duōqíng　proffer a love or affection which is not reciprocated

自作主张 zì zuò zhǔzhāng　act on one's own; decide for oneself: 这件事我们得请示, 不能～。We can't decide this for ourselves; we must ask for instructions.

恣 zì　① throw off restraint; do as one pleases: 得以自～ be able to do as one likes (or indulge oneself) ② dial. comfortable: ～得很 very comfortable

恣情 zìqíng　① to one's heart's content; as much as one likes: ～欢笑 laugh heartily ② wanton; arbitrary; wilful

恣肆 zìsì　formal ① unrestrained; self-indulgent; wanton ② (of writing style) forceful and unrestrained; free and natural

恣睢 zìsuī　formal reckless; unbridled: 暴戾恣睢 bàolì-zìsuī

恣行无忌 zì xíng wú jì　act wilfully and unscrupulously; behave recklessly

恣意 zìyì　unscrupulous; reckless; unbridled; wilful: ～践踏 wilfully trample on / ～掠夺别国的资源 indulge in unbridled plunder of the resources of other countries / ～侵犯别国领土 unscrupulously (or wilfully) encroach upon others' territory

恣意妄为 zìyì wàngwéi　act wilfully and wildly; behave unscrupulously

恣纵 zìzòng　formal self-indulgent; undisciplined

渍 zì　① steep; soak; ret: ～麻 ret flax, jute, etc. / 白衬衫被汗水～黄了。The white shirt has yellowed with sweat. ② floodwater on low-lying land: 防洪排～ prevention of floods and drainage of floodwater ③ be soiled (with grease, etc.): 她每天擦机器, 不让～一点油泥。She polishes the machine every day so that there's not a speck of dirt on it. / 烟斗里～了很多油子。The pipe is caked with tar. ④ dial. stain; sludge: 油～ oil sludge / 茶～ tea stains

渍涝 zìlào　waterlogging: ～的低洼地 waterlogged low-lying land

渍染 zìrǎn　dye: 血污～ bloodstained

渍水 zìshuǐ　accumulated water

眦（眥） zì　corner of the eye; canthus

zōng

宗[1] zōng　① ancestor: 祖宗 zǔzōng ② clan: 同宗 tóngzōng ③ sect; faction; school: 正宗 zhèngzōng ④ principal aim; purpose: 开宗明义 kāizōng-míngyì ⑤ (in academic or artistic work) take as one's model: 他的唱工～的是梅派。In singing he takes Mei Lanfang as his model. ⑥ model; great master: 诗宗 shīzōng ⑦ m.: 一～心事 a matter that worries one ⑧ (Zōng) a surname

宗[2] zōng　① old an administrative unit in Xizang, roughly corresponding to the county

宗祠 zōngcí　ancestral hall (or temple)

宗法 zōngfǎ　patriarchal clan system: ～社会 patriarchal society

宗匠 zōngjiàng　great master (in academic or artistic work): 词家～ a great ci master / 一代～ the greatest master of one's time

宗教 zōngjiào　religion: 信仰～ believe in religion

宗教法庭 zōngjiào fǎtíng　the Inquisition (in European history)

宗教改革 zōngjiào gǎigé　the Reformation (in European history)

宗教戒律 zōngjiào jièlǜ　religious taboo

宗教派别 zōngjiào pàibié　religious sect

宗教信仰 zōngjiào xìnyǎng　religious belief

宗教仪式 zōngjiào yíshì　religious rites; ritual

宗筋 zōngjīn　Chin. med. penis

宗庙 zōngmiào　ancestral temple (or shrine) of a ruling house

宗派 zōngpài　faction; sect: ～斗争 factional strife / ～活动 factional activities; sectarian activities

宗派主义 zōngpàizhǔyì　sectarianism; factionalism: ～者 sectarian; factionalist

宗谱 zōngpǔ　family tree; genealogical tree; genealogy

宗亲 zōngqīn　members of the same clan; clansmen

宗社 zōngshè　formal the state; the country

宗师 zōngshī　master of great learning and integrity

宗室 zōngshì　① imperial (or royal) clan ② imperial (or royal) clansman

宗祧 zōngtiāo　the family line: 继承～ carry on the family line

宗仰 zōngyǎng　formal hold in esteem: 海内～ be held in esteem throughout the country

宗支 zōngzhī　(also 宗枝 zōngzhī) descendants of the same clan

宗旨 zōngzhǐ　aim; purpose: 建党～ the aim of Party building / 全心全意地为人民服务是我军的唯一～。To serve the people wholeheartedly is the sole purpose of our army.

宗主国 zōngzhǔguó　suzerain (state); metropolitan state

宗主权 zōngzhǔquán　suzerainty

宗族 zōngzú　① patriarchal clan ② clansman

综 zōng　put together; sum up: ～上所述 to sum up ——see also zèng

综观 zōngguān　make a comprehensive survey: ～全局 take a broad view of the situation

综合 zōnghé　① synthesize: ～群众的意见 synthesize

(*or* sum up) the opinions of the masses ② synthetical; comprehensive; multiple; composite: ～的研究 a synthetical (*or* comprehensive) study

综合报导 zōnghé bàodǎo (also 综合报道 zōnghé bàodào) comprehensive (*or* composite) dispatch; news roundup

综合报告 zōnghé bàogào comprehensive report; summing-up report

综合病征 zōnghé bìngzhēng (also 综合征 zōnghézhēng) syndrome

综合大学 zōnghé dàxué university

综合规划 zōnghé guīhuà unified plan

综合考察 zōnghé kǎochá comprehensive survey

综合利用 zōnghé lìyòng comprehensive utilization; multipurpose use

综合平衡 zōnghé pínghéng overall balance

综合性工厂 zōnghéxìng gōngchǎng multiple-producing factory

综合语 zōnghéyǔ *linguis.* synthetic language

综合治理 zōnghé zhìlǐ tackle a problem in a comprehensive way: 实行山、水、田、林、路～。The problems concerning mountains, rivers, farmland, forests and roads should be tackled in a comprehensive way.

综计 zōngjì sum up; add up: 合理化建议～有九个方面。To sum up, the rationalization proposals fall into nine categories.

综括 zōngkuò sum up: ～起来 to sum up; to state succinctly

综述 zōngshù summarize; sum up: 来稿～ a summary of readers' contributions

棕(椶)

zōng ① palm ② palm fibre; coir: 棕毛 zōngmáo

棕绷 zōngbēng (also 棕绷子 zōngbēngzi) wooden bed frame strung with crisscross coir ropes

棕编 zōngbiān coir-woven articles

棕黑 zōnghēi dark brown

棕红 zōnghóng reddish brown

棕黄 zōnghuáng pale brown

棕榈 zōnglǘ palm

棕榈酸 zōnglǘsuān palmitic (*or* palmic) acid

棕榈油 zōnglǘyóu palm oil; palm butter

棕毛 zōngmáo palm fibre: ～蓑衣 palm rain cape

棕壤 zōngrǎng *agric.* brown earth

棕色 zōngsè brown: ～森林土 brown forest soil

棕绳 zōngshéng coir rope

棕树 zōngshù common name for 棕榈 zōnglǘ

棕毯 zōngtǎn coir-woven blanket

棕箱 zōngxiāng a wooden box with a coir-woven case

棕熊 zōngxióng brown bear

棕衣 zōngyī palm-bark rain cape

踪(蹤)

zōng footprint; track; trace: 跟踪 gēnzōng

踪迹 zōngjì trace; track: 他不见了，未留下任何～。He disappeared without a trace. / 警察紧跟罪犯的～追到山里去。The police followed the criminal's tracks into the mountains.

踪影 zōngyǐng (usu. used in the negative) trace; sign: 杀人犯毫无～。There is no trace of the murderer. / 我已好几天不见她的～了。I haven't seen a trace of her for several days now.

鬃

zōng hair on the neck of a pig, horse, etc.: 猪鬃 zhūzōng

鬃刷 zōngshuā bristle brush

zǒng

总 (總、緫)

zǒng ① assemble; put together; sum up: ～起来说 to sum up / 把两笔帐～到一块算 settle the two accounts together ② general; overall; total: ～产量 total output / ～趋势 general trend / ～根源 root cause / ～的说来 generally speaking; by and large ③ chief; head; general: ～头目 chief boss; chieftain ④ *adv.* always; invariably: 我一去那儿天～下雨。It invariably rains when I go there. / 我不是～在这儿。I am not always here. ⑤ *adv.* anyway; after all; eventually; sooner or later: 问题～是要解决的。The problem will be settled sooner or later. / 你～会成功的。You're bound to succeed. / 他～还是个孩子，哪能像大人那样有力气? After all, he's only a child. How can he possibly be as strong as a grown-up? ⑥ *adv.* surely; certainly; probably: 她说的你～不会相信吧? You don't believe what she said, surely? / 他～不大可能写这样一封信。It's most unlikely that he should have written such a letter. / 明天他～该回来了。He certainly ought to be back tomorrow. / 他～有一千多块钱了。He probably has more than 1,000 *yuan*.

总罢工 zǒngbàgōng general strike

总编辑 zǒngbiānjí editor in chief

总部 zǒngbù general headquarters

总裁 zǒngcái director-general (of a political party); president (of a company); governor (of a bank)

总参谋部 zǒngcānmóubù the Headquarters of the General Staff

总参谋长 zǒngcānmóuzhǎng chief of the general staff

总产值 zǒngchǎnzhí gross output value; total output value: 工农业年～ gross annual value of industrial and agricultural output (*or* production)

总成 zǒngchéng ① *old* help (sb. to achieve his aim) ② *mech.* assembly

总赤字 zǒngchìzì total deficit

总得 zǒngděi must; have to; be bound to: ～想个办法 have got to find a way out / 他今天～来一趟。He's bound to come today.

总店 zǒngdiàn main store (of a business)

总动员 zǒngdòngyuán general (*or* total) mobilization

总督 zǒngdū ① (in the Qing Dynasty) governor-general (of two provinces, except for the metropolitan province of Zhili 直隶, now Hebei Province, which had a governor-general to itself): 两广～ Governor-General of Guangdong and Guangxi ② (in British colonies and dominions) viceroy; governor-general; governor: 印度～ (formerly) Viceroy of India / 加拿大～ Governor-General of Canada / 香港～ Governor of Hong Kong / 澳大利亚联邦～ Governor-General of the Commonwealth of Australia

总队 zǒngduì a unit in an army corresponding to a regiment or division

总额 zǒng'é total: 存款～ total deposits / 工资～ total wages; payroll

总而言之 zǒng ér yán zhī in short; in a word; in brief; to make a long story short: ～，这电影我一点也不喜欢。In short, I didn't like the film at all. / ～，我们要有准备。有了准备就能应付各种局面。In short, we must be prepared. Being prepared, we shall be able to deal with all kinds of situations.

总方针 zǒngfāngzhēn general policy; general principle: 经济工作的～ the general policy guiding economic work / 外交政策～ general principles of foreign policy

总纲 zǒnggāng general programme; general principles: 党章～ the general programme of the Party Constitu-

tion／中华人民共和国宪法～ the General Principles of the Constitution of the People's Republic of China

总工程师 zǒnggōngchéngshī chief engineer

总工会 zǒnggōnghuì federation of trade unions: 中华全国～ All-China Federation of Trade Unions

总公司 zǒnggōngsī head office (of a corporation)

总攻 zǒnggōng *mil.* general offensive

总供给 zǒnggōngjǐ aggregate supply

总共 zǒnggòng *adv.* in all; altogether; in the aggregate: ～约五千人 about five thousand people in all／这个地区～有二百二十家工厂。There are altogether 220 factories in this area.

总管 zǒngguǎn ① take overall responsibility ② *old* steward; butler

总归 zǒngguī *adv.* anyway; after all; eventually: 困难～是可以克服的。Difficulties can after all be overcome.／事实～是事实。After all, facts are facts.／他可能迟到，来～会来的。He will probably be late but he'll come eventually.

总行 zǒngháng head office (of a bank)

总合 zǒnghé sum up; add up

总和 zǒnghé sum; total; sum total: 头三个月产量的～ the total output of the first three months／无数相对的真理之～，就是绝对的真理。The sum total of innumerable relative truths constitutes absolute truth.／对世界政治、经济的～进行具体的分析 make a concrete analysis of world politics and economics as a whole／各部分的～ summation of individual parts

总后方 zǒnghòufāng rear area (in wartime)

总后勤部 zǒnghòuqínbù the General Logistics Department

总汇 zǒnghuì ① (of streams) come or flow together: ～入海 flow into the sea together ② confluence; concourse; aggregate: 人民是智慧的海洋，力量的～。The people are a sea of wisdom and the aggregation of strength.／李时珍的《本草纲目》是当时中国药物学的～。*Compendium of Materia Medica* by Li Shizhen (1518-1593) was a comprehensive summary of all pharmacological knowledge accumulated in China up to his time.

总机 zǒngjī switchboard; telephone exchange

总集 zǒngjí general collection; general anthology (e.g. 萧统《文选》Xiao Tong's *General Anthology of Prose and Verse*)

总计 zǒngjì ① *math.* grand total ② amount to; add up to; total: ～一千元。It amounts to 1,000 *yuan. or* It adds up to 1,000 *yuan.*／观众～有十万人。The audience totalled 100,000. *or* There were 100,000 spectators in all.

总价 zǒngjià total (price)

总监 zǒngjiān inspector general; chief inspector

总角 zǒngjiǎo *formal* a child's hair twisted in a knot—childhood

总角之交 zǒngjiǎo zhī jiāo childhood friend

总结 zǒngjié ① sum up; summarize: ～经验 sum up one's experience／～工作 summarize one's work ② summary; summing-up: 作～ make a summary／哲学是关于自然知识和社会知识的概括和～。Philosophy is the generalization and summation of the knowledge of nature and society.

总结报告 zǒngjié bàogào summary (*or* final, concluding) report

总结会 zǒngjiéhuì summing-up meeting

总经理 zǒngjīnglǐ general manager; president

总开关 zǒngkāiguān master switch

总括 zǒngkuò sum up: ～起来 to sum up; to state succinctly

总揽 zǒnglǎn assume overall responsibility; take on everything: ～大权 have overall authority; assume a dominant role

总理 zǒnglǐ premier; prime minister: 国务院～ the Premier of the State Council／副～ Vice-Premier

总领事 zǒnglǐngshì consul general

总领事馆 zǒnglǐngshìguǎn consulate general

总路线 zǒnglùxiàn general line

总论 zǒnglùn introduction (at the beginning of a book)

总目 zǒngmù general table of contents; general catalogue:《四库全书～》*General Catalogue for the Complete Collection in Four Treasuries*／全书分订五册，除分册目录外，第一册前面还有全书～。The book is in five volumes. There is a table of contents for each volume, and also a general one for the whole book in the first volume.

总平面图 zǒngpíngmiàntú general layout

总评 zǒngpíng general comment; overall appraisal

总谱 zǒngpǔ *mus.* score

总其成 zǒng qí chéng assume overall responsibility for sth. and bring it to completion

总书记 zǒngshūjì secretary-general; general secretary

总数 zǒngshù total; sum total

总司令 zǒngsīlìng commander in chief

总司令部 zǒngsīlìngbù general headquarters

总算 zǒngsuàn *adv.* ① at long last; finally: 会议一再延期，现在～开成了。The meeting has come off at last, after being postponed again and again.／他想来想去，最后～想出了一个好主意。He thought it over and over and finally hit upon a good idea. ② considering everything; all things considered; on the whole: 小孩子的字能写成这样，～不错了。For a child's handwriting, it's quite good.

总体 zǒngtǐ overall; total: ～规划 overall plan／～设计 master design／～战略 total strategy／～外交 total diplomacy

总体战争 zǒngtǐ zhànzhēng total war

总统 zǒngtǒng president (of a republic)

总统府 zǒngtǒngfǔ presidential palace; the residence and／or office of a president

总统选举 zǒngtǒng xuǎnjǔ presidential election

总统制 zǒngtǒngzhì presidential government; presidential system

总危机 zǒngwēijī general crisis

总务 zǒngwù ① general affairs ② person in charge of general affairs

总务处 zǒngwùchù general affairs department

总务科 zǒngwùkē general affairs section

总务司 zǒngwùsī general service department

总需求 zǒngxūqiú aggregate demand

总则 zǒngzé general rules; general principles; general provisions

总闸门 zǒngzhámén *petroleum* master valve; master gate

总长 zǒngzhǎng ① cabinet minister (a name used 1912-1927; now called 部长 bùzhǎng) ② *inf.* (short for 总参谋长) chief of the general staff

总帐 zǒngzhàng general ledger

总政治部 zǒngzhèngzhìbù the General Political Department: ～主任 Director of the General Political Department

总之 zǒngzhī *conj.* ① in a word; in short; in brief: 我是既没工夫又没兴趣，～，我不干。I have neither the time nor the inclination; in short, I refuse. ② anyway; anyhow: 确切地址我记不清了，～是在颐和园附近。I can't remember the exact address. Anyway, it's somewhere near the Summer Palace.

总支 zǒngzhī general branch: 党总支 dǎngzǒngzhī

总值 zǒngzhí total (*or* gross) value: 生产～ total output value／进(出)口～ gross import (export) value

总指挥 zǒngzhǐhuī ① commander in chief ② general

director
总指挥部　zǒngzhǐhuībù　general headquarters
总状花序　zǒngzhuàng huāxù　*bot.* raceme

偬(傯)　zǒng　see 倥偬 kǒngzǒng

zǒng

纵[1](縱)　zǒng　① from north to south or from south to north: 纵贯 zòngguàn ② vertical; longitudinal; lengthwise: 纵深 zòngshēn / 纵剖面 zòngpōumiàn ③ short for 纵队 zòngduì②

纵[2](縱)　zǒng　① release; set free: 欲擒故纵 yù qín gù zòng ② indulge; let loose; let oneself go: 纵声 zòngshēng ③ jump up; jump into the air: 他向前一～，就把球接住了。He leaped forward and caught the ball.

纵[3](縱)　zǒng　*conj. formal* even if; even though: ～有千难万险，也挡不住英勇的勘探队员。Even though there are myriad hardships and hazards, they can't stop the dauntless prospectors.

纵[4](縱)　zǒng　*dial.* creased; crumpled: 衣服压～了。The dress is crumpled.

纵波　zòngbō　*phys.* longitudinal wave
纵步　zòngbù　① stride: ～向前走去 stride forward ② jump; bound: 他一个～跳过了小河。He crossed the brook in one big jump.
纵断面　zòngduànmiàn　same as 纵剖面 zòngpōumiàn
纵队　zòngduì　① column; file: ～队形 column formation / 一路～ column of files; single file / 二路～ column of twos ② a military unit during the War of Liberation, equivalent to an army; column
纵隔　zònggé　*physiol.* mediastinum: ～炎 mediastinitis
纵观　zòngguān　take a sweeping view; make a general survey: ～全局 make a general survey of the situation / ～时势 give a broad overview of the trend of the age
纵贯　zòngguàn　pass through from north to south or from south to north: ～两省的铁路 a railway passing through two provinces from north to south / 大运河～河北、山东、江苏、浙江四省。The Grand Canal flows southwards through the four provinces of Hebei, Shandong, Jiangsu and Zhejiang.
纵横　zònghéng　① in length and breadth; vertically and horizontally: ～数百里的山区 a mountainous area several hundred *li* in length and breadth ② with great ease; freely: 笔意～ write with great ease ③ sweep over; march over unhindered
纵横捭阖　zònghéng-bǎihé　manoeuvre among various states or political groupings
纵横驰骋　zònghéng chíchěng　(of an army) move about freely and quickly; sweep through the length and breadth of: 八路军在华北平原～，歼灭大量敌人。The Eighth Route Army, sweeping through the length and breadth of the north China plain, wiped out large numbers of enemy troops. / 青年们可以在广阔的科学领域里～。The length and breadth of the whole realm of science is open for our youth to explore and conquer.
纵横家　Zònghéngjiā　Political Strategists (in the Warring States Period, 475–221 B.C.)
纵横交错　zònghéng jiāocuò　crisscross: ～的水渠 a crisscross network of irrigation channels
纵虎归山　zòng hǔ guī shān　let the tiger return to the mountains—cause calamity for the future
纵火　zònghuǒ　set on fire; commit arson: ～犯 arsonist

纵酒　zòngjiǔ　drink to excess
纵览　zònglǎn　look far and wide; scan: ～四周 look all round / ～群书 read extensively
纵令[1]　zònglìng　*conj.* even if; even though
纵令[2]　zònglìng　give free rein to; indulge; connive
纵论　zònglùn　talk freely; have a wide-ranging discussion: ～天下大事 talk freely about world events / ～史事 give a talk that ranges over the whole span of history
纵目　zòngmù　look as far as one's eyes can see: ～四望 look far into the distance in all directions
纵剖面　zòngpōumiàn　vertical section
纵切面　zòngqiēmiàn　same as 纵剖面 zòngpōumiàn
纵情　zòngqíng　to one's heart's content; as much as one likes: ～歌唱 sing to one's heart's content; sing heartily
纵然　zòngrán　*conj.* even if; even though: ～成功的希望不大，我们也要试试。We will try even if there isn't much hope of success. / 今天～有雨，也不会很大。Even if it rains today, it can't be a heavy rain.
纵容　zòngróng　connive; wink at: 在某人～下 with the connivance of sb. / 受到～和庇护 be winked at and shielded
纵射　zòngshè　*mil.* enfilade
纵身　zòngshēn　jump; leap: ～一跳 jump into the air; jump up / ～上马 leap onto a horse
纵深　zòngshēn　*mil.* depth: 向～发展 develop in depth / 对敌人的补给线进行～阻截 carry out a deep interdiction of enemy supply routes / ～防御 defence in depth
纵声　zòngshēng　at the top of one's voice: ～大笑 laugh heartily / ～歌唱 sing lustily
纵使　zòngshǐ　*conj.* even if; even though
纵视图　zòngshìtú　longitudinal view
纵谈　zòngtán　talk freely: ～国内外大好形势 talk freely about the excellent internal and external situation
纵眺　zòngtiào　look as far as one's eyes can see: ～黄山景色 scan the scenery of Huangshan
纵向　zòngxiàng　vertical; longitudinal; lengthwise: ～结合 vertical integration (as of enterprises)
纵欲　zòngyù　give way to one's carnal desires; indulge in sensual pleasures
纵恣　zòngzì　*formal* self-indulgent; undisciplined; wanton
纵坐标　zòngzuòbiāo　*math.* ordinate

粽(糉)　zǒng　see 粽子 zòngzi
粽子　zòngzi　a pyramid-shaped dumpling made of glutinous rice wrapped in bamboo or reed leaves (eaten during the Dragon Boat Festival)

zōu

邹(鄒)　Zōu　a surname

诹　zōu　*formal* consult; seek advice from
诹访　zōufǎng　*formal* consult; seek advice from
诹吉　zōují　*formal* pick an auspicious day (for a marriage, etc.)

陬　zōu　*formal* ① corner ② foot of a hill

zǒu

走　zǒu　① walk; go: 这孩子还不会～。The baby cannot walk yet. / 一直往前～ go straight ahead / 很

远的路 walk a long distance / ～社会主义道路 take the socialist road / ～群众路线 follow the mass line / ～下主席台 step down from the rostrum / ～在游行队伍的前列 march in the van of the procession / ～遍全国 travel the length and breadth of the whole country / ～前人没有～过的道路 break new paths; take paths never trodden before / 这船一小时～十五海里。 The ship makes 15 knots. ② run; move: 钟不～了。 The clock has stopped. / 这个表～得很准。 This watch keeps good time. / 打得赢就打, 打不赢就～。 Fight when you can win, move away when you can't. / 你这步棋～坏了。 You've made a bad move. ③ leave; go away: ～开! Get away! *or* Clear off! / 我们该～了。 It's time for us to leave. *or* We must be off now. / 他已经把蓝图拿～了。 He's taken the blueprint away. ④ visit; call on: 他们两家～得很近。 The two families often visit each other. ⑤ through; from: 咱们～这个门进去吧。 Let's go in through this door. ⑥ leak; let out; escape: ～气了。 The gas is leaking. *or* The air is escaping. ⑦ depart from the original; lose the original shape, flavour, etc.: 把原来的意思讲～了 fail to get across the original meaning

走板 zǒubǎn ① (of opera singing) be out of tune ② digress from the subject; stray from the point

走背运 zǒu bèiyùn have bad luck; be out of luck; be down on one's luck

走笔 zǒubǐ *formal* write rapidly: ～疾书 write rapidly (*or* swiftly)

走边 zǒubiān (of actors playing military roles in traditional opera) walk with a light, cautious tread to suggest travel by night

走镖 zǒubiāo (in former times) act as an armed escort for a convoy

走步 zǒubù *basketball* walking

走村串寨 zǒucūn-chuànzhài go from village to village

走刀量 zǒudāoliàng *mech.* feed

走道 zǒudào ① pavement; sidewalk ② path; walk; footpath

走道儿 zǒudàor *inf.* walk: 小孩子刚会～。 The baby has just learned to toddle.

走电 zǒudiàn *dial.* leakage of electricity

走调儿 zǒudiàor out of tune: 她唱歌爱～。 Her singing often gets out of tune.

走动 zǒudòng ① walk about; stretch one's legs: 坐了一整天了, 出去～～吧。 We've been sitting all day long. Let's go out for a stroll. / 病人能～了。 The invalid is able to get about now. ② (of relatives and friends) visit each other: 他们两家关系不错, 常常～。 The two families are on good terms and often visit each other.

走读 zǒudú attend a day school

走读生 zǒudúshēng day student; nonresident student

走访 zǒufǎng ① interview; have an interview with: 本报记者～了几位著名的小说家。 Our reporter interviewed several famous novelists. ② pay a visit to; go and see

走风 zǒufēng let out a secret; leak out

走钢丝 zǒu gāngsī *acrob.* wirewalking

走狗 zǒugǒu running dog; lackey; flunkey; stooge; servile follower

走关节 zǒu guānjié get round (laws, rules, etc.) by bribery

走过场 zǒu guòchǎng do sth. as a mere formality; go through the motions; do sth. perfunctorily or superficially

走红 zǒuhóng (also 走红运 zǒu hóngyùn) have good luck; be in luck

走后门 zǒu hòumén get in by the back door—get sth. done through pull; secure advantages through influence

走话 zǒuhuà *dial.* let out a secret; leak out

走火 zǒuhuǒ ① *elec.* sparking ② (of firearms) discharge accidentally: 他一时不慎, 枪～了。 He wasn't careful and his rifle went off accidentally. ③ go too far in what one says; put sth. too strongly; overstate ④ catch fire; be on fire: 仓库～了。 The storehouse is on fire.

走江湖 zǒu jiānghú wander from place to place and earn a living by juggling, fortune-telling, etc.; become a vagrant

走口 zǒukǒu *dial.* make a slip of the tongue; let slip an inadvertent remark

走廊 zǒuláng corridor; passage; passageway

走漏 zǒulòu ① leak out; divulge: ～风声 divulge a secret; leak information / 这话我只告诉你。你可不能～半点消息。 This is strictly confidential. Don't breathe a word of it to anyone. ② smuggling and tax evasion

走路 zǒulù ① walk; go on foot: 孩子已经学会～了。 The baby has learned to walk. / 你们是坐车去还是～去? Will you go there by bus or on foot? / 过去打运动战, ～的时间常多于作战的时间。 In mobile warfare, we used to spend more time in moving than in fighting. ② leave; go away

走马 zǒumǎ ① gallop or trot along on horseback ② a fine horse

走马灯 zǒumǎdēng running horse lantern (a lantern on the top band of which are decorative figures, which revolve as the hot air ascends): 人员不断更换, 就像～似的。 Personnel were shifted about as often as if they were on a running horse lantern (*or* a merry-go-round).

走马疳 zǒumǎgān *med.* noma; gangrenous stomatitis

走马换将 zǒumǎ-huànjiàng change of command; reshuffle of personnel: 领导班子～后, 工作有了起色。 Things are looking up as a result of a reshuffle of the leading group.

走马看花 zǒumǎ kàn huā (also 走马观花 zǒumǎ guān huā) look at flowers while riding a horse—gain a shallow understanding from a fleeting glance

走马上任 zǒumǎ shàngrèn go to one's post; take up (*or* assume) office

走门路 zǒu ménlu (also 走门子 zǒu ménzi) solicit help from potential backers; gain one's end through pull

走南闯北 zǒunán-chuǎngběi journey north and south; travel widely: 我～, 也没见过这么能干的妇女。 I've been everywhere, but never have I seen a woman as capable as her.

走内线 zǒu nèixiàn take the inner line—use private influence to achieve one's end (e.g. seek sb.'s favour by approaching his confidants or members of his family); go through private channels

走娘家 zǒu niángjia (of a married woman) visit her parents' home

走俏 zǒuqiào (of goods) sell well; be in great demand

走亲戚 zǒu qīnqi call on relatives

走禽 zǒuqín Cursores; cursorial birds

走人 zǒurén *inf.* go away; leave: 咱们～, 不等他了。 Let's go now and not wait for him any more. / 叫他卷铺盖～。 Tell him to pack up and quit.

走色 zǒushǎi lose colour; fade: 这件衣服穿了两年了, 还没有～。 The jacket hasn't lost colour though I've been wearing it for two years.

走扇 zǒushàn (of a door or window) won't shut properly (due to warping)

走墒 zǒushāng evaporation of water in soil

走神儿 zǒushénr (of one's attention) wander; be absent-minded: 她一～漏了一针。 She dropped a stitch the moment her attention began to wander.

走绳 zǒushéng (also 走索 zǒusuǒ) *acrob.* rope-dancing; ropewalking

走失 zǒushī　① wander away; be lost; be missing: 一只羊～了。A sheep has wandered away from the flock. / 我们一起出去的, 半路上他～了。We went out together and he got lost on the way. ② fail to keep; lose: 译文～原意。The original meaning is lost in the translation.

走时 zǒushí　(also 走时运 zǒu shíyùn) *dial.* have good luck; be in luck

走事儿 zǒushìr　*dial.* use one's head; ponder (or think over) a problem

走兽 zǒushòu　four-footed animals; quadrupeds; beasts

走水 zǒushuǐ　① leak water: 房顶～了。The roof is leaking. ② (of water) flow; run: 渠道～很通畅。Water runs well in the canal. ③ *euph.* be on fire; catch fire

走私 zǒusī　smuggle: ～的货物 smuggled goods

走题 zǒutí　(of a speech, etc.) digress from the subject; stray from the point: 说话～儿 speak beside the point; wander from the subject

走投无路 zǒu tóu wú lù　have no way out; be in an impasse; come to a dead end: 逼得～ be driven (or pushed) to the wall / 穷困潦倒, ～ be down-and-out and have no place to turn

走味儿 zǒuwèir　lose flavour: 茶叶～了。The tea has lost its flavour.

走下坡路 zǒu xiàpōlù　go downhill; be on the decline: 清朝自乾隆以后就开始～。After the reign of Emperor Qianlong, the power of the Qing Dynasty began to decline.

走险 zǒuxiǎn　take a risk; make a reckless move

走乡随乡 zǒu xiāng suí xiāng　same as 随乡入乡 suí xiāng rù xiāng

走向 zǒuxiàng　① run; trend; alignment: 矿脉的～ the run of the ore vein / 海岸线～ the trend of the coastline / 确定两国边界线的全部～ determine the entire alignment of the boundary line between the two countries / 横断山脉是南北～的山脉。The Hengduan Mountains run from south to north. ② *geol.* strike: ～断层 strike fault / ～节理 strike joint ③ move towards; head for; be on the way to: ～大治 move towards great order / ～胜利 advance towards victory; march to victory / ～反面 change (or turn) into one's opposite / ～死亡 head for one's doom; go down to one's doom / 世界一定要～进步, ～光明, 而决不是～反动, ～黑暗。The world will surely move towards progress and light, and definitely not towards reaction and darkness.

走相 zǒuxiàng　become deformed

走形 zǒuxíng　be out of shape

走形式 zǒu xíngshì　do sth. as a mere formality; go through the motions

走穴 zǒuxué　*inf.* (esp. of a performer) moonlight

走眼 zǒuyǎn　see wrong: 拿着好货当次货, 你可看走了眼了。You've seen wrong. You took superior goods for inferior goods.

走样 zǒuyàng　lose shape; go out of form; be different from what is expected or intended: 放上鞋楦免得鞋～。Use shoe trees to keep your shoes from losing shape. / 这事让他给说～了。His account presented a distorted picture of the matter.

走一步, 看一步 zǒu yī bù, kàn yī bù　take one step and look around before taking another—proceed without a plan, or with caution

走油 zǒuyóu　(of oily food) go rancid

走运 zǒuyùn　have good luck; be in luck: 不～ have bad luck (or fortune) / 咱们真～! We're really in luck. / 祝你～。Good luck to you. or Good luck!

走着瞧 zǒuzheqiáo　wait and see: 咱们～! We'll see (who's right).

走资派 zǒuzīpài　(used during the Great Cultural Revolution) capitalist-roader; person in power taking the capitalist road

走字 zǒuzì　*dial.* have good luck; be in luck

走走 zǒuzou　① take a stroll: 我们出去～吧。Let's take a stroll. ② come or go in a general sense: 有空常来～。Drop in when you are free.

走卒 zǒuzú　pawn; cat's-paw; lackey; stooge

走嘴 zǒuzuǐ　make a slip of the tongue; let slip an inadvertent remark: 她说着说着就走了嘴了。As she talked on and on, she blurted the secret out.

zòu

奏 zòu　① play (music); perform (on a musical instrument): ～国歌 play the national anthem / ～哀乐 play funeral music / 当贵宾进入宴会厅时, 乐队开始～迎宾曲。The band struck up a tune of welcome when the distinguished guests entered the banquet hall. ② achieve; produce: 奏功 zòugōng ③ present a memorial to an emperor: 奏本 zòuběn

奏案 zòu'àn　a table at which an emperor examined memorials

奏报 zòubào　① present a memorial to the emperor (or throne) ② a memorial to the emperor (or throne)

奏本 zòuběn　present a memorial to the emperor (or throne): 奏某人一本 impeach sb. in a memorial to the emperor (or throne)

奏功 zòugōng　yield result; produce effects; prove effective: 应手～ produce an instant effect

奏技 zòujì　*formal* (of singers, dancers, etc.) perform

奏捷 zòujié　win a battle; score a success: ～归来 return in triumph

奏凯 zòukǎi　win victory; be victorious; triumph

奏鸣曲 zòumíngqǔ　*mus.* sonata: 小～ sonatina

奏鸣曲式 zòumíngqǔshì　*mus.* sonata form

奏疏 zòushū　a memorial to the emperor (or throne)

奏效 zòuxiào　prove effective; be successful; get the desired result: 这个队换用了4-2-4阵式, 这一着果然～。The team changed its formation to a 4-2-4 one, which sure enough proved effective. / 这药服了马上～。This medicine will have immediate efficacy. / 这个办法能～吗? Will this method work?

奏议 zòuyì　① a memorial to the emperor (or throne) ② general name for various memorials to the emperor (or throne)

奏乐 zòuyuè　play music; strike up a tune

奏章 zòuzhāng　a memorial to the emperor (or throne)

奏折 zòuzhé　a memorial to the throne (as written on paper folded in accordion form)

揍 zòu　① *inf.* beat; hit; strike: 把他～一顿 beat him up / 挨～ get a thrashing ② *dial.* smash; break: 他把碗给～了。He smashed the bowl. / 小心别把玻璃～了。Be careful not to break the glass.

zū

租 zū　① rent; hire; charter: ～三间房 rent three rooms / ～一条小船 hire a boat / ～一架飞机 charter a plane ② rent out; let out; lease: 这块地已经～给人了。This piece of land has been leased out. ③ rent: 收～ collect rent ④ land tax

租船 zūchuán　*com.* chartering: ～代理 chartering agent / ～契约 charter party; charter / ～人 charterer / ～市场 chartering market

租佃 zūdiàn　(of a landlord) rent out land to tenants:

～关系 tenancy relationship / ～制度 tenancy system

租户 zūhù ① tenant (of a building or part of it); lessee; leaseholder ② hirer (of a thing)

租价 zūjià rent; rental

租界 zūjiè concession (in former times, a tract of land in a Chinese port or city supposedly on lease to, but actually seized by, an imperialist power and put under its colonial rule); settlement

租借 zūjiè rent; hire; lease: ～人 leaseholder; lessee; tenant; hirer

租借地 zūjièdì leased territory; leasehold

租金 zūjīn rent; rental: 这套房间每月～八元。The rent for this flat is eight *yuan* a month.

租赁 zūlìn rent; lease; hire: ～服装和道具 rent costumes and stage properties / ～合同 contract for lease

租米 zūmǐ (in former times) rice paid as land rent by peasants to landlords

租钱 zūqian *inf.* rent; rental

租让 zūràng lease

租书处 zūshūchù book rental

租税 zūshuì (in former times) land tax and other levies

租用 zūyòng rent; hire; take on lease: ～家具 rent furniture / ～礼堂 hire a hall / ～人 leaseholder; lessee; tenant; hirer

租约 zūyuē lease: ～什么时候到期? When does the lease expire? / 短期～ short term tenancy

租债 zūzhài rent and debt: 逼还～ press for rent and debt payments

租子 zūzi *inf.* land rent; ground rent; rent

zú

足[1] zú ① foot; leg: ～不出户 never go out of one's room; stay indoors / 自首至～ from head to foot ② leg (of certain utensils)

足[2] zú ① enough; ample; sufficient: ～吃～喝 eat and drink to one's satisfaction / 赚～了钱 made plenty of money / 工人们生产劲头很～。The workers are full of drive in their work. ② *adv.* fully; as much as: 路上～～走了两个钟头。The journey took fully two hours. / 从这里到邮局～有二里路。It's a good two *li* from here to the post office. ③ *adv.* (usu. used in the negative) enough; sufficiently: 无～挂齿 not worth mentioning

足本 zúběn an unabridged version (of a novel, etc.)

足秤 zúchèng full measure (by a steelyard)

足尺 zúchǐ full measure (by a rule)

足赤 zúchì pure gold; solid gold

足跟 zúgēn heel

足够 zúgòu enough; ample; sufficient: 有～的时间吗? Is there enough time? / ～用十个月的燃料 sufficient fuel to last ten months / 我们对困难要有～的估计。We must take full account of our difficulties.

足迹 zújì footmark; footprint; track: 雪地上的～ footprints (*or* tracks) in the snow / 祖国各个角落都有地质勘探队员的～。In every corner of our country there are footmarks left by our geological prospectors.

足见 zújiàn it serves to show; one can well perceive: 他的发言内容丰富，～他是作了认真准备的。His speech is substantial, which shows he took great pains to prepare it.

足金 zújīn pure gold; solid gold

足球 zúqiú ① soccer; football: 踢～ play soccer (*or* football) / 美国式～ American football / 英国式～ soccer; association football / ～队 football team; eleven / ～运动员 footballer ② football (the ball used in playing either soccer or American football)

足色 zúsè (of gold or silver) of standard purity

足实 zúshí *dial.* ① sufficient; adequate; ample ② full and round; well-developed; full-grown

足岁 zúsuì actual age

足坛 zútán the football world: ～名将 a football star / ～劲旅 a strong football team

足下 zúxià a polite form of address between friends (used mostly in letters): ～以为如何? I wonder what you think of this.

足以 zúyǐ *adv.* enough; sufficiently: 你的话不～说服她。What you say isn't enough to convince her. / 他游得很快,～通过测试。He swam quickly enough to pass the test. / 他挣的不多,但～应付生活所需。He does not earn a large salary but it is adequate for his needs.

足音 zúyīn (sound of) footsteps: 杂乱的～ hurried footsteps

足银 zúyín pure silver

足月 zúyuè (of a foetus) born after the normal period of gestation; mature

足智多谋 zúzhì-duōmóu wise and full of strategems; wise and resourceful

卒[1] zú ① soldier; private: 士卒 shìzú ② servant: 走卒 zǒuzú ③ pawn, one of the pieces in Chinese chess

卒[2] zú ① finish; end: ～其事 finish the job; wind up the business ② finally; at last: ～底于成 finally achieve success ③ die: 病～ die of illness / ～于1986年 died in 1986
　　——see also cù

卒岁 zúsuì *formal* get through the year: 聊以～ just to tide over the year

卒业 zúyè *formal* graduate; finish a course of study

卒子 zúzi ① *old* rank-and-file soldier ② pawn, one of the pieces in Chinese chess

族 zú ① clan: 合～ all the members of a clan; the whole clan ② a death penalty in ancient China, imposed on an offender and his whole family, or even the families of his mother and wife ③ race; nationality: 汉族 Hànzú ④ a class or group of things with common features: 猫～ the cat tribe / 碱土～ alkaline earth family

族类 zúlèi the same clan

族灭 zúmiè (also 族诛 zúzhū) same as 族 zú[2]

族亲 zúqīn members of a clan; clansmen

族权 zúquán clan authority; clan power

族人 zúrén clansman

族长 zúzhǎng clan elder; the head of a clan

镞 zú *formal* arrowhead: 箭镞 jiànzú

zǔ

阻 zǔ hinder; block; obstruct: 拦阻 lánzǔ / 险阻 xiǎnzǔ

阻碍 zǔ'ài hinder; block; impede: ～交通 block the traffic / 遇到～ meet with obstruction / ～生产力的发展 hinder the development of the productive forces / 他由于缺乏自信而～了事业的发展。He was impeded in his career by a lack of belief in himself.

阻挡 zǔdǎng stop; stem; resist; obstruct: 不可～的历史潮流 an irresistible historical trend / 他要那么干,谁也～不住。You can't stop him from doing that.

阻挡犯规 zǔdǎng fànguī *basketball* blocking

阻断 zǔduàn　stop; obstruct; block

阻遏 zǔ'è　check; stop; hold back; stem

阻隔 zǔgé　separate; cut off: 山川～ be separated by mountains and rivers

阻梗 zǔgěng　*formal* block; obstruct; clog: 交通～。The traffic is held up. *or* There's a traffic jam.

阻击 zǔjī　*mil.* block; check: 我军以一部～南线之敌。Our army used part of its forces to check the enemy coming from the south. / ～战 blocking action / ～阵地 blocking position

阻截 zǔjié　stop; obstruct; bar the way

阻绝 zǔjué　block; obstruct; clog

阻抗 zǔkàng　*elec.* impedance: 反射～ reflected impedance / ～匹配 impedance matching

阻拦 zǔlán　stop; obstruct; bar the way: 他决心要走，我们也不好～。As he was determined to go, we thought it better not to stop him.

阻力 zǔlì　① obstruction; resistance: 改革在这个地区遇到了一些～。The reform programme met with some resistance in that area. / 冲破各种～ break through all kinds of obstructions ② *phys.* resistance; drag: 空气～ air resistance / 迎面～ frontal resistance / 摩擦～ friction drag

阻难 zǔnàn　thwart; obstruct; make things difficult for sb.

阻挠 zǔnáo　obstruct; thwart; stand in the way; put a spoke in sb.'s wheel: 条约的履行受到了～。The execution of the treaty was obstructed. / ～两国关系正常化 stand in the way of the normalization of relations between the two countries

阻尼 zǔní　*phys.* damping: ～器 damper / ～振荡 damped oscillation

阻塞 zǔsè　block; obstruct; clog: 交通～。The traffic is held up. *or* There's a traffic jam. / 脏东西把管子～了。The pipe is clogged with dirt.

阻塞振荡器 zǔsè zhèndàngqì　blocking oscillator

阻抑 zǔyì　prevent; stop; restrain; check

阻雨 zǔyǔ　*formal* be stopped by rain

阻援 zǔyuán　hold off (*or* delay) enemy reinforcements

阻止 zǔzhǐ　prevent; stop; hold back: ～事态的恶化 prevent the situation from deteriorating / 别～他，让他去吧。Don't try to stop him. Let him go. / ～敌军前进 check the enemy's advance / 任何反动势力都不能～人类历史的前进。No force of reaction can arrest the progress of human history.

阻滞 zǔzhì　check; stop; hold back; stem

诅

诅 zǔ　*formal* curse; swear; wish sb. evil

诅骂 zǔmà　curse; swear; abuse; revile

诅咒 zǔzhòu　curse; swear; wish sb. evil; imprecate

组

组 zǔ　① organize; form: 改组 gǎizǔ ② group: 读报～ a newspaper-reading group ③ *m.* set; series; battery: 两～发电机 two generators / 一～邮票 a set of stamps

组胺 zǔ'àn　*chem.* histamine

组编 zǔbiān　put together (material); fit together: 抓住这个主题，把所有的材料～起来，成为一个整体。Keep to the theme; put all relevant material together and work it into a unified, organic whole.

组成 zǔchéng　form; make up; compose: ～新的国务院 form a new State Council / ～统一战线 form a united front / 水的～ the composition of water / 每五个人～一组。Every five persons constitute a group. / 主席团由一百四十八位代表～。The presidium consists of 148 delegates. / 党组织是由无产阶级先进分子～的。The Party organization is composed of the advanced elements of the proletariat.

组成部分 zǔchéng bùfen　component part; component; ingredient

组分 zǔfèn　component part; component

组稿 zǔgǎo　(of editors) commission authors to write on given topics; solicit contributions

组歌 zǔgē　suite of songs

组阁 zǔgé　form (*or* set up, organize) a cabinet

组合 zǔhé　① make up; compose; constitute: 这本集子是由诗、散文和短篇小说三部分～而成的。This collection is made up of three parts: poems, essays and short stories. / 各种政治力量的重新～ a realignment of various political forces ② association; combination: 词组是词的～。A phrase is a group of words. ③ *math.* combination

组合车床 zǔhé chēchuáng　combined lathe

组合家具 zǔhé jiājù　composite furniture; component furniture

组合理论 zǔhé lǐlùn　*math.* combinatorial theory

组合体 zǔhétǐ　*mech.* assembly

组合音响 zǔhé yīnxiǎng　hi-fi stereo component system; hi-fi (set, equipment)

组合钻床 zǔhé zuànchuáng　combination drilling machine

组画 zǔhuà　a series of paintings

组件 zǔjiàn　*elec.* package; module: 微型～ micromodule; module

组建 zǔjiàn　put together (a group); form: ～剧团 put a theatre group together

组接 zǔjiē　*film* montage; film editing

组曲 zǔqǔ　*mus.* suite

组态 zǔtài　*phys.* configuration: 平衡～ configuration of equilibrium

组织 zǔzhī　① organize; form: ～劳力 organize a labour force; organize labour power / ～一个登山队 form a mountaineering team / ～一次座谈 organize a discussion / ～一次演出 get up a performance / 把他们的积极性～到建设祖国的伟大事业中去 enlist their initiative in the great cause of reconstructing the nation / 这篇文章～得很好。This article is well-organized. ② organization; organized system: 党团～ Party and Youth League organizations / 群众～ mass organizations / 给予～处分 take disciplinary measures against a member of an organization / ～条例 organic rules / ～委员 committee member in charge of organizational work / ～委员会 organizing committee / 党的～原则是民主集中制。The organizational principle of the Party is democratic centralism. ③ *text.* weave: 平纹～ plain weave / 斜纹～ twill weave / 缎纹～ satin weave ④ *physiol.* tissue: 神经～ nerve (*or* nervous) tissue

组织胺 zǔzhī'àn　same as 组胺 zǔ'àn

组织法 zǔzhīfǎ　rules of organization; organic law; constituent act

组织关系 zǔzhī guānxi　credentials showing membership in an organization; membership credentials

组织疗法 zǔzhī liáofǎ　tissue therapy; histotherapy

组织生活 zǔzhī shēnghuó　regular activities of an organization

组织学 zǔzhīxué　*physiol.* histology

组织液 zǔzhīyè　*physiol.* tissue fluid

组装 zǔzhuāng　put together; assemble

组字游戏 zǔzì yóuxì　crossword puzzle

祖

祖 zǔ　① grandfather: 祖父 zǔfù ② ancestor: 远祖 yuǎnzǔ ③ founder (of a craft, religious sect, etc.); originator: 鼻祖 bízǔ ④ (Zǔ) a surname

祖辈 zǔbèi　ancestors; forefathers; ancestry

祖本 zǔběn　the first edition (of a block-printed book) or the first rubbing (taken from a stone inscription)

祖妣 zǔbǐ　*formal* one's deceased (paternal) grandmother

祖产 zǔchǎn　property handed down from one's ancestors; ancestral estate

祖传 zǔchuán　handed down from one's ancestors

祖传秘方 zǔchuán mìfāng　a secret prescription handed down in the family from generation to generation

祖代 zǔdài　for generations; from generation to generation: ～务农 have been farmers for generations

祖坟 zǔfén　ancestral grave

祖父 zǔfù　(paternal) grandfather

祖国 zǔguó　one's country; homeland; native land; motherland; fatherland

祖籍 zǔjí　original family home; ancestral home; the land of one's ancestors

祖饯 zǔjiàn　*formal* give a farewell dinner

祖居 zǔjū　① ancestral home ② same as 祖籍 zǔjí ③ have one's ancestral home at; be a native of: ～绍兴 be a native of Shaoxing

祖考 zǔkǎo　*formal* ① one's deceased (paternal) grandfather ② same as 祖先 zǔxiān

祖鲁语 Zǔlǔyǔ　Zulu (language)

祖率 zǔlǜ　*math.* the approximate ratio of the circumference of a circle to its diameter as calculated by Zu Chongzhi (祖冲之, 429–500), i.e. between 3.1415926 and 3.1415927

祖母 zǔmǔ　(paternal) grandmother

祖母绿 zǔmǔlǜ　emerald

祖上 zǔshàng　ancestors; forefathers; forbears

祖师 zǔshī　(also 祖师爷 zǔshīyé) ① the founder of a school of learning, a craft, etc. ② the founder of a sect of Buddhism or Taoism

祖述 zǔshù　follow the example of (former worthies)

祖孙 zǔ-sūn　grandparent and grandchild: ～三代 three generations

祖先 zǔxiān　ancestry; ancestors; forbears; forefathers

祖业 zǔyè　① same as 祖产 zǔchǎn ② ancestors' meritorious achievements

祖遗 zǔyí　inherited from one's ancestors: ～的房产 house property inherited from one's ancestors

祖荫 zǔyìn　*formal* ancestors' protection or blessing

祖茔 zǔyíng　ancestral grave

祖宗 zǔzong　forefathers; ancestry; forbears: ～崇拜 ancestor (or ancestral) worship

祖祖辈辈 zǔzǔbèibèi　for generations; from generation to generation: 我家～都是种地的。Our family have been farmers for generations. or I come from a long line of farmers.

俎 zǔ　① an ancient sacrificial utensil ② a kind of chopping block used in ancient times

俎豆 zǔdòu　① sacrificial vessels; ritual vessels ② *formal* sacrifices

俎上肉 zǔshàngròu　*formal* meat on the chopping block—a helpless victim

zuān

钻(鑽) zuān　① drill; bore: ～孔 drill a hole / ～木取火 drill wood to make fire ② get into; go through; make one's way into: ～进密林深处 go deep into a forest / 火车走这条线得～许多山洞。The train has to pass through quite a few tunnels on this railway line. / 月亮从云缝里～了出来。The moon broke through the clouds. ③ study intensively; dig into: ～书本 dig into books / ～业务 study one's trade; dig into one's job or a subject; work hard to perfect oneself professionally ——see also zuàn

钻刺 zuāncì　*formal* ① ridicule; satirize ② curry favour with sb. in authority for personal gain; secure personal gain

钻狗洞 zuān gǒudòng　worm one's way into a doghole—manoeuvre for advantage; fool around with men or women

钻故纸堆 zuān gùzhǐduī　bury oneself in outdated writings; delve into musty old books

钻劲 zuānjìn　application to studies; studiousness: 科研工作需要～, 不能突击。Scientific research demands close application rather than spurts of effort.

钻空子 zuān kòngzi　avail oneself of loopholes (in a law, contract, etc.); exploit an advantage: 不让对方～ leave no loopholes for the other side to exploit / 被人钻了空子 be taken advantage of; be tricked / 严防坏人～ take strict precautions against giving bad people an opening

钻门子 zuān ménzi　*inf.* jockey for favours; manoeuvre for advantage

钻谋 zuānmóu　use pull to get what one wants

钻牛角尖 zuān niújiǎojiān　(also 钻牛角 zuān niújiǎo) ① take unnecessary pains to study an insignificant or insoluble problem; split hairs ② get into a dead end (or a blind alley)

钻圈 zuānquān　*acrob.* jumping (or plunging) through hoops

钻探 zuāntàn　(exploration) drilling: 海底～ offshore drilling / ～设备 drilling equipment / ～工 driller

钻探机 zuāntànjī　drilling machine

钻天柳 zuāntiānliǔ　lombardy poplar (*Populus nigra* var. *italica*)

钻天杨 zuāntiānyáng　*Chosenia macrolepis*

钻头觅缝 zuāntóu-mìfèng　(also 钻天觅缝 zuāntiān-mìfèng) worm oneself into every crack and crevice—try all possible means: 他想长工资, ～地往上巴结。He wants a rise in his pay, and so he's currying favour with the boss by all possible means.

钻心 zuānxīn　① (of pain, itching, etc.) unbearable: 他感到浑身～的疼。He was seized with sharp pains all over his body. ② sneak in; infiltrate: ～战术 the tactic of taking the fortress from within

钻心虫 zuānxīnchóng　*zool.* borer

钻研 zuānyán　study intensively; dig into: ～国际法 assiduously study international law / ～技术 perfect one's skill; master technique / 努力～业务 endeavour to gain professional proficiency / 她学习物理很～。She is a serious student of physics.

钻营 zuānyíng　curry favour with sb. in authority for personal gain; secure personal gain

蹿 zuān　① jump up ② dash forward: 燕子～天儿。The swallow dashed (or shot) through the air.

zuǎn

缵 zuǎn　inherit

纂[1] zuǎn　*formal* compile; edit: 编纂 biānzuǎn

纂[2](鬘) zuǎn　*dial.* a woman's hair worn in a knot at the nape; bun

纂修 zuǎnxiū　compile; edit

zuàn

钻(鑽) zuàn　① drill; auger: 手摇～ hand

drill; drill ② diamond; jewel: 十九～的手表 a 19-jewel watch ③ bore; drill: 在木头上～个眼 bore a hole in wood ——see also zuān

钻床 zuànchuáng　*mech.*　drilling machine; driller: 龙门～ planer drilling machine

钻杆 zuàngǎn　*petroleum*　drill rod (*or* pipe)

钻机 zuànjī　*petroleum*　(drilling) rig; drilling machine: 安装～ rig up / 拆卸～ rig down / 旋转～ rotary rig

钻戒 zuànjiè　diamond ring

钻井 zuànjǐng　well drilling: 构造～ core drilling / 海洋～ offshore drilling / ～船 oil rig / ～队 drilling crew (*or* team) / ～工人 driller / ～记录 drill log

钻具 zuànjù　*petroleum*　drilling tool; drilling rig

钻模 zuànmú　*mech.*　(drill) jig: 分度～ indexing jig

钻石 zuànshí　① diamond ② jewel (used in a watch)

钻塔 zuàntǎ　*min.*　boring tower; derrick

钻铤 zuàntǐng　*petroleum*　drill collar

钻头 zuàntóu　bit (of a drill): 装上～ brace a bit / 卸下～ break out a bit / 三牙轮～ three cone bit

钻压 zuànyā　*petroleum*　bit pressure; bit weight

赚　zuàn　*dial.*　kid; deceive; hoax ——see also zhuàn

赚弄 zuànnong　*dial.*　deceive; hoax; kid

攥　zuàn　*inf.*　hold; grip; grasp: 手里～着一把斧子 hold an axe in one's hand / ～紧拳头 clench one's fist / 一把～住他的手 clasp him by the hand

zuǐ

咀　zuǐ　a popular form for 嘴 zuǐ ——see also jǔ

嘴　zuǐ　① mouth: 闭上～ keep one's mouth shut / ～上说说而已 pay lip service / 你这张～啊! What a tongue you've got! ② anything shaped or functioning like a mouth: 茶壶～儿 the spout of a teapot / 瓶～儿 the mouth of a bottle

嘴把式 zuǐbǎshì　*dial.*　a person given to idle talk

嘴巴 zuǐbā　① *dial.*　mouth: 张开～。 Open your mouth. ② *inf.*　(usu. used in) 打～ slap sb. in the face; box sb.'s ears / 挨了个～ get a slap in the face

嘴笨 zuǐbèn　inarticulate; clumsy of speech

嘴馋 zuǐchán　fond of good food; greedy; voracious: 他把东西全吃了,他不是饿,是～。He ate all the food. He was not hungry, just greedy. / 他一见有好吃的东西就～。He will start drooling at the sight of good food.

嘴敞 zuǐchǎng　*dial.*　have a loose tongue

嘴唇 zuǐchún　lip: 上(下)～ the upper (lower) lip / 咬着～ bite one's lips

嘴乖 zuǐguāi　*inf.*　(of children) clever and pleasant when speaking to elders: 这小姑娘～,挺逗人喜欢。What a dear little girl, talking so sweetly!

嘴尖 zuǐjiān　① sharp-tongued; cutting in speech: 他这个人～,说的话真刺耳。He's sharp-tongued and what he says is often very biting. ② be choosy about what one eats: 别～了,给你什么你吃什么。Don't be so choosy. Take what you're given.

嘴角 zuǐjiǎo　corners of the mouth: 他～叼着一支烟走了进来。He came in with a cigarette dangling from a corner of his mouth. / 他的～渐渐露出了一丝狡黠的笑意。A slow sly smile was creeping around the corners of his mouth.

嘴紧 zuǐjǐn　tight-lipped; closemouthed

嘴啃泥 zuǐkěnní　fall on one's face: 他脚底一滑,摔了个～。He slipped and fell on his face.

嘴快 zuǐkuài　have a loose tongue: 她～,跟谁都会说。

She has a loose tongue and will tell everybody.

嘴懒 zuǐlǎn　not inclined to talk much

嘴冷 zuǐlěng　*dial.*　blunt: 我这话可有点～,请您原谅。Please excuse me for speaking so bluntly.

嘴脸 zuǐliǎn　*derog.*　face; features; countenance: 一副丑恶～! What a hideous face! / 他那副～真难看。He had a very nasty look on his face. / 社会上各种人物的～被区别得清清楚楚。All sorts of people in society have been clearly shown up for what they are.

嘴皮子 zuǐpízi　*inf. derog.*　lips (of a glib talker): 他那两片～可能说了。He has a ready tongue. *or* He can argue on any side of any question. ——see also 耍嘴皮子 shuǎ zuǐpízi

嘴贫 zuǐpín　(also 嘴频 zuǐpín) loquacious; garrulous

嘴勤 zuǐqín　fond of talking; chatty

嘴软 zuǐruǎn　afraid to speak out: 吃人～。A guest can't speak against his host.

嘴上没毛,办事不牢 zuǐ shàng méi máo, bànshì bù láo　a man too young to grow a beard is not dependable; a man with downy lips is bound to make slips

嘴松 zuǐsōng　have a loose tongue: 性直～ have a candid nature and a loose tongue

嘴碎 zuǐsuì　loquacious; garrulous

嘴损 zuǐsǔn　*dial.*　sharp-tongued; sarcastic

嘴甜 zuǐtián　ingratiating in speech; smooth-tongued; honeymouthed

嘴稳 zuǐwěn　able to keep a secret; discreet in speech

嘴严 zuǐyán　tight-lipped; closemouthed

嘴硬 zuǐyìng　stubborn and reluctant to admit mistakes or defeats: 知道错了,就别～。You know you're wrong, so don't stubbornly insist that you aren't.

嘴直 zuǐzhí　outspoken; plainspoken

嘴子 zuǐzi　① *dial.*　anything shaped or functioning like a mouth: 山～ the tip of a foothill ② *mus.*　mouthpiece (of a wind instrument)

zuì

最　zuì　*adv.*　① (used before an adjective or a verb) most; -est: ～大 the biggest / ～小 the smallest / ～美 the most beautiful / ～不发达国家 the least developed country / ～基本的条件 fundamental prerequisites / 他～不讲道理。He's most unreasonable. / 我～喜欢吃巧克力冰淇淋。I like chocolate ice cream best. ② (used before a noun of locality or a place word) farthest to or nearest (a place): ～上头 farthest to (*or* nearest) the top; at the very top / ～东头 farthest to the east; at the very east end

最初 zuìchū　initial; first: ～阶段 the initial stage / ～的印象 first impressions / ～的计划 the original plan; the first and earliest plan / ～她不想来,后来改变了主意。At first she didn't want to come, but later she changed her mind. / 我～认识他是在1958年。I first got to know him in 1958.

最大公约数 zuìdà gōngyuēshù　*math.*　greatest common divisor

最低 zuìdī　lowest; minimum

最低纲领 zuìdī gānglǐng　minimum programme

最低价格 zuìdī jiàgé　lowest price; bottom price; bedrock price

最多 zuìduō　most; at (the) most; maximum: 哪个学生看的书～? Which of the students has read the most books? / 屋里～不过十个人。There were at most ten people in the room. / 这个礼堂～能容纳一千人。This hall can hold a maximum of one thousand people. / 这所学校学生～的时候有三千人。The school's enrolment at its height reached 3,000. / 我～只能等半个小时。I

can wait half an hour at the longest.

最高 zuìgāo highest; supreme; tallest: ～国家权力机关 the highest organ of state power / 达到～峰 reach the climax (*or* peak); reach a culminating point / 创造历史上～纪录 hit an all-time high / ～年产量 peak annual output / ～权力 supreme power / ～速度 maximum speed / ～限额 ceiling

最高点 zuìgāodiǎn *statistics* peak

最高纲领 zuìgāo gānglǐng maximum programme

最高国务会议 zuìgāo guówù huìyì the Supreme State Conference

最高级 zuìgāojí ① highest; summit: ～会谈 top-level talks; summit talks ② *gram.* the superlative degree

最高级会议 zuìgāojí huìyì summit meeting

最高人民法院 zuìgāo rénmín fǎyuàn supreme people's court

最高统帅 zuìgāo tǒngshuài supreme commander

最高限价 zuìgāo xiànjià ceiling price

最好 zuìhǎo ① best; first-rate: ～的办法 the best way / 质量～ best in quality / ～的干部 first-rate cadres ② had better; it would be best: 你～今天把它搞完。You'd better finish it today. / 我们～在天黑以前赶到目的地。It would be best if we could reach our destination before dark.

最后 zuìhòu final; last; ultimate: ～胜利 final victory / ～解决问题 bring the issue to a final solution; settle the question once and for all / 作～挣扎 make a last-ditch struggle / 坐在～一排 sit in the last row / 他们的建议～被采纳了。Their suggestion was eventually accepted. / ～，我想谈一下学习问题。Lastly, I would like to touch on the problem of study.

最后条款 zuìhòu tiáokuǎn final provisions; final articles

最后通牒 zuìhòu tōngdié ultimatum

最后议定书 zuìhòu yìdìngshū final protocol

最后议事录 zuìhòu yìshìlù *precés-verbal final*

最惠国 zuìhuìguó most-favoured-nation: ～税率 most-favoured-nation rate / ～条款 most-favoured-nation clause

最惠国待遇 zuìhuìguó dàiyù most-favoured-nation (MFN) treatment; MFN trading status: 给以～ accord (a country) most-favoured-nation treatment

最佳 zuìjiā ① *phys.* optimum: ～数 optimum number / ～谐振 optimum resonance ② the best: 提供～服务 provide the best service / ～运动员 the best athlete (*or* player)

最近 zuìjìn ① recently; lately; of late: 我～很忙。I've been very busy recently. / ～几天 in the last few days / ～的消息 the latest news; recent news / ～一期的《英语学习》 the current issue of *English Language Learning* ② in the near future; soon: ～要上演许多新电影。Many new films will be released soon.

最轻量级 zuìqīngliàngjí *sports* bantamweight

最少 zuìshǎo least; at (the) least; minimum: 他做的事～。He did the least work. / 这东西～得五块钱。It costs at least 5 *yuan.* / 票价～也得十块钱。Tickets will cost a minimum of 10 *yuan.*

最为 zuìwéi *adv.* (used before disyllabic adjectives or verbs) most; extremely: ～重要 most (*or* extremely) important / ～可疑 most suspicious

最小二乘法 zuìxiǎo èrchéngfǎ *math.* least square method

最小公倍数 zuìxiǎo gōngbèishù *math.* least (*or* lowest) common multiple

最终 zuìzhōng final; ultimate: ～结果 the final outcome / 党的～目的，是实现共产主义。The ultimate aim of the Party is the realization of communism.

罪（皐）
zuì ① crime; guilt: 贪污～ crimes of corruption / 受贿～ crimes of accepting bribes / ～上

加～ be doubly guilty ② fault; blame: 归罪 guīzuì ③ suffering; pain; hardship: 受罪 shòuzuì ④ put the blame on: 罪己 zuìjǐ

罪案 zuì'àn details of a criminal case; case

罪不容诛 zuì bùróng zhū even death cannot atone for the offence; be guilty of crimes for which even death is insufficient punishment

罪大恶极 zuìdà-èjí be guilty of the most heinous crimes

罪恶 zuì'è crime; evil: ～多端 be guilty of all kinds of evil / ～滔天 be guilty of monstrous crimes

罪恶昭彰 zuì'è zhāozhāng (also 罪恶昭著 zuì'è zhāozhù) have committed flagrant crimes

罪犯 zuìfàn criminal; offender; culprit

罪该万死 zuì gāi wàn sǐ be guilty of a crime for which one deserves to die ten thousand deaths; be guilty of a crime for which even death cannot atone

罪过 zuìguo ① fault; offence; sin: 这是我的～。It's my fault. / 他有什么～要受这样的苦? What sin has he committed to deserve all this? ② *hum.* thanks, but this is really more than I deserve

罪己 zuìjǐ ① bear the blame oneself; take the blame on oneself ② (of a ruler) take the blame for misgovernment or natural calamities: 下～诏 (of a ruler) issue a penitential decree

罪迹 zuìjì crime; guilt; offence

罪咎 zuìjiù fault; offence; error

罪款 zuìkuǎn a list of crimes committed

罪魁 zuìkuí chief criminal (*or* culprit, offender); arch-criminal

罪魁祸首 zuìkuí-huòshǒu chief culprit (*or* offender); arch-criminal

罪戾 zuìlì *formal* sin; crime

罪名 zuìmíng charge; accusation: 偷窃的～ a charge of theft

罪莫大焉 zuì mòdà yān there is no greater crime than this

罪孽 zuìniè wrongdoing that brings retribution; sin: ～深重 sinful

罪愆 zuìqiān *formal* fault; offence; sin

罪情 zuìqíng details of a criminal case; case

罪人 zuìrén guilty person; offender; sinner: 历史～ a person condemned by history

罪刑 zuìxíng crime and punishment

罪行 zuìxíng crime; guilt; offence: 他的～较轻。His offence is a minor one.

罪尤 zuìyóu *formal* fault; offence; sin

罪有应得 zuì yǒu yīng dé one deserves one's punishment; the punishment fits the crime

罪责 zuìzé responsibility for an offence: ～难逃 cannot escape the responsibility for the offence (*or* crime); cannot get away with it

罪证 zuìzhèng evidence of a crime; proof of one's guilt

罪状 zuìzhuàng facts about a crime; charges in an indictment: 反革命分子的～ the crimes of a counterrevolutionary / 党八股的八大～ the eight indictments against stereotyped Party writing (*or* Party jargon)

醉
zuì ① drunk; intoxicated; tipsy: 他喝～了。He's tipsy. *or* He's had a drop too much. ② (of some kinds of food) liquor-saturated; steeped in liquor: ～蟹 liquor-saturated crab / ～虾 wine-soaked shrimp

醉笔 zuìbǐ same as 醉墨 zuìmò

醉步 zuìbù the reeling steps of a drunken man

醉鬼 zuìguǐ drunkard; sot; inebriate

醉汉 zuìhàn drunkard; drunken man

醉红 zuìhóng deep red; crimson: 在秋风里，成排的枫树颤动着～的叶子。There were rows of maple trees with red leaves tremulous in the autumn breeze.

醉酒 zuìjiǔ　drunk; intoxicated: 〜的人犯罪, 应当负刑事责任。An intoxicated person who commits a crime shall bear criminal responsibility. /《贵妃〜》*Drunken Beauty* (an operatic dance drama)

醉猫儿 zuìmāor　drunken cat—a person acting oddly under the influence of liquor

醉墨 zuìmò　painting or calligraphy done under the influence of liquor

醉拳 zuìquán　drunken boxing (a form of boxing with movements suggesting a drunken man reeling along)

醉生梦死 zuìshēng-mèngsǐ　live as if drunk or dreaming; lead a befuddled life

醉态 zuìtài　the state of being drunk; drunkenness

醉翁之意不在酒 zuìwēng zhī yì bù zài jiǔ　the Old Tippler's delight does not reside in wine—have other things in mind; have ulterior motives: 〜, 在乎山水之间也。山水之乐, 得之心而寓之酒也。(欧阳修) The Old Tippler's delight resides not in wine but in the mountains and waters. The joy of mountains and waters he holds in his heart and he finds expression for it in wine.

醉乡 zuìxiāng　a drunken stupor: 沉入〜 fall into a drunken stupor

醉心 zuìxīn　be bent on; be wrapped up in: 他〜于数学的研究。He's deeply engrossed in mathematical research. /〜名利 be infatuated with fame and gain

醉醺醺 zuìxūnxūn　sottish; drunk; tipsy

醉眼 zuìyǎn　*formal* eyes showing the effects of drink: 〜朦胧 drunken and bleary-eyed

醉意 zuìyì　signs or feeling of getting drunk: 他已经有几分〜了。He is a bit tipsy.

---

zūn

尊[1]　zūn　① senior; of a senior generation: 尊长 zūnzhǎng ② respect; venerate; honour: 自尊 zìzūn ③ *honour*. your: 〜夫人 your wife / 〜姓大名? May I know your name? ④ *m.*: 一〜佛像 a statue of a Buddha /五十〜大炮 fifty artillery pieces

尊[2]　zūn　same as 樽 zūn

尊称 zūnchēng　① a respectful form of address; honorific title: "您"是"你"的〜。您(nin) is an honorific form for 你(ni "you"). ② address sb. respectfully: 人们〜他为郭老。People respectfully called him the venerable Guo.

尊崇 zūnchóng　worship; revere; venerate

尊甫 zūnfǔ　*formal honor*. your father

尊府 zūnfǔ　① *honor*. your residence; your home ② *formal honor*. your father

尊公 zūngōng　*formal honor*. ① your father ② you

尊贵 zūnguì　honourable; respectable; respected: 〜的客人 an honoured guest

尊号 zūnhào　a respectful title conferred on an emperor or empress

尊驾 zūnjià　*honor*. you: 恭候〜光临。We request the pleasure of your company.

尊敬 zūnjìng　respect; honour; esteem: 我们都非常〜他。We have the greatest esteem for him. /〜父母 honour one's parents /〜的来宾们 Distinguished Guests (a form of address)

尊命 zūnmìng　*honor*. your instructions

尊亲 zūnqīn　one's senior relatives

尊荣 zūnróng　rank and honour

尊容 zūnróng　distinguished face (usu. used ironically): 瞧他那副〜, 还打扮呢! What a face he's got, and he pays so much attention to dress.

尊尚 zūnshàng　uphold; advocate

尊师爱生 zūnshī-àishēng　respect the teacher and love the student; students respecting teachers and teachers loving students

尊师重道 zūnshī-zhòngdào　honour the teacher and revere his teachings

尊堂 zūntáng　*formal honor*. your mother

尊翁 zūnwēng　*formal honor*. your father

尊严 zūnyán　dignity; honour: 国家〜 national dignity /维护法律的〜 guard the sanctity of the law

尊意 zūnyì　*honor*. your opinion: 不知〜如何? I'd like to hear your opinion.

尊长 zūnzhǎng　elders and betters

尊重 zūnzhòng　① respect; value; esteem: 互相〜 respect each other /〜少数民族的风俗习惯 respect the habits and customs of the minority nationalities /〜群众的首创精神 value the initiative of the masses /〜科学 have a high regard for science /这位老教师很受人们的热爱和〜。The old teacher was much loved and esteemed. ② serious; proper: 放〜些! Behave yourself!

遵　zūn　abide by; obey; observe; follow: 〜纪爱民 observe discipline and cherish the people /〜医嘱 follow the doctor's advice

遵办 zūnbàn　act in compliance with instructions

遵从 zūncóng　defer to; comply with; follow: 〜上级的指示 in compliance with the directives of the leadership /〜全国人民的愿望 in deference to the desire of the people of the whole country /〜老师的教导 follow the teacher's advice

遵奉 zūnfèng　*formal* act on; follow

遵命 zūnmìng　*pol.* comply with your wish; obey your command: 〜办理 act in compliance with your instructions /给我弄两张音乐会的票。——〜。Get me two tickets for the concert.—Whatever you say.

遵守 zūnshǒu　observe; abide by; comply with: 〜劳动纪律 observe labour discipline /〜公共秩序 observe public order /〜时间 be on time; be punctual /〜法律 abide by the law /〜并执行协议 comply with and carry out the agreement /〜交通规则 observe traffic regulations /〜规章制度 abide by rules and regulations

遵行 zūnxíng　act on; follow: 〜一贯的原则 act according to one's consistent principles

遵循 zūnxún　follow; abide by; adhere to: 〜和平共处的原则 follow the principle of peaceful coexistence /制定一个章程, 使大家有所〜 work out a set of rules so that people will have something to go by

遵依 zūnyī　obey; conform to; comply with; act in accordance with

遵义会议 Zūnyì Huìyì　the Zunyi Meeting (the historic meeting in Zunyi, Guizhou Province, held in January 1935, which put an end to the domination of the "Left" opportunist line in the Party Central Committee and established Chairman Mao's leadership in the whole Party)

遵照 zūnzhào　obey; conform to; comply with; act in accordance with: 〜上级的命令 in obedience to orders from above /〜党中央制定的政策办事 act in accordance with the policies formulated by the Party Central Committee

樽（罇）　zūn　a kind of wine vessel used in ancient times

鳟　zūn　trout

---

zǔn

撙　zǔn　save: 每月〜下一些钱 save some money

every month

撙节 zǔnjié　retrench; practise economy: 〜开支 retrench; cut down expenses

zuō

作 zuō　workshop: 木工〜 carpenters' workshop / 洗衣〜 laundry ——see also zuó; zuò

作场 zuōchǎng　*dial.* workshop

作坊 zuōfang　workshop: 生产纺织品的〜 a workshop for manufacturing textiles

嘬 zuō　*inf.* suck: 小孩儿〜奶。The baby is sucking its mother's breast.

嘬瘪子 zuō biězi　*dial.* feel embarrassed; be nonplussed

嘬牙花子 zuō yáhuāzi　*dial.* be at a loss what to do; feel quite helpless

zuó

作 zuó　same as 作 zuò, limited to use in the following entry words ——see also zuō; zuò

作践 zuójian　*inf.* ① spoil; waste: 〜东西 spoil things ② run sb. down; disparage: 他这不是故意〜人吗? Didn't he say that just to run me down? ③ humiliate; insult

作料 zuóliao　condiments; seasoning

作兴 zuó·xīng　*dial.* ① (usu. used in the negative) there's reason to; it's justifiable (*or* permissible) to: 可不〜骂人。It's not right to swear at people. ② perhaps; possibly; maybe: 〜要下雨。Maybe it's going to rain.

昨 zuó　① yesterday: 昨天 zuótiān ② the past: 昨非 zuófēi

昨儿 zuór　(also 昨儿个 zuórge) *inf.* yesterday: 〜晚上 yesterday evening; last night

昨非 zuófēi　*formal* past mistakes

昨日 zuórì　yesterday

昨天 zuótiān　yesterday

昨晚 zuówǎn　yesterday evening; last night

昨叶荷草 zuóyèhécǎo　same as 瓦松 wǎsōng

昨夜 zuóyè　yesterday evening; last night

捽 zuó　*dial.* seize; grasp: 小孩儿〜住妈妈的衣服。The child held tightly to his mother's dress.

琢 zuó　see below ——see also zhuó

琢磨 zuómo　think over; turn over in one's mind; ponder: 你〜〜。You think it over. / 〜问题 turn a problem over in one's mind / 〜出个办法 figure out a way (to do sth.) / 这件事她〜了很久。She pondered over the matter for a long time. / 他的用意何在, 我正在〜。I'm trying to figure out what he's driving at. ——see also zhuómó

zuǒ

左 zuǒ　① the left side; the left: 〜上方 the upper left / 〜转弯 turn to the left; turn left ② east: 山〜 areas east of the Taihang Mountains, specifically Shandong Province ③ the Left: 凡有人群的地方, 都有〜、中、

右。Wherever there are masses of people they are invariably divided into the Left, the middle and the Right. ④ queer; unorthodox; heretical: 左脾气 zuǒpíqi ⑤ wrong; incorrect: 你想〜了。You're not thinking in the right way. *or* You've got a wrong idea. ⑥ different; contrary; opposite: 相左 xiāngzuǒ ⑦ (Zuǒ) a surname

左膀右臂 zuǒbǎng-yòubì　right-hand man; a capable assistant

左边锋 zuǒbiānfēng　*football* outside left; left wing

左边 zuǒbian　the left; the left (*or* left-hand) side: 房子〜有一棵榆树。There's an elm tree on the left of the house.

左不过 zuǒbuguò　*adv.* ① anyway; anyhow; in any event: 他说来说去, 〜是这么个意思。He put it this way and that, but anyway that's what it boils down to. ② only; merely; just: 你怎么啦?—没什么, 〜有点头痛。What's the matter with you?—Nothing serious. Just a slight headache.

左侧 zuǒcè　same as 左边 zuǒbian

左道旁门 zuǒdào-pángmén　① heretical sect; heterodox school ② heresy; heterodoxy

左舵 zuǒduò　left standard rudder; left rudder: 〜十度! Port 10 degrees!

左锋 zuǒfēng　*basketball* left forward

左顾右盼 zuǒgù-yòupàn　glance right and left; look around: 他〜, 像是在找人。Casting glances here and there, he seemed to be looking for somebody.

左后卫 zuǒhòuwèi　*football* left back

左强 zuǒjiàng　*old* cantankerous; crotchety

左近 zuǒjìn　in the vicinity (*or* neighbourhood); nearby: 〜有邮局吗? Is there a post office in the vicinity? / 他就住在〜。He lives nearby.

左邻右舍 zuǒlín-yòushè　neighbours

左轮 zuǒlún　revolver

左面 zuǒmiàn　the left (*or* left-hand) side; the left

左内锋 zuǒnèifēng　*football* inside left

左派 zuǒpài　① the Left; the left wing: 〜势力 Left forces; forces of the Left ② Leftist

左脾气 zuǒpíqi　have a queer temperament

左撇子 zuǒpiězi　left-handed person; left-hander; lefty

左迁 zuǒqiān　*formal* demote

左前卫 zuǒqiánwèi　*football* left halfback; left half

左倾 zuǒqīng　left-leaning; progressive; inclined towards the revolution

"左"倾 zuǒqīng　"Left" deviation: 〜空谈 "Left" phrase-mongering / 〜机会主义 "Left" opportunism / 〜冒险主义 "Left" adventurism

左券 zuǒquàn　see 稳操左券 wěn cāo zuǒquàn

左嗓子 zuǒsǎngzi　① sing out of key ② a person who sings out of key

左手 zuǒshǒu　① the left hand ② same as 左首 zuǒshǒu

左首 zuǒshǒu　the left-hand side; the left: 坐在我的〜 sit on my left

左思右想 zuǒsī-yòuxiǎng　think over from different angles; turn sth. over in one's mind: 她躺在床上〜, 一夜也没合眼。She lay awake all night, thinking the matter over and over again.

左袒 zuǒtǎn　*formal* take sides with; be partial to

左提右挈 zuǒtí-yòuqiè　① help each other; give mutual help ② guide and support; give guidance and help to

左舷 zuǒxián　port (of a ship)

左性 zuǒxing　(also 左性子 zuǒxìngzi) stubborn; pigheaded; wilful

左旋糖 zuǒxuántáng　another name for 果糖 guǒtáng

左翼 zuǒyì　① *mil.* left wing; left flank ② the left wing; the Left: 〜分子 Leftist; Left-winger / 〜文艺运动 the Left-wing movement in literature and art

左翼作家联盟 Zuǒyì Zuòjiā Liánméng　the League of Lef-

tist Writers (organized in 1930)

左右 zuǒyòu ① the left and right sides: 主席台～, 红旗迎风飘扬. Red flags are fluttering on both sides of the rostrum. / ～摇摆 vacillate now to the left and now to the right ② (used after a numeral) about; or so: 八点钟～ around eight o'clock / 一个月～ a month or so / 价值十元～. It's worth about 10 *yuan*. / 身高一米七～ be about 1.70 metres in height ③ master; control; influence: ～局势 be master of the situation / 为人所～ be controlled by sb.; fall under sb.'s influence / 他这个人不是别人能～得了的. He is not a man who can be influenced by others. ④ those in close attendance; retinue: 屏退～ order one's attendants to clear out ⑤ *adv. dial.* anyway; anyhow; in any case: 我～闲着没事, 就陪你走一趟吧. Anyway I'm free now. Let me go with you.

左…右… zuǒ…yòu… over and over again: 左劝右劝 try again and again to persuade sb. / 左一条清规, 右一条戒律 one taboo after another / 左一趟右一趟地去请他 go several times to invite him

左右逢源 zuǒ-yòu féng yuán ① be able to achieve success one way or another ② gain advantage from both sides

左右开弓 zuǒ-yòu kāi gōng shoot first with one hand, then with the other; use both hands alternately in quick succession; be ambidextrous: ～连续抽打 attack with a volley of forehand and backhand smashes / ～打人嘴巴 slap sb. on both cheeks

左右手 zuǒyòushǒu right-hand man: a capable assistant

左右袒 zuǒyòutǎn take sides with; be partial to: 不为～ refuse to take sides; remain neutral

左右为难 zuǒ-yòu wéinán in a dilemma; in an awkward predicament: 我想去看看她, 可是不是时候. 不去吧, 又不放心. 真是～. I'd like to go and see her myself, though it isn't an appropriate time. But I'll never stop worrying if I don't go. It really is difficult to decide what to do for the best.

左证 zuǒzhèng evidence; proof

左支右绌 zuǒzhī-yòuchù find it hard to cover expenses; be in straitened circumstances; have too many problems to cope with

佐

佐 zuǒ ① assist: 辅佐 fǔzuǒ ② assistant: 僚佐 liáozuǒ

佐餐 zuǒcān be eaten together with rice or bread; go with rice or bread

佐酒 zuǒjiǔ *formal* ① drink with sb. ② (of food) go with wine: ～佳肴 delicacies that go with wine

佐理 zuǒlǐ assist sb. with a task

佐料 zuǒliào same as 作料 zuóliao

佐命 zuǒmìng *formal* an aid to the founder of a dynasty

佐药 zuǒyào *med.* adjuvant

佐证 zuǒzhèng same as 左证 zuǒzhèng

撮

撮 zuǒ *m.* (for hair) tuft: 一～黑毛 a tuft of black hair / 一～山羊胡子 a goatee ——see also cuō

撮子 zuǒzi *inf.* tuft (of hair): 剪下一～头发 cut off a tuft of hair

zuò

坐

坐 zuò ① sit: 请～. Please sit down. / 请进来～～. Please come in and sit for a while. / 我愿意站着, 你～下吧. I like to stand, you sit down. / 他忽然～起来了. He sat up suddenly. ② travel by or on (any conveyance except those which one straddles): ～火车

(公共汽车) ride on a train (bus) / ～火车 (公共汽车) 去 go by train (bus) / ～电梯上去 go up by lift / 进来～～. Come in and sit down for a while. ③ (of a building) have its back towards: 这所房子～北朝南. This house faces south. ④ put (a pan, pot, kettle, etc.) on a fire: 把壶～上 put the kettle on (the fire) ⑤ same as 座① zuò ⑥ (of a building) sink; subside: 这个房子向后～了. This house is beginning to slope backwards. ⑦ (of rifles, guns, etc.) recoil; kick back: 坐力 zuòlì ⑧ bear; fruit: 坐果 zuòguǒ ⑨ be punished: 反坐 fǎnzuò ⑩ *formal* because; for the reason that: ～此解职 be dismissed on this account

坐班 zuòbān keep office hours

坐标 zuòbiāo *math.* coordinate: ～轴 coordinate axis

坐不下 zuòbuxià (of a vehicle, table, room, etc.) have not enough seats for (a certain number of people); cannot seat: 这车～这么多人. This car can't seat so many people.

坐不住 zuòbuzhù cannot sit still; be restless; fidget: 我们一听说有新任务, 就～了. When we learnt that we'd been given a new task, we just couldn't sit still any longer. / 大伙儿听他讲了三个小时都～了. After listening to him for three hours they became restless.

坐草 zuòcǎo *formal* confinement in childbirth; lying-in

坐禅 zuòchán *Buddhism* sit in meditation

坐场诗 zuòchǎngshī same as 定场诗 dìngchǎngshī

坐吃山空 zuò chī shān kōng if left to sit idle, one can even consume a mountain; sit idle and eat, and in time your whole fortune will be used up

坐次 zuòcì order of seats; seating arrangements

坐大 zuòdà *formal* (of localist forces, etc.) be left to grow strong and insubordinate

坐待 zuòdài sit back and wait

坐得下 zuòdexià (of a vehicle, table, room, etc.) have seats for (a certain number of people); seat: 这车～四十五人. This bus seats 45 people. / 这桌子～八人. This table seats eight.

坐得住 zuòdezhù can sit still; can sit for long: 大伙儿都出去玩儿了, 你还～啊? How can you sit in here when everybody is out playing? / 她～, 当编辑挺合适. She has sedentary habits; she is fit to be an editor.

坐等 zuòděng sit back and wait: ～胜利 sit back waiting for victory with folded arms

坐地分赃 zuò dì fēn zāng (of a ringleader, criminal, receiver of stolen goods, etc.) take a share of the spoils without participating in the robbery

坐地虎 zuòdìhǔ local tyrant (*or* despot)

坐垫 zuòdiàn cushion

坐定[1] zuòdìng take a seat; be seated

坐定[2] zuòdìng *dial.* be destined; be doomed

坐而论道 zuò ér lùn dào sit back and pontificate

坐根儿 zuògēnr *dial.* at all; simply

坐骨 zuògǔ ischium

坐骨神经 zuògǔ shénjīng sciatic nerve: ～痛 sciatica

坐观成败 zuò guān chéng-bài wait to see what will come of another's venture; look on coldly; be a mere onlooker

坐馆 zuòguǎn *old* ① be a private tutor ② be a *yamen* clerk

坐果 zuòguǒ bear fruit; fructify

坐化 zuòhuà (of Buddhist monks) pass away (*or* die) in a sitting posture

坐家女 zuòjiānǚ *dial.* an unmarried woman

坐监 zuòjiān (also 坐监狱 zuò jiānyù) be in prison; be in jail; be imprisoned

坐劲[1] zuòjìn give strong support; back up; bolster and pep up

坐劲[2] zuòjìn recoil (of a gun); kick: 这枝步枪的～儿不

小。 This rifle has a terrible kick.

坐禁闭 zuò jìnbì　be placed in confinement (as a disciplinary measure)

坐井观天 zuò jǐng guān tiān　look at the sky from the bottom of a well—have a very narrow view

坐具 zuòjù　a thing to sit on; seat

坐科 zuòkē　undergo professional training at an old-type opera school

坐困 zuòkùn　be confined; be walled in; be shut up: ~金陵一年余 be confined within the walls of Jinling city for over a year

坐困愁城 zuòkùn chóuchéng　be walled in by one's own worries

坐蜡 zuòlà　dial.　be in trouble; be on the spot

坐牢 zuòláo　be in prison; be in jail; be imprisoned: 他坐了三年牢。 He's been in prison for three years.

坐冷板凳 zuò lěngbǎndèng　sit on a cold bench—hold an unimportant post and be neglected; be kept waiting for an assignment or an audience with a VIP

坐力 zuòlì　recoil (of a gun); kick

坐立不安 zuò-lì bù ān　feel uneasy whether sitting or standing; be fidgety; be on tenterhooks: [关]公退，寻思去计，~《三国演义》 Guan Yu withdrew feeling that he must evolve some scheme of departure without further loss of time. It caused him much uneasiness.

坐落 zuòluò　(of a building) be situated; be located: 我们工厂~在山脚下。 Our factory is located at the foot of a hill.

坐骑 zuòqí　saddle horse; mount

坐蓐 zuòrù　formal　confinement in childbirth; lying-in

坐山雕 zuòshāndiāo　zool.　cinereous vulture

坐山观虎斗 zuò shān guān hǔ dòu　sit on top of the mountain to watch the tigers fight—watch in safety while others fight, then reap the spoils when both sides are exhausted

坐商 zuòshāng　tradesman; shopkeeper

坐失良机 zuò shī liángjī　let slip a golden opportunity; lose a good chance

坐实 zuòshí　① clear and definite ② confirm; substantiate

坐食 zuòshí　formal　sit idle and eat; be a parasite

坐视 zuòshì　sit by and watch; sit tight and look on: ~不理 sit by idly and remain indifferent

坐视不救 zuòshì bù jiù　sit back and watch without going to the rescue: 奈关公是吾叔父，安忍坐视而不救乎?《三国演义》 But Guan Yu is my uncle, and I cannot bear to sit still and not try to save him. / 既蜀中危急，孤岂可~?《三国演义》 The land of Shu being in danger, I cannot sit and look on unconcerned.

坐收渔利 zuò shōu yúlì　(also 坐收渔人之利 zuò shōu yúrén zhī lì) reap the spoils of victory without lifting a finger; profit from others' conflict; reap thirdparty profit ——see also 鹬蚌相争, 渔翁得利 yù bàng xiāng zhēng, yúwēng dé lì

坐守 zuòshǒu　defend tenaciously; be firmly entrenched in

坐索 zuòsuǒ　(also 坐讨 zuòtǎo) stay at sb.'s house demanding payment of a debt

坐探 zuòtàn　an enemy agent planted within one's own ranks

坐桶 zuòtǒng　nightstool; closestool; commode

坐位 zuòwei　① a place to sit; seat: 留几个~ reserve some seats / 排~ make seating arrangements / 回到你的~上去。 Go back to your place. ② a thing to sit on; seat: 给我搬个~儿来。 Get (or Fetch, Bring) me a seat.

坐卧不宁 zuò-wò bù níng　(also 坐卧不安 zuò-wò bù'ān) be unable to sit down or sleep at ease; feel restless; be on tenterhooks

坐误 zuòwù　let slip (an opportunity): 因循坐误 yīnxún

坐席 zuòxí　① take one's seat at a banquet table ② attend a banquet

坐享其成 zuò xiǎng qí chéng　sit idle and enjoy the fruits of others' work; reap where one has not sown

坐药 zuòyào　Chin. med.　suppository

坐以待毙 zuò yǐ dài bì　sit still waiting for death; await one's doom; resign oneself to death: 与其~, 不如先下手打他个措手不及。 It is better for us to go into action now and take the enemy by surprise, rather than wait passively until the enemy comes and seizes us.

坐以待旦 zuò yǐ dài dàn　sit up and wait for daybreak

坐月子 zuòyuèzi　inf.　confinement in childbirth; lying-in

坐赃 zuòzāng　dial.　plant stolen or banned goods on sb.

坐镇 zuòzhèn　(of a commander) personally attend to garrison duty; assume personal command

坐庄 zuòzhuāng　① be a resident buyer of a business firm ② be the banker or dealer (in a gambling game)

坐罪 zuòzuì　formal　pass sentence; condemn

作

作 zuò　① rise; grow: 枪声大~。 Heavy firing broke out. ② write; compose: ~诗 compose a poem / ~书一封 write a letter / ~画 paint a picture ③ writings; work: 新~ a new work / 成功之~ a successful work ④ pretend; affect: 故~怒容 pretend to be angry ⑤ regard as; take sb. or sth. for: 看作 kànzuò / 作废 zuòfèi ⑥ feel; have: 作呕 zuò'ǒu ——see also zuō; zuó

作案 zuò'àn　commit a crime or an offence: ~时被捕 be caught in the act; be caught red-handed

作罢 zuòbà　drop; relinquish; give up: 双方意见不一, 事情只好~。 Since the two sides couldn't agree, the matter had to be dropped.

作保 zuòbǎo　be sb.'s guarantor; go bail for sb.; sponsor sb.

作弊 zuòbì　practise fraud; cheat; indulge in corrupt practices

作壁上观 zuò bìshàngguān　watch the fighting from the ramparts—sit by and watch; be an onlooker (or bystander)

作别 zuòbié　formal　bid farewell; take one's leave: 与亲友~ take leave of one's relatives and friends

作瘪子 zuò biězi　same as 嘬瘪子 zuō biězi

作成 zuòchéng　dial.　help (sb. to achieve his or her aim)

作词 zuòcí　write words (for a song): 李红~ words by Li Hong

作大 zuòdà　same as 做大 zuòdà

作抖 zuòdǒu　dial.　shiver; shake; tremble

作对 zuòduì　① set oneself against; oppose: 他没有理由和你~。 He has no reason to oppose you. ② pair off in marriage

作恶 zuò'è　do evil: ~多端 do all kinds of evil; be steeped in iniquity ② formal　gloomy; melancholy

作伐 zuòfá　formal　act as matchmaker

作法¹ zuòfǎ　exercise magic

作法² zuòfǎ　① way of doing things; course of action; practice: 习惯~ a habitual practice / 这种~已经很普遍了。 This has become a common practice. / 他现在的~是行不通的。 His present course of action will get him nowhere. ② technique of writing: 文章~ technique of writing; art of composition

作法自毙 zuò fǎ zì bì　make a law only to fall foul of it oneself; be hoist with one's own petard; get caught in one's own trap

作废 zuòfèi　become invalid: 声明~ declare invalid / 宣布条约~ declare a treaty null and void

作风 zuòfēng　style; style of work; way: 工作~ style of

work / ～正派 be honest and upright in one's ways; have moral integrity / 资产阶级生活～ bourgeois way of life; bourgeois life-style / 推广民主～ develop a democratic style of work / 实事求是的～ a practical and realistic way of doing things / 永远保持艰苦奋斗的～ always keep to the style of hard struggle and plain living

作复 zuòfù write in reply; write back: 迟未～ have not been able to reply sooner

作梗 zuògěng obstruct; hinder; create difficulties

作古 zuògǔ *formal euph.* die; pass away

作怪 zuòguài do mischief; make trouble: 保守思想在他们头脑中～。Conservative ideas are doing mischief in their minds.

作害 zuò·hài (of birds and beasts) damage (crops, etc.); make havoc of

作耗 zuòhào *dial.* make trouble; create a disturbance

作合 zuòhé make a match; act as go-between

作家 zuòjiā writer; author: 巴金是中国的著名～。Ba Jin is a famous Chinese writer. / 多产～ a prolific writer (*or* author)

作家协会 Zuòjiā Xiéhuì the Writers' Union

作假 zuòjiǎ ① counterfeit; falsify ② cheat; play tricks ③ behave affectedly

作价 zuòjià fix a price for sth.; evaluate: 合理～, 公平交易 fair pricing and square dealing / 旧水泵～五百元 appraise the old pump at 500 *yuan*

作奸犯科 zuòjiān-fànkē violate the law and commit crimes; commit offences against law and discipline

作茧自缚 zuò jiǎn zì fù spin a cocoon around oneself; get enmeshed in a web of one's own spinning

作件 zuòjiàn workpiece; work

作劲 zuòjìn *dial.* ① exert all one's strength: ～干活儿 work hard ② support; back up; bolster up

作客 zuòkè *formal* sojourn: ～他乡 sojourn in a strange land

作客思想 zuòkè sīxiǎng feeling of not belonging; guest mentality

作困兽斗 zuò kùnshòu dòu fight like a cornered beast; fight back at bay

作乐 zuòlè make merry; enjoy oneself; have a good time ——see also zuòyuè

作冷 zuòlěng feel a chill

作脸 zuòliǎn *dial.* win honour (*or* glory) for; try to make a good showing

作乱 zuòluàn stage an armed rebellion

作美 zuòměi (usu. used in the negative) (of weather, etc.) help; cooperate; make things easy for sb.: 天公不作美 tiāngōng bù zuòměi

作幕 zuòmù be an assistant to a ranking official or general in old China

作难 zuònán ① feel embarrassed; feel awkward; find oneself in a predicament ② make things difficult for sb.

作难 zuònàn *formal* start a revolt; rise in revolt

作鸟兽散 zuò niǎo-shòu sàn scatter like birds and beasts; flee helter-skelter; stampede

作孽 zuòniè do evil; commit a sin

作弄 zuònòng tease; make a fool of; play a trick on; poke fun at

作呕 zuò'ǒu feel sick; feel like vomiting; be overcome by nausea

作派 zuò·pài ① same as 做功 zuògōng ② manner; style; way

作陪 zuòpéi help entertain the guest of honour; be invited along with the chief guest

作品 zuòpǐn works (of literature and art)

作畦 zuòqí *agric.* bedding: ～机 bedder

作情 zuòqíng *dial.* ① admire ② send gifts; make a

gift of sth. ③ mediate; arbitrate ④ feel grateful to sb.; appreciate the kindness ⑤ be affected or pretentious; strike a pose

作曲 zuòqǔ ① write music; compose: 莫扎特五岁就开始～了。Mozart began to compose when he was five years old. ② write music (for a song): 王芳～ music by Wang Fang

作曲家 zuòqǔjiā composer

作人 zuòrén ① act as becomes a man; get along with other people; conduct oneself ② *formal* rear people; nurture talent

作如是观 zuò rúshì guān view the matter in this light

作色 zuòsè show signs of anger; get worked up: 愤然～ flush with indignation

作势 zuòshì assume a posture; attitudinize

作手 zuòshǒu *formal* writer

作数 zuòshù count; be valid: 怎么昨天说的, 今天就不～了? How is it that what you said yesterday no longer counts today? / 那条旧规定不～了。That old rule doesn't hold any longer. / 他讲的话作得了数。What he says counts.

作耍 zuòshuǎ *dial.* ① make fun of; play tricks on; tease; kid ② joke: 这种事不是～的。This is no joking matter (*or* no joke).

作死 zuòsǐ seek death; take the road to ruin; look for trouble: 天这么冷不穿棉衣, 你～呀! Are you tired of life that you don't wear padded clothes in such cold weather?

作速 zuòsù lose no time; hasten: ～处理 deal with the matter as soon as possible; settle the matter quickly

作算 zuòsuàn *dial.* ① even; even if; even though ② count; hold; stand

作祟 zuòsuì ① (of ghosts, spirits, etc.) haunt ② make mischief; cause trouble; exercise evil influence: 这都是利己主义在～。All this trouble is caused by selfishness.

作态 zuòtài pose; affect; strike an attitude: 忸怩作态 niǔní zuòtài

作田 zuòtián *dial.* till (*or* cultivate) land; go in for farming

作痛 zuòtòng have a pain; ache: 周身的筋骨隐隐～ feel a dull pain all over

作威作福 zuòwēi-zuòfú tyrannically abuse one's power; ride roughshod over others; act like a tyrant: 骑在人民头上～ ride roughshod over the people; lord it over the people

作为[1] zuòwéi ① conduct; deed; action: 从他的～可以看出他的态度。From his deeds we can discern his attitude. ② accomplishment; achievement: 这位新经理很有～。The new manager is a dynamic and able man. ③ scope for one's abilities or talents: 大有作为 dà yǒu zuòwéi

作为[2] zuòwéi ① regard as; look on as; take as: 把他～靠山 look on him as a prop / 把那个～借口 use it as an excuse ② in the capacity, character, or role of; as: ～你的朋友, 我得劝劝你。As your friend, I have to give you some advice. / 你～领导, 就要以身作则。As a leader, you should set a good example to the others.

作伪 zuòwěi fake (works of art, cultural relics, etc.); make an imitation; forge

作文 zuòwén ① (of students) write a composition ② composition

作文章 zuò wénzhāng same as 做文章 zuò wénzhāng

作务 zuòwù *dial.* take care of; manage; look after

作物 zuòwù crop: 高产～ high-yield crops; highly productive crop

作息 zuò-xī work and rest: 按时～ work and rest according to schedule

作息时间表 zuò-xī shíjiānbiǎo daily schedule; work

schedule; timetable

作响 zuòxiǎng make a sound: 大车在路上辘辘～。The cart rumbled on the road. / 风吹树叶沙沙～。The leaves rustled in the wind.

作想 zuòxiǎng *dial.* think over; consider

作学问 zuò xuéwèn same as 做学问 zuò xuéwèn

作痒 zuòyǎng have an itch; itch: 头皮～ have an itch in one's scalp / 全身～ itch (*or* feel itchy) all over

作业 zuòyè ① school assignment: 做～ do one's assignment / 改～ correct students' papers ② work; task; operation; production: 水下～ underwater operation / 野外～ fieldwork; field operation / 农业主要～机械化 mechanization in all major processes of farm work / ～班 work team / ～计划 production plan / ～区 operation area / ～线 production line

作揖 zuòyī make a slight bow with hands folded in front

作艺 zuòyì *old* (of artists) perform; put on a show

作俑 zuòyǒng *formal* create a bad precedent ——see also 始作俑者 shǐ zuòyǒng zhě

作用 zuòyòng ① act on; affect: 外界事物～于我们的感官,在我们的头脑中形成印象。External things act on our sense organs and give rise to impressions in our brains. ② action; function: 化学～ chemical action / 心脏的～ the function of the heart ③ effect: 起～ be effective / 起积极～ play a positive role / 不起～ be ineffective; won't work ④ purpose; intention; motive: 他说那句话有什么～? What was his purpose in saying that? / 他那样说是有他的～的。He had an axe to grind when he said that.

作用力 zuòyònglì *phys.* acting force

作乐 zuòyuè *formal* play music ——see also zuòlè

作战 zuòzhàn fight; conduct operations; do battle: 英勇～ fight heroically / 大规模～ conduct large-scale operations / 积极对敌～ active warfare against the enemy / ～部队 combat (*or* fighting) troops / ～部署 operational preparations / ～地图 battle map; operation map / ～方案 battle plan; line of action / ～方法 method of fighting; tactics in operations / ～方式 mode of operations / ～方针 concept of operations; operational principles; operational policy / ～基地 operational base; base of operations / ～技术 fighting technique / ～命令 combat (*or* operation) order / ～区域 theatre of war / ～线 battle line / ～效能 fighting efficiency / ～指挥部 operational headquarters

作者 zuòzhě author; writer:《儒林外史》的～是吴敬梓。Wu Jingzi was the author of *The Scholars*. / ～赠 From the author / ～不详 by an anonymous author; authorship unknown / 本文～ the present writer

作证 zuòzhèng ① be used as evidence ② testify; give evidence; bear witness: 在法庭上～ bear witness in a lawcourt

作中 zuòzhōng act as an intermediary; be a middleman

作准 zuòzhǔn ① same as 作数 zuòshù ② valid; authentic: ～文本 authentic text

怍 zuò *formal* ashamed: ～色 blush of shame

祚 zuò *formal* ① blessing ② throne

柞 zuò common name for 栎 ——see also zhà

柞蚕 zuòcán tussah

柞蚕丝 zuòcánsī tussah silk

柞栎 zuòlì *bot.* toothed oak

柞丝绸 zuòsīchóu tussah silk; pongee

胙 zuò sacrificial meat (in ancient times)

座[1]（坐） zuò seat; place: 这个剧场有五千个～儿。The theatre seats 5,000.

座[2] zuò ① stand; pedestal; base: 花瓶～儿 vase stand / 塑像～儿 pedestal for a statue ② *astron.* constellation: 大熊座 Dàxióngzuò ③ *m.* (for mountains, buildings, and other similar immovable objects): 一～山 a mountain / 一～楼 a building / 一～桥 a bridge / 一～铜像 a bronze statue

座舱 zuòcāng ① passenger cabin (in an airliner) ② cockpit (of a fighter)

座车 zuòchē (railway) carriage

座次 zuòcì same as 坐次 zuòcì

座号 zuòhào seat number

座机 zuòjī sb.'s private plane

座落 zuòluò same as 坐落 zuòluò

座上客 zuòshàngkè guest of honour; honoured guest

座谈 zuòtán have an informal discussion

座谈会 zuòtánhuì forum; symposium; informal discussion: 文艺～ forum on literature and art / 新针疗法～ symposium on new acupuncture therapy

座位 zuòwèi a place to sit; seat: 这个体育馆有一万八千个～。The stadium seats 18,000.

座无虚席 zuò wú xūxí all seats are occupied; there are no empty seats: 剧场内～。There was a full house.

座右铭 zuòyòumíng motto; maxim: "为人民服务"是我们的～。"Serve the people" is our motto.

座钟 zuòzhōng desk clock

座子 zuòzi ① stand; pedestal; base ② saddle (of a bicycle, motorcycle, etc.)

唑 zuò see 咔唑 kǎzuò; 噻唑 sāizuò

做（作） zuò ① do; make; produce; manufacture: ～结论 pass a verdict; reach a conclusion / ～长期打算 plan on a long-term basis / ～衣服 make clothes / 这种糖是甜菜～的。This sugar is made from beets. / 这是你自己～的吗? Did you make this yourself? ② cook; prepare: ～菜 cook a dish ③ do; act; engage in: 好本职工作 do one's best at one's own job / 从点滴的事情～起 start with little things / 大事～不来, 小事又不～ be unable to do big jobs and look down on small ones / 照正确的意见去～ act upon correct views / 共～了两万多个劳动日 did a total of more than 20,000 workdays / 我们正在～我们的前人从来没有～过的极其光荣伟大的事业。We are now engaged in a great and most glorious cause, never undertaken by our forefathers. ④ be; become: ～演员 become an actor or actress; go on the stage / 后来她～保育员了。Later she became a child-care worker. / 今天开会由你～主席。You'll be the chairman at today's meeting. ⑤ write; compose: ～一首诗 write a poem ⑥ hold a family (*or* home) celebration: 做寿 zuòshòu ⑦ be used as: 这篇文章可以～教材。This article may be used as teaching material. / 树皮可以～造纸的原料。Bark may be used as one of the raw materials for paper. ⑧ form or contract a relationship: ～朋友 make friends with / ～对头 set oneself against sb.

做爱 zuò'ài make love

做伴 zuòbàn keep sb. company: 我也来, 和你做个伴儿。I'll come too, and keep you company.

做操 zuòcāo do gymnastics; do callisthenics; do exercises

做大 zuòdà *old* put on airs; give oneself airs

做到 zuòdào accomplish; achieve: 我们应当～增产不增人。We should manage to increase production without taking on new hands. / 外国科学家～的, 中国科学家一定能够～, 而且做得更好。What foreign scientists have

accomplished, Chinese scientists can also accomplish, and can even do a better job of it.

做东 zuòdōng play the host; host sb.; act as host to sb.: 咱们找个馆子庆祝一下, 我来～。 We should find a restaurant and celebrate a little. It is my treat.

做法 zuòfǎ way of doing or making a thing; method of work; practice: 惯常的～ the usual practice; the usual way of doing sth.

做饭 zuòfàn do the cooking; prepare a meal: ～的 a cook

做工 zuògōng ① do manual work; work: 她在纺织厂～。 She works in a textile mill. ② charge for the making of sth.: 这套衣服～十块钱。 The charge for the tailoring of this suit was ten *yuan*. ③ workmanship: ～精美 of excellent workmanship

做工夫 zuò gōngfu ① put in time and energy; concentrate one's efforts ② do manual labour; work

做公的 zuògōngde *old* runner or baliff in a feudal *yamen*

做功 zuògōng (also 做工 zuògōng) acting (in traditional opera); business

做官 zuòguān be an official; secure an official position: ～当老爷 act like high officials and overbearing bureaucrats; act as bureaucrats and overlords

做鬼 zuòguǐ play tricks; play an underhand game; get up to mischief

做好人 zuò hǎorén try to be a good fellow; try to get along with everyone (often at the expense of principle)

做好做歹 zuòhǎo-zuòdǎi ① try every possible way to persuade sb. or to mediate

做活儿 zuòhuór do manual labour; work: 他们一块儿在地里～。 They worked together in the fields.

做活局子 zuò huójúzi gang up to cheat

做绝 zuòjué leave no room for manoeuvre: 把事情～ get things into an impasse; leave oneself no avenue of retreat; pass the point of no return / 坏事～ perpetrate every kind of villainy

做客 zuòkè be a guest: 我昨天到一个老朋友家里去～。 I was a guest at an old friend's yesterday.

做礼拜 zuò lǐbài go to church; be at church

做买卖 zuò mǎimai do business; carry on trade: 做成一笔买卖 make a deal; strike a bargain / ～的 businessman; trader; merchant

做满月 zuò mǎnyuè celebrate a baby's birth when he is one month old

做媒 zuòméi be a matchmaker (or go-between)

做梦 zuòmèng ① have a dream; dream: 昨晚我做了一个可怕的梦。 I had a terrible dream last night. / 我们～也没有想到有今天。 We never dreamt that we would be as we are today. ② have a pipe dream; daydream: 他岂不是在～吗? Isn't he just daydreaming?

做派 zuò·pài same as 做功 zuògōng

做亲 zuòqīn ① (of two families) become related by marriage ② get married

做圈套 zuò quāntào set a trap (to deceive sb.)

做人 zuòrén ① conduct oneself; behave: 懂得如何～处世 know how to conduct oneself in society ② be an

upright person: 重新做人 chóngxīn zuòrén

做人情 zuò rénqíng do sb. a favour

做生活 zuò shēnghuó *dial.* do manual labour; work

做生日 zuò shēngri celebrate sb.'s birthday

做生意 zuò shēngyì do business; carry on trade: 做成一笔生意 make a deal; strike a bargain

做声 zuòshēng make a sound (as when speaking, coughing, etc.): 别～! Keep quiet!

做事 zuòshì ① do work; do a deed; handle affairs: 他在你们厂做什么事? What sort of work does he do in your factory? / 他～做得很好。 He does his work well. / 热心为群众～ be enthusiastic in rendering services to the masses / ～不能只凭动机, 不问效果。 Actions shouldn't be guided solely by motive without any attention to effect. ② work; have a job: 他在钢铁厂～。 He works in an iron and steel mill. / 他没～。 He doesn't have a job.

做手脚 zuò shǒujiǎo juggle things; put up a job

做寿 zuòshòu celebrate the birthday (usu. of elderly people); hold a birthday party

做文章 zuò wénzhāng ① write a composition ② make an issue of sth.; make a fuss about sth.: 抓住一点小事～ seize on a trifle and make an issue of it; make a fuss about something trivial / 执政党每犯一点错误, 反对党就大～。 Whenever the party in power made the slightest mistake, the opposition made much of it.

做戏 zuòxì ① put on a play; act in a play ② playact; pretend

做小 zuòxiǎo be sb.'s concubine

做学问 zuò xuéwèn engage in scholarship; do research: 他是～的人, 不会做买卖。 He's a scholar and no businessman.

做眼色 zuò yǎnsè *dial.* tip sb. the wink; wink at sb.

做样子 zuò yàngzi make a show; go through the motions

做一天和尚撞一天钟 zuò yītiān héshang zhuàng yītiān zhōng go on tolling the bell as long as one is a monk —do the least that is expected of one; take a passive attitude towards one's work

做贼心虚 zuò zéi xīnxū have a guilty conscience like a thief; have sth. on one's conscience: 他们推三阻四, 正好暴露了他们～。 In making so many excuses, they revealed their own guilty conscience.

做针线 zuò zhēnxiàn do needlework; sew: 她坐在窗口～。 She sat sewing by the window.

做主 zuòzhǔ ① decide; take the responsibility for a decision: 我做不了主。 I am not in a position to decide. / 这件事是他自己～办的。 He did it on his own responsibility. / 只能做一半主 have only half the say ② back up; support

做作 zuòzuo affected; artificial: 他老是那么～。 He's always affected. *or* He's never natural. / 她唱得还可以, 就是演得太～。 Her singing is all right, but her acting is overdone.

酢 zuò see 酬酢 chóuzuò ——see also cù

附录一
Appendix 1

汉字简化字和繁体字对照表
The Simplified Chinese Characters and
Their Original Complex Forms

[说明]　　根据国务院于 1986 年 6 月 24 日批准重新发表《简化字总表》的通知以及国家语言文字工作委员会于 1986 年 10月10 日公布的〈关于重新发表《简化字总表》的说明〉, 本《修订本》对原《汉英词典》的"汉字简化字和繁体字对照表"作了以下几点更动:

1. 删去原第一表中的"迭 [叠]" "象 [像]"两个简化字。"叠""像"不再作为繁体字处理。第一表原收 352 个字, 现收 350 个字。

2. 原第一表的"复 [[復] [複] [覆]"中删去 [覆]。"覆"不再作为繁体字处理。

3. 原第二表的"罗 [羅] [囉]"中删去 [囉]。"罗"只作为 [羅] 的简化字。[囉] 的简化字改为"啰"。

4. 鉴于本《修订本》中简化字单字条目已加注繁体字, 原从简体查繁体的第三表, 改为从繁体查简体的繁简字对照表。此外, 根据国家语言文字工作委员会公布的〈关于重新发表《简化字总表》的说明〉, 对一部分需加以说明的简化字加了注释, 附于总表后面。

第一表 Table 1
不作简化偏旁用的简化字

A
碍[礙] 肮[骯] 袄[襖]

B
坝[壩] 板[闆] 办[辦] 帮[幫] 宝[寶] 报[報] 币[幣] 毙[斃] 标[標] 表[錶] 别[彆] 卜[蔔] 补[補]

C
才[纔] 蚕[蠶] 灿[燦] 层[層] 搀[攙] 谗[讒] 馋[饞] 缠[纏] 忏[懺] 偿[償] 厂[廠] 彻[徹] 尘[塵] 衬[襯] 称[稱] 惩[懲] 迟[遲] 冲[衝] 丑[醜] 础[礎] 处[處] 触[觸] 辞[辭] 聪[聰] 丛[叢]

D
担[擔] 胆[膽] 导[導] 灯[燈] 邓[鄧] 敌[敵] 籴[糴] 递[遞] 点[點] 淀[澱] 电[電] 冬[鼕] 独[獨] 吨[噸] 夺[奪] 堕[墮]

E
儿[兒]

F
矾[礬] 范[範] 飞[飛] 坟[墳] 奋[奮] 粪[糞] 凤[鳳] 肤[膚] 妇[婦] 复[復][複]

G
盖[蓋] 干[乾][幹] 赶[趕] 个[個] 巩[鞏] 沟[溝] 构[構] 购[購] 谷[穀] 顾[顧] 刮[颳] 关[關] 观[觀] 柜[櫃]

H
汉[漢] 号[號] 合[閤] 轰[轟] 后[後] 胡[鬍] 壶[壺] 沪[滬] 护[護] 划[劃] 怀[懷] 坏[壞] 欢[歡] 环[環] 还[還] 回[迴] 伙[夥] 获[獲][穫]

J
击[擊] 鸡[雞] 积[積] 极[極] 际[際] 继[繼] 家[傢] 价[價] 艰[艱] 歼[殲] 茧[繭] 拣[揀] 硷[鹼] 舰[艦] 姜[薑] 浆[漿] 桨[槳] 奖[獎] 讲[講] 酱[醬] 胶[膠] 阶[階] 借[藉] 仅[僅] 惊[驚] 竞[競] 旧[舊] 剧[劇] 据[據] 惧[懼] 卷[捲]

K
开[開] 克[剋] 垦[墾] 恳[懇] 夸[誇] 块[塊] 亏[虧] 困[睏]

L
腊[臘] 蜡[蠟] 兰[蘭] 拦[攔] 栏[欄] 烂[爛] 累[纍] 垒[壘] 类[類] 里[裏] 礼[禮] 隶[隸] 帘[簾] 联[聯] 怜[憐] 炼[煉] 练[練] 粮[糧] 疗[療] 辽[遼] 了[瞭] 猎[獵] 临[臨] 邻[鄰] 岭[嶺] 庐[廬] 芦[蘆] 炉[爐] 陆[陸] 驴[驢] 乱[亂]

M
么[麼] 霉[黴] 蒙[矇][懞][濛] 梦[夢] 面[麵] 庙[廟] 灭[滅] 蔑[衊] 亩[畝]

N
恼[惱] 脑[腦] 拟[擬] 酿[釀] 疟[瘧]

P
盘[盤] 辟[闢] 苹[蘋] 凭[憑] 扑[撲] 仆[僕] 朴[樸]

Q
启[啟] 签[籤] 千[韆] 牵[牽] 纤[縴] 窍[竅] 窃[竊] 寝[寢] 庆[慶] 琼[瓊] 秋[鞦] 曲[麯] 权[權] 劝[勸] 确[確]

R
让[讓] 扰[擾] 热[熱] 认[認]

S
洒[灑] 伞[傘] 丧[喪] 扫[掃] 涩[澀] 晒[曬] 伤[傷] 舍[捨] 沈[瀋] 声[聲] 胜[勝] 湿[濕] 实[實] 适[適] 势[勢] 兽[獸] 书[書] 术[術] 树[樹] 帅[帥] 松[鬆] 苏[蘇][囌] 虽[雖] 随[隨]

T
台[臺][颱][檯] 态[態] 坛[壇][罈] 叹[嘆] 誊[謄] 体[體] 粜[糶] 铁[鐵] 听[聽] 厅[廳] 头[頭] 图[圖] 涂[塗] 团[團][糰] 椭[橢]

W
洼[窪] 袜[襪] 网[網] 卫[衛] 稳[穩] 务[務] 雾[霧]

X
牺[犧] 习[習] 系[係][繫] 戏[戲] 虾[蝦] 吓[嚇] 纤[纖] 咸[鹹] 显[顯] 宪[憲] 县[縣] 响[響] 向[嚮] 协[協] 胁[脅] 亵[褻] 衅[釁] 兴[興] 须[鬚] 悬[懸] 选[選] 旋[鏇]

Y
压[壓] 盐[鹽] 阳[陽] 养[養] 痒[癢] 样[樣] 钥[鑰] 药[藥] 爷[爺] 叶[葉] 医[醫] 亿[億] 忆[憶] 应[應] 痈[癰] 拥[擁] 佣[傭] 踊[踴] 忧[憂] 优[優] 邮[郵] 余[餘] 御[禦] 吁[籲] 郁[鬱] 誉[譽] 渊[淵] 园[園] 远[遠] 愿[願] 跃[躍] 运[運] 酝[醞]

Z
杂[雜] 赃[贓] 脏[臟][髒] 凿[鑿] 枣[棗] 灶[竈] 斋[齋] 毡[氈] 战[戰] 赵[趙] 折[摺] 这[這] 征[徵] 症[癥] 证[證] 只[隻][祇] 致[緻] 制[製] 钟[鐘][鍾] 肿[腫] 种[種] 众[衆] 昼[晝] 朱[硃] 烛[燭] 筑[築] 庄[莊] 桩[樁] 妆[妝] 装[裝] 壮[壯] 状[狀] 准[準] 浊[濁] 总[總] 钻[鑽]

第二表 Table 2
可作简化偏旁用的简化字和简化偏旁

A

爱〔愛〕

B

罢〔罷〕
备〔備〕
贝〔貝〕
笔〔筆〕
毕〔畢〕
边〔邊〕
宾〔賓〕

C

参〔參〕
仓〔倉〕
产〔產〕
长〔長〕
尝〔嘗〕
车〔車〕
齿〔齒〕
虫〔蟲〕
刍〔芻〕
从〔從〕
窜〔竄〕

D

达〔達〕
带〔帶〕
单〔單〕
当〔當〕
〔噹〕
党〔黨〕
东〔東〕
动〔動〕
断〔斷〕
对〔對〕
队〔隊〕

E

尔〔爾〕

F

发〔發〕
〔髮〕
丰〔豐〕
风〔風〕

G

冈〔岡〕
广〔廣〕
归〔歸〕
龟〔龜〕
国〔國〕
过〔過〕

H

华〔華〕
画〔畫〕
汇〔匯〕
〔彙〕
会〔會〕

J

几〔幾〕
夹〔夾〕
戋〔戔〕
监〔監〕
见〔見〕
荐〔薦〕
将〔將〕
节〔節〕
尽〔盡〕
〔儘〕
进〔進〕
举〔舉〕

K

壳〔殼〕

L

来〔來〕
乐〔樂〕
离〔離〕
历〔歷〕
〔曆〕
丽〔麗〕
两〔兩〕
灵〔靈〕
刘〔劉〕
龙〔龍〕
娄〔婁〕
卢〔盧〕
虏〔虜〕
卤〔鹵〕
〔滷〕
录〔錄〕
虑〔慮〕
仑〔侖〕
罗〔羅〕

M

马〔馬〕
买〔買〕
卖〔賣〕
麦〔麥〕
门〔門〕
黾〔黽〕

N

难〔難〕
鸟〔鳥〕
聂〔聶〕
宁〔寧〕
农〔農〕

Q

齐〔齊〕
岂〔豈〕
气〔氣〕
迁〔遷〕
佥〔僉〕
乔〔喬〕
亲〔親〕
穷〔窮〕
区〔區〕

S

啬〔嗇〕
杀〔殺〕
审〔審〕
圣〔聖〕
师〔師〕
时〔時〕
寿〔壽〕
属〔屬〕
双〔雙〕
肃〔肅〕
岁〔歲〕
孙〔孫〕

T

条〔條〕

W

万〔萬〕
为〔爲〕
韦〔韋〕
乌〔烏〕
无〔無〕

X

献〔獻〕
乡〔鄉〕
写〔寫〕
寻〔尋〕

Y

亚〔亞〕
严〔嚴〕
厌〔厭〕
尧〔堯〕
业〔業〕
页〔頁〕
义〔義〕
艺〔藝〕
阴〔陰〕
隐〔隱〕
犹〔猶〕
鱼〔魚〕
与〔與〕
云〔雲〕

Z

郑〔鄭〕
执〔執〕
质〔質〕
专〔專〕

简化偏旁

讠〔言〕
饣〔食〕
纟〔糸〕
収〔𡊍〕
芇〔𤇾〕
𡿨〔𢀖〕
只〔戠〕
钅〔金〕
𭕄〔興〕
𦍌〔翠〕
圣〔巠〕
亦〔䜌〕
呙〔咼〕

第三表 Table 3

繁简字对照表

7画

*〔車〕车
*〔夾〕夹
*〔貝〕贝
*〔見〕见
〔壯〕壮
〔妝〕妆

8画

【一】
*〔長〕长①
*〔亞〕亚
〔軋〕轧
*〔東〕东
*〔兩〕两
〔協〕协
*〔來〕来
*〔戔〕戋
【丨】
*〔門〕门
*〔岡〕冈
【丿】
*〔侖〕仑
*〔兒〕儿
【丶】
〔衹〕只
【フ】
〔狀〕状
〔糾〕纠

9画

【一】
〔剋〕克
〔軌〕轨
〔厙〕厍
*〔頁〕页
〔郟〕郏
〔剄〕刭
〔勁〕劲
【丨】
〔貞〕贞
〔則〕则
〔閂〕闩
〔迴〕回
【丿】
〔俠〕侠
〔係〕系
〔鳧〕凫
〔帥〕帅㉞
〔後〕后
〔釓〕钆
〔釔〕钇
〔負〕负
*〔風〕风
【丶】
〔訂〕订
〔計〕计
〔訃〕讣
〔軍〕军
【フ】
〔陣〕阵
*〔韋〕韦
〔陝〕陕
〔陘〕陉
〔飛〕飞
〔紆〕纡
〔紅〕红
〔紂〕纣
〔紈〕纨
〔級〕级
〔約〕约
〔紇〕纥
〔紀〕纪
〔紉〕纫

10画

【一】
*〔馬〕马②
〔挾〕挟
〔貢〕贡
*〔華〕华
〔莢〕荚
〔莖〕茎
〔莧〕苋
〔莊〕庄③
〔軒〕轩
〔連〕连
〔軔〕轫
〔劃〕划
【丨】
〔鬥〕斗
*〔時〕时
*〔畢〕毕
〔財〕财
〔覎〕觃
〔閃〕闪
〔唄〕呗
〔員〕员
*〔豈〕岂
〔峽〕峡
〔峴〕岘
〔剛〕刚
〔剮〕剐
【丿】
*〔氣〕气
〔郵〕邮
〔倀〕伥
〔倆〕俩
*〔條〕条④
〔們〕们
〔個〕个
〔倫〕伦
〔隻〕只
〔島〕岛
*〔烏〕乌⑤
*〔師〕师㉞
〔徑〕径
〔釘〕钉
〔針〕针
〔釗〕钊
〔釙〕钋
〔釕〕钌
*〔殺〕杀
*〔倉〕仓
〔脅〕胁
〔狹〕狭
〔狽〕狈
*〔芻〕刍
【丶】
〔訐〕讦
〔訌〕讧
〔討〕讨
〔訕〕讪
〔訖〕讫
〔訓〕训
〔這〕这
〔訊〕讯
〔記〕记
〔凍〕冻
〔畝〕亩
〔庫〕库
〔浹〕浃
〔涇〕泾
【フ】
〔書〕书
〔陸〕陆
〔陳〕陈
*〔孫〕孙
*〔陰〕阴
〔務〕务
〔紜〕纭
〔純〕纯
〔紕〕纰
〔紗〕纱
〔納〕纳
〔紝〕纴
〔紛〕纷
*〔紙〕纸
〔紋〕纹
〔紡〕纺
〔紖〕纼
〔紐〕纽
〔紓〕纾

11画

【一】
〔責〕责
〔現〕现
〔匭〕匦
〔規〕规
*〔殼〕壳⑥
〔埡〕垭
〔掗〕挜
〔捨〕舍
〔捫〕扪
〔掆〕㧏
〔堝〕埚
〔頂〕顶
〔掄〕抡
*〔執〕执
〔捲〕卷
〔掃〕扫
〔堊〕垩
〔萊〕莱
〔萵〕莴
〔乾〕干⑦
〔梘〕枧
〔軛〕轭
〔斬〕斩
〔軟〕软
*〔專〕专
*〔區〕区⑧
〔堅〕坚
*〔帶〕带
〔厠〕厕
〔硃〕朱
*〔麥〕麦
〔頃〕顷
【丨】
*〔鹵〕卤
〔處〕处
〔敗〕败
〔販〕贩
〔貶〕贬
〔啞〕哑
〔閉〕闭
〔問〕问
*〔婁〕娄
〔啢〕唡
*〔國〕国
〔喎〕㖞
〔帳〕帐
〔崬〕岽
〔崍〕崃
〔崗〕岗
〔圇〕囵
*〔過〕过
【丿】
〔氫〕氢
*〔動〕动
〔偵〕侦
〔側〕侧
〔貨〕货
*〔進〕进
〔梟〕枭
*〔鳥〕鸟⑨
〔偉〕伟
〔徠〕徕
〔術〕术⑩
*〔從〕从
〔釷〕钍
〔釺〕钎
〔釧〕钏
〔釤〕钐
〔釣〕钓
〔釩〕钒
〔釹〕钕
〔釵〕钗
〔貪〕贪
〔覓〕觅
〔飥〕饦
〔貧〕贫
〔脛〕胫
*〔魚〕鱼
【丶】
〔詎〕讵
〔訝〕讶
〔訥〕讷
〔許〕许
〔訛〕讹
〔訢〕䜣
〔訩〕讻
〔訟〕讼
〔設〕设
〔訪〕访
〔訣〕诀
*〔產〕产
〔牽〕牵
〔烴〕烃
〔淶〕涞
〔淺〕浅
〔渦〕涡
〔淪〕沦
〔悵〕怅
〔鄆〕郓
〔啓〕启
〔視〕视
【フ】
*〔將〕将⑪
〔晝〕昼
〔張〕张
〔階〕阶
〔陽〕阳
*〔隊〕队
〔婭〕娅
〔媧〕娲
〔婦〕妇
〔習〕习
*〔參〕参
〔紺〕绀
〔紲〕绁
〔紱〕绂
〔組〕组
〔紳〕绅
〔紬〕䌷
〔細〕细
〔終〕终
〔絆〕绊
〔紼〕绋
〔絀〕绌
〔紹〕绍
〔紿〕绐
〔貫〕贯
*〔鄉〕乡

12画

【一】
〔貳〕贰
〔預〕预
*〔堯〕尧⑫
〔揀〕拣
〔馭〕驭
〔項〕项
〔賁〕贲
〔場〕场
〔揚〕扬
〔塊〕块
*〔達〕达
〔報〕报
〔揮〕挥
〔壺〕壶
〔惡〕恶
〔葉〕叶⑬
〔貰〕贳
*〔萬〕万
〔葷〕荤
〔喪〕丧
〔葦〕苇
〔葒〕荭
〔葤〕荮
〔棖〕枨
〔棟〕栋
〔棧〕栈
〔棡〕㭎
〔極〕极
〔軲〕轱
〔軻〕轲
〔軸〕轴
〔軼〕轶
〔軤〕轷
〔軫〕轸
〔軺〕轺
*〔畫〕画
〔腎〕肾
〔棗〕枣
〔硨〕砗
〔硤〕硖
〔硯〕砚
〔殘〕残
*〔雲〕云
【丨】
〔覘〕觇
〔睏〕困
〔貼〕贴
〔貺〕贶
〔貯〕贮
〔貽〕贻
〔閏〕闰
〔開〕开
〔閑〕闲
〔間〕间
〔閔〕闵
〔悶〕闷
〔貴〕贵
〔鄖〕郧
〔勛〕勋
*〔單〕单
〔喲〕哟
*〔買〕买
〔剴〕剀
〔凱〕凯
〔幀〕帧
〔嵐〕岚
〔幃〕帏
〔圍〕围
【丿】
*〔無〕无⑭
〔氬〕氩
*〔喬〕乔
*〔筆〕笔
*〔備〕备
〔貸〕贷
〔順〕顺
〔傖〕伧
〔㑳〕㑇
〔傢〕家
〔鄔〕邬
〔衆〕众

*表示按《简化字总表》规定可作偏旁使用的字。

①②③……表示注释，释文附于表末（第 1397 页）。

〔復〕复	〔渢〕沨	〔蓽〕荜	〔僂〕偻	〔誠〕诚	**14画**	〔曄〕晔	〔鉻〕铬
〔須〕须	〔渾〕浑	〔夢〕梦	〔賃〕赁	〔誅〕诛	【一】	〔夥〕伙⑳	〔錚〕铮
〔鈃〕钘	〔愜〕惬	〔蒼〕苍	〔傷〕伤	〔話〕话	〔瑪〕玛	〔賑〕赈	〔銫〕铯
〔鈣〕钙	〔惻〕恻	〔幹〕干	〔傭〕佣	〔誕〕诞	〔璉〕琏	〔賒〕赊	〔鉸〕铰
〔鈈〕钚	〔惲〕恽	〔蓀〕荪	〔裊〕袅	〔詬〕诟	〔瑣〕琐	〔嘆〕叹	〔銥〕铱
〔鈦〕钛	〔惱〕恼	〔蔭〕荫	〔頎〕颀	〔詮〕诠	〔瑲〕玱	〔暢〕畅	〔銃〕铳
〔鈁〕钫	〔運〕运	〔蒓〕莼	〔鈺〕钰	〔詭〕诡	〔駁〕驳	〔嘜〕唛	〔銨〕铵
〔鈍〕钝	〔補〕补	〔楨〕桢	〔鉦〕钲	〔詢〕询	〔摶〕抟	〔閨〕闺	〔銀〕银
〔鈔〕钞	〔禍〕祸	〔楊〕杨	〔鉗〕钳	〔詣〕诣	〔摳〕抠	〔聞〕闻	〔銣〕铷
〔鈉〕钠	【フ】	〔嗇〕啬	〔鈷〕钴	〔淨〕净	〔趙〕赵	〔閩〕闽	〔餳〕饧
〔鈴〕铃	*〔尋〕寻	〔楓〕枫	〔缽〕钵	〔該〕该	〔趕〕赶	〔閫〕阃	〔餌〕饵
〔欽〕钦	〔費〕费	〔軾〕轼	〔鉅〕钜	〔詳〕详	〔摟〕搂	〔閬〕阆	〔蝕〕蚀
〔鈞〕钧	〔違〕违	〔輊〕轾	〔鈳〕钶	〔詫〕诧	〔摑〕掴	〔閣〕阁	〔餉〕饷
〔鈎〕钩	〔韌〕韧	〔輅〕辂	〔鈸〕钹	〔詡〕诩	〔臺〕台	〔閡〕阂	〔餄〕饸
〔鈧〕钪	〔隕〕陨	〔較〕较	〔鉞〕钺	〔裏〕里	〔墊〕垫	〔嘔〕呕	〔餎〕饹
〔鈁〕钫	〔賀〕贺	〔豎〕竖	〔鉬〕钼	〔準〕准	*〔壽〕寿	〔蝸〕蜗	〔餃〕饺
〔鈥〕钬	*〔發〕发	〔買〕买	〔鉭〕钽	〔頏〕颃	〔摺〕折⑱	〔團〕团	〔餏〕饻
〔鈄〕钭	〔綁〕绑	*〔匯〕汇	〔鉀〕钾	〔資〕资	〔摻〕掺	〔嘍〕喽	〔餅〕饼
〔鈕〕钮	〔絨〕绒	〔電〕电	〔鈾〕铀	〔羥〕羟	〔摜〕掼	〔鄲〕郸	〔領〕领
〔鈀〕钯	〔結〕结	〔頓〕顿	〔鈿〕钿	*〔義〕义⑯	〔勩〕勚	〔鳴〕鸣	〔鳳〕凤
〔傘〕伞	〔絝〕绔	〔盞〕盏	〔鉑〕铂	〔煉〕炼	〔蔞〕蒌	〔幘〕帻	〔颱〕台
〔爺〕爷	〔經〕经	【丨】	〔鈴〕铃	〔煩〕烦	〔蔦〕茑	〔嶄〕崭	〔獄〕狱
〔創〕创	〔絎〕绗	*〔歲〕岁	〔鉛〕铅	〔煬〕炀	〔蓯〕苁	〔嶇〕岖	【丶】
〔飩〕饨	〔給〕给	*〔虜〕虏	〔鉚〕铆	〔塋〕茔	〔蔔〕卜	〔罰〕罚	〔誡〕诫
〔飪〕饪	〔絢〕绚	*〔業〕业	〔鈰〕铈	〔熒〕荥	〔蔣〕蒋	〔嶁〕嵝	〔誣〕诬
〔飫〕饫	〔絳〕绛	*〔當〕当	〔鉉〕铉	〔煒〕炜	〔薌〕芗	〔幗〕帼	〔語〕语
〔飭〕饬	〔絡〕络	〔睞〕睐	〔鉈〕铊	〔遞〕递	〔構〕构	〔圖〕图	〔誚〕诮
〔飯〕饭	〔絞〕绞	〔賊〕贼	〔鉍〕铋	〔溝〕沟	〔樺〕桦	【丿】	〔誤〕误
〔飲〕饮	〔統〕统	〔賄〕贿	〔鈮〕铌	〔漣〕涟	〔橈〕桡	〔製〕制	〔誥〕诰
*〔爲〕为	〔絕〕绝	〔賂〕赂	〔鈹〕铍	〔滅〕灭	〔覡〕觋	〔種〕种	〔誘〕诱
〔脹〕胀	〔絲〕丝	〔賅〕赅	*〔僉〕佥	〔湞〕涢	〔槍〕枪	〔稱〕称	〔誨〕诲
〔腖〕胨	*〔幾〕几	〔嗎〕吗	*〔會〕会	〔滌〕涤	〔輒〕辄	〔箋〕笺	〔誑〕诳
〔腡〕脶		〔嘩〕哗	*〔亂〕乱	〔溮〕浉	〔輔〕辅	〔僥〕侥	〔説〕说
〔勝〕胜	**13画**	〔嗊〕唝	〔飾〕饰	〔塗〕涂	〔輕〕轻	〔僨〕偾	〔認〕认
*〔猶〕犹	【一】	〔暘〕旸	〔飽〕饱	〔滄〕沧	〔塹〕堑	〔僕〕仆㉑	〔誦〕诵
〔貿〕贸	〔項〕项	〔閘〕闸	〔飼〕饲	〔愷〕恺	〔匱〕匮	〔僑〕侨	〔誒〕诶
〔鄒〕邹	〔琿〕珲	*〔黽〕黾⑮	〔飿〕饳	〔愾〕忾	*〔監〕监	〔僞〕伪	*〔廣〕广
【丶】	〔瑋〕玮	〔暈〕晕	〔飴〕饴	〔愴〕怆	〔緊〕紧	〔銜〕衔	〔麼〕么㉒
〔詁〕诂	〔載〕载	〔號〕号	〔頌〕颂	〔窩〕窝	〔厲〕厉	〔鍘〕铡	〔廎〕顷
〔訶〕诃	〔馱〕驮	〔園〕园	〔頒〕颁	〔禎〕祯	*〔厭〕厌	〔銬〕铐	〔瘧〕疟
〔評〕评	〔馴〕驯	〔蛺〕蛱	〔腸〕肠	〔禕〕祎	〔碩〕硕	〔銠〕铑	〔瘍〕疡
〔詛〕诅	〔馳〕驰	〔蜆〕蚬	〔腫〕肿	【フ】	〔碭〕砀	〔鉺〕铒	〔瘋〕疯
〔調〕调	〔塒〕埘	*〔農〕农	〔腦〕脑	*〔肅〕肃⑰	〔颯〕飒	〔銪〕铕	〔塵〕尘
〔詐〕诈	〔塤〕埙	〔嗩〕唢	〔魛〕鱽	〔裝〕装	〔奩〕奁	〔鋁〕铝	〔颶〕飓
〔訴〕诉	〔損〕损	〔嘜〕唛	〔鳩〕鸠	〔遜〕逊	*〔爾〕尔	〔銅〕铜	〔適〕适㉓
〔診〕诊	〔遠〕远	〔嗚〕呜	〔獅〕狮	〔際〕际	〔奪〕夺	〔銦〕铟	*〔齊〕齐
〔詆〕诋	〔塏〕垲	〔嗆〕呛	〔猻〕狲	〔媽〕妈	〔殞〕殒	〔銖〕铢	〔養〕养
〔詞〕词	〔勢〕势	〔圓〕圆	【丶】	〔預〕预	〔鳶〕鸢	〔銑〕铣	〔鄰〕邻
〔詘〕诎	〔搶〕抢	〔骯〕肮	〔誆〕诓	〔綆〕绠	〔瘞〕瘗	〔銩〕铥	*〔鄭〕郑
〔詔〕诏	〔搗〕捣	【丿】	〔誄〕诔	〔綃〕绡	【丨】	〔鋌〕铤	〔燁〕烨
〔詒〕诒	〔塢〕坞	〔筧〕笕	〔試〕试	〔絹〕绢	*〔對〕对	〔銓〕铨	〔熗〕炝
〔馮〕冯	〔壺〕壶	*〔節〕节	〔詿〕诖	〔綉〕绣	〔幣〕币	〔鉿〕铪	〔榮〕荣
〔痙〕痉	*〔聖〕圣	*〔與〕与	〔詩〕诗	〔綏〕绥	〔彆〕别	〔銚〕铫	〔滎〕荥
〔勞〕劳	〔蓋〕盖	〔債〕债	〔詰〕诘	〔綈〕绨	*〔嘗〕尝⑲	〔銘〕铭	〔犖〕荦
〔湞〕浈	〔蓮〕莲	〔僅〕仅	〔誇〕夸	〔彙〕汇	〔嘖〕啧		〔熒〕荧
〔測〕测	〔蒔〕莳	〔傳〕传	〔詼〕诙				〔漢〕汉
〔湯〕汤		〔傴〕伛					〔滿〕满
〔淵〕渊		〔傾〕倾					

〔漸〕渐
〔漚〕沤
〔滯〕滞
〔滷〕卤
〔漊〕溇
〔漁〕渔
〔滸〕浒
〔滬〕沪
〔滬〕沪
〔漲〕涨
〔滲〕渗
〔慚〕惭
〔慪〕怄
〔慳〕悭
〔慟〕恸
〔慘〕惨
〔慣〕惯
〔寬〕宽
*〔賓〕宾
〔窪〕洼
*〔寧〕宁㉔
〔寢〕寝
〔實〕实
〔皸〕皲
〔複〕复
【フ】
〔劃〕划
*〔盡〕尽
〔屢〕屡
〔獎〕奖⑪
〔墮〕堕
〔隨〕随
〔皺〕皱
〔墜〕坠
〔嫗〕妪
〔頗〕颇
〔態〕态
〔鄧〕邓
〔緒〕绪
〔綾〕绫
〔綺〕绮
〔綫〕线
〔緋〕绯
〔綽〕绰
〔緄〕绲
〔綱〕纲
〔網〕网
〔維〕维
〔綿〕绵
〔綸〕纶
〔綬〕绶
〔綳〕绷
〔綢〕绸
〔綹〕绺
〔綣〕绻
〔綜〕综
〔綻〕绽
〔綰〕绾

15画

【一】
〔鬧〕闹㉕
〔璡〕琎
〔靚〕靓
〔髮〕发
〔撓〕挠
〔墳〕坟
〔撻〕挞
〔駔〕驵
〔駛〕驶
〔駟〕驷
〔駙〕驸
〔駒〕驹
〔駐〕驻
〔駝〕驼
〔駘〕骀
〔撲〕扑
〔頡〕颉
〔撣〕掸
*〔賣〕卖㉖
〔撫〕抚
〔撟〕挢
〔撳〕揿
〔熱〕热
〔鞏〕巩
〔摯〕挚
〔撈〕捞
〔穀〕谷
〔慤〕悫
〔撏〕挦
〔撥〕拨
〔蕘〕荛
〔蕆〕蒇
〔蕓〕芸
〔邁〕迈
〔黃〕黄
〔蕪〕芜
〔蕎〕荞
〔蕕〕莸
〔蕩〕荡
〔蕁〕荨
〔樁〕桩
〔樞〕枢
〔標〕标
〔樓〕楼
〔樅〕枞
〔麩〕麸
〔賫〕赍
〔樣〕样
〔橢〕椭

〔輛〕辆
〔輥〕辊
〔輞〕辋
〔槧〕椠
〔暫〕暂
〔輪〕轮
〔輬〕辌
〔輜〕辎
〔甌〕瓯
〔歐〕欧
〔毆〕殴
〔賢〕贤
*〔遷〕迁
〔鴇〕鸨
〔憂〕忧
〔碼〕码
〔磑〕硙
〔確〕确
〔賚〕赉
〔遼〕辽
〔殤〕殇
〔鴉〕鸦
【丨】
〔輩〕辈
〔劌〕刿
*〔齒〕齿
〔劇〕剧
〔膚〕肤
*〔慮〕虑
〔鄴〕邺
〔輝〕辉
〔賞〕赏㉗
〔賦〕赋
〔賭〕赌
〔賬〕账
〔賠〕赔
〔賙〕赒
〔賜〕赐
〔賧〕赕
〔嘵〕哓
〔噴〕喷
〔噠〕哒
〔噁〕恶
〔闋〕阕
〔闌〕阑
〔闃〕阒
〔闈〕闱
〔數〕数
〔踐〕践
〔遺〕遗
〔蝦〕虾
〔嘸〕呒
〔嘮〕唠
〔噦〕哕
〔嘰〕叽
〔嶢〕峣
〔嶠〕峤

*〔罷〕罢
〔嶠〕峤
〔嶔〕嵚
〔幟〕帜
〔嶗〕崂
【ノ】
〔頲〕颋
〔篋〕箧
〔範〕范
〔價〕价
〔儂〕侬
〔儉〕俭
〔儈〕侩
〔億〕亿
〔儀〕仪
〔皚〕皑
*〔樂〕乐
*〔質〕质
〔徵〕征㉘
〔衝〕冲
〔慫〕怂
〔徹〕彻
〔衛〕卫
〔盤〕盘
〔鋪〕铺
〔鋏〕铗
〔鋱〕铽
〔銷〕销
〔鋥〕锃
〔鋰〕锂
〔鋇〕钡
〔鋤〕锄
〔鋯〕锆
〔鋨〕锇
〔銹〕锈
〔銼〕锉
〔鋒〕锋
〔鋅〕锌
〔銳〕锐
〔銻〕锑
〔銀〕银
〔鋝〕锊
〔鋼〕钢
〔劍〕剑
〔劊〕刽
〔鄶〕郐
〔餑〕饽
〔餓〕饿
〔餒〕馁
〔膞〕䏝
〔腡〕脶
〔膠〕胶
〔鴰〕鸹
〔魷〕鱿

〔魴〕鲂
〔穎〕颖
〔颳〕刮
*〔劉〕刘
〔鱍〕鲅
【丶】
〔請〕请
〔諸〕诸
〔諏〕诹
〔諾〕诺
〔諑〕诼
〔誹〕诽
〔課〕课
〔諉〕诿
〔誰〕谁
〔論〕论
〔諗〕谂
〔調〕调
〔諂〕谄
〔諒〕谅
〔諄〕谆
〔誶〕谇
〔談〕谈
〔誼〕谊
〔廟〕庙
〔廠〕厂
〔廡〕庑
〔瘞〕瘗
〔瘡〕疮
〔慶〕庆㉚
〔廢〕废
〔敵〕敌
〔頦〕颏
〔導〕导
〔瑩〕莹
〔潔〕洁
〔澆〕浇
〔潿〕涠
〔潤〕润
〔澗〕涧
〔潰〕溃
〔潷〕滗
〔潙〕沩
〔澇〕涝
〔潯〕浔
〔潑〕泼
〔憒〕愦
〔憫〕悯
〔憤〕愤
〔憚〕惮
〔憮〕怃
〔憐〕怜
*〔寫〕写㉛
*〔審〕审
*〔窮〕穷

〔褳〕裢
〔褲〕裤
〔鳩〕鸠
〔遲〕迟
〔層〕层
〔彈〕弹
〔選〕选
〔槳〕桨⑪
〔漿〕浆⑪
〔險〕险
〔嬈〕娆
〔嫻〕娴
〔駕〕驾
〔嬋〕婵
〔嫵〕妩
〔嬌〕娇
〔嬀〕妫
〔嫿〕婳
〔駑〕驽
〔翬〕翚
〔毿〕毵
〔緙〕缂
〔緗〕缃
〔練〕练
〔緘〕缄
〔緬〕缅
〔緹〕缇
〔緲〕缈
〔緝〕缉
〔緦〕缌
〔緞〕缎
〔緱〕缑
〔縋〕缒
〔緩〕缓
〔締〕缔
〔編〕编
〔緡〕缗
〔緯〕纬
〔緣〕缘

16画

【一】
〔璣〕玑
〔墻〕墙
〔駱〕骆
〔駭〕骇
〔駢〕骈
〔擓〕㧟
〔擄〕掳
〔擋〕挡
〔擇〕择
〔頰〕颊
〔撿〕捡
〔擔〕担
〔壇〕坛

〔擁〕拥
〔據〕据
〔薔〕蔷
〔薑〕姜
〔薈〕荟
〔薊〕蓟
*〔薦〕荐
〔蕭〕萧
〔頤〕颐
〔鴣〕鸪
〔薩〕萨
〔蕷〕蓣
〔橈〕桡
〔樹〕树
〔樸〕朴
〔橋〕桥
〔機〕机
〔輳〕辏
〔輻〕辐
〔輯〕辑
〔輸〕输
〔賴〕赖
〔頭〕头
〔醞〕酝
〔醜〕丑
〔勵〕励
〔磧〕碛
〔磚〕砖
〔磣〕碜
*〔歷〕历
〔曆〕历
〔奮〕奋
〔頷〕颔
〔殨〕㱮
〔殫〕殚
〔頸〕颈
【丨】
〔頻〕频
*〔盧〕卢
〔曉〕晓
〔瞞〕瞒
〔縣〕县㉜
〔瞘〕眍
〔瞜〕䁖
〔睞〕睐
〔鴨〕鸭
〔閾〕阈
〔閹〕阉
〔閶〕阊
〔閿〕阌
〔閽〕阍
〔閻〕阎
〔閼〕阏
〔曇〕昙
〔噸〕吨
〔鴞〕鸮
〔噥〕哝
〔踴〕踊

〔螞〕蚂
〔蟎〕螨
〔蟈〕蝈
〔噹〕当
〔罵〕骂
〔噥〕哝
〔戰〕战
〔噲〕哙
〔鴦〕鸯
〔曖〕暧
〔嘯〕啸
〔還〕还
〔嶧〕峄
〔嶼〕屿
【ノ】
〔積〕积
〔頹〕颓
〔穌〕稣
〔篤〕笃
〔築〕筑
〔篳〕筚
〔篩〕筛
*〔舉〕举
〔興〕兴
〔嶨〕峃
〔學〕学
〔儔〕俦
〔憊〕惫
〔儕〕侪
〔儐〕傧
*〔儘〕尽
〔鴕〕鸵
〔艙〕舱
〔錶〕表
〔鍺〕锗
〔錯〕错
〔鍩〕锘
〔錨〕锚
〔錛〕锛
〔錸〕铼
〔錢〕钱
〔鍀〕锝
〔錁〕锞
〔錕〕锟
〔鍆〕钔
〔錫〕锡
〔錮〕锢
〔鍋〕锅
〔錘〕锤
〔錐〕锥
〔錦〕锦
〔鍁〕锨
〔錠〕锭
〔鍵〕键
*〔錄〕录
〔鋸〕锯
〔錳〕锰

〔鎦〕镏 ／ *〔龍〕龙 ／ 〔趨〕趋 ／ 〔闈〕闱 ／ 〔膿〕脓 ／ 【フ】 ／ 〔轉〕转

〔覵〕觍 ／ 〔劑〕剂 ／ 〔擱〕搁 ／ 〔闆〕板 ／ 〔臉〕脸 ／ 〔屨〕屦 ／ 〔轆〕辘

〔墾〕垦 ／ 〔燒〕烧 ／ 〔擬〕拟 ／ 〔闊〕阔 ／ 〔膾〕脍 ／ 〔彌〕弥 ／ 〔醫〕医

〔餞〕饯 ／ 〔燜〕焖 ／ 〔擴〕扩 ／ 〔闈〕闱 ／ 〔膽〕胆 ／ 〔嬪〕嫔 ／ 〔礎〕础

〔餜〕餜 ／ 〔熾〕炽 ／ 〔壙〕圹 ／ 〔暖〕暖 ／ 〔謄〕誊 ／ 〔績〕绩 ／ 〔殯〕殡

〔餛〕馄 ／ 〔螢〕萤 ／ 〔擠〕挤 ／ 〔蹕〕跸 ／ 〔鮭〕鲑 ／ 〔縹〕缥 ／ 〔霧〕雾

〔餡〕馅 ／ 〔營〕营 ／ 〔蟄〕蛰 ／ 〔蹌〕跄 ／ 〔鮚〕鲒 ／ 〔縷〕缕

〔館〕馆 ／ 〔縈〕萦 ／ 〔縶〕絷 ／ 〔蟎〕螨 ／ 〔鮪〕鲔 ／ 〔縵〕缦 ／ 【丨】

〔頜〕颌 ／ 〔燈〕灯 ／ 〔擲〕掷 ／ 〔螻〕蝼 ／ 〔鮦〕鲖 ／ 〔縲〕缧 ／ *〔豐〕丰㊴

〔鴿〕鸽 ／ 〔濛〕蒙 ／ 〔擯〕摈 ／ 〔蟈〕蝈 ／ 〔鮫〕鲛 ／ 〔總〕总 ／ 〔覷〕觑

〔膩〕腻 ／ 〔燙〕烫 ／ 〔擰〕拧 ／ 〔雖〕虽 ／ 〔鮮〕鲜 ／ 〔縱〕纵 ／ 〔懟〕怼

〔鷗〕鸥 ／ 〔澠〕渑 ／ 〔轂〕毂 ／ 〔嚀〕咛 ／ 〔颶〕飓 ／ 〔縴〕纤㊼ ／ 〔叢〕丛

〔鮍〕鲏 ／ 〔濃〕浓 ／ 〔聲〕声 ／ 〔覬〕觊 ／ 〔獷〕犷 ／ 〔縮〕缩 ／ 〔矇〕蒙

〔鮃〕鲆 ／ 〔澤〕泽 ／ 〔藉〕借㉝ ／ 〔嶺〕岭㊳ ／ 〔獰〕狞 ／ 〔繆〕缪 ／ 〔題〕题

〔鮎〕鲇 ／ 〔濁〕浊 ／ 〔聰〕聪 ／ 〔嶸〕嵘 ／ 【丶】 ／ 〔繅〕缫 ／ 〔蹺〕跷

〔鮓〕鲊 ／ 〔澮〕浍 ／ 〔聯〕联 ／ 〔點〕点 ／ 〔講〕讲 ／ 〔嚮〕向 ／ 〔瞼〕睑

〔穌〕稣 ／ 〔澱〕淀 ／ 〔艱〕艰 ／ 【ノ】 ／ 〔謨〕谟 ／ 〔闖〕闯

〔鮒〕鲋 ／ 〔澦〕滪 ／ 〔藍〕蓝 ／ 〔矯〕矫 ／ 〔謖〕谡 ／ 18画 ／ 〔闔〕阖

〔鯽〕鲫 ／ 〔懞〕蒙 ／ 〔舊〕旧㉞ ／ 〔鶻〕鹘 ／ 〔謝〕谢 ／ 〔闐〕阗

〔鮑〕鲍 ／ 〔憚〕惮 ／ 〔薺〕荠 ／ 〔簀〕箦 ／ 〔謠〕谣 ／ 【一】 ／ 〔闕〕阙

〔鮁〕鲅 ／ 〔憶〕忆 ／ 〔藎〕荩 ／ 〔簍〕篓 ／ 〔謅〕诌 ／ 〔耮〕耢 ／ 〔顓〕颛

〔鮐〕鲐 ／ 〔憲〕宪 ／ 〔韓〕韩 ／ 〔輿〕舆 ／ 〔謗〕谤 ／ 〔瓊〕琼 ／ 〔曠〕旷

〔鴝〕鸲 ／ 〔窺〕窥 ／ 〔隸〕隶 ／ 〔歟〕欤 ／ 〔謚〕谥 ／ 〔攆〕撵 ／ 〔蹣〕蹒

〔獲〕获 ／ 〔窶〕窭 ／ 〔檉〕柽 ／ 〔鵂〕鸺 ／ 〔謙〕谦 ／ 〔鬆〕松 ／ 〔嚙〕啮

〔穎〕颖 ／ 〔褻〕亵 ／ 〔檣〕樯 ／ *〔龜〕龟 ／ 〔謐〕谧 ／ 〔翹〕翘 ／ 〔壘〕垒

〔獨〕独 ／ 〔褸〕褛 ／ 〔檟〕槚 ／ 〔優〕优 ／ 〔氈〕毡 ／ 〔擷〕撷 ／ 〔蟯〕蛲

〔獫〕猃 ／ 〔禪〕禅 ／ 〔檔〕档 ／ 〔償〕偿 ／ 〔應〕应 ／ 〔擾〕扰 ／ *〔蟲〕虫

〔獪〕狯 ／ 【フ】 ／ 〔櫛〕栉 ／ 〔儲〕储 ／ 〔癘〕疠 ／ 〔騏〕骐 ／ 〔蟬〕蝉

〔鴛〕鸳 ／ *〔隱〕隐 ／ 〔檢〕检 ／ 〔魎〕魉 ／ 〔療〕疗 ／ 〔騎〕骑 ／ 〔蟣〕虮

【丶】 ／ 〔嬙〕嫱 ／ 〔檜〕桧 ／ 〔禦〕御 ／ 〔癇〕痫 ／ 〔騍〕骒 ／ 〔嚕〕噜

〔謀〕谋 ／ 〔嬡〕嫒 ／ 〔麯〕曲 ／ 〔聳〕耸 ／ 〔癉〕瘅 ／ 〔騅〕骓 ／ 〔顛〕颠

〔諶〕谌 ／ 〔縉〕缙 ／ 〔轅〕辕 ／ 〔鵃〕鸼 ／ 〔癆〕痨 ／ 〔擻〕擞 ／ 【ノ】

〔諜〕谍 ／ 〔縝〕缜 ／ 〔轄〕辖 ／ 〔償〕偿 ／ 〔齋〕斋 ／ 〔攄〕摅 ／ 〔鵲〕鹊

〔謊〕谎 ／ 〔縛〕缚 ／ 〔輾〕辗 ／ 〔鵊〕鹣 ／ 〔糞〕粪 ／ 〔擺〕摆 ／ 〔鵝〕鹅

〔諫〕谏 ／ 〔縟〕缛 ／ 〔擊〕击 ／ 〔鍥〕锲 ／ 〔糝〕糁 ／ 〔贄〕贽 ／ 〔穫〕获

〔諧〕谐 ／ 〔緻〕致 ／ 〔臨〕临㉞ ／ 〔鍇〕锴 ／ 〔燦〕灿 ／ 〔燾〕焘 ／ 〔穡〕穑

〔謔〕谑 ／ 〔縧〕绦 ／ 〔磽〕硗 ／ 〔鍘〕铡 ／ 〔燭〕烛 ／ *〔聶〕聂 ／ 〔穢〕秽

〔謁〕谒 ／ 〔縫〕缝 ／ 〔壓〕压㉟ ／ 〔錫〕锡 ／ 〔燴〕烩 ／ 〔職〕职 ／ 〔簡〕简

〔謂〕谓 ／ 〔縐〕绉 ／ 〔礄〕硚 ／ 〔鍚〕钖 ／ 〔鴻〕鸿 ／ *〔藝〕艺 ／ 〔簣〕篑

〔諤〕谔 ／ 〔縭〕缡 ／ 〔磯〕矶 ／ 〔鍔〕锷 ／ 〔濤〕涛 ／ 〔覲〕觐 ／ 〔簞〕箪

〔諭〕谕 ／ 〔縑〕缣 ／ 〔鴯〕鸸 ／ 〔鍤〕锸 ／ 〔濫〕滥 ／ 〔鞦〕秋 ／ *〔雙〕双

〔諼〕谖 ／ 〔縊〕缢 ／ 〔邇〕迩 ／ 〔鍬〕锹 ／ 〔濕〕湿 ／ 〔藪〕薮 ／ 〔軀〕躯

〔諷〕讽 ／ 〔尷〕尴 ／ 〔鍾〕钟 ／ 〔濘〕泞 ／ 〔蠆〕虿 ／ *〔邊〕边

〔諮〕谘 ／ 17画 ／ 〔鷙〕鸷 ／ 〔鍛〕锻 ／ 〔濟〕济 ／ 〔繭〕茧 ／ *〔歸〕归㉞

〔諳〕谙 ／ 〔殮〕殓 ／ 〔鎪〕锼 ／ 〔濱〕滨 ／ 〔藥〕药 ／ 〔鏵〕铧

〔諺〕谚 ／ 【一】 ／ 【丨】 ／ 〔鍬〕锹 ／ 〔濘〕泞 ／ 〔藶〕苈 ／ 〔鎮〕镇

〔諦〕谛 ／ 〔耬〕耧 ／ 〔齔〕龀 ／ 〔鍰〕锾 ／ 〔濰〕潍 ／ 〔顒〕颙 ／ 〔鏈〕链

〔謎〕谜 ／ 〔環〕环 ／ 〔戲〕戏 ／ 〔鍍〕镀 ／ 〔懨〕恹 ／ 〔檯〕台 ／ 〔鎘〕镉

〔諢〕诨 ／ 〔贅〕赘 ／ 〔虧〕亏 ／ 〔鎂〕镁 ／ 〔賽〕赛 ／ 〔櫃〕柜 ／ 〔鎖〕锁

〔諱〕讳 ／ 〔璦〕瑷 ／ 〔斃〕毙 ／ 〔鎡〕镃 ／ 〔襇〕裥 ／ 〔檻〕槛 ／ 〔鎧〕铠

〔諝〕谞 ／ 〔覯〕觏 ／ 〔瞭〕了㊱ ／ 〔鎇〕镅 ／ 〔襆〕幞 ／ 〔檳〕槟 ／ 〔鎳〕镍

〔憑〕凭 ／ 〔黿〕鼋 ／ 〔顆〕颗 ／ 〔懇〕恳 ／ 〔禮〕礼 ／ 〔檸〕柠 ／ 〔鎢〕钨

〔鄺〕邝 ／ 〔幫〕帮 ／ 〔購〕购 ／ 〔餷〕馇 ／ 〔鵜〕鹈 ／ 〔櫚〕榈 ／ 〔鎩〕铩

〔瘻〕瘘 ／ 〔騁〕骋 ／ 〔賻〕赙 ／ 〔斂〕敛 ／ 〔鵠〕鹄 ／ 〔鎵〕镓

〔瘮〕瘆 ／ 〔駸〕骎 ／ 〔嬰〕婴 ／ 〔鴿〕鸽 ／ 〔鵒〕鹆 ／ 〔鎬〕镐

*〔親〕亲 ／ 〔駿〕骏 ／ 〔賺〕赚 ／ 〔禮〕礼

〔辦〕办 ／ 〔嚇〕吓㊲

〔闌〕阑

〔鏘〕锵

〔鎰〕镒

〔鎵〕镓

〔饃〕馍

〔餼〕饩

〔餾〕馏

〔饈〕馐

〔臍〕脐

〔鯁〕鲠

〔鯉〕鲤

〔鯀〕鲧

〔鯇〕鲩

〔鯢〕鲵

〔颸〕飔

〔颺〕飏

〔觴〕觞

〔獵〕猎

〔雛〕雏

〔臏〕膑

【丶】

〔謹〕谨

〔謳〕讴

〔謾〕谩

〔謫〕谪

〔謭〕谫

〔謬〕谬

〔癤〕疖

〔雜〕杂

*〔離〕离

〔顏〕颜

〔糧〕粮

〔燼〕烬

〔鵜〕鹈

〔瀆〕渎

〔懣〕懑

〔濾〕滤

〔鯊〕鲨

〔濺〕溅

〔瀏〕浏

〔濼〕泺

〔瀉〕泻

〔瀋〕沈

*〔竄〕窜

〔竅〕窍

〔額〕额

〔禰〕祢

〔襠〕裆

〔襝〕裣

〔禱〕祷

【フ】

〔醬〕酱⑪

〔韞〕韫

〔隴〕陇

〔嬸〕婶

〔繞〕绕

〔繚〕缭
〔織〕织
〔繕〕缮
〔繒〕缯
*〔斷〕断

19画

【一】
〔鵡〕鹉
〔鶄〕鶄
〔鬍〕胡
〔騙〕骗
〔騷〕骚
〔壢〕坜
〔壚〕垆
〔壞〕坏㊵
〔攏〕拢
〔擇〕择
*〔難〕难
〔鵲〕鹊
〔藶〕苈
〔蘋〕苹
〔蘆〕芦
〔鶓〕鹋
〔藺〕蔺
〔蘄〕蕲
〔勸〕劝
〔蘇〕苏
〔藹〕蔼
〔蘢〕茏
〔顛〕颠
〔櫝〕椟
〔櫟〕栎
〔櫓〕橹
〔櫞〕橼
〔轎〕轿
〔鏨〕錾
〔轍〕辙
〔轔〕辚
〔繫〕系㊶
〔鶇〕鸫
*〔麗〕丽㊷
〔厴〕厣
〔礪〕砺
〔礙〕碍
〔礦〕矿
〔贋〕赝
〔願〕愿
〔鶴〕鹤
〔璽〕玺
〔豶〕豮
【丨】
〔贈〕赠
〔闞〕阚
〔關〕关

〔曖〕暧
〔疇〕畴
〔蹺〕跷
〔蟶〕蛏
〔蠅〕蝇
〔蟻〕蚁
*〔嚴〕严
〔獸〕兽
〔嚨〕咙
〔羆〕罴
*〔羅〕罗
【丿】
〔氈〕毡
〔犢〕犊
〔贊〕赞
〔穩〕稳
〔簽〕签
〔簾〕帘
〔簫〕箫
〔牘〕牍
〔懲〕惩
〔鐯〕锗
〔鏗〕铿
〔鏢〕镖
〔鏜〕镗
〔鏤〕镂
〔鏝〕镘
〔鏰〕镚
〔鏞〕镛
〔鏡〕镜
〔鏟〕铲
〔鏑〕镝
〔鏃〕镞
〔鏇〕旋
〔鏘〕锵
〔辭〕辞
〔饉〕馑
〔饅〕馒
〔鵬〕鹏
〔臘〕腊
〔鯖〕鲭
〔鯪〕鲮
〔鯫〕鲰
〔鯡〕鲱
〔鯤〕鲲
〔鯧〕鲳
〔鯢〕鲵
〔鯰〕鲶
〔鯛〕鲷
〔鯨〕鲸
〔鯔〕鲻
〔獺〕獭
〔鵮〕鹐
〔颼〕飕
【丶】
〔譚〕谭
〔譖〕谮
〔譙〕谯

〔識〕识
〔譜〕谱
〔證〕证
〔譎〕谲
〔譏〕讥
〔鶉〕鹑
〔廬〕庐
〔癟〕瘪
〔癢〕痒
〔龐〕庞
〔壟〕垄
〔鶥〕鹛
〔類〕类㊸
〔爍〕烁
〔瀟〕潇
〔瀨〕濑
〔瀝〕沥
〔瀕〕濒
〔瀘〕泸
〔瀧〕泷
〔懶〕懒
〔懷〕怀
〔寵〕宠
〔襪〕袜㊹
〔襤〕褴
【ㄱ】
〔韜〕韬
〔騭〕骘
〔騖〕骛
〔鶩〕鹜
〔顙〕颡
〔繮〕缰
〔繩〕绳
〔繾〕缱
〔繰〕缲
〔繹〕绎
〔繯〕缳
〔繳〕缴
〔繪〕绘

20画

【一】
〔瓏〕珑
〔驁〕骜
〔驊〕骅
〔騮〕骝
〔騸〕骟
〔驂〕骖
〔攖〕撄
〔攔〕拦
〔攙〕搀
〔聹〕聍
〔顢〕颟
〔驀〕蓦
〔蘭〕兰
〔蘞〕蔹
〔蘚〕藓
〔鶘〕鹕

〔飄〕飘
〔櫪〕枥
〔櫨〕栌
〔櫸〕榉
〔礬〕矾
〔麵〕面
〔櫬〕榇
〔櫳〕栊
〔礫〕砾
【丨】
〔鹹〕咸
〔齟〕龃
〔齡〕龄
〔齣〕出
〔齙〕龅
〔齠〕龆
*〔獻〕献
*〔黨〕党
〔懸〕悬
〔鶪〕䴗
〔罌〕罂
〔贍〕赡
〔闥〕闼
〔闡〕阐
〔鶡〕鹖
〔蠣〕蛎
〔蠐〕蛴
〔蠑〕蝾
〔嚶〕嘤
〔鶚〕鹗
〔髏〕髅
〔鶻〕鹘
【丿】
〔犧〕牺
〔籌〕筹
〔籃〕篮
〔譽〕誉
〔覺〕觉
〔嚳〕喾
〔衊〕蔑
〔艦〕舰
〔鐃〕铙
〔鐝〕镢
〔鐐〕镣
〔鏷〕镤
〔鐦〕锎
〔鐧〕锏
〔鐘〕钟
〔鐥〕鐥
〔鐠〕镨
〔鐒〕铹
〔鐋〕铴
〔錯〕错
〔鐨〕镄
〔鐙〕镫
〔鏺〕鏺
【ㄱ】
〔鵬〕鹏
〔騖〕鹜
〔纊〕纩
〔繽〕缤
〔繼〕继
〔饗〕飨
〔鐥〕鐥
〔響〕响

21画

【一】

〔鐽〕钑
〔釋〕释
〔饒〕饶
〔饊〕馓
〔饋〕馈
〔饌〕馔
〔饑〕饥
〔臚〕胪
〔朧〕胧
〔騰〕腾
〔鰆〕䲠
〔鰈〕鲽
〔鰂〕鲗
〔鰛〕鳁
〔鰓〕鳃
〔鰐〕鳄
〔鰍〕鳅
〔鰒〕鳆
〔鰉〕鳇
〔鰁〕鳈
〔鯿〕鳊
〔獼〕猕
〔觸〕触
【丶】
〔護〕护
〔譴〕谴
〔譯〕译
〔譫〕谵
〔議〕议
〔癥〕症
〔辮〕辫
〔龑〕䶮
〔競〕竞
〔贏〕赢
〔糲〕粝
〔糰〕团
〔鷀〕鹚
〔爐〕炉
〔瀾〕澜
〔瀲〕潋
〔瀰〕弥
〔懺〕忏
〔寶〕宝
〔騫〕骞
〔竇〕窦
〔襬〕摆
【ㄱ】
〔鵬〕鹏
〔鶩〕鹜
〔纊〕纩
〔繽〕缤
〔繼〕继
〔饗〕飨
〔鐥〕鐥
〔響〕响

21画

【一】

〔瓔〕璎
〔釋〕释
〔饒〕饶
〔鰭〕鳍
〔鰱〕鲢
〔鰣〕鲥
〔鰨〕鳎
〔騾〕骡
〔驅〕驱
〔驃〕骠
〔驄〕骢
〔攛〕撺
〔韃〕鞑
〔鞽〕鞒
〔歡〕欢
〔權〕权
〔櫻〕樱
〔欄〕栏
〔轟〕轰
〔覽〕览
〔酈〕郦
〔飆〕飙
〔殲〕歼
【丨】
〔齜〕龇
〔齦〕龈
〔齬〕龉
〔贐〕赆
〔囁〕嗫
〔囈〕呓
〔闢〕辟
〔囀〕啭
〔顥〕颢
〔躊〕踌
〔躋〕跻
〔躑〕踯
〔躍〕跃
〔纍〕累
〔蠟〕蜡
〔囂〕嚣
〔巋〕岿
〔髒〕脏
【丿】
〔儺〕傩
〔儷〕俪
〔儼〕俨
〔鷂〕鹞
〔鐵〕铁
〔鑊〕镬
〔鐳〕镭
〔鐲〕镯
〔鐮〕镰
〔鐿〕镱
〔鑄〕铸
〔鐸〕铎
〔鐺〕铛
〔鷚〕鹨
〔霽〕霁

〔鴿〕鸽
〔臟〕脏
〔臕〕膘
〔鰭〕鳍
〔鰱〕鲢
〔鰥〕鳏
〔鰟〕鳑
〔鰜〕鳒
〔鰢〕鳚
〔鰰〕鰰
〔鱅〕鳙
〔鰾〕鳔
〔鰻〕鳗
〔鱂〕鳉
〔鰼〕鳛
〔玀〕猡
【丶】
〔讀〕读
〔讅〕审
〔巒〕峦
〔彎〕弯
〔孿〕孪
〔變〕变
〔顫〕颤
〔鷓〕鹧
〔癭〕瘿
〔癬〕癣
〔聾〕聋
〔龔〕龚
〔襲〕袭
〔灑〕洒
〔竊〕窃
【ㄱ】
〔鷚〕鹨
〔轡〕辔

22画

【一】
〔鬚〕须
〔驍〕骁
〔驕〕骄
〔攤〕摊
〔攢〕攒
〔鷙〕鸷
〔聽〕听
〔蘿〕萝
〔驚〕惊
〔轢〕轹
〔鷗〕鸥
〔鑒〕鉴
〔邐〕逦
〔驚〕鸶
〔霽〕霁

〔癲〕癫
〔癗〕癗
〔癮〕瘾
〔斕〕斓
〔爛〕烂
〔鶯〕莺
〔灄〕滠
〔灃〕沣
〔灘〕滩
〔灕〕漓
〔懼〕惧
〔懾〕慑
〔竈〕灶
〔顧〕顾
〔襯〕衬
〔鶴〕鹤
【ㄱ】
*〔屬〕属
〔纈〕缬
〔續〕续
〔纏〕缠㊺

22画

【一】
〔鬚〕须
〔驍〕骁
〔驕〕骄
〔攤〕摊
〔攢〕攒
〔鷙〕鸷
〔聽〕听
〔蘿〕萝
〔驚〕惊
〔轢〕轹
〔鷗〕鸥
〔鑒〕鉴
〔邐〕逦
〔驚〕鸶
〔霽〕霁

第八栏（续）

〔鱉〕鳖
〔黷〕黩
〔躚〕跹
〔躓〕踬
〔蠨〕蟏
〔囌〕苏
〔囉〕啰
〔巔〕巅
〔邏〕逻
〔體〕体
【丿】
〔罎〕坛
〔籜〕箨
〔籟〕籁
〔籠〕笼
〔繁〕鳘
〔儻〕傥
〔艫〕舻
〔鑄〕铸
〔鑌〕镔
〔鑔〕镲
〔龕〕龛
〔鱈〕鳕
〔鰌〕鳝
〔鰍〕鳜
〔鱒〕鳟
【丶】
〔讀〕读
〔讅〕审
〔巒〕峦
〔彎〕弯
〔孿〕孪
〔變〕变
〔顫〕颤
〔鷓〕鹧
〔癭〕瘿
〔癬〕癣
〔聾〕聋
〔龔〕龚
〔襲〕袭
〔灘〕滩
〔灑〕洒
〔竊〕窃
【ㄱ】
〔鷚〕鹨
〔轡〕辔

23画

【一】

1396

〔瓉〕瓒
〔驛〕驿
〔驗〕验
〔攪〕搅
〔欏〕椤
〔轤〕轳
〔臕〕膘
〔魘〕魇
〔鷜〕鹡
〔鍵〕键
〔顲〕颥
【丨】
〔曬〕晒
〔鷴〕鹇
〔顯〕显
〔蠱〕蛊
〔髖〕髋
〔髕〕髌
【丿】
〔籤〕签
〔讎〕雠㊻
仇
〔鷦〕鹪

〔黴〕霉
〔鑠〕铄
〔鑕〕锧
〔鑥〕镥
〔鑢〕镰
〔鑱〕镵
〔臟〕脏
〔鱲〕鱲
〔鱔〕鳝
〔鱗〕鳞
〔鱒〕鳟
【丶】
〔讌〕谳
〔欒〕栾
〔攣〕挛
〔變〕变
〔戀〕恋
〔鷟〕鸷
〔癰〕痈
〔廱〕廱
〔讋〕詟
【乛】
〔鷓〕鹧

24画

【一】
〔鬢〕鬓
〔攬〕揽
〔驟〕骤
〔壩〕坝
〔韆〕千
〔觀〕观
〔鹽〕盐
〔釀〕酿
〔靂〕雳
*〔靈〕灵
〔蠶〕蚕㊽
【丨】
〔豔〕艳
〔顰〕颦
〔齲〕龋

〔齷〕龌
〔鹼〕硷
〔臢〕臜
〔鷺〕鹭
〔囑〕嘱
〔羈〕羁
【丿】
〔籩〕笾
〔籬〕篱
〔籪〕簖
〔黌〕黉
〔鱟〕鲎
〔鱠〕鲙
〔鱨〕鲿
【丶】
〔讕〕谰
〔讖〕谶
〔讒〕谗
〔讓〕让
〔鸊〕䴙
〔鷹〕鹰
〔癱〕瘫
〔癲〕癫
〔鱭〕鲚

〔贛〕赣
〔灝〕灏
【乛】
〔矚〕瞩

25画

【一】
〔韉〕鞯
〔欖〕榄
〔靉〕叆
【丨】
〔顱〕颅
〔躡〕蹑
〔躕〕蹰
〔鼉〕鼍
【丿】
〔籮〕箩
〔鑭〕镧
〔鑰〕钥
〔鑲〕镶
〔饞〕馋
〔鱭〕鲚
〔鱷〕鳄

【丶】
〔蠻〕蛮
〔臠〕脔
〔廳〕厅㊾
〔灣〕湾
【乛】
〔糶〕粜
〔纘〕缵

26画

【一】
〔驥〕骥
〔驢〕驴
〔趲〕趱
〔顴〕颧
〔黶〕黡
〔釅〕酽
【丨】
〔矚〕瞩
〔躑〕踯
〔躓〕踬
〔躦〕躜
【丿】

〔邐〕逦
〔鑷〕镊
〔鑹〕镩
【丶】
〔灤〕滦

27画

【一】
〔顳〕颞㉕
〔驤〕骧
〔顥〕颢
【丨】
〔鸕〕鸬
〔黷〕黩
【丿】
〔鑼〕锣
〔鑽〕钻
〔鱸〕鲈
【丶】
〔讞〕谳
〔讜〕谠
〔鑾〕銮
〔豓〕滟
【乛】
〔纜〕缆

28画

【丶】
〔鸛〕鹳
〔欞〕棂
〔鑿〕凿
〔鸚〕鹦
〔钂〕锐
〔钂〕镬
〔戇〕戆

29画

〔驪〕骊
〔鬱〕郁

30画

〔鸝〕鹂
〔饢〕馕
〔鱺〕鲡
〔鸞〕鸾

32画

〔籲〕吁㊿

注　释

①长：四笔。笔顺是：ノ⊂乄长。

②马：三笔。笔顺是：丆马马。

③庄：六笔。下从土，不从圡。

④条：上从夂，三笔，不从夂。

⑤鸟：四笔。笔顺是：ノ勹乌乌。

⑥壳：八笔。上从士，下从几。

⑦乾坤、乾隆的乾读qián（前），不简化。

⑧区：不作区。

⑨鸟：五笔。笔顺是：ノ勹勺鸟鸟。

⑩中药苍术、白术的术读zhú（竹），异体为朮。

⑪将、浆、桨、奖、酱：右上角从夕，不从夕或夗。

⑫尧：六笔。右上作戈，无点；不可误作戈。

⑬叶韵的叶读xié（协）。

⑭无：四笔。上从二，不可误作旡。

⑮黾：从口从电。

⑯义：从乂（读yì）加点。不可误作叉（读chā）。

⑰肃：中间一竖下面的两边从八，下半中间不从米。

⑱在折和摺意义可能混淆时，摺仍用摺。

⑲尝：不是赏的简化字。赏的简化字是赏。

⑳作多解的夥不简化。

㉑前仆后继的仆读pū（扑）。

㉒么读me轻声。读yāo（夭）的么应作幺，么为异体。吆（吆）喝的吆为异体，应作吆。麼读mó（摩）时不简化，如幺麼小丑。

㉓古人南宫适、洪适的适（古字罕用）读kuò（括）。此适字本作适，为了避免混淆，可恢复本字适。

㉔作门屏之间解的宁（古字罕用）读zhù（柱）。为避免此宁字与宁的简化字混淆，原读zhù的宁作㝉，如伫（㐰）立。

㉕門字头的字，一般也写作門字头，如鬧、鬮、鬩也可写作閙、鬮、閲。因此，这些鬥字头的字可简化作门字头。但鬥争的鬥应简作斗。

㉖卖：从十从买，上不从士或土。

㉗赏：不可误作尝。尝是嘗的简化字。

㉘宫商角徵羽的徵读zhǐ（止），不简化。

㉙在余和馀意义可能混淆时，仍用馀。如文言句"馀年无多"。

㉚庆：下从大，不从犬。

㉛写：上从冖，不从宀。

㉜县：七笔。上从且。

㉝藉口、凭藉的藉简化作借；慰藉、狼藉等的藉仍用藉。

㉞临：左从一短竖一长竖，不从丨。归、帅、师不同，左从丨。旧与归也不同，左一竖，右从日。

㉟压：六笔。土的右旁有一点。

㊱瞭：读liǎo（了解）时，简作了；读liào（瞭望）时仍作瞭，不简化。

㊲恐吓的吓读hè（赫）。

㊳岭：不作岺，免与岑混。

㊴四川省酆都县已改丰都县。姓酆的酆不简化。

㊵坏（壞），不作坯。坯是砖坯的坯，读pī（批）。坏坯二字不可互混。

㊶系带子的系读jì（计）。

㊷丽：七笔。上边一横，不作两小横。

㊸类：下从大，不从犬。

㊹袜：从末，不从未。

㊺缠：右从厘，不从厘。

㊻雠：用于校雠、雠定、仇雠等。表示仇恨、仇敌义时用仇。

㊼纤维的纤读xiān（先）。拉纤的纤读qiàn（欠）。

㊽蚕：上从天，不从夭。

㊾厅：从厂，不从广。

㊿喘吁吁、长吁短叹的吁读xū（虚）。

附录二

Appendix 2

汉语拼音方案

The Chinese Phonetic System

1. 字母表　　The Chinese Phonetic Alphabet

字母	名称		字母	名称		字母	名称	
	国际音标	注音字母		国际音标	注音字母		国际音标	注音字母
Aa	[a]	ㄚ	Jj	[tɕiɛ]	ㄐ丨ㄝ	Ss	[ɛs]	ㄝㄙ
Bb	[pɛ]	ㄅㄝ	Kk	[kʻɛ]	ㄎㄝ	Tt	[tʻɛ]	ㄊㄝ
Cc	[tsʻɛ]	ㄘㄝ	Ll	[ɛl]	ㄝㄌ	Uu	[u]	ㄨ
Dd	[tɛ]	ㄉㄝ	Mm	[ɛm]	ㄝㄇ	*Vv	[vɛ]	ㄪㄝ
Ee	[ɤ]	ㄜ	NN	[nɛ]	ㄋㄝ	Ww	[wa]	ㄨㄚ
Ff	[ɛf]	ㄝㄈ	Oo	[o]	ㄛ	Xx	[ɕi]	ㄒ丨
Gg	[kɛ]	ㄍㄝ	Pp	[pʻɛ]	ㄆㄝ	Yy	[ja]	丨ㄚ
Hh	[xa]	ㄏㄚ	Qq	[tɕʻiou]	ㄑ丨ㄡ	Zz	[tsɛ]	ㄗㄝ
Ii	[i]	丨	Rr	[ar]	ㄚㄦ			

＊v 只用来拼写外来语、少数民族语言和方言。

2. 声母表　　Initials of the Chinese Phonetic System

声母	读音			声母	读音		
	国际音标	注音字母	汉字		国际音标	注音字母	汉字
b	[p]	ㄅ	玻	j	[tɕ]	ㄐ	基
p	[pʻ]	ㄆ	坡	q	[tɕʻ]	ㄑ	欺
m	[m]	ㄇ	摸	x	[ɕ]	ㄒ	希
f	[f]	ㄈ	佛	zh	[tʂ]	ㄓ	知
d	[t]	ㄉ	德	ch	[tʂʻ]	ㄔ	痴
t	[tʻ]	ㄊ	特	sh	[ʂ]	ㄕ	诗
n	[n]	ㄋ	讷	r	[ʐ]	ㄖ	日
l	[l]	ㄌ	勒	z	[ts]	ㄗ	资
g	[k]	ㄍ	哥	c	[tsʻ]	ㄘ	雌
k	[kʻ]	ㄎ	科	s	[s]	ㄙ	思
h	[x]	ㄏ	喝				

＊ng[ŋ]在一些方言中作声母；在普通话中只出现在韵尾，不作声母。注音字母用兀表示这个音。

3. 韵母表 Finals of the Chinese Phonetic System

无韵头组			i 韵头组			u 韵头组			ü 韵头组		
韵 母			韵 母			韵 母			韵 母		
注音字母	国际音标	汉字	注音字母	国际音标	汉字	注音字母	国际音标	汉字	注音字母	国际音标	汉字
			i(yi)			u(wu)			ü(yu)		
			ㄧ	[i]	衣	ㄨ	[u]	乌	ㄩ	[y]	迂
a			ia(ya)			ua(wa)					
ㄚ	[a]	啊	ㄧㄚ	[ia]	呀	ㄨㄚ	[ua]	蛙			
o						uo(wo)					
ㄛ	[o]	喔				ㄨㄛ	[uo]	窝			
e											
ㄜ	[ɤ]	鹅									
ê			ie(ye)						üe(yue)		
ㄝ	[ɛ]	欸	ㄧㄝ	[iɛ]	耶				ㄩㄝ	[yɛ]	约
er											
ㄦ	[ər]	耳									
ai						uai(wai)					
ㄞ	[ai]	哀				ㄨㄞ	[uai]	歪			
ei						ui(wei)					
ㄟ	[ei]	欸				ㄨㄟ	[uei]	威			
ao			iao(yao)								
ㄠ	[au]	奥	ㄧㄠ	[iau]	腰						
ou			iu(you)								
ㄡ	[ou]	欧	ㄧㄡ	[iou]	忧						
an			ian(yan)			uan(wan)			üan(yuan)		
ㄢ	[an]	安	ㄧㄢ	[iɛn]	烟	ㄨㄢ	[uan]	弯	ㄩㄢ	[yɛn]	冤
en			in(yin)			un(wen)			ün(yun)		
ㄣ	[ən]	恩	ㄧㄣ	[in]	因	ㄨㄣ	[uən]	温	ㄩㄣ	[yn]	晕
ang			iang(yang)			uang(wang)					
ㄤ	[aŋ]	昂	ㄧㄤ	[iaŋ]	央	ㄨㄤ	[uaŋ]	汪			
eng			ing(ying)			ueng(weng)					
ㄥ	[əŋ] 亨的韵母		ㄧㄥ	[iŋ]	英	ㄨㄥ	[ueŋ][uəŋ]	翁			
ong			iong(yong)								
ㄨㄥ	[uŋ] 轰的韵母		ㄩㄥ	[iuŋ][yŋ]	雍						

*(1)zi(资)、ci(雌)、si(思)的韵母读作[ɿ],但写作 i;zhi(知)、chi(痴)、shi(诗)、ri(日)的韵母读作[ʅ],但写作 i。

(2)韵母儿(耳、二等)写成 er;用做韵尾时写成 r。例如,"儿童"拼作 ertong,"花儿"拼作 huar。

(3)韵母ㄝ[ɛ]单用的时候写成 ê。

(4)i 韵头的韵母,前面没有声母时,写成:yi(衣),ya(呀),ye(耶),yao(腰),you(忧),yan(烟),yin(因),yang(央),ying(英),yong(雍)。

u 韵头的韵母,前面没有声母时,写成:wu(乌),wa(蛙),wo(窝),wai(歪),wei(威),wan(弯),wen(温),wang(汪),weng(翁)。

ü韵头的韵母,前面没有声母时,写成:yu(迂),yue(约),yuan(冤),yun(晕),ü上两点省略。ü韵头的韵母跟声母 j,q,x 拼的时候,写成:ju(居),qu(区),xu(虚),ü上两点也省略;但是跟声母 n,l 拼的时候,仍然写成 nü(女),lü(吕)。

4. 声调符号　　Signs for the Four Tones

阴平	阳平	上声	去声
ˉ	ˊ	ˇ	ˋ

声调符号标在音节的基本韵母上, 轻声不标。例如:

妈 mā	麻 má	马 mǎ	骂 mà	吗 ma
(阴平)	(阳平)	(上声)	(去声)	(轻声)

5. 隔音符号　　Syllable Division Sign

a, o, e开头的音节连接在其他音节后面的时候, 如果音节的界限发生混淆, 用隔音符号(')隔开, 例如: pi'ao(皮袄), ming'e(名额), Yan'an(延安)。

附录三
Appendix 3
世界各国家、地区、首都(或首府)及货币名称表
Countries, Regions, Capitals and Currencies

国家、地区 Country, Region	全称 Official Name	首都(首府) Capital	货币 Currency	地理位置 Location
阿尔巴尼亚 Albania	阿尔巴尼亚共和国 the Republic of Albania	地拉那 Tirana	列克 Lek	欧洲 Europe
阿尔及利亚 Algeria	阿尔及利亚民主人民共和国 the Democratic People's Republic of Algeria	阿尔及尔 Algiers	阿尔及利亚第纳尔 Algerian Dinar (DA)	非洲 Africa
阿富汗 Afghanistan	阿富汗共和国 the Republic of Afghanistan	喀布尔 Kabul	阿富汗尼 Afghani (Af)	亚洲 Asia
阿根廷 Argentina	阿根廷共和国 the Republic of Argentina	布宜诺斯艾利斯 Buenos Aires	奥斯特拉尔 Austral (A)	拉丁美洲 Latin America
阿拉伯联合酋长国 the United Arab Emirates	阿拉伯联合酋长国 the United Arab Emirates	阿布扎比 Abu Dhabi	迪拉姆 Dirham (Dh)	亚洲 Asia
阿鲁巴(荷) Aruba	阿鲁巴(荷) Aruba	奥兰也斯塔德 Oranjestad	阿鲁巴盾或弗罗林 Aruban Guilder or Florin (AFl)	拉丁美洲 Latin America
阿曼 Oman	阿曼苏丹国 the Sultanate of Oman	马斯喀特 Muscat	阿曼里亚尔 Omani Rial (RO)	亚洲 Asia
阿塞拜疆 Azerbaijan	阿塞拜疆共和国 the Azerbaijani Republic	巴库 Baku	卢布 Rouble (Rubl)	欧洲 Europe
埃及 Egypt	阿拉伯埃及共和国 the Arab Republic of Egypt	开罗 Cairo	埃及镑 Egyptian Pound	非洲 Africa
埃塞俄比亚 Ethiopia	埃塞俄比亚人民民主共和国 the People's Democratic Republic of Ethiopia	亚的斯亚贝巴 Addis Ababa	比尔 Birr	非洲 Africa
爱尔兰 Ireland	爱尔兰共和国 the Republic of Ireland	都柏林 Dublin	爱尔兰镑 Irish Pound (I$)	欧洲 Europe
爱沙尼亚 Estonia	爱沙尼亚共和国 the Republic of Estonia	塔林 Tallinn	卢布 Rouble (Rubl)	欧洲 Europe
安道尔 Andorra	安道尔公国 the Principality of Andorra	安道尔城 Andorra la Vella	西班牙比塞塔和法国法郎 Spanish Peseta and French Franc	欧洲 Europe
安哥拉 Angola	安哥拉人民共和国 the People's Republic of Angola	罗安达 Luanda	宽扎 Kwanza (K)	非洲 Africa
安圭拉(英) Anguilla	安圭拉(英) Anguilla	瓦利 Valley	东加勒比元 East Caribbean Dollar (EC$)	拉丁美洲 Latin America

国家、地区 Country, Region	全称 Official Name	首都(首府) Capital	货币 Currency	地理位置 Location
安提瓜岛和巴布达 Antigua and Barbuda	安提瓜岛和巴布达 Antigua and Barbuda	圣约翰 St. John's	东加勒比元 East Caribbean Dollar (EC$)	拉丁美洲 Latin America
澳大利亚 Australia	澳大利亚联邦 the Commonwealth of Australia	堪培拉 Canberra	澳大利亚元 Australian Dollar ($A)	大洋洲及太平 洋岛屿 Oceania and the Pacific Islands
奥地利 Austria	奥地利共和国 the Republic of Austria	维也纳 Vienna	奥地利先令 Austrian Schilling	欧洲 Europe
巴巴多斯 Barbados	巴巴多斯 Barbados	布里奇顿 Bridgetown	巴巴多斯元 Barbados Dollar	拉丁美洲 Latin America
巴布亚新几内亚 Papua New Guinea	巴布亚新几内亚独立国 the Independent State of Papua New Guinea	莫尔兹比港 Port Moresby	基那 Kina (K)	大洋洲及太平 洋岛屿 Oceania and the Pacific Islands
巴哈马 the Bahamas	巴哈马联邦 the Commonwealth of the Bahamas	拿骚 Nassau	巴哈马元 Bahamian Dollar (B$)	拉丁美洲 Latin America
巴基斯坦 Pakistan	巴基斯坦伊斯兰共和国 the Islamic Republic of Pakistan	伊斯兰堡 Islamabad	巴基斯坦卢比 Pakistan Rupee	亚洲 Asia
巴拉圭 Paraguay	巴拉圭共和国 the Republic of Paraguay	亚松森 Asunción	瓜拉尼 Guarani (G)	拉丁美洲 Latin America
巴勒斯坦 Palestine	巴勒斯坦国 the State of Palestine			亚洲 Asia
巴林 Bahrain	巴林国 the State of Bahrain	麦纳麦 Manama	巴林第纳尔 Bahrain Dinar (BD)	亚洲 Asia
巴拿马 Panama	巴拿马共和国 the Republic of Panama	巴拿马城 Panama City	巴波亚 Balboa (B)	拉丁美洲 Latin America
巴西 Brazil	巴西联邦共和国 the Federative Republic of Brazil	巴西利亚 Brasilia	克罗扎多 Cruzado (CZ$)	拉丁美洲 Latin America
白俄罗斯 Belarus	白俄罗斯共和国 the Republic of Belarus	明斯克 Minsk	卢布 Rouble (Rubl)	欧洲 Europe
百慕大群岛(英) Bermuda	百慕大群岛(英) the Bermuda Islands	哈密尔顿 Hamilton	百慕大元 Bermuda Dollar (B$)	北美洲 North America
保加利亚 Bulgaria	保加利亚共和国 the Republic of Bulgaria	索非亚 Sofia	列弗 Lev	欧洲 Europe
北马里亚纳(美) the Northern Mariana Islands	北马里亚纳联邦(美) the Commonwealth of the Northern Mariana Islands	塞班 Saipan	美元 United States Dollar ($)	大洋洲及太平 洋岛屿 Oceania and the Pacific Islands

国家、地区 Country, Region	全称 Official Name	首都(首府) Capital	货币 Currency	地理位置 Location
贝劳 Belau	贝劳共和国 the Republic of Belau	科罗尔 Koror	美元 United States Dollar ($)	大洋洲及太平洋岛屿 Oceania and the Pacific Islands
贝宁 Benin	贝宁共和国 the Republic of Benin	波多诺伏 Porto Novo	非洲金融共同体法郎 Franc de la Communauté Financière Africaine (CFAF)	非洲 Africa
比利时 Belgium	比利时王国 the Kingdom of Belgium	布鲁塞尔 Brussels	比利时法郎 Franc Belge (FB)	欧洲 Europe
秘鲁 Peru	秘鲁共和国 the Republic of Peru	利马 Lima	新索尔 New Sol	拉丁美洲 Latin America
冰岛 Iceland	冰岛共和国 the Republic of Iceland	雷克雅未克 Reykjàvik	冰岛克朗 Icelandic Króna (IKr)	欧洲 Europe
波多黎各岛 Puerto Rico	波多黎各自由联邦 the Commonwealth of Puerto Rico	圣胡安 San Juan	美元 United States Dollar ($)	拉丁美洲 Latin America
波黑 Bosnia-Herzegovena	波斯尼亚-黑塞哥维那共和国 the Republic of Bosnia-Herzegovena	萨拉热窝 Sarajevo	第纳尔 Dinar	欧洲 Europe
波兰 Poland	波兰共和国 the Republic of Poland	华沙 Warsaw	兹罗提 Zloty (Zl)	欧洲 Europe
玻利维亚 Bolivia	玻利维亚共和国 the Republic of Bolivia	拉巴斯(政府所在地) La Paz 苏克雷(法定首都) Sucre	玻利维亚诺 Boliviano (B)	拉丁美洲 Latin America
博茨瓦纳 Botswana	博茨瓦纳共和国 the Republic of Botswana	哈博罗内 Gaborone	普拉 Pula (P)	非洲 Africa
伯利兹 Belize	伯利兹 Belize	贝尔莫潘 Belmopan	伯利兹元 Belizean Dollar (BZ$)	拉丁美洲 Latin America
不丹 Bhutan	不丹王国 the Kingdom of Bhutan	廷布 Thimphu	努尔特鲁姆 Ngultrum (Nu)	亚洲 Asia
布基纳法索 Burkina Faso	布基纳法索 Burkina Faso	瓦加杜古 Ouagadougou	非洲金融共同体法郎 Franc de La Communauté Financière Africaine (CFAF)	非洲 Africa
布隆迪 Burundi	布隆迪共和国 the Republic of Burundi	布琼布拉 Bujumbura	布隆迪法郎 Burundi Franc (FBu)	非洲 Africa
朝鲜 Korea	朝鲜民主主义人民共和国 the Democratic People's Republic of Korea	平壤 Pyongyang	圆 Won	亚洲 Asia
赤道几内亚 Equatorial Guinea	赤道几内亚共和国 the Republic of Equatorial Guinea	马拉博 Malabo	中非金融合作法郎 Franc de la Coopération Financière en Afrique Centrale (CFAF)	非洲 Africa

国家、地区 Country, Region	全称 Official Name	首都(首府) Capital	货币 Currency	地理位置 Location
丹麦 Denmark	丹麦王国 the Kingdom of Denmark	哥本哈根 Copenhagen	丹麦克朗 Danish Krone (DKr)	欧洲 Europe
德国 Germany	德意志联邦共和国 the Federal Republic of Germany	波恩 Bonn	德意志马克 Deutsche Mark (DM)	欧洲 Europe
东帝汶 East Timor	东帝汶民主共和国 the Democratic Republic of East Timor	帝力 Dili	印度尼西亚盾 Indonesian Rupiah(Rp)	亚洲 Asia
东萨摩亚(美) Eastern Samoa	东萨摩亚(美) Eastern Samoa	帕果-帕果 Pago-Pago	美元 United States Dollar ($)	大洋洲及太平洋岛屿 Oceania and the Pacific Islands
多哥 Togo	多哥共和国 the Republic of Togo	洛美 Lomé	非洲金融共同体法郎 Franc de la Communauté Financière Africaine (CFAF)	非洲 Africa
多米尼加岛 Dominica	多米尼加联邦 the Commonwealth of Dominica	罗索 Roseau	东加勒比元 East Caribbean Dollar (EC$)	拉丁美洲 Latin America
多米尼加共和国 the Dominican Republic	多米尼加共和国 the Dominican Republic	圣多明各 Santo Domingo	比索 Peso	拉丁美洲 Latin America
俄罗斯 Russia	俄罗斯联邦 the Russian Federation	莫斯科 Moscow	卢布 Rouble (Rubl)	欧亚 Europe, Asia
厄瓜多尔 Ecuador	厄瓜多尔共和国 the Republic of Ecuador	基多 Quito	苏克雷 Sucre (s)	拉丁美洲 Latin America
厄立特里亚 Eritrea	厄立特里亚 Eritrea	阿斯马拉 Asmara	比尔 Birr	非洲 Africa
法国 France	法兰西共和国 the Republic of France	巴黎 Paris	法郎 Franc	欧洲 Europe
法罗群岛(丹) the Faeroe Islands	法罗群岛(丹) the Faeroe Islands	曹斯哈恩 Tórshavn	法罗克朗 Faeroe Krone	欧洲 Europe
法属波利尼西亚 French Polynesia	法属波利尼西亚 French Polynesia	帕皮提 Papeete	太平洋结算法郎 Franc des Comptoirs Francais du Pacifique (CFP Franc)	大洋洲及太平洋岛屿 Oceania and the Pacific Islands
梵蒂冈 the Vatican	梵蒂冈城国 the Vatican City State	梵蒂冈城 the Vatican City	意大利里拉 Italian Lira	欧洲 Europe
菲律宾 the Philippines	菲律宾共和国 the Republic of the Philippines	马尼拉 Manila	菲律宾比索 Philippine Peso(P)	亚洲 Asia

国家、地区 Country, Region	全称 Official Name	首都(首府) Capital	货币 Currency	地理位置 Location
斐济 Fiji	斐济共和国 the Republic of Fiji	苏瓦 Suva	斐济元 Fiji Dollar ($F)	大洋洲及太平洋岛屿 Oceania and the Pacific Islands
芬兰 Finland	芬兰共和国 the Republic of Finland	赫尔辛基 Helsinki	芬兰马克 Finnish Markka (FIM)	欧洲 Europe
佛得角 Cape Verde	佛得角共和国 the Republic of Cape Verde	普拉亚 Praia	佛得角埃斯库多 Cape Verde Escudo (C.V.Esc)	非洲 Africa
冈比亚 the Gambia	冈比亚共和国 the Republic of the Gambia	班珠尔 Banjul	达拉西 Dalasi	非洲 Africa
刚果 the Congo	刚果共和国 the Republic of the Congo	布拉柴维尔 Brazzaville	中非金融合作法郎 Franc de la Coopéra-tion Financière en Afri-que Centrale (CFAF)	非洲 Africa
哥伦比亚 Colombia	哥伦比亚共和国 the Republic of Colombia	圣非波哥大 Santa Fe Bogotá	比索 Peso	拉丁美洲 Latin America
哥斯达黎加 Costa Rica	哥斯达黎加共和国 the Republic of Costa Rica	圣何塞 San José	科郎 Colón (₡)	拉丁美洲 Latin America
格林纳达 Grenada	格林纳达 Grenada	圣乔治 St. George's	东加勒比元 East Caribbean Dollar (EC$)	拉丁美洲 Latin America
格陵兰(丹) Greenland	格陵兰(丹) Greenland	戈特霍普 Godthaab	丹麦克朗 Danish Krone (DKr)	欧洲 Europe
格鲁吉亚 Georgia	格鲁吉亚共和国 the Republic of Georgia	第比利斯 Tbilisi	卢布 Rouble(Rubl)	欧洲 Europe
古巴 Cuba	古巴共和国 the Republic of Cuba	哈瓦那 La Havana	比索 Peso	拉丁美洲 Latin America
瓜德罗普(法) Guadeloupe	瓜德罗普(法) Guadeloupe	巴斯特尔 Basse-Terre	法国法郎 French Franc	拉丁美洲 Latin America
关岛(美) Guam	关岛(美) Guam	阿加尼亚 Agaña	美元 United States Dollar ($)	大洋洲及太平洋岛屿 Oceania and the Pacific Islands
圭亚那 Guyana	圭亚那合作共和国 the Cooperative Republic of Guyana	乔治敦 Georgetown	圭亚那元 Guyana Dollar ($G)	拉丁美洲 Latin America
圭亚那(法) French Guiana	圭亚那(法) French Guiana	卡宴 Cayenne	法国法郎 French Franc	拉丁美洲 Latin America
哈萨克斯坦 Kazakhstan	哈萨克斯坦共和国 the Republic of Kazakhstan	阿拉木图 Alma-Ata	卢布 Rouble (Rubl)	亚洲 Asia

国家、地区 Country, Region	全称 Official Name	首都(首府) Capital	货币 Currency	地理位置 Location
海地 Haiti	海地共和国 the Republic of Haiti	太子港 Port-au-Prince	古德 Gourde	拉丁美洲 Latin America
韩国 Korea	大韩民国 the Republic of Korea	汉城 Seoul	元 Won	亚洲 Asia
豪兰岛和贝克岛(美) Howland Island and Baker Island	豪兰岛和贝克岛(美) Howland Island and Baker Island		美元 United States Dollar ($)	大洋洲及太平洋岛屿 Oceania and the Pacific Islands
荷兰 the Netherlands	荷兰王国 the Kingdom of the Netherlands	阿姆斯特丹 Amsterdam 海牙(政府所在地) The Hague (the seat of government)	荷兰盾 Guilder or Florin (FI)	欧洲 Europe
荷属安的列斯 Netherlands Antilles	荷属安的列斯 Netherlands Antilles	威廉斯塔德 Willemstad	荷属安的列斯盾 Netherlands Antilles Guilder or Florin (NAFI)	拉丁美洲 Latin America
洪都拉斯 Honduras	洪都拉斯共和国 the Republic of Honduras	特古西加尔巴 Tegucigalpa	伦皮拉 Lempira (L)	拉丁美洲 Latin America
基里巴斯 Kiribati	基里巴斯共和国 the Republic of Kiribati	塔拉瓦 Tarawa	澳大利亚元 Australian Dollar ($A)	大洋洲及太平洋岛屿 Oceania and the Pacific Islands
吉布提 Djibouti	吉布提共和国 the Republic of Djibouti	吉布提 Djibouti	吉布提法郎 Djibouti Franc (DF)	非洲 Africa
吉尔吉斯斯坦 Kirghizstan	吉尔吉斯斯坦共和国 the Republic of Kirghizstan	比什凯克 Bishkek	卢布 Rouble (Rubl)	亚洲 Asia
几内亚 Guinea	几内亚共和国 the Republic of Guinea	科纳克里 Conakry	几内亚法郎 Guinea Franc (GF)	非洲 Africa
几内亚比绍 Guinea-Bissau	几内亚比绍共和国 the Republic of Guinea-Bissau	比绍 Bissau	比索 Peso	非洲 Africa
加拿大 Canada	加拿大 Canada	渥太华 Ottawa	加拿大元 Canadian Dollar (C$)	北美洲 North America
加纳 Ghana	加纳共和国 the Republic of Ghana	阿克拉 Accra	塞迪 Cedi	非洲 Africa
加蓬 Gabon	加蓬共和国 the Gabonese Republic	利伯维尔 Libreville	中非金融合作法郎 Franc de la Coopération Financière en Afrique Centrale (CFAF)	非洲 Africa
柬埔寨 Cambodia	柬埔寨 Cambodia	金边 Phnom Penh	瑞尔 Riel	亚洲 Asia
捷克 Czech	捷克共和国 the Czech Republic	布拉格 Prague	克朗 Koruna	欧洲 Europe

国家、地区 Country, Region	全称 Official Name	首都(首府) Capital	货币 Currency	地理位置 Location
津巴布韦 Zimbabwe	津巴布韦共和国 the Republic of Zimbabwe	哈拉雷 Harare	津巴布韦元 Zimbabwe Dollar (Z$)	非洲 Africa
喀麦隆 Cameroon	喀麦隆共和国 the Republic of Cameroon	雅温得 Yaoundé	中非金融合作法郎 Franc de la Coopéra-tion Financière en Afri-que Centrale (CFAF)	非洲 Africa
卡塔尔 Qatar	卡塔尔国 the State of Qatar	多哈 Doha	卡塔尔里亚尔 Qatar Riyal (QR)	亚洲 Asia
开曼群岛(英) Cayman Islands	开曼群岛(英) Cayman Islands	乔治敦 Georgetown	开曼元 Cayman Dollar (C$)	拉丁美洲 Latin America
科摩罗 the Comoros	科摩罗伊斯兰联邦共和国 the Federal Islamic Repub-lic of the Comoros	莫罗尼 Moroni	科摩罗法郎 Comoros Franc	非洲 Africa
科特迪瓦 Côte d'Ivoire	科特迪瓦共和国 the Republic of Côte d'Ivoire	亚穆苏克罗 Yamoussoukro	非洲金融共同体法郎 Franc de la Com-munauté Financière Afri-caine (CFAF)	非洲 Africa
科威特 Kuwait	科威特国 the State of Kuwait	科威特城 Kuwait City	科威特第纳尔 Kuwaiti Dinar (KD)	亚洲 Asia
克罗地亚 Croatia	克罗地亚共和国 the Republic of Croatia	萨格勒布 Zagreb	第纳尔 Dinar	欧洲 Europe
肯尼亚 Kenya	肯尼亚共和国 the Republic of Kenya	内罗毕 Nairobi	肯尼亚镑 Kenya Pound (K£)	非洲 Africa
库克群岛(新) the Cook Islands	库克群岛(新) the Cook Islands	阿瓦鲁阿 Avarua	新西兰元 New Zealand Dollar ($NZ)	大洋洲及太平洋岛屿 Oceania and the Pacific Islands
拉脱维亚 Latvia	拉脱维亚共和国 the Republic of Latvia	里加 Riga	卢布 Rouble (Rubl)	欧洲 Europe
莱索托 Lesotho	莱索托王国 the Kingdom of Lesotho	马塞卢 Maseru	洛蒂 Loti	非洲 Africa
老挝 Laos	老挝人民民主共和国 the Lao People's Democra-tic Republic	万象 Vientiane	基普 Kip	亚洲 Asia
黎巴嫩 Lebanon	黎巴嫩共和国 the Republic of Lebanon	贝鲁特 Beirut	黎巴嫩镑 Lebanese Pound (£L)	亚洲 Asia
立陶宛 Lithuania	立陶宛共和国 the Republic of Lithuania	维尔纽斯 Vilnius	卢布 Rouble (Rubl)	欧洲 Europe
利比里亚 Liberia	利比里亚共和国 the Republic of Liberia	蒙罗维亚 Monrovia	利比里亚元 Liberian Dollar (L$)	非洲 Africa
利比亚 Libya	大阿拉伯利比亚人民社会主义民众国 the Great Socialist People's Libyan Arab Jamahiriya	的黎波里 Tripoli	利比亚第纳尔 Libyan Dinar (LD)	非洲 Africa

国家、地区 Country, Region	全称 Official Name	首都(首府) Capital	货币 Currency	地理位置 Location
列支敦士登 Liechtenstein	列支敦士登公国 the Principality of Liechten-stein	瓦杜兹 Vaduz	瑞士法郎 Swiss Franc (SF)	欧洲 Europe
留尼汪岛(法) Réunion	留尼汪岛(法) Réunion	圣但尼 Saint-Denis	法国法郎 French Franc	非洲 Africa
卢森堡 Luxembourg	卢森堡大公国 the Grand Duchy of Luxem-bourg	卢森堡 Luxembourg-Ville	卢森堡法郎 Franc Luxembour-geois	欧洲 Europe
卢旺达 Rwanda	卢旺达共和国 the Republic of Rwanda	基加利 Kigali	卢旺达法郎 Rwanda Franc	非洲 Africa
罗马尼亚 Romania	罗马尼亚 Romania	布加勒斯特 Bucharest	列伊 Leu	欧洲 Europe
马达加斯加 Madagascar	马达加斯加民主共和国 the Democratic Republic of Madagascar	塔那那利佛 Antananarivo	马达加斯加法郎 Franc Malgache (Franc MG)	非洲 Africa
马尔代夫 Maldives	马尔代夫共和国 the Republic of Maldives	马累 Malé	拉菲亚 Rufiyaa	亚洲 Asia
马耳他 Malta	马耳他共和国 the Republic of Malta	瓦莱塔 Valletta	马耳他里拉 Malta Lira (LM)	欧洲 Europe
马尔维纳斯群岛(阿、英争议) Islas Malvinas (福克兰群岛) (the Falkland Islands)	马尔维纳斯群岛 Islas Malvinas (福克兰群岛) (the Falkland Islands)	斯坦利港 Stanley	福克兰镑 Falkland Islands Pound (FIS)	拉丁美洲 Latin America
马拉维 Malawi	马拉维共和国 the Republic of Malawi	利隆圭 Lilongwe	马拉维克瓦查 Malawi Kwacha (K)	非洲 Africa
马来西亚 Malaysia	马来西亚 Malaysia	吉隆坡 Kuala Lumpur	林吉特或称马来西亚元 Ringgit or Malaysian Dollar (M$)	亚洲 Asia
马里 Mali	马里共和国 the Republic of Mali	巴马科 Bamako	非洲金融共同体法郎 Franc de la Com-munauté Financière Afri-caine (CFAF)	非洲 Africa
马其顿共和国 the Republic of Mace-donia	前南斯拉夫马其顿共和国 the Former Yugoslavia Republic of Macedonia	斯科普里 Skoplje	第纳尔 Dinar	欧洲 Europe
马绍尔群岛 the Marshall Islands	马绍尔群岛共和国 the Republic of the Marshall Islands	马朱罗 Majuro	美元 United States Dollar ($)	大洋洲及太平洋岛屿 Oceania and the Pacific Islands
马提尼克(法) Martinique	马提尼克(岛)(法) Martinique	法兰西堡 Fort-de-France	法国法郎 French Franc	拉丁美洲 Latin America
马约特岛(法) Mayotte	马约特岛(法) Mayotte	扎乌兹 Dzaoudzi	法国法郎 French Franc	非洲 Africa
毛里求斯 Mauritius	毛里求斯 Mauritius	路易港 Port Louis	毛里求斯卢比 Mauritius Rupee	非洲 Africa

国家、地区 Country, Region	全称 Official Name	首都(首府) Capital	货币 Currency	地理位置 Location
毛里塔尼亚 Mauritania	毛里塔尼亚伊斯兰共和国 the Islamic Republic of Mauritania	努瓦克肖特 Nouakchott	乌吉亚 Ouguiya	非洲 Africa
美国 the United States	美利坚合众国 the United States of America	华盛顿哥伦比亚特区 Washington D.C.	美元 United States Dollar ($)	北美洲 North America
美属维尔京群岛 Virgin Islands of the United States	美属维尔京群岛 the Virgin Islands of the United States	夏洛特阿马利亚 Charlotte Amalie	美元 United States Dollar ($)	拉丁美洲 Latin America
蒙古 Mongolia	蒙古 Mongolia	乌兰巴托 Ulan Bator	图格里克 Tögrög (Tughrik)	亚洲 Asia
蒙特塞拉特岛(英) Montserrat	蒙特塞拉特岛(英) Montserrat	普利茅斯 Plymouth	东加勒比元 East Caribbean Dollar (EC$)	拉丁美洲 Latin America
孟加拉国 Bangladesh	孟加拉人民共和国 the People's Republic of Bangladesh	达卡 Dhaka	塔卡 Taka	亚洲 Asia
密克罗尼西亚 Micronesia	密克罗尼西亚联邦 the Federated States of Micronesia	科洛尼亚 Kolonia	美元 United States Dollar ($)	大洋洲及太平 洋岛屿 Oceania and the Pacific Islands
缅甸 Myanmar	缅甸联邦 the Union of Myanmar	仰光 Yangon	缅元 Kyat	亚洲 Asia
摩尔多瓦 Moldova	摩尔多瓦共和国 the Republic of Moldova	基希讷乌 Kishinev	卢布 Rouble (Rubl)	欧洲 Europe
摩洛哥 Morocco	摩洛哥王国 the Kingdom of Morocco	拉巴特 Rabat	摩洛哥迪拉姆 Moroccan Dirham	非洲 Africa
摩纳哥 Monaco	摩纳哥公国 the Principality of Monaco	摩纳哥城 Monaco-Ville	法国法郎 French Franc	欧洲 Europe
莫桑比克 Mozambique	莫桑比克共和国 the Republic of Mozambique	马普托 Maputo	梅蒂卡尔 Metical	非洲 Africa
墨西哥 Mexico	墨西哥合众国 the United Mexican States	墨西哥城 Mexico City	比索 Peso	拉丁美洲 Latin America
纳米比亚 Namibia	纳米比亚共和国 the Republic of Namibia	温得和克 Windhoek	兰特 Rand (R)	非洲 Africa
南非 South Africa	南非共和国 the Republic of South Africa	比勒陀利亚 Pretoria	兰特 Rand (R)	非洲 Africa
南斯拉夫 Yugoslavia	南斯拉夫联盟共和国 the Federal Republic of Yugoslavia	贝尔格莱德 Belgrade	第纳尔 Dinar	欧洲 Europe
瑙鲁 Nauru	瑙鲁共和国 the Republic of Nauru	亚伦区(行政管理中心) Yaren District	澳大利亚元 Australian Dollar ($A)	大洋洲及太平 洋岛屿 Oceania and the Pacific Islands

国家、地区 Country, Region	全称 Official Name	首都(首府) Capital	货币 Currency	地理位置 Location
尼泊尔 Nepal	尼泊尔王国 the Kingdom of Nepal	加德满都 Kathmandu	尼泊尔卢比 Nepalese Rupee (NR)	亚洲 Asia
尼加拉瓜 Nicaragua	尼加拉瓜共和国 the Republic of Nicaragua	马那瓜 Managua	科多巴 Córdoba	拉丁美洲 Latin America
尼日尔 Niger	尼日尔共和国 the Republic of Niger	尼亚美 Niamey	非洲金融共同体法郎 Franc de la Communauté Financière Africaine (CFAF)	非洲 Africa
尼日利亚 Nigeria	尼日利亚联邦共和国 the Federal Republic of Nigeria	阿布贾 Abuja	奈拉 Naira (N)	非洲 Africa
纽埃岛(新) Niue Island	纽埃岛(新) Niue Island	阿洛菲 Alofi	新西兰元 New Zealand Dollar ($NZ)	大洋洲及太平洋岛屿 Oceania and the Pacific Islands
挪威 Norway	挪威王国 the Kingdom of Norway	奥斯陆 Oslo	挪威克朗 Norwegian Krone	欧洲 Europe
诺福克岛(澳) Norfolk Island	诺福克岛(澳) Norfolk Island	金斯敦 Kingston	澳大利亚元 Australian Dollar ($A)	大洋洲及太平洋岛屿 Oceania and the Pacific Islands
皮特克恩岛(英) Pitcairn Island	皮特克恩岛(英) Pitcairn Island	亚当斯敦 Adamstown	新西兰元 New Zealand Dollar ($NZ)	大洋洲及太平洋岛屿 Oceania and the Pacific Islands
葡萄牙 Portugal	葡萄牙共和国 the Republic of Portugal	里斯本 Lisbon	埃斯库多 Escudo	欧洲 Europe
日本 Japan	日本国 Japan	东京 Tokyo	日元 Yen (￥)	亚洲 Asia
瑞典 Sweden	瑞典王国 the Kingdom of Sweden	斯德哥尔摩 Stockholm	瑞典克朗 Swedish Krona	欧洲 Europe
瑞士 Switzerland	瑞士联邦 the Swiss Confederation	伯尔尼 Bern	瑞士法郎 Swiss Franc	欧洲 Europe
萨尔瓦多 El Salvador	萨尔瓦多共和国 the Republic of El Salvador	圣萨尔瓦多 San Salvador	科郎 Colón	拉丁美洲 Latin America
塞拉利昂 Sierra Leone	塞拉利昂共和国 the Republic of Sierra Leone	弗里敦 Freetown	利昂 Leone (Le)	非洲 Africa
塞内加尔 Senegal	塞内加尔共和国 the Republic of Senegal	达喀尔 Dakar	非洲金融共同体法郎 Franc de la Communauté Financière Africaine (CFAF)	非洲 Africa

国家、地区 Country, Region	全称 Official Name	首都(首府) Capital	货币 Currency	地理位置 Location
塞浦路斯 Cyprus	塞浦路斯共和国 the Republic of Cyprus	尼科西亚 Nicosia	塞浦路斯镑 Cyprus Pound (Cyprus £)	亚洲 Asia
塞舌尔 Seychelles	塞舌尔共和国 the Republic of Seychelles	维多利亚 Victoria	塞舌尔卢比 Seychelles Rupee	非洲 Africa
沙特阿拉伯 Saudi Arabia	沙特阿拉伯王国 the Kingdom of Saudi Arabia	利雅得 Riyadh	沙特里亚尔 Saudi Riyal	亚洲 Asia
圣多美和普林西比 São Tomé and Príncipe	圣多美和普林西比民主共和国 the Democratic Republic of São Tomé and Príncipe	圣多美 São Tomé	多布拉 Dobra (Db)	非洲 Africa
圣赫勒拿岛(英) St. Helena, Ascension Island, etc.	圣赫勒拿岛附阿森松岛等(英) St. Helena, Ascension Island, etc.	詹姆斯敦 Jamestown	圣赫勒拿镑(与英镑等值) St. Helena Pound (= Pound Sterling £)	非洲 Africa
圣基茨和尼维斯 St. Kitts and Nevis	圣基茨和尼维斯联邦 the Federation of St. Kitts and Nevis	巴斯特尔 Basseterre	东加勒比元 East Caribbean Dollar (EC$)	拉丁美洲 Latin America
圣卢西亚岛 St. Lucia	圣卢西亚岛 St. Lucia	卡斯特里 Castries	东加勒比元 East Caribbean Dollar (EC$)	拉丁美洲 Latin America
圣马力诺 San Marino	圣马力诺共和国 the Republic of San Marino	圣马力诺 San Marino	意大利里拉 Italian Lira	欧洲 Europe
圣皮埃尔岛和密克隆群岛(法) St. Pierre and Miquelon Islands	圣皮埃尔岛和密克隆群岛(法) St. Pierre and Miquelon Islands	圣皮埃尔 St. Pierre	法国法郎 French Franc	北美洲 North America
圣文森特岛和格林纳丁斯 St. Vincent and the Grenadines	圣文森特岛和格林纳丁斯 St. Vincent and the Grenadines	金斯敦 Kingstown	东加勒比元 East Caribbean Dollar (EC$)	拉丁美洲 Latin America
斯里兰卡 Sri Lanka	斯里兰卡民主社会主义共和国 the Democratic Socialist Republic of Sri Lanka	科伦坡 Colombo	斯里兰卡卢比 Sri Lanka Rupee	亚洲 Asia
斯洛伐克 Slovakia	斯洛伐克共和国 the Republic of Slovakia	布迪斯拉发 Bratislava	克朗 Koruna	欧洲 Europe
斯洛文尼亚 Slovenia	斯洛文尼亚共和国 the Republic of Slovenia	卢布尔雅那 Ljubljana	第纳尔 Dinar	欧洲 Europe
斯威士兰 Swaziland	斯威士兰王国 the Kingdom of Swaziland	姆巴巴纳 Mbabane	里兰吉尼 Lilangeni	非洲 Africa
苏丹 the Sudan	苏丹共和国 the Republic of the Sudan	喀土穆 Khartoum	苏丹镑 Sudanese Pound (£S)	非洲 Africa
苏里南 Surinam	苏里南共和国 the Republic of Surinam	帕拉马里博 Paramaribo	苏里南盾或弗罗林 Surinam Guilder or Florin (SFI)	拉丁美洲 Latin America

国家、地区 Country, Region	全称 Official Name	首都(首府) Capital	货币 Currency	地理位置 Location
所罗门群岛 Solomon Islands	所罗门群岛 Solomon Islands	霍尼亚拉 Honiara	所罗门岛元 Solomon Islands Dollar (SI$)	大洋洲及太平洋岛屿 Oceania and the Pacific Islands
索马里 Somalia	索马里民主共和国 the Somali Democratic Republic	摩加迪沙 Mogadishu	索马里先令 Somali Shilling (So. Sh.)	非洲 Africa
塔吉克斯坦 Tadzhikistan	塔吉克斯坦共和国 the Republic of Tadzhikistan	杜尚别 Dushanbe	卢布 Rouble (Rubl)	亚洲 Asia
泰国 Thailand	泰王国 the Kingdom of Thailand	曼谷 Bangkok	铢 Baht	亚洲 Asia
坦桑尼亚 Tanzania	坦桑尼亚联合共和国 the United Republic of Tanzania	达累斯萨拉姆 Dar es Salaam	坦桑尼亚先令 Tanzania Shilling	非洲 Africa
汤加 Tonga	汤加王国 the Kingdom of Tonga	努库阿洛法 Nukuoalofa	潘加或汤加元 Pa'anga or Tongan Dollar ($T)	大洋洲及太平洋岛屿 Oceania and the Pacific Islands
特克斯群岛和凯科斯群岛(英) Turks and Caicos Islands	特克斯群岛和凯科斯群岛(英) Turks and Caicos Islands	科伯恩城 Cockburn Town	美元 United States Dollar ($)	拉丁美洲 Latin America
特立尼达和多巴哥 Trinidad and Tobago	特立尼达和多巴哥共和国 the Republic of Trinidad and Tobago	西班牙港 Port of Spain	特立尼达和多巴哥元 Trinidad and Tobago Dollar (TT$)	拉丁美洲 Latin America
突尼斯 Tunisia	突尼斯共和国 the Republic of Tunisia	突尼斯 Tunis	第纳尔 Dinar (TD)	非洲 Africa
图瓦卢(英) Tuvalu	图瓦卢(英) Tuvalu	富纳富提 Funafuti	澳大利亚元和图瓦鲁硬币 Australian Dollar and Tuvaluan Dollar	大洋洲及太平洋岛屿 Oceania and the Pacific Islands
土耳其 Turkey	土耳其共和国 the Republic of Turkey	安卡拉 Ankara	土耳其里拉 Turkish Lira (TL)	亚洲 Asia
土库曼斯坦 Turkmenistan	土库曼斯坦共和国 the Republic of Turkmenistan	阿什哈巴德 Ashkhabad	卢布 Rouble (Rubl)	亚洲 Asia
托克劳群岛(新) Tokelau Islands	托克劳群岛(新) Tokelau Islands	法考福 Fakaofo	新西兰元 New Zealand Dollar ($NZ)	大洋洲及太平洋岛屿 Oceania and the Pacific Islands
瓦利斯群岛和富图纳群岛(法) Wallis and Futuna	瓦利斯群岛和富图纳群岛(法) Wallis and Futuna	马塔乌图 Mata-Utu	太平洋结算法郎 Franc des Comptoirs Francais du Pacifique (CFP Franc)	大洋洲及太平洋岛屿 Oceania and the Pacific Islands

国家、地区 Country, Region	全称 Official Name	首都(首府) Capital	货币 Currency	地理位置 Location
瓦努阿图 Vanuatu	瓦努阿图共和国 the Republic of Vanuatu	维拉港 Port Vila	瓦图 Vatu	大洋洲及太平洋岛屿 Oceania and the Pacific Islands
危地马拉 Guatemala	危地马拉共和国 the Republic of Guatemala	危地马拉城 Guatemala City	格查尔 Quetzal	拉丁美洲 Latin America
威克岛(美) Wake Island	威克岛(美) Wake Island		美元 United States Dollar ($)	大洋洲及太平洋岛屿 Oceania and the Pacific Islands
委内瑞拉 Venezuela	委内瑞拉共和国 the Republic of Venezuela	加拉加斯 Caracas	玻利瓦尔 Bolivar	拉丁美洲 Latin America
文莱 Brunei	文莱达鲁萨兰国 Negava Brunei Darussalam	斯里巴加湾市 Bandar Seri Begawan	文莱元 Brunei Dollar (Br$)	亚洲 Asia
乌干达 Uganda	乌干达共和国 the Republic of Uganda	坎帕拉 Kampala	乌干达新先令 New Uganda Shilling	非洲 Africa
乌克兰 Ukraine	乌克兰 Ukraine	基辅 Kiev	卢布 Rouble (Rubl)	欧洲 Europe
乌拉圭 Uruguay	乌拉圭东岸共和国 the Oriental Republic of Uruguay	蒙得维的亚 Montevideo	新比索 New Peso	拉丁美洲 Latin America
乌兹别克斯坦 Uzbekistan	乌兹别克斯坦共和国 the Republic of Uzbekistan	塔什干 Tashkent	卢布 Rouble (Rubl)	亚洲 Asia
西班牙 Spain	西班牙王国 the Kingdom of Spain	马德里 Madrid	比塞塔 Peseta	欧洲 Europe
西撒哈拉 Western Sahara	西撒哈拉 Western Sahara	阿尤恩 Lá Youne		非洲 Africa
西萨摩亚 Western Samoa	西萨摩亚独立国 the Independent State of Western Samoa	阿皮亚 Apia	塔拉或西萨摩亚元 Tala or Western Samoa Dollar (WS$)	大洋洲及太平洋岛屿 Oceania and the Pacific Islands
希腊 Greece	希腊共和国 the Hellenic Republic	雅典 Athens	德拉克马 Drachma	欧洲 Europe
锡金 Sikkim	锡金 Sikkim	甘托克 Gangtok	印度卢比 Indian Rupee	亚洲 Asia
新加坡 Singapore	新加坡共和国 the Republic of Singapore	新加坡 Singapore City	新加坡元 Singapore Dollar (S$)	亚洲 Asia
新喀里多尼亚(法) New Caledonia	新喀里多尼亚(法) New Caledonia	努美阿 Nouméa	太平洋结算法郎 Franc des Comptoirs Francais du Pacifique (CFP Franc)	大洋洲及太平洋岛屿 Oceania and the Pacific Islands

国家、地区 Country, Region	全称 Official Name	首都（首府） Capital	货币 Currency	地理位置 Location
新西兰 New Zealand	新西兰 New Zealand	惠灵顿 Wellington	新西兰元 New Zealand Dollar ($NZ)	大洋洲及太平洋岛屿 Oceania and the Pacific Islands
匈牙利 Hungary	匈牙利共和国 the Republic of Hungary	布达佩斯 Budapest	福林 Forint	欧洲 Europe
叙利亚 Syria	阿拉伯叙利亚共和国 the Syrian Arab Republic	大马士革 Damascus	叙利亚镑 Syrian Pound (£S)	亚洲 Asia
牙买加 Jamaica	牙买加 Jamaica	金斯敦 Kingston	牙买加元 Jamaican Dollar (J$)	拉丁美洲 Latin America
亚美尼亚 Armenia	亚美尼亚共和国 the Republic of Armenia	埃里温 Yerevan	卢布 Rouble (Rubl)	亚洲 Asia
也门 Yemen	也门共和国 the Republic of Yemen	萨那 San'a	（北方）也门里亚尔 Yemeni Rial (YRI) （南方）也门第纳尔 Yemeni Dinar (YD)	亚洲 Asia
伊拉克 Iraq	伊拉克共和国 the Republic of Iraq	巴格达 Baghdad	伊拉克第纳尔 Iraqi Dinar	亚洲 Asia
伊朗 Iran	伊朗伊斯兰共和国 the Islamic Republic of Iran	德黑兰 Teheran	里亚尔 Rial	亚洲 Asia
以色列 Israel	以色列共和国 the State of Israel	耶路撒冷 Jerusalem	新以色列谢克尔 New Israel Shekel	亚洲 Asia
意大利 Italy	意大利共和国 the Italian Republic	罗马 Rome	里拉 Lira	欧洲 Europe
印度 India	印度共和国 the Republic of India	新德里 New Delhi	印度卢比 Indian Rupee	亚洲 Asia
印度尼西亚 Indonesia	印度尼西亚共和国 the Republic of Indonesia	雅加达 Jakarta	印度尼西亚盾 Indonesian Rupiah (Rp)	亚洲 Asia
英国 the United Kingdom	大不列颠及北爱尔兰联合王国 the United Kingdom of Great Britain and Northern Ireland	伦敦 London	英镑 Pound Sterling (£)	欧洲 Europe
英属维尔京群岛 British Virgin Islands	英属维尔京群岛 the British Virgin Islands	罗德城 Road Town	美元 United States Dollar ($)	拉丁美洲 Latin America
约旦 Jordan	约旦哈希姆王国 the Hashemite Kingdom of Jordan	安曼 Amman	约旦第纳尔 Jordanian Dinar	亚洲 Asia
约翰斯顿岛（美） Johnston Island	约翰斯顿岛（美） Johnston Island		美元 United States Dollar ($)	大洋洲及太平洋岛屿 Oceania and the Pacific Islands

国家、地区 Country, Region	全称 Official Name	首都(首府) Capital	货币 Currency	地理位置 Location
越南 Viet Nam	越南社会主义共和国 the Socialist Republic of Viet Nam	河内 Hanoi	越盾 Dong	亚洲 Asia
赞比亚 Zambia	赞比亚共和国 the Republic of Zambia	卢萨卡 Lusaka	克瓦查 Kwacha	非洲 Africa
扎伊尔 Zaïre	扎伊尔共和国 the Republic of Zaïre	金沙萨 Kinshasa	扎伊尔 Zaïre	非洲 Africa
乍得 Chad	乍得共和国 the Republic of Chad	恩贾梅纳 N'Djamena	中非金融合作法郎 Franc de la Coopération Financière en Afrique Centrale (CFAF)	非洲 Africa
直布罗陀(英、西) Gibraltar	直布罗陀(英、西) Gibraltar	直布罗陀城 the City of Gibraltar	直布罗陀镑和比塞塔 Pound (£) and Peseta	欧洲 Europe
智利 Chile	智利共和国 the Republic of Chile	圣地亚哥 Santiago	比索 Peso	拉丁美洲 Latin America
中非 Central Africa	中非共和国 the Central African Republic	班吉 Bangui	中非金融合作法郎 Franc de la Coopération Financière en Afrique Centrale (CFAF)	非洲 Africa
中国 China	中华人民共和国 the People's Republic of China	北京 Beijing	人民币元 Renminbi Yuan (RMB ¥)	亚洲 Asia
中途岛(美) Midway Island	中途岛(美) Midway Island		美元 United States Dollar ($)	大洋洲及太平洋岛屿 Oceania and the Pacific Islands

本表所据资料截止至1993年7月

附录四
Appendix 4
国家机关、政党、人民团体
State Organs, Political Parties
and People's Organizations

1. **全国人民代表大会** **National People's Congress (NPC)**

主席团 Presidium

办公厅 General Office

秘书处 Secretariat

代表资格审查委员会 Credentials Committee

提案审查委员会 Motions Examination Committee

全国人民代表大会常务委员会 Standing Committee of the National People's Congress

全国人民代表大会各委员会 (Committees of the NPC):

民族委员会 Nationalities Committee

法律委员会 Law Committee

财政经济委员会 Finance and Economic Committee

教育、科学、文化和卫生委员会 Education, Science, Culture and Public Health Committee

外事委员会 Foreign Affairs Committee

华侨委员会 Overseas Chinese Affairs Committee

内务司法委员会 Committee for Internal and Judicial Affairs

人大常委法制工作委员会 Commission of Legislative Affairs

人大常委办公厅 General Office

特定问题调查委员会 Committee of Inquiry into Specific Questions

宪法修改委员会 Committee for Revision of the Constitution

2. **中华人民共和国主席** **President of the People's Republic of China**

副主席 Vice-President

3. **中华人民共和国中央军事委员会** **Central Military Commission of the People's Republic of China**

4. **最高人民法院** **Supreme People's Court**

5. **最高人民检察院** **Supreme People's Procuratorate**

6. **国务院(即中央人民政府)** **State Council (the Central People's Government)**

(1) 国务院办公厅 General Office of the State Council

(2) 国务院各部委 Ministries and Commissions of the State Council

外交部 Ministry of Foreign Affairs

亚洲司 Department of Asian Affairs

非洲司 Department of African Affairs

西亚北非司 Department of West Asian and North African Affairs

西欧司 Department of West European Affairs

东欧中亚司 Department of East European and Central Asian Affairs

美洲大洋洲司 Department of the Affairs of the Americas and Oceania

领事司 Department of Consular Affairs

礼宾司 Protocol Department

国际司 Department of International Organizations and Conferences

条法司	Department of Treaty and Law	对外贸易管理局	Foreign Trade Administration
新闻司	Information Department	进出口局	Import and Export Department
国防部	Ministry of National Defence	对外援助局	Department of Foreign Aid
国家计划委员会	State Planning Commission	国外经济合作局	Department of Foreign Economic Cooperation
国家经济贸易委员会	State Economic and Trade Commission		
国家经济体制改革委员会	State Commission for Economic Restructuring	外资管理局	Foreign Investment Administration
国家教育委员会	State Education Commission	技术进出口局	Technology Import and Export Department
国家科学技术委员会	State Science and Technology Commission	国际组织联络局	Department of Relations with International Organizations
国防科学技术工业委员会	Commission of Science, Technology and Industry for National Defence	地区政策局	Department for Regional Policy
国家民族事务委员会	State Nationalities Affairs Commission	国家进出口商品检验局	State Administration for the Inspection of Import and Export Commodities
公安部	Ministry of Public Security		
国家安全部	Ministry of State Security	条法局	Department of Treaty and Law
监察部	Ministry of Supervision		
民政部	Ministry of Civil Affairs	文化部	Ministry of Culture
司法部	Ministry of Justice	广播电影电视部	Ministry of Radio, Film and Television
财政部	Ministry of Finance		
人事部	Ministry of Personnel	卫生部	Ministry of Public Health
劳动部	Ministry of Labour	国家体育运动委员会	State Physical Culture and Sports Commission
地质矿产部	Ministry of Geology and Mineral Resources		
建设部	Ministry of Construction	国家计划生育委员会	State Family Planning Commission
电力工业部	Ministry of Power Industry		
煤炭工业部	Ministry of Coal Industry	中国人民银行	People's Bank of China (China's Central Bank)
机械工业部	Ministry of Machine-Building Industry		
电子工业部	Ministry of Electronics Industry	审计署	Auditing Administration
		(3) 国务院直属机构	Organizations Directly under the State Council
冶金工业部	Ministry of Metallurgical Industry	国家统计局	State Statistical Bureau
化学工业部	Ministry of Chemical Industry	国家物价局	State Bureau of Commodity Prices
铁道部	Ministry of Railways	国家建筑材料工业局	State Bureau of Building Materials Industry
交通部	Ministry of Communications		
邮电部	Ministry of Posts and Telecommunications	国家医药管理局	State Pharmaceutical Administration
水利部	Ministry of Water Resources	中华人民共和国海关总署	General Administration of Customs of the P. R. C.
农业部	Ministry of Agriculture		
林业部	Ministry of Forestry	国家技术监督局	State Bureau of Technical Supervision
国内贸易部	Ministry of Internal Trade	中华人民共和国国家工商行政管理局	State Administration for Industry and Commerce of the P. R. C.
对外贸易经济合作部	Ministry of Foreign Trade and Economic Cooperation		
		国家环境保护局	State Bureau of Environmental Protection

中国民用航空局	Civil Aviation Administration of China (CAAC)		of China
中华人民共和国国家旅游局	National Tourism Administration of the P. R. C.	国家外国专家局	State Bureau of Foreign Experts Affairs
国家海洋局	National Bureau of Oceanography	国家中医药管理局	State Administration of Traditional Chinese Medicine
国家气象局	State Meteorological Administration	国家语言文字工作委员会	State Language Work Committee
国家地震局	State Seismological Bureau	国家烟草专卖局	State Tobacco Monopoly Bureau
国家土地管理局	State Bureau of Land Administration	国家国有资产管理局	State Administration of State Property
中华人民共和国新闻出版署	The Press and Publications Administration of the P. R. C.	国家黄金管理局	State Gold Administrative Bureau
		国家核安全局	State Bureau of Nuclear Safety
国家档案局	State Archives Bureau	国家测绘局	State Bureau of Surveying and Mapping
国务院宗教事务局	Bureau of Religious Affairs of the State Council	国家矿产储量管理局	State Administration on Mineral Resources
国务院参事室	Counsellors' Office of the State Council	国家文物局	State Cultural Relics Bureau
国务院机关事务管理局	Bureau of Government Offices Administration	国家保密局	State Secrets Bureau
		国家外汇管理局	State Administration of Exchange Control
(4) 国务院办事机构	Administrative Bodies under the State Council	国家进出口商品检验局	State Administration for the Inspection of Import and Export Commodities
国务院法制局	Bureau of the Legislative Affairs under the State Council		
		国家版权局	State Copyright Bureau
国务院外事办公室	Office of Foreign Affairs under the State Council	国家粮食储备局	State Grain Reserve Administration
国务院侨务办公室	Office of Overseas Chinese Affairs under the State Council	(6) 国务院事业单位	Institutions under the State Council
		新华通讯社	Xinhua News Agency
国务院港澳办公室	Hongkong and Macao Affairs Office of the State Council	中国科学院	Chinese Academy of Sciences
		中国社会科学院	Chinese Academy of Social Sciences
国务院特区办公室	Office of Special Economic Zones under the State Council	国务院经济技术社会发展研究中心	Research Centre to Advise on Economic, Technological and Social Development
国务院台湾事务办公室	Taiwan Affairs Office of the State Council	国务院农村发展研究中心	Rural Development Research Centre
国务院新闻办公室	Information Office of the State Council		
(5) 部委归口管理的国家局	State Bureaus under the Jurisdiction of Ministries and Commissions	7. 中国人民政治协商会议（政协）	Chinese People's Political Consultative Conference (CPPCC)
		全国委员会	The CPPCC National Committee
国家税务局	State Administration of Taxation		
中国专利局	Patent Office of the People's Republic	全国政协常务委员会	The Standing Committee of the CPPCC National Committee

8. 中国共产党 — **The Communist Party of China (CPC)**

中共中央委员会	Central Committee of the Communist Party of China
中央政治局	Political Bureau of the Central Committee
中央政治局常务委员会	Standing Committee of the Political Bureau of the Central Committee
中央书记处	Secretariat of the Central Committee
中央整党工作指导委员会	Central Party Consolidation Guidance Commission
中共中央办公厅	General Office of the CPC Central Committee
中央组织部	Organization Department of the CPC Central Committee
中央宣传部	Propaganda Department of the CPC Central Committee
中央统一战线部	United Front Work Department of the CPC Central Committee
中央对外联络部	International Liaison Department of the CPC Central Committee
中央军事委员会	Military Commission of the CPC Central Committee
中央党的建设工作领导小组	Party Building Directorate of the CPC Central Committee
中央宣传思想工作领导小组	Propaganda and Ideological Work Directorate of the CPC Central Committee
中央政法委员会	Commission of Politics and Law of the CPC Central Committee
中央爱国卫生运动委员会	Central Patriotic Public Health Campaign Committee
中央党校	Party School of the CPC Central Committee
中央绿化委员会	Central Afforestation (Greening) Committee
中央文献研究室	Party Literature Research Centre of the CPC Central Committee
中央政策研究室	Policy Research Centre of the CPC Central Committee
中央党史研究室	Party History Research Centre of the CPC Central Committee
中共党史人物研究会	Society on the Historical Figures of the CPC
中央文献编辑委员会	Editorial Committee on Party Literature of the Central Committee
中央编译局	Compilation and Translation Bureau of the CPC Central Committee
中央档案馆	Central Archives
中央国家机关工作委员会	Work Committee of Central Government Departments
中共中央直属机关工作委员会	Work Committee of Departments under the Central Committee
中共中央纪律检查委员会	Central Commission for Discipline Inspection of the CPC

9. 民主党派 — **Democratic Parties**

中国国民党革命委员会	Revolutionary Committee of the Chinese Kuomintang
中国民主同盟(民盟)	China Democratic League
中国民主建国会(民建)	China Democratic National Construction Association
中国民主促进会(民进)	China Association for Promoting Democracy
中国农工民主党	Chinese Peasants' and Workers' Democratic Party
中国致公党	China Zhi Gong Dang
九三学社	Jiu San Society
台湾民主自治同盟	Taiwan Democratic Self-Government League

10. 军事机构 — **Military Establishments**

中国人民解放军	Chinese People's Liberation Army (PLA)
中央军事委员会	Central Military Commission of the P. R. C.
中国人民解放军各总部:	PLA General Departments:
总参谋部	Headquarters of the General Staff
总政治部	General Political Department
总后勤部	General Logistics Department
中国人民解放军军事法院	PLA Military Court

中国人民解放军军事检察院	PLA Military Procuratorate	警备区	PLA
中国人民解放军体育运动委员会	PLA Physical Culture and Sports Committee	**11. 人民团体**	**People's Organizations**
中国人民解放军各军兵种:	PLA Arms and Services:	测绘学会	Society of Geodesy, Photogrammetry and Cartography
中国人民解放军海军	PLA Navy	地震学会	Seismological Society
北海舰队	North China Sea Fleet	工程热物理学会	Engineering Thermophysics Society
南海舰队	South China Sea Fleet	国际金融学会	International Finance Society
东海舰队	East China Sea Fleet	国际战略问题学会	Institute for International Strategic Studies
中国人民解放军空军	PLA Air Force		
中国人民解放军炮兵	PLA Artillery Forces	海洋学会	Society of Oceanography
中国人民解放军第二炮兵	PLA Second Artillery Forces	环境管理、经济与法学学会	Society to Study Environmental Management, Economics and Law
中国人民解放军装甲兵	PLA Armoured Forces		
中国人民解放军通信兵	PLA Signal Forces	科普学会	Popular Science Society
中国人民解放军工程兵	PLA Engineering Corps	全国儿童和少年工作协调委员会	National Children's Work Coordination Committee
中国人民解放军基本建设工程兵	PLA Capital Construction Engineering Corps	全国少年儿童文化艺术委员会	National Council on Cultural and Art Work for Children
中国人民解放军军事院校:	PLA Military Academies:	全国史学会	China Society of History
中国人民解放军国防大学	PLA University of National Defence	少年科学奖基金会	Children's Science Achievement Award Fund
中国人民解放军军事科学院	PLA Academy of Military Sciences	宋庆龄基金会(全称: 纪念宋庆龄国家名誉主席基金会)	Soong Ching Ling Foundation
中国人民解放军军事学院	PLA Military Academy	中国奥林匹克委员会	Chinese Olympic Committee
中国人民解放军政治学院	PLA Political Academy	中国笔会中心	Chinese Pen Centre
中国人民解放军后勤学院	PLA Logistics Academy	中国标准化协会	China Association for Standardization
中国人民解放军各部队:	PLA Units:	中国财政学会	Chinese Finance Society
中国人民解放军北京军区	PLA Beijing Military Area Command	中国残疾人福利基金会	China Welfare Fund for the Handicapped
中国人民解放军沈阳军区	PLA Shenyang Military Area Command	中国道教协会	Chinese Taoist Association
中国人民解放军南京军区	PLA Nanjing Military Area Command	中国电影评论学会	China Film Critics Society
中国人民解放军济南军区	PLA Jinan Military Area Command	中国法律咨询中心	Chinese Legal Consultancy Centre
中国人民解放军广州军区	PLA Guangzhou Military Area Command	中国法学会	China Law Society
中国人民解放军成都军区	PLA Chengdu Military Area Command	中国翻译工作者协会	Translators' Association of China
中国人民解放军兰州军区	PLA Lanzhou Military Area Command	中国佛教协会	Chinese Buddhist Association
中国人民解放军北京卫戍区	Beijing Garrison of the PLA	中国福利会	China Welfare Institute
		中国歌剧研究会	Chinese Opera Research Institute
中国人民解放军上海警备区	Shanghai Garrison of the PLA	中国共产主义青年团	Communist Youth League of China
中国人民解放军天津	Tianjin Garrison of the	中国国际法学会	Chinese Society of Inter-

	national Law	中国天主教教务委员会	National Administrative Commission of the Chinese Catholic Church
中国国际交流协会	Association for International Understanding of China		
中国衡器协会	Weights and Measures Association of China	中国天主教主教团	Chinese Catholic Bishops College
中国红十字会总会	Red Cross Society of China	中国文学艺术界联合会	China Federation of Literary and Art Circles
中国基督教"三自"爱国运动委员会	Three-Self Patriotic Movement Committee of the Protestant Churches of China	中国电视艺术家协会	Chinese Television Artists Association
		中国电影家协会	China Film Association
中国基督教协会	China Christian Council	中国美术家协会	Chinese Artists Association
中国计量测试学会	Chinese Society for Measurement	中国民间文艺家协会	China Society for the Study of Folk Literature and Art
中国教育学会	Chinese Education Society		
中国金融学会	Chinese Monetary Society	中国曲艺家协会	Chinese Ballad Singers Association
中国抗癌协会	Chinese Anti-Cancer Association		
中国考古学会	Archaeological Society of China	中国摄影家协会	Chinese Photographers Society
中国科学技术普及及创作协会	Chinese Association of Popular Science Writers	中国书法家协会	Chinese Calligraphers Association
中国科学技术史学会	Chinese Society of Science and Technology History	中国舞蹈家协会	Chinese Dancers Association
		中国戏剧家协会	Chinese Dramatists Association
中国科学技术协会	China Science and Technology Association	中国音乐家协会	Chinese Musicians Association
中国会计学会	Chinese Accounting Society	中国杂技艺术家协会	Chinese Acrobats Association
中国联合国教科文组织全国委员会	National Commission of the People's Republic of China for UNESCO	中国作家协会	Chinese Writers Association
		中国伊斯兰教协会	Chinese Islamic Association
中国联合国协会	United Nations Association of the People's Republic of China	中国医学会	Chinese Medical Association
中国盲人聋哑人协会	China Association For the Blind and the Deaf-Mutes	中国政法学会	China Society of Political Science and Law
		中华全国妇女联合会	All-China Women's Federation
中国企业管理协会	China Enterprise Management Association	中华全国工商联合会	All-China Federation of Industry and Commerce
中国人民保卫儿童全国委员会	Chinese People's National Committee for Defence of Children	中华全国归国华侨联合会	All-China Federation of Returned Overseas Chinese
中国人民对外友好协会	Chinese People's Association for Friendship with Foreign Countries	中华全国集邮联合会	All-China Philatelic Federation
		中华全国青年联合会	All-China Youth Federation
中国人民外交学会	Chinese People's Institute of Foreign Affairs	中华全国世界语协会	All-China Esperanto League
中国少年儿童基金会	Children's Foundation of China	中华全国台湾同胞联谊会	All-China Federation of Taiwan Compatriots
中国少年先锋队	China Young Pioneers		
中国天主教爱国会	Chinese Patriotic Catholic Association	中华全国体育总会	Ali-China Sports Federa-

	tion
中华全国新闻工作者协会	All-China Journalists' Association
中华全国学生联合会	All-China Students' Federation
中华全国总工会	All-China Federation of Trade Unions

12. 其他涉外机构和公司 — **Other Organizations and Corporations Concerning Foreign Affairs**

保利科技有限公司	Poly Technologies Inc.
北京国际经济信息中心	Beijing Centre for International Economic Information
北京科技协作中心	Beijing Scientific and Technical Cooperation Centre
对外贸易仲裁委员会	Foreign Trade Arbitration Commission (FTAC)
光大实业公司	Everbright Industrial Company
国际问题研究所	Institute of International Studies
国际信托服务公司	International Trust and Service Company
国际招标公司	International Tendering Company
国际政治和经济研究中心	Centre for the Study of International Politics and Economy
海事仲裁委员会	Maritime Arbitration Commission (MAC)
外国企业服务公司	Foreign Enterprises Service Corporation
中国成套设备出口公司	China National Complete Plant Export Corporation
中国出版对外贸易公司	China National Publishing Industry Trading Corporation
中国船舶公司	China Shipping Industrial Company
中国电影发行放映公司	China Film Distribution and Exhibition Corporation
中国电子技术进出口公司	China National Electronics Import and Export Corporation
中国对外翻译出版公司	China Translation and Publishing Corporation
中国对外贸易运输公司	China National Foreign Trade Transportation Corporation
中国纺织品进出口公司	China National Textiles Import and Export Corporation
中国工艺品进出口公司	China National Arts and Crafts Import and Export Corporation
中国国际经济技术交流中心	China International Centre for Economic and Technical Exchanges
中国国际经济咨询公司	China International Economic Consultants Inc. (CIEC)
中国国际科技会议中心	China International Conference Centre for Science and Technology (CICCST / CAST)
中国国际贸易促进会	China Council for the Promotion of International Trade (CCPIT)
中国国际贸易中心	China International Trade Centre
中国国际图书贸易总公司(国际书店)	China International Book Trading Corporation (Guoji Shudian)
中国国际文化交流中心	International Cultural Exchange Centre of China (ICEC)
中国国际信托投资公司	China International Trust and Investment Corporation (CITIC)
中国航空工业服务公司	China Industrial Aviation Service Company
中国航空技术进出口公司	China National Aero-Technology Import and Export Corporation (CATIC)
中国化工建设总公司	China National Chemical Construction Corporation
中国化工进出口公司	China National Chemicals Import and Export Corporation
中国机械进出口公司	China National Machinery Import and Export Corporation
中国机械设备进出口公司	China National Machinery and Equipment Import and Export Corporation
中国技术进出口总公司	China National Technical Import and Export Corporation (CNTIC)
中国经济贸易咨询公司	China Economic and Trade Consultants Cor-

中国精密机械公司	poration China National Precision Machinery Corporation
中国救助打捞公司	Chinese Shipwreck Rescue and Salvage Company
中国科学技术情报研究所	Scientific and Technical Information Institute of China
中国科学技术咨询服务中心	China Science and Technology Consultancy Service Centre
中国粮油食品进出口公司	China National Cereals, Oils and Foodstuffs Import and Export Corporation
中国轻工业品进出口公司	China National Light Industrial Products Import and Export Corporation
中国人民保险公司	People's Insurance Company of China
中国石油公司	Petroleum Company of the People's Republic of China
中国石油公司海洋分公司	Offshore Branch of the Petroleum Company of the P. R. C.

中国缩微出版物进出口公司	China National Microforms Import and Export Corporation
中国图书进出口总公司	China National Publications Import and Export Corporation
中国土产畜产进出口公司	China National Native Produce and Animal By-products Import and Export Corporation
中国外轮代理公司	China Ocean Shipping Agency
中国五金矿产进出口公司	China National Metals and Minerals Import and Export Corporation
中国仪器进出口公司	China National Instruments Import and Export Corporation
中国邮票总公司	China Stamps Company
中国远洋运输公司	China Ocean Shipping Company
中国租船公司	China National Ship Chartering Corporation

附录五
Appendix 5
联合国主要机构
Main Organizations of the United Nations

中文全称	中文简称	英文全称	英文简称
安全理事会	安理会	Security Council	SC
关税及贸易总协定	关贸总协定	General Agreement on Tariffs and Trade	GATT
国际电信联盟	国际电联	International Telecommunications Union	ITU
国际法院		International Court of Justice	ICJ
国际复兴开发银行（又称 世界银行）	复兴开发银行	International Bank for Reconstruction and Development (*also* World Bank)	IBRD
国际海事组织	海事组织	International Maritime Organization	IMO
国际货币基金组织	货币基金组织	International Monetary Fund	IMF
国际金融公司	金融公司	International Finance Corporation	IFC
国际开发协会	开发协会	International Development Association	IDA
国际劳工组织	劳工组织	International Labour Organization	ILO
国际民用航空组织	国际民航组织	International Civil Aviation Organization	ICAO
国际农业发展基金	农发基金	International Fund for Agricultural Development	IFAD
国际原子能机构	原子能机构	International Atomic Energy Agency	IAEA
经济及社会理事会	经社理事会	Economic and Social Council	ESC; ECOSOC
联合国大会	大会	General Assembly	GA
联合国大学		United Nations University	UNU
联合国儿童基金会	儿童基金会	United Nations Children's Fund	UNICEF
联合国工业发展组织	工发组织	United Nations Industrial Development Organization	UNIDO
联合国环境规划署	环境规划署	United Nations Environment Programme	UNEP
联合国教育、科学及文化组织	教科文组织	United Nations Educational, Scientific and Cultural Organization	UNESCO
联合国开发计划署	开发计划署	United Nations Development Pro-gramme	UNDP
联合国粮食及农业组织	粮农组织	Food and Agricultural Organization of the United Nations	FAO
联合国贸易和发展会议	贸发会议	United Nations Conference on Trade and Development	UNCTAD
联合国难民事务高级专员办事处	难民专员办事处	Office of the United Nations High Commissioner for Refugees	UNHCR
联合国人口活动基金	人口活动基金	United Nations Fund for Population Activities	UNFPA

中文全称	中文简称	英文全称	英文简称
联合国特别基金		United Nations Special Fund	UNSF
联合国训练研究所	训研所	United Nations Institute for Training and Research	UNITAR
秘书处		Secretariat	
世界粮食理事会	粮食理事会	World Food Council	WFC
世界气象组织	气象组织	World Meteorological Organization	WMO
世界卫生组织	卫生组织	World Health Organization	WHO
世界知识产权组织		World Intellectual Property Organization	WIPO
托管理事会		Trusteeship Council	TC
万国邮政联盟		Universal Postal Union	UPU

附录六
Appendix 6
中国法定计量单位简表(公制)
Weights and Measures (the Metric System)

一、长度单位表
Units of Length

名称 Name	符号 Symbol	等数 Equivalents
微米 micron	μ; mu	
毫米 millimetre	mm	1毫米=1000微米
厘米 centimetre	cm	1厘米=10毫米
分米 decimetre	dm	1分米=10厘米
米 metre	m	1米=10分米
十米 decametre	dam	十米=10米
百米 hectometre	hm	1百米=100米
千米(公里) kilometre	km	1千米(公里)=1000米

二、面积单位表
Units of Square Measure

名称 Name	符号 Symbol	等数 Equivalents
平方毫米 square millimetre	mm^2	
平方厘米 square centimetre	cm^2	1平方厘米=100平方毫米
平方分米 square decimetre	dm^2	1平方分米=100平方厘米
平方米 square metre	m^2	1平方米=100平方分米
平方千米 (平方公里) square kilometre	km^2	1平方千米(平方公里)=1000000平方米

三、体积单位表
Units of Cubic Measure

名称 Name	符号 Symbol	等数 Equivalents
立方毫米 cubic millimetre	mm³	
立方厘米 cubic centimetre	cm³	1立方厘米＝1000立方毫米
立方分米 cubic decimetre	dm³	1立方分米＝1000立方厘米
立方米 cubic metre	m³	1立方米＝1000立方分米

四、容积单位表
Units of Capacity

名称 Name	符号 Symbol	等数 Equivalents
毫升 millilitre	ml	
厘升 centilitre	cl	1厘升＝10毫升
分升 decilitre	dl	1分升＝10厘升
升 litre	l	1升＝10分升
十升 decalitre	dal	十升＝10升
百升 hectolitre	hl	1百升＝100升
千升 kilolitre	kl	1千升＝1000升

五、质量单位表
Units of Weight

名称 Name	符号 Symbol	等数 Equivalents
毫克 milligram	mg	
厘克 centigram	cg	1厘克＝10毫克
分克 decigram	dg	1分克＝10厘克
克 gram	g	1克＝10分克
十克 decagram	dag	十克＝10克
百克 hectogram	hg	1百克＝100克
千克(公斤) kilogram	kg	1千克(公斤)＝1000克
吨 ton	t	1吨＝1000千克(公斤)

附一：市制计量单位表
The *Shi* System of Weights and Measures

长度 Length	市毫 *hao*	
	市厘 *li*	1市厘＝10市毫
	市分 *fen*	1市分＝10市厘
	市寸 *cun*	1市寸＝10市分
	市尺 *chi*	1市尺＝10市寸
	市丈 *zhang*	1市丈＝10市尺
	市里 *li*	1市里＝150市丈
面积 Area	平方市毫 square *hao*	
	平方市厘 square *li*	1平方市厘＝100平方市毫
	平方市分 square *fen*	1平方市分＝100平方市厘
	平方市寸 square *cun*	1平方市寸＝100平方市分
	平方市尺 square *chi*	1平方市尺＝100平方市寸
	平方市丈 square *zhang*	1平方市丈＝100平方市尺
	平方市里 square *li*	1平方市里＝22500平方市丈
地积 Area	市毫 *hao*	
	市厘 *li*	1市厘＝10市毫
	市分 *fen*	1市分＝10市厘
	市亩 *mu*	1市亩＝10市分
	市顷 *qing*	1市顷＝100市亩
容量 Capacity	市撮 *cuo*	
	市勺 *shao*	1市勺＝10市撮
	市合 *ge*	1市合＝10市勺
	市升 *sheng*	1市升＝10市合
	市斗 *dou*	1市斗＝10市升
	市石 *dan*	1市石＝10市斗
质量(重量) Mass (Weight)	市丝 *si*	
	市毫 *hao*	1市毫＝10市丝
	市厘 *li*	1市厘＝10市毫
	市分 *fen*	1市分＝10市厘
	市钱 *qian*	1市钱＝10市分
	市两 *liang*	1市两＝10市钱
	市斤 *jin*	1市斤＝10市两
	市担 *dan*	1市担＝100市斤

附二：计量单位换算表
Conversion Tables

长度单位换算表
Conversion Tables of Units of Length

1千米(公里)(kilometre)＝2市里(*li*)＝0.621英里(mile)＝0.540海里(nautical mile) 1米(metre)　　　＝3市尺(*chi*)＝3.281英尺(feet)
1市里(*li*)＝0.54米(公里)(kilometre)＝0.311英里(mile)＝0.270海里(nautical mile) 1市尺(*chi*)＝0.333米(metre)＝1.094英尺(feet)
1英里(mile)＝1.609千米(公里)(kilometres)＝3.218市里(*li*)＝0.869海里(nautical mile) 1英尺(foot)＝0.305米(metre)＝0.914市尺(*chi*)
1海里(nautical mile)＝1.852千米(公里)(kilometres)＝3.704市里(*li*)＝1.150英里(miles)

地积单位换算表
Conversion Tables of Units of Area

1公顷(hectare)＝15市亩(*mu*)＝2.471英亩(acres)
1市亩*(*mu*)＝6.667公亩(ares)＝0.165英亩(acre) 1英亩(acre)＝0.405公顷(hectare)＝6.070市亩(*mu*)

*本表1市亩按60平方市丈计算

质量(重量)单位换算表
Conversion Tables of Units of Weight

1千克(公斤)(kilogram)＝2市斤(*jin*)＝2.205英磅(pounds)
1市斤(*jin*)＝0.5千克(公斤)(kilogram)＝1.102英磅(pounds)
1英磅(pound)＝0.454千克(公斤)(kilogram)＝0.907市斤(*jin*)

容量单位换算表
Conversion Tables of Units of Capacity

1升(litre)＝1市升(*sheng*)＝0.22加仑(gallon)
1加仑(gallon)＝4.546升(litres)＝4.546市升(*sheng*)

附录七
Appendix 7
中国历史年代简表
A Brief Chinese Chronology

夏 Xia Dynasty		C. 2100— C. 1600 B.C.		北 齐 Northern Qi	550—577
商 Shang Dynasty		C. 1600— C. 1100 B.C.		西 魏 Western Wei	535—556
周 Zhou Dynasty	西 周 Western Zhou Dynasty	C.1100— 771 B.C.		北 周 Northern Zhou	557—581
	东 周 Eastern Zhou Dynasty	770—256 B.C.		隋 Sui Dynasty	581—618
	春 秋 Spring and Autumn Period	770—476 B.C.		唐 Tang Dynasty	618—907
	战 国 Warring States	475—221 B.C.	五 代 Five Dynasties	后 梁 Later Liang	907—923
秦 Qin Dynasty		221—206 B.C.		后 唐 Later Tang	923—936
汉 Han Dynasty	西 汉 Western Han	206B.C.—24A.D.		后 晋 Later Jin	936—946
	东 汉 Eastern Han	25—220 A.D.		后 汉 Later Han	947—950
三 国 Three Kingdoms	魏 Wei	220—265		后 周 Later Zhou	951—960
	蜀 汉 Shu Han	221—263	宋 Song Dynasty	北 宋 Northern Song Dynasty	960—1127
	吴 Wu	222—280		南 宋 Southern Song Dynasty	1127—1279
西 晋 Western Jin Dynasty		265—316		辽 Liao Dynasty	916—1125
东 晋 Eastern Jin Dynasty		317—420		金 Jin Dynasty	1115—1234
南 北 朝 Northern and Southern Dynasties	南 朝 Southern Dynasties — 宋 Song	420—479		元 Yuan Dynasty	1271—1368
	齐 Qi	479—502		明 Ming Dynasty	1368—1644
	梁 Liang	502—557		清 Qing Dynasty	1644—1911
	陈 Chen	557—589		中华民国 Republic of China	1912—1949
	北 朝 Northern Dynasties — 北 魏 Northern Wei	386—534		中华人民共和国 People's Republic of China	1949—
	东 魏 Eastern Wei	534—550			

附录八

Appendix 8

中国军衔表

Ranks in the Chinese Armed Forces

中文名称 Terms in Chinese	陆 军 Army	空 军 Air Force	海 军 Navy
一级上将	General, First Class	General, First Class	Admiral, First Class
上将	General	General	Admiral
中将	Lieutenant General	Lieutenant General	Vice Admiral
少将	Major General	Major General	Rear Admiral
大校	Senior Colonel	Senior Colonel	Senior Captain
上校	Colonel	Colonel	Captain
中校	Lieutenant Colonel	Lieutenant Colonel	Commander
少校	Major	Major	Lieutenant Commander
上尉	Captain	Captain	Lieutenant
中尉	First Lieutenant	First Lieutenant	Lieutenant, Junior Grade
少尉	Second Lieutenant	Second Lieutenant	Ensign
军士长	Master Sergeant	Master Sergeant	Chief Petty Officer
专业军士	Specialist Sergeant	Specialist Sergeant	Specialist Petty Officer
上士	Sergeant, First Class	Technical Sergeant	Petty Officer, First Class
中士	Sergeant	Staff Sergeant	Petty Officer, Second Class
下士	Corporal	Staff Sergeant	Petty Officer, Third Class
上等兵	Private, First Class	Airman, First Class	Seaman, First Class
列兵	Private	Airman, Second Class	Seaman, Second Class

附录九

Appendix 9

天干地支

The Heavenly Stems and Earthly Branches

天干 The Heavenly Stems	地支 The Earthly Branches
甲 the first of the ten Heavenly Stems	子 the first of the twelve Earthly Branches
乙 the second of the ten Heavenly Stems	丑 the second of the twelve Earthly Branches
丙 the third of the ten Heavenly Stems	寅 the third of the twelve Earthly Branches
丁 the fourth of the ten Heavenly Stems	卯 the fourth of the twelve Earthly Branches
戊 the fifth of the ten Heavenly Stems	辰 the fifth of the twelve Earthly Branches
己 the sixth of the ten Heavenly Stems	巳 the sixth of the twelve Earthly Branches
庚 the seventh of the ten Heavenly Stems	午 the seventh of the twelve Earthly Branches
辛 the eighth of the ten Heavenly Stems	未 the eighth of the twelve Earthly Branches
壬 the ninth of the ten Heavenly Stems	申 the ninth of the twelve Earthly Branches
癸 the last of the ten Heavenly Stems	酉 the tenth of the twelve Earthly Branches
	戌 the eleventh of the twelve Earthly Branches
	亥 the last of the twelve Earthly Branches

附录十

Appendix 10

二十四节气

The Twenty-four Solar Terms

名称 Name	开始日期 Beginning
立春 the Beginning of Spring (lst solar term)	Feb. 3, 4, or 5
雨水 Rain Water (2nd solar term)	Feb. 18, 19, or 20
惊蛰 the Waking of Insects (3rd solar term)	Mar. 5, 6, or 7
春分 the Spring Equinox (4th solar term)	Mar. 20 or 21
清明 Pure Brightness (5th solar term)	Apr. 4, 5, or 6
谷雨 Grain Rain (6th solar term)	Apr. 19, 20, or 21
立夏 the Beginning of Summer (7th solar term)	May 5, 6, or 7
小满 Lesser Fullness of Grain (8th solar term)	May 20, 21, or 22
芒种 Grain in Beard (9th solar term)	Jun. 5, 6, or 7
夏至 the Summer Solstice (10th solar term)	Jun. 21 or 22
小暑 Lesser Heat (11th solar term)	Jul. 6, 7, or 8
大暑 Greater Heat (12th solar term)	Jul. 22, 23, or 24
立秋 the Beginning of Autumn (13th solar term)	Aug. 7, 8, or 9
处暑 the End of Heat (14th solar term)	Aug. 22, 23, or 24
白露 White Dew (15th solar term)	Sep. 7, 8, or 9
秋分 the Autumn Equinox (16th solar term)	Sep. 22, 23, or 24
寒露 Cold Dew (17th solar term)	Oct. 8 or 9
霜降 Frost's Descent (18th solar term)	Oct. 23 or 24
立冬 the Beginning of Winter (19th solar term)	Nov. 7 or 8
小雪 Lesser Snow (20th solar term)	Nov. 22 or 23
大雪 Greater Snow (21st solar term)	Dec. 6, 7, or 8
冬至 the Winter Solstice (22nd solar term)	Dec. 21, 22, or 23
小寒 Lesser Cold (23rd solar term)	Jan. 5, 6, or 7
大寒 Greater Cold (24th solar term)	Jan. 20 or 21

附录十一
Appendix 11
化学元素表
A Table of Chemical Elements

中文 in Chinese	汉语拼音 in Hanyu Pinyin	英文 in English	符号 Symbol	原子序数 Atomic Number	中文 in Chinese	汉语拼音 in Hanyu Pinyin	英文 in English	符号 Symbol	原子序数 Atomic Number
锕	ā	actinium	Ac	89	硅	guī	silicon	Si	14
锿	āi	einsteinium	Es	99	铪	hā	hafnium	Hf	72
砹	ài	astatine	At	85	氦	hài	helium	He	2
钯	bǎ	palladium	Pd	46	𨭆	hǎn	hahnium	Ha	105
钡	bèi	barium	Ba	56	钬	huǒ	holmium	Ho	67
铋	bì	bismuth	Bi	83	镓	jiā	gallium	Ga	31
铂	bó	platinum	Pt	78	钾	jiǎ	potassium	K	19
钚	bù	plutonium	Pu	94	金	jīn	gold	Au	79
氮	dàn	nitrogen	N	7	锔	jú	curium	Cm	96
锝	dé	technetium	Tc	43	锎	kāi	californium	Cf	98
镝	dī	dysprosium	Dy	66	钪	kàng	scandium	Sc	21
碲	dì	tellurium	Te	52	氪	kè	krypton	Kr	36
碘	diǎn	iodine	I	53	铼	lái	rhenium	Re	75
铥	diū	thulium	Tm	69	镧	lán	lanthanum	La	57
氡	dōng	radon	Rn	86	铹	láo	lawrencium	Lw	103
锇	é	osmium	Os	76	铑	lǎo	rhodium	Rh	45
铒	ěr	erbium	Er	68	镭	léi	radium	Ra	88
钒	fán	vanadium	V	23	锂	lǐ	lithium	Li	3
钫	fāng	francium	Fr	87	钌	liǎo	ruthenium	Ru	44
镄	fèi	fermium	Fm	100	磷	lín	phosphorus	P	15
氟	fú	fluorine	F	9	硫	liú	sulphur	S	16
钆	gá	gadolinium	Gd	64	𬬻	lú	rutherfordium	Rf	104
钙	gài	calcium	Ca	20	镥	lǔ	lutetium	Lu	71
锆	gào	zirconium	Zr	40	铝	lǚ	aluminium	Al	13
镉	gé	cadmium	Cd	48	氯	lù	chlorine	Cl	17
铬	gè	chromium	Cr	24	镅	méi	americium	Am	95
汞	gǒng	mercury	Hg	80	镁	měi	magnesium	Mg	12
钴	gǔ	cobalt	Co	27	钔	mén	mendelevium	Md	101

元 素 名 称 Name			符 号 Symbol	原子序数 Atomic Number	元 素 名 称 Name			符 号 Symbol	原子序数 Atomic Number
中文 in Chinese	汉语拼音 in Hanyu Pinyin	英文 in English			中文 in Chinese	汉语拼音 in Hanyu Pinyin	英文 in English		
锰	měng	manganese	Mn	25	钛	tài	titanium	Ti	22
钼	mù	molybdenum	Mo	42	钽	tǎn	tantalum	Ta	73
镎	ná	neptunium	Np	93	碳	tàn	carbon	C	6
钠	nà	sodium	Na	11	铽	tè	terbium	Tb	65
氖	nǎi	neon	Ne	10	锑	tī	antimony	Sb	51
铌	ní	niobium	Nb	41	铁	tiě	iron	Fe	26
镍	niè	nickel	Ni	28	铜	tóng	copper	Cu	29
钕	nǔ	neodymium	Nd	60	钍	tǔ	thorium	Th	90
锘	nuò	nobelium	No	102	钨	wū	tungsten	W	74
锫	péi	berkelium	Bk	97	硒	xī	selenium	Se	34
硼	péng	boron	B	5	锡	xī	tin	Sn	50
铍	pí	beryllium	Be	4	氙	xiān	xenon	Xe	54
钋	pō	polonium	Po	84	锌	xīn	zinc	Zn	30
钷	pǒ	promethium	Pm	61	溴	xiù	bromine	Br	35
镁	pú	protactinium	Pa	91	氩	yà	argon	Ar	18
镨	pǔ	praseodymium	Pr	59	氧	yǎng	oxygen	O	8
铅	qiān	lead	Pb	82	铱	yī	iridium	Ir	77
氢	qīng	hydrogen	H	1	钇	yǐ	yttrium	Y	39
铷	rú	rubidium	Rb	37	镱	yì	ytterbium	Yb	70
铯	sè	cesium	Cs	55	铟	yīn	indium	In	49
钐	shān	samarium	Sm	62	银	yín	silver	Ag	47
砷	shēn	arsenic	As	33	铀	yóu	uranium	U	92
铈	shì	cerium	Ce	58	铕	yǒu	europium	Eu	63
锶	sī	strontium	Sr	38	锗	zhě	germanium	Ge	32
铊	tā	thallium	Tl	81					

赵 验
二 01